Tolley's Yellow Tax Handbook 2004–05

44th Edition

Part 2

Supplementary material relating to—
income tax
corporation tax
capital gains tax

Statutory Instruments, EC legislation, Revenue Concessions, Statements of Practice, Interpretations, Decisions, Press Releases and Destination Tables

CONSULTANT EDITOR

Anne Redston MA(Oxon), FCA, FTII

Tax Partner

Ernst & Young

LexisNexis™ UK

Members of the LexisNexis Group worldwide

United Kingdom	LexisNexis UK, a Division of Reed Elsevier (UK) Ltd, Halsbury House, 35 Chancery Lane, LONDON, WC2A 1EL, and 4 Hill Street, EDINBURGH EH2 3JZ
Argentina	LexisNexis Argentina, BUENOS AIRES
Australia	LexisNexis Butterworths, CHATSWOOD, New South Wales
Austria	LexisNexis Verlag ARD Orac GmbH & Co KG, VIENNA
Canada	LexisNexis Butterworths, MARKHAM, Ontario
Chile	LexisNexis Chile Ltda, SANTIAGO DE CHILE
Czech Republic	Nakladatelství Orac sro, PRAGUE
France	Editions du Juris-Classeur SA, PARIS
Germany	LexisNexis Deutschland GmbH, FRANKFURT and MUNSTER
Hong Kong	LexisNexis Butterworths, HONG KONG
Hungary	HVG-Orac, BUDAPEST
India	LexisNexis Butterworths, NEW DELHI
Ireland	LexisNexis, DUBLIN
Italy	Giuffrè Editore, MILAN
Malaysia	Malayan Law Journal Sdn Bhd, KUALA LUMPUR
New Zealand	LexisNexis Butterworths, WELLINGTON
Poland	Wydawnictwo Prawnicze LexisNexis, WARSAW
Singapore	LexisNexis Butterworths, SINGAPORE
South Africa	LexisNexis Butterworths, DURBAN
Switzerland	Stämpfli Verlag AG, BERNE
USA	LexisNexis, DAYTON, Ohio

First published in 1962

Published by LexisNexis UK

A CIP Catalogue record for this book is available from the British Library.

ISBN 0406973938

Typeset, printed and bound in Great Britain by William Clowes Limited, Beccles and London.

Visit LexisNexis UK at www.lexisnexis.co.uk or email on: yellowandorange@lexisnexis.co.uk

CONTENTS

Tolley's Yellow Tax Handbook 2004–05

FINANCE ACT 2004—KEY DATES

Budget Day	17 March 2004
Finance Act 2004 passed	22 July 2004

PREFACE

Every year, tax legislation becomes more voluminous, and the Yellow Book expands. This edition is no exception. The Government has introduced radical anti-avoidance provisions, a reform of the trust tax system, novel income tax penalties for inheritance tax planning, and a new Construction Industry Scheme.

As complexity increases, the challenge for practitioners grows. We complain, but we are not surprised: we have become inured over time. Tax credits, however, have extended fiscal concepts to a much wider population, many of whom cannot afford to take professional advice. Previously these people may have paid tax, but were sheltered from the full rigours of the system by PAYE, and the deduction of tax at source rules. The introduction of tax credits significantly increases the need for tax simplification.

In this context, Finance Act 2004 contains some glimmers of hope. The new pensions legislation is a radical improvement on the many-layered regimes of the past. Rules for company vans have been simplified. ITEPA has made income tax law more accessible – but also laid bare many areas which are ripe for reform.

In the meantime, the quantity of change and its complexity means that practitioners have an even greater need for appropriate, up-to-date, technical guidance. The Yellow Book contains statutes, regulations and Statements of Practice together with other important supporting documentation, in easily accessible form. Each edition is organised, cross-referenced, and updated for the many changes and additions since the last version, so that it is as easy as possible to use.

We believe that the 2004–05 Yellow Book has met the challenge posed by the legislators, and trust that it will continue to do so in the future. But one day, I hope, the calls for simplification will be heard, the Yellow Book's ever-increasing girth will reduce, and citizens may understand their own tax position.

Anne Redston

PUBLISHERS' NOTE

Tax legislation

Tolley's Yellow and Orange Tax Handbooks are indispensable to the practitioner who needs to refer to the tax legislation as currently in force. Each year the legislation is augmented and amended by one or more Finance Acts and lesser amendments are made from time to time by a variety of other statutes. An increasing amount of the detailed regulation of taxes is contained in statutory instruments—orders or regulations—which are also amended frequently. The Handbooks are normally published annually. They contain the text of the relevant statutes and statutory instruments as amended together with current texts of extra-statutory concessions, statements of practice, published official interpretations and decisions, selected press releases and internal guidance where available.

The Yellow Tax Handbook covers income tax, corporation tax, capital gains tax (in Parts 1a, 1b and 2), and inheritance tax, national insurance contributions, tax credits and petroleum revenue tax (in Part 3). The companion volume, Tolley's Orange Tax Handbook, covers value added tax, stamp duties, insurance premium tax, landfill tax, aggregates levy and climate change levy.

This edition of the Yellow Tax Handbook contains texts in the version applicable to the year 2004–05 as known at the date when the Finance Act 2004 was passed. It does not take account of any changes made after that date.

Organisation

The text of the Handbook is arranged in the following order—Parts 1a and 1b: UK statutes relating to income tax, corporation tax, and capital gains tax including FA 2004, Part 2: statutory instruments, EC legislation, concessions, statements of practice, official interpretations and decisions, selected press releases, miscellaneous non-statutory material and destination tables for consolidation statutes; Part 3: inheritance tax, national insurance contributions, tax credits, petroleum revenue tax. National insurance contributions and tax credits material, which were formerly in the Orange Tax Handbook, now appear in Part 3 of Yellow. This is due to the transfer of functions from the DSS to the Inland Revenue in relation to NIC matters. It also reflects practitioners' needs, particularly those dealing with PAYE who want to see income tax and NICs together. Inheritance tax and petroleum revenue tax have also been moved from the Orange Tax Handbook to Part 3 of this handbook as they are direct taxes and therefore more appropriately positioned here.

Within each category, items are printed in chronological order. To enable individual items to be located quickly, an item reference is printed in bold type in the outside top corner of each page.

Amendments and modifications

Amendments to existing legislation which take effect for the current year are made in the text of the amended legislation. An **Amendment** note under the amended text indicates the authority for the amendment and, where appropriate, the timing of its commencement. All relevant provisions of the current Finance Act are reproduced in full but otherwise the text of provisions which merely amend other Acts is generally omitted and replaced by a note indicating the legislation amended.

Sometimes the effect of a provision is modified by a later Act or statutory instrument but the scope of the modification is limited in some way so that the original provision remains generally unaffected. In this case, the original provision is printed without modification but a **Cross reference** to the later Act or statutory instrument is provided, see below.

Prospective amendments

The Handbook sets out the text of the legislation as it applies for the current tax year. Amendments which are stated to come into effect on a specified date after the end of that year are therefore strictly outside the scope of the current edition and are not made in the text of the Act affected. However, a **Prospective amendment** note is provided to indicate the existence of the amendment and the provision making the prospective amendment is retained in full in successive editions of the Handbook until the amendment becomes effective.

Retrospective amendments

For the tax legislation as it applied in an earlier year, reference should be made to the appropriate earlier edition of the Yellow Tax Handbook. Care must be taken, however, to ensure that amendments made retrospectively are not overlooked. A list of provisions affected by amendments made retrospectively by this year's Finance Act is provided at the front of this edition. Similar lists are provided for amendments made by each year's Finance Act(*s*) in the corresponding earlier editions.

Repealed legislation

Generally, repealed legislation is omitted. Exceptionally, where it may be necessary to refer to the repealed text in dealing with tax liabilities for the current year, the text is retained and is printed in italics.

Defined terms

Where a word or phrase used in the main Acts has been defined elsewhere, a cross-reference to the definition is provided in a **Definitions** note below the text.

Cross references

The notes under each section or Schedule paragraph include references to commentary in *Simon's Direct Tax Service* and to other relevant statutory provisions, statutory instruments, tax cases, published Revenue practice and other published or unpublished official and professional bodies' views. These are presented under the following headings—

Commentary—refers to paragraph number for commentary relating to the provision in *Simon's Direct Tax Service.*

Concession; Statement of Practice; Revenue interpretation; Revenue decision—refer to published official practice separately reproduced in this Handbook.

Revenue & other press releases—refer to published or unpublished official and professional bodies' views reproduced in this Handbook or *WJB Chiltern's Yellow Tax Guide* or elsewhere.

Revenue Internal Guidance—refers to published Revenue views expressed in the Revenue Internal Guidance Manuals not reproduced in this Handbook.

Cross reference—refers to provisions in the same or another Act or statutory instrument.

Simon's Tax Cases—provides references to the most significant cases reported in *Simon's Tax Cases* and *Simon's Tax Cases Special Commissioners' Decisions*. Cases decided on the previous corresponding statutory provision are marked by an asterisk.

Note—introduces other references not within any of the above categories.

August 2004

MEANING OF "THE TAXES ACTS"

- Taxes Acts[1]
  - TMA 1970
  - Tax Acts[2]
    - TA 1988 and other provisions of the Income Tax Acts[3]
    - TA 1988 and other provisions of the Corporation Tax Acts[4]
  - TCGA 1992 and other enactments relating to capital gains tax
  - DLTA 1976 and other enactments relating to development land tax[5]

[1] Defined in TMA 1970 s 118(1).
[2] Defined in TA 1988 s 831(2).
[3] Defined in TA 1988 s 831(1)(*b*).
[4] Defined in TA 1988 s 831(1)(*a*).
[5] Repealed with effect generally from 19 March 1985 by FA 1985 s 93, Sch 25 Pt I and Sch 27 Pt X.

LIST OF ABBREVIATIONS

AEA 1925	=	Administration of Estates Act 1925
ACT	=	Advance Corporation Tax
APRT	=	Advanced petroleum revenue tax
art	=	article(*s*)
BES	=	Business Expansion Scheme
CAA	=	Capital Allowances Act
CCAB	=	Consultative Committee of Accountancy Bodies
C&E	=	Customs & Excise
CGT	=	Capital gains tax
CGTA 1979	=	Capital Gains Tax Act 1979
Ch	=	Chapter of statute
col	=	column(*s*)
Comrs	=	Commissioners
CPA 1947	=	Crown Proceedings Act 1947
CRT	=	Composite rate tax
CSPSSA 2000	=	Child Support, Pensions and Social Security Act 2000
CT	=	Corporation tax
CTD	=	Certificates of tax deposit
CTT	=	Capital transfer tax
CTTA 1984	=	Capital Transfer Tax Act 1984
Dir	=	EC Directive
DLT	=	Development land tax
DLTA 1976	=	Development Land Tax Act 1976
DSS	=	Department of Social Security
DTI	=	Department of Trade and Industry
DTR	=	Double taxation relief
EC	=	European Community/Communities
edn	=	edition
EEC	=	European Economic Community
EEIG	=	European Economic Interest Grouping
EIS	=	Enterprise Investment Scheme
ESC	=	Extra-statutory concession
ESOT	=	Employee share ownership trust
et seq	=	(et sequens) and the following
EU	=	European Union
FA	=	Finance Act
FII	=	Franked investment income
FIMBRA	=	Financial Intermediaries, Managers and Brokers Regulatory Association
F(No 2)A	=	Finance (No 2) Act
FSA	=	Friendly Societies Act
FYA	=	first-year allowance
HA 1988	=	Housing Act 1988
HL	=	House of Lords
HM	=	Her Majesty
HMSO	=	Her Majesty's Stationery Office
IA	=	Interpretation Act
IA 1986	=	Insolvency Act 1986
ICAEW	=	Institute of Chartered Accountants in England & Wales
IHT	=	Inheritance tax
IHTA 1984	=	Inheritance Tax Act 1984
IR Comrs	=	Commissioners of Inland Revenue
IR	=	Inland Revenue
IRRA 1890	=	Inland Revenue Regulation Act 1890
IT	=	Income tax
ITEPA 2003	=	Income Tax (Earnings and Pensions) Act 2003
LAUTRO	=	Life Assurance and Unit Trust Regulatory Organisation
LIFFE	=	London International Financial Futures and Options Exchange

MIRAS	=	Mortgage interest relief at source
NB	=	(nota bene) note well
NHA 1980	=	National Heritage Act 1980
NI	=	National insurance
NIC	=	National insurance contributions
OJ	=	Official Journal of the European Communities
OTA	=	Oil Taxation Act
para	=	paragraph(*s*)
PAYE	=	Pay as you earn
PCTA 1968	=	Provisional Collection of Taxes Act 1968
PEP	=	Personal equity plan
PR	=	Press release
PRP	=	Profit-related pay
PRT	=	Petroleum revenue tax
PSO	=	Pension Schemes Office
Pt	=	Part(*s*)
QCB	=	Qualifying corporate bond
r		rule(*s*)
RD	=	Revenue decision
reg	=	regulations
RI	=	Revenue Interpretation
s	=	section(*s*)
SAYE	=	Save as you earn
Sch	=	Schedule
SSA	=	Social Security Act
SSAA 1992	=	Social Security Administration Act 1992
SS(C)A	=	Social Security (Contributions) Act
SSCBA 1992	=	Social Security Contributions and Benefits Act 1992
SSCPA 1992	=	Social Security (Consequential Provisions) Act 1992
SS(No 2)A	=	Social Security (No 2) Act
SSHBA	=	Social Security and Housing Benefits Act
SS(MP)A	=	Social Security (Miscellaneous Provisions) Act
SSPA 1975	=	Social Security Pensions Act 1975
SSPA 1991	=	Statutory Sick Pay Act 1991
SI	=	Statutory Instrument
SP	=	Statement of Practice
SSAP	=	Statement of Standard Accounting Practice
sub-para	=	sub-paragraph(*s*)
sub-s	=	sub-section(*s*)
TA	=	Income and Corporation Taxes Act
TCGA 1992	=	Taxation of Chargeable Gains Act 1992
TCA 1999	=	Tax Credits Act 1999
TESSA	=	Tax-exempt special savings account
TMA 1970	=	Taxes Management Act 1970
TR	=	Technical release
TSBA	=	Trustee Savings Banks Act
UCITS	=	Undertakings for Collective Investment in Transferable Securities
UK	=	United Kingdom
VAT	=	Value added tax
VATA 1994	=	Value Added Tax Act 1994
VCT	=	Venture capital trust
vol	=	volume(*s*)
WDA	=	writing down allowance

STATUTORY INSTRUMENTS

CHRONOLOGICAL LIST OF PRINTED STATUTORY INSTRUMENTS

Note—For a chronological list of current and amending statutory instruments, and an alphabetical list of the printed statutory instruments, *see below*.

SI Year/No	Title
SI 1956/1230	IT (Purchased Life Annuities) Regulations 1956
SI 1961/580	*Visiting Forces and Allied Headquarters (Income Tax and Death Duties) (Designation) Order 1961*
SI 1964/924	*Visiting Forces (Income Tax and Death Duties) (Designation) Order 1964*
SI 1967/149	Capital Gains Tax Regulations 1967
SI 1970/488	DTR (Taxes on Income) (General) Regulations 1970
SI 1971/1035	Mineral Royalties (Tax) Regulations 1971
SI 1973/317	*DTR (Taxes on Income) (General) (Dividend) Regulations 1973* (revoked)
SI 1977/1143	Friendly Societies (Life Assurance Premium Relief) Regulations 1977
SI 1977/1144	Industrial Assurance (Life Assurance Premium Relief) Regulations 1977
SI 1978/1159	IT (Life Assurance Premium Relief) Regulations 1978
SI 1980/1947	Friendly Societies (Life Assurance Premium Relief) (Change of Rate) Regulations 1980
SI 1980/1948	Industrial Assurance (Life Assurance Premium Relief) (Change of Rate) Regulations 1980
SI 1981/233	Crown Proceedings (Northern Ireland) Order 1981
SI 1982/1236	IT (Interest Relief) Regulations 1982
SI 1984/1801	Income Tax (Prescribed Deposit-takers) (No 1) Order 1984
SI 1984/2060	Capital Allowances (Vehicles for the Disabled) (Similar Payments) Order 1984
SI 1985/994	Films (Certification) Regulations 1985
SI 1985/1696	Income Tax (Composite Rate) (Prescribed Deposit-takers) Order 1985
SI 1986/387	CGT (Parallel Pooling) Regulations 1986
SI 1986/2211	Charitable Deductions (Approved Schemes) Regulations 1986
SI 1987/352	Pension Scheme Surpluses (Administration) Regulations 1987
SI 1987/412	Pension Scheme Surpluses (Valuation) Regulations 1987
SI 1987/530	IT (Entertainers and Sportsmen) Regulations 1987
SI 1987/1513	Occupational Pension Schemes (Maximum Rate Lump Sum) Regulations 1987
SI 1987/1749	Occupational Pension Schemes (Additional Voluntary Contributions) Regulations 1987
SI 1987/1765	Personal Pension Schemes (Provisional Approval) Regulations 1987
SI 1988/88	*DTR (Taxes on Income) (Foreign Loan Interest) Regulations 1988* (revoked)
SI 1988/266	CGT (Definition of Unit Trust Scheme) Regulations 1988
SI 1988/267	IT (Definition of Unit Trust Scheme) Regulations 1988
SI 1988/1012	Personal Pension Schemes (Minimum Contributions under the Social Security Act 1986) Regulations 1988
SI 1988/1013	Personal Pension Schemes (Relief at Source) Regulations 1988
SI 1988/1014	Personal Pension Schemes (Transfer Payments) Regulations 1988 (revoked)
SI 1988/1347	IT (Interest Relief) (Housing Associations) Regulations 1988
SI 1988/1436	Occupational Pension Schemes (Transitional Provisions) Regulations 1988
SI 1989/469	Personal Equity Plan Regulations 1989
SI 1989/1297	Taxes (Interest Rate) Regulations 1989
SI 1989/1299	*IT (Stock Lending) Regulations 1989* (revoked)
SI 1989/2387	Private Medical Insurance (Tax Relief) Regulations 1989
SI 1990/586	Retirement Benefits Schemes (Tax Relief on Contributions) (Disapplication of Earnings Cap) Regulations 1990
SI 1990/1671	Movements of Capital (Required Information) Regulations 1990
SI 1990/2101	Retirement Benefit Schemes (Continuation of Rights of Members of Approved Schemes) Regulations 1990
SI 1990/2231	IT (Building Societies) (Dividends and Interest) Regulations 1990
SI 1990/2232	IT (Deposit-takers) (Interest Payments) Regulations 1990
SI 1990/2361	Tax-exempt Special Savings Account Regulations 1990
SI 1990/2529	Debts of Overseas Governments (Determination of Relevant Percentage) Regulations 1990
SI 1991/512	IT (Building Societies) (Annual Payments) Regulations 1991
SI 1991/1614	Retirement Benefits Schemes (Restriction on Discretion to Approve) (Small Self-administered Schemes) Regulations 1991
SI 1992/10	IT (Building Societies) (Audit Powers) Regulations 1992
SI 1992/12	IT (Deposit-takers) (Audit Powers) Regulations 1992
SI 1992/14	IT (Deposit-takers) (Non-residents) Regulations 1992
SI 1992/15	IT (Interest Payments) (Information Powers) Regulations 1992
SI 1992/42	Taxes (Relief for Gifts) (Designated Educational Establishments) Regulations 1992
SI 1992/568	IT (Dealers in Securities) Regulations 1992

SI Year/No	Title
SI 1992/569	*IT (Dividend Manufacturing) Regulations 1992* (revoked)
SI 1992/734	*Vocational Training (Public Financial Assistance and Disentitlement to Tax Relief) Regulations 1992* (lapsed)
SI 1992/746	*Vocational Training (Tax Relief) Regulations 1992* (lapsed)
SI 1992/1655	*Friendly Societies (Modification of the Corporation Tax Acts) Regulations 1992* (revoked)
SI 1992/2074	*IT (Manufactured Interest) Regulations 1992* (revoked)
SI 1992/2326	Insurance Companies (Pension Business) (Transitional Provisions) Regulations 1992
SI 1992/2744	IT (Insurance Companies) (Expenses of Management) Regulations 1992
SI 1992/3066	Corporation Tax Acts (Provisions for Payment of Tax and Returns) (Appointed Days) Order 1992
SI 1992/3234	IT (Prescribed Deposit-takers) Order 1992
SI 1993/743	IT (Sub-contractors in the Construction Industry) Regulations 1993
SI 1993/744	IT (Employments) Regulations 1993
SI 1993/950	Capital Gains Tax (Gilt-edged Securities) Order 1993
SI 1993/1957	Double Taxation Relief (Taxes on Income) (General) (Manufactured Overseas Dividends) Regulations 1993
SI 1993/2004	IT (Manufactured Overseas Dividends) Regulations 1993
SI 1993/3016	Retirement Benefits Schemes (Restriction on Discretion to Approve) (Additional Voluntary Contributions) Regulations 1993
SI 1993/3112	*Friendly Societies (Provisional Repayments for Exempt Business) Regulations 1993* (revoked)
SI 1994/236	Distraint by Collectors (Fees, Costs and Charges) Regulations 1994
SI 1994/777	*IT (Car Benefits) (Replacement Accessories) Regulations 1994* (revoked)
SI 1994/778	*IT (Replacement Cars) Regulations 1994* (revoked)
SI 1994/1212	IT (Employments) (Notional Payments) Regulations 1994
SI 1994/1518	Private Medical Insurance (Disentitlement to Tax Relief and Approved Benefits) Regulations 1994
SI 1994/1811	Special Commissioners (Jurisdiction and Procedure) Regulations 1994
SI 1994/1812	General Commissioners (Jurisdiction and Procedure) Regulations 1994
SI 1994/2318	IT (Authorised Unit Trusts) (Interest Distributions) Regulations 1994
SI 1994/2656	Capital Gains Tax (Gilt-edged Securities) Order 1994
SI 1994/3226	Exchange Gains and Losses (Transitional Provisions) Regulations 1994
SI 1994/3227	Exchange Gains and Losses (Alternative Method of Calculation of Gain or Loss) Regulations 1994
SI 1994/3228	Exchange Gains and Losses (Referral of Gains and Losses) Regulations 1994
SI 1994/3229	Exchange Gains and Losses (Excess Gains and Losses) Regulations 1994
SI 1994/3230	Local Currency Elections Regulations 1994
SI 1994/3231	Exchange Gains and Losses (Insurance Companies) Regulations 1994
SI 1995/171	*Friendly Societies (Taxation of Transfers of Business) Regulations 1995* (revoked)
SI 1995/351	Lloyd's Underwriters (Tax) Regulations 1995
SI 1995/352	*Lloyd's Underwriters (Tax) (1992–93 to 1996–97) Regulations 1995* (spent)
SI 1995/353	Lloyd's Underwriters (Special Reserve Funds) Regulations 1995
SI 1995/917	Profit-Related Pay (Shortfall Recovery) Regulation 1995
SI 1995/1370	Deposit-takers (Interest Payments) (Discretionary or Accumulation Trusts) Regulations 1995
SI 1995/1730	Insurance Companies (Taxation of Reinsurance Business) Regulations 1995
SI 1995/1979	Venture Capital Trust Regulations 1995
SI 1995/2050	IT (Dealers in Securities) (Tradepoint) Regulations 1995
SI 1995/2052	*IT (Manufactured Dividends) (Tradepoint) Regulations 1995* (revoked)
SI 1995/2902	Taxation of Income from Land (Non-residents) Regulations 1995
SI 1995/2934	IT (Gilt-edged Securities) (Gross Payments of Interest) Regulations 1995
SI 1995/3036	Manufactured Payments and Transfer of Securities (Tax Relief) Regulations 1995
SI 1995/3103	Retirement Benefits Schemes (Information Powers) Regulations 1995
SI 1995/3192	Retirement Age of General Commissioners Order 1995
SI 1995/3220	Sale and Repurchase of Securities (Modification of Enactments) Regulations 1995
SI 1995/3223	*Insurance Companies (Gilt-edged Securities) (Periodic Accounting for Tax on Interest) Regulations 1995* (revoked)
SI 1995/3224	Gilt-edged Securities (Periodic Accounting for Tax on Interest) Regulations 1995
SI 1995/3225	Lloyd's Underwriters (Gilt-edged Securities) (Periodic Accounting for Tax on Interest) Regulations 1995
SI 1995/3237	Insurance Companies (Overseas Life Assurance Business) (Compliance) Regulations 1995

SI Year/No	Title
SI 1995/3238	Insurance Companies (Overseas Life Assurance Business) (Tax Credit) Regulations 1995
SI 1995/3239	Tax-exempt Special Savings Account (Relevant European Institutions) Regulations 1995
SI 1996/21	*Friendly Societies (Gilt-edged Securities) (Periodic Accounting for Tax on Interest) Regulations 1996* (revoked)
SI 1996/805	Personal Pension Schemes (Deferred Annuity Purchase) (Acceptance of Contributions) Regulations 1996
SI 1996/1031	Capital Gains Tax (Gilt-edged Securities) Order 1996
SI 1996/1179	European Investment Bank (Designated International Organisation) Order 1996
SI 1996/1311	Personal Pension Schemes (Tables of Rates of Annuities) Regulations 1996
SI 1996/1323	*Capital Allowances Act 1990, section 33A, (Appointed Day) Order 1996*
SI 1996/1582	Retirement Benefits Schemes (Restriction on Discretion to Approve) (Excepted Schemes) Regulations 1996
SI 1996/1583	Capitals Gains Tax (Pension Funds Pooling Schemes) Regulations 1996
SI 1996/1585	Income Tax (Pension Funds Pooling Schemes) Regulations 1996
SI 1996/1654	Income Tax (Payments on Account) Regulations 1996
SI 1996/1826	Manufactured Overseas Dividends (French Indemnity Payments) Regulations 1996
SI 1996/2396	Taxation of Benefits under Pilot Schemes (Earnings Top-up) Order 1996
SI 1996/2645	Income and Corporation Taxes Act 1988, section 737A, (Appointed Day) Order 1996
SI 1996/2991	Insurance Companies (Reserves) (Tax) Regulations 1996
SI 1997/57	Electronic Lodgement of Tax Returns Order 1997
SI 1997/133	Finance Act 1996, Schedule 35, (Appointed Day) Order 1997
SI 1997/168	International Organisations (Miscellaneous Exemptions) Order 1997
SI 1997/265	Life Assurance and Other Policies (Keeping of Information and Duties of Insurers) Regulations 1997
SI 1997/405	Lloyd's Underwriters (Double Taxation Relief) Regulations 1997
SI 1997/473	Friendly Societies (Modification of the Corporation Tax Acts) Regulations 1997
SI 1997/991	Finance Act 1997, Schedule 10, (Appointed Day) Order 1997
SI 1997/992	Manufactured Interest (Tax) Regulations 1997
SI 1997/993	Manufactured Dividends (Tax) Regulations 1997
SI 1997/1154	Open-ended Investment Companies (Tax) Regulations 1997
SI 1997/1158	Income Tax (Schedule 22 to the Finance Act 1995) (Prescribed Amounts) Regulations 1997
SI 1997/2681	Lloyd's Underwriters (Scottish Limited Partnerships) (Tax) 1997
SI 1997/2708	Finance Act 1989 Section 178(1) (Appointed Day) Order 1997
SI 1998/311	Finance Act 1989 Section 178(1) (Appointed Day) Order 1998
SI 1998/729	Retirement Benefits Schemes (Restriction on Discretion to Approve) (Excepted Provisions) Regulations 1998
SI 1998/1513	Visiting Forces and Allied Headquarters (Income Tax and Capital Gains Tax) (Designation) Order 1998
SI 1998/1514	Visiting Forces (Income Tax and Capital Gains Tax) (Designation) Order 1998
SI 1998/1868	Gifts for Relief in Poor Countries (Designation) Order 1998
SI 1998/1870	Individual Savings Account Regulations 1998
SI 1998/1871	Individual Savings Account (Insurance Companies) Regulations 1998
SI 1998/2620	Finance Act 1995, Section 139(3), (Appointed Day) Order 1998
SI 1998/3081	Controlled Foreign Companies (Excluded Countries) Regulations 1998
SI 1998/3132	Civil Procedure Rules 1998 (Orders 53, 55, 77 and 91 only)
SI 1998/3173	Finance Act 1994, Section 199, (Appointed Day) Order 1998
SI 1998/3175	Corporation Tax (Instalment Payments) Regulations 1998
SI 1998/3177	European Single Currency (Taxes) Regulations 1998
SI 1998/3178	Scotland Act 1998 (Commencement) Order 1998
SI 1999/358	Corporation Tax (Treatment of Unrelieved Surplus Advance Corporation Tax) Regulations 1999
SI 1999/498	Insurance Companies (Capital Redemption Business) (Modification of the Corporation Tax Acts) Regulations 1999
SI 1999/564	Finance Act 1993, Section 86(2), (Fish Quota) Order 1999
SI 1999/619	Finance Act 1998, Section 37, (Appointed Day) Order 1999
SI 1999/622	Friendly Societies (Provisional Repayments for Exempt Business) Regulations 1999
SI 1999/623	Insurance Companies (Gilt-edged Securities) (Periodic Accounting for Tax on Interest) Regulations 1999
SI 1999/624	Friendly Societies (Gilt-edged Securities) (Periodic Accounting for Tax on Interest) Regulations 1999
SI 1999/881	Overseas Insurers (Tax Representatives) Regulations 1999
SI 1999/1029	Personal Portfolio Bonds (Tax) Regulations 1999

SI Year/No	Title
SI 1999/1408	Non-resident Companies (General Insurance Business) Regulations 1999
SI 1999/1964	Retirement Benefits Schemes (Restriction on Discretion to Approve) (Additional Voluntary Contributions) (Amendment) Regulations 1999
SI 1999/2118	Gifts for Relief in Poor Countries (Designation of Kosovo) Order 1999
SI 1999/2119	Finance Act 1998, Section 83(1), (Appointed Day) Order 1999
SI 1999/2155	Income Tax (Employments) (Amendment No 3) Regulations 1999
SI 1999/2156	Finance Act 1995, Section 139(3), (Appointed Day) Order 1999
SI 1999/2975	Corporation Tax (Simplified Arrangements for Group Relief) Regulations 1999
SI 1999/3308	Lloyd's Underwriters (Special Reserve Funds) Regulations 1999
SI 1999/3330	DTR (Taxes on Income) (Foreign Interest and Dividends) Regulations 1999
SI 2000/600	Income Tax (Charge to Tax)(Payments out of Surplus Funds) (Relevant Rate) Order 2000
SI 2000/921	Income and Corporation Taxes Act 1988, Section 559(4A), Order 2000
SI 2000/922	Finance Act 1995, Section 139(3), (Appointed Day) Order 2000
SI 2000/944	Education (Student Loans) (Repayment) Regulations 2000
SI 2000/945	Income Tax (Electronic Communications) Regulations 2000
SI 2000/1085	Retirement Benefits Schemes (Sharing of Pensions on Divorce or Annulment) Regulations 2000
SI 2000/1087	Retirement Benefits Schemes (Restriction on Discretion to Approve) (Excepted Provisions) Regulations 2000
SI 2000/1093	Finance Act 1999, Schedule 10, Paragraph 18, (First and Second Appointed Days) Order 2000
SI 2000/2004	Finance Act 1999, Section 59(3)(*b*), (Appointed Day) Order 2000
SI 2000/2074	Donations to Charity by Individuals (Appropriate Declarations) Regulations 2000
SI 2000/2076	Individual Learning Accounts (Separate Employers Under the Crown) Regulations 2000
SI 2000/2080	Income Tax (Benefits in Kind) (Exemption for Welfare Counselling) Regulations 2000
SI 2000/2081	*Research and Development (Prescribed Activities) Regulations 2000* (revoked)
SI 2000/2082	Finance Act 2000, Section 108(3), (Appointed Day) Order 2000
SI 2000/2089	Insurance Companies (Overseas Life Assurance Business) (Excluded Business) Regulations 2000
SI 2000/2090	Employee Share Ownership Plans (Partnership Shares—Notice of Effects on Benefits, Statutory Sick Pay and Statutory Maternity Pay) Regulations 2000
SI 2000/2129	Tonnage Tax (Training Requirement) Regulations 2000
SI 2000/2303	Tonnage Tax Regulations 2000
SI 2000/2314	Personal Pension Schemes (Restriction on Discretion to Approve) (Establishment of Schemes under Trusts) Regulations 2000
SI 2000/2316	Personal Pension Schemes (Information Powers) Regulations 2000
SI 2000/2318	Personal Pension Schemes (Concurrent Membership) Order 2000
SI 2000/2319	Finance Act 1998, Section 96(4), (Appointed Day) Order 2000
SI 2000/2875	Orders for the Delivery of Documents (Procedure) Regulations 2000
SI 2000/3158	Controlled Foreign Companies (Designer Rate Tax Provisions) Regulations 2000
SI 2000/3315	Exchange Gains and Losses (Miscellaneous Modifications) Regulations 2000
SI 2001/56	Income Tax (Electronic Communications) (Incentive Payments) Regulations 2001
SI 2001/117	Personal Pension Schemes (Restriction on Discretion to Approve) (Permitted Investments) Regulations 2001
SI 2001/118	Personal Pension Schemes (Conversion of Retirement Benefits Schemes) Regulations 2001
SI 2001/119	Personal Pension Schemes (Transfer Payments) Regulations 2001
SI 2001/253	Finance Act 1989, Section 178(1), (Appointed Day) Order 2001
SI 2001/391	Investment Trusts (Approval of Accounting Methods for Creditor Relationships) Order 2001
SI 2001/1122	Capital Gains Tax (Gilt-edged Securities) Order 2001
SI 2001/1123	Income Tax (Car Benefits) (Reduction of Value of Appropriate Percentage) Regulations 2001
SI 2001/1156	Double Taxation Relief (Taxes on Income) (Underlying Tax on Dividends and Dual Resident Companies) Regulations 2001
SI 2001/1163	Double Taxation Relief (Surrender of Relievable Tax Within a Group) Regulations 2001
SI 2001/1304	General Commissioners of Income Tax (Costs) Regulations 2001
SI 2001/1757	General Insurance Reserves (Tax) Regulations 2001
SI 2001/2541	Capital Allowances (Energy-saving Plant and Machinery) Order 2001
SI 2001/3643	Finance Act 1996, Section 167, (Appointed Day) Order 2001

SI Year/No	Title
SI 2001/3973	Friendly Societies (Provisional Repayments for Exempt Business) (Amendment) Regulations 2001
SI 2001/3974	Individual Savings Account (Insurance Companies) (Amendment) Regulations 2001
SI 2001/4024	Referrals to the Special Commissioners Regulations 2001
SI 2002/205	Income Tax (Exemption of Minor Benefits) Regulations 2002
SI 2002/653	Scottish Water (Transfer of Functions, etc) (Tax Provisions) Order 2002
SI 2002/680	Income Tax (Employments and Electronic Communications) (Miscellaneous Provisions) Regulations 2002
SI 2002/1596	Income Tax (Benefits in Kind) (Exemption for Employment Costs resulting from Disability) Regulations 2002
SI 2002/1966	Relief for Community Amateur Sports Clubs (Designation) Order 2002
SI 2002/1967	Corporation Tax (Finance Leasing of Intangible Assets) Regulations 2002
SI 2002/1968	Income Tax (Prescribed Deposit-takers) Order 2002
SI 2002/1969	Exchange Gains and Losses (Transitional Provisions and Savings) Regulations 2002
SI 2002/1970	Exchange Gains and Losses (Bringing into Account Gains or Losses) Regulations 2002
SI 2002/2661	Venture Capital Trust (Exchange of Shares and Securities) Regulations 2002
SI 2002/2849	Capital Gains Tax (Gilt-edged Securities) Order 2002
SI 2002/3047	Statutory Payment Schemes (Electronic Communications) Regulations 2002
SI 2003/96	Community Investment Tax Relief (Accreditation of Community Development Finance Institutions) Regulations 2003
SI 2003/282	Income and Corporation Taxes (Electronic Communications) Regulations 2003
SI 2003/1828	Insurance Companies (Taxation of Reinsurance Business) (Amendment) Regulations 2003
SI 2003/1830	Income Tax (Authorised Unit Trusts) (Interest Distributions) Regulations 2003
SI 2003/2076	Capital Allowances (Environmentally Beneficial Plant and Machinery) Order 2003
SI 2003/2082	Insurance Companies (Calculation of Profits: Policy Holders' Tax) Regulations 2003
SI 2003/2172	Finance Act 1995, Section 127(12) (Designated Transactions) Regulations 2003
SI 2003/2173	Finance Act 2003, Schedule 26 Paragraph 3(3) (Designated Transactions) Regulations 2003
SI 2003/2339	Taxation of Benefits under Government Pilot Schemes (Return to Work Credit and Employment Retention and Advancement Schemes) Order 2003
SI 2003/2495	Income Tax (Incentive Payments for Voluntary Electronic Communication of PAYE Returns) Regulations 2003
SI 2003/2682	Income Tax (Pay As You Earn) Regulations 2003 [with destination table]
SI 2003/2714	Non-resident Insurance Companies Regulations 2003
SI 2003/3075	Money Laundering Regulations 2003
SI 2003/3143	Income and Corporation Taxes (Electronic Certificates of Deduction of Tax and Tax Credit) Regulations 2003
SI 2003/3297	Reporting of Savings Income Information Regulations 2003
SI 2004/438	Capital Gains Tax (Gilt-edged Securities) Order 2004
SI 2004/439	Urban Regeneration Companies (Tax) (Designation) Order 2004
SI 2004/674	Recovery of Duties and Taxes etc Due in Other Member States (Corresponding UK Claims, Procedure and Supplementary) Regulations 2004
SI 2004/712	Research and Development (Prescribed Activities) Regulations 2004
SI 2004/1450	Child Trust Funds Regulations 2004
SI 2004/1865	Tax Avoidance Schemes (Promoters and Prescribed Circumstances) Regulations 2004
SI 2004/1819	Thalidomide Children's Trust (Application of Section 329AA of the Income and Corporation Taxes Act 1988) Order 2004
SI 2004/1863	Tax Avoidance Schemes (Prescribed Descriptions of Arrangements) Regulations 2004
SI 2004/1864	Tax Avoidance Schemes (Information) Regulations 2004

CHRONOLOGICAL LIST OF STATUTORY INSTRUMENTS

Note—The following is the list of current and amending instruments.
For the list of current instruments which are reproduced in this work, *see above*.
For an alphabetical list, *see below*.

SI Year/No	Title
SI 1956/1230	IT (Purchased Life Annuities) Regulations 1956
SI 1960/2308	*IT (Purchased Life Annuities) (Amendment) Regulations 1960* (amend SI 1956/1230)
SI 1961/580	*Visiting Forces and Allied Headquarters (Income Tax and Death Duties) (Designation) Order 1961*
SI 1964/924	*Visiting Forces (Income Tax and Death Duties) (Designation) Order 1964*
SI 1967/149	Capital Gains Tax Regulations 1967
SI 1970/488	DTR (Taxes on Income) (General) Regulations 1970
SI 1971/1035	Mineral Royalties (Tax) Regulations 1971
SI 1973/317	*DTR (Taxes on Income) (General) (Dividend) Regulations 1973* (revoked)
SI 1977/1143	Friendly Societies (Life Assurance Premium Relief) Regulations 1977
SI 1977/1144	Industrial Assurance (Life Assurance Premium Relief) Regulations 1977
SI 1978/1159	IT (Life Assurance Premium Relief) Regulations 1978
SI 1978/1160	*Friendly Societies (Life Assurance Premium Relief) (Amendment) Regulations 1978* (amend SI 1977/1143)
SI 1978/1161	*Industrial Assurance (Life Assurance Premium Relief) (Amendment) Regulations 1978* (amend SI 1977/1144)
SI 1979/346	*IT (Life Assurance Premium Relief) Regulations 1979* (amend SI 1978/1159)
SI 1979/1576	*Tax, Consumer Credit and Judicature (Northern Ireland Consequential Amendments) Order 1979* (amends SI 1978/1159)
SI 1980/1947	Friendly Societies (Life Assurance Premium Relief) (Change of Rate) Regulations 1980
SI 1980/1948	Industrial Assurance (Life Assurance Premium Relief) (Change of Rate) Regulations 1980
SI 1982/1236	IT (Interest Relief) Regulations 1982
SI 1983/311	*IT (Interest Relief) (No 2) Regulations 1983* (amend SI 1982/1236)
SI 1984/322	*Industrial Assurance (Life Assurance Premium Relief) (Amendment) Regulations 1984* (amend SI 1977/1144)
SI 1984/323	*Friendly Societies (Life Assurance Premium Relief) (Amendment) Regulations 1984* (amend SI 1977/1143)
SI 1984/1801	Income Tax (Prescribed Deposit-takers) (No 1) Order 1984
SI 1984/2060	Capital Allowances (Vehicles for the Disabled) (Similar Payments) Order 1984
SI 1985/994	Films (Certification) Regulations 1985
SI 1985/1252	*IT (Interest Relief) (No 3) Regulations 1985* (amend SI 1982/1236)
SI 1985/1696	Income Tax (Composite Rate) (Prescribed Deposit-takers) Order 1985
SI 1986/387	CGT (Parallel Pooling) Regulations 1986
SI 1986/482	*IT (Building Societies) Regulations 1986* (*see* SI 1990/2231; SI 1991/512)
SI 1986/2211	Charitable Deductions (Approved Schemes) Regulations 1986
SI 1987/352	Pension Scheme Surpluses (Administration) Regulations 1987
SI 1987/412	Pension Scheme Surpluses (Valuation) Regulations 1987
SI 1987/530	IT (Entertainers and Sportsmen) Regulations 1987
SI 1987/844	*IT (Building Societies) (Amendment) Regulations 1987* (amend SI 1986/482)
SI 1987/1513	Occupational Pension Schemes (Maximum Rate Lump Sum) Regulations 1987
SI 1987/1749	Occupational Pension Schemes (Additional Voluntary Contributions) Regulations 1987
SI 1987/1765	Personal Pension Schemes (Provisional Approval) Regulations 1987
SI 1988/88	*DTR (Taxes on Income) (Foreign Loan Interest) Regulations 1988* (revoked)
SI 1988/266	CGT (Definition of Unit Trust Scheme) Regulations 1988
SI 1988/267	IT (Definition of Unit Trust Scheme) Regulations 1988
SI 1988/504	*Occupational Pension Schemes (Rate of Tax under Paragraph 2(2) of Part II of Schedule 5 to the Finance Act 1970) Order 1988* (*see* TA 1988 s 598)
SI 1988/993	*Personal Pension Schemes (Establishment of Schemes) Order 1988* (amends TA 1988 s 632)
SI 1988/1012	Personal Pension Schemes (Minimum Contributions under the Social Security Act 1986) Regulations 1988
SI 1988/1013	Personal Pension Schemes (Relief at Source) Regulations 1988
SI 1988/1014	*Personal Pension Schemes (Transfer Payments) Regulations 1988* (revoked)
SI 1988/1347	IT (Interest Relief) (Housing Associations) Regulations 1988
SI 1988/1436	Occupational Pension Schemes (Transitional Provisions) Regulations 1988
SI 1989/469	Personal Equity Plan Regulations 1989

SI Year/No	Title
SI 1989/992	*Transfer of Functions (Economic Statistics) Order 1989* (amend SI 1987/412)
SI 1989/1115	Personal Pension Schemes (Transfer Payments) (Amendment) Regulations 1989 (amend SI 1988/1014) (revoked)
SI 1989/1297	Taxes (Interest Rate) Regulations 1989
SI 1989/1299	IT (Stock Lending) Regulations 1989 (revoked)
SI 1989/2290	*Pension Scheme Surpluses (Valuation) (Amendment) Regulations 1989* (amend SI 1987/412)
SI 1989/2387	Private Medical Insurance (Tax Relief) Regulations 1989
SI 1990/585	*Occupational Pension Schemes (Additional Voluntary Contributions) (Amendment) Regulations 1990* (amend SI 1987/1749)
SI 1990/586	Retirement Benefits Schemes (Tax Relief on Contributions) (Disapplication of Earnings Cap) Regulations 1990
SI 1990/626	*IT (Purchased Life Annuities) (Amendment) Regulations 1990* (amend SI 1956/1230)
SI 1990/678	*Personal Equity Plan (Amendment) Regulations 1990* (amend SI 1989/469)
SI 1990/1671	Movements of Capital (Required Information) Regulations 1990
SI 1990/2101	Retirement Benefit Schemes (Continuation of Rights of Members of Approved Schemes) Regulations 1990
SI 1990/2231	IT (Building Societies) (Dividends and Interest) Regulations 1990
SI 1990/2232	IT (Deposit-takers) (Interest Payments) Regulations 1990
SI 1990/2361	Tax-exempt Special Savings Account Regulations 1990
SI 1990/2529	Debts of Overseas Governments (Determination of Relevant Percentage) Regulations 1990
SI 1990/2546	*Life Assurance (Apportionment of Receipts of Participating Funds) (Applicable Percentage) (Amendment) Order 1990* (amend SI 1990/1541)
SI 1991/512	IT (Building Societies) (Annual Payments) Regulations 1991
SI 1991/733	*Personal Equity Plan (Amendment) Regulations 1991* (amend SI 1989/469)
SI 1991/889	*Taxes (Interest Rate) (Amendment) Regulations 1991* (amend SI 1989/1297)
SI 1991/1614	Retirement Benefits Schemes (Restriction on Discretion to Approve) (Small Self-administered Schemes) Regulations 1991
SI 1991/1997	*Companies Act 1989 (Eligibility for Appointment as Company Auditor) (Consequential Amendments) Regulations 1991* (amend SI 1985/994)
SI 1991/2774	*Personal Equity Plan (Amendment No 2) Regulations 1991* (amend SI 1989/469)
SI 1991/2808	*IT (Purchased Life Annuities) (Amendment) Regulations 1991* (amend SI 1956/1230)
SI 1992/10	IT (Building Societies) (Audit Powers) Regulations 1992
SI 1992/11	*IT (Building Societies) (Dividends and Interest) (Amendment) Regulations 1992* (amend SI 1990/2231)
SI 1992/12	IT (Deposit-takers) (Audit Powers) Regulations 1992
SI 1992/13	*IT (Deposit-takers) (Interest Payments) (Amendment) Regulations 1992* (amend SI 1990/2232)
SI 1992/14	IT (Deposit-takers) (Non-residents) Regulations 1992
SI 1992/15	IT (Interest Payments) (Information Powers) Regulations 1992
SI 1992/42	Taxes (Relief for Gifts) (Designated Educational Establishments) Regulations 1992
SI 1992/568	IT (Dealers in Securities) Regulations 1992
SI 1992/569	IT (Dividend Manufacturing) Regulations 1992 (revoked)
SI 1992/571	*IT (Definition of Unit Trust Scheme) (Amendment) Regulations 1992* (amend SI 1988/267)
SI 1992/623	*Personal Equity Plan (Amendment) Regulations 1992* (amend SI 1989/469)
SI 1992/734	*Vocational Training (Public Financial Assistance and Disentitlement to Tax Relief) Regulations 1992* (lapsed)
SI 1992/746	*Vocational Training (Tax Relief) Regulations 1992* (lapsed)
SI 1992/1311	*Transfer of Functions (National Heritage) Order 1992* (amend SI 1985/994)
SI 1992/1655	*Friendly Societies (Modification of the Corporation Tax Acts) Regulations 1992* (revoked)
SI 1992/2074	*IT (Manufactured Interest) Regulations 1992* (revoked)
SI 1992/2075	*Taxes (Interest Rate) (Amendment No 3) Regulations 1992* (amend SI 1989/1297)
SI 1992/2326	Insurance Companies (Pension Business) (Transitional Provisions) Regulations 1992
SI 1992/2744	IT (Insurance Companies) (Expenses of Management) Regulations 1992
SI 1992/2915	*IT (Building Societies) (Dividends and Interest) (Amendment No 2) Regulations 1992* (amend SI 1990/2231)
SI 1992/3066	Corporation Tax Acts (Provisions for Payment of Tax and Returns) (Appointed Days) Order 1992

SI Year/No	Title
SI 1992/3133	*IT (Definition of Unit Trust Scheme) (Amendment No 2) Regulations 1992* (amend SI 1988/267)
SI 1992/3234	IT (Prescribed Deposit-takers) Order 1992
SI 1993/561	*Taxes (Relief for Gifts) (Designated Educational Establishments) (Amendment) Regulations 1993* (amend SI 1992/42)
SI 1993/743	IT (Sub-contractors in the Construction Industry) Regulations 1993
SI 1993/744	IT (Employments) Regulations 1993
SI 1993/756	*Personal Equity Plan (Amendment) Regulations 1993* (amend SI 1989/469)
SI 1993/950	Capital Gains Tax (Gilt-edged Securities) Order 1993
SI 1993/1074	*Vocational Training (Public Financial Assistance and Disentitlement to Tax Relief) (Amendment) Regulations 1993 (amend SI 1992/734* (lapsed))
SI 1993/1082	*Vocational Training (Tax Relief) (Amendment) Regulations 1993* (amend SI 1992/746 (lapsed))
SI 1993/1623	*Debts of Overseas Governments (Determination of Relevant Percentage) (Amendment) Regulations 1993* (amend SI 1990/2529)
SI 1993/1957	Double Taxation Relief (Taxes on Income) (General) (Manufactured Overseas Dividends) Regulations 1993
SI 1993/2004	IT (Manufactured Overseas Dividends) Regulations 1993
SI 1993/2212	*Taxes (Interest Rate) (Amendment No 3) Regulations 1993* (amend SI 1989/1297)
SI 1993/2276	*IT (Employments) (Amendment) Regulations 1993* (amend SI 1993/744)
SI 1993/3016	Retirement Benefits Schemes (Restriction on Discretion to Approve) (Additional Voluntary Contributions) Regulations 1993
SI 1993/3109	*Insurance Companies (Pension Business) (Transitional Provisions) (Amendment) Regulations 1993* (amend SI 1992/2326)
SI 1993/3112	*Friendly Societies (Provisional Repayments for Exempt Business) Regulations 1993* (revoked)
SI 1993/3118	*Vocational Training (Tax Relief) (Amendment No 2) Regulations 1993* (amend SI 1992/746 (lapsed))
SI 1993/3219	*Occupational Pension Schemes (Transitional Provisions) (Amendment) Regulations 1993* (amend SI 1988/1436)
SI 1993/3220	*Retirement Benefits Schemes (Continuation of Rights of Members of Approved Schemes) (Amendment) Regulations 1993* (amend SI 1990/2101)
SI 1993/3221	*Retirement Benefits Schemes (Tax Relief on Contributions) (Disapplication of Earnings Cap) (Amendment) Regulations 1993* (amend SI 1990/586)
SI 1994/236	Distraint by Collectors (Fees, Costs and Charges) Regulations 1994
SI 1994/295	*IT (Deposit-takers) (Interest Payments) (Amendment) Regulations 1994* (amend SI 1990/2232)
SI 1994/296	*IT (Building Societies) (Dividends and Interest) (Amendment) Regulations 1994* (amend SI 1990/2231)
SI 1994/775	*IT (Employments) (Amendment) Regulations 1994* (amend SI 1993/744)
SI 1994/777	IT (Car Benefits) (Replacement Accessories) Regulations 1994 (revoked)
SI 1994/778	IT (Replacement Cars) Regulations 1994 (revoked)
SI 1994/1212	IT (Employments) (Notional Payments) Regulations 1994
SI 1994/1307	*Taxes (Interest Rate) (Amendment) Regulations 1994* (amend SI 1989/1297)
SI 1994/1479	*IT (Definition of Unit Trust Scheme) (Amendment) Regulations 1994* (amend SI 1988/267)
SI 1994/1518	Private Medical Insurance (Disentitlement to Tax Relief and Approved Benefits) Regulations 1994
SI 1994/1527	*Private Medical Insurance (Tax Relief) (Amendment) Regulations 1994* (amend SI 1989/2387)
SI 1994/1567	*Taxes (Interest Rate) (Amendment No 2) Regulations 1994* (amend SI 1989/1297)
SI 1994/1811	Special Commissioners (Jurisdiction and Procedure) Regulations 1994
SI 1994/1812	General Commissioners (Jurisdiction and Procedure) Regulations 1994
SI 1994/1813	*General and Special Commissioners (Amendment of Enactments) Regulations 1994* (amend SI 1967/149, SI 1993/744)
SI 1994/2318	IT (Authorised Unit Trusts) (Interest Distributions) Regulations 1994
SI 1994/2656	Capital Gains Tax (Gilt-edged Securities) Order 1994
SI 1994/3036	*Insurance Companies (Pension Business) (Transitional Provisions) (Amendment) Regulations 1994* (amend SI 1992/2326)
SI 1994/3226	Exchange Gains and Losses (Transitional Provisions) Regulations 1994
SI 1994/3227	Exchange Gains and Losses (Alternative Method of Calculation of Gain or Loss) Regulations 1994
SI 1994/3228	Exchange Gains and Losses (Deferral of Gains and Losses) Regulations 1994
SI 1994/3229	Exchange Gains and Losses (Excess Gains and Losses) Regulations 1994
SI 1994/3230	Local Currency Elections Regulations 1994
SI 1994/3231	Exchange Gains and Losses (Insurance Companies) Regulations 1994

SI Year/No	Title
SI 1994/3232	*Exchange Gains and Losses (Debts of Varying Amounts) Regulations 1994* (insert FA 1993 s 136A)
SI 1994/3233	*Currency Contracts and Options (Amendment of Enactments) Order 1994* (amends FA 1993 s 126, FA 1994 s 150)
SI 1994/3278	*Overseas Life Assurance Fund (Amendment) Order 1994* (amends TA 1988 Sch 19AA)
SI 1995/171	*Friendly Societies (Taxation of Transfers of Business) Regulations 1995* (revoked)
SI 1995/351	Lloyd's Underwriters (Tax) Regulations 1995
SI 1995/352	*Lloyd's Underwriters (Tax) (1992–93 to 1996–97) Regulations 1995* (spent)
SI 1995/353	Lloyd's Underwriters (Special Reserve Fund) Regulations 1995
SI 1995/408	*Exchange Gains and Losses (Transitional Provisions) (Amendment) Regulations 1995* (amend SI 1994/3226)
SI 1995/447	*IT (Employments) (Amendment No 2) Regulations 1995* (amend SI 1993/744)
SI 1995/448	*IT (Sub-contractors in the Construction Industry) (Amendment No 2) Regulations 1995* (amend SI 1993/743)
SI 1995/853	*IT (Employments) (Incapacity Benefit) Regulations 1995* (amend SI 1993/744)
SI 1995/917	Profit-Related Pay (Shortfall Recovery) Regulation 1995
SI 1995/1184	*IT (Building Societies) (Dividends and Interest) (Amendment) Regulations 1995* (amend SI 1990/2231)
SI 1995/1185	*Lloyd's Underwriters (Special Reserve Funds) (Amendment) Regulations 1995* (amend SI 1995/353)
SI 1995/1211	*Life Assurance (Apportionment of Receipts of Participating Funds) (Applicable Percentage) (Amendment) Order 1995* (amend SI 1990/1541)
SI 1995/1212	*IT (Interest Relief) (Housing Associations) (Amendment) Regulations 1995* (amend SI 1988/1347)
SI 1995/1213	*IT (Interest Relief) (Amendment) Regulations 1995* (amend SI 1982/1236)
SI 1995/1223	*IT (Employments) (Amendment No 3) Regulations 1995* (amend SI 1993/744)
SI 1995/1284	*IT (Employments) (Amendment No 4) Regulations 1995* (amend SI 1993/744)
SI 1995/1324	*IT (Manufactured Overseas Dividends) (Amendment) Regulations 1995* (amend SI 1993/2004)
SI 1995/1370	Deposit-takers (Interest Payments) (Discretionary or Accumulation Trusts) Regulations 1995
SI 1995/1539	*Personal Equity Plan (Amendment) Regulations 1995* (amend SI 1989/469)
SI 1995/1551	*Double Taxation Relief (Manufactured Overseas Dividends) (Amendment) Regulations 1995* (amend SI 1993/1957)
SI 1995/1730	Insurance Companies (Taxation of Reinsurance Business) Regulations 1995
SI 1995/1929	*Tax-exempt Special Savings Account (Amendment) Regulations 1995* (amend SI 1990/2361)
SI 1995/1979	Venture Capital Trust Regulations 1995
SI 1995/2050	IT (Dealers in Securities) (Tradepoint) Regulations 1995
SI 1995/2052	*IT (Manufactured Dividends) (Tradepoint) Regulations 1995* (revoked)
SI 1995/2151	*Distraint by Collectors (Fees, Costs and Charges) (Amendment) Regulations 1995* (amend SI 1994/236)
SI 1995/2902	Taxation of Income from Land (Non-residents) Regulations 1995
SI 1995/2934	IT (Gilt-edged Securities) (Gross Payments of Interest) Regulations 1995
SI 1995/3036	Manufactured Payments and Transfer of Securities (Tax Relief) Regulations 1995
SI 1995/3103	Retirement Benefits Schemes (Information Powers) Regulations 1995
SI 1995/3134	*Insurance Companies (Pension Business) (Transitional Provisions) (Amendment) Regulations 1995* (amend SI 1992/2326)
SI 1995/3192	Retirement Age of General Commissioners Order 1995
SI 1995/3220	Sale and Repurchase of Securities (Modification of Enactments) Regulations 1995
SI 1995/3224	Gilt-edged Securities (Periodic Accounting for Tax on Interest) Regulations 1995
SI 1995/3225	Lloyd's Underwriters (Gilt-edged Securities) (Periodic Accounting for Tax on Interest) Regulations 1995
SI 1995/3237	Insurance Companies (Overseas Life Assurance Business) (Compliance) Regulations 1995
SI 1995/3238	Insurance Companies (Overseas Life Assurance Business) (Tax Credit) Regulations 1995
SI 1995/3239	Tax-exempt Special Savings Account (Relevant European Institutions) Regulations 1995
SI 1995/3274	*Vocational Training (Public Financial Assistance and Disentitlement to Tax Relief) (Amendment) Regulations 1995* (amend SI 1992/734 (lapsed))

SI Year/No	Title
SI 1995/3287	*Personal Equity Plan (Amendment No 2) Regulations 1995* (amend SI 1989/469)
SI 1996/1	*Insurance Companies (Pension Business) (Transitional Provisions) (Amendment) Regulations 1996* (amend SI 1992/2326)
SI 1996/223	*IT (Building Societies) (Dividends and Interest) (Amendment) Regulations 1996* (amend SI 1990/2231)
SI 1996/673	*Exchange Gains and Losses (Insurance Companies) (Amendment) Regulations 1996* (amend SI 1994/3231)
SI 1996/781	*Lloyd's Underwriters (Tax) (Amendment) Regulations 1996* (amend SI 1995/351)
SI 1996/782	*Lloyd's Underwriters (Tax) (1992–93 to 1996–97) (Amendment) Regulations 1996* (amend SI 1995/352 (spent))
SI 1996/783	*Double Taxation Relief (Taxes on Income) (General) (Amendment) Regulations 1996* (amend SI 1970/488)
SI 1996/804	*IT (Employments) (Amendment) Regulations 1996* (amend SI 1993/744)
SI 1996/805	Personal Pension Schemes (Deferred Annuity Purchase) (Acceptance of Contributions) Regulations 1996
SI 1996/844	*Tax-exempt Special Savings Account (Amendment) Regulations 1996* (amend SI 1990/2361)
SI 1996/846	*Personal Equity Plan (Amendment) Regulations 1996* (amend SI 1989/469)
SI 1996/980	*IT (Employments) (Amendment No 2) Regulations 1996* (amend SI 1993/744)
SI 1996/981	*IT (Sub-contractors in the Construction Industry) (Amendment) Regulations 1996* (amend SI 1993/743)
SI 1996/1014	*Lloyd's Underwriters (Gilt-edged Securities) (Periodic Accounting for Tax on Interest) (Amendment) Regulations 1996* (amend SI 1995/3225)
SI 1996/1015	*Gilt-edged Securities (Periodic Accounting for Tax on Interest) (Amendment) Regulations 1996* (amend SI 1995/3224)
SI 1996/1031	Capital Gains Tax (Gilt-edged Securities) Order 1996
SI 1996/1179	European Investment Bank (Designated International Organisation) Order 1996
SI 1996/1181	*Gilt-edged Securities (Periodic Accounting for Tax on Interest) (Amendment No 2) Regulations 1996* (amend SI 1995/3224)
SI 1996/1182	*Lloyd's Underwriters (Gilt-edged Securities) (Periodic Accounting for Tax on Interest) (Amendment No 2) Regulations 1996* (amend SI 1995/3225)
SI 1996/1184	*Income Tax (Interest Relief) (Amendment) Regulations 1996* (amend SI 1982/1236)
SI 1996/1185	*Vocational Training (Tax Relief) (Amendment) Regulations 1996* (amend SI 1992/746 (lapsed))
SI 1996/1229	*Income Tax (Manufactured Overseas Dividends) (Amendment) Regulations 1996* (amend SI 1993/2004)
SI 1996/1311	Personal Pension Schemes (Tables of Rates of Annuities) Regulations 1996
SI 1996/1312	*Income Tax (Employments) (Amendment No 3) Regulations 1996* (amend SI 1993/744)
SI 1996/1323	Capital Allowances Act 1990, section 33A, (Appointed Day) Order 1996
SI 1996/1347	*Exchange Gains and Losses (Alternative Method of Calculation of Gain or Loss) (Amendment) Regulations 1996* (amend SI 1994/3227)
SI 1996/1348	*Exchange Gains and Losses (Deferral of Gains and Losses) (Amendment) Regulations 1996* (amend SI 1994/3228)
SI 1996/1349	*Exchange Gains and Losses (Transitional Provisions) (Amendment) Regulations 1996* (amend SI 1994/3226)
SI 1996/1355	*Personal Equity Plan (Amendment No 2) Regulations 1996* (amend SI 1989/469)
SI 1996/1485	*Exchange Gains and Losses (Insurance Companies) (Amendment No 2) Regulations 1996* (amend SI 1994/3231)
SI 1996/1582	Retirement Benefits Schemes (Restriction on Discretion to Approve) (Excepted Schemes) Regulations 1996
SI 1996/1583	Capital Gains Tax (Pension Funds Pooling Schemes) Regulations 1996
SI 1996/1585	Income Tax (Pension Funds Pooling Schemes) Regulations 1996
SI 1996/1621	*Insurance Companies (Taxation of Reinsurance Business) (Amendment) Regulations 1996* (amend SI 1995/1730)
SI 1996/1654	Income Tax (Payments on Account) Regulations 1996
SI 1996/1780	*Income Tax (Paying and Collecting Agents) Regulations 1996* (lapsed)
SI 1996/1826	Manufactured Overseas Dividends (French Indemnity Payments) Regulations 1996
SI 1996/2381	*Income Tax (Employments) (Amendment No 4) Regulations 1996* (amend SI 1993/744)
SI 1996/2396	Taxation of Benefits under Pilot Schemes (Earnings Top-up) Order 1996

SI Year/No	Title
SI 1996/2645	Income and Corporation Taxes Act 1988, section 737A, (Appointed Day) Order 1996
SI 1996/2554	*Income Tax (Employments) (Amendment No 5) Regulations 1996* (amend SI 1993/744)
SI 1996/2616	*Income Tax (Interest Relief) (Housing Associations) (Amendment) Regulations 1996* (amend SI 1988/1347)
SI 1996/2631	*Income Tax (Employments) (Amendment No 6) Regulations 1996* (amend SI 1993/744)
SI 1996/2642	*Manufactured Overseas Dividends (French Indemnity Payments) (Amendment) Regulations 1996* (amend SI 1996/1826)
SI 1996/2643	*Income Tax (Manufactured Overseas Dividends) (Amendment No 2) Regulations 1996* (amend SI 1993/2004)
SI 1996/2645	*Income and Corporation Taxes Act 1988, section 737A (Appointed Day) Order 1996* (*see* TA 1988 s 737A)
SI 1996/2646	*Finance Act 1996, section 159, (Appointed Day) Order* (*see* FA 1996 s 159)
SI 1996/2654	*Double Taxation Relief (Manufactured Overseas Dividends) (Amendment) Regulations 1996* (amend SI 1993/1957)
SI 1996/2953	*Income Tax (Furnished Accommodation) (Basic Amount) Order 1996* (*see* F(No 2)A 1992 Sch 10 para 6)
SI 1996/2969	*Income Tax (Employments) (Notional Payments) (Amendment) Regulations 1996* (amend SI 1994/1212)
SI 1996/2991	Insurance Companies (Reserves) (Tax) Regulations 1996
SI 1996/3049	*Vocational Training (Public Financial Assistance and Disentitlement to Tax Relief) (Amendment) Regulations 1996* (amend SI 1992/734 (lapsed))
SI 1996/3113	*Retirement Benefits Schemes (Tax Relief on Contributions) (Disapplication of Earnings Cap) (Amendment) Regulations 1996* (amend SI 1990/586)
SI 1996/3114	*Retirement Benefit Schemes (Continuation of Rights of Members of Approved Schemes) (Amendment) Regulations 1996* (amend SI 1990/2101)
SI 1996/3115	*Occupational Pension Schemes (Transitional Provisions) (Amendment) Regulations 1996* (amend SI 1988/1436)
SI 1996/3187	*Taxes (Interest Rate) (Amendment No 4) Regulations 1996* (amend SI 1989/1297)
SI 1996/3233	*Retirement Benefit Schemes (Continuation of Rights of Members of Approved Schemes) (Amendment No 2) Regulations 1996* (amend SI 1990/2101)
SI 1996/3234	*Occupational Pension Schemes (Transitional Provisions) (Amendment No 2) Regulations 1996* (amend SI 1988/1436)
SI 1997/57	Electronic Lodgement of Tax Returns Order 1997
SI 1997/133	Finance Act 1996, Schedule 35, (Appointed Day) Order 1997
SI 1997/168	International Organisations (Miscellaneous Exemptions) Order 1997
SI 1997/212	*Authorised Unit Trusts (Interest Distributions) (Qualifying Investments) Order 1997* (amends TA 1988 s 468L)
SI 1997/213	*Unit Trust Schemes and Offshore Funds (Non-qualifying Investments Test) Order 1997* (amends FA 1996 Sch 10 para 8)
SI 1997/214	*Income Tax (Employments) (Amendment) Regulations 1997* (amend SI 1993/744)
SI 1997/265	Life Assurance and Other Policies (Keeping of Information and Duties of Insurers) Regulations 1997
SI 1997/405	Lloyd's Underwriters (Double Taxation Relief) Regulations 1997
SI 1997/473	Friendly Societies (Modification of the Corporation Tax Acts) Regulations 1997
SI 1997/474	*Friendly Societies (Provisional Repayments for Exempt Business) (Amendment) Regulations 1997* (amend SI 1993/3112, now revoked)
SI 1997/480	*Personal Pension Schemes (Transfer Payments) (Amendment) Regulations 1997* (amend SI 1988/1014) (revoked)
SI 1997/481	*Insurance Companies (Overseas Life Assurance Business) (Compliance) (Amendment) Regulations 1997* (amend SI 1995/3237)
SI 1997/511	*Personal Equity Plan (Amendment) Regulations 1997* (amend SI 1989/469)
SI 1997/635	*Vocational Training (Public Financial Assistance and Disentitlement to Tax Relief) (Amendment) Regulations 1997* (amend SI 1992/734 (lapsed))
SI 1997/661	*Vocational Training (Tax Relief) (Amendment) Regulations 1997* (amend SI 1992/746 (lapsed))
SI 1997/987	*Stock Lending and Manufactured Payments (Revocations and Amendments) Regulations 1997* (revoke/amend numerous Statutory Instruments)
SI 1997/988	*Income Tax (Manufactured Overseas Dividends) (Amendment) Regulations 1997* (amend SI 1993/2004)
SI 1997/991	Finance Act 1997, Schedule 10, (Appointed Day) Order 1997
SI 1997/992	Manufactured Interest (Tax) Regulations 1997
SI 1997/993	Manufactured Dividends (Tax) Regulations 1997

SI Year/No	Title
SI 1997/1154	Open-ended Investment Companies (Tax) Regulations 1997
SI 1997/1155	*Exchange Gains and Losses (Insurance Companies) (Amendment) Regulations 1997* (amend SI 1994/3231)
SI 1997/1158	Income Tax (Schedule 22 to the Finance Act 1995) (Prescribed Amounts) Regulations 1997
SI 1997/1603	*Finance Act 1997, Section 110, (Appointed Day) Order 1997* (*see* FA 1997 s 110)
SI 1997/1681	*Taxes (Interest Rate) (Amendment) Regulations 1997* (amend SI 1989/1297)
SI 1997/1715	*Open-ended Investment Companies (Tax) (Amendment) Regulations 1997* (amend SI 1997/1154)
SI 1997/1716	*Personal Equity Plan (Amendment No 2) Regulations 1997* (amend SI 1989/469)
SI 1997/2388	*Personal Pension Schemes (Establishment of Schemes) Order 1997* (amends TA 1988 s 632)
SI 1997/2491	*Income Tax (Payments on Account) (Amendment) Regulations 1997* (amend SI 1996/1654)
SI 1997/2668	*Building Societies Act 1997 (Commencement No 3) Order 1997* (see TA 1988 Sch 12(2))
SI 1997/2681	Lloyd's Underwriters (Scottish Limited Partnerships) (Tax) 1997
SI 1997/2706	*Income Tax (Manufactured Overseas Dividends) (Amendment No 2) Regulations 1997* (amend SI 1993/2004)
SI 1997/2707	*Taxes (Interest Rate) (Amendment No 2) Regulations 1997* (amend SI 1989/1297)
SI 1997/2708	Finance Act 1989 Section 178(1) (Appointed Day) Order 1997
SI 1997/2781	Transfer of Functions (Insurance) Order 1997 (amends TA 1998 s 431(2))
SI 1997/2865	*Insurance Companies (Pension Business) (Transitional Provisions) (Amendment) Regulations 1997* (amend SI 1992/2326)
SI 1997/2877	*Friendly Societies (Modification of the Corporation Tax Acts) (Amendment No 2) Regulations 1997* (amend SI 1997/473)
SI 1998/311	Finance Act 1989 Section 178(1) (Appointed Day) Order 1998
SI 1998/354	*Police Act 1997 (Commencement No 5 and Transitional Provisions) Order 1998* (*see* TA 1988 s 842A)
SI 1998/728	*Retirement Benefits Schemes (Restriction on Discretion to Approve) (Small Self-administered Schemes) (Amendment) Regulations 1998* (amend SI 1991/1614)
SI 1998/729	Retirement Benefits Schemes (Restriction on Discretion to Approve) (Excepted Provisions) Regulations 1998
SI 1998/1315	*Retirement Benefits Schemes (Restriction on Discretion to Approve) (Small Self-administered Schemes) (Amendment No 2) Regulations 1998* (amend SI 1991/1614)
SI 1998/1513	Visiting Forces and Allied Headquarters (Income Tax and Capital Gains Tax) (Designation) Order
SI 1998/1514	Visiting Forces (Income Tax and Capital Gains Tax) (Designation) Order
SI 1998/1868	Gifts for Relief in Poor Countries (Designation) Order 1998
SI 1998/1869	*Personal Equity Plan (Amendment) Regulations 1998* (amend SI 1989/469)
SI 1998/1870	Individual Savings Account Regulations 1998
SI 1998/1871	*Individual Savings Account (Insurance Companies) Regulations 1998* (amend SI 1995/3036 and SI 1997/473)
SI 1998/1872	*Insurance Companies (Overseas Life Assurance Business) (Compliance) (Amendment) Regulations 1998* (amend SI 1995/3237)
SI 1998/1891	*Income Tax (Employments) (Notional Payments) (Amendment) Regulations 1998* (amend SI 1994/1212)
SI 1998/2484	*Income Tax (Employments) (Amendment) Regulations 1998* (amend SI 1993/744)
SI 1998/2620	Finance Act 1995, Section 139(3), (Appointed Day) Order 1998
SI 1998/2622	*Income Tax (Sub-contractors in the Construction Industry) (Amendment) Regulations 1998* (amend SI 1993/743)
SI 1998/3081	Controlled Foreign Companies (Excluded Countries) Regulations 1998
SI 1998/3132	Civil Procedure Rules 1998 (Orders 53, 55, 77 and 91 only)
SI 1998/3173	Finance Act 1994, Section 199, (Appointed Day) Order 1998
SI 1998/3174	*Individual Savings Account (Amendment) Regulations 1998* (amend SI 1998/1870 and SI 1998/1871)
SI 1998/3175	Corporation Tax (Instalment Payments) Regulations 1998
SI 1998/3176	*Taxes (Interest Rate) (Amendment No 2) Regulations 1998* (amend SI 1989/1297)
SI 1998/3177	European Single Currency (Taxes) Regulations 1998
SI 1998/3178	Scotland Act 1998 (Commencement) Order 1998

SI Year/No	Title
SI 1999/70	*Income Tax (Employments) (Amendment) Regulations 1999* (amend SI 1993/744)
SI 1999/358	Corporation Tax (Treatment of Unrelieved Surplus Advance Corporation Tax) Regulations 1999
SI 1999/418	*Social Security Act 1998 (Commencement No 3) Order 1999* (*see* TA 1988 s 172)
SI 1999/419	*Taxes (Interest Rate) (Amendment) Regulations 1999* (amend SI 1989/1297)
SI 1999/498	Insurance Companies (Capital Redemption Business) (Modification of the Corporation Tax Acts) Regulations 1999
SI 1999/564	Finance Act 1993, Section 86(2), (Fish Quota) Order 1999
SI 1999/597	*Income Tax (Indexation) Order 1999* (*see* TA 1988 ss 1, 257, 257A, 265(1))
SI 1999/619	Finance Act 1998, Section 37, (Appointed Day) Order 1999
SI 1999/620	*Gilt-edged Securities (Periodic Accounting for Tax on Interest) (Amendment) Regulations 1999* (amend SI 1995/3224)
SI 1999/621	*Manufactured Dividends (Tax) Amendment Regulations 1999* (amend SI 1997/993)
SI 1999/622	Friendly Societies (Provisional Repayments for Exempt Business) Regulations 1999
SI 1999/623	Insurance Companies (Gilt-edged Securities) (Periodic Accounting for Tax on Interest) Regulations 1999
SI 1999/624	Friendly Societies (Gilt-edged Securities) (Periodic Accounting for Tax on Interest) Regulations 1999
SI 1999/819	*Venture Capital Trusts (Amendment) Regulations 1999* (amends SI 1995/1979)
SI 1999/824	*Income Tax (Employments) (Amendment No 2) Regulations 1999* (amend SI 1993/744)
SI 1999/825	*Income Tax (Sub-contractors in the Construction Industry) (Amendment) Regulations 1999* (amend SI 1993/743)
SI 1999/881	Overseas Insurers (Tax Representatives) Regulations 1999
SI 1999/1029	Personal Portfolio Bonds (Tax) Regulations 1999
SI 1999/1408	Non-resident Companies (General Insurance Business) Regulations 1999
SI 1999/1643	*Insurance Companies (Loan Relationships) (Election for Accruals Basis) Order 1999* (amends FA 1996 Sch 11 para 5(6))
SI 1999/1927	*Double Taxation Relief (Taxes on Income) General (Dividend) (Revocation) Regulations 1999* (revoke SI 1973/317)
SI 1999/1928	*Taxes (Interest Rate) (Amendment No 2) Regulations 1999* (amend SI 1989/1297)
SI 1999/1929	*Corporation Tax (Instalment Payments) (Amendment) Regulations 1999* (amend SI 1998/3175)
SI 1999/1953	*Capital Gains Tax (Definition of Permanent Interest Bearing Share) Regulations 1999* (amend TCGA 1992 s 117)
SI 1999/1963	*Retirement Benefits Schemes (Continuation of Rights of Members of Approved Schemes) (Amendment) Regulations 1999* (amend SI 1990/2101)
SI 1999/1964	*Retirement Benefits Schemes (Restriction on Discretion to Approve) (Additional Voluntary Contributions) (Amendment) Regulations 1999* (amend SI 1993/3106)
SI 1999/2118	Gifts for Relief in Poor Countries (Designation of Kosovo) Order 1999
SI 1999/2119	Finance Act 1998, Section 83(1), (Appointed Day) Order 1999
SI 1999/2155	*Income Tax (Employments) (Amendment No 3) Regulations 1999* (amend SI 1993/744)
SI 1999/2156	Finance Act 1995, Section 139(3), (Appointed Day) Order 1999
SI 1999/2159	*Income Tax (Sub-contractors in the Construction Industry) (Amendment No 2) Regulations 1999* (amend SI 1993/743)
SI 1999/2224	*Films (Certification) (Amendment) Regulations 1999* (amend SI 1985/994)
SI 1999/2334	*Films (Certification) (Amendment) (No 2) Regulations 1999* (amend SI 1985/994)
SI 1999/2386	*Films (Modification of the Definition of ''British Film'') Order 1999* (*see* Film Act 1985 Sch 1)
SI 1999/2538	*Taxes (Interest Rate) (Amendment No 3) Regulations 1999* (amend SI 1989/1297)
SI 1999/2636	*Friendly Societies (modification of the Corporation Tax Acts) (Amendment) Regulations 1999* (amend SI 1997/473)
SI 1999/2637	*Taxes (Interest Rate) (Amendment No 4) Regulations 1999* (amend SI 1989/1297)
SI 1999/2839	*Insurance Companies (Overseas Life Assurance Business) (Compliance) (Amendment) Regulations 1999* (amend SI 1995/3237)
SI 1999/2975	Corporation Tax (Simplified Arrangements for Group Relief) Regulations 1999

SI Year/No	Title
SI 1999/3038	*Income Tax (Indexation) (No 2) Order 1999* (*see* TA 1988 s 257)
SI 1999/3292	*Special Commissioners (Jurisdiction and Procedure) (Amendment) Regulations 1999* (amend SI 1994/1811)
SI 1999/3293	*General Commissioners (Jurisdiction and Procedure) (Amendment) Regulations 1999* (amend SI 1994/1812)
SI 1999/3308	Lloyd's Underwriters (Special Reserve Funds) Regulations 1999
SI 1999/3309	*Welfare Reform and Pensions Act 1999 (Commencement No 1) Order 1999* (not reproduced)
SI 1999/3330	DTR (Taxes on Income) (Foreign Interest and Dividends) Regulations 1999
SI 1999/3420	Welfare Reform and Pensions Act 1999 (Commencement No 2) Order 1999
SI 2000/221	*Civil Procedure (Amendment) Rules 2000* (amend SI 1998/3132)
SI 2000/288	*Special Commissioners (Jurisdiction and Procedure) (Amendment) Regulations 2000* (amend SI 1994/1811)
SI 2000/600	Income Tax (Charge to Tax) (Payments out of Surplus Funds) (Relevant Rate) Order 2000
SI 2000/629	*Welfare Reform and Pensions Act 1999 (Commencement No 3) Order 2000* (not reproduced)
SI 2000/756	*Films (Modification of the Definition of ''British Film'') Order 2000* (*see* Film Act 1985 Sch 1)
SI 2000/759	*Charitable Deductions (Approved Schemes) (Amendment) Regulations 2000* (amend SI 1986/2211)
SI 2000/806	*Income Tax (Indexation) Order 2000* (*see* TA 1988 ss 1, 257, 257A, 265(1))
SI 2000/807	*Retirement Benefits Schemes (Indexation of Earnings Cap) Order 2000* (*see* TA 1988 s 590C)
SI 2000/808	*Capital Gains Tax (Annual Exempt Amount) Order 2000* (*see* TCGA 1992 s 3)
SI 2000/809	*Individual Savings Account (Amendment) Regulations 2000* (amend SI 1998/1870)
SI 2000/810	*Income Tax (Cash Equivalents of Car Fuel Benefits) Order 2000* (amends TA 1988 s 158(2))
SI 2000/892	*Corporation Tax (Instalment Payments) (Amendment) Regulations 2000* (amend SI 1998/3175)
SI 2000/893	*Taxes (Interest Rate) (Amendment) Regulations 2000* (amend SI 1989/1297)
SI 2000/921	Income and Corporation Taxes Act 1988, Section 559(4A), Order 2000
SI 2000/922	Finance Act 1995, Section 139(3), (Appointed Day) Order 2000
SI 2000/944	Education (Student Loans) (Repayment) Regulations 2000
SI 2000/945	Income Tax (Electronic Communications) Regulations 2000
SI 2000/1047	*Welfare Reform and Pensions Act 1999 (Commencement No 4) Order 2000* (not reproduced)
SI 2000/1085	Retirement Benefits Schemes (Sharing of Pensions on Divorce or Annulment) Regulations 2000
SI 2000/1086	*Retirement Benefits Schemes (Restriction on Discretion to Approve) (Small Self-administered Schemes) (Amendment) Regulations 2000* (amend SI 1991/1614)
SI 2000/1087	Retirement Benefits Schemes (Restriction on Discretion to Approve) (Excepted Provisions) Regulations 2000
SI 2000/1088	*Retirement Benefits Schemes (Restriction on Discretion to Approve) (Additional Voluntary Contributions) Regulations 2000* (amend SI 1993/3016)
SI 2000/1093	Finance Act 1999, Schedule 10, Paragraph 18, (First and Second Appointed Days) Order 2000
SI 2000/1116	*Welfare Reform and Pensions Act 1999 (Commencement No 5) Order 2000* (not reproduced)
SI 2000/1151	*Income Tax (Sub-contractors in the Construction Industry) (Amendment) Regulations 2000* (amend SI 1993/743)
SI 2000/1152	*Income Tax (Employments) (Amendment) Regulations 2000* (amend SI 1993/744)
SI 2000/1382	*Welfare Reform and Pensions Act 1999 (Commencement No 7) Order 2000* (not reproduced)
SI 2000/1880	*Income Tax (Sub-contractors in the Construction Industry) (Amendment No 2) Regulations 2000* (amend SI 1993/743)
SI 2000/1973	*Pollution Prevention and Control (England and Wales) Regulations 2000* (amend ICTA 1988 s 91A)
SI 2000/2004	Finance Act 1999, Section 59(3)(*b*), (Appointed Day) Order 2000
SI 2000/2074	Donations to Charity by Individuals (Appropriate Declarations) Regulations 2000
SI 2000/2075	*Individual Savings Account (Insurance Companies) (Amendment) Regulations 2000* (amend SI 1998/1871)

SI Year/No	Title
SI 2000/2076	Individual Learning Accounts (Separate Employers Under the Crown) Regulations 2000
SI 2000/2079	*Individual Savings Account (Amendment No 2) Regulations 2000* (amend SI 1998/1870)
SI 2000/2080	Income Tax (Benefits in Kind) (Exemption for Welfare Counselling) Regulations 2000
SI 2000/2081	*Research and Development (Prescribed Activities) Regulations 2000* (revoked)
SI 2000/2082	Finance Act 2000, Section 108(3), (Appointed Day) Order 2000
SI 2000/2083	Charitable Deductions (Approved Schemes) (Amendment No 2) Regulations 2000
SI 2000/2089	Insurance Companies (Overseas Life Assurance Business) (Excluded Business) Regulations 2000
SI 2000/2090	Employee Share Ownership Plans (Partnership Shares—Notice of Effects on Benefits, Statutory Sick Pay and Statutory Maternity Pay) Regulations 2000
SI 2000/2104	*Insurance Companies (Overseas Life Assurance Business) (Compliance) (Amendment) Regulations 2000* (amend 1995/3237)
SI 2000/2129	Tonnage Tax (Training Requirement) Regulations 2000
SI 2000/2188	*Overseas Life Assurance Fund (Amendment) Order 2000* (amends TA 1988 Sch 19AA)
SI 2000/2303	Tonnage Tax Regulations 2000
SI 2000/2314	Personal Pension Schemes (Restriction on Discretion to Approve) (Establishment of Schemes under Trusts) Regulations 2000
SI 2000/2315	*Personal Pension Schemes (Relief at Source) (Amendment) Regulations 2000* (amend SI 1988/1013)
SI 2000/2316	Personal Pension Schemes (Information Powers) Regulations 2000
SI 2000/2317	*Personal Pension Schemes (Establishment of Schemes) Regulations 2000* (amends TA 1988 s 632)
SI 2000/2318	Personal Pension Schemes (Concurrent Membership) Order 2000
SI 2000/2319	Finance Act 1998, Section 96(4), (Appointed Day) Order 2000
SI 2000/2550	*Capital Gains Tax (Definition of Unit Trust Scheme) (Amendment) Regulations 2000* (amend SI 1988/266)
SI 2000/2551	*Income Tax (Definition of Unit Trust Scheme) (Amendment) Regulations 2000* (amend SI 1988/267)
SI 2000/2710	Friendly Societies (Modification of the Corporation Tax Acts) (Amendment) Regulations 2000 (amend SI 1997/473)
SI 2000/2742	Income Tax (Sub-contractors in the Construction Industry and Employments) (Amendment) Regulations 2000 (amend SI 1993/743, 744)
SI 2000/2875	Orders for the Delivery of Documents (Procedure) Regulations 2000
SI 2000/2958	Welfare Reform and Pensions Act 1999 (Commencement No 9, and Transitional and Savings Provisions) Order 2000 (not reproduced)
SI 2000/2996	Income Tax (Indexation) (No 2) Order 2000 (see TA 1988 ss 257, 257A)
SI 2000/3109	Personal Equity Plan (Amendment) Regulations 2000 (amend SI 1989/469)
SI 2000/3112	Individual Savings Account (Amendment No 3) Regulations 2000 (amend SI 1998/1870)
SI 2000/3158	Controlled Foreign Companies (Designer Rate Tax Provisions) Regulations 2000
SI 2000/3228	Corporation Tax (Simplified Arrangements for Group Relief) (Amendment) Regulations 2000 (amend SI 1999/2975)
SI 2000/3315	Exchange Gains and Losses (Miscellaneous Modifications) Regulations 2000
SI 2001/56	Income Tax (Electronic Communications) (Incentive Payments) Regulations 2001
SI 2001/117	Personal Pension Schemes (Restriction on Discretion to Approve) (Permitted Investments) Regulations 2001
SI 2001/118	Personal Pension Schemes (Conversion of Retirement Benefits Schemes) Regulations 2001
SI 2001/119	Personal Pension Schemes (Transfer Payments) Regulations 2001
SI 2001/204	Taxes (Interest Rate) (Amendment No 1) Regulations 2001 (amend SI 1989/1297)
SI 2001/253	Finance Act 1989, Section 178(1), (Appointed Day) Order 2001
SI 2001/254	Taxes (Interest Rate) (Amendment No 2) Regulations 2001 (amend SI 1989/1297)
SI 2001/391	Investment Trusts (Approval of Accounting Methods for Creditor Relationships) Order 2001
SI 2001/403	IT (Manufactured Overseas Dividends) (Amendment) Regulations 2001 (amend SI 1993/2004)

SI Year/No	Title
SI 2001/404	IT (Building Societies) (Dividends and Interest) (Amendment) Regulations 2001 (amend SI 1990/2231)
SI 2001/405	IT (Interest Payments) (Information Powers) (Amendment) Regulations 2001 (amend SI 1992/15)
SI 2001/406	IT (Deposit-takers) (Interest Payments) (Amendment) Regulations 2001 (amend SI 1990/2232)
SI 2001/635	Income Tax (Cash Equivalents of Car Fuel Benefits) Order 2001 (amends TA 1988 s 158(2))
SI 2001/636	Capital Gains Tax (Annual Exempt Amount) Order 2001 (see TCGA 1992 s 3)
SI 2001/637	Retirement Benefits Schemes (Indexation of Earnings Cap) Order 2001 (see TA 1988 s 590C)
SI 2001/638	*Income Tax (Indexation) Order 2001* (see TA 1988 ss 1, 265(1))
SI 2001/908	Individual Savings Account (Amendment) Regulations 2001 (amend SI 1998/1870)
SI 2001/923	Personal Equity Plan (Amendment) Regulations (amend SI 1989/469)
SI 2001/1081	Income Tax (Electronic Communications) (Miscellaneous Amendments) Regulations (amend SI 2000/945 and SI 2001/56)
SI 2001/1122	Capital Gains Tax (Gilt-edged Securities) Order 2001
SI 2001/1123	Income Tax (Car Benefits) (Reduction of Value of Appropriate Percentage) Regulations 2001
SI 2001/1149	Postal Services Act 2000 (Consequential Modifications No 1) Order, SI 2001/1149 (amends TA 1988 ss 376, 481)
SI 2001/1156	Double Taxation Relief (Taxes on Income) (Underlying Tax on Dividends and Dual Resident Companies) Regulations 2001
SI 2001/1163	Double Taxation Relief (Surrender of Relievable Tax Within a Group) Regulations 2001
SI 2001/1304	General Commissioners of Income Tax (Costs) Regulations 2001
SI 2001/1531	Income Tax (Sub-contractors in the Construction Industry) (Amendment) Regulations 2001 (amend SI 1993/743)
SI 2001/1757	General Insurance Reserves (Tax) Regulations 2001
SI 2001/2541	Capital Allowances (Energy-saving Plant and Machinery) Order 2001
SI 2001/2724	Personal Portfolio Bonds (Tax) (Amendment) Regulations 2001 (amend SI 1999/1029)
SI 2001/2726	Overseas Insurers (Tax Representatives) (Amendment) Regulations 2001 (amend SI 1999/881)
SI 2001/3500	*Transfer of Functions (Miscellaneous) Order 2001* (amends the Human Rights Act 1998)
SI 2001/3629	Financial Services and Markets Act 2000 (Consequential Amendments) (Taxes) Order 2001
SI 2001/3643	Finance Act 1996, Section 167, (Appointed Day) Order 2001
SI 2001/3773	Income Tax (Indexation) (No 2) Order 2001
SI 2001/3777	Personal Equity Plan (Amendment No 2) Regulations 2001 (amend SI 1989/469)
SI 2001/3778	Individual Savings Account (Amendment No 2) Regulations 2001 (amend SI 1998/1870)
SI 2001/3799	Enterprise Management Incentives (Gross Asset Requirement) Order 2001 (amends FA 2000, Sch 14, para 16)
SI 2001/3860	Taxes (Interest Rate) (Amendment No 3) Regulations 2001
SI 2001/3873	Double Taxation Relief (Surrender of Relievable Tax Within a Group) (Amendment) Regulations 2001 (amend SI 2001/1163)
SI 2001/3973	Friendly Societies (Provisional Repayments for Exempt Business) (Amendment) Regulations 2001 (amend SI 1999/622)
SI 2001/3974	Individual Savings Account (Insurance Companies) (Amendment) Regulations 2001 (amend SI 1998/1871)
SI 2001/3975	Friendly Societies (Modification of the Corporation Tax Acts) (Amendment) Regulations 2001 (amend SI 1997/473)
SI 2001/4024	Referrals to the Special Commissioners Regulations 2001
2002/205	Income Tax (Exemption of Minor Benefits) Regulations 2002
SI 2002/653	Scottish Water (Transfer of Functions, etc) (Tax Provisions) Order 2002
SI 2002/680	Income Tax (Employments and Electronic Communications) (Miscellaneous Provisions) Regulations
SI 2002/1397	Secretaries of State for Education and Skills and for Work and Pensions Order 2002 (amends SI 1993/743 and SI 1993/744)
SI 2002/1409	Financial Services and Markets Act 2000 (Consequential Amendments) (Taxes) Order 2002
SI 2002/1596	Income Tax (Benefits in Kind) (Exemption for Employment Costs resulting from Disability) Regulations 2002

SI Year/No	Title
SI 2002/1818	Capital Allowances (Energy-saving Plant and Machinery) (Amendment) Order 2002 (amends SI 2001/2541)
SI 2002/1963	Controlled Foreign Companies (Excluded Countries) (Amendment) Regulations 2002 (amend SI 1998/3081)
SI 2002/1966	Relief for Community Amateur Sports Clubs (Designation) Order 2002
SI 2002/1967	Corporation Tax (Finance Leasing of Intangible Assets) Regulations 2002
SI 2002/1968	Income Tax (Prescribed Deposit-takers) Order 2002
SI 2002/1969	Exchange Gains and Losses (Transitional Provisions and Savings) Regulations 2002
SI 2002/1970	Exchange Gains and Losses (Bringing into Account Gains or Losses) Regulations 2002
SI 2002/1971	European Single Currency (Taxes) (Amendment) Regulations 2002 (amend SI 1998/3177)
SI 2002/1973	Open-ended Investment Companies (Tax) (Amendment) Regulations 2002 (amend SI 1997/1154)
SI 2002/1974	Individual Savings Account (Amendment No 2) Regulations 2002 (amend SI 1998/1870)
SI 2002/2058	Civil Procedure (Amendment) Rules 2002 (amend SI 1998/3132)
SI 2002/2225	Income Tax (Sub-contractors in the Construction industry) (Amendment) Regulations 2002 (amend SI 1993/743)
SI 2002/2406	Controlled Foreign Companies (Excluded Countries) (Amendment No. 2) Regulations 2002 (amend SI 1998/3081)
SI 2002/2661	Venture Capital Trust (Exchange of Shares and Securities) Regulations 2002
SI 2002/2849	Capital Gains Tax (Gilt-edged Securities) Order 2002
SI 2002/2930	Income Tax (Indexation)(No2) Order 2002
SI 2002/2931	Income and Corporation Taxes Act 1988, Section 349B(3) Order 2002
SI 2002/2976	General Commissioners and Special Commissioners (Jurisdiction and Procedure) (Amendment) Regulations 2002
SI 2002/3047	Statutory Payment Schemes (Electronic Communications) Regulations 2002
SI 2002/3158	*Individual Savings Account (Amendment No 3) Regulations 2002* (amend SI 1998/1870)
SI 2003/23	Friendly Societies (Modification of the Corporation Tax Acts) (Amendment) Regulations 2003
SI 2003/88	Finance Act 2002, Section 57(3) and 4(*a*), (Appointed Day) Order 2003
SI 2003/96	Community Investment Tax Relief (Accreditation of Community Development Finance Institutions) Regulations 2003
SI 2003/282	Income and Corporation Taxes (Electronic Communications) Regulations 2003
SI 2003/536	*Income Tax (Sub-contractors in the Construction Industry and Employments) (Amendment) Regulations 2003* (amend SI 1993/743 and SI 1993/744)
SI 2003/843	*Retirement Benefits Schemes (Indexation of Earnings Cap) Order* 2003 (see TA 1988 s 590C)
SI 2003/1361	*Income Tax (Exemption of Minor Benefits) (Increase in Sums of Money) Order 2003* (amends ITEPA 2003)
SI 2003/1434	*Income Tax (Exemption of Minor Benefits) (Amendment) Regulations 2003* (amend SI 2002/205)
SI 2003/1652	*Income Tax (Professional Fees) Order 2003* (amends ITEPA 2003 s 343(2)).
SI 2003/1744	*Capital Allowances (Energy-saving Plant and Machinery) (Amendment) Order 2003* (amends SI 2001/2541)
SI 2003/1745	*Charitable Deductions (Approved Schemes) (Amendment) Regulations 2003* (amend SI 1986/2211)
SI 2003/1828	*Insurance Companies (Taxation of Reinsurance Business) (Amendment) Regulations 2003* (amend SI 1995/1730)
SI 2003/1829	*Double Taxation Relief (Surrender of Relievable Tax Within a Group) (Amendment) Regulations 2003* (amend SI 2001/1163)
SI 2003/1830	Income Tax (Authorised Unit Trusts) (Interest Distributions) Regulations 2003
SI 2003/1831	*Open-ended Investment Companies (Tax) (Amendment) Regulations 2003* (amend SI 1997/1154)
SI 2003/1860	*Life Assurance (Apportionment and Receipts of Participating Funds)(Applicable Percentage) Order 2003* (revokes SI 1990/1541)
SI 2003/1861	*Corporation Tax (Treatment of Unrelieved Surplus Advance Corporation Tax) (Amendment) Regulations 2003* (amend SI 1999/358)
SI 2003/2066	*Collective Investment Schemes (Miscellaneous Amendments) Regulations 2003* (amend SI 1989/469)
SI 2003/2076	Capital Allowances (Environmentally Beneficial Plant and Machinery) Order 2003

SI Year/No	Title
SI 2003/2082	Insurance Companies (Calculation of Profits: Policy Holders' Tax) Regulations 2003
SI 2003/2172	Finance Act 1995, Section 127(12) (Designated Transactions) Regulations 2003
SI 2003/2173	Finance Act 2003, Schedule 26 Paragraph 3(3) (Designated Transactions) Regulations 2003
SI 2003/2339	Taxation of Benefits under Government Pilot Schemes (Return to Work Credit and Employment Retention and Advancement Schemes) Order 2003
SI 2003/2494	*Income Tax (Employments) (Amendment) Regulations 2003 (amend SI 1993/744)*
SI 2003/2495	Income Tax (Incentive Payments for Voluntary Electronic Communication of PAYE Returns) Regulations 2003
SI 2003/2573	*Insurance Companies (Taxation of Reinsurance Business) (Amendment No 2) Regulations 2003* (amend SI 1995/1730)
SI 2003/2581	*Double Taxation Relief (Manufactured Overseas Dividends) (Revocation) Regulations 2003* (revoke SI 1993/1957)
SI 2003/2582	*Income Tax (Manufactured Overseas Dividends) (Amendment) Regulations 2003* (amend SI 1993/2004)
SI 2003/2642	*Insurance Companies (Taxation of Reinsurance Business) (Amendment No 3) Regulations 2003* (amend SI 1995/1730)
SI 2003/2682	Income Tax (Pay As You Earn) Regulations 2003
SI 2003/2714	Non-resident Insurance Companies Regulations 2003
SI 2003/2747	*Individual Savings Account (Amendment) Regulations 2003* (amend SI 1998/1870)
SI 2003/2748	*Personal Equity Plan (Amendment) Regulations 2003* (amend SI 1989/469)
SI 2003/3075	Money Laundering Regulations 2003
SI 2003/3143	Income and Corporation Taxes (Electronic Certificates of Deduction of Tax and Tax Credit) Regulations 2003
SI 2003/3215	*Income Tax (Indexation) (No 2) Order 2003* (amend TA 1988)
SI 2003/3297	Reporting of Savings Income Information Regulations 2003
SI 2004/438	Capital Gains Tax (Gilt-edged Securities) Order 2004
SI 2004/439	Urban Regeneration Companies (Tax) (Designation) Order 2004
SI 2004/674	Recovery of Duties and Taxes etc Due in Other Member States (Corresponding UK Claims, Procedure and Supplementary) Regulations 2004
SI 2004/712	Research and Development (Prescribed Activities) Regulations 2004
SI 2004/851	*IT (PAYE) (Amendment) Regulations 2004* (amend SI 2003/2682)
SI 2004/1075	*Income Tax (Sub-contractors in the Construction Industry) (Amendment) Regulations 2004* (amend SI 1993/743)
SI 2004/1450	Child Trust Funds Regulations 2004
SI 2004/1676	*Personal Equity Plan (Amendment) Regulations 2004* (amend SI 1989/469)
SI 2004/1677	*Individual Savings Account (Amendment) Regulations* (amend SI 1998/1870)

ALPHABETICAL LIST OF PRINTED STATUTORY INSTRUMENTS

Note—For the chronological list, *see above*.

SI Year/No	Title
SI 1996/1323	*Capital Allowances Act 1990, section 33A, (Appointed Day) Order 1996*
SI 2001/2541	Capital Allowances (Energy-saving Plant and Machinery) Order 2001
SI 2003/2076	Capital Allowances (Environmentally Beneficial Plant and Machinery) Order 2003
SI 1984/2060	Capital Allowances (Vehicles for the Disabled) (Similar Payments) Orders 1984
SI 1988/266	Capital Gains Tax (Definition of Unit Trust Scheme) Regulations 1988
SI 1993/950	Capital Gains Tax (Gilt-edged Securities) Order 1993
SI 1994/2656	Capital Gains Tax (Gilt-edged Securities) Order 1994
SI 1996/1031	Capital Gains Tax (Gilt-edged Securities) Order 1996
SI 2001/1122	Capital Gains Tax (Gilt-edged Securities) Order 2001
SI 2002/2849	Capital Gains Tax (Gilt-edged Securities) Order 2002
SI 2004/438	Capital Gains Tax (Gilt-edged Securities) Order 2004
SI 1986/387	Capital Gains Tax (Parallel Pooling) Regulations 1986
SI 1996/1583	Capital Gains Tax (Pension Funds Pooling Schemes) Regulations 1996
SI 1967/149	Capital Gains Tax Regulations 1967
SI 1986/2211	Charitable Deductions (Approved Schemes) Regulations 1986
SI 2004/1450	Child Trust Funds Regulations 2004
SI 1998/3132	Civil Procedure Rules 1998 (Orders 53, 55, 77 and 91 only)
SI 2003/96	Community Investment Tax Relief (Accreditation of Community Development Finance Institutions) Regulations 2003
SI 2000/3158	Controlled Foreign Companies (Designer Rate Tax Provisions) Regulations 2000
SI 1998/3081	Controlled Foreign Companies (Excluded Countries) Regulations 1998
SI 1992/3066	Corporation Tax Acts (Provisions for Payment of Tax and Returns) (Appointed Days) Order 1992
SI 2002/1967	Corporation Tax (Finance Leasing of Intangible Assets) Regulations 2002
SI 1998/3175	Corporation Tax (Instalment Payments) Regulations 1998
SI 1999/2975	Corporation Tax (Simplified Arrangements for Group Relief) Regulations 1999
SI 1999/358	Corporation Tax (Treatment of Unrelieved Surplus Advance Corporation Tax) Regulations 1999
SI 1981/233	Crown Proceedings (Northern Ireland) Order 1981
SI 1990/2529	Debts of Overseas Governments (Determination of Relevant Percentage) Regulations 1990
SI 1995/1370	Deposit-takers (Interest Payments) (Discretionary or Accumulation Trusts) Regulations 1995
SI 1994/236	Distraint by Collectors (Fees, Costs and Charges) Regulations 1994
SI 2000/2074	Donations to Charity by Individuals (Appropriate Declarations) Regulations 2000
SI 2001/1163	Double Taxation Relief (Surrender of Relievable Tax Within a Group) Regulations 2001
SI 1988/88	*Double Taxation Relief (Taxes on Income) (Foreign Loan Interest) Regulations 1988* (revoked)
SI 1973/317	*Double Taxation Relief (Taxes on Income) (General) (Dividend) Regulations 1973* (revoked)
SI 1993/1957	Double Taxation Relief (Taxes on Income) (General) (Manufactured Overseas Dividends) Regulations 1993
SI 1970/488	Double Taxation Relief (Taxes on Income) (General) Regulations 1970
SI 1999/3330	DTR (Taxes on Income) (Foreign Interest and Dividends) Regulations 1999
2001/1156	Double Taxation Relief (Taxes on Income) (Underlying Tax on Dividends and Dual Resident Companies) Regulations 2001
SI 2000/944	Education (Student Loans) (Repayment) Regulations 2000
SI 1997/57	Electronic Lodgement of Tax Returns Order 1997
SI 2000/2090	Employee Share Ownership Plans (Partnership Shares—Notice of Effects on Benefits, Statutory Sick Pay and Statutory Maternity Pay) Regulations 2000
SI 1996/1179	European Investment Bank (Designated International Organisation) Order 1996
SI 1998/3177	European Single Currency (Taxes) Regulations 1998
SI 1994/3227	Exchange Gains and Losses (Alternative Method of Calculation of Gain or Loss) Regulations 1994
SI 2002/1970	Exchange Gains and Losses (Bringing into Account Gains or Losses) Regulations 2002
SI 1994/3229	Exchange Gains and Losses (Excess Gains and Losses) Regulations 1994

SI Year/No	Title
SI 1994/3231	Exchange Gains and Losses (Insurance Companies) Regulations 1994
SI 2000/3315	Exchange Gains and Losses (Miscellaneous Modifications) Regulations 2000
SI 1994/3228	Exchange Gains and Losses (Referral of Gains and Losses) Regulations 1994
SI 2002/1969	Exchange Gains and Losses (Transitional Provisions and Savings) Regulations 2002
SI 1994/3226	Exchange Gains and Losses (Transitional Provisions) Regulations 1994
SI 1985/994	Films (Certification) Regulations 1985
SI 1997/2708	Finance Act 1989 Section 178(1) (Appointed Day) Order 1997
SI 1998/311	Finance Act 1989 Section 178(1) (Appointed Day) Order 1998
SI 2001/253	Finance Act 1989, Section 178(1), (Appointed Day) Order 2001
SI 1999/564	Finance Act 1993, Section 86(2), (Fish Quota) Order 1999
SI 1998/3173	Finance Act 1994, (Appointed Day) Order 1998
SI 2003/2172	Finance Act 1995, Section 127(12) (Designated Transactions) Regulations 2003
SI 1998/2620	Finance Act 1995, Section 139(3), (Appointed Day) Order 1998
SI 1999/2156	Finance Act 1995, Section 139(3), (Appointed Day) Order 1999
SI 2000/922	Finance Act 1995, Section 139(3), (Appointed Day) Order 2000
SI 1997/133	Finance Act 1996, Schedule 35, (Appointed Day) Order 1997
SI 2001/3643	Finance Act 1996, Section 167, (Appointed Day) Order 2001
SI 1997/991	Finance Act 1997, Schedule 10, (Appointed Day) Order 1997
SI 1999/619	Finance Act 1998, Section 37, (Appointed Day) Order 1999
SI 1999/2119	Finance Act 1998, Section 83(1), (Appointed Day) Order 1999
SI 2000/2319	Finance Act 1998, Section 96(4), (Appointed Day) Order 2000
SI 2000/1093	Finance Act 1999, Schedule 10, Paragraph 18, (First and Second Appointed Days) Order 2000
SI 2000/2004	Finance Act 1999, Section 59(3)(*b*), (Appointed Day) Order 2000
SI 2000/2082	Finance Act 2000, Section 108(3), (Appointed Day) Order 2000
SI 2003/2173	Finance Act 2003, Schedule 26 Paragraph 3(3) (Designated Transactions) Regulations 2003
SI 1996/21	*Friendly Societies (Gilt-edged Securities) (Periodic Accounting for Tax on Interest) Regulations 1996* (revoked)
SI 1999/624	Friendly Societies (Gilt-edged Securities) (Periodic Accounting for Tax on Interest) Regulations 1999
SI 1977/1143	Friendly Societies (Life Assurance Premium Relief) Regulations 1977
SI 1980/1947	Friendly Societies (Life Assurance Premium Relief) (Change of Rate) Regulations 1980
SI 1992/1655	*Friendly Societies (Modification of the Corporation Tax Acts) Regulations 1992* (revoked)
SI 1997/473	Friendly Societies (Modification of the Corporation Tax Acts) Regulations 1997
SI 1993/3112	*Friendly Societies (Provisional Repayments for Exempt Business) Regulations 1993* (revoked)
SI 2001/3973	Friendly Societies (Provisional Repayments for Exempt Business) (Amendment) Regulations 2001
SI 1999/622	Friendly Societies (Provisional Repayments for Exempt Business) Regulations 1999
SI 1995/171	*Friendly Societies (Taxation of Transfers of Business) Regulations 1995* (revoked)
SI 1994/1812	General Commissioners (Jurisdiction and Procedure) Regulations 1994
SI 2001/1304	General Commissioners of Income Tax (Costs) Regulations 2001
SI 2001/1757	General Insurance Reserves (Tax) Regulations 2001
SI 1999/2118	Gifts for Relief in Poor Countries (Designation of Kosovo) Order 1999
SI 1998/1868	Gifts for Relief in Poor Countries (Designation) Order 1998
SI 1995/3224	Gilt-edged Securities (Periodic Accounting for Tax on Interest) Regulations 1995
SI 2000/921	Income and Corporation Taxes Act 1988, Section 559(4A), Order 2000
SI 1996/2645	Income and Corporation Taxes Act 1988, section 737A, (Appointed Day) Order 1996
SI 2003/3143	Income and Corporation Taxes (Electronic Certificates of Deduction of Tax and Tax Credit) Regulations 2003
SI 2003/282	Income and Corporation Taxes (Electronic Communications) Regulations 2003
SI 1994/2318	*Income Tax (Authorised Unit Trusts) (Interest Distributions) Regulations 1994* (revoked)
SI 2003/1830	Income Tax (Authorised Unit Trusts) (Interest Distributions) Regulations 2003
SI 2002/1596	Income Tax (Benefits in Kind) (Exemption for Employment Costs resulting from Disability) Regulations 2002

SI Year/No	Title
SI 2000/2080	Income Tax (Benefits in Kind) (Exemption for Welfare Counselling) Regulations 2000
SI 1991/512	Income Tax (Building Societies) (Annual Payments) Regulations 1991
SI 1992/10	Income Tax (Building Societies) (Audit Powers) Regulations 1992
SI 1990/2231	Income Tax (Building Societies) (Dividends and Interest) Regulations 1990
SI 2001/1123	Income Tax (Car Benefits) (Reduction of Value of Appropriate Percentage) Regulations 2001
SI 1994/777	Income Tax (Car Benefits) (Replacement Accessories) Regulations 1994 (revoked)
SI 2000/600	Income Tax (Charge to Tax) (Payments out of Surplus Funds) (Relevant Rate) Order 2000
SI 1985/1696	Income Tax (Composite Rate) (Prescribed Deposit-takers) Order 1985
SI 1992/568	Income Tax (Dealers in Securities) Regulations 1992
SI 1995/2050	Income Tax (Dealers in Securities) (Tradepoint) Regulations 1995
SI 1988/267	Income Tax (Definition of Unit Trust Scheme) Regulations 1988
SI 1992/12	Income Tax (Deposit-takers) (Audit Powers) Regulations 1992
SI 1990/2232	Income Tax (Deposit-takers) (Interest Payments) Regulations 1990
SI 1992/14	Income Tax (Deposit-takers) (Non-residents) Regulations 1992
SI 1992/569	*Income Tax (Dividend Manufacturing) Regulations 1992* (revoked)
SI 2000/945	Income Tax (Electronic Communications) Regulations 2000
SI 2001/56	Income Tax (Electronic Communications) (Incentive Payments) Regulations 2001
SI 1999/2155	Income Tax (Employments) (Amendment No 3) Regulations 1999
SI 2002/680	Income Tax (Employments and Electronic Communications) (Miscellaneous Provisions) Regulations, SI 2002/680
SI 1993/744	Income Tax (Employments) Regulations 1993
SI 1994/1212	Income Tax (Employments) (Notional Payments) Regulations 1994
SI 1987/530	Income Tax (Entertainers and Sportsmen) Regulations 1987
SI 2002/205	Income Tax (Exemption of Minor Benefits) Regulations 2002
SI 1995/2934	Income Tax (Gilt-edged Securities) (Gross Payments of Interest) Regulations 1995
SI 2003/2495	Income Tax (Incentive Payments for Voluntary Electronic Communication of PAYE Returns) Regulations 2003
SI 1992/2744	Income Tax (Insurance Companies) (Expenses of Management) Regulations 1992
SI 1992/15	Income Tax (Interest Payments) (Information Powers) Regulations 1992
SI 1982/1236	Income Tax (Interest Relief) Regulations 1982
SI 1988/1347	Income Tax (Interest Relief) (Housing Associations) Regulations 1988
SI 1978/1159	Income Tax (Life Assurance Premium Relief) Regulations 1978
SI 1995/2052	*Income Tax (Manufactured Dividends) (Tradepoint) Regulations 1995* (revoked)
SI 1992/2074	*Income Tax (Manufactured Interest) Regulations 1992* (revoked)
SI 1993/2004	Income Tax (Manufactured Overseas Dividends) Regulations 1993
SI 2003/2682	Income Tax (Pay As You Earn) Regulations 2003
SI 1996/1654	Income Tax (Payments on Account) Regulations 1996
SI 1996/1585	Income Tax (Pension Funds Pooling Schemes) Regulations 1996
SI 1984/1801	Income Tax (Prescribed Deposit-takers) (No 1) Order 1984
SI 1992/3234	Income Tax (Prescribed Deposit-takers) Order 1992
SI 2002/1968	Income Tax (Prescribed Deposit-takers) Order 2002
SI 1956/1230	Income Tax (Purchased Life Annuities) Regulations 1956
SI 1994/778	*Income Tax (Replacement Cars) Regulations 1994 (revoked)*
SI 1997/1158	Income Tax (Schedule 22 to the Finance Act 1995) (Prescribed Amounts) Regulations 1997
SI 1989/1299	*Income Tax (Stock Lending) Regulations 1989* (revoked)
SI 1993/743	Income Tax (Sub-contractors in the Construction Industry) Regulations 1993
SI 2000/2076	Individual Learning Accounts (Separate Employers Under the Crown) Regulations 2000
SI 1998/1870	Individual Savings Account Regulations 1998
SI 1998/1871	Individual Savings Account (Insurance Companies) Regulations 1998
SI 2001/3974	Individual Savings Account (Insurance Companies) (Amendment) Regulations 2001
SI 1977/1144	Industrial Assurance (Life Assurance Premium Relief) Regulations 1977
SI 1980/1948	Industrial Assurance (Life Assurance Premium Relief) (Change of Rate) Regulations 1980
SI 2003/2082	Insurance Companies (Calculation of Profits: Policy Holders' Tax) Regulations 2003
SI 1999/498	Insurance Companies (Capital Redemption Business) (Modification of the Corporation Tax Acts) Regulations 1999

SI Year/No	Title
SI 1995/3223	*Insurance Companies (Gilt-edged Securities) (Periodic Accounting for Tax on Interest) Regulations 1995* (revoked)
SI 1999/623	Insurance Companies (Gilt-edged Securities) (Periodic Accounting for Tax on Interest) Regulations 1999
SI 1995/3237	Insurance Companies (Overseas Life Assurance Business) (Compliance) Regulations 1995
SI 2000/2089	Insurance Companies (Overseas Life Assurance Business) (Excluded Business) Regulations 2000
SI 1995/3238	Insurance Companies (Overseas Life Assurance Business) (Tax Credit) Regulations 1995
SI 1992/2326	Insurance Companies (Pension Business) (Transitional Provisions) Regulations 1992
SI 1996/2991	Insurance Companies (Reserves) (Tax) Regulations 1996
SI 1995/1730	Insurance Companies (Taxation of Reinsurance Business) Regulations 1995
SI 2003/1828	Insurance Companies (Taxation of Reinsurance Business) (Amendment) Regulations
SI 1997/168	International Organisations (Miscellaneous Exemptions) Order 1997
SI 2001/391	Investment Trusts (Approval of Accounting Methods for Creditor Relationships) Order 2001
SI 1997/265	Life Assurance and Other Policies (Keeping of Information and Duties of Insurers) Regulations 1997
SI 1997/405	Lloyd's Underwriters (Double Taxation Relief) Regulations 1997
SI 1995/3225	Lloyd's Underwriters (Gilt-edged Securities) (Periodic Accounting for Tax on Interest) Regulations 1995
SI 1997/2681	Lloyd's Underwriters (Scottish Limited Partnerships) (Tax) 1997
SI 1995/351	Lloyd's Underwriters (Tax) Regulations 1995
SI 1995/352	*Lloyd's Underwriters (Tax) (1992–93 to 1996–97) Regulations 1995* (spent)
SI 1995/353	Lloyd's Underwriters (Special Reserve Funds) Regulations 1995
SI 1999/3308	Lloyd's Underwriters (Special Reserve Funds) Regulations 1999
SI 1994/3230	Local Currency Elections Regulations 1994
SI 1997/993	Manufactured Dividends (Tax) Regulations 1997
SI 1997/992	Manufactured Interest (Tax) Regulations 1997
SI 1996/1826	Manufactured Overseas Dividends (French Indemnity Payments) Regulations 1996
SI 1995/3036	Manufactured Payments and Transfer of Securities (Tax Relief) Regulations 1995
SI 1971/1035	Mineral Royalties (Tax) Regulations 1971
SI 2003/3075	Money Laundering Regulations 2003
SI 1990/1671	Movements of Capital (Required Information) Regulations 1990
SI 1999/1408	Non-resident Companies (General Insurance Business) Regulations 1999
SI 2003/2714	Non-resident Insurance Companies Regulations 2003
SI 1987/1749	Occupational Pension Schemes (Additional Voluntary Contributions) Regulations 1987
SI 1987/1513	Occupational Pension Schemes (Maximum Rate Lump Sum) Regulations 1987
	Occupational Pension Schemes (Rate of Tax under FA 1970 Sch 5 Part II Para 2) Orders (*see* TA 1988 s 598)
SI 1988/1436	Occupational Pension Schemes (Transitional Provisions) Regulations 1988
SI 1997/1154	Open-ended Investment Companies (Tax) Regulations 1997
SI 2000/2875	Orders for the Delivery of Documents (Procedure) Regulations 2000
SI 1999/881	Overseas Insurers (Tax Representatives) Regulations 1999
SI 1987/352	Pension Scheme Surpluses (Administration) Regulations 1987
SI 1987/412	Pension Scheme Surpluses (Valuation) Regulations 1987
SI 1989/469	Personal Equity Plan Regulations 1989
SI 2000/2318	Personal Pension Schemes (Concurrent Membership) Order 2000
SI 2001/118	Personal Pension Schemes (Conversion of Retirement Benefits Schemes) Regulations 2001
SI 1996/805	Personal Pension Schemes (Deferred Annuity Purchase) (Acceptance of Contributions) Regulations 1996
SI 2000/2316	Personal Pension Schemes (Information Powers) Regulations 2000
SI 1988/1012	Personal Pension Schemes (Minimum Contributions under the Social Security Act 1986) Regulations 1988
SI 1987/1765	Personal Pension Schemes (Provisional Approval) Regulations 1987
SI 1988/1013	Personal Pension Schemes (Relief at Source) Regulations 1988
SI 2000/2314	Personal Pension Schemes (Restriction on Discretion to Approve) (Establishment of Schemes under Trusts) Regulations 2000
SI 2001/117	Personal Pension Schemes (Restriction on Discretion to Approve) (Permitted Investments) Regulations 2001

SI Year/No	Title
SI 1996/1311	Personal Pension Schemes (Tables of Rates of Annuities) Regulations 1996
SI 1988/1014	*Personal Pension Schemes (Transfer Payments) Regulations 1988* (revoked)
SI 2001/119	Personal Pension Schemes (Transfer Payments) Regulations 2001
SI 1999/1029	Personal Portfolio Bonds (Tax) Regulations 1999
SI 1994/1518	Private Medical Insurance (Disentitlement to Tax Relief and Approved Benefits) Regulations 1994
SI 1989/2387	Private Medical Insurance (Tax Relief) Regulations 1989
SI 1995/917	Profit-Related Pay (Shortfall Recovery) Regulation 1995
SI 2004/674	Recovery of Duties and Taxes etc Due in Other Member States (Corresponding UK Claims, Procedure and Supplementary) Regulations 2004
SI 2001/4024	Referrals to the Special Commissioners Regulations 2001
SI 2002/1966	Relief for Community Amateur Sports Clubs (Designation) Order 2002
SI 2003/3297	Reporting of Savings Income Information Regulations 2003
SI 2000/2081	*Research and Development (Prescribed Activities) Regulations 2000* (revoked)
SI 2004/712	Research and Development (Prescribed Activities) Regulations 2004
SI 1995/3192	Retirement Age of General Commissioners Order 1995
SI 1990/2101	Retirement Benefits Schemes (Continuation of Rights of Members of Approved Schemes) Regulations 1990
SI 1995/3103	Retirement Benefits Schemes (Information Powers) Regulations 1995
SI 1993/3016	Retirement Benefits Schemes (Restriction on Discretion to Approve (Additional Voluntary Contributions) Regulations 1993
SI 1999/1964	Retirement Benefits Schemes (Restriction on Discretion to Approve) (Additional Voluntary Contributions) (Amendment) Regulations 1999
SI 1998/729	Retirement Benefits Schemes (Restriction on Discretion to Approve) (Excepted Provisions) Regulations 1998
SI 2000/1087	Retirement Benefits Schemes (Restriction on Discretion to Approve) (Excepted Provisions) Regulations 2000
SI 1996/1582	Retirement Benefits Schemes (Restriction on Discretion to Approve) (Excepted Schemes) Regulations 1996
SI 1991/1614	Retirement Benefits Schemes (Restriction on Discretion to Approve) (Small Self-administered Schemes) Regulations 1991
SI 1990/586	Retirement Benefits Schemes (Tax Relief on Contributions) (Disapplication of Earnings Cap) Regulations 1990
SI 2000/1085	Retirement Benefits Schemes (Sharing of Pensions on Divorce or Annulment) Regulations 2000
SI 1995/3220	Sale and Repurchase of Securities (Modification of Enactments) Regulations 1995
SI 2002/653	Scottish Water (Transfer of Functions, etc) (Tax Provisions) Order 2002
SI 1998/3178	Scotland Act 1998 (Commencement) Order 1998
SI 1994/1811	Special Commissioners (Jurisdiction and Procedure) Regulations 1994
SI 2002/3047	Statutory Payment Schemes (Electronic Communications) Regulations 2002
SI 2003/2339	Taxation of Benefits under Government Pilot Schemes (Return to Work Credit and Employment Retention and Advancement Schemes) Order 2003
SI 1996/2396	Taxation of Benefits under Pilot Schemes (Earnings Top-up) Order 1996
SI 1995/2902	Taxation of Income from Land (Non-residents) Regulations 1995
SI 2004/1864	Tax Avoidance Schemes (Information) Regulations 2004
SI 2004/1863	Tax Avoidance Schemes (Prescribed Descriptions of Arrangements) Regulations 2004
SI 2004/1865	Tax Avoidance Schemes (Promoters and Prescribed Circumstances) Regulations 2004
SI 1990/2361	Tax-exempt Special Savings Account Regulations 1990
SI 1995/3239	Tax-exempt Special Savings Account (Relevant European Institutions) Regulations 1995
SI 1989/1297	Taxes (Interest Rate) Regulations 1989
SI 1992/42	Taxes (Relief for Gifts) (Designated Educational Establishments) Regulations 1992
SI 2004/1819	Thalidomide Children's Trust (Application of Section 329AA of the Income and Corporation Taxes Act 1988) Order 2004
SI 2000/2303	Tonnage Tax Regulations 2000
SI 2000/2129	Tonnage Tax (Training Requirement) Regulations 2000
SI 2004/439	Urban Regeneration Companies (Tax) (Designation) Order 2004
SI 1995/1979	Venture Capital Trust Regulations 1995
SI 2002/2661	Venture Capital Trust (Exchange of Shares and Securities) Regulations 2002
SI 1998/1513	Visiting Forces and Allied Headquarters (Income Tax and Capital Gains Tax) (Designation) Order 1998

SI Year/No	Title
SI 1961/580	*Visiting Forces and Allied Headquarters (Income Tax and Death Duties) (Designation) Order 1961*
	Visiting Forces (Designation) Orders (*see* TA 1988, s 323)
SI 1998/1514	Visiting Forces (Income Tax and Capital Gains Tax) (Designation) Order 1998
SI 1964/924	*Visiting Forces (Income Tax and Death Duties) (Designation) Order 1964*
SI 1992/734	*Vocational Training (Public Financial Assistance and Disentitlement to Tax Relief) Regulations 1992* (lapsed)
SI 1992/746	*Vocational Training (Tax Relief) Regulations 1992* (lapsed)

STATUTORY INSTRUMENTS

1956/1230
Income Tax (Purchased Life Annuities) Regulations 1956

Made by the Commissioners of Inland Revenue under FA 1956 s 28, now TA 1988 s 658; see TA 1988 Sch 30 para 21

Made . . . . *8 August 1956*

Commentary—*Simon's Direct Tax Service* **B5.314**.

1 These Regulations may be cited as the Income Tax (Purchased Life Annuities) Regulations, 1956, and shall come into operation on the fifteenth day of August, 1956.

2 In these Regulations—

''the principal section'' means section 27 of the Finance Act, 1956[a];

''payee'' means the person beneficially entitled for the time being to the payments on account of an annuity;

''payer'' means any person resident in the United Kingdom by whom, or any branch or agency in the United Kingdom of a person not so resident (being a branch or agency through which that person carries on life assurance business) through which, an annuity is paid.

Other expressions have the same meaning as in the Income Tax Acts.

Note—[a] TA 1988 ss 656, 657.

3 The Interpretation Act, 1889[a], shall apply to these Regulations as it applies to an Act of Parliament.

Note—[a] Interpretation Act 1978.

4 A claim for the application of the principal section to an annuity shall be made in writing to the Inspector by the payee, and shall give the particulars set out in the Schedule to these Regulations.

5 The Inspector may by notice require the payer of an annuity to furnish such particulars relating to the annuity as he may require, including the age of the person during whose life the annuity is payable, if known to him, the amount or value of the consideration given for the grant of the annuity, and particulars of any other matter appearing to him to be relevant for the purposes of the principal section.

6 On the receipt of a claim under Regulation 4, the Inspector shall determine whether the annuity is a purchased life annuity to which the principal section applies and, if so, what proportion of each payment on account of the annuity constitutes the capital element. The prescribed tables of mortality to be used for this purpose shall be [the tables comprised in Table A8 set out in Appendix A on pages 113 to 115 of the booklet entitled ''Continuous Mortality Investigation Reports Number 10'' published by the Institute of Actuaries and the Faculty of Actuaries in 1990][1] ... [2] The Inspector shall serve a notice of his determination (hereinafter referred to as ''the original determination'') upon the payee and, unless the payer is not entitled or required to deduct tax from the annuity, upon the payer of the annuity. The determination shall thereupon become effective, and a payer upon whom such notice is served shall be treated as having been notified in the prescribed manner for the purposes of subsection (4) of the principal section.

Amendments—[1] Words substituted by the IT (Purchased Life Annuities) (Amendment) Regulations, SI 1991/2808 reg 3 so far as concerns any purchased life annuity in respect of which the first annuity payment begins to accrue on or after 1 March 1992.
[2] Words revoked by SI 1991/2808 reg 3.

7 If the payee is dissatisfied with the original determination he may, within [thirty days][1] from the date of service upon him of notice thereof, or such further time as the Special Commissioners shall allow, give notice to the Inspector of his intention to appeal against the determination, and such notice of intention to appeal shall specify the grounds of the appeal.

Amendments—[1] Words substituted by the IT (Purchased Life Annuities) (Amendment) Regulations, SI 1960/2308 reg 3.

8 Section 510 of the Income Tax Act, 1952[a] (which relates to the settling of appeals by agreement) shall, with any necessary modifications, apply to notices of appeal under the last preceding Regulation.

Note—[a] TMA 1970 s 54.

9 If an appeal under Regulation 7 is not settled by agreement it shall be heard by the Special Commissioners, who shall for this purpose have all such powers as they have in relation to appeals against assessments to income tax under Schedule D.

10 Section 64 of the Income Tax Act, 1952[a] (which relates to the statement of a case on a point of law for the opinion of the High Court), shall, with any necessary modifications, apply to appeals under these Regulations as it applies to appeals against assessments to income tax.

Note—[a] TMA 1970 s 56.

11 If the original determination is amended as the result of an appeal, the Inspector shall, unless the payer is not entitled or required to deduct tax from the annuity or any part of it, immediately serve a notice of the determination as so amended upon the payer of the annuity. The revised determination shall become effective as soon as the appeal has been determined and any notice as aforesaid has been served, and shall supersede any earlier determination in relation to the first payment made thereafter on account of the annuity, and, subject to the next following Regulation, to all subsequent such payments.

12 If, at any time after a determination has become effective and at least one payment on account of the annuity has been made thereafter, the Inspector or the payee alleges that that determination is erroneous whether by reason of an error or mistake in a claim by the payee or otherwise, the Inspector may make, or the payee may make a claim for, a revised determination. If the Inspector makes a revised determination in accordance with the claim he shall serve notice upon the payee accordingly. If he makes a revised determination without the payee having claimed it, or if he makes a revised determination which is not in accordance with the payee's claim, or if on receipt of the payee's claim he refuses to make a revised determination, he shall serve notice upon the payee accordingly, and Regulations 7, 8, 9 and 10 shall apply, with any necessary modifications, as they apply in relation to the original determination.

13—(1) As soon as the time limit for appealing against a revised determination made under Regulation 12 has expired or, if there is an appeal, as soon as the appeal has been determined, the Inspector shall, unless the payer is not entitled or required to deduct tax from the annuity or any part of it, serve notice of the said determination or, as may be appropriate, of that determination as amended on appeal, upon the payer of the annuity. The determination shall thereupon become effective and shall supersede any earlier determination in relation to the first payment made thereafter on account of the annuity, and, subject to Regulation 12, to all subsequent such payments.

(2) If by virtue of Regulation 7 the Special Commissioners extend the time limited for an appeal, the notice of appeal shall be treated as a claim made under Regulation 12 and that Regulation and paragraph (1) of this Regulation shall apply accordingly.

14 Where any effective determination is amended on appeal, whether by agreement, or by the Special Commissioners, or by order of the High Court, any amount by which the tax deducted from or assessed and charged upon payments on account of the annuity by reference to the said determination exceeds the tax that would have been deducted or assessed and charged if the determination as amended on appeal had applied to those payments shall, subject to Regulation 19, be repaid to the payee by the Commissioners of Inland Revenue. Any amount by which the tax so deducted or assessed and charged falls short of the tax that would have been deducted or assessed and charged if the determination as amended on appeal had applied to those payments shall, subject to Regulation 19, be assessed and charged on the payee under Case VI of Schedule D for the years of assessment in which the said payments were made.

15 Where—

(*a*) income tax has been deducted from or assessed and charged upon the whole of any payments on account of an annuity and subsequently an original determination becomes effective, or

(*b*) a revised determination becomes effective,

the difference between (1) the tax which the payer was entitled to deduct and did in fact deduct from payments on account of the annuity falling due after 5th April, 1956, but made before the said determination became effective, or the tax assessed and charged upon those payments and (2) the tax that would have been deducted from or assessed and charged upon those payments if it had been deducted or assessed and charged in accordance with the said determination shall, except in so far as it has been repaid or assessed and charged under Regulation 14, and subject to Regulation 19, be repaid to the payee by the Commissioners of Inland Revenue or be assessed and charged upon the payee under Case VI of Schedule D for the years of assessment in which the said payments were made, as the circumstances may require, whether or not, in cases within (*b*) hereof, the determination in force before the revised determination became effective had been made or confirmed by the Special Commissioners on an appeal to them:

Provided that—

(i) no repayment shall be made under this Regulation in respect of tax deducted or deductible from or assessed and charged upon any payment on account of the annuity which fell due in a year of assessment which ended more than six years before the beginning of the year of assessment in which the claim which gave rise to the said determination was made, or, in a case where the Inspector initiated a revised determination, before the beginning of the year of assessment in which the Inspector served notice upon the payee under Regulation 12;

(ii) no assessment shall be made under this Regulation in respect of any payment on account of the annuity which fell due as aforesaid, except that, where any form of fraud or wilful default has been committed by or on behalf of any person in connection with or in relation to the taxation of the annuity, an assessment may be made at any time:

But provided always that no repayment or assessment shall be made under this Regulation in respect of tax deducted from or assessed and charged upon any payment on account of the annuity made before the date of the claim which gave rise to the said determination or, as the case may be, the date of the Inspector's revised determination under Regulation 12 if that deduction or assessment and charge was in fact made on the basis or in accordance with the practice generally prevailing at the time when the said payment was made.

16 In relation to an annuity paid by a person not resident in the United Kingdom, otherwise than through a branch or agency through which that person carries on life assurance business in the United Kingdom, to a payee who is resident in the United Kingdom, the foregoing Regulations, except Regulation 5, shall apply as they apply in relation to an annuity paid by a person who is resident in the United Kingdom, with the modification that Regulation 12 shall apply as though the reference to at least one payment having been made on account of the annuity were a reference to at least one first assessment having been made on the payee in respect of the annuity.

17 Where, in a case to which the last preceding Regulation applies, tax is deducted from payments on account of the annuity, whether by virtue of section 188 or 189 of the Income Tax Act, 1952[a], or otherwise, the Commissioners of Inland Revenue shall, subject to Regulation 19, repay to the payee any tax which would not have been deducted if the person paying the annuity had been a payer resident in the United Kingdom upon whom the notices referred to in Regulations 6, 11 and 13 had been served.

Note—[a] TA 1988 s 123(2) and (3).

18 Any assessment required by Regulation 14 or 15 shall be made in accordance with those Regulations notwithstanding anything in the Income Tax Acts.

19—[(1)][1] Where [this paragraph applies and][1] the payee is a married woman living with her husband, any reference in these Regulations to repaying tax to the payee or to charging tax on the payee shall, unless an application for separate assessment under section 355 of the Income Tax Act, 1952[a], is in force, be read as requiring tax to be repaid to, or charged on, her husband.

[(2) Paragraph (1) of this regulation applies in relation to the repaying or charging of tax in respect of any payment or part of any payment on account of an annuity which, by virtue of section 279 of the Income and Corporation Taxes Act 1988 as it has effect for years of assessment before 1990–91, is deemed to be the income of her husband or would have been so deemed but for the operation of section 656(1) of that Act.][2]

Note—[a] TA 1988 s 283.

Amendments—[1] Regulation as originally enacted renumbered as para (1) and words in para (1) inserted by the IT (Purchased Life Annuities) (Amendment) Regulations, SI 1990/626 reg 3.

[2] Para (2) added SI 1990/626 reg 3, with effect from 6 April 1990.

20 A determination that becomes effective under these Regulations shall, except to the extent that it may be varied under these Regulations, be final and conclusive for all the purposes of the Income Tax Acts.

21 Where a determination is varied on appeal or by virtue of Regulation 12, and any tax deducted from or assessed and charged upon a payment on account of the annuity is repaid under Regulation 14, 15 or 17, a corresponding adjustment shall be made in estimating for the purposes of the Income Tax Acts the total income of the payee (or, [in respect of years of assessment before 1990–91,][1] if the payee is a married woman living with her husband, of her husband) for the year in which the payment fell due, and, notwithstanding anything in the Income Tax Acts, such consequential adjustments of his liability to income tax (including surtax) as may be necessary shall be made by assessment or by repayment, as the case may require.

Amendments—[1] Words inserted by the IT (Purchased Life Annuities) (Amendment) Regulations, SI 1990/626 reg 4.

22 Any notice or other document authorised or required to be served on any person under these Regulations by the Inspector may be served by post by letter addressed to such person at his usual or last known place of business or abode, or, where such person is a company, by letter addressed to the secretary of the company at its registered office.

23 Anything which is authorised or required by these Regulations to be done by the Inspector shall be done by such Inspector as the Commissioners of Inland Revenue may direct.

SCHEDULE

PARTICULARS TO BE GIVEN BY THE PAYEE IN MAKING A CLAIM UNDER REGULATION 4

PART I

Particulars to be given in all cases

1 The name of the payer.

2 The number by which the annuity contract is identified.

3 The amount of each payment on account of the annuity.

4 The frequency with which payments on account of the annuity are made.

5 The name of the person or persons on whose life or lives the annuity depends.

6 The name and address of the annuitant ...[1]

Amendments—[1] Words revoked by the IT (Purchased Life Annuities) (Amendment) Regulations, SI 1990/626 reg 5 with effect from 6 April 1990.

7 Such particulars of the occupation of the annuitant ...[1] as the Commissioners of Inland Revenue consider necessary to determine which Inspector should deal with the claim.

Amendments—[1] Words revoked by the IT (Purchased Life Annuities) (Amendment) Regulations, SI 1990/626 reg 5 with effect from 6 April 1990.

8 Such particulars as are necessary to determine whether subsection (8) of the principal section applies to the annuity.

PART II

Additional particulars to be given where the person paying the annuity is not within the definition of payer in Regulation 2

1 The amount of value of the consideration given for the grant of the annuity.

2 The date of birth of each person on whose life the annuity depends.

3 Whether the final payment on account of the annuity will be calculated by reference to the actual date of any person's death.

4 Particulars of any contingencies other than the death of a person on the happening of which the annuity will terminate.

1961/580

Visiting Forces and Allied Headquarters (Income Tax and Death Duties) (Designation) Order 1961

Made by the Commissioners of Inland Revenue under FA 1960, s 73; now TA 1988 s 323

Made . . . . *24 March 1961*

1 Each of the countries specified in the First Schedule to this Order and each of the allied headquarters specified in the Second Schedule to this Order is hereby designated for the purposes of Section 73 of the Finance Act, 1960[a].

Note—[a] TA 1988 s 323.

2 This Order may be cited as the Visiting Forces and Allied Headquarters (Income Tax and Death Duties) (Designation) Order, 1961, and shall come into operation on the 30th day of March, 1961.

FIRST SCHEDULE

Article 1

Belgium, Canada, Denmark, France, Greece, Italy, Luxembourg, the Netherlands, Norway, Portugal, Turkey, and the United States of America.

SECOND SCHEDULE

Article 1

Channel Committee.

Channel Command.

Eastern Atlantic Area Command.

Supreme Headquarters Allied Powers Europe.

Allied Command Atlantic Headquarters.

1964/924
Visiting Forces (Income Tax and Death Duties) (Designation) Order 1964

Made under FA 1960, s 73; now TA 1988 s 323

Made . . . . *23 June 1964*

1 The Federal Republic of Germany is hereby designated for the purposes of section 73 of the Finance Act 1960[a].

Note—[a] TA 1988 s 323.

2 This Order may be cited as the Visiting Forces (Income Tax and Death Duties) (Designation) Order 1964, and shall come into operation on the 30th June 1964.

1967/149
Capital Gains Tax Regulations 1967

Made by the Commissioners of Inland Revenue under FA 1965 Sch 10 para 2, now TMA 1970 s 57; see TA 1970 s 539(1), (3), (5) and TA 1988 Sch 30 para 21

Made . . . . *9 February 1967*

Citation and commencement

1 These Regulations may be cited as the Capital Gains Tax Regulations 1967, and shall come into operation on 16th February 1967.

Interpretation

2—(1) In the Regulations, unless the context otherwise requires—

''appeal'' means an appeal against an assessment to capital gains tax or against a decision on a claim relating to capital gains tax;

''The Board'' means the Commissioners of Inland Revenue;

''Commissioners'' means (subject to Regulation 17) General Commissioners or Special Commissioners;

''third party'' means a third or subsequent party joined under Regulation 8;

references to the Income Tax Management Act 1964[a] are references to that Act as applied in relation to capital gains tax by paragraph 1 of Schedule 10 to the Finance Act 1965[b];

references to Part III of the Finance Act 1965[b] include Schedules 6 to 10 to that Act and any other enactment to be construed as one with the said Part III;

subject to Regulation 15, other expressions have the same meaning as in Part III of the Finance Act 1965[b].

(2) The Interpretation Act 1889[c] shall apply to these Regulations as it applies to an Act of Parliament.

Note—[a] TMA 1970.
[b] TCGA 1992.
[c] Interpretation Act 1978.

Notices of appeals against assessments

3 ...[1]

Amendments—[1] Revoked by FA 1969 Sch 21 Pt VIII.

Choice of appeal Commissioners

4 ...[1]

Amendments—[1] Revoked by FA 1969 Sch 21 Pt VIII.

Assignment of appeals to General Commissioners

5 ...[1]

Amendments—[1] Revoked by FA 1969 Sch 21 Pt VIII.

Representations in writing

6 ...[1]

Amendments—[1] Revoked by the General and Special Commissioners (Amendment of Enactments) Regulations, SI 1994/1813 reg 2, Sch 1 para 27, Sch 2 with effect from 1 September 1994.

Representation of the inspector

7 ...[1]

Amendments—[1] Revoked by the General and Special Commissioners (Amendment of Enactments) Regulations, SI 1994/1813 reg 2, Sch 1 para 27, Sch 2 with effect from 1 September 1994.

Joinder of third parties in appeals

8—(1) Where the market value of an asset on a particular date or the apportionment of any amount or value is a material question in an appeal any person whose liability to capital gains tax for any period may be affected by that market value or by the manner in which that amount or value is apportioned may apply under this Regulation to be joined as a party in the appeal.

(2) An application under this Regulation to be joined as a party in an appeal shall be made in writing to the inspector stating—

(*a*) the name and address of the applicant;
(*b*) the question which may affect his liability to capital gains tax;
(*c*) how his liability may be affected; and
(*d*) his contention with regard to that question.

(3) The inspector shall send a copy of the application to the appellant and to any other party to the appeal.

(4) If the application is received by the inspector not later than thirty days before the date fixed for the hearing of the appeal (or of the question), or if when he receives the application no date has been fixed, he shall, if he is satisfied that it is proper to join the applicant as a party in the appeal, join him as a third party and give notice of the joinder to the appellant and any other party to the appeal.

(5) If the application is received by the inspector later than thirty days before the date fixed for the hearing of the appeal (or of the question) but before it has been determined, or if he is not satisfied that it is proper to join the applicant as a party in the appeal, he shall refer the application to the Commissioners before whom the appeal is brought, and those Commissioners may in their discretion allow or refuse the application.

(6) ...[1]

Provided that an appeal shall not be so transferred unless the Commissioners to whom the application is made are satisfied that the balance of convenience to the parties is in favour of the transfer.

(7) At the hearing and on the determination of the appeal or of any question in the appeal a third party shall, so far as relates to the question in which he is interested, have the same rights as an appellant, including any right to require the statement of a case for the opinion of any Court.

(8) ...[1]

(9) A person entitled under section 26(5) of the Finance Act 1965[a] (proceedings consequent on death) to be a party to an appeal shall, if he wishes to be made a party, apply to be joined under this Regulation.

Note—[a] TCGA 1992.

Revenue Internal Guidance—Capital Gains Tax manual CG 16432–16434 (common examples of interested parties include vendor and purchaser in relation to the same transaction; joint owners of assets; but owner of a similar asset is not an interested party).

Amendments—[1] Paras (6), (8) revoked by the General and Special Commissioners (Amendment of Enactments) Regulations, SI 1994/1813 reg 2, Sch 1 para 27, Sch 2 with effect from 1 September 1994.

Applications for determination of market value

9—(1) Where the market value of an asset on a particular date or the apportionment of any amount or value may affect the liability to capital gains tax for any period (and whether for the same or different periods) of two or more persons and is not (and has not been) a material question in an appeal already brought by any of them, any of those persons may apply to the Commissioners to determine that market value or the manner in which that amount or value should be apportioned.

(2) An application under this Regulation shall be made by notice in writing sent to the inspector stating the question for determination and (to the best of the applicant's knowledge) the names and addresses of the other persons whose liability to capital gains tax may be affected by the question.

(3) In relation to proceedings under this Regulation references in Schedule 3 to the Income Tax Management Act 1964[a] (rules for assigning proceedings to Commissioners) to the place where the appellant ordinarily resided in the year of assessment to which the proceedings relate shall, in cases where the application does not relate to any ascertained year of assessment, be construed as references to the place where the applicant ordinarily resides at the time of making the application.

(4) The inspector shall be a party to proceedings under this Regulation.

(5) An election to bring proceedings under this Regulation before the Special Commissioners instead of before the General Commissioners (or, if the proceedings are in Northern Ireland, before a county court instead of before the Special Commissioners) shall, if not made in the notice of application, be made by notice in writing to the inspector within thirty days thereafter.

(6) Subject to paragraphs (1) to (5) above, these Regulations, Part III of the Finance Act 1965[b] and any enactment directly or indirectly applied by the said Part III shall, so far as they are applicable and with any necessary modifications, apply in relation to proceedings under this Regulation as they apply in relation to an appeal against an assessment to capital gains tax.

Note—[a] TMA 1970 Sch 3.
[b] TMA 1970 s 47.

References of questions of value to other tribunals

10—(1)–(3) ...[1, 2]

Amendments—[1] Para (2) revoked by FA 1969 Sch 21 Pt VIII.
[2] Paras (1), (3) revoked by the General and Special Commissioners (Amendment of Enactments) Regulations, SI 1994/1813 reg 2, Sch 1 para 27, Sch 2 with effect from 1 September 1994.

Conclusive effect of a determination on appeal

11—(1) Where the market value of an asset on a particular date or the apportionment of any amount or value (being a market value or apportionment affecting or which may affect the liability to capital gains tax of two or more persons) is finally determined on an appeal that determination shall, subject to Regulation 14, be in all proceedings relating to capital gains tax conclusive between the Board or any officer of the Board and the following persons—

(*a*) parties to the appeal; and

(*b*) any person who was entitled to apply to be joined as a third party in the appeal, and had notice, in reasonable time for making such application, of the appeal and of the question in the appeal entitling him so to apply, not being a person who did so apply without undue delay and whose application was not allowed.

(2) For the purposes of these Regulations—

(*a*) the determination of an appeal or a question in an appeal shall be treated as final when the determination can no longer be varied by the tribunal making it or by the order of any court;

(*b*) the market value of an asset on a particular date or the apportionment of any amount or value shall be deemed to have been finally determined on an appeal notwithstanding that there was no dispute concerning that market value or apportionment if the market value or apportionment was a material question in the appeal and the appeal has been finally determined.

(3), (4) ...[1]

Amendments—[1] Paras (3), (4) revoked by the General and Special Commissioners (Amendment of Enactments) Regulations, SI 1994/1813 reg 2, Sch 1 para 27, Sch 2 with effect from 1 September 1994.

Agreements in writing of market value or apportionment

12—(1) An agreement or notification which apart from this Regulation would have effect under section 510 of the Income Tax Act 1952[a] (settlement of appeals by agreement or withdrawal) as if an appeal had been determined by Commissioners shall not have that effect in relation to any appeal in which a third party has been joined unless, at the time when such agreement is made or notification is given, the question in which the third party is interested has been finally determined on the appeal or disposed of by an agreement made in accordance with paragraph (2) below.

(2) Where the market value of an asset on a particular date or the apportionment of any amount or value may affect the liability to capital gains tax of two or more persons and is a material question in an appeal, then if the market value or apportionment is agreed in writing between the inspector or any other officer of the Board and all the parties to the appeal whose liability may be affected by it the agreement shall in all proceedings relating to the capital gains tax be conclusive between the Board or any officer of the Board and the following persons—

(*a*) parties to the agreement; and

(*b*) any person who was entitled, in respect of the question in the appeal to which the agreement relates, to apply to be joined as a third party in the appeal, and had notice of the appeal and of the question in the appeal not less than thirty days before the agreement was made, not being a person who did so apply before the agreement was made.

(3) A document purporting to be an agreement made in accordance with paragraph (2) above and produced from proper custody may be received in evidence in any proceedings relating to capital gains tax without further proof as such an agreement made by the persons by whom it purports to be signed.

Note—[a] TMA 1970 s 54.

Persons affected by a determination or agreement in writing

13—(1) A determination or agreement which is by virtue of these Regulations conclusive against or in favour of any person shall to the same extent be conclusive against or in favour of his personal representatives and his trustee or assignee in bankruptcy or under a deed of arrangement.

(2) A determination or agreement relating to any settled property which is by virtue of these Regulations conclusive against or in favour of the trustees of the settlement shall to the same extent be conclusive against or in favour of any person becoming absolutely entitled to that property as against the trustees.

(3) A determination or agreement relating to an asset comprised in the estate of a deceased person, or in a testamentary disposition made by him, which is by virtue of these Regulations conclusive against or in favour of his personal representatives shall to the same extent be conclusive against or in favour of any person acquiring the asset as legatee.

(4) Where paragraph 20 of Schedule 7 to the Finance Act 1965[a] (disposals between husband and wife) or section 31(4) of that Act[b] (disposals of certain works of art, etc) applies in respect of the disposal of an asset, a determination or agreement relating to the asset which is by virtue of these Regulations conclusive against or in favour of the person making the disposal shall to the same extent be conclusive against or in favour of the person acquiring the asset.

Note—[a] TCGA 1992 s 58.
[b] TCGA 1992 s 258.

Fraud or wilful default

14 A determination or agreement shall not by virtue of these Regulations be conclusive in favour of any person if it is shown that any form of fraud or wilful default committed by or on behalf of that person procured or contributed to procure the determination or agreement.

Interpretation of certain expressions

15 For the purposes of these Regulations—

(*a*) The market value of an asset or the apportionment of any amount or value is a material question in an appeal notwithstanding that there is no dispute thereon between the appellant and the inspector if the adoption of a different market value or of a different apportionment might produce a different determination on the appeal.

(*b*) A person shall not be treated as being at any date a person whose liability to capital gains tax may be affected by the market value of an asset or by the apportionment of any amount or value paid, payable or ascertained in connection with an asset unless—

(i) on or before that date, but since 6th April 1965, there has been (or is deemed to have been) a disposal or acquisition of the asset by him, or by personal representatives from whom he may acquire the asset as legatee, or by a company or trustees whose chargeable gains may to any extent be treated as having accrued to him under section 41 or 42 of the Finance Act 1965[a] (non-resident companies and trusts); and

(ii) he is at that date, or was during the year of assessment in which any such disposal or acquisition was made, resident or ordinarily resident in the United Kingdom or carrying on a trade in the United Kingdom:

Provided that section 10(3) of the Finance Act 1956[b] (determination of questions of ordinary residence) shall not apply to a question arising under this paragraph.

(*c*) Personal representatives or trustees who are for the purposes of Part III of the Finance Act 1965[c] treated as a single and continuing body of persons shall be treated as a single person distinct from the persons who may from time to time be the personal representatives or trustees, and if the same persons are personal representatives or trustees in respect of more than one estate or settlement they shall be treated as a separate person in respect of each estate or settlement.

Note—[a] TCGA 1992 s 13.
[b] TA 1988 s 207.
[c] TCGA 1992.

Revenue Internal Guidance—Capital gains tax manual CG 16432–16434 (common examples of interested parties include vendor and purchaser in relation to the same transaction; joint owners of assets; but owner of a similar asset is not an interested party).

Notification of third parties

16 Where it appears to the inspector that a person is entitled to apply to be joined as a third party in an appeal the inspector may, and at that person's request shall, notify him of the appeal and disclose to him (so far as relevant to his interest in that appeal) the market value of any asset or the apportionment of any amount or value used in making the assessment or decision from which the appeal is brought.

Proceedings in Northern Ireland

17 (Spent).

Service by post

18 Any notice or other document to be given, served, sent or delivered under these Regulations may be served by post.

1970/488
Double Taxation Relief (Taxes on Income) (General) Regulations 1970

Made by the Commissioners of Inland Revenue under Income Tax Act 1952 s 351 and FA 1965 s 64, now TA 1988 s 791; see TA 1970 s 539 and TA 1988 Sch 30 para 21

Made . . . . *24 March 1970*

1—(1) These Regulations may be cited as the Double Taxation Relief (Taxes on Income) (General) Regulations 1970 and shall come into operation on 6th April 1970.

(2) The Interpretation Act 1889[a] shall apply to these Regulations as it applies to an Act of Parliament.

(3) In these Regulations "the Board" means the Commissioners of Inland Revenue; "year" means year of assessment.

(4) Except in relation to payments which are income of the year 1969–70 or an earlier year the Double Taxation Relief (Taxes on Income) (General) Regulations 1966 shall cease to have effect from 6th April 1970:

Provided that any notice, direction or claim given or made under Regulation 2, 9 or 11 of the said Regulations of 1966 (including any notice, direction or claim having effect as if so given or made) which was in force immediately before the coming into operation of these Regulations shall continue in force as if given or made under the corresponding provision of these Regulations and the following provisions of these Regulations shall apply accordingly.

Note—[a] Interpretation Act 1889.

2—(1) The following provisions of these Regulations shall have effect where, under arrangements having effect under section 497 of the Income and Corporation Taxes Act 1970[a], persons resident in the territory with the government of which the arrangements are made are entitled to exemption or partial relief from United Kingdom income tax in respect of any income from which deduction of tax is authorised or required by the Income Tax Acts.

(2) Any person who pays any such income (referred to in these Regulations as "the United Kingdom payer") to a person in the said territory who is beneficially entitled to the income (such person being referred to in these Regulations as "the non-resident") may be directed by a notice in writing given by or on behalf of the Board that in paying any such income specified in the notice to the non-resident he shall—

(*a*) not deduct tax, or

(*b*) not deduct tax at a higher rate than is specified in the notice, or

(*c*) deduct tax at a rate specified in the notice instead of at the [lower or basic][1] rate otherwise appropriate;

and where such notice is given, any income to which the notice refers, being income for a year for which the arrangements have effect, which the United Kingdom payer pays after the date of the notice to the non-resident named therein shall, subject to the following provisions of these regulations, be paid as directed in the notice:

Provided that income specified in a notice given under this paragraph shall not include distributions in respect of which income tax is chargeable under Schedule F.

Note—[a] TA 1988 s 788.

Amendments—[1] Words substituted by the Double Taxation Relief (Taxes on Income) (General) (Amendment) Regulations, SI 1996/783 reg 2 with effect from 6 April 1996.

3 Where a notice given under Regulation 2(2) directs the United Kingdom payer to deduct tax at a rate specified in the notice, the provisions of the Income Tax Acts under which he would, but for the notice, have been chargeable with or liable to account for all or part of any tax deducted at the [lower or basic][1] rate shall apply as if those Acts required him to deduct tax at the rate so specified.

Amendments—[1] Words substituted by the Double Taxation Relief (Taxes on Income) (General) (Amendment) Regulations, SI 1996/783 reg 2 with effect from 6 April 1996.

4—(1) Where but for a notice given under Regulation 2(2) the United Kingdom payer would have been entitled to retain any income tax deductible on making any payment, there shall be made to him again the income tax otherwise payable by him for the relevant year an allowance equal to the amount of tax which, but for the notice, he would have been entitled to retain on making the payment but in compliance with the notice has not deducted.

(2) "The relevant year" means the year the [lower or basic][1] standard rate for which would (but for the notice) have determined the amount of the deduction authorised.

Amendments—[1] Words substituted by the Double Taxation Relief (Taxes on Income) (General) (Amendment) Regulations, SI 1996/783 reg 2 with effect from 6 April 1996.

5 The United Kingdom payer shall not, in respect of any payment, be charged with or liable to account for any tax which, but for a notice given under Regulation 2(2), he would have been required by the Income Tax Acts to deduct and account for on making the payment but in compliance with the notice has not deducted.

6 Where in compliance with a notice given under Regulation 2(2) a company makes the payment without deducting tax which, but for the notice, it would have been required to deduct in accordance with section 53 or 54 of the Income and Corporation Taxes Act 1970[a] the payment shall be treated for the purposes of section 248(4) of that Act[b] (which prohibits certain payments from being treated as charges on income for corporation tax) as if the company had deducted that tax in accordance with the said section 53 or 54 and had accounted for it under Part XI of that Act.

Note—[a] TA 1988 s 349.
[b] TA 1988 s 338(4).

7 Where, but for a notice given under Regulation 2(2), a person would have been chargeable with tax under section 53 of the Income and Corporation Taxes Act 1970[a] in respect of any such payment as is mentioned in subsection (1) thereof, the provisions of the Income Tax Acts relating to relief for losses shall apply as if the tax which he would have been so chargeable but in accordance with Regulation 5 is not so chargeable had been paid by him under an assessment under the said section 53.

Note—[a] TA 1988 s 349.

8 Any notice given under Regulation 2(2) may be expressed to become ineffective if certain specified events happen, or, whether so expressed or not, may be cancelled by a notice of cancellation given by or on behalf of the Board, and if to the knowledge of the United Kingdom payer any of those events happens or if such notice of cancellation is given, any payment made to the non-resident by the United Kingdom payer after the happening of that event becomes known to the United Kingdom payer or after the receipt of that notice, as the case may be, shall be subject to deduction of tax in accordance with the Income Tax Acts.

9 If it is discovered after a notice has been given under Regulation 2(2) that the non-resident is not entitled to exemption or partial relief from tax in respect of income referred to in the notice, any tax which, but for the notice, would have been deductible from any payment made to the non-resident by the United Kingdom payer but in compliance with the notice has not been so deducted—

(*a*) may be assessed on the non-resident under Case VI of Schedule D by an Inspector, or

(*b*) shall, if a direction to that effect is given by or on behalf of the Board, be deducted by the United Kingdom payer out of so much of the first payment made to the non-resident after the date of the direction as remains after the deduction of any tax deductible therefrom under the Income Tax Acts, and any balance which cannot be deducted out of the first such payment shall be deducted, subject to the same limitation, out of the next such payment, and so on until the whole of the tax (the amount of which shall be specified in the direction) has been deducted.

Any tax which the United Kingdom payer is required to deduct under paragraph (*b*) of this Regulation shall be accounted for as if it was tax deductible under section 53 of the Income and Corporation Taxes Act 1970[a] in respect of the payment from which it is deducted.

Note—[a] TA 1988 s 349.

10 A notice may be given under Regulation 2(2) where income is paid to a person authorised to receive that income on behalf of the non-resident, and in such a case the references in these Regulations to payment to the non-resident shall be treated as including references to payment to that person.

11 Regulations 2(2) and 8 shall not apply to payments in respect of coupons for any interest, but any such payments may, under arrangements approved by the Board, be made without deduction of tax or with tax deducted at a rate specified in the arrangements, if the non-resident or any person acting on his behalf makes a claim to the United Kingdom payer to that effect in such form as may be prescribed by the Board, and in the case of any payments so made Regulations 3 to 7 inclusive and Regulation 9 shall, with any necessary modifications, apply as if the claim were a notice given under Regulation 2(2).

1971/1035
Mineral Royalties (Tax) Regulations 1971

Made by the Commissioners of Inland Revenue under FA 1970 s 29(6), now TA 1988 s 122(5); see TA 1988 Sch 30 para 21

Made . . . . *23 June 1971*
Coming into Operation . . . . *1 July 1971*

Commentary—*Simon's Direct Tax Service* **B3.416**.

1—(1) These Regulations may be cited as the Mineral Royalties (Tax) Regulations 1971, and shall come into operation on 1st July 1971.

(2) The Interpretation Act 1889[a] shall apply for the interpretation of these Regulations as it applies for the interpretation of an Act of Parliament.

(3) In these Regulations:—

the "principal section" means section 29 of the Finance Act 1970[b];
"agreement" means a mineral lease or agreement, as defined in the principal section;
"specified operations" means the winning and working, grading, washing, grinding and crushing of minerals, but in relation to any particular agreement, includes only such of those operations as are in fact authorised by the agreement;
"rights" includes liberties.

Note—[a] Interpretation Act 1978.
[b] TA 1988 s 122.

2 Subject to Regulation 3 below, where a payment is made on or after 6th April 1970 in respect of a sum receivable on or after that date under an agreement which relates both to the winning and working of minerals and to other matters, then, notwithstanding any allocation of the payment under the terms of the agreement, so much but no more of the payment is to be treated for the purposes of the principal section as mineral royalties as might reasonably have been expected to be provided for by the agreement if—

(*a*) it conferred only the right to carry out specified operations in relation to minerals in or under the land to which the agreement relates; and
(*b*) any buildings, structures, roads, shafts, adits or other works existing on the land at the time when the agreement was granted or made were not in existence.

Provided that no such payments are to be treated as mineral royalties unless minerals in or under the land are being or have been won and worked pursuant to rights conferred by or under the agreement, or there is reasonable prospect of their being so won and worked.

3 The whole of a payment under an agreement shall for the purposes of the principal section be treated as a mineral royalty if under Regulation 2 above nine-tenths or more of it would be so treated.

4 Nothing in these Regulations applies to any periodical payments such as are referred to in subsection (9)(*b*) of the principal section[a] (payments made under certain statutes in Northern Ireland).

Note—[a] TA 1988 s 122(2)(*b*).

1973/317
Double Taxation Relief (Taxes on Income) (General) (Dividend) Regulations 1973

Made by the Commissioners of Inland Revenue under TA 1970 s 517, now TA 1988 s 791; see TA 1988 Sch 30 para 21

Made . . . . *27 February 1973*

Commentary—*Simon's Direct Tax Service* **D1.609.**
Revocation—These Regulations revoked by the Double Taxation Relief (Taxes on Income) (General) (Dividend) (Revocation) Regulations, SI 1999/1927 regs 1, 2 with effect from 21 July 1999.

1977/1143
Friendly Societies (Life Assurance Premium Relief) Regulations 1977

Made by the Chief Registrar of Friendly Societies under FA 1976 Sch 4 para 13, now TA 1988 Sch 14 para 3; see TA 1988 Sch 30 para 21

Made . . . . *7 July 1977*
Laid before Parliament . . . . . *18 July 1977*
Coming into Operation . . . . . . *18 August 1977*

Commentary—*Simon's Direct Tax Service* **E2.1031**.
Cross references—See the Friendly Societies (Life Assurance Premium Relief) (Change of Rate) Regulations, SI 1980/1947.

Citation and Commencement

1 These Regulations may be cited as the Friendly Societies (Life Assurance Premium Relief) Regulations 1977, and shall come into operation on 18th August 1977.

Interpretation

2—(1) In these Regulations—

["friendly society", subject to paragraph (1A) of this regulation, means a friendly society, not being a collecting society, registered under the Friendly Societies Act 1974 and includes a Northern Ireland Friendly Society.][1]
"collecting society" has the meaning assigned by section 1 of the Industrial Assurance Act 1923 as amended by Schedule 6 to the Companies Act 1967;

[''Northern Ireland Friendly Society'' means a friendly society, not being a collecting society, which is registered in Northern Ireland for purposes corresponding to the Friendly Societies Act 1974.][1]

''friendly society contract'' means a contract made by a friendly society with a member of the society in the course of its business in Great Britain, whether contained in the rules of the society or not;

''the prescribed scheme'' means the scheme prescribed in Schedule 1 to these Regulations;

''an approved scheme'' means a special scheme approved by the Chief Registrar of Friendly Societies in the circumstances provided for in regulation 7 of these Regulations;

''actuary'' means an actuary having the qualifications which are prescribed by the Friendly Societies (Qualifications of Actuaries) Regulations 1968;

''net contribution'' has the meaning assigned in paragraph 3 of Schedule 1 to these Regulations;

''gross contribution'' means the contribution of the amount payable under the contract;

''parent'' includes a stepfather or stepmother.

[(1A) References in these Regulations to a friendly society shall include references to a branch thereof registered under the Friendly Societies Act 1974.][1]

(2) The rules for the construction of Acts of Parliament contained in the Interpretation Act 1889[a] shall apply for the purposes of the interpretation of these Regulations.

Note—[a] Interpretation Act 1978.
Amendments—[1] In para (1) definition ''friendly society'' substituted, definition ''Northern Ireland Friendly Society'' inserted, and para (1A) inserted, by the Friendly Societies (Life Assurance Premium Relief) (Amendment) Regulations, SI 1978/1160 reg 2, with effect from 4 September 1978.

Adoption of a scheme

3—(1) A friendly society may by resolution of its committee of management passed before 1st October 1978 adopt—

(*a*) the prescribed scheme, or
(*b*) an approved scheme

for the purpose of securing that in the case of friendly society contracts to which the scheme so adopted applies amounts equal to 17½ per cent of the contributions payable are retained by or refunded to the persons paying the contributions.

(2) Where a friendly society has adopted any such scheme amounts equal to 17½ per cent of the contributions payable under contracts [made before 14th March 1984][1] to which the scheme applies shall be retained by or refunded to the persons paying the contributions as provided in the scheme so adopted.

(3) Written notice of a resolution adopting the prescribed or an approved scheme shall within fourteen days of the passing thereof be sent by the society to the Chief Registrar of Friendly Societies.

(4) Where a friendly society has resolved to adopt the prescribed or an approved scheme any right conferred by section 21 of the Friendly Societies Act 1974 on any person to receive a copy of the rules of the society shall be extended so as to include the right to receive a copy of the resolution and of the scheme adopted by the resolution.

Amendments—[1] Words in para (2) inserted by the Friendly Societies (Life Assurance Premium Relief) (Amendment) Regulations, SI 1984/323 reg 3(*a*), with effect from 14 March 1984.

Increase in contribution

4—(1) A resolution adopting the prescribed scheme may provide that in respect of any specified class of contract made by the society before 6th April 1979 to which the scheme applies under which the contribution does not exceed £4 every four weeks the contribution shall be increased with effect from that date to such sum as after deduction of 17½ per cent thereof equals the amount expressed in the contract to be the contribution.

(2) Where such provision is made the resolution shall operate so as to effect the above mentioned increase in the contribution payable under every contract of a class to which the provision relates, and the prescribed scheme shall take effect accordingly.

Corresponding increase in sum assured

5—(1) Where an increase in contribution has been effected under regulation 4 the sum assured or guaranteed by the contract under which the increased contribution is payable shall be increased by an amount determined in accordance with rules which have been certified by an actuary to be fair in relation to the increased contribution payable and have been approved by the Chief Registrar of Friendly Societies.

(2) Where the sum assured or guaranteed by a contract is increased by virtue of the preceding paragraph the society shall on being requested in writing to do so by the person by whom the increased contribution is payable notify him in writing of the amount of the increase in the sum assured or guaranteed.

6—(1) Where a friendly society has adopted the prescribed scheme by a resolution making such provision as is referred to in regulation 4(1) the member insured under a contract of a class specified in the provision which was made before 6th April 1979 and under which the contribution exceeds £4 every four weeks may before that date irrevocably elect, in the form set out in Schedule 2 to these Regulations or in a form to the like effect, that the contribution payable under the contract under which he is insured shall be increased with effect from 6th April 1979 to such sum as is mentioned in regulation 4(1).

(2) Where such election has been made the increase in contribution shall be effective as from 6th April 1979 as if it had been effected under regulation 4(2), and regulation 5 shall apply in respect of an increase in contribution under this regulation as it applies in relation to an increase under regulation 4.

Approved schemes

7 The Chief Registrar of Friendly Societies may before 1st October 1978 approve a special scheme intended to be adopted by a friendly society for the purposes mentioned in regulation 3 if in his opinion in view of the manner in which the business of the society is conducted, or any other relevant matter, it is expedient that the special scheme should be adopted.

Notice to contribution payers

8 Every friendly society which carries on life or endowment business shall take all reasonable steps to ensure that every person who on 31st December 1978 is paying contributions under a friendly society contract which forms part of such business receives a notice in a form approved by the Chief Registrar of Friendly Societies setting out—

(*a*) the effect of these Regulations,
(*b*) whether the society has adopted the prescribed or an approved scheme, and
(*c*) the effect of the scheme which has been adopted;

and, as regards contracts made between 1st January 1979 and 5th April 1979, that such notice is received by the prospective contribution payer before the contract is made.

Amendment of rules

9 Notwithstanding anything contained in the rules of a friendly society which has adopted the prescribed scheme or an approved scheme, the committee of management of the society may by resolution passed before 6th April 1979 make amendments to the rules of the society in connection with the adoption by the society of any such scheme.

Modification of enactments

10 The enactments mentioned in Schedule 3 to these Regulations shall have effect subject to the adaptations and modifications set out in that Schedule.

SCHEDULE 1

PRESCRIBED SCHEME

Regulation 2

1 The scheme applies to every friendly society contract [made before 14th March 1984][2] assuring life or endowment benefits under which contributions are payable to a friendly society which has adopted the scheme in accordance with regulation 3.

2 Where the member is resident in the United Kingdom and entitled to relief under section 19 of the Income and Corporation Taxes Act 1970[a] the liability of the member in respect of any contribution [due and payable after 5th April 1979][1] under a contract to which the scheme relates shall be discharged by payment of the net contribution; and any payment made on account of such a contribution shall be deemed to have been made after deducting $17\frac{1}{2}$ per cent from an amount payable in respect of the gross contribution.

Note—[a] TA 1988 s 266.

3 The net contribution shall be a sum equal to $82\frac{1}{2}$ per cent of the gross contribution, except that—

(*a*) where the gross contribution does not exceed £4 every four weeks and the said sum is not a multiple of one halfpenny, the said sum shall be rounded off to the nearer halfpenny, or, if the said sum is a multiple of one half of one halfpenny, to the nearer penny, and
(*b*) where the gross contribution exceeds £4 every four weeks and the said sum is not a multiple of one penny, the said sum shall be rounded off to the nearer penny, or, if the said sum is a multiple of one halfpenny, to the nearer even penny.

Amendments—[1] Words in para 2 substituted by the *Friendly Societies (Life Assurance Premium Relief) (Amendment) Regulations*, SI 1978/1160 reg 2, with effect from 4 September 1978.
[2] Words in para 1 inserted by the Friendly Societies (Life Assurance Premium Relief) (Amendment) Regulations, SI 1984/323 reg 3(*b*), with effect from 14 March 1984.

SCHEDULE 2

LIFE ASSURANCE PREMIUM RELIEF FORM OF ELECTION BY MEMBERS

Regulation 6

To: (Name of friendly society)
I (Name) of (Address)
irrevocably choose that as from 6th April 1979 the tax relief to which I shall be entitled in respect of the contributions paid by me in respect of the contract particulars of which are set out below shall take the form of an increase in the sum assured of an amount determined in accordance with rules approved by the Chief Registrar of Friendly Societies.
I understand that if I do not sign this form I shall be entitled to deduct and retain $17\frac{1}{2}$ per cent of the contributions at present payable under the contract.
Signature of member
Date:
Particulars of Contract
Number, if any, and date of contract
Amount of contribution and interval at which payable

SCHEDULE 3

ADAPTATIONS AND MODIFICATIONS OF ENACTMENTS

Regulation 10

This Schedule contains incidental provisions and makes consequential adaptations and modifications to enactments relating to friendly societies.

1977/1144
Industrial Assurance (Life Assurance Premium Relief) Regulations 1977

Made by the Industrial Assurance Commissioner under FA 1976 Sch 4 para 13, now TA 1988 Sch 14 para 3; see TA 1988 Sch 30 para 21

Made	*7 July 1977*
Laid before Parliament	*18 July 1977*
Coming into Operation	*18 August 1977*

Cross references—See the Industrial Assurance (Life Assurance Premium Relief) (Change of Rate) Regulations, SI 1980/1948 reg 3 (amendment of a scheme adopted in accordance with these Regulations).

Citation and Commencement

1 These Regulations may be cited as the Industrial Assurance (Life Assurance Premium Relief) Regulations 1977, and shall come into operation on 18th August 1977.

Interpretation

2—(1) In these Regulations—

"industrial assurance company" and "collecting society" have the meanings assigned by section 1 of the Industrial Assurance Act 1923 as amended by Schedule 6 to the Companies Act 1967;

"industrial assurance contract" means a contract of assurance made by an industrial assurance company in the course of its industrial assurance business in Great Britain or a contract made by a collecting society with a member of the society in the course of its industrial assurance business in Great Britain, whether contained in the rules of the society or not;

"collecting society contract" means a contract, other than an industrial assurance contract, made by a collecting society with a member of the society in the course of business in Great Britain, whether contained in the rules of the society or not;

"the prescribed scheme" means the scheme prescribed in Schedule 1 to these Regulations;

"an approved scheme" means a special scheme approved by the Industrial Assurance Commissioner in the circumstances provided for in regulation 7 of these Regulations;

"actuary" means an actuary having the qualifications which are prescribed by the Friendly Societies (Qualifications of Actuaries) Regulations 1968;

"net premium" has the meaning assigned in paragraph 3 of Schedule 1 to these Regulations;

"gross premium" means the premium of the amount payable under the policy or contract;

"parent" includes a stepfather and a stepmother.

(2) The rules for the construction of Acts of Parliament contained in the Interpretation Act 1889[a] shall apply for the purposes of the interpretation of these Regulations.

Note—[a] Interpretation Act 1978.

Adoption of a scheme

3—(1) An industrial assurance company or collecting society may by resolution of its board of directors or, as the case may be, of its committee of management, passed before 1st October 1978, adopt—

(*a*) the prescribed scheme, or
(*b*) an approved scheme

for the purpose of securing that in the case of policies or contracts to which the scheme so adopted applies amounts equal to 17½ per cent of the premiums payable are retained by or refunded to the persons paying the premiums.

(2) Where an industrial assurance company or collecting society has adopted any such scheme amounts equal to 17½ per cent of the premiums payable under—

[(*a*) policies in respect of assurances made before 14th March 1984, or
(*b*) contracts made before that date, to which][1]

the scheme applies shall be retained by or refunded to the persons paying the premiums as provided in the scheme so adopted.

(3) Written notice of a resolution adopting the prescribed or an approved scheme shall within fourteen days of the passing thereof be sent by the industrial assurance company or collecting society to the Industrial Assurance Commissioner.

(4) Where a collecting society has resolved to adopt the prescribed or an approved scheme any right conferred by section 21 of the Friendly Societies Act 1974 or section 10(1) of the Industrial Assurance and Friendly Societies Act 1948 on any person to receive a copy of the rules of the society or of an amendment thereof shall be extended so as to include the right to receive a copy of the resolution and of the scheme adopted by the resolution.

Amendments—[1] Words in para (2) substituted by the Industrial Assurance (Life Assurance Premium Relief) (Amendment) Regulations, SI 1984/322 reg 3(*a*), with effect from 14 March 1984.

Increase in premium

4—(1) A resolution adopting the prescribed scheme may provide that in respect of any specified class of policy or contract issued or made by the company or society before 6th April 1979 to which the scheme applies under which the premium does not exceed £4 every four weeks the premium shall be increased with effect from that date to such sum as after deduction of 17½ per cent thereof equals the amount expressed in the policy or contract to be the premium.

(2) Where such provision is made the resolution shall operate so as to effect the above mentioned increase in the premium payable under every policy or contract of a class to which the provision relates, and the prescribed scheme shall take effect accordingly.

Cross references—See the Industrial Assurance (Life Assurance Premium Relief) (Change of Rate) Regulations, SI 1980/1948 regs 4, 5 (amendment of gross premium and corresponding amendment to sum assured).

Corresponding increase in sum assured

5—(1) Where an increase in premium has been effected under regulation 4 the sum assured or guaranteed by the policy or contract under which the increased premium is payable shall be increased by an amount determined in accordance with rules which have been certified by an actuary to be fair in relation to the increased premium payable and have been approved by the Industrial Assurance Commissioner.

(2) Where the sum assured or guaranteed by a policy or contract is increased by virtue of the preceding paragraph the company or society shall on being requested in writing to do so by the person by whom the increased premium is payable notify him in writing of the amount of the increase in the sum assured or guaranteed.

6—(1) Where an industrial assurance company or collecting society has adopted the prescribed scheme by a resolution making such provision as is referred to in regulation 4(1), the person insured under a policy or contract of a class specified in the provision which was issued or made before 6th August 1979 and under which the premium exceeds £4 every four weeks may before that date irrevocably elect, in the form set out in Schedule 2 to these Regulations or in a form to the like effect, that the premium under the contract under which he is insured shall be increased with effect from 6th April 1979 to such sum as is mentioned in regulation 4(1).

(2) Where such election has been made the increase in premium shall be effective as from 6th April 1979 as if it had been effected under regulation 4(2), and regulation 5 shall apply in respect of an increase in premium under this regulation as it applies in relation to an increase under regulation 4.

Cross references—See the Industrial Assurance (Life Assurance Premium Relief) (Change of Rate) Regulations, SI 1980/1948 reg 7 (amendment of gross premium and corresponding amendment to sum assured).

Approved schemes

7 The Industrial Assurance Commissioner may before 1st October 1978 approve a special scheme intended to be adopted by an industrial assurance company or collecting society for the purposes mentioned in regulation 3 if in his opinion, in view of the manner in which the business of the company or society is conducted, or any other relevant matter, it is expedient that the special scheme should be adopted.

Cross references—See the Industrial Assurance (Life Assurance Premium Relief) (Change of Rate) Regulations, SI 1980/1948 reg 8 (amendment of approved schemes).

Notice to premium payers

8 Every industrial assurance company and collecting society shall take all reasonable steps to ensure that every person who on 31st December 1978 is paying premiums under an industrial assurance or collecting society contract made by it receives a notice in a form approved by the Industrial Assurance Commissioner setting out—

(*a*) the effect of these Regulations,
(*b*) whether the company or society has adopted the prescribed or an approved scheme, and
(*c*) the effect of the scheme which has been adopted;

and, as regards contracts made between 1st January 1979 and 5th April 1979, that such notice is received by the prospective premium payer before the contract is made.

Amendment of rules

9 Notwithstanding anything contained in the rules of a collecting society which has adopted the prescribed scheme or an approved scheme, the committee of management of the society may by resolution passed before 6th April 1979 make amendments to the rules of the society in connection with the adoption by the society of any such scheme.

Modification of enactments

10 The enactments mentioned in Schedule 3 to these Regulations shall have effect subject to the adaptations and modifications set out in that Schedule.

SCHEDULE 1

PRESCRIBED SCHEME

Regulation 2

1 The scheme applies to every industrial assurance or collecting society contract [made before 14th March 1984][1] under which premiums are payable to an industrial assurance company or collecting society which has adopted the scheme in accordance with regulation 3.

Amendments—[1] Words in para 1 inserted by the Industrial Assurance (Life Assurance Premium Relief) (Amendment) Regulations, SI 1984/322 reg 3(*b*), with effect from 14 March 1984.

2 Where the person assured or member, as the case may be, is resident in the United Kingdom and entitled to relief under section 19 of the Income and Corporation Taxes Act 1970[a] the liability of that person or member in respect of any premium [due and payable after 5th April 1979][1] under a contract to which the scheme relates shall be discharged by payment of the net premium; and any payment made on account of such a premium shall be deemed to have been made after deducting $17\frac{1}{2}$ per cent from an amount payable in respect of the gross premium.

Note—[a] TA 1988 s 266.
Amendments—[1] Words in para 2 substituted by the Industrial Assurance (Life Assurance Premium Relief) (Amendment) Regulations, SI 1978/1161 reg 2, with effect from 4 September 1978.

3 The net premium shall be a sum equal to $82\frac{1}{2}$ per cent of the gross premium, except that—

(*a*) in relation to an industrial assurance contract, where the said sum is not a multiple of one halfpenny, it shall be rounded off to the nearer halfpenny, or, if the said sum is a multiple of one half of one halfpenny, to the nearer penny; and
(*b*) in relation to a collecting society contract, where the said sum is not a multiple of one penny, it shall be rounded off to the nearer penny, or, if the said sum is a multiple of one halfpenny, to the nearer even penny.

SCHEDULE 2

LIFE ASSURANCE PREMIUM RELIEF

Regulation 6

Form of election by Policyholder

To: (Name of industrial assurance company or collecting society)

I (Name) of (Address)

irrevocably choose that as from 6th April 1979 the tax relief to which I shall be entitled in respect of the premiums paid by me in respect of the policy particulars of which are set out below shall take the form of an increase in the sum assured of an amount determined in accordance with rules approved by the Industrial Assurance Commissioner.

I understand that if I do not sign this form I shall be entitled to deduct and retain $17\frac{1}{2}$ per cent of the premium at present payable under the policy.

Date: Signature

Particulars of Policy

Number (if any) and date of policy

Amount of premium and interval at which payable

SCHEDULE 3

ADAPTATIONS AND MODIFICATIONS OF ENACTMENTS

Regulation 10

This Schedule contains incidental provisions and makes consequential adaptations and modifications to enactments relating to industrial assurance and friendly societies.

1978/1159

Income Tax (Life Assurance Premium Relief) Regulations 1978

Made by the Commissioners of Inland Revenue under FA 1976 Sch 4 para 16 (as amended by FA 1978 Sch 3 para 10), now TA 1988 Sch 14 para 7; see TA 1988 Sch 30 para 21

Made . . . . 4 *August 1978*

Coming into Operation . . . . 6 *April 1979*

Commentary—*Simon's Direct Tax Service* **E2.1044**.

Citation and commencement

1 These Regulations may be cited as the Income Tax (Life Assurance Premium Relief) Regulations 1978, and shall come into operation on 6th April 1979.

Interpretation

2—(1) In these Regulations unless the context otherwise requires—

"the Board" means the Commissioners of Inland Revenue;

"authorised officer" in relation to a life office means an official authorised for the purposes of these Regulations by resolution of the life office's Board, except that—

(*a*) in relation to a registered friendly society, it means an official so authorised by resolution of the society's committee of management, and

(*b*) in relation to underwriters falling within subsection (2)(*a*)(ii) of section 19 of the Income and Corporation Taxes Act 1970[a] it means the underwriting agent through whom their business is carried on;

"deficiency" means a deficiency recoverable under paragraph 5(*b*) of Schedule 4[b];

"financial year" in relation to a life office means a period for which the office makes up its accounts;

"four-weekly accounting period" means the period of 28 days commencing on 1 January in a calendar year, and each succeeding period throughout the year being a period of 28 days, except that a period including 29 February and the period commencing on 3 December shall be extended to 29 days;

"income tax month" means the period beginning on the 6th day of any calendar month and ending on the 5th day of the following calendar month; and in Regulations 6 and 7 below, in relation to an income tax month—

(*a*) "relevant calendar month" means a calendar month falling partly in the income tax month, and (*b*) "component part" means the part falling within it of a relevant calendar month;

"industrial branch business" means [any such business carried on before 1st December 2001 as was][2] industrial assurance business as defined in section 1(2) of the Industrial Assurance Act 1923 or [Art 3(1) of the Industrial Assurance (Northern Ireland) Order 1979][1];

"insurance" includes a contract for a deferred annuity;

"life office" means any such body as is mentioned in section 19(*a*) of the Income and Corporation Taxes Act 1970[c] as amended by paragraph 3 of Schedule 4;

"net of deduction" means net of the deduction authorised by paragraph 5 of Schedule 4[d] (or by that paragraph as modified by Regulation 4 below);

"ordinary branch business" means life assurance business other than industrial branch business;

"Schedule 4" means Schedule 4 to the Finance Act 1976.

(2) The Interpretation Act 1889[e] shall apply for the interpretation of these Regulations as it applies for the interpretation of an Act of Parliament.

Notes—[a] TA 1988 s 266(2)(*a*)(ii).
[b] TA 1988 s 266(5)(*b*).
[c] TA 1988 266(2)(*a*).
[d] TA 1988 s 266(5).
[e] Interpretation Act 1978.

Amendments—[1] Words in the definition of "industrial branch business" in para (1) substituted by the Tax, Consumer Credit and Judicature (Northern Ireland Consequential Amendments) Order, SI 1979/1576 arts 1(2), 3, with effect from 3 January 1980.
[2] Words in the definition of "industrial branch business" in para (1) inserted by the Financial Services and Markets Act 2000 (Consequential Amendments) (Taxes) Order, SI 2001/3629 art 110 with effect from 1 December 2001, immediately after the coming into force of the Financial Services and Markets Act 2000 ss 411, 432(1), Sch 20 (and SI 2001/3629 Pts 1 and 2).

Information to be given to the life office

3—(1) A life office may at any time by notice in writing require an individual who pays or proposes to pay premiums net of deduction to furnish to the life office a statement under this Regulation.

(2) A statement under this Regulation shall be in such form and contain such particulars as the Board prescribe, and the particulars prescribed shall be such as are necessary for determining whether the person paying the premiums is or will be entitled to pay them net of deduction.

(3) Where an individual has been required to furnish a statement under this Regulation in relation to any insurance and has not furnished it then (until he does so)—

(*a*) if the statement was required before the first premium in respect of that insurance became due, he shall not be entitled to pay any premiums in respect of that insurance net of deduction, and

(*b*) in any other case, he shall not be entitled to pay net of deduction any premiums in respect of that insurance falling due more than 60 days after the date on which the notice requiring the statement was issued.

(4) If notwithstanding the furnishing of a statement under this Regulation in relation to any insurance the life office concerned is not satisfied that the premiums are properly payable net of deduction, and the person paying them does not agree to pay them without deduction, the life office shall notify the Board forthwith.

(5) Without prejudice to the generality of paragraph (1) above—

(*a*) a life office shall not accept payment of premiums net of deduction in respect of any insurance without first obtaining a statement under this Regulation in relation to that insurance, unless the particulars required in the statement are already in the possession of the life office [or the Board have by notice in writing to the life office dispensed with the requirement of this sub-paragraph in relation to that insurance][1] and

(*b*) where premiums in respect of any insurance are being paid net of deduction and it appears to the life office that they are no longer properly so payable, the life office shall require a statement under this Regulation unless the person paying the premiums agrees to pay them without deduction.

(6) Paragraph (5)(*a*) above shall not apply to insurances made before 1 September 1978 if the life office concerned has established to the satisfaction of the Board that on the basis of the information in the hands of the life office there is not a probability of more than one in ten that the amount claimed to be recoverable for any period under paragraph (5)(*b*) of Schedule 4 in respect of such insurances will exceed by more than 0·5 per cent the amount properly recoverable.

(7) Paragraphs (5)(*a*) and (6) above shall not apply to an insurance made before 6 April 1979 to which paragraph 11 of Schedule 4[a] applies.

Note—[a] TA 1988 Sch 14, para 2.

Amendments—[1] Words in para (5)(*a*) inserted by the IT (Life Assurance Premium Relief) Regulations, SI 1979/346, with effect from 6 April 1979.

Rounding of sums payable by way of net premium

4—(1) This Regulation has effect for adjusting in certain cases the net amount payable by way of premium after the deduction authorised under paragraph 5 of Schedule 4[a], and in those cases the amount treated as deducted and retained under that paragraph shall also be adjusted accordingly.

(2) In the case of—

(*a*) an industrial assurance contract, as defined in any Regulations made under paragraph 13 of Schedule 4[b], or

(*b*) a friendly society contract, as defined in any such Regulations, in respect of which the premiums do not (before any deduction under paragraph 5 of Schedule 4[a]) exceed £4 every four weeks,

if the net amount payable is otherwise not a multiple of one new halfpenny it shall be adjusted and shall—

(i) where the premium is one to which a scheme adopted under Regulations made under paragraph 13 of Schedule 4[b] applies, be the amount payable in accordance with the scheme, and

(ii) in any other case be rounded to the nearer new halfpenny or, if it is a multiple of one half of one new halfpenny, to the nearer new penny.

(3) In the case of any insurance not included in paragraph (2)(*a*) or (*b*) above, if the net amount payable is otherwise not a multiple of one new penny it shall be rounded to the nearer new penny or, if it is a multiple of one new halfpenny, to the nearer even new penny.

Note—[a] TA 1988 s 266(5).
[b] TA 1988 Sch 14, para 3.

Deficiency claims: introductory

5—(1) Sums recoverable by a life office under paragraph 5(*b*) of Schedule 4[a] shall be recovered on a claim made to the Board for the purpose under these Regulations.

(2) A claim for any period allowed by these Regulations shall be a claim relating to the deficiency arising in respect of premiums received in that period, and accordingly references to premiums "for" a period are to premiums received in that period.

(3) Subject to paragraph (4) below a claim shall be for the claimant's financial year, and is referred to in these Regulations as an "annual claim".

(4) A claim may also be made in accordance with Regulation 6 or 8 below for a period shorter than the claimant's financial year, and is referred to in these Regulations as an "interim claim".

(5) A life office which carries on both industrial branch business and ordinary branch business may make annual and interim claims separately for business of each branch.

Note—[a] TA 1988 s 266(5)(*b*).

Interim claims in advance

6—(1) An interim claim for a period allowed by paragraphs (2) and (3) below may be made at any time within one month before the period for which it is made, and is referred to in these Regulations as an "interim claim in advance".

(2) The three kinds of period for which an interim claim in advance may be made are:—

(*a*) a calendar month, or

(*b*) an income tax month, or

(*c*) in the case of a claim relating to industrial branch business only, a four-weekly accounting period.

(3) Interim claims in advance made by one life office may not (except where a change is authorised by prior approval of the Board) be made for periods of different kinds: Provided that if the first claim made for industrial branch business (or the first such claim made after an authorised change) is a separate claim made for a four-weekly accounting period, this paragraph shall then apply separately in relation to industrial branch business and ordinary branch business.

(4) An interim claim in advance for a period shall be based on an estimate of the deficiency that will arise in respect of premiums for that period, and the estimate shall be certified by an authorised officer of the claimant as being the best estimate that can reasonably be made of the deficiency; and if the claim is for an income tax month the estimate shall show the part of the deficiency attributed to each component part of the month.

(5) If the Board are satisfied with the estimate they shall pay the estimated amount of the deficiency to the claimant before the end of the period for which the claim is made; if they are not so satisfied, they shall pay to the claimant before the end of the period such lesser amount if any as in their estimation will approximate to the deficiency.

Supplementary statements

7—(1) When a payment has been made to a life office under Regulation 6(5) above on an interim claim in advance, the life office shall deliver to the Board a supplementary statement under this Regulation, and (except where paragraph (5)(*b*) below applies) shall deliver the statement within two months after the end of the period for which the claim was made.

(2) The supplementary statement shall be a statement correcting (or confirming) the estimate of the deficiency given in accordance with Regulation 6(4) above, and shall—

(*a*) be based as far as possible on the amount of the premiums actually received in the period covered by the statement, and only as far as may be necessary on a revised estimate, and

(*b*) (subject to paragraph (5) below) be for the same period as the interim claim in advance;

and any estimate contained in the supplementary statement shall be certified by an authorised officer of the life office as the best estimate that can reasonably be made.

(3) If the supplementary statement shows a deficiency greater than the payment made under Regulation 6(5), the Board shall if satisfied with the statement pay the amount of the difference to the life office forthwith by way of supplementary payment on the claim; if the supplementary statement shows a deficiency less than the payment made under Regulation 6(5), the life office shall repay the amount of the difference to the Board with the statement.

(4) If in respect of an interim claim on which a payment has been made under Regulation 6(5) above a life office fails to deliver a supplementary statement within the time required by this Regulation, the amount of the payment shall immediately be recoverable by the Board in the same manner as tax charged by an assessment which has become final and conclusive.

(5) Where the interim claim in advance was for an income tax month the life office shall (instead of delivering a statement for that month) deliver a supplementary statement for each of the relevant calendar months, and the supplementary statement for a relevant calendar month shall—

(*a*) provide the information required by paragraph (2) above in respect of that month, and

(*b*) be delivered within two months and five days after the end of that month.

Interim claims in arrear

8—(1) An interim claim for a period allowed by paragraph (2) below may be made at any time within six months after the end of the period for which it is made.

(2) The period for which a claim may be made under this Regulation shall be one which—

(*a*) is not shorter than one calendar month, and

(*b*) falls wholly within the claimant's same financial year, and

(*c*) does not include any part of a period in respect of which a payment was made under Regulation 6(5) above (unless the payment in respect of that period or that part was recovered under Regulation 7(4) above).

(3) A claim under this Regulation may only be made to recover the deficiency arising in respect of premiums actually received and may not be based on an estimate.

(4) If the deficiency claimed is established to the Board's satisfaction, they shall pay the amount of the deficiency to the claimant; if they are not so satisfied they shall pay to the claimant any lesser amount established to their satisfaction.

Annual claims

9—(1) An annual claim for the claimant's financial year may, subject to paragraph (2) below, be made at any time within six years after the end of the financial year.

(2) Where in relation to any financial year a life office has received and not repaid any payment on a relevant interim claim, it shall within one year after the end of the financial year make an annual claim to establish the deficiency for that year.

In this Regulation "relevant interim claim" means, in relation to a financial year, an interim claim for a period falling wholly or partly within that year.

(3) An annual claim shall be a claim to establish and, so far as not already recovered, to recover the deficiency arising in respect of premiums actually received in the year and may not be based on an estimate.

(4) An annual claim required under paragraph (2) above shall bring into account payments made on relevant interim claims, and shall apportion as may be necessary any payment made on a relevant interim claim for any period falling partly in a different year; and for the purpose of this Regulation the "aggregate of the relevant interim payments" means the aggregate of the payments made (and not repaid) on relevant interim claims but excluding any part of a payment apportioned to a different year.

(5) Where the aggregate of the relevant interim payments shown by a claim exceeds the deficiency for the year shown by the claim, the life office shall repay the amount of the excess to the Board with the claim.

(6) If a life office fails to make an annual claim required under paragraph (2) above within the time limited by that paragraph, the Board may issue a notice to the life office showing the aggregate of the relevant interim payments for the year, and stating that the Board are not satisfied that the deficiency for the year exceeds a lower amount stated in the notice.

(7) If an annual claim is not delivered to the Board within two weeks after the issue of a notice under paragraph (6) above the amount of the difference between the aggregate and the lower amount stated in the notice shall immediately be recoverable by the Board in the same manner as tax charged by an assessment which has become final and conclusive.

(8) Where an annual claim has been made and the claimant subsequently discovers that an error or mistake has been made in the claim, the claimant may make a supplementary claim within the time allowed by paragraph (1) above.

SIs

Deficiency claims: supplementary provisions

10—(1) Section 42 of the Taxes Management Act 1970 shall not apply to claims under these Regulations.

(2) No appeal shall lie from the Board's decision on an interim claim.

(3) An appeal shall lie to the Special Commissioners from the Board's decision on an annual claim, and the appeal shall be brought by giving written notice to the Board within 30 days of receipt of written notice of the decision.

(4) No payment or repayment made or other thing done on or in relation to an interim claim or a notice under Regulation 9(6) above shall prejudice the decision on an annual claim.

(5) Part V of the Taxes Management Act 1970 (appeals and other proceedings) shall apply to an appeal under paragraph (3) above, and on an appeal the Special Commissioners may vary the decision appealed against whether or not the variation is to the advantage of the appellant.

(6) All such payments and repayments shall be made as are necessary to give effect to the Board's decision on an annual claim, or to any variation of that decision on appeal.

(7) Claims and supplementary statements under these Regulations shall be in such form and contain such particulars as the Board prescribe and shall be signed by an authorised officer of the life office; and forms prescribed for annual claims may require a report to be given by the life office's auditor.

(8) Where for the purposes of an annual claim for a financial year it is necessary to apportion any payment made on an interim claim for a period falling partly within and partly outside that year, the apportionment shall be made in such manner as the Board prescribe.

Simon's Tax Cases—reg 10(6), *United Friendly Insurance plc v IRC* [1998] STC 621.

Information from policyholders

11 The Board may by notice in writing require any person who has or had a policy of life insurance or contract for a deferred annuity with a life office or who pays or paid premiums under such a policy or contract to furnish them within such time as they may direct with such information (including copies of relevant documents) as they require for the purposes of section 19 of the Income and Corporation Taxes Act 1970 or of Schedule 4.[a]

Note—[a] TA 1988 s 266 and Sch 14.

12—(1) Every person to whom premiums are paid in respect of which a claim is made under these Regulations shall, whenever required to do so, make available for inspection by an authorised officer of the Board all such books, documents and other records in his possession or under his control containing information relating to—

(*a*) such premiums and the policies or contracts under which such premiums are paid, or
(*b*) the persons holding such policies or contracts or paying such premiums,

as may reasonably be required for determining whether the deficiency for which any claim is made under these Regulations is properly recoverable.

(2) Where records are maintained by computer the person required to make them available for inspection shall provide the officer making the inspection with all facilities necessary for obtaining information from them.

(3) Every statement made under Regulation 3 above shall be preserved by the life office to which it is made (or which is the insurer for the time being), in such manner as may be approved by the Board so as to be available for inspection under this Regulation, until three years after the termination of the insurance or contract to which it relates.

1980/1947

Friendly Societies (Life Assurance Premium Relief) (Change of Rate) Regulations 1980

Made by the Chief Registrar of Friendly Societies under FA 1976 Sch 4 para 13, now TA 1988 Sch 14 para 3; see TA 1988 Sch 30 para 21

Made	*15 December 1980*
Laid before Parliament	*29 December 1980*
Coming into Operation	*20 January 1981*

Commentary—*Simon's Direct Tax Service* **E2.1031**.

Citation and commencement

1 These Regulations may be cited as the Friendly Societies (Life Assurance Premium Relief) (Change of Rate) Regulations 1980, and shall come into operation on 20th January 1981.

Interpretation

2 In these Regulations—

"the 1977 Regulations" means the Friendly Societies (Life Assurance Premium Relief) Regulations 1977;

"friendly society" means a friendly society, not being a collecting society, registered under the Friendly Societies Act 1974 or a branch so registered under that Act of a friendly society so registered;

"collecting society" [means a society which before 1st December 2001 was a collecting society within][1] the meaning assigned by section 1 of the Industrial Assurance Act 1923 as amended by Schedule 6 to the Companies Act 1967;

"the prescribed scheme" means the scheme prescribed in Schedule 1 to the Friendly Societies (Life Assurance Premium Relief) Regulations 1977;

"an approved scheme" means a special scheme approved by the Chief Registrar of Friendly Societies in the circumstances provided for in regulation 7 of the Friendly Societies (Life Assurance Premium Relief) Regulations 1977;

"gross contribution" means the contribution of the amount payable under the contract;

"actuary" means an actuary having the qualifications which are prescribed by the Friendly Societies (Qualifications of Actuaries) Regulations 1968;

"the authorised percentage" means the percentage for the time being in force under paragraph 5(*a*) of Schedule 4 to the Finance Act 1976;

"the effective date" means the date on which a change in the authorised percentage takes effect;

"parent" includes a stepfather and a stepmother.

Amendments—[1] Words in the definition of "collecting society" substituted by the Financial Services and Markets Act 2000 (Consequential Amendments) (Taxes) Order, SI 2001/3629 art 111 with effect from 1 December 2001, immediately after the coming into force of the Financial Services and Markets Act 2000 ss 411, 432(1), Sch 20 (and SI 2001/3629 Pts 1 and 2).

Amendment of a scheme

3—(1) Where a friendly society has adopted the prescribed scheme or an approved scheme in accordance with the provisions of the 1977 Regulations the society may, by resolution of its committee of management passed within eight months of the passing of any Act making a change in the authorised percentage, amend any such scheme so that amounts equal to the authorised percentage of the gross contributions due and payable on or after the effective date under contracts to which the scheme applies shall be retained by or refunded to the persons paying the contributions.

(2) Where a friendly society has amended any such scheme, amounts equal to the authorised percentage of the gross contributions payable under contracts to which the scheme applies shall be retained by or refunded to the persons paying the contributions as provided in the scheme so amended.

(3) Written notice of a resolution amending the prescribed scheme or an approved scheme shall within fourteen days of the passing thereof be sent by the society to the Chief Registrar of Friendly Societies.

(4) Where a friendly society has resolved to amend the prescribed scheme or an approved scheme any right conferred by section 21 of the Friendly Societies Act 1974 on any person to receive a copy of the rules of the society shall be extended so as to include the right to receive a copy of the resolution and of the amended scheme adopted by the resolution.

Amendment of gross contribution

4—(1) Where, by virtue of regulation 4 of the 1977 Regulations, a resolution adopting the prescribed scheme provided that the gross contribution was to be increased with effect from 6th April 1979 in respect of any specified class of contract, a resolution amending the prescribed scheme may also amend the gross contribution so that with effect from the effective date the gross contributions shall be amended to such sum as after deduction of the authorised percentage thereof equals the amount expressed in the contract to be the contribution.

(2) Where such an amendment is made, the resolution shall operate so as to effect the above mentioned amendment in the gross contribution payable under every contract of a class to which the provision relates, and the prescribed scheme as amended shall take effect accordingly.

Corresponding amendment to sum assured

5 Where a gross contribution has been amended under regulation 4, the sum assured or guaranteed by the contract may be amended by an amount determined in accordance with rules which have been certified by an actuary to be fair in relation to the gross contribution payable and have been approved by the Chief Registrar of Friendly Societies.

6 Where the gross contribution is amended in accordance with these Regulations, the society shall, on being requested in writing after 5th April 1981 to do so by the person by whom the contribution is payable, notify him in writing of the amount of the effect of the amendment on the sum assured or guaranteed or of any other effect.

7 Where by virtue of regulation 6 of the 1977 Regulations a person insured under a contract irrevocably elected that the contribution under the contract under which he was insured should be increased with effect from 6th April 1979, the amendment to the gross contribution shall apply as from the effective date as if it had been effected under regulation 4(2), and regulations 5 and 6 shall apply in respect of an amended contribution under this regulation as they apply in relation to an amendment under regulation 4.

Amendment of approved scheme

8 Where a friendly society adopted an approved scheme under regulation 7 of the 1977 Regulations the Chief Registrar of Friendly Societies may, within eight months of the passing of any Act making a change in the authorised percentage, approve any amendment to the scheme which in his view is expedient or necessary to give effect to the change in the authorised percentage.

Notice or advertisement

9 Where a friendly society has, in accordance with the provisions of these Regulations, amended the prescribed scheme or an approved scheme adopted by it, as soon as is reasonably practicable it shall either:

(*a*) serve upon every person paying contributions to the society who is affected by the amendment a notice containing a statement setting out the effects thereof; or

(*b*) publish or cause to be published such notice by advertisement in one or more newspapers in general circulation in the area where the society carries on business.

Amendment of rules

10 Notwithstanding anything contained in the rules of a friendly society which has amended the prescribed scheme or an approved scheme, the committee of management of the society may, by resolution passed before the effective date, make amendments to the rules of the society in connection with the amendment by the society of any such scheme.

Modification of enactments

11 The enactments mentioned in the Schedule to these Regulations shall have effect subject to the adaptations and modifications set out in that Schedule.

SCHEDULE

ADAPTATIONS AND MODIFICATIONS OF ENACTMENTS

Regulation 11

This Schedule contains incidental provisions and makes consequential adaptations and modifications to enactments relating to friendly societies.

1980/1948

Industrial Assurance (Life Assurance Premium Relief) (Change of Rate) Regulations 1980

Made by the Chief Registrar of Friendly Societies under FA 1976 Sch 4 para 13, now TA 1988 Sch 14 para 3; see TA 1988 Sch 30 para 21

Made	*15 December 1980*
Laid before Parliament	*29 December 1980*
Coming into Operation	*20 January 1981*

Commentary—*Simon's Direct Tax Service* **E2.1031, 1039**.

Citation and commencement

1 These Regulations may be cited as the Industrial Assurance (Life Assurance Premium Relief) (Change of Rate) Regulations 1980, and shall come into operation on 20th January 1981.

Interpretation

2 In these Regulations—

"the 1977 Regulations" means the Industrial Assurance (Life Assurance Premium Relief) Regulations 1977;

"industrial assurance company" and "collecting society" have the meanings assigned by section 1 of the Industrial Assurance Act 1923 as amended by Schedule 6 to the Companies Act 1967;

"the prescribed scheme" means the scheme prescribed in Schedule 1 to the Industrial Assurance (Life Assurance Premium Relief) Regulations 1977;

"an approved scheme" means a special scheme approved by the Industrial Assurance Commissioner in the circumstances provided for in regulation 7 of the Industrial Assurance (Life Assurance Premium Relief) Regulations 1977;

"actuary" means an actuary having the qualifications which are prescribed by the Friendly Societies (Qualifications of Actuaries) Regulations 1968;

"net premium" has the meaning assigned in paragraph 3 of Schedule 1 to the Industrial Assurance (Life Assurance Premium Relief) Regulations 1977;

"gross premium" means the premium of the amount payable under the policy or contract;

"the authorised percentage" means the percentage for the time being in force under paragraph 5(*a*) of Schedule 4 to the Finance Act 1976;

"the effective date" means the date on which a change in the authorised percentage takes effect;

"amended net premium" shall be a sum equal to the gross premium less the authorised percentage, such sum to be rounded off in accordance with the principles set out in Schedule 1 of the 1977 Regulations;

"parent" includes a stepfather and a stepmother.

Amendment of a scheme

3—(1) Where an industrial assurance company or collecting society has adopted the prescribed scheme or an approved scheme in accordance with the provisions of the 1977 Regulations the company or society may, by resolution of its board of directors or, as the case may be, of its committee of management, passed within eight months of the passing of any Act making a change in the authorised percentage, amend any such scheme so that amounts equal to the authorised percentage of the gross premiums due and payable on or after the effective date under policies or contracts to which the scheme applies shall be retained by or refunded to the persons paying the premiums.

(2) Where an industrial assurance company or collecting society has amended any such scheme, amounts equal to the authorised percentage of the gross premiums payable under policies or contracts to which the scheme applies shall be retained by or refunded to the persons paying the premiums as provided in the scheme so amended.

(3) Written notice of a resolution amending the prescribed scheme or an approved scheme shall within fourteen days of the passing thereof be sent by the industrial assurance company or collecting society to the Industrial Assurance Commissioner.[1]

(4) Where a collecting society has resolved to amend the prescribed scheme or an approved scheme any right conferred by section 21 of the Friendly Societies Act 1974 or section 10(1) of the Industrial Assurance and Friendly Societies Act 1948 on any person to receive a copy of the rules of the society or of an amendment thereof shall be extended so as to include the right to receive a copy of the resolution and of the amended scheme adopted by the resolution.

Amendments—[1] Reference to Industrial Assurance Commissioner to be construed as reference to Friendly Societies Commission, by virtue of the Friendly Societies Act 1992 (Transitional and Consequential Provisions) Regulations, SI 1995/710.

Amendment of gross premium

4—(1) Where, by virtue of regulation 4 of the 1977 Regulations, a resolution adopting the prescribed scheme provided that the gross premium was to be increased with effect from 6th April 1979 in respect of any specified class of policy or contract, a resolution amending the prescribed scheme may also amend the gross premium so that with effect from the effective date the gross premium shall be amended to such sum as after deduction of the authorised percentage thereof equals the amount expressed in the policy or contract to be the premium.

(2) Where such an amendment is made, the resolution shall operate so as to effect the above mentioned amendment in the gross premium payable under every policy or contract of a class to which the provision relates, and the prescribed scheme as amended shall take effect accordingly.

Corresponding amendment to sum assured

5 Where a gross premium has been amended under regulation 4, the sum assured or guaranteed by the policy or contract may be amended by an amount determined in accordance with rules which have been certified by an actuary to be fair in relation to the gross premium payable and have been approved by the Industrial Assurance Commissioner[1].

6 Where the gross premium is amended in accordance with these Regulations, the industrial assurance company or collecting society shall, on being requested in writing after 5th April 1981 to do so by the person by whom the premium is payable, notify him in writing of the effect of the amendment on the sum assured or guaranteed or of any other effect.

7 Where by virtue of regulation 6 of the 1977 Regulations a person insured under a policy or contract irrevocably elected that the premium under the contract under which he was insured should be increased with effect from 6th April 1979, the amendment to the gross premium shall apply as from the effective date as if it had been effected under regulation 4(2), and regulations 5 and 6 shall apply in respect of an amended premium under this regulation as they apply in relation to an amendment under regulation 4.

Amendments—[1] Reference to Industrial Assurance Commissioner to be construed as reference to Friendly Societies Commission, by virtue of the Friendly Societies Act 1992 (Transitional and Consequential Provisions) Regulations, SI 1995/710.

Amendment of approved schemes

8 Where an industrial assurance company or a collecting society adopted an approved scheme under regulation 7 of the 1977 Regulations, the Industrial Assurance Commissioner[1] may, within eight months of the passing of any Act making a change in the authorised percentage, approve any amendment to the scheme which in his view is expedient or necessary to give effect to the change in the authorised percentage.

Amendments—[1] Reference to Industrial Assurance Commissioner to be construed as reference to Friendly Societies Commission, by virtue of the Friendly Societies Act 1992 (Transitional and Consequential Provisions) Regulations, SI 1995/710.

Notice or advertisement

9 Where an industrial assurance company or collecting society has, in accordance with the provisions of these regulations, amended the prescribed scheme or an approved scheme adopted by it, as soon as is reasonably practicable it shall either:

(*a*) serve upon every person paying premiums to the company or society who is affected by the amendment a notice containing a statement setting out the effects thereof; or

(*b*) publish or cause to be published such notice by advertisement in one or more newspapers in general circulation in the area where the company or society carries on business.

Amendment of rules

10 Notwithstanding anything contained in the rules of a collecting society which has amended the prescribed scheme or an approved scheme, the committee of management of the society may, by resolution passed before the effective date, make amendments to the rules of the society in connection with the amendment by the society of any such scheme.

Modifications of enactments

11 The enactments mentioned in the Schedule to these Regulations shall have effect subject to the adaptations and modifications set out in that Schedule.

SCHEDULE

ADAPTATIONS AND MODIFICATIONS OF ENACTMENTS

Regulation 11

This Schedule contains incidental provisions and makes consequential adaptations and modifications to enactments relating to friendly societies.

1981/233

Crown Proceedings (Northern Ireland) Order 1981

Made by Order in Council under the Crown Proceedings Act 1947 s 53

Made . . . . *18 February 1981*

PART I

General

1—(1) This Order may be cited as the Crown Proceedings (Northern Ireland) Order 1981 and ... shall come into operation on 19th March 1981.

(2) In this Order "the Act" means the Crown Proceedings Act 1947.

(5) This Order extends only to Northern Ireland.

Note—Words omitted are outside the scope of this work.

PART II

Extension of the Act to Northern Ireland

2 The provisions of the Act shall extend to Northern Ireland—

(*a*) in relation to Her Majesty's Government in the United Kingdom, with the additions, exceptions and modifications set out in Part III of this Order;

(*b*) in relation to Her Majesty's Government in Northern Ireland, with those additions, exceptions and modifications, but subject to the further additions, exceptions and modifications set out in Part IV of this Order.

PART III

Additions and exceptions to, and modifications of, the Act in its application to the Crown in right of both Her Majesty's government in the United Kingdom and (subject to Part IV) Her Majesty's government in Northern Ireland

3 For any reference to the commencement of the Act there shall be substituted a reference to 1st January 1950 (the date of coming into operation of the Northern Ireland (Crown Proceedings) Order 1949).

Regulations—Northern Ireland (Crown Proceedings) Order, SI 1949/1836.

8 In section 13, the words from ''In this section'' to the end shall be excepted.

10 In section 15(1) after ''civil proceedings'' there shall be inserted ''by or''.

11 For section 16 there shall be substituted the following section:

''16 Interpleader

The Crown may obtain relief by way of interpleader proceedings, and may be made a party to such proceedings, in the same manner in which a subject may obtain relief by way of such proceedings or be made a party thereto; and the provisions of Article 44 of the Judgments Enforcement (Northern Ireland) Order 1981 relating to interpleader proceedings shall, subject to the provisions of this Act, have effect accordingly.''.

12—(1) For section 17(1) there shall be substituted the following subsection:

''(1) The Department of the Civil Service for Northern Ireland shall publish a list specifying the several departments of the Government of the United Kingdom which are authorised departments for the purposes of this Act in Northern Ireland, and the name and address for service of the person who is, or is acting for the purposes of this Act as, the solicitor in Northern Ireland for each such department, and may from time to time amend or vary the said list. The said list may in relation to any such department specify different solicitors for different types of proceedings.

Any document purporting to be a copy of a list published under this section and purporting to be printed under the superintendence or the authority of His Majesty's Stationery Office shall in any legal proceedings be received as evidence for the purpose of establishing what departments are authorised departments for the purposes of this Act, and what person is, or is acting for the purposes of this Act as, the solicitor in Northern Ireland for any such department.''.

(2) After section 17(3) there shall be inserted the following subsection:

''(3A) Civil proceedings against the Crown may be instituted in Northern Ireland against the Attorney General if the alleged liability arises out of the performance of any function pursuant to an agency arrangement or the person instituting the proceedings has any reasonable doubt whether the alleged liability of the Crown arises in respect of His Majesty's Government in the United Kingdom or in respect of His Majesty's Government in Northern Ireland.''.

13 In section 18 for ''the Solicitor for the affairs of His Majesty's Treasury'' there shall be substituted ''the Crown Solicitor for Northern Ireland''.

14 Section 19(1) shall be excepted.

15 In section 20(2) the words ''or transfer'' shall be excepted, for ''transfer'' where secondly occurring there shall be substituted ''remittal'' ...

Note—Words omitted are outside the scope of this work.

17 In section 22 after ''execution'' there shall be inserted ''and all enactments and Judgment Enforcement Rules relating to stay of enforcement of judgments''.

18 For section 23(3) there shall be substituted the following subsection:

''(3) Notwithstanding anything in the preceding provisions of this section, the provisions of this Part of this Act shall not have effect with respect to any of the following proceedings brought by or against the Crown in right of His Majesty's Government in the United Kingdom, that is to say:

(*a*) proceedings brought by the Attorney General on the relation of some other person;
(*b*) proceedings by or against the Public Trustee;
(*c*) proceedings by or against the Land Purchase Trustee for Northern Ireland.''.

19—(1) For section 24(1) there shall be substituted the following subsection:

''(1) Article 127 of the Judgments Enforcement (Northern Ireland) Order 1981 (which provides that a money judgment shall, subject to certain exceptions and to any contrary provision in the judgment, carry interest) shall apply to money judgments given against or in favour of the Crown.''.

(2) Section 24(2) shall be excepted.

(3) In section 24(3) for the reference to section 3 of the Law Reform (Miscellaneous Provisions) Act 1934 there shall be substituted a reference to section 17 of the Law Reform (Miscellaneous Provisions) Act (Northern Ireland) 1937.

20 In section 25—

(*a*) in subsection (1) for "in any proceedings on the Crown side of the King's Bench Division" there shall be substituted "on any application for judicial review pursuant to section 18 of the Judicature (Northern Ireland) Act 1978";

(*b*) in subsection (4) for "no execution or attachment or process in the nature thereof shall be issued out of any court" there shall be substituted "no order or process in the nature of execution shall be made by or issued out of any court, and no enforcement order shall be made by the Enforcement of Judgments Office,".

21 For section 26(2) there shall be substituted the following subsections—

"(2) Without prejudice to the generality of subsection (1) above, the Judgments Enforcement (Northern Ireland) Order 1981, Judgment Enforcement Rules and rules of court shall, save as otherwise provided by any statutory provision within the meaning of that Order, apply to judgments given in favour of the Crown.

(2A) Articles 106 and 107 of that Order of 1981 (which relate respectively to limitation on arrest and imprisonment of debtors and to committal for default) shall apply to sums of money payable and debts due to the Crown.

(2B) Articles 115 and 125 of that Order of 1981 (which relate respectively to committal for contempt in certain cases of default and to the effect of imprisonment under Article 107 or 115) shall—

(*a*) have effect in relation to sums of money payable and debts due to the Crown; and

(*b*) have effect as if those provisions in terms applied to default in payment of any sum payable in respect of estate duty."

24 In section 35 in subsection (2)(*a*) after "Kingdom" there shall be inserted "or, in the case of county court rules, are not resident in Northern Ireland", and in subsection (2)(*d*), for "and for enabling any such proceedings to be put in proper cases into any special list which may be kept for the trial of short causes in which leave to defend is given under any such rule of court as aforesaid" there shall be substituted "or of any county court rule providing for process by default".

26—(1) In section 38(2) the following definitions shall be inserted at the appropriate points in alphabetical order—

"Agency arrangement" means an arrangement such as is mentioned in section 11 of the Northern Ireland Constitution Act 1973;

"Attorney General" means the Attorney General for Northern Ireland;

"County court" means a county court in Northern Ireland;

"County court rules" has the same meaning as in section 21(5) of the Interpretation Act (Northern Ireland) 1954;

"Department of Finance" means the Department of Finance for Northern Ireland;

"High Court" (except in a reference to that court as a prize court) means the High Court of Justice in Northern Ireland;

"Royal Courts of Justice" means those courts at Belfast;

"Rules of court" has the same meaning as in section 21(4) of the Interpretation Act (Northern Ireland) 1954.

(2) In section 38(2)—

(*a*) in the definition of "Civil proceedings" for "proceedings on the Crown side of the King's Bench Division" there shall be substituted "an application for judicial review pursuant to section 18 of the Judicature (Northern Ireland) Act 1978";

(*b*) at the end of the definition of "Order" there shall be inserted "or a dismiss by a county court";

(*c*) in the definition of "Statutory duty" for "Act of Parliament" there shall be substituted "enactment".

(3) At the end of section 38 there shall be added the following subsection:

"(7) Any reference (however expressed) in this Act to an enactment or an Act includes an enactment of the Irish Parliament, the Parliament of Northern Ireland or the Northern Ireland Assembly or an enactment contained in an Order in Council made under section 1(3) of the Northern Ireland (Temporary Provisions) Act 1972 or paragraph 1 of Schedule 1 to the Northern Ireland Act 1974.".

27—(1) In section 40(2), after "without prejudice to the general effect of the foregoing provision" there shall be inserted "but subject to the provisions of section 17(3A) and section 37(3) of this Act".

28 Part V and section 52 shall be excepted.

PART IV

Further additions and exceptions to, and modifications of, the Act in its application to the Crown in right of Her Majesty's government in Northern Ireland

29 The following provisions of the Act, that is to say,—

..., in section 17(5) the words ''or an authorised Government department'' and the words from ''or in'' onwards, section 26(2B)(*b*), ... section 38(3) ... and in Schedule 1, paragraph 2(1), the words from ''including'' onwards,

shall be excepted from the Act in its application to the Crown in right of Her Majesty's Government in Northern Ireland.

Note—Words omitted are outside the scope of this work.
For s 26(2B)(*b*) see Art 21.

30—(1) For any reference (except in section 17(3A), ... or section 53 and except the second reference in section 32) to the Crown (including, except as aforesaid, any express reference which is to be construed as one to the Crown in right of Her Majesty's Government in the United Kingdom) there shall be substituted a reference to be construed as one to the Crown in right of Her Majesty's Government in Northern Ireland; for any reference which is to be construed as one to Her Majesty in right of Her Government in the United Kingdom there shall be substituted a reference to be construed as one to Her Majesty in right of Her Government in Northern Ireland; for any reference to a Government department there shall be substituted a reference to a Northern Ireland department; and for any reference which is to be construed as one to an officer, servant or agent of Her Majesty or an officer, servant or agent of the Crown or for any reference to a Minister of the Crown (except the references in sections 36 and 40(3) to the Secretary of State) there shall be substituted respectively a reference to be construed as one to an officer, servant or agent of Her Majesty's Government in Northern Ireland or a reference to the Head of a Northern Ireland department.

Note—Words omitted are outside the scope of this work.
For s 17(3A) see Art 12(2).

32 In section 17(1) the words ''in Northern Ireland'', where first occurring, shall be excepted.

Note—For s 17(1) see Art 12.

33 For section 23(3) there shall be substituted the following subsection—

''(3) Notwithstanding anything in the preceding provisions of this section, the provisions of this Part of this Act shall not have effect with respect to any of the following proceedings brought by or against the Crown in right of His Majesty's Government in Northern Ireland, that is to say—

(*a*) proceedings brought by the Attorney General on the relation of some other person;
(*b*) proceedings in respect of charities by or against the Attorney General;
(*c*) proceedings by or against the Department of Finance acting in pursuance of any enactment relating to charities;
(*d*) proceedings by or against the Registrar of Titles in Northern Ireland or any officers of the Land Registry of Northern Ireland or proceedings for compensation under section 71 of the Land Registration Act (Northern Ireland) 1970''.

Note—For s 23(3) see Art 18.

1982/1236
Income Tax (Interest Relief) Regulations 1982

Made by the Commissioners of Inland Revenue under FA 1982 s 29(3), now TA 1988 s 378; see TA 1988 Sch 30 para 21

Made	*31 August 1982*
Laid before the House of Commons	*1 September 1982*
Coming into Operation	*1 October 1982*

Commentary—*Simon's Direct Tax Service* **A3.431–433**.

Citation and commencement

1 These Regulations may be cited as the Income Tax (Interest Relief) Regulations 1982, and shall come into operation on 1st October 1982.

Interpretation

2—(1) In these Regulations unless the context otherwise requires—

''authorised officer'' means the official registered by the Board as being authorised for the purposes of these Regulations by the lender;

''the Board'' means the Commissioners of Inland Revenue;

"financial year" in relation to a lender means a period of 12 months or the period (not necessarily a period of 12 months) for which the lender makes up its accounts;

"lender" means a qualifying lender for the purposes of section 26;

"limited loan" means a loan to which either paragraph 5(1) or (2) or paragraph 24(3) of Schedule 1 to the Finance Act 1974[a] applies;

"a qualifying borrower" has the meaning given by Part III of Schedule 7[b] [which shall be deemed to include, for the application to them of sections 26 and 28 and Schedule 7[c] and these regulations those personal representatives and trustees to whom reference is made in Regulation 7A below, so long as they are all resident in the United Kingdom and in Regulation 7B below, so long as the conditions in that Regulation are fulfilled][1];

"relevant loan interest" has the meaning given by Part I of Schedule 7;[d]

"Schedule 7" means Schedule 7 to the Finance Act 1982;[e]

"section 26" means section 26 of the Finance Act 1982;[f]

"section 28" means section 28 of the Finance Act 1982;[g]

"tax year" means a period of 12 months ending on 5th April.

(2) In the application of these Regulations to Scotland—

(*a*) "a freehold or leasehold estate" means any interest in land; and

(*b*) any reference to a loan on the security of such an estate is a reference to a loan upon a heritable security within the meaning of section 9(8)(*a*) of the Conveyancing and Feudal Reform (Scotland) Act 1970.

Notes—[a] TA 1988 s 357(1) or s 365(3).
[b] TA 1988 s 376.
[c] TA 1988 ss 369–377.
[d] TA 1988 ss 370–373.
[e] TA 1988 ss 370–376.
[f] TA 1988 s 369.
[g] TA 1988 s 377.

Cross references—IT (Interest Relief) (Housing Associations) Regulations, SI 1988/1347 reg 3 (a housing association borrowing from a qualifying lender on the security of a freehold or leasehold estate treated as a qualifying borrower).

Amendments—[1] Words in the definition of "a qualifying borrower" in para (1) inserted by the IT (Interest Relief) (No 2) Regulations, SI 1983/311 reg 3, with effect from 15 March 1983.

Loans which the borrower may bring within the tax deduction scheme

3—(1) Loans the interest on which paid by a qualifying borrower is relevant loan interest are loans specified for the purposes of paragraph 7(1)(*a*) of Schedule 7[a] except—

(*a*) loans in respect of property which is used as the only or main residence of a dependent relative or former or separated spouse of his;

[(*b* loans the interest on which is eligible for relief under paragraph 4A of the Schedule 1 to the Finance Act 1974[b]; or][1]

(*c*) loans to which the provisions of sub-paragraphs (*b*), (*c*) or (*d*) of the said paragraph 7(1) apply.

(2) ...[2]

(3) Where the borrower is unable to provide the lender with the notice to which the said paragraph 7(1)(*a*) refers he may, if he considers that the interest payable on his loan is or will be relevant loan interest, apply to the Board for a notice under paragraph 7(1)(*b*) of Schedule 7 and the Board shall notify him of their decision on his application.

Notes—[a] TA 1988 s 374(1)(*a*).
[b] TA 1988 s 356.

Cross references—See the IT (Interest Relief) (Housing Associations) Regulations, SI 1988/1347 reg 8 (for the purposes of this regulation, a housing association is a borrower to whom only para (3) of this regulation applies).

Amendments—[1] Para (1)(*b*) substituted by the IT (Interest Relief) (No 2) Regulations, SI 1983/311 reg 4, with effect from 15 March 1983.

[2] Para (2) revoked by the IT (Interest Relief) (Amendment) Regulations, SI 1995/1213 reg 3, with effect from 4 May 1995.

Loans made before tax year 1983–84 which the lender may bring within the tax deduction scheme

4 Loans of the following descriptions, not being loans to which the interest on which paragraph 2(3) of Schedule 7[a] applies, are specified for the purposes of paragraph 7(1)(*d*)[b] of Schedule 7—

(*a*) a loan secured on a freehold or leasehold estate in respect of property in relation to which the loan was granted in which the borrower (and in the case of joint borrowers each of them), or a dependent relative, or former or separated spouse of his, is residing at the time when the loan is made, or will so reside within 12 months of that time; being a loan

(i) which is not a limited loan (unless it is a limited loan in respect of which notice has been given to the Board under Regulation 7(1) before 1st December 1982);

(ii) in respect of which the lender has undertaken

(*a*) to inform the Board that it is a loan to which this Regulation applies together with the name and address of each borrower, and where known the Tax District to which he makes his return together with his tax reference; and (*b*) to notify the borrower, not later than 30 days before the first payment of relevant loan interest falls due, that interest payable on the loan appears to be relevant loan interest; and

(iii) in respect of which the lender has not been notified that the interest is not relevant loan interest;

(*b*) a loan which is not a limited loan but otherwise qualifies for relief under the provisions of paragraph 24 of Schedule 1 to the Finance Act 1974[c].

Notes—[a] TA 1988 s 370(3).
[b] TA 1988 s 374(1)(*d*).
[c] TA 1988 s 365.

Cross references—See the IT (Interest Relief) (Housing Associations) Regulations, SI 1988/1347 reg 9 (modification of this regulation for the purposes of reg 3 of those Regulations).

Commencement of tax deduction scheme before tax year 1983–84 in certain cases

5 ...

Application of tax deduction scheme to home improvement loans

6 Where before 1st December in any year a lender notifies the Board that it wishes home improvement loans which it has made to which paragraph 4(1)(*b*) of Schedule 7[a] applies to be brought within the tax deduction scheme, the scheme shall begin to apply to relevant loan interest payable on such loans in the tax year beginning in the next following year; but in the case of home improvement loans to be made on or after the date of the lender's notice to the Board it shall begin to apply from the date specified in the notice.

Note—[a] TA 1988 s 372(1)(*b*).

Application of tax deduction scheme to limited loans

7—(1)

[(*a*) Subject to the provisions of sub-paragraph (*b*)—

(i) where before 1st October in any year a lender notifies the Board that it wishes limited loans which it has made to be brought within the tax deduction scheme, the scheme shall begin to apply in the tax year beginning in the next following year to the relevant loan interest payable on those loans in respect of which the Board has given notice as provided by paragraph 7(1)(*b*) of Schedule 7[a]; but in the case of limited loans which the lender makes on or after the date of the lender's notice the scheme shall begin to apply to the relevant loan interest payable on those loans after the date specified in the notice, not being a date earlier than 30 days after the date of that notice;

(ii) where at any time a lender notifies the Board of its wish to bring within the tax deduction scheme only those limited loans which it will make on or after the date of the lender's notice to the Board the scheme shall begin to apply to the relevant loan interest payable on those loans after the date specified in the notice, not being a date earlier than 30 days after the date of that notice].[1]

(*b*) within 30 days of the lender's giving such a notice the Board may notify the lender that the scheme shall not begin to apply in accordance with its notice and, where the Board so notifies the lender, the scheme shall begin to apply only on the date and to the loans which the Board has in writing authorised.

(2) Where a lender has not so notified the Board under paragraph (1)(*a*) the tax deduction scheme shall not begin to apply in the following circumstances—

(*a*) for the tax year 1983–84, in respect of interest on a loan which was a limited loan

(i) when the interest was last charged by the lender to the borrower's account in its records before February 1983, or

(ii) in the case of a loan made after January 1983, when the loan was made;

[(*b*) for any tax year after 5th April 1984 in respect of interest on a loan which was a limited loan

(i) when the interest was last charged by the lender to the borrower's account in its records at any time before March in the previous tax year, or

(ii) in the case of a loan made after the date when the qualifying lender last charged interest to borrowers' accounts in its records at any time before March in the previous tax year, when the loan was made.][2]

Notes—[a] TA 1988 s 374(1)(*b*).

Amendments—[1] Para (1)(*a*) substituted by the IT (Interest Relief) (No 3) Regulations, SI 1985/1252 reg 3, with effect from 1 September 1985.
[2] Para (2)(*b*) substituted by the IT (Interest Relief) (No 2) Regulations, SI 1983/311 reg 5, with effect from 15 March 1983.

[Application of tax deduction scheme to certain personal representatives and trustees

7A Interest which is paid and payable in the United Kingdom by persons as personal representatives of a deceased person or as trustees of a settlement made by his will the whole of which would have been eligible for relief under section 75 of the Finance Act 1972[a] (by virtue of paragraph 8 of Schedule 1 to the Finance Act 1974[b]), apart from section 26(1)[c] and paragraph 5 of Schedule 1 to the Finance Act 1974[d] is relevant loan interest within the meaning of Part I of Schedule 7[e] (but as if sub-paragraph (3) of paragraph 2 of that Schedule[f] were omitted) to which section 26(1)[g] applies.][1]

Note—[a] TA 1988 s 353.
[b] TA 1988 s 358.
[c] TA 1988 s 369(1).
[d] TA 1988 s 357.
[e] TA 1988 ss 370–373.
[f] TA 1988 s 370(3).
[g] TA 1988 s 369(1).
Amendments—[1] This regulation inserted by the IT (Interest Relief) (No 2) Regulations, SI 1983/311 reg 6, with effect from 15 March 1983.

[7B In determining whether loan interest paid and payable by trustees to whom reference is made in section 24(4) of the Housing Subsidies Act 1967 (option mortgages) or Article 143(6) of the Housing (Northern Ireland) Order 1981 (option mortgages in Northern Ireland) is relevant loan interest, Schedule 7[a] shall have effect as if for sub-paragraph (3) of paragraph 2 there were substituted the words—

"(3) This sub-paragraph applies to interest payable by trustees which becomes due on or after 1st April 1983 and is payable on a loan—

(*a*) in respect of which there is in force on 31st March 1983 an option notice given under section 24(2) of the 1967 Act (option mortgages) or under Article 142(2) of the 1981 Order which has effect by virtue of section 24(4) of that Act or, as the case may be, by virtue of Article 143(6) of that Order; and

(*b*) which relates to a dwelling in respect of which, at the time the interest is paid and on the assumption that one of those provisions continues to be applicable, the conditions in section 24(4) of the 1967 Act, or, as the case may be, Article 143(6) of the 1981 Order are fulfilled."][1]

Notes—[a] TA 1988 ss 370–376.
Amendments—[1] This regulation inserted by the IT (Interest Relief) (No 2) Regulations, SI 1983/311 reg 6, with effect from 15 March 1983.

Variation of repayment terms of certain loans

8—(1) Expressions used in this Regulation have the same meaning as in section 28[a].

(2) Subject to the provisions of this Regulation the amount of each combined payment and the date on which it becomes due from a borrower, to whom a specified lender has given a notice under section 28(2)(*a*)[b] to vary the terms of repayment of the loan, shall be notified to the borrower by the lender.

(3) The notice under section 28(2)(*a*)[b] shall be in a form prescribed or authorised by the Board but shall not have effect unless—

(*a*) it contains a statement of the borrower's right under section 28(2)(*b*)[c] to give a counter notice; and

(*b*) there is a period of not less than 30 days between the giving of the notice and the due date for the first of the combined payments to which the notice relates.

(4) A borrower shall be entitled to give a counter notice under section 28(2)(*b*)[c] not later than 3 months after the due date for the first combined payment to which paragraph (2) above refers.

(5) On receipt of the borrower's counter notice under section 28(2)(*b*)[b] the lender shall give notice to the borrower of—

(*a*) the amount of the combined payments which will be due from him after taking account of the requirements of section 28(4)[d];

(*b*) the due date for the first such combined payment which shall be—

(i) where the borrower gives a counter notice under section 28(2)(*b*)[c] within 30 days of the lender's notice under section 28(2)(*a*)[b], the due date for the first combined payment to which paragraph (2) above refers; or

(ii) in any other case, a date not later than what apart from the borrower's counter notice, would have been the date of the second of his combined payments falling due after the date of that counter notice;

(*c*) an estimate of the total period which, assuming there is no change in the amount of the borrower's combined payments, will be required to satisfy the principal and the interest on the loan by means of those payments; and

(*d*) a statement of the borrower's right under section 28(4)[d] to make additional repayments of capital.

Notes—[a] TA 1988 s 377.
[b] TA 1988 s 377(2)(*a*).
[c] TA 1988 s 377(2)(*b*).
[d] TA 1988 s 377(4).

[Repayment claims by certain borrowers

8A—(1) Where in a tax year a borrower has not been able to deduct the full amount of the sums deductible under the provisions of section 26(1)[a] from payments of relevant loan interest by reason of the circumstances described in paragraph 11 of Schedule 7,[b] he may make a claim to the Board for payment of a sum equal to the amount which he has not been able to deduct.

(2) Section 42 of the Taxes Management Act 1970 shall not apply to such a claim.

(3) The Board shall notify the borrower of its decision on the claim.][1]

Notes—[a] TA 1988 s 369(1).
[b] TA 1988 s 375(8).
Amendments—[1] This regulation inserted by the IT (Interest Relief) (No 2) Regulations, SI 1983/311 reg 7, with effect from 15 March 1983.

[8B—(1) This regulation applies in any case where an amount to which a borrower is not entitled is paid to him by the Board pursuant to a claim under regulation 8A.

(2) An officer of the Board may make such assessments as may in his judgment be required for recovering that amount from the borrower.

(3) [The Taxes Management Act 1970 shall apply to an assessment under paragraph (2) as if it were an assessment to income tax for the year of assessment for which the payment was made.][2]

(4) If in a case to which paragraph (1) applies, the borrower fraudulently or negligently makes any false statement or representation in connection with the making of a claim under regulation 8A, he shall be liable to a penalty not exceeding the amount referred to in that paragraph.

(5) If in a case to which paragraph (1) applies, the borrower is required to give notice under subsection (1) of section 375 of the Income and Corporation Taxes Act 1988, and there is any unreasonable delay in the giving of the notice, he shall be liable to a penalty not exceeding so much of the amount referred to in that paragraph as is attributable to that delay.][1]

Amendments—[1] This regulation inserted by the IT (Interest Relief) (Amendment) Regulations, SI 1995/1213 reg 4, with effect from 4 May 1995.
[2] Para (3) substituted by the IT (Interest Relief) (Amendment) Regulations, SI 1996/1184 reg 3, with effect in any case where an assessment is made on or after 20 May 1996 and is for the year 1996–97 or any subsequent year of assessment.
Para (3) is also substituted by the IT (Interest Relief) (Amendment) Regulations, SI 1996/1184 reg 4, with effect in any case where an assessment is made on or after 6 April 1988 and is for the year 1995–96 or any earlier year of assessment, as follows:
"(3) The Taxes Management Act 1970 shall apply to an assessment under paragraph (2) as if it were an assessment to income tax for the year of assessment for which the payment was made and as if the assessment were among those specified in section 55(1) of that Act (recovery of tax not postponed).".

Repayment claims by lenders: introductory

9—(1) Sums recoverable by a lender under section 26(7)[a] shall be recovered on a claim to the Board for the purpose under these Regulations.

(2) Subject to paragraph (3) a claim shall be for the lender's financial year, and is referred to in these Regulations as an "annual claim".

(3) A claim may also be made in accordance with Regulations 10 or 12 for a period shorter than the claimant's financial year and is referred to in these Regulations as an "interim claim".

(4) No payment in respect of sums recoverable on such a claim shall be made to a lender before 1st April 1983.

Note—[a] TA 1988 s 369(6).

Interim claims in advance

10—(1) An interim claim for a period allowed by paragraphs (2) and (3) may be made not later than 1 month, or such shorter period as the Board may allow, before the date to which paragraph (5) refers, and is referred to in these Regulations as an "interim claim in advance".

(2) The periods for which an interim claim in advance may be made are—

(*a*) 1 calendar month; or
(*b*) 3 calendar months.

(3) Interim claims in advance made by a lender may not (except where authorised by prior written approval of the Board) be made for different periods.

(4) An interim claim in advance for a period shall be based on an estimate of the amount deductible by borrowers in respect of payments of relevant loan interest to the lender falling due in that period, and the estimate shall be certified by an authorised officer of the lender as being the best estimate that can reasonably be made of the amount deductible.

(5) If the Board are satisfied with the estimate they shall pay a sum equal to the estimated amount deductible on the date prescribed in paragraph (6) or where it is not a working day the next following working day; if they are not so satisfied they shall pay the lender such lesser sum, if any, as in their estimation will approximate to the amount deductible.

(6) Subject to paragraph (7), the date referred to in paragraph (5) is—

(*a*) in the case of a claim for 1 calendar month the 23rd of the month;
(*b*) in the case of a claim for 3 calendar months the 15th of the second of those months.

(7) In the case of a claim for 1 calendar month, if the lender so claims and satisfies the condition in paragraph (8), the date referred to in paragraph (5) above is the 2nd, 9th or 15th instead of the 23rd of the month.

(8) The condition mentioned in paragraph (7) is that the lender's mean repayment date is closer to the date on which repayment is claimed than each of the other 3 dates and the lender's ''mean repayment date'' means—

(*a*) the date which is found by multiplying the date of each day of the months of April to September in the previous year by the payments of interest due on that day, adding together the products so calculated for all the days of those 6 months, and dividing the total of those products by the total of all payments of interest due in those months; or
(*b*) a date arrived at on some other basis which is authorised by the Board.

Supplementary statements

11—(1) When a payment has been made to a lender under Regulation 10(5) on an interim claim in advance, the lender shall deliver to the Board a supplementary statement under this Regulation and (except when paragraph (5) below applies) shall deliver the statement within 4 months after the end of the period for which the claim was made.

(2) The supplementary statement shall be a statement correcting (or confirming) the estimate of the amount deductible given in accordance with Regulation 10(4) above, and shall—

(*a*) be based as far as possible on the amount of relevant loan interest which actually fell due in the period covered by the statement, and only as far as may be necessary on a revised estimate; and
(*b*) be for the same period as the interim claim in advance;

and any estimate contained in the supplementary statement shall be certified by an authorised officer of the lender as the best estimate that can reasonably be made.

(3) If the supplementary statement shows that the amount deductible was greater than the payment made under Regulation 10(5) the Board shall, if satisfied with the statement, pay the amount of the difference to the lender by way of supplementary payment on the claim, but if the supplementary statement shows that the amount deductible was less than the payment made under Regulation 10(5) the lender shall repay the amount of the difference to the Board with the statement.

(4) If in respect of an interim claim on which a payment has been made under Regulation 10(5) a lender fails to deliver a supplementary statement within the time required by this Regulation, the amount of the payment shall immediately be recoverable by the Board in the same manner as tax charged by an assessment on the lender which has become final and conclusive.

(5) Where the lender debits interest in arrear to a borrower's account in its records and at intervals of more than a month the supplementary statement shall, if this date is later than the date in paragraph (1) above, be delivered not later than 5 months after the end of the month in which interest is so debited.

Interim claims in arrear

12—(1) An interim claim for a period allowed by paragraph (2) may be made by a lender within 6 months after the end of the period for which it is made.

(2) The period for which a claim may be made under this Regulation shall be one which—

(*a*) is not shorter than 1 calendar month;
(*b*) falls within the lender's same financial year; and
(*c*) does not include any part of a period in respect of which a payment was made under Regulation 10(5) (unless the payment in respect of the period or that part was recovered under Regulation 11(4)).

(3) A claim under this Regulation may not be based on an estimate but may only be made to recover the amount deductible in respect of interest which fell due in the period.

(4) If the amount claimed is established to the Board's satisfaction they shall pay the amount to the claimant; if they are not so satisfied they shall pay to the claimant any lesser amount established to their satisfaction.

Annual claims

13—(1) An annual claim for the lender's financial year may not be made at any time more than 6 years after the end of the financial year.

(2) Except where in relation to any financial year a lender repays all the payments made to it on relevant interim claims, it shall within 1 year after the end of the financial year make an annual claim to establish the amount deductible for that financial year.

In this Regulation ''relevant interim claim'' means, in relation to a financial year, an interim claim for a period falling wholly or partly within that financial year.

[(3) The annual claim may not be based on an estimate and shall, unless the lender makes an election under paragraph (4), include only the tax deducted from interest payments due from borrowers during the financial year to which the claim relates and paid not later than 4 months after the end of that year.][1]

(4) Where however a loan is secured on a freehold or leasehold estate in respect of property in relation to which the loan is made, the lender may in respect of any such loan elect to include in an annual claim the amount of tax deductible in respect of interest payments due from the borrower in the year, but always excluding the amounts of tax deductible in respect of interest written off as a bad debt in the accounts of the lender for the financial year to which the claim relates.

(5)

(*a*) Where in a tax year before the passing of the Act imposing tax for that year any deduction has been made in accordance with section 26[a] from a payment of interest at a rate in excess of that rate of tax ultimately so imposed, the lender may include in his annual claim the amount of the excess not recovered where—

(i) the loan has been repaid before the passing of the said Act, and

(ii) the lender has not been able to recover from the borrower the excess so deducted by the end of its financial year or within 6 months of the deduction whichever is the later.

(*b*) The amount included in respect of the excess shall be repaid to the lender by the Board as if it were an amount deductible from relevant loan interest in accordance with section 26[a] and the Board shall be entitled to recover from the borrower the amount so repaid in the same manner as tax charged by an assessment on the borrower which has become final and conclusive.

(6) An annual claim shall bring into account payments made on relevant interim claims, and shall apportion as may be necessary any payment made on such [a] claim for any period falling partly in a different financial year, and for the purpose of this Regulation the ''aggregate of the relevant interim payments'' means the aggregate of the payments made (and not repaid) on relevant interim claims but excluding any part of a payment relating to a different financial year.

(7) Where the aggregate of the relevant interim payments shown by an annual claim exceeds the amount deductible for the financial year shown on the claim, the lender shall repay the amount of the excess to the Board with the claim.

(8) If a lender fails to make an annual claim required under paragraph (2) within the time limited by that paragraph, the Board may issue a notice to the lender showing the aggregate of the relevant interim payments for the year, and stating that the Board are not satisfied that the amount due to the lender for the year exceeds the lower amount stated in the notice.

(9) If an annual claim is not delivered to the Board within 14 days after the issue of such a notice under paragraph (8) the amount of the difference between the aggregate and the lower amount stated in the notice shall immediately be recoverable by the Board in the same manner as tax charged by an assessment on the lender which has become final and conclusive.

(10) Where an annual claim has been made and the lender subsequently discovers that an error or mistake has been made in the claim the lender may make a supplementary annual claim within the time allowed in paragraph (1).

Notes—[a] TA 1988 s 369.

Amendments—[1] Para (3) substituted by the IT (Interest Relief) (No 2) Regulations, SI 1983/311 reg 8, with effect from 15 March 1983.

Lender's claims: supplementary provisions

14—(1) Section 42 of the Taxes Management Act 1970 shall not apply to claims under these Regulations.

(2) No appeal shall lie from the Board's decision on an interim claim.

(3) An appeal shall lie to the Special Commissioners from the Board's decision on an annual claim, and the appeal shall be brought by giving written notice to the Board within 30 days of receipt of written notice of the decision.

(4) No payment or repayment made or other thing done on or in relation to an interim claim or a notice under Regulation 13(8) shall prejudice the decision on an annual claim.

(5) Part V of the Taxes Management Act 1970 (appeals and other proceedings) shall apply to an appeal under paragraph (3) above, and on an appeal the Special Commissioners may vary the decision appealed against whether or not the variation is to the advantage of the appellant.

(6) All such assessments, payments and repayments shall be made as are necessary to give effect to the Board's decision on an annual claim, or to any variation of that decision on appeal.

(7) Claims and supplementary statements under these Regulations shall be in such form and contain such particulars as the Board prescribe and shall be signed by an authorised officer of the lender; and forms prescribed for annual claims may require a report to be given by the lender's auditor.

(8) Where for the purposes of an annual claim for a financial year it is necessary to apportion any amount included in an interim claim for a period falling partly within and partly outside the financial year, the apportionment shall be made in such manner as the Board may prescribe.

Information to be provided to borrowers by lenders

15 A lender shall, at his request, provide the borrower with a certificate showing in respect of a tax year the amount of relevant loan interest due from and paid by the borrower and the amount of tax deducted from that interest.

Information to be provided to the Board

16 The Board may by notice in writing require any person who is a party to a loan agreement to which section 26 applies, or could in the opinion of the Board apply, to furnish them, within such time (not being less than 14 days) as may be provided by the notice, such information (including copies of any relevant documents or records) as they may reasonably require for the purposes of section 26 or Schedule 7.

Cross references—See the IT (Interest Relief) (Housing Associations) Regulations, SI 1988/1347 reg 10 (modification of this Regulation in its application to housing associations).

Inspection of records

17—(1) Every person to whom payments of interest are made in respect of which a repayment claim is made by a lender under these Regulations shall, whenever required to do so, make available for inspection by an officer of the Board authorised for that purpose all such books, documents and other records in his possession or under his control containing information relating to—

(*a*) such interest and the terms of the loans (including relevant contracts or deeds) under which such interest is paid or,

(*b*) the persons holding such contracts or deeds or paying such interest

as may reasonably be required for determining whether the amount for which any such claim is made is properly recoverable.

(2) Where records are maintained by computer the person required to make them available for inspection shall provide the officer making the inspection with all facilities necessary for obtaining information from them.

(3)

(*a*) Every notice given to it by the borrower under paragraph 7(1)(*a*) of Schedule 7[a] shall be preserved by the lender to whom it is given and in such manner as may be approved by the Board, so as to be available for inspection under this Regulation, until two years after the termination of the loan or, if earlier, the date from which the interest ceases to be relevant loan interest;

(*b*) a copy of the notice shall on its written request be made available to the Board.

Note—[a] TA 1988 s 374(1)(*a*).

Application of penalty provisions of the Taxes Management Act 1970

18 (Inserts words in second column of Table in TMA 1970 s 98.)

Borrowers' appeals: supplementary provisions

19—(1) An appeal by a borrower shall lie to the General Commissioners except that the borrower may elect (in accordance with section 46(1) of the Taxes Management Act 1970) to bring his appeal before the Special Commissioners—

(*a*) from the Board's decision on his application under Regulation 3(3);

(*b*) from a notice issued to him by the Board under paragraph 7(1)(*b*) of Schedule 7[a] (notice that interest may be paid under deduction of tax); ...[1]

(*c*) from a notice issued to him by the Board under paragraph 10 of Schedule 7[b] (notice that interest is not relevant loan interest [and][1]

[(*d*) from a decision on his claim under Regulation 8A].

(2) An appeal shall be brought by giving written notice to the Board within 30 days of the receipt by the borrower of the Board's decision or the notice as the case may be.

(3) Part V of the Taxes Management Act 1970 (appeals and other proceedings) shall apply to an appeal under this Regulation, and on an appeal the General or Special Commissioners may vary the decision or notice appealed from whether or not the variation is to the advantage of the appellant.

(4) All such ...[2] payments or repayments shall be made by the inspector as are necessary to give effect to the Board's decision or notice or to any variation of that decision or notice on appeal.

(5), (6) ...[2]

Notes—[a] TA 1988 s 374(1)(*b*).
[b] TA 1988 s 375(6) and (7).

Amendments—[1] Word at end of para (1)(*b*) revoked and para (1)(*d*) and the preceding word ''and'' inserted by the IT (Interest Relief) (No 2) Regulations, SI 1983/311 reg 9, with effect from 15 March 1983.

[2] Word in para (4), and paras (5), (6), revoked by the IT (Interest Relief) (Amendment) Regulations, SI 1995/1213 reg 5, with effect from 4 May 1995.

1984/1801
Income Tax (Prescribed Deposit-takers) (No 1) Order 1984

Made by the Treasury under FA 1984 Sch 8 para 2(1)(*f*): see now ICTA 1988 ss 481(2)(*f*)

Made . . . . *20 November 1984*

1 This Order may be cited as the Income Tax (Prescribed Deposit-Takers) Order 1984 and shall come into operation on 6 April 1985.

2 The following persons are prescribed for the purposes of section 27 of and Sch 8 to the Finance Act 1984[a]:

The British Railways Board or any wholly-owned subsidiary of theirs within the meaning of section 92(1) of the Transport Act 1962 for the time being exercising the powers conferred by section 32 of the British Railways Act 1966 to establish and maintain a savings bank.

Note—[a] TA 1988 s 479, 481 and 482.

1984/2060
Capital Allowances (Vehicles for the Disabled) (Similar Payments) Order 1984

Made by the Treasury under FA 1971 s 43(3) and FA 1980 s 64(12), now CAA 1990 ss 22(6)(*d*), 36(4)(*d*); see CAA 1990 s 163 [now CAA 2001 s 82(4)(*d*)]

Made . . . . *19 December 1984*
Coming into Operation . . . . . . *1 February 1985*

Commentary—*Simon's Direct Tax Service* **B2.332**.

1 This Order may be cited as the Capital Allowances (Vehicles for the Disabled) (Similar Payments) Order 1984 and shall come into operation on 1st February 1985.

2 In this Order—

''army inter-war pensioners'' means former members of Her Majesty's military forces in receipt of a disability pension paid by the Secretary of State for Defence on account of disability attributable to injury sustained after 30th September 1921 but before 3rd September 1939.

3 The following payments are hereby specified as appearing to be of a similar kind to payments within paragraphs (*a*), (*b*) and (*c*) of subsection 3 of the said section 43 and of subsection 12 of the said section 64 for the purposes of the making of first-year allowances in respect of capital expenditure on the provision of mechanically propelled road vehicles, that is to say—

(1) mobility supplement paid under the Naval and Marine Pay and Pensions (Disablement Awards) Order 1984 or under the Naval and Marine Pay and Pensions (Disablement Awards) (No 2) Order 1984;

(2) mobility supplement paid under Queen's Regulations for the Royal Air Force; and

(3) supplementary allowance paid under Royal Warrant dated 30th December 1949 to army inter-war pensioners equivalent to the mobility supplement provided for by Article 26A of the Naval Military and Air Forces etc (Disablement and Death) Services Pensions Order 1983.

4 This Order has effect in relation to expenditure incurred on or after 21st November 1983.

1985/994
Films (Certification) Regulations 1985

Made by the Secretary of State under the Films Act 1985 Sch 1 para 10(1), (4) and (5)

Commentary—*Simon's Direct Tax Service* **B3.1307**.

Citation and commencement

1 These Regulations may be cited as the Films (Certification) Regulations 1985 and shall come into operation on 23rd July 1985.

Interpretation

2 In these Regulations—

''acquirer'' in relation to a film, means any person who has acquired any description of rights in it;

''the Act'' means the Films Act 1985[, as amended][1];

''co-production film'' means a film which by virtue of any Order in Council made under paragraph [4(7)][1] of Schedule 1 to the Act is to be treated as if it were a British film for the purposes of Schedule 1 to the Act;

''group of companies'' means a company and all other companies which are its subsidiaries within the meaning of section 736 of the Companies Act 1985;

...[2]

...[2]

Amendments—[1] Words inserted and substituted by the Films (Certification) (Amendment) Regulations, SI 1999/2224 regs 2, 3(*a*), (*b*) with effect from 27 August 1999.

[2] Definitions ''Member State'' and ''television film'' revoked by SI 1999/2224 regs 2, 3(*c*) with effect from 27 August 1999

Applications

3 An application under paragraph 2(1) of Schedule 1 to the Act for the certification of a master negative, master tape or master disc of a film, other than a co-production film, as a qualifying film, qualifying tape or qualifying disc shall be made in writing to the Secretary of State and be [addressed to the Department of National Heritage][1].

Amendments—[1] Words substituted by the Transfer of Functions (National Heritage) Order, SI 1992/1311 Sch 2 with effect from 3 July 1992.

Particulars

[**4** The application shall set out the particulars of the film described in Regulation 6 below.][1]

Amendments—[1] This regulation substituted by the Films (Certification) (Amendment) Regulations, SI 1999/2224 regs 2, 4 with effect from 27 August 1999.

Evidence

5 The application shall be accompanied by:

(*a*) a statutory declaration made by the applicant as to the truth of the particulars given in the application; and

[(*b*) a report to the Secretary of State prepared by a person referred to in (*c*) below:

(i) verifying particulars G and H set out in regulation 6, and

(ii) stating whether, in the opinion of that person the criteria set out in sub-paragraphs 4(3) and 4(4) of Schedule 1 to the Act have been satisfied in relation to the film.][1]

[(*c*) the persons referred to in regulation 5(*b*) are:

(i) an accountant who is a member of a body of accountants for the time being recognised for the purposes of section 389(1)(*a*) of the Companies Act 1985, or

(ii) a person authorised under section 389(1)(*b*) of that Act to be appointed as auditor of a company

and who in either case is not and was not at any time while the film was being made in partnership with, nor in the employment of the maker of the film or, where the maker is a company, is not and was not at any time while the film was being made—

(iii) an officer or servant of that company or, if that company is a member of a group of companies, of any other company in that group; or

(iv) in partnership with or in the employment of, any such officer or servant.][1]

Amendments—[1] Para (*b*) substituted, and para (*c*) inserted, by the Films (Certification) (Amendment) Regulations, SI 1999/2224 regs 2, 5 with effect from 27 August 1999.

List of particulars

6 The particulars referred to in Regulation 4 above are as follows—

[A

(i) The title of the film or, in the case of a series of films or a part thereof, the title of the series or part,

(ii) whether the applicant for certification has incurred expenditure on the production or the acquisition of the master negative, master tape or master disc of the film,

(iii) if the applicant is not the maker of the film:

(*a*) the applicant's name and principal place of business, and

(*b*) if the applicant has incurred expenditure on the production of the master negative, master tape or master disc of the film, a brief description (including the amount) of that expenditure, and

(iv) the total playing time in minutes and seconds of the film, including credits and titles.][1]

B The following details about the maker ...[3] of the film—

(i) in the case of an individual:

(*a*) his name and nationality, ...[3]

(*b*) the address of his principal place of business[, and][1]

[(*c*) the State in which he was ordinarily resident throughout the period during which the film was being made;][2]

(ii) in the case of a partnership:

(*a*) the name of the partnership,
(*b*) the name and nationality of each partner, ...[3]
(*c*) the address of the partnership's principal place of business; [and][2]
[(*d*) in respect of each partner, the State in which he was ordinarily resident throughout the period during which the film was being made;][2]

(iii) in the case of a company:
(*a*) the name of the company,
(*b*) the address of the company's principal place of business,
(*c*) the address of the company's registered office throughout the time the film was made,
(*d*) the country under the laws of which the company was incorporated, ...[3]
(*e*) the names and nationalities of its directors throughout the time the film was being made[, and][1]
[(*f*) the State in which the central management and control of the company's business was exercised throughout the period during which the film was being made.][2]

[BA Whether the individual, partnership or company referred to in B(i), (ii) or (iii) above undertook the arrangements necessary for the making of the film.][2]

[C The date on which production of the film began.

D The date on which production of the film was completed for the purposes of Schedule 1 to the Act.][1]

[DA If the applicant seeks treatment of a series of films as a single film in reliance upon paragraph 1(4) of Schedule 1 to the Act:

(i) the number of parts in the series,
(ii) the combined playing time in minutes and seconds of those parts, including credits and titles, and
(iii) the reasons why the series constitutes a self-contained work or is a series of documentaries with a common theme.][1]

[E A statement showing:

(i) the total expenditure incurred in the production of the film;
(ii) the percentage of the total expenditure referred to in (i) above that was incurred on film production activity carried out in the United Kingdom;
(iii) how the figures given in response to (i) and (ii) above were arrived at, with reference to different categories of expenditure, the amount of expenditure in each category and where the relevant film production activity was carried out;
(iv) all amounts of expenditure deducted from the total expenditure referred to in (i) above in reliance upon paragraph 4(5) of Schedule 1 to the Act, and the reason for the deduction of each amount.][1]

[F If any part of the film is derived from any other film ("the other film"):

(i) for each part of the film so derived and in respect of which:
(*a*) the maker of the other film is not the maker of the film, or
(*b*) the master negative, tape or disc of the other film is certified under paragraph 3(1) of Schedule 1 to the Act,

the playing time in minutes and seconds of that part;
(ii) the combined playing time in minutes and seconds of all of the parts referred to in (i) above; and
(iii) if the applicant seeks to rely upon paragraph 5(2) of Schedule 1 to the Act:
(*a*) a statement of the reasons why the film should be considered to be a documentary, and
(*b*) a statement of the reasons why the subject matter of the film makes it appropriate for paragraph 5(1) of Schedule 1 to the Act not to be applied.][1]

G, H, I ...[3]

[G][1] Whether all persons who were directly engaged in the making of the film were:

— Commonwealth citizens, or
— citizens of a Member State, or
— persons ordinarily resident in a Commonwealth country or a Member State,

and if so:

...[3]the total amount paid or payable in respect of labour or services,

...[3]

including all deferred and contingent payments and where the precise amount of any such payment will not be known till later an estimate must be made.

[H][1] Where there were persons in both the following classes directly engaged in the making of a film:

Class A Commonwealth citizens, citizens of a Member State and persons ordinarily resident in a Commonwealth country or a Member State

[*Class B* Other persons, not being persons in respect of whom deductions are made in reliance upon paragraph 7(2)(*a*) or (*b*) of Schedule 1 to the Act][1]

or only in Class B, then the amounts paid or payable in respect of the labour or services of the [categories of persons referred to in (i) and (ii) below][1], specifying in each case separate figures for persons who are in Class A and those who are in Class B and including deferred and contingent payments and where the precise amount of such payments will not be known till later an estimate must be made:

(i) Persons (subject to any election under (iv) below) in respect of whom the total amount paid or payable amounts to at least 1 per cent of the total labour costs or [£10,000][1] whichever is the less except where the total labour costs are less than [£20,000][1] in which case persons earning more than [£200][1]; the total figures shall be broken down into separate sub-totals for:

(*a*) actors, actresses and musicians,
(*b*) all other persons;

and a list shall be provided giving the name, functions, nationality, permanent place of residence and amount paid or payable to each of the persons in this category, indicating in which of the sub-totals for (*a*) or (*b*) the payment has been included;

(ii) Persons (subject to any election under (iv) below) other than those mentioned under (i) above; the total figures shall be broken down into separate sub-totals for:

(*a*) actors, actresses and musicians,
(*b*) all other persons, and
(*c*) ...[3];

and in the case of (*a*) the total number of such persons shall be indicated;

[(iii) the total amounts paid to persons in Class A and Class B respectively for living expenses (if not already specified in response to (i) or (ii) above);]

(iv) Whether the applicant elects to deduct from the total labour costs of the film the amounts paid or payable in respect of one person under paragraph 7(2)(*a*) of Schedule 1 to the Act or in respect of any two persons under paragraph 7(2)(*b*) of that Schedule, and if so the name, function, nationality of and amount paid or payable to that person or persons;

(v) The total for Class A and Class B of the labour costs under (i), (ii) and (iii) above, together with the percentage which the total for Class A above is of this combined total;

(vi), (vii) ...[3];

L ...[3]

Amendments—[1] Paras A, C, D, E, F, and words in paras B, G (formerly para J), H (formerly para K) substituted, by the Films (Certification) (Amendment) Regulations, SI 1999/2224 regs 2, 6 with effect from 27 August 1999.
[2] Paras BA, DA, and words in para B, inserted by SI 1999/2224 regs 2, 6 with effect from 27 August 1999.
[3] Paras G, H, I, L, and words in paras B, G (formerly para J), H (formerly para K) revoked, by SI 1999/2224 regs 2, 6 with effect from 27 August 1999.

Statutory declarations

7 A statutory declaration under Regulation 5(*a*) above shall be deemed to have been made by the applicant if:

(*a*) in the case of an application by a partnership, it has been made on behalf of the partnership by one of the partners, or

(*b*) in the case of an application by a company, it has been made on behalf of the company by the Secretary or one of the directors of the company or by any person duly authorised by the company to make the declaration on its behalf.

[Transitional

8 If, following an election by the applicant pursuant to article 1(2) of the Films (Modification of the Definition of "British Film") Order 1999 ("the Order") the application falls to be determined by the Secretary of State in accordance with Schedule 1 to the Films Act 1985 as it stood before the commencement of the Order, these regulations shall apply to the application as if the Films (Certification) (Amendment) Regulations 1999 had not been made.][1]

Amendments—[1] This regulation inserted by the Films (Certification) (Amendment) (No 2) Regulations, SI 1999/2334 reg 2 with effect from 27 August 1999.

1985/1696
Income Tax (Composite Rate) (Prescribed Deposit-takers) Order 1985

Made by the Treasury under FA 1984 Sch 8 para 2: see now TA 1988 ss 481(2)(*f*)

Made . . . . *6 November 1985*

1 This Order may be cited as the Income Tax (Composite Rate) (Prescribed Deposit-takers) Order 1985 and shall come into operation on 6 April 1986.

2 The following persons and classes of persons are prescribed deposit-takers for the purposes of paragraph 2(1)(*f*) of Schedule 8 to the Finance Act 1984[a] in respect of deposits received in the ordinary course of their businesses or activities, apart from any sums borrowed on or before 18

November 1984, under terms (whether as originally agreed or as varied, but as they have effect on that date) under which the earliest date for any repayment is after 5 April 1986:—

(*a*) local authorities in England and Wales (except parish and community councils) within the meaning of the Local Government Act 1972;

(*b*) the Common Council of the City of London;

(*c*) the Council of the Isles of Scilly;

(*d*) Letchworth Garden City Corporation;

(*e*) any new authority or residuary body within the meaning of the Local Government Act 1985;

(*f*) local authorities in Scotland within the meaning of the Local Government (Scotland) Act 1973;

(*g*) district councils in Northern Ireland within the meaning of the Local Government Act (Northern Ireland) 1972.

Notes—[a] TA 1988 s 481(2)(*f*).

1986/387
Capital Gains Tax (Parallel Pooling) Regulations 1986

Made by the Treasury under FA 1985 Sch 19 para 21, now TCGA 1992 s 112; see TCGA 1992 Sch 11 para 29

Made . . . . . *3 March 1986*
Laid before the House of Commons . *4 March 1986*
Coming into Operation . . . *1 April 1986*

Commentary—*Simon's Direct Tax Service* **C2.713**.

Cross references—See TCGA 1992 s 112(1) (these Regulations continue to have effect notwithstanding the repeal by TCGA 1992 Sch 12 of FA 1985 Sch 19 under para 21 of which these Regulations were made and for the purposes of the Interpretation Act 1978 para 21 is deemed not to have been revoked).

1 These Regulations may be cited as the Capital Gains Tax (Parallel Pooling) Regulations 1986 and shall come into operation on 1st April 1986.

2 In these Regulations unless the context otherwise requires—

''new holding'' has the meaning given to it by paragraph 9(3) of Schedule 19 with the omission therefrom of the words ''or sub-paragraph (2)'';

''qualifying securities'' are securities to which Regulation 3 applies;

''relevant securities'' has the meaning given to it by section 88(9) of the Finance Act 1982;

''Schedule 6'' means Schedule 6 to the Finance Act 1983;

''Schedule 19'' means Schedule 19 to the Finance Act 1985;

''1982 holding'' has the meaning given to it by paragraph 6 of Schedule 19;

''1983 holding'' is a holding within the meaning of paragraph 3(3) of Schedule 6.

3 These Regulations shall have effect in relation to a disposal on or after 1st April 1985 of qualifying securities, within the meaning of Schedule 6—

(*a*) in respect of which an election under that Schedule had been made by a company and not revoked on or before 31st March 1987 or such further time as may be allowed by the Board under paragraph 20(1) of Schedule 19; and

(*b*) which, immediately before 1st April 1985, were regarded as indistinguishable parts of a single asset by virtue of paragraph 3 of Schedule 6;

and are designed to enable section 68 of, and Parts I to V of Schedule 19 to, the Finance Act 1985 to have full effect in relation to the qualifying securities concerned.

4 Of qualifying securities in each 1983 holding which is held by a company immediately before 1st April 1985 there shall be identified as at that time for the purposes of these Regulations—

(*a*) by reference to the provisions of Regulations 5, 6, 7 and 8, the 1982 holding and the new holding of such of those securities as are not relevant securities; and

(*b*) by reference to the provisions of Regulations 5, 6 and 9, the 1982 holding (and the securities not in the 1982 holding) of such of those securities as are relevant securities;

and, as modified by these Regulations, the relevant provisions of the said section 68 and Schedule 19 shall apply in relation to the 1982 holdings, the new holdings and the holdings of relevant securities.

5 For the purposes of these Regulations, or, as the case may be, the Schedule hereto, ''A'' to ''H'' shall be identified by reference to the circumstances obtaining in relation to each 1983 holding held by a company immediately before 1st April 1985 as follows—

(*a*) A is the number of qualifying securities in the 1983 holding.

(*b*) B is the amount of the unindexed pool of expenditure (within the meaning of paragraph 6 of Schedule 6) attributable to the 1983 holding.

(*c*) C is the amount of the indexed pool of expenditure attributable to the 1983 holding, computed on the assumption that an operative event within the meaning of paragraph 7(3) of Schedule 6 occurred immediately before 1st April 1985.

(*d*) D is the aggregate of—

(i) A; and

(ii) the number of securities which are of the same class as those to which paragraph (*a*) above refers, but which, because the conditions of paragraph 3(3)(*b*) of Schedule 6 are not fulfilled, do not form part of the 1983 holding.

(*e*) E is the aggregate of—

(i) B; and

(ii) the relevant allowable expenditure in relation to a disposal immediately before 1st April 1985 of the whole of the securities to which paragraph (*d*)(ii) above refers.

(*f*) F is the aggregate of the relevant allowable expenditure in relation to all disposals by the company made after March 1982 and before April 1985 of securities which are of the same class as those to which paragraph (*a*) above refers and which were acquired after 6th April 1965.

(*g*) G is—

(i) the number of securities of that same class which were held by the company immediately before 1st April 1982 and which comprise a holding within the meaning of Part II of Schedule 13 to the Finance Act 1982; or

(ii) where on or after 1st April 1982 there has been a reorganisation of share capital within the meaning of section 77(1) of the Capital Gains Tax Act 1979 the number of shares which (on the assumption that there had been no part disposal of original shares within the meaning of the provisions of that subsection) would comprise a new holding within the meaning of that section.

(*h*) H is the amount which would be the aggregate of the relevant allowable expenditure in relation to a disposal by the company immediately before 1st April 1985 of the whole of the securities to which paragraph (*g*) above refers.

6—(1) J is the number of qualifying securities in the 1982 holding, rounded to the nearest whole number and is given by the formula—

$$G \times \frac{E}{E + F}$$

(2) In relation to a disposal by the company of the whole of the 1982 holding on or after 1st April 1985, K is the relevant allowable expenditure, given by the formula—

$$H \times \frac{E}{E + F}$$

7 In respect of qualifying securities ("the securities")—

(*a*) the number of the securities which fall to be included in the new holding is given by the formula A – J;

(*b*) the relevant allowable expenditure in relation to a disposal by the company of all the securities referred to in paragraph (*a*) above immediately before 1st April 1985 is given by the formula B – K;

(*c*) the indexed pool of expenditure in relation to the securities referred to in paragraph (*a*) above for the purposes of paragraph 13(2) of Schedule 19 is given by the formula—

$$(B - K)\left(\frac{C}{B} + 0{\cdot}05\right)$$

8 In respect of the new holding ("the holding")—

(*a*) the number of securities in the holding is given by the formula D – J;

(*b*) the qualifying expenditure in relation to the holding is given by the formula E – K;

(*c*) the indexed pool of expenditure in relation to the holding is given by the aggregate of—

(i) the amount given by the formula

$$(B - K)\left(\frac{C}{B} + 0{\cdot}05\right)$$

(ii) the relevant allowable expenditure in relation to a disposal by the company immediately before 1st April 1985 of the whole of the securities to which Regulation 5(*d*)(ii) refers; and

(iii) any indexation allowance applicable to such a disposal on the assumption that the amendment of the Finance Act 1982 made by paragraphs 1 and 2 of Schedule 19 had always had effect.

9—(1) This Regulation applies to a holding of relevant securities ("relevant securities holding") which are qualifying securities comprised in a 1983 holding held by the company immediately before 1st April 1985 and, for the purposes of this Regulation, references to qualifying securities in Regulations 5 and 6 shall be treated as references to the relevant securities holding.

(2) In respect of the relevant securities holding—

(*a*) the number of relevant securities in the holding, not being relevant securities in the 1982 holding, is given by the formula A – J;

(*b*) the relevant securities in the holding to which paragraph (*a*) above refers shall be treated for the purposes of the Capital Gains Tax Act 1979 as having been acquired on 31st March 1984;

(*c*) the amount of the relevant allowable expenditure in relation to a disposal on or after 1st April 1985 of all the relevant securities in the holding to which paragraph (*a*) above refers is given by the formula

$$(B - K) \times \frac{C}{B}$$

and shall be apportioned rateably to the relevant securities.

10 The Schedule to these Regulations shall have effect only for providing an example of the operation of the Regulations and, in the event of any conflict between the provisions of the Schedule and the Regulations, the Regulations shall prevail.

SCHEDULE

INTRODUCTORY

In this Schedule—

Part I is a statement of facts which are to be assumed;

Part II is an application of the Regulations to qualifying securities which are not relevant securities;

Part III is an application of the Regulations to qualifying securities which are relevant securities.

PART I

1 QUALIFYING SECURITIES AND EXPENDITURE

PG plc held, acquired or disposed of qualifying securities as follows—

Date		Number of securities	Expenditure/proceeds
31st March 1982	holding	1,000	6,000
1st September 1982	purchased	2,000	12,000
1st March 1983	purchased	3,000	10,000
1st September 1983	rights	6,000	12,000
1st January 1985	sold	3,000	12,000
31st January 1985	purchased	3,000	10,000

2 RETAIL PRICES INDEX

The Retail Prices Index is assumed to be—

March 1982	100	*September 1984*	112
September 1983	107	*January 1985*	114
March 1984	110	*March 1985*	116

3 CALCULATION OF INDEXED POOL OF EXPENDITURE IN ACCORDANCE WITH SCHEDULE 6

	Securities	Expenditure: Excluded from pools £	Expenditure: Unindexed pool £	Expenditure: Indexed pool £
31st March 1982	1,000		6,000	6,000
1st September 1983 indexed rise: $£6,000 \times \frac{107-100}{100}$				
$= £6,000 \times \cdot 070$				420
Additions to 1983 holding	2,000 *(Acquired 1st September 1982)*		12,000	12,000
Rights taken up	3,000	6,000		
	6,000	6,000	18,000	18,420

	Securities	Expenditure Excluded from pools £	Expenditure Unindexed pool £	Expenditure Indexed pool £
1st March 1984 indexed rise: $£18{,}420 \times \dfrac{110-107}{107}$				
$= £18{,}420 \times \cdot 028$				516
Addition (including rights) to 1983 holding	6,000	6,000	10,000	10,000
	12,000	12,000	28,000	28,936
1st September 1984 indexed rise: $£28{,}936 \times \dfrac{112-110}{110}$				
$= £28{,}936 \times \cdot 018$				521
Expiry of 12 months following rights issue; expenditure no longer excluded		(12,000)	12,000	12,000
	12,000	—	40,000	41,457
1st January 1985 indexed rise: $£41{,}457 \times \dfrac{114-112}{112}$ p				
$= £41{,}457 \times \cdot 018$				746
	12,000		40,000	42,203
Disposal	3,000		10,000	10,551
	9,000		30,000	31,652

4 SECURITIES HELD LESS THAN ONE YEAR AT 31ST MARCH 1985

The 3,000 securities acquired on 31st January 1985 for £10,000 do not qualify for inclusion in the 1983 holding on 31st March 1985.

PART II

QUALIFYING SECURITIES WHICH ARE NOT RELEVANT SECURITIES

STEP 1—Regulation 5(*a*)–(*c*)

Index the indexed pool as if an operative event had occurred immediately before 1st April 1985

Indexed pool (see Part I.3, above) £31,652

$£31{,}652 \times \dfrac{116-114}{114} = £31{,}652 \times \cdot 018$ 570

£32,222

Therefore—

A = 9,000

B = 30,000

C = 32,222

STEP 2—Regulation 5(*d*) and (*e*)

Number of securities not within 1983 holding (see Part I.4, above) 3,000

Relevant allowable expenditure £10,000

Therefore—

D = 9,000 + 3,000 = 12,000

E = 30,000 + 10,000 = 40,000.

STEP 3—Regulation 5(*f*)

F = 10,000.

STEP 4—Regulation 5(*g*) and (*h*)

Number of securities held on 31st March 1982	1,000
Rights issue 1 for 1	1,000
	G=2,000
Relevant allowable expenditure on securities	= £6,000
Relevant allowable expenditure on rights 1,000 @ £2 per share	= £2,000
	H=£8,000

STEP 5—Regulation 6

$$J = 2{,}000 \times \frac{40{,}000}{40{,}000 + 10{,}000} = 1{,}600$$

$$K = £8{,}000 \times \frac{40{,}000}{40{,}000 + 10{,}000} = £6{,}400$$

Therefore the 1982 holding comprises:

1,600 shares—relevant allowable expenditure £6,400.

Note: applying the above fraction to the separate components of H (step 4) £4,800 will qualify for indexation from March 1982 and £1,600 from September 1983 for the purposes of section 87 of, and paragraph 5 of Schedule 13 to, the Finance Act 1982.

STEP 6—Regulation 7

Number of securities in the 1983 holding forming part of new holding = 9,000 – 1,600	= 7,400
Relevant allowable expenditure on these securities = £30,000 – £6,400	=£23,600

Aggregate of relevant allowable expenditure and indexation allowance for the purposes of paragraph 13(2), Schedule 19

$$= (30{,}000 - 6{,}400)\left(\frac{32{,}222}{30{,}000} + 0.05\right) = 26{,}528$$

STEP 7—Regulation 8

Number of securities in new holding = 12,000 – 1,600	= 10,400
Qualifying expenditure = £40,000 – £6,400	=£33,600
Relevant allowable expenditure in relation to securities not included in 1983 holding	=£10,000
Indexation allowance	= £180
Indexed pool in relation to the new holding = £26,528 + £10,000 + £180	=£36,708

SUMMARY

1982 holding: 1,600 securities—relevant allowable expenditure £6,400 (of which £4,800 qualifies for indexation from March 1982 and £1,600 from September 1983).

New holding: 10,400 securities—qualifying expenditure £33,600 and indexed pool of expenditure £36,708.

PART III
QUALIFYING SECURITIES WHICH ARE RELEVANT SECURITIES

STEPS 1–5 as in Part II above.

STEP 6—Regulation 9

Number of relevant securities in 1983 holding not forming part of 1982 holding = 9,000 – 1,600 = 7,400

Relevant allowable expenditure

$$= (30{,}000 - 6{,}400) \times \frac{32{,}222}{30{,}000} = £25{,}348$$

Expenditure apportioned to securities

$$\frac{£25{,}348}{7{,}400} = £3.4254$$

Deemed date of acquisition of those securities—31st March 1984.

SUMMARY

1982 holding: 1,600 securities—relevant allowable expenditure £6,400 (of which £4,800 qualifies for indexation from March 1982 and £1,600 from September 1983).

Other relevant securities: 7,400 securities treated as acquired on 31st March 1984—relevant allowable expenditure £25,348.

3,000 securities treated as acquired on 31st January 1986—relevant allowable expenditure £10,000.

1986/2211
Charitable Deductions (Approved Schemes) Regulations 1986

Made by the Treasury under FA 1986 s 28, now TA 1988 s 202(8)–(10); see TA 1988 Sch 30 para 21

Made . . . . 15 December 1986
Laid before the House of Commons . . . 16 December 1986
Coming into Operation . . . . . 8 January 1987

Commentary—*Simon's Direct Tax Service* **E4.948**.

Citation and commencement

1 These Regulations may be cited as the Charitable Deductions (Approved Schemes) Regulations 1986, and shall come into operation on 8th January 1987.

Interpretation

2 In these Regulations unless the context otherwise requires—

"approved agency" means a body approved as agent in accordance with Regulation 5;
"approved scheme" means a scheme approved in accordance with Regulation 3;
"employer" means a person paying emoluments;
"employee" means any person entitled to receive payments of emoluments;
"emoluments" means income to be taken into account in assessing liability to income tax under Schedule E, from payments of which income tax falls to be deducted by virtue of section 204[a] of the Taxes Act and regulations under that section;
"income tax month" means the period beginning on the 6th day of any calendar month and ending on the 5th day of the following calendar month;
"scheme" includes a kind of scheme;
["supplement" means the supplement payable under section 38 of the Finance Act 2000;][1]
"year" means the period beginning on any 6th day of April and ending on the following 5th day of April.

Notes—[a] TA 1988 s 203.
Amendments—[1] Definition of "supplement" substituted by the Charitable Deductions (Approved Schemes) (Amendment) Regulations, SI 2003/1745 reg 3 with effect for supplements payable in respect of sums withheld after 5 April 2003 and before 6 April 2004.

Approval of schemes

3 The Board may grant approval of a scheme for the purposes of section 27 of the Finance Act 1986[a] if it is satisfied on an application by an approved agency that the scheme provides—

(*a*) for a contract between the approved agency and an employer to give effect to the scheme;
(*b*) that any employee to whom the employer pays emoluments on or after 6th April 1987 may ...[2] request the employer, in such form as the Board may approve or prescribe, to withhold from such emoluments such sum as the employee may specify pursuant to the scheme to be paid (subject to the provisions of the scheme) either by way of gift to such charity or charities as the employee may specify or in exchange for vouchers which the employee may surrender by way of gift to the charity or charities of his choice;
(*c*) that under the scheme the employer is constituted the agent of the approved agency in holding moneys withheld from employees pursuant to the scheme;
(*d*) for any minimum sum which may be withheld pursuant to the scheme and for any limit which may be imposed on the number of charities which one employee may specify pursuant to the scheme;
(*e*) ...[2]
(*f*) that no sum so withheld shall be due to the specified charity pursuant to a deed of covenant or, where the sum withheld is paid in exchange for vouchers, that the value of those vouchers shall not be due to the charity or charities to which they are surrendered pursuant to a deed of covenant;
(*g*) that the employer is to be bound to pay over to the approved agency sums withheld from employees pursuant to the scheme in any income tax month within 14 days of the end of that income tax month;
(*h*) that the approved agency will if so requested give written receipts to the employer in respect of sums paid over to it;
(*i*) that in no circumstances will sums duly withheld and paid over to the approved agency be returnable to the employer or to any employee;
(*j*) that the approved agency will, subject to any deduction in respect of its charges, pay sums paid to it by the employer pursuant to the scheme to the charities respectively specified by the employees or provide the employees with vouchers to be surrendered to the charities of their choice;

[(*ja*) that the approved agency will pay to the charities specified by the employees the sums paid to it by the employer pursuant to the scheme within a period which does not exceed the period set out in regulation 4A;][1]

(*k*) that the approved agency will if so requested by an employee at the end of any year give him a certificate of the amounts which the approved agency has paid to charities specified by him in respect of sums withheld from his emoluments in that year and of the maximum time elapsing in any period specified by the employee between the receipt of such sums from the employer and the payment to the charities of amounts in respect of such sums;

(*l*) that if for any reason it becomes impossible for the approved agency to pay any amount to a charity specified by an employee the approved agency shall pay that amount to such other charity as it may consider has objects similar to those of the charity specified by the employee, but so that it shall not in any circumstances appropriate that amount to its own funds; and that on so paying that amount to that other charity the approved agency will give notice to the employee that it has done so;

(*m*) that where an employee has been provided with a voucher by which payment may be made to a charity and that voucher has not been presented to the approved agency by way of payment within a time prescribed by the approved agency the approved agency will pay the amount represented by that voucher to such other charity as it sees fit, but so that it shall not in any circumstances appropriate that amount to its own funds; and that on so paying that amount to that other charity the approved agency will give notice to the employee that it has done so;

(*n*) for the method by which the approved agency's charges in relation to the operation of the scheme will be met and for the determining of the amount of such charges.

Notes—[a] TA 1988 s 202(1)–(7).

Amendments—[1] Para (*ja*) inserted by the Charitable Deductions (Approved Schemes) (Amendment) Regulations, SI 2000/759 reg 3 with effect from 6 April 2000.

[2] Words in para (*b*) and whole of para (*e*) revoked by the Charitable Deductions (Approved Schemes) (Amendment No 2) Regulations, SI 2000/2083 reg 4 with effect from 21 August 2000.

4 Applications by an approved agency in accordance with Regulation 3 shall be in such form as the Board may approve or prescribe.

[Period for payment by agencies to charities

4A—(1) An approved agency shall, notwithstanding anything in the provisions of an approved scheme or in a contract entered into with the employer to give effect to an approved scheme, pay to the charities specified by the employees the sums paid to it by the employer pursuant to the scheme not later than 60 days following either—

(*a*) the date on which it receives the sums paid to it from the employer or, if later,

(*b*) the date on which it receives notification of the charity or charities specified by an employee.

(2) Where an employee has been provided with a voucher by which payment may be made to a charity, the date on which a charity presents that voucher to the approved agency for payment shall be treated for the purposes of paragraph (1)(*b*) as the date on which the approved agency receives notification of the specification of that charity by the employee.][1]

[(3) The prescribed period for the purposes of section 38(1) of the Finance Act 2000 shall be—

(*a*) the period of 7 days following the coming into force of the Charitable Deductions (Approved Schemes) (Amendment) Regulations 2003,

(*b*) if it ends later, the period within which payment of the sums paid to the approved agency by the employer pursuant to the scheme is to be made under this regulation.][2]

Amendments—[1] This regulation inserted by the Charitable Deductions (Approved Schemes) (Amendment) Regulations, SI 2000/759 reg 4 with effect in relation to sums withheld after 5 April 2000.

[2] Para (3) substituted by the Charitable Deductions (Approved Schemes) (Amendment) Regulations, SI 2003/1745 reg 4 with effect for supplements payable in respect of sums withheld after 5 April 2003 and before 6 April 2004.

Approval of agencies

5 The Board may grant approval as an agent for the purposes of section 27 of the Finance Act 1986[a] to any charity which the Board is satisfied is prepared and able to act as an approved agency in relation to approved schemes and to comply with the provisions of these Regulations.

Notes—[a] TA 1988 s 202(1)–(7), (11).

6 Applications by a charity for approval as an agent in accordance with Regulation 5 shall be in such form as the Board may approve or prescribe.

Withdrawal of approval of agencies

7 If at any time the Board is of opinion that an approved agency has ceased to be a charity or has failed to act properly in relation to an approved scheme or has failed to comply with these Regulations, it may give notice of withdrawal of approval to the approved agency and thereupon, from such date as the Board may specify in its notice, the agency shall cease to be approved and all schemes which have been approved on its application shall cease to be approved and all contracts to give effect to such schemes shall determine. When the Board gives such notice it shall inform every employer who has a contract with the approved agency to give effect to an approved scheme that it has so given notice.

Appeals

8—(1) Any person aggrieved by the Board's refusal to grant him approval as an agent in accordance with Regulation 5 or by the Board's withdrawal of such approval in accordance with Regulation 7 may, by notice in writing given to the Board within 30 days from the date on which he is notified of the Board's refusal or withdrawal of approval, require the matter to be determined by the Special Commissioners, and the Special Commissioners shall hear and determine the matter in like manner as an appeal.

(2) Any approved agency aggrieved by the Board's refusal to grant approval of a scheme in accordance with Regulation 3, may, by notice in writing given to the Board within 30 days from the date on which it is notified of the Board's refusal, require the matter to be determined by the Special Commissioners, and the Special Commissioners shall hear and determine the matter in like manner as an appeal.

Information, returns and records

9—(1) Every approved agency shall, within 30 days of entering into a contract with an employer giving effect to an approved scheme, inform the Board, in such form as the Board may approve or prescribe, of the date of the contract and of the name and address of the employer.

(2) Where a contract giving effect to an approved scheme is terminated the approved agency shall, within 30 days, inform the Board of such termination.

[(3) Where an approved agency has not paid to the charities specified by the employees—

(*a*) the sums paid to it by the employer pursuant to the scheme within the period set out in regulation 4A(1) and (2), or

(*b*) any supplements relating to those sums within the period prescribed by regulation 4A(3),

the approved agency shall, not later than 7 days following the last day on which it should have paid those sums or supplements to the charities, inform the Board by furnishing a statement of those sums or supplements and the reasons why it has not been able to comply with regulation 4A.][1]

Amendments—[1] Para (3) substituted by the Charitable Deductions (Approved Schemes) (Amendment) Regulations, SI 2003/1745 reg 5 with effect for supplements payable in respect of sums withheld after 5 April 2003 and before 6 April 2004.

10 On the ending of each year every approved agency shall, within 30 days of the end of such year or within such further time as the Board may allow, furnish a return to the Board, in such form as the Board may approve or prescribe, of the sums received from each employer with whom it has at any time within the year had a subsisting contract to give effect to an approved scheme, of the numbers of employees from whose emoluments such sums have been withheld, of the number of vouchers issued pursuant to any contract and the total values of such vouchers, of the amounts paid by it to each charity in relation to such approved schemes, and of its charges in relation to the operation of schemes.

11—(1) Every approved agency shall retain—

(*a*) records of approved schemes,

(*b*) records of contracts with employers until 3 years from the termination of each contract, ...[1]

(*c*) for not less than 3 years, records of sums received from employers, records of amounts paid to all charities specified by employees, and records of vouchers for charities issued by it to employees pursuant to approved schemes [and

(*d*) for not less than 3 years, records of all supplements paid to charities specified by employees and records of all amounts received from the Board under section 38 of the Finance Act 2000].[2]

(2) Every approved agency, when so required by notice served on it by the Board, shall within 30 days of such service produce for inspection by an officer of the Board all records required to be retained by it by paragraph (1) of this Regulation.

Amendments—[1] Word "and" in para (1)(*b*) revoked and para (1)(*d*) and word "and" preceding it inserted by the Charitable Deductions (Approved Schemes) (Amendment No 2) Regulations, SI 2000/2083 reg 7 with effect for supplements payable in respect of sums withheld after 5 April 2000 and before 6 April 2003.

[2] Para (1)(*d*) and word "and" preceding it substituted by the Charitable Deductions (Approved Schemes) (Amendment) Regulations, SI 2003/1745 reg 6 with effect for supplements payable in respect of sums withheld after 5 April 2003 and before 6 April 2004.

12—(1) Every employer who has entered into a contract with an approved agency pursuant to an approved scheme shall retain—

(*a*) a copy of such contract until 3 years from the termination of the contract,

(*b*) all forms of request to deduct given by employees pursuant to the approved scheme until 3 years from the revocation or lapse of such request and, (*c*) for not less than 3 years, records of all sums withheld from such employees pursuant to the approved scheme and evidence of all payments made to the approved agency pursuant to the approved scheme.

(2) Every employer who has entered into a contract with an approved agency pursuant to an approved scheme, when so required by notice served on him by the Board, shall within 30 days of such service produce for inspection by an officer of the Board all documents and records required to be retained by him pursuant to paragraph (1) of this Regulation.

Termination of contracts

13 If at any time an employer who has contracted to give effect to a scheme has without reasonable excuse failed in a significant respect to give effect to the scheme in accordance with his contract the approved agency shall forthwith give notice to the employer of termination of the contract.

Employee leaving employment

14 Where an employee who has requested his employer to withhold any sum pursuant to an approved scheme leaves his employment, the employer shall provide the employee with a statement, in such form as the Board may approve or prescribe, of the total amount so withheld from the employee's emoluments from that employment in the year in which the employee so leaves his employment.

Service by post

15 Any notice which is authorised or required to be given or served under these Regulations may be sent by post.

[Overpayment of supplement to be treated as unpaid tax

16 Where the Board has made an overpayment under section 38 of the Finance Act 2000 to an approved agent, the amount of that overpayment may be assessed and recovered as if it were an amount of unpaid tax for the purposes of the Taxes Acts.][1]

Amendments—[1] This regulation substituted by the Charitable Deductions (Approved Schemes) (Amendment) Regulations, SI 2003/1745 reg 7 with effect for supplements payable in respect of sums withheld after 5 April 2003 and before 6 April 2004.

1987/352
Pension Scheme Surpluses (Administration) Regulations 1987

Made by the Treasury under FA 1986 Sch 12 Part I, now TA 1988 ss 601(3), 602; see TA 1988 Sch 30 para 21

Made	*3 March 1987*
Laid before the House of Commons	*13 March 1987*
Coming into force	*7 April 1987*

Commentary—*Simon's Direct Tax Service* **E7.238.**

Citation and commencement

1 These Regulations may be cited as the Pension Scheme Surpluses (Administration) Regulations 1987 and shall come into force on 7th April 1987.

Interpretation

2 In these Regulations unless the context otherwise requires—

''administrator'' means the person or persons having the management of an exempt approved scheme;

''the Board'' means the Commissioners of Inland Revenue;

''excluded payment'' has the meaning given to it by regulation 4;

''Schedule 12'' means Schedule 12 to the Finance Act 1986[a];

a ''surplus payment'' means a payment out of funds of an exempt approved scheme which is a payment (not being an excluded payment) to which paragraph 1(1) of Schedule 12 refers;

a ''tax payment'' means the amount equal to 40 per cent of a surplus payment to which paragraph 1(2) of Schedule 12 refers.

Notes—[a] TA 1988 ss 601, 602, Sch 22.

Pension scheme surplus payment—administrator to make return and account for tax payment

3—(1) The administrator shall—

(*a*) on making a surplus payment to an employer deduct out of it the relevant tax payment, and

(*b*) within 14 days after making the surplus payment make a return to the Board in accordance with paragraph (2).

(2) The return to which paragraph (1) refers shall contain the following particulars—

(*a*) the full name or description and tax office reference of the scheme;
(*b*) the name and address and tax office reference of the employer concerned;
(*c*) details of the surplus payment including—

(i) the date when it was made, and
(ii) where the surplus payment (or part) is a transfer of an asset or of money's worth (within the meaning of paragraph 1(9) of Schedule 12[a]) the market value of the asset or money's worth concerned;

(*d*) the amount of the tax payment.

Notes—[a] TA 1988 ss 601(6)(*a*).

Excluded payments

4 An excluded payment is a payment by the administrator which falls within any of the following descriptions—

(*a*) any payment to the employer—

(i) by way of reimbursement of expenditure properly incurred by the employer in respect of an obligation of the administrator in respect of the scheme;
(ii) by way of interest on or repayment of a loan from the employer;
(iii) by way of loan or investment of scheme funds provided it is a loan or investment showing a reasonable commercial return;
(iv) which the administrator is obliged to make under the provisions of a scheme to enable the employer to obtain the discharge by a member of the scheme of some monetary obligation due to the employer which arises out of a criminal, negligent or fraudulent act or omission by the member concerned.

(*b*) a reimbursement of a payment by the employer of a state scheme premium to which section 42 or 45 of the Social Security Pensions Act 1975 applies.

Payment of tax

5—(1) The tax payment shall be due at the time by which the return under regulation 3 is to be made and unless the Board otherwise authorises shall be made with that return.

(2) The tax payment so due shall be payable by the administrator without the making of any assessment.

Assessments of tax upon employer and administrator

6—(1) Subject to the provisions of this Regulation the amount of the tax payment to which regulation 3(1) refers shall be assessed upon the employer under Case VI of Schedule D as an amount of income tax or corporation tax, as the case may be, for the chargeable period in which the surplus payment is made.

(2) The amount of tax charged and due under the assessment under paragraph (1) shall be reduced by the amount paid to the Board by the administrator in respect of the tax payment payable under regulation 5 and, subject to any appeal, the reduced amount shall in all respects be treated as an amount of tax due and payable under an assessment to which paragraph (6) applies and which is final and conclusive.

(3) If, by the end of the sixtieth day after the date of the notice of the assessment to which paragraph (2) refers, the full amount of the tax due and payable under the assessment, together with interest payable, has not been paid to the Board, the amount of tax and interest remaining unpaid may be assessed upon the administrator (under Case VI of Schedule D) in the name of the employer.

(4) The amount of the tax and interest so charged by an assessment upon the administrator shall (subject to any appeal within that period) be due and payable by the administrator within 14 days after the date of the notice of the assessment under paragraph (3) as an amount of tax due and payable under an assessment which is final and conclusive.

(5) Where an amount due and payable under paragraph (3) has been paid by the administrator he may recover a sum equal to that amount from the employer.

(6) The Taxes Management Act 1970 shall apply to any assessment of tax under these Regulations as if—

(*a*) the assessment were an assessment specified in sections 55(1) (recovery of tax not postponed) and 86(2) (interest on tax), and
(*b*) subsections (3) and (4) of section 86 were omitted and "the reckonable date" for the purposes of section 86 were the 30th day after the date when these Regulations come into force or the 15th day after the date when a surplus payment is made (whichever is later).

Other returns

7 Where the Board has reason to believe that a surplus payment has been made to an employer in respect of which no return or an incorrect return has been made under regulation 3, they may, by notice in writing, require the administrator or the employer concerned, within the time limited by the notice, to furnish to the Board a return (or further return) containing the particulars to which regulation 3 refers.

Amounts recoverable to be separate from other amounts recoverable under Tax Acts

8 Any amount recoverable by the Board from an administrator or employer under these Regulations, whether by assessment or otherwise, shall be treated as an amount recoverable from the administrator or employer, as the case may be, in a separate capacity from other amounts which may be recoverable under the Tax Acts.

1987/412
Pension Scheme Surpluses (Valuation) Regulations 1987

Made by the Commissioners of Inland Revenue under FA 1986 Sch 12 Part II, now TA 1988 s 603, Sch 22; see TA 1988 Sch 30 para 21

Made . . . . *13 March 1987*
Laid before the House of Commons . . . *16 March 1987*
Coming into Force . . . *6 April 1987*

Commentary—*Simon's Direct Tax Service* **E7.248, 249**.
Note—The publications to which regulations 5(1) and 6(2) refer may be obtained from—
Institute of Actuaries, Staple Inn Hall, High Holborn, London WC1B 7QJ;
Faculty of Actuaries, 23 St Andrew's Square, Edinburgh EH2 1AQ.

Citation and commencement

1 These Regulations may be cited as the Pension Scheme Surpluses (Valuation) Regulations 1987 and shall come into force on 6th April 1987.

Interpretation

2 In these Regulations unless the context otherwise requires—
''administrator'' means the person or persons having the management of a scheme;
''Board'' means Commissioners of Inland Revenue;
''the effective date'' in relation to a valuation is the date stated to be the effective date in the signed valuation;
''employer'' means employer of members of a scheme;
''indexed-gilt'' means a public sector index-linked security;
''insured scheme'' means a scheme the contributions to which, apart from voluntary contributions made by members, are invested wholly by way of insurance premiums;
a ''Paragraph'' (not being a paragraph of a regulation) means a paragraph of Schedule 12;[a]
''retail prices index'' means the general index of retail prices (for all items) published by the [Central Statistical Office of the Chancellor of the Exchequer][1];
''Schedule 12'' means Schedule 12 to the Finance Act 1986;[a]
''scheme'' means an exempt approved scheme within the meaning of section 21 of the Finance Act 1970;[b]
''self-administered scheme'' means a scheme some or all of the income and other assets of which are invested otherwise than in insurance policies;
''signed valuation'' has the meaning given to it by regulation 9(4);
[''simplified defined contribution scheme'' means a scheme approved by the Board under section 591 of the Income and Corporation Taxes Act 1988 by reference to limitations on—
(*a*) the aggregate amount of the contributions which may be paid by a member and his employer,
(*b*) the maximum lump sum which may be provided under the scheme, and
(*c*) the benefits payable on death which may be provided under the scheme.][2]

Note—[a] TA 1988 ss 601, 602 and Sch 22.
[b] TA 1988 s 592.
Amendments—[1] Words in the definition of ''retail prices index'' substituted by the Transfer of Functions (Economic Statistics) Order, SI 1989/992 Sch 2 para 5(2)(*f*)(iii).
[2] Definition of ''simplified defined contribution scheme'' inserted by the Pension Scheme Surpluses (Valuation) (Amendment) Regulations, SI 1989/2290 reg 3.

Schemes to which Part II of Schedule 12 is to apply

3—(1) With effect from the 6th April 1987 Part II of Schedule 12[a] shall apply, subject to these Regulations, in relation to schemes prescribed by paragraph (2) of this regulation.

(2) Prescribed schemes to which paragraph (1) of this regulation refers are—

[(*a*) self-administered schemes other than schemes which fall within either or both of sub-paragraphs (*a*) and (*b*) of paragraph (3);

(*b*) insured schemes, the policies in respect of which do not provide that levels of contributions require to take account of surpluses, other than schemes—

(i) the policies in respect of which provide only for lump sum benefits for members on death before normal retirement age, or

(ii) which are simplified defined contribution schemes.][1]

[(3) The schemes which fall within this paragraph are schemes which—

(*a*) have less than 12 members,

(*b*) are simplified defined contribution schemes.][2]

Notes—[a] TA 1988 Sch 22.

Amendments—[1] Para (2)(*a*), (*b*) substituted by the Pension Scheme Surpluses (Valuation) (Amendment) Regulations, SI 1989/2290 reg 4, with effect from 28 December 1989.

[2] Para (3) inserted by SI 1989/2290 reg 4.

Actuarial principles and requirements—introductory

4 Regulations 5 to 8 prescribe principles and requirements (based on actuarial principles and practice) in accordance with which valuations of assets and liabilities of a scheme are to be determined for the purposes of Paragraph 5(2).

Valuation of liabilities

5—(1) A valuation of liabilities shall be determined in accordance with the principles described as the ''Projected Accrued Benefit Method'' in the document entitled ''Pension Fund Terminology: Specimen Descriptions of Commonly Used Valuation Methods'' published in 1986 by the Institute of Actuaries and Faculty of Actuaries.

(2) The actuarial assumptions and requirements for the purposes of the valuation to which paragraph (1) of this regulation refers are as follows—

(*a*) *the valuation rate of interest:* the rate assumed to be earned on the investment of the future income of the scheme (net of expenditure) shall be 8·5 per cent per annum;

(*b*) *the net investment yield (pre-retirement):* the margin between the valuation rate of interest to which sub-paragraph (*a*) refers and general increases in salaries must be assumed to be 1·5 per cent per annum;

(*c*) *the net investment yield (post-retirement):*

(i) the valuation rate of interest shall be reduced to take account of pension increases at the rate provided for under the scheme, provided the net investment yield is not so reduced to an amount less than 3 per cent per annum;

(ii) where it is provided under the scheme that there shall be regular reviews of pensions currently payable and for pension increases (not exceeding any relevant increase in the retail prices index) to be given at the discretion of the trustees or employer (subject to availability of funds), paragraph (i) shall apply as if references to increases included references to such discretionary increases;

(iii) the pension increases under paragraph (ii) shall be arrived at after taking account of—

(*a*) the average increase, measured either absolutely or relative to inflation, awarded during the period of 3 years preceding the effective date of the valuation; or

(*b*) such rate of increase notified to the Board under a declaration of intent made jointly by the administrator of the scheme and the employer to pay increases (subject to availability of funds), provided also that the extent of the increase included in the valuation (either by reference to a rate of increase or by a margin in the rate of interest) is disclosed to scheme members;

(iv) where, under the scheme, the rate of pensions increase is effectively linked to increases in the retail prices index, the net investment yield shall be 2 per cent per annum except where the obligation to make an increase is (under the scheme) subject to a stated (or overriding) maximum when an appropriate higher net yield must be used;

(v) no reduction shall be made in the valuation rate of interest unless the requirements of this regulation are fulfilled.

Valuation of liabilities—allowances

6—(1) In calculating liabilities of a scheme an appropriate allowance shall be made for each of the factors described in paragraphs (2) to (4) of this regulation, subject to those provisions and to paragraphs (5) and (6).

(2) *Pensioners mortality*: unless based upon experience of the operation of the scheme or other like schemes where mortality is not expected to be different, the mortality assumptions to be used for the purposes of the valuation, are those in the PA (90) Mortality Table, published in 1979 by the Institute of Actuaries and the Faculty of Actuaries, rated down by one year.

(3) *Salary scales*: any assumption in respect of career escalation in respect of salaries shall be based, where there is such a scale, upon a specifically constructed scale, but, where there is no such scale, an amount not exceeding 1 per cent shall instead be deducted from the net investment yield.

(4) *Expenses:* where the cost of administration of a scheme is borne by the scheme under the terms of the trust deed provision shall be made for future costs by taking account of the average of such costs incurred over the three years preceding the effective date of the valuation, and whether or not contributions are being paid to the scheme.

(5) *Other factors:* assumptions may be made, where appropriate, in respect of staff turnover and other factors relating to the particular circumstances of a scheme.

(6) Changes in actuarial assumptions from those used in the previous valuation may be made where they are justified and any such change shall be notified in writing to the Board at or before the time when the valuation is produced or the certificate is given under Paragraph 5.

Valuation of assets

7—(1) For the purposes of a valuation of assets the following requirements shall be fulfilled—

(*a*) future income [and, where appropriate, capital receipts][1] of the scheme shall be discounted at a rate of 8·5 per cent per annum;

(*b*) scheme income [and capital receipts][1] from indexed-gilts shall be assumed to increase at the rate of 5·3 per cent per annum;

(*c*) income [and, where appropriate, capital receipts][1] from variable interest investments (not being indexed-gilts) shall be assumed to increase at a rate of 3·5 per cent per annum.

(2)

(*a*) Subject to sub-paragraph (*b*), instead of a valuation of the actual assets of a scheme the valuation may be made on the assumption that the scheme assets comprised an appropriate standardised portfolio of the market value of the actual assets at the effective valuation date, and

(*b*) any change in the valuation methods to which sub-paragraph (*a*) refers and any change in the assumed composition of the said appropriate standardised portfolio from whatever was, in either case, assumed for the previous valuation, may be made where it is justified, and any such change shall be notified in writing to the Board at or before the time when the valuation is produced or the certificate is given under Paragraph 5.

Amendments—[1] Words in para (1)(*a*)–(*c*) inserted by the Pension Scheme Surpluses (Valuation) (Amendment) Regulations, SI 1989/2290 reg 5, with effect from 28 December 1989.

Valuation of insurance policies of a scheme

8—(1) Where the assets of a scheme comprise or include contracts of insurance of the kind described in paragraph (2) of this regulation that paragraph shall apply for the purposes of the valuation of those contracts.

(2)

(*a*) *Pension fund management contracts:* the requirements of regulation 7 shall be applicable;

(*b*) *Deposit administration contracts:* the value of the contract shall be taken to be the value of the fund accumulated under the contract;

(*c*)

(i) *Deferred annuity contracts (with profits):* the value of the contract shall be ascertained by estimating future proceeds (assuming future bonus levels consistent with an annual rate of interest of 8·5 per cent) and discounting them at 8·5 per cent per annum,

(ii) *Cash accumulation contracts (with profits):* paragraph (i) shall apply;

(*d*) *Non-profit contracts:* the proceeds shall be discounted at 8·5 per cent per annum.

Periodic actuarial valuations

9—(1) This regulation prescribes the circumstances and the time to which Paragraph 5(1) refers (for the purposes of producing a valuation or giving a certificate to the Board).

(2)

(*a*) Subject to the provisions of this regulation, whenever a valuation of assets and liabilities of the scheme is made the administrator shall in those circumstances, produce a written valuation (''signed valuation'') or give a certificate to the Board which fulfils the requirements of these Regulations, and

(*b*) a signed valuation or a certificate shall in any event be produced or given to the Board by the administrator having an effective date not later than 3 years and 6 months after—

(i) the effective date of the previous valuation or certificate, or

(ii) (where there is no previous valuation or certificate) the date when the scheme was established.

(3) Paragraph (2)(*b*)(i) of this regulation shall apply to a scheme which is a ''public service scheme'' which fulfils the conditions of section 66(1) of the Social Security Pensions Act 1975 with the substitution for ''3 years and 6 months'' of ''5 years''.

(4) A "signed valuation" to which paragraph (2) refers shall be produced to the Board, dated and signed by—

(*a*) a Fellow of the Institute of Actuaries; or
(*b*) a Fellow of the Faculty of Actuaries; or
(*c*) a person with other actuarial qualifications who has been approved as being a proper person to act for the purposes of regulation 8 of the Occupational Pension Schemes (Disclosure of Information) Regulations 1986 in connection with the scheme.

(5) A date to which sub-paragraph (*b*)(i) or (ii) of paragraph (2) refers may be a date (where appropriate) before these Regulations come into force.

Certificate, valuation—other prescribed requirements

10—(1) Subject to regulation 11, for the purposes of Paragraph 6(1) the prescribed period is six months after the date of signing of the valuation or certificate.

(2) For the purposes of Paragraph 6(2)(*a*) *the prescribed periods shall be—*

(*a*) 6 months where Paragraph 6(3)(*a*) applies;
(*b*) 6 months where the proposals (to which Paragraph 6(2) refers) are to enhance the accrued benefits under the scheme and Paragraph 6(3)(*d*) or (*e*) applies;
(*c*) 5 years or such lesser period as may be agreed between the administrator and the Board where Paragraph 6(3)(*b*) or (*c*) applies;
(*d*) in other cases whatever period is agreed between the administrator and the Board;

[and, unless it is otherwise agreed,][1] the periods referred to above shall begin 30 days after the date on which the Board notify to the administrator in writing their approval of proposals made under Paragraph 6(1), or, where there is an appeal, the date of the final determination of the appeal.

(3) In a case to which Paragraph 6(2)(*b*) applies, where the proposals for reducing or eliminating an excess include the provision for any payment to an employer, the proposals may not have the effect of reducing the assets of the scheme to an amount less than is equal to 5 per cent in excess of the liabilities.

(4) For the purposes of Paragraphs 5(3), 6(1), 6(2)(*a*), 8(3)(*a*) and 8(3)(*b*) [of Schedule 12 and paragraph 7(10) of Schedule 22 to the Income and Corporation Taxes Act 1988][2] "the prescribed maximum" is 5 per cent.

[(5) For the purposes of paragraph 7(1) of Schedule 22 to the Income and Corporation Taxes Act 1988 "the prescribed percentage" is 5 per cent.][2]

Amendments—[1] Words in para (2) substituted by the Pension Scheme Surpluses (Valuation) (Amendment) Regulations, SI 1989/2290 reg 6.
[2] Words in para (4), and whole of para (5), inserted by SI 1989/2290 reg 6.

Reduction and elimination of excess—special provisions

11—(1) This regulation prescribes for the purposes of Paragraph 6(4) modifications subject to which the provisions of Paragraph 6(3) are to apply for the reduction or elimination of the excess (within the meaning of that Paragraph).

(2)

(*a*) In the case of a scheme which has been in existence for less than 15 years the excess may be eliminated within a period of five years or by the end of 15 years from the commencement of the scheme whichever is the longer;
(*b*) sub-paragraph (*a*) does not apply to a scheme established to provide benefits for some or all members of an existing or former scheme—
  (i) of the employer, or
  (ii) to which the employer concerned had made contributions.

(3) Where a scheme has ceased to admit new members the excess may be reduced or eliminated over the period terminating with the end of the service of the last member.

(4) Where a scheme, being the only scheme of an employer, has less than 30 members the excess may be reduced or eliminated over the period terminating with the end of the service of the last member.

(5) Where in respect of a scheme to which this regulation applies the excess is being reduced or eliminated over a period in excess of 5 years, no payment under Paragraph 6(3)(*a*) shall be made to the employer unless a suspension of contributions would not reduce the excess to 5 per cent or less of the value of the liabilities of the scheme.

Self-administered schemes and insured schemes—special provisions

12—(1) Where—

(*a*) a self-administered scheme or an insured scheme does not fulfil the conditions of regulation 3, and
(*b*) the administrator intends to make a payment to an employer out of funds which, if made, would be a payment to which Paragraph 1(1) applies,

unless such a scheme is being wound up and not replaced, Paragraph 5(2) shall apply for the purposes of a valuation of assets and liabilities.

(2) Where a valuation to which paragraph (1) of this regulation refers shows that the value of the assets exceeds the value of the liabilities these Regulations and Paragraphs 7, 8(1) and (2) and 11 shall apply to the scheme.

Prescribed periods for the purposes of Schedule 12

13 The following table sets out in the second column prescribed periods for the purposes of the Paragraphs mentioned in the first column—

TABLE

Paragraph	*Period*
5(1)	within 3 months after the date when the valuation or certificate is signed
6(5)	within 6 months after the receipt of the proposals submitted to the Board
7(1)	within 30 days
7(2)	within 60 days
7(3)	within 30 days
8(1)	within 6 months after the receipt by the Board of— (*a*) particulars under Paragraph 7(1), (*b*) a written valuation under Paragraph 7(2), or (*c*) particulars under Paragraph 7(3)
8(3)	within 3 months after the date of the notice to which Paragraph 8(1) refers or, where there is an appeal, 30 days after the final determination of the appeal
8(4)	within 6 months after the receipt of the proposals submitted to the Board.

Appeals procedure and consequences of appeal

14—(1) An appeal may be brought by the administrator against a notice under Paragraph 8(1)(*b*) by a notice in writing given to the Board within 30 days after the date of their notice.

(2) During the period beginning with the receipt by the Board of the notice of appeal to which paragraph (1) of this regulation refers and ending with the determination of the appeal the conditions of Paragraph 8(3) and (4) shall not require to be fulfilled.

Certificate—prescribed form

15—(1) The certificate to which Paragraph 5(3) refers shall be in the form prescribed in the Schedule to these Regulations.

(2) The values of the assets and liabilities which the certificate states (for the purposes of Paragraph 5(3)) shall be determined in accordance with the principles and requirements prescribed by these Regulations for valuations.

(3) The certificate shall be signed by a person who is qualified under regulation 9(4) to sign a valuation.

SCHEDULE

GENERAL

Regulation 15

This certificate is given to the Commissioners of Inland Revenue for the purposes of paragraph 5(3) of Schedule 12 to the Finance Act 1986 [TA 1988 Sch 22 para 2(3)].

Name/description of scheme

Inland Revenue Reference No

A I hereby certify that—

(1) in my opinion as at (date) the value of the assets of the scheme exceeded/did not exceed* 105 per cent of the value of the liabilities of the scheme;

(*delete as necessary)

(2) the assets and liabilities to which paragraph (1) refers have been determined in accordance with principles and requirements prescribed by the Pension Scheme Surpluses (Valuation) Regulations 1987.

B (To be completed if the value of the assets in paragraph A(1) above exceeds 105 per cent.)

	£	£
Actuarial Value of Assets		
Actuarial Value of Liabilities		
5 per cent of value of liabilities		
Surplus		

Signature — Date
Name — Qualification
Address — Name of employer (if applicable)

1987/530
Income Tax (Entertainers and Sportsmen) Regulations 1987

Made by the Treasury under FA 1986 Sch 11, now TA 1988 ss 555–558; see TA 1988 Sch 30 para 21

Made	*26 March 1987*
Laid before the House of Commons	*26 March 1987*
Coming into Force	*1 May 1987*

Commentary—*Simon's Direct Tax Service* **E5.802–807**.

Citation and commencement

1 These Regulations may be cited as the Income Tax (Entertainers and Sportsmen) Regulations 1987 and shall come into force on 1st May 1987.

Interpretation

2—(1) In these Regulations unless the context otherwise requires—

''associate'' has the meaning given to it by section 303(3) of the Taxes Act;[a]

''Board'' means Commissioners of Inland Revenue;

''control'' shall be construed in accordance with section 302(2) to (6) of the Taxes Act;[b]

''entertainer'' means any description of individuals (and whether performing alone or with others) who give performances in their character as entertainers or sportsmen in any kind of entertainment or sport; and ''entertainment or sport'' in this definition includes any activity of a physical kind, performed by such an individual, which is or may be made available to the public or any section of the public and whether for payment or not;

''Management Act'' means the Taxes Management Act 1970;

a payment or transfer to which regulation 3 applies is described as ''connected'';

''relevant activity'' has the meaning given to it by regulation 6;

''Schedule 11'' means Schedule 11 to the Finance Act 1986;[c]

''the Taxes Act'' means the Income and Corporation Taxes Act 1970;

''the Tax Acts'' has the meaning given to it by section 526(2) of the Taxes Act;[d]

''tax payment'' has the meaning given to it by regulation 4;

''tax year'' means year of assessment;

''value transferred'' in relation to a transfer means the gross amount to which regulation 17(1) refers.

(2) Section 533 of the Taxes Act[e] (meaning of connected persons) applies for the purposes of these Regulations.

Notes—[a] TA 1988 s 417(3).
[b] TA 1988 s 416(2)–(6).
[c] TA 1988 ss 555–558.
[d] TA 1988 s 831(2).
[e] TA 1988 s 839.

Payments or transfers with prescribed connection

3—(1) This regulation applies for the purposes of and subject to the provisions of paragraph 2 of Schedule 11[a], the other provisions of that Schedule and these Regulations.

(2) Subject to paragraph (3) a payment or a transfer made for, in respect of, or which in any way derives either directly or indirectly from, the performance of a relevant activity, has a connection of a prescribed kind with the relevant activity.

(3) The following are descriptions of payments to which paragraph (2) shall not apply—

(*a*) a payment out of which a sum representing tax is or falls to be deducted under the Taxes Act apart from Schedule 11[b] or these Regulations;

(*b*)

(i) a payment (to which paragraph (ii) applies) made to a person who is resident and ordinarily resident in the United Kingdom, not being a person who is connected with or an associate of the entertainer concerned;

(ii) a payment to which paragraph (i) refers is a payment—

(*a*) which falls to be made for the provision of services ancillary to the performance of a relevant activity, and

(*b*) which is of an amount or value which does not exceed what would be reasonable for that provision between persons dealing with each other at arms' length;

(*c*) any payment made to an entertainer in respect of the proceeds of sale of records deriving from a sound recording made by the entertainer, being payments calculated by reference to those proceeds or payments on accounts of those proceeds.

Notes—[a] TA 1988 s 555(2)–(6).
[b] TA 1988 ss 555–558.

Tax payments—rules for calculation

4—(1) Each of the sums mentioned in paragraph 2(2) and (3) of Schedule 11[a] (''tax payment'') shall be calculated in accordance with the rules prescribed by this regulation.

(2) Except where it is otherwise provided by these Regulations or there is an arrangement to which this regulation refers, the tax payment shall be a proportion of the connected payment or of the value transferred by a connected transfer equal to the basic rate of income tax for the tax year in which the payment or transfer is made.

(3)

(*a*) Subject to sub-paragraph (*b*), where the connected payments and the value transferred by connected transfers for a tax year made to an entertainer, or to a person who is connected with him or who is an associate of his, do not together exceed £1000 the tax payment shall be a nil amount;

(*b*) connected payments and the value transferred by connected transfers made by any person who is connected with any other person by whom connected payments or connected transfers are made to the entertainer, or by any associate of such other person, shall together be treated as constituting a single connected payment in determining whether they exceed £1000.

(4) An arrangement to which paragraph (2) refers is an arrangement in writing between the Board and the person by whom the connected payment or connected transfer is made, the entertainer, or the recipient of the connected payment or connected transfer, made following a decision by the Board on an application to which regulation 5 refers, under which the tax payment is an amount which, as a proportion of the connected payment or value transferred by the connected transfer, is an amount less than the said basic rate (''reduced tax payment'').

(5) The reduced tax payment may be arrived at by reference to a percentage of the connected payment or of the value transferred by a connected transfer or as a lump sum calculated without reference to any such percentage.

(6) In making an arrangement of the kind to which paragraph (2) refers the Board—

(*a*) shall, subject to sub-paragraph (*b*) and paragraph (7) below, at all times aim at securing that the tax payment shall be, as nearly as may be, the amount of the liability to tax of the entertainer or other person arising in relation to the connected payment or connected transfer under the Tax Acts, Schedule 11[b] and these Regulations, and

(*b*) may take into account the fact that the liability to the Board for tax has, in a manner satisfactory to them, been secured or otherwise provided for, whether by a guarantee (of whatever person) or other means.

(7) Where—

(*a*) a person makes a connected payment or connected transfer in relation to a relevant activity, and

(*b*) in respect of the same relevant activity that person has received a connected payment or connected transfer in respect of which the amount of the tax payment has been paid under these Regulations,

the person concerned shall not be required to deduct out of the connected payment or pay in respect of the connected transfer (to which sub-paragraph (*a*) refers) any sum to which paragraph 2 of Schedule 11[c] applies unless, and to the extent that, the tax payment which then falls to be made exceeds the amount of the tax payment to which sub-paragraph (*b*) refers.

Notes—[a] TA 1988 s 555(3).
[b] TA 1988 ss 555–558.
[c] TA 1988 s 555(2)–(6).

Reduced tax payment—application to be made to the Board

5—(1) Where a connected payment or connected transfer falls to be made subject to a tax payment to which regulation 4(2) refers the person by whom the connected payment or connected transfer is made, the entertainer, or recipient of the connected payment or connected transfer, may make an application in writing to the Board, not later than 30 days before the connected payment or connected transfer falls to be made, that it shall be subject instead to a reduced tax payment (within the meaning of regulation 4).

(2) Unless and until there is in force an arrangement under which such a reduced tax payment falls to be made regulation 4(2) shall at all times continue to apply to the connected payment or connected transfer.

Relevant activity

6—(1) Subject to this regulation, any activity performed in the United Kingdom by an entertainer (whether alone or involving others) of any of the descriptions in paragraph (2) is an activity of a prescribed description (''relevant activity'') for the purposes of paragraph 1 of Schedule 11[a], that Schedule and these Regulations.

(2) A relevant activity to which paragraph (1) refers is an activity performed in the United Kingdom by an entertainer in his character as entertainer on or in connection with a commercial occasion or event and includes—

(*a*) any appearance of the entertainer by way of or in connection with the promotion of any such occasion or event;

(*b*) any participation by the entertainer in or for sound recording, films, videos, radio, television or other similar transmissions (whether live or recorded).

(3) A commercial occasion or event to which paragraph (2) refers includes any description of occasion or event—

(*a*) for which an entertainer (or other person) might receive or become entitled, for or by virtue of the entertainer's performance of the activity, to receive anything by way of cash or any other form of property; or

(*b*) which is designed to promote commercial sales or activity by advertising, the endorsement of goods or services, sponsorship, or other promotional means of any kind.

(4) For the purpose of this regulation—

''film'' includes any record (with or without sound), however made, of a sequence or series of one or more visual images, which is a record capable of being used as a means of showing part or all of that sequence or series as a moving or still picture, and ''record'' in this definition includes video.

Notes—[a] TA 1988 s 555(1).

Persons other than entertainers receiving connected payments or transfers

7—(1) Any description of person in paragraph (2) is a person (not being the entertainer) to whom paragraph 7(1) of Schedule 11[a] refers.

(2) The descriptions of persons to whom paragraph (1) refers are—

(*a*) any person who is under the control of the entertainer;

(*b*) any person who is—

(i) not resident in the United Kingdom, and

(ii) not liable to tax by reason of residence, domicile, place of management or otherwise, in a territory outside the United Kingdom where the rate of tax charged on the profits or income of such a person is a rate exceeding 25 per cent;

(*c*)

(i) subject to paragraph (ii), any person in receipt (whether directly or indirectly) of a connected payment or value transferred by a connected transfer which is, is treated as, or falls to be included in the computation of, income arising under a settlement in relation to which the entertainer is a settlor;

(ii) for the purposes of paragraph (i)—

''income arising under a settlement'' and ''settlor'' have the meanings given to them by section 454 of the Taxes Act[b], and

''settlement'' has the meaning given to it by section 444(2) of the Taxes Act[c];

(*d*)

(i) any person to whom paragraph (2) of this regulation does not otherwise apply who receives any connected payment or connected transfer (whether directly or indirectly) at or in respect of a time when there is in force between that person and the entertainer concerned a contract or arrangement to which paragraph (ii) applies;

(ii) a contract or arrangement to which paragraph (i) refers is a contract or arrangement by or under which it is reasonable to suppose that the entertainer (or other person who is connected with or is an associate of the entertainer) is, will or may become, entitled to receive amounts, whether by way of cash or other value, not substantially less than the appropriate amount of profits or gains arising from the connected payment or connected transfer to which paragraph 8(1) of Schedule 11[d] applies.

Notes—[a] TA 1988 s 556(2).
[b] TA 1988 s 681.
[c] TA 1988 s 670.
[d] TA 1988 s 557(1).

Computation of profits arising from certain payments and transfers attributed to entertainer

8—(1) Subject to the provisions of these Regulations, the profits or gains (to which paragraph 7(2) of Schedule 11[a] refers) arising from the connected payment or connected transfer (to which paragraph 7(1) of that Schedule[b] refers) shall be computed in accordance with the provisions of the Taxes Act relating to the charging of profits or gains under Case I or II (as the case may be) of Schedule D, so that a just and reasonable amount of such a payment or value transferred by such a transfer is charged to tax as such profits or gains; and

(2) Notwithstanding any provision of the Taxes Act, in computing the said profits or gains such deductions of expenses incurred by any person (not being the entertainer) in relation to the payment or transfer concerned shall be made as are just and reasonable.

Notes—[a] TA 1988 s 556(3)(*a*).
[b] TA 1988 s 556(2).

Returns of information to be furnished by maker of connected payments or connected transfers

9—(1) A person who makes a connected payment or connected transfer shall, in accordance with this regulation, make a return to the Board of the connected payment or connected transfer which he makes and of any tax payment (including a nil amount) for which he is accountable to the Board.

(2) A return shall be made in the tax year for each successive period ending on 30th June, 30th September, 31st December and 5th April.

(3) The return for each period shall be made within 14 days after the end of the period.

(4) The Board may by notice in writing require any person who makes a connected payment or connected transfer, within such time as may be specified in the notice, to furnish to them particulars of such payments or transfers including—

(*a*) the dates and the amounts of each payment;
(*b*) the dates of and the value transferred by each transfer;
(*c*) a sufficient description to enable any asset or money's worth transferred to be identified;
(*d*) the business and private name and address of the person to whom each payment or transfer was made;
(*e*) the name and address of the entertainer concerned;
(*f*) the relevant activity to which the payment or transfer relates, including full particulars of all performances.

(5) The Management Act shall apply to a return to which this regulation relates as it applies to a return under the Taxes Acts.

Tax payments—due date

10—(1) A tax payment (including any reduced tax payment), whether any deduction out of a connected payment or provision in respect of a connected transfer has been made or not, shall be due at the time by which the return under regulation 9(1) is to be made ("the due date") and payment shall be made before, or at the time when, that return is made.

(2) A payment at any time so due shall be payable by the person who makes the connected payment or connected transfer concerned, without the making of any assessment in respect of it.

(3) Subject to the provisions of regulation 11, tax which has become due and payable under this regulation (whether or not it has been paid when the assessment is made) may be assessed on the person from whom it is due if that tax, or any part of it, is not paid on or before the due date.

Assessment of tax payments

11—(1) Assessments in respect of any tax due and payable in respect of any period to which regulation 9(2) refers may be made by the Board in relation to a tax year or to the period in question.

(2) Notwithstanding that an assessment under paragraph (1) may be said to relate to a period which is not a tax year—

(*a*) all the provisions of the Income Tax Acts as to the time within which an assessment may be made or the tax year to which an assessment relates shall apply to such an assessment, and
(*b*) the provisions of sections 36 and 37 of the Management Act as to the circumstances in which an assessment may be made out of time shall apply accordingly, but on the footing that the assessment relates to the tax year in which the period (to which regulation 9(2) refers) ends.

(3) Any tax which becomes due under an assessment made under paragraph (1)—

(*a*) shall be payable on or before whichever is earlier of the due date to which regulation 10(1) refers or the 14th day after the date of the notice of the assessment, and
(*b*) shall be treated for all the purposes of Parts VI and IX of the Management Act (including the purposes of section 69 of that Act) as tax with which the person assessed is charged by an assessment to income tax under Schedule D.

Tax liabilities and tax payments—supplementary

12—(1) Where under these Regulations there is accounted for and paid to the Board an amount of tax which is—

(*a*) in respect of a connected payment or connected transfer, or

(*b*) paid under an assessment made under regulation 11,

that amount shall, subject to this regulation, be treated as a payment of tax on account of the tax liability (of whatever person) in respect of the connected payment or connected transfer concerned.

(2) Where, in respect of a connected payment or connected transfer, there is a liability to tax under the Tax Acts as well as under Schedule 11[a] or these Regulations, the Board shall allocate any payment made to them to which paragraph (1) refers as is just and reasonable in discharge of some or all of those liabilities of the entertainer or other person concerned to whom these Regulations apply.

(3) Where—

(*a*) by virtue of paragraph 8 of Schedule 11[b] and these Regulations a connected payment or the value transferred by a connected transfer falls to be included in the amount of profits or gains to which paragraph 8(1)(*a*)[c] refers, and

(*b*) the amount of the connected payment or the value transferred (or an amount in respect of that value) is charged to tax under Schedule E

the amount charged under Schedule E (to which sub-paragraph (*b*) refers) shall be treated as expenditure which falls to be deducted in computing the profits or gains to which sub-paragraph (*a*) refers.

(4) Where a payment is a connected payment—

(*a*) which is, is treated as, or falls to be included in a computation of, income of the entertainer chargeable to tax by virtue of the provisions of Part XVI of the Taxes Act[d], or

(*b*) which is a receipt of a company which provides the services of the entertainer to perform the relevant activity, being a receipt which falls to be included in the computation of its profits which are chargeable to tax under Schedule D,

the charge under Schedule 11[a] shall have effect and the charges to which sub-paragraphs (*a*) and (*b*) refer shall be disregarded.

(5) A person making a connected payment or connected transfer in respect of which a tax payment has been made by virtue of these Regulations shall furnish the recipient with a certificate showing the gross amount of the payment or the value transferred, the amount of the tax payment, and the amount actually paid.

Notes—[a] TA 1988 ss 555–558.
[b] TA 1988 s 557.
[c] TA 1988 s 557(1)(*a*).
[d] TA 1988 Pt XV.

Claim that tax payment excessive to be made to Board

13—(1) Notwithstanding any other provision of these Regulations, where there has been made to a recipient a connected payment or connected transfer in respect of which a tax payment has been made, the entertainer or any person who, by virtue of Schedule 11[a] or these Regulations is, or is treated as, the person to whom (in relation to the connected payment or connected transfer) any tax liability arises may, by a claim in writing made to the Board, claim that the amount of the tax payment made is excessive.

(2) Subject to paragraph (3) the claim shall be treated as a claim made to an inspector to which section 42 of the Management Act applies.

(3) The claim shall be made not before, but within six years after, the end of the tax year in which the connected payment or connected transfer was made.

Notes—[a] TA 1988 ss 555–558.

Administration of tax—supplementary

14—(1) Nothing in these Regulations shall be taken to prejudice any powers conferred by or under the Tax Acts for the recovery of tax, penalties or interest by means of an assessment or otherwise.

(2) Subject to the provisions of these Regulations, the Management Act shall apply in relation to any tax assessable under these Regulations as if—

(*a*) an assessment of such tax was an assessment specified in section 55(1) (recovery of tax not postponed); and

(*b*) section 87 of that Act applied—

(i) with the insertion of the words ''or the Income Tax (Entertainers and Sportsmen) Regulations 1987'' after ''Finance Act 1972'' in subsection (1), and after ''Schedule 20'' in subsections (2)(*b*), (5) and (6),

(ii) with the insertion after ''company'' in subsection (5) of the words ''or individual'', and

(iii) with the insertion after ''Schedules'' in subsection (7) of the words ''or those Regulations''.

Modifications and adaptations of enactments in relation to trades etc

15—(1) In this regulation—

(*a*) "world-wide trade" means a trade of an entertainer which is a trade apart from Schedule 11[a] and these Regulations, and a "Schedule 11 trade" means a trade which is a separate trade of an entertainer only by virtue of Schedule 11[a] and these Regulations;

(*b*) "trade" includes profession or vocation.

(2) For the purposes of section 171 of the Taxes Act[b] (carry forward of losses) the world-wide trade and the Schedule 11 trade shall be treated as the same trade.

(3) For the purposes of section 174 of the Taxes Act[c] (carry back of terminal losses) a loss sustained for any relevant period under a Schedule 11 trade (to which otherwise that section would apply) shall not be a terminal loss except where the world-wide trade is permanently discontinued in that period, in which case such a loss in either trade shall be available under that section to be deducted or set off against profits or gains of those trades.

(4) For the purposes of section 30 of the Finance Act 1978[d] (losses in early years of trade) the world-wide trade and the Schedule 11 trade shall be treated as the same trade, but that section shall apply to any such loss of an entertainer only in the tax year in which the world-wide trade was first carried on and in the next 3 succeeding tax years.

Notes—[a] TA 1988 ss 555–558.
[b] TA 1988 s 385.
[c] TA 1988 ss 388, 389.
[d] TA 1988 ss 381–383.

Apportionment of payments, transfers etc

16—(1) The provisions of paragraph (2) are by way of supplementation of the provisions of section 127 of the Taxes Act[a].

(2) Where, in the case of any payment, value transferred or profits or gains to which Schedule 11[b] or these Regulations apply, it is necessary, in order to arrive at the appropriate amount of such payment, value or profits or gains for any tax year or other period, to make any apportionment, division or aggregation of any amounts or values, any such apportionment, division or aggregation, shall be made as is just and reasonable.

Notes—[a] TA 1988 s 72.
[b] TA 1988 ss 555–558.

Value of transfers—rules for calculation and grossing up

17—(1)

(*a*) The actual worth of what is transferred by a transfer to which paragraph 2(3) of Schedule 11[a] applies ("the net value") shall be treated as a net amount corresponding to a gross amount from which income tax at the basic rate has been deducted; and

(*b*) the said gross amount shall be treated as the value of what is transferred for the purposes of paragraph 2(4) of Schedule 11[b].

(2)

(*a*) The net value to which paragraph (1) refers shall be the cost of what is transferred, and

(*b*) the cost of what is transferred to which sub-paragraph (*a*) refers is the cost in or in connection with its provision (including its provision to the person who makes the transfer) or transfer, less so much of that cost which has been borne by the entertainer.

Notes—[a] TA 1988 s 555(3).
[b] TA 1988 s 555(4).

1987/1513

Occupational Pension Schemes (Maximum Rate Lump Sum) Regulations 1987

Made by the Commissioners of Inland Revenue under F(No 2)A 1987 Sch 3 para 20(4), now TA 1988 Sch 23 para 3; see TA 1988 Sch 30 para 21

Made	*26 August 1987*
Coming into Force	*28 August 1987*

Commentary—*Simon's Direct Tax Service* **E7.227**.

1 These Regulations may be cited as the Occupational Pension Schemes (Maximum Rate Lump Sum) Regulations 1987 and shall come into force on 28th August 1987.

2 These Regulations determine the amount of a maximum rate lump sum for the purposes of paragraphs 20 and 21 of Schedule 3 to the Finance (No 2) Act 1987[a].

3 The amount of a maximum rate lump sum shall be the appropriate fraction of the employee's relevant annual remuneration ascertained from the Table in the Schedule to these Regulations by reference to the period of the employee's service with the employer.

Notes—[a] TA 1988 Sch 23 paras 3, 4.

SCHEDULE

Regulation 3

Table

Period of Service			*Fraction of relevant remuneration*
Years	*Months*	*Days*	*Eightieths*
1–8			1 for every 4 months
8	2		25
8	4		26
8	6		27
8	8		28
8	10		29
9			30
9	2		31
9	4		32
9	6		33
9	8		34
9	10		35
10			36
10	2		37
10	4		38
10	6		39
10	8		40
10	10		41
11			42
11	2		43
11	4		44
11	6		45
11	8		46
11	10		47
12			48
12	2		49
12	4		50
12	6		51
12	8		52
12	10		53
13			54
13	1	10	55
13	2	20	56
13	4		57
13	5	10	58
13	6	20	59
13	8		60
13	9	10	61
13	10	20	62
14			63
14	1	10	64
14	2	20	65
14	4		66
14	5	10	67
14	6	20	68
14	8		69
14	9	10	70
14	10	20	71
15			72
15	1	10	73
15	2	20	74
15	4		75
15	5	10	76
15	6	20	77
15	8		78
15	9	10	79
15	10	20	80
16			81
16	1	10	82

Years	*Period of Service* *Months*	*Days*	*Fraction of relevant remuneration Eightieths*
16	2	20	83
16	4		84
16	5	10	85
16	6	20	86
16	8		87
16	9	10	88
16	10	20	89
17			90
17	1	10	91
17	2	20	92
17	4		93
17	5	10	94
17	6	20	95
17	8		96
17	9	10	97
17	10	20	98
18			99
18	1	10	100
18	2	20	101
18	4		102
18	5	10	103
18	6	20	104
18	8		105
18	9	10	106
18	10	20	107
19			108
19	1		109
19	2		110
19	3		111
19	4		112
19	5		113
19	6		114
19	7		115
19	8		116
19	9		117
19	10		118
19	11		119
20 or more			120

1987/1749
Occupational Pension Schemes (Additional Voluntary Contributions) Regulations 1987

Made by the Commissioners of Inland Revenue under FA 1970 Sch 5 para 10, now TA 1988 s 612(3); see TA 1988 Sch 30 para 21

Made	*5 October 1987*
Laid before the House of Commons	*5 October 1987*
Coming into Force	*26 October 1987*

Commentary—*Simon's Direct Tax Service* **E7.221**.

ARRANGEMENT OF REGULATIONS

Citation and commencement

1 These Regulations may be cited as the Occupational Pension Schemes (Additional Voluntary Contributions) Regulations 1987 and shall come into force on 26th October 1987.

Interpretation

2—(1) In these Regulations unless the context otherwise requires—

''the Board'' means the Commissioners of Inland Revenue;

[''permitted maximum contributions'' in relation to a year of assessment means—

(*a*) 15 per cent of a scheme member's remuneration, or

(*b*) if section 592(8B) of the Income and Corporation Taxes Act 1988 has effect as regards a scheme member's remuneration, 15 per cent of his permitted maximum remuneration;

''permitted maximum remuneration'' in relation to a year of assessment means the figure found for that year by virtue of section 592(8D) and (8E) of the Income and Corporation Taxes Act 1988;

''remuneration'' shall be interpreted in accordance with section 612(1) of the Income and Corporation Taxes Act 1988;][1]

''scheme administrator'' means the administrator of a scheme;

''scheme member'' means a member of a scheme;

''section'' means a section of the Finance Act 1970;

''tax month'' means a period beginning on the 6th day of any month and ending on the 5th day of the following month;

''the Schedule'' means Part II of Schedule 5 to the Finance Act 1970;

''year of assessment'' means a year beginning with 6th April in any year and ending with 5th April in the following year.

[(1A) For the purposes of these Regulations a person is a controlling director of a company if he is a director (as defined by section 612(1) of the Income and Corporation Taxes Act 1988), and he is within paragraph (*b*) of section 417(5) of that Act, in relation to the company.][2].

(2) The Table below indexes other definitions in these Regulations—

Term defined	Regulation
annual claim	6
interim claim	6
scheme	4

Amendments—[1] Definitions of ''permitted maximum contributions'', ''permitted maximum remuneration'' and ''remuneration'' in para (1) inserted by the Occupational Pension Schemes (Additional Voluntary Contributions) (Amendment) Regulations, SI 1990/585 reg 3.

[2] Para (1A) inserted by SI 1990/585 reg 3.

Prescribed cases and conditions: introductory

3 Regulations 4 and 5 respectively prescribe the cases in which, and the conditions subject to which, relief under section 21(4) shall be given in accordance with sub-paragraphs (2) and (3) of paragraph 6A of the Schedule[a].

Notes—[a] TA 1988 s 593.

Prescribed cases

[**4** The prescribed cases are cases where an employee contributes as a scheme member to a retirement benefits scheme which—

(*a*) is one to which his employer is not a contributor and which provides benefits additional to those provided by a retirement benefits scheme or a relevant statutory scheme to which his employer is a contributor, and

(*b*) is an ''exempt approved scheme'' within the meaning of section 592(1) of the Income and Corporation Taxes Act 1988;

and in these Regulations unless the context otherwise requires references to a ''scheme'' shall be construed as references to such a scheme and references to ''his employer'' shall be construed as references to any employer of the scheme member to whom paragraph (*a*) applies.][1]

Amendments—[1] This regulation substituted by the Occupational Pension Schemes (Additional Voluntary Contributions) (Amendment) Regulations, SI 1990/585 reg 4, with effect from 4 April 1990.

Prescribed conditions

5—[(1) The prescribed conditions are that the scheme member has—

(*a*) at or before the time at which he first pays a contribution from which he deducts an amount equal to income tax at the basic rate on the contribution; and

(*b*) at any time after that time, within 30 days of having been required to do so by notice in writing given by the scheme administrator;

furnished to the scheme administrator in writing the particulars, declarations and undertaking specified in paragraphs (2), (3) and (4) respectively; and references in those paragraphs to his remuneration, or his permitted maximum remuneration, are to that for the year of assessment in which he first pays such a contribution, or for the year of assessment specified in the notice, as the case may require.][1]

(2) The particulars specified in this paragraph are—

(*a*) his full name and address;

[(*aa*)] his date of birth;][2]

(*b*) his national insurance number and tax office reference;

(*c*) an estimate of his remuneration ...[3];

(*d*) the full name and address of his employer [who makes contributions to—

(i) a retirement benefits scheme approved under section 591 of the Income and Corporation Taxes Act 1988

(ii) a retirement benefits scheme which is before the Board in order for them to decide whether to give approval under the said section 591, or

(iii) a relevant statutory scheme within the meaning of section 611A of the said Act;][4]

(*e*) the full name and address of the scheme administrator of any retirement benefits scheme referred to in sub-paragraph (*d*) and the full name or title of any such scheme;

[(*f*) the amount, expressed as a monetary sum or as a percentage of—

(i) his remuneration, or,

(ii) if section 592(8B) of the said Act has effect as regards his remuneration, his permitted maximum remuneration,

which he is paying for the relevant year of assessment to the retirement benefits scheme or relevant statutory scheme referred to in sub-paragraph (*d*).][2]

[(3) The declarations specified in this paragraph are declarations signed by the scheme member that to the best of his knowledge and belief—

(*a*) benefits are currently accruing to him under the retirement benefits scheme or relevant statutory scheme referred to in paragraph (2)(*d*);

(*b*) the aggregate of all contributions—

(i) made to the scheme in relation to which the declaration is made, and

(ii) made by him to the retirement benefits scheme or relevant statutory scheme referred to in paragraph (2)(*d*),

will not exceed and, unless the declaration is made in the circumstances described in paragraph (1)(*a*), has not exceeded his permitted maximum contributions;

(*c*) he is neither—

(i) paying contributions to any other scheme which provides benefits additional to those provided by the retirement benefits scheme or relevant statutory scheme referred to in paragraph (2)(*d*), nor

(ii) where his employer is a company, a controlling director of the company;

(*d*) the particulars specified in paragraph (2) and furnished by him to the scheme administrator are correct and complete.][2]

[(4) The undertaking specified in this paragraph is an undertaking by the scheme member that he will within 30 days give notice in writing to the scheme administrator if—

(*a*) he ceases to be employed by the employer referred to in paragraph (2)(*d*), or

(*b*) benefits cease to accrue to him under the retirement benefits scheme or relevant statutory scheme referred to in paragraph (2)(*d*), or

(*c*) where his employer is a company, he becomes a controlling director of the company.][2]

Amendments—[1] Para (1) substituted by the Occupational Pension Schemes (Additional Voluntary Contributions) (Amendment) Regulations, SI 1990/585 reg 5, with effect from 4 April 1990.

[2] Paras (2)(*aa*), (*f*), (3), (4) inserted by SI 1990/585 reg 5.

[3] Words in para (2)(*c*) revoked by SI 1990/585 reg 5.

[4] Words in para (2)(*d*) substituted by SI 1990/585 reg 5.

Claims: introductory

6—(1) Amounts recoverable by a scheme administrator under paragraph 6A(3)(*b*) of the Schedule shall be recovered on a claim made to the Board for the purpose of these Regulations.

(2) Subject to paragraph (3), a claim shall be for a year of assessment (''annual claim'').

(3) A claim may also be made in accordance with regulation 7 for a tax month (''interim claim'').

(4) Notwithstanding the provisions of any other enactment, the Board shall not be under an obligation to make any payment under regulation 7 or 8 earlier than the end of the month following the month in which the claim is received.

Notes—[a] TA 1988 s 593(3)(*b*).

Interim claims

7—(1) Subject to paragraph (3), an interim claim for a tax month may be made by a scheme administrator within 6 months after the end of the tax month for which it is made.

(2) A claim under this regulation may not be based on an estimate but may only be made to recover an amount deducted in respect of contributions paid in the tax month.

(3) An interim claim may not be made for the tax month ending 5th October or any subsequent month until the annual claim for the preceding year of assessment has been made by the scheme administrator and received by the Board.

(4) If the amount claimed is established to the Board's satisfaction they shall pay the amount to the claimant; if they are not so satisfied they shall pay to the claimant any lesser amount established to their satisfaction.

(5) Where a scheme administrator discovers that an amount paid to him under paragraph (4) was excessive he shall bring into account in the interim claim made by him next after the discovery (in this regulation referred to as "the subsequent claim") the amount of the excess; and if that amount exceeds the amount deducted in respect of the tax month for which the subsequent claim is made—

(*a*) the scheme administrator shall repay the amount of the excess to the Board with the claim; and

(*b*) if he fails so to do that amount shall immediately be recoverable by the Board in the same manner as tax charged by an assessment on the scheme administrator which has become final and conclusive.

Annual claims

8—(1) An annual claim for a year of assessment may, subject to paragraph (2), be made at any time within 6 years after the end of the year of assessment.

(2) Where in relation to any year of assessment a scheme administrator has received and not repaid in full any amount on an interim claim he shall within 6 months after the end of the year of assessment make an annual claim.

(3) A claim under this regulation—

(*a*) may not be based on an estimate but may only be made to recover an amount deducted in respect of contributions paid in the year of assessment, and

(*b*) shall bring into account payments made in respect of the year of assessment; and for the purpose of this regulation "aggregate interim payments" means the aggregate of payments made (and not repaid) on interim claims.

(4) Where the aggregate interim payments shown by an annual claim exceeds the amount deducted for the year of assessment—

(*a*) the scheme administrator shall repay the amount of the excess to the Board with the claim; and

(*b*) if he fails so to do, that amount shall immediately be recoverable by the Board in the same manner as tax charged by an assessment on the scheme administrator which has become final and conclusive.

(5) If a scheme administrator fails to make an annual claim under paragraph (2) within the time limited by that paragraph, the Board may issue a notice to the scheme administrator showing the aggregate interim payments for the year, and stating that the Board are not satisfied that the amount due to the scheme administrator for the year of assessment exceeds the lower amount stated in the notice.

(6) If an annual claim is not delivered to the Board within 14 days after the issue of a notice under paragraph (5), the amount of the difference between the aggregate amount and the amount stated in the notice shall immediately be recoverable by the Board in the same manner as tax charged by an assessment on the scheme administrator which has become final and conclusive.

(7) Where an annual claim has been made and the scheme administrator subsequently discovers that an error or mistake has been made in the claim the scheme administrator may make a supplementary claim within the time limited by paragraph (1).

Claims: supplementary provisions

9—(1) Section 42 of the Taxes Management Act 1970 (procedure for making claims) shall not apply to a claim under these Regulations.

(2) No appeal shall lie from the Board's decision on an interim claim.

(3) An appeal shall be to the Special Commissioners from the Board's decision on an annual claim, and the appeal shall be brought by giving written notice to the Board within 30 days of receipt of written notice of the decision.

(4) No payment made or other thing done on or in relation to an interim claim shall prejudice the decision on an annual claim.

(5) Part V of the Taxes Management Act 1970 (appeals and other proceedings) shall apply to an appeal under paragraph (3), and on an appeal the Special Commissioners may vary the decision appealed against whether or not the variation is to the advantage of the appellant.

(6) All such assessments, payments and repayments shall be made as are necessary to give effect to the Board's decision on an annual claim, or to any variation of that decision on appeal.

(7) Claims under these Regulations—

(*a*) shall contain such information and be in such form as the Board may prescribe (and forms prescribed for annual claims may require a report to be given by the scheme administrator's auditor);

(*b*) shall contain declarations to the effect that—

(i) sufficient records in respect of the scheme are maintained so as to enable the requirements of these Regulations to be satisfied, and

(ii) the information contained in the claim (including the declaration referred to in paragraph (i)) is correct; and

(*c*) shall be signed by the scheme administrator or by an authorised representative in the service of the scheme administrator.

Recovery on withdrawal of approval of schemes

10 Where a scheme administrator furnishes to the Board information in accordance with regulation 12(2) he shall at the time that he furnishes the information—

(*a*) pay to the Board the amount (if any) referred to in regulation 12(3)(*d*); and

(*b*) if he fails so to do, that amount shall immediately be recoverable by the Board in the same manner as tax charged by an assessment on the scheme administrator which has become final and conclusive.

Recovery of amounts by assessment

11—(1) Section 30 of the Taxes Management Act 1970 (recovery of overpayment of tax, etc) shall apply in relation to the payment by the Board of an amount—

(*a*) paid under these Regulations to which a scheme administrator was not entitled, or

(*b*) recoverable from a scheme administrator under regulation 7(5), regulation 8(4) or (6) or regulation 10,

as if it had been income tax repaid to the scheme administrator to which he was not entitled.

(2) An assessment made by virtue of this regulation shall be made by the Board and, subject to the provisions of these Regulations, the Taxes Management Act 1970 shall apply as if the assessment were an assessment to tax for the year of assessment in respect of which the amount was paid or is recoverable.

Information

12—(1) The Board may by notice in writing require any person who is, or who at any time has been,—

(*a*) a scheme administrator to whom contributions have been paid under paragraph 6A(2) and (3) of the Schedule[a], or

(*b*) a scheme member who has paid such contributions,

to furnish to them within such time (not being less than 14 days) as may be provided in the notice such information and in such form as may be prescribed in the notice.

(2) If the Board by notice under section 19(3)[b] withdraw their approval of a scheme in relation to which contributions have been paid under paragraph 6A(2) and (3)[a] of the Schedule, the scheme administrator shall within 30 days furnish to the Board in relation to that scheme the information prescribed in paragraph (3).

(3) The information prescribed in this paragraph is—

(*a*) the full name, address, national insurance number and tax office reference of each scheme member who has paid contributions after the date specified in the notice (in this regulation referred to as ''the relevant contributions'');

(*b*) the amount of the relief obtained under section 21(4)[c] by means of the relevant contributions;

(*c*) the amount of such relief actually due; and

(*d*) the difference between the relief referred to in sub-paragraph (*b*) and that referred to in sub-paragraph (*c*).

(4) If a scheme member who has paid contributions under paragraph 6A(2) and (3)[a] of the Schedule fails to comply with the requirements of regulation 5(1)(*b*), the scheme administrator to whom such contributions have been made shall within 30 days furnish to the Board the information prescribed in paragraph (5).

(5) The information prescribed in this paragraph is—

(*a*) the full name, address, national insurance number and tax office reference of the scheme member;

(*b*) the amount of relief obtained by him under section 21(4)[c] by means of such contributions;

(*c*) the amount of such relief actually due; and

(*d*) the difference between the relief referred to in sub-paragraph (*b*) and that referred to in sub-paragraph (*c*).

Notes—[a] TA 1988 s 593(2), (3).
[b] TA 1988 s 590(3).
[c] TA 1988 s 592(7).

Inspection of records

13—(1) Every scheme administrator to whom contributions have been paid under paragraph 6A(2) and (3) of the Schedule[a] shall, whenever required so to do, make available for inspection by a person authorised by the Board for that purpose all books, documents and other records (including all particulars furnished under regulation 5) in his possession or under his control relating to—

(*a*) such contributions paid to him,

(*b*) the scheme to which the contributions relate, and

(*c*) the scheme member who paid the contributions.

(2) Where records are maintained by computer the scheme administrator shall provide the person making the inspection with all facilities necessary to obtain information from them.

(3) Subject to paragraph (4) all books, documents and records referred to in paragraph (1), shall be preserved by the scheme administrator in such manner as may be approved by the Board so as to be available for inspection under this regulation for a period of three years following the termination of the scheme to which they relate.

(4) All particulars[, declarations and undertakings][1] furnished under regulation 5 shall be so preserved for a period of [six years][2] following the date on which the scheme member to whom they relate ceased to [pay contributions to a scheme][2].

Notes—[a] TA 1988 s 593(2), (3).
Amendments—[1] Words in para (4) inserted by the Occupational Pension Schemes (Additional Voluntary Contributions) (Amendment) Regulations, SI 1990/585 reg 6, with effect from 4 April 1990.
[2] Words in para (4) substituted by SI 1990/585 reg 6.

1987/1765

Personal Pension Schemes (Provisional Approval) Regulations 1987

Made by the Treasury under F(No 2)A 1987, s 56(2), now TA 1988 s 655(5)

Made . . . . *8 October 1987*
Laid before the House of Commons . . *8 October 1987*
Coming into Force . . . . . . *29 October 1987*

Citation and commencement

1 These Regulations may be cited as the Personal Pension Schemes (Provisional Approval) Regulations 1987 and shall come into force on 29th October 1987.

Interpretation

2 In these Regulations unless the context otherwise requires—

''Act'' means the Finance (No 2) Act 1987;
''the Board'' means the Commissioners of Inland Revenue;
''scheme'' means a personal pension scheme.

Provisional approval: conditions

3 Where an application to the Board for their approval of a scheme under section 19 of the Act is made before [1st February 1990][1] and[, subject to regulation 3A][1] is accompanied by—

(*a*) written undertakings by the scheme administrator that—

(i) to the best of his belief the application for approval, and the documents which accompany it, are in such form and contain such information that the scheme may be approved,

(ii) the scheme does not make provision for any benefit other than those mentioned in sections 21 to 26 of the Act ...[1], and

(iii) the scheme will be administered in accordance with the provisions contained in Chapter II of Part I of the Act and any regulations made thereunder; and

(*b*) a written undertaking by the person who has power to amend the rules of the scheme that he will comply with a notice given by the Board under regulation 4;

the Board may grant approval of the scheme provisionally notwithstanding that they have not satisfied themselves that the scheme complies with sections 20 to 30 of the Act.

Amendment—[1] Words in square brackets substituted or inserted and words omitted revoked by the Personal Pension Schemes (Provisional Approval) (Amendment) Regulations, SI 1988/1437 reg 3.

[3A Where the scheme is established under a trust, the Board may grant approval of the scheme provisionally if the application is also accompanied by a written undertaking by the scheme administrator that provision is made so as to ensure that neither the capital nor the income of the trust fund is paid to a member of the scheme except by the provision of a benefit referred to in sections 633 to 637 of the Income and Corporation Taxes Act 1988.][1]

Amendment—[1] Inserted by the Personal Pension Schemes (Provisional Approval) (Amendment) Regulations, SI 1988/1437 reg 4.

Amendment of rules

4 If on examination of the application for approval, and the documents which accompany it, the Board are not satisfied that the scheme complies with the requirements of sections 20 to 30 of the Act the Board shall give written notice to the person who has power to amend the rules of the scheme requiring him within a period of 6 months from the date of the notice (or such further time as the Board may allow) to amend the rules of the scheme so that it complies with the requirements of those sections of the Act with effect as from the date of approval of the scheme.

Withdrawal of approval

5—(1) If at the expiration of the period specified in regulation 4 (or at the end of such further time as the Board may have allowed) the Board are not satisfied that a scheme complies with sections 20 to 30 of the Act, the Board shall give written notice to the applicant for approval of the withdrawal of approval as from the date of approval of the scheme.

(2) A notice under paragraph (1) shall state the grounds on which approval is withdrawn.

Appeals

6—

(1) Where the Board withdraw an approval by notice under regulation 5(1) the applicant for approval may appeal to the Special Commissioners against the withdrawal.

(2) An appeal under this regulation shall be made by written notice stating the grounds for the appeal and given to the Board before the end of the period of 30 days beginning with the day on which notice of withdrawal was given to the appellant.

(3) The bringing of an appeal under this regulation shall not affect the validity of the withdrawal pending the determination of the proceedings.

(4) Part V of the Taxes Management Act (appeals and other proceedings) shall apply to an appeal under this regulation.

1988/88
Double Taxation Relief (Taxes on Income) (Foreign Loan Interest) Regulations 1988

Made by the Commissioners of Inland Revenue under FA 1982 s 65(5C), now TA 1988 s 798(9); see TA 1988 Sch 30 para 21

Revocation—These Regulations revoked by the Double Taxation Relief (Taxes on Income) (Foreign Interest and Dividends) Regulations, SI 1999/3330, reg 5(1), subject to transitional provisions, with effect from 3 January 2000.

1988/266
Capital Gains Tax (Definition of Unit Trust Scheme) Regulations 1988

Made by the Treasury under CGTA 1979 s 92, now TCGA 1992 s 99; see TCGA 1992 Sch 11 para 29

Made . . . . *18 February 1988*
Laid before the House of Commons . . . *18 February 1988*
Coming into Force . . . . . . *11 March 1988*

Commentary—*Simon's Direct Tax Service* **C2.735**.

Citation and commencement

1 These Regulations may be cited as the Capital Gains Tax (Definition of Unit Trust Scheme) Regulations 1988 and shall come into force on 11th March 1988.

Interpretation

2 In these Regulations unless the context otherwise requires—

"limited partnership" means a limited partnership registered under the Limited Partnerships Act 1907 and "general partner" and "limited partner" have the same meanings as in that Act;

"limited partnership scheme" means a unit trust scheme of the description specified in regulation 4;

["participant", in relation to a unit trust scheme, shall be construed in accordance with section 235 of the Financial Services and Markets Act 2000;][1]

"the principal Act" means the Capital Gains Tax Act 1979[a];

"scheme property" means, in relation to a unit trust scheme, property of any description, including money, which is held on trust for the participants in the scheme;

"unit trust scheme" means a scheme which, apart from these Regulations, is a unit trust scheme for the purposes of the principal Act.

Notes—[a] TCGA 1992.

Amendments—[1] Definition of "participant" substituted by the Financial Services and Markets Act 2000 (Consequential Amendments) (Taxes) Order, SI 2001/3629 art 116 with effect from 1 December 2001, immediately after the coming into force of the Financial Services and Markets Act 2000 ss 411, 432(1), Sch 20 (and SI 2001/3629 Pts 1 and 2).

Exception of certain unit trust schemes from the principal Act

3 A unit trust scheme which is—

(*a*) a limited partnership scheme, or

(*b*) a profit sharing scheme which has been approved in accordance with Part I of Schedule 9 to the Finance Act 1978[a] [or

(*c*) an employee share ownership plan approved under Schedule 8 to the Finance Act 2000,][1]

shall be treated as not being a unit trust scheme for the purposes of the principal Act.

Notes—[a] TA 1988 Sch 9 Pt 1.

Amendments—[1] Words inserted by the Capital Gains Tax (Definition of Unit Trust Scheme) (Amendment) Regulations, SI 2000/2550 reg 2 with effect from 11 October 2000.

Description of a limited partnership scheme

4 A unit trust scheme is a limited partnership scheme when the scheme property is held on trust for the general partners and the limited partners in a limited partnership.

1988/267
Income Tax (Definition of Unit Trust Scheme) Regulations 1988

Made by the Treasury under TA 1970 s 354A(7), now TA 1988 s 469(7); see TA 1988 Sch 30 para 21

Made	*18 February 1988*
Laid before the House of Commons	*18 February 1988*
Coming into Force	*11 March 1988*

Commentary—*Simon's Direct Tax Service* **D4.419**.

Citation and commencement

1 These Regulations may be cited as the Income Tax (Definition of Unit Trust Scheme) Regulations 1988 and shall come into force on 11th March 1988 and shall have effect in accordance with regulation 9.

Interpretation

2—(1) In these Regulations unless the context otherwise requires—

"charitable unit trust scheme" means a unit trust scheme of one of the descriptions specified in regulation 7;

"enterprise zone" has the same meaning as in section 74 of the Finance Act 1980;

"enterprise zone property scheme" means a unit trust scheme of the description specified in regulation 4;

"inspector" means any inspector of taxes;

"limited partnership" means a limited partnership registered under the Limited Partnerships Act 1907 and "general partner" and "limited partner" have the same meanings as in that Act;

"limited partnership scheme" means a unit trust scheme of the description specified in regulation 8;

["participant", in relation to a unit trust scheme, shall be construed in accordance with section 235 of the Financial Services and Markets Act 2000;][1]

"Schedule A" means the Schedule referred to as Schedule A in section 67(1) of the Taxes Act[a];

"Schedule D" means the Schedule referred to as Schedule D in section 108 of the Taxes Act[b];

"scheme property" means, in relation to a unit trust scheme, property of any description, including money, which is held on trust for the participants in the scheme;

"section 354A" means section 354A of the Taxes Act[c];

"tax year" means a year beginning with 6th April in any year and ending with 5th April in the following year;

"the Taxes Act" means the Income and Corporation Taxes Act 1970;

"trustee" means, in relation to a unit trust scheme, the person holding the scheme property on trust for the participants;

"unit trust scheme" means a scheme which, apart from these Regulations, is a unit trust scheme for the purposes of section 354A[c].

(2) The provisions of section 56 of the Finance Act 1985 shall have effect to determine when capital expenditure is to be taken to be incurred for the purposes of these Regulations.

Notes—[a] TA 1988 s 15(1).
[b] TA 1988 s 18.
[c] TA 1988 s 469.

Amendments—[1] Definition of "participant" substituted by the Financial Services and Markets Act 2000 (Consequential Amendments) (Taxes) Order, SI 2001/3629 art 117 with effect from 1 December 2001, immediately after the coming into force of the Financial Services and Markets Act 2000 ss 411, 432(1), Sch 20 (and SI 2001/3629 Pts 1 and 2).

Exception of certain unit trust schemes from section 354Aa

3 Subject to the provisions of these Regulations, a unit trust scheme which is—

(*a*) an enterprise zone property scheme, or

(*b*) a charitable unit trust scheme, or

(*c*) a limited partnership scheme, or

(*d*) a profit sharing scheme which has been approved in accordance with Part I of Schedule 9 to the Finance Act 1978[b] [or

(*e*) an employee share ownership plan approved under Schedule 8 to the Finance Act 2000,][1]

shall be treated as not being a unit trust scheme for the purposes of section 354A[c].

Notes—[a] TA 1988 s 469.
[b] TA 1988 Sch 9 Pt 1.
[c] TA 1988 s 469.

Amendments—[1] Words inserted by the Income Tax (Definition of Unit Trust Scheme) (Amendment) Regulations, SI 2000/2551 reg 2 with effect from 11 October 2000.

Description of an enterprise zone property scheme

4—(1) A unit trust scheme is an enterprise zone property scheme when it has the characteristics mentioned in paragraph (2) below.

(2) Those characteristics are—

(*a*) that, except as provided in paragraph (3)(*a*) below, the scheme property consists wholly of land (including any buildings or structures on that land)—

(i) the whole or substantially the whole of which, at the time when it became subject to the trusts of the scheme, was situated [or formerly situated][1] in one or more enterprise zones, and

(ii) any part of which not so situated [or formerly situated][1] was contiguous with land forming part of the scheme property which, at that time, was so situated [or formerly situated][1];

(*b*) that, except as provided in paragraph (3)(*b*) below, the contributions of the participants are expended on—

(i) the construction of, or the purchase of interests in, buildings or structures on that land,

(ii) the provision of machinery or plant which is an integral part of such buildings or structures,

as well as on the acquisition of, or of rights in or over, that land;

(*c*) that so much of the expenditure referred to in sub-paragraph (*b*) above as is not—

(i) expenditure on the acquisition of, or of rights in or over, the land itself, or

(ii) expenditure in relation to a building or structure, or to that part of a building or structure, which is not on land situated [or formerly situated][1] in an enterprise zone, or

(iii) expenditure on the provision of machinery or plant,

is expenditure in relation to which Chapter I of Part I of the Capital Allowances Act 1968 applies with the modifications specified in Schedule 13 to the Finance Act 1980[a];

(*d*) that the terms of the scheme secure that—

(i) the contributions of the participants are all to be made within the same tax year and no contributions can be made by participants in any subsequent tax year;

(ii) the capital expenditure referred to in sub-paragraph (*b*) above is to be incurred wholly in the tax year in which the participants make their contributions;

(iii) the nature of the rights and interests of all participants in the scheme is the same;

(iv) the rights and interests of the participants in the scheme cannot be purchased, or otherwise redeemed or cancelled, by the trustee in whole or in part except by way of distribution to the participants generally;

(v) in relation to any arrangements which are entered into after the making of these Regulations, the trustee is irrevocably authorised and obliged to undertake on behalf of the participants the responsibilities specified in regulation 5 and the duty once in every tax year to provide to the inspector in writing the information with respect to the preceding tax year concerning the participants in the scheme which is specified by regulation 6(2).

(3) A unit trust scheme is an enterprise zone property scheme notwithstanding that—

(*a*) the scheme property at any time consists also of—

(i) cash held temporarily by the trustee pending its expenditure as mentioned in paragraph (2)(*b*) above or sub-paragraph (*b*) below, or its distribution to the participants generally;

(ii) cash or other assets held by the trustee in connection with the management of the scheme property; or

(*b*) the contributions of the participants are expended for purposes incidental to, or arising out of, the expenditure referred to in paragraph (2)(*b*) above.

[(4) References in paragraph (2) of this Regulation to land formerly situated in an enterprise zone or in one or more enterprise zones are references to land on which buildings or structures were constructed where the expenditure on such construction was incurred, or was incurred under a contract entered into, at a time when the land was in an enterprise zone, being a time not more than ten years after the land was first included in an enterprise zone.][2]

Notes—[a] CAA 1990 Pt 1.

Amendments—[1] Words in para (2)(*a*)(i), (ii), (*c*)(ii) inserted by the IT (Definition of Unit Trust Scheme) (Amendment) Regulations, SI 1992/571 reg 3, with effect from 31 March 1992.

[2] Para (4) added by SI 1992/571 reg 3, with effect from 31 March 1992.

Responsibilities of trustee of an enterprise zone property scheme

5—(1) The responsibilities of the trustee of an enterprise zone property scheme specified in this regulation are to negotiate and agree with the inspector on behalf of the participants—

(*a*) the amount of any expenditure referred to in regulation 4(2)(*b*) which is—

(i) capital expenditure of each of the participants for a chargeable period in relation to which Chapter I of Part I of the Capital Allowances Act 1968 applies, or applies with the modifications specified in Schedule 13 to the Finance Act 1980[a] and

(ii) capital expenditure of each of the participants on the provision of machinery or plant in respect of which a writing-down allowance is to be or may be made in accordance with section 44 of the Finance Act 1971[b];

(*b*) where, in relation to a building or structure which forms part of the scheme property, an event occurs which gives rise or may give rise to a balancing allowance or a balancing charge to or on each of the participants, the amount of any sale, insurance, salvage or compensation moneys within the meaning of section 86(1) of the Capital Allowances Act 1968[c] relevant to that event;

(*c*) the disposal value, calculated in accordance with section 44(6) of the Finance Act 1971[d] of any plant and machinery forming part of the scheme property which is or may be required to be brought into account by each of the participants for a chargeable period;

(*d*) the amount of any profits or gains arising for each accounting period of the scheme in respect of rents or receipts from the scheme property which are chargeable on the participants under Schedule A;

(*e*) the amount of any interest of money or other annual profits or gains from scheme property which are chargeable on the participants under Schedule D.

(2) The trustee of an enterprise zone property scheme shall also be responsible for providing within three months after the end of each accounting period of the scheme to each person who was a participant in the scheme at any time during that period, or to his personal representative as the case may be, a certificate showing in relation to that participant—

(*a*) the parts of amounts of capital expenditure incurred in that period, and agreed with the inspector in accordance with paragraph (1)(*a*)(i) and (ii) above, which are attributable to his interest in the scheme at the time when the expenditure in question was incurred;

(*b*) the parts of amounts of sale, insurance, salvage or compensation moneys in relation to events occurring in that period, and of the disposal values of plant and machinery agreed with the inspector in accordance with paragraph (1)(*b*) and (*c*) above, which are attributable to his interest in the scheme at the relevant time;

(*c*) the parts of amounts agreed with the inspector to be chargeable under Schedule A or Schedule D, as the case may be, in accordance with paragraph (1)(*d*) and (*e*) above which are attributable to his interest in the scheme for any period in the accounting period in question during which he held that interest.

Notes—[a] CAA 1990 Pt 1.

[b] CAA 1990 s 24.

[c] CAA 1990 s 154(1).

[d] CAA 1990 s 26(1), (2).

Provision of information by trustee of an enterprise zone property scheme

6—(1) The information concerning the participants in an enterprise zone property scheme which the trustee of the scheme shall once in every tax year provide to the inspector in writing with respect to the preceding tax year is that specified by paragraph (2) below.

(2) The information specified by this paragraph is—

(*a*) the name, address and tax office reference, and, if an individual resident in the United Kingdom at any time in the preceding tax year, the national insurance number, of each person who was a participant in the scheme at any time in that tax year;

(*b*) in respect of each such participant, the interest which he had in the scheme at any such time;

(*c*) a copy of any certificate referred to in regulation 5(2) which is supplied to a participant or his personal representative in relation to an accounting period of the scheme ending in, or at the same time as, the preceding tax year.

Descriptions of a charitable unit trust scheme

7—(1) A unit trust scheme is a charitable unit trust scheme if it is of one of the descriptions specified in paragraph (2) below.

(2) Those descriptions are—

(*a*) a common investment fund established under section 22 of the Charities Act 1960 or section 25 of the Charities Act (Northern Ireland) 1964;

[(*aa*) a common deposit fund established under section 22A of the Charities Act 1960;][1]

(*b*) an investment fund or a deposit fund within the meaning of the Scheme scheduled to the Church Funds Investment Measure 1958 or of the scheme contained in the First Schedule to the Methodist Church Funds Act 1960;

(*c*) a fund held by the Church of Scotland Trust under the provisions of section 15 of the Church of Scotland Trust Order 1932 [or under the provisions of the Church of Scotland (Properties and Investments) Order 1994][2];

[(*ca*) a fund held by the Church of Scotland General Trustees or the Church of Scotland Investors Trust under the provisions of the Church of Scotland (Properties and Investments) Order 1994;][2]

(*d*) a unit trust scheme under the terms of which—

(i) the scheme property is held by the trustee on trust for charitable purposes only, and

(ii) the participants are required to be bodies of persons established for charitable purposes only or trustees of trusts so established;

and the income of the participants in which is in either case applied to charitable purposes only.

Amendments—[1] Sub-para (2)(*aa*) inserted by the IT (Definition of Unit Trust Scheme) (Amendment No 2) Regulations, SI 1992/3133, with effect from 1 January 1993.

[2] Words in sub-para (2)(*c*) added and sub-para (2)(*ca*) inserted by the IT (Definition of Unit Trust Scheme) (Amendment) Regulations, SI 1994/1479 reg 2, with effect from 27 June 1994.

Description of a limited partnership scheme

8 A unit trust scheme is a limited partnership scheme when the scheme property is held on trust for the general partners and the limited partners in a limited partnership.

Effect of Regulations

9 These Regulations shall have effect in relation to distribution periods (within the meaning of section 354A[a]) beginning on or after 11th March 1988.

Notes—[a] TA 1988 s 469.

1988/1012

Personal Pension Schemes (Minimum Contributions under the Social Security Act 1986) Regulations 1988

Made by the Commissioners of Inland Revenue under TA 1988 s 649(4)

Made	*9 June 1988*
Laid before the House of Commons	*9 June 1988*
Coming into Force	*1 July 1988*

Commentary—*Simon's Direct Tax Service* **E7.413**.

Citation and commencement

1 These Regulations may be cited as the Personal Pension Schemes (Minimum Contributions under the Social Security Act 1986) Regulations 1988 and shall come into force on 1st July 1988.

Interpretation

2 In these Regulations unless the context otherwise requires—

"the Act" means the Income and Corporation Taxes Act 1988;

"the Board" means the Commissioners of Inland Revenue;

"tax week" means one of the successive periods in a tax year beginning with the first day of that year and every 7th day thereafter; the last day of a tax year (or, in the case of a tax year ending in a leap year, the last 2 days) to be treated accordingly as a separate tax week;

"tax year" means the 12 months beginning with 6th April in any year.

Recovery of any increase attributable to section 649 of the Act by the Secretary of State

3 ...

Amendments—This regulation revoked by the Social Security Contributions (Transfer of Functions, etc) Act 1999 s 26(3), Sch 10 Pt II with effect from 1 April 1999, by virtue of the Social Security Contributions (Transfer of Functions, etc) Act 1999 (Commencement No 1 and Transitional Provisions) Order, SI 1999/527.

Information

4, 5 ...

Amendments—These regulations revoked by the Social Security Contributions (Transfer of Functions, etc) Act 1999 s 26(3), Sch 10 Pt II with effect from 1 April 1999 by virtue of the Social Security Contributions (Transfer of Functions, etc) Act 1999 (Commencement No 1 and Transitional Provisions) Order, SI 1999/527.

Recovery of amounts representing basic rate tax

6—(1) The like provisions as are contained in section 30 of the Taxes Management Act 1970 (recovery of overpayment of tax, etc) shall apply in relation to the payment by the Secretary of State of an amount by way of minimum contributions which—

(*a*) he was not required to pay, or

(*b*) he was required to pay but which he paid to other persons than the trustees or managers of the personal pension scheme to whom he should have made the payment

as if an amount representing income tax at the basic rate on the amount paid had been income tax repaid to the person to, or in respect of, whom the amount was paid to which that person was not entitled.

(2) An assessment made by virtue of this regulation shall be made by the Board and, subject to the provisions of these Regulations, the like provisions as are contained in the Taxes Management Act 1970 shall apply as if the assessment were an assessment to tax for the year of assessment in respect of which the amount was paid.

Northern Ireland

7 In relation to Northern Ireland, these Regulations shall have effect as if—

(*a*) references to the Secretary of State were references to the Department of Health and Social Services for Northern Ireland; ...[1]

(*b*) ...[1]

Amendments—[1] Para (*b*) and the word "and" immediately preceding it revoked by the Social Security Contributions (Transfer of Functions, etc) (Northern Ireland) Order, SI 1999/671 art 24(3) Sch 9 Pt II, with effect from 1 April 1999 (by virtue of the Social Security Contributions (Transfer of Functions, etc) (1999 Order) (Commencement No 1 and Transitional Provisions) Order (Northern Ireland), SR 1999/149, art 2(*c*), Sch 2).

1988/1013
Personal Pension Schemes (Relief at Source) Regulations 1988

Made by the Commissioners of Inland Revenue under TA 1988 s 639

Made	*9 June 1988*
Laid before the House of Commons	*9 June 1988*
Coming into Force	*1 July 1988*

Commentary—*Simon's Direct Tax Service* **E7.407**.

ARRANGEMENT OF REGULATIONS

Citation and commencement

1 These Regulations may be cited as the Personal Pension Schemes (Relief at Source) Regulations 1988 and shall come into force on 1st July 1988.

Interpretation

2—(1) In these Regulations unless the context otherwise requires—

''arrangements'' means approved personal pension arrangements within the meaning of section 630;

[''basis year'' shall be construed in accordance with section 646B;][1]

''the Board'' means the Commissioners of Inland Revenue;

[''earnings threshold'' has the meaning given by section 630(1);][1]

[''electronic signature'' has the meaning given by section 7(2) of the Electronic Communications Act 2000;][1]

''net contribution'' means a contribution from which an individual deducts an amount equal to income tax at the basic rate by virtue of section 639(3) and (4);

[''net relevant earnings'' means relevant earnings computed in accordance with section 646;][2]

[''permitted maximum'' has the meaning given by section 638(4);][2]

[''qualifying post-cessation year'' has the meaning given by section 646D(4) and (5);][2]

[''relevant earnings'' has the meaning given by section 644;][2]

''relevant superannuation scheme'' means a scheme or arrangement as defined in section 645(3);

''retirement annuity contract or trust scheme'' means a retirement annuity contract or trust scheme approved by the Board under Chapter III of Part XIV of the Act;

''scheme'' means an approved personal pension scheme within the meaning of section 630;

''section'' means a section of the Income and Corporation Taxes Act 1988;

''tax month'' means a period beginning on the 6th day of any month and ending with the 5th day of the following month;

''year of assessment'' means a year beginning with 6th April in any year and ending with 5th April in the following year.

(2) The Table below indexes other definitions in these Regulations—

Term defined	*Regulation*
annual claim	8
interim claim	8

Amendments—[1] Definitions of ''basis year'', ''earnings threshold'', ''electronic signature'' inserted by the Personal Pension Scheme (Relief at Source) (Amendment) Regulations, SI 2000/2315 reg 3 with effect for personal pension schemes after 5 April 2001.

[2] Definitions of ''net relevant earnings'', ''permitted maximum'', ''qualifying post-cessation year'', and ''relevant earnings'' substituted for the definitions of ''net relevant Schedule E earnings'' and ''relevant Schedule E earnings'' by , SI 2000/2315 reg 3 with effect for personal pension schemes after 5 April 2001.

Prescribed cases and conditions: introductory

3 Regulation 4 prescribes the cases in which, and regulations 5 to 7 the conditions subject to which, relief under section 639 shall be given in accordance with subsections (3) and (4) of that section.

Prescribed cases

4 The prescribed cases are cases where [an individual is eligible, by virtue of satisfying the provisions of section 632A of the Taxes Act, to make contributions for a year of assessment to the approved personal pension scheme concerned][1]

Amendments—[1] Words substituted by the Personal Pension Scheme (Relief at Source) (Amendment) Regulations, SI 2000/2315 reg 4 with effect for personal pension schemes after 5 April 2001.

Prescribed conditions

5—(1) The condition prescribed in this regulation is that an individual shall furnish ...[1] to the scheme administrator before...[1] the time specified in paragraph (3) the particulars specified in paragraph (2).

(2) The particulars specified in this paragraph are—

(*a*) his full name and [permanent residential address including, where the address is in the United Kingdom, the postcode][1];

(*b*) his date of birth;

(*c*) his national insurance number[, unless aged under 16 or a citizen of a country outside the United Kingdom who is not resident in the United Kingdom,][1] [(*d*) except where the scheme is an occupational pension scheme within the meaning of section 1 of the Pension Schemes Act 1993, the category of status specified in paragraph (2A) that is applicable in his case or, if more than one category is applicable, the one that is his principal source of income;][2]

[(*e*) in the circumstances specified in paragraph (2B), the requisite evidence, that is to say—

(i) a declaration specifying the year of assessment concerned, or an earlier year of assessment not being more than five years preceding that year, as the basis year for the purposes of section 646B (presumption of same level of relevant earnings etc for 5 years);

(ii) where the individual is an employee, the full names and addresses of all those employers who have paid, or will pay, net relevant earnings to him; and

(iii) the particulars specified in paragraph (2C) for the basis year.][2]

[(2A) The categories of status specified in this paragraph for the purposes of paragraph (2)(*d*) are as follows—

(*a*) employed, that is, a person chargeable to tax under Schedule E for the year of assessment concerned in respect of emoluments from an office or employment held by him;

(*b*) a person chargeable to tax under Schedule E for the year of assessment concerned in respect of a pension;

(*c*) self-employed, that is, a person chargeable to tax under Schedule D for the year of assessment concerned in respect of annual profits or gains arising or accruing from any trade, profession or vocation carried on by him;

(*d*) a child under the age of 16;

(*e*) other status not falling within any of sub-paragraphs (*a*) to (*d*) and, in relation to that status, specifying which of the following is applicable in his case or, if more than one, the most applicable—

(i) caring for one or more children aged under 16,

(ii) caring for a person aged 16 or over,

(iii) in full time education,

(iv) unemployed, or

(v) other.][3]

[(2B) The circumstances specified in this paragraph are where the total contributions to be made by the individual and, where he is an employee, his employer for the year of assessment concerned will exceed the earnings threshold, and the year of assessment either—

(*a*) is not a year already specified in a declaration under paragraph (2)(*e*)(i) as the basis year or is not one of the 5 years of assessment following that year, or

(*b*) is such a year but the total contributions to be made by the individual and, where he is an employee, his employer for that year will exceed the permitted maximum based on the net relevant earnings of the individual in the basis year specified in the declaration.][3]

[(2C) The particulars specified in this paragraph are—

(*a*) where the individual is an employee, one of the following—

(i) a copy of his payslip or Inland Revenue Form P60 showing relevant earnings for the basis year;

(ii) a declaration of his employer, signed by the employer or a person nominated by the employer, stipulating the amount of remuneration paid to the employee for the basis year or, where the basis year is the current year, an estimate of the amount of remuneration to be paid to the employee for that year;

(iii) a copy of the self-assessment included in the individual's income tax return for the basis year;

(iv) such other particulars of relevant earnings as may be required by notice in writing given by the Board;

(*b*) where the individual is self-employed, one of the following—

(i) a copy of the accounts for the basis year of the individual's trade, profession or vocation;

(ii) a copy of the income tax return for the basis year of the individual, or of the self-assessment included in that return, showing net relevant earnings of the individual;

(iii) such other particulars of relevant earnings as may be required by notice in writing given by the Board.][3]

[(2D) The reference in paragraph (2C)(*a*)(ii) to a declaration includes a declaration produced in electronic form and incorporating an electronic signature of the employer.][3]

[(3) The time specified in this paragraph is—

(*a*) in relation to the particulars specified in paragraph (2)(*a*) to (*d*), the time at which the individual first pays a net contribution;

(*b*) in relation to the particulars specified in paragraphs (2)(*e*) and (2C), immediately after the expiry of thirty days following the day on which the individual first pays a net contribution for the year of assessment concerned that, when aggregated with previous contributions made by him for that year, exceeds the earnings threshold or, as the case may be, the permitted maximum based on the net relevant earnings of the individual in the basis year.][2]

Amendments—[1] Words revoked in para (1), words substituted in para (2)(*a*), and words added in para (2)(*c*) by the Personal Pension Scheme (Relief at Source) (Amendment) Regulations, SI 2000/2315 regs 5, 6 with effect for personal pension schemes after 5 April 2001.
[2] Sub-paras (2)(*d*), (*e*), and para (3) substituted for paras (2)(*d*) to (*f*) by SI 2000/2315 regs 6, 8 with effect for personal pension schemes after 5 April 2001.
[3] Paras (2A)–(2D) inserted by SI 2000/2315 regs7 with effect for personal pension schemes after 5 April 2001.

6—(1) The condition prescribed in this regulation is that an individual shall furnish to the scheme administrator before...[1] the time specified in paragraph (3) the certificates specified in paragraph (2).

(2) The certificates specified in this paragraph are certificates which show—

(*a*) that, except where subsection (4) or subsection (5) of section 645 applies, the individual is not participating in a relevant superannuation scheme,

(*b*) whether or not the individual is paying contributions under other arrangements or under a retirement annuity contract or trust scheme;

(*c*) that the total contributions which the individual—

(i) is paying under any arrangements or scheme referred to in sub-paragraph (*b*), and

(ii) will pay under the arrangements to which the certificate relates

do not together exceed [the maximum amount permitted under section 640][1];

[(*d*) that the individual's eligibility to make contributions for the year of assessment concerned arises by virtue of section 632A(4) (actual net relevant earnings), the individual does not fulfil any of the conditions in section 632A(6) to (9), and his net relevant earnings do not fall within section 644(5).][2]

[(3) The time specified in this paragraph is—

(*a*) in relation to the certificate specified in paragraph (2)(*a*), (*b*) or (*c*)—

(i) the time at which the individual first pays a net contribution;

(ii) the time at which the individual makes a declaration in accordance with regulation 5(2)(*e*)(i) specifying a year of assessment as the basis year for the purposes of section 646B;

(*b*) in relation to the certificate specified in paragraph (2)(*d*), the time at which the individual first pays a net contribution, being a time when his eligibility to do so arises by virtue of section 632A(4) and he does not fulfil any of the conditions in section 632A(6) to (9).][2]

Amendments—[1] Words in para (1) revoked, and words in para (2)(*c*) substituted by the Personal Pension Scheme (Relief at Source) (Amendment) Regulations, SI 2000/2315 regs 9, 10 with effect for personal pension schemes after 5 April 2001.
[2] Paras (2)(*d*), (3) substituted by SI 2000/2315 regs 10, 11 with effect for personal pension schemes after 5 April 2001.

7—(1) The condition prescribed in this regulation is that on every occasion on which an individual furnishes particulars or a certificate (or both) in accordance with regulation 5 or 6 he shall furnish the declarations specified in paragraph (2).

(2) The declarations specified in this paragraph are declarations ...[1] by the individual to the effect that—

(*a*) in relation to—

(i) the particulars specified in regulation 5(2), they are to the best of the knowledge and belief of the individual correct and complete;

(ii) a certificate specified in regulation 6(2), it is to the best of the knowledge and belief of the individual correct;

[(*b*) the individual will, not later than the date specified in paragraph (3), give notice to the administrator if an event occurs as a result of which the individual, having regard to section 632A(3) to (9), will no longer be eligible to make contributions.][1]

[(3) The date specified for the purposes of sub-paragraph (*b*) of paragraph (2) is the 5th April in the year of assessment in which the event referred to in that sub-paragraph occurs or the date that is 30 days following the occurrence of that event, whichever is the later.][2]

[(4) Certificates furnished under regulation 6, and declarations furnished under this regulation, if in writing, shall be signed by the maker of the certificates or declarations.][2]

[(5) Where particulars, certificates or declarations furnished by an individual under regulation 5 or 6 or this regulation are not in writing, the scheme administrator may—

(*a*) make a declaration in writing on behalf of the individual that the particulars or (as the case may be) the terms of the certificates or declarations so furnished are those recorded in the declaration, and

(*b*) send a copy of the declaration to the individual.][2]

[(6) Subject to any corrections notified by the individual to the scheme administrator within the period of 30 days following the date on which the copy of the declaration referred to in paragraph (5) was sent to the individual, and incorporated in a new declaration made by the scheme administrator, any such declaration shall take effect as from the date on which the copy of it was sent to the individual in accordance with that paragraph.][2]

[(7) Particulars, certificates or declarations furnished by an individual under regulation 5, 6 or this regulation shall be regarded as furnished in writing for the purposes of this regulation if they are furnished—

(*a*) by telephonic facsimile transmission, or

(*b*) by electronic communication containing an electronic signature of the individual.][2]

[(8) Declarations made by the scheme administrator under paragraph (5) of this regulation shall be regarded as made in writing if they are produced by electronic means; and the copy of a declaration to be sent to the individual in accordance with sub-paragraph (*b*) of that paragraph may be sent by telephonic facsimile transmission or by electronic communication.][2]

Amendments—[1] The word "signed" in para (2) revoked, and sub-para (*b*) substituted by the Personal Pension Scheme (Relief at Source) (Amendment) Regulations, SI 2000/2315 reg 12 with effect for personal pension schemes after 5 April 2001.

[2] Paras (3)–(8) added by SI 2000/2315 reg 13 with effect for personal pension schemes after 5 April 2001.

Claims: introductory

8—(1) Amounts recoverable by a scheme administrator under section 639(4)(*b*) shall be recovered on a claim made to the Board for the purpose of these Regulations.

(2) Subject to paragraph (3), a claim shall be for a year of assessment ("annual claim").

(3) A claim may also be made in accordance with regulation 9 for a tax month ("interim claim").

[(3A) No annual claim or interim claim may be made in respect of contributions made by an individual in a year of assessment that exceed the earnings threshold unless that year of assessment is—

(*a*) the basis year specified in a declaration under regulation 5(2)(*e*)(i),

(*b*) one of the 5 years of assessment following that year, or

(*c*) a qualifying post-cessation year.][1]

(4) Notwithstanding the provisions of any other enactment, the Board shall not be under an obligation to make any payment under regulation 9 or 10 earlier than the end of the month following the month in which the claim is received.

Amendments—[1] Para (3A) inserted by the Personal Pension Scheme (Relief at Source) (Amendment) Regulations, SI 2000/2315 reg 14 with effect for personal pension schemes after 5 April 2001.

Interim claims

9—(1) Subject to paragraph (3), an interim claim for a tax month may be made by a scheme administrator within 6 months after the end of the tax month for which it is made.

(2) A claim under this regulation may not be based on an estimate but may only be made to recover an amount deducted in respect of contributions paid in the tax month.

(3) An interim claim may not be made for the tax month ending 5th October or any subsequent month until the annual claim for the preceding year of assessment has been made by the scheme administrator and received by the Board.

(4) If the amount claimed is established to the Board's satisfaction they shall pay the amount to the claimant; if they are not so satisfied they shall pay to the claimant any lesser amount established to their satisfaction.

(5) Where a scheme administrator discovers that an amount paid to him under paragraph (4) was excessive he shall bring into account in the interim claim made by him next after the discovery (in this regulation referred to as "the subsequent claim") the amount of the excess; and if that amount exceeds the amount deducted in respect of the tax month for which the subsequent claim is made—

(*a*) the scheme administrator shall repay the amount of the excess to the Board with the claim; and

(*b*) if he fails so to do that amount shall immediately be recoverable by the Board in the same manner as tax charged by an assessment on the scheme administrator which has become final and conclusive.

Annual claims

10—(1) An annual claim for a year of assessment may, subject to paragraph (2), be made at any time within 6 years after the end of the year of assessment.

(2) Where in relation to any year of assessment a scheme administrator has received and not repaid in full any amount on an interim claim he shall within 6 months after the end of the year of assessment make an annual claim.

(3) A claim under this regulation—

(*a*) may not be based on an estimate but may only be made to recover an amount deducted in respect of contributions [paid in respect of][1] the year of assessment, and

(*b*) shall bring into account payments made in respect of the year of assessment; and for the purpose of this regulation "aggregate interim payments" means the aggregate of payments made (and not repaid) on interim claims.

(4) Where the aggregate of the interim payments shown by an annual claim exceeds the amount deducted for the year of assessment—

SIs

(*a*) the scheme administrator shall repay the amount of the excess to the Board with the claim; and

(*b*) if he fails so to do, that amount shall immediately be recoverable by the Board in the same manner as tax charged by an assessment on the scheme administrator which has become final and conclusive.

(5) If a scheme administrator fails to make an annual claim under paragraph (2) within the time limited by that paragraph, the Board may issue a notice to the scheme administrator showing the aggregate interim payments for the year, and stating that the Board are not satisfied that the amount due to the scheme administrator for the year of assessment exceeds the lower amount stated in the notice.

(6) If an annual claim is not delivered to the Board within 14 days after the issue of a notice under paragraph (5), the amount of the difference between the aggregate amount and the amount stated in the notice shall immediately be recoverable by the Board in the same manner as tax charged by an assessment on the scheme administrator which has become final and conclusive.

(7) Where an annual claim has been made and the scheme administrator subsequently discovers that an error or mistake has been made in the claim the scheme administrator may make a supplementary claim within the time limited by paragraph (1).

Amendments—[1] Words in para (3)(*a*) substituted by the Personal Pension Scheme (Relief at Source) (Amendment) Regulations, SI 2000/2315 reg 15 with effect for personal pension schemes after 5 April 2001.

Claims: supplementary provisions

11—(1) Section 42 of the Taxes Management Act 1970 (procedure for making claims) shall not apply to a claim under these Regulations.

(2) No appeal shall lie from the Board's decision on an interim claim.

(3) An appeal shall be to the Special Commissioners from the Board's decision on an annual claim, and the appeal shall be brought by giving written notice to the Board within 30 days of receipt of written notice of the decision.

(4) No payment made or other thing done on or in relation to an interim claim shall prejudice the decision on an annual claim.

(5) The like provisions as are contained in Part V of the Taxes Management Act 1970 (appeals and other proceedings) shall apply to an appeal under paragraph (3), and on an appeal the Special Commissioners may vary the decision appealed against whether or not the variation is to the advantage of the appellant.

(6) All such assessments, payments and repayments shall be made as are necessary to give effect to the Board's decision on an annual claim, or to any variation of that decision on appeal.

(7) Claims under these Regulations—

(*a*) shall contain such information and be in such form as the Board may prescribe (and forms prescribed for annual claims may require a report to be given by the scheme administrator's auditor);

(*b*) shall contain declarations to the effect that—

(i) sufficient records in respect of the scheme are maintained so as to enable the requirements of these Regulations to be satisfied, and

(ii) the information contained in the claim (including the declaration referred to in paragraph (i)) is correct; and

(*c*) shall be signed by the scheme administrator or by an authorised representative in the service of the scheme administrator.

Recovery on withdrawal of approval of schemes or of arrangements

12 Where a scheme administrator gives to the Board information in accordance with regulation 14(2) he shall at the time that he gives the information—

(*a*) pay to the Board the amount (if any) referred to in regulation 14(3)(*d*); and

(*b*) if he fails so to do, that amount shall immediately be recoverable by the Board in the same manner as tax charged by an assessment on the scheme administrator which has become final and conclusive.

Recovery of amounts by assessment

13—(1) The like provisions as are contained in section 30 of the Taxes Management Act 1970 (recovery of overpayment of tax, etc) shall apply in relation to the payment by the Board of an amount—

(*a*) paid under these Regulations to which a scheme administrator was not entitled, or

(*b*) recoverable from a scheme administrator under regulation 9(5), regulation 10(4) or (6) or regulation 12,

as if it had been income tax repaid to the scheme administrator to which he was not entitled.

(2) An assessment made by virtue of this regulation shall be made by the Board and, subject to the provisions of these Regulations, the like provisions as are contained in the Taxes Management Act 1970 shall apply as if the assessment were an assessment to tax for the year of assessment in respect of which the amount was paid or is recoverable.

Information

14—(1) The Board may by notice in writing require any person who is, or who at any time has been—

(*a*) a Scheme administrator to whom net contributions have been paid, or
(*b*) an individual who has paid such contributions,

to give to them within such time (not being less than 14 days) as may be provided in the notice such information and in such form as may be prescribed in the notice.

(2) If the Board by notice under section 650 withdraw their approval of a scheme, or of arrangements made in accordance with it and under which net contributions have been paid, the scheme administrator shall within 30 days give to the Board in relation to that scheme, or to those arrangements, the information prescribed in paragraph (3).

(3) The information prescribed in this paragraph is—

(*a*) the full name, address, national insurance number, and where known tax office reference of each individual who has paid net contributions after the date specified in the notice in relation to the scheme, or to the arrangements, as the case may be (in this regulation referred to as ''the relevant contributions'');
(*b*) the amount of the relief obtained under section 639(1) by means of the relevant contributions;
(*c*) the amount of such relief actually due; and
(*d*) the difference between the relief referred to in sub-paragraph (*b*) and that referred to in sub-paragraph (*c*).

(4) If an individual who has paid net contributions fails to comply with the requirements of regulations 5 to 7, the scheme administrator to whom such contributions have been made shall within 30 days give to the Board the information prescribed in paragraph (5).

(5) The information prescribed in this paragraph is—

(*a*) the full name, address, national insurance number, and where known tax office reference of the individual;
(*b*) the amount of relief obtained by him under section 639(1) by means of such contributions;
(*c*) the amount of such relief actually due; and
(*d*) the difference between the relief referred to in sub-paragraph (*b*) and that referred to in sub-paragraph (*c*).

Inspection of records

15—(1) Every scheme administrator to whom net contributions have been paid shall, whenever required so to do, make available for inspection by a person authorised by the Board for that purpose all books, documents and other records (including all particulars, certificates and declarations furnished under regulations 5 to 7) in his possession or under his control relating to—

(*a*) such contributions paid to him,
(*b*) the scheme and the arrangements made in accordance with it and under which the contributions were paid, and
(*c*) the individual who paid the contributions.

(2) Where records are maintained by computer the scheme administrator shall provide the person making the inspection with all facilities necessary to obtain information from them.

(3) Subject to paragraph (4), all books, documents and records referred to in paragraph (1), shall be preserved by the scheme administrator so as to be available for inspection under this regulation for a period of six years following the termination of the scheme, or of arrangements made in accordance with it, to which they relate.

(4) All particulars, certificates and declarations furnished under regulations 5 to 7 shall be so preserved for a period of six years following the date on which the individual to whom they relate ceased to make net contributions.

1988/1014

Personal Pension Schemes (Transfer Payments) Regulations 1988

Made by the Commissioners of Inland Revenue under TA 1988 s 638(2)

Made	*9 June 1988*
Laid before the House of Commons	*9 June 1988*
Coming into Force	*1 July 1988*

Commentary—*Simon's Direct Tax Service* **E7.416**.
Amendment—Regulations revoked by the Personal Pension Schemes (Transfer Payments) Regulations, SI 2001/119 reg 15(2) with effect from 6 April 2001.

1988/1347
Income Tax (Interest Relief) (Housing Associations) Regulations 1988

Made by the Treasury under TA 1988 s 378(1)

Made	*29 July 1988*
Laid before the House of Commons	*29 July 1988*
Coming into Force	*1 August 1988*

Commentary—*Simon's Direct Tax Service* **A3.434**.

Citation, commencement and revocations

1—(1) These Regulations may be cited as the Income Tax (Interest Relief) (Housing Associations) Regulations 1988 and shall come into force on 1st August 1988.

(2) The Regulations specified in the Schedule are hereby revoked.

Interpretation

2—(1) In these Regulations unless the context otherwise requires—

"housing association" means a housing association for the time being approved for the purposes of section 488 or a self-build society for the time being approved for the purposes of section 489;

"the Principal Regulations" means the Income Tax (Interest Relief) Regulations 1982;

"qualifying member" means a member of a housing association except a member who, or whose husband or wife, holds an office or employment in respect of the emoluments of which he or she would but for some special exemption or immunity from tax be chargeable to tax under Case I, Case II or Case III of Schedule E;

"section" means a section of the Income and Corporation Taxes Act 1988.

(2) In the application of these Regulations to Scotland—

(*a*) "a freehold or leasehold estate" means any interest in land; and

(*b*) any reference to a loan on the security of such an estate is a reference to a loan upon a heritable security within the meaning of section 9(8)(*a*) of the Conveyancing and Feudal Reform (Scotland) Act 1970.

Introductory

3 Where a housing association borrows or has borrowed from a qualifying lender on the security of a freehold or leasehold estate of that association on land in the United Kingdom sections 369 to 377 and the Principal Regulations shall apply but subject to such modifications and conditions as these Regulations provide and as if, with respect to relevant loan interest on [the loan, the housing association were an individual who is a qualifying borrower within section 376(1).][1]

Amendments—[1] Words substituted by the Income Tax (Interest Relief) (Housing Associations) (Amendment) Regulations, SI 1995/1212 reg 3.

Modification of provisions of Income and Corporation Taxes Act 1988

[**4** Section 369 shall have effect as if for subsection (1) there were substituted the following subsection—

"(1) If a housing association makes a payment of relevant loan interest to which this section applies, it shall be entitled, on making the payment, to deduct and retain out of it a sum equal to the applicable percentage thereof; [and accordingly—

(*a*) subsections (2) and (3) of section 486 (interest paid by registered industrial and provident societies) shall not apply to the payment of that relevant loan interest, and

(*b*) that relevant loan interest shall not be brought into account by way of any debit given for the purposes of Chapter II of part IV of the Finance Act 1996 (loan relationships).][2]."][1]

Amendments—[1] Regulation substituted by the Income Tax (Interest Relief) (Housing Associations) (Amendment) Regulations, SI 1995/1212 reg 4.

[2] Words substituted by the Income Tax (Interest Relief) (Housing Associations) (Amendment) Regulations, SI 1996/2616 regs 2, 3, with effect with respect to any payment of interest made after 3 November 1996.

[**5** Section 370 shall have effect with the modifications specified in regulations 5A to 5D.][1]

Amendments—[1] Regs 5, 5A–5D substituted for reg 5 by the Income Tax (Interest Relief) (Housing Associations) (Amendment) Regulations, SI 1995/1212 reg 5.

[5A For subsections (1) and (2) of section 370 there shall be substituted the following subsections—

"(1) Subject to this section, to sections 372 to 376 and to section 44(6) of the Finance Act 1988, in this Part "relevant loan interest" means interest which is paid and payable in the United Kingdom to a qualifying lender by a housing association and to which subsection (2) or (3) below applies.

(2) This subsection applies to interest if, disregarding section 353(2) and any other provision applying to interest falling to be treated as relevant loan interest—

(*a*) it is interest which would be eligible for relief under section 353 by virtue of section 354 if—

(i) the housing association were an individual who uses the land in question as his only or main residence, and

(ii) in a case falling within section 354(1)(*c*), the other loan there referred to, in so far as it was raised by the housing association, were a loan raised by such an individual; and

(*b*) apart (where applicable) from section 356A the whole of the interest would be eligible for relief for the year in question; and

(*c*) it is interest on a loan to a housing association which is secured on a freehold or leasehold estate of land in the United Kingdom of which the housing association is the owner; and

(*d*) within the period of 12 months following the date on which the interest becomes due, the land (and where it includes separate dwellings each of them)—

(i) is occupied by the housing association, or

(ii) is wholly or to a substantial extent used in qualifying circumstances as the only or main residence of any qualifying member of the housing association or of a dependent relative or former or separated spouse of a qualifying member.

(2A) For the purposes of subsection (2)(*d*) above, the circumstances in which any land or dwelling is used are qualifying circumstances in relation to any interest where they are such (including where the qualifying member resides in accommodation which for him is job-related) that (apart from any modification of this section in relation to housing associations) the interest would be relevant loan interest if—

(*a*) it were paid by the qualifying member who uses the land or dwelling as a residence or whose dependent relative or former or separated spouse so uses the land or dwelling; and

(*b*) the requirements of section 354 were satisfied in relation to payments made by that member.

(2B) In subsections (2) and (2A) above—

(*a*) "dependent relative" and "separated" have the meanings given for the purposes of sections 354 to 366 by section 367(1);

(*b*) "job-related", in relation to any accommodation, shall be construed in accordance with section 356(3).".][1]

Amendments—[1] Regs 5, 5A–5D substituted for reg 5 by the Income Tax (Interest Relief) (Housing Associations) (Amendment) Regulations, SI 1995/1212 reg 5.

[5B In subsection (3)(*b*) of section 370 for the words "is fulfilled" there shall be substituted the words "would be fulfilled if the payment were made by a qualifying member of the housing association who is using the dwelling as his only or main residence, and not by the housing association.".][1]

Amendments—[1] Regs 5, 5A–5D substituted for reg 5 by the Income Tax (Interest Relief) (Housing Associations) (Amendment) Regulations, SI 1995/1212 reg 5.

[5C Subsections (4), (6) and (6A) of section 370 shall be omitted.][1]

Amendments—[1] Regs 5, 5A–5D substituted for reg 5 by the Income Tax (Interest Relief) (Housing Associations) (Amendment) Regulations, SI 1995/1212 reg 5.

[5D In subsection (7) of section 370 for the words "is for the time being fulfilled" there shall be substituted the words "would, if the payment were made as mentioned in that subsection, for the time being be fulfilled".][1]

Amendments—[1] Regs 5, 5A–5D substituted for reg 5 by the Income Tax (Interest Relief) (Housing Associations) (Amendment) Regulations, SI 1995/1212 reg 5.

6 Section 373 shall have effect as if for subsections (1) to (5) there were substituted the words—

"(1) The provisions of this section have effect in relation to a loan or loans by a qualifying lender to a housing association the total amount of which, where applicable, in relation to a loan made on or after 1st August 1988, having regard to section 356A as if that section applied to the housing association, for the time being exceeds the limit ("the aggregate limit") found—

(*a*) in relation to a loan made on or after 1st August 1988 and where qualifying interest is paid by a housing association and another person in relation to a separate dwelling, by dividing the amount of the limit provided by section 357 (the tax relief limit) by the number of persons by whom qualifying interest is payable; and (*b*) except where paragraph (*a*) applies, by multiplying the tax relief limit by the number of separate dwellings provided or to be provided on the land on which the loan is secured and to which the loan relates;

and in this section any such loan is referred to as a "limited loan".

(2) None of the interest on a limited loan is relevant loan interest unless—

(*a*) the loan is made on or after 6th April 1987; or

(*b*) the qualifying lender to whom the interest is payable has given notice to the Board in accordance with regulations that he is prepared to have limited loans of a description which includes that limited loan brought within the tax deduction scheme.

(3) If, in a case where subsection (2) above applies, the total amount of loans to a housing association exceeds the aggregate limit provided by subsection (1) above, none of the interest on the loan which, taken with the amounts of any earlier loans, first exceeds that limit, or on subsequent loans, is relevant loan interest unless it is a loan which was made by the qualifying lender who first gave notice under subsection (2) above or the interest is so designated by the Board.

(4) The reference in subsection (1) above to a loan only part of the interest on which would (apart from section 353(2)) be eligible for relief under section 353 includes a reference to each of two or more loans if, by virtue of subsection (3)(*b*) of section 357, the interest on the loans falls to be treated for the purposes of that section as payable on one loan; but, notwithstanding that each of those loans is accordingly a limited loan for the purposes of this section, none of the interest on any of them is relevant loan interest unless each of the loans was made by the same qualifying lender.

(5) Where the condition in paragraph (*a*) or (*b*) of subsection (2) above is fulfilled and, if subsection (3) or (4) above also applies, the condition in that subsection is also fulfilled only the interest on so much of the total amount to which subsection (1) refers as does not exceed the aggregate limit provided by that subsection is relevant loan interest.".

7 Section 374(1) shall have effect as if for paragraph (*c*) there were substituted the words—

"(*c*) it is interest to which section 370(3) applies in respect of which—

(i) the housing association has given to the lender a certificate in a form prescribed or authorised by the Board that it is a qualifying borrower and that the interest payable on the loan is relevant loan interest; and

(ii) the lender has sent to the Board (or the Board is satisfied that it will send) a copy of the certificate;"

Modification of Principal Regulations

8 For the purposes of Regulation 3 of the Principal Regulations a housing association is a borrower to whom only paragraph (3) of that Regulation applies.

9 Regulation 4 of the Principal Regulations shall have effect as if at the end there were inserted the words—

"(*c*) a loan to a housing association the interest on which is relevant loan interest in respect of which the housing association has given a certificate to the Board that it is a qualifying borrower and that the interest is relevant loan interest.".

10 For Regulation 16 of the Principal Regulations there shall be substituted the words—

"Information to be provided to the Board

16 The Board may by notice in writing require any person who is a party to a loan agreement to which sections 369 to 376 of the Income and Corporation Taxes Act 1988 apply, or could in the opinion of the Board apply, or a member or tenant of a housing association which is a party to such a loan agreement, to furnish them, within such time (not being less than 14 days) as may be provided by the notice, such information (including copies of any relevant documents or records) as they may reasonably require for the purposes of those sections including, in the case of a loan to a housing association, a certificate that all or any specified conditions of the tax deduction scheme are satisfied.".

SCHEDULE

REVOCATIONS

Regulation 1(2)

Note—This Schedule revokes SIs 1983/368, 1984/1653, and 1987/404.

1988/1436
Occupational Pension Schemes (Transitional Provisions) Regulations 1988

Made by the Commissioners of Inland Revenue under TA 1988 Sch 23 para 1(2)

Made . . . . *11 August 1988*
Laid before the House of Commons . . . *11 August 1988*
Coming into Force . . . . *2 September 1988*

Commentary—*Simon's Direct Tax Service* **E7.227**.

Citation and commencement

1 These Regulations may be cited as the Occupational Pension Schemes (Transitional Provisions) Regulations 1988 and shall come into force on 2nd September 1988 but shall have effect in accordance with regulation 12.

Interpretation

2—(1) In these Regulations unless the context otherwise requires—

"the Board" means the Commissioners of Inland Revenue;

"business" includes a trade or profession and includes any activity carried on by a body of persons, whether corporate or unincorporate;

"control", in relation to a body corporate or partnership, has the meaning given to it by section 840; and the definition of "control" in that section applies (with the necessary modifications) in relation to an unincorporated association as it applies in relation to a body corporate;

["the general level of earnings" means the general level of earnings obtaining in Great Britain;][1]

["normal retirement date" means the date specified in the rules of the scheme as the date at which the employee will normally retire;][1]

["pensionable service" means service as an employee of the employer in question in respect of which benefits (other than benefits payable solely on death before retirement) accrue under an approved scheme;][1]

"relevant employer" means—

(*a*) an associated employer, or

(*b*) an employer—

(i) who has acquired, or who has been acquired by, or who has merged with, an employer who had established a scheme before 17th March 1987, or

(ii) who has taken over the whole or part of the business of such an employer;

"section" means a section of, and "Schedule" means Schedule 23 to, the [Taxes Act][2];

["Taxes Act" means the Income and Corporation Taxes Act 1988;][2]

"total pension" means in relation to an employee the aggregate of all benefits (including the value in terms of an annual pension of any lump sum or sums received or receivable by the employee)—

(*a*) from schemes established by his employer, or to which his employer has contributed, and

(*b*) from schemes to which his employer has not contributed and which provide benefits in addition to those provided by schemes to which he has contributed.

(2) For the purpose of these Regulations an employer is associated with another employer if (directly or indirectly) one is controlled by the other or if both are controlled by a third person, and the expression "associated employer" shall be construed accordingly.

Amendments—[1] Definitions in para (1) inserted by the Occupational Pension Schemes (Transitional Provisions) (Amendment) Regulations, SI 1993/3219 regs 1, 2, 3.

[2] In para (1), words "Taxes Act" substituted, and definition of "Taxes Act" inserted, by Occupational Pension Schemes (Transitional Provisions) (Amendment) Regulations, SI 1996/3115 reg 3, with effect from 1 January 1997.

Disapplication of paragraphs 2, 3, 4 and 6 of the Schedule

3—(1) Subject to regulation 4, the provisions contained in paragraphs 2, 3, 4 and 6 of the Schedule shall not apply in the circumstances prescribed in any one or more of paragraphs (2) to [(5)][3] below.

(2) The circumstances prescribed in this paragraph are circumstances where—

(*a*) before 17th March 1987 an employee was a member of a scheme (in this paragraph and in regulation 4 referred to as "the scheme"); and

[(*b*) benefits cease to accrue to the employee under the scheme—

(i) on or after 17th March 1987 and he thereupon becomes a member of another scheme established by his employer or of a scheme established by a relevant employer; or

(ii) by reason of his secondment or posting to a foreign branch of the employer or to another employer and on or after 17th March 1987 the period of his secondment or posting ends and he thereupon becomes a member of a scheme established by the employer by whom he was seconded or posted, or by a relevant employer, and at the time of his secondment or posting he had a definite expectation that he would become a member of such a scheme; or

(iii) by reason of his unpaid absence if, within one month of returning to work, and on or after 17th March 1987, he becomes a member of a scheme established by the employer who established the scheme, or of a scheme established by a relevant employer; or

(iv) by reason of her pregnancy or confinement if, within one month of returning to work, and on or after 17th March 1987, she becomes a member of a scheme established by the employer who established the scheme, or of a scheme established by a relevant employer; or

(v) (where the circumstances are other than those specified in paragraphs (ii), (iii) and (iv)) if, within one month of benefits ceasing so to accrue, and on or after 17th March 1987, benefits again accrue to the employee under that scheme.][1]

(3) The circumstances prescribed in this paragraph are circumstances where an employee was not a member of a scheme before 17th March 1987 but is to be regarded as being a member of that scheme before that date by virtue of regulation 2(2)(*b*) of the Occupational Pension Schemes (Preservation of Benefit) Regulations 1984.

(4) The circumstances prescribed in this paragraph are circumstances where an employer was contractually bound to an employee before 17th March 1987 to provide benefits for him but a scheme had not been established before that date.

[(5) The circumstances prescribed in this paragraph are circumstances where before 17th March 1987 an employee was a member of a scheme and on or after 17th March 1987 the employee becomes a member of a scheme which provides benefits in addition to those under the scheme of which he remains a member.][2]

Amendments—[1] "(5)" in para (1), and whole of para (2)(*b*),substituted by the Occupational Pension Schemes (Transitional Provisions) (Amendment) Regulations, SI 1993/3219 regs 1, 2, 4.
[2] Para (5) added by SI 1993/3219 regs 1, 2, 4.

4—[(1)][1] Regulation 3(1) does not apply in the circumstances prescribed in regulation 3(2) [or (5)][1] so as to disapply paragraph 2 of the Schedule unless on 17th March 1987 the rules of either the scheme or the new scheme or of both schemes allowed for the accrual of benefits in excess of the rate of one-sixtieth of the employee's relevant annual remuneration for each year of service.

[(2) In paragraph (1) above "the new scheme" means another scheme established by the employer or a scheme established by a relevant employer as mentioned in regulation 3(2)(*b*)(i).][1]

Amendments—[1] Regulation renumbered as sub-s (1), words "or (5)" inserted, and para (2) added, by the Occupational Pension Schemes (Transitional Provisions) (Amendment) Regulations, SI 1993/3219 regs 1, 2, 5.

[Disapplication of paragraphs 2, 3, 4 and 6 of the Schedule—further provision][1]

[4ZA—(1) The provisions contained in paragraphs 2, 3, 4 and 6 of the Schedule shall not apply as regards an employee in the circumstances prescribed in paragraph (2) below.

(2) The circumstances prescribed in this paragraph are circumstances where—

(*a*) the employee became a member of a scheme before 17th March 1987 and remained a member until, in the circumstances specified in paragraph (3) below, he ceased to be a member, and

(*b*) by way of compensation for loss suffered, or reasonably likely to be suffered, by the employee as a result of the circumstances specified in paragraph (3) below—

(i) the employee is reinstated as a member of that scheme, or becomes a member of another scheme established by the employer or by an employer who was a relevant employer in relation to that employer, and

(ii) a capital sum is paid [on or after 1st January 1997][2] (whether or not to the trustees of the scheme) in respect of the employee.

(3) The circumstances specified in this paragraph are circumstances where, acting in reliance on bad investment advice at least some of which was given during the period beginning with 29th April 1988 and ending with 30th June 1994, the employee—

(*a*) ceased to be a member of, or to pay contributions to, the scheme and instead became a member of a personal pension scheme or entered into a retirement annuity contract;

(*b*) ceased to be a member of the scheme as a result of the transfer of accrued rights of his under the scheme to a personal pension scheme; or

(*c*) ceased to be a member of the scheme and instead (by virtue of such a provision as is mentioned in section 591(2)(*g*) entered into arrangements for securing relevant benefits by means of an annuity contract.

(4) In paragraph (3) above—

"bad investment advice" means investment advice in respect of which an action against the person who gave it has been, or may be, brought—

(*a*) in or for negligence;

(*b*) for breach of contract;

(*c*) by reason of a breach of a fiduciary obligation; or

[(*d*) by reason of a contravention which is actionable—

(i) under section 62 of the Financial Services Act 1986; or

(ii) under section 150 of the Financial Services and Markets Act 2000;][3]

[''investment advice''—

(*a*) in relation to a time before 1st December 2001, means advice such as is mentioned in paragraph 15 of Schedule 1 to the Financial Services Act 1986; and

(*b*) in relation to a time on or after that date, means advice such as is mentioned in Article 53 of the Financial Services and Markets Act 2000 (Regulated Activities) Order 2001;][3]

''personal pension scheme'' has the meaning given by section 630(1);

''relevant benefits'' has the meaning given by section 612(1);

''retirement annuity contract'' means a contract made before 1st July 1988 and approved by the Board under or by virtue of any provision of Chapter III of Part XIV of the Taxes Act.][1]

Amendments—[1] This regulation inserted by the Occupational Pension Schemes (Transitional Provisions) (Amendment) Regulations, SI 1996/3115 reg 4, with effect from 1 January 1997.

[2] Words in para (2)(*b*)(ii) substituted by Occupational Pension Schemes (Transitional Provisions) (Amendment No 2) Regulations, SI 1996/3234, with effect from 1 January 1997.

[3] In para (4), sub-para (*d*) in definition of ''bad investment advice'' substituted, and definition of ''investment advice'' substituted, by the Financial Services and Markets Act 2000 (Consequential Amendments) (Taxes) Order, SI 2001/3629 art 119 with effect from 1 December 2001, immediately after the coming into force of the Financial Services and Markets Act 2000 ss 411, 432(1), Sch 20 (and SI 2001/3629 Pts 1 and 2).

[Modifications of paragraphs 2 and 9 of the Schedule][1]

4A—(1) In the circumstances prescribed in paragraph (2) below—

(*a*) paragraph 2(2) of the Schedule shall be modified so that the reference to any contrary provision in the rules of the scheme does not include a reference to a provision in the rules allowing a pension to be increased, in accordance with the rules of the scheme, to take account of increases in the cost of living or the general level of earnings;

(*b*) paragraph 9 of the Schedule shall be modified so as to provide in addition that references in the Schedule to ''service'' (other than in relation to the expression ''pensionable service'') shall be deemed to include service that would have been included if the employee had remained in employment until the date specified in the rules of the scheme as the date at which the employee would normally have retired.

(2) The circumstances prescribed in this paragraph are circumstances where an employee takes retirement before his normal retirement date as a result of physical or mental deterioration which is sufficiently serious to prevent him from following his normal employment or which seriously impairs his earning capacity.][1]

Amendments—[1] This regulation inserted by the Occupational Pension Schemes (Transitional Provisions) (Amendment) Regulations, SI 1993/3219 regs 1, 2, 6 with effect from 17 March 1987.

Modification of paragraph 2 of the Schedule

5—(1) In the circumstances prescribed in paragraph (2) below, paragraph 2 of the Schedule shall apply with the modifications prescribed in paragraph (3) below.

(2) The circumstances prescribed in this paragraph are circumstances where a pension attributable to a transfer payment is provided for an employee in respect of service with a former employer of his other than a relevant employer.

(3) The modifications prescribed in this paragraph are that—

(*a*) in paragraph 2 of the Schedule at the end of sub-paragraph (2) there shall be added the words—

''(excluding any pension attributable to a transfer payment provided for the employee in respect of service with a former employer of his other than a relevant employer)'';

and

(*b*) after that sub-paragraph there shall be added the following sub-paragraph—

''(3) In this paragraph a 'relevant employer' has the same meaning as in the Occupational Pension Schemes (Transitional Provisions) Regulations 1988.''.

[5A—(1) In the circumstances prescribed in paragraph (2) below, paragraph 2(2) of the Schedule shall be modified so that the reference to any contrary provision in the rules of the scheme does not include a reference to a provision in the rules allowing a pension to be increased, in accordance with the rules of the scheme, to take account of increases in the cost of living or the general level of earnings.

(2) The circumstances prescribed in this paragraph are circumstances, other than those prescribed in paragraph (2) of regulation 4A, where an employee retires with an immediate pension at or before his normal retirement date.][1]

Amendments—[1] This regulation inserted by the Occupational Pension Schemes (Transitional Provisions) (Amendment) Regulations, SI 1993/3219 regs 1, 2, 7 with effect from 17 March 1987.

[5B—(1) In the circumstances prescribed in paragraph (2) below, paragraph 2(2) of the Schedule shall be modified so that the reference to any contrary provision in the rules of the scheme does not include a reference to a provision in the rules allowing a pension to be increased, in accordance with the rules of the scheme, to take account of increases in the cost of living or the general level of earnings.

(2) The circumstances prescribed in this paragraph are circumstances, other than those prescribed in paragraph (2) of regulation 4A, where an employee leaves pensionable service with an entitlement to a pension from a future date.][1]

Amendments—[1] This regulation inserted by the Occupational Pension Schemes (Transitional Provisions) (Amendment) Regulations, SI 1993/3219 regs 1, 2, 7 with effect from 17 March 1987.

[**5C**—(1) In the circumstances prescribed in paragraph (2) below, paragraph 2(2) of the Schedule shall be modified—

(*a*) so that the reference to any contrary provision in the rules of the scheme does not include a reference to a provision in the rules allowing a pension to be increased, in accordance with the rules of the scheme, to take account of increases in the cost of living or the general level of earnings; and

(*b*) so as to substitute for the reference to a pension exceeding one-thirtieth of the employee's relevant annual remuneration for each year of service up to a maximum of 20 a reference to a pension of the greatest of—

(i) one-thirtieth of his relevant annual remuneration for each year of service up to a maximum of 20,

(ii) one-thirtieth of his relevant annual remuneration for each year of service at the normal retirement date up to a maximum of 20, increased on an actuarial basis in respect of the period from the normal retirement date to the date the payment of the pension commenced,

(iii) one-thirtieth of his relevant annual remuneration for each year of service at the normal retirement date up to a maximum of 20, increased in accordance with the rules of the scheme to take account of increases in the cost of living or general level of earnings from the normal retirement date to the date the payment of the pension commenced, and

(iv) where the employee's total service has exceeded 40 years, the aggregate of one-sixtieth of his relevant annual remuneration for each year of service before the normal retirement date up to a maximum of 40, and of a further one-sixtieth of his relevant annual remuneration for each year of service in respect of the period from the normal retirement date to the date the payment of the pension commenced, subject to an overall maximum of 45 years of service.

(2) The circumstances prescribed in this paragraph are circumstances where an employee continues in service after his normal retirement date.][1]

Amendments—[1] This regulation inserted by the Occupational Pension Schemes (Transitional Provisions) (Amendment) Regulations, SI 1993/3219 regs 1, 2, 7 with effect from 17 March 1987.

[**5D**—(1) In the circumstances prescribed in paragraph (2) below, paragraph 2(2) of the Schedule shall be modified so as to include in the reference to service a reference to service with a relevant employer.

(2) The circumstances prescribed in this paragraph are circumstances where a pension attributable to a transfer payment is provided to an employee in respect of service with a former employer of his who is a relevant employer.][1]

Amendments—[1] This regulation inserted by the Occupational Pension Schemes (Transitional Provisions) (Amendment) Regulations, SI 1993/3219 regs 1, 2, 7 with effect from 17 March 1987.

Disapplication of paragraphs 3, 4, 6 and 7 of the Schedule

6—(1) The provisions contained in paragraphs 3, 4, 6 and 7 of the Schedule shall not apply in the circumstances prescribed in either or both of paragraphs (2) and (4) below.

(2) The circumstances prescribed in this paragraph are circumstances where, subject to paragraph (3) below, the amount of an employee's total pension is not more than £104 a year [or such higher amount as may be prescribed by regulations made under paragraph 15(4) of Schedule 16 to the Social Security Act 1973][1].

(3) In a case where the pension is secured in part by voluntary contributions paid by the employee paragraph 7 shall apply unless the aggregate of the benefits secured for the employee by—

(*a*) the voluntary contributions, and

(*b*) all schemes established by his employer or to which his employer has contributed,

are commuted.

(4) The circumstances prescribed in this paragraph are circumstances where—

(*a*) the rules of a scheme provide that the trustees or administrator of the scheme have power to commute, in whole or in part, the pension secured for an employee if he is in exceptional circumstances of serious ill health, and

(*b*) the trustees or administrator have exercised such power in relation to the employee.

Amendments—[1] Words added by the Occupational Pension Schemes (Transitional Provisions) (Amendment) Regulations, SI 1993/3219 regs 1, 2, 8 with effect from 17 March 1987.

Disapplication of paragraph 5(2) of the Schedule

7—(1) The provision contained in paragraph 5(2) of the Schedule shall not apply in circumstances where—

(*a*) a charge to income tax under Schedule E on an employee arises from the acquisition or disposal of shares or an interest in shares or from a right to acquire shares, and

(*b*) the shares or interest in shares were acquired, or the right to acquire the shares was granted, before 17th March 1987.

(2) For the purposes of this regulation "share" includes stock and this regulation applies in relation to any security (as defined in section 254(1)) issued by a body corporate as it applies to a share in that body corporate.

Disapplication of paragraph 5(3) of the Schedule

8 The provision contained in paragraph 5(3) of the Schedule shall not apply in circumstances where an employee within paragraph (*a*) of sub-paragraph (3) of that paragraph ceased to be a controlling director before 17th March 1987.

Modification of paragraph 5(3) and (4) of the Schedule

9—(1) In the circumstances prescribed in paragraph (2) below, paragraphs 5(3) and (4) of the Schedule shall apply with the modifications prescribed in paragraph (3) below.

(2) The circumstances prescribed in this paragraph are circumstances where the relevant annual remuneration of an employee within paragraph 5(3)(*b*) of the Schedule exceeds the permitted maximum.

(3) The modifications prescribed in this paragraph are that—

(*a*) at the end of paragraph 5(3) of the Schedule there shall be added the words—

"or, in the case of an employee within paragraph (*b*), the permitted maximum if greater"; and

(*b*) in paragraph 5(4) of the Schedule—

(i) for the word "higher" there shall be substituted "highest",

(ii) at the end of paragraph (*a*) the word "and" shall be omitted, and

(iii) at the end of paragraph (*b*) there shall be inserted the words "and, (*c*) the permitted maximum".

Disapplication of paragraph 7 of the Schedule

10—(1) The provisions contained in paragraph 7 of the Schedule shall not apply in the circumstances prescribed in this regulation.

(2) The circumstances prescribed in this regulation are circumstances where—

(*a*) before 8th April 1987 an employee had entered into arrangements for the payment of voluntary contributions (in this paragraph referred to as "the original arrangements"); and

(*b*) on or after that date—

(i) the employee (having ceased to pay voluntary contributions whether or not on or after that date)—

(*a*) recommences to pay such contributions under the original arrangements, or

(*b*) commences to pay such contributions under other arrangements provision for which is made by the rules of a scheme established by his employer; or

(ii) the employee ceases to pay voluntary contributions under the original arrangements and commences to pay such contributions under arrangements provision for which is made by the rules of a scheme established by a relevant employer; or

(iii) any one or more of the terms of the original arrangements in relation to—

(*a*) the amount of the voluntary contributions,

(*b*) the date on which such contributions are paid, or

(*c*) the manner in which such contributions are invested,

is varied.

Authorisation of the Board to direct

11 This regulation authorises the Board to direct that the Schedule or any provision of it shall not apply in any particular case where in the opinion of the Board the facts are such that its application would not be appropriate.

Effect of Regulations and of directions made under regulation 11

12 These Regulations—

(*a*) [except for regulation 4ZA,][1] shall take effect as from 17th March 1987, and

(*b*) authorise any direction given under regulation 11 to take effect as from 17th March 1987 or any later date.

Amendments—[1] Words in para (*a*) inserted by Occupational Pension Schemes (Transitional Provisions) (Amendment) Regulations, SI 1996/3115 reg 5 with effect from 1 January 1997.

1989/469
Personal Equity Plan Regulations 1989

Made by the Treasury under TA 1988 s 333 and CGTA 1979 s 149D, now TCGA 1992 s 151; see TCGA 1992 Sch 11 para 29

Made . . . . 14 March 1989
Laid before the House of Commons . . . . . 14 March 1989
Coming into Force . . . . 6 April 1989

Commentary—*Simon's Direct Tax Service* **Division E3.3**.
Revenue & other press releases—IR Tax Bulletin April 1997 p 418 (explains the rules incorporated into these Regulations whereby certain shares received when a building society or insurance company transfers its business to a company may be transferred into a PEP).

ARRANGEMENT OF REGULATIONS

Citation and commencement

1 These Regulations may be cited as the Personal Equity Regulations 1989 and shall come into force on 6th April 1989.

Interpretation

2—(1) In these Regulations unless the context otherwise requires—

(*a*)

[''approved profit sharing scheme'' [has][12] the same meaning as in Chapter IV of Part V of the Taxes Act;][1]

''the Board'' means the Commissioners of Inland Revenue;

[''building society'' means a building society within the meaning of the Building Societies Act 1986, or the Irish Building Societies Act 1989;][13]

[''company'', except in regulation 6(4), means any body corporate having a share capital other than—

(i) an open-ended investment company, within the meaning given by section [236 of the Financial Services and Markets Act 2000][18],
(ii) a UCITS,
(iii) an industrial and provident society, or
(iv) a body corporate which is a 51 per cent subsidiary of any industrial and provident society;][13]

[''deposit-taker'' has the meaning given by section 481(2) of the Taxes Act;][6]

[''EEA Agreement'' means the Agreement on the European Economic Area signed at Oporto on 2nd May 1992 as adjusted by the Protocol signed at Brussels on 17th March 1993;][5]

[''EEA State'' means a State, other than the United Kingdom, which is a Contracting Party to the EEA Agreement;][5]

[''European institution'' means an EEA firm of the kind mentioned in paragraph 5(*a*), (*b*) or (*c*) of Schedule 3 to the Financial Services and Markets Act 2000 which is an authorised person for the purposes of that Act as a result of qualifying for authorisation under paragraph 12 of that Schedule;][18]

[''51 per cent subsidiary'' and ''75 per cent subsidiary'' have the meaning given by section 838 of the Taxes Act;][4]

[''the former regulation 4(2A)'' and ''the former regulation 4A(2)'' mean, respectively, the former provisions of these Regulations bearing those numbers, as they had effect immediately before the coming into force of the Personal Equity Plan (Amendment) Regulations 2001;][15]

''gains'' means ''chargeable gains'' within the meaning of the [Taxation of Chargeable Gains Act 1992][7];

[''gilt-edged securities'' has the meaning given by paragraphs 1 and 1A of Schedule 9 to the Taxation of Chargeable Gains Act 1992;][15]

[an ''industrial and provident society'' means a society registered or deemed to be registered under the Industrial and Provident Societies Act 1965 or under the Industrial and Provident Societies (Northern Ireland) Act 1969;][15]

...[14]

''investment trust'' has the same meaning as in section 842 of the Taxes Act[, and references to the 'eligible rental income' of an investment trust have the same meaning as in that section][12];

''the Management Act'' means the Taxes Management Act 1970;

''market value'' shall be construed in accordance with [section 272 of the Taxation of Chargeable Gains Act 1992][7];

''notice'' means notice in writing and ''notify'' shall be construed accordingly;

...[14]

[a ''plan investment'' is an investment under the plan which is a qualifying investment for plans within the meaning of regulation 6;][13]

a ''plan investor'' is an individual who subscribes to a plan and who is a qualifying individual within the meaning of regulation 7;

a ''plan manager'' is a person who fulfils the conditions of these Regulations and is approved by the Board for the purposes of these Regulations as a plan manager;

...[14]

[''qualifying distribution'' has the same meaning as in section 832(1) of the Taxes Act;][15]

''recognised stock exchange'' has the same meaning as in section 841 of the Taxes Act;

[''release date'' has the meaning given by section 187(2) of the Taxes Act;][3]

[''relevant authorised person'' has the same meaning as in section 333A(12) of the Taxes Act;][5]

[''savings-related share option scheme'' has the meaning given by paragraph 1 of Schedule 9 to the Taxes Act;][3]

[''security'' means[, except in regulations 6(2)(*c*) to (*e*) and 27(3),][12] any loan stock or similar security of a company whether secured or unsecured;][4]

''share'' includes stock;

...[14]

...[14]

''tax'' where neither income tax nor capital gains tax is specified means either of those taxes;

''tax credit'' means a credit under section 231 of the Taxes Act;

''year'' means a year beginning with 6th April in any year and ending with 5th April in the following year;

''the Taxes Act'' means the Income and Corporation Taxes Act 1988.

...[2]

[(*b*)

[''authorised fund'' means—

(i) an authorised unit trust, or
(ii) an open-ended investment company with variable capital incorporated in the United Kingdom in the case of which an authorisation order made by the Financial Services Authority under regulation 14 of the Open-Ended Investment Companies Regulations 2001 is in force;][18]

''authorised unit trust'' means a unit trust scheme in the case of which an authorisation order made by [the Financial Services Authority][10] under section [243 of the Financial Services and Markets Act 2000][18] is in force;

[a "Chapter 5 UCITS" means—

(i) in relation to any time on or before 12th February 2007, a UCITS complying with Chapter 5 of the Collective Investment Schemes Sourcebook or Chapter 5 of the New Collective Investment Schemes Sourcebook, and

(ii) in relation to any time after 12th February 2007, a UCITS complying with Chapter 5 of the New Collective Investment Schemes Sourcebook;][21]

["the Collective Investment Schemes Sourcebook" means the sourcebook of that name made by the Financial Services Authority under the Financial Services and Markets Act 2000;][19]

["depositary interest" means the rights of the person mentioned in paragraph (*b*), under a certificate or other record (whether or not in the form of a document) acknowledging—

(*a*) that a person holds relevant investments or evidence of the right to them, and

(*b*) that another person is entitled to rights in or in relation to those or identical relevant investments, including the right to receive such investments, or evidence of the right to them or the proceeds from such investments, from the person mentioned in paragraph (*a*).

In this definition "relevant investments" means investments [which are exclusively qualifying investments for plans falling within any of regulation 6(2)(*a*) to (*j*) and (*l*);][12] and the reference to rights in paragraph (*b*) of this definition is a reference to rights which are exclusively rights in or in relation to relevant investments;][11]

["the first condition", and references to the terms of a scheme complying with that condition, mean that the terms of the scheme do not permit any of the investments [of the scheme, or subject to the trusts of the scheme, to consist of units in, or shares of, authorised funds or parts of umbrella schemes which are not securities schemes [, warrant schemes or Chapter 5 UCITS;][21];][18]][15]

["fund of funds scheme"] means—

(i) an [authorised fund][18] which according to the terms of the scheme is a [fund of funds scheme][18] belonging to the category under that name established by [the Financial Services Authority][10], and

(ii) a part of an umbrella scheme which the terms of the scheme identify as a part that would belong to that category if it were itself an [authorised fund][18],

where, in either case, the terms of the scheme [comply with the first condition or the second condition;][12]

["the New Collective Investment Schemes Sourcebook" means the sourcebook of that name made by the Financial Services Authority under the Financial Services Markets Act 2000;][21]

[a "relevant UCITS" means—

(i) a UCITS, situated in a member state other than the United Kingdom, which has been authorised by the competent authorities of the member state in which it is situated, and which is a "recognised scheme" by virtue of section [264 of the Financial Services and Markets Act 2000][18], and

(ii) a part of a UCITS mentioned in paragraph (i), which would be a part of [an umbrella scheme, if the definition of "umbrella scheme" and a part thereof][18] applied to a relevant UCITS,

...[19]

["the second condition", and references to the terms of a scheme complying with that condition, mean that the terms of the scheme only permit any of the investments [of the scheme, or subject to the trusts of the scheme,][18] to consist of units or shares in—

(i) a collective investment scheme which is a "recognised scheme" by virtue of section [270 or 272 of the Financial Services and Markets Act 2000][18], or

[(ii) a part of a scheme mentioned in paragraph (i) which would be a part of an umbrella scheme if the definition of "umbrella scheme" and a part thereof applied to a scheme mentioned in paragraph (i),

where the terms of the scheme mentioned in paragraph (i) identify that scheme, or the part thereof, as the case may be, as a scheme or part that would belong to one of the categories of securities scheme[, warrant scheme or Chapter 5 UCITS][21], if that scheme or part, as the case may be, were independently an authorised fund;][18]][15]

["securities scheme" means—

(i) an authorised fund which according to the terms of the scheme is a securities scheme belonging to the category under that name established by the Financial Services Authority, and

(ii) a part of an umbrella scheme which the terms of the scheme identify as a part which would belong to that category if it were itself an authorised fund;][18]

["UCITS" means undertakings for collective investment in transferable securities within the meaning of Article 1 of [Council Directive 85/611/EEC, as last amended by European Parliament and Council Directive 2001/108/EC][20], and references to—

(i) "the member state in which a UCITS is situated", and

(ii) a UCITS which has been "authorised by the competent authorities of the member state in which it is situated" shall have the same meanings as in Articles 3 and 4 respectively of that Directive;][15]

[''umbrella scheme'' means an authorised fund which according to the terms of the scheme is an umbrella scheme belonging to the category under that name established by the Financial Services Authority, and

(i) in the case of an authorised fund which is an authorised unit trust, references to a part of an umbrella scheme shall be construed in accordance with subsection (8) of section 468 of the Taxes Act, and, in relation to a part of an umbrella scheme, references to investments subject to the trusts of an authorised unit trust and to a unit holder shall be construed in accordance with subsection (9) of that section, and

(ii) in the case of an authorised fund which is an open-ended investment company, references to a part of an umbrella scheme shall be construed in accordance with subsection (18) of section 468 of the Taxes Act as that subsection is added in relation to open-ended investment companies by regulation 10(4) of the 1997 Regulations, and, in relation to a part of an umbrella scheme, references to investments of the company shall be construed in accordance with subsection (12) of that section as so added;][18]

''unit holder'', except in relation to a part of an umbrella scheme, has the meaning given by subsection (6) of section 468 of the Taxes Act;

''unit trust scheme'' has the meaning given by subsection (6) of section 468 of the Taxes Act;

''units'', in relation to an authorised unit trust, means the rights or interests (however described) of the unit holders in that authorised unit trust and, in relation to a part of an umbrella scheme, means the rights or interests for the time being of the unit holders in that part;][8]

[''units in, or shares of, a ...[19] UCITS'' means the rights or interests (however described) of the holders of the units or shares in that ...[19] UCITS;][15]

[''warrant scheme'' means—

(i) an authorised fund which according to the terms of the scheme is a warrant scheme belonging to the category under that name established by the Financial Services Authority, and

(ii) a part of an umbrella scheme which the terms of the scheme identify as a part that would belong to that category if it were itself an authorised fund;][18]

[(*c*)

''open-ended investment company'' [except in sub-paragraph (*a*)][12] has the meaning given by subsection (10) of section 468 of the Taxes Act as that subsection is added in relation to open-ended investment companies by regulation 10(4) of the 1997 Regulations;

...[18]

''shares'' in relation to an open-ended investment company, includes shares of any class and of any denomination of a given class and, in relation to a part of an [umbrella scheme][18], means shares in the company which confer for the time being rights in that part;

...[18]

''the 1997 Regulations'' means the Open-ended Investment Companies (Tax) Regulations 1997.][9]

(2) The Table below indexes other definitions in these Regulations—

[*Term defined*	*Regulation*
Annual claim	20
...[16]	...[16]
Interim claim	19
...[16]	...[16]
...[16]	...[16]
Plan	4(1)
...[16]	...[16]
Qualifying individual	7
Qualifying investments for plans[17]	6[(1)][17]
...[16]	...[16]
Qualifying securities	6(2)[(*b*)][17]
...[16]	...[16]][4]

Amendments—[1] Definition of ''approved profit sharing scheme'' in para (1)(*a*) inserted by the Personal Equity Plan (Amendment) Regulations, SI 1990/678 reg 3, with effect from 6 April 1990.

[2] Definition of ''the 1986 Regulations'' in para (1)(*a*) revoked by the Personal Equity Plan (Amendment) Regulations, SI 1991/733 reg 3, with effect from 6 April 1991.

[3] Definitions of ''release date'', and ''savings-related share option scheme inserted by SI 1991/2774 reg 3, with effect from 1 January 1992.

[4] Definitions of ''51 per cent subsidiary'' and ''75 per cent subsidiary'', and ''security'' inserted, and table in para (2) (as substituted by SI 1991/2774) substituted by the Personal Equity Plan (Amendment) Regulations, SI 1995/1539 reg 3(1), (2) with effect from 6 July 1995.

[5] Definitions of ''EEA Agreement'', ''EEA State'', ''European institution'' and ''relevant authorised person'' inserted by the Personal Equity Plan (Amendment No 2) Regulations, SI 1995/3287 reg 3(*a*), (*b*) with effect from 9 January 1996.

[6] Definition of ''deposit-taker'' in para (1)(*a*) inserted by the Personal Pension Plan (Amendment) Regulations, SI 1996/846 reg 3(1)(*a*), (*c*) with effect from 6 April 1996.

[7] Words in the definitions of ''gains'' and ''market value'' substituted by SI 1996/846, reg 3(1)(*d*), (*e*) with effect from 6 April 1996.

[8] Para (1)(*b*) substituted by SI 1997/1716 reg 3(2) with effect from 8 August 1997.

[9] Para (1)(*c*) added by the Personal Equity Plan (Amendment No 2) Regulations, SI 1997/1716 reg 3(3) with effect from 8 August 1997.

[10] Words in para (1)(*b*), (*c*) substituted by the Personal Equity Plan (Amendment) Regulations, SI 1998/1869 reg 3 with effect from 21 August 1998.
[11] Definition of "depositary interest" in para (1)(*b*) inserted by the Personal Equity Plan (Amendment) Regulations, SI 2000/3109 reg 3 with effect from 13 December 2000.
[12] In para (1)(*a*), word in the definition of "approved profit sharing scheme" substituted for "and 'approved share option scheme' have"; and words in the definitions of "investment trust" and "security" added, in para (1)(*b*), words in the definition of "fund of funds" and "depositary interest" substituted, and in para (1)(*c*), the words "except in sub-paragraph (*a*)" inserted, by the Personal Equity Plan (Amendment) Regulations, SI 2001/923 reg 3 with effect from 6 April 2001.
[13] Definitions of "building society", "company" and "plan investment" in para (1)(*a*) substituted by SI 2001/923 reg 3(2) with effect from 6 April 2001.
[14] Definitions of "general plan", "ordinary share", "portfolio", "single company plan", and "venture capital trust" in para (1)(*a*) revoked by SI 2001/923 reg 3(2)(*c*) with effect from 6 April 2001.
[15] In para (1)(*a*), definitions of "the former regulation 4(2A)" and "the former regulation 4A(2)", "gilt-edged securities", "industrial and provident society", and "qualifying distribution"; and in para (1)(*b*), definitions of "the first condition", "the second condition", "relevant UCITS", "UCITS", "units in, or shares of, a relevant UCITS", "warrant company", and "warrant fund" inserted by SI 2001/923 reg 3 with effect from 6 April 2001.
[16] Words in table in para (2) revoked by SI 2001/923 reg 3(5) with effect from 6 April 2001.
[17] Words and references in table in para (2) substituted by SI 2001/923 with effect from 6 April 2001.
[18] In sub-para (1)(*a*), words in the definition of "company" substituted, definition of "European institution" substituted; in sub-para (1)(*b*), definition of "authorised fund" inserted, words in definitions of "authorised unit trust", "the first condition", "the second condition", and "relevant UCITS" substituted, definition of "fund of funds scheme" substituted for definition of "fund of funds", definition of "securities scheme" substituted for definition of "securities fund", definition of "umbrella scheme" substituted, definition of "warrant scheme" substituted for definitions of "warrant company" and "warrant fund"; in sub-para (1)(*c*), definitions of "securities company" and "umbrella company" revoked, and words in the definition of "shares" substituted, by the Financial Services and Markets Act 2000 (Consequential Amendments) (Taxes) Order, SI 2001/3629 arts 120, 121 with effect from 1 December 2001, immediately after the coming into force of the Financial Services and Markets Act 2000 ss 411, 432(1), Sch 20 (and SI 2001/3629 Pts 1 and 2).
[19] In para (1)(*b*), definitions of "a Chapter 5 UCITS", and "the Collective Investment Schemes Sourcebook" inserted, words in the definition of a "relevant UCITS" revoked, and word "relevant" in definition of "units in, or shares of, a relevant UCITS" revoked, by the PEP (Amendment) Regulations, SI 2003/2748 regs 2, 3 with effect from 17 November 2003.
[20] In para (1)(*b*), words in definition of "UCITS" substituted by the Collective Investment Schemes (Miscellaneous Amendments) Regulations, SI 2003/2066 reg 13 with effect from 13 February 2004.
[21] In para (1)(*b*), definition of "the New Collective Investment Schemes Sourcebook" inserted; definition of a "Chapter 5 UCITS" substituted; in the definition of "the first condition", words substituted for the words "or warrant schemes;"; and in the definition of "the second condition", words substituted for the words "or warrant scheme", by the PEP (Amendment) Regulations, SI 2004/1676 with effect from 22 July 2004.
The definition of a "Chapter 5 UCITS" previously read as follows—

"a 'Chapter 5 UCITS' means a UCITS complying with Chapter 5 of the Collective Investment Schemes Sourcebook;".

Introductory

3 These Regulations provide—

(*a*) for the setting up of plans by plan managers approved by the Board under which individuals may make certain investments, for the conditions under which they may invest and under which those plans are to operate, for relief from tax in respect of plan investments and generally for the administration of tax in relation to plans, ...[1]
(*b*) ...[1]

Amendments—[1] Para (*b*) and the preceding word "and" revoked by the Personal Equity Plan (Amendment) Regulations, SI 1990/678 reg 4 and Schedule, with effect from 6 April 1990.

General conditions for plans and subscriptions to plans

4—(1) A plan is a scheme of investment to which an individual who is a qualifying individual may subscribe [before 6 April 1999][7] and in respect of which ...[2] the following [condition][8] must be fulfilled—

(*aa*) ...[9]
(a) that it is the only [general plan, or as the case may be the only single company plan,]3 to which the qualifying individual subscribes in any year;[9]
[(b) that it is a plan to which only one qualifying individual [subscribed][8]*;]*[1]
(c) that, subject to paragraph (2) and, in the case of a single company plan, to regulation 4A(2), it is a plan to which the qualifying individual subscribes only by payment directly to the plan manager of a sum or sums of the individual's cash which do not in the aggregate exceed the subscription limit, or in the case of a single company plan one half of the subscription limit, in any year.[9]

(2)–(4) ...[10]

(5) A plan must be managed in accordance with these Regulations by a plan manager and under terms agreed in writing between the plan manager and the plan investor.

(6) Apart from other requirements of these Regulations the terms agreed to which paragraph (5) refers shall include the following conditions—

(*a*) that the plan investments shall be in the beneficial ownership of the plan investor;
(*b*) that the title to the plan investments shall be vested in the plan manager or his nominee or jointly in one of them and the plan investor;
(*c*) that[, where a share certificate or other document evidencing title to a plan investment is issued, it][5] shall be held by the plan manager or as he may direct;

[(*d*) that the plan manager shall, if the plan investor so elects, arrange for the plan investor to receive a copy of the annual report and accounts issued to investors by every company, unit trust, open-ended investment company or other entity in which he has plan investments;][6]

[(*e*) that the plan manager shall be under an obligation (subject to any provisions made under any other enactment and if the plan investor so elects) to arrange for the plan investor to be able—

(i) to attend any meetings of investors in companies, unit trusts, open-ended investment companies and other entities in which he has plan investments,

(ii) to vote, and

(iii) to receive, in addition to the documents referred to in sub-paragraph (*d*), any other information issued to investors in such companies, unit trusts, open-ended investment companies and other entities;][6]

[(*ea*) that the plan manager shall satisfy himself that any person to whom he delegates any of his functions or responsibilities under the terms agreed with the plan investor is competent to carry out those functions or responsibilities;][4]

(*f*) that at the request of the plan investor and within such time as shall be agreed[—

(i) a plan, with all rights and obligations of the parties to it, or

(ii) such parts thereof as may be agreed between the plan investor and the plan manager,][8]

may be transferred to another plan manager;

(*g*) that the plan manager shall notify the plan investor if by reason of any failure to satisfy the provisions of these Regulations a plan has or will become void.

Amendments—[1] Para (1)(*b*) substituted by the Personal Equity Plan (Amendment) Regulations, SI 1990/678 reg 5, with effect from 6 April 1990.

[2] Words in para (1) revoked by the Personal Equity Plan (Amendment) Regulations, SI 1991/733 reg 4, with effect from 6 April 1991.

[3] Words in para (1)(*a*) substituted by the Personal Equity Plan (Amendment No 2) Regulations, SI 1991/2774 reg 4.

[4] Para (6)(*ea*) inserted by the Personal Equity Plan (Amendment) Regulations, SI 1993/756 reg 4, with effect from 6 April 1993.

[5] Words in para (6)(*c*) substituted, for the words "the share certificate or other document evidencing title to a plan investment", by the Personal Equity Plan (Amendment No 2) Regulations, SI 1997/1716 reg 4(2)(*a*) with effect from 8 August 1997.

[6] Para (6)(*d*), (*e*) substituted by the Personal Equity Plan (Amendment No 2) Regulations, SI 1997/1716 reg 4(2)(*b*) with effect from 8 August 1997.

[7] Words in para (1) inserted by the Personal Equity Plan (Amendment) Regulations, SI 1998/1869 reg 4 with effect from 21 August 1998.

[8] Words in paras (1), (6)(*f*) substituted by the Personal Equity Plan (Amendment) Regulations, SI 2001/923 reg 4(2) with effect from 6 April 2001.

[9] Para (1)(*aa*), (*a*), (*c*) revoked by SI 2001/923 reg 4(2)(*b*), subject to SI 2001/923 reg 14, with effect from 6 April 2001. SI 2001/923 reg 14 states that the revocation of para (1)(*a*), (*c*) shall not affect any right to treat a plan as void or other penalty or liability relating to events before 6 April 2001.

[10] Paras (2)–(4) revoked by SI 2001/923 reg 4(3) with effect from 6 April 2001. The former para (2A), which is referred to throughout these regulations, read as follows—

"(2A) The circumstances specified in this paragraph are where—

(*a*) in pursuance of a public offer, an application is made by the qualifying individual for the allotment or allocation to him of shares in a company which are [qualifying investments for general plans or, as the case may be, qualifying investments for single company plans within the meaning of regulation 6B(2)], and shares are allotted or allocated to him in consequence of that application; or

(*b*) in connection with the transfer of the whole of the business of a building society ("the society") to a company which has share capital ("the successor company") in accordance with section 97 and the other applicable provisions of the Building Societies Act 1986 shares in the successor company which satisfy the conditions prescribed by paragraph (2B) are allotted or allocated to the qualifying individual by virtue of his being at a relevant time a member of the society or an employee, former employee or pensioner of the society or of a company which is a wholly-owned subsidiary of the society—

(i) in priority to other persons, or

(ii) for consideration of an amount or value lower than the market price of the shares, or

(iii) free, or

(*c*) in connection with the transfer of the whole or part of the business of a mutual insurance company ("the mutual") to a company which has share capital ("the acquiring company") under a scheme to which Schedule 2C to the Insurance Companies Act 1982 applies, or (on the assumption, where it is not in fact the case, that the mutual is carrying on business through a branch in the United Kingdom) would apply but for section 15(1A) of that Act, shares in a company which is either the acquiring company or a company of which the acquiring company is a wholly-owned subsidiary, and which satisfy the conditions prescribed by paragraph (2B), are allotted or allocated to the qualifying individual by virtue of his being at a relevant time a member of the mutual or an employee, former employee or pensioner of the mutual or of a company which is a wholly-owned subsidiary of the mutual—

(i) in priority to other persons, or

(ii) for consideration of an amount or value lower than the market price of the shares, or

(iii) free.".

[Special conditions for single company plans

4A ...[1]

Amendments—[1] This regulation revoked by the Personal Equity Plan (Amendment) Regulations, SI 2001/923 reg 5 with effect from 6 April 2001. The former para (2), which is referred to in these regulations, read as follows—

"(2) Subject to the conditions prescribed by paragraph (3), a single company plan fulfils the condition in regulation 4(1)(*c*) if the qualifying individual subscribes to it by the transfer to the plan manager, or a nominee for the plan manager, of shares in the designated company which the qualifying individual has exercised the right to acquire, or which have been appropriated to the qualifying individual, in accordance with the provisions of a savings-related share option scheme or an approved profit-sharing scheme.".

General investment rules

[5—(1) All transactions by way of purchase by a plan manager of investments under a plan shall be made—

[(*a*) in the case of an authorised fund which is a dual priced unit trust, at the manager's price for the sale of the relevant class of units within the meaning of, and complying with the requirements of, rule 15.4.4 of the Collective Investment Schemes Sourcebook;][10]

[(*b*) in the case of an authorised fund which is a single priced unit trust or an open-ended investment company, at the price of a unit or share within the meaning of, and complying with the requirements of, rule 4.3.11 of the Collective Investment Schemes Sourcebook; and][10]

(*c*) in the case of all other plan investments, at the price for which those investments might reasonably be expected to be purchased in the open market.][7]

[(1ZA) In paragraph (1)(*a*) and (*b*)—

...[11]

''a dual priced unit trust'' means an authorised unit trust in respect of which the manager gives different prices for buying and selling units at the same time;

''a single priced unit trust'' means an authorised unit trust in respect of which the manager gives the same price for buying and selling units at the same time.][10]

[(1A) All other transactions by way of sale or otherwise by a plan manager in investments under a plan shall be made at the price for which those investments might reasonably be expected to be sold or otherwise transacted, as the case may be, in the open market.][7]

(2) Investments, or rights in respect of investments, may not at any time—

(*a*) be purchased or made otherwise than out of cash which a plan manager holds ...[1] under a plan at that time; or

(*b*) be purchased from—

(i) a plan investor, or

(ii) the spouse of a plan investor,

so as to become plan investments under a plan to which the plan investor subscribes or has subscribed.

[(3) [Subject to paragraph (3A),][5] a plan investor's cash subscription and any other cash held by a plan manager under a plan shall be held only in sterling and be deposited in an account with a deposit-taker or [a deposit account or a share account with][4] a building society which is designated [as a ...[8] plan account][3] for the purposes of these Regulations only.][2]

[(3A) A plan manager who is a European institution or a relevant authorised person may hold a plan investor's cash subscription and other cash held under a plan in the currency of the EEA State in which he has his principal place of business and may deposit such cash in an account which is designated as mentioned in paragraph (3) with any person authorised under the law of that State to accept deposits.][6]

[(4) Cash by way of dividends, interest, distributions, and other rights or proceeds in respect of plan investments may be invested only in qualifying investments for plans, or by way of cash deposit in accordance with paragraphs (3) and (3A).][9]

Amendments—[1] Words in para (2)(*a*) revoked by SI 1990/678 reg 6.

[2] Para (3) substituted by the Personal Equity Plan (Amendment) Regulations, SI 1991/733 reg 5, with effect from 6 April 1991.

[3] Words in para (3) inserted by the Personal Equity Plan (Amendment No 2) Regulations, SI 1991/2774 reg 6, with effect from 1 January 1992.

[4] Words in para (3) inserted by the Personal Equity Plan (Amendment) Regulations, SI 1992/623 reg 5, with effect from 6 April 1992.

[5] Words in para (3) inserted by the Personal Equity Plan (Amendment No 2) Regulations, SI 1995/3287 reg 4, with effect from 9 January 1996.

[6] Para (3A) inserted by SI 1995/3287 reg 4.

[7] Paras (1), (1A) substituted for para (1) by the Personal Equity Plan (Amendment) Regulations, SI 2001/923 reg 6(2) with effect from 6 April 2001.

[8] Words in para (3) revoked by SI 2001/923 reg 6(3) with effect from 6 April 2001.

[9] Para (4) substituted for paras (4)–(6) by SI 2001/923 reg 6(4) with effect from 6 April 2001.

[10] Sub-para (1)(*a*), (*b*) substituted, and para (1ZA) inserted, by the Financial Services and Markets Act 2000 (Consequential Amendments) (Taxes) Order, SI 2001/3629 arts 120, 122 with effect from 1 December 2001, immediately after the coming into force of the Financial Services and Markets Act 2000 ss 411, 432(1), Sch 20 (and SI 2001/3629 Pts 1 and 2).

[11] Definition of ''the Collective Investment Schemes Sourcebook'' revoked by the PEP (Amendment) Regulations, SI 2003/2748 regs 2, 4 with effect from 17 November 2003.

[Qualifying investments

6—(1) This regulation specifies the kind of investments (''qualifying investments for plans'') which may be purchased, made or held under a plan.

(2) Qualifying investments for plans to which paragraph (1) refers are—

(*a*) shares, not being shares in an investment trust, issued by a company wherever incorporated and, subject to paragraph (3), officially listed on a recognised stock exchange;

(*b*) securities (''qualifying securities'')—

(i) issued by a company wherever incorporated,

(ii) which satisfy at least one of the conditions specified in paragraph (5) and the condition specified in paragraph (6), and

(iii) in the case of securities of an investment trust, purchased or acquired by the plan manager in circumstances where the trust satisfies the conditions specified in paragraphs (7) and (8);

(*c*) gilt-edged securities which satisfy the condition specified in paragraph (11);

(*d*) any securities issued by or on behalf of a government of any EEA State, which satisfy the condition specified in paragraph (11);

(*e*) any securities which—

(i) in relation to a security mentioned in sub-paragraph (*d*), would be a strip of that security if "strip" had the same meaning as in section 47 of the Finance Act 1942, with the omission of the words "issued under the National Loans Act 1968", and

(ii) satisfy the condition specified in paragraph (11);

(*f*) shares in an investment trust, listed in the Official List of the Stock Exchange, in circumstances where the trust satisfies the conditions specified in paragraphs (7) and (8);

[(*g*) units in, or shares of, a securities scheme or a warrant scheme, in circumstances where the [units or shares satisfy the condition specified in paragraph (13);][6][2]

(*h*) units in, or shares of, a relevant UCITS, in circumstances where the [units or shares satisfy the condition specified in paragraph (13);][6]

[(*j*) units in, or shares of, a fund of funds scheme, in circumstances where the [units or shares satisfy the condition specified in paragraph (13);][6]][2]

[(*ja*) units in, or shares of, a Chapter 5 UCITS, in circumstances where the units or shares satisfy the condition specified in paragraph (13);][4]

(*k*) a depositary interest;

(*l*) shares which—

(i) the qualifying individual exercised the right to acquire in accordance with the provisions of a savings-related share option scheme, or

(ii) were appropriated to the qualifying individual in accordance with the provisions of an approved profit sharing scheme,

where the shares were transferred to the plan manager in the circumstances specified in the former regulation 4A(2) before 6th April 1999;

(*m*) investments which—

(i) were held under the plan on 5th April 2001 (without extending to further investments of a type which was so held),

(ii) immediately before the Personal Equity Plan (Amendment) Regulations 2001 came into force on 6th April 2001, were permitted to be held under the plan by these Regulations, and which (under these Regulations as they had effect immediately before that date) would not subsequently have ceased to be permitted to be so held, and

(iii) do not fall or, having fallen, have not ceased to fall, within any of the other sub-paragraphs of this paragraph;

(*n*) cash deposited in accordance with regulation 5(3) and (3A) which a plan manager holds for the purpose of investment in investments which are qualifying investments for plans falling within any of sub-paragraphs (*a*) to (*k*).

[(*o*) investments which—

(i) were held under the plan on 28th November 2001,

(ii) on that date were admitted to trading on a recognised stock exchange in an EEA State and were not listed by a competent authority in an EEA State for the purposes of Council Directive 2001/34,

(iii) since that date have not ceased to be so admitted and have not become so listed,

(iv) do not fall within any of the other sub-paragraphs of this paragraph, and

(v) are not investments which, having fallen within any of those sub-paragraphs, have ceased so to fall on or after that date.][3]

[(*p*) investments which—

(i) were held under the plan on 6th April 2004; and

(ii) immediately before that date, fell within sub-paragraphs (*g*), (*h*) or (*j*), or sub-paragraph (*k*) so far as the relevant investments (within the meaning in the definition of "depositary interest") fell within any of those sub-paragraphs.][6]

(3) An investment in shares fulfils the condition as to official listing in paragraph (2)(*a*) or (*f*) if—

(*a*) in pursuance of a public offer, the plan manager applies for the allotment or allocation to him of shares in a company or trust which are due to be admitted to such listing within 30 days of the allocation or allotment, and which, when admitted to such listing, would be qualifying investments for plans, and

(*b*) the shares are not allotted or allocated to the plan manager in the circumstances specified in paragraph (4).

(4) The circumstances specified in this paragraph are where—

(*a*) the allotment or allocation of the shares was connected with the allotment or allocation of—

(i) shares in the company or trust of a different class, or
(ii) rights to shares in the company or trust of a different class, or
(iii) shares or rights to shares in another company or trust, or
[(iv) units in or shares in, or rights to units in or shares in, an authorised fund or a part of an umbrella scheme;][2]
(vi) securities or rights to securities of the company or trust, or of another company or trust,

to the plan manager, the plan investor or any other person; and

(*b*) the terms on which the first-mentioned shares in this paragraph were offered were significantly more favourable to the plan manager or plan investor than they would have been if their allotment or allocation had not been connected as described in sub-paragraph (*a*).

(5) The conditions specified in this paragraph are—

(*a*) that the shares in the company issuing the securities are listed on the official list of a recognised stock exchange;

(*b*) that the securities are so listed;

(*c*) that the company issuing the securities is a 75 per cent. subsidiary of a company whose shares are so listed.

(6) The condition specified in this paragraph is that, judged at the date when each of the securities is first held under the plan, the terms on which it was issued do not—

(*a*) require the loan to be repaid or the security to be repurchased or redeemed, or

(*b*) allow the holder to require the loan to be repaid or the security to be repurchased or redeemed except in circumstances which are neither certain nor likely to occur,

within the period of five years from that date.

(7) The condition specified in this paragraph is that the investment trust has no eligible rental income, in its most recent accounting period to end before the date on which the shares in, or securities of, the investment trust first become investments under the plan, provided that the shares or securities shall cease to be qualifying investments for plans if the investment trust has any eligible rental income, in subsequent accounting periods, during which the shares or securities are held.

(8) The condition specified in this paragraph is that not more than 50 per cent in value of the investments of the trust, [scheme][2] or UCITS, or investments subject to the trusts of the scheme, as the case may be, are either—

(*a*) securities which would not be qualifying securities, or

(*b*) securities which would not fall within any of sub-paragraphs (*c*) to (*e*) of paragraph (2),

if paragraph (6), or paragraph (6) as it applies with the modifications in paragraph (11), as the case may be, required the terms on which they were issued to be judged at the date when they first became investments of the trust, [scheme][2] or UCITS or, as the case may be, investments subject to the trusts of the scheme.

[(9) The condition specified in this paragraph is that not more than 50 per cent in value of the investments of the scheme, or subject to the trusts of the scheme, are—

(*a*) units in, or shares of, a securities scheme or a warrant scheme, or

(*b*) units in, or shares of, a relevant UCITS,

where the securities scheme, warrant scheme or UCITS does not satisfy the condition in paragraph (8).][2]

(10) In paragraph (4)(*a*), "company" means any body corporate having a share capital.

(11) The condition specified in this paragraph is the condition specified in paragraph (6), omitting sub-paragraph (*b*) of that paragraph and the word "or" after sub-paragraph (*a*).][1]

[(12) Qualifying investments for plans falling within sub-paragraph (*k*) of paragraph (2), so far as the relevant investments (within the meaning given in the definition of "depositary interest") fall within any of sub-paragraphs (*g*), (*h*), (*j*) or (*ja*) of that paragraph, must satisfy the condition specified in paragraph (13).][5]

[(13) The condition specified in this paragraph is that, during the period of five years from the date on which the qualifying investments in question were first held in the plan, there was no time when—

(*a*) the contract under which the investments were acquired, or any other transaction entered into at any time by the plan investor or any other person, or

(*b*) the nature of the underlying subject matter of the investments,

had the effect that the plan investor was not exposed, or not exposed to any significant extent, to the risk of loss from fluctuations in the value of the investments exceeding 5% of the capital consideration paid or payable for the acquisition of those investments.][5]

[(14) In this regulation references, in relation to qualifying investments, to—

(*a*) the underlying subject matter are references to or to the value of the investments, currencies or other matters to which, or to the value of which, those qualifying investments or their value is referable;

(*b*) the capital consideration paid include the incidental costs of acquisition; and

(*c*) the value are to be construed applying regulation 5(1A), but deducting the incidental costs that would be incurred by a disposal.][5]

Amendments—[1] Regulation substituted by the Personal Equity Plan (Amendment) Regulations, SI 2001/923 reg 7 with effect from 6 April 2001.

[2] Sub-paras 2(*g*), (*j*), and para (9) substituted, sub-para (4)(*a*)(iv) substituted for sub-paras (4)(*a*)(iv), (v), words in para (8) substituted, by the Financial Services and Markets Act 2000 (Consequential Amendments) (Taxes) Order, SI 2001/3629 arts 120, 123 with effect from 1 December 2001, immediately after the coming into force of the Financial Services and Markets Act 2000 ss 411, 432(1), Sch 20 (and SI 2001/3629 Pts 1 and 2).

[3] Sub-para (2)(*o*) added by the Personal Equity Plan (Amendment No 2) Regulations, SI 2001/3777 with effect from 19 December 2001.

[4] Sub-para (2)(*ja*) inserted by the PEP (Amendment) Regulations, SI 2003/2748 regs 2, 5(*c*) with effect from 17 November 2003.

[5] Paras (12)–(14) inserted by the PEP (Amendment) Regulations, SI 2003/2748 regs 2, 6 with effect, so far as relating to SI 1989/469 para (2)(*ja*) above, from 17 November 2003, but otherwise from 6 April 2004.

[6] In sub-para (2), words in sub-para (*g*), (*h*), (*j*) substituted; and sub-para (*p*) inserted, by the PEP (Amendment) Regulations, SI 2003/2748 regs 2, 5(*a*), (*b*), (*d*) with effect from 6 April 2004.

Non-qualifying investments held on 5 April 1990

6A ...[1]

Amendments—[1] Reg 6 substituted for this regulation by the Personal Equity Plan (Amendment) Regulations, SI 2001/923 reg 7 with effect from 6 April 2001.

Qualifying investments for single company plans

6B ...[1]

Amendments—[1] Reg 6 substituted for this regulation by the Personal Equity Plan (Amendment) Regulations, SI 2001/923 reg 7 with effect from 6 April 2001.

Qualifying individuals who may invest under a plan

7—(1) This regulation specifies the description of individual who may invest under a plan ("qualifying individual").

(2) A qualifying individual to whom paragraph (1) refers is an individual—

(*a*) who is 18 years of age or over,

[(*b*) who complied with this sub-paragraph (*b*) as it had effect immediately before the coming into force of the Personal Equity Plan (Amendment) Regulations 2001, and][1]

(*c*)

(i) who is resident and ordinarily resident in the United Kingdom, or

(ii) who, though non-resident, performs duties which by virtue of section 132(4)(*a*) of the Taxes Act (Crown employees serving overseas) are treated as being performed in the United Kingdom.

Amendments—[1] Para (2)(*b*) substituted by the Personal Equity Plan (Amendment) Regulations, SI 2001/923 reg 8 with effect from 6 April 2001.

Plan investor ceasing to qualify

8 Notwithstanding any other provision of these Regulations a plan investor who, after subscribing to a plan, at any time ceases to fulfil the conditions of regulation 7(2)(*c*) may retain the benefits of the plan (including the right to any relief or exemption due under the plan) subsisting at that time ...[1]

Amendments—[1] Words revoked by the Personal Equity Plan (Amendment) Regulations, SI 1998/1869 reg 5, with effect for the year 1999–00 and subsequent years of assessment.

Conditions for application to subscribe to a plan

9 ...

Amendments—This regulation revoked by the Personal Equity Plan (Amendment) Regulations, SI 1998/1869 reg 6, with effect for the year 1999–00 and subsequent years of assessment.

Conditions for application to subscribe to a continuing plan

10 ...

Amendments—This regulation revoked by the Personal Equity Plan (Amendment) Regulations, SI 1998/1869 reg 6, with effect for the year 1999–00 and subsequent years of assessment.

[Application by curator bonis

10A ...

Amendments—This regulation (originally inserted by the Personal Equity Plan (Amendment) Regulations, SI 1996/846 reg 6 with effect from 6 April 1996) revoked by the Personal Equity Plan (Amendment) Regulations, SI 1998/1869 reg 6, with effect for the year 1999–00 and subsequent years of assessment.

Plan manager—qualifications and Board's approval

11—(1) This regulation specifies the circumstances ("qualifying circumstances") in which a person may be approved by the Board as a plan manager.

(2) The qualifying circumstances to which paragraph (1) refers are the following—

(*a*) the person must make written application to the Board for approval in a form prescribed by the Board;

[(*b*) a plan manager must be—

(i) an authorised person within the meaning of [section 31(1)(*a*) or (*c*) of, or Schedule 5 to, the Financial Services and Markets Act 2000 who has permission to carry on one or more of the activities specified in Articles 14, 21, 25, 37, 40, 45, 51 and 53 and, in so far as it applies to any of those activities, Article 64 of the Financial Services and Markets Act 2000 (Regulated Activities) Order 2001][3], or

(ii) a European institution which [carries on one or more of those activities][3]][1]

(*c*) a plan manager must not be prevented from acting as such by [any requirement imposed under section 43 of the Financial Services and Markets Act 2000, or by any prohibition imposed by or under any rules made by the Financial Services Authority under that Act][3] [; and][2]

[(*d*) a plan manager who is a European institution or a relevant authorised person and who does not have a branch or business establishment in the United Kingdom, or has such a branch or business establishment but does not intend to carry out all his functions as a plan manager at that branch or business establishment, must fulfil one of the three requirements specified in regulation 11A.][2]

(3) The terms of the Board's approval may include conditions designed to ensure that the provisions of these Regulations are satisfied.

Amendments—[1] Para (2)(*b*) substituted by the Personal Equity Plan (Amendment No 2) Regulations, SI 1995/3287 reg 5, with effect from 9 January 1996.
[2] Para (2)(*d*) and preceding word "and" inserted by SI 1995/3287 reg 5.
[3] Words in para (2) substituted by the Financial Services and Markets Act 2000 (Consequential Amendments) (Taxes) Order, SI 2001/3629 arts 120, 124 with effect from 1 December 2001, immediately after the coming into force of the Financial Services and Markets Act 2000 ss 411, 432(1), Sch 20 (and SI 2001/3629 Pts 1 and 2).

[Plan manager—appointment of tax representative

11A—(1) The first requirement specified in this regulation is that—

(*a*) a person who falls within subsection (5) of section 333A of the Taxes Act is for the time being appointed by the plan manager to be responsible for securing the discharge of the duties prescribed by paragraph (4) which fall to be discharged by the plan manager, and

(*b*) his identity and the fact of his appointment have been notified to the Board by the plan manager.

(2) The second requirement specified in this regulation is that there are for the time being other arrangements with the Board for a person other than the plan manager to secure the discharge of such duties.

(3) The third requirement specified in this regulation is that there are for the time being other arrangements with the Board designed to secure the discharge of such duties.

(4) The duties prescribed by this paragraph are those that fall to be discharged by a plan manager under these Regulations.

(5) The appointment of a person in pursuance of the first requirement shall be treated as terminated in circumstances where—

(*a*) the Board have reason to believe that the person concerned—

(i) has failed to secure the discharge of any of the duties prescribed by paragraph (4), or

(ii) does not have adequate resources to discharge those duties; and

(*b*) the Board have notified the plan manager and that person that they propose to treat his appointment as having terminated with effect from the date specified in the notice.

(6) Where, in accordance with the first requirement, a person is at any time responsible for securing the discharge of duties, the person concerned—

(*a*) shall be entitled to act on the plan manager's behalf for any of the purposes of the provisions relating to the duties;

(*b*) shall secure (where appropriate by acting on the plan manager's behalf) the plan manager's compliance with and discharge of the duties;

(*c*) shall be personally liable in respect of any failure of the plan manager to comply with or discharge any such duty as if the duties imposed on the plan manager were imposed jointly and severally on the plan manager and the person concerned.][1]

Amendments—[1] This regulation inserted by the Personal Equity Plan (Amendment No 2) Regulations, SI 1995/3287 reg 6, with effect from 9 January 1996.

Plan manager—withdrawal by Board of approval

12—(1) This regulation specifies the circumstances ("the disqualifying circumstances") in which the Board may by notice withdraw their approval of a person as a plan manager in relation to a plan.

(2) The disqualifying circumstances to which paragraph (1) refers are that the Board have reason to believe—

(*a*) that any provision of these Regulations is not or at any time has not been satisfied in respect of a plan managed by the plan manager; or

(*b*) that a person to whom they have given approval to act as a plan manager is not qualified so to act.

(3) The notice to which paragraph (1) refers shall specify—

(*a*) the date from which the Board's approval is withdrawn, and

(*b*) the disqualifying circumstances.

Plan manager—appeal against withdrawal of Board's approval

13—(1) A plan manager to whom notice of withdrawal of approval has been given under regulation 12 may appeal against the withdrawal by notice given to the Board within 30 days after the date of the notice of withdrawal.

(2) The appeal shall be to the Special Commissioners.

(3) The like provisions as are contained in Part V of the Management Act (appeals and other proceedings) shall apply to an appeal and the Special Commissioners shall on appeal to them confirm the notice unless they are satisfied that the notice ought to be quashed.

Plan manager ceasing to act

14 A person shall give notice to the Board and to the subscriber to the plan which he manages of his intention to cease to act as the plan manager [not less than 30 days][1] before he so ceases so that his obligations to the Board under the plan can be conveniently discharged at or about the time he ceases so to act[and the notice to the subscriber shall inform him of his rights to transfer the plan under regulation 16.][1]

Amendments—[1] Words "not less than 30 days" substituted, and words added by the Personal Equity Plan (Amendment) Regulations, SI 2001/923 reg 9 with effect from 6 April 2001.

Plan manager ceasing to qualify

15—[(1)][2] A person shall cease to qualify as a plan manager and shall notify the Board [within 30 days of the relevant event in subparagraphs (*a*) to (*d*), of that relevant event][2] where—

(*a*) the person no longer fulfils the conditions of regulation 11;

(*b*) in the case of an individual, he becomes bankrupt or, in Scotland, his estate is sequestrated, or makes any arrangement or composition with his creditors generally; or

(*c*) in the case of a company a resolution has been passed or a petition has been presented to wind it up [; or][1]

(*d*) in the case of a European institution or a relevant authorised person, action corresponding to that described in paragraph (*b*) or (*c*) has been taken by or in relation to the institution or person under the law of an EEA State.][1]

[(2) On giving the notice referred to in paragraph (1), the person shall also notify the plan investor of his right to transfer the plan under regulation 16, and the notice shall inform the plan investor of his rights under paragraph (3).][2]

[(3) Where the plan investor—

(*a*) receives a notice under paragraph (2), or regulation 14, and

(*b*) within 30 days of the sending of the notice to him, transfers the plan to another plan manager pursuant to regulation 16,

the period between the transferor ceasing to act or qualify as a plan manager, and the transfer to the transferee, shall be ignored in determining whether the plan has at all times been managed by a plan manager.][2]

Amendments—[1] Sub-para (*d*) and preceding word "; or" inserted by the Personal Equity Plan (Amendment No 2) Regulations, SI 1995/3287 reg 7, with effect from 9 January 1996.

[2] Regulation renumbered as para (1), words substituted, and paras (2), (3) inserted by the Personal Equity Plan (Amendment) Regulations, SI 2001/923 reg 10 with effect from 6 April 2001.

Transfer of plans to other plan managers

[**16**—(1) Subject to paragraph (2), where—

(*a*) arrangements are made by a plan investor to transfer a plan[, or the qualifying investments forming part of a plan,][4] from one plan manager ("the transferor") to another plan manager ("the transferee"), or

(*b*) a plan is transferred in consequence of the transferor ceasing to act or to qualify as a plan manager,

the transfer shall have effect and the plan shall not otherwise be affected for the purpose of these Regulations by reason of the transfer.

[(1A) Where part of a plan is transferred, the transferee shall thereafter be the plan manager in relation to the qualifying investments transferred, and all references in these Regulations to the plan manager shall, so far as relates to plan investments transferred, be thereafter taken to be references to the transferee.][5]

(2) The transferor shall within [30][4] days after the date of the transfer give the transferee a notice containing the information specified in paragraph (3) and the declaration specified in paragraph (4).

(3) The information specified in this paragraph is—

(*a*) as regards the plan investor—

(i) his full name,
(ii) the address of his permanent residence, including postcode,
(iii) his date of birth, and
(iv) if he has one, his national insurance number, and

(*b*) as regards the plan[, or the part of the plan being transferred, as the case may be][4]—

(i) ...[4]
(ii) the date of the transfer,
(iii)–(v) ...[3]
(vi) the amount of any dividends on plan investments which are payable to, but have not been received by, the transferor at the date of the transfer,
(vii) the total amount of interest paid or credited in respect of a cash deposit which is a plan investment and has not been itself invested at the date of the transfer,
(viii) the total amount of such interest which has been paid ...[2] to or at the direction of the plan investor or otherwise applied for his benefit from the beginning of the year in which the transfer takes place to the date of the transfer.

(4) The declaration specified in this paragraph is a declaration by the transferor that—

(*a*) he has fulfilled all his obligations to plan investors, to the Board or otherwise, which are imposed by these Regulations;

(*b*) he has transferred to the transferee or a nominee for the transferee any plan investments which are being transferred by virtue of the transfer ...[4] and that, where registration of any such transfer is required, he has taken the necessary steps to ensure that the plan investments can be registered in the name of the transferee or the nominee;

(*c*) that the information contained in the notice is correct.][1]

Amendments—[1] This regulation substituted by the Personal Equity Plan (Amendment) Regulations, SI 1993/756 reg 10, with effect from 6 April 1993.

[2] In para (3)(*b*)(viii) words revoked by the Personal Equity Plan (Amendment) Regulations, SI 1996/846 reg 7 with effect from 6 April 1996.

[3] Para 3(*b*)(iii), (iv), (v) revoked by the Personal Equity Plan (Amendment) Regulations, SI 1998/1869 reg 7, with effect for the year 1999–00 and subsequent years of assessment.

[4] Words in para (1)(*a*) inserted, figure in para (2) substituted, words in para (3)(*b*) inserted, para(3)(*b*)(i) revoked, and words in para 4(*b*) revoked by the Personal Equity Plan (Amendment) Regulations, SI 2001/923 reg 11 with effect from 6 April 2001.

[5] Para (1A) inserted by SI 2001/923 reg 11(3) with effect from 6 April 2001.

Exemption from tax of plan income and gains

17—[(1) Subject to these Regulations—

[(*a*) no tax shall be chargeable on the plan manager or his nominee or on the plan investor—

(i) in respect of interest, dividends, distributions or gains in respect of plan investments, or
(ii) on any annual profits or gains treated by section 714(2) of the Taxes Act as having been received by any of them in respect of plan investments, or
(iii) on an offshore income gain to which a disposal made by any of them of a plan investment gives rise which is treated by section 761(1) of the Taxes Act as constituting profits or gains, or
(iv) on a profit realised by any of them from the discount on a relevant discounted security within the meaning of Schedule 13 to the Finance Act 1996 which is held as a plan investment;][4]

(*b*) losses in respect of plan investments shall be disregarded for the purposes of capital gains tax; and

(*c*) relief in respect of tax shall be given in the manner and to the extent provided by these Regulations.][1]

[(2) Interest on a cash deposit which is a plan investment—

(*a*) where the cash is deposited in an account with a deposit-taker, shall be paid or credited gross and the deposit shall not be treated as a relevant deposit within the meaning of section 481(4) of the [Taxes Act][3] and

(*b*) where the cash is deposited in an account with a building society, shall be treated as a gross payment to which regulation 4 of the Income Tax (Building Societies) (Dividends and Interest) Regulations 1990 applies.][2]

[(3) A plan investor who, after subscribing to a plan at any time, ceases to be resident in the United Kingdom shall be treated for the purposes of determining his entitlement to, and to payment of, tax credits in respect of qualifying distributions so far as they relate to plan investments as if he were so resident.][5]

Statement of Practice SP 2/89, para 2 (xi)—Disposals of shares as part of a PEP investment can be left out of account in deciding when to make capital gains rebasing election under FA 1988 s 96(6).

Note—IT (Building Societies) (Dividends and Interest) Regulations is SI 1990/2231.

Amendments—[1] Para (1) substituted by the Personal Equity Plan (Amendment) Regulations, SI 1995/1539 reg 8, with effect from 6 July 1995.

[2] Para (2) added by the Personal Equity Plan (Amendment) Regulations, SI 1991/733 reg 10, with effect from 6 April 1991.

[3] Words substituted by the Personal Equity Plan (Amendment) Regulations, SI 1996/846 reg 8 with effect from 6 April 1996.

[4] Para (1)(*a*) substituted by the Personal Equity Plan (Amendment No 2) Regulations, SI 1997/1716 reg 10 with effect from 8 August 1997.

[5] Para (3) inserted by the Personal Equity Plan (Amendment) Regulations, SI 1998/1869 reg 8, with effect from 21 August 1998.

[Interest on cash deposits paid to plan investor

17A—(1) When in any year an amount of interest paid or credited in respect of a cash deposit which is a plan investment—

(*a*) is paid by the plan manager to or at the direction of the plan investor or otherwise applied for his benefit, and

(*b*) the aggregate of that amount and of all other amounts so paid in the year [in relation to a particular plan][2] exceeds £180 [(or, where the plan manager is a European institution or a relevant authorised person, its equivalent in the currency of the State in which he has his principal place of business)][3],

paragraph (2) shall apply.

(2) Where this paragraph applies—

(*a*) the plan manager shall pay to the Board a sum representing income tax at the [lower][4] rate in force for the year on—

(i) all amounts paid in that year before this paragraph first applies, and

(ii) the amount referred to in paragraph (1) and each further amount paid in that year [in relation to the plan][2];

(*b*) any sum so payable shall be treated as an amount of tax due under an assessment which is final and conclusive and payable, in the case of the sum payable in respect of the amounts referred to in sub-paragraph (*a*)(i), not later than 30 days after the date on which this paragraph first applies in any year and, in any other case, not later than 30 days after payment of the amount referred to in paragraph (1);

(*c*) the interest referred to in paragraph (1) shall be treated in all other respects as interest of money within the meaning of paragraph (*a*) of Case III of Schedule D in section 18(3) of the Taxes Act and chargeable to tax under that Case for the year in which it arises.

(3) The reference to interest in paragraph (1) includes a reference to any bonus and to a dividend paid or credited in respect of a share account with a building society.][1]

Amendments—[1] This regulation inserted by the Personal Equity Plan (Amendment) Regulations, SI 1991/733 reg 11, with effect from 6 April 1991.

[2] Words in paras (1)(*b*), (2)(*a*)(ii) inserted by the Personal Equity Plan (Amendment No 2) Regulations, SI 1991/2774 reg 12, with effect from 1 January 1992.

[3] Words in para (1)(*b*) inserted by the Personal Equity Plan (Amendment No 2) Regulations, SI 1995/3287 reg 8, with effect from 9 January 1996.

[4] Word substituted by the Personal Equity Plan (Amendment) Regulations, SI 1996/846 regs 1(2), 9 with effect in relation to amounts of interest paid or applied after 5 April 1996.

Tax liabilities and reliefs—plan manager to act on behalf of plan investor

18—(1) A plan manager may under these Regulations make claims, conduct appeals and agree on behalf of the plan investor liabilities for and reliefs from tax in respect of a plan.

(2) Claims shall be made to the Board in accordance with the provisions of regulations 19 and 20.

(3) Where any relief or exemption from tax previously given in respect of a plan has by virtue of these Regulations become excessive, in computing the relief due on any claim there shall be deducted, so that amounts equal to that excess are set-off or repaid to the Board, as the case may be, notwithstanding that those amounts have been invested—

(*a*) any amount repaid in respect of a tax credit;

[(*aa*) any sum representing income tax which is payable under regulation 17A on amounts of interest paid or credited gross and paid by the plan manager to or at the direction of the plan investor or otherwise applied for his benefit;][1]

(*b*) any other amount due to the Board by a plan manager in respect of any tax liability in respect of investments under a plan including (but without prejudice to the making of an assessment under the provisions of that section) any amount falling due in respect of a liability under section 737 of the Taxes Act.

(4) Any amount deducted under paragraph (3) shall be treated as an amount of income tax deducted at source and not repayable within the meaning and for the purposes of section 95(2)(*a*) of the Management Act.

Amendments—[1] Para (3)(*aa*) inserted by the Personal Equity Plan (Amendment) Regulations, SI 1991/733 reg 12, with effect from 6 April 1991.

Repayments in respect of tax to plan manager—interim claims

19—(1) Notwithstanding the provisions of any other enactment, the Board shall not be under an obligation to make any repayment in respect of tax under these Regulations earlier than the end of the month following the month in which the claim for the repayment is received.

(2) A claim for repayment in respect of tax which is not an annual claim (''interim claim'') may be made only for a period of a month (or a number of months not exceeding six) beginning on the 6th day of the month and ending on the 5th day of the relevant following month.

(3) No claim for repayment may be made for the month ending 5th October or any subsequent month until the annual return due in respect of a plan for the preceding year has been duly made by the plan manager and received by the Board.

(4) Where, on the occasion of a claim, there is due to the Board an amount in respect of tax that amount shall be recoverable by the Board in the same manner as tax charged by an assessment on the plan manager which has become final and conclusive.

[(5) ...][1]

Amendments—[1] Para (5) (inserted by the Personal Equity Plan (Amendment) Regulations, SI 1993/756 reg 11, with effect from 6 April 1993) revoked by the Personal Equity Plan (Amendment) Regulations, SI 1998/1869 reg 9, with effect for the year 1999–00 and subsequent years of assessment.

Repayments in respect of tax to plan manager—annual returns and annual claims

20—(1) An annual claim is a claim for repayment in respect of tax for a year and may not be made at any time more than six years after the end of the year.

(2) A plan manager shall within six months after the end of the year make a return of all income and in addition an annual claim to establish the total of repayments due under a plan for that year.

(3) Where the aggregate of the repayments in respect of interim claims for the year shown by an annual claim exceeds the amount repayable for the year shown on the claim, the plan manager shall repay the amount of the excess to the Board with the claim.

(4) If a plan manager fails to make the return and the annual claim required under this regulation within the time limited, the Board may issue a notice to the plan manager showing the aggregate of payments in respect of the interim claims for the year, and stating that the Board are not satisfied that the amount due to the plan manager for that year exceeds the lower amount stated in the notice.

(5) If a return and an annual claim are not delivered to the Board within 14 days after the issue of such a notice under paragraph (4) the amount of the difference between the aggregate and the lower amount stated in the notice shall immediately be recoverable by the Board in the same manner as tax charged by an assessment on the plan manager which has become final and conclusive.

(6) Where a return and an annual claim have been made and the plan manager subsequently discovers that an error or mistake has been made in the return or claim the plan manager may make a supplementary return or annual claim within the time allowed in paragraph (1).

Plan manager's returns and claims—supplementary provisions

21—(1) Section 42 of the Management Act shall not apply to claims under these Regulations.

(2) No appeal shall lie from the Board's decision on an interim claim.

(3) An appeal shall be to the Special Commissioners from the Board's decision on an annual claim, and the appeal shall be brought by giving notice to the Board within 30 days of receipt of notice of the decision.

(4) No payment or repayment made or other thing done on or in relation to an interim claim or a notice under regulation 20(4) shall prejudice the decision on an annual claim.

(5) The like provisions as are contained in Part V of the Management Act (appeals and other proceedings) shall apply to an appeal under paragraph (3) above, and on an appeal the Special Commissioners may vary the decision appealed against whether or not the variation is to the advantage of the appellant.

(6) All such assessments, payments and repayments shall be made as are necessary to give effect to the Board's decision on an annual claim or to any variation of that decision on appeal.

(7) Returns and claims under these Regulations shall be in such form and contain such particulars as the Board prescribe and shall be signed by the plan manager; and forms prescribed for annual claims may require a report to be given by a person qualified for appointment as auditor of a company.

Assessments for withdrawing relief and recovering tax

22—(1) Where—

(*a*) any relief or exemption from tax given in respect of income or gains under a plan is found not to be due or to be excessive, or

(*b*) where the full amount of tax in respect of the income or gains under a plan has not otherwise been fully accounted for and paid to the Board by or on behalf of the plan investor, an assessment to tax may be made by the Board in the amount or further amount which in their opinion ought to be charged.

(2) An assessment to which paragraph (1) refers may be made on the plan manager or on the plan investor.

(3) If the assessment is made to recover tax in respect of income (including any amount in respect of a tax credit) under a plan it shall be made under Case VI of Schedule D.

Records to be kept by plan manager

23—(1) A plan manager shall at all times keep sufficient records in respect of a plan to enable the requirements of these Regulations to be satisfied.

(2) The records shall include a valuation of plan investments at their market value as at 5th April each year.

Information to be given to plan investor by plan manager

24—[(1) ...][1]

(2) A plan manager who makes a payment to a plan investor out of or in respect of which tax has been deducted shall, if the investor so requests in writing, furnish the investor with a statement in writing showing the gross amount of the payment, the amount deducted and the amount actually paid.

(3) On the transfer to a plan investor of a plan investment the plan manager shall provide for the investor details in writing of the market value on the date of transfer.

Amendments—[1] Para (1) (substituted by the Personal Equity Plan (Amendment) Regulations, SI 1993/756 reg 12, with effect from 6 April 1993) revoked by the Personal Equity Plan (Amendment) Regulations, SI 1998/1869 reg 10, with effect for the year 1999–00 and subsequent years of assessment.

[Return of information by plan manager

24A—(1) A plan manager shall within three months after the end of each year (beginning with the year 1993–94) in which he acts as a plan manager, and after ceasing to act or to qualify as a plan manager, deliver to the Board a return for that year, or the part of that year in which he so acted or qualified, signed by him or on his behalf (or, where the return is made on magnetic tape, accompanied by a certificate signed by him or on his behalf as to the contents of the tape) which contains the information specified in paragraphs (2) and (3).

(2) The information specified in this paragraph is information relating to each plan in respect of which he acted as plan manager [at the end of][7] the year or the part of the year for which the return is made as to—

(*a*) as regards the plan investor—

(i) his full name,

(ii) the address of his permanent residence, including postcode,

(iii) his date of birth, and

(iv) if he has one, his national insurance number;

(*b*) as regards all such plans—

(i) the number allocated to the plan by the plan manager,

(ii) ...[7]

[(iii) the market value of the plan investments held under the plan, that value being determined either at 5 April in the year for which, or for part of which, the return is being made or any other valuation date in that year, not falling earlier than 5 October;][6]

(*c*) ...[7]

(3) The information specified in this paragraph is—

[(*a*) the respective market values at the end of the year or the part of the year for which the return is made of plan investments held by him or a nominee for him on behalf of plan investors, under all the plans in respect of which he acted as plan manager in that year or part, with separate values for—

(i) shares, not being shares in an investment trust or in a UCITS,

(ii) qualifying securities,

(iii) shares in investment trusts,

[(iv) units in, or shares of, securities schemes and warrant schemes,][8]

(v) units in, or shares of, a relevant UCITS,

[(vi) units in, or shares of, fund of funds schemes, and][8]

[(via) units in, or shares of, a Chapter 5 UCITS, which satisfy the condition in regulation 6(13);][9]

(vii) cash, including cash represented in share accounts with building societies,

with depositary interests being included in the paragraph to which their relevant investments (referred to in paragraphs (*a*) and (*b*) of the definition of ''depositary interest'') relate; and][7] (*b*) the aggregate market value at that date of all such plan investments held by him or his nominee.

(4) ...[7]

(5) No claim for repayment may be made under regulation 19 for the month ending 5th July or any subsequent month until the return due under this regulation for the preceding year has been duly made by the plan manager and received by the Board.][1]

Amendments—[1] This regulation inserted by the Personal Equity Plan (Amendment) Regulations, SI 1993/756 reg 13, with effect from 6 April 1993.

[2] Para (3)(*ia*) inserted by the Personal Equity Plan (Amendment) Regulations, SI 1995/1539 reg 9, with effect from 6 July 1995.

[3] Words in para (3)(*a*)(i) inserted by the Personal Equity Plan (Amendment) Regulations, SI 1997/511 reg 5, with effect from 20 March 1997.

[4] Words in para (3)(*a*)(ii) substituted, for the words "authorised unit trusts", by the Personal Equity Plan (Amendment No 2) Regulations, SI 1997/1716 reg 12(2)(*a*) with effect from 8 August 1997.

[5] Para (3)(*a*)(iia) inserted by SI 1997/1716 reg 12(2)(*b*) with effect from 8 August 1997.

[6] Para (2)(*b*)(iii) substituted for original para (2)(*b*)(iii), (iv), (v) by the Personal Equity Plan (Amendment) Regulations, SI 1998/1869 reg 11, with effect for the year 1999–00 and subsequent years of assessment.

[7] Words substituted in para (2), para (3)(*a*) substituted, and paras (2)(*b*)(ii), (*c*), and (4) revoked by the Personal Equity Plan (Amendment) Regulations, SI 2001/923 reg 12 with effect from 6 April 2001.

[8] In para (3), sub-paras (*a*)(iv) and (*a*)(vi) substituted by the Financial Services and Markets Act 2000 (Consequential Amendments) (Taxes) Order, SI 2001/3629 arts 120, 125 with effect from 1 December 2001, immediately after the coming into force of the Financial Services and Markets Act 2000 ss 411, 432(1), Sch 20 (and SI 2001/3629 Pts 1 and 2).

[9] Para (3)(*a*)(via) inserted by the PEP (Amendment) Regulations, SI 2003/2748 regs 2, 7 with effect from 6 April 2004.

Information to be provided to the Board

25 The Board may by notice require any person who is or who at any time has been a plan manager or plan investor to furnish them, within such time (not being less than 14 days) as may be provided by the notice, such information about any plan or about any plan investment (including copies of or extracts from any books or other records) as they may reasonably require for the purposes of these Regulations.

Inspection of records by officer of the Board

26—(1) The Board may by notice require any person who is or who at any time has been a plan manager or plan investor, within such time (not being less than 14 days) as may be provided in the notice, to make available for inspection [at a place within the United Kingdom][1] by an officer of the Board authorised for that purpose all documents (including books and other records) in his possession or under his control containing information relating to any plan or to any plan investment.

(2) Where records are maintained by computer the person required to make them available for inspection shall provide the officer making the inspection with all the facilities necessary for obtaining information from them.

Amendments—[1] Words in para (1) inserted by the Personal Equity Plan (Amendment No 2) Regulations, SI 1995/3287 reg 9, with effect from 9 January 1995.

Capital gains tax—adaptation of enactments

27—(1) For the purposes of capital gains tax on the occasion when the title to plan investments is transferred from a plan manager to a plan investor there shall be deemed to be a disposal and reacquisition by him of those investments for a consideration equal to their market value.

[(2) Sections 104 to 114 of the Taxation of Chargeable Gains Act 1992 shall apply for the purposes of pooling and identifying plan investments as if—

(*a*) in section 106A after subsection (11) there were added—

"(12) This section and sections 104, 110, 110A and 114—

(*a*) shall apply separately in relation to any securities which are held by a person as plan investments so long as they are so held, and

(*b*) shall apply in relation to any such securities which became plan investments by being transferred or renounced to a plan manager or to a nominee for a plan manager in the circumstances specified in [the former][2] regulation 4(2A)(*a*), (*b*) or (*c*) or [the former regulation][2] 4A(2) as if they had been plan investments—

(i) in the case of securities which were transferred or renounced in the circumstances specified in [the former][2] regulation 4(2A)(*a*), (*b*) or (*c*), and in the case of securities acquired by that person in accordance with the provisions of a savings-related share option scheme which were transferred in the circumstances specified in [the former][2] regulation 4A(2), from the date of their acquisition by him, or

(ii) in the case of securities appropriated to that person in accordance with the provisions of an approved profit sharing scheme which were transferred in the circumstances specified in [the former][2] regulation 4A(2), from the date when he directed the trustees to transfer the ownership of the securities to him or, if earlier, the release date in relation to those securities, and (*c*) while applying separately to any such securities, shall have effect as if that person held them in a capacity other than that in which he holds any other securities of the same class whether under another such plan or otherwise.

(13) In this section—

(*a*) [''the former regulation 4(2A)(*a*), (*b*) or (*c*)'' (certain public offer shares, certain shares resulting from a building society demutualisation or certain shares resulting from the demutualisation of a mutual insurer), ''the former regulation 4A(2),''][2] ''plan'', ''plan investment'' and ''plan manager'' have the same meanings as in the Personal Equity Plan Regulations 1989 ...[3];

(*b*) ''approved profit sharing scheme'' has the same meaning as in Chapter IV of Part V of the Taxes Act and ''savings-related share option scheme'' has the meaning given by paragraph 1 of Schedule 9 to that Act.''; and

(*b*) in section 110A after subsection (5) there were added—

''(6) Where part of a section 104 holding is treated by section 106A(12)(*b*)(ii) as having been plan investments since a particular date—

(*a*) an operative event shall be regarded as having occurred for the purposes of this section immediately before that date consisting of the disposal of the part of that section 104 holding which is so treated, and

(*b*) this section shall apply in relation to the occurrence of that operative event as it would have applied if it had always applied separately in relation to the part of that section 104 holding which is so treated.''

(3) Section 106A of the Taxation of Chargeable Gains Act 1992 shall apply for the purposes of identifying securities within the meaning of that section which are eligible to become plan investments as if—

(*a*) in subsection (4), there were added at the beginning the words ''Subject to subsection (14) below'';

(*b*) in subsection (6), for the words ''subsections (4) and (5) above'' there were substituted the words ''subsections (4), (5) and (14)''; and

(*c*) after subsections (12) and (13), as added by paragraph (2), there were added—

''(14) Where a person disposes of securities and securities of the same class which were eligible for transfer to a plan under [the former][2] regulation 4(2A)(*a*), (*b*) or (*c*) or [the former regulation][2] 4A(2) were—

(*a*) held by him immediately before that disposal,

(*b*) acquired by him on the same day as that disposal, or

(*c*) acquired by him within the period of thirty days after that disposal,

and those securities were acquired in the circumstances specified in that regulation, he shall be treated as having first disposed of any securities of that class held or acquired by him which were not so eligible.''

(4) Sections 127 to 131 of the Taxation of Chargeable Gains Act 1992 shall not apply in relation to [qualifying investments for plans falling within any of subparagraphs (*a*), (*b*), (*f*) to (*j*), (*l*) or (*m*) of regulation 6(2)][4] which are held under a plan if there is by virtue of any allotment for payment as is mentioned in section 126(2) of that Act a reorganisation affecting those shares or securities.][1]

Note—In relation to any disposal of any securities between 17 March 1998 and 5 April, SI 1998/1869 reg 13 (Personal Equity Plan (Amendment) Regulations 1998) has effect. This inserts the words ''section 124(8) of the Finance Act 1998 had not been enacted and'' after the words ''as if'' in the old para (2A) before the change made by amendment note [1] below.

Amendments—[1] Paras (2), (3), (4) substituted by the Personal Equity Plan (Amendment) Regulations, SI 1998/1869 reg 12, with effect in relation to any disposal of any securities (whenever acquired) from 6 April 1998 (for disposals of securities between 17 March 1998 and 5 April 1998, see note above).

[2] Words in paras (2), (3) inserted by the Personal Equity Plan (Amendment) Regulations, SI 2001/923 reg 13(2) with effect from 6 April 2001.

[3] Words in para (2) revoked by SI 2001/923 reg 13(3)(*b*) with effect from 6 April 2001.

[4] Words in para (4) substituted by SI 2001/923 reg 13(4).

Administration of tax in relation to plans—supplementary

28—(1) Nothing in these Regulations shall be taken to prejudice any powers conferred or duties imposed by or under any enactment in relation to the making of returns of income or gains, or for the recovery of tax, penalties or interest by means of an assessment or otherwise.

(2) Notwithstanding the provisions of these Regulations a plan manager shall not be released from obligations under these Regulations in relation to a plan except under conditions agreed in writing with and notified to that person by the Board.

[(3) The like provisions as are contained in the Management Act shall apply to any assessment under these Regulations as if it were an assessment to tax for the year in which, apart from these Regulations, the plan investor would have been liable (by reason of his ownership of the investments).][1]

[(3A) In the application of the like provisions as are contained in section 86 of the Management Act by virtue of paragraph (3) in relation to any sums due and payable by virtue of an assessment made on a plan manager under these Regulations, the relevant date—

(*a*) is 1st January in the year for which the plan investor would have been liable where the plan manager has made an interim claim for a period falling within that year; and

(*b*) in any other case, is the later of the following dates, that is to say—

(i) 1st January in that year; or

(ii) the date of the making of the repayment by the Board following receipt of the annual claim for that year.][1]

(4) The like provisions as are contained in section 97(1) of the Management Act shall apply as if—

(*a*) there were inserted after the words "sections 95 and 96 above" the words "or the Personal Equity Plan Regulations 1989", and

(*b*) there were inserted after the words "that they were" the words "or have become".

(5) Any form prescribed by the Board for the purposes of these Regulations shall provide for a declaration that all the particulars given in the form are correctly stated to the best of the knowledge and belief of the person concerned.

(6) No obligation as to secrecy imposed by statute or otherwise shall preclude the Board from disclosing to a plan manager or plan investor that any provision of these Regulations has not been satisfied or that relief has been given or claimed in respect of investments under a plan.

Amendments—[1] Paras (3), (3A) substituted for para (3) by the Personal Equity Plan (Amendment) Regulations, SI 1996/842 regs 1(4), 12 with effect from the year 1996–97 and in relation to tax which is charged by an assessment made after 5 April 1998 and is for the year 1995–96 or earlier.

Transitional provisions—plans and plan investors under the 1986 Regulations

29 ...

Amendments—This regulation revoked by the Personal Equity Plan (Amendment) Regulations, SI 1990/678 reg 10 and Schedule, with effect from 6 April 1990.

1989/1297
Taxes (Interest Rate) Regulations 1989

Made by the Treasury under FA 1989 s 178

Made	*27 July 1989*
Laid before the House of Commons	*28 July 1989*
Coming into Force	*18 August 1989*

Commentary—*Simon's Direct Tax Service* **A3.604, 823, 1322; D2.708, 844, 845; E4.632; I11.405, 532.**

Citation and commencement

1 These Regulations may be cited as the Taxes (Interest Rate) Regulations 1989 and shall come into force on 18th August 1989.

Interpretation

2—(1) In these Regulations unless the context otherwise requires—

["the 1998 Regulations" means the Corporation Tax (Instalment Payments Regulations 1998;] [1]

"established rate" means—

(*a*) on the coming into force of these Regulations, 14 per cent per annum; and

(*b*) in relation to any date after the first reference date after the coming into force of these Regulations, the reference rate found on the immediately preceding reference date;

"operative date" means the sixth day of each month [or, where regulation 3ZA or 3BA applies, means the day of each month which is the Monday next following the day referred to in the definition of "reference date" below as "the first Tuesday", and the day of each month which is the Monday next following the day referred to in that definition as "the second Tuesday"] [1];

"reference date" means the day of each month which is the twelfth working day before the sixth day of the following month [or, where regulation 3ZA or 3BA applies, means the day of each month which is the Tuesday next following the day on which the most recent meeting of the Monetary Policy Committee of the Bank of England took place ("the first Tuesday"), and the day of each month which is the Tuesday ("the second Tuesday") occurring two weeks after the first Tuesday] [1];

"section 178" means section 178 of the Finance Act 1989;

"working day" means any day other than a non-business day within the meaning of section 92 of the Bills of Exchange Act 1882.

(2) In these Regulations the reference rate found on a reference date is the percentage per annum found by averaging the base lending rates at close of business on that date of—

(*a*) Bank of Scotland,

(*b*) Barclays Bank plc,

(*c*) Lloyds Bank plc,

(*d*) Midland Bank plc,

(*e*) National Westminster Bank plc, and
(*f*) The Royal Bank of Scotland plc,

[and—

(i) where regulation 3ZA applies, if the result is not a multiple of one-quarter, rounding the result up to the nearest amount which is such a multiple,

(ii) where regulation 3BA applies, if the result is not a multiple of one-quarter, rounding the result down to the nearest amount which is such a multiple,

(iii) in any other case, if the result is not a whole number, rounding the result to the nearest such number, with any result midway between two whole numbers rounded down.][2].

Amendments—[1] Words in para (1) inserted by the Taxes (Interest Rate) (Amendment No 2) Regulations, SI 1998/3176 reg 3 with effect for accounting periods ending on or after 1 July 1999 by virtue of the Finance Act 1994, Section 199 (Appointed Day) Order, SI 1998/3173 art 2.

[2] Words in para (2) substituted by SI 1998/3176 reg 4 with effect for accounting periods ending on or after 1 July 1999 by virtue of SI 1998/3173 art 2.

[Applicable rates of interest on unpaid tax, tax repaid and repayment supplement]1

[3—(1) For the purposes of—

(*a*) [section 86 (except where regulation 3AA(1)(*aa*) applies) and section 88][5] of the Taxes Management Act 1970,

[(*aa*) section 59C of the Taxes Management Act 1970, as it applies to any income tax or capital gains tax which has become payable in accordance with—

(i) section 55 of that Act, so far as it relates to an amendment or an assessment referred to in paragraphs (*a*) and (*b*) of subsection (1) of that section, or

(ii) section 59B of that Act,

(*ab*) section 103A of the Taxes Management Act 1970, so far as it relates to—

(i) any person who may be required by a notice under section 8, 8A or 12AA of that Act (or under any of those sections as extended by section 12 of that Act) to make and deliver a return for a year of assessment or other period, and

(ii) income tax or capital gains tax.][3]

(*b*) [section 118F of, and paragraph 6B of Schedule 3 to][2] the Income and Corporation Taxes Act 1988, ...[4]

[(*ba*) section 71(8A) of the Social Security Administration Act 1992 and section 69(8A) of the Social Security Administration (Northern Ireland) Act 1992, as they have effect in any case where the amount recoverable referred to in each of those sections is in respect of working families' tax credit or disabled person's tax credit, and paragraph 8 of Schedule 4 to the Tax Credits Act 1999;][6]

(*c*) paragraph 6(2)(*a*) of Schedule 1 to the Social Security Contributions and Benefits Act 1992, [and

(*d*) section 15A of the Stamp Act 1891,][4]

the rate applicable under section 178 shall, subject to paragraph (2), be 8.5 per cent per annum.

(2) Where, on a reference date after 1st January 1997, the reference rate found on that date differs from the established rate, the rate applicable under section 178 for the purposes of the enactments referred to in paragraph (1) shall, on and after the next operative date, be the percentage per annum found by applying the formula specified in paragraph (3).

(3) The formula specified in this paragraph is—

$$RR + 2{\cdot}5\,,$$

where RR is the reference rate referred to in paragraph (2).][1]

Note—The rate of interest under this Regulation changes periodically in accordance with the specified formula. Changes are announced by Inland Revenue press release. The rate applicable at any given time can be obtained from *Simon's Direct Tax Service*, Binder 1 and from *Simon's Weekly Tax Intelligence*.

Amendments—[1] This regulation substituted by the Taxes (Interest Rate) (Amendment No 4) Regulations, SI 1996/3187, with effect from 31 January 1997.

[2] Words in sub-para (1)(*b*) inserted by the Taxes (Interest Rate) (Amendment No 2) Regulations, SI 1997/2707 with effect from 9 December 1997.

[3] Sub-paragraphs 3(1)(*aa*) and (*ab*) inserted by the Taxes (Interest Rate) (Amendment) Regulations, SI 1998/310, with effect from 9 March 1998.

[4] In para (1), word "and" in sub-para (*b*) revoked, word "and" in sub-para (*c*), and the whole of sub-para (*d*) inserted by the Taxes (Interest Rate) (Amendment No 3) Regulations, SI 1999/2538 reg 3 with effect from 1 October 1999.

[5] Words in para (1)(*a*) substituted by the Taxes (Interest Rate) (Amendment No 1) Regulations, SI 2001/204 reg 3, with effect from 6 March 2001. Words previously read "sections 86 and 88".

[6] Para (1)(*ba*) inserted by the Taxes (Interest Rate) (Amendment No 2) Regulations, SI 2001/254 reg 3, with effect from 7 March 2001.

[3AA—(1) For the purposes of—

(*a*) sections 86A and 87 of the Taxes Management Act 1970,

[(*aa*) section 86 of the Taxes Management Act 1970 as it has effect in relation to accounting periods of companies ending before 1st October 1993 (interest on unpaid assessed corporation tax),][4]

(*b*) paragraph 3 of Schedule 16A to the Finance Act 1973,

(*c*) paragraphs 15 and 16 of Schedule 2, and paragraph 8 of Schedule 5, to the Oil Taxation Act 1975,

(*d*) paragraph 59 of Schedule 8 to the Development Land Tax Act 1976,

(*e*) ...[2]

(*f*) section 825 of, and paragraph 3 of Schedule 19A to, the Income and Corporation Taxes Act 1988,

rate applicable under section 178 shall, [except where regulation 3AC applies and][3] subject to paragraph (2), [be—

(i) where paragraph (*aa*) above applies, 6.5 per cent per annum;

(ii) in all other cases, 6.25 per cent per annum.][4]

(2) Where, on a reference date after 1st January 1997, the reference rate found on that date differs from the established rate, the rate applicable under section 178 for the purposes of the enactments referred to in paragraph (1) shall, on and after the next operative date, be the percentage per annum found by applying the formula specified in paragraph (3) and, if the result is not a multiple of one-quarter, rounding the result down to the nearest amount which is such a multiple.

(3) The formula specified in this paragraph is—

$$(RR + 2{\cdot}5)\ \frac{(100 - BR)}{100}$$

where RR is the reference rate referred to in paragraph (2) and BR is the percentage at which income tax at the basic rate is charged for the year of assessment in which the reference date referred to in that paragraph falls.][1]

Note—The rate of interest under this Regulation changes periodically in accordance with the specified formula. Changes are announced by Inland Revenue press release. The rate applicable at any given time can be obtained from *Simon's Direct Tax Service*, Binder 1 and from *Simon's Weekly Tax Intelligence*.

Amendments—[1] This regulation inserted by Taxes (Interest Rate) (Amendment No 4) Regulations, SI 1996/3187, with effect from 31 January 1997.

[2] Sub-para (1)(*e*) revoked by the Taxes (Interest Rate) (Amendment No 3) Regulations, SI 1999/2538 reg 4 with effect from 1 October 1999.

[3] Words inserted by Taxes (Interest Rate) (Amendment No 4) Regulations, SI 1999/2637 reg 4 with effect from 14 October 1999.

[4] Para (1)(*aa*) inserted and words at end of para (1) substituted by the Taxes (Interest Rate) (Amendment No 1) Regulations, SI 2001/204 reg 4, with effect from 6 March 2001. Words previously read "be 6.25% per annum".

[3AB—(1) For the purposes of—

(*a*) section 824 of the Income and Corporation Taxes Act 1988,

(*b*) paragraph 6(2)(*b*) of Schedule 1 to the Social Security Contributions and Benefits Act 1992, ...[2]

(*c*) section 283 of the Taxation of Chargeable Gains Act 1992.

[(*d*) section 92 of the Finance Act 1986, and

(*e*) section 110 of the Finance Act 1999,][2]

the rate applicable under section 178 shall, subject to paragraph (2), be 4 per cent per annum.

(2) Where, on a reference date after 1st January 1997, the reference rate found on that date differs from the established rate, the rate applicable under section 178 for the purposes of the enactments referred to in paragraph (1) shall, on and after the next operative date, be the percentage per annum found by applying the formula specified in paragraph (3) and, if the result is not a multiple of one-quarter, rounding the result down to the nearest amount which is such a multiple.

(3) The formula specified in this paragraph is—

$$(RR - 1)\ \frac{(100 - LR)}{100}$$

where RR is the reference rate referred to in paragraph (2) and LR is the percentage at which income tax at the lower rate is charged for the year of assessment in which the reference date referred to in that paragraph falls.][1]

Note—The rate of interest under this Regulation changes periodically in accordance with the specified formula. Changes are announced by Inland Revenue press release. The rate applicable at any given time can be obtained from *Simon's Direct Tax Service*, Binder 1 and from *Simon's Weekly Tax Intelligence*.

Amendments—[1] This regulation inserted by the Taxes (Interest Rate) (Amendment No 4) Regulations, SI 1996/3187, with effect from 31 January 1997.

[2] Word "and" in sub-para (1)(*b*) revoked, and sub-paras (1)(*d*), (*e*) inserted, by the Taxes (Interest Rate) (Amendment No 3) Regulations, SI 1999/2538 reg 5 with effect from 1 October 1999.

[3AC—(1) For the purposes of section 87 of the Taxes Management Act 1970 in so far as it relates to tax that becomes due and payable on or after 14th October 1999, the rate applicable under section 178 shall, subject to paragraph (2), be 7.5 per cent per annum.

(2) Where on a reference date after 14th October 1999 the reference rate found on that date differs from the established rate, the rate applicable under section 178 for the purposes mentioned in paragraph (1) shall, on and after the next operative date, be the percentage per annum found by applying the formula specified in paragraph (3).

(3) The formula specified in this paragraph is—

RR + 2.5

where RR is the reference rate referred to in paragraph (2).][1]

Amendments—[1] This regulation inserted by Taxes (Interest Rate) (Amendment No 4) Regulations, SI 1999/2637 reg 4 with effect from 14 October 1999.

[Applicable rate of interest on overdue corporation tax

[3A—(1) For the purposes of section 87A of the Taxes Management Act 1970 the rate applicable under section 178 shall, [except where regulation 3ZA or 3ZB applies and][2] subject to paragraph(2), be 6·25 per cent per annum.

(2) Where, on a reference date after 1st October 1993, the reference rate found on that date differs from the established rate, the rate applicable under section 178 for the purposes of the enactment referred to in paragraph (1) shall, on and after the next operative date, be the percentage per annum found by applying the formula specified in paragraph (3) and, if the result is not a multiple of one-quarter, rounding the result down to the nearest amount which is such a multiple.

(3) The formula specified in this paragraph is—

$$(RR + 2{\cdot}5)\ \frac{(100 - SCR)}{100}$$

where RR is the reference rate referred to in paragraph (2) and SCR is the percentage at which corporation tax at the small companies' rate is charged for the financial year in which the reference date referred to in that paragraph falls.][1]

Note—The rate of interest under this Regulation changes periodically in accordance with the specified formula. Changes are announced by Inland Revenue press release. The rate applicable at any given time can be obtained from *Simon's Direct Tax Service*, Binder 1 and from *Simon's Weekly Tax Intelligence*.

Amendments—[1] This regulation inserted by the Taxes (Interest Rate) (Amendment No 3) Regulations, SI 1993/2212 with effect from 1 October 1993.

[2] Words in para (1) inserted by the Taxes (Interest Rate) (Amendment No 2) Regulations, SI 1998/3176 reg 5 with effect for accounting periods ending on or after 1 July 1999 by virtue of FA 1994 s 199 (Appointed Day) Order, SI 1998/3173 art 2.

[3ZA—(1) For the purposes of section 87A of the Taxes Management Act 1970 in so far as it relates, by virtue of subsection (1A) of that section, to an amount or amounts treated as becoming due and payable in respect of the total liability of a large company for an accounting period ending on or after 1st July 1999 in accordance with regulation 5 of the 1998 Regulations, the rate applicable under section 178 shall, subject to paragraph (2), be 8.25 per cent per annum.

(2) Where on a reference date after 7th January 1999 the reference rate found on that date differs from the established rate, the rate applicable under section 178 for the purposes mentioned in paragraph (1) shall, on and after the next operative date and as respects the period specified in paragraph (3), be the percentage per annum found by applying the formula specified in paragraph (4).

(3) The period specified in this paragraph is any period falling between—

(*a*) the date on which the first instalment payment is treated as becoming due and payable for the accounting period concerned under regulation 5 of the 1998 Regulations, and

(*b*) the day following the expiry of nine months from the end of that accounting period,

during which any amount treated as becoming due and payable in accordance with regulation 5 of those Regulations for that accounting period remains unpaid.

(4) The formula specified in this paragraph is—

[RR + 1],[2]

where RR is the reference rate referred to in paragraph (2).][1]

Amendments—[1] This regulation inserted by the Taxes (Interest Rate) (Amendment No 2) Regulations, SI 1998/3176 reg 6 with effect for accounting periods ending on or after 1 July 1999 by virtue of FA 1994 s 199 (Appointed Day) Order, SI 1998/3173 art 2.

[2] Formula substituted by the Taxes (Interest Rate) (Amendment) Regulations, SI 2000/893 reg 2(1), with effect as from 20 April 2000 in relation to interest running from before that day as well as to interest running from, or from after, that day.

[3ZB—(1) For the purposes of section 87A of the Taxes Management Act 1970 in so far as it relates to an unpaid amount in respect of the total liability of a company for an accounting period ending on or after 1st July 1999, other than an amount to which regulation 3ZA applies, the rate applicable under section 178 shall, subject to paragraph (2), be 8.5 per cent per annum.

(2) Where on a reference date after 7th January 1999 the reference rate found on that date differs from the established rate, the rate applicable under section 178 for the purposes mentioned in paragraph (1) shall, on and after the next operative date, be the percentage per annum found by applying the formula specified in paragraph (3).

(3) The formula specified in this paragraph is—

RR + 2.5,

where RR is the reference rate referred to in paragraph (2).][1]

Amendments—[1] This regulation inserted by the Taxes (Interest Rate) (Amendment No 2) Regulations, SI 1998/3176 reg 6 with effect for accounting periods ending on or after 1 July 1999 by virtue of FA 1994 s 199 (Appointed Day) Order, SI 1998/3173 art 2.

[Applicable rate of interest on tax overpaid][1]

[3B—(1) For the purposes of section 826 of the Income and Corporation Taxes Act 1988 the rate applicable under section 178 shall, [except where regulation 3BA or 3BB applies and][2] subject to paragraph(2), be 3·25 per cent per annum.

(2) Where, on a reference date after 1st October 1993, the reference rate found on that date differs from the established rate, the rate applicable under section 178 for the purposes of the enactment referred to in paragraph (1) shall, on and after the next operative date, be the percentage per annum found by applying the formula specified in paragraph (3) and, if the result is not a multiple of one-quarter, rounding the result down to the nearest amount which is such a multiple.

(3) The formula specified in this paragraph is—

$$(RR - 1)\,\frac{(100 - CTR)}{100}$$

where RR is the reference rate referred to in paragraph (2) and CTR is the percentage at which corporation tax is charged for the financial year in which the reference date referred to in that paragraph falls.][1]

Note—The rate of interest under this Regulation changes periodically in accordance with the specified formula. Changes are announced by Inland Revenue press release. The rate applicable at any given time can be obtained from *Simon's Direct Tax Service*, Binder 1 and from *Simon's Weekly Tax Intelligence*.

Amendments—[1] This regulation inserted by the Taxes (Interest Rate) (Amendment No 3) Regulations, SI 1993/2212 with effect from 1 October 1993.

[2] Words in para (1) inserted by the Taxes (Interest Rate) (Amendment No 2) Regulations, SI 1998/3176 reg 5 with effect for accounting periods ending on or after 1 July 1999 by virtue of FA 1994 s 199 (Appointed Day) Order, SI 1998/3173 art 2.

[3BA—(1) For the purposes of section 826 of the Income and Corporation Taxes Act 1988 in so far as it relates to an amount paid by a company in respect of its total liability for an accounting period ending on or after 1st July 1999, being an amount falling within paragraph (*d*) of subsection (1) of that section (overpayment) of instalment by large company under regulation 5 of the 1998 Regulations) or an amount falling within paragraph (*e*) of that subsection (payment by company other than large company prior to the day following the expiry of nine months from the end of the accounting period concerned), the rate applicable under section 178 shall, subject to paragraph (2), be 6 per cent per annum.

(2) Where on a reference date after 7th January 1999 the reference rate found on that date differs from the established rate, the rate applicable under section 178 for the purposes mentioned in paragraph (1) shall, on and after the next operative date and as respects the period specified in paragraph (3), be the percentage per annum found by applying the formula specified in paragraph (4).

(3) The period specified in this paragraph is any period falling between—

(*a*) the date on which the first instalment payment is treated as becoming due and payable for the accounting period concerned under regulation 5 of the 1998 Regulations or, in the case of a company other than a large company, the date on which the first instalment payment would be so treated if the company were a large company, and

(*b*) the day following the expiry of nine months from the end of that accounting period,

during which there exists an amount paid by the company in respect of its total liability to which paragraph (1) applies.

(4) The formula specified in this paragraph is—

$$RR - 0.25,$$

where RR is the reference rate referred to in paragraph (2).][1]

Amendments—[1] This regulation inserted by the Taxes (Interest Rate) (Amendment No 2) Regulations, SI 1998/3176 reg 8 with effect for accounting periods ending after 30 June 1999 by virtue of FA 1994 s 199 (Appointed Day) Order, SI 1998/3173 art 2.

[3BB—(1) For the purposes of section 826 of the Income and Corporation Taxes Act 1988 in so far as it relates to an amount overpaid by a company in respect of its total liability for an accounting period ending on or after 1st July 1999, being an amount paid[, or which remains overpaid,][2] on or after the day following the expiry of nine months from the end of that period, the rate applicable under section 178 shall, subject to paragraph (2) [and on and after that day][2], be 5 per cent per annum.

(2) Where on a reference date after 7th January 1999 the reference rate found on that date differs from the established rate, the rate applicable under section 178 for the purposes mentioned in paragraph (1) shall, on and after the next operative date, be the percentage per annum found by applying the formula specified in paragraph (3).

(3) The formula specified in this paragraph is—

RR – 1,

where RR is the reference rate referred to in paragraph (2).][1]

Amendments—[1] This regulation inserted by the Taxes (Interest Rate) (Amendment No 2) Regulations, SI 1998/3176 reg 8 with effect for accounting periods ending on or after 1 July 1999 by virtue of FA 1994 s 199 (Appointed Day) Order, SI 1998/3173 art 2.

[2] Words in para (1) inserted by the Taxes (Interest Rate) (Amendment No 2) Regulations, SI 1999/1928 regs 1, 3 with effect from 28 July 1999.

4 ...

Note—This regulation is reproduced in the IHT section of this publication.

[Applicable rate of official rate of interest

5—(1) For the purposes of section 160 of the Income and Corporation Taxes Act 1988 (''section 160'') the rate applicable under section 178 shall, on and after [6 January 2002] , be ... per cent per annum.

(2) In relation to a loan outstanding for the whole or part of a year of assessment where—

(*a*) the loan was made in the currency of a country or territory specified in the Table below,

(*b*) the benefit of the loan is obtained by reason of the employment of a person who normally lives in that country or territory, and

(*c*) that person has lived in that country or territory at some time in the period of six years ending with that year,

the rate applicable under section 178 for the purposes of section 160 and the date on and after which that rate has effect shall be ascertained from the entries in the Table below relating to the country or territory concerned.

TABLE

Country or territory	*Date on and after which applicable rate has effect*	*Applicable rate*
Japan	6th June 1994	3·9 per cent per annum
Switzerland	[6th July 1994][2]	[5·5 per cent per annum][2]][1]

Note—The rate of interest under this Regulation is subject to occasional changes made by statutory instruments. The rate applicable at any given time may be obtained from *Simon's Direct Tax Service*, Binder 1 and from *Simon's Weekly Tax Intelligence*.

Amendments—[1] This regulation substituted by the Taxes (Interest Rate) (Amendment) Regulations, SI 1994/1307.

[2] Words and percentage in Table substituted by SI 1994/1567.

[3] Date in sub-s (1) substituted by the Taxes (Interest Rate) (Amendment No 3) Regulations, SI 2001/3860 reg 2(*a*) with effect from 6 Janauary 2002.

Effect of change in applicable rate

6 Where the rate applicable under section 178 for the purpose of any of the enactments referred to in regulation [3(1) or 4(1)][1] changes on an operative date by virtue of these Regulations, that change shall have effect for periods beginning on or after the operative date in relation to interest running from before that date as well as from or from after that date.

Amendments—[1] Words substituted by the Taxes (Interest Rate) (Amendment) Regulations, SI 1991/889.

1989/1299
Income Tax (Stock Lending) Regulations 1989

Made by the Treasury under TA 1988 s 129

Revocation—These Regulations revoked by the Stock Lending and Manufactured Payments (Revocations and Amendments) Regulations, SI 1997/987, reg 2, Sch 1, with effect from 1 July 1997 except in relation to any arrangement mentioned in TA 1988 s 129(1), (2) or (2A) (Stock lending) that is entered into before that date.

Made	*27 July 1989*
Laid before the House of Commons	*28 July 1989*
Coming into Force	*18 August 1989*

Commentary—*Simon's Direct Tax Service* **A3.604, 823, 1322; D2.708; E4.632; I11.405, 532**.

Citation and commencement

1 *These Regulations may be cited as the Income Tax (Stock Lending) Regulations 1989 and shall come into force on 18th August 1989.*

Interpretation

2—*(1) In these Regulations, unless the context otherwise requires—*

[“approved agent” means a person who, at the time when the arrangement mentioned in subsection (1) is made, is approved as an agent by the Board for the purposes of these Regulations;][4]

[“approved lender” means a person who, at the time when the arrangement mentioned in subsection (1) is made, is approved as a lender by the Board for the purposes of these Regulations;][4]

[“approved nominee” means a person who, at the time when the arrangement mentioned in subsection (1) is made, is approved as a nominee by the Board for the purposes of these Regulations;][4]

[“approved stock borrowing and lending intermediary” means a person who, at the time when the arrangement mentioned in subsection (1) is made—

(a) is—

(i) a member of the Stock Exchange, and

(ii) a stock borrowing and lending intermediary within the rules of the Stock Exchange acting in that capacity in connection with the arrangement; and

(b) is approved as a stock borrowing and lending intermediary by the Board for the purposes of these Regulations;][4]

“Board” means the Commissioners of Inland Revenue;

[“Board of directors” means the Board of directors of LIFFE (A & M);][1]

[“first borrower” in relation to a chain of arrangements means the person referred to as A in the principal section;][4]

[...;][5]

[“last lender” in relation to a chain of arrangements means the lender at the end of a chain of arrangements that commences with the arrangement between the persons referred to as A and B in the principal section;][5]

[“LIFFE” means The London International Financial Futures and Options Exchange;][1]

[“LIFFE (A & M)” means The London International Financial Futures Exchange (Administration and Management);][1]

“market maker”, in relation to securities of a particular kind or options to buy or sell securities of a particular kind, means a person who—

(a) holds himself out at all normal times in compliance with the rules of the Stock Exchange as willing—

(i) to buy and sell securities of that kind, or

(ii) to grant or take options to buy or sell securities of that kind, or

(iii) to buy and sell options to buy or sell securities of that kind,

at a price specified by him; and

(b) is recognised as doing so by the Council of the Stock Exchange;

[“member” means a member of LIFFE (A & M) who is recognised as such by the Board of directors;][1]

...[1]

“the principal section” means section 129 of the Taxes Act 1988;

[“section 57” means section 57 of the Finance Act 1991;][2]

[“section 271(9)” means section 271(9) of the [1992 Act][4] *;]*[3]

[“subsection (1)”, “subsection (2)”, “subsection (2A)” and “subsection (3)” mean subsection (1), subsection (2), subsection (2A) and subsection (3) of the principal section as the case may be;][3]

“the Taxes Act 1988” means the Income and Corporation Taxes Act 1988;

[“the 1992 Act” means the Taxation of Chargeable Gains Act 1992;][4]

[“United Kingdom equity securities” means shares issued by a company which—

(a) have been admitted to the Official List of the Stock Exchange, or are permitted to be dealt in on the Unlisted Securities Market of the Stock Exchange, or Alternative Investment Market of the Stock Exchange, or

(b) where the company issuing the shares is not resident in the United Kingdom, are registered in a register kept in the United Kingdom by or on behalf of that company,

and, except where comprised in an arrangement falling within regulation 4(1)(b), includes depository receipts for such shares.][7]

(2) For the purposes of paragraph (1) above a depositary receipt for shares ...[8] *is an instrument acknowledging—*

(a) that a person holds such shares ...[8] *or evidence of the right to receive them, and*

(b) that another person is entitled to rights, whether expressed as units or otherwise, in or in relation to shares ...[8] *of the same kind, including the right to receive such shares ...*[8] *(or evidence of the right to receive them) from the person mentioned in sub-paragraph (a) above,*

except that for those purposes a depository receipt for shares ...[8] does not include an instrument acknowledging rights in or in relation to shares ...[8] if they are issued or sold under terms providing for payment in instalments and for the issue of the instrument as evidence that an instalment has been paid.

Amendments—[1] Definitions of "Board of directors", "LIFFE", "LIFFE (A & M)", "member", inserted by the IT (Stock Lending) (Amendment) Regulations, SI 1992/572 reg 3.
[2] Definition of "section 57" inserted by the IT (Stock Lending) (Amendment) Regulations, SI 1993/2003 regs 1–3.
[3] Definitions of "section 271(9)" and "subsection (1) ... subsection (3)" substituted by SI 1993/2003 regs 1–3.
[4] Definitions of "approved agent", "approved lender", "approved nominee", "approved stock borrowing and lending intermediary", "first borrower" and "the 1992 Act" and words in definition of "section 271(9)" inserted by the IT (Stock Lending) (Amendment No 2) Regulations, SI 1995/3219 reg 3, with effect from 2 January 1996.
[5] Definitions of "gilt-edged securities" and "last lender" substituted for former definition "gilt-edged securities" by SI 1995/3219 reg 3; definition of "gilt-edged securities" revoked by the IT (Stock Lending) (Amendment) Regulations, SI 1996/1228 reg 3(*a*), with effect from 28 May 1996.
[6] Definitions of "other United Kingdom securities" and "overseas securities" revoked by SI 1996/1228 reg 3(*a*).
[7] Definition of "United Kingdom equity securities" substituted by SI 1996/1228 reg 3(*b*), with effect from 28 May 1996.
[8] Words revoked by SI 1996/1228 reg 4, with effect from 28 May 1996.

Commencement of the principal section

3 *The date specified by these Regulations for the purpose of the application of the principal section to transfers made in pursuance of an arrangement mentioned in subsection (1) or (2) is 18th August 1989.*

[Commencement of section 57

3A *The date specified by these Regulations for the purpose of the application of section 57 to transfers made in pursuance of an arrangement mentioned in paragraph (a) of subsection (2A) is 30th September 1993.]*[1]

Amendments—[1] This regulation inserted by the IT (Stock Lending) (Amendment) Regulations, SI 1993/2003 regs 1, 2, 4 with effect from 30 September 1993.

[Arrangement for transfer of gilt-edged securities

3B *Where the person referred to as A in the principal section—*

(a) enters into an arrangement mentioned in subsection (1) [for the transfer of securities other than United Kingdom equity securities][2]*, but*

(b) did not enter into the arrangement for the purpose of enabling him to fulfil a contract under which he was required to sell securities,

the principal section shall not be prevented from applying by virtue of subsection (2B) of that section on the grounds that A did not enter into the arrangement for the purpose specified in paragraph (b) above.][1]

Amendments—[1] This regulation inserted by the IT (Stock Lending) (Amendment) Regulations, SI 1995/3219 reg 4, with effect from 2 January 1996.
[2] Words in para (*a*) substituted by the IT (Stock Lending) (Amendment) Regulations, SI 1996/1228 reg 5, with effect from 28 May 1996.

[Replacement loans][1]

[3C—*(1) Where the person referred to as A in the principal section—*

(a) enters into an arrangement mentioned in subsection (1) wholly or partly for the purpose of enabling securities of the same kind as those transferred under a previous stock lending arrangement to which the principal section applies to be returned, and

(b) the arrangement falls within paragraph (2) below,

the principal section shall not be prevented from applying by virtue of subsection (2B) of that section on the grounds that A did not enter into the arrangement for the purpose, or wholly for the purpose, of enabling him to fulfil a contract under which he was required to sell securities.

(2) An arrangement falls within this paragraph if—

(a) the securities to be transferred under the arrangement are of the same kind as the securities transferred under the previous management, and

(b) where the arrangement was not entered into wholly for the purpose mentioned in paragraph (1)(a) above, the sole other purpose was to enable A to fulfil a contract under which he was required to sell securities.][1]

Amendments—[1] This regulation inserted by the IT (Stock Lending) (Amendment) Regulations, SI 1995/3219 reg 4, with effect from 2 January 1996.

[Application of subsection (3) and section 271(9)][1]

[4—*(1) Neither subsection (3) nor section 271(9) shall apply to a transfer, or a disposal and acquisition, made in pursuance of an arrangement mentioned in subsection (1) or (2) unless—*

(a) in relation to an arrangement under which the securities to be transferred are United Kingdom equity securities, not being an arrangement falling within sub-paragraph (b) below, the conditions specified in regulation 6 are fulfilled, or

(b) in relation to an arrangement under which United Kingdom equity securities are to be transferred to a member, the conditions specified in regulation 6A are fulfilled.

(2) Neither subsection (3) nor section 271(9) shall apply to a transfer, or a disposal and acquisition, made in pursuance of an arrangement mentioned in paragraph (a) of subsection (2A), unless the securities to be transferred are securities other than United Kingdom equity securities.][1]

Amendments—[1] This regulation substituted by the IT (Stock Lending) (Amendment) Regulations, SI 1996/1228 reg 6 with effect from 28 May 1996.

Conditions relating to the transfer of gilt-edged securities

5 …

Amendments—This regulation revoked by the IT (Stock Lending) (Amendment No 2) Regulations, SI 1995/3219 reg 6, with effect from 2 January 1996.

Conditions relating to the transfer of other United Kingdom securities

6—*(1) The conditions specified in this regulation in relation to an arrangement mentioned in subsection (1) are—*

[(a) that, subject to sub-paragraph (2) below, the person referred to as A in the principal section is an approved borrower or is both an approved borrower and an approved stock borrowing and lending intermediary;]2

[(b) that the person referred to as B in the principal section—

(i) is an approved stock borrowing and lending intermediary, or

(ii) where A is both an approved borrower and an approved stock borrowing and lending intermediary, is an approved lender, and any person acting for B in connection with the arrangement as an agent or nominee is an approved agent or, as the case may be, an approved nominee;]2

(c) that the arrangement takes a form approved by the Board;

(d) that, where A is an approved borrower by virtue of sub-paragraph (a) of the definition in paragraph (4) below, the contract of sale mentioned in the subsection was entered into by him in the ordinary course of his business;

(e) that, where A is an approved borrower by virtue of sub-paragraph (b) of the definition in paragraph (4) below, the contract of sale mentioned in the subsection was entered into by him in the ordinary course of his business as a market maker in relation to options to buy or sell securities of the kind sold under the contract of sale;

(f) that, where A is an approved borrower by virtue of sub-paragraph (c) of the definition in paragraph (4) below—

(i) the contract of sale mentioned in the subsection was entered into by him in the ordinary course of his business as a market maker in relation to securities carrying rights of subscription for, or conversion into, securities of the kind sold under the contract of sale, and

(ii) he will, by the time that the arrangement is to take effect, have irrevocably exercised rights of subscription for, or conversion into, a quantity of securities of the same kind as those to be transferred by B which is not less than that to be so transferred.

(2) …[4]*.*

(3) The conditions specified in this regulation in relation to an arrangement mentioned in subsection (2) are—

[(a) that B is an approved stock borrowing and lending intermediary, and accordingly the case is not one to which paragraph (1)(b)(ii) above applies;][2]

[(b) that the person referred to as C in the principal section is an approved lender, and any person acting for C in connection with the arrangement as an agent or nominee, is an approved agent or, as the case may be, an approved nominee;][1]

(c) that the arrangement takes a form approved by the Board.

(4) In this regulation—

…[3]

"approved borrower" means a person who, at the time when the arrangement is made—

(a) is a market maker in relation to securities of the kind which are the subject of the arrangement or similar securities, or

(b) is a market maker in relation to options to buy or sell securities of the kind which are the subject of the arrangement, or

(c) is a market maker in relation to securities which carry rights of subscription for, or conversion into, securities of the kind which are the subject of the arrangement,

and for the purposes of this definition securities shall be deemed to be similar if they would be so deemed for the purposes of sections 731 to 734 of the Taxes Act 1988;

…[3]

Amendments—[1] Para (3)(*b*) substituted by the IT (Stock Lending) (Amendment) Regulations, SI 1993/2003 regs 1, 2, 7 with effect from 30 September 1993.
[2] Paras (1)(*a*), (*b*), (3)(*a*) substituted by SI 1995/3219 reg 7, with effect from 2 January 1996.
[3] In para (4) definitions revoked by the IT (Stock Lending) (Amendment No 2) Regulations, SI 1995/3219 reg 7.
[4] Para (2) revoked by the IT (Stock Lending) (Amendment) Regulations, SI 1996/1228 reg 7, with effect from 28 May 1996.

[Conditions relating to the transfer of United Kingdom equity securities to members of LIFFE (A & M)

6A—*(1) The conditions specified in this regulation in relation to an arrangement mentioned in subsection (1) are that—*

[(a) the person referred to as A in the principal section is an approved borrower, or is both an approved borrower and an approved stock borrowing and lending intermediary;][4]

[(b) the person referred to as B in the principal section—

(i) is an approved stock borrowing and lending intermediary, or

(ii) where A is both an approved borrower and an approved stock borrowing and lending intermediary, is an approved lender, and any person acting for B in connection with the arrangement as an agent or nominee is an approved agent or, as the case may be, an approved nominee;][4]

(c) the arrangement takes a form approved by the Board;

(d) the securities to be transferred under the arrangement are United Kingdom equity securities of a particular kind;

(e) save where sub-paragraph (f)(ii) applies, the contract of sale mentioned in subsection (1) is entered into by A—

(i) as an options market maker at the date of the contract by way of a hedge against the likelihood of his being obliged to receive securities of the kind referred to in sub-paragraph (d) on a future exercise of options which he has bought or sold, or

(ii) as an options principal trader at the date of the contract by way of a hedge against the likelihood of his being obliged to receive such securities on a future exercise of options which he has bought or sold;

(f) the arrangement is entered into by A—

(i) for the purposes referred to in paragraphs (i) or (ii) of sub-paragraph (e), or

(ii) in order to meet his obligation to deliver such securities under the contract, where the contract results from the earlier exercise of an option by or against him;

(g) the number of such securities contracted to be sold by A—

(i) where paragraph (i) of sub-paragraph (e) applies, does not result in the total number of securities of that kind contracted to be sold by A under that contract and other like contracts for the purpose referred to in that paragraph, exceeding as at the date of the contract the Max limit applicable on that date in respect of securities of that kind, or

(ii) where paragraph (ii) of sub-paragraph (e) applies, does not result in the total number of securities of that kind contracted to be sold by A under that contract and other like contracts for the purpose referred to in that paragraph exceeding as at the date of the contract the Deltaplus limit applicable on that date in respect of securities of that kind, or the Max limit applicable on that date in respect of securities of that kind to which he would be subject if he were an options market maker, whichever is the less;

(h) the number of such securities to be transferred to A under the arrangement, where paragraph (ii) of sub-paragraph (f) applies, does not exceed the amount, if any, by which the number of securities which he is obliged to deliver for the purpose specified in that paragraph exceeds the number of securities of that kind calculated by reference to the formula—

$$D + E - F$$

where—

D is the number of securities of that kind which he held at the time of exercise of the option referred to in that sub-paragraph, other than securities which he was obliged to deliver at that time as the result of an earlier agreement to sell securities which at the time of the agreement he did not own and had not agreed to purchase, which he had agreed to sell in order to hedge the likelihood of his having to receive such securities on a future exercise of options which he had bought or sold, and which did not exceed the appropriate limit at the time of the agreement,

E is the number of such securities which he was obliged to receive at that time as a result of the earlier exercise of other options by or against him, and

F is the number of such securities which he held at that time as a hedge against the likelihood of his having to deliver such securities on a future exercise of other options which he had bought or sold;

(j) if, following the transfer under the arrangement of such securities to A for the purposes referred to in paragraph (i) or (ii) of sub-paragraph (e), the number of securities so transferred under the arrangement and other like arrangements and not transferred in return under such arrangements exceeds, at any time subsequent to the date of the transfer and for a period of six

consecutive days, the appropriate limit as calculated from day to day in respect of securities of that kind, a contract to purchase such securities in order to enable the amount of the excess to be transferred in return under the arrangement is entered into by A prior to the expiry of the day following the end of that period;

(k) if, following the transfer under the arrangement of such securities to A for the purpose specified in sub-paragraph (f)(ii) above, the number of securities of that kind transferred to him under the arrangement and other like arrangements and not transferred in return under such arrangements, exceeds, for a period of six consecutive days, the sum of—

(i) the appropriate limit, as calculated from day to day, in respect of securities of that kind which are [required to be sold as a hedge against the likelihood of his having to receive][3] *such securities on a future exercise of other options which he had bought or sold, and*

(ii) the number of securities of that kind which are required to meet his obligation to deliver securities resulting from the exercise of other options by or against him,

a contract to purchase such securities in order to enable the amount of the excess to be transferred in return under the arrangement is entered into by A prior to the expiry of the day following the end of that period.

(2) The conditions specified in this regulation in relation to an arrangement mentioned in subsection (2) are—

[(a) that B is an approved stock borrowing and lending intermediary, and accordingly the case is not one to which paragraph (1)(b)(ii) above applies;][4]

[(b) that the person referred to as C in the principal section is an approved lender, and any person acting for C in connection with the arrangement as an agent or nominee is an approved agent or, as the case may be, an approved nominee;][2]

(c) that the arrangement takes a form approved by the Board.][1]

Amendments—[1] This regulation inserted by the IT (Stock Lending) (Amendment) Regulations, SI 1992/572 reg 5, with effect from 22 March 1992.

[2] Para (2)(*b*) substituted by the IT (Stock Lending) (Amendment) Regulations, SI 1993/2003 regs 1, 2, 8, with effect from 30 September 1993.

[3] Words in para (1)(*k*)(i) substituted by the IT (Stock Lending) (Amendment) Regulations, SI 1995/1283 reg 4, with effect from 19 June 1995.

[4] Paras (1)(*a*), (*b*), (2)(*a*) substituted by the IT (Stock Lending) (Amendment No 2) Regulations, SI 1995/3219 reg 8, with effect from 2 January 1996.

[Definitions relating to the conditions specified in regulation 6A

6B *For the purposes of regulation 6A and this regulation—*

''the appropriate limit'' means—

(a) where A is an options market maker in respect of United Kingdom equity securities of a particular kind at the time of the agreement referred to in regulation 6A(1)(h) or, as the case may be, during the period specified in regulation 6A(1)(j) or (k), the Max limit, and

(b) where A is an options principal trader in respect of United Kingdom equity securities of a particular kind at the time or, as the case may be, during the period referred to in paragraph (a), the Deltaplus limit or the Max limit, whichever is the less;

...[2]

''approved borrower'' means a member who buys and sells options to buy or sell United Kingdom equity securities;

...[2]

''the Delta number'' means the number which—

(a) is calculated and published from time to time under the authority of the Board of directors in relation to each type of option and the price at which the option may be exercised, and

(b) reflects the degree of probability of exercise of that option as determined by the Board of directors in the light of the current market price of the shares or stock to which the option relates;

''the Deltaplus limit'' means, in relation to options entered into by A to buy or sell United Kingdom equity securities of a particular kind, the maximum number of such securities which is found by—

(a) subject to paragraph (c), making the following calculation in respect of each relevant expiry month and each designated account—

$$G - H$$

where—

G is the number of such securities which he is likely to receive on the exercise of options expiring within that month, calculated by multiplying the most recently published Delta number by the number of securities in respect of each option which would be transferred if that option were exercised, and H is the number of securities which, adopting the same method of calculation, he is likely to deliver, on the exercise of such options;

(b) increasing the amount calculated in paragraph (a) by 20 per cent of the sum of the number of such securities which he would be entitled or obliged to deliver and the number he would be entitled or obliged to receive, if those options were all exercised;

(c) where at the time of calculation such options would expire, unless previously exercised, within a period of four weeks, making the calculation specified in paragraph (a) of the definition of the Max limit in this regulation in respect of those options for the relevant expiry month instead of the calculation referred to in paragraphs (a) and (b) of this definition;

(d) where the amount calculated by reference to paragraphs (a) and (b) or the amount calculated by reference to paragraph (c) is a negative amount, treating that amount as zero;

(e) aggregating the amounts so calculated in respect of all relevant expiry months and designated accounts;

"designated account" means an account designated for a member by the Board of directors in connection with options to buy or sell United Kingdom equity securities;

"the Max limit" means, in relation to options entered into by A to buy or sell United Kingdom equity securities of a particular kind, the maximum number of such securities which is found by—

(a) making the following calculation in respect of each relevant expiry month and each designated account—

$$J - K$$

where—

J is the number of securities which he is likely to receive, and K is the number of securities which he is likely to deliver, on the exercise of options expiring within that month, on the assumption that—

(i) the market price of the securities is at a figure which, having regard to paragraphs (ii) and (iii), would produce the maximum figure resulting from that calculation,

(ii) such options as give the holder the right to buy such securities at a price above that market price, or to sell such securities at a price below that market price, are not exercised, and

(iii) such options as give the holder the right to buy such securities at a price equal to or below that market price, or to sell such securities at a price equal to or above that market price, are exercised;

(b) where the amount calculated by reference to paragraph (a) is a negative amount, treating that amount as zero;

(c) aggregating the amounts so calculated in respect of all relevant expiry months and designated accounts;

"option" means an option to buy or sell securities which is listed by and traded on LIFFE;

"options market maker" means a member who buys and sells, on his own account, options to buy or sell United Kingdom equity securities and who, at the time specified in regulation 6A(1)(e)(i), or at the times specified in regulation 6A(1)(h), (j) and (k) in connection with the appropriate limit, was recognised by the Board of directors as a market maker in relation to options in respect of United Kingdom equity securities of a particular kind and was acting in the capacity of a market maker in relation to those options;

"options principal trader" means a member who buys and sells, on his own account, options to buy or sell United Kingdom equity securities but who, at the times specified in regulation 6A(1)(e)(ii), or at the times specified in regulation 6A(1)(h), (j) and (k) in connection with the appropriate limit, was not recognised by the Board of directors as a market maker in relation to options in respect of United Kingdom equity securities of a particular kind or, if so recognised, was not acting in the capacity of a market maker in relation to those options;

"relevant expiry month" means a calendar month during which an option to buy or sell United Kingdom equity securities of a particular kind will expire, unless previously exercised.][1]

Amendments—[1] This regulation inserted by the IT (Stock Lending) (Amendment) Regulations, SI 1992/572 reg 5, with effect from 22 March 1992.

[2] Definitions revoked by the IT (Stock Lending) (Amendment No 2) Regulations, SI 1995/3219 reg 9, with effect from 2 January 1996.

Conditions relating to the transfer of overseas securities

7 ...

Amendments—This regulation revoked by the IT (Stock Lending) (Amendment) Regulations, SI 1996/1228 reg 7, with effect from 28 May 1996.

[Conditions relating to the an arrangement mentioned in subsection (2A)

8 ...]

Amendments—This regulation revoked by the IT (Stock Lending) (Amendment) Regulations, SI 1996/1228 reg 7, with effect from 28 May 1996.

[Redemption of securities

9—*(1) The cases specified for the purposes of subsection (4B) of the principal section, in relation to which the principal section shall have effect as mentioned in that subsection, are cases where a person ("the borrower") enters into an arrangement under which—*

(a) another person ("the lender") is to transfer securities to the borrower or his nominee;
(b) the arrangement is to terminate on redemption of the securities; and
(c) on redemption of the securities the borrower is to pay to the lender an amount equivalent to the proceeds of redemption.

(2) Subsection (3) shall not apply to a payment referred to in paragraph (1)(c) above unless the conditions specified in paragraph (4) below are fulfilled.

(3) Section 271(9) shall not apply to any disposal and acquisition made in pursuance of an arrangement mentioned in paragraph (1) above unless the conditions specified in paragraph (4) below are fulfilled.

(4) The conditions specified are that—
(a) the arrangement is part of a chain of arrangements;
(b) the lender is not the last lender in the chain; and
(c) the borrower is not the first borrower in the chain.

(5) Where any of the conditions specified in paragraph (4) above are not fulfilled, the operation of the 1992 Act in relation to disposals and acquisitions made pursuant to the arrangement shall be modified in accordance with paragraph (6), (7) or (8) below (as the case may be).

(6) Where the arrangement is not part of a chain of arrangements—
(a) the lender shall be regarded as having disposed of the securities transferred by him to the borrower pursuant to the arrangement—
(i) on the occasion of the redemption of the securities and not at the time of that transfer, and
(ii) for an amount equivalent to the proceeds of redemption;
(b) the borrower shall be regarded as having acquired the securities transferred to him by the lender pursuant to the arrangement on the occasion and for the amount specified in sub-paragraph (a) above.

(7) Where the lender is the last lender in the chain, he shall be regarded as having disposed of the securities transferred by him to the borrower on the occasion and for the amount specified in paragraph (6)(a) above.

(8) Where the borrower is the first borrower in the chain, he shall be regarded as having acquired the securities transferred to him by the lender pursuant to the arrangement on the occasion and for the amount specified in paragraph (6)(a) above.][1]

Amendments—[1] This regulation inserted by the IT (Stock Lending) (Amendment No 2) Regulations, SI 1995/3219 reg 12, with effect from 2 January 1996.

1989/2387
Private Medical Insurance (Tax Relief) Regulations 1989

Made by the Commissioners of Inland Revenue under FA 1989 ss 54(4), 57

Made	*18 December 1989*
Laid before the House of Commons	*19 December 1989*
Coming into Force	*9 January 1990*

Note—These Regulations lapsed on the repeal of the enabling power by F(No 2)A 1997 s 52, Sch 8, Pt II(2), with effect for the year 1997–98 and subsequent years of assessment, except in relation to the cases in which the relief that has been or may be given under FA 1989 s 54 in respect of any payment is unaffected by the provisions of F(No 2)A 1997 s 17(1).

1990/586
Retirement Benefits Schemes (Tax Relief on Contributions) (Disapplication of Earnings Cap) Regulations 1990

Made by the Commissioners of Inland Revenue under FA 1989 Sch 6 para 18(4)

Made	*13 March 1990*
Laid before the House of Commons	*14 March 1990*
Coming into Force	*4 April 1990*

Commentary—*Simon's Direct Tax Service* **E7.221**.

Citation and commencement

1 These Regulations may be cited as the Retirement Benefits Schemes (Tax Relief on Contributions) (Disapplication of Earnings Cap) Regulations 1990 and shall come into force on 4th April 1990.

Interpretation

2—(1) In these Regulations unless the context otherwise requires—
"the Board" means the Commissioners of Inland Revenue;
"business" includes a trade or profession and includes any activity carried on by a body of persons, whether corporate or unincorporate;

"centralised scheme" has the meaning that it has for the purposes of paragraph 28 of the Schedule;
"exempt approved scheme" means a scheme which is for the time being within paragraph (*a*) or (*b*) of section 592(1) of the [Taxes Act][2];
"relevant statutory scheme" means a scheme within section 611A(1) of the [Taxes Act][2];
"relevant employer" in relation to another employer means—

(*a*) an employer who is associated with the other employer, or
(*b*) an employer—
(i) who has acquired, or who has been acquired by or who has merged with, the other employer in circumstances where the other employer had established an exempt approved scheme before 14th March 1989, or
(ii) who has taken over the whole or part of the business of the other employer in those circumstances;

"the Schedule" means Schedule 6 to the Finance Act 1989.
["the Taxes Act" means the Income and Corporation Taxes Act 1988.][1]

(2) For the purpose of this regulation an employer is associated with another employer if (directly or indirectly) one is controlled by the other or if both are controlled by a third person.

(3) In paragraph (2) above the reference to control—

(*a*) in relation to an employer which is a body corporate and a close company within the meaning of section 414 of the [Taxes Act][2], shall be construed in accordance with section 416 of that Act, and
(*b*) in relation to an employer which is a body corporate other than one mentioned in sub-paragraph (*a*) above or a partnership, shall be construed in accordance with section 840 of that Act;

and the like definition to that in the said section 840 shall apply (with the necessary modifications) in relation to an employer which is an unincorporated association as that definition applies to a body corporate.

(4) In these Regulations references to an exempt approved scheme established by an employer include references to such a scheme to which that employer had contributed.

Amendments—[1] In para (1), definition of "the Taxes Act" inserted by Retirement Benefits Scheme (Tax Relief on Contributions) (Disapplication of Earnings Cap) (Amendment) Regulations, SI 1996/3113 reg 3, with effect from 1 January 1997.
[2] Words "Taxes Act" in paras (1), (3) substituted by Retirement Schemes (Tax Relief on Contributions) (Disapplication of Earnings Cap) (Amendment) Regulations, SI 1996/3113 reg 4, with effect from 1 January 1997.

Exempt approved schemes—disapplication of paragraph 5(4) of the Schedule

3—(1) In relation to any exempt approved scheme of which an employee is a member, the circumstances prescribed for the purposes of paragraph 18(4) of the Schedule as being those in which paragraphs 5(4) of the Schedule shall not have effect as regards that employee's remuneration in respect of an employment are, subject in each case to the satisfaction of one of the conditions contained in paragraph (3) below, any of those specified in paragraph (2) below.

(2) The circumstances specified in this paragraph are the following—

(*a*) before 1st June 1989 the employee became a member of the exempt approved scheme which came into existence before 14th March 1989;
(*b*) on or after 1st June 1989 the employee became a member of the exempt approved scheme which came into existence before 14th March 1989, but before the former date his employer was contractually bound to him to provide the benefits provided by the scheme;
(*c*) the employee became a member of the exempt approved scheme which came into existence on or after 14th March 1989, but before that date his employer was contractually bound to him to provide the benefits provided by the scheme;
(*d*) the employee became a member of a relevant statutory scheme in the circumstances described in regulation 4(2)(*a*), (*b*) or (*c*) below and on or after 1st June 1989—
(i) the office or employment by virtue of which contributions to that scheme were paid became an employment in respect of which the exempt approved scheme was established by his employer, and
(ii) one of the conditions contained in regulation 4(3) below was satisfied at the time in relation to his membership of the relevant statutory scheme;

and in paragraph (3) below "the scheme" means the exempt approved scheme referred to in sub-paragraph (*a*), (*b*), (*c*) or (*d*) above as the case may require.

(3) Subject to paragraph (4) below, the conditions contained in this paragraph are that—

(*a*) at all times since the employee became a member of the scheme benefits have continued to accrue to him under the scheme; or
(*b*) at all times since he became such a member benefits have continued to accrue to him under the scheme except during one or more periods in any of the circumstances specified in paragraph (5)(*b*), (*c*), (*d*) and (*e*) below; or
(*c*) benefits continued to accrue to him under the scheme at all times after he became such a member until they ceased so to accrue and—

(i) he became a member of another exempt approved scheme, whenever it came into existence (in this paragraph and in paragraph (5) below referred to as "the other scheme") in any of the circumstances specified in that paragraph, and

(ii) at all times since benefits have continued to accrue to him under the other scheme, or have continued so to accrue to him except as stated in sub-paragraph (*b*) above,

and this condition shall apply in relation to the cessation of the accrual of benefits under that other scheme (and under any further scheme of which the employee has become a member in any of those circumstances) as it applies in relation to the scheme and for the purposes of that application "the scheme" and "the other scheme" shall be construed accordingly.

(4) Where any of the schemes referred to in paragraph (3) above is a centralised scheme, benefits shall not be regarded as continuing to accrue to an employee under that scheme for the purposes of the relevant condition in that paragraph unless they continue so to accrue by virtue of his being employed by the same employer or by two or more employers who are relevant employers in relation to each other.

(5) The circumstances specified in this paragraph are circumstances where—

(*a*) benefits ceased to accrue to the employee under the scheme and he thereupon became a member of the other scheme which was established by his employer or by an employer who was a relevant employer in relation to his employer;

(*b*) benefits ceased to accrue to the employee under the scheme by reason of his secondment or posting to [a foreign branch of the employer or to][1] another employer and—

(i) at the end of the period of his secondment or posting he again became a member of the scheme or became a member of the other scheme which was established by the employer by whom he was seconded or posted or by an employer who was a relevant employer in relation to that employer, and

(ii) at the time of his secondment or posting he had a definite expectation that the condition contained in paragraph (i) of this sub-paragraph would be fulfilled;

(*c*) benefits ceased to accrue to the employee under the scheme by reason of his unpaid absence and, within one month of returning to work, he again became a member of the scheme or became a member of the other scheme which was established by the employer who established the scheme or by an employer who was a relevant employer in relation to that employer;

(*d*) benefits ceased to accrue to the employee under the scheme by reason of her pregnancy or confinement and, within one month of returning to work, she again became a member of the scheme or became a member of the other scheme which was established by the employer who established the scheme or by an employer who was a relevant employer in relation to that employer;

(*e*) benefits ceased to accrue to the employee under the scheme for a period not exceeding one month in circumstances other than those specified in sub-paragraph (*b*), (*c*) or (*d*) above.

Amendments—[1] Words in para (5)(*b*) inserted by SI 1993/3221, with effect from 11 January 1994.

Relevant statutory schemes—disapplication of paragraph 6(5) of the Schedule

4—(1) In relation to any relevant statutory scheme of which a person is a member, the circumstances prescribed for the purposes of paragraph 18(4) of the Schedule as being those in which paragraph 6(5) of the Schedule shall not have effect as regards that person's remuneration in respect of an office or employment are, subject in each case to the satisfaction of one of the conditions contained in paragraph (3) below, any of those specified in paragraph (2) below.

(2) The circumstances specified in this paragraph are the following—

(*a*) before 1st June 1989 the person became by virtue of his office or employment a member of the relevant statutory scheme which was established before 14th March 1989;

(*b*) on or after 1st June 1989 the person became a member of the relevant statutory scheme which was established before 14th March 1989, but before the former date he was entitled by virtue of his office or employment to be provided with the benefits provided by the scheme;

(*c*) the person became a member of the relevant statutory scheme which was established on or after 14th March 1989, but before that date he was entitled by virtue of his office or employment to be provided with the benefits provided by the scheme;

(*d*) the person became a member of an exempt approved scheme in the circumstances described in regulation 3(2)(*a*), (*b*) or (*c*) above and on or after 1st June 1989—

(i) the employment in respect of which contributions to that scheme were made became an office or employment by virtue of which contributions were paid to the relevant statutory scheme, and

(ii) one of the conditions contained in regulation 3(3) above was satisfied at the time in relation to his membership of the exempt approved scheme;

and in paragraph (3) below "the scheme" means the relevant statutory scheme referred to in sub-paragraph (*a*), (*b*), (*c*) or (*d*) above as the case may require.

(3) The conditions contained in this paragraph are that—

(*a*) at all times since the person became a member of the scheme benefits have continued to accrue to him under the scheme; or

(*b*) at all times since he became such a member benefits have continued to accrue to him under the scheme except during one or more periods in any of the circumstances specified in paragraph (4)(*b*), (*c*), (*d*) and (*e*) below; or

(*c*) if benefits have ceased to accrue to him under the scheme—

(i) he has become a member of another such scheme by virtue of the same office or employment, or of another such scheme having the same rules as the scheme or, where the other such scheme is a scheme established in another part of the United Kingdom, corresponding to the scheme (in this paragraph and in paragraph (4) below referred to in either case as "the other scheme") in any of the circumstances specified in that paragraph, and

(ii) at all times since benefits have continued to accrue to him under the other scheme, or have continued to accrue to him except as stated in sub-paragraph (*b*) above,

and this condition shall apply in relation to the cessation of the accrual of benefits under the other scheme (and under any further scheme of which the person has become a member in any of the circumstances referred to above) as it applies in relation to the scheme and for the purposes of that application "the scheme" and "the other scheme" shall be construed accordingly.

(4) The circumstances specified in this paragraph are where—

(*a*) benefits ceased to accrue to the person under the scheme and he thereupon became a member of the other scheme;

(*b*) benefits ceased to accrue to the person under the scheme by reason of his secondment or posting to another office or employment and—

(i) at the end of the period of his secondment or posting he again became a member of the scheme or became a member of the other scheme, and

(ii) at the time of his secondment or posting he had a definite expectation that the condition contained in paragraph (i) of this sub-paragraph would be fulfilled;

(*c*) benefits ceased to accrue to the person under the scheme by reason of his unpaid absence and, within one month of returning to work, he again became a member of the scheme or became a member of the other scheme;

(*d*) benefits ceased to accrue to the person under the scheme by reason of her pregnancy or confinement and, within one month of returning to work, she again became a member of the scheme or became a member of the other scheme;

(*e*) benefits ceased to accrue to the person under the scheme for a period of time, in circumstances other than those specified in sub-paragraph (*a*), (*b*), (*c*) or (*d*) above, and notwithstanding that period of cessation the person is entitled under the scheme to have remuneration taken into account for any year of assessment in arriving at—

(i) his relevant annual remuneration for the purposes of calculating benefits, and

(ii) his remuneration for that year for the purposes of any restriction on the aggregate amount of contributions payable

in excess of that which, if the scheme were a retirement benefits scheme to which Part II of the Schedule applies, would be the permitted maximum for that year (within the meaning of paragraph 20 of the Schedule).

Additional voluntary contributions—further disapplication of paragraphs 5(4) and 6(5) of the Schedule

5—(1) In relation to an exempt approved scheme or a relevant statutory scheme (in this regulation referred to in either case as "the AVC scheme") which provides benefits in addition to those provided by an exempt approved scheme or a relevant statutory scheme of which an employee or a person is a member, the circumstances prescribed for the purposes of paragraph 18(4) of the Schedule, as being those in which neither paragraph 5(4) nor paragraph 6(5) of the Schedule shall have effect as regards that employee's or that person's remuneration in respect of an office or employment, shall include those specified in paragraph (2) below.

(2) The circumstances specified in this paragraph are where—

(*a*) in relation to the exempt approved scheme which provides benefits to which the benefits provided by the AVC scheme are additional, paragraph 5(4) of the Schedule does not have effect as regards the employee's remuneration in respect of an employment by virtue of regulation 3 above, or

(*b*) in relation to the relevant statutory scheme which provides benefits to which the benefits provided by the AVC scheme are additional, paragraph 6(5) of the Schedule does not have effect as regards the person's remuneration in respect of an office or employment by virtue of regulation 4 above,

and the employee or the person became a member of the AVC scheme in circumstances other than those specified in regulation 3(2) or 4(2) above.

[Mis-sold pension contracts—further disapplication of paragraphs 5(4) and 6(5) of the Schedule

6—(1) In relation to any exempt approved scheme or relevant statutory scheme of which an employee or a person is a member, the circumstances prescribed for the purposes of paragraph 18(4) of the Schedule as being those in which neither paragraph 5(4) nor paragraph 6(5) of the Schedule shall have effect as regards that employee's or that person's remuneration in respect of an office or employment, shall include those prescribed in paragraph (2) below.

(2) The circumstances prescribed in this paragraph are where—

(*a*) the employee or the person concerned either—

(i) was eligible, or reasonably likely to become eligible, to be a member of the scheme before 1st June 1989 but, in the circumstances specified in paragraph (3) below, did not become a member, or

(ii) became a member of the scheme before that date but, in the circumstances specified in paragraph (4) below, ceased to be a member; and

(*b*) by way of compensation for loss suffered, or reasonably likely to be suffered, by that employee or that person as a result of the circumstances specified in paragraph (3) or (4) below—

(i) the employee became or, as the case may be, was reinstated as, a member of the exempt approved scheme, or became a member of another exempt approved scheme established by the same employer or by an employer who was a relevant employer in relation to that employer, or

(ii) the person became or, as the case may be, was reinstated as, a member of the relevant statutory scheme (''the original scheme''), or became a member of another relevant statutory scheme by virtue of the same office or employment, or of another relevant statutory scheme having the same rules as the original scheme or, where the other relevant statutory scheme is a scheme established in another part of the United Kingdom, corresponding to the original scheme, and

(iii) a capital sum was paid (whether or not to the trustees of the exempt approved scheme or relevant statutory scheme concerned) in respect of that employee or that person.

(3) The circumstances specified in this paragraph are where, acting in reliance on bad investment advice at least some of which was given during the period beginning with 29th April 1988 and ending with 31st May 1989, the employee or the person became a member of a personal pension scheme or entered into a retirement annuity contract.

(4) The circumstances specified in this paragraph are where, acting in reliance on bad investment advice at least some of which was given during the period beginning with 29th April and ending with 30th June 1994, the employee or the person—

(*a*) ceased to be a member of, or to pay contributions to, the scheme and instead became a member of a personal pension scheme or entered into a retirement annuity contract;

(*b*) ceased to be a member of the scheme as a result of the transfer of accrued rights of his under the scheme to a personal pension scheme; or

(*c*) ceased to be a member of the scheme and instead (by virtue of such a provision as is mentioned in section 591(2)(*g*) of the Taxes Act) entered into arrangements for securing relevant benefits by means of an annuity contract.

(5) In this regulation—

''bad investment advice'' means investment advice in respect of which an action against the person who gave it has been, or may be brought—

(*a*) in or for negligence;

(*b*) for breach of contract;

(*c*) by reason of a breach of a fiduciary obligation; or

[(*d*) by reason of a contravention which is actionable—

(i) under section 62 of the Financial Services Act 1986; or

(ii) under section 150 of the Financial Services and Markets Act 2000;][2]

[''investment advice''—

(*a*) in relation to a time before 1st December 2001, means advice such as is mentioned in paragraph 15 of Schedule 1 to the Financial Services Act 1986; and

(*b*) in relation to a time on or after that date, means advice such as is mentioned in Article 53 of the Financial Services and Markets Act 2000 (Regulated Activities) Order 2001;][2]

''personal pension scheme'' has the meaning given by section 630(1) of the Taxes Act;

''relevant benefits'' has the meaning given by section 612(1) of the Taxes Act;

''retirement annuity contract'' means a contract made before 1st July 1988 and approved by the Board under or by virtue of any provision of Chapter III of Part XIV of the Taxes Act;

''trustees'', in relation to a scheme which is not set up or established under a trust, means the administrator of the scheme within the meaning given by section 611AA of the Taxes Act in so far as it applies to a non-trust scheme.][1]

Amendments—[1] This regulation added by Retirement Benefits Schemes (Tax Relief on Contributions) (Disapplication of Earnings Cap) (Amendment) Regulations, SI 1996/3113 reg 5, with effect from 1 January 1997.

[2] In para (5), sub-para (*d*) in definition of ''bad investment advice'' substituted; and definition of ''investment advice'' substituted, by the Financial Services and Markets Act 2000 (Consequential Amendments) (Taxes) Order, SI 2001/3629 art 126 with effect from 1 December 2001, immediately after the coming into force of the Financial Services and Markets Act 2000 ss 411, 432(1), Sch 20 (and SI 2001/3629 Pts 1 and 2).

1990/1671
Movements of Capital (Required Information) Regulations 1990

Made by the Commissioners of Inland Revenue under TA 1988 s 765A(2)

Made	*10 August 1990*
Laid before the House of Commons	*13 August 1990*
Coming into Force	*3 September 1990*

Commentary—*Simon's Direct Tax Service* **D4.116A.**
Statement of Practice SP 2/92 para 23—Certain presumptions to apply to determine a company's residence in a member State.
Revenue & other press releases—IR 9-2-94 (per EEA Agreement, these Regulations apply to movements of capital between persons resident in member States on or after 1 January 1994).

Citation and commencement

1 These Regulations may be cited as the Movements of Capital (Required Information) Regulations 1990 and shall come into force on 3rd September 1990.

Interpretation

2 In these Regulations unless the context otherwise requires—

''the Board'' means the Commissioners of Inland Revenue;

''control'' has, in relation to a body corporate, the meaning given by section 840 of the Income and Corporation Taxes Act 1988;

''the Directive'' means the Directive of the Council of the European Communities dated 24th June 1988/88/361/EEC;

''the non-resident body corporate'' means the body corporate which is not resident in the United Kingdom and created or issued shares or debentures, or the shares or debentures of which were transferred to any person, in the course of a relevant transaction;

''the principal section'' means section 765A of the Income and Corporation Taxes Act 1988;

''relevant transaction'' means a movement of capital which would be unlawful under section 765(1) of the Income and Corporation Taxes Act 1988 if Article 1 of the Directive did not apply to it;

''the resident body corporate'' means the body corporate resident in the United Kingdom which has carried out a relevant transaction;

and any question whether a person is connected with another shall be determined in accordance with the like provisions as are contained in section 839(2) to (8) of the Income and Corporation Taxes Act 1988.

Information required for the purposes of the principal section

3—(1) This regulation specifies the information relating to a relevant transaction and the persons connected with it (in this regulation referred to as ''the required information'') which, subject to paragraph (5) below, is required to be given to the Board by the resident body corporate within six months of the carrying out of a relevant transaction.

(2) The required information so far as it relates to the resident body corporate is—

(*a*) its name;
(*b*) the nature of its trade or business;
(*c*) the tax office to which its accounts are submitted and its reference number there.

(3) The required information so far as it relates to the non-resident body corporate is—

(*a*) its name;
(*b*) the territory from the laws of which it derives its status as a body corporate;
(*c*) where the relevant transaction was causing or permitting the non-resident body corporate to issue shares, or to create and issue debentures, the member State in which the non-resident body corporate is claimed to have been resident for the purposes of the Directive at the time of that issue, or of that creation and issue, as the case may be, the grounds on which that claim is made and the facts which support it;
(*d*) the nature of its trade or business;
(*e*) the extent to which the resident body corporate has control over it and the means by which, or the powers by virtue of which, that control is exercisable—

(i) before the relevant transaction was carried out, and
(ii) after the relevant transaction was carried out.

(4) The required information so far as it relates to the relevant transaction is a full description of the transaction and of all steps taken in the course of the transaction and, without prejudice to the generality of that requirement, includes in particular—

(*a*) the date on which the transaction was carried out;
(*b*) the name of any person to whom shares or debentures were issued or transferred;
(*c*) where that person is a body corporate, the territory from the laws of which it derives that status;
(*d*) the member State in which that person is claimed to have been resident for the purposes of the Directive at the time of the issue or transfer, the grounds on which that claim is made and the facts which support it;
(*e*) whether, and if so in what way, any such person is connected with the resident body corporate;
(*f*) where the relevant transaction was causing or permitting the non-resident body corporate to issue shares—

(i) the class or category of those shares,
(ii) the dividend rights attaching to them, and
(iii) if the terms on which they were issued included provision for their redemption, the circumstances in which they can be redeemed;

(*g*) where the relevant transaction was causing or permitting the non-resident body corporate to create and issue debentures—

(i) the rate at which interest is payable on the amount secured by them,
(ii) any amount by which the issue price was less than the amount payable on their redemption, and
(iii) whether any amount payable in respect of the debentures is determined by reference to the movement of an index of prices, earnings or any other indicator of an economic nature published in the United Kingdom or elsewhere;

(*h*) where the relevant transaction was transferring shares or debentures, or causing or permitting shares or debentures to be transferred—

(i) the name of any body corporate making the transfer if that body corporate was not the resident body corporate,
(ii) the territory from the laws of which that body corporate derives that status,
(iii) the member State in which it is claimed to have been resident for the purposes of the Directive at the time of the transfer, the grounds on which that claim is made and the facts which support it;

(*i*) the consideration given for any issue or transfer of shares or debentures and, if that issue or transfer was not for full consideration in money or money's worth, the reason why full consideration was not given;
(*j*) the reason for the transaction and an estimate of the effect of that transaction on the liability to tax in the United Kingdom of the resident body corporate and of any company which would be deemed to be a member of the group of companies which includes the resident body corporate for the purposes of Chapter IV of Part X of the Income and Corporation Taxes Act 1988 if in section 413(3) of that Act the words ''51 per cent subsidiary'' were substituted for the words ''75 per cent subsidiary''.

(5) Where a resident body corporate has caused or permitted shares or debentures to be created, issued or transferred, or has transferred shares or debentures, and another resident body corporate has already given the required information relating to the creation, issue or transfer in question and the persons connected with it, the first mentioned resident body corporate is not required to give any information relating to those matters or those persons.

Statement of Practice SP 2/92 para 23—Certain presumptions to apply to determine a company's residence in a member State.

Notice to give further particulars—prescribed period

4 The period prescribed by this regulation within which the resident body corporate shall give to the Board such further particulars as the Board may require in accordance with subsection (2)(*b*) of the principal section is 60 days from the date of the notice given by the Board under that subsection.

1990/2101
Retirement Benefits Schemes (Continuation of Rights of Members of Approved Schemes) Regulations 1990

Made by the Commissioners of Inland Revenue under FA 1989 Sch 6 para 19(2), (3)

Made	*22 October 1990*
Laid before the House of Commons .	*24 October 1990*
Coming into Force	*14 November 1990*

Commentary—*Simon's Direct Tax Service* **E7.226**.

Citation, commencement and effect

1 These Regulations may be cited as the Retirement Benefits Schemes (Continuation of Rights of Members of Approved Schemes) Regulations 1990 and shall come into force on 14th November 1990 but shall take effect as from 14th March 1989.

Interpretation

2—(1) In these Regulations unless the context otherwise requires—

''approved scheme'' means a retirement benefits scheme approved by the Board for the purposes of Chapter I of Part XIV of the [Taxes Act][2];

[''bad investment advice'' means investment advice in respect of which an action against the person who gave it has been, or may be, brought—

(*a*) in or for negligence;

(*b*) for breach of contract;

(*c*) by reason of a breach of fiduciary obligation; or

[(*d*) by reason of a contravention which is actionable—

(i) under section 62 of the Financial Services Act 1986; or

(ii) under section 150 of the Financial Services and Markets Act 2000;][3]][1]

''the Board'' means the Commissioners of Inland Revenue;

''business'' includes a business carried on in the course of a trade or profession and any activity carried on by a body of persons, whether corporate or unincorporate;

[''investment advice''—

(*a*) in relation to a time before 1st December 2001, means advice such as is mentioned in paragraph 15 of Schedule 1 to the Financial Services Act 1986; and

(*b*) in relation to a time on or after that date, means advice such as is mentioned in Article 53 of the Financial Services and Markets Act 2000 (Regulated Activities) Order 2001;][3]

[''personal pension scheme'' has the meaning given by section 630(1) of the Taxes Act;][1]

''relevant approved scheme'' means an approved scheme which was approved by the Board before 27th July 1989;

''relevant employer'' in relation to another employer means—

(*a*) an employer who is associated with the other employer, or

(*b*) an employer—

(i) who has acquired, or who has been acquired by, or

(ii) who has taken over the whole or part of the business of, or the whole or part of whose business has been taken over by,

the other employer;

''the Schedule'' means Part II of Schedule 6 to the Finance Act 1989.

[''the Taxes Act'' means the Income and Corporation Taxes Act 1988.][1]

(2) For the purpose of this regulation an employer is associated with another employer if (directly or indirectly) one is controlled by the other or if both are controlled by a third person.

(3) In paragraph (2) above the reference to control—

(*a*) in relation to an employer which is a body corporate and a close company within the meaning of section 414 of the [Taxes Act][2], shall be construed in accordance with section 416 of that Act, and

(*b*) in relation to any employer which is a body corporate other than one mentioned in sub-paragraph (*a*) above or a partnership, shall be construed in accordance with section 840 of that Act;

and the like definition to that in the said section 840 shall apply (with the necessary modifications) in relation to an employer which is an unincorporated association as that definition applies to a body corporate.

(4) In these Regulations references to a scheme which was established by an employer include references to a scheme to which that employer had contributed.

Amendments—[1] Definitions in para (1) inserted by the Retirement Benefits Schemes (Continuation of Rights of Members of Approved Schemes) (Amendment) Regulations, SI 1996/3114 reg 3, with effect from 1 January 1997.

[2] Words ''Taxes Act'' in paras (1), (3) substituted by SI 1996/3114 reg 4, with effect from 1 January 1997.

[3] In para (1), sub-para (*d*) in the definition of ''bad investment advice'' substituted; and definition of ''investment advice'' substituted, by the Financial Services and Markets Act 2000 (Consequential Amendments) (Taxes) Order, SI 2001/3629 art 127 with effect from 1 December 2001, immediately after the coming into force of the Financial Services and Markets Act 2000 ss 411, 432(1), Sch 20 (and SI 2001/3629 Pts 1 and 2).

Disapplication of paragraphs 20 and 22 to 26 of the Schedule

3—(1) Paragraphs 20 and 22 to 26 of the Schedule shall not apply as regards an employee in the circumstances prescribed in paragraph (2), (3), (4), (6) or (8) below.

(2) The circumstances prescribed in this paragraph are circumstances where—

(*a*) the scheme came into existence before 14th March 1989, and [(*b*) the employee—

(i) became a member of the scheme on or after 1st June 1989 and within the period of three months following the commencement of the employment, or

(ii) acting in reliance on bad investment advice given on or after that date and within that period, did not become a member of the scheme but became a member of a personal pension scheme on or after that date and within that period;][3]

but before 1st June 1989 the employer was contractually bound to the employee to procure the provision of the benefits which the scheme provided.

(3) The circumstances prescribed in this paragraph are circumstances where—

(*a*) the scheme came into existence on or after 14th March 1989, and

[(*b*) the employee—

(i) became a member of the scheme within the period of three months following that date, or

(ii) acting in reliance on bad investment advice given within that period, did not become a member of the scheme but became a member of a personal pension scheme on or after that date and within that period;][3]

but before 14th March 1989 the employer was contractually bound to the employee to procure the provision of the benefits which the scheme provided.

(4) The circumstances prescribed in this paragraph are circumstances where—

(*a*) the scheme came into existence before 14th March 1989 and the employee became a member of the scheme before 1st June 1989, or

(*b*) the employer was contractually bound to the employee to procure the provision of the benefits which the scheme provided in the circumstances prescribed in paragraph (2) or (3) above,

and the employee's membership of the scheme ceased and he again became a member of that scheme in the circumstances specified in paragraph (5) below.

(5) The circumstances specified in this paragraph are circumstances where—

(*a*) benefits ceased to accrue to the employee under the scheme by virtue of his employment by reason of his secondment or posting to [a foreign branch of the employer or to][1] another employer and—

(i) on or after 1st June 1989 the period of his secondment or posting ended and he again became a member of the scheme, and

(ii) at the time of his secondment or posting he had a definite expectation that he would again become a member of the scheme when the period of his secondment or posting ended; or

(*b*) benefits ceased to accrue to the employee under the scheme by virtue of his employment by reason of his unpaid absence and, on or after 1st June 1989 and within one month of returning to work, he again became a member of the scheme; or

(*c*) benefits ceased to accrue to the employee under the scheme by virtue of her employment wholly or partly because of pregnancy or confinement and, on or after 1st June 1989 and within one month of returning to work in accordance with section 45(1) or (3) of the Employment Protection (Consolidation) Act 1978, she again became a member of the scheme; or

(*d*) benefits ceased to accrue to the employee under the scheme by virtue of his employment (where the circumstances were other than those specified in sub-paragraph (*a*), (*b*) or (*c*) above) and, on or after 1st June 1989 and within one month of benefits ceasing so to accrue, he again became a member of the scheme.

(6) The circumstances prescribed in this paragraph are circumstances where—

(*a*) the employee became a member of a retirement benefits scheme (in this paragraph and in paragraph (7) below referred to as "the original scheme") before 1st June 1989 and at all times when the employee was a member of the original scheme it was either—

(i) a scheme which was before the Board in order for them to decide whether to give approval for the purposes of Chapter I of Part XIV of the [Taxes Act][2], or

(ii) an approved scheme, or

(*b*) the employer was contractually bound to the employee to procure the provision of the benefits which the original scheme provided in the like circumstances to those prescribed in paragraph (2) or (3) above,

and the employee's membership of the original scheme ceased and he became a member of the scheme in the circumstances specified in paragraph (7) below.

(7) The circumstances specified in this paragraph are—

(*a*) circumstances where on or after 1st June 1989 benefits ceased to accrue to the employee under the original scheme by virtue of his employment and he thereupon became a member of the scheme which was established by the employer who established the original scheme or by an employer who was a relevant employer in relation to that employer; or

(*b*) the like circumstances to those specified in paragraph (5)(*a*), (*b*), (*c*) or (*d*) above with the substitution—

(i) for references to benefits ceasing to accrue under the scheme of references to benefits ceasing to accrue under the original scheme;

(ii) for references to again becoming a member of the scheme of references to becoming a member of the scheme which was established by the employer who established the original scheme or by an employer who was a relevant employer in relation to that employer;

(iii) for the reference in sub-paragraph (*d*) of paragraph (5) to the circumstances specified in sub-paragraph (*a*), (*b*) or (*c*) of that paragraph of a reference to the like circumstances to those specified in those sub-paragraphs as modified by paragraphs (i) and (ii) of this sub-paragraph.

(8) The circumstances prescribed in this paragraph are circumstances where—

(*a*) the scheme came into existence before 14th March 1989 and the employee became a member of the scheme before 1st June 1989, or

(*b*) the employer was contractually bound to the employee to procure the provision of the benefits which the scheme provided in the circumstances prescribed in paragraph (2) or (3) above,

and, without benefits ceasing to accrue to the employee under the scheme by virtue of his employment, on or after 1st June 1989 he became a member of another relevant approved scheme which provides benefits which supplement those provided under the scheme.

(9) Where the scheme is a centralised scheme, this regulation shall have effect with the substitution for references to the coming into existence of the scheme of a reference to the commencement of the employer's participation in the scheme; and for the purposes of this paragraph ''a centralised scheme'' has the same meaning as it has for the purposes of paragraph 28 of the Schedule.

Amendments—[1] Words in para (5)(*a*) inserted by the Retirement Benefits Schemes (Continuation of Rights of Members of Approved Schemes) (Amendment) Regulations, SI 1993/3220 regs 1, 2, 3, with effect from 14 March 1989.
[2] Words ''Taxes Act'' in para (6) substituted by the Retirement Benefits Schemes (Continuation of Rights of Members of Approved Schemes) (Amendment) Regulations, SI 1996/3114 reg 4, with effect from 1 January 1997.
[3] Paras (2)(*b*), (3)(*b*) substituted by SI 1996/3114 reg 5, with effect from 1 January 1997.

[Disapplication of paragraphs 20 and 22 to 26 of the Schedule—further provision

3A—(1) Paragraphs 20 and 22 to 26 of the Schedule shall not apply as regards an employee in the circumstances prescribed in paragraph (2) below.

(2) The circumstances prescribed in this paragraph are circumstances where—

(*a*) the employee either—

(i) was eligible, or reasonably likely to become eligible, to be a member of a scheme before 1st June 1989 but, in the circumstances specified in paragraph (3) below, did not become a member, or

(ii) became a member of a scheme before that date but, in the circumstances specified in paragraph (4) below, ceased to be a member; and

(*b*) by way of compensation for loss suffered, or reasonably likely to be suffered, by the employee as a result of the circumstances specified in paragraph (3) or (4) below—

(i) the employee becomes or, as the case may be, is reinstated as, a member of that scheme, or becomes a member of another scheme established by the employer or by an employer who was a relevant employer in relation to that employer, and

(ii) a capital sum is paid [on or after 1st January 1997][2] (whether or not to the trustees of the scheme) in respect of the employee.

(3) The circumstances specified in this paragraph are circumstances where, acting in reliance on bad investment advice at least some of which was given during the period beginning with 29th April 1988 and ending with 31st May 1989, the employee became a member of a personal pension scheme or entered into a retirement annuity contract.

(4) The circumstances specified in this paragraph are circumstances where, acting in reliance on bad investment advice at least some of which was given during the period beginning with 29th April 1988 and ending with 30th June 1994, the employee—

(*a*) ceased to be a member of, or to pay contributions to, the scheme and instead became a member of a personal pension scheme or entered into a retirement annuity contract;

(*b*) ceased to be a member of the scheme as a result of the transfer of accrued rights of his under the scheme to a personal pension scheme; or

(*c*) ceased to be a member of the scheme and instead (by virtue of such a provision as is mentioned in section 591(2)(*g*) of the Taxes Act) entered into arrangements for securing relevant benefits by means of an annuity contract.

(5) In this regulation—

''relevant benefits'' has the meaning given by section 612(1) of the Taxes Act;

''retirement annuity contract'' means a contract made before 1st July 1988 and approved by the Board under or by virtue of any provision of Chapter III of Part XIV of the Taxes Act.][1]

Amendments—[1] This regulation inserted by Retirement Benefits Schemes (Continuation of Rights of Members of Approved Schemes) (Amendment) Regulations, SI 1996/3114 reg 6, with effect from 1 January 1997.
[2] Words in para (2)(*b*)(ii) substituted by Retirement Benefits Schemes (Continuation of Rights of Members of Approved Schemes) (Amendment No 2) Regulations, SI 1996/3233, with effect from 1 January 1997.

[Disapplication of paragraph 21 of the Schedule

3B—(1) Paragraph 21 of the Schedule shall not apply as regards an employee in the circumstances prescribed in paragraph (2) below and as respects the year or years of assessment specified in paragraph (3) below.

(2) The circumstances prescribed in this paragraph are circumstances where—

(*a*) an employee is admitted to membership of the scheme,

(*b*) benefits are to be provided under the scheme in respect of years of service of the employee ending prior to the year of assessment in which he is admitted to membership of the scheme,

(*c*) under the rules of the scheme the employee is required to contribute towards the cost of those benefits, and

(*d*) the annual rate, expressed as a monetary sum or as a percentage of his remuneration, that the employee is required to contribute under the rules of the scheme towards the cost of those benefits either—

(i) is the same as the annual rate that he would have been required to contribute under those rules towards the cost of those benefits if he had been a member of the scheme in the years of service in respect of which those benefits are to be provided, or

(ii) is the same as the annual rate that he is required to contribute under those rules towards the cost of benefits accruing in respect of his current year of service.

(3) The year or years of assessment specified is the year or years of assessment in which the employee makes the contribution referred to in paragraph (2)(*c*) above.][1]

Amendments—[1] This regulation inserted by Retirement Benefits Schemes (Continuation of Rights of Members of Approved Schemes) (Amendment) Regulations, SI 1996/3114 reg 6, with effect from 1 January 1997.

Disapplication of paragraphs 23 and 24 of the Schedule

4—(1) Paragraphs 23 and 24 of the Schedule shall not apply as regards an employee in the circumstances prescribed in paragraph (2), (3) or (4) below.

(2) The circumstances prescribed in this paragraph are circumstances where the scheme of which the employee is a member is a simplified defined contribution scheme.

(3) The circumstances prescribed in this paragraph are circumstances where the amount of the employee's total pension does not exceed £104 per annum or such higher amount as may be prescribed from time to time for the purposes of paragraph 15(4) of Schedule 16 to the Social Security Act 1973 or paragraph 15(4) of Schedule 3 to the Social Security Pensions (Northern Ireland) Order 1975.

(4) The circumstances prescribed in this paragraph are circumstances where—

(*a*) the rules of the scheme provide that the trustees or administrator of the scheme have power to commute, in whole or in part, the pension secured for an employee if he is in exceptional circumstances of serious ill health, and

(*b*) the trustees or administrator have exercised that power in relation to the employee.

(5) In this regulation—

"simplified defined contribution scheme" means a relevant approved scheme which is approved by the Board by virtue of section 591 of the [Taxes Act][1] by reference to limitations on—

(*a*) the aggregate amount of contributions which may be paid by the member and his employer,

(*b*) the maximum lump sum which may be provided under the scheme, and

(*c*) the benefits payable on death which may be provided under the scheme;

"total pension" means in relation to an employee the aggregate of all benefits to him (including the value in terms of an annual pension of any lump sum or sums received or receivable by him)—

(*a*) from approved schemes established by his employer, and

(*b*) from approved schemes to which his employer has not contributed and which, by virtue of contributions made by the employee while he was employed by that employer, provide benefits in addition to those provided by schemes to which his employer has contributed.

Amendments—[1] Words "Taxes Act" in para (5) substituted by Retirement Benefits Schemes (Continuation of Rights of Members of Approved Schemes) (Amendment) Regulations, SI 1996/3114 reg 4 with effect from 1 January 1997.

Modification of paragraph 20 of the Schedule

5—(1) In the circumstances prescribed in paragraph (2) below, paragraph 20 of the Schedule shall be modified so as to contain a provision that the rules of the scheme are to have effect (notwithstanding anything in them to the contrary and notwithstanding the effect of anything in Schedule 23 to the [Taxes Act][1]) as if, for the purpose of calculating benefits under the scheme—

(*a*) the fraction of the employee's relevant annual remuneration derived from added years of service was to be applied separately from the fraction derived from actual years of service, and (*b*) only in the latter case was any excess of what would be his relevant annual remuneration (apart from the said paragraph 20) over the permitted maximum for the year to be disregarded in arriving at that relevant annual remuneration.

(2) The circumstances prescribed in this paragraph are circumstances where—

(*a*) under the rules of the scheme a transfer payment accepted by the scheme has been treated as entitling the employee to be considered as having years of service in addition to his actual years of service; and

(*b*) paragraph 20 of the Schedule did not apply as regards the employee when he was a member of the scheme from which the transfer was accepted;

and in this regulation such additional years are referred to as "added years of service".

Amendments—[1] Words "Taxes Act" in para (1) substituted by Retirement Benefits Schemes (Continuation of Rights of Members of Approved Schemes) (Amendment) Regulations, SI 1996/3114 reg 4, with effect from 1 January 1997.

Modification of paragraph 21 of the Schedule

6—(1) In the circumstances prescribed in paragraph (2) below, paragraph 21(1) of the Schedule shall be modified so that the reference to the amount of contributions payable under the scheme does not include a reference to any of the payments referred to in paragraph (2) below.

(2) The circumstances prescribed in this paragraph are circumstances where the employee—

(*a*) is required by the rules of the scheme as they have effect, and as they had effect on 13th March 1989, to make good a shortfall in contributions by a payment consisting of a single lump sum, or

(*b*) was a member of the scheme on 27th July 1989 and on retirement makes a payment consisting of a lump sum, either directly or by authorising the scheme administrator to deduct it from any lump sum benefit due to him, for the purpose of buying, or completing the purchase of, rights to benefits under the scheme up to the maximum provided under the rules.

[Modification of paragraph 21 of the Schedule—further provision

6A—(1) In the circumstances prescribed in paragraph (2) below, paragraph 21(1) of the Schedule shall be modified so as to substitute for the reference to the limitation of 15 per cent of the employee's remuneration for the year in respect of the employment a reference to a limitation of 15 per cent of what would have been his remuneration for the year in respect of the employment if he had not been temporarily absent throughout, or at any time during, that year.

(2) The circumstances prescribed in this paragraph are circumstances where the employee is temporarily absent throughout, or at any time during, a year of assessment and either—

(*a*) is not paid any remuneration in respect of the employment for the period of absence, or

(*b*) is paid a reduced amount of remuneration for that period.

(3) In this regulation "temporarily absent" in relation to an employee means that the employee—

(*a*) has a definite expectation that he will return to service in the employment, and

(*b*) does not in the course of his absence become a member of—

(i) an approved scheme of another employer who is not a relevant employer, or

(ii) a retirement benefits scheme of another employer who is not a relevant employer, which at the time of his becoming a member was before the Board in order for them to decide whether to give approval for the purposes of Chapter I of Part XIV of the [Taxes Act][2], or

(iii) a personal pension scheme within the meaning of section 630 of the [Taxes Act][2] other than a scheme which permits the acceptance only of minimum contributions paid as mentioned in section 638(6)(*c*) of that Act.][1]

Amendments—[1] The Regulation inserted by the Retirement Benefits Schemes (Continuation of Rights of Members of Approved Schemes) (Amendment) Regulations, SI 1993/3220 regs 1, 2, 4, with effect from 14 March 1989.

[2] Words "Taxes Act" in para (3)(*b*)(ii), (iii) substituted by Retirement Benefits Schemes (Continuation of Rights of Members of Approved Schemes) (Amendment) Regulations, SI 1996/3114 reg 4, with effect from 1 January 1997.

Modification of paragraph 23 of the Schedule

7—(1) In the circumstances prescribed in paragraph (2) below, paragraph 23(2)(*b*) of the Schedule shall be modified so as to include in the reference to the pension payable under the scheme to the employee for the first year in which it is payable a reference to any pension payable to the employee for that year by virtue of voluntary contributions which he had made to an approved scheme while he was employed by his employer.

(2) The circumstances prescribed in this paragraph are circumstances where—

(*a*) the approved scheme referred to in paragraph (1) above is a scheme other than the one which provides the benefits which the voluntary contributions are intended to supplement;

(*b*) the employee is a member of both schemes by virtue of the same employment;

(*c*) the modification of paragraph 23(2)(*b*) of the Schedule made by paragraph (1) above has not already been made in relation to the rules of a relevant approved scheme of which the employee is a member.

[Modification of paragraph 23 of the Schedule—further provision

[7AA—(1) In the circumstances prescribed in paragraph (2) below, paragraph 23 of the Schedule shall be modified so that the references in paragraph 23(2)(*b*) and (3) to the pension payable under the scheme to the employee for the first year in which it is payable shall be construed disregarding the period between the first event and the second event.

(2) The circumstances prescribed in this paragraph are circumstances where a pension becomes payable by virtue of voluntary contributions made to an approved scheme by the employee (in this regulation referred to as "the first event"), before benefits provided for him by—

(*a*) the principal provisions of the scheme, or

(*b*) where the scheme contains provision for the payment of voluntary contributions which is freestanding, the main scheme,

become payable (in this regulation referred to as "the second event").

(3) In this regulation "freestanding", "principal provisions" and "the main scheme" have the same meanings as in paragraph 35 of Schedule 6 to the Finance Act 1989.][1]

Amendments—[1] This regulation inserted by the Retirement Benefits Schemes (Continuation of Rights of Members of Approved Schemes) (Amendment) Regulations, SI 1999/1963 regs 1, 3 with effect from 30 July 1999.

[Modification of paragraphs 23 and 24 of the Schedule

7A—(1) In the circumstances prescribed in paragraph (2) below, paragraphs 23(2) and 24(2) of the Schedule shall be modified so as to substitute for the reference in each of those provisions to years of service a reference to years of service that would have been counted if the employee had remained in employment until his normal retirement date.

(2) The circumstances prescribed in this paragraph are circumstances where the employee retires before his normal retirement date as a result of incapacity.

(3) In this regulation—

(*a*) "normal retirement date" means the date specified in the rules of the scheme as the date at which the employee will normally retire;

(*b*) "incapacity" means physical or mental deterioration which is sufficiently serious to prevent an employee from following his normal employment or which seriously impairs his earning capacity.][1]

Amendments—[1] This regulation inserted by the Retirement Benefits Schemes (Continuation of Rights of Members of Approved Schemes) (Amendment) Regulations, SI 1993/3220 regs 1, 2, 5, with effect from 14 March 1989.

Authorisation of the Board to direct

8 This regulation authorises—

(*a*) the Board to direct that the Schedule or any provision of it shall not apply in any particular case where in the opinion of the Board the facts are such that its application would not be appropriate, and

(*b*) any direction given under this regulation to take effect as from 14th March 1989 or any later date.

1990/2231
Income Tax (Building Societies) (Dividends and Interest) Regulations 1990

Made by the Commissioners of Inland Revenue under TA 1988 s 477A(1) and FA 1990 Sch 5 para 16

Made . . . . *8 November 1990*
Laid before the House of Commons . . *9 November 1990*
Coming into Force . . . . *30 November 1990*

Commentary—*Simon's Direct Tax Service* **A3.120; B5.221–228; D4.727–730, 758.**
Concession A69—Certificate of non-liability to tax etc satisfying conditions of these Regulations given before a building society's conversion to company status.
B13—Untaxed interest paid to non-residents.

Citation, commencement and effect

1 These Regulations may be cited as the Income Tax (Building Societies) (Dividends and Interest) Regulations 1990, shall come into force on 30th November 1990 and shall have effect with respect to the year 1991–92 and subsequent years of assessment.

Interpretation

2—[(1)][4] In these Regulations unless the context otherwise requires—

["the appropriate person" means any person who is beneficially entitled to a payment by a building society of a dividend or interest in respect of an investment, or is entitled to receive any such payment [in his capacity as a personal representative or as a trustee of a discretionary or accumulation trust][5], or to whom any such dividend or interest is payable;][1]

"the Board" means the Commissioners of Inland Revenue;

["discretionary or accumulation trust" means a trust which is such that some or all of any income arising to the trustees would fall (unless treated as income of the settlor or applied in defraying expenses of the trustees) to be comprised for the year in which it arises in income to which section 686 of the Taxes Act (liability to additional rate tax of certain income of discretionary trusts) applies;][6]

"dividend" means any distribution in respect of investments including any qualifying distribution as defined for the purposes of the Corporation Tax Acts and whether described as a dividend or otherwise;

. . .[3]

["electronic communication" includes any communication conveyed by means of an electronic communications network.][8]

["electronic signature" has the meaning given by section 7(2) of the Electronic Communications Act 2000;][7]

"general client account deposit" means a deposit held by a building society in a client account (other than one which is identified by the building society as one in which sums are held only for one or more particular clients of the person whose account it is) in respect of which that person is required by provision made under any enactment to make payments representing interest to some or all of the clients for whom, or on whose account, he received the sums deposited in the account;

"gross payment" means a payment falling within any of the descriptions in regulation 4;

"inspector" includes any officer of the Board;

"investment" includes any shareholding, deposit or loan;

"investor" means the holder of an account with a building society in relation to which a payment of a dividend or interest in respect of an investment is made;

["mental disorder" has the meaning given by section 1(2) of the Mental Health Act 1983 or, in Scotland, section 1(2) of the Mental Health (Scotland) Act 1984 or, in Northern Ireland, Article 3 of the Mental Health (Northern Ireland) Order 1986;][1]

"notice" means notice in writing;

"payment" (except in relation to a payment to the Board) includes "credit" and "paid" shall be construed accordingly;

"payment quarter" means a period of three months ending with the last day of February, May, August or November;

["qualifying certificate of deposit" has the meaning given by section 349(4) of the Taxes Act;][2]

["qualifying deposit right" has the meaning given by section 349(4) of the Taxes Act reading "paid" as "paid or credited";][2]

"qualifying time deposit" in relation to interest paid on a deposit made before 6th April 1991 has the meaning given by regulation 2(1) of the 1986 Regulations, but otherwise has the meaning given by section 482(6) of the Taxes Act;

"the 1986 Regulations" mean the Income Tax (Building Societies) Regulations 1986;

["son or daughter" means a son or daughter aged 16 or over, and includes a stepson or stepdaughter and an adopted or illegitimate son or daughter;][1]

"the Taxes Act" means the Income and Corporation Taxes Act 1988;

"year" means a year beginning with 6th April in any year and ending with 5th April in the following year.

[(2) References in these Regulations to a beneficiary in relation to a discretionary or accumulation trust are references to any person who, as a person falling wholly or partly within any description of actual or potential beneficiaries, is either—

(*a*) a person who is, or will or may become, entitled under the trust to receive the whole or any part of any income under the trust; or

(*b*) a person to or for the benefit of whom the whole or any part of any such income may be paid or applied in exercise of any discretion conferred by the trust.

(3) References in paragraph (2) to income under the trust include references to so much (if any) of any property falling to be treated as capital under the trust as represents amounts originally received by the trustees as income.][6]

Amendments—[1] Definitions of "the appropriate person", "mental disorder", "son or daughter" in para (1) inserted by the IT (Building Societies) (Dividends and Interest) (Amendment) Regulations, SI 1992/11 reg 3.

[2] Definitions of "qualifying certificate of deposit" and "qualifying deposit right" in para (1) substituted for the definition of "qualifying certificate of deposit" by the IT (Building Societies) (Dividends and Interest) (Amendment No 2) Regulations, SI 1992/2915 reg 3, with effect from 14 December 1992.

[3] Definition of "exempt friendly society" revoked by SI 1992/2915 reg 3.

[4] "(1)" at the beginning of the Regulation inserted by the IT (Buildings Societies) (Dividends and Interest) (Amendment) Regulations, SI 1996/223 reg 3(1) with effect from 28 February 1996.

[5] Words in definition of "the appropriate person" in para (1) substituted by SI 1996/223 reg 3(2)(*a*).

[6] Definition of "discretionary or accumulation trust" and paras (2), (3) inserted by SI 1996/223 reg 3(2)(*b*), (3).

[7] Definitions of "electronic communication" and "electronic signature" inserted by the IT (Buildings Societies) (Dividends and Interest) (Amendment) Regulations, SI 2001/404 regs 3, 4, with effect from 9 March 2001.

[8] Definition of "electronic communication" substituted by the Communications Act 2003 (Consequential Amendments) Order, SI 2003/2155 Sch 1 para 24(1)(*a*), (2) with effect from 17 September 2003.

Deduction and payment of income tax

3—(1) In the cases prescribed by paragraph (2) a building society shall, on making any payment of a dividend or interest in respect of shares in, or deposits with or loans to, the society, deduct out of the payment a sum representing the amount of income tax on it for the year in which the payment was made, and shall account for and pay to the Board in accordance with regulation 10 the sum which it was liable to deduct.

[(2) The cases prescribed by this paragraph are all payments of dividends or interest in respect of an investment other than—

(*a*) gross payments, and

(*b*) payments referred to in section 477A(1A) of the Taxes Act.][1].

Amendments—[1] Para (2) substituted by the IT (Building Societies) (Dividends and Interest) (Amendment) Regulations, SI 1992/11 reg 4, with effect from 30 January 1992.

Gross payments

4—(1) A gross payment is a payment by a building society of a dividend or interest in respect of an investment which at the time of payment falls within any of the following descriptions—

(*a*) a payment to an individual beneficially entitled to the payment or to individuals jointly so entitled (including a Scottish partnership, all the partners in which are individuals), being an individual or individuals not ordinarily resident in the United Kingdom;

(*b*) a payment to trustees of a trust in the income of which no person has an interest apart from—

(i) an individual who is not ordinarily resident in the United Kingdom, or

(ii) a Scottish partnership, all the partners in which are such individuals;

[(*bb*) a payment to trustees of a discretionary or accumulation trust in their capacity as such where the trustees are not resident in the United Kingdom and any person who is a beneficiary of the trust is—

(i) an individual who is not ordinarily resident in the United Kingdom, or

(ii) a Scottish partnership, all the partners in which are individuals not ordinarily resident in the United Kingdom, or

(iii) a company within the meaning of section 832(1) of the Taxes Act which is not resident in the United Kingdom;[10]]

(*c*) a payment to personal representatives in respect of an investment forming part of a deceased person's estate which was beneficially owned by the deceased, being an individual not ordinarily resident in the United Kingdom at the time of his death (or in respect of an investment representing that investment or dividends or interest thereon);

(*d*) a payment to a charity in respect of which exemption is granted under section 505(1)(*c*) of the Taxes Act;

...[5]

[(*f*) a payment to an exempt approved scheme within the meaning of subsection (1) of section 592 of the Taxes Act, or to any scheme which is before the Board in order for them to decide whether the scheme qualifies as an exempt approved scheme within the meaning of that subsection;][7]

[(*g*) a payment to a company within the meaning of section 832(1) of the Taxes Act;][6]

(*h*) a payment of interest on a bank loan;

...[5]

(*j*) a payment in respect of a qualifying certificate of deposit[, qualifying deposit right][3] or a qualifying time deposit;

(*k*) a payment for the purposes of approved personal pension arrangements as defined in section 630 of the Taxes Act;

(*l*) a payment in respect of a general client account deposit;

(*m*) ...[2]

(*n*) a payment to or for the benefit of an individual ordinarily resident in the United Kingdom or two or more such individuals jointly in circumstances where the conditions prescribed by regulations 5, 6 and 8 and, where applicable, regulation 9 are fulfilled.

[(*o*) a payment in respect of an investment forming part of a premiums trust fund [(within the meaning of section 184(1) of the Finance Act 1993)][11] of an underwriting member of Lloyd's;][1]

[(*p*) a payment to a local authority within the meaning of section 842A of the Taxes Act.][1]

[(*q*) a payment to a health service body within the meaning of section 519A of the Taxes Act;][4]

[(*r*) a payment to trustees of a unit trust scheme within the meaning of section [237(1) of the Financial Services and Markets Act 2000][13];][4]

[(*s*) a payment in respect of an investment held at a branch of the building society situated outside the United Kingdom.][8]

[(*t*) an amount which is deemed under section 730A(2) of the Taxes Act (treatment of price differential on sale and repurchase of securities) to be a payment of interest.][9]

[(*u*) a payment of interest in respect of an amount of cash which is—

(i) received by the building society in connection with a sale and repurchase agreement in circumstances where section 730A of the Taxes Act (treatment of price differential on sale and repurchase of securities) applies, and

(ii) required as a result of a variation in the value of the securities as security for performance by the parties to the agreement of their obligations under the agreement.][12]

(2)–(4) ...[6]

(5) For the purposes of paragraph (1)(*n*) and subject to paragraph (6), where the conditions prescribed by regulations 5, 6 and 8 and, where applicable, regulation 9 are fulfilled, a building society may, on receipt of the certificate referred to in regulation 5, refund to the investor an amount corresponding to the tax deducted from payments of dividends and interest previously made in the year and shall, on a written application made to the Board, recover a like amount of tax paid in respect of those payments to the amount refunded to the investor.

(6) Paragraph (5) shall not apply where in any year a statement relating to that year has been furnished by the building society to the investor pursuant to section 352 of the Taxes Act prior to receipt of the certificate referred to in regulation 5.

Cross references—See the IT (Building Societies) (Dividends & Interest) Regulations, SI 1990/2231 reg 11 (requirements for declarations confirming the applicability of para (1)(*a*)–(*c*) above).

IT (Building Societies) (Audit Powers) Regulations, SI 1992/10 reg 5 (description of an investment which is an excluded investment for the purposes of those Regulations).

IT (Building Societies) (Audit Powers) Regulations, SI 1992/10 reg 7 (audit conditions to be satisfied for approval of a building society for the purposes of the said Regulations).

Amendments—[1] Para (1)(*o*), (*p*) added by the IT (Building Societies) (Dividends and Interest) (Amendment) Regulations, SI 1992/11 reg 5, with effect from 30 January 1992.

[2] Para. (1)(*m*) revoked by the IT (Building Societies) (Dividends and Interest) (Amendment) Regulations, SI 1992/11 reg 5.

[3] Words in para (1)(*j*) inserted by the IT (Building Societies) (Dividends and Interest) (Amendment No 2) Regulations, SI 1992/2915 reg 4(1) with effect from 14 December 1992.

[4] Para (1)(*q*), (*r*) added by SI 1992/2915 reg 4(1).

[5] Para (1)(*e*), (i) revoked by SI 1992/2915 reg 4(1).

[6] Para (1)(*g*) substituted and paras (2)–(4) revoked by SI 1992/2915 reg 4(1)(ii) with effect from 14 December 1992. Previously para (1)(*g*) and paras (2)–(4) read—

"(*g*) a payment to a company resident in the United Kingdom, which is a 51 per cent subsidiary of the building society making the payment, where the building society and the company have jointly elected that any such payments shall be made gross and the election is in force at the time of the payment;"

"(2) An election under paragraph (1)(*g*)—

(*a*) shall be made by notice to the inspector which shall set out the facts necessary to show that the building society and the company are entitled to make the election,

(*b*) shall cease to be in force if at any time the building society and the company cease to be entitled to make the election and, on that happening the building society and the company shall forthwith notify the inspector, and

(*c*) may be revoked at any time by notice given to the inspector by either the building society or the company making the election; and any such notice shall have effect from the time it is given."

"(3) For the purposes of paragraph (1)(*g*)—

(*a*) a company shall be treated as a 51 per cent subsidiary of a building society if and so long as more than 50 per cent of its ordinary share capital is owned directly or indirectly by the building society;

(*b*) subject to sub-paragraph (*c*), a building society shall be treated as owning share capital directly or indirectly in a company if it would be so treated for the purposes of section 838 of the Taxes Act; and

(*c*) for the purpose of sub-paragraph (*a*), a building society shall be treated as not being the owner—

(i) of any share capital which it owns directly or indirectly in a company which is not resident in the United Kingdom, or

(ii) of any share capital which it owns indirectly and which is owned directly by a company for which a profit on the sale of the shares would be a trading receipt."

"(4) Elections made pursuant to regulation 6(1)(*ff*) of the 1986 Regulations shall have effect as if made pursuant to paragraph (1)(*g*) of this regulation.".

The above amendments do not have effect, by virtue of SI 1992/2915 reg 4(2), in relation to an election made under old sub-paragraph (*g*) which was in force immediately before 14 December 1992, and accordingly such an election shall continue in full force and effect unless and until it ceases to be in force by virtue of paragraph (2) or is revoked pursuant to that paragraph.

[7] Para (1)(*f*) substituted by the IT (Building Societies) (Dividends and Interest) (Amendment) Regulations, SI 1994/296 regs 1–3, with effect from 4 March 1994.

[8] Para (1)(*s*) inserted by SI 1994/296 regs 1–3.

[9] Para (1)(*t*) inserted by the IT (Building Societies) (Dividends and Interest) (Amendment) Regulations, SI 1995/1184 reg 2, with effect from 3 May 1995.

[10] Para (1)(*bb*) inserted by SI 1996/223 reg 4, with effect from 28 February 1996.

[11] Words in para (1)(*o*) substituted by the IT (Building Societies) (Dividends and Interest) (Amendment) Regulations, SI 1996/223 reg 5(1), with effect from 28 February 1996.

[12] Para (1)(*u*) inserted by the IT (Building Societies) (Dividends and Interest) (Amendment) Regulations, SI 2001/404 regs 3, 5 with effect in relation to payments of interest referred to in para (1)(*u*) made after 5 April 2001.

[13] Words in sub-para (1)(*r*) substituted by the Financial Services and Markets Act 2000 (Consequential Amendments) (Taxes) Order, SI 2001/3629 art 128 with effect from 1 December 2001, immediately after the coming into force of the Financial Services and Markets Act 2000 ss 411, 432(1), Sch 20 (and SI 2001/3629 Pts 1 and 2).

Certificate of non-liability to tax

5—(1) Paragraph (2) of this regulation and regulations 6, 8 and 9 prescribe conditions which, if fulfilled, enable a gross payment within paragraph (1)(*n*) of regulation 4 to be made.

(2) The conditions prescribed by this paragraph are—

(*a*) that a certificate is supplied to the building society to the effect that the person beneficially entitled to the payment of a dividend or interest (in this paragraph referred to as "the payment") is unlikely to be liable to pay any amount by way of income tax for the year in which the payment is made;

(*b*) subject to sub-paragraph (*c*), that the certificate is given by—

(i) an investor who was aged 16 or over at the beginning of the year in which the payment is made and who is beneficially entitled to the payment; or

(ii) the parent or guardian of a person beneficially entitled to the payment where that person is under the age of 16 at the beginning of the year in which the payment is made; or

(iii) a person beneficially entitled to the payment where that person is under the age of 16 at the beginning of the year in which the payment is made but will attain that age during the year; or

(iv) the donee of a power of attorney authorising him to administer the financial affairs of a person beneficially entitled to the payment; [or][1]

[(v) a parent, guardian, spouse or son or daughter of a person suffering from mental disorder; or][1]

[(vi) a receiver or other person appointed by any court in the United Kingdom to act in relation to the property and affairs of a person incapable, by reason of mental disorder, of managing and administering his property and affairs;][1] [or][3]

[(vii) a person appointed by the Secretary of State under paragraph (1) of regulation 33 of the Social Security (Claims and Payments) Regulations 1987, whose appointment has not been revoked or terminated, or who has not resigned his office, pursuant to paragraph (2) of that regulation;][3]

(*c*) that the certificate is not given or supplied in circumstances where—

(i) the provisions of section [660B][5] of the Taxes Act apply to the payment, or

(ii) the account to which [the certificate relates][2] is specified in a notice which has been issued under regulation 6(3)(*d*) and which has not been cancelled;

(*d*) that the certificate is given and supplied to the building society—

(i) where paragraph (i), (ii)[, (iv), (v), (vi) or (vii)][4] or (iv) of sub-paragraph (*b*) applies, before the end of the year in which the payment is made, or

(ii) where paragraph (iii) of sub-paragraph (*b*) applies, before the end of the year in which the person beneficially entitled to the payment attains the age of 16; and

(*e*) that the certificate is given [in a form provided or authorised][6] by the Board which contains—

(i) the information specified in the Schedule to these Regulations, and

(ii) an undertaking by the person giving it that if he, being the person beneficially entitled to the payment, or the person so entitled becomes liable to pay any amount by way of income tax for the year in which the payment is made, he will notify the building society ...[6] accordingly, specifying the account to which the certificate relates together with the account number and, where necessary for identifying the account, the branch of the building society where the account is held.

[(3) A certificate given in accordance with paragraph (2), and a notification given under sub-paragraph (*e*) of that paragraph, if in writing, shall be signed by the maker of the certificate or notification ("the relevant person").][7]

[(4) Where a certificate referred to in paragraph (3) is not in writing, the building society concerned may—

(*a*) make a declaration in writing on behalf of the relevant person that the particulars contained in the certificate are those recorded in the declaration, and

(*b*) send a copy of the declaration to the relevant person.][7]

[(5) Subject to any corrections notified by the relevant person to the building society within the period of 30 days following the date on which the copy of the declaration referred to in paragraph (4) was sent to the relevant person, and incorporated in a revised declaration made by the building society, any such declaration shall take effect as from the date on which the copy of it was sent to the relevant person in accordance with that paragraph.][7]

[(6) A certificate or notification referred to in paragraph (3) shall be regarded as being given in writing for the purposes of this regulation if it is given—

(*a*) by telephonic facsimile transmission, or

(*b*) by electronic communication containing an electronic signature of the relevant person.][7]

[(7) A declaration made by the building society in accordance with paragraph (4) shall be regarded as made in writing for the purposes of this regulation if it is produced by electronic means; and the copy of a declaration to be sent to the relevant person in accordance with paragraph (4) may be sent by telephonic facsimile transmission or by electronic communication.][7]

Amendments—[1] Para (2)(*b*)(v), (vi) and the preceding word "or" added by the IT (Building Societies) (Dividends and Interest) (Amendment) Regulations 1992 SI 1992/11 reg 6, with effect from 30 January 1992.

[2] Words in para (2)(*c*)(ii) substituted by SI 1992/11 reg 6.

[3] Para (2)(*b*)(vii) and the preceding word "or" inserted by the IT (Building Societies) (Dividends and Interest) (Amendment) Regulations, SI 1994/296 regs 1, 2, 4, with effect from 4 March 1994.

[4] Numbers in para (2)(*d*)(i) substituted by SI 1994/296 regs 1, 2, 4.

[5] Number in para (2)(*c*)(i) substituted by the IT (Building Societies) (Dividends and Interest) (Amendment) Regulations, SI 1996/223 reg 5(2), with effect from 28 February 1996.

[6] Words substituted in para (2)(*e*), and words "in writing" revoked in sub-para (2)(*e*)(ii) by the IT (Building Societies) (Dividends and Interest) (Amendment) Regulations, SI 2001/404 regs 3, 6 with effect for certificates and notifications referred to in para (3) that are given after 5 April 2001.

[7] Paras (3)–(7) added by SI 2001/404 regs 3, 6 with effect for certificates and notifications referred to in para (3) that are given after 5 April 2001.

Certificate ceasing to be valid

6—(1) The condition prescribed by this regulation is that the certificate referred to in regulation 5 continues in full force and effect and has not ceased to be valid.

(2) A certificate ceases to be valid in any of the circumstances specified in paragraph (3).

(3) The circumstances specified in this paragraph are—

(*a*) the receipt by the building society of information by way of a notification pursuant to regulation 5(2)(*e*)(ii) that the person beneficially entitled to a payment of a dividend or interest arising on an account specified in the notification has become liable to pay an amount by way of income tax for the year in which the payment is made;

(*b*) in the case of a certificate given under regulation 5(2)(*b*)(ii), the end of the year in which the person beneficially entitled to the payment attains the age of 16;

(*c*) the failure by a person who has given a certificate under regulation 5(2)(*b*)(iii), but is not the holder of the account to which the certificate relates, to become the holder before the first payment of a dividend or interest after the end of the year in which he attains the age of 16;

(*d*) where the Board, having reason to believe that a person beneficially entitled to a payment of a dividend or interest is or has become liable to pay an amount by way of income tax, by notice require a building society to deduct tax pursuant to regulation 3 from payments of dividends or interest which—

(i) are made in respect of an account which is held by or on behalf of that person and which, together with the account number and, where necessary for identifying the account, the branch of the building society where the account is held, is specified in the notice, and

(ii) are made to or for the benefit of that person after the expiry of a period of 30 days following the date of issue of the notice [or, if earlier, after it has become reasonably practicable so to deduct tax][1];

(*e*) notification is received by the building society that the person by whom or on whose behalf the certificate was given has died.

Amendments—[1] Words in para (3)(*d*)(ii) added by the IT (Building Societies) (Dividends and Interest) (Amendment) Regulations, SI 1992/11 reg 7, with effect from 30 January 1992.

Consequences of notice under regulation 6(3)(d)

7—(1) Where the Board issue a notice under regulation 6(3)(*d*)—

(*a*) they shall at the same time send a copy to the person referred to in the notice;

(*b*) subject to paragraphs (2) and (3), no further certificate under regulation 5 may be given by or on behalf of the person referred to in the notice in respect of an account specified in the notice;

(*c*) ...[1]

(2) If the Board are satisfied, as a result of information received following the issue of a notice under regulation 6(3)(*d*), that the person referred to in the notice either—

(i) was not liable at the date of the notice, and has not since become liable, to pay an amount by way of income tax, or

(ii) is no longer liable to pay such an amount,

they shall cancel the notice and give notice of the cancellation to the building society and the person referred to in the notice under regulation 6(3)(*d*).

(3) Where a notice of cancellation is issued by the Board under paragraph (2), a further certificate may be given in accordance with the conditions of regulation 5 by or on behalf of the person referred to in the notice under regulation 6(3)(*d*).

Amendments—[1] Para (1)(*c*) revoked by the IT (Building Societies) (Dividends and Interest) (Amendment) Regulations, SI 1992/11 reg 8, with effect from 30 January 1992.

Obsolescent accounts

8—(1) The condition prescribed by this regulation is that, subject to paragraphs (3) and (4), a payment of a dividend or interest arising on an account held with a building society is not a payment in respect of which a written application has been made to the Board by the building society in the circumstances specified in paragraph (2) to the effect that, notwithstanding the provisions of regulations 5 and 9, the payment should be made under deduction of tax pursuant to regulation 3.

(2) The circumstances specified in this paragraph are where—

(*a*) the account to which the payment relates is of a class which, prior to 6th April 1991, had ceased to be available to a person desiring to open a new account;

(*b*) the application, which may relate to more than one such class of account—

(i) gives sufficient particulars of each such class to enable the Board to determine whether the application is validly made, and

(ii) is made not less than 30 days before the first date after 5th April 1991 on which a payment of a dividend or interest arising on any account to which the application relates is to be made.

(3) An application under paragraph (1) shall be of no effect if within 30 days after receipt of the application the Board notify the building society concerned that, having regard to paragraph (2), they are not satisfied that the application is validly made.

(4) A building society may by notice to the Board—

(*a*) cancel an application made under paragraph (1), or

(*b*) vary the application so that it ceases to relate to certain accounts;

and where the application is so cancelled or varied, the condition prescribed by this regulation shall cease to apply to payments of dividends or interest arising on accounts to which the application formerly related and made after the date of the notice.

Joint accounts

9—(1) The conditions prescribed by this regulation apply where more than one person is beneficially entitled to a payment of a dividend or interest arising on an account held with a building society.

(2) The prescribed conditions are that—

(*a*) a certificate referred to in regulation 5 is given by or on behalf of—

(i) each person beneficially entitled to the payment of a dividend or interest, or

(ii) one or more (but not all) of such persons individually; and

(*b*) a notice under paragraph (6) relating to the payment of a dividend or interest—

(i) has not been given to the Board by the building society, or

(ii) has been so given and has subsequently been cancelled by the building society under paragraph (7).

(3) Where the condition in paragraph (2)(*a*)(i) was satisfied but a certificate has ceased to be valid at any time by reason of the occurrence of one of the circumstances specified in sub-paragraph (*a*), (*b*), (*c*) or (*d*) of regulation 6(3), this paragraph shall apply in relation to a payment of a dividend or interest made—

(*a*) after that time, or

(*b*) where sub-paragraph (*d*) of regulation 6(3) applies—

(i) after the expiry of a period of 30 days following the date of issue of the notice referred to in that sub-paragraph, or

(ii) after such date falling within that period as the building society may at its option determine.

(4) Subject to paragraph (6), where the condition in paragraph (2)(*a*)(ii) is satisfied or paragraph (3) applies, for the purposes of these Regulations and of deduction of tax pursuant to regulation 3, it shall be assumed that each person is beneficially entitled in equal shares to the payment of a dividend or interest and accordingly—

(*a*) payment of so much of the dividend or interest as by virtue of this paragraph corresponds to the share of any person by or on behalf of whom a certificate was given shall be made without deduction of tax pursuant to paragraph (1)(*n*) of regulation 4, and

(*b*) payment of the remainder of the dividend or interest shall be made under deduction of tax pursuant to regulation 3.

(5) Tax deducted from a payment within paragraph (4)(*b*) shall, for all the purposes of the Income Tax Acts, be treated as income tax paid by the person or persons to whom the payment is treated as being made.

(6) A building society may by notice inform the Board of its intention that, in circumstances where the condition in paragraph (2)(*a*)(ii) is satisfied or paragraph (3) applies, the whole of a payment of a dividend or interest referred to in the notice shall be made under deduction of tax pursuant to regulation 3 and, subject to paragraph (7), where such notice is given paragraph (4) shall not apply and tax shall accordingly be deducted by the building society from any payment to which the notice relates and which is made after the date of the notice.

(7) A building society may by notice to the Board (in this paragraph referred to as ''the cancellation notice'') cancel a notice given under paragraph (6) and, where a notice is cancelled, paragraph (4) shall apply to any payment of a dividend or interest to which the notice formerly related and which is made after the date of the cancellation notice.

Collection of amounts representing income tax payable by building societies

10—(1) The like provisions as are contained in Schedule 16 to the Taxes Act (''the Schedule 16 provisions'') shall have effect for the purposes of these Regulations but with the modifications specified in the following paragraphs of this regulation.

(2) Any payment by a building society of the following descriptions is, for the purposes of the Schedule 16 provisions, a relevant payment—

(*a*) a payment of a dividend or interest to which regulation 3 applies;

(*b*) a payment of a dividend or interest made after 28th February 1991 and before 6th April 1991 to which regulation 3 of the 1986 Regulations applied.

(3) The Schedule 16 provisions shall have effect in relation to any such relevant payment—

(*a*) with the substitution for any reference to a company of a reference to a building society;

(*b*) as if the amount payable to the Board in respect of any relevant payment made before 6th April 1991 were income tax in respect of the relevant payment;

(*c*) with the omission of paragraph 1 of that Schedule;

(*d*) with the substitution for paragraphs (*a*) to (*c*) of paragraph 2(2) of that Schedule of the words—

"(*a*) each complete payment quarter within the accounting period, beginning with the payment quarter ending 31st May 1991;

(*b*) each part of an accounting period (other than an accounting period ending on or before 22nd March 1991) being a part which begins after February 1991 and which is not a complete payment quarter."; and

(*e*) as if paragraph 5 of that Schedule had effect only in relation to payments—

(i) which are received by the building society after February 1991,

(ii) which fall to be taken into account in computing its income chargeable to corporation tax, and

(iii) in respect of which no claim has previously been made under that paragraph as modified by regulation 7(3)(*e*) of the 1986 Regulations.

(4) Tax which by virtue of this regulation is assessable in accordance with the Schedule 16 provisions is tax assessable in accordance with those provisions for the purposes of section 87 of the Taxes Management Act 1970.

Declarations by investors

11—[(1) A building society may not treat an investment, or any payment of a dividend or interest in respect of it, as being within the provisions of sub-paragraphs (*a*) to (*c*) of paragraph (1) of regulation 4 unless it has received from the appropriate person a declaration ...[9] which can reasonably be taken to indicate that, at the time of the payment, those provisions apply.][1]

[(2) An individual referred to in any of sub-paragraphs (*a*) to (*c*) of paragraph (1) of regulation 4 as not ordinarily resident in the United Kingdom, and a company or trustees referred to in sub-paragraph (*bb*) of that paragraph as not resident in the United Kingdom, may not be treated as not ordinarily resident or, as the case may be, not resident in the United Kingdom unless the declaration specified in paragraph (2AA) containing the undertaking specified in paragraph (2AB) has been made ...[9] by the appropriate person to the building society.][7]

[(2AA) The declaration specified is that—

(*a*) where sub-paragraph (*a*) or (*b*) of regulation 4(1) applies, at the time the declaration is made the individual is not ordinarily resident in the United Kingdom;

(*b*) where sub-paragraph (*bb*) of regulation 4(1) applies, at the time the declaration is made the trustees are not resident in the United Kingdom and do not have any reasonable grounds for believing that any of the beneficiaries of the trust is an individual who is ordinarily resident in the United Kingdom or a company which is resident in the United Kingdom;

(*c*) where sub-paragraph (*c*) of regulation 4(1) applies, the individual was not ordinarily resident in the United Kingdom at the time of his death.][7]

[(2AB) The undertaking specified is that—

(*a*) where sub-paragraph (*a*) or (*b*) of regulation 4(1) applies, the appropriate person will [notify][9] the building society if the individual or any of the individuals in respect of whom the declaration is made becomes ordinarily resident in the United Kingdom;

(*b*) where sub-paragraph (*bb*) of regulation 4(1) applies, the appropriate person will [notify][9] the building society if—

(i) the individual or any of the individuals in respect of whom the declaration is made becomes ordinarily resident in the United Kingdom,

(ii) the trustees or any company in respect of whom the declaration is made become or becomes resident in the United Kingdom, or

(iii) an individual who is ordinarily resident in the United Kingdom or a company which is resident in the United Kingdom becomes or is found to be a beneficiary of the trust to which the declaration relates.][7]

[(2AC) In a case falling within regulation 4(1)(*a*), the declaration required by paragraph (2) must contain—

(*a*) the name and principal residential address of the individual who is beneficially entitled to the payment, or

(*b*) where two or more individuals are so entitled, the name and principal residential address of each of them, or

(*c*) where the person who is so entitled is a Scottish partnership all the partners in which are individuals, the name and principal residential address of each of the individuals.][10]

[(2A) [Subject to paragraph (2B),][4] a building society may not treat an investment, or any payment of a dividend or interest in respect of it, as being within the provisions of [[sub-paragraph][6] (*d*), (*f*), (*g*), (*k*) or (*r*)][5] of paragraph (1) of regulation 4 unless it has received from the investor a declaration ...[9] which can reasonably be taken to indicate that, at the time of the payment, those provisions apply.][3]

[(2B) Paragraph(2A) shall not apply to—

(*a*) a payment of interest made to a building society on a loan made by a building society, or

(*b*) a payment of interest made to a company in relation to which an election under sub-paragraph (*g*) of paragraph (1) of regulation 4 was in force immediately before 14th December 1992 and remains in force at the time of the payment.][4]

[(3) Every declaration shall be made in a form provided or authorised by the Board.][10]

[(3A) A declaration, if made in writing, shall be signed by the maker of the declaration.][10]

[(3B) Where a declaration (''the original declaration'') is not in writing, the building society may—

(*a*) make a declaration in writing (''the building society declaration''), on behalf of the person who made the original declaration, that the particulars contained in the original declaration are those recorded in the building society declaration, and

(*b*) send a copy of the building society declaration to that person.][10]

[(3C) Subject to any corrections notified by that person to the building society within the period of 30 days following the date on which the copy of the building society declaration was sent to that person, and incorporated in a revised declaration made by the building society, the building society declaration shall take effect as from the date on which the copy of it was sent to that person.][10]

[(3D) A declaration shall be regarded as given in writing for the purposes of this regulation if it is given—

(*a*) by telephonic facsimile transmission, or

(*b*) by electronic communication containing an electronic signature of the person making it.][10]

[(3E) A building society declaration made in accordance with paragraph (3B) or (3C) of this regulation shall be regarded as made in writing if it is produced by electronic means; and the copy of the building society declaration to be sent to a person in accordance with paragraph (3B)(*b*) may be sent by telephonic facsimile transmission or by electronic communication.][10]

(4) A building society shall be entitled to act upon a declaration so made unless or until it is in possession of information which can reasonably be taken to indicate that the provisions of regulation 4 specified in [paragraphs (1), (2) or (2A)][2] are not or might not be applicable.

(5) A building society shall, on being so required by notice given to it by the inspector, make any declaration ...[9] to which the notice refers available for inspection by the inspector or by a named officer of the Board, within such time as may be specified in the notice.

(6) The inspector or officer to whom they are to be made available shall be entitled to take copies of, or make extracts from, any declaration ...[9].

(7) Every declaration ...[9] to which this regulation refers shall be preserved by a building society, in such manner as may be approved by the Board, for two years after it has ceased to be otherwise required under the provisions of this regulation.

(8) Declarations ...[9] made pursuant to regulation 8 of the 1986 Regulations shall have effect as if made pursuant to the provisions of this regulation.

Cross references—See the IT (Building Societies) (Audit Powers) Regulations, SI 1992/10 reg 5 (meaning of ''excluded investment'' for the purposes of those Regulations),
regs 6, 7 (audit conditions required to be satisfied for approval of a building society for the purposes of the said Regulations),
reg 8 (termination of approval of a building society approved for the purposes of the said Regulations).

Amendments—[1] Para (1) substituted by the IT (Building Societies) (Dividends and Interest) (Amendment) Regulations, SI 1992/11 reg 9, with effect from 30 January 1992.

[2] Words in para (4) substituted by SI 1992/11 reg 9.

[3] Para (2A) inserted by SI 1992/11 reg 9.

[4] Para (2B) and words in para (2A) inserted by the IT (Building Societies) (Dividends and Interest) (Amendment No 2) Regulations, SI 1992/2915 reg 5, with effect from 14 December 1992.

[5] Words in para (2A) substituted by SI 1992/2915 reg 5.

[6] ''Sub-paragraph'' substituted for ''sub-paragraphs'' by IT (Building Societies) (Dividends and Interest) (Amendment) Regulations, SI 1994/296 reg 5.

[7] Paras (2), (2AA), (2AB), (2AC) substituted for para (2) by the IT (Building Societies) (Dividends and Interest) (Amendment) Regulations, SI 1996/223 reg 6, with effect from 28 February 1996.

[8] Words in para (3) inserted by SI 1996/223 reg 7, with effect from 28 February 1996.

[9] Words in paras (1), (2), (2A), (5)–(8) revoked, and words in para (2AB) substituted by the IT (Building Societies) (Dividends and Interest) (Amendment) Regulations, SI 2001/404 regs 3, 7 with effect for declarations required by paras (1), (2) that are given after 5 April 2001.

[10] Para (2AC) substituted, paras (3)–(3E) substituted for para (3) by the IT (Building Societies) (Dividends and Interest) (Amendment) Regulations, SI 2001/404 regs 3, 7 with effect for declarations required by paras (1), (2) that are given after 5 April 2001.

Returns of dividend and interest payments

12—[(1)][1] [Subject to the provisions of this regulation, the like provisions as are contained in section 17(1), (2), (4) and (4A)][4] of the Taxes Management Act 1970 (interest paid or credited by banks, etc) shall have effect in relation to a building society as if—

(*a*) references to interest included references to dividends within the meaning of these Regulations;

...[6]

[(*b*) for the word ''bank'' in subsection (1) there were substituted ''building society'';][4]

...[4]

...[4]

[(2) A building society shall, if so required by notice from an inspector [and subject to paragraphs (4) and (5)][5], include in a return under the provisions referred to in paragraph (1) the further information specified in paragraph (3).][2]

[(3) The further information specified in this paragraph is—

[(*za*) as regards a gross payment within regulation 4(1)(*a*) in respect of which a declaration under regulation 11 has been made on or after 6th April 2001—

(i) the name and principal residential address of the individual beneficially entitled to the payment or, if more than one, of each individual beneficially entitled to the payment; or

(ii) where the person beneficially entitled to the payment is a Scottish partnership, all the partners in which are individuals, the name and principal residential address of each of the partners; and

(iii) notification of the fact that the account in respect of which the payment was made was one in respect of which a declaration under regulation 11 had been made on or after 6th April 2001;][5]

(*a*) as regards a gross payment within regulation 4(1)(*n*)—

(i) the name and address of the person or, if more than one, each person beneficially entitled to the payment by or on behalf of whom a certificate under regulation 5 has been given (in paragraphs (ii) and (iii) referred to as ''the beneficiary'') if other than the person or persons to whom the payment was made;

(ii) the date of birth of the beneficiary;

(iii) the national insurance number of the beneficiary if furnished to the building society pursuant to regulation 5 of, and the Schedule to, these Regulations;

(iv) notification of the fact that the account in respect of which the payment was made is or was one in connection with which a certificate or certificates under regulation 5 had been given which had not ceased to be valid at the 5th April in the year in which the payment was made or at the date of closure of the account, if earlier in that year;

(v) the reference number of the account referred to in paragraph (iv) and, where necessary for identifying the account, the branch of the building society where the account is held;

(vi) where the payment was made to two or more investors each of whom was beneficially entitled to the payment, notification of that fact and, if known, the number of such persons;

(vii) if furnished to the building society in connection with the account, the dates of birth and national insurance numbers of persons referred to in paragraph (vi) other than the beneficiary referred to in paragraphs (ii) and (iii);

(viii) where a certificate referred to in regulation 5 was given by or on behalf of one or more, but not all, of the persons referred to in paragraph (vi) and had not ceased to be valid at the 5th April in the year in which the payment was made or at the date of closure of the account, if earlier in that year, notification of those facts;

(ix) where the payment was the first payment made in respect of an account, notification of that fact;

(*x*) where the payment was in a currency other than sterling and the amount of the payment is recorded in that currency in a return under the provisions referred to in paragraph (1) of this regulation, notification of the fact that the amount is so recorded and specification of the currency concerned;

(*b*) [as regards any gross payment within regulation 4 other than regulation 4(1)(*n*) that is a payment in respect of an investment, or any payment to which regulation 3 applies that is a payment in respect of an investment][5]—

(i) the reference number of the account in respect of which the payment was made and, where necessary for identifying the account, the branch of the building society where the account is held;

(ii) where the payment was made to two or more investors...[5], notification of that fact and, if known, the number of such persons;

(iii) if furnished to the building society in connection with the account, the date of birth and national insurance number of the person or, where paragraph (ii) applies, each person to whom the payment was made;

(iv) where the payment made in the course of the year was the first payment in respect of an account, notification of that fact;

(v) where the payment was in a currency other than sterling and the amount of the payment is recorded in that currency in a return under the provisions referred to in paragraph (1) of this regulation, notification of the fact that the amount is so recorded and specification of the currency concerned.][2]

[(4) In the cases specified in paragraph (5), a notice under section 17(1) of the Taxes Management Act 1970 shall not require information.][6]

[(5) The cases specified are—

(*a*) a payment in respect of a certificate of deposit within the meaning given by section 56(5) of the Taxes Act;

(*b*) a payment in respect of an investment held by a branch of a building society to whom a notice under paragraph (2) is issued, where the branch is situated in a territory other than the United Kingdom;

(*c*) a payment falling within regulation 4(1)(*a*) in respect of which the information that the notice under section 17(1) of the Taxes Management Act 1970 shall not require is the name and address of the person to whom the dividend or interest was paid or credited, if other than the person beneficially entitled to the dividend or interest;

(*d*) a payment in respect of an account which is a tax exempt special savings account for the purposes of section 326A of the Taxes Act;

(*e*) a payment in respect of an investment under a plan provided for by regulations made under section 333 of the Taxes Act;

(*f*) any other payment not falling within any of sub-paragraphs (*a*) to (*e*) which is specified in a notice under paragraph (2) as being a payment in respect of which information is not required.][6]

Amendments—[1] Figure in para (1) added by the IT (Building Societies) (Dividends and Interest) (Amendment) Regulations, SI 1992/11 reg 10, with effect from 30 January 1992.

[2] Paras (2), (3) added by SI 1992/11 reg 10.

[3] Word "and" in para (1)(*a*) revoked by SI 1992/2915 reg 6.

[4] Words in para (1) substituted, para (1)(*b*) substituted, and paras (1)(*c*), (*d*) revoked by the IT (Building Societies) (Dividends and Interest) (Amendment) Regulations, SI 2001/404 regs 3, 8 with effect for payments of dividends and interest in respect of shares in, or deposits with or loans to, building societies that are made after 5 April 2001.

[5] Words inserted in para (2), para (3)(*za*) inserted, words in para (3)(*b*) substituted, and words in sub-para (3)(*b*)(ii) revoked by SI 2001/404 regs 3, 9, 10 with effect for payments of dividends and interest in respect of shares in, or deposits with or loans to, building societies that are made after 5 April 2001.

[6] Paras (4), 5) added by SI 2001/404 regs 3, 11 with effect for payments of dividends and interest in respect of shares in, or deposits with or loans to, building societies that are made after 5 April 2001.

[Notice under regulation 12—form of return

12A Where a notice under the provisions referred to in regulation 12(1)—

(*a*) requires a return to be made, or

(*b*) specifies any of the further information prescribed by regulation 12(3) and requires it to be contained in the return, and

(*c*) the notice specifies the form in which the return is to be made and delivered,

the return shall be made and delivered in that form.][1]

Amendments—[1] Regulation inserted by the IT (Building Societies) (Dividends and Interest) (Amendment) Regulations, SI 2001/404 regs 3, 12 with effect for payments of dividends and interest in respect of shares in, or deposits with or loans to, building societies that are made after 5 April 2001

Information to be provided to the Board—gross payments

13—(1) This regulation applies to payments of dividends or interest by building societies made without deduction of tax in accordance with regulation 4(1)(*n*); and regulations 5 to 9 (in paragraph (2) referred to as "the gross payments regulations"), including payments made partly without and partly under deduction of tax pursuant to regulation 9(4).

(2) The Board may by notice in writing require any building society to furnish them, within such time (not being less than 14 days) as may be provided by the notice, such information (including copies of any relevant books, documents or other records) as they may reasonably require for the purposes of the gross payments regulations and, in particular, for—

(*a*) verifying payments of dividends or interest by building societies made without deduction of tax in accordance with regulation 4(1)(*n*), and

(*b*) determining whether a person has given or supplied a certificate in compliance with the conditions of regulation 5.

Information to be provided to the Board—net payments

14—(1) This regulation applies to payments of dividends or interest by a building society to which regulation 3 applies.

(2) The Board may by notice require any building society to furnish them, within such time (not being less than 14 days) as may be provided by the notice, such information relating to amounts of dividends or interest paid by the building society to which this regulation applies and to tax deducted by the building society from such payments in accordance with regulation 3 as they may reasonably require for verifying the amount of tax so deducted.

(3) The information which may be required by the Board under paragraph (2) shall include copies of any relevant books, documents or other records of the building society, not being [books, documents or][1] records from which the identity of an investor can be ascertained.

Amendments—[1] Words in para (3) inserted by the IT (Building Societies) (Dividends and Interest) (Amendment) Regulations, SI 1992/11 reg 11.

[Information to be provided to the Board—return under regulation 12

14A The Board may by notice require any building society to furnish them, within such time (not being less than 14 days) as may be provided by the notice, such information (including copies of any relevant books, documents or other records) as they may reasonably require for the purposes of determining whether information contained in a return by the building society by virtue of a notice under the provisions referred to in regulation 12(1) was correct and complete.][1]

Amendment—[1] This Regulation inserted by the IT (Building Societies) (Dividends and Interest) (Amendment) Regulations, SI 2001/404 regs 3, 13 with effect for payments of dividends and interest in respect of shares in, or deposits with or loans to, building societies that are made after 5 April 2001.

Inspection of records

15—(1) Every building society shall, whenever required to do so, make available for inspection by an officer of the Board authorised for that purpose, at such time as that officer may reasonably require, all such [copies of][1] books, documents and other records in its possession or under its control as may be required by the Board under regulations 13 and 14.

(2) Every certificate supplied to a building society pursuant to regulation 5 shall be preserved by the building society in such manner as may be approved by the Board for two years after it has ceased to be otherwise required under the provisions of these Regulations.

Amendments—[1] Words in para (1) inserted by the IT (Building Societies) (Dividends and Interest) (Amendment) Regulations, SI 1992/11 reg 12, with effect from 30 January 1992.

[Inspection of records—return under regulation 12

15A Every building society required to make and deliver a return by virtue of a notice under the provisions referred to in regulation 12(1) shall, whenever required to do so within the period specified in regulation 15B(2), make available for inspection by an officer of the Board authorised for that purpose, at such time as that officer may reasonably require, all such copies of books, documents and other records in its possession or under its control as may be required by the Board under regulation 14A.][1]

Amendment—[1] This Regulation inserted by the IT (Building Societies) (Dividends and Interest) (Amendment) Regulations, SI 2001/404 regs 3, 14 with effect for payments of dividends and interest in respect of shares in, or deposits with or loans to, building societies that are made after 5 April 2001.

[Retention of records—return under regulation 12

15B—(1) A building society required to make and deliver a return by virtue of a notice under the provisions referred to in regulation 12(1) shall retain, for the period specified in paragraph (2), all such books, documents and other records copies of which it may be required to make available for inspection under regulation 15A.

(2) The period specified is the period of two years beginning immediately after the end of the year to which the notice relates.

(3) Paragraphs (1) and (2) are without prejudice to regulations 11(7) and 15(2).][1]

Amendment—[1] This Regulation inserted by the IT (Building Societies) (Dividends and Interest) (Amendment) Regulations, SI 2001/404 regs 3, 14 with effect for payments of dividends and interest in respect of shares in, or deposits with or loans to, building societies that are made after 5 April 2001.

Use of information

16—(1) Subject to paragraph (2) information obtained by the Board [any of regulations 13 to 15A][1]—

(*a*) shall not be used for the purpose of ascertaining the tax liability (if any) of any person other than—

(i) a person beneficially entitled to a payment of a dividend or interest within regulation 13 [or 14][1] to whom the information obtained relates, and
(ii) the building society; and

(*b*) shall otherwise be used only for the purposes of [the provisions referred to in regulation 12(1) and][1] these Regulations.

(2) Paragraph (1) shall not be construed as preventing any disclosure of information within section 182(5) of the Finance Act 1989.

Amendments—[1] Words in sub-paras (1)(*a*)(i) and (*b*) inserted, and words in para (1) substituted by the IT (Building Societies) (Dividends and Interest) (Amendment) Regulations, SI 2001/404 regs 3, 15 with effect for payments of dividends and interest in respect of shares in, or deposits with or loans to, building societies that are made after 5 April 2001.

SCHEDULE

Regulation 5(2)(*e*)(i)

The information referred to in regulation 5(2)(*e*)(i) is—

(*a*) the name, permanent residential address including postcode, and date of birth of the person beneficially entitled to the payment;

(*b*) save where the Board indicate in a particular case that this information is not required, the national insurance number of a person within paragraph (*a*) and aged 16 or over at the beginning of the year in which the payment is made who, at any time within the period of three years ending with the date on which a certificate is signed, has been liable to pay Class 1 or Class 2 contributions within the meaning of section 1(2) of the Social Security Act 1975;

(*c*) the following details relating to the investor's account held with the building society to which the certificate relates—

(i) the name of the building society;

(ii) the branch of the building society where the account is held, if the account cannot otherwise be identified;

(iii) the account number.

1990/2232

Income Tax (Deposit-takers) (Interest Payments) Regulations 1990

Made by the Commissioners of Inland Revenue under TA 1988 ss 480B, 482(11)

Made . . . . *8 November 1990*
Laid before the House of Commons *9 November 1990*
Coming into Force . . . . . *30 November 1990*

Commentary—*Simon's Direct Tax Service* **B5.222–226; D4.1106**.

Citation, commencement and effect

1 These Regulations may be cited as the Income Tax (Deposit-takers) (Interest Payments) Regulations 1990, shall come into force on 30th November 1990 and shall have effect with respect to the year 1991–92 and subsequent years of assessment.

Interpretation

2 In these Regulations unless the context otherwise requires—

"the Board" means the Commissioners of Inland Revenue;

"deposit-taker" and "relevant deposits" have the meanings given by section 481 of the Taxes Act;

"depositor" means the holder of an account with a deposit-taker in relation to which a payment of interest is made;

["electronic communication" includes any communication conveyed by means of an electronic communications network.][3]

["electronic signature" has the meaning given by section 7(2) of the Electronic Communications Act 2000][2]

["mental disorder" has the meaning given by section 1(2) of the Mental Health Act 1983 or, in Scotland, section 1(2) of the Mental Health (Scotland) Act 1984 or, in Northern Ireland, Article 3 of the Mental Health (Northern Ireland) Order 1986;][1]

"notice" means notice in writing;

"payment" (except in relation to a payment to the Board) includes "credit" and "paid" shall be construed accordingly;

"section 480A(1)" means section 480A(1) of the Taxes Act;

["son or daughter" means a son or daughter aged 16 or over, and includes a stepson or stepdaughter, and an adopted or illegitimate son or daughter;][1]

"the Taxes Act" means the Income and Corporation Taxes Act 1988;

"year" means a year beginning with 6th April in any year and ending with 5th April in the following year.

Amendments—[1] Definitions of "mental disorder", "son or daughter" inserted by the IT (Deposit-takers) (Interest Payments) (Amendment) Regulations, SI 1992/13 reg 3.

[2] Definition of "electronic communication" and "electronic signature" inserted by the IT (Deposit-takers) (Interest Payments) (Amendment) Regulations, SI 2001/406 regs 3, 4 with effect for payments of interest by deposit-takers under reg 3 of these Regulations that are made or received after 5 April 2001.

[3] Definition of "electronic communication" substituted by the Communications Act 2003 (Consequential Amendments) Order, SI 2003/2155 Sch 1 para 24(1)(*b*), (2) with effect from 17 September 2003.

Introductory

3 These Regulations apply to payments of interest by deposit-takers in respect of relevant deposits where the persons beneficially entitled to the payments are ordinarily resident in the United Kingdom.

Gross payments

4—(1) The provisions of section 480A(1) shall not apply as regards a payment of interest by a deposit-taker if the conditions prescribed by regulations 5, 6 and 8 and, where applicable, regulation 9 are fulfilled, and accordingly where those conditions are fulfilled such payments shall be made without deduction of tax.

(2) Where paragraph (1) applies and subject to paragraph (3), a deposit-taker may, on receipt of the certificate referred to in regulation 5, refund to the depositor an amount corresponding to the tax deducted from payments of interest previously made in the year and shall, on a written application made to the Board, recover a like amount of tax paid in respect of those payments to the amount refunded to the depositor.

(3) Paragraph (2) shall not apply where in any year a statement relating to that year has been furnished by the deposit-taker to the depositor pursuant to section 352 of the Taxes Act prior to receipt of the certificate referred to in regulation 5.

Certificate of non-liability to tax

5—[(1)][5] The conditions prescribed by this regulation are—

(*a*) that a certificate is supplied to the deposit-taker to the effect that the person beneficially entitled to the payment of interest (in this regulation referred to as ''the payment'') is unlikely to be liable to pay any amount by way of income tax for the year in which the payment is made;

(*b*) subject to paragraph (*c*) that the certificate is given by—

(i) a depositor who was aged 16 or over at the beginning of the year in which the payment is made and who is beneficially entitled to the payment; or

(ii) the parent or guardian of a person beneficially entitled to the payment where that person is under the age of 16 at the beginning of the year in which the payment is made; or

(iii) a person beneficially entitled to the payment where that person is under the age of 16 at the beginning of the year in which the payment is made but will attain that age during the year; or

(iv) the donee of a power of attorney authorising him to administer the financial affairs of a person beneficially entitled to the payment; [or][1]

[(v) a parent, guardian, spouse or son or daughter of a person suffering from mental disorder; or][1]

[(vi) a receiver or other person appointed by any court in the United Kingdom to act in relation to the property and affairs of a person incapable, by reason of mental disorder, of managing and administering his property and affairs ;][1] [or][3]

[(vii) a person appointed by the Secretary of State under paragraph (1) of regulation 33 of the Social Security (Claims and Payments) Regulations 1987, whose appointment has not been revoked or terminated, or who has not resigned his office, pursuant to paragraph (2) of that regulation;][3]

(*c*) that the certificate is not given or supplied in circumstances where—

(i) the provisions of section [660B][5] of the Taxes Act apply to the payment, or

(ii) the account to which [the certificate relates][2] is specified in a notice which has been issued under regulation 6(3)(*d*) and which has not been cancelled;

(*d*) that the certificate is given and supplied to the deposit-taker—

(i) where sub-paragraph (i), (ii)[, (iv), (v), (vi) or (vii)][4] of paragraph (*b*) applies, before the end of the year in which the payment is made, or

(ii) where sub-paragraph (iii) of paragraph (*b*) applies, before the end of the year in which the person beneficially entitled to the payment attains the age of 16; and

(*e*) that the certificate is in such form as the Board may prescribe or authorise and contains—

(i) the information specified in the Schedule to these Regulations, and

(ii) an undertaking by the person giving it that if he, being the person beneficially entitled to the payment, or the person so entitled becomes liable to pay any amount by way of income tax for the year in which the payment is made, he will notify the deposit-taker ...[5] accordingly, specifying the account to which the certificate relates together with the account number and, where necessary for identifying the account, the branch of the deposit-taker where the account is held.

[(2) A certificate given in accordance with paragraph (1), and a notification given under sub-paragraph (*e*) of that paragraph, if in writing, shall be signed by the maker of the certificate or notification (''the relevant person'').][6]

[(3) Where a certificate referred to in paragraph (2) is not in writing, the deposit-taker concerned may—

(*a*) make a declaration in writing on behalf of the relevant person that the particulars contained in the certificate are those recorded in the declaration, and

(*b*) send a copy of the declaration to the relevant person.][6]

[(4) Subject to any corrections notified by the relevant person to the deposit-taker within the period of 30 days following the date on which the copy of the declaration referred to in paragraph (3) was sent to the relevant person, and incorporated in a revised declaration made by the deposit-taker, any such declaration shall take effect as from the date on which the copy of it was sent to the relevant person in accordance with that paragraph.][6]

[(5) A certificate or notification referred to in paragraph (2) shall be regarded as being given in writing for the purposes of this regulation if it is given—

(*a*) by telephonic facsimile transmission, or

(*b*) by electronic communication containing an electronic signature of the relevant person.][6]

[(6) A declaration made by the deposit-taker in accordance with paragraph (3) shall be regarded as made in writing for the purposes of this regulation if it is produced by electronic means; and the copy of a declaration to be sent to the relevant person in accordance with paragraph (3) may be sent by telephonic facsimile transmission or by electronic communication.][6]

Cross references—See the IT (Interest Payments) (Information Powers) Regulations, SI 1992/15 regs 3, 5 (regulatory further information required in a TMA 1970 s 17 return).

Amendments—[1] Para (*b*)(v), (vi) and the preceding word "or" added by the IT (Deposit-takers) (Interest Payments) (Amendment) Regulations, SI 1992/13 reg 4, with effect from 30 January 1992.

[2] Words in para (*c*)(ii) substituted by SI 1992/13 reg 4.

[3] Para (*b*)(vii) and the preceding word "or" added by the IT (Deposit-takers) (Interest Payments) (Amendment) Regulations, SI 1994/295, with effect from 4 March 1994.

[4] Numbers in para (*d*) substituted by SI 1994/295.

[5] Regulation renumbered, in sub-para (1)(*c*)(i), "660B" substituted for "663", and words in sub-para (1)(*e*)(ii) revoked by the IT (Deposit-takers) (Interest Payments) (Amendment) Regulations, SI 2001/406 regs 3, 5, 6 with effect for payments of interest by deposit-takers under reg 3 of these Regulations that are made or received after 5 April 2001.

[6] Paras (2)–(6) added by SI 2001/406 regs 3, 7 with effect for payments of interest by deposit-takers under reg 3 of these Regulations that are made or received after 5 April 2001.

Certificate ceasing to be valid

6—(1) The condition prescribed by this regulation is that the certificate referred to in regulation 5 continues in full force and effect and has not ceased to be valid.

(2) A certificate ceases to be valid in any of the circumstances specified in paragraph (3).

(3) The circumstances specified in this paragraph are—

(*a*) the receipt by the deposit-taker of information by way of a notification pursuant to regulation 5(*e*)(ii) that the person beneficially entitled to a payment of interest arising on an account specified in the notification has become liable to pay an amount by way of income tax for the year in which the payment is made;

(*b*) in the case of a certificate given under regulation 5(*b*)(ii), the ending of the year in which the person beneficially entitled to the payment attains the age of 16;

(*c*) the failure by a person who has given a certificate under regulation 5(*b*)(iii), but is not the holder of the account to which the certificate relates, to become the holder before the first payment of interest after the end of the year in which he attains the age of 16;

(*d*) where the Board, having reason to believe that a person beneficially entitled to a payment of interest is or has become liable to pay an amount by way of income tax, by notice require a deposit-taker to deduct tax pursuant to section 480A(1) from payments of interest which—

(i) are made in respect of an account which is held by or on behalf of that person and which, together with the account number and, where necessary for identifying the account, the branch of the deposit-taker where the account is held, is specified in the notice, and

(ii) are made to or for the benefit of that person after the expiry of a period of 30 days following the date of issue of the notice [or, if earlier, after it has become reasonably practicable so to deduct tax][1];

(*e*) where notification is received by the deposit-taker that the person by whom or on whose behalf the certificate was given has died.

Amendments—[1] Words in para (3)(*d*)(ii) added by the IT (Deposit-takers) (Interest Payments) (Amendment) Regulations, SI 1992/13 reg 5, with effect from 30 January 1992.

Consequences of notice under regulation 6(3)(d)

7—(1) Where the Board issue a notice under regulation 6(3)(*d*)—

(*a*) they shall at the same time send a copy to the person referred to in the notice;

(*b*) subject to paragraphs (2) and (3), no further certificate under regulation 5 may be given by or on behalf of the person referred to in the notice in respect of an account specified in the notice;

(*c*) ...[1]

(2) If the Board are satisfied as a result of information received following the issue of a notice under regulation 6(3)(*d*), that person referred to in the notice either—

(i) was not liable at the date of the notice, and has not since become liable, to pay an amount by way of income tax, or

(ii) is no longer liable to pay such an amount,

they shall cancel the notice and give notice of the cancellation to the deposit-taker and the person referred to in the notice under regulation 6(3)(*d*).

(3) Where notice of cancellation is issued by the Board under paragraph (2), a further certificate may be given in accordance with the conditions of regulation 5 by or on behalf of the person referred to in the notice under regulation 6(3)(*d*).

Amendments—[1] Para (1)(*c*) revoked by the IT (Deposit-takers) (Interest Payments) (Amendment) Regulations, SI 1992/13 reg 6, with effect from 30 January 1992.

Obsolescent accounts

8—(1) The condition prescribed by this regulation is that, subject to paragraphs (3) and (4), a payment of interest arising on an account held with a deposit-taker is not a payment in respect of which a written application has been made to the Board by the deposit-taker in the circumstances specified in paragraph (2) to the effect that, notwithstanding the provisions of regulations 5 and 9, the payment should be made under deduction of tax pursuant to section 480A(1).

(2) The circumstances specified in this paragraph are where—

(*a*) the account to which the payment relates is of a class which, prior to 6th April 1991, had ceased to be available to a person desiring to open a new account;

(*b*) the application, which may relate to more than one such class of account—

(i) gives sufficient particulars of each such class to enable the Board to determine whether the application is validly made, and

(ii) is made not less than 30 days before the first date after 5th April 1991 on which a payment of interest arising on any account to which the application relates is to be made.

(3) An application under paragraph (1) shall be of no effect if within 30 days after receipt of the application the Board notify the deposit-taker concerned that, having regard to paragraph (2), they are not satisfied that the application is validly made.

(4) A deposit-taker may by notice to the Board—

(*a*) cancel an application made under paragraph (1), or

(*b*) vary the application so that it ceases to relate to certain accounts;

and where the application is so cancelled or varied, the condition prescribed by this regulation shall cease to apply to payments of interest arising on accounts to which the application formerly related and made after the date of the notice.

Joint accounts

9—(1) The conditions prescribed by this regulation apply where more than one person is beneficially entitled to a payment of interest arising on an account held with a deposit-taker.

(2) The prescribed conditions are that—

(*a*) a certificate referred to in regulation 5 is given by or on behalf of—

(i) each person beneficially entitled to the payment of interest, or

(ii) one or more (but not all) of such persons individually; and

(*b*) a notice under paragraph (6) relating to the payment of interest—

(i) has not been given to the Board by the deposit-taker, or

(ii) has been so given and has subsequently been cancelled by the deposit-taker under paragraph (7).

(3) Where the condition in paragraph (2)(*a*)(i) was satisfied but a certificate has ceased to be valid at any time by reason of the occurrence of one of the circumstances specified in sub-paragraph (*a*), (*b*), (*c*) or (*d*) of regulation 6(3), this paragraph shall apply in relation to a payment of interest made—

(*a*) after that time, or

(*b*) where sub-paragraph (*d*) of regulation 6(3) applies—

(i) after the expiry of a period of 30 days following the date of issue of the notice referred to in that sub-paragraph, or

(ii) after such date falling within that period as the deposit-taker may at his option determine.

(4) Subject to paragraph (6), where the condition in paragraph (2)(*a*)(ii) is satisfied or paragraph (3) applies, for the purposes of these Regulations and of deduction of tax pursuant to section 480A(1), it shall be assumed that each person is beneficially entitled in equal shares to the payment of interest and accordingly—

(*a*) payment of so much of the interest as by virtue of this paragraph corresponds to the share of any person by or on behalf of whom a certificate was given shall be made without deduction of tax pursuant to regulation 4(1), and

(*b*) payment of the remainder of the interest shall be made under deduction of tax pursuant to section 480A(1).

(5) Tax deducted from a payment within paragraph (4)(*b*) shall, for all the purposes of the Income Tax Acts, be treated as income tax paid by the person or persons to whom the payment is treated as being made.

(6) A deposit-taker may by notice inform the Board of his intention that, in circumstances where the condition in paragraph (2)(*a*)(ii) is satisfied or paragraph (3) applies, the whole of a payment of interest referred to in the notice shall be made under deduction of tax pursuant to section 480A(1), and, subject to paragraph (7), where such notice is given paragraph (4) shall not apply and tax shall accordingly be deducted by the deposit-taker from any payment to which the notice relates and which is made after the date of the notice.

(7) A deposit-taker may by notice to the Board (in this paragraph referred to as "the cancellation notice") cancel a notice given under paragraph (6) and, where a notice is so cancelled, paragraph (4) shall apply to any payment of interest to which the notice formerly related and which is made after the date of the cancellation notice.

Information to be provided to the Board—gross payments

10—(1) This regulation applies to payments of interest made without deduction of tax by deposit-takers in respect of relevant deposits, including payments made partly without and partly under deduction of tax pursuant to regulation 9(4).

(2) The Board may by notice require any deposit-taker to furnish them, within such time (not being less than 14 days) as may be provided by the notice, such information (including copies of any relevant books, documents or other records) as they may reasonably require for the purposes of these Regulations and, in particular, for—

(*a*) verifying payments of interest made without deduction of tax in accordance with these Regulations; and

(*b*) determining whether a person has given or supplied a certificate in compliance with the conditions of regulation 5.

Information to be provided to the Board—net payments

11—(1) This regulation applies to payments of interest by deposit-takers to which regulation 10 does not apply.

(2) The Board may by notice require any deposit-taker to furnish them, within such time (not being less than 14 days) as may be provided by the notice, such information relating to amounts of interest paid by the deposit-taker to which this regulation applies and to tax deducted by the deposit-taker from such payments in accordance with section 480A(1) and these Regulations as they may reasonably require for verifying the amount of tax so deducted.

(3) The information which may be required by the Board under paragraph (2) shall include copies of any relevant books, documents or other records of the deposit-taker, not being [books, documents or][1] records from which the identity of a depositor can be ascertained.

Amendments—[1] Words in para (3) inserted by the IT (Deposit-takers) (Interest Payments) (Amendment) Regulations, SI 1992/13 reg 7.

Inspection of records

12—(1) Every deposit-taker shall, whenever required to do so, make available for inspection by an officer of the Board authorised for that purpose, at such time as that officer may reasonably require, all such [copies of][1] books, documents and other records in his possession or under his control as may be required by the Board under regulations 10 and 11.

(2) Every certificate supplied to a deposit-taker pursuant to regulation 5 shall be preserved by the deposit-taker in such manner as may be approved by the Board for two years after it has ceased to be otherwise required under the provisions of these Regulations.

Amendments—[1] Words in para (1) inserted by the IT (Deposit-takers) (Interest Payments) (Amendment) Regulations, SI 1992/13 reg 8, with effect from 30 January 1992.

Use of information

13—(1) Subject to paragraph (2) information obtained by the Board under regulation 10, 11 or 12—

(*a*) shall not be used for the purpose of ascertaining the tax liability (if any) of any person other than—

(i) a person beneficially entitled to a payment of interest within regulation 10 to whom the information obtained relates, and

(ii) the deposit-taker; and

(*b*) shall otherwise be used only for the purposes of these Regulations.

(2) Paragraph (1) shall not be construed as preventing any disclosure of information within section 182(5) of the Finance Act 1989.

[Form of declaration under section 481(5)(k) of the Taxes Act

14—(1) Notwithstanding section 481(5)(*k*) of the Taxes Act (declaration that person beneficially entitled to deposit interest is not ordinarily resident in the United Kingdom to be made in writing), a declaration under that provision may be made by means of electronic communication.

(2) Where a declaration under that provision ('the original declaration') is not in writing, the deposit-taker may—

(*a*) make a declaration in writing ('the deposit-taker declaration'), on behalf of the person who made the original declaration, that the particulars contained in the original declaration are those recorded in the deposit-taker declaration, and

(*b*) send a copy of the deposit-taker declaration to that person.

(3) Subject to any corrections notified by that person to the deposit-taker within the period of 30 days following the date on which the copy of the deposit-taker declaration was sent to that person, and incorporated in a revised declaration made by the deposit-taker, the deposit-taker declaration shall take effect as from the date on which the copy of it was sent to that person.

(4) A declaration shall be regarded as given in writing for the purposes of this regulation if it is given—

(*a*) by telephonic facsimile transmission, or

(*b*) by electronic communication containing an electronic signature of the person making it.

(5) A deposit-taker declaration made in accordance with paragraph (2) or (3) of this regulation shall be regarded as made in writing if it is produced by electronic means; and the copy of the deposit-taker declaration to be sent to a person in accordance with paragraph (2)(*b*) may be sent by telephonic facsimile transmission or by electronic communication.][1]

Amendments—[1] This Regulation inserted by the IT (Deposit-takers) (Interest Payments) (Amendment Regulations, SI 2001/406 regs 3, 8, with effect for declarations under TA 1988 s 481(5)(*k*) that are made after 5 April 2001.

SCHEDULE

Regulation 5(*e*)(i)

The information referred to in regulation 5(*e*)(i) is—

(*a*) the name, permanent residential address including postcode, and date of birth of the person beneficially entitled to the payment;

(*b*) save where the Board indicate in a particular case that this information is not required, the national insurance number of a person within paragraph (*a*) and aged 16 or over at the beginning of the year in which the payment is made who, at any time within the period of three years ending with the date on which a certificate is signed, has been liable to pay Class 1 or Class 2 contributions within the meaning of section 1(2) of the Social Security Act 1975;

(*c*) the following details relating to the depositor's account held with the deposit-taker to which the certificate relates—

(i) the name of the deposit-taker;

(ii) the branch of the deposit-taker where the account is held, if the account cannot otherwise be identified;

(iii) the account number.

1990/2361

Tax-exempt Special Savings Account Regulations 1990

Made by the Commissioners of Inland Revenue under TA 1988 s 326C(1)

Made . . . . *28 November 1990*
Laid before the House of Commons . . . *28 November 1990*
Coming into Force . . . . . . *19 December 1990*

Commentary—*Simon's Direct Tax Service* **E3.401–405.**

ARRANGEMENT OF REGULATIONS

Citation and commencement

1 These Regulations may be cited as the Tax-exempt Special Savings Account Regulations 1990 and shall come into force on 19th December 1990.

Interpretation

2—[(1)][1] In these Regulations unless the context otherwise requires–

''account'' means a deposit account or share account which is a tax-exempt special savings account for the purposes of section 326A of the Taxes Act;

''account-holder'' means the holder of an account;

''the Board'' means the Commissioners of Inland Revenue;

[''EEA Agreement'' means the Agreement on the European Economic Area signed at Oporto on 2nd May 1992 as adjusted by the Protocol signed at Brussels on 17th March 1993;][4]

[''EEA State'' means a State, other than the United Kingdom, which is a Contracting Party to the EEA Agreement;][4]

[''follow-up account'' has the same meaning as in section 326BB(1) of the Taxes Act;][2]

''notice'' means notice in writing and ''notify'' shall be construed accordingly;

''the principal sections'' means sections 326A[, 326B and 326BB][3] of the Taxes Act;

[a ''relevant European institution'' has the meaning given by section 326A(10) of the Taxes Act;][5]

[a ''society, person or institution'' means a building society or a person falling within section 840A(1)(*b*) of the Taxes Act or a relevant European institution;][6];

''the Taxes Act'' means the Income and Corporation Taxes Act 1988;

''year'' means a year beginning with 6th April in any year and ending with 5th April in the following year.

[(2) For the purposes of these Regulations an account held by an individual matures when a period of five years throughout which the account was a tax-exempt special savings account comes to an end.][2]

Amendments—[1] ''(1)'' at the beginning of the regulation inserted by the Tax-exempt Special Savings Account (Amendment) Regulations, SI 1995/1929 reg 3(1), with effect from 11 August 1995.
[2] Definition of ''follow-up account'' and para (2) inserted by SI 1995/1929 reg 3(2)(*a*), (3).
[3] Words in definition of ''the principal sections'' substituted by SI 1995/1929 reg 3(2)(*b*).
[4] Definitions of ''EEA Agreement'' and ''EEA State'' inserted by the Tax-exempt Special Savings Account (Relevant European Institutions) Regulations, SI 1995/3239 reg 8(*a*), with effect from 2 January 1996.
[5] Definition of a ''relevant European institution'' inserted by SI 1995/3239 reg 8(*b*), (*c*).
[6] Definition of a ''society, person or institution'' substituted for the definition of a ''society or institution'' by the Financial Services and Markets Act 2000 (Consequential Amendments) (Taxes) Order, SI 2001/3629 arts 129, 130 with effect from 1 December 2001, immediately after the coming into force of the Financial Services and Markets Act 2000 ss 411, 432(1), Sch 20 (and SI 2001/3629 Pts 1 and 2).

Introductory

3 These Regulations—

(*a*) prescribe a condition additional to those set out in section 326A of the Taxes Act which must be satisfied if an account is to be or remain a tax-exempt special savings account;

(*b*) make provision for the giving by the Board to societies[, persons][2] and institutions of notices prohibiting them from operating new accounts, including provision about appeals against the giving of notices;

(*c*) require societies[, persons][3] and institutions operating or proposing to operate accounts to give information and send documents to the Board and to make documents available for inspection;

[(*cc*) provide that subsection (2) of section 326BB of the Taxes Act does not apply in relation to a follow-up account unless at the time prescribed by these Regulations the society[, person][2] or institution with which the account is held has a document of a prescribed description containing such information as is prescribed by these Regulations;][1]

[(*cd*) require societies[, persons][2] and institutions operating accounts which mature to give to the individuals, who have held them certificates containing such information as is prescribed by these Regulations;][1]

(*d*) make provision as to the transfer of accounts from one society[, person][2] or institution to another;

(*e*) generally supplement the provisions of the principal sections.

Amendments—[1] Paras (*cc*), (*dd*) inserted by the Tax-exempt Special Savings Account (Amendment) Regulations, SI 1995/1929 reg 4, with effect from 11 August 1995.

[2] Words in paras (*b*), (*c*), (*cd*) inserted by the Financial Services and Markets Act 2000 (Consequential Amendments) (Taxes) Order, SI 2001/3629 arts 129, 133(1)(*a*) with effect from 1 December 2001, immediately after the coming into force of the Financial Services and Markets Act 2000 ss 411, 432(1), Sch 20 (and SI 2001/3629 Pts 1 and 2).

[3] Words in paras (*cc*), (*d*) inserted by SI 2001/3629 arts 129, 133(2)(*a*) with effect from 1 December 2001, immediately after the coming into force of the Financial Services and Markets Act 2000 ss 411, 432(1), Sch 20 (and SI 2001/3629 Pts 1 and 2).

Additional condition as to transferability

4 An account must be transferable from one society[, person][1] or institution to another society[, person][1] or institution which—

(*a*) has notified the Board of its intention to operate accounts,
(*b*) has not ceased, or ceased to be entitled, to operate accounts, and
(*c*) has not been prohibited from operating new accounts by the giving of a prohibition notice which is in force,

but not otherwise, on such terms as may be agreed between the account-holder and any society[, person][1] or institution concerned.

Amendments—[1] Words inserted by the Financial Services and Markets Act 2000 (Consequential Amendments) (Taxes) Order, SI 2001/3629 arts 129, 133(2)(*b*) with effect from 1 December 2001, immediately after the coming into force of the Financial Services and Markets Act 2000 ss 411, 432(1), Sch 20 (and SI 2001/3629 Pts 1 and 2).

Notification by society[, person][3] or institution of intention to operate accounts

5—(1) A society[, person][3] or institution shall before it begins to operate accounts notify the Board of its intention to do so and as part of that notification shall provide the Board with the information specified in paragraph (2) [or, in the case of a relevant European institution, the information specified in paragraph (2A)][1] and a certificate in the terms specified in paragraph (3).

(2) The information specified in this paragraph is—

(*a*) the name under which it is incorporated or registered and, if it is not incorporated or registered in the United Kingdom, the State or territory in which it is incorporated or registered;
(*b*) its principal address in the United Kingdom including postcode;
(*c*) the tax office to which its accounts are submitted and its reference number there; and
(*d*) the date from which it intends to operate accounts.

[(2A) The information specified in this paragraph is–

(*a*) the name under which it is incorporated or registered and the EEA State in which it is incorporated or registered;
(*b*) where it has a branch or business establishment in the United Kingdom and intends to operate all accounts opened with it through that branch or establishment–
   (i) the address of that branch or business establishment including postcode, and
   (ii) the tax office to which its accounts are submitted and its reference number there;
(*c*) where it has a branch or business establishment in the United Kingdom and does not so intend, which of the three requirements in regulation 3 of the Tax-exempt Special Savings Account (Relevant European Institutions) Regulations 1995 it proposes to fulfil;
(*d*) where it does not have a branch or business establishment in the United Kingdom–
   (i) whether it proposes to establish such a branch or business establishment through which it will operate all accounts opened with it, and
   (ii) if not, which of the three requirements mentioned in regulation 3 of the Tax-exempt Special Savings Account (Relevant European Institutions) Regulations 1995 it proposes to fulfil;
(*e*) the date from which it proposes to operate accounts.][1]

(3) The certificate specified in this paragraph is a certificate that the society[, person][3] or institution is a building society or [falls within section 840A(1)(*b*) of the Taxes Act][2] [or is a relevant European institution][1] as the case may be.

Amendments—[1] Words in paras (1), (3), and whole of para (2A), inserted by the Tax-exempt Special Savings Account (Relevant European Institutions) Regulations, SI 1995/3239 reg 9(*a*)–(*c*), with effect from 2 January 1996.

[2] Words in para (3) substituted by the Financial Services and Markets Act 2000 (Consequential Amendments) (Taxes) Order, SI 2001/3629 arts 129, 131 with effect from 1 December 2001, immediately after the coming into force of the Financial Services and Markets Act 2000 ss 411, 432(1), Sch 20 (and SI 2001/3629 Pts 1 and 2).

[3] Word in heading and paras (1), (3) inserted by the Financial Services and Markets Act 2000 (Consequential Amendments) (Taxes) Order, SI 2001/3629 arts 129, 133(2)(*c*) with effect from 1 December 2001, immediately after the coming into force of the Financial Services and Markets Act 2000 ss 411, 432(1), Sch 20 (and SI 2001/3629 Pts 1 and 2).

Conditions for application for an account to be opened

6—(1) An application by an individual for an account to be opened must be made to a society[, person][2] or institution in writing and shall contain the information as to the individual specified in paragraph (2), the declaration by the individual specified in paragraph (3) and the statement specified in paragraph (4).

(2) The information specified in this paragraph is—

(*a*) his full name,

(*b*) his permanent address including postcode,
(*c*) his date of birth, and
(*d*) if he has one, his national insurance number.

(3) The declaration by the individual specified in this paragraph is that—

(*a*) he is aged 18 or more,
[(*b*) he does not hold any other account (with the same or any other society[, person][2] or institution) which will not have matured or have been closed at the time when the account in respect of which the application is made is opened,][1]
[(*c*) he has not made and will not make any other application for an account to be opened (with the same or any other society[, person][2] or institution) which he will hold simultaneously with the account in respect of which the application is made,][1]
(*d*) he will not hold the account on behalf of another person, and
(*e*) to the best of his knowledge all information provided in the application is true.

(4) The statement specified in this paragraph is that false statements made in connection with the application may result in penalties or prosecution.

(5) A society[, person][2] or institution may not accept an application from an individual if it has reason to believe that he—

(*a*) is not, or might not be entitled to, open an account, or
(*b*) has given untrue information in his application.

Amendments—[1] Paras (3)(*b*), (*c*) substituted by the Tax-exempt Special Savings Account (Amendment) Regulations, SI 1995/1929 reg 5, with effect from 11 August 1995.
[2] Words in paras (1), (3)(*b*), (*c*) and (5) inserted by the Financial Services and Markets Act 2000 (Consequential Amendments) (Taxes) Order, SI 2001/3629 arts 129, 133(2)(*d*) with effect from 1 December 2001, immediately after the coming into force of the Financial Services and Markets Act 2000 ss 411, 432(1), Sch 20 (and SI 2001/3629 Pts 1 and 2).

Transfer of accounts

7—(1) Subject to paragraph (2), where—

(*a*) arrangements are made by an account-holder to transfer an account from one society[, person][3] or institution ("the transferor") to another society[, person][3] or institution ("the transferee"), or
(*b*) an account is transferred in consequence of the transferor ceasing, or ceasing to be entitled, to operate accounts,

the transfer shall have effect and the account shall not be otherwise affected for the purposes of the principal sections and these Regulations by reason of the transfer.

(2) The transferor shall within 30 days after the date of transfer give the transferee a notice containing the information specified in paragraph (3) and the declaration specified in paragraph (4) and shall supply the transferee with the original written application made by the account-holder for the account to be opened or a certified copy of that application.

(3) The information specified in this paragraph is—

(*a*) as regards the account-holder—
(i) his full name,
(ii) his permanent address including postcode,
(iii) his date of birth, and
(iv) if he has one, his national insurance number, and
(*b*) as regards the account—
(i) the number allocated to that account by the transferor,
(ii) the date of transfer,
(iii) the date on which the account was opened (whether with the transferor or with any other society[, person][3] or institution which previously operated the account),
(iv) the total of all amounts deposited in, or subscribed for shares in connection with, the account since it was opened,
(v) the total of all amounts of interest, dividend and bonus paid or credited to the account since it was opened,
(vi) the total of all amounts deposited in, or subscribed for shares in connection with, the account in the period beginning with the last anniversary of the opening of the account before the date of transfer and ending with the date of transfer,
(vii) the amount of interest, dividend and bonus paid or credited to the account which was not available for withdrawal at the date of transfer, and
(viii) the amount which was available for withdrawal at that date.

(4) The declaration specified in this paragraph is a declaration by the transferor that—

(*a*) the total of all amounts withdrawn from the account in the period beginning with the date on which it was opened and ending with the date of transfer, together with any fee payable to the transferor in connection with the transfer which is to be paid out of the account, does not exceed the total of all amounts of interest, dividend and bonus paid or credited to the account in that period after deducting income tax from each such amount at the [applicable rate][2];

(*b*) the account-holder has not assigned any rights to the account nor used such rights as security for a loan;

(*c*) the information contained in the notice is to the best of its knowledge correct and that it has fulfilled all its obligations to the account-holder.

[(4A) In paragraph (4)(*a*) "the applicable rate" means—

(*a*) in the case of an amount of interest, dividend or bonus paid or credited before 6th April 1996, the basic rate for the year of assessment in which the amount was paid or credited; and

(*b*) in any other case, the lower rate for the year of assessment in which it was paid or credited.][2]

[(5) Where the account being transferred is a follow-up account, the transferor shall, in addition to satisfying the preceding requirements of this regulation, within 30 days after the date of transfer give the transferee—

(*a*) any document held by him of the description prescribed by regulation 7B(2), or

(*b*) a certified copy of any document of that description previously held by him, or

(*c*) a print-out or other copy of any record constituting a document of that description.][1]

Amendments—[1] Para (5) added by the Tax-exempt Special Savings Account (Amendment) Regulations, SI 1995/1929 reg 6, with effect from 11 August 1995.

[2] Words in para (4)(*a*) substituted and para (4A) inserted by the Tax-exempt Special Savings Account (Amendment) Regulations, SI 1996/844 regs 1(2), 3, with effect as respects transfers of accounts after 5 April 1996.

[3] Word in paras (1)(*a*) and (3)(*b*)(iii) inserted by the Financial Services and Markets Act 2000 (Consequential Amendments) (Taxes) Order, SI 2001/3629 arts 129, 133(2)(*e*) with effect from 1 December 2001, immediately after the coming into force of the Financial Services and Markets Act 2000 ss 411, 432(1), Sch 20 (and SI 2001/3629 Pts 1 and 2).

[Matured accounts

7A—(1) Subject to paragraph (2), a society[, person][2] or institution with which a matured account in respect of which the condition in section 326BB(1)(*b*) of the Taxes Act is satisfied is or has been held shall, if the account-holder so requires by notice to the society[, person][2] or institution, within 30 days after the date of the notice give to the account-holder a certificate containing the information prescribed by paragraph (3) and the declaration prescribed by paragraph (4).

(2) A society[, person][2] or institution shall not give the certificate referred to in paragraph (1)—

(*a*) before the account has matured, or

(*b*) after the expiry of a period of 18 months commencing with the date on which the account matured.

(3) The information prescribed by this paragraph is—

(*a*) as regards the account-holder—

(i) his full name,

(ii) his permanent address including postcode,

(iii) if he has one, his national insurance number, and

(*b*) as regards the account—

(i) the name of the society[, person][2] or institution with which it was held when it matured;

(ii) the number allocated to it by that society[, person][2] or institution;

(iii) the date on which it matured; and

(iv) the total amount deposited in, or subscribed for shares in connection with, the account since it was opened.

(4) The declaration prescribed by this paragraph is a declaration by the society[, person][2] or institution that the account was a tax-exempt special savings account throughout a period of five years and that the information given in the certificate is correct.][1]

Amendments—[1] This regulation inserted by the Tax-exempt Special Savings Account (Amendment) Regulations, SI 1995/1929 reg 7, with effect from 11 August 1995.

[2] Words in paras (1)(*a*), (2), (3)(*b*)(i) and (4) inserted by the Financial Services and Markets Act 2000 (Consequential Amendments) (Taxes) Order, SI 2001/3629 arts 129, 133(2)(*f*) with effect from 1 December 2001, immediately after the coming into force of the Financial Services and Markets Act 2000 ss 411, 432(1), Sch 20 (and SI 2001/3629 Pts 1 and 2).

[Follow-up accounts][1]

[7B—(1) Subsection (2) of section 326BB of the Taxes Act shall not apply to a follow-up account unless, at the time when the total amount deposited in, or subscribed for shares in, the account first exceeds £3,000, the society[, person][2] or institution holds a document of the description prescribed by paragraph (2) containing the information prescribed by that paragraph.

(2) The description prescribed by this paragraph is that the document is either—

(*a*) a certificate given in accordance with regulation 7A(1) and (2) by the society[, person][2] or institution with which the account-holder held a matured account, or

(*b*) where the account-holder holds a follow-up account with the same society[, person][2] or institution with which he held a matured account, a record kept by means of a computer or otherwise which was derived from the records of the society[, person][2] or institution and shows—

(i) as regards the account-holder, the information prescribed by sub-paragraph (*a*) of regulation 7A(3), and

(ii) as regards the matured account, the information prescribed by paragraphs (ii) to (iv) inclusive of sub-paragraph (*b*) of paragraph (3) of that regulation.][1]

Amendments—[1] This regulation inserted by the Tax-exempt Special Savings Account (Amendment) Regulations, SI 1995/1929 reg 7, with effect from 11 August 1995.

[2] Words inserted by the Financial Services and Markets Act 2000 (Consequential Amendments) (Taxes) Order, SI 2001/3629 arts 129, 133(2)(*g*) with effect from 1 December 2001, immediately after the coming into force of the Financial Services and Markets Act 2000 ss 411, 432(1), Sch 20 (and SI 2001/3629 Pts 1 and 2).

Prohibition notices

8—(1) The Board may in the circumstances specified in paragraph (2) give a notice (in this regulation and in regulation 9 referred to as a "prohibition notice") to a society[, person][1] or institution prohibiting the society[, person][1] or institution to which it is given from operating new accounts.

(2) The circumstances specified in this paragraph are where the Board have reason to believe that the society[, person][1] or institution has failed to comply with any provision of the principal sections or of these Regulations.

(3) A prohibition notice shall state—

(*a*) the date from which the society[, person][1] or institution is prohibited from operating new accounts; and

(*b*) the circumstances in which the notice is given.

(4) A prohibition notice shall remain in force until it is cancelled by a further notice given by the Board to the society[, person][1] or institution withdrawing the prohibition from operating new accounts or it is quashed by the Special Commissioners on appeal.

Amendments—[1] Words inserted by the Financial Services and Markets Act 2000 (Consequential Amendments) (Taxes) Order, SI 2001/3629 arts 129, 133(2)(*h*) with effect from 1 December 2001, immediately after the coming into force of the Financial Services and Markets Act 2000 ss 411, 432(1), Sch 20 (and SI 2001/3629 Pts 1 and 2).

Appeals against prohibition notices

9—(1) A society[, person][1] or institution to whom a prohibition notice has been given under regulation 8 may appeal against the notice by notice given to the Board within 30 days after the date of the notice of prohibition.

(2) The appeal shall be to the Special Commissioners.

(3) The like provisions as are contained in Part V of the Taxes Management Act 1970 shall apply to an appeal under this regulation and the Special Commissioners shall on appeal to them confirm the prohibition notice unless they are satisfied that it ought to be quashed.

Amendments—[1] Word in para (1) inserted by the Financial Services and Markets Act 2000 (Consequential Amendments) (Taxes) Order, SI 2001/3629 arts 129, 133(2)(*i*) with effect from 1 December 2001, immediately after the coming into force of the Financial Services and Markets Act 2000 ss 411, 432(1), Sch 20 (and SI 2001/3629 Pts 1 and 2).

Society[, person][1] or institution ceasing to act

10 A society[, person][1] or institution shall give notice to the Board and to the account-holder of its intention to cease to operate an account within a reasonable time before it so ceases so that its obligations in relation to the account (including the transfer of the account to another society[, person][1] or institution) can be conveniently discharged at or about the time it ceases to act.

Amendments—[1] Words inserted by the Financial Services and Markets Act 2000 (Consequential Amendments) (Taxes) Order, SI 2001/3629 arts 129, 133(2)(*i*) with effect from 1 December 2001, immediately after the coming into force of the Financial Services and Markets Act 2000 ss 411, 432(1), Sch 20 (and SI 2001/3629 Pts 1 and 2).

Society[, person][5] or institution ceasing to be entitled to operate accounts

11 A society[, person][5] or institution shall cease to be entitled to operate accounts and shall notify the Board forthwith of that fact where—

(*a*) it ceases to be a building society or, [to [fall within section 840A(1)(*b*) of the Taxes Act][4] or to be a relevant European institution, as the case may be;][1] or

(*b*) its directors have made a proposal under Part I of the Insolvency Act 1986 for a composition in satisfaction of its debts or a scheme of arrangement of its affairs; or

(*c*) [it enters administration][6]; or

(*d*) a receiver or manager of its property has been appointed; or

(*e*) a resolution has been passed or a petition has been presented to wind it up[; or][3]

[(*f*) action has been taken in relation to it under the law of an EEA State corresponding to that described in paragraph (*b*), (*c*), (*d*) or (*e*).][2]

Amendments—[1] Words in para (*a*) substituted by the Tax-exempt Special Savings Account (Relevant European Institutions) Regulations, SI 1995/3239 reg 10(*a*), with effect from 2 January 1996.

[2] Para (*f*) inserted by SI 1995/3239 reg 10(*b*) with effect from 2 January 1996.

[3] Word before para (*f*) inserted by the Tax-exempt Special Savings Account (Amendment) Regulations, SI 1996/844 regs 1(1), 4, with effect from 6 April 1996.

[4] Words in para (*a*) substituted by the Financial Services and Markets Act 2000 (Consequential Amendments) (Taxes) Order, SI 2001/3629 arts 129, 132 with effect from 1 December 2001, immediately after the coming into force of the Financial Services and Markets Act 2000 ss 411, 432(1), Sch 20 (and SI 2001/3629 Pts 1 and 2).

[5] Words inserted by SI 2001/3629 arts 129, 133(2)(*k*) with effect from 1 December 2001, immediately after the coming into force of the Financial Services and Markets Act 2000 ss 411, 432(1), Sch 20 (and SI 2001/3629 Pts 1 and 2).
[6] Words in para (*c*) substituted by the Enterprise Act 2002 (Insolvency) Order, SI 2003/2096 art 6, Schedule para 46 with effect from 15 September 2003.

Return of aggregate information by society[, person][3] or institution

12—(1) A society[, person][3] or institution shall within 30 days after each of the aggregate reporting dates specified in paragraph (2), and after ceasing to or ceasing to be entitled to operate accounts, deliver to the Board a return signed on behalf of the society[, person][3] or institution making it which contains the aggregate information specified in paragraph (3)[, stated separately in relation to accounts in respect of which a document of the description prescribed by regulation 7B(2), or a certified copy of such a document or a print-out or other copy of the record constituting such a document received in connection with the transfer of the account from another society[, person][3] or institution, is held and other accounts][1].

(2) The aggregate reporting dates specified in this paragraph are 31st March, 30th June, 30th September and 31st December in each year that the society[, person][3] or institution operates accounts.

(3) The aggregate information specified in this paragraph is information relating to the period beginning with 1st January 1991, or the date on which the society[, person][3] or institution first began to operate accounts, and ending with the relevant aggregate reporting date or date of cessation, as to—

(*a*) the total number of accounts opened by the society[, person][3] or institution in that period (including accounts transferred to other societies[, persons][2] or institutions but excluding those transferred from other societies[, persons][2] or institutions);

(*b*) the total number of accounts closed in that period, whether at the end of the period of five years beginning with the day on which they were opened or on the earlier death of the account-holder;

(*c*) the total number of accounts, which ceased to be tax-exempt special savings accounts in that period for any of the reasons mentioned in section 326B(1) of the Taxes Act;

(*d*) the total number of accounts transferred to other societies[, persons][2] or institutions in that period;

(*e*) the total amount which in that period was deposited in, or subscribed for shares in connection with, accounts which were being operated by the society[, person][3] or institution at the relevant aggregate reporting date or date of cessation;

(*f*) the total amount of interest, dividends and bonus which in that period was credited to accounts which were being operated by the society[, person][3] or institution at the relevant aggregate reporting date or date of cessation;

(*g*) the total amount held in accounts at the relevant aggregate reporting date or date of cessation; and

(*h*) the total amount of income tax deducted from interest, dividends and bonus paid or credited to accounts which ceased to be tax-exempt special savings accounts for any of the reasons mentioned in section 326B(1) of the Taxes Act.

Amendments—[1] Words inserted in para (1) by the Tax-exempt Special Savings Account (Amendment) Regulations, SI 1995/1929 reg 8, with effect from 11 August 1995.
[2] Words in sub-paras (3)(*a*), (*d*) inserted by the Financial Services and Markets Act 2000 (Consequential Amendments) (Taxes) Order, SI 2001/3629 arts 129, 133(1)(*b*) with effect from 1 December 2001, immediately after the coming into force of the Financial Services and Markets Act 2000 ss 411, 432(1), Sch 20.
[3] Words inserted by SI 2001/3629 arts 129, 133(2)(*l*) with effect from 1 December 2001, immediately after the coming into force of the Financial Services and Markets Act 2000 ss 411, 432(1), Sch 20 (and SI 2001/3629 Pts 1 and 2).

Return of individual information by society[, person][2] or institution

13—(1) A society[, person][2] or institution shall within three months after each of the individual reporting dates specified in paragraph (2), and after ceasing to or ceasing to be entitled to operate accounts, deliver to the Board a return signed on behalf of the society[, person][2] or institution making it (or, where the return is made on magnetic tape, accompanied by a certificate signed on behalf of the society[, person][2] or institution as to the contents of the tape) which contains the individual information specified in paragraph (3).

(2) The individual reporting dates specified in this paragraph are 31st March 1992 and 31st March in each year thereafter.

(3) The individual information specified in this paragraph is information relating to each account operated in the period beginning with the date on which the society[, person][2] or institution began to operate accounts, or with the day following the previous individual reporting date, whichever is the later, and ending with the relevant individual reporting date or date of cessation, as to—

(*a*) as regards the account-holder—
   (i) his full name,
   (ii) his permanent address including postcode,
   (iii) his date of birth, and
   (iv) if he has one, his national insurance number, and

(*b*) as regards the account—

(i) the number allocated to that account by the society[, person][2] or institution,

(ii) the date on which the account was opened (whether with the society[, person][2] or institution making the return or with any other society[, person][2] or institution which previously operated the account),

[(ii*a*) whether the account is one in respect of which a document of the description prescribed by regulation 7B(2), or a certified copy of such a document or a print-out or other copy of the record constituting such a document received in connection with the transfer of the account from another society[, person][2] or institution, is held;][1]

(iii) all amounts deposited in, or subscribed for shares in connection with, the account in the period beginning with the date on which the account was opened and ending with the relevant individual reporting date or date of cessation,

(iv) the balance at the relevant individual reporting date or date of cessation,

(v) in the case of an account which has closed or has ceased to be a tax-exempt special savings account, the date on which that happened, and

(vi) in either of the cases referred to in paragraph (v), whether the account was closed at the end of the period of five years beginning with the day on which the account was opened, or on the earlier death of the account holder, or ceased to be a tax-exempt special savings account for any of the reasons mentioned in section 326B(1) of the Taxes Act, or was transferred to another society[, person][2] or institution.

Amendments—[1] Para (3)(*b*)(ii*a*) inserted by the Tax-exempt Special Savings Account (Amendment) Regulations, SI 1995/1929 reg 9, with effect from 11 August 1995.

[2] Words inserted by the Financial Services and Markets Act 2000 (Consequential Amendments) (Taxes) Order, SI 2001/3629 arts 129, 133(2)(*m*) with effect from 1 December 2001, immediately after the coming into force of the Financial Services and Markets Act 2000 ss 411, 432(1), Sch 20 (and SI 2001/3629 Pts 1 and 2).

Records to be kept by society[, person][2] or institution

[14—(1) A society[, person][2] or institution shall at all times keep sufficient records in respect of each account that it operates to enable the requirements of the principal sections and of these Regulations to be satisfied.

(2) In particular, but without prejudice to the generality of paragraph (1), the society[, person][2] or institution shall preserve so as to be available for inspection under regulation 16 for a period of two years after the account was closed or ceased to be a tax-exempt special savings account—

(*a*) every application made under regulation 6;

(*b*) every document of the description prescribed by regulation 7B(2);

(*c*) every certified copy of such a document or print-out or other copy of the record constituting such a document received in connection with the transfer of the account from another society[, person][2] or institution;

(*d*) a record of amounts deposited in or subscribed in connection with or withdrawn from the account.][1]

Amendments—[1] This regulation substituted by the Tax-exempt Special Savings Account (Amendment) Regulations, SI 1995/1929 reg 10, with effect from 11 August 1995.

[2] Words inserted by the Financial Services and Markets Act 2000 (Consequential Amendments) (Taxes) Order, SI 2001/3629 arts 129, 133(2)(*n*) with effect from 1 December 2001, immediately after the coming into force of the Financial Services and Markets Act 2000 ss 411, 432(1), Sch 20 (and SI 2001/3629 Pts 1 and 2).

Information to be provided to the Board

15 The Board may by notice require any society[, person][1] or institution which operates or which at any time has operated accounts, or any individual who is or has at any time been an account-holder, within such time (not being less than 14 days) as may be provided by the notice, to furnish them with such information (including copies of or extracts from any relevant books or other records) relating to—

(*a*) any account; or

(*b*) any account (not being a tax-exempt special savings account) with which they have reason to believe an account is or may be connected within the meaning of section 326A(8) of the Taxes Act;

as they may reasonably require for the purposes of the principal sections or of these Regulations.

Amendments—[1] Word inserted by the Financial Services and Markets Act 2000 (Consequential Amendments) (Taxes) Order, SI 2001/3629 arts 129, 133(2)(*o*) with effect from 1 December 2001, immediately after the coming into force of the Financial Services and Markets Act 2000 ss 411, 432(1), Sch 20 (and SI 2001/3629 Pts 1 and 2).

Inspection of records by officer of the Board

16 The Board may by notice require any society[, person][2] or institution which operates or which at any time has operated accounts, or any individual who is or has at any time been an account holder, within such time (not being less than 14 days) as may be provided in the notice, to make available for inspection [at a place within the United Kingdom][1] by an officer of the Board authorised for that purpose such documents (including relevant books and other records) as are in that person's possession or under that person's control containing information relating to—

(*a*) any account; or
(*b*) any account (not being a tax-exempt special savings account) with which they have reason to believe an account is or may be connected within the meaning of section 326A(8) of the Taxes Act;

as they may reasonably require for the purposes of the principal sections or of these Regulations.

Amendments—[1] Words inserted by the Tax-exempt Special Savings Account (Relevant European Institutions) Regulations, SI 1995/3239 reg 11, with effect from 2 January 1996.
[2] Word inserted by the Financial Services and Markets Act 2000 (Consequential Amendments) (Taxes) Order, SI 2001/3629 arts 129, 133(2)(*p*) with effect from 1 December 2001, immediately after the coming into force of the Financial Services and Markets Act 2000 ss 411, 432(1), Sch 20 (and SI 2001/3629 Pts 1 and 2).

1990/2529
Debts of Overseas Governments (Determination of Relevant Percentage) Regulations 1990

Made by the Commissioners of the Inland Revenue under TA 1988 s 88B

Made . . . . *10 December 1990*
Coming into Force . . . *11 December 1990*

Commentary—*Simon's Direct Tax Service* **B3.1113.**
Note—TA 1988 s 88B was repealed by FA 1996 ss 104, 105, Sch 41 Pt V(3) with effect for accounting periods ending after 31 March 1996, subject to transitional provisions in FA 1996 Sch 15.

Citation and commencement

1 These Regulations may be cited as the Debts of Overseas Governments (Determination of Relevant Percentage) Regulations 1990 and shall come into force on 11th December 1990.

Interpretation

2—(1) In these Regulations, unless the context otherwise requires—
''the A, B and C factors'' mean the factors so described in Schedule 1 to these Regulations;
''debt'' means a debt to which section 88A(2) of the Income and Corporation Taxes Act 1988 applies;
''overseas state authority'' has the same meaning as in section 88A(4) of the Income and Corporation Taxes Act 1988;
''the principal section'' means section 88B of the Income and Corporation Taxes Act 1988.
(2) For the purposes of these Regulations a debt is connected with a state or territory—
(*a*) in the case of a debt which is owed by, or payment of which is guaranteed by, an overseas state authority, when it is the state or territory by reference to which the overseas state authority is an overseas state authority; and
(*b*) in the case of a debt due payment of which is or may be prevented, restricted or subject to conditions—
(i) by virtue of any law of a state or other territory outside the United Kingdom or any act of an overseas state authority, or
(ii) under any agreement entered into in consequence or anticipation of such a law or act,
when it is the state or territory whose law it is or by reference to which the overseas state authority is an overseas state authority.

Determination of relevant percentage

3—(1) This regulation provides for the determination of the percentage of a debt by reference to the position at the end of a period of account of a company for the purposes of [subsection (2)][1] of the principal section.
[(2) The percentage referred to in paragraph (1) shall be that given by Schedule 2 to these Regulations as corresponding to the number which is found by aggregating the numerical values attributed by Schedule 1 to these Regulations to such of the A, B and C factors as are applicable at the end of the period of account in question in the case of the State or territory with which the debt is connected.][1]

Amendments—[1] Words in para (1) substituted, and para (2) substituted for paras (2)–(5), by the Debts of Overseas Governments (Determination of Relevant Percentage) (Amendment) Regulations, SI 1993/1623 reg 3, with effect from 30 June 1993.

Transitional provisions

4—(1) In relation to the last period of account of a company ending before 20th March 1990, in regulation 3(2) sub-paragraphs (*b*) and (*c*) shall be omitted.
(2) In relation to periods of account of the company—
(*a*) ending on or after 20th March 1990 and before 20th June 1990, in regulation 3(2)(*b*) the words ''each of the four consecutive periods of three months which end with'' shall be omitted;

(*b*) ending on or after 20th June 1990 and before 20th September 1990, in regulation 3(2)(*b*) for the word ''four'' there shall be substituted the word ''two'';

(*c*) ending on or after 20th September 1990 and before 20th December 1990, in regulation 3(2)(*b*) for the word ''four'' there shall be substituted the word ''three''.

(3) Where, in relation to a period of account of the company, regulation 3(2) applies as modified by paragraph (1) or (2), regulation 3(4) shall have effect as if the references in that paragraph to paragraph (2)(*b*) and (*c*) were to those sub-paragraphs as so modified.

SCHEDULE 1

A, B AND C FACTORS

Regulations 2(1) and 3(2)

Introductory

1—(1) In this Schedule—

''arrears'' in relation to repayment of debt, or the payment of interest on debt, do not include arrears arising out of temporary administrative delay which are expected to be corrected within a reasonable period of time and ''in arrear'' shall be construed accordingly;

''external creditor'' in relation to a debt, means a creditor which is an international financial institution, an overseas state authority (other than one which is an overseas state authority by reference to the state or territory with which the debt is connected) and any other creditor who is resident outside the state or territory by reference to which section 88A(2) of the Income and Corporation Taxes Act 1988 applies to the debt;

''international financial institution'' means the International Monetary Fund, the World Bank, the International Bank for Reconstruction and Development, the International Development Agency, the International Finance Corporation and any regional development bank;

''regional development bank'' means any of the European Investment Bank, the African Development Bank, the Asian Development Bank, the Caribbean Development Bank, the Inter-American Development Bank, and any other investment or development bank constituted by international agreement which is [listed in Part I of the Financial Services and Markets Act 2000 (Exemption) Order 2001][2].

(2) References in this Schedule—

(*a*) to the relevant date are references to the end of any period of account ... [1] at which the applicability of the A, B and C factors is in question for the purposes of determining a percentage under these Regulations;

(*b*) to an agreement to reschedule or restructure obligations do not include an agreement by a state or territory to make repayment of debt and payment of outstanding interest in full at an earlier date than the due date or to make future such repayments or payments by reference to earlier dates than the due dates;

(*c*) to the figures for the latest available period and at the latest available date are respectively to the figures for the latest period of twelve months ending before the relevant date for which figures are available and to the figures at the latest date before the relevant date to which figures are available.

Amendments—[1] Words in sub-para (2)(*a*) revoked by the Debts of Overseas Governments (Determination of Relevant Percentage) (Amendment) Regulations, SI 1993/1623, with effect from 30 June 1993.

[2] In para (1), words in the definition of ''regional development bank'' substituted by the Financial Services and Markets Act 2000 (Consequential Amendments) (Taxes) Order, SI 2001/3629 art 134 with effect from 1 December 2001, immediately after the coming into force of the Financial Services and Markets Act 2000 ss 411, 432(1), Sch 20 (and SI 2001/3629 Pts 1 and 2).

The A factors

2 The A factors in the case of a state or territory, which are factors which show the inability or unwillingness of the state or territory to meet its obligations when they are due or thereafter, and the numerical values attributable to them are those given by Table A below.

[Table A

Factor	*Numerical Value*
(1)(*a*) The State or territory has entered into an agreement to reschedule or restructure its obligations as to repayment of debts, or payment of interest on debts, to a general class of external creditors and at the relevant date the agreement was entered into—	
more than fifty four months ago but not more than sixty months ago;	2
more than forty eight months ago but not more than fifty four months ago;	4
more than forty two months ago but not more than forty eight months ago;	6
more than thirty six months ago but not more than forty two months ago;	8
more than thirty months ago but not more than thirty six months ago;	10
more than twenty four months ago but not more than thirty months ago;	12

Factor	*Numerical Value*
more than eighteen months ago but not more than twenty four months ago;	14
more than twelve months ago but not more than eighteen months ago;	16
more than six months ago but not more than twelve months ago;	18
six months ago or less or has only been reached in principle;	20
(*b*) the State or territory within the period of five years preceding the relevant date has refused to co-operate in a rescheduling or restructuring of its obligations as to repayment of debts, or payment of interest on debts, to a general class of external creditors;	20
(*c*) the State or territory within the period of five years preceding the relevant date— (i) has imposed a limit on the performance of its obligations as to repayment of debts, or payment of interest on debts, to a general class of external creditors, without the agreement of those creditors, or (ii) has had severe problems in performing those obligations, or (iii) has both imposed such a limit and had such problems;	20

but so that the numerical value attributable under this factor shall not exceed 20.

(2)(*a*) The State or territory either—

(i) has entered into an agreement to reschedule or restructure its obligations as to repayment of debts, or payment of interest on debts, to a general class of external creditors, under which the creditors have lent further amounts to enable the State or territory to make repayments of debt which are in arrear and pay arrears of interest, or arrears of interest have been added to the amount of outstanding debt or have been paid and immediately lent back to the State or territory, or arrears in repayment of debts which have already been the subject of a rescheduling or restructuring agreement or of unrescheduled debts are rescheduled or restructured, or

(ii) has entered into a further agreement to reschedule or restructure obligations as to repayment of debts to a general class of external creditors which have already been rescheduled or restructured since January 1983,

and at the relevant date the agreement or, as the case may be, the further agreement was entered into—

more than fifty four months ago but not more than sixty months ago;	2
more than forty eight months ago but not more than fifty four months ago;	4
more than forty two months ago but not more than forty eight months ago;	6
more than thirty six months ago but not more than forty two months ago;	8
more than thirty months ago but not more than thirty six months ago;	10
more than twenty four months ago but not more than thirty months ago;	12
more than eighteen months ago but not more than twenty four months ago;	14
more than twelve months ago but not more than eighteen months ago;	16
more than six months ago but not more than twelve months ago;	18
six months ago or less or has only been reached in principle;	20
(*b*) the State or territory within the period of five years preceding the relevant date has refused to co-operate in a rescheduling or restructuring of its obligations as to repayment of debts, or payment of interest on debts, to a general class of external creditors, so that it might have been expected to have entered into an agreement on more than one occasion to reschedule or restructure those obligations and, if it had done so, would be likely still to have arrears of payment at the relevant date;	20
(*c*) the State or territory within the period of five years preceding the relevant date— (i) has imposed a limit on the performance of its obligations as to repayment of debts, or payment of interest on debts, to a general class of external creditors, without the agreement of those creditors, or (ii) has had severe problems in performing those obligations, or (iii) has both imposed such a limit and such problems,	20

so that it might have been expected to have entered into an agreement on more than one occasion to reschedule or restructure those obligations and, if it had done so, would be likely still to have arrears of payment at the relevant date;

but so that the numerical value attributable under this factor shall not exceed 20.][1]

Amendments—[1] Table A substituted by the Debts of Overseas Governments (Determination of Relevant Percentage) (Amendment) Regulations, SI 1993/1623 with effect from 30 June 1993.

The B factors

3 The B factors in the case of a state or territory, which are factors which show that the state or territory has current difficulties in meeting its obligations, and the numerical values attributable to them are those given by Table B below.

[Table B

Factor	*Numerical Value*
(3) The State or territory is in arrear in repaying debt, or in paying interest on debt, to one or more international financial institutions so that, in the case of the International Monetary Fund, it has been declared ineligible to draw on the general resources of that Fund as held in the General Resources Account or any account which may be substituted for it by amendment of the Articles of Agreement of that Fund or, in the case of the World Bank, the International Bank for Reconstruction and Development, the International Development Agency, the International Finance Corporation or a regional development bank, disbursement of loans to it has stopped.	10
(4) The State or territory is in arrear in repaying debt, or in paying interest on debt, to external creditors other than international financial institutions, the arrears have neither been the subject of a rescheduling or restructuring agreement nor been repaid or, as the case may be, paid, and immediately lent back to that State or territory, and at the relevant date they have existed—	
for six months or less;	10
for more than six months but not more than one year;	15
for more than one year.	20][1]

Amendments—[1] Table B substituted by the Debts of Overseas Governments (Determination of Relevant Percentage) (Amendment) Regulations, SI 1993/1623 with effect from 30 June 1993.

The C factors

4 The C factors in the case of a state or territory, which are factors which provide evidence of the likelihood of that state or territory having persistent or future repayment difficulties, and the numerical values attributable to them are those given by Table C below.

[Table C

Factor	*Numerical Value*
(5) The ratio between debt and gross domestic product applicable in the case of the State or territory on the basis of the figures for the latest available period, that is to say the total external debt of the State or territory at the end of that period divided by the annual total of goods produced and services provided in that period, the result being expressed as a percentage and rounded to the nearest one tenth of one percentage point, is—	
between 30 per cent and 49·9 per cent;	2
between 50 per cent and 69·9 per cent;	4
between 70 per cent and 89·9 per cent;	6
between 90 per cent and 109·9 per cent;	8
110 per cent or greater.	10
(6) The ratio between debt and exports applicable in the case of the State or territory on the basis of the figures for the latest available period, that is to say the total external debt of the State or territory at the end of that period divided by the value of exports of goods and services (including interest and net transfer receipts) in that period, the result being expressed as a percentage and rounded to the nearest one tenth of one percentage point, is—	
between 165 per cent and 274·9 per cent;	2
between 275 per cent and 384·9 per cent;	4
between 385 per cent and 494·9 per cent;	6
between 495 per cent and 604·9 per cent;	8
605 per cent or greater.	10
(7) The debt service ratio applicable in the case of the State or territory on the basis of the figures for the latest available period, that is to say the result of dividing the sum of the total amount of the external debt of the State or territory repayable for that period, other than debt which falls to be repaid within twelve months of the date on which it was incurred, and the total amount of interest payable for that period by the value of exports of goods and services (including interest and net transfer receipts) in that period, expressing that result as a percentage and rounding that percentage to the nearest one tenth of one per cent, is—	
between 18 per cent and 29·9 per cent;	2
between 30 per cent and 41·9 per cent;	4
between 42 per cent and 53·9 per cent;	6
between 54 per cent and 65·9 per cent;	8
66 per cent or greater.	10

Factor	*Numerical Value*
(8) The interest service ratio applicable in the case of the State or territory on the basis of the figures for the latest available period, that is to say the result of dividing the total amount of interest payable for that period by the value of exports of goods and services (including interest and net transfer receipts) for the same period, expressing that result as a percentage and rounding that percentage to the nearest one tenth of one per cent, is—	
between 12 per cent and 19·9 per cent;	2
between 20 per cent and 27·9 per cent;	4
between 28 per cent and 35·9 per cent;	6
between 36 per cent and 43·9 per cent;	8
44 per cent or greater.	10
(9) The number of months for which the State or territory has visible import cover at the relevant date, that is to say the result rounded to the nearest one tenth of one month of the formula— $\frac{A}{B} \times 12$ where— A is the amount or value of the assets held by the monetary authorities of the State or territory, which may freely be used to support the exchange value of the currency of that State or territory, on the basis of the figures at the latest available date including assets which may readily be used to obtain such assets and gold valued at 75 per cent of its price expressed in United States dollars per fine troy ounce as declared at the morning fixing in the London Bullion Market on that date; and B is the annual value of imports of goods into the State or territory on the basis of the figure for the latest available period; is—	
between 3·1 and 4 months;	2
between 2·1 and 3 months;	4
between 1·1 and 2 months;	6
between 0·6 of one month and one month;	8
0·5 of one month or less.	10
(10) The State or territory at the relevant date— (*a*) is in breach of performance criteria which were set for it (and which have not been subsequently waived) in an agreement which it has entered into with the International Monetary Fund; or (*b*) has problems in relation to its external debt of such a nature as would justify an approach to the International Monetary Fund for assistance, but— (i) it is unwilling to make such an approach, or (ii) it is unable to make such an approach either because it is not a member of that Fund or because that Fund has refused to have any dealings with that State or territory, or (iii) an approach for assistance having been made, that Fund has refused to discuss the question of assistance with that State or territory.	5
(11) The price expressed as a percentage of its face value which the external debt of the State or territory might reasonably have been expected to fetch on a sale in the open market at the relevant date, that percentage being rounded to the nearest one tenth of one per cent, is—	
between 85·1 per cent and 95 per cent;	2
between 75·1 per cent and 85 per cent;	4
between 65·1 per cent and 75 per cent;	6
between 55·1 per cent and 65 per cent;	8
between 45·1 per cent and 55 per cent;	10
between 35·1 per cent and 45 per cent;	12
between 25·1 per cent and 35 per cent;	14
between 15·1 per cent and 25 per cent;	16
between 5·1 per cent and 15 per cent;	18
5 per cent or less.	20][1]

Amendments—[1] Table C substituted by the Debts of Overseas Governments (Determination of Relevant Percentage) (Amendment) Regulations, SI 1993/1623, with effect from 30 June 1993.

SCHEDULE 2

CORRESPONDING PERCENTAGES

Regulation 3(2)

A percentage shown in column 2 of the table below shall correspond to the number shown opposite to it in column 1.

[Table

(1) Number	(2) Percentage	(1) Number	(2) Percentage
0–9	0	78	53
10–30	5	79	54
31	6	80	55
32	7	81	56
33	8	82	57
34	9	83	58
35	10	84	59
36	11	85	60
37	12	86	61
38	13	87	62
39	14	88	63
40	15	89	64
41	16	90	65
42	17	91	66
43	18	92	67
44	19	93	68
45	20	94	69
46	21	95	70
47	22	96	71
48	23	97	72
49	24	98	73
50	25	99	74
51	26	100	75
52	27	101	76
53	28	102	77
54	29	103	78
55	30	104	79
56	31	105	80
57	32	106	81
58	33	107	82
59	34	108	83
60	35	109	84
61	36	110	85
62	37	111	86
63	38	112	87
64	39	113	88
65	40	114	89
66	41	115	90
67	42	116	91
68	43	117	92
69	44	118	93
70	45	119	94
71	46	120	95
72	47	121	96
73	48	122	97
74	49	123	98
75	50	124	99
76	51	125	100
77	52	126–145	100][1]

Amendments—[1] Table substituted by the Debts of Overseas Governments (Determination of Relevant Percentage) (Amendment) Regulations, SI 1993/1623 with effect from 30 June 1993.

1991/512
Income Tax (Building Societies) (Annual Payments) Regulations 1991

Made by the Commissioners of Inland Revenue under TA 1988 s 350

Made . . . . *6 March 1991*

Commentary—*Simon's Direct Tax Service* **D4.732.**

Citation, commencement and effect

1 These Regulations may be cited as the Income Tax (Building Societies) (Annual Payments) Regulations 1991 and shall come into force on 6th April 1991.

Interpretation

2 In these Regulations unless the context otherwise requires—

''the Board'' means the Commissioners of Inland Revenue;

''payment'' (except in relation to a payment to the Board) includes ''credit'';

''payment quarter'' means a period of three months ending with the last day of February, May, August or November;

''the 1986 Regulations'' mean the Income Tax (Building Societies) Regulations 1986;

''section 349(1) payment'' means a payment by a building society of any annuity or other annual payment from which income tax is deductible under section 349(1) of the Taxes Act and includes such a payment made after 28th February 1991 and before 6th April 1991 to which regulation 3 of the 1986 Regulations applied;

''Schedule 16'' means Schedule 16 to the Taxes Act;

''the Taxes Act'' means the Income and Corporation Taxes Act 1988.

Collection of amounts representing income tax payable by building societies

3—(1) This regulation modifies the provisions of Schedule 16 as they have effect for the purpose of regulating the time and manner in which a building society resident in the United Kingdom—

(*a*) is to account for and pay income tax in respect of a section 349(1) payment, and

(*b*) is to be repaid income tax in respect of payments which it receives.

(2) Schedule 16 shall have effect for those purposes—

(*a*) with the substitution for any reference to a company of a reference to a building society;

(*b*) with the substitution for paragraphs (*a*) to (*c*) of paragraph 2(2) of that Schedule of the words—

''(*a*) each complete payment quarter within the accounting period, beginning with the payment quarter ending 31st May 1991;

(*b*) each part of an accounting period (other than an accounting period ending on or before 22nd March 1991) being a part which begins after February 1991 and which is not a complete payment quarter.'';

(*c*) as if paragraph 5 of that Schedule had effect only in relation to payments—

(i) which are received by the building society after February 1991,

(ii) which fall to be taken into account in computing its income chargeable to corporation tax, and

(iii) in respect of which no claim has previously been made under that paragraph as modified by regulation 7(3)(*e*) of the 1986 Regulations.

Note—The modification of TA 1988 Sch 16, para 5 as mentioned in para (2)(*c*)(iii) above is—

''as if (except for the purposes of Regulation 11) paragraph 5 (set-off against company's income tax payable) applied in relation to payments received by the building society after February 1986 and which fall to be taken into account in computing its income chargeable to corporation tax.''

1991/1614
Retirement Benefits Schemes (Restriction on Discretion to Approve) (Small Self-administered Schemes) Regulations 1991

Made by the Commissioners of Inland Revenue under TA 1988 s 591(6)

Made . . . . *15 July 1991*
Laid before the House of Commons . . . . . *15 July 1991*
Coming into Force . . . . *5 August 1991*

Commentary—*Simon's Direct Tax Service* **E7.217.**

Citation and commencement

1 These Regulations may be cited as the Retirement Benefits Schemes (Restriction on Discretion to Approve) (Small Self-administered Schemes) Regulations 1991 and shall come into force on 5th August 1991.

Interpretation

2—(1) In these Regulations unless the context otherwise requires—

''Act'' means the Income and Corporation Taxes Act 1988;

''actuary'' means—

(*a*) a Fellow of the Institute of Actuaries,

(*b*) a Fellow of the Faculty of Actuaries, or

(*c*) a person with other actuarial qualifications who has been approved as a proper person to act for the purposes of regulation 8 of the Occupational Pension Schemes (Disclosure of Information) Regulations 1986 in connection with the scheme;

...[1]

''the Board'' means the Commissioners of Inland Revenue;

''business'' includes a trade or profession and includes any activity carried on by a body of persons, whether corporate or unincorporate, except the activity of making or managing investments where those investments do not consist of shares in 51 per cent subsidiaries of the body of persons which do not themselves carry on the activity of making or managing investments;

''close company'' has the meaning given by sections 414 and 415 of the Act;

''company'' means any body corporate or unincorporated association, but does not include a partnership;

''control'', in relation to a body corporate or partnership, shall, subject to paragraph (2), be construed in accordance with section 840 of the Act; and the like construction of ''control'' applies (with the necessary modifications) in relation to an unincorporated association as it applies in relation to a body corporate;

''controlling director'' means a director to whom subsection (5)(*b*) of section 417 of the Act (read with subsections (3), (4) and (6) of that section) applies;

''director'' means a director within the meaning of section 612(1) of the Act;

''employer'' in relation to a scheme means an employer who, by virtue of the governing instrument, is entitled to pay contributions to the scheme;

[''ex-spouse'' has the meaning given by section 659D(1) of the Act;][2]

''governing instrument'' in relation to a scheme means a trust deed, or other document by which the scheme is established, and any other document which contains provisions by which the administration of the scheme is governed;

''pensioneer trustee'' means a trustee of a scheme who—

(*a*) is approved by the Board to act as such, and

(*b*) is not connected with—

(i) a scheme member,

(ii) any other trustee of the scheme, or

(iii) a person who is an employer in relation to the scheme.

[''pension sharing order or provision'' means any such order or provision as is mentioned in section 28(1) of the Welfare Reform and Pensions Act 1999 or Article 25(1) of the Welfare Reform and Pensions (Northern Ireland) Order 1999;][2]

''relative'' means brother, sister, ancestor or lineal descendant;

''residential property'' means property normally used, or adapted for use, as one or more dwellings;

''scheme'' means a retirement benefits scheme as defined in section 611(1) of the Act;

[''small self-administered scheme'' means a retirement benefits scheme where—

(*a*) some or all of the income and other assets are invested otherwise than in insurance policies;

(*b*) a scheme member is connected with—

(i) another scheme member, or

(ii) a trustee of the scheme, or

(iii) a person who is an employer in relation to the scheme; and

(*c*) there are fewer than 12 scheme members [to whom benefits are currently accruing as a result of service as employees][2];][1]

[''scheme member'' in relation to a scheme means—

(*a*) a member of the scheme to whom benefit is currently accruing as a result of service as an employee, or

(*b*) a person who is an ex-spouse of a member of the scheme and whose rights under the scheme derive from a pension sharing order or provision;][2]

''shares'' includes stock;

''the trustees'' in relation to a scheme includes any person having the management of the scheme;

''unlisted company'' means a company which is not officially listed on a recognised stock exchange within the meaning of section 841 of the Act;

''51 per cent subsidiary'' has the meaning given by section 838 of the Act.

(2) The interpretation of "control" in paragraph (1) does not apply in relation to a body corporate which is a close company and in relation to such a body corporate "control" shall be construed in accordance with section 416 of the Act.

(3) For the purposes of these Regulations any question whether a person is connected with another shall be determined in accordance with paragraphs (4) to (8) (any provision that one person is connected with another being taken to mean that they are connected with one another).

(4) A person is connected with an individual if that person is the individual's husband or wife, or is a relative, or the husband or wife of a relative, of the individual or of the individual's husband or wife.

(5) Without prejudice to paragraph (4) a person, in his capacity as a scheme member, is connected with an employer in relation to a scheme if—

(*a*) where the employer is a partnership, he is connected with a partner in the partnership, or

(*b*) where the employer is a company, he or a person connected with him is, or at any time during the preceding 10 years has been, a controlling director of the company.

(6) A company is connected with another company—

(*a*) if the same person has control of both, or a person has control of one and persons connected with him, or he and persons connected with him, have control of the other, or

(*b*) if a group of two or more persons has control of each company, and the groups either consist of the same persons or could be regarded as consisting of the same persons by treating (in one or more cases) a member of either group as replaced by a person with whom he is connected.

(7) A company is connected with another person if that person has control of it or if that person and persons connected with him together have control of it.

(8) Any two or more persons acting together to secure or exercise control of a company shall be treated in relation to that company as connected one with another and with any person acting on the directions of any of them to secure or exercise control of the company.

(9) For the purposes of these Regulations a company is associated with an employer if (directly or indirectly) the employer controls that company or that company controls the employer or if both are controlled by a third person.

Amendments—[1] In para (1) words in definition of "administrator" revoked, and definition of "small self-administered scheme" substituted, by the Retirement Benefits Schemes (Restriction on Discretion to Approve) (Small Self-administered Schemes) (Amendment) Regulations, SI 1998/728, 3(*a*), (*b*), with effect from 7 April 1998.

[2] In para (1) definitions of "ex-spouse" and "pension sharing order or provision" inserted and definition of "scheme member" and words in definition of "small self-administered scheme" substituted, by the Retirement Benefits Schemes (Restriction on Discretion to Approve) (Small Self-administered Schemes) (Amendment) Regulations, SI 2000/1086, reg 2 with effect from 10 May 2000.

Restrictions on the Board's discretion

3 The Board shall not exercise their discretion to approve a scheme by virtue of section 591 of the Act in circumstances where the scheme is a small self-administered scheme and—

(*a*) the Board have previously approved such a scheme—

(i) of which an employee of any employer in relation to the scheme has at any time been a scheme member, and

(ii) to which any such employer was entitled to pay contributions, and

(iii) which has not been wound up; or

(*b*) subject to regulation 11, the governing instrument of the scheme does not contain provisions of a description specified in regulations 4 to 10.

Provisions as to borrowing

4—(1) The description of provision specified in this regulation is a provision to the effect that at the time of any borrowing the trustees of the scheme in their capacity as such shall not have borrowed an aggregate amount, including the amount of that borrowing but excluding any amount which has been repaid before that time, in excess of the total of—

(*a*) three times the ordinary annual contribution paid by employers;

(*b*) three times the annual amount of contributions paid by scheme members as a condition of membership in the year of assessment ending immediately before that time;

[(*c*) the amount found by the formula—

$$\frac{(A - B) \times 45}{100}$$

where—

A is the market value of the assets of the scheme at that time, other than assets franking any pension in payment under the rules of the scheme where the purchase of an annuity has been deferred (including any pension that would be payable to a widow or widower of a member of the scheme following the member's death in a case where the rules of the scheme limit such pension to the person to whom the member was married at retirement), and

B is the aggregate of any sums borrowed to purchase those assets [which are outstanding at that time][2], and any other liabilities incurred by the trustees which are outstanding at that time, other than liabilities to pay benefits under the scheme.][1]

(2) In this regulation ''ordinary annual contribution'' means the amount which is the smaller of—

[(*a*) the amount found—

(i) where the scheme has been established for three years or more at the time of any borrowing, by dividing the amount of the contributions paid by employers in the period of three years which ended at the end of the previous accounting period of the scheme by three, or

(ii) where the scheme has been established for less than three years at the time of any borrowing, by dividing the amount of the contributions paid by employers in the period since the scheme was established ending at the time of that borrowing by the number of years falling within that period (a part of a year being counted as one year), and][1]

(*b*) the amount of the annual contributions which, within the period of three years immediately before the date of any borrowing, an actuary has advised in writing would have to be paid in order to secure the benefits provided under the scheme.

Amendments—[1] Paragraphs (1)(*c*) and (2)(*a*) substituted by the Retirement Benefits Schemes (Restriction on Discretion to Approve) (Small Self-administered Schemes) (Amendment) Regulations, SI 1998/728, with effect from 7 April 1998.
[2] Words in paragraph (1)(*c*) inserted by the Retirement Benefits Schemes (Restriction on Discretion to Approve) (Small Self-administered Schemes) (Amendment No 2) Regulations, SI 1998/1315, with effect from 19 June 1998.

Provisions as to investments

5—(1) The description of provision specified in this regulation is a provision to the effect that the trustees of the scheme in their capacity as such shall not directly or indirectly hold as an investment—

(*a*) personal chattels other than choses in action (or, in Scotland, movable property other than incorporeal movable property);

(*b*) residential property other than that specified in paragraph (2);

(*c*) shares in an unlisted company which—

(i) carry more than 30 per cent of the voting power in the company, or

(ii) entitle the holder of them to more than 30 per cent of any dividends declared by the company [in respect of shares of the class held.][1]

(2) The residential property specified in this paragraph is—

(*a*) property which is, or is to be, occupied by an employee who is not connected with his employer and who is required as a condition of his employment to occupy the property; and

(*b*) property which is, or is to be, occupied by a person who is neither a scheme member nor connected with a scheme member in connection with the occupation by that person of business premises held by the trustees of the scheme in their capacity as such.

(3) For the purposes of paragraph (1), trustees shall not be regarded as indirectly holding as an investment residential property other than that specified in paragraph (2) where they hold as an investment units in a unit trust scheme—

(*a*) which is an authorised unit trust within the meaning of section 468(6) of the Act, or

(*b*) where all the unit holders would be wholly exempt from capital gains tax or corporation tax (otherwise than by reason of residence) if they disposed of their units,

and the trustees of the scheme hold such property as an investment subject to the trusts of the scheme.

[(4) For the purposes of paragraph (1), trustees shall not be regarded as indirectly holding as an investment residential property other than that specified in paragraph (2) where—

(*a*) they hold as an investment subject to the trusts of the scheme a right which confers entitlement to receive payment of any rentcharge, ground annual, feu duty or other annual payment reserved in respect of, or charged on or issuing out of, that property, and

(*b*) the property is not occupied by a scheme member or a person connected with him.][1]

Amendments—[1] Words in paragraph (1)(*c*)(ii), and paragraph (4) inserted by the Retirement Benefits Schemes (Restriction on Discretion to Approve) (Small Self-administered Schemes) (Amendment) Regulations, SI 1998/728, with effect from 7 April 1998.

Provisions as to lending and the acquisition of shares

6—(1) The description of provision specified in this regulation is a provision to the effect that the trustees of the scheme in their capacity as such shall not directly or indirectly lend money—

(*a*) to a member of the scheme or a person connected with him, other than an employer in relation to the scheme or any company associated with that employer, or

(*b*) to an employer in relation to the scheme, or any company associated with that employer, unless the lending is within the exception contained in paragraph (2).

(2) Lending is within the exception contained in this paragraph—

(*a*) only if the amount lent is utilised for the purposes of the borrower's business, and

(*b*) if it is—

(i) for a fixed term,

(ii) at a commercial rate of interest, and

(iii) evidenced by an agreement in writing which contains the provisions specified in paragraph (3) and all the conditions on which it is made.

(3) The provisions specified in this paragraph are provisions to the effect that the amount lent shall be immediately repayable—

(*a*) if the borrower—

(i) is in breach of the conditions of the agreement,

(ii) ceases to carry on business, or

(iii) becomes insolvent; or

(*b*) if it is required to enable the trustees to pay benefits which have already become due under the scheme.

(4) Subject to paragraphs (5) and (6), for the purposes of this regulation a borrower shall be taken to have become insolvent if—

(*a*) he has been adjudged bankrupt or has made a composition or arrangement with his creditors;

(*b*) he has died and his estate falls to be administered in accordance with an order under section 421 of the Insolvency Act 1986 or Article 365 of the Insolvency (Northern Ireland) Order 1989;

(*c*) where the borrower is a company, a winding-up order ...[1] has been made with respect to it, [or it has entered administration][1], or a resolution for voluntary winding-up has been passed with respect to it, or a receiver or manager of its undertaking has been duly appointed, or possession has been taken, by or on behalf of the holders of any debentures secured by a floating charge, of any property of the company comprised in or subject to the charge, or a voluntary arrangement is approved under Part I of the Insolvency Act 1986 or Part II of the Insolvency (Northern Ireland) Order 1989.

(5) Until the coming into operation of Article 365 of the Insolvency (Northern Ireland) Order 1989, paragraph (4) above shall have effect in its application to Northern Ireland subject to the following modifications—

(*a*) in sub-paragraph (*b*) of that paragraph for the reference to that Article there shall be substituted a reference to section 30(1) of, and Part I of Schedule 1 to, the Administration of Estates Act (Northern Ireland) 1955; and

(*b*) in sub-paragraph (*c*) of that paragraph the words from "or an administration order" to "to it" (where those words first occur) and the words from "or a voluntary arrangement" onwards shall be omitted.

(6) In the application of this regulation to Scotland, for sub-paragraphs (*a*), (*b*) and (*c*) of paragraph (4) above there shall be substituted the following sub-paragraphs—

(*a*) an award of sequestration has been made on his estate, or he has executed a trust deed for his creditors or has entered into a composition contract;

(*b*) he has died and a judicial factor appointed under section 11A of the Judicial Factors (Scotland) Act 1889 is required by the provisions of that section to divide his insolvent estate among his creditors; or

(*c*) where the borrower is a company, a winding up order ...[1] has been made, or a resolution for voluntary winding-up is passed with respect to it, [or it has entered administration,][1] or a receiver of its undertaking is duly appointed, or a voluntary arrangement for the purposes of Part I of the Insolvency Act 1986 is approved under that part.

(7) For the purposes of this regulation and of regulation 8 a member of a scheme includes—

(*a*) a scheme member;

(*b*) a person who is in receipt of a pension from the scheme;

(*c*) a person who has left the service of the employer but was a scheme member during that service;

(*d*) a person who is in the service of the employer but is no longer a scheme member.

Revenue & other press releases—IR 19-8-98 (Company purchase schemes: collection of outstanding tax—outcome of consultation).

PSO 24-8-98 (Small self-administered schemes (SSASs) (Update 48).

Amendments—[1] Words in para (4)(*c*), (6)(*c*) revoked and inserted by the Enterprise Act 2002 (Insolvency) Order, SI 2003/2096 art 5, Schedule para 51 with effect from 15 September 2003. However, this amendment does not apply in any case where a petition for an administration order was presented before 15 September 2003: SI 2003/2096 art 6.

7—(1) The description of provision specified in this regulation is a provision to the effect that at the time that any money is lent, or any shares in an employer or any company associated with that employer are acquired, the aggregate of—

(*a*) the total amount outstanding of money lent to an employer and any company associated with him in accordance with regulation 6(2) and (3), and

(*b*) the market value of shares in an employer and any company associated with him held by the trustees in their capacity as such.

shall not, where that time is during the period of two years from the date on which the scheme was established, exceed the figure specified in paragraph (2) or, where that time is after the end of that period, exceed the figure specified in paragraph (3).

[(2) The figure specified in this paragraph is the amount found by the formula—

$$\frac{(C-D)\times 25}{100}$$

where—

C is the market value at the time in question of the assets of the scheme which are derived from contributions made by an employer and by employees since the scheme was established, other than assets franking any pension in payment under the rules of the scheme where the purchase of an annuity has been deferred (including any pension that would be payable to a widow or widower of a member of the scheme following the member's death in a case where the rules of the scheme limit such pension to the person to whom the member was married at retirement), and

D is the aggregate of any sums borrowed to purchase those assets [which are outstanding at that time][2], and any other liabilities incurred by the trustees which are outstanding at that time, other than liabilities to pay benefits under the scheme.

(3) The figure specified in this paragraph is the amount found by the formula—

$$\frac{(E-F)\times 50}{100}$$

where—

E is the market value at the time in question of all the assets of the scheme, other than assets franking any pension in payment under the rules of the scheme where the purchase of an annuity has been deferred (including any pension that would be payable to a widow or widower of a member of the scheme following the member's death in a case where the rules of the scheme limit such pension to the person to whom the member was married at retirement), and

F is the aggregate of any sums borrowed to purchase those assets [which are outstanding at that time][2], and any other liabilities incurred by the trustees which are outstanding at that time, other than liabilities to pay benefits under the scheme.][1]

Amendments—[1] Paragraphs (2), (3) substituted by the Retirement Benefits Schemes (Restriction on Discretion to Approve) (Small Self-administered Schemes) (Amendment) Regulations, SI 1998/728, with effect from 7 April 1998.

[2] Words in paragraphs (2), (3) inserted by the Retirement Benefits Schemes (Restriction on Discretion to Approve) (Small Self-administered Schemes) (Amendment No 2) Regulations, SI 1998/1315, with effect from 19 June 1998.

Provisions as to transactions with scheme members and others

8—(1) The description of provision specified in this regulation is a provision to the effect that the trustees of the scheme in their capacity as such shall not directly or indirectly purchase, sell or lease any asset—

(*a*) from or to a member of the scheme or a person connected with him, other than an employer in relation to the scheme or any company associated with that employer, or

(*b*) from or to an employer, or any company associated with that employer, except in accordance with paragraph (2).

(2) A purchase, sale or lease is in accordance with this paragraph only when it is made—

(*a*) after the trustees have obtained independent professional advice in writing, and

(*b*) in accordance with that advice.

(3) For the purpose of this regulation—

(*a*) a purchase by the trustees shall not be regarded as a purchase indirectly from a member of the scheme, or a person connected with him, if the purchase by the trustees took place three years or more after the sale by the member or person connected with him; and

(*b*) a sale by the trustees shall not be regarded as a sale indirectly to a member of the scheme, or a person connected with him, if the purchase by the member or person connected with him took place three years or more after the sale by the trustees.

Provisions as to pensioneer trustees

[**9**—(1) The description of provision specified in this regulation is a provision to the effect that—

(*a*) one of the trustees of the scheme shall be a pensioneer trustee,

(*b*) the appointment of that trustee as a pensioneer trustee, and his obligation and entitlement to act as such, shall be incapable of termination at any time except—

(i) by the death of the trustee,

(ii) by an order of the court,

[(iia)) by virtue of section 3, 4 or 29 of the Pensions Act 1995 or Article 3, 4 or 29 of the Pensions (Northern Ireland) Order 1995 (prohibition, suspension or disqualification),][2]

(iii) by withdrawal by the Board of their approval of the trustee to act as a pensioneer trustee, or

(iv) in the circumstances specified in paragraph (2), and

(*c*) where termination occurs by virtue of any of the events specified in paragraph (1)(*b*)(i) to (iii) or in the circumstances specified in paragraph (2)(*b*), the appointment of a successor to the former pensioneer trustee of the scheme is made no more than 30 days after the termination.

(2) The circumstances specified in this paragraph are where—

(*a*) another trustee is appointed to act as pensioneer trustee in place of the trustee, and the appointment of the other trustee takes effect at the same time as the termination;

(*b*) the trustee has committed a fraudulent breach of trust in relation to the scheme and that is the reason for the termination.][1]

Amendments—[1] This regulation substituted by the Retirement Benefits Schemes (Restriction on Discretion to Approve) (Small Self-administered Schemes) (Amendment) Regulations, SI 1998/728, with effect from 7 April 1998.

[2] Sub-para (1)(*b*)(iia) inserted by the Retirement Benefits Schemes (Restriction on Discretion to Approve) (Small Self-administered Schemes) (Amendment No 2) Regulations, SI 1998/1315, with effect from 19 June 1998.

Provisions as to furnishing of information and documents

10 ...

Amendments—This regulation revoked by the Retirement Benefits Schemes (Restriction on Discretion to Approve) (Small Self-administered Schemes) (Amendment) Regulations, SI 1998/728, with effect from 7 April 1998.

Schemes awaiting approval

11—(1) Where at the date of coming into force of these Regulations a scheme which is a small self-administered scheme is in existence and either—

(*a*) has not yet been submitted to the Board for approval, or

(*b*) is before the Board for approval,

the Board shall not be prevented from approving it by virtue of section 591 of the Act by reason only that it contains a provision or provisions of a description specified in any of sub-paragraphs (*a*), (*b*) and (*c*) of paragraph (2).

(2) The description of provisions specified in this paragraph is—

(*a*) a provision which authorises the trustees of the scheme to retain an investment of a description mentioned in sub-paragraph (*a*), (*b*) or (*c*) of regulation 5(1) which is held by them immediately before the day on which these Regulations were made;

(*b*) a provision which authorises the trustees of the scheme to continue to lend money, or retain shares in an employer or any company associated with that employer, which was being lent or held by them immediately before the day on which these Regulations were made, where at the time the money was first lent or the shares were acquired the aggregate referred to in paragraph (1) of regulation 7 exceeded the figure specified in paragraph (2) of that regulation, but did not exceed the figure specified in paragraph (3) of that regulation, notwithstanding that the loan was made or the shares were acquired during the period of two years from the date on which the scheme was established;

(*c*) a provision which authorises the trustees of the scheme to sell assets held by them immediately before that day to a member of the scheme or a person connected with him.

1992/10

Income Tax (Building Societies) (Audit Powers) Regulations 1992

Made by the Commissioners of Inland Revenue under TA 1988 ss 477A(1), (2), 482A

Made	*8 January 1992*
Laid before the House of Commons	*9 January 1992*
Coming into Force	*30 January 1992*

Commentary—*Simon's Direct Tax Service* **D4.729.**

Citation and commencement

1 These Regulations may be cited as the Income Tax (Building Societies) (Audit Powers) Regulations 1992 and shall come into force on 30th January 1992.

Interpretation

2 In these Regulations unless the context otherwise requires—

"agreement" means agreement in writing and "agree" shall be construed accordingly;

"audit report" means a report made by an auditor in respect of an audit carried out pursuant to these Regulations;

"auditor" means an individual or firm whose name appears in the register of auditors kept pursuant to the Companies Act 1989 (Register of Auditors and Information about Audit Firms) Regulations 1991;

"the Board" means the Commissioners of Inland Revenue;

"the Building Societies Regulations" means the Income Tax (Building Societies) (Dividends and Interest) Regulations 1990;

"deposit-taker" has the meaning given by section 481(2) of the Income and Corporation Taxes Act 1988;

"dividend" means any distribution in respect of an investment, including any qualifying distribution as defined for the purposes of the Corporation Tax Acts and whether described as a dividend or otherwise;

"excluded investment" has the meaning given by regulation 5;

"gross payment" means a payment made without deduction of tax by a building society of a dividend or interest in respect of an investment which at the time of payment falls within any of the descriptions in sub-paragraphs (*a*) to (*l*), (*o*) and (*p*) of regulation 4(1) of the Building Societies Regulations;

"investment" includes any shareholding, deposit or loan;

"notice" means notice in writing;

"payment" (except in relation to a payment to the Board) includes "credit" and "paid" shall be construed accordingly;

"Special Reports booklet" means the booklet entitled "Special Reports of Accountants" published by the Auditing Practices Committee of the Consultative Committee of Accountancy Bodies in 1984.

Information to be provided to the Board—gross payments

3—(1) This regulation applies to gross payments made by building societies in respect of investments which are not excluded investments.

(2) Where this regulation applies, the Board may by notice require a building society to furnish them, within such time (not being less than 14 days) as may be provided by the notice, such information (including copies of any relevant books, documents or other records) as they may reasonably require for the purposes of determining whether payments made by that building society were properly made without deduction of tax.

Inspection of records

4 A building society shall, whenever required to do so, make available for inspection by an officer of the Board authorised for that purpose, at such time as that officer may reasonably require, all such copies of books, documents or other records in its possession or under its control as may be required by the Board under regulation 3.

Excluded investment

5 An investment held with a building society is an excluded investment if—

(*a*) having regard to regulation 11(1) to (4) of the Building Societies Regulations, it falls within any of the descriptions in regulation 4(1)(*a*), (*b*) and (*c*) of those Regulations, and

(*b*) the building society is approved by the Board for the purposes of these Regulations under regulation 6.

Approval of building society

6—(1) A building society shall be approved by the Board for the purposes of these Regulations if the conditions specified in paragraphs (2) and (3) are satisfied with respect to that building society.

(2) The condition specified in this paragraph is that the Board are satisfied that the building society will observe such procedures as will enable it fully to comply with its obligations under regulation 11(4) of the Building Societies Regulations in relation to investments of the kind referred to in regulation 5(*a*) of these Regulations.

(3) The condition specified in this paragraph is that the building society reaches agreement with the Board, on the terms and conditions specified in regulation 7, that it will instruct an auditor—

(*a*) to carry out the audit specified in that regulation, and

(*b*) to make a report in respect of that audit and furnish the report to the Board.

(4) The Board may, if a building society so requests, restrict their approval of that building society under paragraph (1) to either—

(*a*) that part of its business which is carried on through its branches, or

(*b*) the remainder of its business.

(5) If the Board determine to refuse approval of the building society under this regulation, they shall give the building society notice of their determination specifying the reason for their refusal to approve it.

Conditions of audit agreement referred to in regulation 6(3)

7—(1) Paragraph (2) of this regulation specifies the audit, and paragraph (3) the terms and conditions, referred to in regulation 6(3).

(2) The audit specified by this paragraph is an audit consisting of—

(*a*)

(i) a review by the auditor of the procedures put in place by the building society for the purpose of enabling the building society to comply with its obligations under regulation 11(4) of the Building Societies Regulations in relation to investments of the kind referred to in regulation 5(*a*); and

(ii) a check by the auditor of a sample of such investments in order to determine whether the procedures referred to in paragraph (i) have been observed in practice;

(*b*) a check by the auditor of a sample of investments of the kind referred to in regulation 5(*a*) in order to determine whether—

(i) the building society is in possession of valid declarations made pursuant to regulation 11(1) and (2) of the Building Societies Regulations; and, where required by that regulation, certificates in support of those declarations, and

(ii) there is information in the building society's possession which can reasonably be taken to indicate that the provisions of regulation 4(1)(*a*), (*b*) or (*c*) of the Building Societies Regulations are not or might not be applicable with respect to one or more of such investments.

(3) The terms and conditions specified by this paragraph are that—

(*a*) the Board are satisfied that the auditor is experienced in carrying out audits of a building society's or a deposit-taker's business;

(*b*) the auditor is instructed at the building society's expense;

(*c*) the Board, the building society and the auditor reach agreement in relation to—

(i) the aspects of the procedures followed by the building society which are to form the subject of the audit;

(ii) the scope of the information which is to be provided in the audit report made to the Board; and

(iii) the scope of the sample checks referred to in paragraph (2)(*a*)(ii) and (*b*);

(*d*) the building society makes available to the auditor all such books, documents, records and other information as the auditor may reasonably require for the purpose of carrying out the audit and making the audit report;

(*e*) in carrying out the audit and making the audit report, the auditor has regard to the principles set out in the Special Reports booklet and, in particular, paragraphs 24 to 42 of that booklet;

(*f*) the audit is carried out periodically, and the periods to be covered by the audit shall be—

(i) as regards the first audit, the period commencing on such date as the Board and the building society may agree, being not earlier than 6th April 1991, and ending on a date determined by the Board;

(ii) as regards each subsequent audit, the period of one year following the end of the last audit period, or such longer period as the Board and the building society may agree;

(*g*) each audit is carried out, and the audit report furnished to the Board, not later than 180 days after the end of the period covered by that audit;

(*h*) at the same time as he furnishes the audit report to the Board, the auditor sends a copy of the report to the building society;

(*i*) on receipt of the audit report, the Board may require the auditor or the building society to furnish them with such further information as they may reasonably require for the purpose of clarifying any part of the report.

Termination of approval of building society

8—(1) A building society may, by notice to the Board, terminate the approval given by the Board in its case under regulation 6.

(2) The Board and a building society may agree that the approval given by the Board in its case under regulation 6 shall be terminated.

(3) The Board may, by notice to a building society, terminate their approval of the building society in any of the circumstances specified in paragraph (4).

(4) The circumstances specified in this paragraph are where—

(*a*) an auditor has failed to furnish an audit report to the Board in respect of the building society within 180 days after the end of the period covered by the audit;

(*b*) the Board consider that the building society has failed to observe the procedures referred to in regulation 7(2)(*a*);

(*c*) the Board consider that the building society has failed within a reasonable time—

(i) to correct errors and omissions of the building society discovered by the auditor when carrying out an audit, or

(ii) to implement any recommendation made by the auditor for the purpose of remedying a failure on the part of the building society to observe the procedures referred to in regulation 7(2)(*a*);

(*d*) the building society has failed to make available to the auditor any books, documents, records or other information referred to in regulation 7(3)(*d*);

(*e*) the Board consider that the auditor instructed by the building society has failed to discharge his responsibilities in relation to the carrying out of any audit or the making of any audit report pursuant to these Regulations, and the building society fails to instruct another auditor;

(*f*) the Board have grounds for believing, whether in consequence of an audit report or otherwise, that there has been fraudulent conduct or collusion on the part of the building society in relation to any declaration or certificate referred to in regulation 11 of the Building Societies Regulations, or otherwise in connection with any payment of a dividend or interest in respect of any investment.

(5) Subject to paragraph (6), a termination of approval under paragraph (1), (2) or (3) shall have effect from—

(*a*) the last day of the latest period in respect of which an audit report has been furnished to the Board within the time stipulated by regulation 7(3)(*g*); or

(*b*) if the latest period in respect of which an audit report has been so furnished is a period in which the Board consider there to have been a failure on the part of the building society, or fraudulent conduct or collusion on the part of the building society, in one or more of the circumstances specified in paragraph (4)(*b*) to (*f*), the last day of the latest period in which the Board consider that none of those circumstances applies.

(6) If there is no period in which an audit report has been furnished to the Board within the time stipulated by regulation 7(3)(*g*) or the Board consider that there is no period in which one or more of the circumstances specified in paragraph (4)(*b*) to (*f*) does not apply, a termination of approval shall have the like effect as if the building society had not been approved under regulation 6.

Alteration of scope of approval of building society

9—(1) The Board may, by notice to a building society, alter the scope of their approval of the building society under regulation 6 by withdrawing their approval in relation to one or more branches of the building society or an otherwise separately identifiable part of its business in the cases specified in paragraph (2).

(2) The cases specified in this paragraph are cases where the Board consider that one or more of the circumstances specified in regulation 8(4)(*b*) to (*f*) applies to the branch or branches of the building society or the part of its business referred to in paragraph (1), but not to the whole of its business or, as the case may be, the whole of that part of its business approved under regulation 6.

(3) Subject to paragraph (4), an alteration of approval under paragraph (1) shall have effect from—

(*a*) the last day of the latest period in respect of which an audit report has been furnished to the Board within the time stipulated by regulation 7(3)(*g*); or

(*b*) if the latest period in respect of which an audit report has been so furnished is a period in which the Board consider that one or more of the circumstances referred to in paragraph (2) applies to a branch of the building society or a part of its business, the last day of the latest period in which the Board consider that none of those circumstances applies.

(4) If there is no period in which an audit report has been furnished to the Board within the time stipulated by regulation 7(3)(*g*) or the Board consider that there is no period in which one or more of the circumstances referred to in paragraph (2) does not apply to a branch of the building society or a part of its business, an alteration of approval under paragraph (1) shall have the like effect as if, so far as concerns that part of its business from which approval is withdrawn, the building society had not been approved under regulation 6.

Appeals against Board's refusal to approve building society, or termination or alteration of approval

10—(1) A building society to whom notice of the Board's determination to refuse approval under regulation 6(5), or of termination or alteration of approval under regulation 8(3) or 9(1), has been given, may appeal against such refusal, termination or alteration, as the case may be, by notice given to the Board within 30 days of the notice.

(2) The appeal shall be to the Special Commissioners.

(3) The like provisions as are contained in Part V of the Taxes Management Act 1970 shall apply to an appeal under this regulation, and on such an appeal—

(*a*) the jurisdiction of the Special Commissioners shall include jurisdiction to review any relevant decision taken by the Board under regulation 6, 7, 8 or 9, and

(*b*) the Special Commissioners shall confirm the notice unless they are satisfied that the notice ought to be quashed.

Consequences of termination or alteration of approval of building society

11—(1) Subject to paragraph (2), where approval is terminated under regulation 8 or altered under regulation 9—

(*a*) investments of the kind referred to in regulation 5 which are held with the building society whose approval has been terminated or, as the case may be, with a branch or other part of the building society's business from which approval has been withdrawn either—

(i) shall cease to be excluded investments with effect from the appropriate date, or
(ii) where regulation 8(6) or regulation 9(4) applies, shall be treated as if they had never been excluded investments;

(*b*) regulations 3 and 4 shall apply accordingly to such investments;

(*c*) the audit agreement concluded between the Board and the building society pursuant to regulation 6(3) shall cease to have effect in relation to such investments, and accordingly, so far as concerns such investments' no audit shall be carried out by the auditor or audit report furnished to the Board following the termination or alteration of approval.

(2) Where following the termination or alteration of approval of a building society the conditions of regulation 6(2) and (3) are again satisfied with respect to the whole of its business, the Board shall approve the building society under regulation 6 for the purposes of these Regulations.

(3) In this regulation ''the appropriate date'' means—

(*a*) as regards a termination of approval under regulation 8, the date determined by regulation 8(5), and

(*b*) as regards an alteration of approval under regulation 9, the date determined by regulation 9(3).

Use of information

12—(1) Subject to paragraph (2) information obtained by the Board under regulation 3 or 4—

(*a*) shall not be used for the purpose of ascertaining the tax liability (if any) of any person other than—

(i) a person beneficially entitled to a gross payment within regulation 3 to whom the information obtained relates, and
(ii) the building society; and

(*b*) shall otherwise be used only for the purposes of these Regulations.

(2) Paragraph (1) shall not be construed as preventing any disclosure of information within section 182(5) of the Finance Act 1989.

1992/12
Income Tax (Deposit-takers) (Audit Powers) Regulations 1992

Made by the Commissioners of Inland Revenue under TA 1988 ss 482(11)(*aa*), (12), 482A

Made . . . . *8 January 1992*
Laid before the House of Commons . . . . *9 January 1992*
Coming into Force . . . . *30 January 1992*

Commentary—*Simon's Direct Tax Service* **D4.1106**.

Citation and commencement

1 These Regulations may be cited as the Income Tax (Deposit-takers) (Audit Powers) Regulations 1992 and shall come into force on 30th January 1992.

Interpretation

2 In these Regulations unless the context otherwise requires—

''the Act'' means the Income and Corporation Taxes Act 1988;

''agreement'' means agreement in writing and ''agree'' shall be construed accordingly;

''audit report'' means a report made by an auditor in respect of an audit carried out pursuant to these Regulations;

''auditor'' means an individual or firm whose name appears in the register of auditors kept pursuant to the Companies Act 1989 (Register of Auditors and Information about Audit Firms) Regulations 1991;

''the Board'' means the Commissioners of Inland Revenue;

''deposit'', ''deposit-taker'' and ''relevant deposit'' have the meanings given by section 481 of the Act;

''excluded deposit'' has the meaning given by regulation 5;

''notice'' means notice in writing;

''payment'' (except in relation to a payment to the Board) includes ''credit'' and ''paid'' shall be construed accordingly;

''Special Reports booklet'' means the booklet entitled ''Special Reports of Accountants'' published by the Auditing Practices Committee of the Consultative Committee of Accountancy Bodies in 1984.

Information to be provided to the Board—gross payments

3—(1) This regulation applies to payments of interest made without deduction of tax by deposit-takers in respect of deposits which are neither relevant deposits nor excluded deposits.

(2) Where this regulation applies, the Board may by notice require a deposit-taker to furnish them, within such time (not being less than 14 days) as may be provided by the notice, such information (including copies of any relevant books, documents or other records) as they may reasonably require for the purposes of determining whether, having regard to sections 481 and 482 of the Act, payments of interest were properly made without deduction of tax.

Inspection of records

4 A deposit-taker shall, whenever required to do so, make available for inspection by an officer of the Board authorised for that purpose, at such time as that officer may reasonably require, all such copies of books, documents or other records in his possession or under his control as may be required by the Board under regulation 3.

Excluded deposit

5 A deposit held by a deposit-taker is an excluded deposit if—

(*a*) it is not a relevant deposit by reason of a declaration made to the deposit-taker pursuant to section 481(5)(*k*) of the Act which—

(i) is in the form and contains the information and, where applicable, the undertaking required by section 482(2) of the Act, and

(ii) is supported by a certificate where required by the Income Tax (Deposit-takers) (Non-residents) Regulations 1992, and

(*b*) the deposit-taker is approved by the Board for the purposes of these Regulations under regulation 6.

Approval of deposit-taker

6—(1) A deposit-taker shall be approved by the Board for the purposes of these Regulations if the conditions specified in paragraphs (2) and (3) are satisfied with respect to that deposit-taker.

(2) The condition specified in this paragraph is that the Board are satisfied that the deposit-taker will observe such procedures as will enable him fully to comply with his obligations under section 482(5) of the Act in relation to deposits of the kind referred to in regulation 5(*a*) of these Regulations.

(3) The condition specified in this paragraph is that the deposit-taker reaches agreement with the Board, on the terms and conditions specified in regulation 7, that he will instruct an auditor—

(*a*) to carry out the audit specified in that regulation, and

(*b*) to make a report in respect of that audit and furnish the report to the Board.

(4) The Board may, if a deposit-taker so requests, restrict their approval of that deposit-taker under paragraph (1) to either—

(*a*) that part of his business which is carried on through branches, or

(*b*) the remainder of his business.

(5) If the Board determine to refuse approval of the deposit-taker under this regulation, they shall give him notice of their determination specifying the reason for their refusal to approve him.

Conditions of audit agreement referred to in regulation 6(3)

7—(1) Paragraph (2) specifies the audit, and paragraph (3) the terms and conditions, referred to in regulation 6(3).

(2) The audit specified by this paragraph is an audit consisting of—

(*a*)

(i) a review by the auditor of the procedures put in place by the deposit-taker for the purpose of enabling him to comply with his obligations under section 482(5) of the Act in relation to deposits of the kind referred to in regulation 5(*a*), and

(ii) a check by the auditor of a sample of such deposits in order to determine whether the procedures referred to in paragraph (i) have been observed in practice;

(*b*) a check by the auditor of a sample of deposits of the kind referred to in regulation 5(*a*) in order to determine whether—

(i) the deposit-taker is in possession of valid declarations and, where required, certificates in support of those declarations, and

(ii) there is information in the deposit-taker's possession which can reasonably be taken to indicate that one or more of such deposits is or may be a relevant deposit.

(3) The terms and conditions specified by this paragraph are that—

(*a*) The Board are satisfied that the auditor is experienced in carrying out audits of a deposit-taker's business;

(*b*) the auditor is instructed at the deposit-taker's expense;

(*c*) the Board, the deposit-taker and the auditor reach agreement in relation to—

(i) the aspects of the procedures followed by the deposit-taker which are to form the subject of the audit;

(ii) the scope of the information which is to be provided in the audit report made to the Board; and

(iii) the scope of the sample checks referred to in paragraph 2(*a*)(ii) and (*b*).

(*d*) the deposit-taker makes available to the auditor all such books, documents, records and other information as the auditor may reasonably require for the purpose of carrying out the audit and making the audit report;

(*e*) in carrying out the audit and making the audit report, the auditor has regard to the principles set out in the Special Reports booklet and, in particular, paragraphs 24 to 42 of that booklet;

(*f*) the audit is carried out periodically, and the periods to be covered by the audit shall be—

(i) as regards the first audit, the period commencing on such date as the Board and the deposit-taker may agree, being not earlier than 6th April 1991, and ending on a date determined by the Board;

(ii) as regards each subsequent audit, the period of one year following the end of the last audit period, or such longer period as the Board and the deposit-taker may agree;

(*g*) each audit is carried out, and the audit report furnished to the Board, not later than 180 days after the end of the period covered by that audit;

(*h*) at the same time as he furnishes the audit report to the Board, the auditor sends a copy of the report to the deposit-taker;

(*i*) on receipt of the audit report, the Board may require the auditor or the deposit-taker to furnish them with such further information as they may reasonably require for the purpose of clarifying any part of the report.

Termination of approval of deposit-taker

8—(1) A deposit-taker may, by notice to the Board, terminate the approval given by the Board in his case under regulation 6.

(2) The Board and a deposit-taker may agree that the approval given by the Board in his case under regulation 6 shall be terminated.

(3) The Board may, by notice to a deposit-taker, terminate their approval of the deposit-taker in any of the circumstances specified in paragraph (4).

(4) The circumstances specified in this paragraph are where—

(*a*) an auditor has failed to furnish an audit report to the Board in respect of the deposit-taker within 180 days after the end of the period covered by the audit;

(*b*) the Board consider that the deposit-taker has failed to observe the procedures referred to in regulation 7(2)(*a*);

(*c*) the Board consider that the deposit-taker has failed within a reasonable time—

(i) to correct errors and omissions of the deposit-taker discovered by the auditor when carrying out an audit, or

(ii) to implement any recommendation made by the auditor for the purpose of remedying a failure on the part of the deposit-taker to observe the procedures referred to in regulation 7(2)(*a*);

(*d*) the deposit-taker has failed to make available to the auditor any books, documents, records or other information referred to in regulation 7(3)(*d*);

(*e*) the Board consider that the auditor instructed by the deposit-taker has failed to discharge his responsibilities in relation to the carrying out of any audit or the making of any audit report pursuant to these Regulations, and the deposit-taker fails to instruct another auditor;

(*f*) the Board have grounds for believing, whether in consequence of an audit report or otherwise, that there has been fraudulent conduct or collusion on the part of the deposit-taker in relation to any declaration or certificate referred to in regulation 5(*a*), or otherwise in connection with any payment of interest in respect of any deposit.

(5) Subject to paragraph (6), a termination of approval under paragraph (1), (2) or (3) shall have effect from—

(*a*) the last day of the latest period in respect of which an audit report has been furnished to the Board within the time stipulated by regulation 7(3)(*g*); or

(*b*) if the latest period in respect of which an audit report has been so furnished is a period in which the Board consider there to have been a failure on the part of the deposit-taker, or fraudulent conduct or collusion on the part of the deposit-taker, in one or more of the circumstances specified in paragraph (4)(*b*) to (*f*), the last day of the latest period in which the Board consider that none of those circumstances applies.

(6) If there is no period in which an audit report has been furnished to the Board within the time stipulated by regulation 7(3)(*g*) or the Board consider that there is no period in which one or more of the circumstances referred to in paragraph (5)(*b*) does not apply, a termination of approval shall have the like effect as if the deposit-taker had not been approved under regulation 6.

Alteration of scope of approval of deposit-taker

9—(1) The Board may, by notice to the deposit-taker, alter the scope of their approval of the deposit-taker under regulation 6 by withdrawing their approval in relation to one or more branches of the deposit-taker or an otherwise separately identifiable part of his business in the cases specified in paragraph (2).

(2) The cases specified in this paragraph are cases where the Board consider that one or more of the circumstances specified in regulation 8(4)(*b*) to (*f*) applies to the branch or branches of the deposit-taker or the part of his business referred to in paragraph (1), but not to the whole of his business or, as the case may be, the whole of that part of his business approved under regulation 6.

(3) Subject to paragraph (4), an alteration of approval under paragraph (1) shall have effect from—

(*a*) the last day of the latest period in respect of which an audit report has been furnished to the Board within the time stipulated by regulation 7(3)(*g*); or

(*b*) if the latest period in respect of which an audit report has been so furnished is a period in which the Board consider that one or more of the circumstances referred to in paragraph (2) applies to a branch of the deposit-taker or a part of his business, the last day of the latest period in which the Board consider that none of those circumstances applies.

(4) If there is no period in which an audit report has been furnished to the Board within the time stipulated by regulation 7(3)(*g*) or the Board consider that there is no period in which one or more of the circumstances referred to in paragraph (2) does not apply to a branch of the deposit-taker or a part of his business, an alteration of approval under paragraph (1) shall have the like effect as if, so far as concerns that part of his business from which approval is withdrawn, the deposit-taker had not been approved under regulation 6.

Appeals against Board's refusal to approve deposit-taker, or termination or alteration of approval

10—(1) A deposit-taker to whom notice of the Board's determination to refuse approval under regulation 6(5), or of termination or alteration of approval under regulation 8(3) or 9(1), has been given may appeal against such refusal, termination or alteration, as the case may be, by notice given to the Board within 30 days of the notice.

(2) The appeal shall be to the Special Commissioners.

(3) The like provisions as are contained in Part V of the Taxes Management Act 1970 shall apply to an appeal under this regulation, and on such an appeal—

(*a*) the jurisdiction of the Special Commissioners shall include jurisdiction to review any relevant decision taken by the Board under regulation 6, 7, 8 or 9, and

(*b*) the Special Commissioners shall confirm the notice unless they are satisfied that the notice ought to be quashed.

Consequences of termination or alteration of approval of deposit-taker

11—(1) Subject to paragraph (2), where approval is terminated under regulation 8 or altered under regulation 9—

(*a*) deposits of the kind referred to in regulation 5(*a*) which are held by the deposit-taker whose approval has been terminated or, as the case may be, by a branch or other part of the deposit-taker's business from which approval has been withdrawn either—

(i) shall cease to be excluded deposits with effect from the appropriate date, or

(ii) where regulation 8(6) or regulation 9(4) applies, shall be treated as if they had never been excluded deposits;

(*b*) regulations 3 and 4 shall apply accordingly to such deposits;

(*c*) the audit agreement concluded between the Board and the deposit-taker pursuant to regulation 6(3) shall cease to have effect in relation to such deposits, and accordingly, so far as concerns such deposits, no audit shall be carried out by the auditor or audit report furnished to the Board following the termination or alteration of approval.

(2) Where following the termination or alteration of approval of a deposit-taker the conditions of regulation 6(2) and (3) are again satisfied with respect to the whole of his business, the Board shall approve the deposit-taker under regulation 6 for the purposes of these Regulations.

(3) In this regulation "the appropriate date" means—

(*a*) as regards a termination of approval under regulation 8, the date determined by regulation 8(5), and

(*b*) as regards an alteration of approval under regulation 9, the date determined by regulation 9(3).

Use of information

12—(1) Subject to paragraph (2), information obtained by the Board under regulation 3 or 4—

(*a*) shall not be used for the purpose of ascertaining the tax liability (if any) of any person other than—

(i) a person beneficially entitled to a payment of interest within regulation 3 to whom the information obtained relates, and

(ii) the deposit-taker; and

(*b*) shall otherwise be used only for the purposes of these Regulations.

(2) Paragraph (1) shall not be construed as preventing any disclosure of information within section 182(5) of the Finance Act 1989.

1992/14

Income Tax (Deposit-takers) (Non-residents) Regulations 1992

Made by the Commissioners of Inland Revenue under TA 1988 s 482(11), (12)

Made	*8 January 1992*
Laid before the House of Commons	*9 January 1992*
Coming into Force	*30 January 1992*

Commentary—*Simon's Direct Tax Service* **D4.1105.**

Citation and commencement

1 These Regulations may be cited as the Income Tax (Deposit-takers) (Non-residents) Regulations 1992 and shall come into force on 30th January 1992.

Interpretation

2 In these Regulations unless the context otherwise requires—

"the Act" means the Income and Corporation Taxes Act 1988;

"the Board" means the Commissioners of Inland Revenue;

"certificate" means the certificate referred to in section 482(11)(*a*) of the Act;

"declaration" means a declaration under section 481(5)(*k*) of the Act;

"deposit-taker", "deposit" and "relevant deposit" have the meanings given by section 481 of the Act;

"the 1985 Regulations" means the Income Tax (Composite Rate) (Non-residents) Regulations 1985;

"notice" means notice in writing;

"payment" includes "credit".

Requirement for a certificate

3—(1) Every declaration which is in a form prescribed or authorised by the Board under the provisions of section 482(2) of the Act shall, if it does not give the address of the person making it, be supported by a certificate given by the deposit-taker in accordance with paragraph (2) of this regulation and regulations 4 and 5.

(2) The certificate shall be given without delay after receipt of the declaration by the deposit-taker and in any event before the first payment of interest in respect of the deposit to which the declaration relates.

Information to be contained in the certificate

4 The certificate shall—

(*a*) contain the deposit-taker's full name and address;

(*b*) be signed by a duly authorised signatory on behalf of the deposit-taker;

(*c*) state the signatory's office;

(*d*) contain a sufficient description or other identification of the declaration to which the certificate relates;

(*e*) contain a statement that the declaration includes the undertaking required by section 482(2)(*a*) of the Act;

(*f*) contain a statement that the deposit-taker has no reason to believe that any person beneficially entitled to interest in respect of the deposit to which the declaration relates is not resident outside the United Kingdom.

Form of Certificate

5 The certificate shall not be valid for the purposes of these Regulations unless it is in the form prescribed by the Board, or in a form authorised by the Board for those purposes.

Certificate ceasing to be valid

6 When the deposit-taker is in possession of information which can reasonably be taken to indicate that the deposit to which the certificate relates is or may be a relevant deposit, the certificate shall no longer be valid for the purposes of these Regulations and he shall thereupon treat that deposit as a relevant deposit.

Inspection of certificates

7—(1) A deposit-taker shall, on being so required by notice given to him by an inspector, make any certificate to which the notice refers available for inspection by the inspector or by a named officer of the Board within such time as may be specified in the notice.

(2) The inspector or officer to whom a certificate is to be made available under paragraph (1) shall be entitled to take copies of, or make extracts from, that certificate.

(3) A notice under paragraph (1) may be combined with a notice given under section 482(3) of the Act.

Retention of declarations and certificates

8 Every declaration, whether made before or after the coming into force of these Regulations, and every certificate shall be preserved by the deposit-taker in such manner as may be approved by the Board until two years after the deposit has been repaid or has become a relevant deposit.

Revocation of the 1985 Regulations and consequential provision

9—(1) The 1985 Regulations are hereby revoked.

(2) A certificate given in accordance with the 1985 Regulations which was valid for the purposes of those Regulations immediately before the coming into force of these Regulations shall have effect as if given in accordance with regulations 3, 4 and 5, and accordingly, unless the context otherwise requires, references to a certificate in these Regulations shall be construed as including a certificate given in accordance with the provisions of the 1985 Regulations.

1992/15
Income Tax (Interest Payments) (Information Powers) Regulations 1992

Made by the Commissioners of Inland Revenue under TMA 1970 ss 17(5), (6), 18(3B), (3C)

Made	*8 January 1992*
Laid before the House of Commons	*9 January 1992*
Coming into Force	*30 January 1992*

Commentary—*Simon's Direct Tax Service* **A3.120.**

Citation, commencement and effect

1 These Regulations may be cited as the Income Tax (Interest Payments) (Information Powers) Regulations 1992, shall come into force on 30th January 1992 and shall have effect with respect to payments made in the year 1991–92 and subsequent years of assessment.

Interpretation

2 In these Regulations unless the context otherwise requires—

"account-holder" means the holder of an account in relation to which a payment is made;

"the Board" means the Commissioners of Inland Revenue;

["Building Societies Regulations" means the Income Tax (Building Societies) (Dividends and Interest) Regulations 1990;][1]

"deposit-taker" has the meaning given by section 481(2) of the Taxes Act;

"the Deposit-takers Regulations" means the Income Tax (Deposit-takers) (Interest Payments) Regulations 1990;

"the Management Act" means the Taxes Management Act 1970;

"payment" means a payment of interest [(including, in relation to a building society, a payment of a dividend in respect of a share in the building society)][1] and, in relation to a payment in respect of which further information may be required to be contained in a section 17 return pursuant to these Regulations, includes "credit";

"section 17(1)" and "section 18(1)" mean sections 17(1) and 18(1) respectively of the Management Act;

"section 17 return" means a return under section 17(1);

"section 18 information" means information required to be furnished under section 18(1);

"the Taxes Act" means the Income and Corporation Taxes Act 1988;

"year" means a year beginning with 6th April in any year and ending with 5th April in the following year.

Amendments—[1] Definition of "Building Societies Regulations" inserted, and definition of "payment" amended by the IT (Interest Payments) (Information Powers) (Amendment) Regulations, SI 2001/405 regs 2, 3 with effect for payments of interest made, credited or received after 5 April 2001.

[Disapplication of section 17(1) and section 18(1)

3—(1) In the cases prescribed by paragraph (2), a notice under section 17(1) shall not require information.

(2) The cases prescribed are—

(*a*) a payment in respect of a certificate of deposit within the meaning given by section 56(5) of the Taxes Act;

(*b*) a payment in respect of an investment held by a branch of a person to whom a notice under section 17(1) is issued, where the branch is situated in a territory other than the United Kingdom;

(*c*) a payment falling within regulation 6(2)(*ba*) in respect of which the information that the notice under section 17(1) shall not require is the name and address of the person to whom the interest was paid or credited, if other than the person beneficially entitled to the interest;

(*d*) a payment in respect of an account which is a tax exempt special savings account for the purposes of section 326A of the Taxes Act;

(*e*) a payment in respect of an investment under a plan provided for by regulations made under section 333 of the Taxes Act;

(*f*) any other payment not falling within any of sub-paragraphs (*a*) to (*e*) which is specified in the notice under section 17(1) as being a payment in respect of which information is not required.

(3) In the cases prescribed by paragraph (4), a notice under section 18(1) shall not require information.

(4) The cases prescribed are—

(*a*) any amount to which a person holding a relevant discounted security is entitled on the redemption of that security, where the amount is paid or received on or before 5th April 2002;

(*b*) a foreign dividend paid or received on or before 5th April 2002;

(*c*) a payment to or a receipt for a person other than an individual (in whatever capacity the individual is acting), except where the case also falls within regulation 5 or regulation 6(2)(*ba*) or (3)(*d*);

(*d*) a payment information on which is required by a notice under section 17(1) or which is excluded from a notice under section 17(1) by virtue of paragraph (2) above;

(*e*) a payment made in respect of a deposit held at a branch of a person to whom a notice under section 18(1) is issued, where the branch is situated in a territory other than the United Kingdom;

(*f*) a payment falling within regulation 6(2)(*ba*) or (3)(*d*) in respect of which the information that the notice under section 18(1) shall not require is the name and address of the person to whom the interest was paid or credited, if other than the person beneficially entitled to the interest;

(*g*) a payment in respect of an account which is a tax exempt special savings account for the purposes of section 326A of the Taxes Act;

(*h*) a payment in respect of an investment under a plan provided for by regulations made under section 333 of the Taxes Act;

(*i*) any other payment not falling within any of sub-paragraphs (*a*) to (*h*) which is specified in the notice under section 18(1) as being a payment in respect of which information is not required.

(5) In paragraph (4)—

(*a*) ''relevant discounted security'' has the meaning given by paragraph 3 of Schedule 13 to the Finance Act 1996;

(*b*) ''foreign dividend'' means a ''foreign dividend'' within the meaning given by section 18(3G) of the Management Act other than interest.][1]

Amendments—[1] Regulation substituted by the IT (Interest Payments) (Information Powers) (Amendment) Regulations, SI 2001/405 regs 2, 4 with effect for payments of interest made, credited or received after 5 April 2001.

Requirement and conditions for further information

4—(1) Subject to the conditions specified in paragraph (2), a section 17 return shall contain such further information as is prescribed by regulations 5(3) and 6(2) and a person required to furnish section 18 information shall furnish at the same time such further information as is prescribed by regulations 5(3)(*b*) and 6(2) [and (3)][1].

(2) The conditions specified in this paragraph are that—

(*a*) as regards a section 17 return, the notice under section 17(1) requiring the return specifies the further information referred to in paragraph (1) and requires it to be contained in the return;

(*b*) as regards section 18 information, the notice under section 18(1) requiring the section 18 information to be furnished specifies the further information referred to in paragraph (1) and requires it to be furnished at the same time as the section 18 information.

(3) ...[1]

(4) ...[1]

Amendments—[1] Words in para (1) added, and paras (3), (4) revoked, by the IT (Interest Payments) (Information Powers) (Amendment) Regulations, SI 2001/405 regs 2, 5 with effect for payments of interest made, credited or received after 5 April 2001.

Further information—cases where certificate of non-liability to tax is given

5—(1) Paragraph (3) prescribes in relation to the cases specified in paragraph (2) the further information which, subject to [regulations 3 and 4][1], is required to be contained in a section 17 return or to be furnished at the same time as section 18 information.

(2) The cases specified in this paragraph are where a payment is made in circumstances in which a certificate has been given under regulation 5 of the Deposit-takers Regulations that the person beneficially entitled to the payment is unlikely to be liable to pay any amount by way of income tax for the year in which the payment is made.

(3) The further information prescribed by this paragraph is—

(*a*) as regards information to be contained in a section 17 return, the name and address of the person or, if more than one, each person by or on behalf of whom a certificate has been given in connection with the payment (in sub-paragraph (*b*) referred to as "the beneficiary") if other than the person or persons to whom the payment was made;

(*b*) as regards information to be contained in a section 17 return or to be furnished at the same time as section 18 information—

(i) the date of birth of the beneficiary;

(ii) the national insurance number of the beneficiary if furnished to the deposit-taker pursuant to regulation 5 of, and the Schedule to, the Deposit-takers Regulations;

(iii) notification of the fact that the account in respect of which the payment was made is or was one in connection with which a certificate or certificates had been given which had not ceased to be valid at the 5th April in the year in which the payment was made or at the date of closure of the account, if earlier in that year;

(iv) the reference number of the account referred to in paragraph (iii) and, where necessary for identifying the account, the branch of the payer where the account is held;

(v) where the payment was made to two or more account-holders each of whom was beneficially entitled to the payment, notification of that fact and, if known, the number of such persons;

(vi) if furnished to the deposit-taker in connection with the account, the dates of birth and national insurance numbers of persons referred to in paragraph (v) other than the beneficiary referred to in paragraphs (i) and (ii);

(vii) where a certificate was given by or on behalf of one or more, but not all, of the persons referred to in paragraph (v) and had not ceased to be valid at the 5th April in the year in which the payment was made or at the date of closure of the account, if earlier in that year, notification of those facts;

(viii) where the payment was the first payment made in respect of an account, notification of that fact;

(ix) where the payment was in a currency other than sterling and the amount of the payment is recorded in that currency in a section 17 return or as part of section 18 information, notification of the fact that the amount is so recorded and specification of the currency concerned.

Amendments—[1] Words substituted by the IT (Interest Payments) (Information Powers) (Amendment) Regulations, SI 2001/405, regs 2, 6 with effect for payments of interest made, credited or received on or after 5 April 2001.

Further information—other cases

6—(1) Paragraph (2) prescribes in relation to cases to which regulation 5 does not apply the further information [relating to payments in respect of deposits which, subject to regulations 3 and 4,][1] is to be contained in a section 17 return or to be furnished with section 18 information.

[(1A) Paragraph (3) prescribes the further information relating to payments and receipts of interest other than payments in respect of deposits which, subject to regulations 3 and 4, is to be furnished with section 18 information.][1]

(2) The further information prescribed by this paragraph is—

(*a*) the reference number of the account in respect of which a payment was made and, where necessary for identifying the account, the branch of the payer where the account is held;

(*b*) where a payment was made to two or more account-holders ...[1], notification of that fact and, if known, the number of such persons;

[(*ba*) where the payment was made without deduction of tax by virtue of a declaration made after 5th April 2001 under section 481(5)(*k*)(i) of the Taxes Act—

(i) the name and principal residential address of the individual beneficially entitled to the payment or, if more than one, of each individual beneficially entitled to the payment; or

(ii) where the person beneficially entitled to the payment is a Scottish partnership, all the partners in which are individuals, the name and principal residential address of each of the partners;][1]

[(*bb*) in a case falling within sub-paragraph (*ba*), notification of the fact that the account in respect of which the payment was made was one in respect of which a declaration had been made as mentioned in that sub-paragraph;][1]

(*c*) if furnished in connection with the account, the date of birth and national insurance number of the person or, where sub-paragraph (*b*) applies, each person to whom a payment was made;

(*d*) where a payment made in the course of the year was the first payment in respect of an account, notification of that fact;

(*e*) where a payment was in a currency other than sterling and the amount of the payment is recorded in that currency in a section 17 return or as part of section 18 information, notification of the fact that the amount is so recorded and specification of the currency concerned.

[(3) The further information prescribed by this paragraph is—

(*a*) identification of the security or investment in respect of which the payment was made or received;

(*b*) where the payment or receipt was in a currency other than sterling and the amount of the payment or receipt is recorded in that currency as part of section 18 information, notification of the fact that the amount is so recorded and specification of the currency concerned;

(*c*) where the payment was made to, or the receipt was for, two or more persons, notification of that fact and, if known, the number of such persons;

(*d*) where the payment was made without deduction of tax by virtue of a declaration made under—

(i) section 468O(1)(*a*) of the Taxes Act (interest distribution by authorised unit trust—residence condition of unit holder), or

(ii) regulation 3 of the Open-ended Investment Companies (Tax) Regulations 1997 taken together with section 468O(1)(*a*) of the Taxes Act (interest distribution by open-ended investment company—residence condition of owner of share in open-ended investment company),

the name and principal residential address of the person beneficially entitled to the payment or, if more than one, of each person beneficially entitled to the payment;

(*e*) in a case falling within sub-paragraph (*d*), notification of the fact that the unit holder or, as the case may be, the owner of a share was a person in respect of whom a declaration had been made as mentioned in that sub-paragraph.][2]

[(4) In paragraph (1A) the reference to ''interest'' includes a reference to a dividend or other amount treated as interest by virtue of subsection (3E), read with subsections (3F) and (3G), of section 18 of the Management Act.][2]

Amendments—

[1] Words in para (1) substituted, para (1A) inserted, words in para (2)(*b*) revoked, and paras (2)(*ba*), (*bb*) inserted by the IT (Interest Payments) (Information Powers) (Amendment) Regulations, SI 2001/405 regs 2, 7 with effect for payments of interest made, credited or received after 5 April 2001, including dividends or other amounts treated as interest by TMA 1970 s 18(3E)–(3G).

[2] Paras 3, 4 added by SI 2001/405 regs 2, 7(5) with effect for payments of interest made, credited or received after 5 April 2001, including dividends or other amounts treated as interest by TMA 1970 s 18(3E)–(3G).

[Further information—section 17 return – form of information

6A Where a notice under section 17(1)—

(*a*) requires a section 17 return to be made, or

(*b*) specifies the further information prescribed by regulations 5(3) and 6(2) and requires it to be contained in the return, and

(*c*) the notice specifies the form in which the return is to be made and delivered,

the return shall be made and delivered in that form.][1]

Amendments—[1] This Regulation inserted by IT (Interest Payments) (Information Powers) (Amendment) Regulations, SI 2001/405 regs 2, 8 with effect for payments of interest made, credited or received after 5 April 2001.

[Further information—section 18 information—form of information][1]

7 Where a notice under section 18(1)—

(*a*) requires section 18 information to be furnished, or

(*b*) specifies the further information prescribed by regulations 5(3)(*b*) and 6(2) [and (3)][1] and requires it to be furnished with section 18 information, and

(*c*) specifies the form in which information within paragraph (*a*) or (*b*) is to be furnished,

the information shall be furnished in that form.

Amendments—[1] Heading substituted, and words in sub-para (*b*) inserted by the IT (Interest Payments) (Information Powers) (Amendment) Regulations, SI 2001/405 regs 2, 9 with effect for payments of interest made, credited or received after 5 April 2001.

[Information to be provided to the Board—section 17 notice

8 The Board may by notice require a person to furnish them within such time, not being less than 14 days, as may be provided by the notice, such information (including copies of any relevant books, documents or other records) as they may reasonably require for the purposes of determining whether information contained in a section 17 return by that person by virtue of a notice under section 17(1) was correct and complete.][1]

Amendments—[1] This Regulation inserted by IT (Interest Payments) (Information Powers) (Amendment) Regulations, SI 2001/405 regs 2, 10 with effect for payments of interest made, credited or received after 5 April 2001.

[Information to be provided to the Board—section 18 notice

9 The Board may by notice require a person to furnish them within such time, not being less than 14 days, as may be provided by the notice, such information (including copies of any relevant books, documents or other records) as they may reasonably require for the purposes of determining whether information furnished to the inspector by virtue of a notice under section 18(1) was correct and complete.][1]

Amendments—[1] This Regulation inserted by IT (Interest Payments) (Information Powers) (Amendment) Regulations, SI 2001/405 regs 2, 10 with effect for payments of interest made, credited or received after 5 April 2001.

[Inspection of records

10 A person required to make and deliver a section 17 return or to furnish information by virtue of a notice under section 18(1) shall, whenever required to do so within the period specified in regulation 11(2), make available for inspection by an officer of the Board authorised for that purpose, at such time as that officer may reasonably require, all such copies of books, documents or other records in his possession or under his control as may be required by the Board under regulation 8 or, as the case may be, regulation 9.][1]

Amendments—[1] This Regulation inserted by IT (Interest Payments) (Information Powers) (Amendment) Regulations, SI 2001/405 regs 2, 10 with effect for payments of interest made, credited or received after 5 April 2001.

[Retention of records

11—(1) A person required to make and deliver a section 17 return or to furnish information by virtue of a notice under section 18(1) shall retain, for the period specified in paragraph (2), all such books, documents and other records copies of which he may be required to make available for inspection under regulation 10.

(2) The period specified is the period of two years beginning immediately after the end of the year to which the notice under section 17(1) or 18(1) relates.

(3) Paragraphs (1) and (2) are without prejudice to the following provisions—

(*a*) regulations 11(7) and 15(2) of the Building Societies Regulations;
(*b*) regulation 12(2) of the Deposit-takers Regulations;
(*c*) regulation 8 of the Income Tax (Deposit-takers) (Non-residents) Regulations 1992;
(*d*) regulation 8 of the Income Tax (Authorised Unit Trusts) (Interest Distributions) Regulations 1994.][1]

Amendments—[1] This Regulation inserted by IT (Interest Payments) (Information Powers) (Amendment) Regulations, SI 2001/405 regs 2, 10 with effect for payments of interest made, credited or received after 5 April 2001.

[Use of information

12—(1) Subject to paragraph (2), information obtained by the Board under regulations 8 to 10—

(*a*) shall not be used for the purpose of ascertaining the tax liability (if any) of any person other than—

(i) a person beneficially entitled to a payment to whom the information obtained relates, and
(ii) the person by whom the payment was made or received; and

(*b*) shall otherwise be used only for the purposes of—

(i) section 17 or 18 of the Management Act and these Regulations,
(ii) the provisions of Chapter IV of Part XII of the Taxes Act relating to the deduction of tax from payments by building societies and deposit-takers,
(iii) the Building Societies Regulations,
(iv) the Deposit-takers Regulations, and
(v) the Income Tax (Authorised Unit Trusts) (Interest Distributions) Regulations 1994.

(2) Paragraph (1) shall not be construed as preventing any disclosure of information within section 182(5) of the Finance Act 1989.][1]

Amendments—[1] This Regulation inserted by IT (Interest Payments) (Information Powers) (Amendment) Regulations, SI 2001/405 regs 2, 10 with effect for payments of interest made, credited or received after 5 April 2001.

1992/42

Taxes (Relief for Gifts) (Designated Educational Establishments) Regulations 1992

Made by the Secretary of State for Education and Science for England and the Secretaries of State for Scotland and Wales under TA 1988 s 84

Made . . . . *10 January 1992*
Laid before the House of Commons . . . . *14 January 1992*
Coming into Force . . . . . . *4 February 1992*

Commentary—*Simon's Direct Tax Service* **B3.1445.**

1 These Regulations may be cited as the Taxes (Relief for Gifts) (Designated Educational Establishments) Regulations 1992 and shall come into force on 4th February 1992.

2—(1) In these Regulations—

"charity" has the same meaning as in section 506 of the Income and Corporation Taxes Act 1988 and a charity is an educational charity if the charitable purposes for which it is established are exclusively educational purposes;

"the 1980 Act" means the Education (Scotland) Act 1980; and

"the 1989 Act" means the Self-Governing Schools etc (Scotland) Act 1989.

(2) Expressions used in these Regulations in relation to educational establishments in England and Wales have the same meaning as in the Education Acts [1944 to 1992][1].

(3) Expressions used in these Regulations in relation to educational establishments in Scotland have the same meaning as in the 1980 Act or the 1989 Act.

Amendments—[1] Words in para (2) substituted by the Taxes (Relief for Gifts) (Designated Educational Establishments) (Amendment) Regulations, SI 1993/561.

3 The educational establishments and categories of educational establishments specified in the Schedule to these Regulations are hereby designated for the purposes of section 84 of the Income and Corporation Taxes Act 1988.

SCHEDULE

Regulation 3

PART I

SCHOOLS: ENGLAND AND WALES

1 Any school maintained by a local education authority.

2 Any grant-maintained school.

3 Any special school not maintained by a local education authority.

4 Any independent school registered pursuant to section 70 of the Education Act 1944 which is conducted by an educational charity.

5 Any school maintained by the Service Children's Education Authority.

6 The European School established under Article 1 of the Statute of the European School, any school designated as a European School under Article 1 of the Protocol to that Statute and the European School established under article 1 of the Supplementary Protocol to that Statute.

7 Any nursery school recognised by the Secretary of State for the purpose of receiving grant under regulation 5 of the Direct Grant Schools Regulations 1959.

PART II

SCHOOLS: SCOTLAND

1 Any public school.

2 Any self-governing school.

3 Any grant-aided school.

4 Any independent school managed by an educational charity.

PART III

ESTABLISHMENTS OF FURTHER AND HIGHER EDUCATION: ENGLAND AND WALES

1 Any university.

2 [Any institution within the higher education sector (within the meaning of section 91(5) of the Further and Higher Education Act 1992) other than a university.]1

Amendments—[1] This paragraph substituted by the Taxes (Relief for Gifts) (Designated Educational Establishments) (Amendment) Regulations, SI 1993/561, with effect from 1 April 1993.

3 ... [1]

Amendments—[1] This paragraph revoked by the Taxes (Relief for Gifts) (Designated Educational Establishments) (Amendment) Regulations, SI 1993/561, with effect from 1 April 1993.

4 [Any institution of further or higher education (or both) maintained or assisted by a local education authority or in receipt of grant under regulations made under section 100(1)(*b*) of the Education Act 1944.][1]

Amendments—[1] This paragraph substituted by the Taxes (Relief for Gifts) (Designated Educational Establishments) (Amendment) Regulations, SI 1993/561, with effect from 1 April 1993.

5 [Any institution within the further education sector (within the meaning of section 91(3) of the Further and Higher Education Act 1992).][1]

Amendments—[1] This paragraph substituted by the Taxes (Relief for Gifts) (Designated Educational Establishments) (Amendment) Regulations, SI 1993/561, with effect from 1 April 1993.

6–22 ...[1]

Amendments—[1] Paras 6–22 revoked by the Taxes (Relief for Gifts) (Designated Educational Establishments) (Amendment) Regulations, SI 1993/561, with effect from 1 April 1993.

23 Any other establishment providing further or higher education (or both) which is conducted by an educational charity.

PART IV

ESTABLISHMENTS OF FURTHER AND HIGHER EDUCATION: SCOTLAND

1 Any university.

2 Any central institution, college of education or any institution established under section 77 of the 1980 Act.

3 Any establishment for the provision of further education under the management of—

(*a*) an education authority, or
(*b*) a company by virtue of section 65 of the 1989 Act.

4 Any other establishment for the provision of further or higher education (or both) managed by an educational charity.

1992/568
Income Tax (Dealers in Securities) Regulations 1992

Made by the Treasury under TA 1988 s 732

Made	*9 March 1992*
Laid before the House of Commons	*9 March 1992*
Coming into Force	*22 March 1992*

Commentary—*Simon's Direct Tax Service* **B3.727A.**

Citation and commencement

1 These Regulations may be cited as the Income Tax (Dealers in Securities) Regulations 1992 and shall come into force on 22nd March 1992.

Interpretation

2 In these Regulations, unless the context otherwise requires—

"the Board of directors" means the Board of directors of LIFFE (A & M);
"the Delta number" means the number which—

(*a*) is calculated and published from time to time under the authority of the Board of directors in relation to each type of option and the price at which the option may be exercised, and (*b*) reflects the degree of probability of exercise of that option as determined by the Board of directors in the light of the current market price of the shares or stock to which the option relates;

"the Deltaplus limit" has the meaning given by regulation 5(2);

"designated account" means an account designated for a member by the Board of directors in connection with options to buy or sell equity securities;

"equity securities" means securities within the meaning of section 731(9) of the Taxes Act which are issued by a company;

"the first buyer" has the meaning given by section 731(2) of the Taxes Act;

"LIFFE" means The London International Financial Futures and Options Exchange;

"LIFFE (A & M)" means The London International Financial Futures Exchange (Administration and Management);

"the Max limit" has the meaning given by regulation 5(1);

"member" means a member of LIFFE (A & M) who is recognised as such by the Board of directors;

"option" means an option to buy or sell securities which is listed by and traded on LIFFE;

"options market maker" means a member who buys and sells, on his own account, options to buy or sell equity securities and who, at the times specified in regulation 4(3)(*b*) and (4), was recognised by the Board of directors as a market maker in relation to options in respect of equity securities of a particular kind and was acting in the capacity of a market maker in relation to those options;

"options principal trader" means a member who buys and sells, on his own account, options to buy or sell equity securities but who, at the times specified in regulation 4(3)(*b*) and (4), was not recognised by the Board of directors as a market maker in relation to options in respect of equity securities of a particular kind or, if so recognised, was not acting in the capacity of a market maker in relation to those options;

"relevant expiry month" means a calendar month during which an option to buy or sell equity securities of a particular kind will expire, unless previously exercised;

"section 732" means section 732 of the Taxes Act;

"subsection (1)" means subsection (1) of section 732;

"subsection (2A)" means subsection (2A) of section 732;

"the Taxes Act" means the Income and Corporation Taxes Act 1988.

Prescribed persons and date for the purposes of subsection (2A)

3 For the purposes of subsection (2A) this regulation prescribes—

(*a*) The London Clearing House Limited as a recognised clearing house;

(*b*) a member who buys and sells options to buy or sell equity securities as a class or description of member referred to in paragraph (*a*) of that subsection;

(*c*) LIFFE (A & M) as a recognised investment exchange;

(*d*) 22nd March 1992 as the date referred to in paragraph (*b*) of that subsection.

Prescribed circumstances for the purposes of subsection (2A)

4—(1) Paragraphs (2) and (3) of this regulation prescribe for the purposes of subsection (2A) the circumstances in which subsection (1) shall not apply.

(2) If the first buyer is The London Clearing House Limited, the prescribed circumstances are where—

(*a*) the securities referred to in subsection (1) as purchased by the first buyer are equity securities of a particular kind, and

(*b*) those securities were purchased by the London Clearing House Limited as the first buyer acting in its capacity as a person providing clearing services to LIFFE within the meaning of section 38(1) of the Financial Services Act 1986.

(3) If the first buyer is a member, the prescribed circumstances are where—

(*a*) the securities referred to in subsection (1) as purchased by the first buyer are equity securities of a particular kind;

(*b*) those securities were purchased by the member as the first buyer—

(i) as an options market maker at the date of purchase by way of a hedge against the likelihood of his having to deliver such securities on a future exercise of options which he has bought or sold, or

(ii) as an options principal trader at the date of purchase by way of a hedge against the likelihood of his having to deliver such securities on a future exercise of options which he has bought or sold, or

(iii) in order to meet his obligation to deliver securities resulting from the earlier exercise of options by or against him, or

(iv) in order to meet his obligation to receive securities resulting from the earlier exercise of options by or against him;

(*c*) the number of such securities so purchased by the member—

(i) where paragraph (i) of sub-paragraph (*b*) applies, does not result in the total number of securities of that kind held at the date of purchase by the member for the purpose specified in that paragraph exceeding the Max limit applicable on that date in respect of securities of that kind, or

(ii) where paragraph (ii) of sub-paragraph (*b*) applies, does not result in the total number of securities of that kind held at the date of purchase by the member for the purpose specified in that paragraph exceeding the Deltaplus limit applicable on that date in respect of securities of that kind, or the Max limit applicable on that date in respect of securities of that kind to which he would be subject if he were a market maker, whichever is the less, or

(iii) where paragraph (iii) of sub-paragraph (*b*) applies, does not exceed the amount, if any, by which the number of securities which he is so obliged to deliver exceeds the number of securities of that kind calculated by reference to the formula—

$$A + B - C$$

where—

A is the number of securities of that kind which he held at the time of exercise of those options, other than securities which he was obliged to deliver at that time as the result of an earlier agreement to sell securities which at the time of the agreement he did not own and had not agreed to purchase, which he had agreed to sell in order to hedge the likelihood of his having to receive such securities on a future exercise of options which he had bought or sold, and which did not exceed the appropriate limit at the time of the agreement;

B is the number of such securities which he was obliged to receive at that time as a result of the earlier exercise of other options by or against him, and

C is the number of such securities which he held at that time as a hedge against the likelihood of his having to deliver such securities on a future exercise of other options which he had bought or sold;

(*d*) if, following the purchase of such securities by the member in the circumstances referred to in paragraph (i) or (ii) of sub-paragraph (*b*), the number of such securities held by the member, other than securities held in order to meet his obligation to deliver securities as the result of the earlier exercise of options by or against him, exceeds, at any time subsequent to the date of purchase and for a period of six consecutive days, the appropriate limit as calculated from day to day in respect of securities of that kind, the amount of the excess is sold by him prior to the expiry of the day following the end of that period;

(*e*) if, following a purchase of such securities by the member in the circumstances referred to in paragraph (iv) of sub-paragraph (*b*), the number of securities of that kind held by him exceeds, for a period of six consecutive days, the sum of—

(i) the appropriate limit, as calculated from day to day, in respect of securities of that kind which are required as a hedge against the likelihood of his having to deliver such securities on a future exercise of other options which he has bought or sold, and

(ii) the number of securities of that kind required to meet his obligation to deliver securities resulting from the exercise of other options by or against him,

the amount of the excess is sold by him prior to the expiry of the day following the end of that period.

(4) For the purposes of sub-paragraphs (*c*)(iii), (*d*) and (*e*) of paragraph (3), ‘‘the appropriate limit’’ means—

(*a*) as regards a member who is an options market maker in relation to those securities at the time of the agreement referred to in the definition of A in sub-paragraph (*c*)(iii) of paragraph (3) or, as the case may be, during the period specified in sub-paragraph (*d*) or (*e*) of that paragraph, the Max limit, and

(*b*) as regards a member who is an options principal trader in relation to those securities at the time or, as the case may be, during the period referred to in sub-paragraph (*a*) of this paragraph, the Deltaplus limit or the Max limit, whichever is the less.

Meanings of the Max limit and the Deltaplus limit

5—(1) For the purposes of paragraphs (3) and (4) of regulation 4, ‘‘the Max limit’’ means, in relation to options entered into by a member who is an options market maker to buy or sell equity securities of a particular kind, the maximum number of such securities which is found by—

(*a*) making the following calculation in respect of each relevant expiry month and each designated account—

$$D - E$$

where—

D is the number of securities which he is likely to deliver, and

E is the number of securities which he is likely to receive, on the exercise of options expiring within that month, on the assumption that—

(i) the market price of the securities is at a figure which having regard to paragraphs (ii) and (iii) would produce the maximum figure resulting from that calculation,

(ii) such options as give the holder the right to buy such securities at a price above that market price, or to sell such securities at a price below that market price, are not exercised, and

(iii) such options as give the holder the right to buy such securities at a price equal to or below that market price, or to sell such securities at a price equal to or above that market price, are exercised;

(*b*) where the amount calculated by reference to sub-paragraph (*a*) is a negative amount, treating that amount as zero; and

(*c*) aggregating the amounts so calculated in respect of all relevant expiry months and designated accounts.

(2) For the purposes of paragraphs (3) and (4) of regulation 4, "the Deltaplus limit" means, in relation to options entered into by a member who is an options principal trader to buy or sell equity securities of a particular kind, the maximum number of such securities which is found by—

(*a*) subject to sub-paragraph (*c*), making the following calculation in respect of each relevant expiry month and each designated account—

$$F - G$$

where—

F is the number of such securities which he is likely to deliver on the exercise of options expiring within that month, calculated by multiplying the most recently published Delta number by the number of securities in respect of each option which would be transferred if that option were exercised, and

G is the number of securities which, adopting the same method of calculation, he is likely to receive, on the exercise of such options;

(*b*) increasing the amount calculated in sub-paragraph (*a*) by 20 per cent of the sum of the number of such securities which he would be obliged to deliver and the number he would be obliged to receive, if those options were all exercised;

(*c*) where at the time of calculation such options would expire, unless previously exercised, within a period of four weeks, making the calculation specified in paragraph (1)(*a*) of this regulation in respect of those options for the relevant expiry month instead of the calculations referred to in sub-paragraphs (*a*) and (*b*) of this paragraph;

(*d*) where the amount calculated by reference to sub-paragraphs (*a*) and (*b*) or the amount calculated by reference to sub-paragraph (*c*) is a negative amount, treating that amount as zero; and

(*e*) aggregating the amounts so calculated in respect of all relevant expiry months and designated accounts.

1992/569
Income Tax (Dividend Manufacturing) Regulations 1992

Made by the Treasury under TA 1988 s 737(6), (7A), (7B), Sch 23A paras 1(1), 8

Revocation—These Regulations revoked by the Stock Lending and Manufactured Payments (Revocations and Amendments) Regulations, SI 1997/987, reg 3, with effect from 1 July 1997 except in relation to any payment of a manufactured dividend to which these Regulations apply that is made before 1 July 1997.

1992/734
Vocational Training (Public Financial Assistance and Disentitlement to Tax Relief) Regulations 1992

Made by the Treasury under FA 1991 s 32(1), (6), (7)

Made	*12 March 1992*
Laid before the House of Commons	*12 March 1992*
Coming into Force	*6 April 1992*

Commentary—*Simon's Direct Tax Service* **E2.1302, 1303.**
Note—This statutory instrument has lapsed on the repeal of its enabling power by FA 1999 ss 59(2), (3)(*b*), 139, Sch 20 Pt III(15) with effect for payments made after 31 August 2000.

Citation and commencement

1 *These Regulations may be cited as the Vocational Training (Public Financial Assistance and Disentitlement to Tax Relief) Regulations 1992 and shall come into force on 6th April 1992.*

Interpretation

2 *In these Regulations unless the context otherwise requires—*

"the Board" means the Commissioners of Inland Revenue;

"section 32" means section 32 of the Finance Act 1991;

"training payment" means a payment made by an individual in respect of a qualifying course of a vocational training—

(a) in respect of an allowable expense to a person who provides training courses which are qualifying courses of vocational training, or

(b) to a person who—

(i) receives fees for assessment purposes, or

(ii) receives fees payable in connection with the making, as a result of having undertaken the course, of any entry in an official register or any award, or

(iii) receives other fees such as are mentioned in subsection (9) of section 32 in respect of a qualifying course of vocational training provided in the United Kingdom;][1]

["training provider" means a person to whom a training payment is made.][1]

Amendments—Definitions of "training payment" and "training provider" substituted by the Vocational Training (Public Financial Assistance and Disentitlement to Tax Relief) (Amendment) Regulations, SI 1997/635, with effect from 6 April 1997.

Public financial assistance

3—*(1) The descriptions of public financial assistance for the purposes of paragraph (d) of subsection (1) of section 32 are those specified in paragraph (2).*

(2) The descriptions of public financial assistance specified in this paragraph are public financial assistance—

(a) in England and Wales—

(i) under arrangements made under section 2 of the Employment and Training Act 1973 in respect of payments made by the Secretary of State and known by the name of—

(aa) *Youth Training or YT, [or any local name or description of Youth Training,]*[3]

[(bb) *Training for Work,[or any local name or description of Training for Work,]*[3]*]*[1]

(cc) ...[2]

[(dd) *Modern Apprenticeships or Accelerated Modern Apprenticeships,]*[3]

(ee) ...[6] *[...]*[3,6]

[(ff) *Jobmatch,]*[3]

(ii) under regulations made under section 1 of the Education Act 1962 in respect of mandatory awards paid by a local education authority,

(iii) under section 2 of the Education Act 1962 in respect of discretionary awards paid by a local education authority, [and][6]

(iv) ...[6]

(v) under regulations made under section 1 of, and Schedule 2 to, the Education (Student Loans) Act 1990 in respect of loans made to students;

(b) *in Scotland—*

(i) ...[7]

(ii) under arrangements made under section 2(3), (4), (5) and (6) of the Enterprise and New Towns (Scotland) Act 1990 in respect of payments made by Scottish Enterprise or Highlands and Islands Enterprise and known by the name of—

(aa) Youth Training or YT, [or any local name or description of Youth Training,][4]

[(bb) Training for Work, or any local name or description of Training for Work, or][4]

[(cc) Modern Apprenticeships or Accelerated Modern Apprenticeships,][4]

(iii) under regulations made under section 49 of the Education (Scotland) Act 1980 in respect of bursaries administered by Scottish Education Authorities,

(iv) ...[7]

(v) under regulations made under sections 73(f) *and 74(1) of the Education (Scotland) Act 1980 in respect of student allowances for courses of higher education, and*

(vi) under regulations made under section 1 of, and Schedule 2 to, the Education (Student Loans) Act 1990 in respect of loans made to students;

(c) in Northern Ireland—

(i) under arrangements made under sections 1 and 3 of the Employment and Training Act (Northern Ireland) 1950 in respect of which a training allowance is paid,

(ii) under Articles 50 and 51 of the Education and Libraries (Northern Ireland) Order 1986 in respect of mandatory awards paid by Education and Library Boards,

(iii) under Article 50(3) of the Education and Libraries (Northern Ireland) Order 1986 in respect of discretionary awards paid by Education and Library Boards,

(iv) ...[8]

(v) under Article 3 of and Schedule 2 to the Education (Student Loans) (Northern Ireland) Order 1990 in respect of loans made to students; and

[(vi) under the Enterprise Ulster Scheme; and][5]

(d) provided by an overseas government which corresponds to any description of public financial assistance specified in sub-paragraphs (a) *to* (c) *above.*

Amendments—[1] Para (2)(*a*)(i)(*bb*) substituted by the Vocational Training (Public Financial Assistance and Disentitlement to Tax Relief) (Amendment) Regulations, SI 1993/1074 reg 2, with effect from 7 May 1993.

[2] Para (2)(*a*)(i)(*cc*) revoked by the Vocational Training (Public Financial Assistance and Disentitlement to Tax Relief) (Amendment) Regulations, SI 1993/1074 reg 2.
[3] Words in square brackets in para (2)(*a*)(i)(*aa*), (*bb*) and para (2)(*a*)(i)(*ff*) and the word "or" immediately preceding it inserted by the Vocational Training (Public Financial Assistance and Disentitlement to Tax Relief) (Amendment) Regulations, SI 1995/3274 reg 3, with effect from 8 January 1996.
[4] Words in square brackets in para (2)(*b*)(ii)(*aa*) inserted, and para (2)(*b*)(ii)(*bb*) and the word "or" immediately following it, and sub-para (*cc*) substituted by the Vocational Training (Public Financial Assistance and Disentitlement to Tax Relief) (Amendment) Regulations, SI 1995/3274 reg 4, with effect from 8 January 1996.
[5] Para (2)(*c*)(vi) and the word "and" immediately following it inserted by the Vocational Training (Public Financial Assistance and Disentitlement to Tax Relief) (Amendment) Regulations, SI 1995/3274 reg 5, with effect from 8 January 1996.
[6] In para (2), sub-para (*a*)(i)(*ee*), and word "or" immediately following, revoked, word "and" after sub-para (*a*)(iii) inserted, and sub-para (*a*)(iv), and word "and" immediately following, revoked by Vocational Training (Public Financial Assistance and Disentitlement to Tax Relief) (Amendment) Regulations, SI 1996/3049 reg 3, with effect from 1 January 1997.
[7] Para (2)(*b*)(i), (iv) revoked by Vocational Training (Public Financial Assistance and Disentitlement to Tax Relief) (Amendment) Regulations, SI 1996/3049 reg 3, with effect from 1 January 1997.
[8] Para (2)(*c*)(iv), and word "and" immediately following, revoked by Vocational Training (Public Financial Assistance and Disentitlement to Tax Relief) (Amendment) Regulations, SI 1996/3049 reg 3, with effect from 1 January 1997.

Circumstances of disentitlement

4—(1) In the circumstances prescribed by paragraph (2) an individual who has made a training payment shall cease to be and be treated as not having been entitled to relief under subsection (2) of section 32 in respect of the training payment, or of the appropriate part of that training payment.

(2) The circumstances prescribed by this paragraph are where—

(a) the training payment or any part of it is refunded by the training provider, or
(b) any prize, award or other payment is given by the training provider to the individual by virtue merely of the qualifying course of vocational training being undertaken, completed or completed successfully by the individual.

Recovery of tax from training provider

5—(1) This regulation applies where an individual, who by virtue of regulation 4 has ceased to be and is treated as not having been entitled to relief in respect of the training payment or any part of it, has made a training payment to a training provider.

(2) Where this regulation applies, and in the circumstances prescribed by paragraph (3), the training provider [shall, within the period of 90 days following the day on which the individual ceased to be entitled to relief in respect of the training payment, account to the Board for tax relief which has been given on the basis that the individual was so entitled][1].

(3) The circumstances prescribed by this paragraph are where—

(a) the training provider has recovered from the Board an amount equal to any amount deducted and retained by the individual from the training payment in accordance with subsection (4) of section 32, and
(b) that amount has not been repaid to the Board.

Amendments—[1] Words in para (2) substituted by the Vocational Training (Public Financial Assistance and Disentitlement to Tax Relief) (Amendment) Regulations, SI 1996/3049 reg 4, with effect from 1 January 1997.

Adaptation of section 30 of the Taxes Management Act 1970

6—(1) In order to secure the performance of the obligation imposed by regulation 5, section 30 of the Taxes Management Act 1970 shall be adapted so that it applies to the tax for which the training provider is to account to the Board in accordance with that regulation as it applies to tax which has been repaid to a person which ought not to have been repaid to him.

(2) For the purposes of the adaptation required by paragraph (1), any reference in the said section 30 to the repayment of an amount of tax to any person which ought not to have been repaid to him shall be construed as including a reference to tax for which the training provider is to account to the Board in accordance with regulation 5.

1992/746
Vocational Training (Tax Relief) Regulations 1992

Made by the Commissioners of Inland Revenue under FA 1991 ss 32(3), 33(1), (5)

Made	*9 March 1992*
Laid before the House of Commons	*13 March 1992*
Coming into Force	*6 April 1992*

Commentary—*Simon's Direct Tax Service* **E2.1303, 1304.**
Note—This statutory instrument has lapsed on the repeal of its enabling power by FA 1999 ss 59(2), (3)(*b*), 139, Sch 20 Pt III(15) with effect for payments made after 31 August 2000.

Citation and commencement

1 These Regulations may be cited as the Vocational Training (Tax Relief) Regulations 1992 and shall come into force on 6th April 1992.

Interpretation

2 In these Regulations unless the context otherwise requires—

"the Board" means the Commissioners of Inland Revenue;

"section 32" means section 32 of the Finance Act 1991;

"the Taxes Act" means the Income and Corporation Taxes Act 1988;

["training payment" means a payment made by an individual in respect of a qualifying course of vocational training—

(a) in respect of an allowable expense to a person who provides training courses which are qualifying courses of vocational training, or

(b) to a person who—

(i) receives fees for assessment purposes, or

(ii) receives fees payable in connection with the making, as a result of having undertaken the course, of any entry in an official register or any award, or

(iii) receives other fees such as are mentioned in subsection (9) of section 32 in respect of a qualifying course of vocational training provided in the United Kingdom;

"training provider" means a person to whom a training payment is made;][1]

"the Treasury Regulations" means the Vocational Training (Public Financial Assistance and Disentitlement to Tax Relief) Regulations 1992;

"year" means a year beginning with 6th April in any year and ending with 5th April in the following year.

Amendments—[1] Definitions of "training payment" and "training provider" substituted by the Vocational Training (Tax Relief) (Amendment) Regulations, SI 1997/661 reg 3, with effect from 6 April 1997.

Cases and conditions for relief at source

3—*(1) This regulation specifies the cases in which, and the conditions subject to which, relief under subsection (2) of section 32 shall be given at source, that is to say, in accordance with subsections (4) and (5) of that section.*

[(2) Relief shall be given at source in any case where [an individual makes a training payment and][2] *the training provider is resident in the United Kingdom, but subject—*

(a) in a case where the qualifying course of vocational training is such a course by virtue either of paragraph (a) of subsection (10) of section 32, or of both paragraphs (a) and (b) of subsection (10) of section 32, to the conditions specified in paragraph (3); and

(b) in a case where the qualifying course of vocational training is such a course by virtue only of paragraph (b) of subsection (10) of section 32, to the conditions specified in paragraph (4).][1]

(3) The conditions specified in this paragraph are—

(a) that the training provider—

(i) has provided the information specified in paragraph (2) of the notice of entitlement to relief at source specified in regulation 4, and

(ii) has no reason to believe, at the time the training payment is made, that any of the information contained in the notice of entitlement is untrue, and

(b) that the individual making the training payment—

(i) has given a notice of entitlement to relief at source to the training provider, providing the information and certificate specified in paragraphs (3) and (4) of regulation 4, and

(ii) is resident in the United Kingdom at the time of making the training payment or is at that time performing duties which are treated by virtue of section 132(4)(a) of the Taxes Act as performed in the United Kingdom.

[(4) The conditions specified in this paragraph are that the individual making the training payment—

(a) has given a notice of entitlement to relief at source to the training provider providing the information and certificate specified in paragraphs (2) and (3) of regulation 4A, and

(b) is resident in the United Kingdom at the time of making the training payment or is at that time performing duties which are treated by virtue of section 132(4)(a) of the Taxes Act as performed in the United Kingdom.][1]

Amendments—[1] Para (2) substituted and para (4) added by the Vocational Training (Tax Relief) (Amendment) Regulations, SI 1996/1185 reg 3, with effect from 6 May 1996.

[2] Words in para (2) inserted by the Vocational Training (Tax Relief) (Amendment) Regulations, SI 1997/661 reg 4, with effect from 6 April 1997.

Notice of entitlement to relief at source

4—*(1) A notice of entitlement to relief at source shall provide—*

(a) the information specified in paragraph (2) given by the training provider, and

(b) the information specified in paragraph (3) and the certificate in the terms specified in paragraph (4) given by the individual making the training payment.

(2) The information specified in this paragraph is—

(a) the full name of the training provider,
(b) the title and level of the qualifying course of vocational training being undertaken by the individual making the training payment,
(c) the date the training payment was made,
(d) the amount of that training payment, and
(e) the amount deducted and retained out of that training payment by the individual in accordance with subsection (4) of section 32.

(3) The information specified in this paragraph is—

(a) the surname, first name, initials and title of the individual making the training payment,
(b) his address including postcode,
(c) whether he is in paid employment,
(d) whether he is self-employed,
(e) whether he presently pays income tax,
(f) if he has one, his national insurance number,
(g) if he is employed, the name and address of his employer, and
(*h*) if he is self-employed, his business name and address.

(4) The certificate specified in this paragraph is a certificate by the individual who has made the training payment that—

(a) to the best of his knowledge and belief all information provided in the notice is true,
(b) he was resident in the United Kingdom at the time of making the training payment, or was at that time performing duties which were treated by virtue of section 132(4)(a) *of the Taxes Act as performed in the United Kingdom,*
(c) the training payment was made in connection with his own training,
[(ca) at the time the training payment was made, he had attained school-leaving age and, if under the age of nineteen, was not a person who was being provided with full-time education at a school,][1]
[(cb) he has undertaken, or is undertaking, the course neither wholly nor mainly for recreational purposes or as a leisure activity,][1]
(d) at the time the training payment was made, he had not received in relation to the course, and was not entitled to receive in relation to it, any public financial assistance of a description specified in the Treasury Regulations,
(e) he has not received and, to the best of his knowledge and belief, is not entitled to claim, any other relief or deduction in respect of the training payment under any other provision of the Income Tax Acts, and
(f) he has deducted and retained out of the training payment an amount equal to income tax on it at the basic rate for the year in which it was made.

(5) The certificate specified in paragraph (4) shall be signed and dated by the individual making the training payment.

Amendments—[1] Para (4)(*ca*), (*cb*) inserted by the Vocational Training (Tax Relief) (Amendment No 2) Regulations, SI 1993/3118, with effect from 1 January 1994.

[Alternative notice of entitlement to relief at source][1]

[4A—*(1) A notice of entitlement to relief at source shall be given by the individual making the training payment, and shall provide the information specified in paragraph (2) and the certificate specified in paragraph (3).*

(2) The information specified in this paragraph is—

(a) the surname, first name, initials and title of the individual making the training payment,
(b) his address including postcode,
(c) whether he presently pays income tax,
(d) if he has one, his national insurance number,
(e) the name of the training provider,
(f) the title of the qualifying course of vocational training being undertaken by the individual making the training payment,
(g) the date the training payment was made,
(h) the amount of that training payment, and
(i) the amount deducted and retained out of that training payment by the individual in accordance with subsection (4) of section 32.

(3) The certificate specified in this paragraph is a certificate by the individual who has made the training payment that–

(a) to the best of his knowledge and belief all information provided in the notice is true,

(b) he was resident in the United Kingdom at the time of making the training payment, or was at that time performing duties which were treated by virtue of section 132(4)(a) of the Taxes Act as performed in the United Kingdom,

(c) the training payment was made in connection with his own training,

(d) at the time the training payment was made, he had attained the age of thirty,

(e) he has undertaken, or is undertaking, the course neither wholly nor mainly for recreational purposes or as a leisure activity,

(f) at the time the training payment was made, he had not received in relation to the course, and was not entitled to receive in relation to it, any public financial assistance of a description specified in the Treasury Regulations,

(g) he has not received and, to the best of his knowledge and belief, is not entitled to claim, any other relief or deduction in respect of the training payment under any other provision of the Income Tax Acts, and

(h) he has deducted and retained out of the training payment an amount equal to income tax on it at the basic rate for the year in which it was made.

(4) The certificate specified in paragraph (3) shall be signed and dated by the individual making the training payment.][1]

Amendments—[1] This regulation was inserted by the Vocational Training (Tax Relief)(Amendment)Regulations, SI 1996/1185 reg 4, with effect from 6 May 1996.

Refunds of training payments and awards of prizes

5—*(1) This regulation applies where—*

(a) the training payment or any part of it is refunded by the training provider, or

(b) any prize, award or other payment is given to the individual by the training provider by virtue merely of the qualifying course of vocational training being undertaken, completed or completed successfully by the individual.

(2) Where this regulation applies the training provider shall, within 90 days of paying that sum, repay to the Board any amount which he had recovered from the Board on a claim under subsection (5)(b) of section 32 in respect of any sum mentioned in paragraph (1) above.

Claims by training providers—introductory

6—*(1) A claim made by a training provider under subsection (5)(b) of section 32 for the purpose of recovering amounts from the Board shall be made in accordance with this regulation and regulations 8 to 11.*

(2) Subject to paragraph (3) a claim shall be made to the Board in respect of a period of one year and is referred to in these Regulations as an "annual claim".

(3) A claim may also be made to the Board in the manner prescribed by regulations 8, 9 and 10 for a period shorter than a year and is referred to in these Regulations as an "interim claim".

(4) A claim shall be in such form and contain such particulars as the Board may prescribe, shall include a declaration that the records required to be kept by regulation 13 are being kept and shall be signed by the person making it or, where the person is not an individual, by an authorised officer of that person.

(5) Forms prescribed for interim claims may also make provision for the supplementary statement under regulation 9.

(6) Forms prescribed for annual claims may require a report to be given by an approved auditor.

(7) In this regulation "approved auditor" means any person who—

(a) is eligible for appointment as a company auditor under the terms of section 25 of the Companies Act 1989, or

(b) is a member of the Chartered Institute of Public Finance and Accountancy and competent to undertake audit tasks under the rules of that body, or

[(c) is appointed by the Audit Commission or, in Scotland, the Commission for Local Authority Accounts in Scotland or, in Northern Ireland, the Northern Ireland Audit Office, for the purpose of auditing the local authority accounts or, in Northern Ireland, the accounts of an Education and Library Board, relating to the training provider,][1]

and an approved auditor may be a member of the staff of the training provider or an employee of the local authority [or Education and Library Board][2] *mentioned in sub-paragraph (c) above; but a person who is a member of the governing body of the training provider, or who is a proprietor or a director of the training provider, or who is involved in any way with the administration of relief under section 32 may not be an approved auditor.*

Amendments—[1] Para (7)(c) substituted by the Vocational Training (Tax Relief) (Amendment) Regulations, SI 1993/1082 reg 2, with effect from 7 May 1993.

[2] Words in para (7) inserted by SI 1993/1082 reg 2.

Payments by the Board under claims

7—*(1) The Board shall not be under an obligation to make payment to a training provider of any amount claimed—*

(a) earlier than on the 20th day of the month following that in which the claim is received where the claim is received by the 20th day of the month, or

(b) earlier than on the 20th day of the month next following that in which the claim is received, where the claim is received after the 20th day of the month.

(2) The Board shall not be under an obligation to make payment to a training provider of any amount under an interim claim after 5th October in any year unless the annual claim for the preceding year has been received if an interim claim has been made for that preceding year.

(3) No payment in respect of sums recoverable under a claim shall be made to a training provider before 20th May 1992.

Interim claims in advance

8—*(1) An interim claim for a period allowed by paragraph (2) may be made not later than the date specified in paragraph (6) and is referred to in these Regulations as an "interim claim in advance".*

(2) The period for which an interim claim in advance may be made is a period of one month beginning on the 6th day of a month and ending on the 5th day of the following month.

(3) No interim claim in advance may be made for the month ending 5th October or any subsequent month until the [annual claim][1] referred to in regulation 11 has been duly made for the preceding year and received by the Board if an interim claim has been made for that preceding year.

(4) An interim claim in advance shall be based on an estimate of the amount deductible by individuals in respect of training payments to be made in that month, and the estimate shall be certified by an authorised officer of the training provider that to the best of his knowledge and belief the particulars given of the estimate are correct.

(5) The Board shall pay to the training provider—

(a) a sum equal to the estimated amount if they are satisfied with the estimate, or

(b) any lesser amount established to their satisfaction if they are not so satisfied,

on the date specified in paragraph (6) or, where it is not a working day, the next working day.

(6) The date specified in this paragraph is the 20th day of the month.

Amendments—[1] Words in para (3) substituted by the Vocational Training (Tax Relief) (Amendment) Regulations, SI 1997/661 reg 5, with effect from 6 April 1997.

Supplementary statements and claims

9—*(1) When a payment has been made to a training provider under regulation 8(5) on an interim claim in advance, the training provider shall deliver a supplementary statement under this regulation to the Board within 4 months after the end of the period for which the claim was made.*

(2) The supplementary statement shall be a statement correcting (or confirming) the estimate of the amount deductible given in accordance with regulation 8(4), and—

(a) shall be for the same period as the interim claim in advance, and

(b) may not be based on an estimate but shall show the payments actually made during the period covered by the statement.

(3) If the supplementary statement shows that the amount deductible was less than the payment made under regulation 8(5), then the training provider shall repay the amount of the difference to the Board with the statement.

(4) If the supplementary statement shows that the amount deductible was greater than the payment made under regulation 8(5), then the supplementary statement shall constitute an interim claim; and the Board shall pay to the training provider—

(a) the amount of the difference if they are satisfied that the amount claimed was deductible during the period covered by the statement, or

(b) any lesser amount established to their satisfaction if they are not so satisfied.

(5) If in respect of an interim claim on which a payment has been made under regulation 8(5) a training provider fails to deliver a supplementary statement within the time required by this regulation—

(a) the Board shall make no further payment in respect of any interim claim in advance until the supplementary statement has been received; and

(b) the amount of that payment shall immediately be recoverable by the Board in the same manner as tax charged by an assessment on the training provider which has become final and conclusive.

Interim claims in arrear

10—*(1) An interim claim for a period allowed by paragraph (2) may be made and is referred to in these Regulations as an "interim claim in arrear".*

(2) The period for which an interim claim in arrear may be made is one which—

(a) is a period of one month or a number of months beginning on the 6th day of a month and ending on the 5th day of the relevant following month;

(b) falls within the same year; and

(c) does not include any part of a period in respect of which a payment was made under regulation 8(5) (unless the payment in respect of that period or that part was recovered under regulation 9(5)).

(3) No interim claim in arrear may be made for the month ending 5th October or any subsequent month under the [annual claim][1] referred to in regulation 11 has been duly made for the preceding year and received by the Board if an interim claim has been made for that preceding year.

(4) A claim under this regulation may not be based on an estimate but may only be made to recover the amount deducted in respect of the training payments actually made during the period covered by the claim.

(5) If the Board are satisfied that the amount claimed was deductible in the period for which the claim is made they shall pay the amount to the training provider and, if they are not so satisfied, they shall pay any lesser amount which they are satisfied was deductible.

Amendments—[1] Words in para (3) substituted by the Vocational Training (Tax Relief) (Amendment) Regulations, SI 1997/661 reg 5, with effect from 6 April 1997.

Annual claims

11—*(1) An annual claim in respect of a period of one year shall be made—*

(a) within six months after the end of that year if an interim claim has been made, or

(b) within six years after the end of that year if no interim claim has been made.

(2) A claim under this regulation—

(a) may not be based on an estimate but may only be made to recover the amount deducted in respect of the training payments made in the year, and

(b) shall bring into account payments made for the year, and for the purpose of this regulation "aggregate interim payments" means the aggregate of payments made (and not repaid) on interim claims.

(3) If the Board are satisfied that the amount claimed was deductible in the period for which the claim is made they shall pay the amount to the training provider and, if they are not so satisfied, they shall pay any lesser amount which they are satisfied was deductible.

(4) Where the aggregate interim payments shown by an annual claim exceed the amount deducted for the year—

(a) the training provider shall repay the amount of the excess to the Board with the claim, and

(b) if he fails to do so, that amount shall immediately be recoverable by the Board in the same manner as tax charged by an assessment on the training provider which has become final and conclusive.

(5) If a training provider to whom payments are made fails to make an annual claim within the time limited by this regulation, the Board may issue a notice to him showing the aggregate interim payments made to him for the year and stating that the Board are not satisfied that the amount due to him for that year exceeds the lower amount stated in the notice.

(6) If an annual claim for the year is not delivered to the Board within 14 days after the issue of a notice under paragraph (5) the amount of the difference between the aggregate interim payments and the lower amount stated in the notice shall immediately be recoverable by the Board in the same manner as tax charged by an assessment on the training provider which has become final and conclusive.

(7) No payment or repayment made or other thing done on or in relation to an interim claim or a notice under paragraph (5) shall prejudice the decision on an annual claim.

(8) Where an annual claim has been made and the training provider who made it subsequently discovers that an error or mistake has been made in the claim, he may make a supplementary annual claim at any time within six years after the end of the year for which it is made.

[Appeals

11A—*(1) Subject to paragraph (7), a training provider may appeal to the Special Commissioners against the Board's decision on an annual claim by giving notice to the Board within 30 days beginning with the date of the receipt by him of the notice of that decision.*

(2) No appeal shall lie from the Board's decision on an interim claim.

(3) The like provisions as are contained in Part V of the Taxes Management Act 1970 shall apply to the appeal.

(4) On an appeal, the Special Commissioners may vary the decision appealed against whether or not the variation is to the advantage of the appellant.

(5) All such assessments, payments and repayments shall be made as are necessary to give effect to any variation of the Board's decision on appeal.

(6) An assessment made under paragraph (5) shall not be out of time if it is made within six months of the final determination of the appeal.

(7) This regulation shall not apply in relation to claims made before 6th April 1997.][1]

Amendments—[1] This regulation inserted by the Vocational Training (Tax Relief) (Amendment) Regulations, SI 1997/661 reg 6, with effect from 6 April 1997.

Inspection of records kept

12 *The Board may by notice require any person who on or after 6th April 1992 provides (or has at any time on or after 6th April 1992 provided) training courses which are (or were) qualifying courses of vocational training, within 14 days of the notice, to make available for inspection by an officer of the Board authorised for that purpose all documents (including books and other records) in his possession or under his control containing information relating to any qualifying course of vocational training which he has provided or is providing.*

[Keeping of records by training providers

13—*(1) A training provider shall keep sufficient records in respect of qualifying courses of vocational training in respect of which training payments have been made to him to enable the requirements of these Regulations to be satisfied.*

(2) Without prejudice to the generality of paragraph (1), the training provider shall keep every notice of entitlement to relief at source.

(3) A training provider shall keep the records referred to in paragraphs (1) and (2) so as to be available for inspection under these Regulations—

(a) for a period of three years after the end of the year in which the relevant training payment was made, or

(b) for a period of two years after the end of the year in which the annual claim relating to the relevant training payment was made,

whichever period is the later to expire.][1]

Amendments—[1] This regulation substituted by the Vocational Training (Tax Relief) (Amendment) Regulations, SI 1997/661 reg 7, with effect from 6 April 1997.

Provision of information to the Board

14 *The Board may by notice require any training provider to furnish within 14 days of the notice such information about any qualifying course of vocational training [in respect of which a training payment has been made to him]*[1] *as may be reasonably required by them for the purposes of these Regulations.*

Amendments—[1] Words substituted by the Vocational Training (Tax Relief) (Amendment) Regulations, SI 1997/661 reg 8, with effect from 6 April 1997.

1992/1655
Friendly Societies (Modification of the Corporation Tax Acts) Regulations 1992

Made by the Treasury, under TA 1988, s 463

Revocation—These Regulations revoked by the Friendly Societies (Modification of the Corporation Tax Acts) Regulations, SI 1997/473, reg 54(*a*), with effect for accounting periods beginning after 31 December 1994.

1992/2074
Income Tax (Manufactured Interest) Regulations 1992

Made by the Treasury under TA 1988 s 737(6), (7A), (7B), Sch 23A paras 1(1), 8

Revocation—These Regulations revoked by the Stock Lending and Manufactured Payments (Revocations and Amendments) Regulations, SI 1997/987 reg 4, Sch 2, with effect from 1 July 1997 except in relation to any payment of manufactured interest to which these Regulations apply that is made before that date.

1992/2326
Insurance Companies (Pension Business) (Transitional Provisions) Regulations 1992

Made by the Commissioners of Inland Revenue under TA 1988 Sch 19AB paras 4, 5(4)

Made . . . . *29 September 1992*
Laid before the House of Commons *30 September 1992*
Coming into Force . . . . . . *2 October 1992*

Commentary—*Simon's Direct Tax Service* **D4.534.**

Citation and commencement

1 These Regulations may be cited as the Insurance Companies ([Pension][1] Business) (Transitional Provisions) Regulations 1992 and shall come into force on 2nd October 1992.

Amendments—[1] Word substituted by the Insurance Companies (Pension Business) (Transitional Provisions) (Amendment) Regulations, SI 1996/1 reg 3, with effect from 24 January 1996.

Interpretation

2 In these Regulations unless the context otherwise requires—

"accounting period" means any accounting period in relation to which Schedule 19AB has effect;

"the Board" means the Commissioners of Inland Revenue;

"the closing transitional date" shall be construed in accordance with regulation 3(2);

"the corresponding accounting period", in relation to a provisional repayment period, is the accounting period in which that provisional repayment period falls;

"insurance company" means a company to which Part II of the Insurance Companies Act 1982 applies;

"the Management Act" means the Taxes Management Act 1970;

"maximum reduced entitlement" has the meaning given by paragraph 4(6) of Schedule 19AB;

["notional repayment" shall be construed in accordance with paragraph 1A of Schedule 19AB (treated as inserted by regulation 6 of the Insurance Companies (Gilt-edged Securities) (Periodic Accounting for Tax on Interest) Regulations 1995 and, in relation to a notional repayment, "provisional repayment period" shall be construed in accordance with that paragraph of that Schedule;][1]

"the opening transitional date" shall be construed in accordance with regulation 3(1);

"paragraph 4" and "paragraph 5" mean, respectively, paragraph 4 and paragraph 5 of Schedule 19AB;

"provisional repayment" has the meaning given by paragraph 6(1) of Schedule 19AB and[, in relation to a provisional repayment,][1] "provisional repayment period" shall be construed in accordance with paragraph 1 of that Schedule;

"Schedule 19AB" means Schedule 19AB to the Taxes Act;

"the Taxes Act" means the Income and Corporation Taxes Act 1988.

Amendments—[1] Definition "notional repayment" and words in definition of "provisional repayment" inserted by the Insurance Companies (Pension Business) (Transitional Provisions) (Amendment) Regulations, SI 1996/1 reg 4, with effect from 24 January 1996.

Specification of "the opening transitional date" and "the closing transitional date"

3—(1) The date specified by these Regulations as "the opening transitional date" for the purpose of paragraph 4 is 2nd October 1992.

(2) The date specified by these Regulations as "the closing transitional date" for the purpose of paragraph 4 is 1st January 1999.

Reduction of provisional repayment by prescribed percentage

4—(1) This regulation prescribes the percentage by which the amount of any provisional repayment [or any notional repayment][4] to which an insurance company would otherwise be entitled under Schedule 19AB for any [of the accounting periods specified in paragraphs (2) to (5) (being accounting periods ending after the opening transitional date and before the closing transitional date) shall be reduced.][4]

[(2) The prescribed percentage is 7·5 per cent for an accounting period ending after 2nd October 1992 and before 1st January 1994.][1]

[(3) The prescribed percentage is 12·5 per cent for an accounting period ending after 31st December 1993 and before 1st January 1995.][2]

[(4) The prescribed percentage is 10 per cent for an accounting period ending after 31st December 1994 and before 1st January 1996.][3]

[(5) The prescribed percentage is 7·5 per cent for an accounting period ending after 31st December 1995 and before 1st January 1998.][5]

Amendments—[1] Para (2) substituted by the Insurance Companies (Pension Business) (Transitional Provisions) (Amendment) Regulations, SI 1993/3109.

[2] Para (3) substituted by the Insurance Companies (Pension Business) (Transitional Provisions) (Amendment) Regulations, SI 1994/3036 reg 2, with effect from 21 December 1994.

[3] Para (4) substituted (as substituted by SI 1994/3036 reg 2) by the Insurance Companies (Pension Business) (Transitional Provisions) (Amendment) Regulations, SI 1995/3134 reg 2, with effect from 31 December 1995.

[4] Words in para (1) inserted by the Insurance Companies (Pension Business) (Transitional Provisions) (Amendment) Regulations, SI 1996/1 reg 5, with effect from 24 January 1996 and the Insurance Companies (Pension Business) (Transitional Provisions) (Amendment) Regulations, SI 1997/2865 reg 3 with effect from 31 December 1997.

[5] Para (5) substituted by SI 1997/2865 reg 3(*b*), with effect from 31 December 1997.

Requirements to be specified in claim for provisional repayment

5 An insurance company claiming a provisional repayment [or a notional repayment][1] for a provisional repayment period falling within any accounting period [specified in regulation 4][2] shall specify in the claim—

(*a*) the maximum amount to which it could have been entitled by way of provisional repayment [or notional repayment][1] for that provisional repayment period apart from these Regulations;
(*b*) the maximum reduced entitlement for that provisional repayment period; and
(*c*) the amount of the provisional repayment [or the notional repayment][1] claimed for that provisional repayment period.

Amendments—[1] Words inserted by the Insurance Companies (Pension Business) (Transitional Provisions) (Amendment) Regulations, SI 1996/1 reg 6, with effect from 24 January 1996.
[2] Words substituted by the Insurance Companies (Pension Business) (Transitional Provisions) (Amendment) Regulations, SI 1997/2865 reg 4, with effect from 31 December 1997.

Interest where a provisional repayment exceeds the maximum reduced entitlement for a provisional repayment period

6—(1) [Where, in relation to a provisional repayment period falling within an accounting period specified in regulation 4, an insurance company claims, and is paid, by way of provisional repayment an amount in excess of the maximum reduced entitlement for that period][2], interest shall be charged for the period specified in paragraph (2) at the rate specified in paragraph (3).

(2) The period specified in this paragraph is a period beginning on the date on which the amount of the excess is paid to the company and ending on the first occurrence of any of the following—

(*a*) the date on which that amount is repaid to the Board;
(*b*) the date on which the company becomes entitled to that amount when effect is given to a claim such as is mentioned in section 7(6) of the Taxes Act, in section 42(5A) of the Management Act or in sub-paragraph (2) of paragraph 5, made in respect of the corresponding accounting period; [and][1]
(*c*) the date on which the company becomes entitled to that amount when the assessment to corporation tax for the corresponding accounting period becomes final and conclusive.

(3) The rate specified in this paragraph is the rate applicable under section 178 of the Finance Act 1989 for the purposes of section 87A of the Management Act.

(4) Interest charged by virtue of paragraph (1) shall be treated for the purposes of section 30 of the Management Act as if it were an amount of corporation tax which had been repaid and which ought not to have been repaid.

(5) In relation to an amount assessed to corporation tax under section 30 of the Management Act by virtue of these Regulations, section 87A of that Act shall apply with the modifications specified in paragraph (6).

(6) The modifications specified in this paragraph are that—

(*a*) the amount assessed to corporation tax under section 30 of the Management Act by virtue of these Regulations shall be taken to have become due and payable on the date on which that assessment was made; and
(*b*) the words "(in accordance with section 10 of the principal Act)" in subsection (1) shall accordingly be disregarded.

Amendments—[1] "and" substituted for "or" in para (2)(*b*) by the Insurance Companies (Pension Business) (Transitional Provisions) (Amendment) Regulations, SI 1993/3109.
[2] Words in para (1) substituted by the Insurance Companies (Pension Business) (Transitional Provisions) (Amendment) Regulations, SI 1997/2865 reg 5, with effect from 31 December 1997.

Claims during transitional application of pay and file provisions

7 A claim under sub-paragraph (2) of paragraph 5 shall be made at the time of the delivery of the return under section 11 of the Management Act for the accounting period to which the claim relates.

1992/2744

Income Tax (Insurance Companies) (Expenses of Management) Regulations 1992

Made by the Treasury under TA 1988 s 76(7A), (8)

Made	*2 November 1992*
Laid before the House of Commons	*3 November 1992*
Coming into Force	*24 November 1992*

Commentary—*Simon's Direct Tax Service* **D4.504.**

Citation, commencement and effect

1 These Regulations may be cited as the Income Tax (Insurance Companies) (Expenses of Management) Regulations 1992 and shall come into force on 24th November 1992, but shall have effect with respect to sums paid before, as well as after, their coming into force.

Interpretation

2 In these Regulations unless the context otherwise requires—

''LAUTRO'' means the Life Assurance and Unit Trust Regulatory Organisation Limited;

''the Lautro (Compensation Schemes) Rules 1991'' means the rules so entitled which were made by the Board of directors of LAUTRO on 26th November 1991;

''the Lautro Indemnity Scheme'' means the scheme established by rules 8.2 and 8.3 in Part VIII of the Lautro Rules 1988 as amended by the Lautro (Compensation Schemes) Rules 1991;

''the Lautro Rules 1988'' means the rules so entitled which were made by the Board of directors of LAUTRO on 26th April 1988.

Sums treated as expenses of management

3 Any sums paid by a company to which section 76 of the Income and Corporation Taxes Act 1988 applies under a levy imposed under the Lautro Indemnity Scheme established under the rules of LAUTRO shall be treated for the purposes of that section as part of the company's expenses of management.

1992/3066
Corporation Tax Acts (Provisions for Payment of Tax and Returns) (Appointed Days) Order 1992

Made by the Treasury under F(No 2)A 1987 ss 82(1), 83, 85, 86(7), 88(7), 91(4), 95(2), (3), Sch 6 para 7, TA 1988 ss 8(3), 10(1)(*a*), 252(4), 419(1), (3), 584(10), 826(1), (8), (9), FA 1989 s 102(9), TCGA 1992 ss 137(5), 139(8), 180(1)(*b*), 189(6), 190(6)

Made . . . . *7 December 1992*

1 This Order may be cited as the Corporation Tax Acts (Provisions for Payment of Tax and Returns) (Appointed Days) Order 1992.

2—(1) The day appointed for the purposes of the enactments specified in paragraph (2) of this article is 30th September 1993.

(2) The enactments specified in this paragraph are—

(*a*) sections 85, 86, 88 and 91 of, and paragraph 7 of Schedule 6 to, the Finance (No 2) Act 1987;

(*b*) sections 8(3), 10, 252(2) and (3), 419(1) and (3), 584(1), (2) and (5) to (10), and 826, of the Income and Corporation Taxes Act 1988;

(*c*) section 102 of the Finance Act 1989;

(*d*) sections 137(5), 139(8), 179, 189 and 190 of the Taxation of Chargeable Gains Act 1992.

3—(1) The day appointed for the purposes of the enactments specified in paragraph (2) of this article is 31st December 1993.

(2) The enactments specified in this paragraph are sections 82 and 83 of the Finance (No 2) Act 1987.

1992/3234
Income Tax (Prescribed Deposit-takers) Order 1992

Made by the Treasury under TA 1988 s 481(2)(*f*), 482(10)

Made . . . . *17 December 1992*
Laid before the House of Commons . . . . *18 December 1992*
Coming into Force . . . . *1 January 1993*

Commentary—*Simon's Direct Tax Service* **D4.1104.**

1 This Order may be cited as the Income Tax (Prescribed Deposit-takers) Order 1992 and shall come into force on 1st January 1993.

2—(1) For the purposes of paragraph (*f*) of subsection (2) of section 481 of the Income and Corporation Taxes Act 1988 a European deposit-taker is a class of person which is prescribed in relation to all relevant deposits.

[(2) In paragraph (1) above, ''European deposit-taker'' means an EEA firm of the kind mentioned in paragraph 5(*b*) of Schedule 3 to the Financial Services and Markets Act 2000 which has permission under paragraph 15 of that Schedule (as a result of qualifying for authorisation under paragraph 12(1) of that Schedule) to accept deposits.][1]

Amendments—[1] Para (2) substituted by the Financial Services and Markets Act 2000 (Consequential Amendments) (Taxes) Order, SI 2001/3629 art 136 with effect from 1 December 2001, immediately after the coming into force of the Financial Services and Markets Act 2000 ss 411, 432(1), Sch 20 (and SI 2001/3629 Pts 1 and 2).

SI 1993/743: DESTINATION TABLE

This table lists the regulations of the Income Tax (Sub-contractors in the Construction Industry) Regulations 1975, SI 1975 No 1960 and subsequent amending regulations which are consolidated in the Income Tax (Sub-contractors in the Construction Industry) Regulations 1993, SI 1993 No 743.

	Consolidated in SI 1993/743		*Consolidated in SI 1993/743*
IT (Sub-contractors in the Construction Industry) Regulations, SI 1975/1960		IT (Sub-contractors in the Construction Industry) Regulations, SI 1975/1960	
reg 1	reg 1	reg 24	reg 40
reg 2	reg 2	reg 25	reg 39
reg 3	reg 44	reg 26	reg 40
reg 4	reg 43	Schedule	Sch 1
reg 4A	reg 3		
reg 4B	reg 4	IT (Sub-contractors in the Construction Industry) Regulations, SI 1980/1135	
reg 5	reg 5	reg 11	reg 22
reg 5A	reg 5	reg 12	reg 23
reg 6	reg 7		
reg 7	reg 8	IT (Sub-contractors in the Construction Industry) Regulations, SI 1982/1391	
reg 7A	reg 9	reg 23	reg 6
reg 7B	reg 10	reg 24	reg 32
reg 7C	regs 16, 17	Sch 2	Sch 2
reg 7D	reg 18		
reg 8	reg 13	IT (Sub-contractors in the Construction Industry) Regulations, SI 1988/636	
reg 8A	reg 13	reg 7	reg 42
reg 9	reg 19		
reg 10	reg 11		
reg 11	reg 41		
reg 12	reg 14		
reg 12A	reg 15		
reg 13	reg 20		
reg 14	reg 21		
reg 15	reg 24		
reg 16	reg 25		
reg 17	reg 26		
reg 18	reg 27		
reg 19	reg 28		
reg 20	regs 29–31		
reg 21	reg 33		
reg 22	reg 34		
reg 23	regs 35–38		

1993/743

Income Tax (Sub-contractors in the Construction Industry) Regulations 1993

Made by the Commissioners of Inland Revenue under TA 1988 ss 561(5), 562(3)(*b*), (5)(*c*), (11), 563(3)(*c*), (7), 566 and TMA 1970 s 98A(1)

Made	*16 March 1993*
Laid before the House of Commons	*16 March 1993*
Coming into Force	*6 April 1993*

Commentary—*Simon's Direct Tax Service* **Division E5.5.**

ARRANGEMENT OF REGULATIONS

PART I
INTRODUCTORY

PART II
PAYMENTS TO SUB-CONTRACTORS TO WHICH SECTION 559 APPLIES

PART IIA
PAYMENTS EXCEPTED FROM SUBSECTION (1) OF SECTION 559

PART III
SUB-CONTRACTOR'S TAX CERTIFICATES, VOUCHERS AND GUARANTEES

PART IV

PAYMENTS TO SUB-CONTRACTORS USING SUB-CONTRACTOR'S TAX CERTIFICATES

PART V

SUPPLEMENTAL

[PART VI

ELECTRONIC COMMUNICATIONS

The Commissioners of Inland Revenue, in exercise of the powers conferred on them by sections 561(5), 562(3)(*b*), (5)(*c*) and (11), 563(3)(*c*) and (7) and 566 of the Income and Corporation Taxes Act 1988 and by section 98A(1) of the Taxes Management Act 1970 hereby make the following Regulations:

Revenue Internal Guidance—Construction Industry Scheme manual gives a detailed explanation of the provisions of these regulations.

SIs

PART I
INTRODUCTORY

Citation and commencement

1—(1) These Regulations may be cited as the Income Tax (Sub-contractors in the Construction Industry) Regulations 1993.

(2) These Regulations shall come into force on 6th April 1993 immediately after the Income Tax (Sub-contractors in the Construction Industry) (Amendment) Regulations 1993.

Interpretation

2—(1) In these Regulations, unless the context otherwise requires—

[''applicant'', except in regulation 20A, shall be construed in accordance with section 562;][1]

[''approved method of electronic communications'', in relation to the delivery of information or the making of a payment in accordance with a provision of these Regulations, means a method of electronic communications which has been approved, by specific or general directions issued by the Board of Inland Revenue, for the delivery of information of that kind or the making of a payment of that kind under that provision;][6]

''the Board'' means the Commissioners of Inland Revenue;

''business name'' means any name or style under which any business is carried on by a firm or person;

''Class 4 contributions'' means Class 4 contributions within the meaning of the Social Security Contributions and Benefits Act 1992 or, in Northern Ireland, the Social Security Contributions and Benefits (Northern Ireland) Act 1992;

''contract payment'' means any payment such as is mentioned in section 559;

[''education'', includes the training of persons over compulsory school age (in Scotland, school age) for employment in any activities of commerce or industry within the meaning of section 1(1) of the Industrial Training Act 1982, and ''educational institution'' includes the institution by which such training is given;][1]

[''electronic communications'' has the meaning given in section 132(10) of the Finance Act 1999;][6]

''the Management Act'' means the Taxes Management Act 1970;

[''NHS trust'' means a National Health Service trust established under Part I of the National Health Service and Community Care Act 1990 or, as the case may be, under the National Health Service (Scotland) Act 1978;][1]

''national insurance number'' has the same meaning as in the Social Security (Contributions) Regulations 1979 or, in Northern Ireland, the Social Security (Contributions) Regulations (Northern Ireland) 1979;

''nominee'' means any person, other than the sub-contractor, who is nominated to receive a contract payment and to whom such a payment is made;

''notice'' means notice in writing;

''registration number'', in relation to a company, means the distinctive number assigned to a company by the Registrar of Companies on registration under the Companies Act 1985 or, in Northern Ireland, the Companies (Northern Ireland) Order 1986;

...[1]

''sub-contractor's tax certificate'' means a certificate under section 561;

''the Taxes Act'' means the Income and Corporation Taxes Act 1988;

[''user of a registration card'' means the person to whom a registration card which has not expired or been cancelled has been issued, and includes, where a registration card has been issued to a company under regulations 7C(4) and 7D(2), a director or secretary of that company who is authorised to use that registration card;

''user of a sub-contractor's tax certificate'' means a person to whom a sub-contractor's tax certificate which has not expired or been cancelled has been issued, and includes, where a sub-contractor's tax certificate has been issued to a company under regulation 24(5) or (6), a director or secretary of that company who is authorised to use that certificate.][1]

(2) In these Regulations, unless the context otherwise requires, the following expressions have the same meaning as in Chapter IV of Part XIII of the Taxes Act—

...[4]

''construction operations''

''contractor''

[''the qualifying period''

''registration card''

[''relevant liabilities''][5]

''relevant payments''

''a relevant person in relation to the company''][2]

''sub-contractor''.

(3) In these Regulations, unless the context otherwise requires, the following expressions have the same meaning as in the Income Tax (Employments) Regulations 1993—

"collector"
"earnings-related contributions"
"employee"
"income tax month"
"income tax period"
"income tax quarter"
"inspector"
"year".

(4) [The Table below indexes other general definitions in these Regulations:

Term defined	*Regulation*
tax payment voucher	7
the individual turnover threshold	21A(1)
the multiple partnership turnover threshold	21A(2)
the multiple company turnover threshold	21A(3)
the alternative partnership turnover threshold	21A(5)
the alternative company turnover threshold	21A(6)
gross payment voucher	29
construction gross payment voucher	37A.

(5) References, however expressed, in these Regulations to particulars being transmitted electronically by one person ("the transmitter") to another person ("the recipient") are references to any procedure whereby the particulars in question are transmitted by electronic means from the transmitter's computer system to the recipient's computer system and accepted by the recipient's computer system.

(6) In these Regulations, references to a section, without more, are references to that section of the Taxes Act.][3]

Amendments—[1] Definitions in para (1) amended by the Income Tax (Sub-contractors in the Construction Industry) (Amendment) Regulations, SI 1998/2622 reg 3(2), in relation to any application for the issue or renewal of a sub-contractor's tax certificate made with respect to any period beginning after 31 July 1999, and for all other purposes with effect from 1 August 1999.

[2] Words in para (2) inserted by SI 1998/2622 reg 3(3) with effect as in note [1] above.

[3] Para (4) substituted, and paras (5), (6) inserted, by SI 1998/2622 reg 3(4) with effect as in note [1] above.

[4] Reference to "construction contract payments" in para (2) revoked by the Income Tax (Sub-contractors in the Construction Industry) (Amendment No 2) Regulations, SI 1999/2159 reg 3 with effect from 1 August 1999.

[5] In para (2), definition of "relevant liabilities" inserted by the Income Tax (Sub-contractors in the Construction Industry and Employments) (Amendment) Regulations, SI 2003/536 regs 2, 3 with effect from 6 April 2003.

[6] Definitions of "approved method of electronic communications" and "electronic communications" inserted by the Income Tax (Sub-contractors in the Construction Industry) (Amendment) Regulations, SI 2004/1075 regs 2, 3 with effect from 28 April 2004.

PART II
PAYMENTS TO SUB-CONTRACTORS TO WHICH SECTION 559 APPLIES

[Interpretation of Part II

3 In this Part of these Regulations and regulation 40A, "payment to which section 559 applies" means a contract payment, other than—

(*a*) a payment to which section 559 does not apply by virtue of Part IIA of these Regulations; or

(*b*) a payment made to a person excepted from section 559 by virtue of section 561;

and related expressions shall be construed accordingly.][1]

Amendments—[1] This regulation substituted by the Income Tax (Sub-contractors in the Construction Industry) (Amendment) Regulations, SI 1998/2622 reg 4, in relation to any application for the issue or renewal of a sub-contractor's tax certificate made with respect to any period beginning after 31 July 1999, and for all other purposes with effect from 1 August 1999.

[Bodies to which subsection (2) of section 560 applies

3A The bodies which are designated as bodies to which subsection (2) of section 560 applies, being bodies (in addition to those falling within paragraphs (*aa*) to (*e*) of that subsection) which have been established for the purpose of carrying out functions conferred on them by or under any enactment, are those specified in Schedule A1 to these Regulations.][1]

Amendments—[1] This regulation inserted by the Income Tax (Sub-contractors in the Construction Industry) (Amendment) Regulations, SI 1998/2622 reg 4, in relation to any application for the issue or renewal of a sub-contractor's tax certificate made with respect to any period beginning after 31 July 1999, and for all other purposes with effect from 1 August 1999.

Multiple contractors

4—(1) Where a contractor so elects, he shall be treated for all the purposes of this Part of these Regulations as if in respect of each group of sub-contractors specified in the election he were a different contractor, that is to say, as if each group of sub-contractors constituted all the sub-contractors to whom he makes payments to which section 559 applies.

(2) An election under this regulation must be made by notice to the inspector and any such notice shall contain—

(*a*) such information as may be necessary to identify the groups of sub-contractors concerned, and

(*b*) a certificate that the contractor makes no payment to which section 559 applies other than to sub-contractors in the groups so identified.

(3) Subject to paragraph (4), an election shall have effect for the year following that in which it is made and, unless revoked, shall also have effect for any subsequent year.

(4) Where a contractor acquires the whole or a part of the undertaking of another contractor and within 90 days of the acquisition elects under this regulation to be treated as a separate contractor in respect of the group of sub-contractors with whom he contracts for the purposes of the acquired undertaking and in respect of all other sub-contractors to whom he makes payments or, where an election is already in force in respect of them, each group of sub-contractors identified in the existing election, the new election shall have effect for the year in which the acquisition takes place and any subsequent year.

(5) An election in force for any year may be revoked by notice to the inspector and any such revocation shall have effect for the year following that in which notice of it is given and any subsequent year, but shall not prejudice the making of a fresh election for that following or any subsequent year.

Record of individual payment made and of amount deducted

5 ...

Amendments—This regulation revoked by the Income Tax (Sub-contractors in the Construction Industry) (Amendment) Regulations, SI 1998/2622 reg 5, in relation to any application for the issue or renewal of a sub-contractor's tax certificate made with respect to any period beginning after 31 July 1999, and for all other purposes with effect from 1 August 1999.

First payment in year to user of form 714S

6 ...

Amendments—This regulation revoked by the Income Tax (Sub-contractors in the Construction Industry) (Amendment) Regulations, SI 1998/2622 reg 6, in relation to any application for the issue or renewal of a sub-contractor's tax certificate made with respect to any period beginning after 31 July 1999, and for all other purposes with effect from 1 August 1999.

Deduction certificate to be given to sub-contractor

7—(1) Subject to [the following paragraphs of this regulation, in respect][1] of any payment to which section 559 applies, the contractor shall give to the sub-contractor a [tax payment voucher][1], on a form provided by the Board, giving the particulars specified in paragraph (2) and certifying those particulars.

(2) The particulars specified in this paragraph are—

(*a*) the name ...[2] of the sub-contractor to whom, or to whose nominee, the payment is made,
[(*b*) the distinctive reference number taken from that sub-contractor's registration card][2],
[(*c*) the end of the income tax month in which the payment is made][2],
(*d*) the amount of the payment before any deduction is made under section 559,
(*e*) the amount, if any, included in the payment which the contractor has reason to be satisfied represents the direct cost to any person of materials used in carrying out the construction operations to which the contract under which the payment is made relates,
(*f*) the amount from which section 559 requires a sum to be deducted, ...[2]
(*g*) the amount so deducted[, and
(*h*) unless that sub-contractor's registration card is a temporary card, the sub-contractor's national insurance number.][2]

[(3) The contractor shall give a tax payment voucher to the sub-contractor in respect of all such payments made within a period of one income tax month, and the tax payment voucher shall be signed by the contractor and be given to the sub-contractor within 14 days of the end of that income tax month.

(4) Within 14 days of the end of every income tax month the contractor shall either—

(*a*) send the top copy of all tax payment vouchers completed by him in accordance with this regulation to a person nominated by the Board at an address specified by them, or
(*b*) transmit electronically the particulars specified in paragraph (2) to the person so nominated.

(5) Where the contractor transmits the particulars electronically as mentioned in paragraph (4)(*b*), the tax payment voucher shall be a single copy, in the form designated CIS25(E) in Schedule 1 to these regulations, which he shall give to the sub-contractor, but otherwise, the tax payment voucher shall be in triplicate, in the form designated CIS25(I) or CIS25(M) in Schedule 1 to these regulations, and the copy to be given to the sub-contractor shall be the copy marked ''Subcontractor copy''.][3]

Commentary—*Simon's Direct Tax Service* **E5.528.**

Amendments—[1] Words in para (1) amended by the Income Tax (Sub-contractors in the Construction Industry) (Amendment) Regulations, SI 1998/2622 reg 7(2), in relation to any application for the issue or renewal of a sub-contractor's tax certificate made with respect to any period beginning after 31 July 1999, and for all other purposes with effect from 1 August 1999.
[2] Words in para (2) amended by SI 1998/2622 reg 7(3) with effect as in note [1] above.
[3] Paras (3)—(5) substituted by SI 1998/2622 reg 7(4) with effect as in note [1] above.

[Registration cards—powers of inspectors and persons nominated by the Board

7A—(1) The power to issue[, renew][2] or replace a registration card may be exercised either by an inspector or by any person nominated by the Board.

(2) The power to require the surrender of, or cancel, a registration card may be exercised by an inspector.][1]

Amendments—[1] This regulation inserted by the Income Tax (Sub-contractors in the Construction Industry) (Amendment) Regulations, SI 1998/2622 reg 8 with effect from 23 November 1998.
[2] Word in para (1) inserted by the Income Tax (Sub-contractors in the Construction Industry) (Amendment) Regulations, SI 2002/2225 reg 3 with effect from 20 September 2002.

[Registration cards—appeals

7B—(1) Any person aggrieved by the refusal to issue[, renew][2] or replace a registration card under regulation 7A(1) or the cancellation of a registration card under regulation 7A(2) may, by notice given to the Board within 30 days after the refusal or, as the case may be, the cancellation, appeal to the General Commissioners or, if he so elects in the notice, to the Special Commissioners, to determine the matter.

(2) The like provisions as are contained in Part V of the Management Act shall apply, with the appropriate modifications, to an appeal under paragraph (1) as they apply to an appeal against an assessment.][1]

Commentary—*Simon's Direct Tax Service* **E5.520.**
Amendments—[1] This regulation inserted by the Income Tax (Sub-contractors in the Construction Industry) (Amendment) Regulations, SI 1998/2622 reg 8 with effect from 23 November 1998.
[2] Word in para (1) inserted by the Income Tax (Sub-contractors in the Construction Industry) (Amendment) Regulations, SI 2002/2225 reg 4 with effect from 20 September 2002.

[Form of registration card

7C—(1) A registration card shall be prepared by an authorised officer of the Board or any person nominated by the Board—

(*a*) in the case of a temporary registration card, in the form designated CIS4(T), and
(*b*) in any other case, in the form designated CIS4(P),

in Schedule 1 to these regulations.

(2) Where a registration card, other than a temporary registration card, is issued to an individual otherwise than as a partner in a firm, the card shall show—

(*a*) the individual's name,
(*b*) his national insurance number,
(*c*) a facsimile of his usual signature,
(*d*) a full face photograph, being a true likeness of him,
(*e*) the distinctive reference number assigned to the card, and
(*f*) where the individual so wishes, the (or, where there is more than one, a) business name under which his business is carried on.

(3) Where a registration card, other than a temporary registration card, is issued to an individual as a partner in a firm, the card shall show—

(*a*) the individual's name,
(*b*) his national insurance number,
(*c*) a facsimile of his usual signature,
(*d*) a full face photograph, being a true likeness of him,
(*e*) the distinctive reference number assigned to the card,
(*f*) the words 'Acting for',
(*g*) the name of the firm, and
(*h*) subject to paragraph (5), and where the individual so wishes, the (or, where there is more than one, a) business name under which the firm's business is carried on.

(4) Where a registration card, other than a temporary registration card, is issued to a company, the card shall show—

(*a*) the name of the director or secretary of the company who is authorised to use the card,
(*b*) his national insurance number,
(*c*) a facsimile of his usual signature,
(*d*) a full face photograph, being a true likeness of him,
(*e*) the distinctive reference number assigned to the card,
(*f*) the words 'Acting for',
(*g*) the name of the company, and

(*h*) subject to paragraph (5), and where the director or secretary of the company so wishes, the (or, where there is more than one, a) business name under which the company's business is carried on

(5) Where, in a case to which paragraph (3) or (4) applies, the registration card shows a business name under which the firm's or company's business is carried on, that business name shall be the same as that which appears on all other cards that are uncancelled, which have been issued to the partners in the firm or to the company.

(6) A temporary registration card may be issued, showing the same information as is required by paragraph (2), (3) or (4), as the case may be, but with the substitution for sub-paragraph (*b*) in each case of—

"(*b*) the date of its expiry which shall be not more than [twelve or (if the issuer considers it appropriate) thirty six][2] months from the date of its issue,".][1]

Commentary—*Simon's Direct Tax Service* **E5.520.**

Amendments—[1] This regulation inserted by the Income Tax (Sub-contractors in the Construction Industry) (Amendment) Regulations, SI 1998/2622 reg 8 with effect from 23 November 1998.

[2] Word substituted by the Income Tax (Sub-contractors in the Construction Industry) (Amendment) Regulations, SI 2002/2225 reg 5 with effect from 20 September 2002.

[Issue of registration card

7D—(1) A registration card containing the information specified in regulation 7C(2) or (3), as the case may be, shall be issued by an inspector or any person nominated by the Board, to the individual whose name, national insurance number and photograph appear on it.

(2) A registration card containing the information specified in regulation 7C(4) shall be issued by an inspector or any person nominated by the Board, to the company whose name appears on it.][1]

Amendments—[1] This regulation inserted by the Income Tax (Sub-contractors in the Construction Industry) (Amendment) Regulations, SI 1998/2622 reg 8 with effect from 23 November 1998.

[Production for inspection and surrender of a registration card

7E—(1) A user of a registration card, or any person having a registration card in his possession, shall, whenever required to do so by an authorised officer of the Board, produce the registration card to that officer for inspection.

(2) A user of a registration card, or any person having a registration card in his possession, shall, whenever required to do so by an authorised officer of the Board (whether or not by way of notice served on him by that officer), surrender the registration card to the Board or to that officer.

(3) Paragraphs (1) and (2) shall apply whether or not the registration card in question has been cancelled, at the time the requirement is made by the authorised officer of the Board.][1]

Commentary—*Simon's Direct Tax Service* **E5.520.**

Amendments—[1] This regulation inserted by the Income Tax (Sub-contractors in the Construction Industry) (Amendment) Regulations, SI 1998/2622 reg 8 with effect from 23 November 1998.

[Production and verification of a sub-contractor's registration card

7F—(1) Before making any payment to which section 559 applies to a sub-contractor, and unless the circumstances specified in paragraph (3) apply, a contractor shall—

(*a*) ensure that the sub-contractor's registration card is produced to him, and

(*b*) satisfy himself by inspection of the registration card that the person producing it is the user of that registration card.

(2) For the purposes of paragraph (1), the user of the registration card shall, whenever required to do so, produce the registration card for inspection by the contractor or the contractor's authorised representative.

(3) The circumstances specified in this paragraph are that the contractor—

(*a*) has previously caused the sub-contractor's registration card to be produced to him, and

(*b*) thereby satisfied himself as mentioned in paragraph 1(*b*), and

(*c*) has no reason to doubt that the person who produced it remains the user of that registration card.][1]

Amendments—[1] This regulation inserted by the Income Tax (Sub-contractors in the Construction Industry) (Amendment) Regulations, SI 1998/2622 reg 8 with effect from 23 November 1998.

Monthly payment of amounts deducted to collector

8 Subject to regulations 9 and 13(11), the contractor shall pay to the collector within[—

(*a*)][1] 14 days of the end of every income tax month[, or

(*b*) if payment is made by an approved method of electronic communications in respect of amounts deducted from contract payments made by the contractor after 5th April 2004, 17 days of the end of every income tax month.][1]

all amounts which he was liable under section 559 to deduct from payments made by him during that income tax month.

Commentary—*Simon's Direct Tax Service* **E5.532.**
Simon's Tax Cases—reg 8(3), *Slater v Richardson Bottoms Ltd* [1979] STC 630*; *R v Collector of Taxes, ex p Robert Goodall (Builders) Ltd* [1989] STC 206*.
Cross reference—See reg 10(5) (payment by cheque treated as made when cheque received by the collector provided it is paid on first presentation).
Amendments—[1] Para (*a*) numbered as such, and para (*b*) inserted, by the Income Tax (Sub-contractors in the Construction Industry) (Amendment) Regulations, SI 2004/1075 regs 2, 4 with effect from 28 April 2004.

Quarterly payment of amounts deducted to collector

9—(1) Subject to regulation 13(11), where the contractor has reasonable grounds for believing that the condition specified in paragraph (2) applies and so chooses, he shall pay to the collector within[—

(*a*)][2] 14 days of the end of every income tax quarter[, or

(*b*) if payment is made by an approved method of electronic communications in respect of amounts deducted from contract payments made by the contractor after 5th April 2004, 17 days of the end of every income tax quarter,][2]

all amounts which he was liable under section 559 to deduct from payments made by him during that income tax quarter.

[(2) The condition is that, for income tax months falling within the current year, the average monthly amount found by the formula below will be less than £1500.

The formula is—

$$(S + P + N + L) - (C + SP + CD)$$

The expressions used in the formula have the following values.

S is the amount which would be payable by the contractor to the collector under regulation 8.

P is the amount which would be payable by the contractor to the collector under regulation 40 of the Income Tax (Employments) Regulations 1993 if any adjustment to that amount under regulation 7(2) of the Working Tax Credit (Payments by Employers) Regulations 2002 (funding of payment of working tax credit) were disregarded.

N is the amount which would be payable by the contractor to the collector under the Social Security Contributions and Benefits Act 1992 or, in Northern Ireland, the Social Security Contributions and Benefits (Northern Ireland) Act 1992 and (in either case) under the Social Security (Contributions) Regulations 2001 but disregarding—

(*a*) any amount of secondary Class 1 contributions in respect of which liability has been transferred to the employed earner by an election made jointly by the employed earner and the secondary contributor for the purpose of paragraph 3B(1) of Schedule 1 to either of those Acts (transfer of liability to be borne by the earner); and

(*b*) any adjustment to the amount so payable to the collector under regulation 7(2) of the Working Tax Credit (Payments by Employers) Regulations 2002.

L is the amount which would be payable by the contractor to the collector under regulation 39(1) of the Education (Student Loans) (Repayment) Regulations 2000 or of the Education (Student Loans) (Repayment) Regulations (Northern Ireland) 2000 (payment of repayments deducted to the Inland Revenue) if the reduction referred to in paragraph (3) of the respective regulation and in regulation 7(2) of the Working Tax Credit (Payment by Employers) Regulations 2002 were disregarded.

C is the amount which would be payable by the contractor to his employees by way of tax credit under the Working Tax Credit (Payment by Employers) Regulations 2002.

SP is the amount which would be recoverable from the Board by the contractor in respect of payments to his employees by way of statutory sick pay, statutory maternity pay, statutory paternity pay and statutory adoption pay. Here statutory sick say, statutory maternity pay, statutory paternity pay and statutory adoption have the same meanings as they do in the Social Security Contributions and Benefits Act 1992 or the Social Security Contributions and Benefits (Northern Ireland) Act 1992, as the case requires.

CD is—

(*a*) in the case of a company, the amount which others would deduct from payments to it (in its capacity as a sub-contractor) under section 559 of the Taxes Act; and

(*b*) in any other case, nil.][1]

Commentary—*Simon's Direct Tax Service* **E5.532.**
Cross reference—See reg 10(5) (payment by cheque treated as made when cheque received by the collector provided it is paid on first presentation).
Amendments—[1] Para (2) substituted by the Income Tax (Sub-contractors in the Construction Industry and Employments) (Amendment) Regulations, SI 2003/536 regs 2, 4 with effect from 6 April 2003.
[2] In para (1), sub-para (*a*) numbered as such, and sub-para (*b*) inserted, by the Income Tax (Sub-contractors in the Construction Industry) (Amendment) Regulations, SI 2004/1075 regs 2, 5 with effect from 28 April 2004.

Payment of amounts deducted to collector—further provisions

10—(1) The collector shall give a receipt to the contractor for the total amount paid under regulation 8 or 9, if so requested, but if a receipt is given for a total sum paid at the same time which includes that amount and also tax deducted under the Income Tax (Employments) Regulations 1993, or earnings related contributions, or both, then no separate receipt for the total amount so paid need be given.

(2) If the amount specified in regulation 8 or 9(1) which a contractor is liable to pay to the collector exceeds the amount, if any, actually deducted by him from payments made during the relevant income tax period but he satisfies the collector that he took reasonable care to comply with the provisions of section 559 and of these Regulations and that either—

(*a*) the under-deduction or failure to make a deduction was due to an error made in good faith, or

(*b*) in spite of such reasonable care as aforesaid, he had been led to the genuine belief that a payment made by him, which was one to which section 559 applies, was not or was not wholly such a payment,

then the collector may direct that the contractor shall not be liable to pay that excess to the collector.

(3) If the amount specified in regulation 8 or 9(1) which a contractor is liable to pay to the collector exceeds the amount, if any, actually deducted by him from payments made during the relevant income tax period but the inspector (whether or not an assessment under regulation 14 has been made) is satisfied that the person to whom the contractor made such payments either—

(*a*) was not chargeable to income tax or corporation tax in respect of those payments, or

(*b*) has made a return of his income or profits in accordance with section 8 or section 11 of the Management Act, in which those payments were taken into account, and paid the income tax and Class 4 contributions due or corporation tax due in respect of such income or profits,

then the inspector shall, if the contractor so requests, direct that the contractor shall not be liable to pay that excess (or any interest in respect of it) to the collector.

(4) If a contractor is aggrieved by the failure of a collector to make a direction under paragraph (2), he may, by notice to the collector, within 30 days after the date of a notice given after 19th April of a refusal by the collector to make such a direction, appeal to the General Commissioners against that refusal.

[(4A) If a contractor has deducted an amount under section 559, but has not paid it to the collector as required by regulation 8 or 9(1), that amount shall be treated, for the purpose of determining the liability of any sub-contractor in respect of whose liability the sum was deducted, as having been paid to the collector at the time required by regulation 8 or 9(1).][2]

[(5) For the purposes of regulations 8 and 9 and of this regulation, where—

(*a*) any payment to the collector is made by cheque, and

(*b*) the cheque is paid on its first presentation to the banker on whom it is drawn,

the payment shall be treated as made on the day on which the cheque was received by the collector.][1]

Commentary—*Simon's Direct Tax Service* **E5.532.**

Amendments—[1] Para (5) inserted by the IT (Sub-contractors in the Construction Industry) (Amendment) Regulations, SI 1996/981 reg 3 with effect as respects cheques received after 18 April 1996.

[2] Para (4A) inserted by the IT (Sub-contractors in the Construction Industry and Employments) (Amendment) Regulations, SI 2003/536 regs 2, 5 with effect from 6 April 2003.

Return by contractor at end of year

11. ..

Amendments—This regulation revoked by the Income Tax (Sub-contractors in the Construction Industry) (Amendment) Regulations, SI 1998/2622 reg 9 with effect in relation to any period after 31 July 1999.

Notice and certificate in case of contractor failing to pay amounts deducted to collector

12—(1) This regulation applies where, within [17][1] days of the end of any income tax period, the contractor has paid no amount to the collector under regulation 8 or 9 for that income tax period, and the collector is unaware of the amount, if any, which the contractor is liable so to pay.

(2) Where this regulation applies, the collector may give notice to the contractor requiring him to render, within 14 days, a return in such form as the Board may prescribe showing the amount which the contractor is liable to pay to the collector under regulation 8 or 9 in respect of the income tax period in question.

(3) Where a notice given by the collector under paragraph (2) extends to two or more consecutive income tax periods, these Regulations shall have effect as if those consecutive income tax periods were one income tax period.

(4) The collector may give a notice under paragraph (2) notwithstanding that an amount has been paid to him by the contractor under regulation 8 or 9 for an income tax period, if he is not satisfied that the amount so paid is the full amount which the contractor is liable to pay to him for that period, and this regulation shall have effect accordingly.

(5) Upon receipt of a return made by a contractor under paragraph (2), the collector may prepare a certificate showing the amount which the contractor is liable to pay to him for the income tax period in question.

(6) Paragraphs (1) to (5) of regulation 19 shall apply to the amount shown in a certificate under paragraph (5).

(7) The production of the return made by the contractor under paragraph (2) and of the certificate of the collector under paragraph (5) shall be sufficient evidence that the amount shown in the certificate is the amount which the contractor is liable to pay to the collector in respect of the income tax period in question.

(8) Any document purporting to be a certificate under paragraph (5) shall be deemed to be such a certificate until the contrary is proved.

Commentary—*Simon's Direct Tax Service* **E5.532.**

Amendments—[1] In para (1), "17" substituted for "14" by the Income Tax (Sub-contractors in the Construction Industry) (Amendment) Regulations, SI 2004/1075 regs 2, 6 with effect from 28 April 2004.

Notice of specified amount and certificate in case of contractor failing to pay amounts deducted to collector

13—(1) This regulation applies where, after [17][4] days following the end of any income tax period, the contractor has paid no amount to the collector under regulation 8 or 9 for that income tax period ...[1] and there is reason to believe that the contractor is liable so to pay.

(2) Where this regulation applies, the collector, upon consideration of the contractor's record of past payments may to the best of his judgment specify the amount which he considers the contractor is liable to pay, and serve notice on the contractor of that amount.

(3) Where the contractor has paid no amount under regulation 8 or 9 for the relevant income tax periods, the collector may give notice under paragraph (2) which extends to two or more consecutive income tax periods, and these Regulations shall have effect as if those income tax periods were the latest income tax period specified in the notice.

(4) The collector may give a notice under paragraph (2) notwithstanding that an amount has been paid to him by the contractor under regulation 8 or 9 for any income tax period, if he is not satisfied, after seeking the contractor's explanation, that the amount so paid is the full amount which the contractor is liable to pay to him for that income tax period, and this regulation shall have effect accordingly.

(5) If, during the period allowed in a notice given by the collector under paragraph (2), the contractor claims, but does not satisfy the collector, that the payment made in respect of the income tax period specified in the notice is the full amount he is liable to pay to the collector for that income tax period, then—

(*a*) the contractor may require the collector to inspect the contractor's documents and records as if the collector had called upon the contractor to produce those documents in accordance with regulation 41(1); and

(*b*) regulation 41 shall apply to that inspection, and the notice given by the collector under paragraph (2) shall be disregarded.

(6) Subject to paragraph (7), if the specified amount, or any part of it, is unpaid on the expiration of the period of seven days allowed in the notice, [the amount so unpaid—

(*a*) shall be deemed to be an amount which the contractor was liable to pay for that income tax period in accordance with regulation 8 or 9, and

(*b*) may be certified by the collector.][1]

(7) Paragraph (6) shall not apply if, during the period allowed in the notice—

(*a*) the contractor pays the full amount which he is liable to pay to the collector under regulation 8 or 9 for that income tax period, or

(*b*) the contractor satisfies the collector that no amount, or no further amount is due for that income tax period.

[(7A) For the purposes of this regulation, where—

(*a*) any payment to the collector is made by cheque, and

(*b*) the cheque is paid on its first presentation to the banker on whom it is drawn,

the payment shall be treated as made on the day on which the cheque was received by the collector.][2]

(8) ...[1]

(9) The production of a certificate under paragraph (6) shall be sufficient evidence that the contractor is liable to pay the amount shown in the certificate to the collector.

(10) Any document purporting to be a certificate under paragraph (6) shall be deemed to be such a certificate until the contrary is proved.

(11) Notwithstanding anything in this regulation, if the contractor pays any amount certified by the collector under this regulation and that amount exceeds the amount which he would have been liable to pay in respect of that income tax period apart from this regulation, he shall be entitled to set off

such excess against any amount which he is liable to pay to the collector under regulation 8 or 9 for any subsequent income tax period.

(12) If the contractor renders the return required by regulation [40A][3] after the end of the year, and pays the total amount which he is liable to pay, any excess paid and not otherwise recovered by set-off in accordance with this regulation shall be repaid.

Amendments—[1] Words in para (1) revoked, words in para (6) substituted, and para (8) revoked, by the Income Tax (Sub-contractors in the Construction Industry) (Amendment No 2) Regulations, SI 1995/448 reg 2, with effect from 6 April 1995.
[2] Para (7A) inserted by the IT (Sub-contractors in the Construction Industry) (Amendment) Regulations, SI 1996/981 reg 4(1)(*a*), (2), with effect as respects cheques received after 18 April 1996.
[3] Number in para (12) substituted by SI 1998/2622 reg 10, in relation to any application for the issue or renewal of a sub-contractor's tax certificate made with respect to any period beginning after 31 July 1999, and for all other purposes with effect from 1 August 1999.
[4] In para (1), "17" substituted for "14" by the Income Tax (Sub-contractors in the Construction Industry) (Amendment) Regulations, SI 2004/1075 regs 2, 6 with effect from 28 April 2004.

Formal determination of amounts payable by contractor

14—(1) Where—

(*a*) there is a dispute between a contractor and a sub-contractor as to the amount, if any, deductible by the contractor under section 559 from a payment to the sub-contractor or his nominee, or
(*b*) the inspector has reason to believe, as a result of an inspection under regulation 41 or otherwise, that the amount which a contractor is liable to pay to the collector under these Regulations is greater than the amount, if any, which he has so paid, or
(*c*) the inspector considers it necessary to do so in all the circumstances,

the inspector may make an assessment on the contractor in the amount which, according to the best of his judgment, the contractor is liable to pay under these Regulations.

(2) An assessment under paragraph (1) shall be subject to the like provisions as are contained in Parts IV, V and VI of the Management Act as if it were an assessment to income tax and as if the amount assessed were income tax charged on the contractor and the like provisions as are contained in those Parts of the Management Act shall apply accordingly with any necessary modifications, except that the amount charged by the assessment shall be due and payable 14 days after the assessment is made.

(3) Where there is a dispute such as is mentioned in sub-paragraph (*a*) of paragraph (1) and the inspector does not make an assessment on the contractor under that paragraph, either the contractor or the sub-contractor may, on giving notice to the inspector, apply to the General Commissioners to determine the matter.

(4) The like provisions as are contained in Part V of the Management Act shall apply, with the appropriate modifications, to an application under paragraph (3) as they apply to an appeal against an assessment.

(5) Where there is a dispute such as is mentioned in sub-paragraph (*a*) of paragraph (1)—

(*a*) the contractor shall nevertheless make the deduction required by section 559 from the payment, or the part of the payment, to which the dispute relates, and the amount he so deducts shall be treated as a sum which he is liable to pay to the collector under these Regulations; and
(*b*) any amount which, on a final determination of the dispute, is shown not to have been so payable shall[, except where regulation 44B applies, be treated as an overpayment of income tax][1] by the sub-contractor.

Simon's Tax Cases—*Slater v Richardson Bottoms Ltd* [1979] STC 630*; *Burford v Durkin* [1991] STC 7*.
Amendments—[1] Words in para (5)(*b*) substituted by the IT (Sub-contractors in the Construction Industry and Employments) (Amendments) Regulations, SI 2003/536 regs 2, 6 with effect from 6 April 2003.

Interest on amounts overdue which have been formally determined

15—(1) Where an amount is charged by an assessment made in the circumstances specified in paragraph (2), and becomes due and payable, the amount so due and payable shall carry interest at the prescribed rate from the reckonable date until payment.

(2) The circumstances specified in this paragraph are that the assessment is made—

(*a*) by the inspector under regulation 14,
(*b*) at any time after 19th April 1988, and
(*c*) for a year not later than the year ended on 5th April 1992.

(3) Subject to paragraph (4), in this regulation "reckonable date" means the 14th day after the end of the year to which the assessment relates, and for the purposes of this regulation, where the assessment is made in respect of one or more income tax periods, that assessment shall relate to the year of which that period forms part.

(4) Where, at any time after 19th April 1988, an assessment such as is mentioned in paragraph (1) is made in the circumstances specified in paragraph (2), and that assessment relates to a year earlier than the year ended on 5th April 1988, then the amount due and payable under the assessment shall carry interest at the prescribed rate from the 19th April 1988 until payment and in those circumstances that date shall be the reckonable date.

(5) Interest payable under this regulation shall be recoverable as if it were an amount charged by an assessment made under regulation 14.

Cross reference—See reg 17(3) (payment by cheque treated as made when cheque received by the collector provided it is paid on first presentation).

Interest on amounts overdue—general

16—(1) Subject to paragraph (2), where in relation to the year ended on 5th April 1993 or any subsequent year, a contractor has not within[—

(*a*)][1] 14 days after the end of a year[, or

(*b*) if payment is made by an approved method of electronic communications in respect of amounts deducted from contract payments made by the contractor after 5th April 2004, 17 days after the end of a year,][1]

paid to the collector the total amount which he is liable under these Regulations to pay, the amount remaining unpaid shall carry interest at the prescribed rate from the reckonable date until payment.

(2) Paragraph (1) shall not apply to any amount in respect of which a direction under regulation 10(2) or (3) has been made.

(3) In this regulation "the reckonable date" in relation to any year, means the 14th day after the end of that year [or the 17th day after the end of that year if payment is made by an approved method of electronic communications in respect of amounts deducted from contract payments made by the contractor after 5th April 2004][1].

(4) Interest payable under this regulation shall be recoverable as if it were an amount which a contractor is liable under regulation 8 or 9 to pay to the collector.

(5) A certificate of the collector that any amount of interest payable under this regulation has not been paid to him, or, to the best of his knowledge and belief, to any other collector or to any person acting on his behalf or on behalf of another collector, shall be sufficient evidence that the sum mentioned in the certificate is unpaid and due to the Crown.

(6) Any document purporting to be a certificate under paragraph (5) shall be deemed to be such a certificate until the contrary is proved.

Commentary—*Simon's Direct Tax Service* **E5.533.**
Cross reference—See reg 17(3) (payment by cheque treated as made when cheque received by the collector provided it is paid on first presentation).
Amendments—[1] In para (1), sub-para (*a*) numbered as such, and sub-para (*b*) inserted; and words in para (3) inserted, by the Income Tax (Sub-contractors in the Construction Industry) (Amendment) Regulations, SI 2004/1075 regs 2, 7 with effect from 28 April 2004.

Interest on amounts overdue—further provisions

17—(1) In regulations 15 and 16 "the prescribed rate" means the rate applicable under section 178 of the Finance Act 1989 for the purposes of section 86 of the Management Act; and where that rate changes on an operative date within the meaning, given by regulation 2 of the Taxes (Interest Rate) Regulations 1989 by virtue of those Regulations, the change shall have effect for periods beginning on or after the operative date in relation to interest running from before that date as well as from or from after that date.

(2) The amount payable to which regulation 15(1) or 16(1) applies shall carry interest from the reckonable date even if that date is a non-business day within the meaning of section 92 of the Bills of Exchange Act 1882.

[(3) For the purposes of regulations 15 and 16 and of this regulation, where—

(*a*) any payment to the collector is made by cheque, and

(*b*) the cheque is paid on its first presentation to the banker on whom it is drawn,

the payment shall be treated as made on the day on which the cheque was received by the collector.][1]

Commentary—*Simon's Direct Tax Service* **E5.533.**
Amendments—[1] Para (3) inserted by the IT (Sub-contractors in the Construction Industry) (Amendment) Regulations, SI 1996/981 reg 5, with effect as respects cheques received after 18 April 1996.

Interest on amounts overpaid

18—(1) Where an amount paid under these Regulations in respect of the year ended on 5th April 1993 or any subsequent year is repaid to a contractor in the circumstances specified in paragraph (2), the amount repaid shall carry interest at the prescribed rate from the relevant time until the order for the repayment is issued.

(2) The circumstances specified in this paragraph are where the amount is repaid—

(*a*) after the end of the year following that in respect of which the amount was paid, and

(*b*) after the end of the year in which the amount was paid.

(3) In this regulation "the prescribed rate" means the rate applicable under section 178 of the Finance Act 1989 for the purposes of section 824 of the Taxes Act; and where that rate changes on an operative date within the meaning given by regulation 2 of the Taxes (Interest Rate) Regulations

1989 by virtue of those Regulations, the change shall have effect for periods beginning on or after the operative date in relation to interest running from before that date as well as from or from after that date.

(4) In this regulation ''the relevant time'' means—

(*a*) in the case of a repayment of an amount which was paid more than twelve months after the end of the year in respect of which the payment was made, the end of the year in which that amount was paid; and

(*b*) in any other case, the end of the year after the year in respect of which the payment was made.

[(5) For the purposes of this regulation, where—

(*a*) any payment to the collector is made by cheque, and

(*b*) the cheque is paid on its first presentation to the banker on whom it is drawn,

the payment shall be treated as made on the day on which the cheque was received by the collector.][1]

Commentary—*Simon's Direct Tax Service* **E5.533.**

Amendments—[1] Para (5) inserted by the IT (Sub-contractors in the Construction Industry) (Amendment) Regulations, SI 1996/981 reg 4(1)(*b*), (2), with effect as respects cheques received after 18 April 1996.

Recovery of amounts deducted

19—(1) Subject to paragraph (3), the provisions of any enactment relating to the recovery of income tax charged by way of an assessment shall apply to the recovery of the amount specified in paragraph (2) as if that amount had been an amount of income tax charged by way of an assessment on the contractor.

(2) The amount specified in this paragraph is any amount which a contractor is liable under regulation 8 or 9 or is deemed liable under regulation 13 to pay to the collector for any income tax period, and which is not the subject of an assessment under regulation 14 (in this regulation referred to as ''the specified amount'').

(3) Summary proceedings for the recovery of the specified amount may be brought in England, Wales and Northern Ireland at any time before the expiry of twelve months—

(*a*) after the date on which the specified amount became payable, or

(*b*) where a return has been required under regulation 12, after the date of the delivery of that return to the collector.

(4) Proceedings may be brought for the recovery of the specified amount without distinguishing the amounts which the contractor is liable to pay in respect of each sub-contractor and without specifying the sub-contractors in question, and the specified amount shall be one cause of action or one matter of complaint for the purposes of proceedings under sections 65, 66, or 67 of the Management Act.

(5) Nothing in paragraph (4) shall prevent the bringing of separate proceedings for the recovery of each of the several amounts which the contractor is liable to pay for any income tax period in respect of his several sub-contractors.

(6) A certificate of the collector that the specified amount has not been paid to him, or, to the best of his knowledge and belief, to any other collector, or to any person acting on his behalf or on behalf of another collector, shall be sufficient evidence that the sum mentioned in the certificate is unpaid and is due to the Crown.

(7) Any document purporting to be a certificate under paragraph (6) shall be deemed to be such a certificate until the contrary is proved.

Repayment of excess credit

20 ...

Commentary—*Simon's Direct Tax Service* **E5.529.**

Amendments—This regulation revoked by the Income Tax (Sub-contractors in the Construction Industry) (Amendment) Regulations, SI 1998/2622 reg 11, except in relation to companies as respects accounting periods ending before 1 July 1999 (by virtue of the Finance Act 1994, Section 199, (Appointed Day) Order, SI 1998/3173).

[In-year repayments of provisional excess credit

20A—(1) Where—

(*a*) a sub-contractor is an individual or a firm,

(*b*) an application is made by that individual or a partner in the firm (''the applicant'') to the inspector,

(*c*) any income tax and Class 4 contributions due from the applicant, or the sub-contractor, on the applicant's share of the annual profits or gains arising or accruing from the trade, profession or vocation of the sub-contractor, for any earlier year, have been paid,

(*d*) all relevant tax payment vouchers issued to the sub-contractor under regulation 7, and such further evidence as the inspector may require, are produced to the inspector, and

(*e*) the inspector is satisfied by such evidence that the applicant's share of the total of sums deducted under section 559 from payments made to the sub-contractor, in so much of a year as has elapsed at the date when the application is made, exceeds the aggregate of the amounts specified in paragraph (2), the applicant shall, subject to paragraphs (3) and (4), be entitled to repayment of the excess by the inspector.

(2) The amounts specified in this paragraph are—

(*a*) the income tax and any Class 4 contributions payable (whether or not yet due and payable) by the applicant, on his share of the annual profits or gains arising or accruing from the trade, profession or vocation of the sub-contractor which are chargeable to tax for the whole of that year, after deducting any cumulative entitlement of the applicant at the date of the application to an allowance under section 257 or 257A of the Taxes Act;

(*b*) the income tax and any Class 4 contributions payable (whether or not yet due and payable) by the applicant, on any income arising during so much of the year as has elapsed at the date of the application, from which income tax has not been deducted at source, within the meaning given by section 59B(7) of the Management Act; and

(*c*) any sum due and payable to the Board from the sub-contractor under the Tax Acts or the Management Act, and without prejudice to the generality of the foregoing, this shall include any sums deducted by the sub-contractor in the capacity of a contractor, under section 559(4).

(3) Every such application shall be on a form approved by the Board, containing a declaration that all the particulars given in the form are correctly stated to the best of the knowledge and belief of the applicant, and where the application is made by a partner in a firm, the form shall be signed by all the partners in the firm who are individuals and, where a partner is a company, by the secretary or a director of the company.

(4) No repayment under this regulation shall be made after the end of the year to which the application relates.][1]

Commentary—*Simon's Direct Tax Service* **E5.529.**
Amendments—[1] This regulation inserted by the IT (Sub-contractors in the Construction Industry) (Amendment) Regulations, SI 1998/2622 reg 12, in relation to any application for the issue or renewal of a sub-contractor's tax certificate made with respect to any period beginning after 31 July 1999, and for all other purposes with effect from 1 August 1999.

[PART IIA

PAYMENTS EXCEPTED FROM SUBSECTION (1) OF SECTION 559

Small payments

20B—(1) Subsection (1) of section 559 shall not apply to a contract payment if—

(*a*) the conditions prescribed in paragraph (2) in relation to the person making the payment are satisfied, and

(*b*) the condition prescribed in paragraph (3) in relation to the payment is satisfied.

(2) The conditions prescribed in relation to the person making the payment are that—

(*a*) the person is one to whom subsection (2) of section 560 applies by virtue of any of paragraphs (*aa*) to (*f*) of that subsection, and

(*b*) the person has been approved by the inspector for the purposes of this regulation.

(3) The condition prescribed in relation to the payment is that the payment is not one made under a contract in respect of which the total contract payments so made (excluding the direct cost of materials) exceed or are likely to exceed £1000.][1]

Amendments—[1] Part IIA inserted by the IT (Sub-contractors in the Construction Industry) (Amendment) Regulations, SI 1998/2622 reg 13, in relation to any application for the issue or renewal of a sub-contractor's tax certificate made with respect to any period beginning after 31 July 1999, and for all other purposes with effect from 1 August 1999.

PART III

SUB-CONTRACTOR'S TAX CERTIFICATES, VOUCHERS AND GUARANTEES

Powers of inspectors

21 The power to issue, renew, require the surrender of or cancel a sub-contractor's tax certificate or to give directions under subsection (6) of section 561 may be exercised by an inspector.

[Turnover thresholds

21A—(1) The amount specified as the minimum turnover for the purposes of section 562(2A) (in these Regulations referred to as "the individual turnover threshold") is an annual turnover of £30,000.

(2) In these Regulations, "the multiple partnership turnover threshold" for a firm, in relation to a particular period, means an annual turnover equal to the individual turnover threshold multiplied by the total number of times, for that firm, by which the minimum turnover for the purposes of section 562(2A) is to be multiplied pursuant to section 564(2B)(*a*) and (*b*), but identifying and counting the number of partners—

(*a*) in the case of the six month test, according to the maximum number of partners in the firm at any one time during the six consecutive income tax months or lesser consecutive period referred to in regulation 21C(1)(*a*);

(*b*) in the case of the main three year test, according to the maximum number of partners in the firm at any one time in the relevant year referred to in regulation 21D(1)(*a*).

(3) In these Regulations, ''the multiple company turnover threshold'' for a company, in relation to a particular period, means, subject to paragraph (4), an annual turnover equal to the individual turnover threshold multiplied by the number of persons who are relevant persons in relation to the company, but identifying and counting the number of persons who are such relevant persons—

(*a*) in the case of the six month test, according to the maximum number of such relevant persons at any one time during the six consecutive income tax months or lesser consecutive period referred to in regulation 21C(1)(*a*);

(*b*) in the case of the main three year test, according to the maximum number of such relevant persons at any one time in the relevant year referred to in regulation 21D(1)(*a*).

(4) Where—

(*a*) an individual or a firm transfers to a company a business as a going concern, and

(*b*) the business is so transferred wholly or partly in exchange for shares issued by the company to the person transferring the business,

then, in relation to any time prior to the transfer of the business, references in paragraph (3) to ''relevant persons in relation to the company'' shall be construed as references to the individual who, or partners in the firm which, was carrying on the business at that time.

(5) The amount specified for the purposes of section 564(2A)(*b*) (''the alternative partnership turnover threshold'') is £200,000.

(6) The amount specified for the purposes of section 565(2B)(*b*) (''the alternative company turnover threshold'') is £200,000.][1]

Commentary—*Simon's Direct Tax Service* **E5.513, 515, 516.**

Concessions B51—All construction income, net of materials, may form the basis of the turnover which will be counted for the individual, multiple partnership and company turnover tests. This Concession has been classified as obsolete.

B52—Where the multiple partnership and company turnover tests are used on the three year basis, all three years may be based upon the maximum number of partners or directors and shareholders at any point in the last six months of the three year period if that results in lower thresholds. This Concession ceased to apply from 1 August 2001.

Revenue & other press releases—IR 23-10-98 (Worked example of concession B52 for the multiple partnership and company tests).

IR Tax Bulletin December 1998 p 615 (guidance on turnover tests).

IR Tax Bulletin June 1999 p 667 (turnover tests and change in concern).

Amendments—[1] This regulation inserted by the IT (Sub-contractors in the Construction Industry) (Amendment) Regulations, SI 1998/2622 reg 14, in relation to any application for the issue or renewal of a sub-contractor's tax certificate made with respect to any period beginning after 31 July 1999, and for all other purposes with effect from 1 August 1999.

[Prescribed evidence in relation to applications

21B—(1) Paragraph (2) prescribes the evidence by which—

(*a*) an individual must satisfy the Board, as mentioned in section 562(2A), that the individual turnover threshold is likely to be met,

(*b*) the partners in a firm must satisfy the Board, as mentioned in section 564(2A), that the multiple partnership turnover threshold is likely to be met, and

(*c*) a company must satisfy the Board, as mentioned in section 565(2A)(*a*), that the multiple company turnover threshold is likely to be met,

and the matters of which the Board must be satisfied, referred to in sub-paragraph (*a*), (*b*) or (*c*), shall be presumed conclusively from such prescribed evidence.

(2) The evidence prescribed is, subject to paragraph (5), such evidence as complies with either of the six month test or the main three year test.

(3) Paragraph (4) prescribes the evidence by which—

(*a*) the partners in a firm must satisfy the Board, as mentioned in section 564(2A), that the alternative partnership turnover threshold is likely to be met, and

(*b*) a company must satisfy the Board, as mentioned in section 565(2A)(*a*), that the alternative company turnover threshold is likely to be met,

and the matters of which the Board must be satisfied, referred to in sub-paragraph (*a*) or (*b*), shall be presumed conclusively from such prescribed evidence.

(4) The evidence prescribed is such evidence as complies with the alternative three year test.

(5) Where—

(*a*) a person has been a sub-contractor for a continuous period of four years ending with the date of the application for a sub-contractor's tax certificate, and

(*b*) three successive sub-contractor's certificates have been issued to that person, or to a partner in that firm in such capacity, in the circumstances mentioned in regulation 26(2),

paragraph (2) shall apply with the modification that the words 'either of the six month test or' are omitted.][1]

Commentary—*Simon's Direct Tax Service* **E5.514.**
Amendments—[1] This regulation inserted by the IT (Sub-contractors in the Construction Industry) (Amendment) Regulations, SI 1998/2622 reg 14, in relation to any application for the issue or renewal of a sub-contractor's tax certificate made with respect to any period beginning after 31 July 1999, and for all other purposes with effect from 1 August 1999.

[The six month test

21C—(1) The evidence that complies with the six month test is—

(*a*) evidence of turnover of the business mentioned in section 562(2), section 564(2) or section 565(2), as appropriate, during a period of six consecutive income tax months or any lesser consecutive period falling entirely within the year ending with the date of the application;
(*b*) evidence showing that such turnover during the appropriate period mentioned in sub-paragraph (*a*) equalled or exceeded seventy per cent of the relevant turnover threshold; and
(*c*) evidence consisting of tax payment vouchers, gross payment vouchers and construction gross payment vouchers, and documentary evidence of [relevant payments and][2] the direct cost of materials;

(2) In this regulation and in regulations 20B(3), 21A(1) to (3), 21B(1) and (3), 21D[, 21E][3] and 41(4B)—

(*a*) ''the direct cost of materials'' means the direct cost [referred to in section 562(2B)][2];
(*b*) ''turnover'' means [relevant payments][2].

(3) In this regulation and in regulations 21A, 21D and 21E, ''year'' means a period of 365 consecutive days.][1]

Commentary—*Simon's Direct Tax Service* **E5.513.**
Concession B51—All construction income, net of materials, may form the basis of the turnover which will be counted for the individual, multiple partnership and company turnover tests.
Amendments—[1] This regulation inserted by the IT (Sub-contractors in the Construction Industry) (Amendment) Regulations, SI 1998/2622 reg 14, in relation to any application for the issue or renewal of a sub-contractor's tax certificate made with respect to any period beginning after 31 July 1999, and for all other purposes with effect from 1 August 1999.
[2] Words in paras (1)(*d*), (2) substituted by the Income Tax (Sub-contractors in the Construction Industry) (Amendment No 2) Regulations, SI 1999/2159 reg 4(1), (2), (3)(*b*), (*c*) with effect from 1 August 1999.
[3] Word in para (2) inserted by SI 1999/2159 reg 4(1), (3)(*a*) with effect from 1 August 1999.

[The main three year test

21D—(1) The evidence that complies with the main three year test is—

(*a*) evidence of turnover of the business mentioned in section 562(2), 564(2) or 565(2), as appropriate, during a period of three consecutive years falling entirely within the period of four years ending with the date of the application;
(*b*) evidence showing that—

(i) such turnover equalled or exceeded the relevant turnover threshold in at least two out of the three consecutive years mentioned in sub-paragraph (*a*), and
(ii) the average turnover for those three years equalled or exceeded ninety per cent of the average of the relevant turnover threshold in each of those three years; and

(*c*) evidence consisting of accounts covering those three years, tax payment vouchers, gross payment vouchers, construction gross payment vouchers and documentary evidence of [relevant payments and][2] the direct cost of materials.

(2) Where accounts are made up for a period of account which falls partly in one year and partly in another, turnover for that period shall be apportioned on a time basis between the years in which that period falls.][1]

Commentary—*Simon's Direct Tax Service* **E5.513.**
Amendments—[1] This regulation inserted by the IT (Sub-contractors in the Construction Industry) (Amendment) Regulations, SI 1998/2622 reg 14, in relation to any application for the issue or renewal of a sub-contractor's tax certificate made with respect to any period beginning after 31 July 1999, and for all other purposes with effect from 1 August 1999.
[2] Words in para (1)(*c*) substituted by the Income Tax (Sub-contractors in the Construction Industry) (Amendment No 2) Regulations, SI 1999/2159 reg 5 with effect from 1 August 1999.

[The alternative three year test

21E—(1) The evidence that complies with the alternative three year test is—

(*a*) evidence of [turnover][2] received by the business mentioned in section 564(2) or 565(2), as appropriate, during a period of three consecutive years falling entirely within the period of four years ending with the date of the application;
(*b*) evidence showing that—

(i) such [turnover][2] equalled or exceeded the alternative partnership turnover threshold, or the alternative company turnover threshold, as the case may be, in at least two out of the three consecutive years mentioned in sub-paragraph (*a*), and
(ii) the average [turnover][2] received in those three years equalled or exceeded ninety per cent of the average of the relevant turnover threshold in each of those three years; and

(*c*) evidence consisting of accounts covering those three years and documentary evidence of [relevant payments][2], and of the direct cost to the firm or company of materials used or to be used in carrying out the operations in question.

(2) Where accounts are made up for a period of account which falls partly in one year and partly in another, [turnover][2] and the [direct][3] cost of materials for that period shall be apportioned on a time basis between the years in which that period falls.][1]

Commentary—*Simon's Direct Tax Service* **E5.513.**

Concessions B51—All construction income, net of materials, may form the basis of the turnover which will be counted for the individual, multiple partnership and company turnover tests.

B52—Where the multiple partnership and company turnover tests are used on the three year basis, all three years may be based upon the maximum number of partners or directors and shareholders at any point in the last six months of the three year period if that results in lower thresholds.

Revenue & other press releases—IR 23-10-98 (Worked example of concession B52 for the multiple partnership and company tests).

Amendments—[1] This regulation inserted by the IT (Sub-contractors in the Construction Industry) (Amendment) Regulations, SI 1998/2622 reg 14, in relation to any application for the issue or renewal of a sub-contractor's tax certificate made with respect to any period beginning after 31 July 1999, and for all other purposes with effect from 1 August 1999.

[2] Words in paras (1), (2) substituted by the Income Tax (Sub-contractors in the Construction Industry) (Amendment No 2) Regulations, SI 1999/2159 reg 6(*a*), (*b*) with effect from 1 August 1999.

[3] Word in para (2) inserted by SI 1999/2159 reg 6(*c*) with effect from 1 August 1999.

Absence abroad—evidence of living outside the United Kingdom

22—[(1) Where an applicant must satisfy the Board for the purposes of section 562 that he has been outside the United Kingdom for the whole or part of the qualifying period, the evidence by which he is to so satisfy the Board shall be the evidence prescribed in paragraphs (2) and (3).][1]

(2) Subject to paragraph (3), where [the applicant][2] claims to have been employed or self-employed outside the United Kingdom during any part of [the qualifying period][2], the evidence shall be any document from the Revenue Department or equivalent department of the country in which he claims to have been living which confirms his presence there throughout that part of [the qualifying period][2].

(3) Where [the applicant][2] claims—

(*a*) not to have been employed or self-employed while outside the United Kingdom during any part of [the qualifying period][2], or

(*b*) to have been employed or self-employed outside the United Kingdom during any part of [the qualifying period][2] but not to have been liable to tax in the country in which he claims to have been living during that part of [the qualifying period][2],

the evidence shall be any document from the Social Security Department or equivalent department, or from the immigration authorities, or from any other Government department of the country in which he claims to have been living which confirms his presence there throughout that part of [the qualifying period][2].

(4) ...[3]

Amendments—[1] Para (1) substituted by the IT (Sub-contractors in the Construction Industry) (Amendment) Regulations, SI 1998/2622 reg 15(2), in relation to any application for the issue or renewal of a sub-contractor's tax certificate made with respect to any period beginning after 31 July 1999, and for all other purposes with effect from 1 August 1999.

[2] Words in paras (2), (3) substituted by SI 1998/2622 reg 15(3), with effect as in note [1] above.

[3] Para (4) revoked by SI 1998/2622 reg 15(4), with effect as in note [1] above.

Absence abroad—evidence of compliance with tax obligations

23—(1) [Where an applicant must satisfy the Board for the purposes of section 562 that he has complied][1] with any obligations imposed under the tax laws of any country in which he was living during [any part of the qualifying period][1] which are comparable to the obligations mentioned in [subsection (8) of section 562][1], the evidence by which he is so to satisfy the Board shall be the evidence prescribed in paragraph (2).

(2) The evidence shall be such notices or documents issued by the Revenue Department or equivalent department of the country in which [the applicant][2] claims to have been living as confirm that the obligations have been complied with.

(3) ...[3]

Amendments—[1] Words in para (1) amended by the IT (Sub-contractors in the Construction Industry) (Amendment) Regulations, SI 1998/2622 reg 16(2), in relation to any application for the issue or renewal of a sub-contractor's tax certificate made with respect to any period beginning after 31 July 1999, and for all other purposes with effect from 1 August 1999.

[2] Words in para (2) amended by SI 1998/2622 reg 16(3), with effect as in note [1] above.

[3] Para (3) revoked by SI 1998/2622 reg 16(4), with effect as in note [1] above.

[Evidence of unemployment

23A—(1) Where an applicant must satisfy the Board that he was not subject to any one or more of the obligations mentioned in section 562(8) because he was unemployed, the evidence by which he is to so satisfy the Board shall be the evidence prescribed in paragraph (2) or (3) as the case may be.

(2) Where the applicant claims to have been living within the United Kingdom during any period, the evidence shall consist of—

(*a*) a statement from the benefit officer certifying the period during with the applicant was registered as unemployed or,

(*b*) for any period during which the applicant was not registered as unemployed, such other evidence as satisfies the Board that he was unemployed during that period.

(3) Where the applicant claims to have been living outside the United Kingdom during any period, the evidence shall consist of any document from the Social Security Department or equivalent department, or from the immigration authorities, or from any other Government department of the country in which he claims to have been living, which confirms his presence there throughout that period.

(4) In paragraph [(2)][2] above, ''benefit officer'' means the appropriate officer of the [Department for Work and Pensions][3] or, in Northern Ireland, the appropriate officer of the Department of Health and Social Services for Northern Ireland.][1]

Commentary—*Simon's Direct Tax Service* **E5.512.**

Amendments—[1] This regulation inserted by the IT (Sub-contractors in the Construction Industry) (Amendment) Regulations, SI 1998/2622 reg 17, in relation to any application for the issue or renewal of a sub-contractor's tax certificate made with respect to any period beginning after 31 July 1999, and for all other purposes with effect from 1 August 1999.

[2] Word in para (4) substituted by the Income Tax (Sub-contractors in the Construction Industry) (Amendment No 2) Regulations, SI 1999/2159 reg 7 with effect from 1 August 1999.

[3] Words in para (4) substituted by the Secretaries of State for Education and Skills and for Work and Pensions Order, SI 2002/1397 art 12, Schedule para 24 with effect from 27 June 2002.

[Evidence of full-time education

23B—(1) Where an applicant must satisfy the Board that he was not subject to any one or more obligations mentioned in section 562(8) because he was undergoing full-time education, the evidence by which he is to so satisfy the Board shall be the evidence prescribed in paragraph (2) or (3) as the case may be.

(2) Where the applicant claims to have been living within the United Kingdom, the evidence shall consist of a statement from the educational institution which the applicant has attended, certifying the periods during which the applicant was undergoing full-time education at that institution.

(3) Where the applicant claims to have been living outside the United Kingdom, the evidence shall consist of a statement from the educational institution which the applicant has attended, in the country in which the applicant claims to have been living, certifying the periods during which the applicant was undergoing full-time education at that institution.][1]

Commentary—*Simon's Direct Tax Service* **E5.512.**

Amendments—[1] This regulation inserted by the IT (Sub-contractors in the Construction Industry) (Amendment) Regulations, SI 1998/2622 reg 17, in relation to any application for the issue or renewal of a sub-contractor's tax certificate made with respect to any period beginning after 31 July 1999, and for all other purposes with effect from 1 August 1999.

Forms of sub-contractor's tax certificate

24—(1) A sub-contractor's tax certificate shall be prepared by [an authorised officer of the Board or any person nominated by][5] the Board in one of the forms numbered [CIS5[, CIS5 (Partner)][4] and CIS6][1] in Schedule 1 to these Regulations.

(2) Where such a certificate is issued to an individual otherwise than as a partner in a firm ...[2], it shall be in the form numbered [CIS6][1] in Schedule 1; and the certificate shall show—

(*a*) the individual's name,

(*b*) his national insurance number [(or where such a number is not required, a substitute identifying number)][5],

[(*c*) a facsimile of the individual's signature on the application for the certificate,][1]

(*d*) a full face photograph, being a true likeness of him,

(*e*) the date from which the certificate is valid,

(*f*) the date of its expiry,

(*g*) the distinctive number assigned to it, and

(*h*) where the individual so wishes, one business name under which his business is carried on.

(3) ...[3]

(4) [Subject to paragraph (4A), where][4] such a certificate is issued to an individual as a partner in a firm, it shall be in the form numbered [CIS6][1] in Schedule 1; and the certificate shall show—

(*a*) the individual's name,

(*b*) his national insurance number [(or where such a number is not required, a substitute identifying number)][5],

[(*c*) a facsimile of the individual's signature on the application for the certificate,][1]

(*d*) a full face photograph, being a true likeness of him,

(*e*) the date from which the certificate is valid,

(*f*) the date of its expiry,

(*g*) the distinctive number assigned to it, and

(*h*) the words ''Acting for'',

(*j*) the name of the firm, and

(*k*) subject to paragraph (8), and where the individual so wishes, one business name under which the firm's business is carried on.

[(4A) Subject to paragraph (4B), where the inspector considers that in all the circumstances the form of certificate mentioned in paragraph (4) would be inappropriate, he may issue a certificate to the individual in the form numbered CIS5 (Partner) in Schedule 1, and the certificate shall show—

(*a*) a facsimile of the individual's signature on the application for the certificate,
(*b*) the word "Original" (but no copies shall be issued),
(*c*) the date from which the certificate is valid,
(*d*) the date of its expiry,
(*e*) the distinctive number assigned to it,
(*f*) the words "Acting for",
(*g*) the name of the firm, and
(*h*) subject to paragraph (8), and where the individual so wishes, one business name under which the firm's business is carried on.][4]

[(4B) A certificate mentioned in paragraph (4A) shall only be issued to a single partner in a particular firm, in his capacity as such, at any one time.][4]

(5) Subject to paragraph (6), where such a certificate is issued to a company (and more than one such certificate may be issued to a company), it shall be in the form numbered [CIS6][1] in Schedule 1; and the certificate shall show—

(*a*) the name of the secretary or director of the company who is authorised to use the certificate,
[(*aa*) his national insurance number [(or where such a number is not required, a substitute identifying number)][5],
(*b*) a facsimile of his signature on the application for the certificate,][1]
(*c*) a full face photograph, being a true likeness of him,
(*d*) the date from which the certificate is valid,
(*e*) the date of its expiry,
(*f*) the distinctive number assigned to it,
(*g*) the words "Acting for",
(*h*) the name of the company,
(*j*) ...[2]
(*k*) subject to paragraph (8), and where the secretary or director of the company so wishes, one business name under which the company's business is carried on.

(6) If in any case the inspector considers that in all the circumstances the form of certificate mentioned in paragraph (5) would be inappropriate, he may issue a certificate to the company in the form numbered [CIS5][1] in Schedule 1 ...[2]; and the certificate shall also show—

(*a*) [a facsimile of the][1] signature of the secretary of the company at the date of issue,
(*b*) the word "Original",
(*c*) the date from which the certificate is valid,
(*d*) the date of its expiry,
(*e*) the distinctive number assigned to it,
(*f*) the name of the company,
[(*g*) the registration number of the company, and][4]
(*h*) where the secretary of the company so wishes, one business name under which the company's business is carried on.

(7) Where an inspector has issued a certificate under paragraph (6), he may also issue one or more additional certificates to the company and each such additional certificate shall be in the form numbered [CIS5][1] in Schedule 1; and each certificate shall—

(*a*) have its own additional distinctive serial number, and
(*b*) show the particulars mentioned in paragraph (6), except that there shall be substituted for the word "Original" the words "Official Copy".

(8) Where a certificate mentioned in paragraph (4)[, (4A)][4] or (5) shows one business name under which the firm's or company's business is carried on, that business name shall also appear on all other certificates issued to [partners in][4] the firm or company under section 561 and currently in force.

Commentary—*Simon's Direct Tax Service* **E5.517, 518.**

Amendments—[1] Words in paras (1), (2), (4)–(7) substituted by the IT (Sub-contractors in the Construction Industry) (Amendment) Regulations, SI 1998/2622 reg 18(1)–(3), (5)–(8) in relation to any application for the issue or renewal of a sub-contractor's tax certificate made with respect to any period beginning after 31 July 1999, and for all other purposes with effect from 1 August 1999.

[2] In paras (2), (5), words revoked by SI 1998/2622 reg 18(1), (3), (6), (7) with effect as in note [1] above.

[3] Para (3) revoked by SI 1998/2622 reg 18(1), (4), with effect as in note [1] above.

[4] Words in paras (1), (8) inserted, words in para (4) substituted, and paras (4A), (4B), and sub-para (6)(*g*) inserted by the IT (Sub-contractors in the Construction Industry) (Amendment) Regulations, SI 2001/1531 reg 3 with effect from 1 May 2001.

[5] Words in paras (1), (2), (4), (5) inserted by the IT (Sub-contractors in the Construction Industry) (Amendment) Regulations, SI 2002/2225 reg 6 with effect from 20 September 2002.

Issue of sub-contractor's tax certificate

25—(1) A sub-contractor's tax certificate in the form specified in regulation 24(2) ...[1] or (4) shall be issued by an [authorised officer of the Board or any person nominated by the Board][2] to the person whose name, national insurance number and photograph appear on it ...[1]

[(1A) A sub-contractor's tax certificate in the form specified in regulation 24(4A) shall be issued by an [authorised officer of the Board or any person nominated by the Board][2] to the partner who applied for the certificate, and a facsimile of whose signature appears on it.][2]

(2) A sub-contractor's tax certificate in the form specified in regulation 24(5) shall be issued by an [authorised officer of the Board or any person nominated by the Board][2] to the company whose name [appears on it][1].

(3) A sub-contractor's tax certificate in the form specified in regulation 24(6) or (7) shall be issued by an [authorised officer of the Board or any person nominated by the Board][2] to the company whose name [appears on it][1].

Amendments—[1] Words in para (1) revoked, and words in paras (2), (3) substituted, by the Income Tax (Sub-contractors in the Construction Industry) (Amendment) Regulations, SI 1998/2622 reg 19(1)–(3) in relation to any application for the issue or renewal of a sub-contractor's tax certificate made with respect to any period beginning after 31 July 1999, and for all other purposes with effect from 1 August 1999.

[2] Para (1A) inserted by the IT (Sub-contractors in the Construction Industry) (Amendment) Regulations, SI 2001/1531 reg 4 with effect from 1 May 2001.

[3] Words substituted by the IT (Sub-contractors in the Construction Industry) (Amendment) Regulations, SI 2002/2225 reg 7 with effect from 20 September 2002.

[Validity of sub-contractor's tax certificate

26—(1) A sub-contractor's tax certificate shall be valid, during the period prescribed in paragraph (2), (3), (4) or (5), as the case may be, for the purpose of allowing payments to be made to the user of the certificate without the deduction required by sections 559 and for no other purpose.

(2) Subject to paragraph (5), where the Board have been satisfied as mentioned in regulation 21B(1), by evidence complying with the six month test, the period prescribed is one year from the date from which the certificate is valid.

(3) Subject to paragraphs (4) and (5), where the Board have been satisfied as mentioned in regulation 21B(1) or (3), by evidence complying with the main three year test or the alternative three year test, the period prescribed is three years from the date from which the certificate is valid.

(4) Where a certificate is issued, in the circumstances mentioned in paragraph (3), before 1st September 1999, the period prescribed is the period beginning on the date from which the certificate is valid, and ending 2 years and six months, 3 years or 3 years and six months later (according to the expiry date shown on the certificate) so as to secure an even rate of expiry of certificates.

(5) Where a certificate has been issued to a partner in a firm, or to a company, which is uncancelled, and an application is made for the issue of a certificate to a new or other partner, or to the company, for use by a new or other director or secretary of that company, the period prescribed is the period from the date from which the certificate is valid, to the date of expiry which appears on all other certificates that are uncancelled, which have been issued to partners in the firm or to the company, as the case may be.][1]

Commentary—*Simon's Direct Tax Service* **E5.514.**

Amendments—[1] This regulation substituted by the IT (Sub-contractors in the Construction Industry) (Amendment) Regulations, SI 1998/2622 reg 20, in relation to any application for the issue or renewal of a sub-contractor's tax certificate made with respect to any period beginning after 31 July 1999, and for all other purposes with effect from 1 August 1999.

Renewal of sub-contractor's tax certificate

27—(1) At any time within a period of six months before the date of expiry of a sub-contractor's tax certificate, the person to whom it was issued may apply for its renewal.

(2) The provisions of section 561 shall apply to an application for renewal in the same way as they apply to an application for the issue of a sub-contractor's tax certificate.

(3) The provisions of the Taxes Act and of these Regulations shall apply to a renewed certificate in the same way as they apply to a sub-contractor's tax certificate.

Production for inspection and surrender of sub-contractor's tax certificate

28—(1) A [user of a sub-contractor's tax certificate][1] shall produce his sub-contractor's tax certificate for inspection whenever called upon by any authorised officer of the Board.

(2) A [user of a sub-contractor's tax certificate][1] or any person having a sub-contractor's tax certificate in his possession, even though it may have expired or been cancelled, may be required at any time by notice served upon him or whenever called upon him by any authorised officer of the Board to surrender it to them or to that officer.

Amendments—[1] Words in paras (1), (2) substituted by the IT (Sub-contractors in the Construction Industry) (Amendment) Regulations, SI 1998/2622 reg 20, in relation to any application for the issue or renewal of a sub-contractor's tax certificate made with respect to any period beginning after 31 July 1999, and for all other purposes with effect from 1 August 1999.

Form of voucher

29—(1) A [gross payment][1] voucher shall be in the form numbered [CIS24][1] in Schedule 1 and shall show a distinctive number and the further information specified in [paragraph 2][1].

(2) The further information specified in this paragraph is—

(*a*) in the case of an individual, the name and national insurance number of the user,

(*b*) in the case of an individual who is a partner in a firm, the name and national insurance number of the user, the words ''Acting for'' and the name of the firm, and

(*c*) in the case of a company, the name of the secretary or director of the company, the words ''Acting for'' and the name ...[2] of the company.

(3) ...[3]

Amendments—[1] Para (1) amended by the IT (Sub-contractors in the Construction Industry) (Amendment) Regulations, SI 1998/2622 reg 22(2), in relation to any application for the issue or renewal of a sub-contractor's tax certificate made with respect to any period beginning after 31 July 1999, and for all other purposes with effect from 1 August 1999.

[2] Words in para (2) amended by SI 1998/2622 reg 22(3), with effect as in note [1] above.

[3] Para (3) revoked by SI 1998/2622 reg 22(4), with effect as in note [1] above.

Restriction on issue of further vouchers in certain circumstances

30 ...

Amendments—This regulation revoked by the IT (Sub-contractors in the Construction Industry) (Amendment) Regulations, SI 1998/2622 reg 23, in relation to any application for the issue or renewal of a sub-contractor's tax certificate made with respect to any period beginning after 31 July 1999, and for all other purposes with effect from 1 August 1999.

Surrender of voucher

31 A user or any person having a voucher in his possession may be required at any time by notice served upon him or whenever called upon by any authorised officer of the Board to surrender it to them or to that officer.

Guarantees

32 ...

Amendments—This regulation revoked by the IT (Sub-contractors in the Construction Industry) (Amendment) Regulations, SI 1998/2622 reg 24, in relation to any application for the issue or renewal of a sub-contractor's tax certificate made with respect to any period beginning after 31 July 1999, and for all other purposes with effect from 1 August 1999.

PART IV

PAYMENTS TO SUB-CONTRACTORS USING SUB-CONTRACTOR'S TAX CERTIFICATES

Production and verification of sub-contractor's tax certificate

33—(1) On making a contract payment to a sub-contractor using a sub-contractor's tax certificate, and unless the circumstances specified either in regulation 34(2) [or 34A(2)][2] or in paragraph (5) below apply, the contractor shall—

(*a*) satisfy himself of the matters specified in paragraph (2); and

(*b*) ensure that the sub-contractor's tax certificate is produced to him by a person (in this regulation referred to as ''the person in question'') in accordance with paragraphs (3) and (4);

and if the requirements of this paragraph are not complied with, section 559 shall apply to any contract payments made as though the sub-contractor were not excepted from it.

(2) The matters specified in this paragraph are that the contractor shall satisfy himself by inspection of the certificate that the person in question is—

(*a*) the user of the [sub-contractor's tax][1] certificate, where it is in one of the forms specified in paragraphs (2), ...[1] (4)[, (4A)][2] or (5) of regulation 24; or

(*b*) authorised to produce the certificate on behalf of the company which is the user of [the sub-contractor's tax certificate][1], where it is in one of the forms specified in paragraphs (6) or (7) of regulation 24.

(3) Subject to paragraph (4), for the purposes of paragraph (2) above, the person in question shall produce his sub-contractor's tax certificate (or, where sub-paragraph (*b*) of paragraph (2) above applies, one of the company's certificates) for inspection by the contractor or the contractor's authorised representative; and, if he fails to do so, section 559 shall apply as though he, or the company of which he is a director or the secretary, were not excepted from it.

(4) Where the user receives a payment as a nominee, the person who nominated the user shall also produce his sub-contractor's tax certificate for such inspection; and, if he fails to do so, section 559 shall apply to that payment as though neither the nominee nor the person who nominated him were excepted from it.

(5) The circumstances specified in this paragraph are that the contractor has—

(*a*) previously satisfied himself of the matters specified in paragraph (2), and

(*b*) has no reason to doubt that the certificate is still valid.

Commentary—*Simon's Direct Tax Service* **E5.526.**

Amendments—[1] Words in para (2)(*a*), (*b*) amended by the IT (Sub-contractors in the Construction Industry) (Amendment) Regulations, SI 1998/2622 reg 25(2), (3) in relation to any application for the issue or renewal of a sub-contractor's tax certificate made with respect to any period beginning after 31 July 1999, and for all other purposes with effect from 1 August 1999.

[2] Paras (1), (2)(*a*) amended by the IT (Sub-contractors in the Construction Industry) (Amendment) Regulations, SI 2001/1531 reg 5 with effect from 1 May 2001.

Alternative procedure for verification of sub-contractor's tax certificate held by company

34—(1) Where the circumstances specified in paragraph (2) are satisfied, a user specified in paragraph (3) shall give the document specified in paragraph (4) (in this regulation referred to as "the certification document") to the contractor.

(2) The circumstances specified in this paragraph (and which were referred to in regulation 33(1)) are that—

(*a*) the contract payment is made to a company, not being a nominee,

(*b*) the payment is due under a contract made in writing between the contractor and the company,

(*c*) the company has produced the certification document to the contractor,

(*d*) subject to paragraph (5), the contractor has no reason to doubt that the information shown on the certification document is correct,

(*e*) the date of payment is—

(i) not earlier than the date, if any, shown in the certification document as that from which the certificate is valid, and

(ii) not later than the date of expiry shown in the certification document, and

(*f*) the payment is made into a bank account held in the name of the company and specified in the certification document (in this regulation referred to as "the nominated account").

(3) A user specified in this paragraph is a user which—

(*a*) is a company other than a nominee, and

(*b*) has notified the inspector of particulars identifying the nominated account.

(4) The certification document specified in this paragraph is a document signed by the secretary or one of the directors of the company—

(*a*) certifying that the company is the user of a valid sub-contractor's tax certificate in the form specified in paragraph (6) of regulation 24, and

(*b*) specifying—

(i) the name of the user,

(ii) the address of the registered office of the user,

(iii) the registration number of the user,

(iv) the distinctive number of the sub-contractor's tax certificate,

(v) the date, if any, from which the certificate is valid,

(vi) the date of expiry of the certificate,

(vii) particulars identifying the nominated account, and

(viii) where the user so wishes, the business name or names under which the company's business is carried on.

(5) If the contractor has reason to doubt that the information shown on the certification document is correct, he may, within 14 days of the date of receipt of the certification document from the company, apply to the inspector for confirmation that—

(*a*) a valid sub-contractor's tax certificate has been issued in the name of the person to whom the payment is to be made; and

(*b*) the information shown on the certification document agrees with the record held by the inspector;

and, on receipt of such confirmation, the contractor shall have no reason to doubt that the information shown on the certification document is correct.

Commentary—*Simon's Direct Tax Service* **E5.526.**

[Alternative procedure for verification of sub-contractor's tax certificate held by a partner in a firm

34A—(1) Where the circumstances specified in paragraph (2) are satisfied, a partner specified in paragraph (3) shall give the document specified in paragraph (4) (in this regulation referred to as the "certification document") to the contractor.

(2) The circumstances specified in this paragraph (and which were referred to in regulation 33(1)) are that—

(*a*) the contract payment is made to a firm, not being a nominee,

(*b*) the payment is due under a contract made in writing between the contractor and the firm,

(*c*) the partner has produced the certification document to the contractor, (*d*) subject to paragraph (5), the contractor has no reason to doubt that the information shown on the certification document is correct,

(*e*) the date of payment is—

(i) not earlier than the date shown in the certification document as that from which the certificate is valid, and

(ii) not later than the date of expiry shown in the certification document, and

(*f*) the payment is made into a bank account held in the name of the firm and specified in the certification document (''the nominated account'').

(3) A partner specified in this paragraph is –

(*a*) a partner in the firm referred to in paragraph (2)(''the firm''), and

(*b*) one who has notified the inspector of particulars identifying the nominated account.

(4) The certification document specified in this paragraph is a document on the firm's headed notepaper, signed by the partner—

(*a*) certifying that the partner, in his capacity as a partner in the firm, is the user of a valid sub-contractor's certificate in the form specified in paragraph (4A) of regulation 24, and

(*b*) specifying—

(i) the name of the partner,

(ii) the address which is the firm's main place of business,

(iii) the distinctive number of the sub-contractor's tax certificate,

(iv) the date from which the certificate is valid,

(v) the date of expiry of the certificate,

(vi) particulars identifying the nominated account, and

(vii) where the partner so wishes, the business name or names under which the firm's business is carried on.

(5) If the contractor has reason to doubt that the information shown on the certification document is correct, he may, within 14 days of the date of receipt of the certification document from the partner, apply to the inspector for confirmation that—

(*a*) a valid sub-contractor's tax certificate has been issued to the partner, in his capacity as a partner in the firm, to which the payment is to be made, and

(*b*) the information shown on the certification document agrees with the records held by the inspector,

and, on receipt of such confirmation, the contractor shall be presumed to have no reason to doubt that the information shown on the certification document is correct.][1]

Commentary—*Simon's Direct Tax Service* **E5.526.**

Amendments—[1] Inserted by the IT (Sub-contractors in the Construction Industry) (Amendment) Regulations, SI 2001/1531 reg 6 with effect from 1 May 2001.

[Delivery of gross payment voucher by a sub-contractor

35—(1) This regulation applies where—

(*a*) a sub-contractor's tax certificate is issued in one of the forms specified in paragraph (2), (4) or (5) of regulation 24, and

(*b*) a contract payment is made to the relevant sub-contractor, or the user of that sub-contractor's certificate, without the deduction imposed by section 559.

(2) Where this regulation applies, the user of the sub-contractor's tax certificate or, where the sub-contractor is a company, a user who is a director or the secretary of the company, shall—

(*a*) in respect of all contract payments made to the sub-contractor or the user as mentioned in paragraph (1)(*b*), or

(*b*) where the contractor so requests, for each such contract payment made,

within a period of one income tax month, complete in triplicate a gross payment voucher in the form designated CIS24 in Schedule 1, with the particulars mentioned in regulation 38(*a*), signed by him in accordance with regulation 38(*b*) and shall give those copies of the voucher to the contractor no later than fourteen days after the end of the income tax month in question.

(3) The contractor shall complete the copies of the gross payment voucher with his distinctive reference number and shall return the copy of the voucher marked ''Subcontractor copy'' to the sub-contractor, and send the copy of the voucher marked ''Inland Revenue copy'' to a person nominated by the Board, at an address specified by them.

(4) A contractor shall make every effort reasonable in the circumstances to obtain such a gross payment voucher for or in respect of every such payment made by him.][1]

Commentary—*Simon's Direct Tax Service* **E5.527.**

Amendments—[1] This regulation substituted by the IT (Sub-contractors in the Construction Industry) (Amendment) Regulations, SI 1998/2622 reg 26, in relation to any application for the issue or renewal of a sub-contractor's tax certificate made with respect to any period beginning after 31 July 1999, and for all other purposes with effect from 1 August 1999.

Delivery of voucher by sub-contractor to whom section 561(4) of the Taxes Act applies

36 ..

Commentary—*Simon's Direct Tax Service* **E5.527.**
Amendments—This regulation revoked by the IT (Sub-contractors in the Construction Industry) (Amendment) Regulations, SI 1998/2622 reg 27, in relation to any application for the issue or renewal of a sub-contractor's tax certificate made with respect to any period beginning after 31 July 1999, and for all other purposes with effect from 1 August 1999.

Delivery of voucher by sub-contractor which is a company

37 ..

Amendments—This regulation revoked by the IT (Sub-contractors in the Construction Industry) (Amendment) Regulations, SI 1998/2622 reg 28, in relation to any application for the issue or renewal of a sub-contractor's tax certificate made with respect to any period beginning after 31 July 1999, and for all other purposes with effect from 1 August 1999.

[Completion of construction gross payment voucher by contractor where sub-contractor is a company issued with a CIS5 Certificate

37A—(1) This regulation applies where—

(*a*) a sub-contractor's tax certificate is issued to a company in the form specified in paragraph (6) or (7) of regulation 24 [or to an individual as a partner in a firm in the form specified in paragraph (4A) of that regulation][2], and

(*b*) a contract payment is made to the company[, or to that firm, as the case may be][2] without the deduction imposed by section 559.

(2) Where this regulation applies, the contractor shall, in respect of all contract payments made by him as mentioned in paragraph (1)(*b*) within a period of one income tax month, either

(*a*) complete a construction gross payment voucher in the form designated CIS23(M) and CIS23(I) in Schedule 1, containing the particulars specified in paragraph (4) and signed by him, or

(*b*) transmit electronically the particulars specified in paragraph (4) to a person nominated by the Board.

(3) The contractor shall send all construction gross payment vouchers completed by him in accordance with this regulation to a person nominated by the Board, at an address specified by them.

(4) The particulars specified in this paragraph are—

(*a*) the name of the sub-contractor,

[(*b*) in the case of a contract payment to a company, the distinctive number of its subcontractor's tax certificate or, in the case of a contract payment to a firm, the distinctive number of the sub-contractor's tax certificate of the partner in that firm who produced that certificate or a certification document in accordance with regulation 33 or 34A,][2]

(*c*) the end of the income tax month in which the payments were made, and

(*d*) the amount of the payments.][1]

Commentary—*Simon's Direct Tax Service* **E5.527.**
Amendments—[1] This regulation inserted by the IT (Sub-contractors in the Construction Industry) (Amendment) Regulations, SI 1998/2622 reg 29, in relation to any application for the issue or renewal of a sub-contractor's tax certificate made with respect to any period beginning after 31 July 1999, and for all other purposes with effect from 1 August 1999.
[2] Words in para (1) inserted, and sub-para (4)(*b*) substituted, by the IT (Sub-contractors in the Construction Industry) (Amendment) Regulations, SI 2001/1531 reg 7 with effect from 1 May 2001.

Completion and signature of voucher

38 A [gross payment][1] voucher referred to in regulation 35 ...[1] shall be—

(*a*) completed by the user by the insertion of—

(i), (ii) ...[1]

(iii) the name of the contractor,

[(iv) the end of the income tax month in which the contract payments were made,][1]

(v) the amount of the [payments, for or in respect of which the gross payment voucher is given][1]; and

(vi) ...[1]

(*b*) signed by the user on the date the voucher is given.

Amendments—[1] Words "gross payment" inserted, words and sub-paras (i), (ii), (vi) revoked, and sub-para (iv) substituted, by the IT (Sub-contractors in the Construction Industry) (Amendment) Regulations, SI 1998/2622 reg 30, in relation to any application for the issue or renewal of a sub-contractor's tax certificate made with respect to any period beginning after 31 July 1999, and for all other purposes with effect from 1 August 1999.

Return of vouchers

39 Within 14 days of the end of every income tax month a contractor shall forward all [gross payment vouchers and construction gross payment][1] vouchers given to and obtained [or completed by him, in that income tax month, in accordance with regulations 35 and 37A, to a person nominated by the Board, at an address specified by them][1].

SIs

Amendments—[1] Words in this regulation substituted by the IT (Sub-contractors in the Construction Industry) (Amendment) Regulations, SI 1998/2622 reg 31, in relation to any application for the issue or renewal of a sub-contractor's tax certificate made with respect to any period beginning after 31 July 1999, and for all other purposes with effect from 1 August 1999.

Return of payments made without deduction to be made and records of such payments to be kept

40 . . ..

Amendments—This regulation revoked by the IT (Sub-contractors in the Construction Industry) (Amendment) Regulations, SI 1998/2622 reg 32, with effect in relation to any period after 31 July 1999.

PART V

SUPPLEMENTAL

[Returns by contractor at end of year

40A—(1) The contractor shall render a return to the inspector or, if so required, to the collector, not later than 44 days after the end of the year, in such form as the Board may approve or prescribe, containing the particulars specified in paragraph (3) in respect of all sub-contractors not excepted from section 559 to whom payments to which that section applies were made by him during the year.

(2) The contractor shall render a return to the inspector or, if so required, to the collector, not later than 44 days after the end of the year, in such form as the Board may approve or prescribe, containing the particulars specified in paragraph (6) in circumstances where a sub-contractor is excepted from section 559.

(3) The particulars specified in this paragraph are—

(*a*) the year to which the return relates,

(*b*) the total amount of payments to which section 559 applies made by the contractor during the year,

(*c*) the total amount, if any, included in those payments which the contractor is satisfied represents the direct cost to any person other than the contractor of materials used in carrying out the construction operations to which the contracts under which the payments were made related, and

(*d*) the total amount deducted from the payments mentioned in sub-paragraph (*b*) under section 559.

(4) The return required by paragraph (1) shall be supported by the particulars specified in paragraph (5).

(5) The particulars specified in this paragraph are—

(*a*) a list of all sub-contractors not excepted from section 559 to whom payments to which that section applies were made by the contractor during the year, and

(*b*) in respect of each sub-contractor—

(i) the name and distinctive reference number taken from that sub-contractor's registration card,

(ii) the total amount of payments to which section 559 applies made by the contractor to that sub-contractor during the year,

(iii) the total amount, if any, included in those payments which the contractor is satisfied represents the direct cost to any person other than the contractor of materials used in carrying out the construction operations to which the contracts under which the payments were made related, and

(iv) the total amount deducted from the payments in sub-paragraph (ii) under section 559.

(6) The particulars specified in this paragraph are—

(*a*) the total amount of contract payments made by the contractor during the [year—

(i) to firms, a partner in which is excepted from section 559 in his capacity as a partner in the firm and who, in that capacity, holds a sub-contractor's tax certificate in the form numbered CIS5 (Partner) in Schedule 1 to these Regulations, and

(ii)][2] to companies excepted from section 559, which hold a sub-contractor's tax certificate in the form numbered CIS5 in Schedule 1 to these Regulations; and

(*b*) the total amount of contract payments made by the contractor during the year, to persons excepted from section 559, who hold a sub-contractor's tax certificate in the form numbered CIS6 in that Schedule.

(7) The return required by paragraph (2) shall be supported by the particulars specified in paragraph (8).

(8) The particulars specified in this paragraph are—

(*a*) a list of all companies excepted from section 559, who hold a sub-contractor's tax certificate in the form numbered CIS5 in that Schedule, to which the contractor made any contract payment during the year;

[(*aa*) a list of all firms, a partner in which—

(i) is excepted from section 559 in his capacity as a partner in the firm, and

(ii) holds in that capacity a sub-contractor's tax certificate in the form numbered CIS5 (Partner) in that Schedule,

to which the contractor made any contract payment during the year;][2]

(*b*) a list of all persons excepted from section 559, which hold a sub-contractor's tax certificate in the form numbered CIS6 in that Schedule to whom the contractor made any contract payment during the year; and

(*c*) in respect of each of the sub-contractors mentioned in sub-paragraphs (*a*) and (*b*)—

(i) the distinctive reference number taken from that sub-contractor's tax certificate, and

(ii) the total amount paid by the contractor to that sub-contractor in that year, in relation to which the sub-contractor was excepted from section 559.

(9) The particulars specified in paragraphs (5) and (8) either—

(*a*) shall be contained in a document provided by the Board for that purpose or approved by the Board, which shall accompany the relevant return, or

(*b*) not later than the end of the day on which the relevant return is rendered, shall be transmitted electronically to the inspector or collector to whom the return is rendered.

(10) The returns required by paragraphs (1) and (2) shall include a declaration and certificate in the form approved by the Board, stating that—

(*a*) all particulars required to be provided for the year in accordance with this regulation have been provided, and

(*b*) those particulars are complete and accurate to the best of the contractor's knowledge and belief.

(11) A contractor shall make and keep such records as will enable him to comply with the requirements specified in paragraphs (1) to (10) above.

(12) Where the contractor is a company, the declaration and certificate mentioned in paragraph (10) shall be signed either by the secretary or by a director of the company.

(13) If a contractor has failed to pay the total amount which he is liable under these Regulations to pay the collector within 14 days of the end of any year, the collector may prepare a certificate showing the amount remaining unpaid for that year.

(14) Paragraphs (1) to (5) of regulation 19 shall apply to the amount shown on a certificate under paragraph (13) with the modification that summary proceedings for the recovery of that amount or such part of it as remains unpaid may be brought at any time before the expiry of—

(*a*) twelve months after the date limited for delivery of the return mentioned in paragraph (1), or

(*b*) if that return is not delivered by that date, the expiry of twelve months after its delivery.

(15) A certificate of the collector under paragraph (13) that the amount mentioned for that year has not been paid to him, or, to the best of his knowledge and belief, to any other collector, or to any person acting on his behalf or on behalf of another collector, shall be sufficient evidence that the sum mentioned in the certificate is unpaid and is due to the Crown.

(16) Section 98A of the Management Act shall apply to the provisions of paragraphs (1) and (3) to (5), requiring a return to be made.][1]

Commentary—*Simon's Direct Tax Service* **E5.530.**

Amendments—[1] This regulation inserted by the IT (Sub-contractors in the Construction Industry) (Amendment) Regulations, SI 1998/2622 reg 33, in relation to any application for the issue or renewal of a sub-contractor's tax certificate made with respect to any period beginning after 31 July 1999, and for all other purposes with effect from 1 August 1999.

[2] Words in sub-para (6)(*a*) inserted, and sub-para (8)(*aa*) inserted, by the IT (Sub-contractors in the Construction Industry) (Amendment) Regulations, SI 2001/1531 reg 8 with effect from 1 May 2001.

Inspection of records of contractors and sub-contractors

41—(1) Every contractor, whenever called upon to do so by an authorised officer of the Board, shall produce the records specified in paragraph (2) to that officer for inspection, at such time as that officer may reasonably require, at the prescribed place.

(2) The records specified in this paragraph are—

(*a*) all documents and records whatsoever (including vouchers given to the contractor under [regulation 35][1])—

(i) relating to the calculation or payment of all sums paid to sub-contractors (or their nominees) in the years or income tax periods specified by such officer or to deductions from such sums where required under section 559; or

(ii) referred to in regulation [40A][1]; or

[(iii) relating to amounts falling within regulation 40A(6)(*a*) or (*b*); or][1]

(*b*) such of those documents, records and vouchers as may be specified by the authorised officer.

(3) Every person who is or has within the preceding three years been a sub-contractor and who is not the user of a sub-contractor's tax certificate ...[2], whenever called upon to do so by any authorised officer of the Board, shall produce the records specified in paragraph (4) to that officer for inspection, at such time as that officer may reasonably require, at the prescribed place.

(4) The records specified in this paragraph are—

(*a*) all documents and records relating to the calculation or payment of sums paid to him pursuant to any contract or contracts under which he is or was a sub-contractor within the preceding three years; or

(*b*) such of those documents and records as may be specified by the authorised officer.

[(4A) Every person who applies for a sub-contractor's tax certificate, whenever called upon to do so by an authorised officer of the Board, shall produce the records specified in paragraph (4B) to that officer, at such time as that officer may reasonably require, at the prescribed place.

(4B) The records specified in this paragraph are documentary evidence of [relevant payments][5], or of the direct cost of materials, ...[6]][3]

(5) "The prescribed place" mentioned in paragraphs [(1), (3) and (4A)][4] means—

(*a*) such place in the United Kingdom as the contractor or the person mentioned in paragraph (3) (hereafter in this regulation called "the sub-contractor") and the authorised officer may agree upon; or

(*b*) in default of such agreement, the place in the United Kingdom at which the documents and records mentioned in paragraphs (2) and (4) are normally kept; or

(*c*) in default of such agreement and if there is no such place as is referred to in sub-paragraph (*b*) above, the contractor's or the sub-contractor's principal place of business in the United Kingdom.

(6) The authorised officer may—

(*a*) take copies of, or make extracts from, any document produced to him for inspection in accordance with paragraphs [(1) to (4B)][4];

(*b*) remove any document so produced if it appears to him to be necessary to do so, at a reasonable time and for a reasonable period.

(7) Where any document is removed in accordance with paragraph (6)(*b*) the authorised officer shall provide—

(*a*) a receipt for any document so removed; and

(*b*) a copy of the document, free of charge, within seven days to the person by whom it was produced or caused to be produced where the document is reasonably required for the proper conduct of a business.

(8) Where a lien is claimed on a document produced in accordance with paragraphs [(1) to (4B)][4], the removal of the document under paragraph (6)(*b*) shall not be regarded as breaking the lien.

(9) Where records are maintained by computer, the person required to make them available for inspection shall provide the authorised officer with all facilities necessary for obtaining information from them.

(10) By reference to information obtained from an inspection of the documents and records produced under paragraphs [(1) to (4B)][4], the collector may, on the occasion of each inspection, prepare a certificate showing—

(*a*) the amount which it appears from the documents and records so produced that the contractor is liable to pay to the collector under these Regulations for the years or income tax periods covered by the inspection; and

(*b*) any amount which has not been paid to him or, to the best of his knowledge and belief, to any other collector, or to any person acting on his behalf or on behalf of another collector.

(11) Paragraphs (1) to (5) of regulation 19 shall apply to the amount shown in a certificate under paragraph (10), with the modification that summary proceedings for the recovery of that amount, or such part of it as remains unpaid, may be brought at any time before the expiry of twelve months after the date of the certificate.

(12) The production of a certificate under paragraph (10) shall be sufficient evidence that the contractor is liable to pay the amount shown in the certificate under paragraph (10)(*b*) to the collector in respect of the years or income tax periods mentioned in the certificate.

(13) Any document purporting to be a certificate under paragraph (10) shall be deemed to be such a certificate until the contrary is proved.

(14) For the purposes of paragraphs [(1) to (4B)][4], such of the documents and records mentioned in those paragraphs as are not required by other provisions of these Regulations to be sent to the inspector or collector shall be retained by the contractor or the sub-contractor, as the case may be, for not less than three years after the end of the year to which they relate.

Commentary—*Simon's Direct Tax Service* **E5.531.**

Amendments—[1] Para (2) amended by the IT (Sub-contractors in the Construction Industry) (Amendment) Regulations, SI 1998/2622 reg 34(2), in relation to any application for the issue or renewal of a sub-contractor's tax certificate made with respect to any period beginning after 31 July 1999, and for all other purposes with effect from 1 August 1999.

[2] Words in para (3) revoked by SI 1998/2622 reg 34(3), with effect as in note 1 above.

[3] Paras (4A), (4B) inserted by SI 1998/2622 reg 34(4), with effect as in note 1 above.

[4] Words in paras (5), (6), (8), (10), (14) substituted by SI 1998/2622 reg 34(5), (6), with effect as in note 1 above.

[5] Words in para (4B) substituted by the Income Tax (Sub-contractors in the Construction Industry) (Amendment No 2) Regulations, SI 1999/2159 reg 8(*a*) with effect from 1 August 1999.

[6] Words in para (4B) revoked by SI 1999/2159 reg 8(*b*) with effect from 1 August 1999.

[Inspection of records of sub-contractors—additional provisions

41A—(1) Where a sum deducted under section 559 is treated as paid on account of the liabilities mentioned in regulation 44B(2), the sub-contractor, whose liabilities they are, shall—

(*a*) maintain the records specified in paragraph (2); and

(*b*) produce to an authorised officer of the Board for inspection those records, or such of them as may be specified by him, at such time as he may reasonably require, at the prescribed place.

(2) The records are all documents and records relating to the calculation of—

(*a*) the amounts which the sub-contractor would have been liable to pay to the collector in the preceding three years, under the provisions mentioned in regulation 44B(2), but for the withholding by a contractor of sums due to him; and

(*b*) the amounts deducted by a contractor under section 559 which the sub-contractor claims to be entitled to set off against those liabilities.

(3) In this regulation the ''prescribed place'' means—

(*a*) such place in the United Kingdom as the subcontractor and the authorised officer may agree upon; or

(*b*) in default of such agreement, at such place in the United Kingdom where the documents and records mentioned in paragraph (2) are normally kept, or

(*c*) in default of such agreement and if there is no such place referred to in sub- paragraph (*b*), the sub-contractor's principal place of business in the United Kingdom.

(4) The authorised officer may—

(*a*) take copies of, or make extracts from, any document produced to him for inspection in accordance with paragraph (1)(*b*); and

(*b*) remove any document so produced if it appears to him to be necessary to do so, at a reasonable time and for a reasonable period.

(5) Where a lien is claimed on a document produced in accordance with paragraph (1)(*b*), the removal of the document under paragraph (4)(*b*) shall not be treated as breaking the lien.

(6) Where records are maintained by computer, the person required to make them available for inspection shall provide the authorised officer with all facilities necessary for obtaining information from them.][1]

Amendments—[1] This regulation inserted by the IT (Sub-contractors in the Construction Industry and Employments) (Amendment) Regulations, SI 2003/536 regs 2, 7 with effect from 6 April 2003.

Information as to change in control of close company

42—(1) This regulation applies to a company which—

(*a*) is a close company;

(*b*) is a private company limited by shares; and

(*c*) either holds a certificate in force under section 561 or has applied for such a certificate.

(2) Where there is a change in the control of the company by reason of an issue or transfer of shares in the company to a person who was not a shareholder in the company immediately before the issue or transfer, the company shall, within 30 days of the issue or of receiving information as to the transfer, give notice to the inspector of the name and address of the person to whom the shares were issued or transferred.

(3) In this regulation ''control'' has the same meaning as in section 840 of the Taxes Act.

Death of contractor

43 If a contractor dies, anything which he would have been liable to do under these Regulations shall be done by his personal representatives.

Service by post

44 Any notice which is authorised or required to be given, served or issued under these Regulations may be sent by post.

[Electronic transmission

44A—(1) Where a document or particulars are transmitted electronically pursuant to regulations 7(4)(*b*), 37A(2)(*b*) or 40A(9)(*b*), a printed out version of the document or particulars transmitted electronically on that occasion, certified to be such by an officer of, or person nominated by, the Board, shall be conclusive evidence, unless the contrary is proved, that that document or particulars—

(*a*) was transmitted electronically on that occasion, and

(*b*) constitutes the entirety of what was transmitted on that occasion.

(2) Any document purporting to be a certificate in accordance with paragraph (1) shall be deemed to be such a certificate unless the contrary is proved.][1]

Amendments—[1] This regulation inserted by the IT (Sub-contractors in the Construction Industry) (Amendment) Regulations, SI 1998/2622 reg 35, in relation to any application for the issue or renewal of a sub-contractor's tax certificate made with respect to any period beginning after 31 July 1999, and for all other purposes with effect from 1 August 1999.

[Application by the Board of sums deducted under section 559

44B—(1) In the case of sums deducted from payments made to a sub-contractor which is a company ("the qualifying sub-contractor") the following provisions of this regulation apply.

(2) So much of any sum deducted under section 559 by a contractor in a year of assessment and paid to the collector as is required shall be applied by the Board—

(*a*) first, in discharge of any liability of the qualifying sub-contractor to account for primary Class 1 contributions in respect of earnings paid to his employees in that year;

(*b*) second, in discharge of any liability of the qualifying sub-contractor for secondary Class 1 contributions in respect of earnings paid to his employees in that year;

(*c*) third, in discharge of any liability of the qualifying sub-contractor to account for tax deducted from the emoluments of its employees under section 203 of the Taxes Act (pay as you earn) in respect of that year;

(*d*) fourth, in discharge of any liability of the qualifying sub-contractor to account for deductions made by it in that year from the emoluments of its employees in accordance with regulations made under section 22(5) of the Teaching and Higher Education Act 1998, section 73B(3) of the Education Scotland) Act 1980, or Article 3(5) of the Education (Student Support) (Northern Ireland) Order 1998;

(*e*) fifth, in discharge of any liability of the qualifying sub-contractor to refund to the Board any funding payment made by them in respect of statutory sick pay, statutory maternity pay, statutory paternity pay or statutory adoption pay under the relevant recovery provision;

(*f*) sixth, in respect of any liability of the qualifying sub-contractor to account for sums recoverable by the Board in respect of tax credits under regulation 12 of the Tax Credits (Payment by Employers) Regulations 2002; and

(*g*) last, in discharge of any liability of the qualifying sub-contractor to account for sums deducted by it (in its capacity as a contractor) under section 559 from payments made to other sub-contractors.

(3) So much of any sum deducted under section 559 as is not required to discharge the employer's liabilities specified in paragraph (2) shall be repaid to the qualifying sub-contractor.

This is subject to the qualifications in paragraphs (4) and (5).

(4) The Board shall not repay any sum deducted under section 559 to the qualifying sub-contractor until—

(*a*) the year of assessment, in which the deduction was made, has ended; and

(*b*) the qualifying sub-contractor has delivered the return required by regulation 43 of the Income Tax (Employments) Regulations 1993.

(5) If it appears to an officer of the Board that there is an outstanding liability of the qualifying sub-contractor in respect of corporation tax due for an accounting period ending before the relevant payment is made under section 559, the amount required to discharge that liability shall be retained by the Board and applied in discharge of that liability.

(6) In paragraph (2)(*e*) "the relevant recovery provision" means—

(*a*) in respect of statutory paternity pay and statutory adoption pay, regulations 4, 5, 6 and 8 of either the Statutory Paternity Pay and Statutory Adoption Pay (Administration) Regulations 2002 or the Statutory Paternity Pay and Statutory Adoption Pay (Administration) Regulations (Northern Ireland) 2002;

(*b*) in respect of statutory maternity pay, regulations 5, 6, 6A and 7A of the Statutory Maternity Pay (Compensation of Employers) and Miscellaneous Amendment Regulations 1994 or the Statutory Maternity Pay (Compensation of Employers) and Miscellaneous Amendment Regulations (Northern Ireland) 1994.][1]

Amendments—[1] This regulation inserted by the IT (Sub-Contractors in the Construction Industry and Employments) (Amendment) Regulations, SI 2003/536 regs 2, 8 with effect from 6 April 2003.

Revocations

45—(1) The Regulations specified in Schedule 3 to these Regulations are hereby revoked.

(2) ...[1]

Amendments—[1] Para (2) revoked by the IT (Sub-contractors in the Construction Industry) (Amendment) Regulations, SI 1998/2622 reg 36, in relation to any application for the issue or renewal of a sub-contractor's tax certificate made with respect to any period beginning after 31 July 1999, and for all other purposes with effect from 1 August 1999.

General savings

46—(1) In relation to the collection and recovery (whether by assessment or otherwise) of sums required, under the Income Tax (Sub-contractors in the Construction Industry) Regulations 1975, to be deducted from any payments under section 559 made before 6th April 1993, these Regulations shall have effect as if those sums had been liable to be deducted under these Regulations, and accordingly references to any provision of these Regulations shall, where the context so requires, be construed as references to the corresponding provision of the Income Tax (Sub-contractors in the Construction Industry) Regulations 1975.

(2) Anything whatsoever begun under any regulation revoked by these Regulations may be continued under these Regulations as if begun under these Regulations.

[PART 6
ELECTRONIC COMMUNICATIONS][1]

Amendments—[1] This Part inserted by the Income Tax (Sub-contractors in the Construction Industry) (Amendment) Regulations, SI 2004/1075 regs 2, 8 with effect from 28 April 2004.

[Interpretation

47 In this Part—

"official computer system" means a computer system maintained by or on behalf of the Board of Inland Revenue or an officer of the Board;

"PAYE Regulations" means the Income Tax (Pay As You Earn) Regulations 2003;

"specified payment" means the amount due under regulation 8 (monthly payment of amounts deducted to collector) in respect of contract payments made in the tax year to which the e-payment notice issued under regulation 199 of the PAYE Regulations relates;

"tax year" has the meaning given in regulation 2(1) of the PAYE Regulations.][1]

Amendments—[1] This Part inserted by the Income Tax (Sub-contractors in the Construction Industry) (Amendment) Regulations, SI 2004/1075 regs 2, 8 with effect from 28 April 2004.

[Proof of payment sent electronically

48 (1) The use of a method of electronic communications is presumed, unless the contrary is proved, to have resulted in the making of a payment—

(*a*) to the Inland Revenue, if the making of the payment has been recorded on an official computer system;

(*b*) by the Inland Revenue, if despatch of the payment has been recorded on an official computer system.

(2) The use of a method of electronic communications is presumed, unless the contrary is proved, not to have resulted in the making of a payment—

(*a*) to the Inland Revenue, if the making of the payment has not been recorded on an official computer system;

(*b*) by the Inland Revenue, if despatch of the payment has not been recorded on an official computer system.

(3) The time of receipt or despatch of any payment sent by a method of electronic communications is presumed, unless the contrary is proved, to be the time recorded on an official computer system.

(4) In this regulation "the Inland Revenue" means the Board of Inland Revenue or any officer of the Board.][1]

Amendments—[1] This Part inserted by the Income Tax (Sub-contractors in the Construction Industry) (Amendment) Regulations, SI 2004/1075 regs 2, 8 with effect from 28 April 2004.

[Mandatory electronic payment

49 (1) If an e-payment notice has been issued to a contractor in respect of a tax year under regulation 199 of the PAYE Regulations (large employers required to make specified payments under those Regulations electronically), he must pay the specified payment using an approved method of electronic communications.

(2) Paragraph (1) applies regardless of whether a payment of tax is due under regulation 68 of the PAYE Regulations (payment and recovery of tax by employer).

(3) If the Board have given a direction under regulation 199(3) of the PAYE Regulations requiring a particular method of electronic communications to be used in the case of a contractor, he must use that method.][1]

Amendments—[1] This Part inserted by the Income Tax (Sub-contractors in the Construction Industry) (Amendment) Regulations, SI 2004/1075 regs 2, 8 with effect from 28 April 2004.

[Contractor in default if specified payment not received by applicable due date

50 (1) This regulation applies if a contractor is required to make a specified payment by an approved method of electronic communications in accordance with regulation 49.

(2) The contractor is in default if the specified payment is not received in full by the Board (whether by an approved method of electronic communications or otherwise) on or before the date by which that payment is required in accordance with regulation 8 (''the applicable date'').

(3) But the contractor is not in default if—

(*a*) the contractor had a reasonable excuse for failing to make the specified payment in a manner which secures that it is received in full by the Board on or before the applicable due date, and

(*b*) the specified payment is received in full by the Board without unreasonable delay after the excuse ceased.

(4) Inability to pay is not a reasonable excuse for the purposes of sub-paragraph (3)(*a*).

(5) A payment is not treated as received in full by the Board on or before the date by which that payment is required in accordance with regulation 8 unless it is made in a manner which secures (in a case where the payment is made otherwise than in cash) that, on or before that date, all transactions can be completed which need to be completed before the whole amount of the payment becomes available to the Board.][1]

Amendments—[1] This Part inserted by the Income Tax (Sub-contractors in the Construction Industry) (Amendment) Regulations, SI 2004/1075 regs 2, 8 with effect from 28 April 2004.

[Default notice and appeal

51 (1) The Board must issue a default notice to any person who appears to be in default under regulation 50 in respect of a specified payment.

(2) A person may appeal against a default notice by giving notice to the Board within 30 days of the issue of the default notice.

(3) The ground of appeal is that the person is not in default.

(4) If the appeal is successful the default notice must be withdrawn.

(5) Regulation 54 (appeals: supplementary provisions) applies to appeals under this paragraph.][1]

Amendments—[1] This Part inserted by the Income Tax (Sub-contractors in the Construction Industry) (Amendment) Regulations, SI 2004/1075 regs 2, 8 with effect from 28 April 2004.

[Default surcharge

52 (1) A contractor in default in respect of any specified payment to whom—

(*a*) a default notice under regulation 51, and

(*b*) a surcharge notice under regulation 53,

have been issued, is liable to a surcharge.

(2) The surcharge is the sum of the surcharges, calculated in accordance with paragraph (3), in respect of each default relating to the tax year in which were made the contract payments to which the specified payment referred to in paragraph (1) relates.

(3) The surcharge in respect of each default is the specified percentage of (A – B).

(4) In paragraph (3)—

(*a*) A is the total amount the contractor was liable to deduct under section 559 in respect of contract payments made in the tax year in which the contract payments to which the specified payment relates were made;

(*b*) B is the total of the amounts deducted from A under—

(i) rule 5 of regulation 7(2) of the Working Tax Credit (Payment by Employers) Regulations 2002;

(ii) regulations 4, 5 and 6 of the Statutory Maternity Pay (Compensation of Employers) and Miscellaneous Amendment Regulations 1994,

(iii) regulations 3 and 5 of the Statutory Paternity Pay and Statutory Adoption Pay (Administration) Regulations 2002, and

(iv) regulation 44B (application by the Board of sums deducted under section 559);

(*c*) the specified percentage is determined by reference to the number of the default during a surcharge period in accordance with Table 1.

TABLE 1

SPECIFIED PERCENTAGE FOR EACH DEFAULT IN A SURCHARGE PERIOD

1 Default number (within a surcharge period)	*2 Specified percentage*
1st	0%
2nd	0%
3rd	0.17%
4th	0.17%
5th	0.17%
6th	0.33%

1 Default number (within a surcharge period)	*2 Specified percentage*
7th	0.33%
8th	0.33%
9th	0.58%
10th	0.58%
11th	0.58%
12th	0.83%

(5) A surcharge period is a period which—

(*a*) begins on the day following the date by which payment is required in accordance with paragraph 10 for the first specified payment in respect of which the contractor is in default, and

(*b*) ends at the end of a tax year in relation to which the contractor has not been in default in respect of any specified payment.

(6) A surcharge payable under this paragraph is payable 30 days after the issue of the surcharge notice.

(7) Section 102 of the Management Act (mitigation of penalties) applies to a surcharge payable under this paragraph as if it were a penalty.][1]

Amendments—[1] This Part inserted by the Income Tax (Sub-contractors in the Construction Industry) (Amendment) Regulations, SI 2004/1075 regs 2, 8 with effect from 28 April 2004.

[Surcharge notice and appeal

53 (1) The Board must issue a surcharge notice to a contractor who has been in default on three or more occasions during a surcharge period and consequently will be liable to a surcharge under regulation 52.

(2) The surcharge notice must show the total surcharge liability for the tax year.

(3) The surcharge notice must be issued within 6 years of—

(*a*) the end of the tax year, or

(*b*) if earlier, the date on which the contractor delivered a return in accordance with regulation 73 of the PAYE Regulations (annual return of relevant payments liable to deduction of tax (Forms P35 and P14)).

(4) A contractor may appeal against a surcharge notice by giving notice to the Board within 30 days of the issue of the surcharge notice.

(5) The grounds of appeal are—

(*a*) that the numbers of defaults stated in the notice is incorrect, or

(*b*) that the amount of the surcharge is incorrect.

(6) But paragraph (5)(*a*) does not apply in respect of a disputed default which has already been the subject of an appeal under regulation 51, following which the default notice was not withdrawn.][1]

Amendments—[1] This Part inserted by the Income Tax (Sub-contractors in the Construction Industry) (Amendment) Regulations, SI 2004/1075 regs 2, 8 with effect from 28 April 2004.

[Appeals: supplementary provisions

54 (1) The following provisions of the Management Act apply to appeals under regulation 51 (default notices and appeal), as they apply to an appeal under section 31 of that Act—

(*a*) section 31A(5) and (6) (notice of appeal);

(*b*) section 31B (appeals to General Commissioners);

(*c*) section 31D (election to bring appeal before Special Commissioners).

(2) In an appeal under regulation 51 or regulation 53(4) (surcharge notice and appeal), the relevant place for the purposes of paragraph 3(1)(*a*) of Schedule 3 to the Management Act (rules for assigning proceedings to General Commissioners) is the place which at the time of the notice of appeal is—

(*a*) the contractor's place of business in the United Kingdom, or

(*b*) if there is no such place, the contractor's place of residence in the United Kingdom.

(3) In paragraph (2)—

''place of business'' means—

(*a*) the place where the trade, profession, vocation or business with which the proceedings are concerned is carried out, or

(*b*) if more than one such place, the head office or place where it is mainly carried out; and

''place of residence'' means the contractor's usual place of residence or, if that is unknown, the contractor's last known place of residence.][1]

Amendments—[1] This Part inserted by the Income Tax (Sub-contractors in the Construction Industry) (Amendment) Regulations, SI 2004/1075 regs 2, 8 with effect from 28 April 2004.

[SCHEDULE A1

Regulation 3A

BODIES TO WHICH SUBSECTION (2) OF SECTION 560 APPLIES

Amendments—This schedule inserted by the IT (Sub-contractors in the Construction Industry) (Amendment) Regulations, SI 1998/2622 reg 37, in relation to any application for the issue or renewal of a sub-contractor's tax certificate made with respect to any period beginning after 31 July 1999, and for all other purposes with effect from 1 August 1999.

[1 Any NHS trust

2 The Corporate Officers of the House of Commons and the House of Lords

[3 Health and Social Services trusts established under Article 10 of the Health and Personal Social Services (Northern Ireland) Order 1991]1

[4 The Scottish Parliamentary Corporate Body]2

Amendments—[1] Para 3 inserted by the Income Tax (Sub-contractors in the Construction Industry) (Amendment No 2) Regulations, SI 1999/2159 reg 9 with effect from 1 August 1999.

[2] Para 4 inserted by the Income Tax (Sub-contractors in the Construction Industry) (Amendment No 2) Regulations, SI 2000/1880 reg 2 with effect from 6 August 2000.

[SCHEDULE 1

Regulations 7, 7C, 24, 29, 35 and 37A

FORMS OF SUB-CONTRACTOR'S TAX CERTIFICATES, TAX PAYMENT VOUCHERS, GROSS PAYMENT VOUCHERS, CONSTRUCTION GROSS PAYMENT VOUCHERS AND REGISTRATION CARDS]

Amendments—[1] This schedule substituted by the IT (Sub-contractors in the Construction Industry) (Amendment) Regulations, SI 1998/2622 reg 38, in relation to any application for the issue or renewal of a sub-contractor's tax certificate made with respect to any period beginning after 31 July 1999, and for all other purposes with effect from 1 August 1999.

Form CIS6 Face

Inland Revenue

Subcontractors Tax Certificate

[Space for photo image]

Certificate Number:
[space for number]
NI Number:
[space for number]

[space for barcode]

Start date: *[space for date]* Expires end: *[space for date]*
Authorised user: *[space for name]*
Acting for: *[space for name]*
Trading as: *[space for name]*
Authorised user: *[space for signature image]*
CIS6(BMSD8/98)

SPECIMEN

Form CIS6 Reverse

This certificate may be used only by the authorised user in conjunction with subcontractors vouchers issued to him. It must be surrendered on demand by the Inland Revenue. If found please hand in at any Police Station or any Income Tax Office.

Any misuse of this certificate, including allowing any other person to use it, is a serious offence which may lead to penalties or prosecution.

SPECIMEN

Form CIS5 Face

Inland Revenue

Construction
Tax Certificate

[space for barcode]

Certificate Number:
[space for number] *[space for original or copy]*

Company Registration Number: *[space for number]*

Start date: *[space for date]* Expires end: *[space for date]*

Issued to: *[space for name]*

Trading as: *[space for name]*

Company Secretary: *[space for signature image]*

CIS5(BMSD8/98)

Form CIS5 Reverse

This certificate may be used only by the Company named on it. It must be surrendered on demand by the Inland Revenue. If found please hand in at any Police Station or any Income Tax Office.

Any misuse of this certificate, including allowing any other person to use it, is a serious offence which may lead to penalties or prosecution.

Form CIS5(Partner) Face

Inland Revenue

Construction
Tax Certificate

Certificate Number:
[space for number]

[space for original]

[space for barcode]

Start date: *[space for date]* Expires end: *[space for date]*
Acting for: *[space for name]*
Trading as: *[space for name]*

Issued to: *[space for signature image]*

CIS5 (Partner)

SPECIMEN

Form CIS5(Partner) Reverse

This Tax Certificate may be used only by the person to whom it is issued. It must be surrendered on demand by the Inland Revenue. If found please hand in at any Police Station or any Inland Revenue office.

Any misuse of this Tax Certificate, including allowing any other person to use it, is a serious offence which may lead to penalties or prosecution.

(BMSD11/00)

SPECIMEN

Form CIS4(P) Face

Inland Revenue **Registration Card**

[space for barcode]

Card Number:
[space for number]
NI Number:
[space for number]

[Space for photo image]

Authorised user: *[space for name]*
Acting for: *[space for name]*
Trading as: *[space for name]*

Authorised user: *[space for signature image]*

CIS4(P)(BMSD8/98)

SPECIMEN

Form CIS4(P) Reverse

This card may be used only by the named user. It must be surrendered on demand by the Inland Revenue. If found please hand in at any Police Station or any Income Tax Office.

Any misuse of this card, including allowing any other person to use it, is a serious offence which may lead to penalties or prosecution.

SPECIMEN

Form CIS4(T) Face

Revenue

Temporary Registration Card

[space for barcode]

Card Number:
[space for number]

Expires end:
[space for date]

Authorised user: *[space for name]*

Acting for: *[space for name]*

Trading as: *[space for name]*

[Space for photo image]

Authorised user: *[space for signature image]*

CIS4(T)(BMSD8/98)

SPECIMEN

Form CIS4(T) Reverse

This card may be used only by the named user. It must be surrendered on demand by the Inland Revenue. If found please hand in at any Police Station or any Income Tax Office.

Any misuse of this card, including allowing any other person to use it, is a serious offence which may lead to penalties or prosecution.

SPECIMEN

Construction Gross Payment Voucher CIS23 - Manual (M) and Continuous (I) versions

Form CIS23(M) and CIS23(I) — Page 1 Face

Revenue *Construction Industry Scheme*

Construction Gross Payment Voucher □

Voucher number [space for number]

Certificate number [space for number]

I, [space for name of Contractor]

complete and certify this voucher in respect of payment to

Name of Subcontractor to be inserted by Contractor

[space for name of Subcontractor]

It covers payments within the month to 0 5 [space for date]

Gross payment £

SPECIMEN

Contractor's signature [space for signature]

Contractor tax reference [space for number]

CIS23 (BMSD 7/98) **Inland Revenue copy**

Any person involved in the misuse of this document is liable to prosecution □

Form CIS23(M) and CIS23(I) — Page 2 Face

Revenue *Construction Industry Scheme*

Construction Gross Payment Voucher □

Voucher number [space for number]

Certificate number [space for number]

I, [space for name of Contractor]

complete and certify this voucher in respect of payment to

Name of Subcontractor to be inserted by Contractor

[space for name of Subcontractor]

It covers payments within the month to 0 5 [space for date]

Gross payment £

SPECIMEN

Contractor's signature [space for signature]

Contractor tax reference [space for number]

CIS23 (BMSD 7/98) **Contractor copy**

Any person involved in the misuse of this document is liable to prosecution □

Subcontractors Gross Payment Voucher CIS24

Form CIS24 — Page 1 Face

Revenue *Construction Industry Scheme*

Subcontractors Gross Payment Voucher

Voucher number [space for number]

I, [space for name of Subcontractor]

certify that I am the holder of a Gross Payment Certificate which I have produced to

[space for name of Contractor]

Contractor name to be inserted by Subcontractor

Contractor tax reference [space for number]

CIS24 (BMSD 7/98) Inland Revenue copy

Reference number [space for number]

Subcontractors National Insurance number [space for number]

It covers payments within the month to 0 5 [space for date]

Gross amount of payment £ [space for amount]

Subcontractor's signature [space for signature]

Any person involved in the misuse of this document is liable to prosecution

SPECIMEN

Form CIS24 — Page 2 Face

Revenue *Construction Industry Scheme*

Subcontractors Gross Payment Voucher

Voucher number [space for number]

I, [space for name of Subcontractor]

certify that I am the holder of a Gross Payment Certificate which I have produced to

[space for name of Contractor]

Contractor name to be inserted by Subcontractor

Contractor tax reference [space for number]

CIS24 (BMSD 7/98) Subcontractor copy

Reference number [space for number]

Subcontractors National Insurance number [space for number]

It covers payments within the month to 0 5 [space for date]

Gross amount of payment £ [space for amount]

Subcontractor's signature [space for signature]

Any person involved in the misuse of this document is liable to prosecution

SPECIMEN

Form CIS24 — Page 2 Reverse

[space for Subcontractors name and address, to be inserted by Printer]

Form CIS24 — Page 3 Face

Revenue *Construction Industry Scheme*

Subcontractors Gross Payment Voucher

Voucher number [space for number]

I, [space for name of Subcontractor]

certify that I am the holder of a Gross Payment Certificate which I have produced to

[space for name of Contractor]

Contractor name to be inserted by Subcontractor

Contractor tax reference [space for number]

CIS24 (BMSD 7/98) Contractor copy

Reference number [space for number]

Subcontractors National Insurance number [space for number]

It covers payments within the month to 0 5 [space for date]

Gross amount of payment £ [space for amount]

Subcontractor's signature [space for signature]

Any person involved in the misuse of this document is liable to prosecution

SPECIMEN

SIS

Tax Payment Voucher CIS25(E)

Form CIS25(E) Page 1 Face

Revenue *Construction Industry Scheme*

Tax Payment Voucher

Card number [space for number]

Voucher number [space for number]

I, [space for name of Contractor]

complete and certify this voucher in respect of payment to

Name of Subcontractor to be inserted by Contractor

[space for name and address of Subcontractor]

National Insurance number [space for number]

It covers payments within the month to 0 5 [space for date]

Gross amount of payment £ [space for amount] (excl VAT)

Less cost of materials £ [space for amount] (excl VAT)

Amount liable to deduction £ [space for amount]

Amount deducted £ [space for amount] p

Contractor's signature [space for signature]

Contractor tax reference [space for number]

Any person involved in the misuse of this document is liable to prosecution

CIS25(E)(BMSD 7/98) [space for sequential number] [space for "Suncontractor Copy"]

SPECIMEN

Tax Payment Voucher CIS25(I)

Form CIS25(I) **Page 1 Face**

Revenue *Construction Industry Scheme*

Tax Payment Voucher

Card number [space for number]

Voucher number [space for number]

[space for name of Contractor]

complete and certify this voucher in respect of payment to

Name of Subcontractor to be inserted by Contractor

[space for name and address of Subcontractor]

National Insurance number [space for number]

It covers payments within the month to 0 5 [space for date]

Gross amount of payment £ [space for amount] (excl VAT)

Less cost of materials £ [space for amount] (excl VAT)

Amount liable to deduction £ [space for amount]

Amount deducted £ [space for amount] : p

Contractor's signature [space for signature]

Contractor tax reference [space for number]

CIS25(I)(BMSD 7/98) [space for "Inland Revenue Copy"]

Any person involved in the misuse of this document is liable to prosecution

SPECIMEN

Form CIS25(I) **Page 2 Face**

Revenue *Construction Industry Scheme*

Tax Payment Voucher

Card number [space for number]

Voucher number [space for number]

[space for name of Contractor]

complete and certify this voucher in respect of payment to

Name of Subcontractor to be inserted by Contractor

[space for name and address of Subcontractor]

National Insurance number [space for number]

It covers payments within the month to 0 5 [space for date]

Gross amount of payment £ [space for amount] (excl VAT)

Less cost of materials £ [space for amount] (excl VAT)

Amount liable to deduction £ [space for amount]

Amount deducted £ [space for amount] : p

Contractor tax reference [space for number]

CIS25(I)(BMSD 7/98) **Subcontractor copy**

Any person involved in the misuse of this document is liable to prosecution

SPECIMEN

Form CIS25(I) **Page 3 Face**

Revenue *Construction Industry Scheme*

Tax Payment Voucher

Card number [space for number]

Voucher number [space for number]

[space for name of Contractor]

complete and certify this voucher in respect of payment to

Name of Subcontractor to be inserted by Contractor

[space for name and address of Subcontractor]

National Insurance number [space for number]

It covers payments within the month to 0 5 [space for date]

Gross amount of payment £ [space for amount] (excl VAT)

Less cost of materials £ [space for amount] (excl VAT)

Amount liable to deduction £ [space for amount]

Amount deducted £ [space for amount] : p

Contractor's signature [space for signature]

Contractor tax reference [space for number]

CIS25(I)(BMSD 7/98) **Contractors copy**

Any person involved in the misuse of this document is liable to prosecution

SPECIMEN

Tax Payment Voucher CIS25(M)

Form CIS25(M)

Page 1 Face

Revenue *Construction Industry Scheme*

Tax Payment Voucher

Card number [space for number]

Voucher number [space for number]

I, [space for name of Contractor]

complete and certify this voucher in respect of payment to

Name of Subcontractor to be inserted by Contractor

[space for name and address of Subcontractor]

National Insurance number [space for number]

It covers payments within the month to 0 5 [space for date]

Gross amount of payment £ [space for amount] (excl VAT)

Less cost of materials £ [space for amount] (excl VAT)

Amount liable to deduction £ [space for amount]

Amount deducted £ [space for amount] : p

Contractor's signature [space for signature]

Contractor tax reference [space for number]

CIS25(M)(BMSD 7/98) [space for "Inland Revenue Copy"]

Any person involved in the misuse of this document is liable to prosecution

SPECIMEN

Form CIS25(M)

Page 2 Face

Revenue *Construction Industry Scheme*

Tax Payment Voucher

Card number [space for number]

Voucher number [space for number]

I, [space for name of Contractor]

complete and certify this voucher in respect of payment to

Name of Subcontractor to be inserted by Contractor

[space for name and address of Subcontractor]

National Insurance number [space for number]

It covers payments within the month to 0 5 [space for date]

Gross amount of payment £ [space for amount] (excl VAT)

Less cost of materials £ [space for amount] (excl VAT)

Amount liable to deduction £ [space for amount]

Amount deducted £ [space for amount] : p

Contractor tax reference [space for number]

CIS25(M)(BMSD 7/98) Subcontractor copy

Any person involved in the misuse of this document is liable to prosecution

SPECIMEN

Form CIS25(M)

Page 3 Face

Revenue *Construction Industry Scheme*

Tax Payment Voucher

Card number [space for number]

Voucher number [space for number]

I, [space for name of Contractor]

complete and certify this voucher in respect of payment to

Name of Subcontractor to be inserted by Contractor

[space for name and address of Subcontractor]

National Insurance number [space for number]

It covers payments within the month to 0 5 [space for date]

Gross amount of payment £ [space for amount] (excl VAT)

Less cost of materials £ [space for amount] (excl VAT)

Amount liable to deduction £ [space for amount]

Amount deducted £ [space for amount] : p

Contractor's signature [space for signature]

Contractor tax reference [space for number]

CIS25(M)(BMSD 7/98) Contractors copy

Any person involved in the misuse of this document is liable to prosecution

SPECIMEN

SCHEDULE 2

Regulation 32

FORMS OF GUARANTEE

Amendments—Sch 1 above substituted for this Schedule (together with Sch 1 as originally enacted) by the IT (Sub-contractors in the Construction Industry) (Amendment) Regulations, SI 1998/2622 reg 38, in relation to any application for the issue or renewal of a sub-contractor's tax certificate made with respect to any period beginning after 31 July 1999, and for all other purposes with effect from 1 August 1999.

1993/744
Income Tax (Employments) Regulations 1993

Made by the Commissioners of Inland Revenue under TA 1988 ss 203, 204, 824(5) and TMA 1970 s 98A(1)

Made	*16 March 1993*
Laid before the House of Commons	*16 March 1993*
Coming into Force	*6 April 1993*

Amendment—These regulations are revoked by the Income Tax (Pay As You Earn) Regulations, SI 2003/2682 reg 220, Sch 2 with effect from 6 April 2004, subject to the transitional provisions in Sch 1 thereto.

PART I
INTRODUCTORY

Citation and commencement

1—(1) These Regulations may be cited as the Income Tax (Employments) Regulations 1993.

(2) These Regulations shall come into force on 6th April 1993 immediately after the Income Tax (Employments) (No 24) Regulation 1993, the Income Tax (Employments) (No 25) Regulations 1993 and the Income Tax (Employments) (No 26) Regulations 1993.

Interpretation

2—(1) In these Regulations unless the context otherwise requires—

"additional pay" means the appropriate amount required by a code authorisation to be added to the emoluments paid to an employee in order to determine the taxable emoluments;

"allowable superannuation contributions" means any sum paid by an employee by way of contribution towards a superannuation fund or scheme which is allowed to be deducted as an expense under Schedule E;

"basic rate" has the same meaning as in section 832(1) of the Taxes Act;

"the Board" means the Commissioners of Inland Revenue;

"code" means any part of the tax tables in which all the amounts of free emoluments or additional pay for any period have been calculated on the basis of the same total amount for the whole year, and references to code include any designation thereof by numbers and letters, alone or in combination;

"code authorisation" means a notice specifying the appropriate code given by an inspector to an employer;

"collector" means a collector of taxes;

"cumulative additional pay", in relation to any date, means the sum of the additional pay from the beginning of the year up to and including that date;

"cumulative emoluments", in relation to any date, means the sum of all payments of emoluments made by the employer to the employee from the beginning of the year up to and including that date;

"cumulative free emoluments", in relation to any date, means the sum of the free emoluments from the beginning of the year up to and including that date;

"cumulative tax" means the tax due in accordance with the appropriate tax tables in respect of any cumulative taxable emoluments at the relevant date;

"cumulative taxable emoluments", in relation to any date, means the cumulative emoluments reduced by the cumulative free emoluments or, as the case may be, increased by the cumulative additional pay;

"deductions working sheet" means any form of record on or in which are to be kept the matters required by these Regulations in connection with an employee's emoluments and tax, or, in regulations 20 and 104, the form issued by the inspector for the purpose of keeping that record;

"earnings-related contributions" means contributions payable under the Social Security Contributions and Benefits Act 1992 or, in Northern Ireland, the Social Security Contributions and Benefits (Northern Ireland) Act 1992 by or in respect of an employed earner in respect of employed earner's employment;

["electronic communications" has the meaning given by section 132(10) of the Finance Act 1999 [but does not include the electronic transmission of information as defined in paragraph (4);][8] and "approved" in relation to a means of electronic communications means approved by directions issued by or on behalf of the Board;][5]

"emoluments" means the full amount of any income to be taken into account in assessing liability under Schedule E after the deduction of—

(a) allowable superannuation contributions, and

(b) any sum withheld from an employee in accordance with section 202 of the Taxes Act,

...[2];

"employed earner" and "employed earner's employment" have the same meaning as in the Social Security Contributions and Benefits Act 1992 or, in Northern Ireland, the Social Security Contributions and Benefits (Northern Ireland) Act 1992;

"employee" means any person in receipt of emoluments;

"employer" means any person paying emoluments;

"free emoluments" means the appropriate amount of any emoluments of the employee which qualify for relief from income tax;

"higher rate" has the same meaning as in section 832(1) of the Taxes Act;

"income tax month" means the period beginning on the 6th day of any calendar month and ending on the 5th day of the following calendar month;

"income tax period" means income tax quarter where regulation 41 has effect, but otherwise means income tax month;

"income tax quarter" means the period beginning on the 6th day of April and ending on the 5th day of July, or beginning on the 6th day of July and ending on the 5th day of October, or beginning on the 6th day of October and ending on the 5th day of January or beginning on the 6th day of January and ending on the 5th day of April;

"inspector" means an inspector of taxes;

"lower rate" has the same meaning as in section 832(1) of the Taxes Act;

"the Management Act" means the Taxes Management Act 1970;

"notice" means notice in writing;

[''official computer system" means a computer system maintained by or on behalf of the Board for the purpose of the service known as the Internet Service for PAYE;][5]

"overriding limit" means the limit on the amount of tax to be deducted from a payment of emoluments where the tax due in accordance with the appropriate tax tables in respect of any taxable emoluments at the relevant date has been calculated by reference to additional pay, and that limit shall be an amount equal to 50 per cent of the amount of the emoluments paid;

"pension emoluments" means any payment of emoluments comprising a pension or annuity assessable to income tax under Schedule E;

"previous cumulative tax" means the cumulative tax corresponding to the employee's cumulative emoluments at the later of the date of the last preceding payment of emoluments or the date last treated as the occasion on which emoluments were paid;

"reliefs from income tax" includes allowances and deductions but not allowable superannuation contributions;

[''starting rate" has the same meaning as in section 832(1) of the Taxes Act;][4]

"tax not deducted" means tax due in accordance with the appropriate tax tables in respect of any taxable emoluments at the relevant date which as a consequence of the overriding limit has not been deducted;

"tax tables" means the tax tables prepared by the Board under section 203 of the Taxes Act, and "simplified tax tables" means such of those tax tables as are prepared by the Board for use where, under regulation 20, tax is deductible without reference to cumulative emoluments and cumulative tax;

"taxable emoluments" means emoluments reduced by free emoluments or, as the case may be, increased by additional pay;

"the Taxes Act" means the Income and Corporation Taxes Act 1988;

"total net tax deducted", in relation to the emoluments paid to any employee during any period, means the total tax deducted from those emoluments less any tax repaid to the employee;

"trade dispute" has the meaning given by section 27(3) of the Social Security Contributions and Benefits Act 1992 or, in Northern Ireland, section 27(3) of the Social Security Contributions and Benefits (Northern Ireland) Act 1992;

"year" means year of assessment and "current year" shall be construed accordingly.

(2) The table below indexes other general definitions in these Regulations—

Term defined	*Regulation*
the minimum rate	*28(2)*
the prescribed place	*55(3)*
the reckonable date	*51(3).*

[(3) References, however expressed, in these Regulations to payments of emoluments include references to payments on account of emoluments but, except in regulation 46(2)(b), do not include references to payments of emoluments consisting of qualifying removal expenses within the meaning of paragraph 3 of Schedule 11A to the Taxes Act, where the total value to the employee found under paragraph 24(2) of that Schedule exceeds the qualifying limit for the time being specified in paragraph 24(9) of that Schedule and having effect in relation to that employee.][1]

[(4) In these Regulations references to electronic transmission of information, or to something being transmitted electronically are references (and are references only) to the transmission of information—

(a) from a computer system maintained by or on behalf of an officer of the Board to the employer's computer system, or

(b) from the employer's computer system to that maintained by or on behalf of an officer of the Board,

by means of the system operated on behalf of the Board and known as Electronic Data Interchange, and references to a 'transmitter' are references to the person by whom such information is transmitted in that way.

In this paragraph references to the employer's computer system are to the computer system used by or on behalf of the employer for the receipt, processing or storage of payroll information.][6]

[(4A) For the purposes of these Regulations, information shall only be taken—

(a) to have been transmitted electronically, to a computer system maintained by or on behalf of an officer of the Board, or

(b) delivered by means of electronic communications to an official computer system, if it is accepted by the system to which it is transmitted or delivered.][7]

(5) A document certified by an inspector or other officer of the Board to be a printed out version of any particulars transmitted electronically under these Regulations on any occasion shall be conclusive evidence, unless the contrary is proved, that those particulars—

(a) were transmitted electronically on that occasion, and

(b) constitute the entirety of what was transmitted on that occasion.

[(5A) A document certified by an officer of the Board to be a printed-out version of any electronic communication recorded on an official computer system under these Regulations as at a particular date shall be presumed, unless the contrary is proved—

(a) to have been recorded on an official computer system at that date; and

(b) to constitute the entirety of the electronic communication so recorded.][7]

(6) Any document purporting to be a certificate in accordance with paragraph [(5) or (5A)][6] *shall be deemed to be such a certificate unless the contrary is proved.]*[3]

Revenue & other press releases—*ICAEW TR799 June 1990 (the definition of "employer" includes, in the case of a company in administration, the administrator if he pays emoluments to employees of the company; he is liable to deduct and account for PAYE/NIC deductions).*

Share Scheme Lawyer's Group 17-7-95 (Revenue agree that a payment to an employee for cancellation or surrender of share options is not subject to PAYE even though part or all of it may fall within Schedule E).

Simon's Tax Cases—*Booth v Mirror Group Newspapers plc [1992] STC 615*; IRC v Herd [1993] STC 436*.*

Reg 2(1), R v Walton General Comrs, ex p Wilson [1983] STC 464.*

Modification—*Reg 2(1) definition of "total net tax deducted" modified in relation to amounts accounted for in respect of notional payments made under TA 1988 s 203J(3), and the following provisions in this Regulation applied—*

(a) Parts I, III, IV and V

(b) Part VIII regs 99–105

(c) Part IX reg 109

by the IT (Employments) (Notional Payments) Regulations, SI 1994/1212 reg 13(1), (2), (3) with effect from 6 April 1994. Reg 2(1) has effect as if the words ", and the total tax accounted for in accordance with section 203J(3) of the Taxes Act" were added in the definition of "total net tax deducted" after the words "the employee".

Amendments—[1] *Para (3) added by the IT (Employments) (Amendment) Regulations, SI 1993/2276 regs 1, 2, 3, with effect from 12 October 1993.*

[2] *Words in the definition of "emoluments" in para (1) revoked by SI 1993/2276 regs 1, 2, 3.*

[3] *Paras (4), (5) and (6) inserted by the IT (Employments) (Amendment) Regulations, SI 1998/2484 reg 3 with effect from 28 October 1998.*

[4] *Definition "starting rate" inserted by the Income Tax (Employments) (Amendment No 3) Regulations, SI 1999/2155 reg 8 with effect from the year 1999–00.*

[5] *Definition of "electronic communications" and "official computer system" added by the Income Tax (Electronic Communications) (Miscellaneous Amendments) Regulations, SI 2001/1081 regs 7, 8(2) with effect from 9 April 2001.*

[6] *Para (4) and words in para (5) substituted by SI 2001/1081 regs 7, 8(3), (6) with effect from 9 April 2001.*

[7] *Paras (4A), (5A) inserted by SI 2001/1081 regs 7, 8(4), (5) with effect from 9 April 2001.*

[8] *In para (1), words in definition of "electronic communications" inserted, and paras (4A)–(6) repealed by the Income Tax (Employments and Electronic Communications) (Miscellaneous Provisions) Regulations, SI 2002/680 regs 3, 4 with effect from 8 April 2002.*

[Whether information transmitted electronically or delivered by means of electronic communications

2A For the purposes of these Regulations, information shall be taken to have been—

(a) transmitted electronically to a computer system maintained by or on behalf of an officer of the Board, or

(b) delivered to an official computer system by means of electronic communications,

only if it is accepted by the system to which it is transmitted or delivered.][1]

Amendments—[1] *Regs 2A–2E inserted by the Income Tax (Employments and Electronic Communications) (Miscellaneous Provisions) Regulations, SI 2002/680 regs 3, 5 with effect from 8 April 2002.*

[Proof of content of an electronic transmission and of information delivered electronically

2B—(1) A document certified by an officer of the Board to be a printed-out version of any particulars transmitted electronically under these Regulations on any occasion shall be evidence, unless the contrary is proved, that those particulars—

(a) were transmitted electronically on that occasion; and

(b) constitute the entirety of what was transmitted on that occasion.

(2) A document certified by an officer of the Board to be a printed-out version of any information delivered by means of electronic communications under these Regulations on any occasion shall be evidence, unless the contrary is proved, that that information—

(a) was delivered by means of electronic communications on that occasion; and
(b) constitutes the entirety of what was delivered on that occasion.

(3) A document purporting to be a certificate given in accordance with paragraph (1) or (2) shall be presumed to be such a certificate unless the contrary is proved.][1]

Amendments—[1] Regs 2A–2E inserted by the Income Tax (Employments and Electronic Communications) (Miscellaneous Provisions) Regulations, SI 2002/680 regs 3, 5 with effect from 8 April 2002.

[Proof of identity of sender or recipient of information

2C—(1) The identity of—

(a) the sender of any particulars transmitted electronically to an officer of the Board, or
(b) the recipient of any particulars transmitted electronically by an officer of the Board,

shall be presumed, unless the contrary is proved, to be the person recorded as such on the officer of the Board's computer system.

(2) The identity of—

(a) the sender of any information delivered to an official computer system by means of electronic communications under these Regulations; or
(b) the recipient of any information delivered by means of electronic communications from an official computer system,

shall be presumed, unless the contrary is proved, to be the person recorded as such on an official computer system.][1]

Amendments—[1] Regs 2A–2E inserted by the Income Tax (Employments and Electronic Communications) (Miscellaneous Provisions) Regulations, SI 2002/680 regs 3, 5 with effect from 8 April 2002.

[Proof of delivery of information and payments

2D—(1) [Subject to paragraph (4),][2] the use of [a][2] method of electronic communications shall be presumed, unless the contrary is proved, to have resulted in the making of a payment or the delivery of information—

(a) in the case of information falling to be delivered, or a payment falling to be made, to the Board, if the making of the payment or the delivery of the information has been recorded on an official computer system,
(b) in the case of information falling to be delivered, or a payment falling to be made, by the Board, if the despatch of that payment or information has been recorded on an official computer system.

(2) [Subject to paragraph (4),][2] the use of [a][2] method of electronic communications shall be presumed, unless the contrary is proved, not to have resulted in the making of a payment or the delivery of information—

(a) in the case of information falling to be delivered, or a payment falling to be made, to the Board, if the making of the payment or the delivery of the information has not been recorded on an official computer system,
(b) in the case of information falling to be delivered, or a payment falling to be made, by the Board, if the despatch of that payment or information has not been recorded on an official computer system.

(3) [Subject to paragraph (4),][2] the time of receipt of any information or payment sent by [a][2] means of electronic communications shall be presumed, unless the contrary is proved, to be that recorded by an official computer system.][1]

[(4) For the purpose of this regulation the delivery of information must use an approved method of electronic communication.][2]

Amendments—[1] Regs 2A–2E inserted by the Income Tax (Employments and Electronic Communications) (Miscellaneous Provisions) Regulations, SI 2002/680 regs 3, 5 with effect from 8 April 2002.
[2] Words inserted and substituted, and para (4) inserted, by the Income Tax (Employments) (Amendment) Regulations, SI 2003/2494 regs 2, 3 with effect from 20 October 2003.

[Use of unauthorised means of electronic communications

2E—(1) Paragraph (2) applies to information which is required to be delivered to the Board or an officer of theirs under these Regulations.

(2) The use of a means of electronic communications, for the purpose of delivering any information to which this paragraph applies, shall be conclusively presumed not to have resulted in the delivery of that information, unless that means of electronic communications is for the time being approved for delivery of information of that kind.][1]

Amendments—[1] Regs 2A–2E inserted by the Income Tax (Employments and Electronic Communications) (Miscellaneous Provisions) Regulations, SI 2002/680 regs 3, 5 with effect from 8 April 2002.

PART II

GENERAL PROVISIONS RELATING TO EMPLOYERS

Multiple employers

3—(1) [Subject to paragraph (6),][1] where an employer so elects, he shall be treated for all the purposes of these Regulations as if in respect of each group of his employees specified in the election he were a different employer, that is to say, as if each such group constituted all his employees and in particular, but without prejudice to the generality of the foregoing—

(a) each such group shall be treated for those purposes as employed in a separate undertaking from that in which any other such group is employed, and

(b) an employee ceasing to be employed in one such group and commencing employment in another such group shall be treated for those purposes as having ceased to be employed by the employer and having commenced an employment with a new employer.

(2) An election under this regulation must be made by notice to the inspector and any such notice shall contain—

(a) such information as may be necessary to identify the groups of employees concerned, and

(b) a certificate that the employer has no employees other than those in the groups so identified.

(3) Subject to paragraph (4), an election shall have effect for the year following that in which it is made and, unless revoked, shall also have effect for any subsequent year.

(4) Where an employer acquires the whole or a part of any trade, business, concern or undertaking of another employer and within 90 days of the acquisition elects under this regulation to be treated as a separate employer in respect of the group of employees employed in the acquired trade, business, concern or undertaking and his existing employees or, where an election is already in force in respect of them, each group of his existing employees, that election shall have effect for the year in which the acquisition takes place and any subsequent year.

(5) An election in force for any year may be revoked by notice to the inspector and any such revocation shall have effect for the year following that in which notice of it is given and any subsequent year, but shall not prejudice the making of a fresh election for that following or any subsequent year.

[(6) An election made under this regulation shall be disregarded if within 60 days of the election being made an officer of the Board issues a notice to the employer stating that it appears to him that the election is made wholly or mainly for an improper purpose (''an improper purpose notice'').][1]

[(7) For the purpose of this regulation an election is made for an improper purpose if it is made for the purpose of—

(a) avoiding the requirement imposed by regulation 42A of these Regulations;

(b) avoiding the requirement imposed by regulation 46ZC of these Regulations; or

(c) receiving an incentive payment under the Income Tax (Incentive Payments for Voluntary Electronic Communication of PAYE Returns) Regulations 2003.][1]

[(8) An employer may appeal against an improper purpose notice—

(a) by notice to an officer of the Board,

(b) within 30 days of the issue of the improper purpose notice,

(c) on the grounds that—

(i) the election was not made wholly or mainly for an improper purpose, or

(ii) the improper purpose notice was not issued within 60 days of the election, and if the appeal is successful the improper purpose notice shall be withdrawn.][1]

[(9) Regulation 46ZH applies to appeals under paragraph (8).][1]

Revenue & other press releases—*ICAEW TR799 June 1990 (the definition of ''employer'' includes, in the case of a company in administration, the administrator if he pays emoluments to employees of the company; he is liable to deduct and account for PAYE/NIC deductions).*

Amendments—[1] *Words in para (1) inserted, and paras (6)–(9) inserted, by the Income Tax (Employments) (Amendment) Regulations, SI 2003/2494 regs 2, 4 with effect from 20 October 2003.*

Intermediate employers

4—(1) Where an employee works under the general control and management of a person who is not his immediate employer, that person (in this regulation and in regulation 5 referred to as ''the principal employer'') shall be deemed to be the employer for the purposes of these Regulations.

(2) The immediate employer shall furnish the principal employer with such particulars of the employee's emoluments as may be necessary to enable the principal employer to comply with the provisions of these Regulations.

(3) If the employee's emoluments are actually paid to him by the immediate employer, then—

(a) the immediate employer shall be notified by the principal employer of the amount of tax to be deducted or repaid when the emoluments are paid to the employee, and shall deduct or repay the amount so notified to him accordingly; and

(b) the principal employer shall make a corresponding deduction or addition on making to the immediate employer the payment out of which those emoluments will be paid.

Revenue & other press releases—*ICAEW TR799 June 1990 (the definition of "employer" includes, in the case of a company in administration, the administrator if he pays emoluments to employees of the company; he is liable to deduct and account for PAYE/NIC deductions).*

Cross references—*Revocation See FA 1994 s 133. This regulation is revoked with effect from the date of the passing of FA 1994 (ie 3 May 1994), but in relation to any time before its revocation it is deemed to have been validly made. Similar effect applies to SI 1973/334 reg 3 which this regulation re-enacts.*

Troncs

5—(1) This regulation applies where an organised arrangement exists for gratuities or service charges to be shared among two or more employees by any person (the organised arrangement being commonly known as a tronc and the person being commonly known and referred to in this regulation as a tronc-master).

(2) Subject to paragraph (3), where this regulation applies—

(a) every payment to an employee by way of the sharing out of gratuities or service charges by the tronc-master (including the retention by him of his own share if he is also an employee) shall be regarded for the purposes of these Regulations as a payment by him of emoluments; and

(b) to the extent of any such payment, the tronc-master shall be regarded as the employer for the purposes of these Regulations ...[1].

(3) If in any particular case the Board are satisfied that the tronc-master has failed to observe or fulfil the requirements of these Regulations or any of them and they so direct, then—

(a) any gratuities or service charges shared as mentioned in paragraph (1) and paid to the tronc-master through the principal employer shall be dealt with in accordance with [paragraph (4)][2]*, and*

[(b) any share of gratuities or service charges not falling within sub-paragraph (a) above shall be dealt with in accordance with paragraph (4A).][4]

[(4) Where this paragraph applies—

(a) the principal employers shall be deemed to be the employer for the purposes of these Regulations in relation to any gratuities or service charges falling within paragraph (3)(a);

(b) the tronc-master shall furnish the principal employer with such particulars of every payment by way of the sharing out of gratuities or service charges to be made to an employee as may be necessary to enable the principal employer to comply with the provisions of these Regulations;

(c) the principal employer shall, on making any payment of gratuities or service charges to the tronc-master, deduct or repay tax in accordance with these Regulations in respect of the amount of such gratuities or service charges to be paid to each employee, and shall notify the tronc-master of each amount so deducted or repaid.][3]

[(4A) Where this paragraph applies the inspector or other officer of the Board may—

(a) take into account under regulation 7(2)(b) the share of gratuities or service charges referred to in paragraph (3)(b) in his determination of a code, and

(b) where he has not already done so, give notice to the employee under section 8 of the Management Act requiring a return to be made and delivered under that section.][4]

[(5) In paragraphs (3) and (4) "the principal employer" means the person under whose general control and management the employees in question work.][3]

Simon's Tax Cases—*Figael Ltd v Fox [1992] STC 83*.*

Amendments—[1] *Words in para (2)(b) revoked by the IT (Employments) (Amendment) Regulations, SI 1994/775 regs 1–3, with effect from 6 April 1994.*

[2] *Words in para (3)(a) substituted by SI 1994/775 regs 1–3.*

[3] *Paras (4), (5) added by SI 1994/775 regs 1–3.*

[4] *Para (3)(b) substituted and para (4A) inserted by the IT (Employments) (Amendment No 3) Regulations, SI 1996/1312 reg 3, with effect from 5 June 1996.*

PART III

CODING

Deduction and repayment of tax under appropriate code

6—(1) Subject to the conditions specified in paragraph (2), every employer, on making any payment of emoluments to any employee during any year, shall deduct or repay tax in accordance with these Regulations by reference to the appropriate code.

(2) The conditions specified in this paragraph are that—

(a) a code authorisation in respect of the employee has been issued to the employer by the inspector for that year, and

(b) the appropriate code is specified in the code authorisation.

(3) The employer shall act in accordance with this regulation and shall deduct or repay tax by reference to the appropriate code, notwithstanding that that code, as determined by the inspector, may be the subject of an objection or appeal.

[(4) A code authorisation is issued and received for the purposes of these Regulations if either—

(a) it is contained in a document that is sent to the employer by the inspector, ...[2]

(b) it is transmitted to the employer electronically by the inspector.][1] *[or]*[2]

[(c) if the employer has indicated that he is willing for it to be delivered in that way, it is delivered to him [or a person acting on his behalf][3] *by an approved means of electronic communications from an official computer system.]*[2]

Simon's Tax Cases—*Paul Dunstall Organisation Ltd v Hedges [1999] STC (SCD) 26*; DTE Financial Services Ltd v Wilson [1999] STC (SCD) 121.*

Amendments—[1] *Para (4) inserted by the IT (Employments) (Amendment) Regulations, SI 1998/2484 reg 4 with effect from 28 October 1998.*

[2] *Word revoked in para (4)(a), word added in para (4)(b), and para (4)(c) inserted by the Income Tax (Electronic Communications) (Miscellaneous Amendments) Regulations, SI 2001/1081 regs 7, 9 with effect from 9 April 2001.*

[3] *Words in para (4)(c) inserted by the Income Tax (Employments and Electronic Communications) (Miscellaneous Provisions) Regulations, SI 2002/680 regs 3, 6 with effect from 8 April 2002.*

Determination of appropriate code by inspector

7—(1) The appropriate code shall be determined by the inspector, who for that purpose may have regard to any of the matters specified in paragraph (2).

(2) The matters specified in this paragraph are—

(a) subject to paragraph (3), the reliefs from income tax to which the employee is entitled for the year in which the code is determined, so far as his title to those reliefs has been established at the time of the determination,

[(aa) where the code is determined before the beginning of the year for which it is to have effect, any proposed alteration or alterations in the rates for that year of any of the reliefs referred to in sub-paragraph (a);][2]

(b) any income of the employee (other than the emoluments in relation to which the appropriate code is being determined)—

(i) on which the tax will be reduced by any relief for the year for which the code is to have effect, or

(ii) which is otherwise chargeable under Schedule E,

(c) any tax overpaid for any previous year which has not been repaid,

(d) any tax remaining unpaid for any previous year which is not otherwise recovered,

(e) any amount to be recovered as if it were unpaid tax under the provisions of section 30(1) of the Management Act, being an amount of tax .... [1] *repaid to the employee in excess of the amount properly due to him, which is not otherwise recovered, and*

(f) such other adjustments as may be necessary to secure that, so far as possible, the tax in respect of the employee's emoluments for the year for which the code is to have effect shall be deducted from the emoluments paid during that year.

(3) Where the code is determined before the beginning of the year for which it is to have effect, the inspector shall disregard any relief such as is referred to in paragraph (2)(a) if he is not satisfied that the employee will be entitled to it for that year.

Revenue & other press releases—*Hansard 6-3-84 (tips and gratuities are included under para (2)(b) unless paid through PAYE: amount declared is accepted unless the Revenue has reasons to doubt it).*

Simon's Tax Cases—*Reg 7(e), R v Walton General Comrs, ex p Wilson [1983] STC 464*.*

Reg 7(2)(a), (f), Blackburn (Insp of Taxes) v Keeling [2003] STC 639, 1162.

Amendments—[1] *Words revoked by the IT (Employments) (Amendment No 3) Regulations, SI 1996/1312 reg 4, with effect from 5 June 1996.*

[2] *Sub-para (2)(aa) inserted by the IT (Employments) (Amendment No 3) Regulations, SI 1999/2155 reg 3 with effect from 19 August 1999.*

Code applicable where code authorisation is not issued or received

8—(1) Where, under regulation 7, the inspector determines that the appropriate code for any year is not different from the code for the preceding year, he shall not be obliged to issue a code authorisation to the employer.

(2) Subject to paragraphs (3) and (5), if for any year, the employer does not receive a code authorisation for an employee who was in his employment on the 5th April in the year preceding that year, a code authorisation shall be deemed to have been issued by the inspector specifying the code which was appropriate on that 5th April as the appropriate code, and the employer shall act in accordance with regulations 6(1) and 38(1).

(3) If for the year ending on 5th April 1994 the employer does not receive a code authorisation for an employee who was in his employment on 5th April 1993 and the code which was appropriate on that date is no longer valid, a code authorisation shall be deemed to have been issued by the inspector specifying as the appropriate code the code which effects deduction of tax with no personal reliefs at one or more of the rates referred to in paragraph (4), and the employer shall act in accordance with regulations 6(1) and 38(1).

(4) The rates referred to in this paragraph are the lower rate, the basic rate and the higher rate.

(5) In relation to codes for the year ending on 5th April 1995 and subsequent years, where, under regulation 13(4)(b) and (5), a code is deemed to have been determined by the inspector as the

appropriate code for the following year, he shall not be obliged to issue a code authorisation to the employer for that year, but a code authorisation shall be deemed to have been issued by the inspector specifying that code as the appropriate code for that year, and the employer shall act in accordance with regulations 6(1) and 38(1).

Coding at the higher rate or where no tax is deductible

9—(1) The inspector may determine that tax shall be deducted at the higher rate from the whole of any emoluments if he has reason to believe that the employee will be chargeable at the higher rate on some part of his total income.

(2) The inspector may determine that no tax shall be deducted from any emoluments if—

[(a) the emoluments will be taken into account as Schedule D income in any assessment, or][1]

(b) the inspector is not satisfied that the emoluments will be chargeable to tax, or

(c) the inspector has reason to believe that the employee will be entitled to a deduction under section 193(1) of the Taxes Act.

(3) Where paragraph (1) or (2) applies, the inspector shall be deemed to have determined the appropriate code, and all the provisions of these Regulations which relate to objections and appeals against the inspector's determination, or to deduction of tax by reference to the appropriate code, or to the specification of the appropriate code in any code authorisation, return or certificate, shall, with the necessary modifications, have effect accordingly.

Amendments—[1] *Para (2)(a) and the word "or" following it substituted by the IT (Employments) (Amendment No 3) Regulations, SI 1996/1312 reg 5, with effect from 5 June 1996.*

Notice of coding

10—(1) Subject to paragraph (2), the inspector, after he has determined the appropriate code for any year, shall give notice of his determination to the employee if the code so determined is different from the code for the preceding year.

(2) Notice under paragraph (1) need not be given where the change in the code is due to an alteration or alterations[, or proposed alteration or alterations,][1] in the rates of any of the personal reliefs allowable under [sections 257, 257A and 257AA][2] of the Taxes Act or in the tax tables, but the other matters referred to in regulation 7 are not different from those for the preceding year.

Amendments—[1] *Words in para (2) inserted by the Income Tax (Employments) (Amendment No 3) Regulations, SI 1999/2155 reg 4 with effect from 19 August 1999.*
[2] *Words in para (2) substituted by SI 1999/2155 reg 20 with effect from the year 2001–02.*

Objections and appeals against coding

11—(1) The employee may give notice of objection to the inspector stating the ground of his objection if he is aggrieved by the inspector's determination.

(2) On receipt of the notice of objection the inspector may amend his determination by agreement with the employee, and in default of such agreement the employee, on giving notice to the inspector, may appeal against the determination.

(3) Subject to paragraph (4), the appeal shall be heard by the General Commissioners [for the division in which the place of employment is situated].[2]

(4) The like provisions as are contained in section 44(2) of the Management Act shall apply to the appeal as they apply to appeals against assessments.

(5) On appeal, the General Commissioners shall determine the appropriate code, having regard to the same matters as the inspector may have regard to when the appropriate code is determined by him.

(6) The like provisions as are contained in [regulations 20 to 23 of the General Commissioners (Jurisdiction and Procedure) Regulations 1994 and][1] section 56 of the Management Act shall apply to the determination by the General Commissioners.

(7) Subject to paragraph (6) and regulation 12, the determination of the General Commissioners shall be final.

Amendments—[1] *Words in para (6) inserted by the General and Special Commissioners (Amendment of Enactments) Regulations, SI 1994/1813 reg 2(1), Sch 1 para 37, with effect from 1 September 1994.*
[2] *Words in para (3) substituted by the IT (Employments) (Amendment No 3) Regulations, SI 1996/1312 reg 6, with effect from 5 June 1996.*

Amendments of coding

12—(1) If a code is found not to be appropriate because the actual circumstances are different from the circumstances by reference to which it was determined by the inspector or the General Commissioners, the inspector may, and if so required by the employee shall, amend the previous determination by reference to the actual circumstances.

(2) Subject to paragraph (3), the inspector, after he has amended the determination of the code, shall give notice of the amended determination to the employee not later than the date on which the

notice under regulation 13(1) or the code authorisation, as the case may be, is issued to the employer.

(3) Notice under paragraph (2) need not be given where the change in the code is due to an alteration or alterations[, or proposed alteration or alterations,][1] in the rates of any of the personal reliefs allowable under [sections 257, 257A and 257AA][2] of the Taxes Act or in the tax tables, but the other matters referred to in regulation 7 have not changed.

(4) The provisions of regulation 11 regarding objections and appeals shall apply in relation to the amended determination as they apply in relation to the original determination.

Amendments—[1] *Words in para (3) inserted by the Income Tax (Employments) (Amendment No 3) Regulations, SI 1999/2155 reg 4 with effect from 19 August 1999.*
[2] *Words in para (3) substituted by SI 1999/2155 reg 21 with effect from the year 2001–02.*

Notice to employer of amended coding

13—(1) Where a determination of the inspector or the General Commissioners is amended after a code authorisation has been issued or is deemed under these Regulations to have been issued, the inspector shall give notice to the employer [or a person acting on his behalf][3] specifying the code appropriate to the employee's case under the amended determination.

(2) On making any payment of emoluments to the employee after the receipt of the notice mentioned in paragraph (1), the employer shall deduct or repay tax by reference to that code.

(3) In relation to the year ending on 5th April 1994, where there is a change in the rates of any of the personal reliefs allowable under sections 257 to 257F of the Taxes Act, the inspector may give notice requiring the employer to amend specified codes as directed, with effect from the date specified in the notice.

(4) In relation to codes for the year ending on 5th April 1995 and subsequent years, where there is a change[, or proposed change,][1] in the rates of any of the personal reliefs allowable under [sections 257, 257A and 257AA][2] of the Taxes Act—

(a) if the change[, or proposed change,][1] relates to the current year, the inspector may give notice requiring the employer, with effect from the date specified in the notice, to amend specified codes as directed;

(b) if the change relates to the following year, the inspector may give notice requiring the employer to carry forward to the following year and adjust as directed specified codes for the current year.

(5) A code amended by virtue of paragraph (3), or amended by virtue of paragraph (4)(a) in respect of the current year, shall be the appropriate code for that year, and a code carried forward to the following year and adjusted by virtue of paragraph (4)(b) shall be deemed to have been determined by the inspector as the appropriate code for that year, and in any of such cases all the provisions of these Regulations which relate to objections and appeals against the inspector's determination, or to deduction of tax by reference to the appropriate code or to the specification of the appropriate code in any code authorisation, return or certificate, shall, with the necessary modifications, have effect accordingly.

[(6) A notice under this regulation—

(a) may be contained in a document sent to the employer, or a person acting on his behalf, by the inspector;

(b) may be transmitted electronically to the employer, or a person acting on his behalf, by the inspector; or

(c) if the employer has indicated his consent to the delivery of information in that way, and the Board have not been notified that that consent has been withdrawn, may be delivered to the employer, or a person acting on his behalf, by an approved means of electronic communications from an official computer system.][3]

Amendments—[1] *Words in para (4) inserted by the Income Tax (Employments) (Amendment No 3) Regulations, SI 1999/2155 reg 5 with effect from 19 August 1999.*
[2] *Words in para (4) substituted by SI 1999/2155 reg 22 with effect from the year 2001–02.*
[3] *Words in para (1) inserted, and para (6) added, by the Income Tax (Employments and Electronic Communications) (Miscellaneous Provisions) Regulations, SI 2002/680 regs 3, 7 with effect from 8 April 2002.*

PART IV

DEDUCTION AND REPAYMENT OF TAX

DEDUCTION OF TAX—GENERAL

Calculation and making of deduction or repayment

14—(1) Except where these Regulations otherwise provide, the employer shall ascertain, on the occasion of any payment of emoluments to the employee—

(a) the cumulative emoluments of the employee at the date of the payment,

(b) the cumulative free emoluments or, as the case may be, the cumulative additional pay,
(c) the cumulative taxable emoluments, and
(d) the cumulative tax.

(2) If the cumulative tax together with any tax not deducted when the last preceding payment of emoluments was made exceeds the previous cumulative tax—

(a) the employer shall deduct the excess from the emoluments on making the payment in question, but
(b) [except where the deduction is of tax falling to be deducted in respect of a notional payment within the meaning given by section 203J(2) of the Taxes Act it shall][1] *not exceed the overriding limit.*

(3) If the cumulative tax together with any tax not deducted when the last preceding payment of emoluments was made is less than the previous cumulative tax, and subject to regulation 36, the employer shall repay the difference to the employee on making the payment in question.

(4) If the cumulative tax together with any tax not deducted when the last preceding payment of emoluments was made is equal to the previous cumulative tax, no tax shall be either deducted or repaid when the payment in question is made.

Simon's Tax Cases—*reg 14, Paul Dunstall Organisation Ltd v Hedges [1999] STC (SCD) 26*.*
Amendments—[1] *Words in para (2)(b) substituted by the IT (Employments) (Notional Payments) Regulations, SI 1994/1212 reg 9, with effect from 25 May 1994.*
Modification—*Reg 14(2)(b) revoked in relation to amounts accounted for in respect of notional payments made under TA 1988 s 203J(3), and the following provisions in these Regulations applied—*
(a) Parts I, III, IV and V
(b) Part VIII regs 99–105
(c) Part IX reg 109
by the IT (Employments) (Notional Payments) Regulations, SI 1994/1212 regs 13(1), (2), (4) with effect from 6 April 1994.

First payment in the year

15 Where the payment of emoluments is the first payment in the year—

(a) the employer shall deduct the cumulative tax from the emoluments on making the payment in question, and paragraphs (2) to (4) of regulation 14 shall not apply, but
(b) [except where the deduction is of tax falling to be deducted in respect of a notional payment within the meaning given by section 203J(2) of the Taxes Act it shall][1] *not exceed the overriding limit.*

Amendments—[1] *Words in para (b) substituted by the IT (Employments) (Notional Payments) Regulations, SI 1994/1212 reg 9, with effect from 25 May 1994.*
Modification—*Reg 15(2)(b) revoked in relation to amounts accounted for in respect of notional payments made under TA 1988 s 203J(3), and the following provisions in these Regulations applied—*
(a) Parts I, III, IV and V
(b) Part VIII regs 99–105
(c) Part IX reg 109
by the IT (Employments) (Notional Payments) Regulations, SI 1994/1212 regs 13(1), (2), (4) with effect from 6 April 1994.

Deductions in accordance with regulation 9

16—(1) Subject to paragraph (3), this regulation applies where, in accordance with regulation 9, the inspector determines that tax shall be deducted from any emoluments wholly at the higher rate or that no tax shall be deducted from those emoluments.

(2) Where this regulation applies, regulations 14 and 15 shall not apply, but the employer shall—

(a) deduct tax at the higher rate, or shall deduct no tax as the case may require, without regard to the employee's cumulative emoluments or the cumulative tax, and
(b) where tax is deductible at the higher rate, record—
(i) the date of payment,
(ii) the amount of the emoluments, and
(iii) the amount of tax deducted from the emoluments.

(3) Where the inspector's determination that no tax shall be deducted is an amended determination, the employer shall—

(a) if the inspector so directs, make any repayment of tax which may be due by reference to the employee's cumulative emoluments and the corresponding cumulative tax, and
(b) record the particulars specified in regulation 38(3).

Deduction in special cases

17—(1) This regulation applies to—

(a) any payment of emoluments made on 4th or 5th April in a leap year or on 5th April in any other year to an employee who is paid weekly;
(b) any payment of pension emoluments in the year in which retirement takes place unless the inspector directs that regulation 14 shall apply; and
(c) any other payment of emoluments made in any year to any employee to which the inspector directs that this regulation shall apply for that year.

(2) Where this regulation applies regulation 14 shall not apply, but the employer, on making any such payment, shall deduct, by reference to the appropriate code, the amount of tax which would have been deductible if the payment had been made on the preceding 6th April.

(3) On making any such payment the employer shall—

(a) record on the deductions working sheet for that employee—

(i) the date of the payment,
(ii) the amount of the emoluments, and
(iii) the amount of tax, if any, deducted on making the payment; and

(b) either record the particulars specified in paragraph (4) on the deductions working sheet or keep such records as enable the production of those particulars.

(4) The particulars specified in this paragraph are—

(a) the free emoluments, or, as the case may be, the additional pay for the appropriate code,
(b) the taxable emoluments, and
(c) where additional pay has been added, the tax due and the overriding limit.

Emoluments not paid weekly or monthly

18 Where emoluments are paid at regular intervals other than regular intervals of a week or a month—

(a) the employer shall record the actual date of every such payment, and
(b) any payment of such emoluments shall be deemed for the purposes of these Regulations to be made on the date on which it would have been made if a payment had been made in the last day of the preceding year.

Subsidiary emoluments of employee paid monthly or at greater intervals

19—(1) This regulation applies where the employer makes a payment in respect of overtime or other extra earnings to an employee whose main emoluments—

(a) are paid monthly, or
(b) are paid at intervals greater than a month,

at an earlier date than that on which the main emoluments are paid.

(2) Where this regulation applies—

(a) the employer shall not repay tax to the employee on the occasion of the payment, notwithstanding that tax may be repayable under regulation 14; but
(b) regulation 14 shall have effect as if the payment was made on the same date as that on which the main emoluments are next paid.

Employee on fixed pay

20—(1) In the case of an employee who is in receipt of a fixed salary or wage, the inspector may authorise the employer to deduct tax from each payment of emoluments which he makes to the employee by reference only to the amount of that payment, without regard to the cumulative emoluments and cumulative tax.

(2) Where the inspector has authorised the employer in accordance with paragraph (1), the employer shall—

(a) deduct tax accordingly by reference to the appropriate taxable emoluments in the simplified tax tables, and
(b) maintain a record on a deductions working sheet bearing the appropriate code, which the inspector shall issue for that purpose, of—

(i) the date of each such payment,
(ii) the amount of the emoluments,
(iii) the amount of the free emoluments,
(iv) the amount of the taxable emoluments, and
(v) the amount of tax, if any, deducted on making the payment.

(3) If an employer who has been authorised to deduct tax in accordance with paragraph (1) ceases to employ the employee in question, he [shall forthwith—

(a) return the deductions working sheet, duly completed, to the inspector or, if so required, to the collector; or
(b) deliver the information contained in the deductions working sheet by an approved means of electronic communications to an official computer system.][1]

(4) Regulations 6, 14 to 16, 23, 25, 26 and 38(1) shall not apply in cases to which this regulation applies.

Amendments—[1] *Words in para (3) substituted by the Income Tax (Employments and Electronic Communications) (Miscellaneous Provisions) Regulations, SI 2002/680 regs 3, 7 with effect from 8 April 2002.*

Aggregation of emoluments in non-cumulative cases

21 Where under these Regulations tax is deductible otherwise than by reference to cumulative emoluments and cumulative tax, the amount of tax to be deducted in any week or income tax month shall be calculated by reference to the aggregate of the emoluments paid to the employee in that week or month.

Tax-free emoluments

22 Where the employer makes a payment to or for the benefit of the employee in respect of his income tax, the amount of the emoluments which the employer pays to the employee shall be deemed for the purposes of deduction and repayment of tax under these Regulations to be such a sum as will include the amount assessable on the employee in respect of the payment made by the employer in respect of the employee's income tax.

Cessation of employment

23—(1) If the employer ceases to employ an employee in respect of whom a code authorisation has been issued to him, or is deemed under these Regulations to have been issued to him, he shall [forthwith—][2]

[(a) prepare a statement on the form provided containing the particulars specified in paragraph (2) and—

(i) send the statement to the inspector, or

(ii) arrange for the particulars contained in the statement to be transmitted electronically to the inspector; or

(b) deliver a statement containing the particulars specified in paragraph (2) by an approved means of electronic communications to an official computer system.][3]

(2) The particulars specified in this paragraph are—

(a) the name of the employee,

(b) the employee's national insurance number,

(c) any other number used to identify the employee,

(d) the date on which employment ceased,

(e) the code appropriate to the employee,

(f) the week or income tax month in which the last payment of emoluments was made to the employee, or in a case falling within regulation 18 was deemed to be so made,

[(g) the cumulative emoluments at the date of the payment referred to in sub-paragraph (f) above and the corresponding total net tax deducted, and

(h) if the employee has been employed in more than one employment during the year, the cumulative emoluments relating to the last employment, and the corresponding total net tax deducted.][1]

(3) The employer shall make [three][1] copies of the [statement][2] on the form provided, and subject to paragraph (4), shall deliver them to the employee on the day on which the employment ceases.

(4) If the employer fails to deliver the [three][1] copies of the [statement][2] to the employee on the day on which the employment ceases and is so required under regulation 84(8), he shall deliver the [three][1] copies of the [statement][2] to the specified office and not to the employee.

Revenue Internal Guidance—*PAYE Movements manual MV 1-282 (procedures for dealing with changes of employment).*

Amendments—[1] *Para (2)(g), (h) and words in paras (3), (4) substituted by the IT (Employments) (Amendment) Regulations, SI 1996/804 regs 1, 3, with effect from 6 April 1996.*

[2] *Words in paras (1), (3), (4) substituted by the IT (Employments) (Amendment) Regulations, SI 1998/2484 reg 5 with effect from 28 October 1998.*

[3] *Paras (1)(a), (b) substituted by the Income Tax (Electronic Communications) (Miscellaneous Amendments) Regulations, SI 2001/1081 regs 7, 10 with effect from 9 April 2001.*

Emoluments paid after employment ceased

24—(1) This regulation applies where any payment of emoluments is made to an employee—

(a) by an employer after the employee has ceased to be employed by him, or

(b) in respect of an employment which has ceased, by a trustee in bankruptcy, a receiver, a liquidator or any other person making such a payment in respect of an obligation of a former employer,

and the payment has not been included in the [statement][1] issued to the employee in accordance with regulation 23(3).

(2) Where this regulation applies regulation 14 shall not apply, but the person making the payment shall—

(a) deduct tax at the basic rate in force for the year in which the payment is made, and

(b) record on a deductions working sheet (which he shall prepare for the purpose unless he has already prepared one for that year)—

(i) the date of the payment,

(ii) the amount of the emoluments, and

(iii) the amount of tax deducted on making the payment.

Amendments—[1] *Word in para (1) substituted by the IT (Employments) (Amendment) Regulations, SI 1998/2484 reg 6 with effect from 28 October 1998.*

Commencement of subsequent employment

25—(1) Immediately on commencing his next employment, the employee shall deliver ...[1] *two copies of the [statement]*[3] *mentioned in regulation 23(3) to his new employer who, subject to paragraph (8), shall take the action specified in paragraphs (2) to (5).*

(2) The action specified in this paragraph is that the employer shall—

(a) insert on one copy of the [statement][3]*—*

(i) the address of the employee,

(ii) any number used to identify him,

(iii) the date on which the employment commenced, and

(iv) the code in use by the employer in respect of the employee, if other than the code contained in the [statement][3]*, and*

[(b) forthwith either—

(i) send that copy to the inspector by whom code authorisations are normally issued to him, ...[4]

(ii) arrange for both the particulars specified in paragraphs (i) to (iv) of sub-paragraph (a) and the particulars contained in the statement to be transmitted electronically to that inspector][3]*[, or]*[4]

[(iii) deliver a copy of the statement by an approved means of electronic communications to an official computer system.][4]

(3) The action specified in this paragraph is that the employer shall—

(a) prepare a deductions working sheet in accordance with the particulars given on the copies of the [statement][3]*; and*

(b) record on the working sheet the cumulative emoluments shown on the copies of the [statement][3]*.*

(4) The action specified in this paragraph is that the employer shall record on the deductions working sheet or keep such records as enable the production of the following particulars, namely—

(a) save where the code contained in the [statement][3] *reflects additional pay, the cumulative free emoluments, the cumulative taxable emoluments and the corresponding cumulative tax as at the week or month shown on the copies of the [statement]*[3]*;*

(b) where the code contained in the [statement][3] *reflects additional pay, the cumulative additional pay, the cumulative taxable emoluments and either the cumulative tax as at the week or month shown on the copies of the [statement]*[3] *or the total net tax deducted shown on the copies of the [statement]*[3]*, whichever is the less.*

(5) The action specified in this paragraph is that, subject to [paragraph][2] *(7), the employer shall, on making any payment of emoluments to the employee, deduct or repay tax by reference to the appropriate code in accordance with regulation 14, and keep the records required by paragraphs (3) and (4) of regulation 38, as if the cumulative emoluments and cumulative tax shown on the deductions working sheet prepared in accordance with paragraph (3) above represented emoluments paid to the employee by the new employer and tax deducted by him.*

(6) ...[1]

(7) Where the [statement][3] *indicates that regulation 17 has been applied, references in paragraphs (3) to (5) to cumulative emoluments, cumulative free emoluments and cumulative tax shall be disregarded, and regulation 17 shall apply to payments of emoluments made by the new employer.*

(8) Where the two copies of the [statement][3] *show that the last payment of emoluments was in the year preceding that in which the new employment commences, the new employer shall—*

(a) if the date of the commencement of the new employment is within the first seven weeks of the year, comply with paragraphs (1) to (7) with the modification that he shall deduct or repay tax without taking into account the cumulative emoluments and cumulative tax shown on the copies of the [statement][3]*; and*

(b) in any other case, comply with paragraph (2), but deduct tax from each payment of emoluments made by him to the employee, and keep records on a deductions working sheet which he shall prepare for that purpose, as if those payments had been payments to which regulation 30(2) applies.

(9) The delivery of the two copies of the [statement][3] *in accordance with paragraph (1) shall be treated for the purposes of this regulation as the issue of a code authorisation to the new employer in respect of the employee specifying the code contained in the [statement]*[3] *as the appropriate code.*

(10) Where in relation to the year ending on 5th April 1994 the code contained in the [statement][3] *is no longer valid, the code which effects deduction of tax with no personal reliefs at one or more of the rates referred to in regulation 8(4) shall be treated for the purposes of paragraph (9) as if it was the code contained in the [statement]*[3]*.*

(11) If the employee objects to the disclosure of his cumulative emoluments to his new employer, he may deliver the two copies of the [statement][3] to the inspector before he commences his new employment, and the inspector may issue a code authorisation in respect of the employee to the new employer and direct that regulation 17 shall apply to all payments of emoluments which the new employer makes to the employee.

Revenue Internal Guidance—*PAYE Movements manual MV 1-282 (procedures for dealing with changes of employment).*

Amendments—[1] *Word in para (1), and para (6), revoked by the IT (Employments) (Amendment) Regulations, SI 1996/804 regs 1, 4(a), (c), with effect from 6 April 1996.*

[2] *Words in para (5) substituted by SI 1996/804 regs 1, 4(b), with effect from 6 April 1996.*

[3] *Word "statement" substituted for "certificate" wherever occurring, and para (2)(b) substituted, by the IT (Employments) (Amendment) Regulations, SI 1998/2484 reg 7 with effect from 28 October 1998.*

[4] *Word revoked in para (2)(b)(i), word added in para (2)(b)(ii), and para (2)(b)(iii) inserted by the Income Tax (Electronic Communications) (Miscellaneous Amendments) Regulations, SI 2001/1081 regs 7, 11 with effect from 9 April 2001.*

Pension emoluments

26—(1) Retirement on pension shall not be treated as a cessation of employment for the purposes of regulation 23 or of this regulation if the emoluments are paid by the same person both before and after retirement, but any such person shall—

(a) deduct tax in accordance with regulation 17 on making payments of pension emoluments to the employee after retirement; and

[(b) within 14 days after retirement—

(i) prepare a statement on the form provided containing the particulars specified in paragraph (2) ("the statement"),

[(ii) take one of the steps specified in paragraph (1A); and][4]

(iii) deliver a copy of the statement to the employee.][3]

[(1A) The steps referred to in paragraph (1)(b)(ii) are—

(a) sending the statement to the inspector;

(b) arranging for the particulars contained in the statement to be transmitted electronically to the inspector; and

(c) delivering a copy of the statement by an approved means of electronic communications to an official computer system.][5]

(2) The particulars specified in this paragraph are—

(a) the name of the employee,

(b) the employee's national insurance number,

(c) the date of the employee's retirement,

(d) the cumulative emoluments at the date of retirement,

[(e) the emoluments of the employment since the 6th April last to the date of retirement,

(f) the corresponding total net tax deducted, and

(g) the amount of pension payable weekly or monthly as the case may be.][1]

(3) If [two of the][2] copies of the [statement][3] given to the employee in accordance with regulation 23(3) are delivered to an employer who pays or will pay pension emoluments to that employee, the employer shall—

(a) deduct tax by reference to the code shown on the [statement][3] and in accordance with regulation 17; ...[2]

(b) complete one copy of the [statement][3] in accordance with [paragraph (2) of regulation 25 [and take one of the steps specified in paragraph (4); and][4]

(c) make a copy of the [statement][3] on the form provided and deliver it to the employee within 14 days of retirement.][2]

[(4) The steps referred to in paragraph (3)(b) are—

(a) sending the copy of the statement to the inspector mentioned in regulation 25(2)(b)(i);

(b) arranging for the particulars referred to in regulation 25(2)(b)(ii) to be transmitted electronically to that inspector; and

(c) delivering a copy of the statement by an approved means of electronic communications to an official computer system.][5]

Amendments—[1] *Para (2)(e)–(g) substituted for former para (2)(e) and word "and" preceding it by the IT (Employments) (Amendment) Regulations, SI 1996/804 regs 1, 5(a), (b), with effect from 6 April 1996.*

[2] *Words in para (3) substituted, word "and" revoked and sub-para (c) and the word preceding it inserted by SI 1996/804 regs 1, 5(c), with effect from 6 April 1996.*

[3] *Para (1)(b) substituted, and words in para (3) substituted by the IT (Employments) (Amendment) Regulations, SI 1998/2484 reg 8 with effect from 28 October 1998.*

[4] *Para (1)(b)(ii) and words in para (3)(b) substituted by the Income Tax (Electronic Communications) (Miscellaneous Amendments) Regulations, SI 2001/1081 regs 7, 12(2), (4) with effect from 9 April 2001.*

[5] *Paras (1A) inserted, and para (4) added, by SI 2001/1081 regs 7, 12(3), (5) with effect from 9 April 2001.*

Death of employee

27—(1) On the death of an employee in respect of whom a code authorisation has been issued by the inspector, or is deemed under these Regulations to have been issued, the employer shall [forthwith either—

(a) send to the inspector the statement mentioned in regulation 23(1), or the statement mentioned in regulation 30(4), as the case may require, together with the three copies of the statement mentioned in regulation 23(3), and insert on the statement the name and address of the personal representative of the deceased employee, if they are known to him, or

(b) arrange for the particulars contained in that statement, or which would otherwise fall to be inserted or included on that statement in accordance with sub-paragraph (a) of this paragraph or paragraph (2).][1] *[—*

(i) to be transmitted electronically to the inspector, or

(ii) to be delivered by an approved means of electronic communications to an official computer system.][2]

(2) If the employer pays any emoluments after the date of the employee's death in respect of the employee's employment with him, he shall, on making any such payment, deduct or repay tax as if the deceased employee was still in his employment at the date of the payment, and—

(a) if the amount of those emoluments and the date on which they will be paid are known to him at the time he completes the [statement][1] *mentioned in paragraph (1), he shall include on the [statement]*[1] *the amount of the emoluments, the date on which they will be paid, and the amount of tax which will be deducted or repaid; and*

(b) in any other case, he shall indicate on the [statement][1] *that a further payment of emoluments will be made by him.*

Amendments—[1] *Words in para (1) and sub-paras (1)(a) and (b) substituted, and word "statement" in para (2) substituted for "certificate" by the IT (Employments) (Amendment) Regulations, SI 1998/2484 reg 9 with effect from 28 October 1998.*
[2] *Words in sub-para (1)(b) substituted by the Income Tax (Electronic Communications) (Miscellaneous Amendments) Regulations, SI 2001/1081 regs 7, 13 with effect from 9 April 2001.*

DEDUCTION OF TAX WHERE APPROPRIATE CODE NOT KNOWN

Employee for whom appropriate code not known

28—(1) Subject to paragraphs (4) and (5), if the employer makes any payment of emoluments—

(a) to an employee in respect of whom he has not received a code authorisation from the inspector (and in respect of whom no code authorisation is deemed under regulation 8 to have been issued by the inspector), and that payment is equivalent to emoluments at a rate exceeding the minimum rate specified in paragraph (2), or

(b) to a new employee with other employment, or to a new employee to whom neither regulation 29 nor 30 applies, at a rate exceeding £1 a week, or £4 a month,

the employer, on the occasion of any such payment, shall, subject to paragraph (3), [forthwith take one of the steps specified in paragraph (1A).][3]

[(1A) The steps referred to in paragraph (1) are—

(a) providing the inspector with the particulars mentioned in paragraph (1B) in a document provided by the Board or approved by the Board for that purpose;

(b) transmitting those particulars electronically to the inspector; or

(c) delivering those particulars to an official computer system by an approved means of electronic communications.][4]

[(1B) The particulars are the name and address of the employee, the employee's national insurance number, the date on which his employment commenced and such other particulars as may be necessary to enable the determination of the appropriate code in accordance with regulation 7.][4]

(2) "The minimum rate" means—

(a) subject to paragraph (b) below, such sum as represents one fifty-second part of the relief for the time being allowable under section 257(1) of the Taxes Act, rounded to the nearest [£1][2]*, or*

(b) in the case of an employee who is paid monthly or at longer intervals, one twelfth part of the relief for the time being allowable under section 257(1) of the Taxes Act, rounded to the nearest £1.

(3) If the employer, having [provided the inspector with particulars as][1] *mentioned in paragraph (1), makes any subsequent payment of emoluments to the employee, he shall not be required to [provide any further particulars]*[1] *in the same year pursuant to that paragraph.*

(4) This regulation shall not apply where—

(a) the employee has delivered two copies of a [statement][1] *received by him in accordance with regulation 23(3) to his employer immediately on commencing employment; or*

(b) subject to paragraph (5), the employee is resident outside the United Kingdom and the emoluments consist of a pension.

(5) If the employer pays a pension, not being a pension arising wholly from an employment carried on abroad, to a person who is resident outside the United Kingdom in respect of whom he has not received a code authorisation from the inspector, and the payment is equivalent to emoluments at a rate exceeding the minimum rate, the employer shall, on the occasion of the first such payment, [forthwith take one of the steps specified in paragraph (5A).][3]

[(5A) The steps referred to in paragraph (5) are—

(a) providing the inspector with the particulars mentioned in paragraph (5B) in a document provided by the Board or approved for that purpose;

(b) transmitting those particulars electronically to the inspector; or

(c) delivering those particulars to an official computer system by an approved means of electronic communications.][4]

[(5B) The particulars are the name and address of the person entitled to the pension, the date on which the pension commenced and such other particulars as may be necessary to enable the determination of the appropriate code in accordance with regulation 7.][4]

(6) ...[5]

Note—*The Inland Revenue have issued Directions that from 31 May 2001, an employer who is required to deliver information under this regulation is authorised to do so over the internet. The Commissioners of the Inland Revenue further directed that—*

(a) the methods hereby approved by them for—

(i) authenticating the identity of the sender of the relevant information,

(ii) the delivery of the relevant information,

(iii) authenticating the relevant information delivered, and

(b) the form hereby approved by them in which the relevant information is to be delivered

are the methods and the form set out, at the time and for the purposes of the delivery of the relevant information, on the Inland Revenue website.

Simon's Tax Cases—*Booth v Mirror Group Newspapers plc [1992] STC 615*.*

Amendments—[1] *Words in paras (1), (3), (4) and (5) substituted by the IT (Employments) (Amendment) Regulations, SI 1998/2484 reg 10 with effect from 28 October 1998.*

[2] *Sum in para (2)(a) substituted by the Income Tax (Employments) (Amendment No 3) Regulations, SI 1999/2155 reg 6 with effect from 19 August 1999.*

[3] *Words in paras (1), (5) substituted by the Income Tax (Electronic Communications) (Miscellaneous Amendments) Regulations, SI 2001/1081 regs 7, 14(2), (4) with effect from 9 April 2001.*

[4] *Paras (1A), (1B), (5A) and (5B) inserted by SI 2001/1081 regs 7, 14(3), (5) with effect from 9 April 2001.*

[5] *Para (6) revoked by SI 2001/1081 regs 7, 14(6) with effect from 9 April 2001.*

Employee taking up employment after full-time education

29—[(1) This regulation applies to an employee within regulation 28(1)(a) who certifies, on a form provided by the Board [and delivered to the employer—

(a) that he is taking up employment for the first time after a period of full-time education,

(b) that he has not made a claim as defined in regulation 81, and

(c) that he is not in receipt of a pension][1]

(2) If any payment made as described in regulation 28(1) is the first payment of emoluments made by the employer during the year to an employee to whom this regulation applies, and that payment is equivalent to emoluments at a rate exceeding the minimum rate, the employer, on making the payment, shall, on a deductions working sheet which he shall prepare for the purpose, enter cumulative emoluments and cumulative tax before the first payment as nil and deduct tax in accordance with regulation 14, applying the code [which after allowing for the personal relief specified in section 257(1) of the Taxes Act effects deduction of tax at one or more of [the starting rate, the basic rate and the higher rate][3]*]*[2] *as the appropriate code.*

(3) On making any subsequent payment of emoluments to the employee where paragraph (2) applied to the first payment and where a code authorisation has not been issued in respect of the employee, the employer shall deduct or repay tax in accordance with regulation 14, continuing to apply the code [which after allowing for the personal relief specified in section 257(1) of the Taxes Act effects deduction of tax at one or more of [the starting rate, the basic rate and the higher rate][3]*]*[2] *as the appropriate code, and shall keep the records required by paragraphs (3) and (4) of regulation 38.*

Amendments—[1] *Para (1) substituted by the IT (Employments) (Amendment No 5) Regulations, SI 1996/2554 regs 2, 3, with effect from 1 November 1996.*

[2] *Words in paras (2), (3) substituted by the IT (Employments) (Amendment) Regulations, SI 1993/2276 regs 1, 2, 5, with effect from 12 October 1993.*

[3] *Words in paras (2), (3) substituted by the Income Tax (Employments) (Amendment No 3) Regulations, SI 1999/2155 reg 9 with effect from the year 1999–00.*

Employee taking up only or main employment

30—[(1) This regulation applies to an employee within regulation 28(1)(a), who is not within regulation 29, and who certifies, on a form provided by the Board and delivered to the employer—

(a) that the employment is his only or main employment, and

(b) that he is not in receipt of a pension.][1]

(2) If any payment made as described in regulation 28(1) is the first payment of emoluments made by the employer during the year to an employee to whom this regulation applies, and that payment is equivalent to emoluments at a rate exceeding the minimum rate, the employer, on making the payment, shall deduct tax and keep records on a deductions working sheet which he shall prepare for the purpose as if the payment were one to which regulation 17 applied, applying the code [which after allowing for the personal relief specified in section 257(1) of the Taxes Act effects deduction of tax at one or more of [the starting rate, the basic rate and the higher rate][5]*]*[2] *as the appropriate code.*

(3) On making any subsequent payment of emoluments to the employee where paragraph (2) applied to the first payment and where a code authorisation has not been issued in respect of the employee,

the employer shall deduct tax as if such subsequent payment were one to which regulation 17 applied, applying the code [which after allowing for the personal relief specified in section 257(1) of the Taxes Act effects deduction of tax at one or more of [the starting rate, the basic rate and the higher rate][5]][2] as the appropriate code, and shall keep records required by that regulation.

(4) Where paragraph (2) applied to the first payment of emoluments made by the employer to the employee and the employer ceases to employ the employee before a code authorisation has been issued to him by the inspector, then, unless regulation 34 has become applicable, regulations 23 and 25 shall apply, subject to the modifications that—

(a) the [three][3] copies of the [statement][4] of the employer under regulation 23(3) shall not contain particulars of the cumulative emoluments and cumulative tax; and

(b) the new employer, instead of deducting or repaying tax by reference to the cumulative emoluments and cumulative tax, shall deduct tax and keep records in accordance with paragraph (3) as if each payment of emoluments made by him were one to which regulation 17 applied.

Amendments—[1] *Para (1) substituted by the IT (Employments) (Amendment No 5) Regulations, SI 1996/2554 regs 2, 4, with effect from 1 November 1996.*

[2] *Words in paras (2), (3) substituted by the IT (Employments) (Amendment) Regulations, SI 1993/2276 regs 1, 2, 5, with effect from 12 October 1993.*

[3] *Word in para (3) substituted by the IT (Employments) (Amendment) Regulations, SI 1996/804, regs 1, 6, with effect from 6 April 1996.*

[4] *Word "statement" in para (4)(a) substituted by the IT (Employments) (Amendment) Regulations SI 1998/2484 reg 11 with effect from 28 October 1998.*

[5] *Words in paras (2), (3) substituted by the Income Tax (Employments) (Amendment No 3) Regulations, SI 1999/2155 reg 10 with effect from the year 1999–00.*

Other new employees

31—(1) This regulation applies to an employee within regulation 28(1) who is not within regulation 29 or 30.

(2) Subject to paragraph (3), if any payment made as described in regulation 28(1) is the first payment of emoluments made by the employer during the year to an employee to whom this regulation applies, and the payment is at a rate exceeding £1 a week or £4 a month, the employer, on making the payment, shall, on a deductions working sheet which he shall prepare for the purpose, enter cumulative emoluments and cumulative tax before the first payment as nil and deduct tax in accordance with regulation 14, applying the code which effects deduction of tax at the basic rate as the appropriate code.

(3) If the payment is a payment of pension emoluments, then, subject to regulation 28(4) and (5), the employer, on making the payment, shall deduct tax and keep records on a deductions working sheet which he shall prepare for the purpose as if the payment were a payment to which regulation 30(2) applied, and for the purposes of paragraph (4) below, regulation 30(2) shall be treated as having applied to the payment.

(4) On making any subsequent payment of emoluments to the employee where paragraph (2) applied to the first payment and where a code authorisation has not been issued in respect of the employee, the employer shall deduct or repay tax in accordance with regulation 14, continuing to apply the code which effects deduction of tax at the basic rate as the appropriate code, and shall keep the records required by paragraphs (3) and (4) of regulation 38.

Simon's Tax Cases—*Booth v Mirror Group Newspapers plc [1992] STC 615*.*

Initial procedure when payments made to employee for whom appropriate code not known

32 Whenever in accordance with regulation 29, 30, or 31, the employer uses the code [which after allowing for the personal relief specified in section 257(1) of the Taxes Act effects deduction of tax at one or more of [the starting rate, the basic rate and the higher rate][2]][1] or the code which effects deduction of tax at the basic rate, a code authorisation shall, for the purposes of regulations 6, 8, 13(1), 23(1) and 27(1), be deemed to have been issued to the employer by the inspector specifying whichever of those codes applies as the appropriate code.

Amendments—[1] *Words substituted by the IT (Employments) (Amendment) Regulations, SI 1993/2276 reg 5 with effect from 12 October 1993.*

[2] *Words substituted by the Income Tax (Employments) (Amendment No 3) Regulations, SI 1999/2155 reg 11 with effect from the year 1999–00.*

Subsequent procedure on issue of code authorisation

33 On making any payment of emoluments to the employee after a code authorisation has been issued in respect of the employee, the employer shall—

(a) deduct or repay tax by reference to the appropriate code in accordance with regulation 14, and

(b) keep the records required by regulation 38 and for those purposes—

(i) any cumulative emoluments notified to the employer by the inspector shall be treated as if they represented emoluments paid by the employer; and

(ii) the total net tax deducted before the first payment made in accordance with this regulation shall be taken to be the sum of the total net tax deducted, if any, notified to the employer by the inspector and any tax which the employer was liable to deduct from the employee's emoluments under regulation 29, 30 or 31.

Subsequent procedure on presentation of copies of certificate

34—(1) This regulation applies where, after the employer has acted in accordance with regulation 29, 30 or 31—

(a) the employee delivers ...[1] two copies of a [statement][2] received by him in accordance with regulation 23(3) to the employer, and

(b) a code authorisation has not been issued to the employer in respect of the employee.

(2) Where this regulation applies and the [statement][2] relates to an employment in respect of which the last payment of emoluments was made in the year in which the employee delivers the copies then, unless the employer has already ceased to employ the employee, paragraphs (1) to (7) of regulation 25 shall apply as if the employee had delivered the two copies immediately on commencing employment with the employer, and the delivery of the two copies shall be treated as if it were the issue on that day of a code authorisation to the employer in respect of the employee specifying the code shown on the [statement][2] as the appropriate code, except that—

(a) the employer shall not be obliged to prepare a further deductions working sheet if he has already prepared one;

(b) the cumulative emoluments and total net tax deducted immediately before the payment of emoluments following the delivery of the copies shall be taken to be the sum of such cumulative emoluments and total net tax deducted as are shown on the copies, subject to paragraphs (1) to (7) of regulation 25, and such emoluments and tax as have been paid or deducted by the employer since the commencement of the employment;

(c) ...[1]

(3) Where this regulation applies and the [statement][2] relates to an employment in respect of which the last payment of emoluments was made in the preceding year, and the employee delivers the copies—

(a) within the first seven weeks of the year, then, subject to paragraph (4), and unless the employer has already ceased to employ the employee, the employer shall comply with regulation 25(2) and the cumulative emoluments and the total net tax deducted shall be such emoluments and tax as have been paid or deducted by the employer since the commencement of the employment or 6th April whichever was the later and the delivery of the copies shall be treated as if it were the issue on that day of a code authorisation to the employer in respect of the employee specifying the code shown on the [statement][2] as the appropriate code;

(b) after the end of the seventh week of the year, regulation 25 shall not apply.

(4) Where the [statement][2] relates to the year ended 5th April 1993 and the code shown on the [statement][2] is no longer valid, a code authorisation shall be deemed to have been issued on that day to the employer in respect of the employee specifying the code which effects deduction of tax with no personal reliefs at one or more of the rates referred to in regulation 8(4) as the appropriate code.

Amendments—[1] *Word in from para (1)(a), and sub-para (c), revoked by the IT (Employments) (Amendment) Regulations, SI 1996/804 regs 1, 7, with effect from 6 April 1996.*

[2] *Word "statement" substituted for "certificate" wherever occurring by the IT (Employments) (Amendment) Regulations, SI 1998/2484 reg 12 with effect from 28 October 1998.*

REPAYMENT OF TAX

Repayment during absence from work through sickness etc

35—(1) In the circumstances specified in paragraph (2), and on application being made in person by the employee or his authorised representative, the employer shall—

(a) make such repayment of tax to the employee as may be appropriate, having regard to the employee's cumulative emoluments at the date of the pay day in question, the corresponding cumulative tax and any tax not deducted when the last preceding payment of emoluments was made,

(b) record the particulars specified in regulation 38(3), and

(c) record the particulars specified in regulation 38(4) or, as the case may be, keep such records as enable the production of those particulars,

as if the occasion were one on which emoluments had been paid.

(2) The circumstances specified in this paragraph are that, owing to absence from work through sickness or other similar cause, the employee is entitled to receive no emoluments on the usual pay day, and regulation 17 would not apply to a payment made on that day.

(3) If, owing to absence from work otherwise than through sickness or other similar cause, the employee is entitled to receive no emoluments on the usual pay day, then, subject to regulation 36,

the employer shall proceed in accordance with paragraph (1) as if the absence was due to sickness or other similar cause.

Trade disputes

36—(1) This regulation applies where the employee is absent from work in consequence of a trade dispute at his place of employment.

(2) Where this regulation applies, then, subject to paragraph (6), unless the employee is not participating or directly interested in the trade dispute, the employer shall—

(a) on the occasion of any payment of emoluments, calculate the amount of tax to be deducted or repaid, or

(b) if no emoluments are paid on the usual pay day, calculate, in accordance with regulation 35(1), the amount of tax (if any) due to be repaid on that day,

and shall then proceed in accordance with paragraphs (3) to (5) below.

(3) The employer shall—

(a) make no repayment of tax calculated as due to be repaid under paragraph (2) and not yet set off in accordance with sub-paragraph (b) below until—

(i) the employee is no longer so absent, or

(ii) the employer ceases to employ the employee, or

(iii) the employee has become genuinely employed elsewhere in the occupation which he usually follows or has become regularly engaged in some other occupation, or

(iv) the employee dies; but

(b) deduct any tax due to be so deducted except that the deduction shall be reduced by any repayment for the year calculated in accordance with paragraph (2) and not yet paid or set off in accordance with this sub-paragraph.

(4) Where the absence of an employee extends beyond the end of the year, the employer shall—

(a) give notice to the employee of the amount of any repayment of tax calculated in accordance with paragraph (2) which has not been set off against any tax due to be deducted under paragraph (3)(b); and

(b) complete the certificate which is to be given under regulation 39 and the return which is to be rendered under regulation 43 as if that tax had been repaid to the employee.

(5) If he has not made any repayment of tax withheld under paragraph (3) within 42 days after the relevant event specified in sub-paragraph (a) of that paragraph, the employer shall not repay that tax to the employee after that date, but shall proceed in accordance with regulation 42(7).

(6) An employee from whom a repayment of tax has been withheld in accordance with paragraph (3) may request a benefit officer to certify that a determining authority under the Social Security Administration Act 1992 or, in Northern Ireland, the Social Security Administration (Northern Ireland) Act 1992 has decided for the purposes of a claim to benefit that the employee has proved that he is not participating or directly interested in a trade dispute, and if the benefit officer so certifies, the employer shall make such repayment as may be appropriate.

(7) In this regulation—

''benefit'' has the same meaning as in regulation 81;

''benefit officer'' means the appropriate officer of the [Department for Work and Pensions][1] or, in Northern Ireland, the appropriate officer of the Department of Health and Social Services for Northern Ireland;

''place of employment'' has the meaning given by section 27(3) of the Social Security Contributions and Benefits Act 1992 or, in Northern Ireland, section 27(3) of the Social Security Contributions and Benefits (Northern Ireland) Act 1992.

Amendments—[1] *Words in para (7) substituted by the Secretaries of State for Education and Skills and for Work and Pensions Order, SI 2002/1397 art 12, Schedule para 25(1), (2) with effect from 27 June 2002.*

Repayment after cessation of employment

37—(1) This regulation applies in the case of a person who has ceased to be employed.

(2) Where this regulation applies, the person shall, on applying for a repayment, produce to the inspector the ...[1] copies of the [statement][2] delivered in accordance with regulation 23(3)[, or two copies of the certificate delivered in accordance with regulation 89(2),][2] and a certificate that he was not a claimant within the meaning of regulation 81 for the relevant period, together with such evidence of his unemployment as the inspector may require.

(3) Where this regulation applies, and where the person has not made or has ceased to make a claim as defined in regulation 81, any repayment which may be appropriate at any date, having regard to his cumulative emoluments at that date, the corresponding cumulative tax, and any other emoluments paid to the employee for the year but not included in the cumulative emoluments, shall be made to him by the inspector.

Amendments—[1] *In para (2) word revoked by the IT (Employments) (Amendment) Regulations, SI 1996/804 regs 1, 8, with effect from 6 April 1996.*

SIs

[2] *Words in para (2) substituted by the IT (Employments) (Amendment) Regulations, SI 1998/2484 reg 13 with effect from 28 October 1998.*

DOCUMENTS RELATING TO THE DEDUCTION AND REPAYMENT OF TAX

Deductions working sheets etc

38—(1) Subject to the condition specified in regulation 6(2)(a), every employer, on making any payment of emoluments to any employee during any year, shall, if he has not already done so, prepare a deductions working sheet for that employee.

(2) The employer shall record—

(a) the name of the employee,
(b) the employee's national insurance number,
(c) the appropriate code, and
(d) the year to which the working sheet relates,

on each deductions working sheet which he is required to prepare under these Regulations.

(3) The employer shall record—

(a) the date of the payment,
(b) the amount of the emoluments, and
(c) the amount of tax, if any, deducted or repaid on making the payment,

on the deductions working sheet for that employee regarding every payment of emoluments which he makes to the employee.

(4) The employer shall either—

(a) record—

(i) the cumulative emoluments in relation to the date of payment,
(ii) the cumulative free emoluments or, as the case may be, the cumulative additional pay, in relation to that date,
(iii) the cumulative taxable emoluments in relation to that date,
(iv) the corresponding cumulative tax,
(v) where additional pay has been added to the payment, the tax due at that date,
(vi) the overriding limit, if any, in relation to the payment,
(vii) the amount of any tax not deducted at that date as a consequence of the overriding limit, and
(viii) the amount of tax, if any, repayment of which is precluded by regulation 36,

on the deductions working sheet for that employee regarding every payment of emoluments which he makes to the employee; or

(b) keep such records as enable the production of the particulars mentioned in paragraphs (i) to (viii) of sub-paragraph (a) above.

Certificate of tax deducted

39—(1) The employer shall[, not later than 56 days after the end of the year,][1] give a certificate under this regulation to every employee who is in his employment on the last day of the year and from whose emoluments any tax has been deducted during that year.

(2) The certificate shall be in a form provided or authorised by the Board and, subject to regulation 36(4), shall show—

(a) the year to which it relates,
(b) the total amount of the emoluments paid by the employer to the employee during the year, being emoluments which the employer was required to take into account for the purposes of deducting or repaying tax,
(c) the total net tax deducted from the emoluments,
(d) the appropriate code,
(e) the employee's national insurance number,
(f) the name and address of the employer, and
(g) in the case of a form not provided by the Board, that it has been approved by them in substitution for such a form.

(3) In the case of an employee taken into employment after the beginning of the year, the certificate shall include any emoluments paid to the employee by any previous employer and any tax deductible from those emoluments, being emoluments and tax which the employer giving the certificate was required to take into account for the purposes of deducting or repaying tax in the case of emoluments paid by him.

Amendments—[1] *Words in para (1) inserted by the IT (Employments) (Amendment No 4) Regulations, SI 1995/1284 reg 3, with effect from 6 April 1996.*

PART V

PAYMENT AND RECOVERY OF TAX ETC

PAYMENT

Payment of tax monthly by employer

40—(1) Subject to regulations 41 and 48(11), the employer shall pay the amount specified in paragraph (2) to the collector within 14 days of the end of every income tax month [or, where payment is made by an approved method of electronic communications in respect of emoluments paid after 5th April 2004, within 17 days of the end of every income tax month][2].

(2) The amount specified in this paragraph shall be determined by the formula—

$$(A + B) - (C + D)$$

where—

A is all amounts of tax which the employer was liable under these Regulations to deduct from emoluments paid by him in that income tax month;

B is all amounts of tax by which deductions in that income tax month were reduced in accordance with regulation 36(3)(b), being amounts [calculated under regulation 36(2) as due to be repaid in an earlier income tax month but whose repayment was precluded during that income tax month by regulation 36(3)][1]*;*

C is any amounts calculated as due to be repaid in that income tax month, but whose repayment was precluded during that income tax month by regulation 36(3); and

D is any amounts which he was liable to repay in that income tax month (excepting any amounts for which a reduction was claimed in any previous income tax month, or which are being recovered from the Board under regulation 42(6)).

Simon's Tax Cases—*reg 40(4), R v IRC, ex p Chisholm [1981] STC 253*; R v IRC, ex p Sims [1987] STC 211*; R v IRC, ex p Cook [1987] STC 434*.*

Modification—*Reg 40(2) definition of "A" modified in relation to amounts accounted for in respect of notional payments made under TA 1988 s 203J(3), and the following provisions in these Regulations applied—*
(a) Parts I, III, IV and V
(b) Part VIII regs 99–105
(c) Part IX reg 109
by the IT (Employments) (Notional Payments) Regulations, SI 1994/1212 reg 13(1), (2), (5) with effect from 6 April 1994. Reg 40(2) has effect as if after the words "income tax month" in the definition of "A" there were added "and all amounts of tax for which he was liable to account under section 203J(3) of the Taxes Act in respect of notional payments made by him in that month".

Amendments—[1] *Words in para (2) value B substituted by the IT (Employments) (Amendment) Regulations, SI 1993/2276 regs 1, 2, 6, with effect from 12 October 1993.*
[2] *Words in para (1) inserted by the IT (Employments) (Amendment) Regulations, SI 2003/2494 regs 2, 5 with effect from 20 October 2003.*

Payment of tax quarterly by employer

41—(1) Subject to regulation 48(11), the employer shall pay the amount specified in paragraph (2) to the collector within 14 days of the end of every income tax quarter [or, where payment is made by an approved method of electronic communications in respect of emoluments paid after 5th April 2004, within 17 days of the end of every income tax quarter,][3] *where—*

(a) the employer has reasonable grounds for believing that the condition specified in paragraph (3) applies and so chooses, or

(b) regulation 20 applies.

(2) The amount specified in this paragraph shall be determined by the formula—

$$(A + B) - (C + D)$$

where—

A is all amounts of tax which the employer was liable under these Regulations to deduct from emoluments paid by him in that income tax quarter;

B is all amounts of tax by which deductions in that income tax quarter were reduced in accordance with regulation 36(3)(b), being amounts [calculated under regulation 36(2) as due to be repaid in an earlier income tax quarter but whose repayment was precluded during that income tax quarter by regulation 36(3)][1]*;*

C is any amounts calculated as due to be repaid in that income tax quarter, but whose repayment was precluded during that income tax quarter by regulation 36(3); and

D is any amounts which he was liable to repay in that income tax quarter (excepting any amounts for which a reduction was claimed in any previous income tax quarter, or which are being recovered from the Board under regulation 42(6)).

[(3) The condition is that for income tax months falling within the current year, the average monthly amount found by the formula below will be less than £1500.

The formula is—

$$(S + P + N + L) - (C + SP + CD)$$

The expressions used in the formula have the following values.

S is the amount payable by the employer to the collector under sections 559 and 559A of the Taxes Act and regulation 8 of the Income Tax (Sub-contractors in the Construction Industry) Regulations 1993 during the tax month from payments made by him.

P is the amount which would be payable by the employer to the collector under regulation 40 if any adjustment to that amount under regulation 7(2) of the Working Tax Credit (Payments by Employers) Regulations 2002 (funding of payment of working tax credit) were disregarded.

N is the amount which would be payable to the collector under the Social Security Contributions and Benefits Act 1992 or, in Northern Ireland, the Social Security Contributions and Benefits (Northern Ireland) Act 1992 and (in either case) under the Social Security (Contributions) Regulations 2001 but disregarding—

(a) any amount of secondary Class 1 contributions in respect of which liability has been transferred to the employed earner by an election made jointly by the employed earner and the secondary contributor for the purpose of paragraph 3B(1) of Schedule 1 to either of those Acts (transfer of liability to be borne by the earner); and

(b) any adjustment to the amount so payable to the Collector under regulation 7(2) of the Working Tax Credit (Payments by Employers) Regulations 2002;

L is the amount which would be payable by the employer to the collector under regulation 39(1) of the Education (Student Loans) (Repayment) Regulations 2000 or of the Education (Student Loans) (Repayment) Regulations (Northern Ireland) 2000 (payment of repayments deducted to the Inland Revenue) if the reduction referred to in paragraph (3) of the respective regulation and in regulation 7(2) of the Working Tax Credit (Payment by Employers) Regulations 2002 (payment by employers) were disregarded.

C is the amount payable by the employer to his employees by way of tax credit under the Working Tax Credit (Payment by Employers) Regulations 2002.

SP is the amount which would be payable by the employer to his employees by way of statutory sick pay, statutory maternity pay, statutory paternity pay and statutory adoption pay. Here references to statutory sick say, statutory maternity pay, statutory paternity pay and statutory adoption pay are references to payments of that kind under the Social Security Contributions and Benefits Act 1992 or in Northern Ireland under the Social Security Contributions and Benefits (Northern Ireland) Act 1992.

CD is—

(a) if the employer is a company, the amount which others would deduct from payments to it, in its position as a sub-contractor, under section 559 of the Taxes Act; and

(b) in any other case, nil.][2]

Amendments—[1] *Words in para (2) "B" substituted by the IT (Employments) (Amendment) Regulations, SI 1993/2276 regs 1, 2, 7, with effect from 12 October 1993.*

[2] *This regulation inserted by the IT (Sub-contractors in the Construction Industry and Employments) (Amendment) Regulations, SI 2003/536 reg 9 with effect from 6 April 2003.*

[3] *Words in para (1) inserted by the IT (Employments) (Amendment) Regulations, SI 2003/2494 regs 2, 6 with effect from 20 October 2003.*

Payment of tax by employer—further provisions

42—(1) The collector shall give a receipt to the employer for the total amount paid under regulation 40 or 41 if so requested; but if a receipt is given for the total amount of tax and any earnings-related contributions paid at the same time, then no separate receipt for tax only need be given.

(2) If [it appears to the collector that][1] *the amount specified in regulation 40(2) or 41(2) which the employer is liable to pay to the collector exceeds the amount actually deducted by him from emoluments paid during the relevant income tax period, the collector, on being satisfied by the employer that he took reasonable care to comply with these Regulations and that [the failure to deduct the amount which the collector considers should have been but was not deducted ("the excess amount")]*[2] *was due to an error made in good faith, may direct that [the excess amount]*[2] *shall be recovered from the employee, and, where the collector so directs, the employer shall not be liable to pay [the excess amount]*[2] *to the collector.*

(3) [If it appears to the Board that the amount][3] *specified in regulation 40(2) or 41(2) which the employer is liable to pay to the collector exceeds the amount actually deducted by him from emoluments paid during the relevant income tax period, [and the Board]*[3] *are of the opinion that an employee has received his emoluments knowing that the employer has wilfully failed to deduct the amount of tax which he was liable to deduct under these Regulations from those emoluments, [they may direct that the amount which they consider to constitute the excess ("the excess amount")]*[3] *shall be recovered from the employee, and, where the Board so direct, the employer shall not be liable to pay [the excess amount]*[3] *to the collector.*

(4) If tax recoverable from an employee under paragraph (3) does not carry interest under section 88 of the Management Act, it shall carry interest in accordance with regulation 51 from the reckonable date until whichever is the earlier of—

(a) the date on which payment is made, or

(b) the date (if any) immediately before the date on which it begins to carry interest under section 86 of the Management Act.

(5) ...[4]

(6) If the total of the amounts which the employer was liable to repay during any income tax period exceeds the total of the amounts which he was liable to deduct during that income tax period, the employer shall be entitled to deduct the excess from any subsequent payment which he is liable to make to the collector under regulation 40 or 41 or to recover that excess from the Board; but that excess shall not include any amount for which a reduction was made in a payment under regulation 40 or 41 in a previous income tax period, or any amount which is otherwise being recovered from the Board.

(7) If he has not made any repayment of tax withheld under paragraph (3) of regulation 36 within 42 days after the relevant event specified in sub-paragraph (a) of that paragraph, the employer shall pay the tax not repaid to the collector forthwith, and paragraph (1) of this regulation shall apply to the amount paid.

[(7A) For the purposes of regulations 40 and 41 and of this regulation, where—

(a) any payment to the collector is made by cheque, and

(b) the cheque is paid on its first presentation to the banker on whom it is drawn,

the payment shall be treated as made on the day on which the cheque was received by the collector.][5]

(8) A certificate of the collector that any amount of interest payable under paragraph (4) has not been paid to him, or, to the best of his knowledge and belief, to any other collector or to any person acting on his behalf or on behalf of another collector, shall be sufficient evidence that the sum mentioned in the certificate is unpaid and due to the Crown.

(9) Any document purporting to be a certificate under paragraph (8) shall be deemed to be such a certificate until the contrary is proved.

Simon's Tax Cases—*reg 42(3), R v IRC, ex p McVeigh [1996] STC 91; Pawlowski (Collector of Taxes) v Dunnington [1999] STC 550.*

Amendments—[1] *Words in para (2) inserted by the IT (Employments) (Amendment No 2) Regulations, SI 1995/447 reg 3(a)(i), with effect from 6 April 1995.*

[2] *Words in para (2) substituted by the IT (Employments) (Amendment No 2) Regulations, SI 1995/447 reg 3(a)(ii), (iii).*

[3] *Words in para (3) substituted by the IT (Employments) (Amendment No 2) Regulations, SI 1995/447 reg 3(b).*

[4] *Para (5) revoked by the IT (Employments) (Amendment No 2) Regulations, SI 1995/447 reg 3(c).*

[5] *Para (7A) inserted by the IT (Employments) (Amendment No 2) Regulations, SI 1996/980, with effect from 19 April 1996.*

Modification Reg 42(2), (3) revoked in relation to amounts accounted for in respect of notional payments made under TA 1988 s 203J(3), and the following provisions in these Regulations applied—

(a) Parts I, III, IV and V

(b) Part VIII regs 99–105

(c) Part IX reg 109

by the IT (Employments) (Notional Payments) Regulations, SI 1994/1212 regs 13(1), (2), (7) with effect from 6 April 1994.

[Mandatory electronic payment

42A—(1) A large employer to whom an e-payment notice has been issued by 31st December following the specified date is required to use an approved method of electronic communications for the making of specified payments.

(2) For the purposes of—

(a) this regulation and regulation 42B, "specified payments" are payments of tax the employer is due to make under regulation 40 in respect of payments of emoluments in the year following that in which the specified date occurs;

(b) this regulation, regulation 42B and regulation 46ZD, "a large employer" is a person treated as paying PAYE income to 250 or more recipients at the specified date;

(c) this regulation—

(i) "e-payment notice" means a notice issued in respect of a year by an officer of the Board stating that the person appears to be a large employer and accordingly is required to use an approved method of electronic communications for the making of specified payments;

(ii) "the specified date" means such date in the preceding year as is announced annually by means of a direction given by the Board not later than 30th November of the preceding year;

(iii) "the preceding year" means the year preceding the year in which were paid the emoluments to which the specified payments relate.

(3) A person is treated as paying PAYE income to a recipient at the specified date where—

(a) he is required at that date by these Regulations or by regulation 6(6) of the Working Tax Credit (Payment by Employers) Regulations 2002 to prepare or maintain a deductions working sheet in respect of the recipient, and

(b) he has not sent, transmitted or delivered to the inspector a statement required by regulation 23 for the recipient.

(4) A person may appeal against an e-payment notice—

(a) by notice to an officer of the Board,

(b) within 30 days of the issue of the e-payment notice,

(c) on the grounds that the person is not a large employer, and if the appeal is successful the e-payment notice shall be withdrawn.

(5) The Board may give specific or general directions—

(a) suspending, for any period during which the use of an approved method of electronic communications for the making of payments is impossible or impractical, any requirement imposed by these Regulations relating to the use of such means;
(b) substituting alternative requirements for the suspended ones; and
(c) making any provision that is necessary in consequence of the imposition of the substituted requirements.][1]

Amendments—[1] *Regulations 42A, 42B inserted by the IT (Employments) (Amendment) Regulations, SI 2003/2494 regs 2, 7 with effect from 20 October 2003.*

[Default surcharge

42B—(1) Subject to paragraph (4), a person is in default in respect of a specified payment required to be made by an approved method of electronic communications in accordance with regulation 42A where the payment is not received in full by the collector on or before the applicable due date.

(2) For the purpose of this regulation the applicable due date in relation to any specified payment is the date on which payment is required in accordance with regulation 40.

(3) For the purposes of paragraph (1), a payment is not treated as received in full by the collector on or before the applicable due date unless it is made in such manner as secures (in a case where the payment is made otherwise than in cash) that, on or before the applicable due date for payment of that amount, all transactions can be completed that need to be completed before the whole amount of the payment becomes available to the collector.

(4) Subject to paragraph (5), paragraph (1) does not apply if the employer had a reasonable excuse for failing to make the specified payment in such manner as secures it is received in full by the collector on or before the applicable due date and the payment is received in full by the collector without unreasonable delay after the excuse ceased.

(5) Inability to pay the specified payment is not a reasonable excuse for the purposes of paragraph (4).

(6) An officer of the Board shall issue a default notice to any person who appears to be in default in respect of a specified payment.

(7) A person may appeal against a default notice—

(a) by notice to an officer of the Board,
(b) within 30 days of the issue of the default notice,
(c) on the grounds that—

(i) the person is not in default; or
(ii) subject to paragraph (8), the person is not a large employer, and if the appeal is successful the default notice shall be withdrawn.

(8) Paragraph (7)(c)(ii) does not apply where following an appeal under regulation 42A(5) the notice was not withdrawn.

(9) A person in default in respect of any specified payment to whom a default notice and a surcharge notice have been issued is liable to a surcharge equal to the aggregate of the surcharges in respect of every default relating to the year in which were paid the emoluments to which the specified payments relate, calculated in accordance with paragraph (10).

(10) For the purpose of paragraph (9), the surcharge in respect of each default is equal to a specified percentage of the total of—

$$A - B,$$

where—

(a) A is the total amount of tax due for the year in which were paid the emoluments to which the specified payment relates;
(b) B is the total of the amounts deducted from the total amount of tax due for the year in which were paid the emoluments to which the specified payment relates under—

(i) rule 1 of regulation 7(2) of the Working Tax Credit (Payment by Employers) Regulations 2002;
(ii) regulations 3 and 5 of the Statutory Paternity Pay and Statutory Adoption Pay (Administration) Regulations 2002;
(iii) regulations 4, 5 and 6 of the Statutory Maternity Pay (Compensation of Employers) and Miscellaneous Amendment Regulations 1994; and
(iv) regulation 44B of the Income Tax (Sub-contractors in the Construction Industry) Regulations 1993;

(c) the specified percentage is determined by reference to the number of the defaults during the surcharge period in accordance with the Table below;

TABLE

Default number (within the surcharge period)	*Specified percentage*
First	*0%*
Second	*0%*
Third	*0.17%*
Fourth	*0.17%*
Fifth	*0.17%*
Sixth	*0.33%*
Seventh	*0.33%*
Eighth	*0.33%*
Ninth	*0.58%*
Tenth	*0.58%*
Eleventh	*0.58%*
Twelfth and subsequent defaults	*0.83%*

and

(d) the surcharge period is a period which—

(i) begins on the day following the applicable due date for the first specified payment in respect of which the person is in default, and

(ii) ends at the end of a year in which the person has not been in default in respect of any specified payment.

(11) For the purposes of this regulation, a surcharge notice is a notice issued by an officer of the Board within six years of the end of the year or, if earlier, of the employer rendering a return in accordance with regulation 43, to a person liable to a surcharge showing the total surcharge liability for all the defaults relating to that year.

(12) A person may appeal against a surcharge notice—

(a) by notice to an officer of the Board,

(b) within 30 days of the issue of the surcharge notice,

(c) on the grounds that—

(i) subject to paragraph (13), the number of defaults stated in the notice is incorrect; or

(ii) the amount of the surcharge is incorrect.

(13) Paragraph (12)(c)(i) does not apply in respect of a disputed default which has already been the subject of an appeal under paragraph (7) following which the notice was not withdrawn.

(14) Subject to paragraphs (12) and (15), the provisions of Parts 4, 5 and 6 of the Management Act apply to the surcharge notice as if it were an assessment and the amount of the surcharge was tax charged by the assessment.

(15) On an appeal under paragraph (12), section 50(6) to (8) of the Management Act shall not apply but the Commissioners may—

(a) if it appears to them that no surcharge has been incurred, set the surcharge notice aside,

(b) if the amount of the total surcharge liability appears to them to be correct, confirm the surcharge notice, or

(c) if the amount of the total surcharge liability appears to them to be incorrect, increase or reduce it to the correct amount.

(16) A surcharge payable under this regulation is payable 30 days after the issue of the surcharge notice.

(17) Section 102 of the Management Act (mitigation of penalties) applies to a surcharge payable under this regulation as if it were a penalty.][1]

Amendments—[1] *Regulations 42A, 42B inserted by the IT (Employments) (Amendment) Regulations, SI 2003/2494 regs 2, 7 with effect from 20 October 2003.*

DOCUMENTS RELATING TO THE PAYMENT OF TAX

Return by employer at end of year where deductions working sheets required

43—(1) The employer shall [, not later than 44 days after the end of the year—

(a) render a return to the inspector, or, if so required, to the collector;

(b) transmit information electronically to the inspector or, if so required, to the collector; or

(c) deliver a return by an approved means of electronic communications to an official computer system;

in such form as the Board may approve or prescribe, containing the particulars specified in paragraph (1A)][2] *[in respect of all employees in respect of whom the employer was required at any time during the year to prepare or maintain deductions working sheets in accordance with these Regulations.]*[1]

[(1A) The particulars specified in this paragraph are—

(a) the year to which the return relates,

(b) the total amount of the emoluments paid by the employer to the employees during that year, and

(c) subject to regulation 36(4), the total net tax deducted from the emoluments.

(1B) The return required by paragraph (1) shall be supported by the particulars specified in paragraph (2) and, where appropriate, the particulars specified in paragraph (6), in respect of each of the employees to whom the employer paid emoluments during that year.

[(1C) The particulars specified in paragraphs (2) and (6) shall—

(a) be contained in a document, provided by the Board for that purpose or approved by the Board, which shall accompany the return;

(b) be transmitted electronically to the inspector or collector to whom—

(i) the return is rendered, or

(ii) the particulars specified in paragraph (1A) are transmitted; or

(c) be delivered, by such means of electronic communications as may be approved, to an official computer system.][2]

(2) The particulars specified in this paragraph are such particulars as the Board may require for the identification of—

(a) the employee,

(b) the year to which the return [in question][1] *relates,*

(c) the total amount of the emoluments paid by the employer to the employee during that year,

(d) the appropriate code, and

(e) subject to regulation 36(4), the total net tax deducted from the emoluments.

[(3) If a return required by paragraph (1) is delivered to an inspector or collector it shall include the statement and declaration specified in paragraph (4) and the certificate specified in paragraph (5).][2]

[(3A) If particulars required by paragraph (1)—

(a) are transmitted electronically to an inspector or collector; or

(b) are delivered by means of electronic communications to an official computer system;

they shall be accompanied by the statement and declaration specified in paragraph (4) and the certificate specified in paragraph (5).

This is subject to the following qualification.][2]

[(3B) Where paragraph (3A) applies—

(a) paragraphs (4) and (5) shall have effect as if, for 'signed by the employer', there were substituted 'authenticated by or on behalf of the employer in such manner as may be approved by the Board'; and

(b) paragraph (7) shall not apply.][2]

(4) The statement and declaration specified in this paragraph is a statement and declaration, signed by the employer, in the form approved or prescribed by the Board, containing a list of all deductions working sheets on which the employer was required to keep records in accordance with these Regulations in respect of that year.

(5) The certificate specified in this paragraph is a certificate, signed by the employer, showing—

(a) the total net tax deducted or the total net tax repaid in the case of each employee, and

(b) the total net tax deductible or repayable under these Regulations in respect of all his employees,

during that year.

(6) Where an employee has been taken into employment after the beginning of the year, the return made under paragraph (1) shall also [be supported by the following particulars, that is to say,][1] *the total amount of—*

(a) any emoluments paid to the employee by any previous employer, and

(b) any tax deductible or, where required either to be recorded on the deductions working sheet or to be capable of being produced from other records pursuant to regulation 25(4), any tax deducted from those emoluments,

being emoluments and tax which the employer rendering the return was required to take into account for the purposes of deducting or repaying tax in the case of emoluments paid by him.

(7) Where the employer is a body corporate, the statement and declaration specified in paragraph (4) and the certificate specified in paragraph (5) shall be signed either by the secretary or by a director of the body corporate.

(8) If an employer has failed to pay the total net amount of tax which he is liable to pay to the collector within 14 days of the end of any year, the collector may prepare a certificate showing the net amount of tax remaining unpaid for that year.

(9) Paragraphs (1) to (5) of regulation 54 shall apply to the amount shown in a certificate under paragraph (8) with the modification that summary proceedings for the recovery of the net amount of tax or such part of it as remains unpaid may be brought at any time before the expiry of—

(a) twelve months after the date limited for delivery of the statement specified in paragraph (4), or

(b) if that statement is not delivered by that date, the expiry of twelve months after its delivery.

(10) A certificate of the collector under paragraph (8) that the net amount of tax remaining unpaid for that year has not been paid to him, or, to the best of his knowledge and belief, to any other collector or to any person acting on his behalf or on behalf of another collector, shall be sufficient evidence that the sum mentioned in the certificate is unpaid and is due to the Crown.

(11) Any document purporting to be a certificate under paragraph (8) shall be deemed to be such a certificate until the contrary is proved.

(12) Section 98A of the Management Act shall apply in relation to the provisions of paragraph (1) requiring a return to be made.

Concession B46 Revenue will not charge a penalty where employer's return for any year following the year ended 5 April 1995 is received in their hands on or before the last day of business within seven days of the statutory filing date. "Business day" does not include Saturday, Sunday, Christmas Eve, Good Friday or any bank or public holiday.

Cross references—*See Income Tax (Electronic Communications) (Incentive Payments) Regulations, SI 2001/56 reg 4 (incentive payments to be made to individuals and employers who submit returns to the Inland Revenue using electronic communications).*

Amendments—[1] *Words in paras (1), (2)(b), and (6) substituted, and paras (1A)–(1C) inserted by the IT (Employments) (Amendment) Regulations, SI 1998/2484 reg 14 with effect from 28 October 1998.*

[2] *Words in para (1) substituted, para (1C) substituted; and paras (3)–(3B) substituted for para (3) by the Income Tax (Electronic Communications) (Miscellaneous Amendments) Regulations, SI 2001/1081 regs 7, 15 with effect from 9 April 2001.*

[Return by employer where deductions working sheets not required

44—(1) A return shall be made in respect of every employee to whom the employer paid emoluments at any time during the year at a rate exceeding the minimum rate, but in respect of whom the employer was not required under these Regulations to prepare a deductions working sheet.

(2) The employer shall—

(a) render the return mentioned in paragraph (1) to the inspector;

(b) transmit the information contained in the return electronically to the inspector; or

(c) deliver the return by such means of electronic communications as may be approved to an official computer system.][1]

Concession B46—*Revenue will not charge a penalty where employer's return for any year following the year ended 5 April 1995 is received in their hands on or before the last day of business within seven days of the statutory filing date. "Business day" does not include Saturday, Sunday, Christmas Eve, Good Friday or any bank or public holiday.*

Amendments—[1] *Substituted by the Income Tax (Electronic Communications) (Miscellaneous Amendments) Regulations, SI 2001/1081 regs 7, 16 with effect from 9 April 2001.*

Additional return in cases involving a trade dispute

45—(1) In the circumstances specified in paragraph (2), the employer shall forthwith render an additional return containing the particulars specified in paragraph (3) and the statement specified in paragraph (4).

(2) The circumstances specified in this paragraph are where—

(a) the employer has not made any repayment of tax withheld under regulation 36(3) within 42 days after the relevant event specified in regulation 36(3)(a), and

(b) a return has been made under regulation 43 in accordance with regulation 36(4)(b).

(3) The particulars specified in this paragraph are, in respect of each employee, such particulars as the Board may require—

(a) for the identification of the employee,

(b) of the year to which the return relates, and

(c) of the total tax not repaid.

(4) The statement specified in this paragraph is a statement containing—

(a) a list of the names of all employees in respect of whom the additional return is made,

(b) the amount of tax not repaid in respect of each of those employees, and

(c) a total of the tax not repaid by the employer for that year.

[Return of other additional emoluments

46—(1) Subject to paragraph (7), the employer shall [either][3] *[provide the inspector or other officer of the Board, not later than 92 days after the end of the year, with the following particulars]*[2] *[or deliver those particulars in such form and by such means of electronic communications as may be approved to an official computer system]*[3] *in respect of each employee—*

(a) the particulars specified in paragraph (2);

(b) in the case of an employee who is employed in employment to which Chapter II of Part V of the Taxes Act applies, the additional particulars specified in paragraph (3);

(c) in the case of emoluments relating to business entertainment within the meaning of section 577(5) of the Taxes Act, the additional particulars specified in paragraph (4);

(d) in the case of benefits provided for the employee such as give rise to any charge to tax under sections 141, 142, 143, 144A, 145, 146 and 154 to 165 of the Taxes Act (in this regulation referred to as "the relevant sections"), the additional particulars specified in paragraph (5).

[(1A) If the particulars specified in paragraph (1) are provided to the inspector or other officer of the Board they shall either—

(a) be contained in a document provided by the Board or approved by the Board for that purpose; or

(b) be transmitted electronically.][3]

(2) The particulars specified in this paragraph are—

(a) except as regards any emoluments falling within sub-paragraph (b) of this paragraph, particulars of—

(i) any emoluments which the employee receives from the employer or the relevant person otherwise than in money;

(ii) any payments made on behalf of the employee and not repaid;

(iii) any emoluments which the employee is treated by section 141(1) of the Taxes Act as having received in that year by reason of the provision of a non-cash voucher by the employer or the relevant person;

(iv) any emoluments which the employee is treated by section 142(1) of the Taxes Act as having received in that year by reason of the provision of a credit-token by the employer or the relevant person;

(v) the amount of income tax in respect of any notional payment where that amount is treated by section 144A of the Taxes Act as income of the employee arising in that year;

(vi) any living accommodation which has been provided for the employee or for members of his family or household by the employer or the relevant person, and particulars of the amount of any emoluments of which the employee is treated by virtue of section 145 or 146 of the Taxes Act, or by virtue of those sections together, as being in receipt in respect of that accommodation;

(b) particulars of any emoluments consisting of the amount by which the total value to the employee found under paragraph 24(2) of Schedule 11A to the Taxes Act exceeds the qualifying limit for the time being specified in paragraph 24(9) of that Schedule and having effect in relation to that employee.

(3) The particulars specified in this paragraph are—

(a) except as regards any emoluments falling within paragraph (2)(b), particulars of—

(i) any payments made by the employer or the relevant person to the employee by reason of his employment in respect of expenses;

(ii) any sums put by the employer or the relevant person at the disposal of the employee by reason of his employment and paid away by him;

(b) particulars of any benefits provided by the employer or the relevant person for the employee (or for any other person) by reason of his employment such as give rise to any charge to tax under sections 154 to 165 of the Taxes Act, not being benefits which constitute emoluments within paragraph (2)(b).

(4) The particulars specified in this paragraph are particulars showing whether the amount of the emoluments has been or will be disallowed as a deduction or inclusion as mentioned in section 577(1)(a) of the Taxes Act in any tax computation relating to the trade, business, profession or vocation of the employer.

(5) The particulars specified in this paragraph are particulars of the amounts which may be chargeable to tax by virtue of the relevant sections.

(6) In determining for the purposes of paragraph (5) the amounts which may be chargeable to tax by virtue of the relevant sections, the employer—

(a) shall not make—

(i) any deduction or other adjustment which he is unable to show, by reference to information in his possession or otherwise available to him, is authorised or required by the relevant sections; or

(ii) any deduction authorised by sections 141(3), 142(2), 145(3) or 156(8) of the Taxes Act; but

(b) subject to that, shall make all such deductions and other adjustments as may be authorised or required by the relevant sections.

(7) The employer shall not be required[, by virtue of paragraph (1), to provide the inspector or other officer of the Board with][2] *particulars of—*

(a) payments falling within paragraph 1(1)(a) or (b) of Schedule 11A to the Taxes Act, or benefits falling within paragraph 1(1)(c) of that Schedule, where the total value to the employee found under paragraph 24(2) of that Schedule does not exceed the qualifying limit for the time being specified in paragraph 24(9) of that Schedule and having effect in relation to that employee; or

(b) notional payments treated as made by virtue of any of sections 203F to 203H of the Taxes Act in respect of which the employer is under an obligation to deduct or, as the case may be, account for income tax in accordance with section 203J(1) or (3) of that Act.

[(7A) At the same time as he provides the inspector or other officer of the Board with particulars in accordance with this regulation, the employer shall furnish that person with a declaration, in the form provided by the Board, stating that—

(a) all particulars required to be provided for the year in accordance with the regulation have been provided, and

(b) those particulars are complete and accurate to the best of the employer's knowledge and belief.][2]

[(7B) At the same time as he delivers particulars in accordance with this regulation to an official computer system, the employer shall deliver to that system a declaration in such form as may be approved containing the statements specified in sub-paragraphs (a) and (b) of paragraph (7A).][3]

(8) In paragraphs (2) and (3) references to the "the relevant person" are references to any person making payments or providing benefits to an employee as mentioned in those paragraphs where the making or provision of the payments or benefits by that person has been arranged by the employer; and in this paragraph "arranged" includes guaranteed and in any way facilitated.][1]

Note—*The Inland Revenue have issued Directions that from 31 May 2001, an employer who is required to deliver information under this regulation is authorised to do so over the internet. The Commissioners of Inland Revenue further directed that—*

(a) the methods hereby approved by them for—

(i) authenticating the identity of the sender of the relevant information,

(ii) the delivery of the relevant information,

(iii) authenticating the relevant information delivered, and

(b) the form hereby approved by them in which the relevant information is to be delivered

are the methods and the form set out, at the time and for the purposes of the delivery of the relevant information, on the Inland Revenue website.

Revenue & other press releases—*Hansard 14-5-93 (chauffeur-driven cars: where chauffeur drives employee from home to normal place of employment, the costs of the chauffeur should be included on P11D unless the car is a pool car and the home to work journey is merely incidental to the business use of the car).*

Revenue Booklet SAT 3 (1995) (guidance on additional information to be provided for self-assessment returns).

Amendments—[1] *This regulation substituted together with regs 46AA, 46AB for reg 46 as originally enacted by the IT (Employments) (Amendment No 4) Regulations, SI 1995/1284 reg 4, with effect from 6 April 1996.*

[2] *Words in paras (1) and (7) substituted, and paras (1A) and (7A) inserted, by the IT (Employments) (Amendment) Regulations, SI 1998/2484 reg 15 with effect from 28 October 1998.*

[3] *Words inserted in para (1), para (1A) substituted, and para (7B) inserted by the Income Tax (Electronic Communications) (Miscellaneous Amendments) Regulations, SI 2001/1081 regs 7, 17 with effect from 9 April 2001.*

[Other additional emoluments—information to be provided to employee by employer

46AA—(1) Not later than 92 days after the end of the year, the employer shall give the statement specified in paragraph (4) to every current employee in respect of whom [particulars fall to be provided under regulation 46(1)][3] *by him for that year, or in respect of whom information [—*

(a) is furnished by him to the inspector or other officer of the Board; or

(b) is delivered by him to an official computer system by such means of electronic communications as may be approved;

under the FPCS arrangement for that year.][4]

(2) Where a person who was a current employee ceases to be an employee at any time within 92 days of the end of the year, the statement to be given by the employer to that person pursuant to paragraph (1) shall be duly given if it is sent or delivered to, or left at, that person's usual or last known address.

(3) If a former employee in respect of whom [particulars fall to be provided under regulation 46(1)][3] *by the employer for a year, or in respect of whom information is furnished to the inspector or other officer of the Board [or delivered to an official computer system by such means of electronic communications as may be approved]*[4] *by the employer under the FPCS arrangement for a year, so requires by notice to the employer at any time up to three years after the end of the year, the employer shall give the statement specified in paragraph (4) to that former employee within 92 days of the end of the year or within 30 days of receiving the [notice]*[2] *whichever is the later.*

(4) The statement specified in this paragraph shall contain—

(a) the particulars specified in paragraphs (2) to (5) of regulation 46 in so far as those particulars relate to the employee; and

(b) where information is furnished under the FPCS arrangement in respect of the employee, particulars of either—

(i) the amount of the taxable profit, if any, for that year in respect of car allowances and motor mileage allowances paid to the employee in that year for business travel, calculated by reference to the FPCS arrangement; or

(ii) the total amount of the car allowances and motor mileage allowances paid to the employee in that year for business travel, and the total amount of miles covered by the employee in that year in the course of business travel for which the motor mileage allowances were paid.

(5) A former employee who has received a statement from the employer under paragraph (3) in respect of a year may not require a further statement from the employer under that paragraph in respect of the same year.

(6) In this regulation—

"business travel" has the meaning given by section 168(5)(c) of the Taxes Act;

"current employee" means a person who was an employee on the 5th April in the year to which [the particulars provided under regulation 46(1) relate][3];

"former employee" means a person who was an employee during a part of the year to which [the particulars provided under regulation 46(1) relate][3] but who was no longer an employee on the 5th April in that year;

"the FPCS arrangement" means the arrangement known as the Fixed Profit Car Scheme made between the employer and the inspector or other officer of the Board for furnishing information in respect of payments of car allowances and motor mileage allowances made to employees for business travel.][1]

Amendments—[1] *This regulation substituted together with regs 46, 46AB for reg 46 as originally enacted by the IT (Employments) (Amendment No 4) Regulations, SI 1995/1284 reg 4, with effect from 6 April 1996.*

[2] *Word substituted by the IT (Employments) (Amendment No 3) Regulations, SI 1996/1312 reg 7, with effect from 5 June 1996.*

[3] *Words in paras (1), (3) and (6) substituted by the IT (Employments) (Amendment) Regulations, SI 1998/2484 reg 16 with effect from 28 October 1998.*

[4] *Words in para (1) substituted, and words in para (3) inserted by the Income Tax (Electronic Communications) (Miscellaneous Amendments) Regulations, SI 2001/1081 regs 7, 18 with effect from 9 April 2001.*

[Other additional emoluments—information to be provided to employee by other persons

46AB—(1) This regulation applies where—

(a) a person (in this regulation referred to as "the relevant person") has, in any year, made any relevant payments to or on behalf of, or provided any relevant benefits to or in respect of, an employee of another, and

(b) the employer is not required to provide particulars of those payments or benefits ...[2] *under regulation 46(1).*

(2) The relevant person shall give the statement specified in paragraph (3) to the employee not later than 92 days after the end of the year.

(3) The statement specified in this paragraph is a statement containing such of the particulars specified in paragraphs (2), (3) and (5) of regulation 46 as relate to the relevant payments or relevant benefits.

(4) In this regulation—

"relevant benefits" means any benefits particulars of which, if the relevant person had been the employer of the employee in question, would have been required to be provided ...[2] *under regulation 46(1);*

"relevant payments" means any payments particulars of which, if the relevant person had been the employer of the employee in question, would have been required to be provided ...[2] *under regulation 46(1).]*[1]

Amendments—[1] *This regulation substituted together with regs 46, 46AA by the IT (Employments) (Amendment No 4) Regulations, SI 1995/1284 reg 4, with effect from 6 April 1996.*

[2] *Words in paras (1) and (4) revoked by the IT (Employments) (Amendment) Regulations, SI 1998/2484 reg 17 with effect from 28 October 1998.*

[Return where a car is made available][1]

[46A—(1) In the circumstances specified in paragraph (2), the employer shall[, not later than 28 days after the end of each income tax quarter—

(a) provide the inspector with the particulars specified in paragraph (3) in respect of each relevant employee in a document provided or approved by the Board for that purpose;

(b) transmit those particulars to the inspector electronically; or

(c) deliver those particulars by an approved means of electronic communications to an official computer system.][2]

(1A) ...[2]

(2) The circumstances specified in this paragraph are where in any year—

(a) the benefit of a car is chargeable to income tax under system 157 of the Taxes Act as the employee's income, and

(b) one or more of the following occurs in the income tax quarter, namely—

(i) a car which was unavailable becomes available;

(ii) a car which was available becomes unavailable;

(iii) where a car is available to an employee, or to others being members of his family or household, by reason of the employee's employment, the employee becomes a relevant employee.

(3) The particulars specified in this paragraph are particulars of—

(a) the name of the employee;

(b) the employee's national insurance number;
(c) the car which is or becomes available or has become unavailable;
(d) the price of the car;
(e) any capital sum contributed by the employee to expenditure on the provision of the car or on any qualifying accessory which is taken into account in determining the price of the car;
(f) any amount which, as a condition of the car being available for his private use, the employee is required to pay in the year concerned for that use (whether by way of deduction from his emoluments or otherwise);
(g) any provision of fuel for private use.

(4) For the purposes of sub-paragraphs (d) and (e) of paragraph (3) the price of a car shall be determined in accordance with the provisions contained in sections 168A to 168G of the Taxes Act.

(5) In this regulation—

"available" shall be construed in accordance with paragraph 10 of Schedule 6 to the Taxes Act;
"qualifying accessory" has the meaning given by section 168A(10) of the Taxes Act;
a "relevant employee" means an employee who is employed in employment to which Chapter II of Part V of the Taxes Act applies;
"unavailable" shall be construed in accordance with paragraph 9 of Schedule 6 to the Taxes Act.][1]

Amendments—[1] *This regulation inserted by the IT (Employments) (Amendment) Regulations, SI 1994/775 regs 1, 2, 4, with effect from 6 April 1994.*
[2] *Words in para (1) substituted, and para (1A) revoked by the Income Tax (Electronic Communications) (Miscellaneous Amendments) Regulations, SI 2001/1081 regs 7, 19 with effect from 9 April 2001.*

[Termination payments and other benefits—information to be provided

46ZA—(1) Not later than 92 days after the end of a year, being the year 1998–99 or any subsequent year, an employer or former employer shall furnish to the inspector or other officer of the Board in respect of each employee or former employee the information specified in paragraph (2) relating to any award consisting of payments combined with other benefits, or consisting solely of other benefits—

(a) which were awarded in that year in connection with the termination of that person's employment with him or any change in the duties of or emoluments from his employment with him,
(b) which, when provided (whether in that year or a subsequent year), would constitute payments and other benefits received within the meaning of section 148 of the Taxes Act, and
(c) whose total amount, when aggregated with other payments and benefits provided or to be provided (whether in that year or a subsequent year) in respect of the same person as mentioned in paragraph 7(2) of Schedule 11 to the Taxes Act, is estimated by the employer or former employer to exceed £30,000.

(2) The information specified is—

(a) the total amount of the payments and other benefits awarded, calculated as mentioned in paragraph (1)(c);
(b) the total amount of the payments made in that year in connection with the award;
(c) details of the non-cash benefits provided in that year in connection with the award, other than benefits previously contained in a return for that year under regulation 46, and the total amount of the cash equivalents of those benefits (within the meaning of paragraph 12(2) of Schedule 11 to the Taxes Act);
(d) the estimated total number of the years in which payments and other benefits are to be provided in connection with the award and, if the duration of any of those payments and other benefits is capable of being reduced in certain circumstances, details of those circumstances;
(e) the estimated total amount of the payments to be made in subsequent years in connection with the award;
(f) a description of each of the other benefits to be provided in subsequent years in connection with the award, and the terms of their provision.

(3) In calculating the cash equivalents of non-cash benefits for the purposes of paragraphs (1) and (2), the employer or former employer—

(a) shall not make—

(i) any deduction or other adjustment which he is unable to show, by reference to information in his possession or otherwise available to him, is authorised or required by any of the provisions of Chapter II of Part V of the Taxes Act or by section 596B(1)(b) of that Act ("the relevant provisions"), or
(ii) any deduction authorised by section 156(8) of that Act; but

(b) subject to that, shall make all such deductions and other adjustments as may be authorised or required by the relevant provisions.

(4) In calculating the total amount of payments and other benefits for the purposes of paragraphs (1)(c) and (2)(a), the employer or former employer—

(a) shall have regard to the provisions of section 148 of, and Schedule 11 to, the Taxes Act,
(b) shall take into account the matters referred to in paragraph (2)(d), (e) and (f), and

(c) in valuing the amount of non-cash benefits for future years in connection with the award, shall assume that the provisions of the Taxes Act relating to those benefits will remain unchanged with respect to those years.

(5) Paragraph (6) applies where—

(a) information has not been furnished by the employer or former employer under paragraph (1) by the date referred to in that paragraph solely because either—

(i) the total amount of payments and other benefits awarded in the year in respect of the employee or former employee is estimated in accordance with sub-paragraph (c) of that paragraph not to exceed £30,000, or

(ii) the award made in the year consisted of payments only, and did not consist either of payments combined with other benefits or solely of other benefits, but

(b) at some time after that date either—

(i) there is a change in the amount of the payments awarded, or the nature and amounts of other benefits awarded, such that the total amount of those payments and other benefits is estimated in accordance with sub-paragraph (c) of paragraph (1) to exceed £30,000, or

(ii) the nature of the award is changed so that it consists of payments combined with other benefits, or solely of other benefits.

(6) Where this paragraph applies, the employer or former employer shall, not later than 92 days after the end of the year in which the change occurred, furnish to the inspector or other officer of the Board the information specified in paragraph (2) with respect to those payments and other benefits.

(7) Not later than 92 days after the end of a year in which payments and other benefits to which paragraph (1) applies were awarded by an employer or former employer as mentioned in that paragraph or, as the case may be, not later than 92 days after the end of the year in which a change occurred as mentioned in paragraph (5)(b), the employer or former employer shall give to the employee or former employee in relation to whom the award was made a copy of the information specified in paragraph (2) relating to those payments and other benefits that was furnished to the inspector or other officer of the Board in accordance with paragraph (1) or, as the case may be, paragraph (6).

(8) A copy of the information referred to in paragraph (7) shall be duly given to the person concerned if it is sent or delivered to, or left at, that person's usual or last known address.

(9) Where following the furnishing of information by an employer or former employer in accordance with paragraph (1) or (6), there is a material change in the amount of the payments awarded, or the nature and amounts of other benefits awarded, in relation to the employee or former employee, the employer or former employer shall, not later than 92 days after the end of the year in which the material change occurred, give details of the material change to the inspector or other officer of the Board.

(10) Where the payments and other benefits aggregated in accordance with paragraph (1)(c) include payments and other benefits provided in respect of different employments with more than one employer, the employer or former employer by whom information is required to be furnished under paragraph (1), (6) or (9), or a copy of information is required to be given to the employee or former employee under paragraph (7), shall be the employer or the relevant former employer providing the greatest amount of payments and other benefits so aggregated.

(11) Information required to be furnished by an employer or former employer to an inspector or other officer of the Board in accordance with paragraphs (1) and (2) may be so furnished after the award is made but prior to the end of the year in which the payments and benefits are awarded; and in such a case sub-paragraphs (b) and (c) of paragraph (2) shall have effect, so far as concerns the furnishing of information relating to that year, as if they required the amounts and benefits there specified to be estimated by the employer or former employer as accurately as possible.

(12) In this regulation "employment" includes an office, and related expressions have a corresponding meaning.][1]

Amendments—[1] *This regulation inserted by the IT (Employments) (Amendment) Regulations, SI 1999/70 regs 1—3, with effect from 6 April 1999.*

[USE OF ELECTRONIC COMMUNICATIONS AND ELECTRONIC TRANSMISSION OF INFORMATION

Information delivered electronically on another's behalf

46ZB Any information—

(a) delivered by means of the Board's Internet Service for PAYE to an official computer system; or

(b) transmitted electronically to an inspector or collector;

on behalf of any person shall be deemed to have been delivered or transmitted by him unless he proves that they were delivered or transmitted without his knowledge or connivance.][1]

Amendments—*Inserted by the Income Tax (Electronic Communications) (Miscellaneous Amendments) Regulations, SI 2001/1081 regs 7, 20 with effect from 9 April 2001.*

[Mandatory use of electronic communications

46ZC—(1) Specified persons are required to—

(a) transmit the specified information electronically to the inspector or, if so required, the collector, or

(b) deliver the specified information by an approved means of electronic communication to an official computer system.

(2) The specified information may be transmitted or delivered in accordance with paragraph (1) either by the specified person or by another person on his behalf.

(3) The Board may make a general or specific direction requiring a specified person to transmit the specified information electronically or to deliver it by an approved means of electronic communication.

(4) References in regulations 46ZC to 46ZG to information and to the delivery of information shall be construed in accordance with section 135(8) of the Finance Act 2002.][1]

Amendments—[1] *Regulations 46ZC–46ZH inserted by the Income Tax (Employments) (Amendment) Regulations, SI 2003/2494 regs 2, 8 with effect from 20 October 2003.*

[Specified persons

46ZD—(1) A specified person for the purposes of these Regulations is an employer who satisfies the description specified in paragraph (2) or (3) and to whom an e-filing notice has been issued by 31st December following the specified date.

(2) The description specified in this paragraph is that the employer—

(a) is a large employer;

(b) is not an individual who is a practising member of a religious society or order whose beliefs are incompatible with the use of electronic communication;

(c) is not a partnership where all the partners are practising members of a religious society or order whose beliefs are incompatible with the use of electronic communication; and

(d) is not a company where all the directors and the company secretary are practising members of a religious society or order whose beliefs are incompatible with the use of electronic communication.

(3) The description specified in this paragraph is that the employer—

(a) is a large or medium sized employer;

(b) is not an individual who is a practising member of a religious society or order whose beliefs are incompatible with the use of electronic communication;

(c) is not a partnership where all the partners are practising members of a religious society or order whose beliefs are incompatible with the use of electronic communication; and

(d) is not a company where all the directors and the company secretary are practising members of a religious society or order whose beliefs are incompatible with the use of electronic communication.

(4) For the purposes of this regulation—

(a) "company" means any body corporate or unincorporated association but does not include a partnership;

(b) "a large employer" has the meaning given in regulation 42A(2)(b);

(c) "a large or medium sized employer" is a person treated as paying PAYE income to 50 or more recipients at the specified date;

(d) a person is treated as paying PAYE income in the circumstances specified in regulation 42A(3);

(e) "e-filing notice" means a notice issued in respect of a year by an officer of the Board stating that the employer satisfies the description in paragraph (2) or (3) and accordingly is required to use electronic communications for the delivery of specified information;

(f) "the specified date" means such date in the preceding year as is announced annually by means of a direction given by the Board not later than [30th November] of the preceding year;

(g) "the preceding year" means the year preceding that to which the specified information relates.

(5) An employer may appeal against an e-filing notice—

(a) by notice to an officer of the Board,

(b) within 30 days of the issue of the e-filing notice,

(c) on the grounds that the employer does not satisfy the description specified, and if the appeal is successful the e-filing notice shall be withdrawn.][1]

Amendments—[1] *Regulations 46ZC–46ZH inserted by the Income Tax (Employments) (Amendment) Regulations, SI 2003/2494 regs 2, 8 with effect from 20 October 2003.*

[Specified information

46ZE—(1) Subject to paragraph (2), specified information for the purposes of these Regulations is the return and accompanying information required by virtue of regulation 43 of these Regulations (return by employer at end of year)—

(a) for the tax year ending on 5th April 2005, in relation to employers who satisfy the description specified in paragraph (2) of regulation 46ZD; and

(b) for the tax year ending on 5th April 2006 and thereafter, in relation to employers who satisfy the description specified in paragraph (3) of regulation 46ZD.

(2) Specified information does not include information that is supplied in accordance with the provisions and arrangements within regulation 102 of these Regulations (provision for direct collection).][1]

Amendments—[1] *Regulations 46ZC–46ZH inserted by the Income Tax (Employments) (Amendment) Regulations, SI 2003/2494 regs 2, 8 with effect from 20 October 2003.*

[Standards of accuracy and completeness

46ZF—(1) Specified information delivered by means of electronic communications must meet the standards of accuracy and completeness set by specific or general directions given by the Board.

(2) Where the specified information delivered by means of electronic communications fails to meet the standard specified in paragraph (1), that information shall be treated as not having been delivered.][1]

Amendments—[1] *Regulations 46ZC–46ZH inserted by the Income Tax (Employments) (Amendment) Regulations, SI 2003/2494 regs 2, 8 with effect from 20 October 2003.*

[Penalties

46ZG—(1) Subject to paragraph (2), where a specified person or another person on his behalf fails to deliver all or any part of the specified information in accordance with regulation 46ZC(1) he shall be liable to a penalty in accordance with the tables below.

TABLE 1

PENALTY TABLE IN RELATION TO SPECIFIED INFORMATION RELATING TO THE TAX YEAR ENDING 5TH APRIL 2005

Number of employees for whom particulars should have been included with the specified information	*Penalty*
1 to 249	*nil*
250 to 399	*£900*
400 to 499	*£1200*
500 to 599	*£1500*
600 to 699	*£1800*
700 to 799	*£2100*
800 to 899	*£2400*
900 to 999	*£2700*
1000 or more	*£3000*

TABLE 2

PENALTY TABLE IN RELATION TO SPECIFIED INFORMATION RELATING TO THE TAX YEARS ENDING 5TH APRIL 2006 TO 2009

Number of employees for whom particulars should have been included with the specified information	*Penalty*
1 to 49	*nil*
50 to 249	*£600*
250 to 399	*£900*
400 to 499	*£1200*
500 to 599	*£1500*
600 to 699	*£1800*
700 to 799	*£2100*
800 to 899	*£2400*
900 to 999	*£2700*
1000 or more	*£3000*

(2) Paragraph (1) does not apply if the employer had a reasonable excuse for failing to comply with regulation 46ZC(1) and the excuse had not ceased at the time the specified information was delivered.

(3) A notice of appeal against determination under section 100 of the Management Act of a penalty under this regulation can only be on the grounds that—

(a) subject to paragraph (4), the employer is not a specified person;
(b) the employer did comply with regulation 46ZC;
(c) the amount of the penalty is incorrect; or
(d) paragraph (2) applies.

(4) Paragraph (3)(a) does not apply where following an appeal under regulation 46ZD(5) the notice was not withdrawn.][1]

Amendments—[1] *Regulations 46ZC–46ZH inserted by the Income Tax (Employments) (Amendment) Regulations, SI 2003/2494 regs 2, 8 with effect from 20 October 2003.*

[Appeals

46ZH—(1) The following provisions of the Management Act apply to an appeal under regulations 3(8), 42A(4), 42B(7) and 46ZD(5) of these Regulations as they apply to an appeal under section 31 of that Act—

(a) section 31A(5) and (6) (notice of appeal);
(b) section 31B (appeals to General Commissioners);
(c) section 31D (election to bring appeal before Special Commissioners).

(2) Section 103A of the Management Act (interest on penalties) applies to penalties payable under regulation 46ZG.

(3) In an appeal under regulations 3(8), 42A(6), 42B(7) and (12) and 46ZD(5), the relevant place for the purposes of paragraph 3(1)(a) of Schedule 3 to the Management Act (rules for assigning proceedings to General Commissioners) is the place which at the time of the notice of appeal is—

(a) the employer's place of business in the United Kingdom, or
(b) where the employer has no place of business, the employer's place of residence in the United Kingdom.

(4) For the purpose of paragraph (2)—

(a) "place of business" means—

(i) the place where the trade, profession, vocation or business with which the proceedings are concerned is carried on, or
(ii) if the trade, profession, vocation or business is carried on at more than one place, the head office or place where it is mainly carried on;

(b) "place of residence" means the employer's usual place of residence or, if that is unknown, his last known place of residence.][1]

Amendments—[1] *Regulations 46ZC–46ZH inserted by the Income Tax (Employments) (Amendment) Regulations, SI 2003/2494 regs 2, 8 with effect from 20 October 2003.*

UNPAID TAX

Notice and certificate when tax not paid

47—(1) This regulation applies where, within 14 days[, or 17 days where payment is made in respect of emoluments paid after 5th April 2004,][1] *of the end of any income tax period, the employer has paid no amount of tax to the collector under regulation 40 or 41 for that income tax period, and the collector is unaware of the amount, if any, which the employer is liable so to pay.*

(2) Where this regulation applies, the collector may give notice to the employer, requiring him to render, within 14 days, a return in such form as the Board may prescribe showing the amount of tax which the employer is liable to pay to the collector under regulation 40 or 41 in respect of the income tax period in question.

(3) Where a notice given by the collector under paragraph (2) extends to two or more consecutive income tax periods, these Regulations shall have effect as if those consecutive income tax periods were one income tax period.

(4) The collector may give a notice under paragraph (2) notwithstanding that an amount of tax has been paid to him by the employer under regulation 40 or 41 for an income tax period, if he is not satisfied that the amount so paid is the full amount which the employer is liable to pay to him for that income tax period, and this regulation shall have effect accordingly.

(5) Upon receipt of a return made by the employer under paragraph (2), the collector may prepare a certificate showing the amount of tax which the employer is liable to pay to him for the income tax period in question.

(6) Paragraphs (1) to (5) of regulation 54 shall apply to the amount shown in a certificate under paragraph (5).

(7) The production of the return made by the employer under paragraph (2) and of the certificate of the collector under paragraph (5) shall be sufficient evidence that the amount shown in the certificate is the amount of tax which the employer is liable to pay to the collector in respect of the income tax period in question.

(8) Any document purporting to be a certificate under paragraph (5) shall be deemed to be such a certificate until the contrary is proved.

Amendments—[1] *Words in para (1) inserted by the Income Tax (Employments) (Amendment) Regulations, SI 2003/2494 regs 2, 9 with effect from 20 October 2003.*

Notice of specified amount and certificate when tax not paid

48—(1) This applies where, after 14 days[, or 17 days where payment is made in respect of emoluments paid after 5th April 2004,][5] following the end of any income tax period, the employer has paid no amount of tax to the collector under regulation 40 or 41 for that income tax period ...[1] and there is reason to believe that the employer is liable so to pay.

(2) Where this regulation applies, the collector, upon consideration of the employer's record of past payments, may to the best of his judgment specify the amount of tax which he considers the employer is liable to pay, and serve notice on the employer of that amount.

(3) Where the employer has paid no amount under regulation 40 or 41 for the relevant income tax periods, the collector may give a notice under paragraph (2) which extends to two or more consecutive income tax periods, and these Regulations shall have effect as if those income tax periods were the latest income tax period specified in the notice.

(4) The collector may give a notice under paragraph (2) notwithstanding that an amount of tax has been paid to him by the employer under regulation 40 or 41 for any income tax period, if he is not satisfied, after seeking the employer's explanation, that the amount so paid is the full amount which the employer is liable to pay to him for that income tax period, and this regulation shall have effect accordingly.

(5) If, during the period allowed in a notice given by the collector under paragraph (2), the employer claims, but does not satisfy the collector, that the payment made in respect of the income tax period specified in the notice is the full amount he is liable to pay to the collector for that income tax period, then—

(a) the employer may require the collector to inspect the employer's documents and records as if the collector had called upon the employer to produce those documents and records in accordance with regulation 55(1), and

(b) regulation 55 shall apply to that inspection, and the notice given by the collector under paragraph (2) shall be disregarded.

(6) Subject to paragraph (7), if the specified amount of tax, or any part of it, is unpaid on the expiration of the period of seven days allowed in the notice, [the amount so unpaid—

(a) shall be deemed to be an amount of tax which the employer was liable to pay for that income tax period in accordance with regulation 40 or 41, and

(b) may be certified by the collector.][2]

(7) Paragraph (6) shall not apply if, during the period allowed in the notice—

(a) the employer pays the full amount of tax which he is liable to pay to the collector under regulation 40 or 41 for that income tax period, or

(b) the employer satisfies the collector that no amount, or no further amount, is due for that income tax period.

[(7A) For the purposes of this regulation, where—

(a) any payment to the collector is made by cheque, and

(b) the cheque is paid on its first presentation to the banker on whom it is drawn,

the payment shall be treated as made on the day on which the cheque was received by the collector.][4]

(8) ...[3]

(9) The production of a certificate under paragraph (6) shall be sufficient evidence that the employer is liable to pay the amount shown in the certificate to the collector.

(10) Any document purporting to be a certificate under paragraph (6) shall be deemed to be such a certificate until the contrary is proved.

(11) Notwithstanding anything in this regulation, if the employer pays any amount certified by the collector under this regulation and that amount exceeds the amount which he would have been liable to pay in respect of that income tax period apart from this regulation, he shall be entitled to set off such excess against any amount which he is liable to pay to the collector under regulation 40 or 41 for any subsequent income tax period.

(12) If the employer renders the return required by regulation 43(1) after the end of the year, and pays the total net tax which he is liable to pay, any excess of tax paid, and not otherwise recovered by set-off in accordance with this regulation shall be repaid.

Amendments—[1] *In para (1) word revoked by the IT (Employments) (Amendment No 2) Regulations, SI 1995/447 reg 4(a), with effect from 6 April 1995.*

[2] *Words in para (6) substituted by SI 1995/447 reg 4(b).*

[3] *Para (8) revoked by SI 1995/447 reg 4(c).*

[4] *Para (7A) inserted by the IT (Employments) (Amendment No 2) Regulations, SI 1996/980, with effect from 19 April 1996.*

[5] *Words in para (1) inserted by the Income Tax (Employments) (Amendment) Regulations, SI 2003/2494 regs 2, 10 with effect from 20 October 2003.*

Formal determination of tax payable by employer

49—(1) This regulation applies where it appears to the inspector that there may be tax payable under regulation 40 or 41 which—

(a) has not been paid to the collector, and

(b) has not been certified by the collector under regulation 43, 47, 48 or 55.

(2) Where this regulation applies, the inspector may determine the amount of that tax to the best of his judgment, and shall serve notice of his determination on the employer.

(3) A determination under this regulation shall not include tax in respect of which a direction under regulation 42(2) or (3) has been made; and directions under that regulation shall not apply to tax determined under this regulation.

(4) A determination under this regulation may—

(a) cover the tax payable by the employer under regulation 40 or 41 for any one or more income tax periods in a year, and

(b) extend to the whole of that tax or to such part of it as is payable in respect of a class or classes of employees specified in the notice of determination (without naming the individual employees) or of one or more named employees so specified.

(5) Where—

(a) any part of the tax determined under this regulation is not paid within 30 days from the date on which the determination became final and conclusive, and

[(b) the Board are of the opinion that an employee in respect of whose emoluments the determination was made has received his emoluments knowing that the employer has wilfully failed to deduct the amount of tax which he was liable to deduct under these Regulations from those emoluments,][1]

the Board may direct that such part of that tax as it appears to them should have been but was not deducted under these Regulations by the employer on payment of the relevant emoluments shall ...[1] *be recovered from the employee[, and, where the Board so direct, the employer shall not be liable to pay that part of that tax to the collector.]*[1]

(6) If tax recoverable from an employee under paragraph (5) does not carry interest under section 88 of the Management Act, it shall be recoverable from the employee together with interest in accordance with—

(a) regulation 50, in relation to any year not later than the year ended 5th April 1992, from the reckonable date (as defined in that regulation), or

(b) regulation 51, in relation to the year ended 5th April 1993 or any subsequent year, from the reckonable date (as defined in that regulation)

until whichever is the earlier of—

(i) the date on which payment is made, or

(ii) the date (if any) immediately before the date on which it begins to carry interest under section 86 of the Management Act.

(7) A determination under this regulation shall be subject to the like provisions as are contained in [Part IV, Part V (other than section 55 (c)), and Part VI, of the Management Act][3] *as if it was an assessment, and as if the amount of tax determined was income tax charged on the employer, and those Parts of that Act shall apply accordingly with any necessary modifications.*

[(8) An appeal against a determination under this regulation that is to be brought before the General Commissioners shall be brought before the General Commissioners for the division in which the determination was made.][2]

(9) A certificate of the collector that any amount of interest payable under paragraph (6) has not been paid to him, or, to the best of his knowledge and belief, to any other collector or to any person acting on his behalf or on behalf of another collector, shall be sufficient evidence that the sum mentioned in the certificate is unpaid and due to the Crown.

(10) Any document purporting to be a certificate under paragraph (9) shall be deemed to be such a certificate until the contrary is proved.

Simon's Tax Cases—*Wright v Field [1991] STC 18*; Andrews v King [1991] STC 481*.*

Reg 49(5), R v IRC, ex p McVeigh [1996] STC 91; Pawlowski (Collector of Taxes) v Dunnington [1999] STC 550.

Amendments—

[1] *In para (5), sub-para (b) substituted, words revoked, and final words added, by the IT (Employments) (Amendment No 2) Regulations, SI 1995/447 reg 5, with effect from 6 April 1995.*

[2] *Para (8) substituted by the IT (Employments) (Amendment No 3) Regulations, SI 1996/1312 reg 8, with effect in relation to any appeal made on or after 5 June 1996 against a determination in respect of the year 1996-97 or any subsequent year of assessment.*

[3] *Words in para (7) substituted by the Income Tax (Employments) (Amendment No 3) Regulations, SI 1999/2155 reg 7 with effect from 19 August 1999.*

Modification Reg 49(3), (5)(b) words revoked in relation to amounts accounted for in respect of notional payments made under TA 1988 s 203J(3), and the following provisions in these Regulations applied—

(a) Parts I, III, IV and V

(b) Part VIII regs 99–105

(c) Part IX reg 109

by the IT (Employments) (Notional Payments) Regulations, SI 1994/1212 regs 13(1), (2), (7) with effect from 6 April 1994.

Interest on unpaid tax which has been formally determined

50—(1) Where—

(a) an employer has not paid an amount of tax to the collector under regulation 40 or 41, and

(b) the inspector, at any time after 19th April 1988, makes a determination of the amount of such tax under regulation 49, and

(c) the determination does not relate to a year later than the year ended 5th April 1992, and

(d) tax is payable pursuant to that determination,

the tax so payable shall carry interest at the prescribed rate from the reckonable date until payment.

(2) Subject to paragraph (3), in this regulation "the reckonable date" means the 14th day after the end of the year to which the determination relates and, for the purposes of this regulation, where tax payable by the employer for any one or more income tax periods is covered by a determination, that determination shall relate to the year of which that period forms part.

(3) Where, at any time after 19th April 1988, an inspector makes a determination that relates to a year earlier than the year ending on 5th April 1988, then tax payable in accordance with that determination shall carry interest at the prescribed rate from 19th April 1988 until payment and in those circumstances that date shall be the reckonable date.

Interest on tax overdue—general

51—(1) Subject to paragraph (2), where, in relation to the year ended 5th April 1993 or any subsequent year, an employer has not within 14 days[, or 17 days where payment is made by an approved method of electronic communications in respect of emoluments paid after 5th April 2004,][1] *after the end of a year paid to the collector the total net tax deductible by him in respect of all his employees during that year, the tax not so paid shall carry interest at the prescribed rate from the reckonable date until payment.*

(2) Paragraph (1) shall not apply to any tax in respect of which a direction under regulation 42(2) or (3) has been made.

(3) In this regulation "the reckonable date", in relation to any year, means the 14th day after the end of that year [or the 17th day after the end of that year where payment is made by an approved method of electronic communications in respect of emoluments paid after 5th April 2004][1]*.*

(4) A certificate of the collector that any amount of interest payable under this regulation has not been paid to him, or, to the best of his knowledge and belief, to any other collector or to any person acting on his behalf or on behalf of another collector, shall be sufficient evidence that the sum mentioned in the certificate is unpaid and due to the Crown.

(5) Any document purporting to be a certificate under paragraph (4) shall be deemed to be such a certificate until the contrary is proved.

Amendments—[1] *Words in paras (1), (3) inserted by the Income Tax (Employments) (Amendment) Regulations, SI 2003/2494 regs 2, 11 with effect from 20 October 2003.*

Interest on tax overdue—further provisions

52—(1) In regulation 50 and 51 "the prescribed rate" means the rate applicable under section 178 of the Finance Act 1989 for the purposes of section 86 of the Management Act; and where that rate changes on an operative date within the meaning given by regulation 2 of the Taxes (Interest Rate) Regulations 1989 by virtue of those Regulations, the change shall have effect for periods beginning on or after the operative date in relation to interest running from before that date as well as from or from after that date.

(2) The tax payable to which regulation 50(1) or 51(1) applies shall carry interest from the reckonable date even if that date is a non-business day within the meaning of section 92 of the Bills of Exchange Act 1882.

(3) Interest payable under regulation 50 or 51 shall be recoverable as if it were an amount of tax which an employer is liable under regulation 40 or 41 to pay to the collector.

[(4) For the purposes of regulations 50 and 51 and of this regulation, where—

(a) any payment to the collector is made by cheque, and

(b) the cheque is paid on its first presentation to the banker on whom it is drawn, the payment shall be treated as made on the day on which the cheque was received by the collector.][1]

Amendments—[1] *Para (4) inserted by the Income Tax (Employments) (Amendment No 2) Regulations, SI 1996/980 reg 5 with effect from 19 April 1996.*

INTEREST ON TAX OVERPAID

Interest on tax overpaid by employer

53—(1) Where tax in respect of the year ended 5th April 1993 or any subsequent year [not later than the year ended 5th April 1996][2] *is repaid to an employer in the circumstances specified in paragraph (2), the tax repaid shall carry interest at the prescribed rate from the relevant time until the order for the repayment is issued.*

(2) The circumstances specified in this paragraph are where the tax is repaid—

(a) after the end of the year following that in respect of which the tax was paid, and

(b) after the end of the year in which the tax was paid.

(3) In this regulation "the prescribed rate" means the rate applicable under section 178 of the Finance Act 1989 for the purposes of section 824 of the Taxes Act; and where that rate changes on an operative date within the meaning given by regulation 2 of the Taxes (Interest Rate) Regulations 1989 by virtue of those Regulations, the change shall have effect for periods beginning on or after the operative date in relation to interest running from before that date as well as from or from after that date.

(4) In this regulation "the relevant time" means—

(a) in the case of a repayment of tax which was paid more than twelve months after the end of the year in respect of which the payment was made, the end of the year in which that tax was paid; and

(b) in any other case, the end of the year after the year in respect of which the payment was made.

[(5) For the purposes of this regulation, where—

(a) any payment to the collector is made by cheque, and

(b) the cheque is paid on its first presentation to the banker on whom it is drawn,

the payment shall be treated as made on the day on which the cheque was received by the collector.][1]

Amendments—[1] *Para (5) inserted by the IT (Employments) (Amendment No 2) Regulations, SI 1996/980, with effect from 19 April 1996.*

[2] *Words substituted by the IT (Employments) (Amendment No 3) Regulations, SI 1996/1312 reg 9, with effect from 5 June 1996.*

[Interest on tax overpaid by employer—1996-97 and subsequent years][1]

[53A—(1) Where tax in respect of the year ended 5th April 1997 or any subsequent year is repaid to an employer after the end of the year in respect of which the tax was paid, the tax repaid shall carry interest at the prescribed rate—

(a) from the 14th day after the end of the year in respect of which the tax was paid or, if later,

(b) from the date on which the payment of tax for that year was made.

(2) In paragraph (1) "the prescribed rate" means the rate applicable under section 178 of the Finance Act 1989 for the purposes of section 824 of the Taxes Act and where that rate changes on an operative date within the meaning given by regulation 2 of the Taxes (Interest Rate) Regulations 1989 by virtue of those Regulations, the change shall have effect for periods beginning on or after the operative date in relation to interest running from before that date as well as from or from after that date][1]

Amendments—[1] *This regulation inserted by the IT (Employments (Amendment No 3) Regulations, SI 1996/1312 reg 10, with effect from 5 June 1996.*

RECOVERY

Recovery of tax

54—(1) Subject to paragraph (3), the provisions of any enactment relating to the recovery of income tax charged under Schedule E shall apply to the recovery of the amount of tax specified in paragraph (2) (in this regulation referred to as "the amount of tax") as if the amount of tax had been charged under Schedule E by way of an assessment on the employer.

(2) The amount of tax specified in this paragraph is any amount of tax which an employer is liable under regulation 40 or 41, or is deemed liable under regulation 48, to pay to the collector for any income tax period.

(3) Summary proceedings for the recovery of the amount of tax may be brought in England, Wales or Northern Ireland at any time before the expiry of twelve months—

(a) after the date on which the amount of tax became payable, or

(b) where a return has been required under regulation 47, after the date of the delivery of that return to the collector.

(4) Proceedings may be brought for the recovery of the amount of tax without distinguishing the amounts which the employer is liable to pay in respect of each employee and without specifying the employees in question, and the amount of tax shall be one cause of action or one matter of complaint [for the purposes of proceedings under sections 65, 66 and 67 of the Management Act.][1]

(5) Nothing in paragraph (4) shall prevent the bringing of separate proceedings for the recovery of each of the several amounts which the employer is liable to pay for any income tax period in respect of his several employees.

(6) A certificate of the collector that the amount of tax has not been paid to him, or, to the best of his knowledge and belief, to any other collector or to any person acting on his behalf or on behalf of another collector, shall be sufficient evidence that the sum mentioned in the certificate is unpaid and due to the Crown.

(7) Any document purporting to be a certificate under paragraph (6) shall be deemed to be such a certificate until the contrary is proved.

Amendments—[1] *Words in para (4) substituted by the IT (Employments) (Amendment No 3) Regulations, SI 1995/1223 reg 2, with effect from 25 May 1995.*

INSPECTION OF RECORDS

Inspection of employer's records

55—(1) Every employer, whenever called upon to do so by any authorised officer of the Board, shall produce the records specified in paragraph (2) to that officer for inspection, at such time as that officer may reasonably require, at the prescribed place.

(2) The records specified in this paragraph are—

(a) all wages sheets, deductions working sheets, certificates given in accordance with regulations 29(1) and 30(1) (other than those which the employer has sent to the inspector) and other documents and records whatsoever relating to the calculation or payment of the emoluments of his employees in respect of the years or income tax periods specified by such officer or to the deduction of tax from such emoluments; or

[(aa) all documents and records whatsoever relating to any particulars which an employer is required to [provide to the inspector][2] [or deliver by means of electronic communications to an official computer system][3] under regulation 46 in respect of any year specified by the authorised officer; or][1]

(b) such of those wages sheets, deductions working sheets, certificates or other documents and records as may be specified by the authorised officer.

(3) "The prescribed place" mentioned in paragraph (1) means—

(a) such place in the United Kingdom as the employer and the authorised officer may agree upon; or

(b) in default of such agreement, the place in the United Kingdom at which the documents and records referred to in paragraph (2)(a) are normally kept; or

(c) in default of such agreement and if there is no such place as is referred to in sub-paragraph (b) above, the employer's principal place of business in the United Kingdom.

(4) The authorised officer may—

(a) take copies of, or make extracts from, any document produced to him for inspection in accordance with paragraphs (1) and (2);

(b) remove any document so produced if it appears to him to be necessary to do so, at a reasonable time and for a reasonable period.

(5) Where any document is removed in accordance with paragraph (4)(b), the authorised officer shall provide—

(a) a receipt for any document so removed; and

(b) a copy of the document, free of charge, within seven days, to the person by whom it was produced or caused to be produced where the document is reasonably required for the proper conduct of a business.

(6) Where a lien is claimed on a document produced in accordance with paragraphs (1) and (2), the removal of the document under paragraph (4)(b) shall not be regarded as breaking the lien.

(7) Where records are maintained by computer, the person required to make them available for inspection shall provide the authorised officer with all facilities necessary for obtaining information from them.

(8) By reference to the information obtained from an inspection of the documents and records produced under paragraphs (1) and (2), the collector may, on the occasion of each inspection, prepare a certificate showing—

(a) the amount of tax which it appears from the documents and records so produced that the employer is liable to pay to the collector for the years or income tax periods covered by the inspection; and

(b) any amount of such tax which has not been paid to him or, to the best of his knowledge and belief, to any other collector or to any person acting on his behalf or on behalf of another collector.

(9) Paragraphs (1) to (5) of regulation 54 shall apply to the amount shown in a certificate under paragraph (8), with the modification that summary proceedings for the recovery of the amount of tax, or such part of it as remains unpaid, may be brought at any time before the expiry of twelve months after the date of the certificate.

(10) The production of a certificate under paragraph (8) shall be sufficient evidence that the employer is liable to pay the amount shown in the certificate pursuant to paragraph (8)(b) to the collector in respect of the years or income tax periods mentioned in the certificate.

(11) Any document purporting to be a certificate under paragraph (8) shall be deemed to be such a certificate until the contrary is proved.

(12) For the purposes of paragraphs (1) and (2), such of the wages sheets, deductions working sheets, certificates and other documents and records mentioned in those paragraphs as are not required by other provisions of these Regulations to be sent to the inspector or collector shall be retained by the employer for not less than three years after the end of the year to which they relate.

Amendments—[1] *Para (2)(aa) inserted by the IT (Employments) (Amendment No 2) Regulations, SI 1995/447 reg 6, with effect from 6 April 1995.*
[2] *Words in para (2)(aa) substituted by the IT (Employments) (Amendment) Regulations, SI 1998/2484 reg 19 with effect from 28 October 1998.*
[3] *Words in para (2)(aa) inserted by the Income Tax (Electronic Communications) (Miscellaneous Amendments) Regulations, SI 2001/1081 regs 7, 21 with effect from 9 April 2001.*

Modifications—*Reg 55(2)(a) modified in relation to amounts accounted for in respect of notional payments made under TA 1988 s 203J(3), and the following provisions applied—*
(a) Parts I, III, IV and V
(b) Part VIII regs 99–105
(c) Part IX reg 109
by the IT (Employments) (Notional Payments) Regulations, SI 1994/1212 regs 13(1), (2), (8) with effect from 6 April 1994. Reg 55(2)(a) shall have effect as if after "deduction of tax from" there was inserted ", or the accounting of tax in respect of,".

PART VI
SPECIAL PROVISIONS

CHAPTER I
COUNCILLORS' ATTENDANCE ALLOWANCES

Interpretation of Chapter I

56 In this Chapter unless the context otherwise requires—

"attendance allowance" means a payment by way of attendance allowance within section 173(1) of the Local Government Act 1972 regulations made under section 18 of the Local Government and Housing Act 1989 or regulation 4(1) of the Local Government (Payments to Councillors) Regulations (Northern Ireland) 1981;

"council" and "joint committee" shall be construed in accordance with section 148(1) of the Local Government Act (Northern Ireland) 1972;

"councillor" means any person who is entitled to receive a payment by way of attendance allowance by virtue of section 173(1) of the Local Government Act 1972 or regulations made under section 18 of the Local Government and Housing Act 1989 and any member of a council entitled to receive a payment by way of attendance allowance by virtue of regulation 4(1) of the Local Government (Payments to Councillors) Regulations (Northern Ireland) 1981;

"employer" includes the local authority, council, joint authority or joint committee paying the attendance allowance;

"local authority" in England and Wales has the meaning assigned to it by section 270(1) of the Local Government Act 1972 and in Scotland has the meaning assigned to it by section 235(1) of the Local Government (Scotland) Act 1973.

Councillor's option to have tax deducted at basic rate

57—(1) This regulation applies where a councillor is entitled to receive an attendance allowance.

(2) Where a councillor is aggrieved by the inspector's determination under regulation 7 or 9, he may, by notice to the inspector, opt to have income tax deducted from the attendance allowance at the basic rate in force at the time of payment of the attendance allowance.

(3) On receipt of any such notice the inspector shall give notice to the employer of the exercise of the option.

(4) On receipt of a notice given by the inspector to the employer under paragraph (3), and subject to paragraph (5), the employer, on making any payment of an attendance allowance to the councillor, shall deduct income tax at the basic rate in force at the time of that payment.

(5) Where a councillor has exercised his option under paragraph (2) and the inspector considers that the councillor may be obliged to expend money wholly, exclusively and necessarily in the performance of his duties as a councillor, the inspector may direct the employer to disregard an appropriate amount of the councillor's attendance allowance in calculating the tax to be deducted when any payment of attendance allowance is made to the councillor.

(6) Where the inspector has given notice to the employer of the exercise by a councillor of the option in paragraph (2), the employer shall record, on a deductions working sheet, the particulars specified in paragraph (7) regarding every payment of attendance allowance which he makes to the councillor.

(7) The particulars specified in this paragraph are—

(a) the date of the payment,
(b) the amount of the attendance allowance,

(c) where paragraph (5) applies, the net amount of the attendance allowance from which tax has been deducted, and

(d) the amount of tax deducted from the attendance allowance.

Application of Part V of these Regulations

58 Part V of these Regulations shall apply to tax liable to be deducted under regulation 57(4).

CHAPTER II

RESERVE AND AUXILIARY FORCES

Interpretation of Chapter II

59—(1) In this Chapter unless the context otherwise requires—

"the Ministry" means—

(a) in relation to emoluments paid to members of the Merchant Navy Reserve, the [Department of the Environment, Transport and the Regions][2]*, and,*

(b) in all other cases, the Ministry of Defence;

"reserve and auxiliary forces" [means][1] *the forces specified in paragraph (2);*

"reserve pay" means emoluments paid by the Ministry to members of the reserve and auxiliary forces;

"reservist" means any person in receipt of reserve pay other than a person who is not resident in the United Kingdom and is serving outside the United Kingdom.

[(2) The forces specified in this paragraph are—

(a) Royal Naval Reserve (including officers of the retired and emergency lists of the Royal Navy and Royal Marines),

(b) Royal Naval Reserve (including Queen Alexandra's Royal Naval Nursing Service Reserve),

(c) Royal Marines Reserve,

(d) Army Reserve (including Regular Army Reserve of Officers),

(e) Territorial Army,

(f) Air Force Reserve,

(g) Royal Auxiliary Air Force,

(h) Officers, Adult Instructors and Adult Warrant Officers of the Sea Cadet Corps, Army Cadet Force, Air Training Corps or Combined Cadet Force, and

(j) Merchant Navy Reserve.

(3) In paragraph (2)(f) "Air Force Reserve" includes Royal Air Force Reserve of Officers, Royal Air Force Volunteer Reserve (including University Air Squadron members) and Class E Reserve of Airmen.][1]

Amendments—[1] *Words in para (1) substituted, and paras (2), (3) substituted for para (2), by the IT (Employments) (Amendment) Regulations, SI 1997/214, with effect from 1 April 1997.*

[2] *Words in para (1) substituted by the Secretary of State for the Environment, Transport and the Regions Order, SI 1997/2971 reg 6 with effect from 26 January 1998.*

Disapplication of Parts III and IV of these Regulations

60 Parts III and IV of these Regulations shall not apply to reserve pay.

Deduction of tax

61—(1) Subject to paragraph (2), the Ministry, on making any payment of reserve pay to a reservist during any year, shall deduct income tax at the basic rate in force at the time payment is made.

(2) The Ministry shall not deduct income tax if—

(a) it has received notice from the inspector of a determination for that year under any of the following provisions of this Chapter that tax shall not be deducted from reserve pay, and

(b) it has not received notice of any amendment of that determination.

(3) Regulation 8 shall not apply to any notice within paragraph (2).

(4) This regulation shall apply on the making of any payment of reserve pay notwithstanding that an objection or appeal has been made under regulation 63 or 64.

Determination by inspector

62—(1) The inspector may make a determination that tax shall not be deducted from reserve pay if he is satisfied that the reservist will not be liable to income tax on the full amount of the reserve pay in that year, on the footing that any reliefs from income tax to which the reservist is entitled are allowable primarily against his income from other sources.

(2) The inspector may make the determination referred to in paragraph (1) either prior to or at any time during any year.

(3) If the inspector makes the determination referred to in paragraph (1), he shall give notice of that determination to the reservist and to the Ministry.

SIs

Objections and appeals

63—(1) A reservist from whose reserve pay tax has been deducted in accordance with regulation 61 may give notice of objection to the inspector stating the grounds of his objection if he is aggrieved by that deduction.

(2) On receipt of the notice of objection the inspector shall make a determination whether income tax at the basic rate shall be deducted from the reserve pay, and shall give notice of that determination to the reservist.

(3) The inspector may amend his determination by agreement with the reservist, and, in default of such agreement, the reservist, on giving notice to the inspector, may appeal against the determination.

(4) An appeal under paragraph (3) may be made to the General or Special Commissioners.

(5) Subject to paragraph (6), an appeal to the General Commissioners shall be heard [by the General Commissioners for the division in which the reservist's place of residence is situated][1]

(6) The like provisions as are contained in section 44(2) of the Management Act shall apply to the appeal as they apply to appeals against assessments.

(7) On appeal, the Commissioners shall determine whether income tax at the basic rate shall be deducted from the reserve pay having regard to the circumstances by reference to which the inspector may determine under regulation 62 that income tax at the basic rate shall not be deducted from reserve pay.

(8) Subject to regulation 64, the determination of the Commissioners shall be final.

(9) If, on appeal, the Commissioners determine that tax shall not be deducted from the reserve pay, the inspector shall give notice of that determination to the Ministry.

Amendments—[1] *Words substituted by the IT (Employments) (Amendment No 3) Regulations, SI 1996/1312 reg 11, with effect from 5 June 1996.*

Amended determinations

64—(1) If a determination by the inspector or the Commissioners under regulation 62 or 63 is found to be inappropriate because the actual circumstances are different from the circumstances by reference to which it was made, the inspector shall amend that determination.

(2) The inspector shall give notice of his amendment of that determination to the reservist and to the Ministry.

(3) Regulation 63 shall apply in relation to an amendment of a determination as it applies in relation to a determination under regulation 63(2).

Certificate of tax deducted

65—(1) The Ministry may, and [if the reservist so requires][1] *shall, give the reservist a certificate in a form authorised by the Board showing the particulars specified in paragraph (2) in respect of any payment of reserve pay made during the year from which tax is deducted.*

(2) The particulars specified in this paragraph are—

(a) the date of the payment,
(b) the amount of the payment, and
(c) the amount of tax deducted on making the payment.

Amendments—[1] *Words in para (1) substituted by the IT (Employments) (Amendment) Regulations, SI 1993/2276 regs 1, 2, 11, with effect from 12 October 1993.*

Repayment to reservist during the year

66—(1) The Ministry shall not repay tax in respect of reserve pay to a reservist.

(2) On application being made to him by the reservist, the inspector may make such repayment to the reservist as may be appropriate at any time during the year having regard to the matters specified in paragraph (3).

(3) The matters specified in this paragraph are—

(a) the reserve pay of the reservist for the period from the beginning of the year up to and including the date of that application,
(b) the amount of tax deducted from that reserve pay as evidenced by certificates of pay and tax supplied under regulation 65, and
(c) any reliefs from income tax to which the reservist is entitled, and his income for the year from all other sources and his liability to tax on that income, as estimated by the inspector.

Ministry records

67—(1) The Ministry shall record, on a deductions working sheet, the particulars specified in paragraph (2) regarding every payment of reserve pay made to a reservist.

(2) The particulars specified in this paragraph are—

(a) the date of the payment,

(b) the amount of the payment, and
(c) the amount of tax, if any, deducted on making the payment.

End of year certificate

68—(1) [Not later than 56 days after][1] the end of the year the Ministry shall give the certificate specified in paragraph (2) to a reservist to whom paragraph (3) applies.

(2) The certificate specified in this paragraph is a certificate in the form provided or authorised by the Board showing—

(a) the total amount of reserve pay paid by the Ministry to the reservist during the year,
(b) the total tax deducted from the reserve pay,
(c) the force in which the reservist was serving and his service number, and
(d) in the case of a form not provided by the Board, that it has been authorised by them in substitution for such a form.

(3) A reservist to whom this paragraph applies is a reservist who—

(a) is a member of the reserve and auxiliary forces on the last day of the year and from whose reserve pay tax has been deducted during that year, and
(b) has not been given a certificate under regulation 65 in respect of each payment of reserve pay during that year.

Amendments—[1] *Words substituted by the IT (Employments) (Amendment No 3) Regulations, SI 1996/1312 reg 12, with effect from 5 June 1996.*

Application of Parts V and VIII of these Regulations

69—(1) Part V of these Regulations shall apply with any necessary modifications to tax liable to be deducted under regulation 61.

(2) Part VIII of these Regulations shall apply with any necessary modifications to reserve pay.

Other emoluments of reservist

70 Nothing in this Chapter shall affect the application of these Regulations to any other emoluments of a reservist.

CHAPTER III

HOLIDAY PAY

Interpretation of Chapter III

71 In this Chapter unless the context otherwise requires—

''fund'' means a person who pays holiday pay to an individual who is not employed by him (or, on the death of that individual, to some other person);
''holiday pay'' means any payment obtained by an individual (or, on his death, by some other person) in exchange for a voucher, stamp or similar document purchased by a person who employs (or employed) that individual for any holiday period;
''recipient'' means an individual (or, on that individual's death, some other person claiming in respect of that individual's right) who is paid holiday pay by a fund.

Disapplication of Parts III and IV of these Regulations

72 Parts III and IV of these Regulations shall not apply to holiday pay paid by a fund.

Deduction of tax

73 A fund, on making any payment of holiday pay to a recipient, shall deduct income tax at the basic rate in force at the time the payment is made.

Certificate of tax deducted

74—(1) A fund, on making any payment of holiday pay, shall give the recipient a certificate in a form authorised by the Board showing the particulars specified in paragraph (2).

(2) The particulars specified in this paragraph are—

(a) the recipient's name,
(b) the tax year in which the payment is made,
(c) the date of the payment,
(d) the amount of the payment, and
(e) the amount of tax deducted on making the payment.

Repayment to recipient during the year

75—(1) A fund shall not repay tax deducted from a payment of holiday pay to a recipient.

(2) On application being made to him by the recipient, the inspector may make such repayment to the recipient as may be appropriate at any time during the year having regard to the matters specified in paragraph (3).

(3) The matters specified in this paragraph are—

(a) the holiday pay of the recipient (or of the individual in respect of whose right the recipient is paid) for the period from the beginning of the year up to and including the date of that application,

(b) the amount of tax deducted from that holiday pay as evidenced by certificates of pay and tax supplied under regulation 74, and

(c) any reliefs from income tax to which the recipient is (or the individual in respect of whose right the recipient is paid was) entitled, his income for the year from all other sources and his liability to tax on that income, as estimated by the inspector.

Fund records

76—(1) A fund shall record, on a deductions working sheet, the particulars specified in paragraph (2) regarding every payment of holiday pay made to a recipient.

(2) The particulars specified in this paragraph are—

(a) the recipient's name,

(b) the tax year to which the deductions working sheet relates,

(c) the date of the payment,

(d) the amount of the payment, and

(e) the amount of tax deducted on making the payment.

Application of Parts V and VIII of these Regulations

77—(1) Part V of these Regulations shall apply with any necessary modifications to tax liable to be deducted under regulation 73.

(2) Part VIII of these Regulations shall apply with any necessary modifications to holiday pay.

Other emoluments of recipient

78 Nothing in this Chapter shall affect the application of these Regulations to any other emoluments of a recipient.

CHAPTER IV

OTHER CASES

Death of employer

79 If an employer dies, anything which he would have been liable to under these Regulations shall be done by—

(a) his personal representatives, or

(b) where an employer paid emoluments on behalf of another person, the person succeeding him, or

(c) where an employer paid emoluments on behalf of another person and no person succeeds him, the person on whose behalf he paid emoluments.

Succession to a business, etc

80—(1) This regulation applies where there has been a change in the employer from whom an employee receives—

(a) emoluments in respect of his employment in any trade, business, concern or undertaking, or in connection with any property, or

(b) any annuity or pension.

(2) Subject to paragraphs (3) and (4), where this regulation applies—

(a) the change shall not be treated as a cessation of employment for the purposes of regulation 23, but

(b) in relation to any matter arising after the change, the employer after the change shall be liable to do anything which the employer before the change would have been liable to do under these Regulations if the change had not taken place.

(3) The employer after the change shall not be liable for the payment of any tax which was deductible from emoluments paid to the employee before the change took place.

(4) If a trade dispute began, but did not end, before the change took place—

(a) regulations 36(5), 42(7) and 45 shall apply to the employer before the change as though the time limit of 42 days had expired when the change took place, and

(b) the employer after the change shall be liable to make repayment of any tax withheld by the employer before the change in accordance with regulation 36(3) in the year in which the change took place, and regulation 42(6) shall apply in such a case.

(5) The employer before the change shall furnish the employer after the change with such particulars as may be necessary to enable the employer after the change to comply with this regulation.

[Payment for assignment or release of a right to acquire shares

80ZA—(1) This regulation applies where—

(a) the consideration for the assignment or release of a right to acquire shares takes the form of a payment,

(b) the payment is made in the period beginning on 6th April 1998 and ending on 31st July 1998,

(c) so much of that payment ('the relevant amount') as does not exceed the amount assessable by virtue of section 135 of the Taxes Act is treated, in accordance with section 203FB(3)(a) of that Act, as a payment of assessable income of the relevant person, and

(d) the employer would, but for section 67(3) of the Finance Act 1998, have accordingly been liable to deduct an amount of income tax in accordance with these Regulations in respect of the relevant amount.

(2) Regulation 40 shall have effect as if the relevant amount was an amount of emoluments paid by the employer in the income tax month ending on 5th August 1998.''][1]

Amendments—[1] *Regulation inserted by the IT (Employments) (Notional Payments) Regulations, SI 1994/1212 reg 12A (as inserted by SI 1998/1891 reg 8) with effect from 4 August 1998.*

[CHAPTER V
PAYE SETTLEMENT AGREEMENTS]

Statement of Practice SP 5/96—*Explains how PAYE settlement agreements operate.*

Amendments—*This Chapter (regs 80A-80N) inserted by the Income Tax (Employments) (Amendment No 6) Regulations, SI 1996,/2631 regs 2, 4, with effect with respect to any PAYE settlement agreement entered into for the year 1996–97 or any subsequent year, subject to a transitional provision (SI 1996/2631 reg 3), relating to agreements entered into after 5 April 1996 but before 5 November 1996.*

[General provision

80A—(1) The Board and an employer may agree that the employer shall be accountable to the Board in respect of income tax on such emoluments of his employees as are specified in paragraph (3) in accordance with the terms of the agreement and not in accordance with Parts III to V, and Part VIII, of these Regulations.

(2) An agreement falling within paragraph (1) is referred to in this Chapter as a ''PAYE settlement agreement''.

(3) The emoluments specified are emoluments that—

(a) consist of—

(i) sums paid by the employer to an employee or other person in respect of expenses of the employee and falling within section 19 of the Taxes Act as emoluments from the employment,

(ii) any benefit provided for, or made available to, an employee by the employer and falling within section 19 of the Taxes Act as emoluments from the employment,

(iii) sums paid by the employer to an employee in respect of expenses of the employee and falling within section 153 of the Taxes Act, or

(iv) any benefit provided for, or made available to, an employee by the employer and falling within any of sections 141 to 146, or within Chapter II of Part V, of the Taxes Act,

(b) are agreed by the Board and the employer to be—

(i) minor as regards the amount of the sums paid or the type of benefit provided or made available, or

(ii) irregular as regards the frequency in which, or the times at which, the sums are paid or the benefit is provided or made available, or

(iii) paid or (as the case may be) provided or made available in the circumstances specified in paragraph (4); and

(c) are not emoluments to which regulation 80C(2)(a) or (b) applies.

(4) The circumstances specified are where—

(a) in the case of sums paid, deduction of tax by reference to the tax tables is impracticable;

(b) in the case of a benefit provided or made available, the benefit is shared by more than one employee and apportionment of the benefit between the employees concerned is impracticable.

(5) Emoluments comprised in a PAYE settlement agreement shall not be included in a return by the employer under regulation [43, 44 or 45 of these Regulations, or in particulars provided by the employer under regulation 46 of these Regulations][2]*.]*[1]

Amendments—[1] *This Chapter (regs 80A-80N) inserted by the Income Tax (Employments) (Amendment No 6) Regulations, SI 1996/2631 regs 2,4, with effect with respect to any PAYE settlement agreement entered into for the year 1996–97 or any* *subsequent year, subject to a transitional provision (SI 1996/2631 reg 3), relating to agreements entered into after 5 April 1996 but before 5 November 1996.*

[2] *Words in para (5) substituted by the IT (Employments) (Amendment) Regulations, SI 1998/2484 reg 20 with effect from 28 October 1998.*

SIs

[Form of agreement

80B—(1) A PAYE settlement agreement—

(a) shall be in writing, and shall be signed and dated by the employer and by an inspector or other officer of the Board on behalf of the Board, and

(b) shall incorporate, whether by specification or indirect reference, the matters specified in paragraph (2).

(2) The matters specified are—

(a) the emoluments comprised in the agreement;

(b) the method of calculation, determined in accordance with regulation 80F, of the amount of income tax for which the employer is to be accountable to the Board in respect of those emoluments for the year to which the agreement relates;

(c) the date specified in regulation 80G(2) on which income tax in respect of those emoluments is due and payable for the year to which the agreement relates.][1]

Amendments—[1] *This Chapter (regs 80A-80N) inserted by the Income Tax (Employments) (Amendment No 6) Regulations, SI 1996/2631 regs 2,4, with effect with respect to any PAYE settlement agreement entered into for the year 1996–97 or any subsequent year, subject to a transitional provision (SI 1996/2631 reg 3), relating to agreements entered into after 5 April 1996 but before 5 November 1996.*

[Commencement of agreement

80C—(1) A PAYE settlement agreement may be entered into—

(a) at any time before the beginning of the year for which it is intended by the Board and the employer that it should have effect, or

(b) at any time during that year, or

(c) after that year but before 6th July in the following year.

(2) An agreement entered into at a time specified in paragraph (1)(b) or (c) shall not apply to—

(a) emoluments that, at the date the agreement is entered into, have been, or should have been, paid earlier in that year under deduction of tax in accordance with Parts III and IV of these Regulations, or

(b) emoluments consisting of benefits that, at the time the agreement is entered into, are reflected in the employee's code for that year in accordance with Part III of these Regulations.][1]

Amendments—[1] *This Chapter (regs 80A-80N) inserted by the Income Tax (Employments) (Amendment No 6) Regulations, SI 1996/2631 regs 2,4, with effect with respect to any PAYE settlement agreement entered into for the year 1996–97 or any subsequent year, subject to a transitional provision (SI 1996/2631 reg 3), relating to agreements entered into after 5 April 1996 but before 5 November 1996.*

[Variation of agreement

80D—(1) The Board and the employer may, by agreement and consistently with the provisions of this Chapter, and not later than the date specified in paragraph (3), vary the terms of a PAYE settlement agreement entered into by them.

(2) Any such agreement to vary shall be in writing and signed and dated by the employer and by an inspector or other officer of the Board on behalf of the Board.

(3) The date specified is the 6th July in the year following the year to which the PAYE settlement agreement relates.][1]

Amendments—[1] *This Chapter (regs 80A-80N) inserted by the Income Tax (Employments) (Amendment No 6) Regulations, SI 1996/2631 regs 2,4, with effect with respect to any PAYE settlement agreement entered into for the year 1996/97 or any subsequent year, subject to a transitional provision (SI 1996/2631 reg 3), relating to agreements entered into after 5 April 1996 but before 5 November 1996.*

[Emoluments comprised in agreement and liability to tax—consequential provisions

80E—(1) Emoluments of an employee included in a PAYE settlement agreement shall be treated as excluded from his income for the purposes of section 198 of the Taxes Act (relief for necessary expenses) and of otherwise determining the amount of his liability to income tax under Schedule E for the year to which the agreement relates, but not so as to affect the chargeability of those emoluments to income tax or his employer's liability under the agreement to account for income tax in respect of those emoluments.

(2) An employee shall be treated, except for the purposes of the obligations imposed on his employer under regulation 80N, as relieved from any obligations under the Income Tax Acts—

(a) to retain records containing information relating to emoluments included in a PAYE settlement agreement, or

(b) to render returns in respect of those emoluments.

(3) Sums in respect of income tax for which an employer is to be accountable to the Board under a PAYE settlement agreement shall not be treated, for the purposes of these Regulations, as tax deducted from emoluments.

(4) An employee shall have no right to be treated as having paid tax in respect of sums for which his employer is accountable under a PAYE settlement agreement, and accordingly shall not be entitled to claim or receive any refund of tax paid by his employer under the agreement.] [1]

Amendments—[1] *This Chapter (regs 80A-80N) inserted by the Income Tax (Employments) (Amendment No 6) Regulations, SI 1996/2631 regs 2,4, with effect with respect to any PAYE settlement agreement entered into for the year 1996–97 or any subsequent year, subject to a transitional provision (SI 1996/2631 reg 3), relating to agreements entered into after 5 April 1996 but before 5 November 1996.*

[Calculation of tax payable under agreement

80F—(1) A PAYE settlement agreement shall provide for the sums in respect of income tax for which an employer is to be accountable to the Board under the agreement—

(a) to be computed in accordance with the factors specified in paragraph (2), and

(b) to include the amount specified in paragraph (3).

(2) The factors specified are—

(a) in the case of emoluments comprising sums paid in respect of expenses, the estimated aggregate amount of such payments on which income tax is chargeable, reduced by such amount (if any) as would have been deductible under section 198 of the Taxes Act if the emoluments had not been included in the agreement;

(b) in the case of emoluments comprising benefits provided or made available, the estimated aggregate amount of the cash equivalents and other amounts on which income tax is chargeable, reduced by such amount (if any) as would have been deductible under section 198 of the Taxes Act if the emoluments had not been included in the agreement;

(c) the total number of employees in receipt of emoluments comprised in the agreement;

(d) the number of those employees respectively chargeable to income tax—

(i) at [the starting rate][2]*, but not the basic rate or higher rate, for the year to which the agreement relates,*

(ii) at [the starting rate][2]*and the basic rate, but not the higher rate, for that year, and*

(iii) at [the starting rate][2]*, the basic rate and the higher rate for that year;*

(e) such other matters as are agreed by the Board and the employer to be relevant in relation to the emoluments comprised in the agreement.

(3) The amount specified for the purposes of paragraph (1)(b) is an amount equal to income tax on the aggregate of the amounts computed in accordance with paragraph (2)(a) and (b).

(4) The amount specified in paragraph (3) shall be calculated so as to take account of the factor specified in paragraph (2)(d).][1]

Amendments—[1] *This Chapter (regs 80A-80N) inserted by the Income Tax (Employments) (Amendment No 6) Regulations, SI 1996/2631 regs 2,4, with effect with respect to any PAYE settlement agreement entered into for the year 1996–97 or any subsequent year, subject to a transitional provision (SI 1996/2631 reg 3), relating to agreements entered into after 5 April 1996 but before 5 November 1996.*

[2] *Words in para (2)(d) substituted by the Income Tax (Employments) (Amendment No 3) Regulations, SI 1999/2155 reg 12 with effect from the year 1999–00.*

[Payment of tax

80G—(1) An employer shall, on or before the date specified in paragraph (2), pay to the collector the aggregate amount for which he is accountable to the Board under a PAYE settlement agreement for the year to which the agreement relates.

(2) The date specified is the 19th October next following the year concerned.

(3) Subject to paragraph (5), the provisions of any enactment relating to the recovery of income tax charged under Schedule E shall apply to the recovery of the amount specified in paragraph (4) (in this regulation referred to as "the amount of tax") as if that amount had been charged under Schedule E by way of an assessment on the employer.

(4) The amount specified is the aggregate amount referred to in paragraph (1) or any part of that amount.

(5) Summary proceedings for the recovery of the amount of tax may be brought in England, Wales or Northern Ireland at any time before the expiry of 12 months after the date specified in paragraph (2).

(6) Proceedings may be brought for the recovery of the amount of tax without distinguishing the amounts which the employer is liable to pay in respect of each employee under the PAYE settlement agreement and without specifying the employees in question, and the amount of tax shall be one cause of action or one matter of complaint for the purposes of proceedings under sections 65, 66 and 67 of the Management Act.][1]

Amendments—[1] *This Chapter (regs 80A-80N) inserted by the Income Tax (Employments) (Amendment No 6) Regulations, SI 1996/2631 regs 2,4, with effect with respect to any PAYE settlement agreement entered into for the year 1996–97 or any* *subsequent year, subject to a transitional provision (SI 1996/2631 reg 3), relating to agreements entered into after 5 April 1996 but before 5 November 1996.*

[Formal determination of tax payable by the employer

80H—(1) This regulation applies where it appears to an inspector or other officer of the Board that there may be an amount payable to the collector under regulation 80G(1) for any year which has not been paid by the date specified in paragraph (2) of that regulation.

(2) Where this regulation applies, the inspector or officer may determine that amount to the best of his judgment, and shall serve notice of his determination on the employer.

(3) A determination under this regulation shall be subject to the like provisions as are contained in Parts IV, V and VI of the Management Act as if it were an assessment, and as if the amount determined were income tax charged on the employer, and those Parts of that Act shall apply accordingly with any necessary modifications.

(4) Where pursuant to paragraph (3) an appeal against a determination is to the General Commissioners, it shall be brought before the General Commissioners for the division in which the place where the determination was made is situated.][1]

Amendments—[1] *This Chapter (regs 80A-80N) inserted by the Income Tax (Employments) (Amendment No 6) Regulations, SI 1996/2631 regs 2,4, with effect with respect to any PAYE settlement agreement entered into for the year 1996–97 or any subsequent year, subject to a transitional provision (SI 1996/2631 reg 3), relating to agreements entered into after 5 April 1996 but before 5 November 1996.*

[Interest on unpaid tax

80J—(1) Where in respect of the year to which the agreement relates the employer has not paid in full to the collector, on or before the date specified in regulation 80G(2), the amount referred to in paragraph (1) of that regulation, the amount unpaid shall carry interest at the prescribed rate from that date ("the due date") until payment.

(2) Where—

(a) an inspector or other officer of the Board makes a determination of an amount under regulation 80H for any year, and

(b) the amount is payable pursuant to that determination,

the amount so payable shall carry interest at the prescribed rate from the date specified in regulation 80G(2) applicable to that year ("the due date") until payment.

(3) A certificate of the collector that any amount of interest payable under this regulation has not been paid to him or, to the best of his knowledge and belief, to any other collector or to any person acting on his behalf or on behalf of another collector, shall be sufficient evidence that the sum mentioned in the certificate is unpaid and due to the Crown.

(4) Any document purporting to be a certificate under paragraph (3) shall be deemed to be such a certificate until the contrary is proved.

(5) In this regulation "the prescribed rate" means the rate applicable under section 178 of the Finance Act 1989 for the purposes of section 86 of the Management Act; and where that rate changes on an operative date within the meaning given by regulation 2 of the Taxes (Interest Rate) Regulations 1989 by virtue of those Regulations, the change shall have effect for periods beginning on or after the operative date in relation to interest running from before that date as well as from or from after that date.

(6) For the purpose of this regulation, where—

(a) any payment to the collector is made by cheque, and

(b) the cheque is paid on its first presentation to the banker on whom it is drawn,

the payment shall be treated as made on the day on which the cheque was received by the collector.

(7) The amount referred to in paragraph (1) as unpaid and the amount referred to in paragraph (2) as payable shall carry interest from the due date even if that date is a non-business day within the meaning of section 92 of the Bills of Exchange Act 1882.

(8) Interest payable under this regulation shall be recoverable as if it were an amount unpaid as mentioned in paragraph (1).][1]

Amendments—[1] *This Chapter (regs 80A-80N) inserted by the Income Tax (Employments) (Amendment No 6) Regulations, SI 1996/2631 regs 2,4, with effect with respect to any PAYE settlement agreement entered into for the year 1996–97 or any subsequent year, subject to a transitional provision (SI 1996/2631 reg 3), relating to agreements entered into after 5 April 1996 but before 5 November 1996.*

[Interest on overpaid tax

80K—(1) Where tax in respect of the year to which the agreement relates is repaid to the employer after the date specified in regulation 80G(2), the tax repaid shall carry interest at the prescribed rate from that date or, if later, from the date on which the tax was paid until the date on which the order for the repayment is issued.

(2) In paragraph (1) "the prescribed rate" means the rate applicable under section 178 of the Finance Act 1989 for the purposes of section 824 of the Taxes Act; and where that rate changes on an operative date within the meaning given by regulation 2 of the Taxes (Interest Rate) Regulations 1989 by virtue of those Regulations, the change shall have effect for periods beginning on or after the operative date in relation to interest running from before that date as well as from or from after that date.

(3) For the purposes of this regulation, where—

(a) pursuant to paragraph (1) interest is payable from the date on which the tax was paid,

(b) the payment of tax was made to the collector by cheque, and

(c) the cheque was paid on its first presentation to the banker on whom it was drawn.

the payment of tax shall be treated as made on the day on which the cheque was received by the collector.][1]

Amendments—[1] *This Chapter (regs 80A-80N) inserted by the Income Tax (Employments) (Amendment No 6) Regulations, SI 1996/2631 regs 2,4, with effect with respect to any PAYE settlement agreement entered into for the year 1996–97 or any subsequent year, subject to a transitional provision (SI 1996/2631 reg 3), relating to agreements entered into after 5 April 1996 but before 5 November 1996.*

[Review of agreements

80L—(1) An inspector or other officer of the Board shall, on or before the date specified in paragraph (2), review the operation of a PAYE settlement agreement for the year to which the agreement relates.

(2) The date specified is the 6th July next following the year concerned.][1]

Amendments—[1] *This Chapter (regs 80A-80N) inserted by the Income Tax (Employments) (Amendment No 6) Regulations, SI 1996/2631 regs 2,4, with effect with respect to any PAYE settlement agreement entered into for the year 1996–97 or any subsequent year, subject to a transitional provision (SI 1996/2631 reg 3), relating to agreements entered into after 5 April 1996 but before 5 November 1996.*

[Cancellation of Agreement

80M—(1) In the circumstances specified in paragraph (2), the Board may, by notice to an employer, cancel a PAYE settlement agreement entered into by that employer with effect from the date of the notice.

(2) The circumstances specified are where—

(a) there has been serious or persistent failure on the part of the employer—

(i) to account to the Board for sums for which he is accountable under the agreement, or otherwise to comply with the terms of the agreement, or

(ii) to produce records in accordance with regulation 80N, or

(b) there has been serious or persistent failure on the part of the employer with respect to the deduction of, and accounting for, tax in accordance with Parts III to V of these Regulations, or the rendering of returns in accordance with those Parts of these Regulations.

(3) The obligations of the employer contained in Parts III to V, and Part VIII, of these Regulations shall have effect with respect to emoluments to which the cancelled agreement related that are paid or (as the case may be) provided or made available by the employer following the receipt by him of a notice of cancellation pursuant to paragraph (1).][1]

Amendments—[1] *This Chapter (regs 80A-80N) inserted by the Income Tax (Employments) (Amendment No 6) Regulations, SI 1996/2631 regs 2,4, with effect with respect to any PAYE settlement agreement entered into for the year 1996–97 or any subsequent year, subject to a transitional provision (SI 1996/2631 reg 3), relating to agreements entered into after 5 April 1996 but before 5 November 1996.*

[Inspection and retention of records

80N—(1) Every employer, whenever called upon to do so by an inspector or other officer of the Board, shall produce the records specified in paragraph (2) to that person for inspection, at such time as that person may reasonably require, at the prescribed place.

(2) The records specified are—

(a) all books, documents and other records relating to—

(i) the emoluments comprised in a PAYE settlement agreement entered into by the employer,

(ii) the calculation of amounts for which the employer is accountable to the Board in accordance with the agreement in respect of the years specified by the officer, and

(iii) the payment of those amounts to a collector, or

(b) such of those books, documents and other records as may be specified by the inspector or officer.

(3) "The prescribed place" mentioned in paragraph (1) means—

(a) such place in the United Kingdom as the employer and the inspector or officer may agree upon, or

(b) in default of such agreement—

(i) the place in the United Kingdom at which the records specified in paragraph (2) are normally kept, or

(ii) if there is no such place, the employer's principal place of business in the United Kingdom.

(4) The inspector or officer may—

(a) take copies of, or make extracts from, any records produced to him for inspection in accordance with paragraphs (1) and (2);

(b) remove any records so produced if it appears to him to be necessary to do so, at a reasonable time and for a reasonable period.

(5) Where any record is removed in accordance with paragraph (4)(b), the inspector or officer shall provide—

(a) a receipt for the record so removed, and

(b) a copy of the record, free of charge, within seven days, to the person by whom it was produced or caused to be produced where the record is reasonably required for the proper conduct of a business.

(6) Where a lien is claimed on a record produced in accordance with paragraphs (1) and (2), the removal of the document under paragraph (4)(b) shall not be regarded as breaking the lien.

(7) Where records are maintained by computer, the person required to make them available for inspection shall provide the inspector or officer with all facilities necessary for obtaining information from them.

(8) The records specified in paragraph (2)(a) shall be retained by the employer for not less than three years after the end of the most recent year to which they relate.][1]

Amendments—[1] *This Chapter (regs 80A-80N) inserted by the Income Tax (Employments) (Amendment No 6) Regulations, SI 1996/2631 regs 2, 4, with effect with respect to any PAYE settlement agreement entered into for the year 1996–97 or any subsequent year, subject to a transitional provision (SI 1996/2631 reg 3), relating to agreements entered into after 5 April 1996 but before 5 November 1996.*

PART VII

SOCIAL SECURITY BENEFITS

CHAPTER I

GENERAL

Interpretation of Part VII

81 In this Part of these Regulations unless the context otherwise requires—

["benefit" means a payment in accordance with—

(a) the Social Security Act 1986 or the Social Security Contributions and Benefits Act 1992 or, in Northern Ireland, the Social Security (Northern Ireland) Order 1986 or the Social Security Contributions and Benefits (Northern Ireland) Act 1992, or

(b) the Jobseekers Act 1995 or, in Northern Ireland, the Jobseeker's (Northern Ireland) Order 1995,

which includes taxable benefit;][2]

"claim" means a claim to a benefit [or to incapacity benefit][1]*;*

"claimant" means a person who has made a claim and who is not an employed claimant;

"employed claimant" means an employed earner who has made a claim;

["incapacity benefit" means "incapacity benefit" as defined by section 139(5) of Finance Act 1994 which by virtue of subsection(1) of that section, falls to be treated as income for the purposes of the Income Tax Acts and charged to income tax under Schedule E;][1]

"taxable benefit" means income chargeable under section [151A or][2] *617(1) of the Taxes Act; and*

"working sheet" means any form of record on or in which the matters required by this Part of these Regulations are to be kept.

Amendments—[1] *Words in definition of "claim" and definition of "incapacity benefit" inserted by the IT (Employments) (Incapacity Benefit) Regulations, SI 1995/853 reg 4, with effect from 13 April 1995.*

[2] *Definition of "benefit" substituted and words in definition of "taxable benefit" inserted by the IT (Employments) (Amendment No 4) Regulations, SI 1996/2381 reg 3, with effect from 7 October 1996.*

Application of other Parts of these Regulations

82—(1) Parts III to VI of these Regulations shall apply to payments of taxable benefit[, and Parts III to V and Part VIII of these Regulations shall apply to payments of incapacity benefit,][2] *only to the extent and with the modifications set out in this Part of these Regulations.*

(2) To the extent that Parts III to VI [and Part VIII][2] *of these Regulations are [applied by]*[1] *this Part of these Regulations and unless the context otherwise requires—*

"emoluments" shall be interpreted as "taxable benefit" [or, as the case may be, "incapacity benefit"][2]*;*

"employee" shall be interpreted as "claimant";

"employer" shall be interpreted as "the Department";

and related expressions shall be construed accordingly.

Amendments—[1] *Words in para (2) substituted by the IT (Employments) (Amendment) Regulations, SI 1993/2276 regs 1, 2, 12, with effect from 12 October 1993.*

[2] *Words in sub-para (1), (2) inserted by the IT (Employments) (Incapacity Benefit) Regulations, SI 1995/853, with effect from 13 April 1995.*

CHAPTER II

PAYMENTS TO WHOLLY UNEMPLOYED PERSONS

Interpretation of Chapter II

83—(1) In this Chapter "the Department" means—

(a) in Great Britain, the Department of [Social Security][1]*, or*

(b) in Northern Ireland, the Department of Health and Social Services for Northern Ireland.

(2) ...[1]*.*

(3) For the purposes of this Chapter any reference to the deduction or repayment of tax on making any payment shall be taken to refer to the duties imposed upon the Department by regulations 88 and 89.

Amendments—[1] *Words in para (1) substituted and para (2) revoked by the IT (Employments) (Amendment No 4) Regulations, SI 1996/2381 reg 4, with effect from 7 October 1996.*

Procedure on making claim

84—(1) On making a claim after a period of employment to which Part IV of these Regulations applied, the claimant shall deliver to the Department [two of the three][2] *copies of the [statement]*[4] *delivered to him in accordance with regulation 23(3).*

(2) On making a claim after a previous claim to which regulation 89 applied, the claimant shall deliver to the Department [two of the three][2] *copies of the certificate delivered to him in accordance with regulation 89(2)(c).*

(3) The Department shall forthwith—

(a) prepare a deductions working sheet in the form provided or in a form authorised by the Board and in accordance with the particulars given on the copies of the [statement or][4] *certificate, the two copies of which were delivered by the claimant;*

(b) record on the working sheet the cumulative emoluments shown on the [statement or][4] *certificate;*

(c) either record on the working sheet or keep such records as enable the production of the following particulars, namely—

(i) save where the code contained in the [statement or][4] *certificate reflects additional pay, the cumulative free emoluments, the cumulative taxable emoluments and the corresponding cumulative tax as at the week or month shown on the copies of the [statement or]*[4] *certificate;*

(ii) where the code contained in the [statement or][4] *certificate reflects additional pay, the cumulative additional pay, the cumulative taxable emoluments and either the cumulative tax as at the week or month shown on the copies of the [statement or]*[4] *certificate or the total net tax deducted shown on the copies of the [statement or]*[4] *certificate, whichever is the less; and*

(d) supply those particulars to the inspector, in such form as the Board may provide, together with such further information as may be required for the purposes of these Regulations.

(4) ...[2]

(5) If the claim is made within the first seven weeks of the year and a [statement or][4] *certificate, the two copies of which were delivered in accordance with this regulation, shows that the last payment of emoluments or taxable benefit was in the preceding year, the Department shall comply with paragraph (3), but without recording the cumulative emoluments or total net tax deducted (if any) shown on the [statement or]*[4] *certificate.*

(6) The code shown on the [statement or][4] *certificate shall be treated as the appropriate code for the purposes of these Regulations, except that where the [statement or]*[4] *certificate relates to the year ended 5th April 1993 and the code shown on the [statement or]*[4] *certificate is no longer valid, the appropriate code shall be deemed to be the code which effects deduction of tax with no personal reliefs at one or more of the rates referred to in regulation 8(4).*

(7) If, on the making of a claim, no copies of a [statement or][4] *certificate have been delivered in accordance with paragraph [(1) or (2)]*[3]*, or, subject to paragraph (5), the two copies of a [statement or]*[4] *certificate so delivered show that the last payment of emoluments was in a year preceding that in which the claim was made, the Department shall, for the purposes of paragraph (3), record the code [which after allowing for the personal relief specified in section 257(1) of the Taxes Act effects*

deduction of tax at one or more of [the starting rate, the basic rate and the higher rate][5]][1] as the appropriate code.

(8) If, on making a claim, a claimant to whom paragraph (1) applies declares that his last employer has not delivered the [three][3] copies of the [statement][4] referred to in that paragraph to him, the Department may require that last employer to deliver those [three][3] copies to a specified office of the Department.

(9) Subject to paragraph (10), if a claimant has not delivered the two copies of a [statement or][4] certificate in accordance with paragraph (1) or (2) and the two copies of the [statement][4] have not been obtained under paragraph (8) within the period specified by the Board, the Department shall render a return to the inspector, giving the name and address of the claimant, the date of claim and such other particulars as may be necessary to enable the inspector to determine the appropriate code in accordance with regulation 7.

(10) The return referred to in paragraph (9) shall not be rendered if the claimant certifies, in a form provided by the Board, that—

(a) he is undergoing a course of full-time education and has not had regular employment since 6th April, or

(b) he has not had regular employment since the end of his full-time education.

Amendments—[1] *Words in para (7) substituted by the IT (Employments) (Amendment) Regulations, SI 1993/2276 regs 1, 2, 5, with effect from 12 October 1993.*

[2] *Words in paras (1), (2) substituted and para (4) revoked by the IT (Employments) (Amendment) Regulations, SI 1996/804 regs 1, 9(a), (b), with effect from 6 April 1996.*

[3] *Words in paras (7), (8) substituted by the IT (Employments) (Amendment) Regulations, SI 1996/804 regs 1, 9(c), (d), with effect from 6 April 1996.*

[4] *Words in paras (1), (8) and (9) substituted, and words in paras (3), (5)–(7) and (9) inserted by the IT (Employments) (Amendment) Regulations, SI 1998/2484 reg 21 with effect from 28 October 1998.*

[5] *Words in para (7) substituted by the Income Tax (Employments) (Amendment No 3) Regulations, SI 1999/2155 reg 13 with effect from the year 1999–00.*

Determinations and notifications by the inspector

85—(1) The inspector may determine an appropriate code for any claimant in accordance with regulation 7, and if he does so regulations 6, 8 and 10 to 13 inclusive shall apply to that determination.

(2) Any notification of code or amended code, or of cumulative emoluments and total net tax deducted received from the inspector by the Department shall be recorded in substitution for any previous record and shall be used for the purpose of all calculations required under this Chapter.

Quarterly attenders

86—(1) If the Department decides that a claimant may make quarterly declarations in respect of his claim and the claimant has not had regular employment for at least twelve months, these Regulations shall not apply as regards any subsequent payment of benefit or event relating to the claim in question.

(2) If the Department decides that a claimant may make quarterly declarations in respect of his claim on the ground that he is in receipt of a pension in respect of a former employment such that no benefit is payable, the Department shall so notify the inspector.

Determination and recording of amount of taxable benefit

87 On each occasion that a payment of benefit is made to a claimant to whom regulation 86 does not apply, the Department shall determine and record the taxable benefit included in the payment.

End of year

88—(1) [Not later than 56 days after][2] the end of the year the Department shall, in respect of each claimant whose latest claim was not treated as terminated under regulation 89 during the year—

(a) make a tax calculation in accordance with regulation 91;

(b) subject to paragraph (2), issue the certificate specified in paragraph (4) to the claimant; and

(c) render the return specified in paragraph (5) to the inspector.

(2) The Department shall not be required to issue the certificate specified in paragraph (4) if no taxable benefit has been paid and a tax calculation in accordance with regulation 91 is not required.

(3) If a payment of benefit in respect of any year is made after the certificate for that year referred to in paragraph (1) has been rendered or would have been rendered but for paragraph (2), the Department shall proceed under regulation 90 as if further taxable benefit had been paid.

(4) The certificate specified in this paragraph is a certificate in such form as the Board may provide, and shall show as appropriate—

(a) the year to which it relates,

(b) the total benefit for the year excluding any amounts previously notified under regulation 89 or 90,

(c) the taxable benefit included in such total benefit,

(d) the code appropriate to the claimant,
(e) any previous emoluments and any tax deducted from those emoluments which the Department was required to take into account under regulation 91,
(f) the total emoluments for the year and the corresponding total net tax deducted, and
(g) the amount of tax refunded by the Department.

(5) The return specified in this paragraph is a return in such form as the Board may prescribe, and shall show as appropriate—

(a) such particulars as may be required for the identification of the claimant,
(b) the particulars specified in paragraph (4),
(c) ...[1]
(d) the excess (if any) of the total tax due arising from the calculation under regulation 91 over tax previously deducted in the year.

Amendments—[1] *Para (5)(c) revoked by the IT (Employments) (Amendment) Regulations, SI 1996/804 regs 1, 10, with effect from 6 April 1996.*
[2] *Words substituted by the IT (Employments) (Amendment No 3) Regulations, SI 1996/1312 reg 12, with effect from 5 June 1996.*

Termination of claim

89—(1) For the purposes of these Regulations a claim is to be treated as terminated if the claimant—

(a) gives notice of termination, or
(b) fails to make a further claim, or
(c) fails to make a declaration in respect of the claim.

(2) Where a claim is treated as terminated, the Department shall—

(a) make a tax calculation in accordance with regulation 91;
(b) forthwith deliver to the inspector a certificate in such form as the Board may provide containing the following particulars—

(i) such particulars as may be required for the identification of the claimant,
(ii) the last day in accordance with paragraph (3) below,
(iii) the code appropriate to the claimant,
(iv) the cumulative emoluments (including taxable benefit) and the corresponding total net tax deducted at the date of termination or, if regulation 91(4) or (5) applies, the taxable benefit,
(v) the amount of any tax shown by the calculation to be payable in addition to that already paid,
[(vi) if different from the amount referred to in paragraph (iv) above, the amount of taxable benefit paid in the last period of claim,
(vii) if different from the amount of the tax referred to in paragraph (v) above, the amount of tax shown by the calculation to be payable or refundable on the amount of taxable benefit referred to in paragraph (vi) above, and
(viii) the date of issue of the certificate;][1]

(c) make [three][1] *copies of the certificate specified in sub-paragraph (b) above on the form provided, and deliver them to the claimant on the same date as the certificate is delivered to the inspector; and*
(d) give notice to the claimant of—

(i) the total benefit for the year excluding any sums previously notified under this regulation or regulation 90, and
(ii) the taxable benefit included in that total benefit.

(3) Subject to paragraph (4), the relevant date for the purpose of any tax calculation which the Department is required to make under this regulation shall be the last day for which benefit was claimed, and if paid was not recoverable, except that if that last day is 4th or 5th April the relevant date shall be the preceding 3rd April.

(4) The Department shall not be required to amend a tax calculation solely because the date originally treated as the relevant date is subsequently shown to be incorrect.

Amendments—[1] *Para (2)(b)(vi)–(viii) and word in para (2)(c) substituted by the IT (Employments) (Amendment) Regulations, SI 1996/804 regs 1, 11, with effect from 6 April 1996.*

Notification of taxable benefit adjustment

90 If after the issue of a certificate under regulation 88(1) or of a notice under regulation 89(2)(d) or under this regulation, further taxable benefit is paid or taxable benefit overpaid is refunded by the claimant, the Department shall—

(a) give notice to the claimant of the revised figure of total benefit and the taxable benefit included in that revised figure in accordance with the relevant regulation; and
(b) notify the inspector of the sums paid or refunded in such form as the Board may provide.

Tax calculation

91—(1) Subject to paragraphs (4) and (5), whenever the Department is required by these Regulations to make a tax calculation, the Department shall ascertain—

(a) for the year up to the relevant date—

[(zi) the total taxable benefit,][1]

(i) the cumulative emoluments including taxable benefit,

(ii) the cumulative free emoluments or, as the case may be, the cumulative additional pay,

(iii) the cumulative taxable emoluments, and

(iv) the cumulative tax; and

(b) the total net tax deductible at the relevant date, save that where the code reflects additional pay, the total net tax deductible shall not exceed the overriding limit.

(2) If the total net tax deductible calculated in accordance with paragraph (1) exceeds the previous total net tax deducted, the Department shall amend the record of the code as if a direction had been received from the inspector on the relevant date under regulation 17.

(3) If the previous total net tax deducted recorded on the working sheet exceeds the total net tax deductible calculated in accordance with paragraph (1), the Department shall repay the excess to the claimant ...[1]

(4) No tax calculation shall be made if the inspector has made a direction that the provisions of regulation 17 shall apply to the claimant for the relevant year.

(5) Subject to regulation 85(2), the inspector shall be deemed to have made a direction under paragraph (4) where—

(a) regulation 84(7) has been applied and the certificate referred to in regulation 84(10) has not been given, or

(b) the two copies of the [statement or][2] *certificate delivered under regulation 84(1) or (2) do not relate to the claimant's last employment or claim before the present claim, whichever is later, or*

(c) the claimant is in receipt of a pension from a former employer, or

(d) it appears to the Department on the occasion of a claim that a previous claim should have been treated as terminated in accordance with regulation 89, or

(e) the code is one issued under regulation 9.

(6) In this regulation—

"the relevant date" means—

(a) where a calculation is required by regulation 88, the end of the year, and

(b) where a calculation is required by regulation 89, the date specified in regulation 89(3);

"the total net tax deductible" means the total tax due in accordance with the appropriate tax tables in respect of any taxable emoluments at the relevant date.

Amendments—[1] *Para (1)(a)(zi) inserted, and in para (3) words revoked, by the IT (Employments) (Amendment) Regulations, SI 1996/804 regs 1, 12, with effect from 6 April 1996.*

[2] *Words in para (5)(b) inserted by the IT (Employments) (Amendment) Regulations, SI 1998/2484 reg 22 with effect from 28 October 1998.*

Death of claimant

92—(1) On the death of a claimant the Department shall comply with regulation 89 where the name and address of the claimant's personal representative is known, except that—

(a) the [three][2] *copies of the certificate mentioned in regulation 89(2)(c) shall be sent to the inspector together with the certificate under regulation 89(2)(b), and*

(b) the notice referred to in regulation 89(2)(d) shall be sent to the personal representative.

(2) If the Department has not been notified of the name and address of the claimant's personal representative within 30 days of a claimant's death—

(a) the inspector shall be deemed to have made a direction under [regulation 17(1)(c) in relation to any payment of taxable benefit made after the death of the claimant][1]*, and*

(b) the Department shall then proceed as in paragraph (1) above, except that the notice under regulation 89(2)(d) shall not be sent.

Amendments—[1] *Words in para (2)(a) substituted by the IT (Employments) (Amendment) Regulations, SI 1993/2276 regs 1, 2, 13, with effect from 12 October 1993.*

[2] *Words in para (1)(a) substituted by the IT (Employments) (Amendment) Regulations, SI 1996/804 regs 1, 13, with effect from 6 April 1996.*

Finance

93—(1) The Board shall advance monies to the National Insurance Funds of Great Britain and Northern Ireland at intervals to be agreed with the Department of Social Security and the Department of Health and Social Services for Northern Ireland respectively for use in making repayments of income tax under these Regulations.

(2) The Departments mentioned in paragraph (1) shall provide the Board with a quarterly statement of receipts and payments in such form as the Board may require.

CHAPTER III

PAYMENTS TO EMPLOYED PERSONS

Interpretation of Chapter III

94 In this Chapter "the Department" means—

(a) in Great Britain, [the Department for Work and Pensions][1], or

(b) in Northern Ireland, the Department of Health and Social Services for Northern Ireland

by whom a payment of benefit is made.

Amendments—[1] *Words in para (a) substituted by the Secretaries of State for Education and Skills and for Work and Pensions Order, SI 2002/1397 art 12, Schedule para 25(1), (3) with effect from 27 June 2002.*

Benefit paid by the paying Department direct to the claimant

95—(1) If the Department pays benefit directly to an employed claimant—

(a) the Department shall determine and record the amount of taxable benefit, and

(b) the full sum shall be paid without any deduction or repayment of income tax.

Benefit paid by employer

96—(1) If benefit is paid to an employed claimant by his employer on behalf of the Department and the employer calculates the benefit payable by reference to instructions supplied by the Department, the employer shall also calculate the taxable benefit in accordance with those instructions.

(2) If benefit is paid to an employed claimant by his employer on behalf of the Department and paragraph (1) does not apply, the Department shall notify the employer of the amount of benefit and of taxable benefit.

(3) If the employer has undertaken to pay benefit on behalf of the Department, the Department shall pay the full amount of benefit to the employer without any deduction on account of income tax.

(4) Subject to paragraph (5), Parts III to VI of these Regulations shall apply to the taxable benefit paid by the employer on behalf of the Department as if it were a payment of emoluments from the employment.

(5) In any case in which it appears to the Board that deduction of tax from the taxable benefit referred to in paragraph (4) by reference to the tax tables is impracticable, the Board may make such other arrangements as are appropriate for the collection of tax in respect of taxable benefit in such cases.

Termination of claim

97—(1) A claim shall be treated as terminated if the employed claimant—

(a) gives notice of termination, or

(b) fails to make a further claim, or

(c) fails to make a declaration in respect of the claim.

(2) Where a claim is treated as terminated the Department shall notify the inspector and the employed claimant of the total benefit and taxable benefit paid in respect of the claim, showing the amounts appropriate to each year.

Adjustments

98 If, after the payment of benefit by an employer or the Department, the Department recovers part or all of that payment from the employed claimant, the Department shall notify the inspector and the employed claimant of the adjustment to the figure of taxable benefit, showing the amounts appropriate to each year.

[CHAPTER IV

PAYMENTS OF INCAPACITY BENEFIT]

[Interpretation of Chapter IV

98A In this Chapter "the Department" means—

(a) in Great Britain, the Department of Social Security, or

(b) in Northern Ireland, the Department of Health,

by whom a payment of incapacity benefit is made.][1]

Amendments—[1] *This regulation and the heading preceding it inserted by the IT (Employments) (Incapacity Benefit) Regulations, SI 1995/853, with effect from 13 April 1995.*

[Application of other parts of these Regulations

98B Subject to the following provisions of this Chapter, Parts III and IV, Part V except for regulations 47 to 53, and Part VIII of these Regulations shall apply to incapacity benefit paid by the Department as if it were a payment of emoluments from the claimant's employment.][1]

Amendments—[1] *This regulation inserted by the IT (Employments) (Incapacity Benefit) Regulations, SI 1995/853, with effect from 13 April 1995.*

[Deduction where appropriate code not yet determined

98C—(1) On making any payment of incapacity benefit to a claimant—

(a) in respect of whom no code authorisation has been received from the inspector, and
(b) in the circumstances specified in paragraph (2),

the Department shall deduct tax and keep records on a deductions working sheet which it shall prepare for the purpose as if the payment were one to which regulation 17 applied, applying the code which, after allowing for the relevant personal relief, effects deduction of tax at one or both of the rates specified in paragraph (3) as the appropriate code.

(2) The circumstances specified in this paragraph are where for the year in question the claimant is not entitled to receive (in addition to payments of incapacity benefit) any payments of emoluments, or is so entitled but has failed to furnish any details relating to those emoluments when making his claim.

(3) The rates specified in this paragraph are [the starting rate][2] *and the basic rate.*

(4) For the purposes of paragraph (1), the relevant personal relief is any one or more of the following reliefs claimed by the claimant, that is to say—

(a) the relief specified in section 257(1) of the Taxes Act (personal allowance);
[(aa) the relief specified in section 257AA(1) of the Taxes Act (children's tax credit);][4]
(b) ...[3]
(c) the relief specified in section 265(1) of the Taxes Act (blind person's allowance).][1]

Amendments—[1] *This regulation inserted by the IT (Employments) (Incapacity Benefit) Regulations, SI 1995/853, with effect from 13 April 1995.*

[2] *Words in para (3) substituted by the Income Tax (Employments) (Amendment No 3) Regulations, SI 1999/2155 reg 14 with effect from the year 1999–00.*

[3] *Para (4)(b) revoked by the Income Tax (Employments) (Amendment No 3) Regulations, SI 1999/2155 reg 18 with effect from the year 2000–01.*

[4] *Para (4)(aa) inserted by SI 1999/2155 reg 23 with effect from the year 2001–02.*

[Return of payment of incapacity benefit

98D—(1) On the occasion of making any payment of incapacity benefit to a claimant, the Department shall, subject to paragraph (3), forthwith render a return to the inspector containing the particulars specified in paragraph (2).

(2) The particulars specified in this paragraph are—

(a) the name, address and national insurance number of the claimant;
(b) the date on which the claimant's entitlement to incapacity benefit commenced;
(c) the weekly rate of incapacity benefit being paid to the claimant;
(d) where the payment is made in the circumstances specified in regulation 98C(2), details of the code applied to the payment in accordance with paragraph (1) of that regulation.

(3) If the Department, having rendered the return mentioned in paragraph (1), makes any subsequent payment of incapacity benefit to the claimant, it shall not be required to render any further return pursuant to that paragraph unless—

(a) the inspector had earlier made a determination as mentioned in regulation 98G(1) in relation to the payments of incapacity benefit made to the claimant, and
(b) the subsequent payment—
(i) is made at a rate different from the rate subsisting at the time of the determination, and
(ii) is the first payment to be made at the different rate.][1]

Amendments—[1] *This regulation inserted by the IT (Employments) (Incapacity Benefit) Regulations, SI 1995/853, with effect from 13 April 1995.*

[Delivery of certificate relating to cessation of employment

98E—(1) Where—

(a) a claimant has received from an employer on cessation of employment [three][2] *copies of the [statement]*[3] *referred to in regulation 23, and is in possession of those copies immediately before the making of the claim, and*
(b) the claim is made in the circumstances specified in regulation 98C(2),

he shall, subject to paragraph (2), [deliver two of the three copies][2] *to the Department when making the claim, and the Department shall forthwith send the copies to the inspector by whom code authorisations are ordinarily issued to the Department.*

(2) The requirement under paragraph (1) to deliver the two copies of the [statement][3] shall not apply in any case where the claimant has made, or intends to make, a claim for repayment of tax for the year in which the claim to incapacity benefit is made.][1]

Amendments—[1] *This regulation inserted by the IT (Employments) (Incapacity Benefit) Regulations, SI 1995/853, with effect from 13 April 1995.*

[2] *Words in para (1) substituted by the IT (Employments) (Amendment) Regulations, SI 1996/804 regs 1, 14, with effect from 6 April 1996.*

[3] *Words in paras (1)(a) and (2) substituted by the IT (Employments) (Amendment) Regulations, SI 1998/2484 reg 23 with effect from 28 October 1998.*

[Determination of appropriate code by inspector

98F—(1) Following receipt by the inspector of the return referred to in regulation 98D(1), the inspector shall determine the appropriate code for the purposes of these Regulations.

(2) In determining the appropriate code, regulation 7 shall not apply but the inspector shall have regard, subject to paragraph (4), to the reliefs from income tax specified in paragraph (3) to which the claimant is entitled for the year in which the code is determined, so far as his title to those reliefs has been established at the time of the determination.

(3) The reliefs specified in this paragraph are—

(a) the relief specified in section 257(1) of the Taxes Act;

[(b) the relief specified in section 257A(2) of the Taxes Act (married couples allowance);]

(c) the relief specified in section 265(1) of the Taxes Act;

[(ca) the relief specified in section 257AA(1) of the Taxes Act;][3]

(d) ...[2]

(4) Where the code is determined before the beginning of the year for which it is to have effect, the inspector shall disregard any relief specified in paragraph (3) if he is not satisfied that the claimant will be entitled to it for that year.

(5) Regulations 6, 8 and 10 to 13 inclusive shall apply with any necessary modifications to an appropriate code determined by the inspector in accordance with this regulation.][1]

Amendments—[1] *This regulation inserted by the IT (Employments) (Incapacity Benefit) Regulations, SI 1995/853, with effect from 13 April 1995.*

[2] *Para (3)(b) substituted and para (3)(d) revoked by the Income Tax (Employments) (Amendment No 3) Regulations, SI 1999/2155 reg 19 with effect from the year 2000–01.*

[3] *Para (3)(ca) inserted by SI 1999/2155 reg 24 with effect from the year 2001–02.*

[Coding where no tax is deductible

98G—(1) The inspector may determine that no tax shall be deducted from any payment of incapacity benefit made in the circumstances specified in regulation 98C(2) if—

(a) he is not satisfied that the amount of incapacity benefit will be chargeable to tax, or

(b) he considers that the code which would otherwise be the appropriate code would result in too much tax being deducted for the year in question.

(2) Where the inspector determines as mentioned in paragraph (1), he shall be deemed to have determined the appropriate code, and regulations 6, 8 and 10 to 13 inclusive shall apply accordingly with any necessary modifications.][1]

Amendments—[1] *This regulation inserted by the IT (Employments) (Incapacity Benefit) Regulations, SI 1995/853, with effect from 13 April 1995.*

[Subsequent procedure on issue of code authorisation

98H On making any payment of incapacity benefit in the circumstances specified in regulation 98C(2) after a code authorisation has been issued in respect of the claimant, the Department shall, except where the inspector has made a direction under regulation 17(1)(c) in relation to any such payment, deduct or repay tax by reference to the appropriate code in accordance with regulation 14 and keep the records required by regulation 38.][1]

Amendments—[1] *This regulation inserted by the IT (Employments) (Incapacity Benefit) Regulations, SI 1995/853, with effect from 13 April 1995.*

PART VIII

ASSESSMENT AND DIRECT COLLECTION

[Assessment

99 Nothing in these Regulations shall prevent an assessment (whether made under section 9 of the Management Act or otherwise) being made in respect of income assessable to income tax for any year.][1]

Amendments—[1] *This regulation substituted by the IT (Employments) (Amendment No 3) Regulations, SI 1996/1312 reg 13, with effect from 5 June 1996.*

Appeals

100—(1) Subject to paragraph (2), an appeal against an assessment of emoluments shall be heard by the General or Special Commissioners in accordance with the like provisions as are contained in section 31 and Part V of the Management Act.

(2) The appeal shall be brought before the General Commissioners for the division in which the place where the assessment was made is situated and not the General Commissioners for the division in which the place of employment is situated where—

(a) the place of employment referred to in paragraph 3 of Schedule 3 to the Management Act and the place where the assessment was made are not within the same division, and
(b) the inspector so elects by notice given to the employee.1

Simon's Tax Cases—*Murphy v Elders [1974] STC 34*.*
Amendments—[1] *This regulation revoked by the IT (Employments) (Amendment No 3) Regulations, SI 1996/1312 reg 19(1), with effect from 5 June 1996 except so far as concerns any appeal made on or after that date against an assessment for the year 1995-96 or any earlier year.*

Repayment of overpayments and recovery of underpayments

101—(1) If the tax payable under the assessment is less than the total net tax deducted from the employee's emoluments during the year less any subsequent repayments made, the inspector may, and if the person assessed so requires shall, repay the difference to the person assessed instead of taking it into account in determining the appropriate code for a subsequent year.

(2) If the tax payable under the assessment exceeds the total net tax deducted from the employee's emoluments during the year less any subsequent repayments made, the inspector may require the person assessed to pay the excess to the collector instead of taking it into account in determining the appropriate code for a subsequent year, and where the inspector so requires the person assessed shall pay the excess accordingly.

(3) Subject to [paragraphs (5) and (6)][1], for the purpose of determining the amount of the difference mentioned in paragraph (1) or the excess mentioned in paragraph (2), any necessary adjustment shall be made to the total net tax deducted in respect of the matters specified in paragraph (4).

(4) The matters specified in this paragraph are—

(a) any tax which the employer was liable to deduct from the employee's emoluments but failed so to deduct ...[2]
(b) any shortfall in deductions made in accordance with these Regulations from the employee, where—

(i) payments of profit-related pay have been made to the employee in accordance with a profit-related pay scheme registered under Chapter III of Part V of the Taxes Act,
(ii) in consequence of the relief given by that Chapter less tax has been deducted from those payments than would have been deducted if the scheme had not been registered, and
(iii) the registration of the scheme has subsequently been cancelled with effect from a time before that relevant for the purposes of the relief;

(c) any tax overpaid or remaining unpaid for any year; and
(d) any amount to be recovered as if it were unpaid tax under section 30(1) of the Management Act, being an amount of tax ...[1] repaid to the employee in excess of the amount properly due to him, to the extent that the inspector took that amount to be recovered into account in determining the appropriate code and the total net tax deducted was in consequence greater than it would otherwise have been.

(5) An adjustment under sub-paragraph (a) or (b) of paragraph (4) shall be disregarded for the purposes of determining the amount of the difference mentioned in paragraph (1) and of computing any tax overpaid under sub-paragraph (c) of paragraph (4).

[(6) Where a direction is made by the collector under regulation 42(2), or by the Board under regulation 42(3) or 49(5), in relation to the employee and in respect of one or more income tax periods falling within the year—

(a) the employee shall not be entitled to include the amount of tax which is the subject of the direction in calculating the amount of tax referred to in paragraph (4)(a);
(b) if the direction follows the making of the assessment, the amount (if any) shown in the notice of assessment as a deduction from, or a credit against, the tax payable under the assessment shall be taken as reduced by the amount of tax which is the subject of the direction.][3]

[(7) In this regulation—

(a) references to an assessment are references to an assessment other than an assessment under section 9 of the Management Act;
(b) references to "tax payable under the assessment" are references to the amount of tax shown in the assessment as payable without regard to any amount shown in the notice of assessment as a deduction from, or a credit against, the amount of tax payable.][3]

Amendments—[1] *Words in para (3) substituted by the IT (Employments) (Amendment No 2) Regulations, SI 1995/447 reg 7(a), with effect from 6 April 1995.*
[2] *In para (4) words revoked by SI 1995/447 reg 7(b).*

[3] *Paras (6), (7) added by SI 1995/447 reg 7(c); para (7) substituted by the IT (Employments) (Amendment No 3) Regulations, SI 1996/1312 reg 14 (b) with effect from 5 June 1996.*
[4] *Words revoked by SI 1996/1312 reg 14(a).*

[Recovery of overpayments and recovery of underpayments—self-assessments

101A—(1) For the purpose of determining in respect of the year ended 5th April 1997 or any subsequent year—

(a) the amount of any such excess as is mentioned in section 59A(1) of the Management Act, or
(b) the amount of the difference mentioned in section 59B(1) of that Act,

any necessary adjustments in respect of the matters prescribed by paragraph (2) shall be made to the amount of tax deducted at source in accordance with these Regulations in that year.

(2) The matters prescribed are—

(a) the aggregate amount of any repayments of tax deducted at source made to the employee;
(b) the like matters as are specified in paragraph (4) of regulation 101, having regard to paragraphs (5) and (6) of that regulation.

(3) Where the amount of the difference mentioned in section 59B(1) of the Management Act is payable by the employee as mentioned in that section, the inspector or other officer of the Board may—

(a) require the employee to pay that amount to the collector, or
(b) take that amount into account in determining the appropriate code for a subsequent year.

(4) In paragraph (2)(a) the reference to repayments of tax is a reference to any repayments made in the year in which the tax was deducted at source, or after the end of that year but before the employee's return containing his self-assessment is made under section 8 or 8A of the Management Act.][1]

Amendments—[1] *This regulation inserted by the IT (Employments) (Amendment No 3) Regulations, SI 1996/1312 reg 15, with effect from 5 June 1996.*

Provisions for direct collection—general

102—(1) The inspector may proceed in accordance with any of the provisions and arrangements specified in paragraph (2) in any of the cases specified in paragraph (3).

(2) The provisions and arrangements specified in this paragraph are—

(a) the provisions of regulation 103[1]*,*
(b) the provisions of regulation 104, and
(c) arrangements made for the collection of the tax in respect of the emoluments of any employees.

(3) The cases specified in this paragraph are—

(a) cases of casual employment, and
(b) any other case in which the inspector is of opinion that deduction of tax by reference to the tax tables is impracticable.

Amendments—[1] *Words in italics revoked by the IT (Employments) (Amendment No 3) Regulations, SI 1996/1312 reg 16, with effect so far as concerns any action taken by the inspector under this Regulation on or after 5 June 1996 for the year 1996–97 or any subsequent year.*

Direct collection involving assessment

103—(1) As early in the year as may be, the inspector shall make an assessment for that year in the amount specified in paragraph (2).

(2) The amount specified in this paragraph is—

(a) where the assessment is made upon a pension or pensions, the amount receivable in the current year estimated to the best of the inspector's judgment; but if this provision does not apply then
(b) where—

(i) the inspector is unable to ascertain the full amount of the employee's emoluments for the preceding year,
(ii) the inspector is unable to ascertain the full amount of the employee's emoluments for the part of the preceding year during which the employee was in employment, or
(iii) the employee had no emoluments for the previous year,

an amount estimated to the best of the inspector's judgment; but if this provision does not apply then

(c) where the employee was in employment during part only of that preceding year, the amount which bears the same proportion to the amount of the employee's emoluments for the preceding year as a full year bears to the part of that preceding year during which the employee was in employment; but if this provision does not apply then
(d) the amount of the employee's emoluments for the preceding year.

(3) The inspector shall serve a notice of assessment on the employee, and regulation 100 shall apply accordingly as regards appeals.

(4) If the employee has appealed against the assessment, so much of the tax as appears to the inspector to be not in dispute shall be treated as tax payable under the assessment for so long as the appeal remains undetermined; but if the employee considers that a smaller amount is not in dispute, he may require the amount not in dispute to be determined by the Commissioners by whom an appeal against the assessment falls to be determined.

(5) The inspector shall transmit particulars of the tax payable under the assessment to the collector.

(6) The tax payable under the assessment shall be paid to the collector in four equal instalments during the period beginning 30 days after the service of the notice of assessment and ending on the following 5th April, with the first instalment being payable on the last day of the first quarter of that period, the second on the last day of the second quarter of that period, the third on the last day of the third quarter of that period, and the fourth on the following 5th April.

(7) If the employee proves that his emoluments for the period from the beginning of the year to the following 5th July amounted to less than one-quarter of the amount of the assessment, and that the tax paid by him during the first quarter of the period mentioned in paragraph (6) exceeds the tax which would have been payable if the assessment had been made in an amount equal to four times those emoluments, the inspector may direct that the instalment payable during the next quarter of that period shall be reduced by the amount of the excess.

(8) Paragraph (7) shall apply with the necessary modifications where the employee proves that his emoluments for the period from the beginning of the year to the following 5th October or 5th January amounted to less than one-half or three-quarters respectively of the amount of the assessment.

(9) After the end of the year the amount of the employee's emoluments for the year shall be ascertained, and if that amount is—

(a) less than the amount assessed, the assessment shall be reduced accordingly and any tax overpaid shall be repaid;

(b) greater than the amount assessed, a further assessment shall be made, and paragraphs (3), (4) and (5) shall apply to any such further assessment.[1]

Amendments—[1] *This regulation revoked by the IT (Employments) (Amendment No 3) Regulations, SI 1996/1312 reg 19(2) with effect from 5 June 1996 except so far as concerns any assessment made on or after that date for the year 1995–96 or any earlier year.*

Direct collection involving deductions working sheets

104—(1) The inspector may issue a deductions working sheet to the employee specifying—

(a) the name of the employee,

(b) the capacity in which the employee receives emoluments, and

(c) the code appropriate to the employee's case, and

where the inspector does so the following provisions of this regulation shall apply.

(2) Whenever the employee receives any emoluments during the year for which the deductions working sheet was issued, he shall record on the deductions working sheet—

(a) the amount of the emoluments;

(b) the date on which he received the emoluments;

(c) the cumulative emoluments in relation to that date;

(d) the cumulative free emoluments or, as the case may be, the cumulative additional pay in relation to that date according to his code;

(e) the corresponding cumulative tax;

(f) the amount of tax, if any, deducted or repaid on making the payment of emoluments; and

(g) where his code reflects additional pay—

(i) the tax due at the date on which he received the emoluments;

(ii) the overriding limit in relation to the payment; and

(iii) the amount of any tax not deducted as a consequence of the overriding limit.

(3) The employee shall pay the amount specified in paragraph (4) to the collector within 14 days after the end of every income tax quarter.

(4) The amount specified in this paragraph is the amount of the total net tax deducted corresponding to the cumulative emoluments at the last date during the income tax quarter in question on which the employee received emoluments, or in the case of the last income tax quarter of the year corresponding to the cumulative emoluments for the year, reduced by any amounts of tax paid to the collector in respect of previous income tax quarters of the same year.

(5) The collector may proceed in accordance with either paragraph (6) or paragraph (7) if, within 14 days after the end of any income tax quarter—

(a) the employee has paid no amount of tax to the collector for that income tax quarter, and the collector is unaware of the amount, if any, which the employee is liable so to pay, or

(b) an amount has been paid but the collector is not satisfied that it is the full amount which the employee is liable to pay to him for that income tax quarter.

(6) The collector may—

(a) give notice to the employee requiring him to render, within 14 days, a return in such form as the Board may prescribe showing the amount of tax which the employee is liable to pay to the collector under paragraphs (3) and (4) above in respect of the income tax period in question; and

(b) in such a case regulations 47 and 54 shall apply with the necessary modifications for the purposes of ascertaining, certifying and recovering the tax payable by the employee as if it were tax which the employee was liable to deduct from emoluments paid by him.

(7) The collector may—

(a) report the facts to the inspector; and

(b) in such a case the inspector may [by notice under section 8 of the Management Act require the employee to make and deliver a return under that section for the year][1]

(8) ...[2]

(9) If the employee ceases to receive emoluments, he shall forthwith render a return to the inspector or, if so required, to the collector, in such form as the Board may prescribe, showing the particulars specified in paragraph (10).

(10) The particulars specified in this paragraph are such particulars as the Board may require for the identification of—

(a) the employee,

(b) the year to which the return relates,

(c) the last date on which the employee received any emoluments,

(d) the employee's cumulative emoluments at the date referred to in sub-paragraph (c) above, and

(e) the corresponding total net tax deducted.

(11) Not later than 44 days after the end of the year, and [unless he has been required under section 8 of the Management Act to make and deliver a return or he has rendered a return under paragraph (9)][3]*, the employee shall render a return to the inspector, or, if so required, to the collector, in such form as the Board may prescribe, showing the particulars specified in paragraph (12).*

(12) The particulars specified in this paragraph are such particulars as the Board may require for the identification of—

(a) the employee,

(b) the year to which the return relates,

(c) the employee's cumulative emoluments at the end of that year, and

(d) the corresponding total net tax deducted.

(13) Where paragraph (11) applies, paragraphs (8) to (11) of regulation 43 regarding the certification and recovery of tax remaining unpaid by an employer for any year shall apply with the necessary modifications in the case of any tax remaining unpaid by the employee.

(14) If the employee receives emoluments in more than one capacity, no account shall be taken for the purposes of this regulation of the emoluments received by him in any capacity other than that mentioned on the deductions working sheet.

(15) In this regulation "cumulative emoluments" means, in relation to any date, the sum of all emoluments received by the employee from the beginning of the year up to and including that date, irrespective of the person or persons from whom the emoluments were received.

(16) Section 98A of the Management Act shall apply in relation to the provisions of paragraph (11) requiring a return to be made.

Amendments—[1] *Words substituted by the IT (Employments) (Amendment No 3) Regulations, SI 1996/1312 reg 17(1)(a), (2), with effect in any case where a deductions working sheet is issued by the inspector under para (1) of Regulation 104 on or after 5 June 1996 for the year 1996–97 or any subsequent year.*

[2] *Para (8) revoked by the IT (Employments) (Amendment No 3) Regulations, SI 1996/1312 reg 17(1)(b), with effect from 5 June 1996.*

[3] *Words in para (11) substituted by the IT (Employments) (Amendment No 3) Regulations, SI 1996/1312 reg 17(1)(c), with effect from 5 June 1996.*

Recovery of tax from employee

105—(1) Any tax which is payable to the collector by any employee may be recovered in the manner provided by the Income Tax Acts.

(2) Any tax which is payable to the collector under—

(a) regulation 101(2), or

(b) any further assessment made under regulation 103(9),

shall be payable within 14 days of the date on which the collector first makes application for its payment 1

Amendments—[1] *Para (2) revoked by the IT (Employments) (Amendment No 3) Regulations, SI 1996/1312 reg 18, with effect with respect to any tax that becomes payable to the collector by any employee on or after 5 June 1996 for the year 1996–97 or any subsequent year.*

Attribution of repayments

106—(1) A repayment for any year to which section 824(5) of the Taxes Act applies shall, for the purposes of that subsection, be attributed in accordance with paragraphs (2) to (4).

(2) If there is no adjusted overpayment for the previous year, the whole of the repayment shall be attributed to the year for which the repayment is due.

(3) Subject to paragraph (4), if there is an adjusted overpayment for the previous year and the repayment—

(a) does not exceed that adjusted overpayment, the repayment shall be wholly attributed to the previous year;

(b) exceeds that adjusted overpayment, the excess shall be attributed to the year for which the repayment is due, and the balance to the previous year.

(4) If there is an adjusted overpayment for a year earlier than the previous year, paragraph (3) shall apply to so much of the repayment as is, under that paragraph, attributed to the previous year, as though that amount were a repayment due for the previous year, and so on successively until no further attribution is possible under this regulation.

Statement of Practice A9—This Statement (not reproduced) contained examples showing how this regulation worked for 1995—96 and earlier years.

Note This regulation and regs 107, 108 post, being dependent on TA 1988 s 824(5), has lapsed on repeal of that provision (see notes thereto).

Adjustment of overpayments and underpayments

107—(1) In determining, for the purposes specified in paragraph (2), whether for any year there is an adjusted overpayment, and if so its amount, any overpayment or underpayment shall be adjusted, if necessary, in accordance with paragraphs (3) to (7).

(2) The purposes specified in this paragraph are purposes of attributing a repayment (in this regulation referred to as "the relevant repayment") in accordance with regulation 106.

(3) Any tax paid to the collector in respect of an underpayment for any year shall be treated as tax paid for that year and added to the overpayment or deducted from the underpayment for that year.

(4) Paragraphs (5) to (7) apply to a repayment of an overpayment made prior to the relevant repayment if it was a repayment—

(a) for the same year for which the relevant repayment is due, or

(b) for an earlier year which, if paragraphs (5) to (7) applied to it, would affect the attribution of the relevant repayment under regulation 106.

(5) Where this paragraph applies and the repayment was one to which section 824(5) of the Taxes Act applied, any amount attributable to any year under this regulation and regulation 106 shall be deducted from the overpayment or added to the underpayment for that year and any subsequent year for which an adjustment was made under regulation 101(4)(c) in respect of the tax which was repaid.

(6) Where this paragraph applies and the repayment was one to which section 824(5) of the Taxes Act did not apply, it shall be attributed, for the purposes of this regulation, by reference to the circumstances at the time it was made, to such years and in such amounts as the provisions of this regulation and regulation 106 would have required had it been a repayment to which that subsection applied, and any amount so attributed to any year shall be deducted from the overpayment or added to the underpayment for that year and any subsequent year for which an adjustment was made under regulation 101(4)(c) in respect of the tax which was repaid.

(7) If there is more than one repayment to which paragraph (4) applies—

(a) the repayment made first shall be attributed in accordance with paragraph (5) or (6) (as appropriate); and

(b) each repayment made subsequently shall be so attributed successively, starting with the second repayment made, and taking into account any adjustment of any overpayment or underpayment resulting from the attribution under this regulation of any repayment made prior to it.

Note—*See note to reg 106.*

Definitions for the purposes of regulations 106 and 107

108 In regulations 106 and 107—

"adjusted overpayment" means an overpayment adjusted (if necessary) in accordance with regulation 107;

"overpayment" means the difference, calculated in accordance with regulation 101, between the total net tax deducted from an employee's emoluments during any year and the tax payable under an assessment for that year;

"previous year" means, in relation to any year, the last year before that year for which any tax overpaid or remaining unpaid has been included in an adjustment made under regulation 101(4)(c) to the total net tax deducted for that year;

''underpayment'' means the excess, calculated in accordance with regulation 101, of the tax payable under an assessment for any year over the total net tax deducted from an employee's emoluments during that year.

Note See note to reg 106.

PART IX

SUPPLEMENTAL

Service by post

109 Any notice or deductions working sheet which is authorised or required to be given, served or issued under these Regulations may be sent by post.

Revocations

110 The Regulations specified in the Schedule to these Regulations are hereby revoked.

General savings

111 In relation to tax liable, under the Income Tax (Employments) Regulations 1973, the Income Tax (Councillors' Attendance Allowances) Regulations, the Income Tax (Reserve and Auxiliary Forces) Regulations 1975 and the Income Tax (Holiday Pay) Regulations 1981 (''the revoked Regulations'') to be deducted from emoluments paid before 6th April 1993, these Regulations shall have effect as if the tax had been liable to be deducted under these Regulations, and accordingly references to any provision of these Regulations shall, where the context so requires, be construed as references to the corresponding provision of the revoked Regulations.

1993/950

Capital Gains Tax (Gilt-edged Securities) Order 1993

Made by the Treasury under TCGA 1992 Sch 9 para 1

Made . . . . 30 March 1993

1 This Order may be cited as the Capital Gains Tax (Gilt-edged Securities) Order 1993.

2 The following securities are hereby specified for the purposes of Schedule 9 to the Taxation of Chargeable Gains Act 1992—

$8\frac{3}{4}$% Treasury Loan 1997 ''D''

$8\frac{3}{4}$% Treasury Loan 1997 ''E''

$4\frac{5}{8}$% Index-Linked Treasury Stock 1998

$7\frac{1}{4}$% Treasury Stock 1998

9% Conversion Stock 2000 ''C''

$9\frac{3}{4}$% Treasury Stock 2002 ''C''

8% Treasury Stock 2003

10% Treasury Stock 2003 ''B''

$4\frac{3}{8}$% Index-Linked Treasury Stock 2004

$8\frac{1}{2}$% Treasury Loan 2007 ''A''

$8\frac{1}{2}$% Treasury Loan 2007 ''B''

8% Treasury Stock 2009 ''A''

9% Conversion Loan 2011 ''B''

9% Treasury Stock 2012

9% Treasury Stock 2012 ''A''

$8\frac{3}{4}$% Treasury Stock 2017

$8\frac{3}{4}$% Treasury Stock 2017 ''A''

$4\frac{1}{8}$% Index-Linked Treasury Stock 2030.

1993/1957

Double Taxation Relief (Taxes on Income) (General) (Manufactured Overseas Dividends) Regulations 1993

Made by the Commissioners of Inland Revenue under TA 1988 s 791

Made . . . . 2 August 1993

Amendment—These regulations revoked by the Double Taxation Relief (Manufactured Overseas Dividends) (Revocation) Regulations, SI 2003/2581 with effect from 1 November 2003.

SIs

1993/2004
Income Tax (Manufactured Overseas Dividends) Regulations 1993

Made by the Treasury under TA 1988 Sch 23A paras 1(1), 4(6)–(8), 8

Made . . . . 9 August 1993
Laid before the House of Commons . . . 9 August 1993
Coming into Force . . . . 1 October 1993

Commentary—*Simon's Direct Tax Service* **A7.815–823.**
Cross references—See TA 1988 s 737A(5) (sale of securities by a seller and repurchase by him or a connected person).

Citation and commencement

1 These Regulations may be cited as the Income Tax (Manufactured Overseas Dividends) Regulations 1993 and shall come into force on 1st October 1993.

Interpretation

2—[(1)][3] In these Regulations unless the context otherwise requires—

...[2]

''approved United Kingdom collecting agent'' means a person who is [a collecting agent ... [3] and who is][2] resident in the United Kingdom or, if not so resident, is carrying on a trade in the United Kingdom through a [permanent establishment][5] and who [is approved by the Board for the purposes of these Regulations];[2]

''approved United Kingdom intermediary'' means an overseas dividend manufacturer who is resident in the United Kingdom or, if not so resident, is carrying on a trade in the United Kingdom through a [permanent establishment][5] and who is [approved as an intermediary by the Board for the purposes of these Regulations][2]

''the Board'' means the Commissioners of Inland Revenue;

[''chargeable period'' has the meaning given by regulation 2A;][1]

[''collecting agent'' means a person who, in the course of carrying on a trade in the United Kingdom, collects or secures payment of overseas dividends for another person or acts as custodian of any overseas securities;][4]

...[5]

''gross amount of the manufactured overseas dividend'' has the meaning given by paragraph 4(5)(*b*) of Schedule 23A;

''the Income Tax Acts'' has the meaning given by section 831(1)(*b*) of the Taxes Act;

''the Management Act'' means the Taxes Management Act 1970;

''manufactured overseas dividend'' shall be construed in accordance with paragraph 4(1) of Schedule 23A;

''overseas dividend'', ''overseas dividend manufacturer'', ''overseas securities'', ''overseas tax'' and ''overseas tax credit'' have the meanings given by paragraph 1(1) of Schedule 23A;

''relevant withholding tax'' has the meaning given by paragraph 4(5)(*a*) of Schedule 23A;

''Schedule 23A'' means Schedule 23A to the Taxes Act;

''the Taxes Act'' means the Income and Corporation Taxes Act 1988;

''the Tax Acts'' has the meaning given by section 831(2) of the Taxes Act;

...[2]

[''United Kingdom recipient'' shall be construed in accordance with paragraph 4(3A) of Schedule 23A.][5]

[(2) References in regulations 3 to 11, 14 and 15 to manufactured overseas dividends do not include references to manufactured overseas dividends to which regulation 2B applies, and references in those regulations to overseas dividends do not include references to any overseas dividend of which a manufactured overseas dividend to which regulation 2B applies would be representative.][3]

[(3) In these Regulations references to a permanent establishment shall be read, in relation to accounting periods beginning before 1st January 2003, as references to a branch or agency.][5]

Amendments—[1] Definition of ''chargeable period'' substituted by the IT (Manufactured Overseas Dividends) (Amendment) Regulations, SI 1995/1324 reg 3, with effect from 7 June 1995.

[2] Definitions revoked, words in definitions of ''approved United Kingdom collecting agent'' and ''approved United Kingdom intermediary'' inserted or substituted by the IT (Manufactured Overseas Dividends) (Amendment) Regulations, SI 1996/1229 reg 3, with effect from 28 May 1996.

[3] Regulation renumbered as para (1), in definition of ''approved United Kingdom collecting agent'' words revoked and para (2) added, by the IT (Manufactured Overseas Dividends) (Amendment No 2) Regulations, SI 1996/2643 reg 3, with effect from 6 November 1996.

[4] Definition ''collecting agent'' substituted by the IT (Manufactured Overseas Dividends) (Amendment) Regulations, SI 2001/403 reg 2, with effect from 9 March 2001 (previously inserted by SI 1996/2643).

[5] Words in definitions of ''approved United Kingdom collecting agent'' and ''approved United Kingdom intermediary'' substituted; definition of ''the Double Taxation Regulations'' revoked; definition of ''United Kingdom recipient'' substituted; and para (3) inserted; by the IT (Manufactured Overseas Dividends) (Amendment) Regulations, SI 2003/2582 regs 2, 3 with effect from 1 November 2003.

[Chargeable period

2A—(1) In these Regulations ''chargeable period''—

(*a*) as respects a company, means its accounting period for the purposes of corporation tax;

(*b*) as respects a person other than a company who [draws up accounts for any period (''the accounts period''), means][2] one of the periods specified in paragraph (2) below;

(*c*) as respects a person other than a company who [does not draw up accounts, means a year of assessment][2].

(2) The periods specified in this paragraph are—

(*a*) the period which begins at the beginning of the accounts period and ends at the expiration of 12 months from that date or, if earlier, at the end of the accounts period;

(*b*) any subsequent period which—

(i) begins at the end of the immediately preceding period, being a period specified in this paragraph, and

(ii) ends at the expiration of 12 months from that date or, if earlier, at the end of the accounts period.

(3) ...[2]][1]

Amendments—[1] This regulation inserted by the IT (Manufactured Overseas Dividends) (Amendment) Regulations, SI 1995/1324 reg 4, with effect from 7 June 1995.

[2] Words in para (1)(*b*), (*c*) substituted and para (3) revoked by the IT (Manufactured Overseas Dividends) (Amendment) Regulations, SI 1997/988, regs 1, 3, with effect from 1 July 1997.

[Tax treatment of manufactured overseas dividends paid in connection with loan relationships

2B—(1) For the purposes of the provisions of the Tax Acts relating to the charge to tax under Schedule D, paragraph 4(2) and (3) ...[2] of Schedule 23A shall not apply to a manufactured overseas dividend paid in the circumstances prescribed in paragraph (2).

(2) The circumstances prescribed are where the manufactured overseas dividend is representative of an overseas dividend on an overseas security that represents a loan relationship.

(3) Where the payer of a manufactured overseas dividend to which paragraph (2) applies is neither a company nor carrying on a trade in circumstances where the manufactured overseas dividend is taken into account in computing the profits of that trade, the manufactured overseas dividend shall be treated, for the purposes of the provisions of the Tax Acts relating to the charge to tax under Schedule D and so far as the payer is concerned, as if the amount paid was an annual payment, within section 349(1) of the Taxes Act, but so that no amount is required to be deducted on account of income tax from the amount of the payment, or accounted for under section 350 of that Act.

(4) Where the recipient of a manufactured overseas dividend to which paragraph (2) applies is neither a company nor carrying on a trade in circumstances where the manufactured overseas dividend is taken into account in computing the profits of that trade, the manufactured overseas dividend shall be treated, for the purposes of the provisions of the Tax Acts relating to the charge to tax under Schedule D and so far as the recipient is concerned, as an overseas dividend of an amount equal to the amount of the manufactured overseas dividend received by him, but not so as to entitle the recipient to claim relief under Part XVIII of the Taxes Act in respect of any tax attributable to the manufactured overseas dividend received.

(5) For the purposes of paragraph (2), an overseas security shall be taken to represent a loan relationship if a company holding that security would have a loan relationship within the meaning of section 81 of the Finance Act 1996.

(6) References in paragraph (4) to the recipient of a manufactured overseas dividend include references to any person claiming title to the manufactured overseas dividend through or under the recipient.][1]

Amendments—[1] This regulation inserted by the IT (Manufactured Overseas Dividends) (Amendment No 2) Regulations, SI 1996/2643 reg 4, with effect from 6 November 1996.

[2] Words in para (1) revoked by the Stock Lending and Manufactured Payments (Revocations and Amendments) Regulations, SI 1997/987, regs 1, 8, with effect from 1 July 1997.

Prescribed rates of relevant withholding tax

3—(1) Subject to paragraph (4), the rate of relevant withholding tax which is prescribed in relation to any manufactured overseas dividend is the rate which is equal to the rate (or, if more than one, the highest rate) at which tax would have been payable (and not repayable) under the law of the overseas territory specified in paragraph (3) in respect of—

(*a*) an overseas dividend paid on the same date that the manufactured overseas dividend is paid to a person who is—

(i) resident in the United Kingdom and not carrying on a trade outside the United Kingdom through a [permanent establishment][1],

(ii) subject to tax under the law of the United Kingdom, and

(iii) not subject to a special relationship with any other person as respects any commercial or financial dealings, in respect of the same kind of overseas securities as those in respect of which the manufactured overseas dividend was paid, and

(*b*) the overseas tax credit, if any, relating to that overseas dividend.

(2) The reference in paragraph (1) above to tax which would have been payable is a reference to tax which would have been eligible for relief either—

(*a*) pursuant to arrangements made with the government of the overseas territory specified in paragraph (3) which have effect by virtue of section 788 of the Taxes Act and relate to the overseas dividend concerned, or

(*b*) by virtue of other provisions of Part XVIII of the Taxes Act other than section 790(5)(*c*)(ii) of that Act.

(3) The overseas territory specified in this paragraph is the territory of the government or public or local authority which issued the securities in question or, where the securities were issued by any other body of persons not resident in the United Kingdom, the territory under whose law that tax would have been payable.

(4) ...[1]

Amendments—[1] Words in para (1)(*a*)(i) substituted, and para (4) revoked, by the IT (Manufactured Overseas Dividends) (Amendment) Regulations, SI 2003/2582 regs 2, 4 with effect from 1 November 2003.

Tax treatment of approved manufactured overseas dividends paid to approved United Kingdom intermediaries or approved United Kingdom collecting agents

4—(1) For the purposes of the provisions of the Tax Acts relating to the charge to tax under Schedule D other than paragraph 4(3) of Schedule 23A, [a manufactured overseas dividend][1] paid in the circumstances prescribed in paragraph (2)—

(*a*) shall not be treated as an annual payment pursuant to paragraph 4(2) of Schedule 23A;

(*b*) shall be paid without deduction of an amount on account of income tax;

(*c*) where the maker of the payment is an investment company within the meaning of section 130 of the Taxes Act, shall be treated as if it was an expense of management in relation to that company.

[(2) The circumstances prescribed by this paragraph are where—

(*a*) a manufactured overseas dividend is paid to an approved United Kingdom intermediary or an approved United Kingdom collecting agent by an overseas dividend manufacturer who—

(i) is resident in the United Kingdom or, if not so resident, makes the payment in the course of a trade which he carries on through a [permanent establishment][4] in the United Kingdom, and

(ii) is not an approved United Kingdom intermediary; and

(*b*) the manufactured overseas dividend is not representative of the overseas dividend received by the overseas dividend manufacturer.][3]

(3) Subject to paragraph (4), the approved United Kingdom intermediary or approved United Kingdom collecting agent referred to in paragraph (2) shall account for and pay an amount of tax in respect of the manufactured overseas dividend which he receives equal to that which the maker of the payment would have been required to account for and pay had paragraph 4(2) of Schedule 23A applied to the payment.

[(4) Paragraph (3) shall not apply where either paragraph (5) or (6) applies.][4]

[(5) This paragraph applies where the approved United Kingdom intermediary or approved United Kingdom collecting agent pays, in accordance with regulation 5, and without deduction of tax, a manufactured overseas dividend representative of the same overseas dividend as is represented by the manufactured overseas dividend received by him.][4]

[(6) This paragraph applies where the approved United Kingdom collecting agent is required to pay to an approved United Kingdom intermediary a manufactured overseas dividend representative of the same overseas dividend as is represented by the manufactured overseas dividend received by him and the approved United Kingdom intermediary—

(*a*) pays as mentioned in paragraph (5) the manufactured overseas dividend, and

(*b*) issues a notice to the approved United Kingdom collecting agent authorising him to make the payment without deduction of tax.][4]

Amendments—[1] Words substituted by the IT (Manufactured Overseas Dividends) (Amendment) Regulations, SI 1996/1229 reg 4, with effect from 28 May 1996.

[2] Para (4)(*aa*) inserted by the IT (Manufactured Overseas Dividends) (Amendment No 2) Regulations, SI 1996/2643 reg 5, with effect from 6 November 1996.

[3] Para (2) substituted by the IT (Manufactured Overseas Dividends) (Amendment) Regulations, SI 1997/988, regs 1, 4, with effect from 1 July 1997.

[4] Words in para (2)(*a*)(i) substituted, and paras 4–6 substituted for para 4, by the IT (Manufactured Overseas Dividends) (Amendment) Regulations, SI 2003/2582 regs 2, 5 with effect from 1 November 2003.

Tax treatment of approved manufactured overseas dividends paid to persons resident outside the United Kingdom

5—(1) [Subject to paragraph (1A),][3] for the purposes of the provisions of the Tax Acts relating to the charge to tax under Schedule D, [a manufactured overseas dividend][1] paid in [either of the circumstances prescribed by paragraphs (1B) and (2)][3] shall not be treated as an annual payment pursuant to paragraph 4(2) of Schedule 23A, and accordingly shall be paid without deduction of an amount on account of income tax.

[(1A) Where a manufactured overseas dividend is paid in the circumstances prescribed by paragraph (1B) by a person who is not an approved United Kingdom intermediary, the dividend shall be treated, for the purposes of the provisions of the Tax Acts relating to the charge to tax under Schedule D and so far as the payer is concerned, as if the amount paid was an annual payment, within section 349(1) of the Taxes Act, but so that no amount is required to be deducted on account of income tax from the amount of the payment, or accounted for under section 350 of that Act.][3]

[(1B) The circumstances prescribed by this paragraph are where—

(*a*) a manufactured overseas dividend is paid by a person who is resident in the United Kingdom, or, if not so resident, makes the payment in the course of a trade which he carries on through a permanent establishment in the United Kingdom;

(*b*) the payment is to or for the benefit of a person beneficially entitled to it who is not a United Kingdom recipient; and

(*c*) regulation 4(1) does not apply.][3]

(2) The circumstances prescribed by this paragraph are [where—

(*a*) a manufactured overseas dividend is paid by an approved United Kingdom intermediary who, if not resident in the United Kingdom, makes the payment in the course of a trade which he carries on through a permanent establishment in the United Kingdom; and;][3]

(*b*) the payment is made to another approved United Kingdom intermediary or to an approved United Kingdom collecting agent as part of a chain of payments where—

(i) each payment in the chain is a payment by an approved United Kingdom intermediary or an approved United Kingdom collecting agent of [a manufactured overseas dividend][1] representative of the same overseas dividend,

(ii) the maker of the last payment in the chain, if not resident in the United Kingdom, makes the payment in the course of a trade which he carries on through a [permanent establishment in the United Kingdom and makes the payment to or for the benefit of a person beneficially entitled to it who is not a United Kingdom recipient][3], and

(iii) each recipient of payment in the chain has issued a notice to the maker of the payment authorising him to make the payment without deduction of tax.

Amendments—[1] Words substituted by the IT (Manufactured Overseas Dividends) (Amendment) Regulations, SI 1996/1229 reg 4, with effect from 28 May 1996.

[2] Words in sub-para (2)(*b*)(ii) inserted by the IT (Manufactured Overseas Dividends) (Amendment No 2) Regulations, SI 1996/2643 reg 6, with effect from 6 November 1996.

[3] Words in para (1) inserted and substituted, paras (1A), (1B) inserted, and words in para (2) substituted, by the IT (Manufactured Overseas Dividends) (Amendment) Regulations, SI 2003/2582 regs 2, 6 with effect from 1 November 2003.

Retention and record of notices given under regulations 4 and 5

6—(1) A notice given under regulation 4[(6)(*b*)][1] or regulation 5(2)(*b*)(iii) shall be in the form provided, or in a form authorised, by the Board.

(2) A recipient of such a notice—

(*a*) shall retain the notice for a period of six years and, whenever required to do so within that period, shall make it available for inspection by an officer of the Board, and

(*b*) if he receives more than one such notice during any chargeable period, shall in addition maintain a record showing—

(i) the date of each such notice received in that period, and

(ii) a description and the amount of the manufactured overseas dividend referred to in each such notice received in that period.

(3) A person who issues such a notice—

(*a*) shall retain a copy of it for a period of six years and, whenever required to do so within that period, shall make that copy available for inspection by an officer of the Board, and

(*b*) if he issues more than one such notice during any chargeable period, shall in addition maintain a record showing—

(i) the date of each such notice issued in that period, and

(ii) a description and the amount of the manufactured overseas dividend referred to in each such notice issued in that period.

(4) Any record required to be maintained by the recipient of a notice under paragraph (2)(*b*), or by the issuer of a notice under paragraph (3)(*b*), shall be retained by that person for a period of six years from the end of the chargeable period to which the record relates.

[(4A) In the case of a record retained under paragraph (2)(*b*) or (3)(*b*) which is in electronic form the person retaining it shall afford an officer of the Board such assistance and facilities as the officer may reasonably require in order to read the record.][2]

(5) Where the issuer of a notice fails to retain a copy of it for the period specified in paragraph (3)(*a*), or fails to maintain any such record as is specified in paragraph (3)(*b*) or to retain any such record for the period specified in paragraph (4), the Board may require that person to carry out, at his own expense, an audit of manufactured overseas dividends received by that person in order to ascertain the amount of tax, if any, liable to be deducted under paragraph 4(2) of Schedule 23A which was not deducted.

(6) The scope and method of the audit referred to in paragraph (5) shall be agreed between the Board and the issuer of the notice or, in the absence of agreement, determined by the Board, and the issuer of the notice shall account for and pay any tax which on the basis of the findings of the audit was liable to be deducted but which was not deducted from manufactured overseas dividends received by him.

Amendments—[1] Reference in para (1) substituted by the IT (Manufactured Overseas Dividends) (Amendment) Regulations, SI 2003/2582 regs 2, 7 with effect from 1 November 2003.
[2] Para (4A) inserted by the Income and Corporation Taxes (Electronic Certificates of Deduction of Tax and Tax Credit) Regulations, SI 2003/3143 reg 5(1), (2) with effect from 1 January 2004.

[Reduction of tax payable under paragraph 4(3) of Schedule 23A

6A—(1) Where, in a case to which paragraph 4(3) of Schedule 23A applies, overseas tax was charged on, or in respect of, the making of the manufactured overseas dividend received by the United Kingdom recipient, the amount of tax to be accounted for and paid under that provision shall, for the purposes of the provisions of the Tax Acts relating to the charge to tax under Schedule D, be taken as reduced in accordance with paragraph (2) or, as the case may be, paragraph (3).

(2) Where the amount specified in paragraph (4) exceeds the amount specified in paragraph (5), the amount of tax shall be reduced so as to equal the amount of the excess.

(3) Where the amount specified in paragraph (4) is equal to or less than the amount specified in paragraph (5), the amount of tax shall be reduced to nil.

(4) The amount specified in this paragraph is the amount of the manufactured overseas dividend received by the United Kingdom recipient.

(5) The amount specified in this paragraph is the amount which the United Kingdom recipient would have received by way of the overseas dividend of which the manufactured overseas dividend is representative, had the overseas dividend been paid to him.

(6) Relief claimed by the United Kingdom recipient under Part XVIII of the Taxes Act in a case to which paragraph (2) applies, other than relief given by virtue of section 811 of that Act, shall not exceed the aggregate of the amount of tax accounted for and paid by the United Kingdom recipient under paragraph 4(3) of Schedule 23A and the amount of overseas tax charged on, or in respect of, the making of the manufactured overseas dividend received by him.][1]

Amendments—[1] This regulation inserted by the IT (Manufactured Overseas Dividends) (Amendment No 2) Regulations, SI 1996/2643 reg 7, with effect from 6 November 1996.

Disapplication of paragraph 4(3) of Schedule 23A

7—(1) For the purposes of the provisions of the Tax Acts relating to the charge to tax under Schedule D, tax shall not be required to be accounted for and paid pursuant to paragraph 4(3) of Schedule 23A by a United Kingdom recipient of a manufactured overseas dividend which is received by him in any of the circumstances prescribed by paragraph (2).

(2) The circumstances prescribed by this paragraph are where the United Kingdom recipient—

[(*a*) pays, in accordance with regulation 5, and without deduction of tax, a manufactured overseas dividend representative of the same overseas dividend as is represented by the manufactured overseas dividend received by him, or;][4]

(*b*) ...[4]

(*c*) is an approved United Kingdom collecting agent and the person beneficially entitled to the manufactured overseas dividend received by the approved United Kingdom collecting agent is not resident in the United Kingdom, or

(*d*) is an approved United Kingdom collecting agent who is required to pay to an approved United Kingdom intermediary [a manufactured overseas dividend][1] representative of the same overseas dividend as is represented by [the manufactured overseas dividend][1] received by him, the approved United Kingdom intermediary is enabled or authorised as mentioned in sub-paragraph (*a*) above and issues a notice to the approved United Kingdom collecting agent authorising him to pay [the manufactured overseas dividend][1] without deduction of tax.

[or

(*e*) is an approved United Kingdom collecting agent or an approved United Kingdom intermediary in receipt of a manufactured overseas dividend who shows that the overseas dividend manufacturer concerned was entitled to payment of the overseas dividend of which the manufactured overseas dividend is representative either—

(i) as the holder of the overseas securities concerned, or

(ii) directly or indirectly from a person from whom he acquired those securities, or to whom he transferred them, and who was so entitled as the holder of those securities][2]

(3) A notice given under paragraph (2)(*d*) shall be in the form provided, or in a form authorised, by the Board.

[(3A) Where by virtue of paragraph (1) tax is not required to be accounted for and paid pursuant to paragraph 4(3) of Schedule 23A in the circumstances prescribed by paragraph (2)(*e*), paragraph 4(4) of that Schedule shall apply as if the amount of tax required under paragraph 4(3) of that Schedule [were an amount equal to the excess to the gross amount of the overseas dividend over the amount of that overseas dividend received by the overseas dividend manufacturer and][3] had been accounted for and paid.][2]

(4) The United Kingdom recipient—

(*a*) shall maintain a record of all manufactured overseas dividends received by him in any chargeable period in the circumstances prescribed by paragraph (2), showing—

(i) a description and the amount of each such manufactured overseas dividend, and the date on which it was received, and

(ii) the total amount of all such manufactured overseas dividends received in that period;

(*b*) where he is an approved United Kingdom intermediary within sub-paragraph (*b*), or an approved United Kingdom collecting agent within sub-paragraph (*c*), of paragraph (2), shall in addition maintain a record of all manufactured overseas dividends paid by him as mentioned in sub-paragraph (*b*) or, as the case may be, sub-paragraph (*c*), of that paragraph in any chargeable period, showing—

(i) the name and address of the person beneficially entitled to each such payment,

(ii) a description and the amount of each such payment, and the date of the payment, and

(iii) the total amount of all such payments made in that period;

(*c*) shall retain any such record as is specified in sub-paragraph (*a*) or (*b*) of this paragraph for a period of six years from the end of the chargeable period to which the record relates, and shall make any such record available for inspection by an officer of the Board whenever required to do so during the period of retention;

(*d*) where he is an approved United Kingdom collecting agent within sub-paragraph (*d*) of paragraph (2), shall in addition—

(i) retain for a period of six years any notice received by him as mentioned in that sub-paragraph and, whenever required to do so, make it available for inspection by an officer of the Board, and

(ii) if he receives more than one such notice during any chargeable period, maintain a record showing the date of each such notice received in that period and a description and the amount of the manufactured overseas dividend referred to in each such notice, and retain the record for a period of six years from the end of the chargeable period to which the record relates.

[(4A) In the case of a record retained under paragraph (4) which is in electronic form the person retaining it shall afford an officer of the Board such assistance and facilities as the officer may reasonably require in order to read the record.][5]

(5) Where the United Kingdom recipient fails to maintain, or to retain for the requisite period, any such record as is referred to in paragraph (4), or fails to retain for the requisite period any such notice as is referred to in that paragraph, the Board may require that person to carry out, at his own expense, an audit of manufactured overseas dividends received by him in order to ascertain the amount of tax, if any, for which he was liable to account under paragraph 4(3) of Schedule 23A.

(6) The scope and method of the audit referred to in paragraph (5) shall be agreed between the Board and the United Kingdom recipient or, in the absence of agreement, shall be determined by the Board, and the United Kingdom recipient shall account for and pay any tax which on the basis of the findings of the audit he was liable under paragraph 4(3) of Schedule 23A to account for and pay.

Amendments—[1] Words substituted by the IT (Manufactured Overseas Dividends) (Amendment) Regulations, SI 1996/1229 reg 4, with effect from 28 May 1996.

[2] Paras (2)(*e*), (3A) added by the IT (Manufactured Overseas Dividends) (Amendment) Regulations, SI 1996/2643 reg 8, with effect from 6 November 1996.

[3] Words in para (3A) inserted by the IT (Manufactured Overseas Dividends) (Amendment) Regulations, SI 1997/988, regs 1, 5, with effect from 1 July 1997.

[4] In para (2), sub-para (*a*) substituted, and sub-para (*b*) revoked, by the IT (Manufactured Overseas Dividends) (Amendment) Regulations, SI 2003/2582 regs 2, 8 with effect from 1 November 2003.

[5] Para (4A) inserted by the Income and Corporation Taxes (Electronic Certificates of Deduction of Tax and Tax Credit) Regulations, SI 2003/3143 reg 5(1), (3) with effect from 1 January 2004.

[Disapplication of paragraph 5 of Schedule 23A

7A ...

Amendments—[1] This regulation revoked by the Stock Lending and Manufactured Payments (Revocations and Amendments) Regulations, SI 1997/987, regs 1, 8, with effect from 1 July 1997 (previously inserted by the IT (Manufactured Overseas Dividends) (Amendment No 2) Regulations, SI 1996/2643 reg 9).

Tax treatment of manufactured overseas dividends to which regulations 4, 5 and 7 apply—further provision

8 For all purposes of the Tax Acts as they apply in relation to persons resident in the United Kingdom or to persons not so resident but carrying on a business through a [permanent establishment][1] in the United Kingdom, any manufactured overseas dividend to which regulation 4, 5 or 7 applies shall be treated in relation to the recipient, and all persons claiming title through or under him—

(*a*) as if it were an overseas dividend of an amount equal to the amount of the manufactured overseas dividend, or

(*b*) where paragraph (3) of regulation 4 applies and the amount of tax required under that paragraph in respect of the manufactured overseas dividend has been accounted for and paid, as if it were an overseas dividend of an amount equal to the gross amount of the manufactured overseas dividend, but paid after the withholding therefrom, on account of overseas tax, of the amount accounted for and paid; and the amount accounted for and paid shall accordingly be treated in relation to the recipient, and all persons claiming title through or under him, as an amount so withheld instead of an amount on account of income tax.

Amendments—[1] Words substituted by the IT (Manufactured Overseas Dividends) (Amendment) Regulations, SI 2003/2582 regs 2, 9 with effect from 1 November 2003.

Offsetting of tax by overseas dividend manufacturers

9—[(1) In the circumstances prescribed by paragraph (2) and subject to paragraph (4), a person who is an overseas dividend manufacturer in any chargeable period shall be entitled to set off the amounts specified in paragraph (1A) against the sums specified in paragraph (1B)][4]

[(1A) The amounts specified in this paragraph are—

(*a*) amounts of overseas tax in respect of overseas dividends received by the overseas dividend manufacturer in the chargeable period;

(*b*) amounts of overseas tax charged on, or in respect of, the making of manufactured overseas dividends so received by him;

(*c*) amounts deducted under paragraph 4(2) of Schedule 23A from manufactured overseas dividends so received by him;

(*d*) amounts accounted for and paid under paragraph 4(3) of Schedule 23A in respect of manufactured overseas dividends so received by him;

(*e*) amounts accounted for and paid under regulation 4(3) in respect of manufactured overseas dividends so received by him.][4]

[(1B) The sums specified in this paragraph are sums due from the overseas dividend manufacturer on account of the amounts deducted by him under paragraph 4(2) of Schedule 23A from the manufactured overseas dividends paid by him in the chargeable period.][4]

(2) The circumstances prescribed by this paragraph are where—

(*a*) the overseas dividend manufacturer is an approved United Kingdom intermediary,

[(*aa*) ...][1]

(*b*) the overseas dividends and manufactured overseas dividends referred to in [paragraph (1A)][4], if received by an overseas dividend manufacturer within sub-paragraph (*a*) of this paragraph who carries on a business in the ordinary course of which he receives overseas dividends and manufactured overseas dividends and pays manufactured overseas dividends, are such that a profit on the sale of the overseas securities to which those overseas dividends and manufactured overseas dividends relate would form part of the trading profits of that business,

(*c*) ...[2-3]

(*d*) except in a case to which paragraph (3) applies, the overseas dividends or, as the case may be, the manufactured overseas dividends received by him, do not fall to be matched, in accordance with regulation 10(1), against manufactured overseas dividends paid by him in that period.

(3) This paragraph applies to a case where, under regulation 10(1), overseas dividends in respect of which overseas tax is payable received by the overseas dividend manufacturer in any chargeable period, and manufactured overseas dividends so received [on or in respect of the making of which overseas tax has been charged or][4] from which tax has been deducted or in respect of which tax falls to be accounted for and paid as mentioned in [paragraph (1A)][4] above, are matched against manufactured overseas dividends paid by him under deduction of tax in that period.

(4) Where paragraph (3) applies in respect of any chargeable period, the overseas dividend manufacturer shall be entitled to set off against each other—

(*a*) the tax [referred to in that paragraph that is] attributable to the matched overseas dividends and manufactured overseas dividends received, and

(*b*) the tax [referred to in that paragraph that is] attributable to the matched manufactured overseas dividends paid.

[(4A) Subject to paragraphs (4B) and (5), where overseas dividends or manufactured overseas dividends received by the overseas dividend manufacturer in any chargeable period fall to be matched, in accordance with regulation 10(1), against manufactured overseas dividends paid by him in that period, relief under Part XVIII of the Taxes Act may not be claimed by the overseas dividend manufacturer in respect of any tax referred to in paragraph (1A) that is attributable to those overseas dividends or manufactured overseas dividends received.][5]

[(4B) Where overseas dividends or manufactured overseas dividends received by the overseas dividend manufacturer in any chargeable period fall to be matched, in accordance with regulation 10(1), against manufactured overseas dividends to which regulation 5 applies that are paid by him in that period, relief under section 811 of the Taxes Act shall be given to the overseas dividend manufacturer in respect of any tax referred to in paragraph (1A) that is attributable to those overseas dividends or manufactured overseas dividends received.][5]

[(4C) Subject to paragraph (5), where tax referred to in paragraph (1A) that is attributable to overseas dividends or manufactured overseas dividends received by the overseas dividend manufacturer in any chargeable period is set off, in accordance with this regulation, against tax referred to in paragraph (1B) that is attributable to manufactured overseas dividends paid by him in that period, relief under Part XVIII of the Taxes Act may not be claimed by the overseas dividend manufacturer in respect of any tax referred to in paragraph (1A) that is attributable to those overseas dividends or manufactured overseas dividends received.][5]

(5) Except in a case to which paragraph (3) applies, where in accordance with this regulation tax is set off by an overseas dividend manufacturer in any chargeable period and in relation to that period the sum of the overseas tax and amounts referred to in [paragraph (1A)][4] exceeds the total amount of the sums due as mentioned in [paragraph (1B)][4], relief under Part XVIII of the Taxes Act may be claimed by the overseas dividend manufacturer in respect of the amount of the excess.

(6) Where in accordance with this regulation tax is set off by an overseas dividend manufacturer in any chargeable period and in relation to that period the total amount of the sums due from the overseas dividend manufacturer as mentioned in [paragraph (1B)][4] exceeds the sum of the overseas tax and amounts referred to in [paragraph (1A)][4], the amount of the excess shall be payable to the Board.

(7) References to overseas tax in this regulation are references to the amount of such tax which is eligible for relief under Part XVIII of the Taxes Act either—

(*a*) pursuant to arrangements made with the government of the overseas territory specified in paragraph (8) which have effect by virtue of section 788 of the Taxes Act and relate to the overseas dividend [or manufactured overseas dividend] concerned, or

(*b*) by virtue of other provisions of Part XVIII of the Taxes Act other than section 790(5)(*c*)(ii) of that Act.

(8) The overseas territory specified [in this paragraph—

(i) so far as overseas dividends are concerned, is the territory of the government or public or local authority which issued the securities in question or, where the securities were issued by any other body of persons not resident in the United Kingdom, the territory under whose law that tax would have been payable;

(ii) so far as manufactured overseas dividends are concerned, is the territory of the government by which tax is charged on, or in respect of, the making of the manufactured overseas dividend concerned.][4]

Amendments—[1] Para (2)(*aa*) inserted by the IT (Manufactured Overseas Dividends) (Amendment) Regulations, SI 1995/1324 reg 5(*a*), with effect from 7 June 1995, and revoked by the IT (Manufactured Overseas Dividends) (Amendment No 2) Regulations, SI 1996/2643 reg 10(*b*)(i), with effect from 6 November 1996.

[2-3] Para (2)(*c*) and the word "and" immediately following it revoked by the IT (Manufactured Overseas Dividends) (Amendment) Regulations, SI 1996/1229 reg 5, with effect from 28 May 1996.

[4] Paras (1), (1A), (1B) substituted for para (1) and words in paras (2)(*b*), (3), (4)(*a*), (*b*), (5), (6), (7)(A), (8) substituted or inserted by the IT (Manufactured Overseas Dividends) (Amendment No 2) Regulations, SI 1996/2643 reg 10, with effect from 6 November 1996.

[5] Paras (4A), (4B), (4C) substituted for para (4A) by the IT (Manufactured Overseas Dividends) (Amendment) Regulations, SI 1997/988, regs 1, 6, with effect from 1 July 1997.

[Offsetting of tax by overseas dividend manufacturers who are not United Kingdom intermediaries][1]

[9A—(1) An overseas dividend manufacturer who is not an approved United Kingdom intermediary shall be entitled to set off in any chargeable period amounts of overseas tax in respect of overseas dividends received by him in that chargeable period against sums due from him on account of the amounts deducted by him under paragraph 4(2) of Schedule 23A from manufactured overseas dividends paid by him in that chargeable period that are representatives of those overseas dividends.

(2) Where overseas tax referred to in paragraph (1) is set off against sums referred to in that paragraph, relief under Part XVIII of the Taxes Act may not be claimed by the overseas dividend manufacturer in respect of that overseas tax.

[(2A) This paragraph applies where an overseas dividend manufacturer who is not an approved United Kingdom intermediary receives in any chargeable period overseas dividends or manufactured overseas dividends and pays in that period manufactured overseas dividends to which regulation 5 applies that are representative of those overseas dividends or manufactured overseas dividends received.][2]

[(2B) Where paragraph (2A) applies—

(*a*) relief under section 811 of the Taxes Act shall be given to the overseas dividend manufacturer in respect of any tax referred to in regulation 9(1A) that is attributable to the overseas dividends or manufactured overseas dividends received by him; and

(*b*) no other relief under Part 18 of the Taxes Act may be claimed by him in respect of any such tax.][2]

(3) References in this regulation to overseas tax shall be construed in accordance with regulation 9(7).][1]

Amendments—[1] This regulation inserted by the IT (Manufactured Overseas Dividends) (Amendment) Regulations, SI 1997/988, regs 1, 7, with effect from 1 July 1997.

[2] Paras 2A, 2B inserted by the IT (Manufactured Overseas Dividends) (Amendment) Regulations, SI 2003/2582 regs 2, 10 with effect from 1 November 2003.

Matching of dividends and manufactured overseas dividends

10—(1) For the purpose of paragraphs (2)(*d*) and (3) of regulation 9, overseas dividends paid on overseas securities of a particular kind in respect of a particular dividend date which are received in any chargeable period by an overseas dividend manufacturer, and manufactured overseas dividends representative of those overseas dividends which are received by him in that period—

(*a*) shall be matched against manufactured overseas dividends representative of those overseas dividends which are paid by him in that period in accordance with the following order of priority—

(i) manufactured overseas dividends received without deduction of tax [other than manufactured overseas dividends in respect of which tax falls to be accounted for and paid under paragraph 4(3) of Schedule 23A or regulation 4(3)][1]

(ii) overseas dividends received; and

(iii) manufactured overseas dividends received [to which tax referred to in regulation [9(1A)][3] is attributable][2]; and

(*b*) shall first be matched against manufactured overseas dividends paid without deduction of tax under paragraph 4(2) of Schedule 23A [by virtue of regulation 5][4],

and the balance, if any, shall be matched against manufactured overseas dividends paid by him from which tax has been deducted under paragraph 4(2) of Schedule 23A.

[(2) Where under paragraph (1) an overseas dividend or manufactured overseas dividend received is matched with a manufactured overseas dividend paid [to a United Kingdom recipient][4], any voucher relating to the deduction of overseas tax from the overseas dividend shall, subject to paragraph (3), be forwarded to the [United Kingdom recipient][4].

(3) Where under paragraph (1) an overseas dividend received, or a manufactured overseas dividend received on or in respect of the making of which overseas tax has been charged, is matched with more than one manufactured overseas dividend paid [to a United Kingdom recipient][4], the overseas dividend manufacturer—

(*a*) shall endeavour to obtain from the payer of the overseas dividend a voucher corresponding to each such manufactured overseas dividend [so paid][4], or

(*b*) if, despite reasonable attempts to do so, he is unable to obtain such a voucher, shall prepare a voucher corresponding to each such manufactured overseas dividend and showing the following amounts—

(i) so much of the gross amount of the overseas dividend as corresponds to the gross amount of the manufactured overseas dividend [so paid][4],

(ii) so much of the overseas tax in respect of the overseas dividend or manufactured overseas dividend received as would be eligible for relief as mentioned in regulation 9(7) and relates to the amount of the overseas dividend calculated in paragraph (i) above, and

(iii) so much of the actual amount of the overseas dividend or manufactured overseas dividend received as corresponds to the amount of the manufactured overseas dividend [so paid][4], and

(*c*) shall forward the voucher obtained or, as the case may be, prepared by him to the [United Kingdom recipient][4] of the manufactured overseas dividend paid by him to which the voucher relates, instead of the voucher referred to in paragraph (2).][2]

(4) Where a voucher has been forwarded as mentioned in paragraph (3)(*c*) and subsequently a manufactured overseas dividend received by an overseas dividend manufacturer to which that voucher relates is matched under paragraph (1) with more than one manufactured overseas dividend paid [to a United Kingdom recipient][4], the overseas dividend manufacturer—

(*a*) shall endeavour to obtain from the payer of the overseas dividend of which the manufactured overseas dividend received is representative [or (as the case may be) from the payer of the manufactured overseas dividend received][2] a voucher corresponding to each such manufactured overseas dividend [so paid][4], or

(*b*) if, despite reasonable attempts to do so, he is unable to obtain such a voucher, shall prepare a voucher corresponding to each such manufactured overseas dividend [so paid][4] and showing the details specified in paragraphs (i) to (iii) of paragraph (3)(*b*), and

(*c*) shall forward the voucher obtained or, as the case may be, prepared by him to the [United Kingdom recipient][4] of the manufactured overseas dividend to which the voucher relates.

Amendments—[1] Words in para (1)(*a*) (i) substituted by the IT (Manufactured Overseas Dividends) (Amendment) Regulations, SI 1995/1324 reg 6, with effect from 7 June 1995.
[2] Words in para (1)(*a*)(iii), and paras (2), (3), substituted, and words in para (4)(*a*) inserted, by the IT (Manufactured Overseas Dividends) (Amendment No 2) Regulations, SI 1996/2643 reg 11, with effect from 6 November 1996.
[3] Figures in para (1)(*a*)(iii) substituted for "9(3)" by the IT (Manufactured Overseas Dividends) (Amendment) Regulations, SI 1997/988, regs 1, 8, with effect from 1 July 1997.
[4] Words in para (1) substituted, and words in paras (2)–(4) inserted and substituted, by the IT (Manufactured Overseas Dividends) (Amendment) Regulations, SI 2003/2582 regs 2, 11 with effect from 1 November 2003.

Accounting for tax payable under paragraph 4(2) and (3) of Schedule 23A and these Regulations

11—(1) Within 30 days of the end of a chargeable period—

(*a*) an overseas dividend manufacturer shall pay to the Board all amounts which he was liable to deduct under paragraph 4(2) of Schedule 23A on account of income tax from manufactured overseas dividends paid by him in that period;

(*b*) an overseas dividend manufacturer who is an approved United Kingdom intermediary shall pay to the Board the amount of any excess payable under regulation 9(6) attributable to that period;

(*c*) a United Kingdom recipient shall pay to the Board all amounts of tax for which he was liable to account under paragraph 4(3) of Schedule 23A in respect of manufactured overseas dividends received by him in that period;

(*d*) an approved United Kingdom intermediary or an approved United Kingdom collecting agent shall pay to the Board all amounts of tax for which he was liable to account under regulation 4(3) in respect of ...[1] manufactured overseas dividends received by him in that period.

(2) Within [30][2] days of the end of a chargeable period—

(*a*) an overseas dividend manufacturer shall make a return to the Board or an inspector, in such form as the Board may prescribe, showing—

(i) the amounts which he was liable to deduct under paragraph 4(2) of Schedule 23A on account of income tax from ...[1] manufactured overseas dividends paid by him in that period,

(ii) ...[1], and

(iii) the amount of any excess payable under regulation 9(6) attributable to that period;

(*b*) a United Kingdom recipient shall make a return to the Board or an inspector, in such form as the Board may prescribe, showing the amounts of tax for which he was liable to account under paragraph 4(3) of Schedule 23A in respect of manufactured overseas dividends received by him in that period;

(*c*) an approved United Kingdom intermediary or an approved United Kingdom collecting agent shall make a return to the Board or an inspector, in such form as the Board may prescribe, showing the amounts of tax for which he was liable to account under regulation 4(3) in respect of ...[1] manufactured overseas dividends received by him in that period.

(3) Any amount referred to in paragraph (1) shall be due at the end of the period of 30 days specified in that paragraph and shall be payable without the making of any assessment but may be assessed on the overseas dividend manufacturer or, as the case may be, the United Kingdom recipient, approved United Kingdom intermediary or approved United Kingdom collecting agent (whether or not it has been paid when the assessment is made) if it is not paid in full on or before that date.

(4) In any case where—

(*a*) it appears to the inspector that there is—

(i) a manufactured overseas dividend paid, or an overseas dividend or a manufactured overseas dividend received, by an overseas dividend manufacturer in a chargeable period, or

(ii) an overseas dividend or a manufactured overseas dividend received by a United Kingdom recipient, an approved United Kingdom intermediary or an approved United Kingdom collecting agent in a chargeable period,

which ought to have been but which has not been included in a return under paragraph (2) relating to that period, or

(*b*) the inspector is dissatisfied with any return under paragraph (2),

the inspector may make an assessment to the best of his judgment on the overseas dividend manufacturer or, as the case may be, the United Kingdom recipient, approved United Kingdom intermediary or approved United Kingdom collecting agent.

(5) Any income tax due under an assessment made by virtue of paragraph (4) shall be treated for the purposes of interest on unpaid tax as having been payable at the end of the period of 30 days specified in paragraph (1).

(6) Any amount for which an approved United Kingdom intermediary is liable to account under regulation 6(6), and any amount for which a United Kingdom recipient is liable to account under regulation 7(6), in respect of manufactured overseas dividends received by them in a chargeable period, shall be due at the end of the period of 30 days from the end of that period, and shall be payable without the making of any assessment but may be assessed on the approved United Kingdom intermediary or, as the case may be, the United Kingdom recipient (whether or not it has been paid when the assessment is made) if it is not paid in full on or before that date.

(7) The like provisions as are contained in the Income Tax Acts with respect to the time within which an assessment may be made, so far as they refer or relate to the year of assessment for which an assessment is made, or the year to which an assessment relates, shall have effect in relation to an assessment under this regulation notwithstanding that, under this regulation, the assessment may be said to relate to a period which is not a year of assessment; and the like provisions as are contained in section 36 of the Management Act as to the circumstances in which an assessment may be made out of time shall have effect accordingly on the footing that any such assessment relates to the year of assessment in which the period in question ends.

(8) Income tax assessed on a person under this regulation shall be due at the end of the period of 30 days after the issue of the notice of assessment (unless due earlier under paragraph (3) or (6)).

(9) Any tax assessable under any one or more of the provisions of this regulation may be included in one assessment if the tax so included is all due on the same date.

(10) Section 31 and Part V of the Management Act shall apply to an appeal against any assessment to tax under this regulation.

(11) Subsections (1), (7) and (8) of section 87 of the Management Act shall apply to tax assessable under this regulation as they apply to tax assessable in accordance with Schedules 13 and 16 to the Taxes Act, and accordingly those subsections shall have effect as if references to those schedules included references to this regulation.

(12) Section 98 of the Management Act shall apply in relation to a return under paragraph (2) with the modification specified in paragraph (13).

(13) At the end of the second column of the Table in section 98 of the Management Act there shall be inserted—

"Regulation 11(2) of the Income Tax (Manufactured Overseas Dividends) Regulations 1993".

Amendments—[1] Words revoked by the IT (Manufactured Overseas Dividends) (Amendment) (Regulations, SI 1996/1229 reg 6, with effect from 28 May 1996.

[2] Figure in para (2) substituted by the IT (Manufactured Overseas Dividends) (Amendment) Regulations, SI 1997/988, regs 9, with effect in relation to chargeable periods ending on or after 1 July 1997.

Tax treatment of manufactured overseas dividends representative of foreign dividends

12—[(1) This regulation applies to a case where a manufactured overseas dividend is paid to a collecting agent in circumstances where, had it been the overseas dividend of which it is representative, it would have been—

(*a*) a foreign dividend (as defined in section 18(3D) of the Taxes Act, or

(*b*) interest on a quoted Eurobond (as defined by section 124 of that Act) held in a recognised clearing system.][2]

(2) Where this regulation applies—

(*a*) ...[3] deduction of an amount determined by reference to the gross amount of the manufactured overseas dividend shall be made by the ...[2] collecting agent from the manufactured overseas dividend on account of income tax similar to the deduction that would, in the case of the overseas dividend of which the manufactured overseas dividend is representative, have been made under [Chapter VIIA of Part IV of the Taxes Act][1]; and

[(*b*) the provisions of that Chapter relating to collecting agents shall apply in relation to amounts falling to be deducted under sub-paragraph (*a*) as if references in that Chapter to relevant dividends, or the proceeds of sale or other realisation of coupons for relevant dividends, included references to manufactured overseas dividends to which this regulation applies or, as the case may be, the proceeds of sale or other realisation of manufactured overseas dividends to which this regulation applies.][1]

(3) ...[3]

Amendments—[1] Words in sub-para (2)(*a*), and sub-para (2)(*b*), substituted by the IT (Manufactured Overseas Dividends) (Amendment) Regulations, SI 1996/1229 reg 7(*b*), with effect from 28 May 1996.

[2] Para (1) substituted by the IT (Manufactured Overseas Dividends) (Amendment No 2) Regulations, SI 1996/2643 reg 12, with effect from 6 November 1996.

[3] Words in sub-para (2)(*a*) and para (3) revoked by the Income Tax (Manufactured Overseas Dividends) (Amendment No 2) Regulations, SI 1997/2706, with effect from 9 December 1997. Para (3) is rendered obsolete by the Income Tax (Paying and Collecting Agents) (Amendment) Regulations, SI 1997/2705 which come into force on the same day and amend the Income Tax (Paying and Collecting Agents) Regulations, SI 1996/1780.

Further provision relating to manufactured overseas dividends representative of foreign dividends

13 ...

Amendments—This regulation revoked by the IT (Manufactured Overseas Dividends) (Amendment No 2) Regulations, SI 1996/2643 reg 13, with effect from 6 November 1996.

Records to be kept in respect of certain manufactured overseas dividends paid without deduction of tax

14—(1) An overseas dividend manufacturer or an approved United Kingdom collecting agent shall maintain a record in respect of any manufactured overseas dividend paid by him to which this regulation applies showing—

(*a*) the date of payment and the amount of the manufactured overseas dividend,
[(*b*) the name of the person to whom payment was made,][1]
[(*ba*) his grounds for believing that the payment should be made without deduction of tax, and][1]
(*c*) particulars of the overseas securities and the overseas dividend on those securities to which the manufactured overseas dividend relates.

[(2) This regulation applies to any manufactured overseas dividend which an overseas dividend manufacturer or an approved United Kingdom collecting agent, by virtue of regulation 5(1B), pays without deduction of tax.][1]

[(3) An overseas dividend manufacturer or an approved United Kingdom collecting agent—

(*a*) shall retain for a period of six years—
(i) any record required to be maintained by him under paragraph (1), and
(ii) any evidence relevant to his grounds for believing that the payment should be made without deduction of tax; and
(*b*) whenever required to do so within that period, shall make any such record or evidence available for inspection by an officer of the Board.][1]

[(3A) In the case of evidence or a record retained under paragraph (3) which is in electronic form the person retaining it shall afford an officer of the Board such assistance and facilities as the officer may reasonably require in order to read the record or certificate.][2]

(4) Where an overseas dividend manufacturer or an approved United Kingdom collecting agent fails to maintain, or to retain for the requisite period, any such record, or fails to retain any such [evidence][1] for the requisite period, the Board may require that person to carry out, at his own expense, an audit of manufactured overseas dividends paid by him in order to ascertain the amount of tax, if any, liable to be deducted under paragraph 4(2) of Schedule 23A which was not deducted.

(5) The scope and method of the audit referred to in paragraph (4) shall be agreed between the Board and the person concerned or, in the absence of agreement, shall be determined by the Board.

Amendments—[1] Sub-paras (1)(*b*), (*ba*) substituted for sub-para (1)(*b*); paras (2), (3) substituted; and word in sub-para (4) substituted; by the IT (Manufactured Overseas Dividends) (Amendment) Regulations, SI 2003/2582 regs 2, 12 with effect from 1 November 2003.
[2] Para (3A) inserted by the Income and Corporation Taxes (Electronic Certificates of Deduction of Tax and Tax Credit) Regulations, SI 2003/3143 reg 5(1), (4) with effect from 1 January 2004.

Issue of vouchers in respect of manufactured overseas dividends paid under deduction of tax

15—(1) Subject to paragraphs (2) and (3), where an overseas dividend manufacturer makes a payment of a manufactured overseas dividend from which an amount is deducted by him under paragraph 4(2) of Schedule 23A...[1] he shall furnish the recipient of the payment with a voucher showing the details specified in paragraph (4).

(2) ...[1], paragraph (1) shall not apply in any case where, pursuant to paragraph (2), (3)(*c*) or (4)(*c*) of regulation 10, a voucher is forwarded to the recipient of a manufactured overseas dividend.

(3) Where the overseas dividend manufacturer is an approved United Kingdom intermediary, he shall not be required to furnish the recipient of a payment with the voucher referred to in paragraph (1) unless the recipient requests such a voucher.

(4) The details specified in this paragraph are that the voucher shall show—

(*a*) the gross amount of the payment,
(*b*) the amount deducted or, where more than one amount has been deducted, each such amount separately, and
(*c*) the actual amount paid.

(5) An approved United Kingdom collecting agent, where requested to do so by the person beneficially entitled to a manufactured overseas dividend in respect of which tax has been paid or is due to be paid by the approved United Kingdom collecting agent under paragraph 4(3) of Schedule 23A or regulation 4(3), shall furnish that person with a voucher showing—

(*a*) the gross amount of the manufactured overseas dividend received by him,
(*b*) the amount of tax paid or due to be paid by him in respect of the manufactured overseas dividend, and
(*c*) the actual amount paid.

Amendments—[1] Words revoked by the IT (Manufactured Overseas Dividends) (Amendment No 2) Regulations, SI 1996/2643 reg 14, with effect from 6 November 1996.

[Modifications of section 21 of the Management Act in relation to overseas dividend manufacturers][1]

16 ...

Amendments—[1] This regulation revoked by the Stock Lending and Manufactured Payments (Revocations and Amendments) Regulation, SI 1997/987, reg 8(1), (4), (5), with effect in relation to (*a*) transactions entered into on or after 1 July 1997 in respect of which information may be obtained under TMA 1970 s 21, and (*b*) payments made on or after that date (whether under transactions entered into before, or under transactions entered into on or after, that date) in respect of which information may be obtained under that section.

1993/3016

Retirement Benefits Schemes (Restriction on Discretion to Approve) (Additional Voluntary Contributions) Regulations 1993

Made by the Treasury under TA 1988 s 591(6)

Made . . . . *3 December 1993*
Laid before the House of Commons . . . *6 December 1993*
Coming into Force . . . . . *27 December 1993*

Commentary—*Simon's Direct Tax Service* **E7.215, 221.**

Citation and commencement

1 These Regulations may be cited as the Retirement Benefits Schemes (Restriction on Discretion to Approve) (Additional Voluntary Contributions) Regulations 1993 and shall come into force on 27th December 1993.

Interpretation

2—(1) In these Regulations, unless the context otherwise requires—

"approved" in relation to a retirement benefits scheme, means approved by the Board for the purposes of Chapter I of Part XIV of the Taxes Act or before the Board in order for them to decide whether to give approval under section 591;

"benefit certificate" means the certificate referred to in regulation 5(3)(*a*);

"the Board" means the Commissioners of Inland Revenue;

"contributor", in relation to a retirement benefits scheme, means a person who has at any time contributed to the scheme;

"death benefit scheme" means a retirement benefits scheme which provides benefit only on the employee's death;

"freestanding additional voluntary contributions scheme" means a retirement benefits scheme—

(*a*) to which a relevant employer of an employee who contributes to the scheme is not a contributor, and

(*b*) which provides benefits additional to those provided by an approved retirement benefits scheme to which a relevant employer is a contributor or by a relevant statutory scheme;

"leading scheme", in relation to an employee, means—

(*a*) where the employee has paid voluntary contributions to a main scheme or any other scheme established by a relevant employer of the employee or to which a relevant employer is a contributor, that main scheme, and

(*b*) in all other cases, the free-standing additional voluntary contributions scheme from which the main scheme last received a notification in respect of the employee in accordance with regulation 4(2);

"main scheme", in relation to an employee who is a contributor to a freestanding additional voluntary contributions scheme in respect of service with a relevant employer, means—

(*a*) the retirement benefits scheme to which a relevant employer is a contributor and which provides benefits which are supplemented by those provided to the employee by the freestanding additional voluntary contributions scheme; or

(*b*) where there is more than one such retirement benefits scheme, the scheme which provides benefits which are supplemented by those provided by the other schemes;

"notice" means notice in writing and "notify" shall be construed accordingly;

"relevant date" has the meaning given by regulation 5(5)(*c*);

"relevant employer", in relation to an employee, means—

(*a*) the current employer of that employee or, where he has more than one current employer, any of those current employers who are associated, and

(*b*) any of two or more associated employers successively of that employee of whom one is that current employer, or one of those associated current employers, and

(*c*) either of two employers successively of that employee, where one is that current employer, or one of those associated current employers, and one—

(i) has acquired the other, or

(ii) has taken over the whole or part of the business of the other, and (*d*) any of two or more employers successively of that employee, where one is that current employer, or one of those associated current employers, and the Board have agreed that service with each of the employers may be regarded as continuous pensionable service;

"section 591" means section 591 of the Taxes Act;

"simplified defined contribution scheme" means a retirement benefits scheme approved by the Board under section 591 by reference to limitations on—

(*a*) the aggregate amount of contributions which may be paid by a member and his employer,
(*b*) the maximum lump sum which may be provided under the scheme, and
(*c*) the benefits payable on death which may be provided under the scheme;

"surplus funds" has the meaning given by regulation 6(2)(*d*);

"the Taxes Act" means the Income and Corporation Taxes Act 1988.

(2) In these Regulations—

(*a*) references to an employee include references to a deceased employee of an employer and to a person who has been an employee of an employer;

(*b*) references to an employer include references to a person who was an employer of a deceased employee and to a person who has been an employer of an employee;

(*c*) references to a current employer include references to a person who was an employer of a deceased employee at the time of his death;

(*d*) references to a relevant statutory scheme shall be construed in accordance with section 611A of the Taxes Act as if they were references in Chapter I of Part XIV of that Act.

(3) For the purposes of this regulation an employer is associated with another employer if (directly or indirectly) one is controlled by the other or if both are controlled by a third person.

(4) In paragraph (3) the reference to control—

(*a*) in relation to an employer which is a body corporate and a close company within the meaning of section 414 of the Taxes Act, shall be construed in accordance with section 416 of that Act, and

(*b*) in relation to any employer which is a body corporate other than one mentioned in sub-paragraph (*a*) above or a partnership, shall be construed in accordance with section 840 of that Act;

and the like definition to that in the said section 840 shall apply (with the necessary modifications) in relation to an employer which is an unincorporated association as that definition applies to a body corporate.

Introductory

3 These Regulations—

(*a*) are made for the purposes of section 591;

(*b*) restrict the Board's discretion to approve retirement benefits schemes which are not simplified defined contribution schemes or death benefit schemes by reference to the circumstances in which surplus funds arising from the payment of additional voluntary contributions may be repaid to employees;

(*c*) specify the method to be used for calculating the amount of surplus funds.

Restrictions on discretion to approve—freestanding additional voluntary contributions schemes

4—(1) The Board shall not exercise their discretion under section 591 to approve a retirement benefits scheme which is a freestanding additional voluntary contributions scheme unless the rules of the scheme provide that the administrator of the scheme shall comply with the requirements of this regulation and, where the scheme is the leading scheme in relation to an employee, with the requirements of regulation 6 so far as they concern freestanding additional voluntary contributions schemes.

(2) The administrator of the scheme shall—

(*a*) when contributions are first paid to the scheme by an employee to whom benefits are accruing under the main scheme in relation to that employee, and

(*b*) when contributions are first paid by an employee under the scheme following a change of employment as a result of which benefits are accruing to the employee under a different main scheme in relation to that employee, and

(*c*) when the scheme receives a transfer value in respect of an employee from another freestanding additional voluntary contributions scheme and part of that transfer value represents contributions paid during the period that benefits were accruing under the main scheme in relation to the employee,

notify the administrator of that main scheme of the event in question and of the account number of the employee in the scheme within a period of 60 days following receipt by him of the relevant information.

(3) The administrator of the scheme shall keep a separate record of the funds held for the purposes of paying benefits by virtue of the employee's contributions during each period that benefits are accruing under a different main scheme.

(4) [Subject to paragraph (4A), the administrator][1] of the scheme shall not pay any benefit, nor make any repayment of surplus funds to an employee or his personal representative, unless he has received a benefit certificate in respect of that employee from the administrator of the main scheme or, where the scheme is not the leading scheme in relation to the employee, an authorisation from the administrator of that leading scheme.

[(4A) The administrator of the scheme may pay a benefit to an employee in a case where he has not received a benefit certificate from the administrator of the main scheme as mentioned in paragraph (4) or, where the scheme is not the leading scheme in relation to the employee, an authorisation from the administrator of the leading scheme as mentioned in that paragraph, as the case may be, if—

(*a*) the employee has either—

(i) attained the age of 50 years, or

(ii) become incapable through infirmity of body or mind of carrying on his normal occupation or any occupation of a similar nature for which he is trained or fitted, and

(*b*) benefits have neither ceased to accrue to the employee in the circumstances mentioned in regulation 5(5)(*c*)(i) nor become payable to the employee in the circumstances mentioned in regulation 5(5)(*c*)(ii).][1]

[(4B) Where—

(*a*) an employee has notified the administrator of the scheme that he wishes the payment of benefits under the scheme to be deferred until a date after the event referred to in regulation 5(5)(*c*)(ii) (not being a date later than the day on which the employee attains the age of 75 years), and

(*b*) the employee dies after the event referred to in regulation 5(5)(*c*)(ii) but before any payment of benefits under the scheme has been made,

the provisions of regulation 6 (with the exception of sub-paragraphs (*a*) and (*b*) of paragraph (6) of that regulation) shall apply on the assumption (if not otherwise the case) that the scheme is the leading scheme in relation to the employee.][1]

(5) Any payment which is to be made by the administrator of the scheme to or for the benefit of an employee or his personal representative to which section 599A of the Taxes Act applies—

[(*a*) shall be made—

(i) in a case where paragraph (4B) applies, as soon as possible after the administrator has made the calculation required by regulation 6 (as applied by that paragraph), and

(ii) in any other case, as soon as possible following receipt of notice from the leading scheme in relation to the employee of the benefits which may be paid by the scheme;][2]

(*b*) shall be accompanied by a certificate signed by the administrator making the payment showing the amount which, after deduction of income tax at the basic rate for the year of assessment in which the repayment is made, would equal the amount paid to the employee or his personal representative, being the amount which the employee or the personal representative will be required to include in the return of his or the employee's income for that year of assessment.

(6) Where a transfer of accumulated funds is made to another freestanding additional voluntary contributions scheme the administrator of the scheme shall notify the administrator of the main scheme of the date of the transfer within the period of 60 days following that date.

(7) As soon as possible after—

(*a*) any change in the name or address of the administrator of the scheme, or

(*b*) the appointment of a new administrator of the scheme,

the administrator of the scheme shall notify his name and address to the administrator of the main scheme.

Amendments—[1] Words in para (4) substituted for words "The administrator", and sub-paras (4A), (4B) inserted, by the Retirement Benefits Schemes (Restriction on Discretion to Approve) (Additional Voluntary Contributions) Regulations, SI 1999/1964 regs 1, 3 with effect from 30 July 1999.

[2] Para (5)(*a*) substituted by SI 1999/1964 regs 1, 3 with effect from 30 July 1999.

Restriction on discretion to approve—other schemes

5—(1) The Board shall not exercise their discretion under section 591 to approve a retirement benefits scheme, which is not a freestanding additional voluntary contributions scheme, unless the rules of the scheme provide that the administrator of the scheme shall comply with the requirements of this regulation and, where the scheme is the leading scheme in relation to an employee, with the requirements of regulation 6 so far as they concern main schemes.

(2) The administrator of the scheme shall keep for the period of six years following the year of assessment in which the relevant date occurred a record of—

(*a*) any information notified to him by the administrator of a freestanding additional voluntary contributions scheme providing benefits to an employee which are additional to those provided by the scheme as to—

(i) the name of that scheme and the name and address of the administrator of that scheme, and

(ii) the account number of the employee in that scheme; and

(*b*) any information notified to him by the administrator of the leading scheme in relation to an employee as to the kinds and the amounts of benefits that have been secured under every freestanding additional voluntary contributions scheme which provides benefits to the employee which are additional to those provided by the scheme.

(3) Where the scheme is the main scheme in relation to an employee, but is not the leading scheme in relation to that employee, the administrator of the scheme shall—

(*a*) within the period of 30 days following receipt by him of information that the relevant date has passed, provide the administrator of the leading scheme with a certificate showing the information specified in paragraph (4); [*and*][1]

(*b*) at the same time notify the administrator of any other approved freestanding additional voluntary contributions scheme providing benefits which are additional to those provided by the scheme that a benefit certificate has been provided to the administrator of the leading scheme in relation to the employee [and

(*c*) where regulation 4(4B) applies, within 30 days following receipt of a request from the administrator of the scheme referred to in that provision, provide that administrator with a copy of the benefit certificate provided under sub-paragraph (*a*).][1]

(4) The information specified in this paragraph is—

(*a*) the amount of pension and pension equivalent which is payable to the employee, or which will be so payable in the first year for which the pension is payable (on the assumptions that the employee survives to the end of that year and that pension equivalent is, or will be, payable as such) under every scheme established by a relevant employer of the employee or to which a relevant employer is a contributor;

(*b*) the amount of pension which is or will be payable to the widow or widower of the employee in the first year following the death of the employee under every scheme established by a relevant employer of the employee or to which a relevant employer is a contributor;

(*c*) the percentage by which the amounts of pension referred to in sub-paragraphs (*a*) and (*b*) may be increased annually under the rules of the scheme or, where the rules of the schemes do not provide for increases by a specific percentage each year, the average of the percentages by which pensions payable under the schemes referred to in those sub-paragraphs have been increased in each of the three years preceding the relevant date;

(*d*) the maximum amount of pension and pension equivalent which can be paid to the employee in the circumstances described in sub-paragraph (*a*);

(*e*) the maximum amount of pension which can be paid to the widow or widower of the employee in the circumstances described in sub-paragraph (*b*);

(*f*) in relation to the maximum amount referred to in sub-paragraph (*d*), the details of the calculation of that amount and, in particular, whether in calculating that amount he has taken final remuneration to be—

(i) the amount of annual remuneration on which the scheme benefits are calculated, or

(ii) the highest amount of annual remuneration on which, under the rules of the scheme, benefits could be calculated, or

(iii) the average of the total amounts of emoluments paid by a relevant employer to the employee during each of the last three years of assessment from which tax was deducted in accordance with the Income Tax (Employments) Regulations 1973 or the Income Tax (Employments) Regulations 1993, disregarding in calculating those total amounts in relation to an employee to whom section 590C of the Taxes Act applies any excess over the permitted maximum for the year in question which is found for the purposes of that section;

(*g*) where the relevant date is the date of the employee's death, instead of the amount referred to in sub-paragraph (*a*) and the maximum amount referred to in sub-paragraph (*d*), the amount of any benefit consisting of a lump sum payable in that event and the maximum amount of that benefit.

(5) In this regulation—

(*a*) [subject to regulation 5A,][2] ''pension'' means any amount payable by way of a pension or an annuity before any option is exercised to commute any part of that pension or annuity into a lump sum, or to allocate any such part to another person;

(*b*) [subject to regulation 5A,][2] ''pension equivalent'' means the additional amount that would be payable as an annuity if every twelve pounds payable by way of a lump sum under the rules of the scheme (otherwise than by commutation) were payable as an additional annuity of one pound (any amount left over being treated as an annuity of one pound);

(*c*) ''the relevant date'' means the date on which—

(i) benefits cease to accrue to the employee under an approved retirement benefits scheme to which a relevant employer of the employee is a contributor, otherwise than by reason of his unpaid absence, and are not continuing to accrue to him under any other scheme to which a relevant employer is a contributor, or

(ii) benefits become payable to the employee under an approved retirement benefits scheme to which a relevant employer of the employee is a contributor, or

(iii) the employee dies,

whichever occurs first;

(*d*) "scheme" in sub-paragraphs (*a*) and (*b*) of paragraph (4) means—

(i) an approved retirement benefits scheme; or

(ii) a relevant statutory scheme.

(6) The administrator of the scheme shall—

(*a*) notify the administrator of the leading scheme in relation to an employee of any information notified to him as to—

(i) the name of any other approved freestanding additional voluntary contributions scheme providing benefits additional to those provided by the scheme and the name and address of the administrator of the scheme, and

(ii) the account number of the employee in that scheme; and

(*b*) notify the administrator of every approved freestanding additional voluntary contributions scheme providing benefits additional to those provided by the scheme of any change in his name or address.

(7) As soon as possible following his appointment, any new administrator of the scheme shall notify his name and address to the administrator of every approved freestanding additional voluntary contributions scheme providing benefits additional to those provided by the scheme.

Amendments—[1] Word "and" immediately following para (3)(*a*) revoked, and para (3)(*c*) and word "and" immediately preceding it inserted by the Retirement Benefits Schemes (Restriction on Discretion to Approve) (Additional Voluntary Contributions) Regulations, SI 1999/1964 regs 1, 4 with effect from 30 July 1999.

[2] Words inserted by the Retirement Benefits Schemes (Restriction on Discretion to Approve) (Additional Voluntary Contributions) Regulations, SI 2000/1088 reg 3 with effect from 10 May 1999.

[Special rules for determining pension and pension equivalent

5A—(1) This regulation shall apply in determining whether—

(*a*) any amount is payable for the purposes of the meaning of "pension" given by regulation 5(5)(*a*), or

(*b*) any additional amount is payable for the purposes of the meaning of "pension equivalent" given by regulation 5(5)(*b*).

(2) Where the rules of a scheme established by a relevant employer, or to which a relevant employer is a contributor, provide for any benefit payable to any person as the result of a credit under a pension sharing order or provision to be treated as provided separately from any benefits which are provided under the scheme for that person as an employee, any pension sharing order or provision in favour of an employee who is an ex-spouse which affects the amount or additional amount payable shall not be taken into account in relation to that employee.

(3) Subject to paragraph (4), where any pension sharing order or provision made against an employee who is an ex-spouse affects the amount or additional amount payable, the order or provision shall not be taken into account in relation to that employee and accordingly—

(*a*) any amount payable shall be treated as increased by an amount equal to the relevant reduction;

(*b*) any additional amount payable shall be treated as increased by the amount produced by multiplying the relevant reduction by 2·25.

(4) Paragraph (3) shall not apply where the employee is a moderate earner.

(5) In this regulation—

(*a*) "ex-spouse" has the meaning given by section 659D(1) of the Taxes Act;

(*b*) "moderate earner" means an employee—

(i) who is not a controlling director of a company which is his employer, and

(ii) whose earnings at the date at which his marriage was dissolved or annulled were not more than 25 per cent of the permitted maximum for the year of assessment in which the dissolution or annulment occurred;

(*c*) "pension sharing order or provision" means any such order or provision as is mentioned in section 28(1) of the Welfare Reform and Pensions Act 1999 or Article 25(1) of the Welfare Reform and Pensions (Northern Ireland) Order 1999;

(*d*) "the permitted maximum" has the meaning given by section 590C of the Taxes Act 1988;

(*e*) "the relevant date" has the meaning given by regulation 5(5)(*c*);

(*f*) "the relevant reduction" means the total amount by which the employee's benefits or future benefits under the scheme are reduced under section 31 of the Welfare Reform and Pensions Act 1999, or Article 28 of the Welfare Reform and Pensions (Northern Ireland) Order 1999, on the relevant date.

(6) For the purposes of paragraph (5)(*b*)(i), an employee is a controlling director of a company which is his employer if he is a director of the company to whom section 417(5)(*b*) of the Taxes Act 1988 applies either—

(*a*) at the date on which the marriage was dissolved or annulled, or

(*b*) at any time within the period of ten years before that date.

(7) For the purposes of paragraph (5)(*b*)(ii), an ex-spouse's earnings shall be taken to be the total amounts of emoluments—

(*a*) which were paid to the ex-spouse in consequence of pensionable service to which the scheme relates during the year of assessment before the year of assessment in which the marriage was dissolved or annulled, and

(*b*) from which tax was deducted in accordance with the Income Tax (Employments) Regulations 1993.][1]

Amendments—[1] This regulation inserted by the Retirement Benefits Schemes (Restriction on Discretion to Approve) (Additional Voluntary Contributions) Regulations, SI 2000/1088 reg 4 with effect from 10 May 1999.

Calculation of surplus funds

6—(1) As soon as possible following receipt of the benefit certificate [or, where regulation 4(4B) applies, as soon as possible following the death of the employee referred to in sub-paragraph (*b*) of that provision][1] or, where the leading scheme is the main scheme in relation to the employee, as soon as possible after the relevant date referred to in regulation 5(3), the administrator of the leading scheme in relation to the employee ("the leading administrator") shall calculate, in relation to each kind of benefit [being paid or][1] to be provided by every approved freestanding additional voluntary contributions scheme which, in return for contributions paid while the employee was a member of the main scheme, provides benefits which are additional to those provided by the main scheme, the amount (if any) of any over-provision in relation to that kind of benefit at that relevant date.

(2) Where that calculation shows that there is an over-provision in relation to that kind of benefit, the leading administrator shall notify the employee or his personal representative that he may elect within the period of three months following the date of the notification to use the over-provision—

(*a*) to have a benefit provided of a kind not already provided by the scheme, or

(*b*) in the case of a benefit consisting of a pension, to have the pension increased annually by reference to increases not exceeding the increases in the general index of retail prices (for all items) published by the Central Statistical Office of the Chancellor of the Exchequer or at a rate not exceeding the rate of three per cent with yearly rests, or

(*c*) to have the benefit increased by taking final remuneration to be another of the amounts referred to in regulation 5(4)(*f*), or

(*d*) to have the amount of the accumulated funds of the scheme which, in the opinion of the leading administrator, are not required to secure payment of that kind of benefit (in this regulation referred to as "surplus funds") repaid to him, or

(*e*) to have any combination of those courses followed.

(3) If, at the end of the period of three months referred to in paragraph (2), the employee or his personal representative has not notified the leading administrator that he has elected to use the over-provision in one of the ways described in sub-paragraphs (*a*) to (*e*) of that paragraph, the leading administrator shall assume that he has elected to use it in the way described in sub-paragraph (*d*) of that paragraph.

(4) As soon as possible after notification to him of any election to use the over-provision in one of the ways described in sub-paragraphs (*a*) to (*e*) of paragraph (2), or after the expiry of the period of three months referred to in that paragraph, the leading administrator shall notify the administrator of each freestanding additional voluntary contributions scheme referred to in paragraph (1) of the amount of that kind of benefit which is to be provided under that scheme and that any surplus funds are to be repaid to the employee or his personal representative.

(5) Where the leading scheme in relation to the employee is a freestanding additional voluntary contributions scheme, the leading administrator shall notify the administrator of the main scheme of the total amount of each kind of benefit which is to be provided under every freestanding additional voluntary contributions scheme to which the employee has contributed in respect of an employment with a relevant employer.

(6) For the purposes of this regulation there is an over-provision in relation to a kind of benefit where—

(*a*) in the case of a benefit consisting of a pension where a lump sum is not also payable otherwise than by commutation, the amount of pension which is payable to the employee or will be so payable in the first year for which it is payable (on the assumption that the employee survives to the end of that year) under—

(i) every scheme established by a relevant employer of the employee or to which a relevant employer is a contributor, and

(ii) every approved freestanding additional voluntary contributions scheme to which the employee has contributed in respect of an employment with a relevant employer,

exceeds the amount certified under regulation 5(3), or calculated by the leading administrator, to be the maximum amount of pension which can be paid in that year under the main scheme in relation to that employee;

(*b*) in the case of a benefit consisting of a pension and a lump sum which is payable otherwise than by commutation, the amount of pension and pension equivalent which is payable to the employee, or will be so payable in the first year for which the pension is payable (on the assumptions that the employee survives to the end of that year and that pension equivalent is, or will be, payable as such) under every scheme referred to in paragraphs (i) and (ii) of sub-paragraph (*a*) exceeds the amount certified under regulation 5(3), or calculated by the leading administrator, to be the maximum amount of pension and pension equivalent which can be paid under the main scheme in relation to the employee;

(*c*) in the case of a benefit consisting of a pension which is, or will be, payable to the widow or widower of the employee, the amount of pension which is or will be payable in the first year following the death of the employee under every scheme referred to in paragraphs (i) and (ii) of sub-paragraph (*a*) exceeds the amount which can be certified under regulation 5(4)(*e*) as the maximum amount of pension which can be paid to the widow or widower of that employee;

(*d*) in the case of a benefit consisting of a lump sum payable on the death of the employee, the amount payable under every scheme referred to in paragraphs (i) and (ii) of sub-paragraph (*a*) exceeds the amount which can be certified under regulation 5(4)(*g*) as the maximum amount which can be paid.

(7) In paragraph (6), ''pension'' and ''pension equivalent'' have the meanings given by regulation 5(5)(*a*) and (*b*) [respectively, read together with regulation 5A][2] and in sub-paragraph (*a*)(i) of that paragraph ''scheme'' has the meaning given by regulation 5(5)(*d*).

Amendments—[1] Words in para (1) inserted by the Retirement Benefits Schemes (Restriction on Discretion to Approve) (Additional Voluntary Contributions) Regulations, SI 1999/1964 regs 1, 5 with effect from 30 July 1999.
[2] Words in sub-para (7) substituted by the Retirement Benefits Schemes (Restriction on Discretion to Approve) (Additional Voluntary Contributions) Regulations, SI 2000/1088 reg 5 with effect from 10 May 1999.

1993/3112
Friendly Societies (Provisional Repayments for Exempt Business) Regulations 1993

Made by the Treasury under FA 1993, s 121

Amendments—These Regulations revoked by the Friendly Societies (Provisional Repayments for Exempt Business) Regulations, SI 1999/622 reg 13 with effect for accounting periods ending after 30 June 1999.

1994/236
Distraint by Collectors (Fees, Costs and Charges) Regulations 1994

Made by the Treasury under TMA 1970 s 61(6)

Made	*3 February 1994*
Laid before the House of Commons	*4 February 1994*
Coming into Force	*1 March 1994*

Commentary—*Simon's Direct Tax Service* **A3.1412**.

Citation and commencement

1 These Regulations may be cited as the Distraint by Collectors (Fees, Costs and Charges) Regulations 1994 and shall come into force on 1st March 1994.

Interpretation

2 In these Regulations—

''close possession'' means physical possession by the distrainor or a person acting on his behalf of the goods and chattels distrained;

''walking possession'' means possession in accordance with an agreement between the distrainor and the distrainee whereby, in consideration of the distrainor not remaining in close possession, the distrainee undertakes not to dispose of the goods distrained or any part thereof, or permit their removal by any person not authorised by the distrainor to remove them.

Ascertainment of fees, costs and charges

3 The fees chargeable on or in connection with the levying of distress and the costs and charges recoverable where distress has been levied shall be those specified in the Schedule to these Regulations, but subject to any provision of that Schedule.

Deduction of fees, costs and charges by the collector

4 The fees, costs and charges specified in the Schedule to these Regulations shall be deducted by the collector from the sums received on or in connection with the levying of distress or where distress has been levied.

Disputes as to fees, costs and charges

5—(1) In the case of dispute as to any fees chargeable, or costs and charges recoverable under the Schedule to these Regulations, the amount of those fees, costs and charges shall be taxed.

(2) Such a taxation shall be carried out by the district judge of the county court for the district in which the distress is or is intended to be levied, and he may give such directions as to the costs of the taxation as he thinks fit.

(3) In the application of paragraph (2) to Northern Ireland, there shall be substituted for the words "by the district judge of the county court for the district in which the distress is or is intended to be levied" the words "by the Master (Taxing Office)".

SCHEDULE

Regulation 3

Action taken	*Fees, Costs and Charges*
On or in connection with the levying of distress	*Fees*
For making a visit to premises with a view to levying distress (whether the levy is made or not).	[A sum not exceeding £12·50][1].
Levying distress where the total sum charged is £100 or less.	£12·50.
Levying distress where the total sum charged is more than £100.	$12\frac{1}{2}$ per cent on the first £100 of the amount to be recovered; 4 per cent on the next £400; $2\frac{1}{2}$ per cent on the next £1,500; 1 per cent on the next £8,000; $\frac{1}{4}$ per cent on any additional sum.
Where distress has been levied	*Costs and Charges*
1 Taking possession	
Where close possession is taken.	£4·50 for the day of levy only.
Where walking possession is taken.	45p per day, payable for the day the distress is levied and up to 14 days thereafter.
2 Removal and storage of goods	The reasonable costs and charges of removal and storage.
3 Appraisement	The reasonable fees, charges and expenses of the person appraising.
4 Sale	
[Where the sale is held on the auctioneer's premises, for the auctioneer's commission (to include all out-of-pocket expenses other than charges for advertising, removal and storage).	15 per cent on the sum realised plus the reasonable costs of advertising, removal and storage.
Where the sale is held on the debtor's premises, for the auctioneer's commission (not to include out-of-pocket expenses or charges for advertising).	$7\frac{1}{2}$ per cent on the sum realised plus out-of-pocket expenses actually and reasonably incurred and the reasonable costs of advertising.][1]

1 In any case where close possession is taken, an individual left in possession must provide his own board.

2 For the purpose of calculating any percentage fees, costs and charges, a fraction of £1 is to be reckoned as £1, but any fraction of a penny in the total amount so calculated is to be disregarded.

3 In addition to any amount authorised by this Schedule in respect of the supply of goods or services on which value added tax is chargeable there may be added a sum equivalent to value added tax at the appropriate rate on that amount.

Amendments—[1] Words substituted by the Distraint by Collectors (Fees, Costs and Charges) (Amendment) Regulations, SI 1995/2151 reg 2, with effect from 8 September 1995.

1994/777
Income Tax (Car Benefits) (Replacement Accessories) Regulations 1994

Made by the Treasury under TA 1988 s 168E

Made	*15 March 1994*
Laid before the House of Commons	*16 March 1994*
Coming into Force	*6 April 1994*

Commentary—*Simon's Direct Tax Service* **E4.614B**.

Amendments—These Regulations revoked by ITEPA 2003 s 724, Sch 8 with effect, for income tax purposes, from 2003–04; and for corporation tax purposes, for accounting periods ending after 5 April 2003. For transitional provisions and savings see ITEPA 2003 s 723, Sch 7.

Citation and commencement

1 *These Regulations may be cited as the Income Tax (Car Benefits) (Replacement Accessories) Regulations 1994 and shall come into force on 6th April 1994.*

Amendment—These Regulations revoked by ITEPA 2003 s 724, Sch 8 with effect, for income tax purposes, from 2003–04; and for corporation tax purposes, for accounting periods ending after 5 April 2003. For transitional provisions and savings see ITEPA 2003 s 723, Sch 7.

Interpretation

2—*(1) In these Regulations unless the context otherwise requires—*

"accessory" shall be construed in accordance with subsection (11) of section 168A;
"list price" shall be construed in accordance with subsection (2) of section 168A;
"optional accessory" has the meaning given by subsection (9)(d) of section 168A;
"qualifying accessory" has the meaning given by subsection (10) of section 168A;
"the Taxes Act" means the Income and Corporation Taxes Act 1988.

(2) References, however expressed, in these Regulations to sections 168A, 168B, 168C and 168D are references to sections 168A, 168B, 168C and 168D of the Taxes Act.

Cases where replacing accessory not superior to replaced accessory

3—*(1) This regulation applies in any case where—*

(a) a qualifying accessory to which section 168C applies is available with a car which is made available to an employee in any year ("the relevant year"),

(b) the accessory ("the replacing accessory") replaces (whether in the relevant year or earlier) another qualifying accessory ("the replaced accessory"), and

(c) the replacing accessory—

(i) is of the same kind as the replaced accessory, and

(ii) is not superior to the replaced accessory.

(2) Where this regulation applies, the price of the car as regards the relevant year shall be found under the provisions contained in sections 168A to 168D as if the replacement had not been made and the replacing accessory was a continuation of the replaced accessory.

Cases where replacing accessory superior to replaced accessory

4—*(1) This regulation applies in any case where—*

(a) a qualifying accessory to which section 168C applies is available with a car which is made available to an employee in any year ("the relevant year"),

(b) the accessory ("the replacing accessory") replaces (whether in the relevant year or earlier) another qualifying accessory ("the replaced accessory") which—

(i) was an optional accessory, and

(ii) was not a qualifying accessory available with a car with no list price at the time when the car was first made available to the employee,

(c) the replacing accessory—

(i) is of the same kind as the replaced accessory, and

(ii) is superior to the replaced accessory, and

(d) both the replacing accessory and the replaced accessory would, but for paragraph (2) below, be taken into account under the provisions contained in sections 168A to 168C in determining the price of the car as regards the relevant year.

(2) Where this regulation applies, sections 168A to 168D shall apply in determining the price of the car for the relevant year—

(a) as if the replaced accessory was not available with the car in that year, and

(b) where the price of the replaced accessory was included in the list price of the car under subsections (4) and (5) of section 168A, as if the replaced accessory had not been available with the car at the time when the car was first made available to the employee.

Amendment—These Regulations revoked by ITEPA 2003 s 724, Sch 8 with effect, for income tax purposes, from 2003–04; and for corporation tax purposes, for accounting periods ending after 5 April 2003. For transitional provisions and savings see ITEPA 2003 s 723, Sch 7.

Meaning of superior replacing accessory

5—*(1) For the purposes of regulations 3(1)(c)(ii) and 4(1)(c)(ii), a replacing accessory is superior to a replaced accessory if the price of the replacing accessory exceeds either—*

(a) the price of the replaced accessory, or

(b) the price of an accessory which is equivalent to the replaced accessory at the time immediately before the replacing accessory is first made available for use with the car,

whichever is the greater.

(2) References in paragraph (1) above to the price of an accessory are references to the price of an accessory determined in accordance with section 168A or, as the case may be, section 168B or 168C.

Amendment—These Regulations revoked by ITEPA 2003 s 724, Sch 8 with effect, for income tax purposes, from 2003–04; and for corporation tax purposes, for accounting periods ending after 5 April 2003. For transitional provisions and savings see ITEPA 2003 s 723, Sch 7.

1994/778
Income Tax (Replacement Cars) Regulations 1994

Made by the Treasury under TA 1988 Sch 6 para 8

Made . . . . 15 March 1994
Laid before the House of Commons . . . . 16 March 1994
Coming into Force . . . . 6 April 1994

Commentary—*Simon's Direct Tax Service* **E4.614B.**
Amendment—These Regulations revoked by ITEPA 2003 s 724, Sch 8 with effect, for income tax purposes, from 2003–04; and for corporation tax purposes, for accounting periods ending after 5 April 2003. For transitional provisions and savings see ITEPA 2003 s 723, Sch 7.

Citation and commencement

1 These Regulations may be cited as the Income Tax (Replacement Cars) Regulations 1994 and shall come into force on 6th April 1994.

Amendment—These Regulations revoked by ITEPA 2003 s 724, Sch 8 with effect, for income tax purposes, from 2003–04; and for corporation tax purposes, for accounting periods ending after 5 April 2003. For transitional provisions and savings see ITEPA 2003 s 723, Sch 7.

Interpretation

2 *In these Regulations unless the context otherwise requires—*
"paragraph 8" means paragraph 8 of Schedule 6;
"replaced car" means a car normally available to the employee but which for a period of less than 30 days is not available to him;
"replacement car" means a car made available to the employee in order to replace the replaced car for the whole or part of the period during which the replaced car is not available to the employee;
"Schedule 6" means Schedule 6 to the Taxes Act;
"the Taxes Act" means the Income and Corporation Taxes Act 1988.

Amendment—These Regulations revoked by ITEPA 2003 s 724, Sch 8 with effect, for income tax purposes, from 2003–04; and for corporation tax purposes, for accounting periods ending after 5 April 2003. For transitional provisions and savings see ITEPA 2003 s 723, Sch 7.

Modifications of Schedule 6—introductory

3 *Where the conditions specified in paragraphs (a) and (b) of paragraph 8 and the condition prescribed by regulation 4 below are fulfilled, Schedule 6 shall have effect in relation to the cars concerned subject to the modifications prescribed by regulations 5 and 6 below.*

Amendment—These Regulations revoked by ITEPA 2003 s 724, Sch 8 with effect, for income tax purposes, from 2003–04; and for corporation tax purposes, for accounting periods ending after 5 April 2003. For transitional provisions and savings see ITEPA 2003 s 723, Sch 7.

Prescribed condition in relation to replacement cars

4—*(1) The prescribed condition is that—*
(a) the replacement car is of similar quality to the replaced car, or
(b) the replacement car is not made available to the employee under an arrangement of which the main purpose or one of the main purposes is to provide the employee with the benefit of a car which is materially better than the replaced car.

(2) For the purposes of paragraph (1)(a) above the replacement car is of similar quality to the replaced car if it is neither materially better nor materially worse in quality than the replaced car.

(3) For the purposes of paragraph (1)(b) above the replacement car is materially better than the replaced car if—
(a) it is materially better in quality, or
(b) it has a materially higher price.

(4) For the purposes of paragraph (3)(b) above the price of a car shall be determined in accordance with the provisions contained in sections 168A to 168G of the Taxes Act.

Amendments—These Regulations revoked by ITEPA 2003 s 724, Sch 8 with effect, for income tax purposes, from 2003–04; and for corporation tax purposes, for accounting periods ending after 5 April 2003. For transitional provisions and savings see ITEPA 2003 s 723, Sch 7.

Modifications of Schedule 6

5 *[Paragraph 7 shall]*[1] *be modified so as to provide in addition that the paragraph shall be applied as if the replacement had not been made and the replacement car were a continuation of the replaced car.*[2]

Amendments—[1] Words substituted by the Income Tax (Car Benefits) (Reduction of Value of Appropriate Percentage) Regulations, SI 2001/1123 reg 8 with effect from the year 2002–03.
[2] These Regulations revoked by ITEPA 2003 s 724, Sch 8 with effect, for income tax purposes, from 2003–04; and for corporation tax purposes, for accounting periods ending after 5 April 2003. For transitional provisions and savings see ITEPA 2003 s 723, Sch 7.

6 *Paragraph 9 shall be modified so as to provide in addition that, for the purposes of Schedule 6, the replacement car is also to be treated as unavailable for the period during which it replaces the replaced car.*

Amendment—These Regulations revoked by ITEPA 2003 s 724, Sch 8 with effect, for income tax purposes, from 2003–04; and for corporation tax purposes, for accounting periods ending after 5 April 2003. For transitional provisions and savings see ITEPA 2003 s 723, Sch 7.

1994/1212
Income Tax (Employments) (Notional Payments) Regulations 1994

Made by the Commissioners of Inland Revenue under TA 1988 s 203

Made . . . . *4 May 1994*
Laid before the House of Commons . . . . . *4 May 1994*
Coming into Force . . . . *25 May 1994*

Amendment—These regulations are revoked by the Income Tax (Pay As You Earn) Regulations, SI 2003/2682 reg 220, Sch 2 with effect from 6 April 2004, subject to transitional provisions contained in Sch 1 thereto.

Citation, commencement and effect

1 These Regulations may be cited as the Income Tax (Employments) (Notional Payments) Regulations 1994, shall come into force on 25th May 1994, and shall have effect with respect to notional payments made on or after that date.

Interpretation

2—(1) In these Regulations, unless the context otherwise requires—

"assessable" has the meaning given by section 203L(2) of the Taxes Act;[2]
"the Board" means the Commissioners of Inland Revenue;[2]
"cash voucher" means a cash voucher to which section 143(1) of the Taxes Act applies;[2]
"chargeable expense" has the same meaning as in section 141(1) of the Taxes Act;[2]
"cheque voucher" has the meaning given by section 141(7) of the Taxes Act;[2]
"credit-token" has the same meaning as in section 142 of the Taxes Act;[2]
"employee" and "employer" have the meanings given by section 203L(1) of the Taxes Act;[2]
"income tax period" has the meaning given by regulation 2(1) of the principal Regulations;[2]
"non-cash voucher" means a non-cash voucher to which section 141(1) of the Taxes Act applies;[2]
"notional payment" has the meaning given by subsection (2)(a) of section 203J;[2]
"the principal Regulations" means the Income Tax (Employments) Regulations 1993;
...[1]
"the Taxes Act" means the Income and Corporation Taxes Act 1988.[2]

[[(2) In these Regulations references to a section, without more, are to that section of the Taxes Act.][1]*]*[2]

Amendments—[1] *Para (2) inserted, and words in para (1) revoked, by the Income Tax (Employments) (Notional Payments) (Amendment) Regulations, SI 1998/1891, with effect from 4 August 1998.*
[2] *Definitions in italics, and para (2), revoked by ITEPA 2003 s 724, Sch 8 with effect, for income tax purposes, from 2003–04; and for corporation tax purposes, for accounting periods ending after 5 April 2003. For transitional provisions and savings see ITEPA 2003 s 723, Sch 7.*

[Exclusion of property from section 203F

3—*(1) For the purposes of [section 203F, including the purposes of that section as it has effect in accordance with section 203FA(1) and section 203FB(2), (3)(b), (4) and (5),]*[2] *the property described in paragraph (2) below is property of a description excluded from the scope of that section.*

[(2) The property described is—

(a) any shares acquired by the employee (whether or not as a result of the exercise of a right to acquire shares) under a scheme approved by the Board under Schedule 9 to the Taxes Act (approved share option schemes and profit sharing schemes).

(b) any right over or interest in shares obtained or acquired by the employee under such a scheme, and

(c) any shares acquired by the employee as a result of the exercise of a right over shares obtained before 27th November 1996 otherwise than under a scheme approved by the Board under Schedule 9 to the Taxes Act.

where the shares in question form part of the ordinary share capital of—

(i) an employer which is a company (''the employer company''), or
(ii) a company which has control of the employer company, or
(iii) a company which either is, or has control of, a company which is a member of a consortium owning either the employer company or a company having control of the employer company.][1]

(3) For the purposes of paragraph (2) above—

(a) ''company'' has the meaning given by section 832(1) of the Taxes Act;
(b) ''control'' has the meaning given by section 840 of the Taxes Act;
(c) ''ordinary share capital'' has the meaning given by section 832(1) of the Taxes Act;
(d) ''share'' includes stock;
(e) a company is a member of a consortium owning another company if it is one of a number of companies which between them beneficially own not less than three-quarters of the other company's ordinary share capital and each of which beneficially owns not less than one-twentieth of that capital;
[(f) references in paragraph (2) above to shares, or a right over or interest in shares, include references to shares, or a right over or interest in shares, whose value has been enhanced as mentioned in section 203FA.][2]*]*[3]

Commentary—*Simon's Direct Tax Service* **E4.515.**
Revenue & other press releases—*IR Tax Bulletin February 1997 p 385 (interests acquired under long-term incentive plans will not usually be a right over a share within the terms of para (2)(c)).*
Amendments—[1] *Para (2) substituted by the IT (Employments) (Notional Payments) (Amendment) Regulations, SI 1996/2969, with effect from 27 November 1996.*
[2] *Words in para (1) substituted, and para (3)(f) inserted, by the Income Tax (Employments) (Notional Payments) (Amendment) Regulations, SI 1998/1891, with effect from 4 August 1998.*
[3] *This regulation revoked by ITEPA 2003 s 724, Sch 8 with effect, for income tax purposes, from 2003–04; and for corporation tax purposes, for accounting periods ending after 5 April 2003. For transitional provisions and savings see ITEPA 2003 s 723, Sch 7.*

[[Specification of market for the purposes of section 203F(2)(b)

3A The New York Stock Exchange is a market which is specified for the purposes of section 203F(2)(b) (readily convertible assets).][1]*]*[2]

Amendments—[1] *Regulation inserted by the Income Tax (Employments) (Notional Payments) (Amendment) Regulations, SI 1998/1891, with effect from 4 August 1998.*
[2] *This Regulation revoked by ITEPA 2003 s 724, Sch 8 with effect, for income tax purposes, from 2003–04; and for corporation tax purposes, for accounting periods ending after 5 April 2003. For transitional provisions and savings see ITEPA 2003 s 723, Sch 7.*

[[Exclusion of matters from section 203FA

3B—(1) The matter described in paragraph (2) below is a matter of a description excluded from the scope of what constitutes enhancing the value of an asset for the purposes of section 203FA.

(2) The matter described is the enhancement of value arising on the acquisition by the employee (whether or not as a result of the exercise of a right to acquire shares) of—

(a) any shares under a scheme approved by the Board under Schedule 9 to the Taxes Act,
(b) any right over or interest in shares obtained or acquired by the employee under such a scheme, and
(c) any shares acquired by the employee as a result of the exercise of a right over shares obtained before 27th November 1996 otherwise than under a scheme approved by the Board under Schedule 9 to the Taxes Act,

where the shares in question form part of the ordinary share capital of—

(i) an employer which is a company (''the employer company''),
(ii) a company which has control of the employer company, or
(iii) a company which either is, or has control of, a company which is a member of a consortium owning either the employer company or a company having control of the employer company.

(3) Sub-paragraphs (a) to (e) of paragraph (3) of regulation 3 shall apply for the interpretation of paragraph (2) above as they apply for the purposes of paragraph (2) of that regulation.][1]*]*[2]

Amendments—[1] *Regulation inserted by the Income Tax (Employments) (Notional Payments) (Amendment) Regulations, SI 1998/1891, with effect from 4 August 1998.*
[2] *This Regulation revoked by ITEPA 2003 s 724, Sch 8 with effect, for income tax purposes, from 2003–04; and for corporation tax purposes, for accounting periods ending after 5 April 2003. For transitional provisions and savings see ITEPA 2003 s 723, Sch 7.*

Exclusion of use of credit-token from section 203H

4—*(1) The use of a credit-token described in paragraph (2) below is a description of use excluded from the scope of section 203H.*

(2) The use described is the use by an employee of a credit-token to obtain money in circumstances where the money—

(a) is used to defray expenses, and

(b) would not, if it had been paid directly to him by his employer, have been chargeable to income tax under Schedule E except by virtue of section 153 of the Taxes Act.

Amendment—*This Regulation revoked by ITEPA 2003 s 724, Sch 8 with effect, for income tax purposes, from 2003–04; and for corporation tax purposes, for accounting periods ending after 5 April 2003. For transitional provisions and savings see ITEPA 2003 s 723, Sch 7.*

Exclusion of cash vouchers from section 203I

5—*(1) The provision of a cash voucher in either of the descriptions of circumstances specified in paragraphs (2) and (3) below is a provision of a cash voucher excluded from the scope of section 203I.*

(2) The description of circumstances specified in this paragraph is where—

(a) the cash voucher provided for the employee is used to defray expenses, and

(b) the amount for which the voucher is capable of being exchanged would not, if it had been paid directly to the employee by his employer, have been chargeable to income tax under Schedule E except by virtue of section 153 of the Taxes Act.

(3) The description of circumstances specified in this paragraph is where the cash voucher is exchanged for an amount of money which—

(a) is used to defray expenses, and

(b) would not, if it had been paid directly to the employee by his employer, have been chargeable to income tax under Schedule E except by virtue of section 153 of the Taxes Act.

Amendments—*This Regulation revoked by ITEPA 2003 s 724, Sch 8 with effect, for income tax purposes, from 2003–04; and for corporation tax purposes, for accounting periods ending after 5 April 2003. For transitional provisions and savings see ITEPA 2003 s 723, Sch 7.*

Notional payments—non-cash vouchers—time of payment

6—*(1) Paragraphs (2) and (3) below make provision with respect to the time when a notional payment treated as made by virtue of subsection (1) of section 203G (non-cash vouchers) is made.*

(2) Where the non-cash voucher received by the employee is a cheque voucher, the notional payment is made at the time when the voucher is handed over in exchange for money, goods or services.

(3) Where the non-cash voucher received by the employee is a voucher other than a cheque voucher, the notional payment is made at the time when the chargeable expense is incurred or, if later, at the time when the voucher is received by the employee.

(4) For the purposes of paragraph (2) above, a voucher which is posted shall be treated as handed over at the time of posting.

Amendments—*This Regulation revoked by ITEPA 2003 s 724, Sch 8 with effect, for income tax purposes, from 2003–04; and for corporation tax purposes, for accounting periods ending after 5 April 2003. For transitional provisions and savings see ITEPA 2003 s 723, Sch 7.*

Notional payments—deduction of income tax

7—*(1) Paragraph (2) below prescribes the time at which an employer shall deduct income tax in accordance with subsection (1) of section 203J in respect of a notional payment made by him of assessable income of an employee, [not being a notional payment to which regulation 8A applies.]*[1]

(2) The time prescribed is any occasion on or after the time when the notional payment is made and falling within the same income tax period, on which the employer actually makes a payment of, or on account of, assessable income of that employee.[2]

Commentary—*Simon's Direct Tax Service* **E4.949.**

Amendments—[1] *Words in para (1) inserted by the Income Tax (Employments) (Notional Payments) (Amendment) Regulations, SI 1998/1891, with effect from 4 August 1998.*

[2] *This Regulation revoked by ITEPA 2003 s 724, Sch 8 with effect, for income tax purposes, from 2003–04; and for corporation tax purposes, for accounting periods ending after 5 April 2003. For transitional provisions and savings see ITEPA 2003 s 723, Sch 7.*

Notional payments—accounting for income tax where inability to deduct

8—*(1) Paragraph (2) below prescribes the time at which an employer shall account to the Board in accordance with subsection (3) of section 203J for an amount of income tax in respect of a notional payment made by him of assessable income of an employee, [not being a notional payment to which regulation 8A applies.]*[1]*.*

(2) The time prescribed is within 14 days of the end of the income tax period in which the notional payment was made.[2]

Commentary—*Simon's Direct Tax Service* **E4.949.**

Amendments—[1] *Words in para (1) inserted by the Income Tax (Employments) (Notional Payments) (Amendment) Regulations, SI 1998/1891, with effect from 4 August 1998.*

[2] *This Regulation revoked by ITEPA 2003 s 724, Sch 8 with effect, for income tax purposes, from 2003–04; and for corporation tax purposes, for accounting periods ending after 5 April 2003. For transitional provisions and savings see ITEPA 2003 s 723, Sch 7.*

[[Certain notional payments made between 6th April 1998 and 31st July 1998—accounting for income tax

8A—*(1) This regulation applies to any notional payment falling within section 203B (payment by intermediary), section 203C (employee of non-UK employer), section 203F (readily convertible assets), section 203FA (enhancing the value of an asset), section 203FB (gains from share options), section 203G (vouchers and credit-tokens), section 203H (credit-tokens) or section 203I (cash vouchers), where the notional payment—*

(a) is made in the period beginning on 6th April 1998 and ending on 31st July 1998, and

(b) is a notional payment in respect of which the employer would, but for section 65(7), 66(3), 67(3), 68(5) or 69(6) of the Finance Act 1998, have been liable to deduct an amount of income tax in accordance with regulation 7, or to account for an amount of income tax in accordance with regulation 8.

(2) The employer shall be liable to account to the Board, not later than the date specified in paragraph (3) below, for an amount of income tax in respect of the notional payments referred to in paragraph (1) above equal to the amount which he would have been liable to deduct in accordance with regulation 7 or for which he would have been liable to account in accordance with regulation 8.

(3) The date specified is the 19th August 1998.][1] *]*[2]

Amendments—[1] *Regulation inserted by the Income Tax (Employments) (Notional Payments) (Amendment) Regulations, SI 1998/1891, with effect from 4 August 1998.*

[2] *This Regulation revoked by ITEPA 2003 s 724, Sch 8 with effect, for income tax purposes, from 2003–04; and for corporation tax purposes, for accounting periods ending after 5 April 2003. For transitional provisions and savings see ITEPA 2003 s 723, Sch 7.*

Amendments to the principal Regulations—deduction of income tax from notional payments and returns

9 (*Amends SI 1993/744 regs 14(2)(b), 15(b).*)

10–12 (*Superseded.*)

[12A In Chapter IV of the principal Regulations after regulation 80 there shall be inserted—

"Payment for assignment or release of a right to acquire shares

80ZA—(1) This regulation applies where—

(a) the consideration for the assignment or release of a right to acquire shares takes the form of a payment,

(b) the payment is made in the period beginning on 6th April 1998 and ending on 31st July 1998,

(c) so much of that payment ('the relevant amount') as does not exceed the amount assessable by virtue of section 135 of the Taxes Act is treated, in accordance with section 203FB(3)(a) of that Act, as a payment of assessable income of the relevant person, and

(d) the employer would, but for section 67(3) of the Finance Act 1998, have accordingly been liable to deduct an amount of income tax in accordance with these Regulations in respect of the relevant amount.

(2) Regulation 40 shall have effect as if the relevant amount was an amount of emoluments paid by the employer in the income tax month ending on 5th August 1998."][1]

Amendments—[1] *Regulation inserted by the Income Tax (Employments) (Notional Payments) (Amendment) Regulations, SI 1998/1891, with effect from 4 August 1998.*

Application of the principal Regulations to income tax accounted for where inability to deduct

13—(1) The provisions of the principal Regulations specified in paragraph (2) below shall apply to amounts accounted for in respect of notional payments in accordance with subsection (3) of section 203J as they apply in relation to deductions from actual payments, with the modifications specified in paragraphs (3) to (8) below.

(2) The provisions specified are—

(a) all provisions in Parts I, III, IV and V,

(b) regulations 99 to 105 in Part VIII, and

(c) regulation 109 in Part IX.

(3) In regulation 2(1) in the definition of "total net tax deducted" after the words "repaid to the employee" there shall be added the words ", and the total tax accounted for in accordance with section 203J(3) of the Taxes Act".

(4) Regulations 14(2)(b and 15(b) shall be omitted.

(5) In regulation 40(2) in the definition of "A" after the words "income tax month" there shall be added the words ", and all amounts of tax for which he was liable to account under section 203J(3) of the Taxes Act in respect of notional payments made by him in that month".

(6) In regulation 41(2) in the definition of "A" after the words "income tax quarter" there shall be added the words ", and all amounts of tax for which he was liable to account under section 203J(3) of the Taxes Act in respect of notional payments made by him in that quarter".

(7) Regulation 42(2) and (3), and regulation 49(3) and (5)(b), shall be omitted.

(8) In regulation 55(2)(a) after the words "deduction of tax from" there shall be inserted the words ", or the accounting of tax in respect of,".

1994/1518

Private Medical Insurance (Disentitlement to Tax Relief and Approved Benefits) Regulations 1994

Made by the Treasury under FA 1989 ss 54(7), (8), 55(2A), 56(3)

Made	*8 June 1994*
Laid before the House of Commons	*9 June 1994*
Coming into Force	*1 July 1994*

Commentary—*Simon's Direct Tax Service* **E2.904, 905.**

Citation and commencement

1 These Regulations may be cited as the Private Medical Insurance (Disentitlement to Tax Relief and Approved Benefits) Regulations 1994 and shall come into force on 1st July 1994.

Interpretation

2 In these Regulations unless the context otherwise requires—

"the Board" means the Commissioners of Inland Revenue;

"contract" means a contract of private medical insurance;

"hospital" means—

(*a*) any institution for the reception and treatment of persons suffering from illness;

(*b*) any maternity home; or

(*c*) any institution for the reception and treatment of persons during convalescence or of persons requiring medical rehabilitation;

and includes clinics, dispensaries and out-patient departments maintained in connection with any such home or institution;

"indemnity period" means the period, not exceeding one year, for which indemnity is provided under a contract;

"the insured" means any person insured under a contract;

"registered dental practitioner"—

(*a*) in the United Kingdom, means a person registered in the dentists register under the Dentists Act 1984 and

(*b*) in a territory other than the United Kingdom, means a dental practitioner recognised as such by the law of that territory;

"registered medical practitioner"—

(*a*) in the United Kingdom, means a registered medical practitioner within the meaning of Schedule 1 to the Interpretation Act 1978 and

(*b*) in a territory other than the United Kingdom, means a medical practitioner recognised as such by the law of that territory;

"section 54" and "section 55" mean sections 54 and 55 respectively of the Finance Act 1989.

Circumstances of disentitlement to tax relief

3—(1) In the circumstances prescribed by paragraph (2) below, an individual who has made a payment in respect of a premium under a contract shall cease to be, and shall be treated as not having been, entitled to relief under subsection (3) of section 54 in respect of that payment.

(2) The circumstances prescribed by this paragraph are where—

(*a*) at any time after the payment is made the contract is no longer an eligible contract for the purposes of section 54; or

(*b*) the payment is refunded to the individual by the person to whom it was made.

(3) In paragraph (2) above, "eligible contract" has the meaning given by section 55.

Recovery of tax from payee of premium

4—(1) In the circumstances prescribed by paragraph (2) below, the person to whom a payment in respect of a premium under a contract was made by an individual, who by virtue of regulation 3 has ceased to be and is treated as not having been entitled to relief in respect of that payment, shall account to the Board for tax from which relief has been given on the basis that the individual was so entitled.

(2) The circumstances prescribed by this paragraph are where—

(*a*) the person to whom the payment was made has recovered from the Board an amount equal to an amount deducted and retained by the individual from that payment in accordance with subsection (5) of section 54; and

(*b*) that amount has not been repaid to the Board.

Adaptation of section 30 of the Taxes Management Act 1970

5—(1) In order to secure the performance of the obligation imposed by regulation 4, section 30 of the Taxes Management Act 1970 shall be adapted so that it applies to the tax for which a person to whom a payment has been made is to account to the Board in accordance with that regulation as it applies to tax which has been repaid to a person which ought not to have been repaid to him.

(2) For the purposes of the adaptation required by paragraph (1) above, any reference in the said section 30 to the repayment of an amount of tax to any person which ought not to have been repaid to him shall be construed as including a reference to tax for which a person is to account to the Board in accordance with regulation 4.

Approved treatments and associated services

6—(1) Subject to paragraph (5) below, the treatments, medical services and other matters the costs of which may, in the circumstances specified in paragraph (4) below, be indemnified under a contract are those specified in paragraph (2) below.

(2) The treatments, medical services and other matters specified in this paragraph are—

(*a*) treatment of the insured consisting of medical or surgical procedures (including diagnosis), the purpose of which is the relief of illness or injury,

(*b*) services provided to the insured of any of the kinds specified in paragraph (3) below when they are associated with such treatment, and

(*c*) drugs and dressings used in the course of such procedures or services.

(3) The kinds of services specified in this paragraph are—

(*a*) accommodation and other services (including nursing services) provided in a hospital where the insured is accommodated;

(*b*) nursing services provided in the insured's home;

(*c*) accommodation provided for the purposes of convalescence for a period of not more than 14 days immediately following the discharge of the insured from a hospital where the insured has been accommodated;

(*d*) transport by private ambulance (including transport of one other person where medically necessary)—

(i) to or from a hospital where the insured is or has been accommodated, or

(ii) to or from a place where accommodation is provided for the purposes of convalescence;

(*e*) services consisting of—

(i) physiotherapy,

(ii) occupational therapy,

(iii) speech therapy,

(iv) chiropody and podiatry,

(v) prosthesis, and

(vi) orthopty,

including the provision of any equipment necessary for such services.

(4) The circumstances specified in this paragraph are where—

(*a*) treatment is given to the insured in a hospital as a resident or non-resident private patient by, or under the supervision of, a registered medical practitioner or registered dental practitioner, or

(*b*) treatment consisting of surgical procedures performed by a registered medical practitioner providing personal medical services for persons in a particular locality is given to the insured as a private patient of that practitioner, or

(*c*) services consisting of physiotherapy including the provision of any equipment necessary for physiotherapy are provided to the insured and are associated with treatment given to the insured by or under the supervision of a registered medical practitioner.

(5) The treatments specified in this regulation do not include any treatment which, during the period of five years preceding the date the contract was entered into, has not been provided free by the Secretary of State under the National Health Service Act 1977 or the National Health Service (Scotland) Act 1978 or by the Department of Health and Social Services for Northern Ireland under

the Health and Personal Social Services (Northern Ireland) Order 1972, more often than it has been provided in the United Kingdom otherwise than under any of those enactments.

(6) For the purposes of this regulation—

(*a*) a service is associated with treatment if it is provided for the purposes of that treatment or is consequent upon it;

(*b*) references, however expressed, to the insured being accommodated in a hospital are references to the insured—

(i) being accommodated in a hospital as a private patient in circumstances where he is charged for the accommodation, or

(ii) being provided with treatment or services as a private patient in a hospital in circumstances where he is charged for the treatment or services;

(*c*) transport by private ambulance includes transport by air ambulance.

(7) In paragraphs (4) and (6) above "treatment" shall be construed in accordance with paragraph (2)(*a*) above, and in paragraph (6)(*b*)(ii) above "services" shall be construed in accordance with paragraph (2)(*b*) above.

Cash benefits

7—(1) The rules within which a cash benefit provided under a contract is to fall are those specified in paragraph (2) below.

(2) The rules specified in this paragraph are that the benefit may not exceed £5 for each night that the insured is accommodated in a hospital as a private patient in circumstances where he is charged for the accommodation.

Other rights

8—(1) The other rights specified in this regulation which may be conferred by a contract are—

(*a*) a right in the person making payments in respect of a premium under the contract to terminate the contract before the expiry of the indemnity period and to receive a refund of payments made in respect of the period following termination;

(*b*) waiver by the insurer of the right to payment of a premium for any period in which the insured is receiving treatment the cost of which is indemnified under the contract;

(*c*) a right in the person making payments in respect of a premium under the contract to receive a refund of payments made in respect of such a period as is referred to in paragraph (*b*) above; and

(*d*) a right in the person making payments in respect of a premium under the contract to enter into a further contract at the end of the indemnity period.

(2) In paragraph (1)(*b*) above "treatment" shall be construed in accordance with regulation 6(2)(*a*) above.

Revocations

9—(1) The Private Medical Insurance (Disentitlement to Tax Relief and Approved Benefits) Regulations 1989 and the Private Medical Insurance (Disentitlement to Tax Relief and Approved Benefits) (Amendment) Regulations 1992 are hereby revoked.

(2) Anything whatsoever begun under any regulation revoked by these Regulations may be continued under these Regulations as if begun under these Regulations.

1994/1811

Special Commissioners (Jurisdiction and Procedure) Regulations 1994

Made by the Lord Chancellor under TMA 1970 ss 46A, 56B–56D

Made	*6 July 1994*
Laid before Parliament	*14 July 1994*
Coming into Force	*1 September 1994*

Commentary—*Simon's Direct Tax Service* Divisions **A3.5; I11.3**.

Cross reference—see the Miscellaneous section of this publication for the Notes for parties to appeals and other proceedings before the Special Commissioners.

ARRANGEMENT OF REGULATIONS

PART I

INTRODUCTORY

PART II
PREPARATION FOR A HEARING

PART III
HEARING AND DETERMINATION OF PROCEEDINGS

PART IV
SPECIAL PROCEDURE

PART V
MISCELLANEOUS

PART I
INTRODUCTORY

Cross reference—TMA 1970 s 115 (delivery and service of documents).

Citation, commencement and application

1—(1) These Regulations may be cited as the Special Commissioners (Jurisdiction and Procedure) Regulations 1994 and shall come into force on 1st September 1994.

(2) These Regulations do not apply in relation to any proceedings in respect of which notice of the place, date and time of the hearing was given, or a summons was issued, prior to 1st September 1994.

Interpretation

2 In these Regulations unless the context otherwise requires—

"the Board" means the Commissioners of Inland Revenue;

"the Clerk", in relation to any proceedings, means the Clerk to the Special Commissioners;

"costs" includes fees, charges, disbursements, expenses and remuneration;

["the enactments relating to stamp duty" means section 13(4) of the Stamp Act 1891 and Part II of Schedule 17 to the Finance Act 1999;][2]

["the enactments relating to stamp duty land tax" means Part 4 of the Finance Act 2003 and any regulations made under that Part;][5]

"final determination" means the decision finally determining any proceedings before a Tribunal;

"General Commissioners" shall be construed in accordance with section 2(1) of the Management Act;

"inspector" means an inspector of taxes [and in relation to stamp duty land tax means any officer of the Board][5];

"the Management Act" means the Taxes Management Act 1970;

"party" means a party to any proceedings, and for the purposes of these Regulations—

(*a*) where the proceedings relate to an assessment, decision or determination made by the Board, the Board and any inspector or other officer of the Board for the time being concerned with the proceedings shall together constitute a party to those proceedings;

(*b*) where the proceedings relate to an assessment, decision or determination made by an inspector or other officer of the Board, that person and any other inspector or other officer of the Board for the time being concerned with the proceedings shall together constitute a party to those proceedings;

and references to "the Revenue" are references to a party within paragraph (*a*) or, as the case may be, paragraph (*b*) above;

"proceedings" means—

(*a*) any appeal to the Special Commissioners under the Taxes Acts;

(*b*) any proceedings before the Special Commissioners which under the Taxes Acts are to be heard and determined in the same way as such an appeal;

(*c*) any proceedings before the Special Commissioners which relate to a penalty and are not within paragraph (*a*) or paragraph (*b*) above;

(*d*) any appeal to the Special Commissioners relating to inheritance tax;

(*e*) any appeal to the Special Commissioners relating to stamp duty reserve tax;

(*f*) any appeal to the Special Commissioners relating to petroleum revenue tax;

[(*g*) any question in dispute falling to be determined by the Special Commissioners under section 46B or 46C of the Management Act [or regulation 19 of the Stamp Duty Land Tax (Appeals) Regulations 2004][5];

(*h*) any appeal which under regulation 19(3) of the General Commissioners (Jurisdiction and Procedure) Regulations 1994 falls to be determined by the Special Commissioners;][1]

[(*i*) any appeal to the Special Commissioners under the enactments relating to stamp duty;][2]

[(*j*) any appeal to the Special Commissioners under Part II of the Transfer Act or Part III of the Transfer Order;][3]

[(*k*) any appeal to the Special Commissioners under regulation 14(4) of the Working Tax Regulations;][3]

[(*ka*) any appeal to the Special Commissioners under section 320(1) of the Proceeds of Crime Act 2002][4]

[(*l*) any preliminary hearing held under the provisions of regulation 9;][3]

[(*m*) any appeal to the Special Commissioners under the enactments relating to stamp duty land tax;][5]

[(*n*) any proceedings before the Special Commissioners which under any enactments relating to stamp duty land tax are to be heard and determined in the same way as such an appeal or any other proceedings to the Special Commissioners under the enactments relating to stamp duty land tax;][5]

"proceedings in Northern Ireland" means any proceedings (as defined in this regulation)—

(*a*) which fall within the meaning of that expression as defined in section 58(3) of the Management Act, or

(*b*) as respects which an appeal from the determination of the Special Commissioners under any enactment lies to a court in Northern Ireland;

"proceedings in Scotland" means any proceedings (as defined in this regulation) which fall to be determined by reference to the law of Scotland;

["respondent" means—

(*a*) in relation to an appeal under section 320(1) of the Proceeds of Crime Act 2002, the Director of the Assets Recovery Agency;

(*b*) in relation to an appeal under regulation 16 of the Community Investment Tax Relief (Accreditation of Community Development Finance Institutions) Regulations 2003, the Secretary of State;

(*c*) otherwise, the Revenue;][4]

"Special Commissioners" and "the Presiding Special Commissioner" shall be construed in accordance with section 4(1) of the Management Act;

"the Taxes Acts" has the meaning given by section 118(1) of the Management Act;

["the Transfer Act" means the Social Security Contributions (Transfer of Functions, etc) Act 1999;][3]

["the Transfer Order" means the Social Security Contributions (Transfer of Functions, etc) (Northern Ireland) Order 1999;][3]

"Tribunal", in relation to any proceedings, means the Special Commissioner or Special Commissioners by whom the proceedings are [heard;][3]

[“the Working Tax Regulations” means the Working Tax Credit (Payment by Employers) Regulations 2002.][3]

Amendments—[1] Words inserted in definition “proceedings” by the Special Commissioners (Jurisdiction and Procedure) (Amendment) Regulations, SI 1999/3292 reg 3 with effect from 1 January 2000.

[2] Definition “the enactments relating to stamp duty” and words in definition “proceedings” inserted by the Special Commissioners (Jurisdiction and Procedure) (Amendment) Regulations, SI 2000/288 reg 3 with effect from 1 March 2000.

[3] In the definition of “proceedings”, paras (*j*)–(*k*) inserted; word substituted in the definition of “Tribunal”; and definitions of “the Transfer Act”, “the Transfer Order” and “the Working Tax Regulations” inserted, by the General Commissioners and Special Commissioners (Jurisdiction and Procedure) (Amendment) Regulations, SI 2002/2976 regs 2, 3 with effect from 31 December 2002.

[4] In the definition of “proceedings”, para (*ka*) inserted, and definition of “respondent” inserted, by the Special Commissioners (Jurisdiction and Procedure) (Amendment) Regulations, SI 2003/968 regs 2, 3 with effect from 22 April 2003.

[5] Definition of “the enactments relating to stamp duty land tax” inserted; words in definition of “inspector” inserted; in definition of “proceedings”, words in sub-para (*g*) inserted; and sub-paras (*m*), (*n*) inserted; by the SDLT (Appeals) Regulations, SI 2004/1363 reg 24(2) with effect from 11 June 2004.

PART II

PREPARATION FOR A HEARING

Listing and notice of hearing

3—(1) Except in relation to proceedings under section 100C of the Management Act, or section 249 of the Inheritance Tax Act 1984 any party to proceedings which are to be heard by the Special Commissioners may serve notice on the Clerk that he wishes a date for the hearing to be fixed.

(2) On receipt of a notice under paragraph (1) above and on being satisfied that the Special Commissioners have jurisdiction over the proceedings and that he has sufficient particulars of the proceedings and of the issues for determination, the Clerk shall, unless the Presiding Special Commissioner otherwise directs, send notice to each party of the place, date and time of the hearing.

(3) Unless the parties otherwise agree or the Tribunal otherwise directs, the date of the hearing specified in a notice under paragraph (2) above shall be not earlier than twenty eight days after the date on which the notice is sent to the parties.

General power to give directions

4—(1) A Special Commissioner prior to the hearing of any proceedings, for the purpose of enabling the parties to prepare for the hearing or of assisting a Tribunal to determine any of the issues in those proceedings, may on the application of a party or of his own motion, give such directions as he thinks fit.

(2) A Tribunal hearing any proceedings may, for the purpose of assisting the determination of any of the issues in those proceedings, on the application of a party or of its own motion, give such directions as it thinks fit.

(3) An application by a party for any directions under this Part of these Regulations (otherwise than during a hearing) shall be made in writing to the Clerk and, unless it is accompanied by the written consent of all the parties, shall be served by the Clerk on any other party who might be affected by such directions.

(4) If any such other party, by notice to the Special Commissioners and the other party or parties, objects to the directions sought in the application, the Special Commissioner concerned shall consider the objection and, if the application is not one in respect of which the parties are entitled to be heard under these Regulations, shall if he considers it necessary for the determination of the application, give the parties an opportunity to be heard.

Summoning of witnesses

5—(1) Where a party to any proceedings requires the attendance of a person at the hearing of those proceedings to give evidence or to produce any document in his possession, custody or power relevant to the subject matter of the proceedings, a Special Commissioner may, on the application of that party, issue a summons (in this regulation referred to as a “witness summons”) requiring the attendance of that person at the hearing, or the production of the document, wherever that person may be in the United Kingdom.

(2) A witness summons issued under paragraph (1) above shall state the name and address of, or otherwise describe, the person to be served and shall be signed by the Special Commissioner issuing it, and it shall be the responsibility of the party on whose application the summons was issued to serve it on that person.

(3) Service of a witness summons under this regulation shall be effected—

(*a*) in the case of an individual, by leaving a copy of the summons with him;

(*b*) in the case of a body corporate registered in the United Kingdom, by leaving a copy of the summons with the secretary or clerk of the body corporate;

(*c*) in the case of a foreign body corporate with a place of business in the United Kingdom, by leaving a copy of the summons with a person authorised to accept service of process on the body corporate.

(4) A person who in obedience to a witness summons attends the hearing of any proceedings and gives evidence—

(*a*) is a witness of the party on whose application the summons was issued, and

(*b*) may not be cross-examined by that party without the leave of the Tribunal hearing the proceedings.

(5) Leave shall not be given by a Tribunal under paragraph (4)(*b*) above unless the Tribunal decides that the witness may be treated as a hostile witness.

(6) No person shall be required to attend in obedience to a witness summons unless it has been served on him at least seven days before the hearing or, if it has been served on him within that period, he has informed the Clerk that he accepts such service.

(7) No person shall be required to attend and give evidence or to produce any document in obedience to a witness summons unless the party serving the summons either—

(*a*) pays or tenders to that person, at the time when the summons is served on him, a sum sufficient to cover his reasonable expenses of travelling to and from, and his attendance at, the hearing, or

(*b*) has agreed with that person, prior to service of the summons, to pay such a sum to him at a different time.

(8) No person shall be compelled in obedience to a witness summons to give any evidence or produce any document that he could not be compelled to give or produce in an action in a court of law in that part of the United Kingdom by reference to the law of which the proceedings are to be determined.

[(9) No person who has been appointed as an auditor for the purposes of any enactment or who is a tax adviser within the meaning of section 20B(10) of the Management Act or paragraph 26 of Schedule 13 to the Finance Act 2003 shall be compelled in obedience to a witness summons to produce any document if, having regard to section 20B(9) to (13) of that Act, or paragraphs 26 and 27 of Schedule 13 to the Finance Act 2003, he would not be obliged to deliver or make available that document in response to a notice under section 20(3) or (8A) of that Act or paragraphs 6 to 13 of Schedule 13 to the Finance Act 2003.][1]

(10) Where, in the case of any document, a person could under section 20B(14) of that Act [or paragraph 27(3) of Schedule 13 to the Finance Act 2003][1] comply with such a notice by delivering a copy of parts of the document and making those parts available for inspection, he shall not be compelled in obedience to a witness summons to do more at the hearing than—

(*a*) produce a photographic or other facsimile copy of those parts of the document, and

(*b*) make those parts of the document available for inspection by the Tribunal.

(11) On the application, by notice served on the Clerk, of a person on whom a witness summons has been served, a Special Commissioner may set aside the summons in whole or in part; and the party on whose application the summons was issued shall be entitled to be heard on such an application.

(12) This regulation shall apply to proceedings in Scotland—

(*a*) with the omission of paragraphs (4) and (5) above;

(*b*) with the substitution for references to issuing a summons and to a witness summons of references to issuing a citation and to a witness citation.

Amendments—[1] Para (9) substituted, and words in para (10) inserted, by the SDLT (Appeals) Regulations, SI 2004/1363 reg 24(3), (4) with effect from 11 June 2004. Para (9) previously read as follows—

"(9) No person who has been appointed as an auditor for the purposes of any enactment or who is a tax adviser within the meaning of section 20B(10) of the Management Act shall be compelled in obedience to a witness summons to produce any document if, having regard to section 20B(9) to (13) of that Act, he would not be obliged to deliver or make available that document in response to a notice under section 20(3) or (8A) of that Act.".

Agreement of documents

6 If a party agrees a document for the purposes of any proceedings he shall be deemed, subject to the terms of the agreement, to admit for the purposes of those proceedings—

(*a*) that the document was written and signed or executed by the person by whom, and on the date on which, it purports to have been, and

(*b*) if it purports to be a copy of another document, that it is a true copy of that document,

but, subject to any enactment or rule of law, in the absence of an express admission or agreement, he shall not be deemed to admit the truth of the contents of that document.

Proceedings to be heard together or in succession

7—(1) Where two or more proceedings have been brought before, but have not yet been heard by, the Special Commissioners or have been brought before, but have not yet been heard by, the Special Commissioners and any General Commissioners and it appears to [a][1] Special Commissioner—

(*a*) that some common issue arises in both or all of them, or

(*b*) that both or all of them are relevant to some common issue,

[a][1] Special Commissioner may, of his own motion or on application by a party to any of those proceedings, direct that those proceedings be heard at the same time or consecutively and by the same Tribunal.

(2) A direction shall not be given under paragraph (1) above except on notice sent to all the parties to the proceedings in question who shall be entitled to be heard before any direction is given.

(3) On the giving of a direction under paragraph (1) above, the Clerk shall send notice of the date and terms of the direction to all the parties to the proceedings and, where one or more of the proceedings in question was pending before the General Commissioners, to the Clerk to the division or, as the case may be, each division of General Commissioners concerned.

(4) References in this regulation to proceedings pending before the General Commissioners are references to proceedings in relation to which the General Commissioners (Jurisdiction and Procedure) Regulations 1994 apply.

Amendments—[1] Word in para (1) substituted by the General Commissioners and Special Commissioners (Jurisdiction and Procedure) (Amendment) Regulations, SI 2002/2976 regs 2, 4 with effect from 31 December 2002.

[Lead Cases

7A—(1) Where—

(*a*) one or more proceedings under Part II of the Transfer Act or Part III of the Transfer Order have been brought before, but have not yet been heard by, the Special Commissioners; or

(*b*) one or more proceedings under Part II of the Transfer Act or Part III of the Transfer Order have been brought before, but have not yet been heard by, any General Commissioners; and

(*c*) it appears to the Presiding Special Commissioner that those proceedings give rise to common or related issues of fact or law (''same issues proceedings''),

the Presiding Special Commissioner may of his own motion or on application by a party to any of these proceedings direct that one of those proceedings be heard in the first instance as the lead case.

(2) The Presiding Special Commissioner may give such further directions as he also considers appropriate for determination of the lead case and without prejudice to the generality of the foregoing, such further directions may include in particular directions as to—

(*a*) which common or related issues of fact or law (''same issues'') are to be determined in the lead case; or

(*b*) which Tribunal is to hear the lead case.

(3) Subject to paragraph 14 the Presiding Special Commissioner may also direct that pending determination of the lead case all other same issues proceedings before the Special Commissioners, or that were pending before the General Commissioners, shall be stayed.

(4) Directions shall not be given under paragraphs (1) to (3) except on notice to all parties to the proceedings in question who shall be entitled to be heard before any directions are given.

(5) Without prejudice generally to the parties' rights of appeal and to paragraphs (8) and (9) as appropriate, the Tribunal's determination of the same issues in the lead case shall be binding on the parties to each of the same issues proceedings unless the Tribunal or the Presiding Special Commissioner directs otherwise.

(6) On the giving of directions under paragraphs (1) to (3) the Clerk shall send a copy of the directions to all the parties to the same issues proceedings.

(7) Upon determination of the same issues in the lead case the Clerk shall send a copy of that determination to all the parties to the same issues proceedings.

(8) Notwithstanding the provisions of paragraph (5) any party to any of the same issues proceedings may within 21 days beginning with the date on which that party receives notice of the determination of the same issues in the lead case apply to the Presiding Special Commissioner for a direction that the determination as to the same issues in the lead case shall not apply to those proceedings.

(9) Within 28 days beginning with the date of determination of the same issues in the lead case the Presiding Special Commissioner shall—

(*a*) give such further directions as he considers appropriate in relation to the lead case and each of the same issues proceedings stayed pending the determination of the same issues in the lead case; and

(*b*) such directions shall, without prejudice to the generality of the foregoing also include, as appropriate—

(i) directions as to the extent to which the determination of the same issues in the lead case is binding on any subsequent proceedings;

(ii) any further directions required as a result of an application under paragraph (8) which shall include, a direction as to any further hearing required in relation to those proceedings.

(10) On the giving of any further directions under paragraph (9) the Clerk shall send a copy of the relevant directions to each of the parties to the same issues proceedings.

(11) Where one or more of the same issues proceedings or the lead case was pending before the General Commissioners, the Clerk shall also send the notice of the matters specified in paragraphs (1) to (3) and (7) to (9) to the Clerk to the division or, as the case may be, each division of the General Commissioners concerned.

(12) Where a direction has been given for any proceedings to be heard as a lead case and those proceedings are withdrawn or discontinued either before or during the hearing, the Revenue shall—

(*a*) within seven days of withdrawal or discontinuance as the case may be, give notice to—

(i) the Presiding Special Commissioner;
(ii) as appropriate, the Clerk to the relevant division of the General Commissioners;
(iii) all the parties to the same issues proceedings; and

(*b*) the Presiding Special Commissioner may then direct that—

(i) one of the remaining same issues proceedings be substituted as the lead case; and
(ii) may also direct the extent to which any directions made prior to substitution shall be binding in relation to the substituted proceedings.

(13) On the giving of directions under paragraph (12)(*b*) the Clerk shall send a copy of the directions to all the remaining parties to the same issues proceedings and as appropriate, to the Clerks to the relevant divisions of the General Commissioners.

(14) Any same issues proceedings that were pending before the General Commissioners which the Presiding Special Commissioner considers are not appropriate for the lead case procedure shall be remitted to the General Commissioners for determination.

(15) References in this regulation to proceedings pending before the General Commissioners are references to proceedings pending in relation to which the General Commissioners (Jurisdiction and Procedure) Regulations 1994 apply.

(16) References in this regulation to "proceedings" shall for the avoidance of doubt, include more than one appeal against the same decision to the Special Commissioners or the General Commissioners as the case may be.][1]

Amendments—[1] Regulation 7A inserted by the General Commissioners and Special Commissioners (Jurisdiction and Procedure) (Amendment) Regulations, SI 2002/2976 regs 2, 5 with effect from 31 December 2002.

Joining of additional parties

8—(1) If it appears to a Special Commissioner, whether on the application of a party or otherwise, that it is desirable that any person other than the [respondent][1] be made a party to any proceedings, he may direct that such person be joined as a party in the proceedings and may give such further directions for giving effect to, or in connection with, the direction as he thinks fit.

(2) Where—

(*a*) pursuant to a direction under paragraph (1) above a person is joined as a party in any proceedings by reason of a question arising in those proceedings which may affect his liability to tax [or stamp duty land tax][2] or in which he otherwise has an interest, and
(*b*) pursuant to an application under regulation 15(2) by another party the hearing or, as the case may be, part of the hearing of the proceedings is to take place in private,

he shall not be entitled, unless all the other parties consent, to be present at the hearing of the proceedings or, as the case may be, the part of the hearing which is to take place in private except during such part as relates to that question, and a Tribunal shall, if necessary, hear any such question separately from the rest of the proceedings.

(3) Subject to paragraph (4) below, on the application of a person who has been joined as a party in the circumstances specified in paragraph (2) above, a Special Commissioner may, if he is satisfied that it would be to the convenience of the parties to do so, direct that the proceedings be transferred to the General Commissioners for the division in which the applicant ordinarily resided at the date of the application.

(4) No application may be made under paragraph (3) above in any case where the proceedings in question under any enactment lie only to the Special Commissioners and not to the General Commissioners.

Amendments—[1] Words substituted by the Special Commissioners (Jurisdiction and Procedure) (Amendment) Regulations, SI 2003/968 regs 2, 4 with effect from 22 April 2003.
[2] Words in para (2)(*a*) inserted by the SDLT (Appeals) Regulations, SI 2004/1363 reg 24(5) with effect from 11 June 2004.

Preliminary hearing

9—(1) Where it appears to a Special Commissioner that any proceedings would be facilitated by holding a preliminary hearing, he may, on the application of a party or of his own motion, give directions for such a hearing to be held.

(2) The Clerk shall give to the parties not less than fourteen days notice, or such shorter notice as the parties agree or the Special Commissioner sees fit to impose, of the time and place of the preliminary hearing.

(3) On a preliminary hearing the Special Commissioner—

(*a*) shall give all such directions as appear necessary or desirable so as to enable the proceedings to be disposed of expeditiously, effectively and fairly;
(*b*) may, if the parties so agree, determine the proceedings without any further hearing.

Power of Special Commissioners to obtain information

10—(1) A Special Commissioner on a preliminary hearing of any proceedings, or a Tribunal in the course of the hearing of any proceedings, may serve notice on any party...[1] directing that party within the time specified in the notice—

(*a*) to deliver to him or, as the case may be, the Tribunal such particulars as he or the Tribunal may consider are required for the purposes of determining any of the issues in the proceedings, and

(*b*) to make available for inspection by him or the Tribunal, or by [any other party (''inspecting party'')][1], all such books, accounts or other documents in the party's possession or power as may be specified or described in the notice, being books, accounts or other documents which, in the opinion of the Special Commissioner or Tribunal issuing the notice, contain or may contain information relating to the subject matter of the proceedings.

(2) Any [inspecting party][1] may at all reasonable times inspect and take copies of, or extracts from, any particulars delivered under paragraph (1)(*a*) above, and the Special Commissioner or Tribunal who issued the notice, or any [inspecting party][1], may take copies of, or extracts from, any books, accounts or other documents made available for inspection under paragraph (1)(*b*) above.

Revenue Internal Guidance—Inspector's Manual IM4982b (''particulars'' in para (1)(*a*) is a wide term: Commissioners can obtain trading and profit and loss accounts, balance sheets and supporting computations and details of any entry in accounts or returns, but not the completed return itself).

IM4989 (Revenue will consider the cost to the taxpayer of compliance with any order to produce particulars).

Amendments—[1] Words revoked and substituted by the Special Commissioners (Jurisdiction and Procedure) (Amendment) Regulations, SI 2003/968 regs 2, 5 with effect from 22 April 2003.

Postponements and Adjournments

11—(1) A Special Commissioner may postpone the hearing of any proceedings, and the Clerk shall send notice to the parties of the place, date and time of the postponed hearing.

(2) A Tribunal may from time to time adjourn the hearing of any proceedings and, subject to paragraph (3) below, the Clerk shall send notice to the parties of the place, date and time of the adjourned hearing.

(3) If the place, date and time of the adjourned hearing are announced before the adjournment in the presence of the parties, no notice need be sent by the Clerk under paragraph (2) above.

(4) When any hearing is adjourned in order that further information or evidence may be obtained, a Tribunal may give directions regarding the disclosure of such information or evidence to the parties prior to the resumption of the hearing.

Expert evidence

12—(1) Unless a Special Commissioner otherwise directs, no expert evidence may be adduced by a party at the hearing of any proceedings unless—

(*a*) he has agreed with the other party or parties that the substance of the evidence shall be disclosed in the form of a written report or opinion in advance of the hearing and not later than such date as is specified in the agreement, and the substance of the evidence has been so disclosed, or

(*b*) where no such agreement has been reached or where the substance of the evidence has not been so disclosed, an application is made to a Special Commissioner under paragraph (2) below by the party seeking to adduce the evidence to determine whether a direction should be given under paragraph (3) below, and the party seeking to adduce the evidence complies with a direction given under that paragraph.

(2) An application under this paragraph—

(*a*) shall be made not later than twenty one days after the date on which notice is sent by the Clerk under regulation 3(2) or, if the Special Commissioner so permits, at any later time prior to or in the course of the hearing, and

(*b*) shall state whether the party is willing to disclose the substance of the evidence prior to its being given at the hearing and, if not, the reasons for his objection.

(3) On an application under paragraph (2) above, unless he considers that there are special reasons for not doing so, the Special Commissioner shall direct that the substance of the evidence shall be disclosed in the form of a written report or opinion to such other parties and within such period as he may specify.

(4) This regulation shall not apply to proceedings in Scotland.

[Appeals under Proceeds of Crime Act 2002

12A—(1) This regulation applies to an appeal under section 320(1) of the Proceeds of Crime Act 2002.

(2) Paragraphs (3) to (8) apply where the Presiding Special Commissioner nominates an assessor under section 320(2) of that Act in relation to any proceedings.

(3) The assessor shall take such part in the proceedings as the Tribunal may direct and in particular the Tribunal may—

(*a*) direct the assessor to prepare a report for the Tribunal on any matter at issue in the proceedings; and

(*b*) direct the assessor to attend the whole or any part of the hearing or any preliminary hearing.

(4) Not more than 14 days after the nomination of an assessor, the Clerk shall notify each party in writing of the assessor's name.

(5) The Tribunal shall send to the parties a copy of any report prepared by the assessor within 21 days of receiving it.

(6) The parties shall have the opportunity to make observations on the assessor's report within such time and in such manner as the Tribunal shall direct.

(7) The Tribunal shall take any observations made under paragraph (6) into account when making its decision.

(8) The assessor shall not give oral evidence or be open to cross-examination or questioning.][1]

Amendments—[1] Regulation 12A inserted by the Special Commissioners (Jurisdiction and Procedure) (Amendment) Regulations, SI 2003/968 regs 2, 6 with effect from 22 April 2003.

PART III
HEARING AND DETERMINATION OF PROCEEDINGS

Constitution and sittings of Tribunal

13—(1) Any one, two or three of the Special Commissioners shall constitute a Tribunal.

(2) Where any proceedings are before a Tribunal which comprises two or three Special Commissioners—

(*a*) if the Presiding Special Commissioner is one of them, he shall preside at the hearing unless he otherwise directs and, if he is not, one of them shall be nominated by him to preside;

(*b*) the proceedings may be continued by any one or more of them if all the parties give their consent and unless the Presiding Special Commissioner otherwise directs.

Representation at hearing

14 At the hearing of any proceedings before a Tribunal—

(*a*) a party other than the [respondent][1] may be represented by any person whether or not legally qualified, except that if in a particular case the Tribunal is satisfied that there are good and sufficient reasons for doing so, it may refuse to permit a particular person, other than one who is legally qualified or who has been admitted a member of an incorporated society of accountants, to represent a party at the hearing;

(*b*) the [respondent][1] may be represented by a barrister, advocate, solicitor or any officer of the Board.

Amendments—[1] Words substituted by the Special Commissioners (Jurisdiction and Procedure) (Amendment) Regulations, SI 2003/968 regs 2, 7 with effect from 22 April 2003.

[Hearings in public

15—(1) Subject to the following paragraphs of this regulation, hearings before a Tribunal shall be in public.

(2) A Tribunal may direct that all or part of a hearing shall be in private—

(*a*) upon the application of all the parties by notice to the Clerk;

(*b*) upon the application of any party by notice to the Clerk;

(*c*) of its own motion,

if in each case, a Tribunal is satisfied that a hearing in private is necessary—

(i) in the interests of morals, public order, national security, juveniles or for the protection of the private life of the party; or

(ii) it considers that publicity would prejudice the interests of justice.

(3) Before determining an application under paragraph (2)(*b*), or giving a direction under paragraph (2)(*c*), a Tribunal shall give all other parties to the proceedings an opportunity to make representations.

(4) Before giving a direction under paragraph (2) that the entire hearing be in private, a Tribunal shall consider whether only part of the hearing should be heard in private.

(5) The following persons shall be entitled to be present at the hearing of any proceedings before a Tribunal notwithstanding that the hearing or part of the hearing takes place in private, and those referred to in sub-paragraphs (*b*) to (*e*) only may remain during the deliberations of a Tribunal but shall take no part in those deliberations—

(*a*) the parties and their representatives;

[(*aa*) an assessor nominated under section 320(2) of the Proceeds of Crime Act 2002;][2]

(*b*) the Presiding Special Commissioner and any of the Special Commissioners to the extent that they do not constitute the Tribunal or part of the Tribunal for the purpose of the hearing;
(*c*) the Clerk and any of the staff of the Special Commissioners;
(*d*) a member of the Council on Tribunals or of the Scottish Committee of that Council in the capacity of member;
(*e*) a member of the Judicial Studies Board or of one of its committees in the capacity of member.

(6) A Tribunal, with the consent of the parties, may permit any other person to be present at the hearing of proceedings before it which is to take place, or part of which is to take place, in private.

(7) A Tribunal may exclude from the whole or part of a hearing any person whose conduct, in the opinion of a Tribunal, has disrupted or is likely to disrupt the hearing.

(8) Where all or part of a hearing is held or is to be held in private, a Tribunal may direct that information about the whole or part of the proceedings (including information that might help to identify any person) before a Tribunal shall not be made public.

(9) For the purpose of paragraph (2)(i) ''party'' shall not include the Revenue.][1]

Amendments—[1] This regulation substituted by the General Commissioners and Special Commissioners (Jurisdiction and Procedure) (Amendment) Regulations, SI 2002/2976 regs 2, 6 with effect from 31 December 2002.
[2] Sub-para (5)(*aa*) inserted by the Special Commissioners (Jurisdiction and Procedure) (Amendment) Regulations, SI 2003/968 regs 2, 8 with effect from 22 April 2003.

Failure of parties to attend hearing

16—(1) If a party fails to attend or to be represented at a hearing of which he has been duly notified, the Tribunal may—

(*a*) unless it is satisfied that there is good and sufficient reason for such absence, hear and determine the proceedings in the absence of the party or his representative, or
(*b*) postpone or adjourn the hearing.

(2) Before deciding to hear and determine any proceedings in the absence of a party or his representative, the Tribunal shall consider any representations in writing or otherwise submitted by or on behalf of that party in response to the notice of hearing and shall give any party present at the hearing an opportunity to be heard in regard to those representations.

Simon's Tax Cases—*Smith (personal representative of Norcott, dec'd) v IRC* [2002] STC (SCD) 411.

Procedure and evidence at hearing

17—(1) At the beginning of the hearing of any proceedings the Tribunal shall, except where it considers it unnecessary to do so, explain the order of proceeding which it proposes to adopt.

(2) The Tribunal shall conduct the hearing in such manner as it considers most suitable to the clarification and determination of the issues before it and generally to the just handling of the proceedings, and, so far as appears to it appropriate, shall seek to avoid formality in its procedure.

(3) The parties shall be heard in such order as the Tribunal shall determine and shall be entitled—

(*a*) to give evidence,
(*b*) to call witnesses,
(*c*) to question any witnesses including other parties who give evidence, and
(*d*) to address the Tribunal both on the evidence and generally on the subject matter of the proceedings.

(4) In assessing the truth and weight of any evidence, the Tribunal may take account of its nature and source, and the manner in which it is given.

(5) Evidence before the Tribunal may be given orally or, if the Tribunal so directs, by any affidavit or any statement made or recorded in a document, but at any stage of the hearing the Tribunal may, on the application of any party or of its own motion, require the personal attendance as a witness of—

(*a*) the maker of an affidavit, or
(*b*) the maker of such a statement, or
(*c*) in the case of an oral statement recorded in a document, the person by whom the statement was so recorded.

(6) The Tribunal may receive evidence of any fact which appears to the Tribunal to be relevant to the subject matter of the proceedings notwithstanding that such evidence would be inadmissible in proceedings before a court of law in that part of the United Kingdom by reference to the law of which the proceedings before the Tribunal are to be determined, but, save in cases where claims for privilege are allowed (including, in proceedings in Scotland, claims for protection from disclosure by virtue of any rule of law relating to the confidentiality of communications), it shall not refuse to admit any evidence which would be admissible in such proceedings.

(7) The Tribunal may require any witness to give evidence on oath or affirmation and for that purpose there may be administered an oath or affirmation in due form.

Simon's Tax Cases—reg 17(6), *Taylor v Cox* [1998] STC (SCD) 179.

Decisions of Tribunal

18—(1) Where proceedings are before a Tribunal which comprises two or three Special Commissioners, any decision of the Tribunal shall be made by the votes of the Special Commissioners comprising that Tribunal.

(2) Where proceedings are before a Tribunal which comprises two Special Commissioners, in the event of an equality of votes, the Special Commissioner presiding at the hearing shall be entitled to a second or casting vote.

(3) Where proceedings are before a Tribunal which comprises three Special Commissioners, any decision or direction of the tribunal shall be made by the votes of the majority of the Special Commissioners comprising that Tribunal.

(4) The final determination may be given orally by a Tribunal at the end of the hearing or may be reserved and in either event shall be recorded forthwith in a document which, subject to paragraph (7) below, shall contain a statement of the facts found by the Tribunal and the reasons for the determination and shall be signed and dated by the Tribunal.

(5) A Tribunal may, after reserving the final determination—

(*a*) give a written decision in principle on one or more issues arising in the proceedings, and

(*b*) adjourn the making of the final determination until after its decision in principle has been issued and such further questions arising from that decision have been agreed by the parties or, failing agreement, decided by the Tribunal after having heard the parties.

(6) A decision in principle given under paragraph (5)(*a*) above shall contain, in relation to the matters covered by the decision—

(*a*) a statement of the facts found by the Tribunal, and

(*b*) the reasons for the decision.

(7) In any case where a decision in principle has been given under paragraph (5)(*a*) above, the document recording the final determination need not contain a statement of the facts and reasons referred to in paragraph (4) above except in so far as is necessary in order to explain the final determination of the Tribunal on matters not covered in the decision in principle.

(8) The Clerk shall send a copy of the document recording a decision in principle, and a copy of the document recording the final determination, to each party.

(9) Except where the final determination is given at the end of the hearing, it shall be treated as having been made on the date on which a copy of the document recording it is sent to the parties under paragraph (8) above.

(10) Every copy of the document recording the final determination sent to the parties under this regulation[, other than a document recording a final determination made in accordance with regulation 23(2)(*b*),][1] shall be accompanied by a notification of the provisions [as appropriate][2] of—

(*a*) the Management Act [or][2],

[(*aa*) Part 4 of the Finance Act 2003 and any regulations made under Part 4,][2]

(*b*) these Regulations, and

(*c*) rules of court,

relating to appeals from the Special Commissioners, and of the time within which, and the manner in which, such appeals shall be made.

Amendments—[1] In sub-s (10) words inserted by the Special Commissioners (Jurisdiction and Procedure) (Amendment) Regulations, SI 1999/3292 reg 4 with effect from 1 January 2000.

[2] Words in para (10) inserted, and sub-para (*aa*) thereof inserted, by the SDLT (Appeals) Regulations, SI 2004/1363 reg 24(6) with effect from 11 June 2004.

Simon's Tax Cases—*Y Co Ltd v IRC* [1996] STC (SCD) 147.

Review of Tribunal's decision in principle or final determination

19—(1) If, on the application of a party or of its own motion, a Tribunal is satisfied that—

(*a*) a decision in principle or the final determination was wrongly made as a result of an administrative error on the part of the Clerk or any of the staff of the Special Commissioners or a party, or

(*b*) a party, who was entitled to be heard at a hearing but failed to appear or to be represented, had good and sufficient reason for failing to appear or to be represented, or

(*c*) accounts or other information relevant to a party's case had been sent to the Clerk or to the appropriate inspector or other officer of the Board prior to the hearing of the proceedings but had not been received by the Tribunal until after the hearing,

the Tribunal may review and set aside or vary the decision in principle or final determination (or both the decision in principle and the final determination).

(2) An application for the purposes of paragraph (1) above shall be made to the Tribunal not later than fourteen days after the date on which a copy of the document recording the decision in principle or, as the case may be, the final determination was sent to the parties under regulation 18(8), or by such later time as the Tribunal may allow, and shall be in writing stating the grounds in full.

(3) Where the Tribunal proposes to review of its own motion the decision in principle or final determination, it shall serve notice of that proposal on the parties not later than fourteen days after

the date on which a copy of the document recording the decision in principle or, as the case may be, the final determination was sent to the parties under regulation 18(8).

(4) The parties shall have an opportunity to be heard on a review, or in relation to any application or proposal for review, under this regulation and the review shall be determined by the Tribunal which decided the case or, where it is not practicable for it to be heard by that Tribunal, by a Tribunal appointed by the Presiding Special Commissioner; and if, having reviewed the decision in principle or final determination, the Tribunal sets aside that decision or determination, it shall substitute such decision or determination as it thinks fit or order a rehearing before either the same or a differently constituted Tribunal.

(5) Regulation 18 shall apply to a decision by a Tribunal varying a decision in principle or final determination, or substituting a new decision in principle or final determination, as it applies to a decision in principle or final determination.

Revenue Internal Guidance—Inspector's Manual IM4922 (no appeal against decision of Commissioners to reopen appeal).
Simon's Tax Cases—reg 19(1)(*b*) *Phillips v Burrows* [2000] STC (SCD) 112.

Publication of decisions in principle or final determinations

20—(1) The Presiding Special Commissioner may make arrangements for the publication of reports of such of the decisions in principle and final determinations given by Tribunals as he considers appropriate.

(2) Where the Presiding Special Commissioner considers it appropriate to publish a report of a decision in principle or final determination pursuant to paragraph (1) above, and that decision or determination relates to proceedings the whole or part of which were heard in private in accordance with regulation 15(2), he shall ensure that the report is in a form which so far as possible prevents the identification of any person whose affairs are dealt with in the decision or determination.

Revenue Interpretation RI 132—Special Commissioners expect to have attention drawn to any of their previously published decisions where relevant. Revenue view is that decisions do not create legally binding precedent but they may be relevant in other cases, particularly if there is no appeal to a higher court against the decision.
Revenue Internal Guidance—Inspector's Manual IM4952 (decisions of Special Commissioners are not legally binding, but the Commissioners will expect to have relevant published decisions drawn to their attention when deciding a particular case).
Simon's Tax Cases—*Y Co Ltd v IRC* [1996] STC (SCD) 147.

Orders for costs

21—(1) Subject to paragraph (2) below, a Tribunal may make an order awarding the costs of, or incidental to, the hearing of any proceedings by it against any party to those proceedings (including a party who has withdrawn his appeal or application) if it is of the opinion that the party has acted wholly unreasonably in connection with the hearing in question.

(2) No order shall be made under paragraph (1) above against a party without first giving that party an opportunity of making representations against the making of the order.

(3) An order under paragraph (1) above may require the party against whom it is made to pay to the other party or parties the whole or part of the costs incurred by the other party or parties of, or incidental to, the hearing of the proceedings, such costs to be taxed if not otherwise agreed.

(4) Any costs required to be taxed pursuant to an order under this regulation shall be taxed in the county court according to such of the scales prescribed by rules of court for proceedings in the county court as may be directed by the order or, in the absence of any such direction, by the county court.

(5) In the application of this regulation to proceedings in Scotland—

(*a*) any reference to costs shall be construed as a reference to expenses;

(*b*) in paragraph (4) above, for the references to the county court there shall be substituted references to the sheriff court and for the reference to proceedings there shall be substituted a reference to civil proceedings.

(6) In the application of this regulation to proceedings in Northern Ireland, for paragraphs (3) and (4) above there shall be substituted—

"(3) An order under paragraph (1) above may require the party against whom it is made to pay to the other party or parties the whole or part of the costs incurred by that other party or parties of, or incidental to, the hearing of the proceedings, such costs to be taxed in the county court if not determined by the Tribunal or otherwise agreed.

(4) Any costs which may be determined by the Tribunal under paragraph (3) above shall be determined by reference to the scales prescribed by rules of court for proceedings in the county court and any costs required to be taxed pursuant to an order under this regulation shall be taxed in the same manner as costs in equity suits or proceedings in the county court.".

Simon's Tax Cases—reg 21, *Scott (t/a Farthings Steak House) v McDonald* [1996] STC (SCD) 381; *Salt v Young* [1999] STC (SCD) 249; *Carter v Hunt* [2000] STC (SCD) 17; *Phillips v Burrows* [2000] STC (SCD) 107; *Robertson v IRC (No 2)* [2002] STC (SCD) 242.
reg 21(1), *Gamble v Rowe* [1998] STC 1247; *Self-assessed v Insp of Taxes (No 2)* [2000] STC (SCD) 47; *Phillips v Burrows* [2000] STC (SCD) 112; *Powell v Jackman (Insp of Taxes)* [2002] STC (SCD) 488.

PART IV

SPECIAL PROCEDURE

Proceedings relating to tax on chargeable gains

22—(1) Where the market value of an asset on a particular date or the apportionment of an amount or value is a material question in any proceedings relating to tax on chargeable gains, the Tribunal hearing the proceedings shall, if so required by any party, record in its decision in principle or final determination that market value or apportionment.

(2) The final determination on an appeal of the market value of an asset on a particular date or of the apportionment of any amount or value may be proved in any proceedings relating to tax on chargeable gains by a certificate stating the material particulars signed by—

(*a*) an inspector where the appeal was settled by agreement, or

(*b*) the Clerk where the Special Commissioners determined the appeal, or

(*c*) the clerk or registrar of another tribunal where the material question was determined by that other tribunal in accordance with section [46D][1] or 47B of the Management Act or section 222(4A) of the Inheritance Tax Act 1984

and a document purporting to be such a certificate may be received in evidence in any such proceedings without further proof.

(3) In this regulation the expression "final determination on an appeal" shall be construed in accordance with regulation 11(2) of the Capital Gains Tax Regulations 1967, and the expression "material question in any proceedings" shall be construed in accordance with regulation 15(*a*) of those Regulations.

Amendments—[1] In sub-s (2)(*c*) figure substituted by the Special Commissioners (Jurisdiction and Procedure) (Amendment) Regulations, SI 1999/3292 reg 4 with effect from 1 January 2000.

[References of questions to other tribunals

23—(1) A question in an appeal which is required to be determined in accordance with section 46D or 47B of the Management Act or section 222(4A) of the Inheritance Tax Act 1984 [or regulation 6 of the Stamp Duty Land Tax (Appeals) Regulations 2004,][2] shall be referred to the appropriate tribunal by the Tribunal before whom the appeal is brought or, if the hearing of the appeal has not yet begun, by an inspector or other officer of the Board.

(2) Where any question in an appeal has been referred to another tribunal in accordance with paragraph (1) above, the Tribunal before whom the appeal is brought—

(*a*) shall finally determine the remaining question or questions in the appeal without awaiting the determination of the question referred to the other tribunal, and

(*b*) shall make a final determination of the appeal (in accordance with regulation 18) once all the questions in the appeal have been finally determined.

(3) The reference in paragraph (2)(*b*) above to all the questions in the appeal having being finally determined is a reference to a time when no further appeals in relation to those questions under any enactment are pending.][1]

Amendments—[1] This regulation substituted by the Special Commissioners (Jurisdiction and Procedure) (Amendment) Regulations, SI 1999/3292 reg 6 with effect from 1 January 2000.

[2] Words in para (1) inserted by the SDLT (Appeals) Regulations, SI 2004/1363 reg 24(7) with effect from 11 June 2004.

Revenue Internal Guidance—Inspector's Manual IM4919a (appeals to the court on other matters may proceed before the determination of valuations by the Land Tribunal).

Penalty for failure to comply with Tribunal direction

24—(1) If any party or other person fails to comply with any direction of a Tribunal under these Regulations including a direction in a notice under regulation 10, the Tribunal may summarily determine a penalty against that party or other person not exceeding £10,000.

(2) Subject to paragraphs (6) to (11) of regulation 5, if a person on whom a summons is served under that regulation—

(*a*) fails to attend in obedience to the summons, or

(*b*) attends, but refuses to be sworn or to affirm, or

(*c*) refuses to answer any lawful question, or

(*d*) refuses to produce any document which he has been required to produce,

the Tribunal may summarily determine a penalty against him not exceeding £10,000.

(3) Subject to [paragraphs (4) and (5)][1] below, any penalty determined by the Tribunal under paragraph (1) or (2) above shall for all purposes be treated as if it were tax charged in an assessment and due and payable.

(4) Any penalty determined by the Tribunal under paragraph (1) or (2) above in proceedings relating to—

(*a*) an appeal under section 222 of the Inheritance Tax Act 1984 or

(*b*) an appeal under regulation 8 of the Stamp Duty Reserve Tax Regulations 1986, shall for all purposes be treated as if it were tax determined by the Board and due and payable.

[(5) Any penalty determined by the Tribunal under paragraph (1) or (2) above in proceedings relating to an appeal under the enactments relating to stamp duty shall for all purposes be treated as if it were a penalty, other than a penalty under section 15B of the Stamp Act 1891 (penalty on late stamping), determined by an officer of the Board, and due and payable, under those enactments.][1]

Amendments—[1] Words in sub-s (3) substituted and sub-s (5) added by the Special Commissioners (Jurisdiction and Procedure) (Amendment) Regulations, SI 2000/288 reg 4 with effect from 1 March 2000.

PART V
MISCELLANEOUS

Irregularities

25—(1) Any irregularity resulting from any failure to comply with any provision of these Regulations or with any direction given by a Tribunal before the Tribunal has reached its decision shall not of itself render the proceedings void.

(2) Where any such irregularity comes to the attention of a Tribunal, the Tribunal, before reaching its decision, may, and if it considers that any person may have been prejudiced by that irregularity shall, give such directions as it thinks just to cure or waive the irregularity.

(3) Clerical mistakes in any document recording a direction or decision of a Tribunal, or errors arising in such a document from an accidental slip or omission, may be corrected by the Special Commissioner presiding at the hearing or any other of the Special Commissioners comprising the Tribunal, or by the Presiding Special Commissioner if all the Special Commissioners comprising the Tribunal have died or ceased to be Special Commissioners, by certificate under his hand.

Notices

26 Every notice required by these Regulations shall be in writing unless a Tribunal authorises it to be given orally.

Service

27—(1) Any notice or other document (other than a summons under regulation 5) required or authorised by these Regulations to be sent or delivered to, or served on, any person shall be duly sent or delivered to, or served on, that person—

(*a*) if it is sent to him at his proper address by post; or

(*b*) if it is sent to him at that address by facsimile transmission or other similar means which produce a document containing a text of the communication, in which event the document shall be regarded as sent when it is received in a legible form; or

(*c*) if it is delivered to him or left at his proper address.

(2) Any such document may—

(*a*) in the case of a body corporate, be sent or delivered to, or left with, the secretary or clerk of that body;

(*b*) in the case of a foreign body corporate, be sent or delivered to, or left with, the person authorised to accept service of process on it;

(*c*) in the case of a partnership, be sent or delivered to, or left with, any partner;

(*d*) in the case of an unincorporated association other than a partnership, be sent or delivered to, or left with, any member of the governing body of the association.

(3) For the purposes of this regulation, a person's proper address is—

(*a*) in the case of the secretary or clerk of a body corporate registered in the United Kingdom, the address of the registered or principal office of that body corporate;

(*b*) in the case of the person authorised to accept service of process on a foreign body corporate, the address of the principal office or place of business of that body corporate in the United Kingdom;

(*c*) in the case of the Special Commissioners or their Clerk, the address of the Clerk;

(*d*) in the case of any other person, the usual or last known address of that person.

Substituted service

28 If any person to or on whom any notice or other document (other than a summons under regulation 5) is required to be sent, delivered or served for the purposes of these Regulations cannot be found or has died and has no known representative, or is out of the United Kingdom, or if for any other reason service on him cannot be readily effected, a Tribunal may dispense with the requirement that the notice or other document be sent or delivered to, or served on him or may make an order for substituted service on such other person or in such other form (whether by advertisement in a newspaper or otherwise) as the Tribunal may think fit.

1994/1812
General Commissioners (Jurisdiction and Procedure) Regulations 1994

Made by the Lord Chancellor under TMA 1970 ss 46A, 56B

Made	*6 July 1994*
Laid before Parliament	*14 July 1994*
Coming into Force	*1 September 1994*

Commentary—*Simon's Direct Tax Service* Divisions **A3.5**; **A3.7**.

ARRANGEMENT OF REGULATIONS

PART I
INTRODUCTORY

PART II
PREPARATION FOR A HEARING

PART III
HEARING AND DETERMINATION OF PROCEEDINGS

PART IV
SPECIAL PROCEDURE

PART V
MISCELLANEOUS

PART I

INTRODUCTORY

Citation, commencement and application

1—(1) These Regulations may be cited as the General Commissioners (Jurisdiction and Procedure) Regulations 1994 and shall come into force on 1st September 1994.

(2) These Regulations do not apply in relation to—

(*a*) any proceedings in respect of which notice of the place, date and time of the hearing was given or, in the case of more than one such notice, first given by the Clerk prior to 1st September 1994, and in respect of which an election is made by any party to the proceedings, by notice served on the Clerk, that these Regulations shall not apply, or

(*b*) any proceedings under section 100C of the Taxes Management Act 1970 in respect of which a summons was issued prior to 1st September 1994 by the General Commissioners to the defendant (or, in Scotland, the defender) to appear before them at a time and place stated in the summons.

(3) Where these Regulations apply in relation to any proceedings in respect of which notice of the place, date and time of the hearing was given or, as the case may be, first given by the Clerk prior to 1st September 1994, anything done in relation to those proceedings prior to that date which, if the proceedings had been brought before the General Commissioners on or after that date, could have been done pursuant to these Regulations, shall have effect as if done pursuant to these Regulations.

(4) An election under paragraph (2)(*a*) above shall be made prior to the time of commencement of the hearing of the proceedings in question or, in the case of a hearing which commenced before 1st September 1994 but which was adjourned, prior to the time of commencement of the first continuation of the hearing on or after that date, and shall be irrevocable.

Interpretation

2 In these Regulations unless the context otherwise requires—

"the Board" means the Commissioners of Inland Revenue;

"the Clerk", in relation to any proceedings, means the Clerk to the General Commissioners;

"division" shall be construed in accordance with section 2(1) of the Management Act;

"final determination" means the decision finally determining any proceedings before a Tribunal;

"General Commissioners" shall be construed in accordance with section 2(1) of the Management Act, and "the General Commissioners", in relation to any proceedings, means the General Commissioners for a division before whom the proceedings are brought (and references to a General Commissioner are to be read accordingly);

"inspector" means an inspector of taxes [and in relation to stamp duty land tax means any officer of the Board][2];

"the Management Act" means the Taxes Management Act 1970;

"party" means a party to any proceedings, and for the purposes of these Regulations—

(*a*) where the proceedings relate to an assessment, decision or determination made by the Board, the Board and any inspector or other officer of the Board for the time being concerned with the proceedings shall together constitute a party to those proceedings;

(*b*) where the proceedings relate to an assessment, decision or determination made by an inspector or other officer of the Board, that person and any other inspector or other officer of the Board for the time being concerned with the proceedings shall together constitute a party to those proceedings;

and references to "the Revenue" are references to a party within paragraph (*a*) or, as the case may be, paragraph (*b*) above;

"proceedings" means—

(*a*) any appeal to the General Commissioners under the Taxes Acts;

(*b*) any proceedings before the General Commissioners which under the Taxes Acts are to be heard and determined in the same way as such an appeal;

(*c*) any proceedings before the General Commissioners which relate to a penalty and are not within paragraph (*a*) or paragraph (*b*) above;

[(*d*) any appeal to the General Commissioners under Part II of the Transfer Act or Part III of the Transfer Order;][1]

[(*e*) any appeal to the General Commissioners under regulations 8(6) and 14(4) of the Working Tax Regulations;][1]

[(*f*) any appeal to the General Commissioners under the enactments relating to stamp duty land tax;][2]

[(*g*) any proceedings before the General Commissioners which under any enactments relating to stamp duty land tax are to be heard and determined in the same way as such an appeal or any other proceedings to the General Commissioners under the enactments relating to stamp duty land tax;][2]

"proceedings in Northern Ireland" means any proceedings (as defined in this regulation) which fall within the meaning of that expression as defined in section 58(3) of the Management Act;

''proceedings in Scotland'' means any proceedings (as defined in this regulation) which fall to be determined by reference to the law of Scotland;

''Special Commissioners'' shall be construed in accordance with section 4(1) of the Management Act;

[''the enactments relating to stamp duty land tax'' means Part 4 of the Finance Act 2003 and any regulations made under that Part;][2]

''the Taxes Acts'' has the meaning given by section 118(1) of the Management Act;

[''the Transfer Act'' means the Social Security Contributions (Transfer of Functions, etc) Act 1999;][1]

[''the Transfer Order'' means the Social Security Contributions (Transfer of Functions, etc) (Northern Ireland) Order 1999;][1]

''Tribunal'', in relation to any proceedings, means, subject to regulation 11(3), two or more, but not more than five, General Commissioners for a division before whom the proceedings are [brought;][1]

[''the Working Tax Regulations'' means the Working Tax Credit (Payment by Employers) Regulations 2002.][1]

Amendments—[1] In the definition of ''proceedings'', paras (*d*), (*e*) inserted; definitions of ''the Transfer Act'', ''the Transfer Order'', and ''the Working Tax Regulations'' inserted; and in the definition of ''Tribunal'', word substituted, by the General Commissioners and Special Commissioners (Jurisdiction and Procedure) (Amendment) Regulations, SI 2002/2976 regs 7, 8 with effect from 31 December 2002.

[2] Words in definition of ''inspector'' inserted, in definition of ''proceedings'', paras (*f*), (*g*) inserted; and definition of ''the enactments relating to stamp duty land tax'' inserted by the SDLT (Appeals) Regulations, SI 2004/1363 reg 23(2) with effect from 11 June 2004.

PART II
PREPARATION FOR A HEARING

Listing and notice of hearing

3—(1) Except in relation to proceedings under section 100C of the Management Act, any party to proceedings which are to be heard by the General Commissioners may serve notice on the Clerk that he wishes a date for the hearing to be fixed.

(2) On receipt of a notice under paragraph (1) above the Clerk shall send notice to each party of the place, date and time of the hearing.

(3) Unless the parties otherwise agree or a Tribunal otherwise directs, the date of the hearing specified in a notice under paragraph (2) above shall be not earlier than twenty eight days after the date on which the notice is sent to the parties.

Summoning of witnesses

4—(1) Where a party to any proceedings requires the attendance of a person at the hearing of those proceedings to give evidence or to produce any document in his possession, custody or power relevant to the subject matter of the proceedings, a General Commissioner may, on the application of that party, issue a summons (in this regulation referred to as a ''witness summons'') requiring the attendance of that person at the hearing, or the production of the document, wherever that person may be in the United Kingdom.

(2) A witness summons issued under paragraph (1) above shall state the name and address of, or otherwise describe, the person to be served and shall be signed by the General Commissioner issuing it, and it shall be the responsibility of the party on whose application the summons was issued to serve it on that person.

(3) Service of a witness summons under this regulation shall be effected—

(*a*) in the case of an individual, by leaving a copy of the summons with him;

(*b*) in the case of a body corporate registered in the United Kingdom, by leaving a copy of the summons with the secretary or clerk of the body corporate;

(*c*) in the case of a foreign body corporate with a place of business in the United Kingdom, by leaving a copy of the summons with a person authorised to accept service of process on the body corporate.

(4) A person who in obedience to a witness summons attends the hearing of any proceedings and gives evidence—

(*a*) is a witness of the party on whose application the summons was issued, and

(*b*) may not be cross-examined by that party without the leave of the Tribunal hearing the proceedings.

(5) Leave shall not be given by a Tribunal under paragraph (4)(*b*) above unless the Tribunal decides that the witness may be treated as a hostile witness.

(6) No person shall be required to attend in obedience to a witness summons unless it has been served on him at least seven days before the hearing or, if it has been served on him within that period, he has informed the Clerk that he accepts such service.

(7) No person shall be required to attend and give evidence or to produce any document in obedience to a witness summons unless the party serving the summons either—

(*a*) pays or tenders to that person, at the time when the summons is served on him, a sum sufficient to cover his reasonable expenses of travelling to and from, and his attendance at, the hearing, or

(*b*) has agreed with that person prior to service of the summons, to pay such a sum to him at a different time.

(8) No person shall be compelled in obedience to a witness summons to give any evidence or produce any document that he could not be compelled to give or produce in an action in a court of law in that part of the United Kingdom by reference to the law of which the proceedings are to be determined.

[(9) No person who has been appointed as an auditor for the purposes of any enactment or who is a tax adviser within the meaning of section 20B(10) of the Management Act or paragraph 26 of Schedule 13 to the Finance Act 2003 shall be compelled in obedience to a witness summons to produce any document if, having regard to section 20B(9) to (13) of that Act, or paragraphs 26 and 27 of Schedule 13 to the Finance Act 2003, he would not be obliged to deliver or make available that document in response to a notice under section 20(3) or (8A) of that Act or paragraphs 6 to 13 of Schedule 13 to the Finance Act 2003.][1]

(10) Where, in the case of any document, a person could under section 20B(14) of that Act [or paragraph 27(3) of Schedule 13 to the Finance Act 2003][1] comply with such a notice by delivering a copy of parts of the document and making those parts available for inspection, he shall not be compelled in obedience to a witness summons to do more at the hearing than—

(*a*) produce a photographic or other facsimile copy of those parts of the document, and

(*b*) make those parts of the document available for inspection by the Tribunal.

(11) On the application, by notice served on the Clerk, of a person on whom a witness summons has been served, a General Commissioner may set aside the summons in whole or in part; and the party on whose application the summons was issued shall be entitled to be heard on such an application.

(12) Subject to paragraphs (6) to (11) above, if a person on whom a witness summons is served—

(*a*) fails to attend in obedience to the summons, or

(*b*) attends, but refuses to be sworn or to affirm, or

(*c*) refuses to answer any lawful question, or

(*d*) refuses to produce any document which he has been required by the summons to produce,

the Tribunal hearing the proceedings may summarily determine a penalty against him not exceeding £1,000.

(13) Any penalty determined by a Tribunal under paragraph (12) above shall for all purposes be treated as if it were tax charged in an assessment and due and payable.

(14) This regulation shall apply to proceedings in Scotland—

(*a*) with the omission of paragraphs (4) and (5) above;

(*b*) with the substitution for references to issuing a summons and to a witness summons of references to issuing a citation and to a witness citation.

Amendments—[1] Para (9) substituted, and words in para (10) inserted, by the SDLT (Appeals) Regulations, SI 2004/1363 reg 23(3), (4) with effect from 11 June 2004. Para (9) previously read as follows—

"(9) No person who has been appointed as an auditor for the purposes of any enactment or who is a tax adviser within the meaning of section 20B(10) of the Management Act shall be compelled in obedience to a witness summons to produce any document if, having regard to section 20B(9) to (13) of that Act, he would not be obliged to deliver or make available that document in response to a notice under section 20(3) or (8A) of that Act.".

Agreement of documents

5 If a party agrees a document for the purposes of any proceedings he shall be deemed, subject to the terms of the agreement, to admit for the purposes of those proceedings—

(*a*) that the document was written and signed or executed by the person by whom, and on the date on which, it purports to have been, and

(*b*) if it purports to be a copy of another document, that it is a true copy of that document,

but, subject to any enactment or rule of law, in the absence of an express admission or agreement, he shall not be deemed to admit the truth of the contents of that document.

Proceedings to be heard together or in succession

6—(1) Where two or more proceedings have been brought before, but have not yet been heard by, the General Commissioners for one or more divisions and it appears to two or more of the General Commissioners for one of those divisions—

(*a*) that some common issue arises in both or all of them, or

(*b*) that both or all of them are relevant to some common issue,

those Commissioners may, of their own motion or on an application by a party to any of those proceedings, direct that those proceedings be heard at the same time or consecutively and by the same Tribunal within their division.

(2) A direction shall not be given under paragraph (1) above except on notice sent to all the parties to the proceedings in question who shall be entitled to be heard before any direction is given.

(3) On the giving of a direction under paragraph (1) above, the Clerk to the General Commissioners by whom the direction is given shall send notice of the date and terms of the direction to all the parties to the proceedings and, except where all the proceedings have been brought before the General Commissioners for the same division, to the Clerk to the other division or, if more than one, each other division of General Commissioners concerned.

[Lead Cases

6A—(1) Where—

(*a*) one or more proceedings under Part II of the Transfer Act or Part III of the Transfer Order have been brought before, but have not yet been heard, by General Commissioners for one or more divisions, and

(*b*) those proceedings give rise to common or related issues of fact or law (''same issues proceedings'')

the General Commissioners or each of the General Commissioners for each division as the case may be, shall arrange for transfer of those proceedings to the Special Commissioners.

(2) Before transferring any same issues proceedings the appropriate General Commissioners shall give all the parties to the proceedings in question an opportunity to make representations.

(3) For the purpose of this regulation ''proceedings'' shall for the avoidance of doubt, include more than one appeal against the same decision to the General Commissioners.][1]

Amendments—[1] Regulation 6A inserted by the General Commissioners and Special Commissioners (Jurisdiction and Procedure) (Amendment) Regulations, SI 2002/2976 regs 7, 9 with effect from 31 December 2002.

Joining of additional parties

7—(1) If it appears to a Tribunal, whether on the application of a party or otherwise, that it is desirable that any person other than the Revenue be made a party to any proceedings, the Tribunal may order such person to be joined as a party in the proceedings and may give such directions for giving effect to, or in connection with, the order as it thinks fit.

(2) Where pursuant to an order under paragraph (1) above a person is joined as a party in any proceedings by reason of a question arising in those proceedings which may affect his liability to tax [or stamp duty land tax][1] or in which he otherwise has an interest, he shall not be entitled, unless all the other parties consent, to be present at the hearing of the proceedings except during such part of the hearing as relates to that question, and a Tribunal shall, if necessary, hear any such question separately from the rest of the proceedings.

(3) On the application of a person who has been joined as a party in the circumstances specified in paragraph (2) above, a Tribunal may, if it is satisfied that it would be to the convenience of the parties to do so, transfer the proceedings to the General Commissioners for the division in which the applicant ordinarily resided at the date of the application, or to the Special Commissioners.

Amendments—[1] Words in para (2) inserted, by the SDLT (Appeals) Regulations, SI 2004/1363 reg 23(5) with effect from 11 June 2004.

Postponements and Adjournments

8—(1) A Tribunal may postpone the hearing of any proceedings, and the Clerk shall send notice to the parties of the place, date and time of the postponed hearing.

(2) A Tribunal may from time to time adjourn the hearing of any proceedings and, subject to paragraph (3) below, the Clerk shall send notice to the parties of the place, date and time of the adjourned hearing.

(3) If the place, date and time of the adjourned hearing are announced before the adjournment in the presence of the parties, no notice need be sent by the Clerk under paragraph (2) above.

(4) When any hearing is adjourned in order that further information or evidence may be obtained, the Tribunal hearing the proceedings may give directions regarding the disclosure of such information or evidence to the parties prior to the resumption of the hearing.

Expert evidence

9—(1) Unless a Tribunal otherwise directs, no expert evidence may be adduced by a party at the hearing of any proceedings unless—

(*a*) he has agreed with the other party or parties that the substance of the evidence shall be disclosed in the form of a written report or opinion in advance of the hearing and not later than such date as is specified in the agreement, and the substance of the evidence has been so disclosed, or

(*b*) where no such agreement has been reached or where the substance of the evidence has not been so disclosed, an application is made to a Tribunal under paragraph (2) below by the party seeking to adduce the evidence to determine whether a direction should be given under paragraph (3) below, and the party seeking to adduce the evidence complies with a direction given under that paragraph.

(2) An application under this paragraph—

(*a*) shall be made not later than twenty one days after the date on which notice is sent by the Clerk under regulation 3(2) or, if the Tribunal so permits, at any later time prior to or in the course of the hearing, and

(*b*) shall state whether the party is willing to disclose the substance of the evidence prior to its being given at the hearing and, if not, the reasons for his objection.

(3) On an application under paragraph (2) above, unless it considers that there are special reasons for not doing so, the tribunal shall direct that the substance of the evidence shall be disclosed in the form of a written report or opinion to such other parties and within such period as it may specify.

(4) This regulation shall not apply to proceedings in Scotland.

PART III

HEARING AND DETERMINATION OF PROCEEDINGS

Power of Tribunal to obtain information

10—(1) A Tribunal hearing any proceedings may at any time before the final determination of those proceedings serve notice on any party ...[1] directing him within the time specified in the notice—

(*a*) to deliver to it such particulars as it may require for the purpose of determining any of the issues in the proceedings, and

(*b*) to make available for inspection by it, or by [any other party (''inspecting party'')][1], all such books, accounts or other documents in his possession or power as may be specified or described in the notice, being books, accounts or other documents which, in the opinion of the Tribunal, contain or may contain information relevant to the subject matter of the proceedings.

(2) Any [inspecting party][1] may at all reasonable times inspect and take copies of, or extracts from, any particulars delivered under paragraph (1)(*a*) above, and the Tribunal [who issued the notice,][1] or any [inspecting party][1] may take copies of, or extracts from, any books, accounts or other documents made available for inspection under paragraph (1)(*b*) above.

(3) If any person fails to comply with a notice served under this regulation, the Tribunal may summarily determine a penalty against him not exceeding £300 and, if the failure continues after the determination of such penalty, a further penalty or penalties not exceeding £60 for each day on which the failure continues after the day on which the penalty was determined (but excluding any day for which a further penalty has already been determined).

(4) Any penalty determined by the Tribunal under paragraph (3) above shall for all purposes be treated as if it were tax charged in an assessment and due and payable.

Revenue Internal Guidance—Inspector's Manual IM4982b (''particulars'' in para (1)(*a*) is a wide term: Commissioners can obtain trading and profit and loss accounts, balance sheets and supporting computations and details of any entry in accounts or returns, but not the completed return itself).

IM4989 (Revenue will consider the cost to the taxpayer of compliance with any order to produce particulars).

Simon's Tax Cases—*Phipps v New Forest West General Comrs and IRC* [1997] STC 797.

reg 10(1)(*b*), *Johnson v Blackpool General Comrs and IRC* [1997] STC 1202, *Slater Ltd v Comrs for the General Purposes of the Income Tax for the division of Beacontree* [2002] STC 246.

reg 10(3), *Johnson v Blackpool General Comrs and IRC* [1996] STC 277.

Slater Ltd v Comrs for the General Purposes of the Income Tax for the division of Beacontree [2002] STC 246.

Amendments—[1] In para (1), words '', other than the Revenue,'' revoked, and in sub-para (*b*), words substituted for the words ''an officer of the Board''; in para (2), words substituted for the words ''officer of the Board'', and words inserted, by the SDLT (Appeals) Regulations, SI 2004/1363 reg 23(6), (7) with effect from 11 June 2004.

Constitution and sittings of Tribunal

11—(1) A Tribunal hearing any proceedings shall, where possible, comprise at least three General Commissioners but the validity of any proceedings before a Tribunal shall not be challenged where the Tribunal in question is comprised of two General Commissioners.

(2) The General Commissioners comprising a Tribunal shall decide which one of them shall preside at the hearing of proceedings before them.

(3) Proceedings before any Tribunal may be continued by any one or more of the General Commissioners comprising that Tribunal if all the parties give their consent.

Representation at hearing

12 At the hearing of any proceedings before a Tribunal—

(*a*) a party other than the Revenue may be represented by any person whether or not legally qualified, except that if in a particular case the Tribunal is satisfied that there are good and sufficient reasons for doing so, it may refuse to permit a particular person, other than one who is legally qualified or who has been admitted a member of an incorporated society of accountants, to represent a party at the hearing;

(*b*) the Revenue may be represented by a barrister, advocate, solicitor or any officer of the Board.

[Hearings in public

13—(1) Subject to the following paragraphs of this regulation, hearings before a Tribunal shall be in public.

(2) A Tribunal may direct that all or part of a hearing shall be in private—

(*a*) upon the application of all the parties by notice to the Clerk;
(*b*) upon the application of any party by notice to the Clerk;
(*c*) of its own motion,

if in each case, a Tribunal is satisfied that a hearing in private is necessary—

(i) in the interests of morals, public order, national security, juveniles or for the protection of the private life of the party; or
(ii) if it considers that publicity would prejudice the interests of justice.

(3) Before determining an application under paragraph (2)(*b*) or giving a direction under (2)(*c*) a Tribunal shall give all other parties an opportunity to make representations.

(4) Before giving a direction under paragraph (2) that the entire hearing be in private, a Tribunal shall consider whether only part of the hearing should be heard in private.

(5) The following persons shall be entitled to be present at the hearing of any proceedings before a Tribunal notwithstanding that the hearing or part of the hearing takes place in private, and those referred to in sub-paragraphs (*b*) to (*e*) only may remain present during the deliberations of the Tribunal but shall take no part in those deliberations—

(*a*) the parties and their representatives;
(*b*) the Clerk and any of the staff of the General Commissioners;
(*c*) a member of the Council on Tribunals or of the Scottish Committee of that Council in the capacity of member;
(*d*) any of the Special Commissioners;
(*e*) a member of the Judicial Studies Board or of one of its Committees in the capacity of member.

(6) A Tribunal may exclude from the whole or part of a hearing any person whose conduct, in the opinion of a Tribunal, has disrupted or is likely to disrupt the hearing.

(7) A Tribunal, with the consent of the parties, may permit any other person to be present at the hearing of proceedings before it which is to take place, or part of which is to take place, in private.

(8) Where all or part of a hearing is held or is to be held in private, a Tribunal may direct that information about the whole or part of the proceedings (including information that might help to identify any person) before a Tribunal shall not be made public.

(9) For the purposes of paragraph (2)(i) ''party'' shall not include the Revenue.][1]

Amendments—[1] This regulation substituted by the General Commissioners and Special Commissioners (Jurisdiction and Procedure) (Amendment) Regulations, SI 2002/2976 regs 7, 10 with effect from 31 December 2002.

Failure of parties to attend hearing

14—(1) If a party fails to attend or to be represented at a hearing of which he has been duly notified, the Tribunal may—

(*a*) unless it is satisfied that there is good and sufficient reason for such absence, hear and determine the proceedings in the absence of the party or his representative, or
(*b*) postpone or adjourn the hearing.

(2) Before deciding to hear and determine any proceedings in the absence of a party or his representative, the Tribunal shall consider any representations in writing or otherwise submitted by or on behalf of that party in response to the notice of hearing and shall give any party present at the hearing an opportunity to be heard in regard to those representations.

Procedure and evidence at hearing

15—(1) At the beginning of the hearing of any proceedings the Tribunal shall, except where it considers it unnecessary to do so, explain the order of proceeding which it proposes to adopt.

(2) The Tribunal shall conduct the hearing in such manner as it considers most suitable to the clarification and determination of the issues before it and generally to the just handling of the proceedings and, so far as appears to it appropriate, shall seek to avoid formality in its procedure.

(3) The parties shall be heard in such order as the Tribunal shall determine and shall be entitled—

(*a*) to give evidence,
(*b*) to call witnesses,
(*c*) to question any witnesses including other parties who give evidence, and
(*d*) to address the Tribunal both on the evidence and generally on the subject matter of the proceedings.

(4) In assessing the truth and weight of any evidence, the Tribunal may take account of its nature and source, and the manner in which it is given.

(5) Evidence before the Tribunal may be given orally or, if the Tribunal so directs, by affidavit or a statement made or recorded in a document, but at any stage of the hearing the Tribunal may, on the application of any party or of its own motion, require the personal attendance as a witness of—

(*a*) the maker of an affidavit, or
(*b*) the maker of such a statement, or
(*c*) in the case of an oral statement recorded in a document, the person by whom the statement was so recorded.

(6) The Tribunal may receive evidence of any fact which appears to the Tribunal to be relevant to the subject matter of the proceedings notwithstanding that such evidence would be inadmissible in proceedings before a court of law in that part of the United Kingdom by reference to the law of which the proceedings before the Tribunal are to be determined, but, save in cases where claims for privilege are allowed (including, in proceedings in Scotland, claims for protection from disclosure by virtue of any rule of law relating to the confidentiality of communications), it shall not refuse to admit any evidence which would be admissible in such proceedings.

(7) The Tribunal may require any witness to give evidence on oath or affirmation and for that purpose there may be administered an oath or affirmation in due form.

Simon's Tax Cases—reg 15(6), *Walker v Smith* [1999] STC 605.

Decisions of Tribunal

16—(1) Any decision of a Tribunal shall be made by the votes of the majority of the General Commissioners comprising that Tribunal and, in the event of an equality of votes, the General Commissioner presiding at the hearing shall be entitled to a second or casting vote.

(2) The final determination may be given orally by a Tribunal at the end of the hearing or may be reserved and in either event shall be recorded in a document which shall be signed and dated by the Tribunal.

(3) The Clerk shall send to each party a notice setting out the final determination recorded under paragraph (2) above.

(4) Except where the final determination is given at the end of the hearing, it shall be treated as having been made on the date on which the notice is sent to the parties under paragraph (3) above.

(5) Every notice sent to the parties under paragraph (3) above[, other than a notice setting out a final determination made in accordance with regulation 19(2)(*b*),][1] shall be accompanied by a notification of the provisions [as appropriate][2] of—

(*a*) the Management Act [or][2],
[(*aa*) Part 4 of the Finance Act 2003 and any regulations made under that Part,][2]
(*b*) these Regulations, and
(*c*) rules of court,

relating to appeals from the General Commissioners and of the time within which, and the manner in which, such appeals shall be made.

Amendments—[1] In para (5), words inserted by the General Commissioners (Jurisdiction and Procedure) (Amendment) Regulations, SI 1999/3293 reg 3 with effect from 1 January 2000.
[2] In para (5), words inserted, and sub-para (*aa*) inserted, by the SDLT (Appeals) Regulations, SI 2004/1363 reg 23(8) with effect from 11 June 2004.

Review of Tribunal's final determination

17—(1) If, on the application of a party or of its own motion, a Tribunal is satisfied that—

(*a*) the final determination was wrongly made as a result of an administrative error on the part of the Clerk or any of the staff of the General Commissioners or a party, or
(*b*) a party, who was entitled to be heard at a hearing but failed to appear or to be represented, had good and sufficient reason for failing to appear or to be represented, or
(*c*) accounts or other information relevant to a party's case had been sent to the Clerk or to the appropriate inspector or other officer of the Board prior to the hearing of the proceedings but had not been received by the Tribunal until after the hearing,

the Tribunal may review and set aside or vary the final determination.

(2) An application for the purposes of paragraph (1) above shall be made to the Tribunal not later than fourteen days after the date on which notice setting out the final determination was sent to the parties under regulation 16(3), or by such later time as the Tribunal may allow, and shall be in writing stating the grounds in full.

(3) Where the Tribunal proposes to review of its own motion the final determination, it shall serve notice of that proposal on the parties not later than fourteen days after the date on which notice setting out the final determination was sent to the parties under regulation 16(3).

(4) The parties shall have an opportunity to be heard on a review, or in relation to any application or proposal for review, under this regulation and the review shall be determined by the Tribunal which decided the case or, where it is not practicable for it to be heard by that Tribunal, by another Tribunal; and if, having reviewed the final determination, the Tribunal sets aside that determination, it shall

substitute such determination as it thinks fit or order a rehearing before either the same or a differently constituted Tribunal.

(5) Regulation 16 shall apply to a decision by a Tribunal varying a final determination or substituting a new final determination, as it applies to a final determination.

Revenue Internal Guidance—Inspector's Manual IM4922 (no appeal against decision of Commissioners to reopen appeal).

PART IV

SPECIAL PROCEDURE

Proceedings relating to tax on chargeable gains

18—(1) Where the market value of an asset on a particular date or the apportionment of an amount or value is a material question in any proceedings relating to tax on chargeable gains, the Tribunal hearing the proceedings shall, if so required by any party, record in its final determination that market value or apportionment.

(2) The final determination on an appeal of the market value of an asset on a particular date or of the apportionment of any amount or value may be proved in any proceedings relating to tax on chargeable gains by a certificate stating the material particulars signed by—

(*a*) an inspector where the appeal was settled by agreement, or

(*b*) the Clerk where the General Commissioners determined the appeal, or

(*c*) the clerk or registrar of another tribunal where the material question was determined by that other tribunal in accordance with section [46D][1] or 47B of the Management Act,

and a document purporting to be such a certificate may be received in evidence in any such proceedings without further proof.

(3) In this regulation the expression "final determination on an appeal" shall be construed in accordance with regulation 11(2) of the Capital Gains Tax Regulations 1967, and the expression "material question in any proceedings" shall be construed in accordance with regulation 15(*a*) of those Regulations.

Amendments—[1] In sub-s (2)(*c*) figure substituted by the General Commissioners (Jurisdiction and Procedure) (Amendment) Regulations, SI 1999/3293 reg 4 with effect from 1 January 2000.

[References of questions to other tribunals

19—(1) A question in an appeal which is required to be determined in accordance with section 46B, 46C, 46D or 47B of the Management Act [or regulations 6 or 19 of the Stamp Duty Land Tax (Appeals) Regulations 2004][2] shall be referred to the appropriate tribunal by the Tribunal before whom the appeal is brought or, if the hearing of the appeal has not begun, by an inspector or other officer of the Board.

(2) Where any question in an appeal has been referred to another tribunal in accordance with paragraph (1) above, the Tribunal before whom the appeal is brought—

(*a*) shall make a final determination of the remaining question or questions in the appeal, and shall at the request of any party state a case thereon under regulation 22, without awaiting the determination of the question referred to the other tribunal, and

(*b*) shall make a final determination of the appeal (in accordance with regulation 16) once all the questions in the appeal have been finally determined.

(3) Where—

(*a*) a question in an appeal has been referred to the Special Commissioners in accordance with paragraph (1) above, and

(*b*) that question is the sole question in dispute in the appeal,

the proceedings shall be transferred to the Special Commissioners by the Tribunal before whom the appeal is brought or, if the hearing of the appeal has not yet begun, shall be brought before the Special Commissioners by an inspector or other officer of the Board.

(4) The reference in paragraph (2)(*b*) above to all questions in the appeal having been finally determined is a reference to a time when no further appeals in relation to those questions, whether by way of case stated under these Regulations or under any other enactment, are pending.][1]

Revenue Internal Guidance—Inspector's Manual IM4919a (appeals to the court on other matters may proceed before the determination of valuations by the Land Tribunal).

Amendments—[1] This regulation substituted by the General Commissioners (Jurisdiction and Procedure) (Amendment) Regulations, SI 1999/3293 reg 5 with effect from 1 January 2000.

[2] Words in para (1) inserted by the SDLT (Appeals) Regulations, SI 2004/1363 reg 23(9) with effect from 11 June 2004.

Case stated procedure

20—(1) Within thirty days after the final determination of any proceedings falling within paragraph (*a*) or (*b*) of the definition of "proceedings" in regulation 2 is made by a Tribunal[, other than a final determination to which regulation 19(2)(*b*) refers,][1] or, as the case may be, within thirty days after a decision varying such a final determination or substituting for it a new final determination is made by a Tribunal under regulation 17, any party to the proceedings, if dissatisfied with the determination or decision as being erroneous in point of law, may by notice served on the Clerk require the Tribunal to state and sign a case for the opinion of the High Court.

(2) A case stated pursuant to a requirement under paragraph (1) above shall set forth the facts and the final determination of the Tribunal.

(3) After a party has required a case to be stated under paragraph (1) above, the Tribunal may by notice served on him require him [within a period of time stated in the notice, not being less than twenty eight days,][2] to identify the question of law on which he requires the case to be stated.

(4) If a party fails to comply with a notice served under paragraph (3) above, or if the Tribunal is not satisfied that the question identified is a question of law, or until the fee specified in section 56(3) of the Management Act has been paid, the Tribunal may refuse to state a case.

(5) Where a final determination of a Tribunal is set aside or varied under regulation 17, a requirement for a case to be stated in respect of that determination shall cease to be valid.

Revenue Internal Guidance—Inspector's Manual IM4916b (where Commissioners make a decision in principle, a final decision is normally required once figures have been determined if the case is to go to court).

Amendments—[1] Words inserted by the General Commissioners (Jurisdiction and Procedure) (Amendment) Regulations, SI 1999/3293 reg 6(*a*) with effect from 1 January 2000.

[2] Words substituted by SI 1999/3293 reg 6(*b*) with effect from 1 January 2000.

Consideration of draft case

21—(1) Within fifty six days after the receipt of a notice served under regulation 20(1) requiring a case to be stated or, if a notice is served under regulation 20(3), within fifty six days after the day on which a question of law is identified to the satisfaction of the Tribunal, the Clerk shall send a draft of the case to the party who required the case to be stated and to the other party or parties.

(2) Within fifty six days after the draft case is sent to the parties under paragraph (1) above, any party may make representations on the draft to the Clerk in writing and shall at the same time send a copy of any representations so made to the other party or parties.

(3) Within twenty eight days after the latest date on which representations may be made under paragraph (2) above, any party may make further representations on the draft to the Clerk in writing in response to any representations made under paragraph (2) above, and shall at the same time send a copy of such further representations to the other party or parties.

(4) A failure by the Clerk to send a draft case within the time specified in paragraph (1) above, or a failure by a party to make representations within the time specified in paragraph (2) or (3) above, or to send a copy of representations under either of those paragraphs to the other party or parties, shall not affect the validity of the case after it has been stated and signed pursuant to regulation 22, or of any subsequent proceedings in relation to the case.

(5) Where a party fails to send a copy of any representations to another party in accordance with paragraph (2) or (3) above, that other party may apply to the Clerk for a copy of the representations.

Preparation and submission of final case

22—(1) Subject to paragraph (2) below, as soon as may be after the latest date on which representations may be made under regulation 21, the Tribunal whose decision is questioned, after taking into account any representations made under that regulation, shall state and sign the case.

(2) If a member of the Tribunal has died or ceased to be a General Commissioner, then the case shall be stated and signed by the continuing Commissioner or Commissioners or, if there is no continuing Commissioner, by the Clerk.

(3) After the case has been stated and signed the Clerk shall send it to the party who required it to be stated, and shall notify the other party or parties that the case has been sent to that party.

(4) The party requiring the case shall—

(*a*) transmit the case to the High Court within thirty days of receiving it, and

(*b*) at or before the time when he transmits the case to the High Court, send notice of the fact that the case has been stated on his application, together with a copy of the case, to the other party or parties.

Revenue Internal Guidance—Inspector's Manual IM5041 (date of receipt of case stated by the party concerned in para (4)(*a*) is the date on which it is delivered at the place given as his address at the time of requiring the case, unless in the meantime notice of a change of address has been given to the Clerk to the Commissioners).

Simon's Tax Cases—reg 22(1), *McKinney v Hagans Caravans (Manufacturing) Ltd* [1997] STC 1023.
reg 22(4)(*a*), *New World Medical Ltd v Cormack (Insp of Taxes)* [2002] STC 1245.

Case stated procedure—Scotland and Northern Ireland

23—(1) In relation to proceedings in Scotland, references in regulations 20(1) and 22(4) to the High Court shall be taken as references to the Court of Session as the Court of Exchequer.

(2) In relation to proceedings in Northern Ireland—

(*a*) the reference in regulation 20(1) to the High Court shall be taken as a reference to the Court of Appeal in Northern Ireland;

(*b*) the procedure relating to the transmission of a case stated under regulation 22 to the Court of Appeal in Northern Ireland shall be that for the time being in force in Northern Ireland as respects cases stated by a county court in exercise of its general jurisdiction, and regulation 22(4) shall not apply.

PART V
MISCELLANEOUS

Irregularities

24—(1) Any irregularity resulting from any failure to comply with any provision of these Regulations or with any direction given by a Tribunal before the Tribunal has reached its final determination shall not of itself render the proceedings void.

(2) Where any such irregularity comes to the attention of a Tribunal, the Tribunal before reaching its final determination may, and if it considers that any person may have been prejudiced by that irregularity shall, give such directions as it thinks just to cure or waive the irregularity.

(3) Clerical mistakes in any document recording a direction or a decision of a Tribunal, or errors arising in such a document from an accidental slip or omission, may be corrected by the General Commissioner presiding at the hearing or any other of the General Commissioners comprising the Tribunal, or by the Clerk if all the General Commissioners comprising the Tribunal have died or ceased to be General Commissioners, by certificate under his hand.

Notices

25 Every notice required by these Regulations shall be in writing unless a Tribunal authorises it to be given orally.

Service

26—(1) Any notice or other document (other than a summons under regulation 4) required or authorised by these Regulations to be sent or delivered to, or served on, any person shall be duly sent or delivered to, or served on, that person—

(*a*) if it is sent to him at his proper address by post; or
(*b*) if it is sent to him at that address by facsimile transmission or other similar means which produce a document containing a text of the communication, in which event the document shall be regarded as sent when it is received in a legible form; or
(*c*) if it is delivered to him or left at his proper address.

(2) Any such document may—

(*a*) in the case of a body corporate, be sent or delivered to, or left with, the secretary or clerk of that body;
(*b*) in the case of a foreign body corporate, be sent or delivered to, or left with, the person authorised to accept service of process on it;
(*c*) in the case of a partnership, be sent or delivered to, or left with, any partner;
(*d*) in the case of an unincorporated association other than a partnership, be sent or delivered to, or left with, any member of the governing body of the association.

(3) For the purposes of this regulation, a person's proper address is—

(*a*) in the case of the secretary or clerk of a body corporate registered in the United Kingdom, the address of the registered or principal office of that body corporate;
(*b*) in the case of the person authorised to accept service of process on a foreign body corporate, the address of the principal office or place of business of that body corporate in the United Kingdom;
(*c*) in the case of the General Commissioners for a division or their Clerk, the address of the Clerk;
(*d*) in the case of any other person, the usual or last known address of that person.

Substituted service

27 If any person to or on whom any notice or other document (other than a summons under regulation 4) is required to be sent, delivered or served for the purposes of these Regulations cannot be found or has died and has no known representative, or is out of the United Kingdom, or if for any other reason service on him cannot be readily effected, a Tribunal may dispense with the requirement that the notice or other document be sent or delivered to, or served on him or may make an order for substituted service on such other person or in such other form (whether by advertisement in a newspaper or otherwise) as the Tribunal may think fit.

1994/2318
Income Tax (Authorised Unit Trusts) (Interest Distributions) Regulations 1994

Made by the Commissioners of Inland Revenue under TA 1988 ss 468O(3), (4), 468P(8), (9)

Amendment—These regulations are revoked by the IT (Authorised Unit Trusts)(Interest Distributions) Regulations, SI 2003/1830 reg 11 with effect for interest distributions made after 15 October 2002.

1994/2656
Capital Gains Tax (Gilt-edged Securities) Order 1994

Made by the Treasury under TCGA 1992 Sch 9, para 1

Made . . . . . . *11 October 1994*

1 This Order may be cited as the Capital Gains Tax (Gilt-edged Securities) Order 1994.

2 The following securities are hereby specified for the purposes of Schedule 9 to the Taxation of Chargeable Gains Act 1992—

7% Treasury Convertible Stock 1997
$7\frac{1}{4}$% Treasury Stock 1998 "A"
$7\frac{1}{4}$% Treasury Stock 1998 "B"
6% Treasury Stock 1999
Floating Rate Treasury Stock 1999
7% Treasury Stock 2001
7% Treasury Stock 2001 "A"
8% Treasury Stock 2003 "A"
$6\frac{3}{4}$% Treasury Stock 2004
$6\frac{3}{4}$% Treasury Stock 2004 "A"
$7\frac{3}{4}$% Treasury Stock 2006
$8\frac{1}{2}$% Treasury Loan 2007 "C"
9% Treasury Loan 2008 "D"
$6\frac{1}{4}$% Treasury Stock 2010
9% Conversion Loan 2011 "C"
9% Conversion Loan 2011 "D"
8% Treasury Stock 2013.

1994/3226
Exchange Gains and Losses (Transitional Provisions) Regulations 1994

Made by the Treasury under FA 1993 ss 164(14), 165(4), (5), 167(1), (4)–(6), Sch 16

Made . . . . *15 December 1994*
Laid before the House of Commons . . . . *16 December 1994*
Coming into Force . . . . *23 March 1995*

Commentary—*Simon's Direct Tax Service* **D2.975–981.**
Revenue Internal Guidance—Company Taxation Manual COT13730–13800 (detailed explanation of the regulations).
Modification—See the Exchange Gains and Losses (Transitional Provisions and Savings) Regulations, SI 2002/1969 (SI 1994/3226, as modified by SI 2002/1969, to continue to have effect notwithstanding the repeal of FA 1993 ss 164(14), 165(4)–(6), 167(1), (4)–(6), Sch 16 by FA 2002 ss 79(1)(*b*), 141, Sch 40 Pt 3(10) with effect for accounting periods beginning after 30 September 2002).

ARRANGEMENT OF REGULATIONS

PART I
INTRODUCTORY PROVISIONS

PART II
MISCELLANEOUS TRANSITIONAL PROVISIONS

PART III
PRE-COMMENCEMENT GAINS AND LOSSES:
CASE I ASSETS AND LIABILITIES AND CAPITAL ASSETS

PART IV
PRE-COMMENCEMENT GAINS AND LOSSES:
DEBTS OF FIXED AMOUNTS

PART I
INTRODUCTORY PROVISIONS

Citation, commencement and interpretation

1—(1) These Regulations may be cited as the Exchange Gains and Losses (Transitional Provisions) Regulations 1994.

(2) These Regulations shall come into force on 23rd March 1995.

(3) In these Regulations, subject to any contrary intention—

(*a*) ''the 1992 Act'' means the Taxation of Chargeable Gains Act 1992;

(*b*) ''the 1993 Act'' means the Finance Act 1993;

[(*ba*) ''discounted debt'' has the same meaning as ''relevant discounted security'' as that term is defined for the purposes of Schedule 13 to the Finance Act 1996 by paragraphs 3 and 14(1) of that Schedule;][1]

(*c*) any reference to Chapter II is a reference to Chapter II of Part II of the 1993 Act;

(*d*) any reference to a particular section is a reference to that section of that Act;

(*e*) any reference to an exchange gain or loss is a reference to an exchange gain or loss of a trade or part of a trade or a non-trading exchange gain or loss;

(*f*) any reference to an exchange difference is a reference to any gain or loss which is attributable to fluctuations in currency exchange rates;

[(*g*) ''a regulation 6(3) asset'' means an existing asset the basic valuation of which was determined for the purposes of Chapter II in accordance with regulation 6(3) of these Regulations;][2]

(*h*) ''the regulation 2(2) provisions'' means the provisions specified in regulation 2(2) [; and

(*i*) ''the relevant accounting period'', in relation to a company, means the company's first accounting period to begin on or after 1st October 2002.][2]

(4) In determining for the purposes of these Regulations whether any gain or loss or other amount has or has not been taken into account for the purposes of corporation tax in computing a company's profits and gains (or the profits and gains of a trade) for an accounting period, or would have been or would not have been so taken into account if the company had been within the charge to corporation tax at the time the gain or loss accrued, there shall be disregarded, subject to any contrary intention, any insufficiency of profits or gains for that period.

(5) In computing the chargeable profits for an accounting period of a controlled foreign company as respects which—

(*a*) a direction under section 747 of the Income and Corporation Taxes Act 1988 has been given for the company's accounting period which includes the day preceding the day on which these Regulations come into force, or (*b*) it can reasonably be assumed that such a direction would have been given for that accounting period but for the fact that the company pursues, within the meaning of Part I of Schedule 25 to that Act, an acceptable distribution policy,

it shall be assumed for the purposes of these Regulations (if it would not otherwise be so assumed) that the company is resident in the United Kingdom for the period as respects which the computation is being made for any other period (whether earlier or later than the period referred to in paragraph (*a*) or (*b*) above), and any gain or loss or other amount which is, or has been, taken into account in computing the company's chargeable profits for any period (or which would have been so taken into account if such a computation had been made) shall be treated for those purposes as being, or having been, taken into account for the purposes of corporation tax in computing the company's profits and gains for that period.

Amendments—[1] Definition of "discounted debt" inserted by the Exchange Gains and Losses (Transitional Provisions) (Amendment) Regulations, SI 1996/1349 reg 3, with effect from 30 June 1996.
[2] Sub-para (3)(*g*) substituted, and sub-para (3)(*i*) inserted by the Exchange Gains and Losses (Transitional Provisions and Savings) Regulations, SI 2002/1969 regs 2, 3 with effect for accounting periods beginning after 30 September 2002.

Interaction with other Exchange Gains and Losses provisions

2—(1) Subject to any provision to the contrary, in any case where a calculation falls to be made in relation to an existing asset, liability or contract in accordance with any of these Regulations and at the same time or in relation to the same event a calculation also falls to be made in relation to that asset, liability or contract in accordance with any of the provisions specified in paragraph (2) below, then the calculation to be made in accordance with these Regulations shall be made first and shall have effect for the purposes of the calculation falling to be made in accordance with any of those provisions.

(2) The provisions referred to above are the following—

...[1]

The Exchange Gains and Losses (Alternative Method of Calculation of Gain or Loss) Regulations 1994;

...[1]

Amendments—[1] Words revoked by the Exchange Gains and Losses (Transitional Provisions and Savings) Regulations, SI 2002/1969 regs 2, 4 with effect for accounting periods beginning after 30 September 2002.

PART II

MISCELLANEOUS TRANSITIONAL PROVISIONS

Delayed application of Chapter II in relation to certain fluctuating debts

3 ...

Amendment—Regulations 3–6 revoked by the Exchange Gains and Losses (Transitional Provisions and Savings) Regulations, SI 2002/1969 regs 2, 5 with effect for accounting periods beginning after 30 September 2002.

Bad debts

4 ...

Amendment—Regulations 3–6 revoked by the Exchange Gains and Losses (Transitional Provisions and Savings) Regulations, SI 2002/1969 regs 2, 5 with effect for accounting periods beginning after 30 September 2002.

Exchange rate at translation times

5 ...

Amendment—Regulations 3–6 revoked by the Exchange Gains and Losses (Transitional Provisions and Savings) Regulations, SI 2002/1969 regs 2, 5 with effect for accounting periods beginning after 30 September 2002.

Basic valuation

6 ...

Amendment—Regulations 3–6 revoked by the Exchange Gains and Losses (Transitional Provisions and Savings) Regulations, SI 2002/1969 regs 2, 5 with effect for accounting periods beginning after 30 September 2002.

PART III

PRE-COMMENCEMENT GAINS AND LOSSES: CASE I ASSETS AND LIABILITIES AND CAPITAL ASSETS

Revenue Internal Guidance—Company Taxation Manual COT13796 (worked example).

Interpretation

7—(1) For the purposes of any computation required to be made for the purposes of regulation 10 or 11 below, an amount which is a gain shall be taken to be a positive figure and an amount which is a loss shall be taken to be a negative figure, but for the purposes of regulations 12 and 13 all amounts shall be taken to be positive.

(2) In this Part—

"attributed gain", in relation to any asset or liability, means a gain which is attributed to the asset or liability under regulation 8(3) or 9(2) below;

"attributed loss", in relation to any asset or liability, means a loss which is attributed to the asset or liability under regulation 8(3) or 9(2) below;

"current period" has the meaning given by regulation 10 below;

"the cumulative gain" has the meaning given by regulation 10 below;

"the cumulative loss" has the meaning given by regulation 10 below;

"the cumulative taxed gain" has the meaning given by regulation 11 below;

"the cumulative taxed loss" has the meaning given by regulation 11 below;

["the final accounting period", in relation to a company, means the company's accounting period preceding the relevant accounting period;][1]

...[1]

Amendment—[1] In sub-para (2), definition of "the final accounting period" inserted, and words revoked, by the Exchange Gains and Losses (Transitional Provisions and Savings) Regulations, SI 2002/1969 regs 2, 6 with effect for accounting periods beginning after 30 September 2002.

Attributed gains and losses: trade assets and liabilities

8—(1) Paragraph (3) below applies in relation to an existing asset held by a qualifying company—

(*a*) if a profit or loss would have accrued to the company if it had disposed of the asset immediately before the company's commencement day for a consideration equal to the asset's basic valuation; and

(*b*) that profit or loss would have been taken into account in computing for the purposes of corporation tax the profits and gains of a trade carried on by the company for the accounting period which includes the day immediately before the company's commencement day.

(2) Paragraph (3) below applies in relation to an existing liability owed by a qualifying company—

(*a*) if a profit or loss would have accrued to the company—

(i) in a case falling within section 153(2)(*a*), if the liability had been satisfied in full by the company immediately before the company's commencement day, or

(ii) in a case falling within section 153(2)(*c*) or (*d*), if the right to settlement or the share or shares in question (as the case may be) had been acquired by the company immediately before the company's commencement day for a consideration equal to the consideration for the company becoming subject to the liability, and

(*b*) that profit or loss (if it had accrued) would have been taken into account in computing for the purposes of corporation tax the profits and gains of a trade carried on by the company for the accounting period ending immediately before the company's commencement day.

(3) The amount of any such profit or loss as is mentioned in paragraph (1) or (2) above reduced in accordance with paragraph (4) below if applicable, shall be attributed to the asset or liability (as the case may be) and—

(*a*) in the case of a profit shall be attributed as a gain, and

(*b*) in the case of a loss shall be attributed as a loss.

(4) In any case where unrealised exchange differences which have accrued in respect of the asset or liability are taken into account for the purposes of corporation tax for the accounting period ending immediately before the company's commencement day or any earlier accounting period, the amount of the profit or loss referred to in paragraph (3) above shall be reduced by an amount equal to the amount of those differences.

(5) Section 159 applies for the purposes of this regulation as modified by regulation 6 [of these Regulations][1].

Amendment—[1] Words in sub-para (5) substituted by the Exchange Gains and Losses (Transitional Provisions and Savings) Regulations, SI 2002/1969 regs 2, 7 with effect for accounting periods beginning after 30 September 2002.

Attributed gains and losses: regulation 6(3) assets

9—(1) This regulation applies in relation to any regulation 6(3) asset held by a qualifying company a disposal of which by that company immediately before its commencement day at the asset's market value at that time would have given rise to a chargeable gain or allowable loss, but does not apply in any case where any such disposal of the asset by the company would fall within section 116(10)(*b*) of the 1992 Act.

(2) Subject to paragraph (3) below, an amount equal to any chargeable gain or allowable loss (as the case may be) which would have accrued to the company had it disposed of the asset as mentioned in paragraph (1) above shall be attributed to the asset and—

(*a*) if a chargeable gain would have accrued, it shall be attributed as a gain, and
(*b*) if an allowable loss would have accrued, it shall be attributed as a loss.

(3) In any case where—

(*a*) the asset was held by a company which at any time before its commencement day was not resident in the United Kingdom, and
(*b*) if the asset had been disposed of at that time and a gain had accrued to the company on that disposal, it would not have been included in the company's chargeable profits by virtue of section 10(3) of the 1992 Act,

then for the purposes of paragraph (1) above the company shall be deemed to have acquired the asset, at market value, on the first day on which any gain which would have accrued to the company if the asset had been disposed of on that day (assuming that the disposal gave rise to a gain and disregarding any allowable losses which might be available for deduction under section 8(1) of, or Schedule 7A to, the 1992 Act) would have been included in the company's chargeable profits for the purposes of corporation tax (whether because the company became resident or the asset became situated in the United Kingdom on that day or for any other reason).

(4) In any case where the company referred to in paragraph (1) above acquired the asset on a no gain/no loss disposal, then the reference in paragraph (3) above to a company includes the company from which it acquired the asset, and if that company also acquired the asset on such a disposal, to the company from which it acquired the asset, and so on for a series of such disposals.

(5) The disposal referred to in paragraph (1) above shall be taken not to be a no gain/no loss disposal, and for the purposes of this regulation a disposal is a no gain/no loss disposal if, by virtue of any enactment specified in section 35(3)(*d*) of the 1992 Act, neither a gain nor a loss accrues to the person making the disposal.

(6) In any case where section 176 of the 1992 Act would have applied in relation to the disposal referred to in paragraph (1) above if that disposal had actually taken place, that section shall apply for the calculation of any allowable loss for the purposes of that paragraph.

(7) Any expression used in this regulation which is not defined in Chapter II shall have the same meaning as in the 1992 Act.

The cumulative gain and the cumulative loss

10—(1) Subject to regulation 15, in the case of any existing asset or liability held or owed by a company as respects which an initial exchange gain or loss accrues to the company for an accrual period ("the current period"), there shall be calculated the aggregate amount of initial exchange gains and losses which have accrued as respects the asset or liability in question for all earlier accrual periods and for the current period, and that aggregate amount—

(*a*) if positive, shall be the cumulative gain for that asset or liability for the current period, and
(*b*) if negative, shall be the cumulative loss for that asset or liability for the current period,

but in cases where that aggregate amount is zero there shall be either a cumulative gain or a cumulative loss equal to zero for the period, according to whether there was a cumulative gain or a cumulative loss of any amount (including zero) for the accrual period immediately preceding the current period.

(2) For the purposes of paragraph (1) above, the amount of any initial exchange gain or loss shall be determined disregarding the following provisions of this Part and the regulation 2(2) provisions.

[(3) Where—

(*a*) the asset held or the liability owed by the company consists of a discounted debt, and
(*b*) the company did not cease on 31st March 1996 to be entitled to the asset or (as the case may be) subject to the liability,

it shall be regarded, for the purposes of paragraph (1) above the section 158 (translation times and accrual periods), as ceasing on that date to be entitled or subject, and references in this regulation and in regulations 11 and 12 to accrual periods (including references to an accrual period as the current period) shall, as respects that asset or liability, be construed accordingly.][1]

Amendments—[1] Para (3) added by the Exchange Gains and Losses (Transitional Provisions) (Amendment) Regulations, SI 1996/1349 reg 5, with effect from 30 June 1996.

The cumulative taxed gain and the cumulative taxed loss

11—(1) In the case of any asset or liability to which regulation 10 applies, there shall be calculated the aggregate amount of the initial exchange gains and losses which have accrued to the company as respects the asset or liability for accrual periods earlier than the current period, and—

(*a*) if that aggregate amount is positive it shall be the cumulative taxed gain for that asset or liability for the current period,
(*b*) if it is negative it shall be the cumulative taxed loss for that asset or liability for the current period, and
(*c*) if that aggregate amount is zero or, by virtue of regulation 12, there is no aggregate amount, there shall be taken to be a cumulative taxed loss equal to zero for the period.

(2) For the purposes of paragraph (1) above—

(*a*) the question whether any initial exchange gain or loss has accrued for any period other than the current period shall be determined in accordance with this Part but as if the regulation 2(2) provisions had never come into force; and
(*b*) there shall be disregarded any gain or loss which accrued for an accrual period other than the current period unless—

(i) it has been taken into account in computing the profits or gains of the company holding or owing the asset or liability for the purposes of corporation tax for accounting periods ending before the beginning of the current period, or
(ii) it would have been so taken into account if the regulation 2(2) provisions had never come into force; or
(iii) it is equal to zero.

Assets and liabilities as respects which there is an attributed gain or loss

12—(1) Subject to regulation 15, in relation to an asset or liability held or owed by a company as respects which—

(*a*) there is an attributed gain, E, or an attributed loss, F, and
(*b*) an initial exchange gain or loss ("the actual gain or loss") accrues to the company for the current period,

Table A or Table B below (as appropriate) shall apply and in any case falling within the first column of that Table, the actual gain or loss shall be deemed not to accrue but, subject to any conditions specified in the second column, the gain or loss specified in relation thereto in the third column shall be deemed to accrue and shall be an initial exchange gain or loss (as the case may be) accruing in the place of the actual gain or loss.

(2) For the purposes of paragraph (1)(*b*) above, the question whether any initial exchange gain or loss has accrued shall be determined disregarding this Part and the regulation 2(2) provisions.

TABLE A

IF THERE IS AN ATTRIBUTED GAIN E

Case for the current period	Condition	Deemed gain or loss
1 Cumulative loss B and no cumulative taxed gain or loss	B is greater than E	Loss equal to B–E
2 Cumulative loss B and a cumulative taxed loss C	(i) B is not greater than E and C is greater than zero	(i) Gain equal to C
	(ii) B is greater than E and C is less than (B–E)	(ii) Loss equal to (B–E)–C
	(iii) B is greater than E and C is greater than (B–E)	(iii) Gain equal to C–(B–E)
3 Cumulative loss B and a cumulative taxed gain D	(i) B is greater than E	(i) Loss equal to (B–E)+D
	(ii) B is not greater than E	(ii) Loss equal to D
4 Cumulative gain A and a cumulative taxed gain D	(i) A is greater than D	(i) Gain equal to A–D
	(ii) D is greater than A	(ii) Loss equal to D–A
5 Cumulative gain A and a cumulative taxed loss C		Gain equal to C+A

TABLE B

IF THERE IS AN ATTRIBUTED LOSS F

Case for the current period	Condition	Deemed gain or loss
1 Cumulative gain A and no cumulative taxed gain or loss	A is greater than F	Gain equal to A–F
2 Cumulative gain A and a cumulative taxed gain D	(i) A is not greater than F	(i) Loss equal to D
	(ii) A is greater than F and D is less than (A–F)	(ii) Gain equal to (A–F)–D
	(iii) A is greater than F and D is greater than (A–F)	(iii) Loss equal to D–(A–F)
3 Cumulative gain A and a cumulative taxed loss C	(i) A is greater than F	(i) Gain equal to (A–F)+C
	(ii) A is not greater than F and C is greater than zero	(ii) Gain equal to C
4 Cumulative loss B and a cumulative taxed loss C	(i) B is greater than C	(i) Loss equal to B–C
	(ii) C is greater than B	(ii) Gain equal to C–B
5 Cumulative loss B and a cumulative taxed gain D		Loss equal to B+D

Gains and losses on disposal of assets and liabilities

13—(1) Subject to regulations [14 and 14A][1], paragraph (2) or (3) below applies where—

(*a*) an accrual period ends as respects an existing asset or liability held or owed by a company which is the last accrual period as respects that asset or liability, and

(*b*) there is as respects the asset or liability an attributed gain or loss.

[(1A) For the purposes of paragraph (1)(*a*) above, the final accounting period shall be treated as the last accrual period as respects any asset or liability held or owed by the company immediately after the end of the final accounting period.][1]

(2) If there is an attributed gain, E, as respects the asset or liability, then—

(*a*) if there is a cumulative gain, A, as respects the asset or liability for the last period, an amount equal to E shall be deemed to be a relevant gain, accruing to the company as respects that asset or liability immediately [after the end of the final accounting period][1];

(*b*) if there is a cumulative loss, B, as respects the asset or liability for the last period, and E exceeds B, an amount equal to the excess shall be deemed to be a relevant gain, accruing to the company as respects that asset or liability immediately [after the end of the final accounting period][1]; and

(*c*) if there is neither a cumulative loss nor a cumulative gain as respects the asset or liability for the last period, an amount equal to E shall be deemed to be a relevant gain, accruing to the company as respects that asset or liability immediately [after the end of the final accounting period][1].

(3) If there is an attributed loss, F, as respects the asset or liability, then—

(*a*) if there is a cumulative loss, B, as respects the asset or liability for the last period, an amount equal to F shall be deemed to be a relevant loss, accruing to the company as respects that asset or liability immediately [after the end of the final accounting period][1];

(*b*) if there is a cumulative gain, A, as respects the asset or liability for the last period, and F exceeds A, an amount equal to the excess shall be deemed to be a relevant loss, accruing to the company as respects that asset or liability immediately [after the end of the final accounting period][1]; and

(*c*) if there is neither a cumulative loss nor a cumulative gain as respects the asset or liability for the last period, an amount equal to F shall be deemed to be a relevant loss, accruing to the company as respects that asset or liability immediately [after the end of the final accounting period][1].

[(4) In paragraphs (2) and (3) above, a relevant gain or loss in relation to a regulation 6(3) asset is a chargeable gain or an allowable loss.][1]

[(4A) In relation to any asset other than a regulation 6(3) asset or any liability, an amount equal to the amount of any relevant gain or loss that is deemed to accrue to the company under paragraph (2) or (3) above shall be treated for the purposes of Chapter 2 of Part 4 of the Finance Act 1996 (according to whether it is a relevant gain or loss)—

(*a*) as a credit in respect of a loan relationship of the company, or

(*b*) as a debit in respect of a loan relationship of the company,

which falls to be brought into account under section 82(2) of that Act.][1]

(5)–(8) ...[1]

Amendments—[1] Words in sub-paras (1), (2), (3) substituted, sub-para (1A) inserted, sub-paras (4), (4A) substituted for para (4), and sub-paras (5)–(8) revoked, by the Exchange Gains and Losses (Transitional Provisions and Savings) Regulations, SI 2002/1969 regs 2, 8 with effect for accounting periods beginning after 30 September 2002.

[Elections to defer bringing into account relevant gains and losses deemed to accrue immediately after the end of the final accounting period

14—(1) In any case where, apart from this regulation, relevant gains or losses would accrue to a company immediately after the end of the final accounting period by virtue of regulation 13, the company may elect, by notice to the inspector within two years of the end of the final accounting period, that this regulation shall apply as respects—

(*a*) subject to paragraph (3) below, all relevant gains or losses to which paragraph (4) of regulation 13 would apply;

(*b*) all relevant gains or losses to which paragraph (4A) of that regulation would apply; or

(*c*) both.

An election under this paragraph shall be irrevocable.

(2) Where an election is made under paragraph (1) above, every gain or loss to which this regulation applies shall be treated as accruing only when the asset or liability to which the gain or loss relates ceases to be held or owed by the company.

(3) No election may be made under paragraph (1) above as respects relevant gains or losses to which regulation 13(4) would apply if an election under regulation 14A is made as regards such losses.][1]

Amendments—[1] Regulations 14, 14A and 14B substituted for regulation 14 as originally enacted by the Exchange Gains and Losses (Transitional Provisions and Savings) Regulations, SI 2002/1969 regs 2, 9 with effect for accounting periods beginning after 30 September 2002.

[Elections to treat losses deemed to accrue immediately after the end of the final accounting period as debits in respect of loan relationships

14A—(1) In any case where—

(*a*) apart from this regulation, relevant losses would accrue to a company as respects regulation 6(3) assets immediately after the end of the final accounting period by virtue of regulation 13; and

(*b*) if relevant gains would accrue as respects such assets at that time by virtue of that regulation, such losses would exceed them,

the company may elect, by notice to the inspector within two years of the end of the final accounting period, that this regulation shall apply as respects such losses or, in a case where sub-paragraph (*b*) applies, such losses to the extent that they exceed the relevant gains.

An election under this paragraph shall be irrevocable.

(2) Where an election is made under paragraph (1) above, an amount equal to the amount of the losses to which this regulation applies shall be treated for the purposes of Chapter 2 of Part 4 of the Finance Act 1996 as a debit in respect of a loan relationship of the company for the new accounting period and not falling to be brought into account under section 82(2) of that Act.][1]

Amendments—[1] Regulations 14, 14A and 14B substituted for regulation 14 as originally enacted by the Exchange Gains and Losses (Transitional Provisions and Savings) Regulations, SI 2002/1969 regs 2, 9 with effect for accounting periods beginning after 30 September 2002.

[Treatment of losses available to be carried forward at the end of the final accounting period as a result of an election made under regulation 14(5) or 16(1)

14B—(1) This regulation apples where, as a result of an election made under regulation 14(5) or 16(1) of these Regulations, an amount of available losses ("the relevant amount") was available at the end of the final accounting period to be carried forward and, apart from this regulation, to be set against a company's exchange gains.

(2) Where this regulation applies an amount equal to the relevant amount shall be treated for the purposes of Chapter 2 of Part 4 of the Finance Act 1996 as a debit in respect of a loan relationship of the company for the new accounting period and not falling to be brought into account under section 82(2) of that Act.][1]

Amendments—[1] Regulations 14, 14A and 14B substituted for regulation 14 as originally enacted by the Exchange Gains and Losses (Transitional Provisions and Savings) Regulations, SI 2002/1969 regs 2, 9 with effect for accounting periods beginning after 30 September 2002.

Elections to treat pre-commencement day gains and losses as accruing after commencement day over 6 year period

15 ...

Amendment—Regulations 15, 16 revoked by the Exchange Gains and Losses (Transitional Provisions and Savings) Regulations, SI 2002/1969 regs 2, 10 with effect for accounting periods beginning after 30 September 2002.

Set off of certain pre-commencement losses against exchange gains

16 ...

Amendment—[1] Regulations 15, 16 revoked by the Exchange Gains and Losses (Transitional Provisions and Savings) Regulations, SI 2002/1969 regs 2, 10 with effect for accounting periods beginning after 30 September 2002.

PART IV
PRE-COMMENCEMENT GAINS AND LOSSES: DEBTS OF FIXED AMOUNTS

...

Amendment—Pt IV (regs 17–22) revoked by the Exchange Gains and Losses (Transitional Provisions and Savings) Regulations, SI 2002/1969 regs 2, 11 with effect for accounting periods beginning after 30 September 2002.

1994/3227
Exchange Gains and Losses (Alternative Method of Calculation of Gain or Loss) Regulations 1994

Made by the Treasury under FA 1993 ss 164(14), 167(1), (4)–(6), Sch 15

Made . . . . *15 December 1994*
Laid before the House of Commons . . . . *16 December 1994*
Coming into Force . . . . *23 March 1995*

Commentary—*Simon's Direct Tax Service* **D2.930–937.**
Revenue Internal Guidance—Company Taxation Manual COT13660–13723 (detailed explanation of the regulations).
Modification—See the Exchange Gains and Losses (Transitional Provisions and Savings) Regulations, SI 2002/1969 (SI 1994/3227, as modified by SI 2002/1969, to continue to have effect notwithstanding the repeal of FA 1993 ss 164(14), 167(1), (4)–(6), Sch 15 by FA 2002 ss 79, 141, Sch 40 Pt 3(10) with effect for accounting periods beginning after 30 September 2002).

ARRANGEMENT OF REGULATIONS

GENERAL

Citation, commencement and interpretation

1—(1) These Regulations may be cited as the Exchange Gains and Losses (Alternative Method of Calculation of Gain or Loss) Regulations 1994.

(2) These Regulations shall come into force on 23rd March 1995.

(3) In these Regulations "the 1993 Act" means the Finance Act 1993.

ASSETS ETC HELD IN EXEMPT CIRCUMSTANCES

Reduction in exchange gains and losses

2 ...

Amendment—[1] Regulations 2, 3 revoked by the Exchange Gains and Losses (Transitional Provisions and Savings) Regulations, SI 2002/1969 regs 12, 13 with effect for accounting periods beginning after 30 September 2002.

UNREMITTABLE INCOME

Reduction in exchange gains and losses

3 ...

Amendment—Regulations 2, 3 revoked by the Exchange Gains and Losses (Transitional Provisions and Savings) Regulations, SI 2002/1969 regs 12, 13 with effect for accounting periods beginning after 30 September 2002.

MATCHING

Interpretation

4—(1) This regulation has effect for the interpretation of regulations 5 to 11.

(2) In those regulations—

"the Taxes Act" means the Income and Corporation Taxes Act 1988;

"the 1992 Act" means the Taxation of Chargeable Gains Act 1992;

"accounts", in relation to a company, means the accounts of the company prepared in accordance with normal accountancy practice being either—

(i) the annual accounts of the company prepared in accordance with Part VII of the Companies Act 1985 or

(ii) if the company is not required to prepare such accounts, the accounts which it is required to keep under the law of its home State or, if it is not so required to keep accounts, such of its accounts as most closely correspond to accounts which it would have been required to prepare if the provisions of that Part applied to the company;

"a local currency election" means an election under the Local Currency Elections Regulations 1994;

"chargeable gain" has the same meaning as it has for the purposes of the 1992 Act;

"a liability" means—

(*a*) a liability falling within section 153(2)(*a*) of the 1993 Act, or

(*b*) in relation to a currency contract held by a company, the duty of the company under that contract to pay in exchange for one currency an amount of a second currency;

["qualifying asset" shall be construed in accordance with subsection (1) of section 153 of the 1993 Act, read with subsections (3) and (4) of that section][1]

and in relation to a currency contract references to initial exchange gains or losses shall be construed as references to initial exchange gains or losses accruing as regards the second currency.

(3) For the purposes of this regulation and regulations 5 to 11, any reference to an asset being matched in part only shall include a reference to any asset matched in accordance with an election under regulation 10(2)(*c*).

(4) A liability is matched by an asset at any time only to the extent that the value of the liability at that time is matched by the value of the asset at that time and, subject to that, if the election concerned is made under regulation 10(2)(*c*) so that the asset is matched in part only, the liability shall be taken to be matched only to a corresponding extent.

(5) The value of a company's asset or liability at any time shall be taken to be the value attributed to the asset or liability as at that time by the company for the purposes of its accounts for the accounting period which includes that time (expressed in the currency in which those accounts are prepared).

(6) Any reference to the disposal of an asset and to the time of the disposal of an asset shall be construed as a reference to any event which is a disposal for the purposes of the 1992 Act and the time at which the disposal occurs for the purposes of that Act, and for the purposes of the foregoing, any reference to a disposal includes a part disposal.

Revenue Internal Guidance—Company Taxation Manual COT13672 (example on value of matched asset).

Modifications—Para (2) modified by the Exchange Gains and Losses (Miscellaneous Modifications) Regulations, SI 2000/3315 regs 6, 8 with effect for any accounting period of a company beginning after 31 December 1999 for which FA 2000 ss 105, 106 have effect. Para (2) as modified reads as follows—

(2) In those regulations—

''the Taxes Act'' means the Income and Corporation Taxes Act 1988;''the 1992 Act'' means the Taxation of Chargeable Gains Act 1992;''accounts'', in relation to a company, means the accounts of the company prepared in accordance with normal accountancy practice being either—(i) the annual accounts of the company prepared in accordance with Part VII of the Companies Act 1985 or

(ii) if the company is not required to prepare such accounts, the accounts which it is required to keep under the law of its home State or, if it is not so required to keep accounts, such of its accounts as most closely correspond to accounts which it would have been required to prepare if the provisions of that Part applied to the company;

[''branch'' shall be construed in accordance with section 93(7) of the 1993 Act;]...''chargeable gain'' has the same meaning as it has for the purposes of the 1992 Act; ''a liability'' means—(*a*) a liability falling within section 153(2)(*a*) of the 1993 Act, or

(*b*) in relation to a currency contract held by a company, the duty of the company under that contract to pay in exchange for one currency an amount of a second currency;

''qualifying asset'' shall be construed in accordance with subsection (1) of section 153 of the 1993 Act, read with subsections (3) and (4) of that section[''the relevant foreign currency'' has the meaning given by section 93(7) of the 1993 Act.]and in relation to a currency contract references to initial exchange gains or losses shall be construed as references to initial exchange gains or losses accruing as regards the second currency.''**Amendments**—[1] Definition of ''qualifying asset'' added by the Exchange Gains and Losses (Alternative Method of Calculation of Gain or Loss) (Amendment) Regulations, SI 1996/1347 regs 2, 3, with effect from 30 June 1996.

Gains and losses accruing as regards matched liabilities to be found by the alternative method of calculation

5—(1) This regulation applies in any case where—

(*a*) a liability is owed by a company, and

(*b*) the liability is eligible to be matched with an asset on a day which falls within an accrual period for that liability, and

(*c*) an election made under regulation 10 is in effect for that day matching the liability (wholly or in part) with an eligible asset held by the company;

and in this regulation ''the current period'' means that accrual period.

(2) In any case where this regulation applies, then, subject to [paragraphs (3) and (3A)][1] below—

(*a*) the amount of the initial exchange gain or initial exchange loss which, apart from this regulation, would accrue to the company for the current period as respects the liability shall be found in accordance with the alternative method of calculation, and

(*b*) the accrued amount for each day in that period during which the liability and asset are matched shall—

(i) if the whole of the liability is matched, be reduced to nil, or

(ii) if only a proportion of the liability is matched, be reduced by a corresponding proportion.

(3) If in any case where this regulation applies—

(*a*) at any time during the current period there is a major change in the extent to which the liability is matched, and

(*b*) there is a significant change in the rate of exchange relevant to the computation of the accrued amounts during the current period, and

(*c*) that time is not (disregarding this regulation) a translation time as respects the liability,

then[, subject to paragraph (3A) below,] the initial exchange gain or loss as respects the liability for the current period shall be calculated, in accordance with paragraph (2) above, as if that time were a translation time (but not so as to create more than one accrual period) so that separate calculations are made for different parts of the period.

[(3A) If in a case where this regulation applies—

(*a*) only a proportion of a liability owed by the company is matched with an asset, not being an asset that is a ship or an aircraft, or

(*b*) another liability owed by the company is eligible to be matched with that asset at the time the election is made, but is not matched, and

(*c*) an exchange loss in relation to—

(i) the whole of the liability referred to in sub-paragraph (*a*) or (*b*), or

(ii) a proportion of that liability, being in the case of the liability referred to in sub-paragraph (*a*), a greater proportion than the proportion matched,

is shown in the company's accounts for the period which is or includes the current period, in the reserves,

the amount of the initial exchange loss as respects that liability for the current period, calculated in accordance with this regulation, shall be reduced by the amount by which the exchange loss shown in the reserves and relating to that liability exceeds the exchange loss relating to the proportion (if any) of the liability that was matched.][1]

(4) A liability (not being a duty under a currency contract) is eligible to be matched with an asset if—

(*a*) the liability does not represent either—

(i) a duty to settle under a debt in respect of goods or services supplied to the company in the ordinary course of its trade, or

(ii) accrued interest, and

(*b*) the nominal currency of the liability is such that borrowing in that currency could reasonably be expected to eliminate or substantially reduce the economic risk of holding the asset which is attributable to fluctuations in exchange rates.

Where the asset is matched in part only, references in this paragraph to the asset are to the part matched.

(5) In the case of a liability which is a duty under a currency contract, the liability is eligible to be matched with an asset if the second currency to which it relates is such that the company could by entering into that contract reasonably expect to eliminate or substantially reduce the economic risk of holding the asset which is attributable to fluctuations in exchange rates.

Where the asset is matched in part only, references in this paragraph to the asset are to the part matched.

(6) An asset held by a company is an eligible asset at any time if at that time—

(*a*) it is shares in a company which is not resident in the United Kingdom, but this sub-paragraph only applies if at the time the election is made the company is an associated company of the company making the election; or

(*b*) it is shares in a company which—

(i) is resident in the United Kingdom, and

(ii) has made a local currency election and is entitled, by virtue of that election, to have the basic profits and losses of a trade, or part of a trade, which it carries on in the United Kingdom computed in a currency other than sterling, and

(iii) is a 90 per cent subsidiary (within the meaning of paragraph (7) below) of the company making the election; or

(*c*) it is a debt on a security which under the terms of issue can be converted into or exchanged for shares falling within sub-paragraph (*a*) or (*b*) above [and which is not a qualifying asset]; or

(*d*) it is the company's net investment in a branch outside the United Kingdom through which the company carries on a trade or part of a trade and the company has made a local currency election and is entitled, by virtue of that election, to have the basic profits and losses of that trade or that part computed in a currency other than sterling; or

(*e*) it is a ship or an aircraft.

(7) For the purposes of paragraph (6) above—

(*a*) "shares" includes stock but does not include any asset which is a qualifying asset, ...[1]

[(*aa*) all shares in the same company shall constitute a single asset,

(*ab*) all debts on a security issued by the same company shall constitute a single asset, and][1]

(*b*) a company is a 90 per cent subsidiary of another company if it is a 90 per cent subsidiary of that other within the meaning of section 838 of the Taxes Act or would be if "directly or indirectly" were substituted for "directly" in subsection (1)(*c*) of that section.

(8) An asset held by a company is also an eligible asset at any time (whether or not it also falls within any provision of paragraph (6)) if at that time—

(*a*) a gain accruing on the disposal of the asset by a person resident in the United Kingdom would be a chargeable gain, and

(*b*) the asset—

(i) is not a qualifying asset, and

(ii) is held by a branch of the company outside the United Kingdom through which the company carries on a trade or part of a trade and the company is not entitled to have the basic profits and losses of that trade or that part computed in a currency other than sterling by virtue of a local currency election.

(9) For the purposes of paragraphs (6) and (8) above—

(*a*) a company is an associated company of another if that other directly controls 20 per cent or more of the voting power in the company;

(*b*) the net investment of a company in a branch is the value of the assets of that branch less the liabilities of the branch and any other liabilities owed by the company for the purposes of the trade or part trade carried on through the branch.

Revenue Interpretation RI 153—Sets out how the Revenue will apply para (3A).

Revenue Internal Guidance—Company Taxation Manual COT13674 (worked example).

COT13700 (background to sub-para (3A)).

COT13722 (worked example on "economic risk").

Modifications—This regulation modified by the Exchange Gains and Losses (Miscellaneous Modifications) Regulations, SI 2000/3315 regs 6, 8 with effect for any accounting period of a company beginning after 31 December 1999 for which FA 2000 ss 105, 106 have effect. Paras (6), (6A), (8), (9) as modified read as follows—

"(6) An asset held by a company [which prepares its accounts as a whole in sterling] is an eligible asset at any time if at that time—

(*a*) it is shares in a company which is not resident in the United Kingdom, but this sub-paragraph only applies if at the time the election is made the company is an associated company of the company making the election; or

(*b*) it is shares in a company which—

(i) is resident in the United Kingdom, and

[(ii) is a company to which section 93 of the 1993 Act applies by virtue of its accounts as a whole being prepared in a currency other than sterling in accordance with normal accounting practice, and]

(iii) is a 90 per cent subsidiary (within the meaning of paragraph (7) below) of the company making the election; or (*c*) it is a debt on a security which under the terms of issue can be converted into or exchanged for shares falling within sub-paragraph (*a*) or (*b*) above [and which is not a qualifying asset]; or

(*d*) it is the company's net investment [in a branch through which the company carries on a business or part of a business and, by virtue of section 93 of the 1993 Act, the profits and losses of that business or that part are to be computed and expressed in a currency other than sterling]; or

(*e*) it is a ship or an aircraft.

(6A) An asset held by a company which prepares its accounts as a whole in a currency other than sterling is an eligible asset at any time if at that time—

(*a*) it is shares which—

(i) are denominated in a currency other than the relevant foreign currency for the company making the election, and

(ii) are in a company that is not resident in the United Kingdom and is, at the time the election is made, an associated company of the company making the election; or

(*b*) it is shares in a company which—

(i) is resident in the United Kingdom, and

(ii) prepares its accounts as a whole either in sterling or in a currency other than sterling which is not the relevant foreign currency for the company making the election, and

(iii) is a 90 per cent. subsidiary (within the meaning of paragraph (7) below) of the company making the election; or

(*c*) it is a debt on a security which under the terms of issue can be converted into or exchanged for shares falling within sub-paragraph (*a*) or (*b*) above and which is not a qualifying asset; or

(*d*) it is the company's net investment [in a branch through which the company carries on a business or part of a business and, by virtue of section 93 of the 1993 Act, the profits and losses of that business or that part are to be computed and expressed in a currency other than the relevant foreign currency for the company; or

(*e*) it is a ship or an aircraft.''.

''(8) An asset held by a company is also an eligible asset at any time (whether or not it also falls within any provision of paragraph (6)) if at that time—

(*a*) a gain accruing on the disposal of the asset by a person resident in the United Kingdom would be a chargeable gain, and

[(*b*) the asset is not a qualifying asset, and

(*c*) the asset is held by a branch of the company outside the United Kingdom through which the company carries on a business or part of a business, and

(i) where the company prepares its accounts as a whole in sterling, the profits and losses of that business or that part are not to be computed and expressed in a currency other than sterling by virtue of section 93 of the 1993 Act, or

(ii) where the company prepares its accounts as a whole in a currency other than sterling, the profits and losses of that business or that part are not to be computed and expressed in a currency other than the relevant foreign currency for the company by virtue of that section.]

(9) For the purposes of paragraphs [(6), (6A) and (8)] above—

(*a*) a company is an associated company of another if that other directly controls 20 per cent or more of the voting power in the company;

(*b*) the net investment of a company in a branch is the value of the assets of that branch less the liabilities of the branch and any other liabilities owed by the company for the purposes of the [business] or part [business] carried on through the branch.''.

Amendments—[1] Words in para (2) substituted, words in paras (3), (6)(*c*), and paras (3A), (7)(*aa*), (*ab*), inserted, and at the end of para (7)(*a*) word revoked, by the Exchange Gains and Losses (Alternative Method of Calculation of Gain or Loss) (Amendment) Regulations, SI 1996/1347 regs 2, 4, with effect as respects accrual periods ending on or after 30 June 1996.

Controlled foreign companies

6—(1) Where an accounting period of a controlled foreign company is or includes an accrual period, then, for the purposes of computing in accordance with Schedule 24 to the Taxes Act the company's chargeable profits for that accounting period, an election for matching may be made by a company resident in the United Kingdom which has, or jointly by companies resident in the United Kingdom which together have, a majority interest in the foreign company, notwithstanding that in such a case the company owing any liability or acquiring or holding any asset will not be the company making the election.

(2) Paragraph 4(3) and (4) of that Schedule shall apply for the purposes of determining whether one or more companies has a majority interest in another company and, for that purpose, the relevant accounting period is the accounting period referred to in paragraph (1) above.

Deemed gains and losses on disposal of matched assets

7—(1) [Paragraphs (3) to (5) below apply in any case where a disposal of an asset is deemed by virtue of paragraph (1A) below to have been made by a company immediately before the first day of its first accounting period to begin on or after 1st October 2002][1] (''the disposal time'') and at any time before the disposal time it was (to any extent) a matched asset for the purposes of an election for matching made by the company (''the relevant election'').

[(1A) For the purposes of paragraph (1) above, any asset held by the company at the beginning of the first day of its first accounting period to begin on or after 1st October 2002 shall be deemed to have been disposed of by the company immediately before that first day.][1]

(2) ...[1]

(3) There shall be found as respects the liability or liabilities matched with the asset for each accrual period for which the relevant election has had effect—

(*a*) the amount of the initial exchange gain (if any) calculated in accordance with the preceding regulations, and

(*b*) the amount of the initial exchange gain which would have accrued if the relevant election had not had effect;

and the excess of the amount found under sub-paragraph (*b*) over that found under sub-paragraph (*a*), or if no amount is found under sub-paragraph (*a*) the amount found under sub-paragraph (*b*), for each period is referred to below as the amount by which the initial exchange gain for the period has been reduced.

(4) There shall be found as respects the liability or liabilities matched with the asset for each accrual period for which the relevant election has had effect—

(*a*) the amount of the initial exchange loss (if any) calculated in accordance with the preceding regulations, and

(*b*) the amount of the initial exchange loss which would have accrued if the relevant election had not had effect;

and the excess of the amount found under sub-paragraph (*b*) over that found under sub-paragraph (*a*), or if no amount is found under sub-paragraph (*a*) the amount found under sub-paragraph (*b*), for each period is referred to below as the amount by which the initial exchange loss for the period has been reduced.

(5) There shall be found—

(*a*) the aggregate of the amounts by which the initial exchange gains accruing as respects the liability for accrual periods for which the relevant election has effect have been reduced, and

(*b*) the aggregate of the amounts by which the initial exchange losses accruing as respects the liability for accrual periods for which the relevant election has effect have been reduced.

(6)–(8) ...[1]

Amendments—[1] Words in para (1) substituted, para (1A) inserted, paras (2), (6)–(8) revoked, by the Exchange Gains and Losses (Transitional Provisions and Savings) Regulations, SI 2002/1969 regs 12, 14 with effect for accounting periods beginning after 30 September 2002.

Deferral etc of deemed gains and losses in certain cases

8 ...

Amendment—Regulations 8, 9 revoked by the Exchange Gains and Losses (Transitional Provisions and Savings) Regulations, SI 2002/1969 regs 12, 15 with effect for accounting periods beginning after 30 September 2002.

Transactions to which section 116 or 127 of the 1992 Act applies

9 ...

Amendment—Regulations 8, 9 revoked by the Exchange Gains and Losses (Transitional Provisions and Savings) Regulations, SI 2002/1969 regs 12, 15 with effect for accounting periods beginning after 30 September 2002.

Elections for matching

10—(1) Subject to the provisions of these Regulations, an election under this regulation—

(*a*) may be made by notice given to the inspector by the company which owes the liability to be matched by the election,

(*b*) shall have effect as from the day on which it is made, and

(*c*) shall be irrevocable.

(2) An election for matching must identify—

(*a*) ...;[1]

(*b*) the asset to be matched;

(*c*) if the liability [to be matched by the election][1] is not being matched with the whole of the asset either—

(i) a fixed percentage of the asset which is to be available for matching; or

(ii) the value of the whole asset as at the time the election is made and a specific amount which is to be available for matching; or

(iii) a proportion or part of the asset which is to be available for matching where the value of the proportion or part is to be determined by reference to a formula or other method of calculation specified in the election and may vary from time to time in accordance with that formula or other method of calculation;

(*d*) ...;[1]

(*e*) the provision of these Regulations by virtue of which the asset is an eligible asset.

(3) An election under paragraph (2)(*c*)(i) or (ii) above may be varied by a subsequent election under this regulation so as to increase the percentage or amount which is specified in the election.

(4) An election to match a liability with an asset falling within regulation 5(6)(*a*), (*b*), (*c*) or (*d*) or 5(8), shall not have effect for any accrual period for which an initial exchange gain accrues as respects the liability unless—

(*a*) any exchange difference arising in relation to the asset, and

(*b*) at least part of any exchange difference arising in relation to the liability,

are shown, in the company's accounts for the period which is or includes the accrual period in which those differences arise, in the reserves, and if only part of the exchange differences relating to the liability are shown in the reserves, the election shall have effect for that period only to that part.

Where the liability or asset (or both) are matched in part only, references in this paragraph to the liability or asset are to the part matched.

(5) An election shall not cease to have effect at any time by reason only that the liability [matched by][1] the election ceased at that time to match the asset to which the election refers either at all or to the same extent to which it matched it at the time the election was made (either by reason of its ceasing to be owed by the company or because it is reduced or its value changes), but where [in any such case at any time after the election is made or, in the case of an election to which regulation 11(2) applies, has effect, the company is subject to another eligible liability][1] which might have been [matched by][1] the election if the election had been made at that time, the election shall continue to have effect in relation to that other liability.

This paragraph shall apply with the necessary modifications in relation to any such other liability as it applies in relation to the liability originally [matched by][1] the election.

(6) In any case where the asset to which the election refers was original shares as defined by section 126 of the 1992 Act and by reason of a reorganisation (as so defined) the asset ceased at any time to match the liability [matched by][1] the election, then if the whole or any part of the new holding (as so defined) might have been specified in the election if the election had been made at the time of the reorganisation, the election shall not cease to have effect but shall continue to have effect in relation to the new holding or part as the case may be.

(7) Any question as to which liability is matched with which asset shall be determined on a just and reasonable basis.

Revenue Internal Guidance—Company Taxation Manual COT13694 (worked example on sub-para (2)(*c*)).

Modifications—This regulation modified by the Exchange Gains and Losses (Miscellaneous Modifications) Regulations, SI 2000/3315 regs 6, 8 with effect for any accounting period of a company beginning after 31 December 1999 for which FA 2000 ss 105, 106 have effect. Para (4) as modified reads as follows—

"(4) An election to match a liability with an asset falling within regulation 5(6)(*a*), (*b*), (*c*) or (*d*) [or 5(6A)(*a*), (*b*), (*c*) or (*d*)] or 5(8), shall not have effect for any accrual period for which an initial exchange gain accrues as respects the liability unless—

(*a*) any exchange difference arising in relation to the asset, and

(*b*) at least part of any exchange difference arising in relation to the liability,

are shown, in the company's accounts for the period which is or includes the accrual period in which those differences arise, in the reserves, and if only part of the exchange differences relating to the liability are shown in the reserves, the election shall have effect for that period only to that part.".

Amendments—[1] Para (2)(*a*), (*d*) revoked, words in para (2)(*c*) inserted and words in paras (5), (6) substituted, by the Exchange Gains and Losses (Alternative Method of Calculation of Gain or Loss) (Amendment) Regulations, SI 1996/1347 regs 2, 5, with effect from 30 June 1996.

Effectiveness of elections

11—(1) An election which does not comply with regulation 10(2) shall be of no effect.

[(1A) Notwithstanding the following provisions of this regulation, an election made under regulation 10 or this regulation—

(*a*) shall have effect only in relation to accounting periods beginning before 1st October 2002, and

(*b*) an election which specifies a day as the day from which the election is to have effect must specify a day that falls within an accounting period beginning before 1st October 2002.][2]

(2) Notwithstanding regulation 10(1) above, if an election—

(*a*) specifies as an eligible asset an asset which the company acquired not more than 92 days before the day on which the election is made, and

(*b*) specifies the date of acquisition as the date as from which the election is to have effect,

the election shall have effect, so far as it relates to that asset and any liability to be matched with that asset, as from that date.

(3) Notwithstanding regulation 10(1) above, an election under regulation 10(3) may specify a day not more than 92 days earlier than the day on which the election is made as the date as from which the election is to have effect, and in such a case the election shall have effect as from that date.

(4) Notwithstanding regulation 10(1) above, if an election specifies an asset as an eligible asset which the company held on its commencement day and the election is made before the expiry—

(*a*) of the period of 183 days beginning with 23rd March 1995, or

(*b*) of the period of 92 days beginning with the company's commencement day,

whichever is the later, and the election specifies the company's commencement day as the date as from which the election is to have effect, the election shall have effect, so far as it relates to that asset and any liability to be matched with that asset, as from that specified day.

(5) Notwithstanding regulation 10(1) above, an election expressed to be made under this paragraph and made—

(*a*) in pursuance of regulation 6 above in relation to a controlled foreign company as respects which a direction under section 747 of the Taxes Act is given on or after 23rd March 1995 for an accounting period of the company [or, where the direction is given on or after 1st April 1996, no earlier accounting period of that company is an ADP exempt period][1], whenever beginning, (and a direction under that section has not been given with respect to an earlier accounting period of that company), and

(*b*) before the expiry of the period of 92 days beginning with the date of that direction,

shall have effect from the latest of the following days, that is to say, the first day of the first accounting period as respects which the direction has effect, the first day of the first accounting period beginning on or after 23rd March 1995, and the day on which the asset in question is acquired by the company.

[(6) In paragraph (5) above "ADP exempt period" means an accounting period of the company—

(*a*) which begins on or after 28th November 1995, and

(*b*) in respect of which the company has pursued, within the meaning of Part I of Schedule 25 to the Taxes Act, an acceptable distribution policy.][1]

Amendments—[1] Words in para 5(*a*) inserted and para (6) added by the Exchange Gains and Losses (Alternative Method of Calculation of Gain and Loss) (Amendment) Regulations, SI 1996/1347 regs 2, 6, with effect from 30 June 1996.

[2] Para (1A) substituted by the Exchange Gains and Losses (Transitional Provisions and Savings) Regulations, SI 2002/1969 regs 12, 16 with effect for accounting periods beginning after 30 September 2002.

TRANSACTIONS NOT AT ARM'S LENGTH

Disregard of regulations 2 and 4 to 11

12 ...

Amendment—Regulation 12 revoked by the Exchange Gains and Losses (Transitional Provisions and Savings) Regulations, SI 2002/1969 regs 12, 17 with effect for accounting periods beginning after 30 September 2002.

1994/3228
Exchange Gains and Losses (Deferral of Gains and Losses) Regulations 1994

Made by the Treasury under FA 1993 ss 143(7), 164(14), 167(1)

Made . . . . 15 December 1994
Laid before the House of Commons . . . . 16 December 1994
Coming into Force . . . . . . 23 March 1995

Commentary—*Simon's Direct Tax Service* **D2.946–950.**
Revenue Internal Guidance—Company Taxation Manual COT13810–13840 (detailed explanation of the regulations).

Citation, commencement and interpretation

1—(1) These Regulations may be cited as the Exchange Gains and Losses (Deferral of Gains and Losses) Regulations 1994.

(2) These Regulations shall come into force on 23rd March 1995.

(3) In these Regulations, "the 1993 Act" means the Finance Act 1993 and any reference to a particular section, without more, is a reference to that section of that Act.

Settlement and replacement of debts

2—(1) This regulation applies where—

(*a*) a debt held or owed by a company ("the original debt") under which a long-term capital asset or liability ("the original asset or liability") subsists is settled and replaced to any extent by another debt ("the replacement debt") under which another such asset or liability ("the replacement asset or liability") subsists, and

(*b*) (apart from this regulation) an exchange gain or loss accrues to the company for an accrual period ("the settlement period") as respects the original asset or liability which (where the debt is not wholly settled) is attributable to that part of the debt by which its nominal amount is decreased;

and in these Regulations "the replacement debt date" is the date on which that company becomes entitled or subject to the replacement debt.

(2) Subject to paragraph (6) below, in any case where this regulation applies—

(*a*) if the settlement period is the last accrual period as respects the original asset or liability, subject to paragraph (3) below, any exchange gain or loss which accrued for that period as respects that asset or liability shall be deemed to be unrealised, and any such exchange gain shall be deemed not to accrue as respects that asset or liability for that period;

(*b*) if the settlement period is not the last accrual period as respects the original asset or liability, subject to paragraph (3) below, any exchange gain which accrued for that period as respects that asset or liability shall be deemed not to accrue as respects that asset or liability for that period;

(*c*) an amount equal to the amount of any exchange gain falling within sub-paragraph (*a*) or (*b*) above shall be deemed to be an exchange gain accruing as respects the replacement asset or liability for its first accrual period and section 143(2) shall not apply in relation to any gain deemed to accrue by this sub-paragraph;

and sections 139 to 143 (apart from section 143(7)) shall have effect accordingly.

(3) Paragraph (2) does not apply—

(*a*) in relation to any debt unless it falls within paragraph (10) or (11) below;

(*b*) in relation to any debt unless the replacement debt date falls in the period beginning 30 days before the date on which the original debt or part of the original debt was settled and ending 30 days after that date;

(*c*) in relation to any debt as the replacement debt as respects another debt if or to the extent that, for the purposes of this regulation and sections 139 to 143, it replaces a third debt.

(4) Where this regulation applies and the amount by which the original debt is settled exceeds the amount of the replacement debt, then the exchange gain referred to in paragraph (1)(*b*) above shall be apportioned according to the proportion which that excess bears to the amount by which that debt is replaced, and paragraph (2) shall not apply to so much of the exchange gain as corresponds to the excess.

(5) In any case where paragraph (2) above applies and the replacement debt date falls in one accounting period and the settlement of the whole or part of the original debt occurred in a later accounting period, then the reference in paragraph (2)(*c*) above to the first accrual period for the replacement debt shall be construed as a reference to the accrual period for that debt which falls within that later accounting period.

(6) In any case where paragraph (2) above would (but for this paragraph) apply and the settlement of the original debt occurred in one accounting period and the replacement debt date falls in a later accounting period, then that paragraph shall not apply but—

(*a*) if the settlement period is the last accrual period for the asset or liability in question, the exchange gain or loss shall be deemed to be unrealised, and

(*b*) for the purposes of making a claim under section 139 as respects the original debt (or so much of it as is replaced) and the earlier accounting period—

(i) the first accrual period for the replacement debt shall be taken to be the second accrual period for the original debt, and

(ii) section 143(2) shall not apply; and

(*c*) references in section 140(4) to (9) to the asset or liability shall be construed as references to the replacement asset or liability;

and sections 139 to 143 (apart from section 143(7)) shall have effect accordingly.

(7) For the purposes of paragraph (3)(*c*) above—

(*a*) if the whole or part of the original debt is settled but there is more than one new debt held or owed by the company which may be taken to be the replacement debt, then the first of those new debts to which the company became entitled or subject shall be taken to replace the original debt and any later debt may only be taken to replace the original debt if and to the extent that the amount replaced of the original debt exceeds the amount of the earlier debt, and

(*b*) if there is more than one debt which another debt could be taken to replace, that other debt shall be taken to replace the debt which was settled first and shall only be taken to replace the debt settled later if and to the extent that its amount exceeds the amount of the debt settled earlier.

(8) The company may notify the inspector that it wishes one debt to be taken to replace another debt otherwise than in accordance with paragraph (7) above (but subject to paragraph (3)), and if the [notice states][1] that the first mentioned debt in fact replaced the other debt, paragraph (7) shall not apply and that debt shall be taken to replace the other debt in accordance with the notice.

(9) Where paragraph (6), (7) or (8) above applies all such apportionments of gains shall be made for the purposes of this regulation and sections 139 to 143 as may be just and reasonable.

(10) A debt falls within this paragraph if—

(*a*) the maximum amount of the principal is specified at the commencement of the term of the debt and the principal cannot be increased beyond that maximum amount (except as mentioned in sub-paragraph (*c*) below), and

(*b*) any part of the principal once repaid cannot be redrawn, and

(*c*) any interest which, if not paid when due, is to be capitalised or rolled-up, is to be added to the principal on the due date and repayable on the same terms as the principal.

In determining whether a debt falls within this paragraph there shall be disregarded any term in so far as it provides for the principal or any interest to be calculated by reference to any withholding or other tax (including foreign tax).

(11) A debt falls within this paragraph if—

(*a*) it is a debt on a deep gain security for the purposes of paragraph 1 of Schedule 11 to the Finance Act 1989 and the amount payable on redemption is payable on one specified date, or

(*b*) it is a debt on a qualifying indexed security for the purposes of that paragraph, or

(*c*) it is a debt on a deep discount security for the purposes of paragraph 1 of Schedule 4 to the Income and Corporation Taxes Act 1988;

and for the purposes of this regulation the amount of any such debt on the replacement debt date shall be taken to be equal to its basic valuation.

Revenue Internal Guidance—Company Taxation Manual COT13826–13828 (worked examples).

Amendments—[1] Words substituted by the Exchange Gains and Losses) (Deferral of Gains and Losses) (Amendment) Regulations, SI 1996/1348 regs 2, 3, with effect with respect to accounting periods of companies ending on or after 30 June 1996.

Disregard of certain profits in section 141(3) computation

3—(1) This regulation applies in any case where a company's profits for an accounting period which are to be taken into account under section 141(3) of the 1993 Act include any income or chargeable gains which are relevant income or gains for the purposes of section 797 of the Income and Corporation Taxes Act 1988 ("the relevant income or gains").

(2) Where this regulation applies then, for the purposes of section 141(3), the company's profits for the accounting period shall be reduced by an amount equal to the excess of X over Y where—

X is the amount of the relevant income and gains, and

Y is the amount (if any) found under paragraph (4) below.

(3) There shall be found the amount which would be the amount of corporation tax attributable to the relevant income or gains under section 797 if Chapter IV of Part X of the 1988 Act had not been enacted, and the excess of that amount over the amount of the credit for foreign tax allowable against the corporation tax in fact attributable to the relevant income or gain determined in accordance with section 797(2) and (3) shall be the net corporation tax attributable to the relevant income or gain.

(4) There shall be found the gross amount (if any) of income and gains on which an amount of corporation tax equal to that net corporation tax would be charged if the income and gains were chargeable to tax as income and gains of the company for that accounting period at the rate payable by the company (before any credit under Part XVIII of the 1988 Act).

Revenue Internal Guidance—Company Taxation Manual COT13816 (worked example).

Groups of companies

4—(1) For the purposes of this regulation companies are members of a group if by virtue of section 170 of the Taxation of Chargeable Gains Tax Act 1992 they are members of a group for the purposes of sections 171 to 181 of that Act.

(2) This regulation applies to a claim made under section 139 of the 1993 Act as regards an accounting period of the claimant company for the whole or part of which it is a member of a group, and in relation to such a claim subsection (5) of that section shall have effect with the addition at the end of paragraph (*c*) of the words—

"and if the claim is made by a member of a group (within the meaning of section 141 below) it must contain a statement of that fact.".

(3) In relation to a claim to which this regulation applies, section 141 shall have effect subject to the following modifications.

(4) The following subsections shall be substituted for subsection (1)—

"(1) Subject to subsection (1A) below, where a company ("the claimant company") makes a claim under section 139 above ("the current claim") as regards an accounting period of the claimant company for the whole or part of which it is a member of a group ("the relevant accounting period")—

(*a*) an amount is available for relief under that section for that accounting period which is equal to the amount (if any) by which amount A is exceeded by the appropriate proportion of the group B amount, or of the group C amount, if it is lower than the group B amount, and

(*b*) the appropriate proportion is that proportion which amount B3 (as found for the claimant company) bears to amount ΣB3.

(1A) In any case where there is no group B amount or no group C amount, no amount shall be available for relief under section 139.

(1B) For the purposes of this section a company is a member of a group if by virtue of section 170 of the Taxation of Chargeable Gains Tax Act 1992 it is a member of the group for the purposes of sections 171 to 181 of that Act, and references below to a "group company" and "group", in relation to the claimant company, are references to companies belonging to the same group as that company and to that group.".

(5) After subsection (3) there shall be inserted—

"(3A) In any case where an amount equal to the appropriate proportion found under subsection (1) above for the claimant company is equal to at least half of the amount of that company's profits (within the meaning of subsection (3) above disregarding this subsection), subsection (3) shall have effect as if for the reference to the company's profits there were substituted a reference to the [aggregate of the profits of the claimant company and][1] of those group companies to which subsection (3B) below applies for the relevant accounting period.

(3B) This subsection applies as respects a group company for an accounting period if at any time during that period—

(*a*) that group company owes the claimant company qualifying debts the amount outstanding under which is equal to at least one-tenth of the total value outstanding of all the qualifying debts owed by that group company; or

(*b*) the claimant company owes that group company qualifying debts the amount outstanding under which is equal to at least one-tenth of the total value outstanding of all the qualifying debts owed by the claimant company;

and for the purposes of this subsection "qualifying debts" do not include debts due for goods or services supplied to or by the company in the course of its trade.".

(6) The following subsections shall be substituted for subsections (4) and (5)—

"(4) There shall be found for each group company during the relevant accounting period amounts B1 and B2 where—

(*a*) B1 is the total amount of—

(i) unrealised exchange gains which accrue or would (apart from a claim under section 139 above) accrue to the company in an accrual period constituting or falling within the relevant accounting period as regards long-term capital assets or long-term capital liabilities or both,

(ii) less any such exchange gain in so far as it is attributable to that part of the debt by which its nominal amount is decreased, and

(*b*) B2 is the total amount of—

(i) unrealised exchange losses which accrue to the company in an accrual period constituting or falling within the relevant accounting period as regards long-term capital assets or long-term capital liabilities or both,

(ii) less any such exchange loss in so far as it is attributable to that part of the debt by which its nominal amount is decreased,

and the excess of B1 over B2 (if any) is called B3, and the excess of B2 over B1 (if any) is called B4.

(4A) There shall be found the aggregate of the B3 amounts for the group, called ΣB3, and the aggregate of the B4 amounts for the group, called ΣB4, and the excess of ΣB3 over ΣB4 (if any) is called the group B amount.

(4B) There shall be found for each group company during the relevant accounting period amounts C1 and C2 where—

(*a*) C1 is the total amount of the exchange gains which accrue or would (apart from a claim under section 139 above) accrue to the company in an accrual period constituting or falling within the relevant accounting period as regards relevant items, and

(*b*) C2 is the total amount of the exchange losses which accrue to the company in an accrual period constituting or falling within the relevant accounting period as regards relevant items,

and the excess of C1 over C2 (if any) is called C3, and the excess of C2 over C1 (if any) is called C4.

This subsection is subject to subsection (5) below.

(4C) There shall be found the aggregate of the C3 amounts for the group, called ΣC3, and the aggregate of the C4 amounts for the group, called ΣC4, and the excess of ΣC3 over ΣC4 (if any) is called the group C amount.

(4D) In any case where an accrual period for a company falls partly within and partly outside the relevant accounting period, any exchange gains or losses which accrue or would (apart from a claim under section 139) accrue to the company in that accrual period shall be apportioned according to the respective lengths of that part of the accrual period which falls within the relevant accounting period and the remainder of the accrual period, and the proportion of the exchange gains and losses corresponding to the remainder of that period shall be disregarded for the purposes of this section.

(4E) In any case where a company (including the claimant company) ceases to be or becomes a group company during the relevant accounting period—

(*a*) references in subsections (1), (3), (3A), (3B), (4) and (4B) above to that accounting period shall as respects that company be construed as references to that part of that period during which the company was a group company, and

(*b*) the company's profits for that period shall be apportioned according to the respective lengths of that part of the relevant accounting period during which the company was a group company and of the remainder of the accounting period, and

(*c*) the proportion of the profits corresponding to that remainder shall be disregarded for the purposes of this section;

but if it appears that such an apportionment would produce an unreasonable or unjust result, such other method of apportionment shall be used as appears just and reasonable.

(4F) In any case where the accounting period of a group company other than the claimant company does not coincide with the relevant accounting period—

(*a*) references in subsections (1), (3), (3A), (3B), (4) and (4B) above to that accounting period shall as respects that group company be construed as references to so much of its accounting period or periods which fall within the relevant accounting period, and

(*b*) that group company's profits for that period or periods shall be apportioned according to the respective lengths of that part of its accounting period which coincides with the relevant accounting period and the remainder of the accounting period, and

(*c*) the proportion of the profits corresponding to the remainder of that period or periods shall be disregarded for the purposes of this section.

(4G) In any case where subsection (3) or (3A) above has effect subject to regulation 3 of the Exchange Gains and Losses (Deferral of Gains and Losses) Regulations 1994, subsections (4E) and (4F) above shall each have effect with the addition of a reference to that regulation in paragraph (*a*).

(5) For the purposes of subsection (4B) above, in computing the amounts C1 and C2 for any group company which is not the claimant company, there shall be disregarded any exchange gain or loss which has accrued (disregarding section 139 above) as regards an asset, liability or contract if, by virtue of subsection (11) of section 128 above, any gain or loss falling within subsection (12) of that section and accruing to the company as respects that asset, liability or contract would not be taken into account in calculating for the purposes of corporation tax the profits or losses of any period of a trade carried on by the company during the relevant accounting period.''.

(7) In subsection (6) for ''subsections (4) and (5) above'' there shall be substituted ''this section''.

(8) In subsection (7) for ''subsection (5) above'' there shall be substituted ''this section''.

Revenue Internal Guidance—Company Taxation Manual COT13840 (worked example).
Amendments—[1] Words substituted by the Exchange Gains and Losses (Deferral of Gains and Losses) (Amendment) Regulations, SI 1996/1348 regs 2, 4, with effect with respect to accounting periods of companies ending on or after 30 June 1996.

1994/3229
Exchange Gains and Losses (Excess Gains and Losses) Regulations 1994

Made by the Treasury under FA 1993 ss 148, 164(14), 167(1)

Made . . . . *15 December 1994*
Laid before the House of Commons . . . . . *16 December 1994*
Coming into Force . . . . *23 March 1995*

Commentary—*Simon's Direct Tax Service* **D2.965.**
Revenue Internal Guidance—Company Taxation Manual COT13846–13873 (detailed explanation of the regulations).

Citation, commencement and interpretation

1—(1) These Regulations may be cited as the Exchange Gains and Losses (Excess Gains and Losses) Regulations 1994.

(2) These Regulations shall come into force on 23rd March 1995.

(3) In these Regulations ''the 1993 Act'' means the Finance Act 1993.

Non-exchange losses and gains

2—(1) In any case where as respects an asset or liability—

(*a*) an exchange gain has accrued to a qualifying company, and

(*b*) a loss which is not an exchange loss (''the non-exchange loss'') subsequently accrues to the company—

(i) at the time the company ceases to be entitled or subject to the asset or liability or to part of the asset or liability, and

(ii) by virtue of an arm's length transaction, and

(*c*) relief from tax is not (apart from this regulation) available under the Tax Acts in respect of the non-exchange loss,

then, on a claim being made by the company, an initial exchange loss equal in amount to the excess (if any) of A over B or, if less, the amount of the non-exchange loss shall be treated as accruing to the company as respects that asset or liability for the appropriate accrual period.

(2) Paragraph (1) above does not apply in relation to any asset or liability as respects which the loss referred to in paragraph (1)(*b*) accrues to the company if the company acquired the asset or became subject to the liability in pursuance of a transaction which was not an arm's length transaction.

(3) For the purposes of this regulation the amount of any non-exchange loss shall be reduced by the amount, if any, of any insurance or compensation moneys or other sum to which the company is entitled in respect of the loss which do not fall to be taken into account in computing the company's profits for the purposes of corporation tax.

(4) In any case where as respects an asset or liability—

(*a*) an exchange loss has accrued to a qualifying company, and

(*b*) a gain which is not an exchange gain (''the non-exchange gain'') subsequently accrues to the company at the time the company ceases to be entitled or subject to the asset or liability or to part of the asset or liability, and

(*c*) the non-exchange gain is not (apart from this regulation) chargeable to tax under the Tax Acts,

then an initial exchange gain equal in amount to the excess (if any) of B over A or, if less, the amount of the non-exchange gain shall be treated as accruing to the company as respects that asset or liability for the appropriate accrual period.

(5) For the purposes of paragraphs (1) and (4) above—

A is the aggregate amount of any exchange gains which have accrued to the company as respects the asset or liability for all accrual periods since the company's commencement day;
B is the aggregate amount of any exchange losses which have accrued to the company as respects the asset or liability for all accrual periods since the company's commencement day;
"the appropriate accrual period", in relation to any asset or liability—

(i) if the company ceases to be entitled or subject to part only of the asset or liability, means the accrual period in which it ceases to be so entitled or subject, and
(ii) in any other case, means the last accrual period as respects that asset or liability; and

"an arm's length transaction" is any transaction the terms of which are such as might reasonably be expected to have been agreed between parties at arm's length.

(6) The amount of any exchange gain or exchange loss shall not be taken into account under paragraph (1) or (4) above unless by virtue of section 128(4) or (8) or 129(2) or (4) of the 1993 Act the company has been treated as receiving an amount equal to that amount or incurring a loss equal to that loss.

(7) A claim under paragraph (1) above must be made to the inspector before the expiry of the period of two years beginning with the end of the accounting period in which the non-exchange loss accrued to the company.

Revenue Internal Guidance—Company Taxation Manual COT13852–13854 (worked examples).

Cancellation of relief where loss is recovered

3—(1) Where—

(*a*) by virtue of regulation 2(1) an initial exchange loss has been treated as accruing to a company ("the loss making company") as respects an asset or liability by reason of a non-exchange loss accruing as respects that asset or liability, and
(*b*) the whole or part of that non-exchange loss is subsequently recovered by the loss making company, or by another company in the same group, in an accounting period of the loss making company,

an initial exchange gain equal in amount to the amount of the net exchange loss found in accordance with paragraphs (3) and (4) below shall be deemed to accrue to the loss making company.

For the purposes of this paragraph, companies are members of a group if by virtue of section 170 of the Taxation of Chargeable Gains Act 1992 they are members of a group for the purposes of sections 171 to 181 of that Act.

(2) Any initial exchange gain deemed to accrue under paragraph (1) above shall—

(*a*) if the initial exchange loss referred to above was an exchange loss of a trade or part of a trade and the loss making company carries on that trade or part at the time of the recovery, be deemed to be an exchange gain of that trade or part, and section 128 of the 1993 Act shall apply accordingly,
(*b*) if sub-paragraph (*a*) above does not apply, be deemed to be a non-trading exchange gain, and section 129 of the 1993 Act shall apply accordingly,

and in either case the gain shall be deemed to accrue as respects the asset or liability for an accrual period identical to the accounting period in which the time of recovery falls.

(3) For the purposes of paragraph (1) above the net exchange loss shall (subject to paragraph (4) below) be equal to the excess (if any) of A over (B–C) where—

A is the amount of the loss recovered, translated into the company's local currency (if it is not in that currency) using the London closing exchange rates for the two currencies for the date of the recovery,
B is the amount of the non-exchange loss referred to in paragraph (1) above, and
C is the amount of the initial exchange loss deemed to accrue to the company by virtue of regulation 2(1).

(4) Where parts of the loss are recovered at different times, then in relation to any recovery after the first—

(*a*) amount A shall include any amount recovered earlier;
(*b*) the net exchange loss found in accordance with paragraph (3) above shall be reduced by the amount (or aggregate amount, if more than one) of any initial exchange gain deemed to accrue (under paragraph (1) above) in relation to any earlier recovery.

Revenue Internal Guidance—Company Taxation Manual COT13863–13873(worked examples).

1994/3230

Local Currency Elections Regulations 1994

Made by the Treasury under FA 1993 ss 93(1), (6), 94(1)–(3), (11), 95(1)–(3)

Made . . . . 15 *December 1994*
Laid before the House of Commons . . . . 16 *December 1994*
Coming into Force . . . . 23 *March 1995*

Commentary—*Simon's Direct Tax Service* **D2.910, 911.**
Regulations—European Single Currency (Taxes) Regulations SI 1998/3177 regs 41–47.
Revenue Internal Guidance—Company Taxation Manual COT13620–13651 (detailed explanation of the local currency regulations).

Citation and commencement

1—(1) These Regulations may be cited as the Local Currency Elections Regulations 1994.

(2) These Regulations shall come into force on 23rd March 1995.

Definitions

2 In these Regulations, except where the context otherwise requires—

"the 1993 Act" means the Finance Act 1993;

"accounts" in relation to a company, means—

(i) the annual accounts of the company prepared in accordance with Part VII of the Companies Act 1985 or

(ii) if the company is not required to prepare such accounts, the accounts which it is required to keep under the law of its home State or, if it is not so required to keep accounts, such of its accounts as most closely correspond to accounts which it would have been required to prepare if the provisions of that Part applied to the company;

"commencement day", in relation to any company, means the first day of the company's first accounting period beginning on or after 23rd March 1995;

"local currency" means a currency other than sterling;

"overseas branch" means a branch outside the United Kingdom;

"specified", in relation to an election, means specified in the election;

and references to an election are references to an election under regulations 3 or 4.

Elections for trades

3—(1) Subject to the following provisions of these Regulations, a company carrying on a trade may by notice given to the inspector elect to have the basic profits and losses of the trade computed and expressed for the purposes of corporation tax in a specified local currency.

(2) A company may not make an election under this regulation for a trade for an accounting period if there is in force an election under regulation 4 for that accounting period and any part of that trade.

Revenue Internal Guidance—Company Taxation Manual COT13648 (flow chart for determining whether election valid). COT13649, 13651 (worked examples).
Cross reference—See the European Single Currency (Taxes) Regulations, SI 1998/3177 reg 43 (an election made under this regulation in relation to the ecu or a currency participating in the euro shall have affect, inter alia, as if it was made in relation to the euro as well as the ecu or participating currency as the case may be).
Modification—This regulation has effect as if para (2) is substituted and a new para (3) inserted in accordance with the European Single Currency (Taxes) Regulations, SI 1998/3177 reg 45 in relation to local currency elections affected by the introduction of the euro.

Elections for part trades

4—(1) Subject to the following provisions of these Regulations, a company carrying on a trade may by notice given to the inspector elect to have the basic profits and losses of a specified part of the trade computed and expressed for the purposes of corporation tax in a specified local currency.

(2) A company may make an election under this regulation—

(*a*) for a trade which it carries on, wholly or in part, through one or more overseas branches, or

(*b*) for a ring fence trade as respects which the condition mentioned in section 94A(2) of the 1993 Act is fulfilled,

but not in relation to any other trade (and accordingly an election under paragraph (1) of this regulation may, subject to these Regulations, be made for a part of the trade which is carried on in the United Kingdom).

(3) An election under this regulation may specify different currencies for different parts of the trade but if the company makes an election for each part of the trade, at least two currencies must be specified.

(4) Where a company makes more than one election for different parts of one trade, paragraph (3) above shall apply cumulatively to the elections.

(5) Where a company carries on part of a trade through two or more branches situated in the same country, an election under paragraph (2)(*a*) above for that part of the trade must specify the same currency to be used for all those branches, and for the purposes of this paragraph the United Kingdom shall be taken to be one country.

(6) In any case where a company makes an election under this regulation for one or more parts of a trade but not for all the parts of the trade, the basic profits and losses of any part of the trade for which there is no election shall be computed and expressed for the purposes of corporation tax in sterling.

(7) A company may not make an election under this regulation for part of a trade for an accounting period if there is in force an election under regulation 3 for that trade and that accounting period.

Revenue Internal Guidance—Company Taxation Manual COT 13648 (flow chart for determining validity of election).
Cross reference—See the European Single Currency (Taxes) Regulations, SI 1998/3177 reg 43 (an election made under this regulation in relation to the ecu or a currency participating in the euro shall have affect, inter alia, as if it was made in relation to the euro as well as the ecu or participating currency as the case may be).

Factors affecting determination of local currency

5—(1) This regulation applies in relation to any election made by a company for the purpose of determining what currency (if any) may be specified in the election.

(2) A currency may be specified in an election as a local currency if, but only if—

(*a*) it is the currency of the primary economic environment in which the trade or part of the trade is carried on, and
(*b*) one of the conditions set out in paragraphs (3), (4), (5) and (6) below is satisfied.

(3) A currency may be specified in any election as a local currency if the accounts are prepared in that currency in accordance with normal accountancy practice.

(4) A currency may be specified in an election made by a company resident in the United Kingdom as a local currency if the accounts, so far as they relate to the trade or part in question, are prepared from the financial statements relating to the trade or part using the closing rate/net investment method, and those statements are prepared in that currency.

The reference above to the closing rate/net investment method is a reference to that method as described under the title ''Foreign currency translation'' in the Statement of Standard Accounting Practice issued in April 1983 by the Institute of Chartered Accountants in England and Wales.

(5) A currency may be specified in an election made by a company not resident in the United Kingdom as a local currency if it is the currency in which the financial statements relating to that trade or part are prepared in accordance with normal accountancy practice.

(6) Subject to paragraph (7) below, a currency may be specified as a local currency in any election which is not for a trade or part of a trade carried on in the United Kingdom if—

(*a*) the company making the election was within the charge to corporation tax as respects the trade or part in question immediately before its commencement day, and
(*b*) for accounting periods ending within the two years before that day, the basic profits and losses of the trade or part were computed and expressed for corporation tax purposes in that currency.

(7) An election made by virtue of paragraph (6) above shall be of no effect unless it is made before the expiry of the period of 92 days beginning with the company's commencement day.

Modification—This regulation has effect as if para (2) is amended in accordance with the European Single Currency (Taxes) Regulations, SI 1998/3177 reg 42 in relation to local currency elections affected by the introduction of the euro.

Factors relevant to the determination of the primary economic environment

6 In determining whether a currency is the currency of the primary economic environment in which a trade or any part of a trade is carried on, regard shall be had to all relevant circumstances including in particular (in so far as they may be relevant) the following factors, that is to say—

(*a*) the currency in which the net cash flows of the trade or part are generated or expressed in the relevant accounting records;
(*b*) the currency in which the company manages the profitability of the trade or part so far as it is affected by currency exposure;
(*c*) in the case of a company which is resident in the United Kingdom, the currency in which the company's share capital and its reserves are denominated;
(*d*) the currency to which the company, or, where the trade or part is carried on through a branch, that branch, is exposed in its long term capital borrowing (of any kind whatsoever);
(*e*) the currency which is the generally recognised currency in which trading in the principal market of the trade or part is carried on.

Revenue Internal Guidance—Company Taxation Manual COT13631 (text of Public Statement re currency elections).
Modification—This regulation has effect as if the words ''for the purposes of regulation 5(2)(*a*)'' are inserted after the words ''In determining'' in relation to local currency elections affected by the introduction of the euro: see the European Single Currency (Taxes) Regulations, SI 1998/3177 reg 42.

Provisions supplementary to regulations 4, 5 and 6

7—(1) Where the election specifies more than one currency for parts of a trade, regulations 4, 5 and 6 shall apply separately in relation to each currency and each part of the trade.

(2) In regulations 4, 5 and 6, except where the context otherwise requires—

(*a*) any reference to accounts, in relation to an election, is a reference to the accounts of the company making the election for the accounting period for which the election is to have effect; and

(*b*) any reference to relevant accounting records, in relation to an election, is a reference to the accounting records, relating to the trade or that part of a trade to which the election refers, for the accounting period for which the election is to have effect.

Determination of rate of exchange

8—(1) A company may in an election for a trade or part of a trade state that for accounting periods for which the election has effect an average arm's length exchange rate will be used in translating the basic profits or losses of the trade or part into sterling for the purposes of section 93(4) or 94(8) of the 1993 Act (as the case may be).

(2) In paragraph (1) above—

''arm's length exchange rate'' means such exchange rate as might reasonably be expected to be agreed between persons dealing at arm's length; and

''average arm's length exchange rate'' means the rate which represents the average of the arm's length exchange rates for all the days in the accounting period in question.

(3) Subject to paragraph (4) below, where an election contains a statement in accordance with paragraph (1) above, the average arm's length exchange rate shall be used in translating the basic profits or losses of the trade or part into sterling for the purposes of section 93(4) or 94(8) of the 1993 Act (as the case may be) for all accounting periods for which the election has effect.

(4) The company may by notice given to the inspector terminate the statement referred to above with effect from the first day of the first accounting period beginning on or after the date of the notice.

Modification—This regulation has effect in accordance with the modifications made by the European Single Currency (Taxes) Regulations, SI 1998/3177 reg 46 in relation to local currency elections affected by the introduction of the euro.

Periods for which elections have effect

9—(1) Subject to the following provisions of these Regulations, an election for a trade or part of a trade shall have effect as respects that trade or part for all accounting periods beginning on or after the date on which the election is made.

(2) Subject to the following provisions of these Regulations, an election for a trade or part of a trade made by a company which, as respects that trade or part, is within the charge to corporation tax immediately before its commencement day shall have effect as respects that trade or part of all accounting periods beginning on or after that day if the election is made before the end of the period of 92 days beginning with that day.

(3) Subject to the following provisions of these Regulations, an election for a trade or part of a trade made by a company which, as respects that trade or part, is not within the charge to corporation tax immediately before its commencement day shall have effect as respects that trade or part for all accounting periods beginning on or after the first day on which it comes within that charge as respects that trade or part if the election is made before the end of the period of 92 days beginning with that first day.

Modification—This regulation has effect as in accordance with the modifications made by the European Single Currency (Taxes) Regulations, SI 1998/3177 reg 47 in relation to local currency elections affected by the introduction of the euro.

Information to be submitted with elections and effectiveness of elections

10—(1) An election by a company for a trade or part of a trade shall include—

(*a*) a statement of the reasons why the company believes that such of the requirements of these Regulations as are applicable to the election will be met as respects that trade or part for the first accounting period of the company for which the election is to have effect; and

(*b*) particulars of the nature of the trade or part and the place where it is carried on.

(2) An election which does not comply with paragraph (1) above and regulation 5(7) (if applicable) shall be of no effect.

(3) Without prejudice to paragraphs (1) and (2) above, an election made by a company for a trade or part of a trade shall be of no effect if the requirements of regulation 5 (so far as they are applicable to the election) are not complied with as respects that trade or part for the first accounting period of the company for which the election is intended to have effect.

(4) If at any time in an accounting period of the company, the currency specified in an election made by the company ceases to be eligible to be specified in an election as the local currency of the trade or part, the election shall cease to have effect at the end of that accounting period.

(5) In any case where an election has ceased to have effect by virtue of paragraph (4) above, the company shall notify the inspector in writing of that fact as soon as is reasonably practicable after becoming aware of it.

(6) In a case where paragraph (4) above applies the inspector may notify the company in writing that by virtue of that paragraph the election is no longer effective.

1994/3231
Exchange Gains and Losses (Insurance Companies) Regulations 1994

Made by the Treasury under FA 1993 ss 167(1), 168(2)–(5)

Made . . . . *15 December 1994*
Laid before the House of Commons . . . . *16 December 1994*
Coming into Force . . . . *23 March 1995*

Commentary—*Simon's Direct Tax Service* **D2.966.**

Modification—See the Exchange Gains and Losses (Transitional Provisions and Savings) Regulations, SI 2002/1969 (SI 1994/3231 as modified by SI 2002/1969 to continue to have effect, notwithstanding the repeal, with effect for accounting periods beginning after 30 September 2002, of FA 1993 ss 167(1), 168(2)–(5) by FA 2002 ss 79(1)(*b*), 141, Sch 40 Pt 3(10)).

1—(1) These Regulations may be cited as the Exchange Gains and Losses (Insurance Companies) Regulations 1994.

(2) These Regulations shall come into force on 23rd March 1995.

[(3) In these Regulations unless the context otherwise requires—

"basic valuation" shall be construed in accordance with section 159(1) of the 1993 Act;

["the final accounting period", in relation to a company, means the company's accounting period preceding the first accounting period to begin on or after 1st October 2002;][2]

"loan relationship" shall be construed in accordance with the Corporation Tax Acts, except that a relationship shall not be a loan relationship where the profits or gains chargeable to tax under Case III of Schedule D which arise from the relationship are confined to interest;

"new holding" and "original shares" have the meanings given by section 126(1) of the 1992 Act;

"regulation 7 asset" shall be construed in accordance with regulation 7(1);

"the Taxes Act" means the Income and Corporation Taxes Act 1988;

"the 1992 Act" means the Taxation of Chargeable Gains Act 1992;

"the 1993 Act" means the Finance Act 1993.][1]

Amendments—[1] Para (3) substituted by the Exchange Gains and Losses (Insurance Companies) (Amendment) Regulations, SI 1996/673 regs 1, 3.

[2] Definition of "the final accounting period" inserted by the Exchange Gains and Losses (Transitional Provisions and Savings) Regulations, SI 2002/1969 regs 18, 19 with effect for accounting periods beginning after 30 September 2002.

2–5A

Amendment—Regulations 2–5A revoked by the Exchange Gains and Losses (Transitional Provisions and Savings) Regulations, SI 2002/1969 regs 18, 20 with effect for accounting periods beginning after 30 September 2002.

6 ...

Amendments—This para revoked by the Exchange Gains and Losses (Insurance Companies) (Amendment) Regulations, SI 1996/673 regs 1(3), 5, with effect for accounting periods ending after 31 March 1996.

[**7**—[(1) An asset specified by this regulation is referred to in regulations 7A and 8 to 12 as a "regulation 7 asset".][4]

(2) An asset is specified by this regulation if it is an asset which, at the time of its disposal—

(*a*) represents a loan relationship of a company;
(*b*) is an asset to which paragraph (3), (4), (5) or (6) below applies; and
(*c*) is held in exempt circumstances.

(3) This paragraph applies to an asset if—

(*a*) the settlement currency of a debt to which it relates is a currency other than sterling; and
(*b*) that debt is not a debt on a security.

(4) This paragraph applies to an asset if the debt to which it relates is a debt on a security and is in a foreign currency.

(5) This paragraph applies to an asset if it is comprised in a relevant holding and is denominated in a currency other than sterling.

(6) This paragraph applies to an asset if—

(*a*) it is a qualifying corporate bond,
(*b*) it would not, apart from this paragraph, be a regulation 7 asset,
(*c*) it constitutes a new holding, and
(*d*) the original shares, in relation to the new holding, consisted of a regulation 7 asset by virtue of paragraph (3), (4) or (5) above.

(7) For the purposes of paragraph (4) above a debt is a debt in a foreign currency if it is—

(*a*) a debt expressed in a currency other than sterling;
(*b*) a debt the amount of which in sterling falls at any time to be determined by reference to the value at that time of a currency other than sterling; or
(*c*) subject to paragraph (8) below, a debt as respects which provision is made for its conversion into, or redemption in, a currency other than sterling.

(8) A debt is not a debt in a foreign currency for the purposes of paragraph (4) above by reason only that provision is made for its redemption on payment of an amount in a currency other than sterling equal, at the rate prevailing at the date of redemption, to a specified amount in sterling.

(9) For the purposes of paragraph (5) above an asset is comprised in a relevant holding if it consists of—

(*a*) a unit in a unit trust scheme, or
(*b*) a relevant interest in an offshore fund[, or][2]
[(*c*) a share in an open-ended investment company][2]

to which section 212 of the 1992 Act does not apply or would not apply if the asset were an asset of the company's [long-term insurance][3] fund.

(10) For the purposes of paragraph (5) above—

(*a*) a unit in a unit trust scheme, or
(*b*) a right (other than a share in a company) which constitutes a relevant interest in an offshore fund,

shall be taken to be denominated in a currency other than sterling if the price at which it may be acquired from, or disposed of to, persons concerned in the management of the trust or fund is fixed by those persons in a currency other than sterling.

(11) For the purposes of paragraph (5) above shares constituting a relevant interest in an offshore fund shall be taken to be denominated in a currency other than sterling if their nominal value is expressed in such a currency [; and shares of a given class in an open-ended investment company shall be taken to be denominated in a currency other than sterling if the price at which they may be acquired from, or disposed of to, the company or its authorised corporate director is fixed by the company or director in a currency other than sterling, or (as the case may be) the price or prices at which they are quoted in The Stock Exchange Daily Official List is in a currency other than sterling][2].

(12) The reference in paragraph (2)(*c*) above to exempt circumstances shall be construed in accordance with paragraph 3 of Schedule 17 to the 1993 Act, but as if references in that paragraph to a currency were references to the debt to which the relationship relates.

(13) In this regulation—

"debt on a security" shall be construed in accordance with section 132 of the 1992 Act;
"[long-term insurance][3] fund" has the meaning given by section 431(2) of the Taxes Act;
["open-ended investment company" and "authorised corporate director" in relation to such a company have the meanings given by subsection (10) of section 468 of the Taxes Act, read with subsections (11) to (18) of that section, as those sub-sections are added in relation to open-ended investment companies by regulation 10(4) of the Open-ended Investment Companies (Tax) Regulations 1997; and accordingly references in subsections (11) to (16) of that section to "the Tax Acts" shall be construed as if they included references to these Regulations;][2]
"qualifying corporate bond" has the same meaning as in the 1992 Act;
"relevant interest in an offshore fund" has the meaning given by section 212(5) of the 1992 Act;
"security" includes a debenture that is deemed to be a security for the purposes of section 251 of the 1992 Act by virtue of subsection (6) of that section;
"unit trust scheme" shall be construed in accordance with section 99 of the 1992 Act.][1]

Amendments—[1] This regulation inserted by the Exchange Gains and Losses (Insurance Companies) (Amendment) Regulations, SI 1996/673 regs 1(2), 4, with effect for disposals made after 31 March 1996.

[2] Para (9)(*c*) (and word "or" preceding it), words in para (11) and definitions of "open-ended investment company" and "authorised corporate director" in para (13) inserted by the Exchange Gains and Losses (Insurance Companies) (Amendment) Regulations, SI 1997/1155, with effect in relation to disposals taking place on or after 28 April 1997.

[3] Words "long-term insurance" substituted for "long-term business" in paras (9), (13) by the Financial Services and Markets Act 2000 (Consequential Amendments) (Taxes) Order, SI 2001/3629 art 138 with effect from 1 December 2001, immediately after the coming into force of the Financial Services and Markets Act 2000 ss 411, 432(1), Sch 20 (and SI 2001/3629 Pts 1 and 2).

[4] Para (1) substituted by the Exchange Gains and Losses (Transitional Provisions and Savings) Regulations, SI 2002/1969 regs 18, 21 with effect for accounting periods beginning after 30 September 2002.

[7A—(1) An asset shall be deemed to have been disposed of by an insurance company immediately before its first accounting period to begin on or after 1st October 2002 where—

(*a*) the asset was a regulation 7 asset at the time of its deemed disposal, and

(*b*) at that time, the insurance company had made no election under regulation 8A of these Regulations.

(2) Subject to regulation 7B, any chargeable gain or allowable loss accruing on the deemed disposal under paragraph (1) above of an asset shall be brought into account as if it had accrued immediately after the end of the final accounting period.][1]

Amendments—[1] Regulations 7A, 7B inserted by the Exchange Gains and Losses (Transitional Provisions and Savings) Regulations, SI 2002/1969 regs 18, 22 with effect for accounting periods beginning after 30 September 2002.

[7B In any case where, apart from this regulation, chargeable gains or allowable losses would accrue to an insurance company immediately after the end of the final accounting period by virtue of regulation 7A—

(*a*) the insurance company may elect, by notice to the inspector within two years of the end of the final accounting period, that this regulation shall apply as respects all such gains or losses, and

(*b*) where such an election is made, every such gain or loss to which this regulation applies shall be treated as accruing only when the asset or liability to which the gain or loss relates ceases to be held or owed by the insurance company.][1]

Amendments—[1] Regulations 7A, 7B inserted by the Exchange Gains and Losses (Transitional Provisions and Savings) Regulations, SI 2002/1969 regs 18, 22 with effect for accounting periods beginning after 30 September 2002.

[8—(1) The amount of the chargeable gain accruing on the [the deemed disposal under regulation 7A(1) of an asset] shall, subject to paragraphs (5) and (6) below and to [regulations [9][3] to 12][2], be computed by ascertaining the amount specified in paragraph (3) below ("the first amount") and the amount specified in paragraph (4) below ("the second amount").

(2) Where the second amount exceeds the first amount the excess shall be a chargeable gain; where the first amount exceeds the second amount the excess shall be an allowable loss; and where the first amount and the second amount are equal there shall be neither a chargeable gain nor an allowable loss.

(3) The first amount is the basic valuation of the asset translated into sterling at the time immediately after the company becomes entitled to the asset.

(4) The second amount is the basic valuation of the asset translated into sterling at the time immediately before the company ceases to be entitled to the asset.

(5) Where any profit on the sale of a regulation 7 asset would be treated wholly as a receipt falling to be brought into account in computing profits or gains charged under Case I of Schedule D, neither a chargeable gain nor an allowable loss shall be treated as arising.

(6) Where any profit on the sale of a regulation 7 asset would be treated partly as a receipt falling to be brought into account in computing profits or gains charged under Case I of Schedule D, any chargeable gain or allowable loss accruing by virtue of this regulation shall be reduced on a just and reasonable basis.

(7) Any translation into sterling required by this regulation shall be made by reference to the London closing rate.

(8) The provisions of Chapters III and IV of Part II of the 1992 Act shall not apply to any computation required by this regulation.

(9) All regulation 7 assets which are the subject of the computation required by this regulation shall be treated as relevant securities within the meaning given by subsection (1) of section 108 of the 1992 Act; and that section shall apply accordingly.

(10) Nothing in this regulation shall be taken as preventing any gain or loss which is deemed to accrue by virtue of section 116(10)(*b*) of the 1992 Act from being brought into charge to tax.][1]

Amendments—[1] This regulation inserted by the Exchange Gains and Losses (Insurance Companies) (Amendment) Regulations, SI 1996/673 regs 1(2), 4, with effect for disposals made after 31 March 1996.

[2] Words substituted by the Exchange Gains and Losses (Insurance Companies) (Amendment No 2) Regulations, SI 1996/1485 regs 2,4, with effect from 30 June 1996.

[3] Words in para (1) substituted by the Exchange Gains and Losses (Transitional Provisions and Savings) Regulations, SI 2002/1969 regs 18, 23 with effect for accounting periods beginning after 30 September 2002.

8A ...

Amendment—Regulation 8A revoked by the Exchange Gains and Losses (Transitional Provisions and Savings) Regulations, SI 2002/1969 regs 18, 24 with effect for accounting periods beginning after 30 September 2002.

[**9**—(1) This regulation applies in any case where—

(*a*) an insurance company has acquired a regulation 7 asset, and

(*b*) the asset was held by the company immediately before 1st April 1996.

(2) Regulation 8 shall apply on the [deemed disposal under regulation 7A(1) of the asset][2] with the modification that the first amount shall be the basic valuation of the asset translated into sterling by reference to the London closing rate on 1st April 1996.][1]

Amendments—[1] This regulation inserted by the Exchange Gains and Losses (Insurance Companies) (Amendment) Regulations, SI 1996/673 regs 1(2), 4, with effect for disposals made after 31 March 1996.

[2] Words in para (2) substituted by the Exchange Gains and Losses (Transitional Provisions and Savings) Regulations, SI 2002/1969 regs 18, 25 with effect for accounting periods beginning after 30 September 2002.

[**10**—(1) This regulation applies in any case where, for the purposes of sections 126 to 131 of the 1992 Act—

(*a*) a regulation 7 asset constitutes the original shares, and

(*b*) another regulation 7 asset constitutes the new holding.

(2) Regulation 8 shall apply on the disposal of the new holding with the modifications specified in paragraphs (3) and (4) below.

(3) The modification specified in this paragraph is that the first amount shall be the aggregate of—

(*a*) the basic valuation of the original shares translated into sterling at the time immediately after the company became entitled to the original shares, and

(*b*) the basic valuation of the new holding translated into sterling at the time immediately after the company became entitled to the new holding.

(4) The modification specified in this paragraph is that the second amount shall be the aggregate of—

(*a*) the basic valuation of the original shares translated into sterling at the time immediately before the company became entitled to the new holding, and

(*b*) the basic valuation of the new holding translated into sterling at the time immediately before the company ceased to be entitled to the new holding.][1]

Amendments—[1] This regulation inserted by the Exchange Gains and Losses (Insurance Companies) (Amendment) Regulations, SI 1996/673 regs 1(2), 4, with effect for disposals made after 31 March 1996.

[**11**—(1) This regulation applies in any case where—

(*a*) an asset is a regulation 7 asset by virtue of paragraph (5) of that regulation, and

(*b*) the asset has at any time after 31st March 1996 and during the company's period of ownership been an asset which did not represent a loan relationship.

(2) Regulation 8 shall apply on the [deemed disposal under regulation 7A(1) of the asset][2] with the modification that the first amount shall be the basic valuation of the asset translated into sterling at the beginning of the accounting period in which the asset first became a regulation 7 asset by virtue of paragraph (5) of that regulation.][1]

Amendments—[1] This regulation inserted by the Exchange Gains and Losses (Insurance Companies) (Amendment) Regulations, SI 1996/673 regs 1(2), 4, with effect for disposals made after 31 March 1996.

[2] Words in para (2) substituted by the Exchange Gains and Losses (Transitional Provisions and Savings) Regulations, SI 2002/1969 regs 18, 26 with effect for accounting periods beginning after 30 September 2002.

[**12**—(1) This regulation applies in any case where an asset is a regulation 7 asset by virtue of paragraph (6) of that regulation.

(2) Regulation 8 shall apply on the [deemed disposal under regulation 7A(1) of the asset][2] with the modifications that—

(*a*) the first amount shall be the basic valuation of the original shares in relation to the asset translated into sterling at the time immediately after the company became entitled to the original shares, and

(*b*) the second amount shall be the basic valuation of the original shares in relation to the asset translated into sterling at the time immediately before the company ceased to be entitled to the original shares.][1]

Amendments—[1] This regulation inserted by the Exchange Gains and Losses (Insurance Companies) (Amendment) Regulations, SI 1996/673 regs 1(2), 4, with effect for disposals made after 31 March 1996.

[2] Words in para (2) substituted by the Exchange Gains and Losses (Transitional Provisions and Savings) Regulations, SI 2002/1969 regs 18, 27 with effect for accounting periods beginning after 30 September 2002.

1995/171

Friendly Societies (Taxation of Transfers of Business) Regulations 1995

Made by the Treasury, under TA 1988, s 463(2)–(4)

Revocation—These Regulations revoked by the Friendly Societies (Modification of the Corporation Tax Acts) Regulations, SI 1997/473, reg 54(*b*), with effect in relation to transfers, amalgamations and conversions taking place after 31 December 1994.

1995/351
Lloyd's Underwriters (Tax) Regulations 1995

Made by the Commissioners of Inland Revenue under FA 1993 ss 179(2), 179A(3)(*b*), 182(1), (4), (5), 184(1), (3), FA 1994 ss 227(2), 229, 230(1), (3)

Made . . . . 15 February 1995
Laid before the House of Commons . . . . . 16 February 1995
Coming into Force . . . . 9 March 1995

Commentary—*Simon's Direct Tax Service* **E5.613, 614, 619, 619A, 624, 642.**

ARRANGEMENT OF REGULATIONS

PRELIMINARY

Citation, commencement and effect

1 These Regulations may be cited as the Lloyd's Underwriters (Tax) Regulations 1995 and shall come into force on 9th March 1995, but except as otherwise provided shall have effect—

(*a*) in their application to members who are individuals, with respect to the year 1992–93 and subsequent years of assessment;

(*b*) in their application to corporate members, with respect to the underwriting year 1994 and subsequent underwriting years.

Interpretation

2—(1) In these Regulations unless the context otherwise requires—

''ancillary trust fund'' in relation to a member who is an individual has the meaning given by section 184(1) of the Finance Act 1993 and in relation to a corporate member has the meaning given by section 230(1) of the Finance Act 1994;

''the Board'' means the Commissioners of Inland Revenue;

''Chapter III'' means Chapter III of Part II of the Finance Act 1993 and ''Chapter V'' means Chapter V of Part IV of the Finance Act 1994;

''inspector'' includes any officer of the Board;

''Management Act'' means the Taxes Management Act 1970;

''managing agent'' in relation to a member who is an individual has the meaning given by section 184(1) of the Finance Act 1993 as extended by regulation 3, and in relation to a corporate member has the meaning given by section 230(1) of the Finance Act 1994 as extended by that regulation;

''member'' means a member of Lloyd's who is an individual or, as the case may be, a corporate member and who is or has been an underwriting member;

''quota share contract'' in relation to a member who is an individual has the meaning given by section 178(4) of the Finance Act 1993 and in relation to a corporate member has the meaning given by section 225(4) of the Finance Act 1994;

''Schedule 19'' and ''Schedule 20'' mean respectively Schedule 19 and Schedule 20 to the Finance Act 1993;

''the Taxes Act'' means the Income and Corporation Taxes Act 1988;

''section 179'' and ''section 179A'' mean respectively, section 179 and section 179A of the Finance Act 1993;

[''tax credit'' means a tax credit under section 231 of the Taxes Act;][1]

''underwriting business'' in relation to a member who is an individual has the meaning given by section 184(1) of the Finance Act 1993 and in relation to a corporate member has the meaning given by section 230(1) of the Finance Act 1994.

(2) For the purposes of these Regulations an underwriting year and a year of assessment shall be deemed to correspond to each other if the underwriting year ends in the year of assessment.

(3) References in these Regulations to the profits or losses of the underwriting business of a member who is an individual are references to profits or losses of that business within Chapter III, and references to the profits or losses of a corporate member's underwriting business are references to the profits or losses of that business within Chapter V.

Amendments—[1] Definition of ''tax credit'' in sub-para (1) inserted by the Lloyd's Underwriters (Tax) (Amendment) Regulations, SI 1996/781 regs 1, 3 with effect from 5 April 1996.

Managing agents

3—(1) For the purposes of Parts I and III of Schedule 19 and of these Regulations, if the person who is acting as a managing agent in relation to an underwriting year corresponding to a year of assessment (in this regulation referred to as ''the original year of assessment'') is different from the person who was so acting at the end of that underwriting year (in this regulation referred to as ''the original agent''), then ''managing agent'' has the meaning given by sub-paragraph (*a*) or, as the case may be, sub-paragraph (*b*) of paragraph (2) below.

(2) If the original agent ceases so to act—

(*a*) before the beginning of the year of assessment next but two following the original year of assessment, then ''managing agent'' means—

(i) the person who is so acting at the beginning of that year of assessment, or

(ii) if that person ceases so to act, such person as the Board may determine having regard to all the circumstances;

(*b*) after the end of the year of assessment next but one following the original year of assessment, then ''managing agent'' means such person as the Board may determine having regard to all the circumstances.

ASSESSMENT AND COLLECTION OF TAX

Assessment and collection—general

4 Subject to regulations 5 to 8 below and regulations 6 to 12, 14 and 15 of the Lloyd's Underwriters (Tax) (1992–93 to 1996–97) Regulations 1995, the like provisions as are contained in the Management Act and the Tax Acts relating to the assessment and collection of tax shall have effect in relation to tax charged in accordance with section 171 of the Finance Act 1993 or, as the case may be, section 219 of the Finance Act 1994.

Amount payable under stop-loss insurance—individual member

5—(1) This regulation applies where—

(*a*) any insurance money payable to a member under a stop-loss insurance in respect of a loss in his underwriting business, or any amount payable to a member out of the High Level Stop Loss Fund in respect of such a loss, falls to be treated by virtue of section 178(2) of the Finance Act 1993 as a trading receipt in computing the profits arising from the business for the year of assessment which corresponds to the underwriting year in which the loss arose or, as respects an amount payable in respect of a loss declared in the underwriting year 1997 or a subsequent underwriting year, the underwriting year in which the loss was declared;

(*b*) the amount so treated operates to reduce or extinguish the amount of the loss sustained by the member in his underwriting business for that year of assessment;

(*c*) section 178(3) of the Finance Act 1993 does not apply as respects the payment of that amount; and

(*d*) the inspector is precluded—

(i) by section 34 of the Management Act from making an assessment under section 29(3)(*c*) of that Act or, as respects the year 1996–97 and subsequent years of assessment, section 29(1)(*c*) of that Act, in respect of the whole or any part of that amount, or

(ii) by section 30(5) of the Management Act from making an assessment under that section in respect of the whole or any part of that amount.

(2) An assessment under section 29(3)(*c*) or, as the case may be, section 29(1)(*c*) or 30 of the Management Act in respect of the whole or any part of that amount shall not be out of time if made before the end of the underwriting year following the underwriting year in which the amount was received.

Amount payable under stop-loss insurance—corporate member

6—(1) This regulation applies where—

(*a*) any insurance money is payable to a corporate member under a stop-loss insurance in respect of a loss in its underwriting business, and the insurance money or, as the case may be, the apportioned part of the insurance money falls to be treated by virtue of section 225(2) of the Finance Act 1994 as a trading receipt in computing the profits arising from the business for an accounting period;

(*b*) the amount so treated operates to reduce or extinguish the amount of the loss sustained by the corporate member in its underwriting business for that accounting period;

(*c*) section 225(3) of the Finance Act 1994 does not apply as respects the payment of the insurance money; and

(*d*) the inspector is precluded—

(i) by section 34 of the Management Act from making an assessment under section 29(3)(*c*) of that Act or, as respects an accounting period ending on or after such day as is appointed under section 199(3) of the Finance Act 1994 section 29(1)(*c*) of the Management Act, in respect of the whole or any part of the amount so treated, or

(ii) by section 30(5) of the Management Act from making an assessment under that section in respect of the whole or any part of that amount.

(2) An assessment under section 29(3)(*c*) or, as the case may be, section 29(1)(*c*) or 30 of the Management Act in respect of the whole or any part of that amount shall not be out of time if made before the end of the underwriting year following the underwriting year in which the amount was received.

Non-delivery of return—reasonable excuse

7—(1) For the purposes of Schedule 19, a managing agent shall be deemed not to have failed—

(*a*) to deliver a return of a syndicate profit or loss within the time specified in paragraph 2(2) of that Schedule, or

(*b*) to deliver a return apportioning a syndicate profit or loss within the period referred to in paragraph 6(4) of that Schedule,

if he delivered it within such further time, if any, as the inspector may have allowed.

(2) Where a managing agent had a reasonable excuse for not delivering such a return as is mentioned in paragraph (1) above, he shall be deemed not to have failed to deliver it unless the excuse had ceased and, after the excuse ceased, not to have failed to deliver it if he did so without unreasonable delay after the excuse had ceased.

[Payment of income tax—taxed income and tax credits][1]

[7A The like provisions as are contained in sections 59A and 59B of the Management Act shall have effect for the year 1996–97 and subsequent years of assessment in relation to tax which—

(*a*) is charged on income in accordance with section 171 of the Finance Act 1993, being income falling within section 172(1)(*c*) of that Act, and

(*b*) either—

(i) was paid by way of deduction at source, or

(ii) is represented by a tax credit,

as if references to income tax deducted or treated as deducted from any income or treated as paid on any income in respect of a year of assessment were references to income tax deducted or treated as deducted or paid in respect of the underwriting year corresponding to that year of assessment.][1]

Amendments—[1] This regulation inserted by the Lloyd's Underwriters (Tax) (Amendment) Regulations, SI 1996/781 regs 1, 4 with effect from 5 April 1996.

[7B The like provisions as are contained in section 824 of the Taxes Act shall have effect for the year 1996–97 and subsequent years of assessment in relation to—

(*a*) any repayment of tax which was paid by way of deduction at source in respect of income charged to tax in accordance with section 171, and falling within section 172(1)(*c*), of the Finance Act 1993, and

(*b*) any payment of the whole or part of a tax credit (to which section 824 of the Taxes Act applies by virtue of subsection (2) of that section) in respect of such income,

as if the reference in subsection (3)(*b*) of that section to the year of assessment for which the tax was charged was a reference to the year of assessment for which the tax was assessed on the member concerned.][1]

Amendments—[1] This regulation inserted by the Lloyd's Underwriters (Tax) (Amendment) Regulations, SI 1996/781 regs 1, 4 with effect from 5 April 1996.

[Year of assessment to which taxed income and tax credits attributable][1]

[7C The like provision as is contained in paragraph (*a*) of section 835(6) of the Taxes Act (total income) shall have effect for the year 1994–95 and subsequent years of assessment as if it provided that income falling within that paragraph and within section 172(1)(*c*) of the Finance Act 1993 should be deemed to be income of the year of assessment corresponding to the underwriting year in which it was received by the member concerned, and not income of the year of assessment referred to in that paragraph.][1]

Amendments—[1] This regulation inserted by the Lloyd's Underwriters (Tax) (Amendment) Regulations, SI 1996/781 regs 1, 4 with effect from 5 April 1996.

Determinations and notices of determinations

8 The like provisions as are contained in section 113(1B) of the Management Act shall apply to a determination or a notice of a determination under Schedule 19 as if the determination were an assessment and the notice of the determination were a notice of an assessment.

CESSATION OF MEMBER'S UNDERWRITING BUSINESS

Cessation of individual member's underwriting business—final year of assessment

9—(1) Where a member who is an individual ceases to carry on his underwriting business, whether by reason of death or otherwise, the member's final year of assessment shall, in the cases specified in paragraphs (2) to (5) below and subject to subsection (3) of section 179, be ascertained in accordance with the provisions of those paragraphs.

(2) In any case where a letter is issued by the Membership Department of Lloyd's to the member or his agent inviting an application for the repayment of the member's deposit, the member's final year of assessment shall be not later than the year of assessment in which falls the date which is 180 days after the date of issue of the letter.

(3) In any case where the member's deposit at Lloyd's is paid over to a person other than the member or his personal representatives or assigns, the member's final year of assessment shall be that which corresponds to the underwriting year in which his deposit is so paid over or, where paragraph (2) above applies and the year of assessment specified in that paragraph is earlier, that earlier year of assessment.

(4) In any case where the member or another person is released from any arrangement entered into by the member or that person in order to satisfy the requirement on the part of the member to provide a deposit at Lloyd's, the member's final year of assessment shall, except in a case to which paragraph (5) below applies, be that which corresponds to the underwriting year in which the release occurs.

(5) In any case where the member's deposit at Lloyd's is extinguished or released before the last open year of account of any syndicate of which he is a member is closed, the member's final year of assessment shall be either—

(*a*) the year of assessment next following the year of assessment which corresponds to the underwriting year in which the last open year of account of any syndicate of which he is a member is closed or, if later,

(*b*) the year of assessment which corresponds to the underwriting year in which he ceases to be a member of Lloyd's under the rules or practice of Lloyd's.

(6) This regulation has effect in relation to any member—

(*a*) whose deposit at Lloyd's is paid over to him or another person or, as the case may be, released or extinguished, on or after 1st January 1993, and

(*b*) in whose case the last open year of account of any syndicate of which he was a member is closed on or after that date.

(7) For the purposes of this regulation, the last open year of account of a syndicate of which a person is a member shall be regarded as having closed either—

(*a*) when the member is treated under the rules or practice of Lloyd's as having been discharged of all his liabilities in relation to that syndicate, whether by the syndicate closing its accounts or by the member or his personal representatives or assigns entering into a quota share contract, or

(*b*) in a case where the member enters, or his personal representatives or assigns enter, into a quota share contract before the end of the closing year of the syndicate, at the end of the underwriting year in which the contract is made.

Cessation of individual member's underwriting business by reason of death on or after 6th April 1994—date of cessation of business

10—(1) For the purposes of the Income Tax Acts, where a member ceases to carry on his underwriting business by reason of his death, the business shall, in the cases specified in paragraphs (2) to (5) below, be treated as continuing until the date specified in those paragraphs in relation to the appropriate case.

(2) In any case where a letter is issued by the Membership Department of Lloyd's to the member's agent, or his personal representatives or assigns, inviting an application for the repayment of the member's deposit, the member's business shall be treated as continuing until the date which is 180 days after the date of issue of the letter.

(3) In any case where the member's deposit at Lloyd's is paid over to a person other than the member's personal representatives or assigns, the member's business shall be treated as continuing until his deposit is so paid over or, where paragraph (2) above applies and the date specified in that paragraph occurs earlier, that earlier date.

(4) In any case where the member's personal representatives are, or another person is, released from any arrangement entered into by the member or that person in order to satisfy the requirement on the part of the member to provide a deposit at Lloyd's, the member's business shall, except in a case to which paragraph (5) below applies, be treated as continuing until the date on which the release occurs.

(5) In any case where the member's deposit at Lloyd's is extinguished or released before the last open year of account of any syndicate of which he was a member is closed, the member's business shall be treated as continuing until either—

(*a*) the end of the year of assessment next following the year of assessment which corresponds to the underwriting year in which the last open year of account of any syndicate of which he was a member is closed or, if later,

(*b*) the end of the year of assessment which corresponds to the underwriting year in which he ceased to be a member of Lloyd's under the rules or practice of Lloyd's.

(6) For the purposes of paragraph (5) above, the last open year of account of a syndicate of which a person was a member shall be regarded as having closed either—

(*a*) when the member is treated under the rules or practice of Lloyd's as having been discharged of all his liabilities in relation to that syndicate, whether by the syndicate closing its accounts or by the member or his personal representatives entering into a quota share contract, or

(*b*) in a case where the member enters, or his personal representatives enter, into a quota share contract before the end of the closing year of the syndicate, at the end of the underwriting year in which the contract is made.

(7) This regulation has effect in relation to any member whose death occurs on or after 6th April 1994.

Profits and losses arising after death of member before 6th April 1994

11 For the purposes of the provisions of Chapter III other than Schedule 20, where—

(*a*) the death of a member occurred before 6th April 1994;

(*b*) the member's deposit at Lloyd's, if paid over to him or his personal representatives or assigns, was not paid over prior to 1st January 1993; and

(*c*) income arises to, or expenses are incurred or paid by, his personal representatives after his death from the carrying on by them of the member's underwriting business in circumstances where the income or expenses would have been taken into account, by virtue of those provisions, in computing the profits or losses arising to the member from his underwriting business had they arisen or been incurred or paid prior to his death,

the income and expenses shall be regarded as arising to, or incurred or paid by, the member and are accordingly to be taken into account in computing profits or losses arising to the member from his underwriting business for the purposes of those provisions.

Cessation of individual member's underwriting business by reason of death on or after 6th April 1994—profits or losses arising after death

12 For the purposes of the provisions of Chapter III other than Schedule 20, where—

(*a*) the death of a member occurs on or after 6th April 1994; and

(*b*) income arises to, or expenses are incurred or paid by, his personal representatives after his death from the carrying on by them of the member's underwriting business in circumstances where the income or expenses would have been taken into account, by virtue of those provisions, in computing the profits or losses arising to the member from his underwriting business had they arisen or been incurred or paid prior to his death,

the profits or losses arising to the personal representatives from the income and expenses shall be computed as if references in those provisions to profits and losses arising to the member from his underwriting business included references to the profits and losses arising to the personal representatives.

Cessation of individual member's underwriting business—claim for relief where business commenced before 1st January 1972

13—(1) This regulation applies where—

(*a*) a member who is an individual has ceased to be a member of Lloyd's under the rules or practice of Lloyd's or, if earlier, has given notice of resignation of membership under the rules or practice of Lloyd's which has not been withdrawn; and

(*b*) the member's underwriting business as an underwriting member of Lloyd's commenced before 1st January 1972.

(2) The member may claim that—

(*a*) for the last year of assessment in which profits or losses of his underwriting business arising directly from his membership of one or more syndicates, or from assets forming part of a premiums trust fund of one or more syndicates, being profits or losses declared in the underwriting year following the closing year, fall to be included by virtue of the provisions of Chapter III, he shall be charged to tax in respect of those profits on the amount of the actual profits of the period beginning on 6th April and ending on 31st December in that underwriting year (but subject to any deduction or set-off to which he may be entitled under section 385 of the Taxes Act); and

(*b*) for the year of assessment immediately preceding that referred to in subparagraph (*a*) above, there shall be deducted in computing profits arising as mentioned in that sub-paragraph an amount equal to the lesser of—

(i) the amount of those profits, and

(ii) the amount of the profits of his underwriting business for the underwriting year 1972.

(3) For the purposes only of determining the last year of assessment under paragraph (2) above in any case where the member enters into a quota share contract in relation to a syndicate before the end of the closing year of the syndicate, any loss declared by that syndicate following the making of the contract shall be treated as if it were a declared profit.

(4) A member may not make more than one claim under paragraph (2) above.

Cessation of individual member's underwriting business—terminal loss relief

14—(1) This regulation applies where a member ceases to carry on his underwriting business, whether by reason of death or otherwise, and either—

(*a*) his deposit at Lloyd's is paid over to him or his personal representatives or assigns on or after 1st January 1993, or

(*b*) the last open year of account of any syndicate of which he is a member is closed after 31st December 1992.

(2) Notwithstanding section 179 or section 179A, or regulation 9 or 10 of these Regulations, the date on which the member's underwriting business is permanently discontinued for the purposes of section 388 of the Taxes Act (carry-back of terminal losses) shall be deemed to be the 5th April in the last year of assessment in which profits or losses of that business which arise directly from his membership of one or more syndicates, or from assets forming part of a [premium][1] trust fund, fall to be included by virtue of the provisions of Chapter III.

(3) No claim may be made by a member under section 388 of the Taxes Act until—

(*a*) he has ceased to be a member under the rules or practice of Lloyd's or, if earlier,

(*b*) he has given (and not withdrawn) notice of resignation of membership under the rules or practice of Lloyd's.

(4) A member may not make more than one claim under section 388 of the Taxes Act in respect of the same underwriting business.

(5) For the purposes of paragraph (1)(*b*) above, the last open year of account of a syndicate of which a person is a member shall be regarded as having closed either—

(*a*) when the member is treated under the rules or practice of Lloyd's as having been discharged of all his liabilities in relation to that syndicate, whether by the syndicate closing its accounts or by the member or his personal representatives or assigns entering into a quota share contract; or

(*b*) in a case where the member enters, or his personal representatives or assigns enter, into a quota share contract before the end of the closing year of the syndicate, at the end of the underwriting year in which the contract is made.

(6) For the purposes only of determining the last year of assessment under paragraph (2) above in any case where the member enters into a quota share contract in relation to a syndicate before the

end of the closing year of the syndicate, any loss declared by that syndicate following the making of the contract shall be treated as if it were a declared profit.

Amendments—[1] Word in para (2) substituted by the Financial Services and Markets Act 2000 (Consequential Amendments) (Taxes) Order, SI 2001/3629 art 139 with effect from 1 December 2001, immediately after the coming into force of the Financial Services and Markets Act 2000 ss 411, 432(1), Sch 20 (and SI 2001/3629 Pts 1 and 2).

Cessation of individual member's underwriting business by reason of death—winding up of old-style special reserve fund

15—(1) In any case where—

(*a*) a member ceases to carry on his underwriting business by reason of his death;

(*b*) the member's final year of assessment, ascertained in accordance with the provisions of Chapter III and these Regulations, is the year 1992–93 or any subsequent year of assessment; and

(*c*) prior to his death no new-style fund had been set up in relation to the member;

subsection (4) of section 175 of the Finance Act 1993 (winding-up of old-style fund) shall apply as if paragraph (*b*) of that subsection was omitted.

(2) In paragraph (1) above, "new-style fund" and "old-style fund" have the meanings given by paragraph 12(1) of Schedule 20.

Cessation of corporate member's underwriting business—final underwriting year

16—(1) Where a corporate member ceases to carry on its underwriting business, whether by reason of being wound up or otherwise, its final underwriting year shall, in the cases specified in paragraphs (2) to (5) below, be ascertained in accordance with the provisions of those paragraphs.

(2) In any case where a letter is issued by the Membership Department of Lloyd's to the corporate member or its agent inviting an application for the repayment of the corporate member's deposit, the corporate member's final underwriting year shall be not later than the underwriting year in which falls the date which is 180 days after the date of issue of the letter.

(3) In any case where the corporate member's deposit at Lloyd's is paid over to a person other than the corporate member, its final underwriting year shall be the underwriting year in which its deposit is so paid over or, where paragraph (2) above applies and the underwriting year specified in that paragraph is earlier, that earlier underwriting year.

(4) In any case where the corporate member or another person is released from any arrangement entered into by the corporate member or that person in order to satisfy the requirement on the part of the corporate member to provide a deposit at Lloyd's, the corporate member's final underwriting year shall, except in a case to which paragraph (5) below applies, be the underwriting year in which the release occurs.

(5) In any case where the corporate member's deposit at Lloyd's is extinguished or released before the last open year of account of any syndicate of which it is a member is closed, the corporate member's final underwriting year shall be either—

(*a*) the underwriting year next following the underwriting year in which the last open year of account of any syndicate of which it was a member is closed or, if later,

(*b*) the underwriting year in which the corporate member ceases to be a member of Lloyd's under the rules or practice of Lloyd's.

(6) For the purposes of this regulation, the last open year of account of a syndicate of which a person is a corporate member shall be regarded as having closed when the member is treated under the rules or practice of Lloyd's as having been discharged of all its liabilities in relation to that syndicate, whether by the syndicate closing its accounts or by the member entering into a quota share contract.

SUPPLEMENTAL

Revocations

17—(1) The Lloyd's Underwriters (Tax) Regulations 1974, the Lloyd's Underwriters (Tax) (No 2) Regulations 1974 and the Lloyd's Underwriters (Schedule 19A to the Income and Corporation Taxes Act 1988) Regulations 1990 are hereby revoked.

(2) A claim made under regulation 21 of the Lloyd's Underwriters (Tax) Regulations 1974 which was valid for the purposes of that regulation immediately before the coming into force of these Regulations but which had not been finally determined at that time ("a pending claim") shall have effect as if made under regulation 13 of these Regulations, and accordingly references in that regulation to a claim shall be construed as including references to a pending claim.

1995/352
Lloyd's Underwriters (Tax) (1992–93 to 1996–97) Regulations 1995

Note—These Regulations are now spent.

1995/353
Lloyd's Underwriters (Special Reserve Funds) Regulations 1995

Made by the Commissioners of Inland Revenue under FA 1993 ss 182(1)(*c*), (4), 184(1), (3), Sch 20 paras 3(2), 4(8), 5(10), 6(1), (3), 11(5)

Made . . . . 15 February 1995
Laid before the House of Commons . . . . 16 February 1995
Coming into Force . . . . . . 9 March 1995

Commentary—*Simon's Direct Tax Service* **E5.645.**

Citation, commencement and effect

1 These Regulations may be cited as the Lloyd's Underwriters (Special Reserve Funds) Regulations 1995, shall come into force on 9th March 1995 and, except as otherwise provided by these Regulations, shall have effect for the year 1992–93 and subsequent years of assessment.

Interpretation

2 In these Regulations "Schedule 20" means Schedule 20 to the Finance Act 1993.

Syndicate profit or loss—modification of definition—running-off syndicates

3 ...

Note—Reg 3 amends FA 1993 Sch 20, para 1(2).

Cash calls—running-off syndicates—modification of paragraph 4 of Schedule 20

4 ...

Note—Reg 4 amends FA 1993 Sch 20, para 4.

Payments into or out of special reserve fund—prescribed periods

5—(1) The period prescribed for the purposes of paragraph 3(1) of Schedule 20 is the period which begins on 1st January in the calendar year in which the profits and losses comprising the syndicate profit made by the member for the underwriting year concerned are declared and ends on 31st October in that calendar year or, if earlier, on the date on which payment is made to or on behalf of the member of an amount representing any part of the syndicate profit made by the member for that underwriting year.

(2) The period prescribed for the purposes of any payments required by paragraph 4(1) of Schedule 20—

(*a*) where the accounts of the syndicate have remained open beyond the end of the closing year and the cash call concerned is made—

(i) in respect of an underwriting year determined by reference to paragraph 1(2)(*c*) [of Schedule 20][1], and

(ii) in a calendar year ("the relevant calendar year") after the end of the closing year,

is the period which begins on 1st January in the relevant calendar year and ends on the date which is 90 days after the date on which the cash call is made on the member;

(*b*) in any other case, is the period which begins on 1st January in the calendar year next but one preceding the underwriting year which is the closing year for the syndicate concerned and ends on the earlier of the following dates, namely—

(i) the date which is 90 days after the date on which the cash call concerned is made on the member, and

(ii) the date which is 90 days after the end of the closing year.

(3) The period prescribed for the purposes of any payments required by paragraph 4(2) of Schedule 20 is the period which begins on 1st January in the calendar year in which the profits and losses comprising the syndicate profit or loss of the member for the underwriting year concerned are declared and ends on the earlier of the following dates, namely—

(*a*) 31st October in that calendar year;

(*b*) where there is a syndicate profit made by the member for the underwriting year concerned, the date on which payment is made to or on behalf of the member of an amount representing any part of that profit.

(4) The period prescribed for the purposes of any payment required by paragraph 4(3) of Schedule 20 is the period of 90 days following the date on which the stop-loss payment is made to the member in respect of his syndicate loss.

(5) The period prescribed for the purposes of any payments required by paragraph 4(6) of Schedule 20 is the period of 90 days following the date on which the whole or part of the stop-loss payment made to the member is repaid by him.

(6) The period prescribed for the purposes of any payments required by paragraph 5(1) of Schedule 20 is the period which begins on 1st January in the calendar year in which the profits and losses comprising the syndicate loss sustained by the member for the underwriting year concerned are declared and ends on 31st October in that calendar year.

(7) The period prescribed for the purposes of any payment required by paragraph 5(4) of Schedule 20 is the period of 90 days following the date on which the stop-loss payment is made to the member in respect of his syndicate loss.

(8) The period prescribed for the purposes of any payments required by paragraph 5(7) of Schedule 20 is the period of 90 days following the date on which the whole or part of the stop-loss payment made to the member is repaid by him.

(9) The period prescribed for the purposes of any payments required by paragraph 6(2) of Schedule 20 is the period of 90 days following the last day of the underwriting year in respect of which the valuation giving rise to the payments is made.

Amendments—[1] Words in para (2) substituted by the Lloyd's Underwriters (Special Reserve Funds) (Amendment) Regulations, SI 1995/1185 reg 3 with effect from 23 May 1995.

Valuation of special reserve fund

6—(1) Paragraph (2) below prescribes the manner in which the value of a member's special reserve fund as at the end of an underwriting year shall be determined, and paragraph (3) below prescribes the matters which, in addition to the value of the fund, are to be stated by the fund manager in his report to the member of the value of the fund.

(2) The value of the fund shall be determined so as to be in accordance with—

(*a*) the market value of the assets of the fund, and
(*b*) the rules of Lloyd's relating to the method of valuation of the fund.

(3) The matters prescribed are—

(*a*) the amount of any payment made in the underwriting year to which the valuation relates under any of the paragraphs of Schedule 20 specified in paragraph (4) below, and
(*b*) the date on which each such payment was made.

(4) The paragraphs specified are paragraphs 3(1), 4(1), (2), (3) and (6), 5(1), (4) and (7), 6(2) and 7(1).

(5) This regulation shall have effect for the underwriting year 1994 and subsequent underwriting years.

Cessation of underwriting business—modifications of Part I of Schedule 20

[7—(1) For the purposes of the Income Tax Acts and these Regulations—

(*a*) references in paragraphs 1, 3 to 6, 8 and 10 of Schedule 20 to a member, other than references relating to a member's special reserve fund, shall be construed, in the circumstances specified in paragraph (2) below and unless the context otherwise requires, as including references to the member's personal representatives;
(*b*) references in those paragraphs to a member's special reserve fund shall be construed, in the circumstances specified in paragraph (2) below and unless the context otherwise requires, as including references to income arising after the death of the member from assets of the fund and retained by the trustees, and profits arising from the investment of that income.

(2) The circumstances specified in this paragraph are where—

(*a*) the member dies on or after 6th April 1994, and
(*b*) the member's personal representatives carry on his underwriting business after his death.

(3) This regulation shall have effect—

(*a*) in its application to paragraphs 1, 3 to 6 and 8 of Schedule 20, for the year 1994–95 and subsequent years of assessment;
(*b*) in its application to paragraph 10 of Schedule 20, for the year 1997–98 and subsequent years of assessment.][1]

Amendments—This regulation substituted together with reg 7A for reg 7 as originally enacted by the Lloyd's Underwriters (Special Reserve Funds) (Amendment) Regulations, SI 1995/1185 reg 4 with effect from 23 May 1995.

[7A—(1) Paragraph 9 of Schedule 20 (tax exemption for profits arising from assets of fund) shall apply with the modifications specified in paragraphs (2) and (3) below.

(2) In sub-paragraph (1) after the words ''special reserve fund'' there shall be inserted the words ''or arising after the death of the member from the investment of income retained by the trustees''.

(3) In sub-paragraphs (2) and (3) after the words ''special reserve fund'' in both places where they occur there shall be inserted the words ''or arising after the death of the member as mentioned in sub-paragraph (1) above''.

(4) This regulation shall have effect for the year 1994–95 and subsequent years of assessment.][1]

Amendments—[1] This regulation substituted together with reg 7 for reg 7 as originally enacted by the Lloyd's Underwriters (Special Reserve Funds) (Amendment) Regulations, SI 1995/1185 reg 4 with effect from 23 May 1995.

8 ...

Note—Reg 8 amends FA 1993 Sch 20, para 11 (and has been amended by SI 1995/1185 reg 5 with effect from the year 1994–95).

1995/917
Profit-Related Pay (Shortfall Recovery) Regulations 1995

Made by the Commissioners of Inland Revenue under TA 1988 ss 179(2), 203

Made	*29 March 1995*
Laid before the House of Commons	*29 March 1995*
Coming into Force	*19 April 1995*

Commentary—*Simon's Direct Tax Service* **E4.313.**

Citation and commencement

1 These Regulations may be cited as the Profit-Related Pay (Shortfall Recovery) Regulations 1995 and shall come into force on 19th April 1995.

Interpretation

2 In these Regulations—

"the Board" means the Commissioners of Inland Revenue;
"collector" means a collector of taxes;
"the Management Act" means the Taxes Management Act 1970;
"the principal Regulations" means the Income Tax (Employments) Regulations 1993;
"the Taxes Act" means the Income and Corporation Taxes Act 1988;
"year" means year of assessment.

Information

3—(1) Where the registration of a profit-related pay scheme registered under Chapter III of Part V of the Taxes Act is cancelled by the Board, the scheme employer shall, within 60 days of being required by the Board to do so, make a return to the Board, in such form as the Board may prescribe, containing the particulars specified in paragraph (2) below.

(2) The particulars specified in this paragraph are particulars of—

(*a*) the aggregate amount of the shortfall in the deductions made in accordance with the principal Regulations (an amount equal to which is payable by the scheme employer to the Board pursuant to section 179(2) of the Taxes Act);

(*b*) the amount of the shortfall attributable to each year where the shortfall relates to more than one year.

Recovery

4—(1) Within 60 days of his being required to make a return in accordance with regulation 3, the scheme employer shall pay to the Board an amount equal to the aggregate amount of the shortfall shown in the return.

(2) Subject to these Regulations, the amount payable to the Board pursuant to paragraph (1) above shall be recoverable from the scheme employer as if it were an amount of tax which the scheme employer was liable under regulation 40 or 41 of the principal Regulations to pay to the collector.

Evidence

5—(1) Where an amount equal to the aggregate amount of the shortfall shown in a return has not been paid or fully paid within the period specified in regulation 4(1), an officer of the Board may certify the amount due to the collector.

(2) The production of a certificate under paragraph (1) above shall be sufficient evidence that the scheme employer is liable to pay to the collector the amount shown in the certificate.

(3) A certificate of a collector that an amount payable pursuant to regulation 4(1) has not been paid to him or, to the best of his knowledge and belief, to any other collector shall be sufficient evidence that the amount specified in the certificate is unpaid and due to the Crown.

(4) Any document purporting to be a certificate under paragraph (1) or (3) above shall be deemed to be such a certificate until the contrary is proved.

Determinations

6—(1) Where it appears to the Board that there is an amount payable pursuant to regulation 4(1) which has not been paid or fully paid, the Board may determine to the best of their judgment the amount so unpaid, and shall serve notice of the determination on the scheme employer.

(2) A determination under paragraph (1) above shall be subject to the like provisions as are contained in Parts IV, V and VI of the Management Act as if it were an assessment and as if the amount determined were income tax charged on the scheme employer, and those Parts of that Act shall, subject to these Regulations, apply accordingly with any necessary modifications.

(3) An appeal against a determination under paragraph (1) above may be brought before either—

(*a*) the General Commissioners for the division where the trade, profession or vocation of the scheme employer is carried on or in which the head office or principal place of business of the scheme employer is situated, or
(*b*) the Special Commissioners.

Interest on unpaid amounts of shortfall

7—(1) Where—

(*a*) there is an amount payable pursuant to regulation 4(1), or
(*b*) the Board make a determination of an amount under regulation 6, and
(*c*) in either case the amount in question is not paid or fully paid on or before the 14th day after the end of the year to which it is attributable,

the amount shall carry interest at the prescribed rate from the reckonable date until payment.

(2) In paragraph (1) above ''the prescribed rate'' means the rate applicable under section 178 of the Finance Act 1989 for the purposes of section 86 of the Management Act; and where that rate changes on an operative date within the meaning given by regulation 2 of the Taxes (Interest Rate) Regulations 1989 by virtue of those Regulations, the change shall have effect for periods beginning on or after the operative date in relation to interest running from before that date as well as from or from after that date.

(3) In this regulation ''the reckonable date'' means—

(*a*) where the amount referred to in sub-paragraph (*a*) or (*b*) of paragraph (1) above arises from a cancellation by the Board of the registration of a scheme under section 178(3) of the Taxes Act, the day immediately following the last day of the period specified in subsection (2) or, as the case may be, subsection (3) of section 180 of that Act;
(*b*) in any other case, the 14th day after the end of the year to which the amount is attributable.

(4) The amount unpaid referred to in paragraph (1) above shall carry interest from the reckonable date even if that date is a non-business day within the meaning of section 92 of the Bills of Exchange Act 1882.

(5) Interest payable under this regulation shall be recoverable as if it were an amount of tax which an employer is liable under regulation 40 or 41 of the principal Regulations to pay to the collector.

Death of a scheme employer

8 If a scheme employer dies, anything which he would have been liable to do under these Regulations shall be done by his personal representatives.

Revocations

9—(1) The Profit-Related Pay (Shortfall Recovery) Regulations 1988 (''the 1988 Regulations''), so far as not previously revoked, are hereby revoked.

(2) Regulation 14 of the Income Tax (Employments) (Amendment) Regulations 1993 is hereby revoked.

(3) Anything done pursuant to the 1988 Regulations which, if done on or after the coming into force of these Regulations, could have been done pursuant to these Regulations, shall have effect as if done pursuant to these Regulations.

1995/1370
Deposit-Takers (Interest Payments) (Discretionary or Accumulation Trusts) Regulations 1995

Made by the Commissioners of Inland Revenue under TA 1988, s 482(11)(*ab*)

Made . . . . 23 May 1995
Laid before the House of Commons . . . 24 May 1995
Coming into Force . . . . 14 June 1995

Commentary—*Simon's Direct Tax Service* **D4.1105.**

Citation, commencement and effect

1—(1) These Regulations may be cited as the Deposit-takers (Interest Payments) (Discretionary or Accumulation Trusts) Regulations 1995 and shall come into force on 14th June 1995.

(2) These Regulations shall have effect with respect to any payment of interest made on or after 6th April 1996 by a deposit-taker in respect of a deposit made before 6th April 1995 where the interest is income arising to the trustees of a discretionary or accumulation trust.

Interpretation

2 In these Regulations—

''the Board'' means the Commissioners of Inland Revenue;

''discretionary or accumulation trust'' has the meaning given by section 481(4A) of the Taxes Act;

''notice'' means notice in writing;

''payment'' includes ''credit'';

''section 480A(1)'' and ''section 481(5B)'' mean section 480A(1) and section 481(5B) respectively of the Taxes Act;

''the Taxes Act'' means the Income and Corporation Taxes Act 1988.

Discretionary or accumulation trust—form of notification

3 A notification given by any of the trustees of a discretionary or accumulation trust for the purposes of section 481(5B) shall be in the form provided by the Board.

Receipt of notification by deposit-taker

4—(1) On receipt of a notification under section 481(5B), a deposit-taker shall be entitled not to deduct tax pursuant to section 480A(1) from any payment of interest in respect of the deposit to which the notification relates and which is made in the circumstances specified in paragraph (2) below.

(2) The circumstances specified in this paragraph are where the payment is made within the period of 30 days following receipt of the notification, and at the time of the making of the payment it has not become reasonably practicable for the deposit-taker to deduct tax pursuant to section 480A(1).

Cancellation of notification

5 If the Board are satisfied, at any time following the giving of a notification under section 481(5B), that interest in respect of the deposit to which the notification relates is not income arising to the trustees of a discretionary or accumulation trust, they shall cancel the notification and give notice of the cancellation to the deposit-taker concerned.

1995/1730

Insurance Companies (Taxation of Reinsurance Business) Regulations 1995

Made by the Commissioners of Inland Revenue under TA 1988, ss 431C(1), 439A, 442A(2)–(6), FA 1995 Sch 8, para 58

Made	*7 July 1995*
Laid before the House of Commons	*7 July 1995*
Coming into Force	*28 July 1995*

Commentary—*Simon's Direct Tax Service* **D4.509.**

Citation, commencement and effect

1 These Regulations may be cited as the Insurance Companies (Taxation of Reinsurance Business) Regulations 1995, shall come into force on 28th July 1995, and shall have effect with respect to accounting periods beginning on or after 1st January 1995.

Interpretation

2 In these Regulations unless the context otherwise requires—

''accounting period'' means an accounting period of a cedant company during which a reinsurance arrangement is in force;

''basic life assurance and general annuity business'' has the meaning given by section 431F of the Taxes Act;

''the Board'' means the Commissioners of Inland Revenue;

"deposit-back arrangement" means an arrangement whereby an amount is deposited with the cedant company by the reinsurer;

"EEA Agreement" means the Agreement on the European Economic Area signed at Oporto on 2nd May 1992 as adjusted by the Protocol signed at Brussels on 17th March 1993;

"EEA State" means a State, other than the United Kingdom, which is a Contracting Party to the EEA Agreement;

["expense risk" means the risk that the amount of expenses attributable to a policy or contract over its duration is greater than the amount expected by the cedant company when it entered into the policy or contract;][1]

"inspector" includes any officer of the Board;

["insurance business transfer scheme" has the meaning given by section 431(2) of the Taxes Act;][1]

"internal linked fund" means an account to which an insurance company appropriates certain linked assets and which may be subdivided into units the value of which is determined by the company by reference to the value of those assets;

"investment return" means the investment return to be treated as accruing to a cedant company in respect of a policy pursuant to subsection (1) of section 442A in an accounting period;

"linked assets" has the meaning given by section 432ZA(1) of the Taxes Act, and "non-linked assets" means assets other than linked assets;

"linked business" means business which comprises the effecting and carrying out by an insurance company of policies where benefits provided for under each policy are to be determined by reference to the value of linked assets;

"morbidity risk" in relation to a policy means the risk that the person whose life is insured by the policy will suffer any sickness, accident or infirmity;

"mortality risk" in relation to a policy means the risk that the person whose life is insured by the policy will die;

"periodical return" has the meaning given by section 431(2) of the Taxes Act;

"policy" includes an annuity contract;

["the Prudential Sourcebook (Insurers)" has the meaning given by section 431(2) of the Taxes Act;][2]

"reinsurance arrangement" means a reinsurance arrangement to which section 442A applies;

"relevant profits" has the meaning given by section 88(3) of the Finance Act 1989;

"section 431C", "section 439A" and "section 442A" mean respectively section 431C, section 439A and section 442A of the Taxes Act;

"90% subsidiary" means a body corporate 90 per cent or more of whose ordinary share capital is owned directly or indirectly by another body corporate;

"the Taxes Act" means the Income and Corporation Taxes Act 1988.

Amendments—[1] Definitions of "expense risk" and "insurance business transfer scheme" inserted by the Insurance Companies (Taxation of Reinsurance Business) (Amendment No 2) Regulations, SI 2003/2573 regs 2, 3(*a*), (*b*) with effect for periods of account beginning after 31 October 2003: SI 2003/2573 reg 1(2).

[2] Definition of "the Prudential Sourcebook (Insurers)" inserted by SI 2003/2573 regs 2, 3(*c*) with effect for periods of account beginning after 31 December 2000: SI 2003/2573 reg 1(3).

Calculation of investment return in sole accounting period

3—(1) Where the period during which a reinsurance arrangement is in force falls wholly within a single accounting period, the amount of the investment return in that accounting period ("I") shall be calculated in accordance with the formula—

$$I = (C - P) \times R$$

where—

[C is the aggregate of—

(*a*) so much of any amount payable by the reinsurer to the cedant company during that accounting period as a result of the death, illness, or infirmity of, or accident to, any person as does not exceed the amount which would have been paid by the reinsurer if the policy had been surrendered immediately before the death, illness, or infirmity of, or accident to, that person, and

(*b*) other amounts paid by the reinsurer to the cedant company during that accounting period, being sums paid by way of commission or as result of the surrender in whole or in part of the rights under the policy or otherwise, but excluding any sum which forms part of the relevant profits of the cedant company or is paid by way of commission that has been deducted from expenses of management pursuant to section 76(1) (*ca*) of the Taxes Act][1];

P is the aggregate of the sums paid by the cedant company to the reinsurer during that accounting period by way of premium; and

R is the percentage rate of return prescribed by paragraph (2) below.

(2) The percentage rate of return prescribed is 100 per cent.

Amendments—[1] Words substituted by the Insurance Companies (Taxation of Reinsurance Business) (Amendment) Regulation, SI 1996/1621 regs 2, 3, with effect with respect to accounting periods beginning on or after 1 January 1995.

Calculation of investment return in first accounting period

4 Where the period during which a reinsurance arrangement is in force falls within more than one accounting period, the amount of the investment return in the first accounting period ("I_1") shall be calculated in accordance with the formula—

$$I_1 = (P - C) \times R$$

where—

P is the aggregate of the sums paid by the cedant company to the reinsurer during that accounting period by way of premium or otherwise [(but excluding any such sums paid in repayment of a loan or otherwise diminishing a debt such as is mentioned in paragraph 12(4)(*a*)(ii) of Appendix 9.4 of the Prudential Sourcebook (Insurers))][1];

C is the aggregate of the sums paid by the reinsurer to the cedant company during that accounting period by way of commission or as a result of the surrender in part of the rights under the policy or otherwise [(but excluding any such sums paid by way of a loan or otherwise creating a debt such as is mentioned in paragraph 12(4)(*a*)(i) of Appendix 9.4 of the Prudential Sourcebook (Insurers))][1]; and

R is the percentage rate of return prescribed by regulation 7(2);

but where [C is greater than P][1], taking the amount to be zero.

Amendments—[1] Words inserted and substituted by the Insurance Companies (Taxation of Reinsurance Business) (Amendment No 2) Regulations, SI 2003/2573 regs 2, 4 with effect for periods of account beginning after 31 December 2000: SI 2003/2573 reg 1(3).

Calculation of investment return in second and subsequent accounting periods other than final accounting period

5—(1) Where the period during which a reinsurance arrangement is in force falls within more than one accounting period, the amount of the investment return in the second or any subsequent accounting period other than the final accounting period ("I_n") shall be calculated in accordance with the formula—

$$I_n = ((P_n - C_n) + I_{n-1}) \times R$$

where—

P_n is the aggregate of the sums paid by the cedant company to the reinsurer during that accounting period and earlier accounting periods by way of premium or otherwise [(but excluding any such sums paid in repayment of a loan or otherwise diminishing a debt such as is mentioned in paragraph 12(4)(*a*)(ii) of Appendix 9.4 of the Prudential Sourcebook (Insurers))][3];

C_n is the aggregate of the sums paid by the reinsurer to the cedant company during that accounting period and earlier accounting periods by way of commission or as a result of the surrender in part of the rights under the policy or otherwise [(but excluding any such sums paid by way of a loan or otherwise creating a debt such as is mentioned in paragraph 12(4)(*a*)(i) of Appendix 9.4 of the Prudential Sourcebook (Insurers))][3];

I_{n-1} is the aggregate amount of the net investment return in previous accounting periods, that is to say, net of tax [at the appropriate rate or rates prescribed][1] by paragraph (2) below; and

R is the percentage rate of return prescribed by regulation 7(4) or (6), as the case may be;

but where [($(Pn - Cn) + In\text{-}1$)][3] is less than zero, taking the amount to be zero.

[(2) The rates prescribed by this paragraph are—

(*a*) as respects an accounting period ending before the financial year 1996, the rate applicable in accordance with section 88(1) of the Finance Act 1989;

(*b*) as respects an accounting period commencing in or after the financial year 1996 [and ending before the financial year 2003][2], the rate applicable in accordance with section 88A(1) of the Finance Act 1989;

(*c*) as respects an accounting period part of which falls in the financial year 1995 ("the 1995 part") and part in the financial year 1996 ("the 1996 part"), the rate applicable in accordance with section 88(1) of the Finance Act 1989 in relation to the proportion of the amount of the investment return attributable to the 1995 part, and the rate applicable in accordance with section 88A(1) of that Act in relation to the proportion of the amount of the investment return attributable to the 1996 part.][1]

[(*d*) as respects an accounting period commencing in or after the financial year 2003, the rate applicable in accordance with section 88(1) of the Finance Act 1989;][2]

[(*e*) as respects an accounting period part of which falls in the financial year 2002 ("the 2002 part") and part in the financial year 2003 ("the 2003 part"), the rate applicable in accordance with section 88A(1) of the Finance Act 1989 in relation to the proportion of the amount of the investment return attributable to the 2002 part, and the rate applicable in accordance with section 88(1) of that Act in relation to the proportion of the amount of the investment return attributable to the 2003 part.][2]

Amendments—[1] Words in para (1), and para (2), substituted by the Insurance Companies (Taxation of Reinsurance Business) (Amendment) Regulations, SI 1996/1621 regs 2,4, with effect with respect to accounting periods beginning on or after 1 January 1995.

[2] Words in sub-para (2)(*b*) inserted, and sub-paras (2)(*d*), (*e*) inserted, by the Insurance Companies (Taxation of Reinsurance Business) (Amendment) Regulations, SI 2003/1828 regs 1(2), 3 with effect for accounting periods ending in the financial year 2003, and subsequent financial years.

[3] Words inserted and substituted by the Insurance Companies (Taxation of Reinsurance Business) (Amendment No 2) Regulations, SI 2003/2573 regs 2, 5 with effect for periods of account beginning after 31 December 2000: SI 2003/2573 reg 1(3).

Calculation of investment return in final accounting period

6—(1) Where the period during which a reinsurance arrangement is in force falls within more than one accounting period, the amount of the investment return in the final accounting period is the amount by which the profit over the whole period during which the policy and the reinsurance arrangement was in force (''the whole period'') exceeds the aggregate of the amounts of the investment returns [treated as accruing][1] in earlier accounting periods.

(2) For the purposes of paragraph (1) above, the profit over the whole period is the amount by which the aggregate of the amounts specified in paragraph (3) below exceeds the aggregate of all amounts paid to the reinsurer by way of premiums in respect of the policy.

(3) The amounts specified in this paragraph are—

(*a*) any amount payable by the reinsurer to the cedant company as a result of the maturity of the policy concerned;

(*b*) so much of any amount payable by the reinsurer as a result of the death, illness, or infirmity of, or accident to, any person as does not exceed the amount which would have been paid by the reinsurer if the policy had been surrendered immediately before the death, illness, infirmity or accident;

(*c*) any amount payable by the reinsurer as a result of the surrender in whole of the rights conferred by the policy;

(*d*) any amount payable by the reinsurer as a result of the surrender in part of the rights conferred by the policy;

(*e*) any amount not falling within any of sub-paragraphs (*a*) to (*d*) above which is payable by the reinsurer to the cedant company in respect of the policy, other than an amount which—

(i) forms part of the relevant profits of the cedant company, or

(ii) is paid by way of commission that has been deducted from expenses of management pursuant to section 76(1)(*ca*) of the Taxes Act.

[(4) For the purposes of paragraph (1) above, the aggregate of the amounts of the investment returns treated as accruing in earlier accounting periods are the amounts treated as accruing in those accounting periods but—

(*a*) prior to any setting off permitted by regulation 7A(2)(*c*), calculated in accordance with regulations 4 and 5 as if in regulation 7(7) the formula were—
$(X \times 100)/Y$; and

(*b*) in any case falling within paragraph (10)(*b*)(iii) of regulation 7, adjusted by such an amount as the inspector determines to be just and reasonable in the circumstances after taking into account the factor specified in paragraph (12)(*d*) of that regulation.][1]

Amendments—[1] Words inserted, and para (4) inserted, by the Insurance Companies (Taxation of Reinsurance Business) (Amendment No 2) Regulations, SI 2003/2573 regs 2, 6 with effect for periods of account beginning after 31 December 2000: SI 2003/2573 reg 1(3).

Prescribed percentage rates of return for the purposes of regulations 4 and 5

7—(1) Where the period during which a reinsurance arrangement is in force falls within more than one accounting period, the percentage rate of return—

(*a*) in relation to the first accounting period, is the rate prescribed by paragraph (2) below;

(*b*) in relation to any subsequent accounting period other than the final accounting period or an accounting period falling within paragraph (6) below, is the rate prescribed by paragraph (4) below.

(2) The rate prescribed by this paragraph is the rate (''R'') found by the formula—

$$R = \frac{(D - E) \times F}{G}$$

where—

D is such percentage rate as is specified in any of paragraphs (7) to (10) below and is applicable to the reinsurance arrangement concerned and, if more than such rate is so applicable, is the first applicable rate specified in the order of those paragraphs;

E is the percentage rate which results from applying the formula specified in paragraph (3) below;

F is the number of days in the first accounting period falling after the date prescribed by regulation 8(2); and

G is the number of days in that accounting period;

...[2].

(3) The formula specified in this paragraph is—

$$\frac{A}{P-C}$$

where—

A is the amount of any payment made by the reinsurer to the cedant company which forms part of the relevant profits of that company for the first accounting period, other than a payment which falls to be taken into account under these Regulations in calculating the investment return to be treated as accruing to that company in that accounting period; and

P and C have the meanings given by regulation 4.

(4) The rate prescribed by this paragraph is the rate (''R'') found by the formula—

$$R = (D - H)$$

where—

D has the meaning given by paragraph (2) above; and

H is the percentage rate which results from applying the formula specified in paragraph (5) below;

...[2].

(5) The formula specified in this paragraph is—

$$\frac{B}{((P_n - C_n) + I_{n-1})}$$

Where—

B is the amount of any payment made by the reinsurer to the cedant company which forms part of the relevant profits of that company for the subsequent accounting period concerned, other than a payment which falls to be taken into account under these Regulations in calculating the investment return to be treated as accruing to that company in that accounting period; and

P_n, C_n and I_{n-1} have the meanings given by regulation 5(1).

(6) In any case where a subsequent accounting period other than the final accounting period is less than 12 months in duration, the percentage rate of return prescribed in relation to that accounting period is the rate (''R'') found by the formula—

$$R = \frac{J \times K}{365}$$

where—

J is the rate prescribed by paragraph (4) above, and

K is the number of days in that accounting period.

(7) In any case where—

(*a*) assets by reference to the value of which benefits payable under the reinsurance arrangement concerned are to be determined are held by the reinsurer in an internal linked fund, or by another company in an internal linked fund, or

(*b*) such assets are held directly by the reinsurer, that is to say, without being appropriated to an internal linked fund,

the percentage rate of return specified is the rate, expressed as a rate per annum, which is found by the formula—

$$[\left(\frac{X \times 100}{Y}\right) \times \text{the Relevant Fraction}]^2$$

where—

X is the amount of investment income arising from those assets for the accounting period concerned, increased by the amount of any increase in the value of those assets which is identified in the records of the reinsurer or (as the case may be) the other company, or reduced by the amount of any reduction in the value of those assets which is so identified; and

Y is the mean of the value of those assets at the beginning and end of the accounting period concerned, as identified in those records;

...[2]

[(7A) For the purposes of paragraph (7) above, *the Relevant Fraction is*—

(*a*) in a case where, in finding X, the amount of investment income is increased by the amount of an increase in the value of the assets mentioned in sub-paragraphs (*a*) and (*b*) of that paragraph—

$$\frac{(X - X1)}{X}$$

(*b*) in a case where, in finding X, the amount of investment income is decreased by the amount of a reduction in the value of those assets and, after being so decreased, is not less than zero—

$$\frac{(X2 - X1)}{X2}; \text{ or}$$

(*c*) in a case where X is an amount that is less than zero—

$$1+\left\{0.5\times\left(\frac{X1}{X2}\right)\right\}\ ]^{3};$$

where—

X is the same as for the purposes of that paragraph;

X1 is the amount included in the amount of investment income used in finding X which represents dividends and other distributions that are not chargeable to corporation tax by virtue of section 208 of the Taxes Act (which provides that dividends and other distributions of a company resident in the United Kingdom are not generally so chargeable); and

X2 is the amount of investment income before it is decreased by the amount of any reduction in the value of the assets mentioned in sub-paragraphs (*a*) and (*b*) of that paragraph.][2]

(8) In any case where—

(*a*) there is in force a deposit-back arrangement as part of the reinsurance arrangement, and

(*b*) the calculation of the rate of return on the deposit is capable of being expressed as a percentage rate per annum,

the percentage rate of return specified is such of the calculated rates of return on the deposit as is applicable to a period which includes any part of the accounting period concerned and is capable of being expressed not later than six months after the end of that accounting period and, if there is more than one such rate of return, is the average of those rates for periods beginning with the period which includes the date of commencement of the accounting period and ending with the period which includes the date of the end of the accounting period.

(9) In any case where the policy being reinsured provides for a percentage rate of return which is fixed or is capable of being determined for the accounting period concerned not later than six months after the end of that period, the percentage rate of return specified is that percentage rate plus 1 per cent.

(10) In any case not falling within paragraph (7), (8) or (9) above, the percentage rate of return specified is either—

[(*a*) the rate found by expressing the amount of the expected income from non-linked assets for the accounting period concerned as a percentage of the value of the total non-linked assets (other than assets not providing income) as identified in the relevant part of the periodical return of the cedant company specified in paragraph (11) below; or][2]

(*b*) where—

(i) that periodical return contains no relevant part, or

(ii) the cedant company is not required to make a periodical return, or

(iii) the cedant company shows that in the circumstances the calculation specified in sub-paragraph (*a*) above would not produce a reasonable result,

such rate as the inspector determines to be just and reasonable in the circumstances after taking into account the factors specified in paragraph (12) below.

(11) The periodical return specified in this paragraph is the periodical return for the period of account immediately preceding the period of account in which the accounting period concerned falls, and "the relevant part" of that return means—

(*a*) in the case of a cedant company whose head office is in the United Kingdom, the part which shows the expected income from non-linked assets in respect of the whole of the company's [long-term][1] business;

(*b*) in the case of a cedant company which is an overseas life insurance company—

(i) the part which shows the expected income from non-linked assets of the company's [long-term insurance][1] fund relating exclusively to business carried on through a branch or agency in the United Kingdom or, if there is no such part,

(ii) the part which shows the expected income from non-linked assets of the company's [long-term insurance][1] fund relating exclusively to business carried on through branches and agencies in the United Kingdom and EEA States taken together.

(12) The factors specified in this paragraph are—

(*a*) the nature of the policy concerned;

(*b*) the rate of interest assumed by the cedant company in determining the valuation of its liabilities in respect of the policy for the purposes of its periodical return;

(*c*) any undertaking by the cedant company with respect to—

(i) the nature of the assets in which the premiums it receives will be invested, or

(ii) the rate of return which it is offering or has offered on that or any similar policy[;

(*d*) the extent to which the reinsurer is in receipt of dividends and other distributions which—

(i) arise from assets held by the reinsurer which may reasonably be regarded as related to the reinsurance arrangement in question; and

(ii) are not chargeable to corporation tax by virtue of section 208 of the Taxes Act.][2]

(13) An appeal may be brought against a determination of the inspector under [regulation 6(4)(*b*) or][2] paragraph (10)(*b*) above by giving written notice to the inspector within 30 days of receipt of written notice of the decision.

(14) An appeal under paragraph (13) above shall lie to the Special Commissioners who may confirm or vary the determination appealed against (whether or not the variation is to the advantage of the appellant).

Amendments—[1] Words in para (11) substituted by the Financial Services and Markets Act 2000 (Consequential Amendments) (Taxes) Order, SI 2001/3629 art 140 with effect from 1 December 2001, immediately after the coming into force of the Financial Services and Markets Act 2000 ss 411, 432(1), Sch 20 (and SI 2001/3629 Pts 1 and 2).

[2] Words in paras (2), (4), (7) revoked, formula in para (7) substituted, para (7A) inserted, sub-para (10)(*a*) substituted, and sub-para (12)(*d*) and words in para (13) inserted, by the Insurance Companies (Taxation of Reinsurance Business) (Amendment No 2) Regulations, SI 2003/2573 regs 2, 7 with effect for periods of account beginning after 31 December 2000: SI 2003/2573 reg 1(3).

[3] Formula in sub-para (7A)(*c*) substituted by the Insurance Companies (Taxation of Reinsurance Business) (Amendment No 3) Regulations, SI 2003/2642 with effect for periods of account beginning after 31 December 2000.

[Treatment of amounts of investment return which are less than zero

7A—(1) This regulation applies where the amount of investment return on a policy or contract, as calculated in accordance with regulation 3, 4 or 5, is less than zero ("the negative amount").

(2) The negative amount may be set off in the following order against the following amounts—

(*a*) first, the amount of any income (other than any investment return which is treated under these Regulations as accruing) which—

(i) accrues in the same accounting period as that in which the negative amount is treated as accruing; and

(ii) is referable to basic life assurance and general annuity business and is charged to tax under Case VI of Schedule D;

(*b*) secondly, the amount of any investment return which—

(i) is treated under these Regulations as accruing in the same accounting period as that in which the negative amount is treated as accruing; and

(ii) is more than zero; and

(*c*) thirdly, the amount of any investment return which is treated under these Regulations as accruing—

(i) in an accounting period subsequent to that in which the negative amount is treated as accruing; and

(ii) in respect of the same policy or contract as that in respect of which the negative amount is treated as accruing;

and is more than zero.

(3) Any setting off under paragraph (2)(*c*) above shall, so far as possible, reduce amounts accruing in an earlier accounting period before reducing amounts accruing in a later one.

(4) Except as is provided for by paragraph (2) above, the negative amount shall be treated for the purposes of section 396 of the Taxes Act as if it were zero.][1]

Amendments—[1] This regulation inserted by the Insurance Companies (Taxation of Reinsurance Business) (Amendment No 2) Regulations, SI 2003/2573 regs 2, 8 with effect for periods of account beginning after 31 December 2000: SI 2003/2573 reg 1(3).

Ascertainment of investment return—prescribed dates of payments made under reinsurance arrangements

8—(1) For the purposes of ascertaining the investment return in each accounting period, the payments specified in paragraphs (2) to (6) below shall be treated as paid on the dates prescribed by those paragraphs in relation to the payment concerned.

(2) In any case where under the reinsurance arrangement a premium or any other amount is payable to the reinsurer within 30 days of the date on which the first premium is paid to the reinsurer, the date prescribed as the date on which that premium or other amount is to be treated as paid is the date on which the first premium is paid.

(3) In any case where under the reinsurance arrangement commission or any other amount is payable by the reinsurer in respect of the policy concerned at the same time as the first premium is paid to the reinsurer or within 30 days of the date on which the first premium is paid to the reinsurer, the date prescribed as the date on which that commission or other amount is to be treated as paid is the date on which the first premium is paid.

(4) In any case where under the reinsurance arrangement—

(*a*) a premium other than the first premium or a premium falling within paragraph (2) above, or any other amount not being an amount falling within paragraph (2) above, is paid to the reinsurer before the end of the accounting period in which the first premium is paid, or (*b*) commission or any other amount, not being commission or an amount falling within paragraph (3) above, is paid by the reinsurer to the cedant company before the end of that accounting period,

the date prescribed as the date on which that premium or other amount is to be treated as paid to the reinsurer, or that commission or other amount is to be treated as paid by the reinsurer, is the first day of the next accounting period.

(5) The dates prescribed as the dates on which any premium or any other amount paid to the reinsurer under the reinsurance arrangement, other than a premium or amount falling within paragraph (2) or (4)(*a*) above, is to be treated as paid are the following—

(*a*) as to one half of the amount of the premium or other amount, the date on which the premium or other amount is paid;
(*b*) as to the other half, the first day of the accounting period next following that in which the premium or other amount is paid.

(6) The dates prescribed as the dates on which any commission or any other amount paid by the reinsurer under the reinsurance arrangement, not being commission or an amount falling within paragraph (3) or (4)(*b*) above, is to be treated as paid are the following—

(*a*) as to one half of the commission or other amount, the date on which the commission or other amount is paid;
(*b*) as to the other half, the first day of the accounting period next following that in which the commission or other amount is paid.

Exclusion of certain reinsurance arrangements from section 442A

9—(1) There shall be excluded from the operation of section 442A any reinsurance arrangement in respect of a policy which falls within any of the descriptions prescribed by paragraphs (2) to [(4A)][1] below.

(2) The description prescribed by this paragraph is of any reinsurance arrangement where—

(*a*) both the cedant company and the reinsurer are insurance companies which are either resident in the United Kingdom or, as respects the reinsurance arrangement or, as the case may be, the business to which the reinsurance is attributable, are within the charge to corporation tax by virtue of section 11 of the Taxes Act;
(*b*) the cedant company is a 9 per cent subsidiary of the reinsurer, or the reinsurer is a 90 per cent subsidiary of the cedant company, or each is a 9 per cent subsidiary of another body corporate; and
(*c*) the reinsurer is not a company which is charged to tax under Case I of Schedule D.

(3) The description prescribed by this paragraph is of any reinsurance arrangement where—

(*a*) the reinsurer is a company which in the relevant period is chargeable to tax under the laws of the territory in which it is domiciled or resident in respect of amounts to which the reinsurance arrangement gives rise;
(*b*) the head office of the reinsurer is in an EEA State;
(*c*) the charge to tax in the relevant period is such a charge made otherwise than by reference to profits as (by disallowing their deduction in computing the amount chargeable) to require sums payable and other liabilities arising under reinsurance arrangements to be treated as sums or liabilities falling to be met out of amounts subject to tax in the hands of the reinsurer;
(*d*) the rate of tax fixed for the purposes of that charge in relation to the amounts subject to tax in the hands of the reinsurer (not being amounts arising or accruing in respect of investments that are of a particular description for which a special relief or exemption is generally available) has in the relevant period been at least 20 per cent;
(*e*) none of the obligations of the reinsurer under the reinsurance arrangement to pay any sum or meet any other liability, other than obligations in respect of mortality risk or morbidity risk, has itself been the subject of a reinsurance arrangement;
(*f*) no deposit-back arrangements are in force in respect of the reinsurance arrangement; and
(*g*) the reinsurer is not subject in the relevant period to a restriction in the amount of the expenses which may be deducted in computing its liability to tax, where the restriction is calculated by reference to the amount of its profits.

(4) The description prescribed by this paragraph is of any reinsurance arrangement under which—

(*a*)

[(i) the mortality risk or the morbidity risk (but no other risk other than the expense risk) is being reinsured, or both the mortality risk and the morbidity risk (but no other risk other than the expense risk) are being reinsured, and][1]
(ii) no payment by way of surrender value is capable of being made by the reinsurer to the cedant company; or

(*b*) either—

(i) no profit such as is referred to in regulation 6(2) is capable of arising; or

(ii) such profit is capable of arising only as a result of the death, illness or infirmity of, or accident to, a person or the lapsing of the policy.

[(4A) The description prescribed by this paragraph is of any reinsurance arrangement which is not prescribed by paragraph (4) above and consists of a contract which—

(*a*) has the effect of increasing the amount of assets that falls to be included at line 34 of Form 9 in the periodical return of the cedant company (representing assets available to meet its required minimum margin for long-term insurance business); and

(*b*) includes—

(i) terms for the transfer of liabilities to policyholders from the insurer; and

(ii) a provision for the recapture of such liabilities in specified circumstances.][1]

(5) In paragraph (3) above, "the relevant period" means a period for which the reinsurer draws up accounts and which ends in or at the end of an accounting period of the cedant company or, if there is more than one such period ending in or at the end of the same accounting period, the period which is the first to end.

(6) For the purposes of paragraph (4) above, the fact that a premium payable by the cedant company under the reinsurance arrangement is calculated so as to reflect a guarantee by that company under the terms of the policy that it will issue a different policy at a future date shall not be taken to mean that risks other than mortality risk or morbidity risk are being reinsured under the reinsurance arrangement.

Amendments—[1] Reference in para (1) substituted, sub-para (4)(*a*)(i) substituted, and para (4A) inserted, by the Insurance Companies (Taxation of Reinsurance Business) (Amendment No 2) Regulations, SI 2003/2573 regs 2, 9 with effect for periods of account beginning after 31 October 2003: SI 2003/2573 reg 1(2).

Exclusion of policy and contract from section 442A

10[—(1)][1] There shall be excluded from the operation of section 442A—

[(*a*) any policy which evidences a contract of long-term insurance which is neither—

(i) a qualifying contract of insurance, nor

(ii) a reinsurance contract; and][1]

(*b*) any annuity contract under which—

(i) payment of the annuity is to commence not later than 12 months after the date of the contract, and

(ii) no surrender value is capable of being produced.

[(2) In paragraph (1)(*a*) above, "contract of long-term insurance" means any contract which falls within Part 2 of Schedule 1 to the Financial Services and Markets Act 2000 (Regulated Activities) Order 2001 and "qualifying contract of insurance" has the meaning given by article 3(1) of that Order.][1]

Amendments—[1] Para (1) renumbered as such, sub-para (1)(*a*) substituted, and para (2) inserted, by the Financial Services and Markets Act 2000 (Consequential Amendments) (Taxes) Order, SI 2002/1409 art 4 with effect from 2 July 2002.

Exclusion of certain business from section 431C

11 There shall be excluded from section 431C any reinsurance business where—

(*a*) in relation to the reinsurance arrangement—

(i) the cedant company is a 90 per cent subsidiary of the reinsurer, or the reinsurer is a 90 per cent subsidiary of the cedant company, or each is a 90 per cent subsidiary of another body corporate,

(ii) the cedant company is either resident in the United Kingdom or is an overseas life insurance company which, as respects the reinsurance arrangement or, as the case may be, the business being reinsured, is within the charge to corporation tax by virtue of section 11 of the Taxes Act, and

(iii) the business being reinsured is basic life assurance and general annuity business in the hands of the cedant company; or

(*b*) ...[4]

(*c*) the business—

(i) is the reinsurance of the business of a company which is not resident in the United Kingdom,

(ii) is not business [which is overseas life assurance business within the meaning given by section 431D(1)][3] of the Taxes Act[, being business for which the policy or contract concerned was made on or after 1 November 1994][1], and

(iii) is linked business where the linked assets concerned consist wholly or substantially of land in the United Kingdom [or [(*d*) the business is business in relation to which an election under regulation 11A has been made.][4]][2]

Simons Tax Cases—*Royal London Mutual Insurance Society Ltd v Barrett (Insp of Taxes)* [2002] STC(SCD) 61.

Amendments—[1] Words inserted by the Insurance Companies (Taxation of Reinsurance Business) (Amendment) Regulations, SI 1996/1621 regs 2, 5(*a*), with effect with respect to accounting periods ending on or after 15 July 1996.

[2] Para (*d*) and the word "or" preceding it, added by the Insurance Companies (Taxation of Reinsurance Business) (Amendment) Regulations, SI 1996/1621 regs 2, 5(*b*) with effect with respect to accounting periods beginning on or after 1 January 1995.

[3] In sub-paras (*b*), (*c*)(ii), words substituted by the Insurance Companies (Taxation of Reinsurance Business) (Amendment) Regulations, SI 2003/1828 regs 1(3), 4 with effect for any policy or contract for any life assurance business made after 21 August 2000.

[4] Para (*b*) revoked, and para (*d*) substituted, by the Insurance Companies (Taxation of Reinsurance Business) (Amendment No 2) Regulations, SI 2003/2573 regs 2, 10 with effect for periods of account beginning after 31 October 2003: SI 2003/2573 reg 1(2).

[Election for certain business to be excluded from section 431C

11A—(1) A company may make an election under this regulation in relation to—

(*a*) any period of account beginning on or after 1st November 2003; and
(*b*) any of its reinsurance business which is business of the kind specified in paragraph (2), (3) or (4) below.

(2) The business specified in this paragraph is business—

(*a*) which is of any of the descriptions specified in section 431D(1)(*b*) of the Taxes Act, being business for which the policy or contract concerned was made on or after 1st November 1994; and
(*b*) the contract for which was made before the beginning of the company's first period of account to begin on or after 1st November 2003.

(3) The business specified by this paragraph is business the contract for which—

(*a*) was effected by a company resident in the United Kingdom at or through a branch or agency outside the United Kingdom where none, or no significant part, of the reinsurance business carried on relates to life assurance business with policy holders or annuitants residing in the United Kingdom; and
(*b*) was made before 1st November 1994.

(4) The business specified by this paragraph is business the contract for which was made after the beginning of the company's first period of account to begin on or after 1st November 2003 and replaces—

(*a*) a contract made before the beginning of the company's first period of account to begin on or after 1st November 2003 such as is mentioned in paragraph (2) above;
(*b*) a contract made before 1st November 1994 such as is mentioned in paragraph (3) above; or
(*c*) a contract that replaced a contract such as is mentioned in sub-paragraph (*a*) or (*b*).

(5) For the purposes of paragraph (4) above, a contract replaces a contract if it results in—

(*a*) no significant difference in the type of business being reinsured; and
(*b*) no significant variation in the terms on which that business is reinsured.

(6) For the purposes of paragraph (5) above, where more than one contract replaces a contract—

(*a*) there is no significant difference in the type of business being reinsured if the replacement contracts, when taken together, do not result in such a difference; and
(*b*) there is no significant variation in the terms on which business is reinsured if the replacement contracts, when taken together, do not result in such a variation.

(7) Where there is a relevant transfer from one person ("the transferor") to another ("the transferee") and the transferor makes an election under this regulation in relation to that business, the transferee is to be treated for the purposes of these Regulations as making the election.

(8) In paragraph (7) above, "a relevant transfer" means a transfer of reinsurance business that is effected by—

(*a*) novation; or
(*b*) an insurance business transfer scheme.

(9) A company may revoke an election under this regulation with effect for any period of account in relation to which it would have effect.

(10) A revocation under paragraph (9) above must be in respect of all elections under this regulation which a company has made or is treated as having made.][1]

Amendments—[1] This regulation inserted by the Insurance Companies (Taxation of Reinsurance Business) (Amendment No 2) Regulations, SI 2003/2573 regs 2, 11 with effect for periods of account beginning after 31 October 2003: SI 2003/2573 reg 1(2).

Exclusion of certain reinsurance business from section 439A

12 There shall be excluded from section 439A any reinsurance business carried on by a company ("the reinsurer") whose reinsurance business is limited to arrangements where—

(*a*) the cedant company is a 90 per cent subsidiary of the reinsurer, or the reinsurer is a 90 per cent subsidiary of the cedant company, or each is a 90 per cent subsidiary of another body corporate, and

(*b*) the cedant company either—

(i) is resident in the United Kingdom, or

(ii) is not so resident but, as respects all the business reinsured with the reinsurer, is within the charge to corporation tax by virtue of section 11 of the Taxes Act.

[Transfers of reinsurance arrangements effected by novation or insurance business transfer schemes

13—(1) Where a transfer of a reinsurance arrangement from one insurance company ("the transferor") to another ("the transferee") is effected by novation or an insurance business transfer scheme, these Regulations shall apply in relation to the reinsurance arrangement concerned as follows.

(2) Regulation 3 shall not apply.

(3) For the purposes of regulations 4 to 7, an accounting period of the transferor shall be treated as ending with the day of the transfer and a new accounting period of the transferee shall be treated as beginning with that day but—

(*a*) the new accounting period of the transferee so treated as beginning shall not be treated as the first accounting period during which the reinsurance arrangement concerned is in force; and

(*b*) the accounting period of the transferor which is so treated as ending shall not treated as the final accounting period during which the reinsurance arrangement concerned is in force.

(4) For the purposes of regulation 5, 6 and 9, the references in regulations 5(1), 6(3) and 9(6) respectively to the cedant company shall be treated as including (as well as the transferee)—

(*a*) the transferor; and

(*b*) any insurance company from which the reinsurance arrangement concerned was transferred on an earlier transfer effected by novation or an insurance business transfer scheme.

(5) For the purposes of regulation 5, the reference in paragraph (1) of that regulation to previous accounting periods shall be treated as including (as well as the previous accounting periods of the transferee)—

(*a*) previous accounting periods of the transferor; and

(*b*) previous accounting periods of any insurance company from which the reinsurance arrangement concerned was transferred on an earlier transfer effected by novation or an insurance business transfer scheme.

(6) For the purposes of regulation 6, the reference in paragraph (1) of that regulation to the amounts of the investment returns in earlier accounting periods shall be treated as including (as well as the amounts of the investment returns in earlier accounting periods of the transferee)—

(*a*) the amounts of the investment returns in earlier accounting periods of the transferor; and

(*b*) the amounts of the investment returns in earlier accounting periods of any insurance company from which the reinsurance arrangement concerned was transferred on an earlier transfer effected by novation or an insurance business transfer scheme.

[(6A) For the purposes of regulation 7A, any negative amount that is available before the transfer to be set off by the transferor in accordance with paragraph (2)(*c*) of that regulation shall be treated as if it had accrued in an earlier accounting period of the transferee.][2]

(7) The following questions shall be determined in respect of the transferor as the cedant company before the transfer and then, as a separate matter, in respect of the transferee as the cedant company after the transfer—

(*a*) whether the reinsurance arrangement concerned falls within the description prescribed by regulation 9(2);

(*b*) whether, in relation to the reinsurance arrangement concerned, any of the circumstances set out in regulations 11(*a*) and 12 exist.

(8) ...[3].][1]

Amendments—[1] This regulation inserted by the Insurance Companies (Taxation of Reinsurance Business) (Amendment) Regulations, SI 2003/1828 regs 1(4), 5 with effect for transfers of reinsurance arrangements taking place after 31 December 2002.

[2] Para (6A) inserted by the Insurance Companies (Taxation of Reinsurance Business) (Amendment No 2) Regulations, SI 2003/2573 regs 2, 12(1), (2) with effect for transfers of reinsurance arrangements taking place after 31 December 2002: SI 2003/2573 reg 1(4).

[3] Para (8) revoked by the Insurance Companies (Taxation of Reinsurance Business) (Amendment No 2) Regulations, SI 2003/2573 regs 2, 12(1), (3) with effect for periods of account beginning after 31 October 2003: SI 2003/2573 reg 1(2).

1995/1979
Venture Capital Trust Regulations 1995

Made by the Treasury under FA 1995 s 73(1)–(4)

Made . . . . *26 July 1995*
Laid before the House of Commons . . . . . *26 July 1995*
Coming into Force . . . . *16 August 1995*

Commentary—*Simon's Direct Tax Service* **Division E3.6.**

ARRANGEMENT OF REGULATIONS

PART I

INTRODUCTORY

Citation and commencement

1 These Regulations may be cited as the Venture Capital Trust Regulations 1995 and shall come into force on 16th August 1995.

Interpretation

2—(1) In these Regulations unless the context otherwise requires—

"accounting date" has the meaning given by section 834(1);
"the Board" means the Commissioners of Inland Revenue;
"eligible shares" has the meaning given by paragraph 6(1) of Schedule 15B;

[''enduring declaration'' shall be construed in accordance with regulation 12;][1]
''full approval'' means approval in pursuance of subsection (2) of section 842AA;
''investor'' means a person who holds shares in a company which is, or has been, a trust company;
''the Management Act'' means the Taxes Management Act 1970;
''period of account'' has the meaning given by section 834(1);
[''permitted maximum'' shall be construed in accordance with paragraph 8 of Schedule 15B;][1]
''provisional approval'' means approval in pursuance of subsection (4) of section 842AA;
''qualifying holding'' shall be construed in accordance with Schedule 28B;
''trust company'' means a venture capital trust within the meaning given by section 842AA;
''year'' means a year beginning with 6th April in any year and ending with 5th April in the following year.

(2) In these Regulations, any reference to a provision, without more, is a reference to that provision of the Income and Corporation Taxes Act 1988.

Amendments—[1] Definitions of ''enduring declaration'' and ''permitted maximum'' in para (1) revoked by the Venture Capital Trusts (Amendment) Regulations, SI 1999/819 reg 3 with effect for distributions made by a venture capital trust after 5 April 1999.

PART II

APPROVAL OF A COMPANY FOR PURPOSES OF SECTION 842AA

Applications for approval

3—(1) A company making an application for approval as a venture capital trust for the purposes of section 842AA shall apply to the Board in writing.

(2) The application shall be either for full approval or for provisional approval.

(3) An application for full approval shall contain a declaration—

(*a*) that the conditions for full approval were fulfilled in relation to the most recent complete accounting period of the company;

(*b*) that to the best of the company's knowledge and belief, the conditions for full approval will also be fulfilled in relation to the accounting period of the company which is current when the application for full approval is made; and

(*c*) that to the best of the company's knowledge and belief, the particulars given in the application are true and correct.

(4) An application for provisional approval shall contain a declaration that to the best of the company's knowledge and belief—

(*a*) the conditions for full approval will be fulfilled within the periods specified in subsection (4) of section 842AA; and

(*b*) the particulars given in the application are true and correct.

(5) An application for approval for the purposes of section 842AA shall be signed by the secretary or by a director of the company.

Approval of a company

4—(1) The Board's approval of a company as a trust company for the purposes of section 842AA shall be given to the company by notice in writing.

(2) The notice shall specify—

(*a*) the date on which the Board's approval is given, and

(*b*) the date from which the approval shall have effect.

(3) A notice giving provisional approval may include conditions designed to ensure that the company will fulfil the conditions specified in subsection (4) of section 842AA.

(4) The company may appeal to the Special Commissioners against the inclusion of any of the conditions mentioned in paragraph (3) above.

Refusal of approval of a company

5—(1) The Board's refusal of approval of a company as a trust company for the purposes of section 842AA shall be given to the company by notice in writing.

(2) The notice shall specify—

(*a*) the date on which the Board's refusal of approval is given, and

(*b*) the reasons for the Board's refusal of approval.

(3) The company may appeal to the Special Commissioners against the refusal of approval.

Withdrawal of approval of a company

6—(1) The Board's withdrawal of approval of a company as a trust company for the purposes of section 842AA shall be given to the company by notice in writing.

(2) The notice shall specify—

(*a*) the date from which the Board's withdrawal of approval shall have effect, and

(*b*) the reasons for the Board's withdrawal of approval.

(3) The company may appeal to the Special Commissioners against the withdrawal of approval.

Appeals to the Special Commissioners

7—(1) This regulation applies where a company appeals to the Special Commissioners pursuant to regulation 4(4), 5(3) or 6(3).

(2) The appeal shall be made by notice in writing given to the Board before the end of the period of 30 days beginning with the day on which the notice of provisional approval, refusal of approval or withdrawal of approval, as the case may be, was given to the company.

(3) Subject to paragraph (4) below, the Special Commissioners shall on appeal confirm the notice unless they are satisfied that the notice ought to be quashed.

(4) Where the appeal is against the inclusion of any of the conditions mentioned in regulation 4(3), the Special Commissioners may vary any of those conditions.

(5) If the Special Commissioners allow an appeal against a refusal of approval, they shall specify the date from which the approval is to have effect.

Breach of conditions for approval

8—(1) Where—

(*a*) any of the conditions specified in subsection (2) of section 842AA has ceased to be fulfilled, or

(*b*) a resolution has been passed or a petition has been presented to wind up the company,

a trust company which has been given full approval shall forthwith give notice in writing to the Board of that fact.

(2) Where—

(*a*) any of the conditions specified in paragraph (*a*) or (*b*) of section 842AA(4) has not been fulfilled, or

(*b*) any of the conditions included in a notice giving provisional approval and given under regulation 4(3) has been broken, or

(*c*) after fulfilling the conditions specified in paragraphs (*a*) and (*b*) of section 842AA(4), any of the conditions specified in subsection (2) of section 842AA has ceased to be fulfilled, or

(*d*) a resolution has been passed or a petition has been presented to wind up the company,

a trust company which has been given provisional approval shall forthwith give notice in writing to the Board of that fact.

PART III

RELIEF FROM INCOME TAX

CHAPTER I

RELIEF IN RESPECT OF INVESTMENTS IN TRUST COMPANIES

Certificate to be given to investor

9—(1) If an individual to whom eligible shares have been issued so requires, a trust company shall, within 30 days, give him a certificate containing the particulars specified in paragraph (2) below and certifying as specified in paragraph (3) below.

(2) The particulars specified are—

(*a*) the name of the investor,

(*b*) his permanent address including postcode,

(*c*) the date on which the eligible shares were issued to him,

(*d*) the amount payable in respect of those shares and the date on which that amount will be payable, and

(*e*) the amount paid in respect of those shares and the date on which that amount was paid.

(3) The certificate shall certify—

(*a*) that eligible shares have been issued to the investor,

(*b*) that to the best of the trust company's knowledge and belief the shares were both subscribed for and issued as mentioned in paragraph 1(9) of Schedule 15B, and

(*c*) that to the best of the trust company's knowledge and belief the shares were not issued in a case where the investor is not entitled to relief under Part I of Schedule 15B because the case is one to which paragraph 2 of that Schedule applies.

(4) The trust company shall keep a record of the information contained in any certificate given under this regulation.

[CHAPTER II

RELIEF IN RESPECT OF DISTRIBUTIONS BY TRUST COMPANIES][1]

Amendments—[1] Part III Chapter II (regs 10—21) revoked by the Venture Capital Trusts (Amendment) Regulations, SI 1999/819 reg 4 with effect for distributions made by a venture capital trust after 5 April 1999.

[Return containing particulars of amounts subscribed for eligible shares

21A—(1) A company which at any time in the period specified in paragraph (2) below (''the specified period'') is a trust company, shall deliver to the Board, in respect of the specified period and within the time limit specified in paragraph (3) below, a return containing, in respect of each amount subscribed by any investor for eligible shares in the specified period, the particulars specified in paragraph (4) below.

(2) The specified period is—

(*a*) a year, or

(*b*) a period beginning on the 6th April and ending on the day on which that company ceased to be approved as a trust company,

whichever is the shorter.

(3) The time limit specified is—

(*a*) six months after the end of the year, or

(*b*) six months after the day on which the company ceased to be approved as a trust company,

whichever is the earlier.

(4) The particulars specified are—

(*a*) the full name of the investor,

(*b*) his permanent residential address, including postcode,

(*c*) his date of birth,

(*d*) if he has one, his national insurance number,

(*e*) the amount paid in respect of eligible shares subscribed for in that period, and

(*f*) the date on which that amount was paid.

(5) A return under this regulation shall be in such form as the Board may prescribe or authorise.][1]

Amendments—[1] This regulation inserted by the Venture Capital Trusts (Amendment) Regulations, SI 1999/819 reg 5 with effect for distributions made by a venture capital trust after 5 April 1999.

PART IV

RETURN OF PARTICULARS OF INVESTMENTS, KEEPING OF RECORDS AND PROVISION OF INFORMATION

Return containing particulars of investments

22—(1) A company which is, or has been, a trust company shall deliver to the Board, in respect of the period specified in paragraph (2) below (''the specified period''), and within the time limit specified in paragraph (3) below, a return containing the particulars specified in paragraph (4) below, the certificate specified in paragraph (5) below and the declaration specified in paragraph (6) below.

(2) The specified period is—

(*a*) an accounting period of a trust company,

(*b*) a period beginning on the date from which the Board's approval of a company for the purposes of section 842AA has effect and ending on an accounting date of the company, or

(*c*) a period beginning at the commencement of an accounting period of a company and ending on the day on which that company ceased to be approved for the purposes of section 842AA,

whichever is the shortest.

(3) The time limit specified is—

(*a*) twelve months after the end of the accounting period of the trust company, or

(*b*) twelve months after the day on which the company ceased to be approved for the purposes of section 842AA,

whichever is the shorter.

(4) The particulars specified are—

(*a*) in respect of each investment held by the company at the beginning of the specified period, the value of that investment computed in accordance with subsections (5) and (11) of section 842AA;

(*b*) in respect of any new investment made by the company during the specified period—

(i) the date on which that investment was made, and

(ii) the value of that investment together with any revaluation of investments, computed in accordance with subsections (5) and (11) of section 842AA, which is required as a result of the making of that investment;

(*c*) in relation to each investment, whether or not it is a qualifying holding; *[and]*[1]

(*d*) in relation to each qualifying holding—

(i) the name of the company in which the investment has been made, and

(ii) the address of that company's registered or principal office [and

(*e*) in respect of each disposal of an investment by the company during the specified period—

(i) the name of the company in which the investment was held,

(ii) the address of that company's registered or principal office,

(iii) the date of the disposal, and

(iv) the value, immediately after the disposal, computed in accordance with subsections (5) and (11) of section 842AA, of the remainder of any holding of investments from which the disposal was made.][1]

(5) The certificate specified is—

(*a*) where the trust company has been given full approval or has been given provisional approval three years or more before the beginning of the specified period, that the trust company satisfied all the conditions in subsection (2) of section 842AA throughout the specified period; or

(*b*) where the trust company has been given provisional approval less than three years before the beginning of the specified period, that the trust company satisfied all the conditions of subsection (4) of section 842AA and any other conditions attached to the provisional approval throughout the specified period; or

(*c*) that the company has ceased to be approved for the purposes of section 842AA.

(6) The declaration specified, is a declaration that the particulars contained in the return are, to the best of the company's knowledge and belief, true and correct.

(7) The declaration specified in paragraph (6) above shall be signed by the secretary or by a director of the company.

(8) A return under this regulation shall be in such form as the Board may specify or authorise.

Amendments—[1] In reg 22(4), word "and" immediately following sub-para (*c*) revoked, and sub-para (*e*) inserted, by the Venture Capital Trusts (Amendment) Regulations, SI 1999/819 reg 6 with effect for distributions made by a venture capital trust after 5 April 1999.

Records to be kept by trust company

23—(1) A company which is or has been a trust company shall at all times during the relevant period keep sufficient accounts, records and other information to enable the requirements of section 842AA, Schedule 15B and these Regulations to be satisfied.

(2) In paragraph (1) above, the "relevant period" means—

(*a*) in the case of a company which has ceased to be approved for the purposes of section 842AA, the period of six years from the date on which the company ceased to be so approved, and

(*b*) in any other case, the period of six years from the end of the period of account or the year to which the accounts, records and information relate, whichever is the longer.

Information to be provided to the Board

24—(1) The Board may by notice require any company which is or has been a trust company or any person who holds or has held shares in such a company, within such period as may be specified in the notice, to furnish them with such information as they may reasonably require for the purposes of section 842AA, Schedule 15B or these Regulations.

(2) The period specified in a notice given under paragraph (1) above shall be not less than 14 days.

Inspection of records by officer of the Board

25—(1) The Board may by notice require any company which is or has been a trust company or any person who holds or has held shares in such a company, within such period as may be specified in the notice, to make available for inspection by an officer of the Board authorised for that purpose such accounts, records and other information as are in that person's possession or under that person's control as the Board may reasonably require for the purposes of section 842AA, Schedule 15B or these Regulations.

(2) The period specified in a notice given under paragraph (1) above shall be not less than 14 days.

(3) Where records are maintained by computer the person required to make them available for inspection shall provide the officer making the inspection with all the facilities necessary for obtaining information from them.

1995/2050

Income Tax (Dealers in Securities) (Tradepoint) Regulations 1995

Made by the Treasury under TA 1988 s 732(2A), (7)

Made . . . . *1 August 1995*

Laid before the House of Commons . . . . *4 August 1995*

Coming into Force . . . . *25 August 1995*

Commentary—*Simon's Direct Tax Service* **B3.727A.**

Citation and commencement

1 These Regulations may be cited as the Income Tax (Dealers in Securities) (Tradepoint) Regulations 1995 and shall come into force on 25th August 1995.

Interpretation

2 In these Regulations unless the context otherwise requires—

''Board of directors'' means the Board of directors of Tradepoint;

''clearing participant'' means a member (as defined by this regulation) who is also a member of The London Clearing House Limited and who as such is permitted by the Board of directors and that clearing house to clear transactions made on the Exchange for a traded security;

''equity securities'' means securities within the meaning given by section 731(9) of the Taxes Act which are issued by a company;

''the Exchange'' means Tradepoint Investment Exchange;

''first buyer'' shall be construed in accordance with section 731(2) of the Taxes Act;

''member'' in relation to Tradepoint means a person approved by the Board of Directors as a participant in the Exchange;

''subsection (1)'' and ''subsection (2A)'' mean subsection (1) and subsection (2A) respectively of section 732 of the Taxes Act;

''Taxes Act'' means the Income and Corporation Taxes Act 1988;

''Tradepoint'' means Tradepoint Financial Networks plc.

Prescribed persons and date for the purposes of subsection (2A)

3 For the purposes of subsection (2A)—

(*a*) The London Clearing House Limited is a recognised clearing house which is prescribed;

(*b*) Tradepoint is a recognised investment exchange which is prescribed;

(*c*) a member in relation to Tradepoint who is a clearing participant is prescribed as a class or description of member of Tradepoint;

(*d*) the date which is referred to in paragraph (*b*) of subsection (2A) and which is prescribed is 25th August 1995.

Prescribed circumstances for the purposes of subsection (2A)

4—(1) Paragraphs (2) and (3) below prescribe for the purposes of subsection (2A) the circumstances in which subsection (1) shall not apply.

(2) If the first buyer is The London Clearing House Limited, the circumstances prescribed are where—

(*a*) the securities referred to in subsection (1) as purchased by the first buyer are equity securities, and

(*b*) those securities were purchased by The London Clearing House Limited as the first buyer acting in its capacity as a person providing clearing services in connection with a transaction made on the Exchange.

(3) If the first buyer is a member in relation to Tradepoint and is a clearing participant, the prescribed circumstances are where—

(*a*) the securities referred to in subsection (1) as purchased by the first buyer are equity securities, and

(*b*) those securities were purchased by the member as the first buyer and in his capacity as a clearing participant—

(i) from a person in circumstances where the member is required to sell equity securities under a matching transaction to The London Clearing House Limited, or

(ii) from The London Clearing House Limited in circumstances where he is required to sell equity securities under a matching transaction to another person.

(4) In paragraph (3) above ''matching transaction'' means a transaction under which—

(*a*) the equity securities to be sold by the member are of the same kind as the equity securities purchased by him, and

(*b*) the number and price of the equity securities to be sold by the member are identical to the number and price of the equity securities purchased by him.

1995/2052

Income Tax (Manufactured Dividends) (Tradepoint) Regulations 1995

Made by the Treasury under TA 1988, s 737(6), (7A), (7B), Sch 23A, paras 1(1), 8(2), (3)

Revocation—These Regulations revoked by the Stock Lending and Manufactured Payments (Revocations and Amendments) Regulations, SI 1997/987, reg 6, with effect from 1 July 1997 except in relation to any payment of a manufactured dividend to which these Regulations apply that is made before that date.

1995/2902

Taxation of Income from Land (Non-residents) Regulations 1995

Made by the Commissioners of Inland Revenue under TA 1988 s 42A

Made	*10 November 1995*
Laid before the House of Commons	*10 November 1995*
Coming into Force	*1 December 1995*

Revenue & other press releases—IR Booklet IR 140 (non-resident landlords, their agents and tenants).

ARRANGEMENT OF REGULATIONS

PRELIMINARY

Citation, commencement and effect

1—(1) These Regulations may be cited as the Taxation of Income from Land (Non-residents) Regulations 1995 and shall come into force on 1st December 1995.

(2) These Regulations shall have effect with respect to any payment made on or after 6th April 1996 which—

(*a*) constitutes income of a Schedule A business carried on by a non-resident, and
(*b*) either—

(i) is made by a person falling within subsection (2)(*a*) of section 42A who is a prescribed person in respect of the non-resident, or
(ii) is received by an agent who is a prescribed person in respect of the non-resident or by another person at the direction of that agent.

Interpretation

2 In these Regulations unless the context otherwise requires—

"agent" means a person falling within subsection (2)(*b*) of section 42A;

"annual period" means the period commencing on 1st April and ending on the following 31st March;

"the Board" means the Commissioners of Inland Revenue;

"deductible expense" means an expense which is deductible under the Tax Acts in computing the profits or gains of a non-resident's Schedule A business;

"Management Act" means the Taxes Management Act 1970;

"non-resident" means a person who has his usual place of abode outside the United Kingdom;

"notice" means notice in writing;

"prescribed person" means a person prescribed by regulation 3;

"professional trustee" means a person who carries on, or is employed by, a business which consists of or includes the management of trusts, and who acts as trustee in the course of that business or employment;

"quarter" means—

(*a*) the period from 6th April 1996 to 30th June 1996;

(*b*) any subsequent period of 3 months ending with the last day of September, December, March or June;

"section 42A" means section 42A of the Taxes Act;

"Schedule A business" shall be construed in accordance with subsection (8)(*a*) of section 42A;

"Taxes Act" means the Income and Corporation Taxes Act 1988;

"year" means year of assessment.

PRESCRIBED PERSONS

Prescribed persons for the purposes of section 42A

3—(1) In any case where a person falling within subsection 2(*a*) or (*b*) of section 42A is issued with a notice by the Board stating that he is a prescribed person for the purposes of subsection (1) of that section in respect of the Schedule A business of a non-resident, or a part of that business, that person is prescribed for the purposes of subsection (1) of that section in respect of that business or, as the case may be, the part referred to in the notice.

(2) Except where it relates to a part of a non-resident's Schedule A business, a notice under paragraph (1) above need not specify the name of the non-resident concerned or describe his Schedule A business.

(3) In any case where—

(*a*) no notice has been issued by the Board under paragraph (1) above in respect of a non-resident's Schedule A business, or there is a part of his business in respect of which no notice has been issued under that paragraph; and

(*b*) a person whose usual place of abode is in the United Kingdom—

(i) is an agent in respect of that business or that part,

(ii) has power to receive income in respect of that business or that part or has control over the direction of that income, and

(iii) is not an excluded person,

that person is, subject to paragraph (4) below, prescribed for the purposes of subsection (1) of section 42A in respect of that business or, as the case may be, that part.

(4) Where in a case falling within paragraph (3) above there is more than one person to whom sub-paragraph (*b*) of that paragraph applies as respects the same business or the same part of a business, the person who is the elected agent or, if there is no elected agent, the last agent is the person prescribed for the purposes of subsection (1) of section 42A in respect of that business or, as the case may be, that part.

(5) In any case where—

(*a*) no notice has been issued by the Board under paragraph (1) above in respect of a non-resident's Schedule A business, or there is a part of his business in respect of which no notice has been issued under that paragraph;

(*b*) there is no person to whom paragraph (3)(*b*) above applies in respect of that business or that part; and

(*c*) a person whose usual place of abode is in the United Kingdom—

(i) is a tenant of premises owned by the non-resident in connection with that business or that part, and

(ii) is liable to pay to the non-resident in respect of his occupation of those premises sums exceeding in the aggregate £5,200 per annum or, where he occupies the premises for less than one year, the proportionate amount of that sum which is determined by the duration of his occupation, that person is prescribed for the purposes of subsection (1) of section 42A in respect of that business or, as the case may be, that part.

Interpretation of regulation 3

4—(1) In regulation 3—

(*a*) ''excluded person'' means an agent whose activity on behalf of the non-resident in connection with the management or administration of his Schedule A business or part thereof (as the case may be) is confined to the provision of legal advice or legal services;

(*b*) ''elected agent'' means the agent who is elected jointly by the last agent and himself to assume the responsibilities of a prescribed person for the purposes of subsection (1) of section 42A in relation to the Schedule A business or part thereof (as the case may be);

(*c*) ''last agent'' means the agent by whom sums constituting income from the non-resident's Schedule A business or part thereof (as the case may be) are paid directly to the non-resident or to an agent whose usual place of abode is outside the United Kingdom or to a person who is not an agent.

(2) An election shall be made by notice to the Board signed by the last agent and the person to be elected, and any such notice shall state—

(*a*) the name and address of the agent elected, and

(*b*) the date from which the election has effect, not being a date earlier than the first day of the quarter in which the election is made.

(3) An election may be revoked by notice to the Board given by either of the agents who made the election, and any such revocation shall have effect—

(*a*) from the first day of the quarter next following the date on which the notice is received by the Board, or

(*b*) after the expiry of 30 days following the date on which the notice is received by the Board,

whichever is the later to occur.

Partnerships

5 In any case where a liability to make any payment to the Board under these Regulations arises from amounts payable or things done in the course of a business carried on by any persons in partnership, that partnership as such shall be treated for the purposes of these Regulations as a person falling within subsection (2)(*a*) or (*b*) (as the case may be) of section 42A.

Multiple branches

6—(1) In any case where an agent—

(*a*) is a prescribed person by virtue of regulation 3 in respect of the Schedule A business, or part thereof, of more than one non-resident,

(*b*) acts on behalf of those non-residents through branches of his business in circumstances where the average number of non-residents in each branch at the relevant time is not less than five, and

(*c*) is a person approved by the Board for the purposes of this regulation,

that person shall be treated for the purposes of these Regulations as if in respect of each branch he were a separate and distinct person.

(2) An application for approval under paragraph (1) above shall be made to the Board in a form provided or authorised by the Board which shall contain—

(*a*) such information as is necessary to identify the branches concerned,

(*b*) the number of non-residents in each branch, and

(*c*) a declaration by the prescribed person that he does not act on behalf of any non-residents other than those whose business is managed by the branches so identified.

(3) An approval under paragraph (1) above shall, unless revoked or withdrawn, have effect for the quarter following that in which it is given and for any subsequent quarter.

(4) An approval may be revoked by the prescribed person by notice to the Board and, subject to paragraph (5) below, such revocation shall have effect for the quarter following that in which it is given and for any subsequent quarter.

(5) Notwithstanding the revocation of approval under paragraph (4) above, a further application for approval may be made by the prescribed person in accordance with paragraph (2) above at any time following the revocation; and paragraph (3) above shall apply accordingly in relation to an approval given in response to that application.

(6) The Board may, by notice to the prescribed person, refuse approval where they have reason to believe that—

(*a*) the average number of non-residents in each branch is less than five at the relevant time, or

(*b*) there is likely to be a failure on the part of the prescribed person to comply with the obligations imposed on him under these Regulations in relation to any branch, or

(*c*) the declaration given by the prescribed person pursuant to paragraph (2)(*c*) above is incorrect.

(7) The Board may, by notice to the prescribed person, withdraw approval where they have reason to believe that—

(*a*) the average number of non-residents in each branch was at the relevant time, or has since become, less than five, or

(*b*) there has been a failure on the part of the prescribed person to comply with the obligations imposed on him under these Regulations in relation to any branch, or

(*c*) the declaration given by the prescribed person pursuant to paragraph (2)(*c*) above was, or has become, incorrect.

(8) The prescribed person may appeal against a notice under paragraph (6) above refusing approval, or a notice under paragraph (7) above withdrawing approval, by notice to the Board within 30 days of the date of issue of the notice of refusal or, as the case may be, the notice of withdrawal.

(9) The appeal shall be to the General Commissioners except that the prescribed person may elect (in accordance with section 46(1) of the Management Act) to appeal to the Special Commissioners.

(10) The General Commissioners or, as the case may be, the Special Commissioners shall on appeal to them confirm the notice of refusal or withdrawal unless they are satisfied that it ought to be quashed.

(11) In this regulation—

(*a*) references to branches of an agent's business are references to the units (of whatever kind) into which the agent has divided his business;

(*b*) references to "the relevant time" are references to the time at which an application for approval is made by the prescribed person.

Registration by prescribed persons

7—(1) The person prescribed by paragraph (2) below shall, within the period of 30 days following the date specified in paragraph (3) below, register with the Board the following details—

(*a*) his name and address, and

(*b*) his tax office reference, if he has one.

(2) The person prescribed by this paragraph is any person who is—

(*a*) an agent in respect of the Schedule A business, or part thereof, of a non-resident, and

(*b*) a person prescribed by regulation 3 in respect of that business or that part.

(3) The date specified in this paragraph is the date on which the agent became a person prescribed by regulation 3 in respect of that business or that part.

Payment and recovery of tax

Calculation of payment of tax by person falling within subsection (2)(a) of section 42A

8—(1) A person falling within subsection (2)(*a*) of section 42A who is a prescribed person in respect of the Schedule A business, or part thereof, of a non-resident shall calculate for each quarter the amount of any payment to be made to the Board in respect of tax which is or may become chargeable on the income from that business or that part.

(2) The amount of the payment to be calculated by that person is the amount of tax at the basic rate on the aggregate of all income which falls to be treated as a receipt of that business or that part, other than income specified in paragraph (3) below, and which either—

(*a*) was paid by him in the quarter to the non-resident, or

(*b*) was paid by him in the quarter to a person other than the non-resident, not being a payment which he can reasonably be satisfied is a deductible expense.

(3) The income specified in this paragraph is any income which—

(*a*) is attributable to a branch of the non-resident in the United Kingdom, and

(*b*) is chargeable to corporation tax.

Calculation of payment of tax by agent

9—(1) An agent who is a prescribed person in respect of the Schedule A business, or part thereof, of a non-resident shall calculate for each quarter the amount of any payment to be made to the Board in respect of tax which is or may become chargeable on the income from that business or that part.

(2) The amount of the payment to be calculated is the amount of tax at the basic rate on the amount which results after deducting from the income specified in paragraph (3) below—

(*a*) the expenses specified in paragraph (4) below, and

(*b*) any excess amount of expenses falling to be deducted from that income in accordance with paragraph (5) below.

(3) The income specified is all income which falls to be treated as a receipt of that business or that part, other than income specified in regulation 8(3), and which either—

(*a*) was received by the prescribed person in the quarter concerned, or (*b*) was income which it was in his power to receive or over whose direction he had control but which was paid at his direction to another person in that quarter without being received by him.

(4) The expenses specified are all amounts paid in the quarter by the prescribed person or by another person at his direction that he can reasonably be satisfied are deductible under the Tax Acts in computing the profits or gains of that business or that part.

(5) Where in any quarter in an annual period the expenses specified in paragraph (4) above exceed the income specified in paragraph (3) above—

(*a*) the amount of the excess shall first be deducted from the income specified in paragraph (3) above for previous quarters in that annual period, taking later quarters before earlier quarters, and

(*b*) any balance remaining of that amount shall be carried forward and deducted from the income specified in paragraph (3) above for subsequent quarters, including quarters after the end of that annual period, taking earlier quarters before later quarters.

(6) Where an amount paid by a prescribed person in a previous quarter becomes repayable as a result of an excess amount being deducted from income pursuant to paragraph (5)(*a*) above, the amount repayable—

(*a*) shall first be set off by the prescribed person against payments due under this regulation in respect of other non-residents in respect of whose Schedule A business or part thereof he is a prescribed person for the quarter in which the excess amount arises, and

(*b*) any balance remaining shall, on a claim being made to the Board by the prescribed person, be repaid to him.

(7) A claim under paragraph (6)(*b*) above (''a repayment claim'') shall be made in a quarterly return under regulation 10.

(8) An appeal shall lie to the Special Commissioners from the Board's decision on a repayment claim, and the appeal shall be brought by giving notice to the Board within 30 days of receipt of notice of the decision.

(9) All such assessments, payments and repayments shall be made as are necessary to give effect to the Board's decision on a repayment claim or to any variation of that decision on appeal.

Accounting for tax—quarterly returns

10—(1) In the circumstances specified in paragraph (2) below and within 30 days after the end of a quarter, a prescribed person shall make a return to the Board, in such form as the Board may prescribe, containing the information specified in paragraph (3) below and the declaration specified in paragraph (4) below.

(2) The circumstances specified are where—

(*a*) an amount is payable by the prescribed person in respect of the quarter, calculated in accordance with regulation 8 or 9 as the case may be, or

(*b*) a repayment of tax is due under regulation 9(6)(*b*), or

(*c*) the Board have issued a notice to the prescribed person requiring a return to be made in respect of that quarter.

(3) The information specified is—

(*a*) the name and address of the prescribed person;

(*b*) where the prescribed person is a person falling within subsection (2)(*a*) of section 42A, the aggregate of the amounts payable by him for that quarter, calculated in accordance with regulation 8, in respect of all non-residents in respect of whose Schedule A businesses (or parts thereof) he is a prescribed person;

(*c*) where the prescribed person is an agent, the aggregate of the amounts payable by him for that quarter, calculated in accordance with regulation 9, in respect of all non-residents in respect of whose Schedule A businesses (or part thereof) he is a prescribed person, after set off of any amounts repayable pursuant to paragraph (6)(*a*) of that regulation; and

(*d*) a claim for repayment of an amount pursuant to regulation 9(6)(*b*), where appropriate.

(4) The declaration specified is a declaration by the prescribed person that the particulars given in the return are to the best of his knowledge correct and complete.

(5) The aggregate amount referred to in paragraph (3)(*b*) or (*c*) above shall be due at the time by which the return under paragraph (1) above is to be made, and that amount so due—

(*a*) shall be payable by the prescribed person without the making of an assessment, and

(*b*) may be assessed on the prescribed person (whether or not it has been paid when the assessment is made) if it, or any part of it, is not paid on or before the due date.

(6) The amount so due shall carry interest at the rate applicable under section 178 of the Finance Act 1989 to section 87 of the Management Act from the date when the amount becomes due until payment.

(7) Where an amount paid by a prescribed person in a previous quarter is repaid pursuant to a claim under regulation 9(6)(*b*), the repayment shall not affect interest under paragraph (6) above on the amount repaid for such time as is specified in paragraph (8) below but, subject to that, paragraph (6) above shall apply as if any such amount which is repaid had never become payable.

(8) The time for which interest is not affected is—

(*a*) any time before the expiration of the period of 30 days from the end of the quarter in which the excess of expenses giving rise to the repayment arose, unless the return for that quarter is made earlier in that period; and

(*b*) if that return is made earlier in that period, any time ending before the date on which the return is made.

(9) If it appears to the Board that there is an amount which ought to have been but has not been included in a quarterly return as payable to the Board, or if the Board are dissatisfied with any quarterly return, they may make an assessment on the prescribed person to the best of their judgment in respect of that amount.

(10) The like provisions as are contained in paragraph 10 of Schedule 16 to the Taxes Act (assessments and due date of tax) shall have effect in relation to an assessment under paragraph (9) above as if—

(*a*) for references to an assessment under that Schedule there were substituted references to an assessment under paragraph (9) above;

(*b*) the references to paragraphs 4(1) and 9 of that Schedule were omitted;

(*c*) sub-paragraph (5) were omitted.

(11) Any income tax due under an assessment made by virtue of paragraph (9) above shall carry interest at the rate applicable under section 178 of the Finance Act 1989 to section 87 of the Management Act from the date when the tax becomes due until payment; and for that purpose the tax shall be treated as having become due at the time when it would have become due if a correct return had been made.

Annual returns

11—(1) Not later than the 5th July following the end of an annual period, a prescribed person, other than a person specified in paragraph (3) below, shall make a return to the Board for that period—

(*a*) in respect of the non-resident or, if more than one, each non-resident separately, in respect of whose Schedule A business (or part thereof) he was a prescribed person at any time falling within that period, and

(*b*) containing the information specified in paragraph (4) below and the declaration specified in paragraph (5) below.

(2) A return under paragraph (1) above shall be in such form as the Board may prescribe.

(3) The person specified is any tenant who, as a result of a notice given by the Board under regulation 17(5)(*b*), was not obligated to make payments to the Board in respect of any payments made to a non-resident in that period.

(4) The information specified is—

(*a*) the name of the non-resident;

(*b*) where the non-resident is—

(i) an individual, or

(ii) a trustee other than a corporate or a professional trustee,

the principal residential address of the non-resident;

(*c*) where the non-resident is a company, the address of its registered office or its principal place of business;

(*d*) where the non-resident is a professional trustee, the address of his employment or principal place of business;

(*e*) where the prescribed person is an agent, the amount of income which, before deduction of any expenses, fell to be taken into account in the annual period in calculating under regulation 9 amounts of tax payable by him in respect of the Schedule A business (or part thereof) of the non-resident, or which would have fallen so to be taken into account if the non-resident had not been an approved person for the purposes of regulation 17 in that period;

(*f*) where the prescribed person is a person falling within subsection (2)(*a*) of section 42A, the aggregate of the following amounts of income—

(i) the amount of income which fell to be taken into account in the annual period in calculating under regulation 8 amounts of tax payable by him in respect of the Schedule A business (or part thereof) of the non-resident, or which would have fallen so to be taken into account if the non-resident had not been an approved person for the purposes of regulation 17 in that period, and

(ii) the amount of income which did not fall so to be taken into account because it was paid to a person other than the non-resident in circumstances where the prescribed person could reasonably be satisfied that the amount of the payment was a deductible expense;

(*g*) except where the non-resident is an approved person for the purposes of regulation 17, the aggregate of—

(i) all amounts paid during the annual period on behalf of the non-resident by or at the direction of the prescribed person which the prescribed person could reasonably be satisfied constituted deductible expenses, and

(ii) amounts carried forward to that period from a previous period pursuant to regulation 9(5)(*b*);

(*h*) the aggregate of the amounts specified as payable to the Board in quarterly returns made by the prescribed person for the annual period;

(*j*) the reference number relating to an approval by the Board of the non-resident under regulation 17.

(5) The declaration specified is a declaration by the prescribed person that the particulars given in the return are to the best of his knowledge correct and complete.

Certificate of tax liability

12—(1) Not later than the 5th July following the end of an annual period, a prescribed person who is liable under these Regulations to make any payments to the Board for any quarter falling within that period in respect of tax chargeable on the income of a non-resident, shall provide the non-resident with a certificate which shall include the particulars specified in paragraph (2) below and the declaration specified in paragraph (3) below.

(2) The particulars specified are—

(*a*) the name of the non-resident;

(*b*) where the non-resident is—

(i) an individual, or

(ii) a trustee other than a corporate or a professional trustee,

the principal residential address of the non-resident;

(*c*) where the non-resident is a company, the address of its registered office or its principal place of business;

(*d*) where the non-resident is a professional trustee, the address of his employment or principal place of business;

(*e*) the name and address of the prescribed person;

(*f*) the annual period to which the certificate relates;

(*g*) the aggregate amount of the liability referred to in paragraph (1) above for all quarters falling within the annual period.

(3) The declaration specified is a declaration by the prescribed person that the certificate is to the best of his knowledge correct and complete.

PROVISION OF INFORMATION AND INSPECTION AND KEEPING OF RECORDS

Information to be provided to the Board by prescribed persons

13 The Board may by notice require a prescribed person to furnish them, within such time (not being less than 14 days) as may be provided by the notice, such information as they may reasonably require to satisfy themselves that the prescribed person has complied with the requirements of these Regulations.

Inspection of records by officer of the Board

14—(1) The Board may by notice require a prescribed person, within such time (not being less than 14 days) as may be provided by the notice, to make available for inspection by an officer of the Board authorised for that purpose all such books, documents and other records in his possession or under his control as they may reasonably require to satisfy themselves that the prescribed person has complied with the requirements of these Regulations.

(2) Where a document or other record is maintained by computer, the prescribed person shall provide the officer making the inspection with all the facilities necessary for obtaining information from that document or other record.

Keeping of records

15 A prescribed person shall at all times maintain and retain sufficient records to enable an officer of the Board to satisfy himself on inspection of those records that the prescribed person has complied with the requirements of these Regulations.

Use of information

16—(1) Subject to paragraph (2) below, information obtained by the Board under regulation 13 or 14—

(*a*) shall not be used for the purpose of ascertaining the tax liability (if any) of any person other than—

(i) a person whose usual place of abode is outside the United Kingdom, or

(ii) a person falling within subsection (2)(*a*) of section 42A, or

(iii) an agent.

(2) Paragraph (1) above shall not be construed as preventing any disclosure of information within section 182(5) of the Finance Act 1989.

GROSS PAYMENT OF PROPERTY INCOME

Application for gross payment of property income

17—(1) A non-resident may apply to the Board for the obligation imposed under these Regulations to make payments to the Board not to apply in relation to payments falling to be treated as receipts of a Schedule A business carried on by him.

(2) An application under paragraph (1) above shall be made on a form provided by the Board and shall contain the information specified in paragraph (3) below and the undertakings specified in paragraph (4) below.

(3) The information specified is—

(*a*) the name of the applicant;
(*b*) the date of the application;
(*c*) where the applicant is—

(i) an individual, or
(ii) a trustee other than a corporate or a professional trustee,

the principal residential address of the applicant;
(*d*) where the applicant is a company, the address of its registered office or its principal place of business, and the names and principal residential addresses of its directors;
(*e*) where the applicant is a professional trustee, the address of his employment or principal place of business;
(*f*) the applicant's national insurance number, if he has one;
(*g*) the applicant's United Kingdom tax office reference, if he has one;
(*h*) the name and address of the prescribed person or, if more than one, each of the prescribed persons by or through whom payments falling to be treated as receipts of the applicant's Schedule A business are made;
(*j*) a statement that—

(i) the applicant has complied with all obligations imposed on him by or under the Tax Acts or the Management Act prior to the date of the application; or
(ii) the applicant has not had any obligations imposed on him by or under the Tax Acts or the Management Act prior to the date of the application; or
(iii) he does not expect to be liable to pay any amount by way of United Kingdom income tax for the year in which the application is made.

(4) The undertakings specified are that—

(*a*) where the applicant makes a statement falling within paragraph (3)(*j*)(iii) above, he will notify the Board in writing if he becomes liable to pay any such amount;
(*b*) the applicant will fully comply with all obligations imposed on him by or under the Tax Acts or the Management Act;
(*c*) the applicant will inform the Board if his usual place of abode ceases to be outside the United Kingdom.

(5) Where the Board approve an application under paragraph (1) above, they shall give—

(*a*) notice of the approval to the non-resident, and
(*b*) notice to the prescribed person or, if more than one, each prescribed person, specifying the date from which the obligations referred to in paragraph (1) above shall cease to apply in relation to payments falling to be treated as receipts of the applicant's Schedule A business and made on or after that date.

(6) The Board may, by notice to the applicant, refuse an application under paragraph (1) above where—

(*a*) they are not satisfied that the statement contained in the application and falling within paragraph (3)(*j*)(i), (ii) or (iii) above, as the case may be, is correct; or
(*b*) they are not satisfied that the applicant will comply with the undertakings contained in the application.

(7) The applicant may appeal against the Board's refusal of his application under paragraph (6) above by giving notice to the Board within 90 days of receipt of the notice of refusal.

(8) The appeal shall be to the General Commissioners, except that the appellant may elect (in accordance with section 46(1) of the Management Act) to bring the appeal before the Special Commissioners instead of the General Commissioners.

(9) The General Commissioners or the Special Commissioners, as the case may be, shall on appeal to them confirm the notice refusing approval unless they are satisfied that the notice ought to be quashed.

Review of approval under regulation 17—furnishing of information

18 Where the Board have approved an application under regulation 17, they may by notice require the non-resident by whom the application was made to furnish them, within such time (not being less than 42 days) as may be provided by the notice, such information as they may reasonably require to enable them to review the approval.

Withdrawal of approval under regulation 17

19—(1) An approval of an application under regulation 17 may be withdrawn by the Board by notice to the non-resident by whom the application was made specifying—

(*a*) the reasons for the withdrawal, and

(*b*) the date from which the withdrawal of approval shall take effect.

(2) The Board may withdraw their approval of an application where—

(*a*) they cease to be satisfied that the statement contained in the application and falling within regulation 17(3)(*j*)(i), (ii) or (iii), as the case may be, is correct; or

(*b*) they cease to be satisfied that the non-resident will comply with the undertakings contained in the application; or

(*c*) the non-resident fails to furnish information to the Board in accordance with regulation 18.

(3) Where the Board withdraw their approval of an application under paragraph (1) above, they shall give notice to the prescribed person or, if more than one, each prescribed person, specifying the date from which the obligations imposed under these Regulations to make payments to the Board shall apply in relation to payments falling to be treated as receipts of the applicant's Schedule A business and made on or after that date.

(4) A non-resident may appeal against the Board's withdrawal of approval under paragraph (1) above by giving notice to the Board within 90 days of the date of issue of the notice withdrawing approval.

(5) The appeal shall be to the General Commissioners, except that the non-resident may elect (in accordance with section 46(1) of the Management Act) to bring the appeal before the Special Commissioners instead of the General Commissioners.

(6) The General Commissioners or the Special Commissioners, as the case may be, shall on appeal to them confirm the notice withdrawing approval unless they are satisfied that the notice ought to be quashed.

PROVISIONS RELATING TO SELF-ASSESSMENT

Self-assessment—payments on account

20 Section 59A of the Management Act (payments on account of income tax) ("section 59A") shall have effect in relation to payments to be made to the Board by virtue of section 42A in respect of any tax as if any reference in section 59A to income tax deducted at source included a reference to such payments.

Self-assessment—consequential provisions

21—(1) A non-resident may set off against either of the amounts specified in paragraph (2) below the aggregate amount of the payments which—

(*a*) were liable to be made to the Board under these Regulations for each quarter ending in a year by any person who is a prescribed person in respect of the Schedule A business (or part thereof) carried on by the non-resident in that year, and

(*b*) were retained by the prescribed person out of sums due from him to the non-resident in order to meet that liability.

(2) The amounts specified are—

(*a*) the amount in which the non-resident is chargeable to income tax for the year in question, and

(*b*) the amount of the first payment on account of his liability to income tax for that year.

(3) Where pursuant to paragraph (1) above an amount is set off against the amount specified in paragraph (2)(*a*) above, section 59A (as modified by regulation 20) shall have effect as if the reference in subsection (1) of that section to the amount which is the assessed amount were a reference to that assessed amount reduced by the amount set off.

(4) Where pursuant to paragraph (1) above an amount is set off against the amount specified in paragraph (2)(*b*) above, section 59A (as so modified) shall have effect as if the reference in subsection (2) of that section to the first payment on account were a reference to the amount of that payment reduced by the amount set off.

(5) In any case where—

(*a*) by virtue of regulation 17 the obligations imposed under these Regulations to make payments to the Board do not apply in any year in relation to payments falling to be treated as receipts of a Schedule A business carried on by a non-resident in that year, and

(*b*) those obligations applied to such payments in the immediately preceding year, subsection (1) of section 59A (as so modified) shall have effect as if those obligations did not apply in the immediately preceding year.

1995/2934

Income Tax (Gilt-edged Securities) (Gross Payments of Interest) Regulations 1995

Made by the Treasury under TA 1988 s 51A(3)–(5), (9)

Made . . . . *15 November 1995*
Laid before the House of Commons . . . . *15 November 1995*
Coming into Force . . . . *23 November 1995*

Commentary—*Simon's Direct Tax Service* **A7.1105–1109.**

Citation, commencement and effect

1 These Regulations may be cited as the Income Tax (Gilt-edged Securities) (Gross Payments of Interest) Regulations 1995, shall come into force on 23rd November 1995, and shall have effect with respect to any payment of interest on gilt-edged securities which is made on or after 2nd January 1996.

Interpretation

2 In these Regulations unless the context otherwise requires—

"approved CGO member" means a CGO member who is approved by the Board to receive interest on gilt-edged securities without deduction of income tax;

"arrangements" means arrangements under which gilt-edged securities of an eligible person are held;

"the Board" means the Commissioners of Inland Revenue;

"business establishment", in relation to a person having a business establishment in the United Kingdom, means premises which are, or are intended to be, occupied and used with a reasonable degree of permanence;

"CGO" means the Central Gilts Office of the Bank of England;

"CGO member" means a person who has been admitted to membership of the CGO by the Bank of England;

"the Crown Agents" has the meaning given by section 1(2) of the Crown Agents Act 1979;

"EEA Agreement" means the Agreement on the European Economic Area signed at Oporto on 2nd May 1992 as adjusted by the Protocol signed at Brussels on 17th March 1993;

"EEA State" means a State, other than the United Kingdom, which is a Contracting Party to the EEA Agreement;

"eligible person" shall be construed in accordance with subsection (2) of section 51A;

"intermediary" means any person through whom an instruction is passed to a CGO member or another intermediary in connection with the holding of gilt-edged securities of an eligible person;

"notice" means notice in writing;

"recognised intermediary" has the meaning given by regulation 6(2);

"section 51A" means section 51A of the Taxes Act;

"STAR account" means an account designated by the CGO for the holding of gilt-edged securities of an eligible person;

"Taxes Act" means the Income and Corporation Taxes Act 1988.

Conditions relating to arrangements for the holding of gilt-edged securities—general

3 For the purposes of subsection (3)(*a*) of section 51A, the conditions that are to be satisfied in relation to arrangements for the holding of any gilt-edged securities are those specified in regulations 4 to 6.

Condition relating to accounts in which gilt-edged securities are held

4 The condition specified in this regulation is that gilt-edged securities are held under the arrangements in a STAR account.

Condition relating to holder of gilt-edged securities

5—(1) The condition specified in this regulation is that gilt-edged securities are held under the arrangements by a person who—

(*a*) is a CGO member, and

(*b*) is approved by the Board to receive interest on those securities without deduction of income tax.

(2) An application for approval under paragraph (1) above shall be made in writing to the Board.

(3) On receipt of an application under paragraph (2) above, the Board may by notice require the applicant to furnish them with such information as they may reasonably require to enable them to decide whether to give or refuse approval.

(4) The Board shall approve a CGO member under paragraph (1) above if they are satisfied that—

(*a*) he will comply with his obligations as a CGO member under the arrangements and these Regulations, and

(*b*) in the case of a person resident outside the United Kingdom who does not have a business establishment in the United Kingdom by means of which his functions as a CGO member under the arrangements are wholly or mainly carried out, the requirements specified in regulation 7 are fulfilled by him.

(5) The Board may, by notice to the applicant, refuse approval where they have reason to believe that—

(*a*) the applicant is not a CGO member, or

(*b*) the applicant will not comply with his obligations as a CGO member under the arrangements or these Regulations, or

(*c*) in the case of an applicant falling within paragraph (4)(*b*) above, the requirements specified in regulation 7 are not fulfilled by him.

(6) The Board may, by notice to the CGO member concerned, withdraw approval where they have reason to believe that—

(*a*) he is not, or has ceased to be, a CGO member, or

(*b*) he has not complied, or will not comply, with his obligations as a CGO member under the arrangements or these Regulations, or

(*c*) in the case of a CGO member falling within paragraph (4)(*b*) above, the requirements specified in regulation 7 are not fulfilled by him.

(7) A CGO member may appeal against a notice under paragraph (5) above refusing approval, or a notice under paragraph (6) above withdrawing approval, by notice to the Board within 30 days after the date of issue of the notice of refusal or withdrawal.

(8) The appeal shall be to the Special Commissioners who shall confirm the notice of refusal or withdrawal unless they are satisfied that it ought to be quashed.

Condition relating to intermediaries

6—(1) The condition specified in this regulation is that an intermediary is a recognised intermediary.

(2) A recognised intermediary is an intermediary who either—

(*a*) falls within the description of intermediary specified in paragraph (3) below, or

(*b*) is for the time being approved by the Board as a recognised intermediary.

(3) The description of intermediary specified in this paragraph is of an intermediary who—

(*a*) is resident in the United Kingdom or an EEA State,

(*b*) falls within any of the categories specified in paragraph (4) below, and

(*c*) is for the time being registered with the Board in accordance with paragraph (5) below.

(4) The categories specified in this paragraph are—

(*a*) the Bank of England;

(*b*) any bank or other institution authorised under the Banking Act 1987;

(*c*) a European authorised institution within the meaning of the Banking Co-ordination (Second Council Directive) Regulations 1992;

(*d*) the European Investment Bank;

(*e*) a central bank of an EEA State;

(*f*) a building society within the meaning of the Building Societies Act 1986;

(*g*) an investment firm within the meaning of Article 1(2) of Council Directive 93/22/EEC dated 10th May 1993 on investment services in the securities field which is authorised in accordance with that Directive;

(*h*) a member of the Securities and Futures Authority;

(i) a member of a recognised stock exchange situated in the United Kingdom or in an EEA State;

(*j*) the Crown Agents and the Crown Agents Financial Services Limited.

(5) An intermediary registers with the Board for the purposes of paragraph (3)(*c*) above by providing the following information to the Board—

(*a*) the full name and address of the intermediary;

(*b*) the category specified in paragraph (4) above in which the intermediary falls;

(*c*) in the case of an intermediary resident outside the United Kingdom who does not have a business establishment in the United Kingdom by means of which his functions as an intermediary under the arrangements are wholly or mainly carried out, details of the arrangements instituted by that person pursuant to regulation 7.

(6) An application for approval as a recognised intermediary under paragraph (2)(*b*) above shall be made in writing to the Board.

(7) On receipt of an application under paragraph (6) above, the Board may by notice require the applicant to furnish them with such information as they may reasonably require to enable them to decide whether to give or refuse approval.

(8) The Board shall approve an intermediary as a recognised intermediary if they are satisfied that—

(*a*) he will comply with his obligations as a recognised intermediary under the arrangements and these Regulations, and

(*b*) in the case of an intermediary resident outside the United Kingdom who does not have a business establishment in the United Kingdom by means of which his functions as an intermediary under the arrangements are wholly or mainly carried out, the requirements specified in regulation 7 are fulfilled by him.

(9) The Board may, by notice to an intermediary registering with the Board under paragraph (5) above, cancel the registration where they have reason to believe that—

(*a*) that person does not fall within the description of intermediary specified in paragraph (3)(*a*) or (*b*) above, or

(*b*) he has not complied, or will not comply, with his obligations as a recognised intermediary under the arrangements or these Regulations, or

(*c*) in the case of an intermediary falling within sub-paragraph (*c*) of paragraph (5) above, the requirements specified in regulation 7 are not fulfilled by him.

(10) The Board may, by notice to the applicant, refuse approval under paragraph (2)(*b*) above where they have reason to believe that—

(*a*) the applicant will not comply with his obligations as a recognised intermediary under the arrangements and these Regulations, or

(*b*) in the case of an applicant who is an intermediary falling within paragraph (8)(*b*) above, the requirements specified in regulation 7 are not fulfilled by him.

(11) The Board may, by notice to the intermediary concerned, withdraw approval given under paragraph (2)(*b*) above where they have reason to believe that—

(*a*) he has not complied, or will not comply, with his obligations as a recognised intermediary under the arrangements or these Regulations, or

(*b*) in the case of an intermediary falling within paragraph (8)(*b*) above, the requirements specified in regulation 7 are not fulfilled by him.

(12) An intermediary may appeal against a notice under paragraph (9), (10) or (11) above by notice to the Board within 30 days after the date of issue of the notice cancelling the registration or, as the case may be, refusing or withdrawing approval.

(13) The appeal shall be to the Special Commissioners who shall confirm the notice appealed against unless they are satisfied that it ought to be quashed.

(14) The Board shall maintain, and publish in such manner as they consider appropriate, a list of recognised intermediaries registered with, or approved by, them in accordance with this regulation for the use of eligible persons, CGO members and other recognised intermediaries.

Requirements relating to approval and registration of a non-resident under regulations 5 and 6

7—(1) The requirements referred to in regulation 5(4)(*b*), (5)(*c*) and (6)(*c*), and regulation 6(8)(*b*), (9)(*c*), (10)(*b*) and (11)(*b*) are that the non-resident CGO member or, as the case may be, the non-resident intermediary either—

(*a*) appoints a person who falls within paragraph (2) below to be responsible for securing the discharge of the obligations which fall to be discharged by the member or the intermediary under the arrangements, or

(*b*) agrees other arrangements with the Board designed to secure the discharge of those obligations.

(2) A person falls within this paragraph if—

(*a*) he is an individual resident in the United Kingdom, or

(*b*) he is not an individual and has a business establishment in the United Kingdom, or

(*c*) he is a partner whose firm has a business establishment in the United Kingdom.

(3) The appointment of a person under paragraph (1)(*a*) above shall not have effect unless and until notice of the appointment is given by the CGO member or intermediary to the Board.

(4) A person appointed under paragraph (1)(*a*) above—

(*a*) shall be entitled to act on behalf of the CGO member or intermediary concerned in respect of any of his functions or obligations under the arrangements,

(*b*) shall secure the CGO member's or intermediary's compliance with and discharge of any obligations of the member or intermediary under the arrangements, and

(*c*) shall be personally liable in respect of any failure of the CGO member or intermediary to comply with or discharge any of his obligations under the arrangements as if the obligations imposed on the member or intermediary were imposed jointly and severally on the member or intermediary and the person appointed.

(5) The Board may, by notice to the person appointed and the CGO member or intermediary, determine that the appointment shall be treated as not having fulfilled the requirements specified in paragraph (1) above where they have reason to believe that the person appointed either—

(*a*) has failed to secure compliance with the obligations of the member or intermediary under the arrangements, or

(*b*) does not have adequate resources to secure compliance with those obligations or to meet liabilities under the arrangements.

Declarations by eligible persons

8—(1) For the purposes of subsection (3)(*b*) of section 51A, an eligible person other than—

(*a*) an approved CGO member, or

(*b*) a recognised intermediary who gives an instruction in accordance with regulation 10(2)(*b*)(ii),

shall provide a declaration, in a form provided or authorised by the Board, to a CGO member or recognised intermediary containing the information and the undertaking specified in paragraph (2) below.

(2) The declaration shall contain—

(*a*) the full name of the eligible person by whom the declaration is made;

(*b*) the address of the principal place of business of the eligible person or, in the case of an eligible person which is a company resident in the United Kingdom, the address of the registered office;

(*c*) the name of the CGO member or recognised intermediary to whom the declaration is provided;

(*d*) a statement that the gilt-edged securities of the declarant are gilt-edged securities of an eligible person within the meaning of subsection (2) of section 51A;

(*e*) an undertaking by the eligible person that he will notify the CGO member or the recognised intermediary to whom the declaration is provided of any gilt-edged securities which are or have at any time since the making of the declaration been owned by him to which the declaration does not apply or has ceased to apply;

(*f*) a statement that the information contained in the declaration is correct to the best of the eligible person's knowledge and belief.

(3) The declaration shall be signed and dated—

(*a*) by the eligible person, or

(*b*) by an officer or employee of the eligible person authorised for that purpose by the eligible person, stating the capacity in which he signs.

Requirements in relation to functions of approved CGO members

9—(1) An approved CGO member shall not be entitled to place gilt-edged securities in a STAR account unless the requirement specified in paragraph (2) below is satisfied or, as the case may be, the requirements specified in paragraph (3) or (4) below are satisfied.

(2) The requirement specified in this paragraph is that the gilt-edged securities are the securities of the CGO member in his capacity as an eligible person.

(3) The requirements specified in this paragraph are that—

(*a*) the gilt-edged securities are securities in respect of which the CGO member has obtained a declaration completed in accordance with regulation 8,

(*b*) the CGO member has no reason to believe, by reference to information in his possession, that the declaration is, or has become, incorrect, or that it does not apply to the gilt-edged securities concerned, and

(*c*) the eligible person by whom the declaration is made is the person to whom, or on whose direction, interest arising on the gilt-edged securities concerned is to be paid.

(4) The requirements specified in this paragraph are that—

(*a*) the gilt-edged securities are securities in respect of which the CGO member has received an instruction from an intermediary which is given in accordance with regulation 10(5) and contains all the information required by that regulation,

(*b*) the intermediary from whom the instruction is received is, by reference to the list referred to in regulation 6(14), a recognised intermediary, and

(*c*) the CGO member has no reason to believe, by reference to information in his possession, that the gilt-edged securities concerned should not be held in the STAR account.

Requirements in relation to functions of recognised intermediaries

10—(1) A recognised intermediary shall not be entitled to arrange for gilt-edged securities to be placed in a STAR account unless the requirements specified in paragraph (2), (3) or (4) below (as the case may be) are satisfied.

(2) The requirements specified in this paragraph are that—

(*a*) the gilt-edged securities are the securities of the recognised intermediary in his capacity as an eligible person, and

(*b*) the recognised intermediary either—

(i) provides a declaration in accordance with regulation 8, or

(ii) gives an instruction to an approved CGO member or to another recognised intermediary in accordance with paragraph (5) below.

(3) The requirements specified in this paragraph are that—

(*a*) the gilt-edged securities are securities in respect of which the recognised intermediary has obtained a declaration completed in accordance with regulation 8,

(*b*) the recognised intermediary has no reason to believe, by reference to information in his possession, that the declaration is, or has become, incorrect, or that it does not apply to the gilt-edged securities concerned,

(*c*) the eligible person by whom the declaration is made is the person to whom, or on whose direction, interest arising on the gilt-edged securities concerned is to be paid, and

(*d*) the recognised intermediary in receipt of the declaration gives an instruction to an approved CGO member or to another recognised intermediary (as the case may be) in accordance with paragraph (5) below.

(4) The requirements specified in this paragraph are that—

(*a*) the gilt-edged securities are securities in respect of which the recognised intermediary has received an instruction from another recognised intermediary which is given in accordance with paragraph (5) below and contains all the information required by that paragraph,

(*b*) the recognised intermediary in receipt of the instruction has no reason to believe, by reference to information in his possession, that the gilt-edged securities concerned should not be placed in a STAR account, and

(*c*) the recognised intermediary in receipt of the instruction in turn gives an instruction to an approved CGO member or to another recognised intermediary (as the case may be) in accordance with paragraph (5) below.

(5) An instruction given pursuant to this regulation shall contain the following information—

(*a*) identification of the recognised intermediary by whom it is given,

(*b*) identification of the approved CGO member or recognised intermediary to whom the instruction is given,

(*c*) either—

(i) details of the gilt-edged securities to which the instruction relates, or

(ii) details specifying or otherwise describing the contracts or arrangements under which the gilt-edged securities will be received for the recognised intermediary giving the instruction,

(*d*) an instruction to the recipient to arrange for those gilt-edged securities to be placed in a STAR account, and

(*e*) the date of the instruction.

Requirements in relation to the removal of gilt-edged securities from a STAR account

11—(1) In any of the circumstances specified in paragraph (2) below and subject to paragraph (3) below, an approved CGO member or a recognised intermediary shall make arrangements for the immediate removal of the gilt-edged securities concerned from a STAR account in which the securities were placed by the CGO member, or arranged to be placed by the recognised intermediary.

(2) The circumstances specified are where—

(*a*) gilt-edged securities of the CGO member or the intermediary in his capacity as an eligible person are transferred to another person;

(*b*) after the CGO member has placed, or the intermediary has arranged to place, gilt-edged securities in the STAR account in response to a declaration, the CGO member or the intermediary receives a notification from the maker of the declaration pursuant to the undertaking contained in the declaration;

(*c*) after the CGO member has placed, or the intermediary has arranged to place, gilt-edged securities in the STAR account in response to an instruction received from a recognised intermediary, it comes to the attention of the CGO member or the intermediary that another recognised intermediary has been appointed to act in relation to those gilt-edged securities, or an intermediary has been appointed so to act who is not a recognised intermediary;

(*d*) the CGO member or the intermediary receives a notice issued by the Board in accordance with paragraph (4) below requiring the CGO member to remove, or the intermediary to arrange to remove, gilt-edged securities held in a STAR account by the CGO member or on the instruction of the intermediary for a person specified in the notice;

(*e*) the CGO member or the intermediary has reason to believe, by reference to information in his possession, that any gilt-edged securities should not be held in the STAR account.

(3) The obligation under paragraph (1) above to remove gilt-edged securities from a STAR account shall not apply in any case where—

(*a*) the CGO member or the intermediary holds or receives a declaration from another eligible person, or an instruction from a recognised intermediary in accordance with regulation 10(5), relating to those securities, or (*b*) the securities are acquired by the CGO member or the intermediary in his capacity as an eligible person.

(4) A notice issued by the Board as mentioned in paragraph (2)(*d*) above—

(*a*) shall specify the name of the person for whom the CGO member or the intermediary has acted;

(*b*) may stipulate that the CGO member shall not place, or the intermediary arrange to place, any other gilt-edged securities in a STAR account in reliance upon a declaration given by the person specified in the notice;

(*c*) may be revoked by the Board by notice to the CGO member or intermediary to whom it was issued.

Information to be provided to the Board

12—(1) The Board may by notice require any person who is or has at any time been an approved CGO member or a recognised intermediary to furnish them, within such time (not being less than fourteen days) as may be provided in the notice, such information (including copies of or extracts from any books documents or other records) as they may reasonably require for the purpose of satisfying themselves that the requirements of these Regulations have been complied with by that person.

(2) The Board may by notice require a person who has made a declaration in accordance with regulation 8 to furnish them, within such time (not being less than fourteen days) as may be provided in the notice, such information (including copies of or extracts from any books, documents or other records) as they may reasonably require for the purpose of verifying the information contained in the declaration.

Inspection of records by officer of the Board

13—(1) The Board may by notice require any person who is or has at any time been an approved CGO member or a recognised intermediary, within such time (not being less than fourteen days) as may be provided in the notice, to make available for inspection by an officer of the Board authorised for that purpose all such books, documents and other records in his possession or under his control as they may reasonably require for the purpose of satisfying themselves that the requirements of these Regulations have been complied with by—

(*a*) the CGO member or intermediary to whom the notice is issued, or

(*b*) another approved CGO member or recognised intermediary, or

(*c*) a person who has made a declaration in accordance with regulation 8.

(2) Where records are maintained by computer the person required to make them available for inspection shall provide the officer making the inspection with all the facilities necessary for obtaining information from them.

Keeping of records

14 An approved CGO member or a recognised intermediary shall at all times keep sufficient records to enable the Board to satisfy themselves, on inspection of those records, that the requirements of these Regulations have been complied with by him.

Retention of documents

15—(1) An approved CGO member or a recognised intermediary shall retain, for the period specified in paragraph (2) below—

(*a*) any declaration or instruction obtained by him pursuant to these Regulations on the basis of which gilt-edged securities were placed, or arranged to be placed, by him in a STAR account;

(*b*) any document containing details of any contract or arrangements referred to in any such instruction by virtue of which the gilt-edged securities to which the instruction relates were received for the recognised intermediary giving the instruction.

(2) The period specified—

(*a*) in the case of a CGO member, is the period which commences on the date on which the securities were placed in the STAR account and ends on—

(i) the date which is two years after the securities cease to be held in that account in reliance upon the declaration or instruction concerned (whether or not the CGO member ceases to act in that capacity before the end of the period), or

(ii) such earlier date as is agreed between the Board and the CGO member;

(*b*) in the case of a recognised intermediary, is the period which commences on the date on which he gave an instruction for securities to be placed in the STAR account and ends on—

(i) the date which is two years after the securities cease to be held in that account in reliance upon the declaration or instruction concerned (whether or not the intermediary ceases to act in that capacity before the end of the period), or

(ii) such earlier date as is agreed between the Board and the intermediary.

1995/3036
Manufactured Payments and Transfer of Securities (Tax Relief) Regulations 1995

Made by the Treasury under TA 1988 s 730A(7), 737D(1)

Made	*28 November 1995*
Laid before the House of Commons	*28 November 1995*
Coming into Force	*2 January 1996*

Commentary—*Simon's Direct Tax Service* **B3.701.**

Citation, commencement and effect

1—(1) These Regulations may be cited as the Manufactured Payments and Transfer of Securities (Tax Relief) Regulations 1995 and shall come into force on 2nd January 1996.
(2) These Regulations have effect in relation to—
(*a*) any manufactured payment made on or after 2nd January 1996, and
(*b*) any payment of interest deemed to be made on or after that date under an agreement to sell securities entered into on or after 1st May 1995.

Interpretation

2 In these Regulations—
''manufactured payment'' has the meaning given by section 737D(2) of the Taxes Act;
''the Taxes Act'' means the Income and Corporation Taxes Act 1988.

Tax relief for manufactured payments

3—(1) Any manufactured payment made to a person for the benefit of—
(*a*) a scheme referred to in section 592(2) or 643(2) of the Taxes Act, or
(*b*) any fund referred to in section 608(2)(*a*), 613(4), 614(2), (3) or (4) or 620(6) of that Act,
shall be treated as comprised in income of that person that is eligible for relief from tax by virtue of that section.
(2) Any manufactured payment made to an insurance company shall be treated, to the extent of so much of the payment as is referable to the company's pension business [or individual savings account business within the meaning of regulation 3 of the Individual Savings Account (Insurance Companies) Regulations 1998][1], as comprised in income of that company that is eligible for relief from tax by virtue of section 438 of the Taxes Act.

Amendments—[1] Words inserted in para 2 by the Individual Savings Account (Insurance Companies) Regulations, SI 1998/1871, with effect from 6 April 1999.

Tax relief for deemed payments of interest

4—(1) Where, pursuant to section 730A(2) of the Taxes Act (treatment of price differential on sale and repurchase of securities), a payment of interest is deemed to be made to a person in circumstances where, if it were actually made, it would be received by that person for the benefit of—
(*a*) a scheme specified in section 592(2) or 643(2) of the Taxes Act, or
(*b*) any fund referred to in section 608(2)(*a*), 613(4), 614(2), (3) or (4) or 620(6) of that Act,
the amount of the payment shall be treated as comprised in income that is eligible for relief from tax by virtue of that section.
(2) Where, pursuant to section 730A(2) of the Taxes Act, a payment of interest is deemed to be made to an insurance company, it shall be treated, to the extent of so much of the deemed payment as is referable to the company's pension business [or individual savings account business within the meaning of regulation 3 of the Individual Savings Account (Insurance Companies) Regulations 1998][1], as comprised in income that is eligible for relief from tax by virtue of section 438 of the Taxes Act.

Amendments—[1] Words inserted in para 2 by the Individual Savings Account (Insurance Companies) Regulations, SI 1998/1871, with effect from 6 April 1999.

1995/3103
Retirement Benefits Schemes (Information Powers) Regulations 1995

Made by the Commissioners of Inland Revenue under TA 1988 s 605(1A), (1B), (1D), (1E)

Made	*30 November 1995*
Laid before the House of Commons	*30 November 1995*
Coming into Force	*1 January 1996*

Commentary—*Simon's Direct Tax Service* **E7.247.**

PART I

INTRODUCTORY

Citation and commencement

1 These Regulations may be cited as the Retirement Benefits Schemes (Information Powers) Regulations 1995 and shall come into force on 1st January 1996.

Interpretation

2[—(1)][1] In these Regulations unless the context otherwise requires—

"actuary" means—

(*a*) a Fellow of the Institute of Actuaries, or

(*b*) a Fellow of the Faculty of Actuaries, or

(*c*) person with other actuarial qualifications who has been approved as being a proper person to act for the purposes of regulation 8 of the Occupational Pension Schemes (Disclosure of Information) Regulations 1986 in connection with the scheme;

"approved", in relation to a retirement benefits scheme, means—

(*a*) approved by the Board for the purposes of Chapter I, or

(*b*) before the Board in order for them to decide whether to give approval for the purposes of that Chapter;

"the Board" means the Commissioners of Inland Revenue;

"Chapter I" means Chapter I of Part XIV of the Taxes Act;

"company" means any body corporate or unincorporated association, but does not include a partnership;

["controlling director" in relation to a company means a person who is, or was within the ten years immediately preceding the event in question—

(*a*) a director as defined in section 612(1) of the Taxes Act (interpretation for the purposes of Chapter 1 of Part 14), and

(*b*) within paragraph (*b*) of section 417(5) of the Taxes Act (meaning of director for the purposes of provisions about close companies);][1]

["electronic communications" includes any communications conveyed by means of an electronic communications network.][2]

"exempt approved scheme" means an approved scheme which is for the time being within paragraph (*a*) or (*b*) of section 592(1) of the Taxes Act;

"friendly society" has the meaning given by section 116 of the Friendly Societies Act 1992;

["governing instrument" in relation to a retirement benefits scheme means a trust deed, or other document by which the scheme is established, and any other document (except an enactment) which contains provisions by which the administration of the scheme is governed;][1]

"insurance company" has the meaning given by section 659B of the Taxes Act;

"insured scheme" means an approved scheme, the contributions to which, apart from voluntary contributions made by members, are invested wholly by way of insurance premiums, and the policies in respect of which do not provide that levels of contributions require to take account of surpluses, but does not include a scheme—

(*a*) the policies in respect of which provide only for lump sum benefits for members on death before the normal retirement date, or

(*b*) which is a simplified defined contribution scheme;

"large self-administered scheme" means a self-administered scheme which is not a small self-administered scheme and is not a simplified defined contribution scheme;

"member", in relation to a retirement benefits scheme, means a member of the scheme to whom benefit is currently accruing as a result of service as an employee;

"normal retirement date" means the date specified in the rules of a retirement benefits scheme as the date at which an employee will normally retire;

"permitted maximum" has the meaning given by section 590C of the Taxes Act;

"relevant statutory scheme" has the meaning given by section 611A of the Taxes Act;

"retirement benefits scheme" has the meaning given by section 611(1) of the Taxes Act;

"scheme year" means—

(*a*) a year specified for the purposes of the scheme in any document comprising the scheme or, if no year is specified, a period of 12 months commencing on 1st April or on such other date as the trustees select; or

(*b*) such other period (if any) exceeding 6 months but not exceeding 18 months as is selected by the trustees—

(i) in respect of the scheme year in which the scheme commences or terminates, or

(ii) in connection with a variation of the date on which the scheme year is to commence;

"self-administered scheme" means an approved scheme some or all of the income and other assets of which are invested otherwise than in insurance policies;

"shares" includes stock;

[''signed'' in relation to a document includes the incorporation in it, or the logical association with it, of an electronic signature, as defined in section 7(2) of the Electronic Communications Act 2000;][1]

''simplified defined contribution scheme'' means a retirement benefits scheme approved by the Board by reference to limitations on—

(*a*) the aggregate amount of the contributions which may be paid by a member and his employer,

(*b*) the maximum lump sum which may be provided under the scheme, and

(*c*) the benefits payable on death which may be provided under the scheme;

[''small self-administered scheme'' means an approved scheme which is a small self-administered scheme within the meaning given by regulation 2(1) of the 1991 Regulations;][1]

''special contribution'' means any contribution paid to a retirement benefits scheme by an employer which is neither a fixed amount paid annually, whether in instalments or otherwise nor an annual amount, that is payable over a period of three years or more and is calculated on a consistent basis in accordance with actuarial principles by reference to the earnings, contributions or number of members of the scheme;

''Taxes Act'' means the Income and Corporation Taxes Act 1988;

...[1]

''1991 Regulations'' means the Retirement Benefits Schemes (Restriction on Discretion to Approve) (Small Self-administered Schemes) Regulations 1991.

[(2) In these Regulations, a reference to a notice or other document (other than a consent under paragraph (3) below) includes a notice or other document in such form and delivered by such means of electronic communications as the Board may approve by directions.][1]

[(3) The Board or an officer of theirs shall only deliver a notice or other document under these Regulations to a person by means of electronic communications if that person—

(*a*) has given his consent in writing to the delivery of documents by the Board by that means; and

(*b*) has not notified the Board that that consent has been withdrawn.][1]

Amendments—[1] Para (1) renumbered as such, definitions substituted and inserted, definition of ''unlisted company'' revoked, and paras (2), (3) inserted by the Retirement Benefits Schemes (Information Powers) (Amendment) Regulations, SI 2002/3006 reg 3 with effect from 6 April 2003.

[2] In para (2), definition of ''electronic communications'' substituted by the Communications Act 2003 (Consequential Amendments) Order, SI 2003/2155 art 3(1), Schedule 1 para 23(1)(*b*), (2) with effect from 17 September 2003.

PART II
INFORMATION REQUIRED WITHOUT NOTICE

Prescribed person

3 For the purposes of this Part of these Regulations, ''the prescribed person'' in relation to a retirement benefits scheme means—

(*a*) the person who is, or the persons who are, for the time being the administrator in relation to the scheme by virtue of section 611AA of the Taxes Act; or

(*b*) where section 606(1) of the Taxes Act applies at any time in relation to the scheme, the person who is, or the persons who are, by virtue of that section responsible at that time for the discharge of all duties imposed on the administrator under Chapter I (whenever arising) and liable for any tax due from the administrator in the administrator's capacity as such (whenever falling due); or

(*c*) where section 599(7) of the Taxes Act applies in relation to an insurance company, that insurance company.

Actuarial valuation reports—self-administered schemes and insured schemes

4—(1) The prescribed person in relation to a self-administered scheme or an insured scheme shall furnish to the Board, at the time prescribed by paragraph (2) below, any valuation report of the scheme's assets in relation to its liabilities having an effective date that falls on or after the date of coming into force of these Regulations, where the report—

(*a*) was commissioned for the purposes of the scheme, and

(*b*) consists of an actuarial valuation determined and dated and signed by an actuary.

(2) The time prescribed—

(*a*) where the valuation report relates to a large self-administered scheme or an insured scheme, is any time not later than two years after the date stated to be the effective date in the valuation;

(*b*) where the valuation report relates to a small self-administered scheme, is any time not later than one year after the date stated to be the effective date in the valuation.

Investment and borrowing transactions of small self-administered schemes

5—(1) The prescribed person in relation to a small self-administered scheme shall furnish to the Board, at the time prescribed by paragraph (2) below, such information (including copies of any relevant books, documents or other records) as—

(*a*) is specified on the relevant form supplied by [or in the relevant document delivered by][1] the Board, and

(*b*) relates to any transaction that is—

(i) of a kind specified in paragraph (3) below, and

(ii) entered into by or on behalf of the trustees or the administrator of the scheme on or after the date of coming into force of these Regulations.

(2) The time prescribed is any time not later than 90 days after the date of the transaction in question.

(3) The transactions specified in this paragraph are—

(*a*) the acquisition or disposal of land;

(*b*) the lending of money to an employer in relation to the scheme or any company associated with him;

(*c*) the acquisition or disposal of shares in an employer in relation to the scheme or any company associated with him;

(*d*) the acquisition or disposal of shares in an unlisted company;

(*e*) the borrowing of money;

(*f*) the purchase, sale or lease from or to an employer in relation to the scheme, or any company associated with him, of any asset other than one specified in sub-paragraph (*a*), (*c*) or (*d*).

[(4) In paragraph (3) above—

(*a*) ''unlisted company'' means a company which is not listed on a recognised stock exchange within the meaning of section 841(1) of the Taxes Act (recognised stock exchanges and recognised investment exchanges), but does not include an open-ended investment company within the meaning of section 236 of the Financial Services and Markets Act 2000 (meaning of open-ended investment company for the purposes of Part 17 of that Act); and

(*b*) references to a company associated with an employer shall be construed in accordance with regulation 2(9) of the 1991 Regulations.][1]

Revenue & other press releases—PSO 24-8-98 (Small self-administered schemes (SSASs) (Update 48).

Amendments—[1] Words in para (1) inserted, and para (4) substituted, by the Retirement Benefits Schemes (Information Powers) (Amendment) Regulations, SI 2002/3006 reg 4 with effect from 6 April 2003.

Participation of employers in a scheme

6—(1) The prescribed person in relation to an approved scheme shall furnish to the Board, at the time prescribed by paragraph (2) below, such information (including copies of any relevant books, documents or other records) relating to an event specified in paragraph (3) below and occurring on or after the date of coming into force of these Regulations as is specified on the relevant form supplied by [or in the relevant document delivered by][1] the Board.

(2) The time prescribed is any time not later than 180 days after the end of the scheme year in which the event in question occurs.

(3) The events specified in this paragraph are—

(*a*) the admission of a new employer as a participant in the scheme;

(*b*) in relation to any employer who is a participant in the scheme—

(i) a change in his name or address;

(ii) the occasion of his ceasing to carry on a trade or business;

(iii) a change in his association with any other employer who is a participant in the scheme.

(4) For the purposes of paragraph (3)(*b*)(iii) above, an employer is associated with another employer if—

(*a*) the association falls within the meaning given by subsection (3) of section 590A of the Taxes Act, read with subsection (4) of that section, or

(*b*) there exists some other basis of association between the employers which, for the purpose of granting or maintaining approval of the scheme, the Board have accepted as being sufficient to establish a permanent community of interest between the employers, whether by reason of the association falling within any of the situations specified in paragraph (5) below or otherwise.

(5) The situations specified are where—

(*a*) all the employees of the employers are the same individuals;

(*b*) the operations of the employers are interdependent;

(*c*) in the case of employers who are companies, the same individuals comprise the majority of the directors of, or hold the majority of the ordinary share capital in, each of the companies.

Amendments—[1] Words in para (1) inserted by the Retirement Benefits Schemes (Information Powers) (Amendment) Regulations, SI 2002/3006 reg 5 with effect from 6 April 2003.

Special contributions by employers

7—(1) The prescribed person in relation to an exempt approved scheme shall furnish to the Board, at the time prescribed by paragraph (2) below, such information (including copies of any relevant books, documents or other records) relating to the special contribution specified in paragraph (3) below as is specified on the relevant form supplied by [or in the relevant document delivered by][1] the Board.

(2) The time prescribed is any time not later than 180 days after the end of the scheme year[, in which there falls the end of the chargeable period, in the course of][1] which the special contribution was paid to the scheme by the employer.

(3) The special contribution specified in this paragraph is any special contribution paid to the scheme by an employer on or after the date of coming into force of these Regulations, other than a contribution which—

(*a*) has been certified by an actuary as made solely to finance cost of living increases for existing pensioners under the scheme; or

(*b*) when aggregated with other special contributions paid by that employer to the scheme in the same chargeable period other than a contribution falling within sub-paragraph (*a*) above, does not result in an amount which exceeds—

(i) one half of the permitted maximum as at the end of the scheme year referred to in paragraph (2) above, or

(ii) the total contributions, other than special contributions, made by the employer to the scheme in the same chargeable period,

whichever is the greater.

Amendments—[1] Words in para (1) inserted, and words in para (2) substituted, by the Retirement Benefits Schemes (Information Powers) (Amendment) Regulations, SI 2002/3006 reg 6 with effect from 6 April 2003.

Controlling directors as members of schemes

8—(1) The prescribed person in relation to an approved scheme shall furnish to the Board, at the time prescribed by paragraph (2) below, such information (including copies of any relevant books, documents or other records) relating to an event specified in paragraph (3) below and occurring on or after the date of coming into force of these Regulations as is specified on the relevant form supplied by [or in the relevant document delivered by][1] the Board.

(2) The time prescribed is any time not later than 180 days after the end of the scheme year in which the event in question occurs.

(3) The events specified in this paragraph are—

[(*a*) the admission of any person to membership of the scheme who is a controlling director of a company which is an employer in relation to the scheme; or][1]

(*b*) the occasion of an existing member of the scheme becoming a controlling director of a company which is an employer in relation to the scheme.

Amendments—[1] Words in para (1) inserted, and para (3)(*a*) substituted, by the Retirement Benefits Schemes (Information Powers) (Amendment) Regulations, SI 2002/3006 reg 7 with effect from 6 April 2003.

Controlling directors—benefits on retirement due to incapacity or serious ill-health

9—(1) The prescribed person in relation to an approved scheme shall furnish to the Board, at the time prescribed by paragraph (2) below—

(*a*) notification of any proposal such as is specified in paragraph (3) below and is made on or after the date of coming into force of these Regulations, and

(*b*) the information specified in paragraph (4) below.

(2) The time prescribed—

(*a*) in the case of the proposal specified in paragraph (3)(*a*) below, is any time not less than 28 days prior to the proposed payment of the benefits;

(*b*) in the case of the proposal specified in paragraph (3)(*b*) below, is any time not less than 14 days prior to the proposed payment of the benefits.

(3) The proposals specified in this paragraph are—

(*a*) any proposal for the scheme to pay benefits to a person who is a controlling director of a company which is an employer in relation to the scheme in circumstances where that person is to retire on grounds of incapacity prior to the normal retirement date;

(*b*) any proposal for the scheme to pay benefits commuted wholly to lump sum form to a person who is a controlling director of a company which is an employer in relation to the scheme in circumstances where that person is to be retired on grounds of serious ill-health.

(4) The information to be furnished shall be in the form of copies of documents relating to the decision of the administrator of the scheme to permit retirement on grounds of incapacity prior to the normal retirement date or, as the case may be, full commutation of benefits to lump sum form on retirement on grounds of serious ill-health, including copies of medical reports and other documents in the possession or under the control of the prescribed person containing details of the medical evidence which formed the basis of that decision.

(5) In this regulation—

"incapacity" means physical or mental deterioration which is sufficiently serious to prevent a person from following his normal employment or which seriously impairs his earning capacity;

"serious ill-health" means ill-health which is such as to give rise to a life expectancy of less than one year.

Reporting of chargeable events

10—(1) A person who is a prescribed person within regulation 3(*a*) or (*b*) in relation to a retirement benefits scheme which is—

(*a*) an approved scheme, or

(*b*) a relevant statutory scheme established under a public general Act,

shall furnish to the Board, at the time prescribed by paragraph (2) below, such information (including copies of any relevant books, documents or other records) relating to an event specified in paragraph (3) below as is specified on the relevant form supplied by[, or in the relevant document delivered by][1] the Board.

(2) The time prescribed is any time not later than 30 days after the end of the year of assessment in which the event in question occurs.

(3) The events specified in this paragraph are—

(*a*) any repayment under the scheme to which section 598 of the Taxes Act applies (repayment of employee's contributions);

(*b*) any commutation of an employee's pension under the scheme to which section 599 of the Taxes Act applies;

(*c*) any payment under the scheme to which section 599A of the Taxes Act applies (payment to or for the benefit of an employee or his personal representatives out of surplus funds);

(*d*) any payment to an employer to which section 601 of the Taxes Act applies (charge to tax on payments to employer out of funds of an exempt approved scheme).

[(4) In this regulation and regulation 11 references to an approved scheme include a scheme which has at any time been approved.][1]

Amendments—[1] Words in para (1) inserted, and para (4) inserted, by the Retirement Benefits Schemes (Information Powers) (Amendment) Regulations, SI 2002/3006 reg 8 with effect from 6 April 2003.

11—(1) An insurance company which is a prescribed person by virtue of regulation 3(*c*) in relation to a retirement benefits scheme which is—

(*a*) an approved scheme, or

(*b*) a relevant statutory scheme established under a public general Act,

shall furnish to the Board, at the time prescribed by paragraph (2) below, such information (including copies of any relevant books, documents or other records) relating to an event specified in paragraph (3) below as is specified on the relevant form supplied by [or in the relevant document delivered by][1] the Board.

(2) The time prescribed is any time not later than 180 days after the end of the chargeable period of the insurance company in which the event in question occurs.

(3) The events specified in this paragraph are—

(*a*) any repayment under the scheme to which section 598 of the Taxes Act applies;

(*b*) any commutation of an employee's pension under the scheme to which section 599 of the Taxes Act applies;

(*c*) any payment to an employer to which section 601 of the Taxes Act applies.

Amendments—[1] Words in para (1) inserted by the Retirement Benefits Schemes (Information Powers) (Amendment) Regulations, SI 2002/3006 reg 9 with effect from 6 April 2003.

[Reporting transfer payments from approved retirement benefits schemes, relevant statutory schemes or specified annuity contracts

11A—(1) The prescribed person within regulation 3(*a*), (*b*) or (*c*) in relation to—

(*a*) an approved retirement benefits scheme,

(*b*) a relevant statutory scheme, or

(*c*) an annuity contract referred to in section 605(1B)(*c*) of the Taxes Act other than a contract which provides for the immediate payment of benefits,

shall furnish to the Board, at the time prescribed by paragraph (2) below, such information (including copies of any relevant books, documents or other records) relating to an event specified in paragraph (3) below, as is specified by the Board.

(2) The time prescribed is any time not later than 28 days after the event in question.

(3) The event specified in this paragraph is one satisfying all the following conditions.

First condition

A transfer payment ("the payment") is made from—

(*a*) an approved retirement benefits scheme,

(*b*) a relevant statutory scheme, or

(*c*) a fund held subject to an annuity contract falling within paragraph (1)(*c*), ("the paying scheme").

Second condition

The market value of the payment—

(*a*) equals or exceeds £250,000; or

(*b*) when aggregated with the market value of any other payments relating to the same person, made from the paying scheme within any period of 365 days, beginning with the first of those payments and including the date of the payment in question, equals or exceeds £250,000.

Third condition

The payment is not made to a relevant statutory scheme, an approved statutory scheme or an annuity contract which provides for the immediate payment of benefits.][1]

Amendments—[1] Regulations 11A–11C inserted by the Retirement Benefits Schemes (Information Powers) (Amendment) Regulations, SI 2002/3006 reg 10 with effect from 6 April 2003.

[Reporting transfer payments to retirement benefits schemes or specified annuity contracts

11B—(1) The prescribed person within regulation 3(*a*), (*b*) or (*c*) in relation to—

(*a*) a retirement benefits scheme for the time being approved by the Board, other than a statutory scheme, or

(*b*) an annuity contract referred to in section 605(1B)(*c*) of the Taxes Act, other than a contract which provides for the immediate payment of benefits,

shall furnish to the Board, at the time prescribed by paragraph (2) below, such information (including copies of any relevant books, documents or other records) relating to an event specified in paragraph (3) below, as is specified by the Board.

This is subject to the qualification in paragraph (5).

(2) The time prescribed is any time not later than 28 days after the event in question.

(3) The event is one satisfying both of the following conditions.

First condition

A transfer payment ("the payment") is received by—

(*a*) a retirement benefits scheme which is for the time being approved by the Board, or

(*b*) a fund held subject to an annuity contract falling within paragraph (1)(*b*)

("the receiving scheme").

Second condition

The market value of the payment, when aggregated with the market value of any other transfer payments relating to the same person, made to the receiving scheme within a period of 365 days, beginning with the first such payment and including the date of the payment in question, equals or exceeds £250,000.

(4) If a payment has fallen within the second condition in paragraph (3), all subsequent transfer payments made to the receiving scheme within the period referred to in that condition, so far as they relate to the same person, shall be notified individually to the Board by the prescribed person in relation to the receiving scheme.

This is subject to the following qualification.

(5) The prescribed person in relation to the receiving scheme shall not be under an obligation to furnish information under this regulation if the prescribed person in respect of the paying scheme is under an obligation to furnish information in respect of the same transaction under regulation 11A.][1]

Amendments—[1] Regulations 11A–11C inserted by the Retirement Benefits Schemes (Information Powers) (Amendment) Regulations, SI 2002/3006 reg 10 with effect from 6 April 2003.

[Interpretation for the purposes of regulations 11A and 11B

11C—(1) In regulations 11A and 11B—

"market value" has the meaning given in section 272 of the Taxation of Chargeable Gains Act 1992 (valuation: general provisions for the purposes of that Act); and

"transfer payment" includes a payment under paragraph 1(3) of Schedule 5 to the Welfare Reform and Pensions Act 1999 or paragraph 1(3) of Schedule 5 to the Welfare Reform and Pensions (Northern Ireland) Order 1999.

(2) In relation to an annuity contract mentioned in section 605(1B)(*c*) of the Taxes Act, references to a prescribed person within regulation 3 include a reference to the insurance company with which the contract is made.][1]

Amendments—[1] Regulations 11A–11C inserted by the Retirement Benefits Schemes (Information Powers) (Amendment) Regulations, SI 2002/3006 reg 10 with effect from 6 April 2003.

PART III

NOTICES REQUIRING PARTICULARS AND DOCUMENTS

Approved schemes and relevant statutory schemes

12—(1) The Board may by notice require any of the persons prescribed by paragraph (2) below, within the time prescribed by paragraph (3) below, to furnish to the Board such particulars, and to produce to the Board such documents, as they may reasonably require relating to—

(*a*) any monies received or receivable by an approved scheme or a relevant statutory scheme, or
(*b*) any investments or other assets held by that scheme, or
(*c*) any monies paid or payable out of funds held under that scheme.

(2) The persons prescribed are—

(*a*) the person who is, or the persons who are, for the time being by virtue of section 611AA of the Taxes Act the administrator of the scheme which is the subject of the notice;
(*b*) any person who was, or any persons who were, at any time prior to the relevant date by virtue of section 611AA of the Taxes Act the administrator of that scheme, other than an excluded person;
(*c*) the trustee or trustees of that scheme, or any person who was, or any persons who were, at any time prior to the relevant date the trustee or trustees of that scheme, other than an excluded person;
(*d*) any person who is, or has been at any time prior to the relevant date, an employer in relation to that scheme, other than an excluded person;
(*e*) any person who is, or has been at any time prior to the relevant date, a scheme sponsor in relation to that scheme, other than an excluded person;
(*f*) any person who provides, or has at any time prior to the relevant date provided, administrative services to that scheme, other than an excluded person.

(3) The time prescribed is such time (not being less than 28 days) as may be provided by the notice.

(4) A notice under paragraph (1) above may require particulars to be furnished, and documents to be produced, relating to more than one scheme.

[(4A) In paragraph (1) above "approved" has the same meaning as in regulation 10.][1]

(5) In paragraph (2) above—

(*a*) "excluded person" means a person who, on ceasing to act in relation to the scheme or, as the case may be, provide administrative services to the scheme, transferred all documents in his possession or under his control relating to the scheme to another person who succeeded him in acting in relation to the scheme or providing administrative services to the scheme;
(*b*) "the relevant date" means the date on which the time prescribed by regulation 15(3)(*f*) ends.

Amendments—[1] Para (4A) inserted by the Retirement Benefits Schemes (Information Powers) (Amendment) Regulations, SI 2002/3006 reg 11 with effect from 6 April 2003.

Annuity contracts

13—(1) The Board may by notice require any of the persons prescribed by paragraph (2) below, within the time prescribed by paragraph (3) below, to furnish to the Board such particulars, and to produce to the Board such documents, as they may reasonably require relating to any annuity contract issued by that person by means of which benefits provided under an approved scheme or a relevant statutory scheme have been secured.

(2) The persons prescribed are—

(*a*) the insurance company which issued the annuity contract, where that company is a body corporate;
(*b*) the chief executive and the manager, within the meaning of [sections 417(1) and 423 of the Financial Services and Markets Act 2000 respectively][1], of the insurance company which issued the annuity contract;
(*c*) the friendly society which issued the annuity contract, where that friendly society is a society incorporated under the Friendly Societies Act 1992;
(*d*) the chief executive and the secretary, or any assistant or deputy chief executive, or assistant or deputy secretary, of the friendly society which issued the annuity contract.

(3) The time prescribed is such time (not being less than 28 days) as may be provided by the notice.

(4) A notice under paragraph (1) above may require particulars and documents relating to more than one annuity contract.

Amendments—[1] Words in sub-para (2)(*b*) substituted by the Financial Services and Markets Act 2000 (Consequential Amendments) (Taxes) Order, SI 2001/3629 art 141 with effect from 1 December 2001, immediately after the coming into force of the Financial Services and Markets Act 2000 ss 411, 432(1), Sch 20 (and SI 2001/3629 Pts 1 and 2).

PART IV
INSPECTION AND RETENTION OF RECORDS

Inspection of records

14—(1) The Board may by notice require any of the persons prescribed by paragraph (2) below to make available for inspection by an officer of the Board authorised for that purpose, within the time prescribed by paragraph (3) below, all books, documents and other records in his possession or under his control relating to—

(*a*) any monies received or receivable by an approved scheme or a relevant statutory scheme, or
(*b*) any investments or other assets held by that scheme, or
(*c*) any monies paid or payable out of funds held under that scheme, or
(*d*) any annuity contract by means of which benefits provided under that scheme have been secured.

(2) The persons prescribed are—

(*a*) the person who is, or the persons who are, for the time being by virtue of section 611AA of the Taxes Act the administrator of [a scheme][1];
(*b*) any person who was, or any persons who were, at any time prior to the relevant date, by virtue of section 611AA of the Taxes Act the administrator of [a][1] scheme, other than an excluded person;
(*c*) the trustee or trustees of [a][1] scheme, or any person who was, or any persons who were, at any time prior to the relevant date the trustee or trustees of [a][1] scheme, other than an excluded person;
(*d*) any person who is, or has been at any time prior to the relevant date, an employer in relation to [a][1] scheme, other than an excluded person;
(*e*) any person who is, or has been at any time prior to the relevant date, a scheme sponsor in relation to [a][1] scheme, other than an excluded person;
(*f*) any person who provides, or has at any time prior to the relevant date provided, administrative services to [a][1] scheme, other than an excluded person.

(3) The time prescribed is such time (not being less than 28 days) as may be provided by the notice.

(4) A notice under paragraph (1) above may require books, documents and other records relating to more than one scheme to be made available for inspection [and may specify matters falling within paragraph (1)(*a*) to (*d*) by reference to schemes generally, or those of a limited description, without naming individually each scheme which is the subject of the notice.][1]

(5) Where records are maintained by computer the person required to make them available for inspection shall provide the officer making the inspection with all the facilities necessary for obtaining information from them.

(6) The authorised officer may take copies of, or make extracts from, any books, documents or other records made available for inspection in accordance with paragraph (1) above.

(7) In paragraph (2) above "excluded person" and "the relevant date" have the meanings given by regulation 12(5).

Amendments—[1] Words in para (2) substituted, and words in para (4) inserted, by the Retirement Benefits Schemes (Information Powers) (Amendment) Regulations, SI 2002/3006 reg 12 with effect from 6 April 2003.

Retention of records

15—(1) Each of the persons prescribed by paragraph (2) below shall preserve, for the time prescribed by paragraph (3) below, all books, documents and other records in his possession or under his control relating to—

(*a*) any monies received or receivable by an approved scheme or a relevant statutory scheme, or
(*b*) any investments or other assets held by that scheme, or
(*c*) any monies paid or payable out of funds held under that scheme, or
(*d*) any annuity contract by means of which benefits provided under that scheme have been secured, or
(*e*) any person who is, or has been, a controlling director of a company which is an employer in relation to the scheme.

(2) The persons prescribed are—

(*a*) the person who is, or the persons who are, for the time being by virtue of section 611AA of the Taxes Act the administrator of the scheme;
(*b*) any person who was, or any persons who were, at any time prior to the relevant date, by virtue of section 611AA of the Taxes Act the administrator of that scheme, other than an excluded person;
(*c*) the trustee or trustees of that scheme, or any person who was or any persons who were, at any time prior to the relevant date the trustee or trustees of that scheme, other than an excluded person;
(*d*) any person who is, or has been at any time prior to the relevant date, an employer in relation to that scheme, other than an excluded person;
(*e*) any person who is, or has been at any time prior to the relevant date, a scheme sponsor in relation to that scheme, other than an excluded person;

(*f*) any person who provides, or has at any time prior to the relevant date provided, administrative services to that scheme, other than an excluded person.

(3) The time prescribed—

(*a*) in the case of accounts and actuarial valuation reports relating to the scheme, including books, documents and other records on which such accounts or reports are based, is 6 years from the end of the scheme year in which falls the date on which the accounts were signed or, as the case may be, the report was signed;

(*b*) in the case of books, documents or other records containing information which is required to be furnished pursuant to regulation 5, is 6 years from the end of the scheme year in which the transaction in question occurred;

(*c*) in the case of books, documents or other records containing information which is required to be furnished pursuant to regulation 6, 8, [10, 11, 11A or 11B][1], is 6 years from the end of the scheme year in which the event to which the information relates occurred;

(*d*) in the case of books, documents or other records containing information which is required to be furnished pursuant to regulation 7, is 6 years from the end of the scheme year in which the special contribution to which the information relates was paid to the scheme;

(*e*) in the case of books, documents or other records containing information which is required to be furnished pursuant to regulation 9, is 6 years from the end of the scheme year in which the benefits to which the information relates began to be paid;

(*f*) in the case of books, documents or other records relating to an event specified in paragraph (4) below, is 6 years from the end of the scheme year in which the event occurred.

(4) The events specified are—

(*a*) the provision by the scheme of any benefit to an employee, or to the widow, widower, children, dependants, or personal representatives, of an employee;

(*b*) the refund of contributions to a person who left service as an employee without entitlement to benefits under the scheme;

(*c*) the payment of contributions to the scheme by an employer or employee;

(*d*) the making of payments by the scheme to any employer participating in the scheme;

(*e*) the payment of transfer values or the purchase of annuities under the scheme;

(*f*) the acquisition or disposal of any asset by the scheme;

(*g*) the undertaking of any transaction for the purposes of the scheme;

(*h*) the receipt by the scheme of any income resulting from—

(i) the investment of assets held by the scheme, or

(ii) any trading activity carried on by the scheme.

(5) The duty under paragraph (1) above to preserve books, documents and other records may be discharged by the preservation of the information contained in them.

(6) In paragraph (2) above ''excluded person'' and ''the relevant date'' have the meanings given by regulation 12(5).

Amendments—[1] Words in para (3)(*c*) substituted by the Retirement Benefits Schemes (Information Powers) (Amendment) Regulations, SI 2002/3006 reg 13 with effect from 6 April 2003.

1995/3192
Retirement Age of General Commissioners Order 1995

Made under TMA 1970 s 2 and Judicial Pensions and Retirement Act 1993 ss 26(9), 29(3), (4)

Made	*8 December 1995*
Laid before Parliament	*11 December 1995*
Coming into force	*1 January 1996*

Citation and Commencement

Commentary—*Simon's Direct Tax Service* **A2.504.**

1 This Order may be cited as the Retirement Age of General Commissioners Order 1995 and shall come into force on 1st January 1996.

Interpretation

2 In this Order–

(*a*) ''General Commissioner'' means Commissioner for the general purposes of the income tax appointed under section 2 of the 1970 Act;

(*b*) ''the 1970 Act'' means the Taxes Management Act 1970;

(*c*) ''the 1993 Act'' means the Judicial Pensions and Retirement Act 1993.

Amendment of Judicial Pensions and Retirement Act 1993

3 Schedule 5 to the 1993 Act shall be amended by inserting after the entry relating to the office of Deputy Special Commissioner appointed under section 4A of the 1970 Act the words "Commissioner for the general purposes of the income tax appointed under section 2 of the Taxes Management Act 1970".

Application

4 Article 3 shall have effect only in relation to a person appointed to the office of General Commissioner on or after 1st January 1996 and accordingly–

(*a*) section 26(1) of the 1993 Act shall apply only to a General Commissioner appointed on or after 1st January 1996;

(*b*) the following provisions of the 1993 Act shall not apply to a General Commissioner, whenever appointed—

(i) in section 26(3), the words from "subject to" to "but";
(ii) section 26(11); and
(iii) Schedule 7;

(*c*) section 2(7) of the 1970 Act shall continue to have effect only in relation to a General Commissioner appointed on or before 31st December 1995.

5 Section 26(4) to (6) of the 1993 Act shall not apply to a General Commissioner, whenever appointed.

1995/3220
Sale and Repurchase of Securities (Modification of Enactments) Regulations 1995

Made by the Treasury under TA 1988 s 737E(1), (2), (4)

Made	*6 December 1995*
Laid before the House of Commons	*11 December 1995*
Coming into Force	*2 January 1996*

Commentary—*Simon's Direct Tax Service* **A7.3.**

Citation and commencement

1 These Regulations may be cited as the Sale and Repurchase of Securities (Modification of Enactments) Regulations 1995 and shall come into force on 2nd January 1996.

Interpretation

2—(1) In these Regulations unless the context otherwise requires—

"original owner" shall be construed in accordance with subsection (1) of section 730A;
"the Taxes Act" means the Income and Corporation Taxes Act 1988;
"transferor" shall be construed in accordance with subsection (1) of section 727A, or subsection (1) of 737A (as the case may be);
"the 1992 Act" means the Taxation of Chargeable Gains Act 1992.

(2) In these Regulations unless the context otherwise requires, any reference to a particular section, without more, is a reference to that section of the Taxes Act.

Redemption of securities—modification of enactments

3 In relation to any case falling within subsection (2)(*a*) and (*b*) of section 737E (sale and redemption of securities), sections 727A, 730A and 737A shall have effect as if references (however expressed) to a person being required to buy back securities under an agreement included references to that person being entitled under the agreement to an amount equivalent to the proceeds of redemption of the securities concerned; and references in section 730A to "repurchase" and "repurchaser", and in that section and in section 737A to "repurchase price", shall be construed accordingly.

4 In relation to any case where section 730A has effect as modified by regulation 3, section 263A(1) of the 1992 Act shall have effect as if it provided in addition that—

(*a*) the original owner shall be regarded for the purposes of capital gains tax as having disposed of the securities transferred by him to the interim holder pursuant to the arrangements—

(i) on the occasion of the redemption of the securities and not at the time of that transfer, and
(ii) for an amount equivalent to the proceeds of redemption; and

(*b*) the interim holder shall be regarded for the purposes of capital gains tax as having acquired the securities transferred to him pursuant to the arrangements on that occasion and for that amount.

Substituted securities—modification of enactments

5—(1) In the cases specified in paragraph (2) below, the provisions specified in paragraph (3) below shall have effect with the modifications applicable to that provision which are specified in paragraphs (4) to (7) below.

(2) The cases specified are cases involving any arrangement for the sale and repurchase of securities where the arrangement—

(*a*) falls within subsection (1)(*b*) of section 737E, and
(*b*) involves securities ("substituted securities") being substituted for other securities.

(3) The provisions specified are—

(*a*) sections 727A, 730A, 737A and 737C, and
(*b*) section 263A of the 1992 Act.

(4) Sections 727A and 737A shall each have effect as if any reference to securities included a reference to substituted securities.

(5) Section 730A shall have effect—

(*a*) as if any reference to securities included, subject to sub-paragraph (*b*) below, a reference to substituted securities; and
(*b*) in cases where section 737A applies in relation to the repurchase price of the securities, or would apply if it were in force in relation to the securities, as if—
(i) subsection (9) of that section did not apply, but references to the repurchase price of the securities were references to the repurchase price of the securities that were bought back by the original owner under an agreement falling within subsection (1) of section 730A, increased by the aggregate amount specified in paragraph (6)(*c*) below; and
(ii) the securities transferred by the original owner under the agreement were the securities bought back by him.

(6) Section 737C shall have effect as if—

(*a*) any reference to securities included, subject to sub-paragraph (*b*) below, a reference to substituted securities;
(*b*) references to the repurchase price of the securities were references to the repurchase price of the securities that were bought back by the transferor; and
(*c*) the section provided that that repurchase price should be treated as increased, in accordance with subsection (3)(*b*), (9) or (11)(*c*) (as the case may be) of section 737C, by the aggregate of the gross amounts of manufactured payments treated by section 737A(5) as having been made in respect of securities transferred in pursuance of the original sale and substituted securities.

(7) Section 263A of the 1992 Act shall have effect as if it provided that, in the circumstances specified in paragraph (8) below, any reference to securities included a reference to substituted securities.

(8) The circumstances specified are where, as part of the process of substitution, the securities substituted by the substituted securities are returned to the original owner.

1995/3223
Insurance Companies (Gilt-edged Securities) (Periodic Accounting for Tax on Interest) Regulations 1995

Amendments—These Regulations are revoked by the Insurance Companies (Gilt-edged Securities) (Periodic Accounting for Tax on Interest) Regulations, SI 1999/623 reg 10 with effect for accounting periods beginning before 1 April 1999 and ending after 30 June 1999.

1995/3224
Gilt-edged Securities (Periodic Accounting for Tax on Interest) Regulations 1995

Made by the Treasury under TA 1988, s 51B(1)–(4)

Made	*11 December 1995*
Laid before the House of Commons	*11 December 1995*
Coming into Force	*2 January 1996*

Commentary—*Simon's Direct Tax Service* **A7.1115–1120.**

Citation and commencement

1—These Regulations may be cited as the Gilt-edged Securities (Periodic Accounting for Tax on Interest) Regulations 1995 and shall come into force on 2nd January 1996.

Interpretation

2—(1) In these Regulations unless the context otherwise requires—

"amount of manufactured gilt interest paid" means an amount specified in regulation 6(5) or, as the case may be, 7(5);

"amount of manufactured gilt interest received" means an amount specified in regulation 6(3) or, as the case may be, 7(3);

"amount of real gilt interest received" means an amount specified in regulation 6(4) or, as the case may be, 7(4);

"the Board" means the Commissioners of Inland Revenue;

"FOTRA securities" means securities issued with the condition mentioned in section 22(1) of the Finance (No 2) Act 1931 (securities free of tax for residents abroad);

"manufactured payment" means any payment which for the purposes of Schedule 23A is a payment of manufactured interest, and to which paragraph [3A(2)(*a*)][1] of that Schedule applies[, other than a payment made on or after 1st April 1999][2];

"payment on account" shall be construed in accordance with regulation 13(2) or, as the case may be, 14(2);

"the relevant amount of tax" shall be construed in accordance with paragraph (6)(*b*), (8)(*c*) or (10) of regulation 13 or paragraph (6)(*b*), (8)(*c*) or (14) of regulation 14, as the case may be;

"relevant gilt-edged securities" has the meaning given by section 51B(5);

"relevant payment" means any payment which is a relevant payment for the purposes of Schedule 16;

"relevant year of assessment" has the meaning given by section 51B(6);

"return period" shall be construed in accordance with regulation 5(1).

(2) The Table below indexes other general definitions in these Regulations—

Term defined	*Regulation*
aggregate amount of excess gilt interest received	8(3)
amount of excess gilt interest paid	8(2)
amount of excess gilt interest received	8(1)
non-resident company	3(5)
relevant company	3(1)
resident company	3(3).

(3) In these Regulations unless the context otherwise requires, any reference to a particular provision, without more, is a reference to that provision of the Income and Corporation Taxes Act 1988.

Amendments—[1] Figures in definition of "manufactured payment" in para (1) substituted, for "3A", by the Stock Lending and Manufactured Payments (Revocations and Amendments) Regulations, SI 1997/987, regs 1, 7, with effect from 1 July 1997.

[2] Words in para 1 in definition of "manufactured payment" inserted by the Gilt-edged Securities (Periodic Accounting for Tax on Interest) Regulations, SI 1999/620 reg 2 with effect from 30 March 1999.

Relevant companies

3—(1) This regulation specifies the persons to whom—

(*a*) payments of interest on relevant gilt-edged securities are made without deduction of tax, and

(*b*) these Regulations apply;

and any such person is referred to in these Regulations as a "relevant company".

(2) A relevant company shall be either a resident company or a non-resident company.

(3) For the purposes of these Regulations and except as provided in paragraph (4) below, a resident company is a company within the meaning given by section 832 which is resident within the United Kingdom.

(4) Paragraph (3) above shall not apply to any of the following persons, that is to say—

(*a*) any body of persons established for charitable purposes only;

(*b*) a health service body within the meaning given by section 519A(2);

(*c*) a friendly society carrying on a business all of whose profits are exempt from income tax and corporation tax under section 460(1), 461(1) or 461B(1).

(5) For the purposes of these Regulations a non-resident company is a company within the meaning given by section 832 which is not resident in the United Kingdom, but which is carrying on a trade in the United Kingdom through a branch or agency and has a UK representative for the purposes of section 126 of, and Schedule 23 to, the Finance Act 1995.

(6) In paragraph (5) above "UK representative" shall be construed in accordance with section 126 of the Finance Act 1995.

Requirement to make returns

4—(1) A relevant company shall for each of its accounting periods make, in accordance with these Regulations, returns to an officer of the Board of—

(*a*) amounts of any payments of interest on relevant gilt-edged securities made to it without deduction of tax, and (*b*) amounts of tax for which it is to be accountable under these Regulations in respect of those payments.

(2) A return required for the purposes of these Regulations may be combined with a return required for the purposes of Schedule 16.

Cross references—Insurance Companies (Gilt-edged Securities) (Periodic Accounting for Tax on Interest) Regulations, SI 1999/623 reg 3 (return need not include tax on excess gilt interest received which is referable to the insurance company's pension business where that tax is included in a claim for a notional repayment pursuant to TA 1988 Sch 19AB para 1A(1)).
Friendly Societies (Gilt-edged Securities) (Periodic Accounting for Tax on Interest) Regulations, SI 1999/624 reg 3 (return need not include tax on excess gilt interest received which is referable to the friendly society's business where that tax is included in a claim for a notional repayment pursuant to TA 1988 Sch 19AB para 1A(1)).

Return periods and due date for returns

5—(1) A relevant company shall make a return—

(*a*) in the case of a company other than a building society, for the periods specified in paragraph (2) below, and

(*b*) in the case of a building society, for the periods specified in paragraph (3) below, and any such period is referred to in these Regulations as a "return period".

(2) The periods specified in this paragraph are—

(*a*) each complete quarter falling within the accounting period, that is to say, each of the periods of three months ending at the end of March, June, September and December which falls within that period;

(*b*) each part of the accounting period which is not a complete quarter and ends on the first (or only), or begins immediately after the last (or only), of those dates which falls within the accounting period;

(*c*) if none of those dates falls within the accounting period, the whole accounting period.

(3) The periods specified in this paragraph are—

(*a*) each complete quarter falling within the accounting period, that is to say, each of the periods of three months ending at the end of May, August, November and February which falls within that period;

(*b*) each part of the accounting period which is not a complete quarter and ends on the first (or only), or begins immediately after the last (or only), of those dates which falls within the accounting period;

(*c*) if none of those dates falls within the accounting period, the whole accounting period.

(4) A return for any return period specified in this regulation shall be made within 14 days from the end of that period.

Amounts to be shown on returns made by resident companies

6—(1) This regulation applies in the case of a return made by a resident company for a return period.

(2) The return shall show—

(*a*) the aggregate of the amounts specified in paragraphs (3) and (4) below, and
(*b*) the amount specified in paragraph (5) below.

(3) The amount specified in this paragraph is the amount of any manufactured payment received by the company in the return period which is income of the company for the purposes of the Corporation Tax Acts.

(4) The amount specified in this paragraph is the amount of any other payment of interest on relevant gilt-edged securities made without deduction of tax to the company in the return period which is income of the company for the purposes of the Corporation Tax Acts.

(5) The amount specified in this paragraph is the amount of any manufactured payment made by or on behalf of the company in the return period in respect of which the company can claim relief, whether by way of deduction in computing profits or gains or by way of deduction or set off against income or total profits.

Amounts to be shown on returns made by non-resident companies

7—(1) This regulation applies in the case of a return made by a non-resident company for a return period.

(2) The return shall show—

(*a*) the aggregate of the amounts specified in paragraphs (3) and (4) below, and
(*b*) the amount specified in paragraph (5) below.

(3) The amount specified in this paragraph is the amount of any manufactured payment, other than a manufactured payment in respect of FOTRA securities, received by the company in the return period which is income of that company within the charge to corporation tax by virtue of section 11.

(4) The amount specified in this paragraph is the amount of any other payments of interest on relevant gilt-edged securities, other than FOTRA securities, made without deduction of tax to the

company in the return period which is income of that company within the charge to corporation tax by virtue of section 11.

(5) The amount specified in this paragraph is the amount of any manufactured payment, other than a manufactured payment in respect of FOTRA securities, made by or on behalf of the company in the return period in respect of which the company can claim relief for the purposes of corporation tax, whether by way of deduction in computing profits or gains or by way of deduction or set off against income or total profits.

Amounts of excess gilt interest and aggregate amount of excess gilt interest received

8—(1) Where, for any return period, the aggregate of the amount of manufactured gilt interest received and the amount of real gilt interest received exceeds the amount of manufactured gilt interest paid, the amount of the excess is referred to in these Regulations as an "amount of excess gilt interest received".

(2) Where, for any return period, the amount of manufactured gilt interest paid exceeds the aggregate of the amount of manufactured gilt interest received and the amount of real gilt interest received, the amount of the excess is referred to in these Regulations as an "amount of excess gilt interest paid".

(3) Subject to paragraph (4) below, where, at the end of a return period falling within an accounting period, the aggregate of the amounts of manufactured gilt interest received and the amounts of real gilt interest received for return periods which fall within the accounting period exceeds the amounts of manufactured gilt interest paid for return periods which fall within the accounting period, the amount of the excess is referred to in these Regulations as an "aggregate amount of excess gilt interest received".

(4) Paragraph (3) above does not include any amount of interest in respect of which tax has previously been set off under regulation 10.

Tax for which relevant company accountable

9—(1) Subject to [paragraphs (2) and (2A)][1] below and to regulation 12(2), the amount of income tax for which a relevant company is to be accountable under these Regulations in respect of payments of interest on relevant gilt-edged securities made to it without deduction of tax, shall, for each return period, be income tax at the basic rate for the relevant year of assessment on the amount of excess gilt interest received.

(2) [Subject to paragraph (2A) below, where the lower rate][1] changes during a return period, the amount of income tax for which a relevant company is to be accountable pursuant to paragraph (1) above for that return period shall be ascertained after considering the period before 6th April separately from the period after 5th April; and "income tax on the aggregate amount of excess gilt interest received" in paragraphs (2) and (3) of regulation 10 and "income tax nominally attributable to the amount of excess gilt interest paid" in regulations 11(2) and 12(2) shall be construed accordingly.

[(2A) In the case of a return period which begins before but includes 6th April 1996, the amount of income tax for which a relevant company is to be accountable pursuant to paragraph (1) above for that return period shall be ascertained after considering the period before 6th April 1996 separately from the period after 5th April 1996; and "income tax on the aggregate amount of excess gilt interest received" in paragraphs (2) and (3) of regulation 10 and "income tax nominally attributable to the amount of excess gilt interest paid" in regulations 11(2) and 12(2) shall be construed accordingly.][1]

(3) Amounts in respect of which there is an obligation on a relevant company to account for income tax under these Regulations shall be treated for the purposes of the Tax Acts as payments on which the company has borne income tax by deduction.

Amendments—[1] Words in sub-ss (1), (2), and whole of sub-s (2A) substituted, by the Gilt-edged Securities (Periodic Accounting for Tax on Interest) (Amendment No 2) Regulations, SI 1996/1181 regs 3–5 with effect in relation to all payments of interest on relevant gilt-edged securities made without deduction of tax after 5 April 1996.

Set off of tax against tax payable in accordance with Schedule 16

10—(1) This regulation applies in any case where at the end of any return period there is an aggregate amount of excess gilt interest received.

(2) Subject to any claim under paragraph 5 of Schedule 16, the company may claim to have the income tax on the aggregate amount of excess gilt interest received set against any income tax which it is liable to pay under Schedule 16 in respect of relevant payments made by it in that return period.

(3) Subject to paragraph (2) above, the company may claim to have the income tax on the aggregate amount of excess gilt interest received set against any income tax which it was liable to pay under Schedule 16 in respect of relevant payments made by it in previous return periods within the accounting period.

(4) Any claim pursuant to paragraph (2) or (3) above shall be included in the return made under these Regulations for the return period in question, and (where necessary) income tax paid by the company under Schedule 16 and for that accounting period and before the claim is allowed shall be repaid accordingly.

Set off against tax for previous return periods

11—(1) Subject to regulation 10, this regulation applies in any case where for any return period there is an amount of excess gilt interest paid.

(2) The company may claim to have the income tax nominally attributable to the amount of excess gilt interest paid set against any income tax which the company was liable to pay under these Regulations for a previous return period falling within the same accounting period.

(3) Any claim pursuant to paragraph (2) above shall be included in a return made under these Regulations for the return period in question, and (where necessary) income tax paid by the company under these Regulations and for that accounting period and before the claim is allowed shall be repaid accordingly.

Carry forward of tax on excess gilt interest paid

12—(1) Subject to regulation 11, this regulation applies in any case where, for any return period other than the final return period within an accounting period, there is an amount of excess gilt interest paid.

(2) Any income tax for which the company would otherwise be accountable under regulation 9 for subsequent return periods within the accounting period shall be reduced by the income tax nominally attributable to the amount of excess gilt interest paid.

Payments on account and special return—relevant companies other than building societies

13—(1) This regulation applies in the case of a relevant company other than a building society.

(2) Each year, the company shall, on or before 14th March, make a special return to an officer of the Board, in such form as the Board may prescribe or approve, in respect of the period specified in paragraph (4) below ("the special return period") showing, subject to paragraphs (5) to (8) below, the amount of income tax at the [lower rate][1] for the relevant year of assessment on the amount of excess gilt interest received for which the company will be accountable under these Regulations for the special return period, computed to the best of the company's judgment (the "payment on account").

(3) The payment on account shall be due at the time by which the special return is to be made, and sub-paragraphs (*a*) and (*b*) of regulation 16(1) shall apply to the sum so due.

(4) The special return period is—

(*a*) in a case where an accounting period of the company ("the earlier accounting period") ends during March (otherwise than at the end of the month), a period consisting of—

(i) the final return period for the earlier accounting period ("the earlier period"), and

(ii) a period beginning immediately after the end of the earlier accounting period and ending at the end of March ("the later period"); and

(*b*) in any other case, the return period ending at the end of March.

(5) The payment on account shall be computed without reference—

(*a*) to any claim which the company may be entitled to make pursuant to paragraph 5 of Schedule 16 or paragraph 1A(1) of Schedule 19AB (as inserted by regulation 6 of the Insurance Companies (Gilt-edged Securities) (Periodic Accounting for Tax on Interest) Regulations 1995 ("paragraph 1A(1)"), or

(*b*) to any set off which the company may be entitled to claim pursuant to regulation 10 or 11.

(6) In relation to a special return period in a case where paragraph (4)(*a*) above applies, the payment on account shall be separately computed in relation to the earlier period and the later period; and

(*a*) in this regulation the amount of tax for which the company is accountable under these Regulations for the earlier period is referred to as "the earlier relevant amount of tax" and the amount of tax for which the company is accountable under these Regulations for the later period is referred to as "the later relevant amount of tax", and

(*b*) for the purposes of these Regulations "the relevant amount of tax" means, subject to paragraphs (8) and (11) below, the aggregate of the earlier relevant amount of tax and the later relevant amount of tax.

(7) Where, by 14th April, no part of the payment on account has been paid, the company shall be treated as having computed, to the best of its judgment, that the amount of income tax at the [lower rate][1] for the relevant year of assessment on the amount of excess gilt interest received for which the company will be accountable under these Regulations for the special return period is zero.

(8) Where, in relation to a special return period in a case where paragraph (4)(*a*) above applies, no part of the payment on account has been paid by the due date in relation to the earlier period but a payment on account has been paid by the due date in relation to the later period—

(*a*) the company shall be treated, in relation to the earlier period as having computed, to the best of its judgment, that the amount of income tax for the relevant year of assessment on the amount of excess gilt interest received for which the company will be accountable under these Regulations for the earlier period is zero, (*b*) to the extent that the payment on account has been paid before the due date for the later period, it shall, accordingly, be set against the later relevant amount of tax, and

(*c*) for the purposes of these Regulations "the relevant amount of tax" means the later relevant amount of tax.

(9) Where, in relation to a special return period in a case where paragraph (4)(*a*) above applies, the payment on account, to the extent that it has been paid before the due date for the earlier period, shall be set against the earlier relevant amount of tax and the later relevant amount of tax.

(10) Where, in relation to a special return period in a case where paragraph (4)(*b*) above applies, the payment on account, to the extent that it has been paid before 14th April, shall be set against the amount of tax for which the company is accountable under these Regulations for the return period ending on 31st March; and for the purposes of these Regulations "the relevant amount of tax" means, subject to paragraph (11) below, that amount of tax.

(11) The relevant amount of tax and (where necessary) the earlier relevant amount of tax and the later relevant amount of tax shall be computed without reference to any claim which the company may be entitled to make under paragraph 1A(1).

(12) If the amount of the payment on account paid exceeds the relevant amount of tax, the amount of the excess shall be repayable.

Amendments—[1] Words in sub-ss (2), (7) substituted by the Gilt-edged Securities (Periodic Accounting for Tax on Interest) (Amendment No 2) Regulations, SI 1996/1181 reg 6, with effect in relation to all payments of interest on relevant gilt-edged securities made without deduction of tax after 5 April 1996.

Payments on account and special returns—relevant companies which are building societies

14—(1) This regulation applies in the case of a relevant company which is a building society.

(2) Each year, the company shall, on or before 14th March, make a special return to an officer of the Board, in such form as the Board may prescribe or approve, in respect of a period consisting of the month of March ("the special return period") showing, subject to paragraphs (4) to (7) below, the amount of income tax at the [lower rate][1] for the relevant year of assessment on the amount of excess gilt interest received for which the company will be accountable under these Regulations for the special return period, computed to the best of the company's judgment (the "payment on account").

(3) The payment on account shall be due at the time by which the special return is to be made, and sub-paragraphs (*a*) and (*b*) of regulation 16(*1*) shall apply to the sum so due.

(4) The payment on account shall be computed without reference—

(*a*) to any claim which the company may be entitled to make pursuant to paragraph 5 of Schedule 16, or

(*b*) to any set off which the company may be entitled to claim pursuant to regulation 10 or 11.

(5) In a case where an accounting period of the company ("the earlier accounting period") ends during March (otherwise than at the end of the month) the payment on account shall be separately computed in relation to—

(*a*) the final return period for the earlier accounting period ("the earlier period"), and

(*b*) a period beginning immediately after the end of the earlier accounting period and ending at the end of March ("the later period").

(6) Where paragraph (5) above applies—

(*a*) the amount of tax for which the company is accountable under these Regulations for the earlier period is referred to in this regulation as "the earlier relevant amount of tax" and the amount of tax for which the company is accountable under these Regulations for the later period is referred to in this regulation as "the later relevant amount of tax", and

(*b*) for the purposes of these Regulations "the relevant amount of tax" means, subject to paragraph (8) below, the aggregate of the earlier relevant amount of tax and the later relevant amount of tax.

(7) Where, by 14th April, no part of the payment on account has been paid, the company shall be treated as having computed, to the best of its judgment, that the amount of income tax at the [lower rate][1] for the relevant year of assessment on the amount of excess gilt interest received for which the company will be accountable under these Regulations for the special return period is zero.

(8) Where, in relation to a special return period in a case where paragraph (5) above applies, no part of the payment on account has been paid by the due date in relation to the earlier period but a payment on account has been paid by the due date in relation to the later period—

(*a*) the company shall be treated, in relation to the earlier period as having computed, to the best of its judgment, that the amount of income tax for the relevant year of assessment on the amount of excess gilt interest received for which the company will be accountable under these Regulations for the earlier period is zero,

(*b*) to the extent that the payment on account has been paid before the due date for the later period, it shall, accordingly, be set against the later relevant amount of tax, and

(*c*) for the purposes of these Regulations "the relevant amount of tax" means the later relevant amount of tax.

(9) Subject to paragraph (10) below, the company shall, by 14th April, make a further special return to an officer of the Board (a ''special reconciliation return'') in respect of the period specified in paragraph (11) below (''the special reconciliation return period'').

(10) Paragraph (9) above does not apply where—

(*a*) an accounting period of the company ends at the end of March, or

(*b*) the company is not accountable for any income tax under these Regulations for the special reconciliation return period and the company has not made a payment on account—

(i) in a case where paragraph (5) above applies, in respect of the later period, or

(ii) in a case where paragraph (5) above does not apply, in respect of the special return period.

(11) The special reconciliation return period is—

(*a*) in a case where an accounting period of the company ends during March (otherwise than at the end of the month), a period beginning immediately after the end of that accounting period and ending at the end of March, and

(*b*) in any other case, a period consisting of the month of March.

(12) The special reconciliation return shall show—

(*a*) the amounts specified in regulation 6 in respect of the special reconciliation return period, and

(*b*) the amount of income tax at the [lower rate][1] for the relevant year of assessment on the amount of excess gilt interest received for which the company is accountable under these Regulations for the special reconciliation return period in respect of payments of interest on relevant gilt-edged securities made to it without deduction of tax.

(13) Where, in relation to a special return period in a case where paragraph (5) above applies, the payment on account, to the extent that it has been paid before the due date for the earlier period, shall be set against the earlier relevant amount of tax and the later relevant amount of tax.

(14) Where, in relation to a special return period in a case where paragraph (5) above does not apply, the payment on account, to the extent that it has been paid before 14th April, shall be set against the amount of tax for which the company is accountable under these Regulations for the special reconciliation return period; and for the purposes of these Regulations ''the relevant amount of tax'' means that amount of tax.

(15) If the amount of the payment on account paid exceeds the relevant amount of tax, the amount of the excess shall be repayable.

(16) An amount of income tax for which the company is accountable under these Regulations in respect of the special reconciliation return period and which has been paid by the due date for the return for the next return period shall be set against the amount of income tax for which the company is accountable under these Regulations for the next return period.

(17) Where the amount of income tax paid in respect of the special reconciliation return period exceeds the amount of income tax for which the company is accountable under these Regulations for the next return period, the excess shall be repayable.

Amendments—[1] Words in sub-ss (2), (7), (12)(*b*) substituted by the Gilt-edged Securities (Periodic Accounting for Tax on Interest) (Amendment No 2) Regulations, SI 1996/1181 reg 6, with effect in relation to all payments of interest on relevant gilt-edged securities made without deduction of tax after 5 April 1996.

Consequences of set off

15—(1) Income tax set against other tax under regulation 10 shall be treated as repaid.

(2) Income tax set against other tax under regulation 13 or 14 shall be treated as an amount paid in respect of income tax for which the company is accountable under regulation 9.

(3) The same tax shall not be taken into account both under these Regulations and under section 7(2) or 11(3).

Payment of tax

16—(1) Income tax in respect of any payment required to be included in a return under these Regulations shall be due at the time by which the return is to be made, and income tax so due—

(*a*) shall be payable by the relevant company without the making of any assessment; and

(*b*) may be assessed on the company (whether or not it has been paid when the assessment is made) if it, or any part of it, is not paid on or before the due date.

(2) If it appears to the inspector that there is a payment of relevant gilt interest to a relevant company which ought to have been but has not been included in a return, or if the inspector is dissatisfied with any return, he may make an assessment on the company to the best of his judgment; and any income tax due under an assessment made by virtue of this paragraph shall be treated for the purposes of interest on unpaid tax as having been payable at the time when it would have been payable if a correct return had been made.

[(3) For the purposes of this regulation, where—

(*a*) any payment to an officer of the Board is made by cheque, and

(*b*) the cheque is paid on its first presentation to the banker on whom it is drawn, the payment shall be treated as made on the day on which the cheque was received by the officer of the Board.][1]

Amendments—[1] Para (3) added by the Gilt-edged Securities (Periodic Accounting for Tax on Interest) (Amendment) Regulations, SI 1996/1015 reg 2(1), (2)(*a*), (3), with effect as respects cheques received on or after 22 April 1996.

Collection proceedings following claims

17—(1) Where a claim has been made under regulation 10 or 11, no proceedings for collecting tax which would fall to be discharged if the claim were allowed shall be instituted pending the final determination of the claim, but this paragraph shall not affect the date when the tax is due.

(2) When the claim is finally determined any tax underpaid in consequence of paragraph (1) above shall be paid.

(3) Where proceedings are instituted for collecting tax assessed, or interest on tax assessed, under any provision of regulation 16, effect shall not be given to any claim made after the institution of the proceedings so as to affect or delay the collection or recovery of the tax charged by the assessment or of interest thereon, until the claim has been finally determined.

(4) When the claim is finally determined any tax overpaid in consequence of paragraph (3) above shall be repaid.

(5) References in this regulation to proceedings for the collection of tax include references to proceedings by way of distraint or poinding for tax.

Prospective amendments—In sub-s (5) words ''or poinding'' repealed by the Abolition of Poindings and Warrant Sales Act 2001 s 3(1), Schedule, Pt 3 with effect from 31 December 2002 or such earlier date as the Scottish Ministers may by statutory instrument appoint.

Assessments and due date of tax

18—(1) All the provisions of the Income Tax Acts as to the time within which an assessment may be made, so far as they refer or relate to the year of assessment for which an assessment is made, or the year to which an assessment relates, shall apply in relation to any assessment under these Regulations notwithstanding that, under these Regulations, the assessment may be said to relate to a quarter or other period which is not a year of assessment, and the provisions of section 36 of the Taxes Management Act 1970 as to the circumstances in which an assessment may be made out of time shall apply accordingly on the footing that any such assessment relates to the year of assessment in which the quarter or other period ends.

(2) Income tax assessed on a company under these Regulations shall be due within 14 days after the issue of the notice of assessment (unless due earlier under regulation 16(1)).

(3) Paragraph (2) above has effect subject to any appeal against the assessment, but no such appeal shall affect the date when tax is due under regulation 16(1).

(4) On the determination of an appeal against an assessment under these Regulations any tax overpaid shall be repaid.

(5) Any tax assessable under any one or more of the provisions of these Regulations may be included in one assessment if the tax so included is all due on the same date.

Interest payable on amounts of tax unpaid

19—(1) Any amounts of tax which have become due under these Regulations shall carry interest at the specified rate from the date when the amounts become due until payment.

(2) Without prejudice to the generality of paragraph (1) above, where in any year—

(*a*) the payment on account has not been paid, or has not been paid in full, by 14th March, or

(*b*) the relevant amount of tax exceeds the amount of the payment on account,

the amount unpaid or, as the case may be, the amount of the excess, shall carry interest at the specified rate for the specified period.

(3) In this regulation ''the specified rate'' means the rate applicable under section 178 of the Finance Act 1989 for the purposes of section 87 of the Taxes Management Act 1970.

(4) In paragraph (2) above ''the specified period'' means the period from 14th March until either payment or

(*a*) in a case where paragraph (4)(*a*) of regulation 13 applies and in relation to the earlier period referred to in that paragraph, the due date in relation to the earlier period,

(*b*) in a case where paragraph (5) of regulation 14 applies and in relation to the earlier period referred to in that paragraph, the due date in relation to the earlier period, or

(*c*) in any other case, 14 April,

whichever first occurs.

(5) Any sum to which this regulation applies shall carry interest from the due date even if that date is a non-business day within the meaning of section 92 of the Bills of Exchange Act 1882.

[(6) For the purposes of this regulation, where—

(*a*) any payment to an officer of the Board is made by cheque, and (*b*) the cheque is paid on its first presentation to the banker on whom it is drawn,

the payment shall be treated as made on the day on which the cheque was received by the officer of the Board.][1]

Amendments—[1] Para (6) added by the Gilt-edged Securities (Periodic Accounting for Tax on Interest) (Amendment) Regulations, SI 1996/1015 reg 2(1), (2)(*b*), (3), with effect as respects cheques received on or after 22 April 1996.

Interest payable where payment on account excessive

20—(1) This regulation applies in any case where the payment on account paid exceeds the relevant amount of tax.

(2) Section 826 (interest on corporation tax overpaid) shall not apply to a repayment of the amount of the excess, but that amount shall carry interest in accordance with the provisions of this regulation at the specified rate for the period from the opening date until the date on which it is repaid.

(3) In this regulation "the specified rate" means the rate determined in accordance with paragraphs (4) to (7) below.

(4) Subject to paragraph (5) below, the specified rate shall be 4.5 per cent per annum.

(5) Where, on a reference date occurring after 2nd January 1996, the reference rate found on that date differs from the established rate, the specified rate shall, on and after the next operative date, be the percentage per annum found by applying the formula specified in paragraph (6) below; and, if the result is not a multiple of one quarter, rounding the result down to the nearest amount which is such a multiple.

(6) The formula specified is—

$$(RR-1)\ \frac{(100-BR)}{100}$$

where RR is the reference rate referred to in paragraph (5) above and BR is the percentage at which income tax at the basic rate is charged for the year of assessment in which the reference date referred to in that paragraph falls.

(7) In this regulation "established rate", "operative date", "reference date" and "reference rate" shall be construed in accordance with the Taxes (Interest Rate) Regulations 1989.

(8) In this regulation "the opening date" means 14th March or the date on which the payment on account is paid, whichever is the later.

(9) Any sum to which this regulation applies shall carry interest from the opening date even if that date is a non-business day within the meaning of section 92 of the Bills of Exchange Act 1882.

[(10) For the purposes of this regulation, where—

(*a*) any payment to an officer of the Board is made by cheque, and

(*b*) the cheque is paid on its first presentation to the banker on whom it is drawn,

the payment shall be treated as made on the day on which the cheque was received by the officer of the Board.][1]

Amendments—[1] Para (10) added by the Gilt-edged Securities (Periodic Accounting for Tax on Interest) (Amendment) Regulations, SI 1996/1015 reg 2(1), (2)(*c*), (3), with effect as respects cheques received on or after 22 April 1996.

Saving

21 Nothing in these Regulations shall be taken to prejudice any powers conferred by the Income Tax Acts for the recovery of income tax by means of an assessment or otherwise.

1995/3225

Lloyd's Underwriters (Gilt-edged Securities) (Periodic Accounting for Tax on Interest) Regulations 1995

Made by the Treasury under TA 1988 s 51B(1)–(4)

Made	*11 December 1995*
Laid before the House of Commons	*11 December 1995*
Coming into Force	*2 January 1996*

Commentary—*Simon's Direct Tax Service* **A7.1130, 1131.**

Citation and commencement

1 These Regulations may be cited as the Lloyd's Underwriters (Gilt-edged Securities) (Periodic Accounting for Tax on Interest) Regulations 1995 and shall come into force on 2nd January 1996.

Interpretation

2—(1) In these Regulations unless the context otherwise requires—

"the Board" means the Commissioners of Inland Revenue:

"the Management Act" means the Taxes Management Act 1970;

"managing agent"—

(*a*) in relation to a member who is an individual has the meaning given by section 184(1) of the Finance Act 1993 as extended by regulation 3 of the Lloyd's Underwriters (Tax) Regulations 1995, and

(*b*) in relation to a corporate member has the meaning given by section 230(1) of the Finance Act 1994 as extended by that regulation;

"manufactured payment" means any payment which for the purposes of Schedule 23A to the Taxes Act is a payment of manufactured interest, and to which paragraph [3A(2)(*a*)][1] of that Schedule applies;

"members" means a member of Lloyd's who is an individual or, as the case may be, a corporate member and who is or has been an underwriting member;

["premiums trust fund" means any trust fund to which an underwriter is required, by rules made by the Financial Services Authority under Part X of the Financial Services and Markets Act 2000, to carry premiums received by him or on his behalf in respect of the carrying on of any insurance market activity, within the meaning of section 316(3) of that Act;][2]

"relevant gilt-edged securities" and "relevant year of assessment" have the meanings given respectively by subsections (5) and (6) of section 51B;

"section 51B" means section 51B of the Taxes Act;

"Schedule 19" means Schedule 19 to the Finance Act 1993;

"syndicate" means a syndicate of underwriting members of Lloyd's formed for an underwriting year;

"the Taxes Act" means the Income and Corporation Taxes Act 1988;

"trustees" means the trustees of premiums trust funds of members of the syndicate concerned;

"underwriting year" means the calendar year.

(2) The Table below indexes other general definitions in these Regulations—

Term defined	*Regulation*
amount of excess gilt interest paid	4(6)
amount of excess gilt interest received	4(5)
payment on account	7(2)
relevant quarter	7(1)
total amount of tax	7(3)

Amendments—[1] Figures in definition of "manufactured payment" in para (1) substituted, for "3A", by the Stock Lending and Manufactured Payments (Revocation and Amendments) Regulations, SI 1997/987, regs 1, 7, with effect from 1 July 1997.

[2] Definition of "premiums trust fund" in para (1) substituted by the Financial Services and Markets Act 2000 (Consequential Amendments and Repeals) Order, SI 2001/3649 art 519 with effect from 1 December 2001.

Requirement to make returns

3—(1) A managing agent for a syndicate shall for each underwriting year make, in accordance with these Regulations, returns to an officer of the Board of—

(*a*) amounts of any payments of interest on relevant gilt-edged securities which are made without deduction of tax to the trustees of premiums trust funds of members of that syndicate, and

(*b*) amounts of tax for which he is to be accountable under these Regulations in respect of those payments.

(2) Subject to regulation 7(2), a return shall be made for each complete quarter falling within the underwriting year, that is to say, each of the periods of three months ending with 31st March, 30th June, 30th September and 31st December which falls within that underwriting year.

(3) A return for any quarter shall be made within 14 days from the end of that quarter.

Contents of returns

4—(1) The return made by a managing agent for any quarter shall show—

(*a*) the aggregate of the amounts specified in paragraphs (2) and (3) below, and

(*b*) the amount specified in paragraph (4) below.

(2) The amount specified in this paragraph is the aggregate amount of manufactured payments received by the trustees in the quarter which fall to be taken into account in computing the syndicate's profit or loss for the purposes of Schedule 19.

(3) The amount specified in this paragraph is the aggregate amount of other payments of interest on relevant gilt-edged securities made without deduction of tax to the trustees in the quarter which fall to be taken into account in computing the syndicate's profit or loss for the purposes of Schedule 19.

(4) The amount specified in this paragraph is the aggregate amount of manufactured payments made by or on behalf of the trustees in the quarter which fall to be taken into account in computing the syndicate's profit or loss for the purposes of Schedule 19.

(5) Where, for any quarter, the aggregate of the amounts specified in paragraphs (2) and (3) above exceeds the amount specified in paragraph (4) above, the amount of the excess is referred to in these Regulations as an "amount of excess gilt interest received".

(6) Where, for any quarter, the amount specified in paragraph (4) above exceeds the aggregate of the amounts specified in paragraphs (2) and (3) above, the amount of the excess is referred to in these Regulations as an ''amount of excess gilt interest paid''.

Tax for which managing agent accountable

5—(1) Subject to [paragraphs (2) and (2A)][1] below and regulation 6(3), the amount of tax for which a managing agent is to be accountable under these Regulations shall, for each quarter, be the amount of income tax at the [lower rate][1] for the relevant year of assessment on the amount of excess gilt interest received.

(2) [Subject to paragraph (2A) below, where the lower rate][1] changes during the quarter ending on 30th June, the amount of income tax for which the managing agent is to be accountable pursuant to paragraph (1) above for that quarter shall be ascertained after considering the period before 6th April separately from the period after 5th April: and ''income tax nominally attributable to the amount of excess gilt interest paid'' in regulation 6(1) and (3) shall be construed accordingly.

[(2A) In the case of the quarter ending on 30th June 1996, the amount of income tax for which the managing agent is to be accountable pursuant to paragraph (1) above for that quarter shall be ascertained after considering the period before 6th April 1996 separately from the period after 5th April 1996; and ''income tax nominally attributable to the amount of excess gilt interest paid'' in regulation 6(1) and (3) shall be construed accordingly.][1]

(3) Amounts in respect of which there is an obligation on a managing agent to account for tax under paragraph (1) above shall be treated for the purposes of paragraph 13(1)(*a*) of Schedule 19 as payments on which income tax has been borne by deduction.

Amendments—[1] Words in paras (1), (2) substituted and para (2A) inserted by the Lloyd's Underwriters (Gilt-edged Securities) (Periodic Accounting for Tax on Interest) (Amendment No 2) Regulations, SI 1996/1182 regs 2–5, with effect in relation to all payments of interest on relevant gilt-edged securities made without deduction of tax on or after 6 April 1996.

Amount of excess gilt interest paid—set off of tax nominally attributable to that amount against tax for other quarters

6—(1) Where for any quarter in an underwriting year there is an amount of excess gilt interest paid, the managing agent may claim to have the income tax nominally attributable to the amount of excess gilt interest paid set against income tax for which he is liable to account under regulation 5 for a previous quarter falling within the same underwriting year.

(2) Any claim under paragraph (1) above shall be included in a return made for the quarter, and (where necessary) income tax paid by the managing agent under these Regulations for that underwriting year and before the claim is allowed shall be repaid accordingly.

(3) Subject to paragraph (1) above, where for any quarter other than the final quarter in an underwriting year there is an amount of excess gilt interest paid, any income tax for which the managing agent would otherwise be accountable under regulation 5 for subsequent quarters falling within the same underwriting year shall be reduced by the income tax nominally attributable to the amount of excess gilt interest paid.

Payments on account and special returns

7—(1) This regulation applies in the case of the quarter ending on 31st March in each underwriting year (''the relevant quarter'').

(2) A managing agent shall, on or before 14th March, make a special return to the Board, in such form as the Board may prescribe or approve, showing the amount of income tax at the [lower rate][1] (''the payment on account'') for which the managing agent will become accountable under these Regulations in respect of that quarter, computed to the best of his judgment.

(3) To the extent that the payment on account is paid before the date on which the return for the relevant quarter is due in accordance with regulation 3(3)—

(*a*) it shall be set off against the amount of tax for which the managing agent is liable to account under regulation 5 in respect of that quarter (''the total amount of tax''), and

(*b*) the amount of tax against which the payment is set off shall accordingly be treated, for the purposes of these Regulations, as having been paid.

(4) If the amount of the payment on account so paid exceeds the total amount of tax, the amount of the excess shall be repayable.

(5) Where, by 14th April, no part of the payment on account has been paid by the managing agent, he shall be treated as having computed to the best of his judgment, that the amount referred to in paragraph (2) above is zero.

Amendments—[1] Words substituted by the Lloyd's Underwriters (Gilt-edged Securities) (Periodic Accounting for Tax on Interest) (Amendment No 2) Regulations, SI 1996/1182 regs 2, 6, with effect in relation to all payments of interest on relevant gilt-edged securities made without deduction of tax on or after 6 April 1996.

Payment of tax

8—(1) The amount of income tax in respect of any payment required to be included in a return under regulation 3, and the amount of the payment of account required to be shown in a special return under regulation 7(2), shall be due at the time by which the return or the special return (as the case may be) is to be made, and any amount so due

(*a*) shall be payable by the managing agent without the making of any assessment: and

(*b*) may be assessed on the managing agent (whether or not it has been paid when the assessment is made) if it, or any part of it, is not paid on or before the due date.

(2) If it appears to the inspector that there is a payment of relevant gilt interest which ought to have been but has not been included in a return, or if the inspector is dissatisfied with any return, he may make an assessment on the managing agent to the best of his judgment; and any income tax due under an assessment made by virtue of this paragraph shall be treated for the purposes of interest on unpaid tax as having been payable at the time when it would have been payable if a correct return had been made.

(3) Where a managing agent administers more than one syndicate in an underwriting year

(*a*) he may make a single payment in respect of all syndicates administered by him comprising the aggregate of the amounts of income tax required to be included in returns under regulation 3 for each quarter and

(*b*) he may make a single payment in respect of all syndicates administered by him comprising the aggregate of the payments on account required to be shown in special returns under regulation 7(2) for the relevant quarter.

[(4) For the purposes of this regulation, where—

(*a*) any payment to an officer of the Board is made by cheque, and

(*b*) the cheque is paid on its first presentation to the banker on whom it is drawn,

the payment shall be treated as made on the day on which the cheque was received by the officer of the Board.][1]

Amendments—[1] Para (4) added by the Lloyd's Underwriters (Gilt-edged Securities) (Periodic Accounting for Tax on Interest) (Amendment) Regulations, SI 1996/1014 reg 2(1), (2)(*a*), (3), with effect as respects cheques received on or after 22 April 1996.

Collection proceedings following claims

9—(1) Where a claim has been made under regulation 6(1), no proceedings for collecting tax which would fall to be discharged if the claim were allowed shall be instituted pending the final determination of the claim, but this paragraph shall not affect the date when the tax is due.

(2) When the claim is finally determined any tax underpaid in consequence of paragraph (1) above shall be paid.

(3) Where proceedings are instituted for collecting tax assessed, or interest on tax assessed. under any provision of regulation 8, effect shall not be given to any claim made after the institution of the proceedings so as to affect or delay the collection or recovery of the tax charged by the assessment or of interest thereon, until the claim has been finally determined.

(4) When the claim is finally determined any tax overpaid in consequence of paragraph (3) above shall be repaid.

(5) References in this regulation to proceedings for the collection of tax include references to proceedings by way of distraint or [attachment][1] for tax.

Amendments—[1] Word in para (5) substituted by the Debt Arrangement and Attachment (Scotland) Act 2002 s 61, Sch 3 para 35 with effect from 30 December 2002.

Assessments and due date of tax

10—(1) All the provisions of the Income Tax Acts as to the time within which an assessment may be made, so far as they refer or relate to the year of assessment for which an assessment is made, or the year to which an assessment relates, shall apply in relation to any assessment under regulation 8 notwithstanding that, under that regulation, the assessment may be said to relate to a quarter and not a year of assessment, and the provisions of section 36 of the Management Act as to the circumstances in which an assessment may be made out of tins shall apply accordingly on the footing that any such assessment relates to the year of assessment in which the quarter ends.

(2) Income tax assessed on a managing agent under regulation 8 shall be due within 14 days after the issue of the notice of assessment (unless due earlier under regulation 8(1)).

(3) Paragraph (2) above has effect subject to any appeal against the assessment, but no such appeal shall affect the date when tax is due under regulation 8(1).

(4) On the determination of an appeal against an assessment under these Regulations any tax overpaid shall be repaid.

(5) Any tax assessable under any one or more of the provisions of these Regulations may be included in one assessment if the tax so included is all due on the same date.

Interest payable on amounts of tax unpaid

11—(1) Any amounts of tax which have become due under these Regulations shall carry interest at the specified rate from the date when the amounts become due until payment.

(2) Without prejudice to the generality of paragraph (1) above—

(*a*) where in any year the payment on account has not been paid or has not been paid in full, by 14th March, the amount unpaid shall carry interest at the specified rate from 14th March until 14th April or the date on which it is paid, whichever first occurs: and

(*b*) where in any year the total amount of tax exceeds the amount of the payment on account, the excess shall carry interest at the specified rate from 14th March until 14th April or the date on which payment of the excess is made, whichever first occurs.

(3) In this regulation ''the specified rate'' means the rate applicable under section 178 of the Finance Act 1989 for the purposes of section 87 of the Management Act.

(4) Any sum to which this regulation applies shall carry interest from the due date even if that date is a non-business day within the meaning of section 92 of the Bills of Exchange Act 1882.

[(5) For the purposes of this regulation, where—

(*a*) any payment to an officer of the Board is made by cheque and

(*b*) the cheque is paid on its first presentation to the banker on whom it is drawn,

the payment shall be treated as made on the day on which the cheque was received by the officer of the Board.][1]

Amendments—[1] Para (5) added by the Lloyd's Underwriters (Gilt-edged Securities) (Periodic Accounting for Tax on Interest) (Amendment) Regulations, SI 1996/1014 reg 2(1), (2)(*b*), (3), with effect as respects cheques received on or after 22 April 1996.

Interest payable where payment on account excessive

12—(1) This regulation applies in any case where the payment on account paid exceeds the total amount of tax.

(2) Neither section 824 (repayment supplements: individuals and others) nor section 826 (interest on corporation tax overpaid) of the Taxes Act shall apply to a repayment of the amount of the excess, but that amount shall carry interest in accordance with the provisions of this regulation at the specified rate from the opening date until the date on which it is repaid.

(3) In this regulation ''the specified rate'' means the rate determined in accordance with paragraphs (4) to (7) below.

(4) Subject to paragraph (5) below, the specified rate shall be 4.5 per cent per annum.

(5) Where, on a reference date occurring after 2nd January 1996, the reference rate found on that date differs from the established rate, the specified rate shall, on and after the next operative date, be the percentage per annum found by applying the formula specified in paragraph (6) below; and, if the result is not a multiple of one quarter, rounding the result down to the nearest amount which is such a multiple.

(6) The formula specified is—

$$(RR-1)\ \frac{(100-BR)}{100},$$

where RR is the reference rate referred to in paragraph (5) above and BR is the percentage at which income tax at the basic rate is charged for the year of assessment in which the reference date referred to in that paragraph falls.

(7) In this regulation ''established rate'' , ''operative date'', ''reference date'' and ''reference rate'' have the same meanings as in the Taxes (Interest Rate) Regulations 1989.

(8) In this regulation, ''the opening date'' means 14th March or the date on which the payment on account is paid, if later.

(9) Any sum to which this regulation applies shall carry interest from the opening date even if that date is a non-business day within the meaning of section 92 of the Bills of Exchange Act 1882.

[(10) For the purposes of this regulation, where—

(*a*) any payment to an officer of the Board is made by cheque, and

(*b*) the cheque is paid on its first presentation to the banker on whom it is drawn,

the payment shall be treated as made on the day on which the cheque was received by the officer of the Board.][1]

Amendments—[1] Para (10) added by the Lloyd's Underwriters (Gilt-edged Securities) (Periodic Accounting for Tax on Interest) (Amendment) Regulations, SI 1996/1014 reg 2(1), (2)(*c*), (3) with effect as respects cheques received on or after 22 April 1996.

Saving

13 Nothing in these Regulations shall be taken to prejudice any powers conferred by the Income Tax Acts for the recovery of income tax by means of an assessment or otherwise.

1995/3237
Insurance Companies (Overseas Life Assurance Business) (Compliance) Regulations 1995

Made by the Commissioners of Inland Revenue under TA 1988, s 431E and FA 1995 Sch 8, para 58

Made . . . . *12 December 1995*
Laid before the House of Commons . . . . *12 December 1995*
Coming into Force . . . . *2 January 1996*

Commentary—*Simon's Direct Tax Service* **D4.524.**

ARRANGEMENT OF REGULATIONS

Certificates to be obtained on the happening of specified events

Sanctions

Keeping and inspection of records and provision of information

PRELIMINARY

Citation, commencement and effect

1 These Regulations may be cited as the Insurance Companies (Overseas Life Assurance Business) (Compliance) Regulations 1995, shall come into force on 2nd January 1996, and shall have effect in relation to accounting periods beginning on or after 1st November 1994.

Interpretation

2—(1) In these Regulations unless the context otherwise requires—

''basic life assurance and general annuity business'' has the meaning given by section 431F;

[''beneficiary'' has the meaning given by regulation 2 of the Excluded Business Regulations;][4]

''the Board'' means the Commissioners of Inland Revenue;

''branch'' includes agency;

[''company tax return'' has the meaning given by paragraph 3 of Schedule 18 to the Finance Act 1998;

[''excluded business'' means business which is excluded from section 431D (as amended by section 108 of the Finance Act 2000 and from time to time) by the Excluded Business Regulations;

''the Excluded Business Regulations'' means the Insurance Companies (Overseas Life Assurance Business) (Excluded Business) Regulations 2000;][4]

''the first [long-term][6] insurance Directive'' means Council Directive 79/267 of 5th March 1979;][2]

[''individual savings account business'' has the meaning given to it by regulation 3 of the Individual Savings Account (Insurance Companies) Regulations 1998;][1]

''life reinsurance business'' has the meaning given by section 431C;

''pension business'' has the meaning given by section 431B;

''policy holder'' includes annuitant;

''relevant business'' means—

(*a*) in the case of an overseas life insurance company, life assurance business carried on through a branch or agency in the United Kingdom [other than pension business, individual savings account business or][1] life reinsurance business, or

(*b*) in any other case, life assurance business [other than pension business, individual savings account business or][1] life reinsurance business;

''relevant policy'' means any policy or contract, or any underlying policy, which has at any time been treated as relating to overseas life assurance business[, or any policy or contract for business to which regulation 5(3) applies;][2]

''relevant record'' means—

(*a*) any certificate, declaration, undertaking or other document which in these Regulations is either prescribed or specified, or

(*b*) any other document relating to a relevant policy;

...[4]

[[''term assurance business'' means life assurance business in relation to which the policy or contract, or the underlying policy, is one which—

(*a*) is for a specified term; and

(*b*) is not capable of acquiring a surrender value that exceeds the amount of premiums paid;][4]

''the third [long-term][6] insurance Directive'' means Council Directive 92/96 of 10th November 1992;][2]

"underlying policy" means a policy or contract any risk arising from which is reinsured by a reinsurer in a reinsurance arrangement, and "underlying policy holder" shall be construed accordingly.

(2) Subject to paragraph (3) below, in any case where the obligations under any policy or contract of the body that issued, entered into or effected it ("the original insurer") are at any time the obligations of another body ("the transferee") to whom there has been a transfer of the whole or any part of a business previously carried on by the original insurer, any reference to an insurance company (however expressed) shall, unless the context otherwise requires, include the transferee.

(3) Paragraph (2) above does not apply to regulations 5 to [7A][3], 9, 10 or 21 to 23.

(4) In these Regulations any reference to a particular provision, without more, is a reference to that provision of the Income and Corporation Taxes Act 1988.

[(5) Save where otherwise indicated, any reference in these Regulations to any of the provisions of section 431D is a reference to that provision as it had effect prior to the amendment of that section by section 108 of the Finance Act 2000.][5]

Amendments—[1] Definition of "individual savings account business" inserted, and definition of "relevant business" amended in para 1, by the Insurance Companies (Overseas Life Assurance Business) (Compliance) (Amendment) Regulations, SI 1998/1872, with effect from 6 April 1999.

[2] Definitions of "company tax return", "the first long term insurance Directive", "term assurance business" and "the third long term insurance Directive", and words in definition of "relevant policy" inserted, by the Insurance Companies (Overseas Life Assurance Business) (Compliance) (Amendment) Regulations, SI 1999/2839, reg 3(1)–(4), with effect from 8 November 1999.

[3] Reference in para (3) substituted by the Insurance Companies (Overseas Life Assurance Business) (Compliance) (Amendment) Regulations, SI 2000/2104 reg 3(1), (3) with effect for policies or contracts made by, or, as the case may be, transferred to, an insurance company after 7 November 1999.

[4] Definitions of "beneficiary" and "term assurance business" substituted, definitions of "excluded business" and "the Excluded Business Regulations" inserted and definition of "settlor" revoked by SI 2000/2104 reg 3(1), (2), with effect for policies or contracts made by, or, as the case may be, transferred to, an insurance company after 21 August 2000.

[5] Para (5) inserted by SI 2000/2104 reg 3(1), (4) with effect from 23 August 2000.

[6] Words in para (1) substituted by the Financial Services and Markets Act 2000 (Consequential Amendments) (Taxes) Order, SI 2001/3629 art 142(*a*) with effect from 1 December 2001, immediately after the coming into force of the Financial Services and Markets Act 2000 ss 411, 432(1), Sch 20 (and SI 2001/3629 Pts 1 and 2).

Meaning of specified event

3 ...

Amendments—This regulation revoked by the Insurance Companies (Overseas Life Assurance Business) (Compliance) (Amendment) Regulations, SI 1999/2839, reg 4, with effect from 8 November 1999.

[Exclusion of business of friendly society which is exempt from tax][1]

[3A—These Regulations do not apply to any business of a friendly society the profits arising from which are exempt from income tax and corporation tax under section 460(1).][1]

Amendments—[1] This regulation inserted by the Insurance Companies (Overseas Life Assurance Business) (Compliance) (Amendment) Regulations, SI 1997/481, with effect from 19 March 1997 in relation to accounting periods beginning after 31 October 1994.

Business which is overseas life assurance business
General

4—In the circumstances prescribed in regulations 5 to 11, any issue as to whether business is overseas life assurance business shall be determined by reference to the matter prescribed in those regulations.

Business other than reinsurance business effected by a company resident in the United Kingdom outside the United Kingdom

5—(1) This regulation applies in circumstances where—

(*a*) an insurance company has entered into relevant business which is not reinsurance business,
(*b*) that business is with a policy holder not residing in the United Kingdom,
(*c*) the policy or contract for that business was effected by an insurance company resident in the United Kingdom at or through a branch outside the United Kingdom, ...[1]
(*d*) the policy or contract was made on or after 1st January 1996 [and
(*e*) to the best of the company's knowledge and belief the policy or contract is not [for excluded business][3].][1]

[(1A) This regulation also applies in circumstances where—

(*a*) on or after 8th November 1999 business is transferred to an insurance company in accordance with an authorisation granted outside the United Kingdom for the purposes of—

(i) Article 31a.2 of the first [long-term][4] insurance Directive, or
(ii) Article 11 of the third [long-term][4] insurance Directive,

(*b*) that business is with a policy holder not residing in the United Kingdom,
(*c*) that business is, immediately after the transfer, carried on by an insurance company resident in the United Kingdom at or through a branch outside the United Kingdom, and

(*d*) to the best of the company's knowledge and belief the policy or contract [is not for excluded business][3].][1]

[(2) Except in relation to business to which paragraph (3) below applies, the business referred to in paragraphs (1) and (1A) above shall be overseas life assurance business.

(3) This paragraph applies to business—

(*a*) which is not term assurance business, and

(*b*) for which the policy or contract is one—

(i) in respect of which the insurance company completes the certificate prescribed in paragraph (4) below, or

(ii) which falls within a class of policies or contracts in respect of which the company completes the certificate prescribed in paragraph (4A) below.

(4) The certificate prescribed is a certificate—

(*a*) showing the date on which it is given,

(*b*) stating the territory in which the branch is situated, and

(*c*) identifying the policy or contract by stating the name of the policy holder and any unique identifying designation given to the policy or contract.][1]

[(4A) The certificate prescribed is a certificate—

(*a*) stating the territory in which the branch is situated,

(*b*) setting out the unique characteristics of a class of policies or contracts which is not being treated by the insurance company as relating to overseas life assurance business, and

(*c*) confirming that any policy or contract within the class is capable of being identified readily in the books and records of the company by virtue of a unique identifying designation given to policies or contracts within that class.][1]

(5) A certificate under this regulation shall be given by an employee of the insurance company, and shall show the name of that employee and his position within the company.

(6) Paragraph (7) below applies in any case where—

(*a*) policies or contracts for business to which [paragraph (2) above][2] applies were effected at or through a particular branch outside the United Kingdom [or, where paragraph (1A) above applies, transferred to an insurance company so as to be carried on at or through a particular branch outside the United Kingdom,][1], and

(*b*) those policies or contracts were effected by[, or transferred to,][1] an insurance company within the same accounting period.

[(7) The insurance company may combine a certificate under paragraph (3)(*b*)(i) above with another certificate under paragraph (3)(*b*)(i) above in a single document.][1]

(8) The insurance company shall complete the certificate prescribed in this regulation [before the date on which it makes its company tax return for the accounting period in which the policy or contract was made or, where paragraph (1A) above applies, transferred.][2]

Amendments—[1] In para (1)(*d*) word "and" revoked, paras (1)(*e*), (1A), (4), and words in para (6) inserted, and paras (2)–(4), (7) substituted, by the Insurance Companies (Overseas Life Assurance Business) (Compliance) (Amendment) Regulations, SI 1999/2839, reg 5(1)–(5), (7) with effect in relation to accounting periods ending on or after 31 December 1999, or where an insurance company so elects by written notice given to an officer of the Board on or before 31 December 1999, the first accounting period beginning on or after 1 October 1999 and ending after 31 December 1999 and subsequent accounting periods.

[2] In para (6) words substituted for "this regulation", and in para (8) words substituted for "within three months following the end of the insurance company's accounting period in which the policy or contract was made", by SI 1999/2839, reg 5(1), (6), (8) with effect in relation to accounting periods ending on or after 31 December 1999, or where an insurance company so elects by written notice given to an officer of the Board on or before 31 December 1999, the first accounting period beginning on or after 1 October 1999 and ending after 31 December 1999 and subsequent accounting periods.

[3] Words in paras (1)(*e*), (1A)(*d*) substituted by the Insurance Companies (Overseas Life Assurance Business) (Compliance) (Amendment) Regulations, SI 2000/2104 reg 4 with effect for policies or contracts made by, or, as the case may be, transferred to, an insurance company after 21 August 2000.

[4] Words in sub-para (1A)(*a*) substituted by the Financial Services and Markets Act 2000 (Consequential Amendments) (Taxes) Order, SI 2001/3629 art 142(*b*) with effect from 1 December 2001, immediately after the coming into force of the Financial Services and Markets Act 2000 ss 411, 432(1), Sch 20 (and SI 2001/3629 Pts 1 and 2).

Business other than reinsurance business effected either by a company resident in the United Kingdom otherwise than outside the United Kingdom or by an overseas life insurance company—policies or contracts made before 1st January 1996

6—(1) This regulation applies in circumstances where—

(*a*) an insurance company has entered into relevant business which is not reinsurance business,

(*b*) that business is with a policy holder not residing in the United Kingdom,

(*c*) the policy or contract for that business was effected either by an insurance company resident in the United Kingdom otherwise than at or through a branch outside the United Kingdom, or by an overseas life insurance company, and

(*d*) the policy or contract was made before 1st January 1996.

(2) The business shall be overseas life assurance business where the insurance company completes—

(*a*) the certificate prescribed in paragraph (3) below, and

(*b*) the declaration prescribed—

(i) in a case where the policy holder is an individual, in paragraph (4) below, or
(ii) in a case where the policy holder is not an individual, in paragraph (5) below.

(3) The certificate prescribed is a certificate—

(*a*) stating that to the best of the company's knowledge and belief the policy holder was not residing in the United Kingdom on the date the policy or contract was made, and
(*b*) specifying the territory in which to the best of the company's knowledge and belief the policy holder was residing on that date.

(4) The declaration prescribed is a declaration that to the best of the company's knowledge and belief—

(*a*) the policy or contract is not one to which section 431D(2) applies, and
(*b*) where the policy or contract is one to which section 431D(2) does not apply solely by virtue of section 431D(5), that the conditions specified in section 431D(5) are fulfilled.

(5) The declaration prescribed is a declaration that to the best of the company's knowledge and belief—

(*a*) the policy or contract is one to which subsection (5) of section 431D applies and that the conditions specified in that subsection are fulfilled, or
(*b*) the policy or contract is one to which subsection (7) of section 431D applies and that the conditions specified in that subsection are fulfilled.

(6) A certificate or declaration under this regulation shall be given by an employee of the insurance company, and shall show the name of that employee and his position within the company.

(7) The insurance company shall complete any certificate or declaration prescribed in this regulation either within six months following the end of the insurance company's accounting period in which the policy or contract was made, or by 1st March 1996, whichever is the later.

Business other than reinsurance business effected either by a company resident in the United Kingdom otherwise than outside the United Kingdom or by an overseas life insurance company—policies or contracts made on or after 1st January 1996

7—(1) This regulation applies in circumstances where—

(*a*) an insurance company has entered into relevant business which is [neither reinsurance business nor term assurance business][1];
(*b*) that business is with a policy holder[who is an individual not residing in the United Kingdom and either—

(i) is a British citizen, or
(ii) is a person in respect of whose business the company has treated this regulation as applying,][1];

(*c*) the policy or contract for that business was effected either by an insurance company resident in the United Kingdom otherwise than at or through a branch outside the United Kingdom, or by an overseas life insurance company, and
(*d*) the policy or contract was made on or after 1st January 1996.

[(1A) This regulation also applies where—

(*a*) on or after 8th November 1999 relevant business which is neither reinsurance business nor term assurance business is transferred to an insurance company in accordance with an authorisation granted outside the United Kingdom for the purposes of—

(i) Article 31a.2 of the first [long-term][4] insurance Directive, or
(ii) Article 11 of the third [long-term][4] insurance Directive,

(*b*) that business has not been treated by the transferor as relating to overseas life assurance business,
(*c*) that business is with a policy holder who is an individual not residing in the United Kingdom and either—

(i) is a British citizen, or
(ii) is a person in respect of whose business with the company has treated this regulation as applying, and

(*d*) that business is, immediately after the transfer, carried on by an insurance company resident in the United Kingdom otherwise than at or through a branch outside the United Kingdom, or by an overseas life insurance company.][1]

(2) The business shall be overseas life assurance business where the insurance company obtains—

(*a*) the document prescribed in paragraph (3) below from the policy holder, and
(*b*) in any case where [the business is of a description falling within the circumstances set out in regulation 5 of the Excluded Business Regulations][3] and the policy or contract is held otherwise than by the trustees of the trust, the certificate prescribed in paragraph (8) below from the trustees of the trust.

(3) The document prescribed is a document containing—

(*a*) the certificate prescribed in paragraph (4) below,

[(*b*) the declaration prescribed in paragraph (5) below, and][1]
(*c*) the undertaking prescribed in paragraph (7) below.

(4) The certificate prescribed is a certificate—

(*a*) stating that the policy holder was not residing in the United Kingdom on the date the policy or contract was made [or, where paragraph (1A) above applies, transferred][1], and
(*b*) specifying the territory in which the policy holder was residing on that date.

[(5) The declaration prescribed is a declaration that the policy or contract is not for excluded business.][3]

(6) ...[1]

(7) The undertaking prescribed is an undertaking that the policy holder will notify the company if—

(*a*) the policy holder begins residing in the United Kingdom, or
(*b*) the rights conferred by the policy or contract come to be held subject to a trust, or
(*c*) the declaration prescribed in paragraph (5) [above][1] ceases to be true.

[(8) The certificate prescribed is a certificate stating that the circumstances are as set out in paragraph (1)(*b*) or (*c*), as the case may be, of regulation 5 of the Excluded Business Regulations.][3]

(9) The insurance company shall obtain the document prescribed in paragraph (3) above and, in any case where [the business is of a description falling within the circumstances set out in regulation 5 of the Excluded Business Regulations][3] and the policy or contract is held otherwise than by the trustees of the trust, the certificate prescribed in paragraph (8) above, [before the date on which it makes its company tax return for the accounting period in which the policy or contract was made or, where paragraph (1A) above applies, transferred.][1]

Amendments—[1] Words in paras (1)(*a*), (*b*), (7)(*c*), (9), and para (3)(*b*) substituted, para (1A) and words in para (4)(*a*) inserted and para (6) revoked by the Insurance Companies (Overseas Life Assurance Business) (Compliance) (Amendment) Regulations, SI 1999/2839, reg 6, with effect for policies or contracts made by or, as the case may be, transferred to, an insurance company after 7 November 1999.

[3] Words in paras (2)(*b*), (9) and whole of paras (5), (8) substituted by the Insurance Companies (Overseas Life Assurance Business) (Compliance) (Amendment) Regulations, SI 2000/2104 reg 5 with effect for policies or contracts made by, or, as the case may be, transferred to, an insurance company after 21 August 2000.

[4] Words in sub-para (1A)(*a*) substituted by the Financial Services and Markets Act 2000 (Consequential Amendments) (Taxes) Order, SI 2001/3629 art 142(*c*) with effect from 1 December 2001, immediately after the coming into force of the Financial Services and Markets Act 2000 ss 411, 432(1), Sch 20 (and SI 2001/3629 Pts 1 and 2).

[Business other than reinsurance business effected either by a company resident in the United Kingdom otherwise than outside the United Kingdom or by an overseas life insurance company—policy holder not within regulation 7

7A—(1) This regulation applies in circumstances where—

(*a*) an insurance company has entered into relevant business which is neither reinsurance business nor term assurance business,
(*b*) that business is with a policy holder not residing in the United Kingdom who either—

(i) is not an individual, or
(ii) if an individual, is not one falling within regulation 7(1)(*b*)(i) or (ii),

(*c*) the policy or contract for that business was effected either by an insurance company resident in the United Kingdom otherwise than at or through a branch outside the United Kingdom, or by an overseas life insurance company, and
(*d*) the policy or contract was made on or after 8th November 1999.

(2) This regulation also applies where—

(*a*) on or after 8th November 1999 relevant business which is neither reinsurance business nor term assurance business is transferred to an insurance company in accordance with an authorisation granted outside the United Kingdom for the purposes of—

(i) Article 31a.2 of the first [long-term][4] insurance Directive, or
(ii) Article 11 of the third [long-term][4] insurance Directive,

(*b*) that business has not been treated by the transferor as relating to overseas life assurance business,
(*c*) that business is with a policy holder not residing in the United Kingdom who either—

(i) is not an individual, or
(ii) if an individual, is not one falling within regulation 7(1)(*b*)(i) or (ii), and

(*d*) that business is, immediately after the transfer, carried on by an insurance company resident in the United Kingdom otherwise than at or through a branch outside the United Kingdom, or by an overseas life insurance company.

[(3) The business shall be overseas life assurance business where the insurance company completes the certificate prescribed in paragraph (4) or (5) below.][2]

(4) The certificate prescribed is a certificate—

(*a*) showing the date on which it is given,
(*b*) stating the name of the policy holder,
(*c*) stating any unique identifying designation given to the policy or contract,

(*d*) stating the territory which, to the best of the company's knowledge and belief, is the territory in which the policy holder resides,

(*e*) stating that the company has no knowledge of any information making it reasonable for the company to assume that the policy holder was residing in the United Kingdom at the time the policy or contract was made or, where paragraph (2) above applies, transferred,

(*f*) stating that to the best of the company's knowledge and belief the policy or contract is not[for excluded business][2],

(*g*) ...[2]

(*h*) where the company makes the statement mentioned in sub-paragraph [(*f*)][2] above, stating that the company is in possession of information enabling it to make that statement, and stating the nature of that information.

[(5) The certificate prescribed is a certificate—

(*a*) showing the date on which it is given,

(*b*) stating the name of the policy holder,

(*c*) stating any unique identifying designation given to the policy or contract, and

(*d*) stating that to the best of the company's knowledge and belief the policy or contract is for business of a description falling within regulation 7(*b*) of the Excluded Business Regulations.][3]

(6) A certificate under this regulation shall be given by an employee of the insurance company, and shall show the name of that employee and his position within the company.

(7) Paragraph (8) below applies in any case where policies or contracts for business to which this regulation applies were effected by, or where paragraph (2) above applies, transferred to, an insurance company within the same accounting period.

(8) The insurance company may—

(*a*) combine a certificate under paragraph (4) above with another certificate under paragraph (4) above in a single document, or

(*b*) combine a certificate under paragraph (5) above with another certificate under paragraph (5) above in [a single document,][3]

but a certificate under paragraph (4) above shall not be combined with a certificate under paragraph (5) above in a single document.

(9) The insurance company shall complete the certificate prescribed in this regulation before the date on which it makes its company tax return for the accounting period in which the policy or contract was made or, where paragraph (2) above applies, transferred.][1]

Amendments—[1] This regulation inserted by the Insurance Companies (Overseas Life Assurance Business) (Compliance) (Amendment) Regulations, SI 1999/2839, reg 7, with effect in relation to policies or contracts made by or, as the case may be, transferred to, an insurance company after 7 November 1999.

[2] Para (3) and words in para (4)(*f*), (*h*) substituted and para (4)(*g*) revoked by the Insurance Companies (Overseas Life Assurance Business) (Compliance) (Amendment) Regulations, SI 2000/2104 reg 6 with effect for policies or contracts made by, or, as the case may be, transferred to, an insurance company after 21 August 2000.

[3] Para (5) and words in para (8)(*b*) substituted by SI 2000/2104 reg 6(1), (4), (5) with effect from 23 August 2000.

[4] Words in sub-para (2)(*a*) substituted by the Financial Services and Markets Act 2000 (Consequential Amendments) (Taxes) Order, SI 2001/3629 art 142(*d*) with effect from 1 December 2001, immediately after the coming into force of the Financial Services and Markets Act 2000 ss 411, 432(1), Sch 20 (and SI 2001/3629 Pts 1 and 2).

Certain business other than reinsurance business where the company comes into possession of additional information

8—(1) This regulation applies in circumstances where—

(*a*) an insurance company has entered into relevant business which is [neither reinsurance business nor term assurance business][1],

[(*b*) that business was entered into by the insurance company with a policy holder referred to in regulation 7(1)(*b*);][1]

(*c*) the policy or contract for that business was effected either by an insurance company resident in the United Kingdom otherwise than at or through a branch outside the United Kingdom, or by an overseas life insurance company, and

(*d*) the insurance company comes to be in possession of information making it reasonable for the company to assume [either—

(i) that there has been a change in the identity of the policy holder and the new policy holder is a person referred to in regulation 7(1)(*b*), or

(ii) that the policy holder (being a person referred to in regulation 7(1)(*b*)) has ceased to be beneficially entitled to the rights conferred by the policy or contract.][1]

[(1A) This regulation also applies in circumstances where—

(*a*) on or after 8th November 1999 relevant business which is neither reinsurance business nor term assurance business is transferred to an insurance company in accordance with an authorisation granted outside the United Kingdom for the purposes of—

(i) Article 31a.2 of the first [long-term][3] insurance Directive, or

(ii) Article 11 of the third [long-term][3] insurance Directive,

(*b*) that business was entered into with a policy holder referred to in regulation 7(1)(*b*), (*c*) that business is, immediately after the transfer, carried on by an insurance company resident in the United Kingdom otherwise than at or through a branch outside the United Kingdom, or by an overseas life insurance company, and

(*d*) the insurance company to whom the business is transferred comes to be in possession of information making it reasonable for the company to assume either—

(i) that there has been a change in the identity of the policy holder and the new policy holder is a person referred to in regulation 7(1)(*b*), or

(ii) that the policy holder (being a person referred to in regulation 7(1)(*b*)) has ceased to be beneficially entitled to the rights conferred by the policy or contract.][1]

(2) The business shall continue to be overseas life assurance business where the insurance company obtains—

(*a*) the document prescribed in paragraph (3) below from the policy holder, and

(*b*) in any case where [the business is of a description falling within the circumstances set out in regulation 5 of the Excluded Business Regulations][2], the certificate prescribed in paragraph (8) below from the trustees of the trust.

(3) The document prescribed is a document containing—

(*a*) the certificate prescribed in paragraph (4) below,

[(*b*) the declaration prescribed in paragraph (5) below, and]

(*c*) the undertaking prescribed in paragraph (7) below.

(4) The certificate prescribed is a certificate—

(*a*) stating that the policy holder was not residing in the United Kingdom—

(i) in a case where it is reasonable for the company to assume that there has been a change in the identity of the policy holder, on the date he became the policy holder, or

(ii) in a case where it is reasonable for the company to assume that the policy holder has ceased to be beneficially entitled to the rights conferred by the policy or contract, on the date on which he ceased to be beneficially entitled to those rights, and

(*b*) specifying the territory in which the policy holder was residing on that date.

[(5) The declaration prescribed is a declaration that the policy or contract is not for excluded business.][2]

(6) ...[1]

(7) The undertaking prescribed is an undertaking that the policy holder will notify the company if—

(*a*) the policy holder begins residing in the United Kingdom, or

(*b*) the rights conferred by the policy or contract come to be held subject to a trust, or

(*c*) the declaration prescribed in paragraph (5) [above][1] ceases to be true.

[(8) The certificate prescribed is a certificate stating that the circumstances are as set out in regulation 5(1)(*b*) or (*c*) of the Excluded Business Regulations.][2]

(9) The insurance company shall obtain the document prescribed in paragraph (3) above and, in any case where [the business is of a description falling within the circumstances set out in regulation 5 of the Excluded Business Regulations][2] applies, the certificate prescribed in paragraph (8) above, [before the date on which the insurance company makes its company tax return for the accounting period in which][1]the insurance company comes to be in possession of information making it reasonable for the company to assume that there has been a change in the identity of the policy holder or that the policy holder has ceased to be beneficially entitled to the rights conferred by the policy or contract, as the case may be.

Amendments—[1] Words in paras (1), (7)(*c*), (9), and para (3)(*b*) substituted, para (1A) inserted and para (6) revoked, by the Insurance Companies (Overseas Life Assurance Business) (Compliance) (Amendment) Regulations, SI 1999/2839, reg 8, with effect in any case where the date on which the insurance company comes to be in possession of information making it reasonable for the company to assume that there has been a change in the identity of the policy holder, or the policy holder ceased to be beneficially entitled to the rights conferred by the policy or contract, falls after 8 November 1999.

[2] Words in paras (2)(*b*), (9) and whole of paras (5), (8) substituted by the Insurance Companies (Overseas Life Assurance Business) (Compliance) (Amendment) Regulations, SI 2000/2104 reg 7 with effect for policies or contracts made by, or, as the case may be, transferred to, an insurance company after 21 August 2000.

[3] Words in sub-para (1A)(*a*) substituted by the Financial Services and Markets Act 2000 (Consequential Amendments) (Taxes) Order, SI 2001/3629 art 142(*e*) with effect from 1 December 2001, immediately after the coming into force of the Financial Services and Markets Act 2000 ss 411, 432(1), Sch 20 (and SI 2001/3629 Pts 1 and 2).

Reinsurance of business effected by a company resident in the United Kingdom outside the United Kingdom

9—(1) This regulation applies in circumstances where—

(*a*) an insurance company has entered into relevant business [which is not term assurance business][1],

(*b*) that business is reinsurance of life assurance business with a policy holder not residing in the United Kingdom,

(*c*) the underlying policy in relation to that business was effected by an insurance company resident in the United Kingdom at or through a branch outside the United Kingdom, and

(*d*) the underlying policy in relation to that business was made on or after 1st January 1996.

(2) The business shall be overseas life assurance business where the insurance company obtains from the cedant company—

(*a*) the certificate prescribed in paragraph (3) below, and

(*b*) the undertaking prescribed in paragraph (4) below.

(3) The certificate prescribed is a certificate [that—

(*a*) the underlying policy in relation to the business is not one in respect of which the cedant company has completed the certificate prescribed in regulation 5(4) [or (4A)][2], or

(*b*) in relation to an underlying policy which was made in an accounting period for which regulation 5(2) to (4) did not have effect, the cedant company had complied with the requirements of regulation 5(2) as it applied for that accounting period.][1]

(4) The undertaking prescribed is an undertaking that the cedant company will notify the insurance company if the cedant company comes to be in possession of information making it reasonable for the cedant company to assume that—

(*a*) ...[1]

(*b*) the underlying policy in relation to the business has ceased to be life assurance business with a policy holder who was not residing in the United Kingdom at the time the policy or contract was made or at any time within [twelve][1] months thereafter, or

(*c*) the underlying policy holder, not being the person with whom the policy or contract was originally effected, was residing in the United Kingdom at the time the underlying policy was made or at any time thereafter.

(5) The insurance company shall obtain the certificate prescribed in paragraph (3) above and the undertaking prescribed in paragraph (4) above [before the date on which it makes its company tax return for the accounting period in which the reinsurance arrangement was made.][1]

Amendments—[1] In para (1) words inserted, in paras (3), (4), (5) words substituted, and in para (4) words omitted by the Insurance Companies (Overseas Life Assurance Business) (Compliance) (Amendment) Regulations, SI 1999/2839, reg 9(1)–(5), with effect in relation to accounting periods ending on or after 31 December 1999, or where an insurance company so elects by written notice given to an officer of the Board on or before 31 December 1999, the first accounting period beginning on or after 1 October 1999 and ending after 31 December 1999 and subsequent accounting periods.

[2] Words inserted by the Insurance Companies (Overseas Life Assurance Business) (Compliance) (Amendment) Regulations, SI 2000/2104 reg 8 with effect for—

(*a*) accounting periods ending on or after 31st December 1999; or

(*b*) where an insurance company has so elected by written notice given to an officer of the Board on or before 31 December 1999, the first accounting period beginning on or after 1 October 1999 and ending after 31 December 1999 and subsequent accounting periods.

Reinsurance of business effected either by a company resident in the United Kingdom otherwise than outside the United Kingdom or by an overseas life insurance company

10—(1) This regulation applies in circumstances where—

(*a*) an insurance company has entered into relevant business [which is not term assurance business][1],

(*b*) that business is reinsurance of life assurance business with a policy holder [referred to in regulation 7(1)(*b*)][1],

(*c*) the underlying policy in relation to that business was effected either by an insurance company resident in the United Kingdom otherwise than at or through a branch outside the United Kingdom, or by an overseas life insurance company, and

(*d*) the underlying policy in relation to that business was made on or after 1st January 1996.

(2) The business shall be overseas life assurance business where the insurance company obtains from the cedant company—

(*a*) the certificate prescribed in paragraph (3) below, and

(*b*) the undertaking prescribed in paragraph (4) below.

(3) The certificate prescribed is a certificate that the cedant company either—

(*a*) has completed the certificate prescribed in regulation 6(3) and, in any case where section 431D(5) applies, the [declaration prescribed in regulation 6(4) or (5)][1], or

(*b*) has obtained the document prescribed in regulation 7(3) from the underlying policy holder and, in any case [the business is of a description falling within the circumstances set out in regulation 5 of the Excluded Business Regulations][2] and the policy or contract is held otherwise than by the trustees of the trust, the certificate prescribed in regulation 7(8) from the trustees of the trust,

...[1]

(4) The undertaking prescribed is an undertaking that the cedant company will notify the insurance company if the cedant company comes to be in possession of information making it reasonable for the cedant company to assume that—

(*a*) any part of the certificate prescribed in regulation 6(3) or any part of the declarations prescribed in paragraphs (4) and (5) of regulation 6 or, as the case may be, any part of the document prescribed in regulation 7(3) has ceased to be true, or

(*b*) in any case [the business is of a description falling within the circumstances set out in regulation 5 of the Excluded Business Regulations][2] and the policy or contract is held otherwise than by the trustees of the trust, any part of the certificate prescribed in regulation 7(8) has ceased to be true, or

(*c*) the underlying policy in relation to the business has ceased to be life assurance business with a policy holder who was not residing in the United Kingdom at the time the policy or contract was made or at any time within six months thereafter, or

(*d*) the underlying policy holder, not being the person with whom the policy or contract was originally effected, was residing in the United Kingdom at the time the underlying policy was made or at any time thereafter.

(5) The insurance company shall obtain the certificate prescribed in paragraph (3) above and the undertaking prescribed in paragraph (4) above [before the date on which it makes its company tax return for the accounting period in which the reinsurance arrangement was made.][1]

Amendments—[1] Words in para (1)(*a*) inserted, words in paras (1)(*b*), (3), (5) substituted, and words in para (3) revoked, by the Insurance Companies (Overseas Life Assurance Business) (Compliance) (Amendment) Regulations, SI 1999/2839, reg 10, with effect in relation to policies or contracts made by or, as the case may be, transferred to, an insurance company on or after 8 November 1999.

[2] Words in paras (3)(*b*), (4)(*b*) substituted by the Insurance Companies (Overseas Life Assurance Business) (Compliance) (Amendment) Regulations, SI 2000/2104 reg 9 with effect for policies or contracts made by, or, as the case may be, transferred to, an insurance company after 21 August 2000.

[Reinsurance of business effected either by a company resident in the United Kingdom otherwise than outside the United Kingdom or by an overseas life insurance company—policy holder not within regulation 7

10A—(1) This regulation applies in circumstances where—

(*a*) an insurance company has entered into relevant business which is not term assurance business,

(*b*) that business is reinsurance of life assurance business with a policy holder not residing in the United Kingdom who either—

(i) is not an individual, or

(ii) if an individual, is not one falling within regulation 7(1)(*b*)(i) or (ii),

(*c*) the underlying policy in relation to that business was effected either by an insurance company resident in the United Kingdom otherwise than at or through a branch outside the United Kingdom, or by an overseas life insurance company, and

(*d*) the underlying policy in relation to that business was made on or after 8th November 1999.

(2) The business shall be overseas life assurance business where the insurance company obtains from the cedant company—

(*a*) the certificate prescribed in paragraph (3) below, and

(*b*) [where the cedant company has completed the certificate prescribed in regulation 7A(4),][2] the undertaking prescribed in paragraph (4) below.

(3) The certificate prescribed is a certificate that the cedant company has complied with the requirements of regulation 7A(3).

(4) The undertaking prescribed is an undertaking that the cedant company will notify the insurance company if the cedant company comes to be in possession of information making it reasonable for the cedant company to assume that—

(*a*) any part of the certificate prescribed in [regulation 7A(4)][2] has ceased to be true, or

(*b*) the underlying policy in relation to the business has ceased to be life assurance business with a policy holder who was not residing in the United Kingdom at the time the policy or contract was made or at any time within six months thereafter, or

(*c*) the underlying policy holder, not being the person with whom the policy or contract was originally effected, was residing in the United Kingdom at the time the underlying policy was made or at any time thereafter.

(5) The insurance company shall obtain the certificate prescribed in paragraph (3) above and the undertaking prescribed in paragraph (4) above before the date on which it makes its company tax return for the accounting period in which the reinsurance arrangement was made.][1]

Amendments—[1] This regulation inserted by the Insurance Companies (Overseas Life Assurance Business) (Compliance) (Amendment) Regulations, SI 1999/2839, reg 11, with effect in relation to policies or contracts made by or, as the case may be, transferred to, an insurance company on or after 8 November 1999.

[2] Words in para (2)(*b*) inserted and words in para (4) substituted by the Insurance Companies (Overseas Life Assurance Business) (Compliance) (Amendment) Regulations, SI 2000/2104 reg 10 with effect from 23 August 2000.

Certain reinsurance business where the company comes into possession of additional information

11—(1) This regulation applies in circumstances where—

(*a*) an insurance company has entered into relevant business [which is not term assurance business][1],

(*b*) that business is reinsurance of life assurance business [and was entered into by the insurance company with a policy holder referred to in regulation 7(1)(*b*)][1],

(*c*) the underlying policy in relation to that business was effected by an insurance company resident in the United Kingdom otherwise than at or through a branch outside the United Kingdom, or by an overseas life insurance company, and (*d*) the insurance company comes to be in possession of information making it reasonable for the company to assume [either—

(i) that there has been a change in the identity of the underlying policy holder and the new underlying policy holder is a person referred to in regulation 7(1)(*b*), or

(ii) that the underlying policy holder (being a person referred to in regulation 7(1)(*b*)) has ceased to be beneficially entitled to the rights conferred by the policy or contract.][1]

(2) The business shall continue to be overseas life assurance business where the insurance company obtains from the cedant company—

(*a*) the certificate prescribed in paragraph (3) below, and

(*b*) the undertaking prescribed in paragraph (4) below.

(3) The certificate prescribed is a certificate that the cedant company has obtained the document prescribed in regulation 8(3) from the policy holder and, in any case where [the business is of a description falling within the circumstances set out in regulation 5 of the Excluded Business Regulations][2], the certificate prescribed in regulation 8(8) from the trustees of the trust, within six months after the cedant company came to be in possession of information making it reasonable for the cedant company to assume that there had been a change in the identity of the policy holder or that the policy holder had ceased to be beneficially entitled to the rights conferred by the policy or contract, as the case may be.

(4) The undertaking prescribed is an undertaking that the cedant company will notify the insurance company if the cedant company comes to be in possession of information making it reasonable for the cedant company to assume that—

(*a*) any part of the document prescribed in regulation 8(3) has ceased to be true, or

(*b*) in any case where[the business is of a description falling within the circumstances set out in regulation 5 of the Excluded Business Regulations][2], any part of the certificate prescribed in regulation 8(8) has ceased to be true, or

(*c*) the underlying policy in relation to the business has ceased to be life assurance business with a policy holder not residing in the United Kingdom.

(5) The insurance company shall obtain the certificate prescribed in paragraph (3) above and the undertaking prescribed in paragraph (4) above [before the date on which it makes its company tax return for the accounting period in which the reinsurance arrangement was made.][1]

Amendments—[1] Words in para (1)(*a*) inserted, and words in paras (1)(*b*), (*d*), (5) substituted, by the Insurance Companies (Overseas Life Assurance Business) (Compliance) (Amendment) Regulations, SI 1999/2839, reg 12, with effect in any case where the date on which the insurance company comes to be in possession of information making it reasonable for the company to assume that there has been a change in the identity of the policy holder, or the policy holder ceased to be beneficially entitled to the rights conferred by the policy or contract, falls after 8 November 1999.

[2] Words in paras (3), (4)(*b*) substituted by the Insurance Companies (Overseas Life Assurance Business) (Compliance) (Amendment) Regulations, SI 2000/2104 reg 11 with effect for policies or contracts made by, or, as the case may be, transferred to, an insurance company after 21 August 2000.

TERRITORIES IN WHICH POLICY HOLDERS RESIDING

General

12—In the circumstances prescribed in regulations 13 to [16A][1], any issue as to whether a policy holder is residing in the United Kingdom or in some other territory shall be determined by reference to the matters prescribed in those regulations.

Amendments—[1] Reference substituted by the Insurance Companies (Overseas Life Assurance Business) (Compliance) (Amendment) Regulations, SI 2000/2104 reg 12 with effect for policies or contracts made by, or, as the case may be, transferred to, an insurance company after 7 November 1999.

Business other than reinsurance business effected by a company resident in the United Kingdom outside the United Kingdom

13—(1) This regulation applies in circumstances where—

(*a*) an insurance company has entered into relevant business which is not reinsurance business, and

(*b*) the policy or contract for that business was effected by an insurance company resident in the United Kingdom at or through a branch outside the United Kingdom.

[(1A) This regulation also applies where—

(*a*) on or after 8th November 1999 relevant business which is not reinsurance business is transferred to an insurance company in accordance with an authorisation granted outside the United Kingdom for the purposes of—

(i) Article 31a.2 of the first [long-term][5] insurance Directive, or

(ii) Article 11 of the third [long-term][5] insurance Directive, and

(*b*) that business is, immediately after the transfer, carried on by an insurance company resident in the United Kingdom at or through a branch outside the United Kingdom.][1]

(2) Subject to paragraph (3) below, the territory in which the policy holder was residing at the time the policy or contract was made [or, where paragraph (1A) applies, transferred][1] shall be the territory in which the branch was situated.

(3) Where, at the time the policy or contract was made [or transferred][3] or at any time within [eighteen][2] months thereafter, the company was in possession of information making it reasonable for the company to assume that the policy holder was residing in the United Kingdom at the time the policy or contract was made [or transferred][3] or at any time within [twelve][2] months thereafter, the territory in which the policy holder was residing at the time the policy or contract was made [or transferred][3] shall be the United Kingdom.

(4) Where, pursuant to paragraph (2) or (3) above, a policy holder has been treated as residing in a particular territory at the time the policy or contract was made [or transferred][1], the territory in which the policy holder is residing at any time thereafter shall, subject to paragraph (5) below, be that same territory.

(5) Subject to paragraph (3) above, where at any time after the policy or contract was made [or transferred][1] the company comes to be in possession of information making it reasonable for the company to assume that the policy holder, [being neither—

(*a*) the person with whom the policy or contract was originally effected, nor

(*b*) a person to whom the rights conferred by the policy or contract have been assigned in circumstances where the assignment did not constitute a chargeable event within the meaning of section 540, 542 or 545, nor

(*c*) a personal representative in whom those rights have been vested by operation of law][4],

was residing in the United Kingdom at the time he became the policy holder or at any time thereafter, the territory in which the policy holder is residing shall, from the date on which it is reasonable for the company so to assume, be the United Kingdom.

Amendments—[1] Para (1A), and words in para (2), (4), (5), inserted, by the Insurance Companies (Overseas Life Assurance Business) (Compliance) (Amendment) Regulations, SI 1999/2839, reg 13(1)–(3), (5), (6)(*a*), with effect from 8 November 1999.

[2] Words in para (3) substituted by SI 1999/2839, reg 13(1), (4)(*a*), (*b*), with effect in relation to policies or contracts made by or, as the case may be, transferred to, an insurance company on or after 8 November 1999. Words previously read "twelve" and "six" respectively.

[3] Words in para (3) inserted by SI 1999/2839, reg 13(1), (4)(*c*), with effect in relation to policies or contracts made by or, as the case may be, transferred to, an insurance company on or after 8 November 1999.

[4] Words in para (5) substituted by SI 1999/2839, reg 13(1), (6)(*b*), with effect from 8 November 1999.

[5] Words in sub-para (1A)(*a*) substituted by the Financial Services and Markets Act 2000 (Consequential Amendments) (Taxes) Order, SI 2001/3629 art 142(*f*) with effect from 1 December 2001, immediately after the coming into force of the Financial Services and Markets Act 2000 ss 411, 432(1), Sch 20 (and SI 2001/3629 Pts 1 and 2).

Business other than reinsurance business effected either by a company resident in the United Kingdom otherwise than outside the United Kingdom or by an overseas life insurance company

14—(1) This regulation applies in circumstances where—

(*a*) an insurance company has entered into relevant business which is not reinsurance business, and

(*b*) the policy or contract for that business was effected either by an insurance company resident in the United Kingdom otherwise than at or through a branch outside the United Kingdom, or by an overseas life insurance company [and

(*c*) that business is with a policy holder referred to in regulation 7(1)(*b*).][1]

[(1A) This regulation also applies in circumstances where—

(*a*) on or after 8th November 1999 relevant business which is not reinsurance business is transferred to an insurance company in accordance with an authorisation granted outside the United Kingdom for the purposes of—

(i) Article 31a.2 of the first [long-term][6] insurance Directive, or

(ii) Article 11 of the third [long-term][6] insurance Directive,

(*b*) that business has not been treated by the transferor as relating to overseas life assurance business,

(*c*) that business is, immediately after the transfer, carried on either by an insurance company resident in the United Kingdom otherwise than at or through a branch outside the United Kingdom, or by an overseas life insurance company, and

(*d*) that business is with a policy holder referred to in regulation 7(1)(*b*).][1]

(2) Subject to [paragraphs (3) and (3A)][5] below, the territory in which the policy holder was residing at the time the policy or contract was made [or, where paragraph (1A) applies, transferred][1] shall be the territory specified in the certificate prescribed in regulation 6(3) or, as the case may be, 7(4).

(3) Where, at the time the policy or contract was made [or transferred][3] or at any time within [eighteen][2] months thereafter, the company was in possession of information making it reasonable for the company to assume that the policy holder was residing in the United Kingdom at the time the policy or contract was made [or transferred][3] or at any time within [twelve][2] months thereafter, the territory in which the policy holder was residing at the time the policy or contract was made [or transferred][3] shall be the United Kingdom.

[(3A) Subject to paragraph (3) above, where the policy is for term assurance business, the territory in which the policy holder was residing at the time the policy was made or transferred shall be the territory in which, to the best of the company's knowledge or belief, the policy holder was residing at the time the policy was made or transferred.][5]

(4) Where, pursuant to paragraph (2)[, (3) or (3A)][5]above, a policy holder has been treated as residing in a particular territory at the time the policy or contract was made [or transferred][1], the territory in which the policy holder is residing at any time thereafter shall, subject to paragraph (5) below, be that same territory.

(5) Subject to paragraph (3) above, where at any time after the policy or contract was made [or transferred][1] the company comes to be in possession of information making it reasonable for the company to assume that the policy holder, [being neither—

(*a*) the person with whom the policy or contract was originally effected, nor

(*b*) any person to whom the rights conferred by the policy or contract have been assigned in circumstances where the assignment did not constitute a chargeable event within the meaning of section 540, 542 or 545, nor

(*c*) a personal representative in whom those rights have been vested by operation of law][4],

was residing in the United Kingdom at the time he became the policy holder or at any time thereafter, the territory in which the policy holder is residing shall, from the date on which it is reasonable for the company so to assume, be the United Kingdom.

Amendments—[1] Para (1)(*c*) and word "and" preceding it, para (1A), and words in paras (2), (4), (5) inserted, by the Insurance Companies (Overseas Life Assurance Business) (Compliance) (Amendment) Regulations, SI 1999/2839, reg 14(1)–(4), (6), (7)(*a*), with effect from 8 November 1999.

[2] Words in para (3) substituted by SI 1999/2839, reg 14(1), (5)(*a*), (*b*), with effect in relation to policies or contracts made by or, as the case may be, transferred to, an insurance company on or after 8 November 1999. Words previously read "twelve" and "six" respectively.

[3] Words in para (3) inserted by SI 1999/2839, reg 14(1), (5)(*c*), with effect in relation to policies or contracts made by or, as the case may be, transferred to, an insurance company on or after 8 November 1999.

[4] Words in para (5) substituted by SI 1999/2839, reg 14(1), (7)(*b*), with effect from 8 November 1999.

[5] Words in paras (2), (4) substituted and para (3A) inserted by the Insurance Companies (Overseas Life Assurance Business) (Compliance) (Amendment) Regulations, SI 2000/2104 reg 13 with effect for policies or contracts made by, or, as the case may be, transferred to, an insurance company after 21 August 2000.

[6] Words in sub-para (1A)(*a*) substituted by the Financial Services and Markets Act 2000 (Consequential Amendments) (Taxes) Order, SI 2001/3629 art 142(*g*) with effect from 1 December 2001, immediately after the coming into force of the Financial Services and Markets Act 2000 ss 411, 432(1), Sch 20 (and SI 2001/3629 Pts 1 and 2).

[Business other than reinsurance business effected either by a company resident in the United Kingdom otherwise than outside the United Kingdom or by an overseas life insurance company—policy holder not within regulation 7

14A—(1) This regulation applies in circumstances where—

(*a*) an insurance company has entered into relevant business which is not reinsurance business,

(*b*) that business is with a policy holder not residing in the United Kingdom who either—

(i) is not an individual, or

(ii) if an individual, is not one falling within regulation 7(1)(*b*)(i) or (ii),

(*c*) the policy or contract for that business was effected either by an insurance company resident in the United Kingdom otherwise than at or through a branch outside the United Kingdom, or by an overseas life insurance company, and

(*d*) the policy or contract was made on or after 8th November 1999.

(2) This regulation also applies where—

(*a*) on or after 8th November 1999 relevant business which is not reinsurance business is transferred to an insurance company in accordance with an authorisation granted outside the United Kingdom for the purposes of—

(i) Article 31a.2 of the first [long-term][3] insurance Directive, or

(ii) Article 11 of the third [long-term][3] insurance Directive,

(*b*) that business has not been treated by the transferor as relating to overseas life assurance business,

(*c*) that business is with a policy holder not residing in the United Kingdom who either—

(i) is not an individual, or

(ii) if an individual, is not one falling within regulation 7(1)(*b*)(i) or (ii), and

(*d*) that business is, immediately after the transfer, carried on by an insurance company resident in the United Kingdom otherwise than at or through a branch outside the United Kingdom, or by an overseas life insurance company.

(3) Subject to[paragraphs (4), (4A) and (4B) below][2], the territory in which the policy holder was residing at the time the policy or contract was made or, where paragraph (2) above applies, transferred shall be the territory specified in the certificate prescribed in [regulation 7A(4) above][2] or, as the case may be, paragraph (5) of that regulation.

(4) Where, at the time the policy or contract was made or transferred or at any time within eighteen months thereafter, the company was in possession of information making it reasonable for the

company to assume that the policy holder was residing in the United Kingdom at the time the policy or contract was made or transferred or at any time within twelve months thereafter, the territory in which the policy holder was residing at the time the policy or contract was made or transferred shall be the United Kingdom.

[(4A) Subject to paragraph (4) above, where the policy is for term assurance business, the territory in which the policy holder was residing at the time the policy was made or transferred shall be the territory in which, to the best of the company's knowledge or belief, the policy holder was residing at the time the policy was made or transferred.

(4B) Where the policy or contract is for business of a description falling within regulation 7(*b*) of the Excluded Business Regulations, the territory in which the policy holder was residing at the time the policy or contract was made or transferred shall be the territory under the law of which the scheme mentioned in that regulation is established.][2]

(5) Where, pursuant to paragraph (3)[, (4), (4A) or (4B)][2] above, a policy holder has been treated as residing in a particular territory at the time the policy or contract was made or transferred, the territory in which the policy holder is residing at any time thereafter shall, subject to paragraph (6) below, be that same territory.

(6) Subject to paragraph (4) above, where at any time after the policy or contract was made or transferred the company comes to be in possession of information making it reasonable for the company to assume that the policy holder, being neither—

(*a*) the person with whom the policy or contract was originally effected, nor

(*b*) a person to whom the rights conferred by the policy or contract have been assigned in circumstances where the assignment did not constitute a chargeable event within the meaning of section 540, 542 or 545, nor

(*c*) a personal representative in whom those rights have been vested by operation of law,

was residing in the United Kingdom at the time he became the policy holder or at any time thereafter, the territory in which the policy holder is residing shall, from the date on which it is reasonable for the company so to assume, be the United Kingdom.][1]

Amendments—[1] This regulation inserted by the Insurance Companies (Overseas Life Assurance Business) (Compliance) (Amendment) Regulations, SI 1999/2839, reg 15, with effect in relation to policies or contracts made by or, as the case may be, transferred to, an insurance company on or after 8 November 1999.

[2] Words in paras (3), (5) substituted and paras (4A), (4B) inserted by the Insurance Companies (Overseas Life Assurance Business) (Compliance) (Amendment) Regulations, SI 2000/2104 reg 14 with effect for policies or contracts made by, or, as the case may be, transferred to, an insurance company after 21 August 2000.

[3] Words in sub-para (2)(*a*) substituted by the Financial Services and Markets Act 2000 (Consequential Amendments) (Taxes) Order, SI 2001/3629 art 142(*h*) with effect from 1 December 2001, immediately after the coming into force of the Financial Services and Markets Act 2000 ss 411, 432(1), Sch 20 (and SI 2001/3629 Pts 1 and 2).

Reinsurance business effected by a company resident in the United Kingdom outside the United Kingdom

15—(1) This regulation applies in circumstances where—

(*a*) an insurance company has entered into relevant business which is reinsurance business, and

(*b*) the underlying policy in relation to that business was effected by an insurance company resident in the United Kingdom at or through a branch outside the United Kingdom.

(2) Subject to paragraph (3) below, the territory in which the underlying policy holder was residing at the time the underlying policy was made shall be the territory in which the branch was situated.

(3) Where, at the time the underlying policy was made or at any time within [eighteen][1] months thereafter, the company was in possession of information making it reasonable for the company to assume that the underlying policy holder was residing in the United Kingdom at the time the underlying policy was made or at any time within [twelve][1] months thereafter, the territory in which the underlying policy holder was residing at the time the underlying policy was made shall be the United Kingdom.

(4) Where, pursuant to paragraph (2) or (3) above, an underlying policy holder has been treated as residing in a particular territory at the time the underlying policy was made, the territory in which the underlying policy holder is residing at any time thereafter shall, subject to paragraph (5) below, be that same territory.

(5) Subject to paragraph (3) above, where at any time after the underlying policy was made the company comes to be in possession of information making it reasonable for the company to assume that the underlying policy holder, [being neither—

(*a*) the person with whom the policy or contract was originally effected, nor

(*b*) a person to whom the rights conferred by the policy or contract have been assigned in circumstances where the assignment did not constitute a chargeable event within the meaning of section 540, 542 or 545, nor

(*c*) a personal representative in whom those rights have been vested by operation of law][2],

was residing in the United Kingdom at the time he became the underlying policy holder or at any time thereafter, the territory in which the underlying policy holder is residing shall, from the date on which it is reasonable for the company so to assume, be the United Kingdom.

Amendments—[1] Words in para (3) substituted by the Insurance Companies (Overseas Life Assurance Business) (Compliance) (Amendment) Regulations, SI 1999/2839, reg 16(1), (2), with effect in relation to policies or contracts made by or, as the case may be, transferred to, an insurance company on or after 8 November 1999. Words previously read "twelve" and "six" respectively.

[2] Words in para (5) substituted by SI 1999/2839, reg 16(1), (3), with effect from 8 November 1999.

Reinsurance business effected either by a company resident in the United Kingdom otherwise than outside the United Kingdom or by an overseas life insurance company

16—(1) This regulation applies in circumstances where—

(*a*) an insurance company has entered into relevant business which is reinsurance business, and

(*b*) the underlying policy in relation to that business was effected either by an insurance company resident in the United Kingdom otherwise than at or through a branch outside the United Kingdom, or by an overseas life insurance company [and

(*c*) the underlying policy holder in relation to that business is a person referred to in regulation 7(1)(*b*).][1]

(2) Subject to [paragraphs (3) and (3A)][3] below, the territory in which the underlying policy holder was residing at the time the underlying policy was made shall be the territory specified in the certificate prescribed in regulation 6(3) or, as the case may be, 7(4).

(3) Where, at the time the underlying policy was made or at any time within [eighteen][2] months thereafter, the company was in possession of information making it reasonable for the company to assume that the underlying policy holder was residing in the United Kingdom at the time the underlying policy was made or at any time within [twelve][2]months thereafter, the territory in which the underlying policy holder was residing at the time the underlying policy was made shall be the United Kingdom.

[(3A) Subject to paragraph (3) above, where the underlying policy is for term assurance business, the territory in which the policy holder was residing at the time the underlying policy was made or transferred shall be the territory in which, to the best of the company's knowledge or belief, the policy holder was residing at the time the underlying policy was made or transferred.][3]

(4) Where, pursuant to paragraph (2)[, (3) or (3A)][3] above, an underlying policy holder has been treated as residing in a particular territory at the time the underlying policy was made, the territory in which the underlying policy holder is residing at any time thereafter shall, subject to paragraph (5) below, be that same territory.

(5) Subject to paragraph (3) above, where at any time after the underlying policy was made the company comes to be in possession of information making it reasonable for the company to assume that the underlying policy holder, [being neither—

(*a*) the person with whom the policy or contract was originally effected, nor

(*b*) a person to whom the rights conferred by the policy or contract have been assigned in circumstances where the assignment did not constitute a chargeable event within the meaning of section 540, 542 or 545, nor

(*c*) a personal representative in whom those rights have been vested by operation of law][1],

was residing in the United Kingdom at the time he became the underlying policy holder or at any time thereafter, the territory in which the underlying policy holder is residing shall, from the date on which it is reasonable for the company so to assume, be the United Kingdom.

Amendments—[1] Para (1)(*c*) and word "and" preceding it inserted, and words in para (5) substituted by the Insurance Companies (Overseas Life Assurance Business) (Compliance) (Amendment) Regulations, SI 1999/2839, reg 17(1), (2), (4), with effect from 8 November 1999.

[2] Words in para (3) substituted by SI 1999/2839, reg 17(1), (3), with effect in relation to policies or contracts made by or, as the case may be, transferred to, an insurance company on or after 8 November 1999. Words previously read "twelve" and "six" respectively.

[3] Words in paras (2), (4) substituted and para (3A) inserted by the Insurance Companies (Overseas Life Assurance Business) (Compliance) (Amendment) Regulations, SI 2000/2104 reg 15 with effect for policies or contracts made by, or, as the case may be, transferred to, an insurance company after 21 August 2000.

[Reinsurance business effected either by a company resident in the United Kingdom otherwise than outside the United Kingdom or by an overseas life insurance company—policy holder not within regulation 7

16A—(1) This regulation applies in circumstances where—

(*a*) an insurance company has entered into relevant business,

(*b*) that business is reinsurance of life assurance business with a policy holder not residing in the United Kingdom who either—

(i) is not an individual, or

(ii) if an individual, is not one falling within regulation 7(1)(*b*)(i) or (ii),

(*c*) the underlying policy in relation to that business was effected either by an insurance company resident in the United Kingdom otherwise than at or through a branch outside the United Kingdom, or by an overseas life insurance company, and

(*d*) the underlying policy in relation to that business was made on or after 8th November 1999.

(2) Subject to [paragraphs (3), (3A) and (3B)][2] below, the territory in which the underlying policy holder was residing at the time the underlying policy was made shall be the territory specified in the certificate prescribed in [regulation 7A(4) above][2].

(3) Where, at the time the underlying policy was made or at any time within eighteen months thereafter, the company was in possession of information making it reasonable for the company to assume that the underlying policy holder was residing in the United Kingdom at the time the underlying policy was made or at any time within twelve months thereafter, the territory in which the underlying policy holder was residing at the time the underlying policy was made shall be the United Kingdom.

[(3A) Subject to paragraph (3) above, where the underlying policy is for term assurance business, the territory in which the policy holder was residing at the time the underlying policy was made or transferred shall be the territory in which, to the best of the company's knowledge or belief, the policy holder was residing at the time the underlying policy was made or transferred.

(3B) Where the underlying policy is for business of a description falling within regulation 7(*b*) of the Excluded Business Regulations, the territory in which the policy holder was residing at the time the underlying policy was made or transferred shall be the territory under the law of which the scheme mentioned in that regulation is established.][2]

(4) Where, pursuant to paragraph (2)[, (3), (3A) or (3B)][2] above, an underlying policy holder has been treated as residing in a particular territory at the time the underlying policy was made, the territory in which the underlying policy holder is residing at any time thereafter shall, subject to paragraph (5) below, be that same territory.

(5) Subject to paragraph (3) above, where at any time after the underlying policy was made the company comes to be in possession of information making it reasonable for the company to assume that the underlying policy holder, being neither—

(*a*) the person with whom the policy or contract was originally effected, nor

(*b*) a person to whom the rights conferred by the policy or contract have been assigned in circumstances where the assignment did not constitute a chargeable event within the meaning of section 540, 542 or 545, nor

(*c*) a personal representative in whom those rights have been vested by operation of law,

was residing in the United Kingdom at the time he became the underlying policy holder or at any time thereafter, the territory in which the underlying policy holder is residing shall, from the date on which it is reasonable for the company so to assume, be the United Kingdom.][1]

Amendments—[1] This regulation inserted by the Insurance Companies (Overseas Life Assurance Business) (Compliance) (Amendment) Regulations, SI 1999/2839, reg 18, with effect in relation to policies or contracts made by or, as the case may be, transferred to, an insurance company on or after 8 November 1999.

[2] Words in paras (2), (4) substituted and paras (3A), (3B) inserted by the Insurance Companies (Overseas Life Assurance Business) (Compliance) (Amendment) Regulations, SI 2000/2104 reg 16 with effect for policies or contracts made by, or, as the case may be, transferred to, an insurance company after 21 August 2000.

CERTIFICATES TO BE OBTAINED ON THE HAPPENING OF SPECIFIED EVENTS

Business other than reinsurance business effected either by a company resident in the United Kingdom otherwise than outside the United Kingdom or by an overseas life insurance company

17 ...

Amendments—This regulation revoked by the Insurance Companies (Overseas Life Assurance Business) (Compliance) (Amendment) Regulations, SI 1999/2839, reg 4, with effect in relation to specified events occurring after 7 November 1999.

SANCTIONS

Reclassification of policy or contract from date when it was effected

18—(1) Subject to paragraph (2) below, this regulation applies in any case where an insurance company—

(*a*) treats a policy or contract as relating to overseas life assurance business—

(i) in the circumstances prescribed in regulation 6(1) where the insurance company has not completed the certificate prescribed in regulation 6(3) or one of the declarations prescribed in paragraphs (4) and (5) of regulation 6 within the period limited in regulation 6(7), or

(ii) in the circumstances prescribed in regulation 7(1) where the insurance company has not obtained the document prescribed in regulation 7(3) or, in any case where section 431D(5)[, or where the business is of a description falling within the circumstances set out in regulation 5 of the Excluded Business Regulations,][3] applies and the policy or contract is held otherwise than by the trustees of the trust, the certificate prescribed in regulation 7(8) within the period limited in regulation 7(9), or [(iii) in the circumstances prescribed in regulation [7A(1)][4] where the insurance company has not completed the certificate prescribed in regulation 7A(4) or (5) within the period limited in regulation 7A(9), or][1]

[(*aa*) treats an underlying policy as relating to overseas life assurance business in the circumstances prescribed in regulation 9 where the insurance company has not obtained the certificate prescribed in regulation 9(3) or the undertaking prescribed in regulation 9(4) within the period limited in regulation 9(5), or][1]

(*b*) treats an underlying policy as relating to overseas life assurance business in the circumstances prescribed in regulation 10(1) where the insurance company has not obtained the certificate prescribed in regulation 10(3) or the undertaking prescribed in regulation 10(4) within the period limited in regulation 10(5), or

[(*ba*) treats an underlying policy as relating to overseas life assurance business in the circumstances prescribed in regulation 10A(1) where the insurance company has not obtained the certificate prescribed in regulation 10A(3) or the undertaking prescribed in regulation 10A(4) within the period limited in regulation 10A(5), or][1]

(*c*) treats a policy or contract as relating to overseas life assurance business in the circumstances prescribed in regulation 13(3)[, 14(3) or 14A(4)][2], or

(*d*) treats an underlying policy as relating to overseas life assurance business in the circumstances prescribed in regulation 15(3)[, 16(3) or 16A(3)][2], or

(*e*) treats a policy, contract or underlying policy as relating to overseas life assurance business in circumstances where the insurance company, at the time the policy or contract was made [or transferred][1] or the relevant business in relation to that underlying policy was entered into, was in possession of information making it reasonable for the insurance company to assume [that—

(*a*) any of the requirements of section 431D (other than those relating to where the policy holder is residing) was not fulfilled (notwithstanding its possession of any certificate, declaration or other document), or

(*b*) the business was excluded business.][3]

(2) This regulation shall not apply in any case specified in sub-paragraph [(*aa*), (*b*), (*ba*), (*d*) or (*e*)][2] of paragraph (1) above where the insurance company is a company to which section 439A applies.

(3) The company shall—

(*a*) in the case of business other than reinsurance business, treat the policy or contract as relating to basic life assurance and general annuity business from the date the policy or contract was made [or transferred][1], or

(*b*) in the case of reinsurance business, treat the business relating to the underlying policy as basic life assurance and general annuity business from the date the underlying policy was made.

(4) All necessary adjustments, whether by way of assessment [self-assessment,][1] or otherwise, shall be made to give effect to paragraph (3) above; and any such assessment may be made without limits on time.

Amendments—[1] Para 1(*a*)(iii), (*aa*), (*ba*), and words in para (1)(*e*), (3)(*a*), (4), inserted, by the Insurance Companies (Overseas Life Assurance Business) (Compliance) (Amendment) Regulations, SI 1999/2839, reg 19(1)–(4), (7), (9), (10), with effect from 8 November 1999.

[2] Words substituted by SI 1999/2839, reg 19(5), (6), (8), with effect from 8 November 1999.

[3] Words in para (1)(*a*)(ii) inserted and words in para (1)(*e*) substituted by the Insurance Companies (Overseas Life Assurance Business) (Compliance) (Amendment) Regulations, SI 2000/2104 reg 17(1), (2)(*a*), (3) with effect for policies or contracts made by, or, as the case may be, transferred to, an insurance company after 21 August 2000.

[4] Words in para (1)(*a*)(iii) substituted by SI 2000/2104 reg 17(1), (2)(*b*) with effect from 23 August 2000.

[Reclassification of policy or contract as relating to overseas life assurance business from date when it was made or transferred

18A—(1) This regulation applies in any case where an insurance company—

(*a*) does not treat a policy or contract as relating to overseas life assurance business in the circumstances prescribed in regulation 5(1) or (1A), and

(*b*) has not completed the certificate prescribed in regulation 5(4) [or (4A)] within the period limited in regulation 5(8).

(2) The company shall treat the policy or contract as relating to overseas life assurance business from the date the policy or contract was made or transferred.

(3) All necessary adjustments, whether by way of assessment or otherwise, shall be made to give effect to paragraph (2).][1]

Amendments—[1] This regulation inserted by the Insurance Companies (Overseas Life Assurance Business) (Compliance) (Amendment) Regulations, SI 1999/2839, reg 20, with effect from 8 November 1999.

[2] Words in para (1)(*b*) substituted by the Insurance Companies (Overseas Life Assurance Business) (Compliance) (Amendment) Regulations, SI 2000/2104 reg 18 with effect for cases occurring after 7 November 1999.

Reclassification of policy or contract from date after it was effected

19—(1) Subject to paragraph (2) below, this regulation applies in any case where an insurance company—

(*a*) treats a policy or contract as relating to overseas life assurance business in the circumstances prescribed in regulation 8(1) where the insurance company has not obtained the document prescribed in regulation 8(3) or, in any case where section 431D(5) applies[, or the business is of a description falling within the circumstances set out in regulation 5 of the Excluded Business Regulations,][3] the certificate prescribed in regulation 8(8) within the period limited in regulation 8(9), or
(*b*) treats an underlying policy as relating to overseas life assurance business in the circumstances prescribed in regulation 11(1) where the insurance company has not obtained the certificate prescribed in regulation 11(3) or the undertaking prescribed in regulation 11(4) within the period limited in regulation 11(5), or
(*c*) treats a policy or contract as relating to overseas life assurance business in the circumstances prescribed in regulation 13(5)[, 14(5) or 14A(6)][1], or
(*d*) treats an underlying policy as relating to overseas life assurance business in the circumstances prescribed in regulation 15(5)[, 16(5) or 16A(5)][1], or
(*e*) treats a policy, contract or underlying policy as relating to overseas life assurance business in circumstances where the insurance company, at any time after the policy or contract was made [or transferred][1] or the relevant business in relation to that underlying policy was entered into, was in possession of information making it reasonable for the insurance company to assume [that—
(*a*) any of the requirements of section 431D (other than those relating to where the policy holder is residing) was not fulfilled (notwithstanding its possession of any certificate, declaration or other document), or
(*b*) the business was excluded business.][3]

(2) This regulation shall not apply in any case specified in sub-paragraph (*b*), (*d*) or (*e*) of paragraph (1) above where the insurance company is a company to which section 439A applies.

(3) [Subject to [paragraphs (3A) and (3B)][3] below,][1] the company shall—

(*a*) in the case of business other than reinsurance business, treat the policy or contract as relating to basic life assurance and general annuity business from the end of the accounting period in which the relevant date falls, or
(*b*) in the case of reinsurance business, treat the business relating to the underlying policy as basic life assurance and general annuity business from the end of the accounting period in which the relevant date falls.

[(3A) Paragraph (3) above shall not apply where—

(*a*) the case concerned falls within paragraph (1)(*e*) above,
(*b*) section 431D(7) applied to the policy or contract when it was made or transferred, or the underlying policy when it was made,
(*c*) the case falls within paragraph (1)(*e*) above by reason of the fact that, at some time that is—

(i) more than three years after the date on which the policy or contract was made or transferred, or the underlying policy was made, but
(ii) is not earlier than 8th November 1999,

the number of persons for or in respect of whom benefits were to be provided under the policy or contract, or the underlying policy, and who were not relevant overseas employees within the meaning of section 431D(8), became a not insignificant number ('the relevant number') for the purposes of section 431D(7), and
(*d*) the relevant number has at no time exceeded the number which is equal to twenty per cent of the total number of persons for or in respect of whom benefits are to be provided under the policy or contract or the underlying policy.][1]

[(3B) Paragraph (3) above shall not apply where—

(*a*) the case concerned falls within paragraph (1)(*e*) above,
(*b*) the policy or contract fell within the description set out in regulation 7(*c*) of the Excluded Business Regulations when it was made or transferred, or the underlying policy fell within that description when it was made,
(*c*) the case falls within paragraph (1)(*e*) above by reason of the fact that, at some time that is more than three years after the date on which the policy or contract was made or transferred, or the underlying policy was made, the number of persons for or in respect of whom benefits were to be provided under the policy or contract, or the underlying policy, and who were not relevant overseas employees within the meaning of regulation 2 of the Excluded Business Regulations, became a not insignificant number ('the relevant number') for the purposes of regulation 7(*c*) of those Regulations, and
(*d*) the relevant number has at no time exceeded the number which is equal to twenty per cent of the total number of persons for or in respect of whom benefits are to be provided under the policy or contract or the underlying policy.][3]

(4) All necessary adjustments, whether by way of assessment or otherwise, shall be made to give effect to paragraph (3) above; and any such assessment may be made without limits on time.

(5) In paragraph (3) above "the relevant date" means—

(*a*) in any case specified in sub-paragraph (*a*) or (*b*) of paragraph (1) above, the last day by which the insurance company should have obtained any certificate, document or undertaking mentioned in either of those sub-paragraphs, or

(*b*) in any case specified in sub-paragraph (*c*) or (*d*) of paragraph (1) above, the date when it became reasonable for the company to assume as mentioned in regulation 13(5), 14(5), 15(5) or 16(5) as the case may be, or

(*c*) in any case specified in sub-paragraph (*e*) of paragraph (1) above, the date when it became reasonable for the insurance company to assume as mentioned in that sub-paragraph.

Amendments—[1] In para (1)(*c*), (*d*) words substituted for original words "or 14(5)", and "or 16(5)" respectively, and words in para (1)(*e*), (3) and whole of para (3A) inserted, by the Insurance Companies (Overseas Life Assurance Business) (Compliance) (Amendment) Regulations, SI 1999/2839, reg 21, with effect in relation to accounting periods ending on or after 31 December 1999, or where an insurance company so elects by written notice given to an officer of the Board on or before 31 December 1999, the first accounting period beginning on or after 1 October 1999 and ending after 31 December 1999 and subsequent accounting periods.

[2] Words in para (5)(*b*) substituted by the Insurance Companies (Overseas Life Assurance Business) (Compliance) (Amendment) Regulations, SI 2000/2104 reg 19(1), (6) with effect for—

(*a*) accounting periods ending on or after 31st December 1999; or

(*b*) where an insurance company has so elected by written notice given to an officer of the Board on or before 31 December 1999, the first accounting period beginning on or after 1 October 1999 and ending after 31 December 1999 and subsequent accounting periods.

[3] Words in para (1)(*a*) and whole of para (3A) inserted and words in paras (1)(*e*), (3) substituted by SI 2000/2104 reg 19(1)–(5) with effect for policies or contracts made by, or, as the case may be, transferred to, an insurance company after 21 August 2000.

Charge to tax where no certificate under regulation 17

20 ...

Amendments—This regulation revoked by the Insurance Companies (Overseas Life Assurance Business) (Compliance) (Amendment) Regulations, SI 1999/2839, reg 4, with effect in relation to specified events occurring after 7 November 1999.

KEEPING AND INSPECTION OF RECORDS AND PROVISION OF INFORMATION

Records to be kept and transfers of records

21—(1) A company (including any transferee) shall at all times keep sufficient records in respect of each relevant policy to enable the requirements of these Regulations to be satisfied.

(2) Without prejudice to the generality of paragraph (1) above, any relevant record shall be preserved by the company, in such manner as may be approved by the Board, so as to be available for inspection under regulation 23 for a period of six years after the termination of the policy or contract.

(3) In any case where the obligations under any policy or contract of the body that issued, entered into or effected it ("the original insurer") are at any time the obligations of another body (in this regulation and in regulations 22 and 23 referred to as the "transferee") to whom there has been a transfer of the whole or any part of a business previously carried on by the original insurer, the original insurer shall deliver any relevant record to the transferee within the period of three months after the transfer.

(4) Paragraph (3) above has effect in relation to transfers on or after 1st January 1996.

Information to be provided to the Board

22 An officer of the Board authorised for the purposes of this regulation may by notice require any company which has at any time effected a relevant policy or any transferee, within such time as may be provided by the notice (not being less than 30 days), to furnish him with such information relating to any relevant policy as he may reasonably require for the purposes of these Regulations.

Inspection of records

23—(1) An officer of the Board authorised for the purposes of this regulation may by notice require any company which has at any time effected a relevant policy or any transferee, within such time as may be provided in the notice (not being less than 30 days), to make available for inspection by him such books, documents and other records as are in the company's possession or under the company's control containing such information relating to any relevant policy as he may reasonably require for the purposes of these Regulations.

(2) The officer to whom the books, documents and other records are made available shall be entitled to take copies, or make extracts from, any book, document or record made available to him by virtue of paragraph (1) above.

1995/3238
Insurance Companies (Overseas Life Assurance Business) (Tax Credit) Regulations 1995

Made by the Commissioners of Inland Revenue under TA 1988, ss 431E(2), (3), 441A(3)–(5) and FA 1995 Sch 8 para 58

Made . . . . 12 December 1995
Laid before the House of Commons . . . . 12 December 1995
Coming into Force . . . . . . 2 January 1996

Commentary—*Simon's Direct Tax Service* **D4.524.**

Preliminary

Citation, commencement and effect

1 These Regulations may be cited as the Insurance Companies (Overseas Life Assurance Business) (Tax Credit) Regulations 1995, shall come into force on 2nd January 1996, and shall have effect in relation to accounting periods beginning on or after 1st November 1994.

Interpretation

2—(1) In these Regulations unless the context otherwise requires—

''the Board'' means the Commissioners of Inland Revenue;

''branch'' includes agency;

''the Compliance Regulations'' means the Insurance Companies (Overseas Life Assurance Business) (Compliance) Regulations 1995;

''linked liabilities'' means liabilities in respect of benefits to be determined by reference to the value of linked assets;

''policy holder'' includes annuitant;

''relevant overseas policy holders'' shall be construed in accordance with regulation 3;

''relevant tax credit'' has the meaning given by regulation 8;

''tax credit territory'' shall be construed in accordance with regulation 4.

(2) In regulations 9 to 12, in any case where the obligations under any policy or contract of the body that issued, entered into or effected it (''the original insurer'') are at any time the obligations of another body (''the transferee'') to whom there has been a transfer of the whole or any part of a business previously carried on by the original insurer, any reference to an insurance company (however expressed) shall, unless the context otherwise requires, include the transferee.

(3) In these Regulations any reference to a particular provision, without more, is a reference to that provision of the Income and Corporation Taxes Act 1988.

Meaning of relevant overseas policy holders

3—(1) For the purposes of these Regulations, and subject to paragraph (2) below, policy holders are relevant overseas policy holders of a company if—

(*a*) in relation to business other than reinsurance business, the company's life assurance business with them is overseas life assurance business, or

(*b*) in relation to reinsurance business—

(i) the cedant company's life assurance business with them is overseas life assurance business, or

(ii) the reinsurance of the cedant company's business with them is overseas life assurance business.

(2) Policy holders shall not be relevant overseas policy holders where the business is reinsurance of business within sub-paragraph (i) or (ii) of section 431D(1)(*b*).

Meaning of tax credit territory

4 For the purposes of these Regulations a territory is a tax credit territory if an individual resident in the territory and receiving a distribution would be entitled, under arrangements having effect by virtue of section 788, to a tax credit in respect of a qualifying distribution made to him by a company resident in the United Kingdom.

Entitlement to tax credit

5—(1) Subject to paragraph (2) below, an insurance company shall be entitled, under section 441A(3), to an amount of tax credit in the case of a distribution in respect of an asset of the company's overseas life assurance fund if any of the company's relevant overseas policy holders is residing in a tax credit territory.

(2) An insurance company shall not be entitled, under section 441A(3), to an amount of tax credit as mentioned in paragraph (1) above to the extent that the company is entitled to that amount under any other provision of the Corporation Tax Acts.

Amount of tax credit

6—The amount of tax credit to which an insurance company is entitled by virtue of regulation 5 in respect of an asset shall be calculated by—

(*a*) taking, for each tax credit territory in which any of its relevant overseas policy holders is residing, the appropriate fraction of the relevant tax credit, and

(*b*) aggregating the amounts arrived at under paragraph (*a*) above.

Appropriate fraction

7—(1) In regulation 6 "the appropriate fraction" means—

(*a*) in any case where the asset is linked to overseas life assurance business, the fraction specified in paragraph (2) below, and

(*b*) in any case where the asset is not linked to overseas life assurance business, the fraction specified in paragraph (3) below.

(2) The fraction referred to in paragraph (1)(*a*) above is the fraction of which—

(*a*) the numerator is the aggregate amount of the company's linked liabilities which are liabilities in respect of—

(i) its relevant overseas policy holders within regulation 3(1)(*a*) residing in the tax credit territory, or

(ii) its cedant companies in respect of the company's relevant overseas policy holders within regulation 3(1)(*b*) residing in the tax credit territory, and

(*b*) the denominator is the aggregate amount of the company's linked liabilities which are liabilities in respect of—

(i) all its relevant overseas policy holders within regulation 3(1)(*a*), or

(ii) its cedant companies in respect of all the company's relevant overseas policy holders within regulation 3(1)(*b*).

(3) The fraction referred to in paragraph (1)(*b*) above is the fraction of which—

(*a*) the numerator is the aggregate amount of the company's liabilities, other than its linked liabilities, in respect of—

(i) its relevant overseas policy holders within regulation 3(1)(*a*) residing in the tax credit territory, or

(ii) its cedant companies in respect of the company's relevant overseas policy holders within regulation 3(1)(*b*) residing in the tax credit territory, and

(*b*) the denominator is the aggregate amount of the company's liabilities, other than its linked liabilities, in respect of—

(i) all its relevant overseas policy holders within regulation 3(1)(*a*), or

(ii) its cedant companies in respect of all the company's relevant overseas policy holders within regulation 3(1)(*b*).

(4) In its application to an overseas life insurance company this regulation shall be modified so that the word "liabilities" wherever it occurs is construed in accordance with the definition given in paragraph 6(2) of Schedule 19AC.

Relevant tax credit

8 In regulation 6 the "relevant tax credit" means the amount of tax credit which would be paid under arrangements having effect by virtue of section 788, after taking into account any tax to be charged or deducted and any reduction in the amount received to be made by reference to the aggregate of the distribution and tax credit under those arrangements, if the distribution were received by an individual resident in the tax credit territory.

Territories in which policy holders residing

General

9 Any issue as to the territory in which a relevant overseas policy holder is residing for the purposes of these Regulations shall be determined in accordance with regulations 10 to 12.

Policies or contracts effected by a company resident in the United Kingdom outside the United Kingdom

10—(1) This regulation applies in circumstances where a policy or contract is effected by a company resident in the United Kingdom at or through a branch outside the United Kingdom.

(2) Subject to paragraph (3) below, the territory in which the policy holder was residing at the time the policy or contract was made shall be the territory in which the branch was situated.

(3) Where—

(*a*) the policy or contract was made at or through a branch situated in a tax credit territory, and

(*b*) at the time the policy or contract was made the company was in possession of information making it reasonable for the company to assume that the policy holder was residing in a non-qualifying territory at that time,

the territory in which the policy holder was residing at the time the policy was made shall be that non-qualifying territory.

(4) Where, pursuant to paragraph (2) or (3) above, a policy holder has been treated as residing in a territory at the time the policy or contract was made, the territory in which the policy holder is residing at any time thereafter shall, subject to paragraphs (5) and (6) below, be that same territory.

(5) Where—

(*a*) the policy or contract was made at or through a branch situated in a tax credit territory, and

(*b*) at any time after the policy or contract was made the company comes to be in possession of information making it reasonable for the company to assume that the policy holder was residing in a non-qualifying territory at the time the policy or contract was made or at any time thereafter,

the territory in which the policy holder is residing shall, from the relevant date, be that non-qualifying territory.

(6) If at any time after paragraph (5) above has applied, the company comes to be in possession of information making it reasonable for the company to assume that the policy holder, after residing in a non-qualifying territory, has begun residing in a tax credit territory, the territory in which the policy holder is residing shall, from the relevant date, be that tax credit territory.

Policies or contracts effected either by a company resident in the United Kingdom otherwise than outside the United Kingdom or by an overseas life insurance company

11—(1) This regulation applies in circumstances where a policy or contract is effected either by a company resident in the United Kingdom otherwise than at or through a branch outside the United Kingdom, or by an overseas life insurance company.

(2) Subject to paragraph (6) below, in a case where the business is not reinsurance business, the territory in which the policy holder was residing at the time the policy or contract was made shall be the territory specified in the certificate prescribed in regulation 6(3) or, as the case may be, 7(4) of the Compliance Regulations.

(3) Subject to paragraph (4) to (6) below, in a case where the business is reinsurance business, the territory in which the policy holder was residing at the time the policy or contract was made shall be a non-qualifying territory.

(4) Subject to paragraph (6) below, in a case where—

(*a*) the business is reinsurance business, and

(*b*) the relevant overseas policy holder is a policy holder with a cedant company whose business with him is overseas life assurance business,

the territory in which the policy holder was residing at the time the policy or contract was made shall be the territory which the cedant company notifies the company is the territory specified in the certificate prescribed in regulation 6(3) or, as the case may be, 7(4) of the Compliance Regulations.

(5) Subject to paragraph (6) below, in a case where—

(*a*) the business is reinsurance business other than reinsurance business in a case falling within paragraph (4) above, and

(*b*) the reinsurer notifies the company of the territory in which it reasonably believes the relevant overseas policy holder to reside,

the territory in which the policy holder was residing at the time the policy or contract was made shall be the territory notified.

(6) Where, at the time the policy or contract was made, the company was in possession of information making it reasonable for the company to assume that the policy holder was residing in a non-qualifying territory at that time, the territory in which the policy holder was residing at the time the policy or contract was made shall be that non-qualifying territory.

(7) Where, pursuant to any of paragraphs (2) to (6) above, a policy holder has been treated as residing in a territory at the time the policy or contract was made, the territory in which the policy holder is residing at any time thereafter shall, subject to paragraphs (8) and (9) below, be that same territory.

(8) Where, at any time after the policy or contract was made, the company comes to be in possession of information making it reasonable for the company to assume that the policy holder was residing in a non-qualifying territory at the time the policy was made or at any time thereafter, the territory in which the policy holder is residing shall, from the relevant date, be that non-qualifying territory.

(9) If at any time after paragraph (8) has applied, the company comes to be in possession of information making it reasonable for the company to assume that the policy holder, after residing in a non-qualifying territory, has begun residing in a tax credit territory, the territory in which the policy holder is residing shall, from the relevant date, be that tax credit territory.

(10) The company shall obtain the notification mentioned in paragraph (4) above within—

(*a*) nine months following the end of the cedant company's accounting period in which the cedant company entered into the business with the relevant overseas policy holder, or

(*b*) three months following the making of the reinsurance arrangement, or

(*c*) three months following the end of the company's accounting period in which the company first receives a distribution from an asset of its overseas life assurance fund to which a tax credit is attached,

whichever is the last to occur.

Interpretation of regulations 10 and 11

12—(1) In regulations 10 and 11 a "non-qualifying territory" means—

(*a*) the United Kingdom, or

(*b*) a territory which is not a tax credit territory, or

(*c*) a territory which is a tax credit territory, but where the amount of the relevant tax credit is nil.

(2) In each of the provisions to which this paragraph applies, "the relevant date" means the date from which it is reasonable for the company to assume that the policy holder is residing as mentioned in that provision; and this paragraph applies to regulations 10(5), 10(6), 11(8) and 11(9).

Keeping and inspection of records and provision of information

Records to be kept and transfers of records

13—(1) An insurance company (including any transferee) shall at all times keep sufficient records to enable the requirements of these Regulations to be satisfied.

(2) In any case where the obligations under any policy or contract of the body that issued, entered into or effected it ("the original insurer") are at any time the obligations of another body (in this regulation referred to as the "transferee") to whom there has been a transfer of the whole or any part of a business previously carried on by the original insurer, the original insurer shall deliver any relevant record (within the meaning given by the Compliance Regulations) to the transferee within the period of three months after the transfer.

(3) Paragraph (2) above has effect in relation to transfers on or after 1st January 1996.

Information to be provided to the Board

14 An officer of the Board authorised for the purposes of this regulation may by notice in writing require any insurance company to which these Regulations apply or any cedant company with which the insurance company has entered into a reinsurance arrangement, within such time as may be provided by the notice (not being less than 30 days), to furnish him with such information as he may reasonably require for the purposes of these Regulations.

Inspection of records

15—(1) An officer of the Board authorised for the purposes of this regulation may by notice in writing require any insurance company to which these Regulations apply or any cedant company with which the insurance company has entered into a reinsurance arrangement, within such time as may be provided in the notice (not being less than 30 days), to make available for inspection by that officer in the United Kingdom, such books, documents and other records as are in the company's possession or under the company's control containing information relating to the territory in which any policy holder is, or has been, treated under these Regulations as residing.

(2) The officer to whom the books, documents and other records are made available shall be entitled to take copies, or make extracts from, any books, documents or records made available to him by virtue of paragraph (1) above.

1995/3239

Tax-exempt Special Savings Account (Relevant European Institutions) Regulations 1995

Made by the Commissioners of Inland Revenue under TA 1988 s 326C(1), (1A), 326D

Made	*12 December 1995*
Laid before the House of Commons	*12 December 1995*
Coming into Force	*2 January 1996*

Commentary—*Simon's Direct Tax Service* **E3.401.**

PART I

GENERAL

Citation and commencement

1 These Regulations may be cited as the Tax-exempt Special Savings Account (Relevant European Institutions) Regulations 1995 and shall come into force on 2nd January 1996.

Interpretation

2 In these Regulations—

"the Board" means the Commissioners of Inland Revenue;

"notice" means notice in writing and "notify" shall be construed accordingly;

"the principal Regulations" means the Tax-exempt Special Savings Account Regulations 1990;

"a relevant European institution" has the meaning given by section 326A(10) of the Taxes Act:

"the Taxes Act" means the Income and Corporation Taxes Act 1988;

and in Part III of these Regulations "regulation" means a regulation of the principal Regulations.

PART II
TAX REPRESENTATIVES

Accounts held with relevant European institutions

3—(1) An account held with a relevant European institution shall not be a tax-exempt special savings account at the time it is opened, or shall cease to be a tax-exempt special savings account at a given time, unless at the time concerned one of the following three requirements is fulfilled.

(2) The first requirement is that—

(*a*) a person who falls within subsection (5) of section 326D of the Taxes Act is appointed by the institution to be responsible for securing the discharge of the duties prescribed by regulation 4 which fall to be discharged by the institution, and

(*b*) his identity and the fact of his appointment have been notified to the Board by the institution.

(3) The second requirement is that there are other arrangements with the Board for a person other than the institution to secure the discharge of such duties.

(4) The third requirement is that there are other arrangements with the Board designed to secure the discharge of such duties.

Prescribed duties of tax representatives

4 The duties prescribed by this regulation are those that fall to be discharged by a society or institution under the principal Regulations.

Termination of appointment

5 The appointment of a person in pursuance of the first requirement mentioned in regulation 3(2) shall be treated as terminated in circumstances where—

(*a*) the Board have reason to believe that the person concerned—

(i) has failed to secure the discharge of any of the duties prescribed by regulation 4 or

(ii) does not have adequate resources to discharge those duties; and

(*b*) the Board have notified the institution and that person that they propose to treat his appointment as having terminated with effect from the date specified in the notice.

Powers and liabilities of tax representative

6 Where, in accordance with the first requirement mentioned in regulation 3(2), a person is at any time appointed to be responsible for securing the discharge of duties the person concerned—

(*a*) shall be entitled to act on the institution's behalf for any of the purposes of the provisions relating to the duties;

(*b*) shall secure (where appropriate by acting on the institution's behalf) the institution's compliance with and discharge of the duties;

(*c*) shall be personally liable in respect of any failure of the institution to comply with or discharge any such duty as if the duties imposed on the institution were imposed jointly and severally on the institution and the person concerned.

Effect of section 326B(3) of the Taxes Act

7 Section 326B(3) of the Taxes Act shall have effect as if the reference to subsection (1) included a reference to this Part of these Regulations.

PART III
AMENDMENTS TO THE PRINCIPAL REGULATIONS

8–11 (*Amend* the Tax-exempt Special Savings Account Regulations 1990, SI 1990/2361, regs 2(1), 5, 11, 16.)

1996/21
Friendly Societies (Gilt-edged Securities) (Periodic Accounting for Tax on Interest Regulations 1996

Amendments—These Regulations are revoked by the Friendly Societies (Gilt-edged Securities) (Periodic Accounting for Tax on Interest) Regulations, SI 1999/624 reg 9 with effect for accounting periods beginning before 1 April 1999 and ending after 30 June 1999.

1996/805
Personal Pension Schemes (Deferred Annuity Purchase) (Acceptance of Contributions) Regulations 1996

Made by the Commissions of Inland Revenue under TA 1988 s 638(7A)

Made . . . . *13 March 1996*
Laid before the House of Commons . . . . *15 March 1996*
Coming into Force . . . . *6 April 1996*

Commentary—*Simon's Direct Tax Service* **E7.413.**

1 These Regulations may be cited as the Personal Pension Schemes (Deferred Annuity Purchase) (Acceptance of Contributions) Regulations 1996 and shall come into force on 6th April 1996.

2—(1) In these Regulations—

''member'' and ''personal pension scheme'' have the meanings given by section 630(1);

''pension date'' means the date determined in accordance with arrangements made by a member in accordance with a personal pension scheme on which the member elects—

(*a*) to defer the purchase of an annuity such as is mentioned in section 634, and

(*b*) to make income withdrawals in accordance with section 634A.

(2) Any reference in these Regulations to a particular section is a reference to that section of the Income and Corporation Taxes Act 1988.

3—(1) Paragraph (2) prescribes a case for the purpose of section 638(7A) (restriction on approval of personal pension scheme).

(2) The case prescribed is the acceptance by a personal pension scheme after a member's pension date of minimum contributions paid as mentioned in section 638(6)(*c*) in respect of that member.

1996/1031
Capital Gains Tax (Gilt-edged Securities) Order 1996

Made by the Treasury under TCGA 1992 Sch 9 para 1

Made . . . . *3 April 1996*

1 This Order may be cited as the Capital Gains Tax (Gilt-edged Securities) Order 1996.

2 The following securities are hereby specified for the purposes of Schedule 9 to the Taxation of Chargeable Gains Act 1992—

8% Treasury Stock 2000

8% Treasury Stock 2000 ''A''

$8\frac{1}{2}$% Treasury Stock 2005

$7\frac{1}{2}$% Treasury Stock 2006

8% Treasury Stock 2015

8% Treasury Stock 2015 ''A''.

1996/1179
European Investment Bank (Designated International Organisation) Order 1996

Made by the Treasury under TA 1988 ss 349 (3AB), 840A(1)(*d*)

Made . . . . *29 April 1996*

Commentary—*Simon's Direct Tax Service* **D4.1101.**

1 This Order may be cited as the European Investment Bank (Designated International Organisation) Order 1996.

2 In this Order—

''relevant international organisation'' has the meaning given by section 840A(3) of the Taxes Act;

''the Taxes Act'' means the Income and Corporation Taxes Act 1988.

3—(1) The European Investment Bank being a relevant international organisation is designated as a bank for the purposes of any provision to which paragraph (2) of this article applies.

(2) This paragraph applies to any provision in relation to which it is provided that the word "bank" in that provision has the meaning given by section 840A of the Taxes Act.

4 Paragraph (*a*) of section 349(3) of the Taxes Act, being a provision to which article 3(2) applies, shall apply to the European Investment Bank as if the words from "if" to the end were omitted.

1996/1311

Personal Pension Schemes (Tables of Rates of Annuities) Regulations 1996

Made by the Commissioners of Inland Revenue under TA 1988 s 630(4)

Made	*14 May 1996*
Laid before the House of Commons	*15 May 1996*
Coming into Force	*5 June 1996*

Commentary—*Simon's Direct Tax Service* **E7.406.**

1 These Regulations may be cited as the Personal Pension Schemes (Tables of Annuities) Regulations 1996 and shall come into force on 5th June 1996.

2 In these Regulations—

"member" and "personal pension scheme" have the meanings given by section 630(1) of the Taxes Act;

"protected rights" has the meaning given by section 10 of the Pension Scheme Act 1993;

"the Taxes Act" means the Income and Corporation Taxes Act 1988.

3 The tables of rates of annuities mentioned in section 630(2)(*b*) of the Taxes Act, being tables prepared by the Government Actuary for the purposes of Chapter IV of Part XIV of that Act (personal pension schemes), shall be prepared with respect to rights of a member, or of a widow or widower of a member or a dependant of a deceased member, under a pension scheme—

(*a*) where the rights are protected rights, in accordance with the provisions of regulation 5B(2) and (3) of the Personal and Occupational Pension Schemes (Protected Rights) Regulations 1987;

(*b*) where the rights are other than protected rights, in accordance with the basis specified in regulation 4.

4 The basis specified in this regulation is that—

(*a*) separate tables are prepared for men and for women;

(*b*) no distinction is made by reference to the marital status of a member, or the marital status of a widow or widower of a member or of a dependant of a deceased member;

(*c*) no provision is made for annuity payments to continue after death;

(*d*) the annuity is payable monthly in arrears with no guaranteed period of payment;

(*e*) no increases to the annuity are payable.

1996/1323

Capital Allowances Act 1990, section 33A, (Appointed Day) Order 1996

Made by the Treasury under the Capital Allowances Act 1990, s 33F(3)

Made . . . . *16th May 1996*

1 This Order may be cited as the Capital Allowances Act 1990, section 33A, (Appointed Day) Order 1996.

2 The date appointed for the purposes of section 33A of the Capital Allowances Act 1990 as the date before which no claim under that section may be made is 31st May 1996.

1996/1582

Retirement Benefits Schemes (Restriction on Discretion to Approve) (Excepted Schemes) Regulations 1996

Made by the Commissioners of Inland Revenue under TA 1988 s 591A(2)

Made	*18 June 1996*
Laid before the House of Commons	*19 June 1996*
Coming into Force	*10 July 1996*

Commentary—*Simon's Direct Tax Service* **E7.215.**

1 These Regulations may be cited as the Retirement Benefits Schemes (Restriction on Discretion to Approve) (Excepted Schemes) Regulations 1996 and shall come into force on 10th July 1996.

2 In regulation 3 "the Board" means the Commissioners of Inland Revenue.

3 The description of provision specified for the purposes of section 591A(2) of the Income and Corporation Taxes Act 1988 is any provision specified in the Retirement Benefits Schemes

(Restriction on Discretion to Approve) (Additional Voluntary Contributions) Regulations 1993 that must be contained in a retirement benefits scheme before the Board may approve the scheme by virtue of section 591 of that Act.

1996/1583
Capital Gains Tax (Pension Funds Pooling Schemes) Regulations 1996

Made by the Treasury under TCGA 1992 s 99(3)

Made . . . . *19 June 1996*
Laid before the House of Commons . . . . . *19 June 1996*
Coming into Force . . . . . . *11 July 1996*

Commentary—*Simon's Direct Tax Service* **E7.203.**

1 These Regulations may be cited as the Capital Gains Tax (Pension Funds Pooling Schemes) Regulations 1996 and shall come into force on 11th July 1996.

2 In these Regulations—

"pension funds pooling scheme" means a unit trust scheme of the description specified in regulation 4 of the Income Tax (Pension Funds Pooling Schemes) Regulations 1996;

"unit trust scheme" has the meaning given by section [237(1) of the Financial Services and Markets Act 2000][1].

3 A unit trust scheme which is a pension funds pooling scheme shall be treated as not being a unit trust scheme for the purposes of the Taxation of Chargeable Gains Act 1992.

Amendments—[1] Words in definition of "unit trust scheme" substituted by the Financial Services and Markets Act 2000 (Consequential Amendments) (Taxes) Order, SI 2001/3629 art 143 with effect from 1 December 2001, immediately after the coming into force of the Financial Services and Markets Act 2000 ss 411, 432(1), Sch 20 (and SI 2001/3629 Pts 1 and 2).

1996/1585
Income Tax (Pension Funds Pooling Schemes) Regulations 1996

Made by the Treasury under TA 1988 s 469(7), (8)

Made . . . . *19 June 1996*
Laid before the House of Commons . . . . . *19 June 1996*
Coming into Force . . . . . . *11 July 1996*

Commentary—*Simon's Direct Tax Service* **E7.203.**

Citation and commencement

1 These Regulations may be cited as the Income Tax (Pension Funds Pooling Schemes) Regulations 1996 and shall come into force on 11th July 1996.

Interpretation

2—(1) In these Regulations unless the context otherwise requires—

"address" in relation to any person means—

(*a*) where that person is an individual, the address of his principal place of business or, if he has none, his principal residential address;

(*b*) where that person is a company, the address of its registered or principal office;

"the Board" means the Commissioners of Inland Revenue;

"cancellation event" means an occasion when the rights and interests of a participant in the scheme property of a unit trust scheme are wholly redeemed, or otherwise wholly purchased or wholly cancelled, by the trustee of that scheme, other than an occasion when the rights and interests of the participant in the scheme property become the rights and interests of its successor in the scheme property;

"descendant" in relation to a former participant in a unit trust scheme ("the relevant participant") means the participant for the time being in the scheme which is either the successor of the relevant participant or the successor of another former participant in the scheme which, at the time it so participated, was part of the line of succession of participants that commenced with the relevant participant;

"employee" has the meaning given by section 612(1) of the Taxes Act, and "employer" and other cognate expressions shall be construed accordingly;

"notice" means notice in writing;

"overseas scheme" means a pension funds scheme which—

(*a*) is established outside the United Kingdom, and

(*b*) is not an exempt approved scheme but is for the time being accepted by the Board as equivalent to a retirement benefits scheme approved by the Board for the purposes of Chapter I of Part XIV of the Taxes Act;

"pension funds pooling scheme" means a unit trust scheme of the description specified in regulation 4;

"relevant period" in relation to a unit trust scheme means a period which—

(*a*) commences when the trustee of the scheme first incurs expenditure in respect of which an allowance under the 1990 Act is to be, or may be, made, or next incurs such expenditure after the end of a relevant period, and

(*b*) ends when it is first the case that the trustee of the scheme has disposed of all interests in respect of which such expenditure is incurred, unless immediately after that time the scheme incurs further expenditure in respect of which an allowance under the 1990 Act is to be, or may be, made;

"retirement benefits scheme" has the meaning given by subsection (1) of section 611 of the Taxes Act (read with subsections (2) to (5) of that section);

"scheme" in relation to a pension funds scheme shall be construed in accordance with section 611(2) of the Taxes Act;

"scheme property" in relation to a unit trust scheme means property of any description, including money, which is held on trust for the participants in the scheme;

"section 469" means section 469 of the Taxes Act;

"sponsor" in relation to a pension funds scheme means any person who established the scheme or who for the time being has authority to vary the terms of, or to terminate, the scheme, or to appoint or replace a manager of the scheme;

"successor" in relation to a former participant in a unit trust scheme means the participant which—

(*a*) was not a participant in the scheme immediately before the time when that former participant ceased to participate in the scheme, and

(*b*) immediately after that time became entitled to all the rights and interests in the scheme property to which that former participant was entitled immediately before ceasing so to participate;

"tax year" means a year beginning on 6th April and ending on 5th April in the following calendar year;

"Taxes Act" means the Income and Corporation Taxes Act 1988;

"trustee" in relation to a unit trust scheme means the person or persons for the time being holding the scheme property on trust for the participants in that scheme;

"units" and "unit trust scheme" have the meanings given by section [237 of the Financial Services and Markets Act 2000][1];

"1990 Act" means the Capital Allowances Act 1990;

"1992 Act" means the Taxation of Chargeable Gains Act 1992.

(2) References in these Regulations to an exempt approved scheme are references to a retirement benefits scheme which is either—

(*a*) an exempt approved scheme within the meaning given by subsection (1) of section 592 of the Taxes Act, or

(*b*) before the Board in order for them to decide whether the scheme qualifies as an exempt approved scheme within the meaning of that subsection.

(3) References in these Regulations to a superannuation fund are references to a superannuation fund which either—

(*a*) falls within subsection (6) of section 615 of the Taxes Act, or

(*b*) is before the Board in order for them to decide whether the superannuation fund falls within that subsection.

(4) References in these Regulations to an exempt approved scheme, a superannuation fund or an overseas scheme as a participant in a unit trust scheme, are references to the appropriate person or persons specified in paragraph (5) who is or are for the time being a participant or participants in the unit trust scheme [and, for the purposes of this paragraph, "participant" shall be construed in accordance with section 235 of the Financial Services and Markets Act 2000][1].

(5) The persons specified are—

(*a*) in the case of an exempt approved scheme set up under trust or a superannuation fund, the trustees of that scheme or fund;

(*b*) in the case of an exempt approved scheme not set up under trust, the sponsor of that scheme;

(*c*) in the case of an overseas scheme, the persons who are for the time being parties to the arrangements constituting that scheme, other than an employee in his capacity as a beneficiary of the scheme.

(6) The like provisions as are contained in section 159(2) to (8) of the 1990 Act shall have effect to determine when capital expenditure is to be taken to be incurred for the purposes of these Regulations.

Amendments—[1] In para (1), words in definition of "units" and "unit trust scheme", and words in para (4) substituted by the Financial Services and Markets Act 2000 (Consequential Amendments) (Taxes) Order, SI 2001/3629 art 145 with effect from 1 December 2001, immediately after the coming into force of the Financial Services and Markets Act 2000 ss 411, 432(1), Sch 20 (and SI 2001/3629 Pts 1 and 2).

Exception of pension funds pooling scheme from section 469

3 A unit trust scheme which is a pension funds pooling scheme shall be treated as not being a unit trust scheme for the purposes of section 469.

Description of a pension funds pooling scheme

4—(1) Subject to paragraph (2), a unit trust scheme is a pension funds pooling scheme at any time if at that time it has the characteristics specified in paragraph (3).

(2) A unit trust scheme which at any time in a tax year, or at the end of a tax year, ceases to have the characteristics specified in paragraph (3) is not a pension funds pooling scheme as regards that year.

(3) The characteristics specified in this paragraph are that—

(*a*) subject to regulation 9(10) and (11), each participant in the scheme is—

(i) an exempt approved scheme, or

(ii) a superannuation fund, or

(iii) an overseas scheme;

(*b*) each participant in the scheme has been approved by the Board in accordance with regulation 7 as eligible to participate in the scheme and, subject to regulation 9(10) and (11), that approval has not subsequently been revoked or withdrawn under regulation 7(8) or (9);

(*c*) all the participants in the scheme are jointly absolutely entitled as against the trustee of that scheme, within the meaning of section 60 of the 1992 Act, to the scheme property;

(*d*) subject to paragraph (4), the scheme property consists of any or all of the following—

(i) land;

(ii) buildings or structures on land;

(iii) shares, stock or other investments which are the subject of transactions falling within subsection (12) of section 127 of the Finance Act 1995 (read with subsection (13) of that section);

(iv) investments comprising futures contracts or options contracts relating to land (including contracts falling within subsection (13) of that section);

(*e*) except as provided in paragraph (5), the contributions of the participants are expended on any or all of the following—

(i) the acquisition of, or of rights in or over, land, or the management or development of that land;

(ii) the acquisition or construction of, or the purchase of interests in, buildings or structures on land, or the management or development of those buildings or structures;

(iii) the provision of machinery or plant which is an integral part of those buildings or structures, or the management, alteration or improvement of that machinery or plant;

(iv) the making of any investments falling within sub-paragraph (*d*)(iii) or (iv) above, or the management of those investments;

(*f*) where expenditure falling within sub-paragraph (*e*) is expenditure in respect of which an allowance under the 1990 Act is to be, or may be, made, the terms of the scheme secure that the conditions specified in regulation 5 (read with regulation 6) are satisfied;

(*g*) the terms of the scheme secure that no participant has rights or interests in any part of the scheme property that are different in nature from the rights or interests which any other participant has in that part of the scheme property;

(*h*) the terms of the scheme secure that, in relation to any arrangements which are entered into on or after the date of coming into force of these Regulations—

(i) a participant is obliged to give to the trustee of the scheme, in the situation described, and within the period of time specified, in paragraph (1) of regulation 8, the notification specified in that regulation;

(ii) the trustee of the scheme is irrevocably authorised and obliged to undertake on behalf of the participants the responsibilities specified in regulation 10 and the duties specified in regulations 9 and 11;

(*j*) the trustee of the scheme has given notice to the Board electing for the scheme to be treated, pursuant to these Regulations, the Capital Gains Tax (Pension Funds Pooling Schemes) Regulations 1996, and the Stamp Duty and Stamp Duty Reserve Tax (Pension Funds Pooling Schemes) Regulations 1996, as not being a unit trust scheme for the purposes specified in each of the Regulations.

(4) A unit trust scheme is a pension funds pooling scheme notwithstanding that the scheme property at any time consists wholly or partly of—

(*a*) cash held temporarily by the trustee that is subsequently expended as mentioned in sub-paragraph (*e*) of paragraph (3), or for purposes incidental to, or arising out of, any of the expenditure referred to in that sub-paragraph,

(*b*) cash held temporarily by the trustee that is subsequently expended in making payment to a participant or former participant in the scheme following the redemption, purchase or cancellation of any of the rights or interests of that participant or former participant in the scheme property.

(*c*) cash held temporarily by the trustee that is subsequently expended by way of distribution to the participants generally,

(*d*) cash held temporarily by the trustee that is subsequently expended on the management of the scheme, or the management or development of the scheme property,

(*e*) cash held temporarily by the trustee that is subsequently expended on the acquisition or maintenance of assets falling within sub-paragraph (*f*) below, or

(*f*) other assets held by the trustee in connection with the management of the scheme, or the management or development of the scheme property.

(5) A unit trust scheme is a pension funds pooling scheme notwithstanding that the contributions of the participants are expended—

(*a*) for purposes incidental to, or arising out of, the expenditure referred to in paragraph (3)(*e*),

(*b*) for any of the purposes mentioned in sub-paragraphs (*a*) to (*e*) of paragraph (4), or

(*c*) on the acquisition or maintenance of assets falling within sub-paragraph (*f*) of that paragraph.

(6) In this regulation—

''management'' includes insurance, repair and maintenance;

''development'' includes alteration or improvement.

Expenditure qualifying for capital allowances—specification of conditions

5—(1) The conditions specified for the purposes of regulation 4(3)(*f*) are those set out in paragraphs (2) to (6).

(2) The first condition is that each participant in the scheme in a relevant period is either—

(*a*) an enduring participant, or

(*b*) a participant that is a descendant of a former participant in the scheme which was a participant at the commencement of that period.

(3) The second condition is that, during a relevant period, no participant in the scheme is the successor of more than one former participant which ceased to participate in the scheme—

(*a*) immediately before the commencement of that period, or

(*b*) at the time of the commencement of that period, or

(*c*) at any subsequent time before the end of that period.

(4) The third condition is that during a relevant period—

(*a*) an enduring participant's share of the scheme property remains the same as it was at the commencement of that period, and

(*b*) the share of a participant which is a descendant of a former participant which was a participant at the commencement of the relevant period remains the same as the share of that former participant was at the commencement of that period,

until such time as a cancellation event occurs, or, if earlier, the rights and interests in the scheme property of the participant concerned become the rights and interests in the scheme property of its successor.

(5) The fourth condition is that, immediately after the occurrence of a cancellation event during a relevant period, the ratio that the shares of the scheme property belonging to the participants at that time bear to each other is the same as the ratio that the shares of the scheme property belonging to those participants bore to each other immediately before the occurrence of that event.

(6) The fifth condition is that, following the occurrence of a cancellation event during a relevant period, every participant's share of the scheme property remains the same as it was immediately after the occurrence of that event or, where a participant is a descendant of a former participant which was a participant immediately after the occurrence of that event, the same as the share of that former participant was at that time, until that period ends or, if earlier, a further cancellation event occurs or the rights and interests in the scheme property of the participant concerned become the rights and interests in the scheme property of its successor.

(7) In this regulation ''enduring participant'' in relation to a relevant period means a participant which has been a participant since the commencement of that period.

Expenditure qualifying for capital allowances—provisions supplementary to regulation 5

6—(1) Where the rights and interests of a participant in the scheme property become the rights and interests of its successor in the scheme property at the time when a relevant period commences or a cancellation event occurs during a relevant period, those rights and interests shall be treated, for the purposes of regulation 5, as having become the rights and interests of the successor before the commencement of the relevant period or (as the case may be) the occurrence of the cancellation event.

(2) Where the rights and interests of a participant in the scheme property become the rights and interests of its successor in the scheme property at the time when a relevant period ends, those rights and interests shall be treated, for the purposes of regulation 5, as having become the rights and interests of the successor after the end of that period.

(3) Where contributions by participants in the scheme are made at the time when—

(*a*) a relevant period commences, or
(*b*) a cancellation event occurs during a relevant period, or
(*c*) a relevant period ends,

those contributions shall be treated, for the purposes of regulation 5, as having been made before the commencement of the relevant period or the occurrence of the cancellation event, or after the end of the relevant period (as the case may be).

(4) Where during a relevant period the rights and interests of a participant in the scheme property become the rights and interests of its successor in the scheme property at the same time as the trustee of the scheme makes a disposal of any interest or rights in or over an asset which, immediately before that disposal was made, formed part of the scheme property, the disposal shall be treated, for the purposes of regulation 5, as having been made after the participant's rights and interests in the scheme property have become the successor's rights and interests in the scheme property.

(5) Where, as a result of a business reorganisation, amalgamation or other form of reconstruction, a merger of participants occurs, that is, the whole of the rights and interests of two or more participants in the scheme property become the whole of the rights and interests of a single participant in the scheme property, then for the purposes of regulation 5—

(*a*) where the merger occurs at the time when a relevant period commences, it shall be treated as having occurred before that time;
(*b*) where the merger occurs at the time when a relevant period ends, it shall be treated as having occurred after that time;
(*c*) where the merger occurs during a relevant period, it shall be treated as never having occurred.

(6) Where, as a result of a business reorganisation, fragmentation or other form of reconstruction, a demerger relating to participants occurs, that is, the whole of the rights and interests of a single participant in the scheme property (''the demerging participant'') become the whole of the rights and interests of two or more participants in the scheme property (''the replacement participants''), then for the purposes of regulation 5—

(*a*) where the demerger occurs at the time when a relevant period commences or a cancellation event occurs during a relevant period, it shall be treated as having occurred before that time;
(*b*) where the demerger occurs at the time when a relevant period ends, it shall be treated as having occurred after that time;
(*c*) where the demerger occurs during a relevant period, the demerging participant shall be treated as having been comprised of participants whose successors are the replacement participants.

(7) For the purposes of paragraph (6)(*c*), where one of the replacement participants is the demerging participant, that participant shall be treated as if, in its capacity as a replacement participant, it were a separate and distinct participant from the demerging participant.

(8) In paragraph (4) ''disposal'' shall be construed in accordance with the provisions of Chapter II of Part II of the 1992 Act relating to disposals of assets.

(9) Where during a relevant period of a unit trust scheme it first occurs that the scheme has the characteristics specified in regulation 4(3), that period shall be treated, for the purposes of regulation 5 and this regulation, as having commenced at the time of that first occurrence.

Approval of participants

7—(1) An application for approval of a scheme or fund as eligible to participate in a pension funds pooling scheme shall be made in writing by the trustee of that pension funds pooling scheme to the Board and shall contain the information specified in paragraph (2) or, as the case may be, in paragraph (3) or (4).

(2) As regards an exempt approved scheme or a superannuation fund, the information is—

(*a*) the full title of the scheme or fund;
(*b*) the Board's reference number relating to the scheme or fund.

(3) As regards an overseas scheme other than a scheme falling within paragraph (4) below, the information is—

(*a*) the full title of the scheme;
(*b*) where the scheme is established under trust, the names and addresses of the sponsors and trustees of the scheme;
(*c*) where the scheme is not established under trust, the names and addresses of the sponsors and managers of the scheme;
(*d*) the names and addresses of any employers who contribute to, but are not sponsors of, the scheme;
(*e*) where the arrangements constituting the scheme are made between two or more persons, details of any undertakings or promises made between any of those persons that are, or are likely to be, relevant to the custodianship of any rights or interests of that scheme in the pension funds pooling scheme, and the name and address of each of those persons;
(*f*) identification of the legislative and, if applicable, the regulatory provision under which the scheme is authorised for tax or supervisory purposes;

(*g*) a copy of any letter or other document issued by the relevant tax authority or by the relevant supervisory authority confirming the authorised status of the scheme, together with a translation into English where the letter or other document is in a language other than English;

(*h*) the normal age of retirement under the scheme for male employees and female employees respectively;

(*i*) details showing how the amounts of the contributions payable to the scheme by employers and employees are calculated in respect of all employees who are members of the scheme within the meaning given by section 591D(8) of the Taxes Act;

(*j*) details of the amounts of any contributions payable to the scheme by a person in a capacity other than that of employer or employee;

(*k*) details of the amounts of any supplementary voluntary contributions (including single lump sum contributions) which an employee is entitled to pay to the scheme;

(*l*) details of any benefits, including loans, which may be provided by the scheme to or on behalf of an employee on death or on or during retirement;

(*m*) details of any benefits, including loans, which may be provided by the scheme to or on behalf of an employee otherwise than on death or on or during retirement;

(*n*) details of any withdrawals which may be made from the scheme by or on behalf of an employee otherwise than on death or on or during retirement;

(*o*) where the scheme enables loans or other benefits to be provided within sub-paragraph (*m*), or withdrawals to be made within sub-paragraph (*n*), or any other benefits to be provided which are not related to employment, a copy of the rules of the scheme together with a translation into English where the rules are in a language other than English.

(4) As regards an overseas scheme falling within a class or description of scheme in relation to which the Board have announced that they are satisfied, having regard to the legislative provision under which the scheme is established, or the supervisory control of the operation of the scheme by the government of the territory in which it is established, that the information specified in sub-paragraphs (*h*) to (*o*) of paragraph (3) is not required, the information is the like information as that specified in sub-paragraphs (*a*) to (*g*) of that paragraph.

(5) Where the Board determine to approve a scheme or fund pursuant to an application under paragraph (1), they shall give notice of the approval to the trustee of the pension funds pooling scheme.

(6) Approval may be given by the Board in full where they are satisfied that the scheme or fund is eligible to participate in the pension funds pooling scheme, or may be given on a provisional basis—

(*a*) in the case of a scheme falling within paragraph (3), pending the Board's consideration of information received by them pursuant to that paragraph, or

(*b*) in the case of an exempt approved scheme or a superannuation fund which is before the Board for the purpose referred to in regulation 2(2)(*b*) or (3)(*b*) (as the case may be).

(7) On receipt of a notice of approval, the trustee of the pension funds pooling scheme may admit the scheme or fund which is the subject of the notice to be a participant in the pension funds pooling scheme.

(8) The Board shall, by notice to the trustee, either convert to full approval or revoke an approval given on a provisional basis and, where the approval is revoked, the notice shall state the reason why it is considered by the Board that the participant is not eligible to participate in the pension funds pooling scheme.

(9) The Board may, by notice to the trustee, withdraw approval of a participant where they are satisfied that a participant is not eligible to participate in the pension funds pooling scheme, and the notice shall state the reason why it is considered by the Board that the participant is not so eligible.

(10) In this regulation references to a pension funds pooling scheme include references to any arrangements which, although not constituting such a scheme at the time an application for approval is made under paragraph (1), have been entered into with the intention that they will constitute such a scheme, and references to the trustee of a pension funds pooling scheme shall be construed accordingly.

Notification by participant of non-eligibility

8—(1) On becoming aware that, by reason of a change in its circumstances or otherwise, it is not, or may not be, eligible to participate in a pension funds pooling scheme, a participant shall notify the trustee of the scheme in writing of that fact within seven days after its becoming so aware.

(2) A notification under paragraph (1)—

(*a*) shall state the reason why the participant considers that it is not, or may not be, so eligible, and

(*b*) shall be accompanied by a copy of any document in the participant's possession that confirms or suggests that it is not, or may not be, so eligible.

Duties of trustee of a pension funds pooling scheme—participants ceasing to be eligible to participate

9—(1) On receiving a notification by a participant in accordance with regulation 8(1), the trustee of a pension funds pooling scheme shall, within 14 days after the date of receipt of the notification, give notice to the Board that a notification has been received by him.

(2) A notice under paragraph (1) shall state the full title of the participant concerned and, in the case of a notification received from a participant which is an exempt approved scheme or a superannuation fund, the Board's reference number relating to that participant.

(3) A notice under paragraph (1) shall be accompanied by—

(*a*) a copy of the notification received from the participant, and

(*b*) a copy of the information provided by the participant to the trustee in accordance with regulation 8(2)(*b*), together with a translation of that information into English where the document in which the information is comprised is in a language other than English.

(4) Where, as a result of receiving any information, other than information provided in accordance with regulation 8(1), the trustee of a pension funds pooling scheme has reason to believe that—

(*a*) in the case of a participant which is an exempt approved scheme or a superannuation fund, the participant is not eligible to participate in the scheme, or

(*b*) in the case of a participant which is an overseas scheme, the Board would be likely, were they to be in possession of the information received by the trustee, to have reason to revoke or withdraw their approval of the participant under regulation 7(8) or (9),

the trustee shall, within 14 days after the date of receipt of that information, give notice to the Board containing the information specified in paragraph (5).

(5) The information specified in this paragraph is—

(*a*) the full title of the participant,

(*b*) in the case of a participant which is an exempt approved scheme or a superannuation fund, the Board's reference number relating to the scheme or fund concerned,

(*c*) details of the information received by the trustee;

(*d*) a statement setting out the reasons for the trustee's belief that—

(i) in the case of a participant which is an exempt approved scheme or a superannuation fund, the participant is not eligible to participate in the scheme, or

(ii) in the case of a participant which is an overseas scheme, the Board would be likely to have reason to revoke or withdraw their approval of the participant.

(6) A notice under paragraph (4) above shall be accompanied by a copy of any document in the trustee's possession that contains information in support of his belief as mentioned in paragraph (5)(*d*), together with a translation of that information into English where the document is in a language other than English.

(7) Where a notice is given by the trustee under paragraph (1) or (4) in relation to a participant which is an overseas scheme, an officer of the Board may, for the purpose of ascertaining whether or not the participant is eligible to participate in the scheme, by notice require the trustee to furnish him, within such time (not being less than 21 days) as may be provided by the notice, such information relating to the participant as is specified in regulation 7(3) (whether or not the participant is an overseas scheme to which regulation 7(4) applies).

(8) On receiving a notice given by the Board revoking or withdrawing approval under regulation 7(8) or (9), the trustee of the scheme shall forthwith give notice to the participant concerned that every unit in the scheme held by the participant, or by a nominee on its behalf, will be sold or cancelled by the trustee within 28 days after the date on which the notice given by the Board was received by the trustee.

(9) A notice given by the trustee under paragraph (8) shall state the reason why the participant is not eligible to participate in the scheme.

(10) Where all the units referred to in paragraph (8) are sold or cancelled by the trustee within the period of 28 days referred to in that paragraph, the unit trust scheme shall not cease to have the characteristics specified in regulation 4(3)(*a*) and (*b*).

(11) Where any of the units referred to in paragraph (8) are not sold or cancelled by the trustee within the period of 28 days referred to in that paragraph, the unit trust scheme shall be regarded as ceasing to satisfy the characteristics specified in regulation 4(3)(*a*) and (*b*) with effect from the date on which the notice given by the Board under regulation 7(8) or (9) was received by the trustee.

(12) References in this regulation to a participant which is an exempt approved scheme or a superannuation fund include references to a participant which is no longer an exempt approved scheme or a superannuation fund but which was such a scheme or fund at the time when notice of approval was given by the Board to the trustee in accordance with regulation 7(5).

Responsibilities of trustee of a pension funds pooling scheme

10—(1) The trustee of a pension funds pooling scheme shall be responsible for negotiating and agreeing with an officer of the Board on behalf of the participants the matters specified in paragraph (2).

(2) The matters specified in this paragraph are—

(*a*)

(i) a method of calculating the amount of any income arising from the scheme property in each accounting period of the scheme, and of attributing to each participant the appropriate allocation of that amount;

(ii) the amount of any income arising from the scheme property in each accounting period of the scheme, and the amount of that income that is attributable to each participant;

(*b*) the amount of any profits or gains arising in each accounting period of the scheme in respect of rents or receipts from the scheme property in that period that are attributable to each of those participants in the scheme which are chargeable on such profits or gains under Schedule A;

(*c*) the amount of any interest of money or other annual profits or gains from the scheme property arising in each accounting period of the scheme that are attributable to each of those participants in the scheme which are chargeable on such interest or other annual profits or gains under Schedule D;

(*d*) the amount of any dividends or other distributions from the scheme property arising in each accounting period of the scheme that are attributable to each of those participants in the scheme which are chargeable on such dividends or other distributions under Schedule F;

(*e*)

(i) where in an accounting period an event occurs that gives rise, or may give rise, to a balancing allowance or a balancing charge under the 1990 Act to or on those participants which were participants immediately before or immediately after that event, a method of computing the amount of the balancing allowance or charge attributable to each of those participants;

(ii) the amount of the balancing allowance or charge referred to in paragraph (*i*) of this sub-paragraph that is attributable to each of the participants concerned;

(*f*) in relation to expenditure to which regulation 4(3)(*f*) applies, the amount of any such expenditure incurred in each accounting period of the scheme which is—

(i) capital expenditure for a chargeable period in relation to which Part I of the 1990 Act applies, or

(ii) capital expenditure on the provision of machinery or plant in respect of which a writing-down allowance is to be, or may be, made in accordance with sections 24 to 26 of the 1990 Act;

(*g*) the amount of the expenditure calculated in accordance with sub-paragraph (*f*) for an accounting period that is attributable to each participant;

(*h*) where, in relation to a building or structure which forms part of the scheme property, an event occurs in an accounting period which gives rise, or may give rise, to a balancing allowance or a balancing charge under the 1990 Act to or on each of the participants which were participants immediately before or immediately after that event, the amount of any sale, insurance, salvage or compensation moneys within the meaning of section 156 of the 1990 Act which are relevant to that event;

(*j*) the disposal value, calculated in accordance with section 26 of the 1990 Act, of any plant and machinery forming part of the scheme property which is or may be required to be brought into account for a chargeable period;

(*k*) the form of the certificate referred to in paragraph (3).

(3) The trustee of a pension funds pooling scheme shall also be responsible for providing within three months after the end of each accounting period of the scheme to each participant in the scheme in that period, a certificate in relation to that participant showing the information specified in paragraph (4).

(4) The information specified in this paragraph is—

(*a*) the amount of the income agreed with the officer of the Board under paragraph (2)(*a*)(ii) which is attributable to that participant for the accounting period concerned;

(*b*) the amount (if any) agreed with the officer of the Board under paragraph (2)(*b*) to be chargeable under Schedule A which is attributable to that participant for the accounting period concerned;

(*c*) the amount (if any) agreed with the officer of the Board under paragraph (2)(*c*) to be chargeable under Schedule D which is attributable to that participant for the accounting period concerned;

(*d*) the amount (if any) agreed with the officer of the Board under paragraph (2)(*d*) to be chargeable under Schedule F which is attributable to that participant for the accounting period concerned;

(*e*) where in the accounting period concerned an event occurs that gives rise to a balancing allowance or a balancing charge under the 1990 Act, the amount (if any) of that allowance or charge agreed with the officer of the Board under paragraph (2)(*e*)(ii) which is attributable to that participant for that period;

(*f*) the amount (if any) of the expenditure agreed with the officer of the Board under paragraph (2)(*g*) which is attributable to that participant for the accounting period concerned;

(*g*) where applicable, the parts of amounts of sale, insurance, salvage or compensation moneys in relation to events occurring in the accounting period concerned, and of the disposal values of plant and machinery agreed with the officer of the Board under paragraph (2)(*h*) and (*j*), which are attributable to that participant for that period.

(5) In this regulation any reference to a participant in the scheme in relation to an accounting period includes a reference to a participant which, although not a participant throughout that period, was a participant at some time during that period.

Duties of trustee of a pension funds pooling scheme—annual provision of information

11—(1) Where, at the end of a tax year, a unit trust scheme has the characteristics specified in regulation 4(3), the trustee of that scheme shall, within three months after the end of that year ("the relevant year"), provide to an officer of the Board, in a form authorised, or in the form provided, by the Board—

(*a*) the information concerning each participant in the scheme specified in paragraph (2), or, as the case may be, paragraph (3), and

(*b*) a declaration made by the trustee and signed by him or, if the trustee is a company, signed by the company secretary or other person authorised by the company for that purpose, that the information so provided is correct to the best of the declarant's knowledge and belief.

(2) As regards a participant in the relevant year which is an exempt approved scheme or a superannuation fund, the information is—

(*a*) the full title of the scheme or fund;

(*b*) the Board's reference number relating to the scheme or fund;

(*c*) a copy of any certificate referred to in regulation 10(3) which was supplied by the trustee to the participant in respect of any accounting period of the scheme ending in or at the end of the relevant year;

(*d*) where the trustee has in the relevant year received a notice given by the Board under regulation 7(8) or (9) revoking or withdrawing approval in relation to that participant—

(i) a copy of the notice given to the participant by the trustee under regulation 9(8);

(ii) the date or dates (if any), whether during the relevant year or subsequently but prior to the making of the declaration under paragraph (1)(*b*), on which units held by the participant, or by a nominee on its behalf, at the time the notice given by the Board was received by the trustee, were sold or cancelled;

(iii) if applicable, the date on which the participant ceased to participate in the scheme;

(*e*) where the trustee has not, whether in the relevant year or subsequently but prior to the making of the declaration under paragraph (1)(*b*), received a notice given by the Board under regulation 7(8) or (9) revoking or withdrawing approval in relation to that participant, confirmation that the participant had not at any time in that year received notification from the Board that it was not an exempt approved scheme or, as the case may be, a superannuation fund.

(3) As regards a participant in the relevant year which is an overseas scheme, the information is—

(*a*) the full title of the scheme;

(*b*) details of any matters falling within sub-paragraphs (*b*) to (*g*) and, where the scheme is not one to which regulation 7(4) applies, sub-paragraphs (*h*) to (*o*) of regulation 7(3) which, by reason of changes to those matters having occurred in the relevant year, differ from—

(i) the details of those matters which were included in the trustee's application under regulation 7(1) in respect of the participant, or

(ii) (if applicable) the details of those matters which were most recently provided in accordance with this sub-paragraph in respect of the participant in relation to tax years ending before the relevant year;

(*c*) the like information as is specified in paragraph (2)(*c*);

(*d*) if applicable, the like information as is specified in paragraph (2)(*d*).

(4) As regards a participant in the relevant year which is an overseas scheme, an officer of the Board may, at any time after the form referred to in paragraph (1) has been provided to him by the trustee of the scheme, by notice require the trustee to furnish him, within such time (not being less than 21 days) as may be provided by the notice, with a statement in writing setting out details of matters—

(*a*) falling within sub-paragraphs (*b*) to (*g*) and, where the scheme is not one to which regulation 7(4) applies, sub-paragraphs (*h*) to (*o*) of regulation 7(3) with respect to that scheme, and

(*b*) subsisting at any time during the relevant year.

(5) In this regulation any reference to a participant in the relevant year which is an exempt approved scheme or a superannuation fund or an overseas scheme (as the case may be)—

(*a*) includes a reference to a participant which, although not a participant throughout that year, was a participant at some time during that year, and

(*b*) includes a reference to a participant which is no longer an exempt approved scheme or a superannuation fund or an overseas scheme but which was such a scheme or fund at the time when notice of approval was given by the Board to the trustee of the scheme in accordance with regulation 7(5).

1996/1654
Income Tax (Payments on Account) Regulations 1996

Made by the Commissioners of Inland Revenue under TMA 1970 s 59A(1)

Made	*26 June 1996*
Laid before the House of Commons	*26 June 1996*
Coming into Force	*17 July 1996*

Commentary—*Simon's Direct Tax Service* **E1.821.**

1—(1) These Regulations may be cited as the Income Tax (Payments on Account) Regulations 1996 and shall come into force on 17th July 1996.

(2) Regulation 3 shall have effect as respects the year 1996–97 and subsequent years of assessment.

(3) Regulation 4 shall have effect as respects the year 1997–98 and subsequent years of assessment.

2 In these Regulations "subsection (1)" means subsection (1) of section 59A of the Taxes Management Act 1970.

3 The prescribed amount for the purposes of paragraph (*c*) of subsection (1) is the amount of £500.

4 The prescribed proportion for the purposes of paragraph (*d*) of subsection (1), that is to say, the proportion which the relevant amount as mentioned in paragraph (*c*) of subsection (1) bears to the assessed amount as mentioned in paragraph (*b*) of subsection (1), is the proportion of one to [five][1].

Amendments—[1] Amount in regulation 4 substituted by the Income Tax (Payments on Account) (Amendment) Regulations, SI 1997/2491 with effect from 7 November 1997.

1996/1826
Manufactured Overseas Dividends (French Indemnity Payments) Regulations 1996

Made by the Treasury under TA 1988 Sch 23A paras 1(1), 8

Made	*12 July 1996*
Laid before the House of Commons	*15 July 1996*
Coming into Force	*1 August 1996*

Commentary—*Simon's Direct Tax Service* **A7.824.**

Citation and commencement

1 These Regulations may be cited as the Manufactured Overseas Dividends (French Indemnity Payments) Regulations 1996 and shall come into force on 1st August 1996.

Interpretation

2—(1) In these Regulations—

"French equities" means shares of any company resident in France;

"French indemnity payment" means a payment, representative of a dividend on French equities, that a party to a transaction for the sale of those equities is required, under the rules of the Society of French Stock Exchanges, to make to the other party to that transaction;

"manufactured overseas dividend" shall be construed in accordance with paragraph 4(1) of Schedule 23A;

"Schedule 23A" means Schedule 23A to the Taxes Act;

"the Tax Acts" has the meaning given by section 831(2) of the Taxes Act;

"the Taxes Act" means the Income and Corporation Taxes Act 1988.

(2) References in these Regulations to "the dividend concerned" are references to the dividend of which a French indemnity payment is representative.

(3) References in these Regulations to "the sale and repurchase of French equities" shall be construed in accordance with section 730A of the Taxes Act (read with the modifications to that enactment made in relation to the redemption and substitution of securities by regulations 3 and 5 of the Sale and Repurchase of Securities (Modification of Enactments) Regulations 1995).

Tax treatment of French indemnity payments

3—(1) This regulation applies where a person makes or receives a payment of a manufactured overseas dividend that is a French indemnity payment, other than a payment which arises from an arrangement for the sale and repurchase of French equities.

(2) For the purposes of the Tax Acts—

(*a*) [paragraph 4][1] of Schedule 23A shall not apply in relation to the indemnity payment, but where the maker of the payment receives the dividend concerned, he (and no other person) shall be chargeable to tax in respect of that dividend;

(*b*) subject to paragraph (3)—

(i) relief by way of deduction in computing profits or gains, or deduction or set off against income or total profits, shall not be given under any provision of the Tax Acts in respect of the indemnity payment to the maker of the payment, and

(ii) the indemnity payment shall not be chargeable to tax.

(3) For the purposes of the Tax Acts and the Taxation of Chargeable Gains Act 1992 the amount paid or payable in respect of the sale of the French equities to which the dividend concerned relates shall, as respects both the seller and the purchaser of those equities, be taken as reduced by the amount of the indemnity payment.

(4) Any entitlement to relief under Part XVIII of the Taxes Act (double taxation relief) in respect of the indemnity payment shall be extinguished.

Amendments—[1] Words in para (2)(*a*) substituted by the Manufactured Overseas Dividends (French Indemnity Payments) (Amendment) Regulations, SI 1996/2642 reg 2, with effect from 6 November 1996.

4—(1) This regulation applies where a person makes or receives a payment of a manufactured overseas dividend that is a French indemnity payment arising from an arrangement for the sale and repurchase of French equities.

(2) For the purposes of the Tax Acts—

(*a*) [paragraph 4][1] of Schedule 23A shall not apply in relation to the indemnity payment, but where the maker of the payment receives the dividend concerned, he (and no other person) shall be chargeable to tax in respect of that dividend;

(*b*) the indemnity payment shall be treated as an annual payment, within section 349(1) of the Taxes Act, but so that no amount is required to be deducted on account of income tax from the amount of the payment, or accounted for under section 350 of that Act;

(*c*) in relation to a recipient of the indemnity payment, or a person claiming title to it through or under him, who is resident in the United Kingdom or, if not so resident, is carrying on business through a branch or agency in the United Kingdom, the payment shall be treated as if it were an overseas dividend of an amount equal to the amount of the payment, but without prejudice to paragraph (3).

(3) Any entitlement to relief under Part XVIII of the Taxes Act in respect of the indemnity payment shall be extinguished.

Amendments—[1] Words in para (2)(*a*) substituted by the Manufactured Overseas Dividends (French Indemnity Payments) (Amendment) Regulations, SI 1996/2642 reg 2, with effect from 6 November 1996.

1996/2396

Taxation of Benefits under Pilot Schemes (Earnings Top-up) Order 1996

Made by the Treasury under FA 1996 s 151(1)(*a*), (2), (5), (7)

Made . . . . *13 September 1996*
Laid before the House of Commons . . *16 September 1996*
Coming into Force . . . . *8 October 1996*

Commentary—*Simon's Direct Tax Service* **E4.238.**

Citation, commencement and effect

1—(1) This Order may be cited as the Taxation of Benefits under Pilot Schemes (Earnings Top-up) Order 1996 and shall come into force on 8th October 1996.

(2) This Order shall have effect in relation to amounts of Earnings Top-up payable on or after 8th October 1996.

Interpretation

2 In this Order—

"benefit" shall be construed in accordance with section 151(6) of the Finance Act 1996;

"Earnings Top-up" means the benefit payable under that name by virtue of a Government pilot scheme;

"Government pilot scheme" has the meaning given by subsections (3) and (4) of section 151 of the Finance Act 1996.

Exemption of Earnings Top-up from income tax

3 The Income Tax Acts shall have effect in relation to any amount of Earnings Top-up as if it were wholly exempt from income tax and, accordingly, to be disregarded in computing the amount of any receipts brought into account for income tax purposes.

1996/2645
Income and Corporation Taxes Act 1988, section 737A, (Appointed Day) Order 1996

Made by the Treasury under the Income and Corporation Taxes Act 1988, s 737B(9)

Made . . . . *16 October 1996*

1 This Order may be cited as the Income and Corporation Taxes Act 1988, section 737A, (Appointed Day) Order 1996.

2 The day appointed for the purposes of section 737A of the Income and Corporation Taxes Act 1988 in relation to agreements to sell overseas securities entered into on or after that day is 6th November 1996.

1996/2991
Insurance Companies (Reserves) (Tax) Regulations 1996

Made by the Treasury under TA 1988 ss 444BA(10), 444BB(1), (3), (4), (5), 444BC, 444BD(1), (4), (5)

Made . . . . . *27 November 1996*
Laid before the House of Commons . . . *28 November 1996*
Coming into Force . . . . . *23 December 1996*

Commentary—*Simon's Direct Tax Service* **D4.538.**

ARRANGEMENT OF REGULATIONS

PART I
GENERAL

PART II
EQUALISATION RESERVES, ETC

Overall scope

Accounting on a non-annual basis

General provisions

PART III
RESERVES MAINTAINED FOR THE PURPOSES OF CREDIT INSURANCE BUSINESS

PART I

GENERAL

Citation, commencement and effect

1 These Regulations may be cited as the Insurance Companies (Reserves) (Tax) Regulations 1996, shall come into force on 23rd December 1996, and shall have effect for accounting periods of insurance companies ending on or after that day.

Interpretation

2—(1) In these Regulations unless the context otherwise requires—

''the Board'' means the Commissioners of Inland Revenue;

''branch'' includes agency;

[''company tax return'' has the meaning given by paragraph 3(1) of Schedule 18 to the Finance Act 1998;][2]

''credit insurance business'' has the meaning given by subsection (7) of section 444BD;

''credit insurance equalisation reserve'' means a reserve which is an equivalent reserve for the purposes of section 444BD by virtue of subsection (3) of that section;

''double taxation relief'' has the meaning given by subsection (6) of section 444BB;

[''EEA firm'' means an EEA firm of the kind mentioned in paragraph 5(*d*) of Schedule 3 to the Financial Services and Markets Act 2000;][1]

''equivalent reserve'' shall be construed in accordance with section 444BD;

[''equalisation reserves rules'' means the rules in Chapter 6 of the Prudential Sourcebook (Insurers);][2]

...[2]

''paragraph 52 method of accounting on a non-annual basis'' means the method of accounting on a non-annual basis described in paragraph 52 of Schedule 9A to the Companies Act 1985;

[''the Prudential Sourcebook (Insurers)'' means the Interim Prudential Sourcebook for Insurers made by the Financial Services Authority under the Financial Services and Markets Act 2000;][2]

''return period'' means the period covered in a document prepared by an insurance company for the purposes of section [9.3 of the Prudential Sourcebook (Insurers)][2];

...[2]

''section 444BA'', ''section 444BB'', ''section 444BC'' and ''section 444BD'' means sections 444BA, 444BB, 444BC and 444BD respectively of the Taxes Act;

''the Taxes Act'' means the Income and Corporation Taxes Act 1988;

[''Treaty firm'' means a firm which has permission under paragraph 4 of Schedule 4 to the Financial Services and Markets Act 2000 (as a result of qualifying for authorisation under paragraph 2 of that Schedule) to effect or carry out contracts of insurance in the United Kingdom and, in this definition, ''contract of insurance'' has the meaning given by Article 3(1) of the Financial Services and Markets Act 2000 (Regulated Activities) Order 2001;][1]

...[2]

(2) In these Regulations ''statutory accounts'', in relation to a company, means—

(*a*) the annual accounts of the company prepared in accordance with Part VII of the Companies Act 1985, or

(*b*) if the company is not required to prepare such accounts, the accounts which it is required to keep under the law of its home state or, if it is not so required to keep accounts, such of its accounts as most closely correspond to accounts which it would have been required to prepare if the provisions of that Part applied to the company.

(3) For the purposes of these Regulations a return period and an accounting period are related if any day falls within both the return period and the accounting period.

Amendments—[1] Definition of ''EEA firm'' substituted for definition of ''EC company'', and definition of ''Treaty firm'' inserted, by the Financial Services and Markets Act 2000 (Consequential Amendments) (Taxes) Order, SI 2001/3629 art 147(1), (3), (9) with effect from 1 December 2001, immediately after the coming into force of the Financial Services and Markets Act 2000 ss 411, 432(1), Sch 20 (and SI 2001/3629 Pts 1 and 2).

[2] Definition of ''company tax return'', ''equalisation reserve rules'' and ''the Prudential sourcebook (Insurers)'' inserted, definition of ''the Management Act'', ''section 34A regulations, and ''the 1982 Act'' revoked, and words in the definition of ''return period'' substituted, by SI 2001/3629 art 147(1), (2), (4)–(8), (10), (11) with effect for periods of account ending after 30 November 2001.

Differing treatments of reserves

3—(1) This regulation applies in any case where for any accounting period—

(*a*) an insurance company maintains any reserve to which these Regulations apply, and

(*b*) the amount of that reserve for the purposes of the Tax Acts is different from the amount of that reserve as maintained for regulatory purposes.

(2) A separate computation of the amount of the reserve for the purposes of the Tax Acts and of the amount of the reserve as maintained for regulatory purposes shall be made for each accounting period until, in any later accounting period, the two computations produce the same opening balance for the reserve.

(3) For the purposes of this regulation a reserve is maintained by a company for regulatory purposes if it is maintained—

(*a*) by virtue of [equalisation reserves rules][1], or

(*b*) for the purposes of the company's statutory accounts, or

(*c*) for the purposes of any credit insurance business in accordance with requirements specified in subsection (3) of section 444BD.

Amendments—[1] Words in sub-para (3)(*a*) substituted by the Financial Services and Markets Act 2000 (Consequential Amendments) (Taxes) Order, SI 2001/3629 art 151 with effect for periods of account ending after 30 November 2001.

PART II

EQUALISATION RESERVES, ETC

Overall scope

Scope of this Part

4—(1) Subject to paragraph (2), this Part of these Regulations applies to—

(*a*) any equalisation reserve which an insurance company is required to maintain by virtue of [equalisation reserves rules][1], and

(*b*) any reserve which is an equivalent reserve by virtue of subsection (2) of section 444BD.

(2) This part of these Regulations does not apply to any credit insurance equalisation reserve.

Amendments—[1] Words in sub-para (1)(*a*) substituted by the Financial Services and Markets Act 2000 (Consequential Amendments) (Taxes) Order, SI 2001/3629 art 151 with effect for periods of account ending after 30 November 2001.

Accounting on a non-annual basis

Non-annual accounts: tax returns prepared on an annual basis

5—(1) This regulation applies in any case where an insurance company—

(*a*) for the purpose of preparing the documents it is required to prepare for the purposes of section [9.3 of the Prudential Sourcebook (Insurers)][1], has applied a paragraph 52 method of accounting on a non-annual basis for any return period in respect of the whole or any part of its business, and

(*b*) for a related accounting period has submitted to an officer of the Board a [company tax return][1] which is based on accounts prepared on an annual basis in respect of the whole of its business for that accounting period.

(2) The operation of paragraphs (*a*) and (*b*) of subsection (2) of section 444BA shall be modified so as to provide that, for the purposes of the Tax Acts, the amounts which, in accordance with [equalisation reserves rules][2], are transferred into or out of the equalisation reserve in respect of the company's business for the accounting period in question shall be the amounts which would have been transferred into or out of the equalisation reserve if the company had been required, by virtue of [equalisation reserves rules][2], to maintain an equalisation reserve by reference to accounts prepared on an accident year basis.

(3) For the purposes of paragraph (1)(*b*) accounts are prepared on an annual basis where they are prepared otherwise than in accordance with a paragraph 52 method of accounting on a non-annual basis.

(4) For the purposes of paragraph (2) accounts are prepared on an accident year basis where the accounts and statements required to be deposited with the [Financial Services Authority pursuant to Chapter 9 of the Prudential Sourcebook (Insurers)] are prepared using Forms 21, 22 and 23 [prescribed by the Accounts and Statements Rules contained in that Chapter][1].

Amendments—[1] Words in paras (1), (4) substituted by the Financial Services and Markets Act 2000 (Consequential Amendments) (Taxes) Order, SI 2001/3629 art 148 with effect for periods of account ending after 30 November 2001.

[2] Words in para (2) substituted by the Financial Services and Markets Act 2000 (Consequential Amendments) (Taxes) Order, SI 2001/3629 art 151 with effect for periods of account ending after 30 November 2001.

General provisions

Companies carrying on mutual business and business other than mutual business

6—(1) This regulation applies in any case where an insurance company which, in accordance with [equalisation reserves rules][1], is required to make transfers into or out of an equalisation reserve in respect of any business carried on by that company for any accounting period, is carrying on both mutual business and business other than mutual business for the whole or any part of that period.

(2) Paragraphs (*a*) and (*b*) of subsection (2) of section 444BA shall be modified so as to provide that, for the purposes of corporation tax, the amounts of the net premiums earned, the net premiums written and the net claims incurred which, in accordance with [equalisation reserves rules][1], are used for the purpose of computing the amounts transferred into or out of the equalisation reserve or the

amount of the maximum reserve in relation to the equalisation reserve for the accounting period in question, shall be restricted to the amounts attributed to business other than mutual business.

(3) For the purposes of corporation tax, the modifications specified in paragraph (2) shall be made before subsections (4) to (6) of section 444BA are applied.

(4) In paragraph (2) "net premiums earned", "net premiums written", "net claims incurred" and "maximum reserve" have the meanings given by [equalisation reserves rules][1].

Amendments—[1] Words in paras (1), (2) and (4) substituted by the Financial Services and Markets Act 2000 (Consequential Amendments) (Taxes) Order, SI 2001/3629 art 151 with effect for periods of account ending after 30 November 2001.

[EEA firms and Treaty firms][1]

7—(1) This regulation applies in any case where for any accounting period—

(*a*) an equivalent reserve is maintained, otherwise than by virtue of [equalisation reserves rules][3], by an [EEA firm or a Treaty firm][1] carrying on business in the United Kingdom through a branch, and

(*b*) the three conditions specified in paragraphs (2) to (4) are satisfied.

(2) The first condition is that the branch in the United Kingdom has submitted, together with its [company tax return][2], a balance sheet ("the branch balance sheet") in respect of the trade of the branch.

(3) The second condition is that the branch balance sheet includes as a liability an amount in respect of an equalisation reserve which is equal to the amount which it would have been required to include as a liability in respect of an equalisation reserve maintained by virtue of [equalisation reserves rules][3] if the branch had been subject to such [rules][4].

(4) The third condition is that a balance sheet drawn up on the same day as the branch balance sheet for the purposes of the company's statutory accounts ("the company balance sheet"), either—

(*a*) includes as a liability an amount in respect of an equalisation reserve equal to or greater than the amount in respect of the equalisation reserve included in the branch balance sheet, or

(*b*) in a case where the amount in respect of the equalisation reserve included in the branch balance sheet exceeds the amount in respect of the equalisation reserve included in the company balance sheet, shows the amount of the excess in the company balance sheet otherwise than as funds belonging to, or available for distribution either immediately or prospectively to, the proprietors of the company.

(5) For the purpose of calculating the amount of the excess referred to in paragraph (4), any amount in the company balance sheet denominated in a currency other than sterling is to be translated into sterling at the London closing exchange rate on the last day of the accounting period in question.

(6) Section 444BA shall have effect, subject to the modification specified in paragraph (7), in relation to the equalisation reserve included in the branch balance sheet as it has effect in relation to equalisation reserves maintained by virtue of [equalisation reserves rules][3].

(7) Section 444BA shall be modified so as to provide in addition that in any case where, after the conditions specified in paragraphs (2) to (4) have been satisfied in an earlier accounting period, any of those conditions ceases to be satisfied in a later accounting period, then, for the purposes of the Tax Acts—

(*a*) any balance which exists in the reserve at the end of the later accounting period shall be deemed to have been transferred out of the reserve immediately before the end of that accounting period;

(*b*) that transfer shall be deemed to be a transfer in respect of that company's business for that accounting period; and

(*c*) the amount of the reserve shall thereupon be deemed to be nil.

Amendments—[1] Heading and words in sub-para (1)(*a*) substituted by the Financial Services and Markets Act 2000 (Consequential Amendments) (Taxes) Order, SI 2001/3629 art 149(1), (2) with effect from 1 December 2001, immediately after the coming into force of the Financial Services and Markets Act 2000 ss 411, 432(1), Sch 20 (and SI 2001/3629 Pts 1 and 2).

[2] Words in para (2) substituted by SI 2001/3629 art 149(3) with effect for periods of account ending after 30 November 2001.

[3] Words in paras (1)(*a*), (3) and (6) substituted by the Financial Services and Markets Act 2000 (Consequential Amendments) (Taxes) Order, SI 2001/3629 art 151 with effect for periods of account ending after 30 November 2001.

[4] Word in para (3) substituted for "regulations" by the Financial Services and Markets Act 2000 (Consequential Amendments) (Taxes) Order, SI 2002/1409 art 5 with effect from 2 July 2002.

Certain insurance business carried on outside the United Kingdom

8—(1) [Subject to regulation 8B][1] this regulation applies in any case where for any accounting period—

(*a*) an equivalent reserve is maintained, otherwise than by virtue of [equalisation reserves rules][3], in respect of any insurance business ...[2] which is carried on outside the United Kingdom by a company resident in the United Kingdom, and

(*b*) the condition specified in paragraph (2) is satisfied.

(2) The condition is that the company prepares statutory accounts in which the balance sheet includes as a liability an amount in respect of an equalisation reserve which is equal to the amount which it

would have been required to include as a liability in respect of an equalisation reserve maintained by virtue of [equalisation reserves rules][3] if the company had been subject to such [rules][4].

(3) For the purpose of calculating the amount of the liability referred to in paragraph (2), any amount in the company balance sheet denominated in a currency other than sterling is to be translated into sterling at the London closing exchange rate on the last day of the accounting period in question.

(4) Section 444BA shall have effect, subject to the modification specified in paragraph (5), in relation to the equalisation reserve included in the statutory accounts as it has effect in relation to equalisation reserves maintained by virtue of [equalisation reserves rules][3].

(5) Section 444BA shall be modified so as to provide in addition that in any case where, after the condition specified in paragraph (2) has been satisfied in an earlier accounting period, that condition ceases to be satisfied in a later accounting period, then, for the purposes of the Tax Acts—

(*a*) any balance which exists in the reserve at the end of the later accounting period shall be deemed to have been transferred out of the reserve immediately before the end of that accounting period;

(*b*) that transfer shall be deemed to be a transfer in respect of that company's business for that accounting period; and

(*c*) the amount of the reserve shall thereupon be deemed to be nil.

[(6) In paragraph (1)(*a*) ''insurance business'' means business which consists of the effecting or carrying out of contracts of insurance and, for the purposes of this definition, ''contract of insurance'' has the meaning given by Article 3(1) of the Financial Services and Markets Act 2000 (Regulated Activities) Order 2001.][2]

Amendments—[1] Words inserted by the Non-resident Companies (General Insurance Business) Regulations, SI 1999/1408 reg 7(2) with effect from 10 June 1999.

[2] Words in sub-para (1)(*a*) revoked, and para (6) added, by the Financial Services and Markets Act 2000 (Consequential Amendments) (Taxes) Order, SI 2001/3629 art 150 with effect from 1 December 2001, immediately after the coming into force of the Financial Services and Markets Act 2000 ss 411, 432(1), Sch 20 (and SI 2001/3629 Pts 1 and 2).

[3] Words in paras (1)(*a*), (2) and (4) substituted by the Financial Services and Markets Act 2000 (Consequential Amendments) (Taxes) Order, SI 2001/3629 art 151 with effect for periods of account ending after 30 November 2001.

[4] Word in para (2) substituted for ''regulations'' by the Financial Services and Markets Act 2000 (Consequential Amendments) (Taxes) Order, SI 2002/1409 art 5 with effect from 2 July 2002.

[Certain insurance business carried on outside the United Kingdom by a controlled foreign company—non-annual accounts but returns prepared on an annual basis

8A—(1) Subject to regulation 8B, this regulation applies in any case where—

(*a*) paragraphs (1) and (2) of regulation 8 apply in respect of an accounting period of a controlled foreign company,

(*b*) the statutory accounts drawn up by the controlled foreign company for that period use a paragraph 52 method of accounting on a non-annual basis, but

(*c*) returns of chargeable profits of that company for that period are based on accounts prepared on an annual basis.

(2) Paragraph (3) of regulation 8 shall apply in relation to this regulation as it applies in relation to that regulation.

(3) Section 444BA shall have effect, subject to the modifications specified in paragraph (5) of regulation 8 and in paragraph (4) of this regulation, in relation to the equalisation reserve included in the statutory accounts as it has effect in relation to equalisation reserves maintained by virtue of [equalisation reserves rules][2].

(4) The operation of paragraphs (*a*) and (*b*) of subsection (2) of section 444BA shall be modified so as to provide that, for the purposes of the Tax Acts, the amounts which are transferred into or out of the equalisation reserve in respect of the controlled foreign company's business for the accounting period in question shall be the amounts which would have been transferred into or out of the equalisation reserve if the company had been required to maintain an equalisation reserve by reference to accounts prepared on an accident year basis.

(5) The reference in paragraph (1)(*c*) to accounts prepared on an annual basis shall be construed in accordance with regulation 5(3).

(6) The reference in paragraph (4) to accounts prepared on an accident year basis shall be construed in accordance with regulation 5(4).][1]

Amendments—[1] Reg 8A inserted by the Non-resident Companies (General Insurance Business) Regulations, SI 1999/1408 reg 7(3) with effect from 10 June 1999.

[2] Words in para (3) substituted by the Financial Services and Markets Act 2000 (Consequential Amendments) (Taxes) Order, SI 2001/3629 art 151 with effect for periods of account ending after 30 November 2001.

[Disapplication of regulations 8 and 8A where controlled foreign company prepares non-annual accounts and final replacement of the technical provision does not take place in conformity with the Companies Act

8B Regulations 8 and 8A shall not apply in any case where for an accounting period a controlled foreign company—

(*a*) draws up its statutory accounts for that period using a paragraph 52 method of accounting on a non-annual basis, and

(*b*) the final replacement of the technical provision, as described in sub-paragraph (4) of that paragraph does not take place on or before the end of the year referred to in that sub-paragraph as the third year following the underwriting year.][1]

Amendments—[1] Reg 8B inserted by the Non-resident Companies (General Insurance Business) Regulations, SI 1999/1408 reg 7(2) with effect from 10 June 1999.

United Kingdom branches of companies not resident in the United Kingdom which maintain equalisation reserves by virtue of [equalisation reserves rules][1]

9—(1) If the three conditions prescribed in paragraphs (2) to (4) below are satisfied, section 444BA shall have effect in the case of an equalisation reserve maintained by an insurance company which—

(*a*) is not resident in the United Kingdom, and

(*b*) carries on business in the United Kingdom through a branch.

(2) The first condition is that the branch in the United Kingdom has submitted, together with its return under section 11 of the Management Act, a balance sheet (''the branch balance sheet'') in respect of the trade of the branch.

(3) The second condition is that the branch balance sheet includes as a liability an amount in respect of an equalisation reserve maintained by virtue of [equalisation reserves rules][1].

(4) The third condition is that a balance sheet drawn up on the same day as the branch balance sheet for the purposes of the company's statutory accounts (''the company balance sheet''), either—

(*a*) includes as a liability an amount in respect of an equalisation reserve equal to or greater than the amount in respect of the equalisation reserve included in the branch balance sheet, or

(*b*) in a case where the amount in respect of the equalisation reserve included in the branch balance sheet exceeds the amount in respect of the equalisation reserve included in the company balance sheet, shows the amount of the excess in the company balance sheet otherwise than as funds belonging to, or available for distribution either immediately or prospectively to, the proprietors of the company.

(5) For the purpose of calculating the amount of the excess referred to in paragraph (4), any amount in the company balance sheet denominated in a currency other than sterling is to be translated into sterling at the London closing exchange rate on the last day of the accounting period in question.

(6) Where, after the conditions prescribed in paragraphs (2) to (4) have been satisfied in an earlier accounting period, any of those conditions ceases to be satisfied in a later accounting period, then, for the purposes of the Tax Acts—

(*a*) any balance which exists in the reserve at the end of the later accounting period shall be deemed to have been transferred out of the reserve immediately before the end of that accounting period;

(*b*) that transfer shall be deemed to be a transfer in respect of that company's business for that accounting period; and

(*c*) the amount of the reserve shall thereupon be deemed to be nil.

Amendments—[1] Words in heading and para (3) substituted by the Financial Services and Markets Act 2000 (Consequential Amendments) (Taxes) Order, SI 2001/3629 art 151 with effect for periods of account ending after 30 November 2001.

Double taxation relief

10—(1) This regulation applies in any case where an insurance company which, in accordance with [equalisation reserves rules][1], is required to make transfers into or out of an equalisation reserve in respect of any business carried on by that company for any accounting period, is carrying on any business by reference to which double taxation relief is afforded in respect of any income or gains.

(2) Paragraphs (*a*) and (*b*) of subsection (2) of section 444BA shall be modified so as—

(*a*) to require that the amounts which, in accordance with [equalisation reserves rules][1], are transferred into or out of the equalisation reserve in respect of the company's business for the accounting period in question shall be apportioned amongst each branch outside the United Kingdom through which the company carries on business and business which is not carried on through branches outside the United Kingdom; and

(*b*) to provide that only those amounts which, pursuant to sub-paragraph (*a*), are apportioned to each branch outside the United Kingdom through which the company carries on business shall be brought into account for the purposes of computing the profits or losses by reference to which double taxation relief is afforded.

(3) The apportionment of each transfer into the equalisation reserve which is required by this regulation shall be made in accordance with the formula—

$$\frac{A \times B}{C}$$

where—

A is the amount which, in accordance with [equalisation reserves rules][1], is transferred into the equalisation reserve in respect of the company's business for the accounting period in question;
B is the amount of net premiums written by reference to which A is calculated that is attributable to business carried on through the branch outside the United Kingdom for the accounting period in question; and
C is the amount of net premiums written by reference to which A is calculated for the accounting period in question.

(4) In paragraph (3) "net premiums written" means gross premiums written net of reinsurance premiums payable under reinsurance ceded.

(5) The apportionment of each transfer out of the equalisation reserve which is required by this regulation shall be made in accordance with the formula—

$$\frac{D \times E}{F}$$

where—

D is the amount which, in accordance with [equalisation reserves rules][1], is transferred out of the equalisation reserve in respect of the company's business for the accounting period in question;
E is the amount of claims attributable to business carried on through the branch outside the United Kingdom that is to be taken into account in determining whether, by comparison with premiums, any transfer out of the equalisation reserve needs to be made for the period in question; and
F is the amount of claims to be taken into account in determining whether, by comparison with premiums, any transfer out of the equalisation reserve needs to be made for the period in question.

(6) Paragraph (7) applies where—

(*a*) an insurance company carries on business through one or more branches outside the United Kingdom,
(*b*) an amount is transferred into an equalisation reserve in respect of the business of that company for any accounting period, and
(*c*) the company has made an election for the purposes of subsection (4) of section 444BA so that there is an unrelieved transfer in relation to that accounting period.

(7) The company—

(*a*) shall apportion the amount transferred into the equalisation reserve in accordance with paragraph (3) without having regard to the existence of the unrelieved transfer, and
(*b*) may then set the amount of the unrelieved transfer, or any part of that amount, against the amount transferred into the equalisation reserve for that accounting period (and the action of the company under this sub-paragraph is called "the allocation" in paragraph (8)).

(8) The allocation may be made—

(*a*) in such amounts, and
(*b*) in relation to such of the apportioned amounts transferred into the equalisation reserve pursuant to paragraph (7)(*a*) (and whether in relation to business carried on in the United Kingdom or in relation to business which the company carries on through a branch outside the United Kingdom),

as the company thinks fit.

(9) Paragraph (10) applies where—

(*a*) an insurance company carries on business through one or more branches outside the United Kingdom,
(*b*) an amount is transferred out of an equalisation reserve in respect of the business of that company for any accounting period, and
(*c*) the accounting period is one to which any amount representing one or more unrelieved transfers has been carried forward under subsection (4) of section 444BA.

(10) The company—

(*a*) shall ascertain the amount to which the rule mentioned in subsection (2)(*b*) of section 444BA applies by virtue of the operation of subsection (5) of that section (in this paragraph and in paragraph (11) referred to as "the ascertained amount"), and
(*b*) shall then apportion the ascertained amount.

(11) Paragraph (5) shall apply for the purposes of the apportionment of the ascertained amount as it applies for the purposes of the apportionment of each transfer out of the equalisation reserve which is required by this regulation, with the modification that in the formula set out in that paragraph D shall be the ascertained amount.

(12) In paragraphs (6), (7) and (9) "unrelieved transfer" shall be construed in accordance with subsection (4) of section 444BA.

Amendments—[1] Words in para (1), (2)(*a*), (3) and (5) substituted by the Financial Services and Markets Act 2000 (Consequential Amendments) (Taxes) Order, SI 2001/3629 art 151 with effect for periods of account ending after 30 November 2001.

PART III
RESERVES MAINTAINED FOR THE PURPOSES OF CREDIT INSURANCE BUSINESS

Scope of this Part

11 This Part of these Regulations applies to any credit insurance equalisation reserve.

Application of section 444BA

12 Where for any accounting period an insurance company maintains a credit insurance equalisation reserve, section 444BA shall have effect in relation to that reserve as it has effect in relation to equalisation reserves maintained by virtue of [equalisation reserves rules][1].

Amendments—[1] Words substituted by the Financial Services and Markets Act 2000 (Consequential Amendments) (Taxes) Order, SI 2001/3629 art 151 with effect for periods of account ending after 30 November 2001.

Transitional provision

13—(1) This regulation applies in any case where an insurance company was required, pursuant to regulations 76 to 78 of, and Schedule 14 to, the Insurance Companies Regulations 1994, to maintain a credit insurance equalisation reserve.

(2) Paragraph 2(2) of Schedule 2 to the Insurance Companies (Reserves) Regulations 1996 shall be disregarded for the purposes of the Tax Acts in determining how much is required, on any occasion, to be transferred into the credit insurance equalisation reserve.

Application of provisions contained in Part II of these Regulations

14 Subject to regulation 13, regulations 5, 6, 9 and 10 shall have effect in relation to any credit insurance equalisation reserve as they have effect in relation to any reserve to which Part II of these Regulations applies.

1997/57
Electronic Lodgement of Tax Returns Order 1997

Made by the Treasury under TMA 1970 Sch 3A para 2(1)

Made	*15 January 1997*
Laid before the House of Commons	*16 January 1997*
Coming into Force	*1 March 1997*

1 This Order may be cited as the Electronic Lodgement of Tax Returns Order 1997, shall come into force on 1st March 1997 and shall have effect for the year 1996–97 and subsequent years of assessment.

2—(1) The provisions set out in paragraph (2) are, by virtue of paragraph 2(1)(*b*) of Schedule 3A to the Taxes Management Act 1970, specified for the purposes of that Schedule.

(2) The provisions are—

(*a*) section 8 of the Taxes Management Act 1970 (personal return);
(*b*) section 8A of that Act (trustee's return);
(*c*) section 12AA of that Act (partnership return).

3 The day appointed pursuant to paragraph 2(1)(*c*) of Schedule 3A to the Taxes Management Act 1970 in relation to notices requiring returns to be delivered or made under the provisions specified by article 2 is 1st March 1997.

1997/133
Finance Act 1996, Schedule 35, (Appointed Day) Order 1997

Made by the Treasury under the Finance Act, Sch 35, para 7(2)

Made	*23 January 1997*

1 This Order may be cited as the Finance Act 1996, Schedule 35, (Appointed Day) Order 1997.

2 The day appointed for the purposes of paragraph 7(2) of Schedule 35 to the Finance Act 1996 is 31st January 1997.

1997/168
International Organisations (Miscellaneous Exemptions) Order 1997

Made by the Treasury under TA 1988 s 582A(1)

Made . . . . *27 January 1997*

Commentary—*Simon's Direct Tax Service* **D4.339.**

1 This Order may be cited as the International Organisations (Miscellaneous Exemptions) Order 1997.

2 The following international organisations are designated for the purposes of subsections (2) and (4) to (6) of section 582A and subsection (4) of section 118B of the Income and Corporation Taxes Act 1988—

Asian Development Bank
European Bank for Reconstruction and Development
International Bank for Reconstruction and Development
International Development Association
Multilateral Investment Guarantee Agency.

3 The following international organisations are designated for the purposes of subsection (5) of section 582A and subsection (4) of section 118B of the Income and Corporation Taxes Act 1988—

African Development Bank
European Investment Bank
Inter-American Development Bank.

4 The International Organisations (Miscellaneous Exemptions) Order 1991 and the International Organisations (Miscellaneous Exemptions) Order 1992 are hereby revoked.

1997/265
Life Assurance and Other Policies (Keeping of Information and Duties of Insurers) Regulations 1997

Made by the Commissioners of Inland Revenue under TA 1988, s 552(4A)(*b*), (4B), (4C)

Made . . . . *10 February 1997*
Laid before the House of Commons . . . . *10 February 1997*
Coming into Force . . . . *1 April 1997*

Commentary—*Simon's Direct Tax Service* **E3.503.**

Citation and commencement

1 These Regulations may be cited as the Life Assurance and Other Policies (Keeping of Information and Duties of Insurers) Regulations 1997 and shall come into force on 1st April 1997.

Interpretation

2—(1) In these Regulations unless the context otherwise requires—

''the Board'' means the Commissioners of Inland Revenue;

''relevant records'', in respect of a policy or contract, means the books, documents and records specified in regulation 3;

''Schedule 15'' means Schedule 15 to the Taxes Act;

''section 552'' means section 552 of the Taxes Act [and a reference to that section without more includes, where necessary, a reference to section 552ZA of the Taxes Act;][1]

''the Taxes Act'' means the Income and Corporation Taxes Act 1988.

(2) For the purposes of these Regulations, an ''insurer''—

(*a*) in a case where the obligations under any policy or contract of the body that issued, entered into or effected it (''the original insurer'') are at any time the obligations of another body (''the transferee'') to whom there has been a transfer of the whole or any part of a business previously carried on by the original insurer, means the transferee, and

(*b*) in any other case, means the body by or with whom the policy or contract was issued, entered into or effected.

(3) For the purposes of these Regulations and in relation to an insurer, a policy or contract is a relevant policy or contract if, on the happening of a chargeable event within the meaning of Chapter II of Part XIII of the Taxes Act in relation to the policy or contract, the insurer is under the duty to deliver a certificate pursuant to section 552; and, for the purposes of this paragraph, [the words ''unless satisfied that no gain is to be treated as arising by reason of the event'' in subsection (1)(*a*) shall be disregarded][1].

(4) For the purposes of these Regulations and in respect of any policy or contract, any reference to books, documents and records includes books, documents and records (including material prepared for the purposes of advertising or publicity) which contain information—

(*a*) relating to the terms of the policy or contract, or

(*b*) required for the purposes of a certificate to be delivered under section 552.

Amendments—[1] Definition of "section 552" in para (1) amended, and words in para (3) substituted by the Life Assurance and Other Policies (Keeping of Information and Duties of Insurers) (Amendment) Regulations, SI 2002/444 reg 3 with effect from 6 April 2002.

Keeping of records—general

3 An insurer shall, in respect of each relevant policy or contract, keep sufficient books, documents and records to enable the Board—

(*a*) to ascertain the terms of the policy or contract,

(*b*) to ascertain whether there has been or is likely to be any contravention of the requirements of section 552, and

(*c*) to verify any certificate delivered under that section.

Period for which records to be kept

4—(1) Subject to paragraph (2), an insurer shall, in respect of each relevant policy or contract, keep the relevant records for a period of three years after the termination of the policy or contract.

(2) In any case where—

(*a*) a relevant policy is connected with another policy for the purposes of paragraph 13 or 14 of Schedule 15, or

(*b*) in relation to a relevant policy under which a single premium only is payable, liability for that payment is discharged in accordance with paragraph 15(2) of Schedule 15, or

(*c*) a relevant policy is issued in substitution for, or on the maturity of and in consequence of an option conferred by, another policy,

an insurer shall, in respect of each policy, keep the relevant records for a period of three years after the termination of the final policy which is in force.

Transfers of records

5—(1) This regulation applies in any case where the obligations under any policy or contract of the body that issued, entered into or effected it ("the original insurer") are at any time the obligations of another body ("the transferee") to whom there has been a transfer of the whole or any part of a business previously carried on by the original insurer.

(2) The original insurer shall, in respect of that policy or contract, deliver the relevant records to the transferee within the period of three months after the transfer.

(3) This regulation has effect in relation to transfers on or after 1st April 1997.

6—(1) This regulation applies in any case where each of the three conditions specified in paragraphs (2) to (4) is fulfilled.

(2) The first condition is that one policy (the "new policy") is issued in substitution for another policy (the "old policy").

(3) The second condition is that the new policy is issued in substitution for an old policy issued by an insurance company (the "old insurer") which was resident outside the United Kingdom at the time the old policy was issued.

(4) The third condition is that the new policy is issued by an insurance company (the "new insurer") pursuant to arrangements made between the old insurer and the new insurer for the issue of policies in substitution for ones held by persons becoming resident in the United Kingdom.

(5) The new insurer shall, in respect of the old policy, obtain the relevant records from the old insurer within the period of three months after the issue of the new policy.

(6) This regulation has effect in relation to any new policy where the insurance for that new policy is made, and that new policy is issued, on or after 1st April 1997.

7—(1) This regulation applies in any case where each of the conditions specified in paragraphs (2) and (3) is fulfilled.

(2) The first condition is that one policy ("the new policy") is issued in substitution for, or on the maturity of and in consequence of an option conferred by, another policy ("the old policy").

(3) The second condition is that, at the time the new policy is issued, the insurance company issuing the new policy ("the new insurer") and the insurance company which issued the old policy ("the old insurer") are both members of a group of companies.

(4) For the purposes of paragraph (3) two companies are members of a group of companies if one is the 51 per cent subsidiary of the other or both are 51 per cent subsidiaries of a third company.

(5) The original insurer shall, in respect of the old policy, deliver the relevant records to the new insurer within the period of three months beginning with the date on which the new policy was

substituted for the old policy or, as the case may be, the date of the exercise of the option on the maturity of the old policy.

(6) This regulation has effect in relation to any new policy where the insurance for that new policy is made, and that new policy is issued, on or after 1st April 1997.

Information to be provided to the Board

8—(1) The Board may by notice require any person to whom premiums under any policy are or have at any time been payable, within such period as may be specified in the notice, to furnish them with such information as they may reasonably require to enable them—

(*a*) to ascertain whether there has been or is likely to be any contravention of the requirements of section 552, and

(*b*) to verify any certificate delivered under that section.

(2) The period specified in a notice given under paragraph (1) shall be a period of not less than 14 days beginning with the date on which the notice is given.

Inspection of records by officer of the Board

9—(1) The Board may by notice require any person to whom premiums under any policy are or have at any time been payable, to make available for inspection by an officer of the Board authorised for that purpose, at such time as that officer may reasonably require, all such books, documents and records as are in that person's possession or under that person's control and are such as may be required by the Board under regulation 8.

(2) The time specified in a notice given under paragraph (1) shall not fall within the period of 14 days beginning with the date on which the notice is given.

1997/405

Lloyd's Underwriters (Double Taxation Relief) Regulations 1997

Made by the Commissioners of Inland Revenue under FA 1993 s 182(1)

Made	*21 February 1997*
Laid before the House of Commons	*21 February 1997*
Coming into Force	*14 March 1997*

Commentary—*Simon's Direct Tax Service* **E5.651.**

Citation, commencement and effect

1—(1) These Regulations may be cited as the Lloyd's Underwriters (Double Taxation Relief) Regulations 1997 and shall come into force on 14th March 1997.

(2) These Regulations shall have effect for the year 1996–97 and subsequent years of assessment.

Interpretation

2—(1) In these Regulations—

"Canadian tax" means the appropriate income tax or income taxes imposed by the Government of Canada;

"final year of assessment" shall be construed in accordance with section 179(2);

"foreign tax" means tax chargeable under the law of a territory outside the United Kingdom;

"member" means a member of Lloyd's who is an individual and who is or has been an underwriting member;

"Part XVIII" means Part XVIII of the Taxes Act;

"the Taxes Act" means the Income and Corporation Taxes Act 1988;

"United States tax" means the appropriate Federal income tax or Federal income taxes of the United States of America imposed by the Internal Revenue Code.

(2) For the purposes of these Regulations an underwriting year and a year of assessment shall be deemed to correspond to each other if the underwriting year ends in the year of assessment.

(3) References to a section, without more, are references to that section of the Finance Act 1993.

Pooled foreign tax

3—(1) For the purposes of Part XVIII foreign tax paid in respect of profits or losses arising from a member's underwriting business in a year of assessment shall be taken into account in accordance with paragraph (2).

(2) Foreign tax paid as mentioned in paragraph (1) shall be taken into account by reference to the aggregate amount of such amounts of foreign tax as are paid (whether or not under the law of more than one territory outside the United Kingdom) in respect of income that is taken into account in computing the profits or losses of the member's underwriting business; and accordingly the provisions of Part XVIII shall apply as if—

(*a*) references, however expressed, to tax paid under the law of a territory outside the United Kingdom were references to that aggregate amount paid as a single payment in respect of a single source of income, and

(*b*) references to United Kingdom tax chargeable in respect of any income were references to United Kingdom tax chargeable in respect of the total profits of the member's underwriting business.

Allocation of foreign tax to United Kingdom years of assessment—syndicate profits

4—(1) For the purposes of regulation 3, foreign tax referred to in that regulation that is paid in respect of income specified in paragraph (2), other than foreign tax to which regulation 6 or 7 applies, shall be allocated to the year of assessment specified in paragraph (3).

(2) The income specified is the income that is taken into account in computing the profits or losses of the member's underwriting business falling within section 172(1)(*a*) or (*b*).

(3) The year of assessment specified is the same year of assessment as the year of assessment to which, by virtue of section 172, the profits or losses referred to in paragraph (2) relate.

Allocation of foreign tax to United Kingdom years of assessment—non-syndicate profits

5—(1) For the purposes of regulation 3, foreign tax referred to in that regulation that is paid in respect of income specified in paragraph (2), other than foreign tax to which regulation 6 or 7 applies, shall be allocated to the year of assessment specified in paragraph (3).

(2) The income specified is the income that is taken into account in computing the profits or losses of the member's underwriting business falling within section 172(1)(*c*).

(3) The year of assessment specified is the same year of assessment as the year of assessment to which, by virtue of section 172, the profits or losses referred to in paragraph (2) relate.

Allocation of foreign tax to United Kingdom years of assessment—United States tax

6—(1) This regulation applies to foreign tax that is United States tax paid by Lloyd's in accordance with a United States tax return rendered by them for a calendar year in respect of income that is taken into account in computing the profits or losses of the member's underwriting business.

(2) For the purposes of regulation 3 and subject to paragraph (3), United States tax paid as mentioned in paragraph (1) shall be allocated to the year of assessment next but one following the year of assessment to which the underwriting year for which the return is made corresponds.

(3) Where the member's final year of assessment is the year 1996–97, United States tax paid as mentioned in paragraph (1) which under paragraph (2) would have been eligible for relief in a later year of assessment had not the member's final year of assessment been the year 1996–97 and which has not been used for relief in an earlier year of assessment, shall be allocated to the year 1996–97.

Allocation of foreign tax to United Kingdom years of assessment—Canadian tax

7—(1) This regulation applies to foreign tax that is Canadian tax paid by Lloyd's in accordance with a Canadian tax return rendered by them for a calendar year in respect of income that is taken into account in computing the profits or losses of the member's underwriting business.

(2) For the purposes of regulation 3 and subject to paragraph (3), Canadian tax paid as mentioned in paragraph (1) shall be allocated to the year of assessment next following the year of assessment to which the underwriting year for which the return is made corresponds.

(3) Where the member's final year of assessment is the year 1996–97, Canadian tax paid as mentioned in paragraph (1) which under paragraph (2) would have been eligible for relief in a later year of assessment had not the member's final year of assessment been the year 1996–97 and which has not been used for relief in an earlier year of assessment, shall be allocated to the year 1996–97.

Allocation of foreign tax to United Kingdom years of assessment—additional payments of foreign tax

8—(1) Where—

(*a*) payment of foreign tax ("the primary payment") is made for an underwriting year in respect of income that falls to be taken into account in computing the profits or losses of a member's underwriting business, and

(*b*) payment of an additional amount of foreign tax in respect of that income is subsequently required,

then, notwithstanding anything in regulations 4 to 7 but subject to paragraph (2), the additional amount paid shall, for the purposes of regulation 3, be treated as foreign tax paid for the underwriting year in which it was paid and not as foreign tax paid for the underwriting year for which the primary payment was made.

(2) Where the underwriting year in which the additional amount of foreign tax is paid is an underwriting year that is subsequent to the underwriting year corresponding to the member's final

year of assessment, the additional amount paid shall, for the purposes of regulation 3, be treated as foreign tax paid for the underwriting year corresponding to the member's final year of assessment.

Refunds of foreign tax

9—(1) Where—

(*a*) income that is taken into account in computing the profits or losses of a member's underwriting business is treated as reduced by foreign tax under section 811 of the Taxes Act, and

(*b*) an amount of that foreign tax is subsequently repaid to the member,

the amount repaid shall be treated as a payment received as mentioned in section 172(1)(*c*).

(2) Subject to paragraph (3), where—

(*a*) relief for foreign tax is given by way of credit against United Kingdom tax on profits arising from a member's underwriting business, and

(*b*) an amount of that foreign tax is subsequently repaid to the member,

the amount of United Kingdom tax charged on the profits arising from the member's underwriting business for the relevant year of assessment shall be treated as increased by the amount repaid.

(3) Where—

(*a*) relief by way of credit against United Kingdom tax on profits arising from a member's underwriting business is claimed for an amount of foreign tax,

(*b*) relief is given in respect of part only of the amount of the foreign tax claimed, and

(*c*) an amount of the foreign tax claimed is subsequently repaid to the member,

the amount of United Kingdom tax charged on the profits arising from the member's underwriting business for the relevant year of assessment shall be treated as increased by the amount (if any) which is equal to so much of the amount received as exceeds the amount of the foreign tax in respect of which relief was not given.

(4) In paragraphs (2) and (3) ''the relevant year of assessment''—

(*a*) where the underwriting year in which the repayment of foreign tax was received is an underwriting year subsequent to the underwriting year corresponding to the member's final year of assessment, means the member's final year of assessment;

(*b*) in any other case, means the year of assessment corresponding to the underwriting year in which the repayment of foreign tax was received.

1997/473

Friendly Societies (Modification of the Corporation Tax Acts) Regulations 1997

Made by the Treasury under TA 1988 s 463

Made	*25 February 1997*
Laid before the House of Commons	*26 February 1997*
Coming into Force	*20 March 1997*

Commentary—*Simon's Direct Tax Service* **D4.601.**

The Treasury, in exercise of the powers conferred on them by section 463 of the Income and Corporation Taxes Act 1988, hereby make the following Regulations:

Citation, commencement and effect

1—(1) These Regulations may be cited as the Friendly Societies (Modification of the Corporation Tax Acts) Regulations 1997 and shall come into force on 20th March 1997.

(2) Except as otherwise provided these Regulations shall have effect for accounting periods beginning on or after 1st January 1995.

Interpretation

2 In these Regulations—

[''annual return society'' means a friendly society which is required to submit an annual actuarial investigation to the Financial Services Authority under rule 5.1 of the Prudential Sourcebook (Friendly Societies);][3]

...[3]

[''general business'' means business which consists of the effecting or carrying out of contracts that fall within Part I of Schedule 1 to the Financial Services and Markets Act 2000 (Regulated Activities) Order 2001;][2]

''incorporated friendly society'' has the meaning given by section 116 of the Friendly Societies Act 1992;

[''individual savings account business'' has the meaning given to it by regulation 3 of the Individual Savings Account (Insurance Companies) Regulations 1998;][1]

"linked business" means any business [of effecting or carrying out contracts of insurance which fall within paragraph III of Part II of Schedule 1 to the Financial Services and Markets Act 2000 (Regulated Activities) Order 2001][2];

["non annual return society" means a friendly society which is not required to submit an annual actuarial investigation to the Financial Services Authority under rule 5.1 of the Prudential Sourcebook (Friendly Societies);][3]

...[3]

"pension business" has the meaning given by section 431B of the Taxes Act;

["prescribed transactions" means any of the following transactions—

(*a*) the transfer of business as between a friendly society required to keep a separate fund for long-term business and a friendly society not so required,

(*b*) the amalgamation of a friendly society required to keep a separate fund for long-term business and a friendly society not so required,

(*c*) the transfer of the whole or part of the business of a friendly society not required to keep a separate fund for long-term business to a company which is not a friendly society, and

(*d*) the conversion of a friendly society not required to keep a separate fund for long-term business into a company which is not a friendly society,

and the requirement to keep a separate fund for long-term business means a requirement imposed by rule 4.20 of the Prudential Sourcebook (Friendly Societies);][3]

["the Prudential Sourcebook (Friendly Societies)" means the Interim Prudential Sourcebook for Friendly Societies made by the Financial Services Authority under the Financial Services and Markets Act 2000;][3]

...[3]

"the Taxes Act" means the Income and Corporation Taxes Act 1988;

"the 1992 Act" means the Taxation of Chargeable Gains Act 1992.

Amendments—[1] Definition of "individual savings account business" inserted by the Individual Savings Account (Insurance Companies) Regulations, SI 1998/1871, with effect from 6 April 1999.

[2] Definition of "general business" and "relevant section 43 requirements" inserted, words in the definition of "linked business" and "section 37(3) society" substituted, by the Financial Services and Markets Act 2000 (Consequential Amendments) (Taxes) Order, SI 2001/3629 art 153 with effect from 1 December 2001, immediately after the coming into force of the Financial Services and Markets Act 2000 ss 411, 432(1), Sch 20 (and SI 2001/3629 Pts 1 and 2).

[3] Definitions of directive society", "non-directive society", "section 37(3) society", "relevant section 43 requirements", and "specified transactions" revoked; definition of "prescribed transactions" substituted; definitions of "annual return society", "non annual return society" and "the Prudential Sourcebook (Friendly Societies)" inserted, by the Friendly Societies (Modification of the Corporation Tax Acts) (Amendment) Regulations, SI 2004/822 regs 2, 3. The regulations came into force on 8 April 2004, and these amendments have effect for accounting periods beginning after 31 December 2002.

[2A—In the Corporation Tax Acts, in their application to a friendly society—

"insurance business transfer scheme" means a scheme which effects—

(*a*) the transfer of the whole or part of the business of a friendly society to another friendly society,

(*b*) the amalgamation of two or more friendly societies,

(*c*) the transfer of the whole or part of the business of a friendly society to a company which is not a friendly society,

(*d*) the conversion of a friendly society into a company which is not a friendly society, or

(*e*) the transfer of the whole or part of the long-term business of an insurance company to a friendly society.][1]

Amendments—[1] This regulation inserted, by the Friendly Societies (Modification of the Corporation Tax Acts) (Amendment) Regulations, SI 2004/822 regs 2, 4. The regulations came into force on 8 April 2004, and this insertion has effect for accounting periods beginning after 31 December 2002.

Transfer of [long-term] business of an insurance company to a friendly society

3

Amendment—This regulation revoked by the Friendly Societies (Modification of the Corporation Tax Acts) (Amendment) Regulations, SI 2004/822 regs 2, 5. The regulations came into force on 8 April 2004, and this revocation has effect for accounting periods beginning after 31 December 2002.

[Modifications] of section 12 ... of the Taxes Act

4

Amendment—This regulation revoked by the Friendly Societies (Modification of the Corporation Tax Acts) (Amendment) Regulations, SI 2004/822 regs 2, 5. The regulations came into force on 8 April 2004, and this revocation has effect for accounting periods beginning after 31 December 2002.

[Modification of section 43F of the Taxes Act

4A—(1) Paragraph (2) prescribes a modification of section 43F(1) of the Taxes Act so far as it applies to the life or endowment business carried on by friendly societies.

(2) For the words from "required" to the end substitute "made up for the purposes of an investigation into the financial condition of a friendly society under [rule 5.1 or 5.2 of the Prudential Sourcebook (Friendly Societies)].""[2].

(3) This regulation shall have effect in relation to transactions entered into on or after 21st March 2000.][1]

Amendments—[1] Regulation 4A inserted by the Friendly Societies (Modification of the Corporation Tax Acts) (Amendment) Regulations, SI 2000/2710 reg 3 with effect in relation to transactions entered into on or after 21 March 2000 (see para (3) above).

[2] Words substituted by the Friendly Societies (Modification of the Corporation Tax Acts) (Amendment) Regulations, SI 2003/23 reg 3 with effect for accounting periods ending after 30 November 2001.

Modifications of section 76 of the Taxes Act

5—(1) Paragraphs (2) to (6) prescribe modifications of section 76 of the Taxes Act so far as it applies to the life or endowment business carried on by friendly societies.

(2) In subsection (1)(*ca*) after the words "referable to" there shall be inserted the word "taxable".

(3) In subsection (1)(*d*) after the words "referable to" there shall be inserted the words "tax exempt basic life assurance and general annuity business".

(4) In subsection (1)(*e*) after the words "referable to" there shall be inserted the word "taxable".

(5) In subsection (1) at the end there shall be inserted—

"; and in paragraph (*d*) above 'tax exempt basic life assurance and general annuity business' means basic life assurance and general annuity business the profits arising from which fall to be exempted from tax by virtue of section 460(1), and for the purposes of this definition it shall be assumed that the friendly society has made a claim for exemption from tax under that provision".

(6) ...[1]

Amendments—[1] Para (6) revoked by the Financial Services and Markets Act 2000 (Consequential Amendments) (Taxes) Order, SI 2001/3629 art 155 with effect from 1 December 2001, immediately after the coming into force of the Financial Services and Markets Act 2000 ss 411, 432(1), Sch 20 (and SI 2001/3629 Pts 1 and 2).

Modifications of section 431 of the Taxes Act

6—(1) Paragraphs (2) to (7) prescribe modifications of section 431 of the Taxes Act so far as it applies to the life or endowment business carried on by friendly societies.

(2) In subsection (2) the following definitions shall be inserted in the appropriate places in alphabetical order—

["annual return society" means a friendly society which is required to submit an annual actuarial investigation to the Financial Services Authority under rule 5.1 of the Prudential Sourcebook (Friendly Societies);][4]

"incorporated friendly society" has the meaning given by section 116 of the Friendly Societies Act 1992;

["non annual return society" means a friendly society which is not required to submit an annual actuarial investigation to the Financial Services Authority under rule 5.1 of the Prudential Sourcebook (Friendly Societies);][4]

["the Prudential Sourcebook (Friendly Societies)" means the Interim Prudential Sourcebook for Friendly Societies made by the Financial Services Authority under the Financial Services and Markets Act 2000;][1]

"tax exempt basic life assurance and general annuity business" means basic life assurance and general annuity business the profits arising from which are exempt from tax by virtue of section 460(1);

"taxable basic life assurance and general annuity business" means basic life assurance and general annuity business other than tax exempt basic life assurance and general annuity business;

"valuation report"—

(*a*) in the case of [an annual return society][4], means the abstract of the actuary's report referred to in [rule 5.1(2) of the Prudential Sourcebook (Friendly Societies)][1];

(*b*) in the case of a [non annual return society][4], means the abstract of the actuary's report referred to in section [rule 5.2(2) of the Prudential Sourcebook (Friendly Societies)][1];

(3) In subsection (2) for the definition of "liabilities" there shall be substituted—

" 'liabilities'—

(*a*) in relation to [an annual return society][4], means the liabilities of the society estimated as for the purposes of its valuation report (excluding any that have fallen due or been reinsured and any not arising under or in connection with policies or contracts effected as part of the society's insurance business); and

(*b*) in relation to a [non annual return society][4] society—

(i) means, in the case of a society which has sent a valuation report as at the end of an accounting period to the [Financial Services Authority][3], the liabilities of the society estimated as for the purposes of its valuation report (excluding any that have fallen due or been reinsured and any not arising under or in connection with policies or contracts effected as part of the society's insurance business), and

(ii) means, in the case of a society which has not sent a valuation report as at the end of an accounting period to the [Financial Services Authority][3] but has caused the actuary to the society to prepare a report on the same basis as the actuary's report referred to in [rule 5.2(2) of the Prudential Sourcebook (Friendly Societies)][1], the liabilities of the society estimated as for the purposes of that report (excluding any that have fallen due or been reinsured and any not arising under or in connection with policies or contracts effected as part of the society's insurance business), and

(iii) means, in any other case, the liabilities of the society ascertained in accordance with subsections (7) to (10) below;''.

(4) In subsection (2) for the definition of ''[long-term][2] business'' there shall be substituted—

'' '[long-term][2] business' shall be construed in accordance with section 117 of the Friendly Societies Act 1992;''.

[(4A) Where a friendly society is not required to keep a separate fund for long-term business, for the definition of ''long-term insurance fund'' in subsection (2) there shall be substituted—

'' 'long-term insurance fund'' has the meaning given by section 431AB;''.][4]

(5) In subsection (2) for the definition of ''periodical return'' there shall be substituted—

'' 'periodical return'—

(*a*) in the case of [an annual return society][4], [means the FSC1 return within the meaning given in Chapter 5 of the Prudential Sourcebook (Friendly Societies); and][1]

(*b*) in the case of a [non annual return society][4], means [the FSC2 return within the meaning given in that Chapter][1];''.

(6) In subsection (2) for the definition of ''value'' there shall be substituted—

'' 'value'—

(*a*) in relation to the assets of [an annual return society][4], means the value of the assets as taken into account for the purposes of the society's periodical return; and

(*b*) in relation to the assets of a [non annual return society][4]—

(i) means, in the case of a society which has sent a valuation report as at the end of an accounting period to the [Financial Services Authority][3], the value of the assets as taken into account for the purposes of its valuation report,

(ii) means, in the case of a society which has not sent a valuation report as at the end of an accounting period to the [Financial Services Authority][3] but has caused the actuary to the society to prepare a report on the same basis as the actuary's report referred to in [rule 5.2(2) of the Prudential Sourcebook (Friendly Societies)][1], the value of the assets as taken into account for the purposes of that report, and

(iii) means, in any other case, the value of the assets ascertained in accordance with subsections (11) to (14) below;''

(7) At the end of the section the following subsections shall be inserted—

''(7) For the purposes of paragraph (*b*)(iii) of the definition of 'liabilities' in subsection (2) above the closing liabilities of a society for an accounting period ('the relevant accounting period') shall be ascertained in accordance with the formula—

$$L1 + \left((L2 - L1) \times \frac{T1}{T2} \right)$$

where—

L1 is the liabilities as at the end of the last accounting period ('the preceding accounting period') which precedes the relevant accounting period and for which a relevant report is drawn up;

L2 is the liabilities as at the end of the first accounting period ('the subsequent accounting period') which follows the relevant accounting period and for which a relevant report is drawn up;

T1 is the number of days from the end of the preceding accounting period to the end of the relevant accounting period;

T2 is the number of days from the end of the preceding accounting period to the end of the subsequent accounting period;

and where the formula is used to ascertain the closing liabilities for an accounting period, the liabilities so ascertained shall be the opening liabilities for the next accounting period.

(8) Where, for those purposes, it is necessary to ascertain the liabilities in any case where a relevant report has not been drawn up at the end of the relevant accounting period, the liabilities shall be estimated on a basis compatible with that used in the previous relevant report, having regard to any changes in the nature or extent of the society's business since that report.

(9) In any case where subsection (8) above has applied, subsection (7) above shall apply as soon as the society is able to ascertain the closing liabilities in accordance with the formula set out in

that subsection; and all such adjustments to the liability to tax of the society shall be made, whether by assessment or otherwise, as may be required to give effect to subsection (7) above.

(10) In subsections (7) and (8) above a 'relevant report' means a valuation report or the report specified in paragraph (*b*)(ii) of the definition of 'liabilities' in subsection (2) above.

(11) For the purposes of paragraph (*b*)(iii) of the definition of 'value' in subsection (2) above the value of the assets of a society as at the end of an accounting period ('the relevant accounting period') shall be ascertained in accordance with the formula—

$$V1+\left((V2-V1)\times\frac{T1}{T2}\right)$$

where—

V1 is the value of the assets at the end of the last accounting period ('the preceding accounting period') which precedes the relevant accounting period and for which a relevant report is drawn up;

V2 is the value of the assets as at the end of the first accounting period ('the subsequent accounting period') which follows the relevant accounting period and for which a relevant report is drawn up;

T1 is the number of days from the end of the preceding accounting period to the end of the relevant accounting period;

T2 is the number of days from the end of the preceding accounting period to the end of the subsequent accounting period;

and where the formula is used to ascertain the value of the assets as at the end of an accounting period, the value so ascertained shall be the value of the assets at the beginning of the next accounting period.

(12) Where, for those purposes, it is necessary to ascertain the value of the assets in any case where a relevant report has not been drawn up at the end of the relevant accounting period, the value of the assets shall be estimated on a basis compatible with that used in the previous relevant report, having regard to any changes in the nature or extent of the society's business since that report.

(13) In any case where subsection (12) above has applied, subsection (11) above shall apply as soon as the society is able to ascertain the value of the assets in accordance with the formula set out in that subsection; and all such adjustments to the liability to tax of the society shall be made, whether by assessment or otherwise, as may be required to give effect to subsection (11) above.

(14) In subsections (11) and (12) above a 'relevant report' means a valuation report or the report specified in paragraph (*b*)(ii) of the definition of 'value' in subsection (2) above."

Amendments—[1] Words in paras (2), (3), (5) and (6) substituted, and words in para (2) inserted, by the Financial Services and Markets Act 2000 (Consequential Amendments) (Taxes) Order, SI 2001/3629 art 156 with effect for periods of account ending after 30 November 2001.

[2] Words in para (4) substituted by the Financial Services and Markets Act 2000 (Consequential Amendments) (Taxes) Order, SI 2001/3629 art 165(2)(*b*) with effect from 1 December 2001, immediately after the coming into force of the Financial Services and Markets Act 2000 ss 411, 432(1), Sch 20 (and SI 2001/3629 Pts 1 and 2).

[3] Words substituted for the words "Friendly Societies Commission" by the Friendly Societies (Modification of the Corporation Tax Acts) (Amendment) Regulations, SI 2003/23 reg 4 with effect for accounting periods ending after 30 November 2001.

[4] In para (2), definitions of "directive society" and "non-directive society" revoked, and definitions of "annual return society" and non annual return society" inserted, and words in definition of "valuation report" substituted; in para (3), words in definition of "liabilities" substituted; para (4A) inserted; in para (5), words in definition of "periodical return" substituted, and in para (6), words in definition of "value" substituted, by the Friendly Societies (Modification of the Corporation Tax Acts) (Amendment) Regulations, SI 2004/822 regs 2, 6. The regulations came into force on 8 April 2004, and these amendments have effect for accounting periods beginning after 31 December 2002.

7—(1) Paragraph (2) prescribes modifications of section 431(2) of the Taxes Act so far as it applies to the life or endowment business carried on by friendly societies in relation to accounting periods ending on or after 1st September 1996.

(2) The following definitions shall be inserted in the appropriate places in alphabetical order—

" 'tax exempt class IV business' means—

(*a*) business specified in section 466(1)(*d*) the profits arising from which are exempt from tax by virtue of section 460(1), and

(*b*) business other than that specified in section 466(1)(*d*) the profits arising from which are exempt from tax by virtue of section 461(1) or 461B(1);

'taxable class IV business' means business specified in section 466(1)(*d*) other than tax exempt class IV business;".

[7A In the case of a friendly society not required to keep a separate fund for long-term business, the following section shall be treated as inserted after section 431AA of the Taxes Act—

"431AB Friendly societies: meaning of "long-term insurance fund"

(1) "Long-term insurance fund" means the fund made up of—

(*a*) assets held primarily for the purposes of long-term business carried on by a friendly society, and (*b*) the relevant fraction of each asset held neither primarily for the purposes of long-term business nor primarily for the purposes of some other specific business carried on by that society.

(2) For the purposes of subsection (1) "the relevant fraction" means—

((0.5 × (OLB + CLB)) – (0.5 × (OLA + CLA))) / ((0.5 × (OTB + CTB)) – (0.5 × (OTA + CTA)))

where—

OLB and **CLB** are respectively the balances brought forward and carried forward in the fund accounts for those accounts within which the society conducts its long-term business;

OLA and **CLA** are respectively the opening and closing values of the assets already recognised at the beginning and end of the period of account as held for the purposes of long-term business carried on by the society;

OTB and **CTB** are respectively the total balances brought forward and carried forward on all the society's fund accounts; and

OTA and **CTA** are respectively the opening and closing values of the assets already recognised at the beginning and end of the period of account as held for the purposes of long-term business or for the purposes of other specific business carried on by the society.

(3) In calculating the values and balances for the purpose of determining the relevant fraction in subsection (2), a balance on a general management fund or a general reserve fund shall be excluded.

(3) In subsection (2), references to balances brought forward and carried forward are references to balances brought forward and carried forward as shown in the society's periodical return."][1]

Note—Para (4) appears to have been incorrectly numbered above as para (3).

Amendments—[1] This regulation inserted by the Friendly Societies (Modification of the Corporation Tax Acts) (Amendment) Regulations, SI 2004/822 regs 2, 7. The regulations came into force on 8 April 2004, and this insertion has effect for accounting periods beginning after 31 December 2002.

Modification of section 432 of the Taxes Act

8—(1) Paragraph (2) prescribes a modification of section 432 of the Taxes Act so far as it applies to the life or endowment business carried on by friendly societies in relation to accounting periods ending on or after 1st September 1996.

(2) At the end of the section the following subsection shall be inserted—

"(3) Where a friendly society carries on both tax exempt class IV business and taxable class IV business, the business of each such category shall, for the purposes of the Corporation Tax Acts, be treated as though it were a separate business."

Modifications of section 432A of the Taxes Act

9—(1) Paragraph (2) prescribes a modification of section 432A of the Taxes Act so far as it applies to the life or endowment business carried on by friendly societies; and paragraph (3) prescribes a further modification of that section so far as it applies to the life or endowment business carried on by [non annual return societies][3].

(2) After subsection (1) the following subsections shall be inserted—

"(1A) Subsections (1B) to (1D) below apply where a friendly society with branches carries on more than one category of business.

(1B) In a case where—

(*a*) the society has caused the actuary to the society to prepare, as at the end of an accounting period and as at the end of the previous accounting period, reports prepared on the same basis as the society's valuation report but which are limited to an investigation of the matters referred to in [rule 5.1(3) of the Prudential Sourcebook (Friendly Societies)][1] in relation to the central body of the society (and not to any of its branches), and

(*b*) the society so chooses,

the apportionment of the income, gains or losses of the central body shall be determined by reference to the liabilities and the value of the assets estimated for the purposes of those reports.

(1C) Subject to subsection (1B) above, the apportionment shall be of the income, gains or losses of the society, together with all its branches.

(1D) Where, by virtue of this section, income, gains or losses are referable to any of the following categories, namely—

[(*aa*) individual savings account business,][3]

(*a*) pension business,

(*b*) taxable basic life assurance and general annuity business, or

(*c*) taxable class IV business,

that income, or those gains or losses, shall be attributable to the central body of the society and not to any of its branches unless the society shows that any business within any of those categories was written by a branch, in which case the income, gains or losses referable to any of those categories shall be attributed to any such branch in such manner as is just and reasonable."

(3) After subsection (1D) (inserted by paragraph (2)) the following subsection shall be inserted—

"(1E) In a case where, in relation to any period, the [Financial Services Authority, by giving a direction under section 148 of the Financial Services and Markets Act 2000][1], has dispensed with the requirement that a society shall cause such an abstract as is mentioned in [rule 5.2 of the Prudential Sourcebook (Friendly Societies)][1] to be made and sent to the [Authority][2], the definitions of 'liabilities' and 'value' in section 431(2) shall not apply; and any apportionment required by this section shall be made in such manner as is just and reasonable."

Amendments—[1] Words in paras (2), (3) substituted by the Financial Services and Markets Act 2000 (Consequential Amendments) (Taxes) Order, SI 2001/3629 art 157 with effect for periods of account ending after 30 November 2001.

[2] Word substituted for the word "Commission" by the Friendly Societies (Modification of the Corporation Tax Acts) (Amendment) Regulations, SI 2003/23 reg 5 with effect for accounting periods ending after 30 November 2001.

[3] Words in para (1) substituted, and words in para (2) inserted, by the Friendly Societies (Modification of the Corporation Tax Acts) (Amendment) Regulations, SI 2004/822 regs 2, 8. The regulations came into force on 8 April 2004, and these amendments have effect for accounting periods beginning after 31 December 2002.

10—(1) Paragraph (2) prescribes a modification of section 432A(2) of the Taxes Act so far as it applies to the life or endowment business carried on by friendly societies in relation to accounting periods beginning before 1st January 1996.

(2) For paragraphs (*d*) and (*e*) there shall be substituted—

"(*d*) taxable basic life assurance and general annuity business which is not industrial assurance business;

(*da*) tax exempt basic life assurance and general annuity business which is not industrial assurance business;

(*e*) taxable basic life assurance and general annuity business which is industrial assurance business;

(*ea*) tax exempt basic life assurance and general annuity business which is industrial assurance business; and".

11—(1) Paragraph (2) prescribes a modification of section 432A(2) of the Taxes Act so far as it applies to the life or endowment business carried on by friendly societies in relation to accounting periods beginning on or after 1st January 1996.

(2) For paragraph (*d*) there shall be substituted—

"(*d*) taxable basic life assurance and general annuity business;

(*da*) tax exempt basic life assurance and general annuity business;".

12—(1) Paragraph (2) prescribes a modification of section 432A(2) of the Taxes Act so far as it applies to the life or endowment business carried on by friendly societies in relation to accounting periods ending on or after 1st September 1996.

(2) For paragraph (*f*) there shall be substituted—

"(*f*) taxable class IV business; and

(*fa*) tax exempt class IV business."

13—[(1) Where an annual return society is not required to keep a long-term insurance fund, in respect of its life or endowment business section 432A of the Taxes Act shall apply with the following modifications.][6]

(2) For subsection (6) there shall be substituted—

"(6) For the purposes of subsection (5) above 'the relevant fraction', in relation to a category of business, is the fraction of which—

(*a*) the numerator is the mean of the opening and closing liabilities of the category, reduced [(but not below nil)][1] by the mean of the opening and closing [net][1] values of any assets directly referable to the category; and

[(*b*) the denominator is the aggregate of—

(i) the numerator given by paragraph (*a*) above; and

(ii) the numerators given by that paragraph in relation to the other categories of business.][1]

(3) Subsection (8) shall be omitted.

(4) Paragraph (*b*) of subsection (9) shall be omitted.

(5) ...[6]

Amendments—[1] Words in substituted sub-s (6)(*a*) inserted and words in sub-s (6)(*b*) substituted by the Friendly Societies (Modification of the Corporation Tax Acts) (Amendment) Regulations, SI 2000/2710 reg 4 with effect in relation to accounting periods beginning on or after 1 January 2000 and ending after 20 March 2000. Words in sub-s (6) previously read—

"(*b*) the denominator is the mean of the opening and closing liabilities of the long term business, reduced by the mean of the opening and closing value of any assets directly referable to any category of business."

[2] Words in para (5) substituted by the Financial Services and Markets Act 2000 (Consequential Amendments) (Taxes) Order, SI 2001/3629 art 165(1)(*a*) with effect from 1 December 2001, immediately after the coming into force of the Financial Services and Markets Act 2000 ss 411, 432(1), Sch 20 (and SI 2001/3629 Pts 1 and 2).

[3] Words in para (5) substituted by the Financial Services and Markets Act 2000 (Consequential Amendments) (Taxes) Order, SI 2001/3629 art 165(2)(*c*) with effect from 1 December 2001, immediately after the coming into force of the Financial Services and Markets Act 2000 ss 411, 432(1), Sch 20 (and SI 2001/3629 Pts 1 and 2).

[4] Words in para (5) substituted by the Friendly Societies (Modification of the Corporation Tax Acts) (Amendment) Regulations, SI 2001/3975 regs 3, 4 with effect from 1 January 2002.

[5] Para (1)(*a*) substituted by the Friendly Societies (Modification of the Corporation Tax Acts) (Amendment) Regulations, SI 2003/23 reg 6 with effect for accounting periods ending after 30 November 2001.

[6] Para (1) substituted, and para (5) revoked, by the Friendly Societies (Modification of the Corporation Tax Acts) (Amendment) Regulations, SI 2004/822 regs 2, 9. The regulations came into force on 8 April 2004, and these amendments have effect for accounting periods beginning after 31 December 2002.

[Modifications of section 432AA of the Taxes Act

13A—(1) Paragraphs (2) to (4) prescribe modifications of subsection (4) of section 432AA of the Taxes Act so far as it applies to the life or endowment business carried on by friendly societies on and after 1st April 1998, subject to the transitional provisions in Part IV of Schedule 5 to the Finance Act 1998.

(2) In paragraph (*c*) before the words ''basic life assurance'' there shall be inserted the word 'taxable'.

(3) After paragraph (*c*) there shall be inserted the following paragraph—

''(*ca*) tax exempt basic life assurance and general annuity business;''.

(4) For paragraph (*d*) there shall be substituted the following paragraphs—

''(*d*) taxable class IV business;

(*da*) tax exempt class IV business.''][1]

Amendments—[1] This regulation inserted by the Friendly Societies (Modification of the Corporation Tax Acts) (Amendment) Regulations, SI 1999/2636 reg 3 with effect from 13 October 1999.

[Modifications of section 432AB of the Taxes Act

13B—(1) Paragraphs (2) and (3) prescribe modifications of section 432AB of the Taxes Act so far as it applies to the life or endowment business carried on by friendly societies on and after 1st April 1998, subject to the transitional provisions in Part IV of Schedule 5 to the Finance Act 1998.

(2) In subsection (3) before the words ''basic life assurance'' there shall be inserted the word ''taxable''.

(3) In subsection (4) before the words ''basic life assurance'' there shall be inserted the word ''taxable''.][1]

Amendments—[1] This regulation inserted by the Friendly Societies (Modification of the Corporation Tax Acts) (Amendment) Regulations, SI 1999/2636 reg 3 with effect from 13 October 1999.

[**14**—(1) Section 432E of the Taxes Act shall apply to the life or endowment business of a friendly society with the following modifications.

(2) In subsection (1), the words ''or, as the case may be, subsection (2B)'' shall be inserted after the words ''subsections (2) and (2A)''.

(3) After subsection (2A), the following subsection shall be treated as inserted—

''(2B) In a case where an amount is taken into account under subsection (2) of section 83 of the Finance Act 1989 by virtue of subsection (2F) of that section, the amount determined under subsection (2) above is increased by—

$$\left(\frac{CAS}{AS}\right)\times RP$$

where—

CAS and AS have the same meanings as in subsection (2) above; and

RP is the amount taken into account under subsection (2) of section 83 of the Finance Act 1989 by virtue of subsection (2F) of that section.''][1]

Amendments—[1] This regulation substituted by the Friendly Societies (Modification of the Corporation Tax Acts) (Amendment) Regulations, SI 2004/822 regs 2, 10. The regulations came into force on 8 April 2004, and this substitution has effect for accounting periods beginning after 31 December 2002.

Modification of section 432F(1) of the Taxes Act

15

Amendment—This regulation revoked by the Friendly Societies (Modification of the Corporation Tax Acts) (Amendment) Regulations, SI 2004/822 regs 2, 11. The regulations came into force on 8 April 2004, and this revocation has effect for accounting periods beginning after 31 December 2002.

Modification of section 434B(2) of the Taxes Act

16

Amendment—This regulation revoked by the Friendly Societies (Modification of the Corporation Tax Acts) (Amendment No 2) Regulations, SI 1997/2877 reg 3. It follows the repeal of TA 1988 s 434B(2) in relation to accounting periods of insurance companies beginning after 5 March 1997, and has effect in relation to accounting periods of friendly societies beginning after the same date.

Modifications of section 434D of the Taxes Act

17

Amendment—This regulation revoked, together with reg 18, by the Friendly Societies (Modification of the Corporation Tax Acts) (Amendment) Regulations, SI 2001/3975 regs 3, 5 with effect from 1 January 2002.

Modification of section 434E(6) of the Taxes Act

18

Amendment—This regulation revoked, together with reg 17, by the Friendly Societies (Modification of the Corporation Tax Acts) (Amendment) Regulations, SI 2001/3975 regs 3, 5 with effect from 1 January 2002.

Modifications of section 436 of the Taxes Act

19—(1) Paragraph (2) prescribes a modification of section 436 of the Taxes Act so far as it applies to the life or endowment business carried on by [non annual return societies][1] other than societies—

(*a*) which carry on any pension business which is linked business, and

(*b*) to which section 432E of the Taxes Act does not apply.

(2) After subsection (3)(*e*) there shall be inserted the following paragraph—

"and

(*f*) the opening liabilities and the closing liabilities of the society shall be ascertained in accordance with paragraph (*b*) of the definition of 'liabilities' in subsection (2) of section 431, and the definition of 'closing liabilities' in that subsection shall not apply."

Amendments—[1] Words in para (1) substituted by the Friendly Societies (Modification of the Corporation Tax Acts) (Amendment) Regulations, SI 2004/822 regs 2, 12. The regulations came into force on 8 April 2004, and this amendment has effect for accounting periods beginning after 31 December 2002.

[19A—(1) Paragraph (2) prescribes a modification of section 436 of the Taxes Act so far as it applies to the life or endowment business carried on by [non annual return societies][2] other than societies—

(*a*) which carry on any individual savings account business which is linked business, and

(*b*) to which section 432E of the Taxes Act does not apply.

(2) After subsection (3)(*e*) there shall be inserted the following paragraph—

"and

(*f*) the opening liabilities and the closing liabilities of the society shall be ascertained in accordance with paragraph (*b*) of the definition of "liabilities" in subsection (2) of section 431, and the definition of "closing liabilities" in that subsection shall not apply."][1]

Amendments—[1] This regulation inserted by the Individual Savings Account (Insurance Companies) Regulations, SI 1998/1871 reg 25 with effect from 6 April 1999.

[2] Words in para (1) substituted by the Friendly Societies (Modification of the Corporation Tax Acts) (Amendment) Regulations, SI 2004/822 regs 2, 13. The regulations came into force on 8 April 2004, and this amendment has effect for accounting periods beginning after 31 December 2002.

20—(1) Paragraph (2) prescribes a modification of section 436 of the Taxes Act so far as it applies to the life or endowment business carried on by [non annual return societies][1]—

(*a*) which carry on any pension business which is linked business, and

(*b*) to which section 432E of the Taxes Act does not apply,

in relation to accounting periods beginning on or after 1st January 1995; and paragraphs (3) and (4) prescribe further modifications of that section so far as it applies to the life or endowment business carried on by such [non annual return societies][1] in relation to accounting periods ending on or after the date on which these Regulations come into force.

(2) After subsection (5) the following subsections shall be inserted—

"(6) Subsection (7) below applies where the amount shown in respect of Item 3 of Part I of Schedule 7 to the Friendly Societies (Accounts and Related Provisions) Regulations 1994 ('the Item 3 amount') is a positive amount; and subsection (8) below applies where the Item 3 amount is a negative amount.

(7) The amount of the increase in liabilities to policy holders (that is to say, the excess of the society's closing liabilities to policy holders over its opening liabilities to policy holders) that is taken into account for the purpose of computing the profits arising to the society from pension business shall be the Item 3 amount.

(8) The amount of the decrease in liabilities to policy holders (that is to say, the excess of the society's opening liabilities to policy holders over its closing liabilities to policy holders) that is taken into account for the purpose of computing the profits arising to the society from pension business shall be the Item 3 amount."

(3) At the beginning of subsection (6) (inserted by paragraph (2)) there shall be inserted the words "Subject to subsection (9) below,".

(4) After subsection (8) (inserted by paragraph (2)) the following subsections shall be inserted—

"(9) Subject to subsection (11) below, in a case where, for any period of account, income or gains arising to a society—

(*a*) derive directly or indirectly from a transaction or transactions with a member or members of the society, and

(*b*) exceed the amount of the income or gains which would have arisen to the society if any transaction mentioned in paragraph (*a*) above had been a transaction at arm's length,

the closing liabilities of the society shall be reduced by the amount of the excess; but the opening liabilities for the next following period of account shall not be increased by the like amount.

(10) For the purposes of subsection (9) above a person associated with a member shall be treated as a member; and 'associated' shall be construed in accordance with section 783(10).

(11) In any case where—

(*a*) there has been a transaction consisting of the disposal of an asset to a friendly society ('the earlier disposal'),

(*b*) section 17(1)(*a*) of the 1992 Act has applied on the earlier disposal,

(*c*) the friendly society subsequently makes a disposal of the asset ('the later disposal'), and

(*d*) subsection (9) above applies (or would, apart from this subsection, apply) to the later disposal,

any gains accruing to the society on the later disposal shall, for the purposes of subsection (9) above, be reduced by the excess (if any) of the amount treated, by virtue of the application of section 17(1)(*a*) of the 1992 Act, as the consideration for the earlier disposal over the actual amount of the consideration for the earlier disposal."

Amendments—[1] Words in para (1) substituted by the Friendly Societies (Modification of the Corporation Tax Acts) (Amendment) Regulations, SI 2004/822 regs 2, 14. The regulations came into force on 8 April 2004, and this amendment has effect for accounting periods beginning after 31 December 2002.

[20A—(1) Paragraph (2) prescribes a modification of section 436 of the Taxes Act so far as it applies to the life or endowment business carried on by [non annual return societies][1]—

(*a*) which carry on any individual savings account business which is linked business, and

(*b*) to which section 432E of the Taxes Act does not apply.

(2) After subsection (5) the following subsections shall be inserted—

"(6) Subsection (7) below applies where the amount shown in respect of Item 3 of Part I of Schedule 7 to the Friendly Societies (Accounts and Related Provisions) Regulations 1994 ("the Item 3 amount") is a positive amount; and subsection (8) below applies where the Item 3 amount is a negative amount.

(7) The amount of the increase in liabilities to policy holders (that is to say, the excess of the society's closing liabilities to policy holders over its opening liabilities to policy holders) that is taken into account for the purpose of computing the profits arising to the society from individual savings account business shall be the Item 3 amount.

(8) The amount of the decrease in liabilities to policy holders (that is to say, the excess of the society's opening liabilities to policy holders over its closing liabilities to policy holders) that is taken into account for the purpose of computing the profits arising to the society from individual savings account business shall be the Item 3 amount."

Amendments—[1] This regulation inserted by the Individual Savings Account (Insurance Companies) Regulations, SI 1998/1871 reg 25 with effect from 6 April 1999.

[2] Words in para (1) substituted by the Friendly Societies (Modification of the Corporation Tax Acts) (Amendment) Regulations, SI 2004/822 regs 2, 15. The regulations came into force on 8 April 2004, and this amendment has effect for accounting periods beginning after 31 December 2002.

Modifications of section 437 of the Taxes Act

21—(1) Paragraphs (2) to (4) prescribe modifications of section 437 of the Taxes Act so far as it applies to the life or endowment business carried on by friendly societies.

(2) ... [1]

(3) In subsection (1C)(*a*), before the words "basic life assurance" there shall be inserted the word "taxable".

(4) In subsection (1F) at the end there shall be inserted—

" 'taxable basic life assurance and general annuity business' means basic life assurance and general annuity business the profits arising from which do not fall to be exempted from tax by virtue of section 460(1), and for the purposes of this definition it shall be assumed that the friendly society has made a claim for exemption from tax under that provision."

Amendments—[1] Paragraph (2) revoked by the Friendly Societies (Modification of the Corporation Tax Acts) (Amendment No 2) Regulations, SI 1997/2877 reg 4. The modification made by reg 21(2) is rendered obsolete by the substitution in FA 1997 s 67(1) of TA 1988 s 437(1A), with effect in relation to accounting periods of insurance companies beginning after 5 March 1997. SI 1997/2877 reg 4 has effect in relation to accounting periods of friendly societies beginning after the same date.

[Modification of section 438B of the Taxes Act

21A—(1) Paragraphs (2) to (4) prescribe modifications of section 438B of the Taxes Act so far as it applies to friendly societies.

(2) In subsection (1) before the words "basic life assurance and general annuity business" there shall be inserted the word "taxable".

(3) In subsection (3) before the words "basic life assurance and general annuity business" there shall be inserted the word 'taxable'.

(4) ...[2]

(5) This regulation has effect from 6th April 2001.][1]

Amendments—[1] This regulation inserted, together with reg 21B, by the Friendly Societies (Modification of the Corporation Tax Acts) (Amendment) Regulations, SI 2001/3975 regs 3, 16 with effect from 1 January 2002.

[2] Para (4) revoked by the Friendly Societies (Modification of the Corporation Tax Acts) (Amendment) Regulations, SI 2004/822 regs 2, 16 with effect from the financial year 2003.

21B—

Amendment—This regulation revoked by the Friendly Societies (Modification of the Corporation Tax Acts) (Amendment) Regulations, SI 2004/822 regs 2, 17. The regulations came into force on 8 April 2004, and this revocation has effect for accounting periods beginning after 31 December 2002.

Modifications of section 440 of the Taxes Act

22—[(1) The modifications of section 440 of the Taxes Act given in paragraphs (3) and (4) apply—

(*a*) where a friendly society begins or ceases to be required by rule 4.20 of the Prudential Sourcebook (Friendly Societies) to keep a separate fund for long-term business, or

(*b*) in relation to a prescribed transaction.][3]

(3) In subsection (1), before the words "If at any time" there shall be inserted the words "Subject to subsection (4A) below,"

(4) After subsection (4) there shall be inserted—

"(4A) Subsection (1) above shall not have effect in relation to any assets which—

(*a*) cease to be within the category set out in paragraph (*e*) of subsection (4) above and come within the category set out in paragraph (*f*) of that subsection, or

(*b*) cease to be within the category set out in paragraph (*f*) of subsection (4) above and come within the category set out in paragraph (*e*) of that subsection."

Amendments—[1] Words in sub-para (1)(*b*) substituted by the Financial Services and Markets Act 2000 (Consequential Amendments) (Taxes) Order, SI 2001/3629 art 158(1) with effect from 1 December 2001, immediately after the coming into force of the Financial Services and Markets Act 2000 ss 411, 432(1), Sch 20 (and SI 2001/3629 Pts 1 and 2).

[2] Words in sub-para (1)(*b*) substituted by the Financial Services and Markets Act 2000 (Consequential Amendments) (Taxes) Order, SI 2001/3629 art 165(2)(*d*) with effect from 1 December 2001, immediately after the coming into force of the Financial Services and Markets Act 2000 ss 411, 432(1), Sch 20 (and SI 2001/3629 Pts 1 and 2).

[3] Para (1) substituted for paras (1), (2) by the Friendly Societies (Modification of the Corporation Tax Acts) (Amendment) Regulations, SI 2004/822 regs 2, 18. The regulations came into force on 8 April 2004, and this substitution has effect for accounting periods beginning after 31 December 2002.

23—

Amendment—[1] This regulation revoked by the Friendly Societies (Modification of the Corporation Tax Acts) (Amendment) Regulations, SI 2004/822 regs 2, 19. The regulations came into force on 8 April 2004, and this revocation has effect for accounting periods beginning after 31 December 2002.

24—(1) Paragraph (2) prescribes a modification of section 440(4) of the Taxes Act so far as it applies to the life or endowment business carried on by friendly societies.

(2) For paragraph (*d*) there shall be substituted—

"(*d*) assets linked solely to taxable basic life assurance and general annuity business;

(*da*) assets linked solely to tax exempt basic life assurance and general annuity business;".

25—

Amendment—[1] This regulation revoked by the Friendly Societies (Modification of the Corporation Tax Acts) (Amendment) Regulations, SI 2004/822 regs 2, 20. The regulations came into force on 8 April 2004, and this revocation has effect for accounting periods beginning after 31 December 2002. TA 1988 s 440(1) shall not have effect in relation to any transfer of assets by virtue of the revocation.

Modifications of section 440A(2) of the Taxes Act

26—(1) Paragraph (2) prescribes a modification of section 440A(2) of the Taxes Act so far as it applies to the life or endowment business carried on by friendly societies.

(2) In paragraph (*a*), for sub-paragraph (iii) there shall be substituted—

"(iii) taxable basic life assurance and general annuity business, or

(iv) tax exempt basic life assurance and general annuity business,".

27

Amendment—[1] This regulation revoked by the Friendly Societies (Modification of the Corporation Tax Acts) (Amendment) Regulations, SI 2004/822 regs 2, 21. The regulations came into force on 8 April 2004, and this revocation has effect for accounting periods beginning after 31 December 2002.

Modifications of section 441 of the Taxes Act

28—(1) Paragraph (2) prescribes a modification of subsection (4) of section 441 of the Taxes Act so far as it applies to the life or endowment business carried on by [non annual return societies][1]; and paragraph (3) prescribes a modification of that section so far as it applies to the life or endowment business carried on by friendly societies.

(2) Before paragraph (*b*) there shall be inserted—

"(*ab*) the opening liabilities and the closing liabilities of the society shall be ascertained in accordance with paragraph (*b*) of the definition of 'liabilities' in subsection (2) of section 431, and the definition of 'closing liabilities' in that subsection shall not apply, and".

(3) After subsection (4) the following subsections shall be inserted—

"(4A) Profits (or any loss, to be computed on the same basis as the profits) arising to the society from its overseas life assurance business shall be divided into a taxable part and a tax exempt part.

(4B) The division shall be made in the ratio which the mean of the opening and closing liabilities to policy holders in respect of taxable business bears to the mean of the opening and closing liabilities to policy holders in respect of tax exempt business.

(4C) The profits referable to the taxable part or, as the case may be, any loss referable to the taxable part, shall be treated as income within Schedule D, and be chargeable or, as the case may be, allowable, under Case VI of that Schedule.

(4D) In subsection (4B) above and in this subsection 'tax exempt business' means overseas life assurance business the profits arising from which are exempt from tax by virtue of section 460(1); and 'taxable business' means overseas life assurance business other than tax exempt business."

Amendments—[1] Words in para (1) substituted by the Friendly Societies (Modification of the Corporation Tax Acts) (Amendment) Regulations, SI 2004/822 regs 2, 22. The regulations came into force on 8 April 2004, and this amendment has effect for accounting periods beginning after 31 December 2002.

Modification of section 442A(1) of the Taxes Act

29—(1) Paragraph (2) prescribes a modification of section 442A(1) of the Taxes Act so far as it applies to the life or endowment business carried on by friendly societies.

(2) Before the words "basic life assurance" there shall be inserted the word "taxable".

Modification of section 444A(1) of the Taxes Act

30

Amendment—This regulation revoked by the Friendly Societies (Modification of the Corporation Tax Acts) (Amendment) Regulations, SI 2004/822 regs 2, 23. The regulations came into force on 8 April 2004, and this revocation has effect for accounting periods beginning after 31 December 2002.

[Modification of section 460(2) of the Taxes Act

[30A][2]—(1) Paragraph (2) prescribes a modification of section 460(2) of the Taxes Act.

(2) After paragraph (*b*) there shall be inserted the following paragraph—

"(*ba*) shall not apply to profits arising from individual savings account business."][1]

Amendments—[1] This regulation inserted by the Individual Savings Account (Insurance Companies) Regulations, SI 1998/1871 reg 25(5) with effect from 6 April 1999.
[2] Number of regulation substituted by the Individual Savings Account (Amendment) Regulations, SI 1998/3174 reg 13 with effect from 6 April 1999.

[Modification of section 587B of the Taxes Act

30AA—(1) Paragraph (2) prescribes a modification of section 587B of the Taxes Act so far as it applies to the life or endowment business carried on by friendly societies.

(2) In subsection (8)(*b*)(ii) before "basic life assurance" insert "taxable".

(3) This regulation shall have effect in relation to disposals made by friendly societies on or after 1st April 2000.]

Amendments—[1] Regulation 30AA inserted by the Friendly Societies (Modification of the Corporation Tax Acts) (Amendment) Regulations, SI 2000/2710 reg 5 with effect in relation to disposals made by friendly societies after 30 March 2000 (see para (3)).

[Modifications of section 755A of the Taxes Act

30B—(1) Paragraphs (2) to (6) prescribe modifications of section 755A of the Taxes Act so far as it applies to the life or endowment business carried on by friendly societies in relation to accounting periods ending on or after 1st July 1999.

(2) In subsections [(3) and (10)][2] before the words "BLAGAB apportioned profit", in each place where they occur, there shall be inserted the word "taxable".

(3) In subsection (4)—

(*a*) the word "or" immediately following paragraph (*b*) shall be omitted;

(*b*) after paragraph (*c*) there shall be inserted—

"or

(*d*) tax exempt basic life assurance and general annuity business,".

(4) In subsection (6)(*c*) for the words "paragraphs (*a*) to (*c*)" there shall be substituted the words "paragraphs (*a*) to (*d*)".

[(4A) In subsection (11)(*b*), after the word "profit" insert the words "which is taxable".][2]

[(4B) In subsection (11B)(*b*), before the words "BLAGAB profits" insert the word "taxable".][2]

[(4C) In subsection (11C)(*b*), before the words "BLAGAB profits" insert the word "taxable".][2]

(5) In subsection (12)—

(*a*) for the words "BLAGAB apportioned profit" there shall be substituted the words "taxable BLAGAB apportioned profit";

(*b*) before the words "basic life assurance" there shall be inserted the word "taxable".

(6) In subsection (13)—

(*a*) the word "or" immediately following paragraph (*c*) shall be omitted;

(*b*) in paragraph (*d*) before the words "basic life assurance" there shall be inserted the word "taxable";

(*c*) after paragraph (*d*) there shall be inserted—

"or

(*e*) tax exempt basic life assurance and general annuity business,".][1]

Amendments—[1] Regulation 30B inserted by the Friendly Societies (Modification of the Corporation Tax Acts) (Amendment) Regulations, SI 1999/2636 reg 4 with effect from 13 October 1999.

[2] In para (2), references substituted, and paras (4A)–(4C) inserted, by the Friendly Societies (Modification of the Corporation Tax Acts) (Amendment) Regulations, SI 2004/822 regs 2, 24 with effect from the financial year 2003.

[Modifications of section 804B of the Taxes Act

30C—(1) Paragraphs (2) to (4) prescribe modifications of section 804B of the Taxes Act so far as it applies to the life or endowment business carried on by friendly societies.

[(1A) The modification of section 804B(4)(*a*) prescribed by paragraph (2)(*a*) shall not apply where section 804B(4) is applied by virtue of regulation 4(3) and (5) of the Double Taxation Relief (Surrender of Relievable Tax within a Group) Regulations 2001.][2]

(2) In subsection (4)—

(*a*) in paragraph (*a*) before "basic" insert "taxable";

(*b*) for paragraph (*b*) substitute—

"(*b*) taxable class IV business,".

(3) In subsection (5)—

(*a*) in paragraph (*a*) before "basic" insert "taxable";

(*b*) for paragraph (*b*) substitute—

"(*b*) tax exempt basic life assurance and general annuity business; nor

(*c*) taxable class IV business; nor

(*d*) tax exempt class IV business.".

(4) In subsection (9) for the words from "other than" to "credit in respect of" substitute "other than—

(*a*) taxable basic life assurance and general annuity business, or

(*b*) tax exempt basic life assurance and general annuity business, or

(*c*) taxable class IV business, or

(*d*) tax exempt class IV business,

credit in respect of".

(5) This regulation shall have effect in relation to accounting periods beginning on or after 1st April 2000.][1]

Amendments—[1] Regulation 30C inserted by the Friendly Societies (Modification of the Corporation Tax Acts) (Amendment) Regulations, SI 2000/2710 reg 6 with effect for accounting periods beginning after 30 March 2000 (see para (5)).

[2] Para (1A) inserted by the Friendly Societies (Modification of the Corporation Tax Acts) (Amendment) Regulations, SI 2004/822 regs 2, 25. The regulations came into force on 8 April 2004, and these amendments have effect for accounting periods beginning after 31 December 2002.

[Modifications of section 804D of the Taxes Act

30D—(1) Paragraphs (2) to (4) prescribe modifications of section 804D of the Taxes Act so far as it applies to the life or endowment business carried on by [non annual return societies][2].

(2) In subsection (2) for the words from ''by which'' to the end substitute ''by which—

(*a*) so much of the total of the amounts shown, in the society's accounts for that period, in respect of Item 1 of Part I of Schedule 7 to the Friendly Societies (Accounts and Related Provisions) Regulations 1994 as is referable to that category of business exceeds—

(*b*) so much of any commissions payable and any expenses of management incurred in connection with the acquisition of the business, as shown in those accounts in respect of Item 2(*f*) and (*g*) of Part I of that Schedule, as is referable to that category of business.''.

(3) In subsection (4) for the words from ''claims incurred'' to the end substitute ''total income of that category determined under subsection (2) above.''.

(4) Omit subsection (5).

(5) This regulation shall have effect in relation to periods of account beginning on or after 1st April 2000.][1]

Amendments—[1] Regulation 30D inserted by the Friendly Societies (Modification of the Corporation Tax Acts) (Amendment) Regulations, SI 2000/2710 reg 6 with effect for periods of account beginning after 30 March 2000 (see para (5)).
[2] Words in para (1) substituted by the Friendly Societies (Modification of the Corporation Tax Acts) (Amendment) Regulations, SI 2004/822 regs 2, 26. The regulations came into force on 8 April 2004, and these amendments have effect for accounting periods beginning after 31 December 2002.

Modification of paragraph 5 of Schedule 19AA to the Taxes Act

31—(1) Paragraph (2) prescribes a modification of paragraph 5 of Schedule 19AA to the Taxes Act so far as it applies to the life or endowment business carried on by friendly societies.

(2) In sub-paragraph (5) for the words ''or basic life assurance and general annuity business'' there shall be substituted the words '', taxable basic life assurance and general annuity business or tax exempt basic life assurance and general annuity business''.

[32 Where section 82(1)(*b*) of the Finance Act 1989 applies, as originally enacted, by virtue of paragraph 1(6) of Schedule 33 to the Finance Act 2003—

(*a*) in the case of a friendly society, subsection (1)(*b*) of that section shall be modified so that for ''section 9.6 of the Prudential Sourcebook (Insurers)'' substitute ''rule 5.1 of the Prudential Sourcebook (Friendly Societies)'';

(*b*) in the case of a non annual return society, after subsection (8) of that section there shall be treated as inserted—

''(9) Where a period of account ends on a day to which a valuation report has not been prepared, or begins on a day immediately following such a day, the amount of any unappropriated surplus on valuation for the purposes of subsections (1)(*b*) and (4) shall be the amount which was taken into account at the end of the last period of account for which a valuation report was prepared.'']][1]

Amendments—[1] This regulation substituted by the Friendly Societies (Modification of the Corporation Tax Acts) (Amendment) Regulations, SI 2004/822 regs 2, 27. The regulations came into force on 8 April 2004, and this substitution has effect for accounting periods beginning after 31 December 2002.

[32A—(1) In the case of a friendly society, section 82B of the Finance Act 1989 shall apply with the following modifications.

(2) In paragraph (*a*) of subsection 1, for ''section 9.6 of the Prudential Sourcebook (Insurers)'' substitute ''rule 5.1 of the Prudential Sourcebook (Friendly Societies)''.

(3) In paragraph (*b*) of subsection 1, for ''Rule 4.1(6) of the Prudential Sourcebook (Insurers)'' substitute ''Rule 2(6) of Appendix 4 to the Prudential Sourcebook (Friendly Societies)''.

(4) Where that friendly society is a non annual return society—

(*a*) in subsection (2) for ''the period of account immediately preceding the period of account in question'' substitute ''the period of account for which a report was submitted which most closely precedes the period of account in question (''the most closely preceding period of account'')'';

(*b*) in subsection (3), wherever occurring, for ''that immediately preceding period of account'' substitute ''the most closely preceding period of account''.][1]

Amendments—[1] This regulation inserted by the Friendly Societies (Modification of the Corporation Tax Acts) (Amendment) Regulations, SI 2004/822 regs 2, 28. The regulations came into force on 8 April 2004, and this insertion has effect for accounting periods beginning after 31 December 2002.

Modifications of section 83 of the Finance Act 1989

33—(1) Paragraph (2) prescribes a modification of section 83 of the Finance Act 1989 so far as it applies to the life or endowment business carried on by [annual return societies][1].

(2) After subsection [(2E)][1] there shall be inserted the following subsections—

''[(2F)][1] Where, in a case where the expenses charged in the management fund exceed the amount transferred from all revenue account funds, the amount determined in accordance with subsection

[(2G)][1] below shall be taken into account as [an increase in value of the assets of the long-term insurance fund][1].

[(2G)][1] Subject to subsection [(2I)][1] below, that amount is the amount found by—

(*a*) taking the aggregate amount of the society's investment income recognised in the account of the management fund;

(*b*) either adding any increase in value of the assets of the management fund, or subtracting any decrease in value of the assets of the management fund, as the case may be; and

(*c*) multiplying the amount so found by the fraction specified in subsection [(2H)][1] below.

[(2H)][1] That fraction is the fraction of which—

(*a*) the numerator is the amount transferred from the revenue account recognised for the purposes of section 83A(2), and

(*b*) the denominator is the amount transferred from all revenue account funds.

[(2I)][1] Where, apart from this subsection, the amount determined in accordance with subsection [(2G)][1] above would be a negative amount, the amount determined in accordance with that subsection shall be taken to be nil.''

Amendments—[1] Words in para (1) substituted, and words references in para (2) substituted, by the Friendly Societies (Modification of the Corporation Tax Acts) (Amendment) Regulations, SI 2004/822 regs 2, 29. The regulations came into force on 8 April 2004, and this insertion has effect for accounting periods beginning after 31 December 2002.

34

Amendment—Regulations 34, 35 revoked by the Friendly Societies (Modification of the Corporation Tax Acts) (Amendment) Regulations, SI 2004/822 regs 2, 30. The regulations came into force on 8 April 2004, and these revocations have effect for accounting periods beginning after 31 December 2002.

35

Amendment—Regulations 34, 35 revoked by the Friendly Societies (Modification of the Corporation Tax Acts) (Amendment) Regulations, SI 2004/822 regs 2, 30. The regulations came into force on 8 April 2004, and these revocations have effect for accounting periods beginning after 31 December 2002.

Modifications of section 83A of the Finance Act 1989

36—(1) Paragraph (2) prescribes a modification of section 83A of the Finance Act 1989 so far as it applies to the life or endowment business carried on by [annual return societies][3].

(2) For subsection (2) there shall be substituted—

''(2) The accounts recognised for the purposes of those sections are—

(*a*) a revenue account included in, or supplied to the [Financial Services Authority][2] with, the society's valuation report which contains items relating to the society's life or endowment business in respect of the whole of the society's [long-term][1] business;

(*b*) any separate revenue account included in, or supplied to the [Financial Services Authority][2] with, the society's valuation report which contains items relating to the society's life or endowment business in respect of a part of the society's [long-term][1] business.

Paragraph (*b*) above does not include accounts required in respect of internal linked funds.

(2A) In subsection (2) above 'life or endowment business' has the meaning given by section 466(1) of the Taxes Act 1988.''

Amendments—[1] Words in para (2) substituted by the Financial Services and Markets Act 2000 (Consequential Amendments) (Taxes) Order, SI 2001/3629 art 165(2)(*e*) with effect from 1 December 2001, immediately after the coming into force of the Financial Services and Markets Act 2000 ss 411, 432(1), Sch 20 (and SI 2001/3629 Pts 1 and 2).

[2] Words substituted for the words ''Friendly Societies Commission'' by the Friendly Societies (Modification of the Corporation Tax Acts) (Amendment) Regulations, SI 2003/23 reg 8 with effect for accounting periods ending after 30 November 2001.

[3] Words in para (1) substituted by the Friendly Societies (Modification of the Corporation Tax Acts) (Amendment) Regulations, SI 2004/822 regs 2, 31. The regulations came into force on 8 April 2004, and this substitution has effect for accounting periods beginning after 31 December 2002.

37—(1) Paragraphs (2) and (3) prescribe modifications of Section 83A of the Finance Act 1989 so far as it applies to the life or endowment business carried on by [non annual return societies][1].

(2) For subsection (2) there shall be substituted—

''(2) The account recognised for the purposes of those sections is the income and expenditure account prepared in accordance with the requirements of the Friendly Societies (Accounts and Related Provisions) Regulations 1994.''

(3) Subsections (3) to (5) shall be omitted.

Amendments—[1] Words in para (1) substituted by the Friendly Societies (Modification of the Corporation Tax Acts) (Amendment) Regulations, SI 2004/822 regs 2, 32. The regulations came into force on 8 April 2004, and this substitution has effect for accounting periods beginning after 31 December 2002.

Modification of section 85(1) of the Finance Act 1989

38—(1) Paragraph (2) prescribes a modification of section 85(1) of the Finance Act 1989 so far as it applies to the life or endowment business carried on by friendly societies.

(2) Before the words "basic life assurance" there shall be inserted the word "taxable".

Modifications of section 86 of the Finance Act 1989

39—(1) Paragraph (2) prescribes modifications of section 86 of the Finance Act 1989 so far as it applies to the life or endowment business carried on by friendly societies.

(2) In subsections (1) and (5) before the words "basic life assurance" there shall be inserted the word "taxable".

[39A In the case of a friendly society, section 88(3A)(*a*) of the Finance Act 1989 shall be modified by inserting the word "taxable" before the words "basic life assurance and general annuity business".][1]

Amendments—[1] This regulation inserted by the Friendly Societies (Modification of the Corporation Tax Acts) (Amendment) Regulations, SI 2004/822 regs 2, 33 with effect for accounting periods ending after 8 April 2003.

Modifications of section 88A of the Finance Act 1989

40

Amendments—This regulation revoked by the Friendly Societies (Modification of the Corporation Tax Acts) (Amendment) Regulations, SI 2004/822 regs 2, 34. The regulations came into force on 8 April 2004, and this revocation has effect for accounting periods beginning after 31 December 2002.

[40A—(1) In the case of a friendly society, section 89(1B) of the Finance Act 1989 shall be modified by inserting the word "taxable" before the words "basic life assurance and general annuity business", wherever occurring.

(2) This regulation has effect for the purposes of section 210A of the Taxation of Chargeable Gains Act 1992 in relation to any accounting period of a company if it is necessary under that section to determine the company's taxable basic life assurance and general annuity business profits for the period.

(3) Subject to paragraph (2), this regulation has effect for accounting periods ending on or after 9th April 2003."][1]

Amendments—[1] This regulation inserted by the Friendly Societies (Modification of the Corporation Tax Acts) (Amendment) Regulations, SI 2004/822 regs 2, 35. The regulations came into force on 8 April 2004, and this insertion has effect for accounting periods beginning after 31 December 2002.

Modification of section 152A(1) of the Capital Allowances Act 1990

41

Amendment—This regulation revoked by the Friendly Societies (Modification of the Corporation Tax Acts) (Amendment) Regulations, SI 2001/3975 regs 3, 7 with effect from 1 January 2002.

Modification of paragraph 16 of Schedule 7 to the Finance Act 1991

42—(1) Paragraph (2) prescribes a modification of paragraph 16 of Schedule 7 to the Finance Act 1991 so far as it applies to the life or endowment business carried on by friendly societies.

(2) In sub-paragraph (7), in the definition of "general annuity contract", for the words "referable to general annuity business" there shall be substituted the words " 'referable to taxable general annuity business', and 'taxable general annuity business' means general annuity business the profits arising from which do not fall to be exempted from tax by virtue of section 460(1) of the Taxes Act 1988, and for the purposes of these definitions it shall be assumed that the friendly society has made a claim for exemption from tax under that provision".

Modifications of paragraph 17 of Schedule 7 to the Finance Act 1991

43—(1) Paragraph (2) prescribes a modification of paragraph 17 of Schedule 7 to the Finance Act 1991 so far as it applies to the life or endowment business carried on by friendly societies.

(2) In sub-paragraph (4), in the definitions of "X" and "Z", before the words "basic life assurance" there shall be inserted the word "taxable".

[43A—(1) In the case of a friendly society, section 210B of the Taxation of Chargeable Gains Act 1992 shall be modified as follows.

(2) In subsection (7)(*a*), the word "taxable" shall be inserted before the words "BLAGAB internal linked fund".

(3) In subsection (8), for the definition of "BLAGAB internal linked fund" there shall be substituted—

""taxable BLAGAB internal linked fund" means an internal linked fund all the assets appropriated to which are linked solely to taxable basic life assurance and general annuity business,".][1]

Amendments—[1] This regulation inserted by the Friendly Societies (Modification of the Corporation Tax Acts) (Amendment) Regulations, SI 2004/822 regs 2, 36 with effect in accordance with FA 2003 Sch 33 para 15(2), (3).

[Modifications] of section 211... of the 1992 Act

44

Amendment—This regulation revoked by the Friendly Societies (Modification of the Corporation Tax Acts) (Amendment) Regulations, SI 2004/822 regs 2, 37. The regulations came into force on 8 April 2004, and this revocation has effect for accounting periods beginning after 31 December 2002.

[44A—(1) In the case of a friendly society, section 211ZA of the Taxation of Chargeable Gains Act 1992 shall be modified as follows.

(2) In subsection (7), the word "taxable" shall be inserted before the words "basic life assurance and general annuity business".

(3) In subsection (10), the word "taxable" shall be inserted before the words "basic life assurance and general annuity business".][1]

Amendments—[1] This regulation inserted by the Friendly Societies (Modification of the Corporation Tax Acts) (Amendment) Regulations, SI 2004/822 regs 2, 38 with effect for insurance business transfer schemes taking place on after 31 December 2002.

Modifications of section 212 of the 1992 Act

45—(1) Paragraph (2) prescribes a modification of section 212 of the 1992 Act so far as it applies to the life or endowment business carried on by friendly societies...[2].

(2) In subsection (2) before the words "or to assets" there shall be inserted the words ", tax exempt basic life assurance and general annuity business".

(3) ...[2]

Amendments—[1] Words in para (3) substituted by the Financial Services and Markets Act 2000 (Consequential Amendments) (Taxes) Order, SI 2001/3629 art 165(1)(*c*) with effect from 1 December 2001, immediately after the coming into force of the Financial Services and Markets Act 2000 ss 411, 432(1), Sch 20 (and SI 2001/3629 Pts 1 and 2).

[2] Words in para (1) revoked, and para (3) revoked, by the Friendly Societies (Modification of the Corporation Tax Acts) (Amendment) Regulations, SI 2004/822 regs 2, 39. The regulations came into force on 8 April 2004, and these revocations have effect for accounting periods beginning after 31 December 2002.

Modifications of section 213 of the 1992 Act

46—(1) Paragraph (2) prescribes a modification of section 213(1A) of the 1992 Act so far as it applies to the life or endowment business carried on by friendly societies.

(2) In paragraph (*a*) after the words "referable to" there shall be inserted the word "taxable".

47

Amendments—Regulations 47, 49, 50, 50A, 50B, 51, 52, 53D, 53E, 53F, 53G and 53J revoked by the Friendly Societies (Modification of the Corporation Tax Acts) (Amendment) Regulations, SI 2004/822 regs 2, 40. The regulations came into force on 8 April 2004, and these revocations have effect for accounting periods beginning after 31 December 2002.

Modification of section 214(1) of the 1992 Act

48—(1) Paragraph (2) prescribes a modification of section 214(1) of the 1992 Act so far as it applies to the life or endowment business carried on by friendly societies.

(2) In paragraph (*c*) before the words "basic life assurance" there shall be inserted the word "taxable".

Modifications of section 214A of the 1992 Act

49—

Amendments—Regulations 47, 49, 50, 50A, 50B, 51, 52, 53D, 53E, 53F, 53G and 53J revoked by the Friendly Societies (Modification of the Corporation Tax Acts) (Amendment) Regulations, SI 2004/822 regs 2, 40. The regulations came into force on 8 April 2004, and these revocations have effect for accounting periods beginning after 31 December 2002.

50

Amendments—Regulations 47, 49, 50, 50A, 50B, 51, 52, 53D, 53E, 53F, 53G and 53J revoked by the Friendly Societies (Modification of the Corporation Tax Acts) (Amendment) Regulations, SI 2004/822 regs 2, 40. The regulations came into force on 8 April 2004, and these revocations have effect for accounting periods beginning after 31 December 2002.

Modifications of paragraph 17 of Schedule 7AC to the 1992 Act

50A

Amendments—Regulations 47, 49, 50, 50A, 50B, 51, 52, 53D, 53E, 53F, 53G and 53J revoked by the Friendly Societies (Modification of the Corporation Tax Acts) (Amendment) Regulations, SI 2004/822 regs 2, 40. The regulations came into force on 8 April 2004, and these revocations have effect for accounting periods beginning after 31 December 2002.

Modifications of paragraph 10 of Schedule 7AD to the 1992 Act

50B

Amendments—Regulations 47, 49, 50, 50A, 50B, 51, 52, 53D, 53E, 53F, 53G and 53J revoked by the Friendly Societies (Modification of the Corporation Tax Acts) (Amendment) Regulations, SI 2004/822 regs 2, 40. The regulations came into force on 8 April 2004, and these revocations have effect for accounting periods beginning after 31 December 2002.

Modifications of paragraph 1 of Schedule 18 to the Finance Act 1994

51

Amendments—Regulations 47, 49, 50, 50A, 50B, 51, 52, 53D, 53E, 53F, 53G and 53J revoked by the Friendly Societies (Modification of the Corporation Tax Acts) (Amendment) Regulations, SI 2004/822 regs 2, 40. The regulations came into force on 8 April 2004, and these revocations have effect for accounting periods beginning after 31 December 2002.

Modifications of paragraph 12 of Schedule 9 to the Finance Act 1996

52

Amendment—Regulations 47, 49, 50, 50A, 50B, 51, 52, 53D, 53E, 53F, 53G and 53J revoked by the Friendly Societies (Modification of the Corporation Tax Acts) (Amendment) Regulations, SI 2004/822 regs 2, 40. The regulations came into force on 8 April 2004, and these revocations have effect for accounting periods beginning after 31 December 2002.

Modifications of Schedule 11 to the Finance Act 1996

53—(1) Paragraphs (2) and (3) prescribe modifications of Schedule 11 to the Finance Act 1996 so far as it applies to the life or endowment business carried on by friendly societies.

(2) In paragraphs 2(1) and 4(1)(*a*) before the words "basic life assurance" there shall be inserted the word "taxable".

(3) In paragraph 6 the following definition shall be added at the end—

"['taxable basic life assurance and general annuity business'][1] has the meaning given by section 431(2) of the Taxes Act 1988."

Amendments—[1] Words substituted by the Friendly Societies (Modification of the Corporation Tax Acts) (Amendment) Regulations, SI 1999/2636 reg 5(1), (2) with effect for accounting periods ending after 31 March 1996.

[Modifications of Schedule 11 to the Finance Act 1996 as modified in relation to capital redemption business

53ZA—(1) Paragraphs (2) and (3) prescribe modifications of Schedule 11 to the Finance Act 1996—

(*a*) as that Schedule is modified in relation to companies carrying on capital redemption business by regulation 15 of the Insurance Companies (Capital Redemption Business) (Modification of the Corporation Tax Acts) Regulations 1999, and

(*b*) so far as that Schedule (as so modified) applies to the life or endowment business carried on by friendly societies for accounting periods ending on or after 1st July 1999.

(2) In paragraph 2(1) before the words "basic life assurance" there shall be inserted the word "taxable".

(3) In paragraph 4(1), (2)(*a*), (7) and (10) before the words "basic life assurance", wherever they occur, there shall be inserted the word "taxable".]

Amendments—[1] This regulation inserted by the Friendly Societies (Modification of the Corporation Tax Acts) (Amendment) Regulations, SI 1999/2636 reg 6 with effect from 13 October 1999.

Modification of paragraph 18 of Schedule 12 to the Finance Act 1997

53A—(1) Paragraph (2) prescribes a modification of paragraph 18 of Schedule 12 to the Finance Act 1997.

[(2) In sub-paragraph (1) for the words "Chapter 9 of the Prudential Sourcebook (Insurers)" there shall be substituted the words "Chapter 5 of the Prudential Sourcebook (Friendly Societies)"][2]

[(3) In sub-paragraph (2) for the words " 'the Prudential Sourcebook (Insurers)' means the Interim Prudential Sourcebook for Insurers" substitute the words " 'the Prudential Sourcebook (Friendly Societies)' means the Interim Prudential Sourcebook for Friendly Societies".][2]

[4][3] This regulation shall have effect in relation to periods for which accounts of friendly societies are made up ending on or after 26th November 1996.[1]

Amendments—[1] Regulation inserted by the Friendly Societies (Modification of the Corporation Tax Acts) (Amendment No 2) Regulations, SI 1997/2877 reg 5, and modifies FA 1997 Sch 12 para 18. The inserted regulation has effect in relation to periods of account of friendly societies ending on or after 26 November 1996.

[2] Paras (2), (3) substituted for para (2) by the Financial Services and Markets Act 2000 (Consequential Amendments) (Taxes) Order, SI 2001/3629 art 164 with effect for periods of account ending after 30 November 2001.
[3] Paragraph numbering corrected by the Financial Services and Markets Act 2000 (Consequential Amendments) (Taxes) Order, SI 2002/1409 art 6 with effect from 2 July 2002.

[Modifications of paragraph 4 of Schedule 6 to the Finance Act 1999

53B—(1) Paragraphs (2) and (3) prescribe modifications of paragraph 4 of Schedule 6 to the Finance Act 1999 in relation to a reverse premium (within the meaning of that Schedule) received on or after 9th March 1999 by a friendly society carrying on life or endowment business, not being a payment or other benefit to which the friendly society was entitled immediately before that date.

(2) In paragraph (3)(*b*) before the words ''basic life assurance'' there shall be inserted the word ''taxable''.

(3) In paragraph (4) for the words ''basic life assurance and general annuity business'' there shall be substituted the words ''taxable basic life assurance and general annuity business''.]

Amendments—[1] This regulation inserted by the Friendly Societies (Modification of the Corporation Tax Acts) (Amendment) Regulations, SI 1999/2636 reg 7 with effect from 13 October 1999.

[Modification of section 256 of the Capital Allowances Act 2001

53C—(1) Paragraphs (2) and (3) prescribe modifications of section 256 of the Capital Allowances Act 2001 so far as it applies to the life or endowment business carried on by friendly societies for chargeable periods ending on or after 1st April 2001.

(2) In subsection (1)(*a*) before the words ''basic life assurance and general assurance business'' there shall be inserted the word ''taxable''.

(3) In subsection (2)(*a*) before the words ''basic life assurance and general assurance business'' there shall be inserted the word ''taxable''.][1]

Amendments—[1] This regulation inserted, together with reg 53D, by the Friendly Societies (Modification of the Corporation Tax Acts) (Amendment) Regulations, SI 2001/3975 regs 3, 8 with effect from 1 January 2002.

Modification of section 560 of the Capital Allowances Act 2001

53D

Amendments—Regulations 47, 49, 50, 50A, 50B, 51, 52, 53D, 53E, 53F, 53G and 53J revoked by the Friendly Societies (Modification of the Corporation Tax Acts) (Amendment) Regulations, SI 2004/822 regs 2, 40. The regulations came into force on 8 April 2004, and these revocations have effect for accounting periods beginning after 31 December 2002.

Modification of section 66 of the Finance Act 2002

53E

Amendments—Regulations 47, 49, 50, 50A, 50B, 51, 52, 53D, 53E, 53F, 53G and 53J revoked by the Friendly Societies (Modification of the Corporation Tax Acts) (Amendment) Regulations, SI 2004/822 regs 2, 40. The regulations came into force on 8 April 2004, and these revocations have effect for accounting periods beginning after 31 December 2002.

Modification of paragraph 10 of Schedule 22 to the Finance Act 2002

53F

Amendments—Regulations 47, 49, 50, 50A, 50B, 51, 52, 53D, 53E, 53F, 53G and 53J revoked by the Friendly Societies (Modification of the Corporation Tax Acts) (Amendment) Regulations, SI 2004/822 regs 2, 40. The regulations came into force on 8 April 2004, and these revocations have effect for accounting periods beginning after 31 December 2002.

Modifications of paragraph 28 of Schedule 26 to the Finance Act 2002

53G

Amendments—Regulations 47, 49, 50, 50A, 50B, 51, 52, 53D, 53E, 53F, 53G and 53J revoked by the Friendly Societies (Modification of the Corporation Tax Acts) (Amendment) Regulations, SI 2004/822 regs 2, 40. The regulations came into force on 8 April 2004, and these revocations have effect for accounting periods beginning after 31 December 2002.

[Modification of paragraph 36 of Schedule 29 to the Finance Act 2002

53H—(1) Paragraph (2) prescribes a modification of paragraph 36 of Schedule 29 to the Finance Act 2002 so far as it applies to the life or endowment business carried on by friendly societies on or after 1st April 2002, subject to the transitional provisions in Part 14 of that Schedule.

(2) In sub-paragraph (3) after ''carries on'' insert ''taxable''.][1]

Amendments—[1] Regulations 53E–53J inserted by the Friendly Societies (Modification of the Corporation Tax Acts) (Amendment) Regulations, SI 2003/23 reg 10 with effect from 30 January 2003.

Modifications of paragraph 89 of Schedule 29 to the Finance Act 2002

53J

Amendment—Regulations 47, 49, 50, 50A, 50B, 51, 52, 53D, 53E, 53F, 53G and 53J revoked by the Friendly Societies (Modification of the Corporation Tax Acts) (Amendment) Regulations, SI 2004/822 regs 2, 40. The regulations came into force on 8 April 2004, and these revocations have effect for accounting periods beginning after 31 December 2002.

Supersession of earlier Regulations

54 In consequence of the provisions of these Regulations—

(*a*) the Friendly Societies (Modification of the Corporation Tax Acts) Regulations 1992 shall cease to have effect for accounting periods beginning on or after 1st January 1995; and

(*b*) the Friendly Societies (Taxation of Transfers of Business) Regulations 1995 shall cease to have effect in relation to transfers, amalgamations and conversions taking place on or after that date.

1997/991
Finance Act 1997, Schedule 10, (Appointed Day) Order 1997

Made by the Treasury under FA 1997, Sch 10, paras 7(1), 16(1), (2)

Made . . . . *20 March 1997*

1 This Order may be cited as the Finance Act 1997, Schedule 10, (Appointed Day) Order 1997.

2 The day appointed for the purposes of paragraphs 7(1) and 16(1) and (2) of Schedule 10 to the Finance Act 1997 is 1st July 1997.

1997/992
Manufactured Interest (Tax) Regulations 1997

Made by the Treasury under TA 1988 Sch 23A paras 1(1), 8(1), (2)–(4)

Made . . . . *20 March 1997*
Laid before the House of Commons . . . *20 March 1997*
Coming into Force . . . . *1 July 1997*

Commentary—*Simon's Direct Tax Service* **A7.802.**

Citation and commencement

1 These Regulations may be cited as the Manufactured Interest (Tax) Regulations 1997 and shall come into force on 1st July 1997.

Interpretation

2—(1) In these Regulations—

''manufactured interest'' shall be construed in accordance with paragraph 3(1) of Schedule 23A;

''recipient'' in relation to a payment of manufactured interest means a person referred to in paragraph 3(5) of Schedule 23A who is a company.

(2) References to a section or a Schedule, without more, are references to that section of, or that Schedule to, the Income and Corporation Taxes Act 1988.

Application of the Tax Acts to manufactured interest on which recipients are accountable for tax

3—(1) Schedule 16 shall apply in relation to the collection of income tax on payments of manufactured interest to which paragraph (2) applies (''specified payments'') as if references in that Schedule, other than the reference in paragraph 5 of that Schedule, to relevant payments made by a company were references to specified payments.

(2) The payments of manufactured interest specified in this paragraph are payments in relation to which the recipients are liable to account for income tax under paragraph 3(5) of Schedule 23A.

(3) The recipient of a payment of manufactured interest to which paragraph (2) applies (or would apply but for regulation 4(1)) or, as the case may be, any person claiming title through or under him, shall be treated for the purposes of the Tax Acts as if the payment had borne income tax by deduction.

Liability for tax where the manufacturer receives the interest of which the manufactured interest is representative

4—(1) The recipient of a payment of manufactured interest shall not be liable to account for income tax under paragraph 3(5) of Schedule 23A in any case where he shows that—

(*a*) the interest manufacturer was entitled to payment of the interest of which the manufactured interest is representative either—

(i) as the holder of the securities concerned, or

(ii) directly or indirectly from a person from whom he acquired those securities, or to whom he transferred them, and who was so entitled as the holder of those securities, and

(*b*) the amount of the payment of interest actually received by the interest manufacturer does not exceed the amount found by deducting from the gross amount of the interest such tax as would have been deducted if the payment of interest had been made to the recipient.

(2) Where paragraph (1) applies the interest manufacturer shall be liable for tax, in respect of the payment of manufactured interest, in an amount equal to the amount (if any) of relief from United Kingdom tax to which, assuming him to have made a claim under arrangements having effect by virtue of section 788, the interest manufacturer is entitled in respect of the payment of interest received by him.

(3) The amount of tax for which the interest manufacturer is liable shall be set against the amount of relief from United Kingdom tax to which, on the assumption made in paragraph (2), he is entitled as mentioned in that paragraph.

(4) Where paragraph (1) does not apply by reason only of the fact that sub-paragraph (*b*) of that paragraph does not apply, the amount of income tax for which the recipient of the payment of manufactured interest shall be liable to account under paragraph 3(5) of Schedule 23A shall be reduced to an amount equal to the amount by which the amount of the payment of interest actually received by the interest manufacturer exceeds the amount found as mentioned in that sub-paragraph.

1997/993
Manufactured Dividends (Tax) Regulations 1997

Made by the Treasury under TA 1988 Sch 23A paras 1(1), 2(3)–(5), 8(1), (2)–(4)

Made	*20 March 1997*
Laid before the House of Commons	*20 March 1997*
Coming into Force	*1 July 1997*

Commentary—*Simon's Direct Tax Service* **A7.802.**

Citation and commencement

1 These Regulations may be cited as the Manufactured Dividends (Tax) Regulations 1997 and shall come into force on 1st July 1997.

Interpretation

2—(1) In these Regulations unless the context otherwise requires—

''the Board'' means the Commissioners of Inland Revenue;

''chargeable period'' has the meaning given by regulation 3;

''dividend'' means a dividend on United Kingdom equities, not being a foreign income dividend within Chapter VA of Part VI of the Taxes Act;

''the Management Act'' means the Taxes Management Act 1970;

''manufactured dividend'' shall be construed in accordance with paragraph 2(1) of Schedule 23A;

''relevant period'' means—

(*a*) each complete quarter falling within a chargeable period, that is to say, each of the periods of three months ending with 31st March, 30th June, 30th September or 31st December which falls within that period;

(*b*) each part of the chargeable period which is not a complete quarter and ends on the first (or only), or begins immediately after the last (or only), of those dates which falls within the chargeable period;

(*c*) if none of those dates falls within a chargeable period which is an accounting period, the whole chargeable period;

''the Taxes Act'' means the Income and Corporation Taxes Act 1988.

(2) References in these Regulations to a ''creditable amount'' in respect of a dividend or manufactured dividend received in any period—

[(*za*) are references to such amount in respect of a dividend or manufactured dividend other than a dividend or manufactured dividend that is paid on or after 6th April 1999, and either][1]

(*a*) are references to the tax credit in respect of that dividend or manufactured dividend, not being an amount of tax credit to which paragraph (3) applies, or

(*b*) where the recipient of the dividend or manufactured dividend is a company that is not resident in the United Kingdom and the dividend or manufactured dividend is attributable to a branch or agency through which the company trades in the United Kingdom, are references to an amount of tax equal to the amount of advance corporation tax payable in respect of that dividend or manufactured dividend, or (as the case may be) the amount of advance corporation tax that would have been payable in respect of that dividend or manufactured dividend if—

(i) the person by whom the dividend or manufactured dividend was paid were a company resident in the United Kingdom, and

(ii) the manufactured dividend were a distribution by that company.

(3) This paragraph applies to the amount of tax credit in respect of a distribution which—

(*a*) is comprised in the UK distribution income (within the meaning given by paragraph 5B(4) of Schedule 19AC) of an overseas life insurance company falling within that Schedule, and

(*b*) is a distribution in respect of which that company has claimed or may claim the payment of a tax credit under section 438(4) or 441A(7).

(4) References in these Regulations to a section or Schedule, without more, are references to that section of, or that Schedule to, the Taxes Act.

Amendments—[1]Sub-para (*za*) inserted by the Manufactured Dividends (Tax) Amendment Regulations, SI 1999/621 reg 2, with effect from 30 March 1999.

Chargeable period

3—(1) In these Regulations "chargeable period" means—

(*a*) as respects a company, its accounting period;

(*b*) as respects a person other than a company who draws up accounts for any period ("the accounts period"), one of the periods specified in paragraph (2);

(*c*) as respects a person other than a company who does not draw up accounts, a year of assessment.

(2) The periods specified in this paragraph are—

(*a*) the period which begins at the beginning of the accounts period and ends at the expiration of 12 months from that date or, if earlier, at the end of the accounts period;

(*b*) any subsequent period which—

(i) begins at the end of the immediately preceding period, being a period specified in this paragraph, and

(ii) ends at the expiration of 12 months from that date or, if earlier, at the end of the accounts period.

Accountability for tax

4—(1) Where—

(*a*) a manufactured dividend is paid by any person other than a company resident in the United Kingdom, and

(*b*) the payment is one in relation to which either the dividend manufacturer or the recipient of the payment is a person to whom paragraph (2) below applies ("the appropriate person"),

the appropriate person shall be liable to account to the Board, to the extent and in the manner specified in these Regulations, for tax as mentioned in paragraph 2(3) of Schedule 23A.

(2) Subject to regulation 5, the appropriate person is—

(*a*) where paragraph 2(5) of Schedule 23A applies in relation to the manufactured dividend, the dividend manufacturer;

(*b*) where sub-paragraph (*a*) above does not apply in relation to the manufactured dividend and either of the conditions specified in paragraph (3) below applies, the recipient of the payment.

(3) The conditions specified in this paragraph are—

(*a*) that the recipient is a person resident in the United Kingdom;

(*b*) that the recipient is a company that is not so resident but carries on a trade in the United Kingdom through a branch or agency, and the manufactured dividend is attributable to the carrying on of that trade through that branch or agency.

Liability for tax where the manufacturer receives the dividend of which the manufactured dividend is representative

5—(1) Regulation 4(2)(*b*) shall not apply in any case where the recipient of the manufactured dividend shows that—

(*a*) the dividend manufacturer was entitled to payment of the dividend of which the manufactured dividend is representative either—

(i) as the holder of the securities concerned, or

(ii) directly or indirectly from a person from whom he acquired those securities, or to whom he transferred them, and who was so entitled as the holder of those securities, and

(*b*) the aggregate of the amount of the dividend received by the dividend manufacturer and any amount paid to him in respect of a tax credit in relation to that dividend ("the aggregate amount") does not exceed the amount of the dividend.

(2) Where paragraph (1) applies, the dividend manufacturer concerned shall be liable for tax, in respect of the manufactured dividend paid by him, in an amount equal to the amount (if any) of a tax credit in respect of the dividend received by him which, assuming him to have made a claim under

arrangements having effect by virtue of section 788, the dividend manufacturer is entitled to have paid to him in respect of the dividend received by him.

(3) The amount of tax for which the dividend manufacturer is liable shall be set against the amount of the tax credit to which, on the assumption made in paragraph (2), he is entitled as mentioned in that paragraph.

(4) Where paragraph (1) does not apply by reason only of the fact that sub-paragraph (*b*) of that paragraph does not apply, the amount of tax for which the recipient of the manufactured dividend shall be liable to account under paragraph 2(3) of Schedule 23A shall be reduced to an amount equal to the amount by which the aggregate amount exceeds the amount of the dividend.

Accounting for tax by recipients that are United Kingdom resident companies

6—(1) This regulation applies in any case where a recipient of a manufactured dividend—

(*a*) is liable under regulation 4 to account to the Board for any tax in respect of that manufactured dividend, and

(*b*) is a company resident in the United Kingdom.

(2) Paragraphs 1 to 3, 8 and 10 of Schedule 13 (collection of advance corporation tax) and, on or after the appointed day referred to in section 137(2) of the Finance Act 1996, paragraph 7A of that Schedule, shall apply in relation to the amount of tax for which the company is liable to account in respect of that manufactured dividend as if—

(*a*) paragraph 1 of that Schedule required a return under that paragraph to include in addition manufactured dividends received by the company in each of its accounting periods and the tax for which it is liable to account in respect of those manufactured dividends;

(*b*) paragraph 2(1) of that Schedule required a return for any return period to include in addition the amount of any manufactured dividends received by the company in that period, and the amount of tax for which it is liable to account in respect of those manufactured dividends;

(*c*) references in paragraph 3 of that Schedule to franked payments and advance corporation tax in respect of such payments included references to manufactured dividends required to be included in a return under that Schedule by virtue of this regulation and tax for which the company is liable to account in respect of those manufactured dividends;

(*d*) paragraph 8 of that Schedule included a reference to a manufactured dividend included in a return under that Schedule by virtue of this regulation;

(*e*) paragraph 10 of that Schedule included a reference to tax for which the company is liable to account in respect of manufactured dividends received in any accounting period.

Accounting for tax by persons other than United Kingdom resident companies

7—(1) This regulation applies in any case where the payer or recipient of a manufactured dividend ("the relevant person")—

(*a*) is liable under regulation 4 to account to the Board for any tax in respect of that manufactured dividend, and

(*b*) is not a company resident in the United Kingdom.

(2) The relevant person shall be liable to account in respect of any relevant period for an amount of tax equal to the sum of the following—

(*a*) the amount (if any) by which for that period the aggregate amount of tax for which he is accountable in respect of manufactured dividends paid by him exceeds the aggregate amount of creditable amounts in respect of dividends and manufactured dividends received by him, and

(*b*) the amount (if any) for that period of the aggregate amount of tax for which he is accountable in respect of manufactured dividends received by him.

(3) Tax for which the relevant person is accountable under paragraph (2)—

(*a*) shall be due not later than 14 days after the end of the relevant period concerned, and

(*b*) shall be payable without the making of an assessment.

(4) Tax due under paragraph (3) shall, whether or not an assessment is made under paragraph (10) of this regulation or under regulation 8(4), carry interest at the rate applicable under section 178 of the Finance Act 1989 to section 87 of the Management Act from the end of the period of 14 days referred to in that paragraph until payment.

(5) Where the aggregate amount of creditable amounts in respect of dividends and manufactured dividends received by the relevant person in a relevant period exceeds the aggregate amount of tax for which he is accountable in respect of manufactured dividends paid by him in that period, the amount of the excess may be carried forward to any subsequent relevant period falling within the same chargeable period for the purposes of offsetting, pursuant to paragraph (2)(*a*), that excess amount against the aggregate amount of tax for which he is accountable in respect of manufactured dividends paid by him in respect of that subsequent relevant period.

(6) Where—

(*a*) the aggregate amount of tax for which the relevant person is accountable in respect of manufactured dividends paid by him in a relevant period ("the first period") exceeds the aggregate amount of creditable amounts in respect of dividends and manufactured dividends received by him in that period, and

(*b*) in any subsequent relevant period falling within the same chargeable period there is an excess of the aggregate amount of creditable amounts in respect of dividends and manufactured dividends received by him over the aggregate amount of tax for which he is accountable in respect of manufactured dividends paid by him,

that excess amount may be set off, for the purposes of paragraph (2)(*a*), against the aggregate amount of tax for which the relevant person is accountable in respect of manufactured dividends paid by him in the first period, and a repayment of tax shall be made accordingly.

(7) Where—

(*a*) the relevant person is a company that is not resident in the United Kingdom, and

(*b*) the aggregate amount of creditable amounts in respect of dividends and manufactured dividends received by him in a chargeable period exceeds the aggregate amount of tax for which the company is accountable in respect of manufactured dividends paid by him in that period,

the amount of that excess may be carried forward so as to be regarded, for the purposes of paragraph (2), as a creditable amount in respect of dividends or manufactured dividends received by him in the first relevant period of the next chargeable period.

(8) Where—

(*a*) the relevant person was under an obligation to make a return under regulation 20 of the Income Tax (Dividend Manufacturing) Regulations 1992 in respect of the return period ending 30th June 1997, and

(*b*) surplus tax credits received by the relevant person fell to be carried forward on that date to its next accounting period under paragraph (10)(*a*) of that regulation or would have fallen so to be carried forward if its accounting period had ended on that date, references in these Regulations to creditable amounts shall, as respects the relevant period commencing 1st July 1997, be taken as including references to those surplus tax credits.

(9) The same creditable amount shall not be taken into account both under this regulation and under any other provision of the Tax Acts.

(10) Tax which has become due from a person under paragraph (3) may be assessed on that person (whether or not it has been paid when the assessment is made) if that tax, or any part of it, is not paid on or before the due date.

Returns by persons other than United Kingdom resident companies

8—(1) This regulation applies in any case where under regulation 7 the relevant person is liable to account for an amount of tax in respect of any relevant period falling within a chargeable period.

(2) The relevant person shall, within 30 days from the end of the chargeable period, make a return for that period to the Board.

(3) A return under paragraph (2) shall show—

(*a*) the aggregate amount of the manufactured dividends received by the relevant person in the chargeable period in respect of which he is liable to account for tax under regulation 7,

(*b*) the aggregate amount of the manufactured dividends paid by the relevant person in the chargeable period in respect of which he is liable to account for tax under regulation 7,

(*c*) the aggregate amount of creditable amounts in respect of dividends and manufactured dividends received by the relevant person in the chargeable period,

(*d*) the amount of creditable amounts brought forward from the previous chargeable period under regulation 7(7);

(*e*) the amount of creditable amounts carried forward to the next chargeable period under regulation 7(7);

(*f*) the aggregate amount of tax for which he is liable to account under regulation 7 for the chargeable period which is the subject of the return.

(4) If it appears to an officer of the Board that there is a manufactured dividend which ought to have been and has not been included in a return under paragraph (2), or if he is otherwise dissatisfied with any such return, he may make an assessment on the relevant person to the best of his judgment.

(5) Section 98 of the Management Act (''section 98'') shall apply in relation to a return under paragraph (2) with the modification specified in paragraph (6).

(6) At the end of the second column of the Table in section 98 there shall be added—

''Regulation 8(2) of the Manufactured Dividends (Tax) Regulations 1997.''

Set off of tax by companies not resident in the United Kingdom

9—(1) Subject to the modification specified in paragraph (2), the provisions of section 239 other than subsection (7) of that section, section 246(5) and section 797(4) shall apply in relation to the aggregate amount of tax for which a company that is not resident in the United Kingdom is liable in accordance with regulation 7(2)(*a*) to account for all relevant periods falling within any chargeable period in respect of manufactured dividends paid by it, as if that tax were advance corporation tax paid by the company in respect of distributions made by it in that chargeable period.

(2) Subsection (3) of section 239 shall apply as if the reference in that subsection to any of the company's accounting periods beginning in the six years preceding the accounting period concerned were a reference to any of the company's accounting periods ending on or after 1st July 1997 and beginning in the six years preceding that accounting period.

1997/1154
Open-ended Investment Companies (Tax) Regulations 1997

Made by the Treasury under TA 1995 s 152

Made . . . . *3 April 1997*
Laid before the House of Commons . . . *7 April 1997*
Coming into Force . . . . *28 April 1997*

Commentary—*Simon's Direct Tax Service* **D4.447.**

ARRANGEMENT OF REGULATIONS

PART I
INTRODUCTORY

PART II
GENERAL PROVISIONS RELATING TO TAX TREATMENT OF OPEN-ENDED INVESTMENT COMPANIES

PART III
SPECIFIC MODIFICATIONS OF CHAPTER III OF PART XII OF THE TAXES ACT (UNIT TRUST SCHEMES)

PART IV
OTHER SPECIFIC MODIFICATIONS OF THE TAX ACTS

PART V
SPECIFIC MODIFICATIONS OF THE 1992 ACT

PART VI

MISCELLANEOUS PROVISIONS

PART I

INTRODUCTORY

Citation and commencement

1 These Regulations may be cited as the Open-ended Investment Companies (Tax) Regulations 1997 and shall come into force on 28th April 1997.

Interpretation

2—(1) In these Regulations unless the context otherwise requires—

"accumulation share", in relation to an open-ended investment company, means a share in that company in respect of which income is credited periodically to the capital part of the scheme property of the company;

"authorised corporate director", in relation to an open-ended investment company, has the meaning given by subsection (10) of section 468, read with subsections (16) and (17) of that section, as those subsections are added by regulation 10(4);

"authorised unit trust" has the meaning given by subsection (6) of section 468;

"open-ended investment company" has the meaning given by subsection (10) of section 468, read with subsections (11) to (18) of that section, as those subsections are added by regulation 10(4);

"owner of shares", in relation to an open-ended investment company, has the meaning given by subsection (10) of section 468, read with subsection (15) of that section, as those subsections are added by regulation 10(4); and references to "owner of a share" and "owner of the shares" shall be construed accordingly;

"scheme property", in relation to an open-ended investment company, has the meaning given by subsection (10) of section 468, read with subsection (13) of that section, as those subsections are added by regulation 10(4);

"unit holder", in relation to a unit trust scheme, has the meaning given by subsection (6) of section 468; and references to "holder of a unit" and "holders of units" shall be construed accordingly;

"units", in relation to a unit trust scheme, means the rights or interests (however described) of the unit holders in the scheme;

"unit trust scheme" has the meaning given by section 469(7);

"the Taxes Act" means the Income and Corporation Taxes Act 1988;

"the Tax Acts" means the provisions of "the Tax Acts" (as defined by section 831(2)) other than section 152 of the Finance Act 1995;

"the 1992 Act" means the Taxation of Chargeable Gains Act 1992.

(2) For the purposes of the definitions of "authorised corporate director", "open-ended investment company", "owner of shares" and "scheme property" in paragraph (1), references in subsection (11) to (16) of section 468 (as those subsections are added by regulation 10(4)) to "the Tax Acts" shall be construed as if they included references to these Regulations.

(3) In these Regulations references to a section or a Schedule, without more, are references to that section of, or that Schedule to, the Taxes Act.

PART II

GENERAL PROVISIONS RELATING TO TAX TREATMENT OF OPEN-ENDED INVESTMENT COMPANIES

[Tax treatment of open-ended investment companies—general

3—(1) Subject to the modifications and exceptions specified in this Part, and the modifications specified in Parts III to V, of these Regulations, the Tax Acts and the 1992 Act shall have effect in relation to—

(*a*) open-ended investment companies,
(*b*) holdings in, and the assets of, such companies, and

(*c*) transactions involving such companies,

in like manner as the manner in which they have effect in relation to authorised unit trusts, to rights under, and the assets subject to, such trusts and to transactions for purposes connected with such trusts.

(2) References in the Tax Acts and the 1992 Act to companies, to holdings in, and the assets of, companies and to transactions involving companies, shall accordingly have effect (or shall not have effect as the case may be) in relation to open-ended investment companies, to holdings in, and the assets of, such companies, and to transactions involving such companies, in like manner as the manner in which they have effect (or do not have effect) in relation to authorised unit trusts, to rights under, and the assets subject to, such trusts, and to transactions for purposes connected with such trusts.][1]

Amendments—[1]This regulation substituted by the Open-ended Investment Companies (Tax) (Amendment) Regulations, SI 1997/1715 reg 3, with effect from 8 August 1997. (The amendment corrects a printing error and makes a drafting improvement.)

General modifications of the Tax Acts and the 1992 Act

4 The modifications specified in regulations 5 to 8 have effect subject to the modifications specified in Parts III to V of these Regulations.

General modification—authorised unit trust

5—(1) Subject to paragraph (2), the modifications specified in this regulation are that references, however expressed, in the Tax Acts and the 1992 Act to—

(*a*) an authorised unit trust (other than references in a definition of an authorised unit trust, an unauthorised unit trust or a unit trust scheme),

(*b*) a unit trust scheme as denoting or including (whether expressly or by implication) an authorised unit trust (other than references in a definition of an authorised unit trust, an unauthorised unit trust or a unit trust scheme), and

(*c*) the trustees of an authorised unit trust within sub-paragraph (*a*) or of a unit trust scheme within sub-paragraph (*b*),

shall have effect as if they included references to an open-ended investment company.

[(2) Paragraph (1) shall not apply to references in any of the provisions specified in paragraph (3) or to references to provisions which include reference, whether made expressly or by implication, to an open-ended investment company.][1]

(3) The provisions specified in this paragraph are—

(*a*) section 468(1), (4) and (6) to (9);
(*b*) section 468L(8), (9)(*d*) and (10) to (12);
(*c*) section 469(1);
(*d*) section 470;
(*e*) the definition of "company" in section 839(8);
(*f*) paragraph 6 of Schedule 20;
(*g*) section 80 of the Finance Act 1989;
(*h*) *section 152(3) of the Finance Act 1993;*[2]
(*i*) *section 154(2) of the Finance Act 1994;*[2]
(*j*) paragraphs 3 and 8 of Schedule 10 to the Finance Act 1996;
(*k*) sections 99(1), 100(2) and 272(5) of the 1992 Act.

Amendments—[1] Para (2) inserted by the Open-ended Investment Companies (Tax) (Amendment) Regulations, SI 1997/1715 reg 4, with effect from 8 August 1997, having been omitted from the original Regulations in error.
[2] Paras (3)(*h*), (*i*) repealed by the Open-ended Investment Companies (Tax) (Amendment) Regulations, SI 2002/1973 regs 1–3 with effect for accounting period beginning after 30 September 2002.

General modification—manager of authorised unit trust

6—(1) Subject to paragraph (2), the modifications specified in this regulation are that references, however expressed, in the Tax Acts and the 1992 Act to the manager of an authorised unit trust or of a unit trust scheme within regulation 5(1)(*b*) shall have effect as if they included references to the authorised corporate director of the open-ended investment company concerned.

(2) Paragraph (1) shall not apply to section 468(4), to section 272(5) of the 1992 Act, or to references in provisions which include reference, whether made expressly or by implication, to the authorised corporate director of an open-ended investment company.

General modification—unit of authorised unit trust

7—(1) Subject to paragraphs (2) and (3), the modifications specified in this regulation are that—

(*a*) references, however expressed, in the Tax Acts and the 1992 Act to—

(i) a unit or an interest in, or rights under, an authorised unit trust,
(ii) a unit or an interest in, or rights under, a unit trust scheme within regulation 5(1)(*b*), or

(iii) an entitlement to a share of, or in, the investments subject to the trusts of an authorised unit trust or a unit trust scheme within regulation 5(1)(*b*),

shall have effect as if they included references to a share in the open-ended investment company concerned;

(*b*) references, however expressed, in the Tax Acts and the 1992 Act to the holder of a unit within [sub-paragraph][1] (*a*) (other than references in a definition of a unit holder) shall have effect as if they included references to the owner of a share in the open-ended investment company concerned.

(2) Paragraph (1) shall not apply to references in provisions which include reference, whether made expressly or by implication, to shares in, or an owner of shares in, an open-ended investment company.

(3) Paragraph (1) shall in addition not apply to references in any of the provisions specified in paragraph (4).

(4) The provisions specified are—

(*a*) section 468(1), (8) and (9);
(*b*) section 468L(9)(*d*) and (10);
(*c*) the definition of "company" in section 839(8);
(*d*) paragraph 6 of Schedule 20;
(*e*) paragraph 8 of Schedule 10 to the Finance Act 1996;
(*f*) sections 99(1), *117B(3)(a)*[2] and 272(5) of the 1992 Act.

Amendments—[1] Word in para (1)(*b*) substituted by the Open-ended Investment Companies (Tax) (Amendment) Regulations, SI 1997/1715 reg 5, with effect from 8 August 1997, to correct drafting error.
[2] In para 4(*f*), ", 117B(3)(*a*)" repealed by the Open-ended Investment Companies (Tax) (Amendment) Regulations, SI 2002/1973 regs 1, 2, 4 with effect for accounting periods beginning after 30 September 2002.

General modification—registered office of company

8—(1) Subject to paragraph (2), the modifications specified in this regulation are that references in the Tax Acts and the 1992 Act to the registered office of a company shall have effect as if they were references to the head office of an open-ended investment company.

(2) Paragraph (1) shall not apply to references in provisions which include reference, whether made expressly or by implication, to the head office of an open-ended investment company.

PART III
SPECIFIC MODIFICATIONS OF CHAPTER III OF PART XII OF THE TAXES ACT (UNIT TRUST SCHEMES)

General provision

9 Sections 468, *468AA*[1], and 468H to 468R shall have effect with the modifications specified in regulations 10 to 13 and as if—

(*a*) references in those sections to "accumulation units" included references to "accumulation shares";

(*b*) references in those sections to "the company referred to in section 468(1)" included references to the open-ended investment company concerned; and

(*c*) references, however expressed, in those sections to the terms of an authorised unit trust included references to the instrument of incorporation of the open-ended investment company concerned and the prospectus in issue for the time being of that company (including any supplements to that prospectus).

Amendments—[1] Reference to ", 468AA" repealed by the Open-ended Investment Companies (Tax) (Amendment) Regulations, SI 2002/1973 regs 1, 2, 5 with effect for accounting periods beginning after 30 September 2002.

Modifications of section 468

10—(1) Section 468 shall be modified in accordance with paragraphs (2) to (4).

(2) After subsection (3) there shall be inserted the following subsection—

"(3A) Section 234A shall apply in relation to an open-ended investment company."

(3) After subsection (4) there shall be inserted the following subsection—

"(4A) Section 75 shall apply in relation to an open-ended investment company whether or not it is an investment company within the meaning of section 130; and sums appropriated in accordance with the terms of the prospectus in issue for the time being (including any supplements to that prospectus) of an open-ended investment company for such remuneration of its authorised corporate director as is paid in respect of the management of the company's scheme property shall be treated for the purposes of section 75 as sums disbursed as expenses of management."

(4) After subsection (9) there shall be added the following subsections—

"(10) Subject to subsections (11) to (18) below, in this Chapter—

'authorised corporate director' in relation to an open-ended investment company means a corporate director of the company acting in the capacity as the director having responsibility for the management of its scheme property, being an authorised person within the meaning [given by section 31(2) of the Financial Services and Markets Act 2000][1], or if there is no such director, the person for the time being having responsibility for the management of the scheme property of the company and acting in that capacity;

'collective investment scheme' has the meaning given by section [235 of the Financial Services and Markets Act 2000][1];

'open-ended investment company' means an open-ended investment company within the meaning given by section [236 of the Financial Services and Markets Act 2000][1] which is incorporated in the United Kingdom;

'owner of shares' in relation to an open-ended investment company means—

(*a*) the beneficial owner of the shares, or

(*b*) where the shares are held on trust (other than a bare trust), the trustees of the trust, or

(*c*) where the shares are comprised in the estate of a deceased person, the deceased's personal representatives;

'scheme property' in relation to an open-ended investment company means the property subject to the collective investment scheme constituted by the company.

(11) Subject to subsection (17) below, each of the parts of an umbrella company shall be regarded for the purposes of the Tax Acts, except where the context otherwise requires, as an open-ended investment company and the umbrella company as a whole shall not be so regarded and shall not be regarded as being a company for the purposes of the Tax Acts.

(12) In relation to a part of an umbrella company, any reference in this Chapter to investments of an open-ended investment company shall have effect for the purposes of the Tax Acts, except where the context otherwise requires, as a reference to such of the investments as under the arrangements referred to in subsection (18) below form part of the separate pool to which that part of the umbrella company relates.

(13) In relation to a part of an umbrella company, any references in this Chapter to the scheme property of an open-ended investment company shall have effect for the purposes of the Tax Acts, except where the context otherwise requires, as references to such property subject to the collective investment scheme constituted by the umbrella company as is comprised in the separate pool to which that part of the umbrella company relates.

(14) In relation to a part of an umbrella company, any references in this Chapter to the instrument of incorporation or the prospectus in issue for the time being (including any supplements to that prospectus) of an open-ended investment company shall have effect for the purposes of the Tax Acts as references to such parts of the instrument of incorporation or of that prospectus (including any supplements to that prospectus) as apply to that part of the umbrella company.

(15) A person for the time being having rights in a part of an umbrella company shall be regarded for the purposes of the Tax Acts, except where the context otherwise requires, as the owner of shares in the open-ended investment company which that part is deemed to be by virtue of subsection (11) above and not as the owner of shares in the umbrella company itself.

(16) In relation to a part of an umbrella company and subject to subsection (17) below, the authorised corporate director of an umbrella company shall be regarded for the purposes of the Tax Acts, except where the context otherwise requires, as the authorised corporate director of the open-ended investment company which that part is deemed to be by virtue of subsection (11) above and not as the authorised corporate director of the umbrella company itself.

(17) In relation to section 468P (residence declarations)—

(*a*) a declaration under that section made by an owner of shares in an umbrella company shall be made to the umbrella company itself and not to the part or parts of that company in which the owner of the shares concerned is deemed to be an owner of shares by virtue of subsection (15) above;

(*b*) the undertaking contained in that declaration shall be an undertaking to notify the umbrella company and not the part or parts of that company in which the owner of the shares concerned is deemed to be an owner of shares by virtue of subsection (15) above; and

(*c*) subsections (11) and (16) above shall not apply in relation to subsection (8) of that section (regulations requiring information to be supplied and documents to be made available).

(18) In this section 'umbrella company' means a company—

(*a*) which falls within the definition of [an open-ended investment company][1] in section [236 of the Financial Services and Markets Act 2000][1],

(*b*) which is incorporated in the United Kingdom,

(*c*) whose instrument of incorporation provides for arrangements for such pooling as is mentioned in section [235(*a*)][1] of that Act in relation to separate parts of the scheme property of the company, and

(*d*) the owners of shares in which are entitled to exchange rights in one part for rights in another;

and any reference to a part of an umbrella company is a reference to such of the arrangements as relate to a separate pool.''

Amendments—[1] Words in para (4) substituted by the Financial Services and Markets Act 2000 (Consequential Amendments) (Taxes) Order, SI 2001/3629 art 166 with effect from 1 December 2001, immediately after the coming into force of the Financial Services and Markets Act 2000 ss 411, 432(1), Sch 20 (and SI 2001/3629 Pts 1 and 2).

Modifications of section 468AA

11—(1) Section 468AA shall be modified in accordance with paragraphs (2) and (3).

(2) In subsection (1)—

(a) for the word ''Trustees'' (where it first occurs) there shall be substituted the words ''An open-ended investment company'';

(b) [paragraph][1] (b) and the word ''and'' immediately preceding it shall be omitted.

(3) Subsection (3) shall be omitted.

Note—This regulation repealed by the Open-ended Investment Companies (Tax) (Amendment) Regulations, SI 2002/1973 regs 1, 2, 6 with effect for accounting periods beginning after 30 September 2002.

Amendments—[1]Word in para (2)(*b*) substituted by the Open-ended Investment Companies (Tax) (Amendment) Regulations, SI 1997/1715 reg 6, with effect from 8 August 1997, to correct drafting error.

Modifications of section 468I

12—(1) Section 468I shall be modified in accordance with paragraphs (2) and (3).

(2) In subsection (7) there shall be inserted at the beginning the words ''Subject to subsection (9) below,''.

(3) After subsection (7) there shall be added the following subsections—

''(8) Subject to subsection (9) below, where distribution accounts show an amount as available for distribution to owners of shares in any of the ways set out in subsections (2) to (4) above there shall not be any discrimination between owners of shares in respect of different classes of shares.

(9) For the purposes of subsections (7) and (8) above differences in amounts treated as paid in accordance with section 468J(2) or 468K(2), or treated as made in accordance with section 468L(2), to owners of shares in proportion to their rights in respect of different classes of shares shall not be regarded as discriminatory where those differences—

(*a*) are wholly attributable to differences between the amounts or treatment for accounting purposes of the charges or expenses which—

(i) are permitted by the instrument of incorporation of the open-ended investment company concerned or the prospectus in issue for the time being of that company (including any supplements to that prospectus), and

(ii) are payable out of the scheme property of that company in respect of the shares of those classes, and

(*b*) except where the relevant condition is satisfied, are not such as to enable the owners of the shares in any one of those classes to obtain a tax advantage which they would not obtain if there were no differences between the amounts or treatment for accounting purposes of those charges or expenses.

(10) For the purposes of paragraph (*b*) of subsection (9) above the relevant condition is that the company is able to show that the differences between the amounts or treatment for accounting purposes of the charges or expenses referred to in that subsection apply for bona fide commercial reasons.

(11) In paragraph (*b*) of subsection (9) above 'tax advantage' has the same meaning as in Chapter I of Part XVII of the Taxes Act.''

Modifications of section 468L

13—(1) Section 468L shall be modified in accordance with paragraphs (2) to (7).

(2) In subsection (8)—

(*a*) for the words ''authorised unit trust'' there shall be substituted the words ''open-ended investment company'';

(*b*) for the words ''that trust'' there shall be substituted the words ''that company''.

(3) In subsection (9)—

(*a*) for the words ''an authorised unit trust, means the investments of that trust'' there shall be substituted the words ''an open-ended investment company, means the investments of that company'';

(*b*) in paragraph (*d*) for the words ''another authorised unit trust'' there shall be substituted the words ''an authorised unit trust'';

(*c*) in paragraph (*e*) for the words ''an open-ended investment company'' there shall be substituted the words ''another open-ended investment company''.

(4) In subsection (10)—

(*a*) for the words "another authorised unit trust" there shall be substituted the words "an authorised unit trust";

(*b*) for the words "the other authorised unit trust" there shall be substituted the words "that authorised unit trust".

(5) In subsection (11) for the words "the other authorised unit trust" there shall be substituted the words "the authorised unit trust".

(6) In subsection (12B) for the words "subsection (12A) above" there shall be substituted the words "this section".

(7) Subsections (12C) to (12G) shall be omitted.

PART IV
OTHER SPECIFIC MODIFICATIONS OF THE TAX ACTS

Modifications of section 832(1)

14 In section 832(1) after the definition of "notice" where shall be inserted the following definitions—

" 'open-ended investment company', and 'authorised corporate director', 'owner of shares' and 'scheme property' in relation to an open-ended investment company, have the meanings given by subsection (10) of section 468, read with subsections (11) to (18) of that section, as those subsections are added by regulation 10(4) of the Open-ended Investment Companies (Tax) Regulations 1997;".

Modifications of section 839(8)

15 In section 839(8) in the definition of "company" the words "(including an open-ended investment company)" shall be inserted after the word "corporate".

Modification of Schedule 20

16 After paragraph 6 of Schedule 20 there shall be inserted the following paragraph—

"**6A** Shares in an open-ended investment company."

Modification of section 152 of the Finance Act 1993

17 After subsection (2) of section 152 of the Finance Act 1993 there shall be inserted the following subsection—

"(2A) An open-ended investment company is not a qualifying company."

Amendment—Repealed by the Open-ended Investment Companies (Tax) (Amendment) Regulations, SI 2002/1973 regs 1, 2, 6 with effect for accounting periods beginning after 30 September 2002.

Modifications of section 154 of the Finance Act 1994

18—(1) In subsection (1) of section 154 of the Finance Act 1994 after the word "subsections" there shall be inserted the word "(1A),"

(2) After subsection (1) of that section there shall be inserted the following subsection—

"(1A) An open-ended investment company is not a qualifying company for the purposes of this Chapter."

Amendment—Repealed by the Open-ended Investment Companies (Tax) (Amendment) Regulations, SI 2002/1973 regs 1, 2, 6 with effect for accounting periods beginning after 30 September 2002.

Modifications of Schedule 10 to the Finance Act 1996

19—(1) Schedule 10 to the Finance Act 1996 shall be modified in accordance with paragraphs (2) to (10).

(2) Paragraph 2(3) shall be omitted.[1]

(3) In paragraph 8(1)—

(*a*) for the words "a unit trust scheme or offshore fund" there shall be substituted the words "an open-ended investment company";

(*b*) for the words "scheme or fund" there shall be substituted the word "company".

(4) In paragraph 8(2) for the words "a unit trust scheme or offshore fund, means investments of the scheme or fund" there shall be substituted the words "an open-ended investment company, means investments of the company".

(5) Paragraph 8(3A) shall be omitted.

(6) In paragraph 8(4) for the words "sub-paragraphs (3) and (3A)" there shall be substituted the words "sub-paragraph (3)".

(7) Paragraph 8(6A) and (6B) shall be omitted.

(8) In paragraph 8(7) there shall be added at the end the words ", and references in this paragraph to investments of an open-ended investment company shall be construed in accordance with subsection (12) of section 468, read with subsection (18) of that section, as those subsections are added by regulation 10(4) of the Open-ended Investment Companies (Tax) Regulations 1997".

(9) Paragraph 8(7A) to (7D) shall be omitted.

(10) In paragraph 8(8) for the words "a unit trust scheme or offshore fund" there shall be substituted the words "an open-ended investment company".

Amendments—[1] Para (2) repealed by the Open-ended Investment Companies (Tax) (Amendment) Regulations, SI 2002/1973 with effect for accounting periods beginning after 30 September 2002.

PART V
SPECIFIC MODIFICATIONS OF THE 1992 ACT

Modifications of section 99 of the 1992 Act

20 In section 99(2) of the 1992 Act after paragraph (*b*) there shall be added the following paragraph—

"(*c*) 'open-ended investment company' has the meaning given by subsection (10) of section 468 of the Taxes Act, read with subsections (11) to (18) of that section, as those subsections are added by regulation 10(4) of the Open-ended Investment Companies (Tax) Regulations 1997; and accordingly references in subsections (11) to (16) of that section to 'the Tax Acts' shall be construed as if they included references to this Act."

Modification of section 117B of the 1992 Act

21 In section 117B(3) of the 1992 Act there shall be added at the end the words "; and shares of a given class in an open-ended investment company shall be taken to be denominated in a currency other than sterling if the price at which they may be acquired from, or disposed of to, the company or its authorised corporate director is fixed by the company or director in a currency other than sterling, or (as the case may be) the price or prices at which they are quoted in The Stock Exchange Daily Official List is in a currency other than sterling."

Amendments—Repealed by the Open-ended Investment Companies (Tax) (Amendment) Regulations, SI 2002/1973 regs 1, 2, 8 with effect for accounting periods beginning after 30 September 2002.

Modifications of section 272 of the 1992 Act

22 In section 272 of the 1992 Act—

(*a*) in subsection (3)(*a*) after the words "2 figures, or" there shall be added the words "where a single price is shown in the quotations for the shares or securities in The Stock Exchange Daily Official List on the relevant date, that price, or";

(*b*) after subsection (5) there shall be inserted the following subsections—

"(5AA) In this Act 'market value' in relation to shares of a given class in an open-ended investment company the prices of which are published regularly by the authorised corporate director of that company (whether or not those shares are also quoted in The Stock Exchange Daily Official List) shall mean an amount equal to the price so published on the relevant date, or if no price was published on that date, on the latest date before that date.

(5AB) In subsection (5AA) 'authorised corporate director' has the meaning given by subsection (10) of section 468 of the Taxes Act, read with subsections (16) and (17) of that section, as those subsections are added by regulation 10(4) of the Open-ended Investment Companies (Tax) Regulations 1997; and accordingly the reference in subsection (16) of that section to 'the Tax Acts' shall be construed as if it included a reference to this Act."

Modifications of section 288 of the 1992 Act

23 In section 288(8) of the 1992 Act in the Table—

after the expression "'Absolutely entitled as against the trustee'" there shall be inserted the following expression and reference—

"'Authorised corporate director'	s 272(5AB) (as that provision is inserted by regulation 22(*b*) of the Open-ended Investment Companies (Tax) Regulations 1997)";

(*b*) after the expression "'Market value'" there shall be inserted the following expression and reference—

"'Open-ended investment company'	s 99 (as that section is modified by regulation 20 of the Open-ended Investment Companies (Tax) Regulations 1997)".

SIs

PART VI
MISCELLANEOUS PROVISIONS

Ownership of shares in open-ended investment companies

24—(1) Where, in respect of a given class of shares specified in the instrument of incorporation of an open-ended investment company, shares issued of that class consist of both smaller denomination shares and larger denomination shares, and a person owns both smaller denomination shares and larger denomination shares of that class—

(*a*) those shares owned by him shall be treated as being securities of the same class for the purposes of the provisions of the Tax Acts and the 1992 Act relating to ownership of shares in a company,

(*b*) each larger denomination share shall be treated for those purposes as if it were comprised of the relevant number of smaller denomination shares, and

(*c*) the market value of each smaller denomination share shall be taken for those purposes to be the relevant proportion of the market value of each larger denomination share.

(2) In paragraph (1)—

(*a*) ''smaller denomination shares'' means shares to which are attached rights specified in the company's instrument of incorporation that are expressed in the smaller of two denominations, and ''larger denomination shares'' means shares to which are attached rights so specified that are expressed in the larger of two denominations;

(*b*) ''relevant number'' means the number calculated by reference to the relevant proportion;

(*c*) ''relevant proportion'' means the proportion, determined by the company's instrument of incorporation, which the rights attaching to each smaller denomination share bear to the rights attaching to each larger denomination share.

Amalgamation of an authorised unit trust with, and conversion of an authorised unit trust to, an open-ended investment company

25—(1) This regulation applies where, in connection with a scheme of reorganisation—

(*a*) the whole of the scheme property of an authorised unit trust (''the target trust'') that is available for transfer is transferred on a given date (''the transfer date'') under an arrangement to an open-ended investment company (''the acquiring company'');

(*b*) the consideration under the arrangement consists of or includes the issue on that date of shares (''the consideration shares'') in the acquiring company to the holders of units in the target trust in exchange for those units (''the exchanged units'');

(*c*) the consideration shares are issued to those persons in proportion to their holdings of the exchanged units;

(*d*) the consideration under the arrangement does not include anything else in addition to the issue of the consideration shares, other than (where applicable) the assumption or discharge by the acquiring company of liabilities of the trustees of the target trust; and

(*e*) under the arrangement all the units in the target trust are extinguished.

(2) Notwithstanding anything in section 12(1) to (7), an accounting period of the target trust (''the pre-transfer accounting period'') shall end immediately before the transfer date and the whole of the property referred to in paragraph (1) shall be treated, for the purposes of the Corporation Tax Acts, as having been transferred immediately after the end of that accounting period.

(3) Where there is an amount of surplus advance corporation tax in relation to the pre-transfer accounting period of the target trust which—

(*a*) has not been dealt with under section 239(3), and

(*b*) were it not for this provision, would be treated under section 239(4) as if it were advance corporation tax paid in respect of distributions made by the trust in its next accounting period or, where the pre-transfer accounting period is the final accounting period of the trust, in what would have been its next accounting period were the trust to have an accounting period beginning on the transfer date,

that amount—

(i) shall, with effect from the transfer date, be treated under section 239(4) as if it were advance corporation tax paid in respect of distributions made by the acquiring company in the first of its accounting periods to end on or after the transfer date; and accordingly

(ii) where the pre-transfer accounting period is not the final accounting period of the trust, shall not be treated under section 239(4) as if it were advance corporation tax paid in respect of distributions made by the trust in its next accounting period.

(4) Where in respect of the pre-transfer accounting period of the target trust the trustees are entitled under—

(*a*) section 75(3) (carry forward of management expenses and sums treated as management expenses),

(*b*) section 241(3) (carry forward of franked investment income), or

(*c*) section 246F(3) (carry forward of foreign income dividends), to carry forward an excess amount of the next accounting period of the trust or, where the pre-transfer accounting period is the final accounting period of the trust, to what would have been its next accounting period were the trust to have an accounting period beginning on the transfer date, then that entitlement shall be translated with effect from the transfer date into a right in the acquiring company to treat that amount as if it had been carried forward under the provision in question to the first of its accounting periods to end on or after the transfer date.

(5) In a case to which paragraph (4)(*b*) or (*c*) applies, the amount so treated as carried forward shall be treated for the purposes of Schedule 13 as an amount received by the acquiring company on the transfer date.

(6) For the purpose of the operation of sections 242 (set-off of losses against surplus of franked investment income) and 244 in respect of accounting periods of the target trust ending before the transfer date—

(*a*) the target trust shall be regarded as ceasing to exist immediately after the end of its pre-transfer accounting period,

(*b*) the acquiring company shall be regarded as the continuation of that trust with effect from the transfer date, and

(*c*) the pre-transfer accounting period of the target trust shall be regarded as the accounting period ending immediately before the beginning of the first accounting period of the acquiring company to end on or after the transfer date.

(7) For the purposes of elections made under sections 246J(1) and 246P(6), and of claims (including supplementary claims) made under sections 246N and 246Q, in respect of foreign income dividends paid by the target trust in accounting periods ending before the transfer date—

(*a*) the target trust shall be regarded as ceasing to exist immediately after the end of its pre-transfer accounting period,

(*b*) the acquiring company shall be regarded as the continuation of that trust with effect from the transfer date, and

(*c*) the first accounting period of the acquiring company which ends on or after the transfer date shall be regarded as the accounting period which succeeds the pre-transfer accounting period of the target trust.

(8) A declaration under section 468P made before the transfer date by a unit holder to the trustees of the target trust which is treated by them as valid immediately before the transfer date shall be treated for the purposes of that section (as it applies in relation to open-ended investment companies by virtue of these Regulations) as if—

(*a*) it had been made for the purposes of section 468O—

(i) on the transfer date in writing to the acquiring company by the owner of the shares exchanged for the units in question, and

(ii) in such form as may be required or authorised by the Board pursuant to section 468P(1)(*a*),

(*b*) it contained the details or undertakings required by section 468P(1)(*c*), and

(*c*) the undertaking contained in the declaration to notify the trustees of the target trust were an undertaking to notify the acquiring company.

(9) The acquiring company may on or after the transfer date—

(*a*) continue anything which immediately before that date was in the process of being done by the trustees of the target trust for the purposes of tax in relation to accounting periods of the target trust ending before that date and which is not continued by the trustee on or after that date, and

(*b*) do anything which—

(i) immediately before that date was not in the process of being done for the purposes of tax in relation to such accounting periods by the trustees of the target trust, and is not done by them for those purposes, but

(ii) might reasonably have been expected to be done by them for those purposes had the scheme of reorganisation not taken place.

(10) The exchange of units for shares referred to in paragraph (1)(*b*) shall not be treated as being a "transaction in securities" for the purposes of Schedule 7 to the Finance Act 1997.

(11) In paragraph (1)(*a*) "the whole of the scheme property of an authorised unit trust ('the target trust') that is available for transfer" means the whole of the property subject to the trusts of the target trust, other than any property which is retained for the purpose of discharging liabilities of the trustees of the target trust.

Distributions by authorised unit trust after the end of its pre-transfer accounting period

26—(1) Where, in a case to which regulation 25(1) applies, there is in respect of any post-transfer distribution date of the target trust an amount which, were it not for this provision, would be treated for the purposes of the Tax Acts in accordance with subsection (2) of section 468J as dividends on shares paid on that distribution date by the target trust to its unit holders in proportion to their rights, that amount shall instead be treated for those purposes in accordance with that subsection (as it applies in relation to open-ended investment companies by virtue of these Regulations) as dividends on shares paid on that date by the acquiring company to those persons in proportion to their rights.

(2) Where, in a case to which regulation 25(1) applies, there is in respect of any post-transfer distribution date of the target trust an amount which, were it not for this provision, would be treated for the purposes of the Tax Acts in accordance with subsection (2) of section 468K as foreign income dividends on shares paid on that distribution date by the target trust to its unit holders in proportion to their rights, that amount shall instead be treated for those purposes in accordance with that subsection (as it applies in relation to open-ended investment companies by virtue of these Regulations) as foreign income dividends on shares paid on that date by the acquiring company to those persons in proportion to their rights.

(3) In circumstances in which paragraph (1) or (2) applies where—

(*a*) there is an amount of surplus advance corporation tax in relation to the accounting period of the acquiring company in which a post-transfer distribution date of the target trust falls, not being advance corporation tax which has been repaid to that company, and

(*b*) that amount has not been dealt with under section 239(3),

the amount shall, subject to paragraph (4), be treated for the purposes of section 239(3) as if it were an amount of surplus advance corporation tax in relation to the post-transfer accounting period of the target trust.

(4) The aggregate amount of surplus advance corporation tax falling to be treated as mentioned in paragraph (3) in respect of the post-transfer accounting period of the target trust shall not exceed the aggregate amount of advance corporation tax paid in respect of dividends and foreign income dividends treated as paid by the acquiring company by virtue of paragraphs (1) and (2).

(5) For the purposes of sections 246J, 246N, 246P and 246Q, amounts treated by virtue of paragraph (2) as foreign income dividends paid on a distribution date by the acquiring company shall be treated as foreign income dividends paid by the target trust in its pre-transfer accounting period and not as foreign income dividends paid by the acquiring company.

(6) For the purposes of paragraph (5), section 246J shall have effect as if—

(*a*) in subsection (4) the words from ‘‘or for the accounting period’’ to the end were omitted;

(*b*) in subsection (5) the words from ‘‘and no such amount’’ to the end were omitted.

(7) In this regulation—

‘‘post-transfer accounting period’’ in relation to a target trust means the accounting period of that trust which begins on the transfer date and ends, notwithstanding anything in section 12(1) to (7), on the post-transfer distribution date or, where there is more than one post-transfer distribution date, the latest such date;

‘‘post-transfer distribution date’’ of a target trust means a distribution date of that trust which occurs on or after the transfer date and which is the distribution date for a distribution period of the trust ending before the transfer date.

Provisions supplementary to regulations 25 and 26

27—(1) Nothing in regulations 25 and 26 shall have the effect for the purposes of the Tax Acts of enabling any—

(*a*) set-off or matching of an amount to be made,

(*b*) repayment of an amount of tax or payment of an amount of tax credit to be made, or

(*c*) other relief to be given,

more than once in respect of the same amount or relief.

(2) The provisions of regulations 25 and 26 are without prejudice to any enactment of the Tax Acts which provides, where an officer of the Board discovers that a set-off, matching, repayment of tax, or payment of tax credit or provision for relief in any other form ought not to have been made, given or otherwise allowed, or is or has become excessive, for assessments to be made—

(*a*) for recovering any tax that ought to have been paid,

(*b*) for recovering any repayment of tax or payment of tax credit that ought not to have been made,

(*c*) for withdrawing any relief that ought not to have been given, and

(*d*) generally for securing that the resulting liabilities to tax (including interest on unpaid tax) of—

(i) the target trust and the holders of units in the target trust, and

(ii) the acquiring company and the owners of shares in the acquiring company,

are what they would have been if only such set-offs, matchings, repayments, payments or provisions for relief had been made, given or otherwise allowed as ought to have been made, given or otherwise allowed.

[Modifications of the Income Tax (Authorised Unit Trusts) (Interest Distributions) Regulations 2003

28—(1) The Income Tax (Authorised Unit Trusts) (Interest Distributions) Regulations 2003 ("the principal Regulations") shall have effect in relation to open-ended investment companies as they have effect in relation to authorised unit trusts with the modifications specified in paragraphs (3) to (9).

(2) In paragraphs (3) to (9) "regulation", except where the context otherwise requires, means a regulation of the principal Regulations.

(3) Modify regulation 2 as follows—

(*a*) renumber regulation 2 as paragraph (1) of that regulation;
(*b*) in regulation 2(1)—

(i) for the definitions of "authorised unit trust" and "unit holder" substitute the following definition—
"authorised corporate director", in relation to an open-ended investment company, has the meaning given by subsection (10) of section 468 of the Taxes Act without regard to the modification made by subsection (16) of that section, as those subsections are added by regulation 10(4) of the Open-ended Investment Companies (Tax) Regulations 1997"
(ii) after the definition of "interest distribution" insert the following definitions—
"open-ended investment company"—

(*a*) except as regards the reference to that expression in regulation 10(2)(*a*), has the meaning given by subsection (10) of section 468 of the Taxes Act without regard to the modifications made by subsections (11) to (18) of that section, as those subsections are added by regulation 10(4) of the Open-ended Investment Companies (Tax) Regulations 1997;
(*b*) as regards that reference, has the meaning given by subsection (10) of section 468 of the Taxes Act, read with subsections (11) to (18) of that section, as those subsections are added by regulation 10(4) of the Open-ended Investment Companies (Tax) Regulations 1997; "owner of shares", in relation to an open-ended investment company, has the meaning given by subsection (10) of section 468 of the Taxes Act, read with subsection (15) of that section, as those subsection are added by regulation 10(4) of the Open-ended Investment Companies (Tax) Regulations 1997

(iii) after the definition of "the Tax Acts" add the following definition—
""umbrella company" has the meaning given by subsection (18) of section 468 of the Taxes Act, as that subsection is added by regulation 10(4) of the Open-ended Investment Companies (Tax) Regulations 1997, and references to a part of an umbrella company shall be construed in accordance with that subsection.";
(iv) Omit the definition of "unit trust scheme";

(*c*) after paragraph (1) add—

"(2) For the purposes of the definitions of "open-ended investment company" and "owner of shares" in paragraph (1), references in subsections (11) to (16) of section 468 of the Taxes Act (as added by regulation 10(4) of the Open-ended Investment Companies (Tax) Regulations 1997) to "the Tax Acts" shall be construed as if they included references to these Regulations.".

(4) In regulation 5 in the substituted section 468O(1) for the words "a unit holder" substitute the words "an owner of shares".

(5) In regulation 6(*b*) in the substituted section 468P(2)(*c*) for the words "the trustees of the authorised unit trust" substitute the words "the open-ended investment company".

(6) In regulation 7(2) for the words "a unit holder" substitute the words "an owner of shares".

(7) In regulation 8—

(*a*) for the words "the trustees of an authorised unit trust" substitute the words "an open-ended investment company or its authorised corporate director";
(*b*) for the words "that authorised unit trust" substitute the words "that company or, where the open-ended investment company concerned is an umbrella company, the part of that company in question".

(8) In regulation 9 for the words "The trustees of an authorised unit trust" substitute the words "An open-ended investment company or its authorised corporate director".

(9) In regulation 10(2)—

(*a*) in sub-paragraph (*a*) for the words "the trustees of the authorised unit trust" substitute the words "the open-ended investment company";
(*b*) in sub-paragraph (*b*) for the words "a unit holder" substitute the words "an owner of shares"."][1]

Amendments—[1] This regulation substituted by the Open-ended Investment Companies (Tax) (Amendment) Regulations, SI 2003/1831 with effect for interest distributions made after 15 October 2002.

1997/1158
Income Tax (Schedule 22 to the Finance Act 1995) (Prescribed Amounts) Regulations 1997

Made by the Commissioners of Inland Revenue under FA 1995 Sch 22 paras 1(3), 2(4)(*b*), 3(3), 5(4)(*b*), 6(3), 7(3), 9(3)(*a*), 10(3)

Made	*3 April 1997*
Laid before the House of Commons	*4 April 1997*
Coming into Force	*25 April 1997*

Commentary—*Simon's Direct Tax Service* **E1.215, 216.**

Citation and commencement

1 These Regulations may be cited as the Income Tax (Schedule 22 to the Finance Act 1995) (Prescribed Amounts) Regulations 1997 and shall come into force on 25th April 1997.

Interpretation

2—(1) In these Regulations "appropriate period" means—

(*a*) where paragraph 1(3) applies, "the transitional period" within the meaning given by paragraph 1(4);

(*b*) where paragraph 3(3) applies so as to modify paragraph 1(3), "the transitional overlap period" within the meaning given by paragraph 3(4);

(*c*) where paragraph 6(3) applies so as to modify paragraph 1(3), the years of assessment 1995–96 and 1996–97;

(*d*) where paragraph 7(3) applies so as to modify paragraph 1(3), "the transitional overlap period" within the meaning given by paragraph 7(4).

(2) References in these Regulations to a paragraph are to that paragraph of Schedule 22 to the Finance Act 1995.

Amounts prescribed under paragraph 1(3)—persons other than partners

3 As respects a trade, profession or vocation carried on by any person (other than in partnership)—

(*a*) the amount prescribed for the purposes of paragraph 1(3)(*a*) and of that provision as applied by paragraphs 3(3), 6(3) and 7(3) is £10,000;

(*b*) the amount prescribed for the purposes of paragraph 1(3)(*c*) and of that provision as applied by paragraphs 3(3), 6(3) and 7(3) is £50,000.

Amount prescribed under paragraph 1(3)(a)—persons in partnership

4 As respects a trade, profession or vocation carried on by persons in partnership, the amount prescribed for the purposes of paragraph 1(3)(*a*) and of that provision as applied by paragraphs 3(3), 6(3) and 7(3)—

(*a*) where the maximum number of partners comprising the partnership in the appropriate period does not exceed 20, is the amount determined by the formula—

£7,500 . A

where A is the maximum number of partners comprising the partnership in the appropriate period;

(*b*) where the maximum number of partners comprising the partnership in the appropriate period exceeds 20, is the amount determined by the formula—

£150,000 + (£1,000.B)

where B is the number by which the maximum number of partners comprising the partnership in the appropriate period exceeds 20.

Amount prescribed under paragraph 1(3)(c)—persons in partnership

5 As respects a trade, profession or vocation carried on by persons in partnership, the amount prescribed for the purposes of paragraph 1(3)(*c*) and of that provision as applied by paragraphs 3(3), 6(3) and 7(3) is the amount determined by the formula—

£50,000 . C

where C is the maximum number of partners comprising the partnership in the appropriate period.

Amount prescribed under paragraph 2(4)(b)

6 The amount prescribed for the purposes of paragraph 2(4)(*b*) is £15,000.

Amount prescribed under paragraph 5(4)(b)

7 The amount prescribed for the purposes of paragraph 5(4)(*b*) is £7,500.

Amount prescribed under paragraph 9(3)(a)

8 The amount prescribed for the purposes of paragraph 9(3)(*a*) and of that provision as applied by paragraph 10(3) is £7,500.

1997/2681
Lloyd's Underwriters (Scottish Limited Partnerships) (Tax) Regulations 1997

Made by the Commissioners of Inland Revenue under FA 1993 s 182(1) and FA 1994 s 229

Made	*7 November 1997*
Laid before the House of Commons	*10 November 1997*
Coming into force	*1 December 1997*

Commentary—*Simon's Direct Tax Service* **E5.601.**

PRELIMINARY

Citation, commencement and effect

1 These Regulations may be cited as the Lloyd's Underwriters (Scottish Limited Partnerships) (Tax) Regulations 1997, shall come into force on 1st December 1997 and shall have effect with respect to accounting periods of Lloyd's Scottish limited partnerships ending on or after that date.

Interpretation

2—(1) In these Regulations unless the context otherwise requires—

"accounting period" in relation to a Lloyd's Scottish limited partnership has the meaning given by regulation 6(2);

"corporate member" has the meaning given by section 230(1) of the Finance Act 1994;

"Lloyd's Scottish limited partnership" means a limited partnership formed under the laws of Scotland which is a member of Lloyd's;

"member" means a member of Lloyd's who is or has been an underwriting member;

"the Taxes Act" means the Income and Corporation Taxes Act 1988.

(2) For the purposes of these Regulations an underwriting year and a year of assessment shall be deemed to correspond to each other if the underwriting year ends in the year of assessment.

PROVISIONS RELATING TO BOTH INDIVIDUAL AND CORPORATE PARTNERS IN A LLOYD'S SCOTTISH LIMITED PARTNERSHIP

Operation of partnership assessment rules

3—(1) Where section 111(2) of the Taxes Act applies in relation to a Lloyd's Scottish limited partnership—

(*a*) the provisions of Chapter III of Part II of the Finance Act 1993 shall apply, subject to the amendments made by these Regulations, as if the partnership were a member who is an individual;

(*b*) the Lloyd's Underwriters (Tax) Regulations 1995 shall have effect in relation to that partnership—

(i) as if it were a member who is an individual, and

(ii) with the omission of regulations 9 to 17;

(*c*) the Lloyd's Underwriters (Double Taxation Relief) Regulations 1997 shall have effect in relation to that partnership as if it were a member who is an individual.

(2) Where section 114(1) of the Taxes Act applies in relation to a Lloyd's Scottish limited partnership—

(*a*) the provisions of Chapter V of Part IV of the Finance Act 1994 shall apply, subject to the amendments made by these Regulations, as if the partnership were a member which is a corporate member;

(*b*) the Lloyd's Underwriters (Tax) Regulations 1995 shall have effect in relation to that partnership—

(i) as if it were a member which is a corporate member, and

(ii) with the omission of regulations 9 to 17.

Disapplication of cessation provisions

4—(1) Sections 179 and 179A of the Finance Act 1993 shall not apply in relation to a Lloyd's Scottish limited partnership which, by virtue of regulation 3(1), is treated as a member who is an individual.

(2) Section 227 of the Finance Act 1994 shall not apply in relation to a Lloyd's Scottish limited partnership which, by virtue of regulation 3(2), is treated as a member which is a corporate member.

Ancillary trust funds relating to a Lloyd's Scottish limited partnership

5—(1) An ancillary trust fund set up in relation to a Lloyd's Scottish limited partnership shall be regarded as an ancillary trust fund of that partnership, irrespective of whether the fund is established by the partnership itself or by one or more of the partners in the partnership; and, subject to the modification specified in paragraph (2), section 176 of the Finance Act 1993 and section 223 of the Finance Act 1994 shall apply accordingly.

(2) Subsections (3) and (4) of section 176 of the Finance Act 1993 shall be omitted.

(3) In paragraph (1) "ancillary trust fund"—

(*a*) where regulation 3(1) applies, has the meaning given by section 184(1) of the Finance Act 1993;

(*b*) where regulation 3(2) applies, has the meaning given by section 230(1) of the Finance Act 1994.

PROVISIONS RELATING TO INDIVIDUAL PARTNERS IN A LLOYD'S SCOTTISH LIMITED PARTNERSHIP

Basis of assessment

6—(1) Where regulation 3(1) applies in relation to a Lloyd's Scottish limited partnership—

(*a*) section 60(2) to (5), and sections 61 to 63A, of the Taxes Act shall not apply in relation to that partnership;

(*b*) section 172 of the Finance Act 1993 shall apply in relation to that partnership as if—

(i) in each of paragraphs (*a*) and (*b*) of subsection (1) of that section for the reference to the corresponding underwriting year there were substituted a reference to the accounting period ending in the corresponding underwriting year;

(ii) in paragraph (*c*) of that subsection for the reference to profits or losses derived from payments made or received in the corresponding underwriting year there were substituted a reference to profits or losses attributable to the accounting period ending in the corresponding underwriting year.

(2) In paragraph (1)(*b*)(i) and (ii) "accounting period" in relation to a Lloyd's Scottish limited partnership means the period—

(*a*) beginning on the 1st January in each year, or the date on which the partnership was formed (if later in that year), and

(*b*) ending on—

(i) the 31st December in that year, or the date when the partnership is terminated (if earlier), or

(ii) where the partnership was formed later than 1st January in that year, the 31st December in the following year, or the date when the partnership is terminated (if earlier).

Disapplication of section 175 of the Finance Act 1993 (special reserve funds)

7—(1) Section 175 of, and Schedule 20 to, the Finance Act 1993 shall not apply in relation to a Lloyd's Scottish limited partnership which, by virtue of regulation 3(1), is treated as a member who is an individual.

(2) Paragraph (1) shall not prevent the setting up of a special reserve fund in relation to an individual who is both a member of Lloyd's and a partner in a Lloyd's Scottish limited partnership, but in such a case the special reserve fund shall take account only of the underwriting business carried on by that person as a member.

Disapplication of section 180 of the Finance Act 1993 (underwriting profits to be earned income)

8 Section 180 of the Finance Act 1993 shall not apply in relation to the profits arising to an individual as a partner in a Lloyd's Scottish limited partnership.

Death of partner

9—(1) This regulation applies where—

(*a*) regulation 3(1) applies in relation to a Lloyd's Scottish limited partnership, and

(*b*) an individual who is a partner in the partnership dies.

(2) The carrying on of the deceased partner's partnership business by his personal representatives shall not be treated for the purposes of the Income Tax Acts as a change in the persons engaged in the carrying on of that business.

(3) The deceased partner's partnership business shall be treated for the purposes of the Income Tax Acts as continuing until either—

(*a*) any security provided by him in relation to that business is released or repaid by Lloyd's to his personal representatives, or

(*b*) his interest in the partnership is assigned by his personal representatives.

Terminal loss relief

10—(1) This regulation applies where—

(*a*) regulation 3(1) applies in relation to a Lloyd's Scottish limited partnership, and

(*b*) an individual who is a partner in the partnership ceases to carry on his partnership business, whether by reason of death or otherwise.

(2) The date on which the individual's partnership business is permanently discontinued for the purposes of section 388 of the Taxes Act (carry-back of terminal losses) ("section 388") shall be deemed to be the 5th April in the last year of assessment in which his share of the profits or losses of that business arising from the partnership's membership of one or more syndicates, or from assets forming part of a premiums trust fund, fall to be included in a computation under section 111 of the Taxes Act.

(3) A partner may not make more than one claim under section 388 in respect of the same partnership business.

1997/2708
Finance Act 1989, section 178(1), (Appointed Day) Order 1997

Made by the Treasury under FA 1989 s 178(7)

Made . . . . *17 November 1997*

Commentary—*Simon's Direct Tax Service* **A3.1322.**

1 This Order may be cited as the Finance Act 1989, section 178(1), (Appointed Day) Order 1997.

2 The day appointed for section 118F of the Income and Corporation Taxes Act 1988 for periods beginning on or after which section 178(1) of the Finance Act 1989 shall have effect is 9th December 1997.

1998/311
Finance Act 1989, section 178(1) (Appointed Day) Order 1998

Made by the Treasury under FA 1989 s 178(7)

Made . . . . *12 February 1998*

Commentary—*Simon's Direct Tax Service* **A3.1322.**

1 This Order may be cited as the Finance Act 1989, section 178(1), (Appointed Day) Order 1998.

2 The day appointed for sections 59C and 103A of the Taxes Management Act 1970 for periods beginning on or after which section 178(1) of the Finance Act 1989 shall have effect is 9th March 1998.

1998/729
Retirement Benefits Schemes (Restriction on Discretion to Approve) (Excepted Provisions) Regulations 1998

Made by the Commissioners of Inland Revenue, under TA 1988 s 591A(2)

Made . . . . *17 March 1998*
Laid before the House of Commons . . . . *17 March 1998*
Coming into force . . . . *17 April 1998*

Commentary—*Simon's Direct Tax Service* **E7.217.**

Citation and commencement

1 These Regulations may be cited as the Retirement Benefits Schemes (Restriction on Discretion to Approve) (Excepted Provisions) Regulations 1998 and shall come into force on 7th April 1998.

Interpretation

2 In regulations 4 and 5—

"the 1991 Regulations" means the Retirement Benefits Schemes (Restriction on Discretion to Approve) (Small Self-administered Schemes) Regulations 1991;

"the 1998 Regulations" means the Retirement Benefits Schemes (Restriction on Discretion to Approve) (Small Self-administered Schemes) (Amendment) Regulations 1998.

Description of provisions

3 Regulations 4 and 5 specify descriptions of provisions for the purposes of subsection (2) of section 591A of the Income and Corporation Taxes Act 1988, each provision so specified being a provision of a required description within the meaning of subsection (5)(*b*) of that section.

4 The description of provision specified in this regulation is the provision specified in regulation 5 of the 1991 Regulations as amended by regulations 6 and 7 of the 1998 Regulations.

5 The description of provision specified in this regulation is the provision specified in regulation 9 of the 1991 Regulations as substituted by regulation 9 of the 1998 Regulations.

1998/1513

Visiting Forces and Allied Headquarters (Income Tax and Capital Gains Tax) (Designation) Order 1998

Made	*24 June 1998*
Coming into force	*24 June 1998*

Whereas section 323 of the Income and Corporation Taxes Act 1988 provides for certain exemptions from income tax in respect of members of visiting forces of designated countries, members of civilian components of such forces, and persons attached to or employed by designated allied headquarters; and further provides that for the purposes of that section "designated" means designated for the purpose in question by or under any Order in Council made for giving effect to any international agreement:

And whereas section 11(1) of the Taxation of Chargeable Gains Act 1992 extends the said section 323 of the Income and Corporation Taxes Act 1988 so as to provide for exemption from capital gains tax in respect of members of visiting forces of designated countries, members of civilian components of such forces, and persons attached to or employed by designated allied headquarters:

And whereas this Order is an Order made for giving effect to the following international agreements, namely, the Agreement regarding the Status of Forces of Parties to the North Atlantic Treaty dated 19th June 1951, the Protocol on the Status of International Military Headquarters set up Pursuant to the North Atlantic Treaty dated 28th August 1952, and the Agreement among the States Parties to the North Atlantic Treaty and the Other States Participating in the Partnership for Peace regarding the Status of their Forces dated 19th June 1995:

Now, therefore, Her Majesty, in exercise of the powers conferred on Her by the said section 323 of the Income and Corporation Taxes Act 1988 and the said section 11(1) of the Taxation of Chargeable Gains Act 1992, is pleased, by and with the advice of Her Privy Council, to order, and it is hereby ordered, as follows:

1 This Order may be cited as the Visiting Forces and Allied Headquarters (Income Tax and Capital Gains Tax) (Designation) Order 1998 and shall come into force on 24th June 1998.

2 Each of the countries specified in the First Schedule to this Order and each of the allied headquarters specified in the Second Schedule to this Order is hereby designated for the purposes of section 323 of the Income and Corporation Taxes Act 1988 and of section 11(1) of the Taxation of Chargeable Gains Act 1992.

FIRST SCHEDULE

Albania, Bulgaria, the Czech Republic, Estonia, Hungary, Latvia, Lithuania, Poland, Romania, the Slovak Republic, Slovenia, Spain and Sweden.

SECOND SCHEDULE

Headquarters of the Supreme Allied Commander Atlantic (SACLANT).

Headquarters Eastern Atlantic (EASTLANT).

Headquarters Maritime Air Eastern Atlantic (MARAIREASTLANT).

Headquarters Submarine Forces Eastern Atlantic (SUBEASTLANT).

Headquarters Allied Forces North Western Europe (AFNORTHWEST).

Headquarters Allied Naval Forces North Western Europe (NAVNORTHWEST).

Headquarters Allied Air Forces North Western Europe (AIRNORTHWEST).

NATO Airborne Early Warning Force Headquarters and NATO E-3A Component.

Commentary—*Simon's Direct Tax Service* **C1.221; E5.403.**

1998/1514
Visiting Forces (Income Tax and Capital Gains Tax) (Designation) Order 1998

Made . . . . 24 June 1998
Coming into force in relation to each country specified in article 2, the date determined in accordance with article 1(2)

Whereas section 323 of the Income and Corporation Taxes Act 1988 provides for exemptions from income tax in respect of members of visiting forces of designated countries and members of civilian components of such forces; and further provides that for the purposes of that section ''designated'' means designated for the purpose in question by or under any Order in Council made for giving effect to any international agreement:

And whereas section 11(1) of the Taxation of Chargeable Gains Act 1992 extends the said section 323 of the Income and Corporation Taxes Act 1988 so as to provide for exemption from capital gains tax in respect of members of visiting forces of designated countries and members of civilian components of such forces:

And whereas this Order is an Order made for giving effect to the following international agreements, namely, the Agreement regarding the Status of Forces of Parties to the North Atlantic Treaty dated 19th June 1951, and the Agreement among the States Parties to the North Atlantic Treaty and the Other States Participating in the Partnership for Peace regarding the Status of their Forces dated 19th June 1995:

Now, therefore, Her Majesty, in exercise of the powers conferred on Her by the said section 323 of the Income and Corporation Taxes Act 1988 and the said section 11(1) of the Taxation of Chargeable Gains Act 1992, is pleased, by and with the advice of Her Privy Council, to order, and it is hereby ordered, as follows:

1—(1) This Order may be cited as the Visiting Forces (Income Tax and Capital Gains Tax) (Designation) Order 1998 and shall come into force in accordance with the following provisions of this article.

(2) This Order shall come into force, in relation to each of the countries specified in article 2, on whichever is the later of the following dates—

(*a*) the date on which its Government becomes a party to the Agreement among the States Parties to the North Atlantic Treaty and the Other States Participating in the Partnership for Peace regarding the Status of their Forces dated 19th June 1995; and

(*b*) the day after the date on which this Order is made.

(3) The date on which this Order comes into force in relation to each of the countries specified in article 2 shall be notified in the London, Edinburgh and Belfast Gazettes.

2 The following countries are hereby designated for the purposes of section 323 of the Income and Corporation Taxes Act 1988 and section 11(1) of the Taxation of Chargeable Gains Act 1992—

Armenia, Austria, Azerbaijan, Belarus, Finland, Georgia, Kazakhstan, Kyrgyzstan, the Former Yugoslav Republic of Macedonia, Moldova, Russia, Switzerland, Turkmenistan, Ukraine, and Uzbekistan.

Commentary—*Simon's Direct Tax Service* **C1.221; E5.403**.

1998/1868
Gifts for Relief in Poor Countries (Designation) Order 1998

Made by the Treasury under FA 1998 s 47(8) and 48(9)

Made . . . . 31 July 1998
Laid before the House of Commons . . . 31 July 1998
Coming into force . . . . 21 August 1998

Commentary—*Simon's Direct Tax Service* **B3.1445A, D2.212**.
Revenue & other press releases—HMT 31–7–98 (eighty countries eligible for Millennium Gift Aid).

1 This Order may be cited as the Gifts for Relief in Poor Countries (Designation) Order 1998 and shall come into force on 21st August 1998

2 The descriptions of countries specified for the purposes of sections 47 and 48 of the Finance Act 1998 are—

(*a*) the countries included in the lists of countries which are eligible for lending by the International Development Association (''the Association''), and by the Association and the International Bank for Reconstruction and Development (''the Bank''), published by the Association and the Bank (under the name of The World Bank) in Appendix 5 to The World Bank Annual Report 1997, under the headings ''Countries eligible for IDA funds only'' and ''Countries eligible for a blend of IBRD and IDA funds'', and

(*b*) any further countries included in those lists as published in The World Bank Annual Reports issued between the date on which this Order is made and 31st December 2000.

Commentary—*Simon's Direct Tax Service* **B3.1445A; D2.212; E1.504**.
Revenue & other press releases—IR 31-7-98 (Eighty countries eligible for Millennium Gift Aid announced).

1998/1870
Individual Savings Account Regulations 1998

Made by the Treasury under TA 1988 ss 333, 333A and 333B, TCGA 1992 s 151 and FA 1998 ss 75 and 76(3)

Made . . . . *31 July 1998*
Laid before the House of Commons . . . . *31 July 1998*
Coming into force . . . . *In accordance with regulation 1*

Commentary—*Simon's Direct Tax Service* **Division E3.7**.
Revenue & other press releases—IR 31-7-98 (The Individual Savings Account (ISA)—tax regulations).

ARRANGEMENT OF REGULATIONS

Citation and commencement

1 These Regulations may be cited as the Individual Savings Account Regulations 1998 and shall come into force for the purposes of—

(*a*) applications under regulations 12 and 13 relating to the year 1999–00, to subscribe to an account in that year,

(*b*) applications under regulation 14 to be approved as an account manager to manage accounts in the year 1999–00 and subsequent years, and

(*c*) regulations 16 to 18 and 20, so far as they relate to applications referred to in paragraph (*b*),

on 1st October 1998, and for all other purposes on 6th April 1999.

Interpretation

2—(1) In these Regulations unless the context otherwise requires—

(*a*) "account", except in the case of—

(i) an account with a deposit-taker, or

(ii) a tax-exempt special savings account, or
(iii) a share or deposit account with a building society, or
(iv) a deposit account with [a person falling within section 840A(1)(*b*) of the Taxes Act][5], or a relevant European institution,

shall be construed in accordance with regulation 4(1);

an "account investment" is an investment under the account which is a qualifying investment for a stocks and shares component, a cash component or an insurance component, as the case may be, within the meaning of regulation 7, 8 or 9;

an "account investor" is an individual who subscribes to an account and who is a qualifying individual within the meaning of regulation 10;

an "account manager" is a person who fulfils the conditions of these Regulations and is approved by the Board for the purposes of these Regulations as an account manager;

["approved employee share ownership plan", "participant", "plan shares" and (in relation to plan shares) "ceasing to be subject to the plan" shall have the meanings given in Schedule 8 to the Finance Act 2000, except that, in construing "plan shares", paragraph 115(8), and the words "or securities or rights" in paragraph 116(1), of that Schedule, shall be omitted;][3]

"approved profit sharing scheme" has the same meaning as in Chapter IV of Part V of the Taxes Act;

an "assurance undertaking" means an assurance undertaking within the meaning of Article 8 of the First Council Directive 79/267 as extended by the EEA Agreement;

"the Board" means the Commissioners of Inland Revenue;

"building society" means a building society within the meaning of the Building Societies Act 1986, or the Irish Building Societies Act 1989;

"company", except in regulation 7(4), means any body corporate having a share capital other than—

(i) an open-ended investment company, within the meaning given by section [236 of the Financial Services and Markets Act 2000][5],
(ii) a UCITS,
(iii) an industrial and provident society, or
(iv) a body corporate which is a 51 per cent subsidiary of any industrial and provident society;

"deposit-taker" has the meaning given by section 481(2) of the Taxes Act;

["the Director of Savings" has the same meaning as in the National Debt Act 1972;][1]

"EEA Agreement" means the Agreement on the European Economic Area signed at Oporto on 2nd May 1992, as adjusted by the Protocol signed at Brussels on 17th March 1993;

"EEA State" means a State, other than the United Kingdom, which is a Contracting Party to the EEA Agreement;

["European institution" means an EEA firm of the kind mentioned in paragraph 5(*a*), (*b*) or (*c*) of Schedule 3 to the Financial Services and Markets Act 2000 which is an authorised person for the purposes of that Act as a result of qualifying for authorisation under paragraph 12 of that Schedule;][5]

"51 per cent subsidiary" and "75 per cent subsidiary" have the meanings given by section 838 of the Taxes act;

"gains", except in regulations 22(1)(*a*)(ii) to (v) and 35(6), means "chargeable gains" within the meaning of the Taxation of Chargeable Gains Act 1992;

"gilt-edged securities" has the meaning given by [paragraphs 1 and 1A][1] of Schedule 9 to the Taxation of Chargeable Gains Act 1992;

"income tax quarter" has the same meaning as in the Income Tax (Employments) Regulations 1993;

an "incorporated friendly society" means a society incorporated under the Friendly Societies Act 1992;

an "industrial and provident society" means a society registered or deemed to be registered under the Industrial and Provident Societies Act 1965 or under the Industrial and Provident Societies (Northern Ireland) Act 1969;

"investment trust" has the meaning given by section 842 of the Taxes Act, and references to the "eligible rental income" of an investment trust have the same meaning as in that section;

...[5]

"the Management Act" means the Taxes Management Act 1970;

"market value" shall be construed in accordance with section 272 of The Taxation of Chargeable Gains Act 1992;

"notice", except in [regulations 9 and 36][1], means notice in writing and "notify" shall be construed accordingly;

"qualifying distribution" has the same meaning as in section 832(1) of the Taxes Act;

"recognised stock exchange" has the same meaning as in section 841 of the Taxes Act;

a "registered friendly society" has the meaning given by the Friendly Societies Act 1992, and includes any society that by virtue of section 96(2) of that Act is to be treated as a registered friendly society;

"release date" has the meaning given by section 187(2) of the Taxes Act;

"relevant authorised person" has the same meaning as in section 333A(12) of the Taxes Act;

SIs

"relevant European institution" has the meaning given by section 326A(10) of the Taxes Act;
"savings-related share option scheme" has the meaning given by paragraph 1 of Schedule 9 to the Taxes Act;
"security", except in regulations [7(2)(*c*) to (*cb*) and (8)(*b*), 8(2)(*e*) and (*f*)][1], 31(4)(*b*) and 34(3), means any loan stock or similar security of a company whether secured or unsecured;
"tax" where neither income tax nor capital gains tax is specified means either of those taxes;
"tax credit" means a tax credit under section 231 of the Taxes Act;
"the Taxes Act" means the Income and Corporation Taxes Act 1988;
"tax-exempt special savings account" means a deposit account or share account which is a tax-exempt special savings account for the purposes of section 326A of the Taxes Act, and references to—

(i) the day on which such an account "matured",
(ii) "the total amount deposited in the matured account, before it matured", and
(iii) "a follow-up account",

have the same meanings as in section 326BB of the Taxes Act;
"year" means a year of assessment, and "the year 1999–00" means the year of assessment beginning on 6th April 1999;
(*b*) ["authorised fund" means—

(i) an authorised unit trust, or
(ii) an open-ended investment company with variable capital incorporated in the United Kingdom in the case of which an authorisation order made by the Financial Services Authority under regulation 14 of the Open-Ended Investment Companies Regulations 2001 is in force;][5]

"authorised unit trust" means a unit trust scheme in the case of which an authorisation order made by the Financial Services Authority under section [243 of the Financial Services and Markets Act 2000][5] is in force;
[a "Chapter 5 UCITS" means a UCITS complying with Chapter 5 of the Collective Investment Schemes Sourcebook;][6]
["the Collective Investment Schemes Sourcebook" means the sourcebook of that name made by the Financial Services Authority under the Financial Services and Markets Act 2000;][6]
["depositary interest" means the rights of the person mentioned in paragraph (*b*), under a certificate or other record (whether or not in the form of a document) acknowledging—

(*a*) that a person holds relevant investments or evidence of the right to them, and
(*b*) that another person is entitled to rights in or in relation to those or identical relevant investments, including the right to receive such investments, or evidence of the right to them or the proceeds from such investments, from the person mentioned in paragraph (*a*),

where "relevant investments" means investments which are exclusively qualifying investments for a stocks and shares component falling within any of regulation 7(2)(*a*) to (*h*), and the rights mentioned in paragraph (*b*) are exclusively rights in or in relation to relevant investments;][4]
["the first condition", and references to the terms of a scheme complying with that condition, mean that the terms of the scheme do not permit any of the investments [of the scheme, or subject to the trusts of the scheme, to consist of units in, or shares of, authorised funds or parts of umbrella schemes which are not securities schemes or warrant schemes][5]
"the second condition", and references to the terms of a scheme complying with that condition, mean that the terms of the scheme only permit any of the investments [of the scheme, or subject to the trusts of the scheme][5] to consist of units or shares in—

(i) a collective investment scheme which is a "recognised scheme" by virtue of section [270 or 272 of the Financial Services and Markets Act 2000][5], or
[(ii) a part of a scheme mentioned in paragraph (i) which would be a part of an umbrella scheme if the definition of "umbrella scheme" and a part thereof applied to a scheme mentioned in paragraph (i),

where the terms of the scheme mentioned in paragraph (i) identify that scheme, or part thereof, as the case may be, as a scheme or part that would belong to one of the categories of securities scheme or warrant scheme, if that scheme or part, as the case may be, were independently an authorised fund;][5]][2]
["fund of funds scheme"][5], except in regulation 8(2)(*d*), means—

(i) an [authorised fund][5] which according to the terms of the scheme is a [fund of funds scheme][5] belonging to the category under that name established by the Financial Services Authority, and
(ii) a part of an umbrella scheme which the terms of the scheme identify as a part that would belong to that category if it were itself an [authorised fund][5],

where, in either case, the terms of the scheme [comply with the first condition and the second condition][2];
["money market scheme"][5] means—

(i) an [authorised fund][5] which according to the terms of the scheme is a [money market scheme][5] belonging to the category under that name established by the Financial Services Authority, and

(ii) a part of an umbrella scheme which the terms of the scheme identify as a part that would belong to that category if it were itself an [authorised fund][5];

''open-ended investment company'', except in sub-paragraph (*a*), has the meaning given by subsection (10) of section 468 of the Taxes Act as that subsection is added in relation to open-ended investment companies by regulation 10(4) of the 1997 Regulations, and ''shares'', in relation to an open-ended investment company, includes shares of any class and of any denomination of a given class and, in relation to a part of an umbrella company, means shares in the company which confer for the time being rights in that part;

[a ''relevant UCITS'' means—

(i) a UCITS, situated in a member state other than the United Kingdom, which has been authorised by the competent authorities of the member state in which it is situated, and which is a ''recognised scheme'' by virtue of section [264 of the Financial Services and Markets Act 2000][5], and

(ii) a part of a UCITS mentioned in paragraph (i), which would be a part of [an umbrella scheme, if the definition of ''umbrella scheme'' and a part thereof][5] applied to a relevant UCITS,

...[6]

[''securities scheme'' means—

(i) an authorised fund which according to the terms of the scheme is a securities scheme belonging to the category under that name established by the Financial Services Authority, and

(ii) a part of an umbrella scheme which the terms of the scheme identify as a part which would belong to that category if it were itself an authorised fund;][5]

''the 1997 Regulations'' means the Open-ended Investment Companies (Tax) Regulations 1997

''UCITS'' means undertakings for collective investment in transferable securities within the meaning of Article 1 of [Council Directive 85/611/EEC, as last amended by European Parliament and Council Directive 2001/108/EC][7], and references to—

(i) ''the member state in which a UCITS is situated'', and

(ii) a UCITS which has been ''authorised by the competent authorities of the member state in which it is situated''

shall have the same meanings as in Articles 3 and 4 respectively of that Directive;

[''umbrella scheme'' means an authorised fund which according to the terms of the scheme is an umbrella scheme belonging to the category under that name established by the Financial Services Authority, and

(i) in the case of an authorised fund which is an authorised unit trust, references to a part of an umbrella scheme shall be construed in accordance with subsection (8) of section 468 of the Taxes Act, and, in relation to a part of an umbrella scheme, references to investments subject to the trusts of an authorised unit trust and to a unit holder shall be construed in accordance with subsection (9) of that section, and

(ii) in the case of an authorised fund which is an open-ended investment company, references to a part of an umbrella scheme shall be construed in accordance with subsection (18) of section 468 of the Taxes Act as that subsection is added in relation to open-ended investment companies by regulation 10(4) of the 1997 Regulations, and, in relation to a part of an umbrella scheme, references to investments of the company shall be construed in accordance with subsection (12) of that section as so added;][5]

''unit holder'', except in relation to a part of an umbrella scheme, has the meaning given by subsection (6) of section 468 of the Taxes Act;

''unit trust scheme'' has the meaning given by subsection (6) of section 468 of the Taxes Act;

''units'', in relation to an authorised unit trust, means the rights or interests (however described) of the unit holders in that authorised unit trust and, in relation to a part of an umbrella scheme, means the rights or interests for the time being of the unit holders in that part;

''units in, or shares of, a ...[6] UCITS'' means the rights or interests (however described) of the holders of the units or shares in that ...[6] UCITS;

[''warrant scheme'' means—

(i) an authorised fund which according to the terms of the scheme is a warrant scheme belonging to the category under that name established by the Financial Services Authority, and

(ii) a part of an umbrella scheme which the terms of the scheme identify as a part that would belong to that category if it were itself an authorised fund;][5]

(2) The Table below indexes other definitions in these Regulations—

Term defined	*Regulation*
Account	4(1)
Component	4(1)(*a*)
The disqualifying circumstances	17(1)
Interim claim	25
Maxi-account	4(1)(*c*)

Term defined	*Regulation*
Mini-account	4(1)(*d*)
Qualifying circumstances	14(1)
Qualifying individual	10
Qualifying investments for a stock and shares component	7
Qualifying investments for a cash component	8
Qualifying investments for an insurance component	9
Qualifying securities	7(2)(*b*)
Subscription limits	4(2) to (4)
TESSA only account	4(1)(*e*)

Amendments—[1] Words in para (1)(*a*) amended by the Individual Savings Account (Amendment) Regulations, SI 1998/3174 reg 3(2) with effect from 6 April 1999.

[2] Words in para (1)(*b*) amended by SI 1998/3174 reg 3(3) with effect from 6 April 1999.

[3] Definition of ''approved employee share ownership plan'' inserted by the Individual Savings Account (Amendment No 2) Regulations, SI 2000/2079 reg 3 with effect from 21 August 2000.

[4] Definition of ''depositary interest'' inserted by the Individual Savings Account (Amendment No 3) Regulations, SI 2000/3112 reg 3 with effect from 13 December 2000.

[5] In sub-para (1)(*a*), words in the definition of ''account'' and ''company'' substituted, definition of ''European institution'' substituted, and definition of ''long term business'' revoked; in sub-para (1)(*b*), definition of ''authorised fund'' inserted, words in definition of ''authorised unit trust'', ''the first condition'', ''the second condition'', ''fund of funds scheme'', ''money market scheme'', and ''relevant UCITS'' substituted; definition of ''securities scheme'' substituted for definitions of ''securities company'' and ''securities fund'', definition of ''umbrella scheme'' substituted for definitions of ''umbrella scheme'' and ''umbrella company'', and definition of ''warrant scheme'' substituted for definitions of ''warrant company'' and ''warrant fund'', by the Financial Services and Markets Act 2000 (Consequential Amendments) (Taxes) Order, SI 2001/3629 art 169 with effect from 1 December 2001, immediately after the coming into force of the Financial Services and Markets Act 2000 ss 411, 432(1), Sch 20 (and SI 2001/3629 Pts 1 and 2).

[6] Definitions of ''a Chapter 5 UCITS'' and ''the Collective Investment Schemes Sourcebook'' inserted, and words in definition of ''relevant UCITS'' and ''units in, or shares of, a relevant UCITS'' revoked, by the Individual Savings Account (Amendment) Regulations, SI 2003/2747 regs 1(1), (2), 2, 3 with effect from 17 November 2003.

[7] In para (2), words in definition of ''UCITS'' substituted by the Collective Investment Schemes (Miscellaneous Amendments) Regulations, SI 2003/2066 reg 13(4) with effect from 13 February 2004.

Introductory

3 These Regulations provide for the setting up of plans in the form of an account, by account managers approved by the Board, under which individuals may make certain investments, for the conditions under which they may invest and under which those accounts are to operate, for relief from tax in respect of account investments and generally for the administration of tax in relation to such accounts.

General conditions for accounts and subscriptions to accounts

4—(1) An account is a scheme of investment, to which an individual who is a qualifying individual may subscribe, and in respect of which the following conditions must be fulfilled—

(*a*) subject to sub-paragraphs (*c*) to (*e*), that an account is made up of one or more of the following components only, namely—

a stocks and shares component,
a cash component, and
an insurance component;

(*b*) that, on the setting up of the account it is, subject to sub-paragraphs (*c*) to (*e*), designated by the account manager as—

(i) a maxi-account, or
(ii) a mini-account, or
(iii) a TESSA only account,

and such designation shall be treated as continuing to have effect for the year in which the individual first subscribes to the account, and each successive year following that year in which the individual subscribes to the account;

(*c*) that an account which is or has been designated as a maxi-account (a ''maxi-account'') must be—

(i) made up of a stocks and shares component [save that a maxi-account to which the qualifying individual first subscribes when that individual is under the age of 18 years must include a cash component][2] (with or without other components), and

(ii) the only account, other than a TESSA only account, to which the qualifying individual subscribes in any year during which such designation continues to have effect;

(*d*) that an account which is or has been designated as a mini-account (a ''mini-account'') must be—

(i) made up of a single specified component, and

(ii) the only account, other than a mini-account made up of a different type of component to that specified in accordance with paragraph (i) or a TESSA only account, to which the qualifying individual subscribes in any year during which such designation continues to have effect;

(*e*) that an account which is or has been designated as a TESSA only account (a "TESSA only account") must—

(i) be made up of a cash component only, and

(ii) only accept subscriptions made pursuant to regulation 5(1)(*c*);

(*f*) that all cash subscriptions shall, forthwith on payment being made—

(i) in the case of a maxi-account, subject to [paragraph (*ia*) and][2] paragraph (2), be allocated irrevocably to the component agreed between the account investor and the account manager, and

[(ia) in the case of a maxi-account where the qualifying individual is under 18 years of age, be treated as allocated irrevocably to the cash component of the account, and][2]

(ii) in the case of a mini-account, or a TESSA only account, be treated as allocated irrevocably to the single component of the account;

(*g*) that it is an account to which only one qualifying individual subscribes;

(*h*) that, subject to paragraph (4) below and regulation 7(2)(*h*), it is an account to which the qualifying individual subscribes only by payment to the account manager of a sum or sums of the individual's cash which (ignoring transfers and payments from the account manager to the individual) do not in the aggregate in any year exceed the relevant subscription limit.

(2) [Subject to paragraphs (2A) and (2B), the][2] subscription limit for any maxi-account for the purposes of these Regulations is £7,000 for the [years 1999–00 [to 2005–06][2]][1] and £5,000 for subsequent years, of which no more than £3,000 in the [years 1999–00 and [to 2005–06][2]][1], and £1,000 in subsequent years, may be allocated to a cash component, and no more than £1,000 may be allocated in any year to an insurance component.

[(2A) The subscription limit for any maxi-account for any year, at the end of which the qualifying individual is 16 years of age or over but less than 18 years, is £3,000 in the years 2001–02 to 2005–06, and £1,000 in subsequent years.][3]

[(2B) For any year during which the qualifying individual attains the age of 18 years, no more than £3,000 in the years 2001–02 to 2005–06, and £1,000 in subsequent years, may be subscribed before the individual attains that age.][3]

(3) The subscription limit for any mini-account for the purposes of these Regulations is—

(*a*) in the case of an account made up of a cash component, £3,000 for the [years 1999–00 [to 2005–06][2]][1] and £1,000 for subsequent years,

(*b*) in the case of an account made up of an insurance component, £1,000,

(*c*) in the case of an account made up of a stocks and shares component, £3,000.

(4) The subscription limit for any TESSA only account is, assuming that the words "in any year" in paragraph (1)(*h*) were omitted, that contained in paragraph (1)(*e*)(ii) above.

(5) An account must at all times be managed in accordance with these Regulations by an account manager and under terms agreed in a recorded form between the account manager and the account investor.

(6) Apart from other requirements of these Regulations the terms agreed to which paragraph (5) refers shall include the following conditions—

(*a*) that the account investments shall be in the beneficial ownership of the account investor;

(*b*) that, except in relation to qualifying investments for a cash component within regulation 8(2)(*a*), (*b*) or (*e*), and subject to regulation 15—

(i) the title to all account investments shall be vested in the account manager or his nominee or jointly in one of them and the account investor, and

(ii) where a share certificate or other document evidencing title to an account investment is issued, it shall be held by the account manager or as he may direct;

(*c*) that, in relation to a stocks and shares component, and qualifying investments falling within regulation 8(2)(*c*) and (*d*), the account manager shall, if the account investor so elects, arrange for the account investor to receive a copy of the annual report and accounts issued to investors by every company, unit trust, open-ended investment company or other entity in which he has account investments;

(*d*) that, in relation to a stocks and shares component, and qualifying investments falling within regulation 8(2)(*c*) and (*d*), the account manager shall be under an obligation (subject to any provisions made under any enactment and if the account investor so elects) to arrange for the account investor to be able—

(i) to attend any meetings of investors in companies, unit trusts, open-ended investment companies and other entities in which he has account investments,

(ii) to vote, and

(iii) to receive, in addition to the documents referred to in sub-paragraph (*c*), any other information issued to investors in such companies, unit trusts, open-ended investment companies and other entities;

(*e*) that the account manager shall satisfy himself that any person to whom he delegates any of his functions or responsibilities under the terms agreed with the account investor is competent to carry out those functions or responsibilities;

(*f*) that [on the instructions of the account investor ("the transfer instructions") and within such time as is stipulated by the account investor in the transfer instructions]—

(i) an account, with all rights and obligations of the parties to it, or

(ii) such parts thereof as may be agreed between the account investor and the account manager, [shall][4] be transferred to another account manager subject to and in accordance with regulation 21;

(*fa*) that on the instructions, subject to regulation 9(3)(*b*), of the account investor ("the withdrawal instructions") and within such time as is stipulated by the account investor in the withdrawal instructions, account investments, interest, dividends, rights or other proceeds in respect of such investments or any cash shall be transferred or paid to him;][3]

(*g*) that the account manager shall notify the account investor if by reason of any failure to satisfy the provisions of these Regulations an account is or will become no longer exempt from tax by virtue of regulation 22(1).

[(7) The time stipulated in transfer instructions or withdrawal instructions shall be subject to any reasonable business period (not exceeding 30 days) of the account manager required for the practical implementation of the instructions.][3]

Commentary—*Simon's Direct Tax Service* **E3.707, 709, 710.**

Amendments—[1] Words in para (2), (3)(*a*) substituted by the Individual Savings Account (Amendment) Regulations, SI 2000/809 reg 2 with effect from 6 April 2000.

[2] In para (1), words in sub-paras (*c*)(i) and (*f*)(i) inserted, sub-para (*f*)(ia) inserted; in para (2) and (3)(*a*), words substituted by the Individual Savings Account (Amendment) Regulations, SI 2001/908 reg 3 with effect from 6 April 2001.

[3] Paras (2A), (2B) inserted by SI 2001/908 reg 3 with effect from 6 April 2001.

[4] In para 6(*f*), word substituted for the words "at the request of the account investor and within such time as shall be agreed", and for the word "may"; and paras 6(*fa*), (7) inserted by the ISA (Amendment No 2) Regulations, SI 2002/1974 regs 1–3 with effect from 1 October 2002. The amendments apply to all accounts, whether set up before or after that date.

[Repair of certain incompatible accounts

4A—(1) An invalid account is "eligible for repair" if, in relation to the year in which the subscriptions to the account were made ("the relevant year"), it satisfies—

(*a*) the First Condition below, and

(*b*) any one of the Second to Fourth Conditions.

First condition

The account is invalid because it causes the account investor to breach the conditions in regulation 4(1)(*c*)(ii) or (*d*)(ii), as the case may be (which, taken together, allow an individual to subscribe to either one maxi-account, or to single mini-accounts with each of the 3 types of component, during a year), and for no other reason.

Second condition

Subscriptions have been made to the account during the relevant year pursuant to regulation 5(1) (transfers from matured TESSAs), with or without other subscriptions.

Third condition

The account would have been a "first later account" under regulation 4B if that regulation had effect prior to 6th April 2003 (but not earlier than 6th April 2001).

This condition shall not have effect on or after 6th April 2003 (when it is replaced by regulation 4B).

Fourth condition

The account is (disregarding any account which is eligible for repair under the Third Condition) the earliest account in the relevant year, the subscriptions to which caused the account investor to breach the conditions of regulation 4(1)(*c*)(ii) or (*d*)(ii), as the case may be, (that is, it was first subscribed to earlier in that year than any other such account).

(2) In this regulation—

(*a*) where an account investor subscribes to a particular account in more than one year, each year's subscriptions shall be treated as a separate account for the purposes of this regulation, and regulation 4B (except for determining when an account is closed) only;

(*b*) "date of discovery" means the date on which an officer of the Board gives a notice ("notice of discovery") to the account manager or account investor that the account is invalid, and (if appropriate) directions under paragraph (5) below;

(*c*) "counting towards the subscription limits" has the meaning in regulation 5(1);

(*d*) "valid account" means an account which (apart from under this regulation) is exempt from tax under regulation 22(1);

(*e*) "invalid account" means a scheme of investment which is not exempt from tax under these Regulations but which (if so exempt) would be an account within the meaning in regulation 4(1)(*a*) and, in relation to an invalid account, references to an account, a component and subscriptions pursuant to regulation 5(1) have corresponding meanings; and

(*f*) (for the avoidance of doubt) "repair" of an account is without prejudice to loss of, and accounting to the Board for, any relief from tax given for the period up to the date of discovery.

(3) An invalid account which is eligible for repair shall be treated as—

(*a*) exempt from tax under this regulation (as if under regulation 22), and (*b*) complying with the conditions of regulation 4(1)(*c*)(ii) or (*d*)(ii), as the case may be,

as from the date of discovery, to the extent of the relevant proportion mentioned in paragraph (4)(*b*).

(4)—(*a*) Calculate the extent to which the subscriptions made (and counting towards the subscription limits) during the relevant year—

(i) to that account, any other account which is eligible for repair, and any valid account, but
(ii) disregarding any closed account, or subscriptions to a closed account, in relation to which a first later account qualifies for the relief in regulation 4B(2) or satisfies the Third Condition above, taken together, as if they were subscriptions to a single maxi-account and allocations to the corresponding components of that account, do not exceed the subscription and allocation limits in regulation 4(2) to (2B), as the case may be, and

(*b*) an officer of the Board shall apportion that result between the accounts mentioned in sub-paragraph (*a*)(i), and the amount apportioned to the account mentioned in paragraph (3) is the relevant proportion.

(5) The account manager must comply within 30 days with any directions in the notice of discovery which—

(*a*) make the apportionment under paragraph (4)(*b*) and identify the account and component from which excess subscriptions or allocations (if any) are to be removed;
(*b*) direct the removal of subscriptions and proceeds representing them from an account; or
(*c*) direct the removal of subscriptions and proceeds representing them from a component.][1]

Amendments—[1] This regulation inserted by the Individual Savings Account (Amendment No 3) Regulations, SI 2002/3158 regs 1(2)(*a*), 3 with effect where a notice of discovery is given after 7 January 2003, and in relation to subscriptions to accounts made after 5 April 2001.

[Closure of mini-account or TESSA only account prior to the opening of the same type of account to be disregarded once

4B—(1) Where—

(*a*) an account investor, within the same year—

(i) subscribes to a mini-account or TESSA only account,
(ii) then closes it ("the closed account"), and
(iii) subsequently first subscribes to another account which has the same designation and type of component as the closed account, and

(*b*) the closed account was (apart from under this regulation) exempt from tax under regulation 22(1),

the earliest account in that year to fall within the terms of sub-paragraph (*a*)(iii) (the "first later account") shall be eligible for the relief in paragraph (2).

(2) The first later account shall be treated, as from the date of the first subscription to it mentioned in paragraph (1)(*a*)(iii)—

(*a*) in the case of a mini-account, as complying with the conditions of regulation 4(1)(*d*)(ii), and
(*b*) in the case of a TESSA only account, as complying with the conditions of regulation 5(1),

in the same manner as the closed account.

(3) In this regulation, an account is closed where—

(*a*) the account investor withdraws from the account all account investments, other proceeds in respect of such investments and cash, representing subscriptions to the account (and closure shall be treated as occurring at the date of such withdrawal), and
(*b*) no further subscriptions to the account are made during the remainder of the year, after such withdrawal.][1]

Amendments—[1] This regulation inserted by the Individual Savings Account (Amendment No 3) Regulations, SI 2002/3158 regs 1(2)(*b*), 4 with effect for subscriptions to accounts after 5 April 2003.

Transfers from matured tax-exempt special savings accounts

5—(1) Subject to paragraph (3), a qualifying individual whose tax-exempt special savings account matures on or after 6th April 1999, may within the period of six months from the day on which it matured, apply the proceeds from that account, not exceeding the total amount deposited in the matured account, before it matured, in making subscriptions—

(*a*) to a maxi-account held by him, which includes a cash component, to which those subscriptions shall be irrevocably allocated, or
(*b*) to a mini-account made up of a cash component, held by him, or
(*c*) to a TESSA only account held by him,

and such subscriptions shall not count towards the subscription limits in regulation 4(2) and (3)(*a*), as the case may be.

(2) In relation to a qualifying individual, whose tax-exempt special savings account matures on or after 6th January 1999, but before 6th April 1999, and who does not open a follow-up account in relation to that account, paragraph (1) shall apply with the modification that the reference to the

period of six months is replaced with a reference to so much of that period as falls on or after 6th April 1999.

(3) Paragraph (1) shall not apply unless, at the time when the first subscription referred to in paragraph (1) is made, the account manager holds either—

(*a*) a certificate given by the society[, person][1] or institution with which the qualifying individual held the matured account, containing the information prescribed by paragraph (4) and the declaration prescribed by paragraph (5), or

(*b*) where the account manager is the same society[, person][1] or institution with which the qualifying individual held the matured account, a record kept by means of a computer or otherwise which was derived from the records of the society[, person][1] or institution and shows—

(i) as regards the account-holder, the information prescribed by sub-paragraph (*a*) of paragraph (4), and

(ii) as regards the matured account, the information prescribed by paragraphs (ii) to (iv) of sub-paragraph (*b*) of paragraph (4).

(4) The information prescribed by this paragraph is—

(*a*) as regards the account-holder—

(i) his full name,

(ii) his permanent address including postcode, and

(iii) if he has one, his national insurance number, and

(*b*) as regards the matured account—

(i) the name of the society[, person][1] or institution with which it was held when it matured,

(ii) the number allocated to it by that society[, person][1] or institution,

(iii) the date on which it matured, and

(iv) the total amount deposited in, or subscribed for shares in connection with, the account since it was opened.

(5) The declaration prescribed by this paragraph is a declaration by the society[, person][1] or institution that the account was a tax-exempt special savings account throughout a continuous period of five years and that the information given in the certificate is correct.

Commentary—*Simon's Direct Tax Service* **E3.708**.

Amendments—[1] Words inserted by the Financial Services and Markets Act 2000 (Consequential Amendments) (Taxes) Order, SI 2001/3629 art 170 with effect from 1 December 2001, immediately after the coming into force of the Financial Services and Markets Act 2000 ss 411, 432(1), Sch 20 (and SI 2001/3629 Pts 1 and 2).

General investment rules

6—(1) All transactions by way of purchase by an account manager of investments under an account shall be made—

[(*a*) in the case of an authorised fund which is a dual priced unit trust, at the manager's price for the sale of the relevant class of units within the meaning of, and complying with the requirements of, rule 15.4.4 of the Collective Investment Schemes Sourcebook;][2]

[(*b*) in the case of an authorised fund which is a single priced unit trust or an open-ended investment company, at the price of a unit or share within the meaning of, and complying with the requirements of, rule 4.3.11 of the Collective Investment Schemes Sourcebook; and][2]

(*c*) in the case of all other account investments, at the price for which those investments might reasonably be expected to be purchased in the open market.

[(1ZA) In paragraph (1)(*a*) and (*b*)—

…[3]

"a dual priced unit trust" means an authorised unit trust in respect of which the manager gives different prices for buying and selling units at the same time;

"a single priced unit trust" means an authorised unit trust in respect of which the manager gives the same price for buying and selling units at the same time.][2]

(2) All other transactions by way of sale or otherwise by an account manager in investments under an account shall be made at the price for which those investments might reasonably be expected to be sold or otherwise transacted, as the case may be, in the open market.

(3) Investments, or rights in respect of investments, may not at any time—

(*a*) be purchased or made otherwise than out of cash which an account manager holds under an account at that time, and which has been allocated to the particular component of that account, for which those investments or rights are qualifying investments; or

(*b*) be purchased from—

(i) an account investor, or

(ii) the spouse of an account investor,

so as to become account investments under an account to which the account investor subscribes or has subscribed.

(4) Subject to paragraphs (5) and (6), an account investor's cash subscription and any other cash held by an account manager under an account shall be held only in sterling and be deposited in—

(i) an account with a deposit-taker, or a deposit account or a share account with a building society, or

(ii) in the case where the account manager is [the Director of Savings][1], an account with [the Director of Savings][1],

which is designated as an ISA account for the purposes of these Regulations only.

(5) An account manager who is a European institution, a relevant authorised person or an assurance undertaking may hold an account investor's cash subscription and other cash held under an account in the currency of the EEA State in which he has his principal place of business and may deposit such cash in an account, which is designated as mentioned in paragraph (4), with any person authorised under the law of that State to accept deposits.

(6) Cash by way of dividends, interest, distributions, and other rights or proceeds in respect of qualifying investments for any component shall at all times be recorded and accounted for separately from that for any other component, and may be invested only—

(*a*) in qualifying investments for the same component; or

(*b*) by way of cash deposit in accordance with paragraphs (4) and (5).

Commentary—*Simon's Direct Tax Service* **E3.710**.

Amendments—[1] Words in para (4)(ii) substituted by the Individual Savings Account (Amendment) Regulations, SI 1998/3174 reg 4 with effect from 6 April 1999.

[2] Sub-paras (1)(*a*), (*b*) substituted, and para (1ZA) inserted, by the Financial Services and Markets Act 2000 (Consequential Amendments) (Taxes) Order, SI 2001/3629 art 171 with effect from 1 December 2001, immediately after the coming into force of the Financial Services and Markets Act 2000 ss 411, 432(1), Sch 20 (and SI 2001/3629 Pts 1 and 2).

[3] In para (1ZA), definition of ''the Collective Investment Schemes Sourcebook'' revoked by the Individual Savings Account (Amendment) Regulations, SI 2003/2747 regs 1(1), (2), 2, 4 with effect from 17 November 2003.

Qualifying investments for a stocks and shares component

7—(1) This regulation specifies the kind of investments (''qualifying investments for a stocks and shares component'') which may be purchased, made or held under a stocks and shares component, and in this regulation and regulations 31 and 34, ''shares'' without more includes stock.

(2) Qualifying investments for a stocks and shares component to which paragraph (1) refers are—

(*a*) shares, not being shares in an investment trust, issued by a company wherever incorporated and, subject to paragraph (3), officially listed on a recognised stock exchange;

(*b*) securities (''qualifying securities'')—

(i) issued by a company wherever incorporated,

(ii) which satisfy at least one of the conditions specified in paragraph (5) and the condition specified in paragraph (6), and

(iii) in the case of securities of an investment trust, purchased or acquired by the account manager in circumstances where the trust satisfies the conditions specified in paragraphs (7) and (8);

[(*c*) gilt-edged securities which satisfy the condition specified in paragraph (12);

(*ca*) any securities issued by or on behalf of a government of any EEA State, which satisfy the condition specified in paragraph (12);

(*cb*) any securities which—

(i) in relation to security mentioned in sub-paragraph (*ca*), would be a strip of that security if ''strip'' had the same meaning as in section 47 of the Finance Act 1942, with the omission of the words ''issued under the National Loans Act 1968'', and

(ii) satisfy the condition specified in paragraph (12);][1]

(*d*) shares in an investment trust, listed in the Official List of the Stock Exchange, in circumstances where the trust satisfies the conditions specified in paragraphs (7) and (8);

[(*e*) units in, or shares of, a securities scheme or a warrant scheme, in circumstances where the [units or shares satisfy the condition specified in paragraph (15)][11];][6]

(*f*) units in, or shares of, a relevant UCITS, in circumstances where the [units or shares satisfy the condition specified in paragraph (15)][11];

[(*g*) units in, or shares of, a fund of funds scheme, in circumstances where the [units or shares satisfy the condition specified in paragraph (15)][11];[6]

[(*ga*) units in, or shares of, a Chapter 5 UCITS, in circumstances where the units or shares satisfy the condition specified in paragraph (15);][9]

(*h*) subject to the conditions specified in paragraph (10)[—

(i) shares which the qualifying individual has exercised the right to acquire in accordance with the provisions of a savings-related share option scheme,

(ii) shares which have been appropriated to the qualifying individual in accordance with the provisions of an approved profit sharing scheme, or

(iii) plan shares of an approved employee share ownership plan which cease to be subject to the plan but have remained in the beneficial ownership of the participant,][4]

and such shares shall be treated as fulfilling the condition as to payment of cash in regulation 4(1)(*h*);

[(*ha*) a depositary interest;][5]

(*j*) cash deposited in accordance with regulation 6(4) to (6) which an account manager holds for the purpose of investment in investments which are qualifying investments for a stocks and shares component.

[(*k*) investments which—

(i) were held under a stocks and shares component on 28th November 2001,

(ii) on that date were admitted to trading on a recognised stock exchange in an EEA State and were not listed by a competent authority in an EEA State for the purposes of Council Directive 2001/34,

(iii) since that date have not ceased to be so admitted and have not become so listed,

(iv) do not fall within any of the other sub-paragraphs of this paragraph, and

(v) are not investments which, having fallen within any of those sub-paragraphs, have ceased so to fall on or after that date.][7]

[(*l*) investments which—

(i) were held under the stocks and shares component on 6th April 2004; and

(ii) immediately before that date, fell within sub-paragraphs (*e*), (*f*) or (*g*), or sub-paragraph (*ha*) so far as the relevant investments (within the meaning in the definition of ''depositary interest'') fell within any of those sub-paragraphs.][11]

(3) An investment in shares fulfils the condition as to official listing in paragraph (2)(*a*) or (*d*) if—

(*a*) in pursuance of a public offer, the account manager applies for the allotment or allocation to him of shares in a company or trust which are due to be admitted to such listing within 30 days of the allocation or allotment, and which, when admitted to such listing, would be qualifying investments for a stocks and shares component, and

(*b*) the shares are not allotted or allocated to the account manager in the circumstances specified in paragraph (4).

(4) The circumstances specified in this paragraph are where—

(*a*) the allotment or allocation of the shares was connected with the allotment or allocation of—

(i) shares in the company or trust of a different class, or

(ii) rights to shares in the company or trust of a different class, or

(iii) shares or rights to shares in another company or trust, or

[(iv) units in or shares in, or rights to units in or shares in, an authorised fund or a part of an umbrella scheme [, or][8]][6]

(vi) securities or rights to securities of the company or trust, or of another company or trust,

to the account manager, the account investor or any other person; and

(*b*) the terms on which the first-mentioned shares in this paragraph were offered were significantly more favourable to the account manager or account investor than they would have been if their allotment or allocation had not been connected as described in sub-paragraph (*a*).

(5) The conditions specified in this paragraph are—

(*a*) that the shares in the company issuing the securities are listed on the official list of a recognised stock exchange;

(*b*) that the securities are so listed;

(*c*) that the company issuing the securities is a 75 per cent subsidiary of a company whose shares are so listed.

(6) The condition specified in this paragraph is that, judged at the date when each of the securities is first held under the account, the terms on which it was issued do not—

(*a*) require the loan to be repaid or the security to be re-purchased or redeemed, or

(*b*) allow the holder to require the loan to be repaid or the security to be re-purchased or redeemed except in circumstances which are neither certain nor likely to occur.

within the period of five years from that date.

(7) The condition specified in this paragraph is that the investment trust has no eligible rental income, in its most recent accounting period to end before the date on which the shares in, or securities of, the investment trust first become investments under the account, provided that the shares or securities shall cease to be qualifying investments for a stocks and shares component if the investment trust has any eligible rental income, in subsequent accounting periods, during which the shares or securities are held.

(8) The condition specified in this paragraph is that not more than 50 per cent in value of the investments of the trust, [scheme][6] or UCITS, or investments subject to the trusts of the scheme, as the case may be, are [either—

(*a*) securities which would not be qualifying securities, or

(*b*) securities which would not fall within any of sub-paragraphs (*c*) to (*cb*) of paragraph (2),

if paragraph (6), or paragraph (6) as it applies with the modifications in paragraph (12), as the case may be,][2] required the terms on which they were issued to be judged at the date when they first became investments of the trust, [scheme][6] or UCITS or, as the case may be, investments subject to the trusts of the scheme.

[(9) The condition specified in this paragraph is that not more than 50 per cent in value of the investments of the scheme, or subject to the trusts of the scheme, are—

(*a*) units in, or shares of, a securities scheme or a warrant scheme, or

(*b*) units in, or shares of, a relevant UCITS, where the securities scheme, warrant scheme or UCITS does not satisfy the condition in paragraph (8).][6]

(10) The conditions specified in this paragraph are—

(*a*) in relation to shares which the individual has exercised his right to acquire in accordance with the provisions of a savings-related share option scheme, that the shares are transferred to the account manager or his nominee before the expiry of the period of 90 days following the exercise of that right;

(*b*) in relation to shares appropriated to the individual in accordance with the provisions of an approved profit-sharing scheme, that the shares are transferred to the account manager or his nominee before the expiry of the period of 90 days following the date when the individual directed the trustees to transfer the ownership of the shares to him or, if earlier, the release date in relation to the shares;

[(*ba*) in relation to plan shares mentioned in paragraph (2)(*h*)(iii), that the shares are transferred to the account manager or his nominee before the expiry of the period of 90 days following the date when the plan shares ceased to be subject to the plan;][4]

(*c*) that the aggregate market value at the date of transfer of any shares transferred to the account manager or his nominee in accordance with sub-paragraphs [(*a*), (*b*) or (*ba*)][4] in any year, and the individual's cash subscriptions in that year which are allocated to the stocks and shares component of that account—

(i) in the case of a maxi-account do not together exceed the subscription limit in regulation 4(2) in that year, reduced by the cash subscriptions in that year which are allocated to a cash component, or an insurance component, of the account; and

(ii) in the case of a mini-account, do not together exceed the subscription limit in regulation 4(3)(*c*) in that year.

(11) In paragraph (4)(*a*), "company" means any body corporate having a share capital.

[(12) The condition specified in this paragraph is the condition specified in paragraph (6), omitting sub-paragraph (*b*) of that paragraph and the word "or" after sub-paragraph (*a*).][3]

[(13) The references to "shares" in paragraphs (2)(*h*) and (10) shall include references to a depositary interest where the relevant investments in question (referred to in paragraphs (*a*) and (*b*) of the definition of "depositary interest") are shares falling within both paragraphs (2)(*h*) and (10).][5]

[(14) Qualifying investments for a stocks and shares component falling within sub- paragraph (*ha*) of paragraph (2), so far as the relevant investments (within the meaning given in the definition of "depositary interest") fall within any of sub-paragraphs (*e*), (*f*), (*g*) or (*ga*) of that paragraph, must satisfy the condition specified in paragraph (15).][10]

[(15) The condition specified in this paragraph is that, during the period of five years from the date on which the qualifying investments in question were first held in the account, there was no time when—

(*a*) the contract under which the investments were acquired, or any other transaction entered into at any time by the account investor or any other person, or

(*b*) the nature of the underlying subject matter of the investments, had the effect that the account investor was not exposed, or not exposed to any significant extent, to the risk of loss from fluctuations in the value of the investments exceeding 5% of the capital consideration paid or payable for the acquisition of those investments.][10]

[(16) In this regulation references, in relation to qualifying investments, to—

(*a*) the underlying subject matter are references to or to the value of the investments, currencies or other matters to which, or to the value of which, those qualifying investments or their value is referable;

(*b*) the capital consideration paid include the incidental costs of acquisition; and

(*c*) the value are to be construed applying regulation 6(2), but deducting the incidental costs that would be incurred by a disposal.][10]

Commentary—*Simon's Direct Tax Service* **E3.715**.

Amendments—[1] Para (2)(*c*) substituted and para 2(*ca*), (*cb*) inserted by the Individual Savings Account (Amendment) Regulations, SI 1998/3174 reg 5(2) with effect from 6 April 1999.

[2] Words in para (8) substituted by SI 1998/3174 reg 5(3) with effect from 6 April 1999.

[3] Para (12) inserted by SI 1998/3174 reg 5(4) with effect from 6 April 1999.

[4] Words in para (2)(*h*) and (10)(*c*) substituted and para (10)(*ba*) inserted by the Individual Savings Account (Amendment No 2) Regulations, SI 2000/2079 reg 4 with effect from 21 August 2000.

[5] Para (2)(*ha*) inserted and para (13) added by the Individual Savings Account (Amendment No 3) Regulations, SI 2000/3112 reg 4 with effect from 13 December 2000.

[6] Sub-paras (2)(*e*), (*g*) and para (9) substituted, in para(4), sub-para (*a*)(iv) substituted for sub-paras (*a*)(iv) and (*a*)(v), words in sub-para (8) substituted, by the Financial Services and Markets Act 2000 (Consequential Amendments) (Taxes) Order, SI 2001/3629 art 172 with effect from 1 December 2001, immediately after the coming into force of the Financial Services and Markets Act 2000 ss 411, 432(1), Sch 20 (and SI 2001/3629 Pts 1 and 2).

[7] Sub-para (2)(*k*) added by the Individual Savings Account (Amendment No 2) Regulations, SI 2001/3778 art 3 with effect from 19 December 2001.

[8] Word in para (4)(*a*) substituted for ";" by the Financial Services and Markets Act 2000 (Consequential Amendments) (Taxes) Order, SI 2002/1409 art 7 with effect from 2 July 2002.
[9] Sub-para (2)(*ga*) inserted by the Individual Savings Account (Amendment) Regulations, SI 2003/2747 regs 1(1), (2), 2, 5(*c*) with effect from 17 November 2003.
[10] Paras (14)–(16) inserted by SI 2003/2747 regs 1(1), (2), 2, 6 with effect, so far as paras (14)–(16) above relate to sub-para (2)(*ga*), from 17 November 2003, but otherwise from 6 April 2004.
[11] Words in sub-paras (2)(*e*), (*f*), (*g*) substituted, and sub-para (2)(*l*) inserted, by the Individual Savings Account (Amendment) Regulations, SI 2003/2747 regs 1(1), (3), 2, 5(*a*), (*b*), (*d*) with effect from 6 April 2004.

Qualifying investments for a cash component

8—(1) This regulation specifies the kind of investments ("qualifying investments for a cash component") which may be purchased, made or held under a cash component.

(2) Qualifying investments for a cash component to which paragraph (1) refers are, subject to paragraph (3)—

(*a*) cash deposited in a deposit account with a building society, or [a person falling within section 840A(1)(*b*) of the Taxes Act][2] or a relevant European institution;

(*b*) cash deposited in a share account with a building society;

[(*c*) units in, or shares of, a money market scheme;][2]

[(*d*) units in, or shares of, a fund of funds scheme, within the meaning given in regulation 2(1)(*b*), with the modification that for the words from "comply with" to the end there are substituted the words "permit the investments of the scheme, or subject to the trusts of the scheme, to consist only of units in, or shares of, money market schemes";][2]

[(*e*) such investment deposits with the National Savings Bank which, according to the terms and conditions subject to which they are made, are expressly permitted to be held under a cash component of an account;

(*f*) any securities issued under the National Loans Act 1968—

(i) for the purpose of or in connection with raising money under the auspices of the Director of Savings within the meaning of section 11(1)(*a*) of the National Debt Act 1972, and

(ii) other than national savings certificates, premium savings bonds, national savings stamps and national savings gift tokens, which, according to the terms and conditions subject to which they are issued and purchased, are expressly permitted to be held under a cash component of an account.][1]

[(*g*) investments falling within sub-paragraphs (*e*), (*f*), (*g*) or (*ga*) of regulation 7(2), in circumstances where the units or shares do not satisfy the condition specified in regulation 7(15);][3]

[(*h*) a depositary interest (with the references in that definition to a stocks and shares component and to regulation 7(2)(*a*) to (*h*) being replaced with references to a cash component and to regulation 8(2)(*a*) to (*g*))][3]

(3) A deposit account or share account which is a qualifying investment for a cash component falling within paragraph (2)(*a*) or (*b*) respectively must not be connected with any other account falling within the descriptions in those sub-paragraphs, held by the account investor or any other person, and for this purpose such an account is connected with another if—

(*a*) either was opened with reference to the other, or with a view to enabling the other to be opened on particular terms, or with a view to facilitating the opening of the other on particular terms, and

(*b*) the terms on which the first-mentioned account in this paragraph was opened would have been significantly less favourable to the holder if the other had not been opened.

Commentary—*Simon's Direct Tax Service* **E3.716**.
Amendments—[1] Para (2) (*e*) substituted and para 2(*f*) inserted by the Individual Savings Account (Amendment) Regulations, SI 1998/3174 reg 6 with effect from 6 April 1999.
[2] In para (2), words in sub-para (*a*) substituted, and sub-paras (*c*) and (*d*) substituted, by the Financial Services and Markets Act 2000 (Consequential Amendments) (Taxes) Order, SI 2001/3629 art 173 with effect from 1 December 2001, immediately after the coming into force of the Financial Services and Markets Act 2000 ss 411, 432(1), Sch 20 (and SI 2001/3629 Pts 1 and 2).
[3] Sub-paras (2)(*g*), (*h*) inserted by the Individual Savings Account (Amendment) Regulations, SI 2003/2747 regs 1(1), (2), 2, 7 with effect from 17 November 2003.

Qualifying investments for an insurance component

9—(1) This regulation specifies the kind of investments ("qualifying investments for an insurance component") which may be purchased, made or held under an insurance component.

(2) Qualifying investments for an insurance component to which paragraph (1) refers are, subject to paragraphs (4) to (7)—

(*a*) policies of life insurance which satisfy the conditions specified in paragraph (3), and

(*b*) cash deposited in accordance with regulation 6(4) to (6) which an account manager holds for the purpose of investment in investments which are qualifying investments for an insurance component.

(3) The conditions specified in this paragraph are that—

(*a*) the insurance is on the life of the account investor only;

(*b*) the terms and conditions of the policy provide—

(i) that the policy may only be owned or held as a qualifying investment for an insurance component of an account which satisfies the provisions of these Regulations;

(ii) that the policy shall automatically terminate if [it comes to the notice of the account manager, in any manner, that either of the events specified in paragraph (8) has occurred in relation to the policy][1];

(iii) for an express prohibition of any transfer of the policy, or the rights conferred by the policy or any share or interest in the policy or rights respectively, other than the cash proceeds from the termination of the policy or a partial surrender of the rights conferred by the policy, to the account investor; and

(iv) that the policy, the rights conferred by the policy and any share or interest in the policy or rights respectively, shall not be capable of assignment or (in Scotland) assignation, other than that they may be vested in the account investor's personal representatives, and that the title to the policy may be transferred to a new account manager subject to and in accordance with regulations 15 and 21,

[(*c*) the policy evidences or secures a contract of insurance which—

(i) falls within paragraph I or III of Part II of Schedule 1 to the Financial Services and Markets Act 2000 (Regulated Activities) Order 2001, or

(ii) would fall within either of those paragraphs if the insurer was a company with permission under Part 4 of the Financial Services and Markets Act 2000 to effect or carry out contracts of insurance;][4]

(*d*) the policy is not—

(i) a contract to pay an annuity on human life, or

(ii) a personal portfolio bond within the meaning given by [regulation 2(1) of the Personal Portfolio Bonds (Tax) Regulations 1999, or][3]

(iii) a contract, the effecting and carrying out of which constitutes "pension business" within the meaning given by section 431B(1) of the Taxes Act; and

(*e*) after the first payment in respect of a premium in relation to the policy has been made, there is no contractual obligation on any person to make any other such payment.

(4) A policy which is a qualifying investment for an insurance component falling within paragraph (2)(*a*) must not be connected with any other policy ("the linked policy"), held by the account investor or any other person, and for this purpose a policy is connected with another if—

(*a*) either policy was issued in respect of an insurance made with the reference to the other, or with a view to enabling the other to be made on particular terms, or with a view to facilitating the making of the other on particular terms, and

(*b*) the terms on which the first-mentioned policy in this paragraph was issued would have been significantly less favourable to the holder if the linked policy had not been issued.

(5) References to "the linked policy" in paragraph (4) shall include a contract of insurance, and references to the issuing of the linked policy shall include the making of such a contract.

(6) No sum may at any time, at or after the making of the insurance, be lent to or at the direction of the account investor or by arrangement with the insurer for the time being responsible for the obligations under the policy.

[(7) Where either of the events specified in paragraph (8) occurs in relation to a policy, the policy shall nevertheless be treated, for the purposes of these Regulations, excepting paragraphs (3)(*b*)(ii) and (8) and regulation 36, as if it had satisfied the conditions in paragraph (3)(*b*)(i) during the period—

(*a*) commencing at the time at which the specified event occurred, and

(*b*) ending immediately before—

(i) the end of the final year in relation to the policy, within the meaning of section 546(4) of the Taxes Act, or

(ii) the time at which the specified event came to the notice of the account manager, whichever first occurs (the "termination event").

(8) The events specified in this paragraph are—

(*a*) that the policy has ceased to be one in respect of which the conditions in paragraph (3)(*b*)(i) are satisfied: and

(*b*) that those conditions were not satisfied in relation to the policy at the date on which the insurance was made.

(9) Where—

(*a*) it comes to the notice of the account manager, in any manner, that an event specified in paragraph (8) has occurred in relation to a policy, and

(*b*) the account manager is not the insurer for the time being responsible for the obligations under the policy or, where the policy is not still in existence, the person who was the last such insurer, the account manager shall, within 30 days of the event coming to his notice, give notice to that insurer, specifying the event mentioned in sub-paragraph (*a*), and the termination event.][2]

Commentary—*Simon's Direct Tax Service* **E3.717**.

Amendments—[1] Words in para (3)(*b*)(ii) substituted by the Individual Savings Account (Amendment) Regulations, SI 1998/3174 reg 7(2) with effect from 6 April 1999.
[2] Para (7) substituted and paras (8), (9) inserted by SI 1998/3174 reg 7(3) with effect from 6 April 1999.
[3] Words in para (3)(*d*)(ii) substituted by the Individual Savings Account (Amendment) Regulations, SI 2001/908 reg 4 with effect from 6 April 2001.
[4] Sub-para (3)(*c*) substituted by the Financial Services and Markets Act 2000 (Consequential Amendments) (Taxes) Order, SI 2001/3629 art 174 with effect from 1 December 2001, immediately after the coming into force of the Financial Services and Markets Act 2000 ss 411, 432(1), Sch 20 (and SI 2001/3629 Pts 1 and 2).

Qualifying individuals who may invest under an account

10—(1) This regulation specifies the description of individual who may invest under an account ("qualifying individual").

(2) A qualifying individual to whom paragraph (1) refers is an individual—

(*a*) who[, in the cases of a maxi-account or of a mini-account made up of a cash component, is 16 years of age or over and, in any other case,][1] is 18 years of age or over;

(*b*) who, in the case where the account is a maxi-account, has not subscribed, and will not subscribe, to any other account, not being a TESSA only account, in the year in which the subscription is made;

(*c*) who, in the case where the account is a mini-account, has not subscribed, and will not subscribe, to any other account, not being a mini-account made up of a different type of component than the account mentioned in paragraph (1) or a TESSA only account, in the year in which the subscription is made; and

(*d*)

(i) who is resident and ordinarily resident in the United Kingdom, or

(ii) who, though not resident in the United Kingdom, performs duties which by virtue of section 132(4)(*a*) of the Taxes Act (Crown employees serving overseas) are treated as being performed in the United Kingdom[, or

(iii) who, though not resident in the United Kingdom, is married to a person mentioned in paragraph (ii)][1].

Commentary—*Simon's Direct Tax Service* **E3.705**.
Amendments—[1] In para (2), words in sub-para (*a*) inserted, and sub-para (*d*)(iii) added, by the Individual Savings Account (Amendment) Regulations, SI 2001/908 reg 5 with effect from 6 April 2001.

Account investor ceasing to qualify

11 Notwithstanding any other provision of these Regulations an account investor who, after subscribing to an account, at any time ceases to fulfil the conditions of regulation 10(2)(*d*) may retain the benefits of the account (including the right to any relief or exemption due under the account) subsisting at that time but, so long as he fails to fulfil those conditions, shall not be entitled to subscribe further to such an account.

Conditions for application to subscribe to an account

12—(1) An application by an individual to subscribe to an account in the year in which he first subscribes to that account, and in the year following a year in which that individual has not subscribed to the account, must be made to an account manager in a statement and, subject to paragraph (5), must fulfil the conditions specified in paragraphs (2), (3) and (4).

(2) An application must specify the first year to which the application relates.

(3) An application shall provide for a declaration by the applicant that—

(*a*) his application is to subscribe to a maxi-account, a mini-account made up of a specified component or a TESSA only account, as the case may be;

(*b*) the declaration shall have effect for the year to which paragraph (2) refers, and each successive year following that year, in which the applicant subscribes to the account;

(*c*) all cash subscriptions made, and to be made, to the account are the applicant's cash;

(*d*) in the case of a maxi-account, the applicant—

(i) has not subscribed, and will not subscribe, to any other account, not being a TESSA only account, in the year to which paragraph (2) refers, and

(ii) will not subscribe to any other account, not being a TESSA only account, in each successive year following that year, during which the declaration has effect;

(*e*) in the case of a mini-account, the applicant—

(i) has not subscribed, and will not subscribe, to any other account, not being a mini-account made up of a different type of component than that specified in accordance with subparagraph (*a*) or a TESSA only account, in the year to which paragraph (2) refers, and

(ii) will not subscribe to any such other account as is referred to in paragraph (i), in each successive year following that year, during which the declaration has effect;

[(*f*) the applicant is 16 years of age or over, and—

(i) is resident and ordinarily resident in the United Kingdom, or

(ii) is a person who performs duties which, by virtue of section 132(4)(*a*) of the Taxes Act, are treated as being performed in the United Kingdom, or

(iii) is married to a person mentioned in paragraph (ii),

and will inform the account manager if he ceases to be so resident and ordinarily resident, or to perform such duties, or to be married to a person who performs such duties, as the case may be;][1]

(*g*) the applicant authorises the account manager—

(i) to hold the applicant's cash subscription, account investments, interest, dividends and any other rights or proceeds in respect of those investments and any other cash;

(ii) to make on his behalf any claims to relief from tax in respect of account investments;

(iii) on the applicant's request, subject to regulation 9(3)(b), to transfer or pay to him as the case may be, account investments, interest, dividends, rights or other proceeds in respect of such investments or any cash;[2]

(iv) where the application is not in writing, to record the terms of the declaration in a written declaration made on behalf of the applicant.

(4) An application must contain—

(*a*) the applicant's full name,

(*b*) the address of his permanent residence, including postcode,

(*c*) his national insurance number, or confirmation that he does not have one, and

(*d*) his date of birth.

(5) In the case of an application to subscribe by way of applying the proceeds from a matured tax-exempt special savings account within regulation 5(1)(*a*), (*b*) or (*c*) where the account matured on or after 6th January 1999 but before 6th April 1999, the declaration in paragraph (3) shall be modified by including a statement that the applicant has not opened, and will not open, a follow-up account.

(6) An account manager may not accept as an account investor any individual if he has reason to believe that—

(*a*) he is not or might not be a qualifying individual, or

(*b*) he has given untrue information in his application.

(7) Where paragraph (3)(*g*)(iv) applies, the account manager shall make the written declaration therein referred to, and send a copy to the applicant and, subject to any corrections notified by the applicant to the account manager within the period of 30 days from the date the copy is sent, and incorporated in a new declaration made by the account manager, any such declaration shall take effect as from the date on which the original declaration was made as a declaration made on behalf of the applicant.

(8) Section 95 of the Management Act shall have effect as if—

(*a*) the statement and declarations to which paragraphs (1), (3) and (7) refer were a statement or declarations, as the case may be, within the meaning of subsection (1)(*b*), and

(*b*) there were substituted for subsection (3) the following words—

"(3) The relevant years of assessment for the purposes of this section are the year of assessment in respect of which any claim to relief or exemption from tax in connection with which the statement or declarations are relevant, is made, the next following, and any preceding year of assessment."

[(9) An application furnished by an individual under this regulation ...[3] shall be regarded as in writing if it is furnished—

(*a*) by telephonic facsimile transmission containing the signature of the individual, or

(*b*) by electronic communication containing an electronic signature of the individual.][1]

[(10) Declarations made by the account manager under paragraph (3)(*g*)(iv) of this regulation ...[3] shall be regarded as made in writing if they are produced by electronic means, and the copy of a declaration to be sent to the individual in accordance with paragraph (7) of [this regulation][3] may be sent by telephonic facsimile transmission or by electronic communication.][1]

[(11) In this regulation—

["electronic communication" includes any communication conveyed by means of an electronic communications network.][4]

"electronic signature" has the meaning given by section 7(2) of the Electronic Communications Act 2000.][1]

[(12) An application may be made on behalf of an individual who is suffering from mental disorder, by a parent, guardian, spouse, son or daughter of the individual, and shall be treated for the purposes of these Regulations as an application made by the individual.][3]

[(13) In paragraph (12) "mental disorder" has the meaning given by section 1(2) of the Mental Health Act 1983 or, in Scotland, section 1(2) of the Mental Health (Scotland) Act 1984 or, in Northern Ireland Article 3 of the Mental Health (Northern Ireland) Order 1986.][3]

Commentary—*Simon's Direct Tax Service* **E3.706**.

Amendments—[1] Para (3)(*f*) substituted, and paras (9)–(11) added, by the Individual Savings Account (Amendment) Regulations, SI 2001/908 reg 6 with effect from 6 April 2001.

[2] Para 3(*g*)(iii) repealed by the Individual Savings Account (Amendment No 2) Regulations, SI 2002/1974 regs 1, 2, 4 with effect from 1 October 2002. This amendment applies to all accounts, whether set up before or after that date.

[3] Words in paras (9), (10) revoked, words in para (10) substituted, and paras (11), (12) inserted, by the Individual Savings Account (Amendment No 3) Regulations, SI 2002/3158 reg 5 with effect from 8 January 2003.
[4] In para (11), definition of "electronic communication" substituted by the Communications Act 2003 (Consequential Amendments) Order, SI 2003/2155 art 3(2), Schedule 1 para 24 with effect from 17 September 2003.

Application by curator bonis

13 ...[1]

Amendments—[1] Repealed by the Individual Savings Account (Amendment No 3) Regulations, SI 2002/3158 reg 6 with effect from 8 January 2003.

Account manager—qualifications and Board's approval

14—(1) This regulation specifies the circumstances ("qualifying circumstances") in which a person may be approved by the Board as an account manager.

(2) The qualifying circumstances to which paragraph (1) refers are the following—

(*a*) the person must make an application to the Board for approval in a form prescribed by the Board;

(*b*) an account manager must be—

(i) an authorised person within the meaning of [section 31(1)(*a*) or (*c*) of, or Schedule 5 to, the Financial Services and Markets Act 2000 who has permission to carry on one or more of the activities specified in Articles 14, 21, 25, 37, 40, 45, 51 and 53 and, in so far as it applies to any of those activities, Article 64 of the Financial Services and Markets Act 2000 (Regulated Activities) Order 2001 but excluding any person falling within paragraph (iv) below][2]; or

(ii) a European institution which [carries on one or more of those activities][2]; or

(iii) in the case of an account manager approved to set up and administer accounts made up of a cash component only, [the Director of Savings][1], a building society, [a person falling within section 840A(1)(*b*) of the Taxes Act][2] or a relevant European institution; or

(iv) in the case of an account manager approved to set up and administer accounts made up of an insurance component only, an insurance company, within the meaning given by section 431(2) of the Taxes Act, an incorporated friendly society, or a registered friendly society; or

(v) in the case of an account manager approved to set up and administer accounts made up of an insurance component only, an assurance undertaking which does not fall within paragraph (iv) above;

(*c*) an account manager must not be prevented from acting as such by [any requirement imposed under section 43 of the Financial Services and Markets Act 2000, or by any prohibition imposed by or under any rules made by the Financial Services Authority under that Act][2]; and

(*d*) an account manager who—

(i) is a European institution or a relevant authorised person and who does not have a branch or business establishment in the United Kingdom, or has such a branch or business establishment but does not intend to carry out all his functions as an account manager at that branch or business establishment, or

(ii) falls within sub-paragraph (*b*)(v),

must fulfil one of the three requirements specified in regulation 16.

(3) The terms of the Board's approval may—

(*a*) approve a person to set up and administer accounts—

(i) which are made up of a single specified component, or

(ii) which are made up of any two specified components, or

(iii) which are made up of three components; and

(*b*) include conditions designed to ensure that the provisions of these Regulations are satisfied.

Commentary—*Simon's Direct Tax Service* **E3.721, 722.**

Amendments—[1] Words in para (2)(*b*)(iii) substituted by the Individual Savings Account (Amendment) Regulations, SI 1998/3174 reg 8 with effect from 6 April 1999.
[2] Words in sub-paras (2)(*b*), (*c*) substituted by the Financial Services and Markets Act 2000 (Consequential Amendments) (Taxes) Order, SI 2001/3629 art 175 with effect from 1 December 2001, immediately after the coming into force of the Financial Services and Markets Act 2000 ss 411, 432(1), Sch 20 (and SI 2001/3629 Pts 1 and 2).

Special requirements relating to insurer-managers

15 If and so long as a person falling within regulation 14(2)(*b*)(iv) or (v) acts as account manager of an account, and the account investments include a policy of life insurance—

(*a*) the title to all such policies shall be vested in the account investor; and

(*b*) where a policy document or other document evidencing title to such policies of life insurance is issued, it shall be held by the account investor.

Account manager—appointment of tax representative

16—(1) This regulation specifies the requirements mentioned in regulation 14(2)(*d*).

(2) The first requirement specified in this regulation is that—

(*a*) a person who falls within subsection (5) of section 333A of the Taxes Act is for the time being appointed by the account manager to be responsible for securing the discharge of the duties prescribed by paragraph (5) which fall to be discharged by the account manager, and

(*b*) his identity and the fact of his appointment have been notified to the Board by the account manager.

(3) The second requirement specified in this regulation is that there are for the time being other arrangements with the Board for a person other than the account manager to secure the discharge of such duties.

(4) The third requirement specified in this regulation is that there are for the time being other arrangements with the Board designed to secure the discharge of such duties.

(5) The duties prescribed by this paragraph are those that fall to be discharged by an account manager under these Regulations.

(6) The appointment of a person in pursuance of the first requirement shall be treated as terminated in circumstances where—

(*a*) the Board have reason to believe that the person concerned—

(i) has failed to secure the discharge of any of the duties prescribed by paragraph (5), or

(ii) does not have adequate resources to discharge those duties, and

(*b*) the Board have notified the account manager and that person that they propose to treat his appointment as having terminated with effect from the date specified in the notice.

(7) Where, in accordance with the first requirement, a person is at any time responsible for securing the discharge of duties, the person concerned—

(*a*) shall be entitled to act on the account manager's behalf for any of the purposes of the provisions relating to the duties;

(*b*) shall secure (where appropriate by acting on the account manager's behalf) the account manager's compliance with and discharge of the duties; and

(*c*) shall be personally liable in respect of any failure of the account manager to comply with or discharge any such duty as if the duties imposed on the account manager were imposed jointly and severally on the account manager and the person concerned.

Commentary—*Simon's Direct Tax Service* **E3.722**.

Account manager—withdrawal by Board of approval

17—(1) This regulation specifies the circumstances ("the disqualifying circumstances") in which the Board may by notice withdraw their approval of a person as an account manager in relation to an account.

(2) The disqualifying circumstances to which paragraph (1) refers are that the Board have reason to believe—

(*a*) that any provision of these Regulations is not or at any time has not been satisfied in respect of an account managed by the account manager; or

(*b*) that a person to whom they have given approval to act as an account manager is not qualified so to act.

(3) The notice to which paragraph (1) refers—

(*a*) may withdraw an approval in part, that is, in respect of particular types of accounts specified in the notice;

(*b*) shall specify the date from which the Board's approval is withdrawn; and

(*c*) shall specify the disqualifying circumstances.

Commentary—*Simon's Direct Tax Service* **E3.723**.

Account manager—appeal against withdrawal of Board's approval

18—(1) An account manager to whom notice of withdrawal of approval has been given under regulation 17 may appeal against the withdrawal by notice given to the Board within 30 days after the date of the notice of withdrawal.

(2) The appeal shall be to the Special Commissioners.

(3) The like provisions as are contained in Part V of the Management Act (appeals and other proceedings) shall apply to an appeal and the Special Commissioners shall on appeal to them confirm the notice unless they are satisfied that the notice ought to be quashed.

Commentary—*Simon's Direct Tax Service* **E3.723**.

Account manager ceasing to act

19 A person shall give notice to the Board and to the account investor in the account which he manages of his intention to cease to act as the account manager not less than 30 days before he so ceases so that his obligations to the Board under the account can be conveniently discharged at or about the time he ceases so to act, and the notice to the account investor shall inform him of his right to transfer the account under regulation 21.

Commentary—*Simon's Direct Tax Service* **E3.724**.

Account manager ceasing to qualify

20—(1) A person shall cease to qualify as an account manager and shall notify the Board within 30 days of the relevant event in sub-paragraphs (*a*) to (*e*), of that relevant event, where—

(*a*) the person no longer fulfils the conditions of regulation 14; or

(*b*) in the case of an individual, he becomes bankrupt or, in Scotland, his estate is sequestrated, or he makes any arrangement or composition with his creditors generally; or

(*c*) in the case of a company, a resolution has been passed or a petition has been presented to wind it up; or

(*d*) in the case of a building society, [a person falling within section 840A(1)(*b*) of the Taxes Act][1] or a relevant European institution—

(i) it ceases to be a building society or to [fall within section 840A(1)(*b*) of the Taxes Act][1] or to be a relevant European institution, as the case may be; or

(ii) its directors have made a proposal under Part I of the Insolvency Act 1986 for a composition in satisfaction of its debts or a scheme of arrangement of its affairs; or

(iii) [it enters administration][2]; or

(iv) a receiver or manager of its property has been appointed; or

(*e*) in the case of a European institution, a relevant authorised person or an assurance undertaking which falls within regulation 14(2)(*b*)(v), action corresponding to that described in sub-paragraph (*b*), (*c*) or (*d*) has been taken by or in relation to the institution, person or undertaking under the law of an EEA State.

(2) On giving the notice referred to in paragraph (1), the person shall also notify the account investor of his right to transfer the account under regulation 21, and the notice shall inform the account investor of his rights under paragraph (3).

(3) Where the account investor—

(*a*) receives a notice under paragraph (2), or regulation 19, and

(*b*) within 30 days of the sending of the notice to him, transfers the account to another account manager pursuant to regulation 21,

the period between the transferor ceasing to act or qualify as an account manager, and the transfer to the transferee, shall be ignored in determining whether the account has at all times been managed by an account manager.

Commentary—*Simon's Direct Tax Service* **E3.723**.

Amendments—[1] Words in sub-para (1)(*d*) substituted by the Financial Services and Markets Act 2000 (Consequential Amendments) (Taxes) Order, SI 2001/3629 art 176 with effect from 1 December 2001, immediately after the coming into force of the Financial Services and Markets Act 2000 ss 411, 432(1), Sch 20 (and SI 2001/3629 Pts 1 and 2).

[2] Words in para (1)(*d*)(iii) substituted by the Enterprise Act 2002 (Insolvency) Order, SI 2003/2096 art 5, Schedule para 73 with effect from 15 September 2003. However, this amendment does not apply in any case where a petition for an administration order was presented before that date.

Transfer of accounts to other account managers

21—(1) No transfer shall be made of—

(*a*) any subscriptions to the account, made by the account investor in the year in which a transfer under this regulation takes place, but prior to the transfer, or

(*b*) the qualifying investments and other proceeds representing those subscriptions,

except by means of a transfer of the whole of the account pursuant to paragraph (2).

(2) Subject to paragraph (5), where—

(*a*) arrangements are made by an account investor to transfer an account from one account manager ("the transferor") to another account manager ("the transferee"), or

(*b*) an account is transferred in consequence of the transferor ceasing to act or to qualify as an account manager,

the transfer shall have effect and the account, its components and its designation under regulation 4(1)(*b*) shall not otherwise be affected for the purpose of these Regulations by reason of the transfer.

(3) Subject to paragraphs (1), (4) and (5), where arrangements are made by an account investor to transfer the investments forming part of an account, that is—

(*a*) part of the qualifying investments and cash proceeds held under a component, or

(*b*) the whole of the qualifying investments and cash proceeds held under a particular component (where there is more than one component),

of an account held by him from one account manager ("the transferor") to another account manager ("the transferee"), the transfer shall have effect and the account, its components and its designation under regulation 4(1)(*b*) shall not otherwise be affected for the purpose of these Regulations by reason of the transfer.

(4) Where a transfer takes place pursuant to paragraph (3)—

(i) all subscriptions to the account made by the account investor in the year in which the transfer under that paragraph takes place (whether before or after the transfer) must be made to a single account manager, and subject thereto

(ii) the transferee shall thereafter be the account manager in relation to the qualifying investments and cash proceeds transferred, and all references in these Regulations to the account manager shall, so far as relates to account investments transferred under that paragraph, be thereafter taken to be references to the transferee.

(5) The transferor shall within 30 days after the date of the transfer give the transferee a notice containing the information specified in paragraph (6) and the declaration specified in paragraph (7).

(6) The information specified in this paragraph is—

(*a*) as regards the account investor—

(i) his full name,

(ii) the address of his permanent residence, including postcode,

(iii) his date of birth, and

(iv) if he has one, his national insurance number, and

(*b*) as regards an account transferred pursuant to paragraph (2)—

(i) whether the account is a maxi-account, a mini-account made up of a specified component or a TESSA only account,

(ii) the date of the transfer,

(iii) the total amount of cash subscribed to the account during the period from the beginning of the year in which the transfer takes place to the date of the transfer, and the amounts respectively allocated to each component of the account,

(iv) the identification of the assets belonging to each component, where there are more than one component,

(v) the amount of any dividends on account investments which are payable to, but have not been received by, the transferor at the date of the transfer, and

(vi) any amount which is, or will become, due under regulation 23 which has not been paid to the Board at the date of the transfer, and

(*c*) as regards part of an account transferred pursuant to paragraph (3)—

(i) the date of the transfer,

(ii) the identification of the assets belonging to each component, where there are more than one component,

(iii) the amount of any dividends on account investments which are payable to, but have not been received by, the transferor at the date of the transfer, and

(iv) any amount which is, or will become, due under regulation 23 which has not been paid to the Board at the date of the transfer.

(7) The declaration specified in this paragraph is a declaration by the transferor that—

(*a*) he has fulfilled all his obligations to account investors, to the Board or otherwise, which are imposed by these Regulations;

(*b*) he has transferred to the transferee or a nominee for the transferee any account investments which are being transferred by virtue of the transfer and that, where registration of any such transfer is required, he has taken the necessary steps to ensure that those account investments can be registered in the name of the transferee or the nominee;

(*c*) that the information contained in the notice is correct.

Commentary—*Simon's Direct Tax Service* **E3.725**.

Exemption from tax of account income and gains

22—(1) Subject to these Regulations—

(*a*) no tax shall be chargeable on the account manager or his nominee or on the account investor—

(i) in respect of interest, dividends, distributions or gains in respect of account investments, or

(ii) on any annual profits or gains treated by section 714(2) of the Taxes Act as having been received by any of them in respect of account investments, or

(iii) on an offshore income gain to which a disposal made by any of them of an account investment gives rise, which is treated by section 761(1) of the Taxes Act as constituting profits or gains, or

(iv) on a profit realised by any of them from the discount on a relevant discounted security within the meaning of Schedule 13 to the Finance Act 1996, which is held as an account investment, or

(v) in respect of gains treated by section 541 of the Taxes Act as arising in connection with a policy of life insurance which is an account investment held under an insurance component;

(*b*) losses in respect of account investments shall be disregarded for the purposes of capital gains tax;

(*c*) a corresponding deficiency occurring at the end of the final year, within the meaning of section 549(1) of the Taxes Act, so far as it relates to a policy of life insurance which is an account investment held under an insurance component, shall not be allowable as a deduction from the total income of the account investor;

(*d*) relief in respect of tax shall be given in the manner and to the extent provided by these Regulations; and

(*e*) interest on a cash deposit which is an account investment held under a cash component shall not[, except for the purposes of section 660B of the Taxes Act,][1] be regarded as income for any income tax purposes.

(2) An account investor who, after subscribing to an account, at any time ceases to be resident in the United Kingdom, shall be treated as if he were resident in the United Kingdom for the purposes of determining his entitlement to, or to payment of, tax credits in respect of qualifying distributions, so far as they relate to account investments under an account held by him.

Amendments—[1] Words inserted in para (1)(*e*) by the Individual Savings Account (Amendment) Regulations, SI 2001/908 reg 8 with effect from 6 April 2001.

Interest on cash deposits held under a stocks and shares component or insurance component

23—(1) When in any year, a sum of interest is paid or credited in respect of a cash deposit which is held under a stocks and shares component or insurance component in accordance with regulation 6(4) to (6)—

(*a*) no relief from tax shall apply to such interest, but

(*b*) paragraph (2) shall apply, and the amount determined in accordance with that paragraph shall be taken to represent the tax on such interest, in the place of the liabilities to tax which would otherwise arise.

(2) Where this paragraph applies—

(*a*) the account manager shall pay to the Board an amount representing income tax at the lower rate in force for the year on all sums of interest referred to in paragraph (1) paid or credited in that year; and

(*b*) any amount so payable—

(i) may be set-off against any repayment in respect of tax due under regulation 25, and subject thereto

(ii) shall be treated as an amount of tax due under an assessment which is final and conclusive and payable not later than 6 months after the end of the year in which the interest was paid or credited.

(3) The interest referred to in paragraph (1) shall in all other respects be regarded as if it were not income for any income tax purposes, and no repayment of tax or amounts representing tax shall be made to the account investor receiving or entitled to such interest.

(4) The reference to interest in paragraph (1), and in regulation 22, includes a reference to any bonus and to a dividend paid or credited in respect of a share account with a building society.

Commentary—*Simon's Direct Tax Service* **E3.726**.

Tax liabilities and reliefs—account manager to act on behalf of account investor

24—(1) An account manager may under these Regulations make claims, conduct appeals and agree on behalf of the account investor liabilities for and reliefs from tax in respect of an account.

(2) Claims shall be made to the Board in accordance with the provisions of regulations 25 and 26.

(3) Where any relief or exemption from tax previously given in respect of an account has by virtue of these Regulations become excessive, in computing the relief due on any claim there shall be deducted (so that amounts equal to that excess are set-off or repaid to the Board, as the case may be) notwithstanding that those amounts have been invested—

(*a*) any amount repaid in respect of income tax or paid in respect of a tax credit;

(*b*) any sum representing income tax which is payable under regulation 23 on amounts of interest paid or credited as mentioned in that regulation; and

(*c*) any other amount due to the Board by an account manager in respect of any tax liability in respect of account investments under an account including (but without prejudice to the making of an assessment under the provisions of that Schedule) any amount falling due in respect of a liability under paragraph 3 or 4 of Schedule 23A to the Taxes Act.

(4) Any amount deducted under paragraph (3) shall be treated as an amount of income tax deducted at source and not repayable within the meaning and for the purposes of section 95(2)(*a*) of the Management Act.

Commentary—*Simon's Direct Tax Service* **E3.726**.

Repayments in respect of tax to account manager—interim claims

25—(1) Notwithstanding the provisions of any other enactment, the Board shall not be under an obligation to make any repayment in respect of tax under these Regulations earlier than the end of the month following the month in which the claim for the repayment is received.

(2) A claim for repayment in respect of tax which is not an annual claim ("interim claim") may be made only for a period of a month (or a number of months not exceeding six) beginning on the 6th day of the month and ending on the 5th day of the relevant following month.

(3) No claim for repayment may be made for the month ending 5th October or any subsequent month until the annual return under regulation 26(2) due in respect of an account for the preceding year has been duly made by the account manager and received by the Board.

(4) Where, on the occasion of a claim, there is due to the Board an amount in respect of tax, that amount shall be recoverable by the Board in the same manner as tax charged by an assessment on the account manager which has become final and conclusive.

(5) This regulation and regulation 26 shall not apply to any repayment in respect of tax on qualifying investments for an insurance component of any account, or on distributions and other rights or proceeds in respect of the qualifying investments held under any such component [except in so far as regulation 26(2) requires the return of all sums of interest referred to in regulation 23(2)(*a*) and any gain treated as arising in accordance with regulation 36(3)(*a*) or (*b*)][1].

Commentary—*Simon's Direct Tax Service* **E3.726**.

Amendments—[1] Words in para (5) inserted by the Individual Savings Account (Amendment) Regulations, SI 1998/3174 reg 9 with effect from 6 April 1999.

Repayments in respect of tax to account manager—annual returns and annual claims

26—(1) An annual claim is a claim for repayment in respect of tax for a year and may not be made at any time more than six years after the end of the year.

(2) An account manager shall within six months after the end of the year make a return of all income, and of all sums of interest referred to in regulation 23(2)(*a*) [and any gain treated as arising in accordance with regulation 36(3)(*a*) or (*b*)][1], and in addition an annual claim to establish the total of repayments due under an account for that year, and the total amount payable under regulation 23(2)(*a*).

(3) Where the aggregate of the repayments in respect of interim claims for the year shown by an annual claim exceeds the amount repayable for the year shown on the claim, the account manager shall repay the amount of the excess to the Board with the claim.

(4) If an account manager fails to make the return and the annual claim required under this regulation within the time limited, the Board may issue a notice to the account manager showing the aggregate of payments in respect of the interim claims for the year, and stating that the Board are not satisfied that the amount due to the account manager for that year exceeds the lower amount stated in the notice.

(5) If a return and an annual claim are not delivered to the Board within 14 days after the issue of such a notice under paragraph (4) the amount of the difference between the aggregate and the lower amount stated in the notice shall immediately be recoverable by the Board in the same manner as tax charged by an assessment on the account manager which has become final and conclusive.

(6) Where a return and an annual claim have been made and the account manager subsequently discovers that an error or mistake has been made in the return or claim the account manager may make a supplementary return or annual claim within the time allowed in paragraph (1).

Commentary—*Simon's Direct Tax Service* **E3.726**.

Amendments—[1] Words in para (2) inserted by the Individual Savings Account (Amendment) Regulations, SI 1998/3174 reg 10 with effect from 6 April 1999.

Account manager's returns and claims—supplementary provisions

27—(1) Section 42 of the Management Act shall not apply to claims under these Regulations.

(2) No appeal shall lie from the Board's decision on an interim claim.

(3) An appeal shall be to the Special Commissioners from the Board's decision on an annual claim, and the appeal shall be brought by giving notice to the Board within 30 days of receipt of notice of the decision.

(4) No payment or repayment made or other thing done on or in relation to an interim claim or a notice under regulation 26(4) shall prejudice the decision on an annual claim.

(5) The like provisions as are contained in Part V of the Management Act (appeals and other proceedings) shall apply to an appeal under paragraph (3) above, and on appeal the Special Commissioners may vary the decision appealed against whether or not the variation is to the advantage of the appellant.

(6) All such assessments, payments and repayments shall be made as are necessary to give effect to the Board's decision on an annual claim or to any variation of that decision on appeal.

(7) Returns and claims under these Regulations shall be in such form and contain such particulars as the Board prescribe and, subject to regulation 31(1) and (2), shall be signed by the account manager, and forms prescribed for annual claims may require a report to be given by a person qualified for appointment as auditor of a company.

Commentary—*Simon's Direct Tax Service* **E3.726**.

Assessments for withdrawing relief and recovering tax

28—(1) Where—

(*a*) any relief or exemption from tax given in respect of income or gains under an account is found not to be due or to be excessive, or

(*b*) the full amount of tax in respect of the income or gains under an account has not otherwise been fully accounted for and paid to the Board by or on behalf of the account investor,

an assessment to tax may be made by the Board in the amount or further amount which in their opinion ought to be charged.

(2) An assessment to which paragraph (1) refers may be made on the account manager or on the account investor.

(3) If the assessment is made to recover tax in respect of income (including any amount in respect of a tax credit) under an account it shall be made under Case VI of Schedule D.

Commentary—*Simon's Direct Tax Service* **E3.737**.

Records to be kept by account manager

29 An account manager shall at all times keep sufficient records in respect of an account to enable the requirements of these Regulations to be satisfied.

Commentary—*Simon's Direct Tax Service* **E3.730**.

Information to be given to account investor by account manager

30—(1) An account manager shall give notice to the account investor, at the commencement of, and in respect of, each successive year following the year in which the investor first subscribed to the account, during which the declaration referred to in regulation 12(3) has or may have effect, that—

(*a*) in the case of a maxi-account, if the account investor subscribes to that account in the year to which the notice relates, the account investor may not subscribe to any other account, not being a TESSA only account, in that year;

(*b*) in the case of a mini-account, if the account investor subscribes to that account in the year to which the notice relates, the account investor may not subscribe to any other account, not being a mini-account made up of a different type of component than the account to which the notice relates or a TESSA only account, in that year.

(2) An account manager who makes a payment to an account investor out of or in respect of which tax, or a sum representing tax, has been deducted shall, if the account investor so requests in writing, furnish the account investor with a statement in writing showing the gross amount of the payment, the amount deducted and the amount actually paid.

(3) On the transfer to an account investor of an account investment, subject to regulation 9(3)(*b*), the account manager shall provide for the account investor details in writing of the market value on the date of transfer.

Commentary—*Simon's Direct Tax Service* **E3.731**.

Returns of information by account manager

31—(1) An account manager shall within 60 days after the end of each year (beginning with the year 1999–00) in which he acts as an account manager, and after ceasing to act or to qualify as an account manager, deliver to the Board a return for that year, or for the part of that year in which he so acted or qualified, which contains the information specified in paragraphs (3), (4) and (5), and is accompanied by a certificate as to the contents of the return, in the form prescribed by the Board, signed by the account manager or on his behalf.

(2) An account manager shall within one month after the end of each income tax quarter in which he acts as an account manager, and after ceasing to act or to qualify as an account manager, deliver to the Board a return for, cumulatively, all the income tax quarters which have elapsed in that year, or for the part of that period in which he so acted or qualified, which contains the information specified in paragraph (7), and is accompanied by a certificate as to the contents of the return, in the form prescribed by the Board, signed by the account manager or on his behalf.

(3) The information specified in this paragraph is information relating to each account, in respect of which he acted as account manager, in the year or the part of the year for which the return is made, other than accounts transferred to another account manager under Regulation 21(2) in that year or part of a year, as to—

(*a*) as regards the account investor—

(i) his full name,
(ii) the address of his permanent residence, including postcode,
(iii) his date of birth, and
(iv) if he has one, his national insurance number;

(*b*) as regards each such account—

(i) the number allocated to the account by the account manager, and
(ii) the market value of the account investments held under each component of the account, subject to paragraph (6), the value of each account investment being determined either as at 5th April in that year, or any other valuation date in that year, not falling earlier than 5th October, and

(*c*) as regards each such maxi-account or mini-account, to which subscriptions, ...[3] were made in that year or part of a year—

(i) whether the account is a maxi-account or a mini-account made up of a specified component [or a TESSA only account][3],
(ii) the total amount of cash subscribed to the account, other than pursuant to regulation 5(1), in the year or the part of the year for which the return is made, and the amounts respectively allocated to each component of the account,
(iii) the date on which the first subscription (being either cash, ...[3] or shares pursuant to regulation 7(2)(*h*)) was made to the account, in the year or the part of the year for which the return is made, and
(iv) the aggregate market value at the date of transfer of any shares transferred to the account manager or his nominee in accordance with regulation 7(2)(*h*) in the year or the part of the year for which the return is made [and—
(v) the date when any such mini-account or TESSA only account was closed, where that occurred during the year or the part of the year for which the return was made][3].

(4) The information specified in this paragraph is—

(*a*) the respective market values at the end of the year or the part of the year for which the return is made of account investments held under stocks and shares components, by him or a nominee for him on behalf of account investors, under all the accounts in respect of which he acted as account manager in that year or part, with separate values for—

(i) shares, not being shares in an investment trust or in a UCITS,
(ii) qualifying securities,
(iii) shares in investment trusts,
[(iv) units in, or shares of, securities schemes and warrant schemes,][2]
(v) units in, or shares of, a relevant UCITS,
[(vi) units in, or shares of, fund of funds schemes, and][2]
[(via) units in, or shares of, a Chapter 5 UCITS, which satisfy the condition in regulation 7(15);][4]
(vii) cash, including cash represented in share accounts with building societies,

with depositary interests being included in the paragraph to which their relevant investments (referred to in paragraphs (*a*) and (*b*) of the definition of ''depositary interest'') relate][1];

(*b*) such information in relation to cash components, as if sub-paragraph (*a*) applied to them, with separate values for—

[(i) units in, or shares of, money market schemes and fund of funds schemes within the meaning given by regulation 8(2)(*d*),][2]
[(ia) units in, or shares of, a Chapter 5 UCITS, which do not satisfy the condition in regulation 7(15);][4]
(ii) securities issued under the National Loans Act 1968,
(iii) cash, including cash represented in share accounts with building societies; and

(*c*) the aggregate market value at that date of all such account investments held by him or his nominee.

(5) The information specified in this paragraph is such information in relation to insurance components, as if paragraph (4) applied with the omission of the words ''by him or a nominee for him on behalf of account investors,'' with references to the market value of account investments, in the case of policies of life insurance, being replaced with references to the surrender value of such policies, and as if separate valuations were required of such policies, and of cash.

(6) The reference in paragraph (3)(*b*)(ii) to market value shall, in the case of policies of life insurance, be construed as a reference to their surrender value.

(7) The information specified in this paragraph is information relating to all accounts, in respect of which he was acting as account manager immediately before the end of the period for which the return is made, and to which subscriptions were made in the income tax quarter or other period, for which the return is made, as to—

(*a*) the total number of accounts to which subscriptions were made, with separate figures for—

(i) maxi-accounts,
(ii) mini-accounts, and
(iii) TESSA only accounts; and

(*b*) the total amount of cash subscriptions made in the quarter or other period—

(i) to stocks and shares components of accounts;
(ii) to cash components of accounts; and
(iii) to insurance components of accounts.

(8) No claim for repayment, or repayment, may be made under regulations 25 and 26 until the returns which have become due under this regulation have been duly made by the account manager and received by the Board.

Commentary—*Simon's Direct Tax Service* **E.727–729**.

Amendments—[1] Words in para (4)(*a*) added by the Individual Savings Account (Amendment No 3) Regulations, SI 2000/3112 reg 5 with effect from 13 December 2000.

[2] Sub-paras (4)(*a*)(iv), (vi) and (*b*)(i) substituted by the Financial Services and Markets Act 2000 (Consequential Amendments) (Taxes) Order, SI 2001/3629 art 177 with effect from 1 December 2001, immediately after the coming into force of the Financial Services and Markets Act 2000 ss 411, 432(1), Sch 20 (and SI 2001/3629 Pts 1 and 2).

[3] Words in para (3)(*c*) revoked, words in (3)(*c*)(i) inserted, and para (3)(*c*)(v) inserted, by the Individual Savings Account (Amendment No 3) Regulations, SI 2002/3158 reg 7 with effect from 6 April 2003.

[4] In para (4), sub-paras (*a*)(via), (*b*)((ia) inserted by the Individual Savings Account (Amendment) Regulations, SI 2003/2747 regs 1(1), (3), 2, 8 with effect from 6 April 2004.

Information to be provided to the Board

32 The Board may by notice require any person who is or who at any time has been an account manager or account investor to furnish them, within such time (not being less than 14 days) as may be provided by the notice, such information about any account or about any account investment (including copies of or extracts from any books or other records) as they may reasonably require for the purposes of these Regulations.

Commentary—*Simon's Direct Tax Service* **E3.735**.

Inspection of records by officer of the Board

33—(1) The Board may by notice require any person who is or who at any time has been an account manager or account investor, within such time (not being less than 14 days) as may be provided in the notice, to make available for inspection at a place within the United Kingdom by an officer of the Board authorised for that purpose all documents (including books and other records) in his possession or under his control containing information relating to any account or to any account investment.

(2) Where records are maintained by computer the person required to make them available for inspection shall provide the officer making the inspection with all the facilities necessary for obtaining information from them.

Commentary—*Simon's Direct Tax Service* **E3.736**.

Capital gains tax—adaptation of enactments

34—(1) For the purposes of capital gains tax on the occasion when the title to account investments is transferred from an account manager to an account investor there shall be deemed to be a disposal and reacquisition by the account investor of those investments for a consideration equal to their market value at the date of the transfer.

(2) Sections 104 to 114 of the Taxation of Chargeable Gains Act 1992 shall apply for the purposes of pooling and identifying account investments as if—

(*a*) in section 106A after subsection (11) there were added—

"(12) This section and sections 104, 110, 110A and 114—

(*a*) shall apply separately in relation to any securities which are held by a person as account investments so long as they are so held, and

(*b*) shall apply in relation to any such securities which became account investments by being transferred or renounced to an account manager or to a nominee for an account manager in the circumstances specified in regulation 7(2)(*h*) and [(10)(*a*), (*b*) or (*ba*)][1] as if they had been account investments—

(i) in the case of securities acquired by that person in accordance with the provisions of a savings-related share option scheme, which were transferred in the circumstances specified in regulation [7(2)(*h*)(i)][1] and (10)(*a*), from the date of their acquisition by him, or

(ii) in the case of securities appropriated to that person in accordance with the provisions of an approved profit sharing scheme, which were transferred in the circumstances specified in regulation [7(2)(*h*)(ii)][1] and (10)(*b*), from the date when he directed the trustees to transfer the ownership of the securities to him or, if earlier, the release date in relation to those securities, [or

(iii) in the case of securities which were plan shares of an approved employee share ownership plan before being transferred in the circumstances specified in regulation 7(2)(*h*)(iii) and (10)(*ba*), from the date when the securities ceased to be subject to the plan, and][1]

(*c*) while applying separately to any such securities, shall have effect as if that person held them in a capacity other than that in which he holds any other securities of the same class whether under another such account or otherwise.

(13) In this section—

(*a*) ''account'', ''account investment'' and ''account manager'' have the same meanings as in the Individual Savings Account Regulations 1998 and ''regulation'' means a regulation of those Regulations;

(*b*) ''approved profit sharing scheme'' has the same meaning as in Chapter IV of Part V of the Taxes Act and ''savings-related share option scheme'' has the meaning given by paragraph 1 of Schedule 9 to that Act.''; and

[(*c*) ''approved employee share ownership plan'', ''plan shares'' and (in relation to securities which are plan shares) ''ceasing to be subject to the plan'' have the meanings given in Schedule 8 to the Finance Act 2000, except that, in construing ''plan shares'', paragraph 115(8), and the words 'or securities or rights' in paragraph 116(1), of that Schedule shall be omitted.][1]

(*b*) in section 110A after subsection (5) there were added—

''(6) Where part of a section 104 holding is treated by section 106A(12)(*b*)(ii) as having been account investments since a particular date—

(*a*) an operative event shall be regarded as having occurred for the purposes of this section immediately before that date, consisting of the disposal of the part of that section 104 holding which is so treated, and

(*b*) this section shall apply in relation to the occurrence of that operative event as it would have applied if it had always applied separately in relation to the part of that section 104 holding which is so treated.''

(3) Section 106A of the Taxation of Chargeable Gains Act 1992 shall apply for the purposes of identifying securities within the meaning of that section which are eligible to become account investments as if—

(*a*) in subsection (4), there were added at the beginning the words ''Subject to subsection (14) below'';

(*b*) in subsection (6), the words ''subsections (4) and (5) above'' were replaced with the words ''subsections (4), (5) and (14)''; and

(*c*) after subsections (12) and (13), as added by paragraph (2), there were added—

''(14) Where a person disposes of securities and securities of the same class which were eligible for transfer to an account under regulation 7(2)(*h*) were—

(*a*) held by him immediately before that disposal, or

(*b*) acquired by him on the same day as that disposal, or

(*c*) acquired by him within the period of thirty days after that disposal,

and those securities were acquired in the circumstances specified in that regulation, he shall be treated as having first disposed of any securities of that class held or acquired by him which were not so eligible.''

(4) Sections 127 to 131 of the Taxation of Chargeable Gains Act 1992 shall not apply [in relation to qualifying investments falling within any of sub-paragraphs (*a*), (*b*), (*d*), (*e*), (*f*), (*g*) and (*h*) of regulation 7(2)][2] which are held under an account if there is by virtue of any allotment for payment as is mentioned in section 126(2) of that Act a reorganisation affecting those shares or securities.

Amendments—[1] In the provisions treated as added to section 106A, words in para (12)(*b*) substituted and para (13)(*c*) added by the Individual Savings Account (Amendment No 2) Regulations, SI 2000/2079 reg5 with effect from 21 August 2000.
[2] Words in para (4) substituted by the Financial Services and Markets Act 2000 (Consequential Amendments) (Taxes) Order, SI 2001/3629 art 178 with effect from 1 December 2001, immediately after the coming into force of the Financial Services and Markets Act 2000 ss 411, 432(1), Sch 20 (and SI 2001/3629 Pts 1 and 2).

Administration of tax in relation to accounts—supplementary

35—(1) Nothing in these Regulations shall be taken to prejudice any powers conferred or duties imposed by or under any enactment in relation to the making of returns of income or gains, or for the recovery of tax, penalties or interest by means of an assessment or otherwise.

(2) Notwithstanding the provisions of these Regulations an account manager shall not be released from obligations under these Regulations in relation to an account except under conditions agreed in writing with and notified to that person by the Board.

(3) The like provisions as are contained in the Management Act shall apply to any assessment under these Regulations as if it were an assessment to tax for the year in which, apart from these Regulations, the account investor would have been liable (by reason of his ownership of the investments).

(4) In the application of the like provisions as are contained in section 86 of the Management Act by virtue of paragraph (3) in relation to any sums due and payable by virtue of an assessment made on an account manager under these Regulations, the relevant date—

(*a*) is the 1st January in the year for which the account investor would have been liable where the account manager has made an interim claim for a period falling within that year; and

(*b*) in any other case, is the later of the following dates, that is to say—

(i) the 1st January in that year; or

(ii) the date of the making of the repayment by the Board following receipt of the annual claim for that year.

(5) The like provisions as are contained in section 97(1) of the Management Act shall apply as if—

(*a*) there were inserted after the words "sections 95 and 96 above" the words "or the Individual Savings Account Regulations 1998", and

(*b*) there were inserted after the words "that they were" the words "or have become".

[(6) If—

(*a*) a chargeable event, within the meaning given by Chapter 2 of Part 13 of the Taxes Act, has happened in relation to a policy of life insurance which is an account investment held under an insurance component; and

(*b*) the body by whom the policy was issued is satisfied that no gain is to be treated as chargeable to tax on the happening of the event by virtue of regulation 22(1)(*a*)(v),

the body shall not be obliged to deliver the certificates mentioned in section 552(1) of that Act.

This paragraph does not prevent the operation of section 552(1) in a case to which regulation 36(1) applies.][1].

(7) A termination of a policy of insurance pursuant to regulation 9(3)(*b*)(ii) shall be treated as the surrender in whole of the rights conferred by the policy, for the purposes of section 540(1)(*a*)(iii) of the Taxes Act.

(8) Where there are in force relevant insurances within the meaning given by section 552A of the Taxes Act then, so far as they consist of policies of life insurance which are account investments held under an insurance component, they shall be disregarded in calculating the amount or value of gross premiums, for the purposes of subsection (4)(*b*) of that section.

(9) Any form prescribed by the Board for the purposes of these Regulations shall provide for a declaration that all the particulars given in the form are correctly stated to the best of the knowledge and belief of the person concerned.

(10) No obligation as to secrecy imposed by statute or otherwise shall preclude the Board from disclosing to an account manager or account investor that any provision of these Regulations has not been satisfied or that relief has been given or claimed in respect of investments under an account.

Commentary—*Simon's Direct Tax Service* **E3.737**.

Amendments—[1] Para (6) substituted by the Individual Savings Account (Amendment) Regulations, SI 2002/453 regs 3, 4 with effect from 6 April 2002 for the tax year 2002–03 and subsequent tax years.

[Application of the provisions of Chapter II of Part XIII of the Taxes Act to policies where an investor ceases to be or was not entitled to relief from tax

36—(1) This paragraph applies to a case where—

(*a*) an event specified in regulation 9(8) has occurred in relation to a policy of life insurance, and

(*b*) a termination event within the meaning given by regulation 9(7) occurs in relation to that policy.

(2) Where—

(*a*) there is a case to which paragraph (1) applies, and

(*b*) a chargeable event in relation to the policy, within the meaning given by section 540 of the Taxes Act, has occurred prior to the time at which the termination event mentioned in paragraph (1)(*b*) occurs,

the account investor shall cease to be, and shall be treated as not having been, entitled to relief from tax under regulation 22(1)(*a*)(v), in respect of gains treated as arising on the occurrence of any chargeable event mentioned in sub-paragraph (*b*).

(3) The provisions of Chapter II of Part XIII of the Taxes Act shall apply, in a case to which paragraph (1) applies, to—

(*a*) the termination event mentioned in paragraph (1)(*b*), and

(*b*) any chargeable event mentioned in paragraph (2)(*b*),

with the modifications provided for in regulation 35(7) and paragraphs (4) to (7) of this regulation, and the account investor and the account manager shall account to the Board in accordance with this regulation for tax from which relief under regulation 22(1)(*a*)(v) has been given on the basis that the account investor was so entitled, or in circumstances such that the account investor was not so entitled.

(4) In section 547(5) of the Taxes Act, for the words after "total income" (where it first appears) there shall be substituted the words "that gain shall be chargeable to tax under Case VI of Schedule D".

(5) Relief under section 550 of the Taxes Act shall be computed as if paragraph (4) had not been enacted.

[(6) In section 552 of the Taxes Act—

(*a*) in subsection (1)(*b*) for the words "policy holder" there shall be substituted "account investor";

(*b*) in subsection (3)—

(i) in the words "(or, where the appropriate policy holder is a company, the corresponding financial year)" shall be omitted;

(ii) for the words "the name and address of the appropriate policy holder" there shall be substituted "the name and address of the account investor";

(iii) the words "and the corresponding financial year," shall be omitted;

(*c*) in subsection (5)—

(i) for the words "the appropriate policy holder" there shall be substituted "the account investor";

(ii) sub-paragraph (*b*)(ii) shall be omitted;

(iii) paragraph (*c*) shall be omitted;

(iv) in paragraph (*d*) the words "except where paragraph (*c*) above applies," shall be omitted; and

(v) paragraph (*f*) shall be omitted;

(*d*) in subsection (6)—

(i) paragraph (*b*) shall be omitted;

(ii) for paragraph (*c*) there shall be substituted—

"(*c*) if the event is a death, the period of three months beginning with the receipt of written notification of the death;";

(iii) after paragraph (*c*) there shall be inserted—

"(*d*) [if the event is—

(i) a termination event, or

(ii) a chargeable event preceding such a termination event (as mentioned in regulation 36(2) of the Individual Savings Account Regulations 1998), the period of three months beginning with the date on which the insurer received notice under regulation 9(9)(*b*) of those Regulations or, if earlier, actual notice of the termination event.][3]";

(*e*) in subsection (7)—

(i) in paragraph (*a*) for the words "assessment, or, where the policy holder is a company, the financial year," there shall be substituted "assessment";

(ii) paragraph (*b*) shall be omitted;

(iii) for paragraph (*c*) there shall be substituted—

"(*c*) if the event is a death, the period of three months beginning with the receipt of written notification of the death;";

(iv) after paragraph (*c*) there shall be inserted—

"(*ca*) [if the event is—

(i) a termination event, or

(ii) a chargeable event preceding such a termination event (as mentioned in regulation 36(2) of the Individual Savings Account Regulations 1998), the period of three months beginning with the date on which the insurer received notice under regulation 9(9)(*b*) of those Regulations or, if earlier, actual notice of the termination event.]";[3] and

(v) in paragraph (*d*) for the words "paragraph (*c*)" there shall be substituted "paragraph (*c*) or (*ca*)";

(*f*) in subsection (8)—

(i) in paragraph (*b*) for "policy holder" there shall be substituted "account investor in respect";

(ii) in paragraph (*c*) the words from "or" to the end of the paragraph shall be omitted;

(*g*) in subsection (9) the words "or financial year" shall be omitted in each place where they occur;

(*h*) in subsection 10—

(i) before the definition of "amount" there shall be inserted—

""account investor" has the same meaning as in the Individual Savings Account Regulations 1998;

(ii) the definition of "appropriate policy holder" shall be omitted;

(iii) the definition of "financial year" shall be omitted;

(iv) for the definition of "the relevant year of assessment" there shall be substituted—

""the relevant year of assessment", in the case of any gain, means the year of assessment to which the gain is attributable;" and

(v) after the definition of "section 546 excess" there shall be inserted—

""termination event" has the same meaning as in the Individual Savings Account Regulations 1998;"; and

(*i*) subsection (11) shall be omitted.][2]

[(6A) In section 552ZA of the Taxes Act—

(*a*) in subsection (2)(*b*) the words "or an assignment" shall be omitted; and (*b*) subsections (3) and (4) shall be omitted.][2]

(7) ...[2]

(8) The account manager shall account for and pay income tax at the basic rate in force for the year of assessment in which the termination event, or the chargeable event mentioned in paragraph (2)(*b*), occurred, as the case may be, and any amount so payable—

(*a*) may be set off against any repayment in respect of tax due under regulation 25 or regulation 26 and, subject thereto

(*b*) shall be treated as an amount of tax due not later than 6 months after the end of the year in which the event specified in regulation 9(8) came to the notice of the account manager, and

(*c*) shall be payable without the making of an assessment.

(9) Where tax is charged in accordance with paragraph (3)(*a*) or (*b*)—

(*a*) an assessment to income tax at the basic rate in force for the relevant year of assessment may be made on the account manager or on the account investor, and

(*b*) an assessment to income tax at the higher rate within the meaning of section 832(1) of the Taxes Act, for that year of assessment, may be made on the account investor, within five years after the 31st January next following that year of assessment, and regulation 28 shall not apply.]

Commentary—*Simon's Direct Tax Service* **E3.738**.

Amendments—[1] This regulation inserted by the Individual Savings Account (Amendment) Regulations, SI 1998/3174 reg 12 with effect from 6 April 1999.

[2] Para (6) substituted, para (6A) inserted, and para (7) revoked, by the Individual Savings Account (Amendment) Regulations, SI 2002/453 regs 3, 5 with effect from 6 April 2002 for the tax year 2002–03 and subsequent tax years.

[3] Words in para (6) substituted by the Individual Savings Account (Amendment No. 3) Regulations, SI 2002/3158 reg 8 with effect from 8 January 2003.

1998/1871
Individual Savings Account (Insurance Companies) Regulations 1998

Made by the Treasury under TA 1988 s 333B

Made	*31 July 1998*
Laid before the House of Commons . .	*31 July 1998*
Coming into force . . .	*6 April 1999*

Commentary—*Simon's Direct Tax Service* **Division E3.7**.
Revenue & other press releases—IR 31-7-98 (The Individual Savings Account (ISA)—tax regulations).

Citation and commencement

1 These Regulations may be cited as the Individual Savings Account (Insurance Companies) Regulations 1998 and shall come into force on 6th April 1999.

Interpretation

2 In these Regulations—

''individual savings account business'' has the meaning given by regulation 3;

''the principal Regulations'' means the Individual Savings Accounts Regulations 1998;

''the Taxes Act'' means the Income and Corporation Taxes Act 1988.

Individual savings account business

3 For the purposes of these Regulations ''individual savings account business'' in relation to an insurance company means so much of that company's life assurance business as is referable to any policy of life insurance, or to the reinsurance of liabilities under any such policy, where the policy is, on the date on which the insurance is made, a qualifying investment for an insurance component within the meaning of regulation 9 of the principal Regulations.

Tax credits on distributions to insurance companies

4—(1) The repeal by section 30(4) of the Finance (No 2) Act 1997 of section 231(2) of the Taxes Act (payment of tax credit to a company resident in the United Kingdom) shall not have effect in relation to any distribution made to an insurance company on or after 6th April 1999 but before 6th April 2004 which is a distribution received by the insurance company in respect of investments of so much of its [long-term insurance][1] fund as is referable to its individual savings account business.

(2) Schedule 4 to the Finance (No 2) Act 1997 shall have effect in relation to a distribution to which paragraph (1) applies with the following modifications—

(*a*) paragraph 2 shall be omitted;

(*b*) in paragraph 3(2) for ''1999'' there shall be substituted ''2004''.

Amendments—[1] Words in para (1) substituted by the Financial Services and Markets Act 2000 (Consequential Amendments) (Taxes) Order, SI 2001/3629 art 179 with effect from 1 December 2001, immediately after the coming into force of the Financial Services and Markets Act 2000 ss 411, 432(1), Sch 20 (and SI 2001/3629 Pts 1 and 2).

Modifications of the Taxes Act

5 Regulations 6 to 21 specify modifications of provisions of the Taxes Act so far as concerns individual savings account business of insurance companies.

6 In section 76(1)(*d*) after the words "pension business," there shall be inserted "individual savings account business,".

7 In section 431(2) after the definition of "foreign income dividends" there shall be inserted—

"'individual savings account business' has the meaning given by regulation 3 of the Individual Savings Account (Insurance Companies) Regulations 1998;".

8 In sections 431C(1) and 431D(1) after the words "pension business", in both places where they occur, there shall be inserted ", individual savings account business".

9 In section 431F after the words "pension business," there shall be inserted "individual savings account business,".

10 In section 432A(2) after paragraph (*a*) there shall be inserted—

"(*aa*) individual savings account business;".

11 In section 432AA(4) after paragraph (*a*) there shall be inserted—

"(*aa*) individual savings account business;".

12 In sections 432C(1), 432D(1) and 434D(5) after the words "pension business,", in each place where they occur, there shall be inserted "individual savings account business,".

[12A—In section 434(1A) there shall be added at the end the words "but this subsection shall not apply in relation to distributions in respect of which an insurance company is entitled to a tax credit in respect of its individual savings account business".][1]

Amendments—[1] This regulation inserted by the Individual Savings Account (Insurance Companies) (Amendment) Regulations, SI 2000/2075 reg 3 with effect from 22 August 2000.

13 In section 436—

(*a*) after the words "pension business", in each place where they occur, there shall be inserted "or individual savings account business";

(*b*) in subsection (1)(*a*) for the words "that business" there shall be substituted "the business of each such class".

[14 In section 438—

(*a*) in subsection (1) there shall be added at the end the words "or individual savings account business";

(*b*) subsection (4) shall be omitted.][1]

Amendments—[1] This regulation substituted by the Individual Savings Account (Insurance Companies) (Amendment) Regulations, SI 2000/2075 reg 4 with effect from 22 August 2000.

15 In section 440(4)(*a*) there shall be added at the end "or individual savings account business, or assets linked both to pension business and individual savings account business but not to any other category of business".

16 In section 440A(2)(*a*)(i) after the words "pension business" there shall be inserted "or individual savings account business, or both pension business and individual savings account business".

17 In section 466(2) after the definition of "incorporated friendly society" there shall be inserted—

"'individual savings account business' shall be construed in accordance with section 431;".

18 In section 755A after paragraph (*a*) in each of subsections (4) and (13) there shall be inserted—

"(*aa*) individual savings account business,".

19 In paragraph 5(5) of Schedule 19AA after the words "pension business," there shall be inserted "individual savings account business,".

20—(1) Schedule 19AB, other than paragraphs [2, 4, and 6(4) to (6)][1], as it has effect in relation to provisional repayment periods falling in accounting periods ending on or after the day appointed under section 199 of the Finance Act 1994 for the purposes of Chapter III of Part IV of that Act (corporation tax self-assessment), shall apply in relation to individual savings account business of insurance companies ...[1], with the modifications specified in regulation 21.

(2) ...[1]

Note—The text of TA 1988 Sch 19AB as modified by the Individual Savings Accounts (Insurance Companies) (Amendment) Regulations, SI 2001/3974 is reproduced in SI 2001/3974 Schedule.

Amendments—[1] In para (1), figures substituted, and words revoked; and para (2) revoked by the Individual Savings Accounts (Insurance Companies) (Amendment) Regulations, SI 2001/3974 reg 3 with effect for accounting periods of insurance companies beginning after 31 December 2001.

[21—(1) The amendments made to Schedule 19AB by paragraphs 10 and 11 of Schedule 3 to the Finance (No 2) Act 1997, other than the amendment made by paragraph 10(4) of that Schedule, shall not have effect.

(2) In the heading to Schedule 19AB for the words "pension business—payments on account of tax credits and deducted tax" there shall be substituted the words "individual savings account business—payments on account of tax credits".

(3) In paragraphs 1(1), (2), (5) and (7) and 3(1A) for the words "pension business" wherever they occur there shall be substituted the words "individual savings account business".

(4) In paragraph 1(1)—

(*a*) for the words ", subject to paragraph 2 below, to the aggregate of" there shall be substituted the word "to";

(*b*) paragraph (*a*) shall be omitted.

(5) Paragraph 1(3) shall be omitted.

(6) Paragraph 1(4) shall be omitted.

(7) After paragraph 1(4) the following paragraphs shall be inserted—

"(4A) The provisional fraction for the purposes of this paragraph for a relevant accounting period shall be such fraction as the company may reasonably estimate, being a fraction which is not likely to be greater than the relevant fraction for its individual savings account business which would be determined in accordance with subsections (5) to (9B) of section 432A for that accounting period.

(4B) In sub-paragraph (4A) above 'relevant accounting period' means—

(*a*) the accounting period in which 6th April 1999 falls, or

(*b*) any succeeding accounting period which begins before 6th April 2004."

(8) In paragraph 1(5)(*b*) the words "payment or" in each place where they occur shall be omitted.

(9) In paragraph 1(7)—

(*a*) the words "or repaid" shall be omitted;

(*b*) paragraph (*a*) shall be omitted;

(*c*) for "9(2)" there shall be substituted "9(3)";

(*d*) the words "or section 42(4) of the Management Act" shall be omitted.

(10) Paragraph 1(10) and (11) shall be omitted.

(11) In paragraph 3(1A)—

(*a*) for the words "assumptions in sub-paragraphs (1B) and (1C)" there shall be substituted the words "assumption in sub-paragraph (1B)";

(*b*) the words "or repaid" shall be omitted;

(*c*) for '9(2)' there shall be substituted '9(3)';

(*d*) the words "or section 42(4) of the Management Act" shall be omitted;

(*e*) paragraph (*a*) shall be omitted.

(12) In paragraph 3(1B)—

(*a*) the words "or repayments" shall be omitted;

(*b*) paragraph (*a*) shall be omitted;

(*c*) in paragraph (*b*) for the words "that sub-paragraph" there shall be substituted the words "sub-paragraph (1A) above".

(13) Paragraph 3(1C) shall be omitted.

(14) In paragraph 3(8)—

(*a*) the words "or repaid" shall be omitted;

(*b*) paragraph (*a*) shall be omitted;

(*c*) in paragraph (*b*) for the words "that sub-paragraph" there shall be substituted the words "sub-paragraph (1A) above".

(15) In paragraph 6(1) in the definition of "provisional fraction" for the words "paragraphs 1(4) and 2" there shall be substituted "paragraph 1(4A)".

(16) In paragraphs (3) to (15) of this regulation a reference to a paragraph, without more, is a reference to that numbered paragraph of Schedule 19AB.][1]

Note—The text of TA 1988 Sch 19AB as modified by the Individual Savings Accounts (Insurance Companies) (Amendment) Regulations, SI 2001/3974 is reproduced in SI 2001/3974 Schedule.

Amendments—[1] Substituted by the Individual Savings Accounts (Insurance Companies) (Amendment) Regulations, SI 2001/3974 reg 4 with effect for accounting periods of insurance companies beginning after 31 December 2001.

[21A—In paragraph 9(1) of Schedule 19AC, in the notionally inserted subsection (1D) of section 434, there shall be added at the end the words "but this subsection shall not apply in relation to distributions in respect of which an overseas life insurance company is entitled to a tax credit in respect of its individual savings account business.".][1]

Amendments—[1] This regulation inserted by the Individual Savings Account (Insurance Companies) (Amendment) Regulations, SI 2000/2075 reg 5 with effect from 22 August 2000.

Modifications of the Taxation of Chargeable Gains Act 1992

22 Regulation 23 specifies modifications of provisions of the Taxation of Chargeable Gains Act 1992 so far as concerns individual savings account business of insurance companies.

23 In sections 212(2) and 214A(11)(*a*) after the words "pension business", in both places where they occur, there shall be inserted ", individual savings account business".

Amendments to the Manufactured Payments and Transfer of Securities (Tax Relief) Regulations 1995

24 (1) The Manufactured Payments and Transfer of Securities (Tax Relief) Regulations 1995 shall be amended as follows.

(2) In regulations 3(2) and 4(2) after the words "pension business", in both places where they occur, there shall be inserted the words "or individual savings account business within the meaning of regulation 3 of the Individual Savings Account (Insurance Companies) Regulations 1998".

Amendments to the Friendly Societies (Modification of the Corporation Tax Acts) Regulations 1997

25—(1) The Friendly Societies (Modification of the Corporation Tax Acts) Regulations 1997 shall be amended as follows.

(2) In regulation 2 after the definition of "incorporated friendly society" there shall be inserted the following definition—

"'individual savings account business' has the meaning given by regulation 3 of the Individual Savings Account (Insurance Companies) Regulations 1998;".

(3) (*inserts* SI 1997/473 reg 19A)

(4) (*inserts* SI 1997/473 reg 20A)

(5) (*inserts* SI 1997/473 reg 30A)

1998/2620

Finance Act 1995, Section 139(3), (Appointed Day) Order 1998

Made by the Treasury under FA 1995 s 139(3) and FA 1998 Sch 8 para 7

Made . . . . *23 October 1998*

Commentary—*Simon's Direct Tax Service* **E5.501, 502**.

1 This Order may be cited as the Finance Act 1995, Section 139(3), (Appointed Day) Order 1998.

2 The day appointed for the purposes of sub-paragraphs (2) and (3)(*b*) of paragraph 3 of Schedule 27 to the Finance Act 1995 is 23rd November 1998.

3 The day appointed for the purposes of paragraphs 1, 2, 3(1) and 4 to 7 of Schedule 27 to the Finance Act 1995 is 1st August 1999.

4 Certificates under section 561 of the Income and Corporation Taxes Act 1988 which have been issued or renewed before the date on which this Order is made, for periods ending on or after the day appointed in paragraph 3 of this Order, shall cease to have effect at the end of the day preceding that appointed day.

1998/3081

Controlled Foreign Companies (Excluded Countries) Regulations 1998

Made by the Commissioners of Inland Revenue under TA 1988 s 748(1)(*e*) and TA 1988 s (1A)

Made . . . . . . *9 December 1998*
Laid before the House of Commons . . *10 December 1998*
Coming into force . . . . . *31 December 1998*

Commentary—*Simon's Direct Tax Service* **D4.1243**.
Revenue & other press releases—IR 5-10-93 (non-statutory excluded countries list for accounting periods ending before 1 July 1999).

Citation, commencement and effect

1—(1) These Regulations may be cited as the Controlled Foreign Companies (Excluded Countries) Regulations 1998, shall come into force on 31st December 1998, and shall have effect with respect to any appropriate accounting period of a relevant company.

(2) In this regulation—

"appropriate accounting period" means an accounting period ending on or after the day to be appointed under section 199 of the Finance Act 1994 (corporation tax self-assessment);

"relevant company" means a company resident in the United Kingdom that had a relevant interest in a controlled foreign company at any time during an accounting period of the controlled foreign company ending in an appropriate accounting period of the relevant company;

"relevant interest" shall be construed in accordance with section 752A of the Taxes Act.

Note—The day appointed for the purpose of "appropriate accounting period" in reg 1 is 1 July 1999 by virtue of FA 1994 s 199 (Appointed Day) Order SI 1998/3173 art 2.

Interpretation

2—(1) In these Regulations unless the context otherwise requires—

"controlled foreign company" shall be construed in accordance with section 747(2) of the Taxes Act;

"gains" in relation to a controlled foreign company means any gains of that company other than a gain accruing to the company on a disposal of an asset which, on the assumption that the company was within the charge to corporation tax, would have fallen to be treated as a chargeable gain and would not have been taken into account as a receipt in computing the company's income or profits or gains or losses for the purposes of the Income Tax Acts;

"insurance company" means a company carrying on [the business of effecting or carrying out contracts which fall within Part I or II of Schedule 1 to the Financial Services and Markets Act 2000 (Regulated Activities) Order 2001][1];

"Schedule 1" and "Schedule 2" mean Schedule 1 and Schedule 2 respectively to these Regulations;

"section 748(1)(*e*)" means section 748(1)(*e*) of the Taxes Act;

"the Taxes Act" means the Income and Corporation Taxes Act 1988.

(2) For the purposes of these Regulations a company is resident in a territory if—

(*a*) by reason of the law of that territory relating to domicile, residence or place of management, the company is liable to tax in that territory, or

(*b*) if there is either no such law or such law does not apply to the company, the company is incorporated in that territory;

and references in these Regulations to the territory of residence of a company shall be construed accordingly.

(3) For the purposes of these Regulations a controlled foreign company is resident in a territory, within the meaning of paragraph (2), in an accounting period only if it is so resident throughout that accounting period.

(4) References in these Regulations to a branch or agency of a controlled foreign company are references to a branch or agency situated in a territory other than the territory of residence of the controlled foreign company.

Amendments—[1] In para (1), words in definition of "insurance company" substituted by the Financial Services and Markets Act 2000 (Consequential Amendments) (Taxes) Order, SI 2001/3629 art 180 with effect from 1 December 2001, immediately after the coming into force of the Financial Services and Markets Act 2000 ss 411, 432(1), Sch 20 (and SI 2001/3629 Pts 1 and 2).

Limitation on apportionment of chargeable profits of a controlled foreign company—specified territories

3 The territory in which a controlled foreign company is required to be resident as respects an accounting period for the purposes of section 748(1)(*e*) is—

(*a*) as respects an accounting period beginning before 9th July 1998, any territory specified in Part I or in Part II of Schedule 1;

(*b*) as respects an accounting period beginning on or after that date, any territory specified in Part I or in Part II of Schedule 2.

Limitation on apportionment of chargeable profits of a controlled foreign company—conditions to be satisfied

4—(1) Paragraph (2) specifies the condition which is required to be satisfied as respects an accounting period, for the purposes of section 748(1)(*e*), by a controlled foreign company which is resident in a territory specified in Part I of Schedule 1 or, as the case may be, in Part I of Schedule 2, in that accounting period.

(2) The condition specified is that the requirement with respect to the controlled foreign company's income and gains specified in regulation 5 is satisfied by the controlled foreign company in relation to that accounting period.

(3) Paragraph (4) specifies the conditions which are required to be satisfied as respects an accounting period, for the purposes of section 748(1)(*e*), by a controlled foreign company which is resident in a territory specified in column 1 of Part II of Schedule 1 or, as the case may be, in column 1 of Part II of Schedule 2, in that accounting period.

(4) The conditions specified in this paragraph are that the controlled foreign company—

(*a*) satisfies the requirement with respect to its income and gains specified in regulation 5 in relation to that accounting period, and

(*b*) at no time during that accounting period—

(i) is entitled to any tax exemption, tax reduction or other benefit, or

(ii) falls within any condition,

specified in column 2 of Part II of Schedule 1 or, as the case may be, in column 2 of Part II of Schedule 2, opposite the specification of the territory in which the controlled foreign company is resident.

Income and gains requirement

5—(1) The requirement with respect to the income and gains of a controlled foreign company as respects an accounting period is that the amount of its non-local source income arising in that accounting period does not exceed whichever is the greater of—

(*a*) £50,000 or, where that accounting period is less than twelve months in duration, that amount proportionately reduced, and
(*b*) an amount equal to ten per cent of its commercially quantified income arising in that accounting period.

(2) In paragraphs (1) and (3) "commercially quantified income" means the amount of profits of the controlled foreign company before tax, determined in accordance with generally accepted accounting standards other than an equity basis of accounting, but disregarding capital profits or losses.

(3) Subject to paragraph (4) (special rules for banks and insurance companies), for the purposes of paragraph (1) the amount of a controlled foreign company's non-local source income arising in an accounting period is the aggregate of the following amounts, namely—

(*a*) the gross amount of income consisting of distributions recognised as income in computing the commercially quantified income of that company for that period from the profits of companies not resident in the territory of residence of that company, other than branch or agency income;
(*b*) the gross amount of income and gains recognised as income in computing the commercially quantified income of that company for that period and deriving from loans to, or deposits with, persons not resident in the territory of residence of that company, or branches or agencies situated outside that territory of companies resident in that territory, other than branch or agency income and gains;
(*c*) the gross amount of income and gains recognised as income in computing the commercially quantified income of that company for that period in relation to royalties payable by persons not resident in the territory of residence of that company, or by branches or agencies situated outside that territory of companies resident in that territory, other than branch or agency income and gains;
(*d*) the gross amount of income and gains recognised as income in computing the commercially quantified income of that company for that period in relation to premiums and rents payable in respect of property situated outside the territory of residence of that company by persons not resident in that territory, or by branches situated outside that territory of companies resident in that territory, other than branch or agency income and gains;
(*e*) the amount of any branch or agency income and gains recognised as income in computing the commercially quantified income of that company for that period, calculated in accordance with regulation 6;
(*f*) the gross amount of any income not falling within any of sub-paragraphs (*a*) to (*e*) above that is recognised as income in computing the commercially quantified income of that company for that period and does not constitute income which either—

(i) is treated under the laws of the territory of residence of that company as accruing or arising in, or derived from, that territory, or
(ii) where there are no laws of that territory treating that income as accruing or arising in, or derived from, that territory or another territory, would be treated as accruing or arising in, or derived from, that territory if there were such laws in force in that territory and those laws were identical to the laws of the United Kingdom treating income as accruing or arising in, or derived from, a territory for the purposes of the Corporation Tax Acts, and which
(iii) in either case is within that territory's charge to tax.

(4) Where—

(*a*) the controlled foreign company concerned is an institution carrying on the business of banking, or an assurance company, and
(*b*) income of that company falling within any of sub-paragraphs (*a*) to (*d*) of paragraph (3)—

(i) is an integral part of income arising or accruing to the company from the trade of banking or insurance carried on by the company, being income which, if the company were resident in the United Kingdom, would be income arising to the company from a trade for the purposes of the Corporation Tax Acts, and
(ii) is within the charge to tax of the territory of residence of that company,

the aggregate amount of that income shall be disregarded in computing the aggregate amount of the company's non-local source income.

Branch or agency income and gains

6—(1) The amount of any branch or agency income and gains as mentioned in regulation 5(3)(*e*) is—

(*a*) where the conditions specified in paragraph (2) are satisfied with respect to the branch or agency for the accounting period concerned, the amount (being not more than 10 per cent of the net amount of the profits of that branch or agency for that period) by reference to which the condition specified in sub-paragraph (*d*) of that paragraph is satisfied by that branch or agency;

(*b*) where the conditions specified in paragraph (2) are not satisfied with respect to the branch or agency for the accounting period concerned, the net amount or, where paragraph (3) applies, the gross amount of the branch or agency income and gains for that accounting period.

(2) The conditions specified in this paragraph are that—

(*a*) the branch or agency is situated in a territory specified in Part I or in Part II of Schedule 1 or, as the case may be, in Part I or in Part II of Schedule 2, and where the territory is one specified in Part II of Schedule 1 or in Part II of Schedule 2, at no time during the accounting period—

(i) is entitled to any tax exemption, tax reduction or other benefit, or

(ii) falls within any condition,

specified in column 2 of that Part opposite the specification of that territory;

(*b*) the profits of the branch or agency are within the charge to tax of that territory;

(*c*) the profits attributed to the branch or agency for tax purposes in that territory are those which it might be expected to make if it were a distinct and separate enterprise from the company of which it is a branch or agency, engaged in the same or similar activities under the same or similar conditions and dealing wholly independently with the company of which it is a branch or agency;

(*d*) not more than 10 per cent of the net amount of the profits of the branch or agency for the accounting period would, on the assumption that the branch or agency was not a branch or agency of the controlled foreign company but a separate controlled foreign company, be attributable to the aggregate of the gross amounts of any income and gains falling within any of sub-paragraphs (*a*) to (*d*) of regulation 5(3) and arising outside the territory in which the branch or agency is situated;

(*e*) amounts falling to be deducted in computing the taxable profits of the branch or agency, being amounts which are paid to, or are in respect of costs incurred by, the head office of the company of which it is a branch or agency, either—

(i) are liable to tax, or are disallowed as an expense, in the territory of residence of that company, or

(ii) where that company is liable to tax in its territory of residence in respect of the whole of its profits wherever arising, are not allowed as a deduction in computing the taxable profits of that company except where the amount in question is paid by that company to another person.

(3) This paragraph applies to a case where the net amount of the income and gains referred to in paragraph (1) in the accounting period concerned does not exceed an amount which would be equal to the aggregate of the gross amounts of any income and gains falling within any of sub-paragraphs (*a*) to (*d*) of regulation 5(3) in that period if branch or agency income and gains fell within those sub-paragraphs.

Interpretation of regulations 5 and 6

7—(1) In regulation 5(2) "capital profits or losses" means profits or losses arising in relation to chargeable assets.

(2) In regulations 5(3) and 6 references to "branch or agency income" or to "branch or agency income and gains" are references to income and gains that—

(*a*) arise in or are derived from any branch or agency of a controlled foreign company, and

(*b*) fall within sub-paragraph (*e*) of regulation 5(3) in the accounting period concerned.

(3) In regulation 5(3)—

(*a*) the reference to "the gross amount" of any income in sub-paragraphs (*a*) and (*f*) are references to the amount of that income before deduction of expenses or reserves;

(*b*) the reference to "the gross amount" of any income and gains in sub-paragraph (*b*) is a reference to the amount of that income and those gains found—

(i) after excluding any gain or loss arising on any loan or deposit referred to in that sub-paragraph which is offset by a loss or gain on a contract ancillary to that loan or deposit which [is a derivative contract][1], and

(ii) after deducting any exchange losses attributable to the loans or deposits referred to in that sub-paragraph to the extent that those losses have not already been excluded by virtue of paragraph (i) above, but

(iii) before deducting other expenses or reserves;

(*c*) the references to "the gross amount" of any income and gains in sub-paragraphs (*c*) and (*d*) are references to the amount of that income and those gains found after deducting any exchange losses attributable to the royalties, premiums or rents referred to in those sub-paragraphs but before deducting other expenses or reserves;

and the references to "the gross amounts" in regulation 6(2)(*d*) and (3) shall be construed accordingly.

(4) In regulation 5(3) references to persons not resident in the territory of residence of a controlled foreign company do not include references to a company not so resident in circumstances where—

(*a*) the branch or agency of the company is situated in that territory, and

(*b*) the transaction giving rise to the income and gains in question of the controlled foreign company is made with that branch or agency.

(5) In regulation 6(1)(*b*) the reference to the gross amount of income and gains is a reference to the amount of that income or of those gains before deduction of expenses or reserves.

(6) In regulation 6(1)(*b*) the reference to "the net amount" of the branch or agency income and gains, and in regulation 6(2)(*d*) the reference to "the net amount" of the profits of the branch or agency concerned, are references to the amount of that income, or of those profits, after deduction of expenses but before tax, as determined in accordance with a generally accepted method of accounting for profits of branches or profits of agencies of companies.

(7) In paragraph (1) of this regulation a "chargeable asset" is any asset in the case of which one of the following conditions is satisfied, that is to say—

(*a*) a gain accruing to the company on a disposal of that asset on or after the date of coming into force of these Regulations would, on the assumption that the company was within the charge to corporation tax, have fallen to be treated in relation to the company as a chargeable gain and would not have been taken into account as a receipt in computing the company's income or profits or gains or losses for the purposes of the Income Tax Acts;

(*b*) a chargeable gain or allowable loss would, on the assumption mentioned in sub-paragraph (*a*), be deemed to have accrued to the company on any disposal of that asset on or after the date mentioned in that sub-paragraph.

(8) In paragraph (3)(b)(i) of this regulation—

"qualifying company"—

(a) as respects a contract falling within section 126(1) of the Finance Act 1993, has the meaning given by section 152 of that Act;

(b) as respects a contract falling within section 147(1) of the Finance Act 1994, has the meaning given by section 154 of that Act;

"qualifying contract" means a contract falling within section 126(1) of the Finance Act 1993 or section 147(1) of the Finance Act 1994, as the case may be, other than a contract which, in the case of branch or agency income or gains which would be income or gains falling within sub-paragraph (b) of regulation 5(3) if branch or agency income and gains fell within that sub-paragraph, is not entered into by the branch or agency concerned.

Amendments—[1] In para 3(*b*)(i), words substituted for the words "would be a qualifying contract if the company were a qualifying company", and para (8) revoked, by the Controlled Foreign Companies (Excluded Countries) (Amendment) Regulations, SI 2002/1963 with effect for accounting periods beginning after 30 September 2002.

SCHEDULE 1—REGULATIONS 3, 4 AND 6(2)(*a*)

ACCOUNTING PERIODS BEGINNING BEFORE 9TH JULY 1998

PART I

SPECIFIED TERRITORIES

Australia
Austria
Bangladesh
Bolivia
Botswana
Brazil
Canada
Colombia
Czech Republic
Denmark
Dominican Republic
Falkland Islands
Fiji
Finland
France
Gambia
Germany
Ghana
Honduras
Hungary
Iceland
India
Indonesia
Ivory Coast
Japan
Korea, Republic of
Lesotho
Malawi
Mexico
New Zealand
Nigeria
Norway
Papua New Guinea
Poland
Romania
Senegal
Sierra Leone
Slovak Republic
Solomon Islands
South Africa
Spain
Swaziland
Sweden
Trinidad and Tobago
Turkey
Zambia
Zimbabwe

PART II

SPECIFIED TERRITORIES WITH QUALIFICATIONS

Argentina Companies obtaining exemption from tax on income from transactions, activities or operations carried on in, or from goods located in, tax free areas in accordance with Law 19640 of 16th May 1972.

Belgium—1 Companies which are regarded as Foreign Sales Corporations in section 922(*a*) of the United States Internal Revenue Code 1954 and which accordingly qualify for reduced Belgian taxation.

2 Companies approved under Royal Decree No 187 of 30th December 1982 as Co-ordination Centres.

Brunei Companies qualifying as "pioneer companies" under the Investment Incentives Enactment 1975.

Bulgaria Any company obtaining a tax benefit under Article 111 of Decree 56 of 9th January 1989 (Free Zone legislation).

Chile Companies obtaining exemption from tax under Law 16,441 of 1st March 1966 on income from property located in the Department of Isla da Pascua or from activities developed in that Department.

China Companies deriving income in or from the Hong Kong Special Administrative Region and submitting tax returns to the authorities of that Region.

Egypt Companies which do not fall within the scope of Article 111, Book 2 of Law 157 of 1981 because they do not operate in Egypt.

Faroe Islands Companies deriving interest from Faroese financial institutions from which tax is deducted at source under Law 4 of 26th March 1953.

Greece—1 Companies whose profits are exempt from tax under Article 6(2)(*c*) of Law 3843/1958 (profits from the operation of ships under the Greek flag).

2 Companies having profits exempt from company income tax by virtue of Article 25 of Law 25/1975 or by virtue of Law 89/1967 (profits from shipping and associated activities).

Ireland—1 Companies obtaining relief or exemption from tax under Chapters 1 and 2 of Part 14 of the Taxes Consolidation Act 1997.

2 Holding companies having income exempted from tax under section 44 in Chapter 3 of Part 3 of the Taxes Consolidation Act 1997.

Italy Companies benefiting from paragraphs 12 to 14 of Article 11 of Law 413 of 30th December 1991 (Trieste Free Zone Financial and Insurance Centre).

Kenya Companies having income exempted from tax under paragraph 11 of Schedule 1 to the Income Tax Act 1973.

Luxembourg—1 Companies obtaining any special tax benefit under the Law of 31st July 1929, the decree of 17th December 1938 or the Grand Ducal Regulation of 29th July 1977 (holding companies).

2 Any reinsurance company established in Luxembourg requiring authorisation under Article 92 of the Law of 6th December 1991.

Malaysia—1 Companies exempt from tax in accordance with section 54A of the Income Tax Act 1967 (shipping).

2 Companies subject to tax at 5 per cent in accordance with sections 60A and 60B of the Income Tax Act 1967 (inward reinsurance and offshore insurance).

3 Companies deriving dividends from a company or companies deriving income from one or more of the activities referred to in paragraphs 1 and 2 above.

4 Companies obtaining a tax benefit under the Offshore Companies Act (Island of Labuan) 1990.

Malta—1 Companies entitled to exemption or relief from tax under section 11(2) of the Income Tax Act 1948.

2 Companies obtaining exemption from tax under section 86 of the Merchant Shipping Act 1973.

3 Companies obtaining exemption or relief from tax under section 30 of the Malta International Business Activities Act 1988.

4 Companies obtaining exemption or relief from tax under section 18 of the Malta Freeports Act 1989.

Morocco Companies receiving a tax benefit under Law 58-90 of 1992 (offshore financial centres).

Netherlands Companies which are regarded as Foreign Sales Corporations under section 922(*a*) of the United States Internal Revenue Code 1954.

Pakistan Companies deriving royalties, commissions or fees which are exempt from tax under paragraph 139 in Part I of the second Schedule to the Income Tax Ordinance 1979.

Philippines—1 Companies authorised under Presidential Decree 1034 of 30th September 1976, or under Presidential Decree 1035 of 30th September 1976, to operate an offshore Banking Unit or a Foreign Currency Deposit Unit as defined in those Decrees.

2 Companies receiving interest on deposits with a Foreign Currency Deposit Unit, or other interest subject to the reduced rates of tax under section 27(D) of the National Internal Revenue Code 1997.

Portugal Companies obtaining tax benefits under Decree Law 502/85 of 30th December 1985, Articles 41 and 51(*g*) of the Tax Benefits statute (EBF) approved by Decree Law 215/90 of 31st August 1989 (free zone in Madeira), or Decree Law 501/85 of 28th December 1985 as implemented by Decree Law 63/87 of 5th February 1987 (free zone in the Azores).

Puerto Rico—1 Companies obtaining a tax benefit under section 2(*o*) of the Industrial Incentive Act 1978 (designated service industries).

2 Companies obtaining a tax benefit under section 25 of the International Banking Centre Regulatory Act 1989 (International Banking Entities).

Singapore—1 Any company obtaining tax concessions under Ministry of Finance Regulations pursuant to section 43A, and sections 43C to 43J, of the Income Tax Act.

2 Companies obtaining exemption from tax on the income of a shipping enterprise in accordance with section 13A of the Income Tax Act.

3 Companies obtaining relief from tax in accordance with sections 45 to 55 (international trade incentives), and sections 75 to 84 (warehouse and service incentives), of the Economic Expansion Incentives (Relief from Income Tax) Act.

4 Companies deriving dividends from a company or companies deriving income from one or more of the activities falling within paragraphs 1 to 3 above.

Sri Lanka Companies obtaining relief or exemption from income tax under any of the following provisions of the Inland Revenue Act 1979—

(*a*) section 8(*c*)(iv) (foreign currency banking units);
(*b*) sections 10(*d*) and 15(*b*) (income derived from approved bank accounts);
(*c*) section 10(*e*) (interest of newly resident companies);
(*d*) section 15(*cc*) (services rendered outside Sri Lanka);
(*e*) section 15(*p*) (re-export of approved products).

Tanzania Companies relieved or exempted from income tax under section 15(1) or (1A) of the Income Tax Act 1973.

Thailand Companies obtaining a tax benefit under Royal Decree 280 of 22nd September 1992 (offshore banking units).

Tunisia Companies obtaining exemption from, or reduction of, tax under Law 76-63 of 12th July 1976 (financial and banking institutions dealing with non-residents).

United States Domestic International Sales Corporations as defined in section 992(*a*) of the Internal Revenue Code 1954.

SCEHDULE 2—REGULATIONS 3, 4 AND 6(2)(*a*)

ACCOUNTING PERIODS BEGINNING ON OR AFTER 9TH JULY 1998

PART I

SPECIFIED TERRITORIES

Australia
Austria
Bangladesh
Bolivia
Botswana
Brazil
Bulgaria
Canada
Colombia
Czech Republic
Denmark
Dominican Republic
Falkland Islands
Fiji
Finland
France
Gambia
Germany
Ghana
Honduras
Iceland
India
Indonesia
Ivory Coast
Japan
Korea, Republic of
Lesotho
Malawi
Mexico
New Zealand
Nigeria
Norway
Papua New Guinea
Poland
Romania
Senegal
Sierra Leone
Slovak Republic
Solomon Islands
South Africa
Swaziland
Sweden
Trinidad and Tobago
Turkey
Zambia
Zimbabwe

PART II

SPECIFIED TERRITORIES WITH QUALIFICATIONS

Argentina Companies obtaining exemption from tax on income from transactions, activities or operations carried on in, or from goods located in, tax free areas in accordance with Law 19640 of 16th May 1972.

Belgium—1 Companies which are regarded as Foreign Sales Corporations in section 922(*a*) of the United States Internal Revenue Code 1954 and which accordingly qualify for reduced Belgian taxation.

2 Companies approved under Royal Decree No 187 of 30th December 1982 as Co-ordination Centres.

Brunei Companies qualifying as ''pioneer companies'' under the Investment Incentives Enactment 1975.

Chile Companies obtaining exemption from tax under Law 16,441 of 1st March 1966 on income from property located in the Department of Isla da Pascua or from activities developed in that Department.

China—1 Companies deriving income in or from the Hong Kong Special Administrative Region and submitting tax returns to the authorities of that Region.

2 From 20th December 1999, companies deriving income in or from the Macao Special Administrative Region and submitting tax returns to the authorities of that Region.

Egypt Companies which do not fall within the scope of Article 111, Book 2 of Law 157 of 1981 because they do not operate in Egypt.

Faroe Islands Companies deriving interest from Faroese financial institutions from which tax is deducted at source under Law 4 of 26th March 1953.

Greece—1 Companies whose profits are exempt from tax under Article 6(2)(*c*) of Law 3843/1958 (profits from the operation of ships under the Greek flag).

2 Companies having profits exempt from company income tax by virtue of Article 25 of Law 25/1975 or by virtue of Law 89/1967 (profits from shipping and associated activities).

Hungary Companies benefiting from the reduced rate of tax for extra-territorial companies under section 19(2) of Act LXXXI of 1996 on Corporate Tax and Dividend Tax.

...[1]

Italy Companies benefiting from paragraphs 12 to 14 of Article 11 of Law 413 of 30th December 1991 (Trieste Free Zone Financial and Insurance Centre).

Kenya Companies having income exempted from tax under paragraph 11 of Schedule 1 to the Income Tax Act 1973.

Luxembourg—1 Companies obtaining any special tax benefit under the Law of 31st July 1929, the decree of 17th December 1938 or the Grand Ducal Regulation of 29th July 1977 (holding companies).

2 Any reinsurance company established in Luxembourg requiring authorisation under Article 92 of the law of 6th December 1991.

Malaysia—1 Companies exempt from tax in accordance with section 54A of the Income Tax Act 1967 (shipping).

2 Companies subject to tax at 5 per cent in accordance with sections 60A and 60B of the Income Tax Act 1967 (inward reinsurance and offshore insurance).

3 Companies deriving dividends from a company or companies deriving income from one or more of the activities referred to in paragraphs 1 and 2 above.

4 Companies obtaining a tax benefit under the Offshore Companies Act (Island of Labuan) 1990.

Malta—1 Companies entitled to exemption or relief from tax at the discretion of the Minister responsible for finance under section 12(2) of the Income Tax Act 1948.

2 Companies obtaining exemption from tax under section 86 of the Merchant Shipping Act 1973.

3 Companies obtaining exemption or relief from tax under section 30 of the Malta International Business Activities Act 1988 or section 30 of the Malta Financial Services Centre Act 1988.

4 Companies obtaining exemption or relief from tax under section 18 of the Malta Freeports Act 1989.

Morocco Companies receiving a tax benefit under Law 58-90 of 1992 (offshore financial centres).

Netherlands 1 Companies which are regarded as Foreign Sales Corporations under section 922(*a*) of the United States Internal Revenue Code 1954.

2 A company ("the first company") receiving interest, rents or royalties in an accounting period directly or indirectly from a Dutch company ("the second company") which is connected with the first company within the meaning of section 839 of the Taxes Act, in circumstances where—

(*a*) the second company does not satisfy the income and gains requirement in regulation 5 as respects its accounting period in which the interest, rents or royalties were paid, and

(*b*) the aggregate of the non-local source income of the first company in its accounting period in question and the interest, rents and royalties received by it from the second company in that period exceeds whichever is the greater of—

(i) £50,000 or, where that period is less than twelve months in duration, that amount proportionately reduced, and

(ii) an amount equal to ten per cent of its commercially quantified income arising in that period.

Pakistan Companies deriving royalties, commissions or fees which are exempt from tax under paragraph 139 in Part I of the second Schedule to the Income Tax Ordinance 1979.

Philippines—1 Companies authorised under Presidential Decree 1034 of 30th September 1976, or under Presidential Decree 1035 of 30th September 1976, to operate an offshore Banking Unit or a Foreign Currency Deposit Unit as defined in those Decrees.

2 Companies receiving interest on deposits with a Foreign Currency Deposit Unit, or other interest subject to the reduced rates of tax under section 27(D) of the National Internal Revenue Code 1997.

Portugal Companies obtaining tax benefits under Decree Law 502/85 of 30th December 1985, Articles 41 and 51(*g*) of the Tax Benefits statute (EBF) approved by Decree Law 215/90 of 31st August 1989 (free zone in Madeira), or Decree Law 501/85 of 28th December 1985 as implemented by Decree Law 63/87 of 5th February 1987 (free zone in the Azores).

Puerto Rico—1 Companies obtaining a tax benefit under section 2(*o*) of the Industrial Incentive Act 1978 (designated service industries).

2 Companies obtaining a tax benefit under section 25 of the International Banking Centre Regulatory Act 1989 (International Banking Entities).

Singapore—1 Any company obtaining tax concessions under Ministry of Finance Regulations pursuant to section 43A, and sections 43C to 43K, of the Income Tax Act.

2 Companies obtaining exemption from tax on the income of a shipping enterprise in accordance with section 13A of the Income Tax Act.

3 Companies obtaining relief from tax in accordance with sections 45 to 55 (international trade incentives), and sections 75 to 84 (warehouse and service incentives), of the Economic Expansion Incentives (Relief from Income Tax) Act.

4 Companies deriving dividends from a company or companies deriving income from one or more of the activities falling within paragraphs 1 to 3 above.

Spain—1 Companies which are registered in the official register of the Canary Islands Special Zone (Zona Especial Canaria) established under Law 19/1994 and which benefit from the special low tax rate applied to such companies.

2 Companies benefiting from the alternative taxation regime for co-ordination centres established by the provincial governments of the Basque Country under laws pursuant to Norma Foral 3/1996 of 26th June 1996, Norma Foral 7/1996 of 4th July 1996, and Norma Foral 24/1996 of 5th July 1996.

Sri Lanka Companies obtaining relief or exemption from income tax under any of the following provisions of the Inland Revenue Act 1979—

(*a*) section 8(*c*)(iv) (foreign currency banking units);
(*b*) sections 10(*d*) and 15(*b*) (income derived from approved bank accounts);
(*c*) section 10(*e*) (interest of newly resident companies);
(*d*) section 15(*cc*) (services rendered outside Sri Lanka);
(*e*) section 15(*p*) (re-export of approved products).

Tanzania Companies relieved or exempted from income tax under section 15(1) or (1A) of the Income Tax Act 1973.

Thailand Companies obtaining a tax benefit under Royal Decree 280 of 22nd September 1992 (offshore banking units).

Tunisia Companies obtaining exemption from, or reduction of, tax under Law 76-63 of 12th July 1976 (financial and banking institutions dealing with non-residents).

United States Domestic International Sales Corporations as defined in section 992(*a*) of the Internal Revenue Code 1954.

Amendments—[1] Entry in respect of Ireland revoked by the Controlled Foreign Companies (Excluded Countries) (Amendment No. 2) Regulations, SI 2002/2406 with effect for accounting periods beginning after 10 October 2002.

1998/3132
The Civil Procedure Rules 1998

Made . . . . *10 December 1998*
Laid before Parliament . . . . . . *17 December 1998*
Coming into force . . . . *26 April 1999*

Note—These rules superseded the Rules of the Supreme Court (Revision), SI 1965/1776, with effect from 26 April 1999.

[PART 54
[JUDICIAL REVIEW AND STATUTORY REVIEW][2]][1]

Amendments—[1] This Part inserted by the Civil Procedure (Amendment No 4) Rules, SI 2000/2092, r 22, Schedule with effect from 2 October 2000 except in relation to an application for permission to make an application for judicial review in accordance with RSC Order 53 before that date.
[2] Part heading substituted by the Civil Procedure (Amendment) Rules, SI 2003/364 r 3 with effect from 1 April 2003 (by virtue of SI 2003/754).

Scope and interpretation

54.1—(1) [This Section of this Part][2] contains rules about judicial review.
(2) [In this Section][2]—

(*a*) a "claim for judicial review" means a claim to review the lawfulness of—
  (i) an enactment; or
  (ii) a decision, action or failure to act in relation to the exercise of a public function.

(*b*) an order of mandamus is called a "mandatory order";
(*c*) an order of prohibition is called a "prohibiting order";
(*d*) an order of certiorari is called a "quashing order";
(*e*) "the judicial review procedure" means the Part 8 procedure as modified by [this Section][2];
(*f*) "interested party" means any person (other than the claimant and defendant) who is directly affected by the claim; and
(*g*) "court" means the High Court, unless otherwise stated.

(Rule 8.1(6)(*b*) provides that a rule or practice direction may, in relation to a specified type of proceedings, disapply or modify any of the rules set out in Part 8 as they apply to those proceedings)][1]

Amendments—[1] Rule inserted as stated in note at the start of this Part, see above.
[2] Words substituted by the Civil Procedure (Amendment) Rules, SI 2003/364 r 5(*a*), (*b*) with effect from 1 April 2003 (by virtue of SI 2003/754).

[When this [Section][2] must be used

54.2 The judicial review procedure must be used in a claim for judicial review where the claimant is seeking—
(*a*) a mandatory order;
(*b*) a prohibiting order;
(*c*) a quashing order; or
(*d*) an injunction under section 30 of the Supreme Court Act 1981 (restraining a person from acting in any office in which he is not entitled to act).][1]

Amendments—[1] Rule inserted as stated in note at the start of this Part, see above.
[2] Word in heading substituted by the Civil Procedure (Amendment) Rules, SI 2003/364 r 5(*c*) with effect from 1 April 2003 (by virtue of SI 2003/754).

[When this [Section][2] may be used

54.3—(1) The judicial review procedure may be used in a claim for judicial review where the claimant is seeking—
(*a*) a declaration; or
(*b*) an injunction.

(Section 31(2) of the Supreme Court Act 1981 sets out the circumstances in which the court may grant a declaration or injunction in a claim for judicial review)

(Where the claimant is seeking a declaration or injunction in addition to one of the remedies listed in rule 54.2, the judicial review procedure must be used)

(2) A claim for judicial review may include a claim for damages but may not seek damages alone.

(Section 31(4) of the Supreme Court Act 1981 sets out the circumstances in which the court may award damages on a claim for judicial review)][1]

Amendments—[1] Rule inserted as stated in note at the start of this Part, see above.
[2] Word in heading substituted by the Civil Procedure (Amendment) Rules, SI 2003/364 r 5(*c*) with effect from 1 April 2003 (by virtue of SI 2003/754).

[Permission required

54.4 The court's permission to proceed is required in a claim for judicial review whether started under this [Section][2] or transferred to the Administrative Court.][1]

Amendments—[1] Rule inserted as stated in note at the start of this Part, see above.
[2] Word substituted by the Civil Procedure (Amendment) Rules, SI 2003/364 r 5(*d*) with effect from 1 April 2003 (by virtue of SI 2003/754).

[Time limit for filing claim form

54.5—(1) The claim form must be filed—
(*a*) promptly; and
(*b*) in any event not later than 3 months after the grounds to make the claim first arose.

(2) The time limit in this rule may not be extended by agreement between the parties.

(3) This rule does not apply when any other enactment specifies a shorter time limit for making the claim for judicial review.][1]

Amendments—[1] Rule inserted as stated in note at the start of this Part, see above.

[Claim form

54.6—(1) In addition to the matters set out in rule 8.2 (contents of the claim form) the claimant must also state—
(*a*) the name and address of any person he considers to be an interested party;
(*b*) that he is requesting permission to proceed with a claim for judicial review; and
(*c*) any remedy (including any interim remedy) he is claiming.

(Part 25 sets out how to apply for an interim remedy)

(2) The claim form must be accompanied by the documents required by the relevant practice direction.][1]

Amendments—[1] Rule inserted as stated in note at the start of this Part, see above.

[Service of claim form

54.7 The claim form must be served on—

(*a*) the defendant; and

(*b*) unless the court otherwise directs, any person the claimant considers to be an interested party,

within 7 days after the date of issue.][1]

Amendments—[1] Rule inserted as stated in note at the start of this Part, see above.

[Acknowledgement of service

54.8—(1) Any person served with the claim form who wishes to take part in the judicial review must file an acknowledgement of service in the relevant practice form in accordance with the following provisions of this rule.

(2) Any acknowledgement of service must be—

(*a*) filed not more than 21 days after service of the claim form; and

(*b*) served on—

(i) the claimant; and

(ii) subject to any direction under rule 54.7(*b*), any other person named in the claim form,

as soon as practicable and, in any event, not later than 7 days after it is filed.

(3) The time limits under this rule may not be extended by agreement between the parties.

(4) The acknowledgement of service—

(*a*) must—

(i) where the person filing it intends to contest the claim, set out a summary of his grounds for doing so; and

(ii) state the name and address of any person the person filing it considers to be an interested party; and

(*b*) may include or be accompanied by an application for directions.

(5) Rule 10.3(2) does not apply.][1]

Amendments—[1] Rule inserted as stated in note at the start of this Part, see above.

[Failure to file acknowledgement of service

54.9—(1) Where a person served with the claim form has failed to file an acknowledgement of service in accordance with rule 54.8, he—

(*a*) may not take part in a hearing to decide whether permission should be given unless the court allows him to do so; but

(*b*) provided he complies with rule 54.14 or any other direction of the court regarding the filing and service of—

(i) detailed grounds for contesting the claim or supporting it on additional grounds; and

(ii) any written evidence,

may take part in the hearing of the judicial review.

(2) Where that person takes part in the hearing of the judicial review, the court may take his failure to file an acknowledgement of service into account when deciding what order to make about costs.

(3) Rule 8.4 does not apply.][1]

Amendments—[1] Rule inserted as stated in note at the start of this Part, see above.

[Permission given

54.10—(1) Where permission to proceed is given the court may also give directions.

(2) Directions under paragraph (1) may include a stay of proceedings to which the claim relates.

(Rule 3.7 provides a sanction for the non-payment of the fee payable when permission to proceed has been given)][1]

Amendments—[1] Rule inserted as stated in note at the start of this Part, see above.

[Service of order giving or refusing permission

54.11 The court will serve—

(*a*) the order giving or refusing permission; and

(*b*) any directions,

on—

(i) the claimant;
(ii) the defendant; and
(iii) any other person who filed an acknowledgement of service.][1]

Amendments—[1] Rule inserted as stated in note at the start of this Part, see above.

[Permission decision without a hearing

54.12—(1) This rule applies where the court, without a hearing—

(*a*) refuses permission to proceed; or
(*b*) gives permission to proceed—
(i) subject to conditions; or
(ii) on certain grounds only.

(2) The court will serve its reasons for making the decision when it serves the order giving or refusing permission in accordance with rule 54.11.

(3) The claimant may not appeal but may request the decision to be reconsidered at a hearing.

(4) A request under paragraph (3) must be filed within 7 days after service of the reasons under paragraph (2).

(5) The claimant, defendant and any other person who has filed an acknowledgement of service will be given at least 2 days' notice of the hearing date.][1]

Amendments—[1] Rule inserted as stated in note at the start of this Part, see above.

[Defendant etc may not apply to set aside

54.13 Neither the defendant nor any other person served with the claim form may apply to set aside an order giving permission to proceed.][1]

Amendments—[1] Rule inserted as stated in note at the start of this Part, see above.

[Response

54.14—(1) A defendant and any other person saved with the claim form who wishes to contest the claim or support it on additional grounds must file and serve—

(*a*) detailed grounds for contesting the claim or supporting it on additional grounds; and
(*b*) any written evidence,

within 35 days after service of the order giving permission.

(2) The following rules do not apply—

(*a*) rule 8.5(3) and 8.5(4) (defendant to file and serve written evidence at the same time as acknowledgement of service); and
(*b*) rule 8.5(5) and 8.5(6) (claimant to file and serve any reply within 14 days).][1]

Amendments—[1] Rule inserted as stated in note at the start of this Part, see above.

[Where claimant seeks to rely on additional grounds

54.15 The court's permission is required if a claimant seeks to rely on grounds other than those for which he has been given permission to proceed.][1]

Amendments—[1] Rule inserted as stated in note at the start of this Part, see above.

[Evidence

54.16—(1) Rule 8.6[(1)][2] does not apply.

(2) No written evidence may be relied on unless—

(*a*) it has been served in accordance with any—
(i) rule under this [Section][3]; or
(ii) direction of the court; or
(*b*) the court gives permission.][1]

Amendments—[1] Rule inserted as stated in note at the start of this Part, see above.
[2] Figure inserted by the Civil Procedure (Amendment) Rules, SI 2002/2058 r 21 with effect from 2 December 2002.
[3] Word substituted by the Civil Procedure (Amendment) Rules, SI 2003/364 r 5(*d*) with effect from 1 April 2003 (by virtue of SI 2003/754).

[Court's powers to hear any person

54.17—(1) Any person may apply for permission—

(*a*) to file evidence; or
(*b*) make representations at the hearing of the judicial review.

(2) An application under paragraph (1) should be made promptly.][1]

Amendments—[1] Rule inserted as stated in note at the start of this Part, see above.

[Judicial review may be decided without a hearing

54.18 The court may decide the claim for judicial review without a hearing where all the parties agree.][1]

Amendments—[1] Rule inserted as stated in note at the start of this Part, see above.

[Court's powers in respect of quashing orders

54.19—(1) This rule applies where the court makes a quashing order in respect of the decision to which the claim relates.

(2) The court may—

(*a*) remit the matter to the decision-maker; and

(*b*) direct it to reconsider the matter and reach a decision in accordance with the judgment of the court.

(3) Where the court considers that there is no purpose to be served in remitting the matter to the decision-maker it may, subject to any statutory provision, take the decision itself.

(Where a statutory power is given to a tribunal, person or other body it may be the case that the court cannot take the decision itself)][1]

Amendments—[1] Rule inserted as stated in note at the start of this Part, see above.

[Transfer

54.20 The court may—

(*a*) order a claim to continue as if it had not been started under this [Section][2]; and

(*b*) where it does so, give directions about the future management of the claim.

(Part 30 (transfer) applies to transfers to and from the Administrative Court)][1]

Amendments—[1] Rule inserted as stated in note at the start of this Part, see above.
[2] Word substituted by the Civil Procedure (Amendment) Rules, SI 2003/364 r 5(*e*) with effect from 1 April 2003 (by virtue of SI 2003/754).

(Section II of this Part is not relevant to this work, and has therefore been omitted)

SCHEDULE 1

Rule 50(3)

RSC ORDER 53
APPLICATIONS FOR JUDICIAL REVIEW[1]

Amendments—[1] This order revoked by the Civil Procedure (Amendment No 4) Rules, SI 2000/2092, r 23 with effect from 2 October 2000 except in relation to an application for permission to make an application for judicial review in accordance with this order before that date.

Cases appropriate for application for judicial review

Rule 1—*(1) An application for—*

(a) an order of mandamus, prohibition or certiorari, or

(b) an injunction under section 30 of the Act restraining a person from acting in any office in which he is not entitled to act,

shall be made by way of an application for judicial review in accordance with the provisions of this Order.

(2)—An application for a declaration or an injunction (not being an injunction mentioned in paragraph (1)(b)) may be made by way of an application for judicial review, and on such an application the Court may grant the declaration or injunction claimed if it considers that, having regard to—

(a) the nature of the matters in respect of which a remedy may be granted by way of an order of mandamus, prohibition or certiorari;

(b) the nature of the persons and bodies against whom a remedy may be granted by way of such an order; and

(c) all the circumstances of the case,

it would be just and convenient for the declaration or injunction to be granted on an application for judicial review.[1]

Simon's Tax Cases—r 1(2), *IRC v National Federation of Self-Employed and Small Businesses Ltd* [1981] STC 260.
Amendments—[1] Rule revoked as stated in note to start of this Order, see above.

Joinder of claims for relief

Rule 2—*On an application for judicial review any remedy mentioned in rule 1 (1) or (2) may be claimed as an alternative or in addition to any other remedy so mentioned if it arises out of or relates to or is connected with the same matter.*[1]

Amendments—[1] Rule revoked as stated in note to start of this Order, see above.

Grant of leave to apply for judicial review

Rule 3—*(1) No application for judicial review shall be made unless the permission of the Court has been obtained in accordance with this rule.*

(2) An application for permission must be made without notice being served on any other party to a Judge by filing in the Crown Office—

(a) an application notice in Form No. 86A containing a statement of

(i) the name and description of the applicant;

(ii) the relief sought and the grounds upon which it is sought;

(iii) the name and address of the applicant's solicitors (if any); and

(iv) the applicant's address for service; and

(b) written evidence verifying the facts relied on.

(3) The Judge may determine the application without a hearing, unless a hearing is requested in the notice of application, and need not sit in public; in any case, the Crown Office shall serve a copy of the Judge's order on the applicant.

(4) Where the application for permission is refused by the Judge, or is granted on terms, the applicant may renew it by applying—

(a) in any criminal cause or matter, to a Divisional Court of the Queen's Bench Division;

(b) in any other case, to a single Judge sitting in public or, if the Court so directs, to a Divisional Court of the Queen's Bench Division:

Provided that no application for permission may be renewed in any non-criminal cause or matter in which the Judge has refused permission under paragraph (3) after a hearing.

(5) In order to renew his application for permission the applicant must, within 10 days of being served with notice of the Judge's refusal, lodge in the Crown Office notice of his intention in Form No 86B.

(6) The Court hearing an application for permission may allow the applicant's statement to be amended, whether by specifying different or additional grounds or relief or otherwise, on such terms, if any, as it thinks fit.

(7) The Court shall not grant permission unless it considers that the applicant has a sufficient interest in the matter to which the application relates.

(8) Where permission is sought to apply for an order of certiorari to remove for the purpose of its being quashed any judgment, order, conviction or other proceeding which is subject to appeal and a time is limited for the bringing of the appeal, the Court may adjourn the application for permission until the appeal is determined or the time for appealing has expired.

(9) If the Court grants permission, it may impose such terms as to costs and as to giving security as it thinks fit.

(10) Where permission to apply for judicial review is granted, then—

(a) if the relief sought is an order of prohibition or certiorari and the Court so directs, the grant shall operate as a stay of the proceedings to which the application relates until the determination of the application or until the Court otherwise orders;

(b) if any other relief is sought, the Court may at any time grant in the proceedings interim remedies in accordance with CPR Part 25.[1]

Simon's Tax Cases—r 3(5), *IRC v National Federation of Self-Employed and Small Businesses Ltd* [1981] STC 260
Amendments—[1] Rule revoked as stated in note to start of this Order, see above.

Delay in applying for relief

Rule 4—*(1) An application for permission to apply for judicial review shall be made promptly and in any event within three months from the date when grounds for the application first arose unless the Court considers that there is good reason for extending the period within which the application shall be made.*

(2) Where an order of certiorari is sought in respect of any judgment, order, conviction or other proceeding, the date when grounds for the application first arose shall be taken to be the date of that judgment, order, conviction or proceeding.

(3) Paragraph (1) is without prejudice to any statutory provision which has the effect of limiting the time within which an application for judicial review may be made.[1]

Simon's Tax Cases—*R v Special Comr, ex p Moschi* [1981] STC 465; *R v IRC, ex p Allen* [1997] STC 1141.
Amendments—[1] Rule revoked as stated in note to start of this Order, see above.

Mode of applying for judicial review

Rule 5—*(1) In any criminal cause or matter, where permission has been granted to make an application for judicial review, the application shall be made to a Divisional Court of the Queen's Bench Division.*

(2) In any other such cause or matter, the application shall be made to a judge sitting in open Court, unless the Court directs that it shall be made—

(a) to a Judge in private; or
(b) to a Divisional Court of the Queen's Bench Division.

(2A) An application for judicial review shall be made by the issue of a claim form.

(3) The claim form must be served on all persons directly affected and where it relates to any proceedings in or before a Court and the object of the application is either to compel the Court or an officer of the Court to do any act in relation to the proceedings or to quash them or any order made therein, the claim form must also be served on the Clerk or Registrar of the Court and, where any objection to the conduct of the Judge is to be made, on the Judge.

(4) Unless the Court granting permission has otherwise directed, there must be at least 10 days between the service of the claim form and the hearing.

(5) The application must be entered for hearing within 14 days after the grant of permission.

(6) Written evidence giving the names and addresses of, and the places and dates of service on, all persons who have been served with the claim form must be filed before the application is entered for hearing and, if any person who ought to be served under this rule has not been served, the written evidence must state that fact and the reason for it; and shall be before the Court on the hearing of the application.

(7) If on the hearing of the application the Court is of opinion that any person who ought, whether under this rule or otherwise, to have been served has not been served, the Court may adjourn the hearing on such terms (if any) as it may direct in order that the claim form may be served on that person.[1]

Amendments—[1] Rule revoked as stated in note to start of this Order, see above.

Statements and evidence

Rule 6—*(1) Copies of the statement in support of an application for permission under rule 3 must be served with the claim form and, subject to paragraph (2) no grounds shall be relied upon or any remedy sought at the hearing except the grounds and remedies set out in the statement.*

(2) The Court may on hearing of the application for judicial review allow the applicant to amend his statement, whether by specifying different or additional grounds or otherwise, on such terms, if any, as it thinks fit and may allow further written evidence to be relied on by him.

(3) Where the applicant intends to ask to be allowed to amend his statement or to rely on further written evidence he shall give notice of his intention and of any proposed amendment to every other party.

(4) Any respondent who intends to use written evidence at the hearing shall file it in the Crown Office and give notice thereof to the applicant as soon as practicable and in any event, unless the Court otherwise directs, within 56 days after service upon him of the documents required to be served by paragraph (1).

(5) Each party to the application must supply to every other party on demand and on payment of the proper charges copies of any written evidence which he proposes to rely on at the hearing, including, in the case of the applicant, the written evidence in support of the application for permission under rule 3.[1]

Amendments—[1] Rule revoked as stated in note to start of this Order, see above.

Claim for damages

Rule 7—*(1) On an application for judicial review the Court may, subject to paragraph (2) award damages to the applicant if—*

(a) he has included in the statement in support of his application for permission under rule 3 a claim for damages arising from any matter to which the application relates; and
(b) the Court is satisfied that, if the claim had been made in proceedings for damages begun by the applicant at the time of making his application for judicial review, he could have been awarded damages.

(2) CPR Part 16 shall apply to a statement relating to a claim for damages as it applies to a statement of case.[1]

Amendments—[1] Rule revoked as stated in note to start of this Order, see above.

Application for disclosure, further information, cross-examination, etc

Rule 8—*(1) Unless the Court otherwise directs, any interlocutory application in proceedings on an application for judicial review may be made to any judge or a master of the Queen's Bench Division, notwithstanding that the application for judicial review has been made to and is to be heard by a Divisional Court.*

In this paragraph "interlocutory application" includes an application for an order under CPR Part 31 or CPR Part 18 or for an order for permission to cross-examine any person who has given written evidence or for an order dismissing the proceedings by consent of the parties.

[(2) Any appeal from an order made by a Master pursuant to paragraph (1) shall lie to a Divisional Court and not to a Judge.][2]

(3) This rule is without prejudice to any statutory provision or rule of law restricting the making of an order against the Crown.[1]

Amendments—[1] Rule revoked as stated in note to start of this Order, see above.
[2] Para (2) substituted by the Civil Procedure (Amendment) Rules, SI 2000/221 with effect from 2 May 2000.

Hearing of application for judicial review

Rule 9—*(1) On the hearing of any application for judicial review under rule 5, any person who desires to be heard in opposition to the application, and appears to the Court to be a proper person to be heard, shall be heard, notwithstanding that he has not been served with the claim form.*

(2) Where the remedy sought is or includes an order of certiorari to remove any proceedings for the purpose of quashing them, the applicant may not question the validity of any order, warrant, commitment, conviction, inquisition or record unless before the hearing of the application he has filed in the Crown Office a copy thereof verified by witness statement or affidavit or accounts for his failure to do so to the satisfaction of the Court hearing the application.

(3) Where an order of certiorari is made in any such case as is referred to in paragraph (2) the order shall, subject to paragraph (4) direct that the proceedings shall be quashed forthwith on their removal into the Queen's Bench Division.

(4) Where an order of certiorari is sought and the Court is satisfied that there are grounds for quashing the decision to which the application relates, the Court may, in addition to quashing it, remit the matter to the Court, tribunal or authority concerned with a direction to reconsider it and reach a decision in accordance with the findings of the Court.

(5) Where the remedy sought is a declaration, an injunction or damages and the Court considers that it should not be granted on an application for judicial review but might have been granted if it had been sought in a claim begun by the applicant at the time of making his application for judicial review, the Court may, instead of refusing the application, order the judicial review proceedings to continue as proceedings brought under CPR Part 7 and if it does so may give any directions it considers appropriate.[1]

Amendments—[1] Rule revoked as stated in note to start of this Order, see above.

Saving for person acting in obedience to mandamus

Rule 10 *No action or proceeding shall be begun or prosecuted against any person in respect of anything done in obedience to an order of mandamus.*[1]

Amendments—[1] Rule revoked as stated in note to start of this Order, see above.

Proceedings for disqualification of member of local authority

Rule 11—*(1) Proceedings under section 92 of the Local Government Act 1972 must be begun by the issue of a claim form and brought before a Divisional Court of the Queen's Bench Division.*

(1A) Unless otherwise directed, there must be at least 10 days between the service of the claim form and the hearing.

(2) The claim form must set out the name and description of the applicant, the remedy sought and the grounds on which it is sought, and must be supported by written evidence verifying the facts relied on.

(3) Copies of any written evidence must be filed in the Crown Office before the proceedings are entered for hearing and must be supplied to any other party on demand and on payment of the proper charges.

(4) The provisions of rules 5, 6 and 9 (1) as to the persons on whom the claim form is to be served and as to the hearing shall apply, with the necessary modifications, to proceedings under the said section 92 as they apply to an application for judicial review.[1]

Amendments—[1] Rule revoked as stated in note to start of this Order, see above.

Consolidation of applications

Rule 12 *Where there is more than one application pending under section 30 of the Act, or section 92 of the Local Government Act 1972, against several persons in respect of the same office, and on the same grounds, the Court may order the applications to be consolidated.*[1]

Amendments—[1] Rule revoked as stated in note to start of this Order, see above.

Appeal from Judge's order

Rule 13 *No appeal shall lie from an order made under paragraph (3) of rule 3 on an application for leave which may be renewed under paragraph (4) of that rule.*[1]

Amendments—[1] Rule revoked as stated in note to start of this Order, see above.

Meaning of "Court"

Rule 14 *In relation to the hearing by a Judge of an application for leave under rule 3 or of an application for judicial review, any reference in this Order to "the Court" shall, unless the context otherwise requires, be construed as a reference to the Judge.*[1]

Amendments—[1] Rule revoked as stated in note to start of this Order, see above.

RSC ORDER 55

APPEALS TO HIGH COURT FROM COURT, TRIBUNAL OR PERSON: GENERAL

Amendments—This order revoked by the Civil Procedure (Amendment) Rules, SI 2000/221, r 41 Sch 8 with effect from 2 May 2000.

RSC ORDER 77

PROCEEDINGS BY AND AGAINST THE CROWN

Application and interpretation

Rule 1—(1) These rules apply to civil proceedings to which the Crown is a party subject to the following rules of this Order.

(2) In this Order—

"civil proceedings by the Crown", "civil proceedings against the Crown" and "civil proceedings by or against the Crown" have the same respective meanings as in Part II of the Crown Proceedings Act 1947[142], and do not include any of the proceedings specified in section 23(3) of that Act;

"civil proceedings to which the Crown is a party" has the same meaning as it has for the purposes of Part IV of the Crown Proceedings Act 1947, by virtue of section 38 (4) of that Act;

"order against the Crown" means any order (including an order for costs) made in any civil proceedings by or against the Crown or in any proceedings on the Crown side of the Queen's Bench Division, or in connection with any arbitration to which the Crown is a party, in favour of any person against the Crown or against a government department or against an officer of the Crown as such;

"order" includes a judgment, decree, rule, award or declaration.

Transfer of proceedings

Rule 2—(1) Subject to paragraph (2) in civil proceedings by or against the Crown no order shall be made under CPR Part 30 for the transfer of the proceedings, or of any application therein, from the Royal Courts of Justice to a district registry, except with the consent of the Crown.

(2) In any civil proceedings against the Crown begun by the issue of a claim form out of a district registry the Crown may acknowledge service of the claim form either in the district registry or, at the option of the Crown, in the appropriate office of the Supreme Court at the Royal Courts of Justice, and where service is acknowledged in an office of the Supreme Court at the Royal Courts of Justice the claim shall thereafter proceed in the Royal Courts of Justice and no order shall be made under CPR Part 30 for the transfer of any proceedings before the trial from the Royal Courts of Justice to a district registry.

Particulars to be included in claim form

Rule 3—(1) In the case of a claim form which begins civil proceedings against the Crown the contents of the claim form required by CPR rule 16.2 shall include a statement of the circumstances in which the Crown's liability is alleged to have arisen and as to the government department and officers of the Crown concerned.

(2) If in civil proceedings against the Crown a defendant considers that the claim form does not contain a sufficient statement as required by this rule, he may, before the expiration of the time limited for acknowledging service of the claim form, apply to the claimant by notice for a further and better statement containing such information as may be specified in the notice.

(3) Where a defendant gives a notice under this rule, the time limited for acknowledging service of the claim form shall not expire until 4 days after the defendant has notified the claimant in writing that the defendant is satisfied with the statement supplied in compliance with the notice or 4 days after the Court has, on the application of the claimant in accordance with CPR Part 23, decided that no further information as to the matters referred to in paragraph (1) is reasonably required.

(3A) An application notice under paragraph (3) shall be served on the defendant not less than 7 days before the hearing.

Service on the Crown

Rule 4—(1) Order 11 and any other provision of these rules relating to service out of the jurisdiction shall not apply in relation to the service of any process by which civil proceedings against the Crown are begun.

(2) Personal service of any document required to be served on the Crown for the purpose of or in connection with any civil proceedings is not requisite; but where the proceedings are by or against the Crown service on the Crown must be effected—

(*a*) by leaving the document at the office of the person who is in accordance with section 18 of the Crown Proceedings Act 1947, to be served, or of any agent whom that person has nominated for the purpose, but in either case with a member of the staff of that person or agent; or

(*b*) by posting it in a prepaid envelope addressed to the person who is to be served as aforesaid or to any such agent as aforesaid.

(3) Any document (other than a claim form) service of which is effected under paragraph 2(*a*) between 12 noon on a Saturday and midnight on the following day or after 4 in the afternoon on any other weekday shall, for the purpose of computing any period of time after service of that document, be deemed to have been served on the Monday following that Saturday or on the day following that other weekday, as the case may be.

(4) Where by virtue of these rules any document is required to be served on any person but is not required to be served personally and at the time when service is to be effected that person is in default as to acknowledgment of service or has no address for service, the document need not be served on that person unless the Court otherwise directs or any of these rules otherwise provides.

(5)

(*a*) No process shall be served or executed within the jurisdiction on a Sunday except, in case of urgency, with the permission of the Court.

(*b*) For the purposes of this rule ''process'' includes a claim form, judgment, application or other notice, order, petition, or warrant.

Counterclaim and set-off

Rule 6—(1) A person may not in any proceedings by the Crown make any counterclaim or claim a set-off in his statement of case if the proceedings are for the recovery of, or the counterclaim or set-off arises out of a right or claim to repayment in respect of, any taxes, duties or penalties.

(2) No counterclaim may be made, or set-off claimed in its statements of case, without the permission of the Court, by the Crown in proceedings against the Crown, or by any person in proceedings by the Crown—

(*a*) if the Crown is sued or sues in the name of a Government department and the subject-matter of the counterclaim or set-off does not relate to that department; or

(*b*) if the Crown is sued or sues in the name of the Attorney-General.

(3) Any application for permission under this rule must be made by in accordance with CPR Part 23.

Summary judgment

Rule 7—(1) No application shall be made against the Crown—

(*a*) under CPR Part 24 ...[1] in any proceedings against the Crown,

(*b*) for summary judgment on a counterclaim under CPR Part 24 in any proceedings by the Crown.

(2) Where an application is made by the Crown under CPR Part 24 ...[1] the affidavit or witness statement required in support of the application must be made by—

(*a*) the solicitor acting for the Crown, or

(*b*) an officer duly authorised by the solicitor so acting or by the department concerned

and the witness statement or affidavit shall be sufficient if it states that in the belief of the witness the applicant is entitled to the relief claimed and there is no defence to the claim or part of a claim to which the application relates or no defence except as to the amount of any damages claimed.

Amendments—[1] Words in paras (1), (2) revoked by the Civil Procedure (Amendment) Rules, SI 1999/1008 r 39(*a*) with effect from 26 April 1999.

Summary applications to the Court in certain revenue matters

Rule 8—(1) This rule applies to applications under section 14 of the Crown Proceedings Act 1947.

(2) An application to which this rule applies shall be made by claim form.

(3) The person from whom any account or information or payment is claimed or by whom any books are required to be produced must be made a defendant to the application.

(4) A claim form under this rule—

(*a*) must be entitled in the matter or matters out of which the need for the application arises and in the matter of the Crown Proceedings Act 1947; and

(*b*) must refer to the enactment under which the account or information or payment or the production of books is claimed and, where information is claimed, must show (by appropriate questions or otherwise) what information is required.

(5) Upon any application to which this rule applies, a witness statement or affidavit by a duly authorised officer of the Government department concerned setting out the state of facts upon which the application is based and stating that he has reason to think that those facts exist shall be evidence of those facts; and if evidence is filed disputing any of those facts, further evidence may be filed and the Court may either decide the matter upon the witness statements or affidavits (after any cross-examination that may have been ordered) or may direct that it be decided by oral evidence in Court.

(6) An order in favour of the Crown on an application to which this rule applies shall, unless the Court otherwise determines, name a time within which each of its terms is to be complied with.

(8) Nothing in this rule shall, in relation to any case in which the only remedy claimed by the Crown is the payment of money, be construed as requiring the Crown to proceed by way of an application to which this rule applies or as preventing the Crown from availing itself of any other procedure which is open to it under these rules.

Note—This Order does not include rule 8(7).

Joinder of Commissioners of Inland Revenue

Rule 8A Nothing in CPR rule 19.3 shall be construed as enabling the Commissioners of Inland Revenue to be added as a party to any proceedings except with their consent signified in writing or in such manner as may be authorised.

Judgment in default

Rule 9—(1) Except with the permission of the Court, no judgment in default under CPR Part 12 shall be entered against the Crown in civil proceedings against the Crown.

(2) Except with the permission of the Court, a defendant shall not enter default judgment against the Crown as a third party.

(3) An application for permission under this rule may be made by an application in accordance with CPR Part 23 and the application notice must be served not less than 7 days before the return day.

Third party notices

Rule 10—(1) A Part 20 claim for service on the Crown, where the Crown is not already a party shall not be issued without the permission of the Court, and the application for the grant of such permission must be made by application in accordance with CPR Part 23, and the application notice must be served on the claimant and the Crown.

(2) Permission to issue such a claim for service on the Crown shall not be granted unless the Court is satisfied that the Crown is in possession of all such information as it reasonably requires as to the circumstances in which it is alleged that the liability of the Crown has arisen and as to the departments and officers of the Crown concerned.

Interpleader: application for order against Crown

Rule 11 No order shall be made against the Crown under Order 17, rule 5 (3) except [by application, notice of which must be][1] served not less than 7 days before the return day.

Amendments—[1] Words substituted by the Civil Procedure (Amendment) Rules, SI 1999/1008 r 39(*b*) with effect from 26 April 1999.

Disclosure and further information

Rule 12—(3) Where in any proceedings an order of the Court directs that a list of documents made in answer to an order for disclosure against the Crown shall be verified by witness statement or affidavit, the witness statement or affidavit shall be made by such officer of the Crown as the Court may direct.

(4) Where in any proceedings an order is made under the said section 28 for further information to be provided by the Crown, the Court shall direct by what officer of the Crown the further information is to be provided.

Place of trial

Rule 13—(1) Civil proceedings by or against the Crown shall not, except with the consent of the Crown, be directed to be tried elsewhere than at the Royal Courts of Justice.

(2) Nothing in any of these rules shall prejudice the right of the Crown to demand a local venue for the trial of any proceedings in which the Attorney General has waived his right to a trial at bar.

Evidence

Rule 14—(1) Civil proceedings against the Crown may be instituted to perpetuate any testimony in any case in which the Crown is alleged to have an interest or estate in the honour, title, dignity or office or property in question.

(2) For the avoidance of doubt it is hereby declared that any powers exercisable by the Court in regard to the taking of evidence are exercisable in proceedings by or against the Crown as they are exercisable in proceedings between subjects.

Execution and satisfaction of orders

Rule 15—[(1) Nothing in—

(*a*) CPR Parts [69][2] to 73; and

(*b*) Orders 45 to 47 ... and 52,

shall apply in respect of any order against the Crown.][1]

(2) An application under the proviso to subsection (1) of section 25 of the Crown Proceedings Act 1947, for a direction that a separate certificate shall be issued under that subsection with respect to the costs (if any) ordered to be paid to the applicant, may be made to the Court without notice being served on any other party.

(3) Any such certificate must be in Form No. 95 or 96 in the relevant Practice Direction, whichever is appropriate.

Amendments—[1] Para (1) substituted by the Civil Procedure (Amendment) Rules, SI 2001/2792 rr 1(*c*), 9(*a*), 24 with effect from 25 March 2002 (except in relation to any enforcement proceedings which are issued before that date).

[2] In sub-para (1)(*a*), figure substituted; and in sub-para (1)(*b*), figure revoked by the Civil Procedure (Amendment) Rules, SI 2002/2058 r 31(*a*) with effect from 2 December 2002.

Attachment of debts, etc

Rule 16—(1) No order—

(*a*) for the attachment of debts [under CPR Part 72][3], or

(*b*) for the appointment of a sequestrator under Order 45, or

(*c*) for the appointment of a receiver under [CPR Part 69][2],

shall be made or have effect in respect of any money due or accruing due, or alleged to be due or accruing due, from the Crown.

(1A) No application shall be made under paragraph (2) unless the order of the court to be enforced is for a sum of money amounting in value to at least £50.

(2) Every application to the Court for an order under section 27 (1) of the Crown Proceedings Act 1947 restraining any person from receiving money payable to him by the Crown and directing payment of the money to the applicant or some other person must be made by claim form and, unless the Court otherwise directs, served—

(*a*) on the Crown at least 15 days before the return day, and

(*b*) on the person to be restrained or his solicitor at least 7 days after the claim form has been served on the Crown and at least 7 days before the return day.

(2A) An application under paragraph (2) must be supported by a witness statement or affidavit—

(*a*) setting out the facts giving rise to the application;

(*b*) stating the name and last known address of the person to be restrained;

(*c*) identifying the order to be enforced and stating the amount of such order and the amount remaining unpaid under it at the time of the application, and

(*d*) identifying the particular debt from the Crown in respect of which the application is made.

(2B) Where the debt from the Crown in respect of which the application is made is money payable by the Crown to a person on account of a deposit in the National Savings Bank, the witness statement or affidavit must state the name and address of the branch ...[1] at which the account is believed to be held and the number of that account or, if it be the case, that all or part of this information is not known to the witness.

(2C) A Master, the Admiralty Registrar and a district judge of the Family Division shall have power to hear an application under paragraph (2).

SIs

[(3) CPR rule 72.8 shall apply in relation to such an application as is mentioned in paragraph (2) for an order restraining a person from receiving money payable to him by the Crown as that rule applies to an application under CPR rule 72.2 for a third party debt order, except that the court shall not have power to order enforcement to issue against the Crown][3].

Amendments—[1] Words in para (2B) repealed by the Postal Services Act 2000 (Consequential Modifications No 1) Order, SI 2001/1149 art 3(2), Sch 2 with effect from 26 March 2001.
[2] In sub-para (1)(*c*), words substituted by the Civil Procedure (Amendment) Rules, SI 2002/2058 r 31(*b*) with effect from 2 December 2002.
[3] Words in para (1) substituted, and para (3) substituted, by the Civil Procedure (Amendment No 4) Rules, SI 2001/2792 r 9(*b*) with effect from 25 March 2002, except in relation to any enforcement proceedings issued before that date.

Proceedings relating to postal packets

Rule 17—(1) An application by any person under [section 92 of the Postal Services Act 2000][1], for permission to bring proceedings in the name of the sender or addressee of a postal packet or his personal representatives must be made by claim form in the Queen's Bench Division.

(2) The Crown and the person in whose name the applicant seeks to bring proceedings must be made defendants to a claim under this rule.

Amendment—[1] Words substituted by the Postal Services Act 2000 (Consequential Modifications No 1) Order, SI 2001/1149 art 3(1), Sch 1 para 123(1), (2) with effect from 26 March 2001.

Applications under ss 17 and 29 of Crown Proceedings Act

Rule 18—(1) Every application to the Court under section 17 (4) of the Crown Proceedings Act 1947, must be made by claim form.

(2) An application such as is referred to in section 29 (2) of the Crown Proceedings Act 1947, may be made to the Court at any time before trial in accordance with CPR Part 23, or may be made at the trial of the proceedings.

RSC ORDER 91

REVENUE PROCEEDINGS

Amendment—Revoked by the Civil Procedure (Amendment No 4) Rules, SI 2003/2113 r 19(*a*) with effect from 6 October 2003.

1998/3173

Finance Act 1994, Section 199, (Appointed Day) Order 1998

Made by the Treasury under FA 1994 s 199(3)

Made . . . . *17 December 1998*

Commentary—*Simon's Direct Tax Service* **D2.801**.

1 This Order may be cited as the Finance Act 1994, Section 199, (Appointed Day) Order 1998.

2 The day appointed for the purposes of Chapter III of Part IV of the Finance Act 1994 (corporation tax self-assessment) is 1st July 1999.

1998/3175

Corporation Tax (Instalment Payments) Regulations 1998

Made by the Treasury under TMA 1970 ss 59DA(8) and 59E, TA 1988 s 826A and FA 1998 s 30

Made . . . . *17 December 1998*
Laid before the House of Commons . . . . . *17 December 1998*
Coming into force . . . . *7 January 1999*

Commentary—*Simon's Direct Tax Service* **D2.842**.
Revenue and other press releases—IR Tax Bulletin April 2001 p 831 (discussion of some practical issues regarding quarterly interest payments and group payment arrangements).

Citation, commencement and effect

1—(1) These Regulations may be cited as the Corporation Tax (Instalment Payments) Regulations 1998 and shall come into force on 7th January 1999.

(2) These Regulations have effect in relation to accounting periods of companies ending on or after 1st July 1999.

Interpretation

2—(1) In these Regulations unless the context otherwise requires—
"the Board" means the Commissioners of Inland Revenue;

"large company" has the meaning given by regulation 3;
"Management Act" means the Taxes Management Act 1970;
"Schedule 18" means Schedule 18 to the Finance Act 1998;
"the Taxes Act" means the Income and Corporation Taxes Act 1988.

(2) References in these Regulations to profits of a company in any accounting period are references to the aggregate of—

(*a*) the amount of profits chargeable to corporation tax shown in the company's assessment or determination under Schedule 18 for that accounting period, and on which corporation tax finally falls to be charged, and

(*b*) the amount of the company's franked investment income in that period other than franked investment income which the company (if a member of a group) receives from companies within the group within the meaning of section 13(7) of the Taxes Act.

(3) References in these Regulations to the total liability of a company for an accounting period are references to the amount of tax payable for that period by the company as calculated in accordance with paragraph 8(1) of Schedule 18, reduced by the amount (if any) of deductions from payments made in that period to which section 559 of the Taxes Act (payments to sub-contractors) applies.

Large companies

3—(1) Subject to [paragraphs (2) to (3A),][2], a large company is a company whose profits in any accounting period exceed the upper relevant maximum amount in force at the end of that period.

(2) A company is not a large company as respects an accounting period if the amount of its total liability for that period does not exceed [£10,000][1] or, where the accounting period is less than twelve months, that amount proportionately reduced.

(3) A company is not a large company as respects an accounting period if—

(*a*) its profits for that accounting period do not exceed £10,000,000, and

(*b*) apart from this paragraph, it was not a large company in the twelve months preceding that accounting period.

[(3A) Any question whether a company is, or is not, a large company as respects an accounting period beginning on or after 17th April 2002 shall, so far as not falling to be determined by reference to the company's total liability, be determined as it would have been determined apart from section 501A of the Taxes Act (supplementary charge in respect of ring fence trades).][2]

(4) In paragraph (1) "upper relevant maximum amount" shall be construed in accordance with section 13 of the Taxes Act but disregarding section 434(3A) and (3B) of the Taxes Act and section 88(4) of the Finance Act 1989 (amounts to be left out of account in determining profits for the purposes of section 13 of the Taxes Act).

(5) Subsections (3) to (8) of section 13 of the Taxes Act (reduction of lower and upper relevant maximum amounts by reference to whether a company has one or more associated companies and length of company's accounting period) shall apply so as to reduce the amount specified in paragraph (3)(*a*) in accordance with those subsections as they apply so as to reduce the lower and upper relevant maximum amounts, except that—

(*a*) the number of associated companies referred to in subsection (3) of that section shall be determined by reference to the number existing at the end of the immediately preceding accounting period of the company or, if there is no immediately preceding accounting period or the immediately preceding accounting period did not end on the day before the accounting period concerned commenced, by reference to the number existing at the commencement of the accounting period concerned;

(*b*) section 434(3A) and (3B) of the Taxes Act and section 88(4) of the Finance Act 1989 shall be disregarded.

(6) For the purposes of paragraph (3)(*b*) a company shall be treated as not being a large company in the period of twelve months preceding the accounting period in question in either of the following circumstances—

(*a*) during any part of the period of twelve months it either did not exist or did not have an accounting period;

(*b*) a relevant accounting period of the company either falls within or ends in that period of twelve months.

(7) In paragraph (6) "relevant accounting period" means an accounting period as respects which, by virtue of the provisions of this regulation other than paragraph (3), the company was not a large company.

Amendments—[1] Sum in para (2) substituted by the Corporation Tax (Instalment Payments) (Amendment) Regulations, SI 2000/892 reg 2, with effect for accounting periods ending on or after 1 July 2000.
[2] In sub-para (1), words substituted for the words "paragraphs (2) and (3)" and sub-para (3A) inserted by FA 2002 s 92(5)–(7).

Instalment payments—transitional provision

4—(1) In relation to an accounting period of a large company ending on or after 1st July 1999 but before 1st July 2000—

(*a*) an amount equal to 60 per cent of the company's total liability for that period shall be treated as becoming due and payable in accordance with regulation 5;

(*b*) the balance of the company's total liability for that period shall be payable in accordance with section 59D(1) of the Management Act, that is, on the day following the expiry of nine months from the end of the accounting period ("the due and payable date").

(2) In relation to an accounting period of a large company ending on or after 1st July 2000 but before 1st July 2001—

(*a*) an amount equal to 72 per cent of the company's total liability for that period shall be treated as becoming due and payable in accordance with regulation 5;

(*b*) the balance of the company's total liability for that period shall be payable on the due and payable date.

(3) In relation to an accounting period of a large company ending on or after 1st July 2001 but before 1st July 2002—

(*a*) an amount equal to 88 per cent of the company's total liability for that period shall be treated as becoming due and payable in accordance with regulation 5;

(*b*) the balance of the company's total liability for that period shall be payable on the due and payable date.

Instalment payments—principal provision

5—(1) Save as regards any amount falling within regulation 4(1)(*b*), (2)(*b*) or (3)(*b*), amounts in respect of the total liability of a large company for an accounting period shall be treated as becoming due and payable as follows.

(2) Subject to paragraph (4), the amount of the company's total liability for that period or, as the case may be, the specified percentage amount shall be treated as becoming due and payable in instalments (not exceeding four) on the dates specified in paragraph (3).

(3) The first instalment payment shall be treated as becoming due and payable on the date which is six months and thirteen days from the start of the accounting period.

The final instalment payment shall be treated as becoming due and payable on the date which is three months and fourteen days from the end of the accounting period.

An additional instalment payment or additional instalment payments shall, where the length of the accounting period so allows, each be treated as becoming due and payable on the date which is three months after the date of the immediately preceding instalment payment.

(4) Where the length of the accounting period is such that the date which is three months and fourteen days from the end of the accounting period falls earlier than the date which is six months and thirteen days from the start of the accounting period, the amount of the company's total liability for that period or, as the case may be, the specified percentage amount shall be treated as becoming due and payable on the date which is three months and fourteen days from the end of the accounting period.

(5) Where in accordance with paragraph (2) amounts in respect of the amount of the company's total liability for an accounting period or in respect of the specified percentage amount are treated as becoming due and payable in instalments, the amount treated as becoming due and payable on any instalment payment date shall be calculated in accordance with paragraphs (6) to (8) and by reference to the formula—

$$3 \times \frac{CTI}{n}$$

where—

CTI is the amount of the company's total liability for that accounting period or the specified percentage amount, and

n is the number of whole months falling within that accounting period plus the appropriate decimal.

(6) The amount treated as becoming due and payable on the first instalment payment date is the smaller of CTI and the amount resulting from the formula specified in paragraph (5).

(7) The amount treated as becoming due and payable on each subsequent instalment payment date other than the final instalment payment date is the smaller of—

(*a*) the balance of the company's total liability for that accounting period or of the specified percentage amount carried forward from the immediately preceding instalment payment date, and

(*b*) the amount resulting from the formula specified in paragraph (5).

(8) The amount treated as becoming due and payable on the final instalment payment date is the balance of the company's total liability for that accounting period or of the specified percentage amount carried forward from the immediately preceding instalment payment date.

(9) In this regulation—

"the appropriate decimal" is a decimal, calculated to two places rounded arithmetically where necessary, representing the number of days in the accounting period falling outside the whole months falling within that period and corresponding to the fraction of which the numerator is the number of those days and the denominator is 30;

"the specified percentage amount" means an amount equal to the percentage specified in regulation 4(1)(*a*), (2)(*a*) or (3)(*a*), as the case may be.

Repayment of amounts in respect of a large company's total liability for an accounting period

6—(1) This regulation applies where a large company—

(*a*) has paid an amount or amounts by way of instalments in respect of its total liability for an accounting period in accordance with regulation 5, and

(*b*) subsequently has grounds for believing that, by reason of a change in the circumstances of the company since the payment or payments were made—

(i) the amount of its total liability for that period is likely to be less than previously calculated, and

(ii) the aggregate amount so paid exceeds the aggregate amount ("the revised aggregate amount") that would have been treated as becoming due and payable by the relevant date having regard to the revised calculation of that liability.

(2) The company may, by notice given to an officer of the Board, make a claim to an officer of the Board for the repayment of so much of the aggregate amount so paid as in the company's view exceeds the revised aggregate amount.

(3) The notice under paragraph (2) must state—

(*a*) the amount which the company considers should be repaid, and

(*b*) the grounds referred to in paragraph (1)(*b*).

(4) If the company has appealed against an amendment of an assessment, or an assessment, in respect of the amount of its total liability for the accounting period concerned, and the appeal has not been finally determined, it may apply to the Commissioners to whom the appeal stands referred for a determination of the amount which should be repaid to the company pending determination of the amount of its total liability for that accounting period.

(5) Any claim under paragraph (2) or application under paragraph (4) shall be heard and determined in the same way as an appeal.

(6) If the company makes an application under section 55(3) or (4) of the Management Act (application to postpone payment pending determination of appeal), that application may be combined with an application under paragraph (4).

(7) In paragraph (1)(*b*) "the relevant date" means the date on which a claim under paragraph (2) is made.

(8) Section 59DA of the Management Act (claim for repayment in advance of liability being established) shall not apply in any case where this regulation applies.

Interest on unpaid amounts of a large company's total liability for an accounting period

7—(1) Section 87A of the Management Act shall apply in relation to any unpaid amount in respect of the total liability of a large company for an accounting period, with the modifications specified in paragraphs (2) to (5).

(2) After subsection (1) there shall be inserted the following subsection—

"(1A) An amount or amounts treated as becoming due and payable in respect of the total liability of a large company for an accounting period in accordance with regulation 5 of the Corporation Tax (Instalment Payments) Regulations 1998 shall carry interest at the rate applicable under section 178 of the Finance Act 1989 from the date or dates specified in that regulation as the date or dates when that amount or those amounts are treated as becoming due and payable until payment."

(3) In subsection (2)—

(*a*) for the words "Subsection (1) above applies" there shall be substituted "Subsections (1) and (1A) above apply";

(*b*) for the words "that subsection" there shall be substituted "those subsections".

(4) In subsection (3) there shall be added at the end the words ", and the reference in subsection (1A) above to the date or dates when an amount or amounts are treated as becoming due and payable in respect of the total liability of a large company for an accounting period is a reference to the date or dates when that amount or those amounts are treated as having become due and payable by the company".

(5) After subsection (9) there shall be added—

"(10) In subsections (1A) and (3) above "large company" has the meaning given by regulation 3 of the Corporation Tax (Instalment Payments) Regulations 1998."

Interest on overpaid amounts of a company's total liability for an accounting period

8—(1) Section 826 of the Taxes Act shall apply in relation to—

(*a*) an amount or amounts paid by a large company in accordance with regulation 5 in respect of its total liability for an accounting period, and

(*b*) an amount or amounts paid by a company that is not a large company in an accounting period in respect of its total liability for that accounting period, where the payment is made prior to the day following the expiry of nine months from the end of that accounting period,

with the modifications specified in paragraphs (2) and (3).

(2) In subsection (1)—

(*a*) after paragraph (*c*) there shall be inserted "[or

(*d*) the total amount paid by a large company (as defined in regulation 3 of the Corporation Tax (Instalment Payment) Regulations 1998) up to a point in time in respect of its total liability for an accounting period in accordance with regulation 5 of those Regulations exceeds the amount that is treated as having become due and payable by the company for that period at that time in accordance with that regulation, or

(*e*) an amount paid by a company that is not a large company in an accounting period in respect of the amount of its total liability for that period is paid prior to the day following the expiry of nine months from the end of that period ('the normal due date'),";

(*b*) for the words "the repayment or payment shall" there shall be substituted the words "or, in a case to which paragraph (*d*) above applies, until the date on which the excess amount arising as mentioned in that paragraph is extinguished or, in a case to which paragraph (*e*) above applies, until the normal due date, the repayment or payment or excess amount shall"

(3) After subsections (3) there shall be inserted—

"(3A) In relation to an excess amount in respect of a company's total liability arising as mentioned in subsection (1)(*d*) above, the material date is the date on which the first instalment payment for the accounting period concerned is treated as becoming due as mentioned in regulation 5(3) of the Corporation Tax (Instalment Payments) Regulations 1998 or, if later, the date on which the excess amount arises.

(3B) In relation to a case falling within subsection (1)(*e*) above—

(*a*) if the payment for the accounting period concerned was made on or before the date which, if the company had been a large company, would have been the date on which the first instalment payment for that accounting period would have been treated as becoming due as mentioned in regulation 5(3) of the Regulations referred to in subsection (3A) above, the material date is that date, or

(*b*) if the payment for the accounting period concerned was made later than the date referred to in paragraph (*a*) above, the material date is the date on which that payment was made."

Consequential amendment of section 102 of the Finance Act 1989

9—(1) Section 102 of the Finance Act 1989 (surrender of company tax refund within group) shall apply [with the modifications specified in paragraphs (2) to (4) in any case where a tax refund falls to be made to the surrendering company in respect of an amount paid in respect of its total liability for an accounting period and—

(*a*) either the surrendering company or the recipient company referred to in that section is a large company as respects that accounting period, or

(*b*) both the surrendering company and the recipient company so referred to are large companies as respects that accounting period][1].

(2) In subsection (3), in the definition of "tax refund relating to an accounting period"—

(*a*) the word "or" immediately following paragraph (*b*) shall be omitted;

[(*b*) after paragraph (*c*) of that definition there shall be added "or

(*d*) the repayment of the whole or any part of any amount paid by way of an instalment under the Corporation Tax (Instalment Payments) Regulations 1998 in respect of the company's total liability for the period."][1].

[(3) In subsection (5) after the word "refund" there shall be inserted the words "other than a refund of instalment corporation tax".][1]

[(4) After subsection (5) there shall be inserted the following subsections—

"(5A) In subsection (4) above "the relevant date", in relation to a refund of instalment corporation tax, means—

(*a*) in so far as the refund falls to be treated in accordance with subsections (5C) to (5E) below as consisting of a repayment of the whole or any part of a payment made on or before the earliest due date, that date; and

(*b*) in so far as the refund falls to be treated in accordance with those subsections as consisting of the repayment of the whole or any part of a payment made after the earliest due date, the date on which the payment was made.

(5B) For the purposes of subsection (5A) above the earliest due date, in relation to a refund of instalment corporation tax, is—

(*a*) where the surrendering company is a large company for the relevant accounting period, the earliest date on which any amount is treated as having become due and payable by that company under regulation 5 of the Corporation Tax (Instalment Payments) Regulations 1998 in respect of that company's total liability for that period; and

(*b*) where the surrendering company is not a large company for that accounting period, the date that would have been the earliest due date under paragraph (*a*) above had it been a large company for that period.

(5C) For the purposes of subsection (5A) above the surrendering company shall, at the same time as the giving of the notice under subsection (2) above in the case of any refund of instalment corporation tax relating to any accounting period, give notice to the inspector identifying the extent to which it requires the refund to be treated as consisting of amounts comprised in any payment or payments made for that period.

(5D) Where, in a case to which subsection (5C) above applies, the inspector notifies the surrendering company that the amount of the refund of instalment corporation tax relating to the accounting period is less than the aggregate of the amounts identified under that subsection, that company shall, not later than thirty days after the notification, give a revised notice under that subsection to the inspector.

(5E) Where, in a case to which subsection (5D) above applies—

(*a*) a notification has been given to the surrendering company under that subsection, and

(*b*) the surrendering company fails to give a revised notice in accordance with the requirements of that subsection,

the same consequences shall follow as if no notice had been given in accordance with subsection (2) above in relation to the refund.

(5F) In this section—

(*a*) references to a refund of instalment corporation tax are references to any such refund of tax for any accounting period as falls in relation to that accounting period within paragraph (*d*) of the definition of "tax refund relating to an accounting period" in subsection (3) above;

(*b*) references to a large company shall be construed in accordance with regulation 3 of the Corporation Tax (Instalment Payments) Regulations 1998;

(*c*) references to the total liability of a company for an accounting period shall be construed in accordance with regulation 2(3) of those Regulations."][1]

Revenue and other press releases—IR Tax Bulletin April 2001 p 831 (discussion of the effect of a Group Payment Arrangement (GPA) on the operation of this regulation and FA 1989 s 102).

Amendments—[1] Words in sub-paras (1), (2), and sub-paras (3)—(5), substituted by the Corporation Tax (Instalment Payments) (Amendment) Regulations, SI 1999/1929 regs 1, 3 with effect for accounting periods ending after 30 June 1999.

Information to be provided to the Board

10—(1) The Board may, at any time following the relevant date, by notice require any company to furnish them, within such time (not being less than thirty days) as may be provided by the notice—

(*a*) such information relating to the computation of any amount paid in respect of the company's total liability for an accounting period in accordance with regulation 5 as they may reasonably require for ascertaining whether the amount of the payment was consistent with the quality and quantity of the information available to the company, at the time the payment was due, regarding its total liability for that period;

(*b*) such information as they may reasonably require for ascertaining the reasons for non-payment by the company at any time in accordance with regulation 5 of any amount in respect of the company's total liability for an accounting period;

(*c*) such information as they may reasonably require for ascertaining whether a claim for repayment of an amount under regulation 6(2) was properly made.

(2) In paragraph (1) "the relevant date" means the date specified in paragraph 14(1) of Schedule 18 as the filing date for the company tax return for the accounting period concerned.

Revenue & other press releases—IR 8-6-99 (the Revenue will only use their information powers contained in this regulation where there are indications that a company may have deliberately or recklessly failed to comply with its payment obligations, or fraudulently or negligently made a claim for repayment).

Production of records

11—(1) The Board may, at any time following the relevant date, by notice require a company to produce, within such time (not being less than thirty days) as may be provided by the notice—

(*a*) all such books, documents and other records in its possession or power relating to the computation of any amount paid in respect of the company's total liability for an accounting period in accordance with regulation 5 as they may reasonably require for ascertaining whether the amount of the payment was consistent with the quality and quantity of the information available to the company, at the time the payment was due, regarding its total liability for that period;

(*b*) all such books, documents and other records in its possession or power as they may reasonably require for ascertaining the reasons for non-payment by the company at any time in accordance with regulation 5 of any amount in respect of the company's total liability for an accounting period;

(*c*) all such books, documents and other records in its possession or power as they may reasonably require for ascertaining whether a claim for repayment of an amount under regulation 6(2) was properly made.

(2) In complying with a notice under paragraph (1) copies of books, documents and other records may be produced instead of originals, but—

(*a*) the copies must be photographic or other facsimiles, and

(*b*) an officer of the Board may require the original to be made available for inspection in accordance with regulation 12.

(3) In paragraph (1) "the relevant date" has the same meaning as in regulation 10.

Revenue & other press releases—IR 8-6-99 (the Revenue will only use their information powers contained in this regulation where there are indications that a company may have deliberately or recklessly failed to comply with its payment obligations, or fraudulently or negligently made a claim for repayment).

Inspection of records

12—(1) An officer of the Board authorised to do so may, at any time following the relevant date, require a company [by notice][1] to make available for inspection, at such time as that officer may reasonably require, all such books, documents and other records in its possession or power as could be required to be produced by notice by the Board under regulation 11.

(2) Where records are maintained by computer the officer making the inspection shall be provided by the company with all the facilities necessary for obtaining information from them.

(3) In paragraph (1) "the relevant date" has the same meaning as in regulation 10.

Revenue & other press releases—IR 8-6-99 (the Revenue will only use their information powers contained in this regulation where there are indications that a company may have deliberately or recklessly failed to comply with its payment obligations, or fraudulently or negligently made a claim for repayment).

Amendments—[1] Words in para (1) inserted by the Corporation Tax (Instalment Payments) (Amendment) Regulations, SI 1999/1929 regs 1, 4 with effect for accounting periods ending after 30 June 1999.

Penalty for unpaid tax

13 The circumstances prescribed for the purposes of section 59E(4) of the Management Act (penalty not exceeding twice the amount of interest charged by virtue of regulation 7 on any unpaid amount in respect of the total liability of a company for an accounting period) are where—

(*a*) the company, or a person acting on its behalf, deliberately or recklessly fails to pay the amount in question in accordance with regulation 5;

(*b*) the company, or a person acting on its behalf, fraudulently or negligently makes a claim for repayment of an amount under regulation 6(2).

Revenue & other press releases—IR 8-6-99 (the Revenue will seek a penalty under TMA 1970 s 59E(4) in only the most serious cases involving flagrant abuse of the regulations).

Anti-avoidance provision

14—(1) This regulation applies where, on or after 25th November 1997 and before 30th June 2002—

(*a*) a company does one or both of the following, that is to say—

(i) otherwise than in any of the circumstances specified in paragraph (6), causes the date or dates on which any of its relevant accounting periods begins or ends to be changed,

(ii) otherwise than in either of the circumstances specified in paragraph (7), enters into any arrangements or transactions the effect of which is to transfer the amount of its taxable profits to another company which belongs to the same group, other than a company specified in paragraph (8), and

(*b*) the result is that, on the assumptions specified in paragraph (9), an amount or amounts of corporation tax in respect of the taxable profits of the company for any part of an accounting period beginning after 1st July 1998 and ending on or before 30th June 2002 becomes, or is treated as becoming, due and payable, in accordance with regulations 4 and 5 or section 59D(1) of the Management Act, on a date or dates ("the actual date or dates") later than the date or dates ("the hypothetical date or dates") on which, but for the action taken by the company as mentioned in sub-paragraph (*a*), they would have become, or would be treated as having become, due and payable in accordance with those regulations or that section.

(2) The company shall be liable to pay to the Board, in respect of the accounting period referred to in paragraph (1)(*b*), an amount computed in accordance with paragraph (3).

(3) The amount payable shall be computed—

(*a*) by reference to—

(i) the amount, or (as the case may be) the aggregate of the amounts, of corporation tax referred to in paragraph (1)(*b*), and

(ii) the interval of time elapsing between the hypothetical date or dates and the actual date or dates;

(*b*) so as to allow for accelerated as well as deferred amounts of corporation tax (but not to the extent that it results in an amount falling to be paid by the Board); and

(*c*) as if it were interest on the amount, or the aggregate of the amounts, of corporation tax referred to in paragraph (1)(*b*).

(4) Interest referred to in paragraph (3)(*c*)—

(*a*) shall be at the rate applicable under section 178 of the Finance Act 1989, and

(*b*) shall be treated as if it were tax charged and due and payable under an assessment.

(5) For the purposes of this regulation a relevant accounting period is an accounting period which, but for the action taken by the company as mentioned in paragraph (1)(*a*)(i)—

(*a*) would have ended on 25th November 1997 or after that date but on or before 30th June 2002, and

(*b*) would have been of twelve months duration and commenced immediately following the end of the previous accounting period.

(6) The circumstances specified in this paragraph for the purposes of paragraph (1)(*a*)(i) are where the change in question—

(*a*) derives from a decision made before, or facts in existence prior to, 25th November 1997; or

(*b*) arises as a result of the accounting period concerned ending by reason of—

(i) the occurrence of any of the events specified in paragraphs (*c*) to (*e*) of subsection (3) of section 12 of the Taxes Act, except where the event in question occurs by reason of the transfer of the company's activities to a company which belongs to the same group, or

(ii) the transfer of the whole or part of the [long-term][1] business of an insurance company to another company as mentioned in subsection (7A) of that section; or

(*c*) arises as a result of—

(i) a change in the ultimate control of the company giving rise to the alignment of the company's accounting period with that of its new ultimate parent company, where the alignment is effected prior to the end of the accounting period of the new ultimate parent company in which the change occurs, or

(ii) a notice by the company under section 224(2) of the Companies Act 1985 (specification of accounting reference date not later than nine months after the date of incorporation) giving rise to such alignment as is mentioned in paragraph (i).

(7) The circumstances specified in this paragraph for the purposes of paragraph (1)(*a*)(ii) are where—

(*a*) the accounting period of the company to whom the profits are transferred begins and ends on the same dates as the accounting period of the transferor company and the case is not one where the transferor company has effected a change falling within paragraph (1)(*a*)(i) in the date or dates of any of its relevant accounting periods;

(*b*) as a result of the transfer of profits, the profits of the transferor company for the accounting period in which the transfer is effected or for any subsequent accounting period are reduced by an amount not exceeding £5,000,000 or, where that accounting period is a period of less than twelve months, that amount proportionately reduced.

(8) The company specified in this paragraph for the purposes of paragraph (1)(*a*)(ii) is any company which—

(*a*) is resident outside the United Kingdom, and

(*b*) either—

(i) is not trading in the United Kingdom through a branch or agency, or

(ii) if so trading, is not a company in the case of which the taxable profits transferred form part of the taxable profits of that branch or agency.

(9) The assumptions specified in this paragraph for the purposes of paragraph (1) are that, if the company had not taken the action referred to in sub-paragraph (*a*) of that paragraph—

(*a*) reliefs available to the company or to the group to which the company belongs in calculating liability to corporation tax would have been allocated so as to result in that liability arising later rather than sooner,

(*b*) any profits covered or, as the case may be, not covered by reliefs would similarly have been covered or not covered, and

(*c*) in calculating the amount or amounts of corporation tax which would have become due and payable, or would be treated as having become due and payable on the hypothetical date or dates, not more than twelve months' taxable profits would have been allocated to any of the years falling within regulation 4, that is, the year from 1st July 1999 to 30th June 2000, the year from 1st July 2000 to 30th June 2001, and the year from 1st July 2001 to 30th June 2002, allocating taxable profits for actual accounting periods before taxable profits for relevant accounting periods.

(10) In calculating, for the purposes of this regulation, the hypothetical date or dates, it shall be assumed that—

(*a*) where necessary, taxable profits are apportioned between a company's accounting periods (including its relevant accounting periods) on a time basis or, where that basis would be unjust and unreasonable, on such basis as would be just and reasonable;

(*b*) those dates are determined as if the taxable profits concerned were the only taxable profits for an accounting period.

(11) In this regulation—

(*a*) "control" shall be construed in accordance with section 416 of the Taxes Act;

(*b*) "group" means a company which has one or more 51 per cent subsidiaries together with that or those subsidiaries;

(*c*) "hypothetical date or dates" shall be construed in accordance with paragraph (1)(*b*);

(*d*) the reference in paragraph (6)(*c*) to a change in the ultimate control of the company ("the relevant company") is a reference to the situation arising where—

(i) the company which was previously not under the control of any other company in the group ("the ultimate parent company"), while retaining control of the relevant company, itself comes under the control of another company ("the new ultimate parent company") otherwise than as a result of a reorganisation, or

(ii) the relevant company ceases to be controlled by the ultimate parent company and comes under the control of another company ("the new ultimate parent company") which is not under the control of any other company in the group, or

(iii) otherwise than as a result of a reorganisation, the relevant company comes under the control of a company which is not itself under the control of any other company;

and the reference in paragraph (6)(*c*) to "new ultimate parent company" shall be construed accordingly;

(*e*) references to "51 per cent subsidiary" shall be construed in accordance with section 838(1)(*a*) of the Taxes Act.

Amendments—[1] Word in sub-para (6)(*b*)(ii) substituted by the Financial Services and Markets Act 2000 (Consequential Amendments) (Taxes) Order, SI 2001/3629 art 181 with effect from 1 December 2001, immediately after the coming into force of the Financial Services and Markets Act 2000 ss 411, 432(1), Sch 20 (and SI 2001/3629 Pts 1 and 2).

Insurance companies and friendly societies—supplementary provision

15—(1) This regulation applies where—

(*a*) an insurance company or friendly society is entitled to a provisional repayment under Schedule 19AB to the Taxes Act (including a provisional repayment under that Schedule as modified by the Friendly Societies (Provisional Repayment for Exempt Business) Regulations 1993),

(*b*) an amount of corporation tax ("the relevant amount") is treated as becoming due and payable in accordance with regulation 5 of these Regulations on the date which is the fourteenth day after the end of the provisional repayment period to which the provisional repayment relates, and

(*c*) the whole or part of the provisional repayment is set off against the relevant amount.

(2) For the purposes of calculating—

(*a*) the amount of interest (if any) on the provisional repayment, and

(*b*) the amount of interest (if any) payable on the relevant amount,

the amount so set off shall be treated, unless the company elects otherwise, as—

(i) a provisional repayment under Schedule 19AB to the Taxes Act, and

(ii) a payment on account of the relevant amount,

deemed, in each case, to have been made on the date referred to in paragraph (1)(*b*).

1998/3177
European Single Currency (Taxes) Regulations 1998

Made by the Treasury under FA 1993 ss 93(1) and (6), 94(1), (2), (3) and (11) and 95(1), (2) and (3) and FA 1998 s 163

Made . . . . *17 December 1998*
Laid before the House of Commons . . . *17 December 1998*
Coming into force . . . . *1 January 1999*

ARRANGEMENT OF REGULATIONS

PART I
INTRODUCTORY

PART II
DEDUCTIBILITY OF COSTS OF EUROCONVERSION OF SHARES AND OTHER SECURITIES

PART III
EXCHANGE GAINS AND LOSSES, INTEREST RATE AND CURRENCY CONTRACTS AND OPTIONS, DEBT CONTRACTS AND OPTIONS, AND RELEVANT DISCOUNTED SECURITIES

PART IV
AGREEMENTS FOR SALE AND REPURCHASE OF SECURITIES

PART V
STOCK LENDING ARRANGEMENTS

PART VI
REPURCHASES AND STOCK LENDING—STAMP DUTY AND STAMP DUTY RESERVE TAX

PART VII
ACCRUED INCOME SCHEME

PART VIII
CHARGEABLE GAINS

PART I

INTRODUCTORY

Citation and commencement

1 These Regulations may be cited as the European Single Currency (Taxes) Regulations 1998 and shall come into force on 1st January 1999.

Interpretation

2—(1) In these Regulations unless the context otherwise requires—

"commodity or financial futures" has the meaning given by subsection (2)(*a*) of section 143 of the 1992 Act, and references in these Regulations to commodity or financial futures include references to a commodity or financial futures contract referred to in subsection (7)(*a*) or (*b*);

"debt", other than a debt on a security, includes a debt owed by a bank which is not in sterling and which is represented by a sum standing to the credit of a person in an account in the bank;

"derivative" means any commodity or financial futures or an option;

"ecu" shall be construed in accordance with section 95(5) of the Finance Act 1993;

"euro" means the single currency adopted or proposed to be adopted as its currency by a member State in accordance with the Treaty establishing the European Community;

"euroconversion" has the meaning given by regulation 3;

"long-term capital asset" and "long-term capital liability" have the meaning given in relation to both those expressions by section 143(4) of the Finance Act 1993;[1]

"member State" means a member State other than the United Kingdom;

"participating member State" means a member State that adopts the euro as its currency;

"qualifying contract" shall be construed in accordance with sections 147, 147A and 148 of the Finance Act 1994;[1]

"reconventioning" in relation to a relevant asset means a change, consequent on simple redenomination, in the terms of the asset as a result of which the new terms become aligned to the prevailing terms of equivalent marketable relevant assets denominated in euro;

"relevant asset" means a debt (whether or not a debt on a security), a long-term capital asset, a long-term capital liability, an option, a qualifying contract, or any commodity or financial futures;[1]

"renominalisation" in relation to a relevant asset means a change, consequent on simple redenomination, in the minimum nominal amount in which the asset can be held or traded to a new round amount;

"security" has the meaning given by section 132(3)(*b*) of the 1992 Act;

"simple redenomination" means the conversion of the currency in which an asset, liability, contract or instrument is expressed from the currency of a participating member State into euro, and any rounding of the resulting amount to the nearest euro cent;

"the Taxes Act" means the Income and Corporation Taxes Act 1988;

"the 1992 Act" means the Taxation of Chargeable Gains Act 1992.

(2) In these Regulations references to an option, without more, are references to an option to which section 144 or 144A of the 1992 Act applies.

Amendments—Definitions repealed by the European Single Currency (Taxes) (Amendment) Regulations, SI 2002/1971 with effect for accounting periods beginning after 30 September 2002.

Definition of euroconversion

3—(1) "Euroconversion" means—

(*a*) in relation to any currency, or an amount expressed in any currency, of a participating member State, the conversion or restating of that currency or that amount into euro and any rounding of the resulting amount within a euro;

(*b*) in relation to any asset, liability, contract or instrument—

(i) the simple redenomination of that asset, liability, contract or instrument, or

(ii) in the case of a relevant asset, the simple redenomination of that asset accompanied by either or both of renominalisation and reconventioning, or

(iii) the substitution (whether by way of exchange, conversion, replacement or otherwise) for the asset, liability, contract or instrument of an equivalent replacement asset, liability, contract or instrument.

(2) An equivalent replacement asset, liability, contract or instrument means an asset, liability, contract or instrument whose amount, terms and conditions are identical to what is reasonable to assume would be the amount, terms and conditions of the original asset, liability, contract or instrument were it to undergo a simple redenomination, or (in the case of a relevant asset) a simple redenomination accompanied by either or both of renominalisation and reconventioning.

(3) For the purposes of paragraphs (1) and (2) a simple redenomination is accompanied (in the case of a relevant asset) by renominalisation or reconventioning if either—

(*a*) the renominalisation or reconventioning is effected simultaneously, or

(*b*) it is effected within a period of time following the simple redenomination which is such as to enable it reasonably to be inferred that the renominalisation or reconventioning is associated with the simple redenomination.

PART II

DEDUCTIBILITY OF COSTS OF EUROCONVERSION OF SHARES AND OTHER SECURITIES

Commentary—*Simon's Direct Tax Service* **B3.1203, D4.408, D4.504.**

Interpretation

4 References in this Part of these Regulations to a euroconversion in relation to shares and other securities of a company ("the original shares and other securities") are references to a euroconversion that is effected solely by the issue of shares and other securities in replacement of the original shares and other securities.

Trading companies

5 Costs incurred in respect of a euroconversion of its shares or other securities by a company carrying on a trade shall be deductible in computing the amount of its profits chargeable to corporation tax under Case I of Schedule D as if those costs constituted money wholly and exclusively laid out or expended for the purposes of the trade within section 74(1)(*a*) of the Taxes Act.

Investment companies and insurance companies—deemed expenses of management

6—(1) Costs which—

(*a*) are incurred by an investment company or a company carrying on life assurance business in respect of a euroconversion of its shares or other securities, and

(*b*) except where the costs are referable to life assurance business of a company whose profits in relation to that business are charged to tax otherwise than under Case I of Schedule D, are not deductible under regulation 5,

shall be treated as sums disbursed as expenses of management to which section 75(1) of the Taxes Act (deduction in computing total profits of an investment company for an accounting period) applies.

(2) Costs incurred by a company carrying on life assurance business in respect of a euroconversion of its shares or other securities shall be deductible in computing the profits of that company chargeable to corporation tax under Case VI of Schedule D as if those costs were allowances falling to be made under Part II of the Capital Allowance Act 1990 and referred to in subsection (4) of section 434D of the Taxes Act; and accordingly those costs shall be apportioned in accordance with that subsection between the different classes of life assurance business carried on by that company.

(3) Section 76 of the Taxes Act (expenses of management: insurance companies) shall have effect as if the reference in subsection (1)(*d*) of that section (disallowance of certain expenses of management) to expenses referable to different classes of life assurance business included a reference to costs apportioned to those classes of business under paragraph (2).

(4) In this regulation—

"investment company" has the meaning given by section 130 of the Taxes Act;
"life assurance business" shall be construed in accordance with section 431(2) of the Taxes Act.

PART III

EXCHANGE GAINS AND LOSSES, INTEREST RATE AND CURRENCY CONTRACTS AND OPTIONS, DEBT CONTRACTS AND OPTIONS, AND RELEVANT DISCOUNTED SECURITIES

Commentary—*Simon's Direct Tax Service* B3.1805, 1807, D2.911, 925.

Deferral of unrealised gains

7—(1) Where, as a result of a euroconversion of a long-term capital asset or of a long-term capital liability, that asset ("the original long-term capital asset") or that liability ("the original long-term capital liability") is replaced by a new long-term capital asset or a new long-term capital liability—

(a) the new long-term capital asset or the new long-term capital liability shall be treated as if it were the same asset or liability as the original long-term capital asset or the original long-term capital liability, acquired when the original long-term capital asset or the original long-term capital liability was acquired; and

(b) any gain which accrued as respects the original long-term capital asset or the original long-term capital liability for the accrual period in which the euroconversion of that asset or liability took place shall, without prejudice to regulation 2 of the Exchange Gains and Losses (Deferral of Gains and Losses) Regulations 1994 (settlement and replacement of debts), be deemed to be unrealised, and sections 139 to 143 (apart from section 143(7)) of the Finance Act 1993 shall have effect accordingly.

(2) In paragraph (1) "accrual period" shall be construed in accordance with section 158(4) of the Finance Act 1993.

Amendment—Regulations 7–11 repealed by the European Single Currency (Taxes) (Amendment) Regulations, SI 2002/1971 regs 1, 2, 4 with effect for accounting periods beginning after 30 September 2002.

Interest rate contracts (including options)—change in rate of interest

8 Where, as a result of the adoption of the euro by a member State—

(a) there is a change in the variable rate of interest resulting in a change in the variable rate payment specified in a contract ("the original contract") in accordance with subsection (2) of section 149 of the Finance Act 1994, and

(b) the change in the variable rate payment is such as to result in the rescission of the original contract and the making of a new contract,

the new contract shall be treated for the purposes of that section as if it were the same contract as the original contract, made when the original contract was made.

Amendment—Regulations 7–11 repealed by the European Single Currency (Taxes) (Amendment) Regulations, SI 2002/1971 regs 1, 2, 4 with effect for accounting periods beginning after 30 September 2002.

Currency contracts (including options)—change in rate of interest

9 Where, as a result of the adoption of the euro by a member State—

(a) there is a change in the rate of interest specified in a currency contract ("the original contract") in accordance with subsection (3) of section 150 of the Finance Act 1994, and

(b) the change is such as to result in the rescission of the original contract and the making of a new contract,

the new contract shall be treated for the purposes of that section as if it were the same contract as the original contract, made when the original contract was made.

Amendment—Regulations 7–11 repealed by the European Single Currency (Taxes) (Amendment) Regulations, SI 2002/1971 regs 1, 2, 4 with effect for accounting periods beginning after 30 September 2002.

Currency contracts (including options)—conversion into euro

10—(1) This regulation applies in a case where, as a result of the adoption of the euro by member States—

(a) the amounts of both the currencies specified in a currency contract referred to in section 126 of the Finance Act 1993 ("section 126"), or in a currency contract referred to in section 150 of the Finance Act 1994 ("section 150"), are converted into euro, and

(b) the effect is that the currency contract ("the original currency contract") is rescinded and replaced by a new contract which, but for the adoption of the euro, would have been a currency contract.

(2) This regulation also applies in a case where—

(a) one of the currencies ("the former currency") specified in a currency contract referred to in section 126 or section 150 is in a currency other than euro and the other currency is either in euro or expressed to be in the single currency,

(b) as a result of the adoption of the euro by a member State, the former currency is converted into euro, and

(c) the effect is that the currency contract ("the original currency contract") is rescinded and replaced by a new contract which, but for the adoption of the euro, would have been a currency contract.

(3) In each of the cases referred to in paragraphs (1) and (2) the new contract shall be treated for the purposes of section 126 or, as the case may be, section 150 as if it were a currency contract and were the same contract as the original currency contract, made when the original contract was made.

Amendment—Regulations 7–11 repealed by the European Single Currency (Taxes) (Amendment) Regulations, SI 2002/1971 regs 1, 2 ,4 with effect for accounting periods beginning after 30 September 2002.

Debt contracts (including options)—conversion into euro

11—(1) Where as a result of the adoption of the euro by a member State—

(a) there is a euroconversion of the loan relationship to which, under a debt contract, a qualifying company has any entitlement, or is subject to any duty, to become a party, or

(b) a qualifying company has any entitlement, or is subject to any duty, to become treated as a person with rights and liabilities corresponding to those of a party to a loan relationship and there is a euroconversion of any of those rights and liabilities, and

(b) in either of the cases referred to in sub-paragraphs (a) and (b) the effect is that the original debt contract is rescinded and replaced by a new debt contract,

the new debt contract shall be treated for the purposes of section 150A of the Finance Act 1994 (debt contracts and options) as if it were the same contract as the original debt contract, made when the original debt contract was made.

(2) In paragraph (1)—

"debt contract" has the meaning given by section 150A(1) and (2) of the Finance Act 1994;

"loan relationship" has the meaning given by section 81 of the Finance Act 1996, read with section 150A(10) of the Finance Act 1994;

"qualifying company" shall be construed in accordance with section 154 of the Finance Act 1994.

Amendment—Regulations 7–11 repealed by the European Single Currency (Taxes) (Amendment) Regulations, SI 2002/1971 regs 1, 2, 4 with effect for accounting periods beginning after 30 September 2002.

Exchange or conversion of relevant discounted securities

12—(1) A euroconversion of relevant discounted securities that is effected solely by means of an exchange or conversion of those securities shall be treated as not constituting either—

(*a*) a transfer of those securities within the meaning of paragraph 4 of Schedule 13 to the Finance Act 1996 ("Schedule 13"), or

(*b*) a conversion of those securities for the purposes of paragraph 5 of Schedule 13.

(2) The relevant discounted securities ("the new securities") resulting from the exchange or conversion referred to in paragraph (1) shall be deemed for the purposes of Schedule 13 to have been acquired for the amount resulting from the formula—

A – B

Where—

A is the amount equal to the acquisition cost of the relevant discounted securities replaced by the new securities, and

B is the amount of any cash payment received by a person in respect of the euroconversion, to the extent that that amount does not exceed A.

(3) Where a cash payment is received by a person in respect of relevant discounted securities as a result of a euroconversion of those securities which—

(*a*) involves a simple redenomination of those securities, accompanied by either or both of renominalisation and reconventioning as a consequence of that simple redenomination, and

(*b*) is effected otherwise than by means of—

(i) a transfer of those securities, or

(ii) an exchange or conversion of those securities,

those securities shall be deemed for the purposes of Schedule 13 to have been acquired for the amount resulting from the formula—

C – D

where—

C is the amount equal to the acquisition cost of the relevant discounted securities, and—

D is the amount of the cash payment received, to the extent that that amount does not exceed C.

(4) Where—

(*a*) the amount of the cash payment referred to in the description of B in paragraph (2) exceeds the amount referred to in the description of A in that paragraph, or

(*b*) the amount of the cash payment referred to in the description of D in paragraph (3) exceeds the amount referred to in the description of C in that paragraph,

an amount equal to the excess in either case shall constitute a profit realised by a person from the discount on a relevant discounted security for the purposes of paragraph 1 of Schedule 13 (charge to tax on realised profit comprised in discount).

(5) In this regulation "relevant discounted security" has the meaning given by paragraph 3 of Schedule 13.

PART IV
AGREEMENTS FOR SALE AND REPURCHASE OF SECURITIES

Commentary—*Simon's Direct Tax Service* **Division A7.2.**

Interpretation

13 In this Part of these Regulations—

"capital payment" means any payment on the euroconversion of securities other than any interest, dividend or other annual payment payable in respect of the securities;

"original owner" and "interim holder" shall be construed in accordance with section 730A(1) of the Taxes Act;

"transferor" shall be construed in accordance with sections 727A(1) and 737A(1) of the Taxes Act.

Replacement of securities in a euroconversion

14—(1) This regulation applies in a case where—

(*a*) there is an agreement for the sale of securities, and

(*b*) there is a euroconversion of the securities to which the agreement relates ("the old securities"), effected wholly or in part by the issue of new securities to replace them.

(2) The new securities which replace the old securities shall be regarded for the purposes of sections 727A(1), 730A(1) and 737A(1) of the Taxes Act, and section 263A(1) of the 1992 Act, as similar securities in relation to the old securities.

(3) In paragraph (2) the reference to similar securities shall be construed in accordance with section 727A(4), 730B(4) or 737B(6), as the case may be.

Payment or benefit received by interim holder on euroconversion

15—(1) This regulation applies in a case where—

(*a*) there is an arrangement for the sale and repurchase of securities to which section 263A(1) of the 1992 Act applies,

(*b*) a capital payment, but for the arrangement, would be received by the original owner on the euroconversion of those securities,

(*c*) the interim holder is not required under the arrangement to pay to the original owner an amount representative of that capital payment, and an amount representative of that capital payment is not required under the arrangement to be taken into account in computing the repurchase price of the securities, and

(*d*) the amount of the capital payment would not exceed 500 euros.

(2) The interim holder shall not be regarded, for the purposes of section 263A of the 1992 Act, as receiving a benefit under subsection (3)(*b*) of that section equal to the amount of the capital payment.

Payment deemed to be made by interim holder on euroconversion

16—(1) This regulation applies in a case where—

(*a*) there is an arrangement for the sale and repurchase of securities to which section 730A(1) of the Taxes Act, or section 263A(1) of the 1992 Act, applies, or to which section 730A(1) of the Taxes Act would apply if the sale price and the repurchase price were different,

(*b*) there is a euroconversion of those securities prior to their being repurchased, and

(*c*) it is reasonable to assume that an amount that is representative of a capital payment in respect of the euroconversion is taken into account in computing the repurchase price of those securities.

(2) The amount referred to in paragraph (1)(*c*) shall be treated as if it were a separate representative payment in respect of the euroconversion made by the interim holder to the person required or entitled under the arrangement to repurchase the securities.

(3) The repurchase price of the securities shall be treated, for the purposes of section 730A of the Taxes Act and the 1992 Act, as increased by an amount equal to the amount of the separate payment treated as made by paragraph (2).

Renominalisation resulting in new minimum denomination in which securities can be held or traded

17—(1) This regulation applies in a case where—

(*a*) there is an arrangement for the sale and repurchase of securities to which section 730A(1) or 737A(1) of the Taxes Act, or section 263A(1) of the 1992 Act, applies, or to which section 730A(1) of the Taxes Act would apply if the sale price and the repurchase price were different,

(*b*) there is a euroconversion of those securities prior to their being repurchased,

(*c*) the aggregate nominal value (expressed in euros) of the securities sold, or of securities issued to replace them in a euroconversion is, as a result of renominalisation, not a whole multiple of the new minimum denomination in which those securities can be traded at the time of repurchase under the arrangement,

(*d*) securities the aggregate nominal value of which is equal to the largest whole multiple of the new minimum denomination which does not exceed the aggregate nominal value referred to in sub-paragraph (*c*) are required under the arrangement to be sold back to the original owner or the transferor or a person connected with him, and

(*e*) the interim holder is required under the arrangement to pay to the original owner or transferor, or person connected with him, an amount which either—

(i) is equal to the amount of what would, but for the arrangement, have been the proceeds of disposal of the remainder of the securities on the renominalisation received by the original owner, or

(ii) is equal to the value, at the time of the repurchase of securities pursuant to the arrangement, of the remainder if the remainder could still be held at that time though not traded.

(2) Where this regulation applies, the requirement for payment of the amount specified in paragraph (1)(*e*) is to be regarded for the purposes of sections 727A, 730A and 737A of the Taxes Act, and section 263A of the 1992 Act, as equivalent to a requirement on the original owner, transferor or person connected with him to repurchase the remainder of the securities.

(3) The value referred to in paragraph (1)(*e*)(ii) is the appropriate proportion (based on nominal value) of the market value of the minimum amount of the original securities that, at the time of the repurchase of the securities pursuant to the arrangement, could be traded.

(4) Where the amount calculated in accordance with sub-paragraph (*e*) of paragraph (1) does not exceed 500 euros, and the arrangement does not require payment of a sum equal to this amount, this regulation shall have effect as if the amount calculated in accordance with that sub-paragraph were nil and the requirement specified in that sub-paragraph were satisfied.

(5) Where, in a case to which paragraph (1)(*a*) to (*d*) applies—

(*a*) no amount is paid as mentioned in paragraph (1)(*e*) by the interim holder to the original owner, transferor or person connected with him in respect of securities that, as a result of the renominalisation, could not be traded, but

(*b*) it is reasonable to assume that an amount that is representative of an amount that could have been paid as mentioned in sub-paragraph (*a*) was taken into account in computing the repurchase price of the securities,

that amount shall be treated as if it were a separate payment made by the interim holder to the original owner, transferor or person connected with him that is representative of a capital payment on the euroconversion of the securities, and the repurchase price of the securities shall be treated as increased by an amount equal to the amount of that separate payment so treated as made.

Payment made or deemed to be made by interim holder in respect of euroconversion—chargeable gains consequences

18—(1) This regulation applies in a case where—

(*a*) there is an arrangement for the sale and repurchase of securities to which section 263A(1) of the 1992 Act applies, and

(*b*) as a result of a euroconversion of those securities, a payment representative of a capital payment is made, or treated under regulation 16(2) or 17(5) as made (''deemed payment''), by the interim holder to the original owner or the transferor or a person connected with him.

(2) The payment or deemed payment shall be treated, for the purposes of the 1992 Act—

(*a*) where the original owner and the repurchaser are the same person, as a capital payment received by the original owner in respect of the euroconversion of the securities concerned on such date as, on a just and reasonable view, may be inferred from the terms of the arrangement to be the date when the original owner would, but for the arrangement, have received a capital payment in respect of which the payment or deemed payment is made;

(*b*) where the original owner and the repurchaser are not the same person and so far as concerns persons other than the interim holder, as reducing the repurchase price; and

(*c*) as deductible by the interim holder in computing any capital gain arising—

(i) on a disposal of the securities received by the interim holder under the arrangement, or
(ii) where there has been an exchange of those securities as a result of the euroconversion, on a disposal of the securities received by the interim holder in exchange for the original securities received by him under the arrangement.

Euroconversion—loan relationships consequences

19—(1) Paragraph 15 of Schedule 9 to the Finance Act 1996 (loan relationships—repo transactions and stock-lending) shall have effect as if the definition of ''repo or stock-lending arrangements'' in sub-paragraph (3) of that paragraph also included provision under an agreement or series of agreements for the original owner, or a person connected with him, subsequently to be or become entitled, or required, to have transferred to him either—

(*a*) the rights accruing on a euroconversion of the loan relationship, or
(*b*) where the rights include a payment on the euroconversion, other than interest, of an amount which, when aggregated with all other payments on the euroconversion of loan relationships with equivalent rights which are the subject of the same repo or stock-lending arrangement, results in an aggregate amount that does not exceed 500 euros, either the whole of those rights or the whole of those rights apart from that payment.

(2) In paragraph (1)(*b*) ''equivalent rights'' shall be construed in accordance with paragraph 15(4) of Schedule 9 to the Finance Act 1996.

PART V
STOCK LENDING ARRANGEMENTS

Commentary—*Simon's Direct Tax Service* **B3.1007**.

Interpretation

20 In this Part of these Regulations—

''capital payment'' means any payment on the euroconversion of securities other than any interest, dividend or other annual payment payable in respect of the securities;
''stock lending arrangement'', ''borrower'' and ''lender'' have the meanings given by section 263B(1) of the 1992 Act.

Deemed capital payment

21—(1) This regulation applies in a case where—

(*a*) there is a stock lending arrangement in relation to securities,
(*b*) a capital payment resulting from the euroconversion of those securities would, but for the arrangement, be received by the lender, and
(*c*) the stock lending arrangement does not include a requirement for the borrower to make a payment to the lender that is representative of the capital payment referred to in sub-paragraph (*b*).

(2) Subject to paragraph (3), the lender shall be treated, for all purposes of the Taxes Acts, as having received a capital payment in respect of the euroconversion of the securities concerned—

(*a*) on such date as it is reasonable to assume would have been, but for the arrangement, the first date on which the lender could have received the payment mentioned in paragraph (1)(*b*), and
(*b*) in an amount equal to the amount of the payment he could have received.

(3) Paragraph (2) shall not apply where the amount of the capital payment that the lender could have received is less than 500 euros.

Renominalisation resulting in new minimum amount in which securities can be held or traded

22—(1) This regulation applies in a case where—

(*a*) there is a stock lending arrangement in relation to securities,
(*b*) there is a euroconversion of those securities prior to their being transferred back to the lender under the arrangement,
(*c*) the aggregate nominal value (expressed in euros) of the securities transferred to the borrower under the arrangement, or of the securities issued to replace them in the euroconversion, is, as a result of renominalisation, not a whole multiple of the new minimum denomination in which those securities can be traded at the time of the transfer of securities back to the lender under the arrangement,
(*d*) securities the aggregate nominal value of which is equal to the largest whole multiple of the new minimum denomination which does not exceed the aggregate nominal value referred to in sub-paragraph (*c*) are transferred back to the lender pursuant to the arrangement, and
(*e*) the borrower is required under the arrangement to pay to the lender an amount which either—

(i) is equal to the amount of what would, but for the arrangement, have been the proceeds of disposal of the remainder of the securities on the renominalisation received by the lender, or

(ii) is equal to the value, at the time of the transfer of securities back to the lender under the arrangement, of the remainder of the securities if the remainder could still be held at that time though not traded.

(2) Where this regulation applies, the requirement for payment of the amount specified in paragraph (1)(*e*) is to be regarded for the purposes of section 263B of the 1992 Act as a requirement on the part of the borrower to transfer the remainder of the securities back to the lender.

(3) The value referred to in paragraph (1)(*e*)(ii) is the appropriate proportion (based on nominal value) of the market value of the minimum amount of the original securities that, at the time of the transfer back of securities to the lender under the arrangement, could be traded.

(4) Where the value, or proceeds of disposal, of the remainder of the securities referred to in sub-paragraph (*e*) of paragraph (1) does not exceed 500 euros, and the arrangement does not require payment of a sum equal to this amount, this regulation shall have effect as if the amount calculated in accordance with that sub-paragraph were nil and the requirement specified in that sub-paragraph were satisfied.

Payment made by borrower to lender in respect of euroconversion—chargeable gains consequences

23—(1) This regulation applies in a case where—

(*a*) there is a stock lending arrangement in relation to securities, and

(*b*) a payment representative of a capital payment resulting from a euroconversion of those securities is made by the borrower to the lender.

(2) The representative payment shall be treated, for all purposes of the Taxes Acts—

(*a*) as a capital payment received by the lender in respect of the euroconversion of the securities concerned on such date as it is reasonable to assume would have been, but for the arrangement, the first date on which the lender could have received the capital payment, and

(*b*) as deductible by the borrower in computing any capital gain arising—

(i) on a disposal of the securities received by the borrower under the arrangement, or

(ii) where the euroconversion is effected by means of an exchange of securities, on a disposal of the securities received by the borrower in exchange for the original securities received by him under the arrangement.

PART VI

REPURCHASES AND STOCK LENDING—STAMP DUTY AND STAMP DUTY RESERVE TAX

24—30*[Not reproduced. See Orange Tax Handbook Stamp Duty section.]*

PART VII

ACCRUED INCOME SCHEME

Commentary—*Simon's Direct Tax Service* **Division A7.5.**

Interpretation

31 In this Part of these Regulations—

"the accrued amount" has the meaning given by section 713(4) of the Taxes Act;

"the accrued income provisions" means sections 710 to 728 of the Taxes Act;

"interest period" shall be construed in accordance with section 711(3) and (4) of the Taxes Act except that, where securities are issued on an exchange of securities to which regulation 32 (exchange of securities resulting from euroconversion) applies, paragraph (*a*) of section 711(3) of that Act (commencement of interest period) shall have effect for the purposes of regulation 33 as if the reference in that paragraph to the day following that on which securities are issued were a reference to the day on which they are issued;

"the rebate amount" has the meaning given by section 713(5) of the Taxes Act;

"securities" has the meaning given by section 710(2) to (4) of the Taxes Act;

"transfer" in relation to a transfer of securities has the meaning given by subsection (5), read with subsection (13), of section 710 of the Taxes Act.

Disapplication of accrued income provisions in respect of an exchange or conversion of securities resulting from a euroconversion

32 An exchange or conversion of securities that arises solely as a result of actions to effect a euroconversion of those securities shall not constitute, or be treated as, a transfer of those securities for the purposes of the accrued income provisions.

Disapplication of variable interest rate provision in certain circumstances

33—(1) This regulation applies in a case where, solely to provide for actions reasonably required to effect a euroconversion of a security—

(*a*) there may be a change in the rate of interest carried by the security in relation to the interest period in which the euroconversion occurs, or

(*b*) there may be a change in the rate of interest carried by the security in relation to subsequent periods but, throughout the subsequent periods, the new rate of interest falls within one, and one only, of the categories specified in paragraphs (*a*) to (*c*) of section 717(2) of the Taxes Act, or

(*c*) there may be a change in the rate of interest as mentioned in sub-paragraph (*a*) and a change in the rate of interest as mentioned in sub-paragraph (*b*).

(2) The provision for change in the rate of interest referred to in paragraph (1)(*a*) or (*b*) shall not cause the security concerned to be one to which section 717 of the Taxes Act applies.

Calculation of accrued amount or rebate amount in the event of a euroconversion of securities

34—(1) This regulation applies in a case where—

(*a*) there is a transfer of securities at any time in an interest period, and

(*b*) at any time in that interest period there is a euroconversion of the securities transferred in that period.

(2) The accrued amount or, as the case may be, the rebate amount arising in respect of the transferred securities on the transfer shall be such amount as is just and reasonable.

Treatment of capital sum receivable on euroconversion of securities

35—(1) This regulation applies in a case where—

(*a*) otherwise than as a result of a transfer of securities that is not an exchange or conversion of securities to which regulation 32 applies, a person becomes entitled in an interest period to a capital sum in connection with a euroconversion of securities, and

(*b*) any part of that sum is, on a just and reasonable view—

(i) attributable to a reduction in the interest payable on those securities, or

(ii) by way of compensation for a deferral of the interest payable on those securities.

(2) The person entitled to a capital sum in an interest period as mentioned in paragraph (1)(*a*) shall be regarded as entitled in that interest period to a sum on the securities, for the purposes of section 713(2)(*a*) or (3)(*a*), in an amount equal to the part of the sum referred to in paragraph (1)(*b*).

PART VIII

CHARGEABLE GAINS

Commentary—*Simon's Direct Tax Service* **C2.724**.

Equation of holding of non-sterling currency with new euro holding on euroconversion

36 A euroconversion of currency ("the original currency") shall not be treated for the purposes of the 1992 Act as involving any disposal of the original currency or any acquisition of the new euro holding or any part of it, but the original currency (taken as a single asset) and the new euro holding (taken as a single asset) shall be treated for those purposes as the same asset acquired as the original currency was acquired.

Equation of debt (other than a debt on a security) on euroconversion

37 A euroconversion of a debt other than a debt on a security ("the original debt") shall not be treated for the purposes of the 1992 Act as involving any disposal of that debt by the creditor or any acquisition by him of a new debt or any part of it, but the original debt and the new debt shall be treated for those purposes (to the extent that they are not already so treated) as the same asset acquired as the original asset was acquired.

Derivatives over assets the subject of euroconversion

38—(1) This regulation applies where—

(*a*) a derivative represents rights or obligations in respect of any asset or liability or other amount ("the underlying asset"),

(*b*) there is a euroconversion of the underlying asset,

(*c*) a transaction is entered into in relation to that derivative that would, but for this regulation, result in a disposal for the purposes of the 1992 Act of the derivative ("the original derivative") and the acquisition of a new derivative,

(*d*) the terms of the new derivative differ from the terms of the original derivative only to the extent necessary to reflect the euroconversion of the underlying asset, and

(*e*) no party to the transaction receives any consideration in respect of the original derivative other than the new derivative.

(2) The transaction described at paragraph (1)(*c*) shall not be treated for the purposes of the 1992 Act as involving any disposal of the original derivative or any acquisition of the new derivative, but the original derivative and the new derivative shall be treated for those purposes as the same asset acquired as the original derivative was acquired.

Cash payments received on euroconversion of securities

39—Chapter II of Part IV of the 1992 Act shall have effect as if after section 133 of that Act (premiums on conversion of securities) there were inserted the following section—(*inserts* TCGA 1992 s 133A).

PART IX

CONTROLLED FOREIGN COMPANIES

Commentary—*Simon's Direct Tax Service* **D4.1210**.

Replacement of currency used in accounts of controlled foreign company by euro

40—(1) This regulation applies in a case where, as a result of the adoption of the euro by a participating member State, the currency used in the accounts of a controlled foreign company for the first relevant accounting period of the company is to be replaced by the euro.

(2) Section 747A(2) of the Taxes Act shall have effect as if it provided that—

(*a*) where the currency used in the accounts of the controlled foreign company for the first relevant accounting period was the ecu, the chargeable profits for any subsequent accounting period ending on or after 1st January 1999 should be computed and expressed in the euro;

(*b*) where the currency used in the accounts of the controlled foreign company for the first relevant accounting period was a currency other than the ecu—

(i) the chargeable profits for any subsequent accounting period in which, or in any part of which, the currency continues to exist as a legal sub-unit of the euro should be computed and expressed in either the currency so used or the euro;

(ii) the chargeable profits for any accounting period beginning after the end of the latest accounting period referred to in paragraph (i) should be computed and expressed in the euro.

PART X

AMENDMENTS TO THE LOCAL CURRENCY ELECTIONS REGULATIONS

Commentary—*Simon's Direct Tax Service* **D2.911, 925**.

Amendments—This Part revoked by the Exchange Gains and Losses (Miscellaneous Modifications) Regulations, SI 2000/3315 reg 10 to the extent that it is not previously revoked with effect for any accounting period of a company beginning after 31 December 1999 for which FA 2000 ss 105, 106 have effect.

Introductory

41—*(1) The Local Currency Elections Regulations 1994 ("the 1994 Regulations") shall have effect in relation to the adoption of the euro by a member State with the modifications specified in regulations 42 to 47.*

(2) Except where otherwise defined in these Regulations, expressions used in this Part of these Regulations have the meanings given by the 1994 Regulations, and references to a regulation in regulations 42 to 47 are references to a regulation of the 1994 Regulations.

Amendments—This regulation revoked by the Exchange Gains and Losses (Miscellaneous Modifications) Regulations, SI 2000/3315 reg 10 with effect for any accounting period of a company beginning after 31 December 1999 for which FA 2000 ss 105, 106 have effect.

Period for determining validity of elections

42—*(1) In regulation 5(2)—*

(a) in sub-paragraph (a) after the words "trade is carried on" there shall be inserted ", determined—

(i) at the beginning of the first accounting period to which the election applies and at any time thereafter, or

(ii) where the election is for a part of a trade which the company begins to carry on at a time in the first accounting period to which the election applies which is not the beginning of that accounting period, at the time the part of the trade commences and at any time thereafter";

(b) in sub-paragraph (b) there shall be added at the end "as regards the first accounting period to which the election applies and subsequent accounting periods".

(2) In regulation 6 after the words "In determining" there shall be inserted "for the purposes of regulation 5(2)(a)".

Amendments—This regulation revoked by the Exchange Gains and Losses (Miscellaneous Modifications) Regulations, SI 2000/3315 reg 10 with effect for any accounting period of a company beginning after 31 December 1999 for which FA 2000 ss 105, 106 have effect.

Existing election for ecu or participating currencies

43—*(1) An election made by a company under regulation 3 or 4 in relation to—*

(a) the ecu, or

(b) a currency participating in the euro,

shall have effect for the purposes of the 1994 Regulations on and after 1st January 1999 or, if later, the date on which the euro is adopted by the participating member State concerned, as if the election—

(a) continued on or after that date, and

(b) was made in relation to the euro as well as in relation to the ecu or, as the case may be, the participating currency concerned.

(2) In paragraph (1) the reference to a currency participating in the euro (or the participating currency) is a reference to the currency of a participating member State which, as a result of the adoption of the euro by that member State, is replaced by the euro but continues to exist as a legal sub-unit of the euro.

Amendments—This regulation revoked by the Exchange Gains and Losses (Miscellaneous Modifications) Regulations, SI 2000/3315 reg 10 with effect for any accounting period of a company beginning after 31 December 1999 for which FA 2000 ss 105, 106 have effect.

Treatment of existing part trade elections in participating currencies

44—*(1) Where prior to 1st January 1999 or, if later, prior to the date on which the euro is adopted by the participating member State concerned—*

(a) a company makes more than one election under regulation 4 for different parts of its trade,

(b) the currency specified in each election—

(i) as at 1st January 1999, is a participating currency, or

(ii) as at the later date on which the euro is adopted by the participating member State concerned, is either a participating currency or the euro, and

(c) the elections taken together cover the whole of the company's trade,

the elections shall be treated on and after 1st January 1999 or, as the case may be, the later date referred to above, for the purposes of the 1994 Regulations, as if they together constituted a single election for the euro as well as for the participating currency concerned under regulation 3 in respect of the whole of the company's trade.

(2) Where prior to 1st January 1999 or, if later, prior to the date on which the euro is adopted by the participating member State concerned—

(a) a company makes more than one election under regulation 4 for different parts of its trade,

(b) the currency specified in more than one of its elections—

(i) as at 1st January 1999, is a participating currency, or

(ii) as at the later date on which the euro is adopted by the participating member State concerned, is either a participating currency or the euro, and

(c) the elections taken together do not cover the whole of the company's trade,

all the elections referred to in sub-paragraph (b) shall be treated on and after 1st January 1999 or, as the case may be, the later date referred to above, for the purposes of the 1994 Regulations, as if they together constituted a single election for the euro as well as for the participating currency concerned under regulation 4 in respect of part of the company's trade.

Amendments—This regulation revoked by the Exchange Gains and Losses (Miscellaneous Modifications) Regulations, SI 2000/3315 reg 10 with effect for any accounting period of a company beginning after 31 December 1999 for which FA 2000 ss 105, 106 have effect.

Election for whole trade where part trade election already exists

45 *For regulation 3(2) there shall be substituted—*

"(2) An election made by a company under this regulation for a trade for an accounting period shall be of no effect if—

(a) an election ("the previous election") has previously been made by the company under regulation 4 in a different currency for that accounting period and any part of that trade, and

(b) the previous election remains in force as respects that trade and that accounting period.

(3) Where—

(a) an election ("the new election") is made by a company under this regulation for a trade for an accounting period, and

(b) an election ("the previous election") has previously been made by the company under regulation 4 in the same currency for that accounting period and any part of that trade,

SIs

the new election shall be taken to replace the previous election with effect from the beginning of the first accounting period to which the new election applies.''

Amendments—This regulation revoked by the Exchange Gains and Losses (Miscellaneous Modifications) Regulations, SI 2000/3315 reg 10 with effect for any accounting period of a company beginning after 31 December 1999 for which FA 2000 ss 105, 106 have effect.

Determination of rate of exchange where part trade election replaced by whole trade election or combined part trade election

46—*(1) In regulation 8—*

(a) in paragraph (1) at the beginning there shall be inserted ''Subject to paragraph (5) below,'';

(b) after paragraph (4) there shall be added—

''(5) Where, as a result of the adoption of the euro by one or more participating member States—

(a) elections by a company for parts of its trade under regulation 4 are treated under regulation 44 of the European Single Currency (Taxes) Regulations 1998 as a single election by the company for the euro under regulation 3 in respect of the whole of its trade for an accounting period beginning on or after 1st January 1999 or, if later, on or after the date of adoption of the euro by the member State concerned,

(b) elections by a company for parts of its trade under regulation 4 are treated under regulation 44 of those Regulations as a single election by the company for the euro under regulation 4 in respect of part of its trade for an accounting period beginning on or after 1st January 1999 or, if later, on or after the date of adoption of the euro by the member State concerned,

the company shall, unless it makes a new statement under paragraph (1) above for that accounting period not later than the date specified in paragraph (6) below, be treated in relation to that accounting period and thereafter as using for the purposes of that paragraph the London closing exchange rate.

(6) The date specified is the date which is 92 days after the date of adoption of the euro by the member State concerned.

(7) In paragraphs (5) and (6) above references to the euro are references to the single currency adopted by a member State other than the United Kingdom in accordance with the Treaty establishing the European Community.''

Amendments—This regulation revoked by the Exchange Gains and Losses (Miscellaneous Modifications) Regulations, SI 2000/3315 reg 10 with effect for any accounting period of a company beginning after 31 December 1999 for which FA 2000 ss 105, 106 have effect.

Part trade elections for new part trades

47—*(1) In regulation 9 after paragraph (3) there shall be added—*

''(4) Subject to the following provisions of these Regulations, an election for a part of a trade which a company begins to carry on at a time (''the relevant time'') in an accounting period that is not the beginning of that accounting period shall have effect as respects that part for all accounting periods beginning on or after the relevant time if the election is made before the relevant time.''

Amendments—This regulation revoked by the Exchange Gains and Losses (Miscellaneous Modifications) Regulations, SI 2000/3315 reg 10 with effect for any accounting period of a company beginning after 31 December 1999 for which FA 2000 ss 105, 106 have effect.

1998/3178

Scotland Act 1998 (Commencement) Order 1998

Made by the Secretary of State for Scotland under the Scotland Act 1998 ss 115(2), 126(1) and 130

Made . . . . *16 December 1998*

Citation and interpretation

1—(1) This Order may be cited as the Scotland Act 1998 (Commencement) Order 1998.

(2) In this Order, ''the Act'' means the Scotland Act 1998.

Appointed days

2—(1) All the provisions of the Act, so far as not then in force, shall come into force on 1st July 1999, except the provisions specified in Schedule 5 to this Order.

(2) The provisions of the Act, specified in column 1 of any of the Schedules to this Order and the subject matter of which is described in column 2 of that Schedule shall, so far as not then in force, come into force on the day appointed in relation to that Schedule in the Table below but, where a particular purpose is specified in relation to any provision in column 3 of that Schedule, that provision shall come into force on that day only for that purpose.

TABLE

Schedule	*Appointed day*
1	25th January 1999
2	1st April 1999
3	6th May 1999
4	20th May 1999
5	1st April 2000

Principal Appointed Day

3 The principal appointed day is 1st July 1999.

SCHEDULE 3

Article 2(2)

PROVISIONS OF THE ACT WHICH COME INTO FORCE ON 6TH MAY 1999

Column 1 *Provisions of the Act*	*Column 2* *Subject matter*	*Column 3* *Purpose*
...		
Part IV	The tax-varying power	

1999/358
Corporation Tax (Treatment of Unrelieved Surplus Advance Corporation Tax) Regulations 1999

Made by the Treasury under FA 1998 s 32

Made	*15 February 1999*
Laid before the House of Commons	*16 February 1999*
Coming into force	*9 March 1999*

Commentary—*Simon's Direct Tax Service* **D1.310–312.**
Revenue & other press releases—IR 16–2–99 (regulations for relief of past surplus ACT).

Citation and commencement

1 These Regulations may be cited as the Corporation Tax (Treatment of Unrelieved Surplus Advance Corporation Tax) Regulations 1999 and shall come into force on 9th March 1999.

Introductory

2—(1) These Regulations make provision for and in connection with enabling unrelieved surplus ACT that a company has as at 6th April 1999 to be set against its liability to corporation tax on profits charged to corporation tax for an accounting period beginning on or after that date, other than an accounting period that is subsequent to the company's final accounting period.

(2) In paragraph (1) the reference to unrelieved surplus ACT of a company includes, where the company is a member of a group at any time in an accounting period to which that paragraph applies, a reference to unrelieved surplus ACT that another company, which is a member of the same group at any time in that accounting period, has as at 6th April 1999.

Interpretation

3—(1) In these Regulations unless the context otherwise requires—

''accounting period'' shall be construed in accordance with regulation 2(1);

''ACT'' means advance corporation tax;

''the Board'' means the Commissioners of Inland Revenue;

''distribution'' has the meaning given by section 832(1);

''final accounting period'' shall be construed in accordance with regulations 4 and 5;

''franked distribution'' means the sum of the amount or value of a relevant distribution and such proportion of that amount or value as corresponds to the rate of shadow ACT specified in regulation 11(9), and references in these Regulations to any accounting period in which a franked distribution is made are references to the accounting period in which the relevant distribution in question is made;

''franked investment income'' means income of a company resident in the United Kingdom which consists of a distribution in respect of which the company is entitled to a tax credit (and which accordingly represents income equal to the aggregate of the amount or value of the distribution and the amount of that credit), except that it does not include income to which regulation 7, 8(4) or 9 refers, or income falling within regulation 10 to which paragraph (4) of that regulation does not apply;

"group" has the meaning given by regulation 6;

"notification" means notification in writing;

"parent company" in relation to a group shall be construed in accordance with regulation 6(1) to (7); and "immediate parent company" shall be construed in accordance with regulation 6(8);

"relevant distribution" means a distribution made on or after 6th April 1999;

"shadow ACT" means a notional amount of ACT treated as paid by a company in respect of a relevant distribution and computed in accordance with regulation 11;

"straddling accounting period" means an accounting period beginning before, and ending on or after, 6th April 1999, and includes a separate accounting period mentioned in sections 245(2), 245A(2) and 245B(2);

"surplus franked investment income"—

(*a*) as respects an accounting period beginning on or after 6th April 1999, has the meaning given by regulation 11(13);

(*b*) as respects an accounting period beginning before that date, has the meaning given by section 238(1A);

"surplus shadow ACT" means the excess amount of shadow ACT over the total amount of shadow ACT set against a company's liability to corporation tax for an accounting period in accordance with regulation 12(1);

"the Taxes Act" means the Income and Corporation Taxes Act 1988;

"unrelieved surplus ACT" means the ACT (if any) which, apart from sub-paragraph (3) of paragraph 12 of Schedule 3 to the Finance Act 1998 but otherwise in accordance with that paragraph, would be treated by virtue of section 239(4) as paid in respect of distributions made by a company in the first accounting period of the company to begin on or after 6th April 1999.

(2) References in these Regulations to the profits of a company charged to corporation tax for any accounting period are references to the amount of the company's profits for that period on which corporation tax falls finally to be borne.

(3) References in these Regulations, however expressed, to a company's liability to corporation tax for an accounting period include references to a company's liability in respect of any sums chargeable on the company for that period under section 747(4)(*a*) (controlled foreign companies).

(4) For the purposes only of these Regulations, a straddling accounting period shall be treated as if—

(*a*) it were composed of two accounting periods, the one ending on 5th April 1999 and the other beginning on 6th April 1999;

(*b*) there were apportioned to each of those accounting periods the proportionate part of the profits of the company charged to corporation tax for the straddling accounting period.

(5) References in these Regulations to an accounting period beginning on or after 6th April 1999 include references to—

(*a*) an accounting period deemed by virtue of paragraph (4) of this regulation to begin on 6th April 1999, and

(*b*) a separate accounting period referred to in regulations 16(2) and 17(2) that begins on or after that date.

(6) References in these Regulations, other than the reference in paragraph (4)(*b*) above, to a requirement for profits charged to corporation tax for an accounting period to be apportioned between two separate parts of that accounting period are references to a requirement for those profits to be apportioned either—

(*a*) on a time basis, or

(*b*) where that basis would be unjust and unreasonable, on such basis as would be just and reasonable.

(7) In these Regulations any reference to a particular provision, without more, is a reference to that provision of the Taxes Act.

Definition of final accounting period—company not a member of a group

4—(1) For the purpose of regulation 2(1) and subject to paragraphs (3) to (5) of this regulation and to regulation 5(10), where a company is not a member of a group at any time in the relevant accounting period, the final accounting period of that company is the accounting period beginning in the period of twelve months immediately following the end of the relevant accounting period or, if there is more than one accounting period beginning in that period of twelve months, the latest accounting period beginning in that period.

(2) In paragraph (1) "the relevant accounting period" is the first accounting period of the company after which no amount of unrelieved surplus ACT is available to be set against the company's liability to corporation tax in accordance with these Regulations.

(3) Paragraph (1) shall not apply where, at any time in the first of its accounting periods to begin on or after 6th April 1999, the company notifies an officer of the Board that it will not seek or, as the

case may be, will cease to seek recovery of unrelieved surplus ACT in respect of that accounting period or any subsequent accounting period.

(4) Where, otherwise than in a case to which paragraph (3) applies, the company notifies an officer of the Board at any time in an accounting period that it wishes that accounting period to be its final accounting period and that it will not seek recovery of unrelieved surplus ACT in respect of any subsequent accounting period, the final accounting period of that company is, subject to paragraph (5), the accounting period in which the notification is made.

(5) Where—

(*a*) there is an amount of surplus shadow ACT in respect of an accounting period of the company beginning in the period of twelve months ("the relevant period") immediately following the end of the accounting period in which the company notifies an officer of the Board as mentioned in paragraph (4) or, if there is more than one such accounting period, the latest accounting period beginning in the relevant period, and

(*b*) that amount or any part of it falls to be carried back in accordance with regulation 12(7) to the accounting period in which that notification is made,

the final accounting period shall be the accounting period or, as the case may be, the latest accounting period beginning in the relevant period from which an amount of surplus shadow ACT falls to be carried back as mentioned in sub-paragraph (*b*) of this paragraph, and not the accounting period in which the notification is made.

Definition of final accounting period—company a member of a group

5—(1) For the purpose of regulation 2 and subject to paragraphs (3) to (10), where a company is a member of a group at any time in the relevant accounting period, the final accounting period of that company in its capacity as a member of that group is the accounting period beginning in the period of twelve months immediately following the end of the relevant accounting period or, if there is more than one accounting period beginning in that period of twelve months, the latest accounting period beginning in that period.

(2) In paragraph (1) "the relevant accounting period" is the first accounting period of the company after which no amount of unrelieved surplus ACT belonging to the company or any other company which is a member of the group at any time in that accounting period is available to be set against any liability to corporation tax in accordance with these Regulations; and for this purpose unrelieved surplus ACT belonging to another company that is a member of the group at any time in that accounting period shall be regarded as so available until the end of that other company's accounting period.

(3) Paragraph (1) shall not apply where—

(*a*) the company is a member of the group as at 6th April 1999, and

(*b*) at any time in the first accounting period of the parent company of the group to begin on or after that date, the parent company notifies an officer of the Board on behalf of the group that the group will not seek or, as the case may be, will cease to seek recovery of unrelieved surplus ACT in respect of any accounting period of any member of the group that begins on or after that date.

(4) A notification made in accordance with paragraph (3) shall, subject to paragraph (9), be binding on each company that was a member of the group as at 6th April 1999.

(5) Where, otherwise than in a case to which paragraph (3) applies, at any time in an accounting period of the parent company of the group the parent company notifies an officer of the Board on behalf of the group that the group wishes the accounting period of any member of the group in which the notification is made to be the final accounting period of that member and that it will not seek recovery of amounts of unrelieved surplus ACT available to that member in respect of any subsequent accounting period, the final accounting period of that member and the final accounting period of the parent company is, subject to paragraphs (7) to (10), the accounting period of the parent company in which the notification by the parent company is made.

(6) A notification made in accordance with paragraph (5) shall, subject to paragraph (10), be binding on each company that was a member of the group when the notification was made or that subsequently becomes a member of the group prior to the end of the parent company's final accounting period.

(7) Where paragraph (5) applies and the accounting period of a company in the group other than the parent company that would otherwise be its final accounting period in accordance with that paragraph begins before the end of, but ends after, the accounting period of the parent company in which the notification by the parent company is made, the accounting period of the company concerned shall be treated as if the part ending with the last day of the parent company's accounting period, and the part after, were two separate accounting periods; and the part ending with the last day of the parent company's accounting period shall, subject to paragraph (10), be treated as the company's final accounting period for the purposes of this regulation.

(8) Where—

(*a*) there is an amount of surplus shadow ACT in respect of an accounting period of any company that is a member of the group beginning in the period of twelve months ("the relevant period") immediately following the end of the accounting period of the company in which the parent company notifies an officer of the Board as mentioned in paragraph (5), and

(*b*) all or any part of that surplus amount falls to be carried back under regulation 12 or 13 to an accounting period of a company that is a member of the group ending before the relevant period of the company referred to in sub-paragraph (*a*),

the final accounting period of any company that is a member of the group at any time in the relevant period shall, subject to paragraph (10), be the accounting period or, if more than one, the latest accounting period beginning in the relevant period from which an amount of surplus shadow ACT falls to be carried back as mentioned in sub-paragraph (*b*) of this paragraph, and not the accounting period referred to in paragraph (5).

(9) Where in an accounting period (''the material period'') subsequent to the accounting period in which the parent company notifies an officer of the Board as mentioned in paragraph (3), a company which has an amount of unrelieved surplus ACT becomes a member of the group, these Regulations shall apply in relation to the material period (but not earlier accounting periods) as if no notification had been made in accordance with that paragraph, but not so as to entitle any company to whom that notification, when made, applied to seek recovery of any amount of unrelieved surplus ACT.

(10) Where in an accounting period (''the material period'') subsequent to the final accounting period as determined in accordance with paragraph (1), (5), (7) or (8), a company which has an amount of unrelieved surplus ACT becomes a member of the group, these Regulations shall apply in relation to the material period (but not earlier accounting periods) as if the final accounting period had not yet been determined in accordance with any of those paragraphs, but not so as to entitle a company whose final accounting period had previously been determined in accordance with those provisions to seek recovery of any amount of unrelieved surplus ACT.

(11) Where—

(*a*) a company is a member of two or more groups,

(*b*) its final accounting period as a member of one or more, but not all, of the groups concerned has been determined in accordance with the previous provisions of this regulation, and

(*c*) at least one of those determinations is as a result of a notification made by a parent company in accordance with paragraph (5) of this regulation,

these Regulations shall have effect in relation to the group or groups in respect of which the final accounting period of the company has not been determined as if the total amount of its unrelieved surplus ACT had been set against its liability to corporation tax in accordance with regulation 14.

Definition of group

6—(1) In these Regulations ''group'' means a company resident in the United Kingdom (''the parent company'') which has one or more 51 per cent subsidiaries together with that or those subsidiaries.

(2) For the purposes of paragraph (1)—

(*a*) ''51 per cent subsidiary'' means a 51 per cent subsidiary that is a company resident in the United Kingdom;

(*b*) a company is not the parent company within a group if—

(i) it has no 51 per cent subsidiary but is itself a 51 per cent subsidiary of another company, or

(ii) it and its 51 per cent subsidiaries are all members of another group;

(*c*) the question whether a company is a 51 per cent subsidiary of the parent company shall be determined, subject to paragraph (3), in accordance with section 838, except that the parent company shall be treated as not being the owner—

(i) of any share capital which it owns directly in a company if a profit on the sale of the shares would be treated as a trading receipt of its trade; or

(ii) of any share capital which it owns indirectly, and which is owned directly by a body corporate for which a profit on the sale of the shares would be treated as a trading receipt of its trade; or

(iii) of any share capital which it owns directly or indirectly in a body corporate not resident in the United Kingdom.

(3) Where a company would otherwise not be a 51 per cent subsidiary, but—

(*a*) persons, whether company members or not, enjoy extraordinary rights or powers under the articles of association or under any other document regulating the company, and

(*b*) because of that fact, ownership of the ordinary share capital (for the purposes of the definition of ''51 per cent subsidiary'' in section 838(1)(*a*)) may not be an appropriate test of whether a company is a 51 per cent subsidiary of the parent company,

then in considering whether a company is a 51 per cent subsidiary of the parent company for the purposes of paragraph (1), holdings of all kinds of share capital, including preference shares, or of any particular category of share capital, or voting power or any other kind of special power may be taken into account instead of ordinary share capital.

(4) Notwithstanding that, apart from this paragraph, a company ("the subsidiary company") would at any time be a 51 per cent subsidiary of the parent company for the purposes of this regulation, the subsidiary company shall not be treated at that time as a 51 per cent subsidiary for those purposes—

(*a*) if arrangements are in existence by virtue of which any person has or could obtain, or any persons together have or could obtain, control of the subsidiary company but not of the parent company; and

(*b*) unless the following conditions are also fulfilled, namely—

(i) that the parent company is beneficially entitled to more than 50 per cent of any profits available for distribution to equity holders of the subsidiary company; and

(ii) that the parent company would be beneficially entitled to more than 50 per cent of any assets of the subsidiary company available for distribution to its equity holders on a winding up.

(5) In paragraph (4)—

"arrangements" means arrangements of any kind, whether in writing or not, other than arrangements whose sole or main purpose is to reduce the amount of surplus shadow ACT available to be utilised by a company other than the subsidiary company in accordance with regulation 13;

"control" has the meaning given by section 840.

(6) Where by virtue of any enactment a Minister of the Crown or Northern Ireland department has power to give directions to a statutory body as to the disposal of assets belonging to, or to a subsidiary of, that body, the existence of that power shall not be regarded as constituting (or as having at any time constituted) an arrangement within the meaning of paragraph (4)(*a*).

(7) The provisions of Schedule 18 shall apply for the purposes of paragraph (4)(*b*) as if—

(*a*) for any reference to section 413(7) to (9) there were substituted a reference to paragraph (4)(*b*);

(*b*) paragraph 7(1) of that Schedule were omitted and for any reference to "the relevant accounting period" there were substituted a reference to the accounting period current at the time in question.

(8) For the purposes of these Regulations, a company ("A") is the "immediate parent company" of another company ("B") if, disregarding any other company of which B is a 51 per cent subsidiary by virtue of section 838 and this regulation, A would be the parent company of B by virtue of section 838 and this regulation.

Restriction on franked investment income—replacement of income

7 Where a company takes any action the effect of which is that income consisting of interest to which a company is or will be entitled becomes or is replaced by income consisting of a distribution, and the main purpose of that action is to reduce the amount of shadow ACT which it would be treated as having paid under regulation 11 for an accounting period, the income consisting of the distribution shall not be regarded for the purposes of these Regulations as franked investment income.

Restriction on franked investment income—arrangements to pass on value of franked investment income

8—(1) This regulation applies in any case where—

(*a*) a person ("A") who is a company is entitled to franked investment income;

(*b*) arrangements subsist such that another person ("B") obtains, whether directly or indirectly, a payment representing any of the value of that franked investment income, in excess of the payment that would have been made in the circumstances specified in paragraph (2);

(*c*) the arrangements (whether or not made directly between A and B) were entered into for an unallowable purpose, and

(*d*) neither A nor B is a company whose final accounting period has been determined in accordance with regulation 4 or 5.

(2) The circumstances specified in this paragraph are where—

(*a*) the payment representing any of the value of that franked investment income was made under a transaction between persons at arm's length both of whom were companies;

(*b*) neither company was or had been at any time a member of a group, and

(*c*) neither company was entitled to an amount of unrelieved surplus ACT as at 6th April 1999.

(3) This regulation does not apply if and to the extent that any provision of the Tax Acts has the effect of cancelling or reducing the tax advantage which would otherwise be obtained by virtue of the arrangements.

(4) Where this regulation applies, the franked investment income referred to in paragraph (1) shall not be regarded for the purposes of these Regulations as franked investment income.

(5) For the purposes of this regulation, the question whether any arrangements were entered into for an "unallowable purpose" shall be determined in accordance with paragraphs (6) and (7).

(6) Arrangements are entered into for an unallowable purpose if the purposes for which A is a party to the arrangements include the purpose of reducing the amount of shadow ACT treated as paid, in accordance with regulation 11, on relevant distributions made—

(*a*) by A, or

(*b*) where A is a member of a group, by any other company which is a member of that group, at any time in, or after the end of, the accounting period in which the arrangements are entered into.

(7) In determining for the purposes of paragraph (6) whether a company could have used franked investment income for the purpose of reducing shadow ACT, the company shall be taken to use its actual franked investment income for that purpose before using the franked investment income in question.

(8) In this regulation—

"arrangements" means arrangements of any kind, whether in writing or not (and includes a series of arrangements, whether or not between the same parties);

"tax advantage" has the same meaning as in Chapter I of Part XVII of the Taxes Act.

Restriction on franked investment income—dealers

9—(1) Where a dealer receives—

(*a*) a distribution which is made by a company resident in the United Kingdom ("a UK distribution"), or any payment which is representative of a UK distribution, and

(*b*) the distribution or, as the case may be, the payment is taken into account in computing the profits of the dealer which are chargeable to tax in accordance with the provisions of the Taxes Act applicable to Case I or II of Schedule D,

the distribution or payment shall not be regarded for the purposes of these Regulations as franked investment income.

(2) In paragraph (1) "dealer" means a person who is a dealer in relation to a distribution within the meaning of section 95(2).

Restriction on franked investment income—intra-group distributions

10—(1) A distribution received by a company which is a member of a group from another company within the group, or from another company in the circumstances specified in paragraph (2) or (3) shall, subject to paragraph (4), not be regarded for the purposes of these Regulations as franked investment income.

(2) The circumstances specified in this paragraph are where the company making the distribution in question is not a member of the group at the time the distribution is received but arrangements in place at that time are such as to give rise to a reasonable expectation that the company will join or, as the case may be, rejoin the group.

(3) The circumstances specified in this paragraph are where the distribution in question was made by reference to the shareholdings existing at a time when both the company making the distribution and the company owning the shares at that time were members of the same group.

(4) Where the distribution is a relevant distribution and the company making the relevant distribution has elected as mentioned in regulation 11(3)(*b*), paragraph (1) of this regulation shall not apply to so much of the franked distribution in respect of which that election is made.

Computation of shadow ACT

11—(1) Where a company resident in the United Kingdom makes a relevant distribution, other than a relevant distribution to which paragraph (2) applies, shadow ACT shall, for the purposes of determining the amount of unrelieved surplus ACT that may be set against a company's liability to corporation tax for an accounting period in accordance with regulation 14, be treated as having been paid by the company in accordance with the provisions of this regulation.

(2) This paragraph applies to a relevant distribution—

(*a*) which is a manufactured dividend to which paragraph 2(2) of Schedule 23A applies, or

(*b*) which is made, otherwise than in the circumstances specified in paragraph (3), by a company that is a member of a group to another company within the group.

(3) The circumstances specified in this paragraph are where the company making the distribution—

(*a*) has received, in the accounting period in which the distribution is made, franked investment income of an amount sufficient to ensure that the amount of shadow ACT that, apart from paragraph (2)(*b*), would be treated as having been paid in respect of that distribution would have been less than it would have been had the company not received that amount of franked investment income;

(*b*) has elected in its tax return for the accounting period in which the distribution is made, or in an amendment to that tax return, that an amount of the franked distribution equal to the whole or a stated amount of that franked investment income (multiplied by nine-eighths) should not be excluded in computing its shadow ACT for that period; and (*c*) has informed the company receiving the distribution that sub-paragraphs (*a*) and (*b*) of this paragraph apply in relation to the distribution, and of the amount of the distribution to which the election under sub-paragraph (*b*) applies.

(4) An election to which paragraph (3)(*b*) refers—

(*a*) shall be made not later than two years after the end of the accounting period in which the distribution is made, and

(*b*) shall be irrevocable.

(5) Where a relevant distribution to which paragraph (1) applies does not fall within an accounting period of the company making the distribution, it shall be treated, for all purposes of these Regulations, as falling within an accounting period that—

(*a*) begins—

(i) on the same date as the date on which the accounting period of the company's immediate parent company in which the distribution falls begins or, if later

(ii) on the date immediately following the end of the last accounting period of the company making the distribution that precedes the date on which the distribution is made, and

(*b*) ends—

(i) on the same date as the date on which the accounting period of the company's immediate parent company in which the distribution falls ends or, if earlier

(ii) on the date immediately before the beginning of an accounting period of the company making the distribution.

(6) For the purposes of paragraph (5), where the distribution referred to in that paragraph is made at a time when there is no accounting period of the company's immediate parent company, that paragraph shall have effect as if for the references to the accounting period of the company's immediate parent company there were substituted references to the accounting period of the immediate parent company of the company's immediate parent company (and so on until the accounting period of an immediate parent company in which the distribution falls is found).

(7) Where a company ceases to be a member of a group, shadow ACT shall be computed in accordance with paragraph (1) in relation to the accounting period of the company in which it ceases to be a member of the group as if the part ending on the date on which the company ceases to be member of the group, and the part after, were two separate accounting periods.

(8) Where there is a change of ownership of a company and the change—

(*a*) is not such as to cause the company to cease to be a member of a group, but

(*b*) occurs in circumstances where either regulation 16 or regulation 17 applies,

shadow ACT shall be computed in accordance with paragraph (1) in relation to the accounting period of the company in which the change occurs as if the part ending with the change, and the part after, were two separate accounting periods.

(9) Subject to paragraphs (10) to (12), for the financial year 1999 and any subsequent financial year, shadow ACT shall be treated as having been paid at the rate of 25 per cent on an amount equal to the amount or value of the relevant distribution.

(10) Where in any accounting period a company receives franked investment income, subject to regulation 22(1), shadow ACT shall not be treated as having been paid by the company in respect of relevant distributions made by it in that period unless the amount of franked distributions made by it in that period exceeds the aggregate of—

(*a*) nine-eighths of the amount of franked investment income consisting of distributions made to the company in that period, and

(*b*) the amount of any surplus of franked investment income carried forward from the previous accounting period in accordance with paragraph (12).

(11) If in an accounting period there is such an excess, shadow ACT shall be treated as having been paid on an amount which, when the shadow ACT treated as having been paid thereon is added to it, is equal to the excess.

(12) Where a company has a surplus of franked investment income in any accounting period, the surplus shall be carried forward to the next accounting period for the purposes of paragraphs (3), (10) and (13).

(13) A company has a surplus of franked investment income in an accounting period for the purposes of paragraph (12) if an amount equal to the aggregate of nine-eighths of the franked investment income consisting of distributions made to the company in that period and the surplus of franked investment income carried forward from the previous accounting period in accordance with paragraph (12) exceeds the amount of the franked distributions made by it in that period; and the amount of that excess shall be regarded as the amount of the surplus of franked investment income for the purposes of paragraph (12).

(14) In the application of paragraphs (12) and (13) to a straddling accounting period of a company, or to the case where an accounting period of a company ends on 5th April 1999 and its next accounting period begins on 6th April 1999—

(*a*) there shall be ascertained the amount of surplus franked investment income in the accounting period ending or, in the case of a straddling accounting period, deemed by virtue of regulation 3(4) to end, on 5th April 1999;
(*b*) that amount shall be treated as carried forward to the accounting period beginning or, in the case of a straddling accounting period, deemed by virtue of regulation 3(4) to begin, on 6th April 1999 and shall be treated as mentioned in paragraph (10).

Utilisation of shadow ACT

12—(1) Shadow ACT which a company is treated as having paid in accordance with regulation 11 in respect of any relevant distribution made by it in an accounting period shall, for the purposes mentioned in regulation 11(1) and in accordance with the provisions of this regulation, be set against the company's liability to corporation tax on any profits charged to corporation tax for that accounting period, but not so as to reduce the amount of that liability.

(2) Subject to paragraph (7)(*b*), shadow ACT shall be utilised as mentioned in paragraph (1) before any amount of unrelieved surplus ACT is set against a company's liability to corporation tax in accordance with regulation 14.

(3) The amount of shadow ACT to be set against a company's liability for any accounting period under paragraph (1)—

(*a*) shall not exceed the amount of shadow ACT that would have been treated as paid (apart from regulation 11(10) to (12)) in respect of a relevant distribution made at the end of that period of an amount which, together with the shadow ACT treated as paid in respect of it, is equal to the company's profits charged to corporation tax for that period;
(*b*) shall be computed, where applicable, by reference to the like provisions with respect to separate accounting periods on a change of ownership of a company that are contained in regulations 16 and 17 for the purposes of computing the amount of unrelieved surplus ACT to be set against the company's liability for an accounting period.

(4) Where an amount of credit for foreign tax falls to be allowed in accordance with section 797 against corporation tax attributable to any income or chargeable gain ("the relevant income or gain"), then—

(*a*) paragraph (3) shall have effect only in relation to so much of the company's profits chargeable to corporation tax for the relevant accounting period as does not include the relevant income or gain;
(*b*) in so far as the company's liability to corporation tax for the relevant accounting period relates to the relevant income or gain, it shall be taken to be reduced by the amount of the credit for foreign tax attributable to that income or gain, as determined in accordance with subsections (2) and (3) of section 797; and
(*c*) the amount of shadow ACT which may be set against that liability, so far as it relates to the relevant income or gain, shall not exceed whichever is the lower of the limits specified in paragraph (5).

(5) The limits specified in this paragraph are—

(*a*) the limit which would apply under paragraph (3) if the amount of the relevant income or gain, determined in accordance with subsection (3) of section 797, were the company's only income or gain for the relevant accounting period; and
(*b*) the amount of corporation tax for which, after taking account of the reduction mentioned in paragraph (4)(*b*), the company is liable in respect of that income or gain.

(6) In paragraph (4) "the relevant accounting period" shall be construed in accordance with subsection (2) of section 797.

(7) Where in respect of any accounting period of a company ("the principal period") there is an amount of surplus shadow ACT, that amount shall be treated as if it were shadow ACT which the company is treated as having paid in respect of relevant distributions made by it in any of its accounting periods beginning on or after 6th April 1999 and in the six years preceding the principal period, but so that that amount—

(*a*) is set, so far as possible, against the company's liability for a more recent accounting period before a more remote one,
(*b*) does not cause the amount of shadow ACT specified in paragraph (3)(*a*) as respects an accounting period of the company to be exceeded,
(*c*) where the company is a member of a group, is not set against the liability of another company in the group for an accounting period, and,
(*d*) except in relation to the period beginning twenty four months before the end of the principal period and ending the day before the commencement of the principal period, does not displace any amount of unrelieved surplus ACT that, by virtue of regulation 14, is set against the company's liability for an accounting period.

(8) For the purposes of paragraph (7)—

(a) the reference to any of the company's accounting periods beginning on or after 6th April 1999 includes a reference to a separate accounting period mentioned in regulations 16 and 17 beginning on or after that date;

(b) where an accounting period begins before, but ends during, the period of twenty four months referred to in sub-paragraph (d) of that paragraph, the amount of unrelieved surplus ACT falling to be displaced as mentioned in that sub-paragraph shall be proportionately reduced by reference to the part of that accounting period that falls outside the period of twenty four months.

(9) Subject to regulation 13 (intra-group allocation of shadow ACT), where in respect of any accounting period of a company there is an amount of surplus shadow ACT which has not been dealt with under paragraph (7), that amount shall be treated for the purposes of this regulation (including any further application of this paragraph) as if it were shadow ACT which the company is treated as having paid in the next accounting period.

Intra-group allocation of surplus shadow ACT

13—(1) Where in respect of any accounting period of a company that is a member of a group at any time in that accounting period, there is an amount of surplus shadow ACT that has not been utilised as mentioned in regulation 12(7), the whole or part of that amount shall, for the purposes mentioned in regulation 11(1) and in accordance with the provisions of this regulation, be allocated by the parent company to another company, or other companies, that are members of the group ("the potential recipients").

(2) Where an amount of surplus shadow ACT is allocated to another company in the group under paragraph (1), that amount shall be set against the balance (if any) of that company's liability to corporation tax on any profits charged to corporation tax for an accounting period to which that amount is attributed in accordance with paragraph (8), that remains after the amount of that company's shadow ACT in respect of its own distributions for that period (together with the amount of any surplus shadow ACT treated as belonging to that company under paragraph (6)) has been set against that liability in accordance with regulation 12(1), but not so as to reduce the amount of that liability or so as to exceed the capacity of that company to utilise that amount.

(3) No company that is a member of a group at any time in an accounting period shall be entitled to set an amount of unrelieved surplus ACT against its liability to corporation tax for that accounting period in accordance with regulation 14 until all surplus shadow ACT of that company for that period has been allocated under paragraph (1).

(4) Where the amount of surplus shadow ACT referred to in paragraph (1) is insufficient in relation to the capacity of all the potential recipients fully to utilise surplus shadow ACT, the parent company in the group shall determine the recipients to whom that amount shall be allocated under that paragraph, and the proportion of that amount to be allocated to each of those recipients in accordance with the capacity of each of those recipients to utilise that amount.

(5) Where the amount referred to in paragraph (1) exceeds the amount which could be utilised by all the potential recipients—

(a) so much of that amount as is able to be utilised by the potential recipients shall be allocated to them by the parent company under that paragraph in accordance with the capacity of each of the potential recipients to utilise that amount, and

(b) the balance shall, subject to paragraph (6), be retained by the company in which the amount arose and shall be treated by that company (in accordance with regulation 12(9)) as if it were shadow ACT which the company is treated as having paid in the next accounting period.

(6) Where, in a case to which paragraph (1) applies, the company concerned ceases to be a member of the group, otherwise than by reason of a transaction or arrangements between that company or that company's immediate parent company (or the latter company's immediate parent company and so on) and another person who is not connected with that company within the meaning of section 839, the amount of surplus shadow ACT shall be treated for the purposes of this regulation as belonging to the immediate parent company of that company at the time it ceases to be a member of the group or, where the immediate parent company ceases to be a member of the group at the same time as that company, as belonging to the next immediate parent company (and so on as necessary until an immediate parent company is found who has not ceased to be a member of the group at the same time as that company).

(7) An amount of surplus shadow ACT allocated to a company under paragraph (1) may subsequently be reallocated at any time under that paragraph, but not so as to reduce the amount allocated to a company to an amount below its capacity to utilise surplus shadow ACT after the time limit for amending that company's tax return has expired.

(8) Where the whole or part of an amount of surplus shadow ACT is allocated to a company under paragraph (1), it shall be attributed to a relevant accounting period, or relevant accounting periods, of that company in the following order—

(a) an accounting period beginning and ending on the same dates as, or otherwise contained within, the accounting period of the company whose surplus shadow ACT is allocated ("the transferring company's accounting period");

(*b*) an accounting period beginning before, but ending in, the transferring company's accounting period;

(*c*) an accounting period beginning in, but ending after, the end of the transferring company's accounting period;

(*d*) any further period (whether the whole or part of an accounting period) beginning twenty four months or less prior to the end of the transferring company's accounting period.

(9) In paragraph (8) "relevant accounting period" means an accounting period in which both the transferring company and the company receiving the amount were at some time members of the group.

(10) Where the further period referred to in paragraph (8)(*d*) is a part of an accounting period, the capacity of the company to utilise the amount attributed to that further period shall be proportionately reduced by reference to the part of its accounting period which falls outside that further period.

(11) Where in accordance with paragraph (8) amounts of surplus shadow ACT in respect of accounting periods of two or more companies are attributed to a relevant accounting period, or relevant accounting periods, of a company, the parent company in the group shall determine the order of priority in which those amounts are attributed, and the order of priority so determined shall apply on any subsequent reallocation of those amounts.

(12) Where a company is a member of more than one group and there is an allocation to that company under paragraph (1) of an amount of surplus shadow ACT by the parent company of more than one group, the order of priority in which allocations are attributed to an accounting period, or accounting periods, of that company in accordance with paragraph (8) shall be determined by reference to the date on which an allocation is made (an earlier allocation having priority over a later allocation).

(13) Where in accordance with paragraph (8) an amount falls to be attributed to an accounting period which is either the first or the last accounting period in which both the transferring company and the company receiving the amount were members of the group, then for the purpose of determining the amount to be attributed to that accounting period—

(*a*) the capacity of the company receiving the amount to utilise the amount to be attributed to that accounting period—

(i) shall be proportionately reduced by reference to the part of that period during which the transferring company and the company receiving the amount were not both members of the group, and

(ii) shall be further reduced by any prior attribution to that period by reason of the allocation to the company receiving the amount of the surplus shadow ACT of another company, and

(*b*) the amount shall be treated as attributable to a separate accounting period comprising the part of that accounting period during which both the transferring company and the company receiving the amount were members of the group.

(14) Where in accordance with paragraph (8) an amount is attributed to a relevant accounting period referred to in sub-paragraph (*b*) or (*d*) of that paragraph, that amount—

(*a*) shall displace any amount of unrelieved surplus ACT that, by virtue of regulation 14, was set against the company's liability to corporation tax on any profits charged to corporation tax for that accounting period, but

(*b*) shall not displace any amount of surplus shadow ACT that, in accordance with regulation 12, has previously been set against that company's liability for corporation tax for that accounting period or (as the case may be) has been treated as shadow ACT which that company is treated as having paid in respect of any relevant distributions made by the company in that accounting period.

(15) Where the parent company fails to allocate an amount of surplus shadow ACT in accordance with this regulation—

(*a*) that amount may be allocated in accordance with this regulation by an officer of the Board;

(*b*) if that amount is subsequently allocated by the parent company in accordance with this regulation, any allocation by an officer of the Board under sub-paragraph (*a*) shall be treated as if it had not been made.

Set-off of unrelieved surplus ACT against liability to corporation tax

14—(1) Subject to paragraphs (2) to (4), a company's unrelieved surplus ACT shall be set against its liability to corporation tax on any profits charged to corporation tax for an accounting period beginning on or after 6th April 1999, and shall accordingly discharge a corresponding amount of that liability.

(2) Unrelieved surplus ACT shall not be set against a company's liability to corporation tax for an accounting period under paragraph (1) to the extent that it can be set against the company's liability to corporation tax for an earlier accounting period.

(3) Where section 116(2) applies in relation to a company which is a member of a partnership, no unrelieved surplus advance corporation tax may be set against its liability to corporation tax on its share in the profits of the relevant accounting period of the partnership.

(4) The amount of unrelieved surplus ACT to be set against a company's liability for an accounting period under paragraph (1) shall not exceed the amount calculated in accordance with the formula—

$$A - B$$

where—

A is the amount of the company's capacity to utilise unrelieved surplus ACT calculated in accordance with regulation 12, and

B is the amount of any shadow ACT attributed to that period in accordance with regulations 12 and 13.

(5) References to "the relevant accounting period" in paragraph (3) shall be construed in accordance with section 116(3).

Restriction on set-off of company's unrelieved surplus ACT against subsidiary company's liability to corporation tax

15—(1) Subject to paragraph (2) and regulation 17, unrelieved surplus ACT consisting of ACT which a subsidiary is treated as having paid by virtue of section 240(2) shall be set off against the subsidiary's liability to corporation tax for an accounting period in accordance with regulation 14 before unrelieved surplus ACT consisting of ACT paid in respect of any distribution made by the subsidiary.

(2) No unrelieved surplus ACT consisting of ACT which a subsidiary is treated as having paid by virtue of section 240(2) shall be set against the subsidiary's liability to corporation tax in accordance with regulation 14 for any accounting period in which, or in any part of which, it was not a subsidiary of the surrendering company, unless throughout that period or part both companies were subsidiaries of a third company.

(3) In this regulation "surrendering company" and "subsidiary" have the same meanings as in section 240.

Calculation of unrelieved surplus ACT on change of ownership of company

16—(1) This regulation applies where—

(*a*) within any period of three years there is both a change in the ownership of a company and, either earlier or later in that period, or at the same time, a major change in the nature or conduct of a trade or business carried on by the company; or

(*b*) at any time after the scale of the activities in a trade or business carried on by a company has become small or negligible, and before any considerable revival of the trade or business, there is a change in the ownership of the company.

(2) Regulation 14 shall apply in relation to an accounting period in which the change of ownership occurs as if the part ending with the change of ownership, and the part after, were two separate accounting periods; and for that purpose the profits of the company charged to corporation tax for the accounting period shall be apportioned between those parts.

(3) No unrelieved surplus ACT of the company shall be set off against the company's liability to corporation tax on any profits charged to corporation tax for an accounting period ending after the change of ownership; and for this purpose an accounting period in which the change of ownership occurs shall be treated as if the part ending with the change of ownership, and the part after, were two separate accounting periods.

(4) Paragraph (3) applies to unrelieved surplus ACT consisting of ACT which a subsidiary is treated as having paid by virtue of section 240(2) as it applies to unrelieved surplus ACT consisting of ACT paid in respect of any distribution made by the subsidiary.

(5) Sections 768(8) and (9) and 769 shall apply for the purposes of this regulation as if in subsection (3) of section 769 the reference to the benefit of the losses were a reference to the benefit of unrelieved surplus ACT.

(6) In paragraph (1) "a major change in the nature or conduct of a trade or business" includes—

(*a*) a major change in the type of property dealt in, or services or facilities provided, in the trade or business;

(*b*) a major change in customers, outlets or markets of the trade or business;

(*c*) a change whereby the company ceases to be a trading company and becomes an investment company or vice versa; or

(*d*) where the company is an investment company, a major change in the nature of the investments held by the company;

and this paragraph applies even if the change is the result of a gradual process which began outside the period of three years mentioned in paragraph (1).

(7) In this regulation—

"trading company" means a company whose business consists wholly or mainly in the carrying on of a trade or trades;

"investment company" means a company (other than a holding company) whose business consists wholly or mainly in the making of investments and the principal part of whose income is derived therefrom;

"holding company" means a company whose business consists wholly or mainly in the holding of shares or securities of companies which are its 90 per cent subsidiaries and which are trading companies;

"90 per cent subsidiary" has the meaning given by section 838.

Restriction on application of regulation 15 on change of ownership of company

17—(1) This regulation applies where—

(*a*) there is a change in the ownership of a company ("the relevant company"),

(*b*) there is an amount of unrelieved surplus ACT which the relevant company, as a subsidiary company, is treated as having paid by virtue of section 240(2), and

(*c*) within the period of six years beginning three years before the change, there is a major change in the nature or conduct of a trade or business of the company which is for the purposes of regulation 15 the surrendering company in relation to that amount.

(2) The amount of unrelieved surplus ACT referred to in paragraph (1)(*b*) shall not be set off in accordance with regulation 14 against the relevant company's liability to corporation tax on profits charged to corporation tax for an accounting period ending after the change of ownership; and for this purpose an accounting period in which the change of ownership occurs shall be treated as if the part ending with the change of ownership, and the part after, were two separate accounting periods.

(3) Paragraphs (5) to (7) of regulation 16 shall apply for the purposes of this regulation as they apply for the purposes of that regulation and as if the reference in paragraph (6) of regulation 16 to the period of three years mentioned in paragraph (1) of that regulation were a reference to the period mentioned in paragraph (1)(*c*) of this regulation.

Restriction on set-off under regulation 14 where asset transferred after change of ownership of company

18—(1) This regulation applies where—

(*a*) there is a change in the ownership of a company ("the relevant company"),

(*b*) after the change the relevant company acquires an asset from another company in circumstances such that section 171(1) of the Taxation of Chargeable Gains Act 1992 applies to the acquisition, and

(*c*) a chargeable gain accrues to the relevant company on the disposal of the asset within the period of three years beginning with the change of ownership.

(2) For the purposes of paragraph (1)(*c*) an asset acquired by the relevant company as mentioned in paragraph (1)(*b*) shall be treated as the same as an asset owned at a later time by that company if the value of the second asset is derived in whole or in part from the first asset, and in particular where the second asset is a freehold, and the first asset was a leasehold and the lessee has acquired the reversion.

(3) In relation to the accounting period in which the chargeable gain accrues to the relevant company ("the relevant period"), regulation 14 shall have effect as if the limit imposed by paragraph (4) of that regulation on the amount of unrelieved surplus ACT to be set against the relevant company's liability to corporation tax were reduced by an amount equal to 20 per cent of the amount of the chargeable gain.

(4) Paragraph (5) of regulation 16 shall apply for the purposes of this regulation as it applies for the purposes of that regulation.

Recovery of unrelieved surplus ACT wrongly set off

19 If an officer of the Board discovers that any set off of unrelieved surplus ACT of a company by virtue of regulation 14 ought not to have been made, or has become excessive, the officer may make any such assessments as may in his judgment be required for recovering any tax that ought to have been paid and generally for securing that the resulting liability to tax (including interest on unpaid tax) of the company is what it would have been if only such set off had been made as ought to have been made.

Set off of unrelieved surplus ACT against liability to corporation tax on profits of a controlled foreign company apportioned to a company

20—(1) In any case where—

(*a*) an amount of chargeable profits ("Chapter IV profits") of a controlled foreign company is apportioned to a company resident in the United Kingdom under the provisions of Chapter IV of Part XVII of the Taxes Act, and

(*b*) the company to whom the amount is apportioned has an amount of surplus shadow ACT, calculated in accordance with regulation 12 and (where applicable) regulation 13, available to be

SIs

set against the company's liability to corporation tax for the appropriate accounting period (including, by virtue of regulation 3(3), its liability to tax under section 747(4)(*a*) for that period),

then so much of that amount as does not exceed the relevant maximum shall be set against the company's liability to tax under that section in respect of the Chapter IV profits.

(2) So much of any unrelieved surplus ACT of the company as does not exceed the relevant amount may be set against the company's liability to tax in respect of the Chapter IV profits.

(3) Where—

(*a*) the whole of the amount of the company's surplus shadow ACT has not been set off against the company's liability to tax as mentioned in paragraph (1), and

(*b*) the company is a member of a group,

the part of that amount that has not been so utilised may be allocated by the parent company to any other company in the group to whom an amount of Chapter IV profits has been apportioned, and the provisions of this regulation shall apply accordingly to that other company.

(4) In this regulation—

(*a*) "the appropriate accounting period" has the same meaning as in paragraph 1 of Schedule 26;

(*b*) "the relevant amount" is the amount (if any) which is the difference between the amount of the relevant maximum and the amount of surplus shadow ACT set against the company's liability in respect of the Chapter IV profits in accordance with paragraph (1);

(*c*) "the relevant maximum" is the amount calculated in accordance with the formula—

$$C - D$$

where—

C is the amount of shadow ACT that would have been treated as paid (apart from regulation 11(10) to (12)) in respect of a relevant distribution made at the end of the company's appropriate accounting period of an amount which, together with the shadow ACT treated as paid in respect of it, is equal to the amount calculated in accordance with the formula specified in paragraph (5), and

D is the portion of the controlled foreign company's creditable tax (if any) which is apportioned to the company for that accounting period as mentioned in section 747(4)(*a*).

(5) The formula specified in this paragraph is—

$$E - F$$

where—

E is the amount of the Chapter IV profits on which the company is chargeable to corporation tax for the appropriate accounting period, and

F is the total of any relevant allowances which are to be regarded, by virtue of paragraph 1(5) of Schedule 26, as having been allowed as a deduction against the company's profits together with any such additional amount as would fall to be so regarded if a claim under paragraph 1(1) of Schedule 26 were made in respect of all relevant allowances that are available under that paragraph.

Displacement of unrelieved surplus ACT—consequential provision

21—(1) Where, with respect to an accounting period of a company ("the affected company") that is a member of a group at any time in that accounting period—

(*a*) an amount of unrelieved surplus ACT is displaced under regulation 12(7)(*d*) or 13(8)(*b*) or (*d*), and

(*b*) as a consequence the affected company is assessed to, or an amendment of its self-assessment is made in respect of, an amount of corporation tax for that accounting period,

then, if the whole of that amount of corporation tax is not paid by the affected company within six months from the date determined under paragraph (2), any other company that is a member of the group at any time in that accounting period may, at any time within two years from that date, be assessed and charged (in the name of the affected company) to the whole or, as the case may be, the unpaid part of that amount; and a company paying any amount of corporation tax under this paragraph shall be entitled to recover from the affected company a sum equal to the aggregate of the amount paid and any interest paid by the company under section 87A of the Taxes Management Act 1970 on that amount.

(2) The date referred to in paragraph (1) is whichever is the later of—

(*a*) the date when the amount of corporation tax became due and payable by the affected company or, as the case may be, the date when that amount is treated as having become due and payable under the Corporation Tax (Instalment Payments) Regulations 1998; and

(*b*) the date when an amendment of the affected company's self-assessment was made.

Life assurance companies

22—(1) [So much of the policy holder's franked investment income from investments of a company's long-term insurance fund as is referable to its][1] life assurance business—

(*a*) shall not be used (for the purposes of computing the amount of shadow ACT which the company is treated as having paid for an accounting period under regulation 11(10)) to frank relevant distributions made by the company in that period;

(*b*) shall be disregarded in determining whether the company has a surplus of franked investment income as mentioned in regulation 11(13), or the amount of the surplus.

(2) For the purposes of regulations 12 to 14, the profits charged to corporation tax for any accounting period of a company carrying on life assurance business shall be reduced by deducting the policy holders' share of the relevant profits.

(3) In this regulation—

"life assurance business" [and "long-term insurance fund"][1] shall be construed in accordance with section 431(2);

"policy holders' share of the franked investment income" shall be construed in accordance with section 434(6A)(*a*);

"policy holders' share of the relevant profits" shall be construed in accordance with section 89 of the Finance Act 1989.

Amendments—[1] Words in para (1) substituted, and words in para (2) inserted by the Corporation Tax (Treatment of Unrelieved Surplus Advance Corporation Tax) (Amendment) Regulations, SI 2003/1861 with effect for distributions made after 8 April 2003 in accounting periods beginning before, as well as accounting periods ending on or after, 7 August 2003.

Cancellation of tax advantage

23—(1) Section 704 shall have effect in relation to any relevant distribution with the modification specified in paragraph (2).

(2) In paragraph A after sub-paragraph (*d*) there shall be inserted—

"(*da*) the application of franked investment income for the purpose of regulations made under section 32 of the Finance Act 1998, or".

1999/498

Insurance Companies (Capital Redemption Business) (Modification of the Corporation Tax Acts) Regulations 1999

Made by the Treasury under TA 1988 s 458A

Made	*1 March 1999*
Laid before the House of Commons	*2 March 1999*
Coming into force	*23 March 1999*

Commentary—*Simon's Direct Tax Service* **D4.503, 530**.

Citation, commencement and effect

1 These Regulations may be cited as the Insurance Companies (Capital Redemption Business) (Modification of the Corporation Tax Acts) Regulations 1999, shall come into force on 23rd March 1999 and shall have effect with respect to accounting periods of insurance companies ending on or after 1st July 1999.

Interpretation

2 In these Regulations—

"capital redemption business" means any capital redemption business within the meaning of section 458 of the Taxes Act, other than business referred to in subsection (4) of that section;

"the life assurance provisions of the Corporation Tax Acts" shall be construed in accordance with section 458A(4) of the Taxes Act;

"the Taxes Act" means the Income and Corporation Taxes Act 1988.

Application of life assurance provisions of the Corporation Tax Acts to capital redemption business

3 The life assurance provisions of the Corporation Tax Acts specified in regulations 4 to 16 shall have effect in relation to any insurance company carrying on capital redemption business—

(*a*) as if the company's capital redemption business were life assurance business; and

(*b*) as respects its capital redemption business, with the modifications provided for in those regulations.

Modifications of section 76 of the Taxes Act

4—(1) Section 76 of the Taxes Act shall be modified as follows.

(2) Subsection (5A) shall be omitted.

(3) In subsection (6) the words from "or to any" to the end shall be omitted.

(4) In subsection (8) the definition of "capital redemption business" shall be omitted.

Modifications of section 431 of the Taxes Act

5—(1) Section 431 of the Taxes Act shall be modified as follows.

(2) In subsection (2)—

(*a*) after the definition of "basic life assurance and general annuity business" there shall be inserted the following definition—

"'capital redemption business' has the same meaning as in section 458;";

(*b*) in the definition of "life assurance business" there shall be added at the end the words "and capital redemption business".

Modification of section 431B of the Taxes Act

6—(1) Section 431B of the Taxes Act shall be modified as follows.

(2) In subsection (1) after the words "life assurance business" there shall be inserted the words ", other than its capital redemption business,".

Modification of section 458 of the Taxes Act

7—(1) Section 458 of the Taxes Act shall be modified as follows.

(2) Subsections (1) and (2) shall be omitted.

Modification of Schedule 19AC to the Taxes Act

8—(1) Schedule 19AC to the Taxes Act shall be modified as follows.

(2) In paragraph 5(1), in paragraph (*a*) of the subsection (6A) notionally inserted in section 76 of the Taxes Act, the words "or capital redemption business" shall be omitted.

Modification of section 44 of the Finance Act 1989

9—(1) Section 44 of the Finance Act 1989 shall be modified as follows.

(2) After subsection (12) there shall be inserted the following subsection—

"(12A) In subsection (12) above 'life assurance business' has the same meaning as in Chapter I of Part XII of the Taxes Act 1988."

Modification of section 82 of the Finance Act 1989

10—(1) Section 82 of the Finance Act 1989 shall be modified as follows.

(2) After subsection (8) there shall be added the following subsection—

"(9) In this section and in sections 83, 83AA(*d*) , 85, 86, 88, 88A(*e*) and 89, and in paragraph 1A(1) of Schedule 8A(*f*) , 'life assurance business' has the same meaning as in Chapter I of Part XII of the Taxes Act 1988."

Modification of section 213 of the Taxation of Chargeable Gains Act 1992

11—(1) Section 213 of the Taxation of Chargeable Gains Act 1992shall be modified as follows.

(2) In subsection (1A) for the words from "which" to the end there shall be substituted the words "which are referable to basic life assurance and general annuity business".

Modification of section 214 of the Taxation of Chargeable Gains Act 1992

12—(1) Section 214 of the Taxation of Chargeable Gains Act 1992 shall be modified as follows.

(2) In subsection (1)(*c*) (definition of "relevant linked liabilities") after the words "general annuity business" there shall be inserted the words ", other than capital redemption business,".

Modification of section 65 of the Finance (No 2) Act 1992

13—(1) Section 65 of the Finance (No 2) Act 1992 shall be modified as follows.

(2) In subsection (3)(*b*) there shall be added at the end the words "and capital redemption business".

Modification of Schedule 18 to the Finance Act 1994

14—(1) Schedule 18 to the Finance Act 1994 shall be modified as follows.

(2) In paragraph 1A(1) the words "or capital redemption business" shall be omitted.

Modifications of Schedule 11 to the Finance Act 1996

15—(1) Schedule 11 to the Finance Act 1996 shall be modified as follows.

(2) In paragraph 1(1)(*a*) and (2) the words "or capital redemption business", in both places where they occur, shall be omitted.

(3) In paragraph 2—

(*a*) for sub-paragraph (1) there shall be substituted the following paragraph—

"(1) Where an insurance company carries on basic life assurance and general annuity business, a separate computation, using only the non-trading credits and non-trading debits referable to that business, shall be made for the purposes of this Chapter in relation to that business.";

(*b*) in sub-paragraph (3) for the words from "Where" to "capital redemption business," there shall be substituted the words "Where an insurance company carries on life assurance business or any category of life assurance business,".

(4) In paragraph 4—

(*a*) in sub-paragraph (1) for the words from "paragraph 2 above" to "capital redemption business," there shall be substituted the words "paragraph 2 above for basic life assurance and general annuity business,";
(*b*) in sub-paragraph (2)(*a*) for the words "the relevant category of business" there shall be substituted the words "basic life assurance and general annuity business";
(*c*) in sub-paragraph (7) for the words "the relevant category of business" there shall be substituted the words "its basic life assurance and general annuity business";
(*d*) in sub-paragraph (10) for the words "the relevant category of business" there shall be substituted the words "basic life assurance and general annuity business";
(*e*) in sub-paragraph (16) the definition of "the relevant category of business" and the word "and" immediately preceding it shall be omitted.

(5) In paragraph 6—

(*a*) the definition of "capital redemption business" shall be omitted;
(*b*) in the definition of "life assurance business" after the words "annuity business" there shall be inserted the words "or capital redemption business".

Modification of paragraph 19 of Schedule 12 to the Finance Act 1997

16—(1) Paragraph 19 of Schedule 12 to the Finance Act 1997 shall be modified as follows.

(2) After sub-paragraph (4) there shall be added the following sub-paragraph—

"(5) In this paragraph 'life assurance business' has the same meaning as in Chapter I of Part XII of the Taxes Act 1988."

1999/564
Finance Act 1993, Section 86(2), (Fish Quota) Order 1999

Made by the Treasury under FA 1993 s 86(2)

Made	*3 March 1999*
Laid before the House of Commons	*8 March 1999*
Coming into force	*29 March 1999*

Commentary—*Simon's Direct Tax Service* **C3.301—303**.

1—(1) This Order may be cited as the Finance Act 1993, Section 86(2), (Fish Quota) Order 1999 and shall come into force on 29 March 1999.

(2) This Order shall have effect—

(*a*) in a case where the old assets (but not the new assets) referred to in section 152(1) are fish quota, where the disposal of the old assets takes place on or after the day on which this Order comes into force;
(*b*) in a case where the new assets (but not the old assets) referred to in section 152(1) are fish quota, where the acquisition of the new assets takes place on or after the day on which this Order comes into force; and
(*c*) in a case where both the old assets and the new assets referred to in section 152(1) are fish quota, where both the disposal of the old assets and the acquisition of the new assets take place on or after the day on which this Order comes into force.

2 In this Order, "section 152(1)" and "section 155" mean section 152(1) and 155 of the Taxation of Chargeable Gains Act 1992, respectively.

3 (*inserts* TCGA 1992 s 155 Class 7).

1999/619
Finance Act 1998, Section 37, (Appointed Day) Order 1999

Made by the Treasury under FA 1998 s 37(3)

Made . . . . *9 March 1999*

Commentary—*Simon's Direct Tax Service* **A7.1102, 1115.**

1 This Order may be cited as the Finance Act 1998, Section 37, (Appointed Day) Order 1999.

2 The day appointed for the purposes of section 37 of the Finance Act 1998 (abolition of periodic accounting of tax on interest on gilt-edged securities) is 1st April 1999.

1999/622
Friendly Societies (Provisional Repayments for Exempt Business) Regulations 1999

Made by the Treasury under FA 1993 s 121

Made . . . . *9 March 1999*
Laid before the House of Commons . . . . *9 March 1999*
Coming into force . . . . *30 March 1999*

Commentary—*Simon's Direct Tax Service* **D4.534, 602.**

Modifications—Application of these Regulations, with modifications, in relation to cases where payments of interest on relevant gilt-edged securities are made without deduction of tax to friendly societies carrying on exempt business for accounting periods beginning before 1 April 1999 and ending after 30 June 1999: see the Friendly Societies (Gilt-edged Societies) (Periodic Accounting for Tax on Interest) Regulations, SI 1999/624 regs 4—8.

Note—These Regulations are amended by the Friendly Societies (Provisional Repayment for Exempt Business) (Amendment) Regulations, SI 2001/3973, as detailed below, with effect for accounting periods of friendly societies beginning after 31 December 2001. The text of TA 1988 Sch 19AB as modified by SI 1999/622 (and amended by SI 2001/3973) is reproduced in SI 2001/3973, Schedule.

Citation, commencement and effect

1—(1) These Regulations may be cited as the Friendly Societies (Provisional Repayments for Exempt Business) Regulations 1999 and shall come into force on 30th March 1999.

(2) These Regulations shall have effect in relation to accounting periods of friendly societies ending on or after 1st July 1999.

Interpretation

2 In these Regulations unless the context otherwise requires—

"exempt business" means any business of a friendly society the profits arising from which are exempt from income tax and corporation tax under section 460(1)...[1] of the Taxes Act, not being a business carried on by a friendly society all of whose profits are so exempt;

"Schedule 3" means Schedule 3 to the Finance (No 2) Act 1997;

"Schedule 19AB" means Schedule 19AB to the Taxes Act;

"the Taxes Act" means the Income and Corporation Taxes Act 1988.

Amendments—[1] Words revoked by the Friendly Societies (Provisional Repayments for Exempt Business) (Amendment) Regulations, SI 2001/3973 reg 3 with effect for accounting periods of friendly societies beginning after 31 December 2001.

Application of Schedule 19AB—general

3—(1) Schedule 19AB shall have effect, in accordance with paragraphs (2) and (3) below, in relation to exempt business of a friendly society ...[1].

(2) Schedule 19AB, as it is deemed to have effect, by virtue of paragraph 12(1) of Schedule 3 for the purposes of section 121 of the Finance Act 1993, without the amendments made by Schedule 3, shall have effect as mentioned in paragraph (1) above with the modifications and exceptions specified in regulations 4, 5 and 8 to 12.

(3) ...[1].

Amendments—[1] Words in para (1) revoked, and para (3) revoked by the Friendly Societies (Provisional Repayments for Exempt Business) (Amendment) Regulations, SI 2001/3973 regs 4, 5 with effect for accounting periods of friendly societies beginning after 31 December 2001.

Substitution of paragraph 1(1) of Schedule 19AB (as unamended by Schedule 3)

4—(1) Paragraph (2) substitutes the following sub-paragraph for sub-paragraph (1) of paragraph 1 of Schedule 19AB (as unamended by Schedule 3) in relation to exempt business of a friendly society.

(2) For that sub-paragraph (1) there shall be substituted—

"(1) A friendly society carrying on both tax exempt business and business other than tax exempt business shall for each provisional repayment period in an accounting period be entitled on a claim made in that behalf to a payment (in this Schedule referred to as a 'provisional repayment') of an amount equal to ...[1]—

(*a*) ...[1]

(*b*) ...[1]

(*c*) as respects any distribution made on or after 6th April 1999 and before 6th April 2004 that—

(i) is received by the society in that provisional repayment period, [and][1]

(ii) is referable to its tax exempt business, ...[1]

(iii) ...[1]

the appropriate portion of any tax credit in respect of that distribution.''

Amendments—[1] In para (2) words revoked, and word inserted, by the Friendly Societies (Provisional Repayments for Exempt Business) (Amendment) Regulations, SI 2001/3973 reg 6 with effect for accounting periods of friendly societies beginning after 31 December 2001.

Substitution of paragraph 1(5) of Schedule 19AB where regulation 4 applies

5—(1) Paragraph (2) substitutes the following sub-paragraphs for sub-paragraph (5) of paragraph 1 of Schedule 19AB in circumstances where regulation 4(2) applies.

(2) For sub-paragraph (5) there shall be substituted—

''(5) ...[2]

(5A) In sub-paragraph (1)(*c*) above 'the appropriate portion' means—

(*a*) where the distribution in question is income arising from assets linked to tax exempt basic life assurance and general annuity business or to tax exempt class IV business the profits of which are exempt from tax by virtue of section 460(1) ('section 460(1) exempt business'), the whole;

(*b*) where the distribution in question is income arising from assets of the society's overseas life assurance fund, the fraction whose numerator is the mean of the opening and closing liabilities to policyholders in respect of the society's tax exempt overseas life assurance business and whose denominator is the opening and closing liabilities to policyholders in respect of the whole of the society's overseas life assurance business;

(*c*) if and to the extent that the distribution in question is income arising from assets of the society's [long-term insurance fund][1] but, on the assumption that section 460(1) exempt business were a separate category of business within section 432A, is not referable to a category of business by virtue of subsection (3) or (4) of that section, the provisional fraction;

(*d*) except as provided by paragraph (*a*), (*b*) or (*c*) above, none.

(5B) ...[2]

(5C) In determining the provisional fraction for the purposes of sub-paragraph (5A)(*c*) above, tax exempt basic life assurance and general annuity business and section 460(1) exempt business shall be taken to be a single category for the purposes of section 432A(5).

(5D) In [sub-paragraph] [2](5A) above references to assets of the society's [long-term insurance fund][1]—

(*a*) as respects societies to which regulation 13(1) of the Friendly Societies (Modification of the Corporation Tax Acts) Regulations 1997 applies, shall be construed in accordance with the definition in subsection (11) of section 432A, read with subsections (12) to (14) of that section, as those subsections are added by regulation 13(5) of those Regulations;

(*b*) as respects other societies, shall be construed in accordance with the definitions of '[long-term][1] business' (as substituted by regulation 6(4) of those Regulations) and '[long-term insurance fund][1]' in section 431(2).

(5E) In sub-paragraphs [(5A) and][2] (5C) above—

'tax exempt basic life assurance and general annuity business' shall be construed in accordance with the definition inserted in section 431(2) by regulation 6(2) of the Friendly Societies (Modification of the Corporation Tax Acts) Regulations 1997;

'tax exempt class IV business' shall be construed in accordance with the definition inserted in section 431(2) by regulation 7(2) of those Regulations;

'tax exempt overseas life assurance business' shall be construed in accordance with section 441(4D).''

Amendments—[1] Words in para (2) substituted by the Financial Services and Markets Act 2000 (Consequential Amendments) (Taxes) Order, SI 2001/3629 art 182 with effect from 1 December 2001, immediately after the coming into force of the Financial Services and Markets Act 2000 ss 411, 432(1), Sch 20 (and SI 2001/3629 Pts 1 and 2).

[2] Words substituted and revoked by the Friendly Societies (Provisional Repayments for Exempt Business) (Amendment) Regulations, SI 2001/3973 reg 7 with effect for accounting periods of friendly societies beginning after 31 December 2001.

Substitution of paragraph 1(1) of Schedule 19AB (as amended by Schedule 3)

6 ...[1]

Amendment—[1] Revoked by the Friendly Societies (Provisional Repayments for Exempt Business) (Amendment) Regulations, SI 2001/3973 reg 8 with effect for accounting periods of friendly societies beginning after 31 December 2001.

Substitution of paragraph 1(5) of Schedule 19AB where regulation 6 applies

7 ...[1]

Amendment—[1] Revoked by the Friendly Societies (Provisional Repayments for Exempt Business) (Amendment) Regulations, SI 2001/3973 reg 8 with effect for accounting periods of friendly societies beginning after 31 December 2001.

Modifications of paragraph 1(2) to (4), (7), (10) and (11) of Schedule 19AB

8—(1) Paragraphs (2) to (7) specify modifications of sub-paragraphs (2) to (4), (7), (10) and (11) of paragraph 1 of Schedule 19AB in relation to exempt business of a friendly society.

(2) In sub-paragraph (2)—

(*a*) for the words "a company" there shall be substituted the words "a society";

(*b*) for paragraph (*a*) there shall be substituted—

"(*a*) shall begin whenever—

(i) the society begins, at a time when it is carrying on only tax exempt business, to carry on business other than tax exempt business;

(ii) the society begins, at a time when it is carrying on only business other than tax exempt business, to carry on tax exempt business;

(iii) an accounting period of the society begins at a time when the society is carrying on both tax exempt business and business other than tax exempt business; or

(iv) a provisional repayment period of the society ends, at a time when the society is carrying on both tax exempt business and business other than tax exempt business; and";

(*c*) in paragraph (*b*)(ii) for the word "company" there shall be substituted the word "society".

[(3) Sub-paragraph (3) shall be omitted.][1]

[(4) For sub-paragraph (4) there shall be substituted the following sub-paragraph—

"(4) The provisional fraction for the purposes of this paragraph for an accounting period which begins before 6 April 2004 shall be such fraction as the society may reasonably estimate, being a fraction which is not likely to be greater than the relevant fraction for its tax exempt business which would be determined in accordance with subsections (5) to (9B) of section 432A for that accounting period."][1]

(5) In sub-paragraph (7)—

(*a*) for the words "pension business" (wherever occurring) there shall be substituted the words "tax exempt business";

(*b*) for the word "company" (wherever occurring) there shall be substituted the word "society".

[(*c*) the words "or repaid" shall be omitted;][1]

[(*d*) paragraph (*a*) shall be omitted;][1]

[(*e*) for "9(2)" there shall be substituted "9(3)";][1]

[(*f*) the words "or section 42(4) of the Management Act" shall be omitted.][1]

[(6) Paragraphs (10) and (11) shall be omitted.][1]

Modifications—Insertion of paras (2A), (2B) in applying these Regulations in relation to cases where payments of interest on relevant gilt-edged securities are made without deduction of tax to friendly societies carrying on exempt business for accounting periods beginning before 1 April 1999 and ending after 30 June 1999: see the Friendly Societies (Gilt-edged Societies) (Periodic Accounting for Tax on Interest) Regulations, SI 1999/624 regs 4, 5.

Amendments—[1] Paras (3), (4) substituted, para (5)(*c*)–(*f*) added, and para (6) substituted for paras (6), (7), by the Friendly Societies (Provisional Repayments for Exempt Business) (Amendment) Regulations, SI 2001/3973 reg 9 with effect for accounting periods of friendly societies beginning after 31 December 2001.

[Modifications of paragraph 1A of Schedule 19AB]

[8A—(1)—(7) ...]

Modifications—This regulation is treated as inserted in applying these Regulations in relation to cases where payments of interest on relevant gilt-edged securities are made without deduction of tax to friendly societies carrying on exempt business for accounting periods beginning before 1 April 1999 and ending after 30 June 1999: see the Friendly Societies (Gilt-edged Societies) (Periodic Accounting for Tax on Interest) Regulations, SI 1999/624 regs 4, 6.

[Disapplication of Paragraph 2 of Schedule 19AB

9 Paragraph 2 of Schedule 19AB shall not apply to exempt business of a friendly society.][1]

Amendments—[1] Substituted by the Friendly Societies (Provisional Repayments for Exempt Business) (Amendment) Regulations, SI 2001/3973 reg 10 with effect for accounting periods of friendly societies beginning after 31 December 2001.

Modifications of paragraph 3 of Schedule 19AB

10—(1) Paragraphs (2) to (7) specify modifications of paragraph 3 of Schedule 19AB in relation to exempt business of a friendly society.

(2) In sub-paragraph (1)—

(*a*) for the words "an insurance company's" there shall be substituted the words "a friendly society's";

(*b*) for the words "the company" there shall be substituted the words "the society";

(*c*) for the words "the insurance company" there shall be substituted the words "the friendly society".

(3) In sub-paragraph (1A)—

(*a*) for the word "company" (wherever occurring) there shall be substituted the word "society";
(*b*) for the words "pension business" (wherever occurring) there shall be substituted the words "tax exempt business".
[(*c*) for the words "assumptions in sub-paragraphs (1B) and (1C)" there shall be substituted the words "assumption in sub-paragraph (1B)";][1]
[(*d*) the words "or repaid" shall be omitted;][1]
[(*e*) for "9(2)" there shall be substituted "9(3)";][1]
[(*f*) the words "or section 42(4) of the Management Act" shall be omitted;][1]
[(*g*) paragraph (*a*) shall be omitted.][1]

(4) In sub-paragraph (1B)—

(*a*) for the words "the company" there shall be substituted the words "the society";
(*b*) for the words "the company's" there shall be substituted the words "the society's".
[(*c*) the word "first" shall be omitted;][1]
[(*d*) the words "or repayments" shall be omitted;][1]
[(*e*) paragraph (*a*) shall be omitted;][1]
[(*f*) in paragraph (*b*) for the words "that sub-paragraph" there shall be substituted the words "sub-paragraph (1A) above."][1]

[(5) Sub-paragraph (1C) shall be omitted.][1]

(6) In sub-paragraph (5) for the word "company" there shall be substituted the word "society".

[(7) In sub-paragraph (8)—

(*a*) for the word "company" (wherever occurring) there shall be substituted the word "society";
(*b*) the words "or repaid" shall be omitted;
(*c*) paragraph (*a*) shall be omitted;
(*d*) in paragraph (*b*) for the words "that sub-paragraph" there shall be substituted the words 'sub-paragraph (1A) above."][1]

Modifications—Insertion of para (5A), and words in paras (2)(*b*), (6), in applying these Regulations in relation to cases where payments of interest on relevant gilt-edged securities are made without deduction of tax to friendly societies carrying on exempt business for accounting periods beginning before 1 April 1999 and ending after 30 June 1999: see the Friendly Societies (Gilt-edged Societies) (Periodic Accounting for Tax on Interest) Regulations, SI 1999/624 regs 4, 8.

Amendments—[1] Paras (3)(*c*)–(*g*) and (4)(*c*)–(*f*) added, and paras (5) and (7) substituted, by the Friendly Societies (Provisional Repayments for Exempt Business) (Amendment) Regulations, SI 2001/3973 reg 11 with effect for accounting periods of friendly societies beginning after 31 December 2001.

Disapplication of paragraphs 4 and 5 of Schedule 19AB

11 Paragraphs 4 and 5 of Schedule 19AB shall not apply to exempt business of a friendly society.

Modifications of paragraph 6 of Schedule 19AB

12—(1) Paragraphs (2) and (3) specify modifications of paragraph 6 of Schedule 19AB in relation to exempt business of a friendly society.

(2) In sub-paragraph (1) [—

(*a*)][1] after the definition of "provisional repayment period" there shall be added the following definition—

"'tax exempt business' means any business of a friendly society the profits arising from which are exempt from income tax and corporation tax under section 460(1), ...[1]."

[(*b*) in the definition of "provisional fraction" for the words "paragraphs 1(4) and 2" there shall be substituted "paragraph 1(4)".][1]

[(3) Sub-paragraphs (4) to (6) shall be omitted.][1]

Amendments—[1] Para (2)(*a*) numbered as such, para (2)(*b*) added, and para (3) substituted, by the Friendly Societies (Provisional Repayments for Exempt Business) (Amendment) Regulations, SI 2001/3973 reg 12 with effect for accounting periods of friendly societies beginning after 31 December 2001.

Revocations

13 The Friendly Societies (Provisional Repayments for Exempt Business) Regulations 1993 and the Friendly Societies (Provisional Repayments for Exempt Business) (Amendment) Regulations 1997 are hereby revoked as respects accounting periods in relation to which, by virtue of regulation 1(2), these Regulations have effect.

1999/623
Insurance Companies (Gilt-edged Securities) (Periodic Accounting for Tax on Interest) Regulations 1999

Made by the Treasury under TA 1988 s 51B(1)–(4)

Made . . . . *9 March 1999*
Laid before the House of Commons . . . . *9 March 1999*
Coming into force . . . . . *30 March 1999*

Commentary—*Simon's Direct Tax Service* **A7.1125**.

Citation, commencement and effect

1—(1) These Regulations may be cited as the Insurance Companies (Gilt-edged Securities) (Periodic Accounting for Tax on Interest) Regulations 1999 and shall come into force on 30th March 1999.
(2) These Regulations have effect as respects payments of interest on relevant gilt-edged securities made without deduction of tax to an insurance company carrying on pension business that fall within an accounting period of that company beginning before 1st April 1999 and ending on or after 1st July 1999, not being payments to which section 51B(5A) of the Taxes Act refers.

Interpretation

2 In these Regulations unless the context otherwise requires—
"amount of excess gilt interest received" has the same meaning as in the Gilts Regulations;
"the Gilts Regulations" means the Gilt-edged Securities (Periodic Accounting for Tax on Interest) Regulations 1995;
"pension business" has the meaning given by section 431B of the Taxes Act;
"relevant gilt-edged securities" has the meaning given by section 51B(5) of the Taxes Act;
"return period" has the same meaning as in the Gilts Regulations;
"Schedule 19AB" means Schedule 19AB to the Taxes Act;
"the Taxes Act" means the Income and Corporation Taxes Act 1988.

Basic rule

3—(1) Notwithstanding the provisions of the Gilts Regulations, an insurance company carrying on pension business shall not be required to include in its return for a return period—
(*a*) the amount of tax on the amount of excess gilt interest received in relation to which the condition specified in paragraph (2) below is satisfied, or
(*b*) the appropriate portion of the amount of excess gilt interest received.
(2) The condition specified is that the amount of tax referred to in paragraph (1)(*a*) above is identified in a claim, made by the specified date, for a notional repayment made pursuant to paragraph 1A(1) of Schedule 19AB (as inserted by regulation 6 of these Regulations).
(3) In paragraph (1)(*b*) above "the appropriate portion" has the meaning given by paragraph 1A(7) of Schedule 19AB (as so inserted).
(4) In paragraph (2) above "the specified date" means—
(*a*) the date which is 14 days after the end of the return period, or
(*b*) where the return for the return period is made on a date less than 14 days after the end of the return period, that date.

Modifications of Schedule 19AB

4 Regulations 5 to 9 make provision modifying the operation of Schedule 19AB in relation to cases where payments of interest on relevant gilt-edged securities are made without deduction of tax to an insurance company carrying on pension business.

5—(1) Paragraphs (2) and (3) below specify modifications of paragraph 1 of Schedule 19AB.
(2) In sub-paragraph (2), before the words "For the purposes of this paragraph" there shall be inserted the words "Subject to sub-paragraphs (2A) and (2B) below,".
(3) After sub-paragraph (2) there shall be inserted the following sub-paragraphs—

"(2A) Sub-paragraph (2B) below has effect where payments of interest on relevant gilt-edged securities are made without deduction of tax to insurance companies carrying on pension business.
(2B) For the purposes of this paragraph, a 'provisional repayment period' of a company—
(*a*) shall begin—
(i) on the date on which the company begins to carry on pension business; or
(ii) on the date on which the accounting period of the company beginning before 1st April 1999 and ending on or after 1st July 1999 begins, where the company is carrying on pension business at that time; or

(iii) if different from either of the dates referred to in sub-paragraphs (i) and (ii) above, on 1st October 1998 or 1st January 1999, where that date falls within the accounting period referred to in sub-paragraph (ii) above; and

(*b*) shall end on the expiration of a period ending on 30th September 1998, 31st December 1998 or 31st March 1999, where that date falls within the accounting period referred to in paragraph (*a*)(ii) above.''

(4) Where by virtue of paragraph 1(2B)(*b*) of Schedule 19AB (inserted by paragraph (3) above) a provisional repayment period of a company ends on 31st March 1999, being a time when the company is carrying on pension business, a provisional repayment period of the company shall be taken also to have ended on that date for the purposes of paragraph 1(2)(*a*)(iii) of that Schedule.

6 After paragraph 1 of Schedule 19AB there shall be inserted the following paragraph—

''*Entitlement to certain notional payments on account*

1A—(1) An insurance company carrying on pension business shall for each provisional repayment period in its accounting period beginning before 1st April 1999 and ending on or after 1st July 1999 be entitled on a claim made in that behalf by the specified date to a notional payment (in this Schedule referred to as a 'notional repayment') of an amount equal, subject to paragraph 2 below, to the tax on the appropriate portion of the amount of excess gilt interest received in that provisional repayment period and referable to its pension business, or to a notional repayment of such lesser amount as may be specified in the claim.

(2) No repayment shall be made to a company in respect of any claim to a notional repayment; but the notional repayment shall be taken to be the amount of tax referred to in regulation 3(1) of the Insurance Companies (Gilt-edged Securities) (Periodic Accounting for Tax on Interest) Regulations 1999.

(3) For the purposes of this paragraph a 'provisional repayment period' of a company—

(*a*) shall begin—

(i) on the date on which the company begins to carry on pension business; or

(ii) on the date on which the accounting period of the company beginning before 1st April 1999 and ending on or after 1st July 1999 begins, where the company is carrying on pension business at that time; or

(iii) if different from either of the dates referred to in sub-paragraphs (i) and (ii) above, on 1st October 1998 or 1st January 1999, where that date falls within the accounting period referred to in sub-paragraph (ii) above; and

(*b*) shall end on the expiration of a period ending on 30th September 1998, 31st December 1998 or 31st March 1999, where that date falls within the accounting period referred to in paragraph (*a*)(ii).

(4) In sub-paragraph (1) above 'the specified date' means the earlier of the following dates—

(*a*) the date which is 14 days after the end of a provisional repayment period, or

(*b*) where a provisional repayment period coincides with a return period within the meaning of the Gilts Regulations and the return for the return period is made on a date less than 14 days after the end of the return period, that date.

(5) In the application of subsections (5) to (9) of section 432A for the purpose of determining the amounts to which a company is entitled by way of notional repayments, the reference in subsection (5) to 'the relevant fraction' shall be taken as a reference to the fraction determined in accordance with subsections (6) to (9)—

(*a*) for the latest preceding accounting period of the company for which an inspector is satisfied that the company has supplied him with such information as would enable the relevant fraction for that accounting period to be estimated with reasonable accuracy, and

(*b*) by reference to that information,

and, subject to sub-paragraph (6)(*b*) below, any reference in this paragraph to 'the provisional fraction' is a reference to the fraction so determined.

(6) For the purposes of sub-paragraph (5) above—

(*a*) 'information' means any information, accounts, statements or reports delivered under section 11 of the Management Act; and

(*b*) unless and until an inspector is satisfied as mentioned in paragraph (*a*) of that sub-paragraph, the provisional fraction shall be taken to be nil;

but this sub-paragraph is subject to paragraph 2 below.

(7) In sub-paragraph (1) above 'the appropriate portion' means—

(*a*) in the case of an insurance company carrying on pension business and no other category of long term business, the whole; and

(*b*) in the case of an insurance company carrying on more than one category of long term business—

(i) where the payment in question is of interest on relevant gilt-edged securities arising from an asset linked to pension business, the whole;

(ii) where the payment in question is an amount of manufactured gilt interest received derived from an asset which at the time of its transfer (being the transfer referred to in paragraph 3 of Schedule 23A) was linked to pension business, the whole;

(iii) where the payment in question is an amount of manufactured gilt interest paid in respect of an asset linked to pension business, the whole;

(iv) if and to the extent that the payment in question is income which is not referable to a category of business by virtue of subsection (3) or (4) of section 432A, the provisional fraction, and

(v) except as provided by sub-paragraphs (i) to (iv) above, none.

(8) For the purposes of sub-paragraph (7)(*b*)(iv) above and in relation to a manufactured payment, the provisional fraction shall be found by applying subsections (5) to (9) of section 432A to the payment as if it were an amount of income arising from the assets of the company's long term fund.

(9) In sub-paragraph (1) above 'the amount of excess gilt interest received', in relation to a provisional repayment period, means the amount ascertained in accordance with the formula—

$$(A + B) - C$$

where—

A is the amount of manufactured gilt interest received in that provisional repayment period;
B is the amount of real gilt interest received in that provisional repayment period; and
C is the amount of manufactured gilt interest paid in that provisional repayment period;

and where the aggregate of A and B exceeds C.

(10) Where a claim made pursuant to sub-paragraph (1) above is for a lesser amount as mentioned in that sub-paragraph, the appropriate portion of each of the amounts A, B and C specified in sub-paragraph (9) above shall be ascertained in accordance with the formula—

$$D/E$$

where—

D is the lesser amount of the notional repayment claimed, and
E is the maximum amount of the notional repayment which it is possible for the company to claim.

(11) Paragraphs 57 to 60 of Schedule 18 to the Finance Act 1998 (general provisions as to procedure on claims and elections) shall not apply to a claim for a notional repayment.

(12) A claim for a notional repayment shall be in such form as the Board may determine and the form of claim shall provide for a declaration to the effect that all the particulars given in the form are correctly stated to the best of the knowledge and belief of the person making the claim.

(13) In this paragraph 'manufactured payment' means any payment which for the purposes of Schedule 23A is a payment of manufactured interest, and to which paragraph 3A(2)(*a*) of that Schedule applies.''

7—(1) Paragraphs (2) to (6) below specify modifications of paragraph 2 of Schedule 19AB.

(2) In sub-paragraph (1)(*a*) and (*c*), after the words ''a provisional repayment'', in both places where they occur, there shall be inserted the words ''or a notional repayment''.

(3) In sub-paragraph (2)(*a*)—

(*a*) after the words ''any provisional repayment'' there shall be inserted the words ''or notional repayment'';

(*b*) after the words ''sub-paragraph (3)'' there shall be inserted the words ''or (3A)''.

(4) In sub-paragraph (3), at the beginning, there shall be inserted the words ''In the case of provisional repayments,''.

(5) After sub-paragraph (3) there shall be inserted the following sub-paragraphs—

''(3A) In the case of notional repayments, the amount referred to in sub-paragraph (2)(*a*) above is the amount (if any) by which total notional entitlement exceeds total notional past payments, and for this purpose—

'total notional entitlement' means the aggregate of the notional repayments to which the company would have been entitled (apart from this paragraph) for—

(*a*) the provisional repayment period to which the claim relates, and

(*b*) any earlier provisional repayment period in the same accounting period,

had the substituted provisional fraction been the provisional fraction for the accounting period as from the beginning of that period; and

'total notional past payments' means the aggregate of any amounts already taken into account by way of notional repayments for provisional repayment periods falling within that accounting period.

(3B) In a case where, following the application of sub-paragraph (3A) above, the notional repayment for a provisional repayment period is less than the amount to which the company would be entitled for that provisional repayment period (apart from that sub-paragraph), the appropriate portion of each of the amounts A, B and C specified in paragraph 1A(9) above shall be ascertained in accordance with the formula—

$$F/G$$

where—

F is the amount of any notional repayment ascertained in accordance with sub-paragraph (3A) above, and

G is the maximum amount of the notional repayment which it is possible for the company to claim (apart from that sub-paragraph).''

(6) In sub-paragraph (4), at the end there shall be added ''; and expressions used in this paragraph and in paragraph 1A above have the same meaning in this paragraph as they have in that paragraph''.

8—(1) Paragraphs (2) to (5) below specify modifications of paragraph 3 of Schedule 19AB.

(2) In sub-paragraph (1), for paragraph (*b*) there shall be substituted the following paragraph—

''(*b*) the aggregate amount of the provisional repayments made to the company for that accounting period and of the notional repayments to which the company is entitled in respect of that accounting period exceeds the aggregate of the appropriate amount and the relevant final amount,''.

(3) After sub-paragraph (1C) there shall be inserted the following sub-paragraph—

''(1CA) For the purposes of sub-paragraph (1)(*b*) above, the relevant final amount for the accounting period of a company is the amount (if any) which, on the assumptions in sub-paragraphs (1B) and (1C) above, the company would have been entitled to be repaid, when its self-assessment for the period became final, in respect of income tax borne by deduction on the amount of manufactured gilt interest received and real gilt interest received if those amounts had been paid under deduction of tax, in respect of its pension business for that accounting period on a claim such as is mentioned in section 7.''

(4) In sub-paragraph (5), at the end there shall be added—

''; and so much of the principal as does not exceed the amount of the last notional repayment made to the company for the accounting period in question shall be taken to have become outstanding on the date on which the company made the claim referred to in paragraph 1A(1) above''.

(5) In sub-paragraph (6)—

(*a*) in paragraph (*a*), after the words ''provisional repayment'' there shall be inserted the words ''or, as the case may be, notional repayment,'';

(*b*) in paragraph (*b*), after the words ''preceding provisional repayment'' there shall be inserted the words ''or, as the case may be, preceding notional repayment,'';

(*c*) after the words ''that preceding provisional repayment'' there shall be inserted the words ''or, as the case may be, that preceding notional repayment,'';

(*d*) after the words ''any preceding provisional repayments'' there shall be inserted the words ''or, as the case may be, any preceding notional repayments''.

9—(1) Paragraphs (2) and (3) below specify modifications of paragraph 6 of Schedule 19AB.

(2) In sub-paragraph (1)—

(*a*) before the definition of ''provisional fraction'' there shall be inserted the following definitions—

'''the Gilts Regulations' means the Gilt-edged Securities (Periodic Accounting for Tax on Interest) Regulations 1995;

'notional repayment' means a notional repayment under paragraph 1A above;'';

(*b*) in the definition of ''provisional fraction'' after ''1(4)'' there shall be inserted '', 1A(7) and (9)'';

(*c*) in the definition of ''provisional repayment period'' after ''1'' there shall be inserted ''or 1A'';

(*d*) at the end there shall be added the following definitions—

'''relevant gilt-edged securities' has the meaning given by section 51B(5);

'amount of manufactured gilt interest paid', 'amount of manufactured gilt interest received' and 'amount of real gilt interest received' have the same meanings in this Schedule in relation to a provisional repayment period as they have in the Gilts Regulations in relation to a return period''.

(3) After sub-paragraph (2) there shall be inserted the following sub-paragraph—

''(2A) Any reference in this Schedule to a notional repayment for an accounting period is a reference to a notional repayment for a provisional repayment period falling within that accounting period.''

Revocations

10—(1) The Regulations referred to in paragraph (2) below are, to the extent specified in that paragraph, hereby revoked as respects any payments of interest on relevant gilt-edged securities to which, by virtue of regulation 1(2) of these Regulations, these Regulations apply.

(2) The Regulations referred to are—

(*a*) the Insurance Companies (Gilt-edged Securities) (Periodic Accounting for Tax on Interest) Regulations 1995—the whole;
(*b*) the Insurance Companies (Gilt-edged Securities) (Periodic Accounting for Tax on Interest) (Amendment) Regulations 1996—the whole;
(*c*) the Stock Lending and Manufactured Payments (Revocations and Amendments) Regulations 1997—regulation 7(2)(*c*).

SIs

1999/624
Friendly Societies (Gilt-edged Securities) (Periodic Accounting for Tax on Interest) Regulations 1999

Made by the Treasury under TA 1988 s 51B(1)–(4) and FA 1993 s 121

Made . . . . 9 *March 1999*
Laid before the House of Commons . . . 9 *March 1999*
Coming into force . . . . . 30 *March 1999*

Commentary—*Simon's Direct Tax Service* **A7.1135.**

Citation, commencement and effect

1—(1) These Regulations may be cited as the Friendly Societies (Gilt-edged Securities) (Periodic Accounting for Tax on Interest) Regulations 1999 and shall come into force on 30th March 1999 immediately after the coming into force of the Insurance Companies (Gilt-edged Securities) (Periodic Accounting for Tax on Interest) Regulations 1999 and the Friendly Societies (Provisional Repayments for Exempt Business) Regulations 1999.

(2) These Regulations have effect as respects payments of interest on relevant gilt-edged securities made without deduction of tax to a friendly society that fall within an accounting period of that society beginning before 1st April 1999 and ending on or after 1st July 1999, not being payments to which section 51B(5A) of the Taxes Act refers.

Interpretation

2 In these Regulations unless the context otherwise requires—

''amount of excess gilt interest received'' has the same meaning as in the Gilts Regulations;

''exempt business'' means any business of a friendly society the profits arising from which are exempt from income tax and corporation tax under section 460(1), 461(1) or 461B(1) of the Taxes Act, not being a business carried on by a friendly society all of whose profits are so exempt;

''the Friendly Societies Regulations'' means the Friendly Societies (Provisional Repayments for Exempt Business) Regulations 1999;

''the Gilts Regulations'' means the Gilt-edged Securities (Periodic Accounting for Tax on Interest) Regulations 1995;

''relevant gilt-edged securities'' has the meaning given by section 51B(5) of the Taxes Act;

''return period'' has the same meaning as in the Gilts Regulations;

''Schedule 19AB'' means Schedule 19AB to the Taxes Act;

''the Taxes Act'' means the Income and Corporation Taxes Act 1988.

Basic rule

3—(1) Notwithstanding the provisions of the Gilts Regulations, a friendly society carrying on both exempt business and business other than exempt business shall not be required to include in its return for a return period—

(*a*) the amount of tax on the amount of excess gilt interest received in relation to which the condition specified in paragraph (2) below is satisfied, or

(*b*) the appropriate portion of the amount of excess gilt interest received.

(2) The condition specified is that the amount of tax referred to in paragraph (1)(*a*) above is identified in a claim, made by the specified date, for a notional repayment made pursuant to paragraph 1A(1) of Schedule 19AB (as inserted by regulation 6 of the Insurance Companies (Gilt-edged Securities) (Periodic Accounting for Tax on Interest) Regulations 1999).

(3) In paragraph (1)(*b*) above ''the appropriate portion'' has the meaning given by paragraph 1A(7) of Schedule 19AB (as so inserted).

(4) In paragraph (2) above ''the specified date'' means—

(*a*) the date which is 14 days after the end of the return period, or

(*b*) where the return for the return period is made on a date less than 14 days after the end of the return period, that date.

Modifications of the Friendly Societies Regulations

4 In relation to cases where payments of interest on relevant gilt-edged securities are made without deduction of tax to friendly societies carrying on exempt business, the Friendly Societies Regulations shall have effect with the modifications specified in regulations 5 to 8.

5—(1) Paragraph (2) below specifies a modification of regulation 8.

(2) After paragraph (2) of that regulation there shall be inserted the following paragraphs—

"(2A) In sub-paragraph (2A) for the words 'insurance companies carrying on pension business' there shall be substituted the words 'friendly societies carrying on tax exempt business'.

(2B) In sub-paragraph (2B)—

(*a*) for the words 'a company' there shall be substituted the words 'a society';

(*b*) for paragraphs (*a*) and (*b*) there shall be substituted the following paragraphs—

"(*a*) shall begin whenever—

(i) the society begins, at a time when it is carrying on only tax exempt business, to carry on business other than tax exempt business;

(ii) the society begins, at a time when it is carrying on only business other than tax exempt business, to carry on tax exempt business; or

(iii) the accounting period of the society beginning before 1st April 1999 and ending on or after 1st July 1999 begins, at a time when the society is carrying on both tax exempt business and business other than tax exempt business; and

(*b*) shall end on 31st March 1999."

6 After regulation 8 there shall be inserted the following regulation—

"Modifications of paragraph 1A of Schedule 19AB

8A—(1) Paragraphs (2) to (10) specify modifications of paragraph 1A of Schedule 19AB in relation to exempt business of a friendly society.

(2) In sub-paragraph (1)—

(*a*) for the words "An insurance company carrying on pension business" there shall be substituted the words "A friendly society carrying on both tax exempt business and business other than tax exempt business";

(*b*) for the words "its pension business" there shall be substituted the words "its tax exempt business".

(3) For sub-paragraph (2) there shall be substituted the following sub-paragraph—

"(2) No repayment shall be made to a society in respect of any claim to a notional repayment; but the notional repayment shall be taken to be the amount of tax referred to in regulation 3(1) of the Friendly Societies (Gilt-edged Securities) (Periodic Accounting for Tax on Interest) Regulations 1999."

(4) In sub-paragraph (3)—

(*a*) for the words "a company" there shall be substituted the words "a society";

(*b*) for paragraphs (*a*) and (*b*) there shall be substituted the following paragraphs—

"(*a*) shall begin whenever—

(i) the society begins, at a time when it is carrying on only tax exempt business, to carry on business other than tax exempt business;

(ii) the society begins, at a time when it is carrying on only business other than tax exempt business, to carry on tax exempt business; or

(iii) the accounting period of the society beginning before 1st April 1999 and ending on or after 1st July 1999 begins, at a time when the society is carrying on both tax exempt business and business other than tax exempt business; and

(*b*) shall end on 31st March 1999."

(5) In sub-paragraph (5) for the word "company" (wherever occurring) there shall be substituted the word "society".

(6) For sub-paragraph (7) there shall be substituted the following paragraphs—

"(7) In sub-paragraph (1) above 'the appropriate portion' means—

(*a*) where the payment in question is either an amount of manufactured gilt interest received or an amount of real gilt interest received and is income arising from—

(i) assets linked to tax exempt basic life assurance and general annuity business or to tax exempt class IV business, or

(ii) assets other than those of the society's long term business fund,

the whole;

(*b*) where the payment in question is as mentioned in paragraph (*a*) above but is income arising from the society's overseas life assurance fund, the fraction whose numerator is the mean of the opening and closing liabilities to policyholders in respect of the society's tax exempt overseas life assurance business and whose denominator is the mean of the opening and closing liabilities to policyholders in respect of the whole of the society's overseas life assurance business;

(*c*) where the payment in question is as mentioned in paragraph (*a*) above but is not referable to a category of business by virtue of subsection (3) or (4) of section 432A, the provisional fraction;

(*d*) where the payment in question is an amount of manufactured gilt interest paid in respect of—

(i) assets linked to tax exempt basic life assurance and general annuity business or to tax exempt class IV business, or

(ii) assets other than those of the society's long term business fund,

the whole;

(*e*) where the payment in question is as mentioned in paragraph (*d*) above but is paid in respect of income arising from assets of the society's overseas life assurance fund, the fraction whose numerator is the mean of the opening and closing liabilities to policyholders in respect of the society's tax exempt overseas life assurance business and whose denominator is the mean of the opening and closing liabilities to policyholders in respect of the whole of the society's overseas life assurance business;

(*f*) where the payment in question is as mentioned in paragraph (*d*) above but is not referable to a category of business by virtue of subsection (3) or (4) of section 432A, the provisional fraction;

(*g*) except as provided by paragraphs (*a*) to (*f*) above, none.

(7A) In determining the provisional fraction for the purposes of sub-paragraph (7)(*c*) and (*f*) above, tax exempt basic life assurance and general annuity business and tax exempt class IV business shall be taken to be a single category for the purposes of section 432A(5).

(7B) In sub-paragraph (7) above references to assets of the society's long term business fund—

(*a*) as respects societies referred to in paragraph (1) of regulation 13 of the Friendly Societies (Modification of the Corporation Tax Acts) Regulations 1997, shall be construed in accordance with the definition in subsection (11) of section 432A, read with subsections (12) to (14) of that section, as those subsections are added by paragraph (5) of regulation 13 of those Regulations;

(*b*) as respects other societies, shall be construed in accordance with the definitions of 'long term business' (as substituted by regulation 6(4) of those Regulations) and 'long term business fund' in section 431(2).

(7C) In sub-paragraphs (7) and (7A) above—

'tax exempt basic life assurance and general annuity business' shall be construed in accordance with the definition inserted in section 431(2) by regulation 6(2) of the Friendly Societies (Modification of the Corporation Tax Acts) Regulations 1997;

'tax exempt class IV business' shall be construed in accordance with the definition inserted in section 431(2) by regulation 7(2) of those Regulations;

'tax exempt overseas life assurance business' shall be construed in accordance with section 441(4D).''

(7) In sub-paragraph (8)—

(*a*) for the words 'sub-paragraph (7)(*b*)(iv)' there shall be substituted the words 'sub-paragraph (7)(*c*) and (*f*)';

(*b*) for the word 'company's' there shall be substituted the word 'society's'.''

7—(1) Paragraph (2) below specifies a modification of regulation 9.

(2) In paragraph (2) of that regulation after ''(3)'' there shall be inserted '', (3A) and (3B)''.

8—(1) Paragraphs (2) to (4) below specify modifications of regulation 10.

(2) In paragraph (2)(*b*) of that regulation after the words '''the company''' there shall be inserted the words ''(wherever occurring)''.

(3) After paragraph (5) of that regulation there shall be inserted the following paragraph—

''(5A) In sub-paragraph (1CA)—

(*a*) for the word 'company' (wherever occurring) there shall be inserted the word 'society';

(*b*) for the words 'pension business' there shall be substituted the words 'tax exempt business'.''

(4) In paragraph (6) of that regulation after the word ''company'' there shall be inserted the words ''(wherever occurring)''.

Revocations

9 The Friendly Societies (Gilt-edged Securities) (Periodic Accounting for Tax on Interest) Regulations 1996 and the Friendly Societies (Gilt-edged Securities) (Periodic Accounting for Tax on Interest) (Amendment) Regulations 1997 are hereby revoked as respects any payments of interest on relevant gilt-edged securities in relation to which, by virtue of regulation 1(2) of these Regulations, these Regulations have effect.

1999/881
Overseas Insurers (Tax Representatives) Regulations 1999

Made by the Commissioners of Inland Revenue under TA 1988 s 552A

Made	*18 March 1999*
Laid before the House of Commons	*18 March 1999*
Coming into force	*6 April 1999*

Commentary—*Simon's Direct Tax Service* **D4.524, E3.503**.

Citation and commencement

1 These Regulations may be cited as the Overseas Insurers (Tax Representatives) Regulations 1999 and shall come into force on 6th April 1999.

Interpretation

2 In these Regulations—

''the Board'' means the Commissioners of Inland Revenue;

''EEA Agreement'' means the Agreement on the European Economic Area signed at Oporto on 2nd May 1992 as adjusted by the Protocol signed at Brussels on 17th March 1992;

''EEA State'' means a State which is a Contracting Party to the EEA Agreement other than the United Kingdom;

''the Management Act'' means the Taxes Management Act 1970;

[''notice'' means notice given either in writing or in such form and by such means of electronic communications as may be approved by directions given by the Board, and 'notify' and 'notification' shall be construed accordingly;][1]

''the relevant duties'' has the meaning given for the purposes of section 552B by subsection (2) of that section;

''. . .''[1];

''the Taxes Act'' means the Income and Corporation Taxes Act [1988, and a reference to a numbered section, without more, is a reference to the section of the Taxes Act bearing that number.][1]

Amendments—[1] Definition of ''notice'' substituted, definitions of ''section 552A'' and ''section 552B'' revoked, and definition of ''the Taxes Act'' amended, by the Overseas Insurers (Tax Representatives) (Amendment) Regulations, SI 2002/443 regs 3, 4 with effect from 6 April 2002 in respect of chargeable events occurring after 5 April 2002.

Designated day

3 The day specified for the purpose of the definition of ''the designated day'' in subsection (12) of section 552A is 6th April 1999.

Nomination of tax representative by overseas insurer

4—(1) A nomination to the Board of a tax representative by an overseas insurer must be in writing and must contain the following information—

(*a*) the full name or title under which the overseas insurer is registered in the country in which his principal place of business is situated and the address in that country of that principal place of business;

(*b*) the business address of any branch or agency which the overseas insurer has in the United Kingdom;

(*c*) the name of the person nominated and—

(i) if he is an individual, the address of that person's fixed place of residence in the United Kingdom, or

(ii) if he is not an individual, the address of his business establishment in the United Kingdom;

(*d*) the consent of the person nominated that he is willing to secure that the relevant duties are discharged by or on behalf of the overseas insurer signed—

(i) if he is an individual, by that individual, or

(ii) if he is not an individual, by the proper officer of the company as defined for the purposes of section 108 of the Management Act by subsection (3) of that section in the case of a company and by any partner who is an individual in the case of a partnership;

(*e*) the Inland Revenue office to which, and the tax reference under which, the person nominated submits tax returns.

(2) A nomination which does not contain the information required by paragraph (1) is invalid.

Board's decision on nomination

5—(1) Within the period of thirty days after receipt of a nomination the Board must give notice to the overseas insurer and the person nominated that they—

(*a*) approve the person nominated by the overseas insurer as his tax representative; or

(*b*) refuse to approve the person nominated by the overseas insurer as his tax representative on one or more of the grounds specified in sub-paragraphs (*a*), (*b*) and (*c*) of paragraph (4); or

(*c*) require the overseas insurer or the person nominated or both of them to supply within the period of thirty days after the date of the notice such further information as may be reasonably required before the Board can be satisfied that the person nominated is a fit and proper person to be a tax representative.

(2) A notice under sub-paragraph (*c*) of paragraph (1) must specify the information that the Board require.

(3) Where the overseas insurer or the person nominated, or both of them, supplies information pursuant to a notice under sub-paragraph (*c*) of paragraph (1), the Board must within the period of thirty days after receiving the information—

(*a*) give notice to the overseas insurer and the person nominated—

(i) that they approve the person nominated, or

(ii) that they refuse to approve the person nominated, stating on which of the grounds specified in sub-paragraphs (*a*), (*b*) and (*c*) of paragraph (4) they rely, or

(*b*) give a further notice under sub-paragraph (*c*) of paragraph (1).

(4) The grounds on which the Board may refuse to approve the person nominated by the overseas insurer as his tax representative are that—

(*a*) he does not satisfy the requirements of subsection (7) of section 552A;

(*b*) they have reason to believe that he cannot or will not secure that the relevant duties are properly discharged by or on behalf of the overseas insurer;

(*c*) information which was specified by a notice given under sub-paragraph (*c*) of paragraph (1) has not been supplied.

(5) If at any time there is a change in the information required by regulation 4, or in the further information required by paragraph (1)(*c*) of this regulation, the overseas insurer must notify the Board of that change.

(6) Where the Board have refused to approve the person nominated, and subject to paragraph (5) of regulation 13, the overseas insurer must nominate another person to be his tax representative within the period of three months after the date of the notice of that refusal.

(7) Where the overseas insurer nominates another person in accordance with paragraph (6) that nomination must contain the information required by regulation 4 and paragraphs (1) to (4) of this regulation apply to that nomination in the same way that they applied to the original nomination.

(8) Where the Board approve the person nominated the date of his appointment is the date on which notice was given under paragraph (1) or (3).

Termination by the Board of appointment of person nominated

6—(1) The Board may at any time give notice to both the overseas insurer and the person nominated that they have decided to withdraw the approval which they have given to the person nominated on the grounds that—

(*a*) he no longer satisfies the requirements of subsection (7) of section 552A; or

(*b*) they have reason to believe that he cannot or will not secure that the relevant duties are properly discharged by or on behalf of the overseas insurer; or

(*c*) they have reason to believe that he has failed to secure that relevant duties have been properly discharged by or on behalf of the overseas insurer.

(2) Where the Board have given notice of their decision to withdraw their approval under paragraph (1) of a person nominated—

(*a*) that person continues to be the tax representative of the overseas insurer until they give notice of their approval of the nomination of another person or themselves appoint another person in his place;

(*b*) subject to paragraph (5) of regulation 13, the overseas insurer must nominate another person to be his tax representative within the period of three months after the date on which the Board gave notice of their decision; and

(*c*) any such nomination must contain the information required by regulation 4 and the Board must give their decision on that nomination in accordance with regulation 5.

Termination by overseas insurer of appointment of person nominated

7—(1) The overseas insurer may at any time after the Board have approved the person nominated by him as his tax representative give notice to the Board that he no longer wishes that person to be his tax representative.

(2) Where notice is given by the overseas insurer under paragraph (1), the appointment of the person nominated continues until such time as the Board approve the nomination of another person in his place.

(3) At the same time as the Board give notice of their decision approving the nomination of another person they must give notice to the person originally nominated that his appointment ceased on the date of that notice.

Termination by person nominated of his appointment

8—(1) The person nominated may at any time after the Board have approved him as the tax representative of the overseas insurer give notice to the Board and to the overseas insurer that he no longer wishes to be the overseas insurer's tax representative and in that event the overseas insurer must nominate another person to be his tax representative within the period of three months after the date of that notice.

(2) Where the overseas insurer nominates another person in accordance with paragraph (1), that nomination must contain the information required by regulation 4 and the Board must give their decision on that nomination in accordance with regulation 5.

(3) At the same time as the Board give notice of their decision approving the nomination of another person they must give notice to the person originally nominated that his appointment ceased on the date of that notice.

Termination of appointment on bankruptcy or death or on dissolution or winding-up of a company or partnership

9—(1) Where the person nominated by an overseas insurer is an individual who becomes bankrupt, or in Scotland his estate is sequestrated, or makes any arrangement or composition with his creditors generally or dies, or is a company or a partnership which is dissolved or wound up, the appointment of that person ceases and the overseas insurer must nominate another person to be his tax representative within the period of three months after the event in question.

(2) Any such nomination must contain the information required by regulation 4 and the Board must give their decision on that nomination in accordance with regulation 5.

Appointment by the Board of an overseas insurer's tax representative

10—(1) In circumstances where the overseas insurer has failed—

(*a*) to nominate a person to be his tax representative in accordance with subsection (6) of section 552A; or

(*b*) following the refusal of the Board to approve a person nominated by him, to nominate another person to be his tax representative in accordance with paragraph (6) of regulation 5; or

(*c*) following the withdrawal by the Board of their approval of a person nominated, to nominate another person to be his tax representative in accordance with paragraph (2)(*b*) of regulation 6; or

(*d*) following the notification by a person nominated under paragraph (1) of regulation 8 that he no longer wishes to be the overseas insurer's tax representative or on the occurrence of one of the events described in paragraph (1) of regulation 9, to nominate another person in accordance with the paragraph in question; or

(*e*) following the giving of a notice by the Board in accordance with paragraph (3) of regulation 11, to nominate a person to be his tax representative in accordance with paragraph (4) of that regulation; or

(*f*) following—

(i) the refusal of the Board to agree to release him from the requirement that there be a tax representative, or

(ii) the disclosure to the Board of information with respect to relevant insurances ceasing to be a criminal offence under the law of the EEA State in which he is resident, or

(iii) notification by him to the Board that the total amount or value of gross premiums paid under relevant insurances is £1 million or more, or

(iv) the giving of a notice by the Board of their intention to withdraw from their agreement to release him from the requirement that there be a tax representative,

to nominate a person to be his tax representative in accordance with paragraph (9) of regulation 12; or

(*g*) to notify the Board that the total amount or value of gross premiums paid under relevant insurances is £1 million or more; or

(*h*) following the termination of the appointment of a person appointed under this paragraph, to nominate another person in accordance with paragraph (4) of this regulation;

the Board may appoint a person who satisfies the description in paragraph (2) to be the overseas insurer's tax representative.

(2) A person appointed by the Board to be the tax representative of an overseas insurer must be a person who has a significant business or economic connection with the overseas insurer and may in particular (but without prejudice to the generality of the preceding words) be—

(*a*) a company which is connected with the overseas insurer within the meaning of section 839 ...[1] (connected persons); or

(*b*) the branch or agency in the United Kingdom of any such company.

(3) The Board must give notice of their decision to the person appointed under this regulation and to the overseas insurer and, subject to paragraph (6) of regulation 13, the date of the appointment is the date of the notice.

(4) The Board may at any time terminate the appointment of the person appointed by them as the tax representative of an overseas insurer by giving notice to the person appointed and to the overseas insurer and in that event the overseas insurer must nominate another person to be his tax representative within the period of three months after the date of that notice.

(5) The overseas insurer may at any time nominate a person to be his tax representative in place of the person appointed by the Board and, if the Board approve the nomination of that person, at the same time as the Board give notice of their decision approving the nomination they must give notice to the person appointed by them that his appointment ceased on the date of the notice.

(6) Where the overseas insurer nominates another person in accordance with paragraph (4) or (5), that nomination must contain the information required by regulation 4 and the Board must give their decision on that nomination in accordance with regulation 5.

Amendments—[1] Words "of the Taxes Act" in para (2)(*a*) revoked by the Overseas Insurers (Tax Representatives) (Amendment) Regulations, SI 2002/443 regs 3, 5 with effect from 6 April 2002 in respect of chargeable events occurring after 5 April 2002.

Other arrangements

11—(1) An overseas insurer may make other arrangements with the Board for the purpose of securing the discharge by him or on his behalf of the relevant duties.

(2) Where such arrangements have been made with the Board by the overseas insurer, section 552A is to be regarded as never having applied to the overseas insurer so long as those arrangements remain in force.

(3) If the Board have reason to believe that any arrangements which have been made do not secure the discharge by the overseas insurer or on his behalf of the relevant duties, they may give notice to the overseas insurer that those arrangements are no longer in force with effect from the date of the notice.

(4) Where notice is given by the Board in accordance with paragraph (3)—

(*a*) subject to paragraph (5) of regulation 13, the overseas insurer must nominate a person to be his tax representative within the period of three months after the date of the notice;

(*b*) that nomination must contain the information required by regulation 4; and

(*c*) the Board must give their decision on that nomination in accordance with regulation 5.

Release of overseas insurer from requirement to nominate a tax representative

12—(1) The Board may agree to release an overseas insurer to whom section 552A applies from the requirement that there must be a tax representative where—

(*a*) the overseas insurer is resident in an EEA State and the disclosure by him to the Board of information with respect to holders of relevant insurances is a criminal offence under the law of that State and was such an offence on 17th March 1998; or

(*b*) subject to the condition specified in paragraph (2), at any time after section 552A first applies to the overseas insurer the total amount or value of the gross premiums paid under the relevant insurances referred to in paragraph (*b*) of subsection (4) of that section is nil or a negligible amount; or

(*c*) subject to paragraph (5), the overseas insurer enters into an undertaking—

(i) in relation to relevant insurances referred to in paragraph (3), in the terms set out in Part II of the Schedule;

(ii) in relation to relevant insurances referred to in paragraph (4), in the terms set out in Part III of the Schedule.

(2) The condition specified in this paragraph is that the overseas insurer gives notice of the fact to the Board forthwith if, at any time following the agreement to release the overseas insurer from the requirement that there must be a tax representative, the total amount or value of the gross premiums paid under the relevant insurances referred to in paragraph (*b*) of subsection (4) of section 552A is £1 million or more.

(3) The relevant insurances referred to in this paragraph are—

(*a*) policies of life insurance issued in respect of insurances made before 6th April 2000;

(*b*) contracts for life annuities made before 6th April 2000;

(*c*) capital redemption policies where the contract was effected before 6th April 2000.

(4) The relevant insurances referred to in this paragraph are—

(*a*) policies of life insurance issued in respect of insurances made on or after 6th April 2000;

(*b*) contracts for life annuities made on or after 6th April 2000;

(*c*) capital redemption policies where the contract was effected on or after 6th April 2000.

(5) The Board may at any time give notice to the overseas insurer of their decision to withdraw from their agreement to release him from the requirement that there be a tax representative where that agreement has been given in the circumstances described in sub-paragraph (*c*) of paragraph (1).

(6) An application by an overseas insurer to be released from the requirement that there must be a tax representative must be by notice to the Board specifying which of the circumstances described in sub-paragraphs (*a*), (*b*) and (*c*) of paragraph (1) apply to his case and the Board must, within the period of thirty days after the receipt of the notice of any such application, give notice to the overseas insurer that they—

(*a*) agree to release him from the requirement that there be a tax representative, or

(*b*) refuse to agree to release him from that requirement, or

(*c*) require him to supply within the period of thirty days after the date of that notice such information as may be reasonably required before they can be satisfied that he comes within the relevant circumstances.

(7) A notice under sub-paragraph (*c*) of paragraph (6) must specify the information which the Board require.

(8) Where the overseas insurer supplies information pursuant to a notice under sub-paragraph (*c*) of paragraph (6), the Board must within the period of thirty days after receiving the information—

(*a*) give notice to the insurer that they agree or refuse to agree to release him from the requirement that there be a tax representative, or

(*b*) give a further notice under sub-paragraph (*c*) of paragraph (6).

(9) Where—

(*a*) the Board give notice that they refuse to agree to release the overseas insurer from the requirement that there be a tax representative, or

(*b*) it ceases to be a criminal offence under the law of the EEA State in which the overseas insurer is resident for him to disclose to the Board information with respect to the holders of relevant insurances, or

(*c*) the overseas insurer gives notice to the Board in accordance with the condition in paragraph (2) that the total amount or value of the gross premiums paid under relevant insurances is £1 million or more, or

(*d*) the Board give notice to the overseas insurer of their decision to withdraw from their agreement to release him from the requirement that there be a tax representative,

and subject to paragraph (5) of regulation 13, the overseas insurer must nominate a person to be his tax representative within the period of three months after the date of the notice or the date when disclosure to the Board ceased to be criminal offence, as the case may be.

(10) Where the overseas insurer nominates a person to be his tax representative in accordance with paragraph (9), that nomination must contain the information required by regulation 4 and the Board must give their decision in accordance with regulation 5.

Note—The Overseas Insurers (Tax Representatives) (Amendment) Regulations, SI 2002/443 reg 10 provides that for the purposes of para (1)(*c*) above, an undertaking given by an overseas insurer before the coming into force of those Regulations, which complied with the terms of SI 1999/881 Schedule Pts II and III as then in force, shall have effect as if it were an undertaking in the terms required by the Schedule as amended by SI 2002/443. Accordingly, any agreement by the Board to release the insurer under para (1)(*c*) above given before the coming into force of SI 2002/443 shall continue to have effect until the Board give notice of their decision to withdraw from it. SI 2002/443 has effect from 6 April 2002 in respect of chargeable events occurring after 5 April 2002.

Appeals against decisions of the Board

13—(1) An overseas insurer to whom notice has been given of a decision of the Board—

(*a*) refusing to approve a person nominated by him as his tax representative,

(*b*) withdrawing their approval of a person nominated by him as his tax representative,

(*c*) appointing a person to be his tax representative,

(*d*) that arrangements made under regulation 11 are no longer in force,

(*e*) refusing to agree to release him from the requirement that there be a tax representative, or

(*f*) to withdraw from their agreement to release him from the requirement that there be a tax representative,

may appeal against the decision contained in that notice by notice given to the Board within the period of thirty days after the date of the notice of the decision in question.

(2) A person to whom notice has been given of a decision of the Board appointing him to be the tax representative of an overseas insurer under regulation 10 may appeal against the decision contained in that notice within the period of thirty days after the date of the notice of that decision.

(3) An appeal under paragraph (1) or (2) is to the Special Commissioners.

(4) The like provisions as are contained in Part V of the Management Act (appeals and other proceedings) and in regulations made under sections 56B to 56D of that Act apply to an appeal under this regulation and the Special Commissioners must on appeal to them confirm the decision contained in the notice unless they are satisfied that it ought to be quashed.

(5) Where an overseas insurer appeals against a decision of the Board referred to in sub-paragraph (*a*), (*b*), (*d*), (*e*) or (*f*) of paragraph (1), and the decision of the Board is confirmed on appeal, the period of three months within which he must nominate another person, or a person, as his tax representative does not begin until such time as there is no possibility of a further appeal against that decision.

(6) Where an overseas insurer appeals against a decision of the Board appointing a person to be his tax representative, or the person appointed by the Board to be the tax representative of an overseas insurer appeals against the decision of the Board appointing him, and the decision of the Board is confirmed on appeal, the date of the appointment of that person is the first date on which there is no possibility of a further appeal against that decision.

(7) Where an overseas insurer appeals against a decision of the Board referred to in sub-paragraph (*a*) of paragraph (1) and the decision of the Board is quashed on appeal, the date of the appointment of the person nominated as the tax representative of the overseas insurer is the first date on which there is no possibility of a further appeal against the decision quashing the decision of the Board.

SCHEDULE

Regulation 12(1)(*c*)

PART I

INTERPRETATION

1 In this Schedule—

"basic rate limit" has the meaning given by section 1(3)(*a*) of the Taxes Act;

"financial year" means a period of twelve months beginning with 1st April;

"gain" means a gain which is treated as arising in connection with a policy or contract under section 541, [543, 545 or 546C][1] ...[2];

"inspector" means any inspector of taxes or other officer of the Board;

"year of assessment" means a period of twelve months beginning with 6th April.

Amendments—[1] In the definition of gain, "543, 545 or 546C" substituted by the Overseas Insurers (Tax Representatives) (Amendment) Regulations, SI 2001/2726 reg 2 with effect from 17 August 2001.

[2] In the definition of "gain", words "of the Taxes Act" revoked by the Overseas Insurers (Tax Representatives) (Amendment) Regulations, SI 2002/443 regs 3, 6 with effect from 6 April 2002 in respect of chargeable events occurring after 5 April 2002.

2 For the purposes of this Schedule a year of assessment corresponds to the financial year which ends in that year of assessment.

PART II

UNDERTAKING BY OVERSEAS INSURER—PRE 6TH APRIL 2000 INSURANCES

3 The terms of the undertaking referred to in regulation 12(1)(*c*)(i) are that the overseas insurer undertakes, within three months after the end of each year of assessment, or where the policy holder is a company each financial year, to supply to the inspector the information referred to in paragraph 6 about relevant events occurring in that year of assessment or financial year in connection with a policy or contract held by a policy holder where to the best of the overseas insurer's information and belief the policy holder was resident in the United Kingdom immediately before the relevant event occurred.

4 For the purposes of this undertaking a relevant event is a chargeable event within the meaning of Chapter II of Part XIII of the Taxes Act—

(*a*) in respect of which an insurer is under an obligation to deliver a certificate under [section 552 (as read with section 552ZA)][1];

(*b*) which occurs three months or more after section 552A first applies to the overseas insurer;

(*c*) which is the last such event to occur in relation to the policy or contract;

(*d*) by reason of which the aggregate sum payable, or other benefits to be conferred, by the overseas insurer exceeds twice the basic rate limit for—

(i) the year of assessment in which it occurs, or

(ii) where the policy holder is a company, the year of assessment corresponding to the financial year in which it occurs.

Amendments—[1] In sub-para (*a*), words substituted by the Overseas Insurers (Tax Representatives) (Amendment) Regulations, SI 2002/443 regs 3, 7 with effect from 6 April 2002 in respect of chargeable events occurring after 5 April 2002.

5 In determining whether the aggregate sum payable, or other benefits to be conferred, by reason of a relevant event exceeds twice the basic rate limit for the year of assessment in which it occurs, or for the year of assessment corresponding to the financial year in which it occurs, as the case may be, all sums payable and benefits to be conferred are to be taken into account which are payable or to be conferred by reason of relevant events occurring in that year of assessment or that financial year in connection with policies or contracts—

(*a*) under which immediately before the relevant event in question the same insurer has obligations, and

(*b*) which are held by the same policy holder.

6 The information referred to in this paragraph is—

(*a*) the name and address of the policy holder;
(*b*) any unique identifying designation given to the policy or contract in connection with which a relevant event has occurred;
(*c*) the date and nature of each such relevant event;
(*d*) the aggregate of the sums payable, or other benefits to be conferred, as a result of all such relevant events.

PART III
UNDERTAKING BY OVERSEAS INSURER—POST 5TH APRIL 2000 INSURANCES

7 The terms of the undertaking referred to in regulation 12(1)(*c*)(ii) are that the overseas insurer undertakes—

(*a*) within three months after a relevant event occurs in connection with a policy or contract, to deliver to the policy holder a certificate containing the information referred to in paragraph 10; and
(*b*) within three months after the end of each year of assessment, or where the policy holder is a company each financial year, in which such a certificate is delivered, and in the circumstances described in paragraph 9, to supply to the inspector a copy of that certificate;

where to the best of the overseas insurer's information and belief the policy holder was resident in the United Kingdom immediately before the relevant event occurred.

[**8** For the purpose of this undertaking a relevant event is—

(*a*) a chargeable event within the meaning of Chapter 2 of Part 13 of the Taxes Act; or
(*b*) a chargeable event which is treated as occurring by reason of regulation 6(1) of the Personal Portfolio Bonds (Tax) Regulations 1999,

in respect of which an insurer is under an obligation to deliver a certificate under section 552.][1]

Amendments—[1] This paragraph substituted by the Overseas Insurers (Tax Representatives) (Amendment) Regulations, SI 2002/443 regs 3, 8 with effect from 6 April 2002 in respect of chargeable events occurring after 5 April 2002.

9 The circumstances described in this paragraph are where the aggregate amount of connected gains in the year of assessment or financial year exceeds one half of the basic rate limit for that year of assessment or for the year of assessment corresponding to that financial year and, for the purposes of this paragraph, a gain is connected with another gain where—

(*a*) both gains arise in connection with policies or contracts containing obligations which, immediately before the relevant event in question, were obligations of the same overseas insurer;
(*b*) the policy holder of those policies and contracts is the same; and
(*c*) both gains arise in the same year of assessment or, where the policy holder is a company, the same financial year.

10 The information referred to in this paragraph is—

(*a*) the name and address of the policy holder;
(*b*) any unique identifying designation given to the policy or contract in connection with which the relevant event has occurred;
(*c*) the date and nature of the relevant event;
(*d*) the amount of the gain;
(*e*) the number of years relevant for computing the appropriate fraction of the gain for the purposes of section 550(3)[, apart from section 553(3)][1];
(*f*) whether the policy holder is to be treated as having paid income tax at the basic rate on the amount of the gain in accordance with section 547(5)(*a*)[, apart from section 553(8)][1].

Amendments—[1] Words in paras (*e*) and (*f*) substituted by the Overseas Insurers (Tax Representatives) (Amendment) Regulations, SI 2002/443 regs 3, 9 with effect from 6 April 2002 in respect of chargeable events occurring after 5 April 2002.

1999/1029
Personal Portfolio Bonds (Tax) Regulations 1999

Made by the Treasury under TA 1988 s 553C

Made	*30 March 1999*
Laid before the House of Commons	*30 March 1999*
Coming into force	*6 April 1999*

Commentary—*Simon's Direct Tax Service* **E1.726, E3.512.**

Citation, commencement and effect

1—(1) These Regulations may be cited as the Personal Portfolio Bonds (Tax) Regulations 1999 and shall come into force on 6th April 1999.

(2) These Regulations shall have effect, in relation to personal portfolio bonds, with respect to any year ending on or after 6th April 2000.

Interpretation

2—(1) In these Regulations unless the context otherwise requires—

"building society" means a building society within the meaning of the Building Societies Act 1986, or the Irish Building Societies Act 1989;

"collective investment scheme" has the meaning given by section [235 of the Financial Services and Markets Act 2000][1], and "interest" in relation to a collective investment scheme means the beneficial entitlement (however described) of a participant (within the meaning of that section);

"company" has the meaning given by section 832(1) and (2) of the Taxes Act;

"insurance company" means [an undertaking carrying on the business of effecting or carrying out contracts of insurance and, for the purposes of this definition, "contract of insurance" has the meaning given by Article 3(1) of the Financial Services and Markets Act 2000 (Regulated Activities) Order 2001][1];

"internal linked fund" has the meaning given by [section 11.1 of the Prudential Sourcebook (Insurers) and in this definition "the Prudential Sourcebook (Insurers)" means the Interim Prudential Sourcebook for Insurers made by the Financial Services Authority under the Financial Services and Markets Act 2000][2];

"market value" shall be construed in accordance with section 272 of the Taxation of Chargeable Gains Act 1992;

"personal portfolio bond" has the meaning given by regulation 4, subject to regulation 3;

"policy holder", except in regulation 4(1), includes a holder of a life annuity contract;

"recognised stock exchange" has the meaning given by section 841 of the Taxes Act;

"security" has the same meaning as in section 132(3)(*b*) of the Taxation of Chargeable Gains Act 1992;

"share" includes stock;

"the Taxes Act" means the Income and Corporation Taxes Act 1988;

"unit trust scheme" has the meaning given by subsection (6) of section 468 of the Taxes Act;

"warrant" has the same meaning as in [paragraph 14 of Schedule 2 to the Financial Services and Markets Act 2000][1];

"year" in relation to a personal portfolio bond means a year as defined in section 546(4) of the Taxes Act, and "the final year" has the meaning given by that section.

(2) In these Regulations references to the premium paid, or the amount of the premium paid, include—

(*a*) references to lump sum, or any other, consideration,

(*b*) where more than one amount is payable by way of premium in respect of the policy or contract, references to the aggregate of the premiums paid, and

(*c*) references to the market value at the date of transfer of any property other than cash transferred to the insurance company in satisfaction of any premium.

(3) In these Regulations references to a section, without more, are to that section of the Taxes Act.

Amendments—[1] In para (1) words in the definition of "collective investment scheme", "insurance company" and "warrant" substituted by the Financial Services and Markets Act 2000 (Consequential Amendments) (Taxes) Order, SI 2001/3629 arts 183, 184(1), (2), (4), (5) with effect from 1 December 2001, immediately after the coming into force of the Financial Services and Markets Act 2000 ss 411, 432(1), Sch 20 (and SI 2001/3629 Pts 1 and 2).

[2] In para (1) words in the definition of "internal linked fund" substituted by SI 2001/3629 arts 183, 184(3), (6) with effect for periods of account ending after 30 November 2001.

Policies or contracts issued or made before 17th March 1998 which are the subject of special exclusions from being personal portfolio bonds

3—(1) A policy or contract is not a personal portfolio bond if it is a policy or contract—

(*a*) which, in the case of a policy, was issued in respect of an insurance made before 17th March 1998 and, in the case of a contract, was made before 17th March 1998,

(*b*) whose terms are not varied on or after 16th July 1998 so as to increase the benefits secured or to extend the term of the policy or contract (any exercise of rights conferred by the policy or contract being regarded for this purpose as a variation), and

(*c*) which is a policy or contract to which either paragraph (2) or paragraph (3) applies.

(2) This paragraph applies to a policy or contract under whose terms the benefits have at no time during its existence been capable of being determined either in whole or in part by reference to any index other than those referred to in regulation 4(7), or to any property other than—

(*a*) shares or securities listed on a recognised stock exchange;

(*b*) shares or securities of a company which are dealt in on the Unlisted Securities Market or the Alternative Investment Market, and which satisfy the conditions specified in paragraph (4); and

(*c*) property described in regulation 4(3) and (4).

(3) This paragraph applies to a policy or contract—

(*a*) under whose terms the benefits were at some time during its existence capable of being determined either in whole or in part by reference to property other than that referred to in paragraph (2)(*a*), (*b*) and (*c*), or by reference to an index other than those referred to in regulation 4(7), but at no time during its existence have been so determined, and

(*b*) whose terms are varied before the end of the first year, in relation to that policy or contract, which commences on or after 6th April 1999, subject to paragraph (5), so that the only property that may be selected as mentioned in regulation 4(1) consists of property referred to in paragraph (2)(*a*), (*b*) and (*c*), and the only index that may be so selected consists of an index referred to in regulation 4(7).

(4) The conditions specified in this paragraph are that—

(*a*) any holding of shares or securities of a company, by reference to which any benefits under the policy or contract are or have been capable of being determined during any period, does not at any time during that period exceed 10 per cent. of the issued share capital of the company concerned; and

(*b*) the amount invested in any shares or securities of a single company to which this condition applies does not at any time exceed 10 per cent. of the premium paid in respect of the policy or contract (and ''amount invested'' includes the market value at the date of transfer of any property other than cash transferred to the insurance company in satisfaction of any premium).

(5) In a case where—

(*a*) the policy holder was not resident in the United Kingdom on 17th March 1998, and

(*b*) after that date, the policy holder is at any time resident in the United Kingdom,

paragraph (3)(*b*) shall apply with the modification that, for the year mentioned in that sub-paragraph, there is substituted a reference to whichever is the later of that year, and the first year, in relation to that policy or contract, which commences after the time mentioned in sub-paragraph (*b*) of this paragraph or, where there is more than one such time, the earliest such time.

(6) Any reference in paragraphs (2) and (3) to the period of existence of a policy or contract, or to a period in paragraph (4), or to a time during either such period, shall be construed ignoring any such period or time before 6th April 1994, but shall include any other such period or time (whether before or after the coming into force of these Regulations).

(7) Any reference in paragraphs (2)(*a*) and (*b*) and (4) to shares or securities, or to a holding of shares or securities, includes a reference to any option, warrant or other right to acquire shares or securities.

Definition of personal portfolio bond (applying to all policies or contracts whenever issued or made)

4—(1) Subject to paragraph (2) and regulation 3, ''personal portfolio bond'' means a policy of life insurance, contract for a life annuity or capital redemption policy under whose terms—

(*a*) some or all of the benefits are determined by reference to the value of, or the income from, property of any description (whether or not specified in the policy or contract) or fluctuations in, or in an index of, the value of property of any description (whether or not so specified); and

(*b*) some or all of the property, or such an index, may be selected by, or by a person acting on behalf of, the holder of the policy or contract or a person connected with him (or the holder of the policy or contract and a person connected with him).

(2) A policy or contract is not a personal portfolio bond if—

(*a*) the only property which may be selected as mentioned in paragraph (1)(*b*) is of the description prescribed by either or both of paragraphs (3) and (4), and

(*b*) the only index which may be selected as mentioned in paragraph (1)(*b*) is of the description prescribed by paragraph (7).

(3) The description prescribed by this paragraph is of property which the insurance company has appropriated to an internal linked fund, where the property satisfies the condition specified in paragraph (5).

(4) The description prescribed by this paragraph is of property consisting of any of the following—

(*a*) units in an authorised unit trust within the meaning of subsection (6) of section 468, read with subsections (7) to (9) of that section,

(*b*) shares in an investment trust within the meaning of section 842,

(*c*) shares in an open-ended investment company within the meaning of section [236 of the Financial Services and Markets Act 2000][1]

(*d*) cash, including cash deposited in a deposit account or share account with a building society, or in a bank account or similar account, except where the acquisition of the cash was made wholly or partly for the purpose of realising a gain from the disposal of it,

(*e*) policies or contracts to which Chapter II of Part XIII of the Taxes Act applies, which satisfy the conditions specified in paragraph (6), and

(*f*) an interest in a collective investment scheme which is constituted by—

(i) a company, not being an open-ended investment company, which is resident outside the United Kingdom,

(ii) a unit trust scheme the trustees of which are not resident in the United Kingdom, or

(iii) any arrangements which do not fall within paragraph (i) or (ii), which take effect by virtue of the law of a territory outside the United Kingdom and which, under that law, create rights in the nature of co-ownership (without restricting that expression to its meaning in the law of any part of the United Kingdom),

where the property concerned satisfies, or further satisfies, as the case may be, the condition specified in paragraph (5).

(5) The condition specified in this paragraph is that, at the time when the property is available to be selected, the opportunity to select property of the same description as the first-mentioned property is available to, or to persons acting on behalf of, all the policy holders of the insurance company concerned or one, or more than one, class of policy holders of that insurance company, as mentioned in paragraph (8)(*a*) to (*c*).

(6) The conditions specified in this paragraph are that neither—

(*a*) the policy or contract, nor

(*b*) any property by reference to which the value of any benefits under the policy or contract is or has been directly or indirectly capable of being determined, nor

(*c*) any property which, in relation to the policy or contract, or the premium paid in respect thereof, is ''derived property'' within the meaning of section 660A(10) of the Taxes Act,

is a personal portfolio bond.

(7) The description prescribed by this paragraph is of indices consisting of any of the following—

(*a*) the retail prices index,

(*b*) any similar general index of prices which is published by the government of any foreign state, or by an agent of such a government, or

(*c*) any published index of prices of shares listed on a recognised stock exchange,

in circumstances where, at the time when the index is available to be selected, the opportunity to select the same index is available to, or to persons acting on behalf of, all the policy holders of the insurance company concerned or one, or more than one, class of policy holders of that insurance company, as mentioned in paragraph (8)(*a*) to (*c*).

(8) In paragraphs (5) and (7) a ''class'' of policy holders means a number of policy holders to whom the opportunity is given to select property or an index as mentioned in paragraphs (5) and (7) in circumstances where—

(*a*) that opportunity is clearly identified in marketing or other promotional literature published by the insurance company concerned to members of the public, or members of the public who are intending investors, as available generally to any person falling within its terms,

(*b*) the class and the opportunity are not limited to connected persons, and

(*c*) the composition of the class (which means the inclusion in or exclusion from the class of any person, or the ability of that person to take the opportunity, if he so chooses) is determined by the insurance company alone.

Amendments—[1] Words in sub-para (4)(*c*) substituted by the Financial Services and Markets Act 2000 (Consequential Amendments) (Taxes) Order, SI 2001/3629 arts 183, 185 with effect from 1 December 2001, immediately after the coming into force of the Financial Services and Markets Act 2000 ss 411, 432(1), Sch 20 (and SI 2001/3629 Pts 1 and 2).

Personal portfolio bonds - computation of gain

5—(1) This regulation makes provision for amounts to be treated as gains arising in connection with a personal portfolio bond in any year ending on or after 6th April 2000 other than the final year (a ''relevant year'') for the purposes of charging those gains to tax in accordance with the provisions of Chapter II of Part XIII of the Taxes Act applied (with modifications) by regulation 6.

[(2) There shall be treated as a gain arising in a relevant year the amount calculated in accordance with the formula—

$$0.15 \times (A + B - C)$$

Here—

A is the amount of the premium paid in respect of the personal portfolio bond;

B is the sum of the amounts found by applying the formula at the end of each of the previous years during which the personal portfolio bond was in existence in succession starting with the first such year; and

C is the amount calculated in accordance with the formula in paragraph (2A).][1]

[(2A) **C** is the amount calculated in accordance with the formula—

$$R - G$$

(*a*) at the end of the year immediately preceding the relevant year if the calculation produces an excess; and

(*b*) at the end of any earlier year during the existence of the bond when the calculation produces an excess; and

(*c*) adding together all the amounts produced by sub-paragraphs (*a*) and (*b*).

Here—

R is the reckonable aggregate value mentioned in section 546(2); and

G is the allowable aggregate amount referred to in section 546(3).][1]

[(2B) For the purposes of the computation of **C**—

(*a*) section 546(1)(*a*) shall be read as if the words "or assignment" and "assigned for money or money's worth, or" and sub-paragraph (ii) and the word "; or" preceding it were omitted;

(*b*) section 546(6) shall be disregarded; and

(*c*) sections 546B to 546D shall be disregarded.][1]

(3) The gain calculated in accordance with paragraph (2) shall be treated as arising at the end of the relevant year [concerned.

This is subject to paragraphs (4) and (4A).][1]

(4) The references—

(*a*) in paragraph (3) to the end of a relevant year, and

(*b*) in paragraph (2), in the definition of "B", to the end of any previous year,

shall each be construed as a reference to the time immediately before any gain treated as arising in connection with the same policy or contract at the end of that year under section 541, 543 or 545, on the occurrence of such an excess as is mentioned in section 540(1)(*a*)(v), 542(1)(*c*) or 545(1)(*d*).

[(4A) For the purposes of paragraphs (2) to (3), any gain treated as arising under section 546C shall be treated as arising immediately after the gain calculated in accordance with paragraph (2).][1]

(5) Where the terms of a policy or contract, to which regulation 3(3) applies as modified by regulation 3(5), are varied, within the alternative period permitted by regulation 3(5), (that is, the first year which commences after the time mentioned in regulation 3(5)(*b*) falls later than the year mentioned in regulation 3(3)(*b*)), no gain shall be treated as arising under paragraph (2) at the end of the first year, in relation to the policy or contract, which ends after the time mentioned in regulation 3(5)(*b*).

Amendments—[1] Paras (2), (2A) and (2B) substituted for para (2), words in para (3) substituted, and para (4A) inserted, by the Personal Portfolio Bonds (Tax) Regulations, SI 2001/2724 regs 2, 3 with effect for gains treated as arising after 16 August 2001.

Application of Chapter II of Part XIII of the Taxes Act

6—(1) The gain treated as arising in accordance with regulation 5(2) shall be treated, for the purposes of section 547 and paragraph (2) (other than sub-paragraph (*b*) of that paragraph), as arising on the happening of a chargeable event, which takes place at the time given by regulation 5(3) and (4).

(2) The provisions of Chapter II of Part XIII of the Taxes Act (other than section 553C) shall, so far as concerns policies or contracts that are also personal portfolio bonds, apply, subject to the omissions and modifications specified in paragraphs (3) to (8), both in relation to—

(*a*) the gain treated as arising on the happening of a chargeable event in accordance with regulation 5(2) and paragraph (1), and

(*b*) other gains treated as arising in accordance with that Chapter.

(3) In section 547 (method of charging gain to tax)—

(*a*) in subsection (1) after "[545 or 546C]"[1] there shall be inserted the words "or regulations 5(2) and 6(1) of the Personal Portfolio Bonds (Tax) Regulations 1999";

(*b*) in each of subsections (5A) and (7) after "[543 or 546C(7)(*b*)]"[1] there shall be inserted the words "or regulations 5(2) and 6(1) of the Personal Portfolio Bonds (Tax) Regulations 1999".

(4) In each of paragraphs (*a*), (*b*) and (*c*) of section 541(1), after sub-paragraph (ii) there shall be added—

"and

(iii) the total amount treated under regulation 5 of the Personal Portfolio Bonds (Tax) Regulations 1999 as a gain arising in a relevant year in relation to the policy, prior to the happening of the chargeable event;"

(5) In each of paragraphs (*a*) and (*b*) of section 543(1), after sub-paragraph (ii) there shall be added—

"and

(iii) the total amount treated under regulation 5 of the Personal Portfolio Bonds (Tax) Regulations 1999 as a gain arising in a relevant year in relation to the contract, prior to the happening of the chargeable event;"

(6) Section 550 (relief where gain charged at a higher rate) shall be omitted.

[(7) In section 552—

(*a*) in subsection (1)—

(i) in paragraph (*a*) the words "unless satisfied that no gain is to be treated as arising by reason of the event," shall be omitted;

(ii) in paragraph (*b*), for "paragraph (*a*) or (*b*) of subsection (2)" there shall be substituted "subsection (2)";

(*b*) for subsection (2) there shall be substituted—

"(2) For the purposes of this section the condition is that the amount of the gain, or the aggregate amount of the gain and any other gains connected with it, exceeds one half of the basic rate limit for the relevant year of assessment.

(*c*) in subsection (5)—

(i) for paragraph (*b*) there shall be substituted—

"(*b*) the nature of the chargeable event and the date on which it is treated as having happened;

(ii) paragraph (*c*) shall be omitted;

(iii) for paragraph (*d*) there shall be substituted—

"(*d*) the amount of the gain treated as arising in accordance with regulations 5(2) and 6(1) of the Personal Portfolio Bonds (Tax) Regulations 1999;

(iv) in paragraph (*f*)(ii) the words ", except in a case where paragraph (*c*) above applies," shall be omitted;

(*d*) for subsection (6) there shall be substituted—

"(6) For the purposes of subsection (1)(*a*) above, the relevant three month period is the period of three months beginning with the time given by regulation 5(3), (4) and (4A) of the Personal Portfolio Bonds (Tax) Regulations 1999.

(*e*) for subsection (7) there shall be substituted—

"(7) For the purposes of subsection (1)(*b*) above, the relevant three month period is whichever of the following periods ends later—

(*a*) the period of three months following the end of the year of assessment or, where the policy holder is a company, the financial year, in which the event happened; or

(*b*) if a certificate under subsection (1)(*b*) would not be required in respect of the event apart from the happening of another event, and that other event is a death or an assignment, the period of three months beginning with receipt of written notification of the death or the assignment.

(*f*) for subsection (9) there shall be substituted—

"(9) For the purposes of this section, the year of assessment or financial year to which a gain is attributable is the year in which the gain, treated as arising under regulations 5(2) and 6(1) of the Personal Portfolio Bonds (Tax) Regulations 1999, is treated as arising in accordance with regulation 5(3), (4) and (4A) of those Regulations.

(*g*) in subsection (10)—

(i) for the definition of "appropriate policy holder" there shall be substituted—

""appropriate policy holder" means the person who is the policy holder immediately before the happening of the event; and

(ii) the definition of "section 546 excess" shall be omitted; and

(*h*) each of the references to a chargeable event shall be taken to include a reference to the chargeable event treated as occurring by reason of paragraph (1).][2]

[(7A) In section 552ZA subsection (3) shall be omitted.][2]

(8) In section 553—

(*a*) in each of subsections (3) and (6) after "section [541 or 546C(7)(*b*)]"[1] there shall be inserted the words "or regulations 5(2) and 6(1) of the Personal Portfolio Bonds (Tax) Regulations 1999"; and

(*b*) in subsection (10) after "[545 or 546C(7)(*a*)]"[1] there shall be inserted the words "or, in relation to a gain treated as arising in relation to a policy under regulations 5(2) and 6(1) of the Personal Portfolio Bonds (Tax) Regulations 1999, the same meaning as in section 553C(4)(*b*)."

Amendments—[1] Words in paras (3), (8) substituted by the Personal Portfolio Bonds (Tax) (Amendment) Regulations, SI 2001/2724 regs 2, 4 with effect for gains treated as arising after 16 August 2001.

[2] Paras (7), (7A) substituted for para (7) by the Personal Portfolio Bonds (Tax) (Amendment) Regulations, SI 2002/455 with effect from 6 April 2002, as respects gains treated as arising after 5 April 2002.

1999/1408

Non-resident Companies (General Insurance Business) Regulations 1999

Made by the Treasury under TA 1988 ss 444BB(5), 444BD(1), (4), (5), 755B(5) and 755C

Made . . . . *20 May 1999*

Laid before the House of Commons . . . *20 May 1999*

Coming into force . . . . *10 June 1999*

Commentary—*Simon's Direct Tax Service* **D4.1220**.

Citation, commencement and effect

1—(1) These Regulations may be cited as the Non-resident Companies (General Insurance Business) Regulations 1999 and shall come into force on 10th June 1999.

(2) These Regulations have effect with respect to any appropriate accounting period of a relevant company.

Interpretation

2—(1) In these Regulations unless the context otherwise requires—

"appropriate accounting period" means an accounting period ending on or after 1st July 1999;

"controlled foreign company" shall be construed in accordance with section 747(2);

"general insurance business" has the meaning given by section 755B(6);

"non-resident company" means a company resident outside the United Kingdom;

"relevant company" means a company resident in the United Kingdom that had a relevant interest in a non-resident company at any time during an accounting period of the non-resident company ending in an appropriate accounting period of the relevant company;

"relevant interest" shall be construed in accordance with section 752A on the assumption that the non-resident company is a controlled foreign company;

"the Taxes Act" means the Income and Corporation Taxes Act 1988.

(2) In these Regulations references to a particular provision, without more, are references to that provision of the Taxes Act.

Modifications of Chapter IV of Part XVII of the Taxes Act

3 Chapter IV of Part XVII of the Taxes Act shall have effect with the modifications prescribed in regulations 4 to 6 in any case where a non-resident company—

(*a*) carries on general insurance business, and

(*b*) draws up accounts relating to that business using a method falling within subsection (2) of section 755B.

4 After section 754A there shall be inserted—

"Returns where it is not established whether a non-resident company carrying on general insurance business is a controlled foreign company

754AA—(1) This section applies where—

(*a*) if an apportionment were made in accordance with section 747 of the chargeable profits for an accounting period of a company resident outside the United Kingdom ('the non-resident company'), a company resident in the United Kingdom ('the UK company') would be chargeable to tax by virtue of subsection (5) of that section with reference to the whole or a part of the non-resident company's chargeable profits for that accounting period ('the relevant accounting period');

(*b*) the non-resident company carries on general insurance business within the meaning given by section 755B(6) and draws up accounts relating to that business using a method falling within section 755B(2);

(*c*) the UK company delivers a company tax return for the accounting period in which the relevant accounting period of the non-resident company ends; and

(*d*) at the time when the UK company delivers the company tax return for that accounting period, it is not established whether in the relevant accounting period the non-resident company is subject to a lower level of taxation in the territory in which it is resident so as to constitute a controlled foreign company.

(2) Prior to delivering its company tax return for the accounting period mentioned in paragraph (1)(*c*), the UK company shall consider whether or not the non-resident company is likely, in the relevant accounting period, to be subject to a lower level of taxation in the territory in which it is resident so as to constitute a controlled foreign company.

(3) If the UK company is of the opinion that in the relevant accounting period the non-resident company is likely to be subject to a lower level of taxation in the territory in which it is resident so as to constitute a controlled foreign company, the UK company shall make the company tax return on the basis that the relevant accounting period is an accounting period of a company which is a controlled foreign company.

(4) If the UK company is of the opinion that in the relevant accounting period the non-resident company is not likely to be subject to a lower level of taxation in the territory in which it is resident so as to constitute a controlled foreign company, the UK company shall make the company tax return on the basis that the relevant accounting period is an accounting period of a company which is not a controlled foreign company.

(5) In any case where—

(*a*) the UK company makes the company tax return on the basis mentioned in subsection (3) above, but

(*b*) it becomes established that in the relevant accounting period the non-resident company is not subject to a lower level of taxation in the territory in which it is resident,

the UK company shall amend the company tax return on the basis that the relevant accounting period is an accounting period of a company which is not a controlled foreign company.

(6) In any case where—

(*a*) the UK company makes the company tax return on the basis mentioned in subsection (4) above, but

(*b*) it becomes established that in the relevant accounting period the non-resident company is subject to a lower level of taxation in the territory in which it is resident,

the UK company shall amend the company tax return on the basis that the relevant accounting period is an accounting period of a company which is a controlled foreign company.

(7) Any amendment required to be made to the company tax return by virtue of subsection (5) or (6) above shall be made by the UK company before the expiration of the period commencing immediately following the close of the underwriting year and ending on the date which is eighteen months plus thirty days thereafter.

(8) Subject to subsection (9) below, an amendment of a company tax return in accordance with subsection (7) above is subject to, and must be in accordance with, the other provisions of the Corporation Tax Acts as they apply for the purposes of this Chapter.

(9) The time limits otherwise applicable to amendment of a company tax return do not apply to an amendment of a company tax return in accordance with subsection (7) above.

(10) A company which fails to make an amendment required by subsection (6) above in accordance with subsection (7) above shall be liable to a tax-related penalty under paragraph 20 of Schedule 18 to the Finance Act 1998 (penalty, not exceeding amount of tax understated, for incorrect or uncorrected return).

(11) In subsection (7) above 'the close of the underwriting year' means—

(*a*) the date on which final replacement of the technical provision, as described in sub-paragraph (4) of paragraph 52 of Schedule 9A to the Companies Act 1985, takes place, or

(*b*) where there is no final replacement of the technical provision in the three years following the underwriting year, the date referred to in section 755B(4), that is, the end of the third year following the underwriting year."

5—(1) Section 755B shall be modified as follows.

(2) After subsection (4) there shall be inserted—

"(4A) Where in accordance with subsection (4) above the technical provision is treated as finally replaced by a provision for estimated claims outstanding ('the deemed provision'), the amount of the deemed provision which may be deducted from the chargeable profits of the controlled foreign company for the accounting period concerned shall not exceed the amount that, on the assumptions in Schedule 24, would have been deductible from those profits if the deemed provision had been an actual provision as mentioned in subsection (2)(*a*) above."

6—(1) Paragraph 2 of Schedule 25 shall be modified as follows.

(2) In sub-paragraph (1), in each of paragraphs (*b*) and (*d*) there shall be inserted at the beginning "subject to sub-paragraphs (1AA) to (1AC) below,".

(3) After sub-paragraph (1) there shall be inserted—

"(1AA) Sub-paragraph (1AB) below applies where, in a case to which section 754AA(1) applies—

(*a*) a company resident in the United Kingdom ('the UK company') either—

(i) has made a company tax return for an accounting period on the basis mentioned in section 754AA(3), that is, that an accounting period of a non-resident company ('the relevant accounting period') ending in the accounting period of the UK company for which the company tax return is made is an accounting period of a controlled foreign company, and has not subsequently been required to amend the company tax return in accordance with section 754AA(5) on the basis that the relevant accounting period of the non-resident company is an accounting period of a company which is not a controlled foreign company, or

(ii) has made a company tax return for an accounting period on the basis mentioned in section 754AA(4), that is, that the relevant accounting period of a non-resident company is an accounting period of a company which is not a controlled foreign company, but has subsequently amended the company tax return in accordance with section 754AA(6) to (8) on the basis that the relevant accounting period of the non-resident company is an accounting period of a controlled foreign company; and

(*b*) the final replacement of the technical provision in the accounts of the non-resident company for the relevant accounting period—

(i) takes place on a date falling within the period of three years ('the three year period') following the relevant accounting period, or

(ii) where no final replacement of the technical provision takes place in the three year period, is treated by virtue of section 755B(4) as having taken place on the date that is the end of that period,

and each of those dates is referred to in sub-paragraphs (1AB), (1AD) and (1AE) below as 'the close of the underwriting year'.

(1AB) Where this sub-paragraph applies—

(*a*) the dividend referred to in sub-paragraph (1) above shall be due on or before the date which is eighteen months after the close of the underwriting year, or on or before such later date as the Board may, in any particular case, allow;

(*b*) the amount of the dividend or, if there is more than one, of the aggregate of those dividends which is paid to persons resident in the United Kingdom is the aggregate of the following amounts—

(i) an amount equal to 90 per cent of the company's net chargeable profits for the relevant accounting period or, where sub-paragraph (4) or (5) below applies, of the appropriate portion of those profits, and

(ii) in respect of each dividend that is paid to persons resident in the United Kingdom later than the date which is eighteen months after the end of the relevant accounting period, an amount calculated at the date of the dividend concerned in accordance with the formula—

$$\frac{D \times i}{(1+i)}$$

(1AC) In sub-paragraph (1AB) above—

(*a*) D is the amount of the dividend concerned, and

(*b*) 'i' is the interest factor calculated in accordance with the rates applicable under section 178 of the Finance Act 1989 to section 87A of the Management Act from the date that is eighteen months after the end of the relevant accounting period until the date of payment of that dividend.

(1AD) Where—

(*a*) sub-paragraphs (1AA) to (1AC) above apply in relation to an accounting period of the UK company,

(*b*) the UK company has made a company tax return for that accounting period on the basis that the dividend referred to in sub-paragraph (1) above will be paid to persons resident in the United Kingdom not later than the date which is eighteen months after the close of the underwriting year or not later than the date allowed by the Board as mentioned in sub-paragraph (1AB)(*a*) above, and

(*c*) that dividend is not paid on or before that date,

the UK company shall amend the company tax return so as to record that the controlled foreign company has not pursued an acceptable distribution policy in respect of the relevant accounting period.

(1AE) An amendment required to be made to the company tax return by virtue of sub-paragraph (1AD) above shall be made by the UK company before the expiration of the period of thirty days next following the date which is eighteen months after the close of the underwriting year or next following the date allowed by the Board as mentioned in sub-paragraph (1AB)(*a*) above.

(1AF) A company which fails to make an amendment required by sub-paragraph (1AD) above before the expiry of the period specified in sub-paragraph (1AE) above shall be liable to a tax-related penalty under paragraph 20 of Schedule 18 to the Finance Act 1998.''

Amendments to the Insurance Companies (Reserves) (Tax) Regulations 1996

7—(1) The Insurance Companies (Reserves) (Tax) Regulations 1996 shall be amended as follows.

(2) (*amends* SI 1996/2991 reg 8(1)).

(3) (*inserts* SI 1996/2991 regs 8A, 8B).

1999/1964

Retirement Benefits Schemes (Restriction on Discretion to Approve) (Additional Voluntary Contributions) (Amendment) Regulations 1999

Made by the Commissioners of Inland Revenue under TA 1988 ss 591(6) and 591A(2)

Made	*9 July 1999*
Laid before the House of Commons	*9 July 1999*
Coming into force	*30 June 1999*

Commentary—*Simon's Direct Tax Service* **E7.215, 221**.

Citation and commencement

1 These Regulations may be cited as the Retirement Benefits Schemes (Restriction on Discretion to Approve) (Additional Voluntary Contributions) (Amendment) Regulations 1999 and shall come into force on 30th July 1999.

Interpretation

2 In these Regulations, unless the context otherwise requires, ''the principal Regulations'' means the Retirement Benefits Schemes (Restriction on Discretion to Approve) (Additional Voluntary Contributions) Regulations 1993 and ''regulation'' means a regulation of the principal Regulations.

Amendments to the principal Regulations

3–5 (*amend* SI 1993/3016 regs 4, 5(3), 6(1))

Disapplication of section 591A(2) of the Income and Corporation Taxes Act 1988

6 The provisions contained in regulations 3(2) to 5 of these Regulations are specified provisions of a required description for the purposes of subsection (2) of section 591A of the Income and Corporation Taxes Act 1988.

1999/2118
Gifts for Relief in Poor Countries (Designation of Kosovo) Order 1999

Made by the Treasury under FA 1998 s 48(9) and FA 1999 s 56(8)

Made . . . . *27 July 1999*
Laid before the House of Commons . . . . . *27 July 1999*
Coming into force . . . . *21 August 1999*

Commentary—*Simon's Direct Tax Service* **E1.504**.

1 This Order may be cited as the Gifts for Relief in Poor Countries (Designation of Kosovo) Order 1999 and shall come into force on 21st August 1999, but shall have effect in relation to gifts made on or after 6th April 1999.

2 This Order designates Kosovo (in the Federation of Yugoslavia) as a territory for the purposes of paragraph (*c*) of section 48(2) of the Finance Act 1998.

1999/2119
Finance Act 1998, Section 83(1), (Appointed Day) Order 1999

Made by the Treasury under FA 1998 s 83(1)

Made . . . . *27 July 1999*

Commentary—*Simon's Direct Tax Service* **B2.323**.

1 This Order may be cited as the Finance Act 1998, Section 83(1), (Appointed Day) Order 1999.

2 The day appointed for the purposes of section 83(1) of the Finance Act 1998 is 27th July 1999.

1999/2155
Income Tax (Employments) (Amendment No 3) Regulations 1999

Made by the Commissioners of Inland Revenue under TA 1988 s 203

Made . . . . *29 July 1999*
Laid before the House of Commons . . . . . *29 July 1999*
Coming into force . . . . *19 August 1999*

Amendment—These regulations are revoked by the Income Tax (Pay As You Earn) Regulations, SI 2003/2682 reg 220, Sch 2 with effect from 6 April 2004, subject to transitional provisions contained in Sch 1 thereto.

Citation, commencement and effect

1—(1) These Regulations may be cited as the Income Tax (Employments) (Amendment No 3) Regulations 1999 and shall come into force on 19th August 1999.

(2) Regulations 8 to 14 shall have effect in relation to the year 1999–00 and subsequent years of assessment.

(3) Regulations 15 to 17 shall have effect in relation to the year of assessment 2000–01.

(4) Regulations 18 and 19 shall have effect in relation to the year 2000–01 and subsequent years of assessment.

(5) Regulations 20 to 24 shall have effect in relation to the year 2001–02 and subsequent years of assessment.

Interpretation

2 In these Regulations "the principal Regulations" means the Income Tax (Employments) Regulations 1993 and "regulation" means a regulation of the principal Regulations.

Amendments to the principal Regulations

3–7 (Amend SI 1993/744, regs 7(2), 10(2), 12(3), 13(4), 28(2), reg 49(7).)

SIs

Amendments to the principal Regulations having effect in relation to the year 1999–00 and subsequent years of assessment

8–14 (Amend SI 1993/744, regs 2(1), 29(2), (3), 30(2), (3), 32, 80F(2), 84(7), 98C(3).)

Amendments to the principal Regulations having effect in relation to the year of assessment 2000–01

15–17 (Amend SI 1993/744, regs 10(2), 12(3), 13(4).)

Amendments to the principal Regulations having effect in relation to the year 2000–01 and subsequent years of assessment

18, 19 (Amend SI 1993/744, regs 98C(4), 98F(3).)

Amendments to the principal Regulations having effect in relation to the year 2001–02 and subsequent years of assessment

20 In regulation 10(2) for the words ''sections 257 to 257F or 259'' there shall be substituted the words ''sections 257, 257A and 257AA''.

21 In regulation 12(3) for the words ''sections 257 to 257F or 259'' there shall be substituted the words ''sections 257, 257A and 257AA''.

22 In regulation 13(4) for the words ''sections 257 to 257F'' there shall be substituted the words ''sections 257, 257A and 257AA''.

23 In regulation 98C(4) after sub-paragraph (a) there shall be inserted—

''(aa) the relief specified in section 257AA(1) of the Taxes Act (children's tax credit);''.

24 In regulation 98F(3) after sub-paragraph (c) there shall be inserted—

''(ca) the relief specified in section 257AA(1) of the Taxes Act;''.

1999/2156

Finance Act 1995, Section 139(3), (Appointed Day) Order 1999

Made by the Treasury under FA 1995 s 139(3), Sch 29 Part VIII(21).

Made . . . . *29 July 1999*

Commentary—*Simon's Direct Tax Service* **E5.501**.

1 This Order may be cited as the Finance Act 1995, Section 139(3), (Appointed Day) Order 1999.

2 The day appointed for the purposes of the repeals effected by Part VIII(21) of Schedule 29 to the Finance Act 1995—

(*a*) in or of subsections (1), and (3) to (6) of section 561 of the Income and Corporation Taxes Act 1988, and

(*b*) of section 28 of the Finance Act 1988,

is 6th August 1999.

1999/2975

Corporation Tax (Simplified Arrangements for Group Relief) Regulations 1999

Made by the Treasury under FA 1998 Sch 18 para 77.

Made . . . . *1 November 1999*
Laid before the House of Commons . . . . *2 November 1999*
Coming into force . . . . *23 November 1999*

Commentary—*Simon's Direct Tax Service* **D2.630**.

Citation and commencement

1 These Regulations may be cited as the Corporation Tax (Simplified Arrangements for Group Relief) Regulations 1999 and shall come into force on 23rd November 1999.

Introductory

2 These Regulations make provision for arrangements for the surrendering and claiming of group relief in relation to any accounting period of a claimant company ending on or after 1st July 1999.

Interpretation

3—(1) In these Regulations unless the context otherwise requires—

"the arrangements" means the arrangements made by these Regulations as mentioned in regulation 2;

"authorised company" has the meaning given by regulation 4;

"authorising companies" has the meaning given by regulation 5;

"the Board" means the Commissioners of Inland Revenue;

"claimant company" has the meaning given by section 402(1);

"consortium company" has the meaning given by section 406(1)(*b*);

"group of companies" means a collection of companies such that every pair of companies within that collection comprises companies that are members of the same group of companies within the meaning of section 413(3)(*a*);

"group relief" has the meaning given by subsection (1) of section 402, read with subsection (2) of that section (group claim) and subsection (3) of that section and section 406 (consortium claim);

"insolvency practitioner" in relation to a company means a liquidator, provisional liquidator, administrator, administrative receiver, or a supervisor of a voluntary arrangement under Part I of the Insolvency Act 1986;

"the Management Act" means the Taxes Management Act 1970;

"member of the consortium" shall be construed in accordance with section 413(6);

"Schedule 18" means Schedule 18 to the Finance Act 1998;

"three month date" shall be construed in accordance with regulation 7(1).

(2) In these Regulations references to a section, without more, are to that section of the Income and Corporation Taxes Act 1988.

Authorised company

4 A company is an "authorised company" for the purposes of these Regulations if—

(*a*) it is authorised by companies within regulation 5 to act on their behalf in relation to the arrangements, and

(*b*) it is a member of the same group of companies as that referred to in regulation 5(1)(*a*).

Authorising company

5—(1) In these Regulations an "authorising company" means a company which for the time being—

(*a*) is a member of a group of companies, or

(*b*) is a consortium company in circumstances where a company falling within sub-paragraph (*a*) is a member of the consortium concerned, and

(*c*) in either case satisfies one of the conditions specified in paragraph (2).

(2) Those conditions are that the company—

(*a*) is one of the companies named in the application made by the authorised company in accordance with regulation 6;

(*b*) following the making of that application, is treated for the purposes of these Regulations, by agreement between the company, the authorised company and the Board, as if it had been one of the companies named in that application.

Application by authorised company

6—(1) An application by the authorised company on behalf of itself and the authorising companies to enter into the arrangements must be made in writing to an officer of the Board.

(2) The application must specify—

(*a*) the name and the tax office reference of the authorised company,

(*b*) the names and the tax office references of the authorising companies, and

(*c*) details relating to the authorised company and each of the authorising companies that are sufficient to demonstrate that the company concerned is a member of the group of companies or, as the case may be, a consortium company.

(3) The application must contain a statement by the authorised company and the authorising companies that they agree to be covered by the arrangements and to be bound by claims, surrenders and withdrawals made under the arrangements.

(4) The application must be accompanied—

(*a*) by a specimen copy of the statement referred to in regulation 10(2) that the authorised company proposes to use for the purpose of making and withdrawing surrenders and claims on behalf of itself and the authorising companies;

(*b*) in the case of a company which is a consortium company, by an agreement, signed by each member of the consortium and the consortium company, consenting to the authorised company acting on their behalf in relation to the arrangements.

(5) The application must be signed on behalf of each of the companies concerned by a person referred to in section 108(1) of the Management Act as a person through whom that company may act.

(6) The application must be sent to the tax office dealing with the tax affairs of the authorised company.

Matters consequential to the making of an application

7—(1) Except where paragraph (2), (3) or (4) applies and subject to regulation 9, the authorised company may enter into the arrangements on behalf of itself and the authorising companies at any time on or after the date ("the three month date") that is three months after the date on which the application is delivered to the tax office in accordance with regulation 6(6).

(2) An officer of the Board may, prior to the three month date, accept the application and permit the authorised company to enter into the arrangements on behalf of itself and the authorising companies with effect from the date notified to the authorised company by the officer of the Board.

(3) An officer of the Board may, prior to the three month date, accept the application and permit the authorised company to enter into the arrangements with effect from the date notified to the company by the officer of the Board, but exclude from the arrangements any of the authorising companies on the grounds that he has reason to believe that that company—

(*a*) has failed to comply with its obligations under the Corporation Tax Acts in relation to any accounting period (whether an accounting period ending before, or on or after, 1st July 1999), or

(*b*) is a company in relation to which a person is acting as an insolvency practitioner.

(4) An officer of the Board may, prior to the three month date, refuse the application on the grounds that—

(*a*) he has reason to believe that one or more of the companies named in the application is not a member of a group of companies, or is not a consortium company in circumstances where a company which is a member of that group is a member of the consortium concerned,

(*b*) he has reason to believe that one or more of the companies named in the application has failed to comply with its obligations under the Corporation Tax Acts in relation to any accounting period (whether an accounting period ending before, or on or after, 1st July 1999),

(*c*) the case is not one in which all, or substantially all, of the companies named in the application deliver their company tax returns to the same tax office, or

(*d*) the specimen copy of the statement referred to in regulation 6(4)(*a*) is not adequate for the purpose of enabling an officer of the Board to deal with claims for group relief.

(5) Where following the making of an application by an authorised company under regulation 6 a company is treated by agreement in accordance with regulation 5(2)(*b*) as if it had been one of the companies named in the application, the authorised company may enter into the arrangements on behalf of that company from the date of the agreement.

Change in members of consortium

8—(1) Where following the making of an application under regulation 6 there is a change in the members of the consortium referred to in paragraph (4)(*b*) of that regulation, as from the date of the change the authorised company may not act in accordance with the provisions of regulation 10 in relation to the consortium company concerned unless it takes the action specified in paragraph (2).

(2) The action specified in this paragraph is that the company must ensure that a new agreement, signed by the consortium company concerned and each company that is a member of the consortium immediately after the change, consenting to the authorised company acting on their behalf in relation to the arrangements, is sent to the tax office referred to in regulation 6(6).

(3) Where in accordance with paragraph (2) a new agreement is entered into and sent to the tax office, that agreement is effective for the purposes of the arrangements as from the date on which acceptance of the agreement is notified by an officer of the Board to the authorised company.

Exclusion of company from the arrangements

9—An officer of the Board may, at any time on or after the three month date or, if earlier, the date on which an application under regulation 6 was accepted, exclude from the arrangements a company named, or treated under regulation 5(2)(*b*) as named, in that application, on the grounds that he has reason to believe that that company—

(*a*) is not an authorising company at that time by reason of the company not falling within regulation 5(1)(*a*) or (*b*);

(*b*) has failed to comply with its obligations under the Corporation Tax Acts in relation to any accounting period (whether an accounting period ending before, or on or after, 1st July 1999); or

(*c*) is a company in relation to which a person is acting as an insolvency practitioner.

[Group relief claims under the arrangements not accompanied by copy of notice of consent to surrender

9A—(1) Where an application by an authorised company is accepted by an officer of the Board under regulation 7, any of the authorising companies may make a claim for group relief in accordance with the following provisions of this regulation.

(2) A claim may be made without being accompanied by the copy of the notice of consent required under paragraph 70(4) of Schedule 18 if the authorised company gives authority for the claim being so made.

(3) The authority given by the authorised company must—

(*a*) be included in the company tax return of the authorising company for the accounting period for which the claim is made,
(*b*) be included in that return as originally made, and
(*c*) be signed on behalf of the authorised company by a person referred to in section 108(1) of the Management Act as a person through whom that company may act.][1]

Amendments—[1] Regulation 9A inserted by the Corporation Tax (Simplified Arrangements for Group Relief) (Amendment) Regulations, SI 2000/3228, reg 2 with effect from 29 December 2000.

Group relief claims and surrenders under the arrangements

10—(1) Where an application by an authorised company is accepted by an officer of the Board under regulation 7, the authorised company may act in accordance with the following provisions of this regulation in relation to itself and to any of the authorising companies, other than a company excluded from the arrangements in accordance with regulation 7(3) or 9.

(2) The authorised company may from time to time furnish to an officer of the Board on behalf of itself and the authorising companies a statement in writing, in the form provided, or in a form authorised, by the Board, containing information necessary for the amendment in accordance with the provisions of Part VIII of Schedule 18 of the company tax returns of itself and the authorising companies for the purpose of making and withdrawing claims and surrenders of group relief.

(3) Where a statement is furnished to an officer of the Board as mentioned in paragraph (2)—

(*a*) the provisions of Part VIII of Schedule 18, other than paragraph 70(4) (claim for group relief ineffective unless accompanied by copy of notice of consent to surrender) and paragraph 71(4) (notice of withdrawal of consent to surrender ineffective unless accompanied by notice of consent of claimant company to withdrawal), shall apply in relation to the authorised company as if references to the claimant company and the surrendering company included references to the authorised company;
(*b*) amendments made in accordance with the provisions of Part VIII of Schedule 18 to the company tax returns of the authorising companies in reliance on the information contained in the statement shall have effect for the purposes of the Corporation Tax Acts as if the amendments had been made by those companies.

(4) Without prejudice to the generality of paragraph (2), the information to be contained in the statement must include in particular—

(*a*) as regards the amount claimed, the same information as is specified in paragraph 68 of Schedule 18,
(*b*) as regards the amount surrendered, the same information as is specified in paragraph 71(1) of Schedule 18,
(*c*) where applicable, details showing the effect of the claim on each company's self-assessment included in its company tax return, and
(*d*) where applicable, details showing which of the company tax returns of the companies concerned are returns into which an enquiry is in progress under Part IV of Schedule 18.

(5) A statement provided under paragraph (2) that does not contain information that is sufficient for the amendment of the company tax returns of the authorised company and the authorising companies in accordance with the provisions of Part VIII of Schedule 18 is ineffective.

(6) An authorising company remains liable, in accordance with the provisions of Schedule 18, for any incorrect claim or incorrect company tax return arising from a statement provided by the authorised company under paragraph (2).

Termination of arrangements and exclusion of applicant company from arrangements

11—(1) Either the Board or the authorised company may at any time give notice in writing to the other terminating the arrangements with effect from the date of issue of the notice.

(2) The authorised company may at any time give notice in writing to the Board excluding an authorising company from the arrangements with effect from the date of issue of the notice.

1999/3308
Lloyd's Underwriters (Special Reserve Funds) Regulations 1999

Made by the Commissioners of Inland Revenue under FA 1993 s 182(1)(*b*), (*c*)

Made . . . . 9 *December 1999*
Laid before the House of Commons . . 10 *December 1999*
Coming into force . . . . 31 *December 1999*

Citation, commencement and effect

1—(1) These Regulations may be cited as the Lloyd's Underwriters (Special Reserve Funds) Regulations 1999.

(2) These Regulations shall come into force on 31st December 1999, but except for regulation 3 shall have effect—

(*a*) for the year 2000–01 and subsequent years of assessment, and
(*b*) in relation to payments and transfers of assets made on or after 1st January 2000.

Interpretation

2 In these Regulations ''Schedule 20'' means Schedule 20 to the Finance Act 1993.

Amendments to and modifications of Schedule 20

3–5 (*Amend FA 1993, Sch 20, paras 6(2), 8(1), 10(4).*)

6—(1) Paragraph 11 of Schedule 20 is modified as follows.

(2) In sub-paragraph (2)—

(*a*) for the words ''any payment which is'' there shall be substituted the words ''the aggregate of any payments which are'';
(*b*) after the word ''above'' there shall be inserted the words ''(except where they are also made under paragraph 6(2) above)'';
(*c*) in paragraph (*a*) at the beginning there shall be inserted the words ''subject to sub-paragraph (2A) below,'';
(*d*) in paragraph (*b*) after the words ''being a'' there shall be inserted the word ''single''.

(3) After sub-paragraph (2) the following sub-paragraph shall be inserted—

''(2A) Where the member ceases to carry on his underwriting business by reason of his death, any payment falling within sub-paragraph (2) above shall be treated, for the purposes of sections 59C and 86 of the Management Act, as if made immediately after the commencement of his final year of assessment.''.

(4) In sub-paragraph (3)—

(*a*) in paragraph (*b*) after the word ''paragraph'' there shall be inserted ''3(1),'';
(*b*) the word ''and'' which immediately follows paragraph (*b*) shall be omitted;
(*c*) at the end the following paragraphs shall be added—

''(*d*) as increased by an amount equal to any profits, and reduced by an amount equal to any losses, arising to the trustees from assets after the end of that year (excluding any gains or losses on assets whose transfer is treated as an acquisition by sub-paragraph (4)(*a*) or (*b*) below); and
(*e*) as increased by the aggregate amount of any payments made—

(i) by the trustees to the member or his personal representatives or assigns,
(ii) out of his special reserve fund under paragraph 7(1) above (except where they are also made under paragraph 6(2) above), or otherwise than out of his special reserve fund, and
(iii) before the end of that year,

and for this purpose the amount of any payment which is made by way of the transfer of an asset shall be taken to be the market value of the asset at the date of the transfer and 'market value' shall be construed in accordance with section 272 of the Taxation of Chargeable Gains Act 1992.''

(5) In sub-paragraph (4)—

(*a*) after the word ''above'' there shall be inserted the words ''or otherwise than out of his special reserve fund'';
(*b*) for the words from '', to be'' to the end there shall be substituted—

''—

(*a*) in a case where the asset was held by the trustees at the end of the penultimate underwriting year, as an acquisition of the asset by the member or his personal representatives or assigns at the end of that year for a consideration equal to its market value at that time;
(*b*) in a case where the asset was acquired by the trustees after the end of the penultimate underwriting year, as an acquisition of the asset by the member or his personal representatives or assigns, at the date on which, and for the consideration for which, the asset was acquired by the trustees; and

(*c*) in a case where the asset was both acquired by the trustees and transferred by them to the member or his personal representatives or assigns before the end of the penultimate underwriting year, as an acquisition of the asset by the member or his personal representatives or assigns at the date of the transfer and for a consideration equal to its market value at that time.''.

1999/3330
Double Taxation Relief (Taxes on Income) (Foreign Interest and Dividends) Regulations 1999

Made by the Commissioners of Inland Revenue under the Income and Corporation Taxes Act 1988, s 798B(4)

Made	*13 December 1999*
Laid before the House of Commons	*13 December 1999*
Coming into force	*3 January 2000*

Citation and commencement

1 These Regulations may be cited as the Double Taxation Relief (Taxes on Income) (Foreign Interest and Dividends) Regulations 1999 and shall come into force on 3rd January 2000.

Interpretation

2—(1) In these Regulations unless the context otherwise requires—

''the cost of acquiring the asset'', in relation to a foreign dividend, means—

(*a*) the cost of acquiring the right to the dividend (if any), and

(*b*) the cost of acquiring the stocks, funds, shares or securities (if any) out of which, or in respect of which, the dividend is paid;

''interbank market'' means the market that exists between banks in a particular place for the purpose of borrowing and lending funds and dealing in currencies, and ''the relevant interbank market'' means the interbank market which is most appropriate in relation to a loan having regard to all the terms on which it was made;

''interest period'', in relation to a loan, means—

(*a*) any period specified in the loan agreement as a period for which interest is to be calculated, or, as the case may be, selected in accordance with that agreement by one of the parties thereto, beginning either on the date on which the loan was first made or on the expiry of the preceding interest period; or

(*b*) where no such period is specified in the loan agreement, but interest is to be calculated under that agreement by reference to a period of at least 360 days, and is payable on two or more specified dates within that period, any period beginning immediately after one and ending on the next of those dates; or

(*c*) in any other case, any period not exceeding one year which is appropriate in the circumstances of the loan;

''loan agreement'' means, in relation to a loan, any agreement in pursuance of which the loan is made;

''qualifying taxpayer'' has the meaning given by section 798(4) and (5);

''the specified circumstances'' means circumstances in which—

(*a*) section 798 applies, and

(*b*) the amount of the qualifying taxpayer's financial expenditure in relation to the earning of the foreign interest or foreign dividends in question is not readily ascertainable;

''subsection (3)'' means subsection (3) of section 798B.

(2) References in these Regulations to a particular section, without more, are to that section of the Income and Corporation Taxes Act 1988.

Determination of the sum which it is just and reasonable to attribute to the earning of foreign interest or foreign dividends—matters to be taken into account

3—(1) This regulation specifies, for the purpose of supplementing subsection (3), matters to be taken into account in determining such sum as it is just and reasonable to attribute to the earning of foreign interest or foreign dividends, in the specified circumstances.

(2) Subject to paragraph (6), in relation to a loan there shall be taken into account (whether or not the interest rate payable is determined by reference to rates at which deposits are offered in an interbank market) the interbank bid rates, determined in accordance with regulation 4, which at any time are most appropriate in the circumstances of the loan, having regard to—

(*a*) the amount of principal outstanding on the loan during each interest period,

(*b*) the currency in which the loan is denominated, and

(*c*) the length of each interest period.

(3) In relation to foreign interest other than loan interest, paragraph (2), regulation 4 and the definitions of "interbank market", "the relevant interbank market" and "interest period" shall apply, with the modifications that—

(*a*) references to the loan, or to the loan agreement, are replaced with references to the obligations, under which the right to interest arises;

(*b*) the reference to the date on which the loan was first made is replaced with a reference to the date on which any of those obligations first came into existence; and

(*c*) the reference to principal outstanding is replaced with a reference to any amount other than interest which is owing (whether or not yet due and payable) by the payer of the foreign interest to the qualifying taxpayer.

(4) In relation to foreign dividends, paragraph (2), regulation 4 and the definitions of "interbank market" and "the relevant interbank market" shall apply as if—

(*a*) so much of the cost of acquiring the asset as has not been repaid to the qualifying taxpayer represented a loan from the payee of the dividend to the payer thereof and the dividend represented interest on that loan;

(*b*) the date on which any of the cost of acquiring the asset was first expended by the qualifying taxpayer were the date on which that loan was made; and

(*c*) the interest periods were periods of one year, beginning either—

(i) on the date on which the loan is treated as made by sub-paragraph (*b*), or

(ii) on the expiry of the preceding interest period,

except in a case where the loan so treated as made subsists for less than a year, where the interest period shall be equal to the period for which the loan so treated as made subsists.

(5) Where, in relation to a loan it would be impracticable to establish the interbank bid rates, there shall be taken into account such amount as would, when deducted from the foreign interest payable on the loan in the interest period, provide the lender with a margin no greater than would be usual in the case of loans of that description.

(6) Where a qualifying taxpayer establishes to the satisfaction of the inspector that, in relation to all loans, obligations and assets referred to in this regulation ("arrangements") made or held by him, on which foreign interest or foreign dividends arose in any chargeable period, the sums attributable under paragraphs (2) to (5) would be greater than the total amount of the expenditure incurred in financing those arrangements, there shall be taken into account the best estimate of such total expenditure, and in determining that figure, regard is to be had to the cost to the qualifying taxpayer of obtaining funds for such financing, to the terms on which the arrangements were made and to any other relevant matters.

Determination of interbank bid rates of interest

4 The interbank bid rates referred to in regulation 3(2) shall be taken to be the average of the bids that would be made in relation to each interest period applicable to the loan in the relevant interbank market on terms corresponding to the terms of the loan.

Revocation

5—(1) (*Revokes the Double Taxation Relief (Taxes on Income) (Foreign Loan Interest) Regulations, SI 1988/88.*)

(2) Anything whatsoever begun under any regulation revoked by these Regulations may be continued under these Regulations as if begun under these Regulations.

2000/600

Income Tax (Charge to Tax) (Payments out of Surplus Funds) (Relevant Rate) Order 2000

Made by the Treasury under TA 1988 s 599A(4)

Made	*6 March 2000*
Laid before the House of Commons	*7 March 2000*
Coming into force	*6 April 2000*

1 This Order may be cited as the Income Tax (Charge to Tax) (Payments out of Surplus Funds) (Relevant Rate) Order 2000 and shall come into force on 6th April 2000.

2 The relevant rate for the purposes of section 599A(2) of the Income and Corporation Taxes Act 1988 shall, in relation to payments made on or after 6th April 2000, be 32 per cent.

SIs

2000/921
Income and Corporation Taxes Act 1988, Section 559(4A), Order 2000

Made by the Treasury under TA 1988 s 599(4A)

Made	*30 March 2000*
Laid before the House of Commons	*31 March 2000*
Coming into force	*6 April 2000*

Commentary—*Simon's Direct Tax Service* **E5.528.**

1 This Order may be cited as the Income and Corporation Taxes Act 1988, Section 559(4A), Order 2000 and shall come into force on 6th April 2000 immediately after the bringing into effect of section 139(1) of the Finance Act 1995.

2 The relevant percentage determined for the purposes of section 559(4) and (4A) of the Income and Corporation Taxes Act 1988 is 18 per cent.

2000/922
Finance Act 1995, Section 139(3), (Appointed Day) Order 2000

Made by the Treasury under FA 1995 s 139(3)

Made	*30 March 2000*

Commentary—*Simon's Direct Tax Service* **E5.528.**

1 This Order may be cited as the Finance Act 1995, Section 139(3), (Appointed Day) Order 2000.

2 The day appointed for the purposes of section 139(1) of the Finance Act 1995 is 6th April 2000.

2000/944
Education (Student Loans) (Repayment) Regulations 2000

Made by the Secretary of State for Education and Employment under the Teaching and Higher Education Act 1998 ss 22, 42(6) and the Education (Scotland) Act 1980 ss 73(*f*), 73B

Made	*31 March 2000*
Coming into force	*1 April 2000*

ARRANGEMENT OF REGULATIONS

PART I
GENERAL

PART II
PROVISIONS APPLICABLE TO ALL REPAYMENTS

PART III
REPAYMENTS BY ASSESSMENT TO INCOME TAX

PART I

GENERAL

Citation, commencement and extent

1—(1) These Regulations may be cited as the Education (Student Loans) (Repayment) Regulations 2000, and shall come into force on 1st April 2000.

(2) Subject to paragraph (3) these Regulations extend to England and Wales only.

(3) These Regulations extend to all of the United Kingdom in so far as they impose any obligation or confer any power on the Board, an employer or a borrower in relation to repayments under Part III or IV.

Interpretation

2—In these Regulations—

''the Act'' means the Teaching and Higher Education Act 1998;

''the 1970 Act'' means the Taxes Management Act 1970 as amended from time to time both before and after the date of these Regulations;

''the 1988 Act'' means the Income and Corporation Taxes Act 1988 as amended from time to time both before and after the date of these Regulations;

''the Board'' means the Commissioners of Inland Revenue;

''borrower'' means a person to whom the Secretary of State has lent money pursuant to regulations made under section 22 of the Act and who has not received a notice from him that it has been repaid in full or cancelled, and also has the meaning given it in regulation 3(3);

''collector'' means a Collector of Taxes;

''inspector'' means an Inspector of Taxes;

''repayment'' means a repayment of a student loan;

"Secretary of State" includes any person exercising functions on behalf of a Secretary of State pursuant to section 23(4) of the Act, and also has the meanings given it in regulation 3(3) and (5);

"student loan" means the total outstanding principal, interest, penalties and charges owed by a borrower to the Secretary of State pursuant to these or any other regulations made under section 22 of the Act, excluding any interest, penalties or charges payable under Part III or IV, and also has the meaning given to it in regulation 3(3);

"year of assessment" means the period 6th April to the following 5th April.

Application

3—(1) These Regulations apply to repayments of student loans made under the Act.

(2) Where the Scottish Ministers have determined that repayments of student loans made under the Education (Scotland) Act 1980 shall be collected by the Board under Parts III and IV they shall give notices to the borrower and to the Board in accordance with regulation 11.

(3) Where the Scottish Ministers have given notices in accordance with regulation 11 (5)(*a*) or (*b*) Parts III and IV, and the provisions of Parts I and II so far as they relate to the application of Parts III and IV, shall apply to repayments of students loans made under the Education (Scotland) Act 1980 as they apply to student loans made under the Act, and for those purposes in these Regulations—

"borrower" means a person to whom the Secretary of State or the Scottish Ministers have lent money pursuant to regulations made under section 73(*f*) of the Education (Scotland) Act 1980 and who has not received a notice from them that it has been repaid in full or cancelled;

"Secretary of State" means, other than in this regulation and regulation 4, the Scottish Ministers, and includes any person exercising functions on behalf of the Secretary of State or the Scottish Ministers pursuant to section 73A(4) of the Education (Scotland) Act 1980; and

"student loan" means the total outstanding principal, interest and charges owed by a borrower to the Scottish Ministers pursuant to regulations made under section 73(*f*) of the Education (Scotland) Act 1980, excluding any interest, penalties or charges payable under Part III or IV.

Functions of the Inland Revenue

4—(1) The Board shall collect repayments from borrowers in accordance with Parts III and IV, and the provisions of section 1 of the 1970 Act shall apply for those purposes as they apply for the purposes of income tax.

(2) The Board shall, at such times and in such manner as the Treasury may direct, account to the Secretary of State for, and pay to him the sums estimated by the Board (in the manner so directed) to have been collected by them as repayments in accordance with Parts III and IV.

(3) Repayments shall not include any interest, penalties or charges payable under Part III or IV, and the Board shall cause any such sums which they recover to be paid, at such times and under such regulations as the Treasury may from time to time prescribe, to accounts, to be intituled "The Account of Her Majesty's Exchequer", at the Bank of England, and the sums so paid shall form part of the Consolidated Fund.

Inspectors and collectors

5—Any legal proceedings or administrative act authorised by or done for the purposes of these Regulations and begun by one inspector or collector may be continued by another inspector or, as the case may be, collector; and any inspector or collector may act for any division or other area.

Service by post

6—Any notice or other document which is authorised or required to be given, served or issued under these Regulations may be sent by post.

Penalties etc in relation to Parts III and IV

7—(1) Section 98 of the 1970 Act (special returns etc) shall apply for the purposes of repayments under Part III or IV as if any reference to a provision in the Table in that section were a reference to a provision in those Parts other than regulation 16.

(2) Section 99 of the 1970 Act (assisting in the preparation of incorrect returns etc) shall apply in the case of returns, statements, declarations, accounts, information or documents for the purposes of repayments under Part III or IV as they apply for the purposes of income tax.

(3) Sections 100 and 100A (determination of penalties by officer of Board), 100B (appeals against penalty determinations), 100C (penalty proceedings before Commissioners), 100D (penalty proceedings before court), 102 (mitigation of penalties), 103(3) and (4) (time limits for penalties), 103A (interest on penalties), 104 (savings for criminal proceedings) and 105 (evidence in case of fraudulent conduct) of the 1970 Act shall apply to penalties in connection with repayments under Part III or IV as they apply to penalties in connection with income tax.

(4) Sections 112 to 115A of and Schedule 3A to the 1970 Act (documents) shall apply to assessments, returns or any other documents made, required, issued, served, sent or lodged for the purposes of or in connection with repayments under Part III or IV as they apply to documents for the purposes of or in connection with income tax.

(5) Section 118(2) of the 1970 Act (failure to act within limited time) shall apply in relation to anything required to be done under Part III or IV as it applies in relation to anything required to be done under that Act.

(6) For the purposes of these Regulations the amount of a repayment covered by any assessment under Part III shall not be deemed to be finally determined until that assessment can no longer be varied, whether by any Commissioners on appeal or by the order of any court.

PART II
PROVISIONS APPLICABLE TO ALL REPAYMENTS

Interpretation

9—(1) In this Part—

''date of receipt'' in relation to a repayment shall be construed in accordance with paragraphs (2) and (3);

''disability related benefit'' means long term incapacity benefit or short term incapacity benefit at the higher rate, severe disablement allowance, disability living allowance, industrial injuries benefit and disability working allowance, all payable under the Social Security Contributions and Benefits Act 1992, or the amount of any disability premium and severe disability premium included in the applicable amount in calculating the income support payable under the Income Support (General) Regulations 1987.

(2) For the purposes of this Part a repayment shall be considered to have been paid by the borrower and received by the Secretary of State as follows:

(*a*) where an amount is paid by the borrower directly to the Secretary of State, a repayment of that amount shall be considered to have been received by him on the date on which the amount is in fact received;

(*b*) where the Board has notified the Secretary of State that an amount has become payable to the Board in respect of a year of assessment under Part III, a repayment of that amount shall be considered to have been received by him on 31st January following the year of assessment, whether or not the borrower has in fact paid any or all of that amount to the Board; and

(*c*) where an amount is deducted by an employer under Part IV that amount shall be aggregated with all other such amounts deducted in the same year of assessment and repayments of the aggregate amount shall be considered to have been received by the Secretary of State in equal instalments received on the days during the year of assessment which are—

(i) the last days of a month,

(ii) days after the date on which the Secretary of State has given notice under regulation 11(5)(*b*) that payment should be deducted, and

(iii) days before the date on which he has given notice under regulation 11(5)(*e*) that payment should cease to be deducted.

Interest and penalties

10—(1) Interest or penalties charged under Parts III or IV shall not be added to the principal outstanding, and payment of such interest or penalties shall not be credited against the principal outstanding.

(2) Any repayment received by the Secretary of State shall be applied by him in reduction or in satisfaction of:

(*a*) first, any outstanding penalties or charges under Part V,

(*b*) second, any outstanding interest, and

(*c*) third, any outstanding principal, which shall be reduced or satisfied from the date of receipt.

Time for repayments

11—(1) A borrower may repay all or any part of his student loan to the Secretary of State at any time.

(2) A borrower shall not be required to repay any of his student loan before 6th April 2000.

(3) A borrower shall not be required to repay such part of his student loan as relates to a particular notification of eligibility under the Education (Student Support) Regulations 1999(*a*) until the year of assessment beginning after the date on which that eligibility terminates under regulation 8 of those Regulations.

(4) A borrower—

(*a*) whose student loan was made in connection with his attendance at a course for the initial training of teachers, other than a course leading to a first degree; and (*b*) who has notified the Secretary of State in writing that he does not wish to repay that loan during any period in which he is required to repay a loan made under the Education (Student Loans) Act 1990 or the Education (Student Loans) (Northern Ireland) Order 1990;

shall not be required to repay any of his student loan during any such period.

(5) Subject to paragraph (7) the Secretary of State shall notify the borrower and the Board of—

(*a*) the first, or as the case may be next, year of assessment in respect of which the borrower may be required to make repayments under Part III;

(*b*) the date on and after which a borrower may be required to make repayments by way of deduction from his emoluments under Part IV;

(*c*) where the borrower has given the Secretary of State notification in accordance with paragraph (4), the year of assessment in respect of which the borrower shall cease to be required to make repayments under Part III;

(*d*) the final year of assessment in respect of which the borrower shall be required to make repayments under Part III because—

(i) the loan has been repaid to the Secretary of State in full, or

(ii) an amount sufficient to repay the balance owing to the Secretary of State in full is likely to be received by the Board under Part IV and by the Secretary of State under Part V by the 30th April following the date of issue of the notice, or

(iii) the loan has been cancelled; and

(*e*) the date after which a borrower shall not be required to make repayments by way of deduction from his emoluments under Part IV because—

(i) the loan has been repaid to the Secretary of State in full, or

(ii) an amount sufficient to repay the balance owing to the Secretary of State in full is likely to be received by the Board under Parts III and IV and by the Secretary of State under Part V by that date, or

(iii) the loan has been cancelled; or

(iv) the borrower has given the Secretary of State notification in accordance with paragraph (4).

(6) The Secretary of State shall not issue a notice under paragraph (5)(*d*) after the end of the calendar year during which the final year of assessment specified in the notice ends.

(7) Where the Secretary of State has notified a borrower and the Board that repayments under Parts III and IV shall no longer be made but at a later date it appears to him that the student loan has not been fully repaid he may give further notices in accordance with paragraph (5).

(8) The Secretary of State shall not be required to give notices under paragraph (5)(*a*) or (*b*) where the borrower's student loan does not exceed £120.

(9) Where under paragraph (8) the Secretary of State is not required to give notices under paragraph (5)(*a*) or (*b*) he may require the borrower to repay his student loan in such manner and over such period of time as in all the circumstances seems appropriate.

Cancellation

12—(1) Subject to paragraph (4) where a borrower is not in breach of any obligation to repay his loan in accordance with Part V or in breach of any obligation to repay any other loan mentioned in paragraph (2) and the Secretary of State is satisfied that he—

(*a*) has died;

(*b*) has attained the age of 65; or

(*c*) receives a disability related benefit and because of his disability he is permanently unfit for work

the Secretary of State shall cancel his liability to repay his student loan.

(2) The loans mentioned in this paragraph are loans made under the Education (Student Loans) Act 1990, the Education (Student Loans) (Northern Ireland) Order 1990, the Education (Scotland) Act 1980 and regulations made thereunder and the Education (Student Support) (Northern Ireland) Order 1998 and regulations made thereunder.

(3) For the purposes of this Part the cancellation of a student loan shall have effect on the date on which it is cancelled, not on the date the event giving rise to the right to cancellation takes place.

(4) The cancellation of a borrower's liability to repay his student loan under paragraph (1) shall not affect his liability to make repayments under Part III subject to and in accordance with that Part in respect of any year of assessment—

(*a*) in the case of cancellation under paragraph (1)(*a*) during which the borrower was alive; and

(*b*) in any other case preceding the year of assessment during which the loan is cancelled.

(5) The cancellation of a borrower's liability to repay his student loan under paragraph (1) shall not affect his liability to make repayments by way of deductions made under Part IV subject to and in accordance with that Part in respect of any earnings period ending before the date of cancellation.

Refunds

13—(1) Where the Secretary of State has received a repayment either directly from the borrower or from the Board under Part IV—

(*a*) which results in the student loan being paid in full, or

(*b*) when the student loan has already been paid in full

he shall refund to the borrower any amount not required to repay the loan in full together with interest calculated as if it were the principal of a student loan outstanding from the date of receipt of the repayment to the date of the refund.

(2) Where the Secretary of State is considered to have received a payment from the Board under Part III in respect of a year of assessment—

(*a*) which results in the student loan being paid in full, or

(*b*) when the student loan has already been paid in full

the repayment shall be considered to have been received by the Secretary of State on the 31st January next following the year of assessment in accordance with regulation 9(2)(*b*), and the Secretary of State shall refund to the Board for the account of the borrower any overpayment which results from the receipt.

(3) A refund under paragraph (2) shall not carry interest, and the Board shall be considered to have received the refund on the date on which the amount refunded was considered to have been received by the Secretary of State in accordance with regulation 9.

(4) Where in accordance with Part IV the Secretary of State has received a repayment by way of deduction from a borrower's emoluments for a year of assessment and those emoluments do not exceed £10,000 the Secretary of State shall on application by the borrower refund the amount deducted.

PART III

REPAYMENTS BY ASSESSMENT TO INCOME TAX

Repayments of student loans by persons required to submit a tax return

14 Repayments by a borrower who in respect of any year of assessment is required to make and deliver to the Board a return under section 8 of the 1970 Act shall be made, accounted for and recovered in like manner as income tax payable under the Taxes Acts; and in such case the provisions of this Part (which with extensions and modifications include provisions of the Taxes Acts) shall apply to and for the purposes of such repayments.

Time for and amount of repayments

15—(1) Every borrower who has received notice from the Secretary of State under regulation 11(5)(*a*) that he may be required to make repayments of his student loan shall make a repayment in respect of any year of assessment—

(*a*) which is specified in a notice under regulation 11(5)(*a*) or which, subject to paragraph (2), is any subsequent year up to and including any year specified in a notice under regulation 11(5)(*d*); and

(*b*) in respect of which he has been required to make and deliver a return under section 8 of the 1970 Act.

(2) A borrower shall not be required to make repayments in respect of any year of assessment specified in a notice under regulation 11(5)(*c*) or any subsequent year falling before a year specified in a subsequent notice under regulation 11(5)(*a*).

(3) The repayment shall be an amount equal to the 9% of the borrower's total income for that year calculated in accordance with the Taxes Acts.

(4) In calculating a borrower's total income for the purposes of paragraph (1) any deduction which falls to be made by way of personal reliefs provided for in Chapter I of Part VII of the 1988 Act shall not be made.

(5) In calculating a borrower's total income for the purposes of paragraph (1) there shall be excluded:

(*a*) the first £10,000 of that income;

(*b*) income on which the borrower could not become liable to tax under a self-assessment made under section 9 of the 1970 Act for that year;

(*c*) unearned income unless the amount of such income for that year exceeds £2,000;

(*d*) incapacity benefit payable under the Social Security Contributions and Benefits Act 1992;

(*e*) amounts chargeable to tax under sections 145,146,154,157,158, 159AA, 159A, 160 or 162 of the 1988 Act (benefits in kind);

(*f*) amounts in respect of which relief is given under Part XIV of the 1988 Act (pension schemes, social security benefits, life annuities etc);

(*g*) the amount of any loss in respect of which relief is given under section 380 of the 1988 Act (trade etc losses set-off against general income); and (*h*) the amount of any payment in respect of which relief is given under section 109A of the 1988 Act (relief for post-cessation expenditure).

(6) For the purposes of this regulation unearned income is income other than—

(*a*) earned income within the meaning of section 833(4) and (5) of the 1988 Act;

(*b*) income referred to in section 127(1) of that Act (enterprise allowance);

(*c*) the profits arising from a business chargeable to tax under Case I of Schedule D pursuant to section 503(1) of that Act (furnished holiday accommodation);

(*d*) payments and other benefits chargeable to tax under section 148(1) of that Act (payments and benefits in connection with termination of employment);

(*e*) income treated as earned income under section 107 of that Act (receipts after cessation of trade);

(*f*) sums treated as earned income under section 491(5) of that Act (certain receipts from bodies corporate carrying on mutual business);

(*g*) an amount treated as earned income under section 531(6) of that Act (consideration in respect of the disposal of know-how);

(*h*) any annuity treated as earned income of the annuitant under section 619(1)(*b*) of that Act (certain retirement annuities); and

(*i*) annual payments treated as earned income under section 628(1) of that Act (partnership annuities).

Personal return

16—For the purposes of establishing the amount of the repayment which a borrower is required to make for a year of assessment under regulation 14 an inspector or an officer of the Board may require him—

(*a*) to include in a return required to be made and delivered under section 8 of the 1970 Act such information as may reasonably be required, and

(*b*) to deliver with the return such accounts, statements and documents, relating to information contained in the return by virtue of sub-paragraph (*a*), as may reasonably be required.

Returns to include self-assessment

17—(1) Subject to subsection (2), every return made and delivered by a borrower under section 8 of the 1970 Act shall include a self-assessment, that is to say—

(*a*) an assessment of the amount of the repayment which, on the basis of the information contained in the return and taking into account any relief or allowance mentioned in regulation 15 he is required to make for the year of assessment under regulation 15; and

(*b*) an assessment of the amount payable by him by way of repayment, that is to say, the difference between the amount of the repayment which he is assessed to make for the year of assessment under sub-paragraph (*a*) and the aggregate amount of any repayments deducted from emoluments under Part IV during that year.

(2) Section 9(2) to (6) (self-assessment) and section 9A (power to enquire into returns) of the 1970 Act shall apply to a self-assessment under this regulation as they apply to a self-assessment under section 9(1) of that Act, and any reference in the Taxes Acts to those sections shall be construed as a reference to them as extended by this regulation.

Records

18 Section 12B of the 1970 Act (records to be kept for the purposes of returns) shall apply in the case of a borrower as if any reference to a return includes reference to a return including the information required by regulation 16(*a*).

Other returns and information

19—(1) Part III of the 1970 Act (other returns and information) shall apply for the purposes of establishing the amount of the repayment a borrower may be required to make under this Part as it applies for the purposes of establishing the amounts in which a person is chargeable to income tax.

(2) Section 19A of the 1970 Act (power to call for documents for purposes of certain enquiries) shall apply where an officer of the Board gives notice under section 9A(1) of that Act in relation to a self-assessment under regulation 16 of these Regulations as it applies to a self-assessment under section 9 of that Act.

Assessments, claims and appeals

20—(1) Subject to paragraph (2) Parts IV (assessment and claims) and V (appeals and other proceedings) of the 1970 Act shall apply with any necessary modifications for the purposes of—

(*a*) assessing the amount of the repayment a borrower is required to make under this Part,

(*b*) claims or other matters concerning any such assessment, and

(*c*) appeals against any such assessment

as if any reference to an assessment or a self-assessment included a reference to an assessment or self-assessment for the purposes of this Part.

(2) An officer of the Board shall not make a determination of the amount of a repayment a borrower may be required to make under this Part under section 28C of the 1970 Act (determination of tax where no return delivered).

Payment

21—(1) Any repayment by a borrower under this Part shall be paid as if the repayment were an amount of income tax payable by him under section 59B of the 1970 Act (payment of income tax and capital gains tax) in accordance with the following paragraphs.

(2) In a case where the borrower—

(*a*) gave the notice required by section 7 of that Act within six months from the end of the year of assessment, but

(*b*) was not given notice under section 8 of that Act until after the 31st October next following that year

any repayment by a borrower shall be made at the end of the period of three months beginning with the day on which the notice under section 8 was given.

(3) In any other case the repayment shall be made on or before the 31st January next following the year of assessment.

(4) Section 59B(4A), (5) or (6) of that Act shall apply where an enquiry, an amendment of a self-assessment or an assessment is made in respect of a repayment under this Part respectively, and any reference to tax payable in those subsections shall be treated as a reference to a repayment by a borrower.

(5) Section 59B(5A), (7) and (8) of that Act shall not apply for the purposes of this regulation.

Surcharges

22 Section 59C of the 1970 Act (surcharges on unpaid income tax and capital gains tax) shall apply to repayments which have become payable by a borrower under this Part as it applies to income tax payable in accordance with section 55 or 59B of that Act.

Collection and recovery

23 Part VI of the 1970 Act (collection and recovery) shall apply to repayments, interest and penalties which have become due and payable by a borrower under this Part as it applies to income tax and interest charged and penalties imposed under that Act.

Persons chargeable in a representative capacity

24 Sections 72 (trustees, guardians, etc of incapacitated persons), 74 (personal representatives), 75 (receivers appointed by a court) and 76 (protection for certain trustees, agents and receivers) of the 1970 Act shall apply in the case of repayments due and payable by a borrower under this Part as they apply in the case of income tax chargeable to any person.

Interest

25—(1) Any repayment due and payable under this Part shall carry interest at the rate applicable under section 178 of the Finance Act 1989 for the purposes of section 86 of the 1970 Act from whichever of the following days is applicable—

(*a*) the last day of the period referred to in regulation 21(2), or

(*b*) the date mentioned in regulation 21(3),

until payment, whether or not the applicable day is a non-business day within the meaning of section 92 of the Bills of Exchange Act 1882.

(2) Sections 90 and 91 of the 1970 Act shall apply to interest under this regulation as they apply to interest on income tax.

(3) A refund by the Board to a borrower of an overpayment of amounts payable under this Part shall carry interest at the rate applicable under section 178 of the Finance Act 1989 from the date on which the overpayment arose to the date on which the order for the refund is issued.

Penalties

26—(1) Section 93 of the 1970 Act (failure to make return for income tax and capital gains tax) shall apply to returns under section 8 of that Act which are required to include information under regulation 16 as it applies to any other such returns.

(2) In the case of such returns the references in section 93 to liability to tax which would have been shown in the return shall be references to the aggregate of the amounts which, if a proper return had been delivered on the filing date, would have been payable—

(*a*) by the taxpayer under section 59B of the Act (payment of income tax and capital gains tax), and

(*b*) where the taxpayer is a borrower by way of a repayment under regulation 15.

(3) Section 95 of the 1970 Act (incorrect return or accounts for income tax or capital gains tax) shall apply in relation to anything done for the purposes of or in connection with the ascertainment of liability of a borrower to make a repayment under this Part as it applies for the purposes of or in connection with the ascertainment of liability to income tax, and for that purpose the difference referred to in section 95(2) shall be the difference between—

(*a*) the amount calculated under regulation 15(1) and

(*b*) the amount which would have been the amount so calculated if the return, statement, declaration or accounts as made or submitted by the borrower had been correct.

(4) Section 97 (incorrect return or accounts: supplemental) of the 1970 Act shall apply in the case of returns, statements, declarations, accounts, information or documents for the purposes of repayments under this Part as they apply for the purposes of income tax.

PART IV
DEDUCTION OF REPAYMENTS BY EMPLOYERS

Interpretation

27 In this Part—

"the Contributions Regulations" means the Social Security (Contributions) Regulations 1979;

"deductions working sheet" means any form of record on or in which are to be kept the matters required by the Contributions Regulations in connection with an employee's emoluments and deductions;

"emoluments" means, subject to regulation 30 of these Regulations, such sums as—

(*a*) constitute earnings for the purposes of section 3 of the Social Security Contributions and Benefits Act 1992(*h*) as calculated for the purposes of the Contributions Regulations as amended from time to time, and

(*b*) are to be taken into account for the purposes of the computation of secondary Class 1 contributions under section 9 of the Social Security Contributions and Benefits Act 1992;

"employee" means any person in receipt of emoluments;

"employer" means any person paying emoluments to an employee, including the Crown;

"income tax month" means the period beginning on the 6th day of any calendar month and ending on the 5th day of the following calendar month;

"income tax period" means income tax quarter where regulation 39(2) has effect, but otherwise means income tax month;

"income tax quarter" means the period beginning on 6th April and ending on 5th July, or beginning on 6th July and ending on 5th October, or beginning on 6th October and ending on 5th January, or beginning on 6th January and ending on 5th April;

"the Income Tax Regulations" means the Income Tax (Employments) Regulations 1993;

"national insurance number" means the national insurance number allocated within the meaning of the Contributions Regulations.

Repayment of student loans by employees

28 Repayments by a borrower who is an employee shall be made, accounted for and recovered in like manner as income tax deducted from the emoluments of an office or employment by virtue of regulations under section 203 of the 1988 Act; and in such case the provisions contained in this Part (which with extensions and modifications include provisions of the Income Tax Regulations) shall apply to and for the purposes of such repayments.

Amount of repayments

29—(1) The repayment deducted shall be 9% of any emoluments paid to, or provided to or for the benefit of, the borrower in respect of the employment which exceed the threshold specified in paragraph (2).

(2) The threshold shall be—

(*a*) where the earnings period specified in respect of those emoluments is a year, £10,000; or

(*b*) in any other case, the amount which bears the same relation to £10,000 as the number of days, weeks or months of the earnings period specified in respect of those emoluments bears to the number of days, weeks or months in the year respectively.

(3) Where a repayment calculated under paragraph (1) includes pence as well as pounds the pence shall be ignored.

(4) In the alternative the repayment specified in the last preceding paragraph may be calculated in accordance with the appropriate scale prepared by the Secretary of State.

(5) Where the amount of emoluments to which the appropriate scale is to be applied does not appear in the scale, the amount of the repayment shall be calculated by reference to the next smaller amount of emoluments in the appropriate column in the scale.

(6) Where a scale would, but for the period to which it relates, be appropriate and the earnings period in question is a multiple of the period in the scale, the scale shall be applied by dividing the emoluments in question so as to obtain the equivalent emoluments for the period to which the scale relates and by multiplying the amount of repayments shown in the scale as appropriate to those equivalent emoluments by the same factor as the earnings were divided.

Calculation of emoluments

30—(1) In calculating emoluments for the purposes of these Regulations emoluments paid to or for the benefit of an employee shall be aggregated or not aggregated as they are for the purposes of the Contributions Regulations.

(2) The Board may, where they are satisfied as to the existence of any practice in respect of the payment of emoluments whereby the incidence of repayments is avoided or reduced by means of the payment of emoluments to or for the benefit of an employee by different persons in respect of different employments, give directions for securing that such repayments are made as if that practice were not followed.

(3) The Board may, where they are satisfied as to the existence of any practice in respect of the payment of emoluments whereby the incidence of repayments is avoided or reduced by means of irregular or unequal payments, give directions for securing that such repayments are made as if that practice were not followed.

Earnings periods

31—(1) The amount of repayments, if any, which shall be deducted by the employer shall, subject to the provisions of paragraphs (2) and (3), be calculated by reference to the amount of emoluments paid to, or provided to or for the benefit of, the borrower in respect of the employment, in the earnings period specified or determined in respect of those emoluments for the purposes of the Contributions Regulations.

(2) Where emoluments in respect of two or more employments—

(*a*) fall to be aggregated for the purposes of the Contributions Regulations; and

(*b*) the earnings periods in respect of those emoluments are, by virtue of the Contributions Regulations, of different lengths

the earnings period specified in respect of the aggregated emoluments shall be the shorter or shortest of those earnings periods.

(3) Regulation 6B of the Contributions Regulations shall not apply in determining the earnings period specified in respect of a payment of statutory maternity pay or statutory sick pay.

Multiple employers

32—(1) Where an employer has made an election under regulation 3 of the Income Tax Regulations to be treated as a different employer in respect of each group of employees specified in the election, he shall be treated as having made an election for the purposes of these Regulations.

(2) Where emoluments in respect of two or more employments fall to be aggregated under regulation 12(1)(*a*) of the Contributions Regulations, the amount to be deducted shall be apportioned between the employers in the same proportions as secondary Class 1 contributions are apportioned between them under that regulation.

Intermediate employers

33—(1) Where an employee works for a person who is not his immediate employer, that person (''the principal employer'') shall be deemed to be the employer for the purposes of these Regulations, and the immediate employer shall furnish the principal employer with such particulars of the employee's emoluments as may be necessary to enable the principal employer to comply with these Regulations.

(2) If the employee's emoluments are actually paid to him by the immediate employer—

(*a*) the immediate employer shall be notified by the principal employer of the amount of repayments which shall be deducted when the emoluments are paid to the employee, and shall deduct the amount so notified to him accordingly; and

(*b*) the principal employer may make a corresponding deduction on making to the immediate employer the payment out of which the said emoluments will be paid.

(3) Paragraphs (1) and (2) apply only in the circumstances that a direction has been given by the Board under section 203E of the 1988 Act (PAYE: mobile UK workforce)

(4) In paragraphs (1) and (2)—

(*a*) "the principal employer" means the person specified as the relevant person in the direction referred to in paragraph (3), and

(*b*) "the immediate employer" means the person specified as the contractor in that direction.

Notice to employers

34—(1) Where the Board have been given notice by the Secretary of State under regulation 11(5)(*b*) that a borrower may be required to make repayments under this Part on and after a specified date the Board shall give notice to any person who to their knowledge is an employer of the borrower requiring the employer to make deductions of repayments from emoluments paid to the borrower in accordance with these Regulations.

(2) A notice under paragraph (1) shall contain—

(*a*) the employee's name;

(*b*) his national insurance number;

(*c*) the date on and after which the employer is required to make deductions.

(3) Where the Board have been given notice by the Secretary of State under regulation 11(5)(*e*) that repayments shall no longer be required to be made by a borrower under this Part after a particular date the Board shall give notice to any person who to their knowledge is an employer of that borrower requiring him not to make deductions, or to cease making such deductions accordingly.

(4) A notice under paragraph (3) shall contain—

(*a*) the employee's name;

(*b*) his national insurance number;

(*c*) the date on and after which no deduction is required to be made.

Deduction of repayments

35—(1) Every employer who has received notice that an employee is required to make repayments, either from the Board under regulation 34(1) or by receiving a certificate under regulation 25 of the Income Tax Regulations (form P45), which contains a statement under regulation 50 of those Regulations, shall on making to that employee any payment of emoluments on or after the date referred to in paragraph (2) and before the date referred to in paragraph (3) deduct the appropriate repayment in accordance with these Regulations.

(2) The date referred to in this paragraph is—

(*a*) where the employer has received notice from the Board under regulation 34(1) the date specified in the notice as the date on or after which he is required to make deductions; or

(*b*) where the employer has received a certificate under regulation 25 of the Income Tax Regulations the date on which he first receives the certificate.

(3) The date referred to in this paragraph is the date specified in the notice given by the Board under regulation 34(3) as the date on or after which he is required not to make or to cease to make deductions.

(4) The date specified in a notice under paragraph (2)(*a*) or (3) shall—

(*a*) where the employee's pay period is one week or shorter, be 14 days or more from the date of issue of the notice, or

(*b*) in all other cases, be 42 days or more from the date of issue of the notice.

(5) Where two or more payments of emoluments fall to be aggregated for the purposes of calculating the amount of a repayment required to be deducted the employer may deduct that amount either wholly from one such payment or partly from one and partly from the other or any one or more of the others.

(6) If the employer on making any payment of emoluments to an employee does not deduct from it the full amount of a repayment he was required to deduct he may deduct the amount so underdeducted from any subsequent payment or payments of emoluments to that employee during the same year of assessment but—

(*a*) a subsequent deduction shall not be made after the date referred to in paragraph (3); and

(*b*) the amount of any subsequent deduction shall be an amount in addition to but not in excess of the amount deductible from the payment under the other provisions of this Part.

(7) If the employer deducts any repayment from the emoluments of an employee who is a borrower in accordance with these Regulations he shall not be required to repay any amount to the employee only because that amount was not owed by the employee to the Secretary of State as all or part of a student loan

Priority where other deductions required

36—(1) Where an employer is required to deduct repayments from a payment under regulation 35 but the aggregate of the deduction and any deductions on account of income tax and national insurance contributions exceeds the amount of the payment he shall make the deductions on account of income tax and national insurance first, and the amount of the repayment required to be deducted shall be the remaining balance.

(2) Where an employer is required to deduct repayments from a payment under regulation 35 and is also required to comply with one or more—

(*a*) attachment of earnings orders made under the Attachment of Earnings Act 1971 ("the 1971 Act"), the Community Charge (Administration and Enforcement) Regulations 1989 ("the Community Charge Regulations"), the Council Tax (Administration and Enforcement) Regulations 1992 ("the Council Tax Regulations"), the Judgements Enforcement (Northern Ireland) Order 1981, the Magistrates' Courts (Northern Ireland) Order 1981; or

(*b*) deduction of earnings orders made under the Child Support (Collection and Enforcement) Regulations 1992,

or with one or more of both types of order paragraph (3) shall apply.

(3) An employer shall deduct repayments as if they were amounts required to be deducted pursuant to an order under the 1971 Act which—

(*a*) was not made to secure the repayment of a judgment debt or payments under an administration order,

(*b*) was the most recent order under that Act not so made, and

(*c*) specifies a protected earnings rate equal to the protected earnings rate specified in the most recent attachment of earnings order or deductions of earnings order not so made which specifies such a rate, unless there is no such order.

(4) Where under paragraph (3) an employer is required to comply with an attachment of earnings order made under the Community Charge Regulations or the Council Tax Regulations before deducting a repayment under regulation 35, he shall not deduct any repayment.

(5) Where an employer is required to deduct repayments from a payment under regulation 35 and is also required to comply with one or more earnings arrestments, current maintenance arrestments or conjoined arrestment orders within the meaning of the Debtors (Scotland) Act 1987 (whether or not he is also required to comply with an attachment of earnings order or a deduction of earnings order), he shall not deduct repayments under that regulation.

Deductions working sheet

37—(1) The employer shall record on the deductions working sheet for an employee the amount of any deduction from any payment of emoluments under these Regulations.

(2) Where two or more payments of emoluments fall to be aggregated for the purposes of calculating the amount of repayments required to be deducted the employer, instead of recording separate amounts in respect of each such payment shall record a single amount, being the total of the amount required to be deducted in respect of the aggregated payments.

Certificate of repayments

38—(1) Where the employer is required to give an employee a certificate in accordance with regulation 39 of the Income Tax Regulations or paragraph 25 of Schedule 1 to the Contributions Regulations (form P60) he shall enter thereon in respect of the year to which the certificate relates the amount of repayments deducted by him.

(2) Where the employer is not required to give an employee who is in his employment on the last day of the year a certificate as described in paragraph (1) but has deducted repayments in respect of a year the employer shall nevertheless give the employee such a certificate showing thereon the amount of repayments deducted.

Payment of repayments deducted to the Inland Revenue

39—(1) Subject to paragraphs (2) and (3) the employer shall pay an amount equal to the repayments—

(*a*) which he has deducted under these Regulations during an income tax month, or

(*b*) which he is required to deduct under these Regulations during that income tax month,

whichever is the smaller amount, to the collector within 14 days of the end of that month.

(2) Subject to paragraph (3) the employer shall pay an amount equal to the repayments—

(*a*) which he has deducted during an income tax quarter, or

(*b*) which he is required to deduct during that quarter,

whichever is the smaller amount, to the collector within 14 days of the end of that quarter where under paragraph 26A of Schedule 1 to the Contributions Regulations he is required to pay national insurance contributions due in respect of emoluments paid in that quarter within 14 days of its end.

(3) Where the employer has, under regulation 7(2) of the Tax Credit (Payment by Employers) Regulations 1999, funded the payment of tax credit out of repayments deducted under these Regulations, the amount required to be paid to the collector under paragraph (1) or (2) shall be reduced by the amount of tax credit which the employer has so funded in the income tax period.

(4) If the employer has paid to the collector on account of repayments under this regulation an amount which he was not liable to pay, the amounts which he is liable to pay subsequently in respect of other payments of emoluments made by him during the same year shall be reduced by the amount overpaid, so however that if there was a corresponding overdeduction from any payment of

emoluments to an employee the provisions of this paragraph shall apply only in so far as the employer has reimbursed the employee for that overdeduction.

Recovery of repayments deducted

40—(1) The provisions of the Taxes Acts and of any regulations under section 203 of the 1988 Act relating to the recovery of tax shall apply to the recovery of any amount which the employer is liable to pay to the collector under regulation 39 as if that amount had been tax charged by way of an assessment on the employer under Schedule E.

(2) In the application to any proceedings taken by virtue of this regulation of any provisions referred to in paragraph (1) limiting the amount which is recoverable in those proceedings, there shall be disregarded any amount of tax which may by virtue of the following paragraph be included as part of the cause of action or matter of complaint in those proceedings.

(3) Proceedings may be brought for the recovery of—

(*a*) the total amount which the employer is liable to pay to the collector under regulation 39, or

(*b*) the total amount which the employer is liable to pay to the collector under regulation 39 in addition to any tax which the employer is liable to pay to the collector for any income tax period, or

(*c*) the total amount which the employer is liable to pay to the collector under regulation 39 in addition to any national insurance contributions which the employer is liable to pay to the collector, or

(*d*) the total amount which the employer is liable to pay to the collector under regulation 39 in addition to any national insurance contributions and tax which the employer is liable to pay to the collector

without specifying the respective amounts or distinguishing the amounts which the employer is liable to pay in respect of each employee and without specifying the employees in question, and for the purposes of proceedings under section 66 or 67 of the 1970 Act (including proceedings under that section as applied by the provisions of this regulation) and for the purposes of summary proceedings (including in Scotland proceedings in the sheriff court), the said total amount shall, subject to the provisions of paragraph (2), be one cause of action or one matter of complaint; but nothing in this paragraph shall prevent the bringing of separate proceedings for the recovery of each of the several amounts referred to in this paragraph which is liable to pay to the collector for any income tax period in respect of his several employees.

Interest on unpaid repayments

41—(1) Where an employer has not on or before the 14th day after the end of a year of assessment paid an amount which he is liable to pay to the collector under regulation 39 in that year that amount shall carry interest at the rate applicable under section 178 of the Finance Act 1989 for the purposes of section 86 of the 1970 Act from that date until payment.

(2) Interest payable under this regulation shall be recoverable as if it were an amount which the employer is liable to pay under regulation 39.

(3) An amount to which paragraph (1) applies shall carry interest from the day mentioned in that paragraph even if that date is a non-business day within the meaning of section 92 of the Bills of Exchange Act 1882.

(4) A certificate of the collector that any amount of interest payable under this regulation has not been paid to him, or to the best of his knowledge and belief, to any other collector or to any person acting on his behalf or on behalf of another collector, shall be sufficient evidence that the employer is liable to pay to the collector the amount of interest shown on the certificate and that the sum is unpaid and due to be paid, and any document purporting to be such a certificate shall be deemed to be a certificate until the contrary is proved.

(5) Where an employer has paid interest on an amount under this regulation and it is found not to have been due to be paid, although the amount in respect of which it was paid was due to be paid, that interest shall be repaid to him.

Returns by employers

42—(1) Not later than 44 days after the end of the year of assessment the employer shall render to the inspector or, if so required to the collector in such form as the Board may approve or prescribe, a return showing in respect of each employee, in respect of whom he was required at any time during the year of assessment to prepare or maintain a deductions working sheet in accordance with regulation 37—

(*a*) such particulars as the Board may require for the identification of the employee,

(*b*) the year of assessment to which the return relates, and

(*c*) the total amount of repayments deducted for the year of assessment from the emoluments paid to the employee.

(2) The return required by paragraph (1) shall include a statement and declaration in the form approved or prescribed by the Board containing a list of all deductions working sheets on which the

employer was obliged to keep records in accordance with these Regulations in respect of the year of assessment, and shall also include a certificate showing the total amount of repayments deducted for the year of assessment in respect of each employee.

(3) Where the employer is a body corporate, the declaration and the certificate referred to in paragraph (2) shall be signed by the secretary or by a director of the body corporate.

(4) If within 14 days of the end of any year of assessment an employer has failed to pay to the collector the total amount of repayments he is liable to pay under regulation 39 the collector may prepare a certificate showing the amount of repayments remaining unpaid for the year of assessment in question, and the provisions of regulation 40 shall apply with any necessary modifications to the amount shown in the said certificate.

(5) Where an employer fails to make a return in accordance with paragraph (1) he shall be liable—

(*a*) to a penalty or penalties of the relevant monthly amount for each month (or part of a month) during which the failure continues, but excluding any month after the twelfth or for which a penalty under this paragraph has already been imposed, and

(*b*) if the failure continues beyond twelve months, without prejudice to any penalty under paragraph (*a*) above, to a penalty not exceeding so much of the amount payable by him in accordance with the regulations for the year of assessment to which the return relates as remained unpaid at the end of the 19th April after the end of that year.

(6) For the purposes of subsection (5) the relevant monthly amount in the case of a failure to make a return—

(*a*) where the number of persons in respect of whom particulars should be included in the return is fifty or less, £100, and

(*b*) where that number is greater than fifty, is £100 for each fifty such persons and an additional £100 where that number is not a multiple of fifty.

(7) Where a return under this regulation is required to be made—

(*a*) at the same time as—

(i) any specified return required to be made in accordance with regulations made by the Inland Revenue under section 203(2) (PAYE) or 566(1) (sub-contractors) of the 1988 Act to which section 98A of the 1970 Act (penalties) applies; or

(ii) any specified return required to be made in accordance with regulations made by the Secretary of State under paragraph 6 of Schedule 1 to the Social Security Contributions and Benefits Act 1992 in respect of which section 98A of the 1970 Act has been applied by such regulations, or

(*b*) if the circumstances are such that a return mentioned in paragraph (*a*) does not fall to be made, at a time defined by reference to the time for making that return, had it fallen to be made

and a person has been required to pay a penalty under section 98A(2)(*a*) of the 1970 Act (first twelve months' default in consequence of a failure in respect of a tax return) in respect of the tax return or in respect of the national insurance contributions return or in respect of both he shall not also be required to pay a penalty in respect of any failure to submit the return under this regulation.

(8) Where an employer fraudulently or negligently makes an incorrect return under paragraph (1) he shall be liable to a penalty not exceeding £3,000 for each employee in respect of whom incorrect particulars are included in the return.

Inspection of employer's records

43—(1) Every employer, whenever called upon to do so by an officer authorised by the Board, shall produce to that officer for inspection, at such time as that officer may reasonably require, at the prescribed place—

(*a*) all wages sheets, deductions working sheets, and other documents and records whatsoever relating to the calculation of payment of the emoluments of his employees in respect of the years of assessment specified by such officer or to the amount of the repayments required to be deducted in respect of those emoluments under these Regulations;

(*b*) all wages sheets, deductions working sheets, and other documents and records whatsoever relating to the amount of repayments in fact deducted during the years of assessment specified by such officer; or

(*c*) such of those wages sheets, deductions working sheets or other documents and records as may be specified by such officer.

(2) In paragraph (1) ''the prescribed place'' means—

(*a*) such place in the United Kingdom as the employer and the authorised officer may agree upon; or

(*b*) in default of such agreement, the place in the United Kingdom at which the documents and records referred to in paragraph (1) are normally kept; or

(*c*) in default of such agreement and if there is no such place as is referred to in sub-paragraph (*b*), the employer's principal place of business in the United Kingdom.

(3) The authorised officer may—

(*a*) take copies of, or make extracts from, any documents produced to him for inspection in accordance with paragraph (1);

(*b*) if it appears to him to be necessary to do so, at a reasonable time and for a reasonable period, remove any document so produced, and, if he does so, shall provide a receipt for any documents so removed; and where a lien is claimed on a document produced in accordance with paragraph (1), the removal of the document under this sub-paragraph shall not be regarded as breaking the lien;

and where a document removed in accordance with sub-paragraph (1) is reasonably required for the proper conduct of a business the authorised officer shall within 7 days provide a copy of the document, free of charge, to the person by whom it was produced or caused to be produced.

(4) Where records are maintained by computer, the person required to make them available for inspection shall provide the authorised officer with all facilities necessary for obtaining information from them.

(5) For the purposes of paragraph (1) the wages sheets, deductions working sheets (not being deductions working sheets issued under regulation 21 of the Income Tax Regulations) and other documents and records therein mentioned shall be retained by the employer for not less than three years after the end of the year of assessment to which they relate.

(6) Section 98 of the 1970 Act (penalties for failure to furnish information) shall apply in relation to an employer's duties under this regulation as they apply to a person's duties under provisions specified in the Table below section 98.

Powers to obtain information

44—(1) Section 20 of the 1970 Act (power to call for documents etc), and section 20B of that Act (restrictions on powers) so far as relating to section 20, shall apply in relation to an employer's compliance with this Part as they apply in relation to a person's tax liability or its amount.

(2) Those sections as they so apply shall have effect as if—

(*a*) any reference to the taxpayer, a taxpayer or a class of taxpayer were a reference to the employer, an employer or a class of employers;

(*b*) any reference to any provision of the Taxes Acts were a reference to this Part;

(*c*) any reference to the proper assessment or collection of tax were a reference to the proper repayment of student loans;

(*d*) the reference in section 20(8) to the taxpayer with whose liability the inspector or the Board is concerned were a reference to the employer with whose compliance with this Part the inspector or the Board is concerned;

(*e*) the reference in section 20B(2) to an appeal relating to tax were a reference to an appeal relating to compliance with this Part; and

(*f*) the reference in section 20B(6) to reasonable ground for believing that tax has, or may have been, lost to the Crown owing to the fraud of the taxpayer were a reference to reasonable ground for believing that student loan repayments have, or may have been, incorrectly deducted owing to the fraud of the employer.

(3) Section 20BB of the 1970 Act (falsification etc of documents) shall apply in relation to documents to be delivered, or to be delivered or made available for inspection, under section 20 or 20B(1) as applied by this regulation.

Formal determination of repayments payable by employer

45—(1) This regulation applies where it appears to the inspector that there may be repayments payable by an employer under regulation 39 which—

(*a*) have not been paid to the collector, and

(*b*) have not been certified by the collector under regulation 42.

(2) Where this regulation applies, the inspector may determine the amount of those repayments to the best of his judgment, and shall serve notice of his determination on the employer.

(3) A determination under this regulation may—

(*a*) cover the repayments payable by the employer under regulation 39 for any one or more tax periods in a year, and

(*b*) extend to the whole of the repayments or to such part of them as is payable in respect of a class or classes of employees specified in the notice of determination (without naming the individual employees) or of one or more named employees so specified.

(4) A determination under this regulation shall be subject to the like provisions as are contained in Parts IV (Assessments and Claims), V (Appeals and Other Proceedings), except section 55, and VI (Collection and Recovery) of the 1970 Act as if it were an assessment, and as if the amount of repayments determined was income tax charged on the employer, and those Parts of that Act shall apply with any necessary modifications.

(5) An appeal against a determination under this regulation that is to be brought before the General Commissioners shall be brought before the General Commissioners for the division in which the determination was made.

Interest on unpaid repayments which have been formally determined

46—(1) Where—

(*a*) an employer has not paid an amount of repayments to the collector under regulation 39, and

(*b*) the inspector makes a determination of the amount of such repayments under regulation 45, and

(*c*) repayments are payable pursuant to that determination,

the repayments so payable shall carry interest at the applicable rate under section 178 of the Finance Act 1989 for the purposes of section 86 of the 1970 Act from the 14th day after the end of the year of assessment in which they are payable until payment.

(2) Interest payable under this regulation shall be recoverable as if it were an amount which the employer is liable to pay under regulation 39.

Death of employer

47 If an employer dies, anything which he would have been liable to do under these Regulations shall be done by his personal representative, or in the case of an employer who paid emoluments on behalf of another person, by the person succeeding him, or if no person succeeds him, the person on whose behalf he paid emoluments.

Succession to a business

48—(1) This regulation applies where there has been a change in the employer from whom an employee receives emoluments in respect of his employment in any trade, business, concern or undertaking, or in connection with any property, or from whom an employee receives any annuity other than a pension.

(2) Subject to paragraph (3), where this regulation applies in relation to any matter arising after the change the employer after the change shall be liable to do anything which the employer before the change would have been liable to do under these Regulations if the change had not taken place.

(3) An employer after the change shall not be liable for the payment of any repayment which was deductible from emoluments paid to the employee before, unless they are also deductible from emoluments paid to the employee after, the change took place.

Payment by cheque

49 For the purposes of regulations 39 to 41 where—

(*a*) any payment to the collector is made by cheque, and

(*b*) the cheque is paid on its first presentation to the banker on whom it is drawn, the payment shall be treated as paid on the day on which the cheque was received by the collector, and ''pay'', ''paid'', ''unpaid'' and ''overpaid'' shall be construed accordingly.

Cessation of employment

50 Where an employer sends a certificate under regulation 23(1) of the Income Tax Regulations (form P45) if on the date of the certificate he—

(*a*) has received notice that the employee is a borrower as described in regulation 34(1); and

(*b*) he has not received notice from the Board under regulation 34(3) requiring him to cease making deductions on and after a date which is before the date on which he ceased to employ the employee

he shall include in the statement a statement that the employee is a borrower.

Penalties

51—(1) Where in the case of any employee an employer fraudulently or negligently—

(*a*) makes incorrect deductions, or

(*b*) makes or receives incorrect payments in a year of assessment

in pursuance of this Part he shall be liable to a penalty not exceeding £3,000 for each employee in respect of whom incorrect deductions or payments are made.

(2) A penalty under paragraph (1) shall not be imposed before the end of the year of assessment in question; and no more than one such penalty may be imposed by reference to any one employee in relation to any year of assessment.

Collection and Recovery of Penalties

52 Section 69 of the 1970 Act (recovery of penalties etc) shall apply to penalties imposed under this Part as it applies to penalties imposed under that Act.

2000/945
Income Tax (Electronic Communications) Regulations 2000

Made by the Commissioners of Inland Revenue under the Finance Act 1999 ss 132 and 133(2)

Made . . . . 3 *April 2000*
Laid before the House of Commons . . . . 3 *April 2000*
Coming into force . . . . 24 *April 2000*

Commentary—*Simon's Direct Tax Service* **E1.806, 820.**
Amendments—These Regulations have been revoked by the Income and Corporation Taxes (Electronic Communications) Regulations, SI 2003/282 reg 11 with effect from 5 March 2003. However, any direction given by the Board under these Regulations, to the extent that it could be given under SI 2003/282, shall continue to have effect as if given under SI 2003/282.

PART 1
INTRODUCTION

Citation, commencement and interpretation

1—(1) These Regulations may be cited as the Income Tax (Electronic Communications) Regulations 2000 and shall come into force on 24th April 2000.

(2) In these Regulations—

"the Board" means the Commissioners of Inland Revenue; and

"official computer system" means a computer system maintained by or on behalf of the Commissioners—

(a) to send or receive information or payments, or

(b) to process or store information.

(3) References in these Regulations to the delivery of information and to information shall be construed in accordance with 132(8) of the Finance Act 1999.

Note—These Regulations have been revoked by the Income and Corporation Taxes (Electronic Communications) Regulations, SI 2003/282 reg 11 with effect from 5 March 2003. However, any direction given by the Board under these Regulations, to the extent that it could be given under SI 2003/282, shall continue to have effect as if given under SI 2003/282.

Scope of these regulations

2—(1) These Regulations apply to—

(a) the delivery of information, to or by the Board, the delivery of which is authorised or required by or under section 8, 9 or 9A of the Taxes Management Act 1970 and

(b) the making of any payment or repayment of tax or other sums in connection with the operation of those sections.

(2) Nothing in these Regulations affects the operation of the Electronic Lodgement of Tax Returns Order 1997.

Note—These Regulations have been revoked by the Income and Corporation Taxes (Electronic Communications) Regulations, SI 2003/282 reg 11 with effect from 5 March 2003. However, any direction given by the Board under these Regulations, to the extent that it could be given under SI 2003/282, shall continue to have effect as if given under SI 2003/282.

PART 2
ELECTRONIC COMMUNICATIONS—GENERAL PROVISIONS

Restrictions on the use of electronic communications

3—(1) The Board may use electronic communications in connection with the matters referred to in regulation 2(1).

(2) A person other than the Board may only use electronic communications in connection with the matters referred to in regulation 2(1) if the conditions specified in paragraphs (3) to (6) are satisfied.

(3) The first condition is that the person is for the time being permitted to use electronic communications by an authorisation given by means of a direction of the Board.

(4) The second condition is that the person uses—

(a) an approved method for authenticating the identity of the sender of the communication;

(b) an approved method of electronic communications; and

(c) an approved method for authenticating any information delivered by means of electronic communications.

(5) The third condition is that any information or payment sent by means of electronic communications is in a form approved for the purpose of these Regulations.

(6) The fourth condition is that the person maintains such records in written or electronic form as may be specified in a general or specific direction given by the Board.

(7) In this regulation "approved" means approved for the purposes of these Regulations and for the time being by means of a general or specific direction of the Board.

Note—These Regulations have been revoked by the Income and Corporation Taxes (Electronic Communications) Regulations, SI 2003/282 reg 11 with effect from 5 March 2003. However, any direction given by the Board under these Regulations, to the extent that it could be given under SI 2003/282, shall continue to have effect as if given under SI 2003/282.

Cross references—Revenue Directions (21 August 2001) The Revenue direct that after 20 August 2001, an agent who delivers information on behalf of another person which the other ("the taxpayer") is required to deliver by virtue of a notice under TMA 1970 s 8 is authorised to do so over the internet provided the following conditions are met—

(*a*) that the agent is authorised to act for the taxpayer to whom the return relates—

(i) by means of a form 64-8 signed by the taxpayer; or

(ii) by means of an on-line authorisation given by the taxpayer on the Government Gateway website;

(*b*) that—

(i) the agent makes a copy of the information before it is sent; and

(ii) the copy is authenticated by the taxpayer by means of a signature confirming that the information is correct to the best of the taxpayer's knowledge and belief before the information is sent by the agent; and

(*c*) that for the purpose of the electronic communication, the agent uses software approved by the Commissioners of Inland Revenue.

The Revenue further direct that—

(*a*) the methods approved by them for—

(i) authenticating the identity of the individual sending the relevant information, and

(ii) the delivery of the relevant information;

(*b*) the form approved by them in which the relevant information is to be delivered; and

(*c*) the software products approved for this purpose,

are the methods, form and software products set out, at the time of, and for the purposes of, the delivery of the relevant information, on the Inland Revenue website.

Use of intermediaries

4 The Board may use intermediaries in connection with—

(a) the delivery of information, or the making of payments by means of electronic communications; and

(b) the authentication or security of anything transmitted by any such means,

and may require other persons to use intermediaries in connection with those matters.

Note—These Regulations have been revoked by the Income and Corporation Taxes (Electronic Communications) Regulations, SI 2003/282 reg 11 with effect from 5 March 2003. However, any direction given by the Board under these Regulations, to the extent that it could be given under SI 2003/282, shall continue to have effect as if given under SI 2003/282.

PART 3
ELECTRONIC COMMUNICATIONS—EVIDENTIAL PROVISIONS

Effect of delivering information by means of electronic communications

5—(1) Information to which these Regulations apply and which is delivered by means of electronic communications shall be treated as having been delivered, in the manner or form required by any provision of the Taxes Acts if, but only if, all the conditions imposed by—

(a) these Regulations,

(b) any other applicable enactment, and

(c) any specific or general direction given by the Board,

are satisfied.

(2) Information delivered by means of electronic communications shall be treated as having been delivered on the day on which the last of the conditions imposed as mentioned in paragraph (1) is satisfied.

This is subject to the qualification in paragraph (3).

(3) The Board may by a general or specific direction provide for information to be treated as delivered upon a different date (whether earlier or later) than that given by paragraph (2).

Note—These Regulations have been revoked by the Income and Corporation Taxes (Electronic Communications) Regulations, SI 2003/282 reg 11 with effect from 5 March 2003. However, any direction given by the Board under these Regulations, to the extent that it could be given under SI 2003/282, shall continue to have effect as if given under SI 2003/282.

Proof of identity of sender or recipient of information

6 If it is necessary to prove, for any purpose, the identity of—

(a) the sender of any information delivered by means of electronic communications to an official computer system, or

(b) the recipient of any information delivered by means of electronic communications from an official computer system,

the sender or recipient (as the case may be) shall be ... presumed to be the person recorded as such on an official computer system[, unless the contrary is proved].

Note—These Regulations have been revoked by the Income and Corporation Taxes (Electronic Communications) Regulations, SI 2003/282 reg 11 with effect from 5 March 2003. However, any direction given by the Board under these Regulations, to the extent that it could be given under SI 2003/282, shall continue to have effect as if given under SI 2003/282.

Proof of delivery of information and payments

7—(1) If it is necessary to prove, for any purpose, that the use of electronic communications has resulted in the making of any payment to or by the Board, or the delivery of any information, this shall be ... presumed—

(a) in the case of information delivered, or payments made, to the Board, if the making of the payment or the delivery of the information has been recorded on an official computer system,

(b) in the case of information delivered, or payments made, by the Board, if the despatch of that payment or information has been recorded on an official computer system, and

(c) not to be the case if it has not been so recorded[,

unless the contrary is proved.]

(2) If it is necessary to prove, for any purpose when any information or payment sent by means of electronic communications has been received, the time of receipt shall be ... presumed to be that recorded by an official computer system [unless the contrary is proved.]

Note—These Regulations have been revoked by the Income and Corporation Taxes (Electronic Communications) Regulations, SI 2003/282 reg 11 with effect from 5 March 2003. However, any direction given by the Board under these Regulations, to the extent that it could be given under SI 2003/282, shall continue to have effect as if given under SI 2003/282.

Proof of content of information

8 If it is necessary to prove, for any purpose, the content of any information sent by means of electronic communications, the content shall be ... presumed to be that recorded on an official computer system [unless the contrary is proved].

Note—These Regulations have been revoked by the Income and Corporation Taxes (Electronic Communications) Regulations, SI 2003/282 reg 11 with effect from 5 March 2003. However, any direction given by the Board under these Regulations, to the extent that it could be given under SI 2003/282, shall continue to have effect as if given under SI 2003/282.

[Certificates as to official records

9 A document certified by an officer of the Board to be a printed-out version of any electronic communication recorded on an official computer system as at a particular date shall be presumed, unless the contrary is proved—

(a) to have been recorded on an official computer system at that date; and

(b) to constitute the entirety of the electronic communication so recorded.]

Note—These Regulations have been revoked by the Income and Corporation Taxes (Electronic Communications) Regulations, SI 2003/282 reg 11 with effect from 5 March 2003. However, any direction given by the Board under these Regulations, to the extent that it could be given under SI 2003/282, shall continue to have effect as if given under SI 2003/282.

[Presumption as to certificates

10 A document purporting to be a certificate issued by an officer of the Board under regulation 9 shall be presumed to be such a certificate unless the contrary is proved.]

Note—These Regulations have been revoked by the Income and Corporation Taxes (Electronic Communications) Regulations, SI 2003/282 reg 11 with effect from 5 March 2003. However, any direction given by the Board under these Regulations, to the extent that it could be given under SI 2003/282, shall continue to have effect as if given under SI 2003/282.

2000/1085
Retirement Benefits Schemes (Sharing of Pensions on Divorce or Annulment) Regulations 2000

Made by the Commissioners of Inland Revenue under FA 1999 Sch 10 para 18(10), (11)

Made	*14 April 2000*
Laid before the House of Commons . . .	*19 April 2000*
Coming into force	*10 May 2000*

Commentary—*Simon's Direct Tax Service* **E7.105, 201, 214.**

Revenue and other press releases—Inland Revenue: Pension sharing on divorce to begin 1 December 2000 (19 April 2000).

Citation, commencement and effect

1—(1) These Regulations may be cited as the Retirement Benefits Schemes (Sharing of Pensions on Divorce or Annulment) Regulations 2000 and shall come into force on 10th May 2000.

(2) Regulations 3 to 8 have effect in relation to schemes which have been approved by the Board under section 591 of the Taxes Act 1988 before 10th May 2000.

Interpretation

2 In these Regulations—

"the Board" means the Commissioners of Inland Revenue;

"director" has the meaning given by section 612(1) of the Taxes Act 1988;

"ex-spouse" has the meaning given by section 659D(1) of the Taxes Act 1988;

"moderate earner" has the meaning given by regulation 5(4) to (6);

"pension sharing order or provision" means any such order or provision as is mentioned in section 28(1) of the Welfare Reform and Pensions Act 1999 or Article 25(1) of the Welfare Reform and Pensions (Northern Ireland) Order 1999;

"the permitted maximum" has the meaning given by section 590C of the Taxes Act 1988;

"Schedule 10" means Schedule 10 to the Finance Act 1999;

"scheme" means a retirement benefits scheme;

"simplified defined contribution scheme" has the meaning given by regulation 2(1) of the Retirement Benefits Schemes (Restriction on Discretion to Approve) (Additional Voluntary Contributions) Regulations 1993;

"the Taxes Act 1988" means the Income and Corporation Taxes Act 1988.

Prescribed modifications of Schedule 10 in prescribed circumstances

3 Regulations 4 to 8 prescribe circumstances in which Schedule 10 shall apply with the modifications prescribed by those regulations in the case of schemes approved by the Board before 10th May 2000.

Modification of Schedule 10 in relation to simplified defined contribution schemes

4—(1) In the circumstances prescribed by paragraph (2), Schedule 10 shall apply to a scheme with the modification prescribed by paragraph (3).

(2) The circumstances prescribed by this paragraph are circumstances where a scheme is a simplified defined contribution scheme.

(3) The modification prescribed by this paragraph is that paragraph 18(5) of Schedule 10 shall be omitted.

Modifications of Schedule 10 as regards members of schemes who are moderate earners

5—(1) In the circumstances prescribed by paragraph (2), Schedule 10 shall apply to a scheme as regards an employee within that paragraph with the modification prescribed by paragraph (3).

(2) The circumstances prescribed by this paragraph are circumstances where the employee—

(*a*) is a member of a scheme which is not a simplified defined contribution scheme;

(*b*) is an ex-spouse whose rights under the scheme have been debited as a consequence of a pension sharing order or provision; and

(*c*) is a moderate earner.

(3) The modification prescribed by this paragraph is that paragraph 18(5) of Schedule 10 shall be omitted.

(4) In this regulation, and in regulations 6 to 8, "moderate earner" means an employee—

(*a*) who is not a controlling director of a company which is his employer, and

(*b*) whose earnings at the date at which his marriage was dissolved or annulled were not more than 25 per cent of the permitted maximum for the year of assessment in which the dissolution or annulment occurred.

(5) For the purposes of paragraph (4)(*a*), an employee is a controlling director of a company which is his employer if he is a director of the company to whom section 417(5)(*b*) of the Taxes Act 1988 applies either—

(*a*) at the date on which the marriage was dissolved or annulled, or

(*b*) at any time within the period of ten years before that date.

(6) For the purposes of paragraph (4)(*b*), an ex-spouse's earnings shall be taken to be the total amounts of emoluments—

(*a*) which were paid to the ex-spouse in consequence of pensionable service to which the scheme relates during the year of assessment before the year of assessment in which the marriage was dissolved or annulled, and

(*b*) from which tax was deducted in accordance with the Income Tax (Employments) Regulations 1993.

Modifications of Schedule 10 as regards members who are not moderate earners—schemes providing lump sum retirement benefits only

6—(1) In the circumstances prescribed by paragraph (2), Schedule 10 shall apply to a scheme as regards an employee within that paragraph with the modification prescribed by paragraph (3).

(2) The circumstances prescribed by this paragraph are circumstances where the employee—

(*a*) is a member of a scheme which—

(i) is not a simplified defined contribution scheme; and

(ii) provides him with lump sum retirement benefits only which do not exceed three eightieths of his final remuneration for each year of service up to a maximum of 40;

(*b*) is an ex-spouse whose rights under the scheme have been debited as a consequence of a pension sharing order or provision; and

(*c*) is not a moderate earner.

(3) The modification prescribed by this paragraph is that in paragraph 18(5) of Schedule 10 the words "and (*da*)" shall be omitted.

Modifications of Schedule 10 as regards members who are not moderate earners—schemes providing lump sums otherwise than by the commutation of a part of a pension

7—(1) In the circumstances prescribed by paragraph (2), Schedule 10 shall apply to a scheme as regards an employee within that paragraph with the modification prescribed by paragraph (3).

(2) The circumstances prescribed by this paragraph are circumstances where the employee—

(*a*) is a member of a scheme which—

(i) is not a simplified defined contribution scheme; and

(ii) provides him with a lump sum otherwise than by the commutation of a part of a pension;

(*b*) is an ex-spouse whose rights under the scheme have been debited as a consequence of a pension sharing order or provision;

(*c*) is not a moderate earner; and

(*d*) is not an employee within regulation 8(2)(*b*).

(3) The modifications prescribed by this paragraph are that—

(*a*) in paragraph 18(5) of Schedule 10—

(i) the words "and (*da*)" shall be omitted; and

(ii) at the end after the words "the Taxes Act 1988" there shall be added the words "and provision of the description set out in sub-paragraph (5A) below"; and

(*b*) after paragraph 18(5) of Schedule 10 there shall be inserted the following sub-paragraph—

"(5A) The description of provision referred to in sub-paragraph (5) above is provision providing that in a case in which—

(*a*) a lump sum may be obtained otherwise than by the commutation of a part of a pension provided for an employee, and

(*b*) the amount of that pension is affected by the making of a pension sharing order or provision,

the lump sum does not exceed the sum produced by multiplying by 3 the amount which (after effect has been given to the pension sharing order or provision) is the amount of the pension for the first year in which it is payable calculated in accordance with section 590(4E) of the Taxes Act 1988."

Modifications of Schedule 10 as regards members of schemes who are not moderate earners and to whom paragraphs 2, 3, 4 and 6 of Schedule 23 to the Taxes Act 1988 do not apply

8—(1) In the circumstances prescribed by paragraph (2), Schedule 10 shall apply to a scheme as regards an employee within that paragraph with the modifications prescribed by paragraph (3).

(2) The circumstances prescribed by this paragraph are circumstances where—

(*a*) the employee is a member of a scheme which—

(i) is not a simplified defined contribution scheme; and

(ii) provides for a lump sum either by the commutation of a part of a pension or otherwise; and

(*b*) the employee—

(i) in the case of a scheme approved by the Board before 23rd July 1987, was a member of the scheme before 17th March 1987; or

(ii) is an employee as regards whom the provisions contained in paragraphs 2, 3, 4 and 6 of Schedule 23 to the Taxes Act 1988 are disapplied either by regulation 3 or 4ZA of the Occupational Pension Schemes (Transitional Provisions) Regulations 1988 or by virtue of a direction of the Board made under regulation 11 of those Regulations; or

(iii) is an employee who—

(*a*) was a member of a scheme before 17th March 1987, and

(*b*) on or after 17th March 1987 becomes a member of another scheme to which Schedule 23 to the Taxes Act 1988 does not apply,

and whom the Board, in exercising their discretion under section 591 of the Taxes Act 1988, allow to be treated as having been a member of that other scheme before 17th March 1987; and

(*c*) the employee—

(i) is an ex-spouse whose rights under the scheme have been debited as a consequence of a pension sharing order or provision; and

(ii) is not a moderate earner.

(3) The modifications prescribed by this paragraph are that—

(*a*) in paragraph 18(5) of Schedule 10—

(i) the words "and (*da*)" shall be omitted; and

(ii) at the end after the words "the Taxes Act 1988" there shall be added the words "and provision of the description set out in sub-paragraph (5AA) below"; and

(*b*) after paragraph 18(5) of Schedule 10 there shall be inserted the following sub-paragraphs—

"(5AA) The description of provision referred to in sub-paragraph (5) above is provision providing that in a case in which—

(*a*) a lump sum may be obtained either by the commutation of a part of a pension provided for an employee or otherwise, and

(*b*) the amount of the pension is affected by the making of a pension sharing order or provision,

the lump sum shall not exceed the greater of either A or B.

(5B) In sub-paragraph (5AA) above, A is the sum produced by multiplying by either—

(*a*) 2·25, in the case of a scheme which provides for a lump sum by the commutation of a part of a pension, or

(*b*) 3, in the case of a scheme which provides for a lump sum otherwise than by the commutation of a part of a pension,

the amount which (after effect has been given to the pension sharing order or provision) is the amount of the pension for the first year in which it is payable calculated in accordance with section 590(4E) of the Taxes Act 1988.

(5C) In sub-paragraph (5AA) above, B is the sum produced by the following formula—

C – D

Where—

C is the amount of the lump sum determined in accordance with the rules of the scheme as if no pension sharing order or provision had been made, and

D is the sum produced by multiplying by either—

(*a*) 2·25, in the case of a scheme which provides for a lump sum by the commutation of a part of a pension, or

(*b*) 3, in the case of a scheme which provides for a lump sum otherwise than by the commutation of a part of a pension,

the amount by which the employee's benefits or future benefits under the scheme are reduced under section 31 of the Welfare Reform and Pensions Act 1999 or Article 28 of the Welfare Reform and Pensions (Northern Ireland) Order 1999."

2000/1087

Retirement Benefits Schemes (Restriction on Discretion to Approve) (Excepted Provisions) Regulations 2000

Made by the Commissioners of Inland Revenue under the Income and Corporation Taxes Act 1988, s 591A(2)

Made	*14 April 2000*
Laid before the House of Commons	*19 April 2000*
Coming into force	*10 May 2000*

Commentary—*Simon's Direct Tax Service* **E7.105, 215.**
Revenue and other press releases—IR 19-4-2000: Pension sharing on divorce to begin 1 December 2000

Citation and commencement

1 These Regulations may be cited as the Retirement Benefits Schemes (Restriction on Discretion to Approve) (Excepted Provisions) Regulations 2000 and shall come into force on 10th May 2000 immediately after the coming into force of the 2000 Regulations and the second 2000 Regulations.

Interpretation

2 In these Regulations—

"the 1991 Regulations" means the Retirement Benefits Schemes (Restriction on Discretion to Approve) (Small Self-administered Schemes) Regulations 1991;

"the 1993 Regulations" means the Retirement Benefits Schemes (Restriction on Discretion to Approve) (Additional Voluntary Contributions) Regulations 1993;

"the 2000 Regulations" means the Retirement Benefits Schemes (Restriction on Discretion to Approve) (Small Self-administered Schemes) (Amendment) Regulations 2000;

"the second 2000 Regulations" means the Retirement Benefits Schemes (Restriction on Discretion to Approve) (Additional Voluntary Contributions) (Amendment) Regulations 2000.

Description of provisions

3 Regulations 4 and 5 specify descriptions of provisions for the purposes of subsection (2) of section 591A of the Income and Corporation Taxes Act 1988, each provision so specified being a provision of a required description within the meaning of subsection (5)(*b*) of that section.

4 The description of provision specified in this regulation consists of the provisions specified in regulations 4 to 9 of the 1991 Regulations, read together with paragraph (1) of regulation 2 of the 1991 Regulations as that paragraph is amended by regulation 2 of the 2000 Regulations.

5 The description of provision specified in this regulation consists of—

(*a*) the provisions specified in regulation 5 of the 1993 Regulations as amended by regulation 3 of the second 2000 Regulations; and

(*b*) the provisions specified in regulations 4 and 5 of the 1993 Regulations, read together with regulation 6 of the 1993 Regulations as that regulation is amended by regulation 4 of the second 2000 Regulations.

2000/1093
Finance Act 1999, Schedule 10, Paragraph 18, (First and Second Appointed Days) Order 2000

Made by the Treasury under FA 1999 Sch 10 para 18(1)

Made . . . . *18 April 2000*

Commentary—*Simon's Direct Tax Service* **E7.105, 202, 401.**
Revenue and other press releases—IR 19-4-2000: Pension sharing on divorce to begin 1 December 2000.

1 This Order may be cited as the Finance Act 1999, Schedule 10, Paragraph 18, (First and Second Appointed Days) Order 2000.

2 For the purposes of paragraph 18 of Schedule 10 to the Finance Act 1999—

(*a*) the day appointed as "the first appointed day" is 10th May 2000;
(*b*) the day appointed as "the second appointed day" is 1st December 2000.

2000/2004
Finance Act 1999, Section 59(3)(*b*), (Appointed Day) Order 2000

Made by the Treasury under FA 1999 s 59(3)(*b*)

Made . . . . *25 July 2000*

Commentary—*Simon's Direct Tax Service* **E2.1301.**

1 This Order may be cited as the Finance Act 1999, Section 59(3)(*b*) (Appointed Day) Order 2000.

2 The day appointed for the purposes of section 59(2) and (3)(*b*) of the Finance Act 1999 is 1st September 2000.

2000/2074
Donations to Charity by Individuals (Appropriate Declarations) Regulations 2000

Made by the Commissioners of Inland Revenue under FA 1990 s 25(3), (3A) FA 1999 ss 132(1)(*a*), (2)(*a*), (8), (9), (10), 133(1) and (2) and FA 2000 s 39(10)

Made . . . . *28 July 2000*
Laid before the House of Commons . . . *31 July 2000*
Coming into force . . . . *21 August 2000*

Commentary—*Simon's Direct Tax Service* **E1.504.**

Citation, commencement and effect

1—(1) These Regulations may be cited as the Donations to Charity by Individuals (Appropriate Declarations) Regulations 2000 and shall come into force on 21st August 2000.

(2) These Regulations shall have effect in relation to—

(*a*) gifts made on or after 6th April 2000 which are not covenanted payments; and
(*b*) covenanted payments falling to be made on or after that date.

Interpretation

2 In these Regulations—

"appropriate declaration" has the same meaning as in section 25(1)(*c*) of the Finance Act 1990;
"the Board" means the Commissioners of Inland Revenue;
"donor" has the same meaning as in section 25(1) of the Finance Act 1990;

SIs

[''electronic communications'' includes any communications conveyed by means of an electronic communications network.][1]

Amendments—[1] Definition of ''electronic communications'' substituted by the Communications Act 2003 (Consequential Amendments) Order, SI 2003/2155 art 3(1), Schedule para 23(1)(*c*), (2) with effect from 17 September 2003.

Manner in which an appropriate declaration may be given

3 An appropriate declaration may be given by a donor to a charity—

(*a*) in writing;
(*b*) orally; or
(*c*) by means of electronic communications.

Statements to be contained in declarations

4—(1) An appropriate declaration must contain the following statements which are prescribed by this regulation for the purposes of section 25(3)(*b*) of the Finance Act 1990—

(*a*) the name and address of the donor;
(*b*) the name of the charity;
(*c*) a description of the gift or gifts to which the declaration relates;
(*d*) a statement that the gift or gifts to which the declaration relates are to be treated as qualifying donations for the purposes of section 25 of the Finance Act 1990; and
(*e*) where the declaration is given in writing to the charity, a statement explaining the effect of section 25(8) of the Finance Act 1990.

(2) Where a donor who has given an appropriate declaration to a charity notifies the charity of any change to the statements prescribed by paragraph (1)(*a*), the charity must keep a record of those changes with the appropriate declaration.

Declarations given orally

5—(1) Where a donor gives an appropriate declaration orally to a charity, the charity must make a record in writing of—

(*a*) the statements prescribed by regulation 4(1)(*a*) to (*d*); and
(*b*) a statement explaining the effect of section 25(8) of the Finance Act 1990;

and the charity must send that record (referred to in this regulation and in regulation 6 as ''the written record'') to the donor.

(2) The written record must state the date on which the charity sends it to the donor.

(3) A donor who gives an appropriate declaration orally to a charity is entitled to cancel that declaration by giving notice in writing to the charity not later than 30 days following the day on which the charity sends him the written record, and every written record must contain a statement that the donor is entitled to do so.

Prescribed circumstances in which appropriate declarations given orally are deemed never to have had effect

6—(1) For the purposes prescribed by paragraph (2), an appropriate declaration shall be treated as never having had effect in the circumstances prescribed by paragraph (3) or (4).

(2) The purposes prescribed by this paragraph are any purposes of the Taxes Acts.

(3) The circumstances prescribed by this paragraph are where an appropriate declaration has been given orally by a donor in respect of which the charity has not sent the written record to the donor.

(4) The circumstances prescribed by this paragraph are where an appropriate declaration has been given orally by a donor which the donor cancels by giving notice to the charity in accordance with regulation 5(3).

Prescribed circumstances in which appropriate declarations cease to have effect

7—(1) For the purposes prescribed by paragraph (2), an appropriate declaration shall cease to have effect in, and in accordance with, the circumstances prescribed by paragraph (3).

(2) The purposes prescribed by this paragraph are any purposes of the Taxes Acts.

(3) The circumstances prescribed by this paragraph are where a charity receives notification from a donor of the cancellation of an appropriate declaration with effect from either the receipt of that notification by the charity or such later date as is specified in that notification.

2000/2076
Individual Learning Accounts (Separate Employers Under the Crown) Regulations 2000

Made by the Treasury under ICTA 1988 s 200G(3)

Made	*28 July 2000*
Laid before the House of Commons	*31 July 2000*
Coming into force	*21 August 2000*

Commentary—*Simon's Direct Tax Service* **E4.422.**

1 These Regulations may be cited as the Individual Learning Accounts (Separate Employers under the Crown) Regulations 2000 and shall come into force on 21st August 2000.

2—(1) For the purposes of section 200G of the Income and Corporation Taxes Act 1988, Crown servants mentioned in paragraphs (2) and (3) shall be treated as holding office or employment in accordance with those paragraphs.

(2) Any Crown servant who is in—

(*a*) employment under or for the purposes of a Government department,
(*b*) service as a member of staff of the Scottish Administration, or holds an office in that Administration which is not a ministerial office,
(*c*) service as a member of the staff of the National Assembly for Wales,
(*d*) employment under or for the purposes of a Northern Ireland department, or
(*e*) service as a member of staff of the Northern Ireland Assembly, shall be treated as holding office or employment under the organisation concerned.

(3) Service as a member of—

(*a*) the Royal Navy and Royal Marines,
(*b*) the Military Forces of the Crown, or
(*c*) the Regular Air Force,

shall be treated as employment of the organisation concerned (and each of those organisations shall be treated as an entity for the purposes of these Regulations).

2000/2080
Income Tax (Benefits in Kind) (Exemption for Welfare Counselling) Regulations 2000

Made by the Treasury under TA 1988 s 155ZB

Made	*28 July 2000*
Laid before the House of Commons	*31 July 2000*
Coming into force	*21 August 2000*

Commentary—*Simon's Direct Tax Service* **E4.612.**

1 These Regulations may be cited as the Income Tax (Benefits in Kind) (Exemption for Welfare Counselling) Regulations 2000 and shall come into force on 21st August 2000.

2—(1) There shall be exempted from section 154 of the Income and Corporation Taxes Act 1988 a benefit consisting of welfare counselling that is made available to an employer's employees generally on similar terms.

(2) In paragraph (1) "welfare counselling" means counselling of any kind other than—

(*a*) medical treatment of any kind, or
(*b*) advice specified in paragraph (3).

(3) The advice specified in this paragraph is advice on finance (other than on debt problems), advice on tax, or on leisure or recreation, and legal advice.

2000/2081
Research and Development (Prescribed Activities) Regulations 2000

Made by the Treasury under TA 1988 s 837A(3) and (4)

Made	*28 July 2000*
Laid before the House Of Commons	*31 July 2000*
Coming into force	*21 August 2000*

Commentary—*Simon's Direct Tax Service* **B2.702, 703.**
Note—These regulations are revoked by the Research and Development (Prescribed Activities) Regulations, SI 2004/712, with effect from 1 April 2004.

Citation and commencement

1 These Regulations may be cited as the Research and Development (Prescribed Activities) Regulations 2000 and shall come into force on 21st August 2000.

Interpretation

2 In these Regulations—

"the Guidelines" means the "Guidelines on the Meaning of Research and Development (R&D) for Tax Purposes" which were issued for the purposes of section 837A by the Secretary of State for the Department of Trade and Industry on 28th July 2000;

"section 837A" means section 837A of the Income and Corporation Taxes Act 1988.

Prescribed activities

3—(1) The activities prescribed by paragraph (2) of this regulation are not "research and development" for the purposes of section 837A and the activities prescribed by paragraph (3) of this regulation are "research and development" for those purposes.

(2) The activities prescribed by this paragraph are activities that fall to be treated as not being research and development in accordance with the Guidelines.

(3) The activities prescribed by this paragraph are activities that fall to be treated as research and development in accordance with the Guidelines.

2000/2082
Finance Act 2000, Section 108(3), (Appointed Day) Order 2000

Made by the Treasury under FA 2000 s 108(3)

Made . . . . *28 July 2000*

Commentary—*Simon's Direct Tax Service* **D4.524.**

1 This Order may be cited as the Finance Act 2000, Section 108(3), (Appointed Day) Order 2000.

2 The day appointed for the purposes of section 108(3) of the Finance Act 2000 is 22nd August 2000.

2000/2089
Insurance Companies (Overseas Life Assurance Business) (Excluded Business) Regulations 2000

Made by the Commissioners of Inland Revenue under TA 1988 s 431D

Made . . . . *1 August 2000*
Laid before the House of Commons . . . . *1 August 2000*
Coming into force . . . . *22 August 2000*

Commentary—*Simon's Direct Tax Service* **D4.524.**

Citation, commencement and effect

1—(1) These Regulations may be cited as the Insurance Companies (Overseas Life Assurance Business) (Excluded Business) Regulations 2000 and shall come into force on 22nd August 2000.

(2) These Regulations shall have effect in relation to policies or contracts made by an insurance company on or after 22nd August 2000.

Interpretation

2—(1) In these Regulations—

"beneficiary" means any person who is, or will or may become, entitled to any benefit under a trust, including—

(*a*) any person who may become so entitled on the exercise of a discretion; and

(*b*) a settlor who has an interest in the trust property for the purpose of section 660A;

"the Board" means the Commissioners of Inland Revenue;

"charity" means a person or body of persons established for charitable purposes only;

"collective investment scheme" has the meaning given by section [235 of the Financial Services and Markets Act 2000][1];

"discretionary trust" means any trust under which—

(*a*) the income arising to the trustees is to be accumulated and no person other than the trustees is entitled to that income before it is distributed; or (*b*) the beneficiaries may become entitled to a benefit on the exercise of a discretion (whether or not the trustees have power to accumulate income) and no person is entitled to any benefit before the exercise of that discretion;

"holding company" means a company whose assets all, or all but an insignificant part, consist of shares in companies which, for the purposes of the Tax Acts, are deemed to be its 51 per cent subsidiaries by virtue of section 838;

"investment company" means any company whose business consists wholly or mainly in the making of investments and the principal part of whose income is derived therefrom, but excludes any holding company or collective investment scheme;

"relevant overseas employees" means persons who are not residing in the United Kingdom and are—

(*a*) employees of a policy holder or annuitant; or
(*b*) employees of a person connected with a policy holder or annuitant; or
(*c*) employees in respect of whose employment there is established a superannuation fund to which section 615(3) applies;

and, for the purpose of paragraph (*b*), whether a person is connected with a policy holder or annuitant shall be determined in accordance with section 839;

"relevant former employees" means—

(*a*) former employees of a policy holder or annuitant; or
(*b*) former employees of a person connected with a policy holder or annuitant; or
(*c*) former employees in respect of whose employment there is established a superannuation fund to which section 615(3) applies;

and, for the purpose of paragraph (*b*), whether a person is connected with a policy holder or annuitant shall be determined in accordance with section 839;

"settlor" means the person, or each of the persons, by whom the trust was directly or indirectly created, and for this purpose a person shall, in particular, be regarded as having created a trust if he provided or undertook to provide funds directly or indirectly for the purposes of the trust, or made with any other person a reciprocal arrangement for that other person to create the trust;

"term assurance business" means life assurance business in relation to which the policy or contract, or the underlying policy, is one which—

(*a*) is for a specified term; and
(*b*) is not capable of acquiring a surrender value that exceeds the amount of premiums paid.

(2) In these Regulations any reference to a particular provision, without more, is a reference to that provision of the Income and Corporation Taxes Act 1988.

Amendments—[1] In para (1), words in definition of "collective investment scheme" substituted by the Financial Services and Markets Act 2000 (Consequential Amendments) (Taxes) Order, SI 2001/3629 art 187 with effect from 1 December 2001, immediately after the coming into force of the Financial Services and Markets Act 2000 ss 411, 432(1), Sch 20 (and SI 2001/3629 Pts 1 and 2).

Life assurance business excluded from section 431D

3—(1) Subject to paragraph (2), life assurance business is excluded from section 431D (meaning of "overseas life assurance business") if it is of a description that does not fall within any of the circumstances set out in regulations 4 to 7.

(2) Where a policy or contract for business is owned by two or more policy holders or annuitants who do not hold the policy or contract as trustees of the same trust, the business is excluded from section 431D where, if any of the policy holders or annuitants were the only policy holder or annuitant, paragraph (1) would exclude it from that section.

Circumstances where business not excluded from section 431D

4 The circumstances set out in this regulation are where—

(*a*) the business is with a policy holder or annuitant who—

(i) is not a company, or
(ii) is a company which holds the policy or contract for the business in a fiduciary or representative capacity;

(*b*) the rights conferred by the policy or contract for the business are not held subject to a trust; and

(*c*) not less than 65 per cent of any benefit under the policy or contract for the business is payable to—

(i) persons residing outside the United Kingdom; and
(ii) charities.

5—(1) The circumstances set out in this paragraph are where—

(*a*) the rights conferred by the policy or contract for the business are held subject to a trust;
(*b*) in the case of a discretionary trust, each beneficiary is either an individual not residing in the United Kingdom or a charity; and
(*c*) in the case of a non-discretionary trust, beneficiaries who are—

(i) not residing in the United Kingdom, or
(ii) charities,

have an interest in not less than 65 per cent of the capital of the trust;

(2) For the purposes of paragraph (1)(*b*), an individual who, as a trustee of any trust, is a beneficiary under the trust referred to in paragraph (1)(*a*) shall not be regarded as an individual.

6—(1) The circumstances set out in this paragraph are where—

(*a*) the business is with a policy holder or annuitant which—

(i) is a company, and
(ii) does not hold the policy or contract for the business in a fiduciary or representative capacity;

(*b*) in a case where the company is an investment company which is not controlled, or is not treated as controlled, by the trustees of any trust, the company is not controlled, or is not treated as controlled, by persons residing in the United Kingdom; and

(*c*) in a case where the company is an investment company which is controlled, or is treated as controlled, by the trustees of any trust, the business would, if the trustees were the policy holders or the annuitants, be of a description falling within the circumstances set out in regulation 5.

(2) For the purposes of paragraph (1)(*b*), whether a company is not controlled, or is not treated as controlled, by persons residing in the United Kingdom shall be determined in accordance with section 416 but as if in subsection (6) of that section the words "five or fewer participators" read "persons residing in the United Kingdom".

(3) For the purposes of paragraph (1)(*c*), whether a company is controlled, or is treated as controlled, by the trustees of any trust shall be determined in accordance with section 416 but as if in subsection (6) of that section the words "five or fewer participators" read "the trustees of any trust".

7 The circumstances set out in this regulation are where—

(*a*) the business is term assurance business; or

(*b*) the policy or contract for the business is held for the purposes of, or in connection with, a scheme where the Board—

(i) have approved schemes of the same class or description for the purposes of the Income Tax (Pension Funds Pooling Schemes) Regulations 1996; or
(ii) have been satisfied that schemes of the same class or description are such as are mentioned in section 596(2)(*b*); or

(*c*) the policy or contract for the business is held solely to provide benefits for or in respect of—

(i) persons all, or all but an insignificant number, of whom are relevant overseas employees or relevant former employees, or
(ii) spouses, widows, widowers, children or dependants of such persons.

Trustees residing in the United Kingdom

8—(1) A trustee who is a policy holder or annuitant residing in the United Kingdom shall be treated for the purposes of section 431D as not so residing where the policy or contract for the business is held for the purposes set out in regulation 7(*b*) or (*c*).

(2) Nothing in Chapter II of Part XIII of the Income and Corporation Taxes Act 1988 shall apply to a policy or contract which—

(*a*) constitutes overseas life assurance business by virtue of paragraph (1), and
(*b*) is held for the purposes set out in regulation 7(*b*).

2000/2090

Employee Share Ownership Plans (Partnership Shares—Notice of Effects on Benefits, Statutory Sick Pay and Statutory Maternity Pay) Regulations 2000

Made by the Commissioners of Inland Revenue under FA 2000 s 47, Sch 8 para 38

Made . . . . *1 August 2000*
Laid before the House of Commons . . . . . *1 August 2000*
Coming into force . . . . *22 August 2000*

Commentary—*Simon's Direct Tax Service* **E4.501.**

Citation and commencement

1 These Regulations may be cited as the Employee Share Ownership Plans (Partnership Shares—Notice of Effects on Benefits, Statutory Sick Pay and Statutory Maternity Pay) Regulations 2000 and shall come into force on 4th August 2000.

Prescribed form of notice of effect of deductions from salary on entitlement to social security benefit

2 The form of notice prescribed under paragraph 38 of Schedule 8 to the Finance Act 2000 (employee share ownership plans—notice of possible effect of deductions on benefit entitlement) to be included in a partnership share agreement under the rules of the employee share plan is set out below.

Notice Deductions from your pay to buy partnership shares under this agreement may affect your entitlement to or the level of, some contributory social security benefits, statutory maternity pay and statutory sick pay.

They may also have a similar effect in respect of some contributory social security benefits paid to your wife or husband.

With this agreement you should have been given information on the effect of deductions from your pay to buy partnership shares on entitlement to social security benefits, statutory sick pay and statutory maternity pay. The effect is particularly significant if your earnings are brought below the lower earnings limit for National Insurance purposes, and is explained in the information—it is therefore important that you read it. If you have not been given a copy, ask your employer for it. Otherwise a copy may be obtained from any office of the Inland Revenue, the Department of Social Security, or, in Northern Ireland, the Department for Social Development. You should take the information you have been given into account in deciding whether to buy partnership shares.

2000/2129

Tonnage Tax (Training Requirement) Regulations 2000

Made by the Secretary of State for the Environment, Transport and the Regions under FA 2000 Sch 22 paras 24, 27 to 33, 34(2) and 36

Made . . . . *3 August 2000*
Laid before Parliament . . . . . *9 August 2000*
Coming into force . . . . . . *31 August 2000*

Citation and commencement

1 These Regulations may be cited as the Tonnage Tax (Training Requirement) Regulations 2000 and shall come into force on 31st August 2000.

Interpretation

2 In these Regulations—

"the Act" means the Finance Act 2000;

"back-up officer" means a master or a deck or engineer officer required for the purpose of enabling a ship to be operated on an indefinite basis, allowing for leave, in addition to the officers required by the safe manning document;

"base rate" means the interest rate set by the Bank of England which is used as the basis for other banks' rates;

"British citizen" means a person who is a British citizen within the meaning of the British Nationality Act 1981;

"British citizen from the Channel Islands or Isle of Man" means a person who holds British citizenship by virtue of the fact that he, a parent or grandparent was born, adopted, naturalised or registered in one of those islands, and neither he nor any parent or grandparent was born, adopted, naturalised or registered in the United Kingdom, and he has never been ordinarily resident in the United Kingdom for five years;

"Chamber of Shipping" means the trade association for the United Kingdom shipping industry, incorporated under that name as a company limited by guarantee;

"conversion training" means training of at least ten months' duration for a merchant navy rating, a person formerly employed in Her Majesty's Navy or a skipper or crew member of a fishing vessel, which leads to a first certificate of competency;

"EEA Agreement" means the Agreement on the European Economic Area signed at Oporto on 2nd May 1992 as adjusted by the Protocol signed at Brussels on 17th March 1993;

"EEA State" means a State which is a Contracting Party to the EEA Agreement;

"effective officer complement" means the class comprising the relevant officers and back-up officers for a ship, and is calculated in accordance with regulation 4;

"eligible officer trainee" has the meaning given by regulation 7;

"first certificate of competency" means any of the following certificates referred to in the STCW Convention—

(*a*) the appropriate certificate for an officer in charge of a navigational watch referred to in Regulation II/1.1, II/3.1 or II/3.3, (*b*) the appropriate certificate for an officer in charge of an engineering watch referred to in Regulation III/1.1;

"IMO number" means the number assigned to the ship in accordance with Resolution A.600(15) of 19th November 1987 of the International Maritime Organization;

"Maritime Training Trust" means the body of that name which has been set up by the Chamber of Shipping, the National Union of Marine, Aviation and Shipping Transport Officers (NUMAST) and the National Union of Rail, Maritime and Transport Workers (RMT) to hold and allocate monies contributed by organisations for the purpose of promoting the training of seafarers;

"Merchant Navy Training Board" means the body of that name which is recognised by the Secretary of State under section 2 of the Employment and Training Act 1973 as a national training organisation for maintaining and enhancing skills in the shipping industry;

"nationality groups" means the following groups—

(*a*) British citizens,

(*b*) nationals of EEA States other than the United Kingdom, and

(*c*) people who do not fall within paragraph (*a*) or (*b*);

"Ratings Task Force" means the ad hoc group of that name comprising representatives from industry, trade unions and government and chaired by the Chamber of Shipping;

"relevant course" means a course which leads to a first certificate of competency;

"relevant four month period" means a period of four months commencing 1st October, 1st February or 1st June;

"relevant officer" means a master or a deck or engineer officer;

"safe manning document" means a document described as such or as a safe manning certificate and issued, in the case of a United Kingdom ship, by the Secretary of State, and in the case of any other ship, by or on behalf of the government of the State whose flag the ship is entitled to fly;

"the STCW Convention" means the International Convention on Standards of Training, Certification and Watchkeeping for Seafarers, 1978, as amended on 7th July 1995;

"United Kingdom ship" means a ship registered in the United Kingdom under Part II of the Merchant Shipping Act 1995; and

"year" means a twelve month period beginning on 1 October.

The minimum training obligation

3 The minimum obligations of a tonnage tax company as regards the training of seafarers shall be calculated as set out in regulations 4 and 5.

Revenue Internal Guidance—Tonnage Tax Manual TTM 4001 (outline: condition if entering tonnage tax and minimum training obligation).

4—(1) Subject to the provisions of this regulation—

(*a*) for every 15 posts in the effective officer complement for the qualifying ships operated by the company during a year, and

(*b*) in any case where there are less than 15 posts in that effective officer complement,

a tonnage tax company shall during that year provide the first year of training on a relevant course for not less than one eligible officer trainee.

(2) Where a safe manning document is required to be carried on board a qualifying ship, the number of posts in the effective officer complement shall be calculated by adding the number of relevant officers required by the safe manning document for the ship and the number of back-up officers required for that ship.

(3) Where a safe manning document is not required to be carried on board a qualifying ship, the number of posts in the effective officer complement shall be deemed to be three.

(4) Where the number of posts in the effective officer complement is more than 15 but is not a multiple of 15, the calculation of the number of eligible officer trainees for whom training is to be provided under paragraph (1) is as follows—

(*a*) divide the number of posts in the effective officer complement by 15,

(*b*) if the resulting number involves a fraction of less than a half, round it down to the nearest whole number, and

(*c*) if the resulting number involves a fraction of a half or more, round it up to the nearest whole number.

(5) For the purposes of paragraph (2) and regulation 8(4)(*b*)(iv)(*bb*), the number of back-up officers required for a ship shall be calculated by reference to the ratio of leave to work for officers on that ship, but shall not in any event be less than 50% of the number of relevant officers required by the safe manning document for that ship.

(6) In addition to the training provided under paragraph (1) during a year, the company shall during that year provide training on a relevant course for not less than the same number of eligible officer trainees as the number referred to in paragraph (7).

[(7) The number referred to in paragraph (6) is the total number of eligible officer trainees who, in a previous year when the company was a tonnage tax company—

(*a*) started a relevant course which continues in the year in question; but this shall not include any eligible officer trainee who started a relevant course more than two years before the year in question, or

(*b*) would have started a relevant course which would have continued in the year in question, if the company had provided the first year of training for the minimum number of eligible officer trainees for whom such training was required under paragraph (1); and for these purposes such a course shall be deemed to continue for three years.][1]

(8) Where the training provided for an eligible officer trainee consists of conversion training, the trainee shall count as half a trainee for the purposes of paragraphs (1) and (6).

Revenue Internal Guidance—Tonnage Tax Manual TTM 4001 (outline: condition if entering tonnage tax and minimum training obligation).

Amendments—[1] Para (7) substituted by the Tonnage Tax (Training Requirement) (Amendment) Regulations, SI 2003/2320 reg 3 with effect from 1 October 2003.

5 The Board of directors of a tonnage tax company shall each year review the feasibility of adopting the options agreed by the Ratings Task Force for the training of ratings.

6 Where a company is a member of a tonnage tax group, references in regulations 3, 4 and 5 to "tonnage tax company" and "company" shall be treated as references to "tonnage tax group" and "group" respectively.

Revenue Internal Guidance—Tonnage Tax Manual TTM 4001 (outline: condition if entering tonnage tax and minimum training obligation).

Meaning of "eligible officer trainee"

7 For the purposes of these Regulations, an "eligible officer trainee" means a person on a relevant course who is—

(*a*) a national of an EEA State, or a British citizen from the Channel Islands or Isle of Man, and

(*b*) ordinarily resident in the United Kingdom.

The training commitment

8—(1) Except where paragraph (2) applies, a tonnage tax company shall annually produce a training commitment in respect of the coming year.

(2) Where a company is a member of a tonnage tax group, the tonnage tax group shall annually produce a training commitment in respect of the coming year.

(3) The tonnage tax company in paragraph (1), or the tonnage tax group in paragraph (2), shall submit the training commitment to the Secretary of State for approval.

(4) The training commitment submitted to the Secretary of State shall contain the following information—

(*a*) either—

(i) the total numbers of relevant officers and of ratings, and the breakdowns of these numbers in terms of nationality groups, employed in each ship which the company or group expects to operate as a qualifying ship during the coming year, or

(ii) the total numbers of relevant officers and of ratings, and the breakdowns of these numbers in terms of nationality groups, employed in all ships which the company or group expects to operate as qualifying ships during the coming year;

(*b*) in respect of each ship which the company or group expects to operate as a qualifying ship during the coming year—

(i) the name of the ship,

(ii) the IMO number, if assigned,

(iii) the State or territory in which the ship is registered, or if it is not registered in any State or territory, the State whose flag the ship is entitled to fly,

(iv) where a safe manning document is required to be carried on board the ship—

(*aa*) the number of relevant officers required by that document, and

(*bb*) the figure, calculated by reference to the number of back-up officers required for a ship, by which the number referred to in sub-paragraph (*aa*) is to be multiplied to obtain the number of posts in the effective officer complement, and

(v) the number of posts in the effective officer complement;

(*c*) the total number of eligible officer trainees for whom the company or group expects to provide the first year of training on approved courses during the coming year;

(*d*) details of the company's or group's proposals to meet the minimum training obligation by making payments in lieu of training, and the reasons for meeting the obligation in this way;

(*e*) details of the company's or group's proposals for adopting the options agreed by the Ratings Task Force for the training of ratings or, where applicable, reasons for not adopting those options; and (*f*) the number of ratings who the company or group expects to be involved in the adoption of any options referred to in paragraph (*e*).

(5) In addition to the information required under paragraph (4), the training commitment submitted to the Secretary of State shall contain an undertaking by the company or group—

(*a*) to comply with the minimum training obligation;

(*b*) to exercise best endeavours to provide the training referred to in regulation 4(1) and (6), and to make payments in lieu of training where such training is not provided;

(*c*) to make payments in lieu of training, in any case where—

(i) a qualifying ship is operated by the company or group in addition to those which were expected to be operated, but

(ii) it is not practicable to train the additional trainees required to meet the minimum training obligation; and

(*d*) to comply with the requirements of regulation 12 and with any direction to the company or group under regulation 19.

9 When considering whether to approve a training commitment, the Secretary of State may consult the Merchant Navy Training Board or the Maritime Training Trust or both.

10—(1) Where the Secretary of State is minded not to approve a training commitment, he shall notify the company or group and shall invite representations.

(2) If the Secretary of State and the company or group are unable to reach agreement on the contents of the training commitment by the end of the period of 30 days beginning with the date of the Secretary of State's notification, the Secretary of State may set the training commitment for the year.

(3) On the application of the company or group concerned, made after consultation with the Maritime Training Trust, the Secretary of State may vary the training commitment set by him under paragraph (2).

11—(1) On the application of the company or group concerned, the Secretary of State may adjust a training commitment (to any extent) to take account of changed circumstances.

(2) Such an application shall contain the following information—

(*a*) details of the changed circumstances, and

(*b*) reasons why the training commitment should be adjusted.

(3) When considering an application for adjustment, the Secretary of State may consult the Merchant Navy Training Board or the Maritime Training Trust or both.

"End of period adjustments"

12—(1) A tonnage tax company or tonnage tax group shall make a return (known as an "end of period adjustment") within 30 days after the end of each relevant four month period.

(2) The return shall be made to the Secretary of State and to the Maritime Training Trust.

(3) The return shall contain the following information—

(*a*) the number of eligible officer trainees for whom training on a relevant course has been provided, determined as at the first day of each month in the relevant four month period;

(*b*) where there is an increase in the total number of qualifying ships operated by the company or group, compared with the training commitment, which occurs during the relevant four month period and relates to a period of not less than one month, details of—

(i) the additional ships, and

(ii) any consequent increase in the number of eligible officer trainees for whom training should have been provided in order to meet the minimum training obligation of the company or group referred to in regulation 3; and

(*c*) details of the payments made or proposed to be made in lieu of training in respect of the relevant four month period.

Payments in lieu of training

13 Where a company or group is unable to provide the training required by regulation 4(1) or (6), it may propose in its training commitment to meet the minimum training obligation by making payments in lieu of training.

14 A company or group shall make payments in lieu of training—

(*a*) where its training commitment provides for such payments, or

(*b*) where training is not provided in accordance with its training commitment.

15—(1) The payments in lieu of training shall be calculated in respect of each relevant four month period as follows—

(*a*) in respect of each eligible officer trainee for whom training is required to be provided under regulation 4(1) or (6), calculate the number of months in that period during which—

(i) the training commitment of the company or group provided for payment in lieu of training, or

(ii) the company or group did not provide training in accordance with its training commitment, or both sub-paragraphs (i) and (ii) applied; and

(*b*) multiply that number of months by [£591][1], and the total is the amount of the payments in lieu of training which is due for that period.

(2) For the purposes of the calculation in paragraph (1)(*a*), any surplus (as compared with the requirements in regulation 4(1) and (6)) in the number of months when training is provided during the relevant four month period shall be offset against any shortfall (as compared with those requirements) in that period.

Amendments—[1] Figure in sub-para (1)(*b*) substituted for "£573" by the Tonnage Tax (Training Requirement) (Amendment) Regulations, SI 2003/2320 reg 4 with effect for the purpose of calculating the payments in lieu of training in respect of a relevant four month period falling after 30 September 2003. A "relevant four month period" means a period of four months commencing 1 October, 1 February or 1 June: SI 2003/2320 reg 2.

16 The payments in lieu of training shall be made to the Maritime Training Trust, and shall become due 30 days after the end of each relevant four month period.

17 If in any case there is a failure in relation to a company or group to comply with the requirements of Part IV of Schedule 22 to the Act with respect to—

(*a*) the submission of training commitments, or

(*b*) the making of returns or provision of information,

the Secretary of State may determine to the best of his information and belief the amount of the payments in lieu of training to be made by the company or group.

18—(1) A payment in lieu of training that has become due but is unpaid—

(*a*) is a debt to the Maritime Training Trust, and

(*b*) carries interest at an annual rate equivalent to base rate plus two per cent per annum.

(2) The costs or expenses of any legal or other proceedings for recovering the debt or interest shall be recoverable, and carry interest, in the same way as the debt.

Directions to provide information

19 The Secretary of State may direct any person to provide such information as the Secretary of State may reasonably require for the purposes of ascertaining—

(*a*) what the minimum training obligation of a company or group should be,

(*b*) whether the proposals in a training commitment are adequate to meet the minimum training obligation of a company or group, or

(*c*) whether a company or group has complied with its training commitment.

Audits

20 The Secretary of State may appoint one or more persons to carry out on his behalf an audit of the accounts or other records—

(*a*) of a qualifying single company, or

(*b*) of the qualifying companies in a group,

for the purpose of checking that any return or information provided to the Secretary of State is correct.

Higher rate of payment in case of failure to meet training requirement

21—(1) Subject to paragraph (3), a company or group is to be treated as failing to meet its training commitment in any year where it fails to provide training on a relevant course for at least 50% of the total number of eligible officer trainees for whom the company or group proposed to provide such training in its training commitment.

(2) Subject to paragraph (3)—

(*a*) if a company fails to meet its training commitment in a particular year, the basic rate of any payments in lieu of training that fall to be made by the company in the following year shall be increased by 50%;

(*b*) if a group fails to meet its training commitment in a particular year, the basic rate of any payments in lieu of training that fall to be made by any member of the group in the following year shall be increased by 50%; and

(*c*) if a company or group fails to meet its training commitment in two or more successive years, the basic rate of any payments in lieu of training shall be increased by 100% in the third and subsequent years.

(3) The higher rate shall not be payable where the Secretary of State is satisfied that there are mitigating circumstances for the company's or group's failure to meet the training commitment.

(4) For the purposes of paragraph (2), "the basic rate" is [£538][1] per eligible officer trainee per month.

Amendments—[1] Figure in sub-para (4) substituted for "£522" by the Tonnage Tax (Training Requirement) (Amendment) Regulations, SI 2003/2320 reg 5 with effect for the purpose of calculating the payments in lieu of training in respect of a relevant four month period falling after 30 September 2003. A "relevant four month period" means a period of four months commencing 1 October, 1 February or 1 June: SI 2003/2320 reg 2.

Certificate of non-compliance

22—(1) The Secretary of State may issue a certificate of non-compliance in respect of a single company if—

(*a*) the company fails to meet its training commitment for successive periods amounting to not less than two years, or

(*b*) the company, or any of its officers, commits an offence under Schedule 22 to the Act.

(2) The Secretary of State may issue a certificate of non-compliance in respect of a group if—

(*a*) the group fails to meet its training commitment for successive periods amounting to not less than two years, or

(*b*) a member of the group, or an officer of a member, commits an offence under Schedule 22 to the Act.

(3) The Secretary of State shall issue a certificate of non-compliance if any circumstances referred to in paragraph (1) or (2) arise, unless the Secretary of State is satisfied that there are good reasons why a certificate should not be issued.

23—(1) A company or group in respect of which a certificate of non-compliance has been issued may apply to the Secretary of State to cancel the certificate.

(2) Any such application shall contain information showing that—

(*a*) the training commitment has been complied with for at least one year since the period in relation to which the certificate was issued, and

(*b*) the company or group has made arrangements to ensure that its training commitment for the current and future years will be complied with.

24 When considering an application to cancel a certificate of non-compliance, the Secretary of State may consult the Merchant Navy Training Board or the Maritime Training Trust or both.

Disclosure of information

25 For the purposes of paragraph 34(2) of Schedule 22 to the Act, the following persons are prescribed persons involved in the training of seafarers—

(*a*) the Merchant Navy Training Board, and

(*b*) the Maritime Training Trust.

2000/2303
Tonnage Tax Regulations 2000

Made by the Commissioners of Inland Revenue under FA 2000 Sch 22 paras 47, 85(3), 112(7), 113(4), 130–136

Made	*24 August 2000*
Laid before the House of Commons	*25 August 2000*
Coming into force	*31 August 2000*

Statement of Practice SP 4/00—General operation of the tonnage tax regime.

Citation and commencement

1 These Regulations may be cited as the Tonnage Tax Regulations 2000 and shall come into force on 31st August 2000.

Interpretation

2—(1) In these Regulations—

"corporate partner" means a company which carries on activities in partnership;

"the 1990 Act" means the Capital Allowances Act 1990;

"the paragraph 85(2)(*a*) amount", in relation to an asset, means the amount determined under paragraph 85(2)(*a*) of Schedule 22 for that asset, subject to regulation 8(2)(*a*), and "the paragraph 112(2) amount" and "the paragraph 113(2) amount" shall have corresponding meanings;

"qualifying expenditure" has the meaning in paragraph 135 of Schedule 22;

"Schedule 22" means Schedule 22 to the Finance Act 2000;

"Schedule 28AA" means Schedule 28AA to the Taxes Act;

"the 75% limit" has the meaning given in paragraph 37(4) of Schedule 22;

"the Taxes Act" means the Income and Corporation Taxes Act 1988.

(2) In these Regulations, the following expressions have the same meaning as in Schedule 22—

"bareboat charter terms"

"company"

"core qualifying activities"

"group" (and "member" of a group)

"leaving tonnage tax"
"operating (a ship)"
"qualifying company"
"qualifying ship"
"relevant shipping profits"
"ship"
"ship-related activities"
"subject to tonnage tax"
"tonnage tax company"
"tonnage tax group" (and "member" of such a group)
"tonnage tax profits"
"tonnage tax trade".

(3) References in regulation 3(3)(*a*) to (*j*) and (4) to a qualifying ship operated by a company, where the company is a member of a tonnage tax group, include references to a qualifying ship operated by another qualifying company in the same tonnage tax group.

(4) For the purposes of the definition of "arm's length provision" (regulation 3(3)(*a*)(ii)), where any provision is made or imposed as between a company's tonnage tax trade and other activities carried on by it, the assumptions in paragraph 59(1)(*a*) to (*c*) of Schedule 22 and paragraph 1(3) of Schedule 28AA shall apply.

Qualifying secondary activities

3—(1) The descriptions of activity to be regarded as qualifying secondary activities shall be determined in accordance with the following paragraphs.

(2) A tonnage tax company's qualifying secondary activities means its ship-related activities, other than commercial activities which form part of the operation of a port carried on for profit, that—

(*a*) have a substantial connection with the company's core qualifying activities or, where the company is a member of a tonnage tax group, the core qualifying activities of another qualifying company in that group,

(*b*) fall within the descriptions in paragraph (3) or (4), and

(*c*) in the case of paragraph (3) are carried on at any level and in the case of paragraph (4) are carried on at the permitted level.

(3) The descriptions in this paragraph are—

(*a*) the carriage of passengers or cargo otherwise than on board a qualifying ship operated by the company, where—

(i) there is a single contract with the customer for a journey which includes a voyage on the qualifying ship, and

(ii) the transport for the remainder of the journey is purchased or obtained by the company by provision ("arm's length provision") which would have been made as between independent enterprises;

(*b*) administrative and insurance services which are directly related to the carriage of passengers or cargo, including under a contract described in sub-paragraph (*a*)(i);

(*c*) the embarkation and disembarkation of passengers on a qualifying ship operated by the company, and the provision of relevant facilities by the company;

(*d*) the provision of excursions for passengers of a qualifying ship operated by the company, where any cabin for the passenger remains available for his exclusive use;

(*e*) the provision of holidays, sold to the customer under a single contract, where—

(i) part of the holiday is a voyage on a qualifying ship operated by the company, and the remaining part is land-based ("the land-based part"),

(ii) the land-based part is purchased or obtained by the company by arm's length provision, and

(iii) the cost to the company of the land-based part in accordance with paragraph (ii) is less than one half of the price paid by the customer under the single contract;

(*f*) sales and facilities which are normally provided to customers by seagoing passenger ships, including—

(i) the provision of food or drink,

(ii) entertainment, but not betting or gambling (see paragraph (4)(*b*)(i)),

(iii) the sale of alcoholic beverages, perfume and tobacco, but not luxury goods (see paragraph (4)(*b*)(ii)),

(iv) the exchange of amounts of different currencies for personal expenditure;

(*g*) the loading and unloading of cargo carried on a qualifying ship operated by the company, and the provision by the company of facilities used exclusively for those purposes;

(*h*) the consolidation or breaking of cargo carried on a qualifying ship operated by the company, immediately before or after the voyage, where the activity is not haulage-related;

(*i*) the temporary placement of cargo carried on a qualifying ship operated by the company, on or at the dockside, where the activity is not part of a long-term storage operation;
(*j*) the rental or provision to customers of containers for goods to be carried on a qualifying ship operated by the company;
(*k*) activities carried on by the company in relation to a qualifying ship operated by another qualifying company in the same tonnage tax group, which would be core qualifying activities of the first-mentioned company if carried on in relation to a qualifying ship operated by that company.

(4) The descriptions and permitted levels in this paragraph are—

(*a*) services which, if carried out in relation to qualifying ships operated by the company, would be core qualifying activities of the company or activities of the company which would fall within the descriptions in paragraph (3), but only to the level where—

(i) the relevant staff and assets are needed by the company to carry out the company's main function, and the services are undertaken to make full use of those staff and assets, and
(ii) the services are minimal compared to the main function;

(*b*) (i) betting or gambling facilities normally offered to customers by seagoing passenger ships for entertainment, and

(ii) the sale to passengers on seagoing ships of luxury goods of a kind normally offered to such passengers,

but only to the level where the turnover from those activities is negligible compared to the turnover from the company's core qualifying activities.

(5) In paragraph (4)(*a*) "the company's main function" means the company's core qualifying activities and those of its activities which fall within the descriptions in paragraph (3).

Plant and machinery other than expensive motor cars and long-life assets—writing-down basis

4—(1) This regulation applies to any asset mentioned in paragraph 85(2) of Schedule 22, where the provisions of Part II of the 1990 Act would have applied to the asset on the footing that the company had not been subject to tonnage tax ("the tax condition"), other than—

(*a*) a motor car, to which the provisions of section 34 of the 1990 Act (expensive motor cars) would have effect on that condition, or
(*b*) a long-life asset, where Chapter IVA of Part II of the 1990 Act would have applied to the capital expenditure incurred on the provision of the asset, on that condition.

(2) The written down value of the paragraph 85(2)(*a*) amount for the asset shall be determined by multiplying that amount by the percentage given by the table in paragraph (3).
(3) That table is as follows—

Length of qualifying holding period for the asset	*Percentage of the paragraph 85(2)(a) amount which is qualifying expenditure under Part II of the 1990 Act*
Less than or equal to 1 year	75
1 year and one day to 2 years	55
2 years and one day to 3 years	40
3 years and one day to 4 years	30
4 years and one day to 5 years	25
5 years and one day to 6 years	15
6 years and one day to 7 years	12
7 years and one day to 8 years	10
8 years and one day to 9 years	5
More than 9 years	Nil

(4) References in this regulation and regulations 5 and 6 to the qualifying holding period for an asset are references to the period between—

(*a*) the date on which the expenditure represented by the paragraph 85(2)(*a*) amount, or the part thereof, was incurred, and
(*b*) the date on which the company leaves tonnage tax.

Expensive motor cars—writing-down basis

5—(1) This regulation applies to motor cars described in regulation 4(1)(*a*).

(2) The written down value of the paragraph 85(2)(*a*) amount for the motor car shall be determined in accordance with the following provisions—

Rule 1

The paragraph 85(2)(*a*) amount for the motor car shall be reduced by £3,000 for each complete year in the qualifying holding period, subject to Rule 2.

Rule 2

Rule 1 shall cease to apply at the end of the complete year where the paragraph 85(2)(*a*) amount is first reduced below £12,000, and Rule 3 shall thereafter apply to that amount as reduced at the end of that year (''the reduced amount'').

Rule 3

The table in regulation 4(3) shall apply to the reduced amount, in relation to any subsequent period in the qualifying holding period, as if for the date mentioned in regulation 4(4)(*a*) there were substituted a reference to the end of the year mentioned in Rule 2.

Long-life assets—writing-down basis

6—(1) This regulation applies to long-life assets described in regulation 4(1)(*b*).

(2) The written down value of the paragraph 85(2)(*a*) amount for the asset shall be determined by multiplying that amount by the percentage given by the table in paragraph (3).

(3) That table is as follows—

Length of qualifying holding period for the asset	*Percentage of the paragraph 85(2)(a) amount which is qualifying expenditure under Part II of the 1990 Act*
Less than or equal to 1 year	94
From 1 year and one day to 2 years	88
From 2 years and one day to 3 years	83
From 3 years and one day to 4 years	78
From 4 years and one day to 5 years	73
From 5 years and one day to 6 years	69
From 6 years and one day to 7 years	65
From 7 years and one day to 8 years	61
From 8 years and one day to 9 years	57
From 9 years and one day to 10 years	54
From 10 years and one day to 11 years	51
From 11 years and one day to 13 years	47
From 13 years and one day to 16 years	40
From 16 years and one day to 19 years	33
From 19 years and one day to 22 years	27
From 22 years and one day to 25 years	23
From 25 years and one day to 30 years	18
From 30 years and one day to 35 years	13
From 35 years and one day to 40 years	10

Length of qualifying holding period for the asset	*Percentage of the paragraph 85(2)(a) amount which is qualifying expenditure under Part II of the 1990 Act*
From 40 years and one day to 45 years	7
From 45 years and one day to 50 years	5
From 50 years and one day to 60 years	3
From 60 years and one day to 70 years	2
More than 70 years	Nil

Plant and machinery used for the purposes of the company's offshore activities—writing-down basis

7—(1) This regulation applies to any asset mentioned in paragraph 110(2)(*a*) of Schedule 22, where—

(*a*) the provisions of Part II of the 1990 Act apply to the asset by virtue of paragraph 110(2) of Schedule 22, and

(*b*) the paragraph 112(2) amount or the paragraph 113(2) amount for the asset, as the case may be ("the relevant amount"), falls to be written down under paragraph 112(6) or 113(3) of Schedule 22.

(2) The written down value of the relevant amount shall be determined by applying regulation 4, 5 or 6, as the case may be, as if—

(*a*) the tax condition were omitted,

(*b*) for references to the paragraph 85(2)(*a*) amount there were substituted references to the relevant amount, and

(*c*) for regulation 4(4)(*a*) and (*b*) there were substituted a reference to the period mentioned in paragraph 112(6) or 113(3) of Schedule 22, as the case may be.

Adjustments to be made for capital allowance purposes to the amount of qualifying expenditure for assets where a corporate partner leaves tonnage tax

8—(1) This regulation applies where—

(*a*) a corporate partner leaves tonnage tax,

(*b*) an asset has been used by the corporate partner for the purposes of tonnage tax activities which it carries on as a member of a partnership, and

(*c*) as at the beginning of the partnership chargeable period in which the corporate partner leaves tonnage tax (the beginning of which period is referred to in this regulation as "the relevant time") the asset—

(i) was partnership property of the partnership concerned, or

(ii) would have been so treated by regulation 9(2), or by section 65 of the 1990 Act if the corporate partner had not been subject to tonnage tax,

and applies to the corporate partner and all the other members of the partnership.

In this paragraph "the partnership chargeable period" means the accounting period or period of account used by the partnership in its partnership computation under section 114(1) of the Taxes Act or section 111(2) of that Act, as the case may be.

(2) In relation to any asset mentioned in paragraph (1)(*b*) and (*c*)—

(*a*) there shall be determined the amount for that asset which is referred to in paragraph 85(2)(*a*) of Schedule 22 (which amount is referred to in this regulation as "the paragraph 85(2)(*a*) amount" for the asset), on the assumptions—

(i) that the corporate partner left tonnage tax at the relevant time, and

(ii) (where it is not otherwise the case) that the asset was held by the corporate partner at that time; and

(*b*) where the asset is counted in a calculation under paragraphs (3) to (7) of this regulation, it shall not be counted again in any determination under paragraph 85(1) of Schedule 22 on the same occasion of the corporate partner leaving tonnage tax.

(3) In the following paragraphs of this regulation—

"unrelieved qualifying expenditure", in relation to an asset, means the balance of qualifying expenditure attributable to that asset that would otherwise have been carried forward under Part II of the 1990 Act, including postponed allowances attributable to that asset; and

"postponed allowances" means qualifying expenditure which is unrelieved by virtue of notice having been given under—

(*a*) section 30(1) of the 1990 Act (postponement or reduction of first allowances), or (*b*) section 31(3) of that Act (postponement of writing-down allowance in respect of expenditure in single ship pool).

(4) The unrelieved qualifying expenditure for any asset mentioned in paragraph (1)(*b*) and (*c*), so far as it is not represented by postponed allowances, that would otherwise have been carried forward as at the relevant time, shall be adjusted to the amount resulting from the calculation in paragraph (5) or (6), as the case may be.

(5) Except in the case described in paragraph (6), the calculation is—

$$(A\% \times B) + ((100\% - A\%) \times C)$$

where—

A equals the corporate partner's share (expressed as a percentage) in the partnership property of the partnership concerned at the relevant time, subject to paragraph (8);

B equals the written down value of the paragraph 85(2)(*a*) amount for the asset calculated by applying regulation 4, 5 or 6, as the case may be—

(*a*) as if for regulation 4(4)(*b*), there were substituted a reference to the relevant time; and

(*b*) on the assumptions contained in paragraph (2)(*a*) where applicable;

C equals the unrelieved qualifying expenditure for the asset, so far as it is not represented by postponed allowances, as at the relevant time.

(6) In a case where all the members of the partnership other than the corporate partner are—

(*a*) persons who (within the meaning in section 161 of the 1990 Act) are not within the charge to tax in the United Kingdom on the profits of the trade carried on in the partnership in question, or

(*b*) companies which are subject to tonnage tax,

the calculation is of B, which has the same meaning as in paragraph (5).

(7) The unrelieved qualifying expenditure for any asset mentioned in paragraph (1)(*b*) and (*c*), so far as it is represented by postponed allowances, that would otherwise have been carried forward as at the relevant time (the amount of which is referred to as "D" in this paragraph), shall be reduced to the percentage of D which is represented by the following calculation—

$$(100\% - A\%) \times D$$

where A has the same meaning as in paragraph (5).

(8) Where the share of the corporate partner in the partnership property (expressed as a proportion of the whole) varied during the period—

(*a*) beginning on the last to occur of—

(i) the date on which the corporate partner became a member of the partnership concerned,

(ii) the date on which the corporate partner entered tonnage tax, or

(iii) the date six years before the relevant time, and

(*b*) ending at the relevant time,

the calculation of A in paragraphs (5) and (7) shall be made according to the average of the corporate partner's interest in the property of the relevant partnership during that period, and any necessary apportionment on a daily basis shall be made.

(9) A payment made by a corporate partner to another corporate partner in the same partnership which is compensation for any adjustment carried out under paragraphs (4) to (7)—

(*a*) shall not be taken into account in computing profits or losses of either company for corporation tax purposes, and

(*b*) shall not for any of the purposes of the Corporation Tax Acts, (within the meaning in section 831(1)(*a*) of the Taxes Act) be regarded as a distribution or a charge on income.

Corporate partners—modifications of the requirements for being a qualifying company (with supplementary provision relating to finance leases)

9—(1) Paragraphs (1) to (3), (5) and (6) of this regulation prescribe modifications to the requirements for determining whether—

(*a*) a corporate partner operates qualifying ships within the meaning in paragraphs 16(1)(*b*) and 18(1) to (4) of Schedule 22, and

(*b*) those ships are strategically and commercially managed in the United Kingdom within the meaning in paragraph 16(1)(*c*) of Schedule 22.

(2) Where—

(*a*) a qualifying ship is owned by, or (other than by a charter described in paragraph (3)) chartered to, one or more of the members of a partnership but is not partnership property, and

(*b*) activities of the partnership business which, if carried on by a tonnage tax company, would be tonnage tax activities, are carried on in relation to the ship,

the ship shall be treated as if it were owned by, or chartered to, all the partners, as the case may be, and as if everything done by or to any of the partners in relation to it had been done by or to all the partners.

(3) Any charter of a ship from one or more members of the partnership to the other partners, or to the partnership, for use in the tonnage tax activities carried on in that partnership, shall be treated for the purposes of paragraph 18(4) of Schedule 22 as a charter to a person who is not a third party.

(4) A finance lease (within the meaning in section 82A of the 1990 Act) of a qualifying ship where the lessee is one or more members of a partnership which includes a tonnage tax company as a member, or is such a partnership, and the ship is used in the tonnage tax activities which the tonnage tax company carries on as a member of the partnership, shall be treated for the purposes of Part X of Schedule 22 as if—

(*a*) the qualifying ship were provided (within the meaning in paragraph 89(1) of Schedule 22) to the tonnage tax company;

(*b*) the tonnage tax company were the ''lessee'' for the purposes of paragraphs 98 and 99 of Schedule 22; and

(*c*) the references in paragraph 92 of Schedule 22 to the ship being owned by a tonnage tax company included references to the ship being owned by one or more of the partners, or by the partnership.

(5) Paragraph 16(1)(*c*) of Schedule 22 shall be modified as if, in relation to activities carried on by a corporate partner in a partnership, the reference to those ships were replaced with a reference to the requisite proportion of those ships.

(6) In paragraph (5) ''the requisite proportion of those ships'' means a proportion of those ships such that—

$$\frac{E}{F} \text{ is not less than } G$$

where—

E equals the aggregate net tonnage of all the qualifying ships which are—

(*a*) operated by the partners of the partnership concerned, in their capacity as such partners, and

(*b*) strategically and commercially managed in the United Kingdom;

F equals the aggregate net tonnage of all the qualifying ships which are operated by the partners of the partnership concerned, in their capacity as such partners; and

G equals the share of the corporate partner, expressed as a fraction, in the partnership property of the partnership concerned.

Rules for calculating the tonnage tax profits and relevant shipping profits of a corporate partner

10—(1) Paragraph (2) applies to any corporate partner which is a tonnage tax company (but only in relation to the share of profits or losses which such a partner derives from the activities carried on in the partnership concerned).

(2) Section 114 of the Taxes Act shall apply to the profits and losses of the partnership as if the partnership were a tonnage tax company, for the purpose of calculating—

(*a*) the tonnage tax profits, and

(*b*) the relevant shipping profits (or such of the corresponding losses as fall within paragraph 3(2) of Schedule 22),

of any corporate partner to whom this paragraph applies (but not the share of profits or losses of any other partner).

(3) Where a ship falls to be counted as operated by a partnership in a calculation under paragraph (2)(*a*) carried out in relation to a corporate partner, it shall not be counted again in any computation of the tonnage tax profits of that corporate partner, and the same provision shall apply as between a calculation under paragraph (2)(*b*) and the relevant shipping profits (or relevant corresponding losses) of a corporate partner.

Ships chartered to partners—further provision relating to chartering in

11—(1) Where a corporate partner carries on activities in partnership which include the operation of a qualifying ship, the calculation whether the 75% limit is exceeded by—

(*a*) that corporate partner (if it is a single company), or

(*b*) a group of which that corporate partner is a member, so far as the calculation relates to the corporate partner,

shall be made in accordance with this regulation.

(2) The calculation is as follows—

Step One

Find out the aggregate net tonnage of the qualifying ships that are operated by the members of the partnership concerned, in their capacity as such partners.

Step Two

Find out the proportion, in percentage terms, of the result of Step One which represents tonnage of ships which are chartered to the partners, or to the partnership, otherwise than on bareboat charter terms (''chartered in''), ignoring any such charters which are from another qualifying member of any group of which the corporate partner is also a member.

Step Three

Determine the corporate partner's share of the results of Steps One and Two according to the interests of the partners in the partnership property in the accounting period in question, expressed as a figure of net tonnage and the percentage of it which is chartered in.

Step Four

Follow Steps One to Three for each partnership of which the corporate partner is a member and aggregate the results, to arrive at a total figure of net tonnage and the percentage of it which is chartered in.

Step Five

Aggregate the results of Step Four with the results of the calculation for the purposes of paragraph 37(1)(*a*) or (*b*) of Schedule 22, as the case may be, in relation to any ships other than those which the corporate partner operates as a member of a partnership.

Step Six

Apply paragraph 37(1)(*a*) or (*b*) of Schedule 22, as the case may be, to the results of Step Five.

(3) Where the interests of the partners in the partnership property, expressed as a proportion of the whole, vary in the course of an accounting period, the interest of a corporate partner for that period shall be calculated according to the average interest of that partner during that period.

Chargeable gains—use of assets by partnerships which include corporate partners

12 Where—

(*a*) an asset has been used wholly and exclusively for the purposes of activities of a partnership which are (or would be, if the partnership were a tonnage tax company) tonnage tax activities;

(*b*) throughout the period of use of the asset as mentioned in sub-paragraph (*a*), there was a corporate partner member of the partnership which was also a tonnage tax company; and

(*c*) the asset is disposed of by that corporate partner, or by another member of a group of which that corporate partner is a member,

references in paragraph 65(1) and (3) of Schedule 22 to a tonnage tax asset, or to any time at which or period during which an asset was a tonnage tax asset, shall respectively include references to the asset and period mentioned in this regulation, and references to a period during which an asset was not a tonnage tax asset shall be construed accordingly.

Transactions not at arm's length between a partnership (where a corporate partner is a tonnage tax company) and another partner

13—(1) Where a corporate partner which is a tonnage tax company ("the relevant company") carries on tonnage tax activities in partnership, paragraph 58 of Schedule 22 shall apply to provision made or imposed as between—

(*a*) the partnership, and

(*b*) another partner,

if the condition in paragraph (2) is satisfied, and in that event on the assumptions in paragraph (3).

(2) The condition is that the relevant company (in addition to the partner referred to in paragraph (1)(*b*)) is a major participant in the partnership's enterprise, within the meaning of that expression in paragraph 4(7) of Schedule 28AA.

(3) The assumptions are that the partnership—

(*a*) is a tonnage tax company, and

(*b*) is regarded for the purposes of paragraph 58(1)(*a*) of Schedule 22 as carrying on the tonnage tax trade of the relevant company, so far as that trade consists of activities carried on by the relevant company in the partnership in question.

2000/2314

Personal Pension Schemes (Restriction on Discretion to Approve) (Establishment of Schemes under Trusts) Regulations 2000

Made by the Commissioners of Inland Revenue under TA 1988 s 638A

Made	*29 August 2000*
Laid before the House of Commons	*31 August 2000*
Coming into force	*1 October 2000*

Commentary—*Simon's Direct Tax Service* **E7.403, U6537.**

Citation and commencement

1 These Regulations may be cited as the Personal Pension Schemes (Restriction on Discretion to Approve) (Establishment of Schemes under Trusts) Regulations 2000 and shall come into force on 1st October 2000.

Interpretation

2 In these Regulations—

(*a*) "the Board" means the Commissioners of Inland Revenue; and

(*b*) "small self-administered scheme" means a scheme which, had it been a retirement benefits scheme, would have been a small self-administered scheme within the meaning of regulation 2 of the Retirement Benefits Schemes (Restriction on Discretion to Approve) (Small Self-Administered Schemes) Regulations 1991.

Restriction on Board's discretion to approve some trust-based personal pension schemes

3—(1) The Board shall not exercise their discretion to approve a personal pension scheme under section 631 of the Income and Corporation Taxes Act 1988, in circumstances where the scheme is established under a trust or trusts by a person other than one mentioned in section 632(1)(*a*) to (*e*) of that Act, unless either paragraph (2) or (3) of this regulation is satisfied.

(2) This paragraph is satisfied if—

(*a*) the scheme is a trust scheme within the meaning given by section 124(1) of the Pensions Act 1995 or Article 121(1) of the Pensions (Northern Ireland) Order 1995; and

(*b*) the trust deed for the scheme contains a provision that—

(i) applies if the scheme is at any time a small self-administered scheme; and

(ii) falls within the description specified in regulation 9 of the Retirement Benefits Schemes (Restriction on Discretion to Approve) (Small Self-administered Schemes) Regulations 1991.

(3) This paragraph is satisfied if—

(*a*) an application has been made under section 2 of the Welfare Reform and Pensions Act 1999 or article 4 of the Welfare Reform and Pensions (Northern Ireland) Order 1999 for the registration of the scheme as a stakeholder pension scheme; and

(*b*) the approval of the scheme by the Board as a personal pension scheme is conditional on that registration taking place.

Commentary—*Simon's Direct Tax Service* **E7.403, U6537; U6.6537.**

2000/2316

Personal Pension Schemes (Information Powers) Regulations 2000

Made by the Commissioners of Inland Revenue under TA 1988 s 651A

Made	*29 August 2000*
Laid before the House of Commons	*31 August 2000*
Coming into force	*1 October 2000*

Commentary—*Simon's Direct Tax Service* **U6.6537.**

PART I

INTRODUCTORY

Citation and commencement

1 These Regulations may be cited as the Personal Pension Schemes (Information Powers) Regulations 2000 and shall come into force on 1st October 2000.

Interpretation

2—(1) In these Regulations unless the context otherwise requires—

"approved", "member", "personal pension scheme" and "scheme administrator" have the meanings given by section 630(1);

"the Board" means the Commissioners of Inland Revenue;

"excluded person" means any person who, on ceasing to act in relation to the scheme or, as the case may be, provide administrative services to the scheme, transferred all documents in his possession or under his control relating to the scheme to another person who succeeded him in acting in relation to the scheme or in providing administrative services to the scheme;

"friendly society" has the meaning given by section 116 of the Friendly Societies Act 1992;

"insurance company" has the meaning given by section 659B;

"notice" means notice in writing;

"personal pension arrangements" has the meaning given by section 630(1); and references in these Regulations to "arrangements" in connection with personal pension schemes shall be construed accordingly;

"pooled fund" in relation to a personal pension scheme means a fund—

(*a*) which is open to the public and is described in the documents establishing the fund as being a standard fund open to all members, (*b*) in relation to the management of which the scheme administrator is not required to consult with any member of the scheme except to the extent that an investment offers choices that are available to any person (whether or not a member of the scheme), and

(*c*) the value of which is applied to all members and not segregated among certain members or linked to certain members by reason of particular assets comprised in the fund;

"the relevant date" means the date which is 6 years from the end of the scheme year in which an event specified in regulation 9(4) occurs;

"scheme provider" in relation to a personal pension scheme for which there is for the time being no scheme administrator or for which the scheme administrator cannot be traced means—

(*a*) the person who established the scheme, or

(*b*) any person by whom that person has been directly or indirectly succeeded in relation to the provision of benefits under the scheme;

"scheme year" means—

(*a*) a year specified for the purposes of a personal pension scheme in any document comprising the scheme or, if no year is specified, a period of 12 months commencing on 1st April or on such other date as the scheme administrator selects; or

(*b*) such other period (if any) exceeding 6 months but not exceeding 18 months as is selected by the scheme administrator—

(i) in respect of the scheme year in which the scheme commences or terminates, or

(ii) in connection with a variation of the date on which the scheme year is to commence;

"self-invested personal pension scheme" has the meaning given by regulation 3;

"the Taxes Act" means the Income and Corporation Taxes Act 1988.

(2) For the purposes of these Regulations and subject to paragraph (3), any question whether a person is connected with another person shall be determined in accordance with section 839.

(3) A person shall not be regarded as connected with another person for the purposes of these Regulations where the connection arises as a result of a transaction entered into in the course of normal investment management by a scheme in relation to a fund that is a pooled fund.

(4) In these Regulations references to a particular provision, without more, are references to that provision of the Taxes Act.

Definition of self-invested personal pension scheme

3—(1) In these Regulations "self-invested personal pension scheme" means a personal pension scheme the arrangements made in accordance with which by a member—

(*a*) are arrangements under which the member is able to direct the manner in which some or all of the contributions paid to the scheme are to be invested by or on behalf of the scheme administrator, and

(*b*) are not arrangements falling within paragraph (2).

(2) Arrangements fall within this paragraph if they are either—

(*a*) arrangements under which—

(i) all the investments held for the purposes of the scheme comprise contracts of insurance or units in unit trust schemes, and

(ii) in managing those investments, the scheme administrator or the person acting on his behalf does not consult with any member of the scheme except to the extent necessary by virtue of the scheme offering choices that are available to any person (whether or not a member of the scheme); or

(*b*) arrangements under which—

(i) all contributions paid are, after deduction of expenses, invested in deposits with deposit-takers, and

(ii) the payment of interest on those deposits comprises the only income of the scheme from its investments.

PART II
INFORMATION REQUIRED WITHOUT NOTICE

Investment and borrowing transactions of self-invested personal pension schemes

4—(1) The scheme administrator of an approved personal pension scheme that is a self-invested personal pension scheme is a person who is prescribed for the purposes of this regulation.

(2) The scheme administrator of an approved personal pension scheme that is a self-invested personal pension scheme shall furnish to the Board, at the time prescribed by paragraph (3), such information (including copies of any relevant books, documents or other records) as—

(*a*) is specified on the relevant form supplied by the Board, and

(*b*) relates to any transaction entered into by the scheme or under arrangements made in accordance with the scheme that—

(i) is of a kind specified in paragraph (4), and

(ii) is entered into by or on behalf of the scheme administrator on or after the date of coming into force of these Regulations.

(3) The time prescribed is any time not later than 90 days after the date of the transaction in question.

(4) The transactions specified in this paragraph are—

(*a*) the acquisition or disposal of land;

(*b*) the borrowing of money;

(*c*) the purchase, sale or lease of any asset other than land.

Reporting of chargeable event

5—(1) The scheme administrator of an approved personal pension scheme is a person who is prescribed for the purposes of this regulation.

(2) The scheme administrator of an approved personal pension scheme shall furnish to the Board, at the time prescribed by paragraph (3), such information (including copies of any relevant books, documents or other records) relating to the event specified in paragraph (4) as is specified on the relevant form supplied by the Board.

(3) The time prescribed is any time not later than 30 days after the end of the year of assessment in which the event occurs.

(4) The event specified is any payment under arrangements made in accordance with the scheme to which section 648B(1) applies (return of contributions after pension date).

PART III
NOTICES REQUIRING PARTICULARS AND DOCUMENTS

Approved personal pension schemes

6—(1) The Board may by notice require any of the persons prescribed by paragraph (2), within the time prescribed by paragraph (3), to furnish to the Board such particulars, and to produce to the Board such documents, as they may reasonably require relating to—

(*a*) any monies received or receivable by an approved personal pension scheme or under approved personal pension arrangements made in accordance with that scheme, or

(*b*) any investments or other assets held by that scheme or under those arrangements, or

(*c*) any monies paid or payable out of funds held under that scheme or those arrangements, including any monies paid by way of repayment of contributions to a member of that scheme or his employer.

(2) The persons prescribed are—

(*a*) the person who is for the time being the scheme administrator in relation to the scheme concerned;

(*b*) any person who was at any time prior to the relevant date the scheme administrator in relation to that scheme, other than an excluded person;

(*c*) any person who is, or has been at any time prior to the relevant date, a scheme provider in relation to that scheme, other than an excluded person;

(*d*) any person who provides, or has at any time prior to the relevant date provided, administrative services to that scheme, other than an excluded person.

(3) The time prescribed is such time (not being less than 28 days) as is provided by the notice.

(4) A notice under paragraph (1) may require particulars to be furnished, and documents to be produced, relating to more than one scheme.

Annuity contracts

7—(1) The Board may by notice require any of the persons prescribed by paragraph (2), within the time prescribed by paragraph (3), to furnish to the Board such particulars, and to produce to the Board such documents, as they may reasonably require relating to any annuity contract issued by that person by means of which benefits provided under an approved personal pension scheme or under approved personal pension arrangements made in accordance with that scheme have been secured.

(2) The persons prescribed are—

(*a*) the insurance company which issued the annuity contract, where that company is a body corporate;

(*b*) the chief executive and the manager, within the meaning of [sections 417(1) and 423 of the Financial Services and Markets Act 2000 respectively][1], of the insurance company which issued the annuity contract;

(*c*) the person referred to in section 659B(6) or (8);

(*d*) the friendly society which issued the annuity contract, where that friendly society is a society incorporated under the Friendly Societies Act 1992;

(*e*) the chief executive and the secretary, any assistant chief executive and deputy chief executive, and any assistant secretary and deputy secretary, of the friendly society which issued the annuity contract.

(3) The time prescribed is such time (not being less than 28 days) as is provided by the notice.

(4) A notice under paragraph (1) may require particulars and documents relating to more than one annuity contract.

Amendments—[1] Words in sub-para (2)(*b*) substituted by the Financial Services and Markets Act 2000 (Consequential Amendments) (Taxes) Order, SI 2001/3629 art 188 with effect from 1 December 2001, immediately after the coming into force of the Financial Services and Markets Act 2000 ss 411, 432(1), Sch 20 (and SI 2001/3629 Pts 1 and 2).

PART IV
INSPECTION AND RETENTION OF RECORDS

Inspection of records

8—(1) The Board may by notice require any of the persons prescribed by paragraph (2) to make available for inspection by an officer of the Board authorised for that purpose, within the time prescribed by paragraph (3), all books, documents and other records in his possession or under his control relating to—

(*a*) any monies received or receivable by an approved personal pension scheme,

(*b*) any investments or other assets held by that scheme,

(*c*) any monies paid or payable out of funds held under that scheme, or

(*d*) any annuity contract by means of which benefits provided under that scheme have been secured.

(2) The persons prescribed are—

(*a*) the person who is for the time being the scheme administrator in relation to the scheme concerned;

(*b*) any person who was at any time prior to the relevant date the scheme administrator in relation to that scheme, other than an excluded person;

(*c*) any person who is, or has been at any time prior to the relevant date, a scheme provider in relation to that scheme, other than an excluded person;

(*d*) any person who provides, or has at any time prior to the relevant date provided, administrative services to that scheme, other than an excluded person.

(3) The time prescribed is such time (not being less than 28 days) as is provided by the notice.

(4) A notice under paragraph (1) may require books, documents and other records relating to more than one scheme to be made available for inspection.

(5) Where records are maintained by computer the person required to make them available for inspection shall provide the officer making the inspection with all the facilities necessary for obtaining information from them.

(6) The authorised officer may take copies of, or make extracts from, any books, documents or other records made available for inspection in accordance with paragraph (1).

Retention of records

9—(1) Each of the persons prescribed by paragraph (2) shall preserve, for the time prescribed by paragraph (3), all books, documents and other records in his possession or under his control relating to—

(*a*) any monies received or receivable by an approved personal pension scheme or under approved personal pension arrangements made in accordance with that scheme;

(*b*) any investments or other assets held by that scheme or under those arrangements;

(*c*) any monies paid or payable out of funds held under that scheme or those arrangements; or

(*d*) any annuity contract by means of which benefits provided under that scheme or those arrangements have been secured.

(2) The persons prescribed are—

(*a*) the person who is for the time being the scheme administrator in relation to the scheme concerned;

(*b*) any person who was at any time prior to the relevant date the scheme administrator in relation to that scheme, other than an excluded person;

(*c*) any person who is, or has been at any time prior to the relevant date, a scheme provider in relation to that scheme, other than an excluded person;

(*d*) any person who provides, or has at any time prior to the relevant date provided, administrative services to that scheme, other than an excluded person.

(3) The time prescribed—

(*a*) in the case of accounts relating to the scheme, including books, documents and other records on which such accounts are based, is 6 years from the end of the scheme year in which falls the date on which the accounts were signed;

(*b*) in the case of books, documents or other records containing information which is required to be furnished pursuant to regulation 4, is 6 years from the end of the scheme year in which the transaction in question occurred;

(*c*) in the case of books, documents or other records containing information which is required to be furnished pursuant to regulation 5, is 6 years from the end of the scheme year in which the event specified in paragraph (4) of that regulation occurred;

(*d*) in the case of books, documents or other records relating to an event specified in paragraph (4), is 6 years from the end of the scheme year in which the event occurred.

(4) The events specified are—

(*a*) the provision by the scheme or under the arrangements of any benefit to a member of the scheme or other person;

(*b*) the payment of contributions to the scheme by a member or his employer;

(*c*) the repayment to a member or his employer in accordance with section 638(3) of an excess amount of contributions paid to the scheme;

(*d*) the payment of transfer values or the purchase of annuities under the scheme or the arrangements;

(*e*) the acquisition or disposal of any asset by the scheme or under the arrangements;

(*f*) the undertaking of any transaction for the purposes of the scheme or the arrangements;

(*g*) the receipt by the scheme of any income resulting from—

(i) the investment of assets held by the scheme or under the arrangements, or

(ii) any trading activity carried on by the scheme or under the arrangements.

(5) The duty under paragraph (1) to preserve books, documents and other records may be discharged by the preservation of information contained in them.

2000/2318
Personal Pension Schemes (Concurrent Membership) Order 2000

Made by the Treasury under TA 1988 s 632B(4)(*a*), (*b*), (8)

Made . . . *31 August 2000*
Laid before the House of Commons *31 August 2000*
Coming into force . . *6 April 2001*

Commentary—*Simon's Direct Tax Service* **U6.6537, E7.407.**

Citation, commencement and interpretation

1—(1) This Order may be cited as the Personal Pension Schemes (Concurrent Membership) Order 2000 and shall come into force on 6th April 2001 immediately after the coming into force of paragraph 8 of Schedule 13 to the Finance Act 2000.

(2) In this Order, references to a section, without more, are references to that section of the Income and Corporation Taxes Act 1988.

Definition of remuneration

2 For the purposes of section 632B(1)(*d*), a person's "remuneration" from an office or employment means, in relation to a year of assessment, the total amount of the emoluments paid to him by the employer during that year, within the meaning in regulation 39(2)(*b*) of the Income Tax (Employments) Regulations 1993.

Calculation of a person's grossed-up remuneration from an office or employment

3—(1) The figure referred to in section 632B(4)(*a*) shall be determined in accordance with paragraph (2) or (3).

(2) Where the person held the office or employment throughout the year of assessment in question the figure is 1.

(3) In any other case, the figure is determined in accordance with the following calculation—

Step One

Work out the number of months for which the person held the office or employment during the year of assessment in question (and any remaining fraction of a month shall count as a full month for this purpose).

Step Two

Divide the figure 12 by the figure resulting from Step One and round the result up or down (if necessary) to the nearest single decimal place.

The result is the figure to be applied in calculating the grossed-up remuneration of that person from that office or employment in that year of assessment.

Certificates of eligibility under section 632B

4—(1) A member who claims to be eligible to make contributions to a personal pension scheme by virtue of section 632B in a year of assessment (the "relevant year") subject to continued compliance with the requirements of section 632B for the remainder of the relevant year shall, on or before the making of the first such contribution to the scheme in the relevant year, provide to the scheme administrator of the scheme the certificate required by paragraph (3), subject to paragraph (4).

(2) In this article—

"the qualifying year", in relation to a relevant year, means—

(*a*) any one of the five immediately preceding years of assessment (not being earlier than the year 2000–01), and

(*b*) one in which the aggregate referred to in section 632B(1)(*d*) did not exceed the remuneration limit for the relevant year;

"certificated years" means, in a case where a certificate has been given under paragraph (3) identifying the qualifying year, the five years of assessment which immediately succeed that qualifying year, subject to paragraph (4)(*b*).

(3) The certificate required is one—

(*a*) identifying the qualifying year;

(*b*) that, in relation to the qualifying year, the aggregate referred to in section 632B(1)(*d*) did not exceed the remuneration limit for the relevant year;

(*c*) that the total relevant contributions within the meaning of section 632B(*b*) for the relevant year will not exceed the earnings threshold for that year;

(*d*) that the total relevant contributions for any certificated year will not exceed the earnings threshold for that year;

(*e*) stating the full name and address of any person who pays the member the remuneration of any office or employment held by him to which section 645 applies; and

(*f*) stating that he is not, and has not been, a controlling director in the relevant year or any of the five immediately preceding years of assessment (not being earlier than the year 2000–01).

(4) Where the relevant year is a certificated year (as the result of a certificate given in relation to a contribution made in an earlier year of assessment)—

(*a*) the member is not obliged to provide a further certificate under paragraph (3), but

(*b*) if he does so, the earlier certificate shall cease to have effect at the end of the year of assessment immediately preceding the relevant year first mentioned in this paragraph.

2000/2319

Finance Act 1998, Section 96(4), (Appointed Day) Order 2000

Made by the Treasury under FA 1988 s 96(4)

Made . . . . *31 August 2000*

Commentary—*Simon's Direct Tax Service* **U6.6537, E7.417.**

1 This Order may be cited as the Finance Act 1998, Section 96(4), (Appointed Day) Order 2000.

2 The day appointed for the purposes of section 96(2) and (3)(*b*) of, and Part III(21) of Schedule 27 to, the Finance Act 1998 (repeal of section 652 of the Income and Corporation Taxes Act 1988—information about payments under personal pension scheme arrangements) is 1st October 2000.

2000/2875

Orders for the Delivery of Documents (Procedure) Regulations 2000

Made . . . . *23 October 2000*
Laid before Parliament . . . . *23 October 2000*
Coming into force . . . . *13 November 2000*

Commentary—*Simon's Direct Tax Service* **A3.151.**

The Commissioners of Inland Revenue, in exercise of the powers conferred on them by paragraphs 2(2), 3(2), 6, 7(1) and (2), 10 and 11(*a*) of Schedule 1AA to the Taxes Management Act 1970, hereby make the following Regulations:

Citation and commencement

1 These Regulations may be cited as the Orders for the Delivery of Documents (Procedure) Regulations 2000 and shall come into force on 13th November 2000.

Interpretation

2 In these Regulations—

"the appropriate judicial authority" has the meaning given by section 20D(1) of the Management Act;

"the Board" means the Commissioners of Inland Revenue;

"the court" has the meaning given by paragraph 9(2) of Schedule 1AA to the Management Act;

"items subject to legal privilege" has the meaning given by paragraph 5(2) of Schedule 1AA to the Management Act;

"the Management Act" means the Taxes Management Act 1970;

"notice of application" means the notice of intention to apply for an order to which a person is entitled under paragraph 3(1) of Schedule 1AA to the Management Act;

"order" means an order under section 20BA of the Management Act;

"working day" means any day other than a Saturday, Sunday or public holiday.

Approval of decision to apply for an order

3 Before the hearing of an application for an order, an officer of the Board who is a member of the Senior Civil Service in—

(*a*) the Cross-Cutting Policy branch of the Inland Revenue, or

(*b*) the Special Compliance Office of the Inland Revenue,

must approve in writing the decision to apply for that order.

Notice of application

4—(1) Notice of application must be given in writing and must contain the following details—

(*a*) the date, time and place of the hearing of the application;

(*b*) the specifications or descriptions of documents which are the subject of the application;

(*c*) a description of the suspected offence to which the application relates; and

(*d*) the name of the person suspected of committing, having committed or being about to commit the suspected offence.

(2) Notice of application must be given to the person entitled to it not less than five working days before the hearing of the application.

Notice of an order, or notice of application, treated as having been given

5—(1) Where notice of an order, or notice of application, is delivered to a person, or left at his proper address, notice shall be treated as having been given to that person on the day on which it is delivered or left or, where that day is not a working day, on the next working day.

(2) Where notice of application, or notice of an order, is sent to a person's proper address by facsimile transmission or other similar means which produce a document containing a text of the communication, notice shall be treated as given when the text is received in a legible form.

(3) For the purposes of this regulation, a person's proper address is—

(*a*) the usual or last known place of residence, or the place of business or employment, of that person; or

(*b*) in the case of a company, the address of the company's registered office; or

(*c*) in the case of a liquidator of a company, the liquidator's address for the purposes of the liquidation.

Complying with an order

6—(1) A person complies with an order by producing the documents specified or described in the order to the officer of the Board specified in the order within—

(*a*) the period mentioned in section 20BA(2) of the Management Act; or

(*b*) such further period, if any, as is agreed with that officer.

(2) For the purposes of paragraph (1), documents are produced to an officer of the Board if they are either—

(*a*) delivered to the officer; or

(*b*) left for the officer at an address specified in the relevant order.

(3) Where documents are sent to an officer of the Board at the address specified in the relevant order by post, they shall be treated, unless the contrary is proved, as having been produced to the officer—

(*a*) if first class post is used, on the second working day after posting;

(*b*) if second class post is used, on the fourth working day after posting.

Resolution of disputes as to legal privilege

7—(1) This regulation applies where there is a dispute between the Board and a person against whom an order has been made as to whether a document, or part of a document, is an item subject to legal privilege.

(2) The person against whom an order has been made may apply to the appropriate judicial authority to resolve the dispute.

(3) All the documents to which an application under paragraph (2) relates must be lodged in the court at the same time as the application is made and shall be held by the court until the appropriate judicial authority resolves the dispute.

(4) The court shall give the Board notice of an application made under paragraph (2) not less than five working days before the hearing of the application, and the Board shall be entitled to appear and be heard at that hearing in addition to the person making the application.

(5) On the hearing of an application made under paragraph (2), the appropriate judicial authority shall—

(*a*) resolve the dispute by confirming whether the document, or part of the document, is or is not an item subject to legal privilege; and

(*b*) order the costs of the application to be met by the Board except where it holds that no document, or no part of any document, to which the application relates is an item subject to legal privilege.

(6) Where a person makes an application under paragraph (2) within the period mentioned in regulation 6(1), he shall be treated as having complied with the order in relation to the documents to which the application relates until the appropriate judicial authority resolves the dispute.

(7) A dispute may be resolved at any time by the Board and the person against whom an order has been made reaching an agreement, whether in writing or otherwise, and, for all purposes, the consequences of such an agreement shall be the same as those which would have ensued if, at the time when the agreement was reached, the appropriate judicial authority had resolved the dispute.

2000/3158
Controlled Foreign Companies (Designer Rate Tax Provisions) Regulations 2000

Made by the Commissioners of Inland Revenue under TA 1988 s 750A(2) to (4)

Made . . . . 29 November 2000
Laid before the House of Commons . . . . 29 November 2000
Coming into force . . . . 20 December 2000

Commentary—*Simon's Direct Tax Service* **U6.6848, D4.1205.**

Citation, commencement and effect

1—(1) These Regulations may be cited as the Controlled Foreign Companies (Designer Rate Tax Provisions) Regulations 2000 and shall come into force on 20th December 2000.

(2) These Regulations have effect in relation to any accounting period of a company resident outside the United Kingdom which begins on or after 6th October 1999.

Interpretation

2 In these Regulations "the Board" means the Commissioners of Inland Revenue.

Specified designer rate tax provisions

3 For the purposes of section 750A(1) of the Income and Corporation Taxes Act 1988 (deemed lower level of taxation—designer rate tax provisions) the following provisions are specified, being provisions which appear to the Board to be designed to enable companies to exercise significant control over the amount of tax which they pay—

(*a*) the provisions contained in Part XVIIA (international bodies) of the Income Tax (Guernsey) Law, 1975;

(*b*) Article 123B (international business companies) of the Income Tax (Jersey) Law 1961;

(*c*) the provisions contained in Part 1 (International Companies) of the Isle of Man International Business Act 1994, and the provisions contained in Part 3 (Miscellaneous and Supplemental) of that Act so far as relating to Part 1 of that Act;

(*d*) section 41 (rates for qualifying companies) of the Gibraltar Income Tax Ordinance.

2000/3315
Exchange Gains and Losses (Miscellaneous Modifications) Regulations 2000

Made by the Treasury under FA 1993 ss 164(14), 167(1), (4)–(6) and Schs 15, 16 and FA 1998 s 63

Made . . . . 18 December 2000
Laid before the House of Commons . . . . 19 December 2000
Coming into force . . . . 9 January 2001

Commentary—*Simon's Direct Tax Service* **B3.1716, U6.6849.**

Modifications—See the Exchange Gains and Losses (Transitional Provisions and Savings) Regulations, SI 2002/1969 (SI 2000/3315, as modified by SI 2002/1969 to continue to have effect notwithstanding the repeal, with effect for accounting periods beginning after 30 September 2002, of FA 1993 ss 164(14), 167(1), (4)–(6), Schs 15, 16 by FA 2002 ss 79(1)(*b*), 141, Sch 40 Pt 3(10)).

Citation, commencement and effect

1—(1) These Regulations may be cited as the Exchange Gains and Losses (Miscellaneous Modifications) Regulations 2000 and shall come into force on 9th January 2001.

(2) Regulations 2 to 10 shall have effect in relation to any accounting period of a company beginning on or after 1st January 2000 for which sections 105 and 106 of the Finance Act 2000 have effect.

Modification of the Exchange Gains and Losses (Transitional Provisions) Regulations 1994

2–5 (*Modified* the Exchange Gains and Losses (Transitional Provisions) Regulations, SI 1994/3226 regs 17, 18, 22; *repealed by* the Exchange Gains and Losses (Transitional Provisions and Savings) Regulations, SI 2002/1969 regs 28, 29 with effect for accounting periods beginning after 30 September 2002.)

Modification of the Exchange Gains and Losses (Alternative Method of Calculation of Gain or Loss) Regulations 1994

6–9 (*Modify* Exchange Gains and Losses (Alternative Method of Calculation of Gain or Loss) Regulations, SI 1994/3226 regs 4, 5, 10.)

Revocation of the European Single Currency (Taxes) Regulations 1998

10 Part X of the European Single Currency (Taxes) Regulations 1998 is revoked to the extent that it is not previously revoked.

Modification of the effect of section 146 of the Finance Act 1993

11 ...

Amendment—Regulation 11 repealed by the Exchange Gains and Losses (Transitional Provisions and Savings) Regulations, SI 2002/1969 regs 28, 30 with effect for accounting periods beginning after 30 September 2002.

2001/56

Income Tax (Electronic Communications) (Incentive Payments) Regulations 2001

Made by the Commissioners of Inland Revenue under FA 2000 s 143(1) and Sch 38

Made	*11 January 2001*
Laid before the House of Commons	*11 January 2001*
Coming into force	*1 February 2001*

Commentary—*Simon's Direct Tax Service* **E1.806, E1.820, E4.954, E4.965.**

Citation, commencement and effect

1—(1) These Regulations may be cited as the Income Tax (Electronic Communications) (Incentive Payments) Regulations 2001 and shall come into force on 1st February 2001.

(2) Nothing in these Regulations affects the operation of the Electronic Lodgement of Tax Returns Order 1997 or the Income Tax (Electronic Communications) Regulations 2000.

Interpretation

2 In these Regulations—

''the Board'' means the Commissioners of Inland Revenue;

''employer'' means any person paying emoluments;

''Employments Regulations'' means the Income Tax (Employments) Regulations 1993;

''incentive payment'' means a payment by way of an incentive to use electronic communications for the delivery of information under regulation 3, 4 or 5;

''the Management Act'' means the Taxes Management Act 1970;

''tax credit'' means working families' tax credit or, as the case may be, disabled person's tax credit.

Incentive payment—return under sections 8 and 9 of the Management Act

3—(1) The Board shall make an incentive payment in the amount of £10 to any individual who—

(*a*) makes and delivers a return under sections 8 and 9 of the Management Act for a year of assessment using electronic communications, and

(*b*) satisfies the conditions specified in any direction given by the Board under paragraph (2).

(2) The Board may give a direction specifying any or all of the following conditions—

(*a*) a condition that the year of assessment for which the return is to be made and delivered is one specified in the direction,

(*b*) a condition specifying the form of electronic communication by which the return is to be delivered, (*c*) a condition that the individual by whom the return is to be made and delivered is one who is authorised to use the form of electronic communication specified in the direction,

(*d*) a condition that where the individual by whom the return is made and delivered becomes liable to pay an amount by way of income tax for the year of assessment concerned, the payment or, if more than one, at least one of the payments, made by him in meeting that liability is made using one of the forms of electronic payment specified in the direction,

(*e*) a condition that the return is made and delivered using the form of electronic communication specified in the direction,

(*f*) a condition that the return is made and delivered by the individual on or before the day mentioned in section 8(1A) of the Management Act,

(*g*) a condition that any amount payable by way of income tax by the individual for the year of assessment concerned is paid in accordance with the provisions for payment of income tax contained in sections 59A and 59B of the Management Act.

(3) Where an officer of the Board considers that the individual has failed to satisfy one or more of the conditions specified in the direction, he may give notice to the individual that the conditions are not met or, where the incentive payment has already been authorised or made, notice withdrawing the incentive payment.

(4) Where prior to the giving of a notice under paragraph (3) an incentive payment has already been made to the individual, an officer of the Board may recover the amount of the incentive payment in accordance with paragraph (5).

(5) For the purposes of paragraph (4), subsections (1), (4), (5) and (6) of section 30 of the Management Act (recovery of overpayment of tax, etc) and section 30A of that Act (assessing procedure) shall apply as if the amount of the incentive payment to be recovered were an amount of income tax repaid to that individual which ought not to have been repaid to him.

(6) The Board may give a direction relating to appeals against notices under paragraph (3) and appeals against assessments made in pursuance of paragraph (5).

Incentive payment—return under regulation 43 of the Employments Regulations

4—(1) The Board [shall][1] make an incentive payment in the amount of £50 to any employer who—

(*a*) renders a return under regulation 43 of the Employments Regulations for a year of assessment using electronic communications, and

(*b*) satisfies the conditions specified in any direction given by the Board under paragraph (2).

(2) The Board may give a direction specifying any or all of the following conditions—

(*a*) a condition that the year of assessment for which the return is to be rendered is one specified in the direction;

(*b*) a condition specifying the form of electronic communication by which the return is to be rendered,

(*c*) a condition that the employer by whom the return is to be rendered is one who is authorised to use the form of electronic communication specified in the direction,

(*d*) a condition that at least one of the payments made by the employer under regulation 40 or 41 of the Employments Regulations in the year of assessment concerned is made using one of the forms of electronic payment specified in the direction,

(*e*) a condition that the return is rendered by the employer, or by an agent of the employer authorised to render the return, using the form of electronic communication specified in the direction,

(*f*) a condition that, where the return is rendered by the employer's agent on the employer's behalf—

(i) the employer has registered online to use the form of electronic communication specified in the direction,

(ii) the employer has used that form of electronic communication to notify the Board of his agent's name and address, and

(iii) his agent is authorised by him to render the return on his behalf and to use that form of electronic communication,

(*g*) a condition that the return is rendered not later than the end of the period mentioned in regulation 43(1) of the Employments Regulations,

(*h*) a condition that each of the payments required to be made by the employer under regulation 40 or 41 for the year of assessment concerned is made not later than the end of the period mentioned in regulation 40(1) or, as the case may be, regulation 41(1).

(3) Where an officer of the Board considers that the employer has failed to satisfy one or more of the conditions specified in the direction, he may give notice to the employer that the conditions are not met or, where the incentive payment has already been authorised or made, notice withdrawing the incentive payment.

(4) Where prior to the giving of a notice under paragraph (3) an incentive payment has already been made to the employer, an officer of the Board may recover the amount of the incentive payment in accordance with paragraph (5).

(5) For the purposes of paragraph (4), subsections (1), (4), (5) and (6) of section 30 of the Management Act and section 30A of that Act shall apply as if the amount of the incentive payment to be recovered were an amount of income tax repaid to a person which ought not to have been repaid to him.

(6) The Board may give a direction relating to appeals against notices under paragraph (3) and appeals against assessments made in pursuance of paragraph (5).

Amendments—[1] Word substituted by the Income Tax (Electronic Communications) (Miscellaneous Amendments) Regulations, SI 2001/1081 reg 22 with effect from 9 April 2001.

Incentive payment—return of payments of tax credit

5—(1) The Board shall make an incentive payment in the amount of £50 to any employer who—

(*a*) pays tax credit to one or more of his employees during a year of assessment,

(*b*) in accordance with regulation 6(7) of the Tax Credits (Payment by Employers) Regulations 1999 records on the certificate contained in a return under regulation 43 of the Employments Regulations the total tax credit paid to his employees for that year,

(*c*) renders that return using electronic communications, and

(*d*) satisfies the conditions specified in any direction given by the Board under paragraph (2).

(2) The Board may give a direction specifying any or all of the following conditions—

(*a*) a condition that the year of assessment for which the return is to be rendered is one specified in the direction,

(*b*) a condition specifying the form of electronic communication by which the return is to be rendered,

(*c*) a condition that the employer by whom the return is to be rendered is one who is authorised to use the form of electronic communication specified in the direction,

(*d*) a condition that the employer satisfies each of the conditions specified in a direction made under regulation 4(2) of these Regulations,

(*e*) a condition that the employer has paid tax credit in the year of assessment concerned in accordance with regulation 6 of the Tax Credits (Payment by Employers) Regulations 1999 (obligation to pay tax credit on paying emoluments to employees entitled to tax credit).

(3) Where an officer of the Board considers that the employer has failed to satisfy one or more of the conditions specified in the direction, he may give notice to the employer that the conditions are not met or, where the incentive payment has already been authorised or made, notice withdrawing the incentive payment.

(4) Where prior to the giving of a notice under paragraph (3) an incentive payment has already been made to the employer, an officer of the Board may recover the amount of the incentive payment in accordance with paragraph (5).

(5) For the purposes of paragraph (4), subsections (1), (4), (5) and (6) of section 30 of the Management Act and section 30A of that Act shall apply as if the amount of the incentive payment to be recovered were an amount of income tax repaid to a person which ought not to have been repaid to him.

(6) The Board may give a direction relating to appeals against notices under paragraph (3) and appeals against assessments made in pursuance of paragraph (5).

2001/117

Personal Pension Schemes (Restriction on Discretion to Approve) (Permitted Investments) Regulations 2001

Made by the Commissioners of Inland Revenue under TA 1988 s 638A

Made	*23 January 2001*
Laid before the House of Commons	*24 January 2001*
Coming into force	*6 April 2001*

Citation and commencement

1 These Regulations may be cited as the Personal Pension Schemes (Restriction on Discretion to Approve) (Permitted Investments) Regulations 2001 and shall come into force on 6th April 2001.

Interpretation

2—(1) In these Regulations unless the context otherwise requires—

"approved pension arrangement" means a pension scheme—

(*a*) which is an "approved pension arrangement" as defined in section 660A(11), and

(*b*) under which all the benefits that may be provided are money purchase benefits;

"authorised unit trust scheme" means a unit trust scheme in the case of which an order under section [243 of the Financial Services and Markets Act 2000][1] is in force;

"the Board" means the Commissioners of Inland Revenue;

"commercial property" includes land;

"company" means any body corporate or unincorporated association, but does not include a partnership;

"depositary interest" means the rights of the person mentioned in paragraph (*b*) of this definition under a certificate or other record (whether or not in the form of a document) which acknowledges—

(*a*) that a person holds relevant investments or evidence of the right to them, and

(*b*) that another person is entitled to rights in or in relation to those or identical relevant investments, including the right to receive such investments, or evidence of the right to them or the proceeds from such investments, from the person mentioned in paragraph (*a*);

"deposit-taker" has the meaning given by section 481(2);

"EEA Agreement" means the Agreement on the European Economic Area signed at Oporto on 2nd May 1992, as adjusted by the Protocol signed at Brussels on 17th March 1993;

"EEA State" means a State, other than the United Kingdom, which is a Contracting Party to the EEA Agreement;

"employee" includes the holder of an office;

"employer" in relation to a scheme—

(*a*) means an employer who, by virtue of the governing instrument, is entitled to pay contributions to the scheme, and

(*b*) includes a person under whom an office is held;

"feeder fund" means a feeder fund within the meaning (and complying with the requirements) of paragraph 2 of Part I of Schedule 1 to the Personal Pension Schemes (Appropriate Schemes) Regulations 1997 (including a constituent part of an umbrella personal pension unit trust which is regarded as a feeder fund for the purposes of those Regulations);

"governing instrument" in relation to a scheme means a trust deed, or other document by which the scheme is established, and any other document which contains provisions by which the administration of the scheme is governed;

"insurance company" has the meaning given by section 431(2);

"investment company with variable capital" has the meaning given by regulation 3(2) of the Open-Ended Investment Companies (Investment Companies with Variable Capital) Regulations 1996;

"member" in relation to—

(*a*) a personal pension scheme has the meaning given by section 630(1),

(*b*) an approved pension arrangement falling within Chapter I of Part XIV of the Taxes Act, has the same meaning as "scheme member" in section 611(6)(*a*) and (*b*), and

(*c*) an approved pension arrangement approved under Chapter III of Part XIV of the Taxes Act, means an individual referred to in section 618(2);

"open-ended investment company" except in relation to the phrase "qualifying EEA open-ended investment company"—

(*a*) has the meaning given by section 468(10), and

(*b*) also includes a UCITS situated in a member state other than the United Kingdom which has been authorised by the competent authorities of that member state and is a recognised scheme;

"personal pension scheme" has the meaning given by section 630(1), and "scheme" shall be construed accordingly;

"personal pension unit trust" means a personal pension scheme which is an authorised unit trust scheme of a kind mentioned in Part I of Schedule 1 to the Personal Pension Schemes (Appropriate Schemes) Regulations 1997;

"pooled fund" in relation to a personal pension scheme means a fund—

(*a*) which is open to the public and is described in the documents relating to the scheme as being a fund open to all members,

(*b*) in relation to the management of which the scheme administrator is not required to consult with any member of the scheme except to the extent that an investment offers choices that are available to any person (whether or not a member of the scheme), and

(*c*) the value of which is applied to all members and not segregated among certain members or linked to certain members by reason of particular assets comprised in the fund;

"qualifying EEA investment company" means a company—

(*a*) which is formed under the law of an EEA State and complies with the requirements specified in section 266(2) of the Companies Act 1985,

(*b*) which may lawfully offer its shares to the public in an EEA State, and

(*c*) in relation to which, on the basis of its last published annual accounts, the ratio between the company's loan capital and the value of its ordinary shares is 50 per cent or less;

"qualifying EEA open-ended investment company" means an open-ended investment company within the meaning given by section 75(8) of the Financial Services Act 1986 which—

(*a*) is formed under the law of an EEA State,

(*b*) is not a UCITS, and

(*c*) may lawfully offer its shares to the public in an EEA State;

"qualifying UK investment company" means an investment company within the meaning of section 266 of the Companies Act 1985—

(*a*) which is incorporated in the United Kingdom, and

(*b*) in relation to which, on the basis of its last published accounts, the ratio between the company's loan capital and the value of its ordinary shares is 50 per cent or less;

"recognised futures exchange" has the meaning given by section 288(6) of the Taxation of Chargeable Gains Act 1992;

"recognised scheme" has the meaning given by section 86 of the Financial Services Act 1986;

"recognised stock exchange" has the meaning given by section 841;

"relevant investments" in relation to the definition of "depositary interest" means investments listed in the Schedule to these Regulations as investments which are permitted to be held by a self-invested personal pension scheme;

"residential property" means property normally used, or adapted for use, as one or more dwellings;

"scheme administrator" means the person referred to in section 638(1);

"self-invested personal pension scheme" has the meaning given by regulation 3;

"the Taxes Act" means the Income and Corporation Taxes Act 1988;

"UCITS" means an undertaking for collective investment in transferable securities within the meaning of Article 1 of [Council Directive 85/611/EEC, as last amended by European Parliament and Council Directive 2001/108/EC][2];

"umbrella personal pension unit trust" means a personal pension unit trust which is constituted as an umbrella fund within the meaning of the Financial Services (Regulated Schemes) Regulations 1991;

"unauthorised unit trust" has the meaning given by paragraph 2(4) of Schedule 10 to the Finance Act 1996;

"unit trust scheme" has the meaning given by section 75(8) of the Financial Services Act 1986;

"51 per cent subsidiary" has the meaning given by section 838.

(2) For the purposes of these Regulations and subject to paragraph (3), any question whether a person is connected with another person shall be determined in accordance with section 839.

(3) A person shall not be regarded as connected with another person for the purposes of these Regulations where the connection arises as a result of a transaction entered into in the course of normal investment management by a scheme in relation to a fund that is a pooled fund.

(4) References in these Regulations to a freehold or leasehold interest in commercial or residential property include, as respects Scotland, the estate or interest of the proprietor of the dominium utile or, in the case of property other than feudal property, of the owner of such property, and the interest of a tenant in such property subject to a lease.

(5) In these Regulations references to a particular provision, without more, are references to that provision of the Taxes Act.

Amendments—[1] In para (1), words in the definition of "authorised unit trust scheme" substituted by the Financial Services and Markets Act 2000 (Consequential Amendments) (Taxes) Order, SI 2001/3629 art 189 with effect from 1 December 2001, immediately after the coming into force of the Financial Services and Markets Act 2000 ss 411, 432(1), Sch 20 (and SI 2001/3629 Pts 1 and 2).

[2] In para (1), words in the definition of "UCITS" substituted by the Collective Investment Schemes (Miscellaneous Amendments) Regulations, SI 2003/2066 reg 13(6) with effect from 13 February 2004.

Definition of self-invested personal pension scheme

3—(1) In these Regulations "self-invested personal pension scheme" means a personal pension scheme the arrangements made in accordance with which by a member—

(*a*) are arrangements under which the member is able to direct the manner in which some or all of the contributions paid to the scheme are to be invested by the scheme administrator, and

(*b*) are not arrangements falling within paragraph (2).

(2) Arrangements fall within this paragraph if they are either—

(*a*) arrangements under which—

(i) all the investments held for the purposes of the scheme comprise contracts or policies of insurance, units in unit trust schemes or shares in open-ended investment companies, and

(ii) in managing those investments, the scheme administrator does not consult with any member of the scheme except to the extent necessary by virtue of the investment offering choices that are available to any person (whether or not a member of the scheme); or

(*b*) arrangements under which—

(i) all contributions paid are, after deduction of expenses, invested in deposits with deposit-takers, and

(ii) the payment of interest on those deposits comprises the only income of the scheme from its investments.

Definition of individual pension account

4—(1) For the purposes of regulations 6(2) and 7(4) ''individual pension account'' means an account within which investments may be held and which satisfies the following conditions.

(2) The first condition is that the funds of the account consist only of—

(*a*) monies received from the trustees, managers or administrators of approved pension arrangements, or monies held for the purposes of approved pension arrangements that are designated to be held within the account, and

(*b*) income and gains arising from those monies when held as funds of the account.

(3) The second condition is that any monies so received consist of one or more of the following—

(*a*) contributions to an approved pension arrangement by a member, or the employer of a member, of that approved pension arrangement,

(*b*) amounts transferred to an approved pension arrangement from another approved pension arrangement,

(*c*) minimum contributions referred to in section 638(6)(*c*),

(*d*) minimum payments within the meaning given by section 8(2) of the Pension Schemes Act 1993.

(4) The third condition is that the funds and other assets of the account—

(*a*) are held—

(i) by the trustees, managers or administrators of the approved pension arrangements whose members subscribe to the account as account holders, and

(ii) on behalf of the individual account holders as beneficial owners subject to the account rules, or

(*b*) in the case of assets consisting of units in a personal pension unit trust or, where the personal pension unit trust is an umbrella personal pension unit trust, in the respective parts of the umbrella personal pension unit trust—

(i) are registered in the names of the individual account holders, and

(ii) are issued subject to the terms of the trust deed and the rules constituting the personal pension unit trust.

(5) The fourth condition is that the funds and other assets of the account are used only to provide benefits for individual account holders under approved pension arrangements and subject to the limits and rules of those approved pension arrangements.

(6) The fifth condition is that the assets of the account, other than cash awaiting investment, consist of one or more of the following investments—

(*a*) units in an authorised unit trust scheme or in a unit trust scheme that is a recognised scheme,

(*b*) shares in a qualifying EEA open-ended investment company,

(*c*) units in a UCITS formed under the laws of a member state other than the United Kingdom which has been authorised by the competent authorities of that member state and is a recognised scheme,

(*d*) shares in a body corporate which is a qualifying UK investment company,

(*e*) shares in a body corporate which is a qualifying EEA investment company,

(*f*) shares in an investment company with variable capital, and

(*g*) investments falling within paragraph 3 of Part I of Schedule I to the Financial Services Act 1986 (Government and public securities).

(7) The sixth condition is that, where monies are received by the account that comprise an individual's investment in more than one approved pension arrangement, the amount relating to each approved pension arrangement is separately identified by the administrator of the account.

(8) The seventh condition is that, whenever required to do so by an officer of the Board, the administrator of the account has provided to that officer the following information—

(*a*) the names of individuals who are the account holders,

(*b*) details of the approved pension arrangements of which those individuals are members,

(*c*) the amount of the funds, and the description and value of the assets, held on behalf of each account holder,

(*d*) the amount of income and gains accruing to each account holder from funds and assets held on that individual's behalf,

(*e*) transfers of funds to another individual pension account on behalf of an account holder.

(9) The eighth condition is that, whenever required to do so by an officer of the Board, the administrator of the account has enabled that officer to audit and inspect all aspects of the management and administration of the account, including records and systems relating to the management or administration of the account.

(10) The reference in paragraph (6)(*a*) to units in an authorised unit trust scheme, where the authorised unit trust scheme is an umbrella personal pension unit trust that is constituted as a feeder fund or comprises feeder funds, comprises both the units in the feeder fund or feeder funds that are issued to the individual account holder and the underlying units held by the feeder fund or feeder funds.

Restrictions on discretion to approve—general

5 Regulations 6 to 10 impose, subject to regulation 11, restrictions on the Board's discretion to approve personal pension schemes under Chapter IV of Part XIV of the Taxes Act.

Restriction on investments—self-invested personal pension schemes

6—(1) No investments may be held directly or indirectly for the purposes of a self-invested personal pension scheme other than the investments listed in the Schedule to these Regulations.

(2) Investments listed in the Schedule that are also specified in regulation 4(6) may be held within an individual pension account.

(3) Subject to paragraphs (4) to (8), no amount may be borrowed by a self-invested personal pension scheme for any purpose.

(4) A self-invested personal pension scheme may borrow an amount towards the purchase of a freehold or leasehold interest in commercial property to be held directly or indirectly as an investment for the purposes of the scheme, or towards the development of commercial property held directly or indirectly as an investment for the purposes of the scheme, but the amount borrowed—

(*a*) must not exceed 75 per cent of the purchase price of the property concerned, or 75 per cent of the costs of any development,

(*b*) must be secured only on that property or on any other asset of the scheme, and

(*c*) where the property is subsequently sold, must be repaid on completion of the sale of the property.

(5) A self-invested personal pension scheme may borrow an amount to defray any liability to VAT arising on the purchase or development of commercial property in accordance with paragraph (4), but the period over which the amount is borrowed must not exceed—

(*a*) the period commencing on the date on which the purchase or development of the property is completed and ending on the day that is 12 weeks after that date, or

(*b*) the period commencing on the date on which the purchase or development of the property is completed and ending on the day on which the amount of the liability to VAT is refunded to the purchaser,

whichever is the shorter.

(6) A self-invested personal pension scheme may borrow an amount ("a replacement loan") to replace a loan falling within paragraph (4).

(7) The amount of a replacement loan must not exceed the amount outstanding, as at the date on which the replacement loan is made, of the loan that is replaced.

(8) In this regulation—

(*a*) references to the purchase price of commercial property include references to legal and other costs incidental to the purchase of the property;

(*b*) references to the development of commercial property include references to—

(i) the erection of, or extensions to, buildings, or

(ii) the refurbishment or renovation of, or any other improvements to, buildings.

Restriction on investments—personal pension schemes other than self-invested personal pension schemes

7—(1) This regulation applies to personal pension schemes other than self-invested personal pension schemes.

(2) None of the assets specified in paragraph (3) may be held directly or indirectly as an investment by a personal pension scheme.

(3) The assets specified in this paragraph are—

(*a*) any personal chattels other than choses in action (or, in Scotland, any movable property other than incorporeal movable property);

(*b*) any residential property other than that specified in paragraph (5).

(4) Assets which a personal pension scheme is not restricted under paragraph (2) or (3) from holding as an investment and which are also specified in regulation 4(6) may be held within an individual pension account.

(5) The residential property specified in this paragraph is—

(*a*) property which is, or is to be, occupied by an employee, whether or not a member of the personal pension scheme or connected with a member of the scheme, who is not connected with his employer and is required as a condition of his employment to occupy the property, and

(*b*) property which is, or is to be, occupied by a person who is neither a member of the personal pension scheme nor connected with a member of the scheme in connection with the occupation by that person of business premises held as an investment by the scheme.

(6) For the purposes of paragraphs (2) and (3), a personal pension scheme shall not be regarded as indirectly holding as an investment residential property where the scheme holds as an investment units in a unit trust scheme that holds residential property and—

(*a*) is an authorised unit trust scheme or a recognised scheme, or
(*b*) is an unauthorised unit trust whose gains are not chargeable gains by virtue of section 100(2) of the Taxation of Chargeable Gains Act 1992.

(7) For the purposes of paragraphs (2) and (3), a personal pension scheme shall not be regarded as indirectly holding as an investment residential property where—

(*a*) the scheme holds as an investment a right which confers entitlement to receive payment of any ground rent, rentcharge, ground annual, feu duty or other annual payment reserved in respect of, or charged on or issuing out of, that property, and
(*b*) the property is not occupied by a member of the scheme or a person connected with him.

Restrictions on lending

8—(1) A self-invested personal pension scheme may not lend money to any person (whether or not that person is an individual who is a member of the scheme).

(2) A personal pension scheme that is not a self-invested personal pension scheme may not lend money to a member of the scheme or a person connected with him.

(3) A personal pension scheme shall be regarded, for the purposes of paragraphs (1) and (2), as lending money to a member of the scheme or a person connected with him in circumstances where—

(*a*) the scheme holds as an investment, whether directly or indirectly, assets of a person,
(*b*) that person lends money to the member concerned or a person connected with him, and
(*c*) the loan has the effect of limiting or reducing in any way the return on the investment.

Restrictions on transactions with scheme member and others

9—(1) Subject to paragraphs (2) and (3), no interest in an asset may be acquired by a personal pension scheme in circumstances where a member of that scheme, or a person connected with him, has an interest in that asset or, at any time in the period of three years prior to the date of the acquisition, had an interest in that asset.

(2) Paragraph (1) does not apply in relation to the transfer of eligible shares in a company in accordance with section 638(9) and (12).

(3) Paragraph (1) does not apply in relation to the acquisition at market value by a self-invested personal pension scheme (''scheme A'') of an interest in commercial property in which another self-invested personal pension scheme (''scheme B'') also has an interest in circumstances where—

(*a*) the commercial property is leased by scheme A to—
(i) the member of scheme A for the purposes of a trade or profession carried on by him, whether or not in partnership with another person or persons, or
(ii) a company which is connected with the member of scheme A, for the purposes of a business carried on by the company,
(*b*) the lease is granted on normal commercial terms,
(*c*) the amount of the rent payable under the lease accords with a commercial rate and is supported by an independent professional valuation, and
(*d*) either—
(i) the member of scheme A is, or becomes within a reasonable time after the acquisition by scheme A of the interest in the commercial property, a partner in a partnership carrying on the trade or profession in question, and the member of scheme B is also a partner in that partnership, or
(ii) the member of scheme A is, or becomes within a reasonable time after that acquisition, a director of the company to whom the commercial property is leased, and the member of scheme B is also a director of that company.

(4) Except in the circumstances specified in paragraphs (3) and (5), no interest in an asset may directly or indirectly be sold or leased by a personal pension scheme to a member or a person connected with him.

(5) Commercial property an interest in which is acquired at market value by a self-invested personal pension scheme otherwise than in a case to which paragraph (1) applies may, subject to the conditions specified in paragraph (6), be leased by the scheme to—

(*a*) the member for the purposes of a trade or profession carried on by him, whether or not in partnership with another person or persons, or
(*b*) a company which is connected with the member, for the purposes of a business carried on by the company.

(6) The conditions specified in this paragraph are that—

(*a*) the lease is granted on normal commercial terms, and
(*b*) the amount of the rent payable under the lease accords with a commercial rate and is supported by an independent professional valuation.

(7) For the purposes of paragraph (4) a sale by the scheme shall not be regarded as a sale indirectly to a member, or a person connected with him, if the purchase by the member or the person connected with him took place three years or more after the sale by the scheme.

(8) In paragraphs (3) and (5) ''business'' means a trade, profession or any other activity carried on by the company except the activity of making or managing investments unless—

(*a*) those investments consist wholly of shares in 51 per cent subsidiaries of the company, and

(*b*) those subsidiaries do not themselves carry on the activity of making or managing investments.

(9) In this regulation ''market value'' means the price which the interest in the commercial property might reasonably be expected to fetch on a sale in the open market.

Restrictions on investments relating to members of self-invested personal pension schemes

10—(1) A self-invested personal pension scheme may not set up after the pension date of a member of the scheme either—

(*a*) a borrowing arrangement for that member, or

(*b*) in the case of a serialised borrowing arrangement in existence at the time of the pension date, a further instalment of the loan for that member.

(2) Paragraph (1) applies notwithstanding that the purpose of the borrowing arrangement or, as the case may be, the further instalment of the loan would be to acquire particular investments in accordance with the member's direction.

(3) No commercial property may be acquired by a self-invested personal pension scheme in respect of a member of the scheme after the member's pension date or his attaining the age of 65, whichever is the later.

(4) In paragraphs (1) and (2) ''pension date'' has the meaning given by section 630(1).

Schemes awaiting approval

11—(1) Where at the date of coming into force of these Regulations a personal pension scheme is in existence and either—

(*a*) has not yet been submitted to the Board for approval, or

(*b*) is before the Board for approval,

the Board shall not be prevented from approving it under Chapter IV of Part XIV of the Taxes Act by reason only that it contains a provision or provisions of a description specified in any of subparagraphs (*a*) to (*c*) of paragraph (2).

(2) The description of provisions specified in this paragraph is—

(*a*) a provision which authorises the scheme to retain as an investment an asset—

(i) which is held by the scheme immediately before the date on which these Regulations were made, and

(ii) the holding of which directly or indirectly as an investment would, by virtue of regulation 6 or 7, prevent the Board from approving the scheme;

(*b*) a provision which authorises the scheme to continue to lend money to a person in circumstances which, by virtue of regulation 8, would prevent the Board from approving the scheme;

(*c*) a provision which authorises the scheme to acquire, sell or lease any interest in an asset in circumstances which, by virtue of regulation 9, would prevent the Board from approving the scheme.

SCHEDULE

Regulation 6

LIST OF INVESTMENTS THAT MAY BE HELD DIRECTLY OR INDIRECTLY FOR THE PURPOSES OF A SELF-INVESTED PERSONAL PENSION SCHEME

1 Stocks and shares listed or dealt in on a recognised stock exchange.

2 Futures and options, relating to stocks and shares, traded on a recognised futures exchange.

3 Depositary interests.

4 Units in an authorised unit trust scheme.

5 Units in a unit trust scheme which—

(*a*) is an unauthorised unit trust whose gains are not chargeable gains by virtue of section 100(2) of the Taxation of Chargeable Gains Act 1992, and

(*b*) does not hold any freehold or leasehold interest in residential property other than that specified in paragraph 13 or 14 of this Schedule.

6 Eligible shares within the meaning of section 638(11) received by the self-invested personal pension scheme as contributions to the scheme.

7 Shares in an open-ended investment company.

8 Interests (however described) in a collective investment scheme that is either a recognised scheme or a designated scheme within the meaning of section 86 or 87 of the Financial Services Act 1986.

9 Contracts or policies of insurance linked to insurance company managed funds, unit-linked funds or investment funds of an insurance company resident in the United Kingdom or authorised in accordance with Article 6 of Council Directive 79/267 (First Council Directive on Direct Life Assurance).

10 Traded endowment policies transacted with a person regulated by the Financial Services Authority.

11 Deposits in any currency held in deposit accounts with any deposit-taker.

12 A freehold or leasehold interest in commercial property where the interest is acquired from any person other than a member of the scheme or a person connected with him, or the interest is acquired from a member of the scheme or a person connected with him in circumstances in which regulation 9(3) applies.

13 A freehold or leasehold interest in any residential property which is—

(*a*) property which is, or is to be, occupied by an employee, whether or not a member of the self-invested personal pension scheme or connected with a member of the scheme, who is not connected with his employer and is required as a condition of his employment to occupy the property, and

(*b*) property which is, or is to be, occupied by a person who is neither a member of the self-invested personal pension scheme nor connected with a member of the scheme in connection with the occupation by that person of business premises held as an investment by the scheme.

14 Ground rents, rent charges, ground annuals, feu duties or other annual payments reserved in respect of, or charged on or issuing out of, property, except where the property concerned is occupied by a member of the scheme or a person connected with him.

Commentary—*Simon's Direct Tax Service* **E7.405**.

2001/118
Personal Pension Schemes (Conversion of Retirement Benefits Schemes) Regulations 2001

Made by the Commissioners of Inland Revenue under TA 1988 Sch 23ZA paras 2 and 4

Made	*23 January 2001*
Laid before the House of Commons	*24 January 2001*
Coming into force	*6 April 2001*

Citation and commencement

1 These Regulations may be cited as the Personal Pension Schemes (Conversion of Retirement Benefits Schemes) Regulations 2001 and shall come into force on 6th April 2001.

Interpretation

2—(1) In these Regulations—

"administrator"—

(*a*) in relation to a retirement benefits scheme, has the meaning given by section 611AA and, in relation to a scheme which secures relevant benefits falling within section 591(2A) by means of an annuity contract, includes the insurance company with which the contract is made; and

(*b*) in relation to a personal pension scheme, means the person referred to in section 638(1);

"the Board" means the Commissioners of Inland Revenue;

"continuing member" means a person who—

(*a*) is a member of the eligible scheme which is the subject of the application under paragraph 3 of Schedule 23ZA; and

(*b*) is to remain a member of the scheme if it becomes a personal pension scheme;

"controlling director" means a person who is, or was within the ten years immediately preceding the date of the application under paragraph 3 of Schedule 23ZA, in relation to a relevant employer—

(*a*) a director (as defined in section 612(1)); and

(*b*) within paragraph (*b*) of section 417(5);

"conversion assets value" means the sum which has been calculated, within the period of three months ending with the date of the application under paragraph 3 of Schedule 23ZA, as representing a member's benefits under the retirement benefits scheme which is the subject of that application;

"conversion payment" means the amount to be held subject to a personal pension scheme representing an individual member's benefits at the date of change;

"date of change" has the meaning given in paragraph 3(2) of Schedule 23ZA;

"eligible scheme" means a retirement benefits scheme to which Schedule 23ZA applies;

"Part XIV" means Part XIV of the Taxes Act (pension schemes etc);
"permitted amount" has the meaning given by regulation 7(4);
"personal pension scheme" has the meaning given in section 630;
"prescribed member" means a person who falls within one or more of the classes prescribed by regulation 6;
"qualifying scheme" means a retirement benefits scheme which, if the conditions prescribed under paragraph 2(3)(*d*) of Schedule 23ZA were met, would be an eligible scheme;
"relevant employer" means an employer by reference to employment with whom a continuing member is entitled to benefits under the eligible scheme;
"relevant year" means the year of assessment in which the application for approval as a personal pension scheme is made;
"retirement benefits scheme" has the meaning given in section 611; and
"the Taxes Act" means the Income and Corporation Taxes Act 1988.

(2) In these Regulations, except where the context otherwise requires—

(*a*) a reference to a numbered regulation is a reference to the regulation bearing that number in these Regulations;
(*b*) a reference in a regulation to a numbered paragraph is a reference to the paragraph bearing that number in that regulation;
(*c*) a reference in a paragraph to a lettered sub-paragraph is a reference to the sub-paragraph bearing that letter in that paragraph; and
(*d*) a reference to a numbered section or Schedule is a reference to the section of, or Schedule to, the Taxes Act bearing that number.

Application to convert eligible scheme to personal pension scheme

3—(1) The trustees of a qualifying scheme may apply to the Board for approval of the scheme as a personal pension scheme if the conditions prescribed in paragraphs (2) and (3) are satisfied.

(2) The first condition is that regulation 7 (valuation of prescribed member's benefits) has been complied with in respect of each prescribed member of the scheme.

(3) The second condition is that the value of the fund of a prescribed member, who is to be a continuing member of the scheme, does not exceed the permitted amount.

Documents to accompany application

4—(1) An application for approval under paragraph 3 of Schedule 23ZA must—

(*a*) state the date from which the trustees propose the approval should have effect; and
(*b*) be accompanied by the statements specified in paragraph (2) and the documents specified in paragraph (3).

(2) The statements, which must be signed by or on behalf of the trustees, are—

(*a*) a statement that assets have been identified in respect of each continuing member's entitlement under the proposed personal pension scheme;
(*b*) a statement showing how the assets referred to in sub-paragraph (*a*) were identified; and
(*c*) a statement showing for each individual whom the trustees propose should be a continuing member, if approval is given, whether the whole of each asset so identified has been appropriated to that individual's personal pension fund and, if not, what part of the asset has been so appropriated.

(3) The documents are—

(*a*) a copy of the rules and other scheme instruments which the trustees propose should apply to the personal pension scheme if approval is given;
(*b*) the written consent, to the making of the application, of each relevant employer; and
(*c*) documents showing how the requirements of regulations 7 and 8 were satisfied.

Board's discretion to refuse approval—prescribed descriptions of retirement benefits scheme

5—(1) The descriptions of eligible scheme which are prescribed in respect of the Board's discretion to refuse approval under Schedule 23ZA are all descriptions of eligible scheme other than a simplified defined contribution scheme.

(2) In this regulation "simplified defined contribution scheme" has the meaning given by regulation 2 of the Retirement Benefits Schemes (Restriction on Discretion to Approve) (Additional Voluntary Contributions) Regulations 1993.

Board's discretion to refuse approval—prescribed classes of individual member

6—(1) The classes of individual member of an eligible scheme which are prescribed for the purposes of paragraph 4(1) of Schedule 23ZA are—

(*a*) in the case of a scheme of which a controlling director is to be a continuing member, the classes mentioned in paragraph (2); and
(*b*) in any other case, the class mentioned in paragraph (3).

(2) The classes referred to in paragraph (1)(*a*) are those comprising—

(*a*) controlling directors;

(*b*) persons who are connected with a person falling within sub-paragraph (*a*); and

(*c*) members of the scheme—

(i) whose age at the proposed date of change will be not less than 45 years; and

(ii) whose remuneration derived from their employment with the relevant employer is, or was, for any year of assessment falling (wholly or partly) during the period of six years prior to the date on which the application is made, more than the permitted maximum for the year of assessment in which the application is made.

(3) The class referred to in paragraph (1)(*b*) is that comprising members of the scheme—

(*a*) whose age at the proposed date of change will be not less than 45 years; and

(*b*) whose remuneration derived from employment with the relevant employer is, or was, for any year of assessment falling (wholly or partly) during the period of six years prior to the date on which the application is made, more than the permitted maximum for the year of assessment in which the application is made.

(4) For the purposes of paragraph (2) a person is connected with another if he is—

(*a*) that person's husband or wife;

(*b*) that person's brother, sister, parent or remoter forebear, child or remoter lineal descendant;

(*c*) the husband or wife of a brother, sister, parent or remoter forebear, child or remoter lineal descendant of that person; or

(*d*) a brother, sister, parent or remoter forebear, child or remoter lineal descendant of that person's husband or wife.

(5) In this regulation—

"permitted maximum" has the meaning given in section 590C(2); and

"remuneration" has the meaning given in section 612(1).

Valuation of prescribed member's benefits

7—(1) Before making an application for approval as a personal pension scheme, the trustees of a qualifying scheme shall ascertain whether the conversion assets value, in respect of any prescribed member to whom they intend the proposed personal pension scheme to apply, exceeds the permitted amount.

(2) The conversion assets value must be calculated in accordance with normal actuarial practice.

(3) If the conversion assets value in respect of a prescribed member exceeds the permitted amount, regulation 8 applies to that member.

(4) In these Regulations "the permitted amount" means the maximum amount as described in regulation 8(3) of the Personal Pension Schemes (Transfer Payments) Regulations 2001.

Prescribed members whose conversion assets value exceeds permitted amount

8—(1) If—

(*a*) this regulation applies to a prescribed member; and

(*b*) the Board have exercised their discretion under section 611(3) to treat the eligible scheme as two (or more) separate schemes;

the restriction in paragraph (2) applies to the prescribed member.

(2) The restriction is that the prescribed member may not become a member of the resultant personal pension scheme at the date of change, unless, before that date, the value of the prescribed member's fund, calculated in accordance with normal actuarial practice, is shown to be less than or equal to the permitted amount.

Restriction on discretion to approve—conversion of qualifying scheme

9—(1) The Board shall not approve a qualifying scheme as a personal pension scheme unless the proposed personal pension scheme complies with the restrictions imposed by regulations 10 and 11 in the case of an individual to whom paragraph (2) applies.

(2) This paragraph applies to an individual who is a controlling director and whom the trustees of the scheme which is the subject of the application under Schedule 23ZA intend should be a continuing member.

Restriction on discretion to approve—controlling directors' death benefits

10—(1) The restriction imposed by this regulation is that the accumulated value must be applied, after the death of a controlling director, in accordance with paragraph (3) or (4).

(2) In this regulation "the accumulated value" means the total of—

(*a*) the conversion payment; and

(*b*) any sum attributable to growth through investment of the conversion payment.

(3) If the controlling director has died before any benefits have been paid to him under the arrangements represented by the accumulated value, the accumulated value must be applied—

(*a*) wholly to secure the payment of an annuity which satisfies the conditions in section 636 (annuity after death of member);

(*b*) to secure the payment of income withdrawals with respect to which the conditions in section 636A (income withdrawals after death of member) are satisfied and, as to any amount not used for that purpose, to secure the payment of such an annuity as is referred to in sub-paragraph (*a*); or

(*c*) as to not more than 25%, to secure the payment of a lump sum and, as to the balance, to secure the payment of such an annuity as is referred to in sub-paragraph (*a*) or of such income withdrawals and annuity as are referred to in sub-paragraph (*b*).

This paragraph is subject to the qualification in paragraph (4).

(4) If the administrator of a personal pension scheme is satisfied, having taking all reasonable steps—

(*a*) that there is no surviving spouse to whom an annuity referred to in paragraph (3)(*a*), or income withdrawals referred to in paragraph (3)(*b*) can be paid; and

(*b*) if the arrangement so requires, that there is no dependant to whom such an annuity or income withdrawals can be paid;

the whole of the accumulated value may be applied to secure the payment of a lump sum.

Restrictions on discretion to approve—lump sum benefits to controlling directors under proposed personal pension scheme

11—(1) The restrictions imposed by this regulation are those specified in paragraphs (2) and (3).

(2) The restriction specified in this paragraph is that no amount may be paid to a controlling director by way of a lump sum on his pension date (as defined in section 630(1)) out of the conversion payment unless, within six months beginning with the date of change, the administrator of the retirement benefits scheme which is the subject of the application under Schedule 23ZA, has given such a lump sum certificate as would be required under the rules of the retirement benefits scheme if it were making a transfer payment to a personal pension scheme.

(3) The restriction specified in this paragraph is that the amount that may be paid by way of lump sum as mentioned in paragraph (2) shall not exceed the sum found by the formula in paragraph (4).

(4) The formula referred to in paragraph (3) is—

$$B \times EF$$

Here—

B is the amount shown in the certificate mentioned in paragraph (2); and

EF is the greater of 1 and the fraction in paragraph (5).

(5) The fraction referred to in paragraph (4) is—

$$\frac{R1}{R2}$$

Here—

R1 is the value of the retail prices index for the last month for which that index had been published at the date when the lump sum referred to in paragraph (2) was calculated; and

R2 is the value of that index for the last month for which that index had been published at the time of the approval by the Board of the application under Schedule 23ZA.

(6) The references in paragraph (5) to the retail prices index shall be construed in accordance with section 833(2) as if that paragraph were contained in the Income Tax Acts.

Commentary—*Simon's Direct Tax Service* **E7.240**, **E7.416**.

2001/119

Personal Pension Schemes (Transfer Payments) Regulations 2001

Made by the Commissioners of Inland Revenue under TA 1988 s 638(2) and (7A)

Made	*23 January 2001*
Laid before the House of Commons . .	*24 January 2001*
Coming into force	*In accordance with regulation 1*

PART I

INTRODUCTORY

Citation, commencement and effect

1—(1) These Regulations may be cited as the Personal Pension Schemes (Transfer Payments) Regulations 2001 and shall come into force for the purposes of—

(*a*) regulations 13 and 14, and

(*b*) regulation 3 so far as it relates to regulation 13,

on 14th February 2001, and for all other purposes on 6th April 2001.

(2) Regulation 10 shall have effect in accordance with regulation 15(1).

Interpretation

2 In these Regulations, unless the context otherwise requires—

"administrator"—

(*a*) in relation to a retirement benefits scheme has the meaning given by section 611AA of the Taxes Act and, in relation to a scheme which secures relevant benefits falling within section 591(2A) of the Taxes Act by means of an annuity contract, includes the insurance company with which the contract is made, and

(*b*) in relation to a personal pension scheme means the person referred to in section 638(1) of the Taxes Act;

"approved retirement benefits scheme" means a retirement benefits scheme approved by the Board for the purposes of Chapter I of Part XIV and includes an annuity contract which secures relevant benefits as mentioned in paragraph (*a*) of the definition of "administrator";

"the Board" means the Commissioners of Inland Revenue;

"the certificating requirements" means any requirement to give a lump sum certificate—

(*a*) under regulation 5, 6 or 13,

(*b*) under the Personal Pension Schemes (Transfer Payments) Regulations 1988, or

(*c*) under the rules of a scheme or fund making a transfer payment to a personal pension scheme;

"Chapter I" means Chapter I of Part XIV;

"controlling director" means a director within the meaning of section 612(1) of the Taxes Act who falls within the provisions of subsection (5)(*b*) of section 417 of that Act (read with subsections (3), (4) and (6) of that section);

"dependant" and "surviving spouse" have the respective meanings, and shall be determined at the time, given by section 636(2) of the Taxes Act;

"electronic signature" has the meaning given by section 7(2) of the Electronic Communications Act 2000;

"the 1999 Act" means the Welfare Reform and Pensions Act 1999;

"the 1999 Order" means the Welfare Reform and Pensions (Northern Ireland) Order 1999;

"Part XIV" means Part XIV of the Taxes Act;

"pension credit" means a credit under section 29(1)(*b*) of the 1999 Act or Article 26(1)(*b*) of the 1999 Order, "transferee" means the person who becomes entitled to the pension credit under either of those provisions, and "pension debit" means a debit under section 29(1)(*a*) of that Act or Article 26(1)(*a*) of that Order;

"pension date" has the meaning given by section 630(1) of the Taxes Act;

"pension sharing order or provision" means any such order or provision as is mentioned in section 28(1) of the 1999 Act or Article 25(1) of the 1999 Order;

"personal pension scheme", except in regulation 3, means a personal pension scheme approved by the Board for the purposes of Chapter IV of Part XIV;

"personal pension protected rights premium" means a premium payable under section 55(1) of the Pension Schemes Act 1993 or section 51(6)(*d*) of the Pension Schemes (Northern Ireland) Act 1993;

"protected rights" shall be construed in accordance with section 10 of the Pension Schemes Act 1993 and section 6 of the Pension Schemes (Northern Ireland) Act 1993;

"relevant statutory scheme" has the meaning given by section 611A(1) of the Taxes Act;

"remuneration" shall be construed in accordance with section 612(1) of the Taxes Act;

"retirement annuity contract" means a retirement annuity contract approved by the Board under Chapter III of Part XIV, and "trust scheme" means a trust scheme approved by the Board under that Chapter;

"scheme member" in relation to an approved retirement benefits scheme or relevant statutory scheme means—

(*a*) a member of the scheme to whom benefit is currently accruing as a result of service as an employee, or

(*b*) a person who is an ex-spouse of a member of the scheme and whose rights under the scheme derive from a pension sharing order or provision;

"the Taxes Act" means the Income and Corporation Taxes Act 1988;

"transfer payment" in regulations 5 to 7 and 12 includes a payment under paragraph 1(3) of Schedule 5 to the 1999 Act or under paragraph 1(3) of Schedule 5 to the 1999 Order;

"transfer request" means a request in writing in accordance with regulation 4(1), save that a request shall be regarded as in writing if it is furnished by telephonic facsimile transmission, or by electronic communication containing an electronic signature of the individual in question.

Requirements under section 638(2) of the Taxes Act

3 The provision for the making, acceptance and application of transfer payments, which is required to be made by a personal pension scheme, in order that the scheme may be approved by the Board for the purposes of Chapter IV of Part XIV, is the provision set out in regulations 4 to 13 (to be construed using the relevant definitions in regulation 2).

PART II

PROVISION FOR THE MAKING OF TRANSFER PAYMENTS

Basic obligations

4—(1) Subject to paragraph (2) and regulation 8, where the administrator of a personal pension scheme is requested so to do in writing by an individual who is a member of the scheme, he shall make a transfer payment from the scheme to—

(*a*) another personal pension scheme; or

(*b*) an approved retirement benefits scheme of which the individual is an existing scheme member (otherwise than in relation to the transfer payment); or

(*c*) a relevant statutory scheme of which the individual is an existing scheme member (otherwise than in relation to the transfer payment);

but not to any other approved retirement benefits scheme or relevant statutory scheme.

(2) The transfer payment shall, in respect of arrangements made by the individual in accordance with the scheme which are (wholly or partly) the subject of the transfer request, comprise the whole of the accumulated funds held in connection with those arrangements except that, where the fund—

(*a*) includes protected rights, or

(*b*) has been, or will be, used to pay a personal pension protected rights premium,

the amount of the funds which represents those rights or has been, or will be, so used may be excluded from the transfer payment.

(3) Before making a transfer payment the administrator shall take all reasonable steps to ensure that the payment is being made to a scheme referred to in paragraph (1)(*a*) to (*c*).

(4) The reference in the words of paragraph (1) preceding sub-paragraph (*a*) to an individual who is a member of a scheme shall be treated as including a reference to a surviving spouse or dependant mentioned in regulation 14(3)(*c*).

Transfer payments from one personal pension scheme to another—additional obligation to hand over a lump sum certificate where any of the payments originated from certain schemes mentioned in Chapter I

5—(1) Subject to paragraph (2), the administrator of a personal pension scheme ("the paying scheme") from which a transfer payment is made in the circumstances described in paragraph (3) shall, on the making of the payment, give the certificate referred to in paragraph (3)(*b*) to the administrator of the personal pension scheme to which the payment is made ("the receiving scheme").

(2) Where only one (or some) of the arrangements made by the individual in accordance with the scheme is being transferred, the administrator of the paying scheme shall apportion any amount shown on the certificate on a proportionate basis, and shall prepare and sign replacement certificates in respect of each part of the funds (including in a case where the amount is nil), and shall give the replacement certificate relating to the funds transferred to the administrator of the receiving scheme.

(3) The circumstances described in this paragraph are where the transfer payment is made from the paying scheme to another personal pension scheme and—

(*a*) the payment or part of the payment had its origin in a transfer payment ("the original payment") from an approved retirement benefits scheme or a relevant statutory scheme, and

(*b*) the administrator of the paying scheme holds a certificate which was given in relation to the original payment or any other event showing either—

(i) that an amount is payable out of that payment by way of lump sum to the individual in respect of whom the transfer payment will be made, on his pension date, or

(ii) that no amount is payable out of that payment by way of lump sum to that individual on his pension date.

Transfer payments from a personal pension scheme to certain schemes mentioned in Chapter I—additional obligation to hand over a "nil" lump sum certificate where any of the payments originated from such schemes

6—(1) Subject to paragraph (2), the administrator of a personal pension scheme ("the paying scheme") from which a transfer payment is made in the circumstances described in paragraph (3) shall, on the making of the payment, give the certificate referred to in paragraph (3)(*b*) to the administrator of the approved retirement benefits scheme or relevant statutory scheme to which the payment is made ("the receiving scheme").

(2) Where only one (or some) of the arrangements made by the individual in accordance with the scheme is being transferred, the administrator of the paying scheme shall prepare and sign replacement certificates, each in the amount of nil, in respect of each part of the funds, and shall give

the replacement certificate relating to the funds transferred to the administrator of the receiving scheme.

(3) The circumstances described in this paragraph are where the transfer payment is made from the paying scheme to an approved retirement benefits scheme or a relevant statutory scheme and—

(*a*) the payment or part of the payment had its origin in a transfer payment ("the original payment") from an approved retirement benefits scheme or relevant statutory scheme, and

(*b*) the administrator of the paying scheme holds a certificate which was given in relation to the original payment or any other event showing that no amount may be paid out of that payment by way of lump sum to the individual in respect of whom the transfer payment will be made.

PART III
PROVISION FOR THE ACCEPTANCE OF TRANSFER PAYMENTS

Basic obligation

7 Subject to regulations 4 and 8, a personal pension scheme may accept a transfer payment from—

(*a*) another personal pension scheme;

(*b*) an approved retirement benefits scheme;

(*c*) a relevant statutory scheme;

(*d*) a retirement annuity contract or trust scheme; or

(*e*) a fund to which section 608 of the Taxes Act applies;

but shall not accept a transfer payment from any other source without the prior written approval of the Board.

Prohibition of acceptance of certain transfer payments from certain schemes mentioned in Chapter I unless the administrator has obtained a certificate as to the value of the proposed transfer payment

8—(1) A personal pension scheme shall not accept a transfer payment from—

(*a*) an approved retirement benefits scheme (other than an annuity contract securing relevant benefits as described in section 591(2)(*g*) of the Taxes Act where that contract is made before 6 April 2001), or

(*b*) a relevant statutory scheme,

("the paying scheme") in the circumstances described in paragraph (2) unless the administrator of the personal pension scheme has obtained the certificate referred to in paragraph (3) from the administrator of the paying scheme.

(2) The circumstances described in this paragraph are circumstances where, in relation to any employment to which the proposed transfer payment, or any part of it, relates—

(*a*) the individual is, or has been at any time during the period of ten years prior to the date of the proposed transfer payment ("the proposed transfer date"), a controlling director, or

(*b*)

(i) the individual's annual remuneration is, or was, for any year of assessment falling (wholly or partly) during the period of six years prior to the proposed transfer date, more than the allowable maximum (within the meaning of section 640A(2) of the Taxes Act) for the year of assessment in which the proposed transfer date falls, and

(ii) the individual's age at the proposed transfer date will be not less than 45 years.

(3) The certificate referred to in this paragraph is a certificate, signed by the administrator of the paying scheme, which shows that the proposed transfer payment does not exceed the maximum amount which may be transferred from an approved retirement benefits scheme or relevant statutory scheme to a personal pension scheme calculated in accordance with Appendix XI of "Occupational Pension Schemes Practice Notes (IR 12)" published by the Board on 22 January 2001.

PART IV
PROVISION FOR THE APPLICATION OF TRANSFER PAYMENTS

Basic obligations

9 Subject to regulations 10 to 14, any transfer payment accepted by a personal pension scheme in accordance with these Regulations shall only be used for providing benefits listed in section 633(1) of the Taxes Act or for making a further transfer payment subject to the provisions of these Regulations.

Application of transfer payments to a personal pension scheme from or originating from certain schemes mentioned in Chapter I for the provision of "death benefits"

10—(1) Where a personal pension scheme has in the circumstances described in regulation 8(2) (omitting the word "proposed" wherever it occurs) accepted a transfer payment from—

(*a*) an approved retirement benefits scheme, or

(*b*) a relevant statutory scheme, or

(*c*) another personal pension scheme in circumstances where the transfer payment, or part of it, had its origin in a transfer payment from an approved retirement benefits scheme or a relevant statutory scheme,

the accumulated value arising from that transfer payment or, as the case may be, that part shall be applied after the death of the individual referred to in regulation 8(2) in accordance with paragraph (2) or (3), in the events described in paragraph (2).

(2) Where the individual dies before any benefits have been paid to him under an arrangement under which the transfer payment falls to be held, the accumulated value arising from that transfer payment or, as the case may be, that part shall be applied—

(*a*) wholly to secure the payment to a surviving spouse or (if the arrangement so provides) a dependant of an annuity which satisfies the conditions in section 636 of the Taxes Act, or

(*b*) to secure the payment of income withdrawals by the surviving spouse or (if the arrangement so provides) the dependant with respect to which the conditions in section 636A of the Taxes Act are satisfied and, as to any amount not used for that purpose, to secure the payment to the surviving spouse or (if the arrangement so provides) the dependant of such an annuity as is referred to in sub-paragraph (*a*), or

(*c*) as to not more than 25 per cent to secure the payment of a lump sum and as to the balance to secure the payment to the surviving spouse or (if the arrangement so provides) the dependant of such an annuity as is referred to in sub-paragraph (*a*), or of such income withdrawals and annuity as are referred to in sub-paragraph (*b*).

(3) In the events described in the words of paragraph (2) preceding sub-paragraph (*a*), subject to sub-paragraphs (*a*) to (*c*) of that paragraph, the whole of the accumulated value may be applied to secure the payment of a lump sum.

Application of transfer payments to a personal pension scheme from or originating from certain schemes mentioned in Chapter I for the provision of lump sums to the member

11—(1) Where in the circumstances described in regulation 8(2) (omitting the word "proposed" wherever it occurs) a personal pension scheme ("the receiving scheme") accepts a transfer payment from—

(*a*) an approved retirement benefits scheme, or

(*b*) a relevant statutory scheme, or

(*c*) another personal pension scheme in circumstances where the transfer payment or part of it had its origin in a transfer payment ("the original payment") from an approved retirement benefits scheme or a relevant statutory scheme,

("the paying scheme") the provisions of paragraph (2) shall apply.

(2) Where the provisions of this paragraph apply—

(*a*) no amount may be paid to the individual in respect of whom the transfer payment is made by way of lump sum on his pension date out of the transfer payment or, as the case may be, the part of that payment unless the administrator of the receiving scheme has obtained from the administrator of the paying scheme the lump sum certificate required by the certificating requirements; and

(*b*) the amount which may be so paid by way of lump sum may not exceed the aggregate of the amount shown in any such certificate ("the basic amount") and any amount by which the basic amount may be enhanced at the date of payment.

(3) For the purposes of paragraph (2) the amount by which the basic amount may be enhanced is the result of applying to the basic amount the percentage increase in the retail prices index between—

(*a*)

(i) in a case falling within paragraph (1)(*a*) or (*b*), the month in which the transfer payment referred to in the words preceding paragraph (1)(*a*) was received, or

(ii) in a case falling within paragraph (1)(*c*), the month in which the original payment was made, and

(*b*) the last month for which that index had been published at the date of the payment by way of lump sum.

(4) The reference in paragraph (3) to the retail prices index shall be construed in accordance with section 833(2) of the Taxes Act as if it were a reference in the Income Tax Acts.

Application of transfer payments to a personal pension scheme where a "nil" lump sum certificate is held

12 Where—

(*a*) a personal pension scheme has accepted a transfer payment in accordance with regulation 7, and

(*b*) the administrator of the scheme holds a certificate given under any of the certificating requirements with regard to the transfer payment or any other event, showing that no amount is payable out of that payment by way of lump sum to the individual in respect of whom the transfer payment was made on his pension date,

no such lump sum may be paid out of the accumulated value arising from that transfer payment.

Obligations where there is a pension sharing order or provision

13—(1) Where—

(*a*) a transfer payment has been accepted by a personal pension scheme in the circumstances described in regulation 5(3) (omitting sub-paragraph (*b*)(ii) and the word "either" preceding sub-paragraph (*b*)(i)), and

(*b*) a pension sharing order or provision is subsequently made against the individual in respect of whom the payment was made,

the administrator of the receiving scheme shall recalculate the amount shown on the certificate referred to in regulation 5(2) or (3)(*b*), according to any debit to which the individual's rights under the scheme become subject by virtue of that order or provision, and shall prepare and sign a replacement certificate in respect of the individual's rights remaining after the reduction referred to in section 29 of the 1999 Act or Article 26 of the 1999 Order has taken place.

(2) Where—

(*a*) a transfer payment has been accepted by a personal pension scheme in the circumstances described in regulation 5(3) (omitting sub-paragraph (*b*)(i) and the word "either" which precedes it), and

(*b*) a pension sharing order or provision is subsequently made against the individual in respect of whom the payment was made,

the administrator of the receiving scheme shall prepare and sign a certificate in respect of the pension credit to which the transferee becomes entitled, showing that no amount may be paid out of the original payment by way of lump sum to the transferee.

(3) Where, after the date which is a member's pension date in relation to the arrangements in question, a pension sharing order or provision is made against that member, the administrator of the scheme shall prepare and sign a certificate in respect of the pension credit to which the transferee becomes entitled, showing that no amount may be paid out of the pension credit by way of lump sum to the transferee.

(4) The reference in paragraph (1) to a certificate referred to in regulation 5(2) or (3)(*b*) includes a reference to a certificate given under regulation 4 of the Personal Pension Schemes (Transfer Payments) Regulations 1988.

PART V
EXCEPTIONS TO SECTION 638(7A) OF THE TAXES ACT AND SUPPLEMENTAL

Exceptions to section 638(7A) of the Taxes Act

14—(1) Paragraphs (2) and (3) prescribe situations which fall within the exception in section 638(7A) of the Taxes Act with regard to the making of transfer payments.

(2) The first situation is where—

(*a*) the transfer payment is from the personal pension scheme ("the paying scheme") to another personal pension scheme ("the receiving scheme");

(*b*) income withdrawals are being made by the member from the paying scheme with respect to which the conditions in section 634A of the Taxes Act are satisfied, and the period of deferral of the purchase of an annuity has not ended;

(*c*) the transfer payment comprises the whole of the funds held under any arrangement which is the subject of the transfer payment;

(*d*) where any of the funds referred to in sub-paragraph (*c*) was the subject of, or represents the proceeds of, an earlier transfer payment made in accordance with this paragraph ("the earlier transfer payment"), the period between the earlier transfer payment and the transfer payment referred to in sub-paragraph (*a*) is not less than one year;

(*e*) the arrangements made in accordance with the receiving scheme ("the new arrangements") were set up by the member for the purpose of accepting the transfer payment, or a previous or contemporaneous transfer payment which fell or falls within this first situation, and prohibit the acceptance of—

(i) contributions, or

(ii) further transfer payments which do not fall within this first situation;

(*f*) under the new arrangements the member elects to defer the purchase of such an annuity as is mentioned in section 634 of the Taxes Act, and to make income withdrawals as mentioned in sub-paragraph (*b*), and that election takes effect simultaneously with the transfer payment; and

(*g*) no benefit referred to in section 633(1)(*b*) or (*d*) of the Taxes Act is payable under the new arrangements.

(3) The second situation is where—

(*a*) the transfer payment is from the paying scheme to another personal pension scheme ("the receiving scheme");
(*b*) the member referred to in section 634 of the Taxes Act ("the original member") has died;
(*c*) a surviving spouse or dependant referred to in section 636 of the Taxes Act is making income withdrawals from the paying scheme with respect to which the conditions in section 636A of the Taxes Act are satisfied, and the period of deferral of the purchase of an annuity has not ended;
(*d*) the arrangements made in accordance with the receiving scheme by the surviving spouse or dependant ("the substitute member") were set up for the purpose of accepting the transfer payment, or a previous or contemporaneous transfer payment which fell or falls within this second situation, and prohibit the acceptance of—

(i) contributions, or
(ii) further transfer payments which do not fall within this second situation;

(*e*) under the arrangements referred to in sub-paragraph (*d*) ("the new arrangements") the substitute member elects to defer the purchase of an annuity and to make income withdrawals with respect to which the conditions in section 634A of the Taxes Act are satisfied;
(*f*) the income withdrawals referred to in sub-paragraph (*e*) cannot be made after the original member would have attained the age of 75 or, if earlier, after the substitute member attains that age;
(*g*) the election referred to in sub-paragraph (*e*) takes effect simultaneously with the transfer payment;
(*h*) any benefit under the new arrangements corresponds to a benefit which would have been payable to the same person under the paying scheme (and "the same person" means the same individual, without having regard to the way in which that or any other individual is defined in the new arrangements); and
(*i*) the conditions in paragraph (2)(*c*), (*d*) and (*g*) are satisfied (construing the references in paragraph (2)(*d*) to "this paragraph" and "sub-paragraph (*a*)" as if they were references to the present paragraph and sub-paragraph (*a*) of this paragraph).

Revocations and transitional provision

15—(1) Regulations 8 and 9 of the Personal Pension Schemes (Transfer Payments) Regulations 1988 shall cease to have effect where the death of the individual referred to in the former regulation occurs on or after 6 April 2001, and regulation 10 of these Regulations shall have effect where the death of the individual referred to in that regulation occurs on or after 6 April 2001.

(2) The Personal Pension Schemes (Transfer Payments) Regulations 1988, the Personal Pension Schemes (Transfer Payments) (Amendment) Regulations 1989 and the Personal Pension Schemes (Transfer Payments) (Amendment) Regulations 1997 shall otherwise cease to have effect.

(3) Any transfer payment made under, and any certificate supplied or obtained under a provision of, the Personal Pension Schemes (Transfer Payments) Regulations 1988 shall be treated for the purposes of these Regulations as if made, supplied or obtained, as the case may be, under the corresponding provision (if any) of these Regulations.

Commentary—*Simon's Direct Tax Service* **E7.240, E7.417**.

2001/253
Finance Act 1989, Section 178(1), (Appointed Day) Order 2001

Made by the Treasury under FA 1989 s 178(7)

Made . . . . *1st February 2001*

Commentary—*Simon's Direct Tax Service* **A3.1322**.

1 This Order may be cited as the Finance Act 1989, section 178(1), (Appointed Day) Order 2001.

2—(1) The day appointed for the enactments specified in paragraph (2) for periods beginning on or after which section 178(1) of the Finance Act 1989 shall have effect is 7th March 2001.

(2) The enactments specified are—

(*a*) section 71(8A) of the Social Security Administration Act 1992;
(*b*) section 69(8A) of the Social Security Administration (Northern Ireland) Act 1992;
(*c*) paragraph 8 of Schedule 4 to the Tax Credits Act 1999.

2001/391
Investment Trusts (Approval of Accounting Methods for Creditor Relationships) Order 2001

Made by the Treasury under FA 1996 Sch 10 paras 1, 9(1)

Made . . . . *14 February 2001*
Laid before the House of Commons . . . *14 February 2001*
Coming into force . . . . *7 March 2001*

Commentary—*Simon's Direct Tax Service* **D2.1142**.

Citation, commencement and effect

1 This Order may be cited as the Investment Trusts (Approval of Accounting Methods for Creditor Relationships) Order 2001 and shall come into force on 7th March 2001, but shall have effect in relation to accounting periods of investment trusts ending after 31st March 1996.

Interpretation

2—(1) In this Order—

"Chapter II" means Chapter II of Part IV of the Finance Act 1996;
"creditor relationship" has the same meaning as in section 103(1);
"investment trust" has the meaning given by section 842 of the Taxes Act;
"statutory accounts" shall be construed in accordance with section 86(8);
"the Taxes Act" means the Income and Corporation Taxes Act 1988.

(2) References in this Order to a section, or a Schedule, without more, are references to that section of, or that Schedule to, the Finance Act 1996.

Approval of the use of accounting methods

3 The accounting methods that are approved for use for the creditor relationships of investment trusts for the purposes of paragraph 1 of Schedule 10 are—

(*a*) the method ("the main method") contained in a Statement of Recommended Practice issued by the Association of Investment Trust Companies bearing the date December 1995 ("the Statement"), as modified by article 4 of this Order;
(*b*) the method contained in the Statement as varied by a Guidance Note issued by that Association on 8th January 1997 ("the simple method"), and as modified by article 4.

Modifications of the main method and the simple method

4—(1) The main method and the simple method shall be modified as follows.

(2) For paragraph R604 in the Statement there shall be substituted the following paragraph—

"**R604** An ITC shall be under an obligation—

(*a*) to make proper provision for allocating payments under a creditor relationship to accounting periods (and that expression has the same meaning as in sub-section (3) of section 85 of the Finance Act 1996, on the assumption that the words 'loan relationship' in that sub-section were replaced with the words 'creditor relationship'), and
(*b*) not to make any provision (other than provision comprised in authorised arrangements for bad debt, within the meaning in section 85(5)(*a*) of the Finance Act 1996) that gives debits by reference to the valuation at different times of any asset representing a creditor relationship (within the meaning in section 103(1) of the Finance Act 1996)."

(3) Paragraph R606 in the Statement shall be omitted.

(4) In this Order, "the modified main method" and "the modified simple method" mean the main method, and the simple method, as so modified, respectively.

Purposes for which accounting methods are approved

5—(1) his article has effect for the purpose of determining which of the accounting methods approved under article 3 is to be used as respects the creditor relationships of an investment trust.

(2) The same method shall be used as respects all creditor relationships of an investment trust for any single accounting period.

(3) The modified main method shall be used for any accounting period where—

(*a*) the investment trust uses the main method or the modified main method for the purposes of its statutory accounts for that accounting period;
(*b*) the investment trust has in an earlier accounting period (not being an accounting period described in paragraph (4)) used the modified main method as an authorised accounting method for the purposes of Chapter II; or
(*c*) the investment trust has, at any time during the accounting period referred to in the words preceding sub-paragraph (*a*), held—

(i) a relevant discounted security within the meaning of Schedule 13; or
(ii) a security to which section 717 of the Taxes Act applies.

(4) The accounting period described in this paragraph is one—

(*a*) which ended before the coming into force of this Order; and
(*b*) during which the investment trust did not at any time hold any of the securities referred to in paragraph (3)(*c*)(i) or (ii).

2001/1122
Capital Gains Tax (Gilt-edged Securities) Order 2001

Made by the Treasury under TCGA 1992 Sch 9, para 1

Made . . . . *22 March 2001*

1 This Order may be cited as the Capital Gains Tax (Gilt-edged Securities) Order 2001.

2 The following securities are hereby specified for the purposes of Schedule 9 to the Taxation of Chargeable Gains Act 1992—

Floating Rate Treasury Stock 2001

7%	Treasury Stock 2002
$6\frac{1}{2}$%	Treasury Stock 2003
5%	Treasury Stock 2004
$7\frac{1}{4}$%	Treasury Stock 2007
$5\frac{3}{4}$%	Treasury Stock 2009
8%	Treasury Stock 2021
6%	Treasury Stock 2028
$4\frac{1}{4}$%	Treasury Stock 2032.

2001/1123
Income Tax (Car Benefits) (Reduction of Value of Appropriate Percentage) Regulations 2001

Made by the Treasury under TA 1988 Sch 6, paras 5E, 8

Made . . . . *21 March 2001*
Laid before the House of Commons . . . . *22 March 2001*
Coming into force . . . . *12 April 2001*

Citation, commencement and effect

Commentary—*Simon's Direct Tax Service* **E4.626A**.

1—(1) These Regulations may be cited as the Income Tax (Car Benefits) (Reduction of Value of Appropriate Percentage) Regulations 2001 and shall come into force on 12th April 2001.

(2) These Regulations have effect for the year 2002–03 and subsequent years of assessment.

Interpretation

2 In these Regulations—

"bi-fuel car" means a car which is capable of being propelled by petrol and road fuel gas;
"diesel" means any diesel fuel within the definition in Article 2 of Directive 98/70/EC;
"Directive 98/70/EC" means Directive 98/70/EC of the European Parliament and of the Council relating to the quality of petrol and diesel fuels and amending Council Directive 93/12/EEC;
"petrol" has the meaning given by Article 2 of Directive 98/70/EC;
"road fuel gas" has the meaning given by section 168AB(3) of the Income and Corporation Taxes Act 1988;
"Schedule 6" means Schedule 6 to the Income and Corporation Taxes Act 1988;
"the value of the appropriate percentage" means the value of the appropriate percentage as determined in accordance with paragraphs 2 to 5D of Schedule 6.

Prescribed reduction of value of appropriate percentage – cars propelled solely by diesel

3—(1) In the circumstances prescribed by paragraph (2) the value of the appropriate percentage shall be reduced by the amount prescribed by paragraph (3).

(2) The circumstances prescribed by this paragraph are circumstances where the car—

(*a*) is first registered on or after 1st January 1998,
(*b*) is propelled solely by diesel, and
(*c*) has been type-approved to the emission limit values set out in row B of the table in section 5.3.1.4 of Annex I to Council Directive 70/220/EEC as amended.

(3) The amount prescribed is the percentage amount by which the appropriate percentage for the year ascertained in accordance with paragraphs 2 to 5C of Schedule 6 is increased by virtue of paragraph 5D of that Schedule.

Commentary—*Simon's Direct Tax Service* **E4.626A**.

Prescribed reduction of value of appropriate percentage - electrically propelled cars

4—(1) In the circumstances prescribed by paragraph (2) the value of the appropriate percentage shall be reduced by the amount prescribed by paragraph (3).

(2) The circumstances prescribed by this paragraph are circumstances where the car—

(*a*) is first registered on or after 1st January 1998, and
(*b*) is an electrically propelled vehicle for the purposes of Schedule 6.

(3) The amount prescribed by this paragraph is 6%.

Prescribed reduction of value of appropriate percentage – hybrid cars capable of being propelled by electricity and petrol.

Commentary—*Simon's Direct Tax Service* **E4.626A**.

5—(1) In the circumstances prescribed by paragraph (2) the value of the appropriate percentage shall be reduced by the amount prescribed by paragraph (3).

(2) The circumstances prescribed by this paragraph are circumstances where the car—

(*a*) is first registered on or after 1st January 1998, and
(*b*) is capable of being propelled by electricity and petrol.

(3) The amount prescribed by this paragraph shall be determined by the formula—

$$A + B$$

where—

A is 2%, and
B is 1% for each 20 grams per kilometre by which the CO2 emissions figure is less than the lower threshold provided for in the Table in paragraph 4(1) of Schedule 6.

Commentary—*Simon's Direct Tax Service* **E4.626A**.

Prescribed reduction of value of appropriate percentage – cars propelled solely by road fuel gas and bi-fuel cars to which paragraph 5 of Schedule 6 applies

6—(1) In the circumstances prescribed by paragraph (2) the value of the appropriate percentage shall be reduced by the amount prescribed by paragraph (3).

(2) The circumstances prescribed by this paragraph are circumstances where the car—

(*a*) is first registered on or after 1st January 1998 and is propelled solely by road fuel gas, or
(*b*) is a bi-fuel car to which paragraph 5 of Schedule 6 applies.

(3) The amount prescribed by this paragraph shall be determined by the formula—

$$A + B$$

where—

A is 1%, and
B is 1% for each 20 grams per kilometre by which the CO2 emissions figure is less than the lower threshold provided for in the Table in paragraph 4(1) of Schedule 6.

Commentary—*Simon's Direct Tax Service* **E4.626A**.

Prescribed reduction of value of appropriate percentage – bi-fuel cars to which paragraph 5 of Schedule 6 does not apply

7—(1) In the circumstances prescribed by paragraph (2) the value of the appropriate percentage shall be reduced by the amount prescribed by paragraph (3).

(2) The circumstances prescribed by this paragraph are circumstances where the car—

(*a*) is first registered on or after 1st January 1998,
(*b*) is a bi-fuel car either—

(i) on the date on which it is first registered, or
(ii) by virtue of equipment added after the date on which it is first registered, and

(*c*) is not a car to which paragraph 5 of Schedule 6 applies.

(3) The amount prescribed by this paragraph is 1%.

Commentary—*Simon's Direct Tax Service* **E4.626A**.

Amendment to the Income Tax (Replacement Cars) Regulations 1994

8 *(Amended SI 1994/778; revoked by ITEPA 2003 s 724, Sch 8)*

2001/1156

Double Taxation Relief (Taxes on Income) (Underlying Tax on Dividends and Dual Resident Companies) Regulations 2001

Made by the Treasury under TA 1988 s 801(2A)(*b*)

Made	*26 March 2001*
Laid before the House of Commons	*26 March 2001*
Coming into force	*31 March 2001*

Citation, commencement and application

1—(1) These Regulations may be cited as the Double Taxation Relief (Taxes on Income) (Underlying Tax on Dividends and Dual Resident Companies) Regulations 2001.

(2) These Regulations shall come into force on 31st March 2001 and shall apply in relation to any claim for an allowance by way of credit made on or after that date in respect of a dividend paid by an overseas company to a company resident in the United Kingdom, unless the dividend was paid before that date.

Interpretation

2 In these Regulations—

''the Act'' means the Income and Corporation Taxes Act 1988, and a reference to a numbered section is a reference to the section of the Act which is so numbered;

''dual resident company'' means a company which is liable, by reason of its domicile, residence or place of management or of incorporation, or other similar criterion, to tax in two or more territories;

''overseas company'' has the meaning given in section 801(1) (dividends paid between related companies—relief for UK and third country taxes); and

''third company'' means the company referred to as such in section 801(2).

Additional cases prescribed for the purposes of section 801(2) of the Act

3—(1) The cases specified in paragraphs (2) and (3) are prescribed for the purposes of section 801(2) (cases where the overseas company receives a dividend from a related third company and in respect of which relief allowable for underlying tax is subject to a restriction under section 799(1)(*b*)).

(2) The case specified in this paragraph is that the overseas company is a dual resident company as respects an accounting period and, although resident in the same territory as the third company—

(*a*) it is treated for the purposes of Chapter IV of Part XVII of the Act (tax avoidance—controlled foreign companies) as resident in a different territory; or

(*b*) it would be so treated in accordance with paragraphs (*a*) to (*c*) of subsection (3) of section 749 (residence of controlled foreign companies) if that subsection applied to it.

(3) The case specified in this paragraph is that the third company is a dual resident company as respects an accounting period and although resident in the same territory as the overseas company—

(*a*) it is treated for the purposes of Chapter IV of Part XVII of the Act as resident in a different territory; or

(*b*) it would be so treated in accordance with paragraphs (*a*) to (*c*) of subsection (3) of section 749 if that subsection applied to it.

2001/1163

Double Taxation Relief (Surrender of Relievable Tax Within a Group) Regulations 2001

Made by the Commissioners of Inland Revenue under TA 1988 s 806H

Made	*23 March 2001*
Laid before the House of Commons	*26 March 2001*
Coming into force	*31 March 2001*

Citation, commencement and effect

1—(1) These Regulations may be cited as the Double Taxation Relief (Surrender of Relievable Tax Within a Group) Regulations 2001 and shall come into force on 31st March 2001.

(2) These Regulations shall have effect in relation to any claim made on or after 31st March 2001 for the surrender of an amount of EUFT arising in respect of a dividend falling within section 806A(2) that is paid by a company resident outside the United Kingdom to a company resident in the United Kingdom, unless the dividend was paid before that date.

Interpretation

2—(1) In these Regulations—

"EUFT" means eligible unrelieved foreign tax;

"group" shall be construed in accordance with subsection (3)(*a*) of section 413, read with subsections (4), (5) and (7) of that section;

"the Taxes Act" means the Income and Corporation Taxes Act 1988.

(2) In these Regulations the following expressions have the meanings given by section 413(2)—

"claimant company";

"company";

"group relief";

"surrendering company".

(3) In these Regulations references to a section, without more, are to that section of the Taxes Act.

Introductory

3 These Regulations make provision for, and in connection with, allowing a company which is a member of a group to surrender an amount of EUFT arising to it in an accounting period to another company which is a member of the same group.

Amount of EUFT available for surrender

4—(1) Subject to paragraph (2), the amount of EUFT arising in an accounting period in the cases set out in sections 806A and 806B that may be surrendered by the surrendering company to a claimant company must not exceed the amount (if any) that remains ("the remaining amount") after the surrendering company has fully utilised in accordance with the relevant provisions of sections 806D to 806G the EUFT arising in that accounting period.

(2) For the purposes of paragraph (1), where the surrendering company chooses not to utilise section 806D(4)(*c*) or (5)(*c*) (carry back provision), the remaining amount shall be computed in accordance with that paragraph as if the surrendering company had in fact fully utilised that provision.

(3) Where the surrendering company carries on life assurance business, the policy holders' share of the amount of EUFT attributable to BLAGAB may not be surrendered to another company in the group.

(4) Where—

(*a*) an amount of EUFT is surrendered to a claimant company, and

(*b*) the claimant company carries on life assurance business,

the amount surrendered may not be set against the policy holders' share of the corporation tax attributable [by virtue of section 797(1)][1] to any single dividend referable [by virtue of section 432A][1] to the claimant company's BLAGAB.

(5) In this regulation—

...[1].

"BLAGAB" means basic life assurance and general annuity business [within the meaning given by section 431F][1];

["the policy holders' share of the amount of EUFT attributable to BLAGAB" means the relevant fraction of—

(*a*) where all of the company's long-term business within the meaning given by section 431(2) is BLAGAB, the whole of the amount of EUFT;

(*b*) in any other case, so much of the amount of EUFT as is attributable to BLAGAB by virtue of section 804B(3) or (4);

"the policy holders' share of the corporation tax attributable to any single dividend referable to the claimant company's BLAGAB" means the relevant fraction of that tax;

"the relevant fraction" means the fraction arrived at by dividing—

(*a*) the policy holders' share of the company's relevant profits for the relevant accounting period, by

(*b*) the company's BLAGAB profits for that period, and, for the purposes of this definition, "the policy holders' share of the company's relevant profits" shall be construed in accordance with sections 88(3) and 89 of the Finance Act 1989 and "the company's BLAGAB profits" shall be construed in accordance with section 89(1B) of that Act;][1]

"the relevant provisions of sections 806D to 806G" means all provisions of those sections other than section 806D(4)(*b*) and (5)(*b*) (carry forward provision);

"single dividend" has the meaning given by section 806E(6).

Amendments—[1] Words in paras (4), (5) inserted, in para (5), definitions substituted, and definition of attributable repealed, by the Double Taxation Relief (Surrender of Relievable Tax Within a Group) (Amendment) Regulations, SI 2003/1829 with effect for distributions made after 8 April 2003 in accounting periods ending after 6 August 2003.

Claiming of EUFT

5—(1) The claimant company may claim the whole or part of the amount of EUFT available for surrender in accordance with regulation 4.

(2) The amount of EUFT claimed by the claimant company may be utilised by the claimant company in accordance with the provisions of sections 806D to 806G.

Accounting periods of surrendering company and claimant company

6—(1) The surrendering company and the claimant company must be members of the same group throughout the accounting period of the surrendering company in which the amount of EUFT available for surrender arises.

(2) Where the accounting period of the surrendering company in which the amount of EUFT available for surrender arises and the accounting period of the claimant company are not coterminous—

(*a*) the amount of EUFT arising in that accounting period of the surrendering company which is surrendered to the claimant company in accordance with regulations 4 and 5 shall be treated as if it arose on a dividend received by the claimant company, and

(*b*) that dividend shall be treated as arising in that one of the claimant company's accounting periods in which falls the last day of the accounting period of the surrendering company in which the amount of EUFT surrendered arises.

Calculation of Schedule D Case V income when EUFT claimed

7 An amount of EUFT that is utilised by the claimant company in accordance with the provisions of sections 806D to 806G shall not be taken into account as underlying tax under section 795(2)(*b*) in computing the amount of income of the claimant company.

Form of claim and withdrawal of claim

8—(1) The like provisions as those contained in Part VIII of Schedule 18 to the Finance Act 1998 ("Schedule 18") and listed below shall have effect, with necessary modifications, in relation to claims for amounts of EUFT available for surrender as they have effect in relation to claims for group relief.

(2) Those provisions of Schedule 18 are paragraphs 67, 68, 70(1), (3) and (4), 71, 72(1) and (4), 73, 75, 75A and 76.

Time limit for claims

9—(1) A claim for the whole or part of the amount of EUFT available for surrender in an accounting period of the surrendering company may only be made or withdrawn before the expiration of—

(*a*) six years after the expiration of that accounting period or, if later,

(*b*) one year after the end of the accounting period in which the foreign tax in question is paid.

(2) The time limits otherwise applicable to amendment of a company tax return under the Corporation Tax Acts do not apply to an amendment to the extent that it makes or withdraws a claim for the surrender of an amount of EUFT in accordance with these Regulations within the time allowed under paragraph (1).

Miscellaneous provisions

10—(1) The like provisions as those contained in Chapter IV of Part X of the Taxes Act ("Chapter IV") and listed below shall have effect, with necessary modifications, in relation to claims for amounts of EUFT available for surrender as they have effect in relation to claims for group relief.

(2) Those provisions of Chapter IV are sections 402(1), (2), (5) and (6), ...[1] 410(1), (4) and (5) to (7) and 411(1).

Amendments—[1] Figure revoked by the Double Taxation Relief (Surrender of Relievable Tax Within a Group) (Amendment) Regulations, SI 2001/3873 with effect from 5 December 2001.

2001/1304

General Commissioners of Income Tax (Costs) Regulations 2001

Made by the Lord Chancellor under TMA1970 s 2A(4)

Made . . . . *30 March 2001*
Coming into force . . . . *1 April 2001*

Citation and commencement

1 These Regulations may be cited as the General Commissioners of Income Tax (Costs) Regulations 2001 and shall come into force on the second day after the day on which the Regulations are made.

SIS

Interpretation

2 In these Regulations

"claim" means a claim for costs made by the receiving party;

"costs judge" means in England and Wales a taxing master of the Supreme Court, and in Northern Ireland the Master (Taxing Office);

"order" means an order of the court made under section 2A(3) of the Taxes Management Act 1970 that the Lord Chancellor make a payment in respect of the costs of a person in the proceedings;

"proceedings" means proceedings in respect of any act or omission of a General Commissioner in the execution (or purported execution) of his duty as a General Commissioner;

"receiving party" means the person in whose favour the order is made;

"Supreme Court Costs Office" shall be construed, in relation to Northern Ireland, as the Taxing Office of the Supreme Court of Northern Ireland.

The payment of costs by the Lord Chancellor

3 No order shall be made under section 2A(3) of the Taxes Management Act 1970 in favour of—

(*a*) a public authority; or

(*b*) a person acting—

(i) on behalf of a public authority, or

(ii) in his capacity as an official appointed by a public authority.

Determination of costs

4 Where the court makes an order, the amount of costs payable by the Lord Chancellor shall be determined in accordance with these Regulations.

Court order and determination of costs by the court

5—(1) Except as provided for in paragraph (2), when making the order the court shall—

(*a*) determine such an amount as it considers sufficient reasonably to compensate the receiving party for any costs properly incurred by him in the proceedings, and

(*b*) specify that amount in the order.

(2) The amount of costs shall be determined by a costs judge in accordance with regulations 6 and 7 where—

(*a*) the hearing has lasted more than one day or there is insufficient time for the court to determine the costs on the day of the hearing, or

(*b*) the court considers that there is other good reason for the costs judge to determine the amount of costs.

(3) The court shall serve the order on the receiving party and on the Lord Chancellor together with, where paragraph (2) applies, notification that costs will be determined by a costs judge.

Determination of costs by a costs judge

6—(1) Where the amount of costs is to be determined by a costs judge, the receiving party shall, no later than three months from (but excluding) the date on which the order was made, file his claim and a copy of the order in the Supreme Court Costs Office and serve a copy of the claim on the Lord Chancellor.

(2) On the application of the receiving party to the Supreme Court Costs Office, the costs judge may, in exceptional circumstances, extend the period of three months.

(3) A claim shall—

(*a*) summarise the items of work done by a legal representative or the receiving party as a litigant in person, as appropriate;

(*b*) state, where appropriate, the dates on which items of work were done, the time taken and the sums claimed; and

(*c*) specify any disbursements claimed, including counsel's fees, the circumstances in which they were incurred and the amounts claimed in respect of them,

and shall be accompanied by receipts or other evidence of the receiving party's payment of the costs claimed, and any receipts or other documents in support of any disbursements claimed.

(4) If the receiving party wishes to draw any special circumstances to the attention of the costs judge, he shall specify those circumstances in his claim.

(5) If the Lord Chancellor wishes to make any written representations in respect of the claim he shall, no later than one month from (but excluding) the date on which the Lord Chancellor received the claim from the receiving party, file any written representations at the Supreme Court Costs Office and serve a copy of them on the receiving party.

(6) The costs judge may make directions in respect of—

(*a*) the claim;

(*b*) any written representations;
(*c*) the filing and serving of any further particulars or documents; and
(*d*) ensuring that the determination of costs is dealt with justly.

(7) Where the costs judge considers it appropriate, the claim shall be listed for a hearing before him, and the Supreme Court Costs Office shall serve on the receiving party and on the Lord Chancellor notification of the place, date and time of the hearing.

7—(1) The costs judge shall consider the claim and shall allow such costs in respect of -

(*a*) such work as appears to him to have been actually and reasonably done; and
(*b*) such disbursements as appear to him to have been actually and reasonably incurred,

as he considers sufficient reasonably to compensate the receiving party for any expenses properly incurred by him in the proceedings.

(2) In determining costs under paragraph (1) the costs judge shall take into account all the relevant circumstances of the case including the nature, importance, complexity or difficulty of the work and the time involved.

(3) When determining costs for the purposes of this regulation, there shall be allowed a reasonable amount in respect of all costs reasonably incurred and any doubts which the costs judge may have as to whether the costs were reasonably incurred or were reasonable in amount shall be resolved against the receiving party.

(4) When the costs judge has determined the amount of costs payable to the receiving party, the Supreme Court Costs Office shall notify the receiving party and the Lord Chancellor of the amount of costs payable.

2001/1757
General Insurance Reserves (Tax) Regulations 2001

Made by the Commissioners of Inland Revenue under FA 2000 s 107.

Made	*8 May 2001*
Laid before the House of Commons	*8 May 2001*
Coming into force	*29 May 2001*

Citation, commencement and effect

1 These Regulations may be cited as the General Insurance Reserves (Tax) Regulations 2001 and shall come into force on 29th May 2001, and shall have effect for periods of account of general insurers—

(*a*) beginning on or after 1 January 2001, and
(*b*) ending on or after 29th May 2001.

Interpretation

2—(1) In these Regulations unless the context otherwise requires—

''controlled foreign company'' has the meaning in Chapter IV of Part XVII of the Income and Corporation Taxes Act 1988 (''the Taxes Act'');

[''corporate general insurer'' means a general insurer which is a company;][1]

''Schedule 9A'' means Schedule 9A to the Companies Act 1985;

''section 107'' means section 107 of the Finance Act 2000;

other references to a section, without more, are to that section of the Taxes Act; and

''statutory accounts'', in relation to a company other than an underwriting member, has the meaning given by section 86(8)(*a*) and (*c*) to (*e*) of the Finance Act 1996.

(2) References to a company being connected with another company shall be construed in accordance with section 839(5) to (7).

[(3) In these Regulations a reference to a numbered Rule is a reference to the Rule in regulation 3 bearing that number.][1]

Amendments—[1] In para (1), definition of ''corporate general insurer'' inserted, and para (3) inserted, by the General Insurance Reserves (Tax) (Amendment) Regulations, SI 2003/2862 regs 3, 4 with effect from 5 December 2003.

Recalculation of technical provisions for the purposes of section 107

3—(1) This regulation and regulation 4 apply for determining for the purposes of section 107 whether an amount representing the whole or part of the technical provisions made and taken into account in computing for tax purposes the profits of a general insurer other than an underwriting member (see regulation 7(2)) for a period of account was excessive or insufficient, and the amount of the excess or deficiency.

(2) In the following provisions of this regulation and regulation 4—

''the balance sheet date'' means the end of the earlier period of account (as the latter expression is defined in paragraph (3));

"the recalculation date" means the end of the later period of account (as the latter expression is defined in paragraph (3));

["relevant transaction" means any disposal or acquisition (in whole or in part) of the rights or liabilities of—

(*a*) a corporate general insurer under a contract of insurance; or

(*b*) a reinsurer under a contract of reinsurance;][1]

and

"taken into account" means taken into account in computing for tax purposes the profits of the general insurer's trade for the relevant period of account;

and expressions which are used in Schedule 9A have the same meanings as in that Schedule.

(3) As at the end of each period of account which begins on or after 1 January 2001 (and the period which is relevant to the calculation in question is referred to as "the later period of account"), recalculate the provisions for claims outstanding made and taken into account for each earlier period of account which—

(*a*) began on or after 1 January 2000, ...[1]

(*b*) ...[1]

separately for each such period (and the earlier period which is relevant to the calculation in question is referred to as "the earlier period of account"). The recalculation shall be made in accordance with the following rules.

Rule 1

1.1. Subject to regulation 5, the calculation under Rules 2 to 9 shall be carried out in sterling, and the sterling discount rate in paragraph (*a*) of Rule 5.4. shall apply.

Rule 2

2.1. Find out the amount of the provisions for claims outstanding made and taken into account for the earlier period of account which—

[(*a*) where the earlier period of account is the general insurer's first period of account which began on or after 1st January 2000, were provisions made and taken into account for that period, and][1]

(*b*) in any other case, [were provisions][1] made and taken into account for that period for liabilities which (according to their treatment in the statutory accounts of the general insurer) arose in respect of that period.

2.2. The result of this Rule is referred to as "the original provisions for the earlier period of account".

Rule 3

3.1. In relation to the original provisions for the earlier period of account, find out (subject to Rule 4) the cost of settling the liabilities to which the provisions relate, including the amount of—

(*a*) claims paid (gross amount, less reinsurer's share), between the balance sheet date and the recalculation date, (calculated in accordance with Note 4 on the profit and loss account format in section B of Chapter I of Part I of Schedule 9A, but as if the references to the addition and deduction of provisions for claims were omitted),

(*b*) bonuses and rebates (if any), net of reinsurance (calculated in accordance with Note 5 on that profit and loss account format),

(*c*) premiums (if any) paid, or treated as paid, between the balance sheet date and the recalculation date, under a reinsurance to close contract[, qualifying contract or relevant transaction][1], and

(*d*) provisions (if any) for claims outstanding, net of reinsurance, which are carried forward as at the recalculation date (calculated in accordance with paragraphs 43 and 47 of Schedule 9A), and which are taken into account for the later period of account.

3.2. Any such payment, bonus, rebate, deemed payment or provision is referred to in Rule 5 (except in paragraph (*a*) of Rule 5.2.) as a "liability".

Rule 4

[4.1 This Rule applies where either Rule 4.1A or 4.1B is satisfied.][1]

[4.1A This Rule is satisfied if—

(*a*) on or after 1st January 2004 a corporate general insurer enters into a qualifying contract, other than a reinsurance to close contract, with another person ("the reinsurer") and—

(i) the corporate general insurer and the reinsurer are connected companies; or

(ii) the qualifying contract is, or forms part of, a transaction, as a result of which a company connected with the corporate general insurer ("the connected company") directly or indirectly agrees to meet a liability of the corporate general insurer or any further liability representing that liability, through any number of such agreements ("the replacement agreements"); and

(*b*) Rule 4.1C applies.][1]

[4.1B This Rule is satisfied if—

(*a*) on or after 1st January 2004, as a result of—

(i) a relevant transaction between a corporate general insurer and a company with which it is connected (''a connected company''), or

(ii) a series of transactions having the same effect as a relevant transaction between a corporate general insurer and a connected company,

the connected company directly or indirectly replaces the corporate general insurer as a party to a contract of insurance including by way of novation; and

(*b*) Rule 4.1C applies.][1]

[4.1C This Rule applies if the person assuming the liabilities—

(*a*) is not within the charge to corporation tax in respect of income arising from the qualifying contract or the relevant replacement agreement, assuming there were such income; and

(*b*) is not a controlled foreign company in relation to which—

(i) an apportionment under section 747(3) falls to be made regarding, or

(ii) section 748(1)(*a*) applies to,

the accounting period in which the qualifying contract is made.

This is subject to the following qualification.

This Rule applies only to the extent that the qualifying contract reinsures liabilities represented in technical provisions which the corporate general insurer has previously taken into account.

In this Rule ''the person assuming the liabilities'' means, as the case requires, the reinsurer referred to in Rule 4.1A(*a*) or the connected company referred to in Rule 4.1A(*a*)(ii).][1]

4.2. Where, or to the extent that, this Rule applies, the qualifying contract [or the relevant transaction][1] shall be ignored for the purposes of Rule 3, and accordingly—

(*a*) premiums paid under that contract [or that transaction][1] shall be ignored for the purposes of paragraph (*c*) of Rule 3.1, and

(*b*) the claims paid, bonuses and rebates and provisions for claims for the purposes of paragraphs (*a*), (*b*) and (*d*) of Rule 3.1. shall be calculated without deduction for reinsurance, so that each such liability shall be calculated gross.

Rule 5

5.1. Discount the amount of each liability as defined in Rule 3 to the present value of the liability as at the balance sheet date, by the application of a discount factor, reflecting the time value of money between the balance sheet date and the date of payment of the liability (the period between those dates being referred to as ''the discount period''), subject to Rule 5.2.

5.2. The discount period for any liability shall not extend later than 10 years after—

(*a*) the date on which the corresponding liability to which the provisions relate (as referred to in Rule 3.1. in the words preceding paragraph (*a*)) arose (within the meaning in paragraph (*b*) of Rule 2.1.), or

(*b*) the end of the general insurer's first period of account which began on or after 1 January 2000,

whichever is the later.

5.3. It shall be assumed for the purposes of this calculation that the provisions mentioned in paragraph (*d*) of Rule 3.1. were a single payment made by the general insurer on the recalculation date.

5.4. The discount rate for the whole of the discount period to be used in calculating the discount factor shall be determined as follows—

(*a*) in a case where the sterling discount rate is to apply (see Rule 1), the discount rate shall be found from the formula—

(A – 2.3 per cent), or nil per cent, whichever is the greater;

(*b*) in a case [where the calculations under these Regulations are carried out in Australian dollars, Canadian dollars, euro, Japanese yen, Swiss francs or United States dollars (''the relevant foreign currency'')][1], the discount rate shall be found from the formula—

(A – 2.3 per cent) + (B – C), or nil per cent, whichever is the greater.

5.5. In this Rule—

A is the average of the gross redemption yields, expressed as a percentage, applicable to 5–year British Government Stocks as compiled by the Financial Times, the Institute of Actuaries and the Faculty of Actuaries, which were compiled for each of the first five business days beginning with the day on which the balance sheet date fell or, if that day was not a business day, the first business day thereafter;

B is the London Interbank Offered Rate, in the market which exists between banks in London for the purpose of borrowing and lending funds and dealing in currencies, at which deposits for a term of 12 months were offered in the relevant foreign currency on the day on which the balance sheet date fell (or if that day was not a business day, the first business day thereafter) as determined by the British Banking Association; and

C has the same meaning as B, but with the word "sterling" substituted for the words "the relevant foreign currency".

5.6. The discount shall in principle be computed separately for each liability, save that statistical methods may be used where they may be expected to give approximately the same result as individual calculations.

5.7. Aggregate the discounted liabilities and the result is referred to as "the recalculated provisions" for the earlier period of account.

Rule 6

6.1. Compare the difference between—

(*a*) the original provisions for the earlier period of account, and

(*b*) the recalculated provisions for the earlier period of account,

with a margin for error of 5 per cent of the recalculated provisions for the earlier period of account.

Rule 7

7.1. If the amount of the difference does not exceed the margin for error, the difference is assumed to be nil, for the purposes of that period's recalculation.

7.2. If the amount of the difference exceeds the margin for error, deduct the margin for error from the difference, for the purposes of that period's recalculation.

7.3. The result of Rule 7 represents the cumulative excess or deficiency found from the recalculation under this regulation—

(*a*) in the later period of account, and

(*b*) in any periods of account which fell between the earlier period of account and the later period of account ("intervening periods"),

in relation to the same earlier period of account.

Rule 8

8.1. Compare—

(*a*) the result of Rule 7, with

(*b*) the aggregate excess or deficiency found by combining the results of the recalculation under this regulation in any intervening periods in relation to [the same earlier period of account][1]—

(i) ...[1]

(ii) ...[1]

and find out the adjustment (if any) to the amount mentioned in paragraph (*b*) above which is necessary to make it equal the amount mentioned in paragraph (*a*) above. If the adjustment is an excess, that is the amount of the excess referred to in section 107(2). If the adjustment is a deficiency, that is [subject to Rule 8A][1] the amount of the deficiency referred to in section 107(3).

8.2. Where there has been no intervening period (as mentioned in paragraph (*b*) of Rule 7.3.), or the result of paragraph (*b*) of Rule 8.1. is neither an excess nor a deficiency, the result of Rule 7 shall be the amount of the excess referred to in section 107(2), or the amount of the deficiency referred to in section 107(3), as the case may be.

[Rule 8A

8A.1 This Rule applies if, in respect of the provisions made for the earlier period of account—

(*a*) an election has been made under section 107(4) for the earlier period of account in question, and

(*b*) the result of applying Rule 8 is a deficiency.][1]

[8A.2 Where Rule 8A.1 applies, apply Rules 6 to 8 but, in carrying out the calculation made at the end of the later period of account, add to the amount of the original provisions—

(*a*) the amount of any losses set off, under section 393 of the Taxes Act (losses other than terminal losses of a trade) against the trading income of the company's general insurance business for the period of account for which an election under section 107(4) was made in respect of the provisions for the earlier period of account; and

(*b*) any amount which remains to be set off against the profits of the company's general insurance business for the period of account for which an election under section 107(4) was made in respect of the provisions for the earlier period of account under—

(i) section 393A of the Taxes Act (trading losses: set off against the profits of the same or an earlier accounting period);

(ii) Chapter 4 of Part 10 of the Taxes Act (group relief);

(iii) section 83 of, and Schedule 8 to the Finance Act 1996 (non-trading deficit on loan relationships);

(iv) paragraph 35 of Schedule 29 to the Finance Act 2002 (non-trading losses on intangible fixed assets); and

(v) other charges on the income of the company;

after treating any other profits of the general insurer for the earlier period as being reduced in priority to the profits of its general insurance business.

This is subject to the following qualifications.][1]

[8A.3 The qualifications referred to in Rule 8A.2 are that—

(*a*) the total amount added in accordance with it to the provisions for all earlier periods of account taken together shall not exceed the sum of the amounts found under paragraphs (*a*) and (*b*) of that Rule; and

(*b*) the adjustment made under that Rule shall not exceed the amount of the technical provisions for the earlier period of account.][1]

[8A.4 Compare the result of applying Rule 8A.2 with that found before applying it.

If both the amounts are deficiencies, for the purposes only of Rule 9 the smaller deficiency is the amount referred to in section 107(3).

If the result of applying Rule 8A.2 is an excess—

(*a*) it is disregarded for the purposes of section 107(2); and

(*b*) the deficiency produced by Rule 8 is disregarded for the purposes of section 107(3).][1]

[8A.5 If any amount mentioned in Rule 8A.2 is amended in accordance with any provision of the Taxes Act, the adjustment made under that Rule shall be amended accordingly.][1]

Rule 9

9.1. Interest shall be calculated on the amount of the result of Rule 8, [at the rate or rates specified in respect of the period mentioned below][1] in Regulation 3ZA(1) of the Taxes (Interest Rate) Regulations 1989—

(*a*) but as if there were deducted [from the amount of such interest][1] corporation tax at the rate fixed for companies generally (within the meaning in section 13(1) of the Taxes Act) for the later period of account, and

(*b*) save that the rate of interest is a compound rate, with annual rests,

from the date when corporation tax for the earlier period of account became due and payable [until the stop date][1].

[9.1A Interest shall be calculated on the amount of the result of Rule 8 or 8A (as the case requires) in respect of the period—

(*a*) beginning with the stop date, and

(*b*) ending with the date when corporation tax for the later period of account becomes due and payable at the rate specified in regulation 3ZA(1) of the Taxes (Interest Rate) Regulations 1989,

but as if there were deducted from the amount of such interest corporation tax at the rate fixed for companies generally (within the meaning of section 13(1) of the Taxes Act) for the later period of account.][1]

[9.1B In Rules 9.1 and 9.1A the "stop date" is the earlier of—

(*a*) the date when corporation tax for the later period of account becomes due and payable; and

(*b*) the tenth anniversary of the date on which corporation tax for the earlier period of account became due and payable.

Subsection (1) of section 59D of the Taxes Management Act 1970 (day when corporation tax due and payable) applies for the purposes of this Rule and Rules 9.1 and 9.1A as it applies for the purposes of that section but as if the references in that subsection to an accounting period were to a period of account.][1]

9.2. Where the later period of account falls in more than one financial year, the rates of corporation tax for those financial years shall be apportioned to the later period of account on a daily basis.

9.3. The amount of interest so calculated is the amount to be treated as a receipt or an expense, as the case may be, in accordance with section 107, and is the amount of a receipt or expense, as the case may be, referred to, or to be taken into account in a computation of profits and losses under, [sections 92 to 93A][1] of the Finance Act 1993, in a case where those sections apply.

Rule 10

10.1 No amount representing provisions for unearned premiums or provisions for unexpired risks shall be determined as excessive or insufficient for the purposes of section 107.

Amendments—[1] In para (2), definition of "relevant transaction" inserted; sub-para (3)(*b*) and word preceding it revoked; in Rule 2.1, para (*a*) substituted, and words in para (*b*) substituted; words in Rule 3.1 substituted; Rules 4.1–4.1C substituted for Rule 4.1; words in Rules 4.2, 5.4, 8.1 inserted; in Rule 5.4, para (*b*)(i), (ii) revoked; Rules 8A.1 –8A.5, 9.1A, 9.1B inserted; words in Rule 9 substituted; by the General Insurance Reserves (Tax) (Amendment) Regulations, SI 2003/2862 regs 3, 5 with effect from 5 December 2003.

Provisions supplementing regulation 3

4—(1) Paragraph (2) applies where a general insurer ("the transferor") transfers the whole or part of its general business to another body ("the transferee") by—

[(*a*) a transfer effected under a scheme falling within section 105 of the Financial Services and Markets Act 2000, including an excluded scheme falling within Case 2, 3 or 4 of subsection (3) of that section, or][1]

[(*ab*) a scheme which would be an insurance business transfer scheme but for section 105(1)(*b*) of the Financial Services and Markets Act 2000;][3]

[(*b*) a transfer in accordance with an authorisation granted outside the United Kingdom for the purposes of Article 12 of Council Directive 92/49/EC on the co-ordination of the laws, regulations and administrative provisions relating to direct insurance other than life assurance and amending Directives 73/329/EEC and 88/357/EEC,][3]

on or after the date on which these Regulations come into force.

[(1A) Paragraph (2) also applies where, as a result of—

(*a*) a relevant transaction effected after 5th December 2003 between a corporate general insurer and another company—

(i) with which it is connected, and

(ii) which is within the charge to corporation tax in respect of that transaction, or

(*b*) a series of transactions having the same effect as a relevant transaction effected after 5th December 2003 between two companies which—

(i) have been connected with each other at any time in the course of that series of transactions, and

(ii) are within the charge to corporation tax in respect of the relevant transaction,

one of those companies directly or indirectly replaces the other as the insurer under a contract of insurance, or as the reinsurer under a contract of reinsurance, including (in either case) by way of novation.][3]

(2) Where this paragraph applies, the transferor and the transferee shall be treated for the purposes of section 107 and regulation 3 as if—

(*a*) technical provisions made and taken into account by the transferor, so far as they relate to the general business transferred, had been made and taken into account by the transferee, ...[3]

[(*ab*) an election made under section 107(4) by the transferor had been made by the transferee; and][3]

(*b*) any other act or thing mentioned in Rules 1 to 9 in regulation 3(3) and regulation 5 which was done to or by the transferor, so far as it relates to the general business transferred, had been done to or by the transferee.

[(2A) In paragraph (2)(*a*) "technical provisions made and taken into account by the transferor" means, in relation to a period of account in which a transfer of business occurs, the technical provisions which would have been made and taken into account had the transferor's period of account ended immediately before the transfer.

The time at which the technical provisions are treated as made and taken into account by this paragraph shall be treated as the end of a period of account for the purposes of regulation 3(3) (and an election under section 107(4) may accordingly be made in respect of that period).][3]

(3) Where Rule 4 in regulation 3(3) would apply but for the condition in [Rule 4.1C][3] not being satisfied, in a case falling within [Rule 4.1A(*a*)(i)][3] the reinsurer, and in a case falling within [Rule 4.1A(*a*)(ii)][3] the connected company (and the relevant person is referred to as "the transferee"), and [the corporate general insurer][3], shall be treated for the purposes of section 107 and regulation 3 as if—

(*a*) technical provisions made and taken into account by the [corporate][3] general insurer, so far as they relate to the liabilities reinsured, had been made and taken into account by the transferee,

(*b*) premiums paid under the contract were ignored, and

(*c*) any other act or thing mentioned in [Rules 1 to 10][3] in regulation 3(3) and regulation 5 which was done to or by the [corporate][3] general insurer, so far as it relates to the liabilities reinsured, had been done to or by the transferee.

Amendments—[1] Sub-para (1)(*a*) substituted by the Financial Services and Markets Act 2000 (Consequential Amendments) (Taxes) Order, SI 2001/3629 art 193(1)(*a*) with effect from 1 December 2001, immediately after the coming into force of the Financial Services and Markets Act 2000 ss 411, 432(1), Sch 20 (and SI 2001/3629 Pts 1 and 2). The amendment has effect for any transfer under a scheme falling within the Financial Services and Markets Act 2000 s 105, including an excluded scheme falling within Case 2, 3 or 4 of the Financial Services and Markets Act 2000 s 105(3).

[2] Words in sub-para (1)(*b*) substituted by SI 2001/3629 art 193(1)(*b*) with effect from 1 December 2001, immediately after the coming into force of the Financial Services and Markets Act 2000 ss 411, 432(1), Sch 20 (and SI 2001/3629 Pts 1 and 2). The amendment has effect for any transfer in relation to which the Financial Services and Markets Act 2000 s 116 applies.

[3] Para (1)(*ab*), (*b*) substituted for para (1)(*b*); word in para (2)(*a*) revoked; paras (1A), (2)(*ab*), (2A) inserted; and words in para (3) substituted; by the General Insurance Reserves (Tax) (Amendment) Regulations, SI 2003/2862 regs 3, 6 with effect from 5 December 2003.

[Accounting in foreign currencies and relevant discount rates

5—(1) In respect of that part of a general insurer's business to which subsection (1) of section 747A of the Taxes Act applies, any calculation required under these Regulations shall be made in the same currency as that required to be used, for the purposes of Chapter 4 of Part 17 of the Taxes Act, by subsection (2) of that section.

(2) In respect of that part of a general insurer's business to which section 93A of the Finance Act 1993 applies, so much of any calculation required under these Regulations as relates to business in respect of which financial statements and records are prepared in the relevant foreign currency (within the meaning of that section) shall be made in that currency.

(3) In respect of that part of a general insurer's business to which section 93 of the Finance Act 1993 applies—

(*a*) any calculation required under these Regulations shall be made in the relevant foreign currency (within the meaning of that section); and

(*b*) the exchange rate to be used for determining the sterling equivalent of the amount of the receipt or expense found under Rule 9.3 is the London closing exchange rate.

(4) In respect of so much of general insurer's business as does not fall within the previous provisions of this regulation section 94AA of the Finance Act 1993 shall apply to the calculation of an excess or deficiency under regulation 3 as it applies to a computation under section 92(1) of that Act.

(5) If the foreign currency used in the calculations under paragraphs (1) to (3) is one of the currencies mentioned in paragraph (*b*) of Rule 5.4, the discount rate to be applied to those calculations shall be found in accordance with the formula in that paragraph, and in any other case shall be found in accordance with the formula in paragraph (*a*) of Rule 5.4.][1]

Amendments—[1] This regulation substituted by the General Insurance Reserves (Tax) (Amendment) Regulations, SI 2003/2862 regs 3, 7 with effect from 5 December 2003. However, notwithstanding the substitution—

(*a*) an election may be made before 31 December 2003 under this regulation as it stood immediately before the substitution; and

(*b*) if such an election is made (whether before or after the coming into force of SI 2003/2862) the currency chosen under para (5) of the principal Regulations as it stood before the substitution may continue to be used as it might have been had the substitution not occurred.

Excluded descriptions of general insurer

6—[(1)][2] The descriptions of general insurer which are excluded from the operation of section 107(1) to (4) are—

(*a*) a company which [is in][2] insolvent liquidation (within the meaning in section 214(6) of the Insolvency Act 1986 ("the Act") or Article 178(6) of the Insolvency (Northern Ireland) Order 1989 ("the Order")), where the exclusion takes effect from the date on which it goes into liquidation (within the meaning in section 247(2) of the Act or Article 6(2) of the Order);

(*b*) a company in relation to which an administration order has been made under ...[1] Article 21 of the Order [or a company which is in administration within the meaning of Schedule B1 to the Act][1];

(*c*) a company in respect of which a provisional liquidator [is][2] appointed under section 135 of the Act or Article 115 of the Order; and

(*d*) a company in respect of which a relevant arrangement or compromise (within the meaning in section 74(2) of the Taxes Act) [is in force][2].

[This is subject to the following qualification.][2]

[(2) A general insurer is not excluded from the operation of section 107 by virtue of paragraph (1)(*c*) or (*d*) unless—

(*a*) it is insolvent at the time the provisional liquidator is appointed or the relevant arrangement or compromise comes into force; or

(*b*) in a case falling within paragraph (1)(*d*), it would be insolvent but for the relevant arrangement or compromise coming into force.][2]

Amendments—[1] In para (1)(*b*), words revoked and words inserted by the Enterprise Act 2002 (Insolvency) Order, SI 2003/2096 art 5, Schedule para 78 with effect from 15 September 2003. However, this amendment does not apply in any case where a petition for an administration order was presented before 15 September 2003: SI 2003/2096 art 6.

[2] Para (1) numbered as such, words in sub-paras (*a*), (*c*), (*d*) thereof substituted, and words inserted; and para (2) inserted, by the General Insurance Reserves (Tax) (Amendment) Regulations, SI 2003/2862 regs 3, 8 with effect from 5 December 2003.

"Technical provisions" in relation to an underwriting member

7—(1) "Technical provisions" in relation to an underwriting member and the premium paid or treated as paid by him under a reinsurance to close contract means—

(*a*) where the member is a continuing member, that is, a member not only of the syndicate as a member of which he pays, or is treated as paying, the premium ("the reinsured syndicate") but also of the syndicate as a member of which he receives or is treated as receiving it or part of it ("the reinsurer syndicate"), so much of the premium as equals—

(i) the amount of the premium which he pays or is treated as paying, or

(ii) the amount of the premium which he receives or is treated as receiving, whichever is the lesser (subject to sub-paragraph (*b*)); and

(*b*) where the member is not entitled to participate in the underwriting business of the reinsurer syndicate, or his entitlement to participate in either of the reinsured syndicate or the reinsurer syndicate is less than 4 per cent of the whole, none of the premium.

(2) Regulations 3 to 5 shall apply to—

(*a*) any premium or part of a premium treated as "technical provisions" by paragraph (1)(*a*), with the modifications to regulation 3(3) contained in paragraphs (3) to [(5)][1], and

(*b*) any provisions or part of provisions treated as "technical provisions" by paragraph (8), with the modifications contained in paragraphs (3), (4), (5)(*c*) ...[1] and (7).

(3) In regulation 3(3) in the words preceding sub-paragraph (*a*), for the reference to provisions for claims outstanding there shall be substituted a reference to technical provisions.

(4) In Rule 2—

(*a*) for the reference to provisions for claims outstanding, there shall be substituted a reference to technical provisions, and

(*b*) for paragraph (*b*) of Rule 2.1. there shall be substituted—

"(*b*) in any other case, [were provisions][1] for liabilities arising directly from the underwriting member's membership of one or more syndicates, whose closing year was the year immediately preceding the earlier period of account, but excluding liabilities which the member acquired by means of a reinsurance to close contract, the premium for which was treated as a technical provision for the same member for that preceding year.".

(5) In Rule 3—

(*a*) in paragraph (*a*) "claims paid" shall be construed as a reference to claims paid by the member in consequence of his membership of the reinsurer syndicate or of any further syndicate which, directly or indirectly, reinsures the liabilities to which the provisions relate under any further reinsurance to close contracts;

(*b*) where any claim, bonus, rebate or premium was paid by the member as a member of the reinsurer syndicate, the payment shall be treated for the purposes of Rules 3 and 5 as made one year later than the date of the actual payment; and

(*c*) in Rule 3.1.(*d*) for the reference to provisions for claims outstanding, there shall be substituted a reference to provisions made for the unpaid liabilities of the reinsurer syndicate where it is an open syndicate.

(6) ...[1]

(7) The modification contained in this paragraph is the modification to Rule 3 in paragraph (5)(*b*) omitting the words "as a member of the reinsurer syndicate".

(8) "Technical provisions" in relation to an underwriting member and the provisions made for the unpaid liabilities of an open syndicate of which he is a member means—

(*a*) where the member's entitlement to participate in the underwriting business of the open syndicate is equal to or more than 4 per cent of the whole, the share of those provisions which corresponds to his proportionate entitlement; and

(*b*) in any other case, none of the provisions.

(9) In determining a member's entitlement to participate in the business of a syndicate, or share of a premium, for the purposes of paragraphs (1) and (8), there shall be attributed to a member which is a company any entitlement to participate in the relevant syndicate of any company which is connected with the member.

(10) In a case falling within the provisions of both paragraphs (1) and (9), where—

(*a*) there is a change in the entitlement of a company to participate, as between the reinsured syndicate and the reinsurer syndicate, such that,

(*b*) the reinsurance to close contract has the same financial effect as if a liability were transferred from that company to a company connected with it,

the provisions of [sub-paragraphs (*a*), (*ab*) and (*b*) of regulation 4(2)][1] shall to that extent apply as if there were a transfer of business between those companies.

(11) A syndicate's managing agent (within the meaning in Chapter III of Part II of the Finance Act 1993) shall, on request from a member or former member of the syndicate, provide the member with the information which he needs, and which is within the agent's possession or power, to make a recalculation under regulation 3 (as applied by paragraph (2)) in relation to his proportionate entitlement in the syndicate.

Amendments—[1] References in para (2) substituted and revoked; words in paras (4)(*b*), (10) substituted; para (6) revoked; by the General Insurance Reserves (Tax) (Amendment) Regulations, SI 2003/2862 regs 3, 9 with effect from 5 December 2003.

Elections under section 107(4), or paragraph 4(2) of Schedule 24 to the Taxes Act

8—[(1) An election by a general insurer for the purposes of section 107(4) or for the purposes of paragraph 4(2) of Schedule 24 to the Taxes Act may be made or withdrawn at any time up to whichever is the last of the following dates—

(*a*) the first anniversary of the filing date for the company tax return of the company making the election for the period of account in respect of which the election is made;
(*b*) if notice of enquiry is given into that return, 30 days after the enquiry is completed;
(*c*) if, after such an enquiry, the Board amend the return under paragraph 34(2) of Schedule 18 to the Finance Act 1998, 30 days after the notice of the amendment is issued; and
(*d*) if an appeal is brought against such an amendment, 30 days after the date on which the appeal is finally determined.][1]

[(1A) Paragraph (1) applies to an underwriting member other than a body corporate with the substitution for paragraphs (*a*) to (*c*) of—

"(*a*) the first anniversary of 31st January next following the end of the year of assessment in which falls the end of the period of account in respect of which the election is made;
(*b*) if notice of enquiry is given into the underwriting member's tax return for that year of assessment, 30 days after the enquiry is completed;
(*c*) if after such an enquiry the Board amend the return under section 28A of the Taxes Management Act 1970, 30 days after the amendment of the return;".][1]

(2) Where a general insurer delivers a tax return based wholly or partly on accounts drawn up using the method described in paragraph 52 of Schedule 9A (which provides for a technical provision to be made in the accounts which is later replaced by a provision for estimated claims outstanding) the period in [paragraph (1)(*a*)][1] is extended until two years from the date on which the provision was replaced.

(3) Where a general insurer which is a controlled foreign company draws up accounts using a method falling within section 755B(2), the period of twenty months mentioned in paragraph 4(2) of Schedule 24 to the Taxes Act (elections by a United Kingdom resident company or companies) shall be extended until two years immediately following the close of the underwriting year (within the meaning in section 754AA(11)).

[(4) An election under section 107(4) by a controlled foreign company may be communicated, on its behalf, by the person or persons resident in the United Kingdom by whom it is controlled to the Board.][1]

[(5) An election under section 107(4) shall be made in writing and shall specify—

(*a*) the period of account in respect of which the election is made;
(*b*) the earlier period or periods of account to which the technical provisions in question relate;
(*c*) the amount of technical provisions being disclaimed in respect of each such period; and
(*d*) the currency in which the technical provisions being disclaimed are expressed.][1]

Amendments—[1] Paras (1), (1A) substituted for para (1), words in para (2) substituted, and paras (4), (5) inserted; by the General Insurance Reserves (Tax) (Amendment) Regulations, SI 2003/2862 regs 3,10 with effect from 5 December 2003.

Generally

9—For the purposes of any computation under these Regulations any necessary apportionments shall be made and the method of apportionment adopted shall, subject to the express provisions of these Regulations, be just and reasonable.

[Modification: companies subject to these Regulations on or after 5th December 2003

10—(1) Paragraph (2) applies to a company if any of the following Cases applies.

Case 1

The company is one to which these Regulations first apply on or after 5th December 2003 by reason of its becoming—

(*a*) a controlled foreign company on or after that date; or
(*b*) subject to corporation tax for the first time on of after that date.

Case 2

The company, already being subject to corporation tax in respect of its general insurance business, is charged to tax under Case I of Schedule D in respect of that business for the first time for a period of account beginning on or after 5th December 2003.

Case 3

The company is a controlled foreign company and the first period of account in respect of which—

(*a*) an apportionment falls to be made under section 747(3), or
(*b*) section 748(1)(*a*) applies,

is a period of account ending on or after 5th December 2003.

Case 4

The company is one to which these Regulations apply on 5th December 2003 by reason only of the amendments made by regulation 8 of the General Insurance Reserves (Tax) (Amendment) Regulations 2003 to regulation 6 of these Regulations.

(2) In the case of a company to which this paragraph applies, regulations 2 to 9 of these Regulations shall apply as if references to the first earlier period of account were to the period of account preceding that during which the company first becomes subject to these Regulations and references to original technical provisions shall be construed accordingly.

(3) If paragraph (2) applies, an election may be made under section 107(4) in respect of the original technical provisions of the period of account preceding that during which the company in question first becomes subject to these Regulations.][1]

Amendments—[1] This regulation inserted by the General Insurance Reserves (Tax) (Amendment) Regulations, SI 2003/2862 regs 3,11 with effect from 5 December 2003.

2001/2541
Capital Allowances (Energy-saving Plant and Machinery) Order 2001

Made by the Treasury under CAA 2001 ss 45A(3), (4), 45B(1), 45C(2)(*b*), (3)(*b*) and 180A(2)

Made	*16 July 2001*
Laid before the House of Commons	*16 July 2001*
Coming into force	*7 August 2001*

Citation and commencement

1 This Order may be cited as the Capital Allowances (Energy-saving Plant and Machinery) Order 2001 and shall come into force on 7th August 2001.

Interpretation

2 In this Order—

"Capital Allowances Act" means the Capital Allowances Act 2001;

["Energy Technology Criteria List" means the list dated 11th July 2003 and published by the Department for Environment, Food and Rural Affairs on 14th July 2003;][1]

["Energy Technology Product List" means the list dated 11th July 2003 and published by the Department for Environment, Food and Rural Affairs on 14th July 2003;][1]

Amendments—[1] Definitions of "Energy Technology Criteria List" and "Energy Technology Product List" substituted by the Capital Allowances (Energy-saving Plant and Machinery) (Amendment) Order, SI 2003/1744 arts 2, 3 with effect from 5 August 2003.

The definitions previously read as follows—

"Energy Technology Criteria List" means the list dated 12th July 2002 and published by the Department for Environment, Food and Rural Affairs on 15th July 2002;"

"Energy Technology Product List" means the list dated 12th July 2002 and published by the Department for Environment, Food and Rural Affairs on 15th July 2002.".

Description of energy-saving plant and machinery

3—(1) Plant or machinery is energy-saving plant or machinery for the purposes of section 45A of the Capital Allowances Act (expenditure on energy-saving plant or machinery) if—

(*a*) it falls within a technology class specified in the Energy Technology Criteria List,
(*b*) it meets the energy-saving criteria set out in that List, and
(*c*) [subject to [paragraphs (3) and (4)][2]][1] in the case of plant or machinery falling within any of the technology classes specified in paragraph (2), it is of a type that—
  (i) is specified in, and has not been removed from, the Energy Technology Product List, or
  (ii) has been accepted for inclusion in the Energy Technology Product List.

(2) The technology classes specified for the purposes of paragraph (1)(*c*) are—

(*a*) boilers,
(*b*) motors and drives,
(*c*) refrigeration,
(*d*) thermal screens,
[(*e*) heat pumps,][1]
[(*f*) radiant and warm air heaters,][1]
[(*g*) compressed air equipment,][1]
[(*h*) solar thermal systems.][1]
[(*i*) automatic monitoring and targeting equipment.][2]

[(3) In the case of solar thermal systems either the solar thermal system or the solar collector included in the system must be of a type within paragraph (i) or (ii) of article 3(1)(*c*).][1]

[(4) In the case of automatic monitoring and targeting equipment—

(*a*) portable equipment must be of a type within paragraph (i) or (ii) of article 3(1)(*c*),

(*b*) component based fixed systems are within article 4.][2]

Amendments—[1] Words in para (1)(*c*) inserted, and paras (2)(*e*)–(*h*), (3) added, by the Capital Allowances (Energy-saving Plant and Machinery) (Amendment) Order, SI 2002/1818 regs 2, 4 with effect from 5 August 2002.

[2] In para (1)(*c*), words substituted for the words ''paragraph (3)'', and paras (2)(*i*) and (4) inserted, by the Capital Allowances (Energy-saving Plant and Machinery) (Amendment) Order, SI 2003/1744 arts 2, 4 with effect from 5 August 2003.

Certification of energy-saving plant and machinery

4—(1) In the case of plant or machinery—

[(*a*)][1] falling within the technology class ''Combined Heat and Power'' specified in the Energy Technology Criteria List[, or

(*b*) comprising a component based fixed system falling within the technology class ''Automatic Monitoring and Targeting equipment'' specified in the Energy Technology Criteria List][1]

no section 45A allowance may be made unless a relevant certificate of energy efficiency is in force with respect to that plant or machinery.

(2) In paragraph (1) ''section 45A allowance'' and ''relevant certificate of energy efficiency'' have the meanings given by section 45B of the Capital Allowances Act.

Amendments—[1] Para (1)(*a*) numbered as such, and para (1)(*b*) inserted, by the Capital Allowances (Energy-saving Plant and Machinery) (Amendment) Order, SI 2003/1744 arts 2, 5 with effect from 5 August 2003.

Energy-saving components of plant or machinery

5 Where one or more components of certain plant or machinery (but not all of that plant or machinery)—

(*a*) meets the conditions set out in article 3(1)(*a*) to (*c*), and

(*b*) falls within any of the technology classes specified in article 3(2)(*a*) to (*c*) [and (*g*)][1],

the amount specified in respect of each such component for the purposes of section 45C of the Capital Allowances Act is the amount specified in the Energy Technology Product List in relation to that component.

Amendments—[1] Words in para (*b*) inserted by the Capital Allowances (Energy-saving Plant and Machinery) (Amendment) Order, SI 2002/1818 regs 2, 5 with effect from 5 August 2002.

Energy services providers

6 The class of plant or machinery specified for the purposes of section 180A(2) of the Capital Allowances Act is the technology class ''Combined Heat and Power'' specified in the Energy Technology Criteria List.

Commentary—*Simon's Direct Tax Service* **B2.324**.

2001/3643

Finance Act 1996, Section 167, (Appointed Day) Order 2001

Made by the Commissioners of Inland Revenue under FA 1996 s167(11), (12), TA 1988 Sch 14 para 8(8)(*a*), Sch 15 paras 8A, 18(3)(*c*)(i)

Made . . . . *9 November 2001*

1 This Order may be cited as the Finance Act 1996, Section 167, (Appointed Day) Order 2001.

2 The day appointed for the purposes of—

(*a*) section 167(11) and (12) of the Finance Act 1996,

(*b*) paragraph 8(8)(*a*) of Schedule 14 to the Income and Corporation Taxes Act 1988, and

(*c*) paragraphs 8A and 18(3)(*c*)(i) of Schedule 15 to the Income and Corporation Taxes Act 1988,

is 1st December 2001.

2001/3973

Friendly Societies (Provisional Repayments for Exempt Business) (Amendment) Regulations 2001

Made by the Treasury under FA 1993 s 121, FA 2001 s 87(3), (4)

Made . . . . *11 December 2001*
Laid before the House of Commons . . . . *11 December 2001*
Coming into force . . . . *1 January 2002*

Citation, commencement and effect

1 These Regulations may be cited as the Friendly Societies (Provisional Repayments for Exempt Business) (Amendment) Regulations 2001 and shall come into force on 1st January 2002, and shall have effect in relation to accounting periods of friendly societies beginning on or after 1st January 2002.

Interpretation

2 In these Regulations—

"the principal Regulations" means the Friendly Societies (Provisional Repayments for Exempt Business) Regulations 1999;

"Schedule 19AB" means Schedule 19AB to the Income and Corporation Taxes Act 1988.

Amendments to the principal Regulations and further modifications to Schedule 19AB

3 (*amends* SI 1999/622 reg 2).

4 (*amends* SI 1999/622 reg 3(1)).

5 (*omits* SI 1999/622 reg 3(3)).

6 (*amends* TA 1988 Sch 19AB para 1(1) as substituted by SI 1999/622 reg 4(2)).

7 (*amends* TA 1988 Sch 19AB para 1(5)–(5E) as substituted by SI 1999/622 reg 5(2)).

8 (*omits* SI 1999/622 regs 6, 7).

9 (*amends* SI 1999/622 reg 8).

10 (*amends* SI 1999/622 reg 9).

11 (*amends* SI 1999/622 reg 10).

12 (*amends* SI 1999/622 reg 12).

13 In the heading to Schedule 19AB for the words "pension business—payments on account of tax credits and deducted tax" there shall be substituted the words "tax exempt business—payments on account of tax credits".

14 The Schedule to these Regulations sets out the text of Schedule 19AB as applied by the principal Regulations and these Regulations.

SCHEDULE

Regulation 14

[SCHEDULE 19AB TAX EXEMPT BUSINESS—PAYMENTS ON ACCOUNT OF TAX CREDITS

Entitlement to certain payments on account

1—(1) A friendly society carrying on both tax exempt business and business other than tax exempt business shall for each provisional repayment period in an accounting period be entitled on a claim made in that behalf to a payment (in this Schedule referred to as a 'provisional repayment') of an amount equal to—

(*a*)–(*b*) ...

(*c*) as respects any distribution made on or after 6 April 1999 and before 6 April 2004 that—

(i) is received by the society in that provisional repayment period, and

(ii) is referable to its tax exempt business,

(iii) ...

the appropriate portion of any tax credit in respect of that distribution.

(2) For the purposes of this paragraph, a 'provisional repayment period' of a society—

(*a*) shall begin whenever—

(i) the society begins, at a time when it is carrying on only tax exempt business, to carry on business other than tax exempt business;

(ii) the society begins, at a time when it is carrying on only business other than tax exempt business, to carry on tax exempt business;

(iii) an accounting period of the society begins at a time when the society is carrying on both tax exempt business and business other than tax exempt business; or

(iv) a provisional repayment period of the society ends, at a time when the society is carrying on both tax exempt business and business other than tax exempt business; and

(*b*) shall end on the first occurrence of either of the following—

(i) the expiration of three months from the beginning of the provisional repayment period; or

(ii) the end of an accounting period of the society.

(3) ...

(4) The provisional fraction for the purposes of this paragraph for an accounting period which begins before 6 April 2004 shall be such fraction as the society may reasonably estimate, being a fraction which is not likely to be greater than the relevant fraction for its tax exempt business which would be determined in accordance with subsections (5) to (9B) of section 432A for that accounting period.

(5) ...

(5A) In sub-paragraph (1)(*c*) above 'the appropriate portion' means—

(*a*) where the distribution in question is income arising from assets linked to tax exempt basic life assurance and general annuity business or to tax exempt class IV business the profits of which are exempt from tax by virtue of section 460(1) ('section 460(1) exempt business'), the whole;

(*b*) where the distribution in question is income arising from assets of the society's overseas life assurance fund, the fraction whose numerator is the mean of the opening and closing liabilities to policyholders in respect of the society's tax exempt overseas life assurance business and whose denominator is the opening and closing liabilities to policyholders in respect of the whole of the society's overseas life assurance business;

(*c*) if and to the extent that the distribution in question is income arising from assets of the society's long term business fund but, on the assumption that section 460(1) exempt business were a separate category of business within section 432A, is not referable to a category of business by virtue of subsection (3) or (4) of that section, the provisional fraction;

(*d*) except as provided by paragraph (*a*), (*b*) or (*c*) above, none.

(5B) ...

(5C) In determining the provisional fraction for the purposes of sub-paragraph (5A)(*c*) above, tax exempt basic life assurance and general annuity business and section 460(1) exempt business shall be taken to be a single category for the purposes of section 432A(5).

(5D) In sub-paragraph (5A) above references to assets of the society's long term business fund—

(*a*) as respects societies to which regulation 13(1) of the Friendly Societies (Modification of the Corporation Tax Acts) Regulations 1997 applies, shall be construed in accordance with the definition in subsection (11) of section 432A, read with subsections (12) to (14) of that section, as those subsections are added by regulation 13(5) of those Regulations;

(*b*) as respects other societies, shall be construed in accordance with the definitions of 'long term business' (as substituted by regulation 6(4) of those Regulations) and 'long term business fund' in section 431(2).

(5E) In sub-paragraphs (5A) and (5C) above—

'tax exempt basic life assurance and general annuity business' shall be construed in accordance with the definition inserted in section 431(2) by regulation 6(2) of the Friendly Societies (Modification of the Corporation Tax Acts) Regulations 1997;

'tax exempt class IV business' shall be construed in accordance with the definition inserted in section 431(2) by regulation 7(2) of those Regulations;

'tax exempt overseas life assurance business' shall be construed in accordance with section 441(4D).

(6) Paragraphs 57 to 60 of Schedule 18 to the Finance Act 1998 (general provisions as to procedure on claims and elections) do not apply to a claim for a provisional repayment.

(6A) A claim for a provisional repayment shall be in such form as the Board may determine and the form of claim shall provide for a declaration to the effect that all the particulars given in the form are correctly stated to the best of the knowledge and belief of the person making the claim.

(7) A provisional repayment for a provisional repayment period shall be regarded as a payment on account of the amounts (if any) which the society would, apart from this Schedule, be entitled to be paid in respect of its tax exempt business for the accounting period in which that provisional repayment period falls, in respect of—

(*a*) ...

(*b*) tax credits in respect of distributions received by the society in that accounting period and referable to its tax exempt business,

on a claim such as is mentioned in paragraph 9(3) of Schedule 18 to the Finance Act 1998 in respect of that accounting period.

(8)–(11) ...

2 ...

Repayment, with interest, of excessive provisional repayments

3—(1) In any case where—

(*a*) a friendly society's self-assessment for an accounting period becomes final, and

(*b*) the aggregate amount of the provisional repayments made to the society for that accounting period exceeds the appropriate amount,

the excess, together with the amount of any relevant interest, shall be treated for the purposes of paragraph 52 of Schedule 18 to the Finance Act 1998 as if it were an amount of corporation tax for that accounting period which had been repaid to the friendly society and which ought not to have been so repaid.

(1A) For the purposes of sub-paragraph (1)(*b*) above, the appropriate amount for an accounting period of a society is the amount (if any) which, on the assumption in sub-paragraph (1B) below and disregarding any provisional repayments, the society would be entitled to be paid when its self-assessment for the period becomes final, in respect of its tax exempt business for that accounting period on a claim such as is mentioned in paragraph 9(3) of Schedule 18 to the Finance Act 1998 in respect of—

(*a*) ...

(*b*) tax credits in respect of distributions received by the society in that accounting period and referable to its tax exempt business.

(1B) The assumption is that no payments have been made to the society in respect of—

(*a*) ...

(*b*) tax credits such as are mentioned in paragraph (*b*) of sub-paragraph (1A) above,

before the society's self-assessment for the accounting period in question becomes final.

(1C)...

(1D) Paragraph 53 of Schedule 18 to the Finance Act 1998 (time limit for recovery of excessive repayments etc) does not apply to an assessment under paragraph 52 of that Schedule made by virtue of this paragraph.

But such an assessment is not out of time under paragraph 46 of that Schedule (general six year time limit for assessments) if it is made not later than the end of the accounting period following that in which the self-assessment mentioned in sub-paragraph (1)(*a*) above becomes final.

(2) In this paragraph, 'relevant interest' means interest—

(*a*) in so much of the excess referred to in sub-paragraph (1) above as is or was from time to time outstanding,

(*b*) for any period for which it is or was so outstanding, and

(*c*) at the rate applicable under section 178 of the Finance Act 1989 for the purposes of section 87A of the Management Act (interest on overdue corporation tax).

(3) In the application of section 87A of the Management Act in relation to an amount assessed to corporation tax under paragraph 52 of Schedule 18 to the Finance Act 1998 by virtue of this paragraph—

(*a*) the amount so assessed shall be taken to have become due and payable on the date on which that assessment was made; and

(*b*) the words '(in accordance with section 59D of this Act)' in subsection (1) shall accordingly be disregarded.

(4) In determining the amount of any relevant interest, any question whether the excess mentioned in sub-paragraph (1) above (in the following provisions of this paragraph referred to as 'the principal') or any part of it is or was 'outstanding' at any time shall be determined in accordance with sub-paragraphs (5) to (8) below.

(5) So much of the principal as does not exceed the amount of the last provisional repayment made to the society for the accounting period in question shall be taken to have become outstanding on the date on which that provisional repayment was made.

(6) So much (if any) of the principal as—

(*a*) exceeds the amount of the provisional repayment referred to in sub-paragraph (5) above, but

(*b*) does not exceed the amount of the preceding provisional repayment for that accounting period,

shall be taken to have become outstanding on the date on which that preceding provisional repayment was made; and so on with any remaining portion of the principal and any preceding provisional repayments for that accounting period.

(7) So much (if any) of the principal as has become outstanding as mentioned in sub-paragraph (5) or (6) above and has at any time neither been repaid to the Board nor been assessed to corporation tax under paragraph 52 of Schedule 18 to the Finance Act 1998 by virtue of this paragraph shall be taken to remain outstanding at that time (and an amount shall accordingly be taken to cease being outstanding only when it is repaid to the Board or when it is so assessed).

(8) For the purposes of sub-paragraph (7) above, any repayment made by the society in respect of an amount paid to it in respect of—

(*a*) ...

(*b*) tax credits such as are mentioned in paragraph (*b*) of sub-paragraph (1A) above,

shall be treated as a repayment in respect of the principal, taking an earlier such repayment by the society before a later.

(9) In this paragraph 'self-assessment' means an assessment included in a company tax return and includes a reference to such an assessment as amended.

4–5 ...

Interpretation

6—(1) In this Schedule—

'provisional fraction' shall be construed in accordance with paragraph 1(4) above;

'provisional repayment' means a provisional repayment under paragraph 1 above;

'provisional repayment period' shall be construed in accordance with paragraph 1 above;

'tax exempt business' means any business of a friendly society the profits arising from which are exempt from income tax and corporation tax under section 460(1).

(2) Any reference in this Schedule to a provisional repayment for an accounting period is a reference to a provisional repayment for a provisional repayment period falling within that accounting period.

(3)–(6) ..."

2001/3974

Individual Savings Account (Insurance Companies) (Amendment) Regulations 2001

Made by the Treasury under TA 1988 s 333B, FA 2001 s 87(3), (4)

Made	*11 December 2001*
Laid before the House of Commons	*11 December 2001*
Coming into force	*1 January 2002*

Citation, commencement and effect

1 These Regulations may be cited as the Individual Savings Account (Insurance Companies) (Amendment) Regulations 2001 and shall come into force on 1st January 2002, and shall have effect in relation to accounting periods of insurance companies beginning on or after 1st January 2002.

Interpretation

2 In these Regulations—

"the principal Regulations" means the Individual Savings Account (Insurance Companies) Regulations 1998;

"regulation" means a regulation of the principal regulations;

"Schedule 19AB" means Schedule 19AB to the Income and Corporation Taxes Act 1988.

Amendments to the principal Regulations

3, 4 *(amend* SI 1998/1871 regs 20, 21)

5 The Schedule to these Regulations sets out the text of Schedule 19AB as applied by the principal Regulations and these Regulations.

SCHEDULE

Regulation 5

[SCHEDULE 19AB INDIVIDUAL SAVINGS ACCOUNT BUSINESS—PAYMENTS ON ACCOUNT OF TAX CCREDITS

Entitlement to certain payments on account

1—(1) An insurance company carrying on individual savings account business shall for each provisional repayment period in an accounting period be entitled on a claim made in that behalf to a payment (in this Schedule referred to as a 'provisional repayment') of an amount equal to—

(*a*) ...

(*b*) the appropriate portion of any tax credit in respect of a distribution received by the company in that provisional repayment period and referable to its individual savings account business,

or of such lesser amount as may be specified in the claim.

(2) For the purposes of this paragraph, a 'provisional repayment period' of a company—

(*a*) shall begin whenever—

(i) the company begins to carry on individual savings account business;

(ii) an accounting period of the company begins, at a time when the company is carrying on such business; or

(iii) a provisional repayment period of the company ends, at a time when the company is carrying on such business; and

(*b*) shall end on the first occurrence of either of the following—

(i) the expiration of three months from the beginning of the provisional repayment period; or

(ii) the end of an accounting period of the company.

(3)–(4) ...

(4A) The provisional fraction for the purposes of this paragraph for a relevant accounting period shall be such fraction as the company may reasonably estimate, being a fraction which is not likely to be greater than the relevant fraction for its individual savings account business which would be determined in accordance with subsections (5) to (9B) of section 432A for that accounting period.

(4B) In sub-paragraph (4A) above 'relevant accounting period' means—

(*a*) the accounting period in which 6th April 1999 falls, or (*b*) any succeeding accounting period which begins before 6th April 2004.

(5) In sub-paragraph (1) above 'the appropriate portion' means—

(*a*) in the case of an insurance company carrying on individual savings account business and no other category of long term business, the whole; and

(*b*) in the case of an insurance company carrying on more than one category of long term business—

(i) where the distribution in question is income arising from an asset linked to individual savings account business, the whole; and

(ii) if and to the extent that the distribution in question is income which is not referable to a category of business by virtue of subsection (3) or (4) of section 432A, the provisional fraction; and

(iii) except as provided by sub-paragraph (i) or (ii) above, none.

(6) Paragraphs 57 to 60 of Schedule 18 to the Finance Act 1998 (general provisions as to procedure on claims and elections) do not apply to a claim for a provisional repayment.

(6A) A claim for a provisional repayment shall be in such form as the Board may determine and the form of claim shall provide for a declaration to the effect that all the particulars given in form are correctly stated to the best of the knowledge and belief of the person making the claim.

(7) A provisional repayment for a provisional repayment period shall be regarded as a payment on account of the amounts (if any) which the company would, apart from this Schedule, be entitled to be paid in respect of its individual savings account business for the accounting period in which that provisional repayment period falls, in respect of—

(*a*) ...

(*b*) tax credits in respect of distributions received by the company in that accounting period and referable to its individual savings account business,

on a claim such as is mentioned in paragraph 9(3) of Schedule 18 to the Finance Act 1998 in respect of that accounting period.

(8)–(11) ...

2 ...

Repayment, with interest, of excessive provisional repayments

3—(1) In any case where—

(*a*) an insurance company's self-assessment for an accounting period becomes final, and

(*b*) the aggregate amount of the provisional repayments made to the company for that accounting period exceeds the appropriate amount,

the excess, together with the amount of any relevant interest, shall be treated for the purposes of paragraph 52 of Schedule 18 to the Finance Act 1998 as if it were an amount of corporation tax for that accounting period which had been repaid to the insurance company and which ought not to have been so repaid.

(1A) For the purposes of sub-paragraph (1)(*b*) above, the appropriate amount for an accounting period of a company is the amount (if any) which, on the assumption in sub-paragraph (1B) below and disregarding any provisional repayments, the company would be entitled to be paid, when its self-assessment for the period becomes final, in respect of its individual savings account business for that accounting period on a claim such as is mentioned in paragraph 9(3) of Schedule 18 to the Finance Act 1998 in respect of—

(*a*) ...

(*b*) tax credits in respect of distributions received by the company in that accounting period and referable to its individual savings account business.

(1B) The assumption is that no payments have been made to the company in respect of—

(*a*) ...

(*b*) tax credits such as are mentioned in paragraph (*b*) of sub-paragraph (1A) above,

before the company's self-assessment for the accounting period in question becomes final.

(1C) ...

(1D) Paragraph 53 of Schedule 18 to the Finance Act 1998 (time limit for recovery of excessive repayments etc) does not apply to an assessment under paragraph 52 of that Schedule made by virtue of this paragraph.

But such an assessment is not out of time under paragraph 46 of that Schedule (general six year time limit for assessments) if it is made not later than the end of the accounting period following that in which the self-assessment mentioned in sub-paragraph (1)(*a*) above becomes final.

(2) In this paragraph, 'relevant interest' means interest—

(*a*) on so much of the excess referred to in sub-paragraph (1) above as is or was from time to time outstanding,

(*b*) for any period for which it is or was so outstanding, and (*c*) at the rate applicable under section 178 of the Finance Act 1989 for the purposes of section 87A of the Management Act (interest on overdue corporation tax).

(3) In the application of section 87A of the Management Act in relation to an amount assessed to corporation tax under paragraph 52 of Schedule 18 to the Finance Act 1998 by virtue of this paragraph—

(*a*) the amount so assessed shall be taken to have become due and payable on the date on which that assessment was made; and

(*b*) the words '(in accordance with section 59D of this Act)' in subsection (1) shall accordingly be disregarded.

(4) In determining the amount of any relevant interest, any question whether the excess mentioned in sub-paragraph (1) above (in the following provisions of this paragraph referred to as 'the principal') or any part of it is or was 'outstanding' at any time shall be determined in accordance with sub-paragraphs (5) to (8) below.

(5) So much of the principal as does not exceed the amount of the last provisional repayment made to the company for the accounting period in question shall be taken to have become outstanding on the date on which that provisional repayment was made.

(6) So much (if any) of the principal as—

(*a*) exceeds the amount of the provisional repayment referred to in sub-paragraph (5) above, but

(*b*) does not exceed the amount of the preceding provisional repayment for that accounting period,

shall be taken to have become outstanding on the date on which that preceding provisional repayment was made; and so on with any remaining portion of the principal and any preceding provisional repayments for that accounting period.

(7) So much (if any) of the principal as has become outstanding as mentioned in sub-paragraph (5) or (6) above and has at any time neither been repaid to the Board nor been assessed to corporation tax under paragraph 52 of Schedule 18 to the Finance Act 1998 by virtue of this paragraph shall be taken to remain outstanding at that time (and an amount shall accordingly be taken to cease being outstanding only when it is repaid to the Board or when it is so assessed).

(8) For the purposes of sub-paragraph (7) above, any repayment made by the company in respect of an amount paid to it in respect of—

(*a*) ...

(*b*) tax credits such as are mentioned in paragraph (*b*) of sub-paragraph (1A) above,

shall be treated as a repayment in respect of the principal, taking an earlier such repayment by the company before a later.

(9) In this paragraph 'self-assessment' means an assessment included in a company tax return and includes a reference to such an assessment as amended.

4–5 ...

Interpretation

6—

(1) In this Schedule—

'provisional fraction' shall be construed in accordance with paragraph 1(4A) above;

'provisional repayment' means a provisional repayment under paragraph 1 above;

'provisional repayment period' shall be construed in accordance with paragraph 1 above.

(2) Any reference in this Schedule to a provisional repayment for an accounting period is a reference to a provisional repayment for a provisional repayment period falling within that accounting period.

(3)–(6) ...''

2001/4024
Referrals to the Special Commissioners Regulations 2001

Made by the Lord Chancellor under TMA 1970 s 28ZC(1) to (3) and (7)

Made . . . . *12 December 2001*
Laid before Parliament . . . . . . *19 December 2001*
Coming into force . . . . *31 January 2002*

Citation and commencement

1 These Regulations may be cited as the Referrals to the Special Commissioners Regulations 2001 and shall come into force on 31st January 2002.

Interpretation

2 In these Regulations—

''the Act'' means the Taxes Management Act 1970;

"a referral to the Special Commissioners" means a referral to the Special Commissioners under—

(*a*) section 28ZA of the Act, or

(*b*) paragraph 31A of Schedule 18 to the Finance Act 1998.

Application of provisions of the Act with modifications

3—(1) Section 56A of the Act (appeals from the Special Commissioners) applies in relation to a referral to the Special Commissioners with the following modifications.

(2) For subsection (1) substitute—

"(1) If, in the case of a referral to the Special Commissioners under section 28ZA of this Act or paragraph 31A of Schedule 18 to the Finance Act 1998, any party to the referral is dissatisfied in point of law with—

(*a*) the decision of the Special Commissioners determining the question referred; or

(*b*) a decision under regulation 19 of the Special Commissioners Regulations varying that decision or substituting for it a new decision,

he may appeal against that decision to the High Court."

(3) In subsection (2)—

(*a*) for "A party to any appeal in England and Wales" substitute "In the case of any referral in England and Wales, any person";

(*b*) in paragraph (*a*) for "appeal" substitute "referral".

(4) In subsection (3) for "in principle or a decision finally determining an appeal" substitute "determining a question referred".

(5) Subsections (8) and (9) shall be omitted.

(6) After subsection (11) add—

"(12) In this section, "party to a referral" means—

(*a*) in the case of a referral under section 28ZA of this Act, the taxpayer or the officer of the Board; or

(*b*) in the case of a referral under paragraph 31A of Schedule 18 to the Finance Act 1998, the company or the officer of the Board,

who gave notice of referral under that section or paragraph to the Special Commissioners."

4—(1) Section 58 of the Act (proceedings in tax cases in Northern Ireland) applies in relation to a referral to the Special Commissioners with the following modifications.

(2) Subsection (2) shall be omitted.

(3) In subsection (2B)—

(*a*) for "The Taxes Acts" substitute "In their application to Northern Ireland, the Taxes Acts";

(*b*) for "appeal to the Special Commissioners constituting proceedings in Northern Ireland" substitute "referral to the Special Commissioners under section 28ZA of the Taxes Management Act 1970 or paragraph 31A of Schedule 18 to the Finance Act 1998".

(4) In subsection (2C) omit "on a case stated under regulation 22 of the General Commissioners Regulations or".

(5) Omit subsection (3).

2002/205
Income Tax (Exemption of Minor Benefits) Regulations 2002

Made by the Treasury under TA 1988 s 155ZB

Made	*4 February 2002*
Laid before the House of Commons	*5 February 2002*
Coming into force	*6 April 2002*

Citation, commencement and effect

1—(1) These Regulations may be cited as the Income Tax (Exemption of Minor Benefits) Regulations 2002 and shall come into force on 6th April 2002.

(2) These Regulations have effect for the year 2002-03 and subsequent years of assessment.

Interpretation

2 In these Regulations—

"bus" and "minibus" mean a bus, or a minibus, by means of which is provided a works bus service to which [section 242 of ITEPA][1] applies;

"cycle" has the meaning given by section 192(1) of the Road Traffic Act 1988;

"employment" includes an office and related expressions have a corresponding meaning;

["ITEPA" means the Income Tax (Earnings and Pensions) Act 2003;][1]

...[1]

"working day", in relation to an employee, means a day on which his attendance at a workplace is necessary in the performance of the duties of the employment;

"workplace", in relation to an employee, means a place at which his attendance is necessary in the performance of the duties of the employment.

Amendments—[1] Words in definition of "bus" and "minibus" substituted, definition of "ITEPA" inserted, and the definition of "the Taxes Act" revoked, by the IT (Exemption of Minor Benefits) (Amendment) Regulations, SI 2003/1434 reg 2 with effect from 25 June 2003.

Exemption in respect of the provision of qualifying meals

3—[(1) There is no charge to tax under Chapter 10 of Part 3 of ITEPA in respect of the provision for employees of qualifying meals.][1]

(2) ...[1]

(3) For the purposes of this regulation—

(*a*) a "qualifying meal" is any food or drink which—

(i) is provided by an employer to an employee in recognition of the employee having used a cycle on a designated day to make the journey between his home and a workplace for his necessary attendance at the workplace in the performance of the duties of the employment, and

(ii) is provided for consumption by the employee on his arrival at the workplace on that day; and

(*b*) a "designated day" is a day designated by the employer as a day on which a qualifying meal will be provided to any employee who uses a cycle for the purpose mentioned in sub-paragraph (*a*)(i).

Amendments—[1] Para (1) substituted, and para (2) revoked, by the IT (Exemption of Minor Benefits) (Amendment) Regulations, SI 2003/1434 reg 3 with effect from 25 June 2003.

Exemption in respect of the provision of bus or minibus

4—(1) There is no charge to tax under [Chapter 10 of Part 3 of ITEPA][1] in respect of the provision for employees of a bus, or a minibus, for conveying employees of one or more employers on relevant journeys.

(2) For the purposes of this regulation, a "relevant journey", in relation to an employee, is a journey which—

(*a*) is a single journey of a distance of not more than 10 miles;
(*b*) is between his workplace and shops or other amenities; and
(*c*) is made on a working day.

Amendments—[1] Words in para (1) substituted by the IT (Exemption of Minor Benefits) (Amendment) Regulations, SI 2003/1434 reg 3 with effect from 25 June 2003.

2002/653

Scottish Water (Transfer of Functions, etc) (Tax Provisions) Order 2002

Made by the Treasury under the Scotland Act 1998 ss 104(1), 112(1), (5), 126(1)

Made	*11 March 2002*
Laid before Parliament	*11 March 2002*
Coming into force	*1 April 2002*

Citation and commencement

1 This Order may be cited as the Scottish Water (Transfer of Functions, etc) (Tax Provisions) Order 2002 and shall come into force on 1st April 2002.

Interpretation

2 In this Order—

"the Corporation Tax Acts" has the meaning given by section 831(1)(*a*) of the Taxes Act;

"the new water and sewerage authorities" means the bodies established by section 62(1) of the Local Government etc. (Scotland) Act 1994, that is, the East of Scotland Water Authority, the West of Scotland Water Authority and the North of Scotland Water Authority;

"Scottish Water" means the body corporate known as Scottish Water and established by section 20 of, and Schedule 3 to, the Water Industry (Scotland) Act 2002;

"the Taxes Act" means the Income and Corporation Taxes Act 1988.

Tax Provisions consequential on the transfer of functions etc to Scottish Water

3 Articles 4 to 7 make provision in consequence of the transfer on 1st April 2002 of the functions, property and liabilities of the new water and sewerage authorities to Scottish Water by virtue of sections 21 and 22 of the Water Industry (Scotland) Act 2002.

Corporation tax—general

4—(1) For all purposes of the Corporation Tax Acts in relation to accounting periods beginning on or after 1st April 2002—

(*a*) Scottish Water shall be treated as if it were the same person as each of the new water and sewerage authorities, and

(*b*) the new water and sewerage authorities shall be treated as if together they were the same person as Scottish Water.

(2) For the purposes of section 393 of the Taxes Act (losses other than terminal losses) the new water and sewerage authorities shall be treated as if, before 1st April 2002, they had together carried on a single trade.

(3) Section 400 of the Taxes Act (write-off of government investment) shall not apply with regard to any debt transferred to Scottish Water by virtue of section 22 of the Water Industry (Scotland) Act 2002.

(4) For the purposes of section 400 of the Taxes Act the new water and sewerage authorities shall be treated as if, before 1st April 2002, they had together carried on a single trade.

(5) For the purposes of corporation tax on chargeable gains—

(*a*) Scottish Water shall be treated as having acquired all assets transferred from the new water and sewerage authorities by virtue of section 22 of the Water Industry (Scotland) Act 2002 at the time when they were acquired by the new water and sewerage authorities, and

(*b*) on any disposal of any of those assets by Scottish Water, any expenditure incurred by a new water and sewerage authority which would, if the disposal had been made by that authority, have been allowable by virtue of section 38 of the Taxation of Chargeable Gains Act 1992 in computing the chargeable gain or allowable loss on the disposal of the asset shall be treated as though it had been incurred by Scottish Water.

Transfer arrangements

5 The existence or exercise of the powers of the Scottish Ministers under the Water Industry (Scotland) Act 2002 shall not be regarded as constituting or creating arrangements within the meaning of section 410 of the Taxes Act (arrangements for transfer of company to another group or consortium).

Tax-free benefits

6 Nothing in this Order or Part 3 of the Water Industry (Scotland) Act 2002, and nothing done under this Order or that Part, shall be regarded as a scheme or arrangement for the purposes of section 30 of the Taxation of Chargeable Gains Act 1992 (tax-free benefits).

Stamp Duty

7 No transfer from the new water and sewerage authorities to Scottish Water effected by virtue of the Water Industry (Scotland) Act 2002 shall give rise to any liability to stamp duty.

2002/680

Income Tax (Employments and Electronic Communications) (Miscellaneous Provisions) Regulations 2002

Made by the Commissioners of Inland Revenue under TA 1988 s 203(10) and FA 1999 s 132

Made	*13 March 2002*
Laid before the House of Commons	*13 March 2002*
Coming into force	*8 April 2002*

Citation, commencement and interpretation

1—(1) These Regulations may be cited as the Income Tax (Employments and Electronic Communications) (Miscellaneous Provisions) Regulations 2002 and shall come into force on 8th April 2002.

(2) In these Regulations ''the Board'' means the Commissioners of Inland Revenue.

Notices given by the Board under regulation 34 of the Education (Student Loans) (Repayment) Regulations 2000

2—(1) Any notice to be given by the Board under regulation 34 of the Education (Student Loans) (Repayment) Regulations 2000 (notices to employers by the Board to deduct repayments from emoluments) (''regulation 34'') may be given, either to the employer or a person acting on his behalf, in such form and by such means of electronic communications as are for the time being approved by directions issued by the Board if the employer—

(*a*) has given his consent to the delivery of documents by the Board by that means; and
(*b*) has not notified the Board that that consent has been withdrawn.

(2) If it is recorded on an official computer system that a notice under regulation 34 has been given to any person by an approved means of electronic communications, it shall be presumed, unless the contrary is proved, that a notice—

(*a*) was given by that means;
(*b*) was given to the person recorded on that system as the recipient;
(*c*) was given at the time recorded on that system as the time of delivery; and
(*d*) contained the information recorded on that system in respect of that notice.

(3) A document certified by an officer of the Board to be a printed-out version of a notice, given by means of electronic communications in accordance with paragraph (1), which is recorded on an official computer system as at a particular date shall be presumed unless the contrary is proved—

(*a*) to have been recorded on an official computer system at that date;
(*b*) to constitute the entirety of the electronic communication so recorded.

(4) A document purporting to be such a certificate as is mentioned in paragraph (3) shall be presumed to be such a certificate unless the contrary is proved.

(5) For the purposes of this regulation ''employer'' and ''official computer system'' have the same meanings as they have in the Income Tax (Employments) Regulations 1993.

3–8 *(amended SI 1993/744; revoked by SI 2003/2682, subject to transitional provisions contained in Sch 1 thereto)*

2002/1596

Income Tax (Benefits in Kind) (Exemption for Employment Costs resulting from Disability) Regulations 2002

Made by the Treasury under TA 1988 s 155ZB

Made	*18 June 2002*
Laid before the House of Commons	*18 June 2002*
Coming into force	*9 July 2002*

1 These Regulations may be cited as the Income Tax (Benefits in Kind) (Exemption for Employment Costs resulting from Disability) Regulations 2002 and shall come into force on 9th July 2002.

2 In these Regulations—

(*a*) ''the Access to Work programme'' means the programme known by that name and provided in pursuance of arrangements made by or on behalf of the Secretary of State under section 2 of the Employment and Training Act 1973, in Scotland, made under section 2(3) of the Enterprise and New Towns (Scotland) Act 1990 or, in Northern Ireland, made by or on behalf of the Department of Employment and Learning under section 1 of the Employment and Training (Northern Ireland) Act 1950; and
(*b*) any reference to a section, without more, is to that section of the Income and Corporation Taxes Act 1988.

3 There shall be exempted from section 154 any benefit which satisfies each of the following conditions.

Condition 1

The benefit is provided to a disabled employee.

Condition 2

The main purpose of providing the benefit is to enable the employee to perform the duties of his employment.

Condition 3

The benefit consists in the provision of a hearing aid or other equipment, services or facilities, excepting any excluded benefit within the meaning in section 155ZA and Regulations made under that section.

Condition 4

The benefit is provided under, or within the terms of the provisions of, the Disability Discrimination Act 1995, the Access to Work programme, or any other statutory provision or arrangements, whether or not the employer has any legal duty to provide the benefit.

Condition 5

The benefit is made available to the employer's employees generally on similar terms (which include terms identical to Conditions 1 to 4).

2002/1966
Relief for Community Amateur Sports Clubs (Designation) Order 2002

Made	*25 July 2002*
Laid before the House of Commons	*25 July 2002*
Coming into force	*15 August 2002*

1 This Order may be cited as the Relief for Community Amateur Sports Clubs (Designation) Order 2002 and shall come into force on 15th August 2002.

2 A sport is designated as an eligible sport for the purposes of Schedule 18 to the Finance Act 2002 where that sport appears on the list maintained by the National Sports Councils of activities recognised by them.

3 ''The National Sports Councils'' means UK Sport, Sport England, Sport Scotland, the Sports Council of Wales and the Sports Council of Northern Ireland.

2002/1967
Corporation Tax (Finance Leasing of Intangible Assets) Regulations 2002

Made	*25 July 2002*
Laid before the House of Commons	*25 July 2002*
Coming into force	*15 August 2002*

Citation, commencement and effect

1 These Regulations may be cited as the Corporation Tax (Finance Leasing of Intangible Assets) Regulations 2002, shall come into force on 15th August 2002, and shall have effect from 1st April 2002.

Interpretation

2 In these Regulations—

''financial asset'' shall be construed in accordance with paragraph 75 of Schedule 29;

''finance lease'', ''finance lessor'' and ''finance lessee'' shall be construed in accordance with paragraph 104(4) and (5) of Schedule 29;

''Schedule 29'' means Schedule 29 to the Finance Act 2002 (gains and losses of a company from intangible fixed assets).

Application of Schedule 29

3 Schedule 29 shall apply in relation to a company that is the finance lessor of an intangible asset that is the subject of a finance lease as if, notwithstanding that the asset is accounted for by the finance lessor as a financial asset, it were an intangible fixed asset of the lessor and not a financial asset.

4 References in Schedule 29 to capitalised expenditure on an intangible fixed asset shall accordingly be taken as including references to any amount accounted for by the finance lessor as a financial asset as a consequence of the finance lease of the asset, except that—

(*a*) no election may be made under paragraph 10 of Schedule 29 (election for writing down on fixed rate basis) in respect of that amount,

(*b*) that amount is not to be treated as capitalised expenditure for the purposes of paragraph 39(1)(*b*) of Schedule 29 (roll-over relief in case of realisation and reinvestment—conditions to be met in relation to expenditure on other assets), and

(*c*) accordingly any amount treated by paragraph 57(2) of Schedule 29 (roll-over relief on reinvestment—acquisition of group company treated as equivalent to acquisition of underlying assets) as expenditure on acquiring the financial asset is not to be treated as capitalised expenditure for the purposes of paragraph 39(1)(*b*) of that Schedule.

Intangible fixed asset becoming financial asset — consequentials

5 Where an asset formerly recognised by the lessor for accounting purposes as an intangible fixed asset becomes subject to a finance lease (and accordingly comes to be accounted for as a financial asset)—

(*a*) a realisation of the intangible fixed asset shall be treated, for the purposes of Part 4 of Schedule 29 (realisation of intangible fixed assets), as having occurred on the commencement of the finance lease,

(*b*) the accounting value of the financial asset so created shall be recognised as realisation proceeds of the intangible fixed asset for the purposes of that Part, and
(*c*) that amount shall not be taken into account in determining the accounting value of the financial asset immediately after the realisation for the purposes of paragraph 22(2) of that Schedule (apportionment in case of part realisation).

Financial assets excluded from Schedule 29

6—(1) Assets partially excluded from Schedule 29 by virtue of paragraphs 78 to 81 (assets excluded except as regards royalties) shall be entirely excluded from that Schedule as regards the finance lessor if they are subject to a finance lease and are accounted for by the lessor as financial assets. Accordingly in relation to such assets—

(*a*) Schedule 29 applies only to royalties recognised for accounting purposes prior to the asset becoming subject to the finance lease, or after it ceases to be subject to the finance lease,
(*b*) to the extent that such royalties are brought into account for tax purposes under Schedule 29, they shall not be brought into account for tax purposes again, and
(*c*) to the extent that such royalties are brought into account for tax purposes otherwise than under Schedule 29, they shall not be brought into account for tax purposes under that Schedule.

(2) Except for the purposes of regulation 5, an asset shall be excluded from Schedule 29 if it is used by the finance lessee for the purposes of a trade or business in respect of which he is within the charge to income tax.

(3) Nothing in these Regulations shall be read as enabling Schedule 29 to apply to existing assets excluded from the application of that Schedule by paragraph 118 of that Schedule.

(4) An asset shall count as an existing asset in the hands of the finance lessor for the purposes of paragraph 118 of Schedule 29 if the finance lessee—

(*a*) is a company for whom the asset was the whole or part of an existing asset, or
(*b*) is a person who is a related party in relation to such a company.

(5) References in paragraph (1) to royalties being brought into account for tax purposes include references to royalties which would have been so brought into account if the person concerned had been within the charge to corporation tax.

(6) In paragraph (4)(*b*) ‘‘related party’’ shall be construed in accordance with paragraph 95, read with paragraphs 96 to 101, of Schedule 29.

2002/1968
Income Tax (Prescribed Deposit-takers) Order 2002

Made	*25 July 2002*
Laid before the House of Commons	*25 July 2002*
Coming into force	*1 October 2002*

Citation and commencement

1 This Order may be cited as the Income Tax (Prescribed Deposit-takers) Order 2002 and shall come into force on 1st October 2002.

Prescribed deposit-takers

2—(1) For the purposes of section 481(2)(*f*) of the Income and Corporation Taxes Act 1988, a person who is authorised for the purposes of the Financial Services and Markets Act 2000 and whose business consists wholly or mainly of dealing in financial instruments as principal is a class of person prescribed in relation to all relevant deposits.

(2) In paragraph (1) above—

‘‘financial instruments’’ has the same meaning as in section 349(5) and (6) of the Income and Corporation Taxes Act 1988;
‘‘relevant deposits’’ has the same meaning as in section 481(4) of that Act.

2002/1969
Exchange Gains and Losses (Transitional Provisions and Savings) Regulations 2002

Made . . . . *25 July 2002*
Laid before the House of Commons . . . . . *25 July 2002*
Coming into force . . . . *1 October 2002*

PART 1
INTRODUCTION

Citation, commencement and effect

1—(1) These Regulations may be cited as the Exchange Gains and Losses (Transitional Provisions and Savings) Regulations 2002 and shall come into force on 1st October 2002.

(2) These Regulations have effect in relation to accounting periods beginning on or after 1st October 2002.

PART 2
SAVING OF THE EXCHANGE GAINS AND LOSSES (TRANSITIONAL PROVISIONS) REGULATIONS 1994 WITH MODIFICATIONS

Introduction

2 The Exchange Gains and Losses (Transitional Provisions) Regulations 1994 are modified in accordance with regulations 3 to 11 below and, as modified, continue to have effect (notwithstanding the repeal of sections 164(14), 165(4) to (6) and 167(1) and (4) to (6) of, and Schedule 16 to, the Finance Act 1993 by sections 79(1)(*b*) and 141 of, and Part 3(10) of Schedule 40 to, the Finance Act 2002).

Modification of regulation 1

3 In regulation 1(3)—

(*a*) for sub-paragraph (*g*) substitute—

"(*g*) "a regulation 6(3) asset" means an existing asset the basic valuation of which was determined for the purposes of Chapter II in accordance with regulation 6(3) of these Regulations;";

(*b*) at the end of sub-paragraph (*h*) add "; and

"(i) "the relevant accounting period", in relation to a company, means the company's first accounting period to begin on or after 1st October 2002.".

Modification of regulation 2

4 In regulation 2(2)—

(*a*) omit "Sections 136, 137 and 139 to 141 of the 1993 Act;";

(*b*) omit "The Exchange Gains and Losses (Deferral of Gains and Losses) Regulations 1994.".

Omission of regulations 3 to 6

5 Omit regulations 3 to 6.

Modification of regulation 7

6 In regulation 7(2)—

(*a*) after the definition of "the cumulative taxed loss" insert—

""the final accounting period", in relation to a company, means the company's accounting period preceding the relevant accounting period;";

(*b*) omit the words from "and any reference" to the end.

Modification of regulation 8

7 In regulation 8(5) for "above" substitute "of these Regulations".

Modification of regulation 13

8—(1) Modify regulation 13 as follows.

(2) In paragraph (1) for "14(1) and 15(1)" substitute "14 and 14A".

(3) After paragraph (1) insert—

"(1A) For the purposes of paragraph (1)(*a*) above, the final accounting period shall be treated as the last accrual period as respects any asset or liability held or owed by the company immediately after the end of the final accounting period.".

(4) In paragraphs (2)(*a*), (*b*) and (*c*) and (3)(*a*), (*b*) and (*c*) for "before the end of the last accrual period" substitute "after the end of the final accounting period".

(5) For paragraph (4) substitute—

"(4) In paragraphs (2) and (3) above, a relevant gain or loss in relation to a regulation 6(3) asset is a chargeable gain or an allowable loss. (4A) In relation to any asset other than a regulation 6(3) asset or any liability, an amount equal to the amount of any relevant gain or loss that is deemed to accrue to the company under paragraph (2) or (3) above shall be treated for the purposes of Chapter 2 of Part 4 of the Finance Act 1996 (according to whether it is a relevant gain or loss)—

(*a*) as a credit in respect of a loan relationship of the company, or

(*b*) as a debit in respect of a loan relationship of the company,

which falls to be brought into account under section 82(2) of that Act.".

(6) Omit paragraphs (5) to (8).

Substitution of regulation 14

9 For regulation 14 substitute—

"Elections to defer bringing into account relevant gains and losses deemed to accrue immediately after the end of the final accounting period

14—(1) In any case where, apart from this regulation, relevant gains or losses would accrue to a company immediately after the end of the final accounting period by virtue of regulation 13, the company may elect, by notice to the inspector within two years of the end of the final accounting period, that this regulation shall apply as respects—

(*a*) subject to paragraph (3) below, all relevant gains or losses to which paragraph (4) of regulation 13 would apply;

(*b*) all relevant gains or losses to which paragraph (4A) of that regulation would apply; or

(*c*) both.

An election under this paragraph shall be irrevocable.

(2) Where an election is made under paragraph (1) above, every gain or loss to which this regulation applies shall be treated as accruing only when the asset or liability to which the gain or loss relates ceases to be held or owed by the company.

(3) No election may be made under paragraph (1) above as respects relevant gains or losses to which regulation 13(4) would apply if an election under regulation 14A is made as regards such losses.

Elections to treat losses deemed to accrue immediately after the end of the final accounting period as debits in respect of loan relationships

14A—(1) In any case where—

(*a*) apart from this regulation, relevant losses would accrue to a company as respects regulation 6(3) assets immediately after the end of the final accounting period by virtue of regulation 13; and

(*b*) if relevant gains would accrue as respects such assets at that time by virtue of that regulation, such losses would exceed them,

the company may elect, by notice to the inspector within two years of the end of the final accounting period, that this regulation shall apply as respects such losses or, in a case where sub-paragraph (*b*) applies, such losses to the extent that they exceed the relevant gains.

An election under this paragraph shall be irrevocable.

(2) Where an election is made under paragraph (1) above, an amount equal to the amount of the losses to which this regulation applies shall be treated for the purposes of Chapter 2 of Part 4 of the Finance Act 1996 as a debit in respect of a loan relationship of the company for the new accounting period and not falling to be brought into account under section 82(2) of that Act.

Treatment of losses available to be carried forward at the end of the final accounting period as a result of an election made under regulation 14(5) or 16(1)

14B—(1) This regulation apples where, as a result of an election made under regulation 14(5) or 16(1) of these Regulations, an amount of available losses ("the relevant amount") was available at the end of the final accounting period to be carried forward and, apart from this regulation, to be set against a company's exchange gains.

(2) Where this regulation applies an amount equal to the relevant amount shall be treated for the purposes of Chapter 2 of Part 4 of the Finance Act 1996 as a debit in respect of a loan relationship of the company for the new accounting period and not falling to be brought into account under section 82(2) of that Act.".

Omission of regulation 15 and 16

10 Omit regulations 15 and 16.

Omission of Part 4

11 Omit the whole of Part 4.

PART 3
SAVING OF THE EXCHANGE GAINS AND LOSSES (ALTERNATIVE METHOD OF CALCULATION) REGULATIONS 1994 WITH MODIFICATIONS

Introduction

12 The Exchange Gains and Losses (Alternative Method of Calculation) Regulations 1994 are modified in accordance with regulations 13 to 17 below and, as modified, continue to have effect (notwithstanding the repeal of sections 164(14) and 167(1) and (4) to (6) of, and Schedule 15 to, the Finance Act 1993 by sections 79(1)(*b*) and 141 of, and Part 3(10) of Schedule 40 to, the Finance Act 2002).

Omission of regulations 2 and 3

13 Omit regulations 2 and 3.

Modification of regulation 7

14—(1) Modify regulation 7 as follows.

(2) In paragraph (1) for the words from ''Subject to'' to ''by a company at any time'' substitute ''Paragraphs (3) to (5) below apply in any case where a disposal of an asset is deemed by virtue of paragraph (1A) below to have been made by a company immediately before the first day of its first accounting period to begin on or after 1st October 2002''.

(3) After paragraph (1) insert—

''(1A) For the purposes of paragraph (1) above, any asset held by the company at the beginning of the first day of its first accounting period to begin on or after 1st October 2002 shall be deemed to have been disposed of by the company immediately before that first day.''.

(4) Omit paragraph (2).

(5) Omit paragraphs (6) to (8).

Omission of regulations 8 and 9

15 Omit regulations 8 and 9.

Modification of regulation 11

16 In regulation 11 after paragraph (1) insert—

''(1A) Notwithstanding the following provisions of this regulation, an election made under regulation 10 or this regulation—

(*a*) shall have effect only in relation to accounting periods beginning before 1st October 2002, and

(*b*) an election which specifies a day as the day from which the election is to have effect must specify a day that falls within an accounting period beginning before 1st October 2002.''.

Omission of regulation 12

17 Omit regulation 12.

PART 4
SAVING OF THE EXCHANGE GAINS AND LOSSES (INSURANCE COMPANIES) REGULATIONS 1994 WITH MODIFICATIONS

Introduction

18 The Exchange Gains and Losses (Insurance Companies) Regulations 1994 are modified in accordance with regulations 19 to 27 below and, as modified, continue to have effect (notwithstanding the repeal of sections 167(1) and 168(2) to (5) of the Finance Act 1993 by sections 79(1)(*b*) and 141 of, and Part 3(10) of Schedule 40 to, the Finance Act 2002).

Modification of regulation 1

19 In regulation 1 after the definition of ''basic valuation'' insert—

''"the final accounting period'', in relation to a company, means the company's accounting period preceding the first accounting period to begin on or after 1st October 2002;''.

Omission of regulations 2 to 5A

20 Omit regulations 2 to 5A.

Modification of regulation 7

21 In regulation 7 for paragraph (1) substitute—

''(1) An asset specified by this regulation is referred to in regulations 7A and 8 to 12 as a ''regulation 7 asset''.''.

Insertion of regulations 7A and 7B

22 After regulation 7 insert—

''7A—(1) An asset shall be deemed to have been disposed of by an insurance company immediately before its first accounting period to begin on or after 1st October 2002 where—

(*a*) the asset was a regulation 7 asset at the time of its deemed disposal, and

(*b*) at that time, the insurance company had made no election under regulation 8A of these Regulations.

(2) Subject to paragraph 7B, any chargeable gain or allowable loss accruing on the deemed disposal under paragraph (1) above of an asset shall be brought into account as if it had accrued immediately after the end of the final accounting period.

7B In any case where, apart from this regulation, chargeable gains or allowable losses would accrue to an insurance company immediately after the end of the final accounting period by virtue of regulation 7A—

(*a*) the insurance company may elect, by notice to the inspector within two years of the end of the final accounting period, that this regulation shall apply as respects all such gains or losses, and

(*b*) where such an election is made, every such gain or loss to which this regulation applies shall be treated as accruing only when the asset or liability to which the gain or loss relates ceases to be held or owed by the insurance company.''

Modification of regulation 8

23 In regulation 8(1)—

(*a*) for ''disposal of a regulation 7 asset'' substitute ''the deemed disposal under regulation 7A(1) of an asset'';

(*b*) for ''8A'' substitute ''9''.

Omission of regulation 8A

24 Omit regulation 8A.

Modification of regulation 9

25 In regulation 9(2) for ''disposal of the asset'' substitute ''deemed disposal under regulation 7A(1) of the asset''.

Modification of regulation 11

26 In regulation 11(2) for ''disposal of the asset'' substitute ''deemed disposal under regulation 7A(1) of the asset''.

Modification of regulation 12

27 In regulation 12(2) for ''disposal of the asset'' substitute ''deemed disposal under regulation 7A(1) of the asset''.

PART 5

SAVING OF THE EXCHANGE GAINS AND LOSSES (MISCELLANEOUS MODIFICATIONS) REGULATIONS 2000 WITH MODIFICATIONS

Introduction

28 The Exchange Gains and Losses (Miscellaneous Modifications) Regulations 2000(a) are modified in accordance with regulations 29 and 30 below and, as modified, continue to have effect (notwithstanding the repeal of sections 164(14), 167(1) and (4) to (6) of, and Schedules 15 and 16 to, the Finance Act 1993 by sections 79(1)(*b*) and 141 of, and Part 3(10) of Schedule 40 to, the Finance Act 2002).

Omission of regulations 2 to 5

29 Omit regulations 2 to 5.

Omission of regulation 11

30 Omit regulation 11.

2002/1970
Exchange Gains and Losses (Bringing into Account Gains or Losses) Regulations 2002

Made	*25 July 2002*
Laid before the House of Commons	*25 July 2002*
Coming into force	*1 October 2002*

Citation, commencement and effect

1—(1) These Regulations may be cited as the Exchange Gains and Losses (Bringing into Account Gains or Losses) Regulations 2002 and shall come into force on 1st October 2002 immediately after the Exchange Gains and Losses (Transitional Provisions and Savings) Regulations 2002.

(2) These Regulations have effect in relation to accounting periods beginning on or after 1st October 2002.

Interpretation

2—(1) In these Regulations—

''Chapter 2'' means Chapter 2 of Part 4 of the Finance Act 1996;

''chargeable gain'' and ''allowable loss'' have the same meaning as they have for the purposes of the 1992 Act;

''foreign business asset'', in relation to a company, means an asset of part of a business in relation to which the company prepares—

(*a*) accounts using the closing rate/net investment method as mentioned in subsection (2)(*a*) or (3)(*a*) of section 93A of the Finance Act 1993(c), or

(*b*) a return of accounts using that method as mentioned in subsection (2)(*b*) or (3)(*b*) of that section;

''a no gain/no loss disposal'' means a disposal on which neither a gain nor a loss accrues by virtue of any of the following provisions of the 1992 Act—

(*a*) section 139;
(*b*) section 140A;
(*c*) section 171;
(*d*) section 215; and
(*e*) section 216;

''original shares'' and ''new holding'' have the same meaning as in section 127 of the 1992 Act or (as the case may be) that section as applied by virtue of any enactment relating to chargeable gains;

''paragraph 16'' means paragraph 16 of Schedule 26 to the Finance Act 2002;

''section 84A'' means section 84A of the Finance Act 1996;

''the 1992 Act'' means the Taxation of Chargeable Gains Act 1992;

''the 1994 Regulations'' means the Exchange Gains and Losses (Alternative Method of Calculation of Gain or Loss) Regulations 1994.

(2) In these Regulations—

(*a*) any reference to a disposal of an asset shall be construed as a reference to any event which is or is treated as a disposal for the purposes of the 1992 Act; and

(*b*) any reference to the time of the disposal of an asset shall be construed as a reference to the time at which the disposal occurs for the purposes of that Act,

and, for the purposes of this paragraph, any reference to a disposal includes a part disposal.

(3) In these Regulations—

(*a*) any reference to an asset which is a ship or aircraft includes a reference to a contract—

(i) to which section 67 of the Capital Allowances Act 2001 applies; and
(ii) which relates to plant or machinery which is a ship or aircraft; and

(*b*) any reference to a disposal of an asset which is a ship or aircraft by a person includes a reference to the case where a person ceases to be entitled to the benefit of such a contract and does not then in fact become the owner of the plant or the machinery to which the contract relates.

Prescribed circumstances in which regulation 4 applies

3—(1) Regulation 4 applies in either of the circumstances prescribed by paragraphs (2) and (3) below.

(2) The circumstances prescribed by this paragraph are where there is a disposal of an asset by a company and—

(*a*) any exchange gain or loss arose to the company in relation to the asset in an accounting period beginning on or after 1st October 2002; and

(*b*) in accordance with generally accepted accounting practice an amount representing the whole or part of an exchange loss or gain which arises to the company in relation to a liability representing a loan relationship of the company or an obligation under a derivative contract—

(i) was carried to or sustained by the reserve mentioned in subsection (5) of section 84A or sub-paragraph (4) of paragraph 16; and

(ii) was set off by or against an amount which represents the whole or part of an exchange gain or loss arising in relation to the asset and falls within subsection (6) of section 84A or sub-paragraph (5) of paragraph 16.

(3) The circumstances prescribed by this paragraph are where there is a disposal of an asset by a company and there is in relation to the asset any of the following—

(*a*) a deemed disposal under regulation 7(1A) of the 1994 Regulations (as modified by the Exchange Gains and Losses (Transitional Provisions and Savings) Regulations 2002);

(*b*) a deferred gain or loss under regulation 8 of the 1994 Regulations in relation to which paragraph (3) or (4) of that regulation did not apply immediately before the relevant day;

(*c*) a deferred gain or loss under regulation 9 of the 1994 Regulations in relation to which paragraph (3)(*a*) or (*b*) or paragraph (4)(*a*) or (*b*) of that regulation, as the case may be, did not apply immediately before the relevant day.

(4) In paragraph (3)(*b*) and (*c*) above "the relevant day" means the first day of the company's first accounting period to begin on or after 1st October 2002.

General rule for bringing amounts into account

4—(1) For the purposes of the 1992 Act, there shall be brought into account for the accounting period in which the disposal of the asset occurs—

(*a*) as a chargeable gain accruing to the company at the time of the disposal, the amount of any net gain; or

(*b*) as an allowable loss accruing to the company at the time of the disposal, the amount of any net loss.

(2) Paragraph (1) above does not have effect if the asset disposed of—

(*a*) is a foreign business asset immediately before its disposal; or

(*b*) consists of shares or an asset related to shares on the disposal of which no chargeable gain is treated as accruing by virtue of Part 1 of Schedule 7AC to the 1992 Act.

(3) Paragraph (1) above is subject to regulations 6 and 8.

Calculation of the amount of any net gain or net loss for the purposes of regulation 4

5—(1) The amount of any net gain or net loss referred to in regulation 4(1) shall be calculated in accordance with this regulation.

(2) Subject to paragraph (4) below, the amount of any net gain or loss shall be calculated by finding the aggregate of the amounts representing exchange gains or losses which accrued in relation to liabilities matched with the asset disposed of during the period in which the asset was held by the company disposing of it.

(3) The aggregate referred to in paragraph (2) above shall be found in any manner that is just and reasonable having regard to—

(*a*) the effect of regulation 6 in the accounting period in which the disposal occurs or in any earlier accounting period; and

(*b*) the way in which such an aggregate was found for any earlier accounting period in accordance with this regulation.

(4) Notwithstanding that a loss accruing to a company on the disposal of the asset is not deductible except from a chargeable gain of the kind mentioned in section 18(3) of the 1992 Act, where the aggregate referred to in paragraph (2) would be an amount of net gain for the purposes of regulation 4(1) in relation to that disposal, the amount of such a loss may be deducted from the aggregate.

Assets representing certain loan relationships and ships or aircraft

6—(1) This paragraph applies where the asset disposed of—

(*a*) represents a loan relationship of the company other than one which falls within section 92 or 93 of the Finance Act 1996 at the time of the disposal, or

(*b*) is a ship or aircraft.

(2) Where paragraph (1) applies, the amount to be brought into account under regulation 4(1) shall not be brought into account, for the purposes of the 1992 Act, as a chargeable gain or allowable loss but instead, for the purposes of Chapter 2, as a credit or a debit (according to whether it is an amount of net gain or net loss) in respect of the loan relationships of the company.

(3) Where the asset disposed of represents a loan relationship which falls within section 92 of the Finance Act 1996 at the time of the disposal—

(*a*) the amount of any net gain or loss to be brought into account under regulation 4(1) shall be calculated in accordance with regulation 5 only by reference to exchange gains or losses which accrued in relation to liabilities matched with the asset disposed of during accounting periods beginning before 1st October 2002; and

(*b*) for the purposes of Chapter 2—

(i) the amount of any relevant exchange losses shall be brought into account as a credit in respect of the loan relationships of the company; and

(ii) the amount of any relevant exchange gains shall be brought into account as a debit in respect of those loan relationships.

(4) For the purposes of paragraph (3)(*b*) above, relevant exchange gains or, as the case may be, losses in the case of the asset are the amounts of any exchange gains or, as the case may be, losses which, if section 84A(3) of the Finance Act 1996 had not had effect in relation to them—

(*a*) would have been brought into account under subsection (2)(*b*) of section 92 of that Act in respect of the asset; and

(*b*) for the purposes of subsection (5A) of that section would have been relevant exchange gains or, as the case may be, losses in the case of the asset.

Regulations 5 and 6—supplementary

7—(1) This regulation has effect for the purposes of regulations 5 and 6.

(2) References to the asset disposed of include references to any predecessor asset which was—

(*a*) original shares; or

(*b*) ‘‘the old asset’’ construed in accordance with section 116 of the 1992 Act.

(3) References to the company disposing of the asset include references to any predecessor company which was ‘‘the disposing company’’ for the purposes of regulation 8 of the 1994 Regulations.

(4) In respect of any time falling within an accounting period beginning before 1st October 2002 a liability is matched with an asset to the extent that it is matched in accordance with an election under regulation 10 of the 1994 Regulations.

(5) In respect of any time falling within an accounting period beginning on or after 1st October 2002—

(*a*) a liability is fully matched with an asset where an amount representing the whole of an exchange gain or loss arising in relation to the liability is treated as mentioned in subsection (5) of section 84A or sub-paragraph (4) of paragraph 16; and

(*b*) where the amount treated as mentioned in that subsection or that sub-paragraph represents only part of an exchange gain or loss, the liability shall be treated as being matched only to the corresponding extent.

(6) Where in any accounting period beginning on or after 1st October 2002—

(*a*) a company holds more than one asset in relation to which there are amounts falling within subsection (6) of section 84A or sub-paragraph (5) of paragraph 16; and

(*b*) the assets are denominated and the liabilities are expressed in the same currency,

the extent to which an asset is matched shall be determined in accordance with the rules set out in paragraph (7) below.

(7) The following rules shall apply in relation to—

(*a*) any disposal of an asset occurring before the relevant disposal;

(*b*) any asset held at the time of the relevant disposal.

Rule 1

Liabilities are to be regarded as having been matched to the greatest possible extent with assets which—

(*a*) represent loan relationships of the company (other than ones which fall within section 93 of the Finance Act 1996); or

(*b*) are ships or aircraft.

Rule 2

Subject to Rule 1, liabilities are to be regarded as having been matched to the greatest possible extent with assets (other than foreign business assets) on the disposal of which a chargeable gain accrues or would accrue.

Rule 3

Subject to Rules 1 and 2, liabilities are to be regarded as having been matched with assets—

(*a*) on the disposal of which no chargeable gain is treated as accruing by virtue of Part 1 of Schedule 7AC to the 1992 Act;

(*b*) on a disposal of which no chargeable gain would be treated as accruing by virtue of that Part if the disposal were made on a date falling more than twelve months after the date of the relevant disposal but excluding assets which—

(i) are actually disposed of on a date falling less than twelve months after the date of the relevant disposal, and

(ii) have been held for less than twelve months at the date of the actual disposal; or

(*c*) which are foreign business assets held at the time of the relevant disposal.

(8) For the purposes of paragraph (6) above, the currency in which a liability representing a loan relationship is expressed, or for the acquisition of which an obligation under a currency contract provides, is to be treated as the currency in which an asset is denominated if borrowing in, or the acquisition of, that currency could reasonably be expected to eliminate or substantially reduce the economic risk of holding the asset which is attributable to fluctuations in exchange rates.

(9) In paragraph (7) above, "the relevant disposal" means the disposal referred to in regulation 4.

No gain/no loss disposals

8—(1) This regulation applies where the disposal of the asset is a no gain/no loss disposal.

(2) Where this regulation applies, the amount to be brought into account under regulation 4(1) as a chargeable gain or allowable loss—

(*a*) shall not be brought into account for the accounting period in which the disposal of the asset occurs, but instead

(*b*) or the purposes of the 1992 Act, shall be brought into account as a chargeable gain or allowable loss, as the case may be, by the company making the first relevant disposal of the asset for the accounting period in which the first relevant disposal occurs.

(3) In paragraph (2)(*b*) above, in relation to the disposal of an asset which is a no gain/no loss disposal, "the first relevant disposal" means the first subsequent disposal of that asset which is not a no gain/no loss disposal.

Cases where there is no disposal of the asset by virtue of section 116(10) of the 1992 Act

9—(1) This regulation applies in the circumstances prescribed by paragraph (2) below.

(2) The circumstances prescribed by this paragraph are where the circumstances prescribed by regulation 3(2) would exist but for there being no disposal of the asset for the purposes of the 1992 Act by virtue of section 116(10) of that Act ("section 116(10)").

(3) Where this regulation applies, the amount which, but for section 116(10), would be brought into account under regulation 4(1) as a chargeable gain or allowable loss shall be found and paragraph (4) below shall apply.

(4) Where this paragraph applies—

(*a*) if the amount found under paragraph (3) above would be brought into account as a chargeable gain, the market value of the asset shall, for the purposes of paragraph (*a*) of section 116(10), be increased by an amount equal to that amount;

(*b*) if the amount found under paragraph (3) above would be brought into account as an allowable loss—

(i) the market value of the asset shall, for the purposes of paragraph (*a*) of section 116(10), be reduced by an amount equal to that amount; and

(ii) if that amount exceeds the amount of the market value, an allowable loss equal in amount to the excess shall be treated as accruing on the subsequent disposal of the new asset (within the meaning of section 116(4) of the 1992 Act).

Cases where, but for section 116, section 127 of the 1992 Act would apply in relation to assets as regards which paragraph (2)(a), but not paragraph (2)(b), of regulation 8 has had effect

10—(1) This regulation applies in the circumstances prescribed by paragraph (2) below.

(2) The circumstances prescribed by this paragraph are where, but for section 116 of the 1992 Act, section 127 of that Act would apply in relation to a transaction involving original shares which are or include an asset as regards which paragraph (2)(*a*), but not paragraph (2)(*b*), of regulation 8 has had effect.

(3) Where this regulation applies, regulation 9(4) shall apply to the amount which, by virtue of regulation 8(2)(*a*), is not brought into account as a chargeable gain or an allowable loss for the accounting period in which the disposal of the asset occurs in the same way as it applies to an amount found under regulation 9(3).

Cases where there is no disposal of the asset by virtue of section 127 of the 1992 Act

11—(1) This regulation applies in the circumstances prescribed by paragraph (2) below.

(2) The circumstances prescribed by this paragraph are where the circumstances prescribed by regulation 3(2) would exist but for there being no disposal of the asset for the purposes of the 1992 Act by virtue of section 127 of that Act (''section 127'').

(3) Where this regulation applies, the amount which, but for section 127, would be brought into account under regulation 4(1) as a chargeable gain or allowable loss shall be found and paragraph (4) below shall apply.

(4) Where this paragraph applies—

(*a*) if the amount found under paragraph (3) above would be brought into account as a chargeable gain, in computing the amount of any chargeable gain or allowable loss accruing on the subsequent disposal of the new holding, the consideration received on that disposal shall be increased by an amount equal to that amount;

(*b*) if the amount found under paragraph (3) above would be brought into account as an allowable loss—

(i) in computing the amount of any chargeable gain or allowable loss accruing on the subsequent disposal of the new holding, the consideration received on that disposal shall be reduced by an amount equal to that amount; and

(ii) if that amount exceeds the amount of the consideration, an allowable loss equal in amount to the excess shall be treated as accruing on that disposal.

Cases where section 127 of the 1992 Act applies in relation to assets as regards which paragraph (2)(a), but not paragraph (2)(b), of regulation 8 has had effect

12—(1) This regulation applies in the circumstances prescribed by paragraph (2) below.

(2) The circumstances prescribed by this paragraph are where section 127 of the 1992 Act applies in relation to a transaction involving original shares which are or include an asset as regards which paragraph (2)(*a*), but not paragraph (2)(*b*), of regulation 8 has had effect.

(3) Where this regulation applies, regulation 11(4) shall apply to the amount which, by virtue of regulation 8(2)(*a*), has not been brought into account as a chargeable gain or an allowable loss for the accounting period in which the disposal of the asset occurs in the same way as it applies to an amount found under regulation 11(3).

Cases where exchange gains or losses fall within subsection (4) of section 84A

13—(1) This regulation applies in the circumstances prescribed by paragraph (2) below.

(2) The circumstances prescribed by this paragraph are where there is a disposal of an asset by a company and the asset disposed of represents a loan relationship of the company in relation to which exchange gains or losses have fallen within subsection (4) of section 84A.

(3) Where this regulation applies, an amount equal to the amount of any net gain or net loss shall be brought into account, for the purposes of Chapter 2, as a credit or a debit (according to whether it is an amount of net gain or net loss) in respect of the loan relationship for the accounting period in which the disposal occurs.

(4) For the purposes of this regulation, the amount of any net gain or net loss shall be calculated by finding the aggregate of the amounts representing the exchange gains and losses which fell within subsection (4) of section 84A.

2002/2661

Venture Capital Trust (Exchange of Shares and Securities) Regulations 2002

Made by the Treasury under TA 1988 s 842AA(5AD), Sch 28B para 11B

Made . . . . *22 October 2002*
Laid before the House of Commons . . . *23 October 2002*
Coming into force . . . . *13 November 2002*

Citation, commencement and effect

1—(1) These Regulations may be cited as the Venture Capital Trust (Exchange of Shares and Securities) Regulations 2002 and shall come into force on 13th November 2002.

(2) These Regulations have effect in relation to exchanges of shares or securities occurring on or after 21st March 2000.

Interpretation

2—(1) In these Regulations unless the context otherwise requires—

"earn-out right" has the meaning in section 138A(1) of the 1992 Act (references to "debentures" being read as references to "securities" as defined below);

the "issue" of any shares or securities has the meaning in section 135 of the 1992 Act, except for a security consisting in a liability in respect of an unsecured loan where it has effect as a reference to the making of the loan;

"market value" shall be construed in accordance with sections 272 and 273 of the 1992 Act;

"a monetary right" means a right under an agreement to receive a monetary amount at a future time in respect of shares or securities, whether or not the amount is ascertainable at the date of the agreement;

"original shares or securities" has the meaning in paragraph 11B(2) of Schedule 28B;

"recognised stock exchange" has the meaning given by section 841;

"Schedule 28B" means Schedule 28B to the Taxes Act;

"securities" has the meaning given by section 842AA(12);

"the 1992 Act" means the Taxation of Chargeable Gains Act 1992;

"the Taxes Act" means the Income and Corporation Taxes Act 1988;

"venture capital trust" has the meaning given by section 842AA(1).

(2) References in these Regulations (except regulation 5(1)(*a*), (*b*) and (*d*)) to an exchange of shares or securities shall be construed in accordance with paragraph 11B(2) of Schedule 28B, and "exchanged" has a corresponding meaning.

(3) For the purposes of these Regulations, old shares and new shares are matching shares in relation to each other if the old shares are the shares for which the new shares are exchanged under the arrangements, and the same provision shall apply, with any necessary modifications, as between old securities and new securities, and old securities and new shares.

(4) References in these Regulations to a section, without more, are to that section of the Taxes Act.

Scope of Regulations

3 These Regulations apply to any exchange of shares or securities held by a venture capital trust—

(*a*) which falls within the terms of paragraph 11B(1)(*a*) to (*c*) of Schedule 28B,

(*b*) which falls within one of the cases described in regulations 4 to 6, and

(*c*) where the trust company receives, in respect of the old shares or old securities, new shares or new securities, with or without other consideration.

Exchange of shares or securities for those in the same company

4—(1) The case described in this regulation is an exchange of shares or securities where—

(*a*) persons are, whether for payment or not, issued shares in or securities of a company in respect of and in proportion to (or as nearly as may be in proportion to) their holdings of shares in or securities of the company or of any class of shares in or securities of the company,

(*b*) the person in question is a venture capital trust,

(*c*) the new shares are issued in respect of old shares or old securities, and the new securities are issued solely in respect of old securities,

(*d*) immediately after the exchange, the old shares and old securities are cancelled or otherwise extinguished, and

(*e*) the exchange is not an exchange of convertibles for shares to which paragraph 10D of Schedule 28B applies.

(2) In paragraph (1) and regulation 7—

(*a*) expressions have the same meanings as in section 126(2) of the 1992 Act;

(*b*) the shares or securities issued to the trust company are referred to as the "new shares" and the "new securities" respectively, and the trust company's former holding mentioned in paragraph (1)(*a*) is referred to, separately and as the case may be, as the "old shares" and the "old securities" respectively.

Exchange of shares or securities for those in another company

5—(1) The case described in this regulation is where—

(*a*) a company ("company B") issues shares or securities to a person in exchange for the shares in or securities of another company ("company A"),

(*b*) either—

(i) in consequence of the exchange, company B will hold more than 50% of the ordinary share capital of company A, or

(ii) company B issues the shares or securities in exchange for shares in or securities of company A as the result of a general offer made to members of company A or any class of them (with or without exceptions for persons connected with company B), and made in the first instance on a condition such that if it were satisfied company B would have control of company A,

(*c*) the person in question is a venture capital trust,

(*d*) the new shares are issued in exchange for old shares or old securities, and the new securities are issued solely in exchange for old securities, and

(*e*) the arrangements under which the exchange takes place are not arrangements to which paragraph 10C of Schedule 28B (acquisitions for restructuring purpose) applies.

(2) In paragraph (1)(*a*), (*b*) and (*d*) and regulation 8—

(*a*) expressions (other than "securities") have the same meanings as in section 135 of the 1992 Act;

(*b*) the shares in or securities of company B issued to the trust company are referred to as the "new shares" and the "new securities" respectively, and the shares in or securities of company A held by the trust company and mentioned in paragraph (1)(*a*) are referred to as the "old shares" and the "old securities" respectively.

Scheme of reconstruction involving issue of shares or securities

6—(1) The case described in this regulation is where—

(*a*) an arrangement between a company ("company A") and—

(i) the persons holding shares in or securities of the company, or

(ii) where there are different classes of shares in or securities of the company, the persons holding any class of those shares or securities,

is entered into for the purposes of, or in connection with, a scheme of reconstruction,

(*b*) under the arrangement—

(i) another company ("company B") issues shares or securities to those persons in respect of and in proportion to (or as nearly as may be in proportion to) their original holding, but

(ii) the shares in or securities of company A comprised in their original holding are either retained by those persons or cancelled, redeemed or otherwise extinguished,

(*c*) the person in question is a venture capital trust, and

(*d*) the new shares are issued in respect of old shares or old securities, and the new securities are issued solely in respect of old securities.

(2) In paragraph (1) and regulation 9—

(*a*) expressions (other than "securities") have the same meanings as in section 136(1) and (3) to (5) of the 1992 Act (references to "debentures" in those provisions being read as references to "securities" as defined above);

(*b*) the shares in or securities of company B issued to the trust company are referred to as the "new shares" and the "new securities" respectively, and the trust company's original holding in company A is referred to, separately and as the case may be, as the "old shares" and the "old securities" respectively.

Provision where there is an exchange of shares or securities in the same company

7—(1) In relation to any case described in regulation 4 the following paragraphs have effect.

(2) For the purposes of subsection (2)(*b*) to (*d*) of section 842AA, the aggregate value of the new shares and new securities shall be determined, immediately after the exchange and until such time as those shares or securities fall to be revalued in accordance with subsection (5) of that section, in accordance with the following formula:

$$Nv = Ov \times \frac{Nmv}{Nmv + c}$$

where—

Nv is the aggregate value of the new shares and new securities to be determined in accordance with this paragraph,

Ov is the aggregate value of the old shares and old securities when last valued in accordance with subsection (5) of section 842AA ("historic values",

Nmv is the aggregate market value, immediately after the exchange, of the new shares and new securities,

C is the aggregate market value, immediately after the exchange, of—

(i) any monetary amount,

(ii) any monetary right (without any discount for postponement of the right to receive the payment or any part of it), and

(iii) any other consideration or receipt (except the new shares and new securities),

received by the venture capital trust as consideration for, or in respect of, the old shares or old securities, and

"immediately after the exchange" in this regulation means immediately after the events mentioned in regulation 4(1)(*d*).

(3) For the purposes of subsection (2)(*b*) to (*d*) of section 842AA, where the venture capital trust retains original shares or securities in the company which are not included in the exchange of old shares or old securities for new shares or new securities, such original shares or securities shall, immediately after the exchange, continue to be valued at their value, or apportioned value, as the case may be, when last valued before the exchange in accordance with subsection (5) of section 842AA, until such time as they fall to be revalued in accordance with that subsection.

(4) For the purposes of paragraph 10B of Schedule 28B the like provisions as are contained in paragraphs (2) and (3) shall apply (substituting references to valuations in accordance with paragraph 10B for references to valuations in accordance with subsection (5) of section 842AA).

(5) Where the company in which the venture capital trust holds the old shares or old securities is deemed to satisfy the requirements of paragraph 2 of Schedule 28B (unquoted company) by virtue of sub-paragraph (6) of that paragraph for a period of five years after ceasing to be to be an unquoted company, the company shall be deemed to satisfy those requirements in relation to the new shares or new securities for the same five year period.

(6) Subject to paragraph (7), where the old shares or old securities are shares or securities in relation to which the requirements of paragraphs 6 and 8 of Schedule 28B were (or were deemed to be) satisfied to any extent immediately before the exchange, those requirements shall be deemed, at all times after that time, to be satisfied to the same extent in relation to the matching new shares or new securities.

(7) Where there is a time following the exchange when (apart from the exchange) the requirements of paragraph 6 of Schedule 28B would have ceased under—

(*a*) sub-paragraph (2) of that paragraph, or
(*b*) this paragraph,

to be satisfied in relation to the old shares or old securities, those requirements shall cease at that time to be satisfied in relation to the matching new shares or new securities.

(8) For the purposes of paragraph 7 of Schedule 28B any new shares or new securities shall be deemed—

(*a*) to have been issued at the time when the matching old shares or old securities were issued (or, as the case may be, were deemed to have been issued), and
(*b*) by virtue of that issue, to have raised the same amount of money as was raised (or, as the case may be, was deemed to be raised) by virtue of the issue of the matching old shares or old securities.

(9) In determining whether the requirements of paragraph 9 of Schedule 28B are satisfied in relation to the company at any time in the period for giving effect to the exchange, the exchange shall be disregarded.

(10) The reference in paragraph (9) to the period for giving effect to the exchange is to the period which—

(*a*) begins on the day when a shareholder disposes of, redeems or otherwise ceases to possess shares or securities in consequence of the exchange or, where there is more than one exchange of shares or securities involved in a company reorganisation, the exchanges, and is the first shareholder to do so, and
(*b*) ends on the earlier of—
(i) the date when the last of the shares or securities to be issued in consequence of the exchange or exchanges is issued, and
(ii) the day six months after the date in sub-paragraph (*a*) (or such later date as the Board may by notice in writing allow).

Provision where exchange of shares or securities for those in another company

8—(1) In relation to a case described in regulation 5, the following paragraphs have effect.

(2) For the purposes of subsection (2)(*b*) to (*d*) of section 842AA, the aggregate value of the new shares and new securities issued to the venture capital trust shall be determined, immediately after the exchange and until such time as those shares or securities fall to be revalued in accordance with subsection (5) of that section, in accordance with the formula in regulation 7(2) (substituting references to the period for giving effect to the exchange for references to the events mentioned in regulation 4(1)(*d*)).

(3) For the purposes of paragraph 10B of Schedule 28B, the like provisions as are contained in paragraph (2) shall apply (substituting references to valuations in accordance with paragraph 10B for references to valuations in accordance with subsection (5) of section 842AA).

(4) The new shares and new securities held by the venture capital trust shall be treated, during the period for giving effect to the exchange, as meeting the requirements of Schedule 28B.

(5) The requirements of and arrangements referred to in paragraph 9 of Schedule 28B, to the extent that they are incidental to the exchange, shall be disregarded before and during that period.

(6) The new shares and new securities shall be treated at all times following the end of the period for giving effect to the exchange as having met the requirements of paragraphs 6 and 7 of Schedule 28B.

(7) Where, immediately after the end of the period for giving effect to the exchange, any of the new shares or new securities are found not to meet the requirements of paragraph 2 of Schedule 28B, or of that paragraph and any other paragraphs of that Schedule (other than paragraph 6 or 7), those shares or securities shall be treated as meeting those requirements until the end of the period specified in paragraph (8) or the disposal by the venture capital trust of those shares or securities, whichever is the earlier to occur.

(8) The period specified is the period that—

(*a*) begins on the date when new shares or new securities are first issued to the venture capital trust or, if later, on the date on which all the new shares or new securities issued to the venture capital trust become fully tradeable, and

(*b*) ends immediately before the second anniversary of that date.

(9) Where, immediately after the end of the period for giving effect to the exchange, any of the new shares or new securities are found not to meet the requirements of any paragraph of Schedule 28B other than paragraph 2, 6 or 7, those shares or securities shall be treated as meeting those requirements until the end of the period—

(*a*) beginning on the date when new shares or new securities are first issued to the venture capital trust (''the first issue date''), and

(*b*) ending on the earlier of—

(i) the disposal by the venture capital trust of those shares or securities, or

(ii) subject to paragraph (10), in the case of shares, the day 3 years after the first issue date and, in the case of securities, the day 5 years after the first issue date.

(10) Where, in a case falling within the terms of paragraph (9)(*b*)(ii), before the relevant date there mentioned, the new shares or new securities become marketed to the general public (within the meaning of paragraph 2(3) of Schedule 28B), there shall be substituted for that date the second anniversary of the date on which the new shares or new securities became so marketed or, if later, the second anniversary of the date on which those shares or securities became fully tradeable.

(11) References in this regulation to the period for giving effect to the exchange are references to the period which—

(*a*) begins when a shareholder or holder of securities ceases to possess shares in or securities of company A in consequence of the exchange, and is the first shareholder or holder of securities to do so, and

(*b*) ends when the last of the shares in or securities of company B to be issued in consequence of the exchange (excluding shares or securities issued in pursuance of an earn-out right) is issued.

(12) Shares or securities become fully tradeable for the purposes of this regulation and regulation 9 when, in circumstances where they are offered for issue to the shareholders or holders of securities of company A, they cease to be subject to—

(*a*) rules of the recognised stock exchange (or other exchange) governing the offer that prohibit or restrict the disposal of the shares or securities to any other person, and

(*b*) conditions prohibiting or restricting the disposal of the shares or securities to any other person that are contained in any contract entered into by any of the following persons—

(i) company B, or a company disposing of the shares or securities,

(ii) the person or persons sponsoring, underwriting or organising the offer, and

(iii) the venture capital trust in question.

Provision where scheme of reconstruction involving issue of shares or securities

9—(1) In relation to a case described in regulation 6 the following paragraphs have effect as regards—

(*a*) any shares in or securities of company A that are retained by the venture capital trust after the scheme of reconstruction, whether old shares or old securities or original shares or securities, not included in the scheme of reconstruction (the ''company A shares or securities''), and

(*b*) the shares in or securities of company B issued to the venture capital trust as mentioned in regulation 6(2)(*b*) (the ''new shares'' and the ''new securities'' respectively).

(2) For the purposes of subsection (2)(*b*) to (*d*) of section 842AA, the aggregate value of the new shares and new securities and any company A shares or securities shall be determined, immediately after the reorganisation period and until such time as those shares or securities fall to be revalued in accordance with subsection (5) of that section, in accordance with the formula in regulation 7(2) but where—

Nv is the aggregate value of the new shares and new securities, and of the company A shares or securities, to be determined in accordance with that paragraph,

Nmv is the aggregate market value, immediately after the reorganisation period, of the new shares and new securities and the company A shares or securities, and

any reference to events mentioned in regulation 4(1)(*d*) is replaced with a reference to the reorganisation period.

(3) For the purposes of paragraph 10B of Schedule 28B, the like provisions as are contained in paragraph (2) shall apply (substituting references to valuations in accordance with paragraph 10B for references to valuations in accordance with subsection (5) of section 842AA).

(4) The new shares and new securities held by the venture capital trust shall be treated, during the reorganisation period, as meeting the requirements of Schedule 28B.

(5) The requirements of and arrangements referred to in paragraph 9 of Schedule 28B, to the extent that they are incidental to the scheme of reconstruction, shall be disregarded before and during the reorganisation period.

(6) The new shares or new securities held by the venture capital trust shall be treated at all times following the date on which they were issued to the trust company as having met the requirements of paragraphs 6 and 7 of Schedule 28B.

(7) Where, immediately after the date on which the new shares or new securities were issued to the venture capital trust, those shares or securities are found not to meet the requirements of paragraph 2 of that Schedule, or of that paragraph and any other paragraph of that Schedule excepting paragraph 6 or 7, those shares or securities shall be treated as meeting those requirements until the end of the period specified in paragraph (8) or the disposal by the venture capital trust of those shares or securities, whichever is the earlier to occur.

(8) The period specified is the period that—

(*a*) begins on the date on which the new shares or new securities were issued to the venture capital trust or, if later, on the date on which all those shares or securities become fully tradeable, and

(*b*) ends immediately before the second anniversary of that date.

(9) Where, immediately after the date on which the new shares or new securities were issued to the venture capital trust, those shares or securities are found not to meet the requirements of any paragraph of Schedule 28B other than paragraph 2, 6 or 7, those shares or securities shall be treated as meeting the requirements of that Schedule until the end of the period—

(*a*) beginning on the date when new shares or new securities are first issued to the venture capital trust ("the first issue date"), and

(*b*) ending on the earlier of—

(i) the disposal by the venture capital trust of those shares or securities, or

(ii) subject to paragraph (10), in the case of shares, the day 3 years after the first issue date and, in the case of securities, the day 5 years after the first issue date.

(10) Where, in a case falling within the terms of paragraph (9)(*b*)(ii), before the relevant date there mentioned, the new shares or new securities become marketed to the general public (within the meaning of paragraph 2(3) of Schedule 28B), there shall be substituted for that date the second anniversary of the date on which the new shares or new securities became so marketed or, if later, the second anniversary of the date on which those shares or securities became fully tradeable.

(11) In this regulation references to the reorganisation period are to the period which—

(*a*) begins when a shareholder or holder of securities receives shares in or securities of company B in consequence of the scheme of reconstruction, and is the first person to do so, and

(*b*) ends when the last of the shares in or securities of company B to be issued in consequence of the scheme of reconstruction (excluding shares or securities issued in pursuance of an earn-out right) is issued.

Earn-outs

10—(1) Where, in a case described in either regulation 5 or 6—

(*a*) shares in or securities of company B ("earn-out shares or securities") are issued to a venture capital trust in pursuance of an earn-out right, which was conferred on the trust company in exchange for old shares or old securities, and

(*b*) the requirements of regulation 5(1)(*d*) or 6(1)(*d*), as the case may be, would be satisfied if the earn-out right were treated as replaced by the earn-out shares or securities that are issued in pursuance of it—

(i) regulation 8(4) to (12) or regulation 9(4) to (11), as the case may be, shall apply to the earn-out shares and securities as they apply to new shares and new securities; and

(ii) the trust company may elect to recalculate the formula in regulation 7(2) (as applied by regulation 8(2) or (3) or 9(2) or (3)).

(2) The recalculation shall be made—

(*a*) including the earn-out shares and securities in the calculation of Nv and Nmv (but at their market value immediately after they were issued), and

(*b*) omitting the earn-out right from the calculation of C.

(3) An election under this regulation in respect of any right—

(*a*) must be made, by a notice given to an officer of the Board, within the period of one year from the end of the accounting period in which the relevant earn-out shares and securities are issued, and

(*b*) shall be irrevocable.

Apportionment

11—(1) For the purposes of these Regulations (and of subsection (2)(*b*) to (*d*) of section 842AA and paragraph 10B of Schedule 28B), where it is necessary to apportion any value between the new shares or new securities issued to the venture capital trust (or one or more classes thereof), such apportionment shall be carried out—

(*a*) in the first instance, having regard to the historic values of any old shares or old securities in relation to which the new shares or new securities are matching shares or securities,

(*b*) otherwise according to such method as is just and reasonable, and

(*c*) in any event, with a view to securing that the requirements of section 842AA(2)(*b*) to (*d*), or paragraph 10B of Schedule 28B, as the case may be, do not cease to be met.

(2) In the application of paragraph (1) to regulation 9, references to new shares and new securities shall be construed as extending to company A shares or securities (as defined in that regulation) with any necessary modifications.

2002/2849
Capital Gains Tax (Gilt-edged Securities) Order 2002

Made by the Treasury under TCGA 1992 Sch 9

Made . . . . *18 November 2002*

1 This Order may be cited as the Capital Gains Tax (Gilt-edged Securities) Order 2002.

2 The following securities are hereby specified for the purposes of Schedule 9 to the Taxation of Chargeable Gains Act 1992—

5% Treasury Stock 2008
5% Treasury Stock 2012
5% Treasury Stock 2014
5% Treasury Stock 2025
2% Index-linked Treasury Stock 2035.

2002/3047
Statutory Payment Schemes (Electronic Communications) Regulations 2002

Made by the Commissioners of Inland Revenue under FA 1999 ss 132 and 133(2)

Made . . . . *11 December 2002*
Laid before the House of Commons . . . . *11 December 2002*
Coming into force . . . . *1 January 2003*

PART 1
INTRODUCTION

Citation, commencement and interpretation

1—(1) These Regulations may be cited as the Statutory Payment Schemes (Electronic Communications) Regulations 2002 and shall come into force on 1st January 2003.

(2) In these Regulations—

''the Board'' means the Commissioners of Inland Revenue;

''official computer system'' means a computer system maintained by or on behalf of the Board—

(*a*) to send or receive information or payments; or

(*b*) to process or store information; and

''the statutory payments'' means statutory maternity pay, statutory paternity pay and statutory adoption pay.

(3) References in these Regulations to information and to the delivery of information shall be construed in accordance with section 132(8) of the Finance Act 1999.

Scope of these Regulations

2 These Regulations apply to—

(*a*) the delivery of information to or by the Board, the delivery of which is required or authorised in connection with the statutory payments; and

(*b*) the making or recovery of any of the statutory payments or of any other sum in connection with those payments.

PART 2

ELECTRONIC COMMUNICATIONS—GENERAL PROVISIONS

Restrictions on the use of electronic communications

3—(1) The Board may use electronic communications in connection with the matters referred to in regulation 2.

(2) A person other than the Board may only use electronic communications in connection with the matters referred to in regulation 2 if the conditions specified in paragraphs (3) to (6) are satisfied.

(3) The first condition is that the person is for the time being permitted to use electronic communications by an authorisation given by means of a direction of the Board.

(4) The second condition is that the person uses—

(*a*) an approved method for authenticating the identity of the sender of the communication;

(*b*) an approved method of electronic communications; and

(*c*) an approved method for authenticating any information delivered by means of electronic communications.

(5) The third condition is that any information or payment sent by means of electronic communications is in a form approved for the purposes of these Regulations.

(6) The fourth condition is that the person maintains such records in written or electronic form as may be specified in a general or specific direction given by the Board.

(7) In this regulation ''approved'' means approved for the purposes of these Regulations and for the time being by means of a general or specific direction of the Board.

Use of intermediaries

4 The Board may use intermediaries in connection with—

(*a*) the delivery of information about any statutory payment by means of electronic communications;

(*b*) the making or recovery of any statutory payment by those means; and

(*c*) the authentication or security of anything transmitted by any such means,

and may require other persons to use intermediaries in connection with those matters.

PART 3

ELECTRONIC COMMUNICATIONS — EVIDENTIAL PROVISIONS

Effect of delivering information by means of electronic communications

5—(1) Information to which these Regulations apply, and which is delivered by means of electronic communications, shall be treated as having been delivered, in the manner or form required by or under any provision of the Social Security Acts, section 7 or 8 of the Employment Act 2002 or Article 8 or 9 of the Employment (Northern Ireland) Order 2002 if, but only if, all the conditions specified by—

(*a*) these Regulations, and

(*b*) any specific or general direction given by the Board,

are satisfied.

(2) Information delivered by means of electronic communications shall be treated as having been delivered on the day on which the last of the conditions imposed as mentioned in paragraph (1) is satisfied.

This is subject to the following qualification.

(3) The Board may by a general or specific direction provide for information to be treated as delivered upon a different date (whether earlier or later) (than that given by paragraph (2).

(4) In paragraph (1) ''the Social Security Acts'' means the Social Security Contributions and Benefits Act 1992, the Social Security Administration Act 1992, the Social Security Contributions and Benefits (Northern Ireland) Act 1992 and the Social Security Administration (Northern Ireland) Act 1992.

Proof of identity of sender or recipient of information

6 If it is necessary to prove, for any purpose, the identity of—

(*a*) the sender of any information delivered by means of electronic communications to an official computer system, or

(*b*) the recipient of any information delivered by means of electronic communications from an official computer system,

the sender or recipient (as the case may be) shall be presumed to be the person recorded as such on an official computer system unless the contrary is proved.

Proof of delivery of information and payments

7—(1) If it is necessary to prove, for any purpose, that the use of electronic communications has resulted in the making of any payment to or by the Board, or the delivery of any information to or by them, this shall be presumed, unless the contrary is proved—

(*a*) in the case of information delivered or a payment made to the Board, if the making of the payment, or the delivery of the information, has been recorded on an official computer system;
(*b*) in the case of information delivered, or payment made, by the Board, if the despatch of that payment or information has been recorded on an official computer system, and
(*c*) not to be the case if it has not been so recorded.

(2) If it is necessary to prove, for any purpose, when any information or payment sent by electronic communications has been received, the time of receipt shall be presumed to be that recorded on an official computer system unless the contrary is proved.

Proof of content of information

8 If it is necessary to prove, for any purpose the content of any information sent by means of electronic communications, the content shall be presumed to be that recorded on an official computer system unless the contrary is proved.

Certificates as to official records

9 A document certified by an officer of the Board to be a printed-out version of any electronic communication recorded on an official computer system as at a particular date shall be presumed, unless the contrary is proved—

(*a*) to have been recorded on an official computer system at that date; and
(*b*) to constitute the entirety of the electronic communication so recorded.

Presumption as to certificates

10 A document purporting to be a certificate issued by an officer of the Board under regulation 9 shall be presumed to be such a certificate unless the contrary is proved.

2003/96

Community Investment Tax Relief (Accreditation of Community Development Finance Institutions) Regulations 2003

Made by the Treasury under FA 2002 Sch 16 paras 4(2)(*b*), (4), (5), (6) and 5

Made	*23 January 2003*
Laid before Parliament	*23 January 2003*
Coming into force	*13 February 2003*

PART 1
INTRODUCTORY

Citation and commencement

1 These Regulations may be cited as the Community Investment Tax Relief (Accreditation of Community Development Finance Institutions) Regulations 2003 and shall come into force on 13th February 2003.

Interpretation

2 In these Regulations—

''accreditation'' means accreditation as a community development finance institution;
''the Board'' means the Commissioners of Inland Revenue;
''CDFI'' means a body accredited as a community development finance institution under Schedule 16 to the Finance Act 2002;
''the five year period'' has the meaning given in paragraph 3 of Schedule 16 to the Finance Act 2002;
''the Investment Director'' means the Investment Director of the Small Business Service;
''investment'' has the meaning given in paragraph 2 of Schedule 16 to the Finance Act 2002;
''investment fund'' has the meaning given in regulation 9;
''notice'' means notice in writing;
''qualifying enterprise'' has the meaning given in regulation 10;

SIS

"qualifying investment" has the meaning given in paragraph 8 of Schedule 16 to the Finance Act 2002;

"relevant investment" has the meaning given in regulation 11;

"residential property" has the meaning given in Annex D of the Material Concerning the Accreditation of Community Development Finance Institutions published by the Secretary of State;

"retail community development finance institution" shall be construed in accordance with paragraph 4(6) and (7) of Schedule 16 to the Finance Act 2002;

"the Small Business Service" means the entity so named being an executive agency of the Department of Trade and Industry;

"tax relief certificate" has the meaning given in paragraph 12(1) of Schedule 16 to the Finance Act 2002.

PART 2

APPLICATION AND CRITERIA FOR ACCREDITATION

Criteria for accreditation

3 For the purposes of paragraph 4(2)(*b*) of Part 2 of Schedule 16 to the Finance Act 2002 the criteria to be satisfied for accreditation are specified in Part 2 (Application and Criteria for Accreditation) of the Material Concerning the Accreditation of Community Development Finance Institutions published by the Secretary of State.

Notification of accreditation or refusal

4 The Secretary of State must give notice to a body of the grant of an accreditation specifying the date of the grant of accreditation and the date on which the period of accreditation begins.

5 The Secretary of State must give notice to a body of a refusal to grant accreditation specifying the date of the refusal and the reasons for the refusal.

PART 3

TERMS AND CONDITIONS OF ACCREDITATION

6 An accreditation is subject to the terms set out in this Part.

Publication of details

7—(1) It is a term of accreditation that the CDFI agrees to the publication of the information specified in paragraph (2) in a list which the Secretary of State may publish from time to time.

(2) The information specified for the purpose of paragraph (1) is—

(*a*) the name of the CDFI;
(*b*) the business address of the CDFI;
(*c*) the name of an individual who may be contacted at the CDFI;
(*d*) the date the CDFI was granted accreditation; and
(*e*) an outline of the aims and business operations of the CDFI.

(3) The CDFI must give notice to the Secretary of State of—

(*a*) any change to the information specified in subparagraphs (*a*) to (*d*) of paragraph (2), and
(*b*) any material change to the information specified in subparagraph (*e*) of paragraph (2),

within 30 days of the relevant change.

(4) The CDFI is liable to a penalty of £100 payable to the Small Business Service for each failure to notify a change to the specified information in accordance with paragraph (3) unless the Investment Director is satisfied that the CDFI had a reasonable excuse for failing to notify the change.

General CDFI investment terms

8 It is a term of accreditation that—

(*a*) on or before the first anniversary of the date the CDFI was first granted accreditation ("the accreditation date"), at least 25% of the amount of the investment fund is invested in relevant investments in qualifying enterprises;

(*b*) on or before the second anniversary of the accreditation date, at least 50% of the amount of the investment fund is invested in relevant investments in qualifying enterprises; and

(*c*) on or before the third anniversary of the accreditation date and at all times thereafter, at least 75% of the amount of the investment fund is invested in relevant investments in qualifying enterprises.

Meaning of the "investment fund"

9—(1) The amount of the investment fund at a given date ("the relevant date") is the sum of—

$$A - (B+C)$$

Here—

A is the amount of qualifying investments and investments by other CDFIs in the CDFI made on or before the relevant date and held continuously since the investment was made until the relevant date, but does not include any qualifying investments or investments by other CDFIs in the CDFI made at any time during the three months prior to the relevant date;

B is any amount payable by the CDFI at the relevant date or at any time during the three months following the relevant date to repay, redeem or buy-back the capital element of any qualifying investment;

C is the amount of any investment made by the CDFI from the investment fund which has been written-off in accordance with generally accepted accounting practice.

(2) For the purpose of paragraph (1) where a qualifying investment is a loan which authorises the CDFI to draw down amounts of the loan over a period of time, the amount of the qualifying investment is the amount drawn down at the relevant date.

Meaning of "qualifying enterprise"

10—(1) For the purposes of these Regulations an enterprise is a qualifying enterprise if—

(*a*) the enterprise is a small or medium-sized enterprise;

(*b*) the CDFI can demonstrate that at the time the investment in the enterprise was made the enterprise was unable to obtain finance from other sources; and

(*c*) the enterprise falls within one of the following Cases.

Case 1

The enterprise is located in a geographic area identified in Annex A of the Material Concerning the Accreditation of Community Development Finance Institutions published by the Secretary of State.

Case 2

The enterprise is located in an area which the CDFI, by reference to Government-recognised measures of disadvantage relating to—

(i) income;
(ii) employment;
(iii) health, deprivation and disability;
(iv) education, skills and training;
(v) geographical access to services, and
(vi) housing,

can demonstrate has a level of disadvantage comparable to those identified in Annex A of the Material Concerning the Accreditation of Community Development Finance Institutions published by the Secretary of State.

Case 3

The enterprise is owned and operated by, or intended to serve, individuals recognised as being disadvantaged on account of their ethnicity, gender, age, disability or other similar defining characteristic.

(2) For the purpose of paragraph (1)(*a*), a "small or medium sized enterprise" shall be interpreted in accordance with paragraph 2 of Schedule 20 to the Finance Act 2000.

Meaning of "relevant investment"

11—(1) Subject to paragraph (4), for the purposes of these Regulations a relevant investment is an investment made by the CDFI in an enterprise where—

(*a*) it makes a loan (whether secured or unsecured) to the enterprise, or

(*b*) an issue of securities of or shares in the enterprise, for which the CDFI has subscribed, is made to the CDFI.

(2) For the purposes of paragraph (1)(*a*)—

(*a*) the CDFI does not make a loan to an enterprise where—

(i) the enterprise uses overdraft facilities provided by the CDFI, or

(ii) the CDFI subscribes for or otherwise acquires securities of the enterprise;

(*b*) where the loan agreement authorises the enterprise to draw down amounts of the loan over a period of time the loan is treated as made at the time when the first amount is drawn down.

(3) For the purpose of these Regulations where a relevant investment is a loan within paragraph (2)(*b*) the amount of the relevant investment is the amount drawn down at a given date.

(4) The investments specified in Schedule 1 are not relevant investments.

Limits on qualifying investments

12—(1) The CDFI must give notice to the Investment Director at least one month before entering into any arrangements or commitments with the aim of increasing qualifying investments in the CDFI to more than 125% of the amount stated in its application for accreditation (''the 125% limit).

(2) The Investment Director may approve the increase by notice to the CDFI.

(3) Where—

(*a*) the CDFI fails to give notice in accordance with paragraph (1), or

(*b*) the Investment Director does not approve the increase in accordance with paragraph (2),

the Investment Director may treat all or some of the investments made by the CDFI after the date on which the qualifying investments exceed the 125% limit as not being relevant investments for the purposes of regulation 8 up to an amount equal to the amount by which the qualifying investments exceed the 125% limit.

Reporting requirements

13—(1) The CDFI must make an annual report to the Small Business Service—

(*a*) within three months of each anniversary of the date on which the CDFI was last granted accreditation, or

(*b*) subject to paragraph (2), on such other date coincident with the CDFI's reporting cycle and agreed with the Small Business Service.

(2) The first annual report made by the CDFI must be made no later than 18 months after the date accreditation was granted.

(3) The annual report shall be in the form provided by the Secretary of State for this purpose.

(4) Subject to paragraph (5), the CDFI is liable to a penalty of £500 payable to the Small Business Service where the annual report is not made within three months of date on which it was due under paragraph (1).

(5) Paragraph (4) does not apply if in the opinion of the Investment Director the CDFI had reasonable excuse for failing to make an annual return.

Tax relief certificate

14—(1) Subject to paragraph (2), the CDFI must issue a tax relief certificate to the investor or its nominee within 30 days of receiving an investment from an individual or a company.

(2) Where the investment is received before the grant of accreditation but an application for accreditation is made before 6th April 2003, the CDFI must issue a tax relief certificate within 30 days of the grant of accreditation.

PART 4

GENERAL PROVISIONS

Withdrawal of accreditation

15—(1) The Secretary of State must withdraw the CDFI's accreditation—

(*a*) with effect from the time of the failure, where the CDFI fails to satisfy the terms of regulation 8;

(*b*) subject to paragraph (2), where the CDFI makes a direct or indirect investment in residential property from the investment fund; and

(*c*) subject to paragraph (3), where the CDFI fails to make an annual report within 12 months of the date on which it was due under paragraph (1) of regulation 13.

(2) Paragraph (1)(*b*) does not apply where—

(*a*) the CDFI can demonstrate that to the best of its knowledge and belief it had not invested in residential property, and

(*b*) the CDFI divested itself of the investment within three months of—

(i) the date it discovered that the investment was in residential property, or

(ii) the date of receipt of a notice from the Small Business Service that the investment is in residential property,

whichever is the earlier.

(3) Paragraph (1)(*c*) does not apply if in the opinion of the Investment Director the CDFI had reasonable excuse for failing to make an annual return.

(4) A withdrawal of an accreditation must be given by notice by the Secretary of State specifying the date from which accreditation is withdrawn and the reasons for the withdrawal.

(5) The CDFI must within 30 days of receiving notice under paragraph (4) of withdrawal of accreditation give notice to each of the investors to which it has issued a tax relief certificate in respect of investments made within the specified period stating that accreditation has been withdrawn and specifying the date from which accreditation is withdrawn.

(6) For the purpose of paragraph (5) ''specified period'' means the five years immediately preceding the date from which accreditation is withdrawn.

Appeals against refusal to grant accreditation or withdrawal of accreditation

16—(1) An appeal to the Special Commissioners may be brought against a refusal to grant accreditation or a withdrawal of accreditation.

(2) Notice of an appeal under this regulation must be given—

(*a*) in writing,

(*b*) within 30 days of the date of the notification of the refusal under regulation 5 or the withdrawal under regulation 15(4), and

(*c*) to the Investment Director.

(3) The notice of appeal must require the Investment Director to transmit to the Special Commissioners—

(*a*) in an appeal against a refusal to grant accreditation, the application for accreditation, together with any information or particulars provided by the body to the Secretary of State in support of the application, or

(*b*) in an appeal against a withdrawal of accreditation, the notice under regulation 15(4) together with any information or particulars prepared by the Small Business Service leading to the issue of that notice.

(4) The Special Commissioners may allow the appeal and—

(*a*) in an appeal against a refusal to grant accreditation, direct that the Secretary of State accredit the body within 14 days of its decision, or

(*b*) in an appeal against a withdrawal of accreditation, direct that the withdrawal was ineffective.

(5) The decision of the Special Commissioners shall be final.

SCHEDULE 1

Regulation 11(4)

INVESTMENTS WHICH ARE NOT RELEVANT INVESTMENTS

General Investments

1 Any investment which benefits directly or indirectly from the security offered by a Phoenix Fund guarantee or by any similar publicly-funded underwriting or guarantee arrangement.

2—(1) Any loan to a profit-distributing enterprise—

(*a*) which is not made on terms that are equivalent to those offered by conventional sources of finance, or

(*b*) as a consequence of which, and for so long as, the total amount of loans to that enterprise exceeds £100,000 (''the £100,000 limit'').

(2) Where the £100,000 limit is exceeded—

(*a*) by two or more loans made on the same day, or

(*b*) in any other circumstances where it is not possible to establish which loan caused the limit to be exceeded,

the Investment Director shall determine which of those loans shall not constitute relevant investments so that the amount of relevant investments in the enterprise approximates to but does not exceed the £100,000 limit.

3—(1) Any loan to a profit-distributing enterprise which is not made at market rates or above, or, where interest is not charged on loans the fee structure is not at an equivalent level.

(2) In paragraph (1) ''market rate'' means the European Commission's Hurdle Rate, which is the Reference Rate (as published at http://europa.eu.int/comm/competition/state_aid/others/reference_rates.html) plus four percentage points, or more.

4—(1) Any loan to or equity investment in a non-profit-distributing enterprise for the purposes of undertaking community projects as a consequence of which, and for so long as, the total amount invested in that enterprise exceeds £250,000 (''the £250,000 limit'').

(2) For the purpose of paragraph (1) ''community projects'' means—

(*a*) public sector projects,

(*b*) projects which benefit charities and other non-profit distributing bodies which are engaged entirely in public functions, non-competitive and non-commercial activity, or

(*c*) projects which are commercial in the sense that there is remuneration for the service provider and competition for their supply, but which are small-scale and purely local in nature.

(3) Where the £250,000 limit is exceeded—

(*a*) by two or more loans or equity investments made on the same day, or

(*b*) in any other circumstances where it is not possible to establish which loan or investment caused the limit to be exceeded, the Investment Director shall determine which of those loans or investments shall not constitute relevant investments so that the amount of relevant investments in the enterprise approximates to but does not exceed the £250,000 limit.

5 Any investment in an enterprise as a consequence of which, and for so long as, the total amount invested by the CDFI in that enterprise exceeds 20% of the amount of the investment fund at—

(*a*) for the first year following accreditation, the date the investment is made by the CDFI, and

(*b*) thereafter, the immediately preceding anniversary of the accreditation date.

6—(1) Any investment in an enterprise within Case 2 of regulation 10 as a consequence of which, and for so long as—

(*a*) the total amount invested out of the investment fund by the CDFI in enterprises in Case 2 exceeds the amount invested in enterprises within Cases 1 and 3; or

(*b*) the number of investments out of the investment fund by the CDFI in enterprises in Case 2 exceeds the number of investments in enterprises within Cases 1 and 3.

(2) For the purposes of paragraph (1) an investment in an enterprise which is within both Case 2 and Case 3 shall be treated as being only within Case 3.

Property investments, which are not relevant investments

7 Any investment which funds directly or indirectly the acquisition, construction or development of residential property.

8—(1) Any investment which funds directly or indirectly the acquisition, construction or development of non-residential property where, on the next anniversary of the date on which the CDFI was granted accreditation, in consequence of that investment—

(*a*) the total amount of investment within Case 1 below exceeds the amount of relevant investments other than those in Case 1, or

(*b*) the total amount of investment within Case 2 below exceeds one half of the relevant investments within Case 1.

Case 1

1.1 Investment in a non profit-distributing enterprise, the main activity of which is to hold and invest in or to develop non-residential property.

1.2 Investment in a development trust or other social enterprise for the purpose of investment in or development of non-residential property, whether owned by the trust or by others.

Case 2

2.1 Investment in a profit-distributing enterprise, the main activity of which is holding land with the aim of benefiting from capital appreciation of that land, or with the aim of receiving income through the exploitation of an interest in it.

2.2 Investment in a profit-distributing enterprise, the main activity of which is non-residential property development.

(2) For the purposes of paragraph (1) where a investment is a loan which authorises the CDFI to draw down amounts of the loan over a period of time, the amount of the investment is the amount drawn down at the relevant date.

Investments by retail community investment finance institutions

9 Where the CDFI has been accredited as a retail community investment finance institution, any investment in another CDFI or in any other body whose objective is to provide finance for enterprises in or for disadvantaged communities where, as a consequence of that investment, and for so long as, for more than three months the total amount invested in such bodies exceeds 10% of the amount of the investment fund at—

(*a*) for the first year following accreditation, the date the investment is made by the CDFI, and

(*b*) thereafter, the immediately preceding anniversary of the accreditation date.

10 Any investment by a retail community investment finance institution in a body other than a CDFI whose objective is to provide finance for enterprises in or for disadvantaged communities as a consequence of which, and for so long as, the total amount of investment in such enterprises exceeds £250,000.

Investments by wholesale CDFIs

11—(1) Any investment made by a wholesale CDFI in an enterprise where as a consequence of which, and for so long as, the total amount of investment in that enterprise exceeds—

(*a*) 20% of the amount of the investment fund at—

(i) for the first year following accreditation, the date the investment is made by the CDFI, and

(ii) thereafter, the immediately preceding anniversary of the accreditation date, or

(*b*) £2,500,000

whichever is the lesser amount.

(2) Any investment made by a wholesale CDFI in a body other than a CDFI whose objective is to provide finance for enterprises in or for disadvantaged communities as a consequence of which, and for so long as, the total amount invested in that body exceeds £250,000.

(3) A ''wholesale CDFI'' means a CDFI which is not accredited as a retail community investment finance institution.

Commentary—*Simon's Direct Tax Service* **A1.486.**

2003/282
Income and Corporation Taxes (Electronic Communications) Regulations 2003

Made by the Commissioners of Inland Revenue under FA 1999 ss 132, and 133(2)

Made	*12 February 2003*
Laid before the House of Commons	*12 February 2003*
Coming into force	*5 March 2003*

PART 1
INTRODUCTION

Citation, commencement and interpretation

1—(1) These Regulations may be cited as the Income and Corporation Taxes (Electronic Communications) Regulations 2003 and shall come into force on 5th March 2003.

(2) In these Regulations—

''the Board'' means the Commissioners of Inland Revenue;

''the Management Act'' means the Taxes Management Act 1970;

''official computer system'' means a computer system maintained by or on behalf of the Board—

(*a*) to send or receive information or payments, or

(*b*) to process or store information; and ''the Taxes Act'' means the Income and Corporation Taxes Act 1988.

(3) References in these Regulations to information and to the delivery of information shall be construed in accordance with section 132(8) of the Finance Act 1999.

Scope of these Regulations

2—(1) These Regulations apply to—

(*a*) the delivery of information, to or by the Board, the delivery of which is authorised or required by or under—

(i) any provision of section 8, 8A, 9, 9A, 9B, 9C, 9D, 12AA, 12AB 12AC, 12AD, 12AE, 59DA or 59E of the Management Act,

(ii) Schedule 1A to the Management Act,

(iii) section 30 or 36 of the Finance Act 1998, or

(iv) Schedule 18 to the Finance Act 1998; and

(*b*) the making of any payment or repayment of tax or other sums in connection with the operation of those provisions.

(2) Nothing in these Regulations affects the operation of the Electronic Lodgement of Tax Returns Order 1997.

PART 2
ELECTRONIC COMMUNICATIONS—GENERAL PROVISIONS

Restriction on the use of electronic communications

3—(1) The Board may only use electronic communications in connection with the matters referred to in regulation 2(1) if—

(*a*) the recipient has indicated that he consents to the Board using electronic communications in connection with those matters; and

(*b*) the Board have not been informed that that consent has been withdrawn.

(2) A person other than the Board may only use electronic communications in connection with the matters referred to in regulation 2(1) if the conditions specified in paragraphs (3) to (6) are satisfied.

(3) The first condition is that the person is for the time being permitted to use electronic communications for the purpose in question by an authorisation given by means of a direction of the Board.

(4) The second condition is that the person uses—

(*a*) an approved method for authenticating the identity of the sender of the communication;

(*b*) an approved method of electronic communications; and

(*c*) an approved method for authenticating any information delivered by means of electronic communications.

(5) The third condition is that any information or payment sent by means of electronic communications is in a form approved for the purpose of these Regulations.

Here ''form'' includes the manner in which the information is presented.

(6) The fourth condition is that the person maintains such records in written or electronic form as may be specified in a general or specific direction of the Board.

(7) In this regulation ''approved'' means approved, for the purposes of these Regulations and for the time being, by means of a general or specific direction of the Board.

Revenue Directions—(4 March 2003) Companies: returns under paragraph 3 of Schedule 18 to the Finance Act 1998

''The Commissioners of Inland Revenue hereby direct that, on and after 5 March 2003, a company that is required to deliver information in response to a notice under paragraph 3 of Schedule 18 to the Finance Act 1998 ('the relevant information') is authorised to do so over the Internet.

The Commissioners further direct that—

The methods approved by them for—

(*a*) authenticating the identity of the person sending the relevant information,

i. delivery of the relevant information, and

ii. authenticating the relevant information; and

(*b*) the form approved by them in which the relevant information is to be delivered; are the methods and form set out, at the time of, and for the purposes of, the delivery of the relevant information, in the terms and conditions for use of the Internet Corporation Tax Service, on the Inland Revenue website (www.inlandrevenue.gov.uk).''

Agents acting on behalf of companies—returns under paragraph 3 of Schedule 18 to the Finance Act 1998

''The Commissioners of Inland Revenue hereby direct that on and after 5 March 2003 an agent who delivers information on behalf of a company, which the company is required to deliver in response to a notice under paragraph 3 of Schedule 18 to the Finance Act 1998 ('the relevant information'), is authorised to do so over the Internet provided that the following conditions are met.

The first condition is that the agent is authorised to act for the company to which the return relates by means of a form 64-8 signed by a proper officer of the company.

The second condition is that—

(*a*) the agent makes a copy of the relevant information before it is sent; and

(*b*) the copy is authenticated by a proper officer of the company, (or other person authorised to make the return of behalf of the company) by means of a signature confirming that the information is correct to the best of his knowledge and belief before the information is sent by the agent. This condition will not apply where the agent is a person authorised by the company to make the return on its behalf.

The Commissioners further direct that—

(*a*) the methods approved by them for—

i. authenticating the identity of the person sending the relevant information,

ii. delivery of the relevant information, and

iii. authenticating the relevant information; and

(*b*) the form approved by them in which the relevant information is to be delivered; are the methods and form set out, at the time of, and for the purposes of, the delivery of the relevant information, in the terms and conditions for use of the Internet Corporation Tax Service, on the Inland Revenue website (www.inlandrevenue.gov.uk).''

Other communications within the scope of the Income and Corporation Tax (Electronic Communications) Regulations 2003

''The Commissioners of Inland Revenue hereby direct that—

– companies or their agents may use telephonic facsimile for other communications to which the regulations apply, and

– companies or their agents that are participating in the collaborative workspace trial may also use that facility for such communications.''

Use of intermediaries

4 The Board may use intermediaries in connection with—

(*a*) the delivery of information or the making of payments or repayments by means of electronic communications in connection with the matters referred to in regulation 2(1), and

(*b*) the authentication or security of anything transmitted by such means,

and may require other persons to use intermediaries in connection with those matters.

PART 3

ELECTRONIC COMMUNICATIONS—EVIDENTIAL PROVISIONS

Effect of delivering information by means of electronic communications

5—(1) Information to which these Regulations apply, and which is delivered by means of electronic communications, shall be treated as having been delivered, in the manner or form required by any provision of the Taxes Act or the Management Act if, but only if, all the conditions imposed by—

(*a*) these Regulations,

(*b*) any other applicable enactment (except to the extent that the condition thereby imposed is incompatible with these Regulations), and

(*c*) any specific or general direction given by the Board,

are satisfied.

(2) Information delivered by means of electronic communications shall be treated as having been delivered on the day on which the last of the conditions imposed as mentioned in paragraph (1) is satisfied.

This is subject to paragraphs (3) and (4).

(3) The Board may by a general or specific direction provide for information to be treated as delivered upon a different date (whether earlier or later) than that given by paragraph (2).

(4) Information shall not be taken to have been delivered to an official computer system by means of electronic communications unless it is accepted by the system to which it is delivered.

Proof of content

6—(1) A document certified by an officer of the Board to be a printed-out version of any information delivered by means of electronic communications under these Regulations on any occasion shall be evidence, unless the contrary is proved, that that information—

(*a*) was delivered by means of electronic communications on that occasion; and

(*b*) constitutes the entirety of what was delivered on that occasion.

(2) A document purporting to be a certificate given in accordance with paragraph (1) shall be presumed to be such a certificate unless the contrary is proved.

Proof of sender or recipient

7 The identity of—

(*a*) the sender of any information delivered to an official computer system by means of electronic communications under these Regulations, or

(*b*) the recipient of any information delivered by means of electronic communications from an official computer system,

shall be presumed, unless the contrary is proved, to be the person recorded as such on an official computer system.

Information delivered electronically on another's behalf

8 Any information delivered by an approved method of electronic communications on behalf of any person shall be deemed to have been delivered by him unless he proves that it was delivered without his knowledge or connivance.

Proof of delivery of information and payments

9—(1) The use of an authorised method of electronic communications shall be presumed, unless the contrary is proved, to have resulted in the making of a payment or the delivery of information—

(*a*) in the case of information falling to be delivered, or a payment falling to be made, to the Board, if the making of the payment or the delivery of the information has been recorded on an official computer system; and

(*b*) in the case of information falling to be delivered, or a payment falling to be made, by the Board, if the despatch of that payment or information has been recorded on an official computer system.

(2) The use of an authorised method of electronic communications shall be presumed, unless the contrary is proved, not to have resulted in the making of a payment, or the delivery of information—

(*a*) in the case of information falling to be delivered, or a payment falling to be made, to the Board, if the making of the payment or the delivery of the information has not been recorded on an official computer system; and

(*b*) in the case of information falling to be delivered, or a payment falling to be made, by the Board, if the despatch of that payment or information has not been recorded on an official computer system.

(3) The time of receipt of any information or payment sent by an authorised means of electronic communications shall be presumed, unless the contrary is proved, to be that recorded on an official computer system.

Use of unauthorised means of electronic communications

10—(1) Paragraph (2) applies to information which is required to be delivered to the Board in connection with the matters mentioned in regulation 2(1).

(2) The use of a means of electronic communications, for the purpose of delivering any information to which this paragraph applies, shall be conclusively presumed not to have resulted in the delivery of that information, unless—

(*a*) that means of electronic communications is for the time being approved for delivery of information of that kind; and

(*b*) the sender is approved for the use of that means of electronic communications in relation to information of that kind.

PART 4
REVOCATIONS

Revocation and saving

11—(1) There are revoked—

(*a*) the Income Tax (Electronic Communications) Regulations 2000; and

(*b*) Part 2 of the Income Tax (Electronic Communications) (Miscellaneous Amendments) Regulations 2001 and, in regulation 1(2) of those Regulations, the definition of ''the Electronic Communications Regulations''.

(2) Notwithstanding the revocations in paragraph (1), any direction given by the Board under the provisions revoked, to the extent that it could be given under these Regulations, shall continue to have effect as if given under these Regulations.

Commentary—*Simon's Direct Tax Service* **A3.165.**

2003/1830
Income Tax (Authorised Unit Trusts) (Interest Distributions) Regulations 2003

Made by the Commissioners of Inland Revenue under TA 1988 s 468PB

Made	*16 July 2003*
Laid before the House of Commons	*17 July 2003*
Coming into force	*7 August 2003*

Citation, commencement and effect

1—(1) These Regulations may be cited as the Income Tax (Authorised Unit Trusts) (Interest Distributions) Regulations 2003 and shall come into force on 7th August 2003.

(2) These Regulations have effect in relation to interest distributions made on or after 16th October 2002.

Interpretation

2 In these Regulations—

''authorised unit trust'' and ''unit holder'' have the meanings given by section 468(6) of the Taxes Act;

''the Board'' means the Commissioners of Inland Revenue; ''interest distribution'' has the meaning given by section 468L(3) of the Taxes Act; ''the Taxes Act'' means the Income and Corporation Taxes Act 1988 and references to a section number without more are references to a section of that Act; ''the Tax Acts'' has the meaning given by section 831(2) of the Taxes Act; ''unit trust scheme'' has the meaning given by section 469(7) of the Taxes Act.

Modification—See the Open-ended Investment Companies (Tax) Regulations, SI 1997/1154 reg 28(1)–(3) (modification of this regulation in its application to open-ended investment companies).

Modification of sections 468M(1)(a), 468O and 468P in relation to interest distributions made to or received under a trust

3 Except in a case to which regulation 7 applies, section 468M(1)(*a*), section 468O and section 468P shall apply in relation to an interest distribution made to or received under a trust (other than a unit trust scheme) with the modifications specified in regulations 4, 5 and 6.

4 In section 468M(1)(*a*) after the word ''company'' insert the words ''except where the company is the trustee of the trust to which or under which the interest distribution is made or received,''.

5 In section 468O for subsection (1) substitute the following subsection—

''(1) For the purposes of section 468M, the residence condition is fulfilled with respect to a unit holder in the case of an interest distribution made to or received under a trust if there is a valid declaration made by the trustees of that trust that—

(*a*) the trustees are not resident in the United Kingdom, and

(*b*) each beneficiary of the trust is either not ordinarily resident or, in the case of a beneficiary which is a company, not resident in the United Kingdom.

(1ZA) In subsection (1) and in section 468P, references to a beneficiary are references to any person who is known to the trustees of the trust to be either—

(*a*) a person who is, or will or may become, entitled to any income of the trust, whether in the form of income or not, or

(*b*) a person to whom any such income may be paid, or for whose benefit any such income may be applied, whether in the form of income or not, in the exercise of a discretion by them.''.

Modification—See the Open-ended Investment Companies (Tax) Regulations, SI 1997/1154 reg 28(1), (2), (4) (modification of this regulation in its application to open-ended investment companies).

6 In section 468P—

(*a*) in subsection (1)(*c*) for the words "subsections (2) or (3)" substitute the words "subsection (2)";

(*b*) for subsection (2) substitute the following subsection—

"(2) A declaration made as mentioned in section 468O(1) must contain—

(*a*) the names and principal residential addresses of the trustees of the trust or, in the case of a trustee which is a company, the name of the company and the address of its registered or principal office;

(*b*) the names and principal residential addresses of the beneficiaries of the trust or, in the case of a beneficiary which is a company, the name of the company and the address of its registered or principal office; and

(*c*) an undertaking that the trustees of the trust will notify the trustees of the authorised unit trust in question if—

(i) they become resident in the United Kingdom,

(ii) any beneficiary of the trust named in the declaration becomes ordinarily resident or, in the case of a company, resident in the United Kingdom, or

(iii) any person who becomes a beneficiary of the trust after the making of the declaration either is at the time of becoming a beneficiary, or subsequently becomes, ordinarily resident or, in the case of a company, resident in the United Kingdom.";

(*c*) omit subsection (3);

(*d*) in subsection (5)(*a*) for the words "the person in question" substitute the words "the trustees of the trust have become resident in the United Kingdom, or any beneficiary of the trust";

(*e*) in subsection (5)(*b*) for the words "the person in question" substitute the words "the trustees of the trust are or may be resident in the United Kingdom, or any beneficiary of the trust".

Modification—See the Open-ended Investment Companies (Tax) Regulations, SI 1997/1154 reg 28(1), (2), (5) (modification of this regulation in its application to open-ended investment companies).

Modification of section 468O in cases where an interest distribution made to or received under a trust is income of a person other than the trustees

7—(1) This regulation applies in any case where the whole of an interest distribution made to or received under a trust (other than a unit trust scheme) is, or falls to be treated as, or under any provision of the Tax Acts is deemed to be, the income of a person other than the trustees of that trust.

(2) Where this regulation applies, sections 468M, 468O and 468PA shall apply as if references to a unit holder in those sections were references to the person referred to in paragraph (1).

Modification—See the Open-ended Investment Companies (Tax) Regulations, SI 1997/1154 reg 28(1), (2), (6) (modification of this regulation in its application to open-ended investment companies).

Information to be provided to the Board—interest distributions made without deduction of tax

8 The Board may by notice require the trustees of an authorised unit trust, within such time (not being less than 14 days) as may be provided by the notice, to supply them with such information (including copies of any relevant books, documents or other records) as they may reasonably require for the purpose of determining whether, having regard to section 468M, section 468O and section 468P, interest distributions were properly made by that authorised unit trust without deduction of tax.

Modification—See the Open-ended Investment Companies (Tax) Regulations, SI 1997/1154 reg 28(1), (2), (7) (modification of this regulation in its application to open-ended investment companies).

Inspection of records

9 The trustees of an authorised unit trust shall, whenever required to do so, make available for inspection by an officer of the Board authorised for that purpose, at such time as that officer may reasonably require, all such copies of books, documents or other records in their possession or under their control as may be required by the Board under regulation 8.

Modification—See the Open-ended Investment Companies (Tax) Regulations, SI 1997/1154 reg 28(1), (2), (8) (modification of this regulation in its application to open-ended investment companies).

Use of information

10—(1) Subject to paragraph (3), information obtained by the Board under regulation 8 or 9 shall not be used for the purpose of ascertaining the tax liability (if any) of any person other than the persons specified in paragraph (2) and shall otherwise be used only for the purposes of these Regulations.

(2) The persons specified in this paragraph are—

(*a*) the trustees of the authorised unit trust in question;

(*b*) a unit holder beneficially entitled to an interest distribution made without deduction of tax to whom the information obtained relates;

(*c*) where an interest distribution is made to or received under a trust without deduction of tax and sub-paragraph (*d*) does not apply, the trustees of that trust and any beneficiary of the trust to whom the information obtained relates; and

(*d*) where the whole of an interest distribution made to or received under a trust without deduction of tax is, or falls to be treated as, or under any provision of the Tax Acts is deemed to be, the income of a person other than the trustees of that trust, that person in so far as the information obtained relates to him.

(3) Paragraph (1) shall not be construed as preventing any disclosure of information within section 182(5) of the Finance Act 1989.

(4) In paragraph (2)(*c*), "any beneficiary of the trust" means—

(*a*) any person who is, or will or may become, entitled to any income of the trust, whether in the form of income or not, and

(*b*) any person to whom any such income may be paid, or for whose benefit any such income may be applied, whether in the form of income or not, in the exercise of a discretion by the trustees of the trust.

Modification—See the Open-ended Investment Companies (Tax) Regulations, SI 1997/1154 reg 28(1), (2), (9) (modification of this regulation in its application to open-ended investment companies).

Revocation

11 The Income Tax (Authorised Unit Trusts) (Interest Distributions) Regulations 1994 are revoked.

2003/2076
Capital Allowances (Environmentally Beneficial Plant and Machinery) Order 2003

Made by the Treasury under CAA 2001 ss 45H(3), (4), 45J(3)(*b*)

Made	*11 August 2003*
Laid before the House of Commons	*11 August 2003*
Coming into force	*1 September 2003*

Citation and commencement

1 This Order may be cited as the Capital Allowances (Environmentally Beneficial Plant and Machinery) Order 2003 and shall come into force on 1st September 2003.

Interpretation

2 In this Order—

"the Capital Allowances Act" means the Capital Allowances Act 2001;

"the Water Technology Criteria List" means the list dated 8th July 2003 and published by the Department for Environment, Food and Rural Affairs on 30th July 2003;

"the Water Technology Product List" means the list dated 8th July 2003 and published by the Department for Environment, Food and Rural Affairs on 30th July 2003.

Description of environmentally beneficial plant and machinery

3—(1) Plant or machinery is environmentally beneficial plant or machinery for the purposes of section 45H of the Capital Allowances Act (expenditure on environmentally beneficial plant or machinery) if—

(*a*) it falls within a technology class specified in the Water Technology Criteria List,

(*b*) it meets the environmental criteria set out in that List, and

(*c*) in the case of plant or machinery falling within any of the technology classes specified in paragraph (2), it is of a type that—

(i) is specified in, and has not been removed from, the Water Technology Product List, or

(ii) has been accepted for inclusion in the Water Technology Product List.

(2) The technology classes specified for the purposes of paragraph (1)(*c*) are—

(*a*) flow controllers,

(*b*) leakage detection equipment,

(*c*) meters,

(*d*) taps, and

(*e*) toilets.

Environmentally beneficial components of plant or machinery

4 Where one or more components of certain plant or machinery (but not all of that plant or machinery)—

(*a*) meets the conditions set out in article 3(1)(*a*) to (*c*), and

(*b*) falls within any of the technology classes specified in article 3(2)(*a*) to (*c*), the amount specified in respect of each such component for the purposes of section 45J of the Capital Allowances Act is the amount specified in the Water Technology Product List in relation to that component.

2003/2082

Insurance Companies (Calculation of Profits: Policy Holders' Tax) Regulations 2003

Made by the Treasury under FA 1989 s 82A

Made	*11 August 2003*
Laid before the House of Commons	*11 August 2003*
Coming into force	*1 September 2003*

Citation, commencement and effect

1—(1) These Regulations may be cited as the Insurance Companies (Calculation of Profits: Policy Holders' Tax) Regulations 2003 and shall come into force on 1st September 2003.

(2) These Regulations have effect in relation to periods of account beginning on or after 1st January 2003 and ending on or after these Regulations come into force.

Calculation of Profits: Policy Holders' Tax

2 Tax expended on behalf of policy holders or annuitants is allowed as a deduction in calculating the profits for a period of account to the extent permitted by—

(*a*) subject to regulation 5, the basis of deduction specified in regulation 3; and
(*b*) regulation 5.

3 For the purpose of regulation 2 the basis of deduction is—

(*a*) the basis used in the company's latest company tax return to determine the amount of tax expended on behalf of policy holders or annuitants allowed as a deduction in calculating the profits for that accounting period; or
(*b*) where the company has no latest company tax return—

(i) where the company was the transferee of life assurance business under an insurance business transfer scheme, the basis used in the latest company tax return of the transferor company to determine the amount of tax expended on behalf of policy holders or annuitants allowed as a deduction in calculating the profits for that accounting period; or
(ii) in any other case, the basis the company would have used to determine the amount of tax expended on behalf of policy holders or annuitants allowed as a deduction in calculating the profits for an accounting period had it been required to deliver a company tax return for an accounting period beginning before 1st January 2003.

4 In regulation 3—

(*a*) "the latest company tax return" means the company tax return for the latest preceding accounting period of the company or the transferor company for which such a return has been delivered before the day on which these Regulations come into force;
(*b*) "an insurance business transfer scheme" means a scheme falling within section 105 of the Financial Services and Markets Act 2000, including an excluded scheme falling within Case 2, 3 or 4 of subsection (3) of that section.

5 A deduction for tax expended on behalf of policy holders or annuitants but not brought into account shall be allowed but only where such an amount has been included in any value deemed to be brought into account by virtue of section 83(2B) of the Finance Act 1989.

2003/2172

Finance Act 1995, Section 127(12) (Designated Transactions) Regulations 2003

Made by the Treasury under FA 1995 s 127(12)(*c*)

Made	*21 August 2003*
Laid before the House of Commons	*22 August 2003*
Coming into force	*12 September 2003*

Citation and commencement

1 These Regulations may be cited as the Finance Act 1995, Section 127(12) (Designated Transactions) Regulations 2003 and shall come into force on 12th September 2003.

Designated transaction

2—(1) In this regulation "section 127(12)" means section 127(12) of the Finance Act 1995 (meaning of "investment transaction" for the purposes of determining whether person capable of being the UK representative of a non-resident taxpayer).

(2) For the purposes of section 127(12) a transaction falling within paragraph (3) is designated.

(3) A transaction falls within this paragraph if it is a contract, not otherwise falling within section 127(12), whose terms—

(*a*) provide that—

(i) after setting off their obligations to each other under the contract, a cash payment is to be made by one party to the other in respect of the excess, if any, or

(ii) each party is liable to make to the other party one or more cash payments in respect of that party's obligations to the other under the contract, and

(*b*) do not provide for the delivery of any property other than currency.

This is subject to the following qualification.

(4) A transaction does not fall within paragraph (3) if it is—

(*a*) a contract which relates to land;

(*b*) a contract of insurance; or

(*c*) a contract effected in the course of capital redemption business within the meaning of section 458 of the Income and Corporation Taxes Act 1988.

2003/2173
Finance Act 2003, Schedule 26, Paragraph 3(3) (Designated Transactions) Regulations 2003

Made by the Treasury under FA 2003 Sch 26 para 3(3)(*c*)

Made	*21 August 2003*
Laid before the House of Commons	*22 August 2003*
Coming into force	*12 September 2003*

Citation and commencement

1 These Regulations may be cited as the Finance Act 2003, Schedule 26 Paragraph 3(3) (Designated Transactions) Regulations 2003 and shall come into force on 12th September 2003.

Designated transaction

2—(1) In these Regulations "paragraph 3(3)" means paragraph 3(3) of Schedule 26 to the Finance Act 2003 (meaning of "investment transaction" for the purposes of determining whether a person is an agent of independent status in respect of investment transactions).

(2) For the purposes of paragraph 3(3) a transaction falling within paragraph (3) is designated.

(3) A transaction falls within this paragraph if it is a contract, not otherwise falling within paragraph 3(3), whose terms—

(*a*) provide that—

(i) after setting off their obligations to each other under the contract, a cash payment is to be made by one party to the other in respect of the excess, if any, or

(ii) each party is liable to make to the other party one or more cash payments in respect of that party's obligations to the other under the contract, and

(*b*) do not provide for the delivery of any property other than currency.

This is subject to the following qualification.

(4) A transaction does not fall within paragraph (3) if it is—

(*a*) a contract which relates to land;

(*b*) a contract of insurance; or

(*c*) a contract effected in the course of capital redemption business within the meaning of section 458 of the Income and Corporation Taxes Act 1988.

2003/2339
Taxation of Benefits under Government Pilot Schemes (Return to Work Credit and Employment Retention and Advancement Schemes) Order 2003

Commentary—*Simon's Direct Tax Service* **E4.328.**

Made by the Treasury under FA 1996 s 151(1)(*a*), (2), (5) and (7)

Made	*10 September 2003*
Laid before the House of Commons	*10 September 2003*
Coming into force	*1 October 2003*

Citation and commencement

1 This Order may be cited as the Taxation of Benefits under Government Pilot Schemes (Return to Work Credit and Employment Retention and Advancement Schemes) Order 2003 and shall come into force on 1st October 2003.

Interpretation

2 In this Order—

"benefit" has the meaning given by subsection (6) of section 151 of the Finance Act 1996;

"Employment Retention and Advancement Scheme payment" means a payment of benefit under the Government pilot scheme known as the Employment Retention and Advancement Scheme;

"Government pilot scheme" has the meaning given by subsections (3) and (4) of section 151 of the Finance Act 1996; and

"Return to Work Credit payment" means a payment of benefit under the Government pilot scheme known as the Return to Work Credit Scheme.

Exemptions from income tax

3 The Income Tax Acts shall have effect in relation to any amount of an Employment Retention and Advancement Scheme payment, and any amount of a Return to Work Credit Scheme payment, as if that amount were wholly exempt from income tax and accordingly to be disregarded in computing the amount of any receipts brought into account for income tax purposes.

2003/2495

Income Tax (Incentive Payments for Voluntary Electronic Communication of PAYE Returns) Regulations 2003

Made by the Commissioners of Inland Revenue under FA 2000 s 143(1), Sch 38

Made . . . . *29 September 2003*
Laid before the House of Commons . . . . *29 September 2003*
Coming into force . . . . *20 October 2003*

Citation, commencement and interpretation

1—(1) These Regulations may be cited as the Income Tax (Incentive Payments for Voluntary Electronic Communication of PAYE Returns) Regulations 2003 and shall come into force on 20th October 2003.

(2) In these Regulations—

"approved" means approved by means of a general or specific direction of the Board;

"the Board" means the Commissioners of Inland Revenue;

"direction" means a direction given by the Board;

"incentive payment" has the meaning given in Schedule 38;

"the Management Act" means the Taxes Management Act 1970;

"the PAYE Regulations" means the Income Tax (Employments) Regulations 1993;

"Schedule 38" means Schedule 38 to the Finance Act 2000;

"the specified date" means, in relation to a year of assessment, such date in the immediately preceding year of assessment as is announced annually by means of a direction given by the Board not later than 30th November of that preceding year; and

references to the delivery of information have the same meaning as they have in section 132 of the Finance Act 1999.

(3) In these Regulations "a small employer" is a person treated as paying PAYE income to 49 or fewer recipients at the specified date.

A person is treated as paying PAYE income to a recipient at the specified date if at that date—

(*a*) he is required by the PAYE Regulations or by regulation 6(6) of the Working Tax Credit (Payment by Employers) Regulations 2002 to prepare or maintain a deductions working sheet in respect of the recipient; and

(*b*) he has not delivered, sent or transmitted to the inspector a statement required by regulation 23 of the PAYE Regulations for the recipient.

Construction of references to numbers of employees

2—(1) If an election has been made under regulation 3 of the PAYE Regulations (multiple employers) and—

(*a*) no notice under paragraph (6) of that regulation (elections for improper purposes) has been given, or

(*b*) any notice under that paragraph has been withdrawn,

paragraph (2) applies.

(2) Where this paragraph applies, a reference in these Regulations to a number of recipients shall be construed as a reference to the number of such employees treated as employed in a separate undertaking by virtue of regulation 3(1) of the PAYE Regulations.

Scope

3—(1) These Regulations apply to the persons specified in paragraph (2) who deliver, or cause to be delivered, the return and supporting information required under regulation 43 of the PAYE Regulations by an approved method of electronic communications if—

(*a*) the return and that information are delivered in respect of a year of assessment specified in paragraph (3); and

(*b*) the return satisfies the conditions mentioned in regulation 4(1)(*b*).

(2) The persons specified in this paragraph are those who—

(*a*) are small employers on the specified date; or

(*b*) not being small employers on that date, are treated as making payments of PAYE income for the first time after that date.

(3) The years of assessment specified in this paragraph are 2004–05 to 2008–09.

Incentive payment—return under regulation 43 of the PAYE Regulations

4—(1) The Board shall make an incentive payment in the amount prescribed in paragraph (3) to a person specified in regulation 3(2) for the year of assessment in question, if—

(*a*) he delivers, or causes to be delivered, a return under regulation 43 of the PAYE Regulations for that year of assessment by an approved method of electronic communications; and

(*b*) the return satisfies the conditions as to accuracy and completeness specified in any direction given by the Board.

This is subject to the following qualification.

(2) An incentive payment shall not be made in respect of a return which contains only information supplied in accordance with any of the provisions and arrangements mentioned in regulation 102(2) of the PAYE Regulations.

(3) The amounts prescribed are those shown in the Table 1 for the relevant year of assessment.

TABLE 1

AMOUNTS OF INCENTIVE PAYMENT

Year of assessment	*Amount of incentive payment*
2004–05	£250
2005–06	£250
2006–07	£150
2007–08	£100
2008–09	£75

(4) Where an officer of the Board considers that a person, who has claimed to be entitled to an incentive under these Regulations—

(*a*) does not satisfy one or more of the requirements of these Regulations or the directions made under them, or

(*b*) is not entitled to an incentive payment by virtue of paragraph (2),

the officer shall give notice to that person that the conditions are not met or, where the incentive payment has already been authorised or made, notice withdrawing the incentive payment.

(5) Where, prior to the giving of a notice under paragraph (4), an incentive payment has already been made to the person referred to in that paragraph, an office of the Board may recover the amount of the incentive payment in accordance with paragraph (6).

(6) For the purpose of paragraph (5), subsections (1), (4), (5) and (6) of section 30 and section 30A of the Management Act (recovery of overpayment of tax, etc and assessing procedure) shall apply as if the amount to be recovered were an amount of income tax repaid to a person which ought not to have been repaid to him.

Notice of non-entitlement to incentive payment

5 If, during the year of assessment 2003–04, an officer of the Board considers that a person—

(*a*) is not a small employer in respect of the year of assessment 2004–05; but

(*b*) is treated as paying PAYE income to less than 250 employees at the specified date in respect of that year;

the officer shall give notice to that person that he is not entitled to an incentive payment under these Regulations for the year of assessment 2004–05.

Appeals

6—(1) An appeal lies against a decision made by an officer of the Board under regulation 4(4) or 5 and may be brought—

(*a*) by notice to an officer of the Board; and
(*b*) within 30 days of the issue of the officer's notice under that regulation.

(2) An appeal may be brought against an officer's notice under regulation 4(4) on the grounds that the recipient of the notice—

(*a*) has satisfied all the requirements of these Regulations and the directions made under them so far as they apply to him; and
(*b*) is not precluded from receiving an incentive payment by virtue of regulation 4(2).

(3) The recipient of an officer's notice under regulation 5 may appeal against it on the grounds that he is entitled to an incentive payment for the year of assessment 2004–05.

(4) The following provisions of the Management Act apply to an appeal under these Regulations as they apply to an appeal under section 31 of that Act—

(*a*) section 31A(5) and (6) (notice of appeal);
(*b*) section 31B (appeals to General Commissioners); and
(*c*) section 31D (election to bring appeal before Special Commissioners).

(5) Paragraphs 3 and 8 of Schedule 3 to the Management Act (rules for assigning proceedings to General Commissioners) shall apply for the purposes of an appeal under these Regulations as they apply to an appeal under the PAYE Regulations.

(6) In relation to an appeal under these Regulations the "relevant place" for the purposes of paragraph 3 of Schedule 3 to the Management Act (as applied by paragraph (5) of this regulation) is—

(*a*) the appellant's place of business in the United Kingdom; or
(*b*) where the appellant has no place of business in the United Kingdom, the appellant's place of residence in the United Kingdom.

(7) For the purposes of paragraph (6) "place of business" and "place of residence" have the same meanings as they have for the purposes of paragraph 2(2) of Schedule 3 to the Management Act.

INCOME TAX (PAYE) REGULATIONS 2003
TABLE OF DESTINATIONS

This Table shows how the instruments revoked are dealt with by the Income Tax (Pay As You Earn) Regulations 2003.

The following abbreviations are used in the Table—

Statutory Instruments

SI 1993/744	The Income Tax (Employments) Regulations 1993
SI 1993/2276	The Income Tax (Employments) (Amendment) Regulations 1993
SI 1994/775	The Income Tax (Employments) (Amendment) Regulations 1994
SI 1994/1212	The Income Tax (Employments) (Notional Payments) Regulations 1994
SI 1994/1813	The General and Special Commissioners (Amendment of Enactments) Regulations 1994
SI 1995/216	The Income Tax (Employments) (Amendment) Regulations 1995
SI 1995/447	The Income Tax (Employments) (Amendment No 2) Regulations 1995
SI 1995/853	The Income Tax (Employments) (Incapacity Benefit) Regulations 1995
SI 1995/1223	The Income Tax (Employments) (Amendment No 3) Regulations 1995
SI 1995/1284	The Income Tax (Employments) (Amendment No 4) Regulations
SI 1996/804	The Income Tax (Employments) (Amendment) Regulations 1996
SI 1996/980	The Income Tax (Employments) (Amendment No 2) Regulations 1996
SI 1996/1312	The Income Tax (Employments) (Amendment No 3) Regulations 1996
SI 1996/2381	The Income Tax (Employments) (Amendment No 4) Regulations 1996
SI 1996/2554	The Income Tax (Employments) (Amendment No 5) Regulations 1996
SI 1996/2631	The Income Tax (Employments) (Amendment No 6) Regulations 1996
SI 1997/214	The Income Tax (Employments) (Amendment) Regulations 1997
SI 1998/640	The Profit-Related Pay (shortfall Recovery) Regulations 1998
SI 1998/1891	The Income Tax (Employments) (Notional Payments) (Amendment) Regulations 1998
SI 1998/2484	The Income Tax (Employments) (Amendment) Regulations 1998
SI 1999/70	The Income Tax (Employments) (Amendment) Regulations 1999
SI 1999/824	The Income Tax (Employments) (Amendment No 2) Regulations 1999
SI 1999/2155	The Income Tax (Employments) (Amendment No 3) Regulations 1999
SI 2000/1152	The Income Tax (Employments) (Amendment) Regulations 2000
SI 2000/2742	The Income Tax (Sub-contractors in the Construction Industry and Employments) (Amendment) Regulations 2000
SI 2001/1081	The Income Tax (Electronic Communications) (Miscellaneous Amendments) Regulations 2001

SI 2002/680	The Income Tax (Employments and Electronic Communications) (Miscellaneous Provisions) Regulations 2002
SI 2002/1397	The Secretaries of State for Education and Skills and for Work and Pensions Order 2002
SI 2003/536	The Income Tax (Sub-contractors in the Construction Industry and Employments) (Amendment) Regulations 2003
SI 2003/2494	The Income Tax (Employments) (Amendment) Regulations 2003

Other Abbreviations

Change 1 etc	Changes as listed in the Explanatory Notes
para	paragraph
r	regulation
Sch	Schedule

THE INCOME TAX (EMPLOYMENTS) REGULATIONS 1993 (SI 1993/744)

Existing provision		*Rewritten provision*	*Remarks*
1	Citation and commencement		Commencement.
2	Interpretation		
	(1)		
	"additional pay"	2(1) ("additional pay")	
	"allowable Superannuation contributions"	3(2) ("allowable pension contributions")	
	"basic rate"	2(1) ("basic rate")	
	"the Board"	2(1) ("Board of Inland Revenue")	
	"code"	2(1) ("code"), 7(1)	
	"code authorisation"	2(1) ("employee's code"), 8(1)	
	"collector"	2(1) ("Inland Revenue"); Schedule 1 para 28 ("collector")	
	"cumulative additional pay"	2(1) ("total additional pay to date")	
	"cumulative emoluments"	2(1) ("total payments to date")	
	"cumulative free emoluments"	2(1) ("total free pay to date")	
	"cumulative tax"	2(1) ("total tax to date")	
	"cumulative taxable emoluments"	2(1) ("total taxable payments to date")	
	"deductions working sheet"	2(1) ("deductions working sheet")	
	"earnings-related contributions"	69(3) ("earnings-related contributions")	
	"electronic communications"	2(1), 189 ("electronic communications"), 2(1), 189	Inserted SI 2001/1081 r 8(2); amended SI 2002/680 r 4(*a*).
	"approved"	("approved method of electronic communications")	See Change 10.
	"emoluments"	2(1) ("net PAYE income"), 3(1), (2)	Revoked in part SI 1993/2276 r 3(*a*).
	"employed earner", "employed earner's employment"	70(4)	Part unnecessary
	"employee"	2(1) ("agency worker", "employment", "other payee", "payee", "pensioner"), 10(1), (4), 11, 12(1), (2), (4)	See Change 7.

Existing provision		*Rewritten provision*	*Remarks*
	“employer”	2(1) (“agency”, “employment”, “other payer”, “payer”, “pension payer”), 10(1), (4), 11, 12(1), (2)	See Change 7.
	“free emoluments”	2(1) (“free pay”)	
	“higher rate”	2(1) (“higher rate”)	
	“income tax month”	2(1) (“tax month”)	
	“income tax period”	2(1) (“tax period”)	
	“income tax quarter”	2(1) (“tax quarter”)	
	“inspector”	2(1) (“Inland Revenue”); Schedule 1 para 20 (“inspector”)	
	“lower rate”	—	Unnecessary
	“the Management Act”	2(1) (“TMA”)	
	“notice”	2(1) (“notice”)	
	“official computer system”	2(1)) “official computer system”), 189 (“official computer system”)	Inserted SI 2001/1081 r 8(2).
	“overriding limit”	2(1) (“overriding limit”)	
	“pension emoluments”	2(1) (“PAYE pension income”), 6	
	“previous cumulative tax”	23(8) (“previous total tax to date”)	
	“reliefs from income tax”	2(1) (“reliefs from income tax”)	
	“starting rate”	2(1) (“starting rate”)	Inserted SI 1999/2155 r 8.
	“tax not deducted”	2(1) (“tax not deducted because of the overriding limit”)	
	“tax tables”	2(1) (“tax tables”)	
	“simplified tax tables”	34(3) (“simplified tax tables”)	
	“taxable emoluments”	2(1) (“taxable payments”)	
	“the Taxes Act”	2(1) (ICTA)	
	“total net tax deducted”	2(1) (“total net tax deducted”)	
	“trade dispute”	2(1) (“trade dispute”)	
	“year”, “current year”	2(1) (“tax year”)	
	(2)	—	Unnecessary.
	(3)	4(1), (2)	Inserted SI 1993/2276 r 3(*b*).
	(4)	189	Part unnecessary: substituted SI 2001/1081 r 8(3).
	(4A)	—	Revoked SI 2002/680 r 4(*b*).
	(5)	—	Revoked SI 2002/680 r 4(*b*).
	(5A)	—	Revoked SI 2002/680 r 4(*b*).
	(6)	—	Revoked SI 2002/680 r 4(*b*).
2A	Whether information transmitted electronically or delivered by means of electronic communications		
		192	Inserted SI 2002/680 r 5.
2B	Proof of content of an electronic transmission and of information delivered electronically		
			Inserted SI 2002/680 r 5.
	(1)	193(1)	
	(2)	193(1)	
	(3)	193(2)	
2C	Proof of identity of sender or recipient of information		
			Inserted SI 2002/680 r 5.
	(1)	194	
	(2)	194	
2D	Proof of delivery of information and payments		
			Inserted SI 2002/680 r 5.

Existing provision		*Rewritten provision*	*Remarks*
	(1)	196(1), 197(1)	Amended SI 2003/2494 r 3(2).
	(2)	196(2), 197(2)	Amended SI 2003/2494 r 3(2).
	(3)	196(3), 197(3)	Amended SI 2003/2494 r 3(2).
	(4)	196(1), (2), (3)	Inserted SI 2003/2494 r 3(3).
2E	Use of unauthorised means of electronic communications		Inserted SI 2002/680 r 5.
	(1)	198(1)	
	(2)	198(2)	
3	Multiple employers		Amended SI 2003/2494 r 4.
	(1)	98(1), (2), (11)	Amended SI 2003/2494 r 4(2).
	(2)	98(4)	
	(3)	98(5), (8)	
	(4)	98(6), (7)	
	(5)	98(9), (10)	
	(6)	99(1)	Inserted SI 2003/2494 r 4(3).
	(7)	99(2)	Inserted SI 2003/2494 r 4(3).
	(8)	99(3), (4), (5)	Inserted SI 2003/2494 r 4(3).
	(9)	99(6)	Inserted SI 2003/2494 r 4(3).
4	Intermediate employers	—	Revoked FA 1994 s.133(1)
5	Troncs		
	(1)	100(1), (7)	
	(2)	100(3)	Revoked in part SI 1994/775 r 3(*a*).
	(3)	100(4)	Amended SI 1994/775 r 3(*b*); SI 1996/1312 r 3(*a*).
	(4)	100(5)	Inserted SI 1994/775 r 3(*c*).
	(4A)	100(4)	Inserted SI 1996/1312 r 3(*b*). Part unnecessary.
	(5)	100(7)	Inserted SI 1994/775 r 3(*c*).
6	Deduction and repayment of tax under appropriate code		
	(1)	21(1), 62(2)	
	(2)	21(1)	
	(3)	21(2)	
	(4)	8(2), 213(2), Table 11, (4)	Inserted SI 1998/2484 r 4(2); amended SI 2001/1081 r 9; SI 2002/680 r 6.
7	Determination of appropriate code by inspector		
	(1)	13, 14(1)	
	(2)	14(1), (2)	Revoked in part SI 1996/1312 r 4; amended SI 1999/2155 r 3.
	(3)	14(2)	
8	Code applicable where code authorisation is not issued or received		
	(1)	16(1)	
	(2)	16(2)	
	(3)	—	Spent.
	(4)	—	Spent.
	(5)	20(7)	
9	Coding at the higher rate or where no tax is deductible		
	(1)	7(3), 15(1)	
	(2)	7(3), 15(3)	Amended SI 1996/1312 r 5.
	(3)	7(3)	See Change 4.
10	Notice of coding		
	(1)	17(1), (2)	
	(2)	17(2)	Amended SI 1999/2155 r 4, r 20.
11	Objections and appeals against coding		
	(1)	18(1)	
	(2)	18(2), (3)	
	(3)	18(5)	Amended SI 1996/1312 r 6.
	(4)	—	Unnecessary.
	(5)	18(4)	
	(6)	—	Unnecessary; Amended SI 1994/1813 r 2 (1), Sch. 1 para 37.
	(7)	—	Unnecessary.

Existing provision		Rewritten provision	Remarks
12	Amendments of coding		
	(1)	19(1), (2)	
	(2)	19(3)	
	(3)	19(4)	Amended SI 1999/2155 r 4, r 21.
	(4)	19(5)	
13	Notice to employer of amended coding		
	(1)	20(1), (2)	Amended SI 2002/680 r 7(*a*).
	(2)	20(3)	
	(3)	—	Spent.
	(4)	20(4), (5), (6)	Amended SI 1999/2155 r 5, r 22.
	(5)	20(7)	Spent in part.
	(6)	8(1), 20(8), 213(2), Table 11, (4), (5)	Inserted SI 2002/680 r 7(*b*).
14	Calculation and making of deduction or payment		
	(1)	22, 23(2), (3), 31(4)	Part unnecessary. See Change 20.
	(2)	23(2), (4), (5), 28(5), 29(2), 29(5), 34(2)	Amended SI 1994/1212 r 9.
	(3)	23(6)	
	(4)	23(7)	
15	First payment in the year		
		23(2), (4), (5)	Amended SI 1994/1212 r 9.
16	Deductions in accordance with regulation 9		
	(1)	32(1), 33	
	(2)	32(1), 33, 66(3)	
	(3)	33(2)	
17	Deduction in special cases		
	(1)	24(6), 26(1), 31(1), 25(5), 55(2), 56(5)	
	(2)	26(2), 27(1)	
	(3)	66(4), (7)	
	(4)	66(8)	
18	Emoluments not paid weekly or monthly		
		24(1)–(5), 30	
19	Subsidiary emoluments of employee paid monthly or at greater intervals		
	(1)	25(1), (3)	
	(2)	25(2), (4)	
20	Employee on fixed pay		
	(1)	34(1), (3)	
	(2)	34(1), 35(1), (2)	
	(3)	35(4), 211(4), Table 10	Amended SI 2002/680 r 8.
	(4)	35(4), 211(2), (4), Table 10	
21	Aggregation of emoluments in non-cumulative cases		
		29(1), (2), (4), (5), 34(2)	
22	Tax-free emoluments		
		—	Unnecessary. See Change 19.
23	Cessation of employment		
	(1)	2(1) (''Form P45''), 36(1), 211, (2), (4), Table 10, 215	Amended SI 1998/2484 r 5(2); SI 2001/1081 r 10.
	(2)	36(4), Table 2	Amended SI 1996/804 r 3(*a*).
	(3)	36(2), (4), Table 2	Amended SI 1996/804 r 3(*b*); SI 1998/2484 r 5(3).
	(4)	—	Amended SI 1996/804 r 3(*b*); SI 1998/2484 r 5(3). Unnecessary.
24	Emoluments paid after employment ceased		
	(1)	37(1)	Amended SI 1998/2484 r 6(2).
	(2)	37(2)–(6), 62(2)	
25	Commencement of subsequent employment		
	(1)	40(1), 42(1), (3)	Revoked in part SI 1996/804 r 4(*a*); amended SI 1998/2484 r 7(2).
	(2)	42(7), (8), 52(2), (3), 211(2), (4), Table 10	Amended SI 1998/2484 r 7(2), (3); SI 2001/1081 r 11.
	(3)	42(2), 43(1), (3), 52(4), (5)	Amended SI 1998/2484 r 7(2).

Existing provision		*Rewritten provision*	*Remarks*
	(4)	43(4), (5), (6), (7), 52(6), (7), (8), (9)	Amended SI 1998/2484 r 7(2).
	(5)	43(5), 52(10)	Amended SI 1996/804 r 4(*b*).
	(6)	—	Revoked SI 1996/804 r 4(*c*).
	(7)	43(11), 52(13)	Amended SI 1998/2484 r 7(2).
	(8)	42(4), (5), 44(1), 45(1), (2)	Amended SI 1998/2484 r 7(2).
	(9)	43(7), 44(2)	Amended SI 1998/2484 r 7(2).
	(10)	—	Amended SI 1998/2484 r 7(2). Spent.
	(11)	40(4), (5)	Amended SI 1998/2484 r 7(2).
26	Pension emoluments		
	(1)	36(3), 55(1), (2), (3)	Amended SI 1998/2484 r 8(2); SI 2001/1081 r 12(2).
	(1A)	55(3), 211, (2), (4), Table 10	Inserted SI 2001/1081 r 12(3).
	(2)	55(4)	Amended SI 1996/804 r 5(*b*).
	(3)	56(1), (2)	Amended SI 1996/804 r 5(*c*); SI 1998/2484 r 8(3); SI 2001/1081 r 12(4).
	(4)	56(3), 211(2), (4), Table 10	Inserted SI 2001/1081 r 12(5).
27	Death of employee		
	(1)	38(1), (2), 39(1), (2), 180(1), (2), 211(2), (4), Table 10	Amended SI 1998/2484 r 9(2); SI 2001/1081 r 13.
	(2)	38(3), 39(3), (4), (5), 180(3), (4), (5)	Amended SI 1998/2484 r 9(3).
28	Employee for whom appropriate code not known		
	(1)	9(1)–(6), Table 1, (9), 46(1), 47(2), 48(2), 49(2), 58(1)	Amended SI 1998/2484 r 10(2); SI 2001/1081 r 14(2).
	(1A)	46(3), (4), 47(2), 48(2), 49(2), 58(3), (4), 211(2), (4), Table 10	Inserted SI 2001/1081 r 14(3).
	(1B)	46(3), (5), 58(4), (5) Inserted SI 2001/1081 r 14(3).	
	(2)	2(1) ("PAYE threshold"), 9(7), (8)	Amended SI 1999/2155 r 6.
	(3)	—	Amended SI 1998/2484 r 10(3). Unnecessary.
	(4)	46(1), (7), 58(1)	Amended SI 1998/2484 r 10(4).
	(5)	57(1), (2)	Amended SI 1998/2484 r 10(5); SI 2001/1081 r 14(4).
	(5A)	57(2), 211(2), (4), Table 10	Inserted SI 2001/1081 r 14(5).
	(5B)	57(3)	Inserted SI 2001/1081 r 14(5).
	(6)	—	Revoked SI 2001/1081 r 14(6).
29	Employee taking up employment after full-time education		
	(1)	46(2), 47(1), 211(2), Table 10	Substituted SI 1996/2554 r 3.
	(2)	7(3), 47(2)	Amended SI 1993/2276 r 5; SI 1999/2155 r 9.
	(3)	7(3), 47(3)	Amended SI 1993/2276 r 5; SI 1999/2155 r 9.
30	Employee taking up only or main employment		
	(1)	46(2), 48(1), 211(2), Table 10	Substituted SI 1996/2554 r 4.
	(2)	7(3), 48(2)	Amended SI 1993/2276 r 5; SI 1999/2155 r 10.
	(3)	7(3), 48(3)	Amended SI 1993/2276 r 5; SI 1999/2155 r 10.
	(4)	—	Amended SI 1996/804 r 6; SI 1998/2484 r 11(2). Unnecessary.
31	Other new employees		
	(1)	49(1), 58(2)	
	(2)	49(2)	
	(3)	58(2)	
	(4)	49(3), 58(2)	
32	Initial procedure when payments made to employee for whom appropriate code not known	7(3), 45(2), 50, 59	Amended SI 1993/2276 r 5; SI 1999/2155 r 11.
33	Subsequent procedure on issue of code authorisation	53, 61	

Existing provision		*Rewritten provision*	*Remarks*
34	Subsequent procedure on presentation of copies of certificate		Amended SI 1998/2484 r 12(2).
	(1)	51(1), (2), (3), 60(1)	Revoked in part SI 1996/804 r 7(*a*).
	(2)	42(1), (7), 51(5), 52(2), (3), (5), (6), (7), (9), (11), (12), 60(2), (3), (4), (5)	Revoked in part SI 1996/804 r 7(*b*).
	(3)	51(6), (7), 60(2), (3), (4), (5)	
	(4)	—	Spent. See Change 55.
35	Repayment during absence from work through sickness etc		
	(1)	63(1), (2)	
	(2)	63(1)	
	(3)	63(1)	
36	Trade disputes		
	(1)	64(1)	
	(2)	64(1), (2), (3)	
	(3)	64(5), (6), (11)	
	(4)	64(7)	
	(5)	64(8)	
	(6)	64(9), (10)	
	(7)	64(11)	Amended SI 2002/1397 art. 12, Schedule para 25(2).
37	Repayment after cessation of employment		
	(1)	65(1)	
	(2)	65(1), (2), (3), (4), (8)	Revoked in part SI 1996/804 r 8; amended SI 1998/2484 r 13(2).
	(3)	65(5), (6), (7)	
38	Deductions working sheets etc		
	(1)	66(1), (2)	
	(2)	66(3)	
	(3)	66(4)	
	(4)	66(5), (6)	
39	Certificate of tax deducted		
	(1)	67(1)	Amended SI 1995/1284 r 3.
	(2)	67(2), 211(2), Table 10	
	(3)	67(3)	
40	Payment of tax monthly by employer		
	(1)	68(2), (6), 69(1), Schedule 1 paras. 15, 18(2) Amended SI 2003/2494 r 5.	
	(2)	68(2), (4), (5), 71(2), (3), (5)	Amended SI 1993/2276 r 6.
41	Payment of tax quarterly by employer		
	(1)	68(2), (6), 69(1), 70(1), Schedule 1 paras. 15, 18(2)	Amended SI 2003/2494 r 6.
	(2)	68(2), (4), (5), 71(2), (3), (5)	Amended SI 1993/2276 r 7.
	(3)	70(1), (2), (3)	Substituted SI 2003/536 r 9.
42	Payment of tax by employer—further provisions		
	(1)	69(2), (3)	
	(2)	72(1), (2), (3), (5), (6)	Amended SI 1995/447 r 3(*a*).
	(3)	72(1), (2), (4), (5), (6)	Amended SI 1995/447 r 3(*b*).
	(4)	72(7), (8)	
	(5)	—	Revoked SI 1995/447 r 3(*c*).
	(6)	68(3), (4), 71(4)	
	(7)	64(8)	
	(7A)	219(1)	Inserted SI 1996/980 r 3.
	(8)	218(3)	
	(9)	218(6)	
42A	Mandatory electronic payment		Inserted SI 2003/2494 r 7.
	(1)	190(3); 199(1); 200(2)	
	(2)	190(1), (2); 191(1); 199(2); 200(1)	
	(3)	191(3)	
	(4)	200(3), (4), (5)	
	(5)	199(3)	

Existing provision		*Rewritten provision*	*Remarks*
42B	Default surcharge		Inserted SI 2003/2494 r 7.
	(1)	201(1), (2), (3)	
	(2)	201(2)	
	(3)	201(5)	
	(4)	201(3)	
	(5)	201(4)	
	(6)	202(1)	
	(7)	202(2), (3), (4)	
	(8)	202(5)	
	(9)	203(1), (2)	
	(10)	203(3), (4), Table 8, (5)	
	(11)	204(1), (2), (3)	
	(12)	204(4), (5)	
	(13)	204(6)	
	(14)	204(7)	
	(15)	204(8)	
	(16)	203(6)	
	(17)	203(7)	
43	Return by employer at end of year where deductions working sheets required		
	(1)	73(1), 211(2), (4), Table 10	Amended SI 1998/2484 r 14(2); SI 2001/1081 r 15(2).
	(1A)	73(2), (5)	Inserted SI 1998/2484 r 14(3).
	(1B)	73(3), (6)	Inserted SI 1998/2484 r 14(3).
	(1C)	211(2), (4), Table 10	Substituted SI 2001/1081 r 15(3).
	(2)	73(4), (5)	Amended SI 1998/2484 r 14(4).
	(3)	73(7)	Substituted SI 2001/1081 r 15(4).
	(3A)	73(7), (9)	Inserted SI 2001/1081 r 15(4).
	(3B)	73(9), 211(5)	Inserted SI 2001/1081 r 15(4).
	(4)	73(7), (8), 211(2), Table 10	
	(5)	73(7), (8)	
	(6)	73(6)	Amended SI 1998/2484 r 14(5).
	(7)	73(8)	
	(8)	76(1), (2)	
	(9)	84(3) Table 4	
	(10)	218(1)	
	(11)	218(6)	
	(12)	73(10)	
44	Return by employer where deductions working sheets not required		Substituted SI 2001/1081 r 16.
	(1)	74(1), (3), (4)	
	(2)	74(1), 211(4), Table 10	
45	Additional return in cases involving a trade dispute		
	(1)	75(1), (2), (3)	
	(2)	75(1)	
	(3)	75(2)	
	(4)	75(3)	
46	Return of other additional emoluments		Substituted SI 1995/1284 r 4.
	(1)	85(1), 86(1), (2), (3), 87(1), (2), (3), 211(4), Table 10	Amended SI 1998/2484 r 15(2); SI 2001/1081 r 17(2); SI 2003/2494 r 4.
	(1A)	211(2), (4), Table 10	Substituted SI 2001/1081 r 17(3).
	(2)	86(1)	
	(3)	87(1)	
	(4)	86(3), 87(3)	
	(5)	86(1), 87(1)	
	(6)	88(1), (2)	
	(7)	86(2), 87(2), 89	Amended SI 1998/2484 r 15(4).
	(7A)	85(2), 211(2), (4), Table 10	Inserted SI 1998/2484 r 15(5).
	(7B)	85(2), 211(4), Table 10	Inserted SI 2001/1081 r 17(4).
	(8)	86(4), 87(4)	

Existing provision		*Rewritten provision*	*Remarks*
46AA	Other additional emoluments—information to be provided to employee by employer		
			Inserted SI 1995/1284 r 4.
	(1)	94(1), (2)	Amended SI 1998/2484 r 16(2); SI 2001/1081 r 18(2).
	(2)	94(3)	
	(3)	94(4), (5), Schedule 1 para 16(1), (2), (3), (4), (7), 17(1)	Amended SI 1996/1312 r 7; SI 1998/2484 r 16(2); SI 2001/1081 r 18(3).
	(4)	94(2), Schedule 1 para 16(2), 17(2)	
	(5)	94(6), Schedule 1 para 16(5)	
	(6)	94(7), Schedule 1 para 16(1), (6), 17(3), (4)	Amended SI 1998/2484 r 16(3).
46AB	Other additional emoluments—information to be provided to employee by other persons		
			Inserted SI 1995/1284 r 4.
	(1)	95(1), (3)	Revoked in part SI 1998/2484 r 17(2).
	(2)	95(2)	
	(3)	95(2)	
	(4)	95(3)	Revoked in part SI 1998/2484 r 17(2).
46A	Return where a car is made available		
			Inserted SI 1994/775 r 4.
	(1)	90(1), (2), 211(2), (4), Table 10	Amended SI 2001/1081 r 19(2).
	(1A)	—	Revoked SI 2001/1081 r 19(3).
	(2)	90(1)	
	(3)	90(3)	
	(4)	90(3)	
	(5)	90(4)	
46ZA	Termination payments and other benefits—information to be provided		
			Inserted SI 1999/70 r 3.
	(1)	91(1), (2)	
	(2)	91(3)	
	(3)	91(4)	
	(4)	91(5)	
	(5)	92(1), (2)	
	(6)	92(3)	
	(7)	96(1), (2)	
	(8)	96(3)	
	(9)	92(4), (5)	
	(10)	91(8), 92(7), 96(4), 93(1), (2)	
	(11)	91(6), (7)	
	(12)	91(9)	
46ZB	Information delivered electronically on another's behalf		
		195	Inserted SI 2001/1081 r 20.
46ZC	Mandatory use of electronic communications		
			Inserted SI 2003/2494 r 8.
	(1)	205(1)	
	(2)	205(3)	
	(3)	205(2)	
	(4)	205(4)	
46ZD	Specified persons		
			Inserted SI 2003/2494 r 8.
	(1)	206(1)	
	(2)	206(1), (2)	
	(3)	206(2)	
	(4)	190(1), (2), (3); 191(1), (2), (3); 206(1), (3); 208(1)	
	(5)	208(2), (3), (4)	
46ZE	Specified information		
			Inserted SI 2003/2494 r 8.
	(1)	205(5); 207(1)	
	(2)	207(2)	
46ZF	Standards of accuracy and completeness		
			Inserted SI 2003/2494 r 8.
	(1)	209(1)	
	(2)	209(2)	

Existing provision		Rewritten provision	Remarks
46ZG	Penalties		Inserted SI 2003/2494 r 8.
	(1)	210(1), (2), Table 9	
	(2)	210(3)	
	(3)	210(4)	
	(4)	210(5)	
46ZH	Appeals		Inserted SI 2003/2494 r 8.
	(1)	217(1), (2)	
	(2)	210(6)	
	(3)	217(3)	
	(4)	217(4)	
47	Notice and certificate when tax not paid		
	(1)	77(1), (2), Schedule 1 para 18(3)	Amended SI 2003/2494 r 9.
	(2)	77(4), 211(2), Table 10	
	(3)	77(5)	
	(4)	77(3)	
	(5)	77(6)	
	(6)	84(3), Table 4	
	(7)	218(5)	
	(8)	218(6)	
48	Notice of specified amount and certificate when tax not paid		
	(1)	78(1), (2), Schedule 1 para 18(4)	Revoked in part SI 1995/447 r 4(*a*); amended SI 2003/2494 r 10.
	(2)	78(4)	
	(3)	78(5)	
	(4)	78(3)	
	(5)	78(6), (7)	
	(6)	78(4), (8), 84(3), Table 4, 218(1)	Amended SI 1995/447 r 4(*b*).
	(7)	78(9)	
	(7A)	219(1)	Inserted SI 1996/980 r 4(1)(*a*), (2).
	(8)	—	Revoked SI 1995/447 r 4(*c*).
	(9)	218(1)	
	(10)	218(6)	
	(11)	78(10), (11)	
	(12)	78(12), (13)	
49	Formal determination of tax payable by employer		
	(1)	80(1)	
	(2)	80(2)	
	(3)	80(3)	
	(4)	80(4)	
	(5)	81(1), (2), (3), (4), (5)	Amended SI 1995/447 r 5.
	(6)	81(6), (7)	
	(7)	80(5)	Amended SI 1999/2155 r 7.
	(8)	80(6)	Substituted SI 1996/1312 r 8(1).
	(9)	218(3)	
	(10)	218(6)	
50	Interest on unpaid tax which has formally been determined		
	(1)	Schedule 1 para 20(1), (2), (3)	
	(2)	Schedule 1 para 20(9)	
	(3)	Schedule 1 para 20(9)	
51	Interest on tax overdue—general		
	(1)	82(1), (2), (6), Schedule 1 para 19, 21(1), (2), (4)	Amended SI 2003/2494 r 11(2).
	(2)	82(4), Schedule 1 para 21(3)	
	(3)	2(1) (''reckonable date''), 82(8), Schedule 1 para 21(5)	Amended SI 2003/2494 r 11(3).
	(4)	218(3)	
	(5)	218(6)	
52	Interest on tax overdue—further provisions		
	(1)	82(5), (7), Schedule 1 para 20(5), (9)	
	(2)	82(3), Schedule 1 para 20(4)	
	(3)	84(3), Table 4, Schedule 1 para 20(6), (7)	

Existing provision		*Rewritten provision*	*Remarks*
	(4)	219(1), Schedule 1 para 20(8)	Inserted SI 1996/980 r 5.
53	Interest on tax overpaid by employer		
	(1)	Schedule 1 para 23(1), (2)	Amended SI 1996/1312 r 9.
	(2)	Schedule 1 para 23(3)	
	(3)	Schedule 1 para 23(4), (6)	
	(4)	Schedule 1 para 23(6)	
	(5)	Schedule 1 para 23(5)	Inserted SI 1996/980 r 4(1)(*b*), (2).
53A	Interest on tax overpaid by employer—1996–97 and subsequent years		Inserted SI 1996/1312 r 10.
	(1)	83(1), (2), Schedule 1 para 22	
	(2)	83(3), (4)	
54	Recovery of tax		
	(1)	84(1), (2), Schedule 1 para 20(6)	
	(2)	84(1), Schedule 1 para 20(6)	
	(3)	84(3)	
	(4)	84(4), (5)	Amended SI 1995/1223 r 2.
	(5)	84(6)	
	(6)	77(6), 218(1), Schedule 1 para 20(7)	
	(7)	218(6), Schedule 1 para 20(7)	
55	Inspection of employer's records		
	(1)	97(1)	
	(2)	97(1), (2)	Amended SI 1995/447 r 6; SI 1998/2484 r 19(2); SI 2001/1081 r 21.
	(3)	97(3)	
	(4)	97(4)	
	(5)	97(5)	
	(6)	97(6)	
	(7)	97(7)	
	(8)	79(2), 218(1)	
	(9)	84(3), Table 4	
	(10)	218(1)	
	(11)	218(6)	
	(12)	97(8)	
56	Interpretation of Chapter I	118(1), (2)	
57	Councillor's option to have tax deducted at basic rate		
	(1)	119(1)	
	(2)	119(1)	
	(3)	119(2)	
	(4)	119(3)	
	(5)	119(4), (5), (6)	
	(6)	120(1), (2)	
	(7)	120(3)	
58	Application of Part V of these Regulations	—	Unnecessary.
59	Interpretation of Chapter II		
	(1)	122(1)	Amended SI 1997/214 r 3.
	(2)	122(2)	Substituted SI 1997/214 r 4.
	(3)	122(2)	Inserted SI 1997/214 r 4.
60	Disapplication of Parts III and IV of these Regulations	123(1)	
61	Deduction of tax		
	(1)	124(1)	
	(2)	124(2)	
	(3)	—	Unnecessary.
	(4)	124(3)	
62	Determination by inspector		
	(1)	125(1), (2)	
	(2)	125(3)	
	(3)	125(4)	
63	Objections and appeals		
	(1)	126(1)	
	(2)	126(2), (4)	
	(3)	126 (5), (6)	

Existing provision		*Rewritten provision*	*Remarks*
	(4)	126(7)	
	(5)	127(4) Amended SI 1996/1312 r 11.	
	(6)	127(4)	
	(7)	127(1), (2)	
	(8)	—	Unnecessary
	(9)	127(3)	
64	Amended determinations		
	(1)	128(1), (2)	
	(2)	128(3)	
	(3)	128(4)	
65	Certificate of tax deducted		
	(1)	129(1); 211(2), Table 10	Amended SI 1993/2276 r 11.
	(2)	129(2)	
66	Repayment to reservist during the year		
	(1)	130(1)	
	(2)	130(2)	
	(3)	130(3)	
67	Ministry records		
	(1)	131(1)	
	(2)	131(2)	
68	End of year certificate		
	(1)	132(1), (2)	Amended SI 1996/1312 r 12.
	(2)	132(3); 211(2), Table 10	
	(3)	132(1)	
69	Application of Parts V and VIII of these Regulations		
		—	Unnecessary.
70	Other emoluments of reservist		
		133	
71	Interpretation of Chapter III		
		134	
72	Disapplication of Parts III and IV of these Regulations		
		135(1)	
73	Deduction of tax		
		136	
74	Certificate of tax deducted		
	(1)	137(1); 211(2), Table 10	
	(2)	137(2)	
75	Repayment to recipient during the year		
	(1)	138(1)	
	(2)	138(2)	
	(3)	138(3)	
76	Fund records		
	(1)	139(1)	
	(2)	139(2)	
77	Application of Parts V and VIII of these Regulations		
		—	Unnecessary.
78	Other emoluments of recipient		
		140	
79	Death of employer		
		101(1), (2), (3)	
80	Succession to a business, etc		
	(1)	102(1), (2), (9)	
	(2)	102(3), (4)	
	(3)	102(5), (6), (7)	
	(4)	104(1), (2), (3), (4), (5)	
	(5)	102(8)	
80ZA	Payment for assignment or release of a right to acquire shares		
		—	Inserted SI 1994/1212 r 12A. Spent.
80A	General provision		Inserted SI 1996/2631 r 4.
	(1)	105(1), (2)	
	(2)	105(3)	
	(3)	106(1), (2), (3), (5)	
	(4)	106(3)	
	(5)	107(7)	Amended SI 1998/2484 r 20(2).

Existing provision		Rewritten provision	Remarks
80B	Form of agreement		Inserted SI 1996/2631 r 4.
	(1)	111(1), (2)	
	(2)	111(2)	
80C	Commencement of agreement		Inserted SI 1996/2631 r 4.
	(1)	112(1)	
	(2)	112(2)	
80D	Variation of agreement		Inserted SI 1996/2631 r 4.
	(1)	113(1), (3)	
	(2)	113(2)	
	(3)	113(3)	
80E	Emoluments comprised in agreement and liability to tax—consequential provisions		Inserted SI 1996/2631 r 4.
	(1)	107(1), (2)	
	(2)	107(5), (6)	
	(3)	107(3)	
	(4)	107(4)	
80F	Calculation of tax payable under agreement		Inserted SI 1996/2631 r 4.
	(1)	108(1)	
	(2)	108(2)	Amended SI 1999/2155 r 12.
	(3)	108(3)	
	(4)	108(3)	
80G	Payment of tax		Inserted SI 1996/2631 r 4.
	(1)	109(1)	
	(2)	109(2)	
	(3)	109(3)	
	(4)	109(3)	
	(5)	109(4)	
	(6)	109(5), (6)	
80H	Formal determination of tax payable by the employer		Inserted SI 1996/2631 r 4.
	(1)	110(1)	
	(2)	110(2), (3)	
	(3)	110(4)	
	(4)	110(5)	
80J	Interest on unpaid tax		Inserted SI 1996/2631 r 4.
	(1)	115(1), (2)	
	(2)	115(1), (2)	
	(3)	218(3)	
	(4)	218(6)	
	(5)	115(4), (6)	
	(6)	219(1)	
	(7)	115(3)	
	(8)	115(5)	
80K	Interest on overpaid tax		Inserted SI 1996/2631 r 4.
	(1)	116(1), (2)	
	(2)	116(3), (4)	
	(3)	219(1)	
80L	Review of agreements		Inserted SI 1996/2631 r 4.
	(1), (2)	—	Unnecessary.
80M	Cancellation of agreement		Inserted SI 1996/2631 r 4.
	(1)	114(1), (2), (3)	
	(2)	114(1)	
	(3)	114(4)	
80N	Inspection and retention of records		Inserted SI 1996/2631 r 4.
	(1)	117(1)	
	(2)	117(1), (2)	
	(3)	117(3)	

SIs

Existing provision		*Rewritten provision*	*Remarks*
	(4)	117(4)	
	(5)	117(5)	
	(6)	117(6)	
	(7)	117(7)	
	(8)	117(8)	
81	Interpretation of Part VII		
		148 (''claim'', ''claimant'', ''jobseeker's allowance'', ''taxable jobseeker's allowance''), 173 (''claim'', ''claimant'', ''incapacity benefit'', ''taxable incapacity benefit'')	Amended SI 1995/853 r 4; SI 1996/2381 r 3.
82	Application of other Parts of these Regulations		
	(1)	150(1), 174(1)	Amended SI 1995/853 r 5(*a*)
	(2)	150(2), Table 5, 174(2), Table 7	Amended SI 1993/2276 r 12; SI 1995/853 r 5(*b*).
83	Interpretation of Chapter II		
	(1)	148 (''Department'')	Amended SI 1996/2381 r 4.
	(2)	—	Revoked SI 1996/2381 r 4.
	(3)	150(3)	
84	Procedure on making claim		
	(1)	151(1)	Amended SI 1996/804 r 9(*a*); SI 1998/2484 r 21(2).
	(2)	151(1)	Amended SI 1996/804 r 9(*a*).
	(3)	152(1), (2), 153(1), (2), (3), (4), (9)	Amended SI 1998/2484 r 21(3).
	(4)	—	Revoked SI 1996/804 r 9(*b*).
	(5)	153(5), (6)	Amended SI 1998/2484 r 21(3).
	(6)	153(7)	Amended SI 1998/2484 r 21(3).
	(7)	7(3), 152(3), 153(8), 154(1)	Amended SI 1993/2276 r 5; SI 1996/804 r 9(*c*); SI 1998/1484 r 21(3); SI 1999/2155 r 13.
	(8)	151(2)	Amended SI 1996/804 r 9(*d*); SI 1998/2484 r 21(4).
	(9)	154(2)	Amended SI 1998/2484 r 21(5).
	(10)	154(3), 214(1), Table 12	
85	Determinations and notifications by the inspector		
	(1)	150(1)	
	(2)	155(1), (2)	
86	Quarterly attenders		
		—	Unnecessary.
87	Determination and recording of amount of taxable benefit		
		156	
88	End of year		
	(1)	157(1), (2)	Amended SI 1996/1312 r 12.
	(2)	157(3)	
	(3)	160(1)	
	(4)	157(4)	
	(5)	157(5)	Revoked in part SI 1996/804 r 10.
89	Termination of claim		
	(1)	158(1)	See Change 103.
	(2)	215 (''Form P45U''), 158(2), 159(1), (2), (3), (4)	Amended SI 1996/804 r 11.
	(3)	158(3), (4)	
	(4)	158(5)	
90	Notification of taxable benefit adjustment		
		160(1), (2)	
91	Tax calculation		
	(1)	161(1), (2), (5)	Amended SI 1996/804 r 12(*a*).
	(2)	161(4)	
	(3)	161(3)	Revoked in part SI 1996/804 r 12(*b*).
	(4)	158(2), 162(1)	

Existing provision		*Rewritten provision*	*Remarks*
	(5)	162(1), (2), (3)	Amended SI 1998/2484 r 22(2).
	(6)	161(5)	
92	Death of claimant		
	(1)	163(1), (2)	Amended SI 1996/804 r 13.
	(2)	163(3)	Amended SI 1993/2276 r 13.
93	Finance		
	(1)	164(1)	
	(2)	164(2)	
94	Interpretation of Chapter III		
		148 (''Department'')	Amended SI 2002/1397 art. 12, Schedule para 25(3).
95	Benefit paid by the paying Department direct to the claimant		
		166(1), (2)	
96	Benefit paid by employer		
	(1)	167(1)	
	(2)	167(2)	
	(3)	167(3)	
	(4)	168(1)	
	(5)	168(2), (3)	
97	Termination of claim		
	(1)	169	
	(2)	170(2), 171(1)	
98	Adjustments		
		172(1), (2)	
98A	Interpretation of Chapter IV		
		173 (''Department'')	Inserted SI 1995/853 r 6.
98B	Application of other parts of these Regulations		
		174(1), 174(2), Table 7, 174(4), 180(1), (3), (4), (5)	Inserted SI 1995/853 r 6.
98C	Deduction where appropriate code not yet determined		
			Inserted SI 1995/853 r 6.
	(1)	175(1), (2); 7(3) (''emergency IB codes'')	
	(2)	173, 175(1), (''single-income claimant'')	
	(3)	7(3) (''emergency IB codes'')	Amended SI 1999/2155 r 14.
	(4)	7(3) (''emergency IB codes'')	Revoked in part SI 1999/2155 r 18; amended SI 1999/2155 r 23.
98D	Return of payment of incapacity benefit		
			Inserted SI 1995/853 r 6.
	(1)	176(1)	
	(2)	176(2)	
	(3)	177(1), (2), (3)	
98E	Delivery of certificate relating to cessation of employment		
			Inserted SI 1995/853 r 6.
	(1)	178(1), (2)	Amended SI 1996/804 r 14; SI 1998/2484 r 23(2).
	(2)	178(1)	Amended SI 1998/2484 r 23(2).
98F	Determination of appropriate code by inspector		
			Inserted SI 1995/853 r 6.
	(1)	179(1)	
	(2)	179(3), (4)	
	(3)	179(5)	Amended SI 1999/2155 r 19(*a*), r 24; revoked in part SI 1999/2155 r 19(*b*).
	(4)	179(6)	
	(5)	174(1)	
98G	Coding where no tax is deductible		
			Inserted SI 1995/853 r 6.
	(1)	174(1), (3)	
	(2)	174(1)	
98H	Subsequent procedure on issue of code authorisation		
		174(1)	Inserted SI 1995/853 r 6.
99	Assessment		
		—	Substituted SI 1996/1312 r 13. Unnecessary.

Existing provision		*Rewritten provision*	*Remarks*
100	Appeals		
		—	Revoked in part SI 1996/1312 r 19(1).
101	Repayment of overpayments and recovery of underpayments		
			See Schedule 1 para 24(1), (2) for tax years up to 1995-96.
	(1)	—	
	(2)	188(2), (6)	
	(3)	188(3), Schedule 1 para 25	Amended SI 1995/447 r 7(*a*).
	(4)	185(4), (5), 188(3), Schedule 1 para 25	Revoked in part SI 1995/447 r 7(*b*); SI 1996/1312 r 14(*a*)
	(5)	185(5)	
	(6)	185(5), 188(4), (5)	Inserted SI 1995/447 r 7(*c*).
	(7)	188(1), (7)	Substituted SI 1996/1312 r 14(*b*).
101A	Recovery of overpayments and recovery of underpayments—self-assessments		
			Inserted SI 1996/1312 r 15.
	(1)	185(1), (2)	
	(2)	185(3), (4), (5)	
	(3)	186(1)	
	(4)	185(3)	
102	Provisions for direct collection—general		
	(1)	141(1)	
	(2)	141(1)	Revoked in part SI 1996/1312 r 16(1).
	(3)	141(1)	
103	Direct collection involving assessment		
		—	Revoked in part SI 1996/1312 r 19(2). Spent.
104	Direct collection involving deductions working sheets		
	(1)	8(1), 142(1)	
	(2)	143(1), (2), 144(4)	
	(3)	144(2)	
	(4)	144(2)	
	(5)	147(1)	
	(6)	147(2), (3), 214(1), (2), Table 12	
	(7)	—	Amended SI 1996/1312 r 17(1)(*a*). Unnecessary.
	(8)	—	Revoked SI 1996/1312 r 17(1)(*b*).
	(9)	145(1), 214(1), (2), Table 12	
	(10)	145(2)	
	(11)	146(1), (3), 214(1), (2), Table 12	Amended SI 1996/1312 r 17(1)(*c*).
	(12)	146(2)	
	(13)	146(4)	
	(14)	143(4)	
	(15)	143(5)	
	(16)	146(5)	
105	Recovery of tax from employee		
	(1)	—	Unnecessary.
	(2)	Schedule 1 para 24(3).	Revoked in part SI 1996/1312 r 18(1).
106	Attribution of repayments		
		—	See Schedule 1 para 26.
107	Adjustment of overpayments and underpayments		
		—	See Schedule 1 para 26.
108	Definitions for the purposes of regulations 106 and 107		
		—	See Schedule 1 para 26.
109	Service by post		
		216	
110	Revocations		
		—	
111	General Savings		

THE INCOME TAX (EMPLOYMENTS) (AMENDMENT) REGULATIONS 1993 (SI 1993/2276)

Existing provision		Rewritten provision	Remarks
1	Citation and commencement	—	Commencement.
2	Interpretation	—	Unnecessary.
3	Amendment to r 2 SI 1993/744		
	(*a*)	—	Revokes in part SI 1993/744 r 2(1) (''emoluments'').
	(*b*)	—	Inserts SI 1993/744 r 2(3).
4	Amendment to r 29, r 30 SI 1993/744	—	Spent (superseded amendment of SI 1993/744 r 29(1), r 30(1)).
5	Amendment to r 29, r 30, r 32, r 84 SI 1993/744	—	Amends SI 1993/744 r 29(2), 29(3), 30(2), 30(3), 32, 84(7).
6	Amendment to r 40 SI 1993/744	—	Amends SI 1993/744 r 40(2).
7	Amendment to r 41 SI 1993/744	—	Amends SI 1993/744 r 41(2).
8–10	Amendment to r 46 SI 1993/744	—	Spent (superseded amendment of SI 1993/744 r 46).
11	Amendment to r 65 SI 1993/744	—	Amends SI 1993/744 r 65(1).
12	Amendment to r 82 SI 1993/744	—	Amends SI 1993/744 r 82(2).
13	Amendment to r 92 SI 1993/744	—	Amends SI 1993/744 r 92(2).
14	Revoked r 8 SI 1988/640	—	Unnecessary.

THE INCOME TAX (EMPLOYMENTS) (AMENDMENT) REGULATIONS 1994 (SI 1994/775)

Existing provision		Rewritten provision	Remarks
1	Citation and commencement	—	Commencement.
2	Interpretation	—	Unnecessary.
3	Amendment to r 5 SI 1993/744		
	(*a*)	—	Revokes in part SI 1993/744 r 5(2).
	(*b*)	—	Amends SI 1993/744 r 5(3).
	(*c*)	—	Inserts SI 1993/744 r 5(4), (5).
4	Inserted r 46A SI 1993/744	—	Inserts SI 1993/744 r 46A.

THE INCOME TAX (EMPLOYMENTS) (NOTIONAL PAYMENTS) REGULATIONS 1994 (SI 1994/1212)

Existing provision		Rewritten provision	Remarks
1	Citation, commencement and effect	—	Commencement.
2	Interpretation		
	(1)	—	Revoked in part 2003 Sch. 8 Part 2.
	''the Principal Regulations''	—	Unnecessary.
	(2)	—	Revoked 2003 Sch. 8 Part 2.

Existing provision	Rewritten provision	Remarks
3	Exclusion of property from section 203F	
	—	Revoked 2003 Sch. 8 Part 2.
4	Exclusion of credit-token from section 203H	
	—	Revoked 2003 Sch. 8 Part 2.
5	Exclusion of cash vouchers from section 203I	
	—	Revoked 2003 Sch. 8 Part 2.
6	Notional payments—non-cash vouchers—time of payment	
	—	Revoked 2003 Sch. 8 Part 2.
7	Notional payments—deduction of income tax	
	—	Revoked 2003 Sch. 8 Part 2.
8	Notional payments—accounting for income tax where inability to deduct	
	—	Revoked 2003 Sch. 8 Part 2.
8A	Certain notional payments made between 6th April 1998 and 31st July 1998—accounting for income tax	
	—	Revoked 2003 Sch. 8 Part 2.
9	Amendment to r 14, r 15 SI 1993/744	
	—	Amends SI 1993/744 r 14(2), r 15.
10-12	Amendment to r 46 SI 1993/744	
	—	Spent (superseded amendment of SI 1993/744 r 46).
12A	Inserted r 80ZA SI 1993/744	
	—	Inserted SI 1998/1891 r 8; inserts SI 1993/744 r 80ZA.
13	Application of SI1993/744 to income tax accounted for where inability to deduct	
(1)	2(1) (''notional payment''), 35(2), 37(6), 66(4), 185(5), 188(3)	
(2)	—	Unnecessary.
(3)	2(1) (''total net tax deducted'')	
(4)	—	Unnecessary.
(5)	68(4), 71(5), 82(1), (6)	
(6)	68(4), 71(5), 82(1), (6)	
(7)	72(2), 81(3), (4)	
(8)	97(2)	

THE INCOME TAX (EMPLOYMENTS) (AMENDMENT) REGULATIONS 1995 (SI 1995/216)

Existing provision	Rewritten provision	Remarks
1	Citation and commencement	
	—	Commencement.
2	Amendment to r 41 SI 1993/744	
	—	Spent (superseded amendment of SI 1993/744 r 41(3)).

THE INCOME TAX (EMPLOYMENTS) (AMENDMENT NO 2) REGULATIONS 1995 (SI 1995/447)

Existing provision	Rewritten provision	Remarks
1	Citation and commencement	
	—	Commencement.
2	Interpretation	
	—	Unnecessary.
3	Amendment to r 42 SI 1993/744	
(*a*)	—	Amends SI 1993/744 r 42(2).
(*b*)	—	Amends SI 1993/744 r 42(3).
(*c*)	—	Revokes SI 1993/744 r 42(5).
4	Amendment to r 48 SI 1993/744	
(*a*)	—	Revokes in part SI 1993/744 r 48(1).
(*b*)	—	Amends SI 1993/744 r 48(6).

Existing provision		Rewritten provision	Remarks
	(*c*)	—	Revokes SI 1993/744 r 48(8).
5	Amendment to r 49 SI 1993/744	—	Amends SI 1993/744 r 49(5).
6	Amendment to r 55 SI 1993/744	—	Amends SI 1993/744 r 55(2).
7	Amendment to r 101 SI 1993/744		
	(*a*)	—	Amends SI 1993/744 r 101(3).
	(*b*)	—	Revokes in part SI 1993/744 r 101(4).
	(*c*)	—	Inserts SI 1993/744 r 101(6). Spent in part (superseded amendment of SI 1993/744 r 101(7)).

THE INCOME TAX (EMPLOYMENTS) (INCAPACITY BENEFIT) REGULATIONS 1995 (SI 1995/853)

Existing provision		Rewritten provision	Remarks
1	Citation, commencement and effect	—	Commencement.
2	Interpretation	—	Unnecessary.
3	Amendments to SI 1993/744	—	Introductory.
4	Amendment to r 81 SI 1993/744	—	Amends SI 1993/744 r 81.
5	Amendment to r 82 SI 1993/744		
	(*a*)	—	Amends SI 1993/744 r 82(1).
	(*b*)	—	Amends SI 1993/744 r 82(2).
6	Inserted r 98A—r 98H SI 1993/744	—	Inserts SI 1993/744 rr 98A–98H.

THE INCOME TAX (EMPLOYMENTS) (AMENDMENT NO 3) REGULATIONS 1995 (SI 1995/1223)

Existing provision		Rewritten provision	Remarks
1	Citation and commencement	—	Commencement.
2	Amendment to r 54 SI 1993/744	—	Amends SI 1993/744 r 54(4).

THE INCOME TAX (EMPLOYMENTS) (AMENDMENT NO 4) REGULATIONS 1995 (SI 1995/1284)

Existing provision		Rewritten provision	Remarks
1	Citation and commencement	—	Commencement.
2	Interpretation	—	Unnecessary.
3	Amendment to r 39 SI 1993/744	—	Amends SI 1993/744 r 39(1).
4	Inserted r 46—46AB SI 1993/744	—	Substitutes SI 1993/744 r 46; inserts SI 1993/744 r 46AA, r 46AB.

THE INCOME TAX (EMPLOYMENTS) (AMENDMENT) REGULATIONS 1996 (SI 1996/804)

Existing provision		Rewritten provision	Remarks
1	Citation and commencement	—	Commencement.
2	Interpretation	—	Unnecessary.
3	Amendment to r 23 SI 1993/744	—	Amends SI 1993/744 r 23(2), (3), (4).
4	Amendment to r 25 SI 1993/744		
	(*a*)	—	Revokes in part SI 1993/744 r 25(1).
	(*b*)	—	Amends SI 1993/744 r 25(5).
	(*c*)	—	Revokes SI 1993/744 r 25(6).
5	Amendment to r 26 SI 1993/744		
	(*a*)	—	Spent (superseded amendment of SI 1993/744 r 26(1)).
	(*b*)	—	Amends SI 1993/744 r 26(2).
	(*c*)	—	Amends SI 1993/744 r 26(3).
6	Amendment to r 27, r 30 SI 1993/744	—	Amends SI 1993/744 r 30(4). Spent in part (superseded amendment of SI 1993/744 r 27(1)).
7	Amendment to r 34 SI 1993/744		
	(*a*)	—	Revokes in part SI 1993/744 r 34(1).
	(*b*)	—	Revokes in part SI 1993/744 r 34(2).
8	Amendment to r 37 SI 1993/744	—	Revokes in part SI 1993/744 r 37(2).
9	Amendment to r 84 SI 1993/744		
	(*a*)	—	Amends SI 1993/744 r 84(1), (2).
	(*b*)	—	Revokes SI 1993/744 r 84(4).
	(*c*)	—	Amends SI 1993/744 r 84(7).
	(*d*)	—	Amends SI 1993/744 r 84(8).
10	Amendment to r 88 SI 1993/744	—	Revokes in part SI 1993/744 r 88(5).
11	Amendment to r 89 SI 1993/744	—	Amends SI 1993/744 r 89(2).
12	Amendment to r 91 SI 1993/744		
	(*a*)	—	Amends SI 1993/744 r 91(1).
	(*b*)	—	Revokes in part SI 1993/744 r 91(3).
13	Amendment to r 92 SI 1993/744	—	Amends SI 1993/744 r 92(1).
14	Amendment to r 98E SI 1993/744	—	Amends SI 1993/744 r 98E(1).

THE INCOME TAX (EMPLOYMENTS) (AMENDMENT NO 2) REGULATIONS 1996 (SI 1996/980)

Existing provision		Rewritten provision	Remarks
1	Citation, commencement and effect	—	Commencement.
2	Amendments to SI 1993/744	—	Introductory.
3	Amendment to r 42 SI 1993/744	—	Inserts SI 1993/744 r 42(7A).

Existing provision		Rewritten provision	Remarks
4	Amendment to r 48, r 53 SI 1993/744		
	(1)		
	(a)	—	Inserts SI 1993/744 r 48(7A).
	(b)	—	Inserts SI 1993/744 r 53(5).
	(2)	—	Inserts SI 1993/744 r 48(7A), r 53(5).
5	Amendment to r 52 SI 1993/744	—	Inserts SI 1993/744 r 52(4).

THE INCOME TAX (EMPLOYMENTS) (AMENDMENT NO 3) REGULATIONS 1996 (SI 1996/1312)

Existing provision		Rewritten provision	Remarks
1	Citation and commencement	—	Commencement.
2	Interpretation	—	Unnecessary.
3	Amendment to r 5 SI 1993/744		
	(a)	—	Amends SI 1993/744 r 5(3).
	(b)	—	Inserts SI 1993/744 r 5(4A).
4	Amendment to r 7 SI 1993/744	—	Revokes in part SI 1993/744 r 7(2).
5	Amendment to r 9 SI 1993/744	—	Amends SI 1993/744 r 9(2).
6	Amendment to r 11 SI 1993/744	—	Amends SI 1993/744 r 11(3)
7	Amendment to r 46AA SI 1993/744	—	Amends SI 1993/744 r 46AA(3).
8	Amendment to r 49 SI 1993/744		
	(1)	—	Substitutes SI 1993/744 r 49(8).
	(2)	—	Commencement.
9	Amendment to r 53 SI 1993/744	—	Amends SI 1993/744 r 53(1).
10	Inserted r 53A SI 1993/744	—	Inserts SI 1993/744 r 53A.
11	Amendment to r 63 SI 1993/744	—	Amends SI 1993/744 r 63(5).
12	Amendment to r 68, r 88 SI 1993/744	—	Amends SI 1993/744 r 68(1), r 88(1).
13	Substituted r 99 SI 1993/744	—	Substitutes SI 1993/744 r 99.
14	Amendment to r 101 SI 1993/744		
	(a)	—	Revokes in part SI 1993/744 r 101(4).
	(b)	—	Substitutes SI 1993/744 r 101(7).
15	Inserted r 101A SI 1993/744	—	Inserts SI 1993/744 r 101A.
16	Amendment to r 102 SI 1993/744		
	(1)	—	Revokes in part SI 1993/744 r 102(2).
	(2)	—	Commencement.
17	Amendment to r 104 SI 1993/744		
	(1)		
	(a)	—	Amends SI 1993/744 r 104(7).
	(b)	—	Revokes SI 1993/744 r 104(8).
	(c)	—	Amends SI 1993/744 r 104(11).
	(2)	—	Commencement.
18	Amendment to r 105 SI 1993/744		
	(1)	—	Revokes SI 1993/744 r 105(2).
	(2)	—	Commencement.

Existing provision		*Rewritten provision*	*Remarks*
19	Revocations and savings		
	(1)	—	Revokes in part SI 1993/744 r 100.
	(2)	—	Revokes in part SI 1993/744 r 103.

THE INCOME TAX (EMPLOYMENTS) (AMENDMENT NO 4) REGULATIONS 1996 (SI 1996/2381)

Existing provision		*Rewritten provision*	*Remarks*
1	Citation and commencement	—	Commencement.
2	Interpretation	—	Unnecessary.
3	Amendment to r 81 SI 1993/744	—	Amends SI 1993/744 r 81.
4	Amendment to r 83 SI 1993/744		
	(*a*)	—	Amends SI 1993/744 r 83(1).
	(*b*)	—	Revokes SI 1993/744 r 83(2).

THE INCOME TAX (EMPLOYMENTS) (AMENDMENT NO 5) REGULATIONS 1996 (SI 1996/2554)

Existing provision		*Rewritten provision*	*Remarks*
1	Citation and commencement	—	Commencement.
2	Amendments to SI 1993/744	—	Introductory.
3	Amendment to r 29 SI 1993/744	—	Substitutes SI 1993/744 r 29(1).
4	Amendment to r 30 SI 1993/744	—	Substitutes SI 1993/744 r 30(1).

THE INCOME TAX (EMPLOYMENTS) (AMENDMENT NO 6) REGULATIONS 1996 (SI 1996/2631)

Existing provision		*Rewritten provision*	*Remarks*
1	Citation, commencement and effect	—	Commencement.
2	Interpretation	—	Unnecessary.
3	Transitional provision	—	Unnecessary.
4	Inserted rr 80A–80N SI 1993/744	—	Inserts SI 1993/744 rr 80A–80N.

THE INCOME TAX (EMPLOYMENTS) (AMENDMENT) REGULATIONS 1997 (SI 1997/214)

Existing provision		*Rewritten provision*	*Remarks*
1	Citation and commencement	—	Commencement.
2	Interpretation	—	Unnecessary.

Existing provision		*Rewritten provision*	*Remarks*
3	Amendment to r 59 SI 1993/744	—	Amends SI 1993/744 r 59(1).
4	Amendment to r 59 SI 1993/744	—	Substitutes SI 1993/744 r 59(2); inserts SI 1993/744 r 59(3).

THE INCOME TAX (EMPLOYMENTS) (NOTIONAL PAYMENTS) (AMENDMENT) REGULATIONS 1998 (SI 1998/1891)

Existing provision		*Rewritten provision*	*Remarks*
1	Citation and commencement	—	Commencement.
2	Interpretation	—	Unnecessary.
3	Amendment to r 2 SI 1994/1212	—	Spent (superseded amendment of SI 1994/1212 r 2).
4	Amendment to r 3 SI 1994/1212	—	Revoked 2003 Sch. 8 Part 2.
5	Inserted r 3A, r 3B SI 1994/1212	—	Revoked 2003 Sch. 8 Part 2.
6	Amendment to r 7, r 8 SI 1994/1212	—	Revoked 2003 Sch. 8 Part 2.
7	Inserted r 8A SI 1994/1212	—	Spent.
8	Inserted r 12A SI 1994/1212	—	Inserts SI 1994/1212 r 12A.

THE INCOME TAX (EMPLOYMENTS) (AMENDMENT) REGULATIONS 1998 (SI 1998/2484)

Existing provision		*Rewritten provision*	*Remarks*
1	Citation and commencement	—	Commencement.
2	Interpretation	—	Unnecessary.
3	Amendment to r 2 SI 1993/744		
	(1)	—	Introductory.
	(2)	—	Spent (superseded amendment of SI 1993/744 r 2(4), (5), (6)).
4	Amendment to r 6 SI 1993/744		
	(1)	—	Introductory.
	(2)	—	Inserts SI 1993/744 r 6(4).
5	Amendment to r 23 SI 1993/744		
	(1)	—	Introductory.
	(2)	—	Amends SI 1993/744 r 23(1).
	(3)	—	Amends SI 1993/744 r 23(3), (4).
6	Amendment to r 24 SI 1993/744		
	(1)	—	Introductory.
	(2)	—	Amends SI 1993/744 r 24(1).
7	Amendment to r 25 SI 1993/744		
	(1)	—	Introductory.
	(2)	—	Amends SI 1993/744 r 25(1)–(4), (7)–(11).
	(3)	—	Amends SI 1993/744 r 25(2).
8	Amendment to r 26 SI 1993/744		
	(1)	—	Introductory.
	(2)	—	Amends SI 1993/744 r 26(1).
	(3)	—	Amends SI 1993/744 r 26(3).
9	Amendment to r 27 SI 1993/744		
	(1)	—	Introductory.

Existing provision		*Rewritten provision*	*Remarks*
	(2)	—	Amends SI 1993/744 r 27(1).
	(3)	—	Amends SI 1993/744 r 27(2).
10	Amendment to r 28 SI 1993/744		
	(1)	—	Introductory.
	(2)	—	Amends SI 1993/744 r 28(1).
	(3)	—	Amends SI 1993/744 r 28(3).
	(4)	—	Amends SI 1993/744 r 28(4).
	(5)	—	Amends SI 1993/744 r 28(5).
	(6)	—	Spent (superseded amendment of SI 1993/744 r 28(6)).
11	Amendment to r 30 SI 1993/744		
	(1)	—	Introductory.
	(2)	—	Amends SI 1993/744 r 30(4).
12	Amendment to r 34 SI 1993/744		
	(1)	—	Introductory.
	(2)	—	Amends SI 1993/744 r 34.
13	Amendment to r 37 SI 1993/744		
	(1)	—	Introductory.
	(2)	—	Amends SI 1993/744 r 37(2).
14	Amendment to r 43 SI 1993/744		
	(1)	—	Introductory.
	(2)	—	Amends SI 1993/744 r 43(1).
	(3)	—	Inserts SI 1993/744 r 43(1A), (1B). Spent in part (superseded amendment of SI 1993/744 r 43(1C)).
	(4)	—	Amends SI 1993/744 r 43(2).
	(5)	—	Amends SI 1993/744 r 43(6).
15	Amendment to r 46 SI 1993/744		
	(1)	—	Introductory.
	(2)	—	Amends SI 1993/744 r 46(1).
	(3)	—	Spent (superseded amendment of SI 1993/744 r 46(1A)).
	(4)	—	Amends SI 1993/744 r 46(7).
	(5)	—	Inserts SI 1993/744 r 46(7A).
16	Amendment to r 46AA SI 1993/744		
	(1)	—	Introductory.
	(2)	—	Amends SI 1993/744 r 46AA(1), (3).
	(3)	—	Amends SI 1993/744 r 46AA(6).
17	Amendment to r 46AB SI 1993/744		
	(1)	—	Introductory.
	(2)	—	Revokes in part SI 1993/744 r 46AB(1), (4).
18	Amendment to r 46A SI 1993/744		
	(1)	—	Introductory.
	(2)	—	Spent (superseded amendment of SI 1993/744 r 46A(1)).
	(3)	—	Spent (superseded amendment of SI 1993/744 r 46A(1A)).
19	Amendment to r 55 SI 1993/744		
	(1)	—	Introductory.
	(2)	—	Amends SI 1993/744 r 55(2).
20	Amendment to r 80A SI 1993/744		
	(1)	—	Introductory.
	(2)	—	Amends SI 1993/744 r 80A(5).
21	Amendment to r 84 SI 1993/744		
	(1)	—	Introductory.
	(2)	—	Amends SI 1993/744 r 84(1).
	(3)	—	Amends SI 1993/744 r 84(3), (5)–(7).
	(4)	—	Amends SI 1993/744 r 84(8).
	(5)	—	Amends SI 1993/744 r 84(9).
22	Amendment to r 91 SI 1993/744		
	(1)	—	Introductory.
	(2)	—	Amends SI 1993/744 r 91(5)

Existing provision		*Rewritten provision*	*Remarks*
23	Amendment to r 98E SI 1993/744		
	(1)	—	Introductory.
	(2)	—	Amends SI 1993/744 r 98E(1), (2).

THE INCOME TAX (EMPLOYMENTS) (AMENDMENT) REGULATIONS 1999 (SI 1999/70)

Existing provision		*Rewritten provision*	*Remarks*
1	Citation and commencement	—	Commencement.
2	Interpretation	—	Unnecessary.
3	Inserted r 46ZA SI 1993/744	—	Inserts SI 1993/744 r 46ZA.

THE INCOME TAX (EMPLOYMENTS) (AMENDMENT NO 2) REGULATIONS 1999 (SI 1999/824)

Existing provision		*Rewritten provision*	*Remarks*
1	Citation and commencement	—	Commencement.
2	Amendment to r 41 SI 1993/744	—	Spent (superseded amendment of SI 1993/744 r 41(3)).

THE INCOME TAX (EMPLOYMENTS) (AMENDMENT NO 3) REGULATIONS 1999 (SI 1999/2155)

Existing provision		*Rewritten provision*	*Remarks*
1	Citation, commencement and effect	—	Commencement.
2	Interpretation	—	Unnecessary.
3	Amendment to r 7 SI 1993/744	—	Amends SI 1993/744 r 7(2).
4	Amendment to r 10, r 12 SI 1993/744	—	Amends SI 1993/744 r 10(2), r 12(3)
5	Amendment to r 13 SI 1993/744	—	Amends SI 1993/744 r 13(4).
6	Amendment to r 28 SI 1993/744	—	Amends SI 1993/744 r 28(2).
7	Amendment to r 49 SI 1993/744	—	Amends SI 1993/744 r 49(7).
8	Amendment to r 2 SI 1993/744	—	Inserts SI 1993/744 r 2(1) (''starting rate'').
9	Amendment to r 29 SI 1993/744	—	Amends SI 1993/744 r 29(2), (3).
10	Amendment to r 30 SI 1993/744	—	Amends SI 1993/744 r 30(2), (3).
11	Amendment to r 32 SI 1993/744	—	Amends SI 1993/744 r 32.
12	Amendment to r 80F SI 1993/744	—	Amends SI 1993/744 r 80F(2).

Existing provision	Rewritten provision	Remarks
13	Amendment to r 84 SI 1993/744	
	—	Amends SI 1993/744 r 84(7).
14	Amendment to r 98C SI 1993/744	
	—	Amends SI 1993/744 r 98C(3).
15	Amendment to r 10 SI 1993/744	
	—	Amends SI 1993/744 r 10(2)
16	Amendment to r 12 SI 1993/744	
	—	Amends SI 1993/744 r 12(3)
17	Amendment to r 13 SI 1993/744	
	—	Amends SI 1993/744 r 13(4)
18	Amendment to r 98C SI 1993/744	
	—	Revokes in part SI 1993/744 r 98C(4).
19	Amendment to r 98F SI 1993/744	
(*a*)	—	Amends SI 1993/744 r 98F(3).
(*b*)	—	Revokes in part SI 1993/744 r 98F(3).
20	Amendment to r 10 SI 1993/744	
	—	Amends SI 1993/744 r 10(2).
21	Amendment to r 12 SI 1993/744	
	—	Amends SI 1993/744 r 12(3).
22	Amendment to r 13 SI 1993/744	
	—	Amends SI 1993/744 r 13(4).
23	Amendment to r 98C SI 1993/744	
	—	Amends SI 1993/744 r 98C(4).
24	Amendment to r 98F SI 1993/744	
	—	Amends SI 1993/744 r 98F(3).

THE INCOME TAX (EMPLOYMENTS) (AMENDMENT) REGULATIONS 2000 (SI 2000/1152)

Existing provision	Rewritten provision	Remarks
1	Citation and commencement	
	—	Commencement.
2	Amendment of r 41 SI 1993/744	
	—	Spent (superseded amendment of SI 1993/744 r 41(3)).

THE INCOME TAX (SUB-CONTRACTORS IN THE CONSTRUCTION INDUSTRY AND EMPLOYMENTS) (AMENDMENT) REGULATIONS 2000 (SI 2000/2742)

Existing provision	Rewritten provision	Remarks
3	Amendment of r 41 SI 1993/744	
	—	Spent (superseded amendment of SI 1993/744 r 41(3)).

THE INCOME TAX (ELECTRONIC COMMUNICATIONS) (MISCELLANEOUS AMENDMENTS) REGULATIONS 2001 (SI 2001/1081)

Existing provision	Rewritten provision	Remarks
1	Citation, commencement and interpretation	
(2) (words)	—	Unnecessary.
7	Amendments to SI 1993/744	
	—	Introductory.

Existing provision	*Rewritten provision*	*Remarks*
8 Amendment of r 2 SI 1993/744		
(1)	—	Introductory.
(2)	—	Inserts SI 1993/744 r 2(1) (''electronic communications'', ''official computer system'').
(3)	—	Substitutes SI 1993/744 r 2(4).
(4)–(6)	—	Spent (superseded amendment of SI 1993/744 r 2(4A)–(6)).
9 Amendment of r 6 SI 1993/744	—	Amends SI 1993/744 r 6(4).
10 Amendment of r 23 SI 1993/744	—	Amends SI 1993/744 r 23(1).
11 Amendment of r 25 SI 1993/744	—	Amends SI 1993/744 r 25(2).
12 Amendment of r 26 SI 1993/744		
(1)	—	Introductory.
(2)	—	Amends SI 1993/744 r 26(1).
(3)	—	Inserts SI 1993/744 r 26(1A).
(4)	—	Amends SI 1993/744 r 26(3).
(5)	—	Inserts SI 1993/744 r 26(4).
13 Amendment of r 27 SI 1993/744	—	Amends SI 1993/744 r 27(1).
14 Amendment of r 28 SI 1993/744		
(1)	—	Introductory.
(2)	—	Amends SI 1993/744 r 28(1).
(3)	—	Inserts SI 1993/744 r 28(1A), (1B).
(4)	—	Amends SI 1993/744 r 28(5).
(5)	—	Inserts SI 1993/744 r 28(5A), (5B).
(6)	—	Revokes SI 1993/744 r 28(6).
15 Amendment of r 43 SI 1993/744		
(1)	—	Introductory.
(2)	—	Amends SI 1993/744 r 43(1).
(3)	—	Substitutes SI 1993/744 r 43(1C).
(4)	—	Substitutes SI 1993/744 r 43(3); inserts SI 1993/744 r 43(3A), (3B).
16 Amendment of r 44 SI 1993/744	—	Substitutes SI 1993/744 r 44.
17 Amendment of r 46 SI 1993/744		
(1)	—	Introductory.
(2)	—	Amends SI 1993/744 r 46(1).
(3)	—	Substitutes SI 1993/744 r 46(1A).
(4)	—	Inserts SI 1993/744 r 46(7B).
18 Amendment of r 46AA SI 1993/744		
(1)	—	Introductory.
(2)	—	Amends SI 1993/744 r 46AA(1).
(3)	—	Amends SI 1993/744 r 46AA(3).
19 Amendment of r 46A SI 1993/744		
(1)	—	Introductory.
(2)	—	Amends SI 1993/744 r 46A(1).
(3)	—	Revokes SI 1993/744 r 46A(1A).
20 Inserted r 46ZB SI 1993/744	—	Inserts SI 1993/744 r 46ZB.
21 Amendment of r 55 SI 1993/744	—	Amends SI 1993/744 r 55(2).

THE INCOME TAX (EMPLOYMENTS AND ELECTRONIC COMMUNICATIONS) (MISCELLANEOUS PROVISIONS) REGULATIONS 2002 (SI 2002/680)

Existing provision		Rewritten provision	Remarks
3	Amendments to SI 1993/744	—	Introductory.
4	Amendment of r 2 SI 1993/744		
	(*a*)	—	Amends SI 1993/744 r 2(1) ("electronic communications").
	(*b*)	—	Revokes SI 1993/744 r 2(4A)–(6).
5	Inserted rr 2A–2E	—	Inserts SI 1993/744 rr 2A–2E.
6	Amendment of r 6 SI 1993/744	—	Amends SI 1993/744 r 6(4).
7	Amendment of r 13 SI 1993/744		
	(*a*)	—	Amends SI 1993/744 r 13(1).
	(*b*)	—	Inserts SI 1993/744 r 13(6).
8	Amendment of r 20 SI 1993/744	—	Amends SI 1993/744 r 20(3).

THE INCOME TAX (SUB-CONTRACTORS IN THE CONSTRUCTION INDUSTRY AND EMPLOYMENTS) (AMENDMENT) REGULATIONS 2003 (SI 2003/536)

Existing provision		Rewritten provision	Remarks
1	Citation, commencement and interpretation (2) (words)	—	Unnecessary.
9	Amendment of r 41 SI 1993/744	—	Substitutes SI 1993/744 r 41(3).

THE INCOME TAX (EMPLOYMENTS) (AMENDMENT) REGULATIONS 2003 (SI 2003/2494)

Existing provision		Rewritten provision	Remarks
1	Citation and commencement	—	Commencement.
2	Introductory	—	Unnecessary.
3	Amendment of r 2D SI 1993/744	—	Amends SI 1993/744 r 2D(1)–(3); inserts SI 1993/744 r 2D(4)
4	Amendment of r 3 SI 1993/744	—	Amends SI 1993/744 r 3(1); inserts SI 1993/744 r 3(6)–(9)
5	Amendment of r 40 SI 1993/744	—	Amends SI 1993/744 r 40(1).
6	Amendment of r 41 SI 1993/744	—	Amends SI 1993/744 r 41(1).
7	Inserted r 42A and 42B	—	Inserts SI 1993/744 r 42A and 42B
8	Inserted rr 46ZC–46ZH	—	Inserts SI 1993/744 rr 42ZC–46ZH
9	Amendment of r 47 SI 1993/744	—	Amends SI 1993/744 r 47(1)
10	Amendment of r 48 SI 1993/744	—	Amends SI 1993/744 r 48(1)
11	Amendment of r 51 SI 1993/744	—	Amends SI 1993/744 r 51(1) and (3)

2003/2682

Income Tax (Pay As You Earn) Regulations 2003

Made by the Commissioners of Inland Revenue under ITEPA 2003 ss 684, 685(4), 692, 704, 705, 706, 707, 708 and 710; TMA 1970 ss 59A(10), 59B(8), 98A and 113(1); FA 1999 ss 132 and 133(2); FA 2002 s 136 and FA 2003 ss 145(4) and 205.

Made . . . . 21 October 2003
Laid before Parliament . . . . 30 October 2003
Coming into force . . . . . 6 April 2004

ARRANGEMENT OF REGULATIONS

SIs

PART 4
PAYMENTS, RETURNS AND INFORMATION

CHAPTER 1
PAYMENT OF TAX AND ASSOCIATED RETURNS

Payment and recovery of tax by employer

Annual returns of relevant payments and tax

Failure to account for deductible tax

Interest

Recovery

CHAPTER 2
OTHER RETURNS AND INFORMATION

Returns involving PAYE income other than payments

Information to be given to employees

CHAPTER 3
PAYE RECORDS

PART 5

EMPLOYERS

Special arrangements

Death of employer and succession

PART 6

PAYE SETTLEMENT AGREEMENTS

Making and effect of PSA

Payment of tax under PSA

Form and commencement of PSA

Variation and cancellation of PSA

Interest

Records

PART 7

SPECIAL CASES

CHAPTER 1

COUNCILLORS' ALLOWANCES

CHAPTER 2

RESERVE FORCES' PAY

CHAPTER 3

HOLIDAY PAY FUNDS

CHAPTER 4

DIRECT COLLECTION AND SPECIAL ARRANGEMENTS

PART 8

SOCIAL SECURITY BENEFITS

CHAPTER 1

JOBSEEKER'S ALLOWANCE: NORMAL CASES

CHAPTER 2

JOBSEEKER'S ALLOWANCE: SPECIAL CASES

CHAPTER 3

INCAPACITY BENEFIT

CHAPTER 4

INCOME SUPPORT

PART 9

ASSESSMENT AND SELF-ASSESSMENT

PART 10

COMMUNICATIONS

CHAPTER 1

ELECTRONIC COMMUNICATIONS: INTERPRETATION

CHAPTER 2

ELECTRONIC COMMUNICATIONS: GENERAL

CHAPTER 3

ELECTRONIC PAYMENT BY LARGE EMPLOYERS

CHAPTER 4

MANDATORY USE OF ELECTRONIC COMMUNICATIONS

PART 1

INTRODUCTION

Citation and commencement

1 These Regulations may be cited as The Income Tax (Pay As You Earn) Regulations 2003 and shall come into force on 6th April 2004.

Commentary—*Simon's Direct Tax Service* **E4.1101.**

Interpretation

2—(1) In these Regulations, unless the context otherwise requires—

''additional pay'' means the appropriate amount, established from an employee's code (where it is a K code not used on the cumulative basis) and the tax tables, to be added to the relevant payments made to an employee in order to determine the taxable payments;

''agency'' has the meaning given in section 44 of ITEPA;

''agency worker'' means a worker whose services are treated by section 44 of ITEPA as the duties of an employment held with the agency;

''approved method of electronic communications'' has the meaning given in regulation 189;

''basic rate'', in relation to the charging of income tax for any tax year, means the rate of income tax determined under section 1(2)(*a*) of ICTA;

''Board of Inland Revenue'' means the Commissioners of Inland Revenue (as to which see in particular the Inland Revenue Regulation Act 1890);

''code'' and related expressions have the meanings given in regulation 7;

''cumulative basis'' means the basis of deduction or repayment of tax provided for in regulation 23;

''deductions working sheet'' means—

(*a*) any form of record in which are to be kept the matters required by these Regulations in connection with an employee's relevant payments and tax;

(*b*) in regulations 34 and 35 (simplified deduction scheme), and regulations 142 and 143 (direct collection) the form issued by the Inland Revenue for the purpose of keeping those records;

"earnings" has the meaning given in sections 62 and 721(7) of ITEPA;
"electronic communications" has the meaning given in regulation 189;
"employee's code" has the meaning given in regulation 8(1);
"employer reference" means the combination of letters, numbers or both used by the Inland Revenue to identify an employer for the purposes of these Regulations;
"employer's PAYE reference", in relation to an employer, means the combination of the employer's employer reference and the Inland Revenue office number;
"employment", subject to regulations 10 to 12, has the meaning given in sections 4 and 5 of ITEPA; and "employer" and "employee" have corresponding meanings;
"excluded business expenses" has the meaning given in regulation 5;
"family" and "family or household", in relation to a person, have the meanings given in section 721(4) and (5) of ITEPA;
"free pay" means the appropriate amount, established from an employee's code (where not used on the cumulative basis) and the tax tables, to be subtracted from relevant payments to arrive at taxable payments (and accordingly represents an appropriate part of reliefs allowable against those payments);
"general earnings" has the meaning given in section 7(3) of ITEPA;
"higher rate", in relation to the charging of income tax for any tax year, means the rate of income tax determined under section 1(2)(*b*) of ICTA;
"ICTA" means the Income and Corporation Taxes Act 1988;
"Inland Revenue" means any officer of the Board of Inland Revenue;
"Inland Revenue office", in relation to an employer, means the office of the Inland Revenue from which codes are normally issued to the employer;
"Inland Revenue office number" means the number which identifies an employer's Inland Revenue office;
"ITEPA" means the Income Tax (Earnings and Pensions) Act 2003;
"large employer" and "large or medium employer" have the meanings given in regulation 191;
"national insurance number" means the national insurance number allocated within the meaning of regulation 9 of the Social Security (Crediting and Treatment of Contributions, and National Insurance Numbers) Regulations 2001;
"net PAYE income" has the meaning given in regulation 3;
"non-cumulative basis" means the basis of deduction of tax provided for in regulation 27;
"notice" means notice in writing, or in a form authorised (in relation to the case in question) by directions under section 118 of the Finance Act 1998 (which allows certain claims etc to be made by telephone); and "notify" must be read accordingly;
"notional payment" has the meaning given in section 710(2)(*a*) of ITEPA;
"objects" means gives a notice of objection to the Inland Revenue;
"official computer system" has the meaning given in regulation 189;
"other payee" means a person receiving relevant payments in a capacity other than employee, agency worker or pensioner;
"other payer" means a person making relevant payments in a capacity other than employer, agency or pension payer;
"overriding limit" means the limit on the amount of tax to be deducted from a relevant payment, where the tax due in accordance with the appropriate tax tables in respect of any taxable payments or total taxable payments to date at the relevant date has been calculated by reference to additional pay or total additional pay to date, and that limit is an amount equal to 50% of the amount of the relevant payment;
"PAYE income" has the meaning given in section 683 of ITEPA;
"PAYE pension income" has the meaning given in section 683(3) of ITEPA;
"PAYE threshold" must be determined in accordance with regulation 9;
"payee" means an employee, agency worker, pensioner or other payee;
"payer" means an employer, agency, pension payer or other payer;
"pension" means a pension, annuity or other payments of PAYE pension income;
"pensioner" means a person receiving PAYE pension income;
"pension payer" means a person making payments of PAYE pension income;
"PSA" means a PAYE settlement agreement made in accordance with regulation 105;
"qualifying general earnings", in relation to a PSA, has the meaning given in regulation 106;
"reckonable date" has the meaning given in regulation 82(8);
"relevant payments" has the meaning given in regulation 4;
"relevant pension payments" has the meaning given in regulation 6;
"reliefs from income tax" includes allowances and deductions;
"specified date", for the purposes of Chapters 3 and 4 of Part 10, has the meaning given in regulation 190;
"starting rate", in relation to the charging of income tax for any tax year, means the rate of income tax determined under section 1(2)(*aa*) of ICTA;
"taxable payments" means relevant payments reduced by free pay or, as the case may be, increased by additional pay (where the employee's code is not used on the cumulative basis);
"tax month" means the period beginning on the 6th day of a calendar month and ending on the 5th day of the following calendar month;

''tax not deducted because of the overriding limit'' means any tax—

(*a*) which is due at the relevant date in accordance with the appropriate tax tables in respect of any taxable payments or total taxable payments to date, but
(*b*) which has not been deducted because of the overriding limit;

''tax period'' means—

(*a*) tax quarter, if regulation 34 (simplified deduction scheme for personal employees) or regulation 70 (quarterly tax periods) applies, or
(*b*) tax month, in every other case;

''tax quarter'' means any of the following (inclusive) periods—

6th April to 5th July,
6th July to 5th October,
6th October to 5th January, and
6th January to 5th April;

''tax tables'' means the tax tables prepared by the Board of Inland Revenue under section 685 of ITEPA;

''tax week'' means 6th April to 12th April (inclusive) and each successive period of 7 days, except that the final tax week in a tax year (''Week 53'') is just the last day of the tax year (or last 2 days in a leap year);

''tax year'' means a year for which any Act provides for income tax to be charged;

''TMA'' means the Taxes Management Act 1970;

''total additional pay to date'' means the appropriate amount, established from an employee's code (where it is a K code to be used on the cumulative basis) and the tax tables, to be added to the total payments to date in order to determine the total taxable payments to date;

''total free pay to date'', in relation to any date, means the appropriate amount, established from an employee's code (where used on the cumulative basis) and the tax tables, to be subtracted from total payments to date to arrive at total taxable payments to date (and accordingly represents an appropriate part of reliefs allowable against those payments);

''total net tax deducted'', in relation to the relevant payments made to an employee during any period, means the total tax deducted from those payments plus any tax accounted for in accordance with regulation 62(5) (notional payments), less any tax repaid to the employee;

''total payments to date'', in relation to any date, means the sum of all relevant payments made by the employer to the employee from the beginning of the tax year up to and including that date;

''total tax to date'' means the tax due at any date in accordance with the appropriate tax tables in respect of any total taxable payments to date;

''total taxable payments to date'' means total payments to date reduced by total free pay to date or, as the case may be, increased by total additional pay to date (where the employee's code is used on the cumulative basis);

''trade dispute'' has the meaning given in section 35(1) of the Jobseekers Act 1995 or, in Northern Ireland, in article 2(2) of the Jobseekers (Northern Ireland) Order 1995.

(2) References in these Regulations to income tax in respect of PAYE income (however expressed) are references to income tax in respect of that income if reasonable assumptions are, when necessary, made about other income.

Commentary—*Simon's Direct Tax Service* **E4.1103**.
Derivation—The Income Tax (Employments) Regulations, SI 1993/744 reg 2(1); ITEPA 2003 ss 4, 5, 7(3), 62, 683, 684(7B), 720(2), 721(4), (5), (7).
Modifications—See the Income Tax (PAYE) Regulations, SI 2003/2682 reg 150 (modification of this regulation in its application to payments of taxable jobseeker's allowance made to a claimant).
SI 2003/2682 reg 174 (modification of this regulation in its application to payments of taxable incapacity benefit).

Net PAYE income

3—(1) ''Net PAYE income'' means PAYE income less any—

(*a*) allowable pension contributions, and
(*b*) allowable donations to charity.

(2) In paragraph (1)—

''allowable pension contributions'' means any contribution towards a scheme which is withheld from the payment of PAYE income and for which a deduction must be allowed from employment income under section 592(7) or 594(1) of ICTA (exempt approved schemes and exempt statutory schemes);

''allowable donations to charity'' means any donation which is withheld from the payment of PAYE income and for which a deduction must be allowed under section 713 of ITEPA (donations to charity: payroll deduction scheme).

Commentary—*Simon's Direct Tax Service* **E4.1110**.
Derivation—The Income Tax (Employments) Regulations, SI 1993/744 reg 2(1).

Relevant payments

4—(1) In these Regulations, any reference (however expressed) to relevant payments means payments of, or on account of, net PAYE income, except payments of, or on account of,—

(*a*) PAYE social security income, except in so far as it is provided for in Part 8,
(*b*) United Kingdom social security pensions,
(*c*) excluded relocation expenses,
(*d*) excluded business expenses,
(*e*) excluded pecuniary liabilities, and
(*f*) excluded notional payments.

(2) In paragraph (1)—

''excluded business expenses'' has the meaning given in regulation 5;

''excluded notional payments'' means notional payments which an employer is treated as making by section 694 or 695 of ITEPA (non-cash vouchers and credit tokens) as a result of an employee using a non-cash voucher or credit token on behalf of the employer, except where the voucher or token is used as, or as part of, any scheme or arrangement the purpose, or one of the main purposes, of which is—

(*a*) to provide the employee with money or an asset, or
(*b*) to avoid the making of a relevant payment;

''excluded pecuniary liabilities'' means payments made to a person other than an employee to meet the employee's liability to that other person, but which are not made—

(*a*) in fulfilment (in whole or in part) of the employee's right to a sum of money, nor
(*b*) as, or as part of, any scheme or arrangement the purpose, or one of the main purposes, of which is to avoid the making of a relevant payment;

''excluded relocation expenses'' means payments in respect of removal expenses, as defined by section 272 of ITEPA (removal benefits and expenses to which section 271 applies), if, and to the extent that, they are payments of net PAYE income;

''PAYE social security income'' has the meaning given in section 683(5) of ITEPA;

''United Kingdom social security pensions'' means income which is taxable income in accordance with section 578 of ITEPA (UK social security pensions).

Commentary—*Simon's Direct Tax Service* **E4.1110.**
Derivation—The Income Tax (Employments) Regulations, SI 1993/744 reg 2(3).

Excluded business expenses

5—(1) ''Excluded business expenses'' means expenses within Chapter 3 of Part 3 of ITEPA (earnings and benefits treated as earnings) which the Inland Revenue have authorised the employer to exclude from relevant payments in accordance with this regulation.

(2) The Inland Revenue may authorise an employer to exclude any payment of expenses from relevant payments if the Inland Revenue are of the opinion that a deduction or relief will, or is likely to, result in no tax being payable as a result of the payment.

(3) The Inland Revenue may authorise the exclusion of—

(*a*) specific expenses or a class of expenses,
(*b*) expenses paid by a specific employer or a class of employers, and
(*c*) expenses paid to a specific employee or a class of employees.

(4) The Inland Revenue must notify an employer of any excluded business expenses and the date from which the exclusion is to apply.

(5) The Inland Revenue may revoke the authorisation to exclude business expenses by giving notice to the employer specifying the date of the notice or a subsequent date as the date from which the revocation has effect.

Commentary—*Simon's Direct Tax Service* **E4.1110.**

Relevant pension payments

6 In these Regulations, any reference (however expressed) to relevant pension payments means relevant payments in respect of PAYE pension income.

Derivation—The Income Tax (Employments) Regulations, SI 1993/744 reg 2(1).

Meaning of ''code'' etc

7—(1) In these Regulations, ''code'' means—

(*a*) a combination of letters, numbers or both for use in accordance with the tax tables to establish free pay, additional pay, total free pay to date or total additional pay to date;
(*b*) any of the special codes (whether expressed in words or represented by a combination of letters, numbers or both) for use in accordance with the tax tables or otherwise.

(2) ''K code'' means a code which gives rise to additional pay or total additional pay to date.

(3) The special codes are—

(*a*) the basic rate code, which effects deductions of tax wholly at the basic rate;
(*b*) the higher rate code, which effects deductions of tax wholly at the higher rate;
(*c*) the nil tax code, which requires no deductions of tax;
(*d*) the emergency code, which, after allowing for the relief specified in section 257(1) of ICTA (personal allowance), effects deductions of tax at one or more of the starting rate, basic rate and higher rate, so that during the tax year the amounts subject to deductions at the various rates are in accordance with section 1(2) of ICTA;
(*e*) the emergency IB codes which, after allowing for the relief specified in—

(i) section 257(1) of ICTA (personal allowance), and
(ii) section 265(1) of ICTA (blind person's allowance), if claimed,

effect deductions of tax at one or both of the starting rate and basic rate, so that during the tax year the amounts subject to deductions at the various rates are in accordance with section 1(2) of ICTA.

Commentary—*Simon's Direct Tax Service* **E4.1131, 1133.**
Derivation—The Income Tax (Employments) Regulations, SI 1993/744 regs 2(1), 9, 29(2), (3), 30(2), (3), 32, 84(7), 98C(1), (3), (4).

Employee's code

8—(1) An employee's code is the code—

(*a*) issued to an employer for use in respect of the employee for a tax year,
(*b*) applied by these Regulations for use by an employer in respect of the employee, or
(*c*) issued to an employee in accordance with regulation 142 (direct collection).

(2) A code is issued to an employer if it is contained in a document that is sent—

(*a*) to the employer, or
(*b*) to a person acting on behalf of the employer,

by the Inland Revenue, and any code so issued is received by the employer for the purposes of these Regulations.

Commentary—*Simon's Direct Tax Service* **E4.1131.**
Derivation—The Income Tax (Employments) Regulations, SI 1993/744 regs 2(1), 6(4), 13(6), 104(1).

PAYE threshold

9—(1) The rules set out in Table 1 apply in order to determine whether a relevant payment made by an employer to an employee is a relevant payment which exceeds the PAYE threshold.

(2) Rules 1 to 5 apply if the employer normally pays the employee at regular intervals.

(3) If the employer does not normally pay the employee at regular intervals—

(*a*) rule 6 applies to determine whether a relevant payment made less than a week since the previous relevant payment exceeds the PAYE threshold, and
(*b*) rule 7 applies to determine whether any other relevant payment exceeds the PAYE threshold.

TABLE 1
DETERMINATION OF PAYE THRESHOLD

Employee's payment interval	*Rule to determine whether relevant payment exceeds PAYE threshold*
1 Weekly	1 If the sum of the relevant payment and any other relevant payments made earlier in the same tax week is more than the weekly PAYE threshold.
2 Monthly	2 If the sum of the relevant payment and any other relevant payments made earlier in the same tax month is more than the monthly PAYE threshold.
3 Regular intervals which are multiples of a week	3 If the sum of the relevant payment and any other relevant payments made earlier in the same interval is more than the corresponding multiple of the weekly PAYE threshold.
4 Regular intervals, longer than a week, which are fractions or multiples of a month	4 If the sum of the relevant payment and any other relevant payments made earlier in the same interval is more than the corresponding fraction or multiple of the monthly PAYE threshold.

Employee's payment interval	*Rule to determine whether relevant payment exceeds PAYE threshold*
5 Regular intervals, longer than a week, which are not within rules 1 to 4	5 If the sum of the relevant payment and any other relevant payments made earlier in the same interval is more than the corresponding proportion of the weekly PAYE threshold.
6 Intervals shorter than a week, whether regular or irregular	6 If the sum of the relevant payment and any other relevant payments made earlier in the same tax week is more than the weekly PAYE threshold.
7 Irregular intervals longer than a week	7 If the relevant payment is more than the corresponding proportion of the weekly PAYE threshold since— (*a*) any previous relevant payment in the tax year, or (*b*) if none, the start of the employment or the start of the tax year (whichever is later).

(4) Regulations 24 and 30 (employee not paid weekly or monthly)—

(*a*) apply for the purpose of establishing an employee's normal payment interval, but
(*b*) must otherwise be ignored for the purpose of determining whether a relevant payment exceeds the PAYE threshold.

(5) If an employee has more than one normal payment interval in respect of payments made by the same employer, the rules must be applied on the basis of the shorter or shortest of those intervals.

(6) If an employee's normal payment interval is longer than a year, the rules must be applied as if the normal payment interval were a year.

(7) "Weekly PAYE threshold" means 1/52 of the personal allowance specified in section 257(1) of ICTA, rounded to the nearest pound.

(8) "Monthly PAYE threshold" means 1/12 of the personal allowance specified in section 257(1) of ICTA, rounded to the nearest pound.

(9) The "corresponding proportion of the weekly PAYE threshold" is established by dividing the number of days in the payment interval by 7, and multiplying the result by the weekly PAYE threshold.

Commentary—*Simon's Direct Tax Service* **E4.1106.**
Derivation—The Income Tax (Employments) Regulations, SI 1993/744 regs 18, 28(1), (2).

APPLICATION TO PAYERS AND PAYEES

Application to agencies and agency workers

10—(1) For the purposes of these Regulations—

(*a*) agencies are treated as employers; and
(*b*) agency workers are treated as employees.

(2) For the purposes of the regulations listed in paragraph (3), an agency ceases to employ an agency worker at the earlier of—

(*a*) the end of the relationship between the agency and agency worker, or
(*b*) the end of a period of 3 months during which the agency makes no relevant payments to the agency worker,

and not each time the agency worker stops providing services to a client of the agency.

(3) The regulations are—

regulation 36	Cessation of employment: Form P45
regulation 37	PAYE income paid after employment ceased
regulation 46(6)	Employer to ignore code relating to employment which has ceased
regulation 51(5) to (7)	effects of employment ceasing on Form P45 procedure
regulation 94(3) to (7)	Information to former employees of other earnings.

(4) The following regulations do not apply to agencies or agency workers in their capacity as such—

regulation 34	simplified deduction scheme for personal employees
regulation 35	simplified deduction schemes: records
regulation 91	termination awards: information to be provided
regulation 92	termination awards: return if award changes
regulation 93	termination awards: return if more than one employer

regulation 96	termination awards: information to employees
Part 6	PAYE settlement agreements
regulation 167	jobseeker's allowance paid by employer
regulation 168	regulation 167 cases: application of other regulations.

Commentary—*Simon's Direct Tax Service* **E4.1188.**
Derivation—The Income Tax (Employments) Regulations, SI 1993/744 reg 2(1).

Application to pension payers and pensioners

11—(1) For the purposes of these Regulations—

(*a*) pension payers are treated as employers;
(*b*) pensioners are treated as employees; and
(*c*) a pensioner's "employment" with a pension payer starts when the pension starts and ends when the pension ends.

(2) The following regulations do not apply to pension payers or pensioners in their capacity as such—

regulation 25	cumulative basis: subsidiary PAYE income of employee paid weekly or at greater intervals
regulation 34	simplified deduction scheme for personal employees
regulation 35	simplified deduction schemes: records
regulation 38	death of employee (other than pensioner)
Chapter 2 of Part 3	new employees (other than pensioners): Forms P45 and P46
regulation 63	repayment during unpaid leave
regulation 64	trade disputes
regulation 65	repayment if no longer employed
regulation 71	modification of regulation 68 in case of trade dispute
regulation 75	additional return in case of trade dispute
regulations 85 to 89	employers: annual return of other earnings
regulation 90	quarterly return if car becomes available or unavailable
regulation 91	termination awards: information to be provided
regulation 92	termination awards: return if award changes
regulation 93	termination awards: return if more than one employer
regulation 94	employers: information to employees of other earnings
regulation 95	third parties: information to employees of other earnings
regulation 96	termination awards: information to employees
regulation 100	tips: special arrangements
regulation 102(1)	succession to a business etc: employees (other than pensioners)
regulation 104	succession to a business: trade disputes
Part 6	PAYE settlement agreements
Chapter 3 of Part 7	holiday pay funds
regulation 151	obtaining the claimant's Form P45
regulation 167	jobseeker's allowance paid by employer
regulation 168	regulation 167 cases: application of other regulations.

Commentary—*Simon's Direct Tax Service* **E4.1103.**
Derivation—The Income Tax (Employments) Regulations, SI 1993/744 reg 2(1).

Application to other payers and payees

12—(1) For the purposes of these Regulations—

(*a*) other payers are treated as employers;
(*b*) other payees are treated as employees; and
(*c*) an other payee's "employment" with an other payer starts when relevant payments start and ends when relevant payments end.

(2) The following regulations do not apply to other payers or other payees in their capacity as such—

regulation 34	Simplified deduction scheme for personal employees
regulation 35	Simplified deduction schemes: records
regulation 85 to 88	Employers: annual return of other earnings
regulation 90	Quarterly return if car becomes available or unavailable
regulation 91	Termination awards: information to be provided
regulation 92	Termination awards: return if award changes
regulation 93	Termination awards: return if more than one employer
regulation 94	Employers: information to employees of other earnings
regulation 95	third parties: information to employees of other earnings
regulation 96	Termination awards: information to employees
Part 6	PAYE settlement agreements
regulation 134	Interpretation of Chapter 3 (holiday pay funds)
regulation 167	Jobseeker's allowance paid by employer
regulation 168	Regulation 167 cases: application of other regulations.

(3) Paragraph (2) is subject to regulation 91(9) (termination awards: former employers and employees).

(4) The following regulation does not apply to other payees in their capacity as such—
regulation 64 trade disputes.

PART 2

CODES

Commentary—*Simon's Direct Tax Service* **E4.1103.**
Derivation—The Income Tax (Employments) Regulations, SI 1993/744 reg 2(1).
Cross references—See the Income Tax (PAYE) Regulations, SI 2003/2682 reg 123 (this Part does not apply to relevant payments made by the Ministry of Defence to members of the reserve forces specified in SI 2003/2682 reg 122).
SI 2003/2682 reg 135 (this Part does not apply to holiday pay).
SI 2003/2682 reg 168 (subject to SI 2003/2682 reg 168(3), this Part applies to the taxable jobseeker's allowance paid to a Part 8 Chapter 2 (of SI 2003/2682) claimant by the employer on behalf of the Department under SI 2003/2682 reg 167, as if it were a relevant payment from the employment).

DETERMINATION OF CODE

Determination of code by Inland Revenue

13 The Inland Revenue must determine the code for use by an employer in respect of an employee for a tax year.

Commentary—*Simon's Direct Tax Service* **E4.1132.**
Derivation—The Income Tax (Employments) Regulations, SI 1993/744 reg 7(1).

Matters relevant to determination of code

14—(1) If the Inland Revenue determine a code under this regulation, they must have regard to the following matters so far as known to them—

(*a*) the reliefs from income tax to which the employee is entitled for the tax year in which the code is determined, so far as the employee's title to those reliefs has been established at the time of the determination;

(*b*) any PAYE income of the employee (other than the relevant payments in relation to which the code is being determined);

(*c*) any tax overpaid for any previous tax year which has not been repaid;

(*d*) any tax remaining unpaid for any previous tax year which is not otherwise recovered;

(*e*) any tax repaid to the employee in excess of the amount properly due to the employee which may be recovered as if it were unpaid tax under section 30(1) of TMA (recovery of overpayment of tax etc) and which is not otherwise recovered;

(*f*) unless the employee objects, any other income of the employee which is not PAYE income; and

(*g*) such other adjustments as may be necessary to secure that, so far as possible, the tax in respect of the employee's income in relation to which the code is determined will be deducted from the relevant payments made during that tax year.

(2) If the Inland Revenue determine the code before the beginning of the tax year for which it is determined, the Inland Revenue—

(*a*) must have regard to any expected change in the amount of any relief referred to in paragraph (1)(*a*), but

(*b*) may disregard any such relief if they are not satisfied that the employee will be entitled to it for the tax year for which the code is determined.

(3) Paragraphs (1)(*c*) and (*d*) are subject to regulations 186 and 187 (recovery and repayment: adjustment of employee's code).

Commentary—*Simon's Direct Tax Service* **E4.1132.**
Derivation—The Income Tax (Employments) Regulations, SI 1993/744 reg 7(1), (2).
Modifications—See the Income Tax (PAYE) Regulations, SI 2003/2682 reg 150 (modification of this regulation in its application to payments of taxable jobseeker's allowance made to a claimant).

Flat rate codes

15—(1) The Inland Revenue may determine that the code for use by an employer in respect of an employee for a tax year is the higher rate code, if they have reason to believe that the employee will be chargeable at the higher rate on all or a substantial part of the employee's relevant payments.

(2) The Inland Revenue may determine that the code for use by an employer in respect of an employee for a tax year is the basic rate code, if they have reason to believe that the employee will be chargeable at the basic rate on all or a substantial part of the employee's relevant payments.

(3) The Inland Revenue may determine that the code for use by an employer in respect of an employee for a tax year is the nil tax code, if—

(*a*) the employee's PAYE income will be taken into account as taxable income other than PAYE income in any assessment,

(*b*) the Inland Revenue are not satisfied that the employee's income will be chargeable, or

(*c*) the Inland Revenue have reason to believe that the employee will be entitled to a deduction under Chapter 6 of Part 5 of ITEPA (deductions from seafarers' earnings) in respect of the employee's PAYE income or so much of it as remains after any deductions under section 592(7) or 594(1) of ICTA (exempt approved schemes and exempt statutory schemes).

(4) References in this regulation to an employee's relevant payments, PAYE income and income are references to the payments or income in respect of which the employee's code is being determined for the purposes of the employment in question.

Commentary—*Simon's Direct Tax Service* **E4.1131.**
Derivation—The Income Tax (Employments) Regulations, SI 1993/744 reg 9(1), (2).
Modifications—See the Income Tax (PAYE) Regulations, SI 2003/2682 reg 150 (modification of this regulation in its application to payments of taxable jobseeker's allowance made to a claimant).
SI 2003/2682 reg 174 (modification of this regulation in its application to payments of taxable incapacity benefit).
Cross references—See the Income Tax (PAYE) Regulations, SI 2003/2682 reg 34 (this regulation does not apply to cases where SI 2003/2682 regs 34, 35 apply).

Continued application of employee's code

16—(1) If the Inland Revenue determine that the code for use by an employer in respect of an employee for a tax year remains the same as at the previous 5th April, the Inland Revenue need not issue a code to the employer.

(2) If for any tax year the employer does not receive a code for an employee who was in that employer's employment on the previous 5th April, the code which applied on that date is treated as having been issued by the Inland Revenue for the tax year in question.

Commentary—*Simon's Direct Tax Service* **E4.1136.**
Derivation—The Income Tax (Employments) Regulations, SI 1993/744 reg 8(1), (2).
Modifications—See the Income Tax (PAYE) Regulations, SI 2003/2682 reg 150 (modification of this regulation in its application to payments of taxable jobseeker's allowance made to a claimant).
SI 2003/2682 reg 174 (modification of this regulation in its application to payments of taxable incapacity benefit).
Cross references—See the Income Tax (PAYE) Regulations, SI 2003/2682 reg 34 (this regulation does not apply to cases where SI 2003/2682 regs 34, 35 apply).

Notice to employee of code

17—(1) The Inland Revenue must give notice to an employee of the code which they have determined for use in respect of that employee for any tax year.

(2) But notice need not be given if—

(*a*) the code for use in respect of the employee remains the same as at the previous 5th April; or

(*b*) the change in the code is solely because of an alteration or proposed alteration in the rates of any of the personal reliefs allowable under sections 257 and 257A of ICTA (personal allowance and married couple's allowance) or in the tax tables.

Commentary—*Simon's Direct Tax Service* **E4.1136.**
Derivation—The Income Tax (Employments) Regulations, SI 1993/744 reg 10.
Modifications—See the Income Tax (PAYE) Regulations, SI 2003/2682 reg 150 (modification of this regulation in its application to payments of taxable jobseeker's allowance made to a claimant).
SI 2003/2682 reg 174 (modification of this regulation in its application to payments of taxable incapacity benefit).

APPEALS AND AMENDMENT

Objections and appeals against employee's code

18—(1) An employee who objects to the determination of a code must state the grounds of objection.

(2) On receiving the notice of objection the Inland Revenue may amend the determination of the code by agreement with the employee.

(3) If the Inland Revenue and employee do not reach agreement, the employee may appeal to the General Commissioners against the determination of the code by giving notice to the Inland Revenue.

(4) On appeal, the General Commissioners must determine the code in accordance with these Regulations.

(5) For the purposes of paragraph 3(1)(*a*) of Schedule 3 to TMA (rules for assigning proceedings to General Commissioners), the relevant place for an appeal under this regulation is—

(*a*) the place where the employment is situated, or

(*b*) if there is no such place, the place where the employee lives.

Commentary—*Simon's Direct Tax Service* **E4.1137.**
Derivation—The Income Tax (Employments) Regulations, SI 1993/744 reg 11(1), (2), (3), (5).
Modifications—SI 2003/2682 reg 150 (modification of this regulation in its application to payments of taxable jobseeker's allowance made to a claimant).
SI 2003/2682 reg 174 (modification of this regulation in its application to payments of taxable incapacity benefit).
Cross references—See the Income Tax (PAYE) Regulations, SI 2003/2682 reg 19(5) (this regulation applies in relation to an amended code as it does to the original code).

SI 2003/2682 reg 19(6) (this regulation also applies if the Revenue do not agree that circumstances have changed (as provided for in SI 2003/2682 reg 19), and so refuse to amend the code in accordance with SI 2003/2682 reg 19(2)).
SI 2003/2682 reg 50 (procedure in Form P46 cases where code treated as issued by the Revenue: this does not apply for the purposes of this regulation).

Amendment of code

19—(1) Paragraph (2) applies if the code for use by an employer in respect of an employee is found to be inappropriate because the actual circumstances are different from the circumstances by reference to which it was determined, whether by the Inland Revenue or the General Commissioners.

(2) The Inland Revenue may, and if required by the employee must, amend the code by reference to the actual circumstances.

(3) The Inland Revenue must give notice of the amended code to the employee by the date on which the notice under regulation 20(1) is issued to the employer.

(4) But notice need not be given where the change in the code is solely because of an alteration or proposed alteration in the rates of any of the personal reliefs allowable under sections 257 and 257A of ICTA (personal allowance and married couple's allowance) or in the tax tables.

(5) Regulation 18 (objections and appeals) applies in relation to the amended code as it applies in relation to the original code.

(6) Regulation 18 also applies if the Inland Revenue do not agree that the circumstances have changed and so refuse to amend the code in accordance with paragraph (2).

Commentary—*Simon's Direct Tax Service* **E4.1136.**
Derivation—The Income Tax (Employments) Regulations, SI 1993/744 reg 12.
Modifications—See the Income Tax (PAYE) Regulations, SI 2003/2682 reg 150 (modification of this regulation in its application to payments of taxable jobseeker's allowance made to a claimant).
SI 2003/2682 reg 174 (modification of this regulation in its application to payments of taxable incapacity benefit).

Notice to employer of amended code

20—(1) If the code for use by an employer in respect of an employee is amended after notice of it has been issued to the employer, the Inland Revenue must issue the amended code to the employer.

(2) An amended code is issued to an employer if it is contained in a document that is sent to the employer or a person acting on behalf of the employer by the Inland Revenue, and any code so issued is received by the employer for the purposes of these Regulations.

(3) On making any subsequent relevant payment to the employee, the employer must deduct or repay tax by reference to the amended code.

(4) Paragraphs (5) and (6) apply if there is a change or proposed change in the rates of any of the personal reliefs allowable under sections 257 and 257A of ICTA (personal allowance and married couple's allowance).

(5) If the change or proposed change relates to the current tax year, the Inland Revenue may give notice requiring the employer, with effect from the date specified in the notice, to amend specified codes as directed.

(6) If the change relates to the following tax year, the Inland Revenue may give notice requiring the employer to carry forward to the following tax year specified codes of the current tax year and adjust them as directed in the notice.

(7) A code which has—

(*a*) been amended by virtue of paragraph (5) in respect of the current tax year, or
(*b*) been carried forward to the following tax year and adjusted by virtue of paragraph (6),

is treated as having been determined and issued by the Inland Revenue as the employee's code for that tax year.

(8) A notice under paragraphs (5) and (6) may be issued to the employer or to a person acting on behalf of the employer.

Commentary—*Simon's Direct Tax Service* **E4.1136.**
Derivation—The Income Tax (Employments) Regulations, SI 1993/744 regs 8(5), 13(1), (2), (4), 6).
Modifications—See the Income Tax (PAYE) Regulations, SI 2003/2682 reg 150 (modification of this regulation in its application to payments of taxable jobseeker's allowance made to a claimant).
SI 2003/2682 reg 174 (modification of this regulation in its application to payments of taxable incapacity benefit).

PART 3

DEDUCTION AND REPAYMENT OF TAX

Cross references—See the Income Tax (PAYE) Regulations, SI 2003/2682 reg 123 (this Part does not apply to relevant payments made by the Ministry of Defence to members of the reserve forces specified in SI 2003/2682 reg 122).
SI 2003/2682 reg 135 (this Part does not apply to holiday pay).
SI 2003/2682 reg 168 (subject to SI 2003/2682 reg 168(3), this Part applies to the taxable jobseeker's allowance paid to a Part 8 Chapter 2 (of SI 2003/2682) claimant by the employer on behalf of the Department under SI 2003/2682 reg 167, as if it were a relevant payment from the employment).

CHAPTER 1
DEDUCTION AND REPAYMENT

DEDUCTION AND REPAYMENT BY REFERENCE TO EMPLOYEE'S CODE

Deduction and repayment of tax by reference to employee's code

21—(1) On making a relevant payment to an employee during a tax year, an employer must deduct or repay tax in accordance with these Regulations by reference to the employee's code, if the employer has one for the employee.

(2) The employer must deduct or repay tax by reference to the employee's code, even if the code is the subject of an objection or appeal.

Commentary—*Simon's Direct Tax Service* **E4.1102, 1140.**
Derivation—The Income Tax (Employments) Regulations, SI 1993/744 reg 6(1)–(3).
Modifications—See the Income Tax (PAYE) Regulations, SI 2003/2682 reg 150 (modification of this regulation in its application to payments of taxable jobseeker's allowance made to a claimant).
SI 2003/2682 reg 174 (modification of this regulation in its application to payments of taxable incapacity benefit).
Cross references—See the Income Tax (PAYE) Regulations, SI 2003/2682 reg 34 (this regulation does not apply to cases where SI 2003/2682 regs 34, 35 apply).
SI 2003/2682 reg 37 (PAYE income paid after employment ceased: this regulation not to apply)

THE CUMULATIVE BASIS

The cumulative basis

22 An employer must deduct or repay tax on the cumulative basis, unless these Regulations provide otherwise.

Commentary—*Simon's Direct Tax Service* **E4.1146.**
Derivation—The Income Tax (Employments) Regulations, SI 1993/744 reg 14(1).
Modifications—See the Income Tax (PAYE) Regulations, SI 2003/2682 reg 174 (modification of this regulation in its application to payments of taxable incapacity benefit).
Cross references—See the Income Tax (PAYE) Regulations, SI 2003/2682 reg 26(2) (if SI 2003/2682 reg 26 applies, then this regulation does not apply).
SI 2003/2682 reg 32 (if an employee's code is the higher rate code, the employer must deduct tax at the higher rate, and this regulation and SI 2003/2682 reg 26 do not apply).
SI 2003/2682 reg 33 (application of this regulation in the case of a nil tax code).
SI 2003/2682 reg 34 (this regulation does not apply to cases where SI 2003/2682 regs 34, 35 apply).
SI 2003/2682 reg 37 (PAYE income paid after employment ceased: this regulation not to apply)

Cumulative basis: deduction and repayment

23—(1) This regulation provides for deductions and repayments on the basis of total payments to date (the cumulative basis).

(2) In this regulation—

(*a*) TT is the total tax to date relating to an employee;

(*b*) UT is any tax not deducted because of the overriding limit when the last relevant payment was made to the employee, and is nil if the payment in question is the first relevant payment to the employee in any tax year;

(*c*) PT is the previous total tax to date relating to the employee, and is nil if the payment in question is the first relevant payment to the employee in any tax year.

(3) The employer must, before making any relevant payment to the employee, calculate TT.

(4) If TT + UT exceeds PT, the employer must deduct the excess from the relevant payment on making the payment.

(5) But if the employee's code is a K code, the deduction is not to exceed the overriding limit, subject to 62(6) (notional payments).

(6) If TT + UT is less than PT, the employer must repay the difference to the employee on making the payment, subject to regulations 25(4) (extra payment made before main payment) and 64 (trade disputes).

(7) If TT + UT equals PT, the employer must neither deduct nor repay tax when making the payment.

(8) "Previous total tax to date" means the total tax to date corresponding to the employee's total payments to date and the employee's code—

(*a*) at the date of the last preceding relevant payment, or

(*b*) if later, at the date on which the employer complied with this regulation as if a relevant payment had been made.

(9) But—

(*a*) if the employee's code is an amended code, and

(*b*) the employee's previous code was not used on the cumulative basis,

"previous total tax to date" means the total net tax deducted by the employer.

(10) Paragraphs (2)(*c*), (8) and (9) are subject to regulations 43(9) and (10), 52(11) and (12), 53(4) and 61(4) (which modify the meaning of previous total tax to date in certain circumstances).

Commentary—*Simon's Direct Tax Service* **E4.1146.**
Derivation—The Income Tax (Employments) Regulations, SI 1993/744 regs 2(1), 14, 15.
Modifications—See the Income Tax (PAYE) Regulations, SI 2003/2682 reg 174 (modification of this regulation in its application to payments of taxable incapacity benefit).
Cross references—See the Income Tax (PAYE) Regulations, SI 2003/2682 reg 34 (this regulation does not apply to cases where SI 2003/2682 regs 34, 35 apply).
SI 2003/2682 reg 37 (PAYE income paid after employment ceased: this regulation not to apply)

Cumulative basis: employee not paid weekly or monthly

24—(1) This regulation applies if—

(*a*) an employer normally makes main relevant payments to an employee at regular intervals which are longer than a week, other than monthly, and
(*b*) the employee's code is used on the cumulative basis.

(2) The first main relevant payment in a tax year is treated for the purposes of calculating the deduction or repayment of tax as having been made at the end the period which—

(*a*) starts on the first day of the tax year, and
(*b*) finishes at the end of the employee's normal regular payment interval.

(3) Subsequent main relevant payments in the tax year are treated for the purposes of calculating the deduction or repayment of tax as having been made at the end of the period which—

(*a*) starts the day after the date on which the previous main relevant payment is treated as having been made (by paragraph (2) or this paragraph), and
(*b*) finishes at the end of the employee's normal regular payment interval or the last day of the tax year (if earlier).

(4) If the employee's main relevant payments are normally made at regular intervals which are longer than a year, any such payment in a tax year is treated, for the purposes of calculating the deduction or repayment of tax, as made on the last day of that tax year.

(5) But, in every case, the employer must record the actual date of every payment in the deductions working sheet.

(6) This regulation does not apply if the payment falls within regulation 31(1) (payments in short payment periods).

Commentary—*Simon's Direct Tax Service* **E4.1142.**
Derivation—The Income Tax (Employments) Regulations, SI 1993/744 reg 18.
Modifications—See the Income Tax (PAYE) Regulations, SI 2003/2682 reg 174 (modification of this regulation in its application to payments of taxable incapacity benefit).
Cross references—See the Income Tax (PAYE) Regulations, SI 2003/2682 reg 34 (this regulation does not apply to cases where SI 2003/2682 regs 34, 35 apply).

Cumulative basis: subsidiary PAYE income of employee paid weekly or at greater intervals

25—(1) This regulation applies if—

(*a*) an employee's main relevant payments are normally made at regular intervals of a week or more,
(*b*) the employee's code is used on the cumulative basis, and
(*c*) the employer makes a payment in respect of overtime or other extra earnings (the "extra payment").

(2) For the purposes of calculating the deduction or repayment of tax, the extra payment is treated as made on the same date as that on which the main relevant payment in the payment period is due to be paid or is due to be treated as paid by regulation 24 (employee not paid weekly or monthly).

(3) But paragraph (4) applies if the extra payment is actually made before the date on which the main relevant payment in the payment period is due to be paid (disregarding the effects of regulation 24).

(4) A repayment which would (but for this paragraph) be due under regulation 23(6) on making the extra payment must not be paid to the employee, but must instead be added to the previous total tax (as defined by regulation 23(8)) on making the next relevant payment.

(5) This regulation does not apply if the extra payment is made in a short payment period (but regulation 31 applies instead if that period contains an extra pay day).

(6) "Payment period"—

(*a*) in the case of an employee normally paid weekly, means a tax week,
(*b*) in the case of an employee normally paid monthly, means a tax month,
(*c*) in the case of an employee normally paid at other regular intervals, has the meaning given in paragraph (7).

(7) In the case mentioned in paragraph (6)(*c*)—

(*a*) the first payment period in a tax year starts on 6th April and finishes at the end of the employee's normal regular payment interval, and
(*b*) subsequent payment periods in the tax year start the day after the end of the previous payment period and finish—

(i) at the end of the employee's normal regular payment interval, or
(ii) on 5th April (if earlier).

(8) ''Short payment period'' means the last payment period in a tax year if, because of paragraph (7)(*b*)(ii), it is shorter than the previous payment periods.

(9) ''Extra pay day'' has the meaning given in regulation 31(4).

Commentary—*Simon's Direct Tax Service* **E4.1147.**
Derivation—The Income Tax (Employments) Regulations, SI 1993/744 reg 19.
Modifications—See the Income Tax (PAYE) Regulations, SI 2003/2682 reg 174 (modification of this regulation in its application to payments of taxable incapacity benefit).
Cross references—See the Income Tax (PAYE) Regulations, SI 2003/2682 reg 11 (this regulation not to apply to pension payers or pensioners in their capacity as such).
SI 2003/2682 reg 34 (this regulation does not apply to cases where SI 2003/2682 regs 34, 35 apply).

THE NON-CUMULATIVE BASIS

The non-cumulative basis

26—(1) An employer must deduct tax in accordance with regulation 27 (the non-cumulative basis) from any relevant payment made to an employee if—

(*a*) the Inland Revenue direct, or
(*b*) these Regulations provide,

that the non-cumulative basis is to apply.

(2) If this regulation applies then regulation 22 (cumulative basis) does not apply.

Commentary—*Simon's Direct Tax Service* **E4.1136.**
Derivation—The Income Tax (Employments) Regulations, SI 1993/744 reg 17(1), (2).
Modifications—See the Income Tax (PAYE) Regulations, SI 2003/2682 reg 174 (modification of this regulation in its application to payments of taxable incapacity benefit).
Cross references—SI 2003/2682 reg 32 (if an employee's code is the higher rate code, the employer must deduct tax at the higher rate, and this regulation and SI 2003/2682 reg 22 do not apply).
SI 2003/2682 reg 34 (this regulation does not apply to cases where SI 2003/2682 regs 34, 35 apply).
SI 2003/2682 reg 37 (PAYE income paid after employment ceased: this regulation not to apply)

Non-cumulative basis: general rule for deductions

27—(1) On making a relevant payment, the employer must deduct the amount of tax which would have been deductible in accordance with the appropriate tax tables, by reference to the employee's code, if the payment had been made on the first day of the tax year.

(2) This is subject to—

regulation 28	Modification of general rule
regulation 29	Aggregation of payments.

Commentary—*Simon's Direct Tax Service* **E4.1136, 1151, 1153.**
Derivation—The Income Tax (Employments) Regulations, SI 1993/744 reg 17(2).
Modifications—See the Income Tax (PAYE) Regulations, SI 2003/2682 reg 174 (modification of this regulation in its application to payments of taxable incapacity benefit).
Cross references—See the Income Tax (PAYE) Regulations, SI 2003/2682 reg 34 (this regulation does not apply to cases where SI 2003/2682 regs 34, 35 apply).
SI 2003/2682 reg 37 (PAYE income paid after employment ceased: this regulation not to apply)

Non-cumulative basis: modification of general rule

28—(1) Paragraphs (2) to (5) modify the general rule in regulation 27(1) (the non-cumulative basis) in certain circumstances.

(2) If regulation 30 (employee not paid weekly or monthly) applies to the employee's main relevant payments, the employer must deduct from a relevant payment the amount of tax which would have been deductible, by reference to the employee's code, if the payment (whether or not it is a main relevant payment) had been made on the date given by that regulation.

(3) If the employer does not normally make relevant payments to the employee at regular intervals, the employer must deduct from a relevant payment the amount of tax which would have been deductible, by reference to the employee's code—

(*a*) if the payment is the first payment in the tax year, on the date it is made, or
(*b*) in any other case, on the date found by counting forward *x* days starting on 5th April, where *x* is the number of days found by starting with the date of the previous relevant payment and counting forward to the date of the payment in question.

(4) But if two or more relevant payments are made in the same tax week, the employer must deduct from the second or subsequent relevant payment the amount of tax which (subject to regulation 29(5)) would have been deductible, by reference to the employee's code, if that payment were made at the date given by paragraph (3) for the first payment.

(5) If the employee's code is a K code, the deduction is not to exceed the overriding limit, subject to regulation 62(6) (notional payments).

Derivation—The Income Tax (Employments) Regulations, SI 1993/744 regs 14(2), 17(2), 18.
Modifications—See the Income Tax (PAYE) Regulations, SI 2003/2682 reg 174 (modification of this regulation in its application to payments of taxable incapacity benefit).
Cross references—See the Income Tax (PAYE) Regulations, SI 2003/2682 reg 34 (this regulation does not apply to cases where SI 2003/2682 regs 34, 35 apply).

Non-cumulative basis: aggregation of payments

29—(1) Paragraph (2) applies if—

(*a*) relevant payments are normally made to an employee at regular intervals of a week or more, and

(*b*) the employee's code is used on the non-cumulative basis.

(2) If the relevant payment is the second or subsequent relevant payment made to the employee during the payment period (as defined by regulation 25(6)), the amount of tax to be deducted must be—

(*a*) calculated by reference to the aggregate of the relevant payments made to the employee during the payment period (as defined by regulation 25(6)),

(*b*) increased by any tax not deducted because of the overriding limit when the previous relevant payment in that payment period was made to the employee, and

(*c*) reduced by the amount of tax calculated when the employer made the previous relevant payment in that payment period.

(3) But, for the purposes of the aggregate, any effects of regulation 30(2) (regular payments treated as made at later date) must be disregarded.

(4) Paragraph (5) applies if relevant payments to an employee—

(*a*) are normally made at regular intervals of less than a week, or

(*b*) are made at irregular intervals of less than a week.

(5) If the relevant payment is the second or subsequent relevant payment made to the employee during a tax week, the amount of tax to be deducted must be—

(*a*) calculated by reference to the aggregate of the relevant payments made to the employee in the tax week,

(*b*) increased by any tax not deducted because of the overriding limit when the previous relevant payment in that tax week was made to the employee, and

(*c*) reduced by the amount of tax calculated when the employer made the previous relevant payment in that tax week.

Commentary—*Simon's Direct Tax Service* **E4.1151.**
Derivation—The Income Tax (Employments) Regulations, SI 1993/744 regs 14(2), 21.
Modifications—See the Income Tax (PAYE) Regulations, SI 2003/2682 reg 174 (modification of this regulation in its application to payments of taxable incapacity benefit).
Cross references—See the Income Tax (PAYE) Regulations, SI 2003/2682 reg 34 (this regulation does not apply to cases where SI 2003/2682 regs 34, 35 apply).

Non-cumulative basis: employee not paid weekly or monthly

30—(1) This regulation applies if—

(*a*) an employer normally makes main relevant payments to an employee at regular intervals which are longer than a week, other than monthly, and

(*b*) the employee's code is used on the non-cumulative basis.

(2) Each main relevant payment in a tax year is treated for the purposes of calculating the deduction of tax as having been made at the end the period which—

(*a*) starts on 6th April, and

(*b*) finishes at the end of the employee's regular payment interval.

(3) If the employee's main relevant payments are normally made at regular intervals which are longer than a year, any such payment in a tax year is treated, for the purposes of calculating the deduction of tax, as made on 5th April in that tax year.

(4) But, in every case, the employer must record the actual date of every payment in the deductions working sheet.

Derivation—The Income Tax (Employments) Regulations, SI 1993/744 reg 18.
Modifications—See the Income Tax (PAYE) Regulations, SI 2003/2682 reg 174 (modification of this regulation in its application to payments of taxable incapacity benefit).
Cross references—See the Income Tax (PAYE) Regulations, SI 2003/2682 reg 34 (this regulation does not apply to cases where SI 2003/2682 regs 34, 35 apply).

Payments in short payment periods

31—(1) An employer must deduct tax on the non-cumulative basis from any relevant payment made to an employee in a short payment period which includes an extra pay day, even if the employee's code is normally used on the cumulative basis.

(2) Paragraph (1) does not apply if the employee's code is the basic rate code.

(3) If—

(*a*) the employee's total payments to date do not exceed the employee's total free pay to date, and

(*b*) the employee's code is normally used on the cumulative basis,

the employer must not deduct any tax from relevant payments made in a short payment period which includes an extra pay day.

(4) "Extra pay day" means the last day in a tax year on which a main relevant payment is due to be made to an employee if—

(*a*) the employee's main relevant payments are normally made weekly or at greater intervals which results in the number of pay days varying from tax year to tax year (solely because of the number of days in a calendar year), and

(*b*) the day falls in a short payment period.

(5) "Short payment period" has the meaning given in regulation 25(8).

Commentary—*Simon's Direct Tax Service* **E4.1152.**
Derivation—The Income Tax (Employments) Regulations, SI 1993/744 reg 17(1).
Modifications—See the Income Tax (PAYE) Regulations, SI 2003/2682 reg 174 (modification of this regulation in its application to payments of taxable incapacity benefit).
Cross references—See the Income Tax (PAYE) Regulations, SI 2003/2682 reg 24(6) (SI 2003/2682 reg 24 not to apply where a payment falls within para (1) above).
SI 2003/2682 reg 34 (this regulation does not apply to cases where SI 2003/2682 regs 34, 35 apply).

HIGHER RATE AND NIL TAX CODES

Higher rate code: deductions

32 If an employee's code is the higher rate code the employer must deduct tax at the higher rate, and regulations 22 and 26 (cumulative and non-cumulative basis) do not apply.

Commentary—*Simon's Direct Tax Service* **E4.1153.**
Derivation—The Income Tax (Employments) Regulations, SI 1993/744 reg 16(1), (2).
Cross references—See the Income Tax (PAYE) Regulations, SI 2003/2682 reg 34 (this regulation does not apply to cases where SI 2003/2682 regs 34, 35 apply).

Nil tax code: no deductions or repayments

33—(1) If an employee's code is the nil tax code the employer must not deduct or repay any tax, and so regulation 22 (cumulative basis) does not apply.

(2) But—

(*a*) if the nil tax code is an amended code, and

(*b*) the Inland Revenue so direct,

regulation 22 applies to the next relevant payment the employer makes in the same tax year, and the employer must make any repayment of tax due.

Commentary—*Simon's Direct Tax Service* **E4.1153.**
Derivation—The Income Tax (Employments) Regulations, SI 1993/744 reg 16(1), (3).
Modifications—See the Income Tax (PAYE) Regulations, SI 2003/2682 reg 174 (modification of this regulation in its application to payments of taxable incapacity benefit).
Cross references—See the Income Tax (PAYE) Regulations, SI 2003/2682 reg 34 (this regulation does not apply to cases where SI 2003/2682 regs 34, 35 apply).

SIMPLIFIED DEDUCTION SCHEME

Simplified deduction scheme for personal employees

34—(1) The Inland Revenue may authorise the employer of a personal employee to deduct tax from each relevant payment made to the employee by reference to the appropriate taxable payments in the simplified tax tables.

(2) The amount of tax to be deducted must be—

(*a*) calculated by reference to the aggregate of the relevant payments made to the authorised personal employee during the payment period, and

(*b*) reduced by the amount of tax calculated, by reference to that aggregate, when the employer made the previous relevant payment in the same payment period.

(3) In this regulation—

"payment period" means the interval for which free pay is calculated shown on the deductions working sheet issued in accordance with regulation 35(3);

"personal employee" means—

(*a*) a person employed at the employer's home to provide domestic or personal services for the employer or the employer's family, or

(*b*) a person employed to assist the employer with any business, profession or course of study which, solely because of any physical or mental disability, the employer would not be able to carry on without the assistance of the personal employee;

and "authorised personal employee" means a personal employee in respect of whom an authorisation under paragraph (1) is in force;

"simplified tax tables" means the parts of the tax tables which are prepared by the Board of Inland Revenue for use under this regulation.

(4) The following regulations do not apply to cases in which this regulation and regulation 35 apply—

regulation 15	flat rate codes
regulation 16	continued application of employee's code

regulation 21	deduction and repayment of tax by reference to employee's code
regulations 22 to 25	Cumulative basis
regulations 26 to 31	non-cumulative basis
regulations 32 and 33	higher rate and nil tax codes
regulation 36	cessation of employment: Form P45
regulations 42 to 45	employer to complete Form P45
regulation 55	PAYE pension income paid by former employer
regulation 66	Deductions working sheets.

Commentary—*Simon's Direct Tax Service* **E4.11109.**
Derivation—The Income Tax (Employments) Regulations, SI 1993/744 regs 2(1), 14(2), 20(1), (2), (4), 21.
Cross references—See the Income Tax (PAYE) Regulations, SI 2003/2682 reg 10 (this regulation not to apply to agencies or agency workers in their capacity as such).
SI 2003/2682 reg 11 (this regulation not to apply to pension payers or pensioners in their capacity as such).
SI 2003/2682 reg 12 (this regulation not to apply to other payers or other payees in their capacity as such).

Simplified deduction schemes: records

35—(1) The employer must maintain the following records in relation to an authorised personal employee.

(2) The records are—

(*a*) the date of each relevant payment,
(*b*) the amount of the relevant payment,
(*c*) the amount of the free pay,
(*d*) the amount of the taxable payments, and
(*e*) the amount of tax, if any, deducted on making the relevant payment, or to be deducted or accounted for under regulation 62(4) or (5) (notional payments).

(3) The employer must maintain the records in a deductions working sheet which has been issued by the Inland Revenue showing the code for use by the employer in respect of the employee for the tax year.

(4) On ceasing to employ an authorised personal employee, the employer must return the completed deductions working sheet in respect of that employee to the Inland Revenue.

(5) Before 20th May following the end of a tax year, an employer who, at the end of that tax year, was employing one or more authorised personal employees must send to the Inland Revenue—

(*a*) the completed deductions working sheets in respect of those employees, and
(*b*) a return which complies with paragraph (6).

(6) The employer must declare and certify in the return—

(*a*) how many deductions working sheets are being sent,
(*b*) that those are all the deductions working sheets which have been issued to the employer and not already returned to the Inland Revenue, and
(*c*) that the information contained in the deductions working sheets is fully and truly stated to the best of the employer's knowledge and belief.

(7) The return is treated for the purposes of these Regulations as the return required by regulation 73(1) (annual return of relevant payments liable to deduction of tax).

(8) "Personal employee" and "authorised personal employee" have the same meaning as in regulation 34.

Commentary—*Simon's Direct Tax Service* **E4.11109.**
Derivation—The Income Tax (Employments) Regulations, SI 1993/744 regs 20(2), (3), 43(1), (1A), (2), (3), (4); the Income Tax (Employments) Notional Payments, SI 1994/1212 reg 13(1).
Cross references—See the Income Tax (PAYE) Regulations, SI 2003/2682 reg 10 (this regulation not to apply to agencies or agency workers in their capacity as such).
SI 2003/2682 reg 11 (this regulation not to apply to pension payers or pensioners in their capacity as such).
SI 2003/2682 reg 12 (this regulation not to apply to other payers or other payees in their capacity as such).

Cessation of Employment

Cessation of employment: Form P45

36—(1) On ceasing to employ an employee in respect of whom a code has been issued, the employer must complete Form P45.

(2) The employer must then—

(*a*) send Part 1 of that form to the Inland Revenue, and
(*b*) provide Parts 1A, 2 and 3 to the employee,

on the day on which the employment ceases or, if that is not practicable, without unreasonable delay.

(3) Retirement on pension is not a cessation of employment for the purposes of this regulation if the PAYE pension income is paid by the same employer after retirement.

(4) The information listed in column 1 of Table 2 must, subject to the conditions set out in column 2, be provided in the various Parts of Form P45 as indicated in columns 3 to 5.

TABLE 2
INFORMATION WHICH MUST BE PROVIDED IN FORM P45

1 *Information to be provided*	*2* *Conditions*	*3–5* *Form P45 Part*		
		1	*1A*	*2, 3*
1 the employer's PAYE reference		yes	yes	yes
2 the employee's national insurance number	if known	yes	yes	yes
3 the employee's name		yes	yes	yes
4 the date on which the employment ceased		yes	yes	yes
5 the employee's code or, if more than one, the latest code, issued by the Inland Revenue for the tax year during which the employment ceased		yes	yes	yes
6 whether the employee's code is used on the cumulative basis		yes	yes	yes
7 the tax week or month in which the last relevant payment was made to the employee or, in a case falling within regulation 24, was treated as having been made	if the employee's code is used on the cumulative basis	yes	yes	yes
8 the total payments to date and the corresponding total net tax deducted	if the employee's code is used on the cumulative basis	yes	yes	yes
9 the total payments to date relating to the employment in question and the corresponding total net tax deducted	if the employee's code is used on the cumulative basis, and if different from the information supplied under item 8	yes	yes	no
10 the total payments to date relating to the employment in question and the corresponding total net tax deducted	if the employee's code is not used on the cumulative basis	yes	yes	no
11 the number used by the employer to identify the employee	if any	yes	no	no
12 the department or branch in which the employee was employed	if any	yes	no	no
13 the employee's address	if known	yes	no	no
14 the employer's name		yes	yes	no
15 the employer's address		yes	yes	no
16 the date the Form is completed		yes	yes	no

(5) This regulation is subject to regulations 38, 39 and 180 (death of employee etc).

Commentary—*Simon's Direct Tax Service* **E4.1166.**
Derivation—The Income Tax (Employments) Regulations, SI 1993/744 reg 23(1)–(3).
Modifications—See the Income Tax (PAYE) Regulations, SI 2003/2682 reg 174 (modification of this regulation in its application to payments of taxable incapacity benefit).
Cross references—See the Income Tax (PAYE) Regulations, SI 2003/2682 reg 10 (when an agency is treated as ceasing to employ an agency worker).
SI 2003/2682 reg 34 (this regulation does not apply to cases where SI 2003/2682 regs 34, 35 apply).

PAYE income paid after employment ceased

37—(1) This regulation applies if a relevant payment is made to an employee after the employment has ceased—

(*a*) by the former employer in respect of the former employment, or
(*b*) by any other person in respect of an obligation of the former employer,

and the payment has not been included in Form P45.

(2) The person making the payment must deduct tax at the basic rate in force for the tax year in which the payment is made.

(3) But—

(*a*) the payment does not affect the cessation of employment, and
(*b*) the provisions listed in paragraph (4) do not apply.

(4) The provisions are—

regulation 21	Deduction and repayment of tax by reference to employee's code
regulations 22 and 23	Cumulative basis
regulations 26 and 27	non-cumulative basis
Chapters 2 and 3 of this Part	new employees and new pensioners: Forms P45 and P46.

(5) The person making the payment must record the following information in a deductions working sheet (which the person must prepare for the purpose if one has not already been prepared for that tax year).

(6) The information is—

(*a*) the date of the payment,
(*b*) the amount of the relevant payment, and
(*c*) the amount of tax deducted on making the payment, or to be deducted or accounted for under regulation 62(4) or (5) (notional payments).

(7) The person making the payment must also notify the employee of the information mentioned in paragraph (6) without unreasonable delay.

Commentary—*Simon's Direct Tax Service* **E4.1167.**
Derivation—The Income Tax (Employments) Regulations, SI 1993/744 reg 24; the Income Tax (Employments) (Notional Payments) Payments, SI 1994/1212 reg 13(1).
Cross references—See the Income Tax (PAYE) Regulations, SI 2003/2682 reg 10 (when an agency is treated as ceasing to employ an agency worker).

Death of employee

38—(1) On the death of an employee (other than a pensioner) in respect of whom a code has been issued by the Inland Revenue, the employer must—

(*a*) complete Form P45 indicating in Part 1 that the employee has died, and
(*b*) send it to the Inland Revenue.

(2) The employer must comply with paragraph (1)—

(*a*) on the day on which the employer learns of the employee's death, or
(*b*) if that is not practicable, without unreasonable delay.

(3) The employer must, on making a relevant payment after learning of the employee's death but before completing Form P45, deduct or repay tax as if the deceased employee were still alive and employed by the employer at the date of the payment.

(4) Regulation 37(2) to (6) applies to any relevant payment which—

(*a*) is made in respect of the employee's employment after the date of the employee's death, and
(*b*) is not included in Form P45.

Commentary—*Simon's Direct Tax Service* **E4.1168.**
Derivation—The Income Tax (Employments) Regulations, SI 1993/744 reg 27.
Cross references—See the Income Tax (PAYE) Regulations, SI 2003/2682 reg 11 (this regulation not to apply to pension payers or pensioners in their capacity as such).

Death of pensioner

39—(1) On the death of a pensioner in respect of whom a code has been issued by the Inland Revenue, the pension payer must—

(*a*) complete Form P45 indicating in Part 1 that the pensioner has died, and
(*b*) send it to the Inland Revenue.

(2) The pension payer must comply with paragraph (1)—

(*a*) on the day on which the pension payer learns of the pensioner's death, or
(*b*) if that is not practicable, without unreasonable delay.

(3) Paragraph (4) applies if the pension payer makes any relevant pension payments after the date of the pensioner's death—

(*a*) before completing Form P45, or

(*b*) after completing Form P45 but during the tax year in which the pensioner died.

(4) The pension payer must, on making any such payment, deduct or repay tax as if the deceased pensioner were still alive and in receipt of a pension at the date of the payment.

(5) Regulation 37(2) to (6) applies to any relevant pension payment which—

(*a*) is made in a tax year following the tax year in which the pensioner died, and

(*b*) is not included in Form P45.

Commentary—*Simon's Direct Tax Service* **E4.1168.**
Derivation—The Income Tax (Employments) Regulations, SI 1993/744 reg 27.

Employee's duty to provide Form P45

Duty of employee to give new employer Form P45

40—(1) An employee who has Parts 2 and 3 of Form P45 must give them to the new employer on commencing a new employment.

(2) If an employee receives Parts 2 and 3 of Form P45 after commencing a new employment, the employee must immediately give them to the new employer.

(3) But paragraph (4) applies if an employee objects to the disclosure of the total payments to date to the new employer.

(4) The employee may, instead of complying with paragraph (1) or (2), send Parts 2 and 3 of Form P45 to the Inland Revenue before commencing the new employment or as soon as the employee receives Form P45 (as the case may be).

(5) The Inland Revenue—

(*a*) must then issue a code in respect of the employee to the new employer, and

(*b*) may direct that the non-cumulative basis is to apply to all relevant payments which the new employer makes to the employee.

Commentary—*Simon's Direct Tax Service* **E4.1166, 1170.**
Derivation—The Income Tax (Employments) Regulations, SI 1993/744 reg 25(1), (11).

CHAPTER 2

NEW EMPLOYEES (OTHER THAN PENSIONERS): FORMS P45 AND P46

Cross references—See the Income Tax (PAYE) Regulations, SI 2003/2682 reg 11 (this Chapter not to apply to pension payers or pensioners in their capacity as such).
SI 2003/2682 reg 37 (PAYE income paid after employment ceased: this Chapter not to apply).

Scope of Chapter 2

41 This Chapter sets out the procedure to be followed for deductions and repayments (Form P45 and P46 procedure) in cases to which Chapter 3 (new pensioners: Forms P45 and P46) does not apply (see regulation 54).

Procedure if employer receives Form P45

42—(1) This regulation applies—

(*a*) if an employee gives Parts 2 and 3 of Form P45 to the employer on commencing employment, and

(*b*) in the circumstances mentioned in regulation 51(2) (late presentation of Form P45: before employer required to send Form P46).

(2) The new employer must prepare a deductions working sheet and record on it the following information shown in Parts 2 and 3 of Form P45—

(*a*) the employee's name,

(*b*) the employee's national insurance number.

(3) If Parts 2 and 3 of Form P45 show that the earlier employment ended in the current tax year, the new employer must comply with regulation 43.

(4) If—

(*a*) Parts 2 and 3 of Form P45 show that the earlier employment ended in the previous tax year, and

(*b*) the new employment commences on or before 24th May,

the new employer must comply with regulation 44.

(5) If—

(*a*) Parts 2 and 3 of Form P45 show that the employment ended in the previous tax year, and

(*b*) the employment commences after 24th May,

the new employer must comply with regulation 45.

(6) If Parts 2 and 3 of Form P45 show that the employment ended in any earlier tax year, the new employer must comply with regulation 45.

(7) In all cases the new employer must then insert in Part 3 of Form P45—

(*a*) the employer's employer reference,
(*b*) the date on which the new employment commenced,
(*c*) any number used to identify the employee,
(*d*) the employee's code in use by the employer if different from the code shown in Parts 2 and 3 of Form P45,
(*e*) any figure recorded in accordance with paragraph (5)(*c*) or (6)(*c*) of regulation 43 (Form P45 for current tax year), if different from the total tax to date shown on Parts 2 and 3 of Form P45,
(*f*) the employee's address,
(*g*) the employee's date of birth, if known,
(*h*) the employee's job title or description,
(*i*) the employer's name, and
(*j*) the employer's address.

(8) The employer must then send Part 3 of Form P45 to the employer's Inland Revenue office.

Commentary—*Simon's Direct Tax Service* **E4.1170.**
Derivation—The Income Tax (Employments) Regulations, SI 1993/744 reg 25(1)–(3), (8), 34(2).
Cross references—See the Income Tax (PAYE) Regulations, SI 2003/2682 reg 34 (this regulation does not apply to cases where SI 2003/2682 regs 34, 35 apply).

Form P45 for current tax year

43—(1) The new employer must record in the deductions working sheet the code shown in Parts 2 and 3 of Form P45 as the employee's code.

(2) Paragraphs (3) to (10) apply if Parts 2 and 3 of Form P45 show that the cumulative basis was used.

(3) The employer must record in the deductions working sheet the total payments to date (if any) shown in Parts 2 and 3 of Form P45.

(4) The employer must record in the deductions working sheet the following additional information, or keep such records as enable its production.

(5) If the code shown in Parts 2 and 3 of Form P45 is a K code, the additional information is—

(*a*) the total additional pay to date,
(*b*) the total taxable payments to date, and
(*c*) the lower of the total tax to date as at the week or month shown in Parts 2 and 3 of Form P45 and the total net tax deducted shown in it.

(6) In any other case, the additional information is—

(*a*) the total free pay to date,
(*b*) the total taxable payments to date, and
(*c*) the corresponding total tax to date as at the week or month shown in Parts 2 and 3 of Form P45.

(7) The amounts required by paragraphs (5)(*a*) and (*b*) and (6)(*a*) and (*b*) must be arrived at by the employer by reference to the information shown in Parts 2 and 3 of Form P45.

(8) On making any relevant payment to the employee, the employer must deduct or repay tax by reference to the employee's code on the cumulative basis.

(9) For the purposes of—

(*a*) paragraph (8), and
(*b*) item 8 of Table 2 in regulation 36(4) (Form P45), and
(*c*) regulation 55(4)(*f*) (retirement statement),

the total payments to date recorded in the deductions working sheet in accordance with paragraph (3), and the figure recorded in accordance with paragraph (5)(*c*) or (6)(*c*) must be treated as if they were relevant payments made to the employee by, and tax deducted by, the new employer.

(10) For the purposes of regulation 23(8) (cumulative basis: meaning of previous total tax to date) the figure recorded in accordance with paragraph (5)(*c*) or (6)(*c*) must be treated as the previous total tax to date when the employer next makes a relevant payment to the employee.

(11) If Parts 2 and 3 of Form P45 show that the non-cumulative basis has been used, on making any relevant payment to the employee the employer must, subject to regulation 32 (higher rate code: deductions), deduct or repay tax by reference to the employee's code on the non-cumulative basis.

(12) The receipt by the employer of Parts 2 and 3 of Form P45 is treated as the issue by the Inland Revenue of the code shown in Parts 2 and 3 of Form P45 as the code for use in respect of the employee.

Commentary—*Simon's Direct Tax Service* **E4.1170.**
Derivation—The Income Tax (Employments) Regulations, SI 1993/744 regs 25(3), (4), (5), (7), (9), 27(1), 34(2).
Cross references—See the Income Tax (PAYE) Regulations, SI 2003/2682 reg 34 (this regulation does not apply to cases where SI 2003/2682 regs 34, 35 apply).

Form P45 for previous tax year: employment starting on or before 24th May

44—(1) The new employer must—

(*a*) record in the deductions working sheet the code shown in Parts 2 and 3 of Form P45 as the employee's code, and

(*b*) deduct or repay tax by reference to that code on the cumulative basis, subject to regulation 32 (higher rate code: deductions).

(2) The receipt by the employer of Parts 2 and 3 of Form P45 is treated as the issue by the Inland Revenue of the code shown in Parts 2 and 3 of Form P45 as the code for use in respect of the employee.

Commentary—*Simon's Direct Tax Service* **E4.1170.**
Derivation—The Income Tax (Employments) Regulations, SI 1993/744 reg 25(8), (9).
Cross references—See the Income Tax (PAYE) Regulations, SI 2003/2682 reg 34 (this regulation does not apply to cases where SI 2003/2682 regs 34, 35 apply).

Other Forms P45

45—(1) The new employer must—

(*a*) record in the deductions working sheet the emergency code as the employee's code, and

(*b*) deduct tax from each relevant payment using the emergency code on the non-cumulative basis.

(2) The emergency code is treated as having been issued to the employer by the Inland Revenue as the code for use in respect of the employee.

Commentary—*Simon's Direct Tax Service* **E4.1170.**
Derivation—The Income Tax (Employments) Regulations, SI 1993/744 regs 25(8), 32.
Cross references—See the Income Tax (PAYE) Regulations, SI 2003/2682 reg 34 (this regulation does not apply to cases where SI 2003/2682 regs 34, 35 apply).

Form P46 where employer does not receive Form P45 and code not known

46—(1) This regulation applies if—

(*a*) an employee commences employment without giving the employer Parts 2 and 3 of Form P45, and

(*b*) a code in respect of the employee has not otherwise been issued to the employer.

(2) The employee must indicate in Form P46 which (if any) of the following statements apply—

Statement A: that the employee is taking up employment for the first time after a period of full-time education, and has not since received taxable jobseeker's allowance or taxable incapacity benefit (as defined in Part 8),

Statement B: that this is the employee's only or main employment (disregarding any self-employment),

Statement C: that the employee is also receiving a pension,

and must sign and date the form.

(3) The employer must provide the following information in the Form P46—

(*a*) the employee's national insurance number, if known,

(*b*) the employee's name,

(*c*) the employee's address,

(*d*) the employee's date of birth, if known,

(*e*) the employee's sex,

(*f*) any number used by the employer to identify the employee,

(*g*) the employee's job title,

(*h*) the date on which the employment commenced,

(*i*) the employee's code and whether it is being used on the cumulative basis,

(*j*) the employer's PAYE reference,

(*k*) the employer's name,

(*l*) the employer's address, and

(*m*) the date the form was completed.

(4) The employer must keep the Form P46 until required to send it to the Inland Revenue in accordance with regulations 47 to 49.

(5) Before sending the Form P46, the employer must indicate in the Form which code is being used in respect of the employee and whether it is being used on the non-cumulative basis.

(6) For the purposes of paragraph (1)(*b*), the employer must ignore any code issued to the employer in respect of an employee's earlier employment which has ceased.

(7) This regulation ceases to apply in the circumstances mentioned in regulation 51(2) (late presentation of Form P45: before employer required to send Form P46).

Commentary—*Simon's Direct Tax Service* **E4.1171.**
Derivation—The Income Tax (Employments) Regulations, SI 1993/744 regs 28(1), (1A), (1B), (4), 29, 30.

Cross references—See the Income Tax (PAYE) Regulations, SI 2003/2682 reg 10 (when an agency is treated as ceasing to employ an agency worker for the purposes of para (6) above).
SI 2003/2682 reg 50 (procedure in Form P46 cases where code treated as issued by the Revenue: this does not apply for the purposes of this regulation).

Procedure in Form P46 cases: former full-time students

47—(1) This regulation applies in the case of an employee who indicates in the Form P46 that—

(*a*) only Statement A applies, or
(*b*) only Statements A and B apply.

(2) On making the first relevant payment which exceeds the PAYE threshold to the employee, the employer must—

(*a*) send the Inland Revenue the completed Form P46,
(*b*) prepare a deductions working sheet and enter the total payments to date, and
(*c*) deduct tax on the cumulative basis using the emergency code.

(3) On making any subsequent relevant payment before the Inland Revenue issue a code for use in respect of the employee, the employer must continue to deduct or repay tax on the cumulative basis using the emergency code.

Commentary—*Simon's Direct Tax Service* **E4.1153, 1171.**
Derivation—The Income Tax (Employments) Regulations, SI 1993/744 regs 28(1), (1A), 29.
Cross references—See the Income Tax (PAYE) Regulations, SI 2003/2682 reg 50 (procedure in Form P46 cases where code treated as issued by the Revenue: this does not apply for the purposes of this regulation).

Procedure in Form P46 cases: employee taking up only or main employment

48—(1) This regulation applies in the case of an employee who indicates in the Form P46 that only Statement B applies.

(2) On making the first relevant payment which exceeds the PAYE threshold to the employee, the employer must—

(*a*) send the Inland Revenue the completed Form P46,
(*b*) prepare a deductions working sheet and enter the total payments to date, and
(*c*) deduct tax on the non-cumulative basis using the emergency code.

(3) On making any subsequent relevant payment before the employee's code is issued, the employer must continue to deduct or repay tax on the non-cumulative basis using the emergency code.

Commentary—*Simon's Direct Tax* Service **E4.1153, 1171.**
Derivation—The Income Tax (Employments) Regulations, SI 1993/744 regs 28(1), (1A), 30(1)–(3).
Cross references—See the Income Tax (PAYE) Regulations, SI 2003/2682 reg 50 (procedure in Form P46 cases where code treated as issued by the Revenue: this does not apply for the purposes of this regulation).

Procedure in Form P46 cases: other new employees

49—(1) This regulation applies in any case which is not dealt with by regulation 47 or 48 which concerns an employee to whom regulation 46(1) applies.

(2) On making the first relevant payment to the employee, the employer must—

(*a*) send the Inland Revenue the completed Form P46,
(*b*) prepare a deductions working sheet and enter both the total payments to date and the total tax to date before the first payment as nil,
(*c*) deduct tax on the cumulative basis using the basic rate code.

(3) On making any subsequent relevant payment before the employee's code is issued, the employer must continue to deduct tax on the cumulative basis using the basic rate code.

Commentary—Simon's Direct Tax Service **E4.1171.**
Derivation—The Income Tax (Employments) Regulations, SI 1993/744 regs 28(1), (1A), 31(1), (2), (4).
Cross references—See the Income Tax (PAYE) Regulations, SI 2003/2682 reg 50 (procedure in Form P46 cases where code treated as issued by the Revenue: this does not apply for the purposes of this regulation).

Procedure in Form P46 cases: code treated as issued by Inland Revenue

50—(1) The emergency code or the basic rate code used by the employer in accordance with regulations 47 to 49 is treated, for the purposes of Parts 2 to 4 (codes; deduction and repayment of tax; payments, returns and information) as having been issued by the Inland Revenue as the code for use in respect of the employee.

(2) This does not apply for the purposes of regulation 18 (objections and appeals) and regulations 46 to 49 and 51 to 53 (Form P46 procedure and late presentation of Form P45).

Commentary—Simon's Direct Tax Service **E4.1172.**
Derivation—The Income Tax (Employments) Regulations, SI 1993/744 reg 32

Late presentation of Form P45

51—(1) This regulation applies if an employee gives Parts 2 and 3 of Form P45 to the employer after commencing employment.

(2) If the employee gives Parts 2 and 3 of Form P45 to the employer before the employer is required to send the Form P46 to the Inland Revenue under regulation 47 to 49, regulation 42 (procedure if employer receives Form P45) applies.

(3) If the employee gives Parts 2 and 3 of Form P45 to the employer—

(*a*) after the Form P46 is required to have been sent to the Inland Revenue, but
(*b*) before the employee's code has been issued to the employer,

this regulation and regulation 52 (late presentation of Form P45: employer's duties) apply.

(4) If the employee gives Parts 2 and 3 of Form P45 to the employer after the employee's code has been issued to the employer, they must be destroyed.

(5) If Parts 2 and 3 of Form P45 show that the employment ended in the current tax year then, unless the employer has already ceased to employ the employee—

(*a*) the code shown in Parts 2 and 3 of Form P45 is treated as having been issued by the Inland Revenue to the employer on the day the employee gives them to the employer, and
(*b*) the employer must comply with regulation 52.

(6) If Parts 2 and 3 of Form P45 show that the employment ended in the previous tax year and the employee gives them to the employer on or before 24th May then, unless the employer has already ceased to employ the employee—

(*a*) the code shown in Parts 2 and 3 of Form P45 is treated as having been issued by the Inland Revenue to the employer on the day the employee gives them to the employer,
(*b*) the employer must deduct or repay tax by reference to that code using the cumulative basis, subject to regulation 32 (higher rate code: deductions), and
(*c*) the employer must comply with paragraphs (2) and (3) of regulation 52.

(7) Parts 2 and 3 of Form P45 must be destroyed—

(*a*) if they show that the employment ended in the previous tax year and the employee gives them to the employer after 24th May, or
(*b*) if they show that the employment ended in an earlier tax year.

Commentary—Simon's Direct Tax Service **E4.1171**.
Derivation—The Income Tax (Employments) Regulations, SI 1993/744 reg 34(1)–(3).
Cross references—See the Income Tax (PAYE) Regulations, SI 2003/2682 reg 10 (when an agency is treated as ceasing to employ an agency worker for the purposes of para (5)-(7) above).
SI 2003/2682 reg 50 (procedure in Form P46 cases where code treated as issued by the Revenue: this does not apply for the purposes of this regulation).

Late presentation of Form P45: employer's duties

52—(1) This regulation applies in the circumstances mentioned in regulation 51(5); and paragraphs (2) and (3) of this regulation also apply in the circumstances mentioned in regulation 51(6).

(2) The employer must insert in Part 3 of Form P45—

(*a*) the employer's employer reference,
(*b*) the date on which the new employment commenced,
(*c*) any number used to identify the employee,
(*d*) the employee's code in use by the employer if different from the code shown in Parts 2 and 3 of Form P45,
(*e*) if Parts 2 and 3 of the Form P45 show that the cumulative basis has been used, the figure (if any) recorded in accordance with paragraph (7)(*c*) or (8)(*c*) if different from the total tax to date shown on Parts 2 and 3 of Form P45,
(*f*) the employee's address,
(*g*) the employee's date of birth, if known,
(*h*) the employee's job title or description,
(*i*) the employer's name, and
(*j*) the employer's address.

(3) The employer must then send Part 3 of Form P45 to the employer's Inland Revenue office.

(4) The employer must prepare a deductions working sheet (unless the employer has already prepared one) in accordance with the following information shown in Parts 2 and 3 of Form P45—

(*a*) the employee's name,
(*b*) the employee's national insurance number, and
(*c*) the employee's code.

(5) The employer must record in the deductions working sheet the sum of—

(*a*) the total payments to date (if any) shown in Parts 2 and 3 of Form P45, and
(*b*) the relevant payments which have been made by the employer since the employment commenced which have not already been recorded in the deductions working sheet.

(6) If Parts 2 and 3 of Form P45 show that the cumulative basis has been used, the employer must also record the following additional information in the deductions working sheet, or keep such records as enable its production.

(7) If the code shown in Parts 2 and 3 of Form P45 is a K code, the additional information is—

(*a*) the total additional pay to date,
(*b*) the total taxable payments to date, and
(*c*) the lower of the total tax to date as at the week or month shown in Parts 2 and 3 of Form P45 or the total net tax deducted shown in it.

(8) In any other case, the additional information is—

(*a*) the total free pay to date,
(*b*) the total taxable payments to date, and
(*c*) the corresponding total tax to date as at the week or month shown in Parts 2 and 3 of Form P45.

(9) The employer must ascertain the amounts required by paragraphs (7)(*a*) and (*b*) and (8)(*a*) and (*b*) by reference solely to the information shown in Parts 2 and 3 of Form P45.

(10) If Parts 2 and 3 of Form P45 show that the cumulative basis has been used, the employer, on making any subsequent relevant payment to the employee, must deduct or repay tax by reference to the code shown in Parts 2 and 3 of Form P45 on the cumulative basis.

(11) For the purposes of—

(*a*) paragraph (10), and
(*b*) item 8 of Table 2 in regulation 36(4) (Form P45), and
(*c*) regulation 55(4)(*f*) (retirement statement),

the total payments to date recorded in the deductions working sheet in accordance with paragraph (5) and the figure recorded in accordance with paragraph (7)(*c*) or (8)(*c*) must be treated as if they were relevant payments made to the employee by, and tax deducted by, the new employer.

(12) For the purposes of regulation 23(8) (cumulative basis: meaning of previous total tax to date), the figure recorded in accordance with paragraph (7)(*c*) or (8)(*c*) must be added to any actual previous total tax to date, and the total treated as the previous total tax to date when the employer next makes a relevant payment to the employee.

(13) If Parts 2 and 3 of Form P45 show that the non-cumulative basis has been used, on making any relevant payment to the employee, the employer must, subject to regulation 32 (higher rate code: deductions), deduct tax by reference to the code shown in Parts 2 and 3 of Form P45 on the non-cumulative basis.

Commentary—Simon's Direct Tax Service **E4.1171.**
Derivation—The Income Tax (Employments) Regulations, SI 1993/744 regs 25(2), (3), (4), (5), (7), 34(2), (3).
Cross references—See the Income Tax (PAYE) Regulations, SI 2003/2682 reg 50 (procedure in Form P46 cases where code treated as issued by the Revenue: this does not apply for the purposes of this regulation).

Form P46 cases: subsequent procedure on issue of employee's code

53—(1) On making any relevant payment to an employee falling within regulation 47 to 49 (procedure in Form P46 cases) after the Inland Revenue have issued a code to the employer for use in respect of the employee, the employer must deduct or repay tax by reference to that code.

(2) For the purposes of paragraph (1) and regulation 66 (deductions working sheets)—

(*a*) any total payments to date notified to the employer by the Inland Revenue are treated as if they represented relevant payments made by the employer; and
(*b*) the total net tax deducted before the first payment made in accordance with this regulation is taken to be the sum of—
(i) the total net tax deducted, if any, notified to the employer by the Inland Revenue, and
(ii) any tax which the employer was liable to deduct from the employee's relevant payments under regulation 47, 48 or 49.

(3) For the purposes of—

(*a*) item 8 of Table 2 in regulation 36(4) (Form P45), and
(*b*) regulation 55(4)(*f*) (retirement statement),

any total payments to date and total net tax deducted which are notified to the employer by the Inland Revenue must be treated as if they were relevant payments made to the employee by, and tax deducted by, the employer.

(4) If the employee's previous code was used on the cumulative basis, any amount notified to the employer under paragraph (2)(*b*)(i) must be added to the previous total tax to date for the purposes of regulation 23(8) (cumulative basis: meaning of previous total tax to date).

Derivation—The Income Tax (Employments) Regulations, SI 1993/744 reg 33.
Cross references—See the Income Tax (PAYE) Regulations, SI 2003/2682 reg 50 (procedure in Form P46 cases where code treated as issued by the Revenue: this does not apply for the purposes of this regulation).

CHAPTER 3

NEW PENSIONERS: FORMS P45 AND P46

Cross references—See the Income Tax (PAYE) Regulations, SI 2003/2682 reg 37 (PAYE income paid after employment ceased: this Chapter not to apply)

Scope of Chapter 3

54 This Chapter applies (instead of Chapter 2) when a pension starts, if the pension payer will not be making relevant payments other than relevant pension payments to the pensioner.

Commentary—Simon's Direct Tax Service **E4.1175.**

PAYE pension income paid by former employer

55—(1) This regulation applies if the pension payer was, immediately before the pensioner's retirement, the pensioner's employer and so, in accordance with regulation 36(3), no Form P45 was completed.

(2) On making relevant pension payments to the pensioner, the pension payer must deduct tax on the non-cumulative basis, subject to regulation 32 (higher rate code: deductions), for the remainder of the tax year in which the pension starts or until directed otherwise by the Inland Revenue.

(3) Within 14 days after the pensioner's retirement, the pension payer must prepare a retirement statement and—

(*a*) send it to the Inland Revenue, and
(*b*) give a copy to the pensioner.

(4) The retirement statement must contain the following information—

(*a*) the pensioner's name,
(*b*) the pensioner's address, if known,
(*c*) the pensioner's national insurance number, if known,
(*d*) the pension payer's PAYE reference,
(*e*) the date of retirement,
(*f*) the total payments to date at the date of retirement,
(*g*) the total payments to date relating to the employment in question at the date of retirement,
(*h*) the total net tax deducted corresponding to the total payments to date relating to the employment in question,
(*i*) the amount of pension payable and the frequency of the payments,
(*j*) any number used to identify the pensioner,
(*k*) whether the pensioner's code is use on the cumulative basis,
(*l*) the pension payer's name, and
(*m*) the pension payer's address.

(5) Paragraph (4) is subject to regulation 212 (modifications for electronic version of retirement statement delivered to Inland Revenue).

Commentary—Simon's Direct Tax Service **E4.1175.**
Derivation—The Income Tax (Employments) Regulations, SI 1993/744 regs 17, 26(1), (1A), (2).
Modification—See the Income Tax (PAYE) Regulations, SI 2003/2682 reg 212 (modification of this regulation where pensioner's retirement statement delivered by an approved method of electronic communications).
Cross references—See the Income Tax (PAYE) Regulations, SI 2003/2682 reg 34 (this regulation does not apply to cases where SI 2003/2682 regs 34, 35 apply).

PAYE pension income paid by other pension payer

56—(1) This regulation applies if the pensioner gives Parts 2 and 3 of Form P45 to the pension payer when a pension starts.

(2) The pension payer must insert in Part 3 of Form P45—

(*a*) the pensioner's address,
(*b*) any number used to identify the pensioner, and
(*c*) the date on which the pension started.

(3) The pension payer must then send Part 3 of Form P45 to the pension payer's Inland Revenue office.

(4) The receipt by the pension payer of Parts 2 and 3 of Form P45 under paragraph (1) is treated as the issue by the Inland Revenue of the code shown in Parts 2 and 3 of Form P45 as the code for use in respect of the pensioner.

(5) On making relevant pension payments to the pensioner, the pension payer must, subject to regulation 32 (higher rate code: deductions), deduct or repay tax—

(*a*) on the non-cumulative basis, for the remainder of the tax year to which Parts 2 and 3 of Form P45 relate;
(*b*) on the cumulative basis, for subsequent tax years.

(6) Paragraph (5) applies until the pension payer is directed otherwise by the Inland Revenue.

Commentary—Simon's Direct Tax Service **E4.1176.**
Derivation—The Income Tax (Employments) Regulations, SI 1993/744 regs 17(1), 25(2), 26(3).

Information to be provided in Form P46 if code not known: non UK residents

57—(1) This regulation applies if a pension payer pays a pension, which does not arise wholly from an employment carried on abroad, to a pensioner—

(*a*) who is not resident in the United Kingdom,
(*b*) who has not given Parts 2 and 3 of Form P45 to the pension payer, and
(*c*) in respect of whom a code has not otherwise been issued by the Inland Revenue.

(2) On making the first payment which exceeds the PAYE threshold, the pension payer must send to the Inland Revenue the following information in Form P46.

(3) The information is—

(*a*) the pensioner's name,
(*b*) the pensioner's date of birth, if known,
(*c*) the pensioner's sex,
(*d*) the pensioner's address,
(*e*) the pensioner's national insurance number, if known,
(*f*) the date on which the pension started,
(*g*) any number used to identify the pensioner,
(*h*) the pension payer's PAYE reference,
(*i*) the pension payer's name,
(*j*) the pension payer's address, and
(*k*) the date the form was completed.

(4) For the purposes of paragraph (1)(*c*), the pension payer must ignore any code issued to the pension payer in respect of a previous pension of the pensioner which has ended.

Commentary—Simon's Direct Tax Service **E4.1135, 1177.**
Derivation—The Income Tax (Employments) Regulations, SI 1993/744 reg 28(4), (5), (5A), (5B).

Information (Form P46) and procedure if code not known: UK residents

58—(1) This regulation applies if—

(*a*) a pension payer starts to make relevant pension payments to a pensioner,
(*b*) the pensioner is resident in the United Kingdom,
(*c*) the pensioner does not give to the pension payer Parts 2 and 3 of Form P45, and
(*d*) a code in respect of the pensioner has not otherwise been issued to the pension payer.

(2) On making any relevant pension payments to the pensioner before the Inland Revenue issue a code for use in respect of the pensioner, the pension payer must deduct tax on the non-cumulative basis applying the emergency code.

(3) The pension payer must send the Inland Revenue the following information in Form P46.

(4) The information is—

(*a*) the pensioner's name,
(*b*) the pensioner's date of birth, if known,
(*c*) the pensioner's sex,
(*d*) the pensioner's address,
(*e*) the pensioner's national insurance number, if known,
(*f*) the date on which the pension started,
(*g*) any number used to identify the pensioner,
(*h*) the pension payer's name,
(*i*) the pension payer's address,
(*j*) the pension payer's PAYE reference, and
(*k*) the date the form was completed.

(5) The pension payer must also indicate in the Form that the emergency code is being used on the non-cumulative basis.

(6) For the purposes of paragraph (1)(*d*), the pension payer must ignore any code issued to the pension payer in respect of a previous pension of the pensioner which has ended.

Commentary—Simon's Direct Tax Service **E4.1176.**
Derivation—The Income Tax (Employments) Regulations, SI 1993/744 regs 28(1), (1A), (1B), (4), 31(1), (3), (4).

UK resident pensioner's code treated as issued by Inland Revenue

59—(1) The emergency code used by the pension payer in accordance with regulation 58 is treated, for the purposes of Parts 2 to 4 (codes; deduction and repayment of tax; payments, returns and information) as having been issued by the Inland Revenue as the code for use in respect of the pensioner.

(2) This does not apply for the purposes of regulation 18 (objections and appeals) and regulations 58, 60 and 61 (Form P46 procedure, late presentation of Form P45 etc).

Derivation—The Income Tax (Employments) Regulations, SI 1993/744 reg 32.

Late presentation of Form P45

60—(1) Paragraphs (2) to (6) apply if the pensioner gives Parts 2 and 3 of Form P45 to the pension payer after the pension has started but before a code has been issued.

(2) The pension payer must insert in Part 3 of Form P45—

(*a*) the pensioner's address,

(*b*) any number used to identify the pensioner, and

(*c*) the date on which the pension started.

(3) The pension payer must then send Part 3 of Form P45 to the pension payer's Inland Revenue office.

(4) The receipt by the pension payer of Parts 2 and 3 of Form P45 under paragraph (1) is treated, except for the purposes of paragraph (1), as the issue by the Inland Revenue of the code shown in that Form as the pensioner's code.

(5) On making relevant pension payments to the pensioner, the pension payer must, subject to regulation 32 (higher rate code: deductions), deduct or repay tax—

(*a*) on the non-cumulative basis, for the remainder of the tax year to which Parts 2 and 3 of Form P45 relate;

(*b*) on the cumulative basis, for subsequent tax years.

(6) Paragraph (5) applies until the pension payer is directed otherwise by the Inland Revenue.

(7) If Parts 2 and 3 of Form P45 are given to the pension payer after the pension has started and after a code has been issued by the Inland Revenue, they must be destroyed.

Commentary—Simon's Direct Tax Service **E4.1176.**
Derivation—The Income Tax (Employments) Regulations, SI 1993/744 regs 25(2), (5), 34(1), (2), (3).

Subsequent procedure on issue of UK resident pensioner's code

61—(1) On making any relevant pension payment to a pensioner falling within regulation 58 after the Inland Revenue have issued a code to the pension payer for use in respect of the pensioner, the pension payer must deduct or repay tax by reference to that code.

(2) For the purposes of paragraph (1) and regulation 66 (deductions working sheets)—

(*a*) any total payments to date notified to the pension payer by the Inland Revenue are treated as if they represented relevant pension payments made by pension payer; and

(*b*) the total net tax deducted before the first payment made in accordance with this regulation is taken to be the sum of—

(i) the total net tax deducted, if any, notified to the pension payer by the Inland Revenue, and

(ii) any tax which the pension payer was liable to deduct from the pensioner's relevant pension payments under regulation 58.

(3) For the purposes of—

(*a*) item 8 of Table 2 in regulation 36(4) (Form P45), and

(*b*) regulation 55(4)(*f*) (retirement statement),

any total payments to date and total net tax deducted which are which are notified to the employer by the Inland Revenue must be treated as if they were relevant pension payments made to the pensioner by, and tax deducted by, the pension payer.

(4) If the pensioner's previous code was used on the cumulative basis, any amount notified to the pension payer under paragraph (2)(*b*)(i) must be added to the previous total tax to date for the purposes of regulation 23(8) (meaning of previous total tax to date).

Commentary—Simon's Direct Tax Service **E4.1176.**
Derivation—The Income Tax (Employments) Regulations, SI 1993/744 reg 33.

CHAPTER 4

MISCELLANEOUS

Deductions in respect of notional payments

62—(1) This regulation applies if an employer makes a relevant payment which is a notional payment to an employee.

(2) The employer must, so far as possible, deduct tax required to be deducted in respect of a notional payment in accordance with any of the following regulations from any relevant payment or payments which the employer actually makes to the employee at the same time as the notional payment.

(3) The regulations are—

regulations 22 to 25	cumulative basis
regulations 26 to 31	non-cumulative basis
regulation 32	higher rate code: deductions
regulation 34	simplified deduction scheme for personal employees
regulation 37	PAYE income paid after employment ceased.

(4) If the employer cannot deduct the full amount of tax as required by paragraph (2) from another relevant payment made at the same time as the notional payment, the employer must, so far as possible, deduct the tax from any payment or payments which the employer makes later in the same tax period.

SIs

(5) If the relevant payments actually made are insufficient to enable the employer to deduct the full amount of tax due in respect of notional payments, the employer must account to the Board of Inland Revenue for any amount which the employer is unable to deduct.

(6) Regulations 23(5) and 28(5) (deductions on cumulative or non-cumulative basis not to exceed the overriding limit) do not apply to the extent that the tax to be deducted is in respect of a notional payment.

Commentary—Simon's Direct Tax Service **E4.1145.**
Derivation—The Income Tax (Employments) Regulations, SI 1993/744 regs 6(1), 14(2), 24(2).

Repayment during unpaid leave

63—(1) This regulation applies if—

(*a*) an employee is not entitled to receive any relevant payments on a normal pay day because of absence from work,
(*b*) the cumulative basis would have been used in relation to a payment made on that day,
(*c*) the employee does not fall within regulation 64(1) (absence from work due to participation in trade dispute), and
(*d*) the employee, or the employee's authorised representative, makes an application in person to the employer.

(2) The employer must—

(*a*) comply with regulation 23 (cumulative basis: deduction and repayment) and accordingly repay any tax due to the employee, and
(*b*) comply with regulation 66(4) to (6) (completion of deductions working sheet),

as if the pay day were one on which relevant payments of nil had been made.

Commentary—Simon's Direct Tax Service **E4.1161.**
Derivation—The Income Tax (Employments) Regulations, SI 1993/744 reg 35.
Cross references—See the Income Tax (PAYE) Regulations, SI 2003/2682 reg 11 (this regulation not to apply to pension payers or pensioners in their capacity as such).

Trade disputes

64—(1) This regulation applies if an employee—

(*a*) is absent from work because of a trade dispute at the employee's place of work, and
(*b*) is participating or directly interested in the trade dispute.

(2) The employer must—

(*a*) on making any relevant payment, calculate the amount of tax to be deducted or repaid, and
(*b*) comply with paragraphs (5) to (8).

(3) If no relevant payments are to be made on the normal pay day but the employee's code would be used on the cumulative basis if a relevant payment were made on that day, the employer must—

(*a*) calculate, in accordance with regulation 23 (cumulative basis: deduction and repayment) whether any tax is due to be repaid on that day as if it were a day on which relevant payments of nil had been paid, and
(*b*) comply with paragraphs (5) to (8).

(4) Paragraphs (2) and (3) are subject to paragraphs (9) and (10).

(5) The employer—

(*a*) must not repay any tax due to be repaid until the end of the employee's strike action, but
(*b*) must deduct any tax due to be deducted, less any repayment for the tax year which has not been made.

(6) The amount of any repayment—

(*a*) made at the end of the employee's strike action under paragraph (5)(*a*), or
(*b*) set against tax due to be deducted under paragraph (5)(*b*),

must be reduced by any amount previously set off in accordance with paragraph (5)(*b*).

(7) If the absence of an employee extends beyond the end of the tax year, the employer must—

(*a*) before 1st June following the end of the tax year, give notice to the employee of the amount of any repayment of tax for the tax year in question calculated in accordance with paragraph (2) which has not been set off against any tax due to be deducted under paragraph (5)(*b*); and
(*b*) complete the certificate which must be given under regulation 67 (Form P60) and the return which must be sent under regulation 73 (Form P35 and P14) as if that tax had been repaid to the employee.

(8) If the employer has not made any repayment of tax withheld under paragraph (5) within 42 days after the end of the employee's strike action, the employer must instead immediately pay the tax not repaid to the Inland Revenue, and regulation 69(2) (receipt where requested) applies to that payment.

(9) An employee from whom a repayment of tax has been withheld in accordance with paragraph (5) may request a benefit officer to certify that—

(*a*) section 14 of the Jobseekers Act 1995, or

(*b*) in Northern Ireland, article 16 of the Jobseekers (Northern Ireland) Order 1995,

(no allowance to those involved in trade dispute) does not disqualify the employee from receiving jobseeker's allowance, whether or not the employee is in fact entitled to receive jobseeker's allowance.

(10) If a benefit officer certifies in accordance with paragraph (9), the employer must make such repayment to the employee as may be due.

(11) In this regulation—

"benefit officer" means the appropriate officer—

(*a*) of the Department for Work and Pensions or,
(*b*) in Northern Ireland, of the Department for Social Development;

"end of the employee's strike action" means any of the following—

(*a*) the employee is no longer absent from work because of the trade dispute,
(*b*) the employer ceases to employ the employee,
(*c*) the employee has become genuinely employed elsewhere in the occupation which the employee usually follows,
(*d*) the employee has become regularly engaged in some other occupation, or
(*e*) the employee dies;

"jobseeker's allowance" has the same meaning as in regulation 148;
"place of work" has the meaning given in section 14(4) of the Jobseekers Act 1995 or, in Northern Ireland, in article 16(4) of the Jobseekers (Northern Ireland) Order 1995.

Commentary—Simon's Direct Tax Service **E4.1161.**
Derivation—The Income Tax (Employments) Regulations, SI 1993/744 reg 36.
Cross references—See the Income Tax (PAYE) Regulations, SI 2003/2682 reg 11 (this regulation not to apply to pension payers or pensioners in their capacity as such).
SI 2003/2682 reg 12 (this regulation not to apply to other payees in their capacity as such).

Repayment if no longer employed

65—(1) This regulation applies if, in a tax year, a person ("P")—

(*a*) was employed,
(*b*) is no longer employed, and
(*c*) applies for a repayment of tax.

(2) P must give the Inland Revenue—

(*a*) Parts 2 and 3 of Form P45,
(*b*) either certificate A or B, depending on P's circumstances, and
(*c*) such evidence of P's unemployment as the Inland Revenue may require.

(3) Certificate A is one which certifies that P is unemployed and, to the best of P's knowledge and belief, P—

(*a*) will not be a claimant during the period starting with the date on which the application is made and ending at the end of the tax year, and
(*b*) will not be employed during that period.

(4) Certificate B is one which certifies that P is unemployed and is not a claimant when the application is made.

(5) On receiving P's application, the Inland Revenue must make any repayment of tax which is appropriate, having regard to P's employee's code and the following information.

(6) If P gives certificate A the information is—

(*a*) the total payments to date and the corresponding total tax to date as at the week or month shown in Parts 2 and 3 of Form P45 (or, if lower, the total net tax deducted shown in it),
(*b*) any other relevant payments received by P in the tax year to date, and
(*c*) any other payments P will receive in the tax year.

(7) If P does not give certificate A the information is—

(*a*) the total payments to date and the corresponding total tax to date as at the week or month shown in Parts 2 and 3 of Form P45 (or, if lower, the total net tax deducted shown in it), and
(*b*) any other relevant payments received by P in the tax year to date.

(8) For the purposes of this regulation, "claimant" means a person who is—

(*a*) a claimant as defined by regulation 148 (jobseeker's allowance), or
(*b*) a claimant in receipt of taxable benefit as defined by regulation 173 (incapacity benefit).

Commentary—Simon's Direct Tax Service **E4.1162.**
Derivation—The Income Tax (Employments) Regulations, SI 1993/744 reg 37.
Cross references—See the Income Tax (PAYE) Regulations, SI 2003/2682 reg 11 (this regulation not to apply to pension payers or pensioners in their capacity as such).

Deductions working sheets

66—(1) Paragraph (2) applies if a code has been issued to an employer in respect of an employee.

(2) The employer must, on making a relevant payment to the employee, prepare a deductions working sheet (unless the employer has already done so).

(3) The employer must record in the deductions working sheet—

(*a*) the employee's name,
(*b*) the employee's national insurance number, if known,
(*c*) the employee's code, and
(*d*) the tax year to which the deductions working sheet relates.

(4) The employer must record in the deductions working sheet in respect of every relevant payment which the employer makes to the employee—

(*a*) the date of the payment,
(*b*) the amount of the payment, and
(*c*) the amount of tax, if any, deducted or repaid on making the payment, or to be deducted or accounted for under regulation 62(4) or (5) (notional payments).

(5) If the employee's code is used on the cumulative basis, the employer must, in respect of every relevant payment which the employer makes to the employee, either—

(*a*) record the following information in the deductions working sheet, or
(*b*) keep such records as enable its production.

(6) The information is—

(*a*) the total payments to date in relation to the date of payment,
(*b*) the total free pay to date or, as the case may be, the total additional pay to date, in relation to that date,
(*c*) the total taxable payments to date in relation to that date,
(*d*) the corresponding total tax to date,
(*e*) if the employee's code is a K code—
(i) the tax due to be deducted at that date (subject to the overriding limit),
(ii) the overriding limit, if any, in relation to the payment,
(iii) the amount of any tax not deducted at that date because of the overriding limit, and
(*f*) any amount of tax which is not to be repaid because of regulation 64 (trade disputes).

(7) If the employee's code is not used on the cumulative basis, the employer must, in respect of every relevant payment which the employer makes to the employee, either—

(*a*) record the following information in the deductions working sheet, or
(*b*) keep such records as enable its production.

(8) The information is—

(*a*) the free pay, or, as the case may be, the additional pay for the employee's code,
(*b*) the taxable payments, and
(*c*) if the employee's code is a K code, the tax due to be deducted and the overriding limit.

Commentary—Simon's Direct Tax Service **E4.1141.**
Derivation—The Income Tax (Employments) Regulations, SI 1993/744 regs 17(3), (4), 38, (4); the Income Tax (Employments) (Notional Payments) Regulations, SI 1994/1212 reg 13(1), (2).
Modifications—See the Income Tax (PAYE) Regulations, SI 2003/2682 reg 174 (modification of this regulation in its application to payments of taxable incapacity benefit).
Cross references—See the Income Tax (PAYE) Regulations, SI 2003/2682 reg 34 (this regulation does not apply to cases where SI 2003/2682 regs 34, 35 apply).

Information to employees about payments and tax deducted (Form P60)

67—(1) Before 1st June following the end of the tax year, an employer must give a certificate (Form P60) to every employee—

(*a*) who was in the employer's employment on the last day of the tax year, and
(*b*) from whose relevant payments the employer was required to deduct tax at any time during that tax year.

(2) The certificate must show—

(*a*) the tax year to which it relates,
(*b*) the employer's PAYE reference,
(*c*) the employee's name,
(*d*) the employee's national insurance number, if known,
(*e*) any number used by the employer to identify the employee,
(*f*) the total amount of the relevant payments made by the employer to the employee during the tax year in respect of the employment in question,
(*g*) the total net tax deducted in relation to those payments, subject to regulation 64(7)(*b*) (trade disputes),
(*h*) the employee's code,
(*i*) the employer's name, and
(*j*) the employer's address.

(3) In the case of an employee taken into employment after the beginning of the tax year, the certificate must also show—

(*a*) any amounts required by regulation 43(9), 52(11), 53(3) or 61(3) to be treated as relevant payments made by the employer to the employee during the tax year,

(*b*) any amounts treated as tax deducted by the employer at the end of the tax year by any of those regulations,

(*c*) the sum of the figures given under sub-paragraph (*a*) of this paragraph and paragraph (2)(*f*),

(*d*) the sum of the figures given under sub-paragraph (*b*) of this paragraph and paragraph (2)(*g*).

Commentary—Simon's Direct Tax Service **E4.11121.**
Derivation—The Income Tax (Employments) Regulations, SI 1993/744 reg 39.

PART 4
PAYMENTS, RETURNS AND INFORMATION

Modifications—See the Income Tax (PAYE) Regulations, SI 2003/2682 reg 174 (modification of this regulation in its application to payments of taxable incapacity benefit).
Cross references—See the Income Tax (PAYE) Regulations, SI 2003/2682 reg 168 (subject to SI 2003/2682 reg 168(3), this Part applies to the taxable jobseeker's allowance paid to a Part 8 Chapter 2 (of SI 2003/2682) claimant by the employer on behalf of the Department under SI 2003/2682 reg 167, as if it were a relevant payment from the employment).

CHAPTER 1
PAYMENT OF TAX AND ASSOCIATED RETURNS

PAYMENT AND RECOVERY OF TAX BY EMPLOYER

Periodic payments to and recoveries from the Revenue

68—(1) This regulation applies to determine how much an employer must pay or can recover for a tax period.

(2) If A exceeds B, the employer must pay the excess to the Inland Revenue.

(3) But if B exceeds A, the employer may recover the excess either—

(*a*) by deducting it from the amount which the employer is liable to pay under paragraph (2) for a later tax period in the tax year, or

(*b*) from the Board of Inland Revenue.

(4) In this Regulation—

A is—

(*a*) the total amount of tax which the employer was liable to deduct from relevant payments made by the employer in the tax period, plus

(*b*) the total amount of tax for which the employer was liable to account in respect of notional payments made by the employer in that period under regulation 62(5) (notional payments);

B is the total amount which the employer was liable to repay in the tax period.

(5) Paragraphs (2) and (3) are subject to regulation 71 (modification in case of trade disputes).

(6) Paragraph (2) is also subject to regulation 78(11) (entitlement to set off excess payments).

Commentary—Simon's Direct Tax Service **E4.11115.**
Derivation—The Income Tax (Employments) Regulations, SI 1993/744 regs 40, 41(1), (2), 42(6); the Income Tax (Employments) (Notional Payments) Regulations, SI 1994/1212 reg 13(5), (6).
Modifications—See the Income Tax (PAYE) Regulations, SI 2003/2682 reg 71 (modification of this regulation in case of trade dispute).
SI 2003/2682 reg 174 (modification of this regulation in its application to payments of taxable incapacity benefit).
SI 2003/2682 Sch 1 para 15 (for the purposes of giving effect to any enactment or instrument which refers to an amount which is, or would in certain circumstances be, payable to the collector, para (2) above has effect as if that paragraph required payment of the amount to which it refers to the collector).

Due date and receipts for payment of tax

69—(1) An employer must pay amounts due under regulation 68(2)—

(*a*) within 17 days after the end of the tax period, where payment is made by an approved method of electronic communications, or

(*b*) within 14 days after the end of the tax period, in any other case.

(2) The Inland Revenue must give a receipt to the employer for the total amount paid under regulation 68(2) if asked.

(3) But no separate receipt for tax only need be given if a receipt is given for the total amount of tax and any earnings-related contributions (as defined by regulation 1(2) of the Social Security (Contributions) Regulations 2001) paid at the same time.

Commentary—Simon's Direct Tax Service **E4.11115, 11154.**
Derivation—The Income Tax (Employments) Regulations, SI 1993/744 regs 2(1), 40(1), 41(1), 42(1).
Modifications—See the Income Tax (PAYE) Regulations, SI 2003/2682 reg 174 (modification of this regulation in its application to payments of taxable incapacity benefit).

SI 2003/2682 Sch 1 para 18 (modification of this regulation in so far as the provisions apply in relation to tax periods ending before 6 April 2004).
Cross references—See the Income Tax (PAYE) Regulations, SI 2003/2682 reg 219 (for the purposes of this regulation, if payment to the Revenue is made by cheque, and cheque paid on its first presentation to the banker on whom drawn, the payment is treated as made on day cheque received by the Revenue).

Quarterly tax periods

70—(1) This regulation applies, so that the tax period is a tax quarter, if an employer—

(*a*) has reasonable grounds for believing that the average monthly amount will be less than £1,500, and
(*b*) chooses to pay tax quarterly.

(2) ''The average monthly amount'' is the average, for tax months falling within the current tax year, of the amounts found by the formula—

$$(P + N + L + S) - (C + SP + CD).$$

(3) In paragraph (2)—

P is the amount which would be payable to the Inland Revenue under regulation 68 disregarding any WTC adjustment;

N is the amount which would be payable to the Inland Revenue under the SSCBA and the SSC Regulations disregarding—

(*a*) any amount of secondary Class 1 contributions in respect of which liability has been transferred to the employed earner by an election made jointly by the employed earner and the secondary contributor for the purposes of paragraph 3B(1) of Schedule 1 to the SSCBA (transfer of liability to be borne by earner); and
(*b*) any WTC adjustment;

L is the amount which would be payable to the Inland Revenue under regulation 39(1) of the Student Loans Regulations (payment of repayments deducted to the Inland Revenue) disregarding—

(*a*) the reduction referred to in paragraph (3) of that regulation, and
(*b*) any WTC adjustment;

S is the amount which would be payable by the employer to the Inland Revenue under sections 559 and 559A of ICTA (deduction on account of tax etc from payments to certain sub-contractors) and regulation 8 of the Income Tax (Sub-contractors in the Construction Industry) Regulations 1993, disregarding any WTC adjustment;

C is the amount which the employer would be required to pay to employees by way of tax credit under the WTC Regulations;

SP is the amount which would be payable by the employer to employees by way of statutory sick pay, statutory maternity pay, statutory paternity pay and statutory adoption pay under the SSCBA; and

CD is—

(*a*) if the employer is a company, the amount which others would deduct from payments to it, in its position as a sub-contractor, under section 559 of ICTA (deduction on account of tax etc from payments to certain sub-contractors);
(*b*) in any other case, nil.

(4) In this regulation—

''employed earner'' has the same meaning as in the SSCBA;
''SSCBA'' means the Social Security Contributions and Benefits Act 1992 or, in Northern Ireland, the Social Security Contribution and Benefits (Northern Ireland) Act 1992;
''SSC Regulations'' means the Social Security (Contributions) Regulations 2001;
''Student Loans Regulations'' means the Education (Student Loans) (Repayment) Regulations 2000 or, in Northern Ireland, the Education (Student Loans) (Repayment) Regulations (Northern Ireland) 2000;
''WTC adjustment'' means an adjustment to the amount in question under regulation 7(2) of the WTC Regulations (funding of payment of working tax credit);
''WTC Regulations'' means the Working Tax Credit (Payment by Employers) Regulations 2002.

Commentary—Simon's Direct Tax Service **E4.11115.**
Derivation—The Income Tax (Employments) Regulations, SI 1993/744 regs 2(1), 41(1), (3).
Modifications—See the Income Tax (PAYE) Regulations, SI 2003/2682 reg 174 (modification of this regulation in its application to payments of taxable incapacity benefit).

Modification of regulation 68 in case of trade dispute

71—(1) This regulation modifies the amount payable or recoverable by an employer under regulation 68 in cases where regulation 64 (trade disputes) applies—

(*a*) by providing for the amount which would otherwise be payable by the employer for a tax period to be reduced by an amount of repayments (''R'') that cannot be made to employees in the tax period, and
(*b*) by providing—

(i) for amounts which would otherwise be payable in later tax periods to be increased, or
(ii) for amounts which would otherwise be recoverable in later tax periods to be reduced,

by a total of R.

(2) This regulation applies for consecutive tax periods—

(*a*) starting with the first tax period at the end of which there is an amount calculated as due to be repaid but which is required to be withheld by regulation 64(5) (tax to be withheld during strike action), and

(*b*) ending with the next tax period at the end of which no amount is required to be withheld by that regulation.

(3) Column 3 of Table 3 shows the amount payable under regulation 68(2) in the cases set out in column 2 for the first and subsequent tax periods.

TABLE 3
MODIFIED AMOUNT PAYABLE UNDER REGULATION 68

1 Tax period	*2 Case*	*3 Amount payable*
First tax period	if B equals or exceeds A	nil
First tax period	any other case	A – B, reduced by P (or by so much of P as reduces the amount payable to nil)
Subsequent tax periods	if B equals or exceeds (A + Q)	nil
Subsequent tax periods	any other case	(A + Q) – B, reduced by P (or by so much of P as reduces the amount payable to nil).

(4) The amount (if any) recoverable under regulation 68(3) must be reduced to the extent that it includes amounts—

(*a*) for which reduction was made under paragraph (3) in an earlier tax period, or

(*b*) which are otherwise being recovered.

(5) In this regulation—

A is—

(*a*) the total amount of tax which the employer was liable to deduct from relevant payments made by the employer in the tax period, plus

(*b*) the total amount of tax for which the employer was liable to account in respect of notional payments made by the employer in that period under regulation 62(5) (notional payments);

B is the total amount which the employer is liable to repay in the tax period, not including any amounts—

(*a*) for which a reduction was made under paragraph (3) in an earlier tax period; or

(*b*) which are being recovered under paragraph (4);

P is the total of amounts calculated as due to be repaid in the tax period but required to be withheld during that tax period by regulation 64(5);

Q is the total of amounts—

(*a*) which, because of regulation 64(5)(*b*), are set off against tax due to be deducted in the tax period, and

(*b*) which also, under paragraph (3), have reduced the amount payable in an earlier tax period.

Commentary—Simon's Direct Tax Service **E4.11115.**

Derivation—The Income Tax (Employments) Regulations, SI 1993/744 regs 40(2), 41(2), 42(6); the Income Tax (Employments) (Notional Payments) Regulations, SI 1994/1212 reg 13(5), (6).

Cross references—See the Income Tax (PAYE) Regulations, SI 2003/2682 reg 11 (this regulation not to apply to pension payers or pensioners in their capacity as such).

Recovery from employee of tax not deducted by employer

72—(1) This regulation applies if—

(*a*) it appears to the Inland Revenue that the deductible amount exceeds the amount actually deducted, and

(*b*) condition A or B is met.

(2) In this regulation [and regulations 72A and 72B][1]—

"the deductible amount" is the amount which an employer was liable to deduct from relevant payments made to an employee in a tax period;

"the amount actually deducted" is the amount actually deducted by the employer from relevant payments made to that employee during that tax period;

"the excess" means the amount by which the deductible amount exceeds the amount actually deducted.

(3) Condition A is that the employer satisfies the Inland Revenue—

(*a*) that the employer took reasonable care to comply with these Regulations, and
(*b*) that the failure to deduct the excess was due to an error made in good faith.

(4) Condition B is that the Inland Revenue are of the opinion that the employee has received relevant payments knowing that the employer wilfully failed to deduct the amount of tax which should have been deducted from those payments.

(5) The Inland Revenue may direct that the employer is not liable to pay the excess to the Inland Revenue.

[(5A) Any direction under paragraph (5) must be made by notice ("the direction notice"), stating the date the notice was issued, to—

(*a*) the employer and the employee if condition A is met;
(*b*) the employee if condition B is met.][1]

[(5B) A notice need not be issued to the employee under paragraph (5A)(*a*) if neither the Inland Revenue nor the employer are aware of the employee's address or last known address.][1]

(6) If a direction is made, the excess must not be added under regulation 185(5) or 188(3)(*a*) (adjustments to total net tax deducted for self-assessments and other assessments) in relation to the employee.

(7) If condition B is met, tax payable by an employee as a result of a direction carries interest, as if it were unpaid tax due from an employer, in accordance with regulation 82 (interest on tax overdue).

(8) The tax payable carries interest from the reckonable date until whichever is the earlier of—

(*a*) the date on which payment is made, or
(*b*) the date (if any) immediately before the date on which it begins to carry interest under section 86 of TMA.

Commentary—Simon's Direct Tax Service **E4.11117.**
Derivation—The Income Tax (Employments) Regulations, SI 1993/744 regs 42(2), (3), (4), 101(6), 101A(2); the Income Tax (Employments) Regulations, SI 1994/1212 reg 13(7).
Modifications—See the Income Tax (PAYE) Regulations, SI 2003/2682 reg 174 (modification of this regulation in its application to payments of taxable incapacity benefit).
Cross references—See the Income Tax (PAYE) Regulations, SI 2003/2682 reg 218(3), (4) (a certificate of the Inland Revenue that, to the best of their knowledge and belief, any amount of interest payable under para (7) above has not been paid by an employer or employee, is sufficient evidence that the amount mentioned in the certificate is unpaid and due to the Crown).
SI 2003/2682 reg 219 (for the purposes of this regulation, if payment to the Revenue is made by cheque, and cheque paid on its first presentation to the banker on whom drawn, the payment is treated as made on day cheque received by the Revenue).
Amendments—[1] Words in para (2) inserted, and paras (5A), 5B) inserted, by the IT (PAYE) (Amendment) Regulations, SI 2004/851 regs 2, 3 with effect from 12 April 2004.

[Employer's request for a direction and appeal against refusal

72A—(1) In relation to condition A in regulation 72(3), the employer may by notice to the Inland Revenue ("the notice of request") request that the Inland Revenue make a direction under regulation 72(5).

(2) The notice of request must—

(*a*) state—
(i) how the employer took reasonable care to comply with these Regulations; and
(ii) how the error resulting in the failure to deduct the excess occurred;
(*b*) specify the relevant payments to which the request relates;
(*c*) specify the employee or employees to whom those relevant payments were made; and
(*d*) state the excess in relation to each employee.

(3) The Inland Revenue may refuse the employer's request under paragraph (1) by notice to the employer ("the refusal notice") stating—

(*a*) the grounds for the refusal, and
(*b*) the date on which the refusal notice was issued.

(4) The employer may appeal against the refusal notice—

(*a*) by notice to the Inland Revenue,
(*b*) within 30 days of the issue of the refusal notice,
(*c*) specifying the grounds of the appeal.

(5) For the purpose of paragraph (4) the grounds of appeal are that—

(*a*) the employer did take reasonable care to comply with these Regulations, and
(*b*) the failure to deduct the excess was due to an error made in good faith.

(6) If on appeal under paragraph (4) it appears to the Commissioners that the refusal notice should not have been issued they may direct that the Inland Revenue make a direction under regulation 72(5) in an amount the Commissioners determine is the excess for one or more tax periods falling within the relevant tax year.][1]

Amendments—[1] Regulations 72A–72D inserted by the IT (PAYE) (Amendment) Regulations, SI 2004/851 regs 2, 4 with effect from 12 April 2004.

[Employee's appeal against a direction notice where condition A is met

72B—(1) An employee may appeal against a direction notice under regulation 72(5A)(*a*)—

(*a*) by notice to the Inland Revenue,
(*b*) within 30 days of the issue of the direction notice,
(*c*) specifying the grounds of the appeal

(2) For the purpose of paragraph (1) the grounds of appeal are that—

(*a*) the employer did not act in good faith,
(*b*) the employer did not take reasonable care, or
(*c*) the excess is incorrect.

(3) On an appeal under paragraph (1) the Commissioners may—

(*a*) if it appears to them that the direction notice should not have been made, set aside the direction notice; or
(*b*) if it appears to them that the excess specified in the direction notice is incorrect, increase or reduce the excess specified in the notice accordingly.][1]

Amendments—[1] Regulations 72A–72D inserted by the IT (PAYE) (Amendment) Regulations, SI 2004/851 regs 2, 4 with effect from 12 April 2004.

[Employee's appeal against a direction notice where condition B is met

72C—(1) An employee may appeal against a direction notice under regulation 72(5A)(*b*)—

(*a*) by notice to the Inland Revenue,
(*b*) within 30 days of the issue of the direction notice,
(*c*) specifying the grounds of the appeal.

(2) For the purpose of paragraph (1) the grounds of appeal are that—

(*a*) the employee did not receive the payments knowing that the employer wilfully failed to deduct the amount of tax which should have been deducted from those payments, or
(*b*) the excess is incorrect.

(3) On an appeal under paragraph (1) the Commissioners may—

(*a*) if it appears to them that the direction notice should not have been made, set aside the direction notice; or
(*b*) if it appears to them that the excess specified in the direction notice is incorrect, increase or reduce the excess specified in the notice accordingly.][1]

Amendments—[1] Regulations 72A–72D inserted by the IT (PAYE) (Amendment) Regulations, SI 2004/851 regs 2, 4 with effect from 12 April 2004.

[Appeals: supplementary provisions

72D—(1) This regulation applies to appeals under regulations 72A(4), 72B, 72C and 81A.

(2) Subject to paragraph (4), an appeal is to the General Commissioners but the employer or employee as appropriate may elect (in accordance with section 46(1) of TMA) to bring the appeal before the Special Commissioners instead.

(3) Section 31D(2) to (7) of TMA (election to bring appeal before Special Commissioners) has effect in relation to an election under paragraph (2) (as in relation to an election under subsection (1) of that section).

(4) If in respect of the same error by an employer in relation to condition A in regulation 72(3)—

(*a*) more than one employee is appealing under regulation 72B; or
(*b*) there is an appeal by an employer under regulation 72A(4) and by an employee under regulation 72B

the Commissioners who are to determine the appeals are given in paragraphs (5) to (7).

(5) If—

(*a*) the same body of General Commissioners has jurisdiction with respect to all the persons concerned, and
(*b*) none of those persons has elected in accordance with section 46(1) of TMA to bring the appeal before the Special Commissioners

the appeals are to be determined by that body of General Commissioners.

(6) If—

(*a*) different bodies of General Commissioners have jurisdiction with respect to the persons concerned, and
(*b*) none of those persons has elected in accordance with section 46(1) of TMA to bring the appeal before the Special Commissioners

the appeals are to be determined by such of those bodies as the Board of Inland Revenue determine.

(7) In any other case, the appeals are to be determined by the Special Commissioners.

(8) Where paragraph (4) applies or the appeal is material to the liability to tax of the employer and the employee, all the persons concerned are entitled—

(*a*) to appear before and be heard by the Commissioners, or
(*b*) to make representations in writing.

(9) On hearing an appeal the General Commissioners or the Special Commissioners may allow the employer or employee as appropriate to put forward grounds not specified in the notice, and take them into consideration, if satisfied that the omission was not wilful or unreasonable.][1]

Amendments—[1] Regulations 72A–72D inserted by the IT (PAYE) (Amendment) Regulations, SI 2004/851 regs 2, 4 with effect from 12 April 2004.

ANNUAL RETURNS OF RELEVANT PAYMENTS AND TAX

Annual return of relevant payments liable to deduction of tax (Forms P35 and P14)

73—(1) Before 20th May following the end of a tax year, an employer must deliver to the Inland Revenue a return containing the following information.

(2) The information is—

(*a*) the tax year to which the return relates,
(*b*) the total amount of the relevant payments made by the employer during the tax year to all employees in respect of whom the employer was required at any time during that year to prepare or maintain deductions working sheets, and
(*c*) the total net tax deducted in relation to those payments.

(3) The return must be supported by the following information in respect of each of the employees mentioned in paragraph (2)(*b*).

(4) The supporting information is—

(*a*) the employee's name,
(*b*) the employee's address, if known,
(*c*) either—
  (i) the employee's national insurance number, or
  (ii) if that number is not known, the employee's date of birth, if known, and sex,
(*d*) the employee's code,
(*e*) the tax year to which the return relates,
(*f*) the total amount of the relevant payments made by the employer to the employee during that tax year, and
(*g*) the total net tax deducted in relation to those payments.

(5) Paragraphs (2)(*c*) and (4)(*g*) are subject to regulation 64(7) (trade disputes).

(6) If an employee was taken into employment after the beginning of the tax year, the employer must also provide the total amounts of—

(*a*) any amounts required by regulation 43(9), 52(11), 53(3) or 61(3) to be treated as relevant payments made by the employer to the employee during the tax year,
(*b*) any amounts treated as tax deducted by the employer by any of those regulations,
(*c*) the sum of the figures given under sub-paragraph (*a*) of this paragraph and paragraph (4)(*f*),
(*d*) the sum of the figures given under sub-paragraph (*b*) of this paragraph and paragraph (4)(*g*).

(7) The return must include—

(*a*) a statement and declaration containing a list of all deductions working sheets which the employer was required to prepare or maintain at any time during that tax year; and
(*b*) a certificate showing—
  (i) the total net tax deducted or the total net tax repaid in the case of each employee, and
  (ii) the total net tax deducted or repaid in respect of all the employees,

during that tax year.

(8) The statement and declaration and the certificate must be—

(*a*) signed by the employer, or
(*b*) if the employer is a body corporate, signed either by the secretary or by a director.

(9) Paragraph (8) is subject to regulation 211(5) (authentication in approved manner if return sent electronically).

(10) Section 98A of TMA (special penalties in case of certain returns) applies to paragraph (1).

Commentary—Simon's Direct Tax Service **E4.11121, 11122.**
Derivation—The Income Tax (Employments) Regulations, SI 1993/744 reg 43(1)–(1B), (2)–(7), (12).
Modifications—See the Income Tax (PAYE) Regulations, SI 2003/2682 reg 174 (modification of this regulation in its application to payments of taxable incapacity benefit).

Annual return of relevant payments not liable to deduction of tax (Form P38A)

74—(1) Before 20th May following the end of a tax year, an employer must deliver a return to the Inland Revenue in respect of every relevant employee.

(2) The return must contain the following information—

(*a*) the employee's name,
(*b*) the employee's address, if known,
(*c*) the employee's national insurance number, if known,
(*d*) the employee's job title or description,
(*e*) the tax year to which the return relates,
(*f*) the dates during which the employee was employed in the tax year, and
(*g*) the total amount of the relevant payments made by the employer to the employee during the tax year.

(3) A "relevant employee" is one—

(*a*) to whom relevant payments exceeding the PAYE threshold were made at any time during the tax year,
(*b*) who was employed for more than a week, or
(*c*) who was paid more than £100 during the tax year.

(4) But the following are not relevant employees—

(*a*) an employee included on a return under regulation 73 (Forms P35 and P14),
(*b*) an employee who has indicated that statement A or statement B (or both) apply on Form P46 (see regulation 46), and to whom the employer has not made relevant payments exceeding the PAYE threshold at any time during that tax year.

Commentary—Simon's Direct Tax Service **E4.11123.**
Derivation—The Income Tax (Employments) Regulations, SI 1993/744 reg 44.
Modifications—See the Income Tax (PAYE) Regulations, SI 2003/2682 reg 174 (modification of this regulation in its application to payments of taxable incapacity benefit).

Additional return in case of trade dispute

75—(1) An employer must immediately deliver an additional return to the Inland Revenue on each occasion that—

(*a*) the employer has not made any repayment of tax withheld under regulation 64(5) (trade disputes) within 42 days after the end of the employee's strike action, and
(*b*) a return has been made under regulation 73 which, in accordance with regulation 64(7)(*b*), treats that tax as if it were repaid.

(2) The return must contain the following information—

(*a*) the tax year to which it relates,
(*b*) such information as the Board of Inland Revenue may require for identifying each of the employees in question, and
(*c*) the amount of tax not repaid to each of those employees.

(3) The return must be accompanied by a statement containing the following information—

(*a*) a list of all employees in respect of whom the additional return is made,
(*b*) the amount of tax not repaid to each of those employees,
(*c*) the total tax not repaid by the employer to those employees for that tax year.

Commentary—Simon's Direct Tax Service **E4.11127.**
Derivation—The Income Tax (Employments) Regulations, SI 1993/744 reg 45.
Cross references—See the Income Tax (PAYE) Regulations, SI 2003/2682 reg 11 (this regulation not to apply to pension payers or pensioners in their capacity as such).

FAILURE TO ACCOUNT FOR DEDUCTIBLE TAX

Certificate if tax in regulation 73 return is unpaid

76—(1) Paragraph (2) applies if an employer—

(*a*) delivers a return under regulation 73 showing an amount of total net tax deducted by the employer for a tax year, and
(*b*) does not pay that amount to the Inland Revenue before 20th April following the end of the tax year.

(2) The Inland Revenue may prepare a certificate showing how much of that amount remains unpaid.

(3) Regulation 218 deals with the use of certificates as evidence that sums are due and unpaid.

Commentary—Simon's Direct Tax Service **E4.11116.**
Derivation—The Income Tax (Employments) Regulations, SI 1993/744 reg 43(8).
Modifications—See the Income Tax (PAYE) Regulations, SI 2003/2682 reg 174 (modification of this regulation in its application to payments of taxable incapacity benefit).
Cross references—See the Income Tax (PAYE) Regulations, SI 2003/2682 reg 218(1), (2) (a certificate of the Inland Revenue that, to the best of their knowledge and belief, any amount shown in a certificate under this regulation has not been paid by an employer, is sufficient evidence that the amount mentioned in the certificate is unpaid and due to the Crown).

Return and certificate if tax may be unpaid

77—(1) This regulation applies if, 17 days or more after the end of a tax period, condition A or B is met.

(2) Condition A is that—

(*a*) an employer has not paid any tax under regulation 68 for that tax period, and

(*b*) the Inland Revenue are unaware of the amount (if any) which the employer is liable to pay.

(3) Condition B is that—

(*a*) an employer has paid an amount of tax under regulation 68 for that period, but

(*b*) the Inland Revenue are not satisfied that it is the full amount which the employer is liable to pay for that period.

(4) The Inland Revenue may give notice to the employer requiring the employer within 14 days of the issue of the notice to deliver a return showing the amount of tax which the employer is liable to pay under regulation 68 in respect of the tax period.

(5) If the notice extends to two or more consecutive tax periods in a tax year, this regulation has effect as if they were one tax period.

(6) On receiving a return made by the employer under paragraph (4), the Inland Revenue may prepare a certificate showing the amount of tax which the employer is liable to pay for the tax period and how much (if any) of that amount remains unpaid.

(7) Regulation 218 deals with the use of certificates as evidence that sums are due and unpaid.

Commentary—Simon's Direct Tax Service **E4.11116.**
Derivation—The Income Tax (Employments) Regulations, SI 1993/744 reg 47(1)–(5).
Modifications—See the Income Tax (PAYE) Regulations, SI 2003/2682 Sch 1 para 18 (modification of this regulation in so far as the provisions apply in relation to tax periods ending before 6 April 2004).
Cross references—See the Income Tax (PAYE) Regulations, SI 2003/2682 reg 218(1), (2) (a certificate of the Inland Revenue that, to the best of their knowledge and belief, any amount shown in a certificate under para (6) above has not been paid by an employer, is sufficient evidence that the amount mentioned in the certificate is unpaid and due to the Crown).

Notice and certificate if tax may be unpaid

78—(1) This regulation applies if, 17 days or more after the end of a tax period, condition A or B is met.

(2) Condition A is that—

(*a*) an employer has not paid any tax under regulation 68 for that tax period, and

(*b*) the Inland Revenue have reason to believe that the employer is liable to pay an amount of tax.

(3) Condition B is that—

(*a*) an employer has paid an amount of tax under regulation 68 for that tax period, but

(*b*) the Inland Revenue are not satisfied, after seeking the employer's explanation, that it is the full amount which the employer is liable to pay for that period.

(4) The Inland Revenue, on consideration of the employer's record of past payments, may—

(*a*) specify, to the best of their judgment, the amount of tax which they consider the employer is liable to pay, and

(*b*) serve notice on the employer requiring payment of that amount within 7 days of the issue of the notice ("the notice period").

(5) If the notice extends to two or more consecutive tax periods in a tax year, this regulation has effect as if they were the latest tax period specified in the notice.

(6) If, during the notice period, the employer—

(*a*) claims that any payment made in respect of the tax period specified in the notice is the full amount the employer is liable to pay, but

(*b*) does not satisfy the Inland Revenue that this is the case,

the employer may require the Inland Revenue to inspect the employer's PAYE records as if the employer had been required to produce those records in accordance with regulation 97 (inspection of employer's PAYE records).

(7) If there is an inspection by virtue of paragraph (6), regulation 97 applies to that inspection and the notice given by the Inland Revenue under paragraph (4) must be disregarded.

(8) If the amount of tax specified in the notice, or any part of it, is not paid during the notice period—

(*a*) the amount unpaid is treated as an amount of tax which the employer was liable to pay for that tax period under regulation 68, and

(*b*) the Inland Revenue may prepare a certificate showing how much of that tax remains unpaid.

(9) But paragraph (8) does not apply if during the notice period—

(*a*) the employer pays the full amount of tax which the employer is liable to pay under regulation 68 for that tax period, or

(*b*) the employer satisfies the Inland Revenue that no amount, or no further amount, is due for that tax period.

(10) Paragraph (11) applies if the employer pays an amount certified under this regulation which exceeds the amount the employer would have been liable to pay in respect of that tax period apart from this regulation.

(11) The employer is entitled to set off the excess against any amount which the employer is liable to pay under regulation 68 for any subsequent tax period in the tax year.

(12) Paragraph (13) applies if the employer—

(*a*) delivers the return required by regulation 73(1) after the end of the tax year, and

(*b*) pays the total net tax which the employer is liable to pay.

(13) Any excess of tax paid, and not otherwise recovered by set-off in accordance with this regulation, must be repaid.

(14) Regulation 218 deals with the use of certificates as evidence that sums are due and unpaid.

Commentary—Simon's Direct Tax Service **E4.11116.**
Derivation—The Income Tax (Employments) Regulations, SI 1993/744 reg 48(1)–(7), (11), (12).
Modifications—See the Income Tax (PAYE) Regulations, SI 2003/2682 Sch 1 para 18 (modification of this regulation in so far as the provisions apply in relation to tax periods ending before 6 April 2004).
Cross references—See the Income Tax (PAYE) Regulations, SI 2003/2682 reg 218(1), (2) (a certificate of the Inland Revenue that, to the best of their knowledge and belief, any amount shown in a certificate under para (8) above has not been paid by an employer, is sufficient evidence that the amount mentioned in the certificate is unpaid and due to the Crown).
SI 2003/2682 reg 219 (for the purposes of this regulation, if payment to the Revenue is made by cheque, and cheque paid on its first presentation to the banker on whom drawn, the payment is treated as made on day cheque received by the Revenue).

Certificate after inspection of PAYE records

79—(1) This regulation applies if there is an inspection of an employer's PAYE records under regulation 97.

(2) The Inland Revenue may, by reference to the information obtained from the inspection, prepare a certificate showing—

(*a*) the amount of tax which it appears that the employer is liable to pay for the tax years or tax periods covered by the inspection; and

(*b*) any amount of that tax which remains unpaid.

(3) Regulation 218 deals with the use of certificates as evidence that sums are due and unpaid.

Commentary—Simon's Direct Tax Service **E4.11116.**
Derivation—The Income Tax (Employments) Regulations, SI 1993/744 reg 55(8).
Modifications—See the Income Tax (PAYE) Regulations, SI 2003/2682 reg 174 (modification of this regulation in its application to payments of taxable incapacity benefit).
Cross references—See the Income Tax (PAYE) Regulations, SI 2003/2682 reg 218(1), (2) (a certificate of the Inland Revenue that, to the best of their knowledge and belief, any amount shown in a certificate under this regulation has not been paid by an employer, is sufficient evidence that the amount mentioned in the certificate is unpaid and due to the Crown).

Determination of unpaid tax and appeal against determination

80—(1) This regulation applies if it appears to the Inland Revenue that there may be tax payable for a tax year under regulation 68 by an employer which has neither been—

(*a*) paid to the Inland Revenue, nor

(*b*) certified by the Inland Revenue under regulation 76, 77, 78 or 79.

(2) The Inland Revenue may determine the amount of that tax to the best of their judgment, and serve notice of their determination on the employer.

(3) A determination under this regulation must not include tax in respect of which a direction under regulation 72(5) has been made; and directions under that regulation do not apply to tax determined under this regulation.

(4) A determination under this regulation may—

(*a*) cover the tax payable by the employer under regulation 68 for any one or more tax periods in a tax year, and

(*b*) extend to the whole of that tax, or to such part of it as is payable in respect of—

(i) a class or classes of employees specified in the notice of determination (without naming the individual employees), or

(ii) one or more named employees specified in the notice.

(5) A determination under this regulation is subject to Parts 4, 5 (other than section 55) and 6 of TMA (assessment, appeals, collection and recovery) as if—

(*a*) the determination were an assessment, and

(*b*) the amount of tax determined were income tax charged on the employer,

and those Parts of that Act apply accordingly with any necessary modifications.

(6) For the purposes of paragraph 3(1)(*a*) of Schedule 3 to TMA (rules for assigning proceedings to General Commissioners), the relevant place for an appeal against a determination under this regulation is the place where the determination was made.

Commentary—Simon's Direct Tax Service **E4.11116.**
Derivation—The Income Tax (Employments) Regulations, SI 1993/744 reg 49(1)–(4), (7), (8).
Cross references—See the Income Tax (PAYE) Regulations, SI 2003/2682 Sch 1 para 20 (this regulation does not apply in relation to unpaid tax in respect of a tax year ending on or before 5 April 1992).

Employee liability if tax unpaid after regulation 80 determination

81—(1) This regulation applies if—

(*a*) any part of the tax determined under regulation 80 is not paid within 30 days from the date on which the determination became final and conclusive, and
(*b*) condition A or B is met in relation to an employee.

(2) Condition A is that the Inland Revenue are of the opinion that the employee in respect of whose relevant payments the determination was made has received those payments knowing that the employer has wilfully failed to deduct the amount of tax which should have been deducted from those payments.

(3) Condition B is that the unpaid tax represents an amount for which the employer was required to account under regulation 62(5) (notional payments) in relation to a notional payment to the employee.

(4) The Inland Revenue may direct that the employer is not liable to pay the amount of tax which appears to them should have been but was not—

(*a*) deducted on making those relevant payments, or
(*b*) accounted for under regulation 62(5).

[(4A) If condition A or B is met, any direction under paragraph (4) must be made by notice (''the direction notice'') to the employee stating the date the notice was issued.][1]

(5) If a direction is made, the amount of tax must not be added under regulation 185(5) or 188(3)(*a*) (adjustments for self-assessments and other assessments) in relation to the employee.

(6) Tax payable by an employee as a result of a direction carries interest, as if it were unpaid tax due from an employer, in accordance with regulation 82 (interest on tax overdue).

(7) The tax payable carries interest from the reckonable date until whichever is the earlier of—

(*a*) the date on which payment is made, or
(*b*) the date (if any) immediately before the date on which it begins to carry interest under section 86 of TMA.

Commentary—Simon's Direct Tax Service **E4.11117.**
Derivation—The Income Tax (Employments) Regulations, SI 1993/744 reg 49(5), (6), 101(6), 101A(2); the Income Tax (Employments) (Notional Payments) Regulations, SI 1994/1212 reg 13(7).
Cross references—See the Income Tax (PAYE) Regulations, SI 2003/2682 reg 218(3), (4) (a certificate of the Inland Revenue that, to the best of their knowledge and belief, any amount of interest payable under para (6) above has not been paid by an employer or employee, is sufficient evidence that the amount mentioned in the certificate is unpaid and due to the Crown).
Amendments—[1] Para (4A) inserted by the IT (PAYE) (Amendment) Regulations, SI 2004/851 regs 2, 5 with effect from 12 April 2004.

[Employee's appeal against direction notice

81A—(1) An employee may appeal against a direction notice under regulation 81(4A)—

(*a*) by notice to the Inland Revenue,
(*b*) within 30 days of the issue of the direction notice,
(*c*) specifying the grounds of the appeal.

(2) For the purpose of paragraph (1) the grounds of appeal are that—

(*a*) in relation to condition A in regulation 81, the employee did not receive the payments knowing that the employer wilfully failed to deduct the amount of tax which should have been deducted from those payments,
(*b*) in relation to condition B in regulation 81, the relevant payment was not a notional payment, or
(*c*) the excess is incorrect.

(3) On an appeal under paragraph (1) the Commissioners may—

(*a*) if it appears to them that the direction notice should not have been made, set aside the notice; or
(*b*) if it appears to them that the amount of tax specified in the direction notice is incorrect, increase or reduce the amount specified in the notice accordingly.

(4) Regulation 72D applies to appeals under this regulation.][1]

Amendments—[1] This regulation inserted by the IT (PAYE) (Amendment) Regulations, SI 2004/851 regs 2, 6 with effect from 12 April 2004.

INTEREST

Interest on tax overdue

82—(1) This regulation applies if an employer has not paid to the Inland Revenue the total net tax payable in respect of a tax year by the reckonable date.

(2) Any unpaid tax carries interest at the prescribed rate from the reckonable date until payment (''the interest period'').

(3) Paragraph (2) applies even if the reckonable date is a non-business day as defined by section 92 of the Bills of Exchange Act 1882.

(4) But paragraph (2) does not apply to any tax which the employer does not have to pay as a result of a direction made under regulation 72(5) or 81(4).

(5) Any change made to the prescribed rate during the interest period applies to the unpaid tax from the date of the change.

(6) The ''total net tax payable'' in respect of a tax year is—

(*a*) the total of any amounts payable by the employer under regulation 68 for tax periods in the tax year, less
(*b*) the total of any amounts recoverable from the Board of Inland Revenue under regulation 68(3)(*b*) for those tax periods.

(7) The ''prescribed rate'' means the rate applicable under section 178 of the Finance Act 1989 for the purposes of section 86 of TMA.

(8) The ''reckonable date'' means—

(*a*) 17 days after the end of the tax year, if payment is made using an approved method of electronic communications, or
(*b*) 14 days after the end of the tax year, in any other case.

Commentary—Simon's Direct Tax Service **E4.11119, 11143.**
Derivation—The Income Tax (Employments) Regulations, SI 1993/744 reg 51(1)–(3); the Income Tax (Employments) (Notional Payments) Regulations, SI 1994/1212 reg 13(5), (6).
Modifications—See the Income Tax (PAYE) Regulations, SI 2003/2682 Sch 1 para 21 (modification of this regulation for tax years from 1992–93 to 2003–04).
Cross references—See the Income Tax (PAYE) Regulations, SI 2003/2682 Sch 1 para 19 (this regulation does not apply in relation to unpaid tax in respect of a tax year ending on or before 5 April 1992).
SI 2003/2682 reg 218(3), (4) (a certificate of the Inland Revenue that, to the best of their knowledge and belief, any amount of interest payable under this regulation has not been paid by an employer or employee, is sufficient evidence that the amount mentioned in the certificate is unpaid and due to the Crown).
SI 2003/2682 reg 219 (for the purposes of this regulation, if payment to the Revenue is made by cheque, and cheque paid on its first presentation to the banker on whom drawn, the payment is treated as made on day cheque received by the Revenue).

Interest on tax overpaid

83—(1) This regulation applies if tax is repaid to an employer after the end of the tax year in respect of which the tax was paid.

(2) The tax repaid carries interest at the prescribed rate from the later of—

(*a*) 14 days after the end of the tax year, and
(*b*) the date on which the payment of tax for that tax year was made,

until the order for the repayment is issued (''the interest period'').

(3) Any change made to the prescribed rate during the interest period applies to the tax repaid from the date of the change.

(4) ''The prescribed rate'' means the rate applicable under section 178 of the Finance Act 1989 for the purposes of section 824 of ICTA.

Commentary—Simon's Direct Tax Service **E4.11119.**
Derivation—The Income Tax (Employments) Regulations, SI 1993/744 reg 53A.
Cross references—See the Income Tax (PAYE) Regulations, SI 2003/2682 Sch 1 para 22 (this regulation does not apply to tax which was paid by an employer in respect of a tax year ending on or before 5 April 1996).
SI 2003/2682 reg 219 (for the purposes of para (2)(*b*) above, if payment to the Revenue is made by cheque, and cheque paid on its first presentation to the banker on whom drawn, the payment is treated as made on day cheque received by the Revenue).

RECOVERY

Recovery of tax and interest

84—(1) In this regulation, ''the unpaid amount'' means any amount of tax or interest which—

(*a*) an employer is liable to pay under regulation 76(2), 77(6), 78(8), 79(2)(*b*) or 82(2);
(*b*) an employee is liable to pay under regulation 72(7) or regulation 81(6).

(2) Part 6 of TMA (collection and recovery) applies to the recovery of the unpaid amount as if it were income tax charged on the employer or employee (as the case may be) but with the modification indicated in paragraph (3).

(3) Summary proceedings for the recovery of the unpaid amount may be brought in England and Wales or Northern Ireland at any time before the end of the period which applies for the purposes of the regulation in question, as shown in Table 4.

TABLE 4
PERIOD FOR SUMMARY PROCEEDINGS FOR THE RECOVERY OF UNPAID AMOUNT

1 Regulation	*2 Period*
Regulation 76(2)	(*a*) 12 months after the date by which the statement specified in regulation 73(7) must be delivered, or (*b*) if that statement is delivered after that date, 12 months after its delivery.
Regulations 77(6), 78(8) and 82(2)	(*a*) 12 months after the date on which the unpaid amount became payable, or (*b*) if a return has been required under regulation 77, 12 months after the date of the delivery of that return to the Inland Revenue.
Regulation 79(2)(*b*)	12 months after the date of the certificate.
Regulations 72(7) and 81(6)	12 months after the date on which the unpaid amount became payable.

(4) Proceedings against an employer may be brought for the recovery of the unpaid amount without distinguishing the amounts which the employer is liable to pay in respect of each employee and without specifying the employees in question.

(5) The unpaid amount is one cause of action or one matter of complaint for the purposes of proceedings under sections 65, 66 and 67 of TMA (magistrates' courts, county courts and inferior courts in Scotland).

(6) But paragraphs (4) and (5) do not prevent the bringing of separate proceedings for the recovery of each of the amounts which the employer is liable to pay for any tax period in respect of each of the employees.

Commentary—Simon's Direct Tax Service **E4.11118.**
Derivation—The Income Tax (Employments) Regulations, SI 1993/744 regs 43(9), 47(6), 48(6), 52(3), 54(1)–(5), 55(9).
Modifications—See the Income Tax (PAYE) Regulations, SI 2003/2682 reg 174 (modification of this regulation in its application to payments of taxable incapacity benefit).

CHAPTER 2

OTHER RETURNS AND INFORMATION

RETURNS INVOLVING PAYE INCOME OTHER THAN PAYMENTS

Employers: annual return of other earnings (Forms P11D and P9D)

85—(1) Before 7th July following the end of a tax year, the employer must provide the Inland Revenue—

(*a*) with the information listed in regulation 86 for each employee, and
(*b*) with the additional information listed in regulation 87 for each employee whose employment is subject to the benefits code.

(2) At the same time and in the same manner as the employer provides that information, the employer must also provide a declaration stating that—

(*a*) all information required to be provided has been provided, and
(*b*) the information is complete and accurate to the best of the employer's knowledge and belief.

(3) For the purposes of this regulation an employment is "subject to the benefits code" if, for the purposes of the benefits code in ITEPA, it is a taxable employment under Part 2 of ITEPA (as defined by section 66(3) of ITEPA) which is not an excluded employment under section 216(1) of ITEPA (lower-paid employment and certain types of company director).

Commentary—Simon's Direct Tax Service **E4.11124.**
Derivation—The Income Tax (Employments) Regulations, SI 1993/744 reg 46(1), (7A), (7B).
Cross references—See the Income Tax (PAYE) Regulations, SI 2003/2682 reg 11 (this regulation not to apply to pension payers or pensioners in their capacity as such).
SI 2003/2682 reg 12 (this regulation not to apply to other payers or other payees in their capacity as such).

Information employer must provide for each employee

86—(1) Particulars of the following information must be provided in the case of each employee—

(*a*) any earnings which the employee receives from the employer or related third party otherwise than in money, including the amount of those earnings;

(*b*) any payments made on behalf of the employee by the employer or related third party and not repaid, including the amounts;

(*c*) any non-cash voucher provided by the employer or related third party by reason of which the employee is treated by section 87(1) of ITEPA (benefit of non-cash voucher treated as earnings) as receiving earnings in that tax year, including the amount of those earnings;

(*d*) any use of a credit-token provided by the employer or related third party by reason of which the employee is treated by section 94(1) of ITEPA (benefit of credit-token treated as earnings) as receiving earnings in that tax year, including the amount of those earnings;

(*e*) the due amount in respect of any notional payment where that amount is treated by section 222 of ITEPA (payments on account of tax where deduction not possible) as earnings of the employee received in that tax year;

(*f*) any living accommodation which has been provided for the employee or a member of the employee's family or household by the employer or related third party, including the amount that is treated as earnings for that tax year by section 102 of ITEPA (benefit of living accommodation treated as earnings);

(*g*) any earnings consisting of the amount by which the value of the exemption under subsection (2) of section 287 of ITEPA (limit on exemption of removal expenses and removal benefits) exceeds the limit specified in subsection (1) of that section and having effect in relation to the employee.

(2) Particulars of removal expenses and removal benefits to which section 271 of ITEPA (limited exemption of removal benefits and expenses) applies are required—

(*a*) only under paragraph (1)(*g*), and

(*b*) only to the extent that they exceed the limit in section 287(1) of ITEPA which applies to the change of residence of the employee in question.

(3) In the case of any earnings relating to business entertainment, as defined by section 577 of ICTA, the employer must also inform the Inland Revenue whether the amount of the earnings has been or will be disallowed as a deduction or inclusion as mentioned in section 577(1)(*a*) of that Act in any tax computation relating to the trade, business, profession or vocation of the employer.

(4) "Related third party" means a person making payments or providing benefits to an employee, if the making or provision of the payments or benefits by that person has been arranged, guaranteed or in any way facilitated by the employer.

Commentary—Simon's Direct Tax Service **E4.11124.**
Derivation—The Income Tax (Employments) Regulations, SI 1993/744 reg 46(1), (2), (4), (5), (7), (8).
Cross references—See the Income Tax (PAYE) Regulations, SI 2003/2682 reg 11 (this regulation not to apply to pension payers or pensioners in their capacity as such).
SI 2003/2682 reg 12 (this regulation not to apply to other payers or other payees in their capacity as such).

Information employer must also provide for benefits code employees

87—(1) Particulars of the following information must also be provided in the case of each employee whose employment is subject to the benefits code—

(*a*) any payments made by the employer or related third party to the employee by reason of the employment in respect of expenses;

(*b*) any sums put by the employer or related third party at the disposal of the employee by reason of the employment and paid away by the employee;

(*c*) any benefits provided by the employer or related third party for the employee such as give rise to any amount treated by Chapters 6 to 10 of Part 3, and section 223, of ITEPA (cars and vans, loans, shares, other benefits and payments on account of director's tax) as earnings of the employee received in that tax year, including the amount of those earnings.

(2) Particulars are not required under paragraph (1) of removal expenses and removal benefits to which section 271 of ITEPA (limited exemption of removal benefits and expenses) applies (as to which see regulation 86(2)).

(3) In the case of any earnings relating to business entertainment, as defined by section 577 of ICTA, the employer must also inform the Inland Revenue whether the amount of the earnings has been or will be disallowed as a deduction or inclusion as mentioned in section 577(1)(*a*) of that Act in any tax computation relating to the trade, business, profession or vocation of the employer.

(4) "Related third party" has the meaning given in regulation 86(4).

(5) Regulation 85(3) (meaning of employment "subject to benefits code") applies for the purposes of this regulation.

Commentary—Simon's Direct Tax Service **E4.11124.**
Derivation—The Income Tax (Employments) Regulations, SI 1993/744 reg 46(1), (3), (4), (5), (7), (8).
Cross references—See the Income Tax (PAYE) Regulations, SI 2003/2682 reg 11 (this regulation not to apply to pension payers or pensioners in their capacity as such).
SI 2003/2682 reg 12 (this regulation not to apply to other payers or other payees in their capacity as such).

Annual return of other earnings: amounts

88—(1) Paragraph (2) applies if an employer is required by regulations 85 to 87 to provide an amount which is or is treated as earnings.

(2) The employer must make all deductions and other adjustments which the employer is able to show, by reference to information in the employer's possession or otherwise available to the employer, are authorised or required by Part 3 of ITEPA (earnings and benefits etc treated as earnings).

Commentary—Simon's Direct Tax Service **E4.11124.**
Derivation—The Income Tax (Employments) Regulations, SI 1993/744 reg 46(6).
Cross references—See the Income Tax (PAYE) Regulations, SI 2003/2682 reg 11 (this regulation not to apply to pension payers or pensioners in their capacity as such).
SI 2003/2682 reg 12 (this regulation not to apply to other payers or other payees in their capacity as such).

Annual return of other earnings: exclusion for notional payments

89 The employer is not required to provide particulars in the return under regulation 85 of any notional payment which is a relevant payment made by the employer to the employee (as particulars of it may be required under regulation 73 or 74 (annual returns of relevant payments)).

Commentary—Simon's Direct Tax Service **E4.11124.**
Derivation—The Income Tax (Employments) Regulations, SI 1993/744 reg 46(7).
Cross references—See the Income Tax (PAYE) Regulations, SI 2003/2682 reg 11 (this regulation not to apply to pension payers or pensioners in their capacity as such).

Quarterly return if a car becomes available or unavailable (Form P46 (Car))

90—(1) This regulation applies if—

(*a*) section 120 of ITEPA (benefit of car treated as earnings) treats the benefit of a car as giving rise to an amount as earnings of an employee received in a tax year, and

(*b*) one or more of the following occurs in a tax quarter—

(i) the car becomes available;

(ii) the car becomes unavailable;

(iii) the car is available and the employee's employment becomes subject to the benefits code (as defined by regulation 85(3)).

(2) The employer must provide the Inland Revenue with the following information in respect of the employee not later than 28 days after the end of the tax quarter.

(3) The information is—

(*a*) the employee's name,

(*b*) the employee's national insurance number, if known,

(*c*) details of the car in question,

(*d*) the interim sum determined at step 4 of section 121(1) of ITEPA (method of calculating cash equivalent of benefit of a car),

(*e*) any capital sum contributed by the employee to expenditure on the provision of the car or on any qualifying accessory which is taken into account in so determining the interim sum in respect of the car,

(*f*) any amount which, as a condition of the car being available for the employee's private use, the employee is required to pay in the tax year concerned for that use (whether by way of deduction from relevant payments or otherwise),

(*g*) whether any fuel is provided for private use.

(4) In this regulation—

"available" and "unavailable" are to be read in accordance with sections 116(1) and 143(2) of ITEPA (meaning of when car is available and unavailable to employee);

"qualifying accessory" has the meaning given in section 125 of ITEPA (meaning of accessory etc).

Commentary—Simon's Direct Tax Service **E4.11126.**
Derivation—The Income Tax (Employments) Regulations, SI 1993/744 reg 46A.
Cross references—See the Income Tax (PAYE) Regulations, SI 2003/2682 reg 11 (this regulation not to apply to pension payers or pensioners in their capacity as such).
SI 2003/2682 reg 12 (this regulation not to apply to other payers or other payees in their capacity as such).

Termination awards: information to be provided

91—(1) Before 7th July following the end of the tax year, an employer must, in respect of each employee who received a termination award, provide the Inland Revenue with the information specified in paragraph (3) relating to that award.

(2) "Termination award" means an award consisting of payments combined with other benefits, or consisting solely of other benefits—

(*a*) which were awarded in that tax year in connection with the termination of the employee's employment with the employer, or any change in the duties of or earnings from that employment,

(*b*) which when provided (whether in that or a subsequent tax year) would constitute payments and other benefits received to which Chapter 3 of Part 6 of ITEPA applies (payments and benefits on termination of employment etc), and (*c*) the total amount of which is estimated by the employer to exceed £30,000, when aggregated with other payments and other benefits provided or to be provided (whether in that or a subsequent tax year) in respect of the same person as mentioned in section 404(1) of ITEPA (aggregation of payments in respect of other related employments).

(3) The information to be provided is—

(*a*) the total amount of the payments and other benefits awarded;

(*b*) the total amount of the payments made in that tax year in connection with the award;

(*c*) details of the non-cash benefits provided in that tax year in connection with the award, other than benefits previously contained in a return for that tax year under regulation 85, and the total amount of their amounts calculated in accordance with section 415(2) of ITEPA (valuation of benefits);

(*d*) the estimated total number of the tax years in which payments and non-cash benefits are to be provided in connection with the award and, if the duration of any of those payments and non-cash benefits is capable of being reduced in certain circumstances, details of those circumstances;

(*e*) the estimated total amount of the payments to be made in subsequent tax years in connection with the award;

(*f*) a description of each of the other benefits to be provided in subsequent tax years in connection with the award, and the terms of their provision.

(4) In calculating the cash equivalents of non-cash benefits for the purposes of this regulation, the employer must make all deductions and other adjustments which the employer is able to show, by reference to information in the employer's possession or otherwise available to the employer, are authorised or required by any of the provisions of the benefits code as applied by section 415 of ITEPA.

(5) In calculating the total amount of payments and other benefits for the purposes of paragraphs (2)(*c*) and (3)(*a*), the employer—

(*a*) must have regard to the provisions of Chapter 3 of Part 6 of ITEPA,

(*b*) must take into account the matters referred to in paragraph (3)(*d*),(*e*) and (*f*), and

(*c*) in valuing the amount of non-cash benefits for future tax years in connection with the award, must assume that the provisions of ITEPA relating to those benefits will remain unchanged with respect to those years.

(6) Information required to be provided by an employer in accordance with paragraphs (1) and (3) may be provided after the termination award is made but before the end of the tax year in which it is made.

(7) If information is provided in accordance with paragraph (6), paragraph (3)(*b*) and (*c*) have effect, so far as concerns the providing of information relating to the tax year, as if they required the amounts and benefits there specified to be estimated by the employer as accurately as possible.

(8) This regulation is subject to regulation 93 (return if more than one employer).

(9) In this regulation and regulations 92, 93 and 96 (further provisions about termination awards)—

''employee'' includes a former employee; and

''employer'' includes a former employer.

Commentary—Simon's Direct Tax Service **E4.11125.**
Derivation—The Income Tax (Employments) Regulations, SI 1993/744 reg 46ZA(1)–(4), (10)–(12).
Cross references—See the Income Tax (PAYE) Regulations, SI 2003/2682 reg 10 (this regulation not to apply to agencies or agency workers in their capacity as such).
SI 2003/2682 reg 11 (this regulation not to apply to pension payers or pensioners in their capacity as such).
SI 2003/2682 reg 12 (this regulation not to apply to other payers or other payees in their capacity as such).

Termination awards: return if award changes

92—(1) Paragraph (3) applies if—

(*a*) information has not been provided by the employer under regulation 91(1) solely because either—

(i) the total amount of payments and other benefits awarded in the tax year in respect of the employee is estimated in accordance with regulation 91(2)(*c*) not to exceed £30,000, or

(ii) the award made in the tax year consisted of payments only, and

(*b*) there is a change in the award in a subsequent tax year.

(2) ''Change in the award'' means—

(*a*) that there is a change in—

(i) the amount of the payments awarded, or

(ii) the nature and amounts of the other benefits awarded,

so that the total amount of those payments and other benefits is estimated in accordance with regulation 91(2)(*c*) to exceed £30,000; or

(*b*) that the nature of the award is changed so that it consists—

(i) of payments combined with other benefits, or

(ii) solely of other benefits,

estimated in accordance with regulation 91(2)(*c*) to exceed £30,000.

(3) The employer must, before 7th July following the tax year in which the change in the award occurred, provide the Inland Revenue with the information specified in regulation 91(3) with respect to those payments and other benefits.

(4) Paragraph (5) applies if, after the employer has provided information in accordance with regulation 91(1) or paragraph (3) above, there is a material change—

(*a*) in the amount of the payments awarded, or

(*b*) in the nature and amounts of the other benefits awarded,

in relation to the employee.

(5) The employer must, before 7th July following the end of the tax year in which the material change occurred, give details of the material change to the Inland Revenue.

(6) For the avoidance of doubt, an employer is not required to provide details under this regulation of a change which arises solely because of amendments to the provisions of ITEPA which relate to non-cash benefits.

(7) This regulation is subject to regulation 93 (return if more than one employer).

Commentary—Simon's Direct Tax Service **E4.11125.**
Derivation—The Income Tax (Employments) Regulations, SI 1993/744 reg 46ZA(5), (6), (9), (10).
Cross references—See the Income Tax (PAYE) Regulations, SI 2003/2682 reg 10 (this regulation not to apply to agencies or agency workers in their capacity as such).
SI 2003/2682 reg 11 (this regulation not to apply to pension payers or pensioners in their capacity as such).
SI 2003/2682 reg 12 (this regulation not to apply to other payers or other payees in their capacity as such).

Termination awards: return if more than one employer

93—(1) This regulation applies if the payments and other benefits aggregated in accordance with regulation 91(2)(*c*) include amounts in respect of different employments with more than one employer.

(2) The person who must provide information to the Inland Revenue under regulation 91 or 92, or to the employee under regulation 96, is the employer providing the greatest amount of payments and other benefits so aggregated.

Commentary—Simon's Direct Tax Service **E4.11125.**
Derivation—The Income Tax (Employments) Regulations, SI 1993/744 reg 46ZA(10).
Cross references—See the Income Tax (PAYE) Regulations, SI 2003/2682 reg 10 (this regulation not to apply to agencies or agency workers in their capacity as such).
SI 2003/2682 reg 11 (this regulation not to apply to pension payers or pensioners in their capacity as such).
SI 2003/2682 reg 12 (this regulation not to apply to other payers or other payees in their capacity as such).

Information to be given to employees

Employers: information to employees of other earnings (Forms P11D and P9D)

94—(1) Before 7th July following the end of a tax year, the employer must give a statement to every current employee in respect of whom particulars are to be provided under regulation 85(1) by the employer for that tax year.

(2) The statement must contain the particulars provided under regulations 86 and 87 in so far as they relate to the employee.

(3) If a person who was a current employee ceases to be an employee at any time before 7th July following the end of the tax year, the statement is given to the employee if it is sent or delivered to, or left at, that person's usual or last known address.

(4) A former employee in respect of whom particulars are to be provided under regulation 85(1) by the employer for a tax year may by notice require the employer to give the statement specified in paragraph (2) to that former employee—

(*a*) before 7th July following the end of the tax year, or

(*b*) within 30 days of receiving the notice,

whichever is the later.

(5) The notice may be given to the employer at any time up to 3 years after the end of the tax year.

(6) A former employee who has received a statement from the employer under paragraph (4) in respect of a tax year may not require a further statement from the employer under that paragraph in respect of the same tax year.

(7) In this regulation—

''current employee'' means a person who was an employee on 5th April in the tax year to which the particulars provided under regulation 85(1) relate;

''former employee'' means a person who was an employee during a part of the tax year to which the particulars provided under regulation 85(1) relate, but who was no longer an employee on 5th April in that tax year.

Commentary—Simon's Direct Tax Service **E4.11124.**
Derivation—The Income Tax (Employments) Regulations, SI 1993/744 reg 46AA.
Cross references—See the Income Tax (PAYE) Regulations, SI 2003/2682 reg 10 (when an agency is treated as ceasing to employ an agency worker for the purposes of paras (3)–(7) above).
SI 2003/2682 reg 11 (this regulation not to apply to pension payers or pensioners in their capacity as such).
SI 2003/2682 reg 12 (this regulation not to apply to other payers or other payees in their capacity as such).

Third parties: information to employees of other earnings

95—(1) This regulation applies if a person (''the third party'') has, in a tax year—

(*a*) made any unrelated payments to, or on behalf of, another person's employee, or

(*b*) provided any unrelated benefits to, or in respect of, another person's employee.

(2) Before 7th July following the end of the tax year, the third party must give the employee a statement containing such of the particulars specified by regulations 86 and 87 as relate to the unrelated payments or unrelated benefits.

(3) A benefit or payment is ''unrelated'' if—

(*a*) the employee's employer is not required to provide particulars about it under regulation 85(1), and

(*b*) the third party would have been required to provide particulars about it under regulation 85(1) had the third party been the employee's employer.

Commentary—Simon's Direct Tax Service **E4.11124.**
Derivation—The Income Tax (Employments) Regulations, SI 1993/744 reg 46AB.
Cross references—See the Income Tax (PAYE) Regulations, SI 2003/2682 reg 11 (this regulation not to apply to pension payers or pensioners in their capacity as such).
SI 2003/2682 reg 12 (this regulation not to apply to other payers or other payees in their capacity as such).

Termination awards: information to employees

96—(1) This regulation applies if an employer is required to provide the information specified in regulation 91(3) to the Inland Revenue by—

(*a*) regulation 91(1) (termination award), or

(*b*) regulation 92(3) (change in termination award).

(2) The employer must also give a copy of that information to the employee before 7th July following the end of the tax year.

(3) A copy of the information is given to the employee if it is sent or delivered to, or left at, the employee's usual or last known address.

(4) As to the person who is the employer in cases where there is more than one employer, see regulation 93.

Commentary—Simon's Direct Tax Service **E4.11125.**
Derivation—The Income Tax (Employments) Regulations, SI 1993/744 reg 46ZA(7), (8), (10).
Cross references—See the Income Tax (PAYE) Regulations, SI 2003/2682 reg 10 (this regulation not to apply to agencies or agency workers in their capacity as such).
SI 2003/2682 reg 11 (this regulation not to apply to pension payers or pensioners in their capacity as such).
SI 2003/2682 reg 12 (this regulation not to apply to other payers or other payees in their capacity as such).

CHAPTER 3
PAYE RECORDS

Inspection of employer's PAYE records

97—(1) Whenever required do so by an authorised officer of the Board, an employer must produce to that officer all PAYE records, or such PAYE records as may be specified by the officer, for inspection at the prescribed place and at such time as that officer may reasonably require.

(2) ''PAYE records'' means the following documents and records—

(*a*) all wages sheets, deductions working sheets, documents completed under regulation 46 (Form P46) (other than those which the employer has sent to the Inland Revenue), and other documents and records relating to—

(i) the calculation of the PAYE income of the employees,

(ii) relevant payments to the employees, or

(iii) the deduction of tax from, or accounting for tax in respect of, such payments, and

(*b*) all documents and records relating to any information which an employer is required to provide to the Inland Revenue under regulation 85 (Forms P11D and P9D).

(3) ''The prescribed place'' means such place in the United Kingdom as the employer and the authorised officer may agree upon, or in the absence of agreement—

(*a*) the place in the United Kingdom at which the PAYE records are normally kept, or

(*b*) if there is no such place, the employer's principal place of business in the United Kingdom.

(4) The authorised officer may—

(*a*) take copies of, or make extracts from, any document produced for inspection in accordance with paragraph (1);

(*b*) remove any document so produced if it appears to the officer to be necessary to do so, at a reasonable time and for a reasonable period.

(5) If any document is removed in accordance with paragraph (4)(*b*), the authorised officer must provide—

(*a*) a receipt for the document, and

(*b*) a copy of the document, free of charge, to the person by whom it was produced or caused to be produced, within 7 days of that person requesting a copy, if the document is reasonably required for the proper conduct of a business.

(6) If a lien is claimed on a document produced in accordance with paragraph (1), the removal of the document under paragraph (4)(*b*) is not to be regarded as breaking the lien.

(7) If records are maintained by computer, the person required to make them available for inspection must provide the authorised officer with all facilities necessary for obtaining information from them.

(8) For the purposes of this regulation, an employer must keep, for not less than 3 years after the end of the tax year to which they relate, all PAYE records which are not required to be sent to the Inland Revenue by other provisions of these Regulations.

Commentary—Simon's Direct Tax Service **E4.11138, 11139.**
Derivation—The Income Tax (Employments) Regulations, SI 1993/744 reg 55(1)–(7), (12); the Income Tax (Employments) (Notional Payments) Regulations, SI 1994/1212 reg 13(8).
Modifications—See the Income Tax (PAYE) Regulations, SI 2003/2682 reg 150 (modification of this regulation in its application to payments of taxable jobseeker's allowance made to a claimant).
SI 2003/2682 reg 174 (modification of this regulation in its application to payments of taxable incapacity benefit).

PART 5
EMPLOYERS

SPECIAL ARRANGEMENTS
Multiple PAYE schemes

98—(1) An employer may elect, for the purposes of these Regulations, to be treated as different employers in relation to different groups of employees.

(2) Where the employer makes an election, these Regulations apply as if—

(*a*) in respect of each group the employer were a different employer;

(*b*) each group constituted all of the employer's employees;

(*c*) each group were employed in a separate undertaking from the others; and

(*d*) an employee who has moved from one group to another has left one employment and started employment with a new employer.

(3) While an election is in force, an employer must allocate any new employees to one of the groups.

(4) An election must be made by notice to the Inland Revenue containing—

(*a*) such information as may be necessary to identify the groups of employees, and

(*b*) a certificate that each employee falls into one of the groups.

(5) An employer must, subject to paragraph (6), make an election before the beginning of the tax year for which it is to have effect.

(6) An employer who acquires the whole or a part of any business of another employer may, within 90 days of the acquisition, elect—

(*a*) to be treated as a different employer in relation to the acquired employees, or two or more different employers in relation to groups of the acquired employees, whether or not an election is already in force in respect of the existing employees, or

(*b*) to add some or all of the acquired employees to existing groups of employees in respect of whom an election is already in force,

and such an election has effect for the tax year in which the acquisition takes place.

(7) In paragraph (6)—

"business" includes any trade, concern or undertaking;

"acquired employee" means an employee who was employed in the acquired business.

(8) An election continues in effect until revoked by a notice given to the Inland Revenue.

(9) A notice of revocation must be given before the beginning of the tax year for which the election is to be revoked, but the revocation of an election does not prevent the making of a new election for that or a later tax year.

(10) An election which has not yet come into effect may be revoked at any time before the beginning of the tax year for which it is to have effect.

(11) This regulation is subject to regulation 99.

Commentary—Simon's Direct Tax Service **E4.11113.**
Derivation—The Income Tax (Employments) Regulations, SI 1993/744 reg 3.
Modifications—See the Income Tax (PAYE) Regulations, SI 2003/2682 reg 150 (modification of this regulation in its application to payments of taxable jobseeker's allowance made to a claimant).
SI 2003/2682 reg 174 (modification of this regulation in its application to payments of taxable incapacity benefit).

Multiple PAYE schemes: election made for improper purpose ineffective

99—(1) An election made under regulation 98 must be disregarded if the Inland Revenue—

(*a*) issue a notice to the employer stating that it appears to them that the election is made wholly or mainly for an improper purpose ("an improper purpose notice"), and

(*b*) issue the improper purpose notice within 60 days of the making of the election.

(2) An election is made for an "improper purpose" if it is made for the purpose of—

(*a*) avoiding the requirement imposed by regulation 199 (large employers required to make specified payments electronically),

(*b*) avoiding the requirement imposed by regulation 205 (mandatory use of electronic communications), or

(*c*) receiving an incentive payment under the Income Tax (Incentive Payments for Voluntary Electronic Communication of PAYE Returns) Regulations 2003.

(3) An employer may appeal against an improper purpose notice by giving notice to the Inland Revenue within 30 days of the issue of the improper purpose notice.

(4) The grounds of appeal are—

(*a*) that the election was not made wholly or mainly for an improper purpose, or

(*b*) that the improper purpose notice was not issued within 60 days of the election.

(5) If the appeal is successful the improper purpose notice must be withdrawn.

(6) Regulation 217 (appeals: supplementary provisions) applies to appeals under this regulation.

Commentary—Simon's Direct Tax Service **E4.11113.**
Cross reference—See the Income Tax (PAYE) Regulations, SI 2003/2682 reg 217 (TMA 1970 ss 31A(5), (6), 31B and 31D apply to an appeal under para (3) above as they apply to an appeal under TMA1970 s 31).

Tips: special arrangements

100—(1) This regulation applies if an organised arrangement exists for tips to be shared among employees by a person ("T") who is not the principal employer.

(2) On becoming aware of the existence of an arrangement, the principal employer must notify the Inland Revenue about the arrangement giving T's name, if known.

(3) For the purposes of these Regulations—

(*a*) every payment made to an employee by way of the employee's share of tips by T (including the retention by T of T's own share if T is also an employee) is regarded as a relevant payment by T; and

(*b*) to the extent of any such payment, T is regarded as the employer.

(4) But if in any case the Inland Revenue are satisfied that T has failed to comply with any of the requirements of these Regulations and they so direct, then—

(*a*) any tips paid to T through the principal employer for sharing among the employees are to be dealt with in accordance with paragraph (5), and

(*b*) any other tips may be taken into account by the Inland Revenue under regulation 14(1)(*b*) in determining the code for each employee.

(5) If this paragraph applies—

(*a*) the principal employer is treated as the employer for the purposes of these Regulations in relation to the tips;

(*b*) T must, before the principal employer pays any tips to T, give the principal employer such particulars of every payment by way of the sharing of tips to be made to an employee as may be necessary to enable the principal employer to comply with these Regulations;

(*c*) the principal employer must, on making any payment of tips to T, deduct or repay tax in accordance with these Regulations in respect of the amount of such tips to be paid to each employee, and notify T of each amount so deducted or repaid.

(6) Paragraph (2) does not apply if the arrangement came into existence before 6th April 2004.

(7) In this regulation—

"the principal employer" means the person under whose general control and management the employees work;

"tips" means gratuities and service charges.

Commentary—*Simon's Direct Tax Service* **E4.1114.**
Derivation—The Income Tax (Employments) Regulations, SI 1993/744 reg 5.
Cross references—See the Income Tax (PAYE) Regulations, SI 2003/2682 reg 11 (this regulation not to apply to pension payers or pensioners in their capacity as such).

DEATH OF EMPLOYER AND SUCCESSION

Death of employer

101—(1) This regulation applies if an employer dies.

(2) Anything which the employer would have been liable to do under these Regulations must be done by the employer's personal representatives.

(3) But if the employer made payments on behalf of another person (''the principal''), anything which the employer would have been liable to do under these Regulations in respect of or in connection with those payments must be done by the principal.

Commentary—*Simon's Direct Tax Service* **E4.11111.**
Derivation—The Income Tax (Employments) Regulations, SI 1993/744 reg 79.

Succession to a business etc

102—(1) This regulation applies if there is a change in an employee's employer while the employee remains in employment in the same business.

(2) This regulation also applies if there is a change in the pension payer who pays a pension to a pensioner.

(3) The change is not to be treated as a cessation of employment for the purposes of regulation 36 (cessation of employment: Form P45).

(4) The new employer is, in relation to any matter arising after the change, liable to do anything which the former employer would have been liable to do under these Regulations if the change had not taken place.

(5) Paragraph (4) is subject to paragraphs (6) and (7) and regulation 104 (succession to a business: trade disputes).

(6) The new employer is not liable for the payment of any tax which was deductible from relevant payments made to the employee—

(*a*) before the change took place, unless those payments were made by the new employer, or
(*b*) by the former employer after the change took place.

(7) The new employer is not liable for the payment of any tax which was to be deducted or accounted for in accordance with regulation 62(4) or (5) (notional payments) in respect of notional payments made to the employee—

(*a*) before the change took place, unless those payments were made by the new employer, or
(*b*) by the former employer after the change took place.

(8) The former employer must give the new employer any particulars which the new employer needs in order to comply with this regulation.

(9) In paragraph (1), ''business'' includes any trade, concern or undertaking.

Commentary—*Simon's Direct Tax Service* **E4.11112.**
Derivation—The Income Tax (Employments) Regulations, SI 1993/744 reg 80(1)–(3), (5).
Modifications—See the Income Tax (PAYE) Regulations, SI 2003/2682 reg 150 (modification of this regulation in its application to payments of taxable jobseeker's allowance made to a claimant).
SI 2003/2682 reg 174 (modification of this regulation in its application to payments of taxable incapacity benefit).
Cross references—See the Income Tax (PAYE) Regulations, SI 2003/2682 reg 11 (para (1) above not to apply to pension payers or pensioners in their capacity as such).

Death and succession

103—(1) Regulation 101 (death of employer) does not affect the operation of regulation 102 (succession to a business etc) for the purposes of which the deceased employer's personal representative or the principal may also be the new employer.

(2) But paragraph (3) applies where a person (''P'') is both the new employer and also the deceased employer's personal representative or the principal.

(3) Paragraphs (6) and (7) of regulation 102 (new employer not liable for certain payments of tax) do not apply to P in P's capacity as personal representative or principal.

(4) ''Principal'' has the same meaning as in regulation 101.

Commentary—*Simon's Direct Tax Service* **E4.11112.**

Succession to a business: trade disputes

104—(1) This regulation applies if a trade dispute began, but did not end, before a change to which regulation 102 (succession to a business etc) applies took place.

(2) The former employer must comply with regulations 64(8) (trade disputes: payments to Revenue) and 75 (additional return in case of trade dispute) as though the time limit of 42 days ran out on the date on which the change took place.

(3) The new employer is liable to repay, in accordance with regulation 64, any tax that was withheld in the tax year in which the change took place by the former employer.

(4) The new employer may recover from the Board of Inland Revenue an amount repayable under paragraph (3), as if it were an amount recoverable under regulation 68(3)(*b*) (periodic payments to and recoveries from Revenue).

(5) But any amount recovered under paragraph (4) must be ignored when determining how much the new employer must pay or can recover under regulation 68.

Commentary—*Simon's Direct Tax Service* **E4.11112.**
Derivation—The Income Tax (Employments) Regulations, SI 1993/744 reg 80(4).
Cross references—See the Income Tax (PAYE) Regulations, SI 2003/2682 reg 11 (this regulation not to apply to pension payers or pensioners in their capacity as such).

PART 6

PAYE SETTLEMENT AGREEMENTS

Cross references—SI 2003/2682 reg 12 (this Part not to apply to other payers or other payees in their capacity as such).

MAKING AND EFFECT OF PSA

Inland Revenue and employer may make PSA

105—(1) The Inland Revenue and an employer may agree that paragraph (2) applies in respect of income tax on qualifying general earnings of the employer's employees for a tax year.

(2) In relation to qualifying general earnings included in the agreement, the employer is—

(*a*) accountable to the Board of Inland Revenue in accordance with the terms of the agreement and this Part, and

(*b*) not accountable in accordance with the rest of these Regulations.

(3) Such an agreement is referred to as a PAYE settlement agreement ("PSA").

Commentary—*Simon's Direct Tax Service* **E4.11110.**
Derivation—The Income Tax (Employments) Regulations, SI 1993/744 reg 80A(1), (2).

Qualifying general earnings

106—(1) Qualifying general earnings are those general earnings which meet conditions A and B.

(2) Condition A is that the general earnings consist of—

(*a*) taxable benefits provided or made available by reason of employments with the employer, or

(*b*) expenses paid to persons holding those employments.

(3) Condition B is that the employer and the Inland Revenue agree that the general earnings are—

(*a*) minor, as regards the amount of the sums paid or the type of benefit provided or made available,

(*b*) irregular, as regards the frequency in which, or the times at which, the sums are paid or the benefit is provided or made available,

(*c*) paid in circumstances where deduction of tax by reference to the tax tables is impracticable, or

(*d*) in the case of a benefit provided or made available, shared between employees so that apportionment of the benefit between the employees is impracticable.

(4) "Taxable benefit", in relation to an employee, means any benefit provided or made available, other than in the form of a payment of money, to the employee or to a person who is a member of the employee's family or household.

(5) General earnings to which regulation 112(2)(*a*) or (*b*) (pre-agreement general earnings etc) apply are not qualifying general earnings.

Commentary—*Simon's Direct Tax Service* **E4.11110.**
Derivation—The Income Tax (Employments) Regulations, SI 1993/744 reg 80A(3), (4).

Effect of PSA

107—(1) Qualifying general earnings included in the PSA are treated as excluded from an employee's income for the purposes of determining the amount of the employee's liability to income tax for the tax year to which the PSA relates.

(2) But this does not affect—

(*a*) the chargeability of those qualifying general earnings to income tax, or

(*b*) the employer's liability under the PSA to account for income tax in respect of those qualifying general earnings.

(3) Sums in respect of income tax for which an employer is accountable to the Board of Inland Revenue under a PSA are not to be treated, for the purposes of these Regulations, as tax deducted from relevant payments.

(4) An employee has no right to be treated as having paid tax in respect of sums for which the employer is accountable under a PSA, and accordingly is not entitled to claim or receive any refund of tax paid by the employer under the PSA.

(5) An employee must, subject to paragraph (6), be treated as relieved from any obligations under the Income Tax Acts—

(*a*) to keep records containing information relating to qualifying general earnings included in a PSA, or
(*b*) to deliver returns in respect of those qualifying general earnings.

(6) Paragraph (5) does not apply for the purposes of the obligations imposed on the employer under regulation 117 (inspection of PSA records).

(7) Qualifying general earnings comprised in a PSA are not to be included—

(*a*) in a return by the employer under regulation 73, 74, or 75 (returns of relevant payments and tax deducted), nor
(*b*) in particulars provided by the employer under regulation 85 (annual return of other earnings (Forms P11D and P9D)).

Commentary—*Simon's Direct Tax Service* **E4.11110.**
Derivation—The Income Tax (Employments) Regulations, SI 1993/744 regs 80A(5), 80E.

Payment of tax under PSA

Calculation of tax payable under PSA

108—(1) A PSA must provide for the sums in respect of income tax for which an employer is to be accountable to the Board of Inland Revenue under the PSA—

(*a*) to be computed in accordance with the factors specified in paragraph (2), and
(*b*) to be comprised of the amounts specified in paragraph (3).

(2) The factors are—

(*a*) in the case of qualifying general earnings comprising sums paid in respect of expenses, the estimated aggregate amount of such payments on which income tax is chargeable, reduced by such amount (if any) as would have been deductible if the qualifying general earnings had not been included in the PSA;
(*b*) in the case of qualifying general earnings comprising benefits provided or made available, the estimated aggregate amount of the cash equivalents and other amounts on which income tax is chargeable, reduced by such amount (if any) as would have been deductible if the qualifying general earnings had not been included in the PSA;
(*c*) the total number of employees in receipt of qualifying general earnings comprised in the PSA;
(*d*) the number of those employees respectively chargeable to income tax—

(i) only at the starting rate for the tax year to which the PSA relates,
(ii) at both the starting rate and the basic rate for that tax year, and
(iii) at the starting rate, the basic rate and the higher rate for that tax year;

(*e*) such other matters as are agreed by the Inland Revenue and the employer to be relevant in relation to the qualifying general earnings comprised in the PSA.

(3) The amounts specified for the purposes of paragraph (1)(*b*) are—

(*a*) an amount equal to income tax on the aggregate of the amounts computed in accordance with paragraph (2)(*a*) and (*b*), calculated so as to take account of the factor specified in paragraph (2)(*d*); and
(*b*) a further amount reflecting an estimate of the income tax on the benefit to the employees of having no tax liability on the qualifying general earnings included in the PSA.

Commentary—*Simon's Direct Tax Service* **E4.11110.**
Derivation—The Income Tax (Employments) Regulations, SI 1993/744 reg 80F(1)–(3).

Payment of tax and recovery proceedings

109—(1) The employer must pay to the Inland Revenue by the due date the aggregate amount for which the employer is accountable to the Board of Inland Revenue under a PSA.

(2) "The due date" means 19th October following the end of the tax year to which the PSA relates.

(3) Part 6 of TMA (collection and recovery) applies to the recovery of the aggregate amount or any part of it ("the amount of tax") as if it were income tax charged on the employer.

(4) But summary proceedings for the recovery of the amount of tax may be brought in England, Wales or Northern Ireland at any time before the expiry of 12 months beginning with the due date.

(5) Proceedings may be brought for the recovery of the amount of tax without distinguishing the amounts which the employer is liable to pay in respect of each employee under the PSA and without specifying the employees in question.

(6) The amount of tax is one cause of action or one matter of complaint for the purposes of proceedings under sections 65, 66 and 67 of TMA (magistrates' courts, county courts and inferior courts in Scotland).

Commentary—*Simon's Direct Tax Service* **E4.11110.**
Derivation—The Income Tax (Employments) Regulations, SI 1993/744 reg 80G.

Formal determination of tax payable by the employer

110—(1) This regulation applies if it appears to the Inland Revenue that there may be an amount payable under regulation 109(1) for any tax year which has not been paid by the due date (as defined by regulation 109(2)).

(2) The Inland Revenue may determine the amount payable to the best of their judgment.

(3) If a determination is made, the Inland Revenue must serve notice of it on the employer.

(4) A determination under this regulation is subject to Parts 4, 5 and 6 of TMA (assessment, appeals, collection and recovery) as if—

(*a*) the determination were an assessment, and
(*b*) the amount determined were income tax charged on the employer,

and those Parts of TMA apply accordingly with any necessary modifications.

(5) For the purposes of paragraph 3(1)(*a*) of Schedule 3 to TMA (rules for assigning proceedings to General Commissioners), the relevant place for an appeal against a determination is the place where the determination was made.

Commentary—*Simon's Direct Tax Service* **E4.11110.**
Derivation—The Income Tax (Employments) Regulations, SI 1993/744 reg 80H.

FORM AND COMMENCEMENT OF PSA

Statement of Practice—See Statement of Practice 5/96 PAYE Settlement Agreements.

Form of PSA

111—(1) A PSA must be—

(*a*) in writing, and
(*b*) signed and dated by the employer and the Inland Revenue.

(2) A PSA must incorporate, whether by specification or indirect reference—

(*a*) the qualifying general earnings included in the PSA,
(*b*) the method of calculation, determined in accordance with regulation 108, of the amount of income tax for which the employer is to be accountable in respect of those qualifying general earnings, and
(*c*) the due date by which, in accordance with regulation 109, income tax in respect of those qualifying general earnings is due and payable.

Commentary—*Simon's Direct Tax Service* **E4.11110.**
Derivation—The Income Tax (Employments) Regulations, SI 1993/744 reg 80B.

Commencement of PSA

112—(1) A PSA may be entered into at any time before 6th July following the end of the tax year for which it is to have effect ("the year in question").

(2) A PSA entered into after the beginning of the year in question cannot apply to—

(*a*) general earnings which, when the PSA is entered into, have been, or should have been, paid earlier in the year in question under deduction of tax in accordance with Part 3, or
(*b*) general earnings consisting of benefits which, when the PSA is entered into, are or were reflected in the employee's code for the year in question in accordance with Part 2.

Commentary—*Simon's Direct Tax Service* **E4.11110.**
Derivation—The Income Tax (Employments) Regulations, SI 1993/744 reg 80C.

VARIATION AND CANCELLATION OF PSA

Variation of PSA

113—(1) The Inland Revenue and the employer may, by agreement and consistently with the provisions of this Part, vary the terms of a PSA entered into by them.

(2) The agreement must be—

(*a*) in writing, and
(*b*) signed and dated by the employer and by the Inland Revenue.

(3) The last date for variation of a PSA is 6th July following the end of the tax year to which it relates.

Commentary—*Simon's Direct Tax Service* **E4.11110.**
Derivation—The Income Tax (Employments) Regulations, SI 1993/744 reg 80D.

Cancellation of PSA

114—(1) The Inland Revenue may cancel a PSA if the employer has seriously or persistently failed—

(*a*) to account to the Board of Inland Revenue for sums for which the employer is accountable under the PSA, or otherwise to comply with the terms of the PSA,

(*b*) to produce records in accordance with regulation 117 (inspection of PSA records),

(*c*) to deduct, or account for, tax in accordance with Parts 3 and 4 (deduction and repayment of tax; payments, returns and information), or

(*d*) to deliver returns in accordance with Parts 3 and 4.

(2) Cancellation must be effected by notice to the employer.

(3) A cancellation comes into effect from the date of the notice.

(4) If a PSA is cancelled, this Part does not apply to general earnings—

(*a*) to which the cancelled PSA related, and

(*b*) which are paid, or (as the case may be) provided or made available, after the employer receives notice of the cancellation.

Commentary—*Simon's Direct Tax Service* **E4.11110.**
aDerivation—The Income Tax (Employments) Regulations, SI 1993/744 reg 80M.

INTEREST

Interest on unpaid tax

115—(1) This regulation applies if an employer has not paid to the Inland Revenue by the due date (as defined by regulation 109(2)) the full amount for which the employer is liable under this Part.

(2) The unpaid amount carries interest at the prescribed rate from the due date until payment ("the interest period").

(3) Paragraph (2) applies even if the due date is a non-business day as defined by section 92 of the Bills of Exchange Act 1882.

(4) Any change made to the prescribed rate during the interest period applies to the unpaid amount from the date of the change.

(5) Interest is recoverable as if it were an amount payable under the PSA.

(6) "The prescribed rate" means the rate applicable under section 178 of the Finance Act 1989 for the purposes of section 86 of TMA.

Commentary—*Simon's Direct Tax Service* **E4.11110.**
nDerivation—The Income Tax (Employments) Regulations, SI 1993/744 reg 80J(1), (2), (5), (7), (8).
Cross references—See the Income Tax (PAYE) Regulations, SI 2003/2682 reg 218(3), (4) (a certificate of the Inland Revenue that, to the best of their knowledge and belief, any amount of interest payable under this regulation has not been paid by an employer or employee, is sufficient evidence that the amount mentioned in the certificate is unpaid and due to the Crown).
SI 2003/2682 reg 219 (for the purposes of this regulation, if payment to the Revenue is made by cheque, and cheque paid on its first presentation to the banker on whom drawn, the payment is treated as made on day cheque received by the Revenue).

Interest on overpaid tax

116—(1) This regulation applies if tax in respect of the tax year to which a PSA relates is repaid to the employer after the due date (as defined by regulation 109(2)).

(2) The tax repaid carries interest at the prescribed rate from the later of—

(*a*) the due date, and

(*b*) the date on which the tax was paid,

until the order for the repayment is issued ("the interest period").

(3) Any change made to the prescribed rate during the interest period applies to the tax repaid from the date of the change.

(4) "The prescribed rate" means the rate applicable under section 178 of the Finance Act 1989 for the purposes of section 824 of ICTA.

Commentary—*Simon's Direct Tax Service* **E4.11110.**
nDerivation—The Income Tax (Employments) Regulations, SI 1993/744 reg 80K(1), (2).
Cross references—See the Income Tax (PAYE) Regulations, SI 2003/2682 reg 219 (for the purposes of this regulation, if payment to the Revenue is made by cheque, and cheque paid on its first presentation to the banker on whom drawn, the payment is treated as made on day cheque received by the Revenue).

RECORDS

Inspection of PSA records

117—(1) An authorised officer may require an employer who has entered into a PSA to produce all PSA records, or such PSA records as may be specified by the authorised officer, for inspection—

(*a*) at the prescribed place, and

(*b*) at such time as that officer may reasonably require.

(2) "PSA records" means all books, documents and other records relating to—

(*a*) the qualifying general earnings comprised in the PSA,

(*b*) the calculation of amounts for which the employer is accountable to the Board of Inland Revenue in accordance with the PSA, and

(*c*) the payment of those amounts to the Inland Revenue.

(3) "The prescribed place" means such place in the United Kingdom as the employer and the authorised officer may agree upon, or in the absence of agreement—

(*a*) the place in the United Kingdom at which the PSA records are normally kept, or

(*b*) if there is no such place, the employer's principal place of business in the United Kingdom.

(4) The authorised officer may—

(*a*) take copies of, or make extracts from, any records produced for inspection in accordance with paragraph (1);

(*b*) remove any records so produced if the officer considers it necessary to do so, at a reasonable time and for a reasonable period.

(5) If any record is removed in accordance with paragraph (4)(*b*), the authorised officer must provide—

(*a*) a receipt for the record, and

(*b*) a copy of the record, free of charge, to the person by whom it was produced or caused to be produced, within 7 days of that person requesting a copy, if the record is reasonably required for the proper conduct of a business.

(6) If a lien is claimed on a record produced in accordance with paragraph (1), the removal of the document under paragraph (4)(*b*) is not to be regarded as breaking the lien.

(7) If records are maintained by computer, the person required to make them available for inspection must provide the authorised officer with all facilities necessary for obtaining information from them.

(8) An employer must keep PSA records for not less than 3 years after the end of the most recent tax year to which they relate.

Commentary—*Simon's Direct Tax Service* **E4.11110.**
/Derivation—The Income Tax (Employments) Regulations, SI 1993/744 reg 80N.

PART 7
SPECIAL CASES

CHAPTER 1
COUNCILLORS' ALLOWANCES

Interpretation of Chapter 1

118—(1) In this Chapter—

"allowances" means—

(*a*) payments by way of attendance allowance within section 173(1) or 175(1) of the Local Government Act 1972,

(*b*) payments within regulations made under section 18(1) of the Local Government and Housing Act 1989,

(*c*) payments within regulations made under section 100(1)(*a*) or (*c*) of the Local Government Act 2000,

(*d*) payments by way of attendance allowance within section 47(1) of the Local Government (Scotland) Act 1973, or

(*e*) payments within regulation 3(1), 4(1) or 5(1) of the Local Government (Payments to Councillors) Regulations (Northern Ireland) 1999;

"councillor" means a person entitled to receive any allowances;

"local council" means the local authority, council, joint authority or joint committee paying allowances.

(2) For the purposes of paragraph (1)—

"council" and "joint committee" are to be read in accordance with section 148(1) of the Local Government Act (Northern Ireland) 1972; and

"local authority" in England and Wales has the meaning given in section 270(1) of the Local Government Act 1972, and in Scotland has the meaning given in section 235(1) of the Local Government (Scotland) Act 1973.

Commentary—*Simon's Direct Tax Service* **E4.1185.**
Derivation—The Income Tax (Employments) Regulations, SI 1993/744 reg 56.

Councillor's option to have tax deducted at basic rate

119—(1) A councillor may, by notice to the Inland Revenue, opt to have income tax deducted from allowances at the basic rate in force at the time of payment of the allowances (the "basic rate option").

(2) On receiving any such notice the Inland Revenue must give notice to the local council of the councillor's exercise of the basic rate option.

(3) On receiving a notice under paragraph (2), the local council must, when making any payment of allowances to the councillor, deduct income tax at the basic rate in force at the time of that payment on the non-cumulative basis.

(4) Paragraph (5) applies if—

(*a*) a councillor has exercised the basic rate option, and
(*b*) the Inland Revenue consider that the councillor may incur deductible expenses.

(5) The Inland Revenue may direct the local council to disregard an appropriate amount of the allowances in calculating the tax to be deducted.

(6) In paragraph (4)(*b*), ''deductible expenses'' means expenses of a kind which would be deductible under sections 336 to 338 of ITEPA (expenses incurred wholly, exclusively and necessarily in performance of duties, and travel expenses).

Commentary—*Simon's Direct Tax Service* **E4.1185.**
Derivation—The Income Tax (Employments) Regulations, SI 1993/744 reg 57(1), (3)–(5).

Particulars that local council must record

120—(1) This regulation applies if the Inland Revenue have given notice to the local council of the exercise by a councillor of the basic rate option.

(2) The local council must record, in a deductions working sheet (which it must prepare for the purpose unless it has already prepared one) the following particulars about every payment of allowances which it makes to the councillor.

(3) The particulars are—

(*a*) the councillor's name,
(*b*) the councillor's national insurance number, if known,
(*c*) the date of the payment,
(*d*) the amount of the allowances,
(*e*) where regulation 119(5) applies, the net amount of the allowances from which tax has been deducted, and
(*f*) the amount of tax deducted from the allowances.

Commentary—*Simon's Direct Tax Service* **E4.1185.**
o**Derivation**—The Income Tax (Employments) Regulations, SI 1993/744 reg 57(6), (7).

Regulations apply as if basic rate option were issue of code

121 If a councillor exercises the basic rate option, these Regulations apply as if the Inland Revenue had issued the basic rate code in respect of the allowances.

Commentary—*Simon's Direct Tax Service* **E4.1185.**

CHAPTER 2

RESERVE FORCES' PAY

Interpretation of Chapter 2

122—(1) In this Chapter—

''the Ministry'' means the Ministry of Defence;
''reserve forces'' means the forces specified in paragraph (2);
''reserve pay'' means relevant payments made by the Ministry to members of the reserve forces;
''reservist'' means any person in receipt of reserve pay, but does not include a person who is not resident in the United Kingdom and is serving outside the United Kingdom.

(2) The forces specified in this paragraph are—

(*a*) the Royal Naval Reserve (including Queen Alexandra's Royal Naval Nursing Service Reserve),
(*b*) the Royal Marines Reserve,
(*c*) the Territorial Army,
(*d*) the Royal Auxiliary Air Force,
(*e*) the University Air Squadron, and
(*f*) Officers, Adult Instructors and Adult Warrant Officers of the Sea Cadet Corps, Army Cadet Force, Air Training Corps or Combined Cadet Force.

Commentary—*Simon's Direct Tax Service* **E4.1181.**
Derivation—The Income Tax (Employments) Regulations, SI 1993/744 reg 59.

Application of other Parts

123—(1) Parts 2 (codes) and 3 (deduction and repayment of tax) do not apply to reserve pay.

(2) The rest of these Regulations apply as if the Inland Revenue had issued the basic rate code in respect of reserve pay.

Commentary—*Simon's Direct Tax Service* **E4.1181.**
Derivation—The Income Tax (Employments) Regulations, SI 1993/744 reg 60.

Deduction of tax

124—(1) On making any payment of reserve pay to a reservist during a tax year, the Ministry must deduct income tax at the basic rate in force when the payment is made.

(2) But the Ministry must not deduct income tax if—

(*a*) it has received notice from the Inland Revenue of a determination for that tax year under this Chapter that tax is not to be deducted from reserve pay, and

(*b*) it has not received notice of any amendment of that determination.

(3) This regulation applies even if an objection or appeal has been made under this Chapter.

Commentary—*Simon's Direct Tax Service* **E4.1181.**
o**Derivation**—The Income Tax (Employments) Regulations, SI 1993/744 reg 61(1), (2), (4).

Determination by Inland Revenue

125—(1) The Inland Revenue may make a determination that tax is not to be deducted from reserve pay if the Inland Revenue are satisfied that the reservist will not be liable to income tax on the full amount of the reserve pay in a tax year.

(2) For the purpose of making a determination, it must be assumed—

(*a*) that any reliefs from income tax to which the reservist is entitled are allowable primarily against the reservist's PAYE income from other sources, and

(*b*) unless the reservist objects, that the balance (if any) of such reliefs is next allowable against the reservist's income other than PAYE income.

(3) The Inland Revenue may make a determination before, or at any time during, the tax year.

(4) On making a determination the Inland Revenue must notify the reservist and the Ministry.

Commentary—*Simon's Direct Tax Service* **E4.1181.**
Derivation—The Income Tax (Employments) Regulations, SI 1993/744 reg 62.

Objection against deduction of tax

126—(1) A reservist who objects to tax being deducted in accordance with regulation 124 (deduction at basic rate) must state the grounds of objection.

(2) On receiving the notice of objection, the Inland Revenue must make a determination whether income tax at the basic rate is to be deducted from the reserve pay.

(3) Regulation 125(2) (assumptions) applies for the purpose of making the determination.

(4) The Inland Revenue must notify the reservist of the determination.

(5) The Inland Revenue may amend the determination by agreement with the reservist.

(6) If the Inland Revenue and the reservist do not reach agreement, the reservist may appeal against the determination by giving notice to the Inland Revenue.

(7) An appeal under paragraph (6) may be made to the General or Special Commissioners.

Commentary—*Simon's Direct Tax Service* **E4.1181.**
Derivation—The Income Tax (Employments) Regulations, SI 1993/744 reg 63(1)–(4).

Appeal to Commissioners

127—(1) On appeal, the Commissioners must determine whether income tax at the basic rate is to be deducted from the reserve pay.

(2) Regulation 125(2) (assumptions) applies for the purpose of making the determination.

(3) If, on appeal, the Commissioners determine that tax is not to be deducted from the reserve pay, the Inland Revenue must give notice of the determination to the Ministry.

(4) For the purposes of paragraph 3(1)(*a*) of Schedule 3 to TMA (rules for assigning proceedings to General Commissioners), the relevant place for the appeal is the place where the reservist lives.

Commentary—*Simon's Direct Tax Service* **E4.1181.**
Derivation—The Income Tax (Employments) Regulations, SI 1993/744 reg 63(5)–(7), (9).

Amended determinations

128—(1) This regulation applies if a determination by the Inland Revenue or the Commissioners under regulation 125, 126 or 127 is found to be inappropriate because the actual circumstances are different from the circumstances by reference to which it was made.

(2) The Inland Revenue must amend the determination.

(3) The Inland Revenue must give notice of the amended determination to the reservist and the Ministry.

(4) Regulations 126 and 127 apply in relation to an amended determination as they apply in relation to a determination under regulation 126(2).

Commentary—*Simon's Direct Tax Service* **E4.1181.**
Derivation—The Income Tax (Employments) Regulations, SI 1993/744 reg 64.

Certificate of tax deducted

129—(1) On making any payment of reserve pay from which tax is deducted, the Ministry may, and if the reservist so requires must, give the reservist a certificate showing the following particulars.

(2) The particulars are—

(*a*) the reservist's name,
(*b*) the reservist's national insurance number, if known,
(*c*) the date of the payment,
(*d*) the amount of the payment, and
(*e*) the amount of tax deducted.

Commentary—*Simon's Direct Tax Service* **E4.1181.**
Derivation—The Income Tax (Employments) Regulations, SI 1993/744 reg 65.

Repayment to reservist during tax year

130—(1) The Ministry must not repay tax in respect of reserve pay to a reservist.

(2) If a reservist applies for a repayment of tax deducted from reserve pay, the Inland Revenue may make such repayment at any time during the tax year as may be appropriate.

(3) In deciding what is appropriate the Inland Revenue must have regard to—

(*a*) the reserve pay of the reservist for the period from the beginning of the tax year up to and including the date of the application,
(*b*) the amount of tax deducted from the reserve pay as evidenced by certificates of pay and tax supplied under regulation 129,
(*c*) any reliefs from income tax to which the reservist is entitled, and
(*d*) the reservist's other PAYE income for the tax year and, unless the reservist objects, the reservist's income for the tax year from all other sources, and liability to tax on that income, as estimated by the Inland Revenue.

Commentary—*Simon's Direct Tax Service* **E4.1181.**
Derivation—The Income Tax (Employments) Regulations, SI 1993/744 reg 66.

Particulars that Ministry must record

131—(1) The Ministry must record, in a deductions working sheet, the following particulars about every payment of reserve pay made to a reservist.

(2) The particulars are—

(*a*) the reservist's name,
(*b*) the reservist's national insurance number, if known,
(*c*) the tax year to which the deductions working sheet relates,
(*d*) the date of the payment,
(*e*) the amount of the payment, and
(*f*) the amount of tax (if any) deducted on making the payment.

Commentary—*Simon's Direct Tax Service* **E4.1181.**
Derivation—The Income Tax (Employments) Regulations, SI 1993/744 reg 67.

End of year certificate

132—(1) The Ministry must give an end of year certificate to a reservist in respect of whom the Ministry was required to prepare or maintain a deductions working sheet.

(2) The certificate must be given before 1st June following the end of the tax year to which it relates.

(3) The certificate must show—

(*a*) the tax year to which it relates,
(*b*) the reservist's name,
(*c*) the reservist's national insurance number, if known,
(*d*) the total amount of reserve pay paid by the Ministry to the reservist during the tax year,
(*e*) the total tax deducted from the reserve pay,
(*f*) the force in which the reservist was serving, and
(*g*) the reservist's service number.

Commentary—*Simon's Direct Tax Service* **E4.1181.**
Derivation—The Income Tax (Employments) Regulations, SI 1993/744 reg 68.

Other PAYE income of reservist

133 Nothing in this Chapter affects the application of these Regulations to any other PAYE income of a reservist.

Commentary—*Simon's Direct Tax Service* **E4.1181.**
Derivation—The Income Tax (Employments) Regulations, SI 1993/744 reg 70.

CHAPTER 3
HOLIDAY PAY FUNDS

Cross references—See the Income Tax (PAYE) Regulations, SI 2003/2682 reg 11 (this Chapter not to apply to pension payers or pensioners in their capacity as such).

Interpretation of Chapter 3

134—In this Chapter—

"fund" means a person who pays holiday pay—

(*a*) to an individual who is not employed by the person, or

(*b*) in respect of such an individual who has died;

"holiday pay" means—

(*a*) any payment received by an individual in exchange for a voucher, stamp or similar document purchased by a person who employs (or employed) that individual for any holiday period, or

(*b*) if such an individual has died, any payment received by a person claiming in respect of that individual's right to such a payment;

"recipient" means a person who is paid holiday pay.

Commentary—*Simon's Direct Tax Service* **E4.1115.**
Derivation—The Income Tax (Employments) Regulations, SI 1993/744 reg 71.
Cross references—SI 2003/2682 reg 12 (this regulation not to apply to other payers or other payees in their capacity as such).

Application of other Parts

135—(1) Parts 2 (codes) and 3 (deduction and repayment of tax) do not apply to holiday pay.

(2) The rest of these Regulations apply as if the Inland Revenue had issued the basic rate code in respect of holiday pay.

Commentary—*Simon's Direct Tax Service* **E4.1115.**
Derivation—The Income Tax (Employments) Regulations, SI 1993/744 reg 72.

Deduction of tax

136 On making any payment of holiday pay to a recipient, a fund must deduct income tax at the basic rate in force at the time the payment is made.

Commentary—*Simon's Direct Tax Service* **E4.1115.**
Derivation—The Income Tax (Employments) Regulations, SI 1993/744 reg 73.

Certificate of tax deducted

137—(1) On making any payment of holiday pay, a fund must give the recipient a certificate showing the following particulars.

(2) The particulars are—

(*a*) the recipient's name,

(*b*) the recipient's national insurance number, if known,

(*c*) the tax year in which the payment is made,

(*d*) the date of the payment,

(*e*) the amount of the payment, and

(*f*) the amount of tax deducted on making the payment.

Commentary—*Simon's Direct Tax Service* **E4.1115.**
Derivation—The Income Tax (Employments) Regulations, SI 1993/744 reg 74.

Repayment to recipient during tax year

138—(1) A fund must not repay tax deducted from a payment of holiday pay to a recipient.

(2) If a recipient applies for a repayment of tax deducted from holiday pay, the Inland Revenue may make such repayment at any time during the tax year as may be appropriate.

(3) In deciding what is appropriate the Inland Revenue must have regard to—

(*a*) the holiday pay of the recipient for the period from the beginning of the tax year up to and including the date of the application,

(*b*) the amount of tax deducted from the holiday pay as evidenced by certificates supplied under regulation 137,

(*c*) any entitlement of the recipient to relief from income tax, and
(*d*) the recipient's other PAYE income for the tax year and, unless the recipient objects, the recipient's income for the tax year from all other sources, and liability to tax on that income, as estimated by the Inland Revenue.

Commentary—*Simon's Direct Tax Service* **E4.1115.**
Derivation—The Income Tax (Employments) Regulations, SI 1993/744 reg 75.

Particulars that fund must record

139—(1) A fund must record, in a deductions working sheet, the following particulars about every payment of holiday pay made to a recipient.

(2) The particulars are—

(*a*) the recipient's name,
(*b*) the recipient's national insurance number, if known,
(*c*) the tax year to which the deductions working sheet relates,
(*d*) the date of the payment,
(*e*) the amount of the payment, and
(*f*) the amount of tax (if any) deducted on making the payment.

Commentary—*Simon's Direct Tax Service* **E4.1115.**
Derivation—The Income Tax (Employments) Regulations, SI 1993/744 reg 76.

Other PAYE income of recipient

140 Nothing in this Chapter affects the application of these Regulations to any other PAYE income of a recipient.

Commentary—*Simon's Direct Tax Service* **E4.1115.**
Derivation—The Income Tax (Employments) Regulations, SI 1993/744 reg 78.

CHAPTER 4
DIRECT COLLECTION AND SPECIAL ARRANGEMENTS

Direct collection and special arrangements

141—(1) In—

(*a*) cases of casual employment, and
(*b*) any other case in which the Inland Revenue are of the opinion that deduction of tax by reference to the tax tables is impracticable,

the Inland Revenue may proceed in accordance with regulation 142, or make special arrangements for the collection of tax in respect of PAYE income of any employees.

(2) A special arrangement does not apply to PAYE income of an employer's employees if—

(*a*) the arrangement has not been agreed with the employer, and
(*b*) the employer does not proceed in accordance with the arrangement.

Commentary—*Simon's Direct Tax Service* **E4.1144.**
Derivation—The Income Tax (Employments) Regulations, SI 1993/744 reg 102.
Modifications—See the Income Tax (PAYE) Regulations, SI 2003/2682 reg 174 (modification of this regulation in its application to payments of taxable incapacity benefit).

Direct collection: issue of deductions working sheet

142—(1) The Inland Revenue may issue a deductions working sheet to an employee specifying—

(*a*) the employee's name,
(*b*) the capacity in which the employee receives relevant payments,
(*c*) the employee's code, and
(*d*) the tax year to which the deductions working sheet relates.

(2) In such a case regulations 143 to 147 apply unless, within 30 days beginning with the receipt of the deductions working sheet, the employee objects to the use of the direct collection procedure.

Commentary—*Simon's Direct Tax Service* **E4.1144.**
Derivation—The Income Tax (Employments) Regulations, SI 1993/744 reg 104(1).

Direct collection: employee to keep records

143—(1) Whenever the employee receives any relevant payment during the tax year, the employee must record in the deductions working sheet—

(*a*) the amount of the payment,
(*b*) the date on which it was received, and
(*c*) the total payments to date.

(2) In addition, the employee must record in the deductions working sheet in relation to the last date in a tax quarter on which the employee receives a relevant payment—

(*a*) the total free pay to date or, as the case may be, the total additional pay to date in relation to that date according to the employee's code, and

(*b*) the corresponding total tax to date.

(3) If the employee does not receive any relevant payments in a tax quarter, the last day of the quarter must be used for the purposes of paragraph (2).

(4) If the employee receives relevant payments in more than one capacity, no account is to be taken for the purposes of this regulation and regulations 144 to 147 of the relevant payments received by the employee in any capacity other than that mentioned in the deductions working sheet.

(5) In this regulation and regulations 145 and 146, "total payments to date" means, in relation to any date, the sum of all relevant payments received by the employee from the beginning of the tax year up to and including that date, irrespective of the person or persons from whom it was received.

Commentary—*Simon's Direct Tax Service* **E4.1144.**
Derivation—The Income Tax (Employments) Regulations, SI 1993/744 reg 104(2), (14), (15).

Direct collection: payment

144—(1) In this regulation—

"the current total tax" means the total tax to date required to be recorded in the deductions working sheet by an employee under regulation 143(2)(*b*);

"the previous total tax" means the total tax to date (if any) required to be recorded for the previous tax quarter in the tax year.

(2) If, in relation to any tax quarter, the current total tax exceeds the previous total tax, the employee must pay the excess to the Inland Revenue, within 14 days after the end of the tax quarter.

(3) But if, in relation to any tax quarter, the previous total tax exceeds the current total tax, the employee may recover the excess—

(*a*) by deducting it from the amount payable under paragraph (2) for a later quarter in the tax year, or

(*b*) from the Board of Inland Revenue.

(4) If the employee's code is a K code, the amount payable under paragraph (2) is not to exceed the overriding limit in relation to the relevant payments which the employee has received in that tax quarter.

(5) Any amount which is not payable because of the application of paragraph (4) must be added to the current total tax for the purpose of the calculation in paragraph (2) or (3) for the next tax quarter (if any) of that tax year.

Commentary—*Simon's Direct Tax Service* **E4.1144.**
Derivation—The Income Tax (Employments) Regulations, SI 1993/744 reg 104(2), (3).

Direct collection: return when relevant payments cease

145—(1) When no longer receiving relevant payments, the employee must, without unreasonable delay, send a return to the Inland Revenue showing the following particulars.

(2) The particulars are—

(*a*) such particulars as the Board may require for identifying the employee,

(*b*) the tax year to which the return relates,

(*c*) the last date on which the employee received any relevant payments ("the last date"),

(*d*) the employee's total payments to date at the last date,

(*e*) the corresponding total tax to date at the last date, and

(*f*) if the employee's code is a K code, the amount, if any, of that corresponding total tax to date which is not payable because of regulation 144(4) (overriding limit).

Commentary—*Simon's Direct Tax Service* **E4.1144.**
Derivation—The Income Tax (Employments) Regulations, SI 1993/744 reg 104(9), (10).

Direct collection: end of year return

146—(1) Before 20th May following the end of the tax year, the employee must deliver a return to the Inland Revenue.

(2) The return must show—

(*a*) such particulars as the Board may require for identifying the employee,

(*b*) the tax year to which the return relates,

(*c*) the employee's total payments to date at the end of the tax year,

(*d*) the total tax to date calculated for the last tax quarter in the tax year, and

(*e*) if the employee's code is a K code, the amount, if any, of that total tax to date which is not payable because of regulation 144(4) (overriding limit).

(3) But paragraph (1) does not apply if the employee has already delivered a return under regulation 145 or section 8 of TMA (personal returns).

(4) If a return is required by paragraph (1), regulations 76, 84 and 218 (which relate to the certification and recovery of tax remaining unpaid by an employer for any tax year) apply with the necessary modifications in the case of any tax remaining unpaid by the employee.

(5) Section 98A of TMA (special penalties in case of certain returns) applies to paragraph (1).

Commentary—*Simon's Direct Tax Service* **E4.1144.**
aa**Derivation**—The Income Tax (Employments) Regulations, SI 1993/744 reg 104(11)–(13), (16).

Direct collection: failure to pay

147—(1) This regulation applies if, within 14 days after the end of any tax quarter—

(*a*) the employee has not paid any tax for that quarter, and the Inland Revenue are unaware of the amount, if any, which the employee is liable to pay for that quarter, or

(*b*) the employee has paid an amount of tax for that quarter, but the Inland Revenue are not satisfied that it is the full amount which the employee is liable to pay for that quarter.

(2) The Inland Revenue may give notice to the employee requiring the employee, within 14 days of the issue of the notice, to deliver a return showing the amount of tax which the employee is liable to pay under regulation 144(2) in respect of the tax quarter in question.

(3) If such a notice is given, regulations 77, 84 and 218(5) and (6) (which relate to the certification and recovery of tax unpaid by an employer) apply with the necessary modifications for the purposes of ascertaining, certifying and recovering the tax payable by the employee as if it were tax which the employee was liable to deduct from relevant payments paid by the employee.

Commentary—*Simon's Direct Tax Service* **E4.1144.**
Derivation—The Income Tax (Employments) Regulations, SI 1993/744 reg 104(5), (6).

PART 8
SOCIAL SECURITY BENEFITS

CHAPTER 1
JOBSEEKER'S ALLOWANCE: NORMAL CASES

Commentary—*Simon's Direct Tax Service* **E4.11101.**
Cross references—See the Income Tax (PAYE) Regulations, SI 2003/2682 reg 165 (except for SI 2003/2682 reg 148, this Chapter does not apply to claimants under Pt 8 Chapter 2 (jobseekers' allowance: special cases).

Interpretation of Chapters 1 and 2

148 In Chapters 1 and 2—

''award'' means an award of a jobseeker's allowance;

''claim'' means a claim for a jobseeker's allowance;

''claimant'' means a person who has made a claim, or who is treated for the purposes of the JSA Regulations as having made a claim;

''Chapter 2 claimant'' means—

(*a*) a claimant who is entitled to a jobseeker's allowance by virtue of regulation 17 of the JSA Regulations (laid off and short time workers); or

(*b*) a claimant who is a share fisherman, as defined by regulation 156 of the JSA Regulations;

''Department'' means the Department for Work and Pensions or, in Northern Ireland, the Department for Social Development;

''JSA Regulations'' means the Jobseeker's Allowance Regulations 1996 or, in Northern Ireland, the Jobseeker's Allowance Regulations (Northern Ireland) 1996;

''jobseeker's allowance'' means benefit payable under—

(*a*) the Jobseekers Act 1995, or

(*b*) in Northern Ireland, the Jobseekers (Northern Ireland) Order 1995;

''taxable jobseeker's allowance'' means any amount of jobseeker's allowance which is chargeable to income tax under Chapter 2 of Part 10 of ITEPA (tax on social security income).

Commentary—*Simon's Direct Tax Service* **E4.11101.**
Derivation—The Income Tax (Employments) Regulations, SI 1993/744 regs 81, 83(1), 94.

Scope of Chapter 1

149 This Chapter applies to claimants who are not Chapter 2 claimants.

Commentary—*Simon's Direct Tax Service* **E4.11101.**

Application of other regulations

150—(1) The following regulations apply to payments of taxable jobseeker's allowance made to a claimant with the modifications mentioned in paragraphs (2) and (3)—

Regulation 2	interpretation
Regulation 14	matters relevant to determination of code
Regulation 15	flat rate codes
Regulation 16	continued application of employee's code
Regulation 17	notice to employee of code
Regulation 18	objections and appeals against employee's code
Regulation 19	amendment of code
Regulation 20	notice to employer of amended code
Regulation 21	deduction and repayment of tax by reference to employee's code
Regulation 97	inspection of employer's PAYE records
Regulation 98	multiple PAYE schemes
Regulation 102	succession to a business etc
Regulation 185	adjusting total net tax deducted for purposes of sections 59A(1) and 59B(1) TMA
Regulation 188	assessments other than self-assessments
Regulation 211	how information must or may be delivered by employers
Regulation 214	how information must be provided by employees
Regulation 216	service by post.

(2) In the application of those regulations, the expressions listed in column 1 of Table 5 have the meanings shown in column 2 of the table.

TABLE 5
MEANING OF EXPRESSIONS IN APPLICATION OF OTHER REGULATIONS

1 Expression	*2 Meaning for purposes of this Chapter*
Employee	claimant
Employer	Department
Employment	award
Relevant payments	taxable jobseeker's allowance.

(3) In the application of regulations 20 and 21, any reference to the deduction or repayment of tax must be read as a reference to the tax calculation which the Department is required to make at the end of the tax year or on the cessation of an award (by virtue of regulations 157(2)(*a*) and 158(2) respectively).

Commentary—*Simon's Direct Tax Service* **E4.11101.**
Derivation—The Income Tax (Employments) Regulations, SI 1993/744 regs 82, 83(3).

Obtaining the claimant's Form P45

151—(1) A claimant who has Parts 2 and 3 of Form P45 must deliver them to the Department on making a claim for a jobseeker's allowance which includes taxable jobseeker's allowance.

(2) If, on making a claim, the claimant declares that the claimant's last employer did not provide Parts 2 and 3 of Form P45, the Department may require the employer to deliver them to a specified office of the Department.

Commentary—*Simon's Direct Tax Service* **E4.11101.**
Derivation—The Income Tax (Employments) Regulations, SI 1993/744 regs 84(1), (2), (8).
Cross references—See the Income Tax (PAYE) Regulations, SI 2003/2682 reg 11 (this regulation not to apply to pension payers or pensioners in their capacity as such).

Deductions working sheet for claimants awarded taxable jobseeker's allowance

152—(1) The Department must prepare a deductions working sheet in respect of each claimant whose award includes taxable jobseeker's allowance.

(2) If the Department obtains Parts 2 and 3 of Form P45 relating to the claimant, it must immediately prepare the deductions working sheet using the information shown in Parts 2 and 3 of Form P45 in accordance with regulation 153.

(3) If the Department does not obtain Parts 2 and 3 of Form P45 relating to the claimant, it must prepare the deductions working sheet in accordance with regulation 154.

Commentary—*Simon's Direct Tax Service* **E4.11101.**
Derivation—The Income Tax (Employments) Regulations, SI 1993/744 reg 84(3), (7).

Form P45: deductions working sheet and return

153—(1) If Parts 2 and 3 of Form P45 relate to the current tax year, the Department must record in the deductions working sheet the total payments to date shown in Parts 2 and 3 of Form P45.

(2) If Parts 2 and 3 of Form P45 relate to the current tax year and show that the cumulative basis has been used, the Department must also—

(*a*) record the following information from Parts 2 and 3 of Form P45 in the deductions working sheet, or
(*b*) keep such records as enable production of the information.

(3) If the code shown in Parts 2 and 3 of Form P45 is a K code, the information is—

(*a*) the total additional pay to date,
(*b*) the total taxable payments to date, and
(*c*) the lower of the total tax to date as at the week or month shown in Parts 2 and 3 of Form P45 or the total net tax deducted shown in them.

(4) In any other case the information is—

(*a*) the total free pay to date,
(*b*) the total taxable payments to date, and
(*c*) the corresponding total tax to date as at the week or month shown in Parts 2 and 3 of Form P45.

(5) Paragraph (6) applies if—

(*a*) the claim is made by 24th May in a tax year, and
(*b*) Parts 2 and 3 of Form P45 show that the last relevant payment was made in the preceding tax year.

(6) The Department must complete the deductions working sheet but without recording the total payments to date or total net tax deducted (if any) shown in Parts 2 and 3 of Form P45.

(7) In cases falling within paragraphs (1) and (5), the code shown in Parts 2 and 3 of Form P45 must be treated as the claimant's code for the purposes of these Regulations.

(8) If, in a case not falling within paragraph (5), Parts 2 and 3 of Form P45 show that the last relevant payment was made in a tax year preceding that in which the claim was made, the Department—

(*a*) must complete the deductions working sheet but without recording the total payments to date or total net tax deducted (if any) shown in Parts 2 and 3 of Form P45, and
(*b*) must record the emergency code as the claimant's code.

(9) The Department must supply the information recorded under this regulation to the Inland Revenue together with such further information as may be required for the purposes of these Regulations.

Commentary—*Simon's Direct Tax Service* **E4.11101.**
Derivation—The Income Tax (Employments) Regulations, SI 1993/744 reg 84(3), (5)–(7).

No Form P45: deductions working sheet and return

154—(1) In a case falling within regulation 152(3) (no Form P45), the Department must—

(*a*) prepare the deductions working sheet within 14 days of the award of a taxable jobseeker's allowance, and
(*b*) record the emergency code as the claimant's code.

(2) The Department must also deliver a return to the Inland Revenue, giving—

(*a*) the claimant's name,
(*b*) the claimant's national insurance number,
(*c*) the claimant's date of birth, if known,
(*d*) the date on which the claim was made, and
(*e*) the reference number of the benefit office submitting the return.

(3) But the return need not be delivered if the claimant certifies that the claimant—

(*a*) is undergoing a course of full-time education and has not had regular employment since the previous 6th April, or
(*b*) has not had regular employment since finishing full-time education.

Commentary—*Simon's Direct Tax Service* **E4.11101.**
Derivation—The Income Tax (Employments) Regulations, SI 1993/744 reg 84(7), (9), (10).

Claimant's code etc to be used for calculations

155—(1) This regulation applies if, in respect of a claimant, the Department receives notification from the Inland Revenue of—

(*a*) a code or amended code,
(*b*) total payments to date, or
(*c*) total net tax deducted.

(2) The Department must record that notification in substitution for any previous record and use it for the purpose of all calculations required under this Chapter.

Commentary—*Simon's Direct Tax Service* **E4.11101.**
Derivation—The Income Tax (Employments) Regulations, SI 1993/744 reg 85(2).

Recording the amount of taxable jobseeker's allowance

156 Whenever a payment of jobseeker's allowance is made, the Department must record the taxable jobseeker's allowance included in the payment.

Commentary—*Simon's Direct Tax Service* **E4.11101.**
Derivation—The Income Tax (Employments) Regulations, SI 1993/744 reg 87.

Obligations at end of tax year

157—(1) This regulation applies in respect of each award which includes taxable jobseeker's allowance and which continues beyond the end of a tax year.

(2) Before 1st June following the end of the tax year, the Department must—

(*a*) make a tax calculation in accordance with regulation 161 if the claimant's code is used on the cumulative basis;
(*b*) subject to paragraph (3), issue a certificate to the claimant; and
(*c*) deliver a return to the Inland Revenue.

(3) The Department need not issue the certificate if—

(*a*) no taxable jobseeker's allowance has been paid, and
(*b*) a tax calculation in accordance with regulation 161 is not required.

(4) The certificate must show—

(*a*) the tax year to which it relates,
(*b*) the total jobseeker's allowance for the tax year excluding any amounts previously notified under regulation 159(2) or 160(2),
(*c*) the taxable jobseeker's allowance included in the total jobseeker's allowance,
(*d*) the claimant's code,
(*e*) the claimant's national insurance number,
(*f*) the claimant's name,
(*g*) the claimant's address, if known,
(*h*) any previous relevant payments and any tax deducted from those relevant payments which the Department was required to take into account under regulation 161,
(*i*) any total payments to date recorded by the Department in accordance with regulation 153(1) plus the total taxable jobseeker's allowance for the tax year, and the corresponding total net tax deducted, and
(*j*) the amount of tax refunded by the Department.

(5) The return must show—

(*a*) the particulars specified in paragraph (4), and
(*b*) if a calculation is required under regulation 161, any amount of tax outstanding.

Commentary—*Simon's Direct Tax Service* **E4.11101.**
Derivation—The Income Tax (Employments) Regulations, SI 1993/744 reg 88(1), (2), (4), (5).

When an award ceases

158—(1) For the purposes of these Regulations an award ceases when entitlement to a jobseeker's allowance ceases.

(2) When an award of a taxable jobseeker's allowance ceases the Department must make a tax calculation in accordance with regulation 161 if the claimant's code is used on the cumulative basis.

(3) The relevant date for the purposes of that calculation is the date on which the award ceases.

(4) The date on which the award ceases is the last day for which benefit was paid and was not recoverable, except that if the last day is 4th or 5th April the date is the preceding 3rd April.

(5) But the Department need not amend a tax calculation solely because the date used for the purposes of the calculation is subsequently shown to be incorrect.

Commentary—*Simon's Direct Tax Service* **E4.11101.**
Derivation—The Income Tax (Employments) Regulations, SI 1993/744 regs 89, 91(4).

Cessation of award: Form P45U

159—(1) When an award of a taxable jobseeker's allowance ceases the Department must immediately complete Form P45U.

(2) The Department must then—

(*a*) send Part 1 of Form P45U to the Inland Revenue, and
(*b*) provide Part 1A of Form P45U and Parts 2 and 3 of Form P45 to the claimant.

(3) The information listed in column 1 of Table 6 must, subject to the conditions set out in column 2, be provided in Parts 1 and 1A of Form P45U and Parts 2 and 3 of Form P45 as indicated in columns 3 to 5.

TABLE 6

INFORMATION WHICH MUST BE PROVIDED IN FORM P45U

1	2	3	4	5
Information to be provided	*Conditions*	*Form P45U*		*Form P45*
		Part 1	*Part 1A*	*Parts 2 & 3*
1 the tax reference as shown in the deductions working sheet		yes	yes	yes
2 claimant's national insurance number		yes	yes	yes
3 claimant's name		yes	yes	yes
4 the date on which the award ceased		yes	yes	yes
5 the claimant's code or, if more than one, the latest code for the tax year during which the award ceased		yes	yes	yes
6 whether the claimant's code is used on the cumulative basis		yes	yes	yes
7 the tax week or month in which the award ceased	if the claimant's code is used on the cumulative basis	yes	yes	yes
8 the total payments to date (including taxable jobseeker's allowance) at the date the award ceased, and the corresponding total net tax deducted	if the claimant's code is used on the cumulative basis	yes	yes	yes
9 the taxable jobseeker's allowance paid during the tax year by virtue of the award in question	if the claimant's code is used on the cumulative basis, and if different from the information supplied under item 8	yes	yes	no
10 the taxable jobseeker's allowance paid during the tax year by virtue of the award in question	if the claimant's code is not used on the cumulative basis	yes	yes	no
11 any amount of tax outstanding	if the claimant's code is used on the cumulative basis	yes	no	no
12 whether the claimant was self-employed immediately before the claim was made		yes	no	no

1	*2*	*3*	*4*	*5*
Information to be provided	*Conditions*	*Form P45U*		*Form P45*
		Part 1	*Part 1A*	*Parts 2 & 3*
13 whether the claimant is receiving a pension by reason of a former employment		yes	no	no
14 the claimant's address	if known	yes	no	no
15 the address of the benefit officer		yes	yes	no
16 the date the form is completed		yes	yes	no

(4) The Department must also give notice to the claimant of—

(*a*) the total jobseeker's allowance for the tax year excluding any sums previously notified under this regulation or regulation 160, 171 or 172, and

(*b*) the taxable jobseeker's allowance included in that total.

(5) Expressions used in Parts 2 and 3 of Form P45 have the following meanings—

(*a*) "employee" means "claimant",

(*b*) "leaving date" means "date the award ceased", and

(*c*) "pay" means "jobseeker's allowance".

(6) Regulation 163 (death of claimant) modifies the requirements of this regulation if an award of taxable jobseeker's allowance has ceased on the death of the claimant.

Commentary—*Simon's Direct Tax Service* **E4.11101.**
Derivation—The Income Tax (Employments) Regulations, SI 1993/744 reg 89(2).

Notification of taxable jobseeker's allowance adjustment

160—(1) Paragraph (2) applies if—

(*a*) after a certificate under regulation 157(2)(*b*) has been issued (or would have been issued but for regulation 157(3)), or

(*b*) after a notice has been issued under regulation 159(4) or this regulation,

further taxable jobseeker's allowance is paid to, or taxable jobseeker's allowance overpaid is recovered from, the claimant.

(2) The Department must—

(*a*) give notice to the claimant of the revised figure of total jobseeker's allowance and the taxable jobseeker's allowance included in that revised figure in accordance with the relevant regulation, and

(*b*) notify the Inland Revenue of the sums paid or refunded.

Commentary—*Simon's Direct Tax Service* **E4.11101.**
Derivation—The Income Tax (Employments) Regulations, SI 1993/744 regs 88(3), 90.

Tax calculation

161—(1) This regulation applies, subject to regulation 162, if the Department is required by regulation 157 or 158 to make a tax calculation.

(2) The Department must calculate in respect of the claimant as at the relevant date—

(*a*) the total payments to date, and

(*b*) the claimant's total tax.

(3) If the recorded tax exceeds the claimant's total tax, the Department must repay the excess to the claimant.

(4) But if the recorded tax is less than the claimant's total tax—;

(*a*) the difference is tax outstanding for the purposes of regulation 157(5)(*b*) or item 11 of Table 6 in regulation 159(3), and

(*b*) the Department must treat the claimant's code as issued by the Inland Revenue on the non-cumulative basis from the relevant date.

(5) In this regulation—

"claimant's total tax" means—

(*a*) if the claimant's code is a K code, the lesser of—

(i) 50% of the claimant's total payments to date, and

(ii) the tax due in accordance with the appropriate tax tables in respect of the claimant's total taxable payments to date at the relevant date;

(*b*) in any other case, the tax due in accordance with the appropriate tax tables in respect of the claimant's total taxable payments to date at the relevant date;

''recorded tax'' means the total tax to date or (as the case may be) the total net tax deducted which was recorded in accordance with regulation 153(3) or (4) when the claim was made;

''relevant date'' means—

(*a*) the end of the tax year, if the calculation is required by regulation 157;

(*b*) the date used for the purposes of the calculation, if the calculation is required by regulation 158;

''total payments to date'' means any payments to date recorded by the Department in accordance with regulation 153(1), plus the total taxable jobseeker's allowance.

Commentary—*Simon's Direct Tax Service* **E4.11101.**
Derivation—The Income Tax (Employments) Regulations, SI 1993/744 reg 91(1)–(3).
Cross references—See the Income Tax (PAYE) Regulations, SI 2003/2682 reg 162 (cases where a tax calculation under this regulation is not required).

No tax calculation required in certain cases

162—(1) A tax calculation under regulation 161 is not required in any of the following cases—

(*a*) if the claimant does not give the Department Parts 2 and 3 of Form P45, and does not certify in accordance with regulation 154(3) (students etc);

(*b*) if the claimant gives the Department Parts 2 and 3 of Form P45, but they do not relate to the claimant's last employment or award before the present award, whichever is later;

(*c*) if the claimant is in receipt of a pension in respect of a former employment;

(*d*) if it appears to the Department on the occasion of a claim that a previous award should have been treated as having ceased in accordance with regulation 158 (when an award ceases); or

(*e*) if the claimant's code is a nil tax code, basic rate code or higher rate code.

(2) Those cases are treated as if the Inland Revenue had made a direction that the claimant's code must be used on the non-cumulative basis.

(3) Those cases are subject to a notification from the Inland Revenue under regulation 155 that revised particulars are to be substituted and used.

Commentary—*Simon's Direct Tax Service* **E4.11101.**
Derivation—The Income Tax (Employments) Regulations, SI 1993/744 reg 91(4), (5).

Death of claimant

163—(1) On being informed of the death of a claimant whose award included taxable jobseeker's allowance, the Department must send the Inland Revenue the completed Form P45U indicating in Part 1 that the claimant has died.

(2) If the Department knows the name and address of the claimant's personal representative, the Department must send the notice referred to in regulation 159(4) to the personal representative.

(3) But if the Department has not been notified of the name and address of the claimant's personal representative within 30 days of the claimant's death, the Department is not required—

(*a*) to make a tax calculation under regulation 161, nor

(*b*) to issue the notice under regulation 159(4).

Commentary—*Simon's Direct Tax Service* **E4.11101.**
Derivation—The Income Tax (Employments) Regulations, SI 1993/744 reg 92.

Finance

164—(1) The Board of Inland Revenue must advance monies to the National Insurance Funds of Great Britain and Northern Ireland at intervals to be agreed with the Department for use in making repayments of income tax under these Regulations.

(2) The Department must provide the Board with a quarterly statement of receipts and payments.

Commentary—*Simon's Direct Tax Service* **E4.11101.**
Derivation—The Income Tax (Employments) Regulations, SI 1993/744 reg 93.

CHAPTER 2

JOBSEEKER'S ALLOWANCE: SPECIAL CASES

Scope of Chapter 2

165—(1) This Chapter applies only to Chapter 2 claimants (as defined by regulation 148).

(2) Except for regulation 148 (interpretation), Chapter 1 does not apply to Chapter 2 claimants.

Commentary—*Simon's Direct Tax Service* **E4.11101.**

Jobseeker's allowance paid directly to claimant

166—(1) This regulation applies if the Department makes a payment of taxable jobseeker's allowance directly to a Chapter 2 claimant.

(2) The Department must—

(*a*) record the amount, and

(*b*) pay the full sum without any deduction or repayment of income tax.

Commentary—*Simon's Direct Tax Service* **E4.11101.**
Derivation—The Income Tax (Employments) Regulations, SI 1993/744 reg 95.

Jobseeker's allowance paid by employer

167—(1) If—

(*a*) a jobseeker's allowance is paid to a Chapter 2 claimant by the claimant's employer on behalf of the Department, and

(*b*) the employer calculates the jobseeker's allowance payable by reference to instructions supplied by the Department,

the employer must also calculate the taxable jobseeker's allowance in accordance with those instructions.

(2) If—

(*a*) a jobseeker's allowance is paid to a Chapter 2 claimant by the claimant's employer on behalf of the Department, and

(*b*) paragraph (1)(*b*) does not apply,

the Department must notify the employer of the amount of jobseeker's allowance and of taxable jobseeker's allowance.

(3) If the employer has undertaken to pay a jobseeker's allowance on behalf of the Department, the Department must pay the full amount to the employer without any deduction on account of income tax.

Commentary—*Simon's Direct Tax Service* **E4.11101.**
Derivation—The Income Tax (Employments) Regulations, SI 1993/744 reg 96(1)–(3).
Cross references—See the Income Tax (PAYE) Regulations, SI 2003/2682 reg 10 (this regulation not to apply to agencies or agency workers in their capacity as such).
SI 2003/2682 reg 11 (this regulation not to apply to pension payers or pensioners in their capacity as such).
SI 2003/2682 reg 12 (this regulation not to apply to other payers or other payees in their capacity as such).

Regulation 167 cases: application of other regulations

168—(1) Parts 2 to 4 (codes; deduction and repayment of tax; payments, returns and information) apply to the taxable jobseeker's allowance paid to a Chapter 2 claimant by the employer on behalf of the Department under regulation 167, as if it were a relevant payment from the employment.

(2) But this is subject to paragraph (3), which applies in any case in which it appears to the Inland Revenue that deduction of tax from the taxable jobseeker's allowance paid by the employer on behalf of the Department by reference to the tax tables is impracticable.

(3) The Inland Revenue may make such other arrangements as are appropriate for the collection of tax in respect of taxable jobseeker's allowance.

(4) Regulations 170 to 172 (information to be supplied etc) do not apply if—

(*a*) the Chapter 2 claimant's employer has been paying the jobseeker's allowance in accordance with regulation 167, and

(*b*) the employer provides the information in question.

Commentary—*Simon's Direct Tax Service* **E4.11101.**
Derivation—The Income Tax (Employments) Regulations, SI 1993/744 reg 96(4), (5).
Cross references—See the Income Tax (PAYE) Regulations, SI 2003/2682 reg 10 (this regulation not to apply to agencies or agency workers in their capacity as such).
SI 2003/2682 reg 11 (this regulation not to apply to pension payers or pensioners in their capacity as such).
SI 2003/2682 reg 12 (this regulation not to apply to other payers or other payees in their capacity as such).

When a Chapter 2 award ceases

169 For the purposes of this Chapter, an award ceases when entitlement to a jobseeker's allowance which depends on regulation 17 or 156 of the JSA Regulations ceases.

Commentary—*Simon's Direct Tax Service* **E4.11101.**
Derivation—The Income Tax (Employments) Regulations, SI 1993/744 reg 97(1).

Information to be supplied at end of tax year

170—(1) This regulation applies in respect of an award of taxable jobseeker's allowance which continues beyond the end of a tax year.

(2) Before 1st June following the end of the tax year, the Department must give notice to the Inland Revenue and the Chapter 2 claimant of—

(*a*) the total jobseeker's allowance, and

(*b*) the taxable jobseeker's allowance,

paid in respect of the award during that tax year.

Commentary—*Simon's Direct Tax Service* **E4.11101.**
Derivation—The Income Tax (Employments) Regulations, SI 1993/744 reg 97(2).
Cross references—See the Income Tax (PAYE) Regulations, SI 2003/2682 reg 168 (cases where this regulation does not apply).

Information to be supplied when an award of taxable jobseeker's allowance ceases

171—(1) When an award of taxable jobseeker's allowance ceases, the Department must give notice to the Inland Revenue and, except where the Chapter 2 claimant has died, the claimant, of—

(*a*) the total jobseeker's allowance, and

(*b*) the taxable jobseeker's allowance,

paid in respect of the award, showing the amounts appropriate to the award for the tax year in which it ceased.

(2) If the Department has been notified of the name and address of a deceased claimant's personal representative within 30 days of the claimant's death, the Department must send the notice to the personal representative.

Commentary—*Simon's Direct Tax Service* **E4.11101.**
Derivation—The Income Tax (Employments) Regulations, SI 1993/744 reg 97(2).
Cross references—See the Income Tax (PAYE) Regulations, SI 2003/2682 reg 168 (cases where this regulation does not apply).

Adjustments of taxable jobseeker's allowance

172—(1) Paragraph (2) applies if, after the issue of a notice under regulation 170 or 171(1)—

(*a*) further taxable jobseeker's allowance is paid to the Chapter 2 claimant, or

(*b*) taxable jobseeker's allowance overpaid is recovered from the Chapter 2 claimant.

(2) The Department must—

(*a*) notify the Chapter 2 claimant of the revised figure of total jobseeker's allowance and the taxable jobseeker's allowance included in that revised figure, and

(*b*) notify the Inland Revenue of any adjustment to the figure of taxable jobseeker's allowance,

showing the amounts appropriate to each tax year.

Commentary—*Simon's Direct Tax Service* **E4.11101.**
Derivation—The Income Tax (Employments) Regulations, SI 1993/744 reg 98.
Cross references—See the Income Tax (PAYE) Regulations, SI 2003/2682 reg 168 (cases where this regulation does not apply).

CHAPTER 3

INCAPACITY BENEFIT

Interpretation of Chapter 3

173—In this Chapter—

"award" means an award of incapacity benefit;

"claim" means a claim for incapacity benefit;

"claimant" means a person who has made a claim;

"Department" means the Department for Work and Pensions or, in Northern Ireland, the Department for Social Development;

"incapacity benefit" means short-term incapacity benefit or long-term incapacity benefit payable under—

(*a*) sections 30A(1), 30A(5), 40 or 41 of the Social Security Contributions and Benefits Act 1992, or

(*b*) in Northern Ireland, section 30A(1), 30A(5), 40 or 41 of the Social Security Contributions and Benefits (Northern Ireland) Act 1992;

"single-income claimant" means a claimant who, for a tax year—

(*a*) is not entitled to receive any relevant payments in addition to the payments of taxable incapacity benefit, or

(*b*) is so entitled but has failed to provide any details relating to those payments when making the claim,

and who is not a self-employed earner as defined by section 2 of the Social Security Contributions and Benefits Act 1992 or, in Northern Ireland, section 2 of the Social Security Contributions and Benefits (Northern Ireland) Act 1992;

"taxable incapacity benefit" means any amount of incapacity benefit which is chargeable to income tax under Chapter 2 of Part 10 of ITEPA (tax on social security income).

Commentary—*Simon's Direct Tax Service* **E4.11102.**
Derivation—The Income Tax (Employments) Regulations, SI 1993/744 regs 81, 98A, 98C.

Application of other regulations

174—(1) The following regulations apply, subject to this Chapter, to payments of taxable incapacity benefit with the modifications mentioned in paragraphs (2) to (4)—

Regulation 2	Interpretation
Regulation 15	flat rate codes
Regulation 16	Continued application of employee's code
Regulation 17	notice to employee of code
Regulation 18	Objections and appeals against employee's code
Regulation 19	Amendment of code
Regulation 20	notice to employer of amended code
Regulation 21	Deduction and repayment of tax by reference to employee's code
Regulations 22 to 25	Cumulative basis
Regulations 26 to 31	non-cumulative basis
Regulation 33	nil tax code: no deductions or repayments
Regulation 36	Cessation of employment: Form P45
Regulation 66	Deductions working sheets
Regulation 67	Information to employees about payments and tax deducted
Regulation 68	periodic payments to and recoveries from the Revenue
Regulation 69	due date and receipts for payments of tax
Regulation 70	Quarterly tax periods
Regulation 72	Recovery from employee of tax not deducted by employer
Regulation 73	annual return of relevant payments liable to deduction of tax
Regulation 74	annual return of relevant payments not liable to deduction of tax
Regulation 76	Certificate if tax in regulation 73 return is unpaid
Regulation 79	Certificate after inspection of PAYE records
Regulation 84	Recovery of tax and interest
Regulation 97	Inspection of employer's PAYE records
Regulation 98	multiple PAYE schemes
Regulation 102	Succession to a business etc
Regulation 141	direct collection and special arrangements
Regulation 185	Adjusting total net tax deducted for purposes of sections 59A(1) and 59B(1) TMA
Regulation 188	Assessments other than self-assessments
Regulation 211	how information must or may be delivered by employers
Regulation 216	service by post
Regulation 218	Certificate that sum due
Regulation 219	Payment by cheque.

(2) In the application of those regulations, the expressions listed in column 1 of Table 7 have the meanings shown in column 2 of the table.

TABLE 7
MEANING OF EXPRESSIONS IN APPLICATION OF OTHER REGULATIONS

1 Expression	*2 Meaning for purposes of this Chapter*
Employee	Claimant
Employer	Department
Employment	Award
Relevant payments	taxable incapacity benefit.

(3) In regulation 15 (flat rate codes)—

(*a*) omit paragraph (1);
(*b*) omit paragraph (3)(*a*); and
(*c*) for paragraph (3)(*c*) substitute—

"(*c*) the Inland Revenue consider that the code which would otherwise be the claimant's code would result in too much tax being deducted for the tax year in question.".

(4) In regulation 21(1) (deduction and repayment of tax by reference to employee's code), for "in accordance with these Regulations" substitute "in accordance with Chapter 3 of Part 8".

Commentary—*Simon's Direct Tax Service* **E4.11102.**
Derivation—The Income Tax (Employments) Regulations, SI 1993/744 regs 82, 98B, 98G(1).

Emergency IB code to be used before claimant's code issued

175—(1) Paragraph (2) applies if the Department makes a payment of taxable incapacity benefit during a tax year to a single-income claimant before a code has been issued by the Inland Revenue for that year in respect of that award.

(2) The Department must—

(*a*) deduct tax using an emergency IB code on the non-cumulative basis, and
(*b*) keep records in a deductions working sheet which it must prepare for the purpose.

(3) The use of an emergency IB code under this regulation is treated as the issue of a code for the purposes of regulations 21, 36 and 180.

Commentary—*Simon's Direct Tax Service* **E4.11102.**
Derivation—The Income Tax (Employments) Regulations, SI 1993/744 reg 98C(1).

Return in respect of all claimants to taxable incapacity benefit

176—(1) When the Department first makes a payment of taxable incapacity benefit to a claimant it must immediately deliver a return to the Inland Revenue containing the following information.

(2) The information is—

(*a*) the claimant's name,
(*b*) the claimant's address,
(*c*) the claimant's date of birth, if known,
(*d*) the claimant's national insurance number,
(*e*) the date on which the claimant's entitlement to taxable incapacity benefit began,
(*f*) the weekly rate of taxable incapacity benefit being paid to the claimant,
(*g*) if a code is being used for the payment, that code and whether it is used on the non-cumulative basis,
(*h*) if the payment was preceded by payment of incapacity benefit which was not taxable, the date that benefit was first paid, and
(*i*) the claimant's tax reference, if known.

Commentary—*Simon's Direct Tax Service* **E4.11102.**
Derivation—The Income Tax (Employments) Regulations, SI 1993/744 reg 98D(1), (2).

Further return required in certain cases

177—(1) On making a subsequent payment of taxable incapacity benefit to the claimant, the Department must deliver a further return in accordance with regulation 176 as if that subsequent payment were the first payment, if conditions A and B are met.

(2) Condition A is that the Inland Revenue have previously determined the claimant's code in relation to the payments of incapacity benefit to be a nil tax code.

(3) Condition B is that the subsequent payment is the first payment to be made at a different rate from the rate subsisting at the time of that determination.

(4) In addition to providing the information listed in regulation 176(2), the Department must indicate in the further return that the weekly rate of taxable incapacity benefit being paid to the claimant represents a revised amount.

Commentary—*Simon's Direct Tax Service* **E4.11102.**
Derivation—The Income Tax (Employments) Regulations, SI 1993/744 reg 98D(3).

Delivery of Form P45 to Department

178—(1) This regulation applies if a single-income claimant—

(*a*) has Parts 2 and 3 of Form P45, and
(*b*) has not made, and does not intend to make, a claim for repayment of tax.

(2) The claimant must deliver Parts 2 and 3 of Form P45 when making a claim, and the Department must immediately send them to the Inland Revenue office.

Commentary—*Simon's Direct Tax Service* **E4.11102.**
Derivation—The Income Tax (Employments) Regulations, SI 1993/744 reg 98E(1).

Determination of claimant's code by Inland Revenue

179—(1) On receiving a return under regulation 176 relating to a single-income claimant, the Inland Revenue must determine the code for the claimant.

(2) The Inland Revenue may determine the code for a claimant who is not a single-income claimant if they consider that it would be impractical to collect tax arising on the claimant's taxable incapacity benefit by other means.

(3) In determining the code for a claimant under this regulation, regulation 14(1) (matters to which Revenue must have regard in determining an employee's code) does not apply.

(4) If the Inland Revenue are satisfied the claimant is entitled, for the tax year for which the code is determined, to any of the following reliefs from income tax, they must have regard to that relief in determining the code for the claimant under this regulation.

(5) The reliefs are—

(*a*) personal allowance (section 257(1) of ICTA),
(*b*) married couple's allowance (section 257A of ICTA), and
(*c*) blind person's allowance (section 265(1) of ICTA).

(6) If the Inland Revenue determine the code for a claimant before the beginning of the tax year for which it is determined, the Inland Revenue—

(*a*) must have regard to any expected change in the amounts of those reliefs, but
(*b*) may disregard any of those reliefs if they are not satisfied that the claimant will be entitled to it for the tax year for which it is determined.

Commentary—*Simon's Direct Tax Service* **E4.11102.**
Derivation—The Income Tax (Employments) Regulations, SI 1993/744 reg 98F(1)–(4).

Death of claimant

180—(1) On the death of a claimant in respect of whom a code has been issued by the Inland Revenue, the Department must—

(*a*) complete Form P45 indicating in Part 1 that the claimant has died, and
(*b*) send it to the Inland Revenue.

(2) The Department must comply with paragraph (1)—

(*a*) on the day on which it learns of the claimant's death, or
(*b*) if that is not practicable, without unreasonable delay.

(3) Paragraph (4) applies if the Department makes any payment of taxable incapacity benefit after the date of the claimant's death—

(*a*) before completing Form P45, or
(*b*) after completing Form P45 but during the tax year in which the claimant died.

(4) The Department must, on making the payment, deduct or repay tax as if the deceased claimant were still alive and the award had not ceased at the date of payment.

(5) Regulation 37(2) to (6) (PAYE income paid after employment ceased) applies to any payment of taxable incapacity benefit which—

(*a*) is made in a tax year following the tax year in which the claimant died, and
(*b*) is not included in Form P45.

Commentary—*Simon's Direct Tax Service* **E4.11102.**
Derivation—The Income Tax (Employments) Regulations, SI 1993/744 regs 27, 98B.

CHAPTER 4

INCOME SUPPORT

Interpretation of Chapter 4

181—In this Chapter—

''award'' means an award of income support;
''claim'' means a claim for income support;
''claimant'' means a person who has made a claim;
''Department'' means the Department for Work and Pensions or, in Northern Ireland, the Department for Social Development;
''income support'' means benefit payable under—

(*a*) section 124 of the Social Security Contributions and Benefits Act 1992, or
(*b*) in Northern Ireland, section 123 of the Social Security Contributions and Benefits (Northern Ireland) Act 1992;

''taxable income support'' means any amount of income support which is chargeable to income tax under Chapter 2 of Part 10 of ITEPA (tax on social security income).

Recording the amount of taxable income support

182—Whenever the Department makes a payment of taxable income support it must—

(*a*) record the amount, and
(*b*) pay the full sum without any deduction or repayment of income tax.

Information to be supplied when an award of taxable income support ceases

183—(1) This regulation applies when an award of taxable income support ceases.

(2) The Department must give notice to the Inland Revenue and, except where the claimant has died, the claimant of—

(*a*) the total income support, and
(*b*) the taxable income support,

paid in respect of the award showing the amounts appropriate to each tax year.

(3) If the Department has been notified of the name and address of a deceased claimant's personal representative within 30 days of the claimant's death, the Department must send the notice to the personal representative.

Adjustments of taxable income support

184—(1) Paragraph (2) applies if, after the issue of a notice under regulation 183(2)—

(*a*) further taxable income support is paid to the claimant, or
(*b*) taxable income support overpaid is recovered from the claimant.

(2) The Department must—

(*a*) notify the claimant of the revised figure of total income support and the taxable income support included in that revised figure, and
(*b*) notify the Inland Revenue of any adjustment to the figure of taxable income support,

showing the amounts appropriate to each tax year.

PART 9

ASSESSMENT AND SELF-ASSESSMENT

Adjusting total net tax deducted for purposes of sections 59A(1) and 59B(1) TMA

185—(1) This regulation applies for the purpose of determining—

(*a*) the excess mentioned in section 59A(1) of TMA (payments on account of income tax: income tax assessed exceeds amount deducted at source), and
(*b*) the difference mentioned in section 59B(1) of TMA (payments of income tax and capital gains tax: difference between tax contained in self-assessment and aggregate of payments on account or deducted at source).

(2) For those purposes, the amount of income tax deducted at source under these Regulations is the total net tax deducted during the relevant tax year (''A'') after making any additions or subtractions required by paragraphs (3) to (5).

(3) Subtract from A any repayments of A which are made before the taxpayer's return and self-assessment is made under section 8 or 8A of TMA (personal return and trustee's return).

(4) Add to A any overpayment of tax from a previous tax year, to the extent that it was taken into account in determining the taxpayer's code for the relevant tax year.

(5) Add to A any tax treated as deducted, other than any direction tax, but—

(*a*) only if there would be an amount payable by the taxpayer under section 59B(1) of TMA on the assumption that there are no payments on account and no addition to A under this paragraph, and then
(*b*) only to a maximum of that amount.

(6) In this regulation—

''direction tax'' means any amount of tax which is the subject of a direction made under regulation 72(5) or regulation 81(4) in relation to the taxpayer in respect of one or more tax periods falling within the relevant tax year;

''relevant tax year'' means—

(*a*) in relation to section 59A(1) of TMA, the immediately preceding year referred to in that subsection;
(*b*) in relation to section 59B(1) of TMA, the tax year for which the self-assessment referred to in that subsection is made;

''tax treated as deducted'' means any tax which in relation to relevant payments made by an employer to the taxpayer in the relevant tax year—

(*a*) the employer was liable to deduct from payments but failed to do so, or
(*b*) the employer was liable to account for in accordance with regulation 62(5) (notional payments) but failed to do so;

''the taxpayer'' means the person referred to in section 59A(1) of TMA or the person whose self-assessment is referred to in section 59B(1) of TMA (as the case may be).

Commentary—*Simon's Direct Tax Service* **E4.11131.**
Derivation—The Income Tax (Employments) Regulations, SI 1993/744 regs 101(4)–(6), 101A(1), (2), (4); the Income Tax (Employments) (Notional Payments) Regulations, SI 1994/1212 reg 13(1).
Modifications—See the Income Tax (PAYE) Regulations, SI 2003/2682 reg 150 (modification of this regulation in its application to payments of taxable jobseeker's allowance made to a claimant).
SI 2003/2682 reg 174 (modification of this regulation in its application to payments of taxable incapacity benefit).

Recovery: adjustment of employee's code

186—(1) This regulation applies if, on the assumption mentioned in paragraph (2), the difference for a tax year mentioned in section 59B(1) of TMA (difference between tax contained in a self-assessment and aggregate of payments on account) would be payable by the taxpayer.

(2) The assumption is that, in respect of the tax year, nothing will be deducted at source under these Regulations in a subsequent tax year.

(3) The Inland Revenue must have regard to the difference in determining a taxpayer's code for a subsequent tax year under regulation 14 (matters relevant to determination of code) if—

(*a*) it is less than £2,000, and

(*b*) the return for the tax year is—

(i) delivered by an approved method of electronic communications before 31st December following the end of the tax year, or

(ii) delivered by any other method before 1st October following the end of the tax year.

(4) In a case not falling within paragraph (3)(*b*)(i), the Inland Revenue may have regard to the difference in determining a taxpayer's code for a subsequent tax year under regulation 14 if—

(*a*) it is less than £2,000, and

(*b*) the return for the tax year is delivered on or after 1st October following the end of the tax year and the code is determined before 31st December.

(5) But the Inland Revenue must not have regard to the difference if the taxpayer objects at the time the return is delivered or subsequently.

Commentary—*Simon's Direct Tax Service* **E4.11132.**
Derivation—The Income Tax (Employments) Regulations, SI 1993/744 reg 101A(3).

Repayment: adjustment of employee's code

187—(1) This regulation applies if the difference for a tax year mentioned in section 59B(1) of TMA (difference between tax contained in a self-assessment and aggregate of payments on account) is payable to the taxpayer.

(2) The Inland Revenue may have regard to the difference in determining the employee's code for a subsequent tax year under regulation 14 (matters relevant to determination of code).

(3) But the Inland Revenue must not have regard to the difference if the taxpayer objects at the time the return is delivered or subsequently.

Commentary—*Simon's Direct Tax Service* **E4.11132.**

Assessments other than self-assessments

188—(1) In this regulation, "assessment" means an assessment other than one under section 9 of TMA (self-assessment).

(2) The tax payable by the employee is—

A – (B – C)

where

A is the tax payable under the assessment;

B is the total net tax deducted in relation to the employee's relevant payments during the tax year for which the assessment is made, adjusted as required by paragraph (3); and

C is so much, if any, of B as is subsequently repaid.

(3) For the purpose of determining the tax payable by the employee, and subject to paragraphs (4) and (5)—

(*a*) add to B any tax which—

(i) the employer was liable to deduct from relevant payments but failed to do so, or

(ii) the employer was liable to account for in accordance with regulation 62(5) (notional payments) but failed to do so;

(*b*) make any necessary adjustment to B in respect of any tax overpaid or remaining unpaid for any tax year; and

(*c*) make any necessary adjustment to B in respect of any amount to be recovered as if it were unpaid tax under section 30(1) of TMA (recovery of overpayment of tax etc) to the extent that—

(i) the Inland Revenue took that amount into account in determining the employee's code, and

(ii) the total net tax deducted was in consequence greater than it would otherwise have been.

(4) No direction tax is to be included in calculating the amount of tax referred to in paragraph (3)(*a*).

(5) If a direction is made after the making of the assessment, the amount (if any) shown in the notice of assessment as a deduction from, or a credit against, the tax payable under the assessment is to be taken as reduced by so much of the direction tax as was included in calculating the amount of tax referred to in paragraph (3)(*a*).

(6) Instead of requiring payment by the employee, the Inland Revenue may take the tax payable by the employee into account in determining the employee's code for a subsequent tax year.

(7) In this regulation—

"direction" means a direction made under regulation 72(5) or 81(4) in relation to the employee in respect of one or more tax periods falling within the tax year in question;

"direction tax" means any amount of tax which is the subject of a direction;

"tax payable under the assessment" means the amount of tax shown in the assessment as payable without regard to any amount shown in the notice of assessment as a deduction from, or a credit against, the amount of tax payable.

Commentary—*Simon's Direct Tax Service* **E4.11133.**
Derivation—The Income Tax (Employments) Regulations, SI 1993/744 reg 101(2)–(4), (6), (7); the Income Tax (Employments) (Notional Payments) Regulations, SI 1994/1212 reg 13(1).
Modifications—See the Income Tax (PAYE) Regulations, SI 2003/2682 reg 150 (modification of this regulation in its application to payments of taxable jobseeker's allowance made to a claimant).
SI 2003/2682 reg 174 (modification of this regulation in its application to payments of taxable incapacity benefit).
SI 2003/2682 Sch 1 para 25 (overpayments and underpayments of tax: tax years before the tax year ending 5 April 2002: modification of this regulation).

PART 10
COMMUNICATIONS

CHAPTER 1
ELECTRONIC COMMUNICATIONS: INTERPRETATION

Meaning of electronic communications etc

189 In these Regulations—

"approved method of electronic communications", in relation to the delivery of information or the making of a payment in accordance with a provision of these Regulations, means a method of electronic communications which has been approved, by specific or general directions issued by the Board of Inland Revenue, for the delivery of information of that kind or the making of a payment of that kind under that provision;

"electronic communications" has the meaning given in section 132(10) of the Finance Act 1999;

"official computer system" means a computer system maintained by or on behalf of the Board of Inland Revenue or an officer of the Board.

Commentary—*Simon's Direct Tax Service* **E4.11150.**
Derivation—The Income Tax (Employments) Regulations, SI 1993/744 reg 2(1).

Specified date

190—(1) For the purposes of Chapters 3 and 4, the Board of Inland Revenue may announce each tax year a date ("the specified date") for the following tax year.

(2) Any announcement must be made by means of a direction no later than 30th November in a tax year.

(3) The specified date for a tax year applies in respect of specified payments due to be made in respect of that year and specified information required to be delivered in respect of that year.

Commentary—*Simon's Direct Tax Service* **E4.11150.**
Derivation—The Income Tax (Employments) Regulations, SI 1993/744 regs 42A(1), (2), 46ZD(4).

Large and medium sized employers

191—(1) "Large employer" means an employer treated as paying PAYE income to 250 or more employees at the specified date.

(2) "Large or medium sized employer" means an employer treated as paying PAYE income to 50 or more employees at the specified date.

(3) An employer is treated as paying PAYE income to an employee at the specified date if the employer—

(*a*) is required at that date by these Regulations, or by regulation 6(6) of the Working Tax Credit (Payment by Employers) Regulations 2002, to prepare or maintain a deductions working sheet in respect of the employee, and

(*b*) has not sent to the Inland Revenue Part 1 of Form P45 in respect of that employee.

Commentary—*Simon's Direct Tax Service* **E4.11150.**
Derivation—The Income Tax (Employments) Regulations, SI 1993/744 regs 42A(2), (3), 46ZD(4).

CHAPTER 2

ELECTRONIC COMMUNICATIONS: GENERAL

Whether information has been delivered electronically

192 For the purpose of these Regulations, information is taken to have been delivered to an official computer system by an approved method of electronic communications only if it is accepted by that official computer system.

Commentary—*Simon's Direct Tax Service* **E4.11151.**
Derivation—The Income Tax (Employments) Regulations, SI 1993/744 reg 2A.

Proof of content of electronic delivery

193—(1) A document certified by the Inland Revenue to be a printed-out version of any information delivered by an approved method of electronic communications is evidence, unless the contrary is proved, that the information—

(*a*) was delivered by an approved method of electronic communications on that occasion, and
(*b*) constitutes everything which was delivered on that occasion.

(2) A document which purports to be a certificate given in accordance with paragraph (1) is presumed to be such a certificate unless the contrary is proved.

Commentary—*Simon's Direct Tax Service* **E4.11151.**
Derivation—The Income Tax (Employments) Regulations, SI 1993/744 reg 2B.

Proof of identity of person sending or receiving electronic delivery

194—The identity of—

(*a*) the person sending any information delivered by an approved method of electronic communications to the Inland Revenue, or
(*b*) the person receiving any information delivered by an approved method of electronic communications by the Inland Revenue,

is presumed, unless the contrary is proved, to be the person recorded as such on an official computer system.

Commentary—*Simon's Direct Tax Service* **E4.11151.**
Derivation—The Income Tax (Employments) Regulations, SI 1993/744 reg 2C.

Information sent electronically on behalf of a person

195—(1) Any information delivered by an approved method of electronic communications—

(*a*) to the Inland Revenue, or
(*b*) to an official computer system,

on behalf of a person is taken to have been delivered by that person.

(2) But this does not apply if the person proves that the information was delivered without the person's knowledge or connivance.

Commentary—*Simon's Direct Tax Service* **E4.11151.**
Derivation—The Income Tax (Employments) Regulations, SI 1993/744 reg 46ZB.

Proof of delivery of information sent electronically

196—(1) The use of an approved method of electronic communications is presumed, unless the contrary is proved, to have resulted in the delivery of information—

(*a*) to the Inland Revenue, if the delivery of the information has been recorded on an official computer system;
(*b*) by the Inland Revenue, if the despatch of the information has been recorded on an official computer system.

(2) The use of an approved method of electronic communications is presumed, unless the contrary is proved, not to have resulted in the delivery of information—

(*a*) to the Inland Revenue, if the delivery of the information has not been recorded on an official computer system;
(*b*) by the Inland Revenue, if the despatch of the information has not been recorded on an official computer system.

(3) The time of receipt or despatch of any information delivered by an approved method of electronic communications is presumed, unless the contrary is proved, to be the time recorded on an official computer system.

Commentary—*Simon's Direct Tax Service* **E4.11151.**
Derivation—The Income Tax (Employments) Regulations, SI 1993/744 reg 2D.

Proof of payment sent electronically

197—(1) The use of a method of electronic communications is presumed, unless the contrary is proved, to have resulted in the making of a payment—

(*a*) to the Inland Revenue, if the making of the payment has been recorded on an official computer system;

(*b*) by the Inland Revenue, if the despatch of the payment has been recorded on an official computer system.

(2) The use of a method of electronic communications is presumed, unless the contrary is proved, not to have resulted in the making of a payment—

(*a*) to the Inland Revenue, if the making of the payment has not been recorded on an official computer system;

(*b*) by the Inland Revenue, if the despatch of the payment has not been recorded on an official computer system.

(3) The time of receipt or despatch of any payment sent by a method of electronic communications is presumed, unless the contrary is proved, to be the time recorded on an official computer system.

(4) In this regulation, ''the Inland Revenue'' means the Board of Inland Revenue or any officer of the Board.

Commentary—*Simon's Direct Tax Service* **E4.11151.**
Derivation—The Income Tax (Employments) Regulations, SI 1993/744 reg 2D.

Use of unauthorised method of electronic communications

198—(1) This regulation applies to information which is required to be delivered to the Board of Inland Revenue or to the Inland Revenue under a provision of these Regulations.

(2) The use of a method of electronic communications for the purpose of delivering such information is conclusively presumed not to have resulted in the delivery of that information, unless that method of electronic communications is for the time being approved for delivery of information of that kind under that provision.

Commentary—*Simon's Direct Tax Service* **E4.11151.**
Derivation—The Income Tax (Employments) Regulations, SI 1993/744 reg 2E.

CHAPTER 3

ELECTRONIC PAYMENT BY LARGE EMPLOYERS

Large employers required to make specified payments electronically

199—(1) A large employer to whom an e-payment notice in respect of a tax year has been issued must use an approved method of electronic communications to make specified payments.

(2) ''Specified payments'', in this Chapter, means payments of tax under regulation 68 (periodic payments to and recoveries from the Revenue) in respect of tax months in the tax year to which the e-payment notice relates.

(3) The Board of Inland Revenue may give specific or general directions—

(*a*) suspending, for any period during which the use of an approved method of electronic communications for the making of specified payments is impossible or impractical, any requirement imposed by these Regulations relating to the use of such methods,

(*b*) substituting alternative requirements for the suspended ones, and

(*c*) making any provision that is necessary in consequence of the imposition of the substituted requirements.

Commentary—*Simon's Direct Tax Service* **E4.11154.**
Derivation—The Income Tax (Employments) Regulations, SI 1993/744 reg 42A(1), (2), (5).

E-payment notices and appeal

200—(1) ''E-payment notice'' means a notice issued by the Inland Revenue in respect of a tax year that the employer is a large employer and accordingly is required to use an approved method of electronic communications for the making of specified payments.

(2) An e-payment notice in respect of a tax year must be issued by 31st December following the specified date for that tax year.

(3) An employer may appeal against an e-payment notice by giving notice to the Inland Revenue within 30 days of the issue of the e-payment notice.

(4) The grounds of appeal are that the employer is not a large employer.

(5) If the appeal is successful the e-payment notice must be withdrawn.

(6) Regulation 217 (appeals: supplementary provisions) applies to appeals under this regulation.

Commentary—*Simon's Direct Tax Service* **E4.11154.**
Derivation—The Income Tax (Employments) Regulations, SI 1993/744 reg 42A(1), (2).
Cross reference—See the Income Tax (PAYE) Regulations, SI 2003/2682 reg 217 (TMA 1970 ss 31A(5), (6), 31B and 31D apply to an appeal under para (3) above as they apply to an appeal under TMA1970 s 31).

Employer in default if specified payment not received by applicable due date

201—(1) This regulation applies if an employer is required to make a specified payment by an approved method of electronic communications in accordance with regulation 199.

(2) The employer is in default if the specified payment is not received in full by the Inland Revenue (whether by an approved method of electronic communications or otherwise) on or before the date by which that payment is required in accordance with regulation 69 (due date for payments of tax).

(3) But the employer is not in default if—

(*a*) the employer had a reasonable excuse for failing to make the specified payment in a manner which secures that it is received in full by the Inland Revenue on or before the applicable due date, and

(*b*) the specified payment is received in full by the Inland Revenue without unreasonable delay after the excuse ceased.

(4) Inability to pay is not a reasonable excuse for the purposes of paragraph (3)(*a*).

(5) A payment is not treated as received in full by the Inland Revenue on or before the date by which that payment is required in accordance with regulation 69 unless it is made in a manner which secures (in a case where the payment is made otherwise than in cash) that, on or before that date, all transactions can be completed which need to be completed before the whole amount of the payment becomes available to the Inland Revenue.

Commentary—*Simon's Direct Tax Service* **E4.11154.**
Derivation—The Income Tax (Employments) Regulations, SI 1993/744 reg 42B(1), (2), (3), (4), (5).

Default notice and appeal

202—(1) The Inland Revenue must issue a default notice to any person who appears to be in default under regulation 201 in respect of a specified payment.

(2) A person may appeal against a default notice by giving notice to the Inland Revenue within 30 days of the issue of the default notice.

(3) The grounds of appeal are—

(*a*) that the person is not in default, or

(*b*) that the person is not a large employer, subject to paragraph (5).

(4) If the appeal is successful the default notice must be withdrawn.

(5) Paragraph (3)(*b*) does not apply if, following an appeal under regulation 200, the e-payment notice was not withdrawn.

(6) Regulation 217 (appeals: supplementary provisions) applies to appeals under this regulation.

Commentary—*Simon's Direct Tax Service* **E4.11154.**
Derivation—The Income Tax (Employments) Regulations, SI 1993/744 reg 42B(6), (7), (8).
Cross reference—See the Income Tax (PAYE) Regulations, SI 2003/2682 reg 217 (TMA 1970 ss 31A(5), (6), 31B and 31D apply to an appeal under para (2) above as they apply to an appeal under TMA1970 s 31).

Default surcharge

203—(1) An employer in default in respect of any specified payment to whom—

(*a*) a default notice under regulation 202, and

(*b*) a surcharge notice under regulation 204,

have been issued, is liable to a surcharge.

(2) The surcharge is the sum of the surcharges, calculated in accordance with paragraph (3), in respect of each default relating to the tax year in which were made the relevant payments to which the specified payment referred to in paragraph (1) relates.

(3) The surcharge in respect of each default is the specified percentage of (A – B).

(4) In paragraph (3)—

(*a*) A is the total amount of tax due for the tax year in which the relevant payments to which the specified payment relates were made;

(*b*) B is the total of the amounts deducted from A under—

(i) rule 1 of regulation 7(2) of the Working Tax Credit (Payment by Employers) Regulations 2002;

(ii) regulations 4, 5 and 6 of the Statutory Maternity Pay (Compensation of Employers) and Miscellaneous Amendment Regulations 1994,

(iii) regulations 3 and 5 of the Statutory Paternity Pay and Statutory Adoption Pay (Administration) Regulations 2002, and

(iv) regulation 44B of the Income Tax (Sub-contractors in the Construction Industry) Regulations 1993;

(*c*) the specified percentage is determined by reference to the number of the default during a surcharge period in accordance with Table 8.

TABLE 8
SPECIFIED PERCENTAGE FOR EACH DEFAULT IN A SURCHARGE PERIOD

1 Default number (within a surcharge period)	*2 Specified percentage*
1st	0%
2nd	0%
3rd	0.17%
4th	0.17%
5th	0.17%
6th	0.33%
7th	0.33%
8th	0.33%
9th	0.58%
10th	0.58%
11th	0.58%
12th and subsequent defaults	0.83%

(5) A surcharge period is a period which—

(*a*) begins on the day following the date by which payment is required in accordance with regulation 69 for the first specified payment in respect of which the employer is in default, and

(*b*) ends at the end of a tax year in relation to which the employer has not been in default in respect of any specified payment.

(6) A surcharge payable under this regulation is payable 30 days after the issue of the surcharge notice.

(7) Section 102 of TMA (mitigation of penalties) applies to a surcharge payable under this regulation as if it were a penalty.

Commentary—*Simon's Direct Tax Service* **E4.11154.**
Derivation—The Income Tax (Employments) Regulations, SI 1993/744 reg 42B(9), (10), (16), (17).

Surcharge notice and appeal

204—(1) The Inland Revenue must issue a surcharge notice to an employer who has been in default on three or more occasions during a surcharge period and consequently will be liable to a surcharge under regulation 203.

(2) The surcharge notice must show the total surcharge liability for the tax year.

(3) The surcharge notice must be issued within 6 years of—

(*a*) the end of the tax year, or

(*b*) if earlier, the date on which the employer delivered a return in accordance with regulation 73 (annual return of relevant payments liable to deduction of tax (Forms P35 and P14)).

(4) An employer may appeal against a surcharge notice by giving notice to the Inland Revenue within 30 days of the issue of the surcharge notice.

(5) The grounds of appeal are—

(*a*) that the number of defaults stated in the notice is incorrect, or

(*b*) that the amount of the surcharge is incorrect.

(6) But paragraph (5)(*a*) does not apply in respect of a disputed default which has already been the subject of an appeal under regulation 202, following which the default notice was not withdrawn.

(7) Parts 4, 5 and 6 of TMA (assessment, appeals, collection and recovery) apply to the surcharge notice as if it were an assessment and the amount of the surcharge was tax charged by the assessment, subject to paragraphs (4), (5) and (8).

(8) On an appeal section 50(6) to (8) of TMA (procedure) do not apply, but the Commissioners may—

(*a*) if it appears to them that no surcharge has been incurred, set the surcharge notice aside,

(*b*) if the amount of the total surcharge liability appears to them to be correct, confirm the surcharge notice, or

(*c*) if the amount of the total surcharge liability appears to them to be incorrect, increase or reduce it to the correct amount.

(9) Regulation 217(3) (appeals: supplementary provisions) applies to appeals under this regulation.

Commentary—*Simon's Direct Tax Service* **E4.11154.**
Derivation—The Income Tax (Employments) Regulations, SI 1993/744 reg 42B(11), (12), (13), (14), (15).

CHAPTER 4

MANDATORY USE OF ELECTRONIC COMMUNICATIONS

Mandatory use of electronic communications

205—(1) A specified employer must deliver specified information by an approved method of electronic communications to the Inland Revenue.

(2) The Board may make a general or specific direction requiring a specified employer to deliver specified information by a particular approved method of electronic communication.

(3) Specified information may be delivered under this regulation by a person on behalf of a specified employer.

(4) References in this Chapter to information and to the delivery of information must be construed in accordance with section 135(8) of the Finance Act 2002 (mandatory e-filing).

(5) This regulation applies in relation to specified information—

(*a*) in respect of the tax year ending 5th April 2005, for specified employers who are large employers,

(*b*) in respect of the tax year ending 5th April 2006 and subsequent tax years, for specified employers who are large or medium sized employers.

Commentary—*Simon's Direct Tax Service* **E4.11152.**
Derivation—The Income Tax (Employments) Regulations, SI 1993/744 regs 46ZC(1)–(4), 46ZE(1).

Specified employers

206—(1) In this Chapter, "specified employer" means—

(*a*) a large employer, or

(*b*) a large or medium sized employer,

to whom an e-filing notice for a tax year has been issued by 31st December following the specified date for the tax year.

(2) But the following are not specified employers—

(*a*) an individual who is a practising member of a religious society or order whose beliefs are incompatible with the use of electronic communications,

(*b*) a partnership, if all the partners fall within sub-paragraph (*a*), and

(*c*) a company, if all the directors and the company secretary fall within sub-paragraph (*a*).

(3) In paragraph (2)(*c*), "company" means a body corporate or unincorporated association but does not include a partnership.

Commentary—*Simon's Direct Tax Service* **E4.11152.**
Derivation—The Income Tax (Employments) Regulations, SI 1993/744 reg 46ZD(1)–(4).

Specified information

207—(1) In this Chapter, "specified information" means the return and accompanying information required by regulation 73 (annual return of relevant payments liable to deduction of tax (Forms P35 and P14)).

(2) But specified information does not include information supplied under special arrangements for the collection of tax made under regulation 141 (direct collection and special arrangements).

Commentary—*Simon's Direct Tax Service* **E4.11152.**
Derivation—The Income Tax (Employments) Regulations, SI 1993/744 reg 46ZE(1), (2).

E-filing notice and appeals

208—(1) In this Chapter, "e-filing notice" means a notice issued by the Inland Revenue in respect of a tax year that an employer—

(*a*) is a large or a large or medium sized employer, and

(*b*) does not fall within regulation 206(2) (religious objection),

and accordingly is required to use an approved method of electronic communications for the delivery of specified information for the tax year.

(2) An employer may appeal against an e-filing notice by notice to the Inland Revenue within 30 days of the issue of the e-filing notice.

(3) The grounds of appeal are that the employer does not satisfy the description specified.

(4) If an appeal is successful the e-filing notice must be withdrawn.

(5) Regulation 217 (appeals: supplementary provisions) applies to appeals under this regulation.

Commentary—*Simon's Direct Tax Service* **E4.11152.**
Derivation—The Income Tax (Employments) Regulations, SI 1993/744 reg 46ZD(4), (5).
Cross reference—See the Income Tax (PAYE) Regulations, SI 2003/2682 reg 217 (TMA 1970 ss 31A(5), (6), 31B and 31D apply to an appeal under para (2) above as they apply to an appeal under TMA1970 s 31).

Standards of accuracy and completeness

209—(1) Specified information delivered by a method of electronic communications must meet the standards of accuracy or completeness set by specific or general directions given by the Board of Inland Revenue.

(2) Specified information which fails to meet those standards must be treated as not having been delivered.

Commentary—*Simon's Direct Tax Service* **E4.11152.**
Derivation—The Income Tax (Employments) Regulations, SI 1993/744 reg 46ZF(1), (2).

Penalties and appeals

210—(1) A specified employer who fails to deliver specified information or any part of it in accordance with regulation 205 is liable to a penalty.

(2) Table 9 sets out the penalties for specified employers for the tax years ending 5th April 2005 to 5th April 2009, depending on the number of employees for whom particulars should have been included with the specified information.

TABLE 9
PENALTIES: TAX YEARS ENDING 5TH APRIL 2005 TO 5TH APRIL 2009

1 Number of employees for whom particulars should have been included with the specified information	*2 Penalty*
1–49	Nil
50–249	nil for tax year ending 5th April 2005, £600 for subsequent tax years
250–399	£900
400–499	£1,200
500–599	£1,500
600–699	£1,800
700–799	£2,100
800–899	£2,400
900–999	£2,700
1000 or more	£3,000

(3) An employer is not liable to a penalty if the employer had a reasonable excuse for failing to comply with regulation 205 which had not ceased at the time the specified information was delivered.

(4) A notice of appeal against a determination under section 100 of TMA of a penalty under this regulation can only be on the grounds that—

(*a*) the employer is not a specified employer, subject to paragraph (5),
(*b*) the employer did comply with regulation 205,
(*c*) the amount of the penalty is incorrect, or
(*d*) paragraph (3) applies.

(5) An employer may not appeal on the grounds that the employer is not a specified employer if the employer has already appealed under regulation 208(2) (appeal against e-filing notice).

(6) Section 103A of TMA (interest on penalties) applies to penalties payable under this regulation.

Commentary—*Simon's Direct Tax Service* **E4.11152.**
Derivation—The Income Tax (Employments) Regulations, SI 1993/744 reg 46ZG(1)–(4).

CHAPTER 5
METHODS OF PROVIDING INFORMATION ETC

How information must or may be delivered by employers

211—(1) Table 10 applies to determine how employers must or may comply with the requirements of the regulations listed in column 1.

(2) The requirements of the regulation must be complied with in a document or format provided or approved by the Board of Inland Revenue if so indicated in column 4.

(3) Where appropriate, the relevant form number is listed in column 3.

(4) Instead of sending a document to the Inland Revenue, the requirements of the regulation may be complied with by an employer arranging for the information it would contain to be delivered to the Inland Revenue by an approved method of electronic communications if so indicated in column 5.

TABLE 10
REGULATIONS WHICH REQUIRE APPROVED DOCUMENT OR FORMAT, AND WHICH PERMIT ELECTRONIC DELIVERY

1	*2*	*3*	*4*	*5*
Regulation	*Description of information*	*Form number*	*Approved document or format*	*Electronic communications*
35(3), (4), (5)(*a*)	simplified deduction scheme: deductions working sheet	Form P12	yes	Yes
35(5)(*b*)	simplified deductions scheme: annual return of deductions working sheets	Form P37	yes	Yes
36(1), (2)(*a*)	cessation of employment	Form P45, Part 1	yes	Yes
36(1), (2)(*b*)	cessation of employment	Form P45, Parts 1A, 2, 3	yes	No
38(1)	death of employee	Form P45, Part 1	yes	Yes
39(1)	death of pensioner	Form P45, Part 1	yes	Yes
42(8)	procedure if new employer receives Form P45	Form P45, Part 3	yes	Yes
46(4), 47(2)(*a*) 48(2)(*a*) 49(2)(*a*)	information to be provided if code not known	Form P46	yes	Yes
52(3)	late presentation of Form P45	Form P45, Part 3	yes	Yes
55(3)(*a*)	retirement statement	Form P160	no	Yes
56(3)	procedure if new pension payer receives Form P45	Form P45, Part 3	yes	Yes
57(2)	information to be provided if code not known (non-UK resident pensioners)	Form P46	yes	Yes
58(3)	information to be provided if code not known (UK resident pensioners)	Form P46	yes	Yes
60(3)	late presentation of Form P45	Form P45, Part 3	yes	Yes
67(1)	information to employees about payments and tax deducted	Form P60	yes	No
73	annual return of relevant payments liable to deduction of tax	Forms P35 and P14	yes	Yes
74	annual return of relevant payments not liable to deduction of tax	Form P38A	yes	Yes
77(4)	return of tax for which employer is liable under regulation 68	Form P100	yes	No

1	*2*	*3*	*4*	*5*
Regulation	*Description of information*	*Form number*	*Approved document or format*	*Electronic communications*
85(1)(*a*)	employers: annual return of other PAYE income	Form P9D	yes	No
85(1)(*a*) and (*b*)	employers: annual return of other PAYE income: benefits code employee	Form P11D	yes	Yes
85(2)	employers: annual return of other PAYE income: declaration	Form P11D(*b*)	yes	Yes
90(2)	quarterly return of cars becoming available or unavailable	Form P46 (car)	yes	Yes
129(1)	reserve forces' pay: certificate of tax deducted	Form P59	yes	No
132(1)	reserve forces' pay: end of year certificate	Form P60	yes	No
137(1)	holiday pay funds: certificate of tax deducted	Form P403	yes	No
152(2)	deductions working sheet for claimants awarded taxable JSA	Form PB8	yes	No
153(9)	Department's return for claimant who delivers Form P45	Forms PB3 and P45 Part 3	yes	No
154(2)	Department's return for claimant who does not deliver Form P45	Form PB3	yes	No
157(2)(*b*)	claimant's end of year certificate	Form P60U	yes	No
157(2)(*c*)	Department's end of year return	Form P14U	yes	No
159(2)	cessation of award of JSA	Form P45U	yes	No
160(2)(*b*)	Department's notification of taxable JSA adjustment	Form P180	yes	No
164(2)	Department's quarterly statement to Board of receipts and payments in respect of taxable JSA	—	yes	No

(5) If an employer delivers electronically the return required by regulation 73 (annual return of relevant payments liable to deduction of tax (Forms P35 and P14)), the statement and declaration and the certificate must, instead of being signed as required by regulation 73(8), be authenticated by or on behalf of the employer in such manner as may be approved by the Board of Inland Revenue.

Commentary—*Simon's Direct Tax Service* **E4.11150, 11151.**

Derivation—The Income Tax (Employments) Regulations, SI 1993/744 regs 20(2), (3), 23(1), (3), 25(2), 26(1A), (4), 27(1), 28(1A), (5A), 29(1), 30(1), 39(2), 43(1), (1C), (3B), (4), 44(2), 46(1), (1A), (7A), (7B), 46A(1), 47(2), 65(1), 68(2), 74(1), 84(3), 88(4), (5), 89(2), 90, 93(2).

Modifications—See the Income Tax (PAYE) Regulations, SI 2003/2682 reg 150 (modification of this regulation in its application to payments of taxable jobseeker's allowance made to a claimant).

SI 2003/2682 reg 174 (modification of this regulation in its application to payments of taxable incapacity benefit).

Modifications for electronic version of Form P160

212—(1) This regulation applies if instead of sending to the Inland Revenue the statement required by regulation 55(3)(*a*) (pensioner's retirement statement: Form P160) a pension payer delivers the information it would contain to the Inland Revenue by an approved method of electronic communications (as permitted by regulation 211).

(2) For sub-paragraphs (*a*) to (*m*) of regulation 55(4) (information to be provided in retirement statement) substitute—

"(*a*) the pension payer's PAYE reference,
(*b*) the pensioner's name,
(*c*) the date of retirement,
(*d*) the date on which the pension started,
(*e*) the pensioner's code immediately before retirement and whether it was being used on the cumulative basis,
(*f*) if the pensioner's code immediately before retirement was used on the cumulative basis—
(i) the tax week or tax month in which the last relevant payment before retirement was made to the pensioner or, in a case falling within regulation 24, was treated as having been made,
(ii) the total payments to date at the date of retirement,
(iii) the total net tax deducted,
(*g*) any number used to identify the pensioner,
(*h*) the tax code in use for the pensioner, and whether it is being used on the cumulative basis,
(*i*) the pensioner's address, if known,
(*j*) the pensioner's sex,
(*k*) the pensioner's national insurance number, if known,
(*l*) the pensioner's date of birth, if known,
(*m*) the amount of pension payable annually."

Commentary—*Simon's Direct Tax Service* **E4.1175.**
Derivation—The Income Tax (Employments) Regulations, SI 1993/744 reg 26(2).

How information may be delivered by Inland Revenue

213—(1) Table 11 applies to determine how the Inland Revenue may comply with requirements of the regulations listed in column 1.

(2) Instead of sending a document to the employer or (where relevant) the employer's agent, the requirements of the regulation may be complied with by the Inland Revenue arranging for the information it would contain to be delivered to the employer or (where relevant) the employer's agent by an approved method of electronic communications if so indicated in column 4.

(3) The relevant form number is listed in column 3.

TABLE 11
REGULATIONS WHICH PERMIT ELECTRONIC DELIVERY BY INLAND REVENUE

1 *Regulation*	*2* *Description of information*	*3* *Form number*	*4* *Electronic communications*
8(2), 20(2)	issue of code to employer or agent	Form P6 or P9	Yes
20(5), (6)	notice to employer to amend codes	Form P7X or P9X	Yes
53(2)	notice to employer of payments and total net tax deducted	Form P6	Yes
61(2)	notice to pension payer of payments and total net tax deducted	Form P6	Yes

(4) But the Inland Revenue may only deliver information by an approved method of electronic communications if the employer or employer's agent (as the case may be) has consented to delivery of information in that way, and the Inland Revenue have not been notified that the consent has been withdrawn.

(5) References in paragraphs (2) and (4) to an employer's agent are to a person acting on behalf of the employer.

Commentary—*Simon's Direct Tax Service* **E4.11151.**
Derivation—The Income Tax (Employments) Regulations, SI 1993/744 regs 6(4), 13(6), 33.

How information must be provided by employees

214—(1) An employee must comply with the requirements of the regulations listed in column 1 of Table 12 in a document or format provided or approved by the Board of Inland Revenue.

(2) Where appropriate, the relevant form number is listed in column 3 of the Table.

TABLE 12
REGULATIONS WHICH REQUIRE EMPLOYEE TO USE APPROVED DOCUMENT OR FORMAT

1	*2*	*3*
Regulation	*Subject*	*Form number*
46(2)	Form P46 where employer does not receive Form P45 and code not known	Form P46
145(1)	direct collection: return when relevant payments cease	—
146(1)	direct collection: end of year return	Form P14
147(2)	direct collection: return of unpaid tax	—
154(3)	claimant's certificate of full-time education	Form P187

Commentary—*Simon's Direct Tax Service* **E4.11151.**
Derivation—The Income Tax (Employments) Regulations, SI 1993/744 regs 29(1), 30(1), 84(10), 104(6), (9), (11).
Modifications—See the Income Tax (PAYE) Regulations, SI 2003/2682 reg 150 (modification of this regulation in its application to payments of taxable jobseeker's allowance made to a claimant).

Meaning of Form P45 and P46

215—In these Regulations—

"Form P45" means the form provided or approved for use in accordance with regulations 36 (cessation of employment: Form P45), 38 (death of employee) or 39 (death of pensioner);

"Parts 2 and 3 of Form P45" means—

(*a*) the Parts 2 and 3 of the Form P45 provided to the employee or claimant (as the case may be) in accordance with regulation 36, or

(*b*) the Parts 2 and 3 of the Form P45 provided to the claimant in accordance with regulation 159 (cessation of award: Form P45U);

"Form P45U" means the form required to be completed in accordance with regulation 159;

"Form P46" means the form provided or approved for use in accordance with regulations 46, 57 and 58 (Form P46 procedure for employees and pensioners).

Commentary—*Simon's Direct Tax Service* **E4.1166, 1171.**
Derivation—The Income Tax (Employments) Regulations, SI 1993/744 regs 23(1)–(3), 89(2).

Service by post

216 Any notice or deductions working sheet which is authorised or required to be given, served or issued under these Regulations may be sent by post.

Derivation—The Income Tax (Employments) Regulations, SI 1993/744 reg 109.
Modifications—See the Income Tax (PAYE) Regulations, SI 2003/2682 reg 150 (modification of this regulation in its application to payments of taxable jobseeker's allowance made to a claimant).
SI 2003/2682 reg 174 (modification of this regulation in its application to payments of taxable incapacity benefit).

PART 11
SUPPLEMENTARY PROVISIONS

MISCELLANEOUS APPEALS

Appeals: supplementary provisions

217—(1) The following provisions of TMA apply to appeals under the regulations listed in paragraph (2) as they apply to an appeal under section 31 of TMA—

Section 31A(5) and (6)	notice of appeal
Section 31B	appeals to General Commissioners
Section 31D	election to bring appeal before Special Commissioners.

(2) The regulations are—

Regulation 99(3)	appeal against improper purpose notice
Regulation 200(3)	appeal against e-payment notice
Regulation 202(2)	appeal against default notice
Regulation 208(2)	appeal against e-filing notice.

(3) In an appeal under the regulations listed in paragraph (2) and regulation 204(4) (appeal against surcharge notice), the relevant place for the purposes of paragraph 3(1)(*a*) of Schedule 3 to TMA (rules for assigning proceedings to General Commissioners) is the place which at the time of the notice of appeal is—

(*a*) the employer's place of business in the United Kingdom, or

(*b*) if there is no such place, the employer's place of residence in the United Kingdom.

(4) In paragraph (3)—

"place of business" means—

(*a*) the place where the trade, profession, vocation or business with which the proceedings are concerned is carried out, or

(*b*) if more than one such place, the head office or place where it is mainly carried out; and

"place of residence" means the employer's usual place of residence or, if that is unknown, the employer's last known place of residence.

Commentary—*Simon's Direct Tax Service* **E4.11155.**
Derivation—The Income Tax (Employments) Regulations, SI 1993/744 reg 46ZH(1), (3), (4).

CERTIFICATE THAT SUM DUE AND PAYMENT BY CHEQUE

Certificate that sum due

218—(1) A certificate of the Inland Revenue that, to the best of their knowledge and belief, any amount shown in a certificate under the regulations listed in paragraph (2) has not been paid by an employer, is sufficient evidence that the amount mentioned in the certificate is unpaid and due to the Crown.

(2) The regulations are—

Regulation 76	unpaid amounts in regulation 73 return (Form P35)
Regulation 77(6)	unpaid amounts in regulation 77 return
Regulation 78(8)	unpaid amounts from regulation 78 specification
Regulation 79	unpaid amounts following inspection under regulation 97.

(3) A certificate of the Inland Revenue that, to the best of their knowledge and belief, any amount of interest payable under the regulations listed in paragraph (4) has not been paid by an employer or employee is sufficient evidence that the amount mentioned in the certificate is unpaid and due to the Crown.

(4) The regulations are—

Regulation 72(7)	interest consequential on regulation 72 direction
Regulation 81(6)	interest consequential on regulation 81 direction
Regulation 82	interest on overdue tax
Regulation 115	interest on tax overdue under PSA.

(5) The production of—

(*a*) the return made by the employer under paragraph (4) of regulation 77 (return and certificate if tax unpaid), and

(*b*) the certificate of the Inland Revenue under paragraph (6) of that regulation,

is sufficient evidence that the amount shown in the certificate is the amount of tax which the employer is liable to pay to the Inland Revenue in respect of the tax period in question under that regulation.

(6) A document which purports to be a certificate under paragraph (1) or (3), or regulation 77(6), is treated as such a certificate until the contrary is proved.

Derivation—The Income Tax (Employments) Regulations, SI 1993/744 regs 42(8), (9), 43(10), (11), 47(7), (8), 48(6), (9), (10), 49(9), (10), 51(4), (5), 54(6), (7), 55(8), (10), (11), 80J(3), (4).
Modifications—See the Income Tax (PAYE) Regulations, SI 2003/2682 reg 174 (modification of this regulation in its application to payments of taxable incapacity benefit).

Payment by cheque

219—(1) For the purposes of the following provisions, if—

(*a*) any payment to the Inland Revenue is made by cheque, and

(*b*) the cheque is paid on its first presentation to the banker on whom it is drawn,

the payment is treated as made on the day on which the cheque was received by the Inland Revenue.

(2) The provisions are—

Regulation 69	due date and receipts for payments of tax
Regulation 72	recovery from employee of tax not deducted by employer
Regulation 78	notice and certificate if tax may be unpaid
Regulation 82	interest on tax overdue
Regulation 83(2)(*b*)	interest on tax overpaid: date of overpayment
Regulation 115	interest on tax due under PSA
Regulation 116	interest due on tax overpaid under PSA.

Commentary—*Simon's Direct Tax Service* **E4.11115.**
Derivation—The Income Tax (Employments) Regulations, SI 1993/744 regs 42(7A), 48(7A), 52(4), 80J(6), 80K(3).
Modifications—See the Income Tax (PAYE) Regulations, SI 2003/2682 reg 174 (modification of this regulation in its application to payments of taxable incapacity benefit).
SI 2003/2682 Sch 1 para 23 (modification of this regulation in relation to interest on overpaid tax : provisions applying to tax years from 1992–93 to 1995–96).

TRANSITIONAL PROVISIONS, SAVINGS AND REVOCATIONS

Transitional provisions, savings and revocations

220—(1) Schedule 1 (transitional provisions and savings) has effect.

(2) The regulations listed in column 1 of Schedule 2 are revoked to the extent specified in column 3 of that Schedule.

(3) Paragraph (2) is subject to Schedule 1.

SCHEDULE 1

TRANSITIONAL PROVISIONS AND SAVINGS

Regulation 220

PART 1

GENERAL PROVISIONS

Continuity of the law

1 The revocation of provisions and their making in a rewritten form in these Regulations does not affect the continuity of the law.

2 Paragraph 1 does not apply to any change in the law made by these Regulations.

3 Anything which—

(*a*) has been done, or has effect as if done, under or for the purposes of a provision of the revoked Regulations, and

(*b*) is in force or effective immediately before the commencement of these Regulations,

has effect after that commencement as if done under or for the purposes of the corresponding provision of these Regulations.

4 Any reference (express or implied) in these Regulations or any document made under these Regulations to—

(*a*) a provision of these Regulations, or

(*b*) things done or falling to be done under or for the purposes of a provision of these Regulations,

is to be read as including, in relation to times, circumstances or purposes in relation to which any corresponding provision of the revoked Regulations had effect, a reference to the provision of the revoked Regulations or to things done or falling to be done under or for the purposes of the provision of the revoked Regulations.

5 Any reference (express or implied) in these Regulations to relevant payments, relevant payments exceeding the PAYE threshold or similar concepts created by these Regulations is to be read as including, in relation to times, circumstances or purposes in relation to which any corresponding concept of the revoked Regulations had effect, a reference to the concept of the revoked Regulations.

6 Any reference (express or implied) in these Regulations to—

(*a*) a provision of ITEPA, or

(*b*) things done or falling to be done under or for the purposes of a provision of ITEPA,

is to be read as including, in relation to times, circumstances or purposes in relation to which any corresponding provision repealed by ITEPA had effect, a reference to the repealed provision or to things done or falling to be done under or for the purposes of the repealed provision.

7 Any reference (express or implied) in these Regulations to general earnings, PAYE income or similar concepts created by ITEPA is to be read as including, in relation to times, circumstances or purposes in relation to which any corresponding concept which has been superseded by ITEPA had effect, a reference to the superseded concept.

8 Paragraphs 4, 5, 6 and 7 apply only in so far as the context permits.

9 Paragraph 5 is without prejudice to the generality of paragraph 4 and paragraph 7 is without prejudice to the generality of paragraph 6.

10 These Regulations have effect in relation to tax liable, under the Income Tax (Employments) Regulations 1993 or section 710 of ITEPA, to be deducted or accounted for in respect of payments made before 6th April 2004 as if the tax had been liable to be deducted or accounted for under these Regulations.

11 Paragraph 10 is without prejudice to the generality of paragraphs 1 to 9.

12 Paragraphs 1 to 11 have effect instead of paragraph (*b*) of section 17(2) of the Interpretation Act 1978.

General saving for old savings

13—(1) The revocation by these Regulations of a provision previously revoked subject to savings does not affect the continued operation of those savings.

(2) The revocation by these Regulations of a saving on the previous revocation of a provision does not affect the operation of the saving in so far as it is not specifically reproduced in these Regulations but remains capable of having effect.

Interpretation

14 In this Part of this Schedule, "the revoked Regulations" means the Regulations which are revoked by these Regulations.

PART 2

SPECIFIC PROVISIONS

Modification of reference to payment to the Inland Revenue in regulation 68(2)

15 For the purposes of giving effect to any enactment or instrument which refers to an amount which is, or would in certain circumstances be, payable to the collector, paragraph (2) of regulation 68 has effect as if that paragraph required payment of the amount to which it refers to the collector.

Derivation—The Income Tax (Employments) Regulations, SI 1993/744 regs 40(1), 41(1).

FPCS information for the tax year ending 5th April 2002: employees not covered by regulation 46(1) of 1993 Regulations

16—(1) This paragraph applies to a person (a "former FPCS employee")—

(*a*) who was employed by an employer during a part of the tax year ending 5th April 2002, but who was no longer employed by that employer on 5th April 2002, and

(*b*) in respect of whom the employer—

(i) has provided information to the Inland Revenue under the FPCS arrangement for the tax year ending 5th April 2002, or

(ii) has delivered information by an approved method of electronic communications to an official computer system under the FPCS arrangement for the tax year ending 5th April 2002, but

(*c*) in respect of whom no particulars were required to be provided by the employer under regulation 46(1) of the 1993 Regulations for the tax year ending 5th April 2002.

(2) The former FPCS employee may by notice require the employer to give a statement to the former FPCS employee containing—

(*a*) particulars of the amount of the taxable profit, if any, for the tax year ending 5th April 2002 in respect of car allowances and motor mileage allowances paid to the former FPCS employee in the tax year ending 5th April 2002 for business travel, calculated by reference to the FPCS arrangement, or

(*b*) particulars of the total amount of the car allowances and motor mileage allowances paid to the former FPCS employee in the tax year ending 5th April 2002 for business travel, and the total amount of miles covered by the former FPCS employee in the tax year ending 5th April 2002 in the course of business travel for which the motor mileage allowances were paid.

(3) The former FPCS employee may give the notice to the employer at any time before 6th April 2005.

(4) The employer must give the statement to the former FPCS employee within 30 days of receiving the notice.

(5) A former FPCS employee who has received the statement from the employer may not require a further statement from the employer in respect of the tax year ending 5th April 2002.

(6) In this paragraph—

"business travel" has the meaning given by section 168(5)(*c*) of ICTA as that definition had effect for the tax year ending 5th April 2002 by virtue of regulation 46AA(6) of the 1993 Regulations;

"the FPCS arrangement" means the arrangement known as the Fixed Profit Car Scheme made between the employer and the Inland Revenue for providing information in respect of payments of car allowances and motor mileage allowances made to employees for business travel.

(7) The reference in sub-paragraph (1)(*b*)(ii) to the delivery of information by an approved method of electronic communications to an official computer system includes, in relation to information which was delivered before the commencement of these Regulations, a reference to the delivery of information to an official computer system within the meaning of regulation 2(1) of the 1993 Regulations by a means of electronic communications approved for the purposes of regulation 46AA(3) of those Regulations.

Derivation—The Income Tax (Employments) Regulations, SI 1993/744 reg 46AA(3), (4), (5), (6).

FPCS information for the tax year ending 5th April 2002: employees covered by regulation 46(1) of 1993 Regulations

17—(1) This paragraph applies to a former employee who would be a former FPCS employee were it not for the fact that the employer was required under regulation 46(1) of the 1993 Regulations to provide particulars in respect of the former employee for the tax year ending 5th April 2002.

(2) If the former employee gives notice to the employer under paragraph (4) of regulation 94 requiring a statement relating to the tax year ending 5th April 2002, the statement must contain (in addition to the particulars mentioned in paragraph (2) of that regulation)—

(*a*) particulars of the amount of the taxable profit, if any, for the tax year ending 5th April 2002 in respect of car allowances and motor mileage allowances paid to the former employee in the tax year ending 5th April 2002 for business travel, calculated by reference to the FPCS arrangement, or

(*b*) particulars of the total amount of the car allowances and motor mileage allowances paid to the former employee in the tax year ending 5th April 2002 for business travel, and the total amount of miles covered by the former employee in the tax year ending 5th April 2002 in the course of business travel for which the motor mileage allowances were paid.

(3) "Former employee" has the same meaning as in regulation 94(7).

(4) Expressions used in this paragraph which are defined in paragraph 16 have the same meaning in this paragraph as in that paragraph.

Derivation—The Income Tax (Employments) Regulations, SI 1993/744 reg 46AA(3), (4), (6).

Due date for payments of tax in respect of tax periods ending before 6th April 2004

18—(1) The following provisions have effect with the following modifications in so far as the provisions apply in relation to tax periods ending before 6th April 2004.

(2) For sub-paragraphs (*a*) and (*b*) of regulation 69(1) (due date for payments of tax) substitute "within 14 days after the end of the tax period".

(3) In regulation 77(1) (return and certificate if tax may be unpaid) for "17 days" substitute "14 days".

(4) In regulation 78(1) (notice and certificate if tax may be unpaid) for "17 days" substitute "14 days".

Derivation—The Income Tax (Employments) Regulations, SI 1993/744 regs 40(1), 41(1), 47(1), 48(1).

Interest on unpaid tax: disapplication of regulation 82 for tax years before the tax year ending 5th April 1993

19 Regulation 82 (interest on tax overdue) does not apply in relation to unpaid tax in respect of a tax year ending on or before 5th April 1992.

Derivation—The Income Tax (Employments) Regulations, SI 1993/744 reg 51(1).

Interest on unpaid tax: provisions applying to tax years before the tax year ending 5th April 1993

20—(1) This paragraph applies if the Inland Revenue make a determination under regulation 80 (determination of unpaid tax) which relates to tax payable for a tax year ending on or before 5th April 1992.

(2) This paragraph also applies if—

(*a*) the inspector, at any time after 19th April 1988, made a determination under regulation 49 of the 1993 Regulations (determination of tax payable by employer),

(*b*) the determination relates to tax payable for a tax year ending on or before 5th April 1992, and

(*c*) tax remains payable pursuant to the determination immediately before the commencement of these Regulations.

(3) The tax payable pursuant to the determination carries interest at the prescribed rate from the relevant start date until payment ("the interest period").

(4) Sub-paragraph (3) applies even if the relevant start date is a non-business day as defined by section 92 of the Bills of Exchange Act 1882.

(5) Any change made to the prescribed rate during the interest period applies to the tax payable pursuant to the determination from the date of change.

(6) Regulation 84 (recovery of tax and interest) applies to an amount of interest which an employer is liable to pay under this paragraph as if it were the unpaid amount for the purposes of that regulation.

(7) Paragraphs (3) and (6) of regulation 218 (certificate of interest due) apply in relation to an amount which an employer is liable to pay under this paragraph as if this paragraph were a regulation included among those listed in paragraph (4) of that regulation.

(8) Regulation 219 (payment by cheque) applies for determining when a payment is made for the purposes of this paragraph as if this paragraph were included among the provisions listed in paragraph (2) of that regulation.

(9) In this paragraph—

''inspector'' means an inspector of taxes;

''the prescribed rate'' means the rate applicable under section 178 of the Finance Act 1989 for the purposes of section 86 of TMA;

''the relevant start date'' means—

(*a*) in a case where the determination relates to tax payable for a tax year ending on or before 5th April 1988, 19th April 1988, and

(*b*) in a case where the determination relates to tax payable for a tax year ending after 5th April 1988 but on or before 5th April 1992, the 14th day after the end of the tax year to which the determination relates.

Derivation—The Income Tax (Employments) Regulations, SI 1993/744 regs 2(1), 50(1)–(3), 52(1)–(4), 54(1), (2), (6), (7).

Interest on tax overdue: application of regulation 82 to tax years from 1992–93 to 2003–04

21—(1) Regulation 82 (interest on tax overdue) has effect with the following modifications where the tax year in respect of which tax is unpaid is—

(*a*) the tax year ending 5th April 1993, or

(*b*) a tax year ending after 5th April 1993 but on or before 5th April 2004.

(2) In paragraph (1) for ''the total net tax payable in respect of a tax year'' substitute ''the total net tax deductible by him in respect of all of his employees during a tax year''.

(3) In paragraph (4) for ''a direction made under regulation 72(5) or 81(4)'' substitute ''a direction made under regulation 42(2) or (3) or 49(5) of the 1993 Regulations or regulation 72(5) or 81(4) of these Regulations''.

(4) Omit paragraph (6).

(5) For paragraph (8) substitute—

''(8) The ''reckonable date'' means 14 days after the end of the tax year.''

(6) After that paragraph insert—

''(9) ''The 1993 Regulations'' means the Income Tax (Employments) Regulations 1993.''

Derivation—The Income Tax (Employments) Regulations, SI 1993/744 reg 51(1)–(3).

Interest on overpaid tax: disapplication of regulation 83 for tax years before the tax year ending 5th April 1997

22 Regulation 83 (interest on overpaid tax) does not apply to tax which was paid by an employer in respect of a tax year ending on or before 5th April 1996.

Derivation—The Income Tax (Employments) Regulations, SI 1993/744 reg 53A(1).

Interest on overpaid tax: provisions applying to tax years from 1992–93 to 1995–96

23—(1) This paragraph applies in relation to tax which—

(*a*) was paid by an employer in respect of the tax year ending 5th April 1993 or in respect of a tax year ending after 5th April 1993 but on or before 5th April 1996, and

(*b*) is repaid to the employer after the end of the tax year in respect of which the tax was paid.

(2) If the late repayment condition is met, the tax repaid carries interest at the prescribed rate from the relevant time until the order for the repayment is issued (''the interest period'').

(3) The late repayment condition is that the tax is repaid—

(*a*) after the end of the tax year following the tax year in respect of which the tax was paid, and

(*b*) after the end of the tax year in which the tax was paid.

(4) Any change made to the prescribed rate during the interest period applies to the tax repaid from the date of change.

(5) Regulation 219 (payment by cheque) applies for determining when a payment is made for the purposes of this paragraph as if this paragraph were included among the provisions listed in paragraph (2) of that regulation.

(6) In this paragraph—

"the prescribed rate" means the rate applicable under section 178 of the Finance Act 1989 for the purposes of section 824 of ICTA;

"the relevant time" means—

(*a*) in a case where the tax was paid more than twelve months after the end of the tax year in respect of which the payment was made, the end of the tax year in which that tax was paid, and

(*b*) in any other case, the end of the tax year after the tax year in respect of which the payment was made.

Derivation—The Income Tax (Employments) Regulations, SI 1993/744 reg 53(1)–(5).

Overpayments and underpayments of tax: tax years before the tax year ending 5th April 1997

24—(1) Despite the revocations made by these Regulations, regulation 101 of the 1993 Regulations (repayment of overpayments and recovery of underpayments) continues to apply in relation to an assessment for a tax year ending on or before 5th April 1996, but with the modifications mentioned in sub-paragraph (2).

(2) The modifications are—

(*a*) the references in paragraphs (1) and (2) of regulation 101 to the appropriate code for a subsequent year are to be read as references to the employee's code for a subsequent tax year;

(*b*) the references in paragraphs (1) and (2) of that regulation to the inspector and to the collector are to be read as references to the Inland Revenue;

(*c*) the reference in paragraph (6) of that regulation to a direction made by the collector under regulation 42(2) of the 1993 Regulations in relation to the employee and in respect of one or more income tax periods falling within the year is to be read as including a reference to a direction under regulation 72(5) of these Regulations in relation to that employee in respect of one or more tax periods falling within the tax year;

(*d*) the reference in that paragraph to a direction made by the Board under regulation 42(3) of the 1993 Regulations in relation to the employee and in respect of one or more income tax periods falling within the year is to be read as including a reference to a direction under regulation 72(5) of these Regulations in relation to that employee in respect of one or more tax periods falling within the tax year;

(*e*) the reference in that paragraph to a direction made by the Board under regulation 49(5) of the 1993 Regulations in relation to the employee and in respect of one or more income tax periods falling within the year is to be read as including a reference to a direction under regulation 81(4) of these Regulations in relation to that employee in respect of one or more tax periods falling within the tax year.

(3) Any tax which is payable to the Inland Revenue under regulation 101(2) as it continues to have effect by virtue of this paragraph is payable within 14 days of the date on which the Inland Revenue first makes application for its payment.

Derivation—The Income Tax (Employments) Regulations, SI 1993/744 reg 105(2).

Overpayments and underpayments of tax: tax years before the tax year ending 5th April 2002

25—(1) Regulation 188 (assessments other than self-assessments)—

(*a*) does not apply in relation to an assessment for a tax year ending on or before 5th April 1996, and

(*b*) has effect in particular with the following modification in relation to an assessment, other than one under section 9 of TMA, for a tax year beginning on or after 6th April 1996 and ending on or before 5th April 2001.

(2) In paragraph (3), after sub-paragraph (*a*) insert—

"(*aa*) make any necessary adjustment to B in respect of any shortfall in deductions made in accordance with the Income Tax (Employments) Regulations 1993 from the employee, where—

(i) payments of profit-related pay have been made to the employee in accordance with a profit-related pay scheme registered under Chapter 3 of Part 5 of ICTA,

(ii) in consequence of the relief given by that Chapter less tax has been deducted from those payments than would have been deducted if the scheme had not been registered, and

(iii) the registration of the scheme has subsequently been cancelled with effect from a time before that relevant for the purposes of the relief;".

Derivation—The Income Tax (Employments) Regulations, SI 1993/744 reg 101(3), (4).

Attribution of repayments: tax years before the tax year ending 5th April 1997

26—(1) Despite the revocations made by these Regulations, regulations 106 to 108 of the 1993 Regulations (attribution of repayments) continue to apply in relation to a repayment to which section 824(5) of ICTA applies for a tax year ending on or before 5th April 1996, but with the modification mentioned in sub-paragraph (2).

(2) The modification is that the reference to the collector in regulation 107(3) is to be read as including a reference to the Inland Revenue.

Certificate that sum due: certificate of the collector

27—(1) A certificate of the collector that any amount shown in a certificate under the regulations listed in paragraph (2) of regulation 218 has not been paid by an employer to the collector or, to the best of the collector's knowledge and belief, to any other collector or to any person acting on the collector's behalf or on behalf of another collector is sufficient evidence that the amount mentioned in the collector's certificate is unpaid and due to the Crown.

(2) A certificate of the collector that any amount of interest payable under the regulations listed in paragraph (4) of regulation 218 has not been paid by an employer or employee to the collector or, to the best of the collector's knowledge and belief, to any other collector or to any person acting on the collector's behalf or on behalf of another collector is sufficient evidence that the amount mentioned in the certificate is unpaid and due to the Crown.

(3) A document which purports to be a certificate of the collector under sub-paragraph (1) or (2) is treated as such a certificate until the contrary is proved.

Interpretation

28—In this Part of this Schedule—

''the 1993 Regulations'' means the Income Tax (Employments) Regulations 1993;

''collector'' means a collector of taxes.

Derivation—The Income Tax (Employments) Regulations, SI 1993/744 reg 2(1).

SCHEDULE 2

REVOCATIONS

Regulation 220

1 Regulations revoked	*2 Reference*	*3 Extent of revocation*
The Income Tax (Employments) Regulations 1993	SI 1993/744	The whole Regulations.
The Income Tax (Employments) (Amendment) Regulations 1993	SI 1993/2276	The whole Regulations.
The Income Tax (Employments) (Amendment) Regulations 1994	SI 1994/775	The whole Regulations.
The Income Tax (Employments) (Notional Payments) Regulations 1994	SI 1994/1212	The whole Regulations.
The Income Tax (Employments) (Amendment) Regulations 1995	SI 1995/216	The whole Regulations.
The Income Tax (Employments) (Amendment No 2) Regulations 1995	SI 1995/447	The whole Regulations.
The Income Tax (Employments) (Incapacity Benefit) Regulations 1995	SI 1995/853	The whole Regulations.
The Income Tax (Employments) (Amendment No 3) Regulations 1995	SI 1995/1223	The whole Regulations.
The Income Tax (Employments) (Amendment No 4) Regulations 1995	SI 1995/1284	The whole Regulations.
The Income Tax (Employments) (Amendment) Regulations 1996	SI 1996/804	The whole Regulations.
The Income Tax (Employments) (Amendment No 2) Regulations 1996	SI 1996/980	The whole Regulations.
The Income Tax (Employments) (Amendment No 3) Regulations 1996	SI 1996/1312	The whole Regulations.
The Income Tax (Employments) (Amendment No 4) Regulations 1996	SI 1996/2381	The whole Regulations.
The Income Tax (Employments) (Amendment No 5) Regulations 1996	SI 1996/2554	The whole Regulations.

1 Regulations revoked	2 Reference	3 Extent of revocation
The Income Tax (Employments) (Amendment No 6) Regulations 1996	SI 1996/2631	The whole Regulations.
The Income Tax (Employments) (Amendment) Regulations 1997	SI 1997/214	The whole Regulations.
The Income Tax (Employments) (Notional Payments) (Amendment) Regulations 1998	SI 1998/1891	The whole Regulations.
The Income Tax (Employments) (Amendment) Regulations 1998	SI 1998/2484	The whole Regulations.
The Income Tax (Employments) (Amendment) Regulations 1999	SI 1999/70	The whole Regulations.
The Income Tax (Employments) (Amendment No 2) Regulations 1999	SI 1999/824	The whole Regulations.
The Income Tax (Employments) (Amendment No 3) Regulations 1999	SI 1999/2155	The whole Regulations.
The Income Tax (Employments) (Amendment) Regulations 2000	SI 2000/1152	The whole Regulations.
The Income Tax (Sub-contractors in the Construction Industry and Employments) (Amendment) Regulations 2000	SI 2000/2742	Regulation 3.
The Income Tax (Electronic Communications) (Miscellaneous Amendments) Regulations 2001	SI 2001/1081	In regulation 1(2), the definition of ''the Employments Regulations''. Regulations 7 to 21.
The Income Tax (Employments and Electronic Communications) (Miscellaneous Provisions) Regulations 2002	SI 2002/680	Regulations 3 to 8.
The Income Tax (Sub-contractors in the Construction Industry and Employments) (Amendment) Regulations 2003	SI 2003/536	In regulation 1(2), the definition of ''the Employments Regulations''. Regulation 9.
The Income Tax (Employments) (Amendment) Regulations 2003	SI 2003/2494	The whole Regulations.

2003/2714
Non-resident Insurance Companies Regulations 2003

Made by the Inland Revenue under TA 1988 s 11AA(5) and FA 2003 s 149(6)

Made . . . . *22 October 2003*
Laid before the House of Commons . . . . *23 October 2003*
Coming into force . . . . . . *13 November 2003*

1 These Regulations may be cited as the Non-resident Insurance Companies Regulations 2003, shall come into force on 13th November 2003, and have effect in relation to accounting periods of non-resident insurance companies beginning on or after 1st January 2003.

2 In these Regulations—

''non-resident insurance company'' means an insurance company that is not resident in the United Kingdom; and for this purpose ''insurance company'' has the meaning given by section 431(2) of the Income and Corporation Taxes Act 1988.

3—(1) In applying subsection (2) of section 11AA of the Income and Corporation Taxes Act 1988 in relation to a non-resident insurance company, it shall be assumed that the permanent establishment has assets such that its free assets would be not less than they would be in the circumstances specified in that subsection.

(2) ''Free assets'' means the amount by which—

(*a*) the value of the assets of the permanent establishment, exceeds

(*b*) the aggregate of the permanent establishment's loan capital and technical provisions; and for this purpose, the reinsurers' share of technical provisions is not to be included in determining the assets of the permanent establishment.

(3) ''Value'' means the amount that, at the time at which the value falls to be determined, the non-resident insurance company would obtain from an independent person for the transfer of all the company's rights in respect of the asset.

(4) ''Technical provision'' means each of the following—

(*a*) provision for unearned premiums;
(*b*) long term business provision;
(*c*) claims outstanding;
(*d*) provision for bonuses and rebates;
(*e*) provision for unexpired risks;
(*f*) technical provisions for linked liabilities;
(*g*) deposits received from reinsurers; and in the case of the items listed in sub-paragraphs (*a*) to (*f*), the amount to be brought into account is the amount by which the gross amount exceeds the reinsurance amount. In this paragraph expressions also used in Schedule 9A to the Companies Act 1985 have the same meaning as in that Schedule.

4—(1) In accordance with the separate enterprise principle, profits from assets attributable, by virtue of regulation 3, to the permanent establishment of a non-resident insurance company are attributed to that establishment.

(2) "The separate enterprise principle" means the principle in subsection (2) of section 11AA of the Income and Corporation Taxes Act 1988 (read with subsection (3) of that section).

2003/3075
Money Laundering Regulations 2003

Made by the Treasury under the European Communities Act 1972 s 2(2) and the Financial Services and Markets Act 2000 ss 168(4)(*b*), 402(1)(*b*), 417(1) and 428(3)

Made . . . . *28 November 2003*
Laid before Parliament . . . . . *28 November 2003*
Coming into force in accordance with regulation 1(2)

PART I
GENERAL

Citation, commencement etc

1—(1) These Regulations may be cited as the Money Laundering Regulations 2003.

(2) These Regulations come into force—

(*a*) for the purposes of regulation 10 in so far as it relates to a person who acts as a high value dealer, on 1st April 2004;
(*b*) for the purposes of regulation 2(3)(*h*), on 31st October 2004;
(*c*) for the purposes of regulation 2(3)(*i*), on 14th January 2005;
(*d*) for all other purposes, on 1st March 2004.

(3) These Regulations are prescribed for the purposes of sections 168(4)(*b*) and 402(1)(*b*) of the 2000 Act.

(4) The following Regulations are revoked—

(*a*) the Money Laundering Regulations 1993;
(*b*) the Financial Services and Markets Act 2000 (Regulations Relating to Money Laundering) Regulations 2001;
(*c*) the Money Laundering Regulations 2001.

Commentary—*Simon's Direct Tax Service* **A3.1701.**

Interpretation

2—(1) In these Regulations—

"the 2000 Act" means the Financial Services and Markets Act 2000;

"applicant for business" means a person seeking to form a business relationship, or carry out a one-off transaction, with another person acting in the course of relevant business carried on by that other person in the United Kingdom;

"applicant for registration" means an applicant for registration as a money service operator, or as a high value dealer;

"the appropriate judicial authority" means—

(*a*) in England and Wales, a magistrates' court,
(*b*) in Scotland, the sheriff,
(*c*) in Northern Ireland, a court of summary jurisdiction;

"authorised person" has the meaning given by section 31(2) of the 2000 Act;

"the Authority" means the Financial Services Authority;

"the Banking Consolidation Directive" means Directive 2000/12/EC of the European Parliament and of the Council of 20th March 2000 relating to the taking up and pursuit of the business of credit institutions as last amended by Directive 2002/87/EC of the European Parliament and of the Council of 16th December 2002;

"business relationship" means any arrangement the purpose of which is to facilitate the carrying out of transactions on a frequent, habitual or regular basis where the total amount of any payments to be made by any person to any other in the course of the arrangement is not known or capable of being ascertained at the outset;

"cash" means notes, coins or travellers' cheques in any currency;

"the Commissioners" means the Commissioners of Customs and Excise;

"constable" includes a person commissioned by the Commissioners and a person authorised for the purposes of these Regulations by the Director General of the National Criminal Intelligence Service;

"EEA State" means a State which is a contracting party to the agreement on the European Economic Area signed at Oporto on 2nd May 1992 as it has effect for the time being;

"estate agency work" has the meaning given by section 1 of the Estate Agents Act 1979 save for the omission of the words " (including a business in which he is employed)" in subsection (1) and includes a case where, in relation to a disposal or acquisition, the person acts as principal;

"high value dealer" means a person who carries on the activity mentioned in paragraph (2)(*n*);

"the Life Assurance Consolidation Directive" means Directive 2002/83/EC of the European Parliament and of the Council of 5th November 2002 concerning life assurance;

"justice" means a justice of the peace or, in relation to Scotland, a justice within the meaning of section 307 of the Criminal Procedure (Scotland) Act 1995;

"money laundering" means an act which falls within section 340(11) of the Proceeds of Crime Act 2002 or an offence under section 18 of the Terrorism Act 2000;

"the Money Laundering Directive" means Council Directive 91/308/EEC of 10th June 1991 on prevention of the use of the financial system for the purpose of money laundering as amended by Directive 2001/97/EC of the European Parliament and of the Council of 4th December 2001;

"money service business" means any of the activities mentioned in paragraph (2)(*d*) (so far as not excluded by paragraph (3)) when carried on by way of business;

"money service operator" means a person who carries on money service business other than a person who carries on relevant business falling within any of sub-paragraphs (*a*) to (*c*) of paragraph (2);

"nominated officer" has the meaning given by regulation 7;

"officer" (except in regulations 7, 10 and 27) has the meaning given by section 1(1) of the Customs and Excise Management Act 1979;

"officer in overall charge of the investigation" means the person whose name and address are endorsed on the order concerned as being the officer so in charge;

"one-off transaction" means any transaction other than one carried out in the course of an existing business relationship;

"operator" means a money service operator;

"recorded information" includes information recorded in any form and any document of any nature whatsoever;

"registered number" has the meaning given by regulation 9(2);

"relevant business" has the meaning given by paragraph (2);

"the review procedure" means the procedure under regulation 21;

"satisfactory evidence of identity" has the meaning given by paragraphs (5) and (6);

"supervisory authority" has the meaning given by paragraphs (7) and (8);

"tribunal" means a VAT and duties tribunal.

(2) For the purposes of these Regulations, "relevant business" means—

(*a*) the regulated activity of—

(i) accepting deposits;

(ii) effecting or carrying out contracts of long-term insurance when carried on by a person who has received official authorisation pursuant to Article 4 or 51 of the Life Assurance Consolidation Directive;

(iii) dealing in investments as principal or as agent;

(iv) arranging deals in investments;

(v) managing investments;

(vi) safeguarding and administering investments;

(vii) sending dematerialised instructions;

(viii) establishing (and taking other steps in relation to) collective investment schemes;

(ix) advising on investments; or

(*x*) issuing electronic money;

(*b*) the activities of the National Savings Bank;

(*c*) any activity carried on for the purpose of raising money authorised to be raised under the National Loans Act 1968 under the auspices of the Director of Savings;

(*d*) the business of operating a bureau de change, transmitting money (or any representation of monetary value) by any means or cashing cheques which are made payable to customers;

(*e*) any of the activities in points 1 to 12 or 14 of Annex 1 to the Banking Consolidation Directive (which activities are, for convenience, set out in Schedule 1 to these Regulations) when carried on by way of business, ignoring an activity falling within any of sub-paragraphs (*a*) to (*d*);

(*f*) estate agency work;

(*g*) operating a casino by way of business;
(*h*) the activities of a person appointed to act as an insolvency practitioner within the meaning of section 388 of the Insolvency Act 1986 or Article 3 of the Insolvency (Northern Ireland) Order 1989;
(*i*) the provision by way of business of advice about the tax affairs of another person by a body corporate or unincorporate or, in the case of a sole practitioner, by an individual;
(*j*) the provision by way of business of accountancy services by a body corporate or unincorporate or, in the case of a sole practitioner, by an individual;
(*k*) the provision by way of business of audit services by a person who is eligible for appointment as a company auditor under section 25 of the Companies Act 1989 or Article 28 of the Companies (Northern Ireland) Order 1990;
(*l*) the provision by way of business of legal services by a body corporate or unincorporate or, in the case of a sole practitioner, by an individual and which involves participation in a financial or real property transaction (whether by assisting in the planning or execution of any such transaction or otherwise by acting for, or on behalf of, a client in any such transaction);
(*m*) the provision by way of business of services in relation to the formation, operation or management of a company or a trust; or
(*n*) the activity of dealing in goods of any description by way of business (including dealing as an auctioneer) whenever a transaction involves accepting a total cash payment of 15,000 euro or more.

(3) Paragraph (2) does not apply to—
(*a*) the issue of withdrawable share capital within the limit set by section 6 of the Industrial and Provident Societies Act 1965 by a society registered under that Act;
(*b*) the acceptance of deposits from the public within the limit set by section 7(3) of that Act by such a society;
(*c*) the issue of withdrawable share capital within the limit set by section 6 of the Industrial and Provident Societies Act (Northern Ireland) 1969 by a society registered under that Act;
(*d*) the acceptance of deposits from the public within the limit set by section 7(3) of that Act by such a society;
(*e*) activities carried on by the Bank of England;
(*f*) any activity in respect of which an exemption order under section 38 of the 2000 Act has effect if it is carried on by a person who is for the time being specified in the order or falls within a class of persons so specified;
(*g*) any activity (other than one falling within sub-paragraph (*f*)) in respect of which a person was an exempted person for the purposes of section 45 of the Financial Services Act 1986 immediately before its repeal;
(*h*) the regulated activities of arranging deals in investments or advising on investments, in so far as the investment consists of rights under a regulated mortgage contract;
(*i*) the regulated activities of dealing in investments as agent, arranging deals in investments, managing investments or advising on investments, in so far as the investment consists of rights under, or any right to or interest in, a contract of insurance which is not a qualifying contract of insurance; or
(*j*) the Official Solicitor to the Supreme Court when acting as trustee in his official capacity.

(4) The following must be read with section 22 of the 2000 Act, any relevant order under that section and Schedule 2 to that Act—
(*a*) paragraphs (2)(*a*) and (3)(*h*) and (*i*);
(*b*) regulation 25 (authorised persons operating a bureau de change);
(*c*) references in these Regulations to a contract of long-term insurance.

(5) For the purposes of these Regulations, and subject to paragraph (6), "satisfactory evidence of identity" is evidence which is reasonably capable of establishing (and does in fact establish to the satisfaction of the person who obtains it) that the applicant for business is the person he claims to be.

(6) Where the person who obtains the evidence mentioned in paragraph (5) knows or has reasonable grounds for believing that the applicant for business is a money service operator, satisfactory evidence of identity must also include the applicant's registered number (if any).

(7) For the purposes of these Regulations, each of the following is a supervisory authority—
(*a*) the Bank of England;
(*b*) the Authority;
(*c*) the Council of Lloyd's;
(*d*) the Office of Fair Trading;
(*e*) the Occupational Pensions Regulatory Authority;
(*f*) a body which is a designated professional body for the purposes of Part 20 of the 2000 Act;
(*g*) the Gaming Board for Great Britain.

(8) The Secretary of State and the Treasury are each a supervisory authority in the exercise, in relation to a person carrying on relevant business, of their respective functions under the enactments relating to companies or insolvency or under the 2000 Act.

(9) In these Regulations, references to amounts in euro include references to equivalent amounts in another currency.

(10) For the purpose of the application of these Regulations to Scotland, ''real property'' means ''heritable property''.

Commentary—*Simon's Direct Tax Service* **A3.1715.**

PART II

OBLIGATIONS ON PERSONS WHO CARRY ON RELEVANT BUSINESS

Systems and training etc to prevent money laundering

3—(1) Every person must in the course of relevant business carried on by him in the United Kingdom—

(*a*) comply with the requirements of regulations 4 (identification procedures), 6 (record-keeping procedures) and 7 (internal reporting procedures);

(*b*) establish such other procedures of internal control and communication as may be appropriate for the purposes of forestalling and preventing money laundering; and

(*c*) take appropriate measures so that relevant employees are—

(i) made aware of the provisions of these Regulations, Part 7 of the Proceeds of Crime Act 2002 (money laundering) and sections 18 and 21A of the Terrorism Act 2000; and

(ii) given training in how to recognise and deal with transactions which may be related to money laundering.

(2) A person who contravenes this regulation is guilty of an offence and liable—

(*a*) on conviction on indictment, to imprisonment for a term not exceeding 2 years, to a fine or to both;

(*b*) on summary conviction, to a fine not exceeding the statutory maximum.

(3) In deciding whether a person has committed an offence under this regulation, the court must consider whether he followed any relevant guidance which was at the time concerned—

(*a*) issued by a supervisory authority or any other appropriate body;

(*b*) approved by the Treasury; and

(*c*) published in a manner approved by the Treasury as appropriate in their opinion to bring the guidance to the attention of persons likely to be affected by it.

(4) An appropriate body is any body which regulates or is representative of any trade, profession, business or employment carried on by the alleged offender.

(5) In proceedings against any person for an offence under this regulation, it is a defence for that person to show that he took all reasonable steps and exercised all due diligence to avoid committing the offence.

(6) Where a person is convicted of an offence under this regulation, he shall not also be liable to a penalty under regulation 20 (power to impose penalties).

Commentary—*Simon's Direct Tax Service* **A3.1716.**

Identification procedures

4—(1) In this regulation and in regulations 5 to 7—

(*a*) ''A'' means a person who carries on relevant business in the United Kingdom; and

(*b*) ''B'' means an applicant for business.

(2) This regulation applies if—

(*a*) A and B form, or agree to form, a business relationship;

(*b*) in respect of any one-off transaction—

(i) A knows or suspects that the transaction involves money laundering; or

(ii) payment of 15,000 euro or more is to be made by or to B; or

(*c*) in respect of two or more one-off transactions, it appears to A (whether at the outset or subsequently) that the transactions are linked and involve, in total, the payment of 15,000 euro or more by or to B.

(3) A must maintain identification procedures which—

(*a*) require that as soon as is reasonably practicable after contact is first made between A and B—

(i) B must produce satisfactory evidence of his identity; or

(ii) such measures specified in the procedures must be taken in order to produce satisfactory evidence of B's identity;

(*b*) take into account the greater potential for money laundering which arises when B is not physically present when being identified;

(*c*) require that where satisfactory evidence of identity is not obtained, the business relationship or one-off transaction must not proceed any further; and (*d*) require that where B acts or appears to act for another person, reasonable measures must be taken for the purpose of establishing the identity of that person.

Commentary—*Simon's Direct Tax Service* **A3.1717.**

Exceptions

5—(1) Except in circumstances falling within regulation 4(2)(*b*)(i), identification procedures under regulation 4 do not require A to take steps to obtain evidence of any person's identity in any of the following circumstances.

(2) Where A has reasonable grounds for believing that B—

(*a*) carries on in the United Kingdom relevant business falling within any of sub-paragraphs (*a*) to (*e*) of regulation 2(2), is not a money service operator and, if carrying on an activity falling within regulation 2(2)(*a*), is an authorised person with permission under the 2000 Act to carry on that activity;

(*b*) does not carry on relevant business in the United Kingdom but does carry on comparable activities to those falling within sub-paragraph (*a*) and is covered by the Money Laundering Directive; or

(*c*) is regulated by an overseas regulatory authority (within the meaning given by section 82 of the Companies Act 1989) and is based or incorporated in a country (other than an EEA State) whose law contains comparable provisions to those contained in the Money Laundering Directive.

(3) Where—

(*a*) A carries out a one-off transaction with or for a third party pursuant to an introduction effected by a person who has provided a written assurance that evidence of the identity of all third parties introduced by him will have been obtained and recorded under procedures maintained by him;

(*b*) that person identifies the third party; and

(*c*) A has reasonable grounds for believing that that person falls within any of sub-paragraphs (*a*) to (*c*) of paragraph (2).

(4) In relation to a contract of long-term insurance—

(*a*) in connection with a pension scheme taken out by virtue of a person's contract of employment or occupation where the contract of long-term insurance—

(i) contains no surrender clause; and

(ii) may not be used as collateral for a loan; or

(*b*) in respect of which a premium is payable—

(i) in one instalment of an amount not exceeding 2,500 euro; or

(ii) periodically and where the total payable in respect of any calendar year does not exceed 1,000 euro.

(5) Where the proceeds of a one-off transaction are payable to B but are instead directly reinvested on his behalf in another transaction—

(*a*) of which a record is kept; and

(*b*) which can result only in another reinvestment made on B's behalf or in a payment made directly to B.

Commentary—*Simon's Direct Tax Service* **A3.1718.**

Record-keeping procedures

6—(1) A must maintain procedures which require the retention of the records prescribed in paragraph (2) for the period prescribed in paragraph (3).

(2) The records are—

(*a*) where evidence of identity has been obtained under the procedures stipulated by regulation 4 (identification procedures) or pursuant to regulation 8 (casinos)—

(i) a copy of that evidence;

(ii) information as to where a copy of that evidence may be obtained; or

(iii) information enabling the evidence of identity to be re-obtained, but only where it is not reasonably practicable for A to comply with paragraph (i) or (ii); and

(*b*) a record containing details relating to all transactions carried out by A in the course of relevant business.

(3) In relation to the records mentioned in paragraph (2)(*a*), the period is—

(*a*) where A and B have formed a business relationship, at least five years commencing with the date on which the relationship ends; or

(*b*) in the case of a one-off transaction (or a series of such transactions), at least five years commencing with the date of the completion of all activities taking place in the course of that transaction (or, as the case may be, the last of the transactions).

(4) In relation to the records mentioned in paragraph (2)(*b*), the period is at least five years commencing with the date on which all activities taking place in the course of the transaction in question were completed.

(5) Where A is an appointed representative, his principal must ensure that A complies with this regulation in respect of any relevant business carried out by A for which the principal has accepted responsibility pursuant to section 39(1) of the 2000 Act.

(6) Where the principal fails to do so, he is to be treated as having contravened regulation 3 and he, as well as A, is guilty of an offence.

(7) ''Appointed representative'' has the meaning given by section 39(2) of the 2000 Act and ''principal'' has the meaning given by section 39(1) of that Act.

Commentary—*Simon's Direct Tax Service* **A3.1719.**

Internal reporting procedures

7—(1) A must maintain internal reporting procedures which require that—

(*a*) a person in A's organisation is nominated to receive disclosures under this regulation (''the nominated officer'');

(*b*) anyone in A's organisation to whom information or other matter comes in the course of relevant business as a result of which he knows or suspects or has reasonable grounds for knowing or suspecting that a person is engaged in money laundering must, as soon as is practicable after the information or other matter comes to him, disclose it to the nominated officer or a person authorised for the purposes of these Regulations by the Director General of the National Criminal Intelligence Service;

(*c*) where a disclosure is made to the nominated officer, he must consider it in the light of any relevant information which is available to A and determine whether it gives rise to such knowledge or suspicion or such reasonable grounds for knowledge or suspicion; and

(*d*) where the nominated officer does so determine, the information or other matter must be disclosed to a person authorised for the purposes of these Regulations by the Director General of the National Criminal Intelligence Service.

(2) Paragraph (1) does not apply where A is an individual who neither employs nor acts in association with any other person.

(3) Paragraph (1)(*b*) does not apply in relation to a professional legal adviser where the information or other matter comes to him in privileged circumstances.

(4) Information or other matter comes to a professional legal adviser in privileged circumstances if it is communicated or given to him—

(*a*) by (or by a representative of) a client of his in connection with the giving by the adviser of legal advice to the client;

(*b*) by (or by a representative of) a person seeking legal advice from the adviser; or

(*c*) by a person in connection with legal proceedings or contemplated legal proceedings.

(5) But paragraph (4) does not apply to information or other matter which is communicated or given with the intention of furthering a criminal purpose.

(6) ''Professional legal adviser'' includes any person in whose hands information or other matter may come in privileged circumstances.

Commentary—*Simon's Direct Tax Service* **A3.1720.**

Casinos

8—(1) A person who operates a casino by way of business in the United Kingdom must obtain satisfactory evidence of identity of any person before allowing that person to use the casino's gaming facilities.

(2) A person who fails to do so is to be treated as having contravened regulation 3.

Commentary—*Simon's Direct Tax Service* **A3.1717.**

PART III
MONEY SERVICE OPERATORS AND HIGH VALUE DEALERS

REGISTRATION

Registers of money service operators and high value dealers

9—(1) The Commissioners must maintain a register of operators.

(2) The Commissioners must allocate to every registered operator a number, which is to be known as his registered number.

(3) The Commissioners must maintain a register of high value dealers.

(4) The Commissioners may keep the registers in any form they think fit.

Commentary—*Simon's Direct Tax Service* **A3.1721.**

Requirement to be registered

10—(1) A person who acts as an operator or as a high value dealer must first be registered by the Commissioners.

(2) An applicant for registration must—

(*a*) make an application to be registered in such manner as the Commissioners may direct; and

(*b*) furnish the following information to the Commissioners—

(i) his name and (if different) the name of the business;

(ii) his VAT registration number or, if he is not registered for VAT, any other reference number issued to him by the Commissioners;

(iii) the nature of the business;

(iv) the address of each of the premises at which he proposes to carry on the business;

(v) any agency or franchise agreement relating to the business, and the names and addresses of all relevant principals, agents, franchisors or franchisees;

(vi) the name of the nominated officer (if any); and

(vii) whether any person concerned (or proposed to be concerned) in the management, control or operation of the business has been convicted of money laundering or an offence under these Regulations.

(3) At any time after receiving an application for registration and before determining it, the Commissioners may require the applicant for registration to furnish them, within 21 days beginning with the date of being requested to do so, with such further information as they reasonably consider necessary to enable them to determine the application.

(4) Any information to be furnished to the Commissioners under this regulation must be in such form or verified in such manner as they may specify.

(5) In this regulation, ''the business'' means money service business (or, in the case of a high value dealer, the business of dealing in goods) which the applicant for registration carries on or proposes to carry on.

(6) In paragraph (2)(*b*)(vii), the reference to ''money laundering or an offence under these Regulations'' includes an offence referred to in regulation 2(3) of the Money Laundering Regulations 1993 or an offence under regulation 5 of those Regulations.

Commentary—*Simon's Direct Tax Service* **A3.1721.**

Supplementary information

11—(1) If at any time after a person has furnished the Commissioners with any information under regulation 10—

(*a*) there is a change affecting any matter contained in that information; or

(*b*) it becomes apparent to that person that the information contains an inaccuracy;

he must supply the Commissioners with details of the change or, as the case may be, a correction of the inaccuracy (hereafter ''supplementary information'') within 30 days beginning with the date of the occurrence of the change (or the discovery of the inaccuracy) or within such later time as may be agreed with the Commissioners.

(2) The supplementary information must be supplied in such manner as the Commissioners may direct.

(3) The obligation in paragraph (1) applies also to changes affecting any matter contained in any supplementary information supplied pursuant to this regulation.

Commentary—*Simon's Direct Tax Service* **A3.1721.**

Determination of application to register

12—(1) The Commissioners may refuse to register an applicant for registration if, and only if—

(*a*) any requirement of—

(i) paragraphs (2) to (4) of regulation 10 (requirement to be registered);

(ii) regulation 11 (supplementary information); or

(iii) regulation 14 (fees);

has not been complied with; or

(*b*) it appears to them that any information furnished pursuant to regulation 10 or 11 is false or misleading in a material particular.

(2) The Commissioners must, by the end of the period of 45 days beginning with the date on which they receive the application or, where applicable, the date on which they receive any further information required under regulation 10(3), give notice in writing to the applicant for registration of—

(*a*) their decision to register him and, in the case of an applicant for registration as an operator, his registered number; or

(*b*) the following matters—

(i) their decision not to register him;
(ii) the reasons for their decision;
(iii) the review procedure; and
(iv) the right to appeal to a tribunal.

Commentary—*Simon's Direct Tax Service* **A3.1721.**

Cancellation of registration

13—(1) The Commissioners may cancel the registration of an operator or high value dealer if, at any time after registration, it appears to them that they would have had grounds to refuse registration under paragraph (1) of regulation 12 (determination of application to register).

(2) Where the Commissioners decide to cancel the registration of an operator or high value dealer, they must forthwith inform him, in writing, of—

(*a*) their decision and the date from which the cancellation takes effect;
(*b*) the reasons for their decision;
(*c*) the review procedure; and
(*d*) the right to appeal to a tribunal.

Commentary—*Simon's Direct Tax Service* **A3.1721.**

Fees

14—(1) The Commissioners may charge a fee—

(*a*) to an applicant for registration; and
(*b*) to an operator or high value dealer annually on the anniversary of his registration by them under these Regulations.

(2) The Commissioners may charge under paragraph (1) such fees as they consider will enable them to meet any expenses incurred by them in carrying out any of their functions under these Regulations or for any incidental purpose.

(3) Without prejudice to the generality of paragraph (2), a fee may be charged in respect of each of the premises at which the operator, high value dealer or applicant for registration carries on (or proposes to carry on) money service business or relevant business falling within regulation 2(2)(*n*).

Commentary—*Simon's Direct Tax Service* **A3.1721.**

POWERS OF THE COMMISSIONERS

Entry, inspection etc

15—(1) Where an officer has reasonable cause to believe that any premises are used in connection with money service business or relevant business falling within regulation 2(2)(*n*), he may at any reasonable time enter and inspect the premises and inspect any recorded information or currency found on the premises.

(2) An operator or high value dealer must—

(*a*) furnish to an officer, within such time and in such form as the officer may reasonably require, such information relating to the business as the officer may reasonably specify; and
(*b*) upon demand made by the officer, produce or cause to be produced for inspection by the officer at such place, and at such time, as the officer may reasonably require, any recorded information relating to the business.

(3) An officer may take copies of, or make extracts from, any recorded information produced under paragraph (2).

Commentary—*Simon's Direct Tax Service* **A3.1721.**

Order for access to recorded information

16—(1) Where, on an application by an officer, a justice is satisfied that there are reasonable grounds for believing—

(*a*) that an offence under these Regulations is being, has been or is about to be committed by an operator or high value dealer; and
(*b*) that any recorded information which may be required as evidence for the purpose of any proceedings in respect of such an offence is in the possession of any person;

he may make an order under this regulation.

(2) An order under this regulation is an order that the person who appears to the justice to be in possession of the recorded information to which the application relates must—

(*a*) give an officer access to it;
(*b*) permit an officer to take copies of, or make extracts from, any information produced; or
(*c*) permit an officer to remove and take away any of it which he reasonably considers necessary;

not later than the end of the period of 7 days beginning with the date of the order or the end of such longer period as the order may specify.

(3) Where the recorded information consists of information stored in any electronic form, an order under this regulation has effect as an order to produce the information in a form in which it is visible and legible, or from which it can readily be produced in a visible and legible form, and, if the officer wishes to remove it, in a form in which it can be removed.

Commentary—*Simon's Direct Tax Service* **A3.1721.**

Procedure where recorded information is removed

17—(1) An officer who removes any recorded information in the exercise of a power conferred by regulation 16 must, if so requested by a person showing himself—

(*a*) to be the occupier of premises from which the information was removed; or

(*b*) to have had custody or control of the information immediately before the removal;

provide that person with a record of what he has removed.

(2) The officer must provide the record within a reasonable time from the making of the request for it.

(3) Subject to paragraph (7), if a request for permission to be granted access to anything which—

(*a*) has been removed by an officer; and

(*b*) is retained by the Commissioners for the purposes of investigating an offence;

is made to the officer in overall charge of the investigation by a person who had custody or control of the thing immediately before it was so removed or by someone acting on behalf of such a person, that officer must allow the person who made the request access to it under the supervision of an officer.

(4) Subject to paragraph (7), if a request for a photograph or copy of any such thing is made to the officer in overall charge of the investigation by a person who had custody or control of the thing immediately before it was so removed, or by someone acting on behalf of such a person, that officer must—

(*a*) allow the person who made the request access to it under the supervision of an officer for the purpose of photographing it or copying it; or

(*b*) photograph or copy it, or cause it to be photographed or copied.

(5) Where anything is photographed or copied under paragraph (4)(*b*), the photograph or copy must be supplied to the person who made the request.

(6) The photograph or copy must be supplied within a reasonable time from the making of the request.

(7) There is no duty under this regulation to grant access to, or supply a photograph or a copy of, anything if the officer in overall charge of the investigation for the purposes of which it was removed has reasonable grounds for believing that to do so would prejudice—

(*a*) that investigation;

(*b*) the investigation of an offence other than the offence for the purposes of the investigation of which the recorded information was removed; or

(*c*) any criminal proceedings which may be brought as a result of—

(i) the investigation of which he is in charge; or

(ii) any such investigation as is mentioned in sub-paragraph (*b*).

Commentary—*Simon's Direct Tax Service* **A3.1721.**

Failure to comply with requirements under regulation 17

18—(1) Where, on an application made as mentioned in paragraph (2), the appropriate judicial authority is satisfied that a person has failed to comply with a requirement imposed by regulation 17, the authority may order that person to comply with the requirement within such time and in such manner as may be specified in the order.

(2) An application under paragraph (1) may only be made—

(*a*) in the case of a failure to comply with any of the requirements imposed by regulation 17(1) and (2), by the occupier of the premises from which the thing in question was removed or by the person who had custody or control of it immediately before it was so removed;

(*b*) in any other case, by the person who had such custody or control.

(3) In England and Wales and Northern Ireland, an application for an order under this regulation is to be made by complaint; and sections 21 and 42(2) of the Interpretation Act (Northern Ireland) 1954 apply as if any reference in those provisions to any enactment included a reference to this regulation.

Commentary—*Simon's Direct Tax Service* **A3.1721.**

Entry, search etc

19—(1) Where a justice is satisfied on information on oath that there is reasonable ground for suspecting that an offence under these Regulations is being, has been or is about to be committed by an operator or high value dealer on any premises or that evidence of the commission of such an offence is to be found there, he may issue a warrant in writing authorising any officer to enter those premises, if necessary by force, at any time within one month from the time of the issue of the warrant and search them.

(2) A person who enters the premises under the authority of the warrant may—

(*a*) take with him such other persons as appear to him to be necessary;

(*b*) seize and remove any documents or other things whatsoever found on the premises which he has reasonable cause to believe may be required as evidence for the purpose of proceedings in respect of an offence under these Regulations; and

(*c*) search or cause to be searched any person found on the premises whom he has reasonable cause to believe to be in possession of any such documents or other things; but no woman or girl may be searched except by a woman.

(3) The powers conferred by a warrant under this regulation may not be exercised—

(*a*) outside such times of day as may be specified in the warrant; or

(*b*) if the warrant so provides, otherwise than in the presence of a constable in uniform.

(4) An officer seeking to exercise the powers conferred by a warrant under this regulation or, if there is more than one such officer, that one of them who is in charge of the search must provide a copy of the warrant endorsed with his name as follows—

(*a*) if the occupier of the premises concerned is present at the time the search is to begin, the copy must be supplied to the occupier;

(*b*) if at that time the occupier is not present but a person who appears to the officer to be in charge of the premises is present, the copy must be supplied to that person;

(*c*) if neither sub-paragraph (*a*) nor (*b*) applies, the copy must be left in a prominent place on the premises.

Commentary—*Simon's Direct Tax Service* **A3.1721.**

PENALTIES, REVIEW AND APPEALS

Power to impose penalties

20—(1) The Commissioners may impose a penalty of such amount as they consider appropriate, not exceeding £5,000, on a person to whom regulation 10 (requirement to be registered) applies, where that person fails to comply with any requirement in regulation 3 (systems and training etc to prevent money laundering), 10, 11 (supplementary information), 14 (fees) or 15 (entry, inspection etc).

(2) The Commissioners must not impose a penalty on a person where there are reasonable grounds for them to be satisfied that the person took all reasonable steps for securing that the requirement would be complied with.

(3) Where the Commissioners decide to impose a penalty under this regulation, they must forthwith inform the person, in writing, of—

(*a*) their decision to impose the penalty and its amount;

(*b*) their reasons for imposing the penalty;

(*c*) the review procedure; and

(*d*) the right to appeal to a tribunal.

(4) Where a person is liable to a penalty under this regulation, the Commissioners may reduce the penalty to such amount (including nil) as they think proper.

Commentary—*Simon's Direct Tax Service* **A3.1721.**

Review procedure

21—(1) This regulation applies to the following decisions of the Commissioners—

(*a*) a decision under regulation 12 to refuse to register an applicant;

(*b*) a decision under regulation 13 to cancel the registration of an operator or high value dealer;

(*c*) a decision under regulation 20 to impose a penalty.

(2) Any person who is the subject of a decision as mentioned in paragraph (1) may by notice in writing to the Commissioners require them to review that decision.

(3) The Commissioners need not review any decision unless the notice requiring the review is given before the end of the period of 45 days beginning with the date on which written notification of the decision was first given to the person requiring the review.

(4) A person may give a notice under this regulation to require a decision to be reviewed for a second or subsequent time only if—

(*a*) the grounds on which he requires the further review are that the Commissioners did not, on any previous review, have the opportunity to consider certain facts or other matters; and (*b*) he does not, on the further review, require the Commissioners to consider any facts or matters which were considered on a previous review except in so far as they are relevant to any issue to which the facts or matters not previously considered relate.

(5) Where the Commissioners are required under this regulation to review any decision they must either—

(*a*) confirm the decision; or

(*b*) withdraw or vary the decision and take such further steps (if any) in consequence of the withdrawal or variation as they consider appropriate.

(6) Where the Commissioners do not, within 45 days beginning with the date on which the review was required by a person, give notice to that person of their determination of the review, they are to be assumed for the purposes of these Regulations to have confirmed the decision.

Commentary—*Simon's Direct Tax Service* **A3.1721.**

Appeals to a VAT and duties tribunal

22 On an appeal from any decision by the Commissioners on a review under regulation 21, the tribunal have the power to—

(*a*) quash or vary any decision of the Commissioners, including the power to reduce any penalty to such amount (including nil) as they think proper; and

(*b*) substitute their own decision for any decision quashed on appeal.

Commentary—*Simon's Direct Tax Service* **A3.1721.**

MISCELLANEOUS

Prosecution of offences by the Commissioners

23—(1) Proceedings for an offence under these Regulations may be instituted by order of the Commissioners.

(2) Such proceedings may be instituted only against an operator or high value dealer or, where such a person is a body corporate, a partnership or an unincorporated association, against any person who is liable to be proceeded against under regulation 27 (offences by bodies corporate etc).

(3) Any such proceedings which are so instituted must be commenced in the name of an officer.

(4) In the case of the death, removal, discharge or absence of the officer in whose name any such proceedings were commenced, those proceedings may be continued by another officer.

(5) Where the Commissioners investigate, or propose to investigate, any matter with a view to determining—

(*a*) whether there are grounds for believing that an offence under these Regulations has been committed by any person mentioned in paragraph (2); or

(*b*) whether such a person should be prosecuted for such an offence;

that matter is to be treated as an assigned matter within the meaning of the Customs and Excise Management Act 1979.

(6) In exercising their power to institute proceedings for an offence under these Regulations, the Commissioners must comply with any conditions or restrictions imposed in writing by the Treasury.

(7) Conditions or restrictions may be imposed under paragraph (6) in relation to—

(*a*) proceedings generally; or

(*b*) such proceedings, or categories of proceedings, as the Treasury may direct.

Commentary—*Simon's Direct Tax Service* **A3.1721.**

Recovery of fees and penalties through the court

24 Where any fee is charged, or any penalty is imposed, by virtue of these Regulations—

(*a*) if the person from whom it is recoverable resides in England and Wales or Northern Ireland, it is recoverable as a civil debt; and

(*b*) if that person resides in Scotland, it may be enforced in the same manner as an extract registered decree arbitral bearing a warrant for execution issued by the sheriff court of any sheriffdom in Scotland.

Commentary—*Simon's Direct Tax Service* **A3.1721.**

Authorised persons operating a bureau de change

25—(1) No authorised person may, as from 1st April 2004, carry on the business of operating a bureau de change unless he has first informed the Authority that he proposes to do so.

(2) Where an authorised person ceases to carry on that business, he must inform the Authority forthwith.

(3) Any information to be supplied to the Authority under this regulation must be in such form or verified in such manner as the Authority may specify.

(4) Any requirement imposed by this regulation is to be treated as if it were a requirement imposed by or under the 2000 Act.

(5) Any function of the Authority under this regulation is to be treated as if it were a function of the Authority under the 2000 Act.

Commentary—*Simon's Direct Tax Service* **A3.1721.**

PART IV
MISCELLANEOUS

Supervisory authorities etc to report evidence of money laundering

26—(1) Where a supervisory authority, in the light of any information obtained by it, knows or suspects, or has reasonable grounds for knowing or suspecting, that someone has or may have been engaged in money laundering, the supervisory authority must disclose the information to a constable as soon as is reasonably practicable.

(2) Where a supervisory authority passes the information to any other person who has such knowledge or suspicion or such reasonable grounds for knowledge or suspicion as is mentioned in paragraph (1), he may disclose the information to a constable.

(3) Where any person within paragraph (6), in the light of any information obtained by him, knows or suspects or has reasonable grounds for knowing or suspecting that someone has or may have been engaged in money laundering, he must, as soon as is reasonably practicable, disclose that information either to a constable or to the supervisory authority by whom he was appointed or authorised.

(4) Where information has been disclosed to a constable under this regulation, he (or any person obtaining the information from him) may disclose it in connection with the investigation of any criminal offence or for the purpose of any criminal proceedings, but not otherwise.

(5) A disclosure made under this regulation is not to be taken to breach any restriction on the disclosure of information (however imposed).

(6) Persons within this paragraph are—

(*a*) a person or inspector appointed under section 65 or 66 of the Friendly Societies Act 1992;

(*b*) an inspector appointed under section 49 of the Industrial and Provident Societies Act 1965 or section 18 of the Credit Unions Act 1979;

(*c*) an inspector appointed under section 431, 432, 442 or 446 of the Companies Act 1985 or under Article 424, 425, 435 or 439 of the Companies (Northern Ireland) Order 1986;

(*d*) a person or inspector appointed under section 55 or 56 of the Building Societies Act 1986;

(*e*) a person appointed under section 167, 168(3) or (5), 169(1)(*b*) or 284 of the 2000 Act, or under regulations made as a result of section 262(2)(*k*) of that Act, to conduct an investigation; and

(*f*) a person authorised to require the production of documents under section 447 of the Companies Act 1985, Article 440 of the Companies (Northern Ireland) Order 1986 or section 84 of the Companies Act 1989.

Commentary—*Simon's Direct Tax Service* **A3.1722.**

Offences by bodies corporate etc

27—(1) If an offence under regulation 3 committed by a body corporate is shown—

(*a*) to have been committed with the consent or the connivance of an officer; or

(*b*) to be attributable to any neglect on his part;

the officer as well as the body corporate is guilty of an offence and liable to be proceeded against and punished accordingly.

(2) If an offence under regulation 3 committed by a partnership is shown—

(*a*) to have been committed with the consent or the connivance of a partner; or

(*b*) to be attributable to any neglect on his part;

the partner as well as the partnership is guilty of an offence and liable to be proceeded against and punished accordingly.

(3) If an offence under regulation 3 committed by an unincorporated association (other than a partnership) is shown—

(*a*) to have been committed with the consent or the connivance of an officer of the association or a member of its governing body; or

(*b*) to be attributable to any neglect on the part of such an officer or member;

that officer or member as well as the association is guilty of an offence and liable to be proceeded against and punished accordingly.

(4) If the affairs of a body corporate are managed by its members, paragraph (1) applies in relation to the acts and defaults of a member in connection with his functions of management as if he were a director of the body.

(5) In this regulation—

(*a*) "partner" includes a person purporting to act as a partner; and

(*b*) "officer", in relation to a body corporate, means a director, manager, secretary, chief executive, member of the committee of management, or a person purporting to act in such a capacity.

Commentary—*Simon's Direct Tax Service* **A3.1722.**

Prohibitions in relation to certain countries

28—(1) The Treasury may direct any person who carries on relevant business—

(*a*) not to enter a business relationship;

(*b*) not to carry out any one-off transaction; or

(*c*) not to proceed any further with a business relationship or one-off transaction;

in relation to a person who is based or incorporated in a country (other than an EEA State) to which the Financial Action Task Force has decided to apply counter-measures.

(2) A person who fails to comply with a Treasury direction is to be treated as having contravened regulation 3.

Commentary—*Simon's Direct Tax Service* **A3.1722.**

Minor and consequential amendments

29 The provisions mentioned in Schedule 2 to these Regulations have effect subject to the amendments there specified, being minor amendments and amendments consequential on the provisions of these Regulations.

Transitional provisions

30—(1) Nothing in these Regulations obliges any person who carries on relevant business falling within any of sub-paragraphs (*a*) to (*e*) of regulation 2(2) to maintain identification procedures which require evidence to be obtained in respect of any business relationship formed by him before 1st April 1994.

(2) Nothing in these Regulations obliges any person who carries on relevant business falling within any of sub-paragraphs (*f*) to (*n*) of regulation 2(2)—

(*a*) to maintain identification procedures which require evidence to be obtained in respect of any business relationship formed by him before 1st March 2004; or

(*b*) to maintain internal reporting procedures which require any action to be taken in respect of any knowledge, suspicion or reasonable grounds for knowledge or suspicion which came to that person before 1st March 2004.

Commentary—*Simon's Direct Tax Service* **A3.1717, 1720.**

SCHEDULES

SCHEDULE 1

ACTIVITIES LISTED IN ANNEX 1 TO THE BANKING CONSOLIDATION DIRECTIVE

Commentary—*Simon's Direct Tax Service* **A3.1715, 1720.**

Regulation 2(2)(*e*)

1 Acceptance of deposits and other repayable funds.

2 Lending.

3 Financial leasing.

4 Money transmission services.

5 Issuing and administering means of payment (eg credit cards, travellers' cheques and bankers' drafts).

6 Guarantees and commitments.

7 Trading for own account or for account of customers in—

(*a*) money market instruments (cheques, bills, certificates of deposit, etc);

(*b*) foreign exchange;

(*c*) financial futures and options;

(*d*) exchange and interest-rate instruments;

(*e*) transferable securities.

8 Participation in securities issues and the provision of services related to such issues.

9 Advice to undertakings on capital structure, industrial strategy and related questions and advice as well as services relating to mergers and the purchase of undertakings.

10 Money broking.

11 Portfolio management and advice.

12 Safekeeping and administration of securities.

13 Credit reference services.

14 Safe custody services.

SCHEDULE 2

MINOR AND CONSEQUENTIAL AMENDMENTS

Regulation 29

PART I

PRIMARY LEGISLATION

Value Added Tax Act 1994 (c 23)

1—(*amends* VATA 1994 s 83).

Northern Ireland Act 1998 (c 47)

2—(*amends* the Northern Ireland Act 1998 Sch 3 para 25).

PART II

SECONDARY LEGISLATION

(amendments hereby made are beyond the scope of this Publication).

2003/3143

Income and Corporation Taxes (Electronic Certificates of Deduction of Tax and Tax Credit) Regulations 2003

Made by the Commissioners of Inland Revenue under FA 1999 s 132

Made	*4 December 2003*
Laid before the House of Commons	*5 December 2003*
Coming into force	*1 January 2004*

Citation, commencement and interpretation

1—(1) These Regulations may be cited as the Income and Corporation Taxes (Electronic Certificates of Deduction of Tax and Tax Credit) Regulations 2003 and shall come into force on 1st January 2004.

(2) In these Regulations references to the delivery of a document include that document being made available to a person in circumstances where—

(*a*) the sender and that person have agreed to his having access to the document on a website,

(*b*) the document is a document to which the agreement relates; and

(*c*) the person is notified in a manner for the time being agreed for the purpose between him and the sender of—

(i) the placing of the document on the website;

(ii) the address of the website; and

(iii) the place on the website at which, and the manner in which, the document may be accessed. Here ''document'' means anything authorised to be delivered by means of electronic communications under these Regulations.

(3) In these Regulations—

''electronic communications'' has the meaning given by section 132(10) of the Finance Act 1999;

''the sender'' means—

(*a*) in relation to a statement to which regulation 2 applies, the company making the qualifying distribution, or a person acting on its behalf;

(*b*) in relation to a statement to which regulation 3 applies, the person under the duty to furnish the certificate, or another person acting on his behalf; and

(*c*) in relation to statement, notice, certificate or voucher to which regulation 4 applies, the person required or authorised, under the relevant provision mentioned in paragraph (2) of that regulation, to deliver that statement, notice, certificate or voucher, or another person acting on his behalf; and ''the Taxes Act'' means the Income and Corporation Taxes Act 1988.

Delivering information electronically about distributions, dividends, interest payments and associated tax credits

2—(1) A statement under section 234(1) or 234A(2) of the Taxes Act (information relating to distributions, dividends, interest payments and associated tax credits) by a company making a qualifying distribution may be delivered by means of electronic communications if the following conditions are satisfied.

(2) The first condition is that the sender has indicated to the proposed recipient that it intends to use electronic communications for the purposes of delivering statements under those sections.

(3) The second condition is that the proposed recipient has consented to information being delivered by the sender by means of electronic communications, and that consent has not been withdrawn.

(4) The third condition is that the statement is delivered in an electronic format—

(*a*) in which the statement may be stored;

(*b*) which permits a paper copy of the information contained in the statement to be printed; and

(*c*) which is designed to prevent alteration of the contents.

Delivering information electronically about deduction of tax

3—(1) A statement under section 352 of the Taxes Act (certificates of deduction of tax) may be delivered by means of electronic communications if the following conditions are satisfied.

(2) The first condition is that the sender has indicated to the proposed recipient that he intends to use electronic communications to furnish statements under section 352.

(3) The second condition is that the proposed recipient has consented to information being delivered by the sender by means of electronic communications, and that consent has not been withdrawn.

(4) The third condition is that the statement is delivered in an electronic format—

(*a*) in which the statement may be stored;

(*b*) which permits a paper copy of the information contained in the statement to be printed; and

(*c*) which is designed to prevent alteration of the contents.

Sending information electronically about manufactured dividends

4—(1) A statement, notice, certificate or voucher required or authorised to be delivered under the provisions listed in paragraph (2) may be delivered by means of electronic communications if the conditions specified in paragraphs (3) to (5) are satisfied.

(2) The provisions referred to in paragraph (1) are—

(*a*) paragraphs 2(6) and 3(8) of Schedule 23A to the Taxes Act (information about manufactured dividends); and

(*b*) regulations 4(4)(*c*), 5(2)(*b*)(iii), 7(2)(*d*), 10(3)(*b*) and (4)(*b*) and 15(1) and (5) of the Income Tax (Manufactured Overseas Dividends) Regulations 1993.

(3) The first condition is that the sender has indicated to the proposed recipient that he intends to use electronic communications to deliver documents of that type.

(4) The second condition is that the proposed recipient has consented to information being delivered by the sender by means of electronic communications, and that consent has not subsequently been withdrawn.

(5) The third condition is that the document in question is delivered in an electronic format—

(*a*) in which it may be stored;

(*b*) which permits a paper copy of the information contained in it to be printed; and

(*c*) which is designed to prevent alteration of its contents.

Amendments of the Income Tax (Manufactured Overseas Dividends) Regulations 1993

5 (*amends the Income Tax (Manufactured Overseas Dividends) Regulations, SI 1993/1957*).

2003/3297

Reporting of Savings Income Information Regulations 2003

Made by the Treasury under FA 2003 s 199

Made . . . . *16 December 2003*
Laid before the House of Commons . . *17 December 2003*
Coming into force in accordance with regulation 1(2)

PART 1
INTRODUCTORY PROVISIONS

Citation and commencement

1—(1) These Regulations may be cited as the Reporting of Savings Income Information Regulations 2003.

(2) These Regulations shall come into force on such date, being not earlier than 1st January 2005, as is determined by the Treasury and specified by notices in the London, Edinburgh and Belfast Gazettes.

Interpretation

2—(1) In these Regulations—

"the Savings Directive" means Council Directive 2003/48/EC of 3rd June 2003 on taxation of savings income in the form of interest payments and a reference without more to an Article is a reference to that Article of Council Directive 2003/48/EC;

"the Securities Directive" means Directive 2001/34/EC of 28th May 2001 on the admission of securities to official stock exchange listing and on information to be published on those securities as amended;

"the UCITS Directive" means Council Directive 85/611/EEC of 20th December 1985 on the co-ordination of laws, regulations and administrative provisions relating to undertakings for collective investment in transferable securities as amended.

(2) In these Regulations—

"agent" means paying agent or receiving agent as appropriate;

"economic operator" is a person established in another member State who makes savings income payments in the course of his business or profession;

"money debt" is a debt arising from a transaction for the lending of money and which falls to be, or may be, settled—

(*a*) by the payment of money; or

(*b*) by the transfer of a right to settlement under a debt which is itself a money debt,

subject to the qualification in regulation 17;

"paying agent" has the meaning given in regulation 3;

"a prescribed territory" is another member State;

"receiving agent" has the meaning given in regulation 6;

"relevant payee" has the meaning given in regulation 7;

"resident" and "residence" shall be construed in accordance with regulation 9;

"residual entity" has the meaning given in regulation 4;

"savings income" has the meaning given in regulation 8;

"third country" means a territory other than a member State;

"UCITS" means an undertaking for collective investment in transferable securities within the UCITS Directive.

(3) For the purposes of these Regulations a person makes savings income payments to another person if the person—

(*a*) makes payments of savings income to another person, or

(*b*) secures the payment of savings income for the other person.

Meaning of paying agent

3 A paying agent is a person who—

(*a*) is established in the United Kingdom;

(*b*) makes savings income payments in the course of his business or profession; and

(*c*) makes those payments—

(i) for the immediate benefit of a relevant payee; or

(ii) to a residual entity established in a prescribed territory.

Here a "person" includes any officer in any public office or in any government department and any savings income payments made by such a person will be treated as if the payment were made in the course of that person's business or profession.

Meaning of residual entity

4—(1) Subject to paragraph (2) a residual entity is an entity established in a member State other than an entity—

(*a*) which is a legal person;

(*b*) the profits of which are taxed under the general arrangements for business taxation; or

(*c*) which is a UCITS authorised in accordance with the UCITS Directive.

(2) In paragraph (1)(*a*) a legal person excludes—

(*a*) in Finland, avoin yhtiö (Ay) and kommandiittiyhtiö (Ky)/ öppet bolag and kommanditbolag; and

(*b*) in Sweden, handelsbolag (HB) and kommanditbolag (KB).

(3) A paying agent shall regard an entity as a residual entity unless the paying agent has reason to believe, on the basis of official evidence produced by the entity to the paying agent, that sub-paragraph (*a*), (*b*) or (*c*) of paragraph (1) applies.

An entity which presents to the paying agent or economic operator a certificate issued by the member State in which that entity is established to the effect that it is to be treated as if it were a UCITS authorised in accordance with the UCITS Directive shall be treated as such for the purposes of this regulation.

Election by an entity to be treated as a UCITS

5—(1) An entity established in the United Kingdom may obtain a certificate to the effect that it is to be treated as a UCITS authorised in accordance with the UCITS Directive for the purposes of the Savings Directive in accordance with this regulation.

(2) A notice requesting the issue of a certificate shall be given to the Inland Revenue by or on behalf of the entity.

(3) The notice shall include the following information—

(*a*) the name and address of the entity;

(*b*) where the notice is given on behalf of the entity, the name, address and position of the person giving notice;

(*c*) a statement that—

(i) the entity is established in the United Kingdom;

(ii) the entity is not a legal person;

(iii) the entity's profits are not taxed under the general arrangements for business taxation;

(iv) the entity is not a UCITS authorised in accordance with the UCITS Directive; and

(v) the entity elects to be treated as if it were a UCITS authorised in accordance with the UCITS Directive for the purposes of the Savings Directive; and

(*d*) a signed and dated declaration by the person giving notice to the effect that it is to the best of his knowledge correct and complete.

(4) The Inland Revenue will issue a certificate to that entity confirming that it is to be treated as if it were a UCITS authorised in accordance with the UCITS Directive for the purposes of the Savings Directive and that certificate shall have effect from the date specified in that certificate.

Meaning of receiving agent

6 A receiving agent is an entity—

(*a*) which is a residual entity;

(*b*) which is established in the United Kingdom; and

(*c*) to which a savings income payment is made for the benefit of a relevant payee by a person established in a member State in the course of his business or profession.

Meaning of relevant payee

7—(1) The agent shall regard a person as a relevant payee if he is an individual—

(*a*) resident in a prescribed territory; and

(*b*) who has received a savings income payment or for whom a savings income payment has been secured,

unless he provides evidence to the agent that the payment is not received or secured for his own benefit because of one of the reasons listed in paragraph (2).

(2) The reasons referred to in paragraph (1) are that the individual—

(*a*) is acting as paying agent or an economic operator;

(*b*) acts on behalf of a residual entity;

(*c*) acts on behalf of an entity—

(i) which is a legal person;

(ii) the profits of which are taxed under the general arrangements for business taxation;

(iii) which is a UCITS authorised in accordance with the UCITS Directive; or

(iv) which is treated as being a UCITS in accordance with the UCITS Directive for the purposes of the Savings Directive by virtue of Article 4(3); or

(*d*) acts on behalf of another individual for whose benefit the payment is received or secured.

(3) An individual who provides evidence that he is acting on behalf of a residual entity must in addition provide the name and address of that residual entity to the agent.

(4) An individual who provides evidence that he acts on behalf of another individual must in addition provide the agent with the name and address, and where appropriate the tax identification number or date and place of birth, of that individual. The individual providing the evidence must obtain and verify this information in accordance with regulation 9.

(5) If the agent has information which suggests that the individual who receives a savings income payment or for whom a savings income payment is secured may not be the relevant payee for the reason referred to in paragraph (2)(*d*), then paragraph (6) applies.

(6) The agent must take reasonable steps to establish who is the relevant payee and if the agent is unable to identify the relevant payee, he shall treat the individual who receives a savings income payment or for whom a savings income payment is secured as the relevant payee.

Meaning of savings income

8—(1) Subject to paragraphs (3) to (6) and (8) savings income is—

(*a*) interest;

(*b*) interest accrued or capitalised at the sale, refund or redemption of a money debt;

(*c*) income distributed by a collective investment fund which is derived directly or indirectly, via other collective investment funds or residual entities, from interest;

(*d*) income realised upon the sale, refund or redemption of shares or units in a collective investment fund if that fund invests directly or indirectly, via other collective investment funds or residual entities, more than 40% of its assets in money debts.

(2) In paragraph (1) "interest"—

(*a*) includes—

(i) prizes attaching to money debts (including premium bonds);

(ii) premiums and discounts derived from money debts;

(iii) any dividend derived from shares (including permanent interest bearing shares) in a building society; and

(iv) any share interest paid by a registered industrial and provident society; and

(*b*) excludes—

(i) any interest which is not related to a money debt; and

(ii) penalty charges for late payment.

(3) In respect of savings income described in paragraph (1)(*b*), where an agent has no information concerning the amount of interest which is accrued or capitalised at the sale, refund or redemption of a money debt the total amount of the proceeds of the sale, redemption or refund is savings income.

(4) In respect of savings income described in paragraphs (1)(*c*), where an agent has no information concerning the proportion of income which derives from interest the total amount of the income is savings income.

(5) In respect of savings income described in paragraphs (1)(*c*) and (*d*), subject to paragraph (9)—

(*a*) where a collective investment fund established in the United Kingdom has invested 15% or less of its assets directly or indirectly, via other collective investment funds or residual entities, in money debts there is no savings income;

(*b*) where a collective investment fund—

(i) is established in another member State which has derogated from paragraphs (1)(*c*) and (*d*) of Article 6 in accordance with Article 6(6); and

(ii) the collective investment fund has invested 15% or less of its assets in money debts in accordance with the law of that member State in the application of that derogation,

there is no savings income.

(6) In respect of savings income described in paragraph (1)(*d*)—

(*a*) where an agent has no information concerning the percentage of assets invested in money debts or in shares or units in collective investment funds, that percentage shall be considered to be more than 40%;

(*b*) where the agent cannot determine the amount of income realised by the relevant payee, the income shall be deemed to correspond to the proceeds of the sale, refund or redemption of the shares or units.

(7) From 1st January 2011 paragraphs (1)(*d*) and (6)(*a*) shall have the effect with the substitution of "25%" for "40%".

(8) Subject to paragraph (9)—

(*a*) where a residual entity established in the United Kingdom invests 15% or less of its assets directly or indirectly, via collective investment funds or other residual entities, in money debts there is no savings income;

(*b*) where a residual entity—

(i) is established in another member State which has derogated from paragraphs (1)(*c*) and (*d*) of Article 6 in accordance with Article 6(6); and

(ii) the residual entity has invested 15% or less of its assets in money debts in accordance with the law of that member State in the application of that derogation,

there is no savings income.

(9) In the application of paragraphs (5) and (8), where the agent cannot ascertain whether or not the collective investment fund or residual entity, as appropriate, has invested 15% or less of its assets in money debts in accordance with those provisions, there is savings income.

(10) The percentages referred to in this regulation shall be determined by reference to the investment policy as laid down in the fund rules or instruments of incorporation of the collective investment

fund or residual entity concerned and, failing which, by reference to the actual composition of the assets of the collective investment fund or residual entity.

(11) In this regulation a collective investment fund is—

(*a*) a UCITS authorised in accordance with the UCITS Directive;

(*b*) an entity which is treated as being a UCITS authorised in accordance with the UCITS Directive for the purposes of the Savings Directive by virtue of Article 4(3); or

(*c*) an undertaking for collective investment established outside the Community.

This is subject to the following qualification.

If a collective investment fund provides arrangements for separate pooling of the contributions of the participants and the profits or income out of which payments are to be made to them and under which participants are entitled to exchange rights in one pool for rights in another, each separate pool shall be treated as a separate collective investment fund.

(12) In this regulation—

''building society'' means a building society within the meaning of the Building Societies Act 1986;

''permanent interest bearing shares'' has the meaning given in section 117(11) of the Taxation of Chargeable Gains Act 1992;

''registered industrial and provident society'' has the meaning given in section 486(12) of the Income and Corporation Taxes Act 1988 as extended by section 486(9) of that Act; and

''share interest'' has the meaning given in section 486(12) of the Income and Corporation Taxes Act 1988.

PART 2
INFORMATION TO BE OBTAINED, VERIFIED AND REPORTED

Identity and residence of relevant payees

9—(1) Where—

(*a*) a paying agent makes a savings income payment to an individual whom he believes to be a relevant payee, or

(*b*) a receiving agent receives or secures a savings income payment for an individual whom he believes to be a relevant payee,

the agent must establish the identity and country of residence of that individual in accordance with this regulation.

(2) Subject to the conditions set out in this regulation, for the purposes of this regulation the country of residence means the country where the individual has his permanent address.

(3) Where contractual relations between the agent and the individual are entered into before 1st January 2004 the agent must verify the name, address and country of residence of the individual by using the information at its disposal, including information obtained pursuant to the Money Laundering Regulations 1993 and the Money Laundering Regulations 2001.

(4) Where contractual relations between the agent and the individual are entered into, or transactions are carried out in the absence of contractual relations, on or after 1st January 2004, the agent shall obtain and verify—

(*a*) the name, address and the tax identification number allocated by the member State of residence for tax purposes or, if it is not available, the date and place of birth of the individual in accordance with paragraphs (5) to (7); and

(*b*) the country of residence of the individual in accordance with paragraphs (8) and (9).

(5) The information in paragraph (4)(*a*) shall be verified by the presentation by the individual of his passport or official identity card to the agent.

(6) If the address does not appear on that passport or official identity card, it shall be verified by the presentation by the individual of any other documentary proof of identity to the agent.

(7) If the tax identification number is not mentioned on the passport, official identity card or any other documentary proof of identity presented by the individual, the agent shall instead verify the individual's date and place of birth on the basis of his passport or official identity card.

(8) Subject to paragraph (9), the country of residence of the individual shall be determined on the basis of his address verified in accordance with paragraphs (5) and (6).

(9) Where the individual declares his country of residence to be in a third country—

(*a*) if he presents a passport or official identity card issued by a member State, the agent shall establish the country of residence by means of a certificate of residence for tax purposes issued by the competent authority of the third country which the individual claims to be his country of residence;

(*b*) if the individual fails to present such a certificate, the member State that issued the passport or other official identity document shall be considered to be the country of residence.

(10) The individual may present a certified copy of any of the documents referred to in this regulation.

Here ''certified copy'' means a copy certified or otherwise authenticated in such manner as would make it admissible in evidence in proceedings before a court.

(11) In this regulation—

''competent authority'' means the competent authority for the purposes of bilateral or multilateral tax conventions or, failing that, such other authority as is competent to issue certificates of residence for tax purposes;

''other documentary proof of identity'' includes certificates of residence for tax purposes.

Information to be reported to the Inland Revenue by paying agents making payments to relevant payees

10—(1) When a paying agent makes a savings income payment for the immediate benefit of a relevant payee the information prescribed by paragraph (2) must be reported by the paying agent to the Inland Revenue in accordance with regulations 14 and 15.

(2) The information prescribed is—

(*a*) the name and address of the paying agent;

(*b*) the name, address and country of residence of the relevant payee established in accordance with regulation 9;

(*c*) where contractual relations between the relevant payee and the paying agent were entered into, or transactions are carried out in the absence of contractual relations, on or after 1st January 2004, the tax identification number, or if it is not available, the relevant payee's date and place of birth, established in accordance with regulation 9;

(*d*) the account number of the relevant payee or, where there is none, identification of the money debt or other instrument giving rise to the savings income;

(*e*) the amount and category of the savings income payments made to the relevant payee in accordance with regulation 13 and the currency in which they were paid.

Information to be reported to the Inland Revenue by paying agents making payments to residual entities

11—(1) When a paying agent makes a savings income payment to a residual entity established in a prescribed territory the information prescribed by paragraph (2) must be reported by the paying agent to the Inland Revenue in accordance with regulations 14 and 15.

(2) The information prescribed is—

(*a*) the name and address of the paying agent;

(*b*) the name and address of the residual entity (including the territory in which it is established); and

(*c*) the total amount and category of the savings income payments made to the residual entity in accordance with regulation 13 and the currency in which they were paid.

Information to be reported to the Inland Revenue by receiving agents

12—(1) When a receiving agent receives or secures savings income the information prescribed by paragraph (2), in respect of each relevant payee the savings income is attributable to, must be reported by the receiving agent to the Inland Revenue in accordance with regulations 14 and 15.

(2) The information prescribed is—

(*a*) a statement that the savings income has been received or secured by the receiving agent in his capacity as such;

(*b*) the name and address of the receiving agent;

(*c*) the name, address and country of residence of the relevant payee established in accordance with regulation 9;

(*d*) where contractual relations between the relevant payee and the receiving agent were entered into, or transactions are carried out in the absence of contractual relations, on or after 1st January 2004, the tax identification number, or if it is not available, the relevant payee's date and place of birth, established in accordance with regulation 9;

(*e*) the account number of the relevant payee or, where there is none, identification of the money debt or other instrument giving rise to the savings income;

(*f*) the amount and category of the savings income received or secured by the receiving agent in accordance with regulation 13 and the currency in which it was paid.

The amount of savings income to be reported to the Inland Revenue

13—(1) The information concerning the savings income prescribed by paragraph (2) must be reported by the agent to the Inland Revenue.

(2) The agent shall identify under which of the following three categories he is reporting the savings income and where the savings income is of the type prescribed by—

(*a*) regulation 8(1)(*a*), report the amount of savings income;

(*b*) sub-paragraph (*b*) or (*d*) of regulation 8(1), report either the amount of savings income or the full amount of the proceeds from the sale, redemption or refund;
(*c*) regulation 8(1)(*c*), report either the amount of savings income or the full amount of the distribution.

(3) Where the agent has reported savings income under sub-paragraph (*a*) or (*c*) of paragraph (2) no further report of the same savings income is required under sub-paragraph (*b*) of that paragraph.

PART 3

REPORTING THE INFORMATION

Paying and receiving agents to notify the Inland Revenue of reportable payments

14—(1) An agent who must report information to the Inland Revenue in accordance with these Regulations must notify the Inland Revenue in writing that he needs to make a report within 14 days of the end of the tax year in which—

(*a*) in the case of a paying agent, the savings income payment was made, or
(*b*) in the case of a receiving agent, the savings income was secured or received,

unless the agent has already received a notice under regulation 15 from the Inland Revenue in respect of that tax year.

(2) An agent who fails to comply with paragraph (1) is liable to a penalty not exceeding £3000 determined in accordance with section 100 of the Taxes Management Act 1970.

(3) Sections 100A, 100B, 102, 103(4) and 118(2) of the Taxes Management Act 1970 apply to a penalty determined in accordance with paragraph (2).

Reports by paying and receiving agents to the Inland Revenue

15—(1) The Inland Revenue must send a notice to—

(*a*) an agent who has notified the Inland Revenue in accordance with regulation 14(1);
(*b*) any person the Inland Revenue considers should have notified it in accordance with regulation 14(1) but has not done so; and
(*c*) any person who has notified the Inland Revenue in accordance with regulation 14(1) in respect of a previous tax year, unless—
(i) the person has informed the Inland Revenue; or
(ii) an officer of the Inland Revenue has reasonable grounds to believe,

that he is no longer an agent.

(2) The notice must specify—

(*a*) the information prescribed by these Regulations which must be reported;
(*b*) the tax year in respect of which the report must be made and that the report must be in respect of all savings income payments for that tax year;
(*c*) the form in which the report must be made;
(*d*) the address to which the report must be delivered; and
(*e*) the date by which the report must be delivered which shall be a date no earlier than 30 days after the date of the notice.

(3) For the report for the tax year in which the commencement date falls, the reference to the tax year in paragraph (2)(*b*) means the period beginning on the commencement date and ending at the end of the tax year in which the commencement date falls.

Here ''commencement date'' is the date specified in the notices under regulation 1(2).

(4) The notice may be combined with a notice issued under section 17 or 18, or under both of those sections, of the Taxes Management Act 1970.

(5) The agent or person, as appropriate, must make and deliver the report in accordance with the requirements specified in the notice.

(6) Paragraph (5) applies regardless of whether any savings income is reportable in accordance with these Regulations.

PART 4

AUDIT

Audit and related issues

16—(1) An officer of the Inland Revenue may by notice require an agent, or a person who appears to the Revenue to be an agent, to furnish them within such time, not being less than 14 days, as may be provided by the notice, such information (including copies of any relevant books, documents or other records) as they may reasonably require for the purposes of determining whether information contained in a report under these Regulations by that agent or person, as appropriate, was correct and complete.

(2) An agent or person, as appropriate, required to make and deliver a report under these Regulations shall, whenever required to do so within the period specified in paragraph (4)(*c*), make available for inspection by an officer of the Inland Revenue, at such time as that officer may reasonably require, all such copies of books, documents or other records in his possession or under his control as may be required by an officer of the Inland Revenue under paragraph (1).

(3) An agent or person, as appropriate, required to make and deliver a report under these Regulations shall retain, for the period specified in paragraph (4), all such books, documents and other records copies of which he may be required to make available for inspection under paragraph (2). These documents include copies of the documents presented by relevant payees in accordance with regulation 9.

(4) The period specified is—

(*a*) in relation to information concerning the identity and country of residence of a relevant payee the period of two years beginning immediately after the end of the tax year in which transactions between the relevant payee and paying agent cease;

(*b*) in relation to the official evidence referred to in regulation 4(3) the period of two years beginning immediately after the end of the tax year in which transactions between the residual entity and paying agent cease; and

(*c*) in relation to information concerning savings income the period of two years beginning immediately after the end of the tax year to which the notice referred to in regulation 15(1) relates.

(5) Paragraphs (3) and (4) are without prejudice to the following provisions—

(i) regulations 11(7) and 15(2) of the Income Tax (Building Societies) (Dividends and Interest) Regulations 1990;

(ii) regulation 12(2) of the Income Tax (Deposit-takers) (Interest Payments) Regulations 1990;

(iii) regulation 8 of the Income Tax (Deposit-takers) (Non-residents) Regulations 1992;

(iv) regulation 9 of the Income Tax (Authorised Unit Trusts) (Interest Distributions) Regulations 2003 including that regulation as modified by regulation 28(8) of the Open-ended Investment Companies (Tax) Regulations 1997.

(6) Subject to paragraph (7), information obtained by the Inland Revenue under this Regulation—

(*a*) shall not be used for the purpose of ascertaining the tax liability (if any) of any person other than—

(i) a person beneficially entitled to a payment to whom the information obtained relates, and

(ii) the person by whom the payment was made or received; and

(*b*) shall otherwise be used only for the purposes of—

(i) these Regulations, unless the notice issued under regulation 15(1) is combined with a notice under section 17 or 18, or both of those sections, of the Taxes Management Act 1970, in which case only for the purposes of these Regulations and with whichever of those sections the notice was combined,

(ii) the provisions of Chapter 4 of Part 12 of the Income and Corporation Taxes Act 1988 relating to the deduction of tax from payments by building societies and deposit-takers,

(iii) the Income Tax (Building Societies) (Dividends and Interest) Regulations 1990,

(iv) the Income Tax (Deposit-takers) (Interest Payments) Regulations 1990, and

(v) the Income Tax (Authorised Unit Trusts) (Interest Distributions) Regulations 2003 including these Regulations as modified by the Open-ended Investment Companies (Tax) Regulations 1997.

(7) Paragraph (6) shall not be construed as preventing any disclosure of information under section 182(5) of the Finance Act 1989.

PART 5

TRANSITIONAL PROVISIONS

Transitional provisions—negotiable debt securities

17—(1) Until 31st December 2010 negotiable debt securities to which paragraph (2) applies shall not be considered to be money debts.

(2) This paragraph applies to negotiable debt securities—

(*a*) which were first issued before 1st March 2001; or

(*b*) for which the original prospectus was approved before that date by—

(i) the competent authority within the meaning of the Securities Directive; or

(ii) the responsible authorities in third countries,

provided that no further issues of such negotiable debt securities are made on or after 1st March 2002.

(3) Where a further issue is made on or after 1st March 2002 of negotiable debt securities described in paragraphs (2)(*a*) and (*b*) issued by a Government or a related entity acting as a public authority or whose role is recognised by an international treaty, as defined in the Schedule, the entire issue of

such security, consisting of the original issue and any further issue, shall be considered a money debt.

(4) If a further issue is made on or after 1st March 2002 of a negotiable debt security described in paragraphs (2)(*a*) and (*b*) issued by a person not referred to in paragraph (3), such further issue shall be considered a money debt.

(5) Where an agent cannot ascertain whether paragraphs (2) to (4) apply the entire issue of the negotiable debt security shall be considered a money debt.

(6) A negotiable debt security is a security that can be transferred from one creditor to another without the approval of the debtor.

SCHEDULE

NEGOTIABLE DEBT SECURITIES: ENTITIES REFERRED TO IN REGULATION 17(3)

Regulation 17(3)

For the purposes of regulation 17(3), an entity is "a related entity acting as a public authority or whose role is recognised by an international treaty'' if it is listed in Table 1 or Table 2 below or it is situate in a third country and meets the following criteria—

(*a*) the entity is clearly considered to be a public entity according to the national criteria;
(*b*) such public entity is a non-market producer which administers and finances a group of activities, principally providing non-market goods and services, intended for the benefit of the community and which are effectively controlled by general government;
(*c*) such public entity is a large and regular issuer of debt; and
(*d*) the State concerned is able to guarantee that such public entity will not exercise early redemption in the event of gross-up clauses.

TABLE 1

Entities within the European Union

Member State	*Entity*
Belgium	Vlaams Gewest (Flemish Region) Région wallonne (Walloon Region) Région bruxelloise/Brussels Gewest (Brussels Region) Communauté française (French Community) Vlaamse Gemeenschap (Flemish Community) Deutschsprachige Gemeinschaft (German-speaking Community)
France	La Caisse d'amortissement de la dette sociale (CADES) (Social Debt Redemption Fund) L'Agence française de développement (AFD) (French Development Agency) Réseau Ferré de France (RFF) (French Rail Network) Caisse Nationale des Autoroutes (CNA) (National Motorways Fund) Assistance publique Hôpitaux de Paris (APHP) (Paris Hospitals Public Assistance) Charbonnages de France (CDF) (French Coal Board) Entreprise minière et chimique (EMC) (Mining and Chemicals Company)
Greece	Οργαυισμος Τηλεπικοινωνιων Ελλαδος (National Telecommunications Organisation) Οργαυισμος Σιδηροδρομων Ελλαδος (National Railways Organisation) Δημοσια Επιχειρηση Ηλεκτρισμου (Public Electricity Company)
Italy	Regions Provinces Municipalities Cassa Depositi e Prestiti (Deposits and Loans Fund)

Member State	*Entity*
Portugal	Região Autónoma de Madeira (Autonomous Region of Madeira) Região Autónoma dos Açores (Autonomous Region of Azores) Municipalities
Spain	Xunta de Galicia (Regional Executive of Galacia) Junta de Andalucía (Regional Executive of Andalusia) Junta de Extremadura (Regional Executive of Extremadura) Junta de Castilla-La Mancha (Regional Executive of Castilla-La Mancha) Junta de Castilla-León (Regional Executive of Castilla-León) Gobierno Foral de Navarra (Regional Government of Navarre) Govern de les Illes Balears (Government of the Balearic Islands) Generalitat de Catalunya (Autonomous Government of Catalonia) Generalitat de Valencia (Autonomous Government of Valencia) Diputación General de Aragón (Regional Council of Aragon) Gobierno de las Islas Canarias (Government of the Canary Islands) Gobierno de Murcia (Government of Murcia) Gobierno de Madrid (Government of Madrid) Gobierno de la Comunidad Autónoma del País Vasco/ Euzkadi (Government of the Autonomous Community of the Basque Country) Diputación Foral de Guipúzcoa (Regional Council of Guipúzcoa) Diputación Foral de Vizcaya/Bizkaia (Regional Council of Vizcaya) Diputación Foral de Alava (Regional Council of Alava) Ayuntamiento de Madrid (City Council of Madrid) Ayuntamiento de Barcelona (City Council of Barcelona) Cabildo Insular de Gran Canaria (Island Council of Gran Canaria) Cabildo Insular de Tenerife (Island Council of Tenerife) Instituto de Crédito Oficial (Public Credit Institution) Instituto Catalán de Finanzas (Finance Institution of Catalonia) Instituto Valenciano de Finanzas (Finance Institution of Valencia)

TABLE 2

International entities

European Bank for Reconstruction and Development
European Investment Bank
Asian Development Bank
African Development Bank
World Bank/IBRD/IMF
International Finance Corporation
Inter-American Development Bank
Council of Europe Social Development Fund
Euratom
European Community
Corporación Andina de Fomento (CAF) (Andean Development Corporation)
Eurofima
European Coal and Steel Community
Nordic Investment Bank
Caribbean Development Bank

Note: The provisions of regulation 17 are without prejudice to any international obligations that member States may have entered into with respect to the international entities listed in Table 2.

2004/438
Capital Gains Tax (Gilt-edged Securities) Order 2004

Made by the Treasury under TCGA 1992 Sch 9 para 1

Made . . . . *23 February 2004*

1 This Order may be cited as the Capital Gains Tax (Gilt-edged Securities) Order 2004.

2 The following securities are hereby specified for the purposes of Schedule 9 to the Taxation of Chargeable Gains Act 1992—

4% Treasury Stock 2007;
4% Treasury Stock 2009;
4% Treasury Stock 2015.

2004/439
Urban Regeneration Companies (Tax) (Designation) Order 2004

Made by the Treasury under TA 1988 s 79B(5), and according to the criteria listed in s 79B(7)

Made *23 February2004*
Coming into force . . . . *24 February 2004*

Citation, commencement and effect

1—(1) This Order may be cited as the Urban Regeneration Companies (Tax) (Designation) Order 2004 and shall come into force on 24th February 2004.

(2) Article 2 takes effect on 1st April 2003.

(3) Article 3 takes effect on 8th April 2003.

(4) Article 4 takes effect on 17th July 2003.

(5) Article 5 takes effect on 2nd December 2003.

Designation of urban regeneration companies taking effect on 1st April 2003

2 For the purposes of section 79B of the Income and Corporation Taxes Act 1988 the following companies limited by guarantee are designated as urban regeneration companies—

(*a*) Bradford City Centre Urban Regeneration Company Limited;
(*b*) Camborne Pool Redruth Urban Regeneration Company Limited;
(*c*) Corby Urban Regeneration Company Limited;
(*d*) Hull Urban Regeneration Company Limited;
(*e*) Leicester Regeneration Company Limited;
(*f*) Liverpool Vision;
(*g*) New East Manchester Limited;
(*h*) Newport Urban Regeneration Company Limited;
(*i*) Sheffield City Centre Urban Regeneration Company Limited;
(*j*) Sunderland ARC Limited;
(*k*) Swindon Urban Regeneration Company Limited; and
(*l*) Tees Valley Urban Regeneration Company Limited.

Designation of urban regeneration companies taking effect on 8th April 2003

3 For the purposes of section 79B of the Income and Corporation Taxes Act 1988 the following companies limited by guarantee are designated as urban regeneration companies—

(*a*) Derby Cityscape Limited;
(*b*) Sandwell Regeneration Company Limited; and
(*c*) Furness West Cumbria New Vision Urban Regeneration Company Limited.

Designation of urban regeneration company taking effect on 17th July 2003

4 For the purposes of section 79B of the Income and Corporation Taxes Act 1988 Ilex Urban Regeneration Company Limited, a company limited by guarantee, is designated as an urban regeneration company.

Designation of urban regeneration company taking effect on 2nd December 2003

5 For the purposes of section 79B of the Income and Corporation Taxes Act 1988 Walsall Regeneration Company Limited, a company limited by guarantee, is designated as an urban regeneration company.

2004/674
Recovery of Duties and Taxes etc Due in Other Member States (Corresponding UK Claims, Procedure and Supplementary) Regulations 2004

Made by the Treasury under FA 2002 Sch 39 para 3(1),(2),(3) and the Commissioners of Customs and Excise and the Commissioners of Inland Revenue, under FA 2002 Sch 39 paras 2(2) and 3(4)

Made	*9 March 2004*
Laid before the House of Commons	*10 March 2004*
Coming into force	*1 April 2004*

ARRANGEMENT OF REGULATIONS

PART 1
GENERAL

PART 2
CORRESPONDING UK CLAIMS

PART 3
REQUESTS FOR ASSISTANCE

PART 4
INTEREST

PART 5
ENFORCEMENT OF CORRESPONDING CLAIMS

SCHEDULES:

PART 1
GENERAL

Citation and commencement

1 These Regulations may be cited as the Recovery of Duties and Taxes etc. Due in Other Member States (Corresponding UK Claims, Procedure and Supplementary) Regulations 2004 and shall come into force on 1st April 2004.

Interpretation

2 In these Regulations—

(*a*) "the Act" means the Finance Act 2002;

(*b*) "applicant authority" means an authority in a member State which makes a request for assistance under the Mutual Assistance Recovery Directive;

(*c*) "authorised official" means an official of an applicant authority authorised by that authority to make requests for assistance in accordance with the Mutual Assistance Recovery Directive;

(*d*) "the Board" means the Commissioners of Inland Revenue;

(*e*) "Commission" means the Commission of the European Communities;

(*f*) "Commissioners" mean the Commissioners of Customs and Excise;

(*g*) "consolidated claim" means several foreign claims recoverable from the same person;

(*h*) "contested" means an action contesting a foreign claim or the instrument permitting enforcement brought by an interested party before the competent body of the member State in which the applicant authority is situated in accordance with the laws in force there;

(*i*) "a corresponding UK claim" means a claim in the United Kingdom corresponding to the foreign claim;

(*j*) "costs" includes fees, charges, disbursements, expenses and remuneration;

(*k*) "Council Directive 77/388/EEC" means that directive as amended and as last amended by Council Directive 2002/93;

(*l*) "the Directive" means Commission Directive 2002/94/EC laying down detailed rules for implementing certain provisions of the Mutual Assistance Recovery Directive;

(*m*) "electronic means" has the same meaning as in Article 2(1) of the Directive;

(*n*) "enforcement action" means action to enforce a foreign claim by way of legal proceedings, distress, diligence or otherwise as might be taken to enforce a corresponding UK claim;

(*o*) "export duties" has the same meaning as in Article 3 of the Mutual Assistance Recovery Directive;

(*p*) "instrument permitting enforcement" means—

(i) any instrument issued by an applicant authority in any member State in relation to a sum claimed by that authority within the jurisdiction of that State; or

(ii) a decision on that claim given in favour of that authority by a court or tribunal or other competent body in that State which permits recovery of that claim in that State or part thereof;

(*q*) "import duties" has the same meaning as in Article 3 of the Mutual Assistance Recovery Directive;

(*r*) "precautionary measures" means measures taken, or to be taken, in order to secure recovery of a foreign claim;

(*s*) "request for assistance" means a request for information, notification, recovery or precautionary measures within the meaning of the Mutual Assistance Recovery Directive.

PART 2
CORRESPONDING UK CLAIMS

Corresponding UK claims—duties and taxes

3 For the purposes of Schedule 39 to the Act, column 2 of the table in Schedule 1 prescribes the corresponding UK claim in relation to each foreign claim described in column 1.

PART 3
REQUESTS FOR ASSISTANCE

Requests for information

4—(1) A request for information shall be made in writing in the form specified in Annex I to the Directive. If the request cannot be transmitted by electronic means it shall bear the official stamp of the applicant authority and be signed by an authorised official.

(2) A request for information shall relate to—

(*a*) a debtor;

(*b*) a person liable for settlement of the debt under the law in force in the member State in which the applicant authority is situated; or (*c*) any third party holding assets belonging to one of the persons mentioned in sub-paragraph (*a*) or (*b*).

(3) The relevant UK authority shall acknowledge receipt of a request for information in writing not later than seven days from the date of such receipt and as appropriate request the applicant authority to provide any additional information necessary to execute the request.

(4) The relevant UK authority shall, not later than six months from the date of acknowledgement of the request, report to the applicant authority the outcome of the investigations which it has conducted in order to obtain the information requested.

(5) The relevant UK authority shall, within a reasonable period following the date upon which that information was obtained, transmit to the applicant authority the information obtained in accordance with the request.

(6) The relevant UK authority shall not be obliged to supply information where—

(*a*) the request was not made in accordance with this regulation;
(*b*) the relevant UK authority would not be able to obtain that information for the purpose of recovery of a corresponding UK claim;
(*c*) the supply of the requested information would disclose any commercial, industrial or professional secret; or
(*d*) disclosure of the information would prejudice the security of the United Kingdom or otherwise be contrary to the law or public policy of the United Kingdom.

(7) An applicant authority may in writing at any time withdraw a request made under this regulation.

Requests for notification of instruments

5—(1) A request for notification of an instrument shall –

(*a*) be made in writing in duplicate in the form specified in Annex II to the Directive;
(*b*) bear the official stamp of the applicant authority;
(*c*) be signed by an authorised official of that authority;
(*d*) be accompanied by two copies of the instrument to be notified.

(2) A request for notification shall relate to a person specified in regulation 4(2).

(3) The relevant UK authority shall—

(*a*) acknowledge receipt of a request for notification in writing not later than seven days after the date of such receipt;
(*b*) take the necessary measures to effect notification immediately upon receipt of the request for notification in accordance with the law applicable to notification of similar instruments in that part of the UK in which notification is given;
(*c*) confirm to the applicant authority, as soon as reasonably practicable, the date the instrument was notified to the person concerned by returning a copy of the request form with the certificate on the reverse completed;
(*d*) not question the validity of the instrument.

(4) The relevant UK authority may request additional information from the applicant authority for the purpose of effecting notification.

(5) For the purposes of this regulation ''instrument'' means any document or decision including those of a judicial nature which emanate from the member State in which the applicant authority is situated and which relate to a foreign claim.

Requests for recovery or precautionary measures

6—(1) A request for recovery or precautionary measures shall—

(*a*) be made in writing in the form specified in Annex III to the Directive including a declaration that the conditions of the Mutual Assistance Recovery Directive for initiating a request have been fulfilled;
(*b*) bear the official stamp of the applicant authority;
(*c*) be signed by an authorised official of that authority;
(*d*) relate to a person specified in regulation 4(2); and
(*e*) be accompanied by an instrument permitting enforcement.

(2) The amount of the foreign claim stated in the request shall be stated in UK sterling and the currency of the member State in which the applicant authority is situated using the exchange rate specified in regulation 15(2).

(3) The relevant UK authority shall—

(*a*) within seven days of receipt of a request for recovery or precautionary measures—

(i) acknowledge receipt of the request in writing to the applicant authority;
(ii) make a request in writing to the applicant authority to complete the request if it does not contain the full or complete information required by Article 7 of the Mutual Assistance Recovery Directive;

(*b*) where it does not take any enforcement action on a request within three months of receipt, not later than seven days from the end of that period inform the applicant authority in writing of the grounds for its failure to comply with the time limit;

(*c*) within a reasonable time having regard to the particular case, where all or part of the foreign claim cannot be recovered or precautionary measures cannot be taken, so inform the applicant authority, indicating the reasons therefor;

(*d*) no later than at the end of each six month period following the date of acknowledgement of receipt of the request, inform the applicant authority in writing of the status or outcome of any enforcement action;

(*e*) continue, save where prevented by paragraph 4 of Schedule 39 to the Act, any enforcement action or precautionary measures where a request to do so is made by the applicant authority not later than two months from the date of receipt of the notification of the outcome of that action and such request shall be subject to the provisions in these Regulations which applied to the initial request;

(*f*) inform the applicant authority immediately any enforcement action has been taken on a request.

(4) For the purpose of this regulation and regulations 8 to 17 and regulations 20 to 26 a single instrument permitting enforcement which covers more than one foreign claim against a person shall be deemed to constitute a single claim.

(5) A relevant UK authority shall consult the applicant authority where in recovering a foreign claim it intends to allow the debtor time to pay by arrangement or to make payment by instalments (whether or not interest is charged or to be charged on those arrangements).

(6) Except where an enactment or rule of law applicable to a corresponding UK claim requires otherwise, a relevant UK authority shall not be obliged to recover a foreign claim where to do so would, because of the situation of the debtor, create serious economic or social difficulties in the United Kingdom.

Transfer of sums recovered

7—(1) Subject to paragraph (3) the relevant UK authority shall transfer in UK sterling to the applicant authority any sum recovered in respect of a foreign claim not later than one month from the date upon which recovery was effected.

(2) For the purposes of this regulation "sum" shall include any interest including interest charged in the UK.

(3) The relevant UK authority and the applicant authority may agree different arrangements for the transfer of an amount where that amount is less than 1500 Euro.

(4) For the purpose of satisfying a request for recovery any sum recovered shall be deemed to have been recovered in proportion to the foreign claim as expressed in UK sterling.

Contested recovery

8—(1) Any enactment permitting proceedings for the recovery of or precautionary measures in relation to a corresponding UK claim shall apply to a foreign claim which is contested.

(2) ...[1].

Amendments—[1] Para (2) revoked by the Recovery of Agricultural Levies Due in Other Member States Regulations, SI 2004/800 regs 2, 3 with effect from 13 April 2004.

Notice of inability to take action or proceedings upon a request for recovery of a contested claim

9 Where, in accordance with paragraph 4 of Schedule 39 to the Act, the relevant UK authority is not permitted to take action for recovery or for a precautionary measure it shall, in writing, advise the competent authority of the reasons within one month of the receipt of the notification by the applicant authority that the foreign claim or instrument permitting enforcement is contested.

Notice of action contesting recovery

10 The relevant UK authority shall notify the applicant authority in writing of any notice of commencement of action in the UK by a person specified in regulation 4(2) for reimbursement of sums recovered or for compensation in relation to recovery of a contested claim.

Reimbursement of sums recovered and compensation

11 Where the result of contesting a foreign claim or instrument permitting enforcement is favourable to the debtor, the applicant authority shall be liable for the reimbursement of any sums recovered, together with any compensation due, in accordance with any law in force in the relevant part of the UK applicable to the corresponding UK claim.

Reimbursement arrangements

12 Where recovery of a foreign claim poses a specific problem, entails a very large amount in costs or relates to the fight against organised crime the relevant UK authority and the applicant authority may agree reimbursement arrangements specific to the case in question.

Notice of cancellation or payment of a claim

13 Where the relevant UK authority undertakes enforcement action or precautionary measures in relation to that foreign claim it shall, upon receipt of notice in writing from the applicant authority as to—

(*a*) payment in satisfaction of that claim; or

(*b*) cancellation or other reason for termination of that claim;

cease any enforcement action or precautionary measures in relation to that claim.

Adjustment of a foreign claim

14—(1) This regulation applies where the amount of a foreign claim is amended for any reason.

(2) Where the amendment leads to a reduction in the amount of the foreign claim—

(*a*) the relevant UK authority shall continue the action which it has undertaken with a view to recovery or to the taking of precautionary measures, but that action shall be limited to the amount still outstanding;

(*b*) if at the time the relevant UK authority is informed of the reduction in the amount of the foreign claim, an amount exceeding the amount still outstanding has already been recovered by it but the transfer procedure referred to in regulation 7 has not yet been initiated, the relevant UK authority shall repay the amount overpaid to the person entitled thereto.

(3) Where the amendment leads to an increase in the amount of the foreign claim—

(*a*) the additional request shall as far as possible be dealt with by the relevant UK authority at the same time as the original request;

(*b*) where, in view of the state of progress of the existing recovery procedure, consolidation of the additional request with the original request is not possible, the relevant UK authority shall be required to comply with the additional request only if it concerns an amount not less than the threshold amount referred to in regulation 15(1).

Minimum amount on requests for assistance

15—(1) A request for assistance shall not be entertained if the foreign claim (whether a single claim or a consolidated claim) is less than 1500 Euro or the sterling equivalent at the time of request.

(2) The rate of exchange to be used for the purposes of these regulations shall be the latest selling rate recorded on the most representative exchange market or markets of the member State in which the applicant authority is situated on the date when the request for assistance is signed.

Limitation on requests for assistance

16—(1) The relevant UK authority shall not be obliged to entertain a request for assistance if the foreign claim is more than five years old.

(2) The point for commencement and calculation of a period of five years shall be—

(*a*) where a foreign claim is not contested, the date the instrument permitting enforcement was established by the applicant authority in accordance with the law in force in the member State in which that authority is situated; or

(*b*) where a foreign claim is contested, the date upon which the applicant authority establishes that the claim or instrument permitting recovery is no longer contested.

Acceptance and transmission of communications

17—(1) The relevant UK authority shall, as far as possible, accept and transmit all information required to be communicated in writing for the purposes of the Mutual Assistance Recovery Directive by electronic means.

(2) Paragraph (1) does not apply to requests for assistance made in accordance with regulations 5 and 6 and the instrument accompanying those requests unless the relevant UK authority and the applicant authority agree to waive paper communication.

Communication of documents and information

18 Documents and information sent to the relevant UK authority pursuant to the Mutual Assistance Recovery Directive may only be communicated by that authority to—

(*a*) the person mentioned in the request for assistance;

(*b*) those persons and authorities responsible for the recovery of the claims, and solely for that purpose; or

(*c*) the judicial authorities dealing with matters concerning the recovery of claims.

Language requirements

19—(1) Save as otherwise agreed by the relevant UK authority, requests for assistance, the instrument permitting enforcement, and any other relevant document addressed to that authority shall be accompanied by a translation of that document in the English language.

(2) All information and particulars communicated to an applicant authority by the relevant UK authority in relation to a request for assistance shall be conveyed in the English language or such other language as is agreed by that authority with the applicant authority.

Limitation

20—(1) The period of limitation or prescription in relation to any issue arising on the recovery of any foreign claim shall be that applicable under the laws in force in the member State in which the applicant authority is situated.

(2) For the purposes of paragraph (1) any step or act taken by the relevant UK authority in recovery of a foreign claim in pursuance of a request for assistance shall be deemed to have been taken in the member State in which the applicant authority is situated where that step or act would, if it had been taken by that applicant authority, have had the effect of suspending or interrupting the period of limitation or prescription in accordance with the laws in force in that member State.

Notice of refusal of requests for assistance

21—(1) Where in accordance with the Mutual Assistance Recovery Directive and the Directive or these Regulations the relevant UK authority decides not to act upon a request for assistance it shall, as soon as practicable after making its decision to refuse a request and any event within three months of the date of acknowledgement of receipt of the request, notify the applicant authority in writing of the reasons for refusal.

(2) In the cases mentioned in regulations 6(6) and 16 a copy of the reasons for refusal shall also be communicated to the Commission within the period specified in paragraph (1).

PART 4

INTEREST

Adaptations

22 Schedule 2 to these Regulations shall have effect.

Interest enforced by the Board

23—(1) A foreign claim corresponding to a UK claim for income tax, capital gains tax or corporation tax carries interest in respect of the principal and any penalty claimed at the rate applicable to the corresponding UK claim under section 178 of the Finance Act 1989 from the date of recognition until payment.

(2) In this regulation "the date of recognition" means the earlier of—

(*a*) the day following the expiry of three months from the date of receipt by the Board of the request for recovery of the foreign claim; and

(*b*) the date the instrument permitting enforcement of the foreign claim is recognised by the Board as an instrument authorising enforcement of the claim in the United Kingdom.

(3) Paragraph (1) above applies even if the date of recognition is a non-business day within the meaning of section 92 of the Bills of Exchange Act 1882.

(4) Interest is payable under this regulation without any deduction of income tax.

(5) For the purposes of this regulation, where—

(*a*) any payment is made by cheque to—

(i) an officer of the Board, or

(ii) the Board, or

(iii) the applicant authority, and

(*b*) the cheque is paid on its first presentation to the banker on whom it is drawn;

the payment shall be treated as made on the day on which the cheque was received by the officer or the Board or the applicant authority.

(6) Interest payable under this regulation shall be recoverable as if it were interest charged under a provision of the Taxes Management Act 1970.

Interest enforced by the Commissioners

24—(1) A foreign claim corresponding to any UK claim—

(*a*) mentioned in column 2 of Part I of Schedule 1, or

(*b*) for insurance premium tax,

shall carry interest in respect of the principal and any penalty claimed at the rate applicable to the corresponding UK claim under section 197 of the Finance Act 1996 from the date of recognition until payment.

(2) In this regulation "the date of recognition" means the earlier of—

(*a*) the day following the expiry of three months from the date of receipt by the Commissioners of the request for recovery of the foreign claim; and

(*b*) the date the instrument permitting enforcement of the foreign claim is recognised by the Commissioners as an instrument authorising enforcement of the claim in the United Kingdom.

(3) Paragraph (1) above applies even if the date of recognition is a non-business day within the meaning of section 92 of the Bills of Exchange Act 1882

(4) Interest is payable under this regulation without any deduction of income tax.

(5) For the purposes of this regulation, where—

(*a*) any payment is made by cheque to—

(i) an officer of Customs and Excise, or

(ii) the Commissioners, or

(iii) the applicant authority, and

(*b*) the cheque is paid on its first presentation to the banker on whom it is drawn,

the payment shall be treated as made on the day on which the cheque was received by the officer or the Commissioners or the applicant authority.

(6) Interest payable under this regulation shall be notified in writing to the person subject to enforcement action in respect of the foreign claim and may be recovered from that person as a debt due to the Crown.

PART 5
ENFORCEMENT OF CORRESPONDING CLAIMS

Evidence

25—(1) An instrument permitting enforcement of a foreign claim recognised by the Board as an instrument authorising enforcement of the claim in the United Kingdom, together with a certificate of a collector that payment of the claim has not been made to him, or, to the best of his knowledge and belief, to any other collector, or to any person acting on his behalf or on behalf of another collector, or to the applicant authority, is sufficient evidence that the sum mentioned in the instrument is unpaid and is due to that authority.

(2) A certificate of a collector that interest is payable under regulation 23(1) and that payment of the interest has not been made to him, or, to the best of his knowledge and belief, to any other collector, or to any person acting on his behalf or on behalf of another collector, or to the applicant authority, is sufficient evidence that the sum mentioned in the instrument is unpaid and is due to that authority.

(3) For the purposes of this regulation, any document purporting to be such a certificate as is mentioned in paragraph (1) and (2) is deemed to be such a certificate unless the contrary is proved.

Enforcement in Scotland

26—(1) For the purposes of enforcement in Scotland, an original, official or certified copy of a decision on a foreign claim by a court, tribunal or other competent body in the member State in which the applicant authority is situated shall be of the same force and effect as an extract of a decree of the Court of Session for the payment of money bearing a warrant for execution.

(2) For the purposes of paragraph (1), a "decision on a foreign claim" means a decision on a foreign claim which permits recovery of that claim in the member State in which the applicant authority is situated or in part thereof.

SCHEDULE 1

Regulation 3

CORRESPONDING CLAIMS

PART 1

Column 1	Column 2
1. Foreign Claim	*2. Corresponding UK Claim*
Import duties and export duties charged, in any member State other than the United Kingdom	Import and export duties charged in the United Kingdom

Column 1	Column 2
1. Foreign Claim	*2. Corresponding UK Claim*
Value added tax (howsoever described) charged in any member State other than the United Kingdom in accordance with the provisions of Council Directive 77/388/EEC	Value added tax charged, in the United Kingdom in accordance with the Value Added Tax Act 1994
Excise duties (howsoever described) charged in any member State other than the United Kingdom upon, –manufactured tobacco, –alcohol and alcoholic beverages, –mineral oils	Excise duty charged, collected or enforced in the United Kingdom in accordance with the Tobacco Products Duty Act 1979, or the Alcoholic Liquor Duties Act 1979, or the Hydrocarbon Oil Duties Act 1979 upon the items described in column 1

PART 2

Column 1			Column 2
1. Foreign Claim			*2. Corresponding UK claim*
EU Country	**Taxes listed in the Mutual Assistance Directive. 77/799/EEC, as amended**	**English Translation**	
Austria	Einkommensteuer	Income Tax	Income Tax
	Koerperschaftsteuer	Corporation tax	Corporation Tax
	Grundsteuer	Real Estate Tax	Capital Gains Tax
	Bodenwertabgabe	Land value levy	CGT
	Abgabe von land- und forstwirtschaftlichen Betrieben	Levy on agricultural and forestry enterprises	CGT
	Versicherungssteuer	Insurance Tax	Insurance Premium Tax
	Feuerschutzsteuer	Fire insurance tax	Insurance Premium Tax
Belgium	Impôt des personnes physiques/ Personenbelasting	Personal income tax	Income Tax
	Impôt des sociétés/ Vennootschapsbelasting	Corporation tax	Corporation Tax
	Impôt des personnes morales/ Rechtspersonenbelasting	Tax on legal persons	Income Tax
	Impôt des non-résidents/ Belasting der niet-verblijfhouders	Tax on non-residents	Income Tax
	Taxe annuelle sur les contrats d'assurance/ Jaarlijkse tax op de verzekeringscontracten	Annual tax on insurance contracts	Insurance Premium Tax
Denmark	Indkomstskat til staten	State income tax	Income Tax
	Selskabsskat	Corporation tax	Corporation Tax
	Den kommunale indkomstskat	Municipal income tax	Income Tax
	Den amtskommunale indkomstskat	County income tax	Income Tax
	Folkepensionsbidragene	Pensions contribution	Income Tax
	Soemandsskat	Seamen's tax	Income Tax
	Den saerlige indkomstskat	Special income tax	Income Tax
	Kirkeskat	Church tax	Income Tax
	Formueskat til staten	State wealth tax	Capital Gains Tax
	Bidrag til dagpengefonden	Contributions to the sickness per diem fund	Income Tax

Column 1			Column 2
1. Foreign Claim			*2. Corresponding UK claim*
EU Country	**Taxes listed in the Mutual Assistance Directive. 77/799/EEC, as amended**	**English Translation**	
	Afgift af lystfartojsforsikringer	Pleasure craft insurance tax	Insurance Premium Tax
	Afgift af ansvarsforsikringer for motorkoretojer m.v.	Tax on motor vehicle compulsory insurance	Insurance Premium Tax
	Stempelafgift af forsikringspraemier	Stamp duty on insurance premiums	Insurance Premium Tax
Finland	Valtion tuloverot/de statliga inkomstskatterna	State income taxes on earned income	Income Tax
	Yhteisoejen tulovero/ inkomstskatten foer samfund	Corporate income tax	Corporation Tax
	Kunnallisvero/ kommunalskatten	Communal tax on earned income	Income Tax
	Kirkollisvero/kyrkoskatten	Church tax	Income Tax
	Kansanelaekeva- kuutusmaksu/fol kpensionsfoersaekring- spremien	Pension insurance premiums	Income Tax
	Sairausvakuutusmaksu/ sjukfoers aekringspremien	Health insurance premium	Income Tax
	Korkotulon laehdevero/ kaellskatten paa raenteinkomst	Withholding tax at source on interest	Income Tax
	Rajoitetusti verovelvollisen laehdevero/kaellskatten foer begraensat skattskyldig	Non-resident net wealth tax	Capital Gains Tax
	Valtion varallisuusvero/den statliga foermoegenhetsskatten	Net wealth tax	Capital Gains Tax
	Kiinteistoevero/ fastighetsskatten	Real property tax	Capital Gains Tax
	Eraista vakuutsmaksuista Suoritettava Vero/skat pa vissa forsakringspremier	Tax on certain insurance premiums	Insurance Premium Tax
	Palosuojelumaksu/ brandskyddavgift	Fire insurance tax	Insurance Premium Tax
France	Impôt sur le revenu	Personal income tax	Income Tax
	Impôt sur les sociétés	Corporation tax	Corporation Tax
	Taxe professionnelle	Business tax	Corporation Tax
	Taxe foncière sur les propriétés bâties	Property tax on land and buildings	Capital Gains Tax
	Taxe foncière sur les propriétés non bâties	Property tax on land without buildings	Capital Gains Tax
	Taxe sur les conventions d'assurances	Tax on insurance agreements	Insurance Premium Tax
Germany	Einkommensteuer	Income tax	Income Tax
	Koerperschaftsteuer	Corporation tax	Corporation Tax
	Vermoegensteuer	Wealth tax	Capital Gains Tax
	Gewerbesteuer	Tax on industry and trade	Corporation Tax
	Grundsteuer	Real estate tax	Capital Gains Tax
	Versicherungssteuer	Insurance Tax	Insurance Premium Tax
	Feuerschutzsteuer	Fire insurance tax	Insurance Premium Tax
Greece	Φόρος εισοδήματος φυσικών προσώπων	Personal income tax	Income Tax
	Φόρος εισοδήματος νομικών προσώπων	Corporate income tax	Corporation Tax

Column 1			Column 2
1. Foreign Claim			*2. Corresponding UK claim*
EU Country	**Taxes listed in the Mutual Assistance Directive. 77/799/EEC, as amended**	**English Translation**	
	Φόρος ακινήτον περιονσίας	Real estate tax	Capital Gains Tax
	Φόρος κύκλον εργασιών (Φ.Κ.Ε)	Tax on the business cycle	Insurance Premium Tax
	Τέλη Χαρτοσήμον''	Stamp taxes	Insurance Premium Tax
Ireland	Income tax		Income Tax
	Corporation tax		Corporation Tax
	Capital gains tax		Capital Gains Tax
	Wealth tax		Capital Gains Tax
	Levy on insurance premiums		Insurance Premium Tax
Italy	Imposta sul reddito delle persone fisiche	Personal income tax	Income Tax
	Imposta sul reddito delle persone giuridiche	Tax on income of corporations	Corporation Tax
	Imposta locale sui redditi	Local income tax	Income Tax
	Imposte sulle assicurazioni private ed I contratti vitalazi di cui alla legge 29.10.67 no 1216	Tax on private insurance and life annuity contracts as covered by law No 1216 of 29.10.67	Insurance Premium Tax
Luxembourg	Impôt sur le revenu des personnes physiques	Personal income tax	Income Tax
	Impôt sur le revenu des collectivités	Corporation tax	Corporation Tax
	Impôt commercial communal	Communal trade tax	Corporation Tax
	Impôt sur la fortune	Wealth tax	Capital Gains Tax
	Impôt foncier	Tax on land and buildings	Capital Gains Tax
	Impôt sur les assurances	Insurance tax	Insurance Premium Tax
	Impôts dans l'interet du service d'incendie	Taxes levied in the interest of the fire service	Insurance Premium Tax
Netherlands	Inkomstenbelasting	Personal income tax	Income Tax
	Vennootschapsbelasting	Corporation tax	Corporation Tax
	Vermogensbelasting	Wealth tax	Capital Gains Tax
	Assurantiebelasting	Insurance tax	Insurance Premium Tax
Portugal	Contribuição predial	Real estate tax	Income Tax
	Imposto sobre a indústria agrícola	Agricultural tax	Income Tax
	Contribuição industrial	Industrial tax	Income Tax
	Imposto de capitais	Withholding tax	Income Tax
	Imposto profissional	Income tax	Income Tax
	Imposto complementar	Complementary tax	Income Tax
	Imposto de mais-valias	Capital gains tax	Income Tax
	Imposto sobre o rendimento do petróleo	Petroleum revenue tax	Income Tax
	Os adicionais devidos sobre os impostos precedents	Surcharges on the above taxes	Income Tax
	Imposto sobre o rendimento das pessoas singulars	Personal income tax	Income Tax
	Imposto de selo sobre os premios de seguros	Stamp duty on insurance premiums	Insurance Premium Tax
Spain	Impuesto sobre la Renta de las Personas Físicas	Personal income tax	Income Tax
	Impuesto sobre Sociedades	Corporation tax	Corporation Tax

Column 1			Column 2
1. Foreign Claim			*2. Corresponding UK claim*
EU Country	**Taxes listed in the Mutual Assistance Directive. 77/799/EEC, as amended**	**English Translation**	
	Impuesto Extraordinario sobre el Patrimonio de las Personas Físicas	Wealth tax	Capital Gains Tax
	Impuesto sobre la prima de seguros	Insurance premium tax	Insurance Premium Tax
Sweden	Den statliga inkomstskatten	National income tax	Income Tax
	Sjoemansskatten	Seamen's tax	Income Tax
	Kupongskatten	Coupon (dividend) tax	Income Tax
	Den saerskilda inkomstskatten foer utomlands bosatta	Income tax on non-residents	Income Tax
	Den saerskilda inkomstskatten foer utomlands bosatta artister m.fl.	Income tax on non-resident artistes and others	Income Tax
	Den statliga fastighetsskatten	National real property tax	Capital Gains Tax
	Den kommunala inkomstskatten	Communal income tax	Income Tax
	Foermoegenhetsskatten	Wealth tax	Capital Gains Tax

PART 3

Column 1	*Column 2*
1. Foreign claims	**2. Corresponding UK claim**
Refunds, interventions and other measures forming part of the system of total or partial financing of the European Agricultural Guidance and Guarantee Fund (EAGGF), including sums to be collected in connection with these actions charged, levied, collected or paid in any member State other than the United Kingdom.	Those items described in Column 1 charged, levied, collected or paid in the United Kingdom.
Levies and other duties provided for under the common organisation of the market for the sugar sector charged in any member State other than the United Kingdom.	Those items described in Column 1 charged in the United Kingdom.
Interest, administrative penalties or fines incurred in any member State other than the United Kingdom relating to a foreign claim described in Column 1 of Parts 1 to 3 of this Schedule	Such interest, administrative penalties or fines as is chargeable in the United Kingdom relating to a corresponding UK claim described in Column 2 of Parts 1 to 3 of this Schedule

SCHEDULE 2

Regulation 22

Note—Schedule 2 is not relevant to this work.

2004/712
Research and Development (Prescribed Activities) Regulations 2004

Made by the Treasury under TA 1988 s 837A(3)

Made	*11 March 2004*
Laid before the House of Commons	*11 March 2004*
Coming into force	*1 April 2004*

Citation, commencement and effect

1—(1) These Regulations may be cited as the Research and Development (Prescribed Activities) Regulations 2004, come into force on 1st April 2004, and subject to paragraphs (2) to (9) have effect—

(*a*) for the purposes of corporation tax, for accounting periods ending on or after 1st April 2004, and

(*b*) for the purposes of income tax and capital gains tax, in relation to the year 2004–05 and subsequent years of assessment.

(2) These Regulations have effect in relation to shares issued on or after 6th April 2004 in relation to Chapter 3 of Part 7 of the Income and Corporation Taxes Act 1988 (enterprise investment scheme).

(3) Nothing in these Regulations affects the operation of the following provisions in relation to shares issued before 6th April 2004—

(*a*) Chapter 3 of Part 7 of the Income and Corporation Taxes Act 1988 (enterprise investment scheme);

(*b*) sections 573 and 574 of that Act (relief for losses on unlisted shares in trading companies); and

(*c*) Schedule 5B to the Taxation of Chargeable Gains Act 1992 (enterprise investment scheme: re-investment).

(4) These Regulations have effect for the purpose of determining whether shares or securities issued on or after 6th April 2004 are, for the purposes of section 842AA of the Income and Corporation Taxes Act 1988 (venture capital trusts), to be regarded as comprised in a company's qualifying holdings.

(5) Nothing in these Regulations affects the operation of Schedule 28B to the Income and Corporation Taxes Act 1988 as it has effect for the purpose of determining whether shares or securities issued before 6th April 2004 are, for the purposes of section 842AA of the Income and Corporation Taxes Act 1988, to be regarded as comprised in a company's qualifying holdings.

(6) These Regulations have effect in relation to shares issued on or after 6th April 2004 in relation to Schedule 15 to the Finance Act 2000 (corporate venturing scheme).

(7) Nothing in these Regulations affects the operation of the Schedule specified in paragraph (6) in relation to shares issued before 6th April 2004.

(8) In relation to—

(*a*) Chapter 9 of Part 7 of the Income Tax (Earnings and Pensions) Act 2003 (enterprise management incentives), and

(*b*) Part 4 of Schedule 7D to the Taxation of Chargeable Gains Act 1992 (enterprise management incentives), these Regulations have effect in relation to share options granted on or after 6th April 2004.

(9) Nothing in these Regulations affects the operation of the provisions specified in paragraph (8) in relation to share options granted before 6th April 2004.

Activities prescribed as research and development

2 For the purposes of section 837A of the Income and Corporation Taxes Act 1988—

(*a*) activities that fall to be treated as research and development in accordance with the "Guidelines on the Meaning of Research and Development for Tax Purposes" issued by the Secretary of State for Trade and Industry on 5 March 2004, are research and development; and

(*b*) activities that do not fall to be treated as such in accordance with those guidelines are not research and development.

Revocation of the Research and Development (Prescribed Activities) Regulations 2000

3 The Research and Development (Prescribed Activities) Regulations 2000 are revoked.

Commentary—*Simon's Direct Tax Service* **B2.702, 703; D2.1201.**

2004/1450
Child Trust Funds Regulations 2004

Made by the Treasury, in exercise of the powers conferred upon them by the Child Trust Funds Act 2004 ss 3(1) to (5) and (7), 5(1), (4) and (5), 6, 7, 8(1), 9(2) and (10)(*b*), 11(1), 12(2), 13, 15, 16, 23(1) and 28(1) to (4)

Made . . . . 27 *May* 2004
Laid before Parliament . . . . 27 *May* 2004
Coming into force in accordance with regulation 1

PART 1
INTRODUCTORY

Citation and commencement

1 These Regulations may be cited as the Child Trust Funds Regulations 2004 and shall come into force for the purposes of—

(*a*) issuing vouchers (see regulation 3),
(*b*) completing account-opening formalities (see regulation 5),
(*c*) applications under regulation 13 to open an account with effect from the appointed day,
(*d*) applications under regulation 14 to be approved as an account provider to manage accounts from the appointed day,
(*e*) regulation 17, so far as it relates to applications referred to in paragraph (*d*), and
(*f*) making a fortnightly claim and financial return (see regulation 30),

on 1st January 2005, and for all other purposes on the appointed day.

Interpretation

2—(1) In these Regulations—

(*a*) the following expressions have the meanings given in the Child Trust Funds Act 2004 (''the Act'')—
''child''
''child trust fund''
''eligible child''
''Inland Revenue''
''Inland Revenue contributions'' (see section 11(2) of the Act),
''parental responsibility'' (see section 3(9) of the Act);
''relevant person'' (see section 15(2) of the Act),
''responsible person'', in relation to a child under 16 (see section 3(8) of the Act),
''the person entitled to child benefit in respect of the child'' (see section 2(1)(*a*), (4) and (6) of the Act);

(*b*) except where the context otherwise requires—
''account'' means a scheme of investment which (except in regulation 22(1)) qualifies as a child trust fund, other than in the cases of—
(i) an account with a deposit-taker,
(ii) a share or deposit account with a building society, or
(iii) a deposit account with a person falling within section 840A(1)(*b*) of the Taxes Act, or a relevant European institution;
an ''account investment'' is an investment under the account which is a qualifying investment for an account within the meaning of regulation 12;
an ''account provider'' is a person who fulfils the conditions of these Regulations and is approved by the Board for the purpose of these Regulations as an account provider;
''appointed day'' means the day appointed under section 27 of the Act, for the purposes of sections 8 and 9 of the Act;
''assurance undertaking'' has the meaning in Article 2 of the Council Directive of 5th November 2002 concerning life assurance (No. 2002/83);
''the Board'' means the Commissioners of Inland Revenue;
''building society'' means a building society within the meaning of the Building Societies Act 1986, or the Irish Building Societies Act 1989;
''company'', except in regulation 12(4)(*a*), means any body corporate having a share capital other than—
(i) an open-ended investment company, within the meaning given by section 236 of the Financial Services and Markets Act 2000,
(ii) a UCITS,
(iii) an industrial and provident society, or
(iv) a body corporate which is a 51 per cent. subsidiary of any industrial and provident society; ''deposit-taker'' has the meaning given by section 481(2) of the Taxes Act;

"the Director of Savings" has the same meaning as in the National Debt Act 1972;

"the Distance Marketing Directive" means Directive 2002/65/EC of the European Parliament and of the Council of 23rd September 2002, and includes any provisions by which an EEA State or the United Kingdom has transposed the Directive or has corresponding obligations in its domestic law, and "distance contract" has the meaning in that Directive;

"electronic communications" includes any communications by means of a telecommunication system (within the meaning in the Telecommunications Act 1984);

"EEA Agreement" means the Agreement on the European Economic Area signed at Oporto on 2nd May 1992, as adjusted by the Protocol signed at Brussels on 17th March 1993;

"EEA State" means a State, other than the United Kingdom, which is a Contracting Party to the EEA Agreement;

"European institution" means an EEA firm of the kind mentioned in paragraph 5(*a*), (*b*) or (*c*) of Schedule 3 to the Financial Services and Markets Act 2000 which is an authorised person for the purposes of that Act as a result of qualifying for authorisation under paragraph 12 of that Schedule;

"51 per cent. subsidiary" and "75 per cent. subsidiary" have the meanings given by section 838 of the Taxes Act;

"gains", except in regulations 22(1) to (3), 24(*a*)(ii), (iii) and (v), 37(5) and 38, means "chargeable gains" within the meaning in the 1992 Act;

"gilt-edged securities" has the meaning given by paragraphs 1 and 1A of Schedule 9 to the 1992 Act;

"incorporated friendly society" means a society incorporated under the Friendly Societies Act 1992;

"industrial and provident society" means a society registered or deemed to be registered under the Industrial and Provident Societies Act 1965 or under the Industrial and Provident Societies (Northern Ireland) Act 1969;

"investments under the account" has the same meaning as investments under a child trust fund in the Act; "investment trust" has the meaning given by section 842 of the Taxes Act, and references to the "eligible rental income" of an investment trust have the same meaning as in that section;

"the Management Act" means the Taxes Management Act 1970;

"market value" shall be construed in accordance with section 272 of the 1992 Act;

"the 1992 Act" means the Taxation of Chargeable Gains Act 1992;

"notice", except in regulations 12(12) and 37(6)(*a*), means notice in writing;

"recognised stock exchange" has the same meaning as in section 841 of the Taxes Act;

"registered friendly society" has the meaning given by the Friendly Societies Act 1992 and includes any society that by virtue of section 96(2) of that Act is to be treated as a registered friendly society;

"relevant authorised person" has the same meaning as in section 333A(12) of the Taxes Act;

"relevant European institution" has the meaning given by section 326A(10) of the Taxes Act;

"security", means any loan stock or similar security of a company whether secured or unsecured;

"subscriptions" has the meaning in section 12(1) of the Act (but excluding Inland Revenue contributions and income or gains arising from investments under the account);

"tax" where neither income tax nor capital gains tax is specified means either of those taxes;

"the Taxes Act" means the Income and Corporation Taxes Act 1988;

"year", except in the expression "subscription year" in regulations 9, 21(5)(*b*) and 32(2)(*b*)(iv), means a year of assessment (within the meaning in section 832(1) of the Taxes Act, or section 288(1) of the 1992 Act, as the case may be);

(*c*) "authorised fund" means—

(i) an authorised unit trust, or

(ii) an open-ended investment company with variable capital incorporated in the United Kingdom in the case of which an authorisation order made by the Financial Services Authority under regulation 14 of the Open-Ended Investment Companies Regulations 2001 is in force;

"authorised unit trust" means a unit trust scheme in the case of which an authorisation order made by the Financial Services Authority under section 243 of the Financial Services and Markets Act 2000 is in force;

"the Collective Investment Schemes Sourcebook" means the sourcebook of that name made by the Financial Services Authority under the Financial Services and Markets Act 2000;

"depositary interest" means the rights of the person mentioned in paragraph (ii), under a certificate or other record (whether or not in the form of a document) acknowledging—

(i) that a person holds relevant investments or evidence of the right to them; and

(ii) that another person is entitled to rights in or in relation to those or identical relevant investments, including the right to receive such investments, or evidence of the right to them or the proceeds from such investments, from the person mentioned in paragraph (*i*), where "relevant investments" means investments which are exclusively qualifying investments for an account falling within regulation 12(2)(*a*) to (*i*), and the rights mentioned in paragraph (ii) are exclusively rights in or in relation to relevant investments;

"fund of funds scheme" means—

(i) an authorised fund which according to the terms of the scheme is a fund of funds scheme belonging to the category under that name established by the Financial Services Authority; and

(ii) a part of an umbrella scheme which the terms of the scheme identify as a part that would belong to that category if it were itself an authorised fund;

''money market scheme'' means—

(i) an authorised fund which according to terms of the scheme is a money market scheme belonging to the category under that name established by the Financial Services Authority; and

(ii) a part of an umbrella scheme which the terms of the scheme identify as a part that would belong to that category if it were itself an authorised fund;

''open-ended investment company'', except in sub-paragraph (*a*), has the meaning given by subsection (10) of section 468 of the Taxes Act as that subsection is added in relation to open-ended investment companies by regulation 10(4) of the 1997 Regulations, and ''shares'' in relation to an open-ended investment company, includes shares of any class and of any denomination of a given class and, in relation to a part of an umbrella company, means shares in the company which confer for the time being rights in that part; ''securities scheme'' means—

(i) an authorised fund which according to the terms of the scheme is a securities scheme belonging to the category under that name established by the Financial Services Authority, and

(ii) a part of an umbrella scheme which the terms of the scheme identify as a part which would belong to that category if it were itself an authorised fund;

''the 1997 Regulations'' means the Open-ended Investment Companies (Tax) Regulations 1997;

''UCITS'' means undertakings for collective investment in transferable securities within the meaning of Article 1 of Council Directive 85/611; ''umbrella scheme'' means an authorised fund which according to the terms of the scheme is an umbrella scheme belonging to the category under that name established by the Financial Services Authority, and

(i) in the case of an authorised fund which is an authorised unit trust, references to a part of an umbrella scheme shall be construed in accordance with subsection (8) of section 468 of the Taxes Act, and, in relation to a part of an umbrella scheme, references to investments subject to the trusts of an authorised unit trust and to a unit holder shall be construed in accordance with subsection (9) of that section, and

(ii) in the case of an authorised fund which is an open-ended investment company, references to a part of an umbrella scheme shall be construed in accordance with subsection (18) of section 468 of the Taxes Act as that subsection is added in relation to open-ended investment companies by regulation 10(4) of the 1997 Regulations, and, in relation to a part of an umbrella scheme, references to investments of the company shall be construed in accordance with subsection (12) of that section as so added;

''unit holder'', except in relation to a part of an umbrella scheme, has the meaning given by subsection (6) of section 468 of the Taxes Act;

''unit trust scheme'' has the meaning given by subsection (6) of section 468 of the Taxes Act;

''units'', in relation to an authorised unit trust, means the rights or interests (however described) of the unit holders in that unit trust and, in relation to a part of an umbrella scheme, means the rights or interests for the time being of the unit holders in that part;

''warrant scheme'' means—

(i) an authorised fund which according to the terms of the scheme is a warrant scheme belonging to the category under that name established by the Financial Services Authority, and

(ii) a part of an umbrella scheme which the terms of the scheme identify as a part that would belong to that category if it were itself an authorised fund.

(2) The table below indexes other definitions in these Regulations:

Term defined	Regulation
''the applicant''	5
''the commencement date''	7(8)
''description'' of an account	4
''the disqualifying circumstances''	16
''first return period''	30(1)
''fortnightly period''	30(1)
''initial contribution''	7(1)
''interim tax claim''	26(2)
''local authority''	33(1)
''looked after child''	33(1)
''management agreement''	5
''the named child''	5 and 8(1)
''qualifying circumstances''	14
''qualifying investments for an account''	12
''registered contact''	8(1)(*d*)

"second return period"	30(1)
"special contribution"	7(1)
"subscription year"	9(2)
"supplementary contribution"	7(5)
the "termination event"	12(12)
"the transfer instructions"	8(2)(*h*)
"the internal transfer instructions"	8(2)(i)

Vouchers

3—(1) The voucher to be issued under section 5(1) of the Act shall contain the following particulars—

(*a*) the full name of the child,
(*b*) his date of birth,
(*c*) his unique reference number,
(*d*) the expiry date of the voucher, and
(*e*) the amount of the initial contribution (see regulation 7(1)), and a statement that the voucher cannot be exchanged for money.

(2) The voucher shall be sent to the person who is entitled to child benefit in respect of the child (or, in the case of a child who is an eligible child because of section 2(3) of the Act, to a responsible person in relation to the child) by post.

(3) The expiry date (when the voucher shall cease to be valid) shall be whichever is the earlier of—

(*a*) the date 12 months from the date of issue of the voucher, or
(*b*) where the child is over 17 years of age, the date on which he will attain the age of 18 years.

Descriptions of accounts

4—(1) An account may be of either of the following descriptions—

Stakeholder account

Where the account meets the characteristics and conditions in the Schedule to these Regulations.

Non-stakeholder account

Where any of those characteristics or conditions is not met.

(2) Accounts opened by the Inland Revenue (see regulation 6) must be stakeholder accounts.

Opening of account by responsible person or the child

5—(1) For the purposes of these Regulations, subject to paragraph (2), an account is opened for a child ("the named child") with an account provider on the date the last of the following conditions is satisfied (in any order), where "the applicant" means—

(*a*) if the named child is 16 or over, the child; and
(*b*) in any other case, a responsible person in relation to the named child—

Condition 1

The applicant gives the voucher relating to the named child to the account provider.

Condition 2

The applicant enters into an agreement with the account provider (the "management agreement") for the management of the account (see regulation 8(1) and (2)), which includes the application and declaration required by regulation 13.

Condition 3

Where that application is not in writing the applicant has agreed, or is treated as having agreed, the contents of the copy of the declaration required by regulation 13(3).

Condition 4

(*a*) In any case where the management agreement is a distance contract, the agreement must be an initial service agreement for the purposes of the Distance Marketing Directive, and contain the instructions required by regulation 8(1)(*f*), and
(*b*) in every case where there is any right to cancel (or automatic cancellation of) the management agreement, the period during which it may be exercised or occur has expired without that right being exercised or cancellation occurring.

(2) An account must satisfy the requirements that—

(*a*) no subscription to the account is accepted by the account provider until the account has been opened in accordance with paragraph (1); and
(*b*) where the account is so opened before the appointed day, it shall not be treated as open for the purpose of accepting subscriptions until the appointed day.

Opening of account by Inland Revenue—(Revenue allocated accounts)

6—(1) The Board shall apply to open an account for a child to whom section 6 of the Act applies, by forwarding to an account provider the particulars which would be required for a voucher (see regulation 3), but omitting paragraph (1)(*d*) of that regulation.

(2) The account provider shall immediately open a stakeholder account in the name of the child, which shall have the same effect as if a responsible person for the child (or the child if aged 16 or over) had entered into the account provider's standard management agreement for the stakeholder account in question, including the terms mentioned in Condition 2 of regulation 5(1) (but treating the reference to the application and declaration required by regulation 13 as a reference to the authorisation required by regulation 13(4)) and regulation 8(1)(*f*).

(3) The Inland Revenue shall maintain (and update from time to time) a list of account providers who have agreed to accept Revenue allocated accounts under this regulation, in the order of the date of their agreement, and the account provider shall be selected in rotation from the current list.

(4) Where the account provider offers two or more types of stakeholder account, the account to be opened shall be chosen by the account provider in rotation between those types.

Government contributions

7—(1) The amounts of the contribution for the purposes of section 8(1) of the Act are set out in paragraphs (2) to (4), (the amounts set out in paragraphs (2) and (4)(*a*) to be known as the "initial contribution", and the amounts set out in paragraphs (3) and (4)(*b*) as the "special contribution").

(2) Where the child is an eligible child on the appointed day by virtue of section 2(1)(*a*) of the Act (by reason of a child benefit award), and—

(i) was born after 31st August 2002 but before 6th April 2003, the amount is £277,
(ii) was born between 6th April 2003 and 5th April 2004, the amount is £268, and
(iii) was born between 6th April 2004 and the day preceding the appointed day, the amount is £256.

(3) Where the child is an eligible child on the appointed day by virtue of section 2(1)(*b*) of the Act (by reason of being a child in the care of a local authority at that date) and—

(i) was born after 31st August 2002 but before 6th April 2003, the amount is £554,
(ii) was born between 6th April 2003 and 5th April 2004, the amount is £536, and
(iii) was born between 6th April 2004 and the day preceding the appointed day, the amount is £512.

(4) Where the child is born on or after the appointed day and—

(*a*) is first an eligible child by virtue of section 2(1)(*a*) of the Act, the amount is £250, and
(*b*) is first an eligible child by virtue of section 2(1)(*b*) of the Act, the amount is £500.

(5) The amounts of the supplementary contribution for the purposes of section 9(2) of the Act (to be known as the "supplementary contribution") are set out in paragraphs (6) and (7).

(6) Where the child is an eligible child on the appointed day (and is a child to whom section 9 of the Act applies), the amount—

(*a*) if the commencement date was after 31st August 2002 but before 6th April 2003, is £266,
(*b*) if the commencement date was between 6th April 2003 and 5th April 2004, is £258,
(*c*) if the commencement date was between 6th April 2004 and the appointed day, is £250.

(7) Where the child becomes an eligible child after the appointed day (and is a child to whom section 9 of the Act applies), the amount is £250.

(8) The "commencement date", in relation to a child, means the first day for which child benefit was paid (under a decision mentioned in section 2(6) of the Act) in respect of the child, except that—

(*a*) where entitlement to child benefit is wholly excluded by a directly applicable Community provision, it means the date on which that exclusion took effect, and
(*b*) where the child was prevented from being an eligible child by virtue of section 2(5) of the Act, it means the date on which the child became an eligible child.

PART 2

OTHER REQUIREMENTS TO BE SATISFIED IN RELATION TO ACCOUNTS

General requirements for accounts

8—(1) An account must satisfy the requirements that—

(*a*) it is the account for a single child ("the named child");
(*b*) the named child is or has been an eligible child;
(*c*) no child may hold more than one account;
(*d*) at any time—

(i) where the named child is under 16, only a single responsible person in relation to the named child, or

(ii) where the named child is 16 or over, only the child, (''the registered contact'') may give instructions to the account provider with respect to its management;

(*e*) the account must at all times be managed in accordance with these Regulations by an account provider and, subject to regulation 6(2), under terms agreed and recorded in a management agreement made between the account provider and the registered contact (on behalf of the named child where appropriate); and

(*f*) the management agreement must include instructions to the provider as to the manner in which Inland Revenue contributions and any subscriptions made are to be invested under the account.

(2) Apart from other requirements of these Regulations the terms so agreed shall include the conditions that—

(*a*) the account investments shall be in the beneficial ownership of the named child;

(*b*) the title to all account investments, except those falling within regulation 12(2)(*k*), (*l*) or (*m*), shall be vested in the account provider or his nominee, subject to sub-paragraph (*f*);

(*c*) where a share certificate or other document evidencing title to an account investment is issued, it shall be held by the account provider or as he may direct, subject to sub- paragraph (*f*);

(*d*) in relation to qualifying investments falling within regulation 12(2)(*a*), (*b*) and (*f*) to (*j*), the account provider shall, if the registered contact so elects (and subject to any charge for the arrangement), arrange for the registered contact to receive a copy of the annual report and accounts issued to investors by every company, unit trust, open-ended investment company or other entity in which account investments are held;

(*e*) in relation to qualifying investments falling within regulation 12(2)(*a*), (*b*) and (*f*) to (*j*), the account provider shall, if the registered contact so elects (subject to any charge for the arrangement, and to any provisions made under any enactment), be under an obligation to arrange for the registered contact to be able—

(i) to attend any meetings of investors in companies, unit trusts, open-ended investment companies and other entities in which account investments are held,

(ii) to vote, and

(iii) to receive, in addition to the documents referred to in sub-paragraph (*d*), any other information issued to investors in such companies, unit trusts, open-ended investment companies and other entities;

(*f*) if and so long as a person falling within regulation 14(2)(*d*)(iv) acts as account provider of an account, and the account investments include a policy of life insurance—

(i) the title to all such policies shall be vested in the registered contact, and

(ii) where a policy document or other document evidencing title to such policies of life insurance is issued, it shall be held by the registered contact;

(*g*) the account provider shall satisfy himself that any person to whom he delegates any of his functions or responsibilities under the management agreement is competent to carry out those functions or responsibilities;

(*h*) on the instructions of the registered contact (''the transfer instructions'') and within such time as is stipulated by the registered contact in the transfer instructions, the whole of an account, with all rights and obligations of the parties to it, shall be transferred free of expense (except any incidental expenses) to another account provider subject to and in accordance with regulation 21;

(*i*) where the account provider offers accounts of another description or type, on the instructions of the registered contact (''the internal transfer instructions'') and within such time as is stipulated by the registered contact in the internal transfer instructions, the account shall become (free of expense, except any incidental expenses) an account of that other description or type (any necessary change in the investments being made accordingly); and

(*j*) the account provider shall notify the registered contact if by reason of any failure to satisfy the provisions of these Regulations an account is or will become no longer exempt from tax by virtue of regulation 24.

(3) Where the transfer instructions or internal transfer instructions, or any new management agreement entered into by the registered contact with the account provider (or a new account provider) under regulation 8(1)(*e*), is a distance contract, the transfer or internal transfer shall only take effect once those contracts satisfy Condition 4 in regulation 5(1).

(4) The time stipulated in transfer instructions or internal transfer instructions shall be subject to any reasonable business period (not exceeding 30 days) of the account provider required for the practical implementation of the instructions.

(5) In this regulation, ''incidental expenses'' means stamp duty and other dealing costs of disposing of or acquiring investments.

Annual limit on subscriptions

9—(1) Any person (including the child) may make subscriptions to a child's account, subject to paragraphs (2) and (3).

(2) Subscriptions to an account made during any subscription year, that is—

(*a*) the period beginning with the day on which the account is opened (or if opened before the appointed day, opened for the purpose of accepting subscriptions under regulation 5(2)(*b*)), and ending immediately before the child's next birthday, and

(*b*) any succeeding period of twelve months, shall not in aggregate exceed the sum of £1,200.

(3) Where the aggregate of subscriptions in any year falls short of £1,200 or is nil, there shall be no addition to the amount for any succeeding year.

Statements for an account

10—(1) The account provider must issue a statement for the account—

(*a*) annually, and

(*b*) where an account is transferred to another account provider under regulation 21, as at the transfer date.

(2) The statement date in the case of an annual statement must be—

(*a*) any date not more than 60 days before or after the named child's birthday, and

(*b*) not more than 12 months from the previous statement date.

(3) The statement shall be sent—

(*a*) where the named child is the registered contact, to the child,

(*b*) where a responsible person is the registered contact, to the named child care of the registered contact,

(*c*) where the Official Solicitor or Accountant of Court has been appointed under section 3(10) of the Act, to the Official Solicitor or Accountant of Court, on behalf of the child, and

(*d*) in any other case, to the named child, within 30 days of the statement date.

(4) Statements shall include the following information—

(*a*) the full name of the child;

(*b*) his address;

(*c*) his date of birth;

(*d*) his unique reference number;

(*e*) the description of the account (see regulation 4);

(*f*) the name of the registered contact (if any);

(*g*) the statement date;

(*h*) the total market value of the investments under the account at the previous statement date (where the account provider held the account at the named child's previous birthday);

(*i*) the amount of any Government contributions claimed by the account provider under regulation 30, during the period between—

(i) the previous statement date referred to in paragraph (1)(*a*) or (*b*), or the opening of the account (whichever is the later), and

(ii) the statement date;

(*j*) the aggregate amount of subscriptions (if any) received during the period in sub- paragraph (*i*);

(*k*) the total amount of deductions (including management charges) made during the period in sub-paragraph (*i*);

(*l*) the total market value of the investments under the account at the statement date;

(*m*) the number or amount, description and market value of each of the investments under the account at the statement date;

(*n*) the basis used in calculating the market value of each investment under the account (together with a statement of any change from a basis used in the previous statement); and

(*o*) the exchange rate used where any investment is, or is denominated in, a currency other than sterling.

General investment rules

11—(1) All transactions by way of purchase by an account provider of investments under an account shall be made—

(*a*) in the case of an authorised fund which is a dual priced unit trust, at the manager's price for the sale of the relevant class of units within the meaning of, and complying with the requirements of, rule 15.4.4 of the Collective Investment Schemes Sourcebook;

(*b*) in the case of an authorised fund which is a single priced unit trust or an open-ended investment company, at the price of a unit or share within the meaning of, and complying with the requirements of, rule 4.3.11 of the Collective Investment Schemes Sourcebook; and

(*c*) in the case of all other account investments, at the price for which those investments might reasonably be expected to be purchased in the open market.

(2) In paragraph (1)—

"a dual priced unit trust" means an authorised unit trust in respect of which the manager gives different prices for buying and selling units at the same time;

"a single priced unit trust" means an authorised unit trust in respect of which the manager gives the same price for buying and selling units at the same time.

(3) All other transactions by way of sale or otherwise by an account provider in investments under an account shall be made at the price for which those investments might reasonably be expected to be sold or otherwise transacted, as the case may be, in the open market.

(4) Investments, or rights in respect of investments, may not at any time—

(*a*) be purchased or made otherwise than out of cash which an account provider holds under an account at that time; or

(*b*) be purchased from—

(i) the named child, or

(ii) the spouse of the named child, so as to become account investments under the account.

(5) Subject to paragraph (6), contributions, subscriptions and any other cash held by an account provider under an account shall be held only in sterling and be deposited in an account with a deposit-taker, or a deposit account or a share account with a building society, which is designated as a CTF account for the purposes of these Regulations only.

(6) An account provider who is a European institution, a relevant authorised person or an assurance undertaking may hold an account investor's cash subscription and other cash held under an account in the currency of the EEA State in which he has his principal place of business and may deposit such cash in an account, which is designated as mentioned in paragraph (5), with any person authorised under the law of that State to accept deposits.

Qualifying investments for an account

12—(1) This regulation specifies the kind of investments (''qualifying investments for an account'') which may be purchased, made or held under an account.

(2) Qualifying investments for an account to which paragraph (1) refers are—

(*a*) shares, not being shares in an investment trust, issued by a company wherever incorporated and officially listed on a recognised stock exchange (see paragraph (3));

(*b*) securities—

(i) issued by a company wherever incorporated,

(ii) which satisfy at least one of the conditions specified in paragraph (5), and

(iii) in the case of securities of an investment trust, purchased or acquired by the account provider in circumstances where the investment trust satisfies the condition specified in paragraph (6);

(*c*) gilt-edged securities;

(*d*) any securities issued by or on behalf of a government of any EEA State;

(*e*) any securities which, in relation to a security mentioned in sub-paragraph (*d*), would be a strip of that security if ''strip'' had the same meaning as in section 47 of the Finance Act 1942, with the omission of the words ''issued under the National Loans Act 1968'';

(*f*) shares in an investment trust, listed in the Official List of the Stock Exchange (see paragraph (3)), in circumstances where the trust satisfies the condition specified in paragraph (6);

(*g*) units in, or shares of, a securities scheme, warrant scheme or fund of funds scheme;

(*h*) units in, or shares of, a money market scheme;

(*i*) units in, or shares of, a UCITS;

(*j*) a depositary interest;

(*k*) cash deposited in a deposit account with a building society, or a person falling within section 840A(1)(*b*) of the Taxes Act or a relevant European institution, subject to paragraph (8);

(*l*) cash deposited in a share account with a building society, subject to paragraph (8);

(*m*) policies of life insurance which satisfy the conditions specified in paragraphs (9) and (10);

(*n*) any securities issued under the National Loans Act 1968—

(i) for the purpose of or in connection with raising money under the auspices of the Director of Savings within the meaning of section 11(1)(*a*) of the National Debt Act 1972, and

(ii) other than national savings certificates, premium savings bonds, national savings stamps and national savings gift tokens,

which, according to the terms and conditions subject to which they are issued and purchased, are expressly permitted to be held under an account.

(3) An investment in shares fulfils the condition as to official listing in paragraph (2)(*a*) or (*f*) if—

(*a*) in pursuance of a public offer, the account provider applies for the allotment or allocation to him of shares in a company or investment trust which are due to be admitted to such listing within 30 days of the allocation or allotment, and which, when admitted to such listing, would be qualifying investments for an account, and

(*b*) the shares are not allotted or allocated to the account provider in the circumstances specified in paragraph (4).

(4) The circumstances specified in this paragraph are where—

(*a*) the allotment or allocation of the shares was connected with the allotment or allocation of—

(i) shares in the company or investment trust of a different class, or

(ii) rights to shares in the company or investment trust of a different class, or

(iii) shares or rights to shares in another company or investment trust, or

(iv) units in or shares in, or rights to units in or shares in, an authorised fund or a part of an umbrella scheme, or

(v) securities or rights to securities of the company or investment trust, or of another company or investment trust, to the account provider, the registered contact or any other person; and

(*b*) the terms on which the first-mentioned shares in this paragraph were offered were significantly more favourable to the account provider or the named child than they would have been if their allotment or allocation had not been connected as described in sub-paragraph (*a*).

(5) The conditions specified in this paragraph are—

(*a*) that the shares in the company issuing the securities are listed on the official list of a recognised stock exchange;

(*b*) that the securities are so listed;

(*c*) that the company issuing the securities is a 75 per cent. subsidiary of a company whose shares are so listed.

(6) The condition specified in this paragraph is that the investment trust has no eligible rental income, in its most recent accounting period to end before the date on which the shares in, or securities of, the investment trust first become investments under the account, provided that the shares or securities shall cease to be qualifying investments for an account if the investment trust has any eligible rental income, in subsequent accounting periods, during which the shares or securities are held.

(7) In paragraph (4)(*a*), ''company'' means any body corporate having a share capital.

(8) A deposit account or share account which is a qualifying investment for an account falling within paragraph (2)(*k*) or (*l*) must not be connected with any other investment, held by the named child or any other person, and for this purpose such an account is connected with an investment if—

(*a*) either was opened or acquired with reference to the other, or with a view to enabling the other to be opened or acquired on particular terms, or with a view to facilitating the opening or acquisition of the other on particular terms, and

(*b*) the terms on which the account was opened would have been significantly less favourable to the holder if the investment had not been acquired.

(9) The conditions specified in this paragraph are that—

(*a*) the insurance is on the life of the named child only;

(*b*) the terms and conditions of the policy provide—

(i) that the policy may only be owned or held as a qualifying investment for an account which satisfies the provisions of these Regulations;

(ii) that the policy shall automatically terminate if it comes to the notice of the account provider, in any manner, that the event specified in paragraph (11) has occurred in relation to the policy;

(iii) for an express prohibition of any payment of the proceeds from the termination of the policy or a partial surrender of the rights conferred by the policy, to the named child (while he is still a child); and

(iv) that the policy, the rights conferred by the policy and any share or interest in the policy or rights respectively, shall not be capable of assignment or (in Scotland) assignation, other than that they may be vested in the named child's personal representatives, and that the title to the policy may be transferred to a new account provider subject to and in accordance with regulations 8(2)(*f*) and 21;

(*c*) the policy evidences or secures a contract of insurance which—

(i) falls within paragraph 1 or 3 of Part 2 of Schedule 1 to the Financial Services and Markets Act 2000 (Regulated Activities) Order 2001, or

(ii) would fall within either of those paragraphs if the insurer were a company with permission under Part 4 of the Financial Services and Markets Act 2000 to effect or carry out contracts of insurance;

(*d*) the policy is not—

(i) a contract to pay an annuity on human life,

(ii) a personal portfolio bond within the meaning given by regulation 2(1) of the Personal Portfolio Bonds (Tax) Regulations 1999, or

(iii) a contract, the effecting and carrying out of which constitutes ''pension business'' within the meaning given by section 431B(1) of the Taxes Act; and

(*e*) after the first payment in respect of a premium in relation to the policy has been made, there is no contractual obligation on any person to make any other such payment.

(10) The condition specified in this paragraph is that no sum may at any time, at or after the making of the insurance, be lent to or at the direction of the named child or registered contact by or by arrangement with the insurer for the time being responsible for the obligations under the policy.

(11) The event specified in this paragraph is that—

(*a*) there has been a breach of any of the conditions in paragraph (9) or (10), or any of those conditions was not satisfied at the date on which the insurance was made; and

(*b*) the breach or non-compliance cannot be remedied in accordance with regulation 23, or (in any other case), has not been remedied within a reasonable time.

(12) Where the event specified in paragraph (11) occurs in relation to a policy, the policy shall nevertheless be treated, for the purposes of these Regulations, excepting paragraphs (9)(*b*)(ii) and (11), and regulations 37(6) and 38, as if it had satisfied the conditions in paragraphs (9) and (10) during the period—

(*a*) commencing at the time when that specified event occurred, and

(*b*) ending immediately before—

(i) the end of the final year in relation to the policy, within the meaning in section 546(4) of the Taxes Act, or

(ii) the time at which that specified event came to the notice of the account provider, whichever first occurs (the "termination event").

Conditions for application by responsible person or the child to open an account (and changes to an account)

13—(1) An application by a responsible person in relation to a child or the child if 16 or over, as the case may be, ("the applicant") to open an account for the child with an account provider must be made to the account provider in a statement which must satisfy the conditions specified in paragraphs (2) to (6).

(2) An application must specify the description of account applied for.

(3) An application must incorporate a declaration by the applicant that he—

(*a*) is aged 16 years of age or over,

(*b*) is—

(i) (where the child is under 16) a responsible person in relation to the named child (that is, that he has parental responsibility in relation to the child), or

(ii) the child if 16 or over, and

(*c*) is to be the registered contact for the account; and where the application is not in writing, must authorise the account provider to record the terms of the declaration in a written declaration made on behalf of the applicant.

(4) The applicant must authorise the account provider (on behalf of the named child where appropriate)—

(*a*) to hold the child's Inland Revenue contributions, subscriptions, account investments, interest, dividends and any other rights or proceeds in respect of those investments and cash, and

(*b*) to make on his behalf any claims to relief from tax in respect of account investments, and the authority must continue until a further application and declaration is made in accordance with paragraph (10).

(5) An application must contain—

(*a*) the applicant's full name,

(*b*) his address, including postcode,

(*c*) the named child's full name,

(*d*) his address, including postcode, and

(*e*) the child's unique reference number on the voucher.

(6) There may be only one declaration and authorisation under paragraphs (3) to (5) in force for an account at any time.

(7) Except in the case—

(*a*) of the death or incapacity of the registered contact,

(*b*) where the registered contact cannot be contacted,

(*c*) of the bringing to an end of a Court order, under which he is a responsible person for the named child,

(*d*) of the named child attaining the age of 16 years,

(*e*) where the Official Solicitor or Accountant of Court is appointed under section 3(10) of the Act, or

(*f*) where a Court so orders, any change in the identity of the registered contact shall require confirmation by the current registered contact that his declaration and authorisation under paragraphs (3)(*c*) and (4) is cancelled.

(8) An account provider must decline to accept an application if he has reason to believe that—

(*a*) the voucher has expired, or is not or might not be genuine, or

(*b*) the applicant has given untrue information in his application.

(9) Where the application is not in writing, the account provider shall make the written declaration referred to in paragraph (3), and notify the applicant of its contents, and such declaration shall take effect from the date on which the applicant agrees the contents (subject to any corrections), and if he neither agrees or disagrees with the contents within 30 days, he shall be treated as having agreed them.

(10) Where—

(*a*) there is a change in the identity of the registered contact, the new registered contact, or (*b*) an account has been opened by the Inland Revenue under regulation 6 (Revenue allocated accounts) and a responsible person in relation to the child (or the child, if 16 or over) subsequently applies to the account provider to be the registered contact for the account, he, shall make the application and declaration required by paragraphs (3) to (5).

Account provider – qualifications and Board's approval

14—(1) This regulation specifies the circumstances ("qualifying circumstances") in which a person may be approved by the Board as an account provider.

(2) The qualifying circumstances are the following—

(*a*) the person must make an application to the Board for approval in a form specified by the Board;

(*b*) the person must undertake with the Board—

(i) to either offer stakeholder accounts to the general public (whether or not accounts of another description are offered), or to fulfil the requirements in paragraph (3),

(ii) to accept vouchers from any responsible person or the child if 16 or over (subject to regulation 13(8)),

(iii) where the person accepts Revenue allocated accounts, to allow instructions for their management to be made or given by post (whether or not other methods are allowed),

(iv) to publicise (and up-date where appropriate) statements of the minimum amount which may be subscribed to an account on a single occasion, and the permitted means of payment of subscriptions,

(v) to inform persons proposing to make subscriptions to an account (other than the named child) that the subscription is a gift to the child,

(vi) to publicise (and up-date where appropriate) statements of the extent to which social, environmental or ethical decisions are taken into account in selecting, retaining or realising investments,

(vii) that a child's unique reference number shall only be used for the purposes of the child's account (and of fulfilling the requirements of these Regulations with regard to that account), and

(viii) that whether there is an initial contribution or special contribution to an account, whether there is a supplementary contribution to the account, and whether the account is a Revenue allocated account is information held for the purposes mentioned in paragraph (vii) only, and shall not be used for other purposes (including marketing other products);

(*c*) the person must demonstrate to the satisfaction of the Board that the person can correctly operate the procedures in regulation 30;

(*d*) an account provider must be—

(i) an authorised person within the meaning of section 31(1)(*a*) or (*c*) of, or Schedule 5 to, the Financial Services and Markets Act 2000, who has permission to carry on one or more of the activities specified in Articles 14, 21, 25, 37, 40, 45, 51, 53 and (in so far as it applies to any of those activities) 64 of the Financial Services and Markets Act 2000 (Regulated Activities) Order 2001, but excluding any person falling within paragraph (iv) below;

(ii) a European institution which carries on one or more of those activities;

(iii) a building society, a person falling within section 840A(1)(*b*) of the Taxes Act or a relevant European institution; or

(iv) an insurance company within the meaning given by section 431(2) of the Taxes Act, an incorporated friendly society or a registered friendly society, or any other assurance undertaking;

(*e*) an account provider must not be prevented from acting as such by any requirement imposed under section 43 of the Financial Services and Markets Act 2000, or by any prohibition imposed by or under any rules made by the Financial Services Authority under that Act; and

(*f*) an account provider who—

(i) is a European institution or a relevant authorised person and who does not have a branch or business establishment in the United Kingdom, or has such a branch or business establishment but does not intend to carry out all his functions as an account provider at that branch or business establishment, or

(ii) falls within the expression "any other assurance undertaking" in sub-paragraph (*d*)(iv),

must fulfil one of the three requirements specified in regulation 15.

(3) The requirements in this paragraph are that the person provides to any potential applicant for a child trust fund (prior to discussing any application under regulation 13)—

(*a*) a statement that a stakeholder account is available from a named alternative account provider who offers it on the terms in paragraph (2)(*b*)(*i*) (omitting the words from ", or to" to the end);

(*b*) a detailed description of that stakeholder account; and

(*c*) sufficient information (according to the method of communication used, and including documentation where appropriate) to put the potential applicant in the position to make an application to that alternative account provider, complying with regulation 13.

(4) The terms of the Board's approval may include conditions designed to ensure that the provisions of these Regulations are satisfied.

Account provider—appointment of tax representative

15—(1) This regulation specifies the requirements mentioned in regulation 14(2)(*f*).

(2) The first requirement specified in this regulation is that—

(*a*) a person who falls within subsection (5) of section 333A of the Taxes Act is for the time being appointed by the account provider to be responsible for securing the discharge of the duties prescribed by paragraph (5) which fall to be discharged by the account provider, and

(*b*) his identity and the fact of his appointment have been notified to the Board by the account provider.

(3) The second requirement specified in this regulation is that there are for the time being other arrangements with the Board for a person other than the account provider to secure the discharge of such duties.

(4) The third requirement specified in this regulation is that there are for the time being other arrangements with the Board designed to secure the discharge of such duties.

(5) The duties prescribed by this paragraph are those that fall to be discharged by an account provider under these Regulations.

(6) The appointment of a person in pursuance of the first requirement shall be treated as terminated in circumstances where—

(*a*) the Board have reason to believe that the person concerned—

(i) has failed to secure the discharge of any of the duties prescribed by paragraph (5), or

(ii) does not have adequate resources to discharge those duties, and

(*b*) the Board have notified the account provider and that person that they propose to treat his appointment as having terminated with effect from the date specified in the notice.

(7) Where, in accordance with the first requirement, a person is at any time responsible for securing the discharge of duties, the person concerned—

(*a*) shall be entitled to act on the account provider's behalf for any of the purposes of the provisions relating to the duties;

(*b*) shall secure (where appropriate by acting on the account provider's behalf) the account provider's compliance with and discharge of the duties; and

(*c*) shall be personally liable in respect of any failure of the account provider to comply with or discharge any such duty as if the duties imposed on the account provider were imposed jointly and severally on the account provider and the person concerned.

Account provider—withdrawal by Board of approval

16—(1) This regulation specifies the circumstances ("the disqualifying circumstances") in which the Board may by notice withdraw their approval of a person as an account provider in relation to an account.

(2) The disqualifying circumstances are that the Board have reason to believe—

(*a*) that any provision of the Act or these Regulations, or any term of an undertaking given in accordance with regulation 14(2)(*b*) or condition under regulation 14(4), is not or at any time has not been satisfied, either in respect of an account managed by the account provider or otherwise; or

(*b*) that a person to whom they have given approval to act as an account provider is not qualified so to act.

(3) The notice to which paragraph (1) refers shall specify—

(*a*) the date from which the Board's approval is withdrawn; and

(*b*) the disqualifying circumstances.

Account provider—appeal against non-approval or withdrawal of Board's approval

17 A person who has been notified of a decision by the Board not to approve that person as an account provider, or an account provider to whom notice of withdrawal of approval has been given under regulation 16, may appeal against the decision by notice given to the Board within 30 days after the date of the notification or notice.

Permitted withdrawals from an account

18 Withdrawals from an account before the date on which the named child attains the age of 18 years may only be made—

(*a*) by the account provider, to settle any management charges and other incidental expenses, which are due by or under the management agreement, or

(*b*) where the account provider is satisfied that the named child has died under that age.

Account provider ceasing to act (or ceasing to accept Revenue allocated accounts)

19—(1) A person shall give notice to the Board and to the registered contact of the account which he manages (or, if there is no registered contact, the named child) of his intention to cease to act as the account provider not less than 30 days before he so ceases so that his obligations to the Board under the account can be conveniently discharged at or about the time he ceases so to act, and the notice to the registered contact or the named child shall inform him of the right to transfer the account under regulation 21, and of his rights under regulation 20(3).

(2) A person shall also give notice to the Board of his intention to cease to accept further Revenue allocated accounts under regulation 6, not less than 30 days before he so ceases.

Account provider ceasing to qualify

20—(1) A person shall cease to qualify as an account provider and shall notify the Board within 30 days of the relevant event in sub-paragraphs (*a*) to (*f*), of that relevant event, where—

(*a*) the person no longer fulfils the conditions of regulation 14;

(*b*) in the case of an individual, he becomes bankrupt, or the subject of a bankruptcy restrictions order or an interim bankruptcy restrictions order or, in Scotland, his estate is sequestrated;

(*c*) he makes any arrangement or composition with his creditors generally;

(*d*) in the case of a company, a resolution has been passed or a petition has been presented to wind it up;

(*e*) in the case of a building society, a person falling within section 840A(1)(*b*) of the Taxes Act or a relevant European institution—

(i) it ceases to be a building society or to fall within section 840A(1)(*b*) of the Taxes Act or to be a relevant European institution, as the case may be;

(ii) its directors have made a proposal under Part 1 of the Insolvency Act 1986 for a composition in satisfaction of its debts or a scheme of arrangement of its affairs; or

(iii) a receiver or manager of its property has been appointed; or

(*f*) in the case of a European institution, a relevant authorised person or an assurance undertaking which falls within regulation 14(2)(*d*)(iv), action corresponding to any described in sub-paragraph (*b*) to (*e*) has been taken by or in relation to the institution, person or undertaking under the law of an EEA State.

(2) On giving the notice referred to in paragraph (1), the person shall also notify the registered contact (or, if there is no registered contact, the named child) of the right to transfer the account under regulation 21, and the notice shall inform the recipient of the rights under paragraph (3).

(3) Where a registered contact—

(*a*) receives a notice under paragraph (2), or regulation 19(1), and

(*b*) within 30 days of the sending of the notice, transfers the account to another account provider pursuant to regulation 21,

the period between the transferor ceasing to act or qualify as an account provider, and the transfer to the transferee, shall be ignored in determining whether the account has at all times been managed by an account provider.

Transfer of accounts to other account providers

21—(1) Where—

(*a*) arrangements are made by a registered contact to transfer the whole of the investments under an account from one account provider (''the transferor'') to another account provider (''the transferee''), or

(*b*) the whole of the investments under an account are so transferred in consequence of an account provider (''the transferor'') ceasing to act or to qualify as an account provider, the transfer shall be treated as a transfer of the account.

(2) The account and its description under regulation 4 shall not be affected for the purposes of these Regulations by reason of the transfer, save that, where the registered contact specifies in accordance with paragraph (3)(*a*) an account of a different description, the account shall, on the transfer, become an account of that other description.

(3) The registered contact shall make—

(*a*) the application required by regulation 13(2) (modified as if the words ''applied for'' were replaced with ''transferred''), and

(*b*) the application and declaration required by regulation 13(3) to (5),

to the transferee.

(4) The transferor shall on the date of the transfer give the transferee a notice containing the information specified in paragraph (5) and the declaration specified in paragraph (6).

(5) The information specified in this paragraph is—

(*a*) as regards the named child—

(i) his full name,

(ii) his date of birth,
(iii) his unique reference number;

(*b*) as regards the account—

(i) the description of the account,
(ii) the date of the transfer,
(iii) the total amount subscribed to the account during the period from the beginning of the subscription year in which the transfer takes place to the date of the transfer,
(iv) any amount which has been claimed from the Board under regulations 26, 27 or 30 and which has not been paid at the date of the transfer;

(*c*) the full name and address, including postcode, of the registered contact who has made the transfer arrangements.

(6) The declaration specified in this paragraph is a declaration by the transferor that—

(*a*) he has fulfilled all his obligations to the named child, the Board or otherwise, which are imposed by these Regulations;
(*b*) he has transferred to the transferee or his nominee all the account investments and that, where registration of any such transfer is required, he has taken the necessary steps to ensure that those account investments can be registered in the name of the transferee or nominee;
(*c*) he will forward any further payment received in respect of those account investments to the transferee, on receipt of the payment, and
(*d*) the information contained in the notice is correct.

Recoupment of Inland Revenue contributions to void accounts (and other accounts)

22—(1) Where—

(*a*) the named child has never been an eligible child (see regulation 8(1)(*b*)), or
(*b*) there is a breach of regulation 8(1)(*c*) in relation to an account, the account is void, and the persons mentioned in paragraph (3) shall account to the Inland Revenue for Inland Revenue contributions paid in respect of the account, together with income and gains which have arisen in consequence of the crediting of any of those payments to the account.

(2) Where—

(*a*) the condition in section 9(5) of the Act was satisfied in relation to a child, but the determination under sections 18 to 21 of the Tax Credits Act 2002 has been overturned, or
(*b*) the condition in section 9(8) of the Act was satisfied in relation to a child, but it has subsequently been determined that payment of the relevant benefit or tax credit mentioned in that subsection should not have been made, or that the applicable amount or tax credit should not have included an amount or credit in respect of the child, the persons mentioned in paragraph (3) shall account to the Inland Revenue for any supplementary contribution paid in respect of the account, together with income and gains which have arisen in consequence of the crediting of any such payment to the account.

(3) The persons mentioned in paragraphs (1) and (2) are—

(*a*) the account provider (to the extent that he has assets in his possession or control),
(*b*) the registered contact,
(*c*) the named child, and
(*d*) any person in whom the Inland Revenue contributions, income or gains, or any property directly or indirectly representing any of them, is vested (whether beneficially or otherwise)

and they shall be jointly and severally liable.

(4) Where a person accountable under this regulation is notified by the Inland Revenue that an amount is due from him under it, that amount shall be treated for the purposes of Part 6 of the Management Act (collection and recovery) as if it were tax charged in an assessment on that person, and due and payable.

"Repair" of invalid accounts

23—(1) Except in the case of a breach of regulation 8(1)(*b*) or (*c*) (where no repair of an account is possible), it is an overriding requirement to be satisfied in relation to an account that the account provider and registered contact, as the case may be, take any steps necessary to remedy any breach of these Regulations.

(2) Where a breach is remedied as mentioned in paragraph (1), the account shall, to the extent of that breach, be treated as having been a valid account at all times, except for determining whether there has been a breach of these Regulations for the purposes of section 20 of the Act (penalties).

PART 3

TAX AND ADMINISTRATION OF ACCOUNTS

Exemption from tax of account income and gains

24 Subject to compliance with these Regulations (and in particular regulation 9)—

(*a*) no tax shall be chargeable on the account provider or his nominee, or on the named child or registered contact (on his behalf)—

(i) in respect of interest, dividends, distributions or gains in respect of account investments,
(ii) on any annual profits or gains treated by section 714(2) of the Taxes Act as having been received by any of them in respect of account investments,
(iii) on an offshore income gain to which a disposal made by any of them of an account investment gives rise, which is treated by section 761(1) of the Taxes Act as constituting profits or gains,
(iv) on a profit realised by any of them from the discount on a relevant discounted security within the meaning of Schedule 13 to the Finance Act 1996, which is held as an account investment, or
(v) in respect of gains treated by section 541 of the Taxes Act as arising in connection with a policy of life insurance which is an account investment;

(*b*) losses accruing on any disposal of account investments shall be disregarded for the purposes of capital gains tax;

(*c*) section 349B(4) of the Taxes Act shall apply with the following modifications—

(i) for references to a plan manager, substitute references to an account provider,
(ii) for references to a plan, substitute references to an account, and
(iii) for the reference to section 333 of the Taxes Act, substitute a reference to the Act;

(*d*) a corresponding deficiency occurring at the end of the final year, within the meaning of section 549(1) of the Taxes Act, so far as it relates to a policy of life insurance which is an account investment, shall not be allowable as a deduction from the total income of the named child;

(*e*) relief in respect of tax shall be given in the manner and to the extent provided by these Regulations; and

(*f*) income arising from account investments shall not be regarded as income for any income tax purposes (including section 660B of the Taxes Act).

Tax liabilities and reliefs—account provider to act on behalf of the named child

25—(1) An account provider may under these Regulations make tax claims, conduct appeals and agree on behalf of the named child (or of the registered contact in respect of the child) liabilities for and reliefs from tax in respect of an account.

(2) Tax claims shall be made to the Board in accordance with the provisions of regulations 26 and 27.

(3) Where any relief or exemption from tax previously given in respect of an account has by virtue of these Regulations become excessive, in computing the relief due on any claim there shall be deducted (so that amounts equal to that excess are set-off or repaid to the Board, as the case may be) notwithstanding that those amounts have been invested, any other amount of tax due to the Board by the account provider in respect of any tax liability in respect of account investments under an account including (but without prejudice to the making of an assessment under that Schedule) any amount falling due in respect of a liability under paragraph 3 or 4 of Schedule 23A to the Taxes Act.

Repayments in respect of tax to account provider—interim tax claims

26—(1) Notwithstanding the provisions of any other enactment, the Board shall not be under an obligation to make any repayment in respect of tax under these Regulations earlier than the end of the month following the month in which the claim for the repayment is received.

(2) A claim for repayment in respect of tax which is not an annual claim ("interim tax claim") may be made only for a period of a month (or a number of months not exceeding six) beginning on the 6th day of the month and ending on the 5th day of the relevant following month.

(3) No claim for repayment may be made for the month ending 5th October or any subsequent month in a year until the annual claim due under regulation 27(2) in respect of an account for the preceding year has been duly made by the account provider and received by the Board.

(4) Where, on the occasion of a claim, there is due to the Board an amount in respect of tax, that amount shall be recoverable by the Board in the same manner as tax charged by an assessment on the account provider which has become final and conclusive.

(5) This regulation and regulation 27 shall not apply to any repayment in respect of tax on account investments falling within regulation 12(2)(*m*) (life insurance), or on distributions and other rights or proceeds in respect of those investments.

Repayments in respect of tax to account provider – annual tax claims

27—(1) An annual tax claim is a claim for repayment in respect of tax for a year and may not be made at any time more than six years after the end of the year.

(2) Where the account provider—

(*a*) has made at least one interim tax claim during a year, or

(*b*) wishes to reclaim tax, or there is due to the Board an amount in respect of tax, following the end of the year,

the account provider shall within six months after the end of the year make an annual tax claim to establish the total of tax repayments due under an account for that year.

(3) Where the aggregate of the repayments in respect of interim tax claims for the year shown by an annual tax claim exceeds the amount of tax repayable for the year shown on the claim, the account provider shall repay the amount of the excess to the Board with the claim.

(4) If an account provider fails to make the annual tax claim required under paragraph (2)(*a*) within the time limited, the Board may issue a notice to the account provider showing the aggregate of payments in respect of the interim tax claims for the year, and stating that the Board are not satisfied that the amount due to the account provider for that year exceeds the lower amount stated in the notice.

(5) If an annual tax claim is not delivered to the Board within 14 days after the issue of a notice under paragraph (4) the amount of the difference between the aggregate and the lower amount stated in the notice shall immediately become recoverable by the Board in the same manner as tax charged by an assessment on the account provider which has become final and conclusive.

(6) Where an annual tax claim has been made and the account provider subsequently discovers that an error or mistake has been made in the claim the account provider may make a supplementary annual claim within the time allowed in paragraph (1).

Account provider's tax claims—supplementary provisions

28—(1) Section 42 of the Management Act shall not apply to tax claims under these Regulations.

(2) No appeal shall lie from the Board's decision on an interim tax claim.

(3) An appeal shall be to the Special Commissioners from the Board's decision on an annual tax claim, and the appeal shall be brought by giving notice to the Board within 30 days of receipt of notice of the decision.

(4) No payment or repayment made or other thing done on or in relation to an interim tax claim or a notice under regulation 27(4) shall prejudice the decision on an annual tax claim.

(5) The provisions contained in Part 5 of the Management Act (appeals and other proceedings) shall apply to an appeal under paragraph (3) above, and on appeal the Special Commissioners may vary the decision appealed against whether or not the variation is to the advantage of the appellant.

(6) All such assessments, payments and repayments shall be made as necessary to give effect to the Board's decision on an annual tax claim or to any variation of that decision on appeal.

(7) Claims under these Regulations shall be in such form and contain such particulars as the Board prescribe and, subject to regulation 32(1), shall be signed by the account provider, and forms prescribed for annual claims may require a report to be given by a person qualified for appointment as auditor of a company.

Assessments for withdrawing relief and recovering tax

29

(1) Where—

(*a*) any relief or exemption from tax given in respect of income or gains under an account is found not to be due or to be excessive, or

(*b*) the full amount of tax in respect of the income or gains under an account has not otherwise been fully accounted for and paid to the Board on behalf of the named child, an assessment to tax may be made by the Board in the amount or further amount which in their opinion ought to be charged.

(2) An assessment to which paragraph (1) refers may be made on the account provider or on the registered contact (in respect of the child where the child is under the age of 16).

(3) If the assessment is made to recover tax in respect of income under an account it shall be made under Case VI of Schedule D.

(4) Sections 72 and 73 of the Management Act shall be modified in relation to accounts, so that—

(*a*) references to a parent or guardian include a reference to the registered contact for an account held by the named child, and

(*b*) references to an incapacitated person, in relation to Scotland, are to a person under the age of 16 years.

Fortnightly claim and financial returns

30—(1) In this regulation—

"fortnightly period" means a period—

(*a*) beginning on the 1st, and ending on the 15th, day of a calendar month, or

(*b*) beginning on the 16th, and ending on the last, day of a calendar month;

"first return period", in relation to account providers approved with effect from a date between 1st January 2005 and 28th February 2005, means the period beginning on the date on which the approval takes effect and ending on 28th February 2005;

"second return period", in relation to account providers approved with effect from a date between 1st January 2005 and 31st March 2005, means the period beginning on the later of 1st March 2005 and the date on which the approval takes effect, and ending on 31st March 2005;

"initial return period", in relation to account providers approved later, means the period—

(*a*) beginning on the date on which the approval takes effect, or the appointed day (whichever is the later), and

(*b*) ending simultaneously with the end of the current fortnightly period.

(2) The following provisions of this regulation apply to an account provider in relation to—

(*a*) that provider's first, second or initial return period, and

(*b*) each succeeding fortnightly period (other than succeeding a first return period), during which, or during any part of which, he acted as an account provider.

(3) Within—

(*a*) ten days of the end of a provider's first return period (if any), and

(*b*) five days of the end of any other period mentioned in paragraph (2), the account provider shall deliver by means of electronic communications to the Board, a return for that period, in a form specified by the Board.

(4) The return shall include a declaration of the information in paragraph (5), and a claim as mentioned in paragraph (6) (in each case, stated separately for each account, quoting the named child's unique reference number and date of birth).

(5) The information is that, during that period—

(*a*) the account provider has opened an account in accordance with regulation 5 (by means of a voucher);

(*b*) the account provider has opened a Revenue allocated account in accordance with regulation 6;

(*c*) an account has been transferred to the account provider in accordance with regulation 21, and is held with the account provider at the end of the period; or

(*d*) an account has been closed, due to the named child dying under the age of 18 (and the date of death).

(6) The claim is—

(*a*) where paragraph (5)(*a*) or (*b*) applies, a claim for the initial contribution or special contribution due to the account in accordance with regulation 7(1) to (4); and

(*b*) where the Inland Revenue have informed the account provider that section 9 of the Act applies to the named child, a claim for the supplementary contribution due to the account in accordance with regulation 7(5) to (7).

(7) Paragraphs (5)(*a*) and (*b*) and (6)(*a*) and (*b*) shall apply notwithstanding any transfer of the account to another account provider under regulation 21, before the end of the period in question.

Records to be kept by account provider

31—(1) An account provider shall at all times keep sufficient records in respect of an account to enable the requirements of these Regulations to be satisfied.

(2) In particular, an account provider shall produce (when required to do so by an officer of the Board) any—

(*a*) application made under regulation 13(1) or (10),

(*b*) voucher given to him,

(*c*) annual statement issued by him, and

(*d*) transfer notice given to him under regulation 21(4),

or electronic copies, within the period of 3 years from when it was made, issued or given (notwithstanding any transfer of the account under regulation 21).

Returns of information by account provider

32—(1) An account provider shall within 60 days after the end of each year in which he acts as an account provider, and after ceasing to act or to qualify as an account provider, deliver by means of electronic communications to the Board a return for that year, or for the part of that year in which he so acted or qualified, in a form specified by the Board, which contains the information specified in paragraph (2).

(2) The information specified in this paragraph is information relating to each account in respect of which he acted as account provider, in the year or the part of the year for which the return is made, other than accounts transferred to another account provider under regulation 21 in that year or part of a year, as to—

(*a*) as regards the named child—
(i) his full name,
(ii) his date of birth, and
(iii) his unique reference number;

(*b*) as regards each such account—
(i) whether or not the account is a stakeholder account,
(ii) whether or not there is a registered contact for the account,
(iii) the aggregate market value of the account investments held under the account, subject to paragraph (3), the value of each account investment being determined either as at 5th April in that year, or any other valuation date not falling earlier than 5th October in that year, and
(iv) the total amount of cash subscribed to the account, in the subscription year ending during the year or the part of the year for which the return is made.

(3) The reference in paragraph (2)(*b*)(iii) to market value shall be construed—
(*a*) in the case of policies of life insurance, as a reference to their surrender value, and
(*b*) as referring to separate values for—
(*i*) cash falling within regulation 12(2)(*k*) or (*l*), and
(ii) policies of life insurance and all other account investments.

(4) No claim for repayment, or repayment, may be made under regulations 26 and 27 until the returns which have become due under this regulation have been duly made by the account provider and received by the Board.

Information about ''looked after children'' from Local Authorities

33—(1) In this regulation—

''local authority'' includes an authority within the meaning of the Children (Northern Ireland) Order 1995;

''looked after and accommodated child'', in Scotland, means a child who is—
(*a*) both looked after, and provided with or placed in accommodation, by a local authority within the meaning of those expressions in Part 2 of the Children (Scotland) Act 1995, or
(*b*) accommodated by a local authority under section 22 of that Act,

and related expressions shall be construed accordingly;

''looked after child''—
(*a*) in England and Wales, has the meaning in section 22(1) of the Children Act 1989, extended to include a child accommodated by a local authority under section 17 of that Act, and
(*b*) in Northern Ireland, means a child accommodated under Part 4 of the Children (Northern Ireland) Order 1995,

and related expressions shall be construed accordingly;

''return period'' means a period—
(*a*) beginning on the day immediately succeeding the appointed day, and ending one month after the appointed day, and
(*b*) each succeeding period of one month.

(2) Within one month of the appointed day, every local authority shall deliver by means of electronic communications to the Board, a return in a form specified by the Board, which contains the information in paragraph (3) for every child who was—
(*a*) looked after (in Scotland, looked after and accommodated) by the authority on the appointed day, and
(*b*) born after 31st August 2002, or a return stating that there were no such children.

(3) The information in this paragraph is a statement (prepared separately for each child) of—
(*a*) the name of the local authority,
(*b*) its address,
(*c*) the unique identifier for the local authority,
(*d*) the name of the local authority officer responsible for the return,
(*e*) the child's full name, sex and date of birth,
(*f*) the Home Office reference number, if any, of the child, and
(*g*) either—
(i) the full name and address of an individual who has parental responsibility (in Scotland, parental responsibilities) in relation to the child, or
(ii) if paragraph (*i*) is considered inappropriate, a correspondence address for the child.

(4) Within five days of the end of each return period, every local authority shall deliver by means of electronic communications to the Board a return for that period in a form specified by the Board, covering every child—

(*a*) born after 31st August 2002, and

(*b*) who during that period has become a child looked after (in Scotland, looked after and accommodated) by that authority, for the first time since the appointed day, or a return stating that there were no such children.

(5) After 31st August 2009, the return in paragraph (4) shall in addition cover every child who was looked after (in Scotland, looked after and accommodated) on his 7th birthday.

(6) The return in paragraph (4) shall consist of a statement (prepared separately for each child) of—

(*a*) the information in paragraph (3),

(*b*) the date on which the child first became a child looked after (in Scotland, looked after and accommodated) by that authority,

(*c*) where the child has also died during that period, the name and address of his personal representatives.

Information to be provided to the Board

34 The Board may by notice require any relevant person to furnish them, within such time (not being less than 14 days) as may be provided in the notice, such information about any account or about any account investment (including copies of or extracts from any books or other records) as they may reasonably require for the purposes of these Regulations.

Inspection of records by officer of the Board

35—(1) The Board may by notice require any relevant person, within such time (not being less than 14 days) as may be provided in the notice, to make available for inspection at a place within the United Kingdom by an officer of the Board authorised for that purpose all documents (including books and other records) in his possession or under his control relating to any account or to any account investment.

(2) Where records are maintained by computer the person required to make them available for inspection shall provide the officer making the inspection with all the facilities necessary for obtaining information from them.

Capital gains tax—adaptation of enactments

36—(1) For the purposes of capital gains tax—

(*a*) any assets held by a named child as account investments shall be regarded as held by the child in a separate capacity from that in which he holds any other assets of the same description; and

(*b*) the named child shall be treated as having sold all the account investments, and as having reacquired them in his personal capacity, for a consideration equal to their market value, immediately before he attains the age of 18 years (and ceases to be a child).

(2) Sections 127 to 131 of the 1992 Act shall not apply in relation to qualifying investments falling within any of sub-paragraphs (*a*), (*b*), and (*f*) to (*i*) of regulation 12(2) which are held under an account if there is by virtue of any allotment for payment as is mentioned in section 126(2) of that Act a reorganisation affecting those assets.

Administration of tax in relation to accounts—supplementary

37—(1) Nothing in these Regulations shall be taken to prejudice any powers conferred or duties imposed by or under any enactment in relation to the making of returns of income or gains, or for the recovery of tax, penalties or interest by means of an assessment or otherwise.

(2) Notwithstanding the provisions of these Regulations an account provider shall not be released from obligations under these Regulations in relation to an account except under conditions agreed in writing with and notified to that person by the Board.

(3) The provisions contained in the Management Act shall apply to any assessment under these Regulations as if it were an assessment to tax for the year in which, apart from these Regulations, the named child would have been liable (by reason of his ownership of the investments).

(4) No obligation as to secrecy imposed by statute or otherwise shall preclude the Board from disclosing to an account provider or registered contact that any provision of these Regulations has not been satisfied or that relief has been given or claimed in respect of investments under an account.

(5) If—

(*a*) a chargeable event, within the meaning given by Chapter 2 of Part 13 of the Taxes Act, has happened in relation to a policy of life insurance which is an account investment, and

(*b*) the body by whom the policy was issued is satisfied that no gain is to be treated as chargeable to tax on the happening of the event by virtue of regulation 24(*a*)(*v*), the body shall not be obliged to deliver the certificates mentioned in section 552(1) of that Act. This paragraph does not prevent the operation of section 552(1) in a case to which regulation 38(1) applies.

(6) Where—

(*a*) it comes to the notice of the account provider, in any manner, that the event specified in regulation 12(11) has occurred in relation to a policy, and

(*b*) the account provider is not the insurer for the time being responsible for the obligations under the policy or, where the policy is not still in existence, the person who was the last such insurer, the account provider shall, within 30 days of the event coming to his notice give notice to that insurer, specifying the event mentioned in sub-paragraph (*a*) and the termination event.

Application of the provisions of Chapter 2 of Part 13 of the Taxes Act to policies

38

(1) This paragraph applies to a case where—

(*a*) the event specified in regulation 12(11) has occurred in relation to a policy of life insurance, and

(*b*) a termination event within the meaning in regulation 12(12) occurs in relation to that policy.

(2) Where—

(*a*) there is a case to which paragraph (1) applies, and

(*b*) a chargeable event in relation to the policy, within the meaning given by section 540 of the Taxes Act, has occurred prior to the time at which the termination event mentioned in paragraph (1)(*b*) occurs, the named child shall cease to be, and shall be treated as not having been, entitled to relief from tax under regulation 24(*a*)(*v*), in respect of gains treated as arising on the occurrence of any chargeable event mentioned in sub-paragraph (*b*).

(3) The provisions of Chapter 2 of Part 13 of the Taxes Act shall apply, in a case to which paragraph (1) applies, to—

(*a*) the termination event mentioned in paragraph (1)(*b*), and

(*b*) any chargeable event mentioned in paragraph (2)(*b*), with the modifications provided for in paragraphs (4) to (8) of this regulation, and the registered contact and the account provider shall account to the Board in accordance with this regulation for tax from which relief under regulation 24 has been given on the basis that the named child was so entitled, or in circumstances such that the named child was not so entitled.

(4) A termination of a policy of insurance pursuant to regulation 12(9)(*b*)(ii) shall be treated as the surrender in whole of the rights conferred by the policy, for the purposes of section 540(1)(*a*)(iii) of the Taxes Act.

(5) In section 547(5) of the Taxes Act, for the words after ''total income'' (where that expression first appears) substitute ''that gain shall be chargeable to tax under Case VI of Schedule D''.

(6) Relief under section 550 of the Taxes Act shall be computed as if paragraph (5) had not been enacted.

(7) In section 552 of the Taxes Act—

(*a*) in subsection (1)(*b*) for ''policy holder'' substitute ''named child'';

(*b*) in subsection (3)—

(i) omit ''(or, where the appropriate policy holder is a company, the corresponding financial year)'';

(ii) for ''the name and address of the appropriate policy holder'' substitute ''the name and address of the named child'';

(iii) omit ''and the corresponding financial year,'';

(*c*) in subsection (5)—

(i) for ''the appropriate policy holder'' substitute ''the named child'';

(ii) omit sub-paragraph (*b*)(ii);

(iii) omit paragraph (*c*);

(iv) in paragraph (*d*) omit ''except where paragraph (*c*) above applies,'';

(*v*) omit paragraph (*f*);

(*d*) in subsection (6)—

(i) omit paragraph (*b*);

(ii) for paragraph (*c*) substitute—

''(*c*) if the event is a death, the period of three months beginning with the receipt of written notification of the death;'';

(iii) after paragraph (c) insert—

''(*d*) if the event is—

(*i*) a termination event, or

(ii) a chargeable event preceding a termination event (as mentioned in regulation 38(2) of the Child Trust Funds Regulations 2004), the period of three months beginning with the date on which the insurer received notice under regulation 37(6) of those Regulations or, if earlier, actual notice of the termination event.'';

(*e*) in subsection (7)—

(i) in paragraph (*a*) omit ", or, where the policy holder is a company, the financial year,";

(ii) omit paragraph (*b*);

(iii) for paragraph (*c*) substitute—

"(*c*) if the event is a death, the period of three months beginning with the receipt of written notification of the death;";

(iv) after paragraph (*c*) insert—

"(ca) if the event is—

(i) a termination event, or

(ii) a chargeable event preceding such a termination event (as mentioned in regulation 38(2) of the Child Trust Funds Regulations 2004, the period of three months beginning with the date on which the insurer received notice under regulation 37(6) of those Regulations or, if earlier, actual notice of the termination event."; and

(v) in paragraph (*d*) after "paragraph (*c*)" insert "or (ca)";

(*f*) in subsection (8)—

(i) in paragraph (*b*) for "policy holder" substitute "named child in respect";

(ii) in paragraph (*c*) omit the words from "or" to the end;

(*g*) in subsection (9) omit "or financial year" in each place where they occur;

(*h*) in subsection (10)—

(i) before the definition of "amount" insert—

""named child" has the same meaning as in the Child Trust Funds Regulations 2004;";

(ii) omit the definitions of "appropriate policy holder" and "financial year";

(iii) for the definition of "the relevant year of assessment" substitute—

""the relevant year of assessment", in the case of any gain, means the year of assessment to which the gain is attributable;"; and

(iv) after the definition of "section 546 excess" insert—" "termination event" has the same meaning as in the Child Trust Funds Regulations 2004;"; and

(v) omit subsection (11).

(8) In section 552ZA of the Taxes Act—

(*a*) in subsection (2)(*b*) omit the words "or an assignment"; and

(*b*) omit subsections (3) and (4).

(9) The account provider shall account for and pay income tax at the lower rate in force for the year in which the termination event, or the chargeable event mentioned in paragraph (2)(*b*) occurred, as the case may be, and any amount so payable—

(*a*) may be set off against any repayment in respect of tax due under regulation 26 or 27 and subject thereto,

(*b*) shall be treated as an amount of tax due not later than 6 months after the end of the year in which the event specified in regulation 12(11) came to the notice of the account provider, and

(*c*) shall be payable without the making of an assessment.

(10) Where tax is charged in accordance with paragraph (3)(*a*) or (*b*)—

(*a*) an assessment to income tax at the lower rate in force for the relevant year may be made on the account provider or on the registered contact (on behalf of the named child), and

(*b*) an assessment to income tax at the higher rate within the meaning of section 832(1) of the Taxes Act, for that year, may be made on the registered contact (on behalf of the named child) within five years after the 31st January next following that year, and regulation 29 shall not apply.

SCHEDULE

STAKEHOLDER ACCOUNTS

Description of stakeholder account

1 An account is a stakeholder account where it has the characteristics and complies with the conditions set out in paragraph 2.

Characteristics of stakeholder account etc

2—(1) A stakeholder account must have the characteristics set out in sub-paragraph (2) and must comply with the conditions set out in sub-paragraphs (3) to (5).

(2) The characteristics of a stakeholder account are—

(*a*) the account does not directly hold investments of any of the following kinds-

(i) those referred to in regulation 12(2)(*f*) (shares in an investment trust);

(ii) securities of an investment trust;

(iii) rights in with-profits endowment policies;
(iv) rights, under a contract of insurance, in a with-profits fund;
(v) units or shares in a relevant collective investment scheme unless it is a requirement of that scheme that the purchase and sale price of those units or shares shall, at any given time, not differ from each other and that the price must be made available to the public on a daily basis;
(vi) rights under a contract of insurance which are expressed as shares in funds held by the insurer unless it is a requirement of the contract of insurance that the purchase and sale price of those shares shall, at any given time, not differ from each other and that the price must be made available to the public on a daily basis;
(vii) depositary interests, where the investments concerned are investments of any of the kinds listed above in this paragraph;

(*b*) the account provider, and any relevant person, must ensure that, subject to the other provisions of this paragraph, the account has exposure to equities, whether directly or indirectly;

(*c*) the account provider and any relevant person must have regard to—

(i) the need for diversification of investments of the account, in so far as is appropriate to the circumstances of the account; and
(ii) the suitability for the purposes of the account of any investment, investment strategy or investment option proposed; and

(*d*) except where otherwise instructed by the registered contact, the account is subject to lifestyling.

(3) The account provider must permit payment of subscriptions to the account by—

(*a*) cheque;
(*b*) direct debit;
(*c*) standing order;
(*d*) direct credit (other than standing order).

(4) The minimum amount which may be subscribed to the account on a single occasion is £10 except where the account provider permits a smaller amount.

(5) Deductions from the account may only be made in the circumstances, and to the extent, set out in paragraph 3.

(6) In this paragraph—

"equities" means shares issued by a company wherever incorporated and officially listed on a recognised stock exchange;

"insurer" means—

(*a*) a person who has permission under Part 4 of the Financial Services and Markets Act 2000 to effect or carry out contracts of insurance, or
(*b*) an EEA firm of the kind mentioned in paragraph 5(*d*) of Schedule 3 to that Act, which has permission under paragraph 15 of that Schedule (as a result of qualifying for authorisation under paragraph 12 of that Schedule) to effect or carry out contracts of insurance;

"lifestyling" means the process beginning from a date on or before the child is 13 years of age, or from when the account is opened, whichever is later, and continuing until the child is 18 years of age, by which the account provider, and any relevant person, adopts an investment strategy which aims progressively to minimise the variation or potential variation in capital value of the account caused by market conditions from time to time;

"relevant collective investment scheme" means an authorised unit trust scheme, an authorised open-ended investment company or a recognised scheme, as the case may be, as defined in section 237(3) of the Financial Services and Markets Act 2000;

"relevant person" means any person to whom the account provider has delegated any of his functions or responsibilities under the management agreement; and "with-profits fund" means a fund maintained by an insurer in respect of a particular part of its long-term business for which—

(*a*) separate accounting records are maintained by the insurer in respect of all income and expenditure relating to that part of its business; and
(*b*) the benefits payable in respect of policies allocated to that fund are determined partly by reference to a discretion exercisable by any person.

(7) In this paragraph, the definitions of "contract of insurance" and "insurer" must be read with—

(*a*) section 22 of the Financial Services and Markets Act 2000,
(*b*) any relevant order made under that section, and
(*c*) Schedule 2 to that Act.

Stakeholder accounts—charges etc

3—(1) Deductions from a stakeholder account may only be made to the extent set out in this paragraph.

(2) Subject to sub-paragraph (5), charges for the management of, and other expenses in connection with, a stakeholder account may be recovered from the account to the extent that they do not exceed whichever is the greater of—

(*a*) 3/730 per cent of the value of the child's rights in the account for each day on which the account is held; or

(*b*) 3/730 per cent of the value of the investments under the account for each day on which the account is held.

(3) For the purposes of sub-paragraph (2)—

(*a*) the frequency, which must be daily, weekly or monthly, with which rights or investments are to be valued; and

(*b*) where valuation is to take place weekly or monthly, the day of the week or, as the case may be, the date in the month on which it is to take place, must be specified in advance in writing by the account provider to the registered contact, and the specification may not be amended during the period of 12 months after the date on which it is made.

(4) When calculating the value of a child's rights or of investments for the purposes of sub-paragraph (2) where the account provider has specified under sub-paragraph (3) that they are to be valued weekly or monthly—

(*a*) where they are to be valued weekly, they are to be valued on such day of the week ("the specified day") as has been so specified by the account provider (except that, where that day is not a working day, the rights are to be valued on the next working day), and the value of the rights on each subsequent day prior to the next specified day is to be taken to be the value of the rights on the previous specified day; and

(*b*) where they are to be valued monthly, they are to be so valued on such date in each month ("the specified date") as has been so specified by the account provider (except that, where that date is not a working day, the rights are to be valued on the next working day), and the value of the rights on each subsequent day prior to the next specified date is to be taken to be the value of the rights on the previous specified date.

(5) The following charges and expenses may be deducted in full from the account and are not subject to and do not count towards the limit provided for in sub-paragraph (2)—

(*a*) any stamp duty, stamp duty reserve tax or other charges incurred by the account provider directly or indirectly in the sale or purchase of investments held under the account;

(*b*) any charges or expenses incurred by the account provider directly or indirectly in complying with an order of the court or any other requirements imposed by law; and

(*c*) expenses incurred by the account provider in complying with its obligations under regulation 8(2)(*d*) and (*e*).

(6) Valuations for the purpose of sub-paragraph (2) shall be after the deduction of any charges or expenses properly deducted from the account under sub-paragraph (5).

2004/1819

Thalidomide Children's Trust (Application of Section 329AA of the Income and Corporation Taxes Act 1988) Order 2004

Made	*14th July 2004*
Laid before the House of Commons	*15th July 2004*
Coming into force	*5th August 2004*

It appears to the Treasury that the Thalidomide Children's Trust, established by a declaration of trust made on 10th August 1973, makes provision for the making of periodical payments by way of compensation for personal injury;

Accordingly the Treasury, in exercise of the powers conferred upon them by section 329AB(3) of the Income and Corporation Taxes Act 1988, make the following Regulations:

Citation, commencement and interpretation

1—(1) This Order may be cited as the Thalidomide Children's Trust (Application of Section 329AA of the Income and Corporation Taxes Act 1988) Order 2004 and shall come into force on 5th August 2004.

(2) In this Order "the Thalidomide Children's Trust" means the Trust established by that name by a declaration of trust made on the 10th August 1973 by Sir Henry Gordon Willmer, Arthur Halsall Walton and Sir Donald Macleod Douglas.

Modified application of section 329AA of the Income and Corporation Taxes Act 1988

2—(1) Section 329AA of the Income and Corporation Taxes Act 1988 (personal injury damages in the form of periodical payments) applies to periodical payments by the Thalidomide Children's Trust as it applies to payments to which subsection (1) of that section applies, but subject to the following modifications.

(2) In subsection (1)—

(*a*) after "Where" insert "the Thalidomide Children's Trust makes periodical payments to a beneficiary of that Trust"; and

(*b*) omit paragraphs (*a*) and (*b*).

(3) In subsection (2)—

(a) for paragraph *(a)* substitute—
"*(a)* the person ("A") entitled to the payments made by the Thalidomide Children's Trust;";
(b) in paragraphs *(b)* and *(c)* for "whether in pursuance of the agreement or order or otherwise" substitute "whether under the terms of the Thalidomide Children's Trust or otherwise".

(4) In subsection (3) omit ", if the agreement or order mentioned in that subsection or a subsequent agreement so provides,".

(5) For subsection (5) substitute—

"(5) In this section "the Thalidomide Children's Trust" means the Trust established by that name by a declaration of trust made on the 10th August 1973 by Sir Henry Gordon Willmer, Arthur Halsall Walton and Sir Donald Macleod Douglas.".

(6) Omit subsections (6) to (8).

2004/1863
Tax Avoidance Schemes (Prescribed Descriptions of Arrangements) Regulations 2004

Made . . . . *22nd July 2004*
Laid before the House of Commons . . . . *22nd July 2004*
Coming into force . . . . *1st August 2004*

The Treasury, in exercise of the powers conferred upon them by section 306(1)*(a)* and *(b)* of the Finance Act 2004, after Royal Assent to that Act, make the following Regulations:

Citation, commencement and interpretation

1—(1) These Regulations may be cited as the Tax Avoidance Schemes (Prescribed Descriptions of Arrangements) Regulations 2004 and shall come into force on 1st August 2004.

(2) In these Regulations—

"the Act" means the Finance Act 2004 and except where the context otherwise requires "Part 7" means Part 7 of the Act (disclosure of tax avoidance schemes);
"Icta 1988" means the Income and Corporation Taxes Act 1988;
"ITEPA 2003" means the Income Tax (Earnings and Pensions) Act 2003;
"the Board" means the Commissioners of Inland Revenue;
"corporation tax" shall be construed in accordance with section 318(1) of the Act;
"employment" has the same meaning as it has for the purposes of the employment income Parts of ITEPA 2003 (see section 4 of that Act) and includes—

(a) former and prospective employments; and
(b) offices (including former and prospective offices) to which the provisions of those Parts that are expressed to apply to employments apply equally (see section 5 of that Act);

and "employee" and "employer" have corresponding meanings;
"promoter" has the meaning given by section 307 of the Act.

(3) For the purposes of these Regulations, section 839 of ICTA 1988 applies to determine whether persons are connected.

Prescribed descriptions of arrangements in relation to income tax, corporation tax and capital gains tax

2—(1) For the purposes of Part 7, the arrangements specified in the Schedule to these Regulations are prescribed in relation to income tax, corporation tax and capital gains tax.

(2) Part 1 of the Schedule specifies arrangements connected with employment.

(3) Part 2 of the Schedule specifies arrangements in relation to financial products.

(4) If an arrangement—

(a) would, but for some exemption contained in Part 1 of the Schedule, be notifiable by virtue of a provision in that Part, and
(b) would be notifiable by virtue of a provision in Part 2 of the Schedule,

it shall not be notifiable under any provision of that Schedule.

SCHEDULE

ARRANGEMENTS PRESCRIBED BY THESE REGULATIONS

Regulation 2(1)

PART 1
ARRANGEMENTS CONNECTED WITH EMPLOYMENT

Introduction

1—(1) The arrangements specified in this Part are those which satisfy the condition in sub-paragraph (2) and involve—

(a) securities or associated rights (see paragraph 3);
(b) payments to trustees and intermediaries (see paragraph 4); or
(c) loans (see paragraph 5).

(2) The condition is that a tax advantage by way of a reduction in, or deferment of, liability might be expected to be obtained, by virtue of the arrangements, by the employer or the employee, or by any other person by reason of the employee's employment—

(a) where the advantage relates to employment income, in any year of assessment; or
(b) in any other case, in any period of account.

Interpretation for the purposes of this Part

2—(1) In this Part the persons who are associated with each other in relation to arrangements are—

(a) the person who is expected to receive any payment under the arrangements,
(b) the employee, and
(c) any relevant linked person.

(2) A person is a relevant linked person if—

(a) that person (on the one hand), and
(b) either the person who is expected to receive the payment or the employee (on the other),

are or have been connected or (without being or having been connected) are or have been members of the same household.

(3) In this Part ''payment'' includes a transfer of assets and any other transfer of money's worth, including, without prejudice to the foregoing, the doing of anything by means of which the value of an asset is increased, or a liability is reduced.

Arrangements involving securities or associated rights

3—(1) This paragraph applies to any arrangements under which—

(a) securities,
(b) interests in securities,
(c) securities options,
(d) anything the right to which is derived from securities, or
(e) anything the value or amount of which is calculated by reference to securities, interests in securities or securities options, or something the right to which is derived from securities,

are obtained by an employee or any other person, by reason of the employee's employment, but this is subject to sub-paragraphs (3), (5) and (6).

In this sub-paragraph—

''securities'' has the meaning which it would have by virtue of section 420 of ITEPA 2003 were subsection (5) disregarded; and
''securities option'' has the meaning given by subsection (8) of that section.

(2) For the purposes of this paragraph, anything obtained under arrangements by an employee or a person associated with him—

(a) which confer a right or opportunity to obtain anything mentioned in sub-paragraph (1), and
(b) the costs of which are borne wholly or partly and whether directly or indirectly by the employer or a person connected with the employer,

is to be treated as obtained by reason of the employee's employment.

(3) This paragraph does not apply if the arrangements in their entirety constitute—

(a) an approved share incentive plan under Schedule 2 to ITEPA 2003, including any trust established for the purposes of the plan under paragraph 71(3) of that Schedule; or
(b) an approved SAYE option scheme under Schedule 3 to that Act or an approved CSOP scheme under Schedule 4 to that Act, together with any trust established solely for the purposes of that scheme or those schemes.

(4) For the purposes of sub-paragraph (3), a plan or scheme (as the case may be) for which approval has been sought from the Board is to be treated as approved during the period while the application for approval is before them.

(5) This paragraph does not apply to arrangements to the extent that they would involve the issue of shares to persons to whom it is reasonably expected that certificates in relation to those shares would be issued under section 306(2) of ICTA 1988 (including that subsection as it is applied by paragraph 6 of Schedule 5B to the Taxation of Chargeable Gains Act 1992).

(6) This paragraph does not apply if the arrangements in their entirety comprise—

(a) the grant of one or more qualifying options which meet the requirements of Schedule 5 to ITEPA 2003 and fall to be notified to the Board in accordance with Part 7 of that Schedule; or

(b) such a grant as is mentioned in paragraph *(a)* together only with such other steps as are reasonably necessary in all the circumstances for the purpose of facilitating it.

Arrangements involving payments to trustees and intermediaries

4—(1) This paragraph applies to any arrangements under which a payment is to be made by the employer or a person connected with him to—

(a) a trust for the benefit of an employee or a person associated with an employee;

(b) a trust for a class of persons which includes an employee or a person so associated; or

(c) a third party who is entitled or required, under the terms of an employee benefit scheme, within the meaning of Schedule 24 to the Finance Act 2003, to hold or use the payment for or in connection with the provision of benefits to employees of the employer or persons associated with any of those employees.

This is subject to the qualification in sub-paragraph (2).

For the purposes of paragraphs *(a)* and *(b)*, it is immaterial whether the trust is established under the law of any part of the United Kingdom or of a country or territory overseas.

(2) This paragraph does not apply to payments to the extent that they are made to—

(a) a pension fund listed in sub-paragraph (4);

(b) a fund to which section 329AA of ICTA 1988 (personal injury damages in the form of periodical payments) applies;

(c) the trustees of a trust established for the purposes of—

(i) an approved share incentive plan under Schedule 2 to ITEPA 2003; or

(ii) an approved SAYE option scheme under Schedule 3, or an approved CSOP scheme under Schedule 4, to that Act or both.

(3) Paragraph 3(4) applies to the construction of references in sub-paragraph (2)*(c)* to approved share plans and schemes as it applies to such references in paragraph 3(3).

(4) The pensions funds are—

(a) those approved under Chapter 1 of Part 14 of ICTA 1988 (retirement benefit schemes);

(b) relevant statutory schemes within section 611A of ICTA 1988 (definition of relevant statutory scheme);

(c) those approved under Chapter 4 of Part 14 of ICTA 1988 (personal pension schemes); and

(d) overseas pension schemes in respect of which tax relief is granted in the United Kingdom under—

(i) section 615 of ICTA 1988 (exemption from tax for superannuation payments in respect of persons not resident in the United Kingdom or in respect of trades carried on wholly or partly outside the United Kingdom);

(ii) arrangements specified in an Order in Council under section 788 of that Act (double taxation agreements); or

(iii) section 390 of ITEPA 2003 (exception from the charge on payments to non-approved schemes for non-domiciled employees with foreign employers).

(5) For the purposes of paragraphs *(a)* and *(c)* of sub-paragraph (4), a pension fund for which approval has been sought from the Board is to be treated as if it were approved during the period while the application for approval is before them.

Arrangements involving loans

5—(1) This paragraph applies to any arrangements which include the making, release or writing off of any loan by an employer, or a person connected with an employer, to or for the benefit of an employee or any other person by reason of the employee's employment.

This is subject to the following qualification.

(2) This paragraph does not apply if the arrangements are in their entirety ones—

(a) to which Chapter 7 of Part 3 of ITEPA 2003 (employment income: taxable benefits: loans) applies unless it is the intention of the parties to the loan that the loan should not be repaid either in whole or in part; or

(b) in respect of which no liability under that Chapter arises by virtue of section 288 or 289 of that Act (limited exemption for bridging loans connected with employment).

(3) The reference in sub-paragraph (1) to making a loan includes arranging, guaranteeing or in any way facilitating a loan.

PART 2
ARRANGEMENTS IN RELATION TO FINANCIAL PRODUCTS

Introduction

6—(1) The arrangements specified in this Part are those which—

(*a*) satisfy the condition in sub-paragraph (2); and

(*b*) include one or more of the financial products to which paragraph 7 applies,

unless they are arrangements that are excluded by paragraph 8.

(2) The condition is that the tax advantage expected to be obtained under the arrangements arises, to a significant degree, from the inclusion in those arrangements of the financial product or any of the financial products to which paragraph 7 applies.

Specified financial products

7—(1) The financial products to which this paragraph applies are—

(*a*) a loan;

(*b*) a contract which—

(i) is a derivative contract for the purposes of Schedule 26 to the Finance Act 2002;

(ii) would be such a derivative contract if paragraph 4 of that Schedule (contracts excluded by virtue of their underlying subject matter) were omitted; or

(iii) would be a derivative contract falling within sub-paragraph (i) or (ii) if it were a contract of a company;

(*c*) an agreement for the sale and repurchase of securities of the kind described in paragraphs (*a*) to (*c*) of subsection (1) of section 730A of ICTA 1988;

(*d*) a stock lending arrangement within the meaning given by section 263B(1) of the Taxation of Chargeable Gains Act 1992;

(*e*) a share; and

(*f*) a contract, not being one of the above, which, whether alone or in combination with one or more other contracts (including any of the above), in substance represents the making of a loan, or the advancing or depositing of money, whatever its form and falls to be accounted for on that basis.

This sub-paragraph is subject to the following qualifications.

(2) This paragraph does not apply if the only financial products involved in the arrangements are one or both of the following—

(*a*) assets which are held within an account which satisfies the conditions in the Individual Savings Accounts Regulations 1998; and

(*b*) assets which are held as plan investments in a personal equity plan within the meaning of the Personal Equity Plan Regulations 1989.

(3) For the purposes of this paragraph, a contract, or a combination of contracts, falls to be accounted for as a loan, or as the advancing or depositing of money, if the person entering into the arrangements is, in accordance with generally accepted accounting practice, required to treat the contract, or the combination of contracts, as a loan, deposit or other financial asset or obligation (as to which, see section 43A(1) of ICTA 1988), or would be so required if the person were a company to which the Companies Act 1985 applied.

This is subject to the following qualification.

(4) Anything which is a finance lease for the purposes of generally accepted accounting practice does not fall to be accounted for as a loan for the purposes of this paragraph.

(5) In this paragraph "generally accepted accounting practice" has the meaning given by section 836A of ICTA 1988.

Excluded arrangements

8—(1) Arrangements are excluded by this paragraph if—

(*a*) sub-paragraphs (2) and (3) apply; and

(*b*) where, as part of the arrangements, a promoter, or any person connected with a promoter, becomes a party to one or more financial products, sub-paragraph (4) applies.

(2) This sub-paragraph applies where the arrangements are such that it might reasonably be expected that no promoter, and no person connected with a promoter, of arrangements that are the same as, or substantially similar to, the arrangements in question would be able to obtain a premium fee from a person experienced in receiving services of the type being provided.

(3) This sub-paragraph applies where the tax advantage expected to be obtained under the arrangements does not arise from any element of the arrangements (including the way in which they are structured) which, disregarding any duty of confidentiality owed to any person, a promoter might reasonably be expected to wish to keep confidential from other promoters.

(4) This sub-paragraph applies where none of the terms of the financial product or products mentioned in sub-paragraph (1)*(b)* differs significantly from the terms which might reasonably be expected to be offered in the open market to the other party to a product that is, or products that are, the same as, or substantially similar to, the product or products in question.

(5) For the purposes of this paragraph, a premium fee, in relation to any arrangements, is a fee which is chargeable by virtue of any element of the arrangements (including the way in which they are structured) from which the tax advantage expected to be obtained arises and is—

(a) a fee to a significant extent attributable to that tax advantage; or

(b) a fee to any extent contingent upon the obtaining of that tax advantage.

2004/1864
Tax Avoidance Schemes (Information) Regulations 2004

Made . . . . *22 July 2004*
Laid before the House of Commons . . . . *22 July 2004*
Coming into force . . . . *1 August 2004*

The Commissioners of Inland Revenue, in exercise of the powers conferred upon them by section 132 of the Finance Act 1999, section 135 of the Finance Act 2002, and sections 308(1) and (3), 309(1), 310, 312, 313(1), (3) and (4)*(g)*, 317(2) and 318(1) of the Finance Act 2004, make the following Regulations:

Citation, commencement and effect

1—(1) These Regulations may be cited as the Tax Avoidance Schemes (Information) Regulations 2004 and shall come into force on 1st August 2004.

(2) These Regulations do not have effect in respect of proposals or arrangements (as the case may be) which are notifiable by virtue of any of the provisions of Part 2 of the Schedule to the Arrangements Regulations—

(a) for the purposes of section 308(1), if the relevant date in relation to a proposal falls before 22nd June 2004;

(b) for the purposes of section 308(3), if the date on which the promoter first becomes aware of any transaction forming part of arrangements falls before that date;

(c) for the purposes of sections 309 and 310, if the date on which any transaction forming part of arrangements is entered into falls before that date.

Interpretation

2 In the Regulations—

''the Act'' means the Finance Act 2004, and a reference to a numbered section (without more) is a reference to the section of the Act which is so numbered;

''the Arrangements Regulations'' means the Tax Avoidance Schemes (Prescribed Descriptions of Arrangements) Regulations 2004;

''corporation tax'' shall be construed in accordance with section 318(1);

''employment'' has the same meaning as it has for the purposes of the employment income Parts of the Income Tax (Earnings and Pensions) Act 2003 (see section 4 of that Act) and includes offices to which the provisions of those Parts that are expressed to apply to employments apply equally (see section 5 of that Act); and ''employee'' and ''employer'' have corresponding meanings;

''notifiable arrangements'' has the meaning given by section 306(1);

''notifiable proposal'' has the meaning given by section 306(2);

''promoter'' has the meaning given by section 307;

''the prescribed taxes'' means capital gains tax, corporation tax and income tax;

''the relevant date'' has the meaning given by section 308(2).

Prescribed information in respect of notifiable proposals and arrangements

3—(1) The information which must be provided to the Board by a promoter under section 308(1) in respect of a notifiable proposal is sufficient information as might reasonably be expected to enable an officer of the Board to comprehend the manner in which the proposal is intended to operate, including—

(a) the promoter's name and address;

(b) details of the provision of the Arrangements Regulations by virtue of which the proposal is notifiable;

(c) a summary of the proposal and the name (if any) by which it is known;

(d) information explaining each element of the proposed arrangements (including the way in which they are structured) from which the tax advantage expected to be obtained under those arrangements arises; and

(*e*) the statutory provisions, relating to any of the prescribed taxes, on which that tax advantage is based.

(2) The information which must be provided to the Board by a promoter under section 308(3) in respect of notifiable arrangements is sufficient information as might reasonably be expected to enable an officer of the Board to comprehend the manner in which the arrangements are intended to operate, including—

(*a*) the promoter's name and address;

(*b*) details of the provision of the Arrangements Regulations by virtue of which the arrangements are notifiable;

(*c*) a summary of the arrangements and the name (if any) by which they are known;

(*d*) information explaining each element of the arrangements (including the way in which they are structured) from which the tax advantage expected to be obtained under the arrangements arises; and

(*e*) the statutory provisions, relating to any of the prescribed taxes, on which that tax advantage is based.

(3) The information which must be provided to the Board by a client under section 309 (duty of person dealing with promoter outside the United Kingdom) in respect of notifiable arrangements is sufficient information as might reasonably be expected to enable an officer of the Board to comprehend the manner in which the arrangements are intended to operate, including—

(*a*) the client's name and address;

(*b*) the name and address of the promoter;

(*c*) details of the provision of the Arrangements Regulations by virtue of which the arrangements are notifiable;

(*d*) a summary of the arrangements, and the name (if any) by which they are known;

(*e*) information explaining each element of the arrangements (including the way in which they are structured) from which the tax advantage expected to be obtained under the arrangements arises; and

(*f*) the statutory provisions, relating to any of the prescribed taxes, on which that tax advantage is based.

(4) The information which must be provided to the Board by a person obliged to do so by section 310 (duty of parties to notifiable arrangements not involving promoter) is sufficient information as might reasonably be expected to enable an officer of the Board to comprehend the manner in which the arrangements of which that transaction forms part are intended to operate, including—

(*a*) the name and address of the person entering into the transaction;

(*b*) details of the provision of the Arrangements Regulations by virtue of which the arrangements are notifiable;

(*c*) a summary of the arrangements and the name (if any) by which they are known;

(*d*) information explaining each element of the arrangements (including the way in which they are structured) from which the tax advantage expected to be obtained under the arrangements arises; and

(*e*) the statutory provisions, relating to any of the prescribed taxes, on which that tax advantage is based.

Time for providing information under section 308, 309 or 310

4—(1) The period or time (as the case may be) within which the prescribed information under section 308, 309 or 310 must be provided to the Board is found in accordance with the following paragraphs of this regulation.

(2) In the case of a notification under section 308(1), the prescribed period is the period of 5 days beginning with the day after the relevant date.

(3) In the case of a notification under section 308(3), the prescribed period is the period of 5 days beginning with the day after that on which the promoter first becomes aware of any transaction forming part of arrangements to which that subsection applies.

(4) In the case of a notification under section 309(1), the prescribed period is the period of 5 days beginning with the day after that on which the client enters into the first transaction forming part of notifiable arrangements to which that subsection applies.

(5) In the case of a notification under section 310 the prescribed time is any time during the period—

(*a*) beginning with the day after that on which the person enters into the first transaction forming part of the notifiable arrangements; and

(*b*) ending with the latest time at which he would first have had to provide the Board with information under section 313 in accordance with regulation 8.

(6) In reckoning any period under this regulation or regulation 5 any day which is a non-business day within the meaning of section 92 of the Bills of Exchange Act 1882 shall be disregarded.

(7) Where paragraph (2), (3) or (4) applies, if the prescribed period referred to in that paragraph would otherwise end before 30th September 2004, it shall instead end upon that date.

(8) This regulation is subject to regulations 5 (statutory clearances) and 6 (transitional provisions).

Statutory clearances

5—(1) If—

(*a*) a promoter must provide information under subsection (1) of section 308;

(*b*) the relevant date by reference to which he must provide that information is that referred to in subsection (2)(*a*) of that section; and

(*c*) he reasonably expects to make an application on behalf of a client under any of the provisions listed in paragraph (3) ("a clearance application");

the prescribed period is that beginning with the day after the relevant date and ending with the applicable date.

(2) The applicable date is—

(*a*) the date on which the first transaction occurs in pursuance of the arrangements, or

(*b*) if the promoter ceases to hold the reasonable expectation referred to in paragraph (1)(*c*) 5 days after he ceases to hold it.

(3) The provisions are—

(*a*) sections 215, 225, 444A and 707 of the Income and Corporation Taxes Act 1988; and

(*b*) sections 138, 139, 140B and 140D of the Taxation of Chargeable Gains Act 1992.

Time for providing information under section 308, 309 or 310: transitional provisions

6—(1) Where paragraph (2) or (3) applies, the prescribed period or time (as the case may be) to be found in accordance with regulation 4 shall end upon 31st October 2004 instead of the day on which it would end by virtue of that regulation.

(2) This paragraph applies in respect of proposals or arrangements (as the case may be) that are notifiable by virtue of any of the provisions of Part 1 of the Schedule to the Arrangements Regulations—

(*a*) for the purposes of section 308(1), if the relevant date in relation to a proposal falls within the period beginning with 18th March 2004 and ending with 31st July 2004;

(*b*) for the purposes of section 308(3), if the date on which the promoter first becomes aware of any transaction forming part of arrangements falls within the period beginning with 18th March 2004 and ending with 31st July 2004;

(*c*) for the purposes of sections 309 and 310, if the date on which any transaction forming part of arrangements is entered into falls within the period beginning with 23rd April 2004 and ending with 31st July 2004.

(3) This paragraph applies in relation to proposals or arrangements that are notifiable by virtue of any of the provisions of Part 2 of the Schedule to the Arrangements Regulations—

(*a*) for the purposes of section 308(1), if the relevant date in relation to a proposal falls within the period beginning with 22nd June 2004 and ending with 31st July 2004;

(*b*) for the purposes of section 308(3), if the date on which the promoter first becomes aware of any transaction forming part of arrangements falls within the period beginning with 22nd June 2004 and ending with 31st July 2004;

(*c*) for the purposes of sections 309 and 310, if the date on which any transaction forming part of arrangements is entered into falls within the period beginning with 22nd June 2004 and ending with 31st July 2004.

Prescribed information under section 312

7 For the purposes of section 312 (duty of promoter to notify client of number), the prescribed information is the reference number referred to in subsection (1) of that section.

Prescribed information under section 313: timing and manner of delivery

8—(1) For the purposes of section 313 (duty of parties to notifiable arrangements to notify the Board of number, etc)—

(*a*) the prescribed information is—

(i) the reference number allocated by the Board under section 311 to the notifiable arrangements or proposed notifiable arrangements; and

(ii) the year of assessment, tax year or accounting period (as the case may be) in which, or the date on which, the person making the notification expects a tax advantage to be obtained; and

(*b*) the prescribed times at which a person who is a party to notifiable arrangements must provide the Board with information under that section are those specified in whichever of paragraphs (2) to (6) are applicable in his case.

(2) In the case of a person who—

(*a*) expects an advantage to arise in respect of his liability to pay, entitlement to a repayment of, or to a deferment of his liability to pay, income tax or capital gains tax as a result of notifiable arrangements; and (*b*) is required to make a return to the Board by a notice under section 8 or 8A of the Taxes Management Act 1970 (income tax and capital gains tax: personal return and trustee's return), in respect of income tax or capital gains tax,

the prescribed information shall be included in the return under that section which relates to the year of assessment in which he is notified of the reference number under section 311 or 312 (as the case may be), or in which the advantage is expected to arise if earlier; and (in any case) in the return for each subsequent year of assessment until the advantage ceases to apply to him.

This paragraph does not apply if the advantage arises in respect of a partner's share of partnership profits or gains, and is subject to the qualifications in paragraph (6).

(3) In the case of a partnership—

(*a*) which expects an advantage to arise in respect of a partner's liability to pay, entitlement to a repayment of, or to a deferment of the partner's liability to pay any of the prescribed taxes in respect of partnership profits or gains as a result of notifiable arrangements; and

(*b*) in respect of which a return is required to be made to the Board by virtue of a notice under section 12AA of the Taxes Management Act 1970 (partnership return) in respect of any of the prescribed taxes,

the prescribed information shall be included in the returns specified in paragraph (4) covering the period in which the person required to make the return in question is notified of the reference number under section 311 or 312 (as the case may be), or in which the advantage is expected to arise, if earlier; and (in any case) in the return covering each such period until the advantage ceases to apply to the partner in question.

(4) The returns referred to in paragraph (3) are—

(*a*) the partnership's return under section 12AA of the Taxes Management Act 1970, and

(*b*) the return under section 8 or 8A of that Act, or under paragraph 3 of Schedule 18 to the Finance Act 1998, of the partner in respect of whom an advantage is expected.

(5) In the case of a company which—

(*a*) expects a tax advantage to arise in respect of its liability to pay, entitlement to a repayment of, or to a deferment of its liability to pay, corporation tax as a result of notifiable arrangements; and

(*b*) is required to make a return to the Board by a notice under paragraph 3 of Schedule 18 to the Finance Act 1998 (company tax return), in respect of corporation tax,

the prescribed information shall be notified to the Board in the return under that paragraph covering the period in which the company is notified of the reference number under section 311 or 312 (as the case may be), or in which the advantage is expected to arise if earlier; and (in any case) in the return covering each subsequent period until the tax advantage ceases to apply to the company.

This paragraph does not apply if the advantage arises in respect of a partner's share of partnership profits or gains, and is subject to the qualifications in paragraph (6).

(6) In the case of a person who is the employer of an employee, by reason of whose employment a tax advantage is expected to arise to any person in respect of income tax, corporation tax or capital gains tax as a result of notifiable arrangements falling within Part 1 of the Schedule to the Arrangements Regulations, the prescribed information shall be notified to the Board—

(*a*) in the return required under regulation 73 of the Income Tax (Pay As You Earn) Regulations 2003 which relates to the tax year in which—

(i) the employer is notified under section 311 or 312 (as the case may be) of the reference number allocated by the Board under section 311, or

(ii) if earlier in the tax year in which the tax advantage is first expected to arise; and

(*b*) in the return required under that regulation for each subsequent tax year until the tax advantage ceases to apply.

(7) In the case of a person who would be obliged to comply with paragraph (2), (3), (5) or (6), but is not otherwise required, in respect of a year of assessment, accounting period or tax year—

(*a*) in the case of notifiable arrangements to which paragraph (2) applies, to make a return under any of the provisions mentioned in paragraph (2)(*b*),

(*b*) in the case of notifiable arrangements to which paragraph (3) applies, to make a return under any of the provisions referred to in paragraph (4),

(*c*) in the case of notifiable arrangements to which paragraph (5) applies, to make the return mentioned in that paragraph, or

(*d*) in a case to which paragraph (6) applies, to make the return mentioned in that paragraph,

the person must provide the information specified in paragraph (8) to the Board by the appropriate date.

(8) The information specified in this paragraph is—

(*a*) the name and address of the person providing it;

(*b*) any National Insurance number, tax reference number, PAYE reference number or other personal identifier allocated by the Board to the person to whom the information relates;

(*c*) the reference number allocated to the scheme by the Board under section 311;

(*d*) the year of assessment, accounting period or tax year in which, or the date on which, the person providing the information expects to obtain a tax advantage by virtue of the notifiable arrangements;

(*e*) the name of the person providing the declaration as to the accuracy and completeness of the notification;

(*f*) the capacity in which the person mentioned in sub-paragraph (*e*) is acting.

(9) For the purposes of paragraph (7) ''the appropriate date'' is—

(*a*) in a case falling within sub-paragraph (*a*), 31st January next following the end of the tax year in question;

(*b*) in a case falling within sub-paragraph (*b*), the earliest date by which the person in question could be required to file a return under section 12AA of the Taxes Management Act 1970, determined in accordance with whichever of subsections (4) and (5) of that section applies to him;

(*c*) in a case falling within sub-paragraph (*c*), the date defined as the filing date for the purposes of paragraph 14 of Schedule 18 to the Finance Act 1998 in respect of the period of account in question; and

(*d*) in a case falling within sub-paragraph (*d*), the date by which the return under regulation 73 of the Income Tax (Pay As You Earn) Regulations 2003 would be due in respect of the tax year in question.

(10) References in this regulation to information being included in a return include that information being so included by way of an amendment to the return.

Exemption from liability for penalty

9 For the purposes of section 313(4)(*g*) (exemption from liability to penalty under other provisions about returns in respect of duty to notify Board of reference number for notifiable arrangements) section 98A(4) of the Taxes Management Act 1970 is prescribed.

Electronic delivery of information

10—(1) Information required to be delivered to the Board or to any other person by virtue of these Regulations may be delivered in such form and by such means of electronic communications as are for the time being authorised for that purpose.

(2) The use of a particular means of electronic communications is authorised for the purposes of paragraph (1) only if—

(*a*) it is authorised by directions given by the Board under section 132(5) of the Finance Act 1999 (voluntary filing by electronic means of returns and other documents); and

(*b*) the user complies with any conditions imposed by the Board under that section.

(3) Nothing in this regulation prevents the delivery of information by electronic communications if the information is contained in a return which is—

(*a*) authorised to be delivered electronically by virtue of regulations under section 132 of the Finance Act 1999; or

(*b*) required to be so delivered by virtue of regulations under section 135 of the Finance Act 2002 (mandatory e-filing).

2004/1865

Tax Avoidance Schemes (Promoters and Prescribed Circumstances) Regulations 2004

Made	*22nd July 2004*
Laid before the House of Commons	*22nd July 2004*
Coming into force	*1st August 2004*

The Commissioners of Inland Revenue, in exercise of the powers conferred upon them by sections 307(5) and 318(1) of the Finance Act 2004, make the following Regulations:

Citation, commencement and interpretation

1—(1) These Regulations may be cited as the Tax Avoidance Schemes (Promoters and Prescribed Circumstances) Regulations 2004 and shall come into force on 1st August 2004.

(2) In these Regulations—

''notifiable arrangements'' has the meaning given by section 306(1);

''notifiable proposal'' has the meaning given by section 306(2); and

except where the context otherwise requires a reference to a numbered section (without more) is a reference to the section of the Finance Act 2004 which is so numbered.

(3) For the purposes of these Regulations section 839 of the Income and Corporation Taxes Act 1988 applies to determine whether persons are connected.

Persons not to be treated as promoters—groups

2—(1) A person is not to be treated as a promoter where—

(a) the person carrying on the relevant business referred to in section 307(1) is a company (''company A''); and

(b) on the date specified in paragraph (2) the other person (or each of the other persons) to whom company A provides services in connection with a notifiable proposal or notifiable arrangements is a company which is a member of the same group as company A.

(2) The date specified by this paragraph is—

(a) in relation to a notifiable proposal, the relevant date within the meaning given by section 308(2);

(b) in relation to notifiable arrangements, the date mentioned in section 308(3).

(3) For the purposes of this regulation two companies are members of the same group if they would, by virtue of the provisions of section 170 of the Taxation of Chargeable Gains Act 1992, be members of the same group for the purposes of sections 171 to 181 of that Act if section 170 were modified as follows—

(a) for each of the references to a 75 per cent subsidiary there were substituted a reference to a 51 per cent subsidiary;

(b) subsection (3)*(b)* and subsections (6) to (8) were omitted.

Persons not to be treated as promoters—employees

3—(1) A person is not to be treated as a promoter in relation to a notifiable proposal or notifiable arrangements where he is an employee of an employer who is—

(a) a promoter in relation to the proposal or the arrangements; or

(b) a person who—

(i) is to enter into any transaction forming part of the proposed arrangements; or

(ii) enters into any transaction forming part of the arrangements.

(2) In this regulation ''employee'' and ''employer'' have the same meanings as they have for the purposes of the employment income Parts of the Income Tax (Earnings and Pensions) Act 2003 (see section 4 of that Act) and—

(a) ''employee'' includes an office holder to whom the provisions of those Parts that are expressed to apply to employments apply equally (see section 5 of that Act); and

(b) ''employer'' includes a person under whom an office holder holds office and to whom those provisions similarly apply.

(3) For the purposes of this regulation an employee of a person who is connected with another person (''A'') shall be treated as an employee of A.

Persons not to be treated as promoters under section 307(1)(a)(i) or (b)(i)

4—(1) A person is not to be treated as a promoter under section 307(1)*(a)*(i) or *(b)*(i) where paragraph (2), (3) or (4) applies.

(2) This paragraph applies where, in the course of providing tax advice, a person is not responsible for the design of any element of the proposed arrangements or arrangements (including the way in which they are structured) from which the tax advantage expected to be obtained arises.

(3) This paragraph applies where—

(a) a person, in the course of a business that is a relevant business for the purposes of section 307 by virtue of subsection (2)*(a)* of that section, is to any extent responsible for the design of the proposed arrangements or arrangements; but

(b) does not provide tax advice in the course of carrying out his responsibilities in relation to the proposed arrangements or arrangements.

(4) This paragraph applies where a person—

(a) is not responsible for the design of all the elements of the proposed arrangements or arrangements (including the way in which they are structured) from which the tax advantage expected to be obtained arises; and

(b) could not reasonably be expected to have—

(i) sufficient information as would enable him to know whether or not the proposal is a notifiable proposal or the arrangements are notifiable arrangements; or

(ii) sufficient information as would enable him to comply with section 308(1) or (3).

Persons not to be treated as promoters under section 307(1)(b)(ii)

5 A person is not to be treated as a promoter under section 307(1)*(b)*(ii) where he is not connected with another person who is a promoter under section 307(1)*(a)* or *(b)*(i) in relation to—

(a) the arrangements; or

(b) arrangements which are substantially the same as those arrangements.

EC TREATY AND LEGISLATION

CONTENTS

Treaty Establishing the European Community (previously the European Economic Community)

Note—The text of this treaty reflects amendments made by the Treaty of Amsterdam, including the renumbering of articles (OJ C340 10.11.97 p 1). The Treaty of Amsterdam was ratified on 1 May 1999.

PART THREE
COMMUNITY POLICIES

TITLE III—FREE MOVEMENT OF PERSONS, SERVICES AND CAPITAL

Chapter 1
Workers

Article 39 (ex Article 48)

1. Freedom of movement for workers shall be secured within the Community.

2. Such freedom of movement shall entail the abolition of any discrimination based on nationality between workers of the Member States as regards employment, remuneration and other conditions of work and employment.

3. It shall entail the right, subject to limitations justified on grounds of public policy, public security or public health:

(*a*) to accept offers of employment actually made;

(*b*) to move freely within the territory of Member States for this purpose;

(*c*) to stay in a Member State for the purpose of employment in accordance with the provisions governing the employment of nationals of that State laid down by law, regulation or administrative action;

(*d*) to remain in the territory of a Member State after having been employed in that State, subject to conditions which shall be embodied in implementing regulations to be drawn up by the Commission.

4. The provisions of this Article shall not apply to employment in the public service.

Simon's Tax Cases—*Zurstrassen v Administration des Contributions Directes* [2001] STC 1102*; *R (on the application of Professional Contractors Group Ltd and others) v IRC* [2002] STC 165.

Article 40 (ex Article 49)

The Council shall, acting in accordance with the procedure referred to in Article 251 and after consulting the Economic and Social Committee, issue directives or make regulations setting out the measures required to bring about freedom of movement for workers, as defined in Article 39, in particular:

(*a*) by ensuring close co-operation between national employment services;

(*b*) by abolishing those administrative procedures and practices and those qualifying periods in respect of eligibility for available employment, whether resulting from national legislation or from agreements previously concluded between Member States, the maintenance of which would form an obstacle to liberalisation of the movement of workers;

(*c*) by abolishing all such qualifying periods and other restrictions provided for either under national legislation or under agreements previously concluded between Member States as imposed on workers of other Member States conditions regarding the free choice of employment other than those imposed on workers of the State concerned;

(*d*) by setting up appropriate machinery to bring offers of employment into touch with applications for employment and to facilitate the achievement of a balance between supply and demand in the employment market in such a way as to avoid serious threats to the standard of living and level of employment in the various regions and industries.

Article 41 (ex Article 50)

Member States shall, within the framework of a joint programme, encourage the exchange of young workers.

Article 42 (ex Article 51)

The Council shall, acting in accordance with the procedure referred to in Article 251, adopt such measures in the field of social security as are necessary to provide freedom of movement for workers; to this end, it shall make arrangements to secure for migrant workers and their dependants:

(*a*) aggregation, for the purpose of acquiring and retaining the right to benefit and of calculating the amount of benefit, of all periods taken into account under the laws of the several countries;

(*b*) payment of benefits to persons resident in the territories of Member States.

The Council shall act unanimously throughout the procedure referred to in Article 251.

Chapter 2

Right of establishment

Article 43 (ex Article 52)

Within the framework of the provisions set out below, restrictions on the freedom of establishment of nationals of a Member State in the territory of another Member State shall be prohibited. Such prohibition shall also apply to restrictions on the setting-up of agencies, branches or subsidiaries by nationals of any Member State established in the territory of any Member State.

Freedom of establishment shall include the right to take up and pursue activities as self-employed persons and to set up and manage undertakings, in particular companies or firms within the meaning of the second paragraph of Article 48, under the conditions laid down for its own nationals by the law of the country where such establishment is effected, subject to the provisions of the Chapter relating to capital.

Simon's Tax Cases—*R (on the application of Professional Contractors Group Ltd and others) v IRC* [2002] STC 165; *Algemene Maatschappij voor Investering en Dienstverlening NV v Belgian State* [2003] STC 356; *Marks and Spencer plc v Halsey (Insp of Taxes)* [2003] STC (SCD) 70; *Lankhorst-Hohorst GmbH v Finanzamt Steinfurt* [2003] STC 607; *Bosal Holding BV v Staatssecretaris van Financiën* [2003] STC 1483.

Article 44 (ex Article 54)

1. In order to attain freedom of establishment as regards a particular activity, the Council, acting in accordance with the procedure referred to in Article 251 and after consulting the Economic and Social Committee, shall act by means of directives.

2. The Council and the Commission shall carry out the duties devolving upon them under the preceding provisions, in particular:

(*a*) by according, as a general rule, priority treatment to activities where freedom of establishment makes a particularly valuable contribution to the development of production and trade;
(*b*) by ensuring close co-operation between the competent authorities in the Member States in order to ascertain the particular situation within the Community of the various activities concerned;
(*c*) by abolishing those administrative procedures and practices, whether resulting from national legislation or from agreements previously concluded between Member States, the maintenance of which would form an obstacle to freedom of establishment;
(*d*) by ensuring that workers of one Member State employed in the territory of another Member State may remain in that territory for the purpose of taking up activities therein as self-employed persons, where they satisfy the conditions which they would be required to satisfy if they were entering that State at the time when they intended to take up such activities;
(*e*) by enabling a national of one Member State to acquire and use land and buildings situated in the territory of another Member State, insofar as this does not conflict with the principles laid down in Article 33(2);
(*f*) by effecting the progressive abolition of restrictions on freedom of establishment in every branch of activity under consideration, both as regards the conditions for setting up agencies, branches or subsidiaries in the territory of a Member State and as regards the subsidiaries in the territory of a Member State and as regards the conditions governing the entry of personnel belonging to the main establishment into managerial or supervisory posts in such agencies, branches or subsidiaries;
(*g*) by co-ordinating to the necessary extent the safeguards which, for the protection of the interests of members and other, are required by Member States of companies or firms within the meaning of the second paragraph of Article 48 with a view to making such safeguards equivalent throughout the Community;
(*h*) by satisfying themselves that the conditions of establishment are not distorted by aids granted by Member States.

Article 45 (ex Article 55)

The provisions of this Chapter shall not apply, so far as any given Member State is concerned, to activities which in that State are connected, even occasionally, with the exercise of official authority.

The Council may, acting by a qualified majority on a proposal from the Commission, rule that the provisions of this Chapter shall not apply to certain activities.

Article 46 (ex Article 56)

1. The provisions of this Chapter and measures taken in pursuance thereof shall not prejudice the applicability of provisions laid down by law, regulation or administrative action providing for special treatment for foreign nationals on grounds of public policy, public security or public health.

2. The Council shall, acting in accordance with the procedure referred to in Article 251, issue directives for the co-ordination of the abovementioned provisions.

Article 47 (ex Article 57)

1. In order to make it easier for persons to take up and pursue activities as self-employed persons, the Council shall, acting in accordance with the procedure referred to in Article 251, issue directives for the mutual recognition of diplomas, certificates and other evidence of formal qualifications.

2. For the same purpose, the Council shall, acting in accordance with the procedure referred to in Article 251, issue directives for the co-ordination of the provisions laid down by law, regulation or administrative action in Member States concerning the taking-up and pursuit of activities as self-employed persons. The Council, acting unanimously throughout the procedure referred to in Article 251, shall decide on directives the implementation of which involves in at least one Member State amendment of the existing principles laid down by law governing the professions with respect to training and conditions of access for natural persons. In other cases the Council shall act by qualified majority.

3. In the case of the medical and allied and pharmaceutical professions, the progressive abolition of restrictions shall be dependent upon co-ordination of the conditions for their exercise in the various Member States.

Article 48 (ex Article 58)

Companies or firms formed in accordance with the law of a Member State and having their registered office, central administration or principal place of business within the Community shall, for the purposes of this Chapter, be treated in the same way as natural persons who are nationals of Member States.

''Companies or firms'' means companies or firms constituted under civil or commercial law, including co-operative societies, and other legal persons governed by public or private law, save for those which are non-profit-making.

Simon's Tax Cases—*Bosal Holding BV v Staatssecretaris van Financiën* [2003] STC 1483.

CHAPTER 3

SERVICES

Article 49 (ex Article 59)

Within the framework of the provisions set out below, restrictions on freedom to provide services within the Community shall be prohibited in respect of nationals of Member States who are established in a State of the Community other than that of the person for whom the services are intended.

The Council may, acting by a qualified majority on a proposal from the Commission, extend the provisions of the Chapter to nationals of a third country who provide services and who are established within the Community.

Simon's Tax Cases—*R (on the application of Professional Contractors Group Ltd and others) v IRC* [2002] STC 165; *Proceedings brought by Danner* [2002] STC 1283; *Försäkringsaktiebolaget Skandia (publ) and another v Riksskatteverket* [2003] STC 1361.

Article 50 (ex Article 60)

Services shall be considered to be 'services' within the meaning of this Treaty where they are normally provided for remuneration, insofar as they are not governed by the provisions relating to freedom of movement for goods, capital and persons.

''Services'' shall in particular include:

(*a*) activities of an industrial character;
(*b*) activities of a commercial character;
(*c*) activities of craftsmen;
(*d*) activities of the professions.

Without prejudice to the provisions of the Chapter relating to the right of establishment, the person providing a service may, in order to do so, temporarily pursue his activity in the State where the service is provided, under the same conditions as are imposed by that State on its own nationals.

Article 51 (ex Article 61)

1. Freedom to provide services in the field of transport shall be governed by the provisions of the Title relating to transport.

2. The liberalisation of banking and insurance services connected with movements of capital shall be effected in step with the liberalisation of movement of capital.

Article 52 (ex Article 63)

1. In order to achieve the liberalisation of a specific service, the Council shall, on a proposal from the Commission and after consulting the Economic and Social Committee and the European Parliament, issue directives acting by a qualified majority.

2. As regards the directives referred to in paragraph 1, priority shall as a general rule be given to those services which directly affect production costs or the liberalisation of which helps to promote trade in goods.

Article 53 (ex Article 64)

The Member States declare their readiness to undertake the liberalisation of services beyond the extent required by the directives issued pursuant to Article 52(1), if their general economic situation and the situation of the economic sector concerned so permit.

To this end, the Commission shall make recommendations to the Member States concerned.

Article 54 (ex Article 65)

As long as restrictions on freedom to provide services have not been abolished, each Member State shall apply such restrictions without distinction on grounds of nationality or residence to all persons providing services within the meaning of the first paragraph of Article 49.

Article 55 (ex Article 66)

The provisions of Articles 45 to 48 shall apply to the matters covered by this Chapter.

CHAPTER 4—CAPITAL AND PAYMENTS

[Article 56 (ex Article 73b)

1. Within the framework of the provisions set out in this Chapter, all restrictions on the movement of capital between Member States and between Member States and third countries shall be prohibited.

2. Within the framework of the provisions set out in this Chapter, all restrictions on payments between Member States and between Member States and third countries shall be prohibited.][1]

Statement of Practice SP 2/92—Movements of capital between residents of EC Member States.
Simon's Tax Cases—*EC Commission v Belgium* [2000] STC 830.
Amendment—[1] This article substituted by the Treaty on European Union signed at Maastricht on 7 February 1992, with effect from 1 January 1994.

[Article 57 (ex Article 73c)

1. The provisions of Article 56 shall be without prejudice to the application to third countries of any restrictions which exist on 31 December 1992 under national or Community law adopted in respect of the movement of capital to or from third countries involving direct investment—including in real estate—establishment, the provision of financial services or the admission of securities to capital markets.

2. Whilst endeavouring to achieve the objective of free movement of capital between Member States and third countries to the greatest extent possible and without prejudice to the other Chapters of this Treaty, the Council may, acting by a qualified majority on a proposal from the Commission, adopt measures on the movement of capital to or from third countries involving direct investment—including investment in real estate—establishment, the provision of financial services or the admission of securities to capital markets. Unanimity shall be required for measures under this paragraph which constitute a step back in Community law as regards the liberalisation of the movement of capital to or from third countries.][1]

Amendment—[1] This article substituted by the Treaty on European Union signed at Maastricht on 7 February 1992, with effect from 1 January 1994.

[Article 58 (ex Article 73d)

1. The provisions of Article 56 shall be without prejudice to the right of Member States—

(*a*) to apply the relevant provisions of their tax law which distinguish between taxpayers who are not in the same situation with regard to their place of residence or with regard to the place where their capital is invested;

(*b*) to take all requisite measures to prevent infringements of national law and regulations, in particular in the field of taxation and the prudential supervision of financial institutions, or to lay down procedures for the declaration of capital movements for purposes of administrative or statistical information, or to take measures which are justified on grounds of public policy or public security.

2. The provisions of this Chapter shall be without prejudice to the applicability of restrictions on the right of establishment which are compatible with this Treaty.

3. The measures and procedures referred to in paragraphs 1 and 2 shall not constitute a means of arbitrary discrimination or a disguised restriction on the free movement of capital and payments as defined in Article 56.][1]

Simon's Tax Cases—*Royal Bank of Scotland v Greek State* [2000] STC 733.
Amendment—[1] This article substituted by the Treaty on European Union signed at Maastricht on 7 February 1992, with effect from 1 January 1994.

[Article 59 (ex Article 73f)

Where, in exceptional circumstances, movements of capital to or from third countries cause, or threaten to cause, serious difficulties for the operation of economic and monetary union, the Council, acting by a qualified majority on a proposal from the Commission and after consulting the ECB, may take safeguard measures with regard to third countries for a period not exceeding six months if such measures are strictly necessary.][1]

Amendment—[1] This article substituted by the Treaty on European Union signed at Maastricht on 7 February 1992, with effect from 1 January 1994.

[Article 60 (ex Article 73g)

1. If, in the cases envisaged in Article 301, action by the Community is deemed necessary, the Council may, in accordance with the procedure provided for in Article 301, take the necessary urgent measures on the movement of capital and on payments as regards the third countries concerned.

2. Without prejudice to Article 297 and as long as the Council has not taken measures pursuant to paragraph 1, a Member State may, for serious political reasons and on grounds of urgency, take unilateral measures against a third country with regard to capital movements and payments. The Commission and the other Member States shall be informed of such measures by the date of their entry into force at the latest.

The Council may, acting by a qualified majority on a proposal from the Commission, decide that the Member State concerned shall amend or abolish such measures. The President of the Council shall inform the European Parliament of any such decision taken by the Council.][1]

Note—Article 301 is not printed. That Article refers to an action by the Community to interrupt or reduce economic relations with a third country.

Amendment—[1] This article substituted by the Treaty on European Union signed at Maastricht on 7 February 1992, with effect from 1 January 1994.

[TITLE VI (EX TITLE V)—COMMON RULES ON COMPETITION, TAXATION AND APPROXIMATION OF LAWS][1]

CHAPTER 2—TAX PROVISIONS

Article 90 (ex Article 95)

No Member State shall impose, directly or indirectly, on the products of other Member States any internal taxation of any kind in excess of that imposed directly or indirectly on similar domestic products.

Furthermore, no Member State shall impose on the products of other Member States any internal taxation of such a nature as to afford indirect protection to other products.

Simon's Tax Cases—*EC Commission v Kingdom of Spain* [1993] STC 150*; *EC Commission v Hellenic Republic* [1993] STC 160*; *EC Commission v French Republic (Case C-276/91)* [1997] STC 584*; [1997] *Fazenda Pública v Fricarnes SA* [1997] STC 1348*.

Article 91 (ex Article 96)

Where products are exported to the territory of any Member State, any repayment of internal taxation shall not exceed the internal taxation imposed on them, whether directly or indirectly.

Article 92 (ex Article 98)

In the case of charges other than turnover taxes, excise duties and other forms of indirect taxation, remissions and repayments in respect of exports to other Member States may not be granted and countervailing charges in respect of imports from Member States may not be imposed unless the measures contemplated have been previously approved for a limited period by the Council acting by a qualified majority on a proposal from the Commission.

[Article 93 (ex Article 99)

The Council shall, acting unanimously on a proposal from the Commission and after consulting the European Parliament and the Economic and Social Committee, adopt provisions for the harmonisation of legislation concerning turnover taxes, excise duties and other forms of indirect taxation to the extent that such harmonisation is necessary to ensure the establishment and the functioning of the internal market within the time-limit laid down in Article 14.][2]

Note—Article 14 is not printed. The time limit laid down in that Article is 31 December 1992.

Amendments—[1] Title introduced by article G(17) of the Treaty on European Union signed at Maastricht on 7 February 1992.
[2] This article substituted by virtue of the Treaty on European Union signed at Maastricht on 7 February 1992.

EC Material

CHAPTER 3—APPROXIMATION OF LAWS

[Article 94 (ex Article 100)

The Council shall, acting unanimously on a proposal from the Commission and after consulting the European Parliament and the Economic and Social Committee, issue directives for the approximation of such laws, regulations or administrative provisions of the Member States as directly affect the establishment or functioning of the common market.][1]

Amendment—[1] This article substituted by the Treaty on European Union signed at Maastricht on 7 February 1992.

[Article 95 (ex Article 100a)

[1. By way of derogation from Article 94 and save where otherwise provided in this Treaty, the following provisions shall apply for the achievement of the objectives set out in Article 14. The Council shall, acting in accordance with the procedure referred to in Article 251 and after consulting the Economic and Social Committee, adopt the measures for the approximation of the provisions laid down by law, regulation or administrative action in Member States which have as their object the establishment and functioning of the internal market.][2]

2. Paragraph 1 shall not apply to fiscal provisions, to those relating to the free movement of persons nor to those relating to the rights and interests of employed persons.

3. The Commission, in its proposals envisaged in paragraph 1 concerning health, safety, environmental protection and consumer protection, will take as a base a high level of protection, taking account in particular of any new development based on scientific facts. Within their respective powers, the European Parliament and the Council will also seek to achieve this objective.

4. If, after the adoption by the Council or by the Commission of a harmonisation measure, a Member State deems it necessary to maintain national provisions on grounds of major needs referred to in Article 30, or relating to the protection of the environment or the working environment, it shall notify the Commission of these provisions as well as the grounds for maintaining them.

5. Moreover, without prejudice to paragraph 4, if, after the adoption by the Council or by the Commission of a harmonisation measure, a Member State deems it necessary to introduce national provisions based on new scientific evidence relating to the protection of the environment or the working environment on grounds of a problem specific to that Member State arising after the adoption of the harmonisation measure, it shall notify the Commission of the envisaged provisions as well as the grounds for introducing them.

6. The Commission shall, within six months of the notifications as referred to in paragraphs 4 and 5, approve or reject the national provisions involved after having verified whether or not they are a means of arbitrary discrimination or a disguised restriction on trade between Member States and whether or not they shall constitute an obstacle to the functioning of the internal market.

In the absence of a decision by the Commission within this period the national provisions referred to in paragraphs 4 and 5 shall be deemed to have been approved.

When justified by the complexity of the matter and in the absence of danger for human health, the Commission may notify the Member State concerned that the period referred to in this paragraph may be extended for a further period of up to six months.

7. When, pursuant to paragraph 6, a Member State is authorised to maintain or introduce national provisions derogating from a harmonisation measure, the Commission shall immediately examine whether to propose an adaptation to that measure.

8. When a Member State raises a specific problem on public health in a field which has been the subject of prior harmonisation measures, it shall bring it to the attention of the Commission which shall immediately examine whether to propose appropriate measures to the Council.

9. By way of derogation from the procedure laid down in Articles 226 and 227, the Commission and any Member State may bring the matter directly before the Court of Justice if it considers that another Member State is making improper use of the powers provided for in this Article.

10. The harmonisation measures referred to above shall, in appropriate cases, include a safeguard clause authorising the Member States to take, for one or more of the non-economic reasons referred to in Article 30, provisional measures subject to a Community control procedure.][1]

Note—Article 14 is not printed. The objective set out in that Article is that of establishing the internal market.
Article 30 is not printed. The non-economic reasons referred to in that Article are—

> "public morality, public policy or public security; the protection of health and life of humans, animals or plants; the protection of national treasures possessing artistic, historic or archaeological value; or the protection of industrial and commercial property".

Amendments—[1] This article added by the Single European Act 1987 art. 18.
[2] Paragraph 1 substituted by virtue of the Treaty on European Union signed at Maastricht on 7 February 1992.

Article 96 (ex Article 101)

Where the Commission finds that a difference between the provisions laid down by law, regulation or administrative action in Member States is distorting the conditions of competition in the common market and that the resultant distortion needs to be eliminated, it shall consult the Member States concerned.

If such consultation does not result in an agreement eliminating the distortion in question, the Council shall, on a proposal from the Commission, acting by a qualified majority, issue the necessary directives. The Commission and the Council may take any other appropriate measures provided for in this Treaty.

Article 97 (ex Article 102)

1. Where there is reason to fear that the adoption or amendment of a provision laid down by law, regulation or administrative action may cause distortion within the meaning of Article 96, a Member State desiring to proceed therewith shall consult the Commission. After consulting the Member States, the Commission shall recommend to the States concerned such measures as may be appropriate to avoid the distortion in question.

2. If a State desiring to introduce or amend its own provisions does not comply with the recommendation addressed to it by the Commission, other Member States shall not be required, in pursuance of Article 96, to amend their own provisions in order to eliminate such distortion. If the Member State which has ignored the recommendation of the Commission causes distortion detrimental only to itself, the provisions of Article 96 shall not apply.

[TITLE VII (EX TITLE VI)—ECONOMIC AND MONETARY POLICY

[CHAPTER 1—ECONOMIC POLICY

Article 98 (ex Article 102a)

Member-States shall conduct their economic policies with a view to contributing to the achievement of the objectives of the Community, as defined in Article 2, and in the context of the broad guidelines referred to in Article 99(2). The member-States and the Community shall act in accordance with the principle of an open market economy with free competition, favouring an efficient allocation of resources, and in compliance with the principles set out in Article 4.][1]][2]

Amendments—[1] This chapter added by the single European Act 1987 art 20.
[2] This title amended by virtue of the Treaty on European Union signed at Maastricht on 7 February 1992.

PART FIVE
INSTITUTIONS OF THE COMMUNITY

TITLE I—PROVISIONS GOVERNING THE INSTITUTIONS

CHAPTER 1—THE INSTITUTIONS

SECTION 4—THE COURT OF JUSTICE

[Article 220

The Court of Justice and the Court of First Instance, each within its jurisdiction, shall ensure that in the interpretation and application of this Treaty the law is observed.

In addition, judicial panels may be attached to the Court of First Instance under the conditions laid down in Article 225a in order to exercise, in certain specific areas, the judicial competence laid down in this Treaty.][1]

Amendments—[1] This article substituted by the Treaty of Nice Article 2(26). The Treaty was signed at Nice on 26 February 2001. See OJ C 80; 10.03.01, p 1.

[Article 221

The Court of Justice shall consist of one judge per Member State.

The Court of Justice shall sit in chambers or in a Grand Chamber, in accordance with the rules laid down for that purpose in the Statute of the Court of Justice.

When provided for in the Statute, the Court of Justice may also sit as a full Court.][1]

Amendments—[1] This article substituted by the Treaty of Nice Article 2(27). The Treaty was signed at Nice on 26 February 2001. See OJ C 80; 10.03.01, p 1.

[Article 222

The Court of Justice shall be assisted by eight Advocates-General. Should the Court of Justice so request, the Council, acting unanimously, may increase the number of Advocates-General.

It shall be the duty of the Advocate-General, acting with complete impartiality and independence, to make, in open court, reasoned submissions on cases which, in accordance with the Statute of the Court of Justice, require his involvement.][1]

Amendments—[1] This article substituted by the Treaty of Nice Article 2(28). The Treaty was signed at Nice on 26 February 2001. See OJ C 80; 10.03.01, p 1.

[Article 223

The Judges and Advocates-General of the Court of Justice shall be chosen from persons whose independence is beyond doubt and who possess the qualifications required for appointment to the highest judicial offices in their respective countries or who are jurisconsults of recognised competence; they shall be appointed by common accord of the governments of the Member States for a term of six years.

Every three years there shall be a partial replacement of the Judges and Advocates-General, in accordance with the conditions laid down in the Statute of the Court of Justice.

The Judges shall elect the President of the Court of Justice from among their number for a term of three years. He may be re-elected.

Retiring Judges and Advocates-General may be reappointed.

The Court of Justice shall appoint its Registrar and lay down the rules governing his service.

The Court of Justice shall establish its Rules of Procedure. Those Rules shall require the approval of the Council, acting by a qualified majority.][1]

Amendments—[1] This article substituted by the Treaty of Nice Article 2(29). The Treaty was signed at Nice on 26 February 2001. See OJ C 80; 10.03.01, p 1.

[Article 224

The Court of First Instance shall comprise at least one judge per Member State. The number of Judges shall be determined by the Statute of the Court of Justice. The Statute may provide for the Court of First Instance to be assisted by Advocates-General.

The members of the Court of First Instance shall be chosen from persons whose independence is beyond doubt and who possess the ability required for appointment to high judicial office. They shall be appointed by common accord of the governments of the Member States for a term of six years. The membership shall be partially renewed every three years. Retiring members shall be eligible for reappointment.

The Judges shall elect the President of the Court of First Instance from among their number for a term of three years. He may be re-elected.

The Court of First Instance shall appoint its Registrar and lay down the rules governing his service.

The Court of First Instance shall establish its Rules of Procedure in agreement with the Court of Justice. Those Rules shall require the approval of the Council, acting by a qualified majority.

Unless the Statute of the Court of Justice provides otherwise, the provisions of this Treaty relating to the Court of Justice shall apply to the Court of First Instance.][1]

Amendments—[1] This article substituted by the Treaty of Nice Article 2(30). The Treaty was signed at Nice on 26 February 2001. See OJ C 80; 10.03.01, p 1.

[Article 225

1. The Court of First Instance shall have jurisdiction to hear and determine at first instance actions or proceedings referred to in Articles 230, 232, 235, 236 and 238, with the exception of those assigned to a judicial panel and those reserved in the Statute for the Court of Justice. The Statute may provide for the Court of First Instance to have jurisdiction for other classes of action or proceeding.

Decisions given by the Court of First Instance under this paragraph may be subject to a right of appeal to the Court of Justice on points of law only, under the conditions and within the limits laid down by the Statute.

2. The Court of First Instance shall have jurisdiction to hear and determine actions or proceedings brought against decisions of the judicial panels set up under Article 225a.

Decisions given by the Court of First Instance under this paragraph may exceptionally be subject to review by the Court of Justice, under the conditions and within the limits laid down by the Statute, where there is a serious risk of the unity or consistency of Community law being affected.

3. The Court of First Instance shall have jurisdiction to hear and determine questions referred for a preliminary ruling under Article 234, in specific areas laid down by the Statute.

Where the Court of First Instance considers that the case requires a decision of principle likely to affect the unity or consistency of Community law, it may refer the case to the Court of Justice for a ruling.

Decisions given by the Court of First Instance on questions referred for a preliminary ruling may exceptionally be subject to review by the Court of Justice, under the conditions and within the limits laid down by the Statute, where there is a serious risk of the unity or consistency of Community law being affected.][1]

Amendments—[1] This article substituted by the Treaty of Nice Article 2(31). The Treaty was signed at Nice on 26 February 2001. See OJ C 80; 10.03.01, p 1.

[Article 225a

The Council, acting unanimously on a proposal from the Commission and after consulting the European Parliament and the Court of Justice or at the request of the Court of Justice and after consulting the European Parliament and the Commission, may create judicial panels to hear and determine at first instance certain classes of action or proceeding brought in specific areas.

The decision establishing a judicial panel shall lay down the rules on the organisation of the panel and the extent of the jurisdiction conferred upon it.

Decisions given by judicial panels may be subject to a right of appeal on points of law only or, when provided for in the decision establishing the panel, a right of appeal also on matters of fact, before the Court of First Instance.

The members of the judicial panels shall be chosen from persons whose independence is beyond doubt and who possess the ability required for appointment to judicial office. They shall be appointed by the Council, acting unanimously.

The judicial panels shall establish their Rules of Procedure in agreement with the Court of Justice. Those Rules shall require the approval of the Council, acting by a qualified majority.

Unless the decision establishing the judicial panel provides otherwise, the provisions of this Treaty relating to the Court of Justice and the provisions of the Statute of the Court of Justice shall apply to the judicial panels.][1]

Amendments—[1] This article inserted by the Treaty of Nice Article 2(32). The Treaty was signed at Nice on 26 February 2001. See OJ C 80; 10.03.01, p 1.

Article 226 (ex Article 169)

If the Commission considers that a Member State has failed to fulfil an obligation under this Treaty, it shall deliver a reasoned opinion on the matter after giving the State concerned the opportunity to submit its observations.

If the State concerned does not comply with the opinion within the period laid down by the Commission, the latter may bring the matter before the Court of Justice.

Simon's Tax Cases—*EC Commission v Federal Republic of Germany (Case C-74/91)* [1996] STC 843*.

Article 227 (ex Article 170)

A Member State which considers that another Member State has failed to fulfil an obligation under this Treaty may bring the matter before the Court of Justice.

Before a Member State brings an action against another Member State for an alleged infringement of an obligation under this Treaty, it shall bring the matter before the Commission.

The Commission shall deliver a reasoned opinion after each of the States concerned has been given the opportunity to submit its own case and its observations on the other party's case both orally and in writing.

If the Commission has not delivered an opinion within three months of the date on which the matter was brought before it, the absence of such opinion shall not prevent the matter from being brought before the Court of Justice.

[Article 228 (ex Article 171)

1. If the Court of Justice finds that a Member State has failed to fulfil an obligation under this Treaty, the State shall be required to take the necessary measures to comply with the judgment of the Court of Justice.

2. If the Commission considers that the Member State concerned has not taken such measures it shall, after giving that State the opportunity to submit its observations, issue a reasoned opinion specifying the points on which the Member State concerned has not complied with the judgment of the Court of Justice.

If the Member State concerned fails to take the necessary measures to comply with the Court's judgment within the time-limit laid down by the Commission, the latter may bring the case before the Court of Justice. In so doing it shall specify the amount of the lump sum or penalty payment to be paid by the Member State concerned which it considers appropriate in the circumstances.

If the Court of Justice finds that the Member State concerned has not complied with its judgment it may impose a lump sum or penalty payment on it.

This procedure shall be without prejudice to Article 227.][1]

Amendments—[1] This article substituted by virtue of the Treaty on European Union signed at Maastricht on 7 February 1992.

[Article 229 (ex Article 172)

Regulations adopted jointly by the European Parliament and the Council, and by the Council, pursuant to the provisions of this Treaty, may give the Court of Justice unlimited jurisdiction with regard to the penalties provided for in such regulations.][1]

Amendments—[1] This article substituted by virtue of the Treaty on European Union signed at Maastricht on 7 February 1992.

[Article 229a

Without prejudice to the other provisions of this Treaty, the Council, acting unanimously on a proposal from the Commission and after consulting the European Parliament, may adopt provisions to confer jurisdiction, to the extent that it shall determine, on the Court of Justice in disputes relating to the application of acts adopted on the basis of this Treaty which create Community industrial property rights. The Council shall recommend those provisions to the Member States for adoption in accordance with their respective constitutional requirements.][1]

Amendment—[1] This article inserted by the Treaty of Nice Article 2(33). The Treaty was signed at Nice on 26 February 2001. See OJ C 80; 10.03.01, p 1.

[Article 230 (ex Article 173)

The Court of Justice shall review the legality of acts adopted jointly by the European Parliament and the Council, of acts of the Council, of the Commission and of the ECB, other than recommendations and opinions, and of acts of the European Parliament intended to produce legal effects *vis-à-vis* third parties.

[It shall for this purpose have jurisdiction in actions brought by a Member State, the European Parliament, the Council or the Commission on grounds of lack of competence, infringement of an essential procedural requirement, infringement of this Treaty or of any rule of law relating to its application, or misuse of powers.][2]

[The Court of Justice shall have jurisdiction under the same conditions in actions brought by the Court of Auditors and by the ECB for the purpose of protecting their prerogatives.][2]

Any natural or legal person may, under the same conditions, institute proceedings against a decision addressed to that person or against a decision which, although in the form of a regulation or a decision addressed to another person, is of direct and individual concern to the former.

The proceedings provided for in this Article shall be instituted within two months of the publication of the measure, or of its notification to the plaintiff, or, in the absence thereof, of the day on which it came to the knowledge of the latter, as the case may be.][1]

Amendments—[1] This article substituted by virtue of the Treaty on European Union signed at Maastricht on 7 February 1992.
[2] Second and third paragraphs substituted by the Treaty of Nice Article 2(34). The Treaty was signed at Nice on 26 February 2001. See OJ C 80; 10.03.01, p 1.

Article 231 (ex Article 174)

If the action is well founded, the Court of Justice shall declare the act concerned to be void.

In the case of a regulation, however, the Court of Justice shall, if it considers this necessary, state which of the effects of the regulation which it has declared void shall be considered as definitive.

[Article 232 (ex Article 175)

Should the European Parliament, the Council or the Commission, in infringement of this Treaty, fail to act, the Member States and the other institutions of the Community may bring an action before the Court of Justice to have the infringement established.

The action shall be admissible only if the institution concerned has first been called upon to act. If, within two months of being so called upon, the institution concerned has not defined its position, the action may be brought within a further period of two months.

Any natural or legal person may, under the conditions laid down in the preceding paragraphs, complain to the Court of Justice that an institution of the Community has failed to address to that person any act other than a recommendation or an opinion.

The Court of Justice shall have jurisdiction, under the same conditions, in actions or proceedings brought by the ECB in the areas falling within the latter's field of competence and in actions or proceedings brought against the latter.][1]

Amendments—[1] This article substituted by virtue of the Treaty on European Union signed at Maastricht on 7 February 1992.

[Article 233 (ex Article 176)

The institution or institutions whose act has been declared void or whose failure to act has been declared contrary to this Treaty shall be required to take the necessary measures to comply with the judgment of the Court of Justice.

This obligation shall not affect any obligation which may result from the application of the second paragraph of Article 288.

This Article shall also apply to the ECB.][1]

Note—Article 288 is not printed. That Article provides for the Community to make good damage caused by its institutions or servants in the performance of their duties.

Amendments—[1] This article substituted by virtue of the Treaty on European Union signed at Maastricht on 7 February 1992.

[Article 234 (ex Article 177)

The Court of Justice shall have jurisdiction to give preliminary rulings concerning—

(*a*) the interpretation of this Treaty;

(*b*) the validity and interpretation of acts of the institutions of the Community and of the ECB;

(*c*) the interpretation of the statutes of bodies established by an act of the Council, where those statutes so provide.

Where such a question is raised before any court or tribunal of a Member State, that court or tribunal may, if it considers that a decision on the question is necessary to enable it to give judgment, request the Court of Justice to give a ruling thereon.

Where any such question is raised in a case pending before a court or tribunal of a Member State against whose decision there is no judicial remedy under national law, that court or tribunal shall bring the matter before the Court of Justice.][1]

Amendments—[1] This article substituted by virtue of the Treaty on European Union signed at Maastricht on 7 February 1992.

Article 239 (ex Article 182)

The Court of Justice shall have jurisdiction in any dispute between Member States which relates to the subject matter of this Treaty if the dispute is submitted to it under a special agreement between the parties.

Article 240 (ex Article 183)

Save where jurisdiction is conferred on the Court of Justice by this Treaty, disputes to which the Community is a party shall not on that ground be excluded from the jurisdiction of the courts or tribunals of the Member States.

[Article 241 (ex Article 184)

Notwithstanding the expiry of the period laid down in the fifth paragraph of Article 230, any party may, in proceedings in which a regulation adopted jointly by the European Parliament and the Council, or a regulation of the Council, of the Commission or of the ECB is at issue, plead the grounds specified in the second paragraph of Article 230, in order to invoke before the Court of Justice the inapplicability of that regulation.][1]

Amendments—[1] This article substituted by virtue of the Treaty on European Union signed at Maastricht on 7 February 1992.

Article 242 (ex Article 185)

Actions brought before the Court of Justice shall not have suspensory effect. The Court of Justice may, however, if it considers that circumstances so require, order that application of the contested act be suspended.

Article 243 (ex Article 186)

The Court of Justice may in any cases before it prescribe any necessary interim measures.

Article 244 (ex Article 187)

The judgments of the Court of Justice shall be enforceable under the conditions laid down in Article 256.

Note—Article 256 is not printed. That Article provides that enforcement shall be governed by the rules of civil procedure in force in the State in the territory of which it is carried out.

[Article 245 (ex Article 188)

The Statute of the Court of Justice shall be laid down in a separate Protocol.

The Council, acting unanimously at the request of the Court of Justice and after consulting the European Parliament and the Commission, or at the request of the Commission and after consulting the European Parliament and the Court of Justice, may amend the provisions of the Statute, with the exception of Title I.][1]

Amendments—[1] This article substituted by the Treaty of Nice Article 2(35). The Treaty was signed at Nice on 26 February 2001. See OJ C 80; 10.03.01, p 1.

CHAPTER 2—PROVISIONS COMMON TO SEVERAL INSTITUTIONS

[Article 249 (ex Article 189)

In order to carry out their task and in accordance with the provisions of this Treaty, the European Parliament acting jointly with the Council, the Council and the Commission shall make regulations, and issue directives, take decisions, make recommendations or deliver opinions.

A regulation shall have general application. It shall be binding in its entirety and directly applicable in all Member States.

A directive shall be binding, as to the result to be achieved, upon each Member State to which it is addressed, but shall leave to the national authorities the choice of form and methods.

A decision shall be binding in its entirety upon those to whom it is addressed.

Recommendations and opinions shall have no binding force.][1]

Amendments—[1] This article substituted by virtue of the Treaty on European Union signed at Maastricht on 7 February 1992.

[Council Directive of 19 December 1977 concerning mutual assistance by the competent authorities of the Member States in the field of direct taxation, certain excise duties and taxation of insurance premiums][1]

(77/799/EEC)

Note—See OJ L336 27.12.77, p 15.
Amendments—[1] Title substituted by Council Directive 2003/93 art 1(1) (OJ L 264; 15.10.2003 p 23).

The Council of the European Communities,

Having regard to the Treaty establishing the European Economic Community, and in particular Article 100 thereof,

Having regard to the proposal from the Commission,

Having regard to the opinion of the European Parliament (OJ No C293, 13.12.1976, p 34),

Having regard to the opinion of the Economic and Social Committee (OJ No C56, 7.3.1977, p 66),

Whereas practices of tax evasion and tax avoidance extending across the frontiers of Member States lead to budget losses and violations of the principle of fair taxation and are liable to bring about distortions of capital movements and of conditions of competition; whereas they therefore affect the operation of the common market;

Whereas, for these reasons the Council adopted on 10 February 1975 a resolution on the measures to be taken by the Community in order to combat international tax evasion and avoidance (OJ No C35, 14.2.1975, p 1);

Whereas the international nature of the problem means that national measures, whose effect does not extend beyond national frontiers, are insufficient; whereas collaboration between administrations on the basis of bilateral agreements is also unable to counter new forms of tax evasion and avoidance, which are increasingly assuming a multinational character;

Whereas collaboration between tax administrations within the Community should therefore be strengthened in accordance with common principles and rules;

Whereas the Member States should, on request, exchange information concerning particular cases; whereas the State so requested should make the necessary enquiries to obtain such information;

Whereas the Member States should exchange, even without any request, any information which appears relevant for the correct assessment of taxes on income and on capital, in particular where there appears to be an artificial transfer of profits between enterprises in different Member States or where such transactions are carried out between enterprises in two Member States through a third country in order to obtain tax advantages, or where tax has been or may be evaded or avoided for any reason whatever;

Whereas it is important that officials of the tax administration of one Member State be allowed to be present in the territory of another Member State if both the States concerned consider it desirable;

Whereas care must be taken to ensure that information provided in the course of such collaboration is not disclosed to unauthorised persons, so that the basic rights of citizens and enterprises are safeguarded; whereas it is therefore necessary that the Member States receiving such information should not use it, without the authorisation of the Member State supplying it, other than for the purposes of taxation or to facilitate legal proceedings for failure to observe the tax laws of the receiving State; whereas it is also necessary that the receiving States afford the information the same degree of confidentiality which it enjoyed in the State which provided it, if the latter so requires;

Whereas a Member State which is called upon to carry out enquiries or to provide information shall have the right to refuse to do so where its laws or administrative practices prevent its tax administration from carrying out these enquiries or from collecting or using this information for its own purposes, or where the provision of such information would be contrary to public policy or would lead to the disclosure of a commercial, industrial or professional secret or of a commercial process, or where the Member State for which the information is intended is unable for practical or legal reasons to provide similar information;

Whereas collaboration between the Member States and the Commission is necessary for the permanent study of co-operation procedures and the pooling of experience in the fields considered, and in particular in the field of the artificial transfer of profits within groups of enterprises, with the aim of improving those procedures and of preparing appropriate Community rules,

Note—Article 100 of the Treaty establishing the European Economic Community renumbered article 94 by the Treaty of Amsterdam ratified on 1 May 1999.

Has adopted this directive:

Article 1

General provisions

[1. In accordance with the provisions of this Directive the competent authorities of the Member States shall exchange any information that may enable them to effect a correct assessment of taxes on income and capital...][1].

2. There shall be regarded as taxes on income and on capital, irrespective of the manner in which they are levied, all taxes imposed on total income, on total capital, or on elements of income or of capital, including taxes on gains from the disposal of movable or immovable property, taxes on the amounts of wages or salaries paid by enterprises, as well as taxes on capital appreciation.

[3. The taxes referred to in paragraph 2 are at present, in particular:

in Belgium:

Impôt des personnes physiques/Personenbelasting

Impôt des sociétés/Vennootschapsbelasting

Impôt des personnes morales/Rechtspersonenbelasting

Impôt des non-residents/Belasting der niet-verblijfhouders

in Denmark:

Indkomstskaten til staten

Selskabsskat

Den kommunale indkomstskat

Den amtskommunale indkomstskat

Folkepensionsbidragene

Sømandsskatten

Den særlige indkomstskat

Kirkeskat

Formueskat til staten

Bidrag til dagpengefonden

in Germany:

Einkommensteuer

Körperschaftsteuer

Vermögensteuer

Gewerbesteuer

Grundsteuer

in Greece:

Φορος εισοδηματος Φυσικών προσωπων

Φορος εισοδηματος νομικών προσωπων

Φορος ακινητου περιονσιας

in Spain:

Impuesto sobre la Renta de las Personas Físicas

Impuesto sobre Sociedades

Impuesto Extraordinario sobre el Patrimonio de las Personas Fiísicas

in France:

Impôt sur le revenu

Impôt sur les sociétés

Taxe professionnelle

Taxe foncière sur les propriétés bâties

Taxe foncière sur les propriétés non bâties

in Ireland:

Income tax

Corporation tax

Capital gains tax

Wealth tax

in Italy:

Imposta sul reddito delle persone fisiche

Imposta sul reddito persone giuridiche

Imposta locale sui redditi

in Luxembourg:

Impôt sur le revenu des personnes physiques

Impôt sur le revenu de collectivités

Impôt commercial communal

Impôt sur la fortune

Impôt foncier

in the Netherlands:

Inkomstenbelasting

Vennootschapsbelasting

Vermogensbelasting

in Austria:

Einkommensteuer

Köperschaftsteuer

Grandsteuer

Bodenwertabgabe

Abgabe von land- und forstwirtschaftlichen Betrieben

in Portugal:

Contribuiçao predial

Imposto sòbre a indústria agricola

Contribuiçao industrial

Imposto dè capitais

Imposto profissional

Imposto complementar

Imposto de mais-valias

Imposto sobre o rendimento do petróleo

Os adicionais devidos sobre os impostos precedentes

in Finland:

Valtion tuloverot/de statliga inkomstskatterna

Yhteisöjen tulovero/inkomstskatten för samfund

Kunnallisvero/kommunalskatten

Kirkollisvero/kyrkoskatten

Kansaneläkevakuutusmaksu/folkpensionsförsäkringspremien

Sairausvakuutusmaksu/sjukförsäkringspremien

Korkotulon lähdevero/källskatten på ränteinkomst

Rajoitetusti verovelvollisen lähdevero/källskatten för begränsat skattskyldig

Valtion varallisuusvero/den statliga förmögenhetsskatten

Kiinteistövero/fastighetsskatten

in Sweden:

Den statliga inkomstskatten

Sjömansskatten

Kupongskatten

Den särskilda inkomstskatten för utomlands bosatta

Den särskilda inkomstskatten för utomlands bosatta artister m.fl.

Den statliga fastighetsskatten

Den kommunala inkomstskatten

Förmögenhetsskatten

in the United Kingdom:

Income tax

Corporation tax

Capital gains tax

Petroleum revenue tax

Development land tax][2]

[in the Czech Republic:

Danê z príjmu

Daň z nemovitostí

Daň dědická, daň darovací a daň z převodu nemovitostí
Daň z přidané hodnoty
Spotřební daně
in Estonia:
Tulumaks
Sotsiaalmaks
Maamaks
in Cyprus:
Φορος Εισοδηματος
'Εκτακτη Εισφορα για την 'Αμυνα της Δημοκρατιας
Φορος Κεφαλαιουχικών Κερδών
Φορος Ακινητης Ιδιοκτησιας
in Latvia:
iedzývotaju ienakuma nodoklis
nekustama ýpašuma nodoklis
uznemumu ienakuma nodoklis
in Lithuania:
Gyventojų pajamų mokestis
Pelno mokestis
Įmonių ir organizacijų nekilnojamojo turto mokestis
Žemeÿs mokestis
Mokestis už valstybinius gamtos išteklius
Mokestis už aplinkos teršimą
Naftos ir dujų išteklių mokestis
Paveldimo turto mokestis
in Hungary:
személyi jövedelemadó
társasági adó
osztalékadó
általános forgalmi adó
jövedéki adó
építményadó
telekadó
in Malta:
Taxxa fuq l-income
in Poland:
Podatek dochodowy od osób prawnych
Podatek dochodowy od osób fizycznych
Podatek od czynnosći cywilnopranych
in Slovenia:
Dohodnina
Davki obĉanov
Davek od dobiĉka pravnih oseb
Posebni davek na bilanĉno vsoto bank in hranilnic
in Slovakia:
daň z príjmov fyzickych osôb
daň z príjmov právnickych osôb
daň z dedičstva
daň z darovania
daň z prevodu a prechodu nehnutel'ností
daň z nehnutel'ností
daň z pridanej hodnoty
spotrebné dane][3]

4. Paragraph 1 shall also apply to any identical or similar taxes imposed subsequently, whether in addition to or in place of the taxes listed in paragraph 3. The competent authorities of the Member States shall inform one another and the Commission of the date of entry into force of such taxes.

[5. The expression ''competent authority'' means:

in Belgium:

De minister van financiën or an authorised representative

Le ministre des finances or an authorised representative

in Denmark:

Skatteministeren or an authorised representative

in Germany:

Der Bundesminister der Finanzen or an authorised representative

in Greece:

Το Υπουργειο Οικονομικών or an authorised representative

in Spain:

El Ministro de Economía y Hacienda or an authorised representative

in France.

Le ministre de l'économie or an authorised representative

in Ireland

The Revenue Commissioners or their authorised representative

in Italy:

[Il ministro dell'economia e delle finanze or an authorised representative.][3]

in Luxembourg:

Le ministre des finances or an authorised representative

in the Netherlands

De minister van financiën or an authorised representative

in Austria:

Der Bundesminister für Finanzen or an authorised representative

in Portugal:

O Ministro da Finanças e do Plano or an authorised representative

in Finland:

Valtiovarainministeriö or an authorised representative

Finansministeriet or an authorised representative

in Sweden:

Ministern med ansvar för skattefrågor or an authorised representative.

in the United Kingdom

[The Commissioners of Customs and Excise or an authorised representative for information required concerning taxes on insurance premiums and excise duty.

The Commissioners of Inland Revenue or an authorised representative for all other information][3].][2]

[in the Czech Republic:

Ministr financí or an authorised representative][4]

[in Estonia:

Rahandusminister or an authorised representative][4]

[in Cyprus:

Υπουργος Οικονομικϖν or an authorised representative][4]

[in Latvia:

Finanšu ministrs or an authorised representative][4]

[in Lithuania:

Finansu ministras or an authorised representative][4]

[in Hungary:

A pénzügyminiszter or an authorised representative][4]

[in Malta:

Il-Ministru responsabbli ghall-Finanzi or an authorised representative][4]

[in Poland:

Minister Finansów or an authorised representative][4]

[in Slovenia:

Minister za finance or an authorised representative][4]

[in Slovakia:

Minister financii or an authorised representative.][4]

Amendments—[1] Paragraph (1) substituted by Council Directive of 25 February 1992: 92/12/EEC; see OJ L76, 23.3.92 p 1. Words omitted from para (1) are not relevant to this Part of the Handbook.

[2] Article 1(3), (5) substituted by the Act of Accession 1995, art 29, Annex I, see OJ L1, 1.1.95, pp 210, 212.

[3] Words in art 1(5) substituted by Council Directive 2003/93/EC art 1(2) (OJ L 264; 15.10.2003 p 23).
[4] Entries in art 1(3), (5) inserted by the Act of Accession 2003, Annex II Chapter 9 para 4 (see OJ L 236; 23.9.2003 p 555).

Article 2

Exchange on request

1. The competent authority of a Member State may request the competent authority of another Member State to forward the information referred to in Article 1(1) in a particular case. The competent authority of the requested State need not comply with the request if it appears that the competent authority of the State making the request has not exhausted its own usual sources of information, which it could have utilised, according to the circumstances, to obtain the information requested without running the risk of endangering the attainment of the sought after result.

2. For the purpose of forwarding the information referred to in paragraph 1, the competent authority of the requested Member State shall arrange for the conduct of any enquiries necessary to obtain such information.

Article 3

Automatic exchange of information

For categories of cases which they shall determine under the consultation procedure laid down in Article 9, the competent authorities of the Member States shall regularly exchange the information referred to in Article 1 (1) without prior request.

Article 4

Spontaneous exchange of information

1. The competent authority of a Member State shall without prior request forward the information referred to in Article 1 (1), of which it has knowledge, to the competent authority of any other Member State concerned, in the following circumstances:

(*a*) the competent authority of the one Member State has grounds for supposing that there may be a loss of tax in the other Member State;
(*b*) a person liable to tax obtains a reduction in or an exemption from tax in the one Member State which would give rise to an increase in tax or to liability to tax in the other Member State;
(*c*) business dealings between a person liable to tax in a Member State and a person liable to tax in another Member State are conducted through one or more countries in such a way that a saving in tax may result in one or the other Member State or in both;
(*d*) the competent authority of a Member State has grounds for supposing that a saving of tax may result from artificial transfers of profits within groups of enterprises;
(*e*) information forwarded to the one Member State by the competent authority of the other Member State has enabled information to be obtained which may be relevant in assessing liability to tax in the latter Member State.

2. The competent authorities of the Member States may, under the consultation procedure laid down in Article 9, extend the exchange of information provided for in paragraph 1 to cases other than those specified therein.

3. The competent authorities of the Member States may forward to each other in any other case, without prior request, the information referred to in Article 1 (1) of which they have knowledge.

Simon's Tax Cases—Art 4(1)(*a*), *WN v Staatssecretaris van Financien* [2001] STC 974.

Article 5

Time limit for forwarding information

The competent authority of a Member State which, under the preceding Articles, is called upon to furnish information, shall forward it as swiftly as possible. If it encounters obstacles in furnishing the information or if it refuses to furnish the information, it shall forthwith inform the requesting authority to this effect, indicating the nature of the obstacles or the reasons for its refusal.

Article 6

Collaboration by officials of the State concerned

For the purpose of applying the preceding provisions, the competent authority of the Member State providing the information and the competent authority of the Member State for which the information is intended may agree, under the consultation procedure laid down in Article 9, to authorise the presence in the first Member State of officials of the tax administration of the other Member State. The details for applying this provision shall be determined under the same procedure.

Article 7
Provisions relating to secrecy

[1. All information made known to a Member State under this Directive shall be kept secret in that State in the same manner as information received under its national legislation. In any case, such information:

— may be made available only to the persons directly involved in the assessment of the tax or in the administrative control of this assessment,

— may be made known only in connection with judicial proceedings or administrative proceedings involving sanctions undertaken with a view to, or relating to, the making or reviewing the tax assessment and only to persons who are directly involved in such proceedings; such information may, however, be disclosed during public hearings or in judgements if the competent authority of the Member State supplying the information raises no objection,

— shall in no circumstances be used other than for taxation purposes or in connection with judicial proceedings or administrative proceedings involving sanctions undertaken with a view to, or in relation to, the making or reviewing of the tax assessment.

In addition, Member States may provide for the information referred to in the first subparagraph to be used for assessment of other levies, duties and taxes covered by Article 2 of Directive 76/308/EEC.][1]

2. Paragraph 1 shall not oblige a Member State whose legislation or administrative practice lays down, for domestic purposes, narrower limits than those contained in the provisions of that paragraph, to provide information if the State concerned does not undertake to respect those narrower limits.

3. Notwithstanding paragraph 1, the competent authorities of the Member State providing the information may permit it to be used for other purposes in the requesting State, if, under the legislation of the informing State, the information could, in similar circumstances, be used in the informing State for similar purposes.

4. Where a competent authority of a Member State considers that information which it has received from the competent authority of another Member State is likely to be useful to the competent authority of a third Member State, it may transmit it to the latter competent authority with the agreement of the competent authority which supplied the information.

Amendments—[1] Paragraph 1 substituted by Council Directive 2003/93/EC art 1(3) (OJ L 264; 15.10.2003 p 23).

Article 8
Limits to exchange of information

1. This Directive shall impose no obligation to have enquiries carried out or to provide information if the Member State, which should furnish the information, would be prevented by its law or administrative practices from carrying out these enquiries or from collecting or using this information for its own purposes.

2. The provision of information may be refused where it would lead to the disclosure of a commercial, industrial or professional secret or of a commercial process, or of information whose disclosure would be contrary to public policy.

3. The competent authority of a Member State may refuse to provide information where the State concerned is unable, for practical or legal reasons, to provide similar information.

Article 9
Consultations

1. For the purposes of the implementation of this Directive, consultations shall be held, if necessary in a Committee, between:

— the competent authorities of the Member States concerned at the request of either, in respect of bilateral questions,

— the competent authorities of all the Member States and the Commission, at the request of one of those authorities or the Commission, in so far as the matters involved are not solely of bilateral interest.

2. The competent authorities of the Member States may communicate directly with each other. The competent authorities of the Member States may by mutual agreement permit authorities designated by them to communicate directly with each other in specified cases or in certain categories of cases.

3. Where the competent authorities make arrangements on bilateral matters covered by this Directive other than as regards individual cases, they shall as soon as possible inform the Commission thereof. The Commission shall in turn notify the competent authorities of the other Member States.

Article 10
Pooling of experience

The Member States shall, together with the Commission, constantly monitor the co-operation procedure provided for in this Directive and shall pool their experience, especially in the field of transfer pricing within groups of enterprises, with a view to improving such co-operation and, where appropriate, drawing up a body of rules in the fields concerned.

Article 11

Applicability of wider-ranging provisions of assistance

The foregoing provisions shall not impede the fulfilment of any wider obligations to exchange information which might flow from other legal acts.

Article 12

Final provisions

1. Member States shall bring into force, the necessary laws, regulations and administrative provisions in order to comply with this Directive not later than 1 January 1979 and shall forthwith communicate them to the Commission.

2. Member States shall communicate to the Commission the texts of any important provisions of national law which they subsequently adopt in the field covered by this Directive.

Article 13

This Directive is addressed to the Member States.

Done at Brussels, 19 December 1977.

Council Regulation
of 25 July 1985
on the European Economic Interest Grouping (EEIG)

(2137/85/EEC)

Note—See OJ L199, 31.7.85, p 1.

The Council of the European Community,

Having regard to the Treaty establishing the European Economic Community, and in particular Article 235[1] thereof,

Having regard to the proposal from the Commission,

Having regard to the opinion of the European Parliament,

Having regard to the opinion of the Economic and Social Committee,

Whereas a harmonious development of economic activities and a continuous and balanced expansion throughout the Community depend on the establishment and smooth functioning of a common market offering conditions analogous to those of a national market; whereas to bring about this single market and to increase its unity a legal framework which facilitates the adaptation of their activities to the economic conditions of the Community should be created for natural persons, companies, firms and other legal bodies in particular; whereas to that end it is necessary that those natural persons, companies, firms and other legal bodies should be able to cooperate effectively across frontiers;

Whereas cooperation of this nature can encounter legal, fiscal or psychological difficulties; whereas the creation of an appropriate Community legal instrument in the form of a European Economic Interest Grouping would contribute to the achievement of the abovementioned objectives and therefore proves necessary;

Whereas the Treaty does not provide the necessary powers for the creation of such a legal instrument;

Whereas a grouping's ability to adapt to economic conditions must be guaranteed by the considerable freedom for its members in their contractual relations and the internal organisation of the grouping;

Whereas a grouping differs from a firm or company principally in its purpose, which is only to facilitate or develop the economic activities of its members to enable them to improve their own results; whereas, by reason of that ancillary nature, a grouping's activities must be related to the economic activities of its members but not replace them so that, to that extent, for example, a grouping may not itself, with regard to third parties, practise a profession, the concept of economic activities being interpreted in the widest sense;

Whereas access to grouping form must be made as widely available as possible to natural persons, companies, firms and other legal bodies, in keeping with the aims of this Regulation; whereas this Regulation shall not, however, prejudice the application at national level of legal rules and/or ethical codes concerning the conditions for the pursuit of business and professional activities;

Whereas this Regulation does not itself confer on any person the right to participate in a grouping, even where the conditions it lays down are fulfilled;

Whereas the power provided by this Regulation to prohibit or restrict participation in grouping on grounds of public interest is without prejudice to the laws of Member States which govern the pursuit

EC Material

of activities and which may provide further prohibitions or restrictions or otherwise control or supervise participation in a grouping by any natural person, company, firm or other legal body or any class of them;

Whereas, to enable a grouping to achieve its purpose, it should be endowed with legal capacity and provision should be made for it to be represented vis-à-vis third parties by an organ legally separate from its membership;

Whereas the protection of third parties requires widespread publicity; whereas the members of a grouping have unlimited joint and several liability for the grouping's debts and other liabilities, including those relating to tax or social security, without, however, that principle's affecting the freedom to exclude or restrict the liability of one or more of its members in respect of a particular debt or other liability by means of a specific contract between the grouping and a third party;

Whereas matters relating to the status or capacity of natural persons and to the capacity of legal persons are governed by national law;

Whereas the grounds for winding up which are peculiar to the grouping should be specific while referring to national law for its liquidation and the conclusion thereof;

Whereas groupings are subject to national laws relating to insolvency and cessation of payments; whereas such laws may provide other grounds for the winding up of groupings;

Whereas this Regulation provides that the profits or losses resulting from the activities of a grouping shall be taxable only in the hands of its members; whereas it is understood that otherwise national tax laws apply, particularly as regards the apportionment of profits, tax procedures and any obligations imposed by national tax law;

Whereas in matters not covered by this Regulation the laws of the Member States and Community law are applicable, for example with regard to:

—social and labour laws,

—competition law,

—intellectual property law;

Whereas the activities of groupings are subject to the provisions of Member States' laws on the pursuit and supervision of activities; whereas in the event of abuse or circumvention of the laws of a Member State by a grouping or its members that Member State may impose appropriate sanctions;

Whereas the Member States are free to apply or to adopt any laws, regulations or administrative measures which do not conflict with the scope or objectives of this Regulation;

Whereas this Regulation must enter into force immediately in its entirety; whereas the implementation of some provisions must nevertheless be deferred in order to allow the Member States first to set up the necessary machinery for the registration of groupings in their territories and the disclosure of certain matters relating to groupings; whereas, with effect from the date of implementation of this Regulation, groupings set up may operate without territorial restrictions,

Note— Article 235 renumbered article 308 by the Treaty of Amsterdam ratified on 1 May 1999 (OJ C340 10.11.97 p 1).

Has adopted this regulation:

Article 1

1. European Economic Interest Groupings shall be formed upon the terms, in the manner and with the effects laid down in this Regulation.

Accordingly, parties intending to form a grouping must conclude a contract and have the registration provided for in Article 6 carried out.

2. A grouping so formed shall, from the date of its registration as provided for in Article 6, have the capacity, in its own name, to have rights and obligations of all kinds, to make contracts or accomplish other legal acts, and to sue and be sued.

3. The Member States shall determine whether or not groupings registered at their registries, pursuant to Article 6, have legal personality.

Article 2

1. Subject to the provisions of this Regulation, the law applicable, on the one hand, to the contract for the formation of a grouping, except as regards matters relating to the status or capacity of natural persons and to the capacity of legal persons and, on the other hand, to the internal organisation of a grouping shall be the internal law of the State in which the official address is situated, as laid down in the contract for the formation of the grouping.

2. Where a State comprises several territorial units, each of which has its own rules of law applicable to the matters referred to in paragraph 1, each territorial unit shall be considered as a State for the purposes of identifying the law applicable under this Article.

Article 3

1. The purpose of a grouping shall be to facilitate or develop the economic activities of its members and to improve or increase the results of those activities; its purpose is not to make profits for itself.

Its activity shall be related to the economic activities of its members and must not be more than ancillary to those activities.

2. Consequently, a grouping may not:

(*a*) exercise, directly or indirectly, a power of management or supervision over its members' own activities or over the activities of another undertaking, in particular in the fields of personnel, finance and investment;

(*b*) directly or indirectly, on any basis whatsoever, hold shares of any kind in a member undertaking; the holding of shares in another undertaking shall be possible only in so far as it is necessary for the achievement of the grouping's objects and if it is done on its members' behalf;

(*c*) employ more than 500 persons;

(*d*) be used by a company to make a loan to a director of a company, or any person connected with him, when the making of such loans is restricted or controlled under the Member States' laws governing companies. Nor must a grouping be used for the transfer of any property between a company and a director, or any person connected with him, except to the extent allowed by the Member States' laws governing companies. For the purposes of this provision the making of a loan includes entering into any transaction or arrangement of similar effect, and property includes moveable and immovable property;

(*e*) be a member of another European Economic Interest Grouping.

EC Material

Article 4

1. Only the following may be members of a grouping:

(*a*) companies or firms within the meaning of the second paragraph of Article 58[1] of the Treaty and other legal bodies governed by public or private law, which have been formed in accordance with the law of a Member State and which have their registered or statutory office and central administration in the Community; where, under the law of a Member State, a company, firm or other legal body is not obliged to have a registered or statutory office, it shall be sufficient for such a company, firm or other legal body to have its central administration in the Community;

(*b*) natural persons who carry on any industrial, commercial, craft or agricultural activity or who provide professional or other services in the Community.

2. A grouping must comprise at least:

(*a*) two companies, firms or other legal bodies, within the meaning of paragraph 1, which have their central administrations in different Member States, or

(*b*) two natural persons, within the meaning of paragraph 1, who carry on their principal activities in different Member States, or

(*c*) a company, firm or other legal body within the meaning of paragraph 1 and a natural person, of which the first has its central administration in one Member State and the second carries on his principal activity in another Member State.

3. A Member State may provide that groupings registered at its registries in accordance with Article 6 may have no more than 20 members. For this purpose, that Member State may provide that, in accordance with its laws, each member of a legal body formed under its laws, other than a registered company, shall be treated as a separate member of a grouping.

4. Any Member State may, on grounds of that State's public interest, prohibit or restrict participation in groupings by certain classes of natural persons, companies, firms, or other legal bodies.

Note—[1] Article 58 renumbered article 48 by the Treaty of Amsterdam ratified on 1 May 1999.

Article 5

A contract for the formation of a grouping shall include at least:

(*a*) the name of the grouping preceded or followed either by the words "European Economic Interest Grouping" or by the initials 'EEIG', unless those words or initials already form part of the name;

(*b*) the official address of the grouping;

(*c*) the objects for which the grouping is formed;

(*d*) the name, business name, legal form, permanent address or registered office, and the number and place of registration, if any, of each member of the grouping;

(*e*) the duration of the grouping, except where this is indefinite.

Article 6

A grouping shall be registered in the State in which it has its official address, at the registry designated pursuant to Article 39(1).

Article 7

A contract for the formation of a grouping shall be filed at the registry referred to in Article 6.

The following documents and particulars must also be filed at that registry:

(*a*) any amendment to the contract for the formation of a grouping, including any change in the composition of a grouping;

(*b*) notice of the setting up or closure of any establishment of the grouping;
(*c*) any judicial decision establishing or declaring the nullity of a grouping, in accordance with Article 15;
(*d*) notice of the appointment of the manager or managers of a grouping, their names and any other identification particulars required by the law of the Member State in which the register is kept, notification that they may act alone or must act jointly, and the termination of any manager's appointment;
(*e*) notice of a member's assignment of his participation in a grouping or a proportion thereof, in accordance with Article 22(1);
(*f*) any decision by members ordering or establishing the winding up of a grouping, in accordance with Article 31, or any judicial decision ordering such winding up, in accordance with Articles 31 or 32;
(*g*) notice of the appointment of the liquidator or liquidators of a grouping, as referred to in Article 35, their names and any other identification particulars required by the law of the Member State in which the register is kept, and the termination of any liquidator's appointment;
(*h*) notice of the conclusion of a grouping's liquidation, as referred to in Article 35(2);
(*i*) any proposal to transfer the official address, as referred to in Article 14(1);
(*j*) any clause exempting a new member from the payment of debts and other liabilities which originated prior to his admission, in accordance with Article 26(2).

Article 8

The following must be published, as laid down in Article 39, in the gazette referred to in paragraph 1 of that Article:
(*a*) the particulars which must be included in the contract for the formation of a grouping, pursuant to Article 5, and any amendments thereto;
(*b*) the number, date and place of registration as well as notice of the termination of that registration;
(*c*) the documents and particulars referred to in Article 7(*b*) to (*j*).

The particulars referred to in (*a*) and (*b*) must be published in full. The documents and particulars referred to in (*c*) may be published either in full or in extract form or by means of a reference to their filing at the registry, in accordance with the national legislation applicable.

Article 9

1. The documents and particulars which must be published pursuant to this Regulation may be relied on by a grouping as against third parties under the conditions laid down by the national law applicable pursuant to Article 3 (5) and (7) of Council Directive 68/151/EEC of 9 March 1968 on coordination of safeguards which, for the protection of the interests of members and others, are required by Member States of companies within the meaning of the second paragraph of Article 58[1] of the Treaty, with a view to making such safeguards equivalent throughout the Community.

2. If activities have been carried on on behalf of a grouping before its registration in accordance with Article 6 and if the grouping does not, after its registration, assume the obligations arising out of such activities, the natural persons, companies, firms or other legal bodies which carried on those activities shall bear unlimited joint and several liability for them.

Note—[1] Article 58 renumbered article 48 by the Treaty of Amsterdam ratified on 1 May 1999.

Article 10

Any grouping establishment situated in a Member State other than that in which the official address is situated shall be registered in that State. For the purpose of such registration, a grouping shall file, at the appropriate registry in that Member State, copies of the documents which must be filed at the registry of the Member State in which the official address is situated, together, if necessary, with a translation which conforms with the practice of the registry where the establishment is registered.

Article 11

Notice that a grouping has been formed or that the liquidation of a grouping has been concluded stating the number, date and place of registration and the date, place and title of publication, shall be given in the *Official Journal of the European Communities* after it has been published in the gazette referred to in Article 39(1).

Article 12

The official address referred to in the contract for the formation of a grouping must be situated in the Community.

The official address must be fixed either:

(*a*) where the grouping has its central administration, or
(*b*) where one of the members of the grouping has its central administration or, in the case of a natural person, his principal activity, provided that the grouping carries on an activity there.

Article 13

The official address of a grouping may be transferred within the Community.

When such a transfer does not result in a change in the law applicable pursuant to Article 2, the decision to transfer shall be taken in accordance with the conditions laid down in the contract for the formation of the grouping.

Article 14

1. When the transfer of the official address results in a change in the law applicable pursuant to Article 2, a transfer proposal must be drawn up, filed and published in accordance with the conditions laid down in Articles 7 and 8.

No decision to transfer may be taken for two months after publication of the proposal. Any such decision must be taken by the members of the grouping unanimously. The transfer shall take effect on the date on which the grouping is registered, in accordance with Article 6, at the registry for the new official address. That registration may not be effected until evidence has been produced that the proposal to transfer the official address has been published.

2. The termination of a grouping's registration at the registry for its old official address may not be effected until evidence has been produced that the grouping has been registered at the registry for its new official address.

3. Upon publication of a grouping's new registration the new official address may be relied on as against third parties in accordance with the conditions referred to in Article 9(1); however, as long as the termination of the grouping's registration at the registry for the old official address has not been published, third parties may continue to rely on the old official address unless the grouping proves that such third parties were aware of the new official address.

4. The laws of a Member State may provide that, as regards groupings registered under Article 6 in that Member State, the transfer of an official address which would result in a change of the law applicable shall not take effect if, within the two-month period referred to in paragraph 1, a competent authority in that Member State opposes it. Such opposition may be based only on grounds of public interest. Review by a judicial authority must be possible.

Article 15

1. Where the law applicable to a grouping by virtue of Article 2 provides for the nullity of that grouping, such nullity must be established or declared by judicial decision. However, the court to which the matter is referred must, where it is possible for the affairs of the grouping to be put in order, allow time to permit that to be done.

2. The nullity of a grouping shall entail its liquidation in accordance with the conditions laid down in Article 35.

3. A decision establishing or declaring the nullity of a grouping may be relied on as against third parties in accordance with the conditions laid down in Article 9(1).

Such a decision shall not of itself affect the validity of liabilities, owed by or to a grouping, which originated before it could be relied on as against third parties in accordance with the conditions laid down in the previous subparagraph.

Article 16

1. The organs of a grouping shall be the members acting collectively and the manager or managers.

A contract for the formation of a grouping may provide for other organs; if it does it shall determine their powers.

2. The members of a grouping, acting as a body, may take any decision for the purpose of achieving the objects of the grouping.

Article 17

1. Each member shall have one vote. The contract for the formation of a grouping may, however, give more than one vote to certain members, provided that no one member holds a majority of the votes.

2. A unanimous decision by the members shall be required to:

(*a*) alter the objects of a grouping;
(*b*) alter the number of votes allotted to each member;
(*c*) alter the conditions for the taking of decisions;
(*d*) extend the duration of a grouping beyond any period fixed in the contract for the formation of the grouping;
(*e*) alter the contribution by every member or by some members to the grouping's financing;
(*f*) alter any other obligation of a member, unless otherwise provided by the contract for the formation of the grouping;
(*g*) make any alteration to the contract for the formation of the grouping not covered by this paragraph, unless otherwise provided by that contract.

EC Material

3. Except where this Regulation provides that decisions must be taken unanimously, the contract for the formation of a grouping may prescribe the conditions for a quorum and for a majority, in accordance with which the decisions, or some of them, shall be taken. Unless otherwise provided for by the contract, decisions shall be taken unanimously.
4. On the initiative of a manager or at the request of a member, the manager or managers must arrange for the members to be consulted so that the latter can take a decision.

Article 18

Each member shall be entitled to obtain information from the manager or managers concerning the grouping's business and to inspect the grouping's books and business records.

Article 19

1. A grouping shall be managed by one or more natural persons appointed in the contract for the formation of the grouping or by decision of the members.

No person may be a manager of a grouping if:

— by virtue of the law applicable to him, or
— by virtue of the internal law of the State in which the grouping has its official address, or
— following a judicial or administrative decision made or recognised in a Member State

he may not belong to the administrative or management body of a company, may not manage an undertaking or may not act as manager of a European Economic Interest Grouping.
2. A Member State may, in the case of groupings registered at their registries pursuant to Article 6, provide that legal persons may be managers on condition that such legal persons designate one or more natural persons, whose particulars shall be the subject of the filing provisions of Article 7(*d*) to represent them.
If a Member State exercises this option, it must provide that the representative or representatives shall be liable as if they were themselves managers of the groupings concerned.

The restrictions imposed in paragraph 1 shall also apply to those representatives.

3. The contract for the formation of a grouping or, failing that, a unanimous decision by the members shall determine the conditions for the appointment and removal of the manager or managers and shall lay down their powers.

Article 20

1. Only the manager or, where there are two or more, each of the managers shall represent a grouping in respect of dealings with third parties.

Each of the managers shall bind the grouping as regards third parties when he acts on behalf of the grouping, even where his acts do not fall within the objects of the grouping, unless the grouping proves that the third party knew or could not, under the circumstances, have been unaware that the act fell outside the objects of the grouping; publication of the particulars referred to in Article 5(*c*) shall not of itself be proof thereof.

No limitation on the powers of the manager or managers, whether deriving from the contract for the formation of the grouping or from a decision by the members, may be relied on as against third parties even if it is published.

2. The contract for the formation of the grouping may provide that the grouping shall be validly bound only by two or more managers acting jointly. Such a clause may be relied on as against third parties in accordance with the conditions referred to in Article 9(1) only if it is published in accordance with Article 8.

Article 21

1. The profits resulting from a grouping's activities shall be deemed to be the profits of the members and shall be apportioned among them in the proportions laid down in the contract for the formation of the grouping or, in the absence of any such provision, in equal shares.
2. The members of a grouping shall contribute to the payment of the amount by which expenditure exceeds income in the proportions laid down in the contract for the formation of the grouping or, in the absence of any such provision, in equal shares.

Article 22

1. Any member of a grouping may assign his participation in the grouping, or a proportion thereof, either to another member or to a third party; the assignment shall not take effect without the unanimous authorisation of the other members.

2. A member of a grouping may use his participation in the grouping as security only after the other members have given their unanimous authorisation, unless otherwise laid down in the contract for the formation of the grouping. The holder of the security may not at any time become a member of the grouping by virtue of that security.

Article 23

No grouping may invite investment by the public.

Article 24

1. The members of a grouping shall have unlimited joint and several liability for its debts and other liabilities of whatever nature. National law shall determine the consequences of such liability.

2. Creditors may not proceed against a member for payment in respect of debts and other liabilities, in accordance with the conditions laid down in paragraph 1, before the liquidation of a grouping is concluded, unless they have first requested the grouping to pay and payment has not been made within an appropriate period.

Article 25

Letters, order forms and similar documents must indicate legibly:

(*a*) the name of the grouping preceded or followed either by the words ''European Economic Interest Grouping'' or by the initials ''EEIG'', unless those words or initials already occur in the name;
(*b*) the location of the registry referred to in Article 6, in which the grouping is registered, together with the number of the grouping's entry at the registry;
(*c*) the grouping's official address;
(*d*) where applicable, that the managers must act jointly;
(*e*) where applicable, that the grouping is in liquidation, pursuant to Articles 15, 31, 32 or 36.

Every establishment of a grouping, when registered in accordance with Article 10, must give the above particulars, together with those relating to its own registration, on the documents referred to in the first paragraph of this Article uttered by it.

Article 26

1. A decision to admit new members shall be taken unanimously by the members of the grouping.

2. Every new member shall be liable, in accordance with the conditions laid down in Article 24, for the grouping's debts and other liabilities, including those arising out of the grouping's activities before his admission.

He may, however, be exempted by a clause in the contract for the formation of the grouping or in the instrument of admission from the payment of debts and other liabilities which originated before his admission. Such a clause may be relied on as against third parties, under the conditions referred to in Article 9(1), only if it is published in accordance with Article 8.

Article 27

1. A member of a grouping may withdraw in accordance with the conditions laid down in the contract for the formation of a grouping or, in the absence of such conditions, with the unanimous agreement of the other members.

Any member of a grouping may, in addition, withdraw on just and proper grounds.

2. Any member of a grouping may be expelled for the reasons listed in the contract for the formation of the grouping and, in any case, if he seriously fails in his obligations or if he causes or threatens to cause serious disruption in the operation of the grouping.

Such expulsion may occur only by the decision of a court to which joint application has been made by a majority of the other members, unless otherwise provided by the contract for the formation of a grouping.

Article 28

1. A member of a grouping shall cease to belong to it on death or when he no longer complies with the conditions laid down in Article 4(1).

In addition, a Member State may provide, for the purposes of its liquidation, winding up, insolvency or cessation of payments laws, that a member shall cease to be a member of any grouping at the moment determined by those laws.

2. In the event of the death of a natural person who is a member of a grouping, no person may become a member in his place except under the conditions laid down in the contract for the formation of the grouping or, failing that, with the unanimous agreement of the remaining members.

Article 29

As soon as a member ceases to belong to a grouping, the manager or managers must inform the other members of that fact; they must also take the steps required as listed in Articles 7 and 8. In addition, any person concerned may take those steps.

Article 30

Except where the contract for the formation of a grouping provides otherwise and without prejudice to the rights acquired by a person under Articles 22(1) or 28(2), a grouping shall continue to exist for the remaining members after a member has ceased to belong to it, in accordance with the conditions laid down in the contract for the formation of the grouping or determined by unanimous decision of the members in question.

Article 31

1. A grouping may be wound up by a decision of its members ordering its winding up. Such a decision shall be taken unanimously, unless otherwise laid down in the contract for the formation of the grouping.

2. A grouping must be wound up by a decision of its members:

(*a*) noting the expiry of the period fixed in the contract for the formation of the grouping or the existence of any other cause for winding up provided for in the contract, or

(*b*) noting the accomplishment of the grouping's purpose or the impossibility of pursuing it further.

Where, three months after one of the situation referred to in the first subparagraph has occurred, a members' decision establishing the winding up of the grouping has not been taken, any member may petition the court to order winding up.

3. A grouping must also be wound up by a decision of its members or of the remaining member when the conditions laid down in Article 4(2) are no longer fulfilled.

4. After a grouping has been wound up by decision of its members, the manager or managers must take the steps required as listed in Articles 7 and 8. In addition, any person concerned may take those steps.

Article 32

1. On application by any person concerned or by a competent authority, in the event of the infringement of Articles 3, 12 or 31(3), the court must order a grouping to be wound up, unless its affairs can be and are put in order before the court has delivered a substantive ruling.

2. On applications by a member, the court may order a grouping to be wound up on just and proper grounds.

3. A Member State may provide that the court may, on application by a competent authority, order the winding up of a grouping which has its official address in the State to which that authority belongs, wherever the grouping acts in contravention of that State's public interest, if the law of that State provides for such a possibility in respect of registered companies or other legal bodies subject to it.

Article 33

When a member ceases to belong to a grouping for any reason other than the assignment of his rights in accordance with the conditions laid down in Article 22 (1), the value of his rights and obligations shall be determined taking into account the assets and liabilities of the grouping as they stand when he ceases to belong to it.

The value of the rights and obligations of a departing member may not be fixed in advance.

Article 34

Without prejudice to Article 37(1), any member who ceases to belong to a grouping shall remain answerable, in accordance with the conditions laid down in Article 24, for the debts and other liabilities arising out of the grouping's activities before he ceased to be a member.

Article 35

1. The winding up of a grouping shall entail its liquidation.

2. The liquidation of a grouping and the conclusion of its liquidation shall be governed by national law.

3. A grouping shall retain its capacity, within the meaning of Article 1(2), until its liquidation is concluded.

4. The liquidator or liquidators shall take the steps required as listed in Articles 7 and 8.

Article 36

Groupings shall be subject to national laws governing insolvency and cessation of payments. The commencement of proceedings against a grouping on grounds of its insolvency or cessation of payments shall not by itself cause the commencement of such proceedings against its members.

Article 37

1. A period of limitation of five years after the publication, pursuant to Article 8, of notice of a member's ceasing to belong to a grouping shall be substituted for any longer period which may be laid down by the relevant national law for actions against that member in connection with debts and other liabilities arising out of the grouping's activities before he ceased to be a member.

2. A period of limitation of five years after the publication, pursuant to Article 8, of notice of the conclusion of the liquidation of a grouping shall be substituted for any longer period which may be laid down by the relevant national law for actions against a member of the grouping in connection with debts and other liabilities arising out of the grouping's activities.

Article 38

Where a grouping carries on any activity in a Member State in contravention of that State's public interest, a competent authority of that State may prohibit that activity. Review of that competent authority's decision by a judicial authority shall be possible.

Article 39

1. The Member States shall designate the registry or registries responsible for effecting the registration referred to in Articles 6 and 10 and shall lay down the rules governing registration. They shall prescribe the conditions under which the documents referred to in Articles 7 and 10 shall be filed. They shall ensure that the documents and particulars referred to in Article 8 are published in the appropriate official gazette of the Member State in which the grouping has its official address, and may prescribe the manner of publication of the documents and particulars referred to in Article 8(*c*).

The Member States shall also ensure that anyone may, at the appropriate registry pursuant to Article 6 or, where appropriate, Article 10, inspect the documents referred to in Article 7 and obtain, even by post, full or partial copies thereof.

The Member States may provide for the payment of fees in connection with the operations referred to in the preceding subparagraphs; those fees may not, however, exceed the administrative cost thereof.

2. The Member States shall ensure that the information to be published in the *Official Journal of the European Communities* pursuant to Article 11 is forwarded to the Office for Official Publications of the European Communities within one month of its publication in the official gazette referred to in paragraph 1.

3. The Member States shall provide for appropriate penalties in the event of failure to comply with the provisions of Articles 7, 8 and 10 on disclosure and in the event of failure to comply with Article 25.

Article 40

The profits or losses resulting from the activities of a grouping shall be taxable only in the hands of its members.

Article 41

1. The Member States shall take the measures required by virtue of Article 39 before 1 July 1989. They shall immediately communicate them to the Commission.

2. For information purposes, the Member States shall inform the Commission of the classes of natural persons, companies, firms and other legal bodies which they prohibit from participating in groupings pursuant to Article 4(4). The Commission shall inform the other Member States.

Article 42

1. Upon the adoption of this Regulation, a Contact Committee shall be set up under the auspices of the Commission. Its function shall be:

(*a*) to facilitate, without prejudice to Articles 169 and 170[1] of the Treaty, application of this Regulation through regular consultation dealing in particular with practical problems arising in connection with its application;

(*b*) to advise the Commission, if necessary, on additions or amendments to this Regulation.

2. The Contact Committee shall be composed of representatives of the Member States and representatives of the Commission. The chairman shall be a representative of the Commission. The Commission shall provide the secretariat.

3. The Contact Committee shall be convened by its chairman either on his own initiative or at the request of one of its members.

Note—[1] Articles 169 and 170 renumbered articles 226 and 227 respectively by the Treaty of Amsterdam ratified on 1 May 1999.

Article 43

This Regulation shall enter into force on the third day following its publication in the Official Journal of the European Communities.

It shall apply from 1 July 1989, with the exception of Articles 39, 41 and 42 which shall apply as from the entry into force of the Regulation.

This Regulation shall be binding in its entirety and directly applicable in all Member States.

Done at Brussels, 25 July 1985.

Council Directive of 24 June 1988 for the implementation of Article 67 of the Treaty

(88/361/EEC)

Note—See OJ L178 08.07.88, p 5.

Statement of Practice SP 2/92—Transactions within TA 1988 s 765A—movements of capital between residents of EC member states.

Cross references—See the Movements of Capital (Required Information) Regulations, SI 1990/1671, *ante*.

Note—The provisions of this Directive are applied with adaptations to the European Economic Area by the Agreement on the European Economic Area concluded on 13 December 1993 art 40, Annex XII, as amended.

Article 67 was substituted by article 73b by the Treaty on European Union signed at Maastricht on 7 February 1992. Article 73b was renumbered article 56 by the Treaty of Amsterdam, which was ratified on 1 May 1999.

The Council of the European Communities,

Having regard to the Treaty establishing the European Economic Community, and in particular Articles 69 and 70(1)[1] thereof,

Having regard to the proposal from the Commission, submitted following consultation with the Monetary Committee (OJ No C26, 1.2.1988, p 1),

Having regard to the opinion of the European Parliament (opinion delivered on 17 June 1988 (not yet published in the Official Journal)),

Whereas Article 8a[2] of the Treaty stipulates that the internal market shall comprise an area without internal frontiers in which the free movement of capital is ensured, without prejudice to the other provisions of the Treaty;

Whereas Member States should be able to take the requisite measures to regulate bank liquidity; whereas these measures should be restricted to this purpose;

Whereas Member States should, if necessary, be able to take measures to restrict, temporarily and within the framework of appropriate Community procedures, short-term capital movements which, even where there is no appreciable divergence in economic fundamentals, might seriously disrupt the conduct of their monetary and exchange-rate policies;

...[3]

Whereas, since the full liberalisation of capital movements could in some Member States, and especially in border areas, contribute to difficulties in the market for secondary residences; whereas existing national legislation regulating these purchases should not be affected by the entry into effect of this Directive;

Whereas advantage should be taken of the period adopted for bringing this Directive into effect in order to enable the Commission to submit proposals designed to eliminate or reduce risks of distortion, tax evasion and tax avoidance resulting from the diversity of national systems for taxation and to permit the Council to take a position on such proposals;

Whereas, in accordance with Article 70(1)[1] of the Treaty, the Community shall endeavour to attain the highest possible degree of liberalisation in respect of the movement of capital between its residents and those of third countries;

Whereas large-scale short-term capital movements to or from third countries may seriously disturb the monetary or financial situation of Member States or cause serious stresses on the exchange markets; whereas such developments may prove harmful for the cohesion of the European Monetary System, for the smooth operation of the internal market and for the progressive achievement of economic and monetary union; whereas it is therefore appropriate to create the requisite conditions for concerted action by Member States should this prove necessary;

Whereas this Directive replaces Council Directive 72/156/EEC of 21 March 1972 on regulating international capital flows and neutralising their undesirable effects on domestic liquidity (OJ No L91, 18.4.1972, p 13); whereas Directive 72/156/EEC should accordingly be repealed,

Note—[1] Articles 67—73 substituted by articles 73b, 73c, 73d, 73e, 73f and 73g by the Treaty on European Union signed at Maastricht on 7 February 1992. Articles 73b, 73c, 73d, 73f and 73g renumbered articles 56, 57, 58, 59 and 60 respectively, and article 73e repealed, by the Treaty of Amsterdam ratified on 1 May 1999 (OJ C340 10.11.97 p 1).

[2] Article 8a renumbered article 18 by the Treaty of Amsterdam (OJ C340 10.11.97 p 1).

[3] Words omitted are not relevant for the purposes of this work.

Has adopted this directive:

Article 1

1. Without prejudice to the following provisions, Member States shall abolish restrictions on movements of capital taking place between persons resident in Member States. To facilitate application of this Directive, capital movements shall be classified in accordance with the Nomenclature in Annex 1.

2. Transfers in respect of capital movements shall be made on the same exchange rate conditions as those governing payments relating to current transactions.

Statement of Practice SP 2/92—Transactions within TA 1988 s 765A—movements of capital between residents of EC member states.
Simon's Tax Cases—*Staatssecretaris van Financien v Verkooijen* [2002] STC 654.

Articles 2, 3

Note—These articles are not relevant for the purposes of this work.

Article 4

This Directive shall be without prejudice to the right of Member States to take all requisite measures to prevent infringements of their laws and regulations, *inter alia* in the field of taxation and prudential supervision of financial institutions, or to lay down procedures for the declaration of capital movements for purposes of administrative or statistical information.

Application of those measures and procedures may not have the effect of impeding capital movements carried out in accordance with Community law.

Article 5

Note—This article is not relevant for the purposes of this work.

Article 6

1. Member States shall take the measures necessary to comply with this Directive no later than 1 July 1990. They shall forthwith inform the Commission thereof. They shall also make known, by the date of their entry into force at the latest, any new measure or any amendment made to the provisions governing the capital movements listed in Annex I.

2–4. ...

5. The Commission shall submit to the Council, by 31 December 1988, proposals aimed at eliminating or reducing risks of distortion, tax evasion and tax avoidance linked to the diversity of national systems for the taxation of savings and for controlling the application of these systems.

The Council shall take a position on these Commission proposals by 30 June 1989. Any tax provisions of a Community nature shall, in accordance with the Treaty, be adopted unanimously.

Note—Paras 2–4 are not relevant for the purposes of this work.

Article 7

1. In their treatment of transfers in respect of movements of Capital to or from third countries, the Member States shall endeavour to attain the same degree of liberalisation as that which applies to operations with residents of other Member States, subject to the other provisions of this Directive.

The provisions of the preceding subparagraph shall not prejudice the application to third countries of domestic rules or Community law, particularly any reciprocal conditions, concerning operations involving establishment, the provisions of financial services and the admission of securities to capital markets.

2. Where large-scale short-term capital movements to or from third countries seriously disturb the domestic or external monetary or financial situation of the Member States, or of a number of them, or cause serious strains in exchange relations within the Community or between the Community and third countries, Member States shall consult with one another on any measure to be taken to counteract such difficulties. This consultation shall take place within the Committee of Governors of the Central Banks and the Monetary Committee on the initiative of the Commission or of any Member State.

Article 8

At least once a year the Monetary Committee shall examine the situation regarding free movement of capital as it results from the application of this Directive. The examination shall cover measures concerning the domestic regulation of credit and financial and monetary markets which could have a specific impact on international capital movements and on all other aspects of this Directive. The Committee shall report to the Commission on the outcome of this examination.

Article 9

The First Directive of 11 May 1960 and Directive 72/156/EEC shall be repealed with effect from 1 July 1990.

Article 10

This Directive is addressed to the Member States.

Done at Luxembourg, 24 June 1988.

ANNEX 1

NOMENCLATURE OF THE CAPITAL MOVEMENTS REFERRED TO IN ARTICLE 1 OF THE DIRECTIVE

In this Nomenclature, capital movements are classified according to the economic nature of the assets and liabilities they concern, denominated either in national currency or in foreign exchange.

The capital movements listed in this Nomenclature are taken to cover:

— all the operations necessary for the purposes of capital movements: conclusion and performance of the transaction and related transfers. The transaction is generally between residents of different Member States although some capital movements are carried out by a single person for his own account (eg transfers of assets belonging to emigrants),

— operations carried out by any natural or legal person (see Explanatory Notes below), including operations in respect of the assets or liabilities of Member States or of other public administrations and agencies, subject to the provisions of Article 68(3)[1] of the Treaty,

— access for the economic operator to all the financial techniques available on the market approached for the purpose of carrying out the operation in question. For example, the concept of acquisition of securities and other financial instruments covers not only spot transactions but also all the dealing techniques available: forward transactions, transactions carrying an option or warrant, swaps against other assets, etc. Similarly, the concept of operations in current and deposit accounts with financial institutions, includes not only the opening and placing of funds on accounts but also forward foreign exchange transactions, irrespective of whether these are intended to cover an exchange risk or to take an open foreign exchange position,

— operations to liquidate or assign assets built up, repatriation of the proceeds of liquidation thereof (see Explanatory Notes below) or immediate use of such proceeds within the limits of Community obligations,

— operations to repay credits or loans.

This Nomenclature is not an exhaustive list for the notion of capital movements—whence a heading XIII—F "Other capital movements—Miscellaneous". It should not therefore be interpreted as restricting the scope of the principle of full liberalisation of capital movements as referred to in Article 1 of the Directive.

I—DIRECT INVESTMENTS

(see Explanatory Notes below)

1 Establishment and extension of branches or new undertakings belonging solely to the person providing the capital, and the acquisition in full of existing undertakings.

2 Participation in new or existing undertaking with a view to establishing or maintaining lasting economic links.

3 Long-term loans with a view to establishing or maintaining lasting economic links.

4 Reinvestment of profits with a view to maintaining lasting economic links.

A—Direct investments on national territory by non-residents (see Explanatory Notes below).

B—Direct investments abroad by residents (see Explanatory Notes below).

II—INVESTMENTS IN REAL ESTATE (NOT INCLUDED UNDER I)

(see Explanatory Notes below)

A—Investments in real estate on national territory by non-residents

B—Investments in real estate abroad by residents

III—OPERATIONS IN SECURITIES NORMALLY DEALT IN ON THE CAPITAL MARKET (NOT INCLUDED UNDER I, IV AND V)

(*a*) Shares and other securities of a participating nature (see Explanatory Notes below).
(*b*) Bonds (see Explanatory Notes below).

A—Transactions in securities on the capital market

1 Acquisition by non-residents of domestic securities dealt in on a stock exchange (see Explanatory Notes below).

2 Acquisition by residents of foreign securities dealt in on a stock exchange.

3 Acquisition by non-residents of domestic securities not dealt in on a stock exchange (see Explanatory Notes below).

4 Acquisition by residents of foreign securities not dealt in on a stock exchange.

B—Admission of securities to the capital market (see Explanatory Notes below)

(i) *Introduction on a stock exchange* (see Explanatory Notes below).
(ii) *Issue and placing on a capital market.*

1 Admission of domestic securities to a foreign capital market.

2 Administration of foreign securities to the domestic capital market.

IV—OPERATIONS IN UNITS OF COLLECTIVE INVESTMENT UNDERTAKINGS

(see Explanatory Notes below)

(*a*) Units of undertakings for collective investment in securities normally dealt in on the capital market (shares, other equities and bonds).
(*b*) Units of undertakings for collective investment in securities or instruments normally dealt in on the money market.
(*c*) Units of undertakings for collective investment in other assets.

A—Transactions in units of collective investment undertakings

1 Acquisition by non-residents of units of national undertakings dealt in on a stock exchange.

2 Acquisition by residents of units of foreign undertakings dealt in on a stock exchange.

3 Acquisition by non-residents of units of national undertakings not dealt in on a stock exchange.

4 Acquisition by residents of units of foreign undertakings not dealt in on a stock exchange.

B—Administration of units of collective investment undertakings to the capital market

(i) Introduction on a stock exchange.
(ii) Issue and placing on a capital market.

1 Admission of units of national collective investment undertakings to a foreign capital market.

2 Admission of units of foreign collective investment undertakings to the domestic capital market.

V—OPERATIONS IN SECURITIES AND OTHER INSTRUMENTS NORMALLY DEALT IN ON THE MONEY MARKET

(see Explanatory Notes below)

A—Transactions in securities and other instruments on the money market

1 Acquisition by non-residents of domestic money market securities and instruments.

2 Acquisition by residents of foreign money market securities and instruments.

B—Admission of securities and other instruments to the money market

(i) Introduction on a recognised money market.
(ii) Issue and placing on a recognised money market.

1 Admission of domestic securities and instruments to a foreign money market.

2 Admission of foreign securities and instruments to the domestic money market.

VI—OPERATIONS IN CURRENT AND DEPOSIT ACCOUNTS WITH FINANCIAL INSTITUTIONS

(see Explanatory Notes below)

A—Operations carried out by non-residents with domestic financial institutions

B—Operations carried out by residents with foreign financial institutions

VII—CREDITS RELATED TO COMMERCIAL TRANSACTIONS OR TO THE PROVISION OF SERVICES IN WHICH A RESIDENT IS PARTICIPATING

(see Explanatory Notes below)

1 Short-term (less than one year).

2 Medium-term (from one to five years).

3 Long-term (five years or more).

A—Credits granted by non-residents to residents

B—Credits granted by residents to non-residents

VIII—FINANCIAL LOANS AND CREDITS (NOT INCLUDED UNDER I, VII AND XI)

(see Explanatory Notes below)

1 Short-term (less than one year).

2 Medium-term (from one to five years).

3 Long-term (five years or more).

A—Loans and credits granted by non-residents to residents

B—Loans and credits granted by residents to non-residents

IX—SURETIES, OTHER GUARANTEES AND RIGHTS OF PLEDGE

A—Granted by non-residents to residents

B—Granted by residents to non-residents

X—TRANSFERS IN PERFORMANCE OF INSURANCE CONTRACTS

A—Premiums and payments in respect of life assurance

1 Contracts concluded between domestic life assurance companies and non-residents.

2 Contracts concluded between foreign life assurance companies and residents.

B—Premiums and payments in respect of credit insurance

1 Contracts concluded between domestic credit insurance companies and non-residents.

2 Contracts concluded between foreign credit insurance companies and residents.

C—Other transfers of capital in respect of insurance contracts

XI—PERSONAL CAPITAL MOVEMENTS

A—Loans

B—Gifts and endowments

C—Dowries

D—Inheritances and legacies

E—Settlement of debts by immigrants in their previous country of residence

F—Transfers of assets constituted by residents, in the event of emigration, at the time of their installation or during their period of stay abroad

G—Transfers, during their period of stay, of immigrants' savings to their previous country of residence

XII—PHYSICAL IMPORT AND EXPORT OF FINANCIAL ASSETS

A—Securities

B—Means of payment of every kind

XIII—OTHER CAPITAL MOVEMENTS

A—Death duties

B—Damages (where these can be considered as capital)

C—Refunds in the case of cancellation of contracts and refunds of uncalled-for payments (where these can be considered as capital)

D—Authors' royalties: patents, designs, trade marks and inventions (assignments and transfers arising out of such assignments)

E—Transfers of the monies required for the provision of services (not included under VI)

F—Miscellaneous

EXPLANATORY NOTES

For the purposes of this Nomenclature and the Directive only, the following expressions have the meanings assigned to them respectively:

Direct investments

Investments of all kinds by natural persons or commercial, industrial or financial undertakings, and which serve to establish or to maintain lasting and direct links between the person providing the capital and the entrepreneur to whom or the undertaking to which the capital is made available in order to carry on an economic activity. This concept must therefore be understood in its widest sense.

The undertakings mentioned under I–1 of the Nomenclature include legally independent undertakings (wholly-owned subsidiaries) and branches.

As regards those undertakings mentioned under I–2 of the Nomenclature which have the status of companies limited by shares, there is participation in the nature of direct investment where the block of shares held by a natural person of another undertaking or any other holder enables the shareholder, either pursuant to the provisions of national laws relating to companies limited by shares or otherwise, to participate effectively in the management of the company or in its control.

Long-term loans of a participating nature, mentioned under I–3 of the Nomenclature, means loans for a period of more than five years which are made for the purpose of establishing or maintaining lasting economic links. The main examples which may be cited are loans granted by a company to its subsidiaries or to companies in which it has a share and loans linked with a profit-sharing arrangement. Loans granted by financial institutions with a view to establishing or maintaining lasting economic links are also included under this heading.

Investments in real estate

Purchases of buildings and land and the construction of buildings by private persons for gain or personal use. This category also includes rights of usufruct, easements and building rights.

Introduction on a stock exchange or on a recognised money market

Access—in accordance with a specified procedure—for securities and other negotiable instruments to dealings, whether controlled officially or unofficially, on an officially recognised stock exchange or in an officially recognised segment of the money market.

Securities dealt in on a stock exchange (quoted or unquoted)

Securities the dealings in which are controlled by regulations, the prices for which are regularly published, either by official stock exchanges (quoted securities) or by other bodies attached to a stock exchange—eg committees of banks (unquoted securities).

Issue of securities and other negotiable instruments

Sale by way of an offer to the public.

Placing of securities and other negotiable instruments

The direct sale of securities by the issuer of by the consortium which the issuer has instructed to sell them, with no offer being made to the public.

Domestic or foreign securities and other instruments

Securities according to the country in which the issuer has his principal place of business. Acquisition by residents of domestic securities and other instruments issued on a foreign market ranks as the acquisition of foreign securities.

Shares and other securities of a participating nature

Including rights to subscribe to new issues of shares.

Bonds

Negotiable securities with a maturity of two years or more from issue for which the interest rate and the terms for the repayment of the principal and the payment of interest are determined at the time of issue.

Collective investment undertakings

Undertakings:

— the object of which is the collective investment in transferable securities or other assets of the capital they raise and which operate on the principle of risk-spreading, and

— the units of which are, at the request of holders, under the legal, contractual or statutory conditions governing them, repurchased or redeemed, directly or indirectly, out of those undertakings' assets. Action taken by a collective investment undertaking to ensure that the stock exchange value of its units does not significantly vary from their net asset value shall be regarded as equivalent to such repurchase or redemption.

Such undertakings may be constituted according to law either under the law of contract (as common funds managed by management companies) or trust law (as unit trusts) or under statute (as investment companies).

For the purposes of the Directive, ''common funds'' shall also include unit trusts.

Securities and other instruments normally dealt in on the money market

Treasury bills and other negotiable bills, certificates of deposit, bankers' acceptances, commercial paper and other like instruments.

Credits related to commercial transactions or to the provision of services

Contractual trade credits (advances or payments by instalment in respect of work in progress or on order and extended payment terms, whether or not involving subscription to a commercial bill) and their financing by credits provided by credit institutions. This category also includes factoring operations.

Financial loans and credits

Financing of every kind granted by financial institutions, including financing related to commercial transactions or to the provision of services in which no resident is participating.

This category also includes mortgage loans, consumer credit and financial leasing, as well as back-up facilities and other note-issuance facilities.

Residents or non-residents

Natural and legal persons according to the definitions laid down in the exchange control regulations in force in each Member State.

Proceeds of liquidation (of investments, securities, etc)

Proceeds of sale including any capital appreciation, amount of repayments, proceeds of execution of judgements, etc.

Natural or legal persons

As defined by the national rules.

Financial institutions

Banks, savings banks and institutions specialising in the provision of short-term, medium-term and long-term credit, and insurance companies, building societies, investment companies and other institutions of like character.

Credit institutions

Banks, savings banks and institutions specialising in the provision of short-term, medium-term and long-term credit.

Note—[1] Articles 67—73 substituted by articles 73b, 73c, 73d, 73e, 73f and 73g by the Treaty on European Union signed at Maastricht on 7 February 1992. Articles 73b, 73c, 73d, 73f and 73g renumbered articles 56, 57, 58, 59 and 60 respectively, and article 73e repealed, by the Treaty of Amsterdam ratified on 1 May 1999 (OJ C340 10.11.97 p 1).

Statement of Practice SP 2/92—Transactions within TA 1988 s 765A—movements of capital between residents of EC.

ANNEXES II–V

Note—These Annexes are not relevant for the purposes of this work.

Council Directive of 23 July 1990 on the common system of taxation applicable to mergers, divisions, transfers of assets and exchanges of shares concerning companies of different member states

(90/434/EEC)

Note—See OJ L225 20.08.90, p 1.

Cross references—See TA 1988 s 815A (double taxation relief for tax payable in a member state on gains accruing when a UK company transfers its branch or agency in a member state to a company resident in another member state).

The Council of the European Communities,

Having regard to the Treaty establishing the European Economic Community, and in particular Article 100[1] thereof,

Having regard to the proposal of the Commission,

Having regard to the opinion of the European Parliament,

Having regard to the opinion of the Economic and Social Committee,

Whereas mergers, divisions, transfers of assets and exchanges of shares concerning companies of different Member States may be necessary in order to create within the Community conditions analogous to those of an internal market and in order thus to ensure the establishment and effective functioning of the common market; whereas such operations ought not to be hampered by restrictions, disadvantages or distortions arising in particular from the tax provisions of the Member States; whereas to that end it is necessary to introduce with respect to such operations tax rules which are neutral from the point of view of competition, in order to allow enterprises to adapt to the requirements of the common market, to increase their productivity and to improve their competitive strength at the international level;

Whereas tax provisions disadvantage such operations, in comparison with those concerning companies of the same Member State; whereas it is necessary to remove such disadvantages;

Whereas it is not possible to attain this objective by an extension at the Community level of the systems presently in force in the Member States, since differences between these systems tend to produce distortions; whereas only a common tax system is able to provide a satisfactory solution in this respect;

Whereas the common tax system ought to avoid the imposition of tax in connection with mergers, divisions, transfers of assets or exchanges of shares, while at the same time safeguarding the financial interests of the State of the transferring or acquired company;

Whereas in respect of mergers, divisions or transfers of assets, such operations normally result either in the transformation of the transferring company into a permanent establishment of the company receiving the assets or in the assets becoming connected with a permanent establishment of the latter company;

Whereas the system of deferral of the taxation of the capital gains relating to the assets transferred until their actual disposal, applied to such of those assets as are transferred to that permanent establishment, permits exemption from taxation of the corresponding capital gains, while at the same time ensuring their ultimate taxation by the State of the transferring company at the date of their disposal;

Whereas it is also necessary to define the tax regime applicable to certain provisions, reserves or losses of the transferring company and to solve the tax problems occurring where one of the two companies has a holding in the capital of the other;

Whereas the allotment to the shareholders of the transferring company of securities of the receiving or acquiring company would not in itself give rise to any taxation in the hands of such shareholders;

Whereas it is necessary to allow Member States the possibility of refusing to apply this Directive where the merger, division, transfer of assets or exchange of shares operation has as its objective tax evasion or avoidance or results in a company, whether or not it participates in the operation, no longer fulfilling the conditions required for the representation of employees in company organs,

Note—[1] Article 100 renumbered article 94 by the Treaty of Amsterdam ratified on 1 May 1999.

Has adopted this directive:

TITLE I

GENERAL PROVISIONS

Article 1

Each Member State shall apply this Directive to mergers, divisions, transfers of assets and exchanges of shares in which companies from two or more Member States are involved.

Article 2

For the purposes of this Directive:

(*a*) "merger" shall mean an operation whereby:

— one or more companies, on being dissolved without going into liquidation, transfer all their assets and liabilities to another existing company in exchange for the issue to their shareholders of securities representing the capital of that other company, and, if applicable, a cash payment not exceeding 10% of the nominal value, or, in the absence of a nominal value, of the accounting par value of those securities,

— two or more companies, on being dissolved without going into liquidation, transfer all their assets and liabilities to a company that they form, in exchange for the issue to their shareholders of securities representing the capital of that new company, and, if applicable, a cash payment not exceeding 10% of the nominal value, or in the absence of a nominal value, of the accounting par value of those securities,

— a company, on being dissolved without going into liquidation, transfers all its assets and liabilities to the company holding all the securities representing its capital;

(*b*) "division" shall mean an operation whereby a company, on being dissolved without going into liquidation, transfers all its assets and liabilities to two or more existing or new companies, in exchange for the pro rata issue to its shareholders of securities representing the capital of the companies receiving the assets and liabilities, and, if applicable, a cash payment not exceeding 10% of the nominal value or, in the absence of a nominal value, of the accounting par value of those securities;

EC Material

(*c*) ''transfer of assets'' shall mean an operation whereby a company transfers without being dissolved all or one or more branches of its activity to another company in exchange for the transfer of securities representing the capital of the company receiving the transfer;
(*d*) ''exchange of shares'' shall mean an operation whereby a company acquires a holding in the capital of another company such that it obtains a majority of the voting rights in that company in exchange for the issue to the shareholders of the latter company, in exchange for their securities, of securities representing the capital of the former company, and, if applicable, a cash payment not exceeding 10% of the nominal value or, in the absence of a nominal value, of the accounting par value of the securities issued in exchange;
(*e*) ''transferring company'' shall mean the company transferring its assets and liabilities or transferring all or one or more branches of its activity;
(*f*) ''receiving company'' shall mean the company receiving the assets and liabilities or all or one or more branches of the activity of the transferring company;
(*g*) ''acquired company'' shall mean the company in which a holding is acquired by another company by means of an exchange of securities;
(*h*) ''acquiring company'' shall mean the company which acquires a holding by means of an exchange of securities;
(*i*) ''branch of activity'' shall mean all the assets and liabilities of a division of a company which from an organisational point of view constitute an independent business, that is to say an entity capable of functioning by its own means.

Simon's Tax Cases—art 2(*d*), *Leur-Bloem v Inspecteur der Belastingdienst/Ondernemingen Amsterdam 2 (Case C-28/95)* [1997] STC 1205.

Article 3

For the purposes of this Directive, ''company from a Member State'' shall mean any company which:

(*a*) takes one of the forms listed in the Annex hereto;
(*b*) according to the tax laws of a Member State is considered to be resident in that State for tax purposes and, under the terms of a double taxation agreement concluded with a third State, is not considered to be resident for tax purposes outside the Community;
(*c*) moreover, is subject to one of the following taxes, without the possibility of an option or of being exempt;

— impôt des sociétés/vennootschapsbelasting in Belgium,
— selskabsskat in Denmark,
— Körperschaftsteuer in the Federal Republic of Germany,
— φροώ εισοδηματοώ νομικων προσωπων κερδοκοπικον χαρακτηρα, in Greece,
— impuesto sobre sociedades in Spain,
— impôt sur les sociétés in France,
— corporation tax in Ireland,
— imposta sul reddito delle persone giuridiche in Italy,
— impôt sur le revenu des collectivités in Luxembourg,
— vennootschapsbelasting in the Netherlands,
— imposto sobre o rendimento das pessoas colectivas in Portugal,
— corporation tax in the United Kingdom,
— Körperschaftsteuer in Austria,
— Yhteisöjen tulovero/inkomstskatten för samfund in Finland;
— Statlig inkomstskatt in Sweden;][1]
[— Daň z příjmu právnickych osobin the Czech Republic,
— Tulumaks in Estonia,
— Φορος Εισοδηματος in Cyprus,
— uzņēmumu ienākuma nodoklis in Latvia,
— Pelno mokestis in Lithuania,
— Társasági adó in Hungary,
— Taxxa fuq l-income in Malta,
— Podatek dochodowy od osób prawnych in Poland,
— Davek od dobic¡ka pravnih oseb in Slovenia,
— Dan¡ z príjmov právnickych osôb in Slovakia][2]

or to any other tax which may be substituted for any of the above taxes.

Amendments—[1] Words in para (*c*) inserted by the Act of Accession 1995 art 29, Annex I.
[2] Words in para (*c*) inserted by the Act of Accession 2003, Annex II Chapter 9 para 7(*a*) (OJ L 236; 23.9.2003 p 555).

TITLE II
RULES APPLICABLE TO MERGERS, DIVISIONS AND EXCHANGES OF SHARES

Article 4

1. A merger or division shall not give rise to any taxation of capital gains calculated by reference to the difference between the real values of the assets and liabilities transferred and their values for tax purposes. The following expressions shall have the meanings assigned to them:

— value for tax purposes: the value on the basis of which any gain or loss would have been computed for the purposes of tax upon the income, profits or capital gains of the transferring company if such assets or liabilities had been sold at the time of the merger or division but independently of it,

— transferred assets and liabilities: those assets and liabilities of the transferring company which, in consequence of the merger or division, are effectively connected with a permanent establishment of the receiving company in the Member State of the transferring company and play a part in generating the profits or losses taken into account for tax purposes.

2. The Member States shall make the application of paragraph 1 conditional upon the receiving company's computing any new depreciation and any gains or losses in respect of the assets and liabilities transferred according to the rules that would have applied to the transferring company or companies if the merger or division had not taken place.

3. Where, under the laws of the Member State of the transferring company, the receiving company is entitled to have any new depreciation or any gains or losses in respect of the assets and liabilities transferred computed on a basis different from that set out in paragraph 2, paragraph 1 shall not apply to the assets and liabilities in respect of which that option is exercised.

Article 5

The Member States shall take the necessary measures to ensure that, where provisions or reserves properly constituted by the transferring company are partly or wholly exempt from tax and are not derived from permanent establishments abroad, such provisions or reserves may be carried over, with the same tax exemption, by the permanent establishments of the receiving company which are situated in the Member State of the transferring company, the receiving company thereby assuming the rights and obligations of the transferring company.

Article 6

To the extent that, if the operations referred to in Article 1 were effected between companies from the Member State of the transferring company, the Member State would apply provisions allowing the receiving company to take over the losses of the transferring company which had not yet been exhausted for tax purposes, it shall extend those provisions to cover the take-over of such losses by the receiving company's permanent establishments situated within its territory.

Article 7

1. Where the receiving company has a holding in the capital of the transferring company, any gains accruing to the receiving company on the cancellation of its holding shall not be liable to any taxation.

2. The Member States may derogate from paragraph 1 where the receiving company's holding in the capital of the transferring company does not exceed 25%.

Article 8

1. On a merger, division or exchange of shares, the allotment of securities representing the capital of the receiving or acquiring company to a shareholder of the transferring or acquired company in exchange for securities representing the capital of the latter company shall not, of itself, give rise to any taxation of the income, profits or capital gains of that shareholder.

2. The Member States shall make the application of paragraph 1 conditional upon the shareholder's not attributing to the securities received a value for tax purposes higher than the securities exchanged had immediately before the merger, division or exchange.

The application of paragraph 1 shall not prevent the Member States from taxing the gain arising out of the subsequent transfer of securities received in the same way as the gain arising out of the transfer of securities existing before the acquisition.

In this paragraph the expression "value for tax purposes" means the amount on the basis of which any gain or loss would be computed for the purposes of tax upon the income, profits or capital gains of a shareholder of the company.

3. Where, under the law of the Member State in which he is resident, a shareholder may opt for tax treatment different from that set out in paragraph 2, paragraph 1 shall not apply to the securities in respect of which such an option is exercised.

4. Paragraphs 1, 2 and 3 shall not prevent a Member State from taking into account when taxing shareholders any cash payment that may be made on the merger, division or exchange.

TITLE III

RULES APPLICABLE TO TRANSFERS OF ASSETS

Article 9

The provisions of Articles 4, 5 and 6 shall apply to transfers of assets.

TITLE IV

SPECIAL CASE OF THE TRANSFER OF A PERMANENT ESTABLISHMENT

Article 10

1. Where the assets transferred in a merger, a division or a transfer of assets include a permanent establishment of the transferring company which is situated in a Member State other than that of the transferring company, the latter State shall renounce any right to tax that permanent establishment. However, the State of the transferring company may reinstate in the taxable profits of that company such losses of the permanent establishment as may previously have been set off against the taxable profits of the company in that State and which have not been recovered. The State in which the permanent establishment is situated and the State of the receiving company shall apply the provisions of this Directive to such a transfer as if the former State were the State of the transferring company.

2. By way of derogation from paragraph 1, where the Member State of the transferring company applies a system of taxing world-wide profits, that Member State shall have the right to tax any profits or capital gains of the permanent establishment resulting from the merger, division or transfer of assets, on condition that it gives relief for the tax that, but for the provisions of this Directive, would have been charged on those profits or capital gains in the Member State in which that permanent establishment is situated, in the same way and in the same amount as it would have done if that tax had actually been charged and paid.

TITLE V

FINAL PROVISIONS

Article 11

1. A Member State may refuse to apply or withdraw the benefit of all or any part of the provisions of Titles II, III and IV where it appears that the merger, division, transfer of assets or exchange of shares:

(*a*) has as its principal objective or as one of its principal objectives tax evasion or tax avoidance; the fact that one of the operations referred to in Article 1 is not carried out for valid commercial reasons such as the restructuring or rationalisation of the activities of the companies participating in the operation may constitute a presumption that the operation has tax evasion or tax avoidance as its principal objective or as one of its principal objectives;

(*b*) results in a company, whether participating in the operation or not, no longer fulfilling the necessary conditions for the representation of employees on company organs according to the arrangements which were in force prior to that operation.

2. Paragraph (1)(*b*) shall apply as long as and to the extent that no Community law provisions containing equivalent rules on representation of employees on company organs are applicable to the companies covered by this Directive.

Simon's Tax Cases—art 11(1)(*a*), *Leur-Bloem v Inspecteur der Belastingdienst/Ondernemingen Amsterdam 2 (Case C-28/95)* [1997] STC 1205.

Article 12

1. Member States shall bring into force the laws, regulations and administrative provisions necessary to comply with this Directive not later than 1 January 1992 and shall forthwith inform the Commission thereof.

2. By way of derogation from paragraph 1, the Portuguese Republic may delay the application of the provisions concerning transfers of assets and exchanges of shares until 1 January 1993.

3. Member States shall communicate to the Commission the texts of the main provisions of national law which they adopt in the field covered by this Directive.

Article 13

This Directive is addressed to the Member States.

Done at Brussels, 23 July 1990.

ANNEX

List of companies referred to in Article 3(*a*)

(*a*) companies under Belgian law known as ''société anonyme''/''naamloze vennootschap'', ''société en commandite par actions''/''commanditaire vennootschap op aandelen'', ''société privée à responsabilité limitée''/''besloten vennootschap met beperkte aansprakelijkheid'' and those public law bodies that operate under private law;

(*b*) companies under Danish law known as: ''aktieselskab'', ''anpartsselskab'';

(*c*) companies under German law known as: ''Aktiengesellschaft'', ''Kommanditgesellschaft auf Aktien'', ''Gesellschaft mit beschränkter Haftung'', ''bergrechtliche Gewerkschaft'';

(*d*) companies under Greek law known as: ''ανωνυμη εταιρεια'';

(*e*) companies under Spanish law known as: ''sociedad anónima'', ''sociedad comanditaria por acciones'', ''sociedad de responsabilidad limitada'' and those public law bodies which operate under private law;

(*f*) companies under French law known as ''société anonyme'', ''société en commandite par actions'', ''société à responsabilité limitée'' and industrial and commercial public establishments and undertakings;

(*g*) the companies in Irish law known as public companies limited by shares or by guarantee, private companies limited by shares or by guarantee, bodies registered under the Industrial and Provident Societies Acts or building societies registered under the Building Societies Acts;

(*h*) companies under Italian law known as ''società per azioni'', ''società in accomandita per azioni'', ''società a responsabilità limitata'', and public and private entities carrying on industrial and commercial activities;

(*i*) companies under Luxembourg law known as ''société anonyme'', ''société en commandite par actions'', ''société à responsabilité limitée'';

(*j*) companies under Dutch law known as: ''naamloze vennootschap'', ''besloten vennootschap met beperkte aansprakelijkheid'';

(*k*) commercial companies or civil law companies having a commercial form as well as other legal persons carrying on commercial or industrial activities, which are incorporated in accordance with Portuguese law;

(*l*) companies incorporated under the law of the United Kingdom;

[(*m*) companies under Austrian law known as ''Aktiengesellschaft'', ''Gesellschaft mit beschränkter Haftung'';

(*n*) companies under Finnish law known as ''osakeyhtiö/aktiebolag'', ''osuuskunta/andelslag'', ''säästöpankki/sparbank'' and ''vakuutusyhtiö/försäkringsbolag'';

(*o*) companies under Swedish law known as: ''aktiebolag'', ''bankaktiebolag'', ''försäkringsaktiebolag.][1]

[(*p*) companies under Czech law known as: ''akciová společnost'', ''společnost s ručením omezenym'';

(*q*) companies under Estonian law known as: ''täisühing'', ''usaldusühing'', ''osaühing'', ''aktsiaselts'', ''tulundusühistu'';

(*r*) under Cypriot law: ''εταιρειες'' as defined in the Income Tax laws;

(*s*) companies under Latvian law known as: ''akciju sabiedrýba'', ''sabiedrýba ar ierobez¡otu atbildýbu'';

(*t*) companies incorporated under the law of Lithuania;

(*u*) companies under Hungarian law known as: ''közkereseti társaság'', ''betéti társaság'', ''közös vállalat'', ''korlátolt felelõsségű társaság'', ''részvénytársaság'', ''egyesülés'', ''közhasznú társaság'', ''szövetkezet'';

(*v*) companies under Maltese law known as: ''Kumpaniji ta' Responsabilita' Limitata'', ''Socÿjetajiet en commandite li l-kapital taghhom maqsum f'azzjonijiet'';

(*w*) companies under Polish law known as: ''spólka akcyjna'', ''spólka z ograniczoną odpowiedzialnośćia[2]'';

(*x*) companies under Slovenian law known as: ''delniška družba'', ''komanditna družba'', ''družba z omejeno odgovornostjo'';

(*y*) companies under Slovak law known as: ''Akciová spoločnost''', ''Spoločnost' s ručením obmedzenym'', ''Komanditná spoločnost][2]

Amendments—[1] Paras (*m*)–(*n*) inserted by the Act of Accession 1995 art 29, Annex I.
[2] Paras (*o*)–(*y*) inserted by the Act of Accession 2003 Annex II Chapter 9, para 7(*b*) (OJ L 236; 23.9.2003 p 555).

Council Directive
of 23 July 1990
on the common system of taxation applicable in the case of parent companies and subsidiaries of different member states

(90/435/EEC)

Note—See OJ L225 20.08.90, p 6.

The Council of the European Communities,

Having regard to the Treaty establishing the European Economic Community, and in particular Article 100[1] thereof,

Having regard to the proposal of the Commission,

Having regard to the opinion of the European Parliament,

Having regard to the opinion of the Economic and Social Committee,

Whereas the grouping together of companies of different Member States may be necessary in order to create within the Community conditions analogous to those of an internal market and in order thus to ensure the establishment and effective functioning of the common market; whereas such operations ought not to be hampered by restrictions, disadvantages or distortions arising in particular from the tax provisions of the Member States; whereas it is therefore necessary to introduce with respect to such grouping together of companies of different Member States, tax rules which are neutral from the point of view of competition, in order to allow enterprises to adapt to the requirements of the common market, to increase their productivity and to improve their competitive strength at the international level;

Whereas such grouping together may result in the formation of groups of parent companies and subsidiaries;

Whereas the existing tax provisions which govern the relations between parent companies and subsidiaries of different Member States vary appreciably from one Member State to another and are generally less advantageous than those applicable to parent companies and subsidiaries of the same Member State; whereas co-operation between companies of different Member States is thereby disadvantaged in comparison with co-operation between companies of the same Member State; whereas it is necessary to eliminate this disadvantage by the introduction of a common system in order to facilitate the grouping together of companies;

Whereas where a parent company by virtue of its association with its subsidiary receives distributed profits, the State of the parent company must:

—either refrain from taxing such profits,

—or tax such profits while authorising the parent company to deduct from the amount of tax due that fraction of the corporation tax paid by the subsidiary which relates to those profits;

Whereas it is furthermore necessary, in order to ensure fiscal neutrality, that the profits which a subsidiary distributes to its parent company be exempt from withholding tax; whereas, however, the Federal Republic of Germany and the Hellenic Republic, by reason of the particular nature of their corporate tax systems, and the Portuguese Republic, for budgetary reasons, should be authorised to maintain temporarily a withholding tax,

Note—[1] Article 100 renumbered article 94 by the Treaty of Amsterdam ratified on 1 May 1999.

Has adopted this directive:

Article 1

1. Each Member State shall apply this Directive:

— to distributions of profits received by companies of that State which come from their subsidiaries of other Member States,

— to distributions of profits by companies of that State to companies of other Member States of which they are subsidiaries.

[— to distributions of profits received by permanent establishments situated in that State of companies of other Member States which come from their subsidiaries of a Member State other than that where the permanent establishment is situated,

— to distributions of profits by companies of that State to permanent establishments situated in another Member State of companies of the same Member State of which they are subsidiaries.]

2. This Directive shall not preclude the application of domestic or agreement-based provisions required for the prevention of fraud or abuse.

Amendments—[1] Words inserted by Council Directive 2003/123/EC art 1(1) (OJ L 7; 13.1.2004 p 41).

Article 2

[1.][3] For the purposes of this Directive "company of a Member State" shall mean any company which:

(*a*) takes one of the forms listed in the Annex hereto;
(*b*) according to the tax laws of a Member State is considered to be resident in that State for tax purposes and, under the terms of a double taxation agreement concluded with a third State, is not considered to be resident for tax purposes outside the Community;
[(*c*) moreover, is subject to one of the following taxes, without the possibility of an option or of being exempt:

— impôt des sociétés/vennootschapsbelasting in Belgium,
— selskabsskat in Denmark,
— Körperschaftsteuer in the Federal Republic of Germany,
— φροώ εισοδηματοώ νομικων προσωπων κερδοσκοπικον χαρακτηρα, in Greece,
— impuesto sobre sociedades in Spain,
— impôt sur les sociétés in France,
— corporation tax in Ireland,
— imposta sul reddito delle persone giuridiche in Italy,
— impôt sur le revenu des collectivités in Luxembourg,
— vennootschapsbelasting in the Netherlands,
— imposto sobre o rendimento das pessoas colectivas in Portugal,
— corporation tax in the United Kingdom,
— Körperschaftsteuer in Austria,
— Yhteisöjen tulovero/inkomstskatten för samfund in Finland,
— Statlig inkomstskatt in Sweden.][1]
[— Dan¡ z příjmu právnických osob in the Czech Republic
— Tulumaks in Estonia
— Φορος Εισοδηματος in Cyprus
— uzņēmumu ienakuma nodoklis in Latvia
— Pelno mokestis in Lithuania
— Társasági adó, osztalékadó in Hungary
— Taxxa fuq l-income in Malta
— Podatek dochodowy od osób prawnych in Poland
— Davek od dobiĉka pravnih oseb in Slovenia
— daň z príjmov právnických osôb in Slovakia][2]

or to any other tax which may be substituted for any of the above taxes.

[2. For the purposes of this Directive the term "permanent establishment" means a fixed place of business situated in a Member State through which the business of a company of another Member State is wholly or partly carried on in so far as the profits of that place of business are subject to tax in the Member State in which it is situated by virtue of the relevant bilateral tax treaty or, in the absence of such a treaty, by virtue of national law.][3]

Simon's Tax Cases—*Ministerio Publico v Epson Europe BV (Case C-375/98)* [2002] STC 739.
Amendment—[1] Words in para (*c*) inserted by the Act of Accession 1995 art 29, Annex 7.
[2] Words in para (*c*) inserted by the Act of Accession 2003 Annex II Chapter 9, para 8(*a*) (OJ L 236; 23.9.2003 p 555).
[3] Para 1 numbered as such, and para 2 inserted by Council Directive 2003/123/EC art 1(2) (OJ L 7; 13.1.2004 p 41).

Article 3

1. [For the purposes of applying this Directive:

(*a*) the status of parent company shall be attributed at least to any company of a Member State which fulfils the conditions set out in Article 2 and has a minimum holding of 20% in the capital of a company of another Member State fulfilling the same conditions;
such status shall also be attributed, under the same conditions, to a company of a Member State which has a minimum holding of 20 % in the capital of a company of the same Member State, held in whole or in part by a permanent establishment of the former company situated in another Member State;
from 1 January 2007 the minimum holding percentage shall be 15%;
from 1 January 2009 the minimum holding percentage shall be 10%;
(*b*) "subsidiary" shall mean that company the capital of which includes the holding referred to in (*a*).][1]

2. By way of derogation from paragraph 1, Member States shall have the option of:

— replacing, by means of bilateral agreement, the criterion of a holding in the capital by that of a holding of voting rights,
— not applying this Directive to companies of that Member State which do not maintain for an uninterrupted period of at least two years holdings qualifying them as parent companies or to those of their companies in which a company of another Member State does not maintain such a holding for an uninterrupted period of at least two years.

Simon's Tax Cases—art 3(2), *Denkavit Internationaal BV, VITIC Amsterdam BV and Voormeer BV v Bundesamt für Finanzen (Joined cases C-283/94, C-291/94 and C-292/94)* [1996] STC 1445.
Amendment—[1] Para 1 substituted by Council Directive 2003/123/EC art 1(3) (OJ L 7; 13.1.2004 p 41).

EC Material

Article 4

[1. Where a parent company or its permanent establishment, by virtue of the association of the parent company with its subsidiary, receives distributed profits, the State of the parent company and the State of its permanent establishment shall, except when the subsidiary is liquidated, either:

— refrain from taxing such profits, or

— tax such profits while authorising the parent company and the permanent establishment to deduct from the amount of tax due that fraction of the corporation tax related to those profits and paid by the subsidiary and any lower-tier subsidiary, subject to the condition that at each tier a company and its lower-tier subsidiary meet the requirements provided for in Articles 2 and 3, up to the limit of the amount of the corresponding tax due.][1]

[1a. Nothing in this Directive shall prevent the State of the parent company from considering a subsidiary to be fiscally transparent on the basis of that State's assessment of the legal characteristics of that subsidiary arising from the law under which it is constituted and therefore from taxing the parent company on its share of the profits of its subsidiary as and when those profits arise. In this case the State of the parent company shall refrain from taxing the distributed profits of the subsidiary.

When assessing the parent company's share of the profits of its subsidiary as they arise the State of the parent company shall either exempt those profits or authorise the parent company to deduct from the amount of tax due that fraction of the corporation tax related to the parent company's share of profits and paid by its subsidiary and any lower-tier subsidiary, subject to the condition that at each tier a company and its lower-tier subsidiary meet the requirements provided for in Articles 2 and 3, up to the limit of the amount of the corresponding tax due.][1]

2. However, each Member State shall retain the option of providing that any charges relating to the holding and any losses resulting from the distribution of the profits of the subsidiary may not be deducted from the taxable profits of the parent company. Where the management costs relating to the holding in such a case are fixed as a flat rate, the fixed amount may not exceed 5% of the profits distributed by the subsidiary.

3. [Paragraphs 1 and 1a shall apply until the date of effective entry into force of a common system of company taxation.][1]

The Council shall at the appropriate time adopt the rules to apply after the date referred to in the first subparagraph.

Amendment—[1] Para 1 substituted, para 1a inserted, and words in para 3 substituted, by Council Directive 2003/123/EC art 1(4) (OJ L 7; 13.1.2004 p 41).

Article 5

1. [Profits which a subsidiary distributes to its parent company shall be exempt from withholding tax.][1]

2–4. ...[1]

Simon's Tax Cases—*Denkavit Internationaal BV, VITIC Amsterdam BV and Voormeer BV v Bundesamt für Finanzen (Joined cases C-283/94, C-291/94 and C-292/94)* [1996] STC 1445; *Ministerio Publico v Epson Europe BV (Case C-375/98)* [2002] STC 739.

Art 5(1), *IRC v Océ Van Der Grinten NV* [2000] STC 951; *Océ van der Grinten NV v IRC* [2003] STC 1248.

Amendment—[1] Para 1 substituted, and paras 2–4 repealed, by Council Directive 2003/123/EC art 1(5) (OJ L 7; 13.1.2004 p 41).

Article 6

The Member State of a parent company may not charge withholding tax on the profits which such a company receives from a subsidiary.

Article 7

1. The term "withholding tax" as used in this Directive shall not cover an advance payment or prepayment (précompte) of corporation tax to the Member State of the subsidiary which is made in connection with a distribution of profits to its parent company.

2. This directive shall not affect the application of domestic or agreement-based provisions designed to eliminate or lessen economic double taxation of dividends, in particular provisions relating to the payment of tax credits to the recipients of dividends.

Simon's Tax Cases—Art 7(2), *Océ Van Der Grinten NV v IRC* [2000] STC (SCD) 127; *Océ van der Grinten NV v IRC* [2003] STC 1248.

Article 8

1. Member States shall bring into force the laws, regulations and administrative provisions necessary for them to comply with this Directive before 1 January 1992. They shall forthwith inform the Commission thereof.

2. Member States shall ensure that the texts of the main provisions of domestic law which they adopt in the field covered by this Directive are communicated to the Commission.

Article 9

This Directive is addressed to the Member States.

Done at Brussels, 23 July 1990.

ANNEX

[List of companies referred to Article 2(1)(*a*)

(*a*) companies under Belgian law known as ''société anonyme''/''naamloze vennootschap'',''société en commandite par actions''/''commanditaire vennootschap op aandelen'', ''société privée à responsabilité limitée''/''besloten vennootschap met beperkte aansprakelijkheid'', ''société coopérative à responsabilité limitée''/''coöperatieve vennootschap met beperkte aansprakelijkheid'', ''société coopérative à responsabilité illimitée''/''coöperatieve vennootschap met onbeperkte aansprakelijkheid'', ''société en nom collectif''/''vennootschap onder firma'', ''société en commandite simple''/''gewone commanditaire vennootschap'', public undertakings which have adopted one of the abovementioned legal forms, and other companies constituted under Belgian law subject to Belgian corporate tax;

(*b*) companies under Danish law known as ''aktieselskab'' and ''anpartsselskab''. Other companies subject to tax under the Corporation Tax Act, insofar as their taxable income is calculated and taxed in accordance with the general tax legislation rules applicable to ''aktieselskaber'';

(*c*) companies under German law known as ''Aktiengesellschaft'', ''Kommanditgesellschaft auf Aktien'', ''Gesellschaft mit beschränkter Haftung'', ''Versicherungsverein auf Gegenseitigkeit'', ''Erwerbs- und Wirtschaftsgenossenschaft'', ''Betriebe gewerblicher Art von juristischen Personen des öffentlichen Rechts'', and other companies constituted under German law subject to German corporate tax;

(*d*) companies under Greek law known as ''ανϖνυμη εταιρεαι'', ''εταιρεαι περιωρισμενης ευϑυνης (ΕΠΕ)'' and other companies constituted under Greek law subject to Greek corporate tax;

(*e*) companies under Spanish law known as: ''sociedad anónima'', ''sociedad comanditaria por acciones'', ''sociedad de responsabilidad limitada'', public law bodies which operate under private law. Other entities constituted under Spanish law subject to Spanish corporate tax (''Impuesto sobre Sociedades'');

(*f*) companies under French law known as ''société anonyme'', ''société en commandite par actions'', ''société à responsabilité limitée'', ''sociétés par actions simplifiées'', ''sociétés d'assurances mutuelles'', ''caisses d'épargne et de prévoyance'', ''sociétés civiles'' which are automatically subject to corporation tax, ''coopératives'', ''unions de coopératives'', industrial and commercial public establishments and undertakings, and other companies constituted under French law subject to French corporate tax;

(*g*) companies incorporated or existing under Irish law, bodies registered under the Industrial and Provident Societies Act, building societies incorporated under the Building Societies Acts and trustee savings banks within the meaning of the Trustee Savings Banks Act, 1989;

(*h*) companies under Italian law known as ''società per azioni'', ''società in accomandita per azioni'', ''società a responsibilità limitata'', ''società cooperative'', ''società di mutua assicurazione'', and private and public entities whose activity is wholly or principally commercial;

(*i*) companies under Luxembourg law known as ''société anonyme'', ''société en commandite par actions'', ''société à responsabilité limitée'', ''société coopérative'', ''société coopérative organisée comme une société anonyme'', ''association d'assurances mutuelles'', ''association d'épargne-pension'', ''entreprise de nature commerciale, industrielle ou minière de l'Etat, des communes, des syndicats de communes, des établissements publics et des autres personnes morales de droit public'', and other companies constituted under Luxembourg law subject to Luxembourg corporate tax;

(*j*) companies under Dutch law known as ''naamloze vennnootschap'', ''besloten vennootschap met beperkte aansprakelijkheid'', ''Open commanditaire vennootschap'', ''Coöperatie'', ''onderlinge waarborgmaatschappij'', ''Fonds voor gemene rekening'', ''vereniging op coöperatieve grondslag'', ''vereniging welke op onderlinge grondslag als verzekeraar of kredietinstelling optreedt'', and other companies constituted under Dutch law subject to Dutch corporate tax;

(*k*) companies under Austrian law known as ''Aktiengesellschaft'', ''Gesellschaft mit beschränkter Haftung'', ''Versicherungsvereine auf Gegenseitigkeit'', ''Erwerbs- und Wirtschaftsgenossenschaften'', ''Betriebe gewerblicher Art von Körperschaften des öffentlichen Rechts'', ''Sparkassen'', and other companies constituted under Austrian law subject to Austrian corporate tax;

(*l*) commercial companies or civil law companies having a commercial form and cooperatives and public undertakings incorporated in accordance with Portuguese law;

(*m*) companies under Finnish law known as ''osakeyhtiö/aktiebolag'', ''osuuskunta/andelslag'',''säästöpankki/sparbank''and ''vakuutusyhtiö/försäkringsbolag'';

(*n*) companies under Swedish law known as ''aktiebolag'', ''försäkringsaktiebolag'', ''ekonomiska föreningar'', ''sparbanker'', ''ömsesidiga försäkringsbolag'';

(*o*) companies incorporated under the law of the United Kingdom;

(*p*) companies incorporated under Council Regulation (EC) No 2157/2001 of 8 October 2001 on the Statute for a European company (SE) and Council Directive 2001/86/EC of 8 October 2001 supplementing the Statute for a European company with regard to the involvement of employees and cooperative societies incorporated under Council Regulation (EC) No 1435/2003 of 22 July 2003 on the Statute for a European Cooperative Society (SCE) and Council Directive 2003/72/EC of 22 July 2003 supplementing the Statute for a European Cooperative Society with regard to the involvement of employees.][1]

Amendment—[1] Annex substituted by Council Directive 2003/123/EC art 1(6) (OJ L 7; 13.1.2004 p 41).

EC Convention of 23 July 1990 on the elimination of double taxation in connection with the adjustment of profits of associated enterprises

(90/436/EEC)

Note—See OJ L225 20.08.90, p 19.
The Convention entered into force on 1 January 1995.
Cross references—See TA 1988 s 815B (provisions to implement this convention).
FA 1989 s 182A (criminal liability for disclosure of information by member of advisory commission set up under this convention).

CHAPTER I

SCOPE OF THE CONVENTION

Article 1

1. This Convention shall apply where, for the purposes of taxation, profits which are included in the profits of an enterprise of a Contracting State are also included or are also likely to be included in the profits of an enterprise of another Contracting State on the grounds that the principles set out in Article 4 and applied either directly or in corresponding provisions of the law of the State concerned have not been observed.

2. For the purposes of this Convention, the permanent establishment of an enterprise of a Contracting State situated in another Contracting State shall be deemed to be an enterprise of the State in which it is situated.

3. Paragraph 1 shall also apply where any of the enterprises concerned have made losses rather than profits.

Article 2

1. This Convention shall apply to taxes on income.

2. The existing taxes to which this Convention shall apply are, in particular the following:

(*a*) in Belgium:

— *impôt des personnes physiques/personenbelasting,*
— *impôt des sociétés/vennootschapsbelasting,*
— *impôt des personnes morales/rechtspersonenbelasting,*
— *impôt des non-résidents/belasting der niet-verblijfhouders,*
— *taxe communale et la taxe d'agglomération additionnelles à l'impôt des personnes physiques/aanvullende gemeentebelasting en agglomeratiebelasting op de personenbelasting;*

(*b*) in Denmark:

— *selskabsskat,*
— *indkomstskat til staten,*
— *kommunale indkomstskat,*
— *amtskommunal indkomstskat,*
— *særlig indkomstskat,*
— *kirkeskat,*
— *udbytteskat,*
— *renteskat,*
— *royaltyskat,*
— *frigøtorelsesafgift;*

(*c*) in the Federal Republic of Germany:

— *Einkommensteuer,*
— *Körperschaftsteuer,*
— *Gewerbesteuer, in so far as this tax is based on trading profits;*

(*d*) in Greece:

— *φοροώ εισοδηματοω φυσικων προσωπων,*

— φοροώ εισοδηματοώ νομικων προσωπων
— *εισφορα υπερ των επιχειρησεων υδρενσηω και αποχετευσηώ*

(*e*) in Spain:
— *impuesto sobre la renta de las personas fisicas,*
— *impuesto sobre sociedades;*

(*f*) in France:
— *impôt sur le revenu,*
— *impôt sur les sociétés;*

(*g*) in Ireland:
— *Income Tax,*
— *Corporation Tax;*

(*h*) in Italy:
— *imposta sul reddito delle persone fisiche,*
— *imposta sul reddito delle persone giuridiche,*
— *imposta locale sui redditi;*

(*i*) in Luxembourg:
— *impôt sur le revenu des personnes physiques,*
— *impôt sur le revenu des collectivités,*
— *impôt commercial, in so far as this tax is based on trading profits;*

(*j*) in the Netherlands:
— *inkomstenbelasting,*
— *vennootschapsbelasting;*

(*k*) in Portugal:
— *imposto sobre o rendimento das pessoas singulares,*
— *imposto sobre o rendimento das pessoas colectivas,*
— *derrama para os municípios sobre o imposto sobre o rendimento das pessoas colectivas;*

(*l*) in the United Kingdom:
— Income Tax,
— Corporation Tax.

3. The Convention shall also apply to any identical or similar taxes which are imposed after the date of signature thereof in addition to, or in place of existing taxes. The competent authorities of the Contracting States shall inform each other of any changes made in the respective domestic laws.

CHAPTER II
GENERAL PROVISIONS

SECTION I
DEFINITIONS

Article 3

1. For the purposes of this Convention: ''competent authority'' shall mean:

— *in Belgium:*

De Minister van Financiën or an authorised representative,
Le Ministre des Finances or an authorised representative,

— *in Denmark:*

Skatteministeren or an authorised representative,

— *in the Federal Republic of Germany:*

Der Bundesminister der Finanzen or an authorised representative,

— *in Greece:*

ο γπονργοώ των οικονομικων or an authorised representative,

— *in Spain:*

El Ministro de Economía y Hacienda or an authorised representative,

— *in France:*

Le Ministre chargé du budget or an authorised representative,

— *in Ireland:*

The Revenue Commissioners or an authorised representative,

— *in Italy:*

Il Ministro delle Finanze or an authorised representative,

— *in Luxembourg:*

Le Ministre des Finances or an authorised representative,

— *in the Netherlands:*

De Minister van Financiën or an authorised representative,

— *in Portugal:*

O Ministro das Finanças or an authorised representative,

— *in the United Kingdom:*

The Commissioners of Inland Revenue or an authorised representative.

2. Any term not defined in this Convention shall, unless the context otherwise requires, have the meaning which it has under the double taxation convention between the States concerned.

SECTION II

PRINCIPLES APPLYING TO THE ADJUSTMENT OF PROFITS OF ASSOCIATED ENTERPRISES AND TO THE ATTRIBUTION OF PROFITS TO PERMANENT ESTABLISHMENTS

Article 4

The following principles shall be observed in the application of this Convention:

1. Where:

(*a*) an enterprise of a Contracting State participates directly or indirectly in the management, control or capital of an enterprise of another Contracting State, or

(*b*) the same persons participate directly or indirectly in the management, control or capital of an enterprise of one Contracting State and an enterprise of another Contracting State,

and in either case conditions are made or imposed between the two enterprises in their commercial or financial relations which differ from those which would be made between independent enterprises, then any profits which would, but for those conditions, have accrued to one of the enterprises, but, by reason of those conditions, have not so accrued, may be included in the profits of that enterprise and taxed accordingly.

2. Where an enterprise of a Contracting State carries on business in another Contracting State through a permanent establishment situated therein, there shall be attributed to that permanent establishment the profits which it might be expected to make if it were a distinct and separate enterprise engaged in the same or similar activities under the same or similar conditions and dealing wholly independently with the enterprise of which it is a permanent establishment.

Article 5

Where a Contracting State intends to adjust the profits of an enterprise in accordance with the principles set out in Article 4, it shall inform the enterprise of the intended action in due time and give it the opportunity to inform the other enterprise so as to give that other enterprise the opportunity to inform in turn the other Contracting State.

However, the Contracting State providing such information shall not be prevented from making the proposed adjustment.

If after such information has been given the two enterprises and the other Contracting State agree to the adjustment, Articles 6 and 7 shall not apply.

SECTION III

MUTUAL AGREEMENT AND ARBITRATION PROCEDURE

Article 6

1. Where an enterprise considers that, in any case to which this Convention applies, the principles set out in Article 4 have not been observed, it may, irrespective of the remedies provided by the domestic law of the Contracting States concerned, present its case to the competent authority of the Contracting State of which it is an enterprise or in which its permanent establishment is situated. The case must be presented within three years of the first notification of the action which results or is likely to result in double taxation within the meaning of Article 1.

The enterprise shall at the same time notify the competent authority if other Contracting States may be concerned in the case. The competent authority shall then without delay notify the competent authorities of those other Contracting States.

2. If the complaint appears to it to be well-founded and if it is not itself able to arrive at a satisfactory solution, the competent authority shall endeavour to resolve the case by mutual agreement with the competent authority of any other Contracting State concerned, with a view to the elimination of double taxation on the basis of the principles set out in Article 4. Any mutual agreement reached shall be implemented irrespective of any time limits prescribed by the domestic laws of the Contracting States concerned.

Article 7

1. If the competent authorities concerned fail to reach an agreement that eliminates the double taxation referred to in Article 6 within two years of the date on which the case was first submitted to one of the competent authorities in accordance with Article 6(1), they shall set up an advisory commission charged with delivering its opinion on the elimination of the double taxation in question.

Enterprises may have recourse to the remedies available to them under the domestic law of the Contracting States concerned; however, where the case has so been submitted to a court or tribunal, the term of two years referred to in the first subparagraph shall be computed from the date on which the judgment of the final court of appeal was given.

2. The submission of the case to the advisory commission shall not prevent a Contracting State from initiating or continuing judicial proceedings or proceedings for administrative penalties in relation to the same matters.

3. Where the domestic law of a Contracting State does not permit the competent authorities of that State to derogate from the decisions of their judicial bodies, paragraph 1 shall not apply unless the associated enterprise of that State has allowed the time provided for appeal to expire, or has withdrawn any such appeal before a decision has been delivered. This provision shall not affect the appeal if and in so far as it relates to matters other than those referred to in Article 6.

4. The competent authorities may by mutual agreement and with the agreement of the associated enterprises concerned waive the time limits referred to in paragraph 1.

5. In so far as the provisions of paragraphs 1 to 4 are not applied, the rights of each of the associated enterprises, as laid down in Article 6, shall be unaffected.

Article 8

1. The competent authority of a Contracting State shall not be obliged to initiate the mutual agreement procedure or to set up the advisory commission referred to in Article 7 where legal or administrative proceedings have resulted in a final ruling that by actions giving rise to an adjustment of transfers of profits under Article 4 one of the enterprises concerned is liable to a serious penalty.

2. Where judicial or administrative proceedings, initiated with a view to a ruling that by actions giving rise to an adjustment of profits under Article 4 one of the enterprises concerned was liable to a serious penalty, are being conducted simultaneously with any of the proceedings referred to in Articles 6 and 7, the competent authorities may stay the latter proceedings until the judicial or administrative proceedings have been concluded.

Article 9

1. The advisory commission referred to in Article 7(1) shall consist of, in addition to its Chairman:

— two representatives of each competent authority concerned; this number may be reduced to one by agreement between the competent authorities,

— an even number of independent persons of standing to be appointed by mutual agreement from the list of persons referred to in paragraph 4 or, in the absence of agreement, by the drawing of lots by the competent authorities concerned.

2. When the independent persons of standing are appointed an alternate shall be appointed for each of them according to the rules for the appointment of the independent persons in case the independent persons are prevented from carrying out their duties.

3. Where lots are drawn, each of the competent authorities may object to the appointment of any particular independent person of standing in any circumstance agreed in advance between the competent authorities concerned or in one of the following situations:

— where that person belongs to or is working on behalf of one of the tax administrations concerned,

— where that person has, or has had, a large holding in or is or has been an employee of or adviser to one or each of the associated enterprises,

— where that person does not offer a sufficient guarantee of objectivity for the settlement of the case or cases to be decided.

4. The list of independent persons of standing shall consist of all the independent persons nominated by the Contracting States. For this purpose each Contracting State shall nominate five persons and shall inform the Secretary-General of the Council of the European Communities thereof.

Such persons must be nationals of a Contracting State and resident within the territory to which this Convention applies. They must be competent and independent.

The Contracting States may make alterations to the list referred to in the first subparagraph; they shall inform the Secretary-General of the Council of the European Communities thereof without delay.

5. The representatives and independent persons of standing appointed in accordance with paragraph 1 shall elect a Chairman from among those persons of standing on the list referred to in paragraph 4, without prejudice to the right of each competent authority concerned to object to the appointment of the person of standing thus chosen in one of the situations referred to in paragraph 3.

The Chairman must possess the qualifications required for appointment to the highest judicial offices in his country or be a jurisconsult of recognised competence.

6. The members of the advisory commission shall keep secret all matters which they learn as a result of the proceedings. The Contracting States shall adopt appropriate provisions to penalise any breach of secrecy obligations. They shall, without delay inform the Commission of the European Communities of the measures taken. The Commission of the European Communities shall inform the other Contracting States.

7. The Contracting States shall take all necessary steps to ensure that the advisory commission meets without delay once cases are referred to it.

Article 10

1. For the purposes of the procedure referred to in Article 7, the associated enterprises concerned may provide any information, evidence or documents which seem to them likely to be of use to the advisory commission in reaching a decision. The enterprises and the competent authorities of the Contracting States concerned shall give effect to any request made by the advisory commission to provide information, evidence or documents. However, the competent authorities of any such Contracting State shall not be under any obligation:

(*a*) to carry out administrative measures at variance with its domestic law or its normal administrative practice;
(*b*) to supply information which is not obtainable under its domestic law or in its normal administrative practice; or
(*c*) to supply information which would disclose any trade, business, industrial or professional secret or trade process, or information the disclosure of which would be contrary to public policy (*ordre public*).

2. Each of the associated enterprises may, at its request, appear or be represented before the advisory commission. If the advisory commission so requests, each of the associated enterprises shall appear or be represented before it.

Article 11

1. The advisory commission referred to in Article 7 shall deliver its opinion not more than six months from the date on which the matter was referred to it.

The advisory commission must base its opinion on Article 4.

2. The advisory commission shall adopt its opinion by a simple majority of its members. The competent authorities concerned may agree on additional rules of procedure.

3. The costs of the advisory commission procedure, other than those incurred by the associated enterprises, shall be shared equally by the Contracting States concerned.

Article 12

1. The competent authorities party to the procedure referred to in Article 7 shall, acting by common consent on the basis of Article 4, take a decision which will eliminate the double taxation within six months of the date on which the advisory commission delivered its opinion.

The competent authorities may take a decision which deviates from the advisory commission's opinion. If they fail to reach agreement, they shall be obliged to act in accordance with that opinion.

2. The competent authorities may agree to publish the decision referred to in paragraph 1, subject to the consent of the enterprises concerned.

Article 13

The fact that the decisions taken by the Contracting States, concerning the taxation of profits resulting from a transaction between associated enterprises, have become final shall not prevent recourse to the procedures set out in Articles 6 and 7.

Article 14

For the purposes of this Convention, the double taxation of profits shall be regarded as eliminated if either:

(*a*) the profits are included in the computation of taxable profits in one State only; or
(*b*) the tax chargeable on those profits in one State is reduced by an amount equal to the tax chargeable on them in the other.

CHAPTER III

FINAL PROVISIONS

Article 15

Nothing in this Convention shall affect the fulfilment of wider obligations with respect to the elimination of double taxation in the case of an adjustment of profits of associated enterprises resulting either from other conventions to which the Contracting States are or will become parties or from the domestic law of the Contracting States.

Article 16

1. The territorial scope of this Convention shall be that defined in Article 227(1)[1] of the Treaty establishing the European Economic Community, without prejudice to paragraph 2 of this Article.

2. This Convention shall not apply to:

— the French territories referred to in Annex IV to the Treaty establishing the European Economic Community,

— the Faroe Islands and Greenland.

Note—[1] Article 227 renumbered article 299 by the Treaty of Amsterdam ratified on 1 May 1999 (OJ C340 10.11.97 p 1).

Article 17

This Convention will be ratified by the Contracting States. The instruments of ratification will be deposited at the office of the Secretary-General of the Council of the European Communities.

Article 18

This Convention shall enter into force on the first day of the third month following that in which the instrument of ratification is deposited by the last signatory State to take that step. The Convention shall apply to proceedings referred to in Article 6(1) which are initiated after its entry into force.

Article 19

The Secretary-General of the Council of the European Communities shall inform the Contracting States of:

(*a*) the deposit of each instrument of ratification;

(*b*) the date on which this Convention will enter into force;

(*c*) the list of independent persons of standing appointed by the Contracting States and any alterations thereto in accordance with Article 9(4).

[Article 20

This Convention is concluded for a period of five years. It shall be extended for further periods of five years at a time, unless a Contracting State informs the Secretary-General of the Council of the European Union of its objection thereto in writing at least six months before the expiry of any five-year period.] [1]

Amendment—[1] Article substituted by protocol taking effect from 1 January 2000 and entering into force on the first day of the third month following the deposit of the last instrument of ratification, acceptance or approval. See OJ C202, 16.7.99, p 1.

Note—The period between 1 January 2000 and the date of entry into force of the protocol should not be taken into account in determining whether a case has been presented within the time specified in art 6(1).

Article 21

Each Contracting State may, at any time, ask for a revision of this Convention. In that event, a conference to revise the Convention will be convened by the President of the Council of the European Communities.

Article 22

This Convention, drawn up in a single original in the Danish, Dutch, English, French, German, Greek, Irish, Italian, Portuguese and Spanish languages, all 10 texts being equally authentic, shall be deposited in the archives of the General Secretariat of the Council of the European Communities. The Secretary-General shall transmit a certified copy to the Government of each Signatory State.

European Economic Community: Final Act and Declarations of 23 July 1990

The Plenipotentiaries of the High Contracting Parties, meeting at Brussels, on the twenty-third day of July nineteen hundred and ninety, for the signature of the Convention on the elimination of double taxation in connection with the adjustment of profits of associated enterprises, have, on the occasion of signing the said Convention:

(*a*) adopted the following joint Declarations attached to the Final Act:

— Declaration on Article 4(1),

— Declaration on Article 9(6),

EC Material

— Declaration on Article 13;

(*b*) taken note of the following unilateral Declarations attached to this Final Act:

— Declaration of France and the United Kingdom on Article 7,
— Individual Declarations of the Contracting States on Article 8,
— Declaration of the Federal Republic of Germany on Article 16.

Joint Declarations

Declaration on Article 4(1)

The provisions of Article 4(1) shall cover both cases where a transaction is carried out directly between two legally distinct enterprises as well as cases where a transaction is carried out between one of the enterprises and the permanent establishment of the other enterprise situated in a third country.

Declaration on Article 9(6)

The Member States shall be entirely free as regards the nature and scope of the appropriate provisions they adopt for penalising any breach of secrecy obligations.

Declaration on Article 13

Where, in one or more of the Contracting States concerned, the decisions regarding the taxation giving rise to the procedures referred to in Articles 6 and 7 have been altered after the procedure referred to in Article 6 has been concluded or after the decision referred to in Article 12 has been taken and where double taxation within the meaning of Article 1 results, account being taken of the application of the outcome of that procedure or that decision, Articles 6 and 7 shall apply.

Unilateral Declarations

Declaration on Article 7

France and the United Kingdom declare that they will apply Article 7(3).

Individual declarations of the Contracting States on Article 8

Belgium

The term "serious penalty" means a criminal or administrative penalty in cases:

— either of a common law offence committed with the aim of tax evasion,
— or infringements of the provisions of the Code of income tax or of decisions taken in implementation thereof, committed with fraudulent intention or with the intention of causing injury.

Denmark

The concept of "serious penalty" means a penalty for the intentional infringement of provisions of the Criminal Law or of special legislation in cases which cannot be regulated by administrative means.

Cases of infringement of provisions of tax law may, as a general rule, be regulated by administrative means where it is considered that the infringement will not entail a punishment greater than a fine.

Germany

An infringement of the tax laws punishable by a "serious penalty" is constituted by any infringement of the tax laws penalised by detention, criminal or administrative fines.

Greece

Under Greek legislation governing taxation, an undertaking is liable to "severe penalties":

1. if it fails to submit declarations, or submits incorrect declarations, in respect of taxes, charges or contributions which must be withheld and paid to the State under existing provisions, or in respect of value added tax, turnover tax or the special tax on luxury goods, in so far as the total amount of the above taxes, charges and contributions which should have been declared and paid to the State as a result of trade or other activities carried out over a period of six months exceeds an amount of six hundred thousand (600,000) Greek drachmas or one million (1,000,000) Greek drachmas over a period of one calendar year;

2. if it fails to submit a declaration of income tax, in so far as the tax due in respect of the income not declared is more than three hundred thousand (300,000) Greek drachmas;

3. if it fails to supply the taxation details laid down in the Code on Taxation Data;

4. if it supplies details as referred to under the previous case 3, which are incorrect as regards quantity or unit price or value, in so far as the inaccuracy results in a discrepancy which exceeds ten per cent (10%) of the total amount or of the total value of the goods, the provision of services or the trade generally;

5. if it fails to keep accurately the books and records required by the Code on Taxation Data, in so far as that inaccuracy has been noted in the course of a regular check, the findings of which have been confirmed either by administrative resolution of the discrepancy or because the period allowed for an appeal has expired or as a result of a definitive decision by an administrative tribunal, provided that during the management period checked the discrepancy between gross income and the income

declared is more than twenty per cent (20%) and in any case not less than one million (1,000,000) Greek drachmas;

6. if it fails to observe the obligation to keep books and records as laid down in the relevant provisions of the Code on Taxation Data;

7. if it issues false or fictitious—or itself falsifies—invoices for the sale of goods or the supply of services or any other taxation details as referred to in case 3 above.

A taxation document is regarded as false if it has been perforated or stamped in any way without the proper authentication having been entered in the relevant books of the competent tax authority, in so far as failure to make such an entry has occurred in the knowledge that such authentication is required for the taxation document. A taxation document is also regarded as false if the content and other details of the original or the copy differ from those which are recorded on the counterfoil of that document.

A taxation document is regarded as fictitious if it has been issued for a transaction or part of a transaction, transfer or any other reason not recorded in the total or for a transaction carried out by persons different from those recorded in the taxation document;

8. if it is aware of the intention of the action taken and collaborates in any way in the production of false taxation documents or is aware that the documents are false or fictitious and collaborates in any way in their issue or accepts the false, fictitious or falsified taxation documents with the intention of concealing material relevant to taxation.

Spain

The term ''serious penalties'' includes administrative penalties for serious tax infringements, as well as criminal penalties for offences committed with respect to the taxation authorities.

France

The term ''serious penalties'' includes criminal penalties and tax penalties such as penalties for failure to make a tax return after receiving a summons, for lack of good faith, for fraudulent practices, for opposition to tax inspection, for secret payments or distribution, or for abuse of rights.

Ireland

''Serious penalties'' shall include penalties for:

(*a*) failing to make a return;
(*b*) fraudulently or negligently making an incorrect return;
(*c*) failing to keep proper records;
(*d*) failing to make documents and records available for inspection;
(*e*) obstructing persons exercising statutory powers;
(*f*) failing to notify chargeability to tax;
(*g*) making a false statement to obtain an allowance.

The legislative provisions governing these offences, as at 3 July 1990, are as follows:

— Part XXXV of the Income Tax Act 1967
— Section 6 of the Finance Act 1968
— Part XIV of the Corporation Tax Act 1976
— Section 94 of the Finance Act 1983.

Any subsequent provisions replacing, amending or updating the penalty code would also be comprehended.

Italy

The term ''serious penalties'' means penalties laid down for illicit acts, within the meaning of the domestic law, constituting a tax offence.

Luxembourg

Luxembourg considers to be a ''serious penalty'' what the other Contracting State considers to be so for the purposes of Article 8.

Netherlands

The term ''serious penalty'' means a penalty imposed by a judge for any action, committed intentionally, which is mentioned in Article 68 of the General Law on taxation.

Portugal

The terms ''serious penalties'' include criminal penalties as well as the further tax penalties applicable to infringements committed with intent to defraud or in which the fine applicable is of an amount exceeding 1,000,000 (one million) Portuguese escudos.

United Kingdom

The United Kingdom will interpret the term ''serious penalty'' as comprising criminal sanctions and administrative sanctions in respect of the fraudulent or negligent delivery of incorrect accounts, claims or returns for tax purposes.

Declaration by the Federal Republic of Germany on Article 16

The Government of the Federal Republic of Germany reserves the right to declare, when lodging its instrument of ratification, that the Convention also applies to Land of Berlin.

Commission Recommendation of 21 December 1993 on the taxation of certain items of income received by non-residents in a member state other than that in which they are resident

(94/79/EC)

Note—See OJ L039, 10.2.94, p 22.

The Commission of the European Communities,

Having regard to the Treaty establishing the European Community, and in particular the second indent of Article 155[1] thereof,

Whereas the internal market comprises an area without frontiers in which the free movement of goods, persons services and capital is guaranteed;

Whereas the free movement of persons may be impeded by personal income tax arrangements which have the effect of imposing a heavier tax burden on non-residents than on residents in comparable situations;

Whereas steps should be taken to ensure that free movement of persons is fully guaranteed in the interests of the proper functioning of the internal market; whereas it is necessary to bring to the notice of the Member States the provisions which, in the Commission's view, are likely to guarantee that non-residents enjoy the same tax treatment as residents;

Whereas this initiative does not affect the Commission's conduct of policy in the field of infringement procedures to ensure that the fundamental principles of the Treaty are respected;

Whereas no distinction should be made under this approach between the taxation of income from dependent personal services, income from professional activities of a self-employed nature, and income from agricultural and forestry activities and from industrial and commercial activities, the rules of equal treatment and non-discrimination compared to residents applying equally to persons receiving such items of income;

Whereas the principle of equality of treatment stemming from Articles 48 and 52[1] of the Treaty requires that persons receiving the items of income in question should not, where the preponderant part of their income is received in the country of activity, be deprived of the tax reliefs and deductions enjoyed by residents;

Whereas it might reasonably be assumed that a person receives the preponderant part of his income in the country of activity where such income constitutes at least 75% of his total taxable income;

Whereas the Member State in which a natural person is resident should continue to have the option of not granting the deductions or other tax reliefs granted to residents where that person benefits from identical or similar deductions or other reliefs in the Member State of activity;

Whereas the Member States continue to have the option of maintaining or introducing arrangements more favourable to taxpayers than those set out in this recommendation,

Note—[1] Articles 48, 52 and 155 renumbered articles 39, 43 and 211 respectively by the Treaty of Amsterdam ratified on 1 May 1999.

Hereby makes the following recommendation:

Scope

Article 1

1. Member States apply the provisions of this recommendation to natural persons who are residents of one Member State and who are subject to income tax in another Member State, without being resident there, on the following items of income:

— income from dependent personal services,

— pensions and other similar remuneration received in consideration of past employment, including social security pensions,

— income from professional occupations or other self-employed activities, including that of performing artists and sportsmen and sportswomen,

— income from agricultural and forestry activities,

— income from industrial and commercial activities.

2. For the purposes of this recommendation, the term "resident" is to be defined according to the provisions of the double taxation agreements concluded between Member States or, in the absence of any such double taxation agreement, according to national law.

Taxation of the income of non-residents

Article 2

1. Member States do not subject the items of income specified in Article 1(1), in the Member State of taxation, to any heavier taxation than if the taxpayer, his spouse and his children were resident in that Member State.

2. Application of the provisions of paragraph 1 shall be subject to the condition that the items of income specified in Article 1(1) which are taxable in the Member State in which the natural person is not resident constitute at least 75% of that person's total taxable income during the tax year.

The Member State of taxation may ask the natural person in question to provide any evidence necessary to prove that he derives at least 75 % of his income from that Member State.

3. Where a natural person benefiting from the tax treatment referred to in paragraph 1 has, in the Member State of taxation, income other than that referred to in Article 1(1), the provisions of that paragraph shall also apply to that other income.

4. By way of derogation from the provision of paragraph 1, the Member State which taxes the items of income referred to in Article 1(1) may decide not to grant deductions or other tax reliefs connected with income which is not taxable in that Member State.

Double grant of deductions or other tax reliefs

Article 3

The Member State in which a natural person is resident may decide not to grant deductions or other tax reliefs which it normally grants to residents if that person benefits from identical or similar deductions or other reliefs in the Member State which taxes the items of his income specified in Article 1.

More favourable provisions for taxpayers

Article 4

Member States may opt to maintain or introduce more favourable provisions for taxpayers than those set out in this recommendation.

Final provisions

Article 5

Member States are invited to communicate to the Commission before 31 December 1994 the texts of the main laws, regulations and administrative provisions which they adopt pursuant to this recommendation, and to notify the Commission of any subsequent changes in this field.

Article 6

This recommendation is addressed to the Member States.

Done at Brussels, 21 December 1993.

EXPLANATORY MEMORANDUM

I. General conditions

1. Freedom of movement for persons is one of the Community's essential objectives and is enshrined in Articles 3, 48, 49, 52 and 53 of the Treaty of Rome. It is also a fundamental element of the internal market, which the Treaty defines as "an area without internal frontiers in which the free movement of goods, persons, services and capital is ensured in accordance with the provisions of this Treaty".

Freedom of movement for workers and their families is a fundamental right. The Community attaches great importance to the promotion of workers' mobility, in particular in the border regions. The Commission has indeed underlined recently in its White Paper on growth, competitiveness and employment, the need for flexibility in the labour market. It has listed, as a first step in this direction, the need to improve the geographical mobility of workers by suppressing the obstacles that hamper it.

Indeed, freedom of movement for persons is still frustrated by the existence of a number of tax provisions which, when applied, often cause persons exercising freedom of movement for the purpose of carrying on an activity in a Member State other than the one in which they are resident to be taxed in the other Member State in a less favourable manner than the residents of that other Member State.

Hundreds of thousands of people are subject to frequent discriminations. This is testified by the great number of complaints that the Commission receives as well as by petitions addressed to the European Parliament.

The fundamental principle of non-discrimination, being an underlying principle of the Treaty, claims for a quick and clear solution.

The problem affects the following categories of person:

— frontier workers,
— other persons in paid employment,
— recipients of pensions and other similar remuneration in consideration of past employment,

EC Material

— persons exercising a professional activity or some other self-employed activity, including performing artists and sportsmen and sportswomen,
— persons exercising agricultural and forestry activities,
— persons exercising industrial and commercial activities.

2. In principle, such persons are taxed in the country in which they carry on their activity, and most Member States apply to them tax arrangements (the non-residents' regime) which differ from those applied to residents. Generally speaking, under these arrangements, only income from sources within the country in which the activity is exercised is taxed, with no provision being made for tax reliefs on grounds of family circumstances or for the various deductions for which residents are eligible, considering that such advantages should be granted by the country of residence.

These advantages can be grouped in different categories, taking into account the taxpayer's contributive capacity:

— as regards the worker itself, there are, for instance, the basic allowance (which provides a tax exemption for low income), but also specific deductions for medical expenses or for exceptional expenditures,
— if he is married, this statute may offer him a right, depending on the Member State concerned, to a joint assessment with his spouse, through a "splitting" system if relevant, or a family coefficient relief or other allowances,
— as regards children, there are often special deductions, grossed up in the case of handicapped children, deductions for school expenses, etc.

However, the persons in question are very often precluded from the benefit of such reliefs in their country of residence too since they have no or insufficient taxable income in that country.

An exception to this rule is the tax treatment of the income of certain frontier workers in that Member States have concluded bilateral agreements under which such income is taxed in the country in which those workers are resident (of the 26 possible bilateral arrangements, 14 provide for taxation in the country of residence and 12 for taxation in the country of activity). It is only where frontier workers are taxed exclusively in their country of residence that they are not discriminated against, being taxed in the same way as other residents.

By contrast, persons who exercise an activity in an employed or self-employed capacity, agricultural and forestry activities, or industrial and commercial activities in a Member State other than the one in which they are resident and who are taxed in their country of residence are, in most cases, subject to a higher level of taxation than persons exercising the same activities in the country in which they are resident.

3. With a view to correcting this situation, the Commission presented, in 1979, a proposal for a Directive concerning the harmonisation of income taxation provisions with respect to freedom of movement for workers within the Community. The Commission has also initiated infringement proceedings against some Member States with regard to tax provisions which discriminate against the residents.

4. Despite discussions stretching over a period of years, the Council has not been able to act on this proposal since some Member States are opposed to the principle of taxing frontier workers' income in their country of residence. Furthermore, some associations of frontier workers have argued that taxation in the country of residence would lead in many cases, to heavier taxation than under current circumstances (eg under arrangements between Belgium and Luxembourg or between Denmark and Germany).

Finally, many Member States have felt that the general problem of taxing non-resident workers may be more suitably resolved by bilateral agreements.

5. In view of this situation, the Commission last year withdrew its 1979 proposal, and it considers that the time has now come for fresh steps to be taken to encourage Member States to eliminate discriminatory provisions from their legislation on the taxation of non-residents and to amend their laws on the basis of common rules of conduct.

This is made all the more necessary by the fact that some Member States have, at their own initiative, already amended their tax rules in this area, and others are planning to do so.

The Commission therefore believes that, unless guidelines are established at Community level, there is a risk that very divergent new rules will be introduced in various Member States.

6. As regards case law, it should be noted that on 26 January 1993 the Court delivered a judgment on this matter (Case C-112/91, Werner v Finanzamt Aachen-Innenstadt).

The Court held that "Article 52[1] of the EEC Treaty does not prevent a Member State imposing a heavier burden on its own nationals who carry out their professional activity within its territory and who reside in another Member State". In its judgment the Court did not, however, make any statement on the possibility of a Member State treating nationals of other Member States in the same way. A new case has since been referred to the Court for a preliminary ruling (Case C-279/93, *Finanzamt Köln-Altstadt v Schumacker*), in which it must be decided whether application of the non-residents' tax regime to a national of another Member State is compatible with Community law.

Note—[1] Article 52 renumbered article 43 by the Treaty of Amsterdam ratified on 1 May 1999.

7. This recommendation forms an integral part of the action that the Commission intends to pursue actively, so as to ensure, in particular by infringement procedures, that the fundamental principles of the Treaty, which the European citizen should be able to benefit from, are fully respected.

8. For these reasons, the Commission has drawn up the attached recommendation defining the principles and rules should underlie Member States' legislation on the tax treatment of non-residents.

9. It seems pertinent to underline the essential elements of this recommendation.

— Its scope covers the income of all persons, whether salaried or self-employed, pensions and income from other economic activities. Compared to the 1979 proposal, it has thus been extended to cover the self-employed and agricultural, forestry, industrial and commercial activities, about which ever increasing numbers of petitions and complaints are received concerning the tax provisions applying to them.

— The allocation of the right to tax non-residents between the state of activity and the state of residence, as determined by the double-taxation agreements concluded between the Member States, is respected as regards the income of frontier workers. Consequently, they may be taxed either in the state where they work or the state in which they reside.

— Precise rules are laid down to ensure non-discriminatory taxation of non-residents by the state of activity where they are in a comparable position to its own residents. A comparable situation is deemed to exist where the income received in the state of activity is at least 75% of the non-resident's total taxable income.

— The option remains for the Member State of residence not to grant to a taxpayer the benefit of certain reliefs or deductions if these have already been accorded by the state of activity. The aim here is to ensure that the persons covered by the recommendation are not discriminated against, and not that they be placed in a more favourable position that other taxpayers.

The Commission considers that these provisions are clear, balanced and simple to apply, and that they will provide a fair solution to the large majority of problems posed by the taxation of non-residents.

10. Implementation of the mechanism established by the recommendation may, in the Commission's opinion, require a more intensive exchange of information between the tax administration of the taxpayer's country of residence and that of his country of activity. The Commission would stress in this context that the provisions applied under Directive 77/799/EEC[1] allow Member States to exchange any information necessary for that purpose.

If it should emerge that this exchange does not function adequately in practice, the Commission is ready to examine with the Member States the measures required to improve the situation.

11. Given the importance of fully achieving the free movement of persons, which forms a vital element of the single market, the Commission recommends that the Member States adopt the necessary tax measures as quickly as possible.

The Commission will assess the measures taken by the Member States in implementing this recommendation and will decide to take further action if necessary, taking account, *inter alia*, of how the Court's case law develops in this field.

II. Comments on certain Articles

Article 1

12. Paragraph 1 of this Article defines the scope of the recommendation as regards the categories of persons involved. The recommendation covers natural persons who are resident in one of the Member States and subject to income tax in another Member State without being resident there.

Paragraph 1 also lists the categories of income falling within the scope of the recommendation. The first two categories (income from dependent personal services and pensions) were already included in the 1979 proposal for a Directive. Income from professional occupations or other self-employed activities, from agricultural and forestry activities and from industrial and commercial activities has been added in order to ensure that individuals engaged in such occupations or activities are treated in the same way as wage and salary earners and those receiving pensions.

The definitions used for these income categories are based largely on those used in the Organisation for Economic Cooperation and Development Model Convention.

13. Paragraph 2 sets out the criteria for establishing an individual's residence status. For this purpose, reference has to be made first to the relevant provisions of the double taxation agreements concluded between Member States, since those provisions clearly establish the place of residence of a person who has tax links with two Member States.

In the Commission's view, reference to national legislation relating to residence for tax purposes would pose more problems, since such legislation may differ from one Member State to another. Recourse should be had to such legislation only where no agreement has been concluded between the two Member States concerned[2].

EC Material

Article 2

14. Paragraph 1 of this Article establishes the principle that the persons and income covered by Article 1 may not be subjected in the Member State imposing tax to any more burdensome taxation than if the taxpayer were resident in that Member State.

In accordance with that principle, the individuals in question should benefit, in the country of activity, from the same special deductions for determining taxable income and from the other general deductions or tax reliefs granted to residents.

If the Member State of activity applies a special tax system to families (eg splitting allowances for dependants), this advantage should also be applied to the incomes referred to in Article 1[1] obtained by the non-resident in that State. Special systems of this nature are generally linked to aggregate taxation of the individuals concerned (spouse and, in some cases, children), and if this is the case the Member State of activity has the option of taking account of the income of such individuals in determining, the rate of taxation applicable to the incomes which it is entitled to tax.

15. Paragraph 2 of this Article establishes that this principle applies only where the income derived by the individuals in question from the country of activity constitutes at least 75% of their total taxable income.

The Commission considers that treatment identical to that of residents is justified only where non-residents are in a situation comparable to that of residents. Such a situation is deemed to exist where a non-resident derives the preponderant part of his income (ie at least 75% of his total taxable income) in the country of activity. In that case, the amount of income taxable in the country of residence is unlikely to be sufficient for the deductions and other reliefs provided for in that country's legislation to apply.

Where, by contrast, the non-resident derives a large share of his income in his country of residence, it would not seem justified to require the Member State of activity to grant him the deductions applicable thereto. The 75% threshold also offers the advantage that the Member State of activity might abstain from taking into account the income obtained outside the state (in applying progressivity), and the task of the tax administration would thus be made considerably easier.

The Commission considers that this approach would solve virtually all the problems which non-residents encounter when their income is taxed in the country of activity.

The general point should be made that an entirely fair and neutral treatment of all situations in this field is impossible under current circumstances. It would be possible only if income tax legislation were completely harmonised in the Community.

16. In the same second subparagraph of paragraph 2, it is also stipulated that a Member State may ask a non-resident to prove that he derives at least 75% of his income on its territory. In the Commission's opinion, such proof can be provided by means of documents, such as a copy of a tax return, a written statement from an employer, a copy of a balance sheet, etc.

17. Under the terms of Article 1, the tax treatment provided for in the recommendation applies only to income derived from employment or self-employment, and to pensions and the other economic activities mentioned.

It is possible, however, that a person receiving such income in a Member State other than that of his residence may also have other sources of income in that Member State, for example property income. Article 2(3) is designed to ensure that the same tax treatment is applied to those other sources of income.

18. Article 2(4) permits the Member States not to grant deductions or other tax reliefs connected with income which is not taxable in the Member State of activity. It would not seem to be justified to grant certain deductions closely connected with income which is not taxable in that Member State. One example is provided by deductions for the purchase of certain securities, given that income from capital is generally taxable in the country of residence.

Article 3

19. The aim of this recommendation is to ensure that individuals receiving certain types of income in a Member State in which they are not resident are taxed on a fair and non-discriminatory basis.

It is also necessary to ensure, however, that non-residents do not benefit from more favourable tax treatment than other taxpayers. This could happen if they were to benefit, in the Member State of residence, from the same deductions of other tax reliefs which they had already been granted in the Member State of activity.

This Article accordingly makes it possible for the Member State of residence to refuse to grant deductions or other tax reliefs in such cases.

However, the Commission takes the view that application of this option should be limited in practice. It has thus been observed that if the Member State of residence applies the ordinary imputation method to take account income obtained in other States—this method already being applied by most Member States—deduction should not normally occur twice.

Article 4

20. This recommendation lays down minimum conditions for ensuring that non-residents are not taxed in a discriminatory manner in the country of activity.

It does not prevent Member States from retaining or introducing arrangements which are more favourable to taxpayers.

Note—[1] OJ L 336, 27. 12. 77, p. 15.
[2] The following combinations of members states are not covered by bilateral agreements (situation at 1 January 1993): Greece–Portugal, Greece–Spain, Greece–Ireland, Greece–Luxembourg, Portugal–Ireland, Spain–Ireland, Portugal–Luxembourg, Portugal–Netherlands.

Commission Recommendation of 25 May 1994 concerning the taxation of small and medium-sized enterprises (text with EEA relevance)

(94/390/EC)

Note—See OJ L177, 9.7.94, p 1.

The Commission of the European Communities,

Having regard to the Treaty establishing the European Community, and in particular the second indent of Article 155[1] thereof,

Whereas on 28 July 1989 the Council adopted Decision 89/490/EEC[2] on the improvement of the business environment and the promotion of the development of enterprises, and in particular small and medium-sized enterprises, in the Community, as revised by Council Decision 91/319/EEC[3];

Whereas in its resolution of 17 June 1992 on Community action to support enterprises, in particular small medium-sized enterprises, including craft-industry enterprises[4], the Council confirmed its undertaking to support the consolidation of the action taken to help enterprises;

Whereas by its Decision 93/379/EEC[5], the Council adopted, from 1 July 1993, a programme to intensify the priority measures and to ensure the continuity of an enterprise policy; whereas the programme gives priority to improving the legal, fiscal and administrative environment of enterprises;

Whereas sole proprietorships and partnerships make up a large proportion of small and medium-sized enterprises, whose role in the creation of jobs has been emphasised on a number of occasions in different Commission communications, and, more particularly, in the White Paper on growth, competitiveness and employment; whereas it is necessary to promote the investment capacity of these enterprises;

Whereas the method of taxing sole proprietorships and partnerships, which are generally subject to personal income tax, a tax which is progressive in nature in particular by comparison with corporation tax, hampers the development of the self-financing capacity of such enterprises and, in an economic environment where access to external financing is becoming more difficult, consequently restricts their investment capacity;

Whereas the current structure of rates of personal income tax and rates of corporation tax distorts competition between enterprises, depending on their legal form, to the detriment of sole proprietorships and partnerships; whereas it is desirable to work for greater tax neutrality, at least as regards the implications which systems of taxation have for profits reinvested by enterprises and, hence for their self-financing capacity;

Whereas several Member States have already taken measures to limit the existing distortion between taxation systems, according to whether an enterprise's profits are charged to personal income tax or corporation tax, either by granting sole proprietorships and partnerships the right to opt for payment of corporation tax on reinvested profits, or by limiting the progressiveness of personal income tax by comparison with the rates of corporation tax to incorporated companies;

Whereas the incorporation of sole proprietorships or partnerships is likely to resolve, despite its impact on areas unrelated to taxation which affect the entrepreneur and the enterprise, the problem of the level of taxation of the non-distributed profits of these enterprises; whereas such an operation must be carried out without giving rise to a significant revenue cost,

Hereby recommends:

Article 1

Member States are invited to adopt those tax measures necessary to correct the deterrent effects of the progressive income tax payable by sole proprietorships and partnerships in respect of reinvested profits. In particular, they should consider the possibility of:

(*a*) giving these enterprises and partnerships in this respect the right to opt to pay corporation tax; and/or

(*b*) restrict the tax charge on reinvested profits to a rate comparable to that of corporation tax.

EC Material

Article 2

Member States are invited to adopt or extend those measures necessary to eliminate the tax obstacle to changes in the legal form of enterprises, in particular the incorporation of sole proprietorships or partnerships.

Article 3

Member States are invited to communicate, by 31 July 1995, the texts of the main laws, regulations and administrative provisions which they adopt in response to this recommendation and inform the Commission of all subsequent changes made in this field.

Article 4

This recommendation is addressed to the Member States.

Done at Brussels, 25 May 1994.

Note—[1] Article 155 renumbered article 211 by the Treaty of Amsterdam ratified on 1 May 1999 (OJ C340 10.11.97 p 1).
[2] OJ No L 239, 16. 8. 1989, p. 33.
[3] OJ No L 175, 4. 7. 1991, p. 32.
[4] OJ No C 178, 15. 7. 1992, p. 8.
[5] OJ No L 161, 2. 7. 1993, p. 68.

EXPLANATORY MEMORANDUM

The importance of SMEs in creating jobs and stimulating growth has been emphasised on several occasions in declarations and resolutions by the European Council, the Council and Parliament. The European Council in Edinburgh on 11 and 12 December 1992 made a special call for measures to promote private investment, especially investment by SMEs.

The Commission White Paper on growth, competitiveness and employment stressed the responsibility of governments and the Community in creating an environment which is as conducive as possible to the competitiveness of enterprises, and in particular SMEs, given that their dynamism, productivity, flexibility and innovation are vital to the European economy.

The need to create a more favourable environment for enterprises is central to the strategic programme for the internal market[1] drawn up by the Commission. Support for the development of SMEs is essential if the internal market is to be fully effective. And improving the tax environment for SMEs is a key aspect of the initiatives proposed for that purpose.

The Commission has looked into the tax treatment of such enterprises, in line with the thinking put forward in the White Paper, with a view to making it easier for SMEs to meet the new requirements of competitiveness.

A detailed examination of how enterprises are taxed reveals a disparity in tax treatment depending on the legal form under which they operate (see findings in Annex). Because of their legal form, sole proprietorships and partnerships very often have to pay income tax on the whole of their income. The progressiveness of the tax scale means that the marginal rates of tax, while sometimes lower, are generally higher than the rates of corporation tax. This tends to create distortions of competition between enterprises on the basis of their legal form, particularly since the self-financing capacity of sole proprietorships and partnerships is likely to be squeezed compared with that of incorporated enterprises of the same size or even larger, owing to their heavier tax burden. In certain cases this may affect the very development of the enterprise. Given the high proportion of sole proprietorships and partnerships in the European Union (it is often estimated that one out of two firms is not an incorporated enterprise), this tax feature has a quite significant impact.

Some Member States have themselves introduced tax arrangements based on the concept of tax neutrality between incorporated and unincorporated enterprises. While tax neutrality is never complete, better equivalence is achieved and there is minimal interference between these arrangements and the general tax system. This special machinery is designed to ensure more equal tax treatment of firms' reinvested profits, irrespective of their legal form (Denmark and Greece), or place a ceiling on the progressive tax on trading income (Germany).

However, in most Member States, the solution most frequently advocated in such circumstances (even if its implications are complex and affect various fields outside that of taxation, especially the social field) is to turn the sole proprietorship or the partnership into an incorporated enterprise. Tax-relief measures are often available in order to facilitate such operations.

The Commission wishes to promote such arrangements throughout the Union by inviting the Member States which do not yet have provisions of this kind to adopt them or to take measures with equivalent effect.

The ideas outlined in this paper are based on the available data and the answers supplied by Member States to a questionnaire on how enterprises are taxed and what tax provisions are applied when a sole proprietorship or partnership converts into an incorporated company.

Conclusions

Given that the vast majority of small and medium-sized enterprises are unincorporated and considering their prime role in keeping economic activity dynamic in the Community and in creating jobs, the Commission is encouraging the Member States to adopt any measures designed to correct the deterrent effects of current taxation structures on the self-financing of sole proprietorships and partnerships. Greater fairness in the tax treatment of the profits retained or reinvested by those enterprises should, by giving them a chance to improve their self-financing capacity and strengthen their cash position, enable them to deal better with the difficulties typically encountered by SMEs, particularly at the bottom of the economic cycle, and to make the best possible use, thanks to increased capacity for investment, of the opportunities available when the economy recovers. These initiatives would also have the advantage of giving entrepreneurs genuine freedom of choice between the various legal forms under which to carry on their activity reducing the significance of the taxation factor in their choice.

The special systems operated in Denmark and Greece, and the German mechanism, provide an interesting illustration of the possible options. Other measures having equivalent effect are also conceivable (eg a special investment reserve). It is for the Member States to choose those procedures which best suit their domestic taxation systems.

Even if, because of the impact in fields unrelated to taxation, the conversion of sole proprietorships or partnerships into incorporated companies does not necessarily constitute the ideal response to the situation described, it is still a response, and it is desirable for an entrepreneur to be able to choose, throughout the life of his business, the legal form which is best suited to its evolution.

Moreover, this is the preferred approach in a number of Member States. For, while the majority of them consider that, legally speaking, these operations entail the cessation of a business activity, the repercussions which this normally has in tax terms are often attenuated.

An examination of the situation in the Community thus reveals that the tax provisions applied when sole proprietorships and partnerships are incorporated make it possible overall to guarantee a minimum level of tax neutrality when the legal status is changed. Isolated changes in tax legislation are nevertheless desirable, particularly in order to generalise the options for imputation of business losses to the owner or partner, when they cannot be carried over because of the change in legal status. And there is a need for a reduction in transfer taxes levied on contributions of assets which might be modelled on the deferment of taxation of capital gains often granted for the same assets. The Commission invites the Member States to improve the existing mechanisms or to introduce such mechanisms in order to ensure that, from the taxation point of view, the incorporation of sole proprietorships and partnerships can be undertaken as flexibly as possible.

These two approaches should not be regarded as mutually exclusive and the Member States are, in particular, invited to draw on the original ideas developed in certain Community countries, with a view to devising, in partnership with the interested parties, those solutions which are best suited to dealing with the problem of self-financing by small and medium-sized enterprises.

Note—[1] COM(93) 632 final of 22 December 1993—Communication from the Commission to the Council: "Making the most of the internal market": Strategic programme.

ANNEX

I. CURRENT SITUATION AS REGARDS THE TAXATION OF SMES' PROFITS

In view of the importance of SMEs for the European economy and their special nature as an economic and social organisation, their current tax treatment in the Community should be examined to see how their profits are taxed and in particular whether or not there are derogation measures in this field under ordinary law that are designed specifically for SMEs.

1. Taxation of enterprises

How an enterprise is taxed generally depends on its legal form rather than on its size.

In the case of sole proprietorships, the enterprise's and the proprietor's income are taxed together, being charged to personal income tax.

Partnerships are usually taxed applying the principle of tax transparency: the profits are taxable in the hands of the partners in proportion to their rights, even if they did not actually draw on those profits. The conditions governing the taxation of partnerships are in effect very similar to those applying to sole proprietorships.

However, in some Member States these firms are either subject de facto to corporation tax if they are engaged in industrial or commercial activities (Belgium, Spain), or they may opt (France) for the tax regime applicable to incorporated enterprises.

In the case of incorporated enterprises, corporation tax is charged on the profits earned by the enterprise itself. In principle, the shareholders and members of those enterprises are themselves taxable only in respect of the profits distributed to them.

2. Establishing the tax base

The industrial or commercial profits of sole proprietorships or partnerships subject to income tax are, in principle, determined in the same way as the profits of incorporated enterprises liable for corporation tax.

The rules governing exceptions under ordinary law essentially consist in flat-rate calculation of the taxable amount or simplification of the taxation procedures.

In practice, these arrangements generally concern only sole proprietorships in the craft sector or of very small size, given the thresholds for such measures (in France, for example, the flat-rate arrangements are available only to enterprises with a turnover of less than FF 500 000, or FF 150 000 in the case of service enterprises) and the fact that they are rarely adjusted. While they offer the heads of small enterprises the advantage of a genuine simplification of their taxation and accounting obligations, these arrangements have the drawback of not encouraging them to introduce the management tools they might need in order to expand their business. In practice, the enterprises covered are often those operating at a local level.

Enterprises subject to corporation tax are always excluded from the flat-rate arrangements. However, in a number of Member States such companies may, in particular under the fourth accounting Directive, benefit from simplified accounting procedures if they rank as small enterprises. They may for example submit an abridged version of their balance-sheet and profit-and-loss account and supply tax information in a more condensed form, thus reducing the number of forms to be completed at the end of the financial year. However, they still have to comply with the usual accounting principles and valuation methods of the tax regime for industrial and commercial profits.

In practice, in the majority of cases, with the exception of the tax treatment applied to proprietor's remuneration in accordance with the transparency or otherwise of the legal form chosen for the enterprise, there are not fundamental differences in the procedures for determining the basis of assessment for enterprises, large or small, incorporated or unincorporated. There are, however, major differences in the rates applied: the progressive scale of personal income tax, the standard rate of corporation tax, reduced rates, etc.

3. Tax rates

A look at the tax rates (...) shows that, in most Member States, the marginal rates of personal income tax are higher than the standard rate of corporation tax, despite the general trend towards reducing rates for both enterprises and natural persons. Because of their legal form and the absence of any distinction between distributed and reinvested income, sole proprietorships and partnerships are de facto taxed on the whole of their income at marginal income-tax rates which may be higher than the corporation-tax rates.

This results in a distortion of competition between enterprises on account of their legal form, to the detriment of sole proprietorships and partnerships. That distortion is all the greater the wider the difference between the rates of income tax and corporation tax.

The system of taxation applying to sole proprietorships and partnerships acts as a brake on their investment-based development. Their self-financing capacity is reduced owing to the higher rates of tax applied to the top slices of income, which are those which provide the greatest scope for saving and investing.

Yet increasing the self-financing capacity of SMEs is the most viable alternative to their recourse to external sources of finance, access to which can be particularly difficult in the present economic situation, since financial intermediaries sometimes tend—following the euphoria of the 1980s—to be excessively cautious and reluctant to grant additional funding. It is therefore important that enterprises should be able to generate sufficient own funds in order to weather any transitory difficulties resulting from external conjunctural or internal factors. When an enterprise is in a phase of major expansion, the shift in balance which may occur in such circumstances makes it more vulnerable, particularly financially.

Given that sole proprietorships represent, on average, almost half of all the enterprises operating in the Member States of the Community, and that they employ 10–20% of the labour force, the potential impact of this special tax feature is quite appreciable.

Since the various legal forms are unevenly represented in the Community, this tax aspect may influence the optimum level of investment within the single market.

The distribution pattern of incorporated enterprises, partnerships and sole proprietorships varies considerably between the Member States. The number of incorporated enterprises is very low in such countries as Germany and Italy, and particularly high in France, Belgium and the United Kingdom (see table in Note 3, on the size of the enterprise sector in the Member States). It is usually small enterprises which adopt unincorporated legal forms, although the situation varies according to the Member State. In Germany, for example, some large enterprises are run in the form of partnerships; in Belgium, small enterprises do not hesitate to incorporate, while only a limited number of large enterprises use incorporation in Germany.

II. AD HOC SOLUTIONS IN SOME OF THE MEMBER STATES

In *Denmark*, the sole proprietor may, each year, elect to be taxed at the rate of corporation tax on income retained within the firm. Under this special scheme, which has been in force since 1987 (special business arrangement or ''business rules''), a distinction is made, with regard to the nature of the income withdrawn by the entrepreneur, between income from capital and personal income. Income from capital, which is determined by applying the average rate of return on bonds for the year to the enterprise's net assets, qualifies for the preferential tax treatment of dividends (traditionally applied to income from shares). Personal income, ie the income withdrawn by the entrepreneur in addition to the return on capital, is taxed applying the sliding scale of income tax. This method, which is used by about 130,000 firms, makes it possible to achieve equality of tax treatment between sole proprietorships, partnerships and incorporated enterprises as regards income retained within the enterprise, since the latter is taxed at 34%—the same rate as corporation tax. The scheme is described in more detail in Note 4.

Norway and Sweden, too, have schemes which are relatively similar in conception to the Danish one. The downside of this tax arrangement is that it imposes more administrative constraints (principally of an accounting nature) on those enterprises which opt for it.

In *Greece*, the tax reform of June 1992 introduced a related mechanism for enterprises formed as partnerships, limited partnerships or private limited companies; previously, these had been subject to the progressive scale of income tax, ranging from 5% to 40%. Following the reform, their profits will be taxed at the single rate of 35% (as in the case of public limited companies) less the remuneration of partners or managers (natural persons holding at least one third of the partnership's/company's shares). Such remuneration, whether in effect withdrawn or not, is estimated at a flat rate of 50% of the partnership's/company's net income, with the partner or manager liable for personal income tax on it. The advantage of the reform is that it provides for neutral treatment of the profits ploughed back by enterprises in the above categories.

In *Germany*, a provision has been introduced with effect from 1 January 1994 whereby progressiveness of income tax on the profits of sole proprietorships and partnerships is limited, the maximum at marginal rate of tax for this type of income being capped at 47%. By contrast, the highest rate (53%) will continue to apply, where appropriate, to all the other taxable income of taxpayers. The difference between the rate of corporation tax (45% on undistributed profits[1]) and that of the tax on the income of non-incorporated enterprises (47%) will henceforth be only two percentage points; it would have been more than four times greater had it not been capped. While the measure is of a different order to those introduced by Greece and Denmark, in that it covers all the income, whether distributed or undistributed, of the enterprises concerned, it still shows a similar willingness to limit the differences of tax treatment between the ploughed-back profits of incorporated enterprises and those of sole partnerships and partnerships.

These few examples illustrate the solutions which can be applied, either without interfering with the general system of taxation (Denmark and Greece) or without jeopardising the principle of tax transparency traditionally applied to sole proprietorships and partnerships (Germany).

Note—[1] The rate is 30% for distributed profits.

Possible conclusions at Community level

The aim here is not to single out one particular solution as ideal for the Community, since each has its advantages and disadvantages.

Thus, the *Danish* system, which seeks to ensure tax neutrality, is sophisticated and appropriate but complex to administer. The opportunity which the Danish entrepreneur (sole proprietor or partnership) has, each year, to opt either for the special scheme or for normal personal income tax enables him to maximise, depending on the year's results, the enterprise's self-financing capacity by adjusting the level of the tax charge. The special scheme means, however, that the entrepreneur must keep detailed accounts. This is a relative constraint, since the accounting requirement has a pedagogical spin-off: it encourages the entrepreneur to set up the information system necessary for the sound management of the business. Another disadvantage of this maximum tax flexibility is that it carries a not inconsiderable budgetary cost. The introduction of schemes where the option is irreversible or has to be applied for a minimum period (five years or more) would of course make it possible to limit the budgetary cost of such mechanisms. But it would entail higher administrative costs for the tax authorities, strict supervision having to be exercised in order to prevent abuse of preferential schemes of this type.

The advantage of the *Greek* system is that it provides partnerships (sole proprietorships are not eligible for the scheme) with equivalent tax treatment of their undistributed profits to that available for incorporated enterprises, the rate of corporation tax (35%) applying in both cases Nevertheless, the scheme, which is applied automatically, has the relative drawback that it does not allow enterprises to choose: in effect, the smallest enterprises, which were previously taxed at low marginal rates of income tax, may find themselves penalised by the new tax arrangements.

The German mechanism of putting a ceiling on income tax on industrial and commercial income has the advantage that it is simple to implement. On the other hand, it has the drawback that it interferes with the tax system by creating an advantage for the self-employed, as against the salaried, entrepreneur—even though the latter's responsibilities, in his capacity as manager for example, might be the same—since the tax burden on the self-employed entrepreneur may not exceed 47%, while it may be as high as 53% on the salary earner.

These differences are principally the reflection of technical and political choices made in specific national contexts.

Despite their diversity, however, all the solutions have the common benefit of reducing, in the States which have implemented them, the tax charge on the undistributed profits of sole proprietorships and partnerships by bringing the rate applied closer to, or aligning it on, the nominal rates of corporation tax applied in the same circumstances to incorporated companies.

Other variants having an equivalent effect are conceivable: thus, sole proprietorships and partnerships could be afforded tax treatment which was more favourable to investment, involving a distinction between retained/reinvested income and the income withdrawn by the entrepreneur or partners. Income retained within the firm would, on the basis of an option exercised irrevocably or not, by the entrepreneur (or the partners unanimously), be taxed at the rate of corporation tax, and only the income withdrawn would be charged to income tax in the hands of the entrepreneur (or the partners) as industrial or commercial income.

While the Scandinavian examples—particularly the Danish one—show that it is possible to implement schemes of this nature, it should be remembered that certain Member States have reservations about them. Thus, the experience of Germany in the early 1950s and studies conducted by the Inland Revenue in the United Kingdom have led to doubts in these States about the practicality of an optional system of charging corporation tax on the reinvested profits of sole proprietorships and partnerships, especially because of the difficulty of monitoring income flows between the entrepreneur and the enterprise and the risk that the scheme might be diverted from its purpose.

One alternative put forward is to allow such enterprises to build up special investment reserves which will have the effect of increasing the enterprise's self-financing capacity while ensuring that the latter is used to undertake (tangible or intangible) investment. Here again, it is for the Member States to judge how much freedom they want to give enterprises in employing their self-financing capacity and deciding on the use to which it is to be put (eg to improve the cash position or to invest in capital goods).

The approach under the solutions described thus for concentrates on the search for neutral tax treatment of the reinvested profits of the enterprise irrespective of its legal form. The advantage of these mechanisms is that they foster, in tax terms, the enterprise's internal development potential without calling into question the entrepreneur's initial choice, based on tax[1] or other criteria, of a particular legal form. At present, only a minority of Member States have such arrangements.

Most Member States prefer a different approach, which consists in facilitating, in tax terms, a change in the legal form of the enterprise during its lifetime.

[1] As regards the tax factor, the entrepreneur will assess his overall tax position; depending on his current or anticipated aggregate income, he will prefer to form an incorporated or non-incorporated enterprise. In all cases, he will make his choice in the light of his personal circumstances without necessarily being aware of the impact of his decision on the cost of subsequent investments and the enterprise's growth potential.(1) A reduced rate of 20% was recently introduced into the UK's scale of personal income tax rates, but it applies to a very small income band (the lowest £2,000, or about ECU 1,500).(1) OJ L 249, 3. 10. 69, p 25.

III. TAX RELIEF WHEN THE LEGAL FORM OF AN SME IS CHANGED

This system is quite different from the one just described. The two approaches, moreover, are neither mutually exclusive nor incompatible, since Denmark, Germany and Greece, which have the ad hoc tax arrangements just described for unincorporated enterprises, also have different facilities in their legislation which are designed to limit tax disadvantages when a sole proprietorship or a partnership incorporates.

These approaches are not really alternatives, either, since they have different effects on the entrepreneur's rights and obligations. An entrepreneur's decision to carry on his trade by (not) forming an incorporated enterprise is based on many other factors apart from tax. The extent of his personal liability will often be a key element in his decision. Another major factor will be the extent (and cost) of social security cover for the entrepreneur, depending on the legal form chosen. The degree of ''intuitu personae'' will also have a part to play if other people are associated with the project.

It should also be stressed that incorporation has a disadvantage for small enterprises in that it imposes on the head of the enterprise a more burdensome administrative structure than necessary—particularly if the only purpose of incorporation is to improve the firm's tax position—weakening the direct link which exists between entrepreneur and enterprise.

Nevertheless, a solution to the problem of the unequal tax treatment of the profits of enterprises which are not incorporated and the profits of those which are might be to encourage the former to incorporate. While this might seem radical and possibly disproportionate, it would achieve the objective of improving the competitiveness of the enterprises concerned. If a change in legal form is facilitated or even encouraged so that a corporate form more adapted in tax terms to the enterprise's development is used, the tax constraints which may be encountered by an enterprise operated as a sole proprietorship or a partnership as a result of the entrepreneur's initial choice may then fall away.

For this reason, it is important that the tax system should generally offer sufficient flexibility as regards the choice of legal form in which the entrepreneur intends to carry on his trade. While the entrepreneur chooses whether or not to go for incorporation when he starts up his business, a few years later he may want to review his original choice as his business grows.

But it is also true that the tax disadvantage from which the sole proprietorship or the partnership may suffer, as it grows, vis-à-vis an incorporated enterprise materialises when the level of profits generated by the enterprise place it towards the upper end of the scale of personal income tax. Such a situation occurs more often at the end of a strong period of growth than when the enterprise is first set up, the early years of activity being characterised generally by a low, or even negative, rate of return.

While the need for the enterprise to be able to adapt its legal form to the requirements of competitive markets, and the benefits of the transformation, are clear, it is important to ensure that such a change does not entail tax costs which could discourage an enterprise from making it.

In the majority of Member States, however, a change of legal form generally means the cessation of the business, with the tax consequences which that entails, and setting up a new legal person. Immediate taxation of the profits of the financial year, of hidden capital gains and provisions initially set aside free of tax, loss of the opportunity to carry over losses from previous financial years and liability for capital duty are the tax burdens which any enterprise taking this road will normally have to face.

It is not often that an enterprise is allowed to continue, since legal formalism usually prevails over the enterprise's economic situation; most Member States, however, make a distinction according to the type of legal transformation concerned and its precise technicalities. Depending on whether the change is from sole proprietorship to incorporated enterprise, from partnership to incorporated enterprise, or from one form of incorporated enterprise to another, the continuity of the enterprise is accepted by certain Member States. Tax reliefs are also granted if certain conditions associated with the legal transformation are met.

In the case of the incorporation of sole proprietorships, the notion that the business should automatically be wound up—which is what most Member States would argue—may be favourably modified depending on the circumstances: thus, in Belgium, "continuity" of the enterprise is accepted for tax purposes if this is what the entrepreneur wants.

Taking the transformation of a partnership into an incorporated enterprise, some Member States (Italy, Portugal) accept continuity, but most consider that this involves cessation of the enterprise and creation of a new legal person.

However, whatever their attitude in terms of legal formalism (the enterprise may continue or should be wound up), most of the Member States have introduced provisions which make it possible to attenuate the tax consequences of transformation. These measures, the details of which are given in Note 2, Member State by Member State, basically concern the opportunity to defer taxation of the hidden capital gains recorded at the time of transformation and to carry over the provisions relating to the activity without changing their purpose. Certain relaxations of registration duty are also provided for.

It is also interesting to note that the possibility which has been created in France for partnerships to opt (irrevocably) for corporation tax has virtually the same tax effects as transformation into an incorporated enterprise. While the relief procedures are the same, there is the additional advantage that hidden capital gains and profits on which tax has been deferred are not taxed, since no change is made to the accounts and it is still possible to tax capital gains at a later stage.

Possible lessons from these measures for the Community

Legal formalism continues to be the dominant factor in the Member States' assessment of whether an enterprise should continue in business when it wishes to change its form of organisation; however, the tax effects of formalism, which in virtually all cases leads to the winding-up of the enterprise and the creation of a new entity, are attenuated by practical measures designed to reduce or defer a number of taxes.

Virtually all of the Member States thus have provisions which allow the taxation of capital gains to be deferred until they are realised (usually on condition that the entrepreneur undertakes to hold on to the securities received in exchange for the capital contributed to the new entity and that the assets transferred continue to be carried at their accounting value in the new entity's books) or allow the entrepreneur to choose between immediate taxation (which enables the new firm to calculate the depreciation of the transferred assets applying the value at which they were contributed and not the value at which they were carried in the books of the original enterprise) and deferred taxation. Only one country (Portugal) does not permit such choice when sole proprietorships are incorporated.

Similarly, all of the Member States except Portugal allow provisions to be maintained if their object remains unchanged. Virtually all of them also maintain the enterprise's normal deadlines for payments.

By contrast, legal formalism and its reflection in taxation do not allow losses to be carried over following a change in an enterprise's legal form. Some countries (Germany, France, Luxembourg, United Kingdom) have indicated, however, that, in such cases, losses incurred by a sole proprietorship or partnership can be imputed to the entrepreneur or the partners.

As regards capital duties, some Member States still apply relatively high rates to real property contributed to companies (Belgium, Greece, Spain, France, Italy). However, some of these countries have introduced provisions to reduce this tax charge (Belgium, France, Spain) as long as securities are issued in return for the contributions made. General introduction of such mechanisms in the Union would appear desirable.

NOTE 1

Comparison of rate of corporation tax and rate of personal income tax—incidence on the taxation of enterprises.

Comparing rates of corporation tax and personal income tax in the Community, we can identify three typical situations, depending on the Member State concerned (see table). The graphs below illustrate the diversity of situations.

The first situation is found in Member States where the rate of corporation tax is not just lower than the top marginal rate of personal income tax, but is actually lower than the bottom marginal rate; the second situation is found in Member States where the rate of corporation tax is somewhere between the highest and lowest marginal rates of personal income tax; and the third situation is found in Member States where the rate of corporation tax is equal to or higher than the top marginal rate of personal income tax.

— The first situation is observed in Denmark, and (in the manufacturing sector, where a reduced rate of corporation tax is applied) in Ireland. It emerges from a simple comparison of the structure of rates that incorporated enterprises paying corporation tax enjoy a clear advantage, in terms of the tax treatment of their profits, over sole proprietorships and partnerships paying personal income tax. All other things being equal, the tax situation is an undeniable incentive to incorporate enterprises from the outset (provided the inherent administrative costs are not prohibitive).

— This incentive effect is mitigated in the second type of situation, which is that in majority of Member States (Belgium, Spain, France, Greece, Ireland in sectors other than manufacturing, Luxembourg, the Netherlands and the United Kingdom). In this situation, sole proprietorships are in a favourable position as long as taxable profits remain fairly low (and as long as the sole proprietor has no other income from other sources), but as they rise, the threshold effect and the scissors effect due to the greater progressiveness of personal income tax in relation to corporation tax work to the disadvantage of sole proprietorships compared to limited companies for example. The same applies to partnerships liable to pay personal income tax.

Among the Member States in the second category, there are three—Belgium, Luxembourg and the United Kingdom—with a progressive scale of corporation tax.

(*a*) Reduced rates in Belgium are a privilege reserved for SMEs, but elsewhere they are integrated in the normal structures of corporation tax, and are focused more on the low profits of companies whether large or small than on small companies as such, although in practice small companies are statistically the ones most affected. At all events, their effect is to attenuate the tax burden on small companies, thus making it easier for them to get off the ground.

(*b*) The progressiveness of corporation tax in the three countries mentioned may seem comparable to the progressive scale of personal income tax applied to sole proprietors in all the Member States. However, although the reduced rates of corporation tax appear close or equal to the lowest rates of tax on personal incomes in Belgium (28% compared with 26.75%) an the United Kingdom (25% in both cases)[1] the progressiveness of the income brackets to which they apply is quite different. In the three Member States concerned, the lowest corporation tax bracket is equal to or higher than the bracket taxed at the highest marginal rate of personal income tax. In practice, the tax arrangements for small companies are still more favourable than those for sole proprietorships.

(*c*) There is one country in this second category, the Netherlands, that applies a degressive scale of corporation tax; the first Fl 100 000 of profits are taxed at 40%, the remainder is taxed at 35%. These rates compare with a top marginal rate of income tax of 60% on incomes in excess of Fl 85 530. The reason for this system is to avoid too wide a disparity between tax arrangements for limited companies and those for other types of enterprise.

— Finally, the third type of situation exists in Italy and Portugal, where the gap between effective rates of corporation tax and personal income tax (top bracket) is so small that, beyond a certain level of profits, there is a degree of tax neutrality between the different legal forms. Germany has recently amended its tax system so as to comply with the unwritten rule of virtual parallelism between top marginal rates of corporation tax and personal income tax. On 1 January 1994, the corporation tax rate was cut form 36% to 30% on distributed profits and from 50% to 45% on undistributed profits; this would have increased the gap between the top rate of corporation tax and the top marginal rate of personal income tax (53%) from 3 to 8 points if it had not also been decided to limit the rate of personal income tax on commercial and industrial incomes to 47%, so as to maintain some parallelism between the tax burden on enterprises paying corporation tax and those paying personal income tax.

[1] As regards the tax factor, the entrepreneur will assess his overall tax position; depending on his current or anticipated aggregate income, he will prefer to form an incorporated or non-incorporated enterprise. In all cases, he will make his choice in the light of his personal circumstances without necessarily being aware of the impact of his decision on the cost of subsequent investments and the enterprise's growth potential.(1) A reduced rate of 20% was recently introduced into the UK's scale of personal income tax rates, but it applies to a very small income band (the lowest £2,000, or about ECU 1,500).(1) OJ L 249, 3. 10. 69, p 25.

Comparative table of rates of corporation tax and personal income tax: all levels of government (*) (1994)

Country	*Rate of personal income tax*	*Rate of personal income tax*	*Differential (**) pers. inc. tax/ corp. tax*	*Rate of Corporation tax*
	Bottom rate	*Top rate*		
Germany	19	53 (47) (***)	–2	30/45 [1]
Belgium	26.75 [25]	59 [55]	–20	39% Reduced rates for SMEs (2): 28% on profits below £300,000
Denmark	38 (+5 points social security contribution)	58 (+5%)	–24	34
Spain	20	56	–21	35
France	5	56.8	–23.47	33.33
Greece	5	40	–5	35 [3]
Ireland	27	48	–9	40% Reduced rate: 10% for manufacturing companies in certain areas (Shannon, IFSC)
Italy	10	51	+ 1.2	52.2 [36] (4)
Luxembourg	10 (+2.5% contribution to Employment Fund)	50 (+ 2.5%)	–9.17	43.33 (33) (5) Reduced rates: 20% (profits under Lfrs 0.4); progressive rates from 20 to 30% (profits 0.4 to 0.6 million); 30% (Lfrs 0.6 to 1 million); 30–33% (Lfrs 1 to 1.312 million); 33% (over Lfrs 1.312 million)
Netherlands	13 (6)	60	–25	35% (but 40% for the first Fl 100 000 in profits)
Portugal	15	40	–0.4	39.6% [36]

Country	*Rate of personal income tax*	*Rate of personal income tax*	*Differential (**) pers. inc. tax/ corp. tax*	*Rate of Corporation tax*
	Bottom rate	*Top rate*		
United Kingdom	25 (7)	40	–7	33% Reduced rate: 25% on profits below £300 000

(*) Rates shown in square brackets are rates of tax charged by central government. Effective rates include local taxation applied in certain Member States.

(**) The differential between the standard rate of corporation tax applied to undistributed profits and the top marginal rate of personal income tax.

(***) Germany: from 1 January 1994, the rate of personal income tax on commercial or industrial income is limited to 47%; for other types of income, the top marginal rate of 53% continues to apply.

1 Germany: the rate of tax on distributed profits is 36%, that on undistributed profits 50%.

2 Belgium: this reduced rate of taxation applies to incorporated SMEs that fulfil all the following conditions—
(*a*) taxable income below Bfrs 13 million;
(*b*) no more than half their shares held by one or more other incorporated enterprises;
(*c*) investment value of shares held no more than 50% of paid-up capital;
(*d*) distributed profits not exceeding 13% of paid-up capital.

3 Greece: for private limited companies, the 35% rate applies to the net residual profits after deduction of the remuneration of the three main shareholders taking part in the management of the company.

4 Italy: enterprises with no more than three salaried employees in which the owner and members of the owner's family work are not liable to pay the local tax on profits (ILOR).

5 Luxembourg: companies pay an additional contribution of 1% to the Employment Fund and a local profits tax at an average rate of 10%.

6 Netherlands: a social security contribution of 25.55% is added to the bottom rate of income tax, making the effective rate 38.55%.

7 United Kingdom: a reduced rate of 20% was recently introduced into the scale of personal income tax, but only on a very narrow band (the first £2,000, about ECU 1,500).

NOTE 2

Measures to alleviate the tax consequences of the conversion of sole proprietorships or partnerships into incorporated enterprises

Whatever the attitudes adopted by Member States on a formal legal level (continuation or cessation of the business in question), most have introduced arrangements for alleviating the tax consequences of such conversion operations.

With regard to the immediate taxation of profits, the great majority of Member States do not require early declaration of profits for the conversion of a sole proprietorship into a company but apply the normal deadline for the declaration of income (France is an exception in that it requires a return to be submitted within 60 days of conversion; Greece also requires almost immediate payment).

Similarly, the great majority of Member States authorise carry-over of provisions where the purpose of such provisions remains unchanged. This kind of arrangement helps to ensure some degree of tax neutrality in the case of changes of legal structure.

By contrast, the benefit of a possible carry-over of losses is frequently lost on a change of legal structure because the activity is deemed to cease. This applies particularly to conversion into a company; however, there are arrangements in some Member States (eg Germany, France, Ireland, Luxembourg and the United Kingdom) for setting such losses against the personal income of the owner (or of the partners in the case of partnership).

With regard to the taxation of latent capital gains on the conversion of a sole proprietorship into a company, the great majority of Member States permit the business either to defer taxation or to be taxed at a preferential rate; others permit enterprises to choose between immediate and deferred taxation (in France latent capital gains on depreciable assets are automatically taxed on conversion to a company, although the owner may choose between immediate and deferred taxation of latent capital gains on intangible assets). In most Member States, these favourable arrangements are subject, in the case of a conversion operation carried out in the form of transfers of assets, to the transfers being remunerated mainly through shares which the transferor undertakes to retain for a minimum number of years and to the assets being included in the new entity's accounts at their book value.

It should be pointed out with regard to capital duties that the amount of duty payable on the conversion of an enterprise is far from negligible. Transfer duties are frequently levied on transfers of buildings, property rights and goodwill for consideration. The rates of these duties can be very high, particularly in the case of transfers for consideration (this is the case, for example, where the company takes on the liabilities of the transferor; under such circumstances, the transfer operation is normally treated as a sale). Council Directive 69/335/EEC of 17 July 1969[1] does permit Member States to levy transfer duties on transfers of immovable assets to incorporated enterprises at a rate in excess of the maximum harmonised capital-duty rate of 1% applicable to other types of transfers.

However, a number of Member States (for example Belgium, France and Spain) have adopted the principle which is most frequently applied to the taxation of capital gains in connection with a conversion operation: taxation of such gains may be suspended if the transferor is remunerated in the form of shares; similarly, transfer duties may be reduced substantially (application of a flat-rate amount or reduced rate) if, for example, the transfers are remunerated by securities which the transferor undertakes to retain for a minimum period.

Tax treatment applied in the Member States when sole proprietorships or partnerships are converted into incorporated enterprises

[1] As regards the tax factor, the entrepreneur will assess his overall tax position; depending on his current or anticipated aggregate income, he will prefer to form an incorporated or non-incorporated enterprise. In all cases, he will make his choice in the light of his personal circumstances without necessarily being aware of the impact of his decision on the cost of subsequent investments and the enterprise's growth potential.(1) A reduced rate of 20% was recently introduced into the UK's scale of personal income tax rates, but it applies to a very small income band (the lowest £2,000, or about ECU 1,500).(1) OJ L 249, 3. 10. 69, p 25.

Country	*Capital duties*	*Capital gains*	*Immediate taxation of profits*	*Carry-over of losses*	*Carry-over of provisions (*)*
Belgium	0.5%[1] (transfer of assets to an incorporated enterprise in exchange for shares)	16.5% for tangible assets 33% for intangible assets (but temporary exemption if the business has not specifically waived application of the "continuation" arrangements)	no	no	yes
Denmark	1% rate	taxation suspended in the case of payment in the form of securities (equal to at least 75% of transferred assets) and subject to the transferor retaining the securities	no	no	yes
Germany	2% (Grunderwerb-steuer) on transfers of land or buildings to a company	suspension of taxation possible (if historic values are entered in the accounts of the recipient company and if securities are retained by the transferor)	no	no (but can be set against the income of the owner or partners)	yes
Greece	normal rate of 1% but rate varies between 3% and 11% for the transfer of a building for consideration (frequent occurrence in the case of sole proprietorships)	no taxation of unrealised capital gains (except for capital gains on property)	yes	yes	yes (except for certain types of provision: for example provisions for doubtful claims)
Spain	normal rate of 1% (corporate transactions) but 6% for the transfer of a building for consideration	taxation suspended (in the case of transfers of assets, etc)	no	no	yes

EC Material

Country	Capital duties	Capital gains	Immediate taxation of profits	Carry-over of losses	Carry-over of provisions (*)
France	fixed duty of FF 500 where the transferor retains for five years the securities received in return for the transfer (failing that, a special duty of 8.6% for transfers of property and goodwill)	possible deferral of taxation (capital gains on non-depreciable assets) if securities received in payment for the transfer are retained. In the case of capital gains on depreciable assets (taxation effected in the hands of the recipient company), payment of tax is spread over five years	yes (but the transferor is not taxed on profits relating to stocks if included at their book value in the assets of the recipient company)	no (but for sole proprietors and partners the trading deficit of the business transferred is included in the total deficit that can be carried over for five years for income-tax purposes)	yes
Ireland	stamp duty of 1%	taxation of capital gains is suspended if remuneration is in the form of securities provided that the securities are retained by the transferor	no	no (but carry-over possible as part of the overall deficit that can be carried over for income-tax purposes)	yes
Italy	transfers of immovable property to companies (8%)	taxation of capital gains suspended (if assets are carried in the balance sheet at their original value)	not available	not available	not available
Luxembourg	real or personal estate invested: 1% in the case of assets transferred for consideration : from 0.24% to 6% depending on the nature of the assets	no taxation of capital gains if the assets are carried at their book value in the account of the recipient company	no	no (but deductibility is permitted in the hands of the person who has incurred the loss, even if he is no longer the owner; the same applies to partners in a partnership)	yes
Netherlands	not available	not available	not available	not available	not available

Country	*Capital duties*	*Capital gains*	*Immediate taxation of profits*	*Carry-over of losses*	*Carry-over of provisions (*)*
Portugal	duty ("sisa") municipal tax on transfers of immovable property: 4% to 10% depending on the nature and use of the property	—taxation of capital gains (stocks and assets) [2]	no[2]	no[2]	no[2]
		—no taxation (tax neutrality) [3]	—[3]	yes [3]	yes[3]
United Kingdom	stamp duty of 1% (land, buildings, etc)	taxation of companies in principle but relief is available (in the case of payment in the form of shares)	no	yes (on future dividends)	yes

(*) This involves the possibility of carrying over provisions whose purpose remains unchanged.
[1] Temporary exemption from capital duty in the case of transfers to companies established in an employment area, to headquarters of multinational companies established in Belgium, to companies undergoing conversion, to innovative companies and to companies located in a development area.
[2] Tax arrangements applied to the conversion of a sole proprietorship into a company.
[3] Tax treatment applied to the conversion of a partnership into a company.

NOTE 3

Comparative figures on the size of the corporate sector

(The figures in this table are based on 1989 data)

Country	*Number of companies*	*Population (1000s)*	*Number of companies per 1000 head of population*	*Total taxes as % of GDP*	*Corporate income tax as % of GDP*
Belgium	225,640	9,938	22.70	44.3	3.10
Denmark	85,917	5,132	16.74	49.9	2.00
Germany	404,195	62,063	6.50	38.1	1.91
Greece	70,824	10,033	7.05	33.2	1.33
Spain	655,491	38,888	16.86	34.4	2.06
France	699,170	56,423	12.39	43.8	2.19
Ireland	110,418	3,515	31.41	37.6	1.50
Italy	300,000	57,540	5.21	37.8	3.40
Luxembourg	11,941	377	31.67	42.4	7.21
Netherlands	257,000	14,846	17.31	46.0	3.68
Portugal	171,919	9,793	17.55	35.1	n/a
United Kingdom	1,005,300	57,236	17.56	36.5	4.02
Total	3,997,815	325,785			
Average			12.27	39.9	2.95

NOTE 4

Description of the "business rules"—Denmark

1. Natural persons carrying on business independently (as sole proprietors or partners) can opt for the "business rules".

2. The objective of these rules is as follows—

(*a*) to render the business' interest payments fully tax-deductible (as is the case with its other operational expenditure);
(*b*) to ensure that that part of the business' profits constituting a return on its equity is taxed in the same way as other capital gains;
(*c*) to counterbalance cyclical trends;
(*d*) to offer taxation at 34% the same rate as corporation tax.

3.1. The rules require independent businessmen to keep their business and personal finances separate for accounting purposes; distinct accounts must be kept for the business' income and personal finances.

The business income is assessed in accordance with the general rules laid down in the tax legislation.

If, in a particular income year, a business shows a profit, this is divided into an imputed capital gain (ie the return on the business' own capital) and the remaining profit. Capital gains are assessed as income from capital, like other return on capital. The remainder of the profit is assessed as personal income on a sliding scale. However, the profit is only liable to tax when it is withdrawn from the business.

Nevertheless, the taxable person may refrain from withdrawing the profit, or a part thereof, and opt to retain it in the business. In that case it attracts advance tax of 34% (ie at the same rate as corporation tax). It is only when the taxable person withdraws the accumulated profit in a subsequent year that it is finally taxed as personal income. The advance business tax is set off against the taxable person's and his/her spouse's tax for the year in question and the five succeeding years but cannot be disbursed as a cash payment.

If the business shows a loss in an income year, the loss must first be set off against any accumulated profit. In the absence of any accumulated profit, the loss is deducted from the taxpayer's other income. Any remaining loss may be carried forward for deduction against the business' profits and other income in the succeeding five years.

3.2. As a general rule, there are not restrictions on the nature of businesses which can opt for the business rules. Nevertheless, if the business reflects aspects of a private limited company, the option is not available. Income from such companies is taxed as income from capital. Insolvent businesses are likewise excluded from the business rules.

3.3. If the taxable person operates a number of businesses, they must all be subject to the business rules. Under these rules, all such businesses are treated as one business.

If the taxable person is married and his/her spouse operates his/her own business, the spouse must apply either the business rules or the "capital gains rules" to his/her business.

3.4. The taxable person is free to determine each year whether the business is to come under the business rules.

If the taxable person ceases to apply the business rules without transferring the business, any accumulated profit is taxed as personal income in the income year following the income year in which he last applied the business rules.

If the taxable person ceases trading in respect of one of a number of businesses without transferring the business, any retained profits are taxed proportionately.

A taxable person who has previously applied the business rules in respect of a business and who, within the immediately succeeding five income years, resumes application of the rules must, when calculating the business' capital account, assess real property at the value which was indicated when the rules were last applied.

3.5. If the taxable person transfers the business or ceases trading as an independent business, any accumulated profits are taxed as unearned income in the same income year or, if the distinction between the business accounts and the taxpayer's individual accounts are maintained for the rest of the year, the succeeding income year. If the taxable person acquires another business before the end of the succeeding income year, he may apply the business rules uninterrupted, provided that the distinction between the business accounts and his personal accounts is maintained throughout the entire period.

If the taxable person applies the business rules without interruption, the purchase price received on the transfer of the business is subject to the business rules.

Where one of a number of businesses, a business which has been separated from an existing business, or a notional part of a business is transferred, the purchase price received is subject to the business rules. The taxable person may opt to transfer an amount not exceeding the net cash consideration outside the business rules to his individual finances, provided that a corresponding part of any accumulated profits is withdrawn and taxed as personal income in the same income year.

3.6. If a taxable person ceases to be liable to tax in Denmark or in any other respect acquires a tax domicile abroad, any accumulated profit is taxed as personal income in the income year in which he ceases to be liable to tax or changes his tax domicile.

3.7. Businesses subject to the business rules may be transferred and/or transformed in the same way as other businesses. If the business is transferred and deferred taxation applies, taxation of any accumulated profits may also be deferred.

Conclusions of the Ecofin Council Meeting on 1 December 1997 Concerning Taxation Policy

(98/C 2/01)

Note—See OJ C002, 6.1.98, pp 1–6.

The Council held a wide-ranging debate in the light of the Commission communication entitled "A package to tackle harmful tax competition in the European Union", which takes stock of a discussion initiated by the Commission at the informal meeting of Ministers for Economic Affairs and Finance in Verona in April 1996 and given more substantial shape at the informal meeting in Mondorf-les-Bains in September 1997.

That discussion concerned the need for co-ordinated action at European level to tackle harmful tax competition in order to help achieve certain objectives such as reducing the continuing distortions in the single market, preventing excessive losses of tax revenue or getting tax structures to develop in a more employment-friendly way.

In the light of that debate and in a spirit of comprehensiveness of approach, three areas were particularly highlighted: business taxation, taxation of savings income and the issue of withholding taxes on cross-border interest and royalty payments between companies.

Following that debate, the Council and the Representatives of the Governments of the Member States, meeting within the Council, agreed to the Resolution on a code of conduct for business taxation set out in Annex 1;

The Council also:

—approved the text on taxation of savings set out in Annex 2,

—considered that the Commission should submit a proposal for a Directive on interest and royalty payments between companies,

—took note of the Commission's intention to submit rapidly two proposals for Directives on the subjects referred to in the first and second indents above,

—called on the Commission to submit to it each year, together with the report provided for in paragraph N of the code of conduct for business taxation, a progress report on work concerning taxation of savings and interest and royalty payments between companies,

—took note of the Commission's undertaking on fiscal State aid,

—called on the Commission to take forward its work on taxation, continuing to draw on the assistance of the Taxation Policy Group,

—took note of the following statements for the Council minutes:

1. re Annex 1 (code of conduct):

Certain Member States and the Commission consider that special tax arrangements for employees could come within the range of problems covered by the code. They accordingly consider that this question needs to be discussed within the Taxation Policy Group with a view to a possible extension of the code under the review procedure laid down in paragraph N.

The Council and the Representatives of the Governments of the Member States, meeting within the Council, as well as the Commission note that standstill and rollback are closely interrelated and stress the need for a balanced application to comparable situations, without this delaying the implementation of standstill and rollback. They also consider that a period of two years, as a general rule, should be sufficient for rollback. As from 1 January 1998 the actual rollback will have to take place within five years although a longer period may be justified in particular circumstances following an assessment by the Council.

The German delegation, like other delegations, understands point B (3) as including, *inter alia*, the targeted granting of advantages for international mobile activities, where they are not granted for non-mobile activities.

The Commission points out that the authorisation granted in 1987 and extended most recently in 1994 for the arrangements for international financial services centres in Dublin expires in 2005 and that, under that authorisation, no new institutions may benefit from those arrangements after 2000.

2. re Annex 2 (taxation of savings):

The Member States state that, if they were to change their legislation, they should be guided by the points set out in Annex 2 to these conclusions.

The United Kingdom delegation considers that such a Directive should not apply to Eurobonds and similar instruments.

The French delegation considers that the Directive on the taxation of savings should not lay down a rate of withholding tax of less than 25%.

The Netherlands delegation notes that it will assess the proposals in the light of the principle of taxation of savings in the country of residence.

The Luxembourg delegation considers that a Directive on taxation of savings should be accompanied by a Directive on business taxation covering general arrangements for business taxation in the Member States.

The Belgian, Italian and Portuguese delegations state that they will not agree to the Directive on interest and royalty payments between companies before the Directive on the taxation of savings is adopted.

3. The Commission notes the Netherlands delegation's request concerning problems relating in particular to taxation of pensions and insurance benefits; it undertakes to consider the matter with the assistance of the Taxation Policy Group with a view to possibly drawing up a proposal for a Directive.

4. The Commission notes the Belgian delegation's request concerning VAT treatment of cross-border motor vehicle leasing and undertakes to look into it with an open mind. It will in particular consider to what extent the proposals already planned to modernise and streamline the present VAT arrangements can provide a suitable solution.

ANNEX 1

RESOLUTION OF THE COUNCIL AND THE REPRESENTATIVES OF THE GOVERNMENTS OF THE MEMBER STATES, MEETING WITHIN THE COUNCIL OF 1 DECEMBER 1997 ON A CODE OF CONDUCT FOR BUSINESS TAXATION

THE COUNCIL OF THE EUROPEAN UNION AND THE REPRESENTATIVES OF THE GOVERNMENTS OF THE MEMBER STATES, MEETING WITHIN THE COUNCIL,

RECALLING that a comprehensive approach to taxation policy was launched, at the Commission's instigation, at the informal meeting of the Ministers for Economic Affairs and Finance held in Verona in April 1996 and confirmed at the meeting in Mondorf-les-Bains in September 1997 in the light of the consideration that coordinated action at European level is needed in order to reduce continuing distortions in the single market, prevent significant losses of tax revenue and help tax structures develop in a more employment-friendly way,

ACKNOWLEDGING the major contribution made by the Taxation Policy Group to the preparation of this Resolution,

NOTING the Commission communication to the Council and the European Parliament of 5 November 1997,

ACKNOWLEDGING the positive effects of fair competition and the need to consolidate the competitiveness of the European Union and the Member States at international level, whilst noting that tax competition may also lead to tax measures with harmful effects,

ACKNOWLEDGING, therefore, the need for a code of conduct for business taxation designed to curb harmful tax measures,

EMPHASISING that the code of conduct is a political commitment and does not affect the Member States' rights and obligations or the respective spheres of competence of the Member States and the Community resulting from the Treaty,

Hereby adopt the following code of conduct:

CODE OF CONDUCT FOR BUSINESS TAXATION TAX MEASURES COVERED

A. Without prejudice to the respective spheres of competence of the Member States and the Community, this code of conduct, which covers business taxation, concerns those measures which affect, or may affect, in a significant way the location of business activity in the Community.

Business activity in this respect also includes all activities carried out within a group of companies.

The tax measures covered by the code include both laws or regulations and administrative practices.

B. Within the scope specified in paragraph A, tax measures which provide for a significantly lower effective level of taxation, including zero taxation, than those levels which generally apply in the Member State in question are to be regarded as potentially harmful and therefore covered by this code.

Such a level of taxation may operate by virtue of the nominal tax rate, the tax base or any other relevant factor.

When assessing whether such measures are harmful, account should be taken of, *inter alia*:

1. whether advantages are accorded only to non-residents or in respect of transactions carried out with non-residents, or

2. whether advantages are ring-fenced from the domestic market, so they do not affect the national tax base, or

3. whether advantages are granted even without any real economic activity and substantial economic presence within the Member State offering such tax advantages, or

4. whether the rules for profit determination in respect of activities within a multinational group of companies departs from internationally accepted principles, notably the rules agreed upon within the OECD, or

5. whether the tax measures lack transparency, including where legal provisions are relaxed at administrative level in a non-transparent way.

STANDSTILL AND ROLLBACK

Standstill

C. Member States commit themselves not to introduce new tax measures which are harmful within the meaning of this code. Member States will therefore respect the principles underlying the code when determining future policy and will have due regard for the review process referred to in paragraphs E to I in assessing whether any new tax measure is harmful.

Rollback

D. Member States commit themselves to re-examining their existing laws and established practices, having regard to the principles underlying the code and to the review process outlined in paragraphs E to I. Member States will amend such laws and practices as necessary with a view to eliminating any harmful measures as soon as possible taking into account the Council's discussions following the review process.

REVIEW PROCESS

Provision of relevant information

E. In accordance with the principles of transparency and openness Member States will inform each other of existing and proposed tax measures which may fall within the scope of the code. In particular, Member States are called upon to provide at the request of another Member State information on any tax measure which appears to fall within the scope of the code. Where envisaged tax measures need parliamentary approval, such information need not be given until after their announcement to Parliament.

Assessment of harmful measures

F. Any Member State may request the opportunity to discuss and comment on a tax measure of another Member State that may fall within the scope of the code. This will permit an assessment to be made of whether the tax measures in question are harmful, in the light of the effects that they may have within the Community. That assessment will take into account all the factors identified in paragraph B.

G. The Council also emphasises the need to evaluate carefully in that assessment the effects that the tax measures have on other Member States, *inter alia* in the light of how the activities concerned are effectively taxed throughout the Community.

Insofar as the tax measures are used to support the economic development of particular regions, an assessment will be made of whether the measures are in proportion to, and targeted at, the aims sought. In assessing this, particular attention will be paid to special features and constraints in the case of the outermost regions and small islands, without undermining the integrity and coherence of the Community legal order, including the internal market and common policies.

Procedure

H. A group will be set up by the Council to assess the tax measures that may fall within the scope of this code and to oversee the provision of information on those measures. The Council invites each

EC Material

Member State and the Commission to appoint a high-level representative and a deputy to this group, which will be chaired by a representative of a Member State. The group, which will meet regularly, will select and review the tax measures for assessment in accordance with the provisions laid down in paragraphs E to G. The group will report regularly on the measures assessed. These reports will be forwarded to the Council for deliberation and, if the Council so decides, published.

I. The Council invites the Commission to assist the group in carrying out the necessary preparatory work for its meetings and to facilitate the provision of information and the review process. To this end, the Council requests Member States to provide the Commission with the information referred to in paragraph E so that the Commission may coordinate the exchange of such information between the Member States.

State aid

J. The Council notes that some of the tax measures covered by this code may fall within the scope of the provisions on State aid in Articles 92 to 94[1] of the Treaty. Without prejudice to Community law and the objectives of the Treaty, the Council notes that the Commission undertakes to publish guidelines on the application of the State aid rules to measures relating to direct business taxation by mid-1998, after submitting the draft guidelines to experts from the Member States at a multilateral meeting, and commits itself to the strict application of the aid rules concerned, taking into account, *inter alia*, the negative effects of aid that are brought to light in the application of this code. The Council also notes that the Commission intends to examine or re-examine existing tax arrangements and proposed new legislation by Member States case by case, thus ensuring that the rules and objectives of the Treaty are applied consistently and equally to all.

Action to combat tax avoidance and evasion

K. The Council calls on the Member States to co-operate fully in the fight against tax avoidance and evasion, notably in the exchange of information between Member States, in accordance with their respective national laws.

L. The Council notes that anti-abuse provisions or countermeasures contained in tax laws and in double taxation conventions play a fundamental role in counteracting tax avoidance and evasion.

Geographical extension

M. The Council considers it advisable that principles aimed at abolishing harmful tax measures should be adopted on as broad a geographical basis as possible. To this end, Member States commit themselves to promoting their adoption in third countries; they also commit themselves to promoting their adoption in territories to which the Treaty does not apply.

In particular, Member States with dependent or associated territories or which have special responsibilities or taxation prerogatives in respect of other territories commit themselves, within the framework of their constitutional arrangements, to ensuring that these principles are applied in those territories. In this connection, those Member States will take stock of the situation in the form of reports to the group referred to in paragraph H, which will assess them under the review procedure described above.

Monitoring and revision

N. In order to ensure the even and effective implementation of the code, the Council invites the Commission to report to it annually on the implementation thereof and on the application of fiscal State aid. The Council and the Member States will review the provisions of the code two years after its adoption.

Note—[1] Articles 92—94 renumbered articles 87—89 respectively by the Treaty of Amsterdam ratified on 1 May 1999 (OJ C340 10.11.97 p 1).

ANNEX 2

TAXATION OF SAVINGS

To ensure a minimum of effective taxation of savings income within the Community and to prevent undesirable distortion of competition, the Council calls upon the Commission to present a proposal for a Directive on the taxation of savings. The Council considers that the following points might form a basis for that proposal:

I. The scope of such a Directive could be limited to interest paid in one Member State to individuals who are resident in another Member State.

II. As a first step towards effective taxation of savings income throughout the Community, such a Directive could be based on the "coexistence model", under which each Member State would either operate a withholding tax or provide information on savings income to other Member States. A Member State might combine the two. The Directive could contain a review clause, for the purpose of determining to what extent further progress would be conceivable with a view to better effective taxation of savings income.

III. Any withholding tax on interest payments made to residents of other Member States could, in principle, be levied by the paying agent. Refinement of this method might be needed in order to counter tax avoidance and evasion more effectively and to avoid double taxation. The arrangements for checking the residence for tax purposes of beneficiaries should not be too cumbersome.

IV. The provisions of such a Directive should take into account the need to preserve the competitiveness of European financial markets on a global scale.

Furthermore, it would be advisable for the points set out above to be adopted as widely as possible. To this end, Member States should undertake to promote the establishment of equivalent measures in third countries, at the same time as discussions on the Directive are taking place; they should also commit themselves to promoting their adoption in territories to which the Treaty does not apply. In particular, Member States with dependent or associated territories or which have special responsibilities or taxation prerogatives in respect of other territories should commit themselves, within the framework of their constitutional arrangements, to ensuring that equivalent measures are applied in those territories.

The Council should review the issue before adopting such a Directive.

Council Directive of 3 June 2003 on taxation of savings income in the form of interest payments

(2003/48/EC)

Note—Published in OJ L 157/39 26.6.2003.

The council of the european union,

Having regard to the Treaty establishing the European Community, and in particular Article 94 thereof,

Having regard to the proposal from the Commission[1],

Having regard to the opinion of the European Parliament[2],

Having regard to the opinion of the European Economic and Social Committee[3],

Whereas:

(1) Articles 56 to 60 of the Treaty guarantee the free movement of capital.

(2) Savings income in the form of interest payments from debt claims constitutes taxable income for residents of all Member States.

(3) By virtue of Article 58(1) of the Treaty Member States have the right to apply the relevant provisions of their tax law which distinguish between taxpayers who are not in the same situation with regard to their place of residence or with regard to the place where their capital is invested, and to take all requisite measures to prevent infringements of national law and regulations, in particular in the field of taxation.

(4) In accordance with Article 58(3) of the Treaty, the provisions of Member States' tax law designed to counter abuse or fraud should not constitute a means of arbitrary discrimination or a disguised restriction on the free movement of capital and payments as established by Article 56 of the Treaty.

(5) In the absence of any coordination of national tax systems for taxation of savings income in the form of interest payments, particularly as far as the treatment of interest received by non-residents is concerned, residents of Member States are currently often able to avoid any form of taxation in their Member State of residence on interest they receive in another Member State.

(6) This situation is creating distortions in the capital movements between Member States, which are incompatible with the internal market.

(7) This Directive builds on the consensus reached at the Santa Maria da Feira European Council of 19 and 20 June 2000 and the subsequent Ecofin Council meetings of 26 and 27 November 2000, 13 December 2001 and 21 January 2003.

(8) The ultimate aim of this Directive is to enable savings income in the form of interest payments made in one Member State to beneficial owners who are individuals resident in another Member State to be made subject to effective taxation in accordance with the laws of the latter Member State.

(9) The aim of this Directive can best be achieved by targeting interest payments made or secured by economic operators established in the Member States to or for the benefit of beneficial owners who are individuals resident in another Member State.

(10) Since the objective of this Directive cannot be sufficiently achieved by the Member States, because of the lack of any coordination of national systems for the taxation of savings income, and can therefore be better achieved at Community level, the Community may adopt measures in accordance with the principle of subsidiarity as set out in Article 5 of the Treaty. In accordance with the principle of proportionality, as set out in that Article, this Directive confines itself to the minimum

required in order to achieve those objectives and does not go beyond what is necessary for that purpose.

(11) The paying agent is the economic operator who pays interest to or secures the payment of interest for the immediate benefit of the beneficial owner.

(12) In defining the notion of interest payment and the paying agent mechanism, reference should be made, where appropriate, to Council Directive 85/611/EEC of 20 December 1985 on the coordination of laws, regulations and administrative provisions relating to undertakings for collective investment in transferable securities (UCITS)[4].

(13) The scope of this Directive should be limited to taxation of savings income in the form of interest payments on debt claims, to the exclusion, *inter alia*, of the issues relating to the taxation of pension and insurance benefits.

(14) The ultimate aim of bringing about effective taxation of interest payments in the beneficial owner's Member State of residence for tax purposes can be achieved through the exchange of information concerning interest payments between Member States.

(15) Council Directive 77/799/EEC of 19 December 1977 concerning mutual assistance by the competent authorities of the Member States in the field of direct and indirect taxation[5] already provides a basis for Member States to exchange information for tax purposes on the income covered by this Directive. It should continue to apply to such exchanges of information in addition to this Directive insofar as this Directive does not derogate from it.

(16) The automatic exchange of information between Member States concerning interest payments covered by this Directive makes possible the effective taxation of those payments in the beneficial owner's Member State of residence for tax purposes in accordance with the national laws of that State. It is therefore necessary to stipulate that Member States which exchange information pursuant to this Directive should not be permitted to rely on the limits to the exchange of information as set out in Article 8 of Directive 77/799/EEC.

(17) In view of structural differences, Austria, Belgium and Luxembourg cannot apply the automatic exchange of information at the same time as the other Member States. During a transitional period, given that a withholding tax can ensure a minimum level of effective taxation, especially at a rate increasing progressively to 35%, these three Member States should apply a withholding tax to the savings income covered by this Directive.

(18) In order to avoid differences in treatment, Austria, Belgium and Luxembourg should not be obliged to apply automatic exchange of information before the Swiss Confederation, the Principality of Andorra, the Principality of Liechtenstein, the Principality of Monaco and the Republic of San Marino ensure effective exchange of information on request concerning payments of interest.

(19) Those Member States should transfer the greater part of their revenue of this withholding tax to the Member State of residence of the beneficial owner of the interest.

(20) Those Member States should provide for a procedure allowing beneficial owners resident for tax purposes in other Member States to avoid the imposition of this withholding tax by authorising their paying agent to report the interest payments or by presenting a certificate issued by the competent authority of their Member State of residence for tax purposes.

(21) The Member State of residence for tax purposes of the beneficial owner should ensure the elimination of any double taxation of the interest payments which might result from the imposition of this withholding tax in accordance with the procedures laid down in this Directive. It should do so by crediting this withholding tax up to the amount of tax due in its territory and by reimbursing to the beneficial owner any excess amount of tax withheld. It may, however, instead of applying this tax credit mechanism, grant a refund of the withholding tax.

(22) In order to avoid market disruption, this Directive should, during the transitional period, not apply to interest payments on certain negotiable debt securities.

(23) This Directive should not preclude Member States from levying other types of withholding tax than that referred to in this Directive on interest arising in their territories.

(24) So long as the United States of America, Switzerland, Andorra, Liechtenstein, Monaco, San Marino and the relevant dependent or associated territories of the Member States do not all apply measures equivalent to, or the same as, those provided for by this Directive, capital flight towards these countries and territories could imperil the attainment of its objectives. Therefore, it is necessary for the Directive to apply from the same date as that on which all these countries and territories apply such measures.

(25) The Commission should report every three years on the operation of this Directive and propose to the Council any amendments that prove necessary in order better to ensure effective taxation of savings income and to remove undesirable distortions of competition.

(26) This Directive respects the fundamental rights and principles which are recognised, in particular, by the Charter of Fundamental Rights of the European Union,

Has adopted this directive:

Notes—[1] OJ C 270 E, 25.9.2001, p. 259.
[2] OJ C 47 E, 27.2.2003, p. 553.
[3] OJ C 48, 21.2.2002, p. 55.

[4] OJ L 375, 31.12.1985, p. 3. Directive as last amended by Directive 2001/108/EC of the European Parliament and of the Council (OJ L 41, 13.2.2002, p. 35).
[5] OJ L 336, 27.12.1977, p. 15. Directive as last amended by the 1994 Act of Accession.

CHAPTER I
INTRODUCTORY PROVISIONS

Article 1

Aim

1. The ultimate aim of the Directive is to enable savings income in the form of interest payments made in one Member State to beneficial owners who are individuals resident for tax purposes in another Member State to be made subject to effective taxation in accordance with the laws of the latter Member State.

2. Member States shall take the necessary measures to ensure that the tasks necessary for the implementation of this Directive are carried out by paying agents established within their territory, irrespective of the place of establishment of the debtor of the debt claim producing the interest.

Article 2

Definition of beneficial owner

1. For the purposes of this Directive, ''beneficial owner'' means any individual who receives an interest payment or any individual for whom an interest payment is secured, unless he provides evidence that it was not received or secured for his own benefit, that is to say that:

(*a*) he acts as a paying agent within the meaning of Article 4(1); or

(*b*) he acts on behalf of a legal person, an entity which is taxed on its profits under the general arrangements for business taxation, an UCITS authorised in accordance with Directive 85/611/EEC or an entity referred to in Article 4(2) of this Directive and, in the last mentioned case, discloses the name and address of that entity to the economic operator making the interest payment and the latter communicates such information to the competent authority of its Member State of establishment, or

(*c*) he acts on behalf of another individual who is the beneficial owner and discloses to the paying agent the identity of that beneficial owner in accordance with Article 3(2).

2. Where a paying agent has information suggesting that the individual who receives an interest payment or for whom an interest payment is secured may not be the beneficial owner, and where neither paragraph 1(*a*) nor 1(*b*) applies to that individual, it shall take reasonable steps to establish the identity of the beneficial owner in accordance with Article 3(2). If the paying agent is unable to identify the beneficial owner, it shall treat the individual in question as the beneficial owner.

Article 3

Identity and residence of beneficial owners

1. Each Member State shall, within its territory, adopt and ensure the application of the procedures necessary to allow the paying agent to identify the beneficial owners and their residence for the purposes of Articles 8 to 12.

Such procedures shall comply with the minimum standards established in paragraphs 2 and 3.

2. The paying agent shall establish the identity of the beneficial owner on the basis of minimum standards which vary according to when relations between the paying agent and the recipient of the interest are entered into, as follows:

(*a*) for contractual relations entered into before 1 January 2004, the paying agent shall establish the identity of the beneficial owner, consisting of his name and address, by using the information at its disposal, in particular pursuant to the regulations in force in its State of establishment and to Council Directive 91/308/EEC of 10 June 1991 on prevention of the use of the financial system for the purpose of money laundering ([1]);

(*b*) for contractual relations entered into, or transactions carried out in the absence of contractual relations, on or after 1 January 2004, the paying agent shall establish the identity of the beneficial owner, consisting of the name, address and, if there is one, the tax identification number allocated by the Member State of residence for tax purposes. These details shall be established on the basis of the passport or of the official identity card presented by the beneficial owner. If it does not appear on that passport or on that official identity card, the address shall be established on the basis of any other documentary proof of identity presented by the beneficial owner. If the tax identification number is not mentioned on the passport, on the official identity card or any other documentary proof of identity, including, possibly, the certificate of residence for tax purposes, presented by the beneficial owner, the identity shall be supplemented by a reference to the latter's date and place of birth established on the basis of his passport or official identification card.

3. The paying agent shall establish the residence of the beneficial owner on the basis of minimum standards which vary according to when relations between the paying agent and the recipient of the

interest are entered into. Subject to the conditions set out below, residence shall be considered to be situated in the country where the beneficial owner has his permanent address:

(*a*) for contractual relations entered into before 1 January 2004, the paying agent shall establish the residence of the beneficial owner by using the information at its disposal, in particular pursuant to the regulations in force in its State of establishment and to Directive 91/308/EEC;

(*b*) for contractual relations entered into, or transactions carried out in the absence of contractual relations, on or after 1 January 2004, the paying agent shall establish the residence of the beneficial owner on the basis of the address mentioned on the passport, on the official identity card or, if necessary, on the basis of any documentary proof of identity presented by the beneficial owner and according to the following procedure: for individuals presenting a passport or official identity card issued by a Member State who declare themselves to be resident in a third country, residence shall be established by means of a tax residence certificate issued by the competent authority of the third country in which the individual claims to be resident. Failing the presentation of such a certificate, the Member State which issued the passport or other official identity document shall be considered to be the country of residence.

Note—[1] OJ L 166, 28.6.1991, p. 77. Directive as last amended by Directive 2001/97/EC of the European Parliament and of the Council (OJ L 344, 28.12.2001, p. 76).

Article 4

Definition of paying agent

1. For the purposes of this Directive, ''paying agent'' means any economic operator who pays interest to or secures the payment of interest for the immediate benefit of the beneficial owner, whether the operator is the debtor of the debt claim which produces the interest or the operator charged by the debtor or the beneficial owner with paying interest or securing the payment of interest.

2. Any entity established in a Member State to which interest is paid or for which interest is secured for the benefit of the beneficial owner shall also be considered a paying agent upon such payment or securing of such payment. This provision shall not apply if the economic operator has reason to believe, on the basis of official evidence produced by that entity, that:

(*a*) it is a legal person, with the exception of those legal persons referred to in paragraph 5; or

(*b*) its profits are taxed under the general arrangements for business taxation; or

(*c*) it is an UCITS recognised in accordance with Directive 85/ 611/EEC.

An economic operator paying interest to, or securing interest for, such an entity established in another Member State which is considered a paying agent under this paragraph shall communicate the name and address of the entity and the total amount of interest paid to, or secured for, the entity to the competent authority of its Member State of establishment, which shall pass this information on to the competent authority of the Member State where the entity is established.

3. The entity referred to in paragraph 2 shall, however, have the option of being treated for the purposes of this Directive as an UCITS as referred to in 2(*c*). The exercise of this option shall require a certificate to be issued by the Member State in which the entity is established and presented to the economic operator by that entity.

Member States shall lay down the detailed rules for this option for entities established in their territory.

4. Where the economic operator and the entity referred to in paragraph 2 are established in the same Member State, that Member State shall take the necessary measures to ensure that the entity complies with the provisions of this Directive when it acts as a paying agent.

5. The legal persons exempted from paragraph 2(*a*) are:

(*a*) in Finland: avoin yhtiö (Ay) and kommandiittiyhtiö (Ky)/ öppet bolag and kommanditbolag;

(*b*) in Sweden: handelsbolag (HB) and kommanditbolag (KB).

Article 5

Definition of competent authority

For the purposes of this Directive, ''competent authority'' means:

(*a*) for Member States, any of the authorities notified by the Member States to the Commission;

(*b*) for third countries, the competent authority for the purposes of bilateral or multilateral tax conventions or, failing that, such other authority as is competent to issue certificates of residence for tax purposes.

Article 6

Definition of interest payment

1. For the purposes of this Directive, ''interest payment'' means:

(*a*) interest paid or credited to an account, relating to debt claims of every kind, whether or not secured by mortgage and whether or not carrying a right to participate in the debtor's profits, and, in particular, income from government securities and income from bonds or debentures, including premiums and prizes attaching to such securities, bonds or debentures; penalty charges for late payments shall not be regarded as interest payments;

(*b*) interest accrued or capitalised at the sale, refund or redemption of the debt claims referred to in (*a*);

(*c*) income deriving from interest payments either directly or through an entity referred to in Article 4(2), distributed by:

(i) an UCITS authorised in accordance with Directive 85/611/EEC,

(ii) entities which qualify for the option under Article 4(3),

(iii) undertakings for collective investment established outside the territory referred to in Article 7;

(*d*) income realised upon the sale, refund or redemption of shares or units in the following undertakings and entities, if they invest directly or indirectly, via other undertakings for collective investment or entities referred to below, more than 40% of their assets in debt claims as referred to in (*a*):

(i) an UCITS authorised in accordance with Directive 85/611/EEC,

(ii) entities which qualify for the option under Article 4(3),

(iii) undertakings for collective investment established outside the territory referred to in Article 7.

However, Member States shall have the option of including income mentioned under (*d*) in the definition of interest only to the extent that such income corresponds to gains directly or indirectly deriving from interest payments within the meaning of (*a*) and (*b*).

2. As regards paragraph 1(*c*) and (*d*), when a paying agent has no information concerning the proportion of the income which derives from interest payments, the total amount of the income shall be considered an interest payment.

3. As regards paragraph 1(*d*), when a paying agent has no information concerning the percentage of the assets invested in debt claims or in shares or units as defined in that paragraph, that percentage shall be considered to be above 40%. Where he cannot determine the amount of income realised by the beneficial owner, the income shall be deemed to correspond to the proceeds of the sale, refund or redemption of the shares or units.

4. When interest, as defined in paragraph 1, is paid to or credited to an account held by an entity referred to in Article 4(2), such entity not having qualified for the option under Article 4(3), it shall be considered an interest payment by such entity.

5. As regards paragraph 1(*b*) and (*d*), Member States shall have the option of requiring paying agents in their territory to annualise the interest over a period of time which may not exceed one year, and treating such annualised interest as an interest payment even if no sale, redemption or refund occurs during that period.

6. By way of derogation from paragraphs 1(*c*) and (*d*), Member States shall have the option of excluding from the definition of interest payment any income referred to in those provisions from undertakings or entities established within their territory where the investment in debt claims referred to in paragraph 1(*a*) of such entities has not exceeded 15% of their assets. Likewise, by way of derogation from paragraph 4, Member States shall have the option of excluding from the definition of interest payment in paragraph 1 interest paid or credited to an account of an entity referred to in Article 4(2) which has not qualified for the option under Article 4(3) and is established within their territory, where the investment of such an entity in debt claims referred to in paragraph 1(*a*) has not exceeded 15% of its assets.

The exercise of such option by a Member State shall be binding on other Member States.

7. The percentage referred to in paragraph 1(*d*) and paragraph 3 shall from 1 January 2011 be 25%.

8. The percentages referred to in paragraph 1(*d*) and in paragraph 6 shall be determined by reference to the investment policy as laid down in the fund rules or instruments of incorporation of the undertakings or entities concerned and, failing which, by reference to the actual composition of the assets of the undertakings or entities concerned.

Article 7

Territorial scope

This Directive shall apply to interest paid by a paying agent established within the territory to which the Treaty applies by virtue of Article 299 thereof.

CHAPTER II
EXCHANGE OF INFORMATION

Article 8

Information reporting by the paying agent

1. Where the beneficial owner is resident in a Member State other than that in which the paying agent is established, the minimum amount of information to be reported by the paying agent to the competent authority of its Member State of establishment shall consist of:

(*a*) the identity and residence of the beneficial owner established in accordance with Article 3;
(*b*) the name and address of the paying agent;
(*c*) the account number of the beneficial owner or, where there is none, identification of the debt claim giving rise to the interest;
(*d*) information concerning the interest payment in accordance with paragraph 2.

2. The minimum amount of information concerning interest payment to be reported by the paying agent shall distinguish between the following categories of interest and indicate:

(*a*) in the case of an interest payment within the meaning of Article 6(1)(*a*): the amount of interest paid or credited;
(*b*) in the case of an interest payment within the meaning of Article 6(1)(*b*) or (*d*): either the amount of interest or income referred to in those paragraphs or the full amount of the proceeds from the sale, redemption or refund;
(*c*) in the case of an interest payment within the meaning of Article 6(1)(*c*): either the amount of income referred to in that paragraph or the full amount of the distribution;
(*d*) in the case of an interest payment within the meaning of Article 6(4): the amount of interest attributable to each of the members of the entity referred to in Article 4(2) who meet the conditions of Articles 1(1) and 2(1);
(*e*) where a Member State exercises the option under Article 6(5): the amount of annualised interest.

However, Member States may restrict the minimum amount of information concerning interest payment to be reported by the paying agent to the total amount of interest or income and to the total amount of the proceeds from sale, redemption or refund.

Article 9

Automatic exchange of information

1. The competent authority of the Member State of the paying agent shall communicate the information referred to in Article 8 to the competent authority of the Member State of residence of the beneficial owner.

2. The communication of information shall be automatic and shall take place at least once a year, within six months following the end of the tax year of the Member State of the paying agent, for all interest payments made during that year.

3. The provisions of Directive 77/799/EEC shall apply to the exchange of information under this Directive, provided that the provisions of this Directive do not derogate therefrom. However, Article 8 of Directive 77/799/EEC shall not apply to the information to be provided pursuant to this chapter.

CHAPTER III
TRANSITIONAL PROVISIONS

Article 10

Transitional period

1. During a transitional period starting on the date referred to in Article 17(2) and (3) and subject to Article 13(1), Belgium, Luxembourg and Austria shall not be required to apply the provisions of Chapter II.

They shall, however, receive information from the other Member States in accordance with Chapter II.

During the transitional period, the aim of this Directive shall be to ensure minimum effective taxation of savings in the form of interest payments made in one Member State to beneficial owners who are individuals resident for tax purposes in another Member State.

2. The transitional period shall end at the end of the first full fiscal year following the later of the following dates:

— the date of entry into force of an agreement between the European Community, following a unanimous decision of the Council, and the last of the Swiss Confederation, the Principality of Liechtenstein, the Republic of San Marino, the Principality of Monaco and the Principality of Andorra, providing for the exchange of information upon request as defined in the OECD Model Agreement on Exchange of Information on Tax Matters released on 18 April 2002 (hereinafter the ''OECD Model Agreement'') with respect to interest payments, as defined in this Directive, made by paying agents established within their respective territories to beneficial owners resident in the territory to which the Directive applies, in addition to the simultaneous application by those same countries of a withholding tax on such payments at the rate defined for the corresponding periods referred to in Article 11(1),

— the date on which the Council agrees by unanimity that the United States of America is committed to exchange of information upon request as defined in the OECD Model Agreement with respect to interest payments, as defined in this directive, made by paying agents established within its territory to beneficial owners resident in the territory to which the Directive applies.

3. At the end of the transitional period, Belgium, Luxembourg and Austria shall be required to apply the provisions of Chapter II and they shall cease to apply the withholding tax and the revenue sharing provided for in Articles 11 and 12. If, during the transitional period, Belgium, Luxembourg or Austria elects to apply the provisions of Chapter II, it shall no longer apply the withholding tax and the revenue sharing provided for in Articles 11 and 12.

Article 11

Withholding tax

1. During the transitional period referred to in Article 10, where the beneficial owner is resident in a Member State other than that in which the paying agent is established, Belgium, Luxembourg and Austria shall levy a withholding tax at a rate of 15% during the first three years of the transitional period, 20% for the subsequent three years and 35% thereafter.

2. The paying agent shall levy withholding tax as follows:

(*a*) in the case of an interest payment within the meaning of Article 6(1)(*a*): on the amount of interest paid or credited;

(*b*) in the case of an interest payment within the meaning of Article 6(1)(*b*) or (*d*): on the amount of interest or income referred to in those paragraphs or by a levy of equivalent effect to be borne by the recipient on the full amount of the proceeds of the sale, redemption or refund;

(*c*) in the case of an interest payment within the meaning of Article 6(1)(*c*): on the amount of income referred to in that paragraph;

(*d*) in the case of an interest payment within the meaning of Article 6(4): on the amount of interest attributable to each of the members of the entity referred to in Article 4(2) who meet the conditions of Articles 1(1) and 2(1);

(*e*) where a Member State exercises the option under Article 6(5): on the amount of annualised interest.

3. For the purposes of points (*a*) and (*b*) of paragraph 2, withholding tax shall be levied pro rata to the period of holding of the debt claim by the beneficial owner. When the paying agent is unable to determine the period of holding on the basis of information in its possession, it shall treat the beneficial owner as having held the debt claim throughout its period of existence unless he provides evidence of the date of acquisition.

4. The imposition of withholding tax by the Member State of the paying agent shall not preclude the Member State of residence for tax purposes of the beneficial owner from taxing the income in accordance with its national law, subject to compliance with the Treaty.

5. During the transitional period, Member States levying withholding tax may provide that an economic operator paying interest to, or securing interest for, an entity referred to in Article 4(2) established in another Member State shall be considered the paying agent in place of the entity and shall levy the withholding tax on that interest, unless the entity has formally agreed to its name, address and the total amount of interest paid to it or secured for it being communicated in accordance with the last subparagraph of Article 4(2).

Article 12

Revenue sharing

1. Member States levying withholding tax in accordance with Article 11(1) shall retain 25% of their revenue and transfer 75% of the revenue to the Member State of residence of the beneficial owner of the interest.

2. Member States levying withholding tax in accordance with Article 11(5) shall retain 25% of the revenue and transfer 75% to the other Member States proportionate to the transfers carried out pursuant to paragraph 1 of this Article.

3. Such transfers shall take place at the latest within a period of six months following the end of the tax year of the Member State of the paying agent in the case of paragraph 1, or that of the Member State of the economic operator in the case of paragraph 2.

4. Member States levying withholding tax shall take the necessary measures to ensure the proper functioning of the revenue-sharing system.

Article 13

Exceptions to the withholding tax procedure

1. Member States levying withholding tax in accordance with Article 11 shall provide for one or both of the following procedures in order to ensure that the beneficial owners may request that no tax be withheld:

(*a*) a procedure which allows the beneficial owner expressly to authorise the paying agent to report information in accordance with Chapter II, such authorisation covering all interest paid to the beneficial owner by that paying agent; in such cases, the provisions of Article 9 shall apply;

(*b*) a procedure which ensures that withholding tax shall not be levied where the beneficial owner presents to his paying agent a certificate drawn up in his name by the competent authority of his Member State of residence for tax purposes in accordance with paragraph 2.

2. At the request of the beneficial owner, the competent authority of his Member State of residence for tax purposes shall issue a certificate indicating:

(*a*) the name, address and tax or other identification number or, failing such, the date and place of birth of the beneficial owner;
(*b*) the name and address of the paying agent;
(*c*) the account number of the beneficial owner or, where there is none, the identification of the security.

Such certificate shall be valid for a period not exceeding three years. It shall be issued to any beneficial owner who requests it, within two months following such request.

Article 14
Elimination of double taxation

1. The Member State of residence for tax purposes of the beneficial owner shall ensure the elimination of any double taxation which might result from the imposition of the withholding tax referred to in Article 11, in accordance with the provisions of paragraphs 2 and 3.

2. If interest received by a beneficial owner has been subject to withholding tax in the Member State of the paying agent, the Member State of residence for tax purposes of the beneficial owner shall grant him a tax credit equal to the amount of the tax withheld in accordance with its national law. Where this amount exceeds the amount of tax due in accordance with its national law, the Member State of residence for tax purposes shall repay the excess amount of tax withheld to the beneficial owner.

3. If, in addition to the withholding tax referred to in Article 11, interest received by a beneficial owner has been subject to any other type of withholding tax and the Member State of residence for tax purposes grants a tax credit for such withholding tax in accordance with its national law or double taxation conventions, such other withholding tax shall be credited before the procedure in paragraph 2 is applied.

4. The Member State of residence for tax purposes of the beneficial owner may replace the tax credit mechanism referred to in paragraphs 2 and 3 by a refund of the withholding tax referred to in Article 11.

Article 15
Negotiable debt securities

1. During the transitional period referred to in Article 10, but until 31 December 2010 at the latest, domestic and international bonds and other negotiable debt securities which have been first issued before 1 March 2001 or for which the original issuing prospectuses have been approved before that date by the competent authorities within the meaning of Council Directive 80/390/EEC[1] or by the responsible authorities in third countries shall not be considered as debt claims within the meaning of Article 6(1)(*a*), provided that no further issues of such negotiable debt securities are made on or after 1 March 2002. However, should the transitional period referred to in Article 10 continue beyond 31 December 2010, the provisions of this Article shall only continue to apply in respect of such negotiable debt securities:

— which contain gross-up and early redemption clauses and
— where the paying agent as defined in Article 4 is established in a Member State applying the withholding tax referred to in Article 11 and that paying agent pays interest to, or secures the payment of interest for the immediate benefit of, a beneficial owner resident in another Member State.

If a further issue is made on or after 1 March 2002 of an aforementioned negotiable debt security issued by a Government or a related entity acting as a public authority or whose role is recognised by an international treaty, as defined in the Annex, the entire issue of such security, consisting of the original issue and any further issue, shall be considered a debt claim within the meaning of Article 6(1)(*a*).

If a further issue is made on or after 1 March 2002 of an aforementioned negotiable debt security issued by any other issuer not covered by the second subparagraph, such further issue shall be considered a debt claim within the meaning of Article 6(1)(*a*).

2. Nothing in this Article shall prevent Member States from taxing the income from the negotiable debt securities referred to in paragraph 1 in accordance with their national laws.

Note—[1] OJ L 100, 17.4.1980, p. 1. Directive repealed by Directive 2001/34/EC of the European Parliament and of the Council (OJ L 184, 6.7.2001, p. 1).

CHAPTER IV

MISCELLANEOUS AND FINAL PROVISIONS

Article 16

Other withholding taxes

This Directive shall not preclude Member States from levying other types of withholding tax than that referred to in Article 11 in accordance with their national laws or double-taxation conventions.

Article 17

Transposition

1. Before 1 January 2004 Member States shall adopt and publish the laws, regulations and administrative provisions necessary to comply with this Directive. They shall forthwith inform the Commission thereof.

2. Member States shall apply these provisions from 1 January 2005 provided that:

(i) the Swiss Confederation, the Principality of Liechtenstein, the Republic of San Marino, the Principality of Monaco and the Principality of Andorra apply from that same date measures equivalent to those contained in this Directive, in accordance with agreements entered into by them with the European Community, following unanimous decisions of the Council;

(ii) all agreements or other arrangements are in place, which provide that all the relevant dependent or associated territories (the Channel Islands, the Isle of Man and the dependent or associated territories in the Caribbean) apply from that same date automatic exchange of information in the same manner as is provided for in Chapter II of this Directive, (or, during the transitional period defined in Article 10, apply a withholding tax on the same terms as are contained in Articles 11 and 12).

3. The Council shall decide, by unanimity, at least six months before 1 January 2005, whether the condition set out in paragraph 2 will be met, having regard to the dates of entry into force of the relevant measures in the third countries and dependent or associated territories concerned. If the Council does not decide that the condition will be met, it shall, acting unanimously on a proposal by the Commission, adopt a new date for the purposes of paragraph 2.

4. When Member States adopt the provisions necessary to comply with this Directive, they shall contain a reference to this Directive or be accompanied by such a reference on the occasion of their official publication. Member States shall determine how such reference is to be made.

5. Member States shall forthwith inform the Commission thereof and communicate to the Commission the main provisions of national law which they adopt in the field covered by this Directive and a correlation table between this Directive and the national provisions adopted.

Article 18

Review

The Commission shall report to the Council every three years on the operation of this Directive. On the basis of these reports, the Commission shall, where appropriate, propose to the Council any amendments to the Directive that prove necessary in order better to ensure effective taxation of savings income and to remove undesirable distortions of competition.

Article 19

Entry into force

This Directive shall enter into force on the 20th day following that of its publication in the *Official Journal of the European Union*.

Article 20

Addressees

This Directive is addressed to the Member States.

Done at Luxembourg, 3 June 2003.

ANNEX

LIST OF RELATED ENTITIES REFERRED TO IN ARTICLE 15

For the purposes of Article 15, the following entities will be considered to be a ''related entity acting as a public authority or whose role is recognised by an international treaty'':

EC Material

Entities within the European Union

Belgium	Vlaams Gewest (Flemish Region) Région wallonne (Walloon Region) Région bruxelloise/Brussels Gewest (Brussels Region) Communauté française (French Community) Vlaamse Gemeenschap (Flemish Community) Deutschsprachige Gemeinschaft (German-speaking Community)
Spain	Xunta de Galicia (Regional Executive of Galicia) Junta de Andalucía (Regional Executive of Andalusia) Junta de Extremadura (Regional Executive of Extremadura) Junta de Castilla-La Mancha (Regional Executive of Castilla-La Mancha) Junta de Castilla-León (Regional Executive of Castilla-León) Gobierno Foral de Navarra (Regional Government of Navarre) Govern de les Illes Balears (Government of the Balearic Islands) Generalitat de Catalunya (Autonomous Government of Catalonia) Generalitat de Valencia (Autonomous Government of Valencia) Diputación General de Aragón (Regional Council of Aragon) Gobierno de las Islas Canarias (Government of the Canary Islands) Gobierno de Murcia (Government of Murcia) Gobierno de Madrid (Government of Madrid) Gobierno de la Comunidad Autónoma del País Vasco/Euzkadi (Government of the Autonomous Community of the Basque Country) Diputación Foral de Guipúzcoa (Regional Council of Guipúzcoa) Diputación Foral de Vizcaya/Bizkaia (Regional Council of Vizcaya) Diputación Foral de Alava (Regional Council of Alava) Ayuntamiento de Madrid (City Council of Madrid) Ayuntamiento de Barcelona (City Council of Barcelona) Cabildo Insular de Gran Canaria (Island Council of Gran Canaria) Cabildo Insular de Tenerife (Island Council of Tenerife) Instituto de Crédito Oficial (Public Credit Institution) Instituto Catalán de Finanzas (Finance Institution of Catalonia) Instituto Valenciano de Finanzas (Finance Institution of Valencia)
Greece	Οργανισμός Τηλεπικοινωνιών Ελλάδος (National Telecommunications Organisation) Οργανισμός Σιδηροδρόμων Ελλάδος (National Railways Organisation) Δημόσια Επιχείρηση Ηλεκτρισμού (Public Electricity Company)
France	La Caisse d'amortissement de la dette sociale (CADES) (Social Debt Redemption Fund) L'Agence française de développement (AFD) (French Development Agency) Réseau Ferré de France (RFF) (French Rail Network) Caisse Nationale des Autoroutes (CNA) (National Motorways Fund) Assistance publique Hôpitaux de Paris (APHP) (Paris Hospitals Public Assistance) Charbonnages de France (CDF) (French Coal Board) Entreprise minière et chimique (EMC) (Mining and Chemicals Company)

Italy	Regions Provinces Municipalities
	Cassa Depositi e Prestiti (Deposits and Loans Fund)
[Latvia	Pašvaldibas (local governments)][1]
[Poland	gminy (communes) powiaty (districts) województwa (provinces) ązki gmin (associations of communes) iatów (association of districts) ewództw (association of provinces) sto stoleczne Warszawa (capital city of Warsaw) ncja Restrukturyzacji i Modernizacji Rolnictwa (Agency for Restructuring and Modernisation Agriculture) Agencja Nieruchomoœci Rolnych (Agricultural Property Agency)][1]
Portugal	Região Autónoma da Madeira (Autonomous Region of Madeira) Região Autónoma dos Açores (Autonomous Region of Azores) Municipalities
[Slovakia	mestá a obce (municipalities) Železnice Slovenskej republiky (Slovak Railway Company) Štátny fond cestného hospodárstva (State Road Management Fund) Slovenské elektrárne (Slovak Power Plants) Vodohospodárska výstavba (Water Economy Building Company)][1]

International entities

European Bank for Reconstruction and Development
European Investment Bank
Asian Development Bank
African Development Bank
World Bank/IBRD/IMF
International Finance Corporation
Inter-American Development Bank
Council of Europe Soc. Dev. Fund
Euratom
European Community
Corporación Andina de Fomento (CAF) (Andean Development Corporation)
Eurofima
European Coal & Steel Community
Nordic Investment Bank
Caribbean Development Bank

The provisions of Article 15 are without prejudice to any international obligations that Member States may have entered into with respect to the abovementioned international entities.

Entities in third countries

Those entities that meet the following criteria:

1. the entity is clearly considered to be a public entity according to the national criteria;

2. such public entity is a non-market producer which administers and finances a group of activities, principally providing non-market goods and services, intended for the benefit of the community and which are effectively controlled by general government;

3. such public entity is a large and regular issuer of debt; 4. the State concerned is able to guarantee that such public entity will not exercise early redemption in the event of gross-up clauses.

Amendments—[1] Entries inserted by Council Directive 2004/66/EC art 1, Annex, Part V para 2 (OJ L 168; 1.5.2004 p 35).

Council Directive of 3 June 2003 on a common system of taxation applicable to interest and royalty payments made between associated companies of different Member States

(2003/49/EC)

Note—Published in OJ L 157/49 26.6.2003.

The council of the european union,

Having regard to the Treaty establishing the European Community, and in particular Article 94 thereof,

Having regard to the proposal from the Commission[1],

Having regard to the opinion of the European Parliament[2],

Having regard to the opinion of the European Economic and Social Committee[3],

Whereas:

(1) In a Single Market having the characteristics of a domestic market, transactions between companies of different Member States should not be subject to less favourable tax conditions than those applicable to the same transactions carried out between companies of the same Member State.

(2) This requirement is not currently met as regards interest and royalty payments; national tax laws coupled, where applicable, with bilateral or multilateral agreements may not always ensure that double taxation is eliminated, and their application often entails burdensome administrative formalities and cash-flow problems for the companies concerned.

(3) It is necessary to ensure that interest and royalty payments are subject to tax once in a Member State.

(4) The abolition of taxation on interest and royalty payments in the Member State where they arise, whether collected by deduction at source or by assessment, is the most appropriate means of eliminating the aforementioned formalities and problems and of ensuring the equality of tax treatment as between national and crossborder transactions; it is particularly necessary to abolish such taxes in respect of such payments made between associated companies of different Member States as well as between permanent establishments of such companies.

(5) The arrangements should only apply to the amount, if any, of interest or royalty payments which would have been agreed by the payer and the beneficial owner in the absence of a special relationship.

(6) It is moreover necessary not to preclude Member States from taking appropriate measures to combat fraud or abuse.

(7) Greece and Portugal should, for budgetary reasons, be allowed a transitional period in order that they can gradually decrease the taxes, whether collected by deduction at source or by assessment, on interest and royalty payments, until they are able to apply the provisions of Article 1.

(8) Spain, which has launched a plan for boosting the Spanish technological potential, for budgetary reasons should be allowed during a transitional period not to apply the provisions of Article 1 on royalty payments.

(9) It is necessary for the Commission to report to the Council on the operation of the Directive three years after the date by which it must be transposed, in particular with a view to extending its coverage to other companies or undertakings and reviewing the scope of the definition of interest and royalties in pursuance of the necessary convergence of the provisions dealing with interest and royalties in national legislation and in bilateral or multilateral double-taxation treaties.

(10) Since the objective of the proposed action, namely setting up a common system of taxation applicable to interest and royalty payments of associated companies of different Member States cannot be sufficiently achieved by the Member States and can therefore be better achieved at Community level, the Community may adopt measures, in accordance with the principle of subsidiarity as set out in Article 5 of the Treaty. In accordance with the principle of proportionality, as set out in that Article, this Directive does not go beyond what is necessary in order to achieve that objective,

Note—[1] OJ C 123, 22.4.1998, p. 9.
[2] OJ C 313, 12.10.1998, p. 151.
[3] OJ C 284, 14.9.1998, p. 50.

Has adopted this directive:

Article 1

Scope and procedure

1. Interest or royalty payments arising in a Member State shall be exempt from any taxes imposed on those payments in that State, whether by deduction at source or by assessment, provided that the beneficial owner of the interest or royalties is a company of another Member State or a permanent establishment situated in another Member State of a company of a Member State.

2. A payment made by a company of a Member State or by a permanent establishment situated in another Member State shall be deemed to arise in that Member State, hereafter referred to as the ''source State''.

3. A permanent establishment shall be treated as the payer of interest or royalties only insofar as those payments represent a tax-deductible expense for the permanent establishment in the Member State in which it is situated.

4. A company of a Member State shall be treated as the beneficial owner of interest or royalties only if it receives those payments for its own benefit and not as an intermediary, such as an agent, trustee or authorised signatory, for some other person.

5. A permanent establishment shall be treated as the beneficial owner of interest or royalties:

(*a*) if the debt-claim, right or use of information in respect of which interest or royalty payments arise is effectively connected with that permanent establishment; and

(*b*) if the interest or royalty payments represent income in respect of which that permanent establishment is subject in the Member State in which it is situated to one of the taxes mentioned in Article 3(*a*)(iii) or in the case of Belgium to the ''impôt des non-résidents/belasting der niet-verblijfhouders'' or in the case of Spain to the ''Impuesto sobre la Renta de no Residentes'' or to a tax which is identical or substantially similar and which is imposed after the date of entry into force of this Directive in addition to, or in place of, those existing taxes.

6. Where a permanent establishment of a company of a Member State is treated as the payer, or as the beneficial owner, of interest or royalties, no other part of the company shall be treated as the payer, or as the beneficial owner, of that interest or those royalties for the purposes of this Article.

7. This Article shall apply only if the company which is the payer, or the company whose permanent establishment is treated as the payer, of interest or royalties is an associated company of the company which is the beneficial owner, or whose permanent establishment is treated as the beneficial owner, of that interest or those royalties.

8. This Article shall not apply where interest or royalties are paid by or to a permanent establishment situated in a third State of a company of a Member State and the business of the company is wholly or partly carried on through that permanent establishment.

9. Nothing in this Article shall prevent a Member State from taking interest or royalties received by its companies, by permanent establishments of its companies or by permanent establishments situated in that State into account when applying its tax law.

10. A Member State shall have the option of not applying this Directive to a company of another Member State or to a permanent establishment of a company of another Member State in circumstances where the conditions set out in Article 3(*b*) have not been maintained for an uninterrupted period of at least two years.

11. The source State may require that fulfilment of the requirements laid down in this Article and in Article 3 be substantiated at the time of payment of the interest or royalties by an attestation. If fulfilment of the requirements laid down in this Article has not been attested at the time of payment, the Member State shall be free to require deduction of tax at source.

12. The source State may make it a condition for exemption under this Directive that it has issued a decision currently granting the exemption following an attestation certifying the fulfilment of the requirements laid down in this Article and in Article 3. A decision on exemption shall be given within three months at most after the attestation and such supporting information as the source State may reasonably ask for have been provided, and shall be valid for a period of at least one year after it has been issued.

13. For the purposes of paragraphs 11 and 12, the attestation to be given shall, in respect of each contract for the payment, be valid for at least one year but for not more than three years from the date of issue and shall contain the following information:

(*a*) proof of the receiving company's residence for tax purposes and, where necessary, the existence of a permanent establishment certified by the tax authority of the Member State in which the receiving company is resident for tax purposes or in which the permanent establishment is situated;

(*b*) beneficial ownership by the receiving company in accordance with paragraph 4 or the existence of conditions in accordance with paragraph 5 where a permanent establishment is the recipient of the payment;

(*c*) fulfilment of the requirements in accordance with Article 3(*a*)(iii) in the case of the receiving company;

(*d*) a minimum holding or the criterion of a minimum holding of voting rights in accordance with Article 3(*b*);

(*e*) the period for which the holding referred to in (*d*) has existed.

Member States may request in addition the legal justification for the payments under the contract (eg loan agreement or licensing contract).

14. If the requirements for exemption cease to be fulfilled, the receiving company or permanent establishment shall immediately inform the paying company or permanent establishment and, if the source State so requires, the competent authority of that State.

15. If the paying company or permanent establishment has withheld tax at source to be exempted under this Article, a claim may be made for repayment of that tax at source. The Member State may require the information specified in paragraph 13. The application for repayment must be submitted within the period laid down. That period shall last for at least two years from the date when the interest or royalties are paid.

16. The source State shall repay the excess tax withheld at source within one year following due receipt of the application and such supporting information as it may reasonably ask for. If the tax withheld at source has not been refunded within that period, the receiving company or permanent establishment shall be entitled on expiry of the year in question to interest on the tax which is refunded at a rate corresponding to the national interest rate to be applied in comparable cases under the domestic law of the source State.

Article 2

Definition of interest and royalties

For the purposes of this Directive:

(*a*) the term ''interest'' means income from debt-claims of every kind, whether or not secured by mortgage and whether or not carrying a right to participate in the debtor's profits, and in particular, income from securities and income from bonds or debentures, including premiums and prizes attaching to such securities, bonds or debentures; penalty charges for late payment shall not be regarded as interest;

(*b*) the term ''royalties'' means payments of any kind received as a consideration for the use of, or the right to use, any copyright of literary, artistic or scientific work, including cinematograph films and software, any patent, trade mark, design or model, plan, secret formula or process, or for information concerning industrial, commercial or scientific experience; payments for the use of, or the right to use, industrial, commercial or scientific equipment shall be regarded as royalties.

Article 3

Definition of company, associated company and permanent establishment

For the purposes of this Directive:

(*a*) the term ''company of a Member State'' means any company:

(i) taking one of the forms listed in the Annex hereto; and

(ii) which in accordance with the tax laws of a Member State is considered to be resident in that Member State and is not, within the meaning of a Double Taxation Convention on Income concluded with a third state, considered to be resident for tax purposes outside the Community; and

(iii) which is subject to one of the following taxes without being exempt, or to a tax which is identical or substantially similar and which is imposed after the date of entry into force of this Directive in addition to, or in place of, those existing taxes:

— impôt des sociétés/vennootschapsbelasting in Belgium,
— selskabsskat in Denmark,
— Körperschaftsteuer in Germany,
— Φόρος εισοδήματος νομικών προσώπων in Greece,
— impuesto sobre sociedades in Spain,
— impôt sur les sociétés in France,
— corporation tax in Ireland,
— imposta sul reddito delle persone giuridiche in Italy,
— impôt sur le revenu des collectivités in Luxembourg,
— vennootschapsbelasting in the Netherlands,
— Körperschaftsteuer in Austria,
— imposto sobre o rendimento da pessoas colectivas in Portugal,
— yhteisöjen tulovero/inkomstskatten för samfund in Finland,
— statlig inkomstskatt in Sweden,
— corporation tax in the United Kingdom;
[— Daň z příjmù právnických osob in the Czech Republic,
— Tulumaks in Estonia,
— φόρος Εισοδηματος in Cyprus,
— Uzņemumu ienakuma nodoklis in Latvia,
— Pelno mokestis in Lithuania,
— Társasági adó in Hungary,
— Taxxa fuq l-income in Malta,
— Podatek dochodowy od osób prawnych in Poland,
— Davek od dobička pravnih oseb in Slovenia,
— Daò z príjmov právnických osôb in Slovakia][1]

(*b*) a company is an ''associated company'' of a second company if, at least:

(i) the first company has a direct minimum holding of 25% in the capital of the second company, or

(ii) the second company has a direct minimum holding of 25% in the capital of the first company, or

(iii) a third company has a direct minimum holding of 25% both in the capital of the first company and in the capital of the second company.

Holdings must involve only companies resident in Community territory.

However, Member States shall have the option of replacing the criterion of a minimum holding in the capital with that of a minimum holding of voting rights;

(*c*) the term ''permanent establishment'' means a fixed place of business situated in a Member State through which the business of a company of another Member State is wholly or partly carried on.

Amendments—[1] Entries in para (*a*)(iii) inserted by Council Directive 2004/66/EC art 1, Annex, Part V para 3(*a*) (OJ L 168; 1.5.2004 p 35).

Article 4

Exclusion of payments as interest or royalties

1. The source State shall not be obliged to ensure the benefits of this Directive in the following cases:

(*a*) payments which are treated as a distribution of profits or as a repayment of capital under the law of the source State;

(*b*) payments from debt-claims which carry a right to participate in the debtor's profits;

(*c*) payments from debt-claims which entitle the creditor to exchange his right to interest for a right to participate in the debtor's profits;

(*d*) payments from debt-claims which contain no provision for repayment of the principal amount or where the repayment is due more than 50 years after the date of issue.

2. Where, by reason of a special relationship between the payer and the beneficial owner of interest or royalties, or between one of them and some other person, the amount of the interest or royalties exceeds the amount which would have been agreed by the payer and the beneficial owner in the absence of such a relationship, the provisions of this Directive shall apply only to the latter amount, if any.

Article 5

Fraud and abuse

1. This Directive shall not preclude the application of domestic or agreement-based provisions required for the prevention of fraud or abuse.

2. Member States may, in the case of transactions for which the principal motive or one of the principal motives is tax evasion, tax avoidance or abuse, withdraw the benefits of this Directive or refuse to apply this Directive.

Article 6

[Transitional rules for the Czech Republic, Greece, Spain, Latvia, Lithuania, Poland, Portugal and Slovakia][1]

1. Greece, Latvia, Poland and Portugal shall be authorised not to apply the provisions of Article 1 until the date of application referred to in Article 17(2) and (3) of Council Directive 2003/48/EC of 3 June 2003 on taxation of savings income in the form of interest payments*. During a transitional period of eight years starting on the aforementioned date, the rate of tax on payments of interest or royalties made to an associated company of another Member State or to a permanent establishment situated in another Member State of an associated company of a Member State must not exceed 10% during the first four years and 5% during the final four years.

Lithuania shall be authorised not to apply the provisions of Article 1 until the date of application referred to in Article 17(2) and (3) of Council Directive 2003/48/EC. During a transitional period of six years starting on the aforementioned date, the rate of tax on payments of royalties made to an associated company of another Member State or to a permanent establishment situated in another Member State of an associated company of a Member State must not exceed 10%. During the first four years of the six-year transitional period, the rate of tax on payments of interest made to an associated company of another Member State or to a permanent establishment situated in another Member State must not exceed 10%; and for the following two years, the rate of tax on such payments of interest must not exceed 5%.

Spain and the Czech Republic shall be authorised, for royalty payments only, not to apply the provisions of Article 1 until the date of application referred to in Article 17(2) and (3) of Directive 2003/48/EC. During a transitional period of six years starting on the aforementioned date, the rate of tax on payments of royalties made to an associated company of another Member State or to a permanent establishment situated in another Member State of an associated company of a Member State must not exceed 10%. Slovakia shall be authorised, for royalty payments only, not to apply the provisions of Article 1 during a transitional period of two years starting on 1 May 2004.

These transitional rules shall, however, remain subject to the continued application of any rate of tax lower than those referred to in the first, second and third subparagraphs provided by bilateral

EC Material

agreements concluded between the Czech Republic, Greece, Spain, Latvia, Lithuania, Poland, Portugal or Slovakia and other Member States. Before the end of any of the transitional periods mentioned in this paragraph the Council may decide unanimously, on a proposal from the Commission, on a possible extension of the said transitional periods.

2. Where a company of a Member State, or a permanent establishment situated in that Member State of a company of a Member State:

— receives interest or royalties from an associated company of Greece, Latvia, Lithuania, Poland or Portugal,

— receives royalties from an associated company of the Czech Republic, Spain or Slovakia,

— receives interest or royalties from a permanent establishment situated in Greece, Latvia, Lithuania, Poland or Portugal, of an associated company of a Member State, or

— receives royalties from a permanent establishment situated in the Czech Republic, Spain or Slovakia, of an associated company of a Member State,

the first Member State shall allow an amount equal to the tax paid in the Czech Republic, Greece, Spain, Latvia, Lithuania, Poland, Portugal, or Slovakia in accordance with paragraph 1 on that income as a deduction from the tax on the income of the company or permanent establishment which received that income.

3. The deduction provided for in paragraph 2 need not exceed the lower of:

(*a*) the tax payable in the Czech Republic, Greece, Spain, Latvia, Lithuania, Poland, Portugal or Slovakia, on such income on the basis of paragraph 1, or

(*b*) that part of the tax on the income of the company or permanent establishment which received the interest or royalties, as computed before the deduction is given, which is attributable to those payments under the domestic law of the Member State of which it is a company or in which the permanent establishment is situated.][1]

Note—[1] See OJ L 157/38, 26.6.2003.
* OJ L 157; 26.6.2003 p 38.
Amendments—[1] Title and paras 1–3 substituted by Council Directive 2004/76/EC (OJ L 157; 30.4.2004 p 106) as amended by Corrigendum (OJ L195; 2.6.2004 p 33).

Article 7

Implementation

1. Member States shall bring into force the laws, regulations and administrative provisions necessary to comply with this Directive not later than 1 January 2004. They shall forthwith inform the Commission thereof.

When Member States adopt these measures, they shall contain a reference to this Directive or shall be accompanied by such reference on the occasion of their official publication. The methods of making such a reference shall be laid down by the Member States.

2. Member States shall communicate to the Commission the text of the main provisions of national law which they adopt in the field covered by this Directive, together with a table showing how the provisions of this Directive correspond to the national provisions adopted.

Article 8

Review

By 31 December 2006, the Commission shall report to the Council on the operation of this Directive, in particular with a view to extending its coverage to companies or undertakings other than those referred to in Article 3 and the Annex.

Article 9

Delimitation clause

This Directive shall not affect the application of domestic or agreement-based provisions which go beyond the provisions of this Directive and are designed to eliminate or mitigate the double taxation of interest and royalties.

Article 10

Entry into force

This Directive shall enter into force on the day of its publication in the *Official Journal of the European Union*.

Article 11

Addressees

This Directive is addressed to the Member States.

Done at Luxembourg, 3 June 2003.

ANNEX

LIST OF COMPANIES COVERED BY ARTICLE 3(*A*) OF THE DIRECTIVE

(*a*) Companies under Belgian law known as: ''naamloze vennootschap/société anonyme, commanditaire vennootschap op aandelen/société en commandite par actions, besloten vennootschap met beperkte aansprakelijkheid/société privée à responsabilité limitée'' and those public law bodies that operate under private law;

(*b*) companies under Danish law known as: ''aktieselskab'' and ''anpartsselskab'';

(*c*) companies under German law known as: ''Aktiengesellschaft, Kommanditgesellschaft auf Aktien, Gesellschaft mit beschränkter Haftung'' and ''bergrechtliche Gewerkschaft'';

(*d*) companies under Greek law known as: ''ανωνυμη εταιρια'';

(*e*) companies under Spanish law known as: ''sociedad anónima, sociedad comanditaria por acciones, sociedad de responsabilidad limitada'' and those public law bodies which operate under private law;

(*f*) companies under French law known as: ''société anonyme, société en commandite par actions, société à responsabilité limitée'' and industrial and commercial public establishments and undertakings;

(*g*) companies in Irish law known as public companies limited by shares or by guarantee, private companies limited by shares or by guarantee, bodies registered under the Industrial and Provident Societies Acts or building societies registered under the Building Societies Acts;

(*h*) companies under Italian law known as: ''società per azioni, società in accomandita per azioni, società a responsabilità limitata'' and public and private entities carrying on industrial and commercial activities;

(*i*) companies under Luxembourg law known as: ''société anonyme, société en commandite par actions and société à responsabilité limitée'';

(*j*) companies under Dutch law known as: ''naamloze vennootschap'' and ''besloten vennootschap met beperkte aansprakelijkheid'';

(*k*) companies under Austrian law known as: ''Aktiengesellschaft'' and ''Gesellschaft mit beschränkter Haftung'';

(*l*) commercial companies or civil law companies having a commercial form, cooperatives and public undertakings incorporated in accordance with Portuguese law;

(*m*) companies under Finnish law known as: ''osakeyhtiö/aktiebolag, osuuskunta/andelslag, säästöpankki/sparbank'' and ''vakuutusyhtiö/försäkringsbolag'';

(*n*) companies under Swedish law known as: ''aktiebolag'' and ''försäkringsaktiebolag'';

(*o*) companies incorporated under the law of the United Kingdom;

[(*p*) companies under Czech law known as: ''akciová společnost'', ''spoleènost s ruèením omezeným'', ''veøejná obchodní spoleènost'', ''komanditní spoleènost'', ''družstvo'';

(*q*) companies under Estonian law known as: ''täisühing'', ''usaldusühing'', ''osaühing'', ''aktsiaselts'', ''tulundusühistu'';

(*r*) companies under Cypriot law known as: companies in accordance with the Company's Law, Public Corporate Bodies as well as any other Body which is considered as a company in accordance with the Income tax Laws;

(*s*) companies under Latvian law known as: ''akciju sabiedriba'', ''sabiedriba ar ierobežotu atbildibu'';

(*t*) companies incorporated under the law of Lithuania;

(*u*) companies under Hungarian law known as: ''közkereseti társaság'', ''betéti társaság'', ''közös vállalat'', ''korlátolt felelõsségû társaság'', ''részvénytársaság'', ''egyesülés'', ''közhasznú társaság'', ''szövetkezet'';

(*v*) companies under Maltese law known as: ''Kumpaniji ta' Responsabilita' Limitata'', ''Socjetajiet in akkomandita li l-kapital taghhom maqsum f'azzjonijiet'';

(*w*) companies under Polish law known as: ''spólka akcyjna'', ''spólka z ograniczoną odpowiedzialnoscią'';

(*x*) companies under Slovenian law known as: ''delniška družba'', ''komanditna delniška družba'', ''komanditna družba'', ''družba z omejeno odgovornostjo'', ''družba z neomejeno odgovornostjo'';

(*y*) companies under Slovak law known as: ''akciová spoločnos'', ''spoločnost s ručením obmedzeným'', ''komanditná spoločnos'', ''verejná obchodná spoločnos'', ''družstvo''.][1]

Amendments—[1] Entries inserted by Council Directive 2004/66/EC art 1, Annex, Part V para 3(*b*) (OJ L 168; 1.5.2004 p 35).

EC Material

EXTRA-STATUTORY CONCESSIONS

CONTENTS

Note—Obsolete or repealed concessions and concessions or parts thereof not applicable to the current year are not reproduced, but are listed below in italics.
Obsolescent concessions which may have some relevance to the current year are both listed and reproduced in italics.
Concessions which have not been allocated a number by the Revenue are listed on the last page of this list and are reproduced after the numbered concessions in chronological order according to the date of the Inland Revenue Press Release in which they are published. However, concessions which were merely awaiting a number at date of going to press are listed and reproduced as A(new), B(new) etc.

A47 *House purchase loans made by life offices to staffs of insurance associations.* (obsolete)
A48 *Transfer of control and management of a partnership outside the UK.* (obsolete)
A49 Widow's pension paid to widow of Singapore nationality, resident in the UK, whose husband was a UK national employed as a Public Officer by the Government of Singapore.
A50 *Job release scheme.* (obsolete)
A51 *Repayment supplement: life assurance premium relief.* (obsolescent)
A52 *Maintenance payments: concessionary relief.* (obsolete)
A53 *Stock relief: business passing on the death of a trader.* (obsolete)
A54 *Members of Parliament: accommodation allowances and expenses.* (obsolete)
A55 Arrears of foreign pensions.
A56 Benefits in kind: the tax treatment of accommodation in Scotland provided for employees.
A57 *Suggestion schemes.* (obsolete)
A58 *Travelling and subsistence allowance when public transport disrupted.* (obsolete)
A59 *Home to work travel of severely disabled employees.* (obsolete)
A60 Agricultural workers' board and lodgings.
A61 Clergymen's heating and lighting etc expenses.
A62 *Pensions to employees disabled at work.* (obsolete)
A63 *External training courses: expenses borne by employer.* (obsolete)
A64 *External training courses: expenses borne by an employee.* (obsolete)
A65 *Workers on offshore oil and gas rigs or platforms: free transfers from or to mainland.* (obsolete)
A66 *Employees' late night journeys from work to home.* (obsolete)
A67 *Payments to employees moved to higher cost housing areas.* (obsolete)
A68 Payments out of a discretionary trust which are emoluments taxable under Schedule E.
A69 Building societies: conversion to company status.
A70 *Small gifts to employees by third parties and staff Christmas parties.* (obsolete)
A71 *Company cars: family members and shared use.* (obsolete)
A72 *Pension schemes and accident insurance policies.* (obsolete)
A73 *Lloyd's underwriters: repayment of tax withheld where there is an overall loss.* (obsolete)
A74 *Meals provided for employees.* (obsolete)
A75 *Theatrical entertainers: transition to Schedule E.* (obsolescent)
A76 *Business Expansion Scheme and Enterprise Investment Scheme: subscriber shares.* (obsolescent)
A77 *Motor mileage allowances paid to volunteer drivers.* (obsolescent)
A78 Residence in the UK: accompanying spouse.
A79 *Tax exempt special savings accounts (TESSAs).* (obsolescent)
A80 *Blanket partnership continuation elections.* (obsolete)
A81 Termination payments and legal costs.
A82 Repayment supplement to individuals resident in EC member states.
A83 *Benefits under permanent health insurance policies.* (superseded)
A84 *Allowances paid to detached national experts.* (obsolete)
A85 *Transfers of assets by employees and directors to employers and others.* (obsolete)
A86 Blind person's allowance.
A87 *Loss relief on accounts basis.* (obsolete)
A88 *Cessation adjustment where loss relief has been allowed on accounts basis.* (obsolete)
A89 *Mortgage interest relief: property used for residential and business purposes.* (obsolete)
A90 *Jobmatch pilot scheme.* (obsolete)
A91 Living accommodation provided by reason of employment.
A92 *Tax-exempt special savings accounts (TESSAs): European authorised institutions.* (obsolete)
A93 Payments from offshore trusts to minor, unmarried child of settlor: claim by settlor for credit of tax paid by trustees.
A94 Profits and losses of theatre backers (angels).
A95 Small lump sum retirement benefits schemes.
A96 Old life assurance policies: insurer stopping collection of premiums.
A97 Jobmatch programme.
A98 Cessation adjustments under self-assessment transitional rules.
A99 FSA/PIA review of sales of Freestanding Additional Voluntary Contributions Schemes (FSAVCS): tax treatment of compensation.
A100 Tax exemption for compensation paid on bank accounts owned by holocaust victims.
A101 Personal pension schemes—tax relief for contributions.
A102 Contributions to approved personal pension plans from 6 April 2001 under TA 1988 s 639 and age related allowances.
A103 Armed Forces Reservists—Revenue Approved Share Schemes and Enterprise Management Incentives (EMI)

B CONCESSIONS APPLICABLE TO INDIVIDUALS AND COMPANIES (INCOME TAX AND CORPORATION TAX)

ESCs

B52 *Sub-contractors in the construction industry scheme: the multiple turnover tests.* (obsolete)
B53 Non-residents and gains on life insurance policies.
B54 Tax relief on films, tapes and discs.
B55 *Farming losses.* (obsolete)
B56 Herd basis rules: slaughter of immature animals intended to be replacements

C CONCESSIONS APPLICABLE TO COMPANIES ETC (CORPORATION TAX AND INCOME TAX)
C1 Credit for underlying tax: dividends from trade investments in overseas companies.
C2 *Loan and money societies.* (obsolete)
C3 *Holiday clubs and thrift funds.* (obsolete)
C4 Trading activities for charitable purposes.
C5 Industrial and provident societies.
C6 *Close companies: excess of relevant income over distributions: small amounts.* (obsolete)
C7 *Close companies: interest on inter-bank loan.* (superseded)
C8 Close companies: loan creditors.
C9 Associated companies.
C10 Groups of companies: arrangements.
C11 Demergers: TA 1988 s 213(7) & (9).
C12 Retail co-operative societies: accounting periods.
C13 Agricultural co-operative associations ''second and third-tier'' associations.
C14 *Tax credit relief for foreign banks trading in the UK through branches.* (superseded)
C15 Dissolution of unincorporated associations: distributions to members.
C16 Dissolution of companies under the Companies Act 1985 s 652—distributions to shareholders.
C17 *Interest and currency swaps..* (obsolescent)
C18 *TA 1988 s 209.* (obsolete)
C19 *Stock lending by pension funds.* (obsolete)
C20 *Claims to group relief.* (obsolete)
C21 *Life insurance companies: levies under the LAUTRO (Compensation Schemes) Rules.* (obsolete)
C22 *Building societies.* (obsolete)
C23 *Interest payable by banks and similar businesses.* (obsolete)
C24 *General insurance business: claims and elections.* (obsolete)
C25 *Long term insurance business: claims and elections.* (obsolete)
C26 *Interest payable in the UK.* (obsolete)
C27 *Life assurance business: calculation of investment return and profits.* (obsolescent)
C28 *Connection within FA 1996 s 87.* (obsolete)
C29 *Transfers of long- term insurance business: transitional relief for losses incurred in general annuity business.* (obsolete)
C30 Authorised unit trusts and open-ended investment companies: waivers of distributions.
C31 Scientific research associations.
C32 Interest relief—companies with tax and NIC liabilities under the personal service rules where the payments for relevant contracts have been received after deduction of tax by virtue of the Construction Industry Scheme (CIS) provisions

D CONCESSIONS RELATING TO CAPITAL GAINS (INDIVIDUALS AND COMPANIES)
(A19 also applies for the purposes of capital gains tax)
D1 *Insurance recoveries: short leases.* (obsolete)
D2 Residence in the UK: year of commencement or cessation of residence.
D3 Private residence exemption: periods of absence (*a*).
D4 Private residence exemption: periods of absence (*b*).
D5 Private residence exemption: property held by personal representatives.
D6 Private residence exemption: separated couples.
D7 *Retirement relief: business passing to spouse.* (obsolete)
D8 Retirement relief: change in business during ten years before disposal.
D9 Retirement relief: directors of groups of companies.
D10 Unquoted shares acquired before 6 April 1965: disposal following reorganisation of share capital.
D11 Retirement relief: asset owned by a director and used by the company.
D12 Close companies: apportionments of income and the consequentials for capital gains tax: close companies in liquidation.
D13 Retirement relief: sale of assets in anticipation of liquidation.
D14 Retirement relief: sale of assets following cessation of trading.
D15 Relief for the replacement of business assets: unincorporated associations.
D16 Relief for the replacement of business assets: repurchase of the same asset.

D17 Unit trusts for exempt unit holders—TCGA 1992 s 100(2).
D18 Default on mortgage granted by vendor.
D19 Replacement of buildings destroyed.
D20 Private residence exemption: residence occupied by dependent relative.
D21 Private residence exemption: late claims in dual residence cases.
D22 Relief for the replacement of business assets: expenditure on improvements to existing assets.
D23 Relief for the replacement of business assets: partition of land on the dissolution of a partnership.
D24 Relief for the replacement of business assets: assets not brought immediately into trading use.
D25 Relief for the replacement of business assets: acquisition of an interest in an asset already used for the purposes of a trade.
D26 Relief for exchanges of joint interests.
D27 *Earn-outs.* (obsolete)
D28 *Assets of negligible value.* (obsolete)
D29 *Transfers of long-term business under Insurance Companies Act 1982 s 49.* (obsolete)
D30 *Relief for the replacement of business assets.* (obsolete)
D31 *Retirement relief: date of disposal.* (obsolete)
D32 Transfer of a business to a company.
D33 Capital gains tax on compensation and damages.
D34 Rebasing and indexation: shares held at 31 March 1982.
D35 Employee trusts: transfers of assets to beneficiaries.
D36 *Relief for irrecoverable loans to traders: time limits for claims.* (obsolete)
D37 Private residence exemption: relocation arrangements.
D38 *Capital Gains Tax: qualifying corporate bonds.* (obsolescent)
D39 Extension of leases.
D40 Non-resident trusts: definition of participator.
D41 *Non-resident trusts: loans repayable on demand.*
D42 Mergers of leases.
D43 *Settled property.* (obsolescent)
D44 Rebasing and indexation: shares derived from larger holdings held at 31 March 1982.
D45 Rollover into depreciating assets.
D46 *Relief against income for capital losses on the disposal of unquoted shares in a trading company.* (obsolete)
D47 Temporary loss of charitable status due to reverter of school and other sites
D48 *Retirement relief.* (obsolete)
D49 Private residence relief: short delay by owner-occupier in taking up residence.
D50 Treatment of compensation.
D51 Transfers of assets from a close company at undervalue.
D52 Share exchanges, company reconstructions and amalgamations: incidental costs of acquisition and warranty payments.
D53 TCGA 1992 s 50: grants repaid.

ADDITIONAL NOTES

Working rule agreements

Statements of Practice

A CONCESSIONS APPLICABLE TO INDIVIDUALS (INCOME TAX AND INTEREST ON TAX)

A1 *Flat rate allowances for cost of tools and special clothing*

Commentary—*Simon's Direct Tax Service* **E4.706.**
Notes—This concession was classified as obsolete by IR 1 (January 2004). It has been enacted in ITEPA 2003 s 367.

A2 *Meal vouchers*

Commentary—*Simon's Direct Tax Service* **E4.432.**
Revenue internal guidance—Employment Income manual, EIM 02650 (General, including how to pay an employee's tax liability on the excess value of meal vouchers).
Note—This concession was classified as obsolete by IR 1 (January 2004). It has been enacted in ITEPA 2003 s 89.

A3 *Pensions to police officers and firemen*

Note—This concession has been superseded by Concession A62 (now obsolete).

A4 *Travelling expenses of directors and employees earning £8,500 a year or more (See also Inland Revenue Tax Bulletin February 1995, page 196)*

The general rule is that the cost to a UK resident taxpayer of travelling to and from his UK place of business is not allowable as a deduction in computing his tax liability; consequently, the full amount of an allowance paid by a company to a director or senior employee in respect of such expenses is chargeable to tax under the benefits code (formerly TA 1988 Part V Ch II). The rule is modified in the following types of case—

(*a*) A director (whether whole or part-time) of two or more companies within a group of parent and subsidiary or associated companies, whether or not entitled to separate remuneration from each of the companies of which he is a director, is regarded as having one place at which he normally acts as a director of companies within the group, and is entitled to a deduction (or a notice of nil liability under ITEPA 2003 s 65 (formerly TA 1988 s 166(1), (2)) for expenses necessarily incurred in travelling within the UK from that place to other places on the business of the group in the course of his duties as a director. The same principle is applied to an individual who is an employee of one company and a director of another company within the same group of companies. (By ''associated company'' is meant a company on whose board the group is represented because of the group's shareholding or other financial interest.)

(*b*) A director who gives services without remuneration to a company not managed with a view to dividends (eg a company owning a hall or sports ground, or running a club) is not treated as assessable in respect of any travelling expenses paid to him.

(*c*) Where a directorship is held as part of a professional practice (and not, for example, because of some direct or indirect financial interest in the company), expenses incurred by the director in carrying out his duties are allowed as deductions in assessing the profits of the practice under Schedule D, whether the practice is carried on alone or in partnership. Reasonable expenses paid to the director by the company are accordingly not assessed upon the director under Schedule E, provided no claim is made to a deduction under Schedule D.

(*d*) Where a director, or an employee who is paid at the rate of £8,500 a year or more, goes abroad on a business journey and, although fit to carry out his duties at his normal place of work, takes his wife with him because his health is so precarious that he cannot undertake foreign travel unaccompanied, no charge is made in respect of expenses of the wife which may be borne by the employer.

''Travelling expenses'' includes in all cases reasonable hotel expenses necessarily incurred.

Commentary—*Simon's Direct Tax Service* **E4.708, 710.**
Revenue Interpretation RI 105—Concession applies regardless of residence status of individual concerned.
Note—The text of this concession is as it appears in IR 1 (January 2004).

A5 *Expenses allowances and benefits in kind*

Note—This concessionary relief was replaced by statutory relief under TA 1988 ss 191A, 191B, Sch 11A, except for certain employees who had entered into a firm commitment to move before 6 April 1993 and actually started to work at the new location before 1 August 1993. A5 was classified as obsolete by IR 1 (August 2002).

A6 *Miners: free coal and allowances in lieu*

Commentary—*Simon's Direct Tax Service* **E4.464.**
Note—This concession was classified as obsolete by IR 1 (January 2004). It has been enacted in ITEPA 2003 s 306.

A7 *Business or other source of income passing on the death of a husband or wife*

Note—This concession was classified as obsolete by IR 1 Supp (November 2000).

A8 *Loss relief for capital allowances unused on the cessation of a business*

Note—This concession was classified as obsolescent by IR 1 Supp (1995) and as obsolete by IR 1 Supp (November 1998). It is obsolete with effect from 1997/98 with the repeal of TA 1988 s 383 by FA 1994 s 214(1)(*b*).

A9 *Doctors' and dentists' superannuation contributions*

Under TA 1988 s 594, contributions required to be made in pursuance of a public general Act of Parliament by the holder of an office or employment towards the provision of superannuation benefits may be deducted in assessing his general earnings (his emoluments prior to April 2003). This section is in practice treated as extending to assessments under Schedule D on the profits of a medical or dental practitioner who is required to make superannuation contributions in pursuance of National Health Service Acts. Where, however, the practitioner also pays premiums or contributions towards a retirement annuity within TA 1988 ss 619 et seq, a restriction is imposed either on the amount of the deduction for his statutory contribution or on the amount of retirement annuity relief allowable.

For 1980–81 onwards, concessionary relief is allowable on either of the following bases.

Either practitioners may have relief on the amount of their NHS contributions together with a relief on the amount of any retirement annuity premium in relation to their non-NHS earnings. For this purpose—

(*a*) Non-NHS earnings are taken as the amount of net relevant earnings (as defined in TA 1988 s 623) less the sum produced by multiplying the amount of the NHS contributions by $16\frac{2}{3}$.

(*b*) Retirement annuity relief will be allowable within the normal limit of 17.5 per cent (or the higher percentages for older contributors) of the non-NHS earnings plus any unused relief for earlier years. For this purpose unused relief should be calculated on the appropriate concessional basis for years in which relief has been allowed on NHS contributions.

Or, practitioners may have relief on the amount of their NHS contributions together with relief on any retirement annuity premiums paid up to the amount of the largest premium on which tax relief was allowed for any of the three years 1969–70 to 1971–72 but with a restriction, if necessary, to keep the total relief (on NHS contributions and retirement annuity premiums) within the pre-1971–72 limits for retirement annuity relief of 10 per cent of net relevant earnings or £750—or the higher limits permitted to older people. Any surplus of premiums paid over the amount allowable on this basis will not be available for carry-forward.

Finally, practitioners may, instead, have relief on a statutory basis. In this case, they would take retirement annuity relief, up to the limits appropriate for a particular year, on their full net relevant earnings (ie including NHS earnings). But in that event no concessionary relief would be available in respect of NHS contributions.

Commentary—*Simon's Direct Tax Service* **B4.112; E7.322A.**
Note—The text of this concession is as it appears in IR 1 (January 2004).

A10 *Lump sums paid under overseas pension schemes*

Income tax is not charged on lump sum relevant benefits receivable by an employee (or by his personal representatives or any dependant of his) from an overseas retirement benefits scheme or an overseas provident fund where the employee's overseas service comprises—

(*a*) not less than 75 per cent of his total service in that employment; or

(*b*) the whole of the last 10 years of his service in that employment, where total service exceeds 10 years; or

(*c*) not less than 50 per cent of his total service in that employment, including any 10 of the last 20 years, where total service exceeds 20 years.

If an employee's overseas service is less than described above, relief from income tax will be given by reducing the amount of the lump sum which would otherwise be chargeable by the same proportion as the overseas service bears to the employee's total service in that employment.

In addition, income tax is not charged on lump sum relevant benefits receivable by an employee (or by his personal representatives or any dependant of his) from any superannuation fund accepted as being within TA 1988 s 615(6).

For the purposes of this concession the term "relevant benefits" has the meaning given in TA 1988 s 612 and the term "overseas service" shall be construed in accordance with the definition of "foreign service" found at ITEPA 2003 s 413(2) (formerly TA 1988 Sch 11 para 9(2)).

Commentary—*Simon's Direct Tax Service* **E7.267.**
Note—The text of this concession is as it appears in IR 1 (January 2004).

A11 *Residence in the UK: year of commencement or cessation of residence*

The Income and Corporation Taxes Acts make no provision for splitting a tax year in relation to residence and an individual who is resident in the UK for any year of assessment is chargeable on the basis that he is resident for the whole year.
But where an individual—

(*a*) comes to the UK to take up permanent residence or to stay for at least two years; or
(*b*) ceases to reside in the UK if he has left for permanent residence abroad,

liability to UK tax which is affected by residence is computed by reference to the period of his residence here during the year. It is a condition that the individual should satisfy the Board of Inland Revenue that prior to his arrival he was, or on his departure is, not ordinarily resident in the UK. The concession would not apply, for example, where an individual who had been ordinarily resident in the UK left for intended permanent residence abroad but returned to reside here before the end of the tax year following the tax year of departure.

This concession is extended to the years of departure and return where, subject to certain conditions, an individual goes abroad under a contract of employment. These conditions are—

– the individual's absence from the UK and the employment itself both extend over a period covering a complete tax year; and
– any interim visits to the UK during the period do not amount to—
  (i) 183 days or more in any tax year; or
  (ii) an average of 91 days or more in a tax year (the average is taken over the period of absence up to a maximum of four years); and
– for years up to and including 1992–93, all the duties of the employment are performed abroad or any duties the individual performs in the UK are incidental to duties abroad.

Where the concession applies and the tax year is split, FA 1995 s 128 (limit on income chargeable on non-residents—income tax) does not apply for the period for which an individual is treated as not resident. That section only applies to complete years of non-residence.

Commentary—*Simon's Direct Tax Service* **E4.117; E6.120, 122.**
Cross references—See Revenue Interpretation RI 40 (interpretation of the term "full-time").

A12 *Double taxation relief: alimony, etc under UK court order or agreement; payer resident abroad*

Where alimony or maintenance payments are paid under a UK court order or agreement, the income arises from a UK source regardless of the country of residence of the payer. Notwithstanding that the source is in law a UK source, relief by way of credit is, however, allowed where—

(*a*) the individual making the payments has left the UK and become resident in an overseas country;
(*b*) the payments are made out of that individual's income in that country and are subject to tax there;
(*c*) UK income tax if deducted from the payments is duly accounted for; and
(*d*) the payee is resident in the UK and effectively bears the overseas tax.

Commentary—*Simon's Direct Tax Service* **E5.112; F2.106.**

A13 *Administration of estates: deficiencies of income allowed against income of another year*

Note—This concession was superseded by FA 1995 Sch 18 para 4.

ESCs

A14 *Deceased person's estate: residuary income received during the administration period*

A beneficiary who for a year of assessment is not resident or not ordinarily resident in the UK, and is deemed under TA 1988 s 695(4) or s 696(4) to have received income from a UK estate in that year, may claim to have their tax liability on that income from the estate adjusted to what it would be if such income had arisen to them directly and as a result they—

- could claim relief under TA 1988 s 278 (claim to personal reliefs by certain non residents); or
- could claim entitlement to exemption in respect of FOTRA Securities issued in accordance with FA 1996 s 154; or
- could claim relief under the terms of a double taxation agreement; or
- would not have been chargeable to income tax.

Relief or exemption, as appropriate, will be granted to the beneficiary only if the personal representatives of the estate—

- have made estate returns for each and every year for which they are required, and
- have paid all tax due and any interest, surcharges and penalties arising, and
- keep available for inspection any relevant tax certificates, together with copies of the estate accounts for all years of the period of administration showing details of all sources of estate income and payments made to beneficiaries.

Relief or exemption, as appropriate, will be granted to the beneficiary on a claim made within five years and ten months of the end of the year of assessment in which the beneficiary is deemed to have received the income.

No tax will be repayable to the beneficiary in respect of income they are deemed to have received where that income, if received by a UK resident beneficiary of an estate, would fall within the definition of ''a relevant amount'' for the purposes of TA 1988 s 699A.

Commentary—*Simon's Direct Tax Service* **C4.110.**
Note—The text of this concession is as it appears in IR 1 (January 2000).

A15 *Dependent relative allowance*

Note—This concession has been classified as obsolete.

A16 *Annual payments (other than interest) paid out of income not brought into charge to income tax*

When a person deducts tax from annual payments (including annuities) and the payer does not have sufficient income charged to income tax to cover the payment, he has to pay the tax over to the Revenue (TA 1988 ss 349(1), 350(1)).

Where—

- an annual payment is made in a tax year later than the one in which the payment was due to be made,
- in the year it is made the payer does not have sufficient income charged to income tax to cover the payment,
- the payer is an individual

but

- in the year the payment was due the payer *did* have sufficient income charged to income tax to cover the payment,

an allowance is made, in fixing the amount to be paid over to the Inland Revenue, equal to the tax which the payer would have been entitled to deduct and keep if the payment had been made at the due dates.

If hardship would otherwise be caused, a similar allowance is made in the case of a trust or other non-trading institution not within the charge to corporation tax making such an annual payment out of the taxed income of past years.

Commentary—*Simon's Direct Tax Service* **A3.406, 411; E1.312.**
Note—The text of this concession is as it appears in IR 1 (January 2000).

A17 *Death of taxpayer before due date for payment of tax and other liabilities*

TMA 1970 s 86 provides for interest to be charged on the late payment of certain duties.

Where a taxpayer dies before a charge becomes due and his executors or administrators cannot pay the duty before they obtain probate or letters of administration, the relevant due date will be the later of—

– the normal due date; or
– 30 days from the grant of probate or letters of administration.

Commentary—*Simon's Direct Tax Service* **A3.1325.**
Note—The text of this concession is as it appears in IR 1 (January 2004).

A18 *Change of accounting basis on the merger of professional firms*

Note—This concession has been classified as obsolete.

A19 *Giving up tax where there are Revenue delays in using information*

Arrears of income tax or capital gains tax may be given up if they result from the Inland Revenue's failure to make proper and timely use of information supplied by—

– a taxpayer about his or her own income, gains or personal circumstances;
– an employer, where the information affects a taxpayer's coding; or
– the Department for Work & Pensions, about a taxpayer's State retirement, disability or widow's pension.

Tax will normally be given up only where the taxpayer—

– could reasonably have believed that his or her tax affairs were in order; and
– was notified of the arrears more than 12 months after the end of the tax year in which the Revenue received the information indicating that more tax was due, or
– was notified of an over-repayment after the end of the tax year following the year in which the repayment was made.

In exceptional circumstances arrears of tax notified 12 months or less after the end of the relevant tax year may be given up if the Revenue—

– failed more than once to make proper use of the facts they had been given about one source of income;
– allowed the arrears to build up over two whole tax years in succession by failing to make proper and timely use of information they had been given.

Commentary—*Simon's Direct Tax Service* **A3.1314.**

A20 *Cessation of trade, profession or vocation*

Note—This concession has been classified as obsolete.

A21 *Schedule A: deferred repairs: property passing from husband to wife (or vice versa) on death*

Note—This concession was withdrawn with effect from 6 April 1995.

A22 *Long service awards*

Note—This concession was classified as obsolete by IR 1 (January 2004). It has been enacted in ITEPA 2003 s 323.

A23 *Non-domiciled employees of non-resident concerns: reimbursed travelling expenses between overseas country and UK*

Note—This concession was superseded by FA 1986 s 37 (see now TA 1988 s 195).

A24 *Foreign social security benefits*

Commentary—*Simon's Direct Tax Service* **E4.129, 328, 329.**
Notes—This concession was classified as obsolete by IR 1 (January 2004). It has been enacted in ITEPA 2003 ss 645, 681.

ESCs

A25 *Crown servants engaged overseas*

Commentary—*Simon's Direct Tax Service* **E4.122, E6.131.**
Note—This concession was classified as obsolete by IR 1 (January 2004). It has been enacted in ITEPA 2003 s 28.

A26 *Sick benefits*

Note—This concession has been classified as obsolete.

A27 *Mortgage interest relief: temporary absence from mortgaged property*

Under the provisions of TA 1988 ss 354, 355, tax relief for interest paid on a mortgage is given where the loan is applied for the purchase of a property which, at the time the interest is paid, is used as the only or main residence of the borrower.

Temporary absences of up to a year are in practice ignored in determining whether a property is used as an only or main residence. In addition where a person is required by reason of his employment to move from his home to another place, either in the UK or abroad, for a period not expected to exceed four years, any property being purchased with the aid of a mortgage which was being used as his only or main residence before he went away, will still be treated as his only or main residence, provided it can reasonably be expected to be so used again on his return. Where a person has acquired an estate or interest in a property, for example by exchange of contracts, but is prevented by his move from occupying it as his home, he will nevertheless be regarded as having used the property as his home for the purposes of the concession. Relief will not be given beyond a period of four years but if there is a further temporary absence after the property has been reoccupied for a minimum period of three months, the four year test will apply to the new absence without regard to the previous absence.

Where a person by reason of his office or employment has moved his home abroad and that office or employment is an office or employment of the type specified in TA 1988 s 132(4)(a) (certain offices and employments under the Crown), then any property being purchased with the aid of a mortgage which has been used as his only or main residence before he went away will still be treated as his only or main residence, provided it can reasonably be expected to be so used again on his return.

If an individual already on an overseas tour of duty purchases a property in the UK in the course of a leave period and uses that property as an only or main residence for a period of not less than three months before his return to the place of his overseas employment he will be regarded as satisfying the condition that the property was being used as his only or main residence before he went away.

If an individual lets his property while he is absent the benefit of the concession may be claimed, where appropriate, if this is more favourable than claiming a deduction in computing the profits or losses of a Schedule A business.

Commentary—*Simon's Direct Tax Service* **A3.432; E1.535.**
Note—This concession has been classified as obsolescent by IR 1 Supp (November 2000).

A28 *Mortgage interest relief: residents of the Republic of Ireland*

Note—This concession has been rendered obsolete by FA 1994 s 81.

A29 *Farming and market gardening: relief for fluctuating profits*

For the purposes of the averaging provisions in TA 1988 s 96, ''farming'' includes the intensive rearing of livestock or fish on a commercial basis for the production of food for human consumption.

Commentary—*Simon's Direct Tax Service* **B3.541.**

A30 *Interest on damages for personal injuries (foreign court awards)*

TA 1988 s 329 exempts from income tax interest on damages awarded by a court in the UK for personal injuries or the death of any person. This exemption is extended to interest on damages awarded in corresponding circumstances by a foreign court provided the interest is exempt from tax in the country in which the award is made.

Commentary—*Simon's Direct Tax Service* **B5.210.**

A31 *Life assurance premium relief by deduction: pre-marriage policies: premium relief after divorce*

TA 1988 Sch 14 para 1(1) provides for life assurance premium relief to continue after divorce in respect of premiums paid by one party on the life of the other if they were married when the policy was taken out but were divorced after 5 April 1979. By concession this treatment is extended to premiums paid by a divorced person on a policy which was taken out prior to the marriage.

Commentary—*Simon's Direct Tax Service* **E2.1043.**
Note—This concession was classified as obsolescent by IR 1 Supp (1992).
Life assurance premium relief was abolished for policies taken out after 13 March 1984.

A32 *Tax relief for life assurance premiums: position of certain pension schemes which are unapproved after 5 April 1980*

TA 1970 s 19(4)(b) (which allowed life assurance premium relief on certain non-qualifying policies) and s 393(2)(b) (which protected the policyholder from any tax charge on policy gains) were repealed with effect from 6 April 1980 as part of the series of measures introducing the new tax code for superannuation. The result is that premium relief may not be available for 1980–81 and future years and there may be a charge to tax on the surrender etc of the policy. In order to continue the protection afforded by these provisions the Inland Revenue will continue to give relief as though they were still in force. The concession will not apply in the case of a policy issued in connection with a retirement benefit scheme established after 5 April 1980.

Commentary—*Simon's Direct Tax Service* **E2.1032, E3.502.**
Note—This concession was classified as obsolescent by IR 1 Supp (1990).

A33 *Lump sum retirement benefits: changes after 5 April 1980*

Lump sum benefits from "closed" or "frozen" pension schemes which have not sought approval under FA 1970 may continue to enjoy the exemption from tax as employment income under ITEPA 2003 Part 2 (and under Schedule E prior to April 2003) which ceased with the repeal of TA 1970 Chap II, Part IX with effect from 6 April 1980.

Commentary—*Simon's Direct Tax Service* **A7.271.**
Note—The text of this concession is as it appears in IR 1 (January 2003). This concession was classified as obsolescent by IR 1 Supp (1990).

A34 *Ulster savings certificates: certificates encashed after death of registered holder*

Accumulated interest on Ulster savings certificates held by persons resident and domiciled in Northern Ireland is exempt from income tax (TA 1988 s 46). Where repayment is made after the death of the holder exemption is allowed if the deceased was resident and domiciled in Northern Ireland at the time of purchase.

Commentary—*Simon's Direct Tax Service* **A7.912.**
Note—This concession was classified as obsolescent by IR 1 Supp (November 1998).

A35 *Mortgage interest relief: year of marriage*

Note—This concession was superseded by FA 1993 s 57 from 16 March 1993 and was classified as obsolete by IR 1 (1993).

A36 *Close companies in liquidation: distributions in respect of share capital*

Note—Close company apportionment rules were abolished by FA 1989. This concession has been classified as obsolescent by IR 1 Supp (November 2000).

A37 *Tax treatment of directors' fees received by partnerships and other companies*

1 Where fees are received in respect of directorships held by members of a professional partnership they are in strictness assessable on the individual partners under employment income (formerly Schedule E). It is however the practice of the Revenue to accede to a request from the partnership for the inclusion of the fees in the Schedule D assessment provided that—

(*a*) the directorship is a normal incident of the profession and of the particular practice concerned;
(*b*) the fees are only a small part of the profits; and
(*c*) under the partnership agreement the fees are pooled for division among the partners.

Partnerships seeking such treatment are expected to provide the Revenue with a written undertaking that directors' fees received in full will be included in the gross income or receipts of the basis period, whether or not the directorship is still held in the year of assessment and whether or not the partner concerned is still a partner.

2 It is also the practice of the Revenue that, where a company has the right to appoint a director to the board of another company, by virtue of its shareholdings in, or a formal agreement with, the second company then, provided the director is required to hand over to the first company any fees or other earnings received in respect of his directorship with the second company and does so, and the first company is chargeable to corporation tax and agrees to accept liability on the fees, those fees are treated as income of the company and not of the director, and tax is not deducted from the fees under PAYE. Where the first company is chargeable not to corporation tax but to income tax (for example, if it is a non-resident company not trading through a branch or agency in the UK) and agrees to accept liability, tax is deducted at the basic rate of income tax from the fees.

3 With effect from 6 April 1980, the practice described in the previous paragraph will be extended to the case where the first company has no formal right to appoint the director to the board but the director is nevertheless required to (and does) hand over his fees to that company, provided it is—

(*a*) a company resident in the UK liable to UK corporation tax or, if non-resident, is trading through a branch or agency in the UK so that its income is chargeable to corporation tax under TA 1988 s 11 and the fees are included in that income; and
(*b*) not a company over which the director has control. (For this purpose "control" has the meaning given to it by [TA 1988 s 840], but in determining whether the company is controlled by the director the rights and powers of his spouse, his children and their spouses and his parents will also be taken into account.)

Commentary—*Simon's Direct Tax Service* **E4.211, 403; E5.311.**
Revenue internal guidance—Company taxation manual, COT 175, 176 (operation of the concession).
Employment income manual, EIM 02500, 02501 (issue of an "NT" coding for the following income tax year where the conditions of paragraph 1 are satisfied).
Note—The text of this concession is as it appears in IR 1 (January 2004).

A38 *Retirement annuity relief: death and disability benefits*

Where an individual is treated as in pensionable employment solely because provision is made under a scheme or arrangement existing on 14 October 1980 fully or partly at the cost of the employer, for a benefit in pension form payable only on death or disability, the employment will be treated as non-pensionable for any tax year in which the individual has not become entitled to benefit as a result of that provision. In accordance with the provisions of TA 1988 s 619(4), the individual will be entitled to pay a retirement annuity premium in the following tax year and, within that same year to elect to have it related back for tax purposes to the previous year, and set against the earnings from the employment for that year subject to the limits on relief in force.

Relief will be available on a year to year basis for the period of employment or until benefit becomes payable as a result of death or disability. The employment in the tax year in which such a contingency occurs will be regarded as pensionable and retirement annuity relief will not be available for that year, but no attempt will be made to recover retirement annuity relief already given for earlier years in the same employment.

Commentary—*Simon's Direct Tax Service* **E7.302.**
Note—This concession was classified as obsolescent by IR 1 Supp (1991).
This concession only applies to persons who hold retirement annuity contracts made before 1 July 1988.

A39 *Exemption for Hong Kong officials: extension of TA 1988 s 320 relief*

Note—This concession was classified as obsolete by IR 1 Supp (November 1998). It is replaced with effect from 1 July 1997 by the Hong Kong Economic and Trade Office (Exemptions and Reliefs) Order, SI 1997/1334.

A40 *Adoption allowances payable under the Adoption Allowance Regulations 1991 and Adoption (Scotland) Act 1978 s 51*

Income tax is not charged on adoption allowances paid under the provisions of the Adoption Allowance Regulations 1991 or schemes approved by the Secretary of State for Scotland under Adoption (Scotland) Act 1978 s 51.

Commentary—*Simon's Direct Tax Service* **B7.202.**

A41 *Qualifying life assurance policies: statutory conditions*

Life assurance policies which contain minor technical infringements of the qualifying conditions in TA 1988 Sch 15 cannot strictly be treated as qualifying. Similarly, under TA 1988 Sch 15 para 21(1), policies in respect of insurances made on or after 1 April 1976 (or varied on or after that date) are not qualifying policies unless they have been certified as such by the Board, or conform to a certified standard form.

In certain circumstances, the Board may be prepared by concession to relax the strict statutory conditions. These relaxations are as follows—

(*a*) where, under TA 1988 Sch 15 para 1(8), the commencement date of a policy is back-dated by not more than three months, for the purposes of testing varied or substituted policies under para 17(2) of the same Schedule, calculating the chargeable event period under TA 1988 s 540(1) and applying the ''clawback'' provisions of TA 1988 ss 268–270, the earlier date will be treated as the date on which the assurance is made;

(*b*) a reduction in premium level in the first year of a policy will not be regarded as a significant variation, provided that the reduction leads to an appropriate reduction in the sum assured and that any excess of premium is used to pay further premiums within the first year of the policy or returned to the policyholder or retained by the insurer, with no value being credited to the policyholder;

(*c*) certain trivial infringements of the qualifying rules may be disregarded. In such cases, the insurer will be required to give written confirmation that all reasonable steps have been taken to ensure that such errors will not be repeated; and

(*d*) a policy in respect of an insurance made on or after 1 April 1976 (or varied on or after that date) which has not been certified by the Board, but which is capable of certification, may be certified as a qualifying policy from the date when the insurance was made (or the policy varied) and any premium relief already given will normally not be recovered. Uncertified policies which are not capable of being certified will normally be regarded as non-qualifying policies from commencement or, where appropriate, the time at which uncertifiable wording was added.

Commentary—*Simon's Direct Tax Service* **E2.1036, 1037, 1041, 1042, 1051, 1052.**

A42 *Chargeable events: loans to policyholders*

Note—This concession was classified as obsolescent by IR 1 Supp (1992) and obsolete by IR 1 Supp (November 1998). Retirement annuity contracts ceased to be available from 1 July 1988.

A43 *Interest relief—investments in partnerships, co-operatives, close companies, and employee-controlled companies*

1 Under TA 1988 ss 360–363, income tax relief is available for interest paid by an individual on a loan taken out to invest in, or on-lend to, a partnership, a co-operative, a close company, or an employee-controlled company. The relief is subject to various conditions, and ceases to be available when those conditions are no longer met.

2 Relief is also reduced or withdrawn (following s 363) if the borrower recovers any capital from the business without using it to repay the loan—for example by selling or exchanging the interest or shares in that business. Strictly, therefore, relief ceases to be due where—

(*a*) a partnership is incorporated into a co-operative, a close company, or an employee-controlled company; or

(*b*) shares in a co-operative, a close company, or an employee-controlled company are exchanged for, or replaced by, shares in any one of these kinds of company; or

(*c*) there is a partnership reconstruction involving a merger or demerger.

3 Under the terms of this concession, relief for interest on a loan to an individual will not be discontinued in the three kinds of circumstances described above where, in relation to that individual, the conditions for relief would have been met if the loan had been a new loan taken out by that person to invest in the new business entity. The rules restricting or withdrawing relief where the borrower recovers any capital from the business continue to apply in the normal way.

Commentary—*Simon's Direct Tax Service* **E1.548–551.**

A44 *Education allowances under Overseas Service Aid Scheme*

Income tax will not be charged on certain education allowances payable to officers in the public service of certain overseas territories where, as part of an agreement under the Overseas Service Aid Scheme, the UK Government has undertaken to exempt such allowances from UK income tax.

Commentary—*Simon's Direct Tax Service* **E4.325.**

A45 *Life assurance policies: variation of term assurance policies*

If under a term assurance for a term of 10 years or less—

(*a*) the original sum assured is reduced to less than half; or

(*b*) the term is extended to cover an additional period (but the total term is still not more than 10 years);

any resulting reduction in the rate of premium to less than half is not treated as leading to the disqualification of the policy under the rules set out in TA 1988 Sch 15 paras 17(2)(*b*) and 18.

Commentary—*Simon's Direct Tax Service* **E2.1041.**

A46 *Variable purchased life annuities: carry forward of excess of capital element*

If, in the case of a purchased life annuity to which TA 1988 s 656 applies, the amount of an annuity payment depends on a contingency other than the duration of a human life or lives, and the capital element determined in accordance with the provisions of that section exceeds the amount of that payment, then the excess may be carried forward for allowance as an addition to the capital element in the next following payment or payments.

Commentary—*Simon's Direct Tax Service* **B5.314.**

A47 *House purchase loans made by life offices to staffs of insurance associations*

Under TA 1988 s 548, a loan made by a life office to a policyholder in connection with a life policy is normally treated for tax purposes in the same way as a surrender of rights under the policy. This does not, however, apply where (inter alia) the policy is a qualifying life policy and the loan was made before 6 April 2000 by the life office to one of its own full-time employees to buy a house. By concession, the same may apply for such a loan by a life office to a full-time employee of certain insurance associations whose function is to serve the insurance market.

Commentary—*Simon's Direct Tax Service* **B7.515.**
Note—This concession was classified as obsolescent by IR 1 Supp (November 2000).

A48 *Transfer of control and management of a partnership outside the UK*

Note—This concession was classified as obsolete as a result of the abolition of stock relief by FA 1984 s 48.

A49 *Widow's pension paid to widow of Singapore nationality, resident in the UK, whose husband was a UK national employed as a Public Officer by the Government of Singapore*

TA 1988 ss 614, 615 exempt from tax certain overseas pensions, including pensions paid by the UK Government to non-residents in respect of public service with the governments of former colonies. TA 1988 s 616 extends this relief to UK residents, in receipt of pensions transferred to the care of the UK Government, by the Governments of Zambia, Malawi and Trinidad and Tobago. This subsection should be extended to exempt from tax widows' pensions paid to widows of Singapore nationality, who are resident in the UK and whose husbands were UK nationals employed in the service of the Government of Singapore.

Commentary—*Simon's Direct Tax Service* **E4.314.**

A50 *Job release scheme*

Note—This concession has been classified as obsolete.

A51 *Repayment supplement: life assurance premium relief*

The repayment supplement provisions of TA 1988 s 824 are to apply as if the payments were repayments of income tax where:—

(a) excessive clawback under TA 1988 ss 268 and 269 is payable to an individual, or

(b) relief not obtained by deduction has been claimed and payment is made under TA 1988 Sch 14 para 6(1).

Commentary—*Simon's Direct Tax Service* **A3.615.**
Note—This concession was classified as obsolescent by IR 1 Supp (1990).

A52 *Maintenance payments: concessionary relief*

Note—This concession has been classified as obsolete.

A53 *Stock relief: business passing on the death of a trader*

Note—This concession was classified as obsolete as a result of the abolition of stock relief by FA 1984 s 48.

A54 *Members of Parliament: accommodation allowances and expenses*

Note—This concession was made as a transitional arrangement and is now obsolete.

A55 *Arrears of foreign pensions*

Note—This concession was classified as obsolete by IR 1 (January 2004). It has been enacted in ITEPA 2003 ss 575(2)(C), 613(3).

A56 *Benefits in kind: the tax treatment of accommodation in Scotland provided for employees*

1 ITEPA 2003 s 102 (formerly TA 1988 s 145) charges to tax in certain circumstances the benefit of living accommodation provided by reason of a person's employment. The charge is based either on the rent paid by the person providing the accommodation, or the property's ''annual value'' if greater, less any amount made good by the employee.

2 Annual value is defined in ITEPA 2003 s 110 (formerly TA 1988 s 837) in terms similar to the definition of ''gross value'' for rating purposes in the General Rate Act 1967. In practice, therefore, a property's gross rateable value may be taken as its annual value for ITEPA 2003 ss 105, 106 (formerly TA 1988 s 145) purposes where the property is situated in the UK.

3 To avoid unfairness as between taxpayers in different parts of the UK, the Revenue will not assess the benefit arising on property in Scotland in accordance with the 1985 Scottish rating revaluation figures while the future of rating revaluations is under consideration.

4 Instead, the existing 1978 valuations will form the basis of assessment for existing properties for 1985–86 and 1986–87. For 1987–88 and subsequent years and for new properties the Revenue will scale back the 1985 figures by the average increase in rateable values in Scotland between 1978 and 1985 (170 per cent); (for example a 1985 gross rateable value of £270 will be reduced to £100 for the purposes of s 33).

Commentary—*Simon's Direct Tax Service* **E4.613.**
Note—The text of this concession is as it appears in IR 1 (January 2004).

A57 *Suggestion schemes*

Commentary—*Simon's Direct Tax Service* **E4.330, 471.**
Revenue internal guidance—Employment income manual EIM 06600 (suggestion scheme awards—general).
Notes—This concession was classified as obsolete by IR 1 (January 2004). It has been enacted in ITEPA 2003 ss 321, 322.

A58 *Travelling and subsistence allowance when public transport disrupted*

Commentary—*Simon's Direct Tax Service* **E4.441, 612, 805FA.**
Revenue internal guidance—Employment Income manual EIM 10100–10120 (travelling and subsistence payments—disruption to public transport caused by strike—general).
Notes—This concession was classified as obsolete by IR 1 (January 2004). It has been enacted in ITEPA 2003 s 245.

A59 *Disabled persons' home to work travel*

Commentary—*Simon's Direct Tax Service* **E4.328.**
Note—This concession was classified as obsolete by IR 1 (January 2004). It has been enacted in ITEPA 2003 ss 246, 247.

A60 *Agricultural workers' board and lodgings*

Income tax will not be charged on the value of free board and lodging provided for agricultural workers by their employers despite any entitlement to take a higher cash wage in lieu provided by the Agricultural Wages Acts, where all the following conditions are satisfied—

(*a*) the worker is not a director and is in lower-paid employment as defined at ITEPA 2003 s 217(1);

(*b*) the contract with the employer provides for a net cash wage with free board and lodgings;

(*c*) where the board and lodging is not provided in the farmhouse, the employer has a contract with a third party for its provision and payments under the contract are made direct to the third party.

Where instead of being entitled to a net cash wage and free board and lodgings, the worker is entitled to a gross cash wage, he is assessable on the gross amount, even if the employer, with his agreement, deducts a sum to pay for his board and lodgings in the farmhouse or elsewhere.

Commentary—*Simon's Direct Tax Service* **E4.441, 986.**
Note—The text of this concession is as it appears in IR 1 (January 2004).

A61 *Clergymen's heating and lighting etc expenses*

Where a clergyman or minister of any religious denomination is provided, in consequence of his being the holder of such office, with a residence in premises owned or leased by a charity or ecclesiastical corporation from which to perform his duties, no tax is charged on sums paid on his behalf or reimbursed in respect of heating, lighting, cleaning and gardening expenses which are the contractual liability of the clergyman or minister.

Where an allowance is paid to the clergyman etc to meet such costs it will not be taxed except to the extent that it exceeds the costs actually incurred.

The concession does not apply where the clergyman or minister is not in lower-paid employment as defined at ITEPA 2003 s 217(1).

Commentary—*Simon's Direct Tax Service* **E4.412, 712.**
Note—The text of this concession is as it appears in IR 1 (January 2004).

A62 *Pensions to employees disabled at work*

Note—This concession was classified as obsolete by IR 1 (January 2004). It has been enacted in ITEPA 2003 s 644.

A63 *External training courses: expenses borne by employer*

Note—This concession was superseded by TA 1988 ss 200B—200D which were introduced by FA 1997 s 63 with effect from 1997/98. This concession was classified as obsolete by IR 1 Supp (November 1998).

A64 *External training courses: expenses borne by an employee*

Note—This concession has been classified as obsolete by IR 1 Supp (November 2000).

A65 *Workers on offshore oil and gas rigs or platforms: free transfers from or to mainland*

Note—This concession was classified as obsolete by IR 1 (January 2004). It has been enacted in ITEPA 2003 s 305.

A66 *Payments for employees journeys home: late night travel and breakdown in car sharing arrangements*

Notes—This concession was classified as obsolete by IR 1 (January 2004). It has been enacted in ITEPA 2003 s 248.

A67 *Payments to employees moved to higher cost housing areas*

Note—This concession was withdrawn with effect from 6 April 1993 and replaced by the statutory relief under TA 1988 ss 191A, 191B, Sch 11A, except for certain employees who had entered into a firm commitment to move before 6 April 1993 and started work at the new location before 2 August 1993. A67 was classified as obsolete by IR 1 (August 2002).

A68 *Payments out of a discretionary trust which are emoluments taxable under Schedule E*

Employee trusts are discretionary trusts created by funds provided by employers for the benefit of their employees, past, present or future, or for the benefit of any dependants or relations of such employees. Where a payment made by the trustees in exercise of any discretion is treated as an emolument assessable to tax under Schedule E, TA 1988 s 687(2) does not operate to give the recipient credit for the tax at the rate suffered by the trustees. This means the payment is effectively taxed twice.

Subject to a claim by the trustees and the conditions set out below, a payment will be made to them equal to the lesser of—

(*a*) tax on the total payments made in any year of assessment which are treated as emoluments in that way; the rate of tax being the rate applicable to trusts in force for that year, and

(*b*) the total tax which the trustees would have available under s 687(3) to set against any payments made in that year to which s 687(2) applied (so far as not already allowed), the "tax pool".

The conditions are that the trustees must—

– have submitted, for each year for which tax has entered the "tax pool", a return of all trust income received and all payments made to beneficiaries,
– supply evidence that they have paid (by deduction or otherwise) tax of at least the amount to be paid to them, and
– agree that the "tax pool" should be reduced by the amount to be paid.

As the payment is compensation for the lack of a credit to the employees under s 687(2)(*a*), no repayment supplement will be added to it.

Commentary—*Simon's Direct Tax Service* **C4.226.**

A69 *Building societies: conversion to company status*

When a building society converts to company status under the Building Societies Act 1986, certificates of non-liability to tax and declarations by investors given or made prior to conversion which satisfy the conditions of the Income Tax (Building Societies) (Dividends and Interest) Regulations 1990, will be treated as having been given or made to the successor company.

Commentary—*Simon's Direct Tax Service* **D4.771.**

A70 *Small gifts to employees by third parties and staff Christmas parties*

Commentary—*Simon's Direct Tax Service* **E4.464, 805FA.**
Notes—This concession was classified as obsolete by IR 1 (January 2004). It has been enacted in ITEPA 2003 ss 264, 270 and 324.

A71 *Company cars: family members and shared use*

Commentary—*Simon's Direct Tax Service* **E4.625.**
Notes—This concession was classified as obsolete by IR 1 (January 2004). It has been enacted in ITEPA 2003 ss 148, 169.

A72 *Pension schemes and accident insurance policies*

Commentary—*Simon's Direct Tax Service* **E4.612.**
Note—This concession was classified as obsolete by IR 1 (January 2004). It has been enacted in ITEPA 2003 s 307.

A73 *Lloyd's Underwriters: repayment of tax withheld where there is an overall loss*

Note—This concession is now obsolete as a result of the Lloyd's Underwriters (Schedule 19A to the Income and Corporation Taxes Act 1988) Regulations, SI 1990/2524 which amended TA 1988 Sch 19A para 2A with effect for 1988–89 and subsequent years of assessment and is now superseded by FA 1993 Sch 19 para 13 with effect for 1992–93 and subsequent years of assessment.

A74 *Meals provided for employees*

Commentary—*Simon's Direct Tax Service* **E4.441, 612.**
Notes—This concession was classified as obsolete by IR 1 (January 2004). It has been enacted in ITEPA 2003 ss 367.

A75 *Theatrical entertainers: transition to Schedule E*

The earnings of theatrical entertainers were before 6 April 1990 generally taxed under Schedule D. But ''standard contracts'', which are widely used for theatrical engagements are generally contracts of employment and the earnings from them are properly taxable under employment income (formerly Schedule E). From 6 April 1990 earnings from engagements under ''standard contracts'', which are contracts of employment, and from other contracts of employment, are taxed under employment income (formerly Schedule E) except where a theatrical entertainer can claim reserved Schedule D status in accordance with the conditions below. In such cases income from theatrical performances, under ''standard contracts'' or under any other contract of employment, will continue to be taxed under Schedule D.

Entertainers qualify for reserved Schedule D status where one of the following conditions is satisfied either—

– *Schedule D assessments have been made in respect of income from engagements as a theatrical entertainer for at least the three tax years 1986–87, 1987–88 and 1988–89, and an assessment for at least one of those years has been based on accounts or a return of income for that year submitted before 31 May 1989,*

or

– *Schedule D assessments have been made in respect of income from engagements as a theatrical entertainer for at least three of the years 1979–80 to 1988–89 provided that—*
– *there has been a satisfactory history of Schedule D treatment, and*
– *accounts or returns of income for all relevant years up to and including 1986–87 were submitted before 31 May 1989, and*
– *the entertainer's last theatrical engagement which started before 6 April 1990 was dealt with under Schedule D (whether or not it ended before that date).*

These conditions mean that a theatrical entertainer starting in the profession after 5 April 1987 cannot qualify for reserved Schedule D status.

Entertainers qualifying for reserved Schedule D status will only be assessed under Schedule D so long as they continue to meet their tax obligations satisfactorily, and continue their professional activities without a break. If, following a break, professional activities are resumed, employment income treatment will apply to any income from a contract of employment.

For the purposes of this concession—

– *''standard contract'' means a standard contract agreed between theatrical employers and the British Actors Equity Association (Equity),*
– *''theatrical entertainer'' means an actor, singer, dancer, musician or other theatrical entertainer, and includes stage managers,*
– *''break'' in professional activities means a cessation agreed under the Schedule D rules between the Inland Revenue and the theatrical entertainer.*

This concession was announced, in a letter to Associations representing theatrical entertainers and employers, on 25 June 1989.

Note—The text of this concession is as it appears in IR 1 (January 2004).

A76 *Business expansion scheme and enterprise investment scheme: subscriber shares*

Commentary—*Simon's Direct Tax Service* **E3.107, 214.**
Note—This concession is withdrawn for shares issued after 5 April 1998 further to the changes introduced by FA 1998 Sch 13 para 8(1) (IR Press Release 30-11-98). It was classified obsolete by IR 1 Supp (November 1998).

A77 *Motor mileage allowances paid to volunteer drivers*

Commentary—*Simon's Direct Tax Service* **B7.202.**
Note—This concession is of no application for 1995/96 and later years. It was classified as obsolete by IR 1 Supp (November 1998).

A78 *Residence in the UK: accompanying spouse*

1 The residence and ordinary residence status of a husband and wife is determined independently but the circumstances of one spouse may, in certain situations, be taken into account when determining the residence status of the other. This can apply when one spouse goes abroad for full-time employment, or to work full-time in a trade, profession or vocation, and is regarded as not resident and not ordinarily resident from the day following departure to the day before return. The following concession applies where an individual in this position is accompanied, or later joined, by his or her spouse who is not in full-time employment (or working full-time in a trade, profession or vocation) abroad.

2 Where the accompanying spouse is abroad for a complete tax year and interim visits to this country do not amount to—

– 183 days or more in any tax year; or
– an average of 91 days or more in a tax year (the average is taken over the period of absence up to a maximum of four years);

then the accompanying spouse's liability to UK tax which is affected by residence, for the years of departure and return at the beginning and end of the period spent abroad, will be determined by reference to the period of his or her residence here during the year.

3 For years up to and including 1992–93 a further condition applied. If accommodation in the UK was available for the accompanying spouse's use, the tax treatments set out in para 2 above would apply where no visits were made to the UK between the date of departure and the following 5 April or, for the year of return, between 6 April and the date of return.

4 In addition, for years up to and including 1992–93, the accompanying spouse who had available accommodation in the UK would be regarded as not ordinarily resident from the day after leaving the UK to the day before the date of return, provided that the absence was for three years or more and visits here averaged less than 91 days a tax year. If the absence abroad was expected to be for three years or more but was cut short because the period of the spouse's employment was terminated unexpectedly, the shorter absence might qualify for this treatment provided that it included a complete tax year and any visits to the UK averaged less than 91 days a tax year.

Commentary—*Simon's Direct Tax Service* **E6.130.**
Note—The text of this concession is as it appears in IR 1 (January 2000).

A79 *Tax exempt special savings accounts (TESSAs)*

No individual may hold a TESSA on behalf of any other person (TA 1988 s 326A(7)). In England and Wales a person holding a power of attorney may under certain circumstances apply for a TESSA on behalf of an incapacitated person in that person's name. However, in Scotland a curator bonis (an administrator appointed by the court to act generally for a person who is incapacitated) must act in his or her own name, not that of the incapacitated person.

By concession, a curator bonis (whether or not he or she already holds a TESSA in his or her own right) will be able to open a TESSA on behalf of an incapacitated person, provided that that person is aged 18 or over. But in all cases where a TESSA is opened on behalf of an incapacitated person, that person's name should also be shown on the application form. In addition, for the purposes of completing returns of information and transfer forms, where appropriate, the details provided by the bank or building society holding the account should be those of the incapacitated person, not the curator bonis.

Commentary—*Simon's Direct Tax Service* **E3.401.**
Note—The text of this concession is as it appears in IR 1 (January 2000).

A80 *Blanket partnership continuation elections*

Note—This concession has been classified as obsolete.

A81 *Termination payments and legal costs*

1 In taking legal action to recover compensation for loss of employment, employees may succeed in recovering from the former employer some or all of their legal costs. This may occur either because the employee is successful in the court action or because a settlement is reached which provides that costs be reimbursed.

2 In the Inland Revenue's view any payments made by way of recovery of costs are assessable to income tax as is the compensation which the former employer has agreed or is obliged to pay. The charge to tax arises under ITEPA 2003 ss 401–406 (formerly TA 1988 s 148). This applies to payments made directly or indirectly in connection with the termination of the holding of an office or of employment.

3 No deduction is strictly allowable for the legal costs which the former employee or office holder may incur in pursuing the former employer for wrongful dismissal.

4 However, the Inland Revenue have decided that in the following circumstances tax will not be charged on payments of costs to the former employee or office holder.

5 In cases where the dispute is settled without recourse to the courts, no charge will be imposed on payments made by the former employer—

– direct to the former employee's solicitor; and

– in full or partial discharge of the solicitor's bill of costs incurred by the employee only in connection with the termination of his or her employment; and
– under a specific term in the settlement agreement providing for that payment.

6 In cases where the dispute goes to court, no charge will be imposed on payments of costs made by the former employer, even where these are made direct to the employee, in accordance with a court order (whether this is made following judgment or compromise of the action).

7 This concession applies only to legal costs. It does not apply to other professional costs eg accountancy fees nor to legal costs incurred over and above the amount which the former employer may pay in the circumstances mentioned. Inspectors of taxes may ask to see documentary evidence in support of a claim that a payment by a former employer meets the necessary requirements as outlined above.

Commentary—*Simon's Direct Tax Service* **E4.805E.**
Revenue Interpretation RI 61—Termination payments and legal costs.
Revenue & other press releases—Law Society 3-11-93 (where the solicitor's bill relates to other matters as well as to the termination costs, the amount relating to the termination must be clearly identifiable in the bill).
Note—The text of this concession is as it appears in IR 1 (January 2004).

A82 *Repayment supplement to individuals resident in EC member states*

1 TA 1988 s 824 provides, in certain circumstances, for repayment supplement to be paid where income tax paid for a year of assessment for which an individual was resident in the UK is repaid. Under this concession, repayment supplement will also be paid where income tax paid for a year of assessment for which an individual was resident in an EC member state other than the UK is repaid, provided that the other conditions of s 824 are satisfied.

2 The concession will also apply to repayments of income tax which have been made to individuals since 12 July 1987 where the tax relates to a year of assessment for which they were resident in an EC member state other than the UK. Claims should be submitted to—

Financial Intermediaries and Claims Office, Fitz Roy House, PO Box 46, Nottingham NG2 1BD; or Claims (International), St John's House, Merton Road, Bootle, Merseyside L69 9BB.

3 The concession will also apply to partnerships, the trustees of a settlement and personal representatives within the meaning of FA 1981 s 111. This concession does not apply to other non-resident taxpayers.

Note—Under TA 1988 s 824 as amended by FA 1994 s 196, Sch 19 para 41, the payment of repayment supplement no longer depends on an individual's residence status.
The text of this concession is as it appears in IR 1 (January 2000)

A83 *Benefits under permanent health insurance policies*

Note—This concession superseded Concession A26 with effect where a policy holder first becomes entitled to certain insurance benefits after 5 April 1994, and is itself rendered obsolete by TA 1988 s 580A introduced by FA 1996 s 143(1).

A84 *Allowances paid to detached national experts*

Commentary—*Simon's Direct Tax Service* **E5.406.**
Note—This concession was classified as obsolete by IR 1 (January 2004). It has been enacted in ITEPA 2003 s 304.

A85 *Transfers of assets by employees and directors to employers and others (see also Inland Revenue Tax Bulletin April 1995)*

Commentary—*Simon's Direct Tax Service* **E4.613.**
Revenue Interpretation RI 112—Relocation packages and guaranteed selling price schemes.
Revenue internal guidance—Employment income manual EIM 03127 (Removal or transfer costs: sale of property to employer).
Note—This concession was classified as obsolete by IR 1 (January 2004). It has been enacted in ITEPA 2003 s 326.

A86 *Blind person's allowance*

When a person becomes entitled to the blind person's allowance by being included on a register compiled under the National Assistance Act 1948 s 29, then he or she shall (subject to the normal time limits for claims) also be given the blind person's allowance for the previous year if, at the end of that previous year, he or she had already obtained evidence of blindness (such as an ophthalmologist's certificate) upon which the registration was subsequently based.

Commentary—*Simon's Direct Tax Service* **E2.801.**
Note—The text of this concession is as it appears in IR 1 (January 2000).

A87 *Loss relief on accounts basis*

Note—This concession was classified obsolete by IR 1 Supp (November 1998).

A88 *Cessation adjustment where loss relief has been allowed on accounts basis*

Note—This concession was classified obsolete by IR 1 Supp (November 1998).

A89 *Mortgage interest relief: Property used for residential and business purposes*

Where tax relief for interest paid on a loan to buy the borrower's home is given under the provisions of TA 1988 s 353 no deduction is allowed for any of the interest on the loan in a computation of profits or losses for the purposes of a Schedule A or Schedule D Case I or II business (see s 368(4)). Conversely, where a deduction is allowed under Schedule A or Schedule D Case I or II no relief can be claimed under s 353 (see s 368(3)). By concession, however, relief for interest on a loan to buy a property used for both residential and business purposes in the circumstances set out below may be allowed in part under s 353 and in part as a deduction in computing profits or losses.

Similarly, where tax relief for interest paid on a loan to buy the borrower's home is given under the provisions of TA 1988 s 369—the mortgage interest relief at source (MIRAS) arrangements—no deduction is allowed for any of the interest on the loan in a computation of profits or losses for the purposes of a Schedule A or Schedule D Case I or II business (see s 369(3)). By concession, however, relief for interest on a loan to buy property used for both residential and business purposes in the circumstances set out below may be allowed in part under the MIRAS arrangements and in part as a deduction in computing profits or losses, provided the interest on the loan is "relevant loan interest" within the terms of s 370.

The circumstances in which this concession applies are as follows.

Where a part of a property, which is the borrower's only or main residence, is used exclusively for business purposes the loan in question may be apportioned on the basis of the proportion of the property so used. Mortgage interest relief may then be claimed for the interest on the part of the loan attributable to residential use and a deduction may be allowed for the interest on the part of the loan attributable to business use.

Where a part of a property, which is the borrower's only or main residence, is only sometimes used for business purposes (but for a significant amount of time and then exclusively) the loan in question may be apportioned on any reasonable basis that takes account of both the proportion of the property so used and the duration of such use. Mortgage interest relief may then be claimed for the interest on the part of the loan attributable to residential use and a deduction may be allowed for the interest on the part of the loan attributable to business use.

Commentary—*Simon's Direct Tax Service* **E1.526.**
Note—This concession has been classified as obsolescent by IR 1 Supp (November 2000).

A90 *Jobmatch pilot scheme*

Note—This concession has been classified as obsolete.

A91 *Living accommodation provided by reason of employment*

This concession applies to living accommodation treated as earnings under ITEPA 2003 Part 3, Chapter 5. Where ITEPA 2003 s 106 applies and the cash equivalent of the benefit of the accommodation is calculated by reference to the annual rent the property might fetch on the open market, the Inland Revenue will disregard "the additional yearly rent". If "the additional yearly rent" is disregarded then the amount of "the excess rent" is deemed to be nil.

Commentary—*Simon's Direct Tax Service* **E4.412, 413.**
Note—This concession is as shown in IR 1 (January 2004).

A92 *Tax-exempt special savings accounts (TESSAs): European authorised institutions*

Note—This Concession was classified as obsolete by IR 1 (August 2002).

ESCs

A93 *Payments from offshore trusts to minor, unmarried child of settlor: Claim by settlor for credit of tax paid by trustees*

Income arising to a trust within the scope of TA 1988 s 686 is charged to tax on the trustees at the rate applicable to trusts or the Schedule F trust rate. Where such income is distributed to or for the benefit of an unmarried minor child, of the settlor, it is treated as the income of the settlor and becomes chargeable on them for the year in which it is distributed under TA 1988 s 660B.

TA 1988 s 687 provides for the settlor of a resident trust to be given full credit against tax due from them under s 660B for tax paid by the trustees at the rate applicable to trusts in respect of income distributed. TA 1988 s 687 does not, however, apply where the trustees exercise their discretion outside the UK. The settlor of such a trust could therefore be liable to tax under s 660B without being able to claim credit against their liability for any tax paid by the trustees.

By concession, the settlor will be able to claim credit against their liability to tax under s 660B for tax paid by the trustees, as if the payments out of UK income were from a UK resident trust. This will apply to the extent that the distribution is made out of income which arose to the trustees not earlier than six years before the end of the year of assessment in which the distribution was paid.

For this purpose, the distribution will be treated as having been made rateably out of the total of the various sources of income arising to the trustees on a last in first out basis. Credit will be given to the settlor for the tax paid by the trustees on the income to the extent that—

- the distribution is regarded as being made from income chargeable to UK tax; and
- such income has not previously been allocated to earlier distributions on a last in, first out basis.

This concession will only apply where the trustees—

- have made trust returns, giving details of all sources of trust income and payments made to beneficiaries for each and every year for which they are required; and
- have paid all tax due, and any interest, surcharges and penalties arising; and
- keep available for inspection any relevant tax certificates.

Credit will be granted to the settlor on a claim made within five years and ten months of the end of the year of assessment in which the beneficiary received the payment from the trustees.

No credit will be given for UK tax treated as paid on income received by the trustees which would not be available for set-off under s 687(2) if that section applied, and that tax is not repayable (for example on dividends). However, such tax is not taken into account in calculating the gross income treated as taxable on the settlor under this concession.

Commentary—*Simon's Direct Tax Service* **C4.315.**
Note—The text of this concession is as it appears in IR 1 (January 2000).

A94 *Profits and losses of theatre backers (angels)*

An individual who backs a theatrical production, except where such backing activity forms part of a trade or profession within the theatre industry, is a theatre ''angel''. If the show is successful, the money is first repaid, and then the angel receives a share of any profit. If the show fails, the angel may lose not only the hope of a return on the money but also all or part of the original investment. Any return a theatre angel receives over and above the original investment is strictly assessable under Schedule D Case III, and the capital gains tax rules apply to losses.

Despite the strict rules, UK resident angels may, in respect of any particular transaction, treat profits as Schedule D Case VI profits, and losses as Schedule D Case VI losses. Where this concessionary treatment is given, any loss in respect of that transaction cannot also qualify as a capital loss.

Unincorporated payers who make payments liable under Schedule D Case III have the right, but usually no obligation, to deduct tax. Incorporated payers will always have an obligation to deduct tax. The Revenue will not however insist on deduction of tax from payments to theatre angels for their theatrical investments if the angel's usual place of abode is in the UK. Payers who do exercise their right to deduct tax under TA 1988 s 349(1) must account to the Revenue for the tax.

Commentary—*Simon's Direct Tax Service* **B7.204.**

A95 *Small lump sum retirement benefits schemes*

Where a person—

- has paid contributions in, or for, any year of assessment to a retirement annuity contract or to a personal pension scheme out of general earnings chargeable to tax as employment income under ITEPA 2003 Part 2 (formerly under Schedule E) from an office or employment, or out of income from any property which is attached to or forms part of those general earnings; and
- has, for the same year of assessment and in respect of the same office or employment accrued lump sum retirement benefits under a relevant lump sum retirement benefits scheme;

any tax relief given for the contributions paid by that person to the retirement annuity contract or personal pension scheme will not be withdrawn provided that, under the rules of the relevant lump sum retirement benefits scheme, for the period in question—

- he or she waives entitlement to the lump sum retirement benefits; or
- no lump sum retirement benefits accrue; and
- the retirement annuity contract or the arrangements under the personal pension scheme are not cancelled.

For these purposes a relevant lump sum retirement benefits scheme means a retirement benefits scheme which is approved as an exempt approved scheme under TA 1988 Part XIV Chap I; and

- under the rules of which the only benefit which may be provided on retirement (other than benefits from any additional voluntary contributions) is a lump sum which does not exceed £400 for each year of pensionable service; and
- whose rules provide for no such lump sum to accrue (or for that lump sum to be waived) in respect of any period for which the person has paid contributions to a retirement annuity contract or to a personal pension scheme.

References to contributions paid by a person should be taken to include any made by an employer (for the benefit of that person) to a personal pension scheme.

Commentary—*Simon's Direct Tax Service* **E7.406.**
Cross reference—See TA 1988 ss 623(2)(*a*), 644(3) (relief for retirement annuity premiums and personal pension contributions denied where earnings are from pensionable employment).
Note—The text of this concession is as it appears in IR 1 (January 2004).

A96 *Old life insurance policies: insurer stopping collection of premiums*

An alteration to the terms of a life assurance policy may have the effect in contract law of varying the terms of the policy or may result in the replacement of the policy (the "old policy") by a new substitute policy (the "new policy"). The result may be that charges to tax can arise on later events such as the maturity or surrender of the policy under the special regime for taxing gains on life assurance policies (TA 1988 Part XIII Ch II) that would not have arisen in the absence of the alteration. This may be because the policy ceases to be a "qualifying policy", or because the original policy was entirely outside the scope of the regime. Similarly a new policy will often not be a qualifying policy.

By concession and for the purposes of TA 1988 Part XIII Ch II or Sch 15 only, no account will be taken of an alteration if *all* of the following conditions are satisfied—

- the alteration is not itself a "chargeable event" as defined at TA 1988 s 540(1); and
- the alteration results from a decision by the insurer that it will not collect further premiums from any of the holders of a number of policies of the same type provided that a specified period of time has elapsed since the policies were taken out; and
- no premiums are payable or paid after the date of the alteration; and
- the benefits to be provided under the policy after the alteration (which may be a varied policy or a "new policy" depending on the nature of the alteration) are substantially equivalent to those which the policy holder would have enjoyed if no alteration had been made. The benefits will be regarded as substantially equivalent if they are unchanged or if they are unchanged apart from a deduction to take account of the unpaid premiums. This should not exceed the amount of the premiums which would have been payable between the date of the alteration and the date on which the benefits become payable, as reduced by any tax relief which would have been due on the premiums had they been paid; and
- the premiums payable under the policy have not been reduced to a nominal amount (and cannot be so reduced in future) on the exercise of an option, if that reduction is connected with a right to make partial surrenders of the rights conferred by the policy after the date of the reduction; and
- the policy is in respect of an insurance made at least 20 years prior to the date of the alteration.

Commentary—*Simon's Direct Tax Service* **E2.1041.**

A97 *Jobmatch programme*

Income tax is not charged on payments made under the Department for Education and Employment's Jobmatch programme, nor in respect of training vouchers received by participants under the terms of the programme.

Note—The text of this concession is as it appears in IR 1 (January 2000).

ESCs

A98 *Cessation adjustments under self-assessment transitional rules*

This concession applies to trades, professions or vocations which cease trading in 1997–98 and 1998–99 and to which the transitional rules in FA 1994 Sch 20 apply.

Where a business ceases trading in 1997–98 or 1998–99 and an officer of the Board subsequently directs, under FA 1994 Sch 20 para 3, that the liability for 1995–96 and/or 1996–97 should be revised, the revisions could result, in certain circumstances, in a backdated interest charge under TMA 1970 s 86. The interest may arise on the additional profits charged as a result of the direction, and as a result of the consequential effect such additions have on the payments on account for the year following any such revision.

It was not intended that interest charges should be backdated in this way, following an FA 1994 Sch 20 para 3 direction. So s 86 interest will not normally be sought—

- where adjustments are made to the 1996–97 liability as the result of a cessation in 1997–98 or 1998–99;
- where adjustments are made to 1996–97 payments on account because of an adjustment to the 1995–96 liability resulting from a cessation in 1997–98;
- where adjustments are made to 1997–98 payments on account because of an adjustment to the 1996–97 liability resulting from a cessation in 1997–98 or 1998–99.

This concession does not apply to the interest on any additional profits attributable to the correction of any error or omission by the taxpayer, or to adjustments to 1995–96 and 1996–97 following a discovery by an officer of the Board. Nor does it apply to interest on tax paid late resulting from the additional profits brought into charge as a result of the cessation adjustments once the amount of the adjustment and the additional tax payable thereon are known.

The concession does not apply to mandatory adjustments to earlier years, following a cessation in 1996–97.

Under self-assessment interest is charged automatically on any tax paid late, including any additional tax due when the profits for earlier years are revised. But in the circumstances described above the additional tax is only due as a result of a discretion exercised, by the Revenue, after all the relevant returns have been filed. The purpose of this concession is to prevent those people who cease trading during the early years of self-assessment and whose liability for earlier years is subsequently revised as a result of the discretionary transitional rules, being charged interest on overdue tax on either their revised liability or their payments on account as a result of those adjustments.

This concession does not in any way alter or fetter an Inspector's right to issue a direction.

Commentary—*Simon's Direct Tax Service* **A3.1321.**

A99 *FSA/PIA review of sales of freestanding additional voluntary contributions schemes (FSAVCS)—tax treatment of compensation*

1 The Financial Services Authority/Personal Investment Authority (FSA/PIA) issued a policy statement on 28 February 2000 which required a review of specified categories of FSAVCS sold during the period beginning with 28 April 1988 and ending with 15 August 1999. Guidance for the performance of the review was issued by the FSA.

2 A payment within para 3 below which is made as a result of a review of an FSAVC covered by the FSA/PIA policy statement and FSA guidance will not be chargeable to income tax. Nor will the receipt of such payment be regarded for the purposes of capital gains tax as the disposal of an asset.

3 (*a*) The payment is a capital sum by way of compensation which has been determined in accordance with the FSA guidance for the performance of the review.

(*b*) The payment is interest on the whole or part of the capital sum described at (*a*) for a period ending on or before the earliest date on which the capital sum was determined.

Commentary—*Simon's Direct Tax Service* **E7.221.**

Note—The text of this concession is as it appears in IR 1 Supp (November 2000).

A100 *Tax exemption for compensation paid on bank accounts owned by holocaust victims*

Under income tax law, compensation payments made in respect of dormant bank and building society accounts normally represent interest, and are therefore strictly subject to the Tax Deduction Scheme for Interest. That means such interest would generally be paid by a bank or building society net of tax to an individual investor unless the individual:

- is a UK non-taxpayer and has completed a registration form R85 to that effect and handed it to his or her bank or building society; or
- is not ordinarily resident in the UK and a declaration to that effect on form R105 has been obtained by the bank or building society.

Furthermore, death duties (estate duty, capital transfer tax, or inheritance tax, as appropriate) are potentially chargeable on UK account balances at death (even if the accountholder had no other UK connection).

Under an initiative called ''Restore UK'', and announced on 8 May 2000 by the British Bankers' Association, compensation is being paid by banks on unclaimed accounts opened by Holocaust victims and frozen during World War II under the Trading with the Enemy Act 1939. Where the investor of the monies in the unclaimed account was a Holocaust victim, the banks have said they will make an exceptional up-rating payment.

No tax will be payable on any monies paid out by banks or building societies under the ''Restore UK'' initiative to Holocaust victims or their beneficiaries. This exemption will cover income tax liabilities on any compensation payments made on or after 8 May 2000 under the scheme, as well as death duties in respect of the capital held in the accounts.

Commentary—*Simon's Direct Tax Service* **A3.405, B5.222.**
Note—The text of this Concession is as it appears in IR 1 Supp (November 2001).

A101 *Personal pension schemes—tax relief for contributions*

1 TA 1998 s 639 provides the rules for giving tax relief on members' contributions to approved personal pension schemes. It has been amended by FA 2000 Sch 13 para 15 for contributions made in the tax year 2001–02 and subsequent tax years. The new s 639(3) provides for a member to obtain relief at the basic rate by deducting from his or her payment to the scheme administrator an amount equal to basic rate tax on the payment. The new subsection (5A) provides that the basic rate limit is increased by the amount of the payment where the member—

(*a*) is liable to income tax at the higher rate on any income for the tax year in which the payment is made; or
(*b*) would be so liable if the adjustment were not made.

The consequence is that an additional amount of income is charged at the basic rate instead of the higher rate, so that the member obtains relief at the higher rate on some or all of the payment.

2 The rules in s 639 as amended do not, however, provide for any relief to be obtained on the payment at the higher rate where the member, although not liable to any income tax at the higher rate in the tax year in question, would be liable to some capital gains tax at the higher rate in that year. This will happen in any case where the member's income is below the basic rate limit, but some capital gains tax would be charged at the higher rate in accordance with TCGA 1992 s 4. In order that these members should not be disadvantaged by the new rules, the adjustment to the basic rate limit provided by TA 1988 s 639(5A) will also apply in respect of any member who—

(*a*) is liable to capital gains tax at the higher rate on any chargeable gains for the tax year in which the payment in question is made; or
(*a*) would be so liable if the adjustment were not made.

Commentary—*Simon's Direct Tax Service* **E7.407, 417.**

A102 *Contributions to approved personal pension plans from 6 April 2001 under TA 1988 s 639 and age-related allowances*

FA 2000 Sch 13 amended the rules by which someone obtains tax relief on contributions to approved personal pension schemes. As a result of the changes a deduction is no longer given in arriving at total income. This affects the level of an individual's income which determines the age-related personal and married couple's allowances.

This concession allows such contributions from 6 April 2001 to reduce an individual's total income for the purposes only of determining the level of age-related allowances available under TA 1988 ss 257(5), 257A(5).

Commentary—*Simon's Direct Tax Service* **E7.407.**

A103 *Armed forces reservists—Revenue approved share schemes and enterprise management incentives (EMI)*

Where a reservist is called up for service under the Reserve Forces Act 1996, the Inland Revenue by concession will treat the employment with the Ministry of Defence (MOD) as fulfilling the employment conditions for Inland Revenue approved employee share schemes*.

By concession, employers and scheme providers will also be allowed to take such action as is necessary to maintain a reservist's participation in an approved employee share scheme, for the period they are away serving with the MOD and this action will not compromise the approval of the scheme.

The concession applies from 7 January 2003.

ESCs

Commentary—*Simon's Direct Tax Service* **E4.531.**
Note—*For the purposes of this Concession Inland Revenue approved employee share schemes include: company share option plans, share incentive plans, save as you earn schemes and enterprise management incentives.

B CONCESSIONS APPLICABLE TO INDIVIDUALS AND COMPANIES (INCOME TAX AND CORPORATION TAX)

B1 *Machinery or plant: changes from the "renewals" to the capital allowances basis*

Expenditure on machinery or plant which has been the subject of a ''renewals'' deduction does not technically qualify as capital expenditure for the purpose of capital allowances (CAA 2001 s 4(2)). Taxpayers who change from the ''renewals'' to the capital allowances basis are, however, permitted to claim such allowances as if the expenditure did so qualify provided that where they use more than one item of a class of machinery or plant they change from the ''renewals'' basis to the capital allowances basis for all the items in that class.

Commentary—*Simon's Direct Tax Service* **B2.307.**
Note—The text of this Concession is as it appears in IR 1 Supp (November 2001).

B2 *Capital allowances for agricultural buildings and works*

Note—This concession has been classified as obsolete.

B3 *Industrial buildings allowances: private roads on industrial trading estates*

Note—This concession was classified as obsolete by IR 1 Supp (November 2001).

B4 *Maintenance and repairs of property obviated by alterations etc: Schedule A assessments*

Note—This concession was classified as obsolete by IR 1 Supp (November 2001).

B5 *Maintenance expenses of owner-occupied farms not carried on on a commercial basis*

Note—This concession was classified as obsolete by IR 1 Supp (November 2001).

B6 *Deficiency payments in respect of home grown cereals*

Note—This concession has been classified as obsolete—the scheme under which the deficiency payments were made ceased from 1976.

B7 *Benevolent gifts by traders*

TA 1988 s 577(8) provides that in general the cost of gifts is not an admissible deduction in computing profits chargeable under Schedule D or in management expenses claims. TA 1988 s 577(9) removes this restriction for Schedule D in the case of business donations to registered charities (provided the deduction would otherwise be allowable) and a similar approach is taken to management expenses claims. Other expenditure on gifts is not regarded as within s 577 provided that—

(*a*) it is allowable under TA 1988 s 74(1)(*a*) or s 75(1);
(*b*) the gift is made for the benefit of a body or association of persons established for educational, cultural, religious, recreational or benevolent purposes, and the body or association is
  (i) local in relation to the donor's business activities; and
  (ii) not restricted to persons connected with the donor;

(*c*) the expenditure is reasonably small in relation to the scale of the donor's business.

The payment of an ordinary annual subscription to a local trade association by a non-member is similarly not regarded as a gift provided condition (*a*) is met.

Commentary—*Simon's Direct Tax Service* **B3.1441.**

B8 *Double taxation relief: income consisting of royalties and "know-how" payments*

Payments made by a person resident in an overseas country to a person carrying on a trade in the UK as consideration for the use of, or for the privilege of using, in the overseas country any copyright, patent, design, secret process or formula, trademark or other like property may in law be payments the source of which is in the UK, but are nevertheless treated for the purpose of credit (whether under double taxation agreements or by way of unilateral relief) as income arising outside the UK except to the extent that they represent consideration for services (other than merely incidental services) rendered in this country by the recipient to the payer.

Commentary—*Simon's Direct Tax Service* **B3.806, F2.106.**

B9 *Bank interest etc received by charities*

Note—This concession was superseded by FA 1996 s 146.

B10 *Income of contemplative communities or of their members*

The precise legal position regarding the title to such income, which is in fact treated by the community as belonging to the common fund, is often difficult to ascertain. In practice in the case of certain Orders (such as those engaged in charitable work among the poor) relief is given under the provisions relating to charities—in the case of the Contemplative Orders which are not in law capable of being regarded as charities, a proportion of the aggregate income not exceeding a specified sum per monk or nun (representing the amount applied for the maintenance of each individual) is regarded as his or her income for the purpose of relief from tax. With effect from the 1995–96 tax year the allowable figure will be equal to the basic personal tax allowance for each year. Where in any year the aggregate of the "allowable figures" exceeds the community's income, the excess may be set against chargeable gains of that year.

Any excess of the aggregate of "allowable figures" over a community's income or gains may no longer be carried forward and set against gains of a subsequent year. However, any excess amount remaining from years up to and including 1994–95 may be carried forward until exhausted.

Commentary—*Simon's Direct Tax Service* **C4.530.**

B11 *Compensation for compulsory slaughter of farm animals*

Where a farmer receives compensation for the compulsory slaughter of his animals by the order of any Ministry, government department, or local or public authority under the law relating to diseases of animals and the compensation is not payable in respect of animals forming part of a production herd for which an election for the herd basis (TA 1988 Sch 5 para 2) has been, or can be, made, any profits which are attributable to the compensation received may be excluded in computing the profits assessable to tax for the year of assessment during the basis period for which the slaughter took place and may be added in three equal instalments to the profits assessable to tax for the three following years of assessment. (Where compensation is received in these circumstances by a company within the charge to corporation tax the profits may be spread over the three accounting periods following that in which the slaughter took place.) For this purpose the profits attributable to the compensation received are to be taken as the difference between the book value of the slaughtered animals at the beginning of the year of account and the compensation received or, in the case of animals bred or purchased during the year in which the slaughter took place, as the difference between the cost of the animals and the compensation received.

Where the compensation received relates to a period affected by the special rules for assessing the profits where the farming is commenced or is discontinued, or where the accounting date is changed, this concession is modified as appropriate.

Commentary—*Simon's Direct Tax Service* **B3.522.**

B12 *Income from abroad assessable on the remittance basis: compulsory remittances to the UK under the Exchange Control Acts*

Note—This concession lapsed with effect from 24 October 1979.

B13 *Untaxed interest paid to non-residents*

Note—This concession was given statutory effect by FA 1995 s 128 with effect from 1996/97. It is therefore obsolete.

B14 *Capital allowances on replacement of motor cars*

Note—This concession has been classified as obsolete.

B15 *Borrowing and lending of securities*

Note—This concession was superseded with effect from 18 August 1989 by regulations made under TA 1988 s 129 (see the IT (Stock Lending) Regulations, SI 1989/1299).

B16 *Fire safety: capital expenditure incurred on certain trade premises (a) in Northern Ireland and (b) by lessors*

CAA 2001 s 29 provides tax relief (in circumstances where it is not otherwise available) for capital expenditure incurred by traders in meeting the requirements of a fire authority under the Fire Precautions Act 1971 s 5(4), following an application for a fire certificate in respect of trade premises of a type designated under that Act. CAA 2001 s 29 also provides relief for capital expenditure incurred by traders in meeting the requirements of a court order which could be made under the Fire Precautions Act 1971 s 10, prior to its amendment by the Fire Safety and Safety of Places of Sport Act 1987 s 9.

(*A*) NORTHERN IRELAND

The Fire Precautions Act 1971 does not apply in Northern Ireland, and consequently the provisions of s 29 do not apply to any expenditure on fire safety incurred on trade premises in Northern Ireland. In practice, however, tax relief is given in respect of such expenditure, on the same basis as in Great Britain, where it has been incurred—

(i) in respect of a building falling within one of the classes of premises which have been designated under the Fire Precautions Act 1971 s 1;
(ii) on or after the date on which the designation order for the class of premises came into operation;
(iii) in respect of a building which is not a new building or an extension to an existing building; and
(iv) in meeting the requirements of a fire authority under legislation applying in Northern Ireland which corresponds to those provisions of the Fire Precautions Act 1971 under which a fire certificate is required in Great Britain. Examples of such legislation are the Office and Shop Premises Act (Northern Ireland) 1966 s 29 (offices and shops with more than a certain number of employees) and the Fire Services Act (Northern Ireland) 1969 s 11 (hotels and boarding houses above a certain size); and the Fire Service (Northern Ireland) Order 1984 art 26.

Relief is also given, on a similar basis, in respect of expenditure in meeting the requirements of a court order made under provisions corresponding to those of the Fire Precautions Act 1971 s 10, prior to its amendment by the Fire Safety and Safety of Places of Sport Act 1987 s 9 (eg the Fire Services (Northern Ireland) Order 1984 art 33 prior to its amendment by the Fire Services (Amendment) (Northern Ireland) Order 1993 art 12).

Where the expenditure qualifies for relief under CAA 2001 s 271 (hotel buildings allowance) it may nevertheless be treated as above provided the taxpayer renounces his entitlement to relief under that section.

(*B*) LESSORS

Under CAA 2001 s 538 relief is given to lessors who make contributions towards their tenants' or licensees' fire safety expenditure, provided the expenditure satisfies the conditions of CAA 2001 s 29 or, in relation to Northern Ireland, the conditions set out above. In practice, relief is also allowed where the lessor incurs the expenditure himself, if similar expenditure by the tenant or licensee would have qualified for relief.

Commentary—*Simon's Direct Tax Service* **B2.310.**
Notes—The text of this Concession is as it appears in IR 1 Supp (August 2002).

B17 *Capital allowances: sale of invented patent to an associate*

Note—This concession has been classified as obsolete.

B18 *Payments out of discretionary trusts*

UK RESIDENT TRUSTS

A beneficiary may receive from trustees a payment to which TA 1988 s 687(2) applies. Where that payment is made out of the income of the trustees in respect of which, had it been received directly, the beneficiary would—

- have been entitled to exemption in respect of FOTRA securities issued in accordance with FA 1996 s 154; or
- have been entitled to relief under the terms of a double taxation agreement; or
- not have been chargeable to UK tax because of their not resident and/or not ordinarily resident status

the beneficiary may claim that exemption or relief or, where the beneficiary would not have been chargeable, repayment of the tax treated as deducted from the payment (or an appropriate proportion of it). For this purpose, the payment will be treated as having been made rateably out of all sources of income arising to the trustees on a last in first out basis.

Relief or exemption, as appropriate, will be granted to the extent that the payment is out of income which arose to the trustees not earlier than six years before the end of the year of assessment in which the payment was made, provided the trustees—

- have made trust returns giving details of all sources of trust income and payments made to beneficiaries for each and every year for which they are required, and
- have paid all tax due, and any interest, surcharges and penalties arising; and
- keep available for inspection any relevant tax certificates.

Relief or exemption, as appropriate, will be granted to the beneficiary on a claim made within five years and ten months of the end of the year of assessment in which the beneficiary received the payment from the trustees.

NON-RESIDENT TRUSTS

A similar concession will operate where a beneficiary receives a payment from discretionary trustees which is not within TA 1988 s 687(2) (ie where non-resident trustees exercise their discretion outside the UK).

Where a non-resident beneficiary receives such a payment out of income of the trustees in respect of which, had it been received directly, it would have been chargeable to UK tax, then the beneficiary—

- may claim relief under TA 1988 s 278 (personal reliefs for certain non-residents); and
- may be treated as receiving that payment from a UK resident trust but claim credit only for UK tax actually paid by the trustees on income out of which the payment is made.

The beneficiary may also claim exemption from tax in respect of FOTRA securities issued in accordance with FA 1996 s 154 to the extent that the payment is regarded as including interest from such securities.

A UK beneficiary of a non-resident trust may claim appropriate credit for tax actually paid by the trustees on the income out of which the payment is made as if the payments out of UK income were from a UK resident trust and within TA 1988 s 687(1).

This treatment will only be available where the trustees—

- have made trust returns giving details of all sources of trust income and payments made to beneficiaries for each and every year for which they are required; and
- have paid all tax due and any interest, surcharges and penalties arising; and
- keep available for inspection any relevant tax certificates.

Relief or exemption, as appropriate, will be granted to the beneficiary on a claim made within five years and ten months of the end of the year of assessment in which the beneficiary received the payment from the trustees.

No credit will be given for UK tax treated as paid on income received by the trustees which would not be available for set off under s 687(2) if that section applied, and that tax is not repayable (for example on dividends). However, such tax is not taken into account in calculating the gross income treated as taxable on the beneficiary under this concession.

Commentary—*Simon's Direct Tax Service* **C4.227, 423.**
Note—The text of this concession is as it appears in IR 1 (January 2000). It applies from 1999–00 (IR Press Release 1-4-99).

B19 *Capital allowances for buildings: balancing charge after cessation of trade*

Note—This concessionary relief was replaced by statutory relief under CAA 1990 s 15A where the balancing charge falls to be made on or after 29 April 1996.

B20 *Capital allowances for buildings: sales by property developers of buildings which have been let*

Where an industrial building is constructed by a person who is carrying on a trade consisting of the construction of buildings with a view to their sale, and it is sold by that person after having been occupied by a tenant, the purchaser is not entitled to writing down allowances since no capital expenditure has been incurred on the construction of the building, the developer's expenditure having been on revenue account (section 2(1)(c), CAA 1968). In practice writing down allowances are made to the purchaser on the amount of the purchase price (or, if less, the amount of the construction expenditure) on the same basis as if he had purchased the building from an owner who had incurred capital expenditure on its construction.

The same treatment applies to qualifying hotels and commercial buildings in enterprise zones, to which the industrial buildings allowance rules apply in this respect.

Commentary—*Simon's Direct Tax Service* **B2.224.**
Note—This concession was superseded by CAA 1968 s 5A: see now CAA 2001 ss 293, 297(1)–(3), 301(6), Sch 3 para 60.

B21 *The construction industry tax deduction scheme: failure to make deductions from uncertified sub-contractors*

Note—This concession was superseded by the IT (Subcontractors in the Construction Industry) Regulations, SI 1975/1960 reg 7(4), with effect from 19 April 1988: see now SI 1993/743 reg 10(2).

B22 *Close companies: non-resident participators; apportionment*

Note—This concession was classified as obsolete in IR 1 Supp (November 2000).

B23 *The construction industry tax deduction scheme: exclusion of certain small payments*

Note—This concession was superseded by the IT (Sub-contractors in the Construction Industry) Regulations, SI 1993/743 reg 20B, inserted by SI 1998/2622 reg 13; in relation to any application for the issue or renewal of a sub-contractor's tax certificate made with respect to any period beginning after 31 July 1999, and for all other purposes with effect from 1 August 1999. This concession is therefore obsolete.

B24 *Postponement of capital allowances to secure double taxation relief*

Note—For claims made after 5 April 1982, this concession was superseded by FA 1982 s 78 which amended TA 1970 s 515(1) to make the claim available in relation to tax under any Case of Schedule D in respect of a trade; see now TA 1988 s 810.

B25 *Schedule D Case V losses*

Note—This concession has been rendered obsolete by FA 1995 s 41 for individuals for years 1998/99 et seq, and by FA 1998 s 38 and Sch 5 para 28 for companies from 1 April 1998. B25 was classified obsolete by IR 1 Supp (November 1998).

B26 *Capital allowances: assets leased outside the UK—transitional provisions: syndicated leases*

Note—This concession applied to transitional provisions which expired on 31 March 1985 and is therefore obsolete.

B27 *Approved employee share schemes: jointly owned companies*

Commentary—*Simon's Direct Tax Service* **E4.565, 584, 594.**
Note—This concession was classified as obsolete by IR 1 (January 2004). It has been enacted in ITEPA 2003 Sch 3 para 46, Sch 4 para 34.

B28 *Leased cars costing over £12,000: rebate of hire charges*

Note—This concession has been replaced by statutory relief under CAA 1990 s 35(2A) where rebates are made or transactions occur on or after 29 April 1996.

B29 *Treatment of income from caravan sites where there is both trading and associated letting income*

Where the proprietor of a caravan site carries on material activities associated with the operation of that site which constitute trading, there may be included as receipts of that trade any site income from the lettings of pitches for static or touring caravans, and any income from letting caravans where the letting does not of itself amount to a trade.
Commentary—*Simon's Direct Tax Service* **A4.105.**

B30 *Income from property in Scotland: property managed as one estate*

Where the owner of an estate in Scotland has made a one-estate election for property to be treated as a single unit for maintenance purposes, the Revenue will continue for the time being to regard the 1978 gross value for rating purposes as the annual value for assessments under Schedule A.
Commentary—*Simon's Direct Tax Service* **A4.311; E4.613.**
Note—This concession was classified as obsolete by IR 1 Supp (November 2001).

B31 *Capital allowances: plant or machinery which is a fixture in a business building situated within an enterprise zone*

The rate of capital allowances on expenditure on machinery or plant, whether the assets are chattels or fixtures (including parts of a building) is normally 25 per cent of the reducing balance. This is a higher rate than that due on expenditure on the construction of an industrial building (4 per cent straight line) whilst in general no allowances at all are due on the construction of a commercial building. Exceptionally a 100 per cent initial allowance is due on expenditure on the construction of an industrial building or a commercial building in an enterprise zone.
Such expenditure does not, however, include expenditure on the provision of machinery or plant which becomes an integral part of such a building; expenditure on such machinery or plant only qualifies for a 25 per cent writing down allowance. By concession, where a taxpayer is entitled to a 100 per cent initial allowance in respect of expenditure on the construction of an industrial or commercial building in an enterprise zone, he may elect to treat as part of the said expenditure on the provision of machinery or plant which is to be an integral part of such a building.
Commentary—*Simon's Direct Tax Service* **B2.263.**
Note—This concession is obsolescent.

B32 *Payroll giving: administrative costs*

Note—This concession was replaced by statutory relief in FA 1993 with effect for 1993–94 and subsequent years of assessment and is therefore obsolete.

B33 *Profit-related pay: the similar terms requirement*

Note—With effect for schemes registered after 2 February 1989 this concession was superseded by TA 1988 s 177B.

B34 *Unit trusts: relief from liability under TA 1988 s 350*

Note—This concession was classified as obsolete by IR 1 Supp (1995).

B35 *Borrowing and lending of securities: gilt lending to redemption*

Note—This concession was listed as obsolete in IR 1 (1996) by virtue of the IT (Stock Lending) Regulations, SI 1989/1299 reg 9 inserted by SI 1995/3219 reg 12.

B36 *Borrowing and lending of securities: replacement loans*

Note—This concession was listed as obsolete in IR 1 (1996) by virtue of the IT (Stock Lending) Regulations, SI 1989/1299 reg 3C inserted by SI 1995/3219 reg 4.

B37 *The herd basis: shares in animals*

Note—This Concession was classified as obsolete by IR 1 (August 2002).

B38 *Tax concessions on overseas debts*

1 A person resident in the UK who carries on a trade partly overseas and partly in the UK is normally liable to UK income or corporation tax on all the profits from that trade. For this purpose the calculation of profits will include, in respect of overseas transactions—

(i) amounts paid to the trader which are not remittable to the UK, and
(ii) amounts owed to the trader which temporarily cannot be paid, and
(iii) amounts owed to the trader which even when paid will not be remittable to the UK,

solely as a consequence of local foreign exchange control restrictions.

2 Relief from tax is not available for such amounts under TA 1988 s 584 (which provides relief for overseas income which cannot be remitted to this country) because the profits of the trade of which they are a component part do not arise outside the UK. Nor does the fact that the amounts are unremittable to the UK entitle the trader to relief under TA 1988 s 74(1)(*j*) (relief for bad or doubtful debts).

3 But by concession, relief may be claimed for—

- amounts paid to the trader overseas which are not remittable to the UK solely as a result of local foreign exchange control restrictions (''trade receipts'') or
- amounts owed to the trader overseas which temporarily cannot be paid because of local foreign exchange control restrictions (''unpayable trade debts'') or
- amounts owed to the trader overseas in circumstances where, even though the debt could be discharged in the overseas country, the amounts receivable when the debt is discharged will not be remittable to the UK because of local foreign exchange control restrictions (''unpaid trade debts'').

4 Relief for unpayable or unpaid trade debts will be allowed only if it is not possible for the debt to be discharged in the UK; and only for that part of a debt which is not insured.

5 Relief may only be claimed where—

(*a*) the assessment for the year for which relief is claimed is not final and conclusive;
(*b*) the trade has made all reasonable endeavours to transfer the trade receipts to the UK, or, where the debt has not been paid, to secure payment and remittance of the funds to the UK;
(*c*) the trade receipts or the trade debts have not been used to finance expenditure or investment outside the UK (see para 8 below);
(*d*) the trade receipts remain unremittable 12 months after the end of the accounting period in which they were received; or (in the case of an unpayable trade debt) the debt is still unpayable 12 months after the end of the accounting period in which the debt arose; or (in the case of an unpaid trade debt) the amounts prospectively receivable when the debt is discharged are still unremittable 12 months after the end of the accounting period in which the debt arose;
(*e*) the taxpayer confirms in writing to the inspector that he agrees to the withdrawal of the relief in the manner and circumstances described in para 7 below.

6 The relief is allowed by deducting the amount of the trade receipt, or unpayable or unpaid trade debt, from the trading profit of the accounting period in which the receipt or debt is recognised as unremittable. The deduction cannot exceed the taxpayer's trading profit for the particular accounting period, and any excess relief which cannot be allowed in that way may be carried forward and set against trading profits for subsequent accounting periods in turn.

7 The relief will be withdrawn by making an addition to the trading profits of the accounting period in which—

- the trade receipt ceases to be unremittable; or the unpayable trade debt becomes payable and the proceeds are not unremittable; or the amounts receivable when the unpaid trade debt is discharged cease to be unremittable; or

- the trade receipt or trade debt is used to finance expenditure or investment outside the UK (see para 8 below); or
- the trade receipt or trade debt is otherwise applied outside the UK; or
- the trade receipts are exchanged for a remittable currency, or the trade debt is discharged in such a currency.

8 For the purposes of paras 5(*c*) and 7 above, the proceeds of a trade debt will be regarded as having been used to finance expenditure outside the UK to the extent that they are used, or might reasonably have been used, to meet expenditure, or guarantee a liability, incurred in the territory in which the debt arose, by the trader or by a person with whom the trader has a special relationship (because, eg, they are ''connected persons'' within the meaning of TA 1988). A trade debt will also be regarded as having been used to finance expenditure outside the UK if it remains unpaid by reason of a special relationship between the debtor and the trader.

BANKS AND OTHER FINANCIAL CONCERNS

9 This concession applies to interest charged on a loan made in the normal course of trade by a bank or other financial concern, where the interest has been included in the accounts on the accruals basis but cannot be remitted because of overseas exchange control restrictions. It does not apply to the principal of such a loan, or to interest in cases where the bank or other concern has made a loan in a currency other than that of the country imposing the restrictions, the debtor has made payment in local currency and the funds are available to be re-lent in that currency.

10 This concession applies to debts received and receivable by UK taxpayers which would be taken into account in computing income under either Schedule D Case I (trading profits) or Case II (profits from professions or vocations).

Commentary—*Simon's Direct Tax Service* **B3.1462A.**

B39 *Contributions to overseas pension schemes*

Note—This concession has been replaced by FA 1989 s 76(6A) to (6C) inserted by FA 1996 Sch 39 para 2 with effect for expenses incurred after 28 April 1996.

B40 *UK investment managers acting for non-resident clients*

TMA 1970 ss 78(1), 79 each provide for assessments to be made on a non-resident person in the name of a branch or agent. TA 1988 s 59 can also apply with the same effect where a branch or agent receives or is entitled to income chargeable to income tax. The Taxes Acts additionally allow for a non-resident to be assessed directly, whether or not there is a branch or agent in whose name the non-resident can be assessed.

However, where in a case otherwise within TMA 1970 s 78(1) the agent is specifically protected from assessment by the terms of s 78(2) (investment managers) or s 82(1) (brokers and general commission agents), the Revenue neither assesses the non-resident directly nor exercises the option of assessing the agent under TMA 1970 s 79 or TA 1988 s 59.

This concession does not apply—

(*a*) to any income of the non-resident falling within the terms of extra-statutory concession B13 and to which that concession is applied; or

(*b*) if the employment of the agent in the UK is outside or goes beyond the normal use by non-residents of UK investment managers, brokers and other agents within TMA 1970 ss 78(2) and 82(1); or

(*c*) if the non-resident has some other presence or representatives in the UK which carries on activities related to the transactions conducted through the agent, unless that other representative is also protected from assessment by TMA 1970 s 78(2) or s 82(1).

Commentary—*Simon's Direct Tax Service* **B3.118.**
Statement of Practice SP 15/91—Treatment of investment managers and their overseas clients.
SP 1/01—Treatment of investment managers and their overseas clients—this concession to continue to apply for the intended life of the fund when it was marketed but not beyond 5 April 2005.

B41 *Claims to repayment of tax*

Under the Taxes Management Act [TMA 1970], unless a longer or shorter period is prescribed, no statutory claim for relief is allowed unless it is made within six years from the end of the tax year to which it relates.

However, repayments of tax will be made in respect of claims made outside the statutory time limit where an overpayment of tax has arisen because of an error by the Revenue or another Government department, and where there is no dispute or doubt as to the facts.

Commentary—*Simon's Direct Tax Service* **A3.620.**

B42 *"Free gifts" and insurance contracts*

Insurance companies frequently offer incentives in connection with policies of life insurance, contracts for life annuities, and capital redemption policies. These are often described as "free gifts" and may take a variety of forms, such as small consumer goods, store vouchers, or discounts offered by hotels or travel agents.

So long as the aggregate cost to the insurer of all "gifts" provided in connection with an insurance (and for this purpose a cluster of policies will be treated as one insurance) does not exceed £30, no account will be taken of the "gifts" in—

– assessing whether policies are "qualifying" life insurance policies under TA 1988 Sch 15; or
– computing any gain arising under the chargeable event legislation, TA 1988 Part XIII Ch II (ss 539–554).

The concession may apply to current as well as future insurances and also to any tax liabilities in respect of past insurances which are not final at the date of issue of this concession.

Commentary—*Simon's Direct Tax Service* **B7.512.**

B43 *Alterations to old pension schemes*

Where an alteration is made to the terms on which benefits are payable by a fund to which TA 1988 s 608 applies, exemption from tax shall continue to be allowed in respect of the income, commissions, profits and gains applied for the purposes of the fund if—

(i) the alteration provides for pensions in payment to be increased by an amount not exceeding the rise in the retail prices index or at a fixed rate of up to 3% a year compound (whether or not the increase in the retail prices index reaches that level);
(ii) subject to the conditions below, the alteration allows for pensions to be commuted in full to a lump sum where the total benefit payable under all schemes in respect of the employment does not exceed the value of a pension of £260 a year;
(iii) the alteration is in order to give effect to any pension sharing order or provision as is mentioned in Welfare Reform and Pensions Act 1999 s 28(1) (rights under pension sharing arrangement) whereby pension rights are shared on divorce or annulment.

The conditions applying to limb (ii) of this concession are that either—

(*a*) the administrator of the fund should make no reduction in the amount of commutation payment made to the employee on account of any income tax borne by the administrator when making the payment; or
(*b*) the employee, having been made aware of the tax consequences, has agreed to the commutation payment.

Commentary—*Simon's Direct Tax Service* **E7.271; U7.7845.**
Note—This Concession has effect from 1 December 2000.

B44 *Profit-related pay: extraordinary items*

Note—This concession was classified obsolete by IR 1 Supp (November 1998).

B45 *Automatic penalties for late company and employers' and contractors' end-of-year returns*

Note—This concession applied to company returns with a statutory filing date before 1 October 1995 and to employers' and contractors' returns for the year ended 5 April 1995 and is therefore obsolete. It is superseded by Concession B46 below.

B46 *Automatic penalties for late company and employers' and contractors' end-of-year returns*

Under TMA 1970 s 11 any company may be required to deliver a return within a specified time limit and, for returns required by notices served after 31 December 1993, automatic penalties are chargeable under TMA 1970 s 94 if that time limit is not met. Regulations under TA 1988 ss 203(2), 566(1) require employers and contractors respectively to render their returns of sums deducted within 44 days of the end of the tax year, ie by 19 May. Automatic penalties are chargeable under TMA 1970 s 98A where these returns are not received by the statutory filing date.

The Revenue do not propose to charge a penalty in the case of any of these returns received in their hands on or before the last business day within seven days following the statutory filing date. A business day, for these purposes, is any day other than a Saturday, a Sunday, Christmas Eve, Good Friday or any bank or other public holiday. This concession applies to those company returns having a statutory filing date under TMA 1970 s 11(4) after 30 September 1995, and to employers' and contractors' returns for the years following the year ended 5 April 1995. The concession does not apply to any other statutory date which may trigger higher or additional penalties under TMA 1970 ss 94 or 98A.

This concession should not be regarded as an extension of the statutory time limits. It will be kept under review.

Commentary—*Simon's Direct Tax Service* **A3.817; D2.715.**

B47 *Furnished lettings of dwelling houses: wear and tear of furniture*

1 CAA 2001 ss 15(3), 35(2) (formerly CAA 1990 ss 28A(3), 61(2)) specifically exclude a claim for capital allowances on plant or machinery let for use in a dwelling house. Accordingly, capital allowances are not due on furniture and furnishings where the income from letting of furnished houses is assessable under Schedule A (or Schedule D Case VI, for income tax cases up to 1994/95 and periods before 1 April 1988 for corporation tax) and is outside the scope of TA 1988 s 503 (furnished holiday lettings).

2 In practice, an allowance for wear and tear may be made, where capital allowances are not due, by deducting 10 per cent of the net rent received. For this purpose the rent is reduced by any part of the occupier's council tax and water rates which the landlord pays. If the rental includes payments for services which would normally be borne by a tenant and the amounts involved are material, these too should be subtracted before calculating the 10 per cent deduction.

3 Where the 10 per cent deduction is allowed, no further deduction is given for the cost of renewing furniture or furnishings, including suites, beds, carpets, curtains, linen, crockery, or cutlery. Nor is a further deduction allowed for chattels of a type which, in unfurnished accommodation, a tenant would normally provide for himself (for example, cookers, washing machines, dishwashers).

4 However, in addition to the 10 per cent allowance, the landlord can also claim the cost of renewing fixtures which are an integral part of the buildings, and which are revenue repairs to the fabric. These are fixtures which would not normally be removed by either tenant or owner if the property were vacated or sold (for example, baths, washbasins, toilets). Expenditure on renewing such items may be treated as expenditure on repairs even though the 10 per cent allowance has been claimed.

5 As an alternative to the 10 per cent allowance, the actual cost of renewing furniture, furnishings and chattels may be claimed as a deduction. The amount to be allowed is the actual cost of the replacements excluding any additions or improvements, and after deducting the scrap value or sale price of the items replaced. The cost of the original items is not expenditure on renewals and is not allowable.

6 Whichever basis a taxpayer chooses to adopt should be consistently applied to all furnished properties rented out.

7 Before 1975/76, when the 10 per cent basis started, there were several bases in common use. The Revenue will not disturb these so long as the let properties remain in the same ownership. Any properties acquired subsequently should be dealt with on one of the two bases described above.

Commentary—*Simon's Direct Tax Service* **B7.206.**
Notes—Concession B47 reclassifies Statement of Practice A19.
The text of this concession is as it appears in IR 1 (January 2000).

B48 *A deduction for an employer's National Insurance Class 1A contributions when computing profits for tax purposes*

Commentary—*Simon's Direct Tax Service* **B3.1428; E4.721.**
Note—This concession was replaced by TA 1988 s 617(4) as substituted by FA 1997 s 65 in relation to contributions paid on or after 26 November 1996. It was classified obsolete by IR 1 Supp (November 1998).

B49 *CAA 2001 s 532: grants repaid*

Where some or all of the expenditure on the provision of an asset has been met by the Crown, any Government, or any other public or local authority, CAA 2001 ss 532—536 prevents capital allowances from being given on that expenditure. By concession, where the grant is later repaid in whole or in part, the amount repaid will be treated as expenditure on which capital allowances may be given.

Capital allowances are also restricted where expenditure on an asset is met by a person other than the Crown or public body who is entitled to capital allowances or a trading deduction on that amount.

Where a grant which has been deducted from expenditure qualifying for capital allowances under this rule is later repaid in whole or in part, the Revenue will treat the amount repaid as expenditure on which capital allowances may be given provided the repayment falls to be taxed on the person who made the grant through a balancing adjustment or as a trading receipt.

Commentary—*Simon's Direct Tax Service* **B2.111.**
Note—The text of this Concession is as it appears in IR 1 Supp (November 2001).

B50 *Capital allowances for caravans on holiday caravan sites*

Note—This concession was classified as obsolete by IR 1 Supp (November 2001).

B51 *Subcontractors in the construction industry: the turnover test—definition of "turnover"*

Note—This concession was classified obsolete by IR 1 Supp (January 2000).

B52 *Subcontractors in the construction industry: the multiple turnover tests*

Note—This concession has been classified obsolete. See IR Tax Bulletin August 2001 p 879.

B53 *Non-residents and gains on life insurance policies*

Non-UK residents and chargeable event gains on life policies, life annuities and capital redemption policies, the information duties of UK insurers and Personal Portfolio Bonds held by individuals not resident in the UK on 17 March 1998.

PART 1

Non-UK resident individuals and companies and chargeable event gains on life insurance policies, life annuity contracts and capital redemption policies

1 A "gain" may be treated as arising in connection with a policy of life insurance, a life annuity contract or a capital redemption policy when a "chargeable event" occurs or is treated as occurring. TA 1988 Pt XIII Ch II defines "chargeable events" and sets out how a "gain" is calculated. It also contains the other provisions relating to chargeable events referred to below. A gain may also be treated as arising in connection with a personal portfolio bond under the Personal Portfolio Bond (Tax) Regulations, SI 1999/1029 reg 5.

2 This concession is about the circumstances in which a gain may be treated as part of the—

– total income of an individual; or
– income of a company.

These are when—

– an individual or company is beneficial owner of the rights conferred by a policy or contract;
– the rights are held on trusts created by an individual or a company; or
– the rights are held as security for a debt owed by an individual or a company.

3 The provisions that deem a gain to be part of the income of an individual or a company are not restricted to UK residents. Except as set out in para 4, however, the Inland Revenue will not pursue liability to tax on a gain that is treated as income of either an individual or a company that is not resident in the UK at any time during the year of assessment or accounting period, as appropriate, in which the gain is chargeable.

4 A tax liability may arise if a policy or contract is held as property used by, or held by, a UK branch or agency of a company that is not resident in the UK.

5 Nothing in this concession affects—

– a gain that is treated as constituting income payable to non-resident trustees or to a company or other institution resident or domiciled outside the UK; and
– the tax treatment of a benefit that an individual ordinarily resident in the UK receives from the trustees, the company or other institution.

PART 2

The information duties of UK insurers

6 Insurers are required to provide information both to policy holders and to the Inland Revenue when a "chargeable event" occurs or is treated as occurring. The information duties of insurers are at TA 1988 ss 552, 552ZA. The only circumstance in which the insurer does not need to provide information either to the policyholder or to the Inland Revenue is when the insurer is satisfied that no gain arises by reason of the event. The obligation to provide information is not restricted to providing information about gains made by policy holders resident in the UK. Information that an insurer supplies to the Inland Revenue about a gain made by a policy holder resident outside the UK may be exchanged with the fiscal authorities in the country in which the policy holder resides.

7 Unless the circumstances set out in para 8 below apply, a UK insurer must provide information about gains both to policy holders and to the Inland Revenue in accordance with TA 1988 s 552 including gains in connection with policies or contracts attributable to any of its branches outside the UK. Information must be given about all gains made in connection with policies and contracts carried out or administered at the branch and not just those effected at the branch. This includes business transferred to a branch. The insurer may arrange for the branch to provide the information directly to its policy holders and to the Inland Revenue.

8 The circumstances in which an insurer does not have to provide information to the Inland Revenue under TA 1988 s 552 are those where—

- the policy holder does not reside in the UK at any time during the year of assessment or accounting period, as appropriate, in which the gain would be treated as forming part of the income of the policy holder, on the assumption that the policy holder is the person chargeable on the gain under TA 1988 s 547, and either—
  - the insurer has provided information about the gain or the sum payable or other benefits conferred by reason of the event to the fiscal authority of the country in which the policy holder resides or, in the case of branch business, to the fiscal authority of the country in which the branch is situated; or
  - the policy or contract forms part of the business of the company carried out or administered at a branch of the company outside the UK and the business of the branch is not mainly with persons residing in the UK and British citizens. A branch's business is for these purposes mainly with persons residing in the UK and British citizens if more than 50 per cent of the total of the liabilities of the insurer attributable to the branch relate to policies and contracts with such holders.

In this paragraph—

- the liabilities to be taken into account for this purpose are the ''closing liabilities'' within the meaning of TA 1988 s 431(2) as at the end of the latest preceding accounting period for which the insurer has prepared its regulatory return,
- ''policy holder'' includes the holder of a contract for a life annuity contract; and
- ''branch'' includes an agency.

9 The tests whether information should be supplied should be applied to the best of an insurer's knowledge and belief taking account of all information in the insurer's possession, whenever that information was obtained and wherever and in what form it is stored.

10 The Inland Revenue may audit an insurer's books, documents and records to ascertain whether there has been, or is likely to be, any contravention of the information requirements. If an insurer is not supplying information because para 8 above applies, the audit may include an audit of any information in the insurer's possession relevant in demonstrating that the conditions set out in those paragraphs are satisfied. If they are satisfied, the Inland Revenue will not treat the insurer as having contravened the requirements of TA 1988 s 552.

PART 3

Personal portfolio bonds and individuals not resident in the UK on 17 March 1998

11 The Personal Portfolio Bond (Tax) Regulations, SI 1999/1029, impose a yearly charge to tax on policies of life insurance, life annuity contracts and capital redemption policies that are personal portfolio bonds within the meaning of those regulations.

12 In some circumstances it is possible to change the terms of a policy or contract taken out before 17 March 1998 to take it outside the definition of a personal portfolio bond. A person who was not resident in the UK on that day and who later becomes resident has to make the change before the end of either the first ''year'' to begin on or after 6 April 1999 or, if later, the first ''year'' to begin after the policy holder becomes resident in the UK. ''Year'', in this context, is as defined in TA 1988 s 546(4).

13 The Taxes Act makes no provision for splitting tax years in relation to residence. So an individual who becomes resident in the UK during a year of assessment is resident for the whole year. This means that, in an extreme case, the period available to make the change could end very shortly after the policy holder arrives in the UK.

14 By concession, where an individual comes to the UK to take up permanent residence, or to stay for at least two years, the ''year'' before the end of which the change has to be made to the policy or contract will be the first ''year'' to begin on or after the date on which the policy holder first arrives in the UK to take up permanent residence or to stay.

COMMENCEMENT

15 This version of Concession B53 replaces an earlier version published on 22 November 1999.

16 Parts I and II of the concession apply in relation to gains treated as arising when chargeable events occur or are treated as occurring on or after 6 April 2002. The equivalent parts of the earlier version of Concession B53 continue to apply in relation to gains treated as arising when chargeable events occur or are treated as occurring before 6 April 2002.

17 Part III of the concession applies to all policy holders who first arrive in the UK to take up permanent residence, or to stay for at least two years, on or after 6 April 2002.

Commentary—*Simon's Direct Tax Service* **B7.503.**
Note—This concession was revised in March 2002.

B54 *Tax relief on films, tapes and discs*

Notwithstanding section 113(2) of Finance Act 2000, master audio tapes or discs shall be deemed to be included in the definitions in section 68(2) of the Capital Allowances Act 1990[1]. This ensures that treatment of the expenditure on production of master audio tapes or discs will continue to be treated as expenditure of a revenue nature.

Commentary—*Simon's Direct Tax Service* **B3.1307.**
Note—The text of this Concession is as it appears in IR 1 Supp (November 2001).
[1] See now CAA 2001 Sch 2 para 82.

B55 *Farming losses—TA 1988 s 397*

Note—This Concession was classified as obsolete by IR 1 (August 2002).

B56 *Herd basis rules: slaughter of immature animals intended to be replacements*

Where—

- a farmer has disposed of production animals subject to a herd basis election with the intention of replacing them with young animals which would have qualified as replacements when they gave birth to their first young; and
- the intended replacements did not give birth to their first young because they were slaughtered while pregnant as a result of the 2001 foot and mouth disease outbreak;

the intended replacements may be regarded as mature for the purposes of TA 1988 Sch 5 para 8(4).

Commentary—*Simon's Direct Tax Service* **B3.516.**

C CONCESSIONS APPLICABLE TO COMPANIES, ETC (CORPORATION TAX AND INCOME TAX)

C1 *Credit for underlying tax: dividends from trade investments in overseas companies*

(*A*) PORTFOLIO SHAREHOLDERS

Credit is still available under a few double taxation agreements for underlying tax on portfolio investments. Where a UK resident receives dividends on a holding of ordinary shares (including the participating part of participating preference dividends) in a company resident in an overseas territory with which the UK has an agreement which provides for such relief, the credit legally due against the UK tax chargeable on the dividends takes into account, in addition to any direct tax on the dividends, the underlying tax payable in the other country on the company's profits. In practice, provided that the overseas countries concerned have agreements with the UK of the type mentioned above, the credit also takes into account any UK tax or foreign tax in a third country payable by the overseas company on its income; and, when the overseas company's profits include ordinary or participating preference dividends from a second company resident in that or another overseas country, both the direct tax charged on the dividends and the underlying tax payable on the profits of the second company. Relief is given similarly for the tax relating to dividends and profits of companies at further removes along a chain of shareholdings.

(*B*) INSURANCE COMPANIES

Where a UK company is charged to tax under Schedule D Case I in respect of any insurance business which it carries on, then, in computing the credit available to the company in respect of dividends paid to it by a company resident in an overseas territory, any tax payable by the overseas company in respect of its profits (whether in that territory, in the UK or in a third country) is, subject to certain limitations, taken into account—

(i) where such business or any part of it is carried on through a branch or agency in the territory in which the overseas company is resident and the dividend is referable to the insurance business carried on by the UK company which is charged to tax under Schedule D Case I,

and/or

(ii) where the UK company controls not less than one-tenth of the voting power of the overseas company (or not less than one-quarter as respects dividends paid to it before 1 April 1971 by companies resident in certain overseas territories).

Where a UK company is entitled to relief under (i), the credit also takes into account, in practice, any UK or overseas tax paid on its income in the same or another country by any company paying dividends to and resident in the same country as the overseas company; and, similarly, tax relating to dividends and income of companies resident in the same country at further removes along a chain of shareholdings.

Where a UK company controls, directly or indirectly, not less than one-tenth of the voting power of a company resident in an overseas country which carries on insurance business which would have been charged to tax under Schedule D Case I if that company (referred to as ''the operating company'') had been resident in the UK (or not less than one-quarter of the voting power where that proportion would have been required for the purpose of relief under (ii) above), the credit also takes into account, in practice, any UK or overseas tax paid on its income in the same or another country by any company paying dividends to and resident in the same country as the operating company, provided, however, that the tax so available for relief shall be reduced in the proportion which the amount of the operating company's distributable surplus for the year of claim from such insurance business bears to the amount of its total distributable surplus for that year; and, similarly, tax relating to dividends, and income of companies resident in the same country as the operating company at further removes along a chain of shareholdings.

Commentary—*Simon's Direct Tax Service* **F2.209.**

C2 *Loan and money societies*

Note—This concession was classified as obsolete by IR 1 Supp (November 2001).

C3 *Holiday clubs and thrift funds*

Note—This concession was classified as obsolete by IR 1 Supp (November 2001).

C4 *Trading activities for charitable purposes*

Certain events arranged by voluntary organisations or charities for the purpose of raising funds for charity may fall within the definition of ''trade'' in TA 1988 s 832, with the result that any profits will be liable to income tax or corporation tax. Tax will not be charged on such profits provided—

(*a*) the event is of a kind which falls within the exemption from VAT under VATA 1994 Sch 9 Group 12, and

(*b*) the profits are transferred to charities or otherwise applied for charitable purposes.

Commentary—*Simon's Direct Tax Service* **C4.523B**; *De Voil Indirect Tax Service* **V4.171.**
Revenue & other press releases—IR booklet ''Fund-raising for charity'' (guidance on tax treatment of fund-raising for charity).
Revenue internal guidance—Business income manual BIM 24794 (further amplification of conditions).
Note—The text of this concession was revised in an Inland Revenue press release dated 31 March 2000.

C5 *Industrial and provident societies*

TA 1988 s 393(8) enables a company with a trading loss brought forward under TA 1988 s 393(1) to set off the loss not only against the trading income of the accounting period but also against any interest or dividends on investments which would have been taken into account as trading income but for the fact that they are charged to tax under other provisions.

In the case of a registered industrial and provident society carrying on a trade, the following items of income may be regarded as trading income for the purposes of s 393(8)—

ESCs

(*a*) interest brought into the computation of corporation tax profits as income under Schedule D Case III;
(*b*) annual interest received under deduction of tax;
(*c*) *amounts assessable under Schedule D Case V.*

Commentary—*Simon's Direct Tax Service* **D4.625.**

C6 *Close companies: excess of relevant income over distributions—small amounts*

Note—This concession was classified as obsolete by IR 1 Supp (November 2000).

C7 *Close companies: interest on inter-bank loan*

Note—This concession was superseded by FA 1980 s 45 and does not apply for accounting periods ended after 26 March 1980.

C8 *Close companies: loan creditors*

In applying the test of control of a company in TA 1988 s 416(2)(*c*), to determine whether or not a company is a close company, a recognised money broker will not be treated as a participator of a company carrying on a business as a stock jobber solely by reason of short term loans or advances arising in the ordinary course of their respective trades.

Commentary—*Simon's Direct Tax Service* **D3.105.**

C9 *Associated companies*

1 TA 1988 s 13 (small companies' relief) and TA 1988 s 13AA (corporation tax starting rate) contains rules which apply when one company is associated with one or more other companies. Broadly speaking, one company is associated with another if one of the two has control of the other, or both are under the control of the same person or persons. The rules about control are contained in TA 1988 ss 416, 417. The provisions of this concession relate to the application of those rules only for the purpose of TA 1988 ss 13 and 13AA.

2 The Revenue will not, by concession, treat one company as being under the control of another where the first company is only under the control of the second by taking into account fixed rate preference shares (as defined in TA 1988 Sch 28B para 13(6)) which a company possesses. Nor will the Revenue treat one company as associated with another where those companies are only under common control by taking into account fixed rate preference shares which another company possesses. In all cases, this part of the concession applies only when the company possessing the fixed rate preference shares—

– is not a close company, and
– takes no part in the management or conduct of the company which issued the shares, or of the business of that company, and
– subscribed for the shares in the ordinary course of a business carried on by it which includes the provisions of finance.

3 The Revenue will not, by concession, treat one company as being under the control of a loan creditor of that company where there is no past or present connection between the company and the loan creditor other than the loan or loans which cause it to be a loan creditor. Nor will the Revenue treat one company as associated with another where the first company is only associated with the second by being controlled by the same loan creditor provided there is no past or present connection between the companies other than the common loan creditor. In all cases, this part of the concession applies only when the loan creditor—

– is a company which is not a close company, or
– is a bona fide commercial loan creditor.

4 The Revenue will not, by concession, treat one company as being associated with a trustee company (for example, a trustee company of a clearing bank) where the company is only associated with that trustee company because it is under its control by taking into account rights and/or powers the trustee company holds in trust provided there is no past or present connection between the company and the trustee company other than those rights and/or powers. In these circumstances, the Revenue will not, by concession, treat the trustee company as being associated with the other company. Nor will the Revenue treat one company as being associated with another because they are controlled by the same trustee by virtue of rights and/or powers held in trust by that trustee provided there is no past or present connection between the companies other than those rights and/or powers.

5 The Revenue will, by concession, treat the definition of a relative (in TA 1988 s 417(4)) for the purpose of TA 1988 ss 13, 13AA as including only a husband or wife or child who is a minor. This part of the concession applies only in respect of companies where there is no substantial commercial interdependence between them.

Commentary—*Simon's Direct Tax Service* **D2.109; D3.112.**
Revenue internal guidance—Company taxation manual CT 3077, 3077a (para 5: meaning of "substantial commercial interdependence").
Note—The text of this concession is as it appears in IR 1 (January 2000).

C10 *Groups of companies: arrangements*

1 The following provisions of TA 1988 contain special rules which apply if there are "arrangements" in existence which may involve a future change in the ownership of the shares or securities in a company—

- s 240(11)(*a*)—surrender of ACT (in respect of accounting periods ended before 6 April 1999) to a subsidiary company;
- s 247(1A)(*b*)—group income elections in certain consortium cases;
- s 410(1), (2)—group and consortium relief.

In addition, Sch 18 para 5B(1) applies if there are "option arrangements".

JOINT VENTURE COMPANIES

2 But in practice these special rules are not applied in relation to certain types of agreement regulating the affairs of two or more member companies holding shares or securities in a joint venture company carrying on a commercial undertaking. The types of agreement to which the concession applies are ones which could involve the transfer of shares or securities in the joint venture company on, or as the result of, the happening of one or more triggering events. Until such a triggering event occurs, such agreements are not regarded as "arrangements" or "option arrangements".

3 Triggering events are—

(*a*) the voluntary departure of a member;
(*b*) the commencement of liquidation, administration or receivership of a member;
(*c*) a serious deterioration in the financial condition of a member;
(*d*) a change in the control or ownership of a member;
(*e*) a default by a member in performing its obligations under the terms of an agreement between the members or with the joint venture company, including its articles of association;
(*f*) an external change in the commercial circumstances in which the undertaking operates such that its viability is seriously threatened;
(*g*) unresolved disagreement among the members;
(*h*) any contingency of a similar kind provided against, but not intended to happen, when the agreement in question was entered into.

4 The details of such agreements will vary but they will be of a kind (*a*) allowing or requiring remaining members to acquire the holding of a departing company, or (*b*) allowing or requiring a departing company to transfer its holding to remaining members.

5 The transfer of the shares or securities will be on the basis of—

- an offer pro rata to the remaining members' holdings of shares or securities, with price fixed by agreement or independent valuation (which may allow for a penalty against a defaulting company), or
- a competitive tender among the remaining members, or
- a reciprocal process where one member offers to sell its holding to another at a certain price per share, when that other can either accept the offer or require the offeror to buy the offeree's holding at the same price (and the reverse, offer to purchase/call option arrangement), or
- other arrangements designed to ensure that a price appropriate to the commercial circumstances is struck.

6 The Articles of a joint venture company may provide for the suspension of a member's voting rights on the happening of a triggering event. Such a provision is not of itself regarded as "arrangements" before the triggering event occurs.

MORTGAGE OF SHARES OR SECURITIES

7 If shares or securities in a company are used as security under a mortgage (or legal or equitable charge) the mortgage will not by itself be regarded as constituting "arrangements" or "option arrangements" until the default or other triggering event occurs which allows the mortgagee to exercise his rights against the mortgagor. This only applies if prior to default the mortgagee possesses no more control over the shares or securities which are the subject of the mortgage than is required by the mortgagee to protect his interest.

8 If a default occurs but is remedied before the mortgagee exercises his rights, "arrangements" and "option arrangements" will be regarded as not having come into existence as a result of the default.

APPLICATION

9 The concession does not apply when the person or persons standing to acquire shares, securities or control could, alone or with connected persons within the meaning of TA 1988 s 839, dictate the terms or timing of the acquisition in advance of the triggering event having occurred. For this purpose members will not be regarded as connected by reason only of their membership of the joint venture company and a mortgagee will not be regarded as connected with the company whose shares are the subject of the mortgage by reason only of the mortgage.

Commentary—*Simon's Direct Tax Service* **D2.637.**
Statement of Practice SP 3/93—(groups of companies—arrangements).
Note—The text of this concession is as it appears in IR 1 Supp (November 2000).

C11 *Demergers: TA 1988 s 213(7) & (9)*

To satisfy the conditions for relief in a demerger under TA 1988 s 213, the distributing company must after the distribution be either a trading company or the holding company of a trading group.

TA 1988 s 213(7) relaxes that condition if—

(*a*) the transfer relates to two or more 75 per cent subsidiaries of the distributing company; and
(*b*) the distributing company is dissolved without there having been after the distribution any net assets of the company available for distribution in a winding-up or otherwise.

However, a company will not be regarded as failing to comply with the requirements of TA 1988 s 213(7) merely because it retains, after the distribution, sufficient funds to meet the cost of liquidation and to repay a negligible amount of share capital remaining. Share capital will be regarded as negligible if it amounts to £5,000 or less. This concession applies equally to s 213(7) and (9).

Commentary—*Simon's Direct Tax Service* **D1.502.**

C12 *Retail co-operative societies: accounting periods*

Many retail co-operative societies prepare their accounts at half-yearly or quarterly intervals. For corporation tax purposes each period of account would constitute an "accounting period" so that corporation tax payments would fall to be made more often than once a year. In practice, accounts comprising 12 months to an agreed terminal date are to be regarded as one accounting period. This concession does not apply on the occasion of a change of accounting date, a commencement or a cessation (including amalgamations and transfers of engagements) and is subject to an undertaking that, apart from the changes referred to, the society will adhere consistently to the concessional basis.

Commentary—*Simon's Direct Tax Service* **D2.107.**

C13 *Agricultural co-operative associations "second and third-tier" associations*

For the purposes of TA 1988 s 486(9) "second and third-tier" associations of agricultural co-operatives are treated as if the members of the basic level co-operative associations were themselves members of the second and third-tier associations.

Commentary—*Simon's Direct Tax Service* **D4.635.**

C14 *Tax credit relief for foreign banks trading in the UK through branches*

Note—This concession was superseded by FA 1982 s 67 (now TA 1988 s 794) and is obsolete.

C15 *Dissolution of unincorporated associations: distributions to members*

Where a company which is an unincorporated association is dissolved the distribution of its assets to its members is an income distribution within TA 1988 s 209, limited where s 490(1) or (4) of that act applies to the amount distributed out of profits brought into charge to corporation tax or out of franked investment income. If substantially the whole of the association's activities have been of a social or recreational nature, it has not carried on an investment business or a trade other than a mutual trade, and the amount distributed to each member is not large, it is given the option of not having s 209 applied and of having the whole of the amounts distributed treated as capital receipts of the members for the purpose of calculating any chargeable gains arising to them on the disposal of their individual interests in the association.

Commentary—*Simon's Direct Tax Service* **D1.142.**

C16 *Dissolution of companies under the Companies Act 1985 ss 652, 652A: distributions to shareholders*

A distribution of assets to its shareholders by a company which is then dissolved under the Companies Act 1985 s 652 or s 652A (or any comparable provisions) is strictly an income distribution within TA 1988 s 209. In most circumstances and providing that certain assurances are given to the inspector before the event, the Revenue is prepared for tax purposes to regard the distribution as having been made under a formal winding-up so that the proviso to s 209(1) applies. The value of the distribution is then treated as capital receipts of the shareholders for the purpose of calculating any chargeable gains arising to them on the disposal of their shares in the company.

The assurances include—

The company

- does not intend to trade or carry on business in future; and
- intends to collect its debts, pay off its creditors and distribute any balance of its assets to its shareholders (or has already done so); and
- intends to seek or accept striking off and dissolution.

The company and its shareholders agree that

- they will supply such information as is necessary to determine, and will pay, any corporation tax liability on income or capital gains; and
- the shareholders will pay any capital gains tax liability (or corporation tax in the case of a corporate shareholder) in respect of any amount distributed to them in cash or otherwise as if the distributions had been made during a winding-up.

Commentary—*Simon's Direct Tax Service* **D1.142.**
Note—The text of this concession is as it appears in IR 1 (January 2000).

C17 *Interest and currency swaps*

Note—This Concession was classified as obsolete by IR 1 (August 2002).

C18 *TA 1988 s 209*

Note—This concession was listed as obsolete in IR 1 (1996) by virtue of TA 1988 s 209(2)(*da*) and the repeal of s 209(2)(*e*)(iv) by FA 1995 s 87(1),(2)(*b*). For the interpretation of the term "in the ordinary course of business" see Statement of Practice SP 12/91 (now obsolete).

C19 *Stock lending by pension funds*

Note—The Manufactured Payments and Transfer of Securities (Tax Relief) Regulations, SI 1995/3036 exempt from tax, with effect from 2 January 1996, all repo profits and manufactured payments received by any of the pension schemes and funds covered by TA 1988 ss 730A, 737D and such income of life assurance companies to the extent that it is referable to their pension business. This concession is therefore obsolete.

C20 *Claims to group relief*

Note—This concession was classified as obsolete in IR 1 Supp (1995).

C21 *Life insurance companies: levies under the LAUTRO (Compensation Schemes) Rules*

Note—This concession was classified as obsolete in IR 1 Supp (1995).

C22 *Building societies*

Note—This concession has been classified as obsolete.

C23 *Interest payable by banks and similar businesses*

Note—This concession has been classified as obsolete.

ESCs

C24 *General insurance business: claims and elections*

Note—This concession was classified as obsolete in IR 1 Supp (November 2000).

C25 *Long term insurance business: claims and elections*

Note—This concession was classified obsolete by IR 1 Supp (November 2000).

C26 *Interest payable in the UK*

Note—This concession was classified as obsolete by IR 1 Supp (November 1998).

C27 *Life assurance business: calculation of investment return and profits*

Where a company carrying on life assurance business has by virtue of FA 1995 Sch 8 para 53(2)—

- *set [TA 1988] s 432F(2) excesses ("sub-s (2) excesses") arising in accounting periods beginning on or after 1 January 1990 and ending before 1 January 1994 against a s 432F(3) excess ("sub-s (3) excess") arising in an accounting period ending on or after 1 January 1994*
- *and those sub-s (2) excesses are not exhausted by the amount of that sub-s (3) excess*

then in the next accounting period in which a sub-s (3) excess arises in respect of the same category of business, the unexhausted amount of the sub-s (2) excess may be set against that subsequent sub-s (3) excess (but no further carry forward is permitted).

A section 432F(3) excess is the amount by which, in any accounting period, the section 432E(3) amount for any category of business exceeds the section 432E(2) amount for that period.

Commentary—*Simon's Direct Tax Service* **D4.526.**
Note—This concession was listed as obsolescent in IR 1 (1996) because the number of people able to benefit from it is decreasing.

C28 *Connection within FA 1996 s 87*

PREAMBLE

1 Concerns have been expressed that the anti-avoidance provisions in FA 1996 [Pt IV] Chap II, which deal with loan relationships between connected companies, will discourage the provision of venture capital for companies through a mixture of loans and equity investment. In addition, the legislation is seen as putting obstacles in the way of arrangements to rescue companies in trouble by swapping debts for shares in the debtor company.

2 Where companies are connected for the purposes of the loan relationship legislation under FA 1996 s 87, for example, because one company controls the other, the creditor company is denied bad debt relief for any amounts owed to it by the debtor company which are within the scope of that legislation. The definition of control for this purpose is very wide and can apply to a creditor company which holds shares in the debtor company which have only very limited rights or is simply a loan creditor of the debtor company.

3 To alleviate these potential obstacles to the provision of venture capital for companies and to company rescues through the swap of loans for shares (debt/equity swaps) the Revenue will in certain limited circumstances allow bad debt relief for such loan relationships, even where the lender and borrower are connected with one another under FA 1996 s 87.

4 The circumstances in which the concession will apply are set out in full below. In each case the concession applies only for the purpose of determining, for the purposes of FA 1996 Sch 9 paras 5 and 6 as they apply to the creditor company, whether the parties to a loan relationship are connected under FA 1996 s 87. It has no effect in respect of any other legislation. The terms creditor company and debtor company mean respectively a company standing in the position of creditor in respect of the loan relationship and a company standing in the place of a debtor in respect of the loan relationship.

5 The concession has a number of legs. The first two, the disregard of rights of partners in certain circumstances and the disregard of rights as a loan creditor for non-banks, although of general application, will primarily be of benefit to venture capital investors. The first leg will, for example prevent a company which is a general partner in a venture capital partnership automatically being treated as connected under FA 1996 s 87 with the company in which the partnership is investing. The second leg will ensure that, as is already the case for loans made by banks, loans made by concerns in the ordinary course of their business of providing finance will not be taken into account in deciding whether a creditor company is connected with a debtor company.

6 The third leg of the concession is relevant for any company whose business is the provision of finance through loans and subscription for shares. Provided the debtor and creditor companies are connected with one another only through a holding of shares in the debtor company of specified preference shares, with limited rights, those shares will be ignored in determining whether the creditor company is treated as connected with the debtor company under FA 1996 s 87 for the purposes of Sch 9 paras 5, 6. This will be so whether the shares in the debtor company were directly subscribed for or acquired in a debt/equity swap.

7 The effect is that in any of the circumstances described above the creditor company will although technically connected with the debtor company under FA 1996 s 87 continue to obtain bad debt relief in respect of amounts owed by the debtor company and relief for any loss on the disposal of such loans.

8 The consequences of taking advantage of this concession are also set out below. These include accepting any subsequent charges that arise in respect of recoveries, decreases in bad debt provisions or profits on disposal of debts for which bad debt relief has been given for tax purposes under the concession.

9 The consequences for a creditor company, previously within the scope of the concession, of becoming connected under FA 1996 s 87 with a debtor company in circumstances in which the extra-statutory concession does not apply are also set out. Broadly the connection under s 87 will be treated as having taken place at the time when the two companies become connected in such a way that the requirements of the concession are no longer satisfied. No relief for existing or outstanding loans will be due after that date but any tax relief already given in respect of the loans will not be withdrawn except where there is a recovery, decrease in bad debt provision or profit on disposal of debts. The same concessional treatment for continuing loans is available, in certain circumstances, where a company enters into an exchange of loans for ordinary share capital. No relief for loans which have not been exchanged will be due after the date on which the companies become connected but any tax relief already given will not be withdrawn.

10 Finally, the concession allows relief, in certain circumstances, for loans in existence at 1 April 1996 where the creditor is connected with the debtor company as a result of an earlier exchange of loans for shares.

DETAILS OF CONCESSION

A creditor company will be able to choose whether to take advantage of this concession in respect of all its loan relationships within the scope of the concession. Where it does not the provisions of FA 1996 [Pt IV] Chap II will apply to its loan relationships in the usual way.

DISREGARD OF RIGHTS AND POWERS OF PARTNERS IN CERTAIN CIRCUMSTANCES

11 In applying TA 1988 s 416(6) for the purposes of FA 1996 s 87(3)(a), (b) as these affect Sch 9 paras 5, 6, the rights and powers to be attributed to a person will not be taken to include any rights and powers which would not be so attributable if the word partner were omitted from TA 1988 s 417(3)(a).

Where companies which are partners are also associated under any other provision of s 417 their rights and powers, other than as a partner, will continue to be attributed to the creditor company for the purposes of s 87(3).

DISREGARD OF CERTAIN LOANS

12 In applying TA 1988 s 416(2)(c) for the purposes of s 87(3)(a), (b), (c) as these affect Sch 9 paras 5, 6, the rights attributable to a company as a loan creditor in respect of any loan made by the creditor company in the ordinary course of its business of providing finance will not be taken into account.

DISREGARD OF CERTAIN SHAREHOLDINGS

13 In applying TA 1988 s 416(2) for the purposes of s 87(3)(a), (b) as these affect Sch 9 paras 5, 6, a company's possession of, or entitlement to possession of, share capital will not be taken to include possession of, or entitlement to possession of, relevant fixed rate preference shares as defined in TA 1988 Sch 28B para 13(5), where the conditions set out below are satisfied.

The conditions to be satisfied before relevant fixed rate preference shares can be disregarded in deciding whether companies are connected under FA 1996 s 87(3) for the purposes of Sch 9 paras 5, 6 are as follows—

(a) the creditor company is not a close company as defined in TA 1988 s 414; and

(b) the creditor company entered into the loan relationship in question in the ordinary course of its business of providing finance and that company, or a company which is part of the same group for the purposes of TA 1988 Chap IV Part X, subscribed for the relevant fixed rate preference shares of the debtor company in the ordinary course of its business of providing finance; and

(c) where the creditor company, or a company which is part of the same group for the purposes of TA 1988 Chap IV Part X, acquired relevant fixed rate preference shares of the debtor company through the exchange of loans for shares, the acquisition was in the ordinary course of its

ESCs

business of providing finance and the face value of the debt was significantly more than the market value of the shares for which it was exchanged; and

(d) the debtor company is within the charge to corporation tax in respect of any loan relationship which is exchanged for shares and any continuing loan relationship with the creditor company.

BAD DEBT RELIEF

***14** Where a creditor company elects for the effect of connection under FA 1996 s 87 with the debtor company in respect of a loan relationship to be disregarded under this concession, then relief for bad debt will continue to be allowed in accordance with FA 1996 Sch 9 para 5 and Sch 9 para 6(6) will not affect the debit arising when the creditor ceases to be a party to the loan relationship. These reliefs will be available for all the loan relationships between the creditor and the debtor company.*

RECOVERY/REVALUATION OF DEBTS

***15** Where a creditor company elects for the effect of connection under FA 1996 s 87 to be disregarded for the purposes of Sch 9 paras 5, 6 in accordance with this concession then that company must agree that where bad debt relief has been given, any decrease in the bad debt provision or recovery will be treated as if it was an appropriate adjustment under para 5(2), notwithstanding Sch 9 para 6, in the accounting period to which it relates.*

In addition any profit arising when the creditor ceases to be a party to the loan relationship will be treated as if it was a taxable amount except to the extent it represents a provision for which tax relief was denied.

DEBT EQUITY SWAPS—GENERAL

***16** Where a creditor company, which has not previously been connected with the debtor company under FA 1996 s 87, exchanges loans for ordinary share capital of the debtor and as a result of the swap becomes connected with the debtor company under s 87 it is, notwithstanding that connection, entitled to statutory relief under Sch 9 para 6(4) in respect of any loans exchanged for shares. Such relief is due regardless of whether a company chooses to take advantage of this concession.*

A creditor company may also exchange loans for shares which are not ordinary share capital. Fixed rate preference shares of the kind described in para 13 are in this category. The creditor company may also have other outstanding loans to the debtor which are not exchanged for shares of any description. The concession enables creditors to obtain relief both for share swaps which do not meet the statutory conditions in Sch 9 para 6(4) (see para 17) and, in certain circumstances, for outstanding loans (see para 18).

DEBT EQUITY SWAPS INTO FIXED RATE PREFERENCE SHARES

***17** Where holdings of fixed rate preference shares are disregarded, under the terms of the concession, a company which exchanges loans for such shares will not be treated as connected to the debtor company under FA 1996 s 87. The creditor company will therefore be entitled to relief in respect of any difference between the tax value of the loans and the value of the shares for which they were exchanged. In addition the creditor will, under the concession, continue to be entitled to relief under Sch 9 para 5 in respect of any loans which were not exchanged for shares.*

DEBT EQUITY SWAP INTO ORDINARY SHARE CAPITAL—TREATMENT OF NON-SWAPPED LOANS

***18** Where the conditions in para 13(a), (c), (d) are met, except that as a result of the swap the creditor company acquired ordinary share capital not fixed rate preference shares, then in addition to statutory relief for loans which are exchanged the creditor company will, by concession, be entitled to bad debt relief for that part of the accounting period prior to the swap, on any loans which were not exchanged for shares. Any bad debt relief in respect of non-exchanged loans which relates to the period up to the debt equity swap will not be withdrawn solely because the companies are connected as a result of that swap, notwithstanding Sch 9 para 6.*

To take advantage of this concession the creditor company must agree that where bad debt relief has been given in respect of a debt under this concession any decrease in the bad debt provision or recovery will be treated as if it was an appropriate adjustment under para 5(2), notwithstanding Sch 9 para 6, in the accounting period to which it relates. In addition the company must agree that any profit arising when it ceases to be a party to the loan relationship will be treated as if it was a taxable amount except to the extent it represents a provision for which tax relief was denied.

In accordance with Sch 9 para 6 neither bad debt relief nor any loss resulting from the creditor company ceasing to be a party to the loan relationships with the debtor company will be due for any period following the debt/equity swap in respect of any outstanding loans to the debtor company.

CONTROL WITHIN THE TERMS OF THE CONCESSION CHANGING TO OTHER FORMS OF CONTROL

19 A creditor company which has not been regarded as connected with the debtor company under FA 1996 s 87 by virtue of the concession may subsequently become connected with the debtor company in circumstances outside the terms of the concession. This could happen, for example, as a result of a second debt/equity swap into ordinary share capital or through a subscription for ordinary shares.

Where a connection under s 87 which is disregarded under paras 11, 12 and 13 of this concession is replaced by a connection which cannot be so disregarded (for convenience called the non-ESC connection) the effects are as set out in paras 20–23.

NON-ESC CONNECTION—TIMING

20 Where a creditor company which has by virtue of paras 11, 12 and 13 been treated as not connected with the debtor company under s 87, subsequently becomes connected with the debtor company in circumstances which are not within those paras it will be treated for all the purposes of Sch 9 paras 5, 6 as becoming connected with the debtor company at the time at which the subsequent connection occurs.

NON-ESC CONNECTION—EFFECT ON BAD DEBT RELIEF FOR PERIOD IN WHICH CONNECTION OCCURS

21 In the accounting period in which control within the terms of the concession is replaced by control outside its terms the creditor company will, by concession, be entitled to bad debt relief for outstanding loans for that part of the accounting period prior to the non-ESC connection.

NON-ESC CONNECTION—EFFECT ON EARLIER BAD DEBT RELIEF

22 Any bad debt relief given in respect of the loan relationship for periods prior to the non-ESC connection will not be withdrawn solely because of the later connection, notwithstanding Sch 9 para 6.

Any decreases in bad debt provisions or recoveries in respect of those loan relationships will be treated as if they were taxable amounts to the extent that bad debt relief has already been given. Any profit arising when the creditor ceases to be a party to the loan relationship will be treated as if it was a taxable amount except to the extent it represents a provision for which tax relief was denied. In all cases the relevant credit will be chargeable in the accounting period to which it relates.

NON-ESC CONNECTION—EFFECT ON LATER BAD DEBT RELIEF

23 No bad debt relief, or relief for losses arising when the creditor company ceases to be a party to the loan relationship, will be given under this concession for that part of an accounting period after the non-ESC connection occurs or for any subsequent accounting period.

CONNECTION UNDER FA 1996 S 87 AT 1 APRIL 1996

24 A creditor company may be connected under FA 1996 s 87 with a debtor company at 1 April 1996 as a result of an earlier debt/equity swap. Where the creditor company would prior to 1 April 1996 have been entitled to bad debt relief under TA 1988 s 74(1)(j) in respect of a loan relationship with the debtor company in existence at that date and the conditions in para 13(a), (c), (d), are met except that the creditor company (or a company which is part of the same group for the purposes of TA 1988 Chap IV Part X) acquired shares other than fixed rate preference shares, then the creditor company will for loans outstanding at 1 April 1996, by concession, be allowed relief under Sch 9 para 5 and relief for any loss arising when it ceases to be a party to such loans.

To take advantage of this concession the creditor company must agree that where bad debt relief has been given in respect of a debt under this concession any decrease in the bad debt provision or recovery will be treated as if it was an appropriate adjustment under para 5(2), notwithstanding Sch 9 para 6, in the accounting period to which it relates. In addition the company must agree that any profit arising when it ceases to be a party to the loan relationship will be treated as if it was a taxable amount except to the extent it represents a provision for which tax relief was denied.

WHEN THE CONCESSION WILL APPLY

25 This concession will have effect as from 1 April 1996 in respect of loan relationships to which a company is a party on or after that date. A company which wishes to take advantage of the concession will be required to do so in respect of all loan relationships between itself and debtor companies which fall within the terms of the concession.

A company which wishes to take advantage of the concession should notify the office dealing with its tax affairs. The company should then within 12 months of the end of an accounting period notify its office of the relief which it is claiming under the terms of the concession for that accounting period.

Commentary—*Simon's Direct Tax Service* **D2.1122.**
Revenue internal guidance—Company Taxation Manual CT12600–12608 (explanation of the concession).
Note—This concession was classified as obsolete by IR 1 (January 2004). It has been replaced by legislation amending FA 1996 s 87 (FA 2002 ss 82, 141, Sch 25 paras 1, 7, Sch 40 Pt 3(12)) with effect for company accounting periods beginning after 30 September 2002.

C29 *Transfers of long-term insurance business: transitional relief for losses incurred in general annuity business*

Note—This concession was classified as obsolete by IR 1 (January 2004).

C30 *Authorised unit trusts and open-ended investment companies: waivers of distributions*

THE TAX FRAMEWORK FOR DISTRIBUTIONS

1 Under TA 1988 ss 468H, 468I, an authorised unit trust (AUT) is required, for each "distribution period" (as defined in s 468H(3)(*a*)), to show in its "distribution accounts" (defined in s 468H(3)(*b*)) the total amount of income available for distribution to its unit holders. Section 468H(2) provides that, for tax purposes, the making of a distribution to a unit holder includes investing an amount on the unit holder's behalf in respect of his accumulation units.

2 For tax purposes, the total amount shown in the "distribution accounts" as available for distribution to unit holders is, in all cases, treated as though it is actually distributed on the relevant "distribution date" (as defined in s 468H(4)). The trustees are obliged under TA 1988 s 234A to issue appropriate tax vouchers to the unit holders in respect of the distribution.

3 The Open-ended Investment Companies (Tax) Regulations 1997 (SI 1997/1154) provide that the tax rules for open-ended investment companies (OEICs) which are incorporated in the UK have essentially the same effects as the corresponding rules for AUTs. In particular, that means that the total amount shown in the "distribution accounts" of an OEIC as available for distribution to the owners of its shares is treated for tax purposes as though it is distributed to them on the relevant distribution date, and the company has to issue tax vouchers accordingly.

FINANCIAL SERVICES REGULATIONS

4 AUTs and OEICs have to comply with the relevant Financial Services Regulations which have been made by the Securities and Investments Board (SIB). One of the requirements of those Regulations is that, except in the circumstances described in the following paragraph, an AUT or OEIC must, in respect of each of its accounting periods, distribute or, respectively, accumulate the total amount of income which is available for allocation between the holders of its income or accumulation units or shares.

5 An AUT or OEIC does not have to comply with this requirement if having to do so would mean that the average amount of income allocated to the investors would fall below the *de minimis* level specified in the relevant Regulations. In effect, this means that the SIB Regulations permit an AUT or OEIC to waive a distribution (or accumulation) in such circumstances if it so chooses, although the fund does, in fact, have some income available for distribution.

THE STRICT POSITION IN TAX LAW

6 The tax rules relating to the distributions of AUTs and OEICs apply wherever, in respect of a distribution period, a fund has an amount of income available for distribution. In strictness, that means that where, under the terms of the relevant *de minimis* provision in the Financial Services Regulations, an AUT or OEIC chooses to waive a distribution (or accumulation) for a particular accounting period, it is, nevertheless, treated for tax purposes as making distributions of the total amounts shown in the "distribution accounts" as available for distribution to its investors for distribution periods ending in the accounting period in question. The trustees or OEIC are accordingly obliged to issue tax vouchers to the unit holders or shareholders in respect of those deemed distributions.

THE CONCESSIONAL TREATMENT

7 Under the terms of this concession, provided that the conditions specified in para 8 are satisfied or, as the case may be, the condition specified in para 9 is satisfied, the AUT or OEIC concerned will not be treated for tax purposes as making distributions of the total amounts shown in its "distribution accounts" as available for distribution to its investors in respect of a distribution period for which it waives a distribution (or accumulation) in accordance with the *de minimis* provision in the relevant Financial Services Regulations. In such circumstances, the requirement to issue tax vouchers in respect of the waived distribution will be relaxed. The differences between the conditions in para 8 and 9 reflect the differences between the *de minimis* provisions applying to AUTs and OEICs.

8 The conditions applicable to an AUT are—

- no more than 50 per cent by value of its units in issue on the distribution date are held in bearer form; and
- the income property of the AUT for the accounting period concerned does not become part of the capital property of the AUT at the end of that period, but is carried forward to the next accounting period and assimilated in the income property of the AUT for that accounting period.

9 The condition applicable to an OEIC is that no more than 50 per cent by value of its shares in issue on the distribution date are held in bearer form.

10 The relaxations provided under this concession extend no further than modifying the tax treatment of distributions of an AUT or OEIC in the circumstances in which it applies. In particular, the concession does not have the effect of treating income arising to an AUT or OEIC during an accounting period for which a distribution (or accumulation) is waived as though, for tax purposes, it arises later. The fund's liability to corporation tax in respect of that accounting period will be calculated according to the usual rules by reference to its taxable profits for that period.

UMBRELLA SCHEMES AND COMPANIES

11 For the purposes of the Tax Acts, each sub-fund of an AUT which is an umbrella scheme is regarded as an AUT in its own right, and the umbrella scheme itself is not regarded as an AUT. Similarly, each sub-fund of an OEIC which is an umbrella company is regarded as an OEIC in its own right, and the umbrella company itself is not regarded as an OEIC.

12 Where a sub-fund of an umbrella scheme is treated as an AUT for tax purposes, references in this concession to the units in issue of that AUT are to be regarded as references to the rights or interests (however described) of those persons who for the time being have rights in the sub-fund in question. Similarly, where a sub-fund of an umbrella company is treated as an OEIC for tax purposes, references in this concession to the shares in issue of that OEIC are to be regarded as references to the shares in issue of the umbrella company which for the time being confer rights in the sub-fund in question.

Commentary—*Simon's Direct Tax Service* **D4.1336.**
Note—This concession has effect for distribution periods ending on or after 18 July 1997.

ESCs

C31 *Scientific research associations*

Scientific research associations which qualified for tax exemption under TA 1988 s 508 for accounting periods ending on or before 31 December 1996, and which would have—

(i) continued to do so under the practice of the Department of Trade and Industry up to that time; and

(ii) met the requirements of s 508(1)(*b*),

will be treated as eligible for the tax exemptions provided by s 508 and TCGA 1992 s 271(6), for accounting periods beginning before 1 September 1999.

This treatment will also be extended to bodies which were established before 4 September 1998 which would have obtained approval as scientific research associations under the practice of the Department of Trade and Industry up to 31 December 1996.

Payments to bodies treated as eligible for the exemption under s 508 as a result of this concession, will qualify for relief under CAA 1990 s 136, provided the other conditions for relief under that section are satisfied.

Capital gains made on disposals of assets on or after 4 September 1998 will qualify for exemption under this concession provided the proceeds are applied for the purposes of qualifying scientific research by a body approved by the Department of Trade and Industry as a scientific research association for accounting periods beginning on or after 1 September 1999.

Commentary—*Simon's Direct Tax Service* **C4.535.**
Notes—CAA 1990 s 136 was repealed by FA 2000 Sch 40, Pt II(7).

C32 *Interest relief—companies with tax and NICs liabilities under the personal service rules where the payments for relevant contracts have been received after deduction of tax by virtue of the Construction Industry Scheme (CIS) provisions*

Under the service provision rules, intermediaries such as personal service companies are required to account for tax and NICs by 19 April on deemed Schedule E payments arising at 5 April in respect of relevant engagements. If an intermediary is unable to finalise the calculation of its deemed Schedule E payment by 19 April then interest will be charged on any late paid tax and NICs.

The deemed Schedule E payment calculation is based upon the amount the company receives for the relevant engagement(*s*). It is independent of any calculations made for the purposes of the CIS and does not take into account any deductions of tax from payments received. The CIS deduction is treated as Corporation Tax paid in respect of the profits of the company. It is not therefore available for offset against any liability in respect of the deemed Schedule E payment and secondary NICs.

Where an intermediary is subject to the service provision rules in respect of income which it has received under deduction under the CIS then, if the intermediary—

- is a company, and
- is treated as making a deemed Schedule E payment in any tax year, and
- in respect of an accounting period which overlaps with a tax year for which a deemed payment is treated as made, is entitled to a repayment of Corporation Tax as a result of deductions being made under the CIS, then

it may make a claim to set off the CIS repayment due to it against any outstanding tax and NICs due on the deemed Schedule E payment, using 19 April as the effective date of payment for the set off.

Where such a claim is made by 31 January following the 19 April when payment is strictly due and that claim is accepted, then interest will not be charged on the amount of late paid tax and NICs which is matched by the Corporation Tax repayment up to the date of the repayment of the Corporation Tax.

The concession will apply in relation to Schedule E payments deemed to arise at 5 April 2001 on which the tax and NICs is due by 19 April 2001. It will be reviewed for later tax years.

Commentary—*Simon's Direct Tax Service* **E4.1018, E5.529.**
Note—This Concession is as it appears in IR 1 Supp (November 2001).

D CONCESSIONS RELATING TO CAPITAL GAINS (INDIVIDUALS AND COMPANIES)

NOTE: The following concession also applies for the purposes of capital gains tax:

A19 *Giving up tax where there are Revenue delays in using information.*

D1 *Insurance recoveries: short leases*

Note—This concessionary relief was replaced by statutory relief under TCGA 1992 s 23(8) introduced by FA 1996 Sch 39 para 3.

D2 *Residence in the UK: year of commencement or cessation of residence—capital gains tax*

1 An individual who comes to live in the UK and is treated as resident here for any year of assessment from the date of arrival is charged to capital gains tax only in respect of chargeable gains from disposals made after arrival, provided that the individual has not been resident or ordinarily resident in the UK at any time during the five years of assessment immediately preceding the year of assessment in which he or she arrived in the UK.

2 An individual who leaves the UK and is treated on departure as not resident and not ordinarily resident here is not charged to capital gains tax on gains from disposals made after the date of departure, provided that the individual was not resident and not ordinarily resident in the UK for the whole of at least four out of the seven years of assessment immediately preceding the year of assessment in which he or she left the UK.

3 This concession does not apply to any individual in relation to gains on the disposal of assets which are situated in the UK and which, at any time between the individual's departure from the UK and the end of the year of assessment, are either—

(i) used in or for the purposes of a trade, profession or vocation carried on by that individual in the UK through a branch or agency; or

(ii) used or held for, or acquired for use by or for the purposes of, such a branch or agency.

4 This concession does not apply to the trustees of a settlement who commence or cease residence in the UK or to a settlor of a settlement in relation to gains in respect of which the settlor is chargeable under TCGA 1992 ss 77–79, or TCGA 1992 s 86, Sch 5.

5 This revised concession applies to any individual who ceases to be resident or ordinarily resident in the UK on or after 17 March 1998, or becomes resident or ordinarily resident in the UK on or after 6 April 1998.

Commentary—*Simon's Direct Tax Service* **C1.601; E6.123.**
Revenue internal guidance—Capital gains manual CG 25730, 25731 (application of this concession where Concession A11 applies in the case of a contract of employment abroad).
CG 25980–26010 (withholding the benefit of this concession where attempt made to use it for tax avoidance).
Note—The text of this concession is as it appears in IR 1 (January 2000).

D3 *Private residence exemption: periods of absence* (*a*)

In determining how far an individual's gain on the disposal of his residence is exempt from capital gains tax under TCGA 1992 ss 222–226, s 223(3) provides that within specified limits, periods of absence are to be treated as periods of residence if, inter alia, the absence was as a result of his employment. Where in the case of a husband and wife who are living together this condition is satisfied as regards one spouse, it is treated as satisfied as regards the other.

Commentary—*Simon's Direct Tax Service* **C2.1307**.

D4 *Private residence exemption: periods of absence (b)*

In determining how far an individual's gain on the disposal of his home is exempt from capital gains tax under TCGA 1992 ss 222–226, certain periods of absence are treated as periods of residence if he resumes residence there at some time after the absence. This condition will be treated as satisfied where after a period of absence falling within s 223(3)(*b*) (absence on duties overseas) or (*c*) (other absences due to conditions of employment) an individual is unable to resume residence in his previous home because the terms of his employment require him to work elsewhere.

Commentary—*Simon's Direct Tax Service* **C2.1307**.
Cross references—See TCGA s 284A (chargeable gain deemed to arise as a consequence of abuse of concessions).

D5 *Private residence exemption: property held by personal representatives*

TCGA 1992 s 225 extends the exemption from capital gains tax given for private residences to cases where a trustee disposes of a house which has been the only or main residence of an individual entitled to occupy it under the terms of a settlement. Relief is also given where personal representatives dispose of a house which before and after the deceased's death has been used as their only or main residence by individuals who under the will or intestacy are entitled to the whole or substantially the whole of the proceeds of the house either absolutely or for life.

Commentary—*Simon's Direct Tax Service* **C2.1306.**

ESCs

D6 *Private residence exemption: separated couples*

Where a married couple separate or are divorced and one partner ceases to occupy the matrimonial home and subsequently as part of a financial settlement disposes of the home, or an interest in it, to the other partner the home may be regarded for the purposes of TCGA 1992 ss 222–224, as continuing to be a residence of the transferring partner from the date his or her occupation ceases until the date of transfer, provided that it has throughout this period been the other partner's only or main residence. Thus, where a husband leaves the matrimonial home while still owning it, the usual capital gains tax exemption or relief for a taxpayer's only or main residence would be given on the subsequent transfer to the wife, provided she has continued to live in the house and the husband has not elected that some other house should be treated for capital gains tax purposes as his main residence for this period.

Commentary—*Simon's Direct Tax Service* **C2.1305.**

D7 *Retirement relief: business passing to spouse*

Note—CGTA 1979 s 124 was repealed with effect for disposals made after 5 April 1985 and replaced by the retirement relief provisions of FA 1985 ss 69, 70, Sch 20. This concession is therefore obsolete.

D8 *Retirement relief: change in business during ten years before disposal*

Note—CGTA 1979 s 124 was repealed with effect for disposals made after 5 April 1985 and replaced by the retirement relief provisions of FA 1985 ss 69, 70, Sch 20. This concession is therefore obsolete.

D9 *Retirement relief: directors of groups of companies*

Note—CGTA 1979 s 124 was repealed with effect for disposals made after 5 April 1985 and replaced by the retirement relief provisions of FA 1985 ss 69, 70, Sch 20. This concession is therefore obsolete.

D10 *Unquoted shares acquired before 6 April 1965: disposal following reorganisation of share capital*

Where, in consequence of a reorganisation of share capital before 6 April 1965, computation of a gain by reference to value at that date is required by TCGA 1992 Sch 2 para 19(1), or where, under para 19(2) in consequence of such a reorganisation after 6 April 1965 time apportionment applies only to the gain or loss up to the date of reorganisation, capital gains tax is not charged on a disposal of the entire new shareholding on more than the actual gain realised.

For the purposes of this concession, the disposal of the entire new holding by way of a number of separate transactions all within the same income tax year (or, in the case of a company, the same accounting period), will be treated as a single disposal.

Commentary—*Simon's Direct Tax Service* **C2.728.**
Note—The text of this concession is as it appears in IR 1 Supp (November 2000).

D11 *Retirement relief: asset owned by a director and used by the company*

Note—CGTA 1979 s 124 was repealed with effect for disposals made after 5 April 1985 and replaced by the retirement relief provisions of FA 1985 ss 69, 70, Sch 20. This concession is therefore obsolete.

D12 *Close companies: apportionments of income and the consequentials for capital gains tax: close companies in liquidation*

Note—The close company apportionment provisions were repealed by FA 1989 s 103, Sch 17 Part V. This concession is therefore obsolete.

D13 *Retirement relief: sale of assets in anticipation of liquidation*

Note—CGTA 1979 s 124 was repealed with effect for disposals made after 5 April 1985 and replaced by the retirement relief provisions of FA 1985 ss 69, 70, Sch 20. This concession is therefore obsolete.

D14 *Retirement relief: sale of assets following cessation of trading*

Note—CGTA 1979 s 124 was repealed with effect for disposals made after 5 April 1985 and replaced by the retirement relief provisions of FA 1985 ss 69, 70, Sch 20. This concession is therefore obsolete.

D15 *Relief for the replacement of business assets—unincorporated associations*

Rollover relief for the replacement of business assets extends, under TCGA 1992 s 158(1)(*e*), to unincorporated associations not established for profit whose activities are wholly or mainly carried on otherwise than for profit. In cases where the assets are held by a company in which at least 90 per cent of the shares are held by or on behalf of such an association or its members, the relief will be available provided the other conditions for it are satisfied.

Commentary—*Simon's Direct Tax Service* **C3.302.**
Revenue Interpretation RI 211—FA 1999 s 76 to be applied in certain circumstances where a capital gain has been relieved by way of a concession published before 9 March 1999 and the gain is not subsequently returned in accordance with the terms of the concession.

D16 *Relief for the replacement of business assets: repurchase of the same asset*

For the purposes of TCGA 1992 s 152, where a person sells a business, or a business asset, and for purely commercial reasons subsequently repurchases the same asset, that asset will be regarded as a ''new asset''.

Commentary—*Simon's Direct Tax Service* **C3.304.**
Revenue Interpretation RI 211—FA 1999 s 76 to be applied in certain circumstances where a capital gain has been relieved by way of a concession published before 9 March 1999 and the gain is not subsequently returned in accordance with the terms of the concession.
Note—The text of this concession is as it appears in IR 1 Supp (November 2000).

D17 *Unit trusts for exempt unit holders: TCGA 1992 s 100(2)*

Where a unit trust otherwise qualifies for exemption from tax on chargeable gains under TCGA 1992 s 100(2), the exemption is not withheld because of such temporary holding of units by the managers of the trust under the ordinary arrangements of the trust for the issue and redemption of units.

Commentary—*Simon's Direct Tax Service* **D4.1325; E7.233, 249.**

D18 *Default on mortgage granted by vendor*

Where on the sale of an asset at arm's length there has been a default in respect of a loan granted by the vendor to the purchaser of all or part of the proceeds, and as a result the vendor has regained the beneficial ownership of the interest which he has contracted to sell, the vendor may elect that for capital gains tax purposes the gain realised by him on that sale be taken as limited to the amount of the proceeds (net of allowable incidental costs of disposal) retained by him and the loan be treated as never having come into existence. Accordingly the computation of the gain (or loss) on any later sale of that asset will be made by reference to the original date and cost of acquisition. The treatment for income tax purposes of any interest received in respect of the loan will remain unaltered.

Commentary—*Simon's Direct Tax Service* **C1.408.**

D19 *Replacement of buildings destroyed*

Commentary—*Simon's Direct Tax Service* **C2.502, 1107.**
Note—This concessionary relief was replaced by statutory relief under TCGA 1992 s 23(6) to (8) introduced by FA 1996 Sch 39 para 3.

D20 *Private residence exemption: residence occupied by dependent relative*

Where relief is claimed under TCGA 1992 s 226 (CGTA 1979 s 105) in respect of the disposal by an individual of a dwelling house which has at any time been the sole residence of a dependent relative, the condition that the dwelling house must have been provided rent free and without any other consideration will be regarded as satisfied where the dependent relative pays all or part of the occupier's council tax and the cost of repairs to the dwelling house attributable to normal wear and tear.

Additionally, the benefit of the relief will not be lost where the dependent relative makes other payments in respect of the property either to the individual or to a third party, provided that no net income is receivable by the individual, taking one year with another. For this purpose net income will be computed in accordance with the normal rules of Schedule A, except that any mortgage payments (including both income and capital elements) and any other payments made by the dependent relative as consideration for the provision of the property, whether made directly to the mortgagee or other recipient or indirectly via the individual will be credited as receipts. The deductions to be debited will be computed in accordance with the normal rules of Schedule A.

Commentary—*Simon's Direct Tax Service* **C2.1311.**
Note—Relief was withdrawn for disposals after 5 April 1988 except where, before 6 April 1988, the dwelling house was the sole residence of the dependent relative.

D21 *Private residence exemption: late claims in dual residence cases*

Where for any period an individual has, or is treated by the Taxes Acts as having more than one residence, but his interest in each of them, or in each of them except one, is such as to have no more than a negligible capital value on the open market (eg a weekly rented flat, or accommodation provided by an employer) the two year time limit laid down by TCGA 1992 s 222(5)(*a*) for nominating one of those residences as the individual's main residence for capital gains tax purposes will be extended where the individual was unaware that such a nomination could be made. In such cases the nomination may be made within a reasonable time of the individual first becoming aware of the possibility of making a nomination, and it will be regarded as effective from the date on which the individual first had more than one residence.

Commentary—*Simon's Direct Tax Service* **C2.1303.**
Note—The text of this concession is as it appears in IR 1 Supp (November 2000).

ESCs

D22 *Relief for the replacement of business assets: expenditure on improvements to existing assets*

Where a person carrying on a trade uses the proceeds from the disposal of an ''old asset'' on capital expenditure to enhance the value of other assets, such expenditure is treated for the purposes of TCGA 1992 ss 152 to 158 and Sch 4 as incurred in acquiring other assets provided—

(*a*) the other assets are used only for the purposes of the trade, or
(*b*) on completion of the work on which the expenditure was incurred the assets are immediately taken into use and used only for the purposes of the trade.

Commentary—*Simon's Direct Tax Service* **C3.304.**
Revenue Interpretation RI 211—FA 1999 s 76 to be applied in certain circumstances where a capital gain has been relieved by way of a concession published before 9 March 1999 and the gain is not subsequently returned in accordance with the terms of the concession.

D23 *Relief for the replacement of business assets: partition of land on the dissolution of a partnership*

Where land used for the purposes of a trade carried on in partnership is partitioned by the partners, the land acquired is treated for the purposes of TCGA 1992 ss 152–158 as a ''new asset'' provided that the partnership is dissolved immediately thereafter. This concession also applies to other qualifying assets which are acquired on the partition.

Commentary—*Simon's Direct Tax Service* **C3.221, 315.**
Revenue Interpretation RI 211—FA 1999 s 76 to be applied in certain circumstances where a capital gain has been relieved by way of a concession published before 9 March 1999 and the gain is not subsequently returned in accordance with the terms of the concession.
Note—The text of this concession is as it appears in IR 1 Supp (November 2000).

D24 *Relief for the replacement of business assets: assets not brought immediately into trading use*

Where a ''new asset'' is not, on acquisition, immediately taken into use for the purposes of a trade, it will nevertheless qualify for relief under TCGA 1992 ss 152–158 provided—

(*a*) the owner proposes to incur capital expenditure for the purposes of enhancing its value;
(*b*) any work arising from such capital expenditure begins as soon as possible after acquisition, and is completed within a reasonable time;
(*c*) on completion of the work the asset is taken into use for the purpose of the trade and for no other purpose; and
(*d*) the asset is not let or used for any non-trading purpose in the period between acquisition and the time it is taken into use for the purpose of the trade.

Where a person acquires land with a building on it, or with the intention to construct a building on it, the land is treated as qualifying for this concession provided that the building itself qualifies for the relief, whether by this concession or otherwise, and provided the land is not let or used for any non-trading purpose in the period between its acquisition and the time that both it and the building are taken into use for the purposes of the trade.

Commentary—*Simon's Direct Tax Service* **C3.304.**
Revenue Interpretation RI 211—FA 1999 s 76 to be applied in certain circumstances where a capital gain has been relieved by way of a concession published before 9 March 1999 and the gain is not subsequently returned in accordance with the terms of the concession.
Note—The text of this concession is as it appears in IR 1 Supp (November 2000).

D25 *Relief for the replacement of business assets: acquisition of an interest in an asset already used for the purposes of a trade*

Where a person carrying on a trade uses the proceeds from the disposal of an ''old asset'' to acquire a further interest in another asset which is already in use for the purposes of the trade, the further interest is treated for the purposes of TCGA 1992 ss 152–158 as a ''new asset'' which is taken into use for the purposes of the trade.

Commentary—*Simon's Direct Tax Service* **C3.304.**
Revenue Interpretation RI 211—FA 1999 s 76 to be applied in certain circumstances where a capital gain has been relieved by way of a concession published before 9 March 1999 and the gain is not subsequently returned in accordance with the terms of the concession.
Note—The text of this concession is as it appears in IR 1 Supp (November 2000).

D26 *Relief for exchanges of joint interests*

Where interests in land which is in the joint beneficial ownership of two or more persons are exchanged after 19 December 1984, and *either*

- a holding of land is held jointly, and, as a result of the exchange, each joint owner becomes sole owner of part of the land formerly owned jointly, *or*
- a number of separate holdings of land are held jointly, and, as a result of the exchange, each joint owner becomes sole owner of one or more holding,

a relief along the lines of TCGA 1992 ss 247, 248 (relief on compulsory acquisition of land) may be claimed to alleviate the charges to capital gains tax which would otherwise arise.

If the consideration received or deemed to be received for the interest relinquished is less than or equal to the consideration given or deemed to be given for the interest acquired, relief will be allowed on the lines of that provided by TCGA 1992 s 247(2), (5); where [the] consideration is greater, greater relief will be allowed on the lines of s 247(3), (5). For this purpose the interest relinquished will be treated as the ''old land'' and the interest acquired as the ''new land''. ''Land'' includes any interest in or right over land and ''holding of land'' includes an estate or interest in a holding of land, and is to be construed in accordance with TCGA 1992 s 243(3).

Relief will not be allowed to the extent that the ''new land'' is, or becomes, a dwelling house or part of a dwelling house within the meaning of TCGA 1992 ss 222–226. However, where individuals who are joint beneficial owners of dwelling houses which are their respective residences become sole owners of those houses in consequence of an exchange of interests, concessionary relief may be claimed if, by virtue of TCGA 1992 ss 222, 223, each gain accruing on a disposal of each dwelling house immediately after that exchange would be exempt. Each individual must undertake to accept for capital gains tax purposes that he or she is deemed to have acquired the other's interest in the dwelling house at the original base cost and on the original date on which that joint interest was acquired.

Where—

- interests in land are exchanged after 29 October 1987; and
- this concession applies to that exchange; and
- there is a parallel exchange of interests in milk or potato quota associated with the land; and
- after the exchange each joint owner becomes sole owner of the part of the quota relating to the land he now owns;

then this concession will apply to the exchange of interests in quota as it applies to the exchange of interests in the land.

For the purposes of this concession a married couple is treated as an individual, so that an exchange of interests which results in a married couple alone becoming joint owners of land or of a dwelling house will meet the terms of the concession.

Commentary—*Simon's Direct Tax Service* **C2.1104.**
Revenue internal guidance—Capital gains manual CG 65170–65175 (operation of this concession, with worked example).

D27 *Earn-outs*

Note—This concession was superseded by TCGA 1992 s 138A introduced by FA 1997 s 89. It was classified obsolete by IR 1 Supp (November 1998).

D28 *Assets of negligible value*

Note—This concession is replaced by TCGA 1992 s 24(2) substituted by FA 1996 Sch 39 para 4 and is therefore obsolete.

D29 *Transfers of long-term business under Insurance Companies Act 1982 s 49*

This concession was superseded, with effect from 1 January 1990, by legislation introduced by FA 1990 Sch 9 (TA 1970 s 267A, TA 1988 ss 444A, 460(10A), CAA 1990 s 152A) and is therefore obsolete.

D30 *Relief for the replacement of business assets*

Note—This concession is rendered obsolete by FA 1995 s 48 and was classified as obsolete by IR 1 Supp (1995).

D31 *Retirement relief: date of disposal*

Commentary—*Simon's Direct Tax Service* **C3.606.**
Revenue Interpretation RI 202—The effect of the phasing out of retirement relief on claims for relief under this concession.
Note—This concession was classified as obsolete by IR 1 (January 2004).

D32 *Transfer of a business to a company*

Where liabilities are taken over by a company on the transfer of a business to the company, the Revenue are prepared for the purposes of the "rollover" provision in TCGA 1992 s 162, not to treat such liabilities as consideration. If therefore the other conditions of s 162 are satisfied, no capital gain arises on the transfer. Relief under s 162 is not precluded by the fact that some or all of the liabilities of the business are not taken over by the company.

Commentary—*Simon's Direct Tax Service* **C3.404.**
Revenue Interpretation RI 211—FA 1999 s 76 to be applied in certain circumstances where a capital gain has been relieved by way of a concession published before 9 March 1999 and the gain is not subsequently returned in accordance with the terms of the concession.
Note—The text of this concession is as it appears in IR 1 Supp (November 2000).

D33 *Capital gains tax on compensation and damages*

ZIM PROPERTIES LTD—COMPENSATION AND DAMAGES

1 Introduction

A person who receives a capital sum derived from an asset is treated for the purposes of capital gains tax as disposing of that asset. The case of *Zim Properties Ltd v Proctor* 58 TC 371 has established that the right to take court action for compensation or damages is an asset for capital gains tax purposes. It follows that a person who receives compensation or damages, whether by court order or arbitration or by negotiated settlement as a result of a cause of action may be regarded as disposing of the right of action. A capital gain may accrue as a result.

THE STRICT POSITION

2 Cost of acquisition

A capital gain will accrue if the capital sum received as compensation exceeds the amount which may be deducted as the cost of acquiring the right of action. A right of action will almost invariably be acquired otherwise than by way of bargain made at arm's length. Special rules for determining the cost of acquisition apply in these circumstances. Where the right of action was acquired on or before 9 March 1981, it is deemed to have been acquired for a sum equal to its market value on the date of acquisition. Where it was acquired on or after 10 March 1981 and there was no disposal of the right of action corresponding to the claimant's acquisition of it, then where, as is usually the case, the taxpayer gave no consideration to acquire it is treated as having been acquired without cost.

If the cause of action was held on 31 March 1982 and disposed of on or after 6 April 1988, it will, in accordance with the rebasing rules, be deemed to have been disposed of and immediately reacquired at its open market value on 31 March 1982.

If a right of action passes on the death of the claimant, it is treated as acquired at its open market value on the date of death.

In computing the gain or loss, a deduction may be made for any legal and professional fees incurred in pursuing the claim. If the action in respect of a claim of substance fails, or if the expenses exceed the compensation, a capital loss may accrue.

3 Date of acquisition

A right of action accrues and so is acquired by a person for capital gains tax purposes when, for example as a result of a breach of contract or the negligent actions of another person (tort), he or she suffers actual loss or damage.

4 Market Value on acquisition

In practice, where relevant, the Board of Inland Revenue will be prepared to accept a valuation which gives rise to neither chargeable gain nor allowable loss.

5 Date of disposal

The right of action is treated as disposed of when a capital sum derived from it is received, and if a series of capital sums is received, each receipt is the occasion of a separate disposal.

6 Rebasing to 31 March 1982

If an asset which was held on 31 March 1982 is disposed of on or after 6 April 1988, the gain or loss is normally computed as if it had been disposed of and immediately reacquired at its open market value on 31 March 1982. If an underlying asset were held on 31 March 1982, but a right of action related to that asset were acquired after 31 March 1982, the rebasing provisions would apply on the disposal of the underlying asset but not on the disposal of the right of action.

7 Reliefs and exemptions

Some forms of compensation are specifically exempted from liability to capital gains tax (see paragraph 12 below) and these remain exempt despite the decision in *Zim Properties*. But other statutory reliefs and exemptions are not available where the receipt of the compensation is regarded as giving rise to a disposal of the right of action, not of any underlying asset to which the relief or exemption might apply. These include deferment relief for compensation applied in restoring or replacing an asset, roll-over relief for the replacement of business assets, retirement relief and private residence relief.

8 Relief by concession

Where a gain arises on the disposal of a right of action, the case may alternatively, by concession, be treated in accordance with the following paragraphs of this statement.

9 Underlying assets

Where the right of action arises by reason of the total or partial loss or destruction of or damage to a form of property which is an asset for capital gains tax purposes, or because the claimant suffered some loss or disadvantage in connection with such a form of property, any gain or loss on the disposal of the right of action may by concession be computed as if the compensation derived from that asset, and not from the right of action. As a result a proportion of the cost of the asset, determined in accordance with normal part-disposal rules, and indexation allowance, may be deducted in computing the gain. For example if compensation is paid by an estate agent because his negligence led to the sale of a building falling through, an appropriate part of the cost of the building may be deducted in computing any gain on the disposal of the right of action.

The gain may be computed by reference to the original cost of the underlying asset, with time-apportionment if appropriate if the asset was acquired before 6 April 1965 or by reference to its market value on 6 April 1965. For disposals on or after 6 April 1988, the gain may be computed in appropriate cases by reference to the value of the asset on 31 March 1982.

10 Other reliefs and exemptions

If the relief was or would have been available on the disposal of the relevant underlying asset, it will be available on the disposal of the right of action. For example, if compensation is derived from a cause of action in respect of damage to a building suffered by reason of professional negligence, and the compensation is applied in restoring the building, deferment relief under TCGA 1992 s 23 will be available as if the compensation derives from the building itself and not from the right of action.

Other reliefs which may become available in this way include private residence relief, retirement relief and roll-over relief. The Board of Inland Revenue will be prepared to consider extending time limits in cases where because of a delay in obtaining a capital sum in compensation, the normal time limit allowed for a relief has elapsed. If the right of action relates to an asset which is specifically exempt from capital gains tax, such as a motor car, any gain on the disposal of the right of action may be treated as exempt.

11 No underlying asset

A right of action may be acquired by a claimant in connection with some matter which does not involve a form of property which is an asset for capital gains tax purposes. This may be the case where professional advisers are said to have given misleading advice in a tax or other financial matter, or to have failed to claim a tax relief within proper time. Actions may be brought in relation to private or domestic matters. Where the action does not concern loss of or damage to or loss in connection with a form of property which is an asset for capital gains tax purposes, the approach in paragraph 9 above of treating the compensation as deriving from the asset itself is not appropriate. In these circumstances any gain accruing on the disposal of the right of action will be exempt from capital gains tax.

OTHER POINTS

12 Personal compensation or damages

TCGA 1992 s 51(2) provides that "sums obtained by way of compensation or damages for any wrong or injury suffered by an individual in his person or his profession or vocation" are not chargeable to capital gains tax. The words "wrong or injury" include breaches of contractual duties and torts (in Scotland, delicts). If the exemption would have applied to damages received for any

ESCs

wrong or injury, it also applies to any compensation for professional negligence in relation to an action in respect of that wrong or injury.

The words ''in his person'' are to be read in distinction to ''in his finances'' but they embrace more than physical injury so that distress, embarrassment loss of reputation or dignity may all be suffered ''in the person''. Compensation or damages for unfair or unlawful discrimination suffered ''in the person'' and for libel or slander (in Scotland defamation) would thus be included. Similarly the words ''in his profession or vocation'' refer to compensation or damages suffered by an individual in his professional capacity such as unfair discrimination, libel or slander (in Scotland, defamation) as distinct from ''in his finances''. If the compensation is received by the members of a partnership, each member, in Scotland as elsewhere, is treated as receiving a share of the compensation. The exemption is extended by concession to such compensation received by an individual in his trade or employment.

The exemption also extends to compensation received by a person other than the individual who suffered the wrong or injury, such as relatives or personal representatives of a deceased person. It also extends to compensation for emotional distress caused by the death of another person, and compensation for loss of financial support.

It does not apply to compensation for any other wrong or injury suffered by any person other than an individual.

13 Indemnity payments

The principle in *Zim Properties Ltd* is not regarded as applicable to payments made by the vendor to the purchaser of an asset under a warranty or indemnity included as one of the terms of a contract of purchase and sale.

Where such a contractual payment is made, then the cost of the asset to the person acquiring it will, on the occasion of a further disposal be reduced by the sum received. The sale proceeds of the person who makes (or is treated by TCGA 1992 s 171A as making) the disposal of the asset are adjusted under TCGA 1992 s 49 in respect of the sum received. Where a warranty or indemnity payment is not made in accordance with the terms of the contract, the principle in *Zim Properties* may apply and the sums received by the vendor or purchaser as appropriate may be identified as capital sums derived from the asset, or from the right of action, depending on the facts of the case.

14 Date of commencement

The concessions and practices set out in this Statement will apply to all open cases on the date of issue, 19 December 1988.

Commentary—*Simon's Direct Tax Service* **C1.327, 328.**
Note—The text of this concession is as it appears in IR 1 Supp (November 2001).

D34 *Rebasing and indexation: Shares held at 31 March 1982*

Where, for the purposes of the rebasing provisions in TCGA 1992 s 35 and the indexation provisions in TCGA 1992 s 55, it is necessary to determine the market value of shares or securities of the same class in any company on 31 March 1982, all the shares or securities held at that date will be valued as a single holding whether they were acquired on or before 6 April 1965 or after that date.

If the shares or securities in the relevant disposal represent some but not all of those valued at 31 March 1982 then the allowable cost or indexation allowance as appropriate will be based on the proportion that the shares or securities disposed of bears to the total holding at 31 March 1982.

Commentary—*Simon's Direct Tax Service* **C2.704.**
Note—The text of this concession is as it appears in IR 1 Supp (November 2000).

D35 *Employee trusts: transfers of assets to beneficiaries*

If the trustees of an employee trust transfer assets to a beneficiary for no payment there is normally a charge to capital gains tax on the trustees. There may also be a charge under Schedule E on an employee.

Where in such circumstances the employee is liable to income tax on the full market value of the assets transferred the trustees will not also be charged to capital gains tax on any gain arising on the transfer of those assets.

In this context ''employee trust'' means a trust within IHTA 1984 s 86 but without the restriction in sub-s (3), and provided that the employee in question is not a person of the kind described in IHTA 1984 s 28(4) and not excluded by sub-s (5).

This concession does not apply where on a transfer from trustees to a beneficiary special statutory rules restrict either the liability to capital gains tax or the Schedule E liability.

Commentary—*Simon's Direct Tax Service* **C4.207, I5.631.**

D36 *Relief for irrecoverable loans to traders: time limits for claims*

Note—This concession was given statutory effect by TCGA 1992 ss 253 (as amended by FA 1996) and 254 (as amended by FA 1996).

D37 *Private residence exemption: relocation arrangements*

Where work is being relocated, the employer may set up arm's length arrangements under which an employee, who moves home because of the relocation, can sell his or her home to a relocation company or to the employer and have a right to a share in any later profit made when the relocation company or the employer later sells the home. Such arrangements may also exist where employees are required by their employer to transfer within an organisation and as a result have to move home.

In such circumstances, if the home is fully exempt from capital gains tax, the employee's right to the share in any later profit will be exempt too. Some employees' homes may be only partially exempt (for example they may have been used partly for business purposes, or may not have been the main home throughout an employee's period of ownership). In such cases, a corresponding proportion of any gain relating to the right to later profits will also be exempt.

The concession does not apply when the right is held by the employee for more than three years.

Where an employee owns his or her home jointly with others and moves home in the circumstances described above, the concession will apply to the other joint holders in the same way as to the employee.

The concession applies to office holders in the same way as to employees, and to arrangements involving unincorporated relocation businesses in the same way as to those involving relocation companies.

Commentary—*Simon's Direct Tax Service* **C2.1301.**

D38 *Qualifying corporate bonds*

Where a person acquired corporate bonds in respect of shares or securities and those bonds became, or would fall to be treated as, qualifying corporate bonds by virtue only of FA 1989 s 139 (see TCGA 1992 Sch 11 para 16(4)), an allowable loss for capital gains purposes will accrue if—

(a) the qualifying corporate bonds were issued in respect of shares or other securities before 14 March 1989 and were still retained at that date by the person to whom they were issued;

(b) the bonds were acquired in a transaction within TCGA 1992 s 116(1) (FA 1984 s 64(7)) and on disposal on or after 14 March 1989 fall to be treated as qualifying corporate bonds as a result of FA 1989 s 139;

(c) relief under TCGA 1992 s 254 (CGTA 1979 s 136A) would have been available had the loan been a qualifying loan within TCGA 1992 s 254(1);

(d) a taxpayer claiming relief under this concession agrees that if part or all of the amount relieved is subsequently recovered the relief will be clawed back in the same way as if TCGA 1992 s 254 (CGTA 1979 s 136A) had applied, save that in all cases the chargeable gain will be treated as accruing to the claimant;

(e) when this concession applies, any gain or loss on the original shares or securities will be treated as accruing at the same time as the loss on the bonds in accordance with TCGA 1992 s 116(15) (FA 1984 Sch 13 para 12).

The loss is computed in accordance with the rules in TCGA 1992 s 254 (CGTA 1979 s 136A) and will be treated as arising when the benefit of this concession is claimed. However, the Revenue will be prepared to accept that any such loss should be treated as arising in an earlier year of assessment (or accounting period in the case of a company) provided that—

(1) the claim is made not later than two years after the end of that year of assessment (or accounting period), and

(2) all the conditions for the relief are satisfied at the date of claim, and

(3) the relief would have been available at the end of the year of assessment or accounting period for which relief is claimed.

Commentary—*Simon's Direct Tax Service* **C2.804.**
Note—This concession was classified as obsolescent by IR 1 Supp (November 1998).

D39 *Extension of leases*

Where the extension of a lease other than under its original terms involves the surrender of the old lease and the grant of a new lease, a liability to capital gains tax may strictly arise. In an arm's length transaction, the value, if any, of the new lease is taken into account as consideration for the disposal of the old lease.

ESCs

In practice, however, the surrender of a lease before its expiry and the grant of a new lease for a longer term will not be regarded as a disposal or part disposal of the old lease where all the following conditions are met—

- the transaction, whether made between connected or unconnected parties, is made on terms equivalent to those that would have been made between unconnected parties bargaining at arm's length;
- the transaction is not part of, or connected with, a larger scheme or series of transactions;
- a capital sum is not received by the lessee;
- the extent of the property in which the lessee has an interest under the new lease does not differ in any way from that to which the old lease related;
- the terms of the new lease (other than its duration and the amount of rent payable) do not differ from those of the old lease. For this purpose trivial differences will be ignored.

Commentary—*Simon's Direct Tax Service* **C2.1212.**
Revenue Interpretation RI 205—This concession is extended so that it can apply to transactions between connected parties where the terms of the transaction are equivalent to those that would have been made between unconnected parties bargaining at arms length.
Revenue Interpretation RI 211—FA 1999 s 76 to be applied in certain circumstances where a capital gain has been relieved by way of a concession published before 9 March 1999 and the gain is not subsequently returned in accordance with the terms of the concession.
Note—The text of this concession is as it appears in IR 1 (January 2000).

D40 *Non-resident trusts: definition of participator*

TCGA 1992 s 86, Sch 5 provide for a charge to capital gains tax on settlors of certain non- or dual resident trusts arising on trust property which originated from the settlor. Schedule 5 para 8 defines what property originates from the settlor and provides that property put into trust by certain companies is treated as originating from those who control the company in question. Schedule 5 para 9 sets out conditions under which trusts created before 19 March 1991 may fall within the scope of the charge on the settlor, some of which may apply to companies controlled by defined persons.

TCGA 1992 ss 87, 88 charge UK resident beneficiaries to capital gains tax on certain capital payments received from non- or dual resident settlements. Section 96 is concerned with the application of these provisions to capital payments made by companies which are controlled by the trustees and capital payments received by certain non-resident companies.

For the purpose of determining who controls such companies ''participator'' is defined in TA 1988 s 417(1). In applying the provisions of Sch 5 paras 2A(10), 8, 9(11) and s 96 a beneficiary of the trust, by concession, is not regarded as a participator in the company solely because of his status as beneficiary.

Commentary—*Simon's Direct Tax Service* **C4.439.**
Note—The text of this concession is as it appears in IR 1 (January 2000). It applies from 1 April 1999 (IR Press Release 1-4-99).

D41 *Non-resident trusts: loans repayable on demand*

Note—This concession is obsolete because it only applies where action was taken before 31 July 1992.

D42 *Mergers of leases*

Where a leaseholder of land acquires a superior interest in that land (either a superior lease or the freehold reversion) so that the first lease is extinguished the two assets are merged within the meaning of TCGA 1992 s 43. On a subsequent disposal the allowable expenditure will include—

- the cost of the first lease (after exclusion if appropriate of that part ''wasted'' down to the date of acquisition of the superior interest (TCGA 1992 Sch 8) in the case of a lease with 50 years or less to run); and
- the cost of the superior interest.

If the superior interest is itself a lease with 50 years or less to run, the total of these two amounts will be ''wasted'' down to the date of disposal under TCGA 1992 Sch 8.

In strictness, indexation allowance on the total of these two amounts is calculated by reference to the date of acquisition of the superior interest. By concession indexation allowance on the expenditure on the earlier, inferior, lease will be calculated by reference to the date of its acquisition.

For disposals before 29 June 1992, indexation allowance will be given by concession for the total of these two amounts by reference to the date of acquisition of the inferior interest.

Commentary—*Simon's Direct Tax Service* **C2.1212.**
Note—The text of this concession is as it appears in IR 1 Supp (November 2000).

D43 *Settled property*

On the death of a person entitled to a life interest in possession in settled property, as defined in TCGA 1992 s 68 (except where the property reverts to the settlor) the trustees are deemed to have disposed of the property and reacquired it at market value and, subject to TCGA 1992 ss 67, 74—

- *if the property continues to be settled property, by reason of TCGA 1992 s 72, there is no chargeable gain or allowable loss;*
- *if someone becomes absolutely entitled within TCGA 1992 s 71, by reason of TCGA 1992 s 73, there is no chargeable gain or allowable loss.*

By concession these provisions will also be applied on the death of a person with any other type of interest in possession in settled property.

Where property continues to be settled property, the concession may be claimed on the subsequent disposal of that property and the market value on date of death shall be reduced by the amount of any outstanding chargeable gain which was held over when that property was transferred to the trustees. The concession may not be claimed for any assets where there is a charge under TCGA 1992 s 67 or 74 on the subsequent disposal.

If this concession is claimed, it must apply to all of the assets in which the deceased had an interest in possession, other than any assets for which the capital gains tax computations were settled before 17 February 1993 or are subject to a charge under TCGA 1992 s 67 or 74. All references to TCGA 1992 include references to corresponding provisions in earlier legislation.

Commentary—*Simon's Direct Tax Service* **C4.210.**
Note—This concession was superseded by TCGA 1992 ss 72 (as amended by FA 1996) and 73 (as amended by FA 1996) in relation to deaths occurring after 5 April 1996. The concession is therefore obsolescent.

D44 *Rebasing and indexation: shares derived from larger holdings held at 31 March 1982*

For rebasing and indexation purposes, taxpayers are treated as having held an asset at 31 March 1982 if it was acquired after that date by a transfer, or series of transfers, treated as giving rise to neither a gain nor a loss for capital gains purposes, from someone who did hold it at that date. Such "no gain/ no loss" transfers include transfers between spouses and between companies in the same group where transfers fell within TCGA 1992 s 58 or s 171(1) or the predecessors of those sections.

Where, for rebasing and indexation purposes, it is necessary to establish the 31 March 1982 market value of shares or securities of the same class, shares or securities acquired in this way by no gain/ no loss transfer are added to any such shares or securities of the same class actually held by the transferee at 31 March 1982 and valued as a single holding.

For the purposes of this valuation, where a claim is made by the taxpayer, the value of the single holding may be regarded as—

- in the case of a disposal by an individual, the appropriate proportion of the value of any larger holding of shares or securities of the same class which were held by the individual's spouse at 31 March 1982 and from which part or all of the single holding was derived by one or more no gain/no loss transfers within TCGA 1992 s 58;
- in the case of a disposal by a company, the appropriate proportion of the value of any larger holding of shares or securities of the same class which were held by another company at 31 March 1982 and from which part or all of the single holding was derived by one or more no gain/no loss transfers within TCGA 1992 s 171(1).

This extra-statutory concession applies in relation to—

- all relevant disposals made before 16 March 1993 in relation to which a claim is made before liabilities are finally determined; and
- all disposals made on or after 16 March 1993 provided a claim is made within two years of the end of the year of assessment or accounting period in which the disposal is made; or at such later time as the Board of Inland Revenue may allow.

Commentary—*Simon's Direct Tax Service* **C2.704; D2.660.**

D45 *Rollover into depreciating assets*

The cessation of use of an asset for the purposes of a trade carried on by a claimant to rollover relief will not be treated as an occasion of charge to capital gains tax under TCGA 1992 s 154(2)(*b*), where the cessation occurs on death of the claimant.

Commentary—*Simon's Direct Tax Service* **C3.311.**

ESCs

D46 *Relief against income for capital losses on the disposal of unquoted shares in a trading company*

Note—This concession was classified as obsolete by IR 1 Supp (November 2001).

D47 *Temporary loss of charitable status due to reverter of school and other sites*

Land, which was given for educational or certain other charitable purposes, may cease to be used for such purposes. In certain cases, where land was conveyed on terms which provided for it to revert to the donor, Reverter of Sites Act 1987 s 1 applies and the trustees hold the land on a trust for sale for the benefit of the revertee. Unless the revertee is known to be a charity, the property is then no longer held on charitable trusts and there is, for capital gains tax purposes, a deemed disposal and re-acquisition by reason of TCGA 1992 s 256(2) which may give rise to a chargeable gain. In addition, if the revertee has not been immediately identified, chargeable gains may also arise to the trustees if the land or other property in the new trust is sold, or when the revertee is subsequently identified; and any income arising will be liable to income tax.

In certain circumstances, the land, or any sale proceeds, will subsequently come to be held on charitable trusts, or for the benefit of a charity. Consequently, where—

(*a*) the Charity Commissioners make an order under Reverter of Sites Act 1987 s 2, or
(*b*) the Secretary of State makes an order under Education Act 1973 s 2, or
(*c*) the revertee, or one of the revertees, is identified in due course and is a charity, or
(*d*) the revertee, or one of the revertees, is identified in due course and is not a charity but disclaims all entitlement to the property,

there will have been a period during which charitable status has been temporarily lost.

Where any of the four circumstances above apply, provided charitable status is established within six years of the date on which the land ceases to be held on the original charitable trust, any capital gains tax which has been charged under TCGA 1992 s 256(2) on the cessation of the original charitable purpose and on any disposals by the trustees during the relevant period will, by concession, be discharged or to the extent already paid be repaid with repayment supplement. Similarly, any income tax which has been charged on income which the trustees receive during the relevant period from the property, or from the proceeds of sale of the property, will be discharged or to the extent already paid, be repaid with repayment supplement, provided the income is used for charitable purposes. Any income tax suffered at source will also be repaid with repayment supplement. If the property is held only partly for one or more charities or revertees who disclaim entitlement in circumstances (*c*) and (*d*) above, then only the share relating to the charity or charities or the revertees who make the disclaimer will be exempted from capital gains tax and income tax.

As a consequence of this concession, the Board will, at the request of the trustees of a trust where the revertee has not been identified, agree to postpone the collection of any tax charged which may subsequently be discharged by this concession. If the revertee is identified at a later stage and does not have charitable status and does not disclaim entitlement the postponed tax charges will become payable with interest.

This concession applies where the above conditions are met and where the land ceased to be held on charitable trusts on or after 17 August 1987, the commencement date for the Reverter of Sites Act 1987.

Where the revertee is known at date of reverter and is a charity the land will remain on charitable trusts and capital gains tax exemption will be available by virtue of TCGA 1992 ss 256(1), 257(3).

Commentary—*Simon's Direct Tax Service* **C1.220, C4.518.**

D48 *Retirement relief*

Note—This concessionary relief was replaced by statutory relief under TCGA 1992 Sch 6 para 14(7) and (8) introduced by FA 1996 Sch 39 para 7.

D49 *Private residence relief—short delay by owner-occupier in taking up residence*

This concession applies—

– where an individual acquires land on which he has a house built, which he then uses as his only or main residence,
– where an individual purchases an existing house and, before using it as his only or main residence, arranges for alterations or redecorations or completes the necessary steps for disposing of his previous residence.

In these circumstances, the period before the individual uses the house as his only or main residence will be treated as a period in which he so used it for the purposes of TCGA 1992 s 223(1), (2)(*a*), provided that this period is not more than one year. If there are good reasons for this period exceeding one year, which are outside the individual's control, it will be extended up to a maximum of two years.

Where the individual does not use the house as his only or main residence within the period allowed, no relief will be given for the period before it is so used. Where relief is given under this concession it will not affect any relief due on another qualifying property in respect of the same period.

Commentary—*Simon's Direct Tax Service* **C2.1307.**

D50 *Treatment of compensation*

This Concession applies to certain capital sums received as compensation for the loss or deprivation of property which at the time of its confiscation, expropriation or destruction was situated outside the United Kingdom.

A capital sum to which this concession applies shall not include any compensation payment made in respect of any property in consequence of statutory, contractual or other legal rights in force at the time that property was confiscated, expropriated or destroyed. Capital sums to which this concession applies are limited to payments made in recognition of, and in recompense for, the past loss or deprivation of the property in circumstances where no form of legal redress was then available to the owner. Loss or deprivation of property includes the disposal of property at less than market value by reason of a sale under duress.

Capital sums to which this Concession applies are those paid as compensation—

– by virtue of statutory orders under the Foreign Compensation Act 1950 or under directly analogous arrangements set up by foreign governments;
– in consequence of any recommendation of the Spoliation Advisory Panel or of any equivalent body set up outside the United Kingdom;
– in settlement of legal claims, or by the order of any recognised court or legal tribunal with jurisdiction to cover such claims, to the effect that the original seizure of the property was wrongful and should be declared illegal.

A capital sum to which this Concession applies shall not be treated as giving rise to a chargeable gain on the person entitled to receive it provided such person—

– was the owner of the property to which the compensation relates at the time it was confiscated, expropriated or destroyed, or
– acquired their title, directly or indirectly, from the owner of the property at the time it was confiscated, expropriated or destroyed.

This Concession will not apply to exempt a capital sum paid as compensation in the circumstances described above where the person entitled to receive it has acquired, or derived their title from another person who has acquired, the right to receive that compensation for consideration in money or money's worth.

In deciding whether this Concession can apply to any person, transfers of assets or rights between husband and wife and within companies in the same group which have been treated as giving rise to neither a gain nor a loss under sections 58 and 171 of TCGA 1992 respectively, will be ignored.

The value of the compensation received will be taken to be the amount paid in money or money's worth, in respect of the compensation claim under the arrangements for claims settlement. This value shall, where the compensation is in the form of an asset, be taken as the value at which the asset was acquired by the person entitled to the compensation for the purposes of computing any gain or loss on a subsequent disposal of the asset by that person.

OFFSET FOR LOSSES CLAIMED

If a capital gains allowable loss is or has been established as a consequence of—

– the property having been confiscated, expropriated or destroyed, or
– as a result of the abandonment or extinction of the rights in respect of which a claim for the compensation was established,

this Concession is not to apply to so much of the chargeable gain which would arise on the receipt of the compensation if this concession did not apply, as is equal to the allowable loss claimed.

DATE OF APPLICATION

The concession in this form applies to compensation received on or after 20 December 2000 and to any case where compensation was received before that date but where the liability thereon was not finally determined before that date.

Commentary—*Simon's Direct Tax Service* **C1.319.**
Note—The text of this Concession is as it appears in IR 1 (August 2002).

ESCs

D51 *Transfers of assets from a close company at undervalue*

TCGA 1992 s 125 applies if a close company transfers assets to a person at undervalue in a transaction which is not an arm's length bargain. The effect of s 125 is to reduce the allowable acquisition cost of shares held by the shareholders in the company at the date of the transfer. By concession the Revenue will not seek to apply s 125 in two circumstances.

First, where the transferee is a participator or an associate of a participator in the company, and—

– the transfer is treated as an income distribution within TA 1988 s 209(2)(*b*) or (4) or
– the transfer is treated as a capital distribution within TCGA 1992 s 122.

Second, where the transferee is an employee of the company and the employee is assessed under Schedule E on the difference between the market value of the asset and any amount he or she paid for it.

Commentary—*Simon's Direct Tax Service* **D2.318.**

D52 *Share exchanges, company reconstructions and amalgamations: incidental costs of acquisition and warranty payments*

This concession applies to—

– incidental costs of acquisition or disposal which would be allowable under TCGA 1992 s 38(1)(*a*) or (*c*)
– payments in respect of contingent liabilities as defined in TCGA 1992 s 49(1)(*c*)

incurred—

(i) on, or as a result of, an exchange of shares or debentures to which TCGA 1992 s 135 applies, or
(ii) under an arrangement as mentioned in TCGA 1992 s 136(i) which is entered into for the purposes of, or in connection with, a ''scheme of reconstruction'' as defined in TCGA 1992 Sch 5AA in circumstances where TCGA 1992 s 136 applies.

Any such costs or payments attributable to the new holding of the shares and/or debentures may be treated as consideration given for the shares or debentures. In the case of contingent liabilities the total allowed under TCGA 1992 s 49(1)(*c*) and this concession will be restricted to the amount that would have been allowed under s 49(1)(*c*) if TCGA 1992 ss 135 or 136 had not applied.

Commentary—*Simon's Direct Tax Service* **C2.208, 726.**
Note—The text of this concession is as it appears in IR 1 (January 2004).

D53 *TCGA 1992 s 50: grants repaid*

Where some or all of the cost of acquiring an asset is met by the Crown or by, any Government, public or local authority, TCGA 1992 s 50 excludes an amount equal to the grant from the allowable acquisition costs in computing the gain on a subsequent disposal.

By concession, where the grant is later repaid in whole or in part the consideration received on the disposal of the asset may be treated as reduced by an amount equal to the amount repaid.

This concession will also apply to the extent that it can be demonstrated that repayment of the grant has taken place by way of a corresponding reduction in the amount of a later grant which would otherwise have been made.

Commentary—*Simon's Direct Tax Service* **C2.218.**

ADDITIONAL NOTES

1 Working Rule Agreements

There are limited concessionary elements in the tax treatment of travelling and subsistence allowances paid under Working Rule Agreements and, from 6 April 1981, to site based staff employees in the construction and allied industries.

Further information on this tax treatment is given in an Inland Revenue Press Release dated 13 February 1981, available from the Inland Revenue Press Office, G7 New Wing, Somerset House, Strand, London WC2R 1LB.

2 Inland Revenue Statements of Practice

Statements of Practice explain the Inland Revenue's interpretation of legislation and the way the department applies the law in practice. They do not affect a taxpayer's right to argue for a different interpretation, if necessary in an appeal to the General or Special Commissioners.

Some Statements of Practice (SPs) contain a minor concessionary element. They are as follows [see *Statements of Practice*, post]—

SP A30	*Settlements: Benefits to settlor's future spouse* (now obsolete)
SP A34	Relief for interest payments: loans for purchase or improvement of land: inherited properties
SP D1	Part disposals of land
SP D3	Company liquidations: Shareholders' CGT
SP D21	Time limit for an election for valuation on 6 April 1965 under TCGA 1992 Sch 2, para 17 (CGTA 1979 Sch 5, para 12): Company leaving a group: TCGA 1992 s 178(ICTA 1970 s 278)
SP 4/79	Life Assurance premium relief: Children's policies
SP 7/79	*Benefits in kind: Cheap loans: Advances for expenses* (now obsolete)
SP 4/80	Industrial buildings allowance: Industrial workshops constructed for separate letting to small businesses
SP 11/81	Additional redundancy payments
SP 12/81	The Construction Industry Tax Deduction Scheme: Carpet fitting
SP 10/84	Foreign bank accounts
SP 5/85	*Capital gains tax: division of a company on a share for share basis* (now obsolete)
SP 3/87	*Repayment of tax to charities on covenanted and other income* (now obsolete)
SP 4/90	*Charitable covenants* (now obsolete)
SP 8/90	Losses on irrecoverable loans in the form of qualifying corporate bonds: Loss on early redemption
SP 6/92	Accident insurance policies: Chargeable events and gains on policies of life insurance
SP 4/95	Long term insurance business: Computations of profit for tax purposes
SP 4/97	Taxation commission, cashbacks and discounts

INLAND REVENUE STATEMENTS OF PRACTICE

STATEMENTS OF PRACTICE ISSUED BEFORE 18 JULY 1978

Note—Statements of Practice which are obsolete or obsolescent or are not applicable in the current year are listed below in italics, but not printed.

Before 18 July 1978 information on administrative practice was issued in various forms including Parliamentary statements and written answers, and letters to professional bodies and journals. An index of those statements issued before 18 July 1978 which remained valid was published in a Revenue Press Release on 18 June 1979 and revised by further Press Releases dated 29 October 1980 and 23 March 1982. The titles of the statements in that index relevant to this work are listed below.

These statements have no binding force and do not affect a taxpayer's right of appeal on points concerning his liability to tax.

Statements relating to IHT are reproduced in Part 3 of this publication.

A STATEMENTS APPLICABLE TO INDIVIDUALS (INCOME TAX AND INTEREST ON TAX)

A1 *Deeds of covenant.* (obsolete)
A2 *Settlements: TA 1988 Part XV.* (obsolete)
A3 *Barristers: the cash basis.* (obsolete)
A4 *Partnerships: change in membership.* (obsolete)
A5 *Covenants in favour of charities: repayment procedure.* (obsolete)
A6 Employment income: VAT
A7 *Benefits in kind and VAT.* (obsolete)
A8 Stock dividends
A9 *Schedule E assessments 1995—96 and earlier: repayment supplement.* (obsolete)
A10 Airline pilots—residence—incidental duties
A11 *Informal end of year assessments.* (obsolete)
A12 *Assessing tolerance.* (obsolete)
A13 Completion of return forms by attorneys
A14 *Delay in rendering tax returns: interest charge and penalties.* (obsolete)
A15 *Benefits in kind: FA 1976 s 64.* (obsolete)
A16 Living expenses abroad: Schedule D Cases I and II
A17 *Earnings for work done abroad.* (obsolete)
A18 *Partnerships and retirement annuity relief.* (obsolete)
A19 *Furnished lettings: wear and tear allowance.* (obsolete)
A20 *Schedule D Case V losses.* (obsolete)
A21 *Temporary workers engaged through foreign agencies.* (obsolete)
A22 *Solicitors' deposit interest.* (obsolete)
A23 *Correspondence with married women.* (obsolete)
A24 *Benefits in kind: scholarships for employees' children.* (obsolete)
A25 *Separate taxation of wife's earnings, TA 1988 s 288: extension of time limits.* (obsolete)
A26 *Capital allowances on machinery and plant: amendment of claim by an individual trader.* (obsolete)
A27 *Accounts on a cash basis.* (obsolete)
A28 *Accountancy expenses.* (superseded)
A29 *Tax treatment of directors' fees received by professional partnerships.* (obsolete)
A30 *Settlements: benefit to settlor's future spouse.* (obsolete)
A31 *Reimbursement of taxpayers' expenses.* (obsolete)
A32 Goods taken by traders for personal consumption
A33 Relief for interest payments: loans applied in acquiring an interest in a partnership: TA 1988 ss 362, 363
A34 Relief for interest payments: loans for purchase or improvement of land: inherited properties: TA 1988 ss 353, 354

B STATEMENTS APPLICABLE TO INDIVIDUALS AND COMPANIES (INCOME TAX AND CORPORATION TAX)

B1 Treatment of VAT
B2 *Stock relief: treatment of VAT.* (obsolete)
B3 *Stock relief: withdrawal of claim.* (obsolete)
B4 *Stock and work in progress: changes in basis of valuing long term contract work in progress.* (obsolete)
B5 *Stocks and work in progress: changes in accountancy practice (SSAP 9).* (obsolete)
B6 Goods sold subject to reservation of title
B7 *Stock relief: completed work in progress of builders.* (obsolete)

C STATEMENTS APPLICABLE TO COMPANIES, ETC (CORPORATION TAX AND INCOME TAX)

C1 Lotteries and football pools
C2 *Group relief: TA 1988 s 412(1)(c).* (obsolete)
C3 *Close companies: TA 1988 Sch 19 para 3(1)(a): "reasonable time".* (obsolete)
C4 *Close companies: general statement.* (obsolete)

C5	*Interest paid to a bank in the UK on a loan made in foreign currency.* (superseded)
C6	Group relief: TA 1988 s 403C
C7	*Group relief: TA 1988 s 410.* (obsolete)
C8	*Taxation of profits of subsidiaries of UK companies.* (obsolete)
C9	*Company taxation: interest paid in foreign currency.* (obsolete)
C10	General rules as to deductions not allowable: valuation fees for compliance with Companies Act 1985 Sch 7 para 1(2)
C11	*Claims to loss relief under TA 1988 s 393(1)* (obsolete)
D	STATEMENTS RELATING TO TAX ON CAPITAL GAINS (INDIVIDUALS AND COMPANIES)
D1	Part disposals of land
D2	*Superannuation funds: tax on capital gains.* (obsolete)
D3	Company liquidations: tax on shareholders' capital gains
D4	*Short delay by owner-occupier in taking up residence TCGA 1992 ss 222–224.* (superseded)
D5	*Partnerships: assets owned by individuals.* (obsolete)
D6	Replacement of business assets: time limit
D7	Treatment of value added tax
D8	*Houses owned by occupants of tied accommodation.* (superseded)
D9	*Residence exemption: separated couples.* (obsolete)
D10	Termination of life interest in settled property: TCGA 1992 ss 71, 72
D11	Partnership: assets owned by a partner
D12	Partnerships and CGT
D13	*Assets of negligible value: time limit for claims.* (superseded)
D14	*Division of a company on a share for share basis.* (superseded)
D15	*Accommodation let by owner-occupiers.* (superseded)
D16	*Interests in possession.* (obsolete)
D17	*FA 1965 s 29(2).* (obsolete)
D18	Value shifting: TCGA 1992 s 30
D19	Replacement of business assets in groups of companies
D20	*Retirement relief: change in business during 10 years before disposal.* (obsolete)
D21	Time limit for an election for valuation on 6 April 1965 under TCGA 1992 Sch 2 para 17: company leaving a group: TCGA 1992 ss 178, 179
D22	*Transfer of business to a company.* (superseded)
D23	Non-resident company: TCGA 1992 s 13
D24	Initial repairs to property: TCGA 1992 s 38(1)
F	MISCELLANEOUS
F1	*Limitations on Revenue advice to taxpayers.* (superseded)
F2	*UK branches of foreign banks.* (obsolete)
F3	*Close companies: apportionment of income and the consequentials for capital gains tax: close companies in liquidation.* (obsolete)

STATEMENTS OF PRACTICE ISSUED AFTER 17 JULY 1978

Note—Statements of Practice which are obsolete or obsolescent or are not applicable in the current year are listed below in italics, but not printed.

1978

SP 1/78	*Employment Protection Act 1975: maternity pay.* (obsolete)
SP 2/78	*Close companies: non-resident participators: apportionment.* (obsolescent)
SP 3/78	Close companies—Income tax relief for interest on loans applied in acquiring an interest in a close company
SP 4/78	*Mining companies: expenditure on planning permission applications.* (obsolete)
SP 5/78	*Stamp duty: conveyance in consideration of a debt (see the Orange Tax Handbook)*
SP 6/78	*Trade unions: provident benefits: legal expenses paid for members.* (superseded)
SP 7/78	*Capital gains tax: exercise of a power of appointment over settled property.* (obsolete)
SP 8/78	*Building licences granted under the Community Land Act 1975: stock relief.* (obsolete)

1979

SP 1/79	Partnerships: extension of statement of practice D12
SP 2/79	*Development land tax: negotiations on liability.* (obsolete)
SP 3/79	*Payment of life assurance premiums on which commission is payable to the policyholder.* (superseded)
SP 4/79	Life assurance premium relief: children's policies

SP 5/79 *Family company: sale of assets in anticipation of liquidation.* (obsolete)
SP 6/79 *Closure of business followed by sale of assets or liquidation of company.* (obsolete)
SP 7/79 Benefits in kind: cheap loans—advances for expenses
SP 8/79 Compensation for acquisition of property under compulsory powers
SP 9/79 *Expenditure on producing films and certain similar assets.* (superseded)
SP 10/79 *Power for trustees to allow a beneficiary to occupy dwelling house* (see *IHT*)
SP 11/79 Life assurance premium relief: children's policies
SP 12/79 *Investigation settlements: retirement annuity relief.* (obsolete)
SP 13/79 *Flat rate expenses for manual and certain other employees.* (obsolete)
SP 14/79 Unquoted shares or securities held on 6 April 1965

1980
SP 1/80 *Legal entitlement and administrative practices.* (superseded)
SP 2/80 *Statement clarifying the operation of an existing administrative practice: Case V Schedule D losses.* (superseded)
SP 3/80 TA 1988 s 707: cancellation of tax advantages from certain transactions in securities: procedure for clearance in advance
SP 4/80 Industrial buildings allowance: industrial workshops constructed for separate letting to small businesses
SP 5/80 *Group relief: TA 1988 s 410.* (superseded)
SP 6/80 *Small workshops allowance.* (obsolete)
SP 7/80 *Deceased persons' estates: income received during the administration period.* (obsolete)
SP 8/80 *Stock relief: deferment of recovery charges: definition of net indebtedness in FA 1980 Sch 7 para 1(5).* (obsolete)
SP 9/80 *Investigation settlements: retirement annuity relief.* (superseded)
SP 10/80 *Mortgage interest relief: year of marriage.* (obsolete)
SP 11/80 Liability under TA 1988 Part XIII Chapter II, on gains arising on life and capital redemption policies and life annuities. (see Concession B53)
SP 12/80 *Business relief from IHT: "Buy and Sell" agreements (see IHT)*
SP 13/80 Demergers: TA 1988 ss 213–218
SP 14/80 Relief for owner occupiers
SP 15/80 Maintenance payments: payment of school fees
SP 16/80 Lorry drivers: relief for expenditure on meals
SP 17/80 *Flat rate expenses for manual and certain other employees.* (obsolete)
SP 18/80 *Securities dealt in on the Stock Exchange Unlisted Securities Market: status and valuation for tax purposes.* (obsolete)

1981
SP 1/81 *Non-statutory redundancy payments.* (superseded)
SP 2/81 *Contributions to retirement benefit schemes on termination of employment.* (obsolete)
SP 3/81 Individuals coming to the UK: ordinary residence
SP 4/81 *Stock relief: recovery of charges when level of trading is negligible.* (obsolete)
SP 5/81 Expenditure on farm drainage
SP 6/81 *Maintenance payments under court orders: retrospective dating.* (obsolete)
SP 7/81 *Allowable expenditure: expenses incurred by personal representatives.* (obsolete)
SP 8/81 Rollover relief for replacement of business assets: trades carried on successively
SP 9/81 *Exercise of a power of appointment over settled property.* (superseded)
SP 10/81 Payments on account of disability resulting in cessation of employment
SP 11/81 Additional redundancy payments
SP 12/81 The construction industry tax deduction scheme: carpet fitting

1982
SP 1/82 *The interaction of income tax and inheritance tax on assets put into settlements* (obsolete)
SP 2/82 Company's purchase of own shares: TA 1988 (see also Inland Revenue Tax Bulletin Issue 21, February 1996, p 280)
SP 3/82 *Indexation.* (obsolete)

1983
SP 1/83 *Country-risk debts.* (obsolete)
SP 2/83 *Tax treatment of expenditure on films and certain similar assets.* (superseded)
SP 3/83 *Relief for losses on loans to traders: time limit for claims.* (superseded)
SP 4/83 *Approved savings-related share option schemes.* (obsolete)
SP 5/83 *Use of schedules in making personal tax returns.* (obsolete)
SP 6/83 *Company residence.* (superseded)
SP 7/83 *Business expansion scheme: overseas activities.* (obsolete)

1984
SP 1/84 Trade unions: provident benefits: legal and administrative expenses

SPs

SP 2/84	*Payments to redundant steel workers.* (obsolete)
SP 3/84	*Stamp duty: convertible loan stock* (see the *Orange Tax Handbook*)
SP 4/84	*Development land tax: double taxation conventions.* (obsolete)
SP 5/84	Employees resident but not ordinarily resident in the UK: liability under Cases II and III of Schedule E
SP 6/84	Non-resident lessors: TA 1988 s 830
SP 7/84	Exercise of a power of appointment or advance over settled property
SP 8/84	*TA 1988 s 124: interest on quoted Eurobonds.* (obsolete)
SP 9/84	*Stamp duty: treatment of securities dealt in on the Stock Exchange Unlisted Securities Market.* (obsolete)
SP 10/84	Foreign bank accounts
SP 11/84	*Estate duty: calculation of duty payable on a chargeable event affecting heritage objects previously granted conditional exemption* (see *IHT*)

1985

SP 1/85	*Treatment of certain payments to relocated employees.* (superseded)
SP 2/85	*Tax treatment of expenditure on films and certain similar assets.* (superseded)
SP 3/85	*Exchange rate fluctuations.* (superseded)
SP 4/85	*Income tax: relief for interest on loan used to buy land for partnership or company business purposes.* (obsolete)
SP 5/85	*Division of a company on a share for share basis.* (obsolete)
SP 6/85	Incentive awards
SP 7/85	*Reliefs for non-residents: treatment of wife's income.* (obsolete)

1986

SP 1/86	Capital allowances: machinery and plant: short-life assets
SP 2/86	Offshore funds
SP 3/86	Payments to a non-resident from UK discretionary trusts or UK estates during the administration period: double taxation relief
SP 4/86	Scholarship and apprenticeship schemes at universities and technical colleges
SP 5/86	Relief for replacement of business assets: employees and office-holders
SP 6/86	*Investigation settlements: inclusion of interest clause in letter or offer.* (obsolete)
SP 7/86	*Business expansion scheme: overseas activities.* (obsolete)
SP 8/86	*Treatment of income of discretionary trusts* (see *IHT*)
SP 9/86	Partnership mergers and demergers
SP 10/86	*Death benefits under superannuation agreements* (see *IHT*)

1987

SP 1/87	*Exchange rate fluctuations.* (superseded)
SP 2/87	*Close company apportionment.* (obsolete)
SP 3/87	*Repayment of tax to charities on covenanted and other income.* (obsolete)
SP 4/87	*Business expansion scheme: overseas activities.* (obsolete)
SP 5/87	Tax returns: the use of substitute forms
SP 6/87	*Acceptance of property in lieu of IHT, CTT and estate duty (see IHT)*
SP 7/87	*IHT: deduction for reasonable funeral expenses (see IHT)*
SP 8/87	*Close company apportionment: member of a trading group.* (obsolete)
SP 9/87	Capital allowances: hotels
SP 10/87	*Stamp duty: conveyances and leases of building plots. (see Orange Tax Handbook)*

1988

SP 1/88	*Tax treatment of forward currency transactions by investment trusts.* (obsolete)
SP 2/88	Civil tax penalties and criminal prosecution cases
SP 3/88	*Delay in rendering tax returns: interest on overdue tax.* (superseded)
SP 4/88	*Tax treatment of transactions in financial futures and options.* (superseded)
SP 5/88	*Taxation of car telephones provided by employers.* (superseded)
SP 6/88	Double taxation relief: chargeable gains

1989

SP 1/89	Partnerships: further extension of statement of practice D12
SP 2/89	*Rebasing elections (superseded by SP 4/92)*
SP 3/89	*Unit trust and investment trust monthly savings schemes.* (superseded)
SP 4/89	Company's purchase of own shares: capital gains treatment of distribution received by corporate shareholder
SP 5/89	Rebasing and indexation: shares held at 31 March 1982
SP 6/89	Delay in rendering tax returns: interest on overdue tax: TMA 1970 s 88
SP 7/89	Surrender of advance corporation tax
SP 8/89	Independent taxation: mortgage interest relief: time limit for married couple's allocation of interest elections

1990

SP 1/90 Company residence
SP 2/90 Guidance notes for migrating companies: notice and arrangements for payment of tax
SP 3/90 *Stocks and long-term contracts* (obsolete)
SP 4/*90* *Charitable covenants.* (obsolete)
SP 5/90 Accountants' working papers
SP 6/90 *Stamp duty: conveyances and transfers of property subject to a debt: Stamp Act 1891, s 57* (see the *Orange Tax Handbook*)
SP 7/90 *Compulsory acquisition of freehold reversion by tenant.* (superseded)
SP 8/90 Losses on irrecoverable loans in the form of qualifying corporate bonds: loss on early redemption

1991

SP 1/91 Small companies' rate of corporation tax and corporation tax starting rate
SP 2/91 Residence in the UK: visits extended because of exceptional circumstances
SP 3/91 Finance lease rental payments
SP 4/91 *Tax returns.* (obsolete)
SP 5/91 *Investment trusts investing in authorised unit trusts.* (superseded by SP 7/94)
SP 6/91 *Stamp duty and value added tax: interaction* (see the *Orange Tax Handbook*)
SP 7/91 Double taxation: business profits: unilateral relief
SP 8/91 Discovery assessments
SP 9/91 Investigation settlements: retirement annuities and personal pension relief
SP 10/91 Corporation tax: a major change in the nature or conduct of a trade
SP 11/91 *Stamp duty and value added tax: interaction* (see the *Orange Tax Handbook*)
SP 12/*91* *Income tax: "in the ordinary course" of banking business.* (obsolete)
SP 13/91 Ex gratia awards made on termination of an office or employment by retirement or death
SP 14/91 *Tax treatment of transactions in financial futures and options* (superseded by SP 3/02)
SP 15/91 *Treatment of investment managers and their overseas clients* (obsolete)
SP 16/91 Accountancy expenses arising out of accounts investigations
SP 17/91 Residence in the UK: when ordinary residence is regarded as commencing where the period to be spent here is less than three years
SP 18/91 *Foreign earnings deduction.* (obsolete)

1992

SP 1/92 *Directors' and employees' emoluments: extension of time limits for relief on transition to receipts basis of assessment.* (obsolete)
SP 2/92 Transactions within TA 1988 s 765A: movements of capital between residents of EC member States
SP 3/92 *Double taxation relief: status of UK/USSR Convention for the avoidance of double taxation* (superseded by SP 4/01)
SP 4/92 Capital gains tax: rebasing elections
SP 5/92 Non-resident trusts
SP 6/92 Accident insurance policies: chargeable events and gains on policies of life insurance
SP 7/92 *Profit-related pay—use of pool determination formulae.* (obsolete)
SP 8/92 Valuation of assets in respect of which capital gains tax gifts holdover relief is claimed
SP 9/92 *Partnerships: circumstances in which late elections will be accepted.* (obsolete)

1993

SP 1/93 *Tax treatment of expenditure on films and certain similar assets.* (superseded by SP 1/98)
SP 2/93 *IHT: the use of substitute forms (see IHT)*
SP 3/93 Groups of companies: arrangements
SP 4/93 Deceased persons' estates: discretionary interests in residue
SP 5/93 UK/Czechoslovakia Double Taxation Convention
SP 6/93 UK/Yugoslavia Double Taxation Convention
SP 7/93 *Insurance companies: transfers of long term business* (obsolete)
SP 8/93 *Stamp duty: new buildings (see the Orange Tax Handbook)*
SP 9/93 *Corporation tax pay and file: Corporation tax returns* (obsolete)
SP 10/93 *Corporation tax pay and file: special arrangements for groups of companies.* (obsolete)
SP 11/93 *Corporation tax pay and file: claims to capital allowances and group relief made outside the normal time limit.* (obsolete)
SP 12/93 Double taxation: dividend income: tax credit relief
SP 13/93 Compulsory acquisition of freehold or extension of lease by tenant
SP 14/93 Valuation of oil disposed of otherwise than at arm's length: Oil Taxation Act 1975 Sch 3 para 2
SP 15/93 Business tax computations rounded to nearest £1,000

1994

SP 1/94 Non-statutory lump sum redundancy payments

SP 2/94 *Enterprise investment scheme and venture capital trust scheme: location of activity.* (superseded by SP 7/98)

SP 3/94 *Business expansion scheme, enterprise investment scheme, capital gains tax reinvestment relief and venture capital trust scheme: loans to investors.* (superseded by SP 6/98)

SP 4/94 Enhanced stock dividends received by trustees of interest in possession trusts

SP 5/94 Associated companies for small companies relief and corporation tax: holding companies

SP 6/94 Capital allowances: notification of expenditure on machinery and plant made outside the normal time limit

SP 7/94 *Investment trusts investing in authorised unit trusts.* (superseded by SP 3/97)

SP 8/94 Allowable expenditure—expenses incurred by personal representatives and corporate trustees

SP 9/94 *Application of foreign exchange and financial instruments legislation to partnerships which include companies* (superseded by SP 4/98)

1995

SP 1/95 *Interest payable in the UK* (superseded)

SP 2/95 *Payment of tax credits to non-resident companies.* (obsolete)

SP 3/95 *Definition of financial trader for the purposes of FA 1994 s 177(1)* (superseded SP 4/02)

SP 4/95 Long term insurance business: computations of profit for tax purposes

SP 5/95 *Taxation of receipts of insurance and personal pension scheme commissions.* (superseded by SP 4/97)

SP 6/95 Legal entitlement and administrative practices

SP 7/95 *Venture capital trusts: value of "gross assets".* (obsolete)

SP 8/95 Venture capital trusts: default terms in loan agreements

1996

SP 1/96 Notification of chargeability to income tax and capital gains tax for tax years 1995–96 onwards

SP 2/96 Pooled cars—incidental private use

SP 3/96 TA 1988 s 313—termination payments made in settlement of employment claims

SP 4/96 Income Tax: interest paid in the ordinary course of a bank's business

SP 5/96 PAYE settlement agreements

1997

SP 1/97 The electronic lodgement service

SP 2/97 *Authorised unit trusts, approved investment trusts, and open-ended investment companies: monthly savings schemes.* (superseded by SP 2/99)

SP 3/97 Investment trusts investing in authorised unit trusts or open-ended investment companies

SP 4/97 Taxation of commission, cashbacks and discounts

1998

SP 1/98 *Tax treatment of expenditure on films.* (superseded)

SP 2/98 *Business by telephone.* (superseded)

SP 3/98 *Stamp duty: group relief* (see the *Orange Tax Handbook*)

SP 4/98 Application of loan relationships, foreign exchange and financial instruments legislation to partnerships which include companies

SP 5/98 *Venture capital trusts and the enterprise investment scheme: value of "gross assets".* (obsolete)

SP 6/98 Enterprise investment scheme, venture capital trusts, capital gains tax reinvestment relief and business expansion scheme: loans to investors

SP 7/98 *Enterprise investment scheme, venture capital trusts and capital gains tax reinvestment relief: location of activity.* (superseded by 3/00)

SP 8/98 *Business by telephone: East Kilbride call centre.* (superseded)

1999

SP 1/99 Self-assessment enquiries and capital gains tax valuations

SP 2/99 Monthly savings in investment funds

SP 3/99 Advance pricing agreements (APAs)

2000

SP 1/00 Corporate venturing scheme—applications for advance clearance under FA 2000 Sch 15 Pt X

SP 2/00 Venture capital trusts, the enterprise investment scheme, the corporate venturing scheme and enterprise management incentives—value of "gross assets"

IR STATEMENTS ISSUED BEFORE 18 JULY 1978

A STATEMENTS APPLICABLE TO INDIVIDUALS (INCOME TAX AND INTEREST ON TAX)

A1 *Deeds of covenant*

Notes—This statement was classified as obsolete by IR 131 (July 1994). A guidance booklet about tax repayment claims on deeds of covenant is available from Inland Revenue, FICO, St John's House, Merton Road, Bootle, Merseyside L69 9BB.

A2 *Settlements: TA 1988 Part XV*

Note—This statement was classified as obsolete by IR 131 (July 1994).

A3 *Barristers—the cash basis*

Note—This statement was classified as obsolete by IR 131 Supp (November 1998). See now FA 1998 s 48.

A4 *Partnerships: change in membership*

Note—This statement was classified as obsolete by IR 131 (January 2000).

A5 *Covenants in favour of charities: repayment procedure*

Note—This statement was classified as obsolete by IR 131 (July 1994).
New repayment procedures were introduced on 1 July 1992. A booklet explaining them is available from Inland Revenue, FICO, St John's House, Merton Road, Bootle, Merseyside L69 9BB.

A6 *Employment income: VAT*

The introduction of VAT on 1 April 1973 affected, in some instances, the amount of the emoluments chargeable to income tax under Schedule E, and the amount to which the PAYE procedure should be applied. The main circumstances in which this situation will arise are summarised below, and it is anticipated that all of the relevant information will be available to the employer in the records which he will maintain for general VAT purposes.

1 Expenses incurred by employees etc and reimbursed by their employer—

The amount to be entered by an employer on his return of expenses payments on Forms P9D and P11D, or by an employee etc when claiming a deduction for expenses, should include any amount paid in respect of VAT, which is reimbursed, whether or not the employer may subsequently recover all or part of that VAT by repayment or set-off.

2 Benefits etc—

Where a director or employee is liable to income tax in respect of payments made to him on his behalf by his employer or in respect of expenses incurred by the employer in providing him with a benefit the liability is on the full amount of the expenditure incurred, inclusive of VAT. This is so whether or not the employer may subsequently recover all or part of the VAT by repayment or set-off.

3 Sums paid for services to certain professional persons—

VATA 1994 s 94(4) provides that a person who, in the course of carrying on a trade, profession or vocation, accepts an office, other than a public office, is subject to VAT in respect of any services supplied by him as the holder of the office.

Where the earnings payable to such a person are subject to tax as employment income, deductible under PAYE, and also to VAT, the earnings to which PAYE is applied should not include the VAT element of any payment.

Note—This statement was revised in IR 131 (August 2003).

A7 *Benefits in kind and VAT*

Note—This statement was classified as obsolete by IR 131 (August 2003).

SPs

A8 *Stock dividends*

There are special rules when share capital is issued to an individual, personal representative or trustee of an accumulation or discretionary trust in the form of a stock dividend (TA 1988 ss 249–251). Such issues are usually made as an alternative to a cash dividend. The recipient is treated as having received income which has borne an amount of income tax. The amount of that income is the sum of either the cash dividend or the market value of the share capital plus the tax which the income is treated as having borne. For this purpose the amount of the cash dividend is used unless that amount is substantially greater or substantially less than the market value of the share capital (s 251(2)(*a*)). In interpreting "substantially greater or substantially less", the practice of the Inland Revenue is generally to use the market value of the share capital when that value exceeds the amount of the cash dividend by 15 per cent or more of the market value of the share capital, or when that value is less than the amount of the cash dividend by 15 per cent or more of the market value of the share capital. However, the Inland Revenue is normally prepared to use the amount of the cash dividend when the difference between the market value of the share capital and the cash dividend is no more than one or two percentage points greater than 15 per cent. In other cases, the amount of the cash dividend is used.

Commentary—*Simon's Direct Tax Service* **D1.104**.

A9 *Schedule E assessments 1995—96 and earlier: repayment supplement*

Note—This statement, which was reworded by IR 131 Supp (November 1998), does not apply from 1996—97 onwards.

A10 *Airline pilots—residence—incidental duties*

Where only a single take-off and landing in this country occurred in a year, the Revenue will normally disregard this on *de minimis* grounds in considering whether any duties were performed in this country.

A11 *Informal end of year adjustments*

Note—This statement was classified as obsolete by IR 131 (July 1994).

A12 *Assessing tolerance*

Note—This statement was classified as obsolete by IR 131 (November 1996).

A13 *Completion of return forms by attorneys*

TMA 1970 s 8(2) requires that every return should include "a declaration made by the person making the return to the effect that the return is to the best of his knowledge correct and complete". For tax years before the introduction of income tax self assessment (1995–96 and earlier), TMA 1970 s 42(5) provided for a "declaration" by the person making the claim.

The Board of Inland Revenue consider that the obligation to make declarations under these sections is within the class of statutory duties which the person making the return of income, or the claim, cannot delegate. Accordingly, it is the normal practice to insist that the return of income or claim should be signed by the taxpayer or claimant personally, and not by his attorney.

However, the Revenue recognise that there may be difficulties where, owing to the age or physical infirmity of the taxpayer, he is unable to cope adequately with the management of his affairs or where for the same reason the taxpayer's general health might suffer if he were troubled for a personal signature. In such special circumstances the Revenue will be willing to consider the matter sympathetically and where possible accept the signature of the attorney who has full knowledge of the taxpayer's affairs.

Revenue & other press releases—Law Society 18 March 1992 (Revenue accept there will be circumstances where the TMA 1970 s 8 requirement for taxpayers to sign their return is not possible, and are in principle prepared to accept the signature of an attorney in case of physical or mental incapacity).

A14 *Delay in rendering tax returns: Interest charge and penalties*

Note—This statement was classified as obsolete by IR 131 (July 1994).

A15 *Benefits in kind: FA 1976 s 64*

Note—This statement was classified as obsolete by IR 131 (July 1994).

A16 *Living expenses abroad: Schedule D Cases I and II*

Where an individual who is a resident in the UK and assessable under Schedule D Case I or II in respect of a trade, profession or vocation (either alone or in partnership) spends time abroad on business, the costs of living abroad personal to him will not be disallowed under TA 1988 s 74(1)(*a*) or (*b*) if the absence abroad is for the purposes of the trade, profession or vocation. Private expenditure, eg on holidays taken in the course of a business trip, will not be allowed. Living expenses are regarded as including the cost of accommodation, food and drink attributable to the individual, trader or partner. If he is accompanied by his family or other dependants, the costs attributable to them will not be allowed.

A17 *Earnings for work done abroad*

Note—This statement was classified as obsolete by IR 131 (November 1996).

A18 *Partnerships and retirement annuity relief*

Note—This statement was classified as obsolete by IR 131 (July 1994).

A19 *Furnished lettings: wear and tear allowance*

Note—This statement has been replaced by Concession B47.

A20 *Schedule D Case V losses*

Note—Superseded by SP 2/80 which was itself superseded by Concession B25 (which was classified as obsolete by IR 1 Supp (November 1998)).

A21 *Temporary workers engaged through foreign agencies*

Note—This statement was classified as obsolete by IR 131 Supp (October 1995).

A22 *Solicitors' deposit interest*

Note—This statement has been classified as obsolete.

A23 *Correspondence with married women*

Note—This statement has been classified as obsolete.

A24 *Benefits in kind: scholarships for employees' children*

Note—This statement has been classified as obsolete.

A25 *Separate taxation of wife's earnings: TA 1988 ss 287–288 Extension of time limits*

Note—This statement was classified as obsolete by IR 131 Supp (November 1998).

A26 *Capital allowances on machinery and plant: amendment of claim by an individual trader*

Note—This statement has been classified as obsolete.

A27 *Accounts on a cash basis*

Note—This statement was classified as obsolete by IR 131 Supp (November 1998). See now FA 1998 s 48.

A28 *Accounting expenses*

Note—This statement has been superseded by SP 16/91.

A29 *Tax treatment of directors' fees received by professional partnerships*

Note—This practice is now embodied in Concession A37.

A30 *Settlements: benefit to settlor's future spouse*

Cross reference—See TA 1988 s 660A.
Note—This statement was classified as obsolete by IR 131 (August 2003).

A31 *Reimbursement of taxpayers' expenses*

Note—Replaced by Code of Practice 1 ''Mistakes by the Inland Revenue'' published on 17 February 1993.

A32 *Goods taken by traders for personal consumption*

The case of *Sharkey v Wernher* (1955) 36 TC 275, establishes the principle that where a trader takes stock from his business for private use or enjoyment or disposes of stock otherwise than by sale in the normal course of trade, the transfer should be dealt with for taxation purposes as if it were a sale at market value. Inspectors have been authorised to take a reasonably broad view in applying this principle.

The decision is not considered to apply to—

(*a*) services rendered to the trader personally or to his household which should be dealt with in accordance with TA 1988 s 74(1)(*b*);

(*b*) the value of meals provided for the proprietors of hotels, boarding houses, restaurants etc and members of their families which should also be dealt with on the basis that TA 1988 s 74(1)(*b*) applies;

(*c*) expenditure incurred by a trader on the construction of an asset which is to be used as a fixed asset in the trade.

A33 *Relief for interest payments: loans applied in acquiring an interest in a partnership (TA 1988 ss 362, 363)*

The Board are advised that the above provisions extend to salaried partners in a professional firm who are allowed independence of action in handling the affairs of clients and generally so to act that they will be indistinguishable from general partners in their relations with clients.

A34 *Relief for interest payments: loans for purchase or improvement of land: inherited properties (TA 1988 ss 353, 354)*

Where a property subject to mortgage passes from A to B under a will or on intestacy, then if A was entitled to tax relief for the mortgage interest B will also be so entitled; and B will also be entitled (while he remains the owner of the property) to relief for the interest on a fresh loan, whether secured on the property or not, so far as applied in paying off the inherited mortgage. If, however, A was not entitled to relief for the mortgage interest (because the mortgage moneys were not used for a qualifying purpose), B will not be entitled to relief either for that interest or for interest on a fresh loan raised to pay off the mortgage.

Revenue interpretation (RI 15)—Independent taxation—interest paid on certain joint loans.

B STATEMENTS APPLICABLE TO INDIVIDUALS AND COMPANIES (INCOME TAX AND CORPORATION TAX)

B1 *Treatment of value added tax*

A. INCOME TAX AND CORPORATION TAX

1 A person carrying on a business who is not a taxable person for VAT

This broadly covers persons whose output is wholly exempt from VAT and those whose taxable output (including that which is zero-rated) does not exceed a certain limit each year. (This limit is increased periodically.)

Such persons will suffer VAT on much of their business expenditure. Where an item of expenditure is allowable as a deduction in computing income for income tax or corporation tax purposes, the VAT related to that expenditure will also be allowable. If the expenditure qualifies for capital allowances, these allowances will be based on the cost inclusive of the related VAT.

2 A taxable person for VAT whose output is wholly taxable (whether at the standard rate of VAT or zero-rated)

There is no essential difference for this purpose between taxable and zero-rated output. It is expected that in general a VAT account will be kept on the lines recommended in the HM Customs and Excise Notice No 700 setting VAT on outputs against VAT on inputs and accounting for (or reclaiming) the difference. In computing income for direct tax purposes in these circumstances it would be correct to take into account both income and expenditure exclusive of the related VAT. VAT on inputs is set off whether it relates to capital or revenue expenditure and it would follow that capital allowances would be determined upon the cost exclusive of VAT. There are certain categories of VAT on imports which are non-deductible—notably that relating to the cost of motor cars and entertaining. This VAT will no doubt be included in the accounts of the business as a part of the expenditure to which it relates. So far as the motor cars are concerned capital allowances will be computed on the cost inclusive of the VAT and the entertaining expenditure which is not allowed as a deduction for direct tax purposes will be the expenditure inclusive of VAT. If a trading debt becomes bad it may well include the VAT related to the sale. To the extent that this tax has been accounted for to HM Customs and Excise and cannot be recovered from them, the full amount of the debt including VAT may be allowed as a trading expense for direct taxation purposes.

Where a trader does not maintain a separate VAT account the adjustments to be made in computing income and capital allowances for direct taxation purposes would be such as to achieve the corresponding result.

3 A partly exempt person

As explained in HM Customs and Excise Notice No 706, a taxable person whose output is partly exempt and partly taxable may set off only part of his VAT on inputs against his VAT on outputs. In such a case the computation of income for direct tax purposes will follow the general principles set out in 1 and 2 above. The VAT on inputs which cannot be set off may comprise two elements—

(*a*) that which is non-deductible because it relates to motor cars or to business entertainment; and
(*b*) that which is referable to the exempt output.

The treatment for direct tax purposes of non-deductible VAT on inputs under (*a*) will be the same as for a wholly taxable person, as explained above. VAT on inputs within (*b*) should be allocated to the categories of expenditure giving rise to it, and its treatment in computing income for direct tax purposes will be the same as the treatment of the expenditure to which it relates.

In many cases the extent to which a partly exempt person ultimately bears VAT on goods and services supplied to him will be determined in accordance with a working arrangement with HM Customs and Excise (such as the special schemes for retailers set out in Notice No 727). It follows that some approximation may be necessary in allocating the VAT ultimately borne to the various items of expenditure to which it was related. Inspectors of taxes will be prepared to consider any reasonable arrangements for allocation which follow the general principles set out above.

In certain circumstances traders may also decide that the cost of keeping records of some items of VAT on inputs is excessive in relation to the ultimate set-off to be obtained and will not make any claim. Where a trader ultimately bears additional VAT in consequence this may be treated as a part of the relevant expense or capital outlay for direct tax purposes.

B. CAPITAL GAINS TAX

If VAT has been suffered on the purchase of an asset but that VAT is available for set-off in the purchaser's VAT account, the cost of the asset for capital gains tax purposes will be the cost exclusive of VAT. Where no VAT set-off is available, the cost will be inclusive of the VAT borne. Where an asset is disposed of, any VAT chargeable will be disregarded in computing the capital gain.

Note—First published as a Revenue Press Release date 7 May 1973. For the corresponding practice relating to capital gains tax, see SP D7.

B2 *Stock relief: treatment of value added tax*

Note—This statement is obsolete. Its deletion was announced in the Revenue List of pre-1978 Statements published on 14 July 1987.

B3 *Stock relief: withdrawal of claim*

Note—This statement is obsolete. Its deletion was announced in the Revenue List of pre-1978 Statements published on 14 July 1987.

B4 *Stock and work in progress: changes in the basis of valuing long-term contract work in progress*

Note—This statement is obsolete. Its deletion was announced in the Revenue List of pre-1978 Statements published on 14 July 1987.

B5 *Stocks and work in progress: changes in accountancy practice (SSAP9)*

Note—This statement has been superseded by SP 3/90, which was itself classified as obsolete by IR 131 (November 2000).

B6 *Goods sold subject to reservation of title*

Certain traders sell goods on special terms whereby they retain the title to the goods until payment is made. The accountancy bodies have advised their members that, for accountancy purposes, if the circumstances indicate that the reservation of title is regarded by the parties as having no practical relevance except in the event of the insolvency of the buyer, the goods should, notwithstanding the strict legal position, normally be treated as purchases in the accounts of the buyer and sales in the accounts of the supplier.

The Revenue has agreed that for sales subject to reservation of title the above recommended accountancy treatment will be accepted for tax purposes provided that both parties to the contract follow it.

The sale of goods subject to reservation of title as described above is to be distinguished from the supply of goods as consignment stocks eg on a sale or return basis. Goods supplied as consignment stocks are normally to be treated as stock in the hands of the supplier until disposed of by the consignee.

Note—First publication by Consultative Committee of Accountancy Bodies, Technical Release No 192 dated September 1976. Republished in the Revenue Press Release dated 18 June 1979, Appendix B(1).

B7 *Stock relief: completed work in progress of builders*

Note—This statement is obsolete. Its deletion was announced in the Revenue List of pre-1978 Statements published on 14 July 1987.

C STATEMENTS APPLICABLE TO COMPANIES ETC (CORPORATION TAX AND INCOME TAX)

C1 *Lotteries and football pools*

Where a football pool or small lottery is to be run by a supporters' club or other society on the basis that a stated percentage or fraction of the cost of each ticket will be given to a club or body conducted and established wholly or mainly for one or more of the purposes specified in the Lotteries and Amusements Act 1976 s 5(1) the Revenue will accept that the donation element as stated in the cost of each ticket may be excluded in computing for tax purposes the profits of the trade of promoting the pool or lottery.

A football pools run by a supporters' club had its appeal against tax assessment upheld by the Special Commissioners. When this question was raised in Parliament on 14 December 1956, Mr Henry Brooke said:

> "The football pool in this case was organised on the basis that a specified percentage of the sum received from each competitor would be paid as a gift to the football club. The Special Commissioners have held that this donation element formed no part of the receipts to be taken into account in computing for income tax purposes the profits of the trade of promoting the pool. This decision will be accepted by the Revenue as governing all cases where a football pool or small lottery is run by a supporters' club or other society on the basis that a stated percentage or fraction of the cost of each ticket or chance will be given to a club or body established and conducted wholly or mainly for one or more of the purposes specified in the Small Lotteries and Gaming Act 1956 s 1(1)."

C2 *Group relief: TA 1988 s 412(1)(c)*

Note—This statement was classified as obsolete by IR 131 (July 1994).

C3 *Close companies: TA 1988 Sch 19 para 3(1)(a): "reasonable time"*

Note—This statement was classified as obsolete by IR 131 (July 1994).

The close company apportionment provisions (TA 1988 ss 423–430 Sch 19) were repealed by FA 1989 s 103 Sch 17 with effect for accounting periods beginning after 31 March 1989.

C4 *Close companies: general statement*

Note—This statement was classified as obsolete by IR 131 (November 1996).

The close company apportionment provisions (TA 1988 ss 423–430 Sch 19) were repealed by FA 1989 s 103 Sch 17 Part V with effect for accounting periods beginning after 31 March 1989.

C5 *Interest paid to a bank in the UK on a loan made in foreign currency*

Note—This statement has been replaced by SP 1/95, which was itself classified as obsolete in IR 131 (1996).

C6 *Group relief: TA 1988 s 403C*

Under TA 1988 s 403C a consortium member's share in a consortium company for any accounting period is measured by reference to the lowest of the member's percentage interests in the share capital, profits and assets of the consortium company. Where any of those percentages has varied the legislation says that the average percentage over the accounting period concerned should be taken. In determining that average percentage, the Revenue's practice is that a weighted average taking into account the length of time involved should be used.

Note—This statement was reworded in IR 131 (1993), IR 131 Supp (November 2000) and IR 131 Supp (November 2001).

C7 *Group relief: TA 1988 s 410.*

Note—This statement was superseded by SP 5/80 which was itself superseded by SP 3/93.

C8 *Taxation of profits of subsidiaries of UK companies*

Note—This statement was classified as obsolete by IR 131 (July 1994).

C9 *Company taxation: interest paid in foreign currency*

Note—This statement was classified as obsolete by IR 131 (July 1994).

C10 *General rules as to deductions not allowable: valuation fees for compliance with Companies Act 1985 Sch 7 para 1(2)*

Costs incurred by companies for the purpose of valuations made to comply with Companies Act 1985 Sch 7 para 1(2) are regarded as allowable expenses under TA 1988 ss 74(1)(*a*), 75(1).

C11 *Claims to loss relief under TA 1988 s 393(1)*

Note—This statement was classified as obsolete in IR 131 Supp (November 2000).

D STATEMENTS RELATING TO TAX ON CAPITAL GAINS (INDIVIDUALS AND COMPANIES)

D1 *Part disposals of land*

To save work for taxpayers and their advisers where part of an estate is disposed of (eg on the sale of a field) the Board of Inland Revenue will accept that the cost of the part can be calculated on the alternative basis set out in this note instead of under the general rule which requires the unsold part to be valued in order to apportion the total cost of the estate. Instructions about the alternative basis have been issued to inspectors who will be glad to give information about its application to particular cases.

Under the alternative basis the part disposed of will be treated as a separate asset and any fair and reasonable method of apportioning part of the total cost to it will be accepted—eg a reasonable valuation of that part at the acquisition date. Where the market value at 6 April 1965 or 31 March 1982, is to be taken as the cost, a reasonable valuation of the part at that date will similarly be accepted.

The cost of the part disposed of will be deducted from the total cost of the estate (or the balance of total cost) to determine the cost of the remainder of the estate; thus the total of the separate amounts adopted for the parts will not exceed the total cost. The cost attributed to each part must also be realistic in itself.

The taxpayer can always require that the general rule should be applied (except in cases already settled on the alternative basis). If he chooses the general rule it will normally be necessary to apply this rule to all subsequent disposals out of the estate; but where the general rule has been applied for a part disposal before the introduction of the alternative basis and it produced a result broadly the same as under the alternative basis, the alternative basis may be used for subsequent part disposals out of the estate.

So long as disposals out of an estate acquired before 6 April 1965 are dealt with on the alternative basis, each part disposal will carry a separate right to elect for acquisition at market value on 6 April 1965. Similarly where part is sold with development value the mandatory valuation at 6 April will apply only to that part. Even where the part is to be treated as acquired at market value on 6 April 1965 or 31 March 1982, however, it will still be necessary to agree how much of the actual cost should be attributed to the part disposed of; first, to ensure that any allowable loss does not exceed the actual loss, and, secondly, to produce a balance of total cost for subsequent disposals.

The alternative basis will not apply to part disposals between 6 April 1967 and 22 July 1970, where development value was involved; and in other cases the Board reserve the right to apply the general rule if they are not satisfied that the apportionments claimed are fair and reasonable.

Taxpayers who wish to adopt the alternative basis will still be able to claim under existing statutory provisions that certain small disposals out of an estate should be deducted from cost instead of being assessed. The disposal proceeds will then be deducted from the total cost (or balance of total cost) available for subsequent disposals.

D2 *Superannuation funds*

Note—This statement was classified as obsolete by IR 131 (January 2000).

D3 *Company liquidations: shareholders' CGT*

1 During the liquidation of a company the shareholders often receive more than one distribution. For capital gains tax each distribution, other than the final one, is a part disposal of his shares by the shareholder, and the residual value of the shares has to be ascertained in order to attribute a proportion of the cost of the shares to the distribution (unless the inspector accepts that the distribution is "small" and can therefore be deducted from cost). It has been represented to the Board of Inland

Revenue that the making and formal agreement of these valuations is holding up the agreement of liabilities and that little if any change in the total tax is involved in the majority of cases.

2 Where the shares of a company are unquoted at the date of the first or later interim distribution, therefore, the Revenue are prepared to authorise inspectors to accept any valuation by the taxpayer or his agent of the residual value of the shares at the date of the distribution, if the valuation appears reasonable and if the liquidation is expected to be completed within two years of the first distribution (and does not in fact extend much beyond that period). The valuation need not include a discount for deferment; and if the distributions are complete before the capital gains tax assessment is made, the Revenue will accept that the residual value of the shares in relation to a particular distribution is equal to the actual amount of the subsequent distributions. In the normal way the Revenue will not raise the question of capital gains tax on an interim distribution until after two years from the commencement of the liquidation unless the distribution, together with any previous distributions, exceeds the total cost of the shares.

3 Where time apportionment (shares acquired before 6 April 1965) applies to a case within the scope of this practice, the Board are prepared to calculate the gain on each distribution by applying the time apportionment fraction as at the date of the first distribution without further adjustment under TCGA 1992 Sch 2 para 16(8).

D4 *Short delay by owner-occupier in taking up residence: TCGA 1992 ss 222–224*

Note—This statement has been replaced by Concession D49.

D5 *Partnerships: assets owned by individuals*

Note—This statement was classified as obsolete by IR 131 (November 1996).

D6 *Replacement of business assets: time limit*

Where new town corporations and similar authorities acquire by compulsory purchase land for development and then immediately grant a previous owner a lease of the land until they are ready to commence building, the Board will be prepared to extend the time limit for roll-over relief under TCGA 1992 ss 152–158 to three years after the land ceases to be used by the previous owner for his trade, provided that there is a clear continuing intention that the sale proceeds will be used to acquire qualifying assets; assurances will be given in appropriate cases subject to the need to raise a protective assessment if the lease extends beyond the statutory six year time limit for making assessments.

This practice may be applied to all cases where the capital gains tax computations have not been settled at 17 January 1973.

Revenue Internal Guidance—Capital gains manual CG 60660–60665 (operation of this Statement).
Cross references—See TCGA 1992 ss 247, 248 (rollover relief in compulsory acquisition).

SPs

D7 *Treatment of VAT*

If VAT has been suffered on the purchase of an asset but that VAT is available for set-off in the purchaser's VAT account, the cost of the asset for CGT purposes will be the cost exclusive of VAT. Where no VAT set-off is available, the cost will be inclusive of the VAT borne. Where an asset is disposed of, any VAT chargeable will be disregarded in computing the capital gain.

Statement of Practice SP B1—Treatment of VAT for purposes of income tax and corporation tax.

D8 *Houses owned by occupants of tied accommodation*

Note—This statement was superseded by legislation in CGTA 1979 s 101(8), now TCGA 1992 s 222(8). Its deletion was announced in the Revenue List of pre-1978 Statements published on 14 July 1987.

D9 *Residence exemption: separated couples*

Note—This statement duplicates Concession D6. It has therefore been deleted by the Revenue Press Release dated 29 October 1980.

D10 *Termination of an interest in possession in settled property: TCGA 1992 ss 71, 72*

1 Where an interest in possession in part of settled property terminates and the part can properly be identified with one or more specific assets, the Board will accept that the deemed disposals and reacquisitions under TCGA 1992 ss 71, 72 (CGTA 1979 ss 54, 55) apply to those specific assets, and not to any part of the other assets comprised in the settled property. Corresponding treatment will apply where, within a reasonable period (normally three months) immediately following the termination, specific assets are apportioned by trustees to give effect to the termination. In either case, the treatment must be consistent with that adopted for inheritance tax purposes.

2 In particular, inspectors will be prepared to agree with the trustees lists of assets properly identifiable with the termination of an interest in possession, and any such agreement will be regarded as binding on the Revenue and the trustees.

3 This practice applies on any act or event which terminates an interest in possession whether voluntarily or involuntarily.

Commentary—*Simon's Direct Tax Service* **C4.210**.
Note—The text of this statement is as it appears in IR 131 (August 2003).

D11 *Partnership: assets owned by a partner*

Provided that the other conditions of TCGA 1992 ss 152–158 are satisfied, relief is available to the owner of assets which are let to a trading or professional partnership of which he is a member and which are used for the purposes of the partnership trade or profession.

D12 *Partnerships*

This statement of practice was originally issued by the Board of Inland Revenue on 17 January 1975 following discussions with the Law Society and the Allied Accountancy Bodies on the capital gains tax treatment of partnerships. This statement sets out a number of points of general practice which have been agreed in respect of partnerships to which TCGA 1992 s 59 applies.

The enactment of the Limited Liability Partnership Act 2000, has created, from April 2001, the concept of limited liability partnerships (as bodies corporate) in UK law. In conjunction with this, new capital gains tax provisions dealing with such partnerships have been introduced through TCGA 1992 s 59A.

TCGA 1992 s 59A(1) mirrors TCGA 1992 s 59 in treating any dealings in chargeable assets by a limited liability partnership as dealings by the individual members, as partners, for capital gains tax purposes. Each member of a limited liability partnership to which s 59A(1) applies has therefore to be regarded, like a partner in any other (non-corporate) partnership, as owning a fractional share of each of the partnership assets and not an interest in the partnership itself.

This statement of practice will therefore be extended to limited liability partnerships which meet the requirements of TCGA 1992 s 59, 59A(1), such that capital gains of a partnership fall to charged on its members as partners. Accordingly, in the text of the statement of practice, all references to a ''partnership'' or ''firm'' shall be taken as including limited liability partnerships to which TCGA 1992 s 59, 59A(1) applies, and all references to ''partner'' shall be taken as including a member of a limited liability partnership to which TCGA 1992 ss 59, 59A(1) applies.

For the avoidance of doubt, this statement of practice does not apply to the members of a limited liability partnership which ceases to be ''fiscally transparent'' by reason of its not being, or its no longer being, within TCGA 1992 ss 59, 59A(1).

1 VALUATION OF A PARTNER'S SHARE IN A PARTNERSHIP ASSET

Where it is necessary to ascertain the market value of a partner's share in a partnership asset for capital gains tax purposes, it will be taken as a fraction of the value of the total partnership interest in the asset without any discount for the size of his share. If, for example, a partnership owned all the issued shares in a company, the value of the interest in that holding of a partner with a one-tenth share would be one-tenth of the value of the partnership's 100% holding.

2 DISPOSALS OF ASSETS BY A PARTNERSHIP

Where an asset is disposed of by a partnership to an outside party each of the partners will be treated as disposing of his fractional share of the asset. In computing gains or losses the proceeds of disposal will be allocated between the partners in the ratio of their share in asset surpluses at the time of disposal. Where this is not specifically laid down the allocation will follow the actual destination of the surplus as shown in the partnership accounts; regard will of course have to be paid to any agreement outside the accounts. If the surplus is not allocated among the partners but, for example, put to a common reserve, regard will be had to the ordinary profit sharing ratio in the absence of a specified asset-surplus-sharing ratio. Expenditure on the acquisition of assets by a partnership will be allocated between the partners in the same way at the time of the acquisition. This allocation may require adjustment, however, if there is a subsequent change in the partnership sharing ratios (see paragraph 4).

3 PARTNERSHIP ASSETS DIVIDED IN KIND AMONG THE PARTNERS

Where a partnership distributes an asset in kind to one or more of the partners, for example on dissolution, a partner who receives the asset will not be regarded as disposing of his fractional share in it. A computation will first be necessary of the gains which would be chargeable on the individual partners if the asset has been disposed of at its current market value. Where this results in a gain being attributed to a partner not receiving the asset the gain will be charged at the time of the distribution of the asset. Where, however, the gain is allocated to a partner receiving the asset concerned there will be no charge on distribution. Instead, his capital gains tax cost to be carried forward will be the market value of the asset at the date of distribution as reduced by the amount of his gain. The same principles will be applied where the computation results in a loss.

4 CHANGES IN PARTNERSHIP SHARING RATIOS

An occasion of charge also arises when there is a change in partnership sharing ratios including changes arising from a partner joining or leaving the partnership. In these circumstances a partner who reduces or gives up his share in asset surpluses will be treated as disposing of part of the whole of his share in each of the partnership assets and a partner who increases his share will be treated as making a similar acquisition. Subject to the qualifications mentioned at 6 and 7 below the disposal consideration will be a fraction (equal to the fractional share changing hands) of the current balance sheet value of each chargeable asset provided there is no direct payment of consideration outside the partnership. Where no adjustment is made through the partnership accounts (for example, by revaluation of the assets coupled with a corresponding increase or decrease in the partner's current or capital account at some date between the partner's acquisition and the reduction in his share) the disposal is treated as made for a consideration equal to his capital gains tax cost and thus there will be neither a chargeable gain nor an allowable loss at that point. A partner whose share reduces will carry forward a smaller proportion of cost to set against a subsequent disposal of the asset and a partner whose share increases will carry forward a larger proportion of cost.

The general rules in TCGA 1992 s 42 for apportioning the total acquisition cost on a part-disposal of an asset will not be applied in the case of a partner reducing his asset-surplus share. Instead, the cost of the part disposed of will be calculated on a fractional basis.

5 ADJUSTMENT THROUGH THE ACCOUNTS

Where a partnership asset is revalued a partner will be credited in his current or capital account with a sum equal to his fractional share of the increase in value. An upward revaluation of chargeable assets is not itself an occasion of charge. If, however, there were to be a subsequent reduction in the partner's asset-surplus share, the effect would be to reduce his potential liability to capital gains tax on the eventual disposal of the assets without an equivalent reduction of the credit he has received in the accounts. Consequently at the time of the reduction in sharing ratio he will be regarded as disposing of the fractional share of the partnership asset represented by the difference between his old and his new share for a consideration equal to that fraction of the increased value at the revaluation. The partner whose share correspondingly increases will have his acquisition cost to be carried forward for the asset increased by the same amount. The same principles will be applied in the case of a downward revaluation.

6 PAYMENTS OUTSIDE THE ACCOUNTS

Where on a change of partnership sharing ratios payments are made directly between two or more partners outside the framework of the partnership accounts, the payments represent consideration for the disposal of the whole or part of a partner's share in partnership assets in addition to any consideration calculated on the basis described in 4 and 5 above. Often such payments will be for goodwill not included in the balance sheet. In such cases the partner receiving the payment will have no capital gains tax cost to set against it unless he made a similar payment for his share in the asset (for example, on entering the partnership) or elects to have the market value at 6 April 1965 treated as his acquisition cost. The partner making the payment will only be allowed to deduct the amount in computing gains or losses on a subsequent disposal of his share in the asset. He will be able to claim a loss when he finally leaves the partnership or when his share is reduced provided that he then receives either no consideration or a lesser consideration for his share of the asset. Where the payment clearly constitutes payment for a share in assets included in the partnership accounts, the partner receiving it will be able to deduct the amount of the partnership acquisition cost represented by the fraction he is disposing of. Special treatment, as outlined in 7 below, may be necessary for transfers between persons not at arm's length.

SPs

7 TRANSFERS BETWEEN PERSONS NOT AT ARM'S LENGTH

Where no payment is made either through or outside the accounts in connection with a change in partnership sharing ratio, a Capital Gains Tax charge will only arise if the transaction is otherwise than by way of a bargain made at arm's length and falls therefore within TCGA 1992 s 17 for transactions between connected persons. Under TCGA 1992 s 286(4) transfers of partnership assets between partners are not regarded as transactions between connected persons if they are pursuant to genuine commercial arrangements. This treatment will also be given to transactions between an incoming partner and the existing partners.

Where the partners (including incoming partners) are connected other than by partnership (for example, father and son) or are otherwise not at arm's length (for example, uncle and nephew) the transfer of a share in the partnership assets may fall to be treated as having been made at market value. Market value will not be substituted, however, if nothing would have been paid had the parties been at arm's length. Similarly if consideration of less than market value passes between partners connected other than by partnership or otherwise not at arm's length, the transfer will only be regarded as having been made for full market value if the consideration actually paid was less than that which would have been paid by parties at arm's length. Where a transfer has to be treated as if it had taken place for market value, the deemed disposal will fall to be treated in the same way as payments outside the accounts.

8 ANNUITIES PROVIDED BY PARTNERSHIPS

A lump sum which is paid to a partner on leaving the partnership or on a reduction of his share in the partnership represents consideration for the disposal by the partner concerned of the whole or part of his share in the partnership assets and will be subject to the rules in 6 above. The same treatment will apply when a partnership buys a purchased life annuity for a partner, the measure of the consideration being the actual costs of the annuity.

Where a partnership makes annual payments to a retired partner (whether under covenant or not) the capitalised value of the annuity will only be treated as consideration for the disposal of his share in the partnership assets under TCGA 1992 s 37(3) if it is more than can be regarded as a reasonable recognition of the past contribution of work and effort by the partner to the partnership. Provided that the former partner had been in the partnership for at least ten years an annuity will be regarded as reasonable for this purpose if it is no more than two-thirds of his average share of the profits in the best three of the last seven years in which he was required to devote substantially the whole of this time to acting as a partner. In arriving at a partner's share of the profits regard will be had to the partnership profits assessed before deduction of any capital allowances or charges. The ten year period will include any period during which the partner was a member of another firm whose business has been merged with that of the present firm. For lesser periods the following fractions will be used instead of two-thirds—

Complete years in partnership	*Fraction*
1–5	1/60 for each year
6	8/60
7	16/60
8	24/60
9	32/60

Where the capitalised value of an annuity is treated as consideration received by the retired partner, it will also be regarded as allowable expenditure by the remaining partners on the acquisition of their fractional shares in partnership assets from him.

9 MERGERS

Where the members of two or more existing partnerships come together to form a new one, the capital gains tax treatment will follow the same lines as that for changes in partnership sharing ratios. If gains arise for reasons similar to those covered in 5 and 6 above, it may be possible for roll-over relief under TCGA 1992 s 152 to be claimed by any partner continuing in the partnership insofar as he disposes of part of his share in the assets of the old firm and acquires a share in other assets put into the "merged" firm. Where, however, in such cases the consideration given for the shares in chargeable assets acquired is less than the consideration for those disposed of, relief will be restricted under TCGA 1992 s 153.

10 SHARES ACQUIRED IN STAGES

Where a share in a partnership is acquired in stages wholly after 5 April 1965, the acquisition costs of the various chargeable assets will be calculated by pooling the expenditure relating to each asset. Where a share built up in stages was acquired wholly or partly before 6 April 1965 the rules in TCGA 1992 Sch 2 para 18 will normally be followed to identify the acquisition cost of the share in each asset which is disposed of on the occasion of a reduction in the partnership's share; that is, the disposal will normally be identified with shares acquired on a "first in, first out" basis. Special consideration will be given, however, to any case in which this rule appears to produce an unreasonable result when applied to temporary changes in the shares in a partnership, for example those occurring when a partner's departure and a new partner's arrival are out of step by a few months.

11 ELECTIONS UNDER TCGA 1992 SCH 2 PARA 4

Where the assets disposed of are quoted securities eligible for a pooling election under TCGA 1992 Sch 2 para 4 partners will be allowed to make separate elections in respect of shares or fixed interest securities held by the partnership as distinct from shares and securities which they hold on a personal basis. Each partner will have a separate right of election for his proportion of the partnership securities and the time limit for the purposes of Schedule 2 will run from the earlier of—

(*a*) the first relevant disposal of shares or securities by the partnership and
(*b*) the first reduction of the particular partner's share in the partnership assets after 19 March 1968.

12 PARTNERSHIP GOODWILL AND TAPER RELIEF

This paragraph applies where the value of goodwill which a partnership generates in the conduct of its business is not recognised in its balance sheet and where, as a matter of consistent practice, no value is placed on that goodwill in dealings between the partners. In such circumstances, the partnership goodwill will not be regarded as a ''fungible asset'' (and, therefore, will not be within the definition of ''securities'' in TCGA 1992 s 104(3)) for the purpose of capital gains tax taper relief under TCGA 1992 s 2A. Accordingly, on a disposal for actual consideration of any particular partner's interest in the goodwill of such a partnership, that interest will be treated as the same asset (or, in the case of a part disposal, a part of the same asset) as was originally acquired by that partner when first becoming entitled to a share in the goodwill of that partnership.

The treatment described in the preceding paragraph will also be applied to goodwill acquired for consideration by a partnership but which is not, at any time, recognised in the partnership balance sheet at a value exceeding its cost of acquisition nor otherwise taken into account in dealings between partners. However, such purchased goodwill will continue to be treated for the purpose of computing capital gains tax taper relief as assets separate from the partnership's self-generated goodwill. On a disposal or part disposal for actual consideration of an interest in such purchased goodwill by any particular partner, that interest shall be treated for taper relief purposes as acquired either on the date of purchase by the partnership or on the date on which the disposing partner first became entitled to a share in that goodwill, whichever is the later.

Commentary—See *Simon's Direct Tax Service* **C3.231**.
Statements of Practice SP 1/79, SP 1/89—Capital gains tax: partnerships—further extension of SP D12.
Revenue Interpretation RI 9—rebasing elections: assets held by the same person in different capacities.
Note—This statement was revised in IR 131 (August 2003).

D13 *Assets of negligible value: time limit for claims*

Note—This statement has been superseded by Concession D28, which is itself rendered obsolete by FA 1996 Sch 39 para 4 amending TCGA 1992 s 24(2).

D14 *Division of a company in a share for share basis*

Note—This statement has been superseded by SP 5/85 (now obsolete).

D15 *Accommodation let by owner-occupiers*

Note—This statement has been superseded by SP 14/80.

D16 *Interests in possession*

Note—This statement has been deleted (as obsolete) by the Revenue Press Release date 29 October 1980.

D17 *FA 1965 s 29(2)*

Note—This statement is obsolete.

D18 *Value shifting: TCGA 1992 s 30*

The Revenue Law Committee of the Law Society raised with the Board of Inland Revenue a problem arising out of the widely drawn provisions of s 30, which problem was causing concern among those dealing with agricultural properties.

The Committee pointed out that there are instances where a farmer who owns the land he farms may decide to retire and may wish to hand over the farming business, possibly to his son, while raising capital for himself. He therefore enters into two transactions—

(*a*) a lease of the farm at a rack-rent to his son on normal agricultural terms; and

(*b*) a sale of the freehold, subject to the lease to the son, to an outside investor, often an institutional buyer.

The market price paid by the institution is for the tenanted value of the property and this is the value on which the retiring farmer pays capital gains tax. He will undoubtedly have reduced the value of his asset by the grant of the tenancy and as a result paid capital gains tax on a tenanted rather than vacant possession value basis.

The Board of Inland Revenue have now confirmed that in the precise circumstances mentioned above they would take the view that TCGA 1992 s 30 cannot and should not apply and accordingly that they do not regard that section as giving rise to an increased charge to capital gains tax when a farmer enters into the two transactions mentioned.

D19 *Replacement of business assets in groups of companies*

To obtain the benefit of TCGA 1992 s 175, the company making the gain during the replacement of business assets by a group of companies must be a member of a group and the company carrying out the complementary transaction must be a member of the same group, as defined by TCGA 1992 s 170(2) when the transaction is carried out.

The Consultative Committee of Accountancy Bodies has raised with the Revenue the problem of defining the membership of a group of companies for the purpose of replacement of business assets bearing in mind that the replacement acquisition may take place at any time within a period beginning twelve months before and ending three years after the disposal (or such longer period as the Board may by notice in writing allow).

The Revenue take the view that to obtain the benefit of s 175 the company making the gain or the qualifying replacement must be a member of a group and the company carrying out the complementary transaction must be a member of the same group when that transaction is carried out. The concept of "same group" is as defined in TCGA 1992 s 170(10).

Thus, if company A makes a gain at a time when it is a member of the X group of companies then that gain may only be rolled over against an acquisition by company B if at the time of that acquisition company B is a member of the X group.

Therefore, company B need not have been a member of the group at the time that company A made the disposal but must be a member of the group by the time that company B makes its acquisition. Similarly, company A must be a member of the group at the time that it makes its disposal but need not be a member of the group at the time that company B makes the corresponding acquisition.

D20 *Retirement relief: change in business during 10 years before disposal*

Note—This statement was superseded by Concession D8 (now obsolete).

D21 *Time limit for an election for valuation on 6 April 1965 under TCGA 1992 Sch 2 para 17: company leaving a group: TCGA 1992 ss 178, 179*

The time limit for the making of an election for valuation on 6 April 1965 under TCGA 1992 Sch 2 para 17 is two years from the end of the year of assessment or accounting period within which the disposal took place, or such further time as the Board of Inland Revenue may allow. The Board will exercise their discretion under paragraph 17(3) to extend the time limit as appropriate where a company ceases to be a member of a group of companies and as a result a chargeable asset acquired from another member of the group within the past six years is deemed to have been disposed of (and re-acquired) immediately after the acquisition (TCGA 1992 ss 178, 179).

Note—TCGA 1992 s 178 repealed by FA 2000 s 101, Sch 29 para 26.

D22 *Transfer of business to a company*

Note—This statement has been superseded by Concession D22.

D23 *Non-resident company: TCGA 1992 s 13*

Where a UK participator in a non-resident company which would be a close company if resident in the UK is chargeable to capital gains tax on a proportion of a capital gain accruing to that company, tax credit relief may be given against UK capital gains tax for the appropriate proportion of any overseas tax payable by the company in the country where it is resident in respect of its gain TCGA 1992 s 277 (CGTA 1979 s 10); alternatively, under TCGA 1992 s 278 (CGTA 1979 s 11), the appropriate proportion of the overseas tax may be deductible in computing the shareholder's gains to the extent that the overseas tax has not qualified for relief under TCGA 1992 s 277 (CGTA 1979 s 10).

Note—This statement was amended by IR 131 Supp (November 1998).

D24 *Initial repairs to property: TCGA 1992 s 38(1)*

Expenditure on initial repairs to a property (including expenditure on decorations), undertaken in order to put it into a fit state for letting and not allowable for the purposes of Schedule A, is regarded as allowable expenditure for capital gains tax purposes under TCGA 1992 s 38(1).

F MISCELLANEOUS

F1 *Limitations of Revenue advice to taxpayers*

Note—This statement has been superseded by Inland Revenue Code of Practice No 10 ''Information and advice'' published in May 1995.

F2 *UK branches of foreign banks*

Note—This statement was superseded by Concession C14 which was in turn superseded by FA 1982 s 67 (now TA 1988 s 794) and is now obsolete.

F3 *Close companies: apportionment of income and the consequences for capital gains tax: close companies in liquidation*

Note—SP F3 has been superseded by Concessions A36, D12, which are now classified as obsolete.

IR STATEMENTS OF PRACTICE ISSUED AFTER 18 JULY 1978

SP 1/78 (18 July 1978) *Employment Protection Act 1975: maternity pay*

Note—This statement was classified as obsolete by IR 131 (July 1994).
Maternity pay for periods beginning after 5 April 1982 is taxable under Schedule E as earned income (FA 1982 s 31, now TA 1988 s 150). This statement of practice has effect only as regards earlier periods.

SP 2/78 *Close companies—non-resident participators: apportionment*

Note—SP 2/78 has been reclassified as Concession B22 (now obsolescent).

SP 3/78 (19 October 1978) *Close companies: income tax relief for interest on loans applied in acquiring an interest in a close company*

1 TA 1988 s 360 provides, subject to certain conditions, for relief from income tax in respect of interest on a loan applied in acquiring any part of the ordinary share capital of a close company or in lending on for use in the business of that or an associated close company.

2 In paragraph 41 of the Revenue's booklet entitled ''Tax treatment of interest paid'' issued in 1974, it is stated that—

> ''The company must have been a ''close company'' for tax purposes throughout the period beginning immediately after the application of the money and ending with the payment of interest giving rise to the claim for relief.''.

The Board of Inland Revenue have now agreed that the statutory provisions may be interpreted as not requiring the company to be close at the time of paying the interest.

3 In future therefore, TA 1988 s 360 will in effect be construed by the Revenue as applying in relation to a company which has ceased to be close after the application of the loan proceeds as they apply in relation to companies which have remained close throughout, provided that the other conditions for relief are satisfied. Claims which have been determined by an agreement taking effect as the determination of an appeal cannot be reopened for the year or years to which the claim related, but subject to this, claims made on the new basis within the statutory time limit will be admitted for all years.

Commentary—*Simon's Direct Tax Service* **E1.547**.

SP 4/78 *Mining companies: expenditure on planning permission applications*

Note—Relief under the old coal mines and oil wells allowances ceased to apply for expenditure incurred, broadly, after 31 March 1986 by virtue of FA 1986 s 55 Sch 13 (now CAA 1990 ss 98–121).

SP 6/78 (13 November 1978) *Trade unions: provident benefits: legal expenses paid for members*

Note—SP 6/78 has been superseded by SP 1/84.

SP 7/78 (14 November 1978) *Capital gains tax: exercise of a power of appointment over settled property*

Note—This statement was classified as obsolete by IR 131 (November 1996).

SP 8/78 (15 November 1978) *Building licences granted under the Community Land Act 1975: stock relief*

Note—This statement is now obsolete. Its deletion was announced in the Revenue Index to Statements of Practice published on 14 July 1987.

This statement of practice applied only to licences granted under the Community Land Act 1975 which was repealed by the Local Government, Planning and Land Act 1980.

SP 1/79 (12 January 1979) *Partnerships: extension of statement of practice D12*

Paragraph 8 of SP D12 explains the circumstances in which the capitalised value of an annuity paid by a partnership to a retired partner will not be treated as consideration for the disposal of his share in the partnership assets. The Board have now agreed that this practice will be extended to certain cases in which a lump sum is paid in addition to an annuity. Where the aggregate of the annuity and one-ninth of the lump sum does not exceed the appropriate fraction (as indicated in the Statement) of the retired partner's average share of the profits, the capitalised value of the annuity will not be treated as consideration in the hands of the retired partner. The lump sum, however, will continue to be so treated.

This extension of the practice will be applied to all cases in which the liability has not been finally determined at the date of this Notice. See also SP 1/89.

Commentary—*Simon's Direct Tax Service* **C3.225**.
Statement of Practice D12—Capital gains tax partnerships.
SP 1/89—Further extension of SP D12.

SP 2/79 *Development land tax: negotiations on liability*

Note—Development land tax was abolished with effect from 19 March 1985.

SP 3/79 (19 February 1979) *Payment of life assurance premiums on which commission is payable to the policyholder*

Note—This statement was superseded by SP 5/95 (which was itself superseded by SP 4/97).

SP 4/79 (28 February 1979) *Life assurance premium relief—children's policies*

The Board of Inland Revenue have considered the question of premium relief as it relates to policies effected on the lives of children in the light of the new scheme for premium relief by deduction commencing on 6 April 1979.

Relief under TA 1988 s 266 is at present confined to premiums on an "insurance or contract ... made by (the claimant) and as from 6 April 1979, "the individual". Where a child is of "tender years" the Board consider that he cannot reasonably be regarded as having "made" the insurance or contract since he would have insufficient knowledge or understanding of what he was doing. Accordingly the Board have decided that no relief is due in respect of premiums on a policy "taken out" by a child of "tender years". For this purpose they regard "tender years" as including a child of less than 12 years of age.

In applying this ruling the Board have agreed that—

1 Relief will be allowed by deduction on children's policies which satisfy all the other requirements for relief and which are issued by a company within UK jurisdiction before 1 March 1979.

2 New policies taken out on or after 1 March 1979 by a child of "tender years" on his own life, will not be allowed relief whether or not the premiums are paid out of the child's own income.

3 Where relief is refused in respect of a policy taken out on or after 1 March 1979 by a child of "tender years", it may be granted when the child reaches the age of 12 years if the insurance or contract was made before 1 September 1979.

Commentary—*Simon's Direct Tax Service* **E2.1034**.
Note—This statement is only relevant for policies still qualifying for life assurance premium relief. This was withdrawn with effect for policies issued after 13 March 1984.
Statement of Practice SP 11/79—Further consideration by the Revenue of premium relief as it applies in relation to children's policies.

SP 5/79 (30 March 1979) *Family company: sale of assets in anticipation of liquidation*

Note—SP 5/79 was reclassified as Concession D13 (now obsolete).

SP 6/79 (30 March 1979) *Closure of business followed by sale of assets or liquidation of company*

Note—SP 6/79 was reclassified as Concession D14 (now obsolete).

SP 7/79 (11 April 1979) *Benefits in kind: cheap loans—advances for expenses*

Commentary—*Simon's Direct Tax Service* **E4.632**.
Note—This statement was classified as obsolete in IR 131 (August 2003) and only applies up to and including the tax year 2002–03; see now ITEPA 2003 s 179.

SP 8/79 (18 June 1979) *Compensation for acquisition of property under compulsory powers*

1 The Revenue practice—announced in a statement on 13 December 1972—has been that any element of compensation for temporary loss of profits, which is present in the compensation or price payable by an authority possessing compulsory powers for the acquisition of property used for the purposes of a trade or profession, is included as part of the consideration for the resulting disposal for the purposes of capital gains.

2 The Board of Inland Revenue have reconsidered this practice in the light of the decision of the Court of Appeal in the recent case of the *City of Stoke on Trent v Wood Mitchell & Co Ltd* [1979] STC 197 (a Lands Tribunal case). In accordance with this decision any element of compensation received for temporary loss of profits in the circumstances described above falls to be included as a receipt taxable under Schedule D Case I or II. Compensation for losses on trading stock and to reimburse revenue expenditure, such as removal expenses and interest, will be treated in the same way for tax purposes.

3 The practice described in paragraph 2 will also apply in compensation cases where no interest is acquired (eg compensation due to damage, injury or exploitation of land, or to the exercise of planning control).

4 The new practice will apply to all cases in which the liability had not been finally determined at the date of the Court of Appeal's judgment (28 July 1978).

Commentary—*Simon's Direct Tax Service* **C2.1115**.

SP 9/79 (10 August 1979) *Expenditure on producing films and certain similar assets*

Note—This statement has been superseded. See now the IR Business Income Manual 56000–56500).

SP 10/79 (15 August 1979) *Power for trustees to allow a beneficiary to occupy a dwelling house*

Note—Statements relating to IHT are reproduced in Part 3 of this publication.

SP 11/79 (1 November 1979) *Life assurance premium relief: children's policies*

The Board of Inland Revenue have given further consideration to the question of premium relief as it applies to policies effected on the lives of children. They remain of the opinion that (as specified in the statement of practice SP 4/79 issued on 28 February 1979) no relief is in strictness due on premiums on a policy taken out by a child of tender years (ie a child under age 12), but they are prepared to relax somewhat the terms of that Statement.

1 In view of the special problems of industrial branch business the Board will not contest life assurance premium relief on premiums on all industrial branch juvenile policies and similar policies issued by registered Friendly Societies as part of their tax exempt business, subject in each case to the limit in TA 1988 Sch 14 para 2(3).

2 Where an ordinary branch policy other than a Friendly Society policy referred to above is taken out on the life of a child and is assigned to him or he possesses or acquires the whole interest in the policy, relief on premiums paid by the child may be allowed (provided that the other conditions are satisfied)—

(*a*) where the policy was taken out after the child had attained age 12;

(*b*) where the policy was taken out prior to 1 March 1979 and before the child attained age 12;

(*c*) where the policy was taken out on or after 1 March 1979 before the child attained age 12 and he has attained that age.

Commentary—*Simon's Direct Tax Service* **E2.1034**.

Note—This statement is only relevant for policies qualifying for life assurance premium relief which was withdrawn for policies issued after 13 March 1984.

SP 12/79 (30 November 1979) *Investigation settlements: retirement annuity relief*

Note—FA 1980 s 32(4) provided that TA 1970 s 227(3) did not apply to premiums paid after 5 April 1981. Accordingly this statement of practice was withdrawn with effect from that date, see SP 9/80 and SP 9/91.

SP 13/79 (5 December 1979) *Flat rate expenses for manual and certain other employees*

Note—Current allowances appear as an appendix to Concession A1 (which has been given statutory effect as ITEPA 2003 s 367).

SP 14/79 (21 December 1979) *Unquoted shares or securities held on 6 April 1965*

1 This statement concerns the application of TCGA 1992 Sch 2 para 19 to unquoted shares and securities held on 6 April 1965. Where there has been a reorganisation of a company's share capital before 6 April 1965, para 19(1) deems the shares to have been sold and re-acquired at market value on 6 April 1965. Where a reorganisation takes place on or after 6 April 1965, and all or part of the new holding of shares is disposed of without an election for valuation as at 6 April 1965 being made para 19(2) requires the new shares to be valued as at the date of the reorganisation: time apportionment is applied to the gain or loss up to that date and on a disposal this is brought into account as well as the subsequent gain or loss.

2 For the purposes of paras 19(1) and 19(2), ''reorganisation of share capital'' includes not only reorganisation of one company's share capital within TCGA 1992 s 126 or s 132, but also certain takeovers, reconstructions and amalgamations involving more than one company within TCGA 1992 s 135 or s 136.

3 Paragraph 19(3), however, prevents the application of paras 19(1) or 19(2) where the new holding differs only from the original shares in being a different number, whether greater or less, of shares of the same class as the original shares. The Revenue's practice has been to treat para 19(3) as capable of covering reorganisations involving more than one company; for example, the exchange of shares of a certain class in one company for shares of the same class in another company.

4 The Board of Inland Revenue have reconsidered this practice in the light of the case of *IRC v Dr G W Beveridge* [[1979] STC 592]. In accordance with opinions expressed in the Court of Session para 19(3) is no longer considered to apply where the shares comprised in the new holding are shares in a different company from the old shares.

5 This interpretation will be applied to all cases in which the liability had not been finally determined at the date of the Court of Session's judgment (19 July 1979).

Commentary—*Simon's Direct Tax Service* **C2.728**.

SP 1/80 (16 January 1980) *Legal entitlement and administrative practices*

Note—This statement has been superseded by SP 6/95.

SP 2/80 (29 February 1980) *Statement clarifying the operation of an existing administrative practice—Schedule D Case V losses*

Note—This statement has been superseded by Concession B25 (which was classified as obsolete by IR 1 Supp (November 1998)).

SP 3/80 (26 March 1980) TA 1988 s 707: *Cancellation of tax advantages from certain transactions in securities: procedure for clearance in advance*

TA 1988 s 703 and the succeeding sections (which provide for the cancellation of tax advantages from certain transactions in securities) contain safeguards against counteraction being taken unwarrantably in respect of transactions which a taxpayer has carried out. In addition, TA 1988 s 707 provides a procedure for the taxpayer to be told in advance whether the Board of Inland Revenue are satisfied that proposed transactions as described to them, if carried out, would not invoke counteraction.

REASONS FOR REFUSING CLEARANCE

1 Where the Board cannot give clearance under TA 1988 s 707 they are not statutorily required to say why and at one time their practice was to decline to do so. With a view to removing misunderstanding in particular about the scope of TA 1988 s 703 in relation to transactions with a commercial element, they later modified that practice.

Where the applicant has given full reasons for his transactions and clearance has to be refused, the Board indicate, where possible, their main grounds for doing so. In appropriate cases where they do not think it right to give reasons the Board will invite the principals themselves as well as their advisers to an interview so that the Board can be certain they have fully appreciated the position.

SIGNIFICANCE OF REFUSING CLEARANCE

2 The rules of the clearance procedure require the Board to say whether in their view TA 1988 s 703 would not apply. They are not required to say whether in their view the section definitely would apply. It may not always be practicable to do so in advance of the transaction's actually being carried out, eg where the motive for it is a relevant factor. Nonetheless, it is not the practice of the Board to withhold consent under TA 1988 s 707 unless they would, on the information available to them, expect to take counteraction under TA 1988 s 703. The then Financial Secretary to the Treasury stated this practice in the 1966 Finance Bill debates in the following words:

> ''The Revenue's approach is that it will not refuse a [Section 707] clearance unless, having considered the transaction fully and all the circumstances of it, it would itself take action under the section if the transaction were completed.''

[Hansard (13 July 1966) Vol 731 col 1566]

Commentary—*Simon's Direct Tax Service* **A7.122.**
Revenue Decision RD6—Circumstances in which the Revenue may refuse clearance under TA 1988 s 707.

SP 4/80 (26 March 1980) *Industrial buildings allowance: industrial workshops constructed for separate letting to small businesses*

Under the industrial buildings allowance rules (CAA 1990 Part 1) a building only qualifies for relief if it is in use as an industrial building or structure as defined in s 18. Where a number of small workshops which are to be industrial buildings are constructed for separate letting to small businesses, it is thus necessary for the owner of the relevant interest to establish in each case that the tenant is carrying on a qualifying trade. He must also establish, in each case, how much, if any, of the building is used for non-qualifying purposes, such as for offices. These requirements can be burdensome, particularly where tenants change frequently, and further information on these points has to be obtained to establish that each workshop continues to be used in full as an industrial building.

The Revenue have decided that, in future, they will normally be prepared to deal with industrial buildings allowance claims for estates consisting of small industrial workshops on a global instead of individual basis. Where, therefore, individual workshops units of 2,500 square feet or less intended for separate letting as industrial buildings to small businesses are constructed as an estate, the inspector will normally be satisfied with a general description of the uses to which the units will be put and, unless the circumstances suggest the need for further enquiry, will not ask for particulars of the trades carried on by individual tenants or details of the uses to which these premises are put. For the purpose of writing down allowances, the whole of any estate built at one time (or part of an estate where it is constructed in phases) will be regarded as having been brought into use when the first workshop begins to be used.

A sale of the relevant interest in the estate would also be dealt with on a global basis so far as possible, but when only part of the estate is sold, separate computations would normally be necessary to establish the balancing adjustments and the successor's allowances.

This practice is intended to simplify the administration of the industrial buildings allowance rules as they apply to most industrial workshop estates built for letting as separate units to small businesses. It will not apply where, exceptionally, several units in one estate are let to the same tenant or connected tenants; where the estate is to a significant extent used for trades which do not attract industrial buildings allowance; and in any other circumstances where the relief available would be significantly lower on a strict application of the industrial building allowances rules.

SP 5/80 (26 March 1980) *Group relief: TA 1988 s 410*

Note—This statement has been superseded by SP 3/93.

SP 6/80 (9 July 1980) *Small workshops allowance*

Note—This statement was classified as obsolete in IR 131 (November 1996).

SP 7/80 (16 July 1980) *Deceased persons' estates: income received during the administration period*

Concession A14—Deceased person's estates: residuary income received during the administration period. This Concession was announced at the same time as this statement of practice.
Statement of Practice SP 3/86—Payments to a non-resident from UK discretionary trusts or UK estates during the administration period: double taxation relief.
Note—This statement was classified as obsolete in IR 131 (July 1994).

SP 8/80 (13 August 1980) *Stock relief: deferment of recovery charges—definition of net indebtedness in FA 1980 Sch 7 para 1(5)*

Note—FA 1980 Sch 7 para 1(5) was repealed by FA 1981 Sch 19 Part VII in relation to accounting periods beginning after 14 November 1980.

SP 9/80 (19 September 1980) *Investigation settlements: retirement annuity relief*

Note—This statement has been superseded by SP 9/91.

SP 10/80 (24 September 1980) *Mortgage interest relief: year of marriage*

Note—This statement was classified as obsolete by IR 131 (July 1994).

SP 11/80 (9 October 1980) *Liability under TA 1988 Part XIII Chapter II, on gains arising on life and capital redemption policies and life annuities*

Note—This statement has been withdrawn with effect from 5 April 1999. See now Concession B53, para 6.

SP 12/80 (13 October 1980) *Business property relief: "buy and sell" agreements*

Note—Statements relating to IHT are reproduced in Part 3 of this publication.

SP 13/80 (14 October 1980) *Demergers: TA 1988 ss 213–218*

TA 1988 ss 213–218 contain certain tax reliefs where trading activities carried on by a single company or group are divided so as to be carried on by two or more companies not belonging to the same group or by two or more independent groups.

This statement of practice explains how the Revenue will apply certain of the provisions in practice and does not affect the right of appeal on points affecting liability to tax. The references are to TA 1988.

"EXEMPT DISTRIBUTION"

This expression, wherever it appears in TA 1988 ss 213–218, refers only to what would otherwise have been a distribution for the purposes of the Corporation Tax Acts. It does not, for example, apply to a distribution in a winding up.

TA 1988 S 213(3)(*B*)(I)

To satisfy s 213(3)(*b*)(i), a trade (or trades) must be transferred. The Revenue will regard this as satisfied where what is received by the transferee company is a trade. What passes from one company to another will be a parcel of assets comprising what is needed for the carrying on of that trade. The same trade may previously have been carried on as such by the distributing company; but this is not essential. What is transferred may have been part only of a trade carried on by that company, for example, the retail end of a combined manufacturing/retailing trade. Or again the assets being transferred may be being brought together for the first time from one or more trades carried on by the distributing company or in the group of which it is a member; assets may even be included which were not previously used in a trade or held by a trading company, eg property may have been held in a property investment company. What matters is that there should be a division of trading activities and that assets transferred should be transferred to be used in a trade by the transferee company and should be so used. Relief will not be denied solely because some minor asset linked with a trading asset, for example a flat above a shop, is also transferred.

TA 1988 S 213(6)(*A*), (8)(*B*), (*D*) "ORDINARY SHARES"

Relief under s 213(2) is given to a distribution to ordinary shareholders only insofar as it is of shares forming part of ordinary share capital (as defined in s 832) which are transferred or issued. Relief on that distribution will not be denied solely because concurrently there is a transfer or issue, of a kind that does not qualify for relief, of other shares or securities to ordinary shareholders or of shares or securities of any description to preference shareholders (and whether or not that other transfer or issue involves a taxable distribution). Similarly, the words ''substantially the whole'' will be regarded as satisfied even where the shareholders give some consideration. However, these other circumstances will be taken into account in judging whether all the conditions, in particular those of s 213(10), (11), are satisfied.

TA 1988 S 213(6)(*A*), (8)(*B*), (*D*) "SUBSTANTIALLY THE WHOLE"

In the context of these particular provisions, ''substantially the whole'' is taken to mean around 90 per cent or more.

TA 1988 S 213(8)(*A*) "INTEREST ... IN THAT TRADE"

The legislation does not define this expression. In the Revenue's view, it must be given a wide meaning. A company would clearly retain an interest in a trade if it carried it on jointly or otherwise

SPs

had a right to the profits or assets or to any of them. But other circumstances could exist in which it could be said to have an interest, for example, if it was or was entitled to be a main supplier or customer, or possibly as a consequence of the two companies having common management. In these kinds of case, the Revenue would not normally argue that the interest was other than a ''minor interest'' unless the interest effectively gave control of the trade or of its assets, or a material influence on the profits or on their destination. More generally, it will not always be possible to quantify an interest in a trade; but where this can be done, ''minor'' is the opposite of ''substantially the whole'' ie around ten per cent or less.

TA 1988 S 213(6)(*B*), (8)(*C*), (*E*) "AFTER"

In the Revenue's view, these provisions require that the company should be bona fide trading after the distribution; but in this context they do not regard ''after'' as meaning ''for ever after''. If there were any intention that the conditions would cease to be satisfied at some later time, the application of s 213(10), (11) would need to be considered.

TA 1988 S 213(11)(*C*)

The concurrent sale of another company in the same group as a subsidiary being demerged is not necessarily a bar to relief. It would be so, for example, if that were a main purpose of a scheme or arrangement of which the distribution formed a part.

TA 1988 S 213(11)(*D*) "AFTER"

''After'' in this context clearly means ''at any time after''.

TA 1988 S 215

Advice on the method of application under s 215(1) and on the information to be included in it is contained in the Annex to this Statement. Where, exceptionally, it is not possible to explain the purposes of a demerger adequately in writing, the Revenue will invite applicants to an interview. If they have to refuse clearance under these provisions, they will normally state the main reason for doing so.

All general enquiries on the demerger legislation should be directed to Business Tax (Demergers), New Wing, Somerset House, London WC2R 1LB and not to local Inspectors. Particular enquiries on the capital gains aspect should, however, be directed to Capital and Savings Division, Capital Gains Clearance Section at Sapphire House, 550 Streetsbrook Road, Solihull, West Midlands B91 1QU.

TA 1988 S 216(1)

This subsection requires a company making an exempt distribution to make a return giving particulars, inter alia, ''of the circumstances by reason of which it is exempt''. In many cases a clearance notification will previously have been given by the Board under s 215(1). Where the distribution is precisely that for which a clearance application was made, all relevant circumstances being as disclosed in that application, it will suffice to refer to the notification and to confirm that that is so.

TA 1988 S 768

Section 768 provides, broadly, that where within any three year period there is both a change in the ownership of a company *and* a major change in the nature or conduct of a trade carried on by it, then relief cannot be obtained against profits arising after the change of ownership for losses incurred before the change.

The object of the demergers legislation is to make it easier for trading activities to be split (which may involve a change in ownership of a company within the meaning of the section) so that some part of them at least may be managed more dynamically (which may involve a major change in the nature or conduct of the trade). In the meantime, if full details are given, the Revenue will consider sympathetically the application of the section where the reason for s 768 applying is that the ownership of a trade being demerged under these provisions is passing from a company to its shareholders, the underlying ownership of the trade being unchanged (eg the shareholders after the distribution own directly the interests in a company which previously they owned indirectly through the company which made the distribution).

Note Concession C11 provides that a distributing company will not be regarded as failing to meet s 213(7) or (9) merely because it retains, after the distribution, sufficient funds to meet the cost of liquidation and to cover the amount of the share capital remaining, depending on the amount of that remaining share capital. The full text of ESC C11 may be found in Booklet IR1.

ANNEX TO SP 13/80
APPLICATIONS FOR CLEARANCE UNDER S 215(1)

Procedure

Application for clearance under TA 1988 s 215 should be sent to:

If not market sensitive—

Mohini Sawhney,
5th floor,
22 Kingsway,
London
WC2B 6NR.

If market sensitive—
Ray McGann,
5th floor,
22 Kingsway,
London
WC2B 6NR.

Applications under TA 1988 s 215 *and* one or both of TCGA 1992 ss 138, 139 or TA 1988 s 703 can be sent to the same address with a copy of the application and all supporting documents for each clearance sought. Applications will then be forwarded to the relevant offices. Alternatively the other applications may be made directly to:

Inland Revenue, Capital and Savings, Capital Gains Clearance Section, Sapphire House, 550 Streetsbrook Road, Solihull, West Midlands, B91 1QU, and, Inland Revenue, Special Investigations Section, 5th Floor, 22 Kingsway, London WC2B 6NR, respectively.

Form of application

To assist companies in preparing clearance applications under s 215(1) and to facilitate their consideration by the Board, an outline of the basic information needed is given below. It is not an exhaustive statement and each applicant in giving the particulars of the relevant transactions required by s 215(5) must fully and accurately disclose all facts and circumstances material for the decision of the Board (s 215(8)).

This advice refers only to applications under s 215(1). Where a single application is made under that and other provisions, eg TCGA 1992 s 138, it should open by stating clearly the provisions under which it is made and should be expanded to include any additional information needed for the application(*s*) under the other provision(*s*).

It will be helpful if applications follow the order of items below, each item being expanded as necessary and further information being added at the end.

1 *Companies*

The name of each "relevant company" (s 213(3)) showing

(*a*) whether it is a "distributing", "subsidiary" or "transferee" company
(*b*) its tax district and reference
(*c*) whether it is resident in the UK
(*d*) status, ie "holding company" or "trading company" within the s 218(1) definition or some other type of company eg investment company or holding or trading company not within the definition.

2 *Groups*

Where appropriate a statement or diagram showing the shareholding interest of each group company in other group companies. A group for this purpose is the largest 51 per cent group (as defined in s 218(1)) to which the distributing company belongs.

3 *Purpose and benefits*

A statement of the reasons for the demerger, the trading activities to be divided, the trading benefits expected and any other benefits expected to accrue whether or not to the company concerned.

If this can be stated more easily after giving a detailed description of the proposed transactions this item may be included in the application after item 4.

4 *Transactions*

A detailed description of all the proposed transactions including—

(*a*) *Share capital*

Particulars (class, amount and voting rights) of all share capital of the companies in para 1 above, issued (or to be issued) in the course of the demerger showing the shares to be transferred and/or issued (or exchanged) in the demerger and to which shareholders (or classes of shareholders) or companies. Particulars of any changes to be made in shareholders' rights or loan capital arrangements in connection with the demerger should also be given.

SPs

(*b*) *Transfer of trade (as distinct from a trading subsidiary)*
Particulars of the transfer including all trading and other assets and liabilities to be transferred and retained. (Approximate statements of affairs for the distributing and transferee companies before and after the demerger would be helpful.) Particulars of any interest in the trade to be retained by the distributing company or its group should also be given.

(*c*) *Prior transactions*
Particulars of any prior transactions or rearrangements within a group in preparation for the demerger.

The description should make it clear why it is considered that all the relevant conditions of s 213(3)–(10) and (12) are satisfied.

5 *s 213(11) conditions*

Confirmation, together with all relevant information, that the distribution is not part of a scheme etc within s 213(11). A statement should also be given of the circumstances, if any, in which it is envisaged that control of a ''relevant company'' (listed in 1 above) might be acquired by someone other than members of the ''distributing company'' or a trade carried on by one of those companies before or after the demerger might cease or be sold. (Such circumstances might of course exist but not as part of a scheme or arrangement or otherwise to cause any of the qualifying conditions to be failed.)

6 *Balance sheet and profit and loss account*

The latest available balance sheets and profit and loss accounts of the existing companies in para 1 above and in the case of a group the consolidated balance sheet and profit and loss account with a note of any material relevant changes between the balance sheet date and the proposed demerger (the latest balance sheet etc available may of course be later than the last sent to the appropriate tax district).

Commentary—*Simon's Direct Tax Service* **D1.502**.
Concession C11—Demergers: TA 1988 s 213(7), (9).
Note—The text of this statement is as shown in IR 131 (August 2003).

SP 14/80 (14 November 1980) *Relief for owner-occupiers*

FA 1980 introduced a new relief from capital gains tax for owner occupiers who let living accommodation in their homes. The legislation has been consolidated as TCGA 1992 s 223(4). The purpose of this statement is to give to people who are (or are thinking of) letting the whole or a part of their homes an indication whether they are likely to be liable to any capital gains tax when they dispose of them. Anyone who would like further information about the application to his own circumstances of the rules and practice described in this statement is advised to get in touch with his Tax Office which will be pleased to give further help.

1 *Full exemption*

Where the owner of a dwelling house has occupied the whole of it as his only or main residence throughout his period of ownership

– since 6 April 1965 if he acquired it before then and disposed of it before 6 April 1988, or
– since 31 March 1982 if he acquired it before then and disposed of it on or after 6 April 1988.

Any gain on disposal is entirely exempt from capital gains tax.

2 *Lodger living with the family*

Where a lodger lives as a member of the owner's family, sharing their living accommodation and taking meals with them, no part of the accommodation is treated as having ceased to be occupied as the owner's main residence, and the exemption is not restricted at all.

3 *The relief for lettings*

The new relief will apply where the owner disposes, after 5 April 1980, of a dwelling house which has been his only or main residence during his period of ownership but which he has wholly or partly let as residential accommodation. That part of the gain which would be taxable, ignoring the relief for lettings, will now be exempt from capital gains tax up to the lower of—

– £40,000 for disposals on or after 19 March 1991,
– and the amount of the exemption attributable to their own occupation.

The amount of the gain on the let part depends on two things—

(*a*) how much has been let; and
(*b*) the length of time during which it was let.

For example, someone occupies the whole of his home (acquired after 6 April 1982) for six years out of a ten year period of ownership. One-third of it is let throughout the other four years. The gain on the house as a whole is £30,000. Ignoring the relief for lettings, £26,000 would be exempt from capital gains tax and £4,000 (1/3 x 4/10 x £30,000) would be chargeable.

Relief for lettings applies to the £4,000 (which is less than the two limits referred to above) so that the whole of the gain of £30,000 is now exempt.

4 *When relief for lettings will be available*

Whether the let accommodation is part of the owner's dwelling house or is itself a separate dwelling house depends on the facts of particular cases. The Board of Inland Revenue wish to make known, however, their view of the application of the relief to the common case where the owner of a house, which was previously occupied as his (or the family) home, lets part as a flat or set of rooms without structural alteration (or with only minor adaptations). For the purposes of relief for lettings the Board will regard this as a letting of part of the owner's dwelling house, whether or not the tenants have separate washing and cooking facilities. But the relief does not extend to property which, although it may be part of the same building, forms a dwelling house separate from that which is, or has been, the owner's (for example, a fully self-contained flat with its own access from the road etc).

Commentary—*Simon's Direct Tax Service* **C2.1308**.
Notes—FA 1980 referred to above is now TCGA 1992 s 223(4).
This statement is as it appears in IR 131 (August 2002).

SP 15/80 (14 November 1980) *Maintenance payments: payment of school fees*

Where a Court Order requiring a former spouse to make maintenance payments direct to his/her child, who is living with the other spouse, includes an element to cover the cost of school fees of that child it is sometimes the practice for the payment of those fees to be made direct to the school under the Order which would normally be in the following form—

> "that that part of the Order which reflects the school fees shall be paid to the [headmaster] [bursar] [school secretary] as agent for the said child and the receipt of that payee shall be sufficient discharge".

Provided this Order reflects what is happening in practice tax relief will be given to the payer for these payments which will form part of the taxable income of the child. Changes to the taxation of maintenance payments introduced by FA 1988 mean that no relief is available to the payer unless the order requiring payments to the child was made:

(i) by 30 June 1988, on an application to the courts made before 15 March 1988; or
(ii) to replace, vary or supplement such an order which itself requires payment direct to the child.

Where relief is available, the payer's tax relief is limited to that available for 1988–89, even if the payments increase in later years. The child's liability to tax on the income is similarly limited to the amount which was taxable in 1988–89.

The Revenue's views of the circumstances which will properly reflect the presuppositions of such an order and of the responsibility for establishing that such circumstances exist are as follows.

The onus will be on the parties themselves to produce evidence, where requested, that the person receiving the school fees has agreed to act as agent for the child and that the contract for the payment of the fees (which will most easily be proved if in writing) is between the child (not the spouse making the payments) and the school.

Changes to the tax rules for maintenance payments mean that relief for payments direct to children will no longer be available from 6 April 2000.

Commentary—*Simon's Direct Tax Service* **E5.110**.
Notes—The text of this statement is as it appears in IR 131 (January 2000). This statement is now of limited scope, see TA 1988 s 347A.

SP 16/80 (20 November 1980) *Lorry drivers: relief for expenditure on meals*

1 *Employees absent from home and normal place of employment—general*

An employer is allowed to make reimbursement of certain expenses payments without deduction of tax to an employee working temporarily away from home and his normal place of employment. The payments are those which are intended to cover the extra cost of travelling and subsistence which the employee incurs because he is away on duty—but not the cost of his travelling from home to his normal place of work or his usual expenses on food or meals taken when at his normal place of work.

Similarly, where the employee is not reimbursed, a deduction for expenses may be allowed where he is necessarily obliged to incur the extra expense in the performance of his duties.

2 *Travelling appointments*

Where travelling itself is an essential feature of an employee's duties, with the result that he has to spend money on meals in restaurants or cafes above what he would spend if he had a fixed place or area of work or were able to get home for meals, a deduction may be allowed for the extra expenses necessarily incurred in the performance of the duties.

Drivers who qualify for consideration under this heading are those who are engaged full-time in travelling in the performance of their duties. By this is meant employment as a driver throughout the full normal working hours of each day, except those days when the employee is precluded from working by reason of sickness or other reasonable cause, or which are holidays or rest days.

SPs

Employees whose jobs entail only incidental travelling would not be regarded as holding travelling appointments.

Even full-time drivers are excluded from consideration if they travel only in a limited area. This is because they incur no additional expenses when at work from one day to the next, as they have an established pattern of expenditure on meals in the same way as any other employee who has to work at a distance from home and who cannot return home for lunch.

Inspectors of taxes require claimants to give full details of the nature of their duties in addition to providing evidence of the expenditure actually incurred, as described in the following paragraph. In practice, relief is not restricted by reference to amounts of expenditure saved by not having meals at home or a fixed place of work.

3 *Evidence of expenditure*

The amount of relief which can be allowed depends mainly on the bills and vouchers which can be supplied by a driver in support of his claims. Employees who consider that they may have a potential claim should ensure that bills, receipts, etc are available in support of any claim for relief for the current tax year and future years; but if exceptionally they are unable on any occasion to obtain bills or receipts, they must make a note at the time of the date, place and amount spent. [Where the employer makes a contribution in cash or otherwise towards the cost of meals this must be specified and the amount received set off against the expense in arriving at the net amount for which relief is claimed.] An expenses deduction cannot be given in the absence of evidence of expenditure and Tax Districts will not accept estimated figures of outgoings.

Commentary—*Simon's Direct Tax Service* **E4.708**.
Cross references—See TA 1988 ss 141(6C), 142(3C), 200A (exemption for incidental overnight expenses provided to employees during qualifying absences from home, including those paid by means of non-cash voucher or credit-token).

SP 17/80 (5 December 1980) *Flat rate expenses for manual and certain other employees*

Note—The current allowances appear in an Annex to Concession A1 (now obsolete and given statutory effect in ITEPA 2003 s 367).

SP 18/80 *Securities dealt in on the Stock Exchange Unlisted Securities Market: status and valuation for tax purposes*

Note—This statement was rendered obsolete on the closure of the Unlisted Securities market.

SP 1/81 (10 March 1981) *Non-statutory redundancy payments*

Note—This statement is superseded by SP 1/94.

SP 2/81 (10 March 1981) *Contributions to retirement benefit schemes on termination of employment*

Commentary—*Simon's Direct Tax Service* **E4.806**.
Note—This statement has been rewritten as ITEPA 2003 s 408 and was classified as obsolete in IR 131 (August 2003).

SP 3/81 (10 April 1981) *Individuals coming to the UK: ordinary residence*

A person who comes to the UK is not usually regarded as having become ordinarily resident here until he has been in this country for at least three years unless it is clear before then that he intends to be here for three years or more. But in general it is the Board's practice to regard someone who comes to the UK, whether to work here or not, as ordinarily resident for tax purposes—

(*a*) from the date of his arrival if he has, or acquires during the year of arrival, accommodation for his use in the UK which he occupies on a basis that implies a stay in this country of three years or more,

(*b*) from the beginning of the tax year in which such accommodation becomes available.

If in the event an individual, who has been regarded as ordinarily resident solely because he has accommodation here, disposes of the accommodation and leaves the UK within three years of his arrival he would normally be treated as not ordinarily resident for the duration of his stay if this were to his advantage.

Commentary—*Simon's Direct Tax Service* **I9.221**.
Cross reference—See Revenue booklet IR 20 (residence of individuals—Chapter 3).

SP 4/81 (11 August 1981) *Stock relief: recovery charges when level of trading is negligible*

Note—This statement was classified as obsolete by IR 131 Supp (October 1995). Stock relief was abolished by FA 1984 s 48 for accounting periods beginning after 12 March 1984.

SP 5/81 (8 September 1981) *Expenditure on farm drainage*

Land which in the past was reasonably well drained but subsequently becomes wholly or partly waterlogged because the maintenance of efficient drainage was uneconomic is sometimes made available for cultivation by the restoration of drainage or by re-draining. In such case so much of the net expenditure incurred (after crediting any grants receivable) as would be necessary to restore the drainage will be admitted as revenue expenditure in farm accounts provided it excludes—

(*a*) any substantial element of improvement—for example, the substitution of tile drainage for mole drainage, and

(*b*) the capital element in cases in which the present owner is known to have acquired the land at a depressed price because of its swampy condition.

Commentary—*Simon's Direct Tax Service* **B3.506**.
Revenue & other press releases—IR leaflet CA2 October 1972 (''works'' includes drainage or sewerage works).

SP 6/81 (8 September 1981) *Maintenance payments under court orders: retrospective dating*

Note—This statement was classified as obsolete by IR 131 (July 1994).

SP 7/81 (18 September 1981) *Allowable expenditure: expenses incurred by personal representatives*

Note—This statement has been replaced by SP 8/94.

SP 8/81 (18 September 1981) *Rollover relief for replacement of business assets: trades carried on successively*

1 Where a trader ceases carrying on his trade and commences carrying on another trade, there will often be an interval between these events. In such cases, the Board are prepared to regard the trades as having been carried on ''successively'' within the meaning of TCGA 1992 s 152(8), provided that this interval does not exceed three years.

2 If the assets on which the gains accrue are disposed of during this interval, relief under s 152 will nevertheless be available, adjusted as necessary under subsection (7). If the new assets are acquired during the interval, the Board are prepared to allow the gain to be rolled over into them provided that they are not used or leased for any purpose in the period before the new trade commences and are taken into use for the purposes of the trade on its commencement.

3 In relation to a group of companies, TCGA 1992 s 175(1), treats all of the trades of the members of the group as a single trade for the purposes of the relief. FA 1995 s 48 extends TCGA 1992 s 175 to permit the relief to be claimed provided that the relevant conditions are satisfied, where one member of the group makes the disposal and another member makes the acquisition. Where the assets on which the gains accrue are disposed of after the first company has ceased to trade, or where the new assets are acquired before the second company has commenced to trade, the treatment in 2, above, will apply.

4 Nothing in this statement overrides the requirement in s 152(3) for the acquisition to take place in the period beginning twelve months before and ending three years after the disposal (unless the Board by notice in writing extend these time limits).

5 This practice will be applied to all cases in which the amount of the relief has not been finally settled by the date of this statement (18 September 1981). (But see Inland Revenue Press Release of 1 September 1992 on Rollover Relief and Groups of Companies.)

Commentary—*Simon's Direct Tax Service* **C3.302, 306**.
Note—TCGA 1992 s 175 has been amended by FA 1995 s 48.

SP 9/81 (23 September 1981) *Exercise of a power of appointment over settled property*

Note—This statement has been superseded by SP 7/84.

SP 10/81 (3 November 1981) *Payments on account of disability resulting in cessation of employment*

1 ITEPA 2003 s 401 provides for the taxation of those payments on retirement or removal from an office or employment which otherwise are not chargeable to tax. ITEPA 2003 s 406(6) excludes from the ambit of s 401 any payment "made on account of injury to or disability of the holder of an office or employment".

2 The practice of the Revenue prior to 1981 was governed by the view that "disability" used in juxtaposition with the word "injury" meant a loss of physical or mental health with which a person was afflicted suddenly at a particular time and which rendered him physically or mentally incapable of carrying out the duties which he had previously performed. A gradual decline in physical or mental [ability] caused by chronic illness culminating in incapacity to perform the duties of an office or employment was not regarded as "disability".

3 As a result of a decision given by the Special Commissioners on 6 January 1981 the Revenue has reconsidered its practice and now accepts that "disability" covers not only a condition resulting from a sudden affliction but also continuing incapacity to perform the duties of an office or employment arising out of the culmination of a process of deterioration of physical or mental health caused by chronic illness.

Commentary—*Simon's Direct Tax Service* **E4.806**.
Note—This statement was revised in IR 131 (August 2003).

SP 11/81 (6 November 1981) *Additional redundancy payments*

TA 1988 s 90 provides relief to an employer for certain redundancy payments made on or after 1 April 1980, which would otherwise have been treated as non-allowable because they were associated with the actual or notional discontinuance of the trade or business. In the Revenue view, the same principle for disallowing redundancy payments for tax purposes can apply where an identifiable part of a trade is discontinued.

In practice, TA 1988 s 90 will be regarded as applying to a partial, as to a complete, discontinuance where the redundancy payment would satisfy the test of TA 1988 s 74(1)(*a*) but for the fact that it is associated with a partial discontinuance.

Commentary—*Simon's Direct Tax Service* **B3.1477**.

SP 12/81 (20 November 1981) *The construction industry tax deduction scheme: carpet fitting*

The Board of Inland Revenue, up until 20 November 1981, took the view that, where carpet fitting was included in a specification for the construction, alteration or repair of a building, it was an operation included in the deduction scheme by virtue of F(No 2)A 1975 Sch 13 (now TA 1988 s 67(2)). The Board, however, received legal advice on this subject. Although the matter was not free from doubt, they have concluded that carpet fitting, even if included in part of a building contract, is not an operation which forms "an integral part of ..." or is "for rendering complete such operations as are ... described ..." in the Act. Accordingly the Board now treat carpet fitting as an operation outside the scope of the scheme.

Commentary—*Simon's Direct Tax Service* **E5.502**.

SP 1/82 (6 April 1982) *The interaction of income tax and inheritance tax on assets put into settlements*

Note—Statements relating to IHT are reproduced in Part 3 of this publication.

SP 2/82 (July 1994) *Company's purchase of own shares: TA 1988 (See also Inland Revenue Tax Bulletin February 1996, p 280)*

Where a company makes a purchase of own shares which involves a payment in excess of the capital originally subscribed for the shares, the excess constitutes a distribution. However, such a payment is treated as not giving rise to a distribution if, among other conditions, the purchase is made wholly or mainly to benefit a trade carried on by the company, or by one of its 75 per cent subsidiaries. This statement indicates how this test is applied by the Revenue.

The Annex to this statement gives guidance on how companies should apply for a ruling on whether or not a purchase will be treated as a distribution.

TA 1988 S 219(1)(*A*)—THE "TRADE BENEFIT TEST"

1 The Company's sole or main purpose in making the payment must be to benefit a trade carried on by it or by its 75 per cent subsidiary. The condition is not satisfied where, for example, the transaction is designed to serve the personal or wider commercial interests of the vending shareholder (although usually he will benefit from it) or where the intended benefit for the company is to some non-trading activity which it also carries on.

2 If there is a disagreement between the shareholders over the management of the company and that disagreement is having or is expected to have an adverse effect on the company's trade, then the purchase will be regarded as satisfying the trade benefit test provided the effect of the transaction is to remove the dissenting shareholder entirely. Similarly, if the purpose is to ensure that an unwilling shareholder who wishes to end his association with the company does not sell his shares to someone who might not be acceptable to the other shareholders, the purchase will normally be regarded as benefiting the company's trade.

Examples of unwilling shareholders are:

- an outside shareholder who has provided equity finance (whether or not with the expectation of redemption or sale to the company) and who now wishes to withdraw that finance;
- a controlling shareholder who is retiring as a director and wishes to make way for new management;
- personal representatives of a deceased shareholder, where they wish to realise the value of the shares;
- a legatee of a deceased shareholder, where he does not wish to hold shares in the company.

3 If the company is not buying all the shares owned by the vendor or if although the vendor is selling all his shares he is retaining some other connection with the company—for example, a directorship or an appointment as consultant—it would seem unlikely that the transaction could benefit the company's trade, so the trade benefit test will probably not be satisfied. However, there are exceptions; for example, where a company does not currently have the resources to buy out its retiring controlling shareholder completely but purchases as many of his shares as it can afford with the intention of buying the remainder where possible. In these circumstances, it may still be possible for the company to show that the main purpose is to benefit its trade. Also, the Board do not raise any objection if for sentimental reasons it is desired that a retiring director of a company should retain a small shareholding in it, not exceeding 5 per cent of the issued share capital.

ANNEX TO SP 2/82

APPLICATIONS FOR ADVANCE CLEARANCE UNDER TA 1988 S 225

Procedure

If clearance under s 225 is desired the application should be sent to—

Mohini Sawhney,
5th floor,
22 Kingsway,
London
WC2B 6NR.

If clearance is also being sought under TA 1988 s 707 a single application may be made under both provisions and should be directed to the address given above **with an extra copy of the application and enclosures**. Such an application should open by stating clearly the provisions under which it is made and should be expanded to include any additional information needed for the application under the other provision.

Form of application—general

TA 1988 ss 219–229 contain conditions which must be satisfied before the tax treatment afforded by s 219 can apply. A comprehensive application which has regard to each of these conditions will remove the need for lengthy fact finding enquiries and enable the Board to come to a decision on the application with the minimum of delay.

To assist companies in preparing clearance applications under s 225 and to facilitate their consideration by the Board an outline of the basic information needed is given below. However, it is not an exhaustive list, and in giving the particulars of the relevant transactions required by s 225(2) the applicant must fully and accurately disclose all facts and circumstances material for the decision of the Board (s 225(5)).

In what follows, references to purchase of shares include references to repayment or redemption of shares.

It will be helpful if applications follow the order set out below, each item being expanded as necessary and any further information being added at the end.

Application for clearance under TA 1988 s 225(1)(a)

It should be stated at the outset whether the purchase of shares is regarded as falling within s 219(1) by virtue of (*a*) or (*b*). If the purchasing company has previously made any application under s 225 it will be helpful if the Board's reference(*s*) can be quoted.

A. Purchase within TA 1988 s 219(1)(a)

1 *The Company*

(*a*) the name of the company making the purchase;
(*b*) its tax district and reference;
(*c*) confirmation that it is an unquoted company as defined in TA 1988 s 229(1);
(*d*) its status, that is, "trading company" or "holding company of a trading group" within TA 1988 s 229(1) definitions or some other type of company not within the definitions.

2 *Groups*

Where the company is a member of a group (see below):

(*a*) the names of the group companies together with their tax districts and references;
(*b*) a statement or diagram showing the shareholding interests of each group company in other group companies.

A group for the purpose of this paragraph is the largest 51 per cent group to which the purchasing company belongs (TA 1988 s 222(9)), but the meaning of "group" is extended, where appropriate, by TA 1988 s 222(10) and (12)).

3 *The payment*

(*a*) details of the shares to be purchased, the name of their present owner, the purchase price and the method of payment.
(*b*) details of any other transactions between the company and the vendor at or about the same time.
(*c*) confirmation that the company's Articles of Association allow it to purchase its own shares.

4 *Shareholders*

(*a*) a list of the current shareholders in the purchasing company, and where appropriate, in each company in a group as in 2 above, together with particulars (amount, class, dividend rights etc) of their current holdings;
(*b*) a statement of any relationships of the shareholders to each other;
(*c*) where the shareholder is the son or daughter of another shareholder, an indication that he or she is over 18 or else details of their age.

5 *Prior transactions*

Particulars of any prior transactions or rearrangements to be carried out in preparation for the purchase.

6 *Purpose and benefits*

A statement of the reasons for the purchase, the trading benefits expected and any other benefits expected to accrue, whether or not to the purchasing company.

7 *Conditions in TA 1988 s 219*

Confirmation together with all relevant information that the purchase etc does not form part of a scheme or arrangement the main purpose or one of the main purposes of which is to enable the owner of the shares to participate in the profits of the company without receiving a dividend, or the avoidance of tax. Confirmation that the vendor will receive no other payment from the company, or details of any such payment to be made.

8 *Conditions in TA 1988 ss 220–224*

(*a*) the present residence status of the vendor and any intended change (TA 1988 s 220);
(*b*) the tax district, reference and national insurance number of the vendor, or if not known his or her private address (TA 1988 s 220);
(*c*) the period of beneficial ownership by the vendor of the shares to be purchased (TA 1988 s 220(5));
(*d*) confirmation, if appropriate, that the vendor's interest will be "substantially reduced" (TA 1988 s 221(1));
(*e*) confirmation, if appropriate, that the combined interests as shareholders of the vendor and his "associates" (see TA 1988 s 227) will be substantially reduced (TA 1988 s 221(2));
(*f*) confirmation, if appropriate, that the vendor's interest as a shareholder in the group will be substantially reduced (TA 1988 s 222(1));
(*g*) confirmation, if appropriate, that the combined interests as shareholders in the group of the vendor and his associates will be substantially reduced (TA 1988 s 222(3));

(*h*) confirmation that the vendor will not, immediately after the purchase, be "connected with" (see TA 1988 s 228) the company making the purchase or with any company which is a member of the same group as that company (TA 1988 s 223(1));

(*j*) confirmation that the purchase is not part of a scheme or arrangement within TA 1988 s 223(2).

9 *Accounts and other financial information*

The application should be accompanied by—

(*a*) copies of the latest available financial statements for the purchasing company and for any group companies (see paragraph 2 above), and in the case of a group the financial statements for the group;

(*b*) a note of any material relevant changes since the balance sheet date or confirmation that there are none;

(*c*) details of any loan or current account which the vendor maintains with the company or with any group company.

B. Purchase within TA 1988 s 219(1)(b)

1 *Company*

(*a*) The name of the company making the purchase;

(*b*) its tax district and reference;

(*c*) confirmation that it is unquoted as defined in TA 1988 s 229(1);

(*d*) its status, ie "trading company" or "the holding company of a trading group" within the definitions in TA 1988 s 229(1), or some other type of company not within the definitions.

2 *Groups*

Where the company is a member of a group (see A2 above):

(*a*) The names of the group companies together with their Tax Districts and references;

(*b*) a statement or diagram showing the shareholding interests of each group company in other group companies.

3 *The payment*

(*a*) Details of the shares to be purchased, the name of the present owner, the purchase price and method of payment.

(*b*) Details of any other transactions between the company and the vendor at or about the same time;

(*c*) confirmation that the company's Articles of Association allow it to purchase its own shares.

4 *Inheritance tax*

(*a*) The name and date of death of the deceased;

(*b*) the reference of the deceased at the Capital Taxes Office;

(*c*) the amount of the outstanding tax and whether or not liability has been finally agreed;

(*d*) the extent to which the purchase price is to be applied in satisfaction of the tax liability;

(*e*) a full explanation of the circumstances in which there would be "undue hardship" if the tax liability were to be discharged otherwise than through the purchase of own shares from this or another such company;

(*f*) the tax district and reference of the person to whom undue hardship would be caused or if not known the address of that person, and their national insurance number.

5 *Accounts and other financial information*

The application should be accompanied by—

(*a*) copies of the latest available financial statements for the purchasing company and for any group companies (see paragraph A2 above), and in the case of a group the financial statements for the group;

(*b*) a note of any material relevant changes since the balance sheet date or confirmation that there are none.

Applications for clearance under TA 1988 s 225(1)(b)

1 *Company*

(*a*) The name of the company making the purchase;

(*b*) its tax district and reference.

2 *The payment*

(*a*) Details of the shares to be purchased, the vendor, the purchase price and the method of payment.

(*b*) confirmation that the company's Articles of Association allow it to purchase its own shares.

3 *Account and other financial information*

(*a*) Copies of the latest available financial statements for the purchasing company;

(*b*) A note of any material relevant changes since the balance sheet date or confirmation that there are none.

4 A statement of the reasons why it is believed that the proposed payment does not fall within the provisions of TA 1988 s 219.

Commentary—*Simon's Direct Tax Service* **D2.505**.

Note—The text of this statement is as it appears in IR 131 (August 2002).

SP 3/82 (24 November 1982) *Indexation*

Note—This statement was classified as obsolete by IR 131 (January 2000).

SP 1/83 (25 January 1983) *Country-risk debts*

Note—This statement was classified as obsolete by IR 131 (July 1994).

SP 2/83 (28 January 1983) *Tax treatment of expenditure on films and certain similar assets*

Note—See now the IR Business Income Manual 56000–56500.

SP 3/83 (7 February 1983) *Relief for losses on loans to traders: time limit for claims*

Note—This statement has been superseded by Concession D36 which has been given statutory effect by TCGA 1992 ss 253, 254.

SP 4/83 (25 February 1983) *Approved savings-related share option schemes*

Note—This statement has been superseded by legislation in FA 1986 s 25. It was classified as obsolete by IR 131 (July 1994).

SP 5/83 (28 April 1983) *Use of schedules in making personal tax returns*

Note—This statement was classified as obsolete by IR 131 (January 2000).

SP 6/83 (27 July 1983) *Company residence*

Note—This statement has been superseded by SP 1/90.

SP 7/83 (13 September 1983) *Business expansion scheme; overseas activities*

Note—This statement was superseded by SP 7/86, which was in turn superseded by SP 4/87 (which was classified as obsolete by IR 131 Supp (November 1998)).

SP 1/84 (17 February 1984) *Trade unions: provident benefits: legal and administrative expenses*

1 Subject to certain conditions, a registered trade union is entitled under TA 1988 s 467 to exemption from tax in respect of its income and capital gains which, as provided for under the rules of the union, are used for the purpose of provident benefits.

2 The following expenses incurred by a registered trade union are regarded as payments made for the purpose of provident benefits—

(i) Legal expenses in representing members at Industrial Tribunal hearings of cases alleging unfair dismissal.

(ii) Legal expenses in connection with a member's claim in respect of an accident or injury he has suffered.

(iii) General administrative expenses of providing provident benefits.

Commentary—*Simon's Direct Tax Service* **D4.636**.

Note—The Revenue has announced that a trade union which has not already made a claim for relief under TA 1988 s 467 for a chargeable period in respect of any kind of expenditure mentioned in SP 1/84 may make a supplementary claim, provided that the supplementary claim is made within the statutory time limit. The prior agreement of a registered trade union's corporation tax liability does not preclude the admission of such a supplementary claim: Revenue Press Release dated 1 August 1985.

SP 2/84 (24 February 1984) *Payments to redundant steel workers*

Note—This statement was classified as obsolete by IR 131 (July 1994).

SP 4/84 *Development land tax: double taxation conventions*

Note—Development land tax was abolished with effect from 19 March 1985.

SP 5/84 (28 March 1984) *Employees resident but not ordinarily resident in the UK: general earnings under ITEPA 2003 ss 25, 26*

1 Employees who are resident but not ordinarily resident in the UK are liable to UK tax under ITEPA 2003 s 25, on general earnings wherever received for duties performed in the UK. They are also chargeable under ITEPA 2003 s 26, on general earnings for duties performed outside the UK but only to the extent that the earnings are remitted to the UK.

2 Where the duties of a single office or employment are performed both in and outside the UK, an apportionment is required to determine how much of the general earnings are attributable to the UK duties. Apportionment of general earnings is essentially a question of fact, but for many years now the Revenue has accepted time apportionment, based on the number of days worked abroad and in the UK, except where this would clearly be inappropriate. For example, in the case of an employee with 200 working days in the UK and 50 working days outside the UK, the proportion of general earnings attributable to UK duties would be 200/250. This practice does not of course, apply where the charge arises under ITEPA 2003 s 15 or 21, and relief is due under ITEPA 2003, Pt 5, Ch 6 (Deductions from seafarers' earnings).

3 Where an employee resident but not ordinarily resident in the UK performs the duties of a single office or employment both in and outside the UK and is remunerated wholly abroad, he is permitted, by a broad interpretation of the decision in the case of *Sterling Trust Ltd v IRC* 12 TC 868, to say that any remittances made to the UK are made primarily out of general earnings for that year in respect of duties performed in the UK assessable under s 25, and only any balance out of general earnings chargeable under s 26 on remittance.

4 However, where part of the general earnings are remitted to the UK, it has been the practice of the Revenue to regard the proportion of the earnings remitted to the UK, as in respect of duties performed both in and outside the UK, and to treat that proportion of such earnings as is attributable to duties performed outside the UK [as] remitted to the UK for the purposes of s 26.

5 The practice changed with effect from 6 April 1983 when the Revenue introduced a simplified procedure for employees who—

(*a*) are resident but not ordinarily resident in the UK;

(*b*) perform duties of a single employment both in and outside the UK, so that they are potentially chargeable under both ITEPA 2003 ss 25 and 26, in respect of general earnings from that employment; and

(*c*) receive part of their general earnings in the UK and part abroad.

In such cases, provided the general earnings chargeable under s 25 are arrived at in a reasonable manner (ie in the absence of special facts, the proportion of the general earnings, including benefits in kind, relating to UK duties is arrived at on a time basis by reference to working days), the Revenue are prepared to accept that a charge under s 26 will arise only where the aggregate of general earnings remitted to the UK exceeds the amount chargeable under s 25 for that year; and to restrict the charge under s 26 to the excess of the aggregate over the charge under s 25.

Commentary—*Simon's Direct Tax Service* **E4.114**.
Note—This statement was revised in IR 131 (August 2003).

SP 6/84 (31 July 1984) *Non-resident lessors—TA 1988 s 830*

Where mobile drilling rigs, vessels or equipment leased by a non-resident lessor are used in connection with exploration or exploitation activities carried on in the UK or in a designated area, the question of whether the profits or gains arising from the lease constitute income from such activities depends on the facts and circumstances of each particular case. However, the practice of the Revenue is not to seek to charge such profits or gains to tax under TA 1988 s 830 if all of the following conditions are satisfied—

1 the contract is concluded outside the UK and the designated areas;

2 the lessor's obligations are limited to the provision of the asset, eg, a rig on "bare-boat" terms, that is to say, if the lessor has not undertaken to provide any facilities, services or personnel;

3 the lessee takes delivery of the asset outside the designated areas, and is responsible for moving it to the place where it is used, and is not restricted to using it solely in the UK or a designated area;

4 the lessee and lessor are not connected persons, and no facilities, services or personnel related to the operation of the asset are provided by any person connected with the lessor.

Commentary—*Simon's Direct Tax Service* **D4.911**.
Note—This statement is as it appears in IR 131 Supp (November 2000).

SP 7/84 (11 October 1984) *Exercise of a power of appointment or advancement over settled property*

The Board's statement of practice SP 9/81, which was issued on 23 September 1981 following discussions with the Law Society, set out the Revenue's views on the capital gains tax implications of the exercise of a power of appointment or advancement when continuing trusts are declared, in the light of the decision of the House of Lords in *Roome & Denne v Edwards* [1981] STC 96. Those views have been modified to some extent by the decision of the Court of Appeal in *Bond v Pickford* [1983] STC 517.

In *Roome & Denne v Edwards* the House of Lords held that where a separate settlement is created there is a deemed disposal of the relevant assets by the old trustees for the purposes of TCGA 1992 s 71(1) (CGTA 1979 s 54(1)). But the judgements emphasised that, in deciding whether or not a new settlement has been created by the exercise of a power of appointment or advancement, each case must be considered on its own facts, and by applying established legal doctrine to the facts in a practical and commonsense manner. In *Bond v Pickford* the judgements in the Court of Appeal explained that the consideration of the facts must include examination of the powers which the trustees purported to exercise, and determination of the intention of the parties, viewed objectively.

It is now clear that a deemed disposal under TCGA 1992 s 71(1) cannot arise unless the power exercised by the trustees, or the instrument conferring the power, expressly or by necessary implication, confers on the trustees authority to remove assets from the original settlement by subjecting them to the trusts of a different settlement. Such powers (which may be powers of advancement or appointment) are referred to by the Court of Appeal as "powers in the wider form". However, the Board considers that a deemed disposal will not arise when such a power is exercised and trusts are declared in circumstances such that—

(*a*) the appointment is revocable, or

(*b*) the trusts declared of the advanced or appointed funds are not exhaustive so that there exists a possibility at the time when the advancement or appointment is made that the funds covered by it will on the occasion of some event cease to be held upon such trusts and once again come to be held upon the original trusts of the settlement.

Further, when such a power is exercised the Board considers it unlikely that a deemed disposal will arise when trusts are declared if duties in regard to the appointed assets still fall to the trustees of the original settlement in their capacity as trustees of that settlement, bearing in mind the provision in TCGA 1992 s 69(1) (CGTA 1979 s 52(1)) that the trustees of a settlement form a single and continuing body (distinct from the persons who may from time to time be the trustees).

Finally, the Board accept that a power of appointment or advancement can be exercised over only part of the settled property and that the above consequences would apply to that part.

Commentary—*Simon's Direct Tax Service* **C4.208**.

SP 8/84 (18 October 1984) *TA 1988 s 124: interest on quoted Eurobonds*

Note—This statement was classified as obsolete by IR 131 Supp (1997).

SP 10/84 (19 December 1984) *Foreign bank accounts*

1 At present, under TCGA 1992 s 252(1), direct transfers from one foreign bank account to another are treated as a disposal and an acquisition of assets for capital gains tax purposes.

2 Except in relation to an account to which TCGA 1992 s 275(1) applies (accounts held by non-domiciled individuals), a taxpayer may treat all bank accounts in his name containing a particular foreign currency as one account and disregard direct transfers among such accounts for capital gains tax purposes. This practice once adopted must be applied to all future direct transfers among bank accounts in that taxpayer's name containing that particular foreign currency until such time as all debt represented in the bank accounts has been repaid to the taxpayer.

3 This practice may be applied to all cases where the capital gains tax computations have not been settled.

Commentary—*Simon's Direct Tax Service* **C1.608, D2.316**.

SP 11/84 *Estate duty: calculation of duty payable on a chargeable event affecting heritage objects previously granted unconditional exemption.*

Note—Statements relating to IHT are reproduced in Part 3 of this publication.

SP 1/85 (18 January 1985) *Treatment of certain payments to relocated employees*

Note—This statement has been re-published as Concession A67, which was classified as obsolete by IR 1 Supp (November 2001).

SP 2/85 (25 January 1985) *Tax treatment of expenditure on films and certain similar assets*

Note—This statement has been superseded. See now the IR Business Income Manual 56000–56500).

SP 3/85 (25 January 1985) *Exchange rate fluctuations*

Note—This provisional statement has been superseded by SP 1/87.

SP 5/85 (21 May 1985) *Division of a company on a share for share basis*

Note—This statement was classified as obsolete by IR 131 (August 2003).

SP 6/85 (29 July 1985) *Incentive awards*

1 Incentive scheme awards are often provided by way of vouchers. ITEPA 2003 s 87 [formerly TA 1988 s 141] treats as earnings a benefit an employee can obtain with a voucher provided for him by reason of his employment. The measure of the earnings is the "expense incurred by the person providing the voucher in or in connection with the provision of the voucher and the money, goods or services for which it is capable of being exchanged" (ITEPA 2003 s 87 [formerly TA 1988 s 141(1)]).

2 It is not always easy to decide which incentive scheme expenses beyond the direct cost of buying the goods or services provided for the employee have been incurred "in connection with" the voucher and the benefit it provides. In general, the expenses which should be included in the emoluments calculation are those which contribute more or less directly to the advantage enjoyed by the employee. Remoter expenses—for example, the cost of devising and planning an incentive scheme under which vouchers are to be distributed—need not be included. More details are given below.

AWARDS OF GOODS OR SERVICES PROVIDED VIA VOUCHERS

3—(*a*) *Expenses included in the computation of emoluments*

(i) Cost of buying the goods or providing services.
(ii) Cost of selecting and testing those goods or services.
(iii) Cost of storing, distributing and installing the goods or, if appropriate, services.
(iv) Cost of servicing and other "after sales" expenses.
(v) Where a third party is used to distribute the awards or to run an incentive campaign, his fees for handling functions within (i) to (iv) above.

(*b*) *Expenses excluded from the computation of emoluments*

(i) Cost of management time in considering whether or not to launch a scheme involving the provision of vouchers.
(ii) Cost of researching, devising and planning such a scheme.
(iii) Cost of preparing and printing promotional material relating to the provision of the voucher.
(iv) Cost of administration (including the costs of meeting the Revenue's requirements) except for the functions covered in (*a*) above.
(v) Where a third party is involved, as in (*a*)(v) above, his fees for handling functions within (*b*)(i) to (iv) above.

RETAIL VOUCHERS

4 Awards sometimes consist of vouchers which are exchangeable for goods etc at retail shops or stores. Generally, the costs set out in para 3(*a*)(i) to (iv) above will largely consist of the price paid to the shop etc for the vouchers. The cost of distributing the vouchers to award winners and the fees of any third party within para 3(*a*)(v) will also need to be included.

OTHER BENEFITS

5 The computation of the benefit of incentive awards assessable under ITEPA 2003 ss 94, 203 [formerly TA 1988 ss 142, 144, 154] will follow broadly similar principles.

COMPUTATIONS

6 When agreeing the assessable benefit of awards made under incentive schemes the total costs should be analysed between the headings in paras 3(*a*) and (*b*) above.

TAXED AWARD SCHEME

7 On 2 November 1984 a press release announced new voluntary arrangements for collecting tax at the basic rate on non-cash incentive prizes awarded to employees. On 18 January 1990 a Revenue press release announced the arrangements had been extended to cover higher rate liabilities. These are known as ''taxed award schemes''. The approach described above will apply to awards dealt with under such arrangements as well as to all other incentive awards. The Incentive Award Unit will continue to deal with all applications for taxed award schemes and will agree the amounts to be treated as emoluments. Awards under other schemes will be dealt with by the tax office which normally handles the PAYE scheme of the provider of the award. Further details of taxed award schemes may be obtained from: Inland Revenue, Incentive Award Unit, Chapel Wharf Area, Floor 4, Trinity Bridge House, 2 Dearman's Place, Salford M3 5BH, telephone: 0161 261 3269, fax: 0161 261 3354, email: chapelwharf-iau@gtnet.gov.uk.

Commentary—*Simon's Direct Tax Service* **E4.471**.
Revenue & other press releases—IR 18-1-90 (employers may also meet an employee's higher rate liability, in addition to basic rate liability, under a taxed award scheme).
Note—This statement was revised in IR 131 (August 2003).

SP 7/85 (19 December 1985) *Reliefs for non-residents: treatment of wife's income*

Note—This statement was classified as obsolete by IR 131 (July 1994).

SP 1/86 (15 January 1986) *Capital allowances: machinery and plant: short-life assets*

CAA 1990 SS 37, 38

1 Several representative bodies have raised with the Revenue some practical questions arising out of the new rules for capital allowances on certain short-life machinery and plant which come into effect on 1 April 1986. The new rules enable allowances on machinery and plant for which an election is made to be dealt with outside the main capital allowance pool.

2 In discussions between these bodies and the Revenue several areas were identified where businesses and their accountants might find guidance helpful. This note sets out, in broad terms, how they can be dealt with in ways which will be acceptable to local inspectors. In general, inspectors will want to be satisfied that the accounting and other records are adequate to support short-life asset elections and computations and that the new legislation is not being abused.

3 These guidelines are not, however, a substitute for the statutory rules. Their aim is to complement the legislation so that the new arrangements are introduced and continue to operate as efficiently as possible for businesses themselves, their professional advisers and the Revenue. The intention is to review the guidelines when the arrangements have settled in and, if necessary, revise them in the light of experience.

ELECTION FOR SHORT-LIFE ASSET TREATMENT

4 The rules for making elections are set out in CAA 1990 s 37(2). They enable all the machinery and plant acquired in a chargeable period (or its basis period) for which short-life asset treatment is wanted, to be included in one election signed by the taxpayer for that period.

5 In general, inspectors will want to be sure that elections and any supporting material, such as a schedule attached to the election or cross references to schedules or analyses supplied with the accounts, provide sufficient information to minimise the possibility of any difference of view at a later date (for example, on a disposal) about what was and what was not covered by an election for any chargeable period etc and that the assets are not in one of the classes excluded by CAA 1990 s 38.

6 In particular, however, where separate identification of the short-life assets acquired in a chargeable period etc is either impossible or possible but impracticable (for example, similar small or relatively inexpensive assets held in very large numbers perhaps in several locations) then the information on the election about the assets, required by CAA 1990 s 37(2)(*b*), may be provided by reference to batches of acquisitions. Where large numbers of similar short-life assets are acquired throughout a chargeable period etc it will be acceptable if the costs of those assets for the period are aggregated and shown on the election in one sum.

CAPITAL ALLOWANCE COMPUTATIONS

7 The Revenue accept that it may not be practicable for individual capital allowance computations to be maintained for each and every short-life asset especially where the assets are held in very large numbers.

8 Where, therefore, the inspector is satisfied that the *actual* life in the business of a distinct class of assets having broadly similar average lives before they are sold or scrapped is likely to be less than five years (that is, the year of acquisition plus the four following years) computations in the form set out in *Example 1* below will be acceptable. On this basis a balancing allowance will normally become available for the last year of the agreed life of the assets.

9 Where disposal proceeds can be attributed to assets acquired in a particular year they should be brought into the appropriate column(*s*) of the computation relating to those assets for the year(*s*) in which the proceeds are received. If attribution in this way is not possible, disposal proceeds may be credited on a FIFO basis; that is all receipts from disposals in any chargeable period etc are to be regarded as related to the earliest period for which a short-life asset pool on the lines of these arrangements is in existence.

10 This form of computation is intended primarily for short-life assets costing similar amounts which cannot be identified individually. It is possible however that similar arrangements may be helpful where short-life assets which have a separate identity are acquired in large numbers such that the business does not in fact keep track of them individually and it would not be reasonable to expect it to do so. Where this is the case, computations based on the above principles and along the lines of *Example 2* below will normally be acceptable to inspectors.

11 Given the wide variety of potential short-life assets and the widely varying size and circumstances of individual businesses, other forms of computation may also be acceptable.

SUBMISSION OF ELECTION AND COMPUTATIONS TO INSPECTORS

12 It is suggested that either on the first occasion when an election is made or when any abridged or simplified computations are submitted to inspectors for the first time, an explanation of the way in which the computations will be or have been put together is provided together with a description of the underlying records on which they are based. Inspectors will want to be satisfied that, together, the elections and the computations provide the correct statutory result and that if, for any reason, questions are asked about individual items (for example, on a disposal several years after acquisition), sufficient information will be available to the business or to its accountants to enable complete and satisfactory answers to be given.

EXAMPLE 1

Assets held in large numbers with a very short life where individual identification is impossible (eg, returnable containers, linen, tools)

The taxpayer satisfies the inspector that the average actual life (NB not useful life) of tools used in his trade is 3 years; it is therefore reasonable to presume that those items acquired in year 1 are all disposed of in year 4. He elects for short-life asset treatment.

Year of acquisition	1986	1987	1988	1989	*Total each year*
Cost of tools	£1000	£1200	£800	£1000	
1986 WDA	£250				£250
	£750				
1987 WDA	£188	£300			£488
	£562	£900			
1988 WDA	£140	£225	£200		£565
	£422	£675	£600		
1989					
Presumed scrapped					
Disposal value	Nil				
Balancing allowance	£422				
					£991
WDA		£169	£150	£250	
Qualifying expenditure carried forward		£506	£450	£750	

Where scrap or sale proceeds are not in practice taxed as trading receipts and can be identified but not related to particular acquisitions, they should be regarded as disposal value of the earliest period for which a short life asset pool is in existence. For example, if proceeds from the sale of all tools scrapped in 1989 were £50, the balancing allowance in the example would be £372.

EXAMPLE 2

Assets held in large numbers where individual identification is possible but impracticable in the circumstances of the case

The taxpayer uses in his trade large numbers of relatively small items such as scientific or technical instruments, calculators, or amusement machines and elects for short-life asset treatment. His accounting records enable him to identify for each kind the number and cost of acquisition, and both the number and sale proceeds of disposals and the number on hand at the end of the short-life asset period related to those acquisitions.

Technical instruments	*Number*	*Cost*	*Disposal value*
Acquisition in 1986	100	£10,000	
Sold in 1988	20		£500
Sold in 1989	40		£400
On hand 1990	40		
Computation			*Total allowance*
1986 expenditure on 100 instruments		£10,000	
WDA		£2,500	£2,500
		£7,500	
1987 WDA		£1,875	£1,875
		£5,625	
1988 disposal of 20 instruments			
Expenditure unallowed 20/(£5,625 × 100) = £1,125		£1,125	
Disposal value £500			
Balancing allowance £625		£4,500)	£1,750
WDA (80 instruments)		£1,125)	
		£3,375	
1989 disposals: 40 instruments			
Expenditure unallowed 40/(£3,375 × 80) = £1,688		£1,688	
Disposal value £400			
Balancing allowance £1,288			
			£1,710
WDA (40 instruments)		£422)	
		£1,265	
1990 WDA		£314	£314
Expenditure unallowed (40 instruments)		£951	
1991 Transfer to main pool		£951	

It is presumed in this example that all the items cost the same amount; where similar items cost different but broadly similar amounts, this method of computation may still be used.

Commentary—*Simon's Direct Tax Service* **B2.343.**

SP 2/86 (7 March 1986) *Offshore funds*

1 This statement sets out the Revenue's views on the interpretation of certain provisions of this legislation, on which queries have been raised.

MATERIAL INTERESTS IN OFFSHORE FUNDS

2 The legislation applies to ''material interests'' in offshore funds. For such an interest to exist, the investor, at the time of acquiring his investment, must have a reasonable expectation of being able to realise it within seven years for an amount reasonably approximate to that portion which the investment represents of the market value of the entity's underlying assets.

INVESTMENTS IN COMMERCIAL LOANS AND BONDS

3 Normal commercial loans or other debt instruments which entitle the lender to no more than a fixed return of principal on redemption, and which are not geared to the underlying assets value of the borrower's business, would not be regarded as a material interest within the legislation.

STOCK EXCHANGE LISTINGS OF SHARES

4 Where shares in an overseas company are listed on a stock exchange, it is possible that the quoted price will on occasions correspond to underlying net asset value. This will however not of itself make the shares a material interest in an offshore fund. The shares would be considered a material interest only if, at the time they were acquired, the investor had a reasonable expectation of a future sale at or near net asset value. If historically the shares have been habitually traded at or near net asset value an investor is likely to have acquired a material interest.

CONDITIONS FOR DISTRIBUTOR STATUS

5 The legislation divides offshore funds into two groups: distributing funds, which must—

(*a*) meet specified investment restrictions, and

(*b*) distribute at least 85 per cent of their income (as computed in their accounts) and 85 per cent of what would be their taxable profits were they UK-resident companies (the ''UK equivalent profits'');

and other funds.

INVESTMENT RESTRICTIONS: NATIONAL AND SUPRA-NATIONAL BODIES

6 The legislation imposes a limit for distributing funds upon the percentage by value of the fund's assets that may be invested in a single company. National or supra-national bodies which are wholly owned by a government, or by governments jointly, and whose activities are directed not with a view to commercial profit, but to the exercise of a wider social or economic function (which may extend to a public utility), will not be regarded as companies for the purposes of this limit [s 760(3)(*b*)].

INVESTMENT RESTRICTIONS: HOLDINGS IN TRADING COMPANIES

7 The investment restrictions on distributing funds are modified for investments in trading companies. To qualify as a trading company for this purpose, a company's business must (among other things) not consist to any extent of dealing in commodities, currencies or financial assets. Many companies carry on some dealing in commodities, currency and financial assets as a supporting or incidental part of their normal trading operations. Whether or not such dealing activities will prevent the company from counting as a trading company will depend on the facts of each case: but provided that the activities are incidental to the business of the company, they will be disregarded in determining whether the company is trading [Sch 27 para 10].

COMPUTATION OF WHAT WOULD BE THE UK EQUIVALENT PROFITS [SCH 27, PARA 5]

(a) Is the fund trading?

8 Where a fund is regarded as trading, the resulting profits will be brought into the computation of UK equivalent profits. Whether the activities of an offshore fund amount to trading will turn on the facts of the particular case; and it is not possible to give any specific guidance on this aspect. Even a single transaction can on occasion constitute ''an adventure or concern in the nature of trade''; but in general a fund would not normally be regarded as trading in respect of transactions which were relatively infrequent or, for example, where the intention was merely to hedge specific investments which were not associated with activities which themselves constituted trading.

(b) Interest paid by offshore funds to non-residents

9 In arriving at the computation of UK equivalent profits, a deduction is available for interest paid by a fund to a person resident outside the UK in the same way as it would be if the interest were paid to a UK resident.

(c) Income taxed in the UK

10 Where an offshore fund receives income that has suffered tax at source in the UK, it is the net income (rather than the gross) that is included in the calculation of the UK equivalent profit.

11 A deduction will also be available for any tax suffered by direct assessment in the UK. The basis of the relief will be determined by reference to the individual case.

Commentary—*Simon's Direct Tax Service* **B7.402, 407**.

SP 3/86 (2 April 1986) *Payments to a non-resident from UK discretionary trusts or UK estates during the administration period: double taxation relief*

INTRODUCTION

1 This statement explains how relief from UK tax under double taxation agreements will be given in respect of payments made to a non-resident from a UK discretionary trust or a UK estate.

BACKGROUND

Discretionary trusts

2 Generally speaking, a non-resident beneficiary receiving payments from a UK discretionary trust is not entitled to repayment of the tax paid by the trustees on the trust income. However, under extra statutory concession B18 (which embodies a longstanding practice) the Revenue ''looks through'' the trust income to the underlying component parts of that income. The purpose of this ''looking through'' is to allow the recipient of the income any relief that would have been available to him under the Taxes Acts had the income come to him direct instead of through the trustees.

3 Where the beneficiary is resident in a country with which the UK has a double taxation agreement, further relief under the ''looking through'' principle may be due. Thus, for example, if the agreement provides for a withholding rate on interest of 15 per cent and interest liable to UK tax formed part of the trust income which had suffered tax at 34 per cent (ie the rate applicable to trusts) then, under the ''looking through'' principle, the beneficiary would be repaid the amount of tax suffered in excess of the withholding rate, in this case 19 per cent.

4 Some of the UK's double taxation agreements include an ''other income'' Article. The purpose of this Article is to determine in which country income not expressly dealt with elsewhere in the agreement should be taxed. In the UK's agreement the article sometimes gives sole taxing rights in respect of such income to the recipient's country of residence.

5 It has been the practice of the Revenue to apply the ''looking through'' principle to all cases where relief in respect of the discretionary payment was sought and to refuse claims where full repayment of UK tax was claimed under the provision of [the] ''other income'' article in the agreement.

Payments out of UK estates during administration period

6 The same principles set out in paragraphs 2–5 apply in the case of payments to non-resident residuary beneficiaries out of UK estates during the administration period. In these cases, the ''looking through'' concession was explained in statement of practice 7/80 and is now contained in ESC A14 (as amended at 14 May 1985). Again it has been Revenue practice to make repayment to beneficiaries on the ''looking through'' basis in all cases.

CHANGE OF PRACTICE

7 Following a review of its practice in these two areas, the Revenue has accepted that if a payment made by trustees out of a UK discretionary trust falls to be treated as a net amount in accordance with TA 1988 s 687(2), the ''looking through'' principle is not appropriate where the beneficiary is resident in a country with which the UK has a double taxation agreement and the ''other income'' Article gives sole taxing rights in respect of such income to that country. (This will usually be the case where income from trusts is not specifically excluded from the Article.) This means that tax paid by the trustees in respect of the discretionary payment will be repayable to the beneficiary, provided that any conditions set out in the ''other income'' Article are met. For example, the recipient may be required to show that he is subject to tax on the income in his country of residence.

8 The practice set out in paragraph 7 will also be applied to payments from the residuary income of a UK estate during the administration period. Under TA 1988 s 695 or 696, such payments are deemed to be income of the beneficiary which has suffered UK tax at the basic rate (the applicable rate from 1993–94 onwards).

9 Where the ''other income'' Article does not give sole taxing rights to the country of residence in respect of the trust or estate income or there is no double taxation agreement with the country concerned, the existing ''looking through'' practice will continue to be applied where it is to the advantage of the beneficiary.

Claims for relief under the new practice

10 The change in practice will be applied to all new and open claims. The Revenue will also accept supplementary claims which are made within the time limits applicable to the original claim under the provisions of TMA 1970 s 42(8). The normal time limit is six years from the end of the year to which the claim relates but this may be extended by TA 1988 s 700(3) in the case of estates.

Procedure for dealing with claims for previous years

11 The change in practice may require a consequential adjustment to claims under TA 1988 s 278. The Revenue will automatically review a beneficiary's entitlement to this relief and make any adjustments necessary.

Commentary—*Simon's Direct Tax Service* **C4.116, 227**.
Note—SP 3/86 was partially reworded in IR 131 (July 1994) and IR 131 (November 1996).

SP 4/86 (8 August 1986) *Scholarship and apprenticeship schemes at universities and technical colleges*

TA 1988 s 331 exempts from income tax, a scholarship, exhibition etc held by a person receiving full-time instruction at a university, college or school or other educational establishment. This statement of practice indicates the circumstances in which payments made by employers to employees for periods of attendance on a full-time educational course, including "sandwich" courses, are treated in practice as exempt from income tax.

1 Where an employee is released by his employer to take a full-time educational course, including a "sandwich" course, at a university, technical college or similar external educational establishment, payments made to the employee for periods of attendance at the educational establishment (but not for periods spent at work whether during vacations or otherwise) are treated as exempt from income tax where the following conditions are satisfied—

(*a*) the period for which the employee is enrolled at the educational establishment is at least one academic year and the actual full-time attendance at that establishment during that period amounts on average to at least twenty weeks a year;

(*b*) the rate of payment, including lodging, subsistence and travelling allowances but excluding any university, etc, fees payable by the employee, does not exceed the higher of [£7,000 a year (£5,500 prior to 6 April 1992) (£5,000 prior to 5 April 1989 and £5,500 between 6 April 1989 and 5 April 1992)] (or the equivalent monthly or weekly rates) and the rate of payment which an individual in similar personal circumstances would have received as a grant from a public awarding body on a scale fixed by the Secretary of State for Education and Science (eg a studentship from one of the Research Councils).

2 Payments are taxable in full where the rate exceeds that in (*b*) above. An increase in the rate of payment beyond the qualifying limit, part of the way through a course, will not affect any entitlement to exemption for the earlier part of the course, and a period of full-time instruction at a rate of payment not qualifying for exemption will be counted as a period of attendance at an educational establishment for the purposes of (*a*) above.

3 An employer's own internal training school or centre, or one run by an employers' association, etc is not regarded as an educational establishment for the purposes of this Practice. Only recognised universities, technical colleges etc, open to the public at large and offering a range of courses, both practical and academic, qualify.

Commentary—*Simon's Direct Tax Service* **E4.325**.

Note—The limit of £5,000 a year was increased with effect from 6 April 1989 to £5,500, Inland Revenue Press Release, 12 April 1989. The limit was increased with effect from 6 April 1992 to £7,000, Inland Revenue Press Release 18 November 1992.

SP 5/86 (21 August 1986) *Relief for replacement of business assets: employees and office-holders*

Relief which is available to a person carrying on a trade under TCGA 1992 ss 152–156 is extended by TCGA 1992 s 158 (1)(*c*) to include employees and office-holders.

If land or buildings are owned by an employee etc, but made available to the employer for general use in his trade, the employee etc may nonetheless satisfy the occupation test of TCGA 1992 s 155 provided the employer does not make any payment (or give other consideration) for his use of the property nor otherwise occupy it under a lease or tenancy.

The qualifying use of assets by an employee etc for the purposes of TCGA 1992 ss 152 and 153 will include any use or operation of those assets by him, in the course of performing the duties of his employment or office, as directed by the employer.

This practice may be applied to all cases where the capital gains tax computations have not been settled at 21 August 1986.

Commentary—*Simon's Direct Tax Service* **C3.302**.

SPs

SP 6/86 (29 August 1986) *Investigation settlements: inclusion of interest clause in letters of offer*

Note—Replaced by leaflet IR 73, "Inland Revenue Investigations—How settlements are negotiated".

SP 7/86 (12 September 1986) *Business expansion scheme: overseas activities*

Note—This statement superseded SP 7/83 and has itself been superseded by SP 4/87 (which was classified as obsolete by IR 131 Supp (November 1998)).

SP 8/86 (10 November 1986) *Treatment of income of discretionary trusts*

Note—Statements relating to IHT are reproduced in Part 3 of this publication.

SP 9/86 (10 December 1986) *Partnership mergers and demergers*

1 This statement explains the basis on which the Revenue apply the provisions of TA 1988 s 113 (change in ownership of trade, profession or vocation) to mergers and demergers of partnership businesses. In the following paragraphs, the word ''business'' means trades, professions or vocations carried on in partnership.

MERGERS

2 When two businesses which are carried on in partnership and which are different in nature merge, it may be that the result of the merger is a new business, different in nature from either of the previous business. Whether this is so is a question of fact to be determined according to the circumstances of each case. Where it is the case, the old businesses will have been permanently discontinued, and a new business commenced; TA 1988 s 113 will therefore not apply and the normal commencement and cessation provisions will apply to each business respectively.

3 However, where two partnership businesses in different ownership carrying on the same sort of activities are merged and then carried on by the joint owners in partnership, the total activities of both businesses may continue, even though in a merged form, ie the new partnership may succeed to the businesses of the old partnership. In that event TA 1988 s 113 applies to both successions, so that both businesses are deemed to have continued.

4 It will of course be a question of fact whether succession has occurred and in this connection disparity in size between the old partnerships will not of itself be a significant matter.

DEMERGERS

5 When a business carried on in partnership is divided up, and several separate partnerships are formed, it will again be a question of fact, to be determined according to the circumstances of each case, whether any of the separate partnerships carries on the same business as was carried on previously by the original partnership. It might be that one of the businesses carried on after the division was so large in relation to the rest as to be recognisably ''the business'' as previously carried on; but that will frequently not be the case, and if it is not then the business will have ceased.

6 The Revenue would want to look carefully at any case where it was claimed that a demerger of a partnership had occurred but it appeared that the demerger was more apparent than real, and that the demerger seemed to have taken place for fiscal reasons. The Revenue might wish to argue that in such a case the same trade was being carried on after the demerger as before.

Note: Despite the reference to partnership businesses in the text, the Revenue regard the principles set out in SP 9/86 as applying equally where—

- businesses previously carried on by sole traders are merged and are subsequently carried on by a partnership and
- a business carried on by a partnership is demerged and the businesses are subsequently carried on by sole traders.

Commentary—*Simon's Direct Tax Service* **E5.303, 333.**
Note—This statement was amended by IR 131 Supp (October 1995) and IR 131 Supp (November 1998).

SP 10/86 *Death benefits under superannuation arrangements*

Note—Statements relating to IHT are reproduced in Part 3 of this publication.

SP 1/87 (17 February 1987) *Exchange rate fluctuations*

Note—This statement of practice has been replaced by SP 2/02.

SP 2/87 (17 March 1987) *Close company apportionment*

Note—This statement was classified as obsolete by IR 131 (November 1996). The provisions for apportionment of close companies' income were abolished for accounting periods beginning after 31 March 1989: FA 1989 s 103 Sch 17 Part V.

SP 3/87 (26 March 1987) *Repayment of tax to charities on covenanted and other income*

Commentary—*Simon's Direct Tax Service* **C4.541, D2.232**.
Note—This statement was classified as obsolete in IR 131 (August 2003).

SP 4/87 (23 April 1987) *Business expansion scheme: overseas activities*

Notes—BES was abolished from 1-1-94 and replaced by EIS (see TA 1988 ss 289–312).
This statement was classified as obsolete by IR 131 Supp (November 1998).

SP 5/87 (15 June 1987) *Tax returns: the use of substitute forms*

INTRODUCTION

The Revenue have reconsidered their interpretation of TMA 1970 s 113(1) in the light of improvements in office technology and its more widespread adoption, in order to help taxpayers and their professional advisers to benefit fully from such developments. This statement explains the Revenue's current approach towards the acceptance of tax returns and other forms by way of facsimiles or photocopies, as substitutes for officially produced printed forms.

THE LEGISLATION

TMA 1970 s 113(1) says that any returns under the Taxes Acts shall be in such form as the Board prescribe. The Board are satisfied that where a photocopy of an official return or an accurate facsimile are used these will satisfy the requirements of the section. Further details about these two alternatives are given below.

ACCURATE FACSIMILES

For any substitute tax return to be acceptable, it must satisfactorily present to the taxpayer the information which the Board have determined shall be before him when he signs the declaration that the return is correct and complete to the best of his knowledge. Put another way, the form, which need not be colour printed, must otherwise be an accurate facsimile of the official form in terms of the words which appear and the general layout. It should also be readily recognisable as a return when it is received in Revenue Offices, and the entries of the taxpayer's details should be distinguishable from the background text. Recent advances in printing technology now mean that accurate facsimile returns can be produced. The Board will accept such returns if approval of their wording and design has been obtained before they are sent in to Tax Districts. Any substitute which is produced with approval will need to bear an agreed unique imprint of some sort so that its source can be readily identified at all times.

To facilitate the production of substitute returns, the Revenue have arranged for advance copies of the major income tax returns for 1987–88 to be made available to professional bodies and software houses. The Revenue intend that this will become an annual practice so that modifications to the returns can be incorporated in the computer produced facsimiles in time for their submission ....

All applications for approval will be considered as quickly as possible but there may be delays in the immediate run up to the Budget. Applications made before 15 February will be cleared before 6 April in that year.

Applications for approval should be made to—

Inland Revenue Business and Management Services Division
Forms Unit, Fourth Floor
Melbourne House, Aldwych
London
WC2B 4LL
telephone 020 7438 7312.

PHOTOCOPIES

A return made on a photocopy of an official form is a valid return provided that it is identical to the official form. It is sufficient that all of the pages are present and attached in the correct order if the facility to produce double sided photocopies is not available. The Revenue will also accept other types of forms (ie forms which are not strictly speaking returns) which are sent in as photocopies. The requirement for all the pages to be present is important where one side of the form contains notes, as it does in wife's earnings election and separate assessment cases. Any copy which does not also duplicate the notes on the original will not be acceptable. This is because such elections may not be valid in the absence of the notes being before the signatories.

The photocopying of official forms is in strictness a breach of copyright. If this is done on an individual basis the Revenue will however take no action. On the other hand if forms are photocopied on a large scale for commercial gain the Revenue will advise HMSO who will collect copyright fees. In the large majority of cases there is no objection to the copying of another return form where the original is lost. This is not to say that the Revenue actively welcomes photocopies as they can have disadvantages, particularly if colour and size are important features in handling the completed forms.

To avoid any misunderstanding, the Revenue cannot accept a photocopy of a completed return or form. In other words, the document sent in must bear the actual signature of the relevant person.

REFERENCES

Where a facsimile or a photocopy is submitted instead of an official form it is important that it bears the correct reference which appeared on the original form. Additionally where an original form was not supplied it is equally important that the taxpayer's reference should be inserted.

Commentary—*Simon's Direct Tax Service* **A3.111**.
Statement of Practice SP 4/91—Design of and information required in a tax return.
Note—The text of this statement is as it appears in IR 131 (August 2003).

SP 6/87 (8 April 1987) *Acceptance of property in lieu of inheritance tax, capital transfer tax and estate duty*

Note—Statements relating to IHT are reproduced in Part 3 of this publication.

SP 7/87 (15 July 1987) *Deduction for reasonable funeral expenses*

Note—Statements relating to IHT are reproduced in Part 3 of this publication.

SP 8/87 (27 August 1987) *Close company apportionment: member of a trading group*

Note—The provisions for apportionment of close companies' income were abolished for accounting periods beginning after 31 March 1989: FA 1989 s 103 Sch 17 Part V. This statement is therefore obsolete, IR 131 (July 1994).

SP 9/87 (22 September 1987) *Capital allowances: hotels*

1 Under the provisions of CAA 1990 s 7, capital expenditure on the construction of hotels which meet certain requirements qualifies for capital allowances. For expenditure incurred on or after 1 April 1986, the rate of allowance is 4 per cent per annum on the straightline basis.

2 To qualify for the allowances, a hotel must have at least ten letting bedrooms and be open for at least four months in the period April to October. In addition, it must provide certain services for guests. Thus, in addition to the making of beds and cleaning of rooms, services provided must normally include the provision of breakfast and an evening meal.

3 Hitherto, the Revenue view of the meals requirement has been that, while it would not expect that all guests should actually consume such meals, mere availability of breakfast and an evening meal was not sufficient.

4 The Revenue has now decided that it will regard the test as satisfied where the *offering* of breakfast and dinner is a normal event in the hotel's carrying on of its business. The Revenue will not regard it as satisfied where the service of meals is exceptional, eg if either breakfast or an evening meal is available only on request.

5 The practice set out in this statement will apply to years of assessment/accounting periods for which assessments have not become final and conclusive.

Commentary—*Simon's Direct Tax Service* **B2.252**.

SP 1/88 (3 February 1988) *Tax treatment of forward currency transactions by investment trusts*

Note—This statement has been superseded by SP 14/91.

SP 2/88 (10 May 1988) *Civil tax penalties and criminal prosecution cases*

1 TMA 1970 prescribes certain civil monetary penalties as the punishment for tax offences, including fraud.

2 The Board of Inland Revenue are, however, a prosecuting authority, and they have the option of taking proceedings in the criminal courts for offences involving fraud where they consider that it is in the public interest to do so.

3 The Board's previous practice, when they prosecute, has been *not* to seek a civil money penalty, whether for fraud or negligence, in respect of—

(*a*) any offence brought before the court, and

(*b*) any other tax offence committed by the person concerned which was brought to light in the course of the same investigation but which, for some reason, it was not appropriate to bring before the court.

4 In future, the Board's practice will be—

(i) to refrain (as previously) from taking steps to recover civil money penalties on the basis of fraud in respect of an offence which has been before the criminal courts;

(ii) to seek appropriate civil money penalties in respect of any offence which has not been brought before the courts; and

(iii) to reserve the right to seek, where there are grounds to do so, a civil penalty in respect of negligence by a taxpayer who has been acquitted of criminal intent in respect of a prosecution for fraud.

5 In all such cases the taxpayer will be entitled to put his arguments against the imposition of a civil money penalty in proceedings before the Appeal Commissioners.

6 This practice will apply in relation to any criminal prosecution case which comes to court after 10 May 1988.

Commentary—*Simon's Direct Tax Service* **A3.830**.

SP 3/88 (10 May 1988) *Delay in rendering tax returns: interest in overdue tax*

Note—This statement is superseded by SP 6/89 for failures occurring after 26 July 1989.

SP 4/88 (22 July 1988) *Tax treatment of transactions in financial futures and options*

Note—This statement has been superseded by SP 14/91.

SP 5/88 (22 July 1988) *Taxation of car telephones provided by employers*

Note—This statement was superseded by legislative provision: TA 1988 s 159A, which was repealed by FA 1990; the replacement provision, TA 1988 s 155AA, has been repealed by ITEPA 2003 s 722; see now ITEPA 2003 s 319.

SP 6/88 (4 November 1988) *Double taxation relief: chargeable gains*

GENERAL

1 TCGA 1992 s 277 applies to capital gains tax the double taxation provisions set out in TA 1988 ss 788–806, with the necessary modifications. TA 1988 s 797 applies the provisions to corporation tax on chargeable gains.

2 The standard credit article in our double taxation agreements (which are made under TA 1988 s 788) says, in effect, that subject to the provisions of the law of the UK, tax payable under the law of the treaty partner on capital gains from sources within that territory shall be allowed as credit against any UK tax computed by reference to the same gains by reference to which the overseas tax is computed. TA 1988 s 790 allows unilateral relief for overseas tax and s 790(4) is in similar terms to the standard credit article.

3 The principal requirement for the granting of credit for overseas tax against liability to capital gains tax (or corporation tax on chargeable gains) is therefore that the overseas tax should be computed by reference to the same gain as the UK tax. There is no requirement that the respective tax liabilities should arise at the same time nor that they should be charged on the same person.

SPECIFIC EXAMPLES

4 The Revenue's view is that the following sets of circumstances fall within the terms of the standard credit article and TA 1988 s 790 and may therefore give rise to a credit for overseas tax against UK capital gains tax or corporation tax on chargeable gains.

(i) The overseas tax charges capital gains as income.

(ii) Overseas tax is payable on a disposal falling within TCGA 1992 s 171 (transfers within a group of companies treated as taking place on a no gain/no loss basis) and a liability to UK tax arises on a subsequent disposal.

(iii) An overseas trade carried on through a branch or agency is domesticated (ie transferred to a local subsidiary) and relief is given under TCGA 1992 s 140. There is a subsequent disposal of the securities (or the subsidiary disposes of the assets within six years) giving rise to a liability to UK tax and overseas tax is charged in whole or in part by reference to the gain accruing at the date of domestication.

(iv) Overseas tax is payable by reference to increases in the value of assets although there has been no disposal. There is a subsequent disposal of the assets on which a liability to UK tax arises.

5 It will be seen that relief is conditional upon the subject of the overseas tax being identified with the gains on which the UK tax liability arises. In contrast, where roll-over relief is claimed, for example under TCGA 1992 s 152, the gain on disposal of the old asset is not subjected to UK tax. The gain on realisation of the new asset remains a gain separate from that realised on sale of the old asset and overseas tax payable as a result of the sale of the old asset is not creditable against UK tax payable on the gain realised on sale of the new asset. However, in such circumstances TCGA 1992 s 278 allows the overseas tax to be claimed as a deduction in computing the gain for roll-over relief purposes.

Commentary—*Simon's Direct Tax Service* **C1.615; F1.149, 252.**

SP 1/89 (1 February 1989) *Partnerships: further extension of statement of practice D12*

REBASING

The Board of Inland Revenue have agreed that a disposal of a share of partnership assets to which paragraph 4 of the statement of practice D12 applies so that neither a chargeable gain nor an allowable loss accrues (before indexation, for disposals before 6 April 1988), may be treated for the purposes of TCGA 1992 s 35, Sch 3 as if it were a no gain/no loss disposal within TCGA 1992 Sch 3 para 1.

DEFERRED CHARGES

A disposal of a share of partnership assets to which paragraph 4 of the statement of practice D12 applies so that neither a chargeable gain nor an allowable loss accrues (before indexation, for disposals before 6 April 1988) may be treated for the purposes of TCGA 1992 s 36 Sch 4 as if it were a no gain/no loss disposal within TCGA 1992 Sch 3 para 1.

INDEXATION

When, on or after 6 April 1988, a partner disposes of all or part of his share of partnership assets in circumstances to which paragraph 4 of the statement of practice D12 applies so that neither a chargeable gain nor an allowable loss accrues, the amount of the consideration will be calculated on the assumption that an unindexed gain will accrue to the transferor equal to the indexation allowance, so that after taking account of the indexation allowance, neither a gain nor a loss accrues.

Where a partner disposes on or after 6 April 1988 of all or part of his share of partnership assets, and he is treated by virtue of this statement as having owned the share on 31 March 1982, the indexation allowance on the disposal may be computed as if he had acquired the share on 31 March 1982. A disposal of a share in a partnership on or after 31 March 1982 to which paragraph 4 of the statement of practice D12 applies so that neither a chargeable gain nor an allowable loss accrues may be treated for the purposes of TCGA 1992 s 55(5) as if it were a no gain/no loss disposal within TCGA 1992 s 55(5). A special rule will however apply where the share changed hands on or after 6 April 1985 (1 April in the case of an acquisition from a company) and before 6 April 1988: in these circumstances the indexation allowance will be computed by reference to the 31 March 1982 value *but* from the date of the last disposal of the share before 6 April 1988.

Commentary—*Simon's Direct Tax Service* **C3.206**.
Statements of Practice D12, SP 1/79—Capital gains tax: partnerships.
Revenue Interpretation RI 9—Rebasing elections: assets held by the same person in different capacities.

SP 2/89 (1 March 1989) *Rebasing elections*

Note—This statement has been superseded by SP 4/92.

SP 3/89 (20 March 1989) *Unit trust and investment trust monthly savings schemes*

Commentary—*Simon's Direct Tax Service* **C2.736**.
Note—This statement is superseded by SP 2/97 from 18 July 1997.

SP 4/89 (19 April 1989) *Company purchase of own shares: capital gains treatment of distribution received by corporate shareholder*

If the purchase of its own shares by a company resident in the UK gives rise to a distribution, and a shareholder receiving such a distribution is itself a company, the distribution is included in the consideration for the disposal of the shares for the purposes of the charge to corporation tax on chargeable gains. In the Revenue's view the effect of TA 1988 ss 208, 345(3) [now TCGA 1992 s 8(4)] is that the distribution does not suffer a tax charge as income within the terms of TCGA 1992 s 37(1). The Revenue will apply this statement of practice where a company purchases its own shares after 19 April 1989.

Commentary—*Simon's Direct Tax Service* **C2.719, D1.405**.
Simon's Tax Cases—*Strand Options and Futures Ltd v Vojak (Insp of Taxes)* [2002] STC (SCD) 398; [2003] STC 331.

SP 5/89 (25 May 1989) *Rebasing and indexation: shares held at 31 March 1982*

Under TCGA 1992 s 35 Sch 3 a person is treated as having held an asset at 31 March 1982 if he acquired it after that date by a transfer, or series of transfers, treated as giving rise to neither a gain nor a loss for capital gains purposes, from someone who did hold it at that date. Shares or securities of the same class in any company which are acquired in this way will be added to any shares or securities of the same class in the same company held by the transferee at 31 March 1982. Where, for rebasing and indexation purposes, it is necessary to determine the market value of the shares or securities at 31 March 1982 they will be valued as a single holding.

If the shares or securities in the relevant disposal represent some but not all of those valued at 31 March 1982 then the allowable cost or indexation allowance as appropriate will be based on the proportion that the shares or securities disposed of bears to the total holding.

The no gains/no loss transfers relevant in this context are those listed in TCGA 1992 s 35(3)(*d*).

Commentary—*Simon's Direct Tax Service* **C2.704**.

SP 6/89 (31 July 1989) *Delay in rendering tax returns: interest on overdue tax (TMA 1970 s 88)*

1 Where an assessment has been made late or is inadequate because there has been delay in making a tax return, interest is payable (under TMA 1970 s 88) on unpaid tax from the date on which the tax should have been paid. The Board of Inland Revenue, however, have specific discretion under TMA 1970 s 88 to mitigate that interest charge. On 10 May 1977, the Board drew attention—by way of a press notice—to the Department's practice of claiming such interest where the delay was "substantial".

2 Enquiries have been received as to what degree of delay is regarded as "substantial", particularly in relation to returns by individuals of their capital gains.

3 In respect of (i) new sources of income, (ii) continuing sources where inadequate estimated assessments are not appealed against or (iii) chargeable gains, the delay is regarded as "substantial", and consideration will be given to charging interest under TMA 1970 s 88, if the relevant tax return has not been made within 30 days of the date on which it was issued or, if later, by 31 October following the end of the tax year in which the income or chargeable gain arose.

4 Where it is not possible to lodge the return, a section 88 charge will not be raised if the inspector is provided, within these time limits, with sufficient information to enable an adequate estimated assessment to be made—eg, in the case of the disposal of a chargeable asset, at least the sale price of that asset.

5 Section 88 has been repealed for 1996–97 and subsequent years of assessment (1997–98 and subsequent years for partnerships set up before 6 April 1994), and also for 1995–96 and earlier years where an assessment is made on or after 6 April 1998. This statement of practice only applies to assessments where s 88 does apply.

Commentary—*Simon's Direct Tax Service* **A3.820**.
Revenue & other press releases—IR Tax Bulletin May 1993 (Circumstances in which Revenue may seek to charge interest under TMA 1970 s 88 instead of under s 86 (not reproduced)).
Notes—This statement supersedes SP 3/88 for failures occurring after 26 July 1989.
The text of this statement is as it appears in IR 131 (January 2000).

SP 7/89 (12 October 1989) *Surrender of advance corporation tax*

TA 1988 s 240 provides that a company may surrender to a 51 per cent subsidiary the benefit of advance corporation tax (ACT) on dividends. The time limit for claims to surrender is six years from the end of the accounting period in which the dividend was paid. A company can claim to surrender ACT whether or not it is surplus to the amount which under the rules in TA 1988 s 239 can be set against the corporation tax (CT) charged on its own profits for that accounting period.

The Board had taken the view that if ACT had already been set against the tax payable on an assessment which had become final, that ACT could not subsequently be surrendered. Following a decision on an appeal to the Special Commissioners the Board has been advised that the determination of an assessment does not preclude the subsequent surrender of ACT set off in the assessment. This practice will now be applied to all new surrender claims and to existing claims which have not been settled at 12 October 1989.

Commentary—*Simon's Direct Tax Service* **D2.644**.
Note—This text of this statement is as it appears in IR 131 (August 2003). Advance corporation tax was abolished from 6 April 1999 onwards.

SP 8/89 (13 November 1989) *Independent taxation: mortgage interest relief time limit for married couples' allocation of interest elections*

Under TA 1988 s 356B(2)(*a*), (4)(*b*), as inserted by FA 1988 Sch 3 para 14, an election by a married couple to allocate mortgage interest between them, or to revoke such an election, must be made not later than 12 months after the end of the relevant year of assessment or within such longer period as the Board of Inland Revenue may in any particular case allow.

The Board will normally exercise its discretion to extend the time limit where it can be demonstrated that failure to comply with the time limit has been caused by sickness, absence abroad or serious personal difficulties, or by the unavailability (within the time limit) through no fault of taxpayers or their advisers of information essential to the decision to make or revoke an election.

Commentary—*Simon's Direct Tax Service* **E1.539**.

SP 1/90 (9 January 1990) *Company residence*

1 Residence has always been a material factor, for companies as well as individuals, in determining tax liability. But statute law has never laid down comprehensive rules for determining where a company is resident and until 1988 the question was left solely to the courts to decide. FA 1988 s 66 introduced the rule that a company incorporated in the UK is resident here for the purposes of the Taxes Acts. Case law still applies in determining the residence of companies excepted from the incorporation rule or which are not incorporated in the UK.

A. THE INCORPORATION RULE

2 The incorporation rule applies to companies incorporated in the UK subject to the exceptions in FA 1988 Sch 7 for some companies incorporated before 15 March 1988. ... Paragraphs 3 to 8 below explain how the Revenue interpret various terms used in the legislation.

Carrying on business

3 The exceptions from the incorporation test in Sch 7 depend in part on the company carrying on business at a specified time or during a relevant period. The question whether a company carries on business is one of fact to be decided according to the particular circumstances of the company. Detailed guidance is not practicable but the Revenue take the view that "business" has a wider meaning than "trade"; it can include transactions, such as the purchase of stock, carried out for the purposes of a trade about to be commenced and the holding of investments including shares in a subsidiary company. Such a holding could consist of a single investment from which no income was derived.

4 A company such as a shelf company whose transactions have been limited to those formalities necessary to keep the company on the register of companies will not be regarded as carrying on business.

5 For the purposes of the case law test (see B below) the residence of a company is determined by the place where its real business is carried on. A company which can demonstrate that in these terms it is or was resident outside the UK will have carried on business for the purposes of Sch 7.

"Taxable in a territory outside the UK"

6 A further condition for some companies for exception from the incorporation test is provided by Sch 7 paras 1(1)(*c*), 5(1). The company has to be taxable in a territory outside the UK. "Taxable" means that the company is liable to tax on income by reason of domicile, residence or place of management. This is similar to the approach adopted in the residence provisions of many double taxation agreements. Territories which impose tax on companies by reference to incorporation or registration or similar criteria are covered by the term "domicile". Territories which impose tax by reference to criteria such as "effective management", "central administration", "head office" or "principal place of business" are covered by the term "place of management".

7 A company has to be liable to tax on income so that a company which is, for example, liable only to a flat rate fee or lump sum duty does not fulfil the test. On the other hand a company is regarded as liable to tax in a particular territory if it is within the charge there even though it may pay no tax because, for example, it makes losses or claims double taxation relief.

"Treasury Consent"

8 Before 15 March 1988 it was unlawful for a company to cease to be resident in the UK without the consent of the Treasury. Companies which have ceased to be resident in pursuance of a Treasury consent, as defined in Sch 7 para 5(1), are excepted from the incorporation rule subject to certain conditions. A few companies ceased to be resident without Treasury consent but were informed subsequently by letter that the Treasury would take no action against them under the relevant legislation. Such a letter is not a retrospective grant of consent and the companies concerned cannot benefit from the exceptions which depend on Treasury consent.

B. THE CASE LAW TEST

9 This test of company residence is that enunciated by Lord Loreburn in *De Beers Consolidated Mines v Howe* (5 TC 198) at the beginning of this century—

> "A company resides, for the purposes of income tax, where its real business is carried on ... I regard that as the true rule; and the real business is carried on where the central management and control actually abides."

10 The "central management and control" test, as set out in *De Beers*, has been endorsed by a series of subsequent decisions. In particular, it was described by Lord Radcliffe in the 1959 case of *Bullock v Unit Construction Company* (1959) 38 TC 712 at 738 as being—

> "as precise and unequivocal as a positive statutory injunction ... I do not know of any other test which has either been substituted for that of central management and control, or has been defined with sufficient precision to be regarded as an acceptable alternative to it. To me ... it seems impossible to read Lord Loreburn's words without seeing that he regarded the formula he was propounding as constituting *the* test of residence".

Nothing which has happened since has in any way altered this basic principle for a company the residence of which is not governed by the incorporation rule; under current UK case law such a company is regarded as resident for tax purposes where central management and control is to be found.

Place of "central management and control"

11 In determining whether or not an individual company outside the scope of the incorporation test is resident in the UK, it thus becomes necessary to locate its place of "central management and control". The case law concept of central management and control is, in broad terms, directed at the highest level of control of the business of a company. It is to be distinguished from the place where the main operations of a business are to be found, though those two places may often coincide. Moreover, the exercise of control does not necessarily demand any minimum standard of active involvement: it may, in appropriate circumstances, be exercised tacitly through passive oversight.

12 Successive decided cases have emphasised that the place of central management and control is wholly a question of fact. For example, Lord Radcliffe in *Unit Construction* said that "the question where control and management abide must be treated as one of fact or 'actuality'" [(1959) 38 TC 712 at 741]. It follows that factors which together are decisive in one instance may individually carry little weight in another. Nevertheless the decided cases do give some pointers. In particular a series of decisions has attached importance to the place where the company's board of directors meet. There are very many cases in which the board meets in the same country as that in which the business operations take place, and central management and control is clearly located in that one place. In other cases central management and control may be exercised by directors in one country though the actual business operations may, perhaps under the immediate management of local directors, take place elsewhere.

13 But the location of board meetings, although important in the normal case, is not necessarily conclusive. Lord Radcliffe in *Unit Construction* pointed out [(1959) 38 TC 712 at 738] that the site of the meetings of the directors' board had *not* been chosen as "*the* test" of company residence. In some cases, for example, central management and control is exercised by a single individual. This may happen when a chairman or managing director exercises powers formally conferred by the company's Articles and the other board members are little more than cyphers, or by reason of a dominant shareholding or for some other reason. In those cases the residence of the company is where the controlling individual exercises his powers.

14 In general the place of directors' meetings is significant only insofar as those meetings constitute the medium through which central management and control is exercised. If, for example, the directors of a company were engaged together actively in the UK in the complete running of a business which was wholly in the UK, the company would not be regarded as resident outside the UK merely because the directors held formal meetings outside the UK. While it is possible to identify extreme situations in which central management and control plainly is, or is not, exercised by directors in formal meetings, the conclusion in any case is wholly one of fact depending on the relative weight to be given to various factors. Any attempt to lay down rigid guidelines would only be misleading.

15 Generally, however, where doubts arise about a particular company's residence status, the Revenue adopt the following approach—

(i) they first try to ascertain whether the directors of the company in fact exercise central management and control;

(ii) if so, they seek to determine where the directors exercise this central management and control (which is not necessarily where they meet);

(iii) in cases where the directors apparently do *not* exercise central management and control of the company, the Revenue then look to establish where and by whom it is exercised.

Parent/subsidiary relationship

16 It is particularly difficult to apply the "central management and control" test in the situation where a subsidiary company and its parent operate in different territories. In this situation, the parent will normally influence, to a greater or lesser extent, the actions of the subsidiary. Where that influence is exerted by the parent exercising the powers which a sole or majority shareholder has in general meetings of the subsidiary, for example to appoint and dismiss members of the board of the subsidiary and to initiate or approve alterations to its financial structure, the Revenue would not seek to argue that central management and control of the subsidiary is located where the parent company is resident. However, in cases where the parent usurps the functions of the board of the subsidiary (such as *Unit Construction* itself) or where that board merely rubber stamps the parent company's decisions without giving them any independent consideration of its own, the Revenue draw the conclusion that the subsidiary has the same residence for tax purposes as its parent.

17 The Revenue recognise that there may be many cases where a company is a member of a group having its ultimate holding company in another country which will not fall readily into either of the categories referred to above. In considering whether the board of such a subsidiary company exercises central management and control of the subsidiary's business, they have regard to the degree of autonomy which those directors have in conducting the company's business. Matters (among others) that may be taken into account are the extent to which the directors of the subsidiary take decisions on their own authority as to investment, production, marketing and procurement without reference to the parent.

Conclusion

18 In outlining factors relevant to the application of the case law test, this statement assumes that they exist for genuine commercial reasons. Where, however, as may happen, it appears that a major objective underlying the existence of certain factors is the obtaining of tax benefits from residence or non-residence, the Revenue examine the facts particularly closely in order to see whether there has been an attempt to create the appearance of central management and control in a particular place without the reality.

19 The case law test examined in this statement is not always easy to apply. The courts have recognised that there may be difficulties where it is not possible to identify any one country as the seat of central management and control. The principles to apply in those circumstances have not been fully developed in case law. In addition, the last relevant case was decided almost 30 years ago, and there have been many developments in communications since then, which in particular may enable a company to be controlled from a place far distant from where the day-to-day management is carried on. As the statement makes clear, while the general principle has been laid down by the courts, its application must depend on the precise facts.

C. DOUBLE TAXATION AGREEMENTS

20 In general our double taxation agreements do not affect the UK residence of a company as established for UK tax purposes. But where the partner country adopts a different definition of residence, it may happen that a UK resident company is treated, under the partner country's domestic law, as also resident there. In these cases, the agreement normally specifies what the tax consequences of this "double" residence shall be.

21 Under the double taxation agreement with the United States, for example, the UK residence of a company for UK tax purposes is unaffected. But where that company is also a US corporation, it is excluded from some of the reliefs conferred by the agreement. On the other hand, under a double taxation agreement which follows the 1977 OECD Model Taxation Convention, a company classed as resident by both the UK and the partner country is, for the purposes of the agreement, treated as resident where its "place of effective management" is situated.

22 The commentary in Art 4 para 3 of the OECD Model records the UK view that, in agreements (such as those with some Commonwealth countries) which treat a company as resident in a state in which "its business is managed and controlled", this expression means "the effective management of the enterprise". More detailed consideration of the question in the light of the approach of Continental legal systems and of Community law to the question of company residence has led the Revenue to revise this view. It is now considered that effective management may, in some cases, be found at a place different from the place of central management and control. This could happen, for example, where a company is run by executives based abroad, but the final directing power rests with non-executive directors who meet in the UK. In such circumstances the company's place of effective management might well be abroad but, depending on the precise powers of the non-executive directors, it might be centrally managed and controlled (and therefore resident) in the UK.

23 The incorporation rule in FA 1988 s 66(1) determines a residence which supersedes a different place "given by any rule of law". This incorporation rule determines residence under UK domestic law and is subject to the provisions of any applicable double taxation agreement. It does not override the provisions of a double taxation agreement which may make a UK incorporated company a resident of an overseas territory *for the purposes of the agreement* (see paras 20 and 21 above).

[APPENDIX]

The Appendix which contains the text of FA 1988 is not reproduced.

Commentary—*Simon's Direct Tax Service* **D4.104–106**.
Note—This statement supersedes SP 6/83.

SP 2/90 (9 January 1990) *Guidance notes for migrating companies: notice and arrangements for payment of tax*

1 FA 1988 s 130 requires a company to notify the Board of Inland Revenue of its intention to cease to be resident in the UK and to obtain the Board's approval of arrangements for payment of the company's tax liabilities. These notes explain the procedure to be followed, the information required in support of a request for approval and the arrangements which will normally be acceptable to the Board.

2 *Notice*

2.1 A notice under FA 1988 s 130(2)(*a*) should be sent to: Inland Revenue, International Division (Company Migrations), Room 312, Melbourne House, Aldwych, London WC2B 4LL.

The notice should give the intended date of migration (see para 5 below). The information required by s 130(2)(*b*), (*c*) should normally be sent with the notice (ie the statement of tax liabilities and proposals for securing payment—see para 3(*d*) and (*e*) below).

2.2 As the Board will have to check the statement of tax payable with the company's tax district, it would be useful if a copy of the notice and of the tax computation could be sent to the company's tax district at the same time.

3 *Information to be supplied*

(*a*) The name of the company, its address in the UK and its place of incorporation;
(*b*) its tax district and reference number;
(*c*) a copy of the latest available accounts;
(*d*) a detailed statement of all tax liabilities which are or will be due for periods commencing before the date of migration. The statement should cover corporation tax and advance corporation tax and, if relevant, all taxes mentioned in s 130(7) and any accrued interest on tax (s 130(8)). It should include any charges which arise as a consequence of the migration itself eg, under TA 1988 s 337(1) and TCGA 1992 s 185. (If an unlimited guarantee is to be offered—see para 4.3—the statement can be restricted to a brief summary of the tax position.);
(*e*) the company's proposals for securing the payment of tax liabilities. These should include the name and address of the proposed attorney and of the proposed guarantor (see paras 4.1 and 4.2);
(*f*) if a corporate guarantor other than a bank is proposed (see para 4.2), a copy of its memorandum and articles of association.

4 *Arrangements for securing payment of tax*

4.1.a It will normally be necessary to appoint an attorney to act for the company in tax matters, eg to receive notices of assessment. The attorney must be resident in the UK and will usually be an individual who is professionally qualified eg, as a solicitor or accountant. The Board will need to be satisfied that the migrating company has power to appoint an attorney. Further information and drafts of the power of attorney in a form approved by the Board are available from the above address.

4.1.b The capacity of a migrating company to appoint an attorney may be demonstrated by the opinion of a lawyer qualified in the appropriate local law upon the following matters:

(i) That the company has power by its constitution and/or by appropriate local law to appoint an attorney in the terms of the draft power of attorney (see para 4.1a above).

(ii) To know what formalities, if any, are required for a valid exercise of the power to appoint an attorney.

(iii) How the deed in the form of the draft power of attorney should be executed and whether execution should be notarily attested.

4.2 The precise form of the arrangements will vary from case to case. Normally they will take the form of a guarantee from a company which must be either resident in the UK or a UK branch of a foreign bank. A guarantor company must of course have power to act as guarantor and the copy of its current memorandum and articles is required to satisfy the Board of this.

The memorandum and articles should be certified by a solicitor or an officer of the company to be the version currently in force and as filed with the Registrar of Companies.

4.3 The guarantee may be unlimited or limited to a specified sum. An unlimited guarantee is given for the total tax liabilities without specifying the amount. Where the migrating company has an associated UK resident company of sufficient substance the Board will normally look for an unlimited guarantee from that company. Where the guarantee is given by a company not associated with the migrating company, usually by a bank, the Board understand that the guarantor will require the guarantee to be limited to a specified sum. Under FA 1988 s 130(4) any dispute as to the amount can be referred to the Special Commissioners.

4.4 Where it is not possible for a guarantee in one of the forms indicated above to be provided, other arrangements may be acceptable. Further information is available from the above address.

5 *Date of migration*

5.1 The Board will act as speedily as possible to approve the arrangements but the time required will depend on several factors. If possible the intended date of migration should be not less than two months from the date of the notice. If it is necessary to agree values of assets in order to estimate tax liabilities, the time required may be longer and companies should take this into account. However, where an unlimited guarantee is proposed, it will not usually be necessary to estimate the tax liabilities in detail and it may then be possible to approve the arrangements well within two months of the notice.

5.2 A company may decide to change the intended date of migration either for its own reasons or because, for example, the arrangements will clearly not be approved in time to meet the original date. It should then give notice under FA 1988 s 130 of the amended date and provide details of any consequential changes in either the amount of tax and interest to be included in the arrangements or the nature of the arrangements themselves.

6 *Non-compliance*

Where a company migrates without the requirements of s 130 being met, the persons responsible, including individual directors, may be liable for substantial penalties under FA 1988 s 131. Where tax liabilities of a migrating company remain unpaid, those liabilities may also be recovered from related companies, or from certain directors, under s 132.

7 *Telephone enquiries*

An initial enquiry may be made to the Inland Revenue, Somerset House Public Enquiry Room (020 7438 6420/5)—callers should ask for International Division (Company Migrations).

Commentary—*Simon's Direct Tax Service* **D4.131**.
Note—This statement was revised in IR 131 (August 2002).

SP 3/90 (10 January 1990) *Stocks and long-term contracts*

Commentary—*Simon's Direct Tax Service* **B3.1013**.
Note—This statement was classified as obsolete in IR 131 Supp (November 2000).

SP 4/90 (20 March 1990) *Charitable covenants*

Commentary—*Simon's Direct Tax Service* **C4.552**.
Note—This statement was classified as obsolete in IR 131 (August 2003).

SP 5/90 (11 April 1990) *Accountants' working papers*

1 TMA 1970 s 20 gives the Revenue powers to call for information relating to a person's tax affairs. TMA 1970 s 20B, which contains restrictions on the use of s 20 powers, was amended by FA 1989 to bring accountants' working papers, which were previously excluded, within the range of documents which the Revenue may require a third party to deliver or make available for inspection under these powers. This statement explains how the new rules work in relation to accountants' working papers and how the Revenue will use these powers in practice.

2 Three classes of documents are still excluded from the papers which may be called for from a third party. First, there is no change in the protection given to documents brought into existence specifically to support the conduct of a pending appeal. Second, audit papers are protected from disclosure by an auditor. Third, communications relating to giving or obtaining tax advice are protected from disclosure by a tax adviser. The protection given to audit papers and tax advice is limited however where the papers contain essential information about the origin of figures in accounts, returns and other information submitted to the Revenue or the relationship of those figures with the books and records of the taxpayer.

3 In addition, papers for which legal professional privilege could be claimed are protected from disclosure by a lawyer in relation to a client's tax affairs and there are general protections for medical records and other records kept by doctors, counsellors etc relating to an individual's personal welfare and the working papers of a journalist.

AUDIT PAPERS

4 An auditor appointed under any statutory provision, eg Companies Act, Building Societies Act etc is not obliged to disclose audit papers to the Revenue under a third party notice, ie TMA 1970 s 20(3) or s 20(8A). Audit papers are papers which are the property of the person appointed as an auditor under that enactment and which have been prepared by, or for, that person in order to carry out the statutory duties of an auditor under that enactment.

5 In practice the Revenue will allow equivalent protection where an accountant is appointed to carry out a non-statutory, independent audit to standards similar to those required for a Companies Act audit or to standards laid down by the client's professional body, provided the work on the audit is kept separate from any work on the preparation of the accounts.

TAX ADVICE

6 A tax adviser is not obliged to disclose communications relating to the giving or obtaining of tax advice to the Revenue under a third party notice. A tax adviser is any person appointed by a client, either directly by the client or indirectly via another tax adviser, to give advice on the client's tax affairs. The communications which are protected are ones between the tax adviser and the client or another adviser, made for the purposes of giving or obtaining advice about the client's tax affairs, and can include notes of meetings and telephone calls, internal memoranda, copy letters and faxes as well as ordinary correspondence.

RESTRICTIONS ON PROTECTION FOR AUDIT PAPERS AND TAX ADVICE

7 The protection given to audit papers and tax advice is restricted where the auditor or tax adviser has assisted the taxpayer in the preparation of accounts, returns or other information to be used for tax and the papers contain workings or other analytical information showing how an entry in the accounts, returns or other information submitted to the Revenue was arrived at, which has not previously been made available to the Revenue. In that event, the Revenue is entitled to have access to the information showing how the entry was arrived at, although information showing why the entry was arrived at in that way remains protected.

8 Where an auditor or tax adviser wishes to claim protection for part of a paper, a copy, which must be photographic or otherwise by way of facsimile, of the part which is not protected may be supplied to the Revenue. But the original must also be made available for inspection by the Revenue on request, when the protected parts may be kept covered up if the auditor or tax adviser wishes.

9 The protection given to audit papers and tax advice is restricted similarly where the notice is made under TMA 1970 s 20(8A) for information in respect of an unnamed taxpayer or taxpayers and the papers contain details giving the identity or address of any of the unnamed taxpayers or of any person who has acted on their behalf.

USE OF S 20 POWERS IN RESPECT OF ACCOUNTANTS' WORKING PAPERS

10 Accountants' working papers will not be called for on a routine basis. The Revenue will normally do so in connection with enquiries into a client's tax affairs only where they have been unable to satisfy themselves otherwise that the client's accounts or returns are complete and correct. Although the new provisions give the Revenue formal powers to require access to accountants' working papers, this has been given in the past on a voluntary basis where appropriate. The Revenue will

SPs

continue their general policy of seeking access on a voluntary basis and will use their formal powers only where they consider it absolutely necessary.

11 Requests will be limited as far as possible to information explaining specific entries. But there may be occasions when the Revenue will wish to examine the whole or a particular part of the working papers. The Revenue will usually be willing to visit the accountant's office or the client's premises to examine the papers and to take copies or extracts.

ACCOUNTANTS CONVICTED OF A TAX OFFENCE

12 The restrictions on the use of the Revenue's powers to obtain access to an accountant's working papers described above do not apply to the Revenue's powers under TMA 1970 s 20A to require access to the working papers of an accountant who has been convicted of a tax offence or had a penalty awarded against him under TMA 1970 s 99.

DESTRUCTION OF PAPERS

13 It is a criminal offence intentionally to falsify, conceal, destroy or otherwise dispose of documents which the Revenue has called for under TMA 1970 s 20 or s 20A before the Revenue has seen them (TMA 1970 s 20BB). This applies both where an informal request has been made under TMA 1970 s 20B(1), which would be made in writing and clearly identified as such when it was made, and where a formal notice has been given under TMA 1970 s 20 or s 20A.

Commentary—*Simon's Direct Tax Service* **A3.153**.
Cross reference—See TMA 1970 s 19A (power to call for documents).

SP 7/90 (29 October 1990) *Compulsory acquisition of freehold reversion by tenant*

Note—This statement has been superseded by SP 13/93.

SP 8/90 (6 December 1990) *Losses on irrecoverable loans in the form of qualifying corporate bonds: loss on early redemption*

If a qualifying corporate bond becomes of negligible value before its redemption date, relief may be claimed under TCGA 1992 s 254(3) for the loss arising on the underlying loan. In the case of a qualifying corporate bond which ceased to have any value because it was redeemed early, the Inland Revenue accepts that relief under s 254 may be claimed on the basis that the condition in s 254(3)(*a*) is satisfied.

Commentary—*Simon's Direct Tax Service* **C3.712**.
Concession D36—CGT: relief for irrecoverable loans to traders: time limits for claims—rendered obsolete by FA 1996 Sch 39 paras 8, 9.

SP 1/91 (6 March 1991) *Small companies' rate of corporation tax and corporation tax starting rate*

1 TA 1988 s 13 contains the rules for the small companies' rate of corporation tax and marginal relief. If a company's profits for an accounting period do not exceed the lower relevant maximum amount, the company may claim to be taxed at the small companies' rate. If the profits exceed the lower relevant maximum amount but do not exceed the upper relevant maximum amount, the company may make a claim for the marginal relief to apply.

2 Section 13AA ICTA 1988 contains the rules for and Corporation tax starting rate and marginal relief. If a company's profits for an accounting period do not exceed the first relevant amount, the company may claim to be taxed at the Corporation tax starting rate. If the profits exceed the first relevant amount but do not exceed the second relevant amount, the company may make a claim for the marginal relief to apply.

3 The lower and upper relevant maximum amounts (for s 13) and the first and second relevant amounts (for s 13AA) are restricted where the company has one or more associated companies. Two companies are associated if one controls the other or both are under the control of the same person or persons.

4 If a company wishes to take advantage of s 13 or s 13AA, it is necessary for it to make a claim. The Inland Revenue's practice is to accept as a valid claim under TA 1988 s 13 or s 13AA a clear indication in a company's return (or corporation tax computation or accompanying correspondence) for the relevant accounting period that the profits should be charged at the small companies' rate, the corporation tax starting rate or that the marginal relief should be applied. The claim should include a statement of the number of associated companies which the company had in the relevant accounting period. Where the company had no associated companies in the accounting period, the claim should state this.

Commentary—*Simon's Direct Tax Service* **D2.109**.
Note—This statement was revised in IR 131 Supp (November 2001).

SP 2/91 (19 March 1991) *Residence in the UK—visits extended because of exceptional circumstances*

1 Under TA 1988 s 336, an individual is not regarded as resident in the UK in a year of assessment if, broadly,

(*a*) he is in this country for some temporary purpose only and without the intention of establishing his residence here, and

(*b*) he has not, in the aggregate, spent at least six months in the UK in that year.

2 In applying the first condition, one of the considerations is that an individual is regarded as resident in the UK if visits to the UK average at least three months in a tax year; the average is calculated over a maximum of four years. Where this rule applies, any days which are spent in the UK because of exceptional circumstances beyond an individual's control, for example, illness, will be excluded from the calculation.

3 Each case where this relaxation of the normal rules may be appropriate will be considered in the light of its own facts. The statutory condition in paragraph 1(*a*) above must of course continue to be met, and the relaxation does not apply for the purposes of calculating the six months in paragraph 1(*b*) above.

Commentary—*Simon's Direct Tax Service* **E6.121**.
Cross reference—See Revenue booklet IR 20 (residents and non-residents—liability to tax in the UK.

SP 3/91 (11 April 1991) *Finance lease rental payments*

1 This statement sets out the view of the Board of Inland Revenue of the correct treatment, for tax purposes, of rentals payable by a lessee under a finance lease. That view reflects advice the Board have received on the application of the correct principles of commercial accounting and relevant case law. The statement sets out what will be the Inland Revenue's practice in applying tax law to rentals payable under a finance lease, in cases where Statement of Standard Accounting Practice (SSAP) 21 has not been applied and in cases where SSAP 21 has been applied.

A. CASES WHERE SSAP21 IS NOT APPLIED

Accounting treatment

2 The Board are advised that finance lease rentals are revenue payments for the use of the asset over time and, in accordance with the correct principles of commercial accounting, should be allocated to the periods of account for which the asset is leased under the ''accruals'' concept.

3 Where a lease provides not only a primary period (ie the period over which the lessee initially contracts to lease the asset), but also secondary periods (ie periods for which the lessee has the option to continue to lease the asset), then in determining what are the periods of account to which the rentals are to be allocated regard should be had not only to the primary period but also to the economic life of the asset and its likely period of use by the lessee.

Tax treatment

4 The Board are advised that for tax purposes, the rentals are deductible in computing profits on the same basis as they are correctly allocated to the periods of account under the accruals concept.

5 There is no entitlement to deduct the rentals for tax purposes, merely by reference to the due dates of payment.

Revenue practice

6 Inspectors of taxes will normally be prepared to accept, for tax purposes, the lessee's accounting treatment of rental payments where that treatment is consistent with the accounting principles described at paras 2 and 3 above.

7 Where the lessee's treatment of rental payments in the accounts does not accord with the basis indicated above, inspectors will seek to negotiate the computational adjustments necessary to secure for tax purposes, an appropriate spreading of the rental payments, in accordance with the accruals concept.

B. CASES WHERE SSAP21 IS APPLIED

Accounting treatment

8 SSAP 21 recognises the transfer of effective ownership of the asset to the lessee who is required to record the lease in the balance sheet, as the acquisition of the asset subject to a loan. The asset is to be depreciated over its expected useful life in the hands of the lessee. Rentals are treated as comprising a finance charge element and a capital repayment element.

Tax treatment

9 Notwithstanding that SSAP 21 requires a proportion of the rentals payable to be treated as capital repayment, the rentals remain in law revenue payments for the use of the asset, and for tax purposes the whole of the rentals should be allocated to the periods of account for which the asset is leased in accordance with the accruals concept.

Revenue practice

10 Where the lessee has accounted for a lease in accordance with SSAP 21 inspectors of taxes will normally accept for tax purposes, that the finance charge element of the rentals allocated to a period of account is deductible in computing the profits of that period.

11 In determining what proportion of the capital repayment element should be allowed for tax purposes in a period of account, inspectors will normally be prepared to accept that the properly computed commercial depreciation of the asset which is charged to the profit and loss account in that period represents the appropriate amount.

12 Where, however, the depreciation charge is not calculated on normal commercial accounting principles then it will not represent the appropriate proportion of the capital repayment element of the rental. In such cases, the inspector will allow such part of the rentals for the period as represents the properly calculated proportion of the capital repayment element which should be allocated to that period in accordance with the accruals concept.

Timing of introduction

13 The practice described in paras 6–7 and 10–12 above will be applied to leases entered into after the date of this statement, 11 April 1991. See also Inland Revenue Tax Bulletin February 1995, pp 189–193.

Commentary—*Simon's Direct Tax Service* **B3.1310**.
Note—The text of this statement is as shown in IR131 (August 2002).

SP 4/91 (1 May 1991) *Tax returns*

Commentary—*Simon's Direct Tax Service* **A3.106, 108, 109; D4.903**.
Note—This statement was classified as obsolete by IR 131 (January 2000).

SP 5/91 (15 July 1991) *Investment trusts investing in authorised unit trusts*

Note—This statement has been superseded by SP 7/94.

SP 7/91 (16 July 1991) *Double taxation: business profits: unilateral relief*

1 TA 1988 s 790 sets out the basis under which relief (''unilateral relief'') may be given for foreign tax in the absence of a double taxation agreement. The section sets out the conditions precedent to the granting of relief. So far as business profits are concerned the foreign tax is admissible for relief only if it is a tax which is payable under the law of the foreign territory; a tax which is computed by reference to income arising in the foreign territory; a tax which is charged upon income; and a tax which corresponds to income tax or corporation tax.

2 Hitherto the Revenue have interpreted the conditions so as to exclude from relief a number of foreign taxes having characteristics similar to turnover taxes, that is to say taxes computed by reference to a prescribed proportion of a gross amount of fee or contractual sum from which expenses fall to be deducted in arriving both at the commercial profit and at the amount which, in the UK, would be assessable under Case I or II of Schedule D. The taxes excluded from relief were those where the proportion of the gross amount charged to tax prompted the view that the tax could not reasonably be regarded as corresponding to UK income tax or corporation tax charged upon net profits.

3 Following consideration of the point in the High Court (*Yates v GCA International Ltd* (formerly *Gaffney Cline and Associates Ltd)* (64 TC 37)), the Revenue have decided to change their interpretation. In future the question of whether or not a foreign tax is admissible for unilateral relief under TA 1988 s 790 will be determined by examining the tax within its legislative context in the foreign territory and deciding whether it serves the same function as income and corporation tax serve in the UK in relation to the profits of the business. Turnover taxes, as such, are not therefore affected by the revised interpretation and will continue to be inadmissible for relief. The revised interpretation will take effect from Wednesday 13 February 1991 when judgment was given in the High Court, and will apply to claims made on or after that date and to earlier claims unsettled at that date. Taxpayers who would like the Revenue to review a previous decision in respect of a specific foreign tax are invited to address their enquiry to Inland Revenue, International Division, Room 319, Strand Bridge House, 138–142 Strand, London WC2R 1HH.

4 It should be noted however that the admissibility of the foreign tax is only one aspect of unilateral relief which can give rise to disputes between the Revenue and the taxpayer. Relief is only available in respect of the foreign tax on income arising in the foreign territory, and according to the facts of the particular case there may be room for argument as to where the income arose and to the amount of the income, having regard to the different principles of law in the foreign territory and in the UK. In the light of the High Court decision the Revenue practice will continue to be to determine questions of this sort by reference to principles of UK tax law. It follows that the charging of foreign tax upon an amount of income will not of itself be sufficient to establish that income of that amount arose in the foreign territory, and it is necessary to apply principles of UK tax law in order to ascertain the amount of the foreign income. As credit for foreign tax is restricted to the income tax or corporation tax attributable to the foreign income, this last point is one of some importance.

Commentary—*Simon's Direct Tax Service* **F1.149**.
Note—This statement is as shown in IR 131 (August 2003).

SP 8/91 (26 July 1991) *Discovery assessments*

GENERAL

1 This statement of practice explains, in relation to income tax, corporation tax and capital gains tax, the circumstances in which the Revenue seeks to recover tax when a person has not been assessed or has been inadequately assessed. The statement does *not* cover cases where there may have been fraud or negligence by or on behalf of the taxpayer.

2 The statement draws attention to the relevant statute and case law, in particular to the cases of—

– *Cenlon Finance Co Ltd v Ellwood* [[1962] 1 All ER 854; 40 TC 176] and
– *Scorer v Olin Energy Systems Ltd* [[1985] STC 218; 58 TC 592].

3 The following paragraphs should be read as subject to the general proviso that it is fundamental to the operation of the tax system that it is for the taxpayer, who is in possession of the facts, to supply them to the Revenue so that his tax liability may be determined. Case law confirms that, if the relevant facts have not been accurately, fully and clearly disclosed by the taxpayer at the time, the Revenue should not regard agreements reached, or action taken or omitted by its officials as binding it to accept less than the full amount of tax legally due.

4 This statement of practice applies to the following for the years specified—

– Individuals—for returns for years to and including 1995–96.
– Partnerships whose trade, profession [or] business [was] set up and commenced before 6 April 1994—for returns for the years to and including 1996–97.
– For bodies within the charge to corporation tax—for accounting periods ending before 1 July 1999.
– For periods after those referred to above, TMA 1970 s 29, as amended by FA 1994 ss 191, 199, applies, except for companies. In the case of companies FA 1998 Sch 18 paras 41–45 apply.

INSPECTORS' DISCOVERY POWERS

5 TMA 1970 s 29(3) [old version] provides that where, after an assessment has been made or a decision has been taken that an assessment is not required, an inspector discovers that any taxable profits have not been assessed, he may make an assessment in the amount he considers ought to be charged. Similarly, a further assessment may be made if an inspector discovers that an assessment is insufficient or that a relief should be withdrawn. These powers may also be exercised by the Board. There are also other discovery provisions in the Taxes Acts which empower an inspector to make assessments to recover excessive reliefs, tax unpaid and over-repayments of tax, for example TMA 1970 s 30 and TA 1988 ss 252, 412(3). Normally any assessment or further assessment must be made not later than six years after the end of the chargeable period to which it relates (TMA 1970 s 34(1)).

6 The Courts have established that, subject to the decisions in the *Cenlon* and *Olin* cases, a change of opinion can amount to ''discovery''; that discovery can be made by an inspector other than the one who made the first assessment; and that discovery can extend to a finding that the law has been incorrectly applied as well as the coming to light of additional facts. The word has been held to include any situation in which for any reason it newly appears to an inspector that a taxpayer has been undercharged.

SPs

THE MAIN PRINCIPLES

7 Two main principles are relevant in considering whether a discovery assessment may be made in any particular circumstances.

First, the Revenue does not go back on a specific agreement made by an inspector on a particular point and raise a discovery assessment in respect of that point, whether or not the inspector correctly took account of current law and practice in entering into that agreement;

Second, in circumstances where it cannot be said that the particular point was the subject of a specific agreement, the Revenue regards itself as bound by the inspector's acceptance of a computation if the view of the point implicit in the computation was a tenable one.

But the Revenue does not regard itself as bound by any agreement made, or considered to be made, or any decision taken by an inspector, if any of the information supplied on which that agreement or decision was founded was misleading.

THE POSITION IN MORE DETAIL

(i) Specific agreement: appeal cases

Cenlon

8 First, there is the case where there has been a specific agreement made by an inspector on a particular point, ie where an issue has been raised expressly by the inspector, the taxpayer or his agent (whether orally or in writing) and agreement has been reached on the treatment of that issue for tax purposes. The decision in the *Cenlon* case established that, if an assessment has been determined on appeal in accordance with TMA 1970 s 54, a discovery assessment should not be made in respect of any particular point which had been specifically dealt with in the course of the determination of that appeal.

Olin

9 The decision in the *Olin* case gives guidance on deciding whether (in the absence of express words making the position clear) a particular point has been agreed, or could be said to have been agreed, in the course of reaching an overall agreement on a person's tax liability for a particular period. The *Olin* case makes it clear that a particular point agreed may not only be an issue raised expressly by the inspector, the taxpayer, or his agent (whether orally or in writing), but also any point which was fundamental to the whole basis of the computation of the taxpayer's liability, and so clearly and fully described in the accounts or computations that its significance for the computation of the taxpayer's liability was clearly and immediately apparent. In these circumstances the inspector could not reasonably be regarded as having agreed the computation without having appreciated and accepted the point. In other words the inspector must have been clearly put on notice of the point.

10 The question whether a particular point is fundamental to the whole basis of the computation of the liability is one which must depend for its answer on the facts and circumstances of the particular case. At one extreme, there will be cases like *Olin* itself where the claim to set off the losses of the defunct trade against the profits of the continuing trade was fundamental in that it had a major impact on the computation of the liability and, moreover, was so clearly and fully described in the computations that the inspector must have appreciated what was being claimed. In the House of Lords, Lord Keith concluded that the inspector's agreement to the computations would have led a reasonable man to believe that the inspector had decided to admit the claim. In circumstances like these, the Revenue would accept that the particular point was covered by the agreement reached and could not subsequently be the subject of a discovery assessment.

11 At the other extreme, there will be cases in which a point is not fundamental to the basis of the computation, in that it does not have a major impact on the liability, or it is not so clearly and fully described in the accounts or computations that its significance is clearly and immediately apparent from the information supplied. For example, in cases where the taxpayer or his agent are claiming a particular deduction in arriving at profits, and among a multiplicity of items contained in the accounts and supporting material is a piece of information which, if the inspector had studied it in detail and thought through the implications, could have alerted him to the fact that the claim was not valid, the Revenue would not accept that a discovery assessment could not be raised in respect of the particular (incorrect) deduction. Moreover, if further information were needed before the inspector could reasonably be expected to appreciate the significance of the point for the taxpayer's liability, the Revenue would not accept that the inspector should be regarded as having considered and agreed that point.

12 The treatment of cases in between these two extremes must be a matter of judgment, depending on the particular facts. It will be necessary to decide, taking a reasonable and commonsense view of the matter, whether a taxpayer or his adviser would consider that a competent inspector, in examining the accounts and computations, must be considered to have addressed his mind to the point at issue before signifying his agreement to the computation of the liability. This will be so only if the point was both fundamental to the whole basis of the computation, and was so clearly and fully described that its significance for the computation of the taxpayer's liability was clearly and immediately apparent. In these circumstances the inspector could not reasonably be regarded as having agreed the computation without having appreciated and accepted the point.

(ii) Specific agreement: non-appeal cases

13 The principles established in the *Cenlon* and *Olin* cases strictly apply only where there was an appeal against an assessment or an appeal against a decision on a claim given in accordance with TMA 1970 s 42 which was subsequently determined either by the Commissioners or under TMA 1970 s 54. But, even if there was no determination of an appeal, a discovery assessment will not be made if the particular point on which the inspector takes a revised view was, or (as in the *Olin* case, see para [9] above) could be said to have been, the subject of the specific agreement of the final figures for assessment purposes. These circumstances may arise because the figures were agreed before an assessment was made, because the figures were agreed before an assessment was made, because the inspector decided not to make an assessment, or because the inspector's decision on the claim was accepted.

(iii) No specific agreement: appeal and non-appeal cases

14 There will also be circumstances in which the *Cenlon* and *Olin* principles are not applicable. Thus, the particular point on which the inspector subsequently takes a revised view and considers making a discovery assessment may not have been the subject of a specific agreement or, because the point was not fundamental, cannot be said to have been the subject of a specific agreement (see para [9] above). In these circumstances, a discovery assessment will not be made, provided that the inspector's original decision, whether on a claim or on the proper amount of an assessment, was based on a full and accurate disclosure of all the relevant facts and was a tenable view, so that the taxpayer could reasonably have believed that the inspector's decision was correct. And it follows that if the inspector's original decision was consistent with a view of the law and practice generally received or adopted at the time, a discovery assessment would not be made where, for example, there is a subsequent change in that practice—eg following a court decision.

SOME PARTICULAR CIRCUMSTANCES WHERE DISCOVERY ASSESSMENT WILL BE MADE

15 The application in any individual case of the general principles described in the preceding paragraphs will, of course, depend on the particular facts and circumstances. But there are certain specific circumstances in which there will clearly be no grounds for an inspector not to make a discovery assessment, ie where—

- profits or income have not earlier been charged to tax because of any form of fraudulent or negligent conduct;
- the inspector has been misled or misinformed in any way about the particular matter at issue;
- there is an arithmetical error in a computation which had not been spotted at the time agreement was reached, and which can be corrected by the making of an in date discovery assessment;
- an error is made in accounts and computations which it cannot reasonably be alleged was correct or intended, eg the double deduction from taxable profits of a particular item (say group relief).

Commentary—*Simon's Direct Tax Service* **A3.218**.
Revenue Interpretation RI 65—Excessive assessment: treatment of—
(*a*) where it results from an error in taxpayer's return,
(*b*) where it is under negotiation with the Revenue for settlement of appeal.
Note—Legislation on discovery assessments, as they apply under the self-assessment regime, is now in TMA 1970 s 29 as substituted by FA 1994 s 191.
The text of this statement is as shown in IR 131 (August 2002).

SP 9/91 (31 July 1991) *Investigation settlements: retirement annuities and personal pension relief*

1 When an assessment to tax becomes final and conclusive more than six years after the end of the year to which it relates, TA 1988 ss 625(3), 642(4) provide special rules for taking account of any unused personal pension or retirement annuity relief arising from the assessment. In particular the taxpayer may pay contributions to utilise that relief and elect that the relief shall be allowed for the year of assessment in which the contributions are paid. These must be in addition to the normal maximum for that year under either TA 1988 s 619(2) (for retirement annuities) or TA 1988 s 640 (for personal pensions). Both the payment of the contributions and the making of the election must take place within six months of the assessment becoming final.

2 Where incorrect returns and accounts are found to have been submitted, offers in settlement of liability to tax, interest and penalties are often accepted by the Board of Inland Revenue without assessment of all the tax. In such an investigation settlement the absence of assessments means that the conditions for obtaining unused relief under either TA 1988 s 625(3) or 642(4) are not satisfied.

3 Nevertheless, where a settlement is reached in circumstances where—

- assessments which would have given rise to unused relief are not made; or

- assessments have been made and appealed against but not formally determined, and the tax for the years of assessment concerned is included in the settlement;

claims under TA 1988 s 625(3) or 642(4) will be accepted if—

(*a*) the settlement includes tax on relevant earnings for a year of assessment which ended more than six years before the date of the letter accepting the offer and which, if assessed, would give rise to unused relief; and

(*b*) within six months of the date of the letter accepting the offer the taxpayer both—

(i) pays a qualifying contribution or premium to cover all or part of the unused relief, and

(ii) makes a formal election under either TA 1988 s 625(3)(*b*) or s 642(4)(*b*).

4 It should be noted that unused relief carried forward can only be utilised by the payment of contributions or premiums in excess of the maximum applying under whichever is applicable of TA 1988 s 619 or 640. It is only this excess that must be paid within the six months period referred to in para 3(*b*). Contributions or premiums up to the normal limits for the year of assessment may be paid within the normal time span for TA 1988 ss 619, 639 and 641.

Commentary—*Simon's Direct Tax Service* **E7.323, 411**.
Note—This statement superseded SP 9/80 which dealt only with retirement annuity relief.

SP 10/91 (7 August 1991) *Corporation tax: a major change in the nature or conduct of a trade or business*

1 This statement explains the basis on which the Revenue interprets the term ''a major change in the nature or conduct of a trade'' (or, as appropriate, ''business'') for various corporation tax purposes.

2 The term is relevant in the following provisions—

- TA 1988 s 245 which prevents advance corporation tax paid in respect of distributions made, or deemed to be made, in an accounting period before a change of ownership from being carried forward to set against a corporation tax liability in an accounting period after a change of ownership, or carried back from an accounting period after the change of ownership to be set against a corporation tax liability of an accounting period before the change of ownership, when in any period of three years there is a change in the ownership of a company and a major change in the nature or conduct of a trade or business carried on by the company.
- TA 1988 s 245A which prevents advance corporation tax surrendered to a subsidiary company under s 240 from being carried forward from an accounting period before the change of ownership to set against the corporation tax liability in an accounting period after the change of ownership when in a period of six years beginning three years before the change in the ownership there is a change in the ownership of the subsidiary company and a major change in the nature or conduct of a trade or business carried on by the surrendering company.
- TA 1988 s 767A, which prevents the use of company purchase schemes to avoid payment of corporation tax, by enabling the Revenue to collect any unpaid tax from the persons who previously controlled the company, or from companies under the control of such persons. It applies in certain circumstances where there is a change of ownership of a company and there is a major change in the nature or conduct of a trade or business of the company during the period of six years beginning three years before the change in ownership.
- TA 1988 s 768, which prevents a trading loss incurred in an accounting period before the change of ownership from being carried forward to set against trading income of an accounting period after the change of ownership when in any period of three years there is a change in the ownership of a company and a major change in the nature or conduct of a trade carried on by the company.
- TA 1988 s 768A, which prevents a trading loss incurred in an accounting period after the change of ownership from being carried back to set against profits of an accounting period before the change of ownership when in any period of three years there is a change in the ownership of a company and a major change in the nature or conduct of a trade carried on by the company.
- TA 1988 s 768B, which prevents excess management expenses or certain interest whether otherwise allowable as a charge or as a Case III debit from a period before the change of ownership from being deducted in computing the corporation tax profits of a period after the change of ownership, when in a period of six years beginning three years before the change in the ownership there is a major change in the nature or conduct of the business of the company.
- TCGA 1992 Sch 7A, which restricts the set-off of pre-entry capital losses brought by a company into a group. Sch 7A para 7 specifies the gains from which pre-entry losses are deductible and includes special rules for trades. Sch 7A para 8 disregards the existence of a trade in relation to the period before a company joins a group if, within three years before or after that event, there is a major change in the nature or conduct of the trade.

The rules for ascertaining whether there has been a change in the ownership of a company for the purposes of TA 1988 ss 245, 245A, 767A, 768, 768A and 768B and are in s 769. The rules for determining whether a company is a member of a group are in TCGA 1992 s 170. These rules apply for the purposes of Sch 7A subject to certain modifications contained within Sch 7A itself.

3 TA 1988 768(4) sets out some of the circumstances which may amount to a major change in the nature or conduct of a trade for the purposes of ss 768 and 768A.

TA 1988 245(4) sets out some of the circumstances which may amount to a major change in the nature or conduct of a trade or business for the purposes of ss 245, 245A and 767A.

TA 1988 s 768B(3) sets out one of the circumstances which may amount to a major change in the nature or conduct of a business for the purposes of s 768B.

TCGA 1992 Sch 7A para 8(2) sets out some of the circumstances which may amount to a major change in the nature or conduct of a trade for the purposes of Sch 7A.

The Revenue will have regard to any of the circumstances specified in the relevant subsection, such as a major change in services or facilities provided in the trade, or a major change in customers of the trade or a change in the nature of the investments held. The Revenue will also have regard, if appropriate, to changes in other factors, such as the location of the company's business premises, the identity of the company's suppliers, management, or staff, the company's methods of manufacture, or the company's pricing or purchasing policies to the extent that these factors indicate that a major change has occurred.

4 In considering whether there has been a major change in the nature or conduct of a trade or business, the Revenue will have regard to a comparison of the conditions applying at any two points in the three years which includes the date of the change of ownership of the company or, for the purpose of TA 1988 ss 245A, 767A and 768B, at any two points in the period of six years beginning three years before the change of ownership. It will not matter whether the change occurs at a particular point in time or is the result of a gradual process. The gradual process may itself have begun before the beginning of the appropriate three (or six) year period.

5 All of the relevant factors will be evaluated as a whole although, on occasion, a change in one factor may be decisive.

6 In the light of the judgment in the Court of Appeal (Northern Ireland) in the case of *Willis v Peeters Picture Frames Ltd* [1983] STC 453 and the comments on that case in the High Court judgment in *Purchase v Tesco Stores Ltd* [1984] STC 304, the Revenue will have regard to both qualitative issues (such as whether something is or is not a change) and to quantitative issues (such as whether or not a change is a major change). To be a major change, the change must be more than significant (Gibson LJ in *Willis v Peeters Picture Frames Ltd*) though it does not necessarily have to be fundamental (Warner J in *Purchase v Tesco Stores Ltd*).

7 The Revenue will not regard a major change in the nature or conduct of a trade as having occurred when all that happens is that a company makes changes to increase its efficiency, or makes changes which are needed to keep pace with the developing technology in the industry concerned or with developing management techniques.

8 Similarly, the Revenue will not regard a major change in the nature or conduct of a trade as having occurred when all that happens is that a company rationalises its product range by withdrawing unprofitable items and, possibly, replacing them with new items of a kind related to those already being produced.

9 For some tax purposes, where part of a trade is transferred by one company to another in the same ownership, the different parts are treated as separate trades. This occurs in the rules for certain company reconstructions in TA 1988 s 343(8). For the purposes of ss 768, 768A only, where a transfer of part of a trade falls within TA 1988 s 343 the transfer will not, by itself, be regarded as a major change in the nature or conduct of either the part-trade transferred or the part-trade retained by the transferring company, where it is relevant to consider either part separately.

Instead, the trade of each company after the transfer (or, if appropriate, the relevant part of a combined trade) will be compared with the equivalent part of the combined trade before the transfer. This will apply whether the transfer occurs before or after the relevant change in the ownership. Where the transfer occurs *after* the change in the ownership, however, it may be necessary to consider whether it involves a major change in the nature or conduct of the undivided trade, as it subsisted at the date of the change in the ownership. In such cases it may be appropriate to regard the transfer as constituting a major change, depending on the surrounding circumstances. In practice, however, the Revenue would not contend that the transfer constituted a major change if there was no other major change in either the original trade, or the parts into which it became divided, within the relevant three or six year period. The transfer of the whole or part of a trade or business may, however, constitute a major change for the purposes of TA 1988 ss 245, 245A, 767A and 768B and TCGA 1992 Sch 7A.

10 Though the courts have made it clear that each case should be looked at in the light of all its facts, the following may assist in showing where the Revenue regard the borderline falling in particular circumstances—

EXAMPLES WHERE A CHANGE WOULD NOT OF ITSELF BE REGARDED AS A MAJOR CHANGE

(*a*) A company manufacturing kitchen fitments in three obsolescent factories moves production to one new factory (increasing efficiency).

(*b*) A company manufacturing kitchen utensils replaces enamel by plastic, or a company manufacturing time pieces replaces mechanical by electronic components (keeping pace with developing technology).

(*c*) A company operating a dealership in one make of car switches to operating a dealership in another make of car satisfying the same market (not a major change in the type of property dealt in).

(*d*) A company manufacturing both filament and fluorescent lamps (of which filament lamps form the greater part of the output) concentrates solely on filament lamps (a rationalisation of product range without a major change in the type of property dealt in).

(*e*) A company whose business consists of making and holding investments in UK quoted shares and securities makes changes to its portfolio of quoted shares and securities (not a change in the nature of investments held).

EXAMPLES WHERE A MAJOR CHANGE WOULD BE REGARDED AS OCCURRING

(*f*) A company operating a dealership in saloon cars switches to operating a dealership in tractors (a major change in the type of property dealt in).

(*g*) A company owning a public house switches to operating a discotheque in the same, but converted, premises (a major change in the services or facilities provided).

(*h*) A company fattening pigs for their owners switches to buying pigs for fattening and resale (a major change in the nature of the trade, being a change from providing a service to being a primary producer).

(*i*) A company switches from investing in quoted shares to investing in real property for rent (a change in the nature of investments held).

Commentary—*Simon's Direct Tax Service* **D2.410**.
Note—The text of this statement is as it appears in IR 131 (August 2002).

SP 12/91 (9 October 1991) *Income tax: "in the ordinary course" of banking business*

Note—This statement is superseded by SP 4/96 in relation to yearly interest paid on or after 1996 and was classified as obsolete in IR 131 (August 2003).

SP 13/91 (31 October 1991) *Ex gratia awards made on termination of an office or employment by retirement or death*

1 An ex gratia payment made on or in connection with an employee's death or retirement from an office or employment is a ''relevant benefit'' as defined in TA 1988 s 612. (But this term does not include payments made solely because of death or disablement by accident or severance payments on redundancy or loss of office.)

2 An ex gratia payment is made under a retirement benefits scheme if the decision to make the payment involves an arrangement. Self evidently, there will be an ''arrangement'' if the payment flows from any prior formal or informal understanding with the employee. But the term ''arrangement'' in this context goes wider and includes any system, plan, pattern or policy connected with the payment of a gratuity. Some examples are—

(*a*) a decision at a meeting to make an *ex gratia* payment on an employee's retirement; or

(*b*) where, say, a personnel manager makes an *ex gratia* payment under a delegated authority or on the basis of some outline structure or policy; or

(*c*) where it is common practice for an employer to make an *ex gratia* payment to a particular class of employee.

3 There may be some exceptional situations where a gratuity is not paid under an ''arrangement''. The position in individual cases can be determined only on their facts. If an employer is unsure whether a gratuity is paid under an arrangement advice may be sought from the IR Savings Pension Shares Schemes Office at Yorke House, PO Box 62, Castle Meadow Road, Nottingham NG2 1BG. Any such request should give full details of the circumstances in which the gratuity is to be paid.

4 The following paragraphs explain the tax treatment of these ex gratia arrangements. All statutory references are to TA 1988.

PENSIONS

5 An ex gratia pension to an employee or the employee's spouse or dependant will be chargeable to income tax as taxable pension income under ITEPA 2003 Pt 9 whether or not paid under a tax approved scheme.

LUMP SUMS

6 Lump sum relevant benefits are not taxable when paid under an approved scheme. In the past, approval has been given only to contractual schemes. But approval may now be given to certain ex gratia lump sum payments in the circumstances described in para 7; or payments may be treated as from an approved scheme where para 8 applies.

7 An employer may apply for tax approval of an arrangement to pay an ex gratia lump sum relevant benefit. In order to qualify for approval, the payment must—

(*a*) be the only lump sum relevant benefit potentially payable in respect of the employment; in other words the employee should not be a member of either of the following—

(i) a retirement benefits scheme that is either approved or is being considered for approval, or

(ii) a relevant statutory scheme (as defined in s 611A),

unless the payment is made on retirement and the scheme provides benefits only on death in service; and

(*b*) satisfy the normal requirements for tax approval of a retirement benefits scheme (which are described in the booklet ''Practice Notes on Approval of Occupational Pension Schemes'' (IR12)). These include a limit on the amount of lump sum payable. On retirement, for example, the limit is 3/80ths of final salary for each year of service with an employer (up to 40 years), while on death it is normally two times salary, though it can be as high as four times salary.

Details on how to apply for approval may be obtained from the IR Savings Pension Shares Schemes Office in Nottingham (address at para 3 above). Where a payment is made before confirmation of approval is received the employer should deduct tax in accordance with the PAYE system. If and when approval is granted the employee will be able to claim repayment of the tax deducted.

8 In addition, the Revenue will accept that an arrangement to pay a single ex gratia lump sum relevant benefit to a particular employee need not be submitted for approval where—

(*a*) the condition at para 7(*a*) above is satisfied, and

(*b*) the total of all lump sum payments from all associated employers (as defined in s 590A(3)) made in connection with the retirement or death does not exceed one-twelfth of the earnings cap prescribed under s 590C for the year of assessment in which the payments are made. For the year ended 5 April 2004, the limit is £8,250.

In these cases the payments will be treated as from an approved retirement benefits scheme. They will therefore not be chargeable to income tax and so need not be reported by an employer to its tax office.

9 An ex gratia lump sum relevant benefit not falling within para 7 or 8 above will constitute a non-approved retirement benefits scheme. It will be charged to tax as employment income under ITEPA 2003 s 394 on the recipient for the year of assessment in which the benefit is received. When making such payments an employer should deduct tax in accordance with the PAYE system.

PAYMENTS FOR REDUNDANCY OR TERMINATION OF EMPLOYMENT CAUSED BY ACCIDENT

10 An ex gratia payment made to an employee on severance of an employment due to redundancy or loss of office, or because of death or disability due to an accident, is not affected by this statement of practice where the arrangements for making the payment are designed solely to meet such a situation. Nor will the tax treatment of any such payment be affected by the payment of early retirement benefits under other arrangements (such as the employer's approved pension scheme). The taxation of such lump sum payments is not therefore affected by this statement of practice. In particular genuine redundancy payments within the terms of SP 1/94 will be taxed under ITEPA 2003 s 403 (subject to the exemptions in s 403(1)).

Commentary—*Simon's Direct Tax Service* **E4.802, 805B, 805D**.
Revenue and other press releases—Law Society 7-10-92 and ICAEW Tax 15/92 16-11-92 (termination of employment by reason of unfair dismissal does not normally constitute ''retirement'' for the purposes of this statement of practice; an ex-gratia payment made to an individual moving to further full-time employment is not made ''on or in anticipation of retirement''). ICAEW TR 851 6-11-91 (guidance on the tax treatment of ex gratia payments).
Revenue publications—IR 12 (1991) Occupational pension schemes practice notes.
Note—This statement was revised in IR 131 (August 2003).

SP 14/91 (21 November 1991) *Tax treatment of transactions in financial futures and options*

Notes—This statement has been replaced by SP 3/02.

SP 15/91 (29 November 1991) *Treatment of investment managers and their overseas clients*

Note—This statement was classified as obsolete in IR 131 Supp (November 2001) and has been replaced by SP 1/01.

SP 16/91 (3 December 1991) *Accountancy expenses arising out of accounts investigations*

It is the practice to allow, in computing profits assessable under Schedule D Cases I and II, the normal accountancy expenses incurred in preparing accounts and agreeing taxation liabilities. Additional accountancy expenses arising out of an investigation of a particular year's accounts will not be allowed where the investigation reveals discrepancies and additional liabilities for earlier years, or a settlement involving only one year includes interest or interest and penalties. Where, however, the investigation results in no addition to profits, or an adjustment to profits for the year of review only without a charge to interest or interest and penalties, the additional accountancy expenses will normally be allowed.

Commentary—*Simon's Direct Tax Service* **B3.1452**.
Revenue Interpretation RI 192—Schedule D Cases I and II: accountancy expenses arising out of self-assessment enquiries.
Note—This statement supersedes SP A28.

SP 17/91 (4 December 1991) *Residence in the UK: when ordinary residence is regarded as commencing where the period to be spent here is less than three years*

1 The Income and Corporation Taxes Acts do not define the term ''ordinary residence''. The rules for determining the ordinary residence of an individual have been based on decisions of the courts.

2 Where an individual comes to, and remains in, the UK but does not intend to stay for at least three years and accommodation is not bought or acquired on a lease of three years or more, that individual is treated as becoming ordinarily resident from the beginning of the tax year after the third anniversary of arrival.

3 Where any individual comes to the UK and, before the beginning of the tax year after the third anniversary of arrival, either purchases or acquires on a lease of three years or more accommodation for use in the UK or has a change of intention concerning the length of stay, ordinary residence will commence—

- from the day of arrival if one of the above events occurs in the tax year of arrival, or
- from the beginning of the tax year in which one of the above events occurs.

For example, if an individual arrives in the UK in January 1992 and purchases accommodation here in May 1993, ordinary residence commences from 6 April 1993.

Commentary—*Simon's Direct Tax Service* **E6.121**.
See Revenue booklet IR 20 (residents and non-residents—liability to tax in the UK).
Note—The text of this statement is as it appears in IR 131 (November 1996).

SP 18/91 (6 December 1991) *Foreign earnings deduction*

Note—This statement was classified as obsolete by IR 131 Supp (November 1998).

SP 1/92 (3 January 1992) *Directors' and employees' emoluments: extension of time limits for relief on transition to receipts basis of assessment*

Note—This statement was classified as obsolete by IR 131 Supp (November 1998).

SP 2/92 (28 February 1992) *Transactions within TA 1988 s 765A—movements of capital between residents of EC member states*

BACKGROUND

1 Article 67 [1] of the Treaty establishing the European Economic Community provides, inter alia, that member states shall progressively abolish between themselves all restrictions on the movement of capital belonging to persons resident in member states. This provision is implemented by the Directive of the Council of the European Communities 88/361/EEC of 24 June 1988. Article 1 of the Directive requires member states to abolish restrictions on movements of capital taking place between persons resident in member states.

Note—[1] Article 67 substituted by the Treaty on European Union, and renumbered article 56 by the Treaty of Amsterdam.

2 As a consequence, the provisions of TA 1988 s 765, which make certain transactions unlawful if they are carried out without Treasury consent, have been disapplied by TA 1988 s 765A(1) so that as from 1 July 1990, the date from which the Directive took effect, a UK resident body corporate no longer requires Treasury consent before carrying out a transaction which is a movement of capital to which Art 1 of the Directive applies. However, s 765A(2) requires the body corporate to provide the Inland Revenue with information on certain of the transactions within six months of carrying them out.

PURPOSE OF THIS STATEMENT

3 Paragraphs 5–23 of this statement seek to explain the views of the Treasury and the Inland Revenue where there may be doubt as to whether a transaction is a movement of capital to which Art 1 of the Directive applies. Their purpose is to assist UK resident bodies corporate in deciding whether they should seek Treasury consent for a transaction or report it to the Inland Revenue. However, it is the responsibility of the UK resident body corporate which considers that a transaction which it has carried out (or proposes to carry out) is one liberalised by the Directive to justify that view.

4 Paragraphs 24–26 give guidance on procedure to bodies corporate making a report under s 765A(2) in accordance with the Regulations made under the section.

THE CHANNEL ISLANDS, THE ISLE OF MAN AND GIBRALTAR

5 The provisions of the Directive do not apply to movements of capital between residents of member states and residents of the Channel Islands and the Isle of Man. But by virtue of Art 227(4)[1] of the Treaty establishing the EEC, that Treaty applies to Gibraltar, subject to the exceptions mentioned in Art 28 of the Act of Accession of Denmark, Ireland and the United Kingdom. It follows that the Directive is as fully applicable to Gibraltar as to any other community territory. However, Gibraltar is not itself a member state being regarded for the purposes of Community Law as part of the territory of the UK. It follows that, while transactions which are movements of capital between residents of Gibraltar and residents of other member states are within s 765A rather than s 765, movements of capital between residents of Gibraltar and residents of the UK are wholly internal to the UK and are still governed by s 765.

Note—[1] Article 227 renumbered article 299 by the Treaty of Amsterdam (OJ C340 10.11.97 p 1).

DIFFERENCE BETWEEN GENERAL AND SPECIAL CONSENT TRANSACTIONS

6 Section 765 has ceased to apply to *all* transactions which are movements of capital within Art 1 of the Directive. But a body corporate has to report to the Inland Revenue only those transactions for which it would need to apply to the Treasury for *special* consent if they were not movements of capital within the Directive. A transaction which would be covered by a *general* consent if it were not a movement of capital within the Directive would be lawful when carried out even if the Directive did not apply to it and so should not be reported under s 765A(2).

MOVEMENTS OF CAPITAL

7 The nomenclature in Annex 1 to the Directive lists a wide range of operations which are within the Directive. These include ‘‘all the operations necessary for the purpose of capital movements—conclusion and performance of the transaction and related transfers’’ but the list is not exhaustive—the Directive makes clear that it is looking to the principle of full liberalisation of capital movements. The Treasury and the Inland Revenue have been advised that all issues and transfers of shares and debentures within s 765(1) which take place between residents of member states may be considered movements of capital within the Directive subject to the reservation in paras 8 and 9.

8 Section 1 of the nomenclature is concerned with direct investment. The explanatory notes define direct investment generally as ‘‘investments of all kinds by natural persons or commercial, industrial or financial undertakings, and which serve to establish or to maintain lasting and direct links between the person providing the capital and the entrepreneur to whom or the undertaking to which the capital is made available in order to carry on an economic activity’’. The expression ‘‘with a view to establishing or maintaining lasting economic links’’ is also used in the description of certain operations listed in Part I. In the view of the Treasury and Inland Revenue, it can be inferred that a transaction otherwise falling within the description of direct investment which is not carried out with a view to establishing or maintaining such links is not a movement of capital to which the Directive applies.

Revenue Interpretation RI 215—This paragraph does not apply to transactions carried out on or after 1 January 1994 following changes made by the Maastricht Treaty.

9 The Treasury and Inland Revenue recognise that transactions of a direct investment type with companies resident in member states will normally be carried out with a view to establishing or maintaining lasting economic links with those companies. But that may not always be so and the treatment of particular cases will depend on their facts. Where, for example, a company is used as nothing more than a conduit the transaction is unlikely to be carried out with a view to establishing or maintaining such links with that company. This may be the case where a subsidiary resident in another member state issues a debenture to its UK resident parent for a sum which is immediately loaned back to the parent or another member of the UK group.

SPs

Revenue Interpretation RI 215—This paragraph does not apply to transactions carried out on or after 1 January 1994 following changes made by the Maastricht Treaty.

ISSUES AND TRANSFERS OF SHARES AND DEBENTURES BETWEEN RESIDENTS OF MEMBER STATES

10 A transaction is excluded from s 765 by s 765A only if it is a movement of capital *between residents of member states*. Thus, for example, a parent company which is a resident of the UK may hold directly all the shares in a company which is a resident of the Netherlands and all the shares in a US company which is not a resident of a member state. If the parent company transfers its shares in the Netherlands company to the US company that transaction will require Treasury consent because the transfer is not between residents of member states. But if the parent company transfers its shares in the US company to the Netherlands company that transfer is between residents of member states and is within s 765A and so excluded from s 765.

11 Similarly, a subsidiary company which is a non-resident body corporate within s 765(1)(*c*) and a resident of a member state may issue shares at the same time to persons who are residents of member states and to persons who are not so resident. The former issue is a movement of capital between residents of member states and excluded from s 765. But the latter issue is still within s 765 and Treasury consent will be required.

12 Article 67 and consequently Council Directive 88/361/EEC relate to restrictions which apply as between member states. They have no application to movements of capital and restrictions which are wholly internal to a single member state. For example, a company which is a resident of the UK holds all the shares in a US company which is not a resident of a member state. If the UK company transfers the shares to another company which is a resident of the UK that is not a capital movement which is within the terms of the Directive. The transaction will require Treasury consent. (Such transfers will often be within the terms of the general consents.)

13 A transaction for which a UK resident company requires consent under s 765 unless s 765A applies may be a movement of capital between persons resident in the same member state other than the UK. The Treasury and the Inland Revenue regard that transaction as not being wholly internal to a single member state and therefore within s 765A because the body corporate requiring consent is resident in the UK which is a different member state. (Such transactions if consent under s 765 were required would often be within the terms of the general consents.)

RESIDENTS OF MEMBER STATES WITHIN THE MEANING OF THE DIRECTIVE

14 The explanatory notes to the Directive give to ''residents or non-residents'' the meaning of ''natural and legal persons according to the definitions laid down in the Exchange Control Regulations in force in each member state''. ''Natural or legal persons'' are ''as defined by the national rules''. In most cases, the territory where a company or natural person is resident will be self-evident.

15 Some member states still have exchange control regulations in force although that may not always be so. Others, including the UK, have no such regulations. In the view of the Treasury and the Inland Revenue this cannot mean that s 765A and, still less, the Directive will be ineffective. But it does introduce an element of uncertainty into the application of the Directive to transactions within s 765. Paragraphs 16–23 explain the approach of the Treasury and the Inland Revenue to the question of residence for the purposes of determining whether a movement of capital is between residents of different member states so that s 765A applies or whether the movement of capital is wholly within the UK or across the external frontier of the Community so that it is still within s 765.

THE UK RESIDENT BODY CORPORATE IN TA 1988 S 765

16 Since the main effect of the Directive in the UK is to render unlawful the restrictions which are placed by s 765 on bodies corporate which are resident in the UK entering into transactions which are capital movements between member states, it is logical to regard bodies corporate which are resident in the UK for the purposes of that section as being residents of the UK within the meaning of the Directive. Consequently a body corporate will be considered to be a resident for the purposes of the Directive if it is resident in the UK for tax purposes. However, the persons from which those restrictions are lifted by the Directive are not the only persons whose residence has to be ascertained in order to discover the scope of the Directive.

OTHER PERSONS RESIDENT IN MEMBER STATES

17 *Exchange control regulations.* So long as there are exchange control regulations in force in a member state, they will determine residence or non-residence in that state for the purposes of the Directive. As the position of member states on exchange control at the time this statement was prepared was in the process of change, it is not possible to indicate in this statement which states retain regulations.

18 *The relevance of tax residence* If there are no Exchange Control Regulations, the Treasury and Inland Revenue will usually regard a person as resident in a member state (including the UK) if that person is resident in that state for its tax purposes. But there may be circumstances in which tax residence is too restrictive a criterion to determine whether a transaction is a movement of capital to which the Directive applies.

19 *Economic activities* A person who is not a tax resident in a member state may have a presence in a member state for the purpose of a continuing economic activity there. A company may have a branch in a member state (see para 20). Or an individual may have moved to a member state with the intention of remaining there to carry on business but may not yet be resident for tax purposes. If a movement of capital is part of that economic activity it would be regarded as made to or by a person resident in that state for the purpose of determining whether a transaction is within s 765A.

20 *Branches in member states* As para 19 suggests, a transaction carried out by a branch in a member state may be regarded as a transaction by a person resident in that state. For example, a UK company holds all the shares in a US company which is not a resident of a member state and all the shares in a French company which is a resident of a member state. The US company has a branch in the UK and lends money to the French company which issues a debenture. The loan is made by the UK branch of the US company. Normally a transaction between the US company and the French company would not be within the Directive. But the UK branch can be treated as a resident of the UK for the purposes of the Directive and the transaction is therefore within s 765A and Treasury consent is not required. Whether or not a transaction is carried out by a branch will be a question of fact.

21 *Branches not in member states* There may be a movement of capital to or from a branch not in a member state of a company which is resident in a member state. The Treasury and Inland Revenue will regard that as a movement of capital by or to a person resident in the member state unless exchange control regulations in the state in which the company is resident treat branches outside the state as non-resident.

22 *Resident of Gibraltar* Although Gibraltar is not a member state (see para 5 above) it will be necessary under some circumstances to decide if a person is a resident of Gibraltar. In relation to transactions with a member state other than the UK a company will be considered to be resident in Gibraltar if it is liable to tax on income by reason of residence, domicile, place of management or other criterion of a similar nature or the transaction is carried out by the Gibraltar branch of a company which is not otherwise resident in Gibraltar. Whether the transaction is carried out by the Gibraltar branch will be a question of fact. An individual will be resident in Gibraltar for these limited purposes if he or she is resident in Gibraltar for the purposes of Gibraltar tax.

23 *Information on residence* The Movements of Capital (Required Information) Regulations, SI 1990/1671 require the resident body corporate to state, where relevant, the grounds on which a person is claimed to be resident in a member state for the purposes of the Directive. A company which owes its status as a body corporate to the laws of a member state and has its main place of business there will usually be a resident of that state for both exchange control (if any) and tax purposes, as will individuals who have their usual place of residence there. The Treasury and Inland Revenue will normally accept a presumption that such a company or individual is a resident of that state for the purposes of the Directive.

PROCEDURE FOR PROVIDING INFORMATION UNDER TA 1988 S 765A(2)

24 The nature and extent of the information to be reported under s 765A(2) are laid down in the Movements of Capital (Required Information) Regulations, SI 1990/1671. Copies of the Regulations are available from HMSO. The information should be given in a letter addressed to Inland Revenue, International Division, Room 311, Melbourne House, Aldwych, London WC2B 4LL. It would be helpful if an additional copy of the letter could be supplied.

25 Provided all the information required by the Regulations is covered, the letter need not be in any particular form. But it will usually be helpful if it follows broadly the order in which the information is requested in the Regulations.

26 Section 765A requires a transaction to be reported *after* it has taken place. It may be part of a series of transactions for one or more of which the company making the report has obtained Treasury consent under s 765. If in that case part or all of the information required by the Regulations has been given to the Treasury or to the Revenue in connection with the application for consent, it is necessary only to identify in the report under s 765A(2)(*a*) the relevant letters in which the information was given.

Commentary—*Simon's Direct Tax Service* **D4.138**.
Cross references—European Community Capital Movements Directive 88/361 EEC.
Movements of Capital (Required Information) Regulations, SI 1990/1671.
Note—This statement was revised in IR 131 (August 2003).

SP 3/92 (1 May 1992) *Double taxation relief: status of UK/USSR Convention for the avoidance of double taxation*

Note—This statement has been superseded by SP 4/01.

SP 4/92 (14 May 1992) *Capital gains tax: rebasing elections*

1 TCGA 1992 s 35(6) provides that an election under TCGA 1992 s 35(5) should be made within two years of the end of the year of assessment or accounting period in which ''the first relevant disposal'' is made, or such longer period as the Board of Inland Revenue may allow.

2 The Board will always exercise their discretion to extend the time limit to at least the date on which the statutory time limit would expire if disposals of a certain kind did not count as a first relevant disposal of either—

(i) an asset held at 31 March 1982; and

(ii) an asset treated by TCGA 1992 Sch 3 para 1 as having been held at that date.

3 There are three kinds of disposals in relation to which the Board will exercise their discretion in this way.

4 *First*, those on which the gain would not be a chargeable gain by virtue of a particular statutory provision. Such disposals can be left out of account in deciding when to make an election.

5 The main examples of these provisions are in the annex attached to this statement of practice.

6 *Second*, those disposals which *in practice* do not give rise to a chargeable gain or allowable loss. The main examples of such disposals are—

BUILDING SOCIETY ACCOUNTS

Withdrawals from building society accounts on which no chargeable gain or allowable loss arises.

PRIVATE RESIDENCES

The disposal by an individual of his or her dwellinghouse where the *whole* of any gain would qualify for relief under TCGA 1992 s 223(1).

NO GAIN/NO LOSS TRANSFERS

Transfers which give rise to neither a chargeable gain nor an allowable loss by virtue of the operation of statutory ''no gain/no loss'' provisions listed at TCGA 1992 s 35(3)(*d*). These include gifts to charities and transfers between spouses.

7 *Third*, those disposals in respect of which a s 35(5) election cannot be made. These are specified in TCGA 1992 Sch 3 para 7 and are, in general terms, disposals of—

(i) plant and machinery; or

(ii) assets used in connection with a trade of working mineral deposits;

(but in either case only if capital allowances were or could have been given);
or

(iii) oil licences; or

(iv) shares deriving their value from oil exploration or exploitation.

In each case, a rebasing election cannot apply to such disposals, but they will nevertheless count strictly as first relevant disposals. Consequently, in all cases the Board will exercise their discretion to extend the time limit to at least the date on which the statutory time limit would expire if such disposals did not count as a first relevant disposal.

PERSONS BECOMING RESIDENT IN THE UK AFTER 6 APRIL 1988

8 A person who is non UK resident on 6 April 1988 may make a disposal which will count as a first relevant disposal between then and the date on which they first become UK resident. The Board will generally give sympathetic consideration to extending the time limit to the end of the second year of assessment or, in the case of companies, accounting period after the year in which the first disposal is made *after taking up UK residence*. The extension will not normally be available where the taxpayer has disposed of an asset, held on 31 March 1982, within TCGA 1992 s 10 in the period between 6 April 1988 and the date of becoming UK resident.

OTHER SITUATIONS IN WHICH THE STATUTORY TIME LIMIT MAY BE EXTENDED

9 There are a variety of other circumstances in which the Board of Inland Revenue may exercise their discretion to extend the statutory time limit. In all cases an extension will depend on the particular facts and circumstances of each individual case.

WHAT MAY BE REGARDED AS A FIRST RELEVANT DISPOSAL?

10 There are also some circumstances where it may help to clarify what is regarded as a first relevant disposal—

(i) Capacity in which a person makes an election under TCGA 1992 s 35(5).

Where a person makes an election under s 35(5) in relation to assets held in one capacity the election does not apply to assets held in another capacity. This is because of the provisions of s 35(7). For this purpose a person may hold assets in several capacities as, for example, an individual, trustee, partner or member of a European Economic Interest Grouping. It follows that there will be a first relevant disposal and a separate time limit for making an election for each holding of assets which a person holds in different capacities.

Individuals who hold assets in different capacities should indicate at the time they make an election in what capacity it should be regarded as applying.

(ii) Disposals of non UK assets by an individual resident but not domiciled in the UK

In the case of individuals who are resident but not domiciled in the UK a disposal of an asset situated outside the UK may be a first relevant disposal. For TCGA 1992 s 35(5) purposes the date on which the proceeds are *remitted* to the UK is taken to be the date on which the disposal occurs and not the date when the asset was disposed of. This means that the date of the first relevant disposal will therefore be the date on which remittances are received from an overseas gain after 5 April 1988 *or* the date of the first disposal of a UK asset, whichever occurs first.

(iii) Disposals by a UK resident during a period of non-residence

An individual who is UK resident on 6 April 1988 may then have a period of non-residence before resuming UK residence. In these circumstances the first relevant disposal will be treated as the first disposal after 5 April 1988 on which the individual is chargeable to UK capital gains tax. So if, for example, a disposal was made between 6 April 1988 and the date the individual became non-resident that will be treated as the first relevant disposal. If there was no disposal in this period the first relevant disposal will be the first disposal after residence is resumed. Where an individual is not entitled to be treated as resuming residence part-way through a tax year by virtue of extra-statutory concession D2, the first disposal will be the first made in the year in which residence is resumed.

11 This statement of practice provides an indication of the main circumstances where, and the extent to which, the Board of Inland Revenue will or may exercise their discretion under TCGA 1992 s 35(6)(*b*). It is not intended to be an exhaustive list of disposals where, having regard to the individual facts and circumstances, such discretion may be exercised.

ANNEX TO SP 4/92

Disposals on which any gain would not be a chargeable gain by virtue of specific statutory provisions are—

(i) private cars (TCGA 1992 s 263) [formerly CGTA 1979 s 130];

(ii) chattels, including household goods, and personal belongings, but excepting commodity futures and foreign currency, worth less than the chattel exemption at the date of disposal (TCGA 1992 s 262(1)) [formerly CGTA 1979 s 128(1)];

(iii) all chattels that are wasting assets, except plant and machinery used in business (but see also (ii) above and para 7(i) of the statement of practice) and commodity futures (TCGA 1992 s 45(1)) [formerly CGTA 1979 s 127(1)];

(iv) Government non-marketable securities, including savings certificates, premium and British Savings bonds (TCGA 1992 s 121) [formerly CGTA 1979 s 71];

(v) gilt-edged securities and qualifying corporate bonds, except those received in exchange for shares or other securities (TCGA 1992 s 115) [formerly CGTA 1979 s 67];

(vi) life assurance policies and deferred annuity contracts unless purchased from a third party (TCGA 1992 s 210(2)) [formerly CGTA 1979 s 143(2)];

(vii) foreign currency acquired to meet personal or family expenditure abroad (TCGA 1992 s 269) [formerly CGTA 1979 s 133];

(viii) rights to compensation or damages for any wrong or injury suffered by an individual in his person, profession or vocation (TCGA 1992 s 51(2)) [formerly CGTA 1979 s 19(5)];

(ix) debts, other than debts on a security, held by the original creditor, his personal representative or legatee (TCGA 1992 s 251(1)) [formerly CGTA 1979 s 134(1)];

(*x*) business expansion scheme shares in respect of which relief has been given and not withdrawn (TCGA 1992 s 150(2)) [formerly CGTA 1979 s 149C(2)];

(xi) shares held as part of a personal equity plan investment (SI 1989/469 reg 1 as amended);

(xii) gifts of eligible property, including works of art, for the benefit of the public (TCGA 1992 s 258(1), (2)) [formerly CGTA 1979 s 147(1), (2)];

(xiii) decorations for valour or gallantry (TCGA 1992 s 268) [formerly CGTA 1979 s 131];

(xiv) rights to or any part of an allowance, annuity or capital sum from a superannuation fund or any other annuity (except under a deferred annual policy) or annual payments receivable under a covenant which is not secured on property (TCGA 1992 s 237) [formerly CGTA 1979 s 144)].

The disposal of sterling, which is not an asset for capital gains tax purposes (TCGA 1992 s 21(1)) [formerly CGTA 1979 s 19(1)] does not count as a first relevant disposal.

Commentary—*Simon's Direct Tax Service* **C2.604**.
Concession D2—Residence in the UK: year of commencement or cessation of residence.
Note—This statement supersedes SP 2/89.

SP 5/92 (21 May 1992) *Non-resident trusts*

(See also Inland Revenue Tax Bulletin August 1993 and April 1995.)

SPs

I. INTRODUCTION

1 FA 1991 ss 83–92, Sch 16–18 introduced new rules for capital gains of certain offshore trusts. These are now in TCGA 1992 ss 80–98, Sch 5. This statement explains the practice the Revenue will follow in applying the new rules in the circumstances set out below.

II. CHARGE ON MIGRATION—RESIDENCE

2 Under TCGA 1992 s 69, a body of trustees is regarded as capable of changing its residence status part-way through a year of assessment. It must be borne in mind, however, that TCGA 1992 s 2(1) provides that the trustees are liable to tax on all chargeable gains of a tax year during any part of which they are resident or during which they are ordinarily resident in the UK.

3 Trustees who became not resident and not ordinarily resident in the UK between 6 April 1990 and 18 March 1991 (inclusive), and remain so until after 5 April 1991 are not liable to a charge under TCGA 1992 s 80, nor are they regarded as having met the condition in TCGA 1992 Sch 5 para 9(4) for 1990–91.

III. CHARGE ON MIGRATION—PAST TRUSTEES' LIABILITIES

4 TCGA 1992 ss 80–85 impose a capital gains tax charge on the unrealised gains of a UK trust which ceases to be within the UK tax charge. The charge applies to a trust which migrates on or after 19 March 1991. Where the tax which is due under this charge is not paid by the current trustees, TCGA 1992 s 82 enables the Revenue to look to certain former trustees to meet the liability. No liability can be sought from the personal representatives of a former trustee who dies before a notice of liability has been served on him. Those who can show that there was no proposal, at the time of their resignation, that the trustees might become not resident and not ordinarily resident in the UK are not liable under this section.

5 Payment can only be sought from former trustees where the Revenue is unable to obtain payment from current trustees. In the first instance, payment will generally be sought from those persons who resigned as trustees immediately before the trust migrated and then from earlier trustees. Each case will, however, need to be considered in the light of the relevant facts.

6 An amount recovered from present trustees by a former trustee in respect of capital gains tax under TCGA 1992 s 82 is not regarded as a capital payment under s 97. Further, such amounts do not fall within the provisions of TA 1988 Part XV, s 739 or s 740 nor are there any inheritance tax implications.

IV. CHARGE ON THE SETTLOR—SETTLOR'S RIGHT TO REPAYMENT FROM THE TRUSTEES

7 TCGA 1992 s 86, Sch 5 charge settlors to capital gains tax where chargeable gains accrue within certain offshore trusts from which the settlor, members of the settlor's immediate family, or companies which they control, can or do benefit. This goes wider than the provisions of TA 1988 Part XV eg the settlor could be chargeable on gains realised within a trust from which his adult children could benefit even though there was no possible benefit to the settlor, his spouse or minor children.

8 The settlor's right, under TCGA 1992 Sch 5 para 6, to reimbursement (or any payment in reimbursement) of tax paid under that Schedule is not regarded as creating an interest in a trust for the settlor under the provisions of TA 1988 Part XV where the settlor, the settlor's spouse, and any companies in which they are participators cannot otherwise benefit from the trust, eg where the only beneficiaries are the settlor's children. Similarly, this statutory right to, or payment in, reimbursement is not regarded as bringing the settlor within the provisions of TA 1988 ss 677, 739, 740, nor as a capital payment for the purposes of TCGA 1992 s 97.

9 Further, this statutory right is not regarded as a reservation of benefit for inheritance tax purposes; nor is a provision in the trust deed either requiring the trustees to recognise the settlor's right to reimbursement under TCGA 1992 Sch 5 para 6 or to reimburse the settlor. But where a settlor does not pursue the statutory right to reimbursement, the failure to exercise this right may give rise to an inheritance tax claim under IHTA 1984 s 3(3), in which case the usual rules for lifetime transfers would apply.

10 A provision written into a settlement deed requiring the trustees to recognise the settlor's right to reimbursement under TCGA 1992 Sch 5 para 6, or to reimburse the settlor, is not, of itself, regarded as giving the settlor an interest in the settlement for the purposes of Sch 5, nor as bringing into play the provisions of TA 1988 Part XV, s 739 or s 740.

V. CHARGE ON THE SETTLOR—CERTAIN TRUSTS CREATED BEFORE 17 MARCH 1998

11 All trusts are within the scope of Schedule 5, except for those falling within the definition of "a protected settlement" in paragraph 9(10A) at 6 April 1999. A protected settlement has to have been created before 19 March 1991. But a protected settlement will also be within the scope of Schedule 5 where, on or after 19 March 1991, at least one of the conditions listed below is met. Moreover, a settlor is not treated as having an "interest" in a trust created before 17 March 1998 under the terms of which the only "defined persons" (listed in paragraph 2(3)) who can benefit are confined to the grandchildren of the settlor or of the settlor's spouse etc, unless at least one of the conditions listed below is met on or after that date.

The conditions referred to above are—

- subject to certain exclusions, property or income is directly or indirectly provided for the purposes of the trust (paragraphs 2A(2) and 9(3));
- the trustees become non-resident in the UK or fall to be treated as such for the purposes of a double taxation agreement (paragraphs 2A(4) and 9(4));
- the terms of the settlement are varied to admit certain new beneficiaries (paragraphs 2A(5) and 9(5));
- a benefit is enjoyed by a defined person who is not a beneficiary under the terms of the trust (paragraphs 2A(6) and 9(6)).

[Paragraphs 12–37 below only refer to paragraph 9, but the same principles will be followed in deciding whether any of the conditions in paragraphs 2A(2)–(6)are met].

(*a*) TCGA 1992 Sch 5 para 9(3): transactions entered into at arm's length

12 The condition in TCGA 1992 Sch 5 para 9(3) is not met where the property or income is provided to the trust under a transaction entered into at arm's length—see para 9(3)(*a*). This applies irrespective of whether the parties to the transaction are connected persons under TCGA 1992 s 286. Each case depends on its own facts and circumstances but a transaction is, in general, regarded as being at arm's length where all the facts and circumstances of the transaction are such as might have been expected if the parties to the transaction had been independent persons dealing at arm's length ie dealing with each other in a normal commercial manner unaffected by any special relationship between them.

13 Solely for the purposes of TCGA 1992 Sch 5 para 9(3)(*a*), a provision in the document governing the transaction for an appropriate adjustment to the consideration where the value agreed by the Revenue differs from the original consideration arrived at by an independent valuer and specified in the sale document is, in general, regarded as falling within the terms of the above definition of an arm's length transaction. The arm's length value of the transaction is to be determined in accordance with the principles set out in para 12 above. This will usually correspond to the value for capital gains tax purposes except, for example, where TCGA 1992 s 19 would apply.

14 It would also be necessary for the terms of the contract to provide for compensating interest at a commercial rate to be paid in either direction once the arm's length value is determined. For this purpose, the official rate of interest for TA 1988 s 160 purposes will usually be regarded as equivalent to a commercial rate of interest, although a different rate may be accepted as so equivalent if the circumstances of a particular case warrant this treatment.

15 This practice is, however, subject to the consideration passing on sale being realistically based, ie on a third party valuation by a qualified valuer, all the other terms of the transaction being at arm's length and the compensating interest being timeously paid. The position in a particular case depends on all the facts and circumstances.

(*b*) TCGA 1992 Sch 5 para 9(3): close companies

16 The condition in TCGA 1992 Sch 5 para 9(3) may be satisfied where property or income is provided to a company in which the trustees are participators. Where, however, the transaction is carried out with the sole object of leaving funds within the company for the company's purposes and it can be shown that any indirect benefit to the trust is merely incidental to that object, the transaction is disregarded for the purposes of para 9(3).

17 Examples of transactions which may be so disregarded are—

- where another shareholder waives an entitlement to all or part of a dividend; or
- where a director restricts withdrawals of remuneration voted,

in order to assist the company's cash flow, and no payments are made, directly or indirectly, to the trustees as a result of this. All relevant factors will be considered in determining whether it is appropriate to apply this practice in a particular case.

(*c*) TCGA 1992 Sch 5 para 9(3): transactions with wholly-owned companies

18 In general, transactions between trustees and companies which they, directly or indirectly, wholly own, or between such companies, are outside the scope of TCGA 1992 Sch 5 para 9(3) and are not treated as capital payments within TCGA 1992 s 97. For this purpose, a company is treated as directly wholly owned by the trustees where the whole of its issued share capital is directly owned by the trustees of the settlement for the benefit of the beneficiaries of the settlement. A company is treated as indirectly wholly owned by the trustees where the whole of its issued share capital is directly and beneficially owned by a company which is directly wholly owned by the trustees or it is the 100 per cent subsidiary of such a company, or a chain of companies, which is indirectly wholly owned by the trustees. This approach may not, however, be taken where, on the facts of a particular case, it appears that the transaction has been entered into solely or mainly for the purposes of obtaining a UK tax advantage.

(*d*) TCGA 1992 Sch 5 para 9(3): loans made to settlements

(i) Loans made before 19 March 1991

19 A fixed-period loan made, directly or indirectly, to a relevant settlement prior to 19 March 1991 on non-commercial terms, eg at a low or nil rate of interest is, generally, regarded as a provision of property in pursuance of a liability incurred before 19 March 1991, provided the loan remains outstanding on the same terms. As such, it falls within the terms of TCGA 1992 Sch 5 para 9(3)(*b*) and the first condition set out in para 9(3) is not met.

20 There would, however, be a direct or indirect provision of property for the purposes of the settlement where a fixed-period loan falls to be repaid after 18 March 1991 but repayment is not made and so becomes a repayable on demand loan.

21 An extra-statutory concession D41, which is being published at the same time as this statement, sets out the position in the case of non-commercial, repayable on demand, loans for the purposes of applying TCGA 1992 Sch 5 para 9(3).

(ii) Loans made after 19 March 1991

22 A loan made, directly or indirectly to a relevant settlement after 19 March 1991 on non-commercial terms, eg at a low or nil rate of interest is regarded as a provision of funds for the purposes of TCGA 1992 Sch 5 para 9(3). This is the case whether the loan is for a fixed period or repayable on demand.

(*e*) TCGA 1992 Sch 5 para 9(3): loans made by trustees

23 The repayment of any loan made, directly or indirectly, to any person by the trustees is not generally regarded as the provision of funds for the purposes of the settlement under TCGA 1992 Sch 5 para 9(3). This does not, however, apply where more is repaid than is due under the original terms of the loan or, in the case of loans made after 19 March 1991, where the interest charged under the terms of the loan exceeds a commercial rate.

(*f*) TCGA 1992 Sch 5 para 9(3): failure to exercise rights to reimbursement

24 Failure, by or on behalf of any relevant person, to exercise statutory rights to reimbursement, *eg* under TA 1988 Part XV may be regarded as the provision of funds for the purposes of the settlement under TCGA 1992 Sch 5 para 9(3). The settlement could remain outside the terms of para 9(3) where the exercise of the right to reimbursement is unsuccessful, provided it could be shown that there had been a genuine attempt to enforce rights to reimbursement.

(*g*) TCGA 1992 Sch 5 para 9(3): administrative expenses

25 As provided by TCGA 1992 Sch 5 para 9(3), a trust may remain outside the scope of Sch 5 where funds are provided to pay certain expenses which exceed the income of the trust. These expenses are defined as ''expenses relating to administration and taxation''; and could be chargeable either to the income or to the capital of the trust. Only sums provided to meet genuine expenses of administration fall within the terms of the proviso: any payments which exceed such expenses are regarded as meeting the condition in para 9(3) and so bringing the trust within the scope of Sch 5.

26 The following items are not regarded as ''expenses relating to administration'' within the terms of the proviso to TCGA 1992 Sch 5 para 9(3)—

- loan interest (other than interest on a loan taken out to meet expenses of administration within the terms of the proviso);
- the costs of acquiring, enhancing or disposing of an asset;
- expenses incurred in connection with a particular trust asset to the extent that such expenditure can be set against income arising from that asset. For the purpose of the proviso to para 9(3), the measure of the gross income from such a source is net of expenses.

27 The term ''expenses relating to ... taxation'' in TCGA 1992 Sch 5 para 9(3) is regarded as encompassing UK or foreign taxes to which the trustees are liable, along with any interest and penalties due on that tax. It could also include certain costs incurred by the trustees under the terms of the trust in obtaining information regarding the beneficiaries' tax liabilities. One example might be where the trustees, in order to ensure they were acting in a beneficiary's best interests, had to ascertain the tax implications for the beneficiary in adopting a particular course of action.

28 It is only the *settlement's* expenses relating to administration or taxation which are within the terms of the proviso to TCGA 1992 Sch 5 para 9(3). Expenses of, for example, a company wholly owned by the trustees fall outside its scope.

29 An expense on capital account paid out of trust income is not treated as a provision of income by a beneficiary for the purposes of TCGA 1992 Sch 5 para 9(3) provided that either—

- the trust deed permits payment of capital expenses from income and the beneficiary is entitled only to net income after such payments; or

– the trustees borrow money from the income account which is subsequently restored, along with interest over the period of the loan. The appropriate rate of interest is considered to be that which a Court of Equity would order on the replacement of trust income.

30 Normally the specific date on which the liability to an expense relating to administration or taxation was incurred determines the year into which it falls for the purpose of applying the proviso to TCGA 1992 Sch 5 para 9(3). Where, however, the expense is incurred for a period rather than on a specific date, the basis of allocating expenses adopted by the trustees in preparing trust accounts or returns is, generally, regarded as acceptable provided that this basis is consistently adopted and is in accordance with conventional trust accounting practice.

31 Additions to meet the difference between expenses relating to administration and taxation and any income arising to the trust do not have to be made by 5 April in the relevant year of assessment. There must, however, be a clear connection between the amount added and the computed shortfall. Additions should, therefore, be made as soon as the relevant figures are available.

32 Income, for the purposes of the proviso to TCGA 1992 Sch 5 para 9(3), is the total income which arises to the trustees in the relevant year, rather than the income which is (or would be if the trust were resident in the UK) subject to UK tax. Usually, items of income will need to be allocated to the year in which they arise for the purposes of the proviso, but, in practice, income arising from a trade carried on by the trustees may be apportioned on a time basis, provided that this basis is consistently followed.

(*h*) TCGA 1992 Sch 5 para 9(3): life tenants

33 A life tenant is not regarded as having provided income or property for the purposes of the settlement merely because there is an administrative delay in paying out the income that has vested in that beneficiary. If, however, the beneficiary directs the trustees to retain this income on the terms of the settlement, this is regarded as a provision of funds within TCGA 1992 Sch 5 para 9(3).

(i) TCGA 1992 Sch 5 para 9(3): indemnities and guarantees

34 An indemnity given by the new trustees to retiring trustees is not considered as the provision of funds for the purposes of the settlement under TCGA 1992 Sch 5 para 9(3). Other types of indemnity are considered in light of the facts of a particular case.

35 The giving of a guarantee is regarded as an indirect provision of funds under the terms of TCGA 1992 Sch 5 para 9(3). Payment of an obligation under a guarantee given before 9 March 1991 is, in general, regarded as a payment in pursuance of a liability incurred before 19 March 1991 and within para 9(3)(*b*). This may not, however, apply where—

– the contingent liability under the guarantee cannot be quantified with a sufficient degree of accuracy, eg where the guarantee is open-ended or the contingency is remote; or
– the guarantor does not take reasonable steps to pursue his rights against the debtor.

(*j*) TCGA 1992 Sch 5 para 9(5): variations

36 This provision is concerned with situations where the terms of the settlement are varied by the beneficiaries or a court to admit new beneficiaries within the class of persons defined at TCGA 1992 Sch 5 para 9(7) without thereby bringing the settlement to an end and creating a new one. For example, where the terms of the trust include a power to appoint anyone within a specified range to be a beneficiary, exercise of that power after 19 March 1991 will not be regarded as a variation of the settlement. The term ''spouse'' in para 9(7) is not considered to include a widow or a widower.

(*k*) TCGA 1992 Sch 5 para 9(6): ultra vires payments

37 For the purposes of clarification, this condition deals with ''ultra vires'' payments, ie cases where one of the persons defined at TCGA 1992 Sch 5 para 9(7) receives a benefit from the trust for the first time and that person is not a beneficiary under the terms of the trust deed. It may also apply where such a person benefits from a transaction with the settlement carried out, for example, under the trustees' investment powers.

VI. CHARGE ON BENEFICIARIES: INTRAGROUP TRANSFERS

38 TCGA 1992 ss 87–89 charge UK resident beneficiaries to capital gains tax on certain capital payments received from non-resident settlements. TCGA 1992 s 96 is concerned with the application of these provisions to capital payments made by companies which are controlled by the trustees and capital payments received by certain non-resident companies.

39 TCGA 1992 s 96 provides that, where the trustees (or a company which they control) make a payment to a closely-controlled non-resident company, the payment is, broadly, treated as made to those who control the company. This may, for example, mean that a payment made by a wholly-owned subsidiary to its holding company (in which the shares are, say, held 50 per cent by the settlor and 50 per cent by the trustees of a non-resident trust) can be treated as being made by the trustees to the settlor.

40 The payment must, however, be a capital payment within TCGA 1992 s 97(1)—ie it must *not* be chargeable to income tax on the recipient nor be made under a transaction entered into at arm's length. Intragroup payments which are not capital payments, for example a capital distribution on winding up which represents merely a repayment of capital on shares, or a distribution chargeable to corporation tax, do not fall within the ambit of TCGA 1992 s 96.

Commentary—*Simon's Direct Tax Service* **C4.434, 438**.
Concession D40—Non-resident trusts: definition of participators.
Revenue & other press releases—ICAEW TAX 20/92 14-12-92 (Guidance note—non-resident settlements. Revenue comment in respect of this statement).
Note—This statement was revised in IR 131 (August 2002).

SP 6/92 (3 July 1992) *Accident insurance policies—chargeable events and gains on policies of life insurance*

1 The Inland Revenue take the view that certain accident insurance policies which provide protection only, and no investment element, do not give rise to chargeable "gains".

RELEVANT LEGISLATION

2 Liability to tax may arise on the occurrence of a chargeable event in connection with a policy of life insurance. The rules are at TA 1988 Part XIII Ch II [ss 539–554]. "Chargeable event" and the "gain" to be taxed are defined at TA 1988 ss 540, 541 respectively. The meaning of "policy of life insurance" is determined from general law and decisions of the courts.

PRESENT PRACTICE

3 Until now, the Inland Revenue have taken the view that the term "policy of life insurance" included an accident insurance policy providing cover against dying as a result of an accident. On that view, a taxable "gain" may arise in connection with an accident insurance policy.

NEW PRACTICE

4 The Inland Revenue now take the view that an accident insurance policy which provides protection only should not be regarded as a policy of life insurance when applying the rules at TA 1988 Part XIII Ch II. Taxable "gains" will not therefore be treated as arising in connection with an accident insurance policy which—

(*a*) affords protection against the risk of dying only if death is as a result of an accident; and
(*b*) has no investment content; and
(*c*) does not acquire a surrender value (other than one equal to a proportion of the premium paid which is refundable if the policy is terminated early or in other circumstances).

5 The accident insurance policies to which this practice will apply are those written as—

(*a*) "Contracts of general Business" of an insurance company or a friendly society or members of Lloyd's within [Financial Services and Markets Act 2000 (Regulated Activities) Order 2001, SI 2001/1544, Part 1, Sch 1, para 1; or
(*b*) similar protection only policies written by non-resident insurers].

COMMENCEMENT

6 This statement of practice will be applied in settling any tax liability which is not final at the date of issue of this statement. The statutory references applicable for the past are those from which the current provisions are derived.

BACKGROUND

7 The aim of the TA 1988 Part XIII Ch II rules is to charge to tax any investment return in life insurance policy benefits. There is no intention to charge to tax mortality benefits (the protection element in life insurance cover). The "gain" which may be subject to tax is broadly the difference between the premiums paid and the benefits received. But where the chargeable event is death, any "gain" is computed by reference to the surrender value of the policy immediately before death—not the total benefits received on death—so that mortality benefits are not normally charged to tax.

8 The rules make no special provision for group life insurance policies (although some, issued in connection with approved retirement benefit schemes or retirement annuity contracts, are completely outside the scope of the charge under the general exclusion for certain policies of insurance at TA 1988 s 539(2)). If a group life insurance policy gives rise to more than one death benefit some mortality benefits come into the computation of gain. This is a result of the rule dealing with partial surrenders of the rights conferred by a policy. Benefits, including death benefits, paid at any time prior to the "chargeable event" in question are included when computing a "gain".

OTHER POINTS

9 An accident insurance policy which provides cover against disablement only (not death) as a result of an accident has never been considered to be a policy of life insurance. The tax treatment of disability benefits from such a policy is not affected therefore by the new practice.

10 Policy benefits may be otherwise chargeable to tax; for example, as receipts of a trade or profession. Any such charge is unaffected by this statement of practice which is concerned only with the application of the chargeable events legislation at TA 1988 Part XIII Ch II.

Commentary—*Simon's Direct Tax Service* **B7.503**.
Note—This statement was revised in IR 131 (August 2002).

SP 7/92 (3 August 1992) *Profit-related pay—use of pool determination formulae*

Note—This statement has been classified as obsolete by IR 131 (August 2002).

SP 8/92 (26 October 1992) *Valuation of assets in respect of which capital gains tax gifts holdover relief is claimed*

(See also Inland Revenue Tax Bulletin April 1997, page 417).

INTRODUCTION

1 This statement sets out the Revenue's practice for dealing with the valuation of assets in respect of which a claim to capital gains tax gifts holdover relief has been made. It applies to both new claims to holdover relief and existing claims in relation to which valuation negotiations with the Revenue may already have started.

CIRCUMSTANCES IN WHICH CAPITAL GAINS TAX GIFTS HOLDOVER RELIEF IS AVAILABLE

2 Subject to an appropriate claim, gifts holdover relief is available where—

- an individual makes a disposal not at arm's length of—
  - an asset used for the purposes of a trade, profession or vocation carried on by the transferor, his personal company or a member of a trading group of which the holding company is the transferor's ''personal'' company—TCGA 1992 s 165(2)(*a*); or
  - shares in a trading company or holding company of a trading group which are either unlisted or are in the transferor's ''personal'' company—TCGA 1992 s 165(2)(*b*); or
  - agricultural property as defined by IHTA 1984—TCGA 1992 Sch 7 para 1;
- the trustees of a settlement make a disposal of certain settled property—TCGA 1992 Sch 7 paras 2, 3;
- an individual or the trustees of a settlement make a disposal of an asset not at arm's length which is either a chargeable transfer under IHTA 1984; or is one of a specified range of exempt transfers—TCGA 1992 s 260(2).

WHAT IS THE HELD OVER GAIN?

3 In the absence of a claim to holdover relief, TCGA 1992 s 17 would treat both the acquisition and disposal of the assets transferred to be for a consideration equal to their market value. Where a valid claim is made the effect is that the transferor's chargeable gain is reduced to nil and the transferee's acquisition cost is reduced by the amount of the held over gain.

4 The held over gain is the amount of the chargeable gain which would have accrued to the transferor, but for the claim to holdover relief. To compute the chargeable gain, and hence the held over gain, it is necessary to establish the market value of the asset at the date of the transfer.

5 Where no other reliefs are involved, holdover relief will be available where the market value of the asset transferred exceeds the transferor's allowable expenditure and the amount of indexation allowance due up to the date of disposal. If holdover relief is claimed and no consideration is paid then the transferee's acquisition cost will be equal to the sum of the transferor's allowable expenditure plus indexation to the date of transfer. In holdover relief cases, assuming none of the restrictions described in paras 6 and 13 below apply, agreement of the market value of the asset at the date of transfer has no bearing on the immediate capital gains tax liability of the transferor.

POSITION WHERE CONSIDERATION IS PAID BY THE TRANSFEREE

6 Additional rules apply which affect the amount of the held over gain where actual consideration is given to the transferor. Full holdover relief is only available if the actual consideration received does not exceed the transferor's allowable expenditure (TCGA 1992 s 38). If the actual consideration received exceeds the transferor's allowable expenditure on the asset, the holdover relief is restricted by that excess (TCGA 1992 ss 165(7), 260(5)).

7 Where consideration is given, the transferee's acquisition cost will be equivalent to the sum of the transferor's allowable expenditure, the indexation allowance due to the date of disposal by the transferor and the gain immediately chargeable on the transferor.

CIRCUMSTANCES WHERE IN FUTURE MARKET VALUE AT DISPOSAL NEED NOT BE AGREED WITH THE REVENUE

8 Subject to the following conditions, the Revenue will admit a claim for holdover relief without requiring a computation of the held over gain in any case where the transferor and transferee complete the second page of the claim form attached to the Help Sheet IR 295. In particular this requires—

- a joint application by the transferor and the transferee;
- provision of details concerning the asset and its history or alternatively a calculation incorporating informally estimated valuations if necessary; and
- a statement that both parties have satisfied themselves that the value of the asset at the date of transfer was in excess of the allowable expenditure plus indexation to that date.

The further conditions are that—

- once a claim made on this basis has been accepted by the Revenue it may not be subsequently withdrawn;
- if after acceptance by the Revenue it emerges that any information provided or statement made by either the transferor or transferee was incorrect or incomplete, in each case their capital gains tax position in relation to the asset will be computed in accordance with the relevant statutory provisions and assessments made as appropriate.

It should be noted that for years 1996–97 onwards all claims to holdover relief are to be made on the claim form attached to Help Sheet IR 295 or a copy of it.

9 Where, under the terms of this statement of practice, a claim is admitted without the held over gain being computed, this does not mean that the Revenue accepts as factually correct or will subsequently be bound by any information or statements given by any person, whether expressly or by implication, in connection with the claim. Neither the Revenue nor the claimants are bound in any way by any estimated values shown on the claim form or in any calculations.

ASSETS HELD ON 31 MARCH 1982

10 Unless actual consideration is given by the transferee, this practice will also apply to assets held by the transferor on 31 March 1982. It will only be necessary to agree a value at 31 March 1982 when the transferee disposes of the asset.

11 If the transferor has made an election under TCGA 1992 s 35(5), the transferee's acquisition cost of the asset will be equal to the 31 March 1982 value plus indexation up to the date of the transfer. If there is no election under TCGA 1992 s 35(5), the transferee's acquisition cost of the asset will be equal to the transferor's original cost plus indexation up to the date of the transfer or the 31 March 1982 value plus indexation up to the date of transfer—whichever is greater.

12 If the transferee has paid some consideration for the asset it will be necessary to agree the 31 March 1982 value immediately. This is so that the excess over the allowable expenditure—which is chargeable to capital gains tax immediately—can be determined. However, the Revenue will still be prepared to accept a holdover relief claim without undertaking a valuation as at the date of transfer.

CIRCUMSTANCES IN WHICH A VALUATION MAY BE REQUIRED

13 There are certain cases where TCGA 1992 Sch 7 paras 5, 6 or 7 restrict the amount of the heldover gain. These are cases where an asset has at some time during the transferor's ownership been used for non-business purposes, or has only been used in part for business purposes, and cases involving shares etc, in a company which has non-business assets. This statement of practice cannot apply in any of these cases, because it is necessary to compute the chargeable gain before holdover relief. Otherwise, the Revenue's expectation is, subject to the circumstances described in paras 8 and 10 to 12, that it will rarely be necessary to determine the market value at the date of the gift. However, a valuation may become necessary as a result of the interaction of the heldover gain with other capital gains tax reliefs. It is not expected that even in these cases will it be necessary to establish the market value immediately. Instead, it is more likely that a valuation will not be required before, for instance, a later disposal of the asset by the transferee. The following paragraphs cover the more common circumstances.

RETIREMENT RELIEF

14 Holdover relief is not available in the case of a disposal of an asset to the extent that any gain benefits from retirement relief (TCGA 1992 s 165(3)(*a*), (*b*); TCGA 1992 s 260(5) Sch 6). This means that holdover relief may be claimed if the market value at the date of transfer is at least equal to the sum of the transferor's allowable expenditure, indexation allowance to the date of disposal and the retirement relief due.

15 Unless requested by the claimants, the agreement of the market value of the asset will be deferred until either—

– it is necessary to determine the quantum of the retirement relief due. (Normally this will be when the transferor makes another disposal which attracts retirement relief), or
– it is necessary to determine the transferee's cost of the asset.

RELIEF IN RESPECT OF DEFERRED CHARGES ON GAINS BEFORE 31 MARCH 1982 (TCGA 1992 SCH 4)

16 In the case of an asset acquired before 31 March 1982 and transferred before 6 April 1988 it is necessary to compute any held over gain in order to give the benefit of the 50 per cent reduction available under TCGA 1992 Sch 4. To the extent that the market value of the asset at the date of transfer has not already been determined the Revenue is prepared to defer the need for a valuation until disposal by the transferee.

TIME APPORTIONMENT IN THE CASE OF ASSETS HELD ON 6 APRIL 1965

17 In the case of an asset held at 6 April 1965 chargeable gains and allowable losses arising on disposal are ''time apportioned'' so that only those accruing since 6 April 1965 are recognised for capital gains tax purposes. If holdover relief is claimed in relation to the gift of such an asset it is always necessary to agree a valuation at the date of transfer in order to apply time apportionment to the deferred gain. The Revenue are content to defer this valuation until the asset is disposed of by the transferee.

APPLICATION OF STATEMENT OF PRACTICE TO EXISTING HOLDOVER RELIEF CLAIMS

18 In relation to existing holdover relief claims, valuation negotiations with the Revenue may have commenced, but not yet been completed. Taxpayers who want to take advantage of the practice in relation to such claims should write to the inspector of taxes to whom they were submitted.

Commentary—*Simon's Direct Tax Service* **C1.426; C3.503**.
Revenue & other press releases—IR Tax Bulletin April 1997 p 417 (confirms that SP 8/92 continues under self-assessment much as before, and explains the introduction of a new claim form).
Note—This statement was amended by IR 131 Supp (November 1998).

SP 9/92 *Partnerships: Circumstances in which late elections will be accepted*

Commentary—*Simon's Direct Tax Service* **E5.312**.
Note—This statement ceases to apply for 1997—98 onwards.

SP 1/93 (11 January 1993) *Tax treatment of expenditure on films and certain similar assets*

Note—This statement has been superseded. See now the IR Business Income Manual 56000–56500).

SP 2/93 (13 January 1993) *Inheritance tax: the use of substitute forms*

Note—See the Inheritance Tax section, post.

SP 3/93 (13 January 1993) *Groups of companies—arrangements*

INTRODUCTION

1 This statement supersedes statement of practice SP 5/80. Some features of the earlier statement have been omitted or revised but this does not indicate a more restrictive approach on the part of the Revenue.

2 This statement gives general guidance on how the Revenue interpret ''arrangements'' in the following provisions of TA 1988—

– s 240(11)(*a*)—surrender of ACT to a subsidiary company;
– s 247(1A)(*b*)—group income elections in certain consortium cases;

– s 410(1), (2)—group and consortium reliefs; and
''option arrangements'' in—
– Sch 18 para 5B(1)—group and consortium reliefs.

EXTRA-STATUTORY CONCESSION C10

3 Certain types of ''arrangements'' or ''option arrangements'' relating to groups and consortia which fall within the above legislation are in practice excluded from its scope by ESC C10, as revised January 1993.

GENERAL

4 This statement of practice gives general guidance in conjunction with ESC C10. Comprehensive guidance cannot be given about what constitutes ''arrangements'' or ''option arrangements'', nor about precisely when they come into existence. Particular cases depend on the particular relevant facts.

5 As regards ''option arrangements'' the Board's view is that if an agreement provides for the creation of specified option rights exercisable at some future time ''option arrangements'' come into existence when the agreement was entered into.

DISPOSAL OF SHARES OR SECURITIES IN A COMPANY

6 Where a holder of shares or securities in a company is preparing to dispose of them, straightforward negotiations for the disposal will not give rise to the existence of ''arrangements'' before the point at which an offer is accepted subject to contract or on a similar conditional basis. Equally, unless there are exceptional features, an offer made to the public at large of shares or a business will not at that stage bring ''arrangements'' into existence.

7 If a disposal requires the approval of shareholders, operations leading towards disposal will not give rise to the existence of ''arrangements'' before that approval is given or until the directors become aware that it will be given.

8 If following negotiations with potential purchasers a holder of shares or securities concentrates on a particular potential purchaser this will not of itself be regarded as bringing ''arrangements'' into existence. But ''arrangements'' might exist if there were an understanding between the parties in the character of an option. For example, an offer, whether formally made or not, might be allowed to remain open for an appreciable period so that the potential purchaser was allowed to choose the moment to create a bargain.

COMPANY RECONSTRUCTIONS

9 The approval of shareholders for a company reconstruction may be required under company law or to comply with the rules of a stock exchange. ''Arrangements'' will not come into existence before approval is given or until the directors become aware that it will be given.

ENFORCEABILITY

10 ''Arrangements'', though not ''option arrangements'', may exist between parties even though they are not enforceable.

Commentary—*Simon's Direct Tax Service* **D2.637**.

SP 4/93 (16 March 1993) *Deceased persons' estates—discretionary interests in residue*

TA 1988 s 698(3) provides for discretionary payments out of the income of the residue of an estate of a deceased person, whether made directly by the personal representatives, or indirectly through a trustee or other person, to be treated as the income of the recipient for the year in which they are paid.

The Revenue will apply TA 1988 s 698(3) whenever such discretionary payments are made, whether they are payments out of income of the residue as it arises or out of income arising to the personal representatives in earlier years, which has been retained pending the exercise of their discretion.

Where payments are made out of income of the residue of UK estates (as defined in TA 1988 s 701(9)) they are treated—

– for years up to and including 1992–93 as received after deduction of basic rate tax
– for 1993–94 and later years as received after deduction of tax at the applicable rate (as defined in s 701(3A)).

Recipients who are not liable to income tax on the payments, including charities, are entitled to claim repayment of this basic rate tax except where payment is made from a ''relevant amount'' as defined in s 699A.

Where payments are made indirectly through trustees, the trustees may be liable to tax at the rate applicable to trusts (for years of assessment up to 1992–93, the sum of the basic and additional rates) on the payments under TA 1988 s 686. Beneficiaries may be treated as receiving the payments after deduction of tax at the rate applicable to trusts (for years of assessment up to 1992–93, the sum of the basic and additional rates). This tax may be repaid or further tax charged, depending on the beneficiary's marginal rate. The trustees are not chargeable to income tax at the rate applicable to trusts (for years of assessment up to 1992–93, the sum of the basic and additional rates), where a trust is established for charitable purposes only.

With effect from 16 March 1993 the Revenue will apply TA 1988 s 698(3) in this way to all open cases whether this results in repayment of tax or an assessment to income tax at the higher rate. Claims for repayment of tax may also be made for years from 1986–87 onwards, including supplementary claims where an earlier claim was refused under the Revenue's previous practice.

Note—The text of this statement is as it appears in IR 131 (November 1996).

SP 5/93 (19 March 1993) *UK/Czechoslovakia Double Taxation Convention*

1 The Convention, the full title of which is as follows:

> "Convention between the Government of the United Kingdom of Great Britain and Northern Ireland and the Government of the Czech and Slovak Federal Republic for the avoidance of double taxation with respect to taxes on income and capital gains";

was signed in London on 5 November 1990 and entered into force on 20 December 1991. It took effect:

(*a*) in the United Kingdom;

- (i) in respect of income tax and capital gains tax for the year of assessment beginning on 6 April 1992 and subsequent years of assessment; and
- (ii) in respect of corporation tax for the financial year beginning on 1 April 1992 and for subsequent financial years; and

(*b*) in Czechoslovakia, from 1 January 1992.

2 Following the dissolution of the Czech and Slovak Federal Republic and the recognition of the Czech Republic and the Slovak Republic by the United Kingdom as sovereign, independent states, the Board of Inland Revenue have been advised that the Czech Republic and the Slovak Republic have committed themselves to continue to honour all the international obligations of the former Federal Republic and that the provisions of the United Kingdom/Czechoslovakia Double Taxation Convention will be treated as remaining in force between the United Kingdom and, respectively, the Czech Republic and the Slovak Republic.

Commentary—*Simon's Direct Tax Service* **E5.810**.
Cross references—UK/Czechoslovakia Double Taxation Convention of 5 November 1990, SI 1991/2876.

SPs

SP 6/93 (19 March 1993) *UK/Yugoslavia Double Taxation Convention*

1 The Convention, the full title of which is as follows:

> "Convention between the United Kingdom of Great Britain and Northern Ireland and the Socialist Federal Republic of Yugoslavia for the Avoidance of Double Taxation with respect to Taxes on Income";

was signed in London on 6 November 1981 and entered into force on 16 September 1982. It took effect:

(*a*) in the United Kingdom;

- (i) in respect of income tax and capital gains tax for the year of assessment beginning on 6 April 1983 and subsequent years of assessment; and
- (ii) in respect of corporation tax for the financial year beginning on 1 April 1983 and for subsequent financial years; and

(*b*) in Yugoslavia from 1 January 1983.

2 As regards the Republics of Croatia and Slovenia, which have been recognised by the United Kingdom as independent sovereign states, the Board of Inland Revenue have been advised that they have committed themselves to continue to respect and implement all the international obligations of the Socialist Federal Republic of Yugoslavia until such time as new bilateral agreements were signed. The provisions of the UK/Yugoslavia Double Taxation Convention will therefore be treated as remaining in force between the UK and, respectively, Croatia and Slovenia.

3 The position with respect to Bosnia-Hercegovina and the remaining Yugoslav republics is uncertain but a further statement will be issued in due course.

Commentary—*Simon's Direct Tax Service* **E5.810**.
Cross references—UK/Yugoslavia Double Taxation Convention of 6 November 1981, SI 1981/1815.

SP 7/93 (11 June 1993) *Insurance companies: transfers of long term business*

Note—This statement was classified as obsolete in IR 131 Supp (November 2000).

SP 9/93 (8 October 1993) *Corporation tax pay and file: corporation tax returns*

Note—This statement was classified as obsolete in IR 131 Supp (November 2001).

SP 10/93 (8 October 1993) *Corporation tax pay and file: special arrangement for groups of companies*

Note—This statement was classified as obsolete in IR 131 Supp (November 2001).

SP 11/93 (8 October 1993) *Corporation tax pay and file: claims to capital allowances and group relief made outside the normal time limit*

Note—This statement was classified as obsolete by IR 131 (August 2002).

SP 12/93 (27 July 1993) *Double taxation: dividend income—tax credit relief*

1 TA 1988 s 790 sets out the basis under which relief (''unilateral relief'') may be given for foreign tax paid in the absence of a double taxation convention. TA 1988 s 790(5)(*c*) provides that tax credit relief shall not be available for overseas tax on a dividend paid by a company resident in a territory outside the UK unless—

(i) the overseas tax is directly charged on the dividend, whether by charge to tax, deduction of tax at source or otherwise, and the whole of it represents tax which neither the company nor the recipient would have borne if the dividend had not been paid; or

(ii) the dividend is paid to a company within s 790(6); or

(iii) TA 1988 s 802 applies (UK insurance companies trading overseas).

2 TA 1988 s 790(6) provides, among other things, that where a dividend is paid by a company resident in a territory outside the UK to a company resident in the UK which either directly or indirectly controls, or is a subsidiary of a company which directly or indirectly controls, not less than 10 per cent of the voting power in the company paying the dividend, any tax in respect of its profits paid under the law of the territory outside the UK by the company paying the dividend shall be taken into account in considering whether any, and if so what, credit is to be allowed in respect of the dividend.

3 There are similar provisions in a number of double taxation conventions, in which case tax credit relief against UK tax on the dividends concerned is available under those conventions and not under s 790. Typically these conventions provide that where a company which is a resident of the other country pays a dividend to a company resident in the UK which controls directly or indirectly at least 10 per cent of the voting power in the company paying the dividend, the credit for foreign tax shall take into account the tax of the other country payable by the company paying the dividend in respect of the profits out of which the dividend is paid.

4 A number of countries outside the UK operate a ''company tax deducted'' system whereby, when a dividend is paid, tax is accounted for at the standard rate of tax on company profits. In the case of Guernsey, for example, where a company pays a dividend out of profits that will be or have been charged to tax in Guernsey, the company is entitled to deduct tax which it must remit to the tax authorities. That tax is a payment on account of tax charged or chargeable on the profits and gains of the company; and where the amount of tax charged or chargeable on the company's profits and gains is less than the amount of tax deducted from the dividend and remitted to the tax authority, the appropriate repayment is made to the company. The tax deducted and accounted for by the company on making the dividend payments is not tax that is additional to the tax on the company's profits and gains.

5 It has been the practice of the Revenue, when calculating the tax credit relief due under TA 1988 s 790 to a UK company against UK tax on a dividend from a company resident in Guernsey, to allow credit at the rate of "company tax deducted" or at the rate of tax paid by the Guernsey company on its profits (the actual underlying rate), whichever is the greater. A similar practice has operated in respect of dividends received from companies resident in Jersey and, in cases where there is a double taxation convention with a provision along the lines of para 3 above, in respect of dividends received from companies resident in Belize, the Gambia, Malaysia, Malta and Singapore.

6 The matter has been under review and, following further consideration, the Revenue has decided that, as regards dividends declared on or after today, the correct way to give effect to the relief allowable as described in paras 2 and 3 above is, subject to the usual rules governing tax credit relief, to allow relief for the amount of the tax actually paid by the overseas company on the particular profits out of which the dividend is paid. Where those profits are not taxed in the other country, no tax credit relief will be available. The amount of overseas tax available for credit relief will be determined not by reference to what is shown on the dividend voucher but by reference to the tax paid in the other country in respect of its profits by the company paying the dividend. This will be ascertained in the usual way by examination of the overseas company's accounts and tax assessments.

Commentary—*Simon's Direct Tax Service* **F2.106**.
Note—The text of this statement is as it appears in IR 131 Supp (October 1995).

SP 13/93 (17 September 1993) *Compulsory acquisition of freehold or extension of lease by tenant*

1 TCGA 1992 s 247 allows roll-over relief in certain circumstances where a landlord disposes of land to an "authority exercising or having compulsory powers" and acquires replacement land. "Authority" is defined in TCGA 1992 s 243(5) to mean a person or body of persons with compulsory purchase powers.

2 In the Inland Revenue's view, relief under s 247 may be claimed by a landlord—subject to the general conditions of the section—where a tenant exercises the following rights to acquire an interest in the tenanted property from the landlord—

– the right to acquire the freehold reversion or an extension of the lease under the Leasehold Reform Act 1967 or the Leasehold Reform, Housing & Urban Development Act 1993; or
– the right to buy or to acquire the freehold or an extension of the lease under the Housing Acts 1985 to 1996 or the right to purchase tenanted property under the Housing (Scotland) Act 1987.

Commentary—*Simon's Direct Tax Service* **C2.1116**.
Revenue interpretation—Compulsory acquisition of freehold or extension of lease by tenant: tenant's right to buy: statement of practice SP 13/93—TCGA 1992 s 247.
Notes—This statement supersedes SP 7/90. The text of this statement is as it appears in IR 131 (August 2002).

SP 14/93 (30 November 1993) *Valuation of oil disposed of otherwise than at arm's length: Oil Taxation Act 1975 Sch 3 para 2*

Note—Statements relating to PRT are reproduced in Part 3 of this publication.

SP 15/93 *Business tax computations rounded to nearest £1,000*

1 The Revenue are prepared to accept computations of business profits for tax purposes in figures rounded to the nearest £1,000 from single businesses or companies with an annual turnover of not less than £5 million, where rounding at least to that extent has been used in preparing their accounts. (The turnover of members of a group will not be aggregated for applying this £5 million threshold.) Where turnover fluctuates either side of the threshold, rounding can be used for a period of account if the turnover for either that year or the immediately previous year is above the limit. (Turnover comprises gross receipts including investment and estate income, as well as trading receipts.)

2 The Revenue will only accept rounding in any particular case if the basis adopted is satisfactory. Rounded computations from such businesses must be accompanied by a certificate made by the person preparing the computations which:

– states the basis on which the rounding has been done;

SPs

- confirms that this basis is unbiased, that it has been applied consistently and that it has been used in a manner which, in all the circumstances, produces a fair result for tax purposes; and
- if the rounding was done by computer, states the program or software used.

In subsequent years if there have been no changes in the basis or in the software, the certificate need only confirm that the rounding has been done on the same basis as before.

3 The Revenue are prepared to accept rounded figures only in relation to the computation of the profits of the business, including in the case of companies, non-Case I items. They cannot accept rounded figures in relation to the computation of tax payable or of any other figure of tax.

4 Nor can they accept rounded figures, in relation to any other aspect of the tax computations, where rounding would impede the proper application of the relevant legislation or where it would normally be necessary to go back to the underlying records to do the computation, and thus there would be no reduction in the compliance burden in allowing the use of round sums. Rounding is not therefore acceptable in:

- computations of chargeable gains (since precise dates on which expenditure is incurred are needed for indexation allowance purposes); rounding can however be accepted in relation to the incidental costs of acquisition and disposal;
- computations of tax credit relief: while individual items of foreign income (including profits of overseas branches and, for the purpose of calculating underlying tax rates, dividends paid by overseas companies and the profits of those companies) may be rounded, computations of credit relief must continue to distinguish the individual items of income and to show the exact amounts of foreign tax for which credit is claimed so that the rules for limiting the credit can be properly applied;
- computations required for purposes of the Accrued Income Scheme (TA 1988 ss 710–728);
- aspects of capital allowances computations where precise figures are required, for example by the statute or where rounding might work unfairly because more than one taxpayer is involved and different bases could be used by each. One case where the statute requires the use of precise figures is the expensive car provisions in CAA 1990 ss 34–36 [see now CAA 2001, Pt 2, Ch 8]. However in any capital allowances apportionment case it would be open to the taxpayer to demonstrate to the Inspector that, taking all the circumstances into account, including those of any other party, the use of rounded figures did not lead to a result that was materially different from the statutory position. For example, in the case of the industrial builders one-quarter rule (CAA 1990 s 18(7); [CAA 2001 s 283]), the Inspector would want to be satisfied that the use of rounding alone did not reduce the non-qualifying expenditure to one-quarter or less of the total expenditure (and thereby enable the whole of the expenditure to attract allowances);
- the application of the statutory amount in TA 1988 s 748(i)(*d*) in relation to a controlled foreign company.

5 Exceptionally other circumstances may arise where rounding would not satisfy the tests in para 4. In those circumstances the Inspector may insist that roundings are not used.

6 These arrangements will continue into Pay and File. Subject to the exceptions provided in the two previous paragraphs, rounded figures from the accounts may be used in the computation of trading profits and losses, each category of income, management expenses and charges. Where appropriate, these figures will of course require adjustment to the "received" or "paid" basis. Group relief or relief for losses from other periods should be on the actual sums surrendered or brought forward (or carried back). No rounding should take place in the return form itself (for example, in the allocation of profits to financial years) or in any arithmetic that precedes such entries (for example, a computation of marginal small companies relief).

7 Where arrangements on the use of rounding have already been agreed locally with inspectors these may continue to operate in the short term, but must come to an end for all periods ending after 31 May 1995.

Commentary—*Simon's Direct Tax Service* **B3.903B**.

SP 1/94 (17 February 1994) *Non-statutory lump sum redundancy payments*

1 ITEPA 2003 s 309(1), (2) provides that statutory redundancy payments shall be exempt from income tax as employment income, with the exception of any liability under s 401 of that Act.

2 Lump sum payments made under a non-statutory scheme, in addition to, or instead of statutory redundancy pay, will also be liable to income tax only under ITEPA 2003 s 401 provided they are genuinely made solely on account of redundancy as defined in the Employment Rights Act 1996. This will be so whether the scheme is a standing one which forms part of the terms on which the employees give their services or whether it is an ad hoc scheme devised to meet a specific situation such as the imminent closure of a particular factory.

3 However, payments made under a non-statutory scheme which are not genuinely made to compensate for loss of employment through redundancy may be liable to tax in full. In particular, payments which are, in reality, a form of terminal bonus will be chargeable to income tax as earnings under ITEPA 2003 s 62. Payments made for meeting production targets or doing extra work in the period leading up to redundancy are examples of such terminal bonuses. Payments conditional on continued service in the employment for a time will also represent terminal bonuses if calculated by reference to any additional period served following issue of the redundancy notice.

4 The Revenue is concerned to distinguish between payments under non-statutory schemes which are genuinely made to compensate for loss of employment through redundancy and payments which are made as a reward for services in the employment or more generally for having acted as or having been an employee. As arrangements for redundancy can often be complex and provide for a variety of payments, it follows that each scheme must be considered on its own facts. The Revenue's practice, in these circumstances, is to allow employers to submit proposed schemes to their inspectors of taxes for advance clearance.

5 An employer or any other person operating a redundancy scheme, who wishes to be satisfied that lump sum payments under a scheme will be accepted as liable to tax only under ITEPA 2003 s 401 should submit the full facts to the inspector for consideration. Applications for clearance should be made in writing and should be accompanied by the scheme document together with the text of any intended letter to employees which explains its terms.

Commentary—*Simon's Direct Tax Service* **E4.327, 805B**.
Statement of Practice SP 13/91—para 10 redundancy payment for redundancy caused by accident.
Note—The Revenue's practice was revised following the decision of the House of Lords in *Mairs v Haughey* [1993] STC 569, and this statement replaced SP 1/81. This statement was revised in IR 131 (August 2003).

SP 2/94 (14 September 1995) *Enterprise investment scheme and venture capital trust scheme: location of activity*

Commentary—*Simon's Direct Tax Service* **E3.121, 623**.
Note—This statement was superseded by SP 7/98.

SP 3/94 (14 September 1995) *Business expansion scheme, enterprise investment scheme, CGT reinvestment relief and venture capital trust scheme: loans to investors*

Commentary—*Simon's Direct Tax Service* **E3.134, 232, 641**.
Note—This statement was superseded by SP 6/98.

SP 4/94 (17 May 1994) *Enhanced stock dividends received by trustees of interest in possession trusts*

1 This statement of practice sets out the Revenue's views on the tax treatment of enhanced stock dividends received by trustees of trusts in which there is an interest in possession—that is, trusts where one or more beneficiaries have a right to the whole of the income of the trust as it arises. Paragraphs 19–20 deal with the position of Scottish trusts.

2 A company may offer its shareholders the option of taking additional shares rather than a cash dividend. Such issues of shares are described in the statute as stock dividends, although they are also commonly known as scrip dividends. Where the number of shares issued is deliberately set so that their market value exceeds the cash alternative, the issue is known as an enhanced stock dividend (or enhanced scrip dividend).

3 On the principles derived from *IRC v Blott* (8 TC 101), an issue of non-redeemable shares is not a distribution for the purposes of TA 1988 s 209. This means that the shares are received without any sort of tax credit. However, TA 1988 s 249 treats certain recipients of stock dividends within s 249(1) as having received on the due date of issue an amount of income which, if reduced by an amount equal to income tax on that income at the Schedule F ordinary rate, would be equal to the "appropriate amount in cash". This is defined as either—

– the relevant cash dividend; or, if substantially greater or less,
– in the case of a company listed on the Stock Exchange Daily Official List, the market value of the share capital on the date of first dealing, and in other cases on the date of issue.

4 TA 1988 s 249 can apply to an enhanced stock dividend received by trustees of an interest in possession trust ("the trustees") only where the beneficiary with an interest in possession ("the beneficiary") is beneficially entitled to it so that s 249(4) applies (see para 8 below).

5 Where the trustees take an enhanced stock dividend they must consider whether, as a matter of trust law, it should be regarded as income or capital, taking account of—

– all the relevant facts;
– any specific provision in the trust deed.

6 The Revenue can offer no guidance about the application of trust law in any particular case. However, the Revenue will accept whichever of the three approaches described in this statement of

SPs

practice the trustees conclude that they should adopt, provided that their conclusion is supportable on the facts of their particular case.

7 The tax treatment of enhanced stock dividends received by the trustees follows from the trust law position. This statement of practice sets out the tax consequences if an enhanced stock dividend—

- is regarded as income; or
- is regarded as capital; or
- is regarded as capital but the trustees make a payment to the beneficiary in accordance with *Re Malam, Malam v Hitchens* (1894) 3 Ch 578.

(I) ENHANCED STOCK DIVIDEND REGARDED AS INCOME

8 If the enhanced stock dividend is regarded as income the beneficiary is beneficially entitled to the shares comprised in the dividend and TA 1988 s 249(4) applies. The beneficiary is treated as having received income of an amount which, when reduced by an amount equal to income tax at the Schedule F ordinary rate, is equal to the "appropriate amount in cash". No repayment of this tax can be made. The beneficiary has no further income tax to pay if he is a basic rate taxpayer. A higher rate taxpayer has an extra liability equal to the difference between the Schedule F ordinary rate and the Schedule F upper rate on the income that he is treated as having received.

9 For capital gains tax (CGT) purposes, TCGA 1992 s 142 applies. The issue is not a reorganisation. The beneficiary is treated as having acquired the shares for the "appropriate amount in cash". Under TCGA 1992 s 60 any formal transfer by the trustees to the beneficiary is disregarded. If they sell the stock dividend on his behalf, it is treated as a sale by the beneficiary.

(II) ENHANCED STOCK DIVIDEND REGARDED AS CAPITAL

10 If the enhanced stock dividend is regarded as capital there is no income tax liability as TA 1988 s 249(4) does not apply.

11 For CGT purposes, the issue is a reorganisation within TCGA 1992 s 126. The consequences are as follows—

- the newly issued shares are pooled with the shares in respect of which they were issued ("the original shares") to form the new holding;
- the new holding and the original shares are treated as the same asset, acquired when the original shares were acquired (TCGA 1992 s 127).

12 The trustees are not regarded as having made any payment for the shares. Because the reorganisation rules apply, the date of acquisition is the date on which the original shares were acquired.

(III) ENHANCED STOCK DIVIDEND REGARDED AS CAPITAL BUT WITH AN ADJUSTING PAYMENT TO THE BENEFICIARY WITH AN INTEREST IN POSSESSION

13 The trustees may decide that where—

- they have elected to take an enhanced stock dividend in preference to a cash dividend that would have belonged to the beneficiary; and
- the enhanced stock dividend is regarded as capital under trust law

the beneficiary is entitled to some compensation from the trustees for the cash dividend forgone.

14 In these circumstances the tax position of the trustees is as set out in section II above. The payment they make to the beneficiary is an annual payment and tax must be deducted from it at the basic rate in accordance with TA 1988 s 349(1). No income tax is treated as having been paid in respect of the enhanced stock dividend, whether by virtue of a tax credit or otherwise, so the trustees have to account to the Revenue for the whole of the basic rate tax deducted from the payment.

15 The beneficiary is treated as receiving income taxable under Schedule D Case III on which income tax at the basic rate has been paid.

16 This treatment applies whether the payment is made—

- out of the proceeds of the disposal of shares comprised in the enhanced stock dividend;
- out of other capital of the trust;
- in the form of a proportion of shares comprised in the enhanced stock dividend. (TA 1988 s 249(4) does not apply in these circumstances because the beneficiary is not beneficially entitled to the stock dividend.)

17 Whatever form the payment takes, the trustees are treated as having made an annual payment and the beneficiary as having received a net sum after deduction of income tax at the basic rate.

18 For CGT purposes, the treatment described in paras 11, 12 above applies. Where the trustees make the payment to the beneficiary in the form of shares, the transfer constitutes a part-disposal of the new holding.

SCOTTISH INTEREST IN POSSESSION TRUSTS

19 The same income tax treatment applies to Scottish trusts in which a beneficiary has a right to income. Although under Scots law the rights of the income beneficiary are different from those of a beneficiary with an interest in possession in an English trust, for income tax purposes the beneficiary of a Scottish trust is treated as having the same rights by virtue of FA 1993 s 118.

20 (This para reflects the changes in FA 1998) For CGT purposes, where the enhanced stock dividend is dealt with as described in section I above (enhanced stock dividend regarded as income), the position of a Scottish trust is different from that of an English trust. Under Scots law the beneficiary is not absolutely entitled to the enhanced stock dividend. However, since TA 1988 s 249(4) applies to the stock dividend (by virtue of FA 1993 s 118), the trustees are treated as having given ''the appropriate amount in cash'' (see para 8 above) as consideration for the new holding by virtue of TCGA 1992 s 141. This is not a reorganisation. If the enhanced stock dividend is transferred to the beneficiary the trustees make a disposal to the beneficiary, which by reason of the share identification rules in TCGA 1992 s 106A, would normally be a disposal of the shares acquired as a stock dividend.

Commentary—*Simon's Direct Tax Service* **C4.253**.
Note—The text of this statement is as it appears in IR 131 (August 2003).

SP 5/94 (20 July 1994) *Associated companies for small companies' relief and corporation tax starting rate: holding companies*

Under TA 1988 s 13(4), a company which does not carry on any trade or business in an accounting period is disregarded in calculating the profits limits for the small companies' relief of any other company with which it is associated.

A holding company which does not carry on a trade, but which holds the shares in one or more companies which are its 51 per cent subsidiaries, may or may not be carrying on a business in respect of that holding. The Revenue's view is that a company is not carrying on such a business in an accounting period if, throughout that period, all of the following apply—

- it has no assets other than shares in companies which are its 51 per cent subsidiaries; and
- it is not entitled to a deduction, as charges or management expenses, in respect of any outgoings; and
- it has no income or gains other than dividends which it has distributed in full to its shareholders and which are, or could be, franked investment income received by that company (TA 1988 s 832(1), (4A)); and
- the 51 per cent subsidiaries are 51 per cent subsidiaries under TA 1988 s 247(8), (8A) and (9A) [13ZA(1)–(4)].

Commentary—*Simon's Direct Tax Service* **D2.109**.
Note—This text of this statement is as it appears in IR 131 (August 2002).

SP 6/94 (4 August 1994) *Capital allowances: notification of expenditure on machinery and plant made outside the normal time limit*

1 FA 1994 s 118(3), (4) introduced time limits for notifying qualifying expenditure on machinery and plant. The Board of Inland Revenue have power under s 118(5) to extend these limits in exceptional circumstances. This statement explains the general criteria which the Board will apply in considering applications for extended time limits.

THE NOTIFICATION RULES

2 For corporation tax cases, and also for income tax cases for years of assessment until 1995–96, the relevant conditions for notifying qualifying expenditure are fulfilled where—

- for chargeable periods ending on or after 30 November 1993, notice of expenditure is given to the inspector, in such form as the Board may require, not later than two years after the end of that period;
- for chargeable periods ending before 30 November 1993—
  - (*a*) the expenditure was included in a computation which—
    - (i) was required to be made for any tax purpose;
    - (ii) was given before that date to the inspector; and

SPs

(iii) was not contained in a document prepared primarily for a purpose which was not a tax purpose; or

(*b*) notice of the expenditure is given to the inspector, in such form as the Board may require, not later than three years after the end of that period or;

(*c*) if the chargeable period ends on or after 1 December 1990, notice of the expenditure is given before 3 May 1994.

3 For income tax cases for 1996–97 and any earlier years dealt with under self assessment the time limit is 31 January following the first anniversary of the end of the year of assessment in which the period of account ends.

4 In the event that the above time limits have not been met, the capital allowances due on the past expenditure will not usually be lost. These will normally be claimable in the first period for which the time limit has not expired. No relief will be available for assets which have been sold prior to notification.

FORM OF NOTIFICATION REQUIRED BY THE BOARD

5 In view of the great variety of circumstances, the Board do not propose to specify in detail the form notifications should take. Generally, the requirement to notify the inspector will be satisfied where the expenditure is included in a computation prepared for any tax purpose (provided the time limits set out earlier are met). However, it will be advisable to give enough information in the computations to identify the asset for which notification is given, as well as the amount of the expenditure. This does not mean that it will be necessary to list each and every item where large numbers of similar assets are purchased.

6 Where the expenditure is included within the calculation of taxable trading profit (ie as revenue expenditure) but is subsequently recategorised as being expenditure on machinery and plant, the original tax computation will be regarded as notice for the purposes of the new rules.

7 Inclusion of expenditure in a document prepared primarily other than for tax purposes (eg annual accounts of a business, valuation reports, quantity surveyors' reports etc) will not satisfy the requirement.

BOARD'S POLICY ON EXTENDING TIME LIMITS

8 The time limits allowed for giving written notification of qualifying expenditure on machinery and plant described above should generally be adequate and the Board will not make routine use of its powers to extend the notification period outside of these limits. But there may be exceptional circumstances in which notification cannot be made within the time specified. Applications to allow further time in accordance with the power referred to at para 1 above will be considered under the following criteria.

9 In general terms the Board's policy will be to extend the notification time limit only where there is good reason, arising out of circumstances beyond the taxpayer's and his agent's control, why notification could not be given within the statutory time limits.

10 Sometimes a large construction project involving expenditure on a variety of assets, including machinery and plant, extends over several years and it is impossible to complete the final allocation of expenditure between different classes of asset when the normal time limit expires. In such cases, the Board will accept a refinement of the allocation of the overall expenditure between machinery and plant and other assets after the time limit has passed provided—

- reasonable estimates have been made of the expenditure attributable to machinery and plant within the time limit; and
- there is no undue delay in finalising the details.

11 The application for extension and notification of the expenditure involved must be made within a reasonable period (normally not more than three months) after the expiry of the circumstances giving rise to the late notification.

12 What constitute acceptable reasons for late notification will depend upon the particular circumstances of each individual case. Such circumstances do not include the following—

- oversight or negligence on the part of the taxpayer or his agent;
- delay, whether due to pressure of work, the complexity of the facts or to other causes except where the circumstances come within para 9 above;
- the taxpayer was absent or ill, unless—
  - the absence or illness arose at a critical time and prevented the giving of notification within the normal time limit; and
  - there was good reason why notification was not given before the time of the absence or illness; and
  - in the case of absence, there was a good reason why the taxpayer was unavailable; and
  - there was no other person who could have given notification on the taxpayer's behalf within the normal time limit.

PROCEDURE

13 The application to extend the notification period outside the statutory time limits should be sent to the inspector dealing with the taxpayer and must include an explanation as to why notification could not have been given within the statutory time limit.

TMA 1970 S 43A

14 There is a general provision in TMA 1970 s 43A which may extend the time limit for giving a notice where a tax liability arises under an assessment which is made late. The s 43A time limit is one year from the end of the chargeable period in which the assessment is made.
15 It should be noted that—

– section 43A does not apply where the assessment is made to recover tax lost to the Crown because of fraudulent or negligent conduct;
– a notice given within the s 43A time limit cannot reduce the tax due beyond the amount due under the late assessment.

Commentary—*Simon's Direct Tax Service* **B2.333**.
Note—The text of this statement is as it appears in IR 131 (January 2000). See also the IR Tax Bulletin, June 1998, p 551.

SP 7/94 (15 September 1994) *Investment trusts investing in authorised unit trusts*

Note—This statement is superseded by SP 3/97 from 18 July 1997.

SP 8/94 (16 September 1994): *Allowable expenditure—expenses incurred by personal representatives and corporate trustees* (see also SP 7/81)

EXPENSES INCURRED BY PERSONAL REPRESENTATIVES

1 Following discussion with representative bodies, the scale of expenses allowable under TCGA 1992 s 38(1)(*b*), for the costs of establishing title in computing the gains or losses of personal representatives on the sale of assets comprised in a deceased person's estate, has been revised. The Board of Inland Revenue will accept computations based on this scale or on the *actual* allowable expenditure incurred.

2 The revised scale is as follows—

Gross value of estate	*Allowable expenditure*
A Up to £40,000	1·75 per cent of the probate value of the assets sold by the personal representatives.
B Between £40,001 and £70,000	A fixed amount of £700, to be divided between all the assets of the estate in proportion to the probate values and allowed in those proportions on assets sold by the personal representatives.
C Between £70,001 and £300,000	1 per cent of the probate value of the assets sold.
D Between £300,001 and £400,000	A fixed amount of £3,000, to be divided as at B above.
E Between £400,001 and £750,000	0·75 per cent of the probate value of the assets sold.

3 The scale does not extend to gross estates exceeding £750,000 where the allowable expenditure is to be negotiated according to the facts of the particular case by the inspector and the taxpayer.
4 The revised scale takes effect where death occurred after 5 April 1993.

EXPENSES INCURRED BY CORPORATE TRUSTEES

5 Following discussion with representative bodies, the Revenue have agreed the following scale of allowable expenditure under TCGA 1992 ss 38, 64(1)(*b*), for expenses incurred by corporate trustees in the administration of estates and trusts. The Board of Inland Revenue will accept computations based either on this scale or on the *actual* allowable expenditure incurred.

6 The scale is as follows—

(a) Transfers of assets to beneficiaries etc

(i) Quoted stocks and shares	
(A) One beneficiary	£20·00 per holding
(B) More than one beneficiary between whom a holding must be divided	As (A), to be divided in equal shares between the beneficiaries

SPs

(ii) Unquoted shares	As (i) above, with the addition of any exceptional expenditure
(iii) Other assets	As (i) above, with the addition of any exceptional expenditure

(b) Actual disposals and acquisitions

(i) Quoted stocks and shares	The investment fee as charged by the trustee
(ii) Unquoted shares	As (i) above, plus actual valuation costs
(iii) Other assets	The investment fee as charged by the trustee, subject to a maximum of £60, plus actual valuation costs

Where a comprehensive annual management fee is charged, covering both the cost of administering the trust and the expenses of actual disposals and acquisitions, the investment fee for the purposes of (i), (ii) and (iii) above will be taken to be £0·25 per £100 on the sale or purchase moneys.

(c) Deemed disposals by trustees

(i) Quoted stocks and shares	£6 per holding
(ii) Unquoted shares	Actual valuation costs
(iii) Other assets	Actual valuation costs

7 This scale takes effect for acquisitions and disposals, or deemed disposals, by corporate trustees after 5 April 1993.

Commentary—*Simon's Direct Tax Service* **C2.207, 208.**
Note—This statement replaces SP 7/81. The text of this statement is as it appears in IR 131 (November 1996).

SP 9/94 (20 December 1994) *Application of foreign exchange and financial instruments legislation to partnerships which include companies*

Commentary—*Simon's Direct Tax Service* **B3.1711**.
Note—This statement is superseded by SP 4/98 which took effect for accounting periods ending after 31 March 1996.

SP 1/95 (30 January 1995) *Interest payable in the UK*

Concession C26—Interest payable in the UK—now obsolescent.
Note—This statement took effect from 30 January 1995 and revised statement of practice C5. This statement no longer applies in respect of TA 1998 s 349 (3)(*a*) to interest paid on or after 29 April 1996. In respect of TA 1998 ss 337(3), 338(3)(*b*) it no longer applies to accounting periods ending after 1 April 1996.

SP 2/95 (7 February 1995) *Payment of tax credits to non-resident companies*

Commentary—*Simon's Direct Tax Service* **D1.413**.
Note—This statement was classified as obsolete in IR 131 (August 2003).

SP 3/95 (21 March 1995) *Definition of financial trader for the purposes of FA 1994 s 177(1)*

Note—This statement of practice has been replaced by SP 4/02.

SP 4/95 (22 March 1995) *Long-term insurance business: computations of profits for tax purposes*

1 This statement sets out the approach that the Revenue adopts to the computation of the trading profit of companies and friendly societies carrying on long-term insurance business when those insurers draw up their accounts in accordance with company law implementing the EC's Insurance Accounts Directive (the IAD). It applies to any computation made in accordance with the statutory provisions applicable to Schedule D Case I. It is not concerned with the measurement of income, capital gains or expenses in the so-called "I minus E" computation.

Note—The IAD was implemented in UK law by the Companies Act 1985 (Insurance Companies Accounts) Regulations, SI 1993/3246, the Insurance Accounts Directive (Miscellaneous Insurance Undertakings) Regulations, SI 1993/3245, and the Friendly Societies (Accounts and Related Provisions) Regulations, SI 1994/1983.

2 The normal starting point for a computation of trading profits for tax purposes is the balance of profit or loss disclosed by a set of accounts drawn up in accordance with the ordinary principles of commercial accounting. For periods of account beginning after 6 April 1999, there is an additional requirement that the profits must be computed on an accounting basis which gives a true and fair view, subject to any adjustment required or authorised by law—FA 1998 s 42. Section 42 is amended by FA 2002 s 103 to clarify that the true and fair view must be one that is shown by the use of UK generally accepted accounting practice. Before the adoption of the IAD, the absence of a profit or loss in the accounts of companies carrying on long-term insurance business made a different approach necessary, and the convention of using the actuarial surplus as a substitute for the commercial profit has been firmly established for many years.

3 We have received legal advice to the effect that, in relation to life assurance and life annuity business, this convention is implicit in the special statutory rules relating to life assurance business, and in particular in FA 1989 s 83. Accordingly, when it is necessary for any purpose to compute—

- the profits from life assurance business in accordance with Case I rules, or
- the Case VI profits of pension business, ISA business, overseas life assurance business, or life reinsurance business in accordance with Case I principles,

we shall continue to base the computation on that part of the total actuarial surplus for the period that relates to the business in question, although we recognise that in many cases this surplus will not be apparent from the face of the regulatory return and will have to be constructed from the various elements that make it up. In general the treatment of particular items in the published accounts in the IAD format will have no direct bearing on their treatment for tax purposes.

4 Different considerations apply, however, to the *other classes of long-term business*. Here, our legal advice is that once a figure of profit is available from a set of accounts drawn up in accordance with an accepted accounting method that follows the ordinary principles of commercial accounting then, subject to any adjustment required as authorised by law, that figure must be used as the starting point for the Case I computation. This will be so whether or not a separate profit and loss account is prepared for this part of the business.

5 This paragraph explains our view of the way in which the tax computations for long-term business other than life assurance should be derived from the accounting profit described in para 4 above. It is based on the proposition (which the Inland Revenue believes to be correct) that accounts drawn up in accordance with the Companies Act 1985 Sch 9A and the Statement of Recommended Practice ''Accounting for insurance business'' issued by the Association of British Insurers in December 1998 fulfil the requirements of FA 1998 s 42.

- Normally an insurance company carries on a single trade, so strictly there should be a single computation for the whole of the company's business other than life assurance business. There will be no objection in practice to companies preparing separate computations for, say, pre-1938 capital redemption business, permanent health insurance, pension fund management, and any general insurance business which the company may conduct; but the results of these separate computations must then be combined, if necessary with the result of any general insurance business, to determine the overall figure of profit or loss from insurance business other than life assurance business.
- Where it is necessary to make a division of the profit of the whole long-term business the division should, so far as possible, be made on a factual basis so that, for example, premiums referable to permanent health insurance are allocated to that business. Where this is not possible, a reasonable method of apportionment should be adopted. But the total amount of the investment return from the assets of the long-term business fund to be attributed to business other than life assurance business should be determined in accordance with the statutory rules in TA 1988 s 432A.
- Gains and losses from loan relationships, financial instruments (for periods beginning before October 2002) and derivative contracts (for periods on or after that date) should be included in accordance with the relevant accounting method. Until July 2001 the Inland Revenue took the view that in relation to other investments, any profit on the sale of which would fall to be included in the company's trading receipts, only realised gains should be brought into account. On 1 August 2001 the Inland Revenue press release ''Tax and accounting—changes in law and practice'', together with draft clauses published on 9 August 2001, made it clear that where such investments are accounted for using a mark to market basis in which the unrealised profits and losses are taken into account in the company's technical or non-technical account, no adjustment is authorised by law to remove those unrealised gains and losses from the Case I profit figure. The legislation contained in those draft clauses was enacted as FA 2002 ss 65, 66.
- FA 2002 s 65 provides that the previous basis would continue to be sanctioned for all periods of account up to the one in which 1 August 2001 falls. But companies may use mark to market for tax purposes if they wish. Whichever basis is used, the appropriate part of the investment gains from all assets backing the long-term business should be included, regardless of whether these are credited in the ''technical'' or ''non-technical'' part of the profit and loss account.

FA 2002 s 66 permits an insurance company to elect to retain the old basis for assets held on 1 January 2002. Where a company carries on both PHI business and general insurance business, the election may be made only in respect of general business assets. Where this is the case, PHI assets will be accounted for for tax purposes on a mark to market basis, whenever they were acquired.

- The deferral of acquisition costs that is required by the Directive (as implemented in the UK) should be followed in the profit computation.

- Where, unusually, permanent health insurance is written on a with-profits basis no deduction is available for bonuses, following the case of *Last v London Assurance* (2 TC 100). Nor is any deduction available for provisions for future bonuses.
- Movements in reserves held within the long-term funds that are properly regarded as reserves rather than provisions should be excluded from the tax computation, whether or not the movements are dealt with through the ''fund for future appropriations'' in the balance sheet. In the Revenue view contingency, closed fund, resilience and similar reserves which may be included in the statutory liabilities for solvency purposes should normally be regarded as reserves rather than provisions. It will be a question of fact in each case as to what extent such reserves relate to long-term business other than life assurance.

6 Where companies write the type of business known as ''deposit administration'' it will be necessary to determine whether this falls to be treated as life assurance business or as the type of pension fund management that is deemed to be (long-term) insurance business by the Insurance Companies Act 1982 s 95. Following the Privy Council decision in *Colonial Life Insurance Company (Trinidad) Ltd v Board of Inland Revenue* ([1991] STC 503) it seems likely that many deposit administration contracts will properly be classified as contracts for life annuities, so that they should be included in life assurance business. (Contracts of this type will also fall to be included in pension business where they are made with the trustees or administrators of approved pension schemes, provided that the other statutory conditions are met.) But where it is agreed that a deposit administration contract, or any other contract, merely provides for the management of the funds of a pension scheme any method which a company has agreed with its inspector for identifying the profit derived from the business need not be disturbed, so long as it continues to give a reasonable result.

7 The practice set out in this statement will be subject to review in the light of accounting developments. It should not be read as carrying any implications for the way in which the profits of a life office might be measured if the Government decides to introduce legislation designed to move away from the present ''I minus E'' basis of life assurance taxation.

Commentary—*Simon's Direct Tax Service* **D4.513**.
Note—The text of this statement is as it appears in IR 131 (August 2002).

SP 5/95 (31 March 1995) *Taxation of receipts of insurance and personal pension scheme commissions*

Note—This statement is superseded by SP 4/97 and was classified as obsolete by IR 131 Supp (November 1998).

SP 6/95 (31 March 1995) *Legal entitlement and administrative practices*

Where an assessment has been made and this shows a repayment due to the taxpayer, repayment is invariably made of the full amount. In self-assessment where any amount is repayable it will be repaid in full on request. Where the end of the year check applied to Schedule E taxpayers who have not had a tax return for the year in question shows an overpayment of £10 or less, the repayment is not made automatically.

As regards payment of tax assessed, where a payment to the Accounts Offices exceeds the amount due and the discrepancy is not noted before the payment has been processed, the excess is not repaid routinely by the computer system unless it exceeds £0.99, or where clerical intervention is required, unless it exceeds £9.99.

For inheritance tax (and capital transfer tax), assessments that lead to repayments of sums overpaid are not initiated automatically by the Capital Taxes Offices if the amount involved is £25 or less.

The aim of these tolerances is to minimise work which is highly cost-effective; they cannot operate to deny repayment to a taxpayer who claims it.

Commentary—*Simon's Direct Tax Service* **E4.974**.
Note—This statement replaces SP 1/80.

SP 7/95 (14 September 1995) *Venture capital trusts: value of "gross assets"*

Note—This statement applied in respect of holdings of shares issued before 6 April 1998 and was classified as obsolete in IR 131 (August 2002). For the statement concerning holdings of shares issued after 5 April 1998, see SP 5/98.

SP 8/95 (14 September 1995) *Venture capital trusts: default terms in loan agreements*

1 TA 1988 s 842AA(12)(*a*) provides that a loan made by a venture capital trust to a company will qualify as security for the purposes of s 842AA (and in the provisions of s 842 as they apply for the purposes of s 842AA) if certain conditions are met. In particular, the terms of the loan (whether secured or not) must not allow any person to require it to be repaid, or any stock or security relating to that loan to be re-purchased or redeemed, within the period of five years from the making of the loan or, as the case may be, the issue of the stock or security.

2 Provided that the loan is made on normal commercial terms, the Revenue will not regard a standard event of default clause in the loan agreement as a provision which would disqualify that loan from being a security within the meaning of s 842AA(12)(*a*). The purpose of such a clause is to afford protection to the lender by enabling redemption to be enforced in circumstances where the borrower defaults. Such a provision would not be regarded as being standard, however, if it entitled the lender, or a third party, to exercise any action which would cause the borrower to default.

SP 1/96 (1 February 1996) *Notification of chargeability to income tax and capital gains tax for tax years 1995–96 onwards*

INTRODUCTION

This statement sets out the Revenue's views on the changes to the obligation to notify chargeability to income tax and capital gains tax for tax years 1995–96 onwards, which were introduced by FA 1994. The changes affect all taxpayers, but have a particular impact on directors, employees and other persons, such as those receiving pensions, who have PAYE income. That is why the statement concentrates mainly on that area.

BACKGROUND

Present position—general

1 The obligation to notify chargeability to income tax to the Revenue applies to a person for any tax year for which he or she has not been required to complete a tax return by the Revenue within 12 months after the end of the tax year. (There is a similar obligation for capital gains tax.) A tax year begins on the 6 April and ends on 5 April.

2 Shortly after the end of any tax year the Revenue send returns to those known or likely to have income or gains which have not been taxed in full. Those who receive returns have no separate obligation to notify chargeability. But there will be some people who have not received a return who have income or gains which have not been taxed in full. Such individuals are required to notify chargeability.

3 The present obligation to notify chargeability to income tax is under TMA 1970 s 7 which requires individuals who have not received tax returns within 12 months from the end of the tax year to notify the Revenue within that time that they are chargeable to income tax and specify each separate source of income. The requirement does not apply to certain sources, for example where a source only produces taxed income and there is no higher rate liability. The obligation to notify liability to capital gains tax is under TMA 1970 s 11A. Where there is a failure to notify chargeability to income or capital gains tax, a penalty not exceeding the amount of tax due can be sought. But the penalty may be reduced in any particular case.

Present position—income from employments etc

4 The Revenue send tax returns to employees and pensioners on a selective basis. This is because most obtain the benefit of all the reliefs due to them and pay tax on all of their income automatically, through the PAYE system and the taxation of interest and dividends at source and through MIRAS.

5 TMA 1970 s 7 provides that employees and pensioners who do not receive a tax return do not have to notify a source such as a specific employment for a particular tax year if they know all the income from it has been taken into account in making deductions through PAYE. Income includes items such as benefits in kind and expenses payments, as well as wages or salaries. Thus, for example, an employee who receives benefits in any tax year which are taken into account in the code number for that year which is operated in respect of the wages or salary will not have to notify the source. And there is no requirement to notify sources such as national insurance benefits and minor amounts of Schedule D income which are effectively taxed through the PAYE system by being taken into account in setting the PAYE code.

6 By the end of the 12 month period after any tax year persons within the PAYE system whose income is wholly or mainly within Schedule E and who have not received returns should normally know whether or not they need to notify chargeability. This is because any changes in circumstances affecting their liability for the year just ended which they or their employers have notified to the Revenue should be reflected in an assessment and/or in changes to their current and future PAYE code numbers. If for instance a person gets a new and continuing benefit in a tax year the employer should report it to the Revenue by 6 June after the end of the tax year (on form P11D) and the Revenue will usually issue an assessment. The current code number will be revised and, if the Revenue decide to collect the additional tax due for the year just ended through PAYE, the taxpayer will normally be aware of this also as he/she will receive a code number for the following year showing how the extra tax will be collected; the taxpayer will therefore know there is no need to notify chargeability in respect of income from the employment.

FA 1994—CHANGES

General

7 Under self-assessment, for tax year 1996–97 onwards, taxpayers who are sent returns at the normal time, shortly after the end of the tax year, will be required to file those returns by the following 31 January and, at the same time, to pay the balance of any income tax due for the year (unless the additional tax liability is to be collected through PAYE by a coding adjustment.)

8 Because of the new time limits for filing returns and paying tax, taxpayers will be required to notify chargeability no later than six months after the end of the tax year (that is by 5 October). This will allow a taxpayer who has not received a tax return to ask for one, if there is a need to notify chargeability, and to complete it and sent it back to the Revenue (with any payment needed) by the following 31 January. (The new time limit is introduced by FA 1994 Sch 19 para 1 which substitutes a new TMA 1970 s 7.) If a taxpayer wants the Revenue to calculate the tax liability, a return issued on or before 31 July after the end of the tax year has to be filed by 30 September. However a taxpayer can still require the Revenue to calculate the tax liability when a return is issued after 31 July, provided the return is filed by two months from the date of issue.

9 In self-assessment penalties for failure to notify chargeability will be based on the amount of tax that was unpaid at 31 January following the end of the tax year, which is the due date for the balance of tax due. This means that a person who does not notify chargeability within the six month period can reduce or eliminate any penalty by paying some or all the tax due by 31 January. And, as at present, where tax is due any penalties chargeable because of a failure to notify chargeability are mitigable by reference to the amount of tax unpaid, the nature of the disclosure and the level of co-operation given to the Revenue during the course of any resulting enquiry.

10 As now, people with income that is not PAYE income or with capital gains, will need to notify their chargeability to tax. There is likely to be little cause for doubt in their case whether they should notify chargeability. People setting up in business or newly receiving income other than from employment or making capital gains will know by the end of the tax year that they should complete a return for that year. If they do not receive one, they have six months to notify the Revenue of the position and ask for a return. It is not necessary for them to have worked out the amount of the income or gain by that time.

Directors, employees, pensioners etc

11 The change in the time limit for notifying chargeability to six months will have particular impact on those with PAYE income. Paragraph 6 above explained how, within the current 12 month period after any tax year, a taxpayer will normally be aware if liability on an untaxed item such as a new and continuing benefit will be dealt with through PAYE. But the change to a new six month limit means that within that period a taxpayer will not generally be in a position to know for certain whether the Revenue is aware of any changes in his circumstances for the tax year just ended or if his code number will be revised to take account of such changes. Any change to the current code number may have been made before 6 October after the end of the tax year, but the issue of a code change for the following year, to collect tax for the year just ended through PAYE, will not. However the new s 7(5) provides that an employee is relieved of an obligation to notify chargeability if income from a source has been or ''will be'' taxed through PAYE.

12 The PAYE regulations have been changed to give effect to the proposals in the Revenue consultative document ''Self-assessment—what it will mean for employers and employees'', published in May 1994. (The changes are in the Income Tax (Employments) (Amendment No 4) Regulations SI 1995/1284 which come into force on 6 April 1996.) Under the revised regulations those employees who are in employment on the last day of a tax year should be provided by the employer, by the following 6 July, with a copy of the information about expenses payments and benefits which is supplied to the Revenue on form P11D or equivalent. (Employees who left an employment during the course of a tax year can obtain a copy of the P11D information from the employer on request.)

13 Subject to paras 14 and 15 below, the Revenue will accept that employees who receive such a copy of the information on a P11D can assume any items on it which are not already taken into account for PAYE ''will be'' taken into account for PAYE, so that there is no need to notify chargeability because of them.

14 In assuming that chargeability need not be notified in respect of items on the P11D, employees will need to be satisfied the information on the P11D is correct and complete. There may be circumstances where employees are aware that, even though they have a copy of P11D information, the actual P11Ds have not been submitted to the Revenue; in such a case employees are not relieved of any obligation to notify chargeability.

15 There is still an obligation to notify chargeability in respect of any items not shown in the copy of the P11D information. And employees who have not received a copy of the P11D information from their employers, even though they believe a P11D was due, are not relieved of any obligation to notify chargeability. Employees cannot assume they are relieved of any obligation to notify chargeability because information may be supplied by employers to the Revenue on returns other than P11D, for example those in relation to share schemes.

16 In considering whether it was reasonable for an employee to consider that a notification of chargeability was not needed, the Revenue will take into account broadly the same factors as now, that is, where there has been an apparent failure, the Revenue will consider whether any explanation given by the employee is a ''reasonable excuse'' (TMA 1970 s 118), so that, in effect, there has been no failure.

17 Although, as explained at para 7 above, the first full year of self-assessment is tax year 1996–97, the new s 7 applies from tax year 1995–96. Thus the time limit for notifying chargeability for 1995–96 is 5 October 1996. The requirement for employers to provide employees with a copy of the information provided to the Revenue only comes into effect for 1996–97 and later years. Some employees may not receive such information for 1995–96. The Revenue will therefore take the absence of any such information into account as a mitigating factor in looking at any case where there is a failure to notify chargeability on P11D items by an employee for 1995–96.

Commentary—*Simon's Direct Tax Service* **E1.805**.
Note—The text of this statement is as shown in IR 131 (August 2003).

SP 2/96 (29 March 1996) *Pooled cars—incidental private use*

INTRODUCTION

1 This statement explains the Board of Inland Revenue's approach to the question whether any private use by an employee of a car made available by his or her employer is ''merely incidental to'' his or her business use of the car. The same approach is taken to vans.

LEGISLATION

2 No tax charge arises on a car made available by reason of an employment (a ''company car'') if it is a ''pooled car''. ITEPA 2003 s 167(3) [formerly TA 1988 s 159(2)] sets out the conditions which must all be satisfied for a car to qualify as a pooled car. ITEPA 2003 s 169 [formerly TA 1988 s 159 as applied by s 159AB] applies the same conditions for pooled vans.

3 The fourth of the five conditions is that any private use of the car or van by any employee to whom it is available is merely incidental to his or her other (ie business) use of the car or van in the tax year in question (ITEPA 2003 s 167(3)(*d*), 168(3)(*d*) [both formerly TA 1988 s 159(2)(*b*)).

BOARD'S INTERPRETATION

4 The Board have been advised that the expression ''merely incidental to'' requires consideration of whether—

(*a*) the private use of the car is independent of the employee's business use of the car (in which case it is not ''merely incidental'' to it) or

(*b*) the private use follows from the business use (in which case it is).

5 This is a qualitative test which means it is necessary to look at the nature of private use, over the year, by each employee who uses the car.

JOURNEYS STARTING FROM HOME

6 A simple example of the test is where an employee takes a car home in order to make an early start on a business journey the following morning. Where that business journey could not reasonably be undertaken the next day starting from the normal place of work then the journey from work to home, although private, is merely incidental to the business use of the car.

USE WHILE AWAY FROM HOME ON BUSINESS

7 Another example is an employee who is staying away from home overnight on a business trip. She uses the car to go to a nearby restaurant in the evening. This use, while it may not be necessary, can be regarded as merely incidental to the necessary business journey and overnight stay.

AMOUNT OF PRIVATE USE

8 In practice the Inland Revenue find that private use of a car which they accept is a pooled car is usually small in comparison with its business use. But this does not mean a proportion of purely private use can always be allowed. For example, use of a car for an annual holiday would *not* be merely incidental to the business use of the car, even if that use was only small in comparison with the employees' business travel in the car in the year in question.

CARS WITH DRIVERS

9 Particular questions arise where a car and driver are available to employees.

10 First the car and driver may be used to take employees between home and work in order for the employee to work in the car on confidential papers. Travel between home and work is usually private. Working in the car during the journey does not change that. But the Inland Revenue's practice has hitherto been to accept that all such journeys, while private could be merely incidental to the business use of the car *without* regard to the frequency or length of such journeys or the employees' other use of the car.

11 The Inland Revenue now take the view that the fact an employee is carrying confidential papers on which he or she may be working is only one of the factors to be considered, along with others, when deciding whether a journey is private or business; and, if private, whether or not that private use is merely incidental to its business use. It may be relevant where, for example, papers have to be delivered to a client or are needed for a meeting at the employee's home. It may also be relevant where the private use is otherwise close to the limits of what would be accepted as merely incidental use. But carrying such papers and working in the car neither changes a private journey into a business journey nor guarantees its use is merely incidental to the employee's other, business use of the car.

12 Second, a person employed as a chauffeur to drive a pooled car may be obliged to take the car to his home for retention overnight. The chauffeur's use of the car for this purpose does not of itself disqualify the car from treatment as a pooled car. This has been the Inland Revenue's practice since 1976 and will continue to be the practice. This is on the basis that such use is necessary in the performance of the duties of a chauffeur who is required to take a car home in order to collect or deliver passengers from or to various locations.

COMMENCEMENT

13 The statement of practice will be applied in this form for 2002–03 and subsequent years of assessment. It originally applied from 1996–97 when it referred to the previous legislation.

Commentary—*Simon's Direct Tax Service* **E4.630A**.
Note—This statement was revised in IR 131 (August 2003).

SP 3/96 (4 April 1996) *ITEPA 2003 ss 225–226—termination payments made in settlement of employment claims*

1 ITEPA 2003 s 225 imposes a charge as earnings from employment on payments made to individuals for undertakings, given in connection with an employment, which restrict their conduct or activities.

2 A financial settlement relating to the termination of an employment may contain terms whereby the employee agrees to accept the termination package in full and final settlement of his or her claims relating to the employment, and/or may expressly provide that the employee should not commence or, if already commenced, should discontinue legal proceedings in respect of those claims. These may relate to claims at common law arising from the contract of employment or to claims arising under employment protection or other legislation. The settlement, therefore, seeks to avoid legal dispute or proceedings, for example before a court or an industrial tribunal, in connection with those rights. The termination settlement may also reaffirm undertakings about the individual's conduct or activity after termination which formed part of the terms on which the employment was taken up.

The Inland Revenue will accept that no chargeable value will be attributed under ITEPA 2003 s 225(1) to such undertakings by an employee or former employee.

3 But this does not affect the application of ss 225–6 to sums that are attributable to other restrictive undertakings which individuals give in relation to an employment, whether these undertakings are contained in a job termination settlement or otherwise.

Commentary—*Simon's Direct Tax Service* **E4.805C**.
Note—This statement was revised in IR 131 (August 2003).

SP 4/96 (13 May 1996) *Income tax: interest paid in the ordinary course of a bank's business*

INTRODUCTION

1 The Taxes Acts generally require that when yearly interest is paid by a company income tax must be deducted on payment. However, this is modified by TA 1988 s 349(3)(*b*) when yearly interest is paid by a bank in the ordinary course of business. This statement of practice sets out how the Revenue applies the test of "in the ordinary course of business" for the purposes of that section.

2 Section 349(3)(*b*) was amended by FA 1996 Sch 37 para 3(*b*) and now applies, to interest paid by a bank "in the ordinary course of its business".

MEANING OF "BANK"

3 "Bank" for the purposes of s 349(3)(*b*) has the meaning given by TA 1988 s 840A.

INTERPRETATION OF "IN THE ORDINARY COURSE OF ITS BUSINESS"

4 The Revenue will accept that yearly interest is paid in the ordinary course of a bank's business unless that interest falls within one or both of the two circumstances set out immediately below.

(i) Yearly interest will not be regarded as paid in the ordinary course of business where the borrowing relates to the capital structure of the bank. A borrowing will be regarded as relating to the capital structure of the bank if it conforms to any of the definitions of tier 1, 2 or 3 capital adopted by the Bank of England, whether or not the borrowing actually counts towards tier 1, 2 or 3 capital for regulatory purposes.
Where, however, a borrowing within the tier 3 definition arose at a time prior to 1 January 1996 (the date when tier 3 capital was introduced for regulatory purposes) and was in the ordinary course of business at the time it arose, yearly interest on that borrowing will continue to be regarded as within s 349(3)(*b*).

(ii) Yearly interest will not be regarded as paid in the ordinary course of business where the characteristics of the transaction giving rise to the interest are primarily attributable to an intention to avoid UK tax.

APPLICATION

5 This statement supersedes SP 12/91 in relation to yearly interest paid on or after 29 April 1996.

6 Whether or not interest is with the scope of this statement of practice depends both on the date of the transaction giving rise to the interest and on whether the bank was also a bank under the pre-FA 1996 rules, that is, whether it was recognised by the Revenue prior to 29 April 1996 as a bank for the purposes of s 349(3)(*b*).

TRANSACTIONS ENTERED INTO ON OR AFTER 29 APRIL 1996

6.1 This statement of practice applies to all yearly interest paid by the bank on or after 29 April 1996.

TRANSACTIONS ENTERED INTO BEFORE 29 APRIL 1996

6.2 Where the paying bank was recognised by the Revenue prior to 29 April 1996 as a bank for the purposes of s 349(3)(*b*), this statement of practice applies to all yearly interest paid by the bank on or after 29 April 1996. This means that such banks (the majority) will not need to consider whether interest arises on an advance, or whether the bank remains a ''bank carrying on a bona fide banking business in the UK'' under the pre-FA 1996 rules at the time of payment of the interest.

Where the paying bank was not recognised by the Revenue prior to 29 April 1996 as a bank for the purposes of s 349(3)(*b*), the bank must continue to deduct income tax from yearly interest paid on or after 29 April 1996 on advances, as it did from payments made before that date. All other interest paid by the bank, however, on or after 29 April 1996 will be governed by this statement of practice.

Commentary—*Simon's Direct Tax Service* **A3.405**.

SP 5/96 (15 October 1996) *PAYE settlement agreements*

INTRODUCTION

1 PAYE settlement agreements (PSAs)—formerly known as annual voluntary settlements (AVSs)—are arrangements under which employers can settle in a single payment the income tax liability on largely, minor benefits in kind and expenses payments given to their employees.

2 PSAs are potentially available to all employers. They are intended to provide flexibility for those employers who use them because items covered by a PSA do not have to be included on Forms P9D or P11D at the end of the year. Nor do employees have to include them on their tax return, if they receive one. But they are not intended to provide a general alternative to the obligation on an employer to operate PAYE under ITEPA 2003 s 684 or to make a return after the end of the year in relation to benefits in kind and expenses payments. This means that PSAs will not apply to—

- cash payments of wages, salaries or bonuses including those paid to casual employees;
- major benefits provided regularly for the sole use of individual employees—for example, a company car, car fuel, provided accommodation, beneficial loans;
- round sum allowances.

3 However, the key intention of PSAs is flexibility. It is intended that inspectors will regard PSAs as a useful way of reducing burdens for employers and Revenue alike.

4 ITEPA 2003, Pt 2, Ch 5 and the Income Tax (Employments) Regulations, SI 1993/744, Pt VI, Ch 5 [see now the Income Tax (PAYE) Regulations 2003, SI 2003/2682, Pt 6] contain the rules governing PSAs.

SPs

PAYE SETTLEMENT AGREEMENTS

Scope of items which may be covered by a PSA

5 Regulation 80A [see now Income Tax (PAYE) Regulations 2003, SI 2003/2682, Pt 6] describes the emoluments which can be covered by a PSA. This provides for the inclusion of expenses payments and benefits which are ''minor'' or, if not minor, are either payable on an ''irregular'' basis or in circumstances where it is ''impracticable'' to apply PAYE or apportion the value of particular benefits which have been shared by a number of employees.

6 These terms have deliberately not been defined. The regulations require the employer and the inspector to agree where payments are of an amount, or are paid in circumstances, which satisfy one or other of the terms. In discussion with the employer, the inspector will be expected to make a reasonable judgment—based on the natural meaning of the words and taking account of the overall objective of the arrangements—about what may be included in a PSA.

7 Some examples are given below of items which may be suitable for inclusion in a PSA. It is not an exhaustive list. And it will not always be appropriate for an item listed below to be included in a particular PSA. In addition, some items might satisfy more than one term. The following paragraphs indicate some of the factors which an inspector may take into account.

Interpretation of "minor"

8 An expenses payment or benefit in kind can be included in a PSA if it is ''minor'' as regards the sums paid or the type of benefit provided—Regulation 80A(3)(*b*)(i). In agreeing with employers what may be included in a particular PSA, inspectors will take account of the natural meaning of the term ''minor''. The key question is whether on any objective judgment the item in question is minor in value. The nature of the item and the circumstances in which it is paid will normally also need to be taken into account. For example, a gift paid as part of a scheme to reward long service which does not satisfy Concession A22. In deciding what constitutes minor, inspectors will not be influenced by, for example, the comparable earnings of the particular employees concerned or the size of the employer.

9 Some examples of what may constitute a ''minor'' item may help—

- Long service awards outside Concession A22.
- Incentive awards.
- Reimbursement of late night taxi fares home outside Concession A66.
- Personal incidental expenses in excess of the statutory daily limit.
- Present for an employee in hospital.
- Staff entertainment—for example, a ticket for Wimbledon.
- Use of a company van.
- Use of a pool car where the conditions for tax exemption are not satisfied.
- Subscriptions to gyms, sports clubs etc.
- Telephone bills.
- Gift vouchers and small gifts.

10 If it is not possible to accept that an item is ''minor'', it may still be appropriate for inclusion in a PSA because the inspector will then consider whether it is either paid on an irregular basis; or whether it is impracticable to apply PAYE to it or identify the amount to be included on form P11D. The following paragraphs indicate some of the factors inspectors will take into account when deciding if the circumstances satisfy either test.

Interpretation of "irregular"

11 Regulation 80A(3)(*b*)(ii) provides that an item may be included in a PSA if it is paid irregularly to an employee. Whether an item is paid on an ''irregular'' basis will depend on the facts of each case. The inspector will take into account, for example, the nature of the item, the normal frequency of its payment and how often it was paid or given to the individual employee in question. The exclusion of an item given to some employees because it was received regularly by them, would not necessarily mean that the same items received, irregularly by other employees would be excluded from a PSA. In considering if an item is received irregularly, inspectors will primarily consider the frequency at which an item is provided during the year for which the PSA applies. But in appropriate cases, for example the use of the employer's holiday accommodation, the period taken into account may be longer. Items provided to the same employee every year are unlikely to satisfy the irregular test.

12 Relocation expenses where the amounts concerned exceed the £8,000 tax exempt threshold (ITEPA 2003 s 271) are an important example of a range of benefits in kind or expenses which may fail the *minor* test, but will normally qualify for inclusion in a PSA on grounds of irregularity.

13 Other examples may include—

- Occasional attendance at an overseas conference where not all the expenses qualify for relief under ITEPA 2003 Pt 5.
- Expenses of a spouse occasionally accompanying an employee abroad.
- Occasional use of a company holiday flat.

– One-off gifts which are not minor.

Interpretation of "impracticable"

14 The key is whether it is "impracticable" for the employer to operate PAYE on a payment; or to identify precisely how much of a shared benefit should be attributable to each individual employee and included on the Form P9D or P11D. The employer will be expected to demonstrate that it would not be possible to do so without a disproportionate amount of effort or record keeping taking account of the value of the item concerned, the number of employees involved and the nature of the items involved.

15 Examples of what might be impracticable may include—

- Free chiropody care.
- Hairdressing services.
- Shared use of the firm's bus to work.
- Christmas parties and similar entertainment provided by the employer which do not already qualify for relief.
- The cost of shared taxi fares home which do not satisfy Concession A66.
- Shared cars.

16 The flow chart at Annex A summaries the tests of eligibility for inclusion in a PSA.

Overlap with Taxed Award Schemes

17 Currently, employers operating formal incentive award schemes can pay the tax on behalf of their employees by entering into a Taxed Award Scheme (TAS) with the Revenue. A general information pack on Taxed Award Schemes is available from The Incentive Valuation Unit, Chapel Wharf Area, Trinity Bridge House, 2 Dearmans Place, Salford M3 5BH; Tel: 0161 261 3269. Most awards under these schemes will be suitable for inclusion in a PSA if employers wish to use a PSA instead of TAS. A third party who provides awards to the employees of another and who wishes to pay the employees' tax bill cannot use a PSA. A TAS should be used instead.

Calculation of tax payable

18 Regulation 80F provides the basis on which the tax payable by the employer may be computed. In practice, this provides for the tax to be grossed up in a similar way to that already adopted by inspectors for agreeing amounts due under the previous, informal arrangements for AVSs. In calculating the tax payable, the inspector and the employer will take into account—

- the amount of any expenses payments and the value of any benefits in kind provided which are to be included;
- the number of employees receiving the payments or benefits concerned;
- the rates of tax which should be used in "grossing up" the tax due.

19 The tax due should be grossed up taking account the effective marginal rates of tax of the individual employees covered by agreement. So, for example, where an agreement relates to a group of employees some of whom are basic rate taxpayers and some are higher rate taxpayers, the tax due will need to be grossed up separately for the two groups of employees and the results aggregated to give the total tax due. In appropriate cases, the inspector and the employer may agree that the amount of tax payable under a PSA in relation to a large number of employees can be calculated by reference to a sample of the employees concerned. An example of how to calculate the tax payable under a PSA is attached at Annex B.

Record-keeping

20 Once a PSA is agreed the employer no longer has to—

- operate PAYE on agreed items or include the items on the P35 or P14;
- include the expenses and benefits concerned on Forms P9D or P11D.

21 The employer will still need to retain suitable records of what had been provided or paid. In general, it will be sufficient to retain records for three years. Where items are easily attributable to individual employees, the same records otherwise required for the purposes of completing Forms P9D and P11D should be retained. Details of cash payments to individual employees should also be retained. But where it is impracticable to allocate a benefit or payment between employees, a record of the individuals concerned will not be needed. Instead the employer should keep sufficient information about—

- the overall cost of providing the benefits concerned (for example the total cost of providing a party which a number of employees attended);
- the number of employees concerned; and
- an indication of their marginal tax rates.

What employers should consider telling their employees

22 Employees should not include items covered by a PSA in their tax return, if they receive one.

23 Employees who receive tax returns may ask the employer to clarify the position in relation to benefits in kind or expenses payments they have received which are not included on the P11D

SPs

information given to them by their employer. So employers may find it best to tell employees about them at the same time as they issue the P11D information to their employees. And if the PSA is a regular arrangement, employers might find it best to tell employees when they first take up their employment or when employees first receive an item included in the PSA. This may reduce the number of possible queries from employees who are completing their own tax returns.

24 However, there is no statutory requirement for employers to tell their employees about a PSA and the Revenue will not be able to disclose details of agreements they have made with employers to their employees. Nor will it be possible for the Revenue to check that an employee who has completed a tax return may have included such items in error.

Adjustments to the scope of a PSA

25 The inspector will not normally need to adjust a PSA during the year. But employers may ask the inspector to widen the scope of a PSA which applies for a particular year by—

- *during* the year, adding items on which PAYE would otherwise be due—but only ceasing to apply PAYE once the inspector has agreed the extension to the PSA;
- *during* the year, adding items which would otherwise be included on Form P9D or P11D;
- *after* the end of the year, but before 6 July following the end of the year, finalising the PSA by adding items which would otherwise need to be included on Form P9D or P11D.

26 Many employers will want to carry forward their PSA to the following year. Inspectors will invite employers before the beginning of the year to renew their PSA. The PSA will only need to be altered if the employer wishes to make an adjustment to what had previously been agreed or it was justified because there had been a change in the circumstances on which the original PSA had been based.

Payment of tax

27 Regulation 80G [see now the Income Tax (PAYE) Regulations 2003, SI 2003/2682, Pt 6] provides for the payment of tax under a PSA. The employer—not the employee—will always be accountable for tax payable in respect of items included in a PSA (ITEPA 2003 Pt 2 Ch 5 and Reg 80A).

28 The precise amount of tax does not need to be agreed by 6 July when the scope of the PSA has to be finalised. Normally, the tax due will be agreed between the employer and the inspector after 6 July, but in time to ensure that payment is made by the due and payable date of 19 October following the end of the tax year to which the PSA applies. There is nothing to preclude the employer from paying the tax in full before the due date (where it can be established in advance) or making instalment payments during the year. Those who wish to do so should contact the inspector accordingly.

Withdrawal of PSA by the inspector

29 Where the inspector establishes that an employer has operated outside the agreed terms of a PSA he may cancel or adjust the agreement. Employers will then be expected to operate PAYE as appropriate on payments made after the date of cancellation or termination. Similarly, all benefits and expenses provided after that date will need to be returned on Form P9D or P11D at the end of the year.

30 Inspectors may cancel a PSA where there has been a serious or persistent failure to account for the tax under the agreement; or more generally where there has been a failure under PAYE or in relation to the completion of Forms P9D or P11D. An inspector would not normally cancel an agreement because, for example, the employer had made a minor error as to the calculation of the tax payable under a PSA, or in relation to the sums on which tax should be computed.

31 Following a withdrawal, the agreement of a PSA for future years will be at the discretion of the inspector. Each case will be looked at on its own merits. But there would be nothing in principle to prevent an inspector agreeing a PSA for the tax year following a cancellation where he was satisfied that the failure would not re-occur.

Rights of appeal

32 There is no statutory right of appeal against the refusal of the inspector to agree a PSA or the cancellation of a PSA. But if the employer believed that the inspector had acted unreasonably, after review under the Revenue's internal complaints procedures, the matter could be considered by the Adjudicator for the Revenue. Details of the complaints procedures for taxpayers are available in the Inland Revenue leaflet IR 120 ''You and the Inland Revenue''.

33 There is a statutory right of appeal against a determination under reg 80H of the amount of tax payable under a PSA. Under TMA 1970 Sch 3 (as amended by FA 1996 Sch 22 para 10) the employer can elect to have the appeal heard where the place of business is located. In practice, this could be where the company head office is located or where the trade is carried on.

Transitional arrangements

34 The PSA arrangements came into effect from 6 April 1996. The scope of AVSs which have been agreed for 1996–97 but before the regulations came into force will continue to apply for 1996–97 even if they extend to items which would not qualify under the PSA rules. These agreements will be reviewed as they are considered for renewal for 1997–98. Leaving aside those regulations which provide for the scope of PSAs, all agreements that apply for 1996–97 are subject to the other regulations in SI 1996/2631.

Treatment of national insurance contributions under a PSA

From 6 April 1999 Class 1B NICs are not due when a PSA is entered into. IR 155, ''PAYE settlement agreements'', explains how Class 1B NICs are calculated and accounted for.

ANNEX A

FLOW CHART FOR DECIDING WHICH ITEMS CAN BE INCLUDED IN A PSA

1 Are the items wages, salaries or bonuses? → YES → The items *cannot* be covered in a PSA.

↓

NO

↓

2 Are the items *major*, regular expenses or benefits*? → YES → The items *cannot* be covered in a PSA.

↓

NO

↓

3 Are the items "minor" expenses or benefits**?

4 Are the items "irregular"**?

5 Is it "impracticable to operate PAYE", or apportion items between employees**?

If the answer to *all* of questions 3 to 5 is "NO" then → The items *cannot* be covered in a PSA.

If the answer to *any* of questions 3 to 5 is "YES" then

↓ ↓ ↓

The items *can* be covered in a PSA.

Notes—* Major benefits such as sole-use company cars, car fuel and beneficial loans are excluded from the scope of PSAs.
** The terms ''minor'' and ''irregular'' and ''impracticable to operate PAYE or apportion items between employees'' are explained above.
Concessions A22 and A66 have now been classified as obsolete.

ANNEX B

CALCULATING THE TAX PAYABLE UNDER A PSA—EXAMPLE

Smith and Jones Ltd has a work-force of 1,000 employees, all of whom are provided with benefits in kind during the tax year 1996–97 valued at £50 per head. Some 800 of their employees pay tax at the basic rate, the remaining 200 at the higher rate. The tax payable under a PAYE settlement agreement (for 1996–97, and covering the whole work-force) would be calculated as follows—

Value of benefits provided to basic rate employees (800 × £50)		£40,000
Tax due @ 24% on £40,000		£9,600
Grossed up tax	$£9{,}600 \times \frac{100}{100-24}$ =	£12,631·58
Value of benefits provided to higher rate employees (200 × £50)		£10,000
Tax due @ 40% on £10,000		£4,000
Grossed up tax	$£4{,}000 \times \frac{100}{100-40}$ =	£6,666·67
Total tax payable by Smith and Jones Ltd under the PSA		£12,631·58
	+	£6,666·67
		£19,298·25

Alternatively, the value of the benefits could be grossed-up, and tax calculated on that figure in the normal way, with identical results—

Value of benefits provided to basic rate employees (800 × £50)		£40,000
Grossed up value of benefits	$£40{,}000 \times \frac{100}{100-24} = £52{,}631{\cdot}58$	
Tax due @ 24% on £52,631·58		£12,631·58
Value of benefits provided to higher rate employees (200 × £50)		£10,000
Grossed up value of benefits	$£10{,}000 \times \frac{100}{100-40} = £16{,}666{\cdot}67$	
Tax due @ 40% on £16,666·67		£6,666·67
Total tax payable by Smith and Jones Ltd under the PSA		£12,631·58
		+ £6,666·67
		£19,298·25

Commentary—*Simon's Direct Tax Service* **E4.968**.
Regulations—Income Tax (Pay As You Earn) Regulations 2003, SI 2003/2682.
Note—This statement was revised in IR 131 (August 2003).

SP 1/97 (16 January 1997) *The electronic lodgement service*

INTRODUCTION

1 TMA 1970 Sch 3A provides the legislative ground for the new electronic lodgement service (ELS). It enables taxpayers to fulfil their obligation to deliver certain tax returns by arranging for an approved "filer" to transmit the relevant information to the Inland Revenue electronically.

2 Using an approved software package the filer enters the information which is transmitted in a secure manner over public networks through the secure messaging gateway (SMG) to the Revenue gateway. This validates the information and, if accepted, logs its receipt and updates the self-assessment system. An acknowledgement message accepting or rejecting the return is then sent back to the filer. The whole cycle should not take any longer than 24 hours.

3 This statement of practice describes how the Revenue will operate ELS and the more detailed requirements of the service.

LEGISLATION

4 The main elements of Sch 3A are—

- the returns and documents which may be sent via ELS;
- approval of electronic filers;
- the method and content of transmission;
- the hard copy of the information transmitted;
- the Revenue's powers and the taxpayer's rights in relation to the information transmitted electronically;
- the use of the information in proceedings.

THE RETURNS AND DOCUMENTS WHICH MAY BE SENT VIA ELS

5 ELS will be available initially only for returns by individuals under TMA 1970 s 8, partnerships under s 12AA, and trustees under s 8A, due under self-assessment from 6 April 1997. Other returns and amendments to self-assessment returns will not, at this stage, be accepted by ELS. The Revenue will be considering the extension of the service to other returns and forms in the future.

6 The ELS legislation acknowledges, implicitly, that supporting documents may be sent separately (for example by post), subject to meeting the relevant time-limit (TMA 1970 Sch 3A para 3(3)). Although advised that in strictness statutory time-limits for filing a return apply equally to any documents intended to accompany it, the Revenue will accept that any documents submitted within one month of the return "accompany" it for the purpose of making a disclosure within TMA 1970 s 29 if the return indicates that such documents have been, or are to be, submitted. Where documents have been sent outside that time limit, the Revenue will consider sympathetically any request for them to be treated as supporting the return in question for that purpose.

7 ELS will accommodate all the information which may be given on the self-assessment tax return, including any further details in the white space areas provided on the return for additional information. The service will be able to cope with substantial amounts of additional data should that be considered appropriate by the taxpayer or his adviser. However, in the majority of cases, the information from the core return and supplementary pages, together with limited details in the "white space", should facilitate adequate disclosure of the taxpayer's affairs.

APPROVAL OF ELECTRONIC FILERS

8 Any person who is authorised to send information to the Revenue via ELS is described here as a "filer". Those who wish to transmit information in this way, whether on their own or another's behalf, must be approved in writing by the Revenue. Application forms for approval are available from the Inland Revenue ELS business support team at Accounts Office Shipley, West Yorkshire, BD98 8AA (telephone number 01274 539301/539325).

9 Applications for approval will be refused only where there is clear evidence that the applicant has been involved in the evasion of tax. The application will automatically be refused in any case where a conviction in relation to a tax offence or a penalty under TMA 1970 s 99 has been imposed within three years of the application. Where in other cases, refusal is considered, the Revenue will have regard to all relevant facts. Particularly crucial will be any facts suggesting the likely misuse of the ELS system in any way by the applicant.

10 Notices of refusal or withdrawal of approval will be given in writing and will include the grounds underlying the Revenue's decision. Any person refused approval, or who has had their approval withdrawn, has a right of appeal against this decision to the Special Commissioners.

11 The statute requires approval to be considered in relation to any person wishing to make transmissions by ELS. However, subject to their right to request applications by those persons in a business wishing to use ELS, the Revenue are prepared to approve an application by an individual on behalf of the particular business concerned, whether it be a large sole practice, a partnership or a company. An application on this basis must include details of all those within the business who have a responsibility for the ELS link, ie those persons who have a clear role in determining the office procedures under which ELS will be operated. This ultimately is something for each particular organisation to decide, but the Revenue will give advice where necessary.

12 Any changes in those who have been or should be named in an application must be notified at yearly intervals. The Revenue will issue a request once each year for confirmation of such changes. Provided applications are updated in this way it will not be necessary for any concern to seek a fresh approval following each change.

13 Where an application on behalf of a business cannot be approved because of concerns relating to certain persons named in the application, the Revenue may nevertheless grant approval provided an undertaking is given by the applicant that those persons who would not gain approval in their own right, are not permitted to make, or authorise, electronic transmissions via ELS link. Similarly, where a person newly joining the organisation would not gain approval in his or her own right, the Revenue may seek confirmation that he or she will not be permitted to make, or authorise, electronic transmissions via ELS link.

14 The Revenue anticipate receiving applications for approval not only from advisers who wish to file their own clients' returns, but also from persons who intend simply to offer the facility of electronic filing. Such applications will be examined to ensure there is a sufficient degree of contact between the taxpayer and the filer. This contact is important where a return is rejected and the Revenue must be satisfied that the filer's processes ensure that the taxpayer is notified promptly of any messages from the Revenue, including any rejection of the information sent.

15 Any approval of a person will apply to the business or practice which that person represents, regardless of the number of locations from which it is operated.

THE METHOD AND CONTENT OF TRANSMISSION

16 Those persons transmitting information electronically must use approved software. The Revenue will arrange with the software suppliers to ensure that the systems are compatible. Part of this process will allow the software products to carry an indication (a "kitemark") that they are approved for ELS use by the Revenue.

17 Approval will be granted following successful testing between the Revenue and the software house. In addition to assuring all parties that the software performs to specification the Revenue will require proof that the software package produces acceptable hard copy transcripts containing the taxpayer declaration and authority.

18 The technical specifications for the software are—

– Return check sum—this will be an algorithmic value calculated from the numeric values on the return. The requirement is that the sending tax return application calculates the value, using a Revenue published standard. The Revenue will recalculate the value on receipt and compare the result with that received from the filer. The return check sum field will be mandatory within the EDIFACT message. (EDIFACT is the international messaging standard for defining the data format and structure of electronic data interchange.)

– Unique electronic tax return identification number—this will be a number created by the tax return software, by reference to a Revenue published standard. The standard will include date, time and form and taxpayer reference fields as a minimum. The number will be mandatory within the EDIFACT message and will be incorporated, as a further check, in the Revenue acknowledgement message.

- The software applications must result in an electronic return being sent to a defined EDIFACT standard. The return and acknowledgement/rejection messages will be to a defined message type including structure, content and (EDIFACT) code.
- This information will be incorporated in an ELS EDIFACT guide which will provide an overview, sample messages, addressing and batching strategy, data communications overview, forms definition, change control, list of ELS forms and security requirements and measures.
- The above EDIFACT guide will, as stated, include a section confirming and providing details that the required communications protocol must be X.400 (1984 or 1988) conformant.
- The sending applications must be capable of receiving and processing return acceptance or rejection messages.

19 Having prepared a taxpayer's return using an approved software package, the filer must print out a standard hard copy of the information, containing the authentication which the taxpayer must sign before the information is transmitted. This authentication, which replaces the taxpayer's signature on a paper return, effectively represents his authority for the filer to transmit the information. The authentication must be an integral part of the hard copy transcript of the return data to be transmitted.

20 A mandatory part of the electronic return is the filer's confirmation that the hard copy was made and authenticated before the information was transmitted. It will also be necessary for the date on which the taxpayer signed the authority to transmit to be included in the transmission. Where this date is not supplied the return will not be accepted and an appropriate rejection message will be sent to the filer.

21 The Revenue approved software ensures that the hard copy, which the taxpayer endorses as complete and correct contains the information that is transmitted to the Revenue. This will, in part, be achieved by each transmission of a new or corrected return bearing the unique identification number, which is a requirement of the Revenue's approval of the software. This code will be part of the transmission to the Revenue and part of the acknowledgement message.

THE HARD COPY OF THE INFORMATION TRANSMITTED

22 TMA 1970 Sch 3A para 8(1) provides that a hard copy of the information transmitted is made within the terms of the statute if it is made "under arrangements designed to ensure that the information contained in the hard copy is the information in fact transmitted". These arrangements refer to the working practices adopted in relation to electronic filing by filers.

23 As a minimum the Revenue expect that safeguards are put in place to ensure or enable the following—

- the authorisation of the manner in which all electronic transmissions via ELS are made only by those who have been specifically approved, or included in a list of partners in an approved partnership;
- the physical security of the computer system;
- the prevention of earlier or later versions of the return to that authorised by the taxpayer being sent in error;
- only authorised staff have access to computer systems and taxpayer files;
- access to any integrated or separate communications applications for ELS;
- security of back up or archiving data.

THE REVENUE'S POWERS AND THE TAXPAYER'S RIGHTS IN RELATION TO THE INFORMATION TRANSMITTED ELECTRONICALLY

24 The legislation provides that the Revenue shall be able to exercise their powers in respect of the information received electronically, and the taxpayer shall be able to make claims to "error or mistake" relief or to amend a return on the basis of the information transmitted. Furthermore, anyone who has their return filed electronically will not be prevented from exercising any right to which they would have been entitled had the return been submitted in paper form.

THE USE OF THE INFORMATION IN PROCEEDINGS

25 When a tax return is sent to the Revenue in paper form there can be no dispute over what the taxpayer actually approved to be submitted. With the transmission of information in electronic form, bearing no signature, this may not be the case. The signed hard copy of the information is the taxpayer's evidence of the details he authorised to be sent. It is an important document, which the taxpayer is strongly advised to keep, or to have his accountant keep, for the same period that any underlying records need to be retained.

26 In the event of any proceedings in relation to a tax return which was delivered via ELS, the taxpayer will have an opportunity to show that he authenticated a valid hard copy which will then stand as evidence of the information transmitted. Otherwise it will be open to the Revenue to produce their own hard copy of the information which was received. It is expected that these two versions will be identical, but it is clearly in the taxpayer's best interests that his own authenticated hard copy is retained, should there be a need to produce it in proceedings.

MISCELLANEOUS

Availability of network

27 It is expected that the ELS network will be available to filers generally for 24 hours per day. Any unavailability of the system (eg to allow for maintenance), whether or not scheduled, will be notified by the SMG provider to filers. The availability of the network will be subject to a service agreement between the Revenue and the SMG provider.

Acknowledgements

28 Any return received at the SMG should result in an acceptance or rejection message being available for collection by the agent within the next working day. The exact details will depend on the service agreement between the Revenue and SMG provider as well as the computer technologies used.

29 A filer will get a ''non delivery'' report as part of the process where, in exceptional circumstances, the file has not been successfully transmitted to the SMG (for the Revenue). The absence of this message indicates that the package has been received, but not opened, at the SMG. Filers will also be able to optionally request a delivery report confirming that the file containing the return or returns has been received but not yet processed.

Date of receipt

30 The legislation provides that the obligation to deliver a return is not fulfilled until four conditions are met. The first three are the approval of the filer, the approval of the transmission process and the authentication of a hard copy. The fourth condition is that the information transmitted to the Revenue is accepted. That is notified to the filer when the Revenue issue an acceptance signal in respect of the information.

31 It follows that until the Revenue have issued this acceptance of the information, the filing obligation is not fulfilled. For this reason, taxpayers and filers are strongly advised to ensure that the transmission is made at least 24 hours before the end of the day on which the time limit for submitting the return expires.

32 However, it is a feature of the system that the date on which the electronic return is lodged with the SMG is recorded. Provided this date is no later than the end of the period by which the return may be delivered, and that the information is not rejected for any reason, a penalty for late submission will not normally be sought, even though the acceptance signal may be transmitted after the due date. As this inevitably involves a certain degree of risk, taxpayers and filers should not rely on this practice to file returns via ELS on the due date.

33 Where a return is rejected the same rules will apply to the date of its resubmission and final acceptance.

Rejections

34 Where returns are rejected by the ELS system a suitable message will be sent back to the filer. This will detail why the processing of the return has not been possible. The filer can then correct the return and resubmit the information electronically. Where the information changes in any way the resubmission will require a fresh authorisation by the taxpayer.

35 It should be noted that this resubmission does not include the transmission of an amended return (ie one altered other than in response to a rejection message) following a previously accepted one. Amended returns must be submitted on paper.

Commentary—*Simon's Direct Tax Service* **A3.166F**.

SP 2/97 (18 July 1997) *Authorised unit trusts, approved investment trusts, and open-ended investment companies: monthly savings schemes*

Note—This statement has been superseded by SP 2/99.

SP 3/97 (18 July 1997) *Investment trusts investing in authorised unit trusts open-ended investment companies*

INTRODUCTION

1 This statement of practice sets out the Inland Revenue's views on the tax implications of investment by investment trusts in authorised unit trusts (AUTs) or open-ended investment companies (OEICs) incorporated in the UK.

2 For the purposes of the Tax Acts, each sub-fund of an AUT which is an umbrella scheme is regarded as an AUT in its own right, and the umbrella scheme itself is not regarded as an AUT.

Similarly, each sub-fund of an OEIC which is an umbrella company is regarded as an OEIC in its own right, and the umbrella company itself is not regarded as an OEIC.

3 Where a sub-fund of an umbrella scheme is treated as an AUT for tax purposes, references in this statement to the units of that AUT are to be regarded as references to the rights or interests (however described) of those persons who for the time being have rights in the sub-fund in question. Similarly, where a sub-fund of an umbrella company is treated as an OEIC for tax purposes, references in this statement to the shares of that OEIC are to be regarded as references to the shares in issue of the umbrella company which for the time being confer rights in the sub-fund in question.

APPROVAL OF INVESTMENT TRUSTS

4 A company has to satisfy the various tests set out in TA 1988 s 842 for a particular accounting period if it is to be approved by the Inland Revenue as an investment trust for that accounting period. The Inland Revenue accept that units in AUTs and shares in OEICs are to be treated as shares in companies for the purposes of those tests.

5 In the majority of cases, no further point arises, since companies seeking approval as investment trusts do not generally have substantial investments in AUTs or OEICs. However, where there is substantial investment of this sort, the test in s 842(1)(*b*) may be relevant. This is because this test restricts the size of an investment trust's holding in any one company, except in the case of a company that—

- is itself an approved investment trust; or
- would qualify as an investment trust but for the public listing test in TA 1988 s 842(1)(*c*).

6 The Inland Revenue consider that for the purposes of s 842(1)(*b*), an AUT or OEIC can, provided it meets one condition, be regarded as a company which would qualify as an investment trust but for the listing test. As a result there is no restriction on the size of the company's investment in that AUT or OEIC.

7 The condition to be met reflects the test in TA 1988 s 842(1)(*a*). It is that, for the period of time in the investing company's accounting period during which it held investments in an AUT or OEIC, the income of the AUT or OEIC concerned consisted wholly or mainly of ''eligible investment income''.

8 For these purposes, ''eligible investment income'' is income deriving from shares or securities, or ''eligible rental income'' within the meaning of TA 1988 s 508A.

9 The Inland Revenue consider that this condition will always be satisfied where the AUT concerned is—

- a ''securities fund'' for the purposes of the Regulations for AUTs which have been made by the Financial Services Authority (FSA) under FSA 1986; or
- a sub-fund of an authorised umbrella scheme which, according to the terms of the scheme, would be a securities fund if it were itself the subject of an authorisation order.

10 Similarly, the Inland Revenue consider that the condition will always be satisfied where the OEIC concerned is—

- a ''securities company'' for the purposes of the corresponding FSA Regulations for OEICs incorporated in the UK; or
- a sub-fund of an umbrella company which, according to the company's instrument of incorporation, would be a securities company if it were itself the subject of an authorisation order.

11 Where the AUT or OEIC concerned does not fall within the categories described in paragraph 9 or 10 above, the question as to whether the relevant income consisted wholly or mainly of eligible investment income (and so whether that AUT or OEIC could count as the equivalent of an investment trust for the purposes of TA 1988 s 842(1)(*b*)) will be tested by reference to the facts.

12 The Inland Revenue consider that this test has to be applied for each accounting period in which the company investing in an AUT or OEIC continues to be so invested. And, for the purpose of this test, income is regarded as consisting wholly or mainly of eligible investment income if at least 70 per cent of it is eligible investment income.

Commentary—*Simon's Direct Tax Service* **D4.424**.
Notes—This Statement supersedes SP 7/94. The text of this statement is as it appears in IR 131 (January 2000).

SP 4/97 (27 November 1997) *Taxation of commission, cashbacks and discounts*

INTRODUCTION

1 This statement sets out the views of the Board of Inland Revenue of the correct treatment for tax purposes of commission, cashbacks and discounts. The passing on to customers by intermediaries or agents of the whole or part of commission and the payment of cashbacks or the granting of discounts by the providers of goods or services has become increasingly common. These arrangements have given rise to considerable uncertainty about the tax consequences for both customers and intermediaries which previous Statements of Practice were unable to resolve. This statement sets out the Revenue's practice in applying the law to these arrangements and in particular it confirms that most customers are not liable to tax on commission, cashbacks and discounts.

2 Sections A and B (paras 3–10) set out both the different types of receipt and arrangements covered by the statement and when these receipts are not liable to tax.

Section C is concerned with the liability to tax under the different cases of Schedule D. It sets out the circumstances in which commission, cashbacks and similar inducements will be taken into account as receipts—

– in computing taxable profits from a trade or profession under Case I or II of Schedule D (paras 11–15);
– in computing other taxable annual profits under Case VI (para 19).

It also provides guidance on the deductibility of commission etc passed on to the customer—

– in computing profits under Case I or II (para 17); and
– in computing profits under Case VI (para 21).

The rest of the statement is concerned with the tax treatment of persons receiving or becoming entitled to commission or a cashback under—

– Schedule E, covered in section D (paras 23–32).

(The deductibility of commission passed on to the customer and the operation of PAYE are dealt with in paras 33 and 34 respectively);

– capital gains tax, covered in section E (para 35); and
– life insurance and personal pensions, covered in section F (paras 36–41).

A SCOPE

3 This statement covers—

– Commission (meaning a sum paid by the providers of goods, investments or services to agents or intermediaries as reward for the introduction of business). Sometimes, commission is passed on to the customer or to some other person by the agent or intermediary, or the customer may receive commission direct from the provider of the goods or services if that provider would normally pay commission to an agent or intermediary.
– Cashbacks (meaning lump sums received by a customer as an inducement for entering into a transaction for the purchase of goods, investments or services and received as a direct consequence of having entered into that transaction (for example a mortgage)). The payer may be either the provider of the goods, investments or services or another party with an interest in ensuring that the transaction takes place.
– Discounts (meaning that the purchaser's obligation is to pay less than the full purchase price of goods, services or investments, other than as a result of any entitlement to commission or a cashback).

4 It deals with liabilities to income or corporation tax under the rules of Schedule D, Schedule E, capital gains tax or the chargeable events legislation (that is, the rules for taxing gains on certain insurances) and with tax relief in respect of contributions to personal pension schemes.

5 It is not practicable to cover in this statement every situation that may arise. There will be individual cases which do not fall squarely within its terms where the taxation consequences may be different. For example, where inducements or rewards offered to customers take the form of a series of payments (and are not simply capital sums calculated in advance but paid in instalments) they may be taxable as income in the recipients' hands. It is beyond the scope of the statement to give a view on all such cases. They will have to be dealt with on an individual basis and the taxation consequences in each case will depend on the precise nature of the arrangements entered into.

B GENERAL

6 The statement covers the main circumstances in which commission or a cashback is likely to be passed between the parties to a transaction. It deals with arrangements where—

– commission or a cash-back is—
  – received
  – netted-off (meaning that the purchaser's entitlement to commission or a cash-back is set off against the obligation to pay the full purchase price for goods or services so that only the net amount is paid); or
  – invested or applied in some way for the benefit of the purchaser;

or where—
  – a discounted purchase price is paid; or
  – extra value is added to the goods, investments or services obtained for the purchase price where there is no entitlement to commission or a cash-back. An example is the allocation of bonus units in an investment or of a different class of unit where the purchase price remains unchanged. However, where the added value represents a return on the investment, the tax treatment may differ from that dealt with in this statement.

7 In general, ordinary retail customers purchasing goods, investments or services at arm's length will not be liable to income or capital gains tax in respect of any commission, discounts or cashbacks received by them. For example, an ordinary retail customer who, when purchasing a car, negotiates to receive part of the commission earned on the sale by the salesperson will not be liable to income or capital gains tax in respect of that commission.

8 The statement outlines some circumstances in which receipts are treated as tax-free, or in which payments qualify for tax relief. However, the legal analysis, and consequent tax treatment, will not necessarily follow that outlined in the statement where the receipts or payments in question form part of a scheme of tax avoidance. Similarly, the treatment outlined in the statement may not apply where the recipient of a commission, cashback or other benefit is party to an arrangement under which the purchase price for goods, investments or services has been increased.

9 The tax treatment of the person receiving or becoming entitled to the commission or cashback will be considered separately from the treatment of the person paying the commission or cashback.

10 Unless otherwise indicated, all statutory references are to TA 1988.

C SCHEDULE D

Cases I and II—receipts

11 Where the provision of the services remunerated by commission etc is on a sufficiently commercial, regular and organised basis to amount to a trade or profession, commission and similar sums to which the trader or professional person becomes entitled will be receipts from that source. A self-employed insurance or travel agent would normally be in that position.

12 The fact that some or all of the commission etc received by a trader or professional person in the circumstances described in para 11 is passed on to customers does not cause it to cease to be a receipt of that business. See para 17 below regarding the corresponding deduction.

13 Furthermore, commission etc, which would have been taxable if it had actually been received by a trader or professional person, does not necessarily cease to be taxable merely because it goes directly to the customer without first being received by the trader. For example, commission may be passed on by way of a reduction in regular insurance or pension policy premiums or by the allocation of extra value (eg units) to the policy by the insurance company. In those circumstances, the commission remains a taxable business receipt so long as the trader or professional person had an enforceable legal right to receive that commission which he subsequently forgoes in favour of the customer (but as indicated at para 17 below a deduction may be available in respect of the amount forgone).

14 Where the trader or professional person neither receives the commission etc nor has any such entitlement to it, there will be no taxable receipt in respect of that commission. Thus commission or a cashback payable to a trader or professional person within the first indent of para 6 is a taxable business receipt but a discount or added value within the last two items of para 6 above will not be a taxable receipt.

15 Commission etc receivable as an incident in the carrying on of any other business taxable under Cases I and II of Schedule D should be taken into account in computing the profits of the business. For example, the following items should be taken into account in computing the profits of the business—

– insurance commission to which an accountant becomes entitled in the course of the profession;
– commission received in respect of business insurance contracts taken out by, say, a grocer (for example, if the premium paid has been reduced by the commission, by deducting only the net sum);
– a cashback received on a car purchased for business purposes (normally by reducing the cost of the car for the purposes of capital allowances).

16 In strict law commission earned for business introduced in the course of a trade or profession remains a taxable business receipt even where it is derived from a private transaction funded by the trader or professional person. For example, a travel agent may obtain commission for booking a package holiday for himself and his family with a tour operator whose holidays he sells to the public.

But, by concession, there may be excluded from taxable profits so much of any such commission as does not exceed the maximum amount the trader or professional person could reasonably have been expected to pass on to an arm's length customer buying the same services or product.

Case I and II—deductions

17 Commission etc passed on to a customer, or otherwise forgone in the circumstances described in para 13 above, as an inducement to enter into a transaction is deductible if it is laid out wholly and exclusively for the purpose of the trade or profession. The statutory test is very likely to be satisfied if the customer required the commission to be passed on as a condition of entering into the transaction or if the transaction was one between independent parties acting at arm's length.

Presentation of information in tax return and/or accounts

18 This paragraph applies to commission etc which is passed on other than by a separate payment and is to be regarded as a taxable receipt as described in para 13 above. In these circumstances, the calculation of the gross commission received and the amount passed on may not be a straightforward matter. Subject to the conditions described below, the commission applied in this way may be excluded from both commission income and commission expenses in the intermediary's tax return. Those conditions are that either the customer required the commission to be passed on as a condition of entering into the transaction or the transaction was one between independent parties acting at arm's length (see para 17 above).

Case VI—receipts

19 Commission etc may sometimes be received by a person as consideration for introducing a customer to a supplier of goods or services, other than in circumstances where the commission would be taxable as income under Case I or II of Schedule D (see para 11 above) or under Schedule E (see para 25 below). Subject to para 20 below, if the commission arises under an enforceable contract, it should be brought into account as a taxable receipt in calculating the profit from the transaction under Case VI of Schedule D.

20 A sum, however described, which is received by an ordinary retail customer as consideration for the purchase by the customer of goods or services should not be regarded as a taxable receipt in computing profits under Case VI. This is the case whether the payer is the provider of the goods or services or another party with an economic interest in ensuring the transaction takes place.

Case VI—deductions

21 Where, in the circumstances described in para 19 above, some or all of the commission etc in question is passed on to the customer, a deduction is due where the customer requires the commission to be passed on as a condition of entering into the transaction or where for some other reason the payment is necessary to earn the commission.

Building society distributions

22 Cashbacks received from building societies are not required as distributions in respect of investments for the purposes of the Income Tax (Building Societies) (Dividends and Interest) Regulations, SI 1990/2231. Building societies are not therefore required to deduct tax from mortgage cashbacks by virtue of those Regulations.

D SCHEDULE E

23 The word "employee" means office holder or an employee. The word "emolument" defined in s 131 includes such things as salaries, fees, wages and profits.

24 It is a question of fact whether a sum within the scope of this statement is received in the capacity of employee/office holder or in some other capacity such as the purchaser of a policy, goods or services. This part of the statement covers only liability arising on emoluments from employment and liability under the benefits legislation (that is employees earning at the rate of £8,500 or more a year and most directors). In some circumstances liability to tax under Schedule E may arise under other provisions, such as the vouchers legislation or legislation dealing with termination and change payments. Those provisions should be considered even where there is no liability under the provisions considered here.

Commission arising from, and discounts in connection with, goods, investments or services sold to third parties

25 Employees who receive, or are entitled to receive, commission (as emoluments) from their employment in respect of goods, investments or services sold to third parties are assessable under Schedule E on the full amount of that commission. This is so whether or not the commission is passed on by them to the customer and whether the commission is paid by the employer or anyone else.

26 Where an employee consents or directs that commission which is due from his or her employment should be either paid to the customer or anyone else, or invested for his or her own benefit or the benefit of the customer or anyone else, that employee is assessable under Schedule E on that commission (but see para 33 for circumstances where a deduction will be admissible).

27 Where the purchaser pays a discounted price, there is no Schedule E liability on the employer if—

– the purchaser is not a member of the employee's family or household; and
– neither the employee nor any member of his or her family or household receives anything (money or benefits) in consequence.

If the purchaser is a member of the employee's family or household, the provision of goods or services at a discount may constitute a taxable benefit for the employee. However, where the discounted price paid covers the cost of those goods or services to the provider, there will be no taxable benefit.

In all cases the cost of providing goods or services is a question of fact. But where the sale is of an insurance policy there will be no taxable benefit if the discount is no greater than the sum of—

– the commission that would otherwise have been paid by the insurer on selling the policy to the third party; and
– the anticipated profit on the policy.

Commission and discounts in respect of an employee's purchase of goods, investments or services from the employer

28 Paragraphs 29 and 30 below are concerned with cases of commission arising from employment. Where a commission is available to an employee on the same basis as it is available to members of the general public, it will not arise from the employment. Paragraph 31 is concerned with tax charges under the benefits legislation. Where the commission or the net or discounted amount referred to within that paragraph is available on the same basis to members of the general public, no benefit will result.

29 Employees who receive commission (from employment) in respect of their own purchase of goods, investments or services from the employer are liable to tax under Schedule E on the full amount of that commission. Where such a commission is placed at the employee's disposal but the employee requests, permits or is required to accept that the commission is applied in some way for his or her benefit, the commission remains liable to tax under Schedule E.

30 Where an employee does not receive and is not entitled to receive, or to have applied for his or her benefit, a cash commission, but does receive from employment a right which has a monetary value, a liability will arise on that value under Schedule E because that right is an emolument. An example is the case where an additional amount is invested in an employee's investment and that investment can be disposed of or otherwise turned to account.

31 Where an employee within the scope (see para 24 above) of the benefits legislation receives a commission from, or pays a net or discounted amount to, the employer in respect of his or her purchase of goods, investments or services, the employee will be liable to tax on the benefit that has been provided. The charge to tax upon a net or discounted amount is calculated following the principles described in para 27 above. The charge upon a commission, not otherwise chargeable to tax, is calculated by reference to the cost of its provision and will typically be the amount paid.

Services etc provided by persons other than the employer in return for commission, or for a net or discounted purchase price, may give rise to a charge calculated in the same way if the benefit is provided by reason of the employment.

Cashbacks

32 Where an employee receives a cashback from his or her employer or a third party on the same basis as is available to members of the general public, Schedule E liability will not arise if the cashback is received under a contract with the employer or third party dissociated from the contract of employment, and the employee gives fair value for the cashback under that contract or by entering into some other contract with the employer or third party. The cashback will then be neither an emolument from employment (within s 19) nor a benefit (within s 154).

However, if in such circumstances the cashback is provided gratuitously and is received from the employee's employer, liability under the benefits legislation must be considered.

Deductions

33 Where commission etc within the scope of this statement is assessable under Schedule E, a claim for deduction in respect of commission shared with, passed on to, or invested for the benefit of, some other party will be admissible if the employee is obliged to expend the sum wholly, exclusively and necessarily in performing the duties of the office or employment. Such an obligation is likely to exist when the transaction falls within the normal framework of the employer's business and is a transaction between independent parties acting at arm's length.

PAYE

34 PAYE applies where commission etc is paid to an employee or on his or her behalf if it is assessable under Schedule E. This includes amounts relating to commission invested on behalf of the employee if the amount of the commission is taxable. Where commission or other taxable income is provided in the form of tradable assets rather than cash, PAYE applies under s 203F.

E CAPITAL GAINS TAX

35 A cashback does not derive from a chargeable asset for capital gains tax purposes. No chargeable gain therefore arises on receipt of the payment. (A cashback does not include a cash payment by a building society to members etc on take-over by, or conversion to, a bank; or by other mutual organisations such as insurance companies or friendly societies on demutualisation.)

Life insurance and personal pensions

Qualifying life insurance policies

36 Where commission in respect of a policy holder's own qualifying life insurance policy is received, netted off or invested, that policy will not be disqualified as a result of entitlement to that commission if the contract under which commission arises is separate from the contract of insurance. In practice, the Revenue will not seek to read two contracts as one in a way that would lead to the loss of qualifying policy status.

37 Where a policy holder pays a discounted premium in respect of his or her own policy, the premium payable under the policy will be the discounted premium. It is this amount that must be used for the purposes of establishing whether the relevant qualifying rules are met.

Calculation of chargeable event gains in respect of life insurance policies, capital redemption policies and life annuity contracts.

38 Chargeable event gains are computed by reference to the premiums or lump sum consideration paid. The amount paid will be interpreted as follows—

- where a policy holder pays a gross premium and receives commission etc in respect of that policy, the chargeable event gain is calculated using the gross amount paid without taking the commission received into account;
- where an amount of commission etc is received or due under an enforceable legal right and subsequently invested in the policy, that amount is included as a premium paid when calculating the chargeable event gain;
- where a policy holder nets off commission from an insurer in respect of his or her own policy from the gross amount of premium payable and the commission is not taxable as income on the policy holder, the chargeable event gain is calculated using the net amount paid to the insurer;
- where a policy holder pays a discounted premium, the chargeable event gain is calculated using the discounted amount of premium paid;
- where extra value is added to the policy by the insurer (for example by allocation of bonus units), the premium for the purpose of calculating the chargeable event gain is the amount paid by the policy holder without taking the extra value into account.

Tax relief in respect of personal pension contributions

39 Tax relief for contributions to personal pension schemes is due in respect of "a contribution paid by an individual". The amount of the contribution will be interpreted as follows where the contract under which the commission arises is separate from the personal pension scheme contract—

- where a contributor pays a gross contribution and receives commission in respect of that contribution, tax relief is given on the gross amount paid without taking the commission received into account;
- where an amount of commission is received by, or is due under an enforceable legal right to, the contributor and subsequently invested in the personal pension that gave rise to the commission, tax relief is given on that amount;
- where a contributor deducts commission in respect of his or her own pension contribution from the gross amount payable, relief is due on the net amount paid;
- where a contributor pays discounted contributions, tax relief is due on the discounted amount paid;
- where extra value is added to the policy by the insurer (for example by allocation of bonus units), relief is due on the amount paid by the contributor without taking the extra value into account.

40 If commission were to be rebated to the contributor under the same contract as the personal pension contract, this would be an unapprovable benefit (since it would involve leakage of the pension fund to the member) which would jeopardise the tax-approved status of the arrangement.

41 The consequences of paying commission on transfers between tax-approved pension schemes may be different from those outlined if such payment is effectively a benefit not authorised by the rules of the pension scheme. Alternatively, the misrepresentation as an annual premium of any premium applied to new pensions business so that a higher rate of rebated commission is generated will call into question the bona fides of the pension arrangement and jeopardise its approval from inception.

Commentary—*Simon's Direct Tax Service* **B7.203, E4.403.**
Note—This statement supersedes SP 5/95. The text of this statement is as it appears in IR 131 (January 2000).

SP 1/98 (25 March 1998) *Tax treatment of expenditure on films*

Commentary—*Simon's Direct Tax Service* **B2.313; B3.1307, 1307A.**
Note—This statement was withdrawn in April 2003. See now the IR Business Income Manual 56000–56500).

SP 2/98 (24 August 1998) *Business by telephone*

Notes—This statement has been superseded by SP 2/03.

SP 4/98 (16 November 1998) *Application of loan relationships, foreign exchange and financial instruments legislation to partnerships which include companies*

Commentary—*Simon's Direct Tax Service* **D4.812.**
Note—This statement superseded SP 9/94 with effect for accounting periods ending after 31 March 1996 and was classified as obsolete by IR 131 (August 2003).

SP 5/98 (30 November 1998) *Venture capital trusts and the enterprise investment scheme—value of "gross assets"*

Note—This statement, which superseded SP 7/95, was superseded by SP 2/00 and classified as obsolete by IR 131 Supp (November 2000).

SP 6/98 (30 November 1998) *Enterprise investment scheme, venture capital trusts, capital gains tax reinvestment relief and business expansion scheme—loans to investors*

INTRODUCTION

1 The rules for the enterprise investment scheme, venture capital trusts, the business expansion scheme, and capital gains tax reinvestment relief each make provision for the tax relief in question to be withdrawn (or to be unavailable) in certain circumstances where a loan is made to the investor or to an associate of the investor.

2 The circumstances in which these rules apply are where the loan would not have been made, or would not have been made on the same terms, if the investor had not made the investment in the shares for which the relief was to be claimed, or had not been proposing to make that investment. This statement explains the Inland Revenue's understanding of the way in which the provisions operate, and gives examples of instances where the rules have effect to deny or withdraw relief and of instances where they do not.

APPLICATION

3 The way in which these rules are applied in any particular case will depend on the precise facts and circumstances. However, in looking to see whether a given loan falls within the scope of the legislation, the Inland Revenue's primary concern will be with the reason why the lender made the loan rather than why the borrower applied for it. The rules do not necessarily have effect to deny or withdraw relief just because a loan is used to finance the acquisition. Moreover, if the lender learns that the purpose, or one of the purposes, of the loan application is the financing of the acquisition, that does not necessarily mean that the rules have effect to deny or withdraw relief. The test is whether the lender makes the loan on terms which are influenced by the fact that the borrower, or an associate of the borrower, has acquired, or is proposing to acquire, the shares.

4 The rules would not have effect to deny or withdraw relief where a person proposing to acquire shares receives a loan from a bank, if the bank would have made a loan on the same terms to a similar borrower who was intending to use it for a different purpose. But if, for example, a loan is made on a specified security which consists of, or includes, the shares in question, it would be one which would not otherwise have been made on the same terms. In such a case, the loan would be linked with the shares, and the investor would not qualify for relief in respect of them. This would apply only where the shares, or any rights associated with them, are specified as all or part of the security. It would not apply, for example, in any case where the lender had recourse against the borrower's assets generally.

5 In considering the terms of any particular loan, the Inland Revenue will have regard to such features as the qualifying conditions which must be satisfied by the borrower, the existence of incentives or benefits offered to the borrower, the time allowed for repayment, the amount of repayment and interest charged, the timing of interest payments, and the nature of the security pledged.

NOTE

6 The business expansion scheme came to an end for new investment at the end of 1993, and capital gains tax reinvestment relief is not available for shares acquired after 5 April 1998.

Commentary—*Simon's Direct Tax Service* **E3.149, 641.**
Note—This statement superseded SP 3/94.

SP 7/98 (30 November 1998) *Enterprise investment scheme, venture capital trusts and capital gains tax reinvestment relief—location of activity*

Commentary—*Simon's Direct Tax Service* **E3.119, 131, 623.**
Note—This statement, which superseded SP 2/94, is itself superseded by SP 3/00.

SP 8/98 (18 December 1998) *Business by telephone: East Kilbride call centre*

Note—This statement has been superseded by SP 3/03 (September 2003).

SP 1/99 (28 January 1999) *Self-assessment enquiries and capital gains tax valuations*

Self-assessment enquiries—TMA 1970 ss 9A, 12AC: enquiries remaining open after expiry of the period within which a notice of enquiry may be issued solely because of an unagreed valuation for capital gains tax purposes.

The following statement of practice applies where, in the case of an enquiry into a return made under TMA 1970 ss 8, 8A, 12AA—

- an officer of the Board has given notice under TMA 1970 ss 9A(1) or 12AC(1) of his intention to enquire into that return; and
- the enquiry remains open after the expiry of the period within which that notice had to be issued (''enquiry period''); and
- the enquiry remains open solely because of an unagreed valuation for capital gains tax purposes.

In such circumstances the Inland Revenue will not, as a matter of practice, raise further enquiries into matters unrelated to the valuation or the capital gains tax computation unless the circumstances are such that, had the enquiry already been completed, an officer of the Board could have made a discovery within the meaning of TMA 1970 s 29.

This practice applies only to valuations for capital gains tax purposes in respect of individuals, partnerships and trusts.

This practice does not alter or fetter the Inland Revenue's right to ask further questions or make additional enquiries on matters in connection with, or consequential to, the obtaining of the valuation which were not raised when the valuation was first referred to the shares valuation division or the valuation office agency.

Commentary—*Simon's Direct Tax Service* **E1.811.**

SPs

SP 2/99 (31 March 1999) *Monthly savings in investment funds*

INTRODUCTION

1 This statement of practice explains where the Inland Revenue will accept simplified capital gains tax computations from individuals who have disposed of shares or units in investment funds which they acquired through monthly savings schemes before 6 April 1999. The investment funds concerned are authorised unit trusts (AUTs), approved investment trusts (AITs), and open-ended investment companies (OEICs) incorporated in the UK. For capital gains tax purposes, each sub-fund of an AUT which is an umbrella scheme is regarded as an AUT in its own right, and the umbrella scheme itself is not regarded as an AUT. Similarly, each sub-fund of an OEIC which is an umbrella company is regarded as an OEIC in its own right, and the umbrella company itself is not regarded as an OEIC.

2 Where taxpayers ask for the practice to apply, the number of calculations needed to determine their capital gains tax liabilities for the units or shares they acquired through their savings scheme which qualify for indexation allowance will be substantially reduced. This statement does not affect the rights of taxpayers who wish to submit computations made on the normal statutory basis.

3 Although the statement covers a wide variety of circumstances, its basic approach is simple. It applies where an investor saves a fixed sum each month and makes no withdrawals, or only relatively small withdrawals. In these cases, the total of an investor's monthly investments in the fund during its accounting year will be added to the total of any distributions or other allocations of income which are reinvested in the fund on his or her behalf in the accounting year. Any small withdrawals made in that accounting year will be deducted. The resulting figure will be treated for capital gains tax purposes as if it had formed a single investment made on the date on which the seventh monthly investment is made. Suppose, for example, an investor in an AUT saves £50 on the seventh of each month, that no distributions or other income allocations are reinvested in the fund on his or her behalf, and that the AUT has an accounting year ending on 31 December. Capital gains tax computations will be made as if the taxpayer had made a single investment of £600 on 7 July. As a result, only one computation will be needed for the investments in the fund in that year, instead of twelve.

WHO CAN ASK FOR THIS PRACTICE TO APPLY?

4 Individuals who entered before 6 April 1998 into a monthly savings scheme to invest regular monthly sums in an AUT, AIT or OEIC, and dispose of investments on or after 6 April 1988. The practice can be applied in respect of monthly sums invested during those accounting years of the fund concerned which ended before 6 April 1999. The practice cannot be applied in respect of monthly sums invested during accounting years which end on or after 6 April 1999, and the capital gains tax computations for investments made in those periods must be calculated on the normal statutory basis.

5 The appendix at the end of this statement provides an example of a capital gains tax computation where the disposal in question is made by an investor some years after 6 April 1999 of income units in an AUT which were acquired through a savings scheme that began before 6 April 1998. The example illustrates how the practice is used for the period for which it is applicable, and how the computations are made for the period for which the practice does not apply.

HOW SHOULD THE TAXPAYER MAKE THE REQUEST?

6 Taxpayers must write to their tax offices not later than twelve months after 31 January following the end of the first tax year in which they dispose of units or shares acquired via monthly savings schemes, and—

- the resulting gains, together with any other gains made in the year, exceed the capital gains annual exempt amount for that year; or
- the disposal proceeds together with the proceeds of their other disposals exceed twice the annual exempt amount; or
- their other disposals in the year give rise to net losses.

7 Where a taxpayer has monthly savings schemes in more than one AUT, AIT or OEIC, applications for this practice to apply should be made separately for each trust or company. Where a taxpayer has more than one monthly savings scheme in the same AUT, AIT or OEIC, the application will cover all those schemes, and this practice will apply as if they formed a single scheme.

8 Some savings schemes allow an investor to make a single monthly payment which is split between different trusts or companies. If so, the statement will apply as if there were separate savings schemes for each trust or company concerned. Thus, an investor who saves £200 a month, with £100 allocated to XYZ growth unit trust and £100 to XYZ income unit trust, will be treated as having two separate schemes for £100 a month each.

9 Some savings schemes allow investors to vary the fund in which their monthly contributions are invested. An investor who changes the fund in which his or her contributions are invested will be regarded for these purposes as having ceased contributing under one savings scheme and having started a new scheme. This treatment also applies in cases where investors switch their contributions between different sub-funds of an umbrella AUT or OEIC.

WHAT WILL THE SIMPLIFIED COMPUTATION APPLY TO?

10 The rules described below will apply in calculating the gain on the disposal of units or shares in the year of assessment to which the application relates. Where the disposal is a part-disposal, the rules will also apply in determining gains on later disposals of units or shares acquired via the savings scheme, subject to the taxpayer's right to revert to the statutory basis. A taxpayer who has exercised his or her right to revert to the statutory basis for a particular savings scheme may not benefit for a second time from the simplified rules for that scheme.

11 Some taxpayers may have units or shares in a monthly savings scheme for a particular AUT, AIT or OEIC and other units or shares in the same AUT, AIT or OEIC which are acquired by, for example, separate lump sum investment. The practice described in this statement will apply only to the units or shares held in the monthly savings scheme. Any gain on units or shares acquired in other ways will be computed according to normal capital gains rules as if those units or shares formed a holding separate from those acquired through the monthly savings scheme.

THE APPROACH OF THE SIMPLIFIED COMPUTATIONS

12 The general approach treats all investments and withdrawals made in a year during the lifetime of the savings plan as though they were made in a single month of that year.

13 The year will correspond to the accounting year of the fund. This may not always be exactly twelve months, because for some funds the date to which accounts are drawn up varies slightly from year to year. For example, the accounting date may be set as the second Thursday in November (irrespective of the day of the month on which it falls). Apart from such small variations, special rules will apply when the accounting date is changed. These are described later.

14 In the straightforward case where an investor makes regular monthly contributions throughout the accounting year, investments and withdrawals will be treated as made on the day on which the seventh monthly investment in the accounting year is due. The calendar month in which that day falls is referred to in this statement as ''the seventh month''.

15 Where distributions are automatically reinvested to acquire further shares or units, or where the investor uses the savings scheme to acquire accumulation units in an AUT or accumulation shares in an OEIC, the distribution or allocation of income will be treated as invested on the day on which it is credited to the trust or company on the investor's behalf. No adjustment will be made for equalisation. The day on which the investment is treated as made for the final distribution in the accounting year of the trust or company will be determined as follows—

- In cases where distributions are automatically reinvested in the trust or company to acquire further units or shares on the investor's behalf, the final distribution for an accounting year will be credited after the end of that accounting year. This means that final distributions for an accounting year will be regarded for these purposes as reinvested in the following accounting year.
- In the case of accumulation units or shares, on the other hand, the final allocation of income in respect of an accounting period becomes part of the capital property of the AUT or OEIC concerned with effect from the end of the accounting year in question.

EXAMPLE 1

(*a*) An accounting year starts on 1 January 1996.

(*b*) The taxpayer subscribes £100 a month throughout the accounting year in income units in an AUT, on the sixth of each month.

(*c*) The final distribution for the accounting year ending on 31 December 1995 is £25, the interim distribution for the new accounting year is £27, and the final distribution for the new accounting year is £30. The distributions are automatically reinvested in the AUT to acquire further units on the taxpayer's behalf.

In calculating the indexation allowance, the taxpayer will be treated as having made a single investment of £1,252 on 6 July 1996.

EXAMPLE 2

(*a*) An accounting year starts on 1 January 1996.

(*b*) The taxpayer subscribes £100 a month in accumulation shares in an OEIC throughout the accounting year, on the sixth of each month.

(*c*) The final distribution for the accounting year ending on 31 December 1995 is £25, the interim distribution for the new accounting year is £27, and the final distribution for the new accounting year is £30.

In calculating the indexation allowance, the taxpayer will be treated as having made a single investment of £1,257 on 6 July 1996.

EXAMPLE 3

(*a*) An accounting year starts on 20 January 1995 and ends on 19 January 1996.

(*b*) The taxpayer subscribes £100 a month throughout the accounting year in shares in an AIT, on the sixth of each month.

(*c*) The final distribution for the accounting year ending on 19 January 1995 and the interim distribution for the new accounting year are £50 in aggregate and are automatically reinvested in the AIT to acquire further shares on the taxpayer's behalf.

The first monthly contribution in the new accounting year is made on 6 February 1995, and the seventh on 6 August 1995. In calculating the indexation allowance, the taxpayer will be treated as having made a single investment of £1,250 on 6 August 1995.

PRE-1982 HOLDINGS

16 When calculating capital gains tax and indexation on the statutory basis, pre-1982 holdings (acquisitions made on or before 31 March 1982) are treated as a separate pool from the post-1982 pool (acquisitions between 1 April 1982 and 5 April 1998). This will also apply for the purposes of the special treatment provided by the practice described in this Statement. Indexation will be calculated for two separate pools and any withdrawals will be treated as disposals of units or shares from the post-1982 pool first, and when that is exhausted, from the pre-1982 pool. This is in accordance with the existing LIFO (last-in, first-out) rules. The practice will not apply to the pre-1982 holding. Where an accounting year straddles 31 March 1982, the practice will apply as if regular saving began in April 1982, in accordance with para 17 below. It will not apply to investments and withdrawals up to 31 March 1982.

FIRST YEAR OF INVESTMENT

17 Where an investor begins regular saving part-way through an accounting year, his or her investments and any withdrawals in that period will be treated as made on the date of the last monthly contribution in the accounting year.

FINAL YEAR OF MONTHLY SAVING

18 In the accounting period in which regular monthly saving stops, investments will be treated as made on the date of the last regular contribution or, if earlier, in the seventh month.

ONE-OFF EXTRA SAVINGS

19 An investor may sometimes make extra payments into his or her savings scheme in addition to the regular monthly commitment. If, in any month, the extra payment is not more than twice the regular monthly commitment, it will be treated in the same way as the regular monthly savings (and so, in the normal case, as if it were made in the seventh month). If the extra payment exceeds twice the monthly commitment, it will be treated as made in the calendar month in which it is actually made.

20 In some AITs, arrangements for one-off savings are kept separate from the monthly savings schemes. Where that happens, the practice will not apply to shares acquired by one-off savings.

INCREASES IN MONTHLY SAVINGS LEVEL

21 Some investors may increase their monthly savings commitments. If the increase occurs after the seventh month in an accounting year, the extra savings will be deemed to be made at the beginning of the next accounting year, and indexation, where available, runs from the seventh month for that following year.

EXAMPLE 4

(*a*) The accounting year coincides with the calendar year, so that the seventh month is July.

(*b*) From January to August 1990, the taxpayer saves £50 a month.

(*c*) From September 1990, the taxpayer saves £100 a month.

(*d*) The final distribution for 1989, which is automatically reinvested, is £50. There is no interim distribution.

The taxpayer will be deemed to have made a single investment of £650 in July 1990. The extra £200 invested between September and December 1990 will be deemed to be invested in January 1991, and added to the investments made in 1991. Indexation will be given on this amount from July 1991 until April 1998.

WITHDRAWALS AND PART-DISPOSALS

22 Savings schemes often allow taxpayers to make withdrawals. Where the withdrawals in any accounting year do not exceed one quarter of the total amount of regular savings made in that accounting year, the withdrawal or withdrawals will not be treated as involving a disposal, but the amount invested in the accounting year will be reduced by the amount withdrawn.

23 Where withdrawals in any accounting year exceed one quarter of the total amount of regular savings made in the accounting year, the practice does not apply to savings made in that year. However, provided the necessary conditions are satisfied, the practice applies to earlier and later accounting years.

24 Under some AIT savings schemes, an investor wishing to realise part of a holding has to make his or her own arrangements to sell the shares because the scheme does not offer a facility to dispose of shares. In such cases, the practice will apply to part-disposals of shares acquired via the scheme in the same way as to withdrawals. If at the time of a disposal prior to 6 April 1998 the investor also has shares acquired outside the scheme, the disposal will be treated, so far as possible, as being of those other shares. For disposals after 5 April 1998, the normal capital gains tax rules apply to identify the shares which are disposed of.

PART DISPOSALS BEFORE 6 APRIL 1988

25 Where there was a part disposal before 6 April 1988 and the gain either was assessed or would have been calculated on the statutory basis under paras 23 or 27 of this statement had the practice applied at the time, the simplified rules will apply to investments and withdrawals made from the start of the accounting year following the accounting year in which the last such part disposal took place.

SHORT-TERM INVESTORS

26 This practice does not apply where fewer than seven months' regular savings are made.

MISSED MONTHS

27 Some savings schemes allow taxpayers to miss a month of regular saving. This practice will apply in the normal way to any accounting year in which the taxpayer misses only one regular payment. If more than one payment is missed in an accounting year the practice will not operate for investments and withdrawals in that accounting year. However, if the necessary conditions are satisfied, it will apply for earlier and later accounting years.

NON-STANDARD PERIODS OF ACCOUNT

28 Sometimes an AUT, AIT or OEIC may draw up accounts for a period which is less than, or greater than, a year. This will often apply for the first accounting period, and a non-standard period of account will also arise if the accounting date is changed. In these circumstances, special rules apply—

(*a*) if the period of account is less than seven months, investments and withdrawals will be treated as made on the date of the last regular contribution in the period;

(*b*) if the period is at least seven months but does not exceed twelve months, investments and withdrawals will be treated as made in the seventh month (as defined in para 14 above);

(*c*) if the period exceeds twelve months, it will be subdivided. The first twelve months will be treated as if they formed an accounting year, and investments and withdrawals in them will be treated as made in the seventh month. Investments and withdrawals in the remainder of the period will be treated as made on the date of the last regular contribution in the period.

These special rules will not apply where there is a change of accounting date in accordance with a routine formula which merely reflects a variation of the kind referred to in para 13.

LOSS OF APPROVED INVESTMENT TRUST STATUS

29 Investment trusts have to be approved each year by the Inland Revenue. This practice will not apply for an accounting period for which approval is not obtained. But, provided the necessary conditions are satisfied, it will apply for earlier or later periods for which approval is given.

INTERACTION WITH YEARS OF ASSESSMENT

30 An accounting year is unlikely to coincide with a year of assessment. When a taxpayer completes his or her return it may not yet be certain that all the conditions for the operation of this practice will be satisfied for the accounting year straddling the end of the year of assessment concerned. In such circumstances, the return should be completed on the assumptions that—

(*a*) monthly savings will continue at the level applying at the end of the year of assessment; and

(*b*) there will be no withdrawals or one-off extra savings in that part of the straddling accounting year which falls after the year of assessment.

31 The treatment described in para 22 above can be applied only if withdrawals in that part of the straddling accounting year which falls within the year of assessment concerned do not exceed total savings in that part of the straddling accounting year. If it turns out that the conditions for the practice to apply are not, in fact, satisfied in the second part of the straddling accounting year, the treatment of any investments and withdrawals made in the earlier part of the straddling accounting year will not be disturbed.

TRANSFERS OR MERGERS OF FUNDS

32 An investor may enter into a monthly savings scheme with an AUT, AIT or OEIC whose business is later transferred to, or merged with, another trust or company. On the transfer or merger the investor's old units or shares will generally be cancelled, and replaced with units or shares in the new trust or company. Where TCGA 1992 s 136 applies in such cases the investor is treated for capital gains tax purposes as not disposing of his or her original units or shares, or acquiring replacement units or shares in the new trust or company.

Instead, the new units or shares are treated as having been acquired at the same times, and for the same amounts, as the original units or shares.

33 If, where TCGA 1992 s 136 applies to the investor's holding on the transfer or merger, the investor continues to make the same regular monthly payments to the new fund, this practice applies as though no transfer or merger had taken place. The new trust or company may, however, have a different accounting date from the old trust or company. If so, the period from the last accounting date of the old fund, to the next accounting date of the new fund, may—so far as the investor is concerned—be treated simply as a non-standard period of account to which para 27 above applies in relation to the continuing contributions. If, on the other hand, TCGA s 136 does not apply on the transfer or merger, the investor is treated as disposing of his or her units or shares for capital gains tax purposes, and starting a new scheme with the new trust or company at that time. In such cases paras 18 and 17 of the statement will apply instead.

APPENDIX

EXAMPLE

Mary enters into a monthly savings scheme in September 1995 in which she invests £100 a month on the first of each month in income units in an AUT. No distributions or other income allocations are reinvested in the fund on her behalf. The accounting year of the unit trust begins on 1 July each year and ends on 30 June in the following year. She makes her last payment in April 2002, and disposes of all her units on 25 May 2004, having made no withdrawals and no additional investments in the fund in the meantime.

The tables below show the prices she paid for the units she purchased under the scheme, and the number of units purchased.

Month	*Price (p)*	*Units*	*Month*	*Price (p)*	*Units*
Sep 1995	38.22	261.64	Jan 1999	58.61	170.62
Oct	38.71	258.33	Feb	60.14	166.28
Nov	39.30	254.45	Mar	59.59	167.81
Dec	39.98	250.13	Apr	60.62	164.96
Jan 1996	38.26	261.37	May	61.57	162.42
Feb	37.01	270.20	June	62.44	160.15
Mar	37.95	263.50	July	62.87	159.06
Apr	39.43	253.61	Aug	63.54	157.38
May	40.62	246.18	Sep	62.10	161.03
June	40.87	244.68	Oct	60.56	165.13
July	41.79	239.29	Nov	59.62	167.73
Aug	42.65	234.47	Dec	59.27	168.72
Sep	43.08	232.13	Jan 2000	60.28	165.89
Oct	42.81	233.59	Feb	61.37	162.95
Nov	42.92	232.99	Mar	62.84	159.13
Dec	44.05	227.01	Apr	64.15	155.88
Jan 1997	46.43	215.38	May	65.06	153.70
Feb	47.11	212.27	June	68.32	146.37
Mar	47.34	211.24	July	70.14	142.57
Apr	48.93	204.37	Aug	71.28	140.29
May	49.62	201.53	Sep	73.81	135.48
June	47.33	211.28	Oct	74.00	135.14
July	46.87	213.36	Nov	74.81	133.67
Aug	46.69	214.18	Dec	74.97	133.39
Sep	48.31	207.00	Jan 2001	75.33	132.75
Oct	50.15	199.40	Feb	76.41	130.87
Nov	51.41	194.51	Mar	77.99	128.22
Dec	52.60	190.11	Apr	78.45	127.47
Jan 1998	52.88	189.11	May	78.42	127.52
Feb	53.17	188.08	June	79.61	125.61
Mar	53.10	188.32	July	80.15	124.77
Apr	54.63	183.05	Aug	82.22	121.62
May	53.96	185.32	Sep	83.58	119.65
June	53.85	185.70	Oct	83.10	120.34
July	54.29	184.20	Nov	83.85	119.26
Aug	55.62	179.79	Dec	84.07	118.95
Sep	55.81	179.18	Jan 2002	85.21	117.36
Oct	56.78	176.12	Feb	86.32	115.85
Nov	57.18	174.89	Mar	87.19	114.69
Dec	57.73	173.22	Apr	88.04	113.58

The total number of units Mary has acquired through the scheme was 14,319.44 at a total cost of £8,000, and when she sold them the price she obtained for each unit was 101 pence. The consideration she received was, therefore, £14,462.63. We want to calculate the amount of the gain of £6,462.63 which is chargeable.

Calculation

This is done in a number of steps.

The first step is to split the units acquired after 30 June 1998—which is the last day of the final accounting year for which the practice can be applied—into batches according to the number of years' taper relief for which they qualify. The gain, and the amount of it which is chargeable, is then calculated in each case.

(*a*) The 1311.68 units acquired from 1 June 2001 to 1 April 2002 inclusive do not qualify for taper relief, as they were not business assets and Mary had held them for less than three complete years when she disposed of them.

The consideration received for these units was 1311.68 × £1.01 =	£1,324.80
The cost of these units was	£1,100.00
The chargeable gain is	£224.80

(*b*) The 1613.74 units acquired from 1 June 2000 to 1 May 2001 inclusive were held by Mary for three complete years before she disposed of them. They therefore qualify for three years' taper relief as non-business assets. This means that 95% of the gain is chargeable.

The consideration received for these units was 1613.74 × £1.01 =	£1,629.88
The cost of these units was	£1,200.00
The gain is	£429.88
The tapered gain is	£408.39

(*c*) The 1936·75 units acquired from 1 June 1999 to 1 May 2000 inclusive were held by Mary for four complete years before she disposed of them. They therefore qualify for four years' taper relief as non-business assets. This means that 90% of the gain is chargeable.

The consideration received for these units was 1936.75 × £1.01 =	£1,956.12
The cost of these units was	£1,200.00
The gain is	£756.12
The tapered gain is	£680.51

(*d*) The 1899.49 units acquired from 1 July 1998 to 1 May 1999 inclusive were held by Mary for five complete years before she disposed of them. They therefore qualify for five years' taper relief as non-business assets. This means that 85% of the gain is chargeable.

The consideration received for these units was 1899.49 × £1.01 =	£1,918.48	
The cost of these units was		£1,100.00
The gain is		£818.48
The tapered gain is		£695.71

The second step is to apply the practice for those accounting years of the fund for which it can be used. These are the periods ending on 30 June 1996, 30 June 1997, and 30 June 1998.

The rule given in para 17 of the statement provides that the units Mary acquired in the accounting year of the fund which ended on 30 June 1996 are treated as though she acquired them on the date she made her last contribution in that period, namely 1 June 1996. The seventh month rule applies for the accounting years ending on 30 June 1997 and 30 June 1998.

So Mary is treated as acquiring—

– 2564.09 units on 1 June 1996 for £1,000;

– 2655.55 units on 1 January 1997 for £1,200; and

– 2338.14 units on 1 January 1998 for £1,200.

The third step is to calculate the gain on these 7557·78 units and how much of it is chargeable. As these units were all acquired (or are treated as acquired) before 6 April 1998, they are pooled together for capital gains tax purposes. They qualify for indexation allowance to April 1998, and also for a year's head start for taper relief purposes, as Mary is treated as holding all of them on 17 March 1998.

The consideration received for these units was 7557.78 × £1.01 =	£7,633.36
The cost of these units was	£3,400.00
The unindexed gain is	£4,233.36
The indexation allowance in respect of these units is	£149.40
The indexed gain is	£4,083.96

The number of complete years after 5 April 1998 for which these units are held is six years. The effect of the one-year head start is that they qualify for seven years' taper relief. The units are not business assets for taper relief purposes. This means that 75% of the gain is chargeable.

SPs

The tapered gain is: £3,062·97

(The Inland Revenue help sheet IR 284 "Shares and capital gains tax" gives details of how to calculate the indexation allowance on a disposal of shares or units in a pool. You can obtain a copy from the Inland Revenue Orderline by telephoning 0645 000404, writing to PO Box 37, St Austell, Cornwall PL25 5YN, e-mailing saorderline.ir@gtnet.gov.uk, or faxing 0645 000604.)

The final step is to sum—

£224.80
£408.39
£680.51
£695.71
£3,062.97

£5,072.38

So the amount of the gain which is chargeable is **£5,072.38.**

The amount of capital gains tax that Mary will actually have to pay for the year of assessment 2004–05, if any, will depend on a number of factors, including the value of the annual exempt amount at that time, the aggregate amount of chargeable gains which accrue to her in that year, the amount of any allowable losses that she has available to set against untapered gains, and the amount of her taxable income. The Inland Revenue booklet CGT1 "Capital gains tax—an introduction", which is available from any tax enquiry centre or tax office, provides further details about the basic capital gains tax rules for individuals.

Commentary—*Simon's Direct Tax Service* **C2.736b**
Note—This statement supersedes SP 2/97 from 31 March 1999.

SP 3/99 (31 August 1999) *Advance pricing agreements (APAs)*

GENERAL

1 This statement of practice provides detailed guidance about how the Inland Revenue interprets FA 1999 ss 85–87, which provide for advance pricing agreements (APAs) and how it intends applying this legislation in practice.

2 APAs aim to assist businesses in determining complex transfer pricing issues. These may arise in applying the arm's length principle in accordance with domestic legislation, with the guidance provided by the "Transfer pricing guidelines for multinational enterprises and tax administrations" (the "OECD transfer pricing guidelines") published by the Organisation for Economic Co-operation and Development (OECD), and with any arrangements made with foreign governments with a view to affording relief from double taxation (DTAs).

3 APAs allow complex transfer pricing issues to be resolved on a prospective basis. They can provide solutions to situations where there is considerable difficulty or doubt in determining the method by which the arm's length principle should be applied. In such cases, even though the process of reaching an agreement can require significant resources, an APA may prove more efficient than the retrospective examination of major transfer pricing issues and may allow the business to predict tax liabilities with greater certainty.

4 APAs made for the purposes of FA 1999 s 85 are written agreements between a business and the Board of Inland Revenue which determine a method for resolving transfer pricing issues in advance of a return being made. When the terms of the agreement are complied with, they provide assurance that the treatment in accordance with the agreement of those transfer pricing issues will be accepted by both the Revenue and the business for the period covered by the agreement.

TRANSFER PRICING ISSUES

5 FA 1999 s 85(2) sets out the transfer pricing issues which can be the subject matter of an APA. An APA can resolve questions relating to two broad situations giving rise to transfer pricing issues—

(*a*) Transfer pricing between separate business enterprises where questions may arise as to the determination of the arm's length provision under the rules at TA 1988 s 770A/Sch 28AA; this matter is covered by s 85(2)(*d*), (*e*).

(*b*) Transfer pricing between parts of one business enterprise operating in more than one country where questions may arise as to the taxable income to be recognised in any such part. These matters are covered by s 85(2)(*a*), (*b*), (*c*).

In the latter case, the relevant subsection is determined by whether a DTA applies and the location of the parts of the enterprise. Where no DTA applies, the attribution of income to part of a non-resident enterprise operating in the UK is specifically covered by s 85(2)(*a*), and income arising outside the UK from part of a resident enterprise is specifically covered by s 85(2)(*c*); where a DTA applies and income is attributable to a permanent establishment, these matters are specifically covered by s 85(2)(*b*).

6 There may be a question as to the extent to which the scope of an APA extends to include consideration of whether a permanent establishment ("PE") of an enterprise exists. Subsection

(2)(*b*) is predicated on the existence of a PE and so it follows that matters under that subsection are agreed on the basis that a PE exists. What the legislation does not specifically provide for is a determination that a PE does not exist. In applying for an APA, therefore, in circumstances where the applicant is concerned that the Revenue might deem that a foreign associate has a PE in the UK in relation to the issues covered by the APA, the applicant can raise the matter with a view to including as part of the APA a determination that the income to be attributed to the potential PE is nil.

UNILATERAL OR BILATERAL APPLICATIONS?

7 An APA may remain limited to a binding agreement between a UK business and the Inland Revenue in accordance with FA 1999 s 85—this is referred to as a "unilateral APA". However, a unilateral APA can provide only a partial resolution of cross-border transfer pricing issues because, although it confirms the tax treatment in the UK, it does not determine how the issues are to be resolved in the other country involved. Consequently, it does not eliminate the risk of double taxation in relation to the transfer pricing issues it addresses. In order to achieve that comprehensively in the case of cross-border transfer pricing issues where a DTA exists between the UK and the other country containing a mutual agreement procedure article, the Inland Revenue would have to reach agreement also with the tax administration of the other country— this is referred to as a "bilateral APA".

8 The Inland Revenue encourages applications for bilateral APAs in relation to cross-border transfer pricing issues. Bilateral arrangements offer an assurance that the method for dealing with the transfer pricing issues covered in the APA will be accepted by the tax administrations of both countries, thus avoiding potential double taxation. Where an APA application affects a country with which the UK has a DTA containing a mutual agreement procedure article, the Inland Revenue will generally invite the treaty partner to participate under that procedure (and any relevant domestic arrangements governing APAs that the treaty partner may itself have) in order to endeavour to resolve difficulties or doubts as to the interpretation or application of the DTA by mutual agreement. If after a specified period the treaty partner has not indicated a desire to participate, or despite wishing to do so is unable to commit to proceeding within a reasonable timescale, or for some other reason it is not possible to reach agreement on a bilateral process, the Inland Revenue will be prepared to consider a unilateral APA.

9 Nevertheless, the Inland Revenue will take into account any representations from the applicant about the appropriateness of a bilateral APA in the circumstances of the particular application. A unilateral APA may be preferable where the applicant considers that the extension to a bilateral APA would unnecessarily complicate and delay the process in circumstances where, for example, the treaty partner has no APA process or where there is considered to be little extra to be gained by seeking a bilateral agreement. This may occur where the applicant has identified that the most immediate need to determine transfer pricing rests in the UK because, for example, the UK business is at the hub of arrangements with associated enterprises in many different countries and where the individual amounts involved for one particular country are relatively small.

10 Neither a business nor a treaty partner should be disadvantaged by a unilateral rather than a bilateral APA because any APA is required to be modified to give effect to any subsequent mutual agreement reached under the terms of a DTA. Where the relevant treaty country takes action which results or will result in double taxation in respect of the transfer pricing issues addressed by a unilateral APA, the UK business may, as in any instance of taxation not in accordance with the treaty, request competent authority assistance in accordance with existing procedures and the requirements of the DTA or domestic provisions to seek to eliminate the double taxation. As is made clear by FA 1999 s 86(3), the Inland Revenue's ability to give effect to a mutual agreement reached with a treaty partner to eliminate double taxation under the terms of a treaty will not be restricted by the unilateral APA. In addition, where a unilateral APA request involves foreign related parties resident in a country with which the UK has a DTA containing an exchange of information article, the Inland Revenue is not restricted by the APA process in notifying the treaty partner of the request and in providing information relating to the request under that article.

SPs

MULTILATERAL APAS

11 Businesses operating in several countries may wish to seek APAs that involve all the relevant tax administrations affected by the transfer pricing issues. The term, "multilateral APA", has been used to describe such agreements, but in fact there is no mechanism for reaching multilateral agreements, and multilateral APAs in strictness are multiple, bilateral APAs.

12 For example, an application in relation to the licensing of major intangible property from the UK to associated businesses in countries X and Y might lead to applications for two bilateral APAs; one between the Inland Revenue and country X and one between the Inland Revenue and country Y. In such a situation, although there may be a superficial similarity between the two sets of licensing arrangements, there may be differences between the terms of the arrangements and differences between the operations of the two licensees that might mean significantly different pricing approaches are developed. In this situation there may be no need for the Inland Revenue to seek discussions on a trilateral basis with the tax administrations of countries X and Y, although information could be provided to all the tax administrations by the business or exchanged between the tax administrations to the extent provided by the terms of the relevant DTAs.

13 Multilateral agreements may be more appropriate where there is essentially only one activity, but several enterprises or parts of enterprises contribute to it. For example, where an enterprise of the UK is engaged in global financial trading through branches in countries X and Y, it may be appropriate for similar agreements to be reached between the Inland Revenue and country X and the Inland Revenue and country Y in order to determine how the profits from the activity are to be allocated to each of the three countries in order to eliminate double taxation. In such a situation the Inland Revenue would be prepared to seek to adapt the bilateral framework in order to reach agreement on a trilateral basis, subject to the acquiescence of the other tax administrations and any constraints on exchanging information imposed by the relevant DTAs. Any agreed outcome would, however, take the form of two bilateral APAs.

14 Further information about the conduct of multilateral APAs can be given when an applicant expresses an interest in applying for an APA.

EXISTING BILATERAL APAS

15 Any existing APA reached with a treaty partner under the terms of the mutual agreement procedure of the DTA prior to the introduction of FA 1999 ss 85–87 is unaffected by those provisions. However, any renewal of such an agreement falling within the scope of the new provisions should be made in accordance with the new provisions and follow the guidance in this statement of practice.

ADMINISTRATION

16 Since one of the main purposes of the APA process is to eliminate the risk of double taxation by means of a mutual agreement with a treaty partner, the Inland Revenue's International Division has responsibility for all applications except those involving oil taxation. Transfer pricing specialists and delegated competent authority officials from International Division, assisted by the tax office responsible for the business, will be responsible for assessing APA requests. All expressions of interest in and applications for APAs (see paras 30–38 below) should be made, in general, to the Assistant Director (APAs) at International Division, and, in cases involving oil taxation, to the Deputy Director (APAs) in the Oil Taxation Office. They will be responsible for all aspects of the process, including signature on behalf of the Board of Inland Revenue of any resulting agreements. Normally the person responsible for signing the agreement on behalf of the business would be the person responsible for signing the tax return, subject to that person having the necessary authority within the multinational group to commit the group to the terms of the APA.

17 The addresses of the Assistant Director (APAs) in International Division and of the Deputy Director (APAs) in the Oil Taxation Office are [given at para 59].

APPLICANTS

18 An APA may be requested by—

- any UK business, including a partnership, with transactions to which the provisions of TA 1988 s 770A/Sch 28AA apply;
- any non-resident trading in the UK through a branch or agency (or permanent establishment);
- any UK resident trading through a branch (or permanent establishment) outside the UK.

19 Potential applicants need to bear in mind that the process is designed to offer assistance in resolving complex transfer pricing issues. The Inland Revenue does not regard entering into APAs on less complex matters as a sensible use of resources in the absence of significant doubt as to the manner in which the arm's length principle should be applied. It may therefore decline to accept applications that do not satisfy those criteria (see para 52 for more details).

20 As a general guide, where reliable market comparables can be established that enable transfer pricing methods to be accurately employed in accordance with the OECD transfer pricing guidelines, the application of the transfer pricing legislation should not be complex and the clarification in accordance with FA 1999 s 85(1), (5) would not be necessary. Where there is difficulty in establishing reliable market comparables, or doubt about how transfer pricing methods can be accurately employed to determine arm's length conditions, the application of the transfer pricing legislation becomes more complex.

21 Guidance about a potential application may be obtained from the Inland Revenue (see the discussion in para 30 about the expression of interest stage in an application) and this statement of practice also indicates some circumstances in which an application might be declined. The Inland Revenue recognises that complex transfer pricing issues can be encountered by smaller businesses as well as by large multinationals, and applications for APAs will not be declined solely by reference to the size of the transactions giving rise to the transfer pricing issues.

SCOPE

22 The potential scope of an APA is flexible. It may involve transfer pricing methods covering many different types of related party transactions and arrangements, including transfers of tangible or intangible property (in Scotland corporeal or incorporeal property) and the provision of services. The APA may relate to all the transfer pricing issues of the business or be limited to one or more specific issues. The APA may apply to pre-existing issues and there is no requirement that the commencement of an APA should coincide with the commencement of the arrangements which it addresses.

TERM

23 An APA will be operative for a specified period from the date of entry into force as set out in the agreement. The business should propose an initial term for the APA taking into account the period over which it is reasonable to assume that the method for dealing with the relevant transfer pricing issues will remain appropriate in the circumstances. It is expected that the term is likely to be for a minimum of three, and a maximum of five, years. The earliest period covered by the APA is dependent on the date of formal submission of the APA request (see para 34).

RETROSPECTION AND "ROLL-BACK"

24 While an APA will normally operate prospectively in relation to chargeable periods beginning after the time the application is made, it is possible that a chargeable period to which the APA relates may have ended before agreement is reached. FA 1999 s 86(1) allows the APA to be effective for that chargeable period and, in accordance with s 86(7), the agreement may set out any adjustments to be made for tax purposes as a consequence of the agreement.

25 In addition, although a particular agreement does not relate to earlier periods, the agreed transfer pricing methodology may be relevant to a return for an earlier period and to the resolution of any transfer pricing enquiries raised for earlier periods if the particular facts and circumstances surrounding those years are substantially the same. Consequently, in such circumstances, the business may wish to consider using the agreement as a basis for amending a self-assessment return and to request that the method for dealing with transfer pricing issues contained in the APA should be considered for resolving any transfer pricing enquiries to which it is relevant for earlier years. The Inland Revenue may itself also suggest that the "roll-back" of the APA is an appropriate means of resolving a transfer pricing issue in earlier years.

26 Except where "roll-back" is being considered, the request for an APA in respect of future years will not in itself affect any transfer pricing enquiry into earlier years. However, to the extent such an approach is appropriate and feasible, the Inland Revenue will co-ordinate the APA request in respect of future years with any transfer pricing enquiry in respect of prior years in order to improve overall efficiency and reduce duplication of enquiries.

27 Information supplied by the business in relation to an APA request will be kept confidential in accordance with the confidentiality requirements of the Taxes Acts and the terms of any relevant DTA. However, such information will contribute to the pool of information held by the Revenue about that business and no undertaking can be given that it will be taken into account only in relation to the APA. Thus, for example, where information is submitted under an APA which would appropriately enable the re-opening of earlier years for that business under existing law, the fact that the information was submitted under an APA would not in itself prevent reopening. To act otherwise could afford businesses seeking an APA an advantage over other businesses and may give rise to abuses. However, where any businesses are uncertain about a full commitment from the outset to the APA process, an initial approach on an anonymised basis (see para 33 below) may provide businesses with an opportunity to explore the possibility of applying for an APA before disclosing their identity.

SPs

APA REQUESTS

28 As provided by FA 1999 s 85(1)(*c*) the APA process is initiated by the business making an application for clarification by agreement of what the effect would be of the application of the statutory provisions in question.

29 The APA process will typically comprise four stages—expression of interest, formal submission of application for clarification, evaluation, and agreement. However, the details of each stage may vary depending on the particular circumstances of the case.

EXPRESSION OF INTEREST

30 A business interested in applying for an APA may wish to explore and seek to clarify in advance various aspects of a potential application, including its scope and term, and to discuss informally the proposed method for dealing with the transfer pricing issues to which it will relate, the presentation of the formal submission, the extent of the documentation requirements, and other matters. Generally, the Revenue might also wish to have the opportunity to discuss a potential application before detailed work in finalising it is undertaken by the business in order to ensure that the application is one which can be considered for an APA and that the application will be focused on relevant issues. This should ensure that resources of the business are not wasted on the application process.

31 Expressions of interest should cover such relevant information as—

(*a*) the nature and value of the transfer pricing issues to be covered by the APA together with the identification and location of the parties involved;

(*b*) a description of the business activities of the parties and how the transactions concerned relate to these business activities;

(*c*) a description of the proposed transfer pricing method and an explanation of how it is intended to demonstrate that the method accords with the arm's length standard;

(*d*) an indication of the nature of any current transfer pricing enquiries, competent authority claims, and any existing APAs or other APA applications that are relevant to the issues covered by the proposed APA; and

(*e*) in the case of a cross-border transfer pricing issue, confirmation that a bilateral APA is required or reasons why the business considers that only a unilateral APA is appropriate in accordance with this statement of practice.

The information may be provided in writing, or in person at a meeting, or in combination. Generally a meeting is likely to be more productive where some information has been provided in advance. Four copies of any written material should be provided.

32 The Inland Revenue will consider the expression of interest and will indicate whether it is prepared to consider an application for an APA, bearing in mind such factors as those listed in paras 19–21, 52. It will discuss with the business the form of that application and the likely time frame for attempting to reach agreement.

33 The expression of interest can best be evaluated where the identity of the business is known. However, if a business wishes to preserve anonymity until a decision in principle is made to proceed with the application, the Revenue will be prepared to enter discussions without knowing the identity of the business providing all other information relevant to the proper evaluation of the request is supplied.

FORMAL SUBMISSION OF APPLICATION FOR CLARIFICATION

34 Where the business wishes to proceed with the APA proposal and the Revenue has not indicated that it is not able or willing to consider it, a formal written application for clarification incorporating a proposal as to the manner of clarification should then be submitted. The application should ideally be made before the start of the first chargeable period to be covered by the APA, but the Revenue will not rule as out of time applications made before the end of that chargeable period. Four copies should be provided.

35 The application must fulfil the requirements of FA 1999 s 85(5) and set out—

(*a*) the applicant's understanding of the effect of the relevant legislation including the effect of any DTA in relation to the transfer pricing issues under consideration;

(*b*) the areas where, because of the complexity of the transfer pricing issues, clarification of that effect is required; and

(*c*) a proposal for clarifying the effect of the legislation in accordance with the applicant's understanding.

The intention is to ensure that any agreement about the practical treatment of specified transfer pricing issues is formed from a proper understanding of the relevant principles of the Taxes Acts. Thus, where the transfer pricing issue concerns, for example, pricing between associated enterprises, the application might include an explanation of why the transfer pricing rules at TA 1988 s 770A/ Sch 28AA are applicable, and would acknowledge that the effect of those rules, which are to be construed in accordance with OECD principles, is to require the substitution of the arm's length provision for tax purposes. The application might then go on to explain in what ways the establishing of the arm's length provision requires clarification, and submit a proposal for establishing the arm's length provision in accordance with the requirements of the effective provisions. This guidance should be adapted to transfer pricing issues within an enterprise in accordance with the general intention of ensuring that there is a proper understanding of the relevant principles of the applicable law from which an agreement about the practical treatment of a specified issue can be formed.

36 The centre-piece of the proposal will be a description of the method by which it is proposed to determine the transfer pricing issues in accordance with the arm's length principle, and an analysis demonstrating how the application of that method satisfies the terms of the UK's legislation, including the effect of any DTA, and the OECD transfer pricing guidelines. The nature of the detailed information supporting the proposal should be tailored to the specific features of the business and of the transfer pricing issues and should take into account discussions with the Inland Revenue during any expression of interest stage.

37 All proposals will also need to be supported by most of the following information—

(*a*) the identification of the parties and recent accounts (generally for the previous three years);

(*b*) a description of the transfer pricing issues proposed to be covered in the APA and analysis of the functions and risks of the parties and actual and projected financial data of the parties in relation to the issues;

(*c*) a description of the world-wide organisational structure, ownership, and business operations of the group to which the company in question belongs, the place or places where such operations are conducted, and all the major categories of transaction flows of the parties to whom the APA is intended to apply;

(*d*) a description of the records which will be maintained to support the transfer pricing method proposed for adoption in the APA and the information which it is proposed will be supplied each year to demonstrate that the tax return conforms to the terms of the APA;

(*e*) a description of any current tax enquiries or competent authority claims that are relevant to the issues covered by the proposed APA;

(*f*) the chargeable periods to be covered by the APA;

(*g*) the identification of assumptions made in developing the proposed transfer pricing method which are critical to the reliability of its application under the arm's length standard; and

(*h*) in the case of a cross-border transfer pricing issue, a request for competent authority assistance in reaching a bilateral APA or, where a bilateral APA is not being sought, any representations from the business that the Revenue should exercise its discretion and refrain from exchanging particular information under the terms of the applicable DTA because, for example, the business considers the information includes trade secrets which should not be disclosed.

38 In the case of a bilateral APA the business will be asked to ensure that all information supplied to one tax administration is made available at the same time to the other tax administration involved.

CRITICAL ASSUMPTIONS

39 As indicated in para 37(*g*) above, the formal proposal should identify the assumptions made in proposing the method for dealing with the transfer pricing issues and which are critical to the reliability of that method. The method should be sufficiently robust to accommodate some changes in the commercial and economic climate from that reasonably foreseeable when the proposals were made and still be capable of replicating an arm's length outcome. However, the accuracy of the method is likely to be predicated on assumptions in respect of particular factors fundamental to its application, such as the nature of the functions performed, accounting policies and practices, the terms of agreements governing the covered transactions, or market share. Critical assumptions are designed to protect both the business and the Revenue from the risk that the agreement may become inappropriate, but they should not be so tightly drawn that the certainty provided by the agreement is jeopardised. Setting parameters for acceptable divergence for some assumptions can help to retain flexibility. Where there is a change, or a change greater than any relevant parameters set, to circumstances that both parties have identified as critical to the agreement, a reconsideration of the agreement is then activated and may lead to its cancellation or modification in accordance with FA 1999 s 86(2), (6) depending on the terms of the agreement.

EVALUATION

40 On receipt of an application the Inland Revenue will evaluate its contents and will seek clarification and further information from the business as necessary. The examination of the application should be a co-operative process in which the transfer pricing issues are discussed openly and access to relevant supporting information and documentation is made available. Lack of co-operation in these respects may result in the Revenue declining to give any further consideration to the application.

41 Where a bilateral APA is being sought, the Inland Revenue will expect the business to continue to make relevant information available at the same time to each tax administration involved, and in turn will keep the treaty partner informed about the progress of its examination of the APA request, will discuss with the treaty partner the issues arising at an early stage, and will keep the business informed about the progress of the bilateral process. While the finalising of a bilateral agreement with a treaty partner is a government to government process, the Inland Revenue is prepared to consider participating in joint meetings to include the multinational business and the other tax administration(*s*) to assist in the understanding and evaluation of the factual issues.

AGREEMENT

42 Any agreement reached between the business and the Inland Revenue represents a binding undertaking on the parties that the treatment for a specified period of the transfer pricing issues covered by the agreement will be determined in accordance with the agreement (provided that its terms are observed and that none of the provisions leading to revocation, cancellation, or competent authority over-ride as described below are triggered). In the case of a bilateral APA the terms of the agreement between the Inland Revenue and the taxpayer will also reflect the agreement reached between the two tax administrations under the mutual agreement procedure of the relevant treaty in order to provide for the elimination of double taxation.

43 The agreement between the Inland Revenue and the business will be made subject to its terms being observed. The terms will include—

(*a*) a commitment from the business to demonstrate adherence to the agreed method for dealing with the transfer pricing issues during the term of the APA in the form of a regular compliance report (see paras 45, 46 below); and

SPs

(*b*) the identification of critical assumptions bearing materially on the reliability of the method and which, if subject to change, would render the agreement invalid.

A description of the matters that would need to be considered for incorporation in any agreement is included as an annex to this statement.

44 If agreement cannot be reached with the business, the Inland Revenue will issue a formal statement recording the reasons. The Inland Revenue does not have any obligation to continue discussion beyond the point at which it has determined that agreement cannot be reached.

APA MONITORING AND REVIEW

45 The APA will identify the nature of the reports that the business is required to provide pursuant to FA 1999 s 86(4). The timing of the submission of the reports will be set out in the agreement. It is expected that the reports will be required annually and will coincide with the filing date for the tax return. Failure to provide reports may lead the Inland Revenue to determine a penalty under TMA 1970 s 98 in respect of the failure, as provided for by FA 1999 s 86(9). The particular requirements of each report will be set out in the finalised agreement and will focus narrowly on the issue covered by the APA, but, as a general guide, they are likely to include—

(*a*) confirmation that the agreed method was applied during the year;

(*b*) the financial results produced by the method, and reconciliation of those results to entries in the statutory accounts and tax computations;

(*c*) where there was a mismatch between prices charged in relevant transactions during the period and those reflected in the results of applying the arm's length standard under the agreed methodology, details of any compensating adjustments made to conform the operating results of the parties to the results of the method; and

(*d*) an assessment of whether the critical assumptions have proved to be sound and whether they remain so.

46 The APA report is intended to provide the information required by the Inland Revenue to establish that the business has complied with the terms and conditions of the APA and to verify the accuracy of representations made in the APA. Identification of the content of the reports to be submitted over the term of the agreement will assist businesses in fulfilling their compliance obligations.

NULLIFYING AND REVOKING APAS

47 FA 1999 s 86(5) gives the Board of Inland Revenue the power to nullify an APA as if it had never been made where the business has fraudulently or negligently provided false or misleading information in connection with the APA application. When considering using this power the Board of Inland Revenue will also take into account the extent to which the terms of the APA would have been different in the absence of the misrepresentation. In accordance with s 86(2), an APA may be revoked by the Revenue in accordance with its terms, where the business does not comply with the terms and conditions of the agreement, or where the identified critical assumptions cease to be valid. When considering nullifying or cancelling a bilateral APA the Revenue may consult with the competent authority of the treaty partner involved.

REVISING AND RENEWING APAS

48 In some cases the APA may provide for modification of its terms in specific circumstances; for example, a particular agreement may provide that where there has been a change which makes the agreed methodology difficult to apply, but which does not go as far as to invalidate a critical assumption, the agreement may be modified with the consent of the parties to resolve that difficulty. In such cases the APA may be revised in accordance with FA 1999 s 86(6) after consultations between the business and the Inland Revenue and, in the case of bilateral agreements, the competent authority of the other country involved.

49 The business may request renewal of an APA ideally not later than six months before the expiry of its current term, but the Revenue will not rule as out of time requests made before the end of the first chargeable period affected by the renewal. The renewal application should expressly consider any changes or anticipated changes in facts and circumstances since the existing agreement was reached, whether any amendments are required to the agreement on renewal as a result, and should demonstrate how the proposed methodology accords with the arm's length standard.

50 The Revenue will conduct a review of the renewal application, taking into account whatever revisions to the existing APA are necessary and appropriate in the light of any changed facts and circumstances. Where it is agreed that the transfer pricing issues under consideration remain the same and the existing transfer pricing methodology can continue as before but with details updated to ensure continued adherence to the arm's length principle, the agreement will simply be amended and extended for a further term. Where, however, the transfer pricing issues have changed, or a different method is being proposed, the business will be required to make a fresh APA application.

51 In the case of a bilateral APA the business should ensure that the information contained in the renewal application is submitted at the same time to the other tax administration involved.

DECLINING OR WITHDRAWING AN APA REQUEST

52 At the expression of interest stage, or at the stage where a formal proposal is submitted, the Inland Revenue may exercise its discretion by declining the request for an APA. In that event, the Inland Revenue will advise the business of the reasons for doing so, and will allow the business the opportunity to make further representations. A request is likely to be declined if—

- sufficient information for proper and full consideration of the request is not provided;
- the proposal does not comply with the terms of the UK's transfer pricing legislation or with the OECD transfer pricing guidelines;
- the affected transactions are thought to be of a hypothetical nature or not seriously contemplated; or
- it appears to be an inefficient use of resources to pursue an APA (for instance because the relevant transactions are of a very limited nature such as not to warrant the time required to complete an APA or are of limited value relative to the value of the rest of the business, or because determination of the method by which the arm's length standard can reliably be applied is not in material doubt).

The Revenue may decline a request if the business is not co-operating to provide timeously the information necessary to consider the request properly.

53 A business may withdraw an APA request at any time before final agreement is reached.

DISCLOSURE OF APAS

54 The Revenue considers that APA information is subject to the same rules of confidentiality as any other information about taxpayers and that the unauthorised disclosure even of the existence of an APA will be a breach of confidentiality. Information exchanged with treaty partners—for instance, in the course of reaching agreement on bilateral APAs—is also protected from disclosure by the terms of the exchange of information article in the relevant DTA.

PENALTIES

55 Because an APA is an agreement between the Revenue and a business which determines how questions relating to the matters covered by the agreement will be determined for the purposes of the Taxes Acts, a return made on any other basis in relation to those matters during the currency of an APA will constitute an incorrect return. Consequently, a tax-geared penalty will be chargeable where the business has acted fraudulently or negligently in making such an incorrect return and tax has been lost as a result. Where a return is made in accordance with an APA, but it is discovered that false or misleading information was submitted fraudulently or negligently in the course of obtaining the APA, the legislation provides at FA 1999 s 86(5) that the agreement is treated as if it had never been made, with the result that questions relating to the subject matter of the agreement are no longer to be determined in accordance with the agreement. This may mean that returns made in accordance with the nullified APA are incorrect with the consequences for penalties described above.

56 A penalty not exceeding £10,000 may be imposed where false or misleading information is supplied fraudulently or negligently in connection with an application for an APA—FA 1999 s 86(8). There is no requirement for the APA to have been finalised in order to apply this sanction. In practice, where a tax-geared penalty is obtained following the nullifying of an APA as described above, a fixed penalty under s 86(8) will not also be pursued for the same offence. As indicated in para 45 above, TMA 1970 s 98 will apply to information required as part of the process of monitoring an APA where there has been a failure to provide the information or where incorrect information has been fraudulently or negligently provided.

APPEALS

57 In accordance with existing appeal procedures, the business has the right to appeal against the amount of any additions to profits arising as a result of the revocation or cancellation of an APA.

UK/UK TRANSACTIONS

58 When a UK business obtains an APA relating to provision made or imposed with another UK business, FA 1999 s 87 removes any uncertainty about the tax position of that other taxpayer. Where there is a discrepancy between the provision agreed under the terms of the APA and the actual provision between the parties to the disadvantage of the other party, that other party may claim to have profits adjusted on the basis that the agreed provision was charged. However, the Revenue would seek to reduce the scope for such discrepancies by encouraging the business to agree wherever possible that the transfer pricing methodology will determine the commercial charge for the provision as well as the charge for tax purposes. Furthermore, where the parties agree, the Revenue will accept a joint application for an APA from both parties in order to reach consistent agreements as to the measure of each party's profits in relation to the transfer pricing issues. Where these measures are adopted, however, s 87 may still need to be invoked if the APA applies to chargeable periods ending before the making of the agreement.

FURTHER INFORMATION

59 The contact address for more information about APAs and for making an APA application in all cases except those involving oil taxation, is—Assistant Director (APAs), International Division, Inland Revenue, Victory House, 30–34 Kingsway, London WC2B 6ES: telephone—020 7438 7405, fax—020 7438 7511, e-mail (general enquiries)—ahickman.ir.mhl@gtnet.gov.uk/

For APAs involving oil taxation, the contact address is—Deputy Director (APAs), Oil Taxation Office, Melbourne House, Aldwych, London WC2B 4LL: telephone—0171 438 7579, fax—0171 438 6910, e-mail (general enquiries)—oto.ir.mh@gtnet.gov.uk.

ANNEX

ADVANCE PRICING AGREEMENTS (APAS)

Matters to be covered in the written agreement

1 This note provides general guidance about the terms expected to be incorporated in an APA reached between the Inland Revenue and a business under FA 1999 s 85 and in accordance with the statement of practice. The precise form of the agreement may be left to the discretion of the parties.

Declaration

2 A declaration is required by FA 1999 s 85(1)(*d*) that the agreement is one made for the purposes of s 85.

Identification of the persons affected

3 The agreement should identify the persons affected by the APA and provide all relevant information about them for the purposes of the agreement, for example the residence of a company and any branches through which it is engaged in matters covered by the APA. It should also identify all related parties with whom the business or transactions covered by the APA are conducted.

Matters covered

4 The agreement should describe the specific matters within FA 1999 s 85(2) that are covered by the terms of the agreement. The information should be sufficiently detailed and specific as to identify the subject matter of the APA unambiguously.

Term

5 The agreement should state the period for which the agreement is to apply to the matters covered. This will normally correspond to certain specified accounting periods of the business.

Transfer pricing method

6 The particular transfer pricing method will vary from agreement to agreement. In all cases, however, the agreement should describe precisely how it is to apply to determine the treatment of the matters covered. An example would be a description of a method which determines how to calculate a royalty rate by reference to the residual profit of the licensee; this might need to cover the identification of the licensee's profits, the calculation of the residual including the use of defined comparable data and any adjustments to that data, and the determination of the royalty.

7 Most agreements are likely to prescribe a single method to apply throughout the term of the agreement. However, it may be that in appropriate cases a stipulated variation in the circumstances can provide for a specified modification in the method, in which case the agreement should describe the modification and the conditions under which the modification takes effect.

8 All terms used to describe the transfer pricing method should be clearly defined.

Critical assumptions

9 Critical assumptions are the conditions on which the agreement is predicated and, where these conditions are no longer satisfied, FA 1999 s 86(2)(*c*) provides that the agreement no longer has effect. They describe and limit the future facts and circumstances to which the agreement will apply and on which the transfer pricing method depends for its reliability. They protect both the business and the Revenue from the risk that the agreement may become inappropriate.

10 In general terms, critical assumptions should be capable of accommodating acceptable variations in the facts and circumstances relating to the matters covered. On the other hand, they must be able to identify those changes in the factual pattern envisaged in the agreement that render the transfer pricing method inappropriate.

11 Examples of the sorts of issues that can be expected to be subject of critical assumptions are—

- the business activities undertaken by specific entities;
- the centres of operation of a business and the nature of its presence in different countries;
- performance of a product in terms of, for example, volume of sales or market share;

– the financial conditions in which transactions are conducted, for example in relation to foreign exchange or interest rates;
– the nature of accounting methods or other information systems that may provide measurements relevant to the matters covered;
– business practice in relation to factors relevant to the transfer pricing method, for example the compensation policy of a financial trader.

12 This list is purely illustrative and the critical assumptions in any APA will always be particular to that agreement.

Reporting requirements

13 The agreement will specify, and thereby in accordance with FA 1999 s 86(2)(*b*), (4) be conditional on, the satisfaction of certain reporting requirements in relation to the application of the agreed method and the validity of the critical assumptions. These will normally be for specified information to be supplied at the time the business submits its accounts and computations in relation to the relevant transactions or business to the Inland Revenue.

14 The requirements may specify financial or other reports in relation to the application of the agreed method and the validity of the critical assumptions which would not otherwise be submitted with the tax return. As with critical assumptions, however, reporting requirements will be tailored to the particular agreement.

Record-keeping requirements

15 It will sometimes become apparent in the course of reaching an APA that certain records are needed to be kept in order for the agreed method to be properly applied. It might not, however, be necessary to provide such records at the same time as meeting other reporting requirements in order for the Inland Revenue to assess whether the terms of the agreement have been complied with. Such records would thus not be covered in the ''reporting requirements'' of the agreement, but might be required to be retained by the business under the terms of the agreement in case examination of them became necessary.

Roll-back

16 The agreement may specify how any adjustments are to be made to earlier periods in accordance with FA 1999 s 86(7).

Revocation and modification

17 An agreement may be revoked under FA 1999 s 86(2)(*a*) in accordance with its terms. This allows the parties to consider including conditions in the agreement that are not directly linked to assumptions underlying the reliability of the method, but may reflect wider concerns such as providing for revocation in the event of a take-over. An agreement may also provide for modification or revocation in accordance with s 86(6) by, for example, including a provision which allows for modification or revocation where the agreed method is proving difficult to apply.

Mutual agreement procedure

18 The Revenue is given authority by FA 1999 s 86(3) to modify an APA to give effect to an agreement with a treaty partner reached under the mutual agreement procedure of the treaty. There is no need for conditions to be made in an APA to confirm this authority, and the APA itself cannot be conditional on the resolution of any related mutual agreement procedure. However, the business may wish to refer specifically to any mutual agreement issues in the terms of an APA.

Commentary—*Simon's Direct Tax Service* **B3.1851**.
Note—This statement was revised in IR 131 (August 2002).

SPs

SP 1/00 (3 August 2000) *Corporate venturing scheme—applications for advance clearance under FA 2000 Sch 15 Part X*

The corporate venturing scheme provides relief against corporation tax (''investment relief'') in certain circumstances to companies investing in new shares of other companies. Where a company hopes to use the scheme to attract investment, FA 2000 Sch 15 para 89 enables it to apply to the Board of Inland Revenue for an advance clearance notice. Such a notice provides confirmation that the Board consider that the conditions for relief under the scheme, other than those applying to the investor, will be met in relation to the proposed issue of shares at the time the issue is made. In the case of those conditions which have to be met throughout a qualification period, however, there can of course be no certainty until after the end of that period that they will be met.

This statement of practice gives guidance to companies wishing to obtain advance clearance.

All references to paragraphs in this statement are to paragraphs of FA 2000 Sch 15.

PROCEDURE

Applications should be sent to The Small Company Enterprise Centre, Centre for Revenue Intelligence (CRI), Ty Glas, Llanishen, Cardiff CF14 5ZG.

Under FA 2000 Sch 15 para 91 the Board must respond to an application within 30 days after receiving the application. The Board may request further particulars, and if they do their response must be given within 30 days after the last such request was complied with.

CONTENT OF APPLICATION—GENERAL

In order to consider applications the Board need certain basic information and assurances. To assist companies in preparing their applications, an outline of what is needed is given below. However, this is not necessarily an exhaustive list in all cases, and each applicant must fully and accurately disclose all facts and circumstances material for the decision of the Board (FA 2000 Sch 15 para 89). The application will be considered solely by reference to the material provided by the company in its application or in response to a request for further particulars.

It will be helpful if applications follow the order set out below, each item being expanded as necessary and any further information being added at the end. This will enable the Board to come to a decision on the application as soon as possible.

For the purposes of the scheme, an ''issue of shares'' consists of all the shares of the same class which are issued by a company on the same day. An advance clearance notice can be given only in respect of a single issue of shares. If it is expected that there will be more than one issue within a short period of time, please say so. Any clearance will apply only to the issue or issues in respect of which information has been given, so if an advance clearance notice is sought in respect of more than one issue, relevant information must be provided in respect of each of them.

INFORMATION AND DOCUMENTS NEEDED

1 General

The name of the tax office dealing with the company making the application, and the tax reference. If the company is newly formed and the tax office is not yet known, state the address of the registered office.

If the company has previously made any application for an advance clearance notice it will be helpful if the Board's reference(*s*) can be quoted.

2 Accounts and other documents

(*a*) copies of the latest available financial statements for the company, or in the case of a group the financial statements for the group and for each group company;
(*b*) a copy of any prospectus or memorandum or other document to be made available to prospective investors or their advisers (or a draft of any such document);
(*c*) a draft copy of any subscription agreement which is to be made with any investor.

3 Transactions subsequent to accounts

Particulars of any material changes or events which have occurred since the date of the latest balance sheet, or which are expected to occur before the issue takes place.

4 The company

The following particulars are needed in relation to the company which is to issue the shares—

(*a*) confirmation that the ''unquoted status'' requirement set out in FA 2000 Sch 15 para 16 will be satisfied;
(*b*) confirmation that the ''independence'' requirement set out in FA 2000 Sch 15 para 17 will be satisfied when the shares are issued;
(*c*) details of the expected ownership of its ordinary share capital following the issue of the shares, with sufficient information to show that the ''individual-owners'' requirement set out at FA 2000 Sch 15 para 18 will be satisfied at that time;
(*d*) confirmation that the ''partnerships and joint ventures'' requirement set out in FA 2000 Sch 15 para 19 will be satisfied when the shares are issued;
(*e*) if, at the time the shares are issued, it will have any subsidiary or control any other company—
- the name of each such company, together with the name of its tax office and its tax reference or, if there is no tax office, the address of its registered office, and
- a statement or diagram showing the shareholding interests of each group company in other group companies, sufficient to show that all subsidiaries will be ''qualifying subsidiaries'' as defined at FA 2000 Sch 15 para 21;

(*f*) sufficient information to establish whether the ''gross assets'' requirement set out in FA 2000 Sch 15 para 22 will be satisfied (see statement of practice SP 2/00);

(*g*) a description of each activity comprised in any trade carried on, or to be carried on, by the company and, in the case of each subsidiary or controlled company mentioned at (*e*) above, each activity comprised in any trade carried on, or to be carried on, by that subsidiary.

5 The share issue and the money raised

(*a*) details of the total number of shares expected to be issued to investors seeking investment relief (where known), the nominal value of such shares, the rights which they will carry, and the price at which they are expected to be issued;

(*b*) details of the activity or activities for which it is intended that the money raised by the issue will be used;

(*c*) in the case of a company which will have subsidiaries at the time when the shares are issued, the identity of the company or companies which will use that money;

(*d*) confirmation that each trade or other activity for which the money will be used will be carried on wholly or mainly in the UK (see statement of practice SP 3/00).

UNDERTAKINGS NEEDED

(*a*) that the company intends that the money raised by the share issue will be used within the time set out at FA 2000 Sch 15 para 36;

(*b*) that the shares to be issued to corporate investors wishing to obtain investment relief will not be issued unless they have been subscribed for wholly in cash and that cash has actually been paid;

(*c*) that those shares will be issued for commercial purposes and not as part of a scheme or arrangement which has as a main purpose the avoidance of tax;

(*d*) that the issuing arrangements in respect of the shares will not include any arrangements of the kind set out at FA 2000 Sch 15 para 37.

INFORMAL EIS CLEARANCES

Where subscribers to the same issue of shares are expected to include individuals who may wish to claim relief under the enterprise investment scheme, any request for an informal clearance under the EIS should be sent to the Board with the CVS application.

Commentary—*Simon's Direct Tax Service* **D2.1335**.
Note—This statement was revised in IR 131 (August 2002).

SP 2/00 (3 August 2000) *Venture capital trusts, the enterprise investment scheme, the corporate venturing scheme and enterprise management incentives—value of "gross assets"*

GROSS ASSETS RULE

1 TA 1988 Sch 28B para 8 provides that a venture capital trust's holding of shares, or of shares and securities, in a company cannot be part of its qualifying holdings for the purposes of TA 1988 s 842AA if the value of that company's gross assets exceeds—

– £15 million immediately before the issue of the holding in question; or
– £16 million immediately afterwards.

2 TA 1988 s 293(6A) provides that a company cannot be a qualifying company for the purposes of the enterprise investment scheme in relation to an issue of eligible shares if the value of its gross assets exceeds—

– £15 million immediately before the issue of the shares; or
– £16 million immediately afterwards.

3 FA 2000 Sch 15 para 22 provides that a company cannot be a qualifying company for the purposes of the corporate venturing scheme in relation to any shares if the value of its gross assets exceeds—

– £15 million immediately before the issue of the shares; or
– £16 million immediately afterwards.

4 FA 2000 Sch 14 para 16 provides that a company cannot be a qualifying company for enterprise management incentives in relation to a qualifying option, if the value of its gross assets exceeds—

– £15 million at the date the option is granted.

5 Where the company is a member of a group of companies, the limits set out in each of the four preceding paragraphs apply to the aggregate value of the gross assets of all the companies in the group. For this purpose, no account is taken of—

– any assets which consist in rights against another company in the group, or
– any shares in, or securities of, another such company.

SPs

VALUATION OF ASSETS

6 In applying these rules, the Inland Revenue's general approach is that the value of a company's gross assets at any time is the aggregate of the values of the company's gross assets as shown in its balance sheet if the company were to draw one up at that time. ''Gross assets'' means all the assets which would be shown on that balance sheet, without any deduction in respect of liabilities. This approach is subject to the proviso that the balance sheet would be drawn up on a basis consistent with that used in the accounts for preceding periods (if any), and in accordance with normal UK accounting practice. (This is referred to later in this statement as ''the accounting practice proviso''.) This general approach is also subject to what is said in paras 10, 11 below.

7 So if the shares or securities in question were issued, or as the case may be, the option was granted, immediately after the date to which the company's accounts were drawn up, the value of the company's gross assets immediately before the issue, or grant, would be the value shown in the balance sheet (subject to the accounting practice proviso and to paras 10, 11 below). And if the shares or securities were issued, or the option was granted, immediately before the date to which the company's accounts were drawn up, the value of the company's gross assets immediately after the issue, or grant, would be the value shown in the balance sheet (subject to the accounting practice proviso and to paras 10, 11 below).

8 Where shares or securities are issued, or options are granted, at other times, the values will, in the first instance, be based on the values given in the company's latest available balance sheet (subject to the accounting practice proviso and to paras 10, 11 below). However, these values should be updated as precisely as is practicable, taking into account all the relevant information available to the company (and, where applicable, to its subsidiaries). For example, where a company is able to ascertain the amount of trade debts owed to it at any given time, it would be reasonable to take the aggregate amount of such debts outstanding at the time of the issue or grant.

9 When accounts covering—

- the accounting period in which the issue was made or the option was granted, and
- if they were not available at the time of the issue or grant, those for the immediately preceding accounting period,

become available, the values arrived at in the way described in para 8 above may need to be reviewed in the light of the information contained in those accounts.

PAYMENTS IN RESPECT OF SHARES OR SECURITIES

10 The Inland Revenue will not regard the assets of a company immediately before the issue of the shares or securities in question as including any advance payment received by the company in respect of that issue.

11 Where shares or securities are issued partly paid, the right to the unpaid portion will be regarded as an asset of the company. That asset will be taken into account for the purpose of deciding whether the relevant gross assets rule is satisfied, whether it is shown in the company's balance sheet or not.

Commentary—*Simon's Direct Tax Service* **D2.1321; E3.212, 628.**
Note—This statement supersedes SP 5/98.

SP 3/00 (3 August 2000) *Enterprise investment scheme, venture capital trusts, corporate venturing scheme, enterprise management incentives and capital gains tax reinvestment relief*

LOCATION OF ACTIVITY

1 The provisions for—

- the enterprise investment scheme;
- venture capital trusts;
- the corporate venturing scheme;
- enterprise management incentives; and
- capital gains tax reinvestment relief (which is not available for investments made after 5 April 1998)

each include the requirement that a company's trade should, at a certain time or for a certain period, be ''carried on wholly or mainly in the United Kingdom''. This statement explains the way in which the Inland Revenue applies this condition in those contexts.

2 The way in which the requirement is applied in any particular case will depend on the relevant facts and circumstances. A company may at any given time carry on some of the activities of the trade outside the UK and yet satisfy the requirement if the major part of the trade, that is over half of the trading activity, taken as a whole, is at that time carried on within the UK.

3 In considering whether the requirement is satisfied, the Inland Revenue will take into account the totality of the activities of the trade. For example, they will consider where the capital assets of the trade are held, where any purchasing, processing, manufacturing and selling is done, and where the company's employees and other agents are engaged in its trading operations. For trades involving the provision of services, the location of the activities giving rise to the services and the location where they are delivered will both be relevant.

4 No one factor is in itself likely to be decisive in any particular case. In particular, the Inland Revenue will not regard a company's activities as not being carried on in the UK solely because—

– the goods or services which it manufactures or provides are exported or supplied to overseas customers;
– its raw materials are purchased from abroad; or
– its raw materials or products are stored abroad.

5 In the case of a trade consisting of ship chartering, the trade will be considered to satisfy the requirement if all the charters are entered into in the UK and the provision of the crews and the management of the ships while under charter take place mainly in the UK. If these conditions are not met the test may still be satisfied, but this will depend on all the facts and circumstances of the case.

6 The corresponding requirements in certain of the schemes mentioned in relation to research and development and to oil exploration are applied in a similar way.

Commentary—*Simon's Direct Tax Service* **D2.1323; E3.119, 623.**
Note—This statement supersedes SP 7/98.

SP 4/00 (25 August 2000) *Tonnage Tax*

INTRODUCTION

1 This statement covers the general operation of the tonnage tax regime for shipping companies. Unless specifically stated otherwise, any reference to a paragraph or Part number relates to FA 2000 Sch 22.

ALLOCATION OF CASES

2 The Inland Revenue will be allocating existing network cases to a number of tax offices specialising in tonnage tax. They are—

– Liverpool Queensway (for the Northwest, London and Northern Ireland);
– Hull 2 (for the rest of England and Wales);
– Aberdeen St Nicholas (for Scotland).

3 Cases dealt with by the large business office (LBO) will generally remain *in situ*, but one LBO will specialise in tonnage tax groups—

– Liverpool LBO.

4 Oil Taxation Office will continue to work oil industry cases that elect into tonnage tax.

CONTACTING THE INLAND REVENUE

5 Existing shipping companies and their agents should initially contact their current tax office. Transfers of companies/groups will be arranged in accordance with the previous paragraphs.

6 Newly set up businesses, including overseas concerns, considering entering tonnage tax should contact Liverpool large business office. The tonnage tax unit at Liverpool LBO will also act as the technical head office for tonnage tax. It may be contacted at Liverpool Large Business Office, Regian House, James Street, Liverpool L75 1AE; tel: 0151 242 8025; fax: 0151 242 8046; email: JohnHoggart@ir.gsi.gov.uk.

7 A "training commitment" forms a necessary condition of entering the tonnage tax regime. However, the Inland Revenue does not administer the training commitment. Enquiries on training should be addressed to the Department for Transport at Shipping Policy 2A, 2/26 Great Minster House, 76 Marsham Street, London SW1P 4DR; telephone 020 7944 5438/5421/5121/5280; fax 020 7944 2182; email: anne.broome@dft.gsi.gov.uk; peter.mcwilliams@dft.gsi.gov.uk; stephen.eglesfield@dft.gsi.gov.uk; fahima.mahtab@dft.gsi.gov.uk.

CLEARANCE

8 A non-statutory and non-mandatory clearance procedure is available to enable any company or group interested in tonnage tax to discuss its own circumstances with the Inland Revenue in advance of making the initial election or before making its first corporation tax return under the tonnage tax regime. Examples of companies that might find this procedure useful include a company considering an initial tonnage tax election, or a company considering starting up a new shipping business in the UK.

9 The clearance procedure will generally only be available in advance of a company or group's first election into tonnage tax. However, in exceptional circumstances, the Inland Revenue may allow a further clearance application prior to a renewal election being made. For instance, such further clearance may be sought after a major change in the structure of a group, or a major change (temporary or permanent) in its activities, which might create a potential exclusion from tonnage tax.

Companies considering clearance are encouraged to contact the Inland Revenue sooner rather than later.

10 This particular clearance procedure is limited to tonnage tax issues only and does not extend to the mechanics of any reorganisation that may be required to put the group or company into the optimum position to make an election. Examples of issues that could be addressed are—

(i) whether a particular ship is a qualifying ship;
(ii) whether the strategic and commercial management test is met;
(iii) whether an activity is a core or secondary qualifying activity;
(iv) how to deal with potentially non-qualifying secondary activities;
(v) how a service at sea is to be split out from the associated transport;
(vi) whether dividends from an overseas subsidiary qualify as relevant shipping income;
(vii) how the calculation of excess finance costs is to be made;
(viii) how to apply the 75% limit on time charters-in within a tonnage tax group;
(ix) how to record ''offshore'' activities and their treatment in the computation;
(*x*) whether incidental income qualifies as relevant shipping income.

11 The clearance application must include all pertinent information to enable a decision to be made. This should include full details of the tonnage tax group structure (see para 23(iii) below) unless already provided as part of a tonnage tax election.

12 Provided that all pertinent information is given to the Inland Revenue, the treatment agreed will be binding on the Inland Revenue. This will hold until (and unless) company circumstances change such that the original clearance is no longer in point. Reviews to determine whether this is the case may form part of any enquiry into a tonnage tax company's tax return.

13 This clearance facility is likely to be of most use to complex groups, perhaps with substantial non-qualifying activities, with unusual vessels or with offshore activities. However, all interested companies are invited to make use of the facility. The clearance procedure will differ from case to case according to the issues under discussion, but is likely to take the form of correspondence alone or a combination of correspondence and meetings.

14 Clearance applications should be sent initially to the company or group's usual tax district—the Inland Revenue will notify the company or group if the case is then transferred to a specialist district (see para 2 above). Adequate time should be allowed for the Inland Revenue to respond to the application (and for correspondence and meetings) before the expected date for making the election.

FOREIGN COMPANY/GROUP CONSIDERING COMMENCING QUALIFYING ACTIVITIES IN THE UK

15 A foreign company or group considering commencing ship operations in the UK within the tonnage tax regime may seek advice from Liverpool LBO, which will deal with the initial stages of the clearance application.

16 One of the queries most likely to be raised by such a foreign company or group is potential exit charges, should it subsequently cease operations in the UK. Where a branch or a subsidiary company of a foreign ship operator has been set up in the UK and that branch or company subsequently ceases operations in the UK there is unlikely to be a specific exit charge from the tonnage tax regime. There may however be a potential liability to tax on pre-migration capital gains on assets brought into the UK, if those gains have not already crystallised in another country before migration.

GROUP ARRANGEMENTS

17 The Inland Revenue recommends that a tonnage tax group should operate under a group arrangement as set out in FA 2000 Sch 22 para 120. A group arrangement will enable a nominated company to act as a representative of the group. This will reduce (although not eliminate) the need for administrative correspondence between the Inland Revenue and each individual company in the group, and make some aspects of the legislation much simpler to implement, for instance, the provisions of FA 2000 Sch 22 paras 37 (75% limit) and 62 (finance costs).

18 A group arrangement will normally cover the following matters—

(i) dealing with the Inland Revenue on behalf of group companies in respect of clearance applications;
(ii) dealing with the Inland Revenue on behalf of group companies in respect of the tonnage tax election and renewal elections;
(iii) making notifications on behalf of group companies as to whether or not the 75% limit on chartering-in (set out in FA 2000 Sch 22 para 37) has been exceeded and making any appeal under FA 2000 Sch 22 para 43 (against an exclusion from tonnage tax notice);
(iv) preparing and negotiating with the Inland Revenue calculations required under FA 2000 Sch 22 para 62 (finance costs);
(v) dealing with the Inland Revenue on matters arising under FA 2000 Sch 22 para 126(4) (dominant party on a merger) and making an appeal under para 126(5) (against Inland Revenue determination);

(vi) making notifications under FA 2000 Sch 22 para 129 (duty to notify Inland Revenue of group changes);

(vii)the provision of any other information in relation to the tonnage tax regime, which it would be expedient to be provided on a group-wide basis.

19 Notification of a group arrangement will normally include the following details—

(i) the name and unique taxpayer reference of each qualifying company in the group;

(ii) the name and unique taxpayer reference of the representative company;

(iii) a list of the matters to be handled by the representative company on behalf of the group, if different from the list in para 18(i)–(vi) above, or confirmation that the representative company will handle all items in that list;

(iv) a declaration signed by an authorised person for each qualifying company confirming that the representative company is authorised to act on their behalf in respect of these specified matters;

(v) a declaration signed by an authorised person for the representative company confirming that it agrees to act on behalf of the group companies in respect of these specified matters.

20 The Inland Revenue will agree in writing to the proposed group arrangement and the issues to be covered by it, or suggest modifications to the proposals, as appropriate.

21 The group arrangement does not need to be renewed if the composition of the group changes unless there is a change in representative company. FA 2000 Sch 22 para 129 notifications will be accepted as notice of changes to the composition of the group arrangement, provided they include a declaration under FA 2000 Sch 22 para 19(iv) in respect of any new additions to the group.

THE TONNAGE TAX ELECTION (PART II)

22 Where a company is a member of a group of companies, the tonnage tax election must be a group election. It is likely that most tonnage tax election will be group elections. Where, exceptionally, a single company makes a tonnage tax election, none of the information requirements listed below in relation to groups will be relevant, and may be ignored.

23 The initial tonnage tax election should contain the information listed below.

(i) The name and unique taxpayer reference of each qualifying company in the group.

(ii) A name for the tonnage tax group that can be used as convenient shorthand in correspondence and on tax returns. For example, ''XYZ TT Group''. It is suggested that ''TT'' be included in the name, as a tonnage tax group may have a different membership from the UK group for other tax purposes.

(iii) Full details of the tonnage tax group structure, including details of non-qualifying companies. For many groups this will be a straightforward comment to the effect that the group consists of XYZ parent company with 100% subsidiaries A, B and C. However, where control is, for instance, traced through individuals or complex share structures, then appropriate details will be required. For foreign owned groups, the information should include appropriate details of the overseas structure within which the UK companies are placed.

(iv) The accounting period(*s*) from which the election is to take effect. If this is not the period in which the election is made, then further details must be given (see para 26 below for more information).

(v) The signature of an authorised person from each company to confirm that the companies are jointly making the election.

(vi) A declaration confirming that—

(*a*) all companies included on the election are qualifying companies,

(*b*) all qualifying companies in the tonnage tax group are included in the election, and

(*c*) a certificate of approval from the Department of the Environment, Transport and the Regions is in force with respect to the initial training commitment.

24 The 75% limit on chartered-in tonnage is not a qualifying condition for making an election. However, an election made during the initial period will be treated as never having been of effect if the limit is exceeded in the first accounting period after entering tonnage tax.

25 Elections made after the initial period will be treated as never having been of effect, if the 75% limit is exceeded in the each of the first three accounting periods (para 38 refers).

26 However, where an election is made after the end of the initial period and the 75% limit is exceeded only in the first accounting period, or only in the first and second accounting periods, the election does not have effect for the one or two ''exceeded'' accounting periods. Entry is effectively deferred until the first period that the limit is satisfied. In these circumstances, it is essential that the election must still be made within 12 months of becoming a qualifying company.

27 A renewal election should contain similar information to the initial election, with the following changes—

(i) a start date is not required;

(ii) the training declaration should be that a training certificate is in force and that the group or company is not subject to a certificate of non-compliance.

28 An election will usually take effect from the start of the accounting period in which it is made. However, FA 2000 Sch 22 para 12 provides for an election to take effect from the beginning of certain other accounting periods. Where this is subject to the agreement of the Inland Revenue, the election should include details of the commercial reasons why one of these alternative start dates is required. For instance, the group might be carrying out a reorganisation to prepare for tonnage tax, and therefore would not wish the election to take effect until after this reorganisation was complete.

29 In ''exceptional circumstances'', para 12(4) allows the elections made during the initial period to take effect from the second accounting period after the one in which the election is made. The ''exceptional circumstances'' must be such that it is commercially impracticable for the company/group election to take effect at an earlier date. This could include contractual arrangements that affect qualification and which cannot be renegotiated in time, or unusually complex restructuring that will take more than one accounting period to achieve. An example of ''exceptional circumstances'' might be the inability to renegotiate long-term time charters that would push a company or group above the 75% limit on time chartering-in.

30 The Inland Revenue will issue to the representative company an acknowledgement to confirm receipt of the election. The acknowledgement will normally include a statement of the date on which the ten-year period covered by the election will start and end, effectively confirming agreement to any backdating or postponement of the starting date, subject to any necessary enquiry into the date of entry. This acknowledgement will not mean that the Inland Revenue necessarily accepts that the companies, their activities or their vessels qualify for tonnage tax. A group that wishes to have reassurance on this point should take advantage of the clearance procedure discussed above.

31 FA 2000 Sch 22 para 10(3) extends an opportunity for newly qualifying groups of companies to elect into tonnage tax after the initial window of entry. It includes a rule to prevent a group avoiding the normal time restrictions for making an election (para 10(1)—initial period) by making minor changes to the composition of the group. For example, a group that became non-qualifying by divesting itself of its shipping interests and then became qualifying by buying most of them back would be ''substantially the same'' group as before and would not be eligible to make an election.

QUALIFYING COMPANIES AND QUALIFYING SHIPS (PART III)

Ships

32 Paragraph 16(1)(*b*) requires a qualifying company to operate ''qualifying ships''—in this context ''ships'' can mean a single ship.

Strategic and commercial management

33 The definition of a qualifying company in para 16 provides that qualifying ships operated by a company must be strategically and commercially managed in the UK. This is a completely different and separate test from that of ''central management and control'' relevant in determining whether a company is resident in the UK.

34 The ''strategic and commercial management'' test arises from the European Commission's guidelines on state aid in the maritime sector. No specific EC guidance is available on the meaning of strategic and commercial management and the Inland Revenue proposes therefore to adopt a common-sense interpretation, taking into account the various different strands of management activity that can be carried out in respect of a ship. The Inland Revenue is happy to provide guidance on this test as part of the clearance procedure outlined in paras 8–14 above.

35 All elements of management activity relevant to the ships in question will be taken into account in determining whether strategic and commercial management is carried out in the UK may include—

A Strategic functions for the shipping business, including—

(i) location of headquarters, including senior management staff;
(ii) decision-making of the company board of directors;
(iii) decision-making of operational board;
(iv) UK stock exchange listing.

The types of decision included in (ii) and (iii) above include—decisions on significant capital expenditure and disposals (eg purchase and sale of ships); award of major contracts; agreement on strategic alliances (eg shipping conferences and pooling); and the extent to which foreign offices work under the direction of UK-based personnel.

B Commercial management of the ship/fleet, including—
(i) route planning;
(ii) taking bookings for cargo or passengers;
(iii) managing the bunkers, provisioning and victualling requirements;
(iv) personnel management;
(v) training organisation;
(vi) technical management including making decisions on the repair and maintenance of vessels;
(vii) extent to which foreign offices/branches work under the direction of UK-based personnel;
(viii) support facilities in the UK (eg training centre, terminal, etc)

36 The fact that a vessel may be flagged, classed, insured or financed in the UK may add further weight to the indicators in 35(A) and 35(B) above in deciding whether that vessel is strategically and commercially managed in the UK.

37 Elements of each leg of the test, ie both strategic and commercial management, must be demonstrated—the strategic management by features such as in list 35(A) above, and the commercial management by features such as in list 35(B) above.

38 The more elements that are carried out in the UK, the more likely it is that the company will be accepted as satisfying this test. However, the approach will not be purely mechanistic; the weight given to each element will depend on the precise facts of each case. Greater weight will be given to higher levels of decision-making and management, as opposed to routine day-to-day management. The Inland Revenue recognises that a worldwide shipping operation may have many of the lower level activities devolved to local branches. In assessing the weight and relevance of the various elements of commercial management activity, the Inland Revenue will take account of such factors as—
(i) the extent to which each element is carried out in the UK, as compared with the extent that it is carried on elsewhere;
(ii) the nature and extent of the accommodation occupied in the UK;
(iii) the number of employees engaged in these activities in the UK;
(iv) the country of residence of key management staff, including company directors;
(v) for an international group, the extent to which such activities in the UK correspond to the UK's share of the worldwide fleet. If some group functions in relation to the fleet are carried out in the UK and other functions elsewhere, the group may still be seen as commercially managing its fleet from the UK provided there is a reasonable balance of activities in the UK considering the proportion of the worldwide fleet represented by ships within the UK's tonnage tax regime.

39 An activity, such as ship management, contracted out to a third party will still count as a positive indicator, provided that it is carried on in the UK.

40 The test does not require the vessels to be operated in UK waters.

41 FA 2000 Sch 22 para 16(1)(*c*) states that the qualifying ships operated by a UK tonnage tax company must be strategically and commercially managed in the UK. This does not mean that each ship operated by the company from the UK must be managed in like manner and to the same extent as every other one. So long as each ship can satisfy *some* of the criteria in lists A and B above, and the company's fleet *as a whole* is strategically and commercially managed in the UK, the para 16(1)(*c*) test will be satisfied.

Examples of strategic and commercial management

42 Example 1

A wholly UK shipping company, where all management activities in relation to its ships are carried out in the UK.

This company will certainly satisfy the test.

43 Example 2

A company that has no commercial presence in the UK apart from its registered office and the occasional board meeting.

This company will almost certainly not satisfy the test.

44 Example 3

An international group operates a quarter of its fleet from the UK, through a UK sub-group. The UK sub-group has UK premises and employs around 100 staff in the UK. All technical management of the worldwide fleet is carried out in the UK, but personnel management is in the Far East. The booking system for all vessels is intranet-based using a computer in North America, but UK staff contribute a quarter of worldwide bookings. The operational board of the UK sub-group includes directors based in London, but meets at various locations around the world.

The UK ship operating company(ies) would be likely to pass the test, as sufficient activity is carried on in the UK to reflect its share of the ships.

Temporary cessations

45 FA 2000 Sch 22 para 17 is aimed at a single company that temporarily ceases to operate any qualifying ships, perhaps for instance through loss at sea, and allows such a company to remain within tonnage tax throughout the period of temporary cessation. Such a single company would otherwise be excluded from tonnage tax for ten years under the rule in para 140. A group company would not be so excluded, although it may also choose to take advantage of this provision if for example it were to sell all of its qualifying ships at once. The Inland Revenue will generally presume that a cessation of more than three months is permanent, unless there is evidence to the contrary.

46 A company that takes advantage of this provision will calculate its tonnage tax profits as though it still operated the same ships as immediately prior to the cessation. The training obligation will continue to apply.

47 A group election covers all qualifying activities carried on by any company within the group. If one company within the group ceases to operate any qualifying ships, but at least one other company in the group continues to do so, the group election will continue to have effect. If it is still in force, that election will cover the first company if it later starts to operate qualifying ships again.

48 Subject to the rules on mergers in Part XII, the group election also extends to newly acquired companies. If a single company has ceased to have any qualifying activities and is then acquired by a larger group and the company resumes qualifying activities after the merger, it will be within the tonnage tax regime if there is a group election in force. The fact that the group contains what was formerly a single ex-tonnage tax company does not prevent the group making a tonnage tax election or a renewal election (para 140(3) refers).

Seagoing

49 Paragraph 19(1) describes a qualifying ship as a ''seagoing ship of 100 tons or more gross tonnage''. Sub-paragraph (4) defines ''seagoing'' as '' 'certificated' for navigation at sea by the competent authority of any country or territory''. The Inland Revenue will normally accept that a ship is seagoing if it is certificated as such under the International Load Line or the SOLAS (Safety of Life at Sea) conventions.

Excluded vessels

50 Paragraph 19(2) prevents a vessel that is used to provide ''goods or services of a kind normally provided on land'' from being a qualifying ship. Examples of businesses where the Inland Revenue will apply this rule include—

(i) retailers;
(ii) restaurants;
(iii) hotels;
(iv) prisons;
(v) radio stations;
(vi) casinos;
(vii) financial service providers.

This list is not exhaustive.

51 Pleasure craft are excluded from the tonnage tax regime under para 20(1)(*b*). The Inland Revenue accepts that a commercially operated cruise liner, although operated primarily for the recreation of its passengers, is not a ''pleasure craft''. This exclusion will be interpreted so as to exclude a vessel that is chartered as a whole by its passengers (for instance a holiday yacht) but not to exclude a vessel that has individual fare paying passengers. Chartered ''as a whole'' will include charter by a passenger alone, or by passengers acting together, or by a third party acting on behalf of one or more of the passengers.

THE 75% LIMIT (PART V)

52 Where a company or group has breached the 75% limit for chartered-in tonnage under FA 2000 Sch 22 para 37, and the breach has continued for two or more consecutive periods then, in the absence of any mitigating circumstances, the Inland Revenue will consider excluding the company or group from tonnage tax under FA 2000 Sch 22 para 39.

53 If a company or group is to avoid exclusion, there will have to be mitigating circumstances of an exceptional commercial nature and the company or group must demonstrate a reasonable expectation of falling within the limit in the near future. An example of such mitigating circumstances might be the accidental loss of an owned vessel and its temporary replacement with another on time charter.

54 The power to exclude is a permissive one. If the Inland Revenue considers that there is evidence of an attempt to engineer an early exit from the tonnage tax regime, then it may decide not to exercise the power to exclude.

ANTI-AVOIDANCE (PART V)

55 Paragraphs 41, 42 provide that a company or group that abuses the tonnage tax regime may be expelled. The provision is aimed at deliberate cases of serious or repeated abuse and will not be used to attack minor errors in the computations or genuine misunderstandings. Nor will it be used to attack any *bona fide* pre-election restructuring that is required to enable a group to opt for the regime, for instance the divisionalisation of shipping and non-shipping activities.

56 Examples of situations where the provision may bite include—

(i) the artificial engineering of non-qualifying income so that it falls within the tonnage tax ring-fence; for example, including within the sale price of a cruise entitlement to a significant discount on the purchase of goods or services to be provided onshore;
(ii) creating a financing structure that circumvents the rules in para 62;
(iii) involvement in leasing arrangements designed to circumvent the restrictions in Part X on finance leases.

RELEVANT SHIPPING PROFITS (PART VI)

Core qualifying activities

57 Paragraph 46 provides that core qualifying activities include the operation of qualifying ships and activities integral and necessary to such operation.

58 Operation of the ship is defined by FA 2000 Sch 22 para 18 in terms of ownership, but to be qualifying the ship must, under FA 2000 Sch 22 para 19(1), be used for transporting passengers or cargo, providing marine assistance, or providing transport for services at sea.

59 Activities ''necessary and integral'' are those activities that are essential to enable the ship operation to take place. These include ship management operations such as purchasing fuel and hiring crew and commercial management operations such as booking cargo. They do not include activities that are merely customary or desirable, although such activities may count as qualifying secondary activities. For instance, providing food for short sea ferry passengers is not integral and necessary to their transport and is therefore not core. However, it is a wholly qualifying secondary activity.

60 The following paragraphs give guidance on some specific maritime activities.

Tugs

61 The operations of a seagoing tug will normally be accepted as core qualifying activities. These will include—

(i) assistance at sea;
(ii) salvage (but see also para 62 below);
(iii) construction work in the marine environment;
(iv) support activities for seagoing ships.

62 Where a tug is involved in raising sunken cargo, this will be regarded as diving support and will need to be treated under the principles described below for transport for services at sea. Any profits from the sale of salvaged goods will fall outside the tonnage tax ring-fence.

Vessels providing transport for services at sea

63 Vessels providing services at sea include diving support vessels, cable layers and crane barges (or ships performing a similar function). It is necessary to apportion the profits/losses from the operation of such vessels between that attributable to transport and that attributable to the service provided. The Inland Revenue will accept any method of apportionment, which produces a just and reasonable result.

64 For example, the Inland Revenue will accept that the profit from transport will be the income that would be receivable on a time charter of a similarly modified vessel for the duration of the accounting period, less the actual expenses of running the vessel (excluding any expenses relating to the provision of the service). Any remaining profit will be the profit relating to the provision of the service and will remain outside the tonnage tax ring-fence.

65 Alternatively, the reverse of the method in para 64 above could be used. For example, where both divers and a diving support vessel were provided, the income and expenses of providing the divers alone could be deducted from the overall profit or loss. Any remaining amount would then be ''relevant shipping profits'' for tonnage tax.

Merchant adventurers

66 Some ship operators behave as ''merchant adventurers'' by taking full or part ownership of their cargo, rather than simply acting as carriers. If there is a price risk associated with the cargo, then a just and reasonable apportionment of the profit or loss on the voyage must be made. A price risk is any situation where the operator buys and sells the cargo at different prices. The Inland Revenue will accept that where the ship operator does not bear any price risk relating to the cargo, then the whole of any profit or loss on the voyage will be within relevant shipping profits for tonnage tax purposes.

67 Tanker operators provide an example of merchant adventuring. For instance, some tanker owners load their own cargo of oil and transport it to a destination in the hope of reaching the market at the right time to achieve a larger profit. Similarly, oil can be sold on a ''delivered'' basis, where the oil is sold at the end of a voyage at the prevailing price, the price risk remaining fully with the ship operator. In these situations a profit split would need to be made between the non-tonnage tax profit on the oil and the tonnage tax profit on its transportation.

68 However, where the oil is sold FOB (free on board) to the ship operator and then sold on C&F (cost and freight), the ship operator would not have a price risk on the oil itself. In effect, the operator would receive freight income for the route, depending on supply and demand for tankers, plus additional remuneration from the shipper if diversions were made from that route to another port. In such a situation a profit split would not need to be made.

Pooling on liner services

69 A ship operator may form alliances or pools with other companies and share liner routes. It is the nature of a pooled liner service that the cargo, having been booked by the ship operator, may actually be carried in one of the partners' ships. The Inland Revenue accepts that, provided a balance is maintained between the bookings made with originating customers (not being other shipping lines) and the cargo carried in its own ships, then the trade will be regarded as one of ship operation and will be a core qualifying activity.

70 A reasonable balance will be regarded as maintained where in an alliance or pool, over a three year period, the aggregated slots/space allocated for use by originating customers of tonnage tax companies in a UK tonnage tax group match the slots/spaces provided to the alliance or pool in ships operated by those companies. An excess of bookings over cargoes carried of not more than 10% will be disregarded. Where there is consistent structural underprovision of more than 10% cargo carrying on own vessels, bookings over the 10% will be regarded as the carrying on of a separate trade outside tonnage tax.

71 Where similar arrangements exist in other non-liner sectors, similar principles will be applied as appropriate, suitably adapted to the circumstances of the sector.

Secondary activities

72 Qualifying secondary activities are defined in the Tonnage Tax Regulations 2000 (SI 2000/2303). This next section provides guidance on some of the operational aspects of these regulations.

73 Some of the regulations and notes below contain provisions whereby activities are allowed up to a certain limit. Where this limit is breached, then the whole of the profit or loss from that activity will fall outside the tonnage tax ring-fence. However, where the limit is breached to a minimal extent then the Inland Revenue may accept, on *de minimis* grounds, that no adjustment is required. This relaxation is to apply in exceptional circumstances only and will not apply to habitual breaches.

74 Activities that are not listed in the regulations and which are not core qualifying activities will be outside the tonnage tax ring-fence. It is not possible to provide an exhaustive list, but some examples are given below—

(i) The operation of a port or harbour. In small ports where the port and a qualifying wharf/terminal are effectively one and the same, the non-qualifying element should be determined on a just and reasonable basis.

(ii) The processing of goods and materials whether on-board, on the quayside or elsewhere, other than consolidation and breaking of cargo under the regulations. The protection and maintenance of cargo (such as refrigeration or the maintenance of any ripening fruit) will not be regarded as processing.

(iii) The storage of cargo beyond what is immediately necessary whilst awaiting loading onto ships or onward transportation. For example, a warehousing or cold storage trade will not be within tonnage tax.

(iv) The hire of containers to customers for use otherwise than for cargoes booked by the tonnage tax company for transit by sea.

(v) Dealing or speculation in shipping futures or other shipping related financial instruments such as bunkers, not wholly entered into to hedge the company's tonnage tax trade.

(vi) A ship-based holiday where the ship remains moored and there is no sea transportation element.

(vii) Sales where orders are taken on-board for goods to be subsequently delivered to an address provided by the customer or where the goods are not of a customary type for cruise or ferry passengers to purchase.

(viii) Operations that would fall to be treated as a separate trade under normal tax principles. For example, it is accepted the buying and selling ships is part of the normal operation of ships and is a core qualifying activity. However, where the buying and selling takes place to such an extent that the trade effectively becomes one of ship-dealing rather than ship operation, then it would fall outside tonnage tax.

75 The regulations allow activities carried out by one member of a tonnage tax group in connection with qualifying ships operated by another member of the same group to be qualifying secondary activities.

76 The regulations also set out that if such activities are carried out additionally for third parties they may qualify as secondary activities if certain conditions are met. The first condition is that the activities for third parties should only use such staff and resources as are necessary to carry out the main function of the company—that is to say all qualifying activities (core or secondary) which it carries out in respect of qualifying ships that it (or another member of the same tonnage tax group) operates. The second condition is that the level of third party services should be minimal compared with the level of activities carried out in respect of those qualifying ships. These conditions refer to the total of all third party activities, but in most cases, it will be simpler and more practical to apply them on an activity by activity basis. For example if a booking office for a cruise line also sold railway tickets, the level of railway ticket sales which could qualify as secondary activities would depend on the level of staff needed to sell the group's cruise tickets and the comparative volume of railway tickets sold compared with cruise tickets.

77 Companies may prefer to separate out secondary activities carried on for third parties and compute and return the profit on such activities outside the ring-fence. In such cases, the Inland Revenue would only look at the third-party work still conducted within the tonnage tax ring-fence in applying the test to determine whether third-party work was minimal.

78 For example, say a ship operator within tonnage tax has a substantial ship management department providing services to third parties as well as other members of the group. It divides its 32 staff into 12 managing group ships and a dedicated section of 20 staff doing third-party ship management. If the 20 third-party staff do occasional work to help the in-house department, this work should be transfer-priced across the ring-fence. If the 12 in-house staff do occasional work for the third-party department, provided this is minimal in comparison with the level of the in-house work done by those 12 staff, then any profit from that third-party work would be within tonnage tax.

79 In order to determine whether the conditions are met, the level of activity may be determined by any reasonable method including reference to turnover, costs, tonnage of ships or number of TEUs, as appropriate. Only if the conditions are not met will it be necessary to make a full and proper allocation of income and expenditure between secondary activities inside the ring fence and those outside it.

80 Whether the level of an activity is minimal will depend on the measure used and the facts of the case, but the Inland Revenue will not normally accept that third-party activity is minimal in any case where it exceeds 20% of that activity carried out in support of ships operated by the tonnage tax group.

81 Where third party services are provided under a reciprocal arrangement between two operators, the Inland Revenue will accept that third-party services may qualify as secondary activities to the extent that they are reciprocated by the other party.

82 Companies may seek confirmation concerning the extent to which an activity for third parties will qualify as part of the clearance procedure outlined in paras 8–14 above.

83 Where administrative and financial services provided under the regulations also relate to the "non-sea leg" of an inclusively priced journey or, in the case of passengers, to a related excursion or holiday on land, then they will be accepted as being part of the wholly qualifying secondary activity.

Passengers

84 The Inland Revenue will accept that the following activities are carried out in connection with the embarkation or disembarkation of passengers or as part of an inclusive transport service bought in at an arm's length price—

(i) car parking, provided that receipts from non-passengers do not on average exceed 10% of receipts from passengers;

(ii) train, coach, bus or other transport services (including flights) to take passengers to or from the ship or eligible linked holiday; including—

  (*a*) purchase of single seats or block of seats on scheduled services, and

  (*b*) chartered-in transport to and from cruise, provided that only qualifying passengers are carried;

(iii) a single night's accommodation for passengers in transit immediately prior to embarkation or immediately after disembarkation;

(iv) the provision of quayside shopping facilities for passengers, provided that the range of goods available is no wider than would qualify to be sold on board under the regulations.

85 The Inland Revenue will accept that the "provision of excursions for passengers" regulation includes—

(i) excursions on non-qualifying vessels;

(ii) the provision of a shore-based facility for the exclusive use of own passengers;

(iii) trips of longer than a single day provided the cabin on board ship remains "occupied" by the passenger.

Gambling

86 Gambling is to be interpreted broadly and will include slot machines, casino games of chance, raffles, bets on horse racing etc. The Inland Revenue will accept that the turnover from gambling is negligible if it amounts to less than 10% of ticket sales plus receipts from the letting of cabins and sale of food and drink for immediate consumption for that voyage. For the purposes of this test, turnover will be regarded as receipts from gambling after deducting winnings paid out, but before any other expenses. The test applies separately to each individual voyage. In this context, a round-the-world cruise will be viewed as a single voyage.

87 Where the turnover from gambling on a particular voyage is more than negligible, then the whole of the profits from gambling on that particular voyage will fall outside the ring-fence.

88 Where third party concessionaires offer gambling facilities and the ship operator's income from the concessionaire varies partly in relation to turnover, then the ''negligible'' test will also apply to the income from the concessionaire.

Sale of luxury goods

89 Whether or not goods are luxury goods depends upon the standard of goods and services that would normally be expected by the passengers on a particular cruise or journey, and the extent to which they will continue to be enjoyed by the purchaser after completion of the journey. The Inland Revenue will accept that turnover from the sale of luxury goods is negligible if it does not exceed 10% of total ticket sales plus receipts from the letting of cabins and sale of food and drink for immediate consumption for that voyage.

90 Where the turnover from sale of luxury goods on a particular voyage is more than negligible, then the whole of the profits from sale of luxury goods on that particular voyage will fall outside the ring-fence.

91 Where luxury goods are offered for sale on-board by third party concessionaires and the ship operator's income from the concessionaire varies partly in relation to turnover, then the ''negligible'' test will also apply to the income from the concessionaire.

Slot charters

92 Slot charters between shipping companies will be accepted as qualifying secondary activities under the same principles set out in paras 69–71 above on pooled liner services.

Incidental activities

93 This category of income will be very restricted in scope and will deal with minor items of shipping related income that do not fit comfortably into core or secondary categories. The aim will be to prevent what is otherwise a wholly qualifying shipping company from having to apply normal corporation tax rules to insignificant items of ship-related income.

94 Incidental shipping related activities may come within tonnage tax if the turnover from them is less than 0·25% of the turnover from other activities that fall within the tonnage tax ring-fence. Any unused balance of this limit will not be available to set off against non-qualifying secondary activities.

95 However, if ship-related activity which could fall within the definition of ''qualifying incidental activities'' is consistently returned outside the tonnage tax ring-fence, then the Inland Revenue will not argue that it should be treated as a qualifying incidental activity for the purposes of applying the 0·25% of turnover test to other items of incidental income.

Distributions of overseas shipping companies

96 The tests set out in FA 2000 Sch 22 para 49(2) are very strict, in particular the para 49(2)(*d*) requirement that all the overseas company's income is such that it would be relevant shipping income if it were a tonnage tax company. The Inland Revenue appreciates that this test may in practice be very difficult to comply with, particularly where the company is not wholly owned. For instance, dividends from a company with income from a secondary activity in excess of permitted levels could not be included under this provision.

97 Tonnage tax groups wishing to ensure that overseas companies will qualify under para 49(2) should make sure that any non ship-related activities are taken out of those companies. The condition in 49(2)(*d*) will be satisfied if the overseas company has no activities which could generate income other than relevant shipping income. However, the test applies to income and not to activities, and the Inland Revenue will accept that the test is satisfied if effective arrangements are in place to ensure that no income arises which is not relevant shipping income. This will ensure that all profits arising from non-qualifying activities will be taxed outside the tonnage tax ring-fence when paid up to the UK as dividends.

98 The Inland Revenue will accept that the tests should be applied afresh for every period of account of the overseas company. For example, suppose a tonnage tax company has an overseas subsidiary with a December year-end that carries out mixed activities. During 2005, this overseas company sells its non-shipping activities so that in 2006 and 2007 it complies with the para 49(2)(*d*) condition. Half way through 2008, it again becomes a mixed activity company. In this example, dividends declared out of 2006 and 2007 profits paid in either of those two years would meet the conditions. Dividends declared out of profits for 2005 and prior or 2008 and subsequent (whenever paid) would not meet the conditions.

99 The Inland Revenue will also accept that where an overseas company receives minimal levels of non-relevant shipping income, this may be disregarded on *de minimis* grounds when considering the para 49(2)(*d*) condition. Minimal in this case means income up to the level specified in para 48(2), ie 0.25% of turnover from core and qualifying secondary activities.

100 In FA 2000 Sch 22 para 49(2)(*f*) there is a condition that the profits from which the dividends are paid must be subject to tax. This test may still be satisfied even if there is no actual liability to tax on those profits (for example because of the operation of loss relief), so long as the profits in question are "subject to a tax on profits". The rules of computation for tax purposes of those profits are also immaterial—for example, dividends paid by a company within a comparable tonnage tax regime in another country would satisfy the "subject to a tax" test.

101 The Inland Revenue will accept that a qualifying dividend that is credited in the accounts of a tonnage tax company will fall within the tonnage tax ring-fence, even if it is actually received when the company has ceased to be a tonnage tax company. A dividend that is credited in the accounts of a company after it has ceased to be a tonnage tax company will not fall within the tonnage tax ring-fence, even if it meets the conditions of para 49.

102 The Inland Revenue will accept that profits arising on the disposal of all or part of an overseas shipping business may be paid out as dividends under these rules, provided that the overseas company has qualified to pay such dividends (see above paragraphs) for the five years prior to the disposal.

103 Where dividends from overseas shipping companies are regarded as relevant shipping income, the supporting computations must give appropriate details. These should include all the information to justify inclusion within tonnage tax, such as name of ship, IMO number, type of charter, etc plus of copy of the accounts for each foreign company.

Exclusion of interest income etc

104 Under FA 2000 Sch 22 para 50, only such interest, as would under normal corporation tax rules be treated as being trading income arising from the trade consisting of a company's tonnage tax activities, may come within the ring fence as relevant shipping profits.

105 In deciding whether or not interest received would be treated as a trade receipt under normal corporation tax principles, companies should bear in mind the cases of *Nuclear Electric v Bradley* (68 TC 670) and *Bank Line Ltd v IRC* (49 TC 307). In the latter case Lord Avonside commented—

> "Income becomes a trading receipt when it arises from capital actively employed and at risk in the business because it is required for its support or, perhaps, to attract customers looking to the credit of the business. Trading income is 'the fruit' of the capital employed in the business in the present and active sense".

This description would not extend to cover interest arising from the proceeds of ships held on deposit whilst replacement ships are sought.

THE RING-FENCE (PART VII)

Transfer-pricing

106 Paragraphs 58, 59 require adjustments to be made (in accordance with TA 1988 Sch 28AA) where transactions or arrangements involving connected persons, or indeed tonnage tax and non-tonnage tax divisions of the same company, are not on arm's length terms. This applies to all transactions regardless of whether or not a hard charge would normally be made for the goods/services provided. The existence of the special ring-fencing rules for finance costs does not over-ride the requirement to apply the transfer-pricing rules to financial transactions across the ring-fence or with a connected party outside the UK.

Finance costs

107 The Inland Revenue will not insist on "hard charging" for the cost of finance across the ring-fence. However, where finance costs across the ring-fence are at less than arm's length rates, transfer pricing across the ring-fence should be undertaken before reallocation of finance costs is computed.

108 A tonnage tax company or group must ensure that an appropriate proportion of its finance costs, in accordance with FA 2000 Sch 22 para 61 or 62, is included in the company's or group's return(*s*) of profits, if it is not already charged against its relevant shipping profits. Further guidance is available in the annex to this statement of practice.

CAPITAL ALLOWANCES (PART IX)

Transfers of ships within a tonnage tax group

109 TA 1988 s 343 (company reconstructions without a change in ownership) can apply to transfers of shipping trade between members of the same tonnage tax group. Where a shipping business is transferred between members of a tonnage tax group in such circumstances as s 343 would normally apply, the tonnage tax pool relating to that shipping business may be transferred along with the shipping business itself to the new owner.

110 One member of a tonnage tax group may own a ship which it bareboat charters to another member of the same group. The Inland Revenue will accept that this is a trade for the purposes of TA 1988 s 343. If the ship (still subject to the bareboat charter) is transferred to a third company within the group, the tonnage tax pool relating to that ship may also be transferred to the third company.

Industrial buildings

111 Paragraph 82 provides that where an "identifiable" part of a building is used for tonnage tax purposes, then that part of the building will be treated as though it does not qualify for industrial buildings allowances. Normal principles should be followed when applying this rule. For instance, the 25% rule in CAA 1990 s 18 [now CAA 2001 s 283] will apply in the usual manner.

FINANCE LEASING (PART X)

112 Part X applies special rules to ships leased into the tonnage tax regime under finance lease terms. Paragraph 90 prevents a finance lessor claiming capital allowances in respect of the cost of a ship leased to a tonnage tax company where the leasing arrangement includes provision of security to such an extent that most of the non-compliance risk associated with the lease is removed from the lessor.

113 In measuring the "non-compliance risk" it will be necessary to take into account the future realisable value of the ship. This may be derived from a series of valuations carried out as at regular intervals over the length of the lease. For example on a 20–25 year lease, valuations should be made as at intervals of not less than five years. These should be professional valuations taking into account normal valuation principles—factors such as the anticipated state of that sector of the shipping market, the forecast of future trends, the adaptability or otherwise of the ship to other purposes and the dominance of the lessee in that particular sector may be relevant if they are part of a normal valuation process.

114 The valuation should be done from the perspective of day one—if the circumstances subsequently change, the Inland Revenue will not seek to revisit the valuation.

115 The ship should be valued unencumbered by any security sought (such as a mortgage given to a third party guarantor), to avoid any difficulties with circularity.

116 Paragraph 90 will not apply to certain types of security. These are—

(i) any security inherent in the leased ship itself, provided to the lessor or to a third party guarantor, including—

- a mortgage on the leased ship;
- an attachment of the lessee's earnings from the leased ship;
- assignment of any insurance proceeds arising in respect of the leased ship;
- rental rebates arising from the arm's length sale of the leased ship;

(ii) any guarantee or other security which satisfies the conditions set out in para 91(3)–(5).

117 Parental guarantees are also left out of account in considering whether the 50% limit has been breached. In the case of a guarantee by the lessee's parent this is because sub-paras 92(2), 91(3) apply equally to the lessee and a person connected with the lessee. In the case of a guarantee from the lessor's parent, it is by virtue of para 91(6).

118 Whilst FA 2000 Sch 22 para 91 only refers to the security inherent in the leased ship, where more than one ship is leased as part of the same deal, the Inland Revenue will accept that the cross-collateralisation of all the ships leased under that deal falls under this heading.

119 The forms of security listed in para 91 will be completely disregarded in considering whether or not more than 50% of the non-compliance risk associated with the lease is removed from the lessor (or a person connected with the lessor). This means that any such security should not be taken into account in computing the non-compliance risk and furthermore any security within para 91 will be treated as *not* removing any of that non-compliance risk from the lessor.

120 Pre-delivery guarantees, whereby the putative lessor obtains guarantees in respect of interim finance during the construction stage, may also be left out of account in looking at the extent of removal of non-compliance risk from the lessor, since the Inland Revenue accepts that such guarantees are not part of the leasing structure once the ship has been delivered and the lease is in place.

OFFSHORE ACTIVITIES (PART XI)

121 FA 2000 Sch 22 para 103(2) provides that the special rules applicable to offshore activities do not apply unless the number of days in which qualifying ships are operated in offshore activities exceeds 30. The 30 days to be taken into account are the total number of ship-days within the designated area operated by all of a company's vessels in the accounting period. Thus, a company operating two vessels in offshore activities, one for 15 days and the second for 16 days, exceeds the 30 days total and both ships come within the special rules for offshore activities.

122 Qualifying ships engaged in the search for oil or gas on the UK continental shelf, eg a seismic vessel, fall within the description of offshore activities in FA 2000 Sch 22 para 104(1) and, similarly, qualifying ships engaged in the exploitation of UKCS oil or gas eg a pipe-laying vessel also fall within it. However, the term "offshore activities" is much wider than this because of the words "in connection with'' and covers all types of ships used in the actual task of exploring for or exploiting gas or oil either in an ancillary, subordinate or supporting role, eg a diving support vessel.

123 FA 2000 Sch 22 para 105 excludes certain vessels from the special rules for offshore activities. The reference to supply vessels, tugs and anchor handling vessels includes vessels performing one or more of the activities of supply, towage and anchor handling.

124 The period of inactivity referred to in para 106(*a*) will include the period during which the vessel is being commissioned in preparation for its forthcoming operation. Similarly, any decommissioning activity on completion of the contract will also be included.

125 Paragraph 110(4) refers to where plant and machinery ceases permanently to be used for the purposes of offshore activities. In this context the question of whether an item of plant and machinery has permanently ceased to be used for offshore activities purposes is primarily a question of fact. In general the Inland Revenue would be prepared to regard a period of two years or less during which the item of plant and machinery is not used for offshore activities as being merely temporary.

GROUPS, MERGERS AND RELATED MATTERS (PART XII)

126 Paragraph 117(2) provides that a company will not be brought into a tonnage tax group if the individual treated as controlling it does not in practice have any ''significant influence over the affairs of the company in question''. Whether significant influence exists will be interpreted according to the facts of each particular case. It will generally be presumed that where there is a close family relationship, such as husband and wife or parent and minor child, then significant influence will exist. An example of where significant influence may not exist is where there has been a long-term demonstrable family rift and the controlling parties have no contact with each other.

127 Where a foreign group including companies operating qualifying ships comes to the UK for the first time, it will have 12 months to decide whether to elect into tonnage tax under FA 2000 Sch 22 para 10(3). If it decides to elect in, the election will have effect from the time that the group came to the UK. If such an election is made, the group will be considered as a tonnage tax group from the moment it comes to the UK for the purposes of applying the rules on mergers set out in FA 2000 Sch 22 paras 123–126.

CORPORATE PARTNERSHIPS (PART XIII)

128 Companies that are members of a partnership may bring qualifying activities carried on through that partnership into tonnage tax, even if some or all other partners are outside the regime. The detailed rules are contained in paras 130–136 and in the Tonnage Tax Regulations 2000 reg 8 onwards.

129 These rules cover, amongst other things—

(i) the computation of tonnage tax and non-tonnage tax profits,
(ii) the application of the 75% chartering-in limit,
(iii) the computation of chargeable gains, and
(iv) the calculation of capital allowances following a partner's exit from tonnage tax,

and will apply equally to those partnerships that have legal personality (as in Scotland), as they do to partnerships that do not.

130 Broadly speaking, the effect of these provisions will enable a partner which is a tonnage tax company to calculate the partnership profit along tonnage tax lines. Partners, who are not within tonnage tax, will calculate their share of partnership profit by reference to normal UK corporation tax principles. Thus, there may be different parallel computations of the profits of one partnership, eg one on tonnage tax lines and one on normal corporation tax lines. The Tonnage Tax Unit at Liverpool large business office (see para 6 above) will advise on points of concern or difficulty.

EXIT CHARGES (PART XIV)

131 FA 2000 Sch 22 para 137(2) provides that exit charges will apply where a company ceases to be a tonnage tax company ''...for reasons relating wholly or mainly to tax''. This paragraph is aimed at situations where a company or group deliberately engineers an exit from tonnage tax, perhaps through a temporary cessation of all qualifying activities or a deliberate manipulation of corporate structures. The Inland Revenue will not seek to apply exit charges if—

(i) the company has reached the natural expiry date of its election (even if the reason that the company chooses not to renew its election is ''relating wholly or mainly to tax'', for instance, if the reason for not renewing is that it wishes to utilise shipping losses); or
(ii) the company has good commercial reasons, aside from considerations of tax, for leaving tonnage tax; or the company is wound up, except in circumstances where company liquidations are a feature of a group scheme to engineer a deliberate exit from tonnage tax; or
(iii) the company leaves the UK except in circumstances where the change in company residence is a feature of a group scheme to engineer a deliberate exit from tonnage tax; or
(iv) the company ceases to be a tonnage tax company as a result of the operation of the rules on mergers.

ANNEX—FINANCE COSTS

Broad approach of the legislation

1 This statement provides guidance on the implementation of FA 2000 Sch 22 paras 61–63. These require that where a single company or members of a group include an excessive deduction for finance costs in computing profits outside the tonnage tax ring-fence, then additional taxable profits should be brought into account to reflect the excess. The rules will apply to all tonnage tax companies or groups that carry on non-tonnage tax activities and incur finance costs that are deductible for the purposes of corporation tax.

2 A simple example of a situation where an additional charge would normally arise is a diversified group that funds its shipping subsidiaries through equity and its non-shipping subsidiaries through debt.

3 The legislation does not include detailed rules prescribing exactly how the calculation of the additional profits should be carried out. Instead, companies and groups may choose an appropriate methodology for this calculation to ensure a just and reasonable result when their own circumstances are taken into account.

4 This guidance assumes that a tonnage tax group is involved, although the principles can be adapted for a single company, as shown in Example G below. Where a group operates under a group arrangement as described in paras 17–21 above, the Inland Revenue will accept that these calculations should be carried out by the representative company and not by every tonnage tax company in the group. However, any resulting adjustment should be allocated to all the tonnage tax companies, as required by para 62(5).

Computational principles

5 The calculation of the excess finance costs for an accounting period will involve the following stages—

(i) Determine the total UK-deductible finance costs of the tonnage tax group that are taken into account in computing profits arising outside the ring-fence (after any statutory disallowances including transfer-pricing adjustments). Intra-group finance costs with a corresponding direct receipt chargeable to UK corporation tax (outside the ring fence) in the same accounting period elsewhere in the group do not need to be counted for this purpose.

(ii) Determine the total UK-deductible finance costs of the tonnage tax group, as if there were no tonnage tax election in place. This could be approximated by the amount determined in (i) above, plus finance costs charged in the calculation of relevant shipping profits. Intra-group finance costs with a corresponding contemporaneous UK taxable receipt that were not counted under (i) above should again be ignored here.

(iii) Determine the proportionate amount of the costs calculated in (ii) that cannot be regarded as being incurred so as to give rise, directly or indirectly, to relevant shipping profits. This should be done on a just and reasonable basis having regard to the underlying funding and the generation of relevant shipping profits. Further guidance is given below.

(iv) Calculate the excess of (i) over (iii), if any.

(v) Allocate this excess to the tonnage tax companies in proportion to their tonnage tax profits.

6 Stages (i) to (iv) can be represented by the following formulae, which are used to facilitate the examples below—

$$\mathbf{E = A - (F \times B)}$$

$$\text{If } \mathbf{(F \times B) > A} \text{ then } \mathbf{E} = 0$$

where—

E is the excess finance costs to be allocated to the tonnage tax companies.

A is the group finance costs that can be taken into account outside the ring-fence (before the application of para 62).

B is the group finance costs determined as if there were no tonnage tax election in place.

F is a just and reasonable fraction.

7 Where there are non-coterminous accounting periods, then the periods should be matched using any just and reasonable method.

Definition of finance costs

8 Finance costs are defined at para 63. All of the costs arising from debt financing should be included and the Inland Revenue will expect this provision to be interpreted very broadly. It could include off-balance sheet methods of financing. However, finance costs will not normally include costs incurred through the late payment of debts, such as interest paid to trade suppliers or interest on late payments of corporation tax/PAYE/VAT.

Determining the just and reasonable fraction (F)

9 It is not possible to specify a single universally applicable formula for determining **F**, as different groups will have different operational and financial circumstances. Each group will therefore have to devise its own methodology. A group may wish to discuss this with its tax office as part of the clearance procedure.

10 In devising an appropriate methodology, the Inland Revenue will generally expect the following considerations to be taken into account—

(i) The calculations must observe the principle of fungibility. This means that individual items of finance should not be linked with individual activities or individual assets. Instead the financing should be viewed as funding the totality of all the tonnage tax and non-tonnage tax activities of the group's UK companies and those of its overseas subsidiaries.

(ii) Any consideration of tonnage tax activities must include the activities of overseas shipping companies whose dividends would ordinarily be relevant shipping profits under para 49 (and thus subject to UK corporation tax solely under the tonnage tax regime). This is the case irrespective of whether any such dividends are paid during the accounting period under review. This approach is necessary to avoid distortionary tax effects that could otherwise be caused as a result of the group's commercial decisions as to where debt is to be located. See examples I and J below.

(iii) If the funding requirements of a business differ from activity to activity the calculation of **F** should take this into account. Shipping is generally a capital-intensive activity due to the high costs of the assets and would be expected to require greater funding than many other activities.

(iv) The existence of and circumstances surrounding intra-group financing across the ring-fence should be taken into account in considering the nature of the activities outside the ring-fence and in arriving at the adjustment required.

(v) A group that utilises complex international funding structures must take these fully into account in determining whether or not a proposed methodology produces a just and reasonable result.

11 The methodology chosen must be used consistently from period to period, unless group circumstances change so that this would no longer produce a just and reasonable result.

Examples

12 The examples below are designed to demonstrate how a just and reasonable result might be reached. They are not exhaustive and are necessarily simplified.

A A tonnage group carries out wholly qualifying shipping operations and all income and expenses (including £100 finance costs) are accounted for within the tonnage tax ring-fence.

In this situation there are no activities outside the ring-fence and therefore neither para 61 nor para 62 applies.

B The same situation as A, except that the £100 finance costs are borne outside the tonnage tax ring-fence, and the group now has £100 of interest income outside the ring-fence. This interest income is negligible when compared to the rest of the group's activities and therefore any funding used to support the interest bearing deposit will also be negligible.

This means that F is 0% so E is 100. The net result is taxable income outside the ring-fence of £100.

C The same situation as B, except now the £100 of interest income is material to the group, representing 10% of its total income.

It might now be reasonable to regard some of the debt as funding the interest bearing deposit, and therefore F increases to (say) 10% and E reduces to 90.

D The same situation as C, except the £100 of interest income now represents 10% of the group's total profits but only a negligible proportion of its total income.

A just and reasonable view might be that the funding applicable to the interest bearing deposit is negligible compared to the funding for the business as a whole, giving the result that F is 0% and E is 100.

E A tonnage tax group contains two UK companies, one of which is a tonnage tax company carrying out wholly qualifying shipping operations and the other of which is not a tonnage tax company. Both businesses are of similar size with similar funding requirements and therefore it is appropriate for **F** to be 50%. Each company incurs £100 finance costs, of which the tonnage tax company's are inside the ring fence.

In this situation A = 100 and B = 200. This means that E = 0 and no adjustment is required.

F The same situation as E, except that the tonnage tax company is now wholly equity funded and all the finance costs have been charged in the non-tonnage tax company.

Now A = 200, B = 200, F = 50%, and therefore E = 100.

G The same situation as F, except that the tonnage tax group is a single company with two divisions. The finance costs are charged equally inside and outside the ring-fence.

There is already an equal sharing of finance costs on either side of the ring-fence, so E = 0.

H A tonnage tax company decides to increase its borrowings at the same time as it acquires a non-tonnage tax company. Finance costs are £100. Before this borrowing, the group was entirely equity funded. The two businesses are of similar size and with similar funding requirements. The group takes the full £100 into account in computing its profits outside the ring fence.

The principle of fungibility means that the finance costs must be regarded as relating to both businesses. Thus, F = 50%, and A = 100, B = 100 and therefore E = 50.

I A tonnage tax group consists of three companies—one is a tonnage tax company carrying out wholly qualifying shipping operations, another is an overseas company qualifying to pay dividends under the provisions of para 49 and the other is a UK non-shipping company. All three businesses are of similar size and with similar funding requirements. Finance costs of £900 are all taken into account in computing the profits of the non-shipping company. Non-tonnage tax activities account for one third of the group.

The para 49 company counts as tonnage tax for this purpose therefore F = 33%. This means that A = 900, B = 900 and E = 600.

J The same situation as I, except that the finance costs are charged £375 in each UK company and £150 overseas.

This means that A = 375, B = 750 and F = 33% giving E = 125. It can be seen that this gives a net UK deduction of 250/750 outside the ring-fence, which is proportionately the same as the 300/900 in example I. This satisfies the principle at 10(ii) and takes proper account of the fact that overseas debt reduces the extent of the group's UK source financing requirement.

K The same situation as J, except that the non-shipping company is now an overseas company.

This means that A = 0, B = 375 and E = 0 (E cannot be negative).

L The same situation as J, except that additional finance costs of £150 are paid by the non-tonnage tax company to the tonnage tax company.

The interest does not constitute trading income and is therefore taxed outside the ring-fence. A still = 375 (as the additional costs can be ignored), B still = 750 and F = 33% giving E = 125 (as in J).

M The same situation as L, except that the additional finance costs of £150 are paid by the non-tonnage tax UK company to the overseas shipping subsidiary.

A = 525 (the additional costs are now brought into account), B = 900 and F = 33% giving E = 225.

N Mrs X controls a group of UK non-tonnage tax companies that are funded primarily by debt. Her husband controls a group of tonnage tax companies that are funded primarily by equity.

The debt and finance costs in the Mrs X companies must be taken account of in the para 62 calculations.

O A tonnage tax group incurs UK finance costs of £100 outside the ring-fence. **F** is determined at 2/3 which means that **E** = 33.3. The group enters into a financing arrangement whereby equity is invested in a subsidiary in a low tax regime and funds loaned back from this subsidiary to a tonnage tax company.

There are no additional commercial activities created by this transaction and prima facie, F remains at 2/3. Interest paid by the tonnage tax company to the overseas finance company increases B but has no impact on A, thus reducing E. The main benefit of this arrangement to the group is to avoid an additional tax charge. The Inland Revenue would view this as not being a just and reasonable result and would expect a further adjustment to be made.

Note—The text of this statement is as shown in IR 131 (August 2002).

SP 1/01 (February 2001) *Treatment of investment managers and their overseas clients*

1 This statement gives guidance on the application of the rules in FA 1995 regarding the assessment of UK investment managers who act on behalf of overseas clients. In particular, it sets out the Inland Revenue's view on—

(*a*) the extent to which trading in the UK by a non-resident client affects protection from assessment in the name of an investment manager (FA 1995 s 127);

(*b*) the factors to be taken into account in determining whether active management of a portfolio on behalf of a non-resident client constitutes the exercise of a trade in the UK by that client;

(*c*) the circumstances in which an investment manager is considered to be acting in an independent capacity within FA 1995 s 127(3)(*c*), and

(*d*) the application of the 20% rule in FA 1995 s 127(4).

PART I—BACKGROUND

2 TMA 1970 ss 78–85 contained a number of provisions concerning the assessment of a UK agent acting on behalf of a non-resident principal. In particular s 78(2) ensured that certain UK investment managers were not assessable to tax on behalf of their overseas clients. statement of practice 15/91 gave guidance on the application of those provisions.

3 FA 1995 repealed TMA 1970 ss 78–85 and introduced (in ss 126–129 and Sch 23) new provisions which apply to agents generally from April 1996 and in relation to investment managers from April 1995. This statement of practice gives guidance on the application of the FA 1995 provisions.

4 The broad effect of the 1995 legislation is to ensure that non-residents (excluding certain non-resident trustees) are not exposed to any additional liability to tax by using the services of independent investment managers in the UK. This is done by restricting the tax chargeable on the income of non-residents in respect of investment transactions carried out through independent UK investment managers. The tax is restricted to the tax, if any, deducted at source. Special rules apply where the transactions carried out by the UK investment manager amount to the carrying on of the whole or part of the non-resident's financial trade in the UK. These special rules are considered in Part III.

5 The provisions do not apply to income from or connected with a trade carried on in the UK by the non-resident other than through a broker or independent investment manager. For instance income arising from the temporary lodgement of funds used in a manufacturing business carried on in the UK is liable to corporation tax or income tax in the normal way. The same applies where the transactions are part of a wider trade, eg insurance, carried on in the UK whether by the investment manager, another agent, or a branch of the non-resident.

6 Where the limit on charge does not apply to income arising through the UK investment manager, it does not necessarily follow that the non-resident is liable to UK tax on that income. For example certain UK securities are exempt from tax. Also, the non-resident may be able to claim exemption under a double taxation agreement where the investment manager is not a permanent establishment of the non-resident. Exemption under an agreement will depend on both the facts and the terms of the agreement.

7 It is sometimes the case that a non-resident appoints an investment manager overseas who in turn appoints a UK investment manager, often its affiliate, to manage the investment of all or part of the portfolio. In those circumstances the legislation is applied as between UK manager and the non-resident on the basis of looking through the overseas manager. The fee income retained by the overseas investment manager should do no more than reflect the work carried out offshore.

PART II—RELEVANCE OF TRADING

8 FA 1995 s 127 only applies to an investment manager who is carrying on the trade of a non-resident client in the UK. If the non-resident is not trading in the UK then the investment manager cannot be the non-resident's ''UK representative'' within FA 1995 s 126 and cannot be assessed.

9 If the transactions carried out through the investment manager are part of the trade carried on by the non-resident then, unless the conditions in s 127 are satisfied (see Part III), the income from that trade, including any profit from the realisation of securities, etc, is taxable.

10 Whether or not a taxpayer is trading is a question of fact to be determined by reference to all the facts and circumstances of the particular case. This applies as much to financial transactions as to other activities.

11 In determining the question of trading, any transactions carried out through an investment manager are to be considered in the context of the status and worldwide activities of the non-resident. An individual is unlikely to be regarded as trading as a result of purely speculative transactions. For a company, a transaction will generally be either trading or capital in nature. (This may also be the case for non-resident collective investment vehicles whether open-ended or closed). If the main business of a non-resident company is a trade outside the financial area, or an investment holding business, the activities in the UK would normally amount to trading only if they constituted or were part of a separate financial trade. But if, exceptionally, activities which are an integral part of the profit earning activities of a non-financial trade are carried out through a UK investment manager (eg hedging on the London terminal markets by a non-resident dealer in physical commodities), then that might amount to trading here. The view to be taken on a particular case will depend on all the facts of that case.

12 The active management of an investment portfolio of shares, bonds and money market instruments such as bills, certificates of deposit, floating rate notes and commercial paper does not normally constitute a trade. But every case must be considered in the light of its own facts. Where futures and options are concerned, statement of practice 14/91 ''Tax treatment of transactions in financial futures and options'' will be applied to non-resident clients who are collective investment vehicles (whether open-ended or closed), pension funds and other bodies which either do not trade or whose principal trade is outside the financial area.

13 If a non-resident carries on a financial trade outside the UK, any transactions carried out through a UK investment manager are likely to amount to trading in the UK. That is so whether there is a discretionary agreement or whether the manager acts on the instructions of the client. The criteria for deciding whether a non-resident financial company is an investment company or a trading company are the same as those which apply to a resident company.

PART III: PARTICULAR PROVISIONS OF FA 1995 S 127(3)—THE INDEPENDENCE TEST AND THE 20% RULE

14 Where there is trading in the UK, no assessment is due on the investment manager if the provisions of s 127 are satisfied. And, except in the circumstances mentioned in para 5 above, no assessment is due on the non-resident. Liability is instead limited to tax deducted at source.

15 The following paragraphs give guidance on two of the tests that must be passed—the independence test (see para 18 below) and the 20% rule (see para 24 below). These two tests ensure that s 127 does not apply to financial trades carried out through an investment manager who is either not independent of the non-resident or who acts on terms other than would be customary between independent parties acting at arm's length.

16 Application of the investment manager provisions is restricted to transactions in shares, stock, commercial paper and warrants, futures (including forward) contracts, options contracts or securities of any description (but not futures contracts or option contracts relating to land, although futures or options contracts involving indices of land may qualify), interest rate swaps, equity swaps, currency swaps, commodity swaps and commodity index swaps (but not transactions in physical commodities, including gold, nor warrants on the London Metal Exchange which give the holder title to the metal).

17 It is also a requirement that the non-resident does not carry on any other trade through the investment manager.

The independence test

18 The manager must act for the non-resident in an independent capacity. This means ascertaining whether, having regard to its legal, financial and commercial characteristics, the relationship between manager and client is a relationship between persons carrying on independent businesses that deal with each other at arm's length. Where the other conditions of s 127(3) are met, the Revenue will regard the independence test as satisfied where any of the following applies—

(i) the provision of services to the non-resident and persons connected with the non-resident is not a substantial part of the investment management business;

(ii) from the start of a new investment management business provided the above condition was satisfied within 18 months;

(iii) an intention to satisfy either of the above conditions was not met for reasons outside the manager's control, although reasonable steps to fulfil that intention were taken;

(iv) investment management services are provided to a collective fund, the interests in which are quoted on a recognised stock exchange or otherwise freely marketed, for instance as units in a unit trust;

(v) investment management services are provided to a widely held collective fund.

19 The condition in (i) above would be satisfied where that part did not exceed 70% of the investment management business, either by reference to fees or to some other measure where that would be more appropriate. Where investment management services are provided to a collective investment scheme constituted as a partnership, participants in the scheme would not be regarded as connected persons for this purpose solely by reason of membership of the partnership.

20 Most funds which are transparent for UK income tax purposes (ie where the beneficial entitlement to the income rests with the participant rather than the fund itself) will satisfy the condition in (i) above.

21 Condition (v) is likely to apply mainly to overseas funds which are not treated as transparent for UK income tax purposes, eg most funds constituted as limited companies. The condition will be regarded as satisfied if either no majority interest in the fund was held by five or fewer persons and persons connected with them, or no interest of more than 20% was held by a single person and persons connected with that person.

22 The list in para 18 above is not exhaustive. Cases which fall outside these categories would have to be considered on their own facts. A subsidiary may be considered independent of its parent company in this regard notwithstanding the parent's ownership of the share capital.

23 An example of a fund not meeting any of the criteria in para 18, but which is likely to be independent on the facts, would be a company which is not widely held but which is itself a subsidiary of a company that is.

The 20% rule

24 In essence the requirement is that the investment manager and persons connected with him (the definition of connected persons is that in TA 1988 s 839) must not have a beneficial entitlement to more than 20% of the non-resident's taxable income arising from transactions carried out through the investment manager. Professional fees paid to the investment manager and persons connected with him are not included in the 20% provided they are allowable as deductions in arriving at the taxable income. This applies equally to incentive or performance fees which are calculated by reference to any increase in the net asset value or profits of the relevant non-resident.

25 Where the 20% threshold is broken, the part of the income of the non-resident to which the investment manager and connected persons are beneficially entitled is excluded from the limitation of charge. The limitation of charge will apply to the part to which they are not beneficially entitled, provided the other conditions in the investment manager provisions are met.

26 The 20% rule is treated as satisfied throughout any period, not exceeding five years, for which it is met in respect of the total taxable income of the period arising from transactions carried out through the investment manager. It is also treated as satisfied if the manager intended to meet that condition but failed to do so, wholly or partly, for reasons outside the manager's control, having taken any reasonable steps to fulfil that intention. This means that the manager must fulfil the intention to keep the beneficial entitlement within 20% of the total taxable income for the period insofar as it is reasonable to do so, but is not required to get within that figure at any cost, for instance where there are good commercial reasons for not achieving that.

27 Example:

Years	*1*	*2*	*3*	*4*	*5*
Taxable income of non-resident	£100	£200	£200	£250	£250
Entitlement of manager to above	£32	£58	£40	£35	£5
Expressed as percentage for each year	32%	29%	20%	14%	2%
Average percentage over qualifying period	32%	30%	26%	22%	17%

It may be assumed that the test is satisfied for year one because (*a*) in this example it was the manager's intention to have a beneficial entitlement to an average of 20% or less in aggregate over a five-year period and (*b*) that intention was fulfilled. Had the 20% beneficial entitlement been achieved before the five years were up, then that shorter period would have been the qualifying period.

A second qualifying period of up to five years could include years two, three, four, five and six and so on.

28 In relation to a tax-transparent fund (see para 20) having overseas investors, the non-residents will be participants in the fund. In such circumstances the 20% rule would be automatically broken where a non-resident participant is connected to the investment manager since this would mean that all the non-resident participants were connected under s 839(4) by virtue of their being partners in the same partnership. The investment manager and connected persons would then be entitled to all the income of that non-resident. Accordingly, where the investment management services are provided to a collective investment scheme (as defined in the Financial Services and Markets Act 2000), the 20% rule is applied by looking at the scheme as a whole rather than at the individual participators. It is not then relevant that the investment manager may be connected to the non-resident as partner (s 127(10)) or that the non-resident participants themselves carry on a financial trade—the availability of s 127 protection is instead tested solely by reference to the nature of the activities of the notional company represented by the scheme.

29 In certain circumstances the investment manager may be connected with the participants because both are partners in one or more partnerships which have an interest in the fund in question. Where the 20% test is failed as a consequence of aggregating the manager's income with that of certain partners who are not connected persons otherwise than as a result of s 839(4), the failure will be regarded as a failure under s 127(4)(*b*) to fulfil an intention to satisfy the test. In certain situations that failure will be considered as (*a*) attributable to matters outside the control of the manager and persons connected with him and (*b*) as not being the result of a failure to take reasonable steps to mitigate the effect of those matters in relation to the fulfilment of that intention. In those situations the 20% test will therefore be passed (see para 26 above). The legislation will be applied in this way where—

- the connected persons are partners other than solely in a fund under consideration, and
- partnership is the only reason that the manager is connected with them.

30 Where overseas pension funds are set up under trust the trustees do not have beneficial ownership of the pension fund income although they may be the legal owners. The 20% rule will not therefore apply where the trustee is connected to the UK investment manager. In practice it would be unusual for an overseas pension fund to be carrying on a financial trade.

31 Where the establishment of a connected person's relationship depends on the question of whether a person falls to be regarded as having control of a company's affairs within the terms of TA 1988 s 416(2), it is not considered that a person's ability (whether *de facto* or *de jure*) to appoint the majority of the Board of directors will itself constitute control of the company's affairs—unless, that is, the Board exercises powers which would normally be exercised by the shareholders at a general meeting.

Interaction of the independence test and the 20% rule

32 The independence test and the 20% rule apply quite separately. Two examples may help to illustrate this.

(i) A UK investment manager acts for an overseas trading fund constituted as a company which accounts for 75% of the business. The parent of the investment manager is an investor in the fund company. If the investment manager is not acting in an independent capacity in relation to the fund company then the whole of the income of the fund is liable to assessment. If the independence test is satisfied, say because no majority interest in the fund is held by five or fewer persons and persons connected with them, then the 20% test must be separately addressed. If the parent's interest in the fund company is 30% then that share of the fund's trading income is liable to assessment.

(ii) A UK investment manager acts for a transparent trading fund constituted as a collective investment scheme in which its overseas parent company is an investor. The facts may show that the investment manager is acting in an independent capacity (eg because condition (i) in para 18 above is satisfied) in relation to all investors including the parent company. As a separate matter the 20% test is then applied to the share in the whole of the taxable profits of the fund to which the manager and persons connected with him are entitled, so that depending on the level of the investment the test may or may not be satisfied.

Concession B40

33 Exceptionally, income in jointly held funds may have come within concession B40 but not within the provisions of FA 1995. Where this applies and such funds were marketed by means of a prospectus or otherwise before 24 November 1994, concession B40 will continue to apply on the same basis as before for the intended life of the fund when it was marketed (not including renewals or extensions), but not beyond 5 April 2005.

Commentary—*Simon's Direct Tax Service* **B3.125A**.

SP 2/01 (February 2001) *Application of local currency rules in FA 2000 to partnerships which include companies*

GENERAL

1 This statement of practice supplements, and in one respect supersedes, an earlier statement (SP 4/98) in so far as it relates to partnerships with corporate members where either the company or the partnership is subject to FA 1993 ss 93, 94 as amended by FA 2000 s 105. The pre-FA 2000 legislation provided for the right to elect to use a currency other than sterling in certain circumstances for restricted aspects of the calculation of trading profits or losses for tax purposes. The FA 2000 amendments replace this elective approach with a more widely-drawn rule setting out the circumstances in which profits and losses for the purposes of corporation tax should be computed in a currency other than sterling. Accordingly, SP 4/98 para 29, which deals with the making of local currency elections, ceases to be relevant for periods governed by the amended version of FA 1993 ss 93, 94. Otherwise, that earlier statement of practice continues to apply in full.

2 The amended legislation takes effect generally for the purposes of corporation tax in relation to accounting periods of companies beginning on or after 1 January 2000 and ending on or after 21 March 2000. However, any company which did not make a local currency election under the Local Currency Election Regulations, SI 1994/3230 for the immediately preceding accounting period may elect that ss 93, 94, as amended, should not apply to it until its first accounting period beginning on or after 1 July 2000. Such an election must be made on or before 31 August 2000. This statement of practice applies for all accounting periods to which the amended version of FA 1993 ss 93, 94 applies. This means both the accounting periods of corporate members of partnerships and accounting periods of partnerships of which a company is a member.

STATUTORY FRAMEWORK

3 TA 1988 s 8(2) provides that a resident company is chargeable to corporation tax on profits arising to it under any partnership wherever it would be so chargeable if the profits accrued to the company directly. TA 1988 s 11(2) provides that a non-resident company is chargeable to corporation tax on the profits arising to it from a trade carried on in the UK through a branch or agency. A partnership is regarded as a branch or agency for this purpose.

4 TA 1988 s 114 gives the rules for computing not only the profits and losses of a trade or profession carried on by persons in partnership where one member or more of the partnership is a company, but also the profits and losses of such partnerships which carry on non-trading business. In this context the word "business" has a very wide meaning and generally encompasses any activity or venture of a commercial nature. The profits and losses of the partnership are computed, for the purposes of corporation tax, as if the partnership is a company, separate from any company which is a partner. The trade, profession or business carried on is also treated as separate from any trade or business which the company member carries on individually on its own account.

5 For the purposes of corporation tax, s 114 provides that the profits or losses of a partnership with a UK resident corporate member are to be computed as if the partnership were a UK resident company. The corporate member's share of the resultant figure is determined in accordance with its interest in the partnership for the relevant period and charged on the company as if it had been carrying on the business itself.

6 If a corporate member of a partnership is not UK resident, s 114 (read with s 115) provides that the computation of partnership profits is to be made on the basis that the partnership is a non-UK resident company. The corporate member's share of the profit determined in accordance with its interest in the partnership for the period is to be charged on the company as if it was carrying on the business itself through a UK branch. Accordingly, in a partnership involving both UK resident and non-UK resident companies, the profits and losses of the partnership have to be computed on two separate bases for the purposes of arriving at the profits and losses of these two types of corporate partner.

7 The effect of s 114 (as extended by s 115) is to determine the share of the FA 1993 ss 93, 94 profit of partnerships with UK resident corporate members, non-UK resident corporate members or both on which such companies are respectively to be charged to corporation tax.

8 FA 1993 ss 93, 94, as amended by FA 2000 s 105, set out the circumstances in which profits and losses of a business or part of a business for the purposes of corporation tax should be computed in a currency other than sterling and provide for the ways in which this computation may be made. The rules for computing any proportion of chargeable gains or capital losses for corporation tax remain as before, namely all are to be computed in sterling.

9 FA 1998 Sch 18 para 12 provides that the corporate member's company return must include any amount which in "a relevant partnership statement", within the meaning of TMA 1970 s 12AB, is stated to be its share of the partnership results for the period. That statement is not directly concerned with the underlying accounts. But the statement is to form part of the partnership return required by TMA 1970 s 12AA. In accordance with subsections (2), (3) of the latter section an officer of the Board may require the partners, or one of them, to deliver a return of relevant information which may include "accounts, statements and documents".

10 Such a partnership return is only required where the partnership is a UK partnership or a foreign partnership which carries on business in the UK through a branch or agency. A UK company may be a member of a foreign partnership which does not carry on business in the UK. In that case the company's corporation tax return requires it to enclose a copy of the partnership accounts and tax computations showing its share of the partnership's taxable profits and losses for the relevant period.

ELECTION TO DEFER APPLICATION OF THE AMENDED LEGISLATION

11 For the purposes of corporation tax, the profits and losses of partnerships to which s 114 applies for the accounting periods referred to in para 2 above will have to be computed on the basis that FA 1993 ss 93, 94 apply to the partnership. It is the view of the Inland Revenue that, because TA 1988 s 114 provides for computations to be prepared as if a partnership were a company, where at least one of the partners is a qualifying company it is open to that partnership to make an election to defer the application of the new rules to it until its first accounting period beginning on or after 1 July 2000. Such an election—which may only be made if the partnership had not previously elected to use a non-sterling currency in respect of its trade—had to have been made on or before 31 August 2000 and been signed by all partners who, at the time of the election, were subject to UK corporation tax. Without all the signatures, the Inland Revenue will treat the election as not effective.

CASES WHERE AMENDED FA 1993 SS 93, 94 APPLY TO A PARTNERSHIP WITH COMPANY MEMBERS

12 For the purposes of applying TA 1988 s 114 to a UK resident corporate member of a (UK or foreign) partnership, it will be necessary to compute the profits and losses of the partnership's business, or part of its business, in accordance with the rules in FA 1993 ss 93, 94 (as amended) if—

- the partnership prepares its accounts as a whole in a currency other than sterling in accordance with normal accounting practice, or
- although preparing partnership accounts as a whole in sterling, so far as relating to the business or part of its business the partnership accounts are prepared using the closing rate/net investment method from financial statements prepared in a currency other than sterling.

13 For the purposes of applying TA 1988 s 114 to a non-UK resident corporate member of a partnership, it will be necessary to compute the profits and losses of the partnership's business or part of its business in accordance with the rules in FA 1993 ss 93, 94 (as amended) if—

- the partnership prepares its accounts as a whole in a currency other than sterling and uses that, or another, foreign currency in the accounts of the UK part of the business which may be required by TMA 1970 s 12AA, or
- the partnership prepares its accounts as a whole in sterling but, so far as relates to part of its UK business, the accounts are prepared using the closing rate/net investment method from financial statements prepared in a currency other than sterling, or
- the accounts supporting the partnership return required by TMA 1970 s 12AA are in sterling but, so far as they relate to part of its UK business, they are prepared using the closing rate/net investment method from financial statements prepared in a currency other than sterling.

14 It is the view of the Inland Revenue that the profits and losses of the business or part business for the period, as computed in the relevant foreign currency, should be allocated to corporate members of the partnership in accordance with their entitlement to share in the profits of the partnership for that period. This sum should then be adjusted to take account of the corporate partner's share of any of the items mentioned in FA 1993 s 93(4)(*b*) as determined in accordance with its entitlement by reference to its partnership interest in the relevant preceding period. (SP 4/98 para 16 sets out the

Inland Revenue view that the partnership itself cannot carry forward items such as non-trading deficits.)

15 The sterling equivalent of the amount computed as a result of the process outlined in the preceding paragraph should then be found in accordance with the rules in FA 1993 s 94 as amended to the extent necessary to find the company's profits or losses for the period for the purposes of corporation tax.

16 The notices of election to use an average arm's length exchange rate and withdrawal of such an election for which s 94(5) provides will only be accepted by the Revenue where signed by all partners who, at the time of the election, are subject to UK corporation tax. Without all the signatures, the Inland Revenue will treat the notice of election or withdrawal as not effective. A valid election once made will not cease to be effective on subsequent partnership changes, unless validly withdrawn by all partners who at the time of the withdrawal are subject to UK corporation tax. Notices of election and withdrawal will take effect with reference to the accounting period of the partnership and not that of individual corporate partners.

17 Where the accounting period of the partnership differs from the accounting period of a corporate member of the partnership, the sterling figure of the company's share of the results of the partnership's business for the period should be allocated between the company's relevant accounting periods on a just and reasonable basis (normally on a time basis).

18 To the extent that a corporate member of a partnership is entitled to a share of losses (within the meaning of FA 1993 s 93(7)) computed in the relevant foreign currency which are not utilised for the purposes of corporation tax by the company in the company's relevant accounting period or periods, it is the view of the Inland Revenue that these losses should be carried forward in the tax computations of the company to the next accounting period in that currency.

CASES WHERE AMENDED SS 93, 94 APPLY TO NON-PARTNERSHIP INCOME OF A COMPANY MEMBER OF A PARTNERSHIP

19 A company which carries on business in partnership may separately carry on its own business or part of its business in a currency other than sterling and, accordingly, be within the scope of FA 1993 ss 93, 94 as amended in respect of that business or part business. It is possible that the company keeps its own accounts in the same currency as the currency used by the partnership or each may use a different non-sterling currency. Alternatively the company may account in foreign currency for its own business, but the business of the partnership may be accounted for in sterling.

20 Irrespective of the way in which the company accounts for its share of the partnership in any of these situations, it is the view of the Inland Revenue that it is necessary to arrive at the company's share of the partnership profits for the relevant accounting period or periods and losses (to the extent these are brought into account for the purposes of corporation tax in that period) in sterling (by conversion of non-sterling profits and losses as computed above where the figure is not already in sterling). This is because TA 1988 s 114 treats the partnership income of a company as if it were due to an entirely separate company and only brings the two figures of profits together for the purposes of the company's corporation tax computation. The profits and losses of the company in respect of its non-partnership business as computed in any non-sterling currency must be separately computed and converted to sterling in accordance with FA 1993 ss 93, 94 so far as these are brought into account for corporation tax purposes for the accounting period. The two sterling amounts must then be combined to arrive at the final corporation tax liability of the company.

Commentary—*Simon's Direct Tax Service* **D2.912.**

SP 3/01 (November 2001) *Relief for underlying tax*

GENERAL

In addition to tax credit relief for direct foreign tax on a dividend, where the UK resident shareholder is a company controlling directly or indirectly not less than 10% of the voting power in the foreign company paying the dividend, it is entitled to relief for the underlying tax attributable to the dividend. This relief may be due under the terms of a double taxation agreement or, alternatively, on a unilateral basis under TA 1988 s 790(6).

The amount of underlying tax to be taken into account for credit relief purposes is so much as is "properly attributable" to the proportion of the foreign company's relevant profits as is represented by the dividend paid to the UK company (TA 1988 s 799(1)).

A SPLIT RATE TAXES

Under some foreign tax systems the amount of tax charged on company profits is dependent on how much of the profits is distributed. The Revenue's view is that in such circumstances the amount of tax to be taken into account in respect of a particular dividend is the actual tax charged on the portion of the profits that the dividend represents. The amount of underlying tax taken into account will therefore reflect the rate charged on the distributed profits and not the average rate of tax paid at that point on all of the relevant profits.

The Underlying Tax Group will accept computations done on either basis for dividends paid to a UK company between 31 March 2000 and 31 December 2001 inclusive.

EXAMPLE 1

A foreign company has taxable profits of 1,000, and after paying 20% company tax has relevant profits of 800. The company pays a dividend of 400 to a UK resident company. The foreign company pays additional company tax on the dividend at the rate of 10% – 40.

The amount of underlying tax to be taken into account in respect of the dividend of 400 is 140 ((400/800 x 200) + 40).

EXAMPLE 2

A foreign company has taxable profits of 1,000, and after paying 40% company tax has relevant profits of 600. Distributed profits are taxed at 25% and on payment of a dividend of 300 to a UK resident company the foreign company receives a dividend rebate of 100.

The amount of underlying tax to be taken into account in respect of the dividend of 300 is 100 ((300/600 x 400) –100). If the remaining 300 relevant profits are distributed there will be a further rebate of 100, giving underlying tax of 100, calculated in the same way.

B LOSSES

Where the foreign company that pays a dividend has accumulated losses, the Revenue's view is that the relevant profits are the undistributed profits of the most recent period available at the time that the dividend was paid. The Underlying Tax Group will accept computations prepared in accordance with this or in line with previous practice for dividends paid to a UK recipient between 31 March 2000 and 31 December 2001 inclusive.

EXAMPLE 1

The accounts for a foreign company show the following results—

	Year 1	**Year 2**	**Year 3**
Profits/(losses)	1,000	(3,000)	1,500
Accumulated profits/(losses)	1,000	(2,000)	(500)

After the end of Year 3, it pays a dividend of 2,000 out of unspecified profits.

The relevant profits are 1,500 from Year 3 and 500 from Year 1.

Alternatively, if the company pays a dividend of 500 for Year 1, the relevant profits are Year 1 profits.

EXAMPLE 2

	Year 1	**Year 2**	**Year 3**
Profits/(losses)	1,000	(2,000)	1,500
Accumulated profits/(losses)	1,000	(1,000)	500

After the end of Year 3 it pays a dividend of 2,000 out of unspecified profits. The relevant profits are 1,500 from Year 3 and 500 from Year 1.

If the dividend were paid before the end of year 3, the relevant profits would be 1,000 from Year 1 and 1,000 from the most recent preceding profitable period.

Commentary—*Simon's Direct Tax Service* **F2.106.**

SP 4/01 (21 December 2001) *Double taxation relief—status of the UK's double taxation conventions with the former USSR and with newly independent states*

INTRODUCTION

1 This statement of practice replaces and supersedes SP 3/92, which made public the UK's understanding at that time of the status, in relation to those former Soviet Republics that had been recognised by the UK as independent sovereign states, of the UK/USSR Double Taxation Convention ("The Convention between the Government of the UK of Great Britain and Northern Ireland and the Government of the Union of Soviet Socialist Republics for the avoidance of double taxation with respect to taxes on income and capital gains").

WHAT SP 3/92 SAID

2 SP 3/92 confirmed that the UK/USSR convention continued in force for Armenia, Azerbaijan, Belarus, Georgia, Kazakhstan, Kyrgyzstan, Moldova, Russian Federation, Tajikistan, Turkmenistan, Ukraine, and Uzbekistan. It also stated that the position in relation to the Baltic States (Estonia, Lithuania and Latvia) was unknown.

DEVELOPMENTS SINCE

3 The UK has subsequently concluded new, separate, double taxation conventions with Azerbaijan, Belarus (not yet in force), Estonia, Kazakhstan, Latvia, Lithuania (not yet in force), Russian Federation, Ukraine and Uzbekistan. Negotiations for a new double taxation convention are also taking place with Georgia.

4 Details of the new conventions are provided later in this statement. Copies may be obtained from the Stationery Office telephone 0870 600 5522.

5 We now know that the Baltic states have never considered themselves bound by the terms of the UK/USSR convention. It has also been established that, contrary to the previous understanding, Armenia, Georgia, Kyrgyzstan, and Moldova do not consider themselves bound by the UK/USSR convention.

ANNOUNCEMENT

6 In these circumstances, *the UK will not apply the terms of the UK/USSR double taxation convention* in the case of residents of Armenia, Georgia, Kyrgyzstan, Lithuania, and Moldova—

– for profits arising on or after 1 April 2002, in the case of corporation tax; and
– for income and gains arising on or after 6 April 2002, in the case of income tax and capital gains tax.

7 The UK will continue to apply the terms of the UK/USSR double taxation convention in the case of residents of Armenia, Georgia, Kyrgyzstan, Lithuania and Moldova in respect of profits arising *before* 1 April 2002 and income and gains arising *before* 6 April 2002.

8 The position in relation to each of the former Soviet republics is summarised fully below—

Country	*Position*
Armenia	Armenia has indicated that it is not operating the UK/USSR Double Taxation Convention (DTC) in relation to residents of the UK. The UK will cease to operate the UK/USSR DTC in relation to residents of Armenia, in accordance with para 6 of this statement.
Azerbaijan	A new DTC is in force. See the Double Taxation Relief (Taxes on Income) Azerbaijan Order, SI 1995/762.
Belarus	Pending the entry into force of the new UK/Belarus DTC, the Double Taxation Relief (Taxes on Income) (Belarus) Order, SI 1995/2706 both Belarus and the UK will continue to operate the UK/USSR DTC in respect of their residents.
Estonia	A new DTC is in force. See the Double Taxation Relief (Taxes on Income) Estonia Order, SI 1994/3207.
Georgia	Georgia has indicated that it is not operating the UK/USSR DTC in relation to residents of the UK. The UK will cease to operate the UK/USSR DTC in relation to residents of Georgia, in accordance with para 6 of this statement. A new DTC is under negotiation.
Kazakhstan	A new DTC is in force. See the Double Taxation Relief (Taxes on Income) Kazakhstan Order, SI 1994/3211 and the Double Taxation Relief (Taxes on Income) Kazakhstan Order, SI 1998/2567 (Protocol).
Kyrgyzstan	Kyrgyzstan has indicated that it is not operating the UK/USSR DTC in relation to residents of the UK. The UK will cease to operate the UK/USSR DTC in relation to residents of Kyrgyzstan, in accordance with para 6 of this statement.
Latvia	A new DTC is in force. See the Double Taxation Relief (Taxes on Income) Latvia Order, SI 1996/3167.
Lithuania	A new DTC with Lithuania is in force with effect from April 2002. See the Double Taxation Relief (Taxes on Income) Lithuania Order, SI 2001/3925 and the Double Taxation Relief (Taxes on Income) Lithuania Order, SI 2002/2847 (Protocol).
Moldova	Moldova has indicated that it is not operating the UK/USSR DTC in relation to residents of the UK. The UK will cease to operate the UK/USSR DTC in relation to residents of Moldova, in accordance with para 6 of this statement.
Russian Federation	A new DTC is in force. See the Double Taxation Relief (Taxes on Income) Russian Federation Order, SI 1994/3213.
Tajikistan	Both Tajikistan and the UK will continue to operate the UK/USSR DTC in respect of their residents.
Turkmenistan	Both Turkmenistan and the UK will continue to operate the UK/USSR DTC in respect of their residents.
Ukraine	A new DTC is in force. See the Double Taxation Relief (Taxes on Income) Ukraine Order. SI 1993/1803.
Uzbekistan	A new DTC is in force. See the Double Taxation Relief (Taxes on Income) Uzbekistan Order, SI 1994/770.

Note—This statement was revised in IR 131 (August 2003).

SP 5/01 (21 December 2001) *CTSA—claims to loss relief, capital allowances and group relief outside limit*

1 The Board of Inland Revenue have powers under—

- TA 1988 s 393A(10) to admit late claims to set off or carry back losses;
- FA 1998 Sch 18 para 82(2) to allow the late making, amending or withdrawing of claims for capital allowances; and
- FA 1998 Sch 18 para 74(2) to allow the late making or withdrawing of claims for group relief.

In this statement references to making claims should be read accordingly so that—

- for capital allowances, making a claim includes amending or withdrawing a claim; and
- for group relief, making a claim includes withdrawing a claim.

The statement explains the time limit rules, sets out the Board's general approach to late claims and gives details of the procedures to be followed.

THE NORMAL RULES

Loss relief

2 Loss relief claims can be made within two years of the accounting period in which the loss is incurred. A loss relief claim made in a company tax return may be amended at any time up to 12 months from the statutory filing date or, if the claim is within the rules in TMA 1970 Sch 1A within 12 months of making the claim.

Capital allowances

3 Claims to capital allowances under CTSA can be made, amended or withdrawn, up to the latest of—

- the first anniversary of the claimant company's filing date;
- if the Revenue issues a notice of enquiry into the claimant company's return, 30 days after the enquiry is completed;
- if the claimant company's return is amended by the Inland Revenue following an enquiry (under FA 1998 Sch 18 para 34(2)), 30 days after notice of the amendment is issued; or
- if the claimant company appeals against the Revenue's amendment, 30 days after the date on which the appeal is finally determined.

Group relief

4 Claims to group relief under CTSA can be made or withdrawn up to the latest of the following dates—

- the first anniversary of the claimant company's filing date;
- if the Revenue issues a notice of enquiry into the claimant company's return, 30 days after the enquiry is completed;
- if the claimant company's return is amended by the Inland Revenue following an enquiry (under FA 1998 Sch 18 para 34(2)), 30 days after notice of the amendment is issued; or
- if the claimant company appeals against the Revenue's amendment, 30 days after the date on which the appeal is finally determined.

5 In general a claim to group relief can only be made where notice of consent has been given by the surrendering company and the claim must be accompanied by a copy of the notice. But groups may apply to the Board to enter into simplified arrangements for claiming and surrendering group relief (the Corporation Tax (simplified Arrangements for Group Relief) Regulations, SI 2975/199).

Special rules where the Revenue makes certain assessments or amendments

6 Special time limit rules apply where the Revenue makes certain assessments or amendments. They are—

- a Revenue amendment of a company tax return under FA 1998 Sch 18 para 34(2)(*b*);
- a discovery assessment made under FA 1998 Sch 18 para 41 (other than an assessment made in a case involving fraudulent or negligent conduct); and
- an assessment to recover excess group relief made under FA 1998 Sch 18 para 76.

7 Where such an assessment or amendment is made, a company may under FA 1998 Sch 18 para 61 make, revoke or vary certain claims etc. The time limit for these claims is one year from the end of the accounting period in which the closure notice was issued or the assessment was made. Any claims etc. made, given, revoked or varied cannot reduce the combined tax liability of the company and any other persons affected by an amount greater than the additional liability to tax arising from the amendment or assessment.

8 Where the Revenue makes a discovery assessment under FA 1998 Sch 18 para 41 to recover tax lost through fraudulent or negligent conduct, the rule in para 65 applies. It allows the admission of any claims which can be given effect in that assessment regardless of time limit.

Board's approach to extending time limits for making claims

9 The time limits allowed for making claims to loss relief, capital allowances and group relief under CTSA and the further provisions described above should generally be adequate and the Board will not make routine use of its powers to accept claims made outside these limits. But the Board recognises that there may be exceptional reasons why a claim is not made within the time specified. Applications to allow further time in accordance with the powers referred to at paragraph 1 above will be considered with the assistance of the following criteria.

10 In general, the Board's approach will be to admit claims which could not have been made within the statutory time limits for reasons beyond the company's control. This would include, for example, cases where—

– at the date of the expiry of the time limit, the company or its agents were unaware of profits against which the company could claim relief; or
– the amount of a profit or loss depended on discussions with an Inspector which were not complete when the time limit expired, and the delay in agreeing figures is not substantially the fault of the company or its agents.

In such cases the Board's approach will be to admit late claims up to the amount of the profit or loss in question. Where the claim involves the withdrawal of an existing claim and the making of a fresh claim, the Board's approach will be to admit these to the extent of the profit or loss in question. Claims which go beyond this and affect profits which were not in dispute at the time of expiry of the statutory time limits will not be within this approach.

Reasons beyond the company's control would also include a claim where all of the following four features were present—

– an officer of the company was ill or otherwise absent for a good reason;
– the absence or illness arose at a critical time and prevented the making of a claim within the normal time limit;
– there was good reason why the claim was not made before the time of the absence or illness; and
– there was no other person who could have made the claim on the company's behalf within the normal time limit.

11 The Board would not, however, regard the following as reasons beyond the company's control—

– oversight or negligence on the part of a claimant company or its agent;
– failure, without good reason, to compute the necessary figure;
– the wish to avoid commitment pending clarification of the effects of making a claim; or
– illness or absence of an agent or adviser to the company.

12 There may be cases falling outside the general approach outlined in para 10 where it would nevertheless be unreasonable, given the overall circumstances of the case, for the Board to refuse a late claim. It is likely that such cases will involve a combination of factors, but the following criteria may be relevant—

– the reason why a claim is late, where the reason does not in itself warrant admission of the claim under the approach outlined above, it will still be taken into account by the Board in assessing the circumstances as a whole;
– the extent to which it is late;
– the consequences for the company if the claim is refused; and
– any particularly unusual features.

For the purpose of this para and those above, if the late claim forms part of a scheme or arrangement, the main purpose or one of the main purposes of which is the avoidance of tax (including the payment of tax), then that will be taken into account in the Board's approach.

Procedures

13 An application to admit a claim outside the statutory time limits should be sent to the Inspector dealing with the claimant company and should include a full explanation of the circumstances of the case. The explanation should cover, but need not be limited to, all the criteria set out in para 12. The application should be made as soon as possible. Delay in making a late claim after the circumstances which caused the claim to be late have ceased to apply may result in the claim being rejected.

SP 1/02 (13 March 2002) *Corporation tax self-assessment and chargeable gains valuations*

Corporation tax self-assessment enquiries—FA 1998 Sch 18 para 24: enquiries remaining open after expiry of the period within which a notice of enquiry may be issued solely because of an unagreed valuation for chargeable gains purposes.

This statement of practice applies where, in the case of an enquiry into a return made under paragraph FA 1998 Sch 18 para 3—

- the Inland Revenue has given notice under FA 1998 Sch 18 para 24 of their intention to enquire into that return;
- the enquiry remains open after the expiry of the period within which that notice had to be issued ("enquiry period"); and
- the enquiry remains open solely because of an unagreed valuation for chargeable gains purposes.

In such circumstances the Inland Revenue will not, as a matter of practice, raise further enquiries into matters unrelated to the valuation or the chargeable gains computation unless the circumstances are such that, had the enquiry already been completed, an officer could have made a discovery within the meaning of FA 1998 Sch 18 para 41. This practice applies only to valuations made for the purpose of computing chargeable gains of companies and other bodies within the charge to corporation tax.

This practice does not alter or fetter the Inland Revenue's right to ask further questions or make additional enquiries on matters in connection with, or consequential to, the obtaining of the valuation which were not raised when the valuation was first referred to shares valuation division or the valuation office agency.

SP 2/02 (30 September 2002) *Exchange rate fluctuations*

INTRODUCTION

1 This statement of practice sets out the Inland Revenue's practice in relation to the tax treatment of exchange rate fluctuations in the tax computations of persons who are carrying on a trade, other than companies within the charge to corporation tax. It is put forward as a practical guide to facilitate the preparation and agreement of tax computations of such taxpayers, and takes account of case law and of the enactment of FA 1998 s 42 which requires the profits of a trade or profession (and hence, by virtue of TA 1988 s 21A, a property business) to be returned on a basis that reflects a true and fair view. It is not relevant for concerns which are companies within the charge to corporation tax for which the rules relating to exchange differences are contained in FA 1993 ss 92–94A and FA 1996 Pt 4 Ch 2 (loan relationships) and FA 2002 Sch 26 (derivative contracts). The general rules it contains may need to be modified in the way in which they are applied in particular circumstances, for example, where the local currency of an overseas trade or property business is a currency other than sterling.

THE CASE LAW—MARINE MIDLAND

2 The most recent relevant case law on the subject of exchange differences is *Pattison v Marine Midland Ltd* [1984] STC 10, 57 TC 219. In that case a UK resident bank carried on business in international commercial banking. For the purpose of making dollar loans and advances in the course of its banking business, it borrowed 15 million US dollars in the form of subordinated loan stock, redeemable in ten years. As a result of exchange rate fluctuations, the sterling value of the loans to its customers increased, but so also did the liability in sterling terms of the loan stock. Its general aim was to remain matched in each foreign currency and for the most part the dollar borrowings remained invested in dollar assets. After five years the loan stock was repaid out of existing dollar funds and at no time was any of the 15 million dollars converted into sterling.

3 Each year in the accounts, the monetary assets and liabilities denominated in a foreign currency were valued in sterling at the exchange rate at the balance sheet date but to the extent that currency liabilities were matched by currency assets, no profit or loss was shown for accounts purposes. The Court of Appeal and the House of Lords held that in these circumstances no profit or loss arose for tax purposes. On the other hand the company brought into its profit and loss account any increase or decrease in the sterling value of excess dollars—ie to the extent that it was in an unmatched position—and this had been accepted as a profit or loss for tax purposes. Lord Templeman said that this practice "reflected the success or failure of the company in acquiring and holding excess dollars which could be converted into sterling". He noted without disapproval the Revenue's acceptance of the practice and said it was "... not inconsistent with the company's submission that no profit or loss was attributable to dollar assets equal in dollar terms to dollar liabilities".

DEFINITIONS

4 In this statement—

- Translation into sterling is regarded as the valuation of a foreign currency asset or liability in terms of sterling at a particular date;
- Conversion into sterling is the exchange of that asset or liability for sterling;
- Local currency is the currency of the primary economic environment in which the trade or business is carried on and net cash flows are generated.

SPs

THE RECOGNITION OF EXCHANGE DIFFERENCES—ACCOUNTS TREATMENT AND TAX CONSEQUENCES

5 Before the enactment of FA 1998 s 42 (which has effect for periods of account beginning after 6 April 1999) it was the general practice in the case of trading companies to bring exchange translation adjustments, other than those in respect of capital items, into account for tax purposes where they have similarly been brought into account in arriving at the accounting profit or loss. Since the accounting treatment is sanctioned by Statement of Standard Accounting Practice 20 (Foreign Currency Translation) (''SSAP 20''), it follows that accounts which observe this practice are, in this regard, giving a true and fair view, and since there is no rule of law which would overturn this practice, it must be followed for tax purposes.

6 It has also been the practice in some circumstances—mainly in the case of certain overseas trading activities dealt with for accounts purposes on what is now generally referred to as the ''closing rate/net investment'' basis—to translate the net profit or loss for tax purposes (the so called ''profit and loss account'' basis). The Revenue considers that, following FA 1998 s 42, where this basis is used in the accounts in accordance with SSAP 20 it also must be followed for tax purposes.

CAPITAL AND CURRENT LIABILITIES

7 Nothing in FA 1998 s 42 or in the case law regarding the computation of trading profits requires the distinction between capital and revenue items to be decided other than by reference to principles well established in tax case law. In computing trading profits for tax purposes, the question whether a loss or profit on exchange on a foreign currency loan made to the taxpayer is respectively an allowable deduction or assessable receipt is determined by the nature of the loan and whether it is to be properly regarded as a capital or current liability. The case law (such as *Marine Midland* and *Beauchamp v F W Woolworth plc* [1989] STC 510, 61 TC 542) shows that the distinction between capital and current liabilities is essentially between loans providing temporary financial accommodation and loans which can be said to add to the capital of the business. The answer in any particular case must turn on its facts and circumstances, which have to be considered in detail.

8 The Court of Appeal and the House of Lords did not find it necessary to decide whether the borrowing by Marine Midland was a capital or current liability; the House of Lords indicated that it would have needed further evidence and argument to decide the issue. The Commissioners and the High Court, however, agreed with the Revenue's view that the borrowing was a capital liability. The Revenue remains of the view that the liability in question in the *Marine Midland* case was of a capital nature.

MATCHED ASSETS AND LIABILITIES

9 The Court of Appeal and House of Lords judgments in *Marine Midland* indicate that where foreign currency borrowings are matched by assets in the same currency the capital or current nature of the borrowing would no longer be relevant in determining whether adjustments are to be made for the purposes of computing trading profits or losses for tax. In these circumstances exchange differences, whether profits or losses, arising on long-term borrowings are not to be distinguished and adjusted in computing trading profits or losses for tax.

GAINS AND LOSSES TAKEN TO RESERVE

10 Under SSAP 20, some gains and losses on monetary assets and liabilities may be taken to reserve rather than to the profit and loss account. This may happen where paras 27–29 SSAP 20 (liabilities hedging investments in certain equity holdings) and paras 15–20 SSAP 20 (closing rate/net investment method) apply. In such cases, the gains and losses are not recognised for tax purposes even if they are not capital items.

SAME CURRENCY

11 Liabilities and assets of the same trader are regarded as matched in the way described in para 9 above to the extent that foreign currency denominated monetary assets are equalled by liabilities in the same currency and a translation adjustment on one would be cancelled out by a translation adjustment on the other. In general, therefore, where there are transactions in more than one foreign currency the question of matching must be considered separately for each currency (see paras 15–34 below). However, it is possible for assets and liabilities in different currencies to be regarded as effectively matched when hedging transactions, such as forward foreign currency contracts, are taken into account (see paras 41–43 below).

MATCHING OF CAPITAL ASSETS IN FOREIGN CURRENCY WITH CURRENT LIABILITIES

12 There may be circumstances where foreign currency assets which for tax would be treated as capital assets are matched with current liabilities in the same currency—the reverse of the situation in *Marine Midland*. This may arise for example in the case of certain monetary assets, eg where loans to subsidiary companies, which for tax would be treated as capital, are matched by short term currency borrowings, which for tax may fall to be treated as current liabilities. The Revenue takes the view that the *Marine Midland* matching principle applies in such circumstances, with the result that again exchange differences arising on the assets or liabilities are not to be distinguished and adjusted.

ASSETS AND LIABILITIES NOT MATCHED

13 In general, an adjustment is required to the tax computation of trading profits in respect of exchange differences that have been debited or credited to the profit and loss account in respect of capital items. It will be for the trader to demonstrate matching of capital currency liabilities, or assets, by reference to the position both during and at the end of the accounting period; and where such liabilities or assets are wholly or partly matched, to show the effect if any on the tax computation.

14 However, in practice, the extent to which currency assets are matched with currency liabilities will in most cases fluctuate in the course of an accounting period, so that it would be impracticable to measure and take account of such fluctuations on a day-by-day basis in determining what adjustment is required in the tax computation to the net exchange difference debited or credited in the profit and loss account. Instead, the practice outlined in paras 17 and 34 below may be adopted, provided it is applied on a consistent basis from year to year.

A PRACTICAL APPROACH

15 In essence the practice offered at paras 17 and 34 below assumes that the extent to which currency assets and liabilities are matched during an accounting period is reflected in the size of the net exchange difference debited or credited to the profit and loss account. The rules suggested for determining the adjustment to be made for tax purposes in respect of the exchange difference arising on capital assets or liabilities which are unmatched, or only partly matched, are based on the premise that capital liabilities are matched primarily with capital assets in the same currency. Any capital liabilities not matched by capital assets in the same currency are regarded as matched by current assets of the same currency only to the extent that the current assets exceed the current liabilities in that currency.

16 Where this practice is not adopted, capital liabilities and assets will be regarded as matched only to the extent that this can be demonstrated by reference to the trader's currency assets and liabilities during the accounting period.

17 Under the practice referred to in para 15 above, the first step will be to ascertain the aggregate of exchange differences, positive and negative, on capital assets and liabilities in the profit and loss account figure.

A. If there are no such differences then no tax adjustment is necessary.

EXAMPLE 1

An individual normally trading in sterling incurs a liability on a trade debt of $600,000 when $1.5 = £1. The liability is entered in the books in sterling at £400,000. By the accounting date sterling has fallen to $1.25 = £1, so that the sterling value of the liability has increased to £480,000. The exchange loss of £80,000 is charged to the profit and loss account. There were no capital exchange differences. No adjustment is required for tax purposes because the transactions are wholly on revenue account.

B. If the net exchange difference on capital items is a loss and the net difference in the profit and loss account is also a loss, the smaller of the two figures is the amount to be disallowed in the tax computation as relating to capital transactions.

EXAMPLE 2

An individual trader borrows $600,000 on long-term capital account when $1.5 = £1. He retains $150,000 as current assets and converts the balance of $450,000 to £300,000. The books will then show the following entries—

Capital loan ($600,000)	£400,000	Current assets ($150,000)	£100,000
		Cash on hand	£300,000
	£400,000		£400,000

By the accounting date when sterling has fallen to $1.25 = £1 these become—

Capital loan ($600,000)	£480,000	Current assets ($150,000)	£120,000
		Cash on hand	£300,000
		Exchange difference to profit and loss account	£60,000
	£480,000		£480,000

The exchange difference on capital account is £80,000 (£480,000–£400,000) but the tax adjustment is limited to the amount charged to the profit and loss account so that £60,000 is disallowed. This reflects the fact that $150,000 of the liability is matched with $150,000 assets. The whole of the exchange difference £60,000 is attributable to the excess currency liability on capital account, the value of which has increased from £300,000 to £360,000.

EXAMPLE 3

A trader incurs a liability by way of overdraft on current account of $300,000 and borrows $600,000 on capital account when $1.5 = £1. She retains $150,000 as current assets and converts the balance of $750,000 to $500,000. The books will then show the following items—

Capital loan ($600,000)	£400,000	Current assets ($150,000)	£100,000
Overdraft on current account ($300,000)	£200,000	Cash on hand	£500,000
	£600,000		£600,000

By the accounting date sterling has fallen to $1.25 = £1 and the book entries are then—

Capital loan ($600,000)	£480,000	Current basis ($150,000)	£120,000
Overdraft on current account ($300,000)	£240,000	Cash on hand	£500,000
		Exchange difference to profit and loss account	£100,000
	£720,000		£720,000

The net exchange loss of £100,000 in the profit and loss account is made up of £120,000 loss on the liabilities and £20,000 profit on the assets.

The exchange difference on capital account is £80,000 (£480,000–£400,000). This is less than the profit and loss account figure so the £80,000 is disallowed for tax purposes. This reflects the matching of the $150,000 current assets with $150,000 of the current liabilities. The capital liability is therefore wholly unmatched.

C. If the net exchange difference on capital items is a profit and the net difference in the profit and loss account is also a profit, then the smaller of the two figures is the amount to be deducted in the tax computation.

EXAMPLE 4

A trading partnership, consisting of individuals, incurs a liability by way of overdraft on current account of $150,000 and borrows a further £300,000 as a capital loan when $1.5 = £1. It converts the £300,000 to $450,000 and makes a loan (not in the course of trade) of $600,000 to an associated company. The books show the following entries at this point—

Overdraft on current account ($150,000)	£100,000	Capital assets ($600,000)	£400,000
Capital loan	£300,000		
	£400,000		£400,000

By the accounting date sterling has fallen to $1.25 = £1 and the book entries are as follows—

Overdraft on current account ($150,000)	£120,000	Capital assets ($600,000)	£480,000
Capital loan	£300,000		
Exchange difference to profit and loss account	£60,000		
	£480,000		£480,000

The net exchange profit of £60,000 in the profit and loss account comprises £80,000 profit on the assets and £20,000 loss on the liability.

The net capital exchange difference is £80,000 (£480,000–£400,000) but the adjustment for tax purposes is limited to the figure in the profit and loss account of £60,000. This reflects the fact that $150,000 of the assets are matched with the dollar liability. The non-taxable exchange profit is attributable to the excess capital assets, whose sterling value changed from £300,000 to £360,000.

D. Where the net exchange difference on capital items produces a loss but the net difference in the profit and loss account is a credit entry, then no tax adjustment is required. Similarly no adjustment is necessary where there is a profit in respect of exchange differences on capital items but a net loss on exchange is debited to the profit and loss account.

EXAMPLE 5

A partnership of individuals borrows $900,000 on capital account and raises a further sterling loan of £200,000. It converts the £200,000 to $300,000 and makes a loan (not in the course of trade) of $750,000 to an associated company. At this time $1.5 = £1. The balance of $450,000 is retained as a current asset. The books show the following entries at this point—

Capital loan ($900,000)	£600,000	Capital assets ($750,000)	£500,000
Capital loan	£200,000	Current assets ($450,000)	£300,000
	£800,000		£800,000

By the accounting date the exchange rate alters to $1.25 = £1 and the book entries become—

Capital loan ($900,000)	£720,000	Capital assets ($750,000)	£600,000
Capital loan	£200,000	Current assets ($450,000)	£360,000
Exchange difference to profit and loss account	£40,000		
	£960,000		£960,000

The profit and loss account entry for the net exchange profit of £40,000 is made up of £160,000 profit on the assets and £120,000 loss on the liability.

The net capital exchange difference is a debit of £20,000 ie (£720,000–£600,000)–(£600,000–£500,000) but the profit and loss account shows a net credit of £40,000. No adjustment is therefore required for tax purposes. This reflects the matching of the net capital liability of $150,000 with part of the dollar current assets. The taxable exchange profit of £40,000 is attributable to the balance of the dollar current assets, whose value increased from £200,000 to £240,000.

E. It follows that normally the amount of any tax adjustment is limited in each case to the credit or debit for net exchange differences in the profit and loss account.

MORE THAN ONE CURRENCY

Where there are transactions in more than one currency, the same principles will apply but each currency must be considered separately. In such circumstances the exchange difference in the profit and loss account is the aggregate of the net exchange profits and losses arising in the various currencies and the tax computation adjustment is determined by comparing the aggregate exchange difference on capital assets and liabilities in a particular currency with the exchange difference for that currency in the profit and loss figure (but see paras 41–43 below where hedging transactions are involved).

EXAMPLE 6

A partnership of individuals borrows $900,000 on long-term capital account and DM 300,000 on overdraft when £1 = £1.5 = DM 3. 0. It makes a loan of $600,000 to an associated company (not in the course of trade) and converts $300,000 into DM 600,000. It loans DM 500,000 to another associated company (not in the course of trade) and retains the balance of DM 400,000 as a current asset.

Capital loan ($900,000)	£600,000	Capital assets ($600,000)	£400,000
Overdraft (DM 300,000)	£100,000	Capital assets(DM 500,000)	£167,000
		Current assets (DM 400,000)	£133,000
	£700,000		£700,000

By the accounting date sterling has fallen to £1 = $1.20 = DM 2.5 and the book entries are as follows—

Capital loan ($900,000)	£750,000	Capital assets ($600,000)	£500,000
Overdraft (DM 300,000)	£120,000	Capital assets (DM 500,000)	£200,000
		Current assets (DM 400,000)	£160,000
		Exchange difference to profit and loss account	£10,000
	£870,000		£870,000

The net exchange difference of £10,000 comprises £50,000 loss on the Dollar assets and liabilities offset by £40,000 profit on the Deutschmark assets and liabilities.

The Dollar exchange loss is entirely on capital account and should be added back to the tax computation.

The Deutschmark exchange difference comprises £60,000 profit on the assets and £20,000 loss on the liability. The net capital exchange difference on Deutschmark assets and liabilities is a profit of £33,000 ie (£200,000–£167,000) so the adjustment for tax purposes is limited to £33,000. This reflects the fact that the overdraft is matched with Deutschmark current assets and the Deutschmark capital assets are unmatched.

Thus the overall adjustment to the tax computation is an addition of £17,000 ie (£50,000–£33,000).

HEDGING TRANSACTIONS

In considering whether a trader is matched in a particular currency, **forward exchange contracts and currency futures** entered into for hedging purposes may be taken into account, provided the hedging is reflected in the accounts on a consistent basis from year to year and in accordance with accepted accounting practice. For example, where a trading transaction is covered by a related or matching forward contract, under SSAP 20 the transaction may be translated using the rate of exchange specified in the forward contract. Alternatively, the forward contracts open at the balance sheet date may be shown as assets or liabilities, valued on a ''market to market'' basis or by reference

SPs

to the difference between the contracted forward exchange rates and the spot rate on the balance sheet date.

Where a trader enters into a **currency swap agreement** to exchange borrowed currency for an equivalent amount of another currency (including sterling) for a fixed period, the two transactions in the original currency should be treated as matched, so that the underlying liability in the first currency is effectively converted into a liability in the second currency for the duration of the swap. If, when the swap is terminated, the currencies are swapped back at the spot rate of exchange prevailing at the commencement of the swap there will be for Case I purposes no exchange loss or profit in terms of the original currency (but the capital gains consequences of unwinding the swap will need to be taken into account).

In the Revenue's view, where currency assets or liabilities are hedged by transactions in currency options no matching can be said to have taken place and such transactions are unaffected by the *Marine Midland* decision.

EXAMPLE 7

Hedging

The facts are those of example 3 above in the subsequent accounting period at the start of which the book entries are—

Capital loan ($600,000)	£480,000	Current assets ($150,000)	£120,000
Overdraft on current account ($300,000)	£240,000	Cash on hand	£500,000
		Exchange difference b/f	£100,000
	£720,000		£720,000

Three months from the end of the period of accounts (there having been no transactions in the meantime affecting the assets and liabilities referred to in the example), when $1.18 = £1, the trader enters a forward contract to purchase $600,000 at $1.20 = £1 in six months' time, to hedge the capital loan which is repayable on the date the forward contract matures. By the accounting date, when $1.10 = £1, the books show either—

Capital loan ($600,000)*	£500,000	Current assets ($150,000)	£150,000
Overdraft on current account ($300,000)	£300,000	Cash on hand	£500,000
		Exchange difference b/f	£100,000
		Exchange different to profit and loss account	£50,000
	£800,000		£800,000

translated at forward rate $1.20 = £1

or

Capital loan ($600,000)*	£600,000	Current assets ($150,000)	£150,000
Overdraft on current account ($300,000)	£300,000	Cash on hand	£500,000
		Forward contract	£100,000
		Exchange difference b/f	£100,000
		Exchange difference to profit and loss account	£50,000
	£900,000		£900,000

Because the forward contract specifically hedges the capital loan the net exchange loss on capital items on either basis is £20,000 (£500,000–£480,000; or £600,000–£480,000 less £100,000 profit on forward contract).

Because this is less than the overall exchange loss of £50,000, the capital loss of £20,000 is disallowed for tax purposes.

OVERSEAS BRANCHES AND TRADES

18 Where a trade carried on wholly abroad, or an overseas branch of a trade, has a local currency other than sterling, accounts will normally be drawn up in the local foreign currency and translated into sterling using the "closing rate/net investment/" method (SSAP 20 paras 25, 46). In such circumstances, computations taking as their starting point the sterling equivalent of accounts prepared in local currency, translated into sterling using the "closing rate/net investment" method, will be the only acceptable method for tax purposes. Capital allowances and other statutory reliefs and charges must be calculated in sterling.

19 The principles outlined in this statement of practice should be applied in considering to what extent an adjustment for tax purposes should be made to the profit figure to be translated into sterling in respect of an exchange difference in the local foreign currency accounts.

ASSETS HELD ON THE "REALISATION" BASIS

20 Some financial concerns hold assets, the profits on the disposal of which are treated for tax purposes as receipts of their trade but which are not stock in trade. Where the concern does not account for such assets on a mark to market basis, such profits are assessable only when the assets are disposed of (the ''realisation'' basis). Nevertheless it may be the practice for accounting purposes to revalue the assets to reflect exchange rate fluctuations. Where the resulting exchange differences are either taken to profit and loss account or set off against exchange differences on liabilities as part of the matching process, with the result that the profits or losses on realisation are recognised for accounts purposes effectively net of exchange differences, the accounts treatment must be followed for tax purposes. The following example shows how this works.

EXAMPLE 8

A partnership of individuals which is a financial concern borrows $600,000 on capital account and raises a further sterling loan of £200,000. It converts the £200,000 to $300,000 and buys financial assets (realisation basis) for $900,000. At this time $1.5 = £1. The books then show the following entries—

Capital loan ($600,000)	£400,000	Cost of financial assets ($900,000)	£600,000
Capital loan	£200,000		
	£600,000		£600,000

At the accounting date the rate of exchange is $1.25 = £1 so the entries are as follows—

Capital loan ($600,000)	£480,000	Financial assets ($900,000)	£720,000
Capital loan	£200,000		
Exchange difference to profit and loss account	£40,000		
	£720,000		£720,000

Since the capital exchange difference is a debit of £80,000 (£480,000–£400,000) and there is a net exchange profit of £40,000 overall, no tax adjustment to the £40,000 is needed.

At the end of the next accounting period the rate of exchange has altered to $1.2 = £1 and the assets are sold so the entries become—

Capital loan ($600,000)	£500,000	Cash proceeds of sale of financial assets ($1,200,000)	£1,000,000
Capital loan	£200,000		
Exchange difference for Year 2 to profit and loss account	£10,000		
Exchange difference for Year 1 brought forward	£40,000		
* Profit on realisation of assets	£250,000		
	£1,000,000		£1,000,000

*Sale proceeds $1.2m less cost $0. 9m giving a profit on realisation of $0.3m or (at $1.2 = £1) £250,000. The exchange profit from holding the $900,000 assets while the exchange rate moved from $1.5 = £1 to $1.2 = £1 has already been taken into account in the exchange differences.

The capital exchange difference is a loss on the loan of £20,000 (£500,000–£480,000) but there is a profit of £30,000 in respect of current assets, ie £750,000 ($900,000 at $1.2 = £1) – £720,000. Thus, there is no adjustment to the figure in the profit and loss account for the exchange difference.

ACTIVITIES WHICH ARE NOT TRADING

21 The practice outlined above applies to professions and to property business where the profits are computed in accordance with the rules of Case I (Schedule A and overseas property businesses). They have no application outside these contexts. In such cases, the capital gains tax rules will apply to the acquisition and disposal of foreign currency chargeable assets (except where the transactions give rise to profits assessable under Case VI of Schedule D) and exchange fluctuations will generally have no tax consequences outside the capital gains field.

CAPITAL GAINS

22 The decision in *Bentley v Pike* [1981] STC 360; 53 TC 590 established that a gain or loss on an asset should be computed by comparing the sterling value at the date of sale of the sale consideration with the sterling value at the date of acquisition of the acquisition cost. The principle was reaffirmed in *Capcount Trading v Evans* [1993] STC 11, 65 TC 545 and is not affected by the *Marine Midland* decision, by FA 1998 s 42 or this statement.

Commentary—*Simon's Direct Tax Service* **B7.1706, 1707**

SP 3/02 (30 September 2002) *Tax treatment of transactions in financial futures and options*

INTRODUCTION

1 This statement of practice sets out the Inland Revenue's views on the tax treatment of transactions in futures and options of the sorts defined in TCGA 1992 s 143 and relating to shares, securities, foreign currency or other financial instruments. It does not apply to contracts falling within the financial instruments legislation in FA 1994 Pt 4 Ch 2; or, for company accounting periods beginning on or after 1 October 2002, derivative contracts falling within FA 2002 Sch 26. The principles set out are of relevance to—

– UK residents such as unauthorised unit trusts, charities and others (including companies) which either do not trade or whose principal trade is outside the financial area; and
– non-resident collective investment vehicles (whether open or closed-ended), pension funds and others (including companies) which either do not trade or whose principal trade is outside the financial area.

2 This statement does not apply to approved pension schemes, whose profits from futures and options are generally exempt from tax.

3 In relation to companies, this statement will be applicable for accounting periods beginning on or after 1 October 2002 and only in relation to financial futures and options where the underlying subject matter is shares, a holding in an authorised unit trust, or a security to which FA 1996 s 92 or 93 applies.

4 ''Financial futures'' is a wide term. It includes—

– contracts for future delivery of shares, securities, foreign currency or other financial instruments;
– contracts that are settled by payment of cash differences determined by movements in the price of such instruments (including contracts where settlement is based on the application of an interest rate or a financial index to a notional principal amount), as well as contracts settled by delivery; and
– both exchange traded and over the counter contracts.

5 ''Options'' includes—

– both exchange traded and over the counter options;
– options that are settled by a cash payment between the parties, as well as those that provide for delivery; and
– warrants.

RELEVANCE OF TRADING

6 TA 1988 s 128 and TCGA 1992 s 143 provide, broadly, that transactions in financial futures and options will be treated as capital in nature unless they are regarded as profits or losses of a trade. It is immaterial for this purpose whether the profits of the trade are taxed under Case I of Schedule D or otherwise (see *HSBC Life (UK) Ltd and others v Stubbs and others* [2002] STC (SCD) 9).

7 If, under normal statutory and case law principles, profits or losses fall to be treated as trading in nature then TA 1988 s 128 and TCGA 1992 s 143 have no application to those profits or losses. It is therefore necessary first to determine whether or not the taxpayer's transactions in futures and options give rise to trading profits or losses.

8 Whether or not a taxpayer is trading is a question of fact and degree, to be determined by reference to all the facts and circumstances of the particular case. However, the Inland Revenue consider that an individual is unlikely to be regarded as trading as a result of purely speculative transactions in financial futures or options. Transactions in financial futures or options by a company may be either trading or capital in nature.

9 However, a financial futures or options transaction which is clearly ancillary to a trading transaction on current account will give rise to trading profits or losses. In contrast, a financial futures or options transaction which is clearly ancillary to a transaction which is not a trading transaction on current account will be capital.

10 A financial futures or options transaction that is not clearly ancillary to another transaction may be a trading transaction in its own right. Whether this is so will depend on all the facts and circumstances of the case. Consideration will be given to what are known as the ''badges of trade''. In such a case, intention and frequency are important. The transaction will not necessarily be regarded as trading. It may well be regarded as capital in nature, depending on all the facts and circumstances.

ELIMINATION OR REDUCTION OF RISK

11 In determining whether a financial futures or options transaction is ancillary to another transaction the following points are relevant—

– there must be another transaction;
– that other transaction must already have been undertaken, or there must be the intention to undertake it in the future;

- the financial futures or options transaction is ancillary to the other transaction if the intention is to eliminate or reduce risk, or to reduce transaction costs, in respect of that other transaction;
- the financial futures or options transaction must be economically appropriate to the elimination or reduction of risk, or to the reduction of transaction costs;
- the financial futures or options transaction may be ancillary to more than one other transaction, and more than one financial futures or options transaction may be ancillary to another transaction;

it may be necessary to enter into new financial futures or options transactions or to terminate existing ones to reflect changes in the value of the assets or liabilities resulting from the other transaction.

12 These points apply to long and short positions and apply whether the futures position is closed out or held to final maturity, or, in the case of an options position, closed out, exercised or held to final expiry.

13 In considering whether the financial futures or options transaction is ''economically appropriate'' to the elimination or reduction of risk, the Inland Revenue take the view that—

- the transaction must be one which, by virtue of the relationship between fluctuations in its price and any fluctuations in the value of the other transaction, may reasonably be expected to be appropriate to be used in order to eliminate or reduce risk;
- the use of a financial futures or options transaction based on an index of some sort is not regarded as precluding the existence of such a reasonable expectation;

it would not normally be expected that the amount of the principal on which the financial futures or options transaction is based should significantly exceed the principal of the other transaction.

14 There may be cases where a financial futures or options transaction is entered into in order to eliminate or reduce risk, but the other transaction then falls away (or the intention to enter into the other transaction is abandoned). If the financial futures or options transaction is closed out within as short a period as is practicable after this happens the transaction will continue to be treated in accordance with the principles outlined above. If, however, the futures or options transaction is not closed out at that time it may be arguable that any profit or loss arising subsequently is of a trading nature. In practice, where the taxpayer is not otherwise trading, the Inland Revenue would not normally take this point in view of the taxpayer's original intention.

BASE CURRENCY

15 The question may arise as to whether a financial futures transaction to buy or sell currency forward is ancillary to a capital transaction. In many cases the answer will be dependent on which currency is the taxpayer's base currency (that is, the currency in which value is measured).

16 For UK resident taxpayers the base currency will normally (but need not necessarily) be sterling. In determining whether there is a non-sterling base currency the Inland Revenue will have regard to factors such as—

- the currency in which accounts are prepared;
- the currency in which share capital is denominated; and
- evidence of the taxpayer's intentions (for example in a published prospectus).

EXAMPLES

17 The following examples illustrate the above and are not intended to cover every situation that may arise. In the first eight, the assets concerned are held or will be acquired as investments and the financial futures or options transactions would normally be treated as capital (on the assumption that the condition in the first bullet in para 13 above is fulfilled)—

(1) A taxpayer which holds gilts sells gilt futures to protect the value of its capital in the event of a fall in the value of gilt-edged securities generally.

(2) A taxpayer which intends to purchase an asset does so in two stages, by (*a*) purchasing a foreign currency future in advance of the purchase of an asset denominated in that currency, or (*b*) purchasing an option in respect of an underlying asset as a first step towards the acquisition of the asset itself.

(3) A taxpayer which holds a broadly based portfolio of UK equities sells FTSE 100 index futures or purchases FTSE 100 index put options to protect against the risk to the value of the portfolio from a fall in the market.

(4) A taxpayer holding foreign currency assets acquires a futures or options contract to reduce the risk of a fall in the value of the foreign currency assets (as measured in the taxpayer's base currency).

(5) A taxpayer which is intending to acquire a broad range of UK securities buys a call option on an FTSE 100 index to protect against a rise in the price of the securities in the period before they can be acquired.

(6) A taxpayer sells or buys options or futures as an incidental and temporary part of a change in investment strategy, (eg changing the ratio of gilts and equities).

(7) A taxpayer either has existing liabilities (eg loans) denominated in a currency other than its base currency or expects to incur such liabilities (eg as a result of an intention to borrow to

SPs

acquire investments) and uses a futures or options contract to protect itself against a rise in the currency in which the liabilities are or will be denominated.

(8) A taxpayer whose base currency is the dollar holds yen-denominated securities and, in order to eliminate the perceived risk of a fall in their value, enters a forward contract to sell for dollars an amount of yen equivalent to the yen value of the securities. (This is because the forward contract may be regarded as ancillary to the transaction in securities.)

The next two examples involve financial futures or options transactions which would be treated as trading (because they would be ancillary to other trading transactions)—

(9) A taxpayer's futures or options transactions are incidental to its trading activity, for example, a manufacturer entering into transactions to reduce the risk of fluctuations in the price of raw materials. (The profits and losses from these transactions would be taken into account as part of the profits and losses of the trade.)

(10) A taxpayer has borrowed money at a floating rate of interest, for trade purposes, and enters into an interest rate future or option with a view to protecting itself against rises in interest rates. (Receipts or payments relating to the future or option would be taken into account as trading income or expenditure on current account. This is because the future or option is ancillary to a trading transaction ie the payment of interest for trade purposes. Given this, it does not matter whether or not the borrowing is on capital account).

Finally, the three examples below illustrate circumstances where a taxpayer's transactions in financial futures and options will not generally be regarded as ancillary to another transaction. It is therefore necessary to look at the transactions in their own right to see whether they are to be treated as capital or as trading transactions.

(11) A taxpayer uses futures and options in conjunction with a holding of cash, bonds etc so as to create synthetic assets. (On the assumption that, in such circumstances, the financial futures or options transactions cannot all be shown to be ancillary to other transactions).

(12) A taxpayer uses futures and options to take a position in a currency in which it does not have a portfolio, and has no intention of acquiring a portfolio, so as to create an exposure to fluctuations in that currency by reference to its base currency.

(13) A taxpayer whose base currency is sterling holds yen-denominated securities and, in order to eliminate the perceived risk of a fall in their value, enters a financial futures transaction to sell for dollars an amount of yen equivalent to the yen value of the securities. There is no intention of selling the yen-denominated securities and using the proceeds to acquire dollar-denominated securities. (The effect of the financial futures transaction is to increase the taxpayer's dollar exposure and to decrease its yen exposure).

Commentary—*Simon's Direct Tax Service* **C2.1012**

SP 4/02 (30 September 2002) *Definition of financial trader for the purposes of FA 2002 Sch 26 para 31*

GENERAL

1 For accounting periods of companies beginning on or after 1 October 2002, FA 2002 Sch 26 provides rules for the tax treatment of derivative contracts. This means futures, options warrants and contracts for differences, except where the underlying subject matter is—

– land, tangible assets (excluding commodities) or intangible fixed assets; or
– in some cases, shares.

2 An anti-avoidance rule in FA 2002 Sch 26 para 31 applies where certain derivative contracts to which non-residents are also party are entered into by companies to which the Schedule applies. Broadly, this rule (which replaces FA 1994 s 168) disallows any payment to the non-resident which is determined (wholly or mainly) by reference to a rate of interest. This applies for example to periodic payments under an interest rate swap or currency swap. However, para 31(5) of the Schedule provides an exemption where the paying company is a bank, building society, clearing house or financial trader, holding the contract solely for the purposes of a trade carried on by it in the UK, and to which it is party as principal.

DEFINITION OF FINANCIAL TRADER

3 The term "financial trader" is defined in FA 2002 Sch 26 para 54(4) as meaning—

(*a*) any person who—
  (i) falls within FSMA 2002 ss 31(1)(*a*), (*b*) or (*c*); and
  (ii) has permission under that Act to carry on one or more of the activities specified in Art 14 and, in so far as it applies to that Art, Article 64 of the Financial Services and Markets Act 2000 (Regulated Activities) Order, SI 2001/544; or

(*b*) any person not falling within para (*a*) who is approved by the Board of Inland Revenue for the purposes of para 54.

4 The Board's approval under (*b*) above will, for instance, be relevant for a financial trader who does not need to be regulated and so would not qualify automatically as a financial trader by virtue of para (*a*) above. Where an agent is acting for a disclosed principal and the principal is entitled to rights and subject to duties under the contract, the principal, as opposed to the agent, will require approval under (*b*).

5 This statement of practice explains the guidelines which the Board will operate in considering whether any person not within (*a*) above should be approved as a financial trader for the purposes of FA 2002 Sch 26 para 54.

FINANCIAL TRADER GUIDELINES

6 To obtain the Board's approval, a company must demonstrate that—

- it is carrying on a trade, the profits or losses of which would fall to be dealt with under Case I of Schedule D;
- this trade includes the provision of derivative contracts (within the meaning of FA 2002 Sch 26) to counterparties in the normal course of trade; and
- this part of the trade, on its own, satisfies the test in *IRC v Livingston* (11 TC 538)—ie the operations involved must be of the same kind and carried on in the same way as those which are characteristic of ordinary trading in the line of business in which the venture is made.

7 Where a company enters into derivative contracts with associated companies, then it will be easier for it to demonstrate that the third part of this test is satisfied if it also enters into derivative contracts to a significant extent with third parties on the same terms. Failing this, a company will need to produce evidence that it is conducting its operations with its associated customers in the same way as if they had been unconnected. Relevant considerations will include—

- the type and range of contracts into which it enters;
- the management of market risk;
- the assessment of credit risk;
- the level of reward obtained in terms of fees or spread.

Commentary—*Simon's Direct Tax Service* **D2.1010**

SP 5/02 (29 October 2002) *Exemptions for companies' gains on substantial shareholdings—s*ole or main benefit test: TCGA 1992 Sch 7AC Para 5

INTRODUCTION

1 The regime in TCGA 1992 Sch 7AC ("Schedule 7AC") for the exemption of gains on disposals of substantial shareholdings will apply to disposals of shares (or an interest in, or an asset related to, shares) by companies which have held a substantial shareholding for at least 12 months where—

- the company holding the shares (or an interest in, or an asset related to shares) is a trading company or a member of a trading group, and
- the shares in question are shares in a trading company or the holding company of a trading group or subgroup.

2 The exemptions provided by the regime may create opportunities for manipulation. The provisions therefore contain an anti-avoidance rule at paragraph 5 of Schedule 7AC. This is aimed at tax-driven arrangements which are intended to exploit any of the exemptions.

3 We expect cases where the anti-avoidance rule is in point to be unusual and infrequent.

4 In what follows, references to paragraphs are to paragraphs of Schedule 7AC.

OUTLINE OF THE ANTI-AVOIDANCE RULE

5 Paragraph 5 is aimed at "arrangements" from which the "sole or main benefit" that can be expected to be derived is that a gain on a disposal will be exempt by virtue of an exemption in Part 1 of Schedule 7AC. The remedy is to deny exemption on any gain arising on the relevant disposal.

"Arrangements" is defined widely and includes "any scheme, agreement or understanding, whether or not legally enforceable".

6 Paragraph 5(1) provides that certain events must occur in pursuance of the arrangements before the "sole or main benefit test" in paragraph 5(2) can apply—

- an untaxed gain must accrue to a company ("company A") on a disposal of shares, or an interest in shares or an asset related to shares, in another company ("company B"),

and before the gain accrued either—

- company A acquired control of company B, or the same person or persons acquired control of both companies, or

SPs

- there was a significant change of trading activities affecting company B at a time when it was controlled by company A, or when both companies were controlled by the same person or persons.

7 Paragraph 5(5) provides that there is a ''significant change of trading activities affecting company B'' if—

- there is a major change in the nature or conduct of a trade carried on by company B or a 51% subsidiary of company B, or
- there is a major change in the scale of the activities of a trade carried on by company B or a 51% subsidiary of company B, or
- company B or a subsidiary of company B begins to carry on a trade.

8 A ''major change in the nature or conduct of the trade'' in this legislation has the same meaning as in TA 1988 s 768.

9 For the purposes of paragraph 5(1) a gain is ''untaxed'' if the gain, or all of it but a part that is not substantial, represents profits that have not been brought into account (in the UK or elsewhere) for the purposes of tax on profits for a period ending on or before the date of the disposal. ''Profits'' for these purposes means income or gains, including unrealised income or gains. But profits are not ''untaxed profits'' if an amount in respect of these profits is apportioned to and chargeable on a UK-resident company under the controlled foreign company rules for an accounting period of the company ending on or before the date of the disposal.

APPLICATION OF THE RULE

10 It will be a question of fact in any particular case as to whether a gain wholly, or wholly except for a part which is not substantial, represents untaxed profits. Broadly, this will involve looking at how the consideration obtained for the shares is derived from assets held directly or indirectly by company B.

11 It will usually be obvious when profits are ''untaxed'' within the meaning of paragraph 5. For example, unrealised profits on capital assets will be untaxed profits. It is impossible to provide a comprehensive catalogue of all situations where the gain will represent untaxed profits but some examples of situations where the profits will not be untaxed profits for the purpose of paragraph 5 would be—

- a dividend received by a holding company that is paid out of taxed profits of the subsidiary;
- where the profits in question themselves represent an exempt gain on disposal of a substantial shareholding;
- where no tax is payable on profits because they are covered by a specific relief (eg loss relief).

12 In many cases a gain will represent both taxed and untaxed profits. In these circumstances, the gain should be taken as first representing the taxed profits and only any balance which then remains as representing untaxed profits.

13 In the context of this legislation we interpret ''substantial'' as meaning more than 20%.

14 Even if on this basis the gain wholly, or wholly except for a part which is not substantial, represents untaxed profits, the exemption would be denied only if—

- each of the circumstances set out in paragraph 5(1) occurs in pursuance of arrangements, and
- the sole or main benefit that could be expected to arise from the arrangements is that the gain accruing on the disposal would otherwise be exempt under Schedule 7AC, and
- from the outset the sole or main benefit expected to arise from the arrangements is the achievement of that outcome.

SP 2/03 (September 2003) *Business by Telephone—Services for Non Contact Centre Customers*

For the purpose of this statement of practice, the term ''non Contact Centre Customer'' is used to describe callers who contact an Inland Revenue office which is not currently served by a Contact Centre.

The security afforded by Contact Centre technology enables us to offer a wider range of services to customers contacting those centres. We are committed to expand the number of offices which will be served by Contact Centres and we intend that by 2005 nearly all telephone calls will be handled by our Contact Centre network. In the meantime, we are improving the range of services offered to our non Contact Centre Customers.

Previously, statement of practice 2/1998, restricted Business by Telephone to individual customers calling on their own behalf. From today's date, we have extended the service to personal representatives whose identity and credentials can be verified and for whom we hold written evidence of customer consent. We will also now provide some specific information by telephone.

Further guidance will be issued with regard to our contact with voluntary intermediaries (eg welfare organisations such as Citizens Advice Bureaux).

This statement of practice sets out, in full, the extended services which are now available for non Contact Centre Customers. It supersedes SP 2/98.

Another Business by Telephone statement of practice (SP 03/03) is being issued today [see below] and will to apply to customers whose affairs are served by a Contact Centre.

SECURITY AND CONFIDENTIALITY

The Inland Revenue is committed to ensuring the information it receives is accurate and that the privacy of customers' affairs is protected. For the services described in this statement of practice—

- Callers will only be able to supply or amend information concerning individuals' tax affairs.
- We will take steps to check the identity of the caller before discussing a customer's tax affairs.
- Callers who fail to satisfy the identity checks will be asked to put their enquiry in writing.
- We will check that we have the customer's written consent before we discuss their affairs with a personal representative.
- We will carry out sample "call backs" to ensure, amongst other things, that our prescribed security procedures are being followed.

SERVICES AVAILABLE BY TELEPHONE FOR NON CONTACT CENTRE CUSTOMERS

The services described below are available to individual customers calling about their own tax liabilities, and to personal representatives acting on behalf of the customer **providing that we can satisfactorily check the identity of the caller.**

The directions by the Board of Inland Revenue under FA 1998 s 118 which provide for these services are at annex A.

In most cases nothing more than a telephone call will be needed, although the call may lead to further action by the Inland Revenue (for example, sending out a revised PAYE coding notice). Where business cannot be completed by telephone we will send customers any forms or other information they need and explain what they need to do next.

PERSONAL REPRESENTATIVES

Some people prefer to ask a personal representative, such as an accountant, agent or family member, to deal with their tax affairs for them. We will accept some types of information from personal representatives providing that—

- we have been able to check the identity of the personal representative, and
- we hold written evidence that the customer has given their consent for that personal representative to act on their behalf

Further guidance will be issued with regard to our contact with voluntary intermediaries (eg welfare organisations such as Citizens Advice Bureaux).

MATTERS THAT CAN BE DEALT WITH BY TELEPHONE

Personal details

We will accept the following information over the telephone—

- changes to name, address, post code and telephone number,
- changes in personal circumstances such as marriage, separation or divorce,
- other personal information—for example, National Insurance number and date of birth.

Customers can also tell us when a personal representative is no longer acting on their behalf. However, they will need to send us written consent for any new personal representative who starts to act for them.

Employment details

We will accept the following information over the telephone—

- details of a customer's new employer and the date when the new employment began,
- a customer's works or payroll number,
- details of earlier employments.

We will not accept details of pay and tax over the telephone. These details should be notified in writing.

Personal allowances

We will accept current year claims to the following personal allowances by telephone from customers and personal representatives calling on the customer's behalf—

- Personal Allowance,
- Married Couple's Allowance[1].
- Blind Person's Allowance.

[1] This allowance is available for tax year 2000/2001 and later years where either the husband or wife was born before 6 April 1935.

SPs

The level of a person's income affects their entitlement to the age-related allowances. We will accept new estimates of income over the telephone from customers or personal representatives calling on their behalf. And, using the figures provided, we will advise whether the amount of the customer's allowances will change.

All claims for previous years must be made in writing.

Expenses

Some employees are entitled to tax relief for expenses or certain professional subscriptions they incur in carrying out their job. We will accept claims for "flat rate" expenses from customers and personal representatives (Flat rate expenses are fixed amounts we have agreed for certain categories of employees to save them having to make claims for individual amounts.) We will also accept claims for Professional Subscriptions up to a limit of £100. (Most Trade Union subscriptions do not qualify for relief but where, exceptionally, a Trade Union subscription does qualify we will accept claims by telephone.)

We will also accept repeat claims to certain travel expenses, and other necessary expenses of employment where the entitlement has already been agreed in principle.

Employee benefits in kind

A customer, or a personal representative calling on the customer's behalf, can tell us by telephone about any benefit in kind, not just the most common ones such as car benefits and fuel benefits.

We will check the details of benefits in kind later, after the end of the tax year. But, telling us about them earlier will help us to keep PAYE tax codes up to date and help the customer to pay the right amount of tax during the tax year. In some circumstances, for example if a benefit is partly for work purposes or a benefit is shared with other employees, we may ask for the details to be put in writing.

Other information

Customers, or personal representatives calling on their behalf, can also help us keep their PAYE tax codes up to date by telling us about—

- receipt of National Insurance Retirement Pension
- receipt of taxable Incapacity Benefit (Incapacity Benefit paid at the short term lower rate for the first 28 weeks is non-taxable)
- small amounts of income, for example bank or building society interest received gross.

Where callers provide information over the telephone about expenses, benefits in kind or other information we will use this to adjust the customer's PAYE code number for the current year and, if appropriate, the next year. Where we need to make adjustments for earlier tax years customers must put the information in writing.

TIME LIMITS

The same time limits apply to claims and elections made by telephone as when they are made in writing.

Where a claim is made by telephone, it will be treated as made at the time of the call provided all the relevant information can be provided by the customer during that call. And a claim by telephone will, of course, be subject to the same conditions and checks as if it were made on paper.

Where a claim cannot be dealt with by telephone, for example, because the caller does not have all the necessary information, the customer may be asked to make the claim in writing. The written claim must still be made within the usual time limits.

INFORMATION WE WILL GIVE TO CUSTOMERS BY TELEPHONE

We will provide the following details to customers, or personal representatives calling on their behalf—

- the customer's Payments on Account,
- any amounts the customer owes us,
- the amount of a repayment awaiting issue,
- amounts of unpaid tax for earlier years included in the tax code for the current year, and
- amounts of tax due for the current year included in a tax code for a later year

GUIDANCE AND ASSISTANCE

In addition to the services above, non Contact Centre Customers can expect the normal range of help and advice by telephone on general tax matters including—

- general questions about income tax and capital gains tax for individuals,
- help with completing returns and other Inland Revenue forms, and

– requests for leaflets, forms, schedules and other Inland Revenue information.

But, please note requests for supplementary pages to the self-assessment return and the helpsheets mentioned in the tax return guide should be made to the self-assessment Orderline 0845 9000404. The Orderline is open from 8.00 am to 8.00 pm 7 days a week.

ANNEX A—DIRECTIONS UNDER FA 1998 S 118

In the following directions references to TA 1988 mean the Income and Corporation Taxes Act 1988 and references to ITEPA 2003 mean the Income Tax (Earnings and Pensions) Act 2003.

Claims, elections and notifications not included on a return

The Commissioners of Inland Revenue hereby direct that from 1 September 2003 an individual who is not required to make a self assessment return for a year under TMA 1970 s 8(1), or has made a self assessment return but the time limit specified in TMA 1970 s 9ZA has passed, may—

- make the claims or elections specified below, or
- notify the income or benefits specified below

by telephone PROVIDED THAT—

- claims or elections are for the "current year" (that is the year of assessment in which the claim or election is made) or the year following the "current year", AND
- the claim or election is made, or the income or benefit is notified, in the manner authorised below.

The matters to which the directions relate are as follows—

Claims and elections

1 A claim to any of the following personal allowances—

Claims to Personal Allowance	under	TA 1988 s 257(1)
		TA 1988 s 257(2) (claimant 65 or over)
	or	TA 1988 s 257(3) (claimant 75 or over)
Claims to Married Couple's Allowance	under	TA 1988 s 257A(2) This allowance is only available where claimant or wife born before 6 April 1935 but under 75)
	or	TA 1988 s 257A(3) (allowance where claimant or wife 75 or over)
Elections for the transfer of 50% of the married couples allowance from husband to wife	under	TA 1988 s 257BA(1) (An election under this section must be made before the commencement of the tax year to which it will relate. The only exception to this time limit relates to the year of marriage when the election may be made during that tax year).
Claims to Blind Person's allowance	under	TA 1988 s 265(1)
	or	TA 1988 s 265(2) (allowance to spouse)

2 A claim to an income tax reduction under the following provision

Relief for interest paid	Under	TA 1988 s 353

3 A claim to make any of the following deductions from income in respect of expenses,

Relief for professional membership fees and annual subscriptions	under	ITEPA 2003 s 343 or 344
Relief for flat rate deductions within the terms of Extra Statutory Concession A1	under	ITEPA 2003 s 367

4 A claim to make any of the following deductions from income in respect of expenses (providing the same class of expense was claimed the previous year),

Relief for expenses	under	ITEPA 2003 s 336
		ITEPA 2003 s 337
		ITEPA 2003 s 338
		ITEPA 2003 s 341
		ITEPA 2003 s 342
		ITEPA 2003 s 346
		ITEPA 2003 s 352
		ITEPA 2003 s 370
		ITEPA 2003 s 371
		ITEPA 2003 s 373
		ITEPA 2003 s 374
		ITEPA 2003 s 376

Income and benefits

5 Notification of any of the any of the following benefits provided by reason of employment—

Cash vouchers	under	ITEPA 2003 s 81
Non cash vouchers	under	ITEPA 2003 s 87
Credit tokens	under	ITEPA 2003 s 94
Living accommodation	under	ITEPA 2003 s 102
Cars available for private use	under	ITEPA 2003 s 120
Car fuel	under	ITEPA 2003 s 149
Vans available for private use	under	ITEPA 2003 s 154
Beneficial loan arrangements	under	ITEPA 2003 s 173
Benefits in kind	under	ITEPA 2003 s 201
Payments, etc free of tax	under	ITEPA 2003 s 222
Director's tax paid	under	ITEPA 2003 s 223

6 Notification of any income from employment

The manner authorised for dealing with matters by telephone.

Claims and elections

The claims, and elections specified above may be made orally, in a telephone conversation with a tax office, if made by—

- the individual, or
- where the individual has notified the Inland Revenue that a personal representative is authorised to act on his or her behalf, that personal representative.

(The directions do not apply to claims made by an individual in his or her capacity as a trustee or partner. Such claims must be made in writing)

The claim or election will be treated as made on the date the telephone call is made, so long as the caller provides the information requested by the Inland Revenue during the telephone conversation.

If the caller does not provide the information which the Inland Revenue requests during the telephone conversation a valid claim, or election will not have been made. Failure to establish a valid claim, or election by telephone does not prevent the caller from a further attempt to establish the claim or election. But, any subsequent attempt must be made in writing, within the statutory time limit for making the claim or election.

Income and benefits

The income and benefits specified above may be notified to the Inland Revenue orally, in a telephone conversation with a tax office, if notified by—

- the individual, or
- where the individual has notified the Inland Revenue that a personal representative is authorised to act on his or her behalf, that personal representative.

The notification will be treated as given on the date the telephone call is made, so long as the individual, or personal representative, provides the information requested by the Inland Revenue during the telephone conversation.

If an individual, or personal representative, does not provide the information which the Inland Revenue requests during the telephone conversation a valid notification will not have been given. The individual, or personal representative, should then write to the individual's tax office to notify them about the income or benefit

Revocation of previous directions

The Commissioners of Inland Revenue hereby revoke their directions published on 24 August 1998 with effect from 1 September 2003.

Commentary—*Simon's Direct Tax Service* **A2.301.**

SP 3/03 (September 2003) *Business by Telephone—Inland Revenue Contact Centres*

In 1998, we published two Statements of Practice setting out the services available by telephone to individual customers and their agents. In response to the demand for those services, and the success of the first Contact Centre in Scotland, we are now expanding the range of business that may be conducted by telephone and making these services available to a greater number of customers. We will now accept certain information by telephone from personal representatives acting on behalf of customers, and we will now provide some information by telephone. Further guidance will be issued with regard to our contact with voluntary intermediaries (eg welfare organisations such as Citizens Advice Bureaux).

The security afforded by Contact Centre technology enables the Inland Revenue to offer these additional services, and they will therefore be restricted to individual customers whose affairs are dealt with in a tax office which is served by a Contact Centre. However, as we are committed to expanding the number of offices which will be served by Contact Centres, all customers should see the phased introduction of improved services over a period of time. Annex B sets out which customers are currently served by Contact Centres.

This statement of practice sets out, in full, the expanded services which are now available from Contact Centres which deal with the tax affairs of individuals. It supersedes statement of practice 8/98.

Another Business by Telephone statement of practice (SP 02/03) is being issued today [see above] and will to apply to customers whose affairs are not yet served by a Contact Centre.

SECURITY AND CONFIDENTIALITY

The Inland Revenue is committed to ensuring the information it receives is accurate and that the privacy of customers' affairs is protected. For the services described in this statement of practice—

- Callers will only be able to supply or amend information concerning individuals' tax affairs.
- We will take steps to check the identity of the caller before discussing a customer's tax affairs.
- Callers who fail to satisfy the identity checks will be asked to put their enquiry in writing.
- We will check that we have the customer's consent before we discuss their affairs with a personal representative.
- Calls to our Contact Centres will be recorded for training and quality assurance purposes and will be available in case of any disagreement as to what was said.

SERVICES AVAILABLE BY TELEPHONE FROM INLAND REVENUE CONTACT CENTRES

The services described below are available to individual customers calling Inland Revenue Contact Centres about their own tax liabilities, and to personal representatives acting on behalf of the customer **providing that we can satisfactorily check the identity of the caller.**

The directions by the Board of Inland Revenue under FA 1998 s 118 which provide for these services are at annex A. In most cases nothing more than a telephone call will be needed, although the call may lead to further action by the Inland Revenue (for example, sending out a revised PAYE coding notice). Where business cannot be completed by telephone we will send customers any forms or other information they need and explain what they need to do next.

PERSONAL REPRESENTATIVES

Some people prefer to ask a personal representative, such as an accountant, agent or family member, to deal with their tax affairs for them. We will accept some types of information from personal representatives providing that—

- we have been able to check the identity of the personal representative, and
- we hold evidence that the customer has given their consent for that personal representative to act on their behalf

Further guidance will be issued with regard to our contact with voluntary intermediaries (eg welfare organisations such as Citizens Advice Bureaux).

Customers using our Contact Centres can give their consent orally which we will record and accept for the purpose of a "one off" telephone call. We do recognise however, that there will be occasions when the customer cannot be present to give oral consent for the personal representative to act on their behalf. On these occasions we will accept (but not provide) information from the personal representative on a provisional basis and then contact the customer by post to confirm the information. Customers will need to give their consent in writing if they want the personal representative to act on their behalf on any future occasions.

MATTERS THAT CAN BE DEALT WITH BY TELEPHONE

Personal details

We will accept the following information over the telephone—

- changes to name, address, post code and telephone number,
- changes in personal circumstances such as marriage, separation or divorce,
- other personal information—for example, National Insurance number and date of birth.

Customers can also tell us when a personal representative is no longer acting on their behalf. However, they will need to send us written consent for any new personal representative who starts to act for them on future occasions.

Employment details

We will accept the following information over the telephone—

- details of a customer's new employer and the date when the new employment began,

SPs

- a customer's works or payroll number,
- details of earlier employments.

We will not accept details of pay and tax over the telephone. These details should be notified in writing.

Personal allowances

Subject to time limits, we will accept claims to the following personal allowances by telephone from customers and personal representatives calling on the customer's behalf—

- Personal Allowance,
- Married Couple's Allowance[1]
- Blind Person's Allowance.

[1] This allowance is available for tax year 2000/2001 and later years where either the husband or wife was born before 6 April 1935. Prior to 2000/2001 no age restriction applied.

Claims for additional relief in respect of children can also be made subject to certain time limits, (the last year a claim can be made is for the tax year 1999/2000).

The level of a person's income affects their entitlement to the age-related allowances. We will accept new estimates of income over the telephone from customers or personal representatives calling on their behalf. And, using the figures provided, we will advise whether the amount of the customer's allowances will change.

Expenses

Some employees are entitled to tax relief for expenses or certain professional subscriptions they incur in carrying out their job. We will accept claims for ''flat rate'' expenses from customers and personal representatives (Flat rate expenses are fixed amounts we have agreed for certain categories of employees to save them having to make claims for individual amounts.) We will also accept claims for Professional Subscriptions up to a limit of £100. (Most Trade Union subscriptions do not qualify for relief but where, exceptionally, a Trade Union subscription does qualify we will accept claims by telephone.)

We will also accept repeat claims to certain travel expenses, and other necessary expenses of employment where the entitlement has already been agreed in principle.

Employee benefits in kind

A customer, or a personal representative calling on the customer's behalf, can tell us by telephone about any benefit in kind, not just the most common ones such as car benefits and fuel benefits.

We will check the details of benefits in kind later, after the end of the tax year. But, telling us about them earlier will help us to keep PAYE tax codes up to date and help the customer to pay the right amount of tax during the tax year. In some circumstances, for example if a benefit is partly for work purposes or a benefit is shared with other employees, we may ask for the details to be put in writing.

Other information

Customers, or personal representatives calling on their behalf, can also help us keep their PAYE tax codes up to date by telling us about

- receipt of National Insurance Retirement Pension
- receipt of taxable Incapacity Benefit (Incapacity Benefit paid at the short term lower rate for the first 28 weeks is non-taxable)
- small amounts of income, for example bank or building society interest received gross.

Where callers provide information over the telephone about expenses, benefits in kind or other information we will use this to adjust the customer's PAYE code number for the current year and, if appropriate, the next year. Where we need to make adjustments for earlier tax years customers must put the information in writing.

SELF ASSESSMENT RETURNS

Including details of telephone notifications and claims in self-assessment tax returns

The telephone services described above are available to all customers who use Inland Revenue Contact Centres, including those who are required to make a self-assessment return. But customers who make a self-assessment return should also include any claims made, or information provided, by telephone in their return.

Notifying amendments to self-assessment returns by telephone

Customers who have made a self-assessment return for any year have the right to amend their return for example, to correct errors which come to light after it has been sent in. Any amendment must normally be made within 12 months of the filing date for that return. The filing date will usually be 31 January after the end of the tax year to which the return relates.

Customers, or personal representatives calling on their behalf, can make the following amendments to self-assessment returns by telephone—

- amendments to PERSONAL ALLOWANCES within the range of allowances described above;
- on the EMPLOYMENT PAGES of the return;
  - amendments to deductions or expenses which fall within the range of services described above;
  - amendments to employment income or employee benefits in kind;
  - correction of provisional figures or incorrect figures;
- correction of personal or employment details.

Where we have opened an enquiry into a self-assessment return customers can still amend the return within the normal 12-month time limit. Our enquiry may include looking at the amendment. The amendment will be given effect when the enquiry is complete.

Customers, or personal representatives calling on their behalf, can also ask us to—

- repay tax overpaid for the year (where the request was omitted from original return);
- include tax payable in the PAYE tax code for the forthcoming year (subject to time limits);
- reduce their payments on account.

Checking amendments notified by telephone

Amendments to self-assessment returns made by telephone will be checked in the same way as amendments made in writing and in some cases we may enquire into the amendment.

TIME LIMITS

The same time limits apply to claims and amendments made by telephone as when they are made in writing.

Where a claim is made by telephone, it will be treated as made at the time of the call provided all the relevant information can be provided by the customer during that call. And a claim by telephone will, of course, be subject to the same conditions and checks as if it were made on paper.

Where a claim cannot be dealt with by telephone, for example, because the caller does not have all the necessary information, the customer may be asked to make the claim in writing. The written claim must still be made within the usual time limits.

INFORMATION WE WILL GIVE TO CONTACT CENTRE CUSTOMERS BY TELEPHONE

We will provide the following details to customers, or personal representatives calling on their behalf—

- the customer's Payments on Account,
- any amounts the customer owes us,
- the amount of a repayment awaiting issue,
- amounts of unpaid tax for earlier years included in the tax code for the current year, and
- amounts of tax due for the current year included in a tax code for a later year.

GUIDANCE AND ASSISTANCE

In addition to the services above, Contact Centres will provide the normal range of help and advice by telephone on general tax matters including—

- general questions about income tax and capital gains tax for individuals,
- help with completing returns and other Inland Revenue forms, and
- requests for leaflets, forms, schedules and other Inland Revenue information.

But, please note requests for supplementary pages to the self-assessment return and the helpsheets mentioned in the tax return guide should be made to the self-assessment Orderline 0845–9000404. The Orderline is open from 8.00 am to 8.00 pm 7 days a week.

ANNEX A—DIRECTIONS UNDER FA 1998 S 118

In the following directions references to TA 1988 mean the Income and Corporation Taxes Act 1988 and references to ITEPA 2003 mean the Income Tax (Earnings and Pensions) Act 2003.

Claims, elections and notifications not included in a return

The Commissioners of Inland Revenue hereby direct that from 1 September 2003 an individual who is not required to make a self assessment return for a year under section 8(1) of the Taxes Management Act 1970, or has made a self assessment return but the time limit specified in section 9ZA of the Taxes Management Act 1970, for amending a return has passed, may—

- make the claims or elections specified below (providing the time limit for making such a claim or election, for the year in question, has not expired), or

SPs

– notify the income or benefits specified below

by telephone PROVIDED THAT—

- at the time the call is made the individual's tax affairs are dealt with in a tax office served by a contact centre,
- the call is made to the contact centre that serves the tax office for the particular individual,
- claims or elections within sections 2–4, below, are for the "current year" (that is the year of assessment in which the claim or election is made) or the year following the "current year", AND
- the claim or election is made, or the income or benefit is notified, in the manner authorised below.

Claims, elections and notifications included in a return

The Commissioners of Inland Revenue also direct that from 1 September 2003 an individual who has made a self assessment return for any year under section 8(1) of the Taxes Management Act 1970, and who wishes to amend the self-assessment for that year under section 9ZA of the Taxes Management Act, may notify an officer of the Board of both the amendment to the self assessment return and the consequential amendment to the self- assessment, by telephone, PROVIDED THAT—

- at the time the call is made the individual's tax affairs are dealt with in a tax office served by a contact centre,
- the call is made to the contact centre that serves the tax office for the particular individual,
- the amendment is of a type specified below, AND
- the amendment is made in the manner authorised below.

The matters to which the directions relate are as follows—

Claims and elections

1 A claim to any of the following personal allowances (providing the time limit for making any such claim for the year in question has not expired) OR an amendment to a return to make such a claim OR an amendment to any such claim which was made in the original return—

claims to Personal Allowance	under	TA 1988 s 257(1)
		TA 1988 s 257(2) (claimant 65 or over)
	or	TA 1988 s 257(3) (claimant 75 or over)
claims to Married Couple's Allowance	under	TA 1988 s 257A(1) Basic allowance for years to 1999/2000 only
		TA 1988 s 257A(2) (For tax years from 2000/2001—allowance where claimant or wife born before 6 April 1935 but under 75). (For 1999/2000 and earlier—allowance where claimant or wife 65 or over but under 75)
	or	TA 1988 s 257A(3) (allowance where claimant or wife 75 or over)
elections for the transfer of 50% of the married couples allowance from husband to wife	under	TA 1988 s 257BA(1) (An election under this section must be made before the commencement of the tax year to which it will relate. The only exception to this time limit relates to the year of marriage when the election may be made during that tax year).
claims to Additional relief in respect of children (to 1999/2000)	under	TA 1988 s 259(2) (but excluding any such claim where the question of apportionment under TA 1988 s 260 arises and no apportionment has been agreed under Section 260 (3)).
elections where Additional relief in respect of children claimed in year of marriage (to 1999–2000)	under	TA 1988 s 261
including any amount claimed in year of separation (to 1999–2000)	under	TA 1988 s 261A
claims to Blind Person's allowance	under	TA 1988 s 265(1)
	or	TA 1988 s 265(2) (allowance to spouse)

2 A claim to an income tax reduction under the following provision OR an amendment to a return to make such a claim OR an amendment to any such claim which was made in the original return—

relief for interest paid	under	TA 1988 s 353

3 A claim to make any of the following deductions from income in respect of expenses, OR an amendment to a return to make such a deduction OR an amendment to any such deduction which was made in the original return—

Relief for professional membership fees and annual subscriptions	under	ITEPA 2003 s 343 or S344
Relief for flat rate deductions within the terms of Extra Statutory Concession A1	under	ITEPA 2003 s 367

4 A claim to make any of the following deductions from income in respect of expenses (providing the same class of expense was claimed the previous year), OR an amendment to a return to make such a deduction OR an amendment to any such deduction which was made in the original return—

Relief for expenses	under	ITEPA 2003 s 336
		ITEPA 2003 s 337
		ITEPA 2003 s 338
		ITEPA 2003 s 341
		ITEPA 2003 s 342
		ITEPA 2003 s 346
		ITEPA 2003 s 352
		ITEPA 2003 s 370
		ITEPA 2003 s 371
		ITEPA 2003 s 373
		ITEPA 2003 s 374
		ITEPA 2003 s 376

Income and benefits

5 Notification of any of the any of the following benefits provided by reason of employment OR an amendment to return details of such benefits omitted from the original return, OR an amendment to any such benefit included in the original return—

Cash vouchers	under	ITEPA 2003 s 81
Non cash vouchers	under	ITEPA 2003 s 87
Credit tokens	under	ITEPA 2003 s 94
Living accommodation	under	ITEPA 2003 s 102
Cars available for private use	under	ITEPA 2003 s 120
Car fuel	under	ITEPA 2003 s 149
Vans available for private use	under	ITEPA 2003 s 154
Beneficial loan arrangements	under	ITEPA 2003 s 173
Benefits in kind	under	ITEPA 2003 s 201
Payments, etc free of tax	under	ITEPA 2003 s 222
Director's tax paid	under	ITEPA 2003 s 223

6 Notification of any income from employment OR an amendment to return details of any income omitted from the employment pages of the original return.

Other amendments

7 Correction of a provisional figure in the employment pages of the original return to a final figure.

8 Correction of an incorrect figure in the employment pages of the original return.

The manner authorised for dealing with matters by telephone

Amendments, claims and elections

The amendments, claims, and elections specified above may be made orally, in a telephone conversation with a contact centre adviser, if made by—

– the individual, or
– where the individual has notified the Inland Revenue that a third party is authorised to act on his or her behalf, that third party.

(The directions do not apply to amendments made by an individual in his or her capacity as a trustee, partner or personal representative. Such amendments must be made in writing).

The amendment, claim or election will be treated as made on the date the telephone call is made, so long as the caller provides the information requested by the Inland Revenue during the telephone conversation.

If the caller does not provide the information which the Inland Revenue requests during the telephone conversation a valid amendment, claim, or election will not have been made. Failure to establish a valid amendment, claim, or election by telephone does not prevent the caller from a further attempt to establish the amendment, claim or election. But, any subsequent attempt must be made in writing, within the statutory time limit for making the amendment, claim or election.

Income and benefits

The income and benefits specified above may be notified to the Inland Revenue orally, in a telephone conversation with a contact centre adviser, if notified by—

– the individual, or
– where the individual has notified the Inland Revenue that a third party is authorised to act on his or her behalf, that third party.

The notification will be treated as given on the date the telephone call is made, so long as the individual, or third party, provides the information requested by the Inland Revenue during the telephone conversation.

If an individual, or third party, does not provide the information which the Inland Revenue requests during the telephone conversation a valid notification will not have been given. The individual, or third party, should then write to the individual's tax office to notify them about the income or benefit

Revocation of previous directions

The Commissioners of Inland Revenue hereby revoke their directions published on 18 December 1998 with effect from 1 September 2003.

ANNEX B—CONTACT CENTRE CUSTOMERS COVERED BY THIS STATEMENT OF PRACTICE AS AT SEPTEMBER 2003

Belfast Contact Centre 02890 505000	
Old Office Name	New Office Name
Belfast 1	Greater Belfast Area
Belfast 2	Greater Belfast Area
Blackpool Contact Centre 0845 3021482	
Old Office Name	New Office Name
Worcester (792)	Worcester and Hereford Area
Hereford (323)	Worcester and Hereford Area
Ludlow (433)	Worcester and Hereford Area
Evesham (262)	Worcester and Hereford Area
Redditch (612)	Worcester and Hereford Area
Blackpool Contact Centre 0845 3021478	
Old Office Name	New Office Name
Preston (449)	NW Lancashire Area.
Lancaster (385)	NW Lancashire Area.
St Annes (635)	NW Lancashire Area.
Chorley (159)	NW Lancashire Area.
Blackpool (065)	NW Lancashire Area.
Bootle Contact Centre 0845 3003939	
Old Office Name	New Office Name
Bootle 1	Sefton
Bootle Merseyside	Sefton
Bootle Maritime	Sefton
Cardiff Contact Centre 0845 3003949	
Old Office Name	New Office Name
Cardiff 1	South Wales Area

Cardiff 3 (0845 3003948)	South Wales Area
Pontypridd	South Wales Area
Merthyr Tydfil	South Wales Area
Brecon	South Wales Area
Pontypool	South Wales Area
Newport	South Wales Area
PD2	South Wales Area
Bangor	North Wales Area
Colwyn Bay	North Wales Area
Porthmadog	North Wales Area
Rhyl	North Wales Area
Welshpool	North Wales Area
Wrexham 1	North Wales Area
Cardiff Contact Centre 0845 3021483	
Old Office Name	New Office Name
Wrexham 2	North Wales Area
Bridgwater	Somerset Area
Frome	Somerset Area
Taunton	Somerset Area
Wells	Somerset Area
Yeovil	Somerset Area
East Kilbride Contact Centre 0845 0703703	
Old Office Name	New Office Name
Centre 1	Centre 1
Scotland North	Scotland North
Lothians Contact Centre 0845 302 1409	
Old Office Name	New Office Name
London Provincial 21	Lothians
London Provincial 22	Lothians
London Provincial 23	Lothians
London Provincial 24	Lothians
London Provincial 25	Lothians
Lothians Contact Centre 0845 302 1484	
Old Office Name	New Office Name
Edinburgh	Scotland South
Stirling	Scotland South

Falkirk	Scotland South
Hawick	Scotland South
Galashiels	Scotland South
Dundee	Scotland East
Perth	Scotland East
Kirkcaldy	Scotland East
Dunfermline	Scotland East
Manchester Contact Centre 0845 3000627	
Old Office Name	New Office Name
Irwell	Chapel Wharf Area
Trinity	Chapel Wharf Area
Deansgate	Chapel Wharf Area
Parsonage	Chapel Wharf Area
Regent	Chapel Wharf Area
Portsmouth Contact Centre 0845 3000628	
Old Office Name	New Office Name
Portsmouth 1	East Hampshire and Wight
Portsmouth Maritime	East Hampshire and Wight
Isle of Wight	East Hampshire and Wight
Southampton Parkside	West Hampshire
Andover	West Hampshire
Winchester	West Hampshire
Sunderland Contact Centre 0845 3021414	
Old Office Name	New Office Name
Washington	North East Metropolitan
LP34	North East Metropolitan
LP10	North East Metropolitan
Tees Valley	North East Metropolitan
Sunderland Contact Centre 0845 5555555	
Old Office Name	New Office Name
Hull	Humber
Grimsby	Humber
Scunthorpe	Humber
Goole	Humber
Sunderland Contact Centre 0845 302 1473	
Old Office Name	New Office Name

Carlisle	Cumbria
Furness	Cumbria
Kendal	Cumbria
Penrith	Cumbria
West Cumbria	Cumbria

Commentary—*Simon's Direct Tax Service* **A2.301.**

INLAND REVENUE INTERPRETATIONS

LIST OF INTERPRETATIONS

Note—The Revenue interpretations are published in the Inland Revenue Tax Bulletin. The Revenue states that the interpretations will normally be applied in relevant cases, but that this is subject to a number of qualifications. Particular cases may turn on their own facts or context and there may be circumstances in which an interpretation will not apply. There may also be circumstances in which the Board would find it necessary to argue for a different interpretation in appeal proceedings.

Interpretations which have no relevance in the current tax year are not reproduced but are included in italics in the list below. Those which are obsolescent are both listed and reproduced in italics.

The number before each interpretation (eg RI 1) does not appear in the official publications. It has been added by the publishers to distinguish "interpretations" from "decisions" (printed *post*) and to facilitate identification for the purpose of cross references.

RI 1 *Expenditure on training courses for business proprietors.* (obsolete)
RI 2 Business loans used to fund an overdrawn account.
RI 3 *Interest charged to work in progress: property development companies. (obsolescent)*
RI 4 Purchase by a company of its own shares: legal expenses.
RI 5 Rollover relief for business assets: extension of time limit.
RI 6 Retirement relief: ill health claim.
RI 7 Rollover relief for business assets: assets not immediately taken into use.
RI 8 Holdover relief for gifts: agricultural property with development value.
RI 9 Rebasing elections: assets held by same person in different capacities.
RI 10 Capital allowances: abortive expenditure on plant and machinery.
RI 11 Rollover relief for business assets: grant of options over land.
RI 12 Interest relief: loans to invest in close companies.
RI 13 *Incidental costs of obtaining loan finance: life insurance premiums.* (obsolete)
RI 14 *Winding up of BES companies. (obsolescent)*
RI 15 Interest relief: joint loans to spouses.
RI 16 Close company loans to participators.
RI 17 *Loss relief claims: order of priority. (superseded)*
RI 18 *Financial loss allowances: treatment as trading receipts.* (obsolete)
RI 19 *Herd basis: change in persons carrying on farming business.* (superseded)
RI 20 *Mobile telephone: reimbursement by employee for private use.* (obsolete)
RI 21 *Close investment-holding companies.* (obsolete)
RI 22 Private residence exemption: unrelated joint occupiers.
RI 23 Qualifying corporate bonds given to a charity.
RI 24 *Business expansion scheme: private rented housing companies. (obsolete)*
RI 25 *Post-cessation professional indemnity insurance premiums. (superseded)*
RI 26 Indexation and rebasing: assets acquired by no gain/no loss disposal after 31 March 1982.
RI 27 *BES shares issued before 19 March 1986: indexation allowance on disposal. (obsolete)*
RI 28 Rollover relief for business assets: furnished holiday lettings.
RI 29 *Investment managers acting as agents for non-residents. (obsolete)*
RI 30 *Insurance agents' commission receivable on indemnity terms.* (obsolete)
RI 31 *Waste disposal sites: meaning of "site preparation expenditure".* (superseded)
RI 32 *Pre-trading expenditure: expenses incurred by another person.* (obsolete)
RI 33 *Capital allowances for plant or machinery: glasshouses.* (superseded)
RI 34 Small capital distributions.
RI 35 *Schemes of reconstruction.* (obsolete)
RI 36 Qualifying corporate bonds: devolution on death.
RI 37 Set-off of management expenses against surplus franked investment income.
RI 38 Settlements: connected persons and losses.
RI 39 Share exchanges partly in the form of qualifying corporate bonds.
RI 40 Residence and ordinary residence: "full-time" employment abroad.
RI 41 Loans to buy into partnerships.
RI 42 Rollover relief for business assets: depreciating assets.
RI 43 Non-resident companies: attribution of gains to UK shareholders.
RI 44 *Personal pension contributions: treatment in computing profits for Class 4 national insurance contributions. (obsolete)*
RI 45 Benefits in kind: medical check-ups.
RI 46 *Capital allowances: commercial know-how.* (superseded)
RI 47 Claims for unrelieved trading losses to be set against capital gains.
RI 48 *Capital gains tax rates: retrospective changes in individuals' liability. (superseded)*
RI 49 Interest paid to UK branches of non-resident companies.
RI 50 *Release of trading debts—"hive across" transactions.* (obsolete)
RI 51 Self-employed lorry drivers' overnight subsistence.
RI 52 *Sums received under exclusivity agreements.* (superseded)
RI 53 *Deep discount securities: bond stripping.* (obsolete)
RI 54 *Capital allowances—time when expenditure is incurred.* (superseded)
RI 55 *Inheritance tax—gifts with reservation (see IHT section post).*
RI 56 *Expenditure by a trader on computer software.* (superseded)

RI 57 *Bank failures—relief for losses incurred by depositors.* (obsolete)

RI 58 Interest—location of source of income.

RI 59 Deep discount securities issued in a foreign currency.

RI 60 *Deep discount securities with a maturity of less than 12 months.* (obsolete)

RI 61 Termination payments and legal costs.

RI 62 Relief for interest on loan to acquire an interest in a close company.

RI 63 *Capital gains tax: allowable expenditure: costs of making valuations.* (obsolete)

RI 64 Corporation tax on chargeable gains: degrouping charges. (obsolete)

RI 65 Recovery of tax overpaid by error or mistake.

RI 66 Interest arising after due date for payment of tax. (obsolete)

RI 67 Compensation for permanent costs in milk quota.

RI 68 Milk quota—a request to practitioners.

RI 69 Reinvestment relief.

RI 70 Restrictions on setting off capital losses—time limits for elections. (obsolete)

RI 71 Allowance of interest paid by companies with neither trading nor investment status. (obsolete)

RI 72 Visitors to the UK—residence position for tax purposes.

RI 73 Travelling and subsistence expenses—temporary absence from normal place of work. (obsolete)

RI 74 Open offer treated as share reorganisation.

RI 75 *Principal private residence relief.* (obsolete)

RI 76 Charges on income—company paying annuities.

RI 77 *Milk quota—superlevy.* (superseded)

RI 78 Outward investment in the corporate sector. (obsolete)

RI 79 Double taxation—treaty claims and loan interest.

RI 80 *Rent-a-room—accommodation used for trade or business purpose.* (superseded)

RI 81 *Bad and doubtful debts.* (obsolete)

RI 82 Deduction for costs of secretarial assistance and childcare costs.

RI 83 *Motor dealers—stock valuation.* (obsolete)

RI 84 *Trading receipts of members' golf clubs.* (superseded)

RI 85 Beneficial loans—exemption for commercial loans.

RI 86 *Capital allowances—machinery and plant fixtures.* (obsolete)

RI 87 Capital gains tax—apportionment for rollover relief.

RI 88 Capital gains tax—meaning of machinery.

RI 89 Principal private residence relief—residences occupied under licence.

RI 90 Corporation tax—company purchase scheme.

RI 91 *Farming—election for herd basis.* (superseded)

RI 92 Termination payments and legal costs.

RI 93 Transfers of assets at undervalue to employees or directors—disposal consideration.

RI 94 Farming—timing issues relating to grants and subsidies.

RI 95 Inheritance tax—business and agricultural relief. (see IHT section, post)

RI 96 Trading loss relief—late claims.

RI 97 *Relief for trading losses on unquoted shares—transition to new rules.* (obsolete)

RI 98 *Formulae to compute stock provisions and write downs.* (obsolete)

RI 99 *Expenses rule—allowable business travel.* (obsolete)

RI 100 *Relief for maintenance payments under FA 1988 s 38.* (obsolete)

RI 101 Variation of inheritances following a death. (see IHT section, post)

RI 102 Californian tax—tax credit relief.

RI 103 *Redundancy payments and provisions—Schedule D Cases I and II.* (superseded)

RI 104 Qualifying indexed securities. (obsolete)

RI 105 Travelling expenses of directors and employees earning £8,500 a year or more—Concession A4.

RI 106 *Capital allowances: meaning of ''colony''.* (superseded)

RI 107 Corporation tax: company purchase scheme.

RI 108 Interest rates and currency swaps: reduced importance of Concession C17.

RI 109 *VAT repayments received by sports clubs.* (superseded)

RI 110 IHT: valuation of assets at the date of death. (see IHT section, post)

RI 111 Interest relief: provision of certificates of interest paid to borrowers.

RI 112 Schedule E: relocation packages.

RI 113 Foreign exchange and financial instruments: currency contracts—transitional rules. (obsolete)

RI 114 *Foreign exchange and financial instruments: grandfathering and other elections.* (obsolete)

RI 115 Loss relief: cessation adjustments—concession A88. (obsolete)

RI 116 *Schedule D Case I: franchise payments.* (superseded)

RI 117 *Schedule D Case I: pre-trading expenditure.* (superseded)

RI 118 *Unapproved retirement benefit schemes.* (superseded)

RI 119 Capital gains tax: private residence relief—garden or grounds.

RI 120 Enterprise investment scheme: qualifying trades.

RI 1 (November 1991) *Expenditure on training courses for business proprietors*

There is some uncertainty whether the cost of proprietors of a business attending a training course, directly related to the business activity, is deductible in arriving at the profits chargeable to tax under Schedule D Cases I or II.

Where attendance at a course is intended to give business proprietors new expertise, knowledge or skills which they lack, it brings into existence an intangible asset which is of enduring benefit to the business. [The Revenue] take the view that the expenditure is therefore of a capital nature, and deduction is prohibited by TA 1988 s 74(1)(f).

On the other hand, where attendance is merely to update expertise etc which proprietors already possess, the expenditure is normally regarded as revenue expenditure and will be deductible if it satisfies the ''wholly and exclusively ... for the purposes of the trade'' test in TA 1988 s 74(1)(a).

Note—This interpretation is no longer current.
Commentary—*Simon's Direct Tax Service* **B3.1242**.

RI 2 (November 1991) *Business loans used to fund an overdrawn account—revaluation of business assets—TA 1988 s 74(1)(a)*

Where interest is incurred wholly and exclusively for the purposes of a business, it may normally be deducted as an expense in computing the profits or gains arising from the trade, profession or vocation. No deduction is due if the loan upon which the interest is paid is used to fund the proprietor's overdrawn current/capital account.

In considering whether a proprietor has overdrawn his current/capital account, a distinction is drawn between accumulated realised profits (both capital and revenue) upon which a proprietor is free to draw, and anticipated profits. Anticipated profits have not crystallised, do not represent a cash item and may never be realised; they are therefore disregarded in considering whether a proprietor's account is overdrawn.

A revaluation of business assets in advance of disposal is such an anticipation of profit and is therefore disregarded in considering whether a current/capital account is overdrawn. A disallowance of the relevant interest cannot be avoided by crediting revaluation surpluses to an overdrawn account.

RI 3 (November 1991) *Interest charged to work in progress: property development companies*

Unless yearly interest is payable in the UK on an advance from a bank carrying on a bona fide banking business in the UK, it is disallowable in computing a company's Case I profits (TA 1988 s 337(2), (3)).

Where a company trading as a property developer charges such disallowable interest straight to work in progress—so that it does not immediately touch the profit and loss account—and that is in accordance with correct accounting practice, the interest need not be disallowed in the Case I computation until it is effectively charged in the profit and loss account as part of the cost of sales. Records of such interest should be kept, and sufficient information provided to the inspector to ensure that the correct disallowance is made when the interest is charged. If the interest qualifies for relief under TA 1988 s 338 (allowance of charges on income), it is allowable against total profits for the period in which it was paid, as reduced by any other relief from tax other than group relief.

Where interest which is allowable for Case I purposes is charged straight to work in progress in accordance with correct accounting practice, a deduction is not available for that interest until it is charged to the profit and loss account as part of the cost of sales.

Note—For accounting periods ending after 31 March 1996, subject to transitional provisions in FA 1996 Sch 15, the allowability of interest payable by a company is governed by the loan relationships provisions of FA 1996 Pt IV Chapter II (ss 80–105).

RI 4 (November 1991) *Purchase by a company of its own shares: legal expenses—TA 1988 ss 74, 219*

Legal (or other) expenditure incurred by a trading company on the redemption, repayment or purchase of its own shares is considered to be capital expenditure, either on general principles or by reference to TA 1988 s 74(1)(*f*) (deduction for capital not allowable). It is capital expenditure on general principles because it is part of the cost of changing the share capital of the company. It is also a sum in respect of any capital withdrawn, within the terms of TA 1988 s 74(1)(*f*).

The expenditure is also likely to be disallowable by virtue of TA 1988 s 74(1)(*a*), because it is not wholly and exclusively laid out or expended for the purposes of the trade. Even where a redemption etc is made ''wholly or mainly for the purposes of benefiting a trade carried on by the company'' within the terms of TA 1988 s 219 (purchase of own shares by unquoted trading company), it does not follow that the related legal costs are wholly and exclusively for the purposes of the trade.

Commentary—*Simon's Direct Tax Service* **B3.1321; D2.507**.

RI 5 (November 1991) *Rollover relief for business assets: extension of time limit—TCGA 1992 s 152(3)*

TCGA 1992 s 152(3) requires the new assets to be acquired, or an unconditional contract for acquisition to be entered into, during a period beginning one year before and ending three years after the date of disposal of the old asset. The Board has discretion under the legislation to extend the statutory time limit. Each case is judged on its merits.

The length of the extension sought is one factor to take into account, but not necessarily the most important. Where it is shown that taxpayers had a firm intention to acquire the new asset(*s*) within the time limit and were prevented by circumstances outside their control, the Board will consider sympathetically a request for extension of the time limit provided the new assets are acquired as soon as reasonably possible.

Commentary—*Simon's Direct Tax Service* **C3.305.**

RI 6 (November 1991) *Retirement relief: ill-health suffered by someone other than claimant—TCGA 1992 s 163, Sch 6 para 3*

The relevant test for capital gains tax ill-health retirement relief is that claimants have ceased work of the kind which they previously undertook and because of their ill-health they are likely to remain permanently incapable of engaging again in work of the same kind.

[The Revenue's] view is that the retirement must be because of the claimant's own ill-health. It may be, for example, that a partnership business is sold because the ill-health of one partner has forced that partner to retire. While that partner may satisfy the necessary medical conditions and obtain relief, no other partners will be entitled to relief unless they satisfy the necessary medical conditions in their own right.

Commentary—*Simon's Direct Tax Service* **C3.603.**

RI 7 (November 1991) *Rollover relief for business assets: assets not immediately taken into use—TCGA 1992 s 152(1)*

TCGA 1992 s 152(1) applies to assets ''which on the acquisition are taken into use ...''. The phrase ''on the acquisition'' is not defined for s 152(1) purposes but is taken to mean the earliest date upon which the taxpayer could reasonably be expected to take the asset into use. While this cannot be earlier than the time when possession is obtained, it may, in some circumstances, be later.

If the asset is ready to use when acquired [the Revenue] would expect it to be brought into use without delay if it is to qualify for relief. If the asset is not ready for use, relief would not be denied solely on the grounds that it was not brought into use as soon as acquired, provided all reasonable steps were taken to make it ready for use as soon as practicable after acquisition and it was then brought into use without unnecessary delay.

Commentary—*Simon's Direct Tax Service* **C3.304.**

RI 8 (November 1991) *Holdover relief for gifts: agricultural property with development value—IHTA 1984 Part V Ch II, TCGA 1992 s 165, Sch 7 para 1*

[The Revenue] are sometimes asked whether the fact that agricultural property transferred had ''hope'' or ''development'' value would either preclude or restrict capital gains tax gifts holdover relief.

Gifts holdover relief is available under TCGA 1992 s 165, as extended by Sch 7 para 1, where agricultural property is disposed of which is not used for the purposes of a trade carried on by the person making the disposal. Relief is available if, amongst other things, the asset transferred is agricultural property as defined by IHTA 1984 Part V Ch II. Inheritance tax agricultural property relief is available in respect of the agricultural value of property transferred but not in respect of any ''hope'' or ''development'' value which is inherent in the property at the time of its transfer.

In contrast to the inheritance tax legislation the capital gains tax relief is given by reference to the nature of the asset transferred, not the value of the asset transferred. Provided that it is agricultural property within IHTA 1984 Part V Ch II, relief is, in principle, available on the whole of the gain, not just that part which reflects the agricultural value of the property transferred.

Commentary—*Simon's Direct Tax Service* **C3.505, I3.612.**

RI 9 (November 1991) *Rebasing elections: assets held by same person in different capacities*

CAPITAL GAINS TAX—REBASING—EFFECT OF TCGA 1992 S 35(5) ELECTION—TCGA 1992 SS 35(5), (7), 59, 69(1)—STATEMENT D12—STATEMENT OF PRACTICE SP 1/89

For capital gains tax purposes, where an asset is disposed of on or after 6 April 1988, only the gain or loss arising since 31 March 1982 is chargeable or allowable. Assets held on 31 March 1982 are deemed to have been sold and reacquired at market value on that date. However, for computational purposes, a comparison is made between the gain or loss based on the 31 March 1982 value and the gain or loss on the basis of historic cost: only the smaller being chargeable or allowable.

A taxpayer may elect under TCGA 1992 s 35(5) to have all gains or losses computed solely on the 31 March 1982 basis, with no comparison being made, so that pre-1982 records may be dispensed with. An election made by a person in one capacity does not cover disposals made in another capacity (TCGA 1992 s 35(7)). [The Revenue have] been asked whether an election made by a partner in respect of partnership assets also applies to assets held privately by the same individual.

Partners have individual interests in the underlying partnership assets, and each may therefore make an election under TCGA 1992 s 35(5) in respect of any disposal of their interest in partnership assets. It is not necessary for all partners to make elections. Where a person is a member of more than one partnership, a separate election is required for each partnership.

An election made in respect of partnership assets is made by a person in the capacity of partner. So a separate election is required for assets held privately. In the same way, an election for assets held privately will not apply to assets held in the capacity of partner.

An election made by a person as an individual will apply to all assets owned by that person in that capacity. So where assets are held jointly (but without the existence of a partnership) each individual's share or holding would be covered by such an election. And if the individual is a sole trader, an election will apply to the business assets held as a sole trader, as well as those held privately.

If assets are held in a fiduciary capacity then it is the ''body of persons'' provided for by TCGA 1992 s 69(1) which is responsible for lodging any election. A separate election is required in respect of each settlement, even if the same body of persons is trustee for more than one settlement. An election made for one settlement would not be binding on any other.

Commentary—*Simon's Direct Tax Service* **C2.604.**
Statements of Practice D12—(Partnerships: assets owned by a partner).
SP 1/79, SP 1/89—(Capital gains tax—partnerships: extension of statement of practice).

RI 10 (February 1992) *Capital allowances: abortive expenditure on plant and machinery—CAA 1990 ss 24, 26, 60*

The side note to CAA 1990 s 60 identifies its application to transactions of hire purchase. However, in certain circumstances this legislation may also apply to abortive capital expenditure incurred on machinery or plant.

A trader may incur capital expenditure on machinery or plant which is never actually owned—perhaps because the buyer withdraws from the supply contract or because the supplier defaults, or for some other reason. In such cases the trader will not qualify for writing down allowance on the expenditure incurred under CAA 1990 s 24 because it will not be possible to satisfy the ''belonging'' condition in s 24(1)(*b*).

CAA 1990 s 60 deals, however, with a trader who incurs capital expenditure on the provision of machinery or plant for the purposes of the trade ''under a contract providing that he shall or may become the owner of the machinery or plant on the performance of the contract''. If such a contract exists. CAA 1990 s 60(1)(*a*) treats the machinery or plant as belonging to the trader.

In many cases, abortive expenditure—for example a deposit paid on machinery which is never actually supplied—may well be incurred under a contract which provides that the taxpayer ''shall or may become the owner''. If so, that expenditure will qualify for writing down allowance by virtue of s 60(1)(*a*).

CAA 1990 s 60(2) will bring the disposal value of the machinery or plant into account at the time when the taxpayer ceases to be entitled to the benefit of the contract without becoming the owner of the machinery or plant (CAA 1990 s 24(6)(*c*)(i)). The disposal value will be calculated by reference to the rules in CAA 1990 s 26(1).

Commentary—*Simon's Direct Tax Service* **B2.305.**

RI 11 (February 1992) *Rollover relief for business assets: grant of options over land—TCGA 1992 ss 21(1), 144, 152(1), 155*

An option over land gives the grantee an equitable interest in the land itself during the lifetime of the option. It follows that the grantor has made a disposal of part of his equitable interest in the land. For capital gains purposes, however, the grant of an option is treated, by virtue of TCGA 1992 s 144, as a separate disposal of the option itself.

Provided rollover relief would be due on the disposal of the underlying land, which is the subject of the option, it may also be available in respect of the gain which arises on the grant of the option. [It should be remembered] though that for rollover relief purposes land has to be occupied as well as used for the purposes of the claimant's trade in order to qualify for relief.

Commentary—*Simon's Direct Tax Service* **C3.303.**

RI 12 (February 1992) *Interest relief: loans to invest in close companies—TA 1988 ss 360, 363(2)(c)*

A loan to an individual which is applied in acquiring convertible loan stock in a close company is applied "in lending money to such a close company". Interest paid by the individual on the loan qualifies for relief under TA 1988 s 360 provided the other conditions for the granting of relief are satisfied.

One of the other conditions for the granting of relief under s 360(3)(*c*) is that the individual does not recover any capital from the company in the period from the application of the loan to the payment of interest. The recovery of capital from the company is defined at TA 1988 s 363(2) so as to include at sub-para (*c*) an "amount or value for assigning any debt due to him from the close company".

The conversion of the loan stock to ordinary share capital in the close company is such an assignment of a debt due to the individual from the close company. The loan stock is assigned to the company in exchange for shares. The individual has therefore made a recovery of capital from the company and, consequently, interest paid by the individual upon the loan applied in acquiring the loan stock will not qualify for relief under TA 1988 s 360 after the date that loan stock is converted.

Commentary—*Simon's Direct Tax Service* **E1.551.**

RI 13 (February 1992) *Incidental costs of obtaining loan finance: life insurance premiums*

[The Revenue are] sometimes asked whether premiums on a life insurance policy taken out by a trader and required as a condition of obtaining loan finance are "incidental costs" allowable in computing Case I profits under TA 1988 s 77.

TA 1988 s 77 is not regarded as providing specific statutory relief for such premiums as the "incidental costs" of obtaining loan finance. "Incidental costs" are defined in s 77(6) as "fees, commissions, advertising, printing and other incidental matters". The expenses listed are viewed as forming a class which would include any incidental costs of taking out a life insurance policy but not the cost of the policy itself, that is, the premiums.

Note—This interpretation is no longer current.
Commentary—*Simon's Direct Tax Service* **B3.1321**.

RI 14 (February 1992) *Winding up of BES companies—TA 1988 ss 293, 574, TCGA 1992 s 24(2)*

When a company carrying on a trade which has issued shares under the business expansion scheme (BES) runs into financial difficulties and eventually ceases trading, the question arises as to whether the company ceases to satisfy the conditions for being a qualifying company for BES relief purposes. And whether by virtue of TA 1988 s 293(6) (the effect of winding up or dissolution) the disqualification can be ignored.

A company ceases to satisfy the conditions for being a qualifying company when it ceases to trade. The only way it can then maintain its qualifying status is to initiate winding up (TA 1988 s 293(6)). Where this is done as promptly as circumstances permit, the Revenue would ignore any short gap between the cessation of trading and the passing of the winding up resolution. Where winding up is not initiated after cessation of trading the company will lose its qualifying status and the shareholders will cease to be entitled to BES relief in respect of their investments in the company.

The appointment of an Administrative Receiver has no effect on the company's status—it is not the same as commencing proceedings for winding up—so the benefit of TA 1988 s 293(6) does not accrue.

Where shareholders cease to be entitled to BES relief in these circumstances they may be able to make claims under TCGA 1992 s 24(2) on the basis that their shares have become of negligible value. It may then be possible for them to claim relief from income tax under TA 1988 s 574—relief for losses on unquoted shares—in respect of the resulting capital loss.

Note—BES was abolished from 1-1-94 and replaced by EIS; see TA 1988 ss 289–312. It may be advisable to consult the Revenue about the application of this interpretation to EIS.

RI 15 (February 1992) *Interest relief: joint loans to spouses—TA 1988 ss 360, 362*

It may happen that a joint loan is taken out by a husband and wife but that only one spouse meets the qualifying conditions for tax relief in respect of the interest paid on the loan.

Where payments of interest on a joint loan are fully satisfied by the spouse meeting the qualifying conditions—even if the joint liability is satisfied out of a joint account—relief may be given in full to that spouse.

Commentary—*Simon's Direct Tax Service* **E1.547, 550**.

RI 16 (February 1992) *Close company loans to participators etc—application to loans carrying a commercial rate of interest—TA 1988 s 419*

Where a loan is made by a close company to its controlling participator at a commercial rate of interest the question sometimes arises whether the loan comes within the exemption in TA 1988 s 419(1) for loans made in the ordinary course of a business which includes the lending of money.

The exemption in s 419(1) is really two separate tests—a company must carry on a business of lending money and the loan must be made in the ordinary course of that business. As regards the first test there is judicial guidance in the case of *Steen v Law*—

> ''In their Lordships' opinion ... 'the lending of money' to be part of the ordinary business of a company, must be what may be called a lending of money in general, in the sense, for example, that moneylending is part of the ordinary business of a registered moneylender or bank.''

A single loan made by a company to a participator, even on commercial terms, is not adequate evidence of the existence of a commercially constituted business of lending money. Since if the first test fails, the second test automatically becomes redundant. Even in other cases where the first test is met, a loan to a participator still has to be made in the ordinary course of the business, and that would not be the case where the size, terms or conditions of the loan differed from those which normally applied.

Commentary—*Simon's Direct Tax Service* **D3.404**.

RI 17 (May 1992) *Loss relief claims: order of priority*

Note—This interpretation is obsolete following the amendments made to TA 1988 s 380 by FA 1994 s 209 (1).

RI 18 (May 1992) *Financial loss allowances: treatment as trading receipts—TA 1988 s 18*

Members of certain public bodies receive financial loss allowances for loss of remunerative time while engaged on the duties of those bodies. People serving as jurors are one example, and others include members of certain local authorities in Great Britain, of certain National Health Service and nursing bodies, and people serving as magistrates or Justices of the Peace.

Where the recipient is carrying on a trade or profession and received the allowance to compensate for loss of profit, we treat it as a receipt of that trade or profession and accordingly assessable to tax under Schedule D Case I or II.

Note—This interpretation has been superseded by the Business Income Manual BIM40475.
Commentary—*Simon's Direct Tax Service* **B3.931**.

RI 19 (May 1992) *Herd basis: change in persons carrying on farming business*

TA 1988 Sch 5 para 2 permits a farmer to elect for the ''herd basis'' to be applied to particular classes of production herd which that farmer keeps.

Where there is a change in the persons carrying on the farming trade within TA 1988 s 113(1), [the Revenue] consider that there is a different ''farmer'' for Sch 5 purposes after the change. Such a change therefore brings to an end the effect of any herd basis elections made by the ''old'' farmer, and the ''new'' farmer has a fresh right to elect for herd basis treatment, subject to the time limit in Sch 5 para 2(3).

It is not relevant whether an election under TA 1988 s 113(2) is made.

Note—This interpretation has been superseded by the Business Income Manual BIM55610.
Commentary—*Simon's Direct Tax Service* **B3.516; E5.314**.

RI 20 (May 1992) *Mobile telephone: reimbursement by employee for private use*

There are new rules for taxing the private use of a mobile telephone provided by an employer. The cash equivalent of this benefit is reduced to nil if, among other things, the employee is required to and does reimburse the full cost of such private use (TA 1988 s 159A(3)(b)). [The Revenue] have been asked whether the employer must impose this requirement before private use occurs.

In [the Revenue's] view, the employer cannot impose a requirement retrospectively. But there may be cases where an employer could not reasonably have foreseen that taxable private use would occur so as to have imposed the necessary requirement for reimbursement. If therefore it can be shown that the telephone was provided for business use only, and that a particular non-business call was entirely due to an exceptional and genuine emergency, reimbursement for that call will be regarded as satisfying the requirement condition.

...

Commentary—*Simon's Direct Tax Service* **E4.617**.
Note—TA 1988 s 159A was repealed by FA 1999 and replaced by TA 1988 s 155AA, which has been repealed by ITEPA 2003 s 722; see now ITEPA 2003 s 319.

RI 21 (May 1992) *Close investment-holding companies*

A close company is a close investment-holding company (CIC) for any accounting period unless, throughout the period, it exists—as a question of fact—wholly or mainly for any of the purposes specified in TA 1988 s 13A(2). A principal effect of CIC status is that the company is not entitled to claim the small companies' rate of corporation tax for that accounting period.

A company in liquidation is normally a CIC. This is because a company in liquidation exists for the purpose of winding up its affairs and distributing its assets to shareholders. Although during the winding up the company might carry on a trade or business that it had carried on previously, it is unlikely that this will be other than incidental to its main purpose of winding up its affairs.

There is however some uncertainty as to the application of s 13A(4). This provides that where a company in liquidation was not a CIC for the accounting period immediately before the commencement of winding up, that status automatically continues for the first accounting period after the commencement of winding up. A company which had previously carried on a trade but which ceased to carry it on some time before the commencement of winding up, will normally be a CIC for the accounting period immediately before the commencement of winding up. It is unlikely therefore to come within s 13A(4).

It is most unlikely, in any event, that a company in liquidation would be found not to be a CIC for any accounting period following the first accounting period after the commencement of winding up.

Note—This interpretation is now obsolete.
Commentary—*Simon's Direct Tax Service* **D3.202**.

RI 22 (May 1992) *Private residence exemption: unrelated joint occupiers—TCGA 1992 s 222*

There is some uncertainty as to whether joint owner occupiers of a property who are not husband and wife are entitled to full private residence relief. [The Revenue] take the view that in general they will be entitled to relief.

Where people jointly own a home [the Revenue] consider each to have an undivided share in all of the property—see *Tod v Mudd* [[1987] STC 141] for a case involving tenants in common. If they have unrestricted access to the whole property, even though some areas may in practice not be used by all of the joint owners, private residence relief may be available under TCGA 1992 s 222. Provided it is their only or main residence, relief will be available on each owner's share of any gain on disposal in the normal way.

Occasionally property in joint ownership may be divided into separate and identifiable homes, each exclusively occupied. In these cases the statute does not provide relief in respect of any gain on the part not occupied by each owner. Concession D26 [now obsolete] may however enable joint owners to exchange their interests so as to acquire sole ownership of the part each occupies without a charge to capital gains tax.

Commentary—*Simon's Direct Tax Service* **C2.1303**.

RI 23 (May 1992) *Qualifying corporate bonds given to a charity—TCGA 1992 ss 116(10), 257*

The normal share reorganisation rules of TCGA 1992 ss 127–130 do not apply if qualifying corporate bonds are issued in exchange for shares. Instead TCGA 1992 s 116(10) requires the computation of the gain that would have arisen if the shares had been sold at their market value at the date of reorganisation. This gain is deferred and accrues on a later disposal of the qualifying corporate bonds.

Although the point has already received some publicity, there remains some doubt as to [the Revenue's] views where there is a transfer of those bonds to a charity. [The Revenue] can confirm that in [their] view, if the disposal is to a charity such as to come within TCGA 1992 s 257, there will no charge on the deferred gain either on the donor or on the charity on a subsequent disposal of the bonds.

Commentary—*Simon's Direct Tax Service* **C2.804**.

RI 24 (August 1992) *Business expansion scheme: private rented housing companies*

Note—BES was abolished from 1-1-94 and replaced by EIS; see TA 1988 ss 289–312.

RI 25 (August 1992) *Post-cessation professional indemnity insurance premiums—TA 1988 s 105*

Commentary—*Simon's Direct Tax Service* **B4.225**.
Note—This interpretation is superseded by Revenue Interpretation RI 130.

RI 26 (August 1992) *Indexation and rebasing: assets acquired by no gain/no loss disposal after 31 March 1982*

CAPITAL GAINS TAX—INDEXATION AND REBASING—ENHANCEMENT EXPENDITURE ON ASSETS DEEMED TO BE HELD ON 31 MARCH 1982 BY THE PERSON MAKING THE DISPOSAL—TCGA 1992 SS 35(3), 38(1)(*B*), 55(5), (6), 56(2), SCH 3 PARA 1

The general capital gains rebasing rule is that where, on or after 6 April 1988, a person disposes of an asset which they held on 31 March 1982 (and the disposal is not a no gain/no loss disposal), the gain or loss is in the first instance calculated by reference to 31 March 1982 market value. Where the person making the disposal did not personally hold the asset on 31 March 1982, but acquired the asset on a no gain/no loss disposal (or indirectly through an unbroken sequence of no gain/no loss disposals) from a person who did hold the asset on 31 March 1982, the person making the eventual disposal is treated as having held the asset on 31 March 1982 for rebasing purposes. This is the effect of TCGA 1992 Sch 3 para 1. There is a similar provision for indexation purposes in TCGA 1992 s 55(5), (6).

[The Revenue] have been asked what the position is where a person is deemed to have held an asset on 31 March 1982 for indexation or rebasing purposes, and enhancement expenditure was incurred after 31 March 1982 by a previous owner of the asset. The answer is that where for indexation or rebasing purposes a person is deemed to have held an asset on 31 March 1982, that person can also be treated as having incurred expenditure which was in fact incurred after that date by a previous holder of the asset. That expenditure can accordingly be taken into account for indexation or rebasing purposes by the person making the eventual disposal, provided the general conditions for relief in TCGA 1992 s 38(1)(*b*) are met.

EXAMPLE

	£
1 January 1980—acquisition by A	10,000
31 March 1982—market value	12,000
1 January 1985—enhancement expenditure	3,000
31 December 1985—no gain/no loss disposal from A to B	
31 December 1991—third party disposal by B	30,000

The enhancement expenditure incurred by A as the actual owner of the asset is treated as incurred by B where for indexation or rebasing purposes B is deemed to have held the asset on 31 March 1982

The rebasing calculation by reference to 31 March 1982 market value is accordingly—

	£	£
Disposal proceeds		30,000
31 March 1982 market value	12,000	
Enhancement expenditure	3,000	
		15,000
		15,000
Indexation allowance		
on £12,000 (March 1982–December 1991)		
0·708 × £12,000	8,496	
on £3,000 (January 1985–December 1991)		
0·488 × £3,000	1,464	
		9,960
Gain		£5,040

For the purposes of the comparison by reference to historic cost in TCGA 1992 s 35(3) B takes over A's actual cost (£10,000, plus enhancement expenditure £3,000). The indexation included in B's allowable cost on the no gain/no loss disposal by TCGA 1992 s 56(2) is stripped out by TCGA 1992 s 55(6)(*b*), and for indexation purposes B is treated as having held the asset on 31 March 1982.

The calculation by reference to historic cost is accordingly—

	£	£
Disposal proceeds		30,000
Cost (from A)		13,000
		17,000
Indexation allowance		
on £12,000 (March 1982–December 1991)		
0·708 × £12,000	8,496	
on £3,000 (January 1985–December 1991)		
0·488 × £3,000	1,464	
		9,960
Gain		£7,040

The chargeable gain is £5,040 (the smaller of £5,040 and £7,040).

Commentary—*Simon's Direct Tax Service* **C2.607**.

RI 27 (August 1992) *BES shares issued before 19 March 1986: indexation allowance on disposal*

Note—BES was abolished from 1-1-94 and replaced by EIS; see TA 1988 ss 289–312.

RI 28 (August 1992) *Rollover relief for business assets: furnished holiday lettings*

CAPITAL GAINS TAX—ROLLOVER RELIEF—COMMERCIAL LETTING OF FURNISHED HOLIDAY ACCOMMODATION IN EXCESS OF 30 DAYS—TA 1988 SS 503, 504—TCGA 1992 S 152

Rollover relief is available on the disposal of property which has been let commercially as furnished holiday accommodation provided it meets the conditions set out in TA 1988 ss 503, 504.

The conditions to be satisfied in the year include—

- the accommodation is to be available for commercial letting to the public for periods which amount in aggregate to 140 days or more;
- the accommodation is let commercially for 70 days or more; and
- for a period of at least seven months which includes the above period when it is commercially let, it is not normally in the same occupation continuously for periods exceeding 31 days.

Many people in holiday areas let their properties out during the main holiday period on a short-term basis but during the quieter part of the year let on a longer-term basis. We have been asked whether these longer lettings—which may be to the same person for more than 31 days—will of themselves, preclude a claim to rollover relief when the property is subsequently disposed of.

Provided the letting during the main holiday period satisfies the requirements of TA 1988 ss 503, 504, the longer lettings in any other part of the same year of assessment will not preclude relief. We regard the whole of the income derived from the property for that year as arising from commercially let furnished holiday accommodation. So rollover relief will generally be due on the property, subject to the other conditions for the relief being satisfied.

Commentary—*Simon's Direct Tax Service* **C3.319**.

RI 29 (November 1992) *Investment managers acting as agents for non-residents*

Commentary—*Simon's Direct Tax Service* **B3.118.**
Statement of Practice SP 15/91—(Treatment of investment managers and their overseas clients).
Note—TMA 1970 s 78 is repealed by FA 1995 s 162, Sch 29 Pt VIII (16).

RI 30 (November 1992) *Insurance agents' commission receivable on indemnity terms*

Frequently, when an insurance company accepts a new policy the selling agent becomes immediately entitled to most or all of the total commission due on the policy. That commission is calculated on the assumption that the policy will not be allowed to lapse at an early date. If, however, the policy lapses within a specified period the agent may have to repay part of the initial commission received. When should commission which is potentially repayable be recognised as income for tax purposes? And is a provision in respect of the potential liability to repay allowable?

*The time at which such commission is recognised as income for tax purposes depends on the agency contract terms. Under most contracts, however, the agent has done substantially all the work required by the contract when the policy is sold. For instance, the agent is usually entitled at that point to retain the initial commission should the policy run the required term even if the agency is terminated. In all such cases the full initial commission receivable should be recognised as income in the accounting period in which the policy is sold (*IRC v Gardner Mountain and D'Ambrumenil [29 TC 69]*).*

*Where the commission is recognised as income at the outset, a reasonably accurate provision will be accepted for the contingent liability to repay the commission should the policy lapse. A proper valuation rather than a ''speculative estimate'' is required (*Owen v Southern Railway of Peru *[36 TC 602, 634]). For instance the calculation of the provision should take into account the lapse rate amongst customers and the proportion of commission that usually has to be repaid on the relevant policy.*

Note—This interpretation is now obsolete.
Commentary—*Simon's Direct Tax Service* **B3.916, 920**.

RI 31 (November 1992) *Waste disposal sites: meaning of "site preparation expenditure"*

TA 1988 s 91B provides relief for site preparation expenditure in relation to waste disposal sites. [The Revenue] have been asked whether this permits a deduction for expenditure that is of a capital nature. In particular, does it include costs incurred before the disposal licence is granted?

In the case of Rolfe v Wimpey Waste Management Ltd [[1989] STC 454] it was held that all expenditure on preparing or making good a landfall site was capital. TA 1988 s 91B was introduced specifically to permit the deduction of an ''allowable amount'', calculated by reference to site preparation expenditure for which relief would not otherwise be available. (A deduction for restoration expenditure is also permitted, under TA 1988 s 91A.)

Site preparation expenditure includes costs incurred before the disposal licence is granted and, in particular, includes expenses associated with obtaining the licence itself. This is subject to the condition that ''... a relevant licence which is then in force ...'' is held at the time the person first deposits waste materials on the site in question (TA 1988 s 91B(1)(b)).

Expenditure qualifying for capital allowances is not covered by this section and neither is the cost of acquiring the site itself.

Note—This interpretation has been superseded by the Business Income Manual BIM67445.
Commentary—*Simon's Direct Tax Service* **B3.1345**.

RIs

RI 32 (November 1992) *Pre-trading expenditure: expenses incurred by another person*

When a person incurs expenses for the purposes of a trade before trading begins, that person may claim relief for the expenses in the first income tax year of assessment. In the case of a company, the expenses are treated as if they were incurred on the first day of trading.

The expenses, or "pre-trading expenditure", must have been paid out in the five years before the start of the trade (or three years if the trade started before 31 March 1989). They must also be such that they would have been allowable on normal principles if they had been paid out after trading began.

[The Revenue] are sometimes asked if relief for pre-trading expenditure is available on expenses incurred by another person in setting up a trade. It is [the Revenue's] view that relief is not available in these circumstances.

Two examples may help to illustrate the point. If an individual incurs expenses for the purposes of a trade, and then incorporates when trading begins, the company is not entitled to relief for the individual's pre-trading expenditure. Similarly, if one company in a group incurs pre-trading expenditure, and a fellow group company then starts to carry on that trade, neither company will benefit from the relief. In both cases the person incurring the expenditure never begins to trade, and the person trading does not incur the expenditure.

Note—This interpretation is now obsolete.
Commentary—*Simon's Direct Tax Service* **B3.1204**.

RI 33 (November 1992) *Capital allowances for plant or machinery: glasshouses*

In the past couple of years, there has been a great deal of publicity suggesting that in the light of general case law developments [the Revenue] accept that all glasshouses are plant and thus qualify for allowances under CAA 1990 s 24. This is not the case. [The Revenue] consider the majority of glasshouse structures to be the premises or setting in which a grower's trade is carried on, and on that basis that they qualify for agricultural buildings allowance.

However [they] do accept that, in some cases, a glasshouse unit and its attendant machinery are interdependent, forming a single entity which will function as apparatus within a grower's business and as such will be plant.

These units will be of an extremely sophisticated design, including extensive computer controlled equipment, without which the structure cannot operate to achieve the optimum artificial growing environment for the particular crops involved. The equipment will have been permanently installed during the construction of the glasshouses and will normally include a computer system which monitors and controls boiler and piped heating systems, temperature and humidity controls, automatic ventilation equipment and automatic thermal or shade screens.

The availability of machinery and plant allowances, which as with other aspects of the tax system, is of course always under review, will nevertheless continue to depend on the precise facts of the case. This will therefore be a matter for discussion with local inspectors.

Note—This interpretation has been superseded by the Capital Allowances Manual CA22090..
Commentary—*Simon's Direct Tax Service* **B2.306, 314**.

RI 34 (November 1992) *Small capital distributions: direction under TCGA 1992 ss 122(2), 123*

The receipt of a capital distribution from a company in respect of shares in that company is treated as a part disposal of those shares (TCGA 1992 s 122). The inspector may make a direction under TCGA 1992 s 122(2) if he or she is satisfied that the distribution is small compared with the value of the shares. In this context [the Revenue] consider the word "small" to mean 5 per cent or less. The effect of the direction is that the distribution is not treated as a disposal but the amount received is deducted from the recipient's allowable expenditure on the shares.

It is possible that a recipient may want to have a small distribution treated as a disposal and would prefer the inspector not to make a direction under s 122(2). This could be advantageous if, for example, any gain would be covered by the annual exempt amount. [The Revenue] will not insist on the application of s 122(2) if the recipient would prefer to have the distribution treated as a disposal. In practice this is most likely to apply to the sale of rights nil paid which TCGA 1992 s 123 treats as a capital distribution.

Commentary—*Simon's Direct Tax Service* **C2.720**.

RI 35 (November 1992) *Schemes of reconstruction*

Where there is a scheme of reconstruction or amalgamation (and the relevant detailed statutory conditions are met) the shareholders can obtain paper for paper rollover treatment in respect of their shares under TCGA 1992 s 136.

[The Revenue] have been asked if this provision can apply to the following transactions carried out as a scheme of arrangement under the Companies Act 1985 s 425—

- *the shares in company A are cancelled;*
- *new shares in company A are issued to a new company, B;*
- *B issues its own shares to the former members of company A pro rata to their holdings in A.*

[The Revenue] confirm that [they] would regard such a scheme as a scheme of reconstruction for the purposes of the capital gains provisions.

[It] should be noted that the Order under the Companies Act 1985 s 425 may be liable to ad valorem stamp duty.

Clarification can be obtained by sending a copy of the draft order to Paul West, The Stamp Office Information and Compliance Section, Ridgeworth House, Liverpool Gardens, Worthing, West Sussex BN11 1XP.

Note—This interpretation is now obsolete.
Commentary—*Simon's Direct Tax Service* **C2.726**.

RI 36 (November 1992) *Qualifying corporate bonds: devolution on death—TCGA 1992 ss 62, 116*

If qualifying corporate bonds (QCBs) are issued in exchange for shares or securities which are not QCBs and TCGA 1992 ss 127–130 would otherwise apply, TCGA 1992 s 116 requires a computation of the gain that would have arisen if the shares or securities had been sold at their market value. That gain is held over and released on a later disposal of the QCBs.

QCBs with a held over gain may be owned at the date of death and form part of the assets of which the deceased person was competent to dispose. TCGA 1992 s 62(1) provides that these assets are acquired by the personal representatives or other persons on whom they devolve but shall not be deemed to be disposed of by the deceased. Therefore the death of the holder of the QCBs will not trigger the release of any held over gain. The market value of the QCBs will, however, form part of the deceased's estate for inheritance tax purposes.

In [the Revenue's] view, the held over gain is not released if the personal representatives dispose of the QCBs or if they transfer the QCBs to the legatees. Neither would the charge be released on a later disposal by the legatees. The held over gain is in effect wiped out by the death.

The position is different if the share reorganisation to which TCGA 1992 ss 127–130 would otherwise have applied occurs after the shares and securities have been acquired by the personal representatives. In that case the held over gain must be computed. If the personal representatives then dispose of the QCBs the gain is released in the normal way: TCGA 1992 s 116(10)(*b*). If they transfer the QCBs to the legatees the gain is not released: TCGA 1992 s 116(11). However, the gain will be released on a later disposal of the QCBs by the legatees.

Commentary—*Simon's Direct Tax Service* **C2.804**.

RI 37 (February 1993) *Set-off of management expenses against surplus franked investment income*

CORPORATION TAX—INVESTMENT COMPANIES—TIME LIMIT FOR CLAIM TO SET OFF MANAGEMENT EXPENSES AGAINST SURPLUS FRANKED INVESTMENT INCOME—TA 1988 SS 75(3), 242

TA 1988 s 242 provides for a company to claim that its surplus franked investment income (FII) should be treated as profits chargeable to corporation tax so that losses, management expenses etc can effectively be set off against the surplus FII. The tax credit included in the FII is then payable to the company. TA 1988 s 242(8)(*b*) states that the time limit for a claim to set off management expenses is six years from the end of the accounting period in which the expenses were incurred.

This time limit does not sit easily with TA 1988 s 75(3) which provides that excess management expenses (including charges paid wholly and exclusively for the purposes of the company's business) for an accounting period are carried forward to the succeeding accounting period and treated for the purposes of s 75 as if they had been disbursed as management expenses for that later accounting period.

Following consideration of a recent decision of the Special Commissioners, for the purpose of the time limit rule in s 242(8)(*b*), amounts treated as management expenses disbursed in a later accounting period by virtue of s 75(3) are treated as incurred in that accounting period.

So, where excess management expenses have been carried forward to a later accounting period, a claim to set them off against surplus FII can be made within six years of the end of that later accounting period, even if the date of claim is more than six years after the end of the period in which they were originally incurred.

Commentary—*Simon's Direct Tax Service* **D2.413**.

RI 38 (February 1993) *Settlements—connected persons and losses—TCGA 1992 ss 18, 69, 71, 286*

Where a loss accrues to a person on making a disposal to a connected person, under TCGA 1992 s 18(3) that loss may only be deducted from gains on other disposals by that person to the same connected person, unless exceptionally s 18(4) applies (gifts to certain associations).

[The Revenue] have been asked several questions about the application and interpretation of the rules in TCGA 1992 ss 18, 286, in cases involving the trustees of settlements.

Are the settlor and the trustees connected at the moment when the settlement comes into existence and the initial property is transferred to the trustees?

Yes. TCGA 1992 s 18(3) applies to a disposal which brings the settlement into existence. It is not restricted to situations where the parties are already connected before the disposal in question.

Are the trustees and beneficiaries connected after the settlor is dead?

No. If the settlor dies, the connection between the trustees and the relatives and spouse of the settlor is broken. Therefore if, for instance, the beneficiaries of the settlement are the children of the late settlor, the trustees are not connected with those beneficiaries, even if one or more of the children are trustees. The basic rule is that the trustees of a settlement are connected with the settlor, and also with any person connected with the settlor (TCGA 1992 s 286(3)). Under TCGA 1992 s 69(1), the trustees are treated as a single and continuing body distinct from the persons who may be the trustees. Therefore in determining whether s 286(3) applies, the identity of the trustees is disregarded.

If the trustees and beneficiaries are connected, does this affect the transfer of losses under TCGA 1992 s 71(2)?

No. On legal advice, [the Revenue] no longer consider the transfer of losses from trustees to beneficiaries under s 71(2) to be inhibited by s 18(3). Therefore where a beneficiary becomes absolutely entitled against the trustees under TCGA 1992 s 71(1) all the unused losses which have arisen to the trustees in respect of property which is or is represented by the property to which the beneficiary becomes entitled, including any loss accruing on the deemed disposal to the beneficiary, are transferred to the beneficiary under s 71(2).

Commentary—*Simon's Direct Tax Service* **C1.508; C2.110**.

RI 39 (February 1993) *Share exchanges partly in the form of qualifying corporate bonds—TCGA 1992 ss 52, 116, 127–130*

Under TCGA 1992 s 116 the normal share reorganisation rules of TCGA 1992 ss 127–130 do not apply if qualifying corporate bonds are issued in exchange for shares. Instead, s 116(10) requires the computation of the gain that would have arisen if the shares had been sold at their market value at the date of reorganisation. The gain is deferred and crystallises on a later disposal of the qualifying corporate bonds. Where only part of the holding of qualifying corporate bonds is disposed of only a corresponding part of the deferred gain crystallises.

Some doubts have been expressed about the position where on a reorganisation, shares are exchanged for a new holding comprised partly of shares (or other chargeable securities) and partly of qualifying corporate bonds.

TCGA 1992 s 116 applies (by virtue of s 116(1)(*b*)) where the new holding comprises both qualifying corporate bonds and shares. Since the definition of ''the new asset'' in s 116(4) refers only to the qualifying corporate bonds received on the exchange, in [the Revenue's] view the provisions in s 116(5), (10) mean that ss 127–130 are only disapplied to the extent that the consideration takes the form of qualifying corporate bonds.

The same general approach applies to transactions other than share exchanges—for instance, a scheme of reconstruction or amalgamation within TCGA 1992 s 136—where, for the purposes of the share reorganisation rules, there is a new holding which consists partly of qualifying corporate bonds. This means that where the new holding comprises both qualifying corporate bonds and shares, the base cost of the original shares is apportioned between the new shares and the qualifying corporate bonds according to their respective market values at the time of the exchange. The apportionment would be on a just and reasonable basis under TCGA 1992 s 52(4).

The new shares inherit the appropriate proportion of the base cost. And the proportion of the gain calculated at the time of the exchange, and attributable by this approach to the qualifying corporate bonds, is deferred and crystallises under s 116(10) on a later disposal of the bonds.

Commentary—*Simon's Direct Tax Service* **C2.804**.

RI 40 (February 1993) *Residence and ordinary residence— meaning of "full-time" employment abroad—TA 1988 s 335*

The residence and ordinary residence of individuals may depend in certain circumstances on whether they are working ''full-time'' in employment abroad. This note gives some guidance on what [the

Revenue] take the term ''full-time'' to mean for this purpose. It is not concerned with any other instances where the term ''full-time'' appears in statute, for example ''full-time working director'' in TA 1988 Part V Ch II.

There are two situations where the point arises—

- TA 1988 s 335 allows accommodation in the UK available for individuals' use to be ignored in deciding their residence status where they work ''full-time'' in employment, the duties of which are, broadly, performed wholly outside the UK;
- Concession A11 provides (inter alia) that an individual who goes abroad for ''full-time'' service under a contract of employment may be treated as not resident and not ordinarily resident on a ''split year'' basis, where other conditions are met.

There is no statutory definition of ''full-time'' in this context, nor any guidance from the courts. The phrase can only therefore be interpreted in accordance with its ordinary, non-technical meaning. Where an individual is working ''full-time'' in an employment will always depend upon the particular facts of the case.

In general terms, where a job involves a standard pattern of hours and an individual is putting in what a layman would clearly recognise as a full working week, [the Revenue] would accept it as full-time. There is no fixed minimum number of hours for this purpose, but 35–40 hours is obviously a typical UK working week.

Some jobs, however, do not have a straightforward structure. There may, for example, be a mixture of round-the-clock working followed by a rest period; or, in the case of sportsmen, days of playing and training interspersed. Some jobs may not have a formal structure with any fixed number of working days. In deciding whether such jobs are full-time employments, [the Revenue] would look at the nature of the job, and, where appropriate, would take account of local conditions and practices in that particular occupation. Someone who had several part-time jobs overseas concurrently might also be accepted as being in full-time employment. If, for example, they had several appointments with the same employer or group of companies, it might be reasonable to aggregate the total time spent on them for the purposes of the full-time test. This approach could also apply where an individual was simultaneously engaged in employment and self-employment abroad.

Where a person has a main employment abroad but also works in the UK in some unconnected occupation (for example, as director of a family company), [the Revenue] would need to consider whether the extent of the UK activities might cast any doubt on the full-time nature of the main employment outside the UK. Again, [the Revenue] would have to look at the facts of the particular case in reaching a decision.

In [the Revenue's] experience there is rarely in practice much difficulty in deciding whether an individual is working full-time. These notes indicate [their] general approach in the minority of cases at the margins where the position may be less clear.

Commentary—*Simon's Direct Tax Service* **E6.122**.
Concession A11—(Residence in the UK: year of commencement or cessation of residence).

RI 41 (February 1993) *Loans to buy into partnerships—interest paid—TA 1988 s 362*

TA 1988 s 362 provides tax relief for interest paid by an individual on a loan used to acquire an interest in a partnership. The question sometimes arises as to whether tax relief on that interest continues to be available when the individual ceases to be a member of the partnership.

TA 1988 s 362(2)(*a*) makes it clear that the individual has to be a member of the partnership throughout the period from the application of the proceeds of the loan until the interest is paid. It follows that there are no circumstances in which relief can be given after the individual has ceased to be a member of the partnership. This is so even where the former partner is unable to withdraw the capital immediately upon leaving the partnership.

Commentary—*Simon's Direct Tax Service* **E1.550**.

RI 42 (May 1993) *Rollover relief for business assets: depreciating assets—land and buildings—TCGA 1992 ss 44, 152–160, 288*

When a trader replaces an asset used in his or her business with another, rollover relief (TCGA 1992 ss 152–160) enables the gain on the old asset to be deducted from the cost of the new asset. The gain is therefore deferred until the new asset is itself disposed of. If, however, the new asset is a depreciating asset, that is one with a predictable life of 60 years or less (TCGA 1992 s 154(7)), then a limit is set on the period of deferment. In these cases, the gain on the old asset is not deducted from the cost of the new asset but is held over until the earliest of three events. These are set out in s 154(2) and are—

- the disposal of the new asset; or
- the cessation of business use of the new asset; or

– the expiry of ten years from the acquisition of the new asset.

[The Revenue] have been asked whether the following assets will be treated as depreciating assets—

– a building constructed on leasehold land where the lease has 60 years or less to run;
– an item of fixed plant or machinery which has become part of a building.

THE BUILDING

[The Revenue] take the view that if the unexpired period of the lease is 60 years or less at the time the building is constructed then the building will be a depreciating asset for rollover relief purposes. Although both general law and the provisions of TCGA 1992 s 288 treat ''land'' as including any building constructed on the land, this treatment is superseded where rollover relief is involved by the provisions of s 155 which treat land and buildings as separate assets. Where a building is constructed on leasehold land it is the length of the trader's interest in that building which is relevant for rollover relief. It cannot exceed the length of time which is left in the lease since, on the expiry of the lease, both land and building must revert to the landlord.

FIXED PLANT AND MACHINERY

If it is clear that an item of fixed plant or machinery has effectively become a part of the building it will be treated as such for rollover purposes. If therefore the building is held either freehold or on a lease with more than 60 years to run when the plant or machinery is installed, then that item will not be regarded as a depreciating asset for rollover purposes.

An item of plant or machinery is normally regarded as a wasting asset (TCGA 1992 s 44) and is therefore a depreciating asset for rollover purposes. However, s 155 distinguishes between fixed plant and machinery as such and fixed plant and machinery which has become part of a building or structure. The distinction will normally be tested by reference to the size and nature of the item in question; how, if at all, it has become attached to the building and how easily it could be removed without damaging the fabric of the building.

Commentary—*Simon's Direct Tax Service* **C3.311**.

RI 43 (May 1993) *Non-resident companies: attribution of gains to UK shareholders—"non-resident groups"—TCGA 1992 ss 13, 14, 171–174, 175(1), 178–180*

In some circumstances gains realised by non-resident companies may be attributed to shareholders who are resident or ordinarily resident in the UK. The main provisions are in TCGA 1992 s 13. The scope of the legislation is not quite as wide ranging as it may seem because some of the group provisions which apply to UK groups for the taxation of gains—for example those relating to intra-group transfers—are imported for s 13 purposes from elsewhere in TCGA 1992 (see s 14). An intra-group transfer by members of a ''non-resident group'' would thus be treated as taking place at no gain and no loss so there would be no gain on the disposal to attribute to UK shareholders.

In relation to the application of the no gain/no loss rule in these circumstances [the Revenue] have been asked whether the words ''so far as relates to corporation tax on chargeable gains'' in TCGA 1992 s 171 limit its application to situations where the gain on the intra-group transaction would otherwise be within the charge to corporation tax.

In [the Revenue's] view the no gain/no loss rule is not limited in this way. The benefit of the rule is given whether the shareholder is assessable to capital gains tax or to corporation tax. A similar view is also taken when considering the operation of any of the other sections referred to in TCGA 1992 s 14.

RI 44 (May 1993) *Personal pension contributions: treatment in computing profits for Class 4 national insurance contributions*

Schedule D Cases I and II—whether a deduction for personal pension contributions is allowable in arriving at the profit for Class 4 national insurance contribution purposes—TA 1988 ss 60, 639—Social Security Contributions and Benefits Act 1992 Sch 2 paras 2, 3.

Commentary—*Simon's Direct Tax Service* **E7.407**.
Note—This interpretation has been affirmed by legislation (SSC & BA 1992 Sch 2 para 3(2) (*g*)).

RI 45 (May 1993) *Benefits in kind: medical check-ups—TA 1988 ss 19, 154*

[The Revenue] have been asked if employers who provide periodic medical check-ups for staff are providing a benefit in kind which should be reported on form P11D.

[They] take the view, on legal advice, that the provision of routine health checks or medical screening for employees does not confer a chargeable benefit on those employees. This applies whether the check-ups are carried out by an employer's own medical staff or by an outside firm. It follows that routine health checks do not need to be returned on form P11D.

By contrast, where an employer pays for an employee's medical treatment or for diagnosis, a tax charge can arise. Where an employer meets an employee's bill, the employee is chargeable under TA 1988 s 19(1) on the amount paid by the employer. Where the employer arranges and pays for the diagnosis and/or treatment him or herself, there is no charge on employees earning less than £8,500 a year. However directors and employees within TA 1988 Part V Ch II (ss 153–168) are chargeable under TA 1988 s 154 on the amount paid by the employer. Details should then be reported on form P11D.

Commentary—*Simon's Direct Tax Service* **E4.612**.

RI 46 (August 1993) *Capital allowances: commercial know-how*

[The Revenue] are sometimes asked whether capital allowances are available for capital expenditure incurred on the acquisition of commercial know-how.

In [their] view there are no capital allowances available for such expenditure because of the statutory definition of know-how.

TA 1988 s 530 permits capital allowances to be given on capital expenditure incurred on the acquisition of know-how. "Know-how" is defined for s 530 purposes at TA 1988 s 533(7) as "... any industrial information and techniques likely to assist in the manufacture or processing of goods or materials ..." (or in mining, agricultural, forestry or fishing operations).

The terms of this definition accordingly restrict allowances to capital expenditure incurred in acquiring information relevant only to industrial or technical processes. Information relevant to commercial processes is not included.

[The Revenue's] view is that know-how which does not assist directly in the manufacturing and processing operations is commercial know-how. Examples include information about marketing, packaging or distributing a manufactured product. Such information does not assist directly in the manufacture of that product. Rather it is concerned with selling the product once it has been manufactured. As such it is not in [the Revenue's] view within the definition of know-how in TA 1988 s 533(7) and so cannot qualify for allowances under s 530.

Note—This interpretation has been superseded by the Capital Allowances Manual CA70010.
Commentary—*Simon's Direct Tax Service* **B2.615**.

RI 47 (August 1993) *Claims for unrelieved trading losses to be set against capital gains—FA 1991 s 72, TA 1988 s 380*

There is some uncertainty as to whether a trader has to make a claim under FA 1991 s 72 (to have unrelieved trading losses for 1991–92 onwards set against capital gains) at the same time as making a claim under TA 1988 s 380 (to have trading losses set against income).

Where a trader claims relief under s 380 to have trading losses set against general income, FA 1991 s 72 allows a claim to be made to have any balance set against capital gains. In strictness, this claim must be made in the same notice as the TA 1988 s 380 claim (FA 1991 s 72(1)).

However [the Revenue] are prepared to accept a separate claim under FA 1991 s 72 where—

- the trader has previously made a s 380 claim and could have claimed relief under s 72; and
- a separate s 72 claim is made within the time limits for the original s 380 claim; and
- after giving the relief under s 380 there is a balance of trading losses which have not otherwise been relieved; and
- all the other conditions for the relief are satisfied.

Commentary—*Simon's Direct Tax Service* **E1.603**.

RI 48 (August 1993) *Capital gains tax rates: retrospective changes in individuals' liability*

Note—This interpretation is in practice superseded by the introduction of self-assessment for individuals from 1996/97 onwards. See now, for example, TMA 1970 Sch 1B (claims for relief involving two or more years).

RI 49 (August 1993) *Interest paid to UK branches of non-resident companies—TA 1988 ss 11, 349, (2)(c)*

TA 1988 s 349(2)(*c*) imposes a requirement to deduct and account for tax where interest is paid to a person whose ''usual place of abode'' is abroad. The aim of this legislation is to provide an easy way of collecting tax due from someone who is usually outside the UK.

For the purposes of the case law test of company residence—the location of central management and control—a company can generally have only one residence. [The Revenue] have now considered whether the same applies to a company's ''usual place of abode''. Are there circumstances in which a non-resident company which carries on the bulk of its business abroad can nonetheless have a ''usual place of abode'' in the UK?

Where a non-resident company trades in the UK through a branch and the profits of that branch are liable to corporation tax under TA 1988 s 11 (and are not exempted under a treaty) [the Revenue] will accept that this presence in the UK constitutes a ''usual place of abode''. Tax need not therefore be deducted in accordance with s 349(2)(*c*) from payments of interest made to the UK branch of such a company.

Commentary—*Simon's Direct Tax Service* **A3.405**.

RI 50 (August 1993) *Release of trading debts—"hive-across" transactions*

[The Revenue] have been asked whether TA 1988 s 94 (trading debts ''released'' treated as trading receipts) has any implications for a ''hive-across'' within a 100 per cent corporate group. A ''hive-across'' is a relatively common type of transaction undertaken for reasons unconnected with tax, the substance of which is that all of the assets and liabilities of a company are transferred to another company in the same group. The transfer of trading debts from one company to another under this arrangement is in reality a composite transaction in which—

- *the transferee assumes the obligation to repay the creditor; and*
- *the creditor consents to release the transferor from its obligations in return for the transferee accepting them.*

Uncertainty has arisen in this area following the recent decision in the twin cases of Collins v Addies and Greenfield v Bains [[1992] STC 746], both of which were concerned with the meaning of the word ''release'' in the context of TA 1988 s 421 (release of loans to participators in close companies).

In that context it was said that the meaning of ''release'' included circumstances in which the debtor gave full value. Concern has been expressed that this may have implications for the ''hive-across'' situation, resulting in a TA 1988 s 94 charge being levied on the transferor company; notwithstanding that in global terms the debt has not in fact been released and that the old debtor company—the transferor—may have given full consideration in the sense that both assets and liabilities were transferred.

In these circumstances [the Revenue] take the view that while there may have been a ''release'' of a debt, Schedule D Case I principles require the consideration given by the transferor to the transferee for accepting the liabilities to be deducted in computing profits, which include any s 94 receipt. So, in the usual case in which full consideration has been given, there will be no net s 94 charge.

Note—This interpretation is now obsolete.
Commentary—*Simon's Direct Tax Service* **B3.923**.

RI 51 (August 1993) *Self-employed lorry drivers' overnight subsistence—TA 1988 s 74(1)(a)*

In considering the application of TA 1988 s 74(1)(*a*) to the cost of meals taken away from the place of business, the courts have held that no deduction is due because it cannot be said that the expense was incurred wholly and exclusively for the purposes of the trade since everyone must eat in order to live—see *Caillebotte v Quinn* [[1975] STC 265].

However [the Revenue] have long accepted reasonable claims for the cost of evening meals and breakfast taken in conjunction with overnight accommodation if the cost of the accommodation would otherwise be allowable as an expense in carrying on the trade or profession. This practice has received the approval of the courts, most recently in the case of *Watkis v Ashford Sparkes & Harward* [[1985] STC 415].

Long distance self-employed lorry drivers have therefore been able to claim a deduction for the reasonable cost of meals taken in conjunction with overnight accommodation.

[The Revenue] have been asked whether this treatment can be extended to such drivers who spend the night in their cabs rather than take overnight accommodation. [They] have confirmed that it can.

It should be emphasised that it is only "reasonable" expenses which may be allowed and the expenses claimed must be supported by adequate contemporaneous records.

Commentary—*Simon's Direct Tax Service* **B3.1437**.

RI 52 (August 1993) *Sums received under exclusivity agreements-—Schedule D Case I*

The question often arises whether a lump sum payment received under an exclusivity agreement is of capital or revenue character and, if revenue, when it should be recognised as income for tax purposes.

Exclusivity agreements are a common feature of trading arrangements in various trades. They often arise, for example, between petrol suppliers and garages or between breweries and publicans. Under these agreements the trader is tied for a number of years to one supplier of goods or services and in return receives a lump sum payment. Frequently such a sum is potentially repayable but the agreement provides for the periodic waiver of the liability to repay a proportion of the sum provided the terms of the exclusivity contract are adhered to. If the agreement runs its full course, none of the lump sum will be repayable.

[The Revenue's] view is that such an "abatable loan" should be treated in the same way as a grant, its capital or revenue nature being determined by the purpose, in the mind of the payer, for which the trader received that sum. This requires consideration of not only the particular agreement in question but also the correspondence and discussions which supplemented the terms of the agreement.

If the supplier designates the payment for a specific capital purpose, and there is evidence that the recipient has expended it in the manner specified, then it can be accepted as a capital receipt. However, if the recipient is effectively at liberty to spend the money as he or she thinks fit, the receipt is to be regarded as an undifferentiated payment and therefore a taxable revenue receipt. For tax purposes, the reduction in each accounting period of the amount that is repayable should be recognised as a trade receipt of that period. This is consistent with normal accountancy practice.

Note—This interpretation has been superseded by the Business Income Manual BIM40300.
Commentary—*Simon's Direct Tax Service* **A1.203**.

RI 53 (August 1993) *Deep discount securities: bond stripping—TA 1988 Sch 4*

Legislation was introduced in 1985 to amend the tax treatment of investors in deep discount securities where they are issued as part of a bond stripping operation. This legislation is now contained at TA 1988 Sch 4 paras 2, 3.

TAX TREATMENT OF DEEP DISCOUNTS

Normally an investor in deep discount securities is only assessed under Schedule D Case III or IV when the securities are redeemed or they are otherwise disposed of (Sch 4 paras 7, 11). When these rules apply the income elements are not treated as accruing period by period. The normal rules are however disapplied in the circumstances described in Sch 4 para 2(1)–(4) when para 3 provides for investors to be assessed under Schedule D Case III or IV on the accrued income element at the end of each income period. The rules in paras 2 and 3 apply in particular to bond stripping.

BOND STRIPPING

The commonest form of stripping involves the repackaging of a secured fixed interest security with periodical interest payments as what are effectively zero coupon bonds. There would typically be—

- *a series of bonds issued at varying discounts to reflect the maturities of the individual interest payments; and*
- *one bond reflecting the final redemption receipt.*

These zero coupon bonds may be variously described (perhaps as receipts) and will often be issued on the Eurobond market. A company may, for example, invest in a "blue-chip" issue and issue its own receipts using the original issue as security.

INLAND REVENUE'S VIEW

In [the Revenue's] view the zero coupon bonds issued in the circumstances described above will normally be deep discount securities as defined in TA 1988 Sch 4 para 1. It is [their] view that—subject to the detailed provisions of Sch 4—a redeemable security will be a deep discount security if—

- *it is issued by a company or public body; and*

- *it is issued at a "deep discount" (broadly this is a difference between issue price and redemption value of 15 per cent or more of the redemption value or 0.5 per cent of that value for each year of the term of the security); and*
- *it has at the time of issue a fixed yield to maturity. (This contrasts with a deep gain security [FA 1989 Sch 11] which does not require this certainty on issue.)*

Stripped bonds which are deep discount securities are likely to be subject to the rules in TA 1988 Sch 4 paras 2, 3 which are aimed at ensuring that the tax treatment of the bond follows that for the underlying security. The accruing income elements on the deep discount securities would then be assessable on the investors under Schedule D Case III or IV at the end of each income period.

If a security is issued in these circumstances, the information requirements in Sch 4 para 13 should still be complied with. This means that the certificate for each security should show the income element for each income period. Where para 2 applies the certificate should also show that tax will be chargeable in accordance with Sch 4 para 3.

Where, however, such information is not given—as may happen in the case of instruments issued by non-UK residents—the basis of charge is not affected and holders should include the appropriate accruing element in their tax returns.

Guidance on the UK tax treatment of a security included in, for example, a prospectus should not be taken as reflecting [the Revenue's] views unless it is correctly stated that [their] confirmation has been obtained.

Note—TA 1988 Sch 4 has been repealed as part of the "loan relationships" provisions of FA 1996 Pt IV Chapter II. For income tax purposes, the "deep discount security" provisions are superseded by the "discounted securities" provisions of FA 1996 Sch 13. This interpretation is now obsolete.
Commentary—*Simon's Direct Tax Service* **B5.415**.

RI 54 (November 1993) *Capital allowances—time when expenditure is incurred*

CAA 1990 s 159(3) contains the basic rule for determining when expenditure is incurred for the purposes of the Act. That rule may be subject to the further rules in s 159(4) onwards. This note does not address those further rules: it is concerned only with the basic rule in s 159(3).

CAA 1990 s 159(3) states that any amount of expenditure qualifying for capital allowances "is to be taken to be incurred on the date on which the obligation to pay that amount becomes unconditional (whether or not there is a later date on or before which the whole or any part of that amount is required to be paid)".

The date on which an obligation to pay becomes unconditional will depend on the terms of the particular contract for the supply of the asset concerned. The date of the contract for supply or of the issue of an invoice does not settle the point. In many cases a person buying goods is legally required to pay for them on or within a prescribed time of delivery. In such cases, we consider the obligation to pay becomes unconditional when the asset is delivered.

All CAA 1990 s 159(3) does is fix the date expenditure is incurred for the purposes of, for example, CAA 1990 s 24 (machinery or plant allowances) or s 123 (agricultural buildings allowances). The successful claimant of allowances must, of course, satisfy the conditions for obtaining the particular allowance. In the case of machinery or plant allowance, for example, one of the conditions is that the asset on which expenditure is incurred "belongs or has belonged" to the claimant in consequence of incurring the expenditure.

Note—This interpretation has been superseded by the Capital Allowances Manual CA11800.
Commentary—*Simon's Direct Tax Service* **B2.104**.

RI 56 (November 1993) *Expenditure by a trader on computer software—Schedule D Cases I and II*

This article summarises [the Revenue's] current thinking on the treatment of expenditure on computer software in the computation of taxable profits from a trade, profession or vocation.

SOFTWARE ACQUIRED UNDER LICENCE

This is the way that nearly all off-the-shelf software is acquired nowadays. The treatment of expenditure of this nature depends on the form the consideration for the licence takes.

REGULAR PAYMENTS AKIN TO A RENTAL

Payments of this kind are revenue. The timing of deductions will be governed by correct accounting practice which normally requires the rentals to be spread over the useful life of the software in accordance with the fundamental accruals concept in Statement of Standard Accounting Practice No 2. (What is correct accounting practice is ultimately a question of law but the courts are heavily influenced by current generally acceptable practice.)

LUMP SUM

The first question to be asked here is whether the licence is a capital asset in the trade of the licensee. In broad terms a licence is a capital asset if it has a sufficiently enduring nature. This approach has to be applied by reference to the function of the licensed software in the context of the licensee's trade. Very often the expectation will be that the software will function as a tool of the trade for a period of several years. On the other hand, the benefit to be obtained by the licensee in question may be sufficiently transitory to stamp the payment as revenue even though the licence granted is for an indefinite period.

No simple rule of thumb covering every business situation can be successfully devised but, in any event, where software is expected to have a useful economic life of less than two years inspectors will accept that the expenditure is revenue. In these circumstances the timing of the deduction will depend on the correct accounting treatment in the same way as it does for regular payments.

Where the licensed software functions as a capital asset of the licensee's trade capital allowances on plant and machinery will be due under CAA 1990 s 67A. This will be the case whether or not the software comes in a corporeal medium (such as on "floppy discs") separate from the licensee's computer hardware. A short life asset election may be made where appropriate. Computer software is not defined for capital allowances purposes and therefore has its normal meaning which is wide and covers both programs and data (for example books stored in digital form).

EQUIPMENT ACQUIRED AS A PACKAGE

Often computer hardware and the licence to use software are purchased as a package for a single payment. In these circumstances the expenditure between hardware and software should be apportioned. Capital allowances under the ordinary plant and machinery rules will be due on the expenditure attributable to the hardware. The treatment of the balance of the expenditure, attributable to the software licence, will depend on the considerations described above. Where, however, both the hardware and software are acquired on capital account and the expenditure all goes into the general machinery and plant "pool", apportionment will not in practice be necessary.

SOFTWARE OWNED OUTRIGHT

Most widely marketed software is licensed to users and not sold to them outright. But some, particularly larger, concerns may develop their own software. The treatment of expenditure on software acquired outright follows the same principles as those governing the treatment of licensed software. In particular, whether the expenditure concerned (including salaries of in-house computer professionals) is capital or revenue again depends on the economic function of the software in the trade in question as it does for licences acquired for lump sums.

Note—This interpretation has been superseded by the Business Income Manual BIM35800.
Commentary—*Simon's Direct Tax Service* **B2.341; B3.1242, 1310.**

RI 57 (November 1993) *Bank failures—relief for losses incurred by depositors*

In the light of the failure of the Bank of Credit and Commerce International (BCCI) [the Revenue] have been asked whether tax relief will be available under Schedule D Cases I and II for the losses suffered by depositors.

The advice given is that, generally speaking, where the balance in a bank account used for the purposes of a trade, profession or vocation is lost because the bank has failed, the loss will be deductible for the purposes of computing the taxable profit or the allowable loss of that trade, profession or vocation up to a maximum of the amount normally kept in the account to meet the ordinary banking requirements of the business. Similarly, where a provision is made in respect of such a balance because it is expected to be lost, relief will be available for the provision to the extent that it reflects the reasonable expectation of loss.

The loss will also be deductible if the bank account balance was held solely to facilitate the issue of letters of credit or guarantees to trade creditors, provided that the creditors are in respect of debts incurred on revenue account by the trade, profession or vocation which suffered the loss.

In some instances it may be necessary to consider the nature and use of the account and to analyse the balance lost in order to determine the extent to which relief may be available. Moreover, each case inevitably turns on its own facts and there may be particular circumstances in some cases which mean that they do not follow the general rule above.

If, having received a Case I or II deduction, the trader receives money from the Deposit Protection Board in respect of the balance that has been lost, then that distribution would itself be a Case I receipt.

Note—This interpretation is now obsolete.
Commentary—*Simon's Direct Tax Service* **B3.1463.**

RI 58 (November 1993) *Interest—location of source of income*

SCHEDULE D CASE III—MEANING OF "SOURCE"

The availability of relief under TA 1988 s 353 for interest paid and the right (or obligation) to deduct tax from that interest under TA 1988 s 349 may depend on whether interest is annual interest chargeable to tax under Schedule D Case III. Chargeability in turn depends on there being a UK source. The current Revenue view on the location of the source for interest is based on the case of *Westminster Bank Executor and Trustee Company* (*Channel Islands*) *Ltd v National Bank of Greece SA* [46 TC 472]—the Greek Bank case. The factors considered relevant in that case (leading to the conclusion that the income involved did not have a UK source) were—

– there was an obligation undertaken by a principal debtor which was a foreign corporation;
– the obligation was guaranteed by another foreign corporation with no place of business in the UK;
– the obligation was secured on lands and public revenues outside the UK;
– funds for payments by the principal debtor of principal or interest to residents outside Greece would have been provided either by a remittance from Greece or funds remitted by debtors from abroad (even though a cheque might be drawn in London).

Although the Greek Bank case was concerned with income which turned out not to have a UK source, inferences can be drawn from that case about the factors which would support the existence of a UK source and [the Revenue] regard the most important as—

– the residence of the debtor, that is the place in which the debt will be enforced;
– the source from which interest is paid;
– where the interest is paid; and
– the nature and location of the security for the debt.

If all of these are located in the UK then it is likely that the interest will have a UK source.

It is not possible for [the Revenue] to comment individually in advance on the many cases in which the location of the source of interest may be relevant since the precise tax treatment depends on all the factors and on exactly how the transactions are in fact carried out. [The Revenue] hope that this summary of [their] views will assist practitioners and their clients in determining for themselves where the source of interest with which they may be concerned is located.

Commentary—*Simon's Direct Tax Service* **B5.102**.

RI 59 (November 1993) *Deep discount securities issued in a foreign currency—Schedule D Case III*

A deep discount security has to satisfy the rules in TA 1988 Sch 4 in order to benefit from those provisions. In particular there must be a difference between issue price and redemption value of 15 per cent or more of the redemption value or 0·5 per cent of that value for each year of the term of the security. These rules are in TA 1988 Sch 4 para 1(1)(*c*).

A number of people have asked how these rules should apply where a security is issued in a currency other than sterling. Their concern is that in sterling terms the certainty of yield to redemption otherwise required by Sch 4 would not be met if the necessary computations had to be carried out in sterling. If there was uncertainty of yield then the securities would become deep gain securities subject to the less favourable rules in FA 1989 Sch 11.

The Revenue's view is that the test to decide whether a discount is ''deep'' may be carried out in the currency of issue. If, for example, a security is issued in dollars and the provisions in Sch 4 are otherwise satisfied then the fact that it is not possible to calculate in sterling with any certainty either the discount or the yield to redemption will not disqualify the security and will not of itself turn it into a deep gain security.

Commentary—*Simon's Direct Tax Service* **B5.411**.

Note—TA 1988 Sch 4 has been repealed as part of the ''loan relationships'' provisions of FA 1996 Pt IV Chapter II. For income tax purposes, the ''deep discount security'' provisions are superseded by the ''discounted securities'' provisions of FA 1996 Sch 13.

RI 60 (November 1993) *Deep discount securities with a maturity of less than 12 months—Schedule D Case III*

[The Revenue] have been asked whether a security carrying a discount of 15 per cent or less but with a maturity of less than one year can be a deep discount security under the rules in TA 1988 Sch 4.

The potential problem is that where a discount is 15 per cent or less the security can only qualify where the discount exceeds 0·5 of Y per cent of the amount payable on maturity where Y is the number of complete years between the date of issue of the security and the redemption date (TA 1988

Sch 4 para 1(1)(c)(ii)). If the security has a maturity of less than 12 months then there are no complete years.

The Revenue view is that where a security has a maturity of less than 12 months a proportionate part of the complete year will be adopted for the purposes of the formula in Sch 4 para 1(1)(c)(ii). Thus where a security is issued for six months Y would equal 0·5 and consequently any discount exceeding 0·25 per cent would be deep. The adoption of any other interpretation would mean that "Y" in the formula would be zero and this would give peculiar results not intended by the legislation.

Commentary—*Simon's Direct Tax Service* **B5.411**.

Note—TA 1988 Sch 4 has been repealed as part of the "loan relationships" provisions of FA 1996 Pt IV Chapter II. For income tax purposes, the "deep discount security" provisions are superseded by the "discounted securities" provisions of FA 1996 Sch 13.

RI 61 (November 1993) *Termination payments and legal costs—TA 1988 ss 148, 188*

[The Revenue] have been asked about the tax treatment of legal costs incurred by an employee in a court action to recover compensation for loss of employment. On 2 September 1993 [the Revenue] issued a Press Release publicising an extra-statutory concession relating to such costs.

...

TA 1988 s 148 charges tax under Schedule E on payments made directly or indirectly in connection with the termination of the holding of an office or employment. That charge is subject only to the very specific exemptions and reliefs which are contained in TA 1988 s 188.

TA 1988 s 188 does not, for example, allow any deduction for legal costs which the former employer or office holder may incur in pursuing the former employer for wrongful dismissal even though any compensation which may be recovered is taxable under s 148 (see *Warnett v Jones* [[1980 STC 131]).

In taking action to recover compensation for loss of an office or employment an individual may succeed in recovering from the former employer some or all of the costs incurred. This might be because he or she is successful in a court action against the former employer or because a settlement is reached which provides that costs be reimbursed. Any payment made by way of recovery of costs would, in [the Revenue's] view, be assessable to tax under s 148 in addition to the compensation which the former employer agreed or was obliged to pay. The effect of this is that the individual could have a liability to tax on a payment for legal costs even though the actual expense incurred is not tax-deductible.

However [the Revenue] are prepared—in certain circumstances—not to charge tax under s 148 on payments of costs made to (or to the order of) the former employee or office holder.

In cases where the dispute is settled without recourse to the courts no charge will be imposed on payments made by the former employer—

- direct to the former employee's solicitor, and
- in full or partial discharge of the solicitor's bill of costs incurred by the employee only in connection with the termination of his or her employment, and
- under a specific term in the settlement agreement providing for that payment.

In cases where the dispute goes to court no charge will be imposed on payments of costs made by the former employer, even where these are made direct to the employee, in accordance with a court order (whether this is made following judgment or compromise of the action).

[The Revenue] approach applies *only* to legal costs. It does not apply to other professional costs, eg accountancy fees, nor to legal costs incurred over and above the amount which the former employer may pay in the circumstances mentioned. Inspectors may ask to see documentary evidence in support of a claim that a payment by a former employer meets the necessary requirements as outlined above.

Commentary—*Simon's Direct Tax Service* **E4.805E**.

Concession A81—(Termination payments and legal costs).

RI 62 (November 1993) *Relief for interest on loan to acquire an interest in a close company*

INTEREST RELIEF—MEANING OF "ACTUAL MANAGEMENT AND CONDUCT OF THE BUSINESS"—TA 1988 S 360

TA 1988 s 360 describes the conditions which have to be satisfied for an individual to obtain relief for interest on a loan to acquire an interest in a close company. One of the conditions is that the individual either has a material interest in the company or holds ordinary share capital of the company and works for the greater part of his time in the actual management or conduct of the company or of an associated company (TA 1988 s 360(2), (3)).

Questions sometimes arise as to how the phrase "actual management or conduct" is to be interpreted. Individuals will normally be regarded as meeting this requirement if they are directors or have significant managerial or technical responsibilities. Because the statute refers to ''actual management or conduct of the company'' the individual must be involved in the overall running and policy-making of the company as a whole. Managerial or technical responsibility for just one particular area will not be sufficient.

Whether an individual does satisfy the ''actual management or conduct'' test is a question which can only be answered by consideration of the full facts of the particular case.

Commentary—*Simon's Direct Tax Service* **E1.547**.

RI 63 (February 1994) *Capital gains tax: allowable expenditure: costs of making valuations*

In computing the gain arising on the disposal of an asset, the incidental costs of disposal are allowable. Those costs are defined in the legislation—TCGA 1992 s 38(2). They include the reasonable costs incurred in ascertaining the market value of the asset for capital gains tax purposes (for example, a 31 March 1982 valuation for rebasing purposes).

We have been asked in particular whether the costs of agreeing a valuation with the Revenue would be allowed.

In our view, the relevant legislation—TCGA 1992 s 38(2)(b)—allows the reasonable costs incurred in making the valuation, so that the gain can be calculated and returned, to be deducted. Any costs subsequently incurred, for example in negotiating with the District Valuer or with the Shares Valuation Division, or in litigating the matter before any tribunal or in the Courts, are not allowable.

Note—This interpretation is now obsolete.
Commentary—*Simon's Direct Tax Service* **C2.208**.

RI 64 (February 1994) *Corporation tax on chargeable gains: degrouping charges*

We have been asked to explain our views on the accounting periods to which TCGA 1992 ss 178, 179 apply. These provisions impose degrouping charges where a company ceases to be a member of a group of companies.

There is a primary degrouping charge in s 178(3) and s 179(3). This applies where the company leaving the group holds an asset acquired from another group member within the previous six years. It also covers assets held by associated companies leaving the group, and cases where gains on assets have been rolled over under the rules applying to the replacement of business assets.

There is a secondary degrouping charge, with broadly similar main conditions, in s 178(4)–(6) and s 179(5)–(8). This applies where, on a takeover, a company in the group taken over does not become a member of the new enlarged group and, within six years of acquiring the asset, that company ceases to be either a 75 per cent subsidiary or an effective 51 per cent subsidiary of companies in the new group.

Before the capital gains legislation was consolidated in 1992 the provisions covering the primary and secondary degrouping charges, for accounting periods preceding pay and file, were in TA 1970 s 278(3), (3B)–(3D). There were provisions relating only to accounting periods covered by Pay and File in TA 1970 s 278(3A), introduced by F(No 2)A 1987 Sch 6 para 4, and in TA 1970 s 278 (3E), introduced by FA 1989 s 138.

In the 1992 consolidation, the degrouping charge provisions for accounting periods preceding pay and file are in s 178. The degrouping charge provisions for accounting periods covered by pay and file are in s 179. The main difference between these two sets of provisions is the time any gain or loss is treated as arising. In s 178(3), the gain or loss arises at the time of the deemed sale which takes place immediately after the chargeable company acquired the asset. For cases within s 179(3), s 179(4) (as amended by FA 1993 s 89) provides that the gain or loss arises at the beginning of the accounting period in which the chargeable company leaves the group, if this gives a later time than the deemed sale.

It is explicit in TCGA 1992 s 180(1) that the secondary degrouping charge in s 178(4)–(6) only applies before the introduction of pay and file, and that the secondary degrouping charge in s 179(5)–(8) only applies to accounting periods covered by pay and file. But s 180 does not contain an explicit rule dealing with the primary degrouping charge in s 178(3) and s 179(3). However we take the view that TCGA 1992 did not change the result of the pre-consolidation legislation. This means that—

- *for companies leaving groups in accounting periods ending before 1 October 1993, s 178 applies and s 179 does not apply, and*
- *for companies leaving groups in accounting periods ending on or after 1 October 1993, s 179 applies and s 178 does not apply.*

RI 65 (February 1994) *Recovery of tax overpaid by error or mistake*

It is a condition for granting relief under TMA 1970 s 33 that the claimant demonstrates not only that an assessment is excessive but that it is excessive by reason of an error or mistake in a return.

Relief will not be available where the substantive point was squarely in issue in the process of reaching agreement and determining the appeal under TMA 1970 s 54.

In these circumstances the assessment for the year (even if it later proved to be excessive) is not excessive by reason of some error or mistake in the taxpayer's return, but by reason of the taxpayer's failure to pursue his argument through the normal appeal channels.

The inspector is similarly barred (in the absence of new facts) from revisiting his side of the argument. The discovery cases of *Cenlon Finance Co Ltd v Ellwood* [(1962) 40 TC 176] and *Scorer v Olin Energy Systems Ltd* [[1985] STC 218, HL; 58 TC 592] make it clear that discovery assessments could not be raised.

Statement of Practice SP 8/91—(Discovery assessments).
Cross reference—See TMA 1970 s 29 as substituted by FA 1994 s 191 (assessment where loss of tax discovered).

RI 66 (February 1994) *Interest arising after due date for payment of tax*

Note—Not applicable from 1996/97 onwards under self-assessment.

RI 67 (May 1994) *Compensation for permanent cuts in milk quota*

Milk quota, which allows a milk producer to produce a certain amount of milk without paying a supplementary levy, was introduced in 1984.

In June 1991, milk producers in the UK suffered a 2·2 per cent cut in the amount of milk quota they held. They were entitled to compensation for the amount of quota they had lost and the first payment of this was received in June 1992. Further payments may be received in 1993, 1994, 1995 and 1996.

Similar arrangements apply to producers who, as part of the overall process of reducing milk production, elected to cease production completely.

[The Revenue] have been asked how this compensation will be treated for capital gains tax. As it represents a payment for the loss of all or part of a producer's quota, it will be treated as a capital sum derived from an asset and will be chargeable in the year(*s*) of receipt (TCGA 1992 s 22(1)(*a*), (2)).

The treatment of compensation received for cuts in quota which were announced prior to 1991 is not affected by this. Such compensation was taxable in the first year of receipt.

Commentary—*Simon's Direct Tax Service* **B3.510**.

RI 68 (May 1994) *Milk quota—a request to practitioners*

In *Tax Bulletin* Issue 6, February 1993, [the Revenue] explained why we did not consider that the decision in *Faulks v Faulks* [1992] 1 EGLR 9 affected the treatment of milk quota for capital gains tax purposes. Nothing has happened since that article was published to make [the Revenue] alter that view but a case involving the point will be heard by the Commissioners in the near future.

[The Revenue] are asking practitioners who have open cases involving quota if they are prepared to await the outcome of this case and local inspectors are writing to those involved.

Commentary—*Simon's Direct Tax Service* **B3.510**.

RI 69 (May 1994) *Reinvestment relief*

Reinvestment relief is a new relief brought in by FA 1993. The scope of the relief was widened in FA 1994.

Under the relief certain chargeable gains accruing to individuals and trustees of certain settlements may be rolled over if the proceeds from the relevant disposal are reinvested in qualifying shares in an unquoted trading company or the unquoted holding company of a trading group.

[The Revenue] have been asked to explain [their] views on three aspects, in particular, of the legislation which is found in TCGA 1992 ss 164A–164N (subject to the amendments included in FA 1994 Sch 11).

WHAT DOES "THE ACTUAL AMOUNT OR VALUE OF THE CONSIDERATION" MEAN IN SECTION 164A(2)(*A*)(II)?

This question is, briefly, whether the word "actual" means literally that, or whether, in the case of a gift or legacy, it means the market value of the asset (because s 164A(10) applies the market value rules first).

[The Revenue's] view is that "actual" means literally "actual". So, it is not possible to rollover gains on to shares which are inherited or received as a gift.

CAN A REINVESTMENT BE MADE IN A COMPANY WHICH IS NOT RESIDENT IN THE UK?

This question relates to s 164N(2) which applies TCGA 1992 s 170 to the reinvestment relief scheme. Section 170(2)(*a*) requires a company to be resident in the UK for the purpose of interpreting the capital gains group provisions. [The Revenue] have been asked whether this implies that a non-resident company could not be a qualifying company for the purpose of reinvestment relief.

[The Revenue's] view is that a singleton company, that is, a company with no subsidiaries and which is not itself a subsidiary, does not have to be UK resident in order to be a qualifying company.

But, a non-resident holding company will not qualify under s 164G(2). Nor will a non-resident trading company which has trading subsidiaries. And a non-resident company which is itself a subsidiary will be excluded by the rule in s 164G(3)(*b*).

IS RELIEF AVAILABLE ON A CHARGEABLE GAIN WHICH ARISES UNDER S 116(10)(*B*) WHEN A QUALIFYING CORPORATE BOND (QCB) IS DISPOSED OF?

...

Commentary—*Simon's Direct Tax Service* **C3.902, 917**.
Revenue interpretation RI 133—(Capital gains tax: reinvestment relief).
Cross reference—See TCGA 1992 s 164A (2A), (2B) introduced by FA 1996 s 177 (supersedes final part of this interpretation).

RI 70 (May 1994) *Restrictions on setting off capital losses—time limits for elections*

Note—Obsolete after 27 July 1995.

RI 71 (May 1994) *Allowance of interest paid by companies with neither trading nor investment status*

Commentary—*Simon's Direct Tax Service* **D2.211**.
Note—TA 1988 s 338(6) has been repealed for accounting periods ended after 31 March 1996, subject to transitional provisions in FA 1996 Sch 15, as a consequence of the loan relationships provisions in FA 1996 Pt IV Chapter II (ss 80–105).

RI 72 (May 1994) *Visitors to the UK—residence position for tax purposes*

A revised edition of the booklet IR 20, "Residents and non-residents—liability to tax in the UK", was issued last November. This note supplements Chapter 3 of the booklet about determining the residence status of certain individuals coming to the UK.

Where an individual comes to the UK as a *short-term visitor*, he or she will be treated as resident only if visits to this country total 183 days or more in a tax year, or average 91 days or more a year over four years (para 3.3 of booklet IR 20 refers). From 6 April 1993 the fact that a short-term visitor may have accommodation in the UK available for use is no longer relevant in determining residence (FA 1993 s 208).

However, an individual who comes to the UK with the intention of either living here *permanently* or remaining here *for at least three years* is treated as resident from the outset (para 3.1 of booklet IR 20 refers). Where such an intention exists, it is likely that the individual would be regarded as resident even where absent from the UK for part of the time—even if the individual were present here for less than 91 days in a particular year.

If there was no positive intention to remain in the UK for at least three years and the individual has not come to the UK to work for at least two years (para 3.6 of booklet IR 20 refers), such a person would be treated as a short-term visitor. Alternatively, someone might have the intention at the outset of coming to and remaining in the UK for at least three years but subsequently change those plans, for example, in the first year. On the face of it, that individual would initially be treated as a long-term visitor and resident in the UK; but the position would be reviewed when the change of circumstances occurred and this might lead to a revision of residence status.

In determining which category applies in any particular circumstances, it will be necessary to consider all the facts, in particular the individual's intentions and what the normal living pattern will be. For example, someone might come to the UK with the intention of being based here for at least three years, but would nevertheless be treated as a short-term visitor if he or she intended to stay for less than 91 days a year on average.

This could be, say, an individual previously resident in Australia who takes up a post as manager of a group's European operations—a post involving work in several countries and expected to last for five years. He moves his wife and family to the UK. His intention from the outset is to spend two months of each year in the UK and the rest of his time elsewhere in Europe—either working or on holiday. In these circumstances, the visits in each year are for a temporary purpose only and the individual would be treated as a short-term visitor, and not resident in the UK for each year where the limits in para 3.3 of booklet IR 20 were not exceeded. Of course, each decision depends upon its own particular facts.

For brevity, this note does not deal with ordinary residence, but that would be a factor in arriving at an individual's precise tax position.

Commentary—*Simon's Direct Tax Service* **E6.121**.

RI 73 (May 1994) *Travelling and subsistence expenses—temporary absence from normal place of work*

Note—This Interpretation is now obsolete.

RI 74 (August 1994) *Open offer treated as a share reorganisation*

[The Revenue] have been asked for their views on when an open offer is treated as a share reorganisation within TCGA 1992 s 126. An open offer is an arrangement under which a company invites its shareholders to subscribe for shares subject to a minimum entitlement based on their existing shareholdings. The shareholders may also be given the opportunity to subscribe for shares which other shareholders do not want. This may be subject to a maximum.

For capital gains purposes the Revenue will treat any subscription for shares, which is equal to or less than the shareholder's minimum entitlement, as a share reorganisation. Any shares subscribed for in excess of the minimum entitlement will be treated as a separate acquisition.

Commentary—*Simon's Direct Tax Service* **C2.718**.

RI 75 (August 1994) *Principal private residence relief*

[The Revenue] have been asked to clarify [their] interpretation of a number of points that arise on principal private residence relief (TCGA 1992 ss 222–226).

SCOPE OF THE DWELLINGHOUSE—MEANING OF CURTILAGE

Lewis v Rook [[1990] STC 23; rvsd [1992] STC 171, CA] gave guidance on determining whether a building, with one or more ancillary buildings, could together form a single dwellinghouse for the purposes of s 222. In cases where there is an identifiable main house it was held that no building can form part of a dwellinghouse with the main house unless that building is appurtenant to, and within the curtilage of, the main house. Curtilage is defined by the Shorter Oxford Dictionary as ''a small court, yard, or piece of ground, attached to a dwellinghouse and forming one enclosure with it''. This definition has been adopted by the courts in non-tax cases and emphasis is placed on the smallness of the area comprised in the curtilage. Buildings standing around a court yard together with the main house will be within the curtilage of the main house.

Where more dispersed groups of buildings have a clear relationship with each other they will fall within a single curtilage if they constitute an integral whole. In the Leasehold Reform Act case of Methuen-Campbell v Walters [[1979] 1 QB 525, [1979] 1 All ER 606, CA] quoted with approval in Lewis v Rook, the Court held that ''For one corporeal hereditament to fall within the curtilage of another, the former must be so intimately associated with the latter as to lead to the conclusion that the former in truth forms part and parcel of the latter''. Whether one building is part and parcel of another will depend primarily on whether there is a close geographical relationship between them. Furthermore, because the test is to identify an integral whole, a wall or fence separating two buildings will normally be sufficient to establish that they are not within the same curtilage. Similarly, a public road or stretch of tidal water will set a limit to the curtilage of the building.

Buildings which are within the curtilage of a main house will normally pass automatically on a conveyance of that house without having to be specifically mentioned. There is a distinction between the curtilage of a main house and the curtilage of an estate as a whole and the fact that a whole estate may be contained within a single boundary does not mean that the buildings on the estate should be regarded as within the curtilage of the main house.

SALE OF A HOUSE AND GARDEN AFTER IT HAS CEASED TO BE USED AS A RESIDENCE

Varty v Lynes [[1976] STC 508] (51 TC 419) established that no principal private residence relief was due on the sale of a garden where it was sold separately and after the dwellinghouse. Certain dicta in that case also suggested that where a dwellinghouse and garden were sold together, but after the taxpayer had ceased to occupy the property, the sale of the garden would not qualify for relief. This particular point was not directly in issue in that case, and so was not decided by it, but the case provided grounds for taking that view. Since then [the Revenue] have not taken this line in cases where house and garden were sold together and for development. Recently [the Revenue] have received advice that arguments based on those dicta are misconceived and we no longer seek to apply them at all.

[The Revenue] do however apply the decision itself, so that no relief is due on the sale of a garden which takes place after a prior sale of the dwellinghouse.

STATEMENT D4

Statement D4 explains that certain delays in occupying a dwellinghouse as a residence at the start of a period of ownership will be regarded as a period of residence in that dwellinghouse for the purposes of private residence relief. For Statement D4 to apply the delay must not exceed a period of one year, or somewhat longer if there are good reasons for exceptional delay. Where a period of delay falls within Statement D4 the dwellinghouse must be occupied as a residence immediately thereafter. Otherwise no extension to the actual period of residence is allowed.

What constitutes a good reason for exceptional delay is a matter left to the discretion of local district inspectors, subject to an overall time limit of two years. Where the period of delay is greater than two years no extension is allowed. [The Revenue] expect good reasons for exceptional delay to be factors outside the taxpayer's control.

Where Statement D4 does apply, and as a result two houses are treated as residences for the same period, no s 222(5) election is required. Relief can be given on both houses for the period covered by Statement D4.

PERIODS OF ABSENCE

Relief is only due for periods of absence from the home falling within s 223(3) if both before and after the period of absence there was a time when the home was the taxpayer's residence. [The Revenue] take the same view of residence for this purpose as [they] take for determining whether s 222 applies generally, so that the question is whether during the period concerned the property has as a matter of fact been a residence.

A minimum period is not specified and [the Revenue] do not attempt to impose one. [The Revenue] take the view that it is quality of occupation rather than length of occupation which determines whether a dwellinghouse is its owner's residence. As Millet J in Moore v Thompson [[1986] STC 170] 61 TC at p 24 comments—

> *"... the Commissioners were alive to the fact that even occasional and short residence in a place can make that a residence; but the question was one of fact and degree ...".*

APPORTIONMENTS

In broad terms the apportionment rules work as follows—

- *section 222(10) apportions consideration where required;*
- *section 223 apportions the gain over time;*
- *section 224(1) restricts relief to parts of the property not used exclusively for a business etc;*
- *section 224(2) provides for a just and reasonable apportionment to apply where there is a change in use.*

Section 224(1) only applies where the part of the property concerned has been exclusively so used throughout the period of ownership. It does not refer to use only at the date of disposal. Where s 224(1) applies no relief is due on the part of the dwellinghouse used for business etc even for the last three years of ownership. This is because s 224(1) only applies s 223 to the part of the dwellinghouse not exclusively used for business etc. Section 223 specifies how much relief is due, and since it does not apply to the business part no relief can be given for that part for any period.

Section 224(2) provides for a just and reasonable apportionment to apply where there is a change in use, and for this purpose commencement or cessation of use of a dwellinghouse as a residence is not a change of use. Section 223 already gives the rules required for such cases and there is therefore no need to apply s 224(2). Our approach in cases falling within s 224(2) is to deal with each case on its merits, and to produce an adjustment which so far as possible reflects—

- *the extent to which, and*
- *the length of time over which, each part of the dwellinghouse has been used as part of the residence.*

This approach broadly follows the statutory method of apportionment for more straightforward cases set out in ss 223, 224(1). [The Revenue] do not normally consider it is appropriate to take into account intervening market values when apportioning gains to different periods in s 224(2) cases since s 223 clearly provides for time apportionment as the appropriate method.

ELECTIONS BY MARRIED COUPLES

When a couple marry and both spouses own a residence a new two year period for making an election under s 222(5) begins.

Where one spouse owns more than one property, and the other owns no property, and there is no change on marriage, then [the Revenue] take the view that a fresh period does not begin since there has been no change in the combination of residences owned by either spouse, and neither spouse needs to become a party to any existing election to which they had not previously been a party. Section 222(6)(a) only requires a notice to be given by both spouses where it affects them both. Where only one spouse owns property only that spouse is affected and he or she will already have had a two-year period in which to make the election.

Where the spouses jointly own more than one property at marriage but neither separately owns any other property, a new two-year period for making an election would still begin. Although both parties own the same properties as before, and have previously had a two-year period in which to elect, they now have to make a joint election and a new period is required accordingly.

The right to receive a notice under s 222(6)(b) only applies to a spouse who owns a residence. Otherwise a spouse, who had no financial interest in a property, would be given a right of appeal against a determination relating to that property owned by the other spouse, and with possibly adverse consequences for that other spouse.

SUCCESSIVE INTERESTS

Section 222(7)(a) stipulates that where a spouse inherits a dwellinghouse from the other spouse he or she also inherits the other spouse's period of ownership for principal private residence relief purposes. This is not overridden by TCGA 1992 s 62 which provides that a legatee acquires an inherited asset for capital gains tax purposes on the date of death. Section 62 sets out the rules for computing the gain arising to a legatee, but says nothing about how any private residence relief which might be due is to be calculated, the rules for which are in s 222 etc. Thus s 222(7) continues to apply with the result that periods of ownership prior to the death of the first spouse to die fall to be taken into account in determining qualifying periods of residence.

One effect of this is to produce results different to those which would be obtained by only looking at the period after the death of the first spouse to die. This can work to the advantage or to the disadvantage of the taxpayer.

TCGA 1992 S 224(3)

To prevent abuse of principal private residence relief there is anti-avoidance legislation at s 224(3) which is widely drawn. Section 224(3) applies—

- *where a dwellinghouse is acquired wholly or partly for the purpose of realising a gain from its disposal; or*
- *where there is subsequent expenditure on the dwellinghouse wholly or partly for the purpose of realising a gain from its disposal.*

Where the first part of s 224(3) applies no relief is due on any gain arising from the disposal of that dwellinghouse. Where the second part applies no relief is due on any part of the gain attributable to the expenditure.

Anyone who buys a dwellinghouse is likely to hope that, in the fullness of time, they will make a gain on its disposal. One house may be chosen over another because its value is more likely to appreciate over time. These cases could be said to fall within the first part of the section but, if the house was genuinely acquired and used as a residence and the conditions for relief are met, relief will not be restricted. The legislation will only be applied when the primary purpose of the acquisition was an early disposal at a profit. The same approach will be taken when considering whether a restriction of relief is appropriate under the second part of the section.

In many cases in which the first part of s 224(3) would be applied the transaction of purchase and sale will amount to an adventure in the nature of trade. In these cases the charge to income tax will take priority over the charge to capital gains tax. In some cases subsequent expenditure on the dwellinghouse may also be part of an adventure in the nature of trade, giving rise to an income tax charge. The income tax charge will again take priority.

The second part of s 224(3) is more often applied than the first. It denies relief on the part of a gain which is attributable to particular expenditure. Common circumstances in which it may be applied are—

- *acquisition by a leaseholder of a superior interest in the property;*
- *conversion of an undivided dwellinghouse into flats;*
- *barn conversions and other developments of outbuildings or of the land attached to the dwellinghouse.*

The legislation does not dictate how this part of the gain should be computed but in practice it implies a comparison between the gain which accrues and the gain which would have accrued if the relevant expenditure had not been incurred.

In deciding whether a restriction to relief is appropriate under the second part of s 224(3) [the Revenue] ignore cases in which the only relevant expenditure is incurred on—

- *obtaining planning permission; or*
- *removing restrictive covenants.*

Where there is a delay between the expenditure and the disposal the effect of inflation may need to be considered. The part of the gain which is excluded from relief is the part attributable to the expenditure incurred. This part may have been increased by the effect of inflation. If so, the effect of inflation will be mitigated by indexation.

DECEASED PERSON'S ESTATES—CONCESSION D5

Concession D5 provides relief to personal representatives where they dispose of a house which before and after the deceased's death has been used as their only or main residence by individuals who under the will or intestacy are entitled to the whole or substantially the whole of the proceeds of the house. This is aimed at beneficiaries who have been living in the dwellinghouse prior to and at the time of death, where there has therefore been continuity of occupation, and "before" is interpreted accordingly. The intention is that beneficiaries who have lived in the house throughout should not be deprived of relief because their home happened to be sold by the personal representatives rather than by themselves as legatees. It is not intended that relief should as a result be extended to beneficiaries for whom the house has not been their only or main residence. To avoid this would mean insisting that resident beneficiaries should have a 100 per cent interest in the dwellinghouse which in turn could operate harshly against resident beneficiaries with very nearly a 100 per cent interest. Hence the reference to "substantially the whole" which [the Revenue] interpret as 75 per cent or more.

DISPOSALS BY BENEFICIARIES

Where there is a disposal by a beneficiary of an inherited property the combined effect of ss 62(4), 222(7) is that the beneficiary's period of ownership begins on the date of death. Where the beneficiary does not become resident until a later date the period prior to taking up occupation will not qualify for relief (unless it falls within the final 36-month period prior to disposal (s 223(2)).

Note—This interpretation is now obsolete.
Commentary—*Simon's Direct Tax Service* **C2.1301**.
Concession D5—(Private residence exemption: property held by personal representatives).
Concession D49—(private residence relief: short delay by owner-occupier in taking up residence).

RI 76 (August 1994) *Charges on income—company paying annuities*

A decision may be taken to incorporate a business carried on by a partnership, and on incorporation the company may assume a liability to pay an existing annuity to a former partner and reflect this in the agreement for the purchase of the business. The Revenue will accept that TA 1988 s 338(5)(*b*) will not operate to deny relief for what might otherwise be a charge.

If a company takes over a business on incorporation, and will subsequently have to pay an annuity, then if the agreement under which the company takes over the business makes reference to the company having ultimately to pay the annuity, again the annuity will not be prevented by s 338(5)(*b*) from being a charge.

This will be the case only so long as the annuity is commercial in amount. The further question of whether TA 1988 s 125 will apply can only be considered in the light of the particular facts and circumstances of each case, but it has been the Revenue's longstanding practice to regard such payments in respect of a bona fide commercial transaction as outside the scope of that provision.

The circumstances giving rise to a liability of this kind which is then assumed by a company will normally be such that the outlay will not be incurred wholly and exclusively for the purposes of a trade carried on by the company. That being so, any excess of charges paid over profits will not be eligible for carry forward under TA 1988 s 393(9).

If a company takes over a business on incorporation, at a later date pays an annuity and the agreement under which the company takes over the business does not make reference to the company's liability ultimately to pay the annuity, s 338(5)(*b*) will be applicable.

Commentary—*Simon's Direct Tax Service* **D2.210**.

RI 77 (August 1994) *Milk quota—superlevy*

Milk production is limited by quotas but producers can exceed their quota without penalty provided national limits are not exceeded. For the 1993–94 quota year national limits have been exceeded.

Producers who have exceeded their quota will be required to pay superlevy if the excess was more than a threshold. The threshold above which superlevy is payable is based on national results. Calculations will be shown and the superlevy deducted on the September 1994 milk statement for August 1994 deliveries. Producers who exceeded their quota by less than the threshold will not pay superlevy.

[The Revenue] have been asked whether superlevy is an allowable Schedule D Case I deduction. [The Revenue] can confirm that it is.

Some producers bought additional quota in order to ensure that they would not have to pay superlevy. It has been suggested that they can claim a deduction for the amount of superlevy they would have paid if they had not bought the quota or for the sum they would have paid if they had leased quota instead of buying it. [The Revenue] do not accept this. In the hands of a farmer who uses it in the business of milk production quota is a fixed capital asset and the cost of fixed capital assets is not an allowable revenue deduction.

Note—This interpretation has been superseded by the Business Income Manual BIM55340 and 55315.
Commentary—*Simon's Direct Tax Service* **B3.510**.

RI 78 (August 1994) *Outward investment in the corporate sector*

Note—FA 1993 ss 61–66 were repealed for accounting periods ended after 31 March 1996, subject to transitional provisions in FA 1996 Sch 15, as a consequence of the loan relationship provisions in FA 1996 Pt IV Chapter II (ss 80–105).

RI 79 (August 1994) *Double taxation—treaty claims and loan interest*

When a company pays yearly interest to a non-UK resident with some specific exceptions it is obliged to deduct income tax by virtue of TA 1988 s 349(2) and account for that tax to the Revenue.

Where the recipient of the interest is a resident of a territory with which the UK has a double taxation treaty, the UK may, depending on the terms of the appropriate treaty, exempt the interest from UK tax or tax it at a reduced rate.

[The Revenue] give such relief under [their] treaties in one of two ways. Either [the Revenue] repay the non-resident any tax that has been suffered (or the appropriate part of that tax) or [they] issue a notice to the payer of the interest authorising him (under SI 1970/488) to pay interest without deduction of tax (or at a reduced rate) according to the terms of the treaty.

Relief from UK tax under a treaty has to be claimed by the non-resident recipient of the interest in a claim made to the Board (TA 1988 s 788(6)). In the absence of an accepted and agreed claim, the payer of the interest is obliged to deduct and account for income tax under s 349(2) in the normal way.

The Revenue closely monitor treaty claims involving loan interest, to ensure that the interest in question qualifies under the terms of the treaty. [The Revenue] are particularly concerned with the possibility that a loan may be standing in the place of equity, and that the payment of interest should in reality be characterised as a distribution of UK profits or, with the possibility that transactions may fall foul of particular anti-abuse provisions in the treaty.

It is important therefore, that non-resident recipients of loan interest comply with their obligations to make treaty claims. It is also important that such claims are examined as soon as possible after the transaction giving rise to interest etc takes place, so that [the Revenue] can more easily focus on current material relevant to the claim. [The Revenue] often need to establish a company's arm's length borrowing capacity at the time a loan is made and it is helpful to be able to consider contemporaneous information.

[The Revenue] recognise that examination of some treaty claims takes time and [they] do not wish to penalise the overseas recipients of the interest for any delay in processing their claims. Equally, [they] do not wish the UK resident payers to assume the benefit of a treaty by allowing them to pay interest without deduction of income tax, simply provided a claim is made at some time within the statutory period. It is therefore Revenue policy, where a claim under the treaty is accepted as valid, to provide that a notice allowing for treaty relief to be given at source by the payer of interest may have retrospective effect—but only to the date that the certified treaty claim is received by Financial Intermediaries and Claims Office (FICO) (International)—formerly the Inspector of Foreign Dividends—on behalf of the Revenue.

FICO (International) deals with a large number of treaty claims. The vast majority of those claims are made when a loan is put in place, and [the Revenue] are able to issue statutory notices well in advance of interest payment dates. Most borrowers who pay interest before the issue of a notice authorising them to pay interest without deduction of tax (or at a reduced rate of tax), deduct income tax and account for it in the normal way. A problem arises only where a claim is lodged after a payment of interest has been made and the payer has failed to deduct income tax in accordance with its statutory duty.

Where interest is paid before a certified claim is received, the Revenue expects the payer of interest to meet the statutory obligations and deduct income tax. If tax is not deducted then TMA 1970 s 87 interest is exigible irrespective of whether relief, as claimed, is ultimately agreed. In practice, where a claim has been successful, the inspector may arrange for acceptance of payment of the s 87 interest due without raising an assessment to collect the income tax from the UK payer. Of course, an assessment is raised and interest charged, as appropriate, where a payer of interest has failed to deduct income tax, whether before or after the certified claim has been received by the UK Revenue, where the claim is refused in whole or in part.

Treaty claims have to be certified by the Revenue authorities in the recipient's tax territory. There can be delay in such authorities forwarding certified claim forms to FICO (International). It is possible, in cases of extreme urgency, for claimants to recover certified claim forms from the overseas Revenue authorities and to send them to FICO (International) themselves. Indeed some authorities—the German Revenue authorities for example—return claim forms to claimants for this purpose.

FICO (International) intend publishing a leaflet entitled "Double taxation relief inter-company loans and royalties". This will be a guide for those companies resident in a country where [the Revenue] have a double taxation treaty (where the agreement provides for relief from UK tax on interest or royalties) on how to claim repayment of UK tax already deducted and/or relief from UK tax at source in respect of future income.

Once published the leaflet will be obtainable from FICO (International) Fitzroy House, PO Box 46, Castle Meadow Road, Nottingham NG2 1BD, and all local districts will be issued with a small supply.

Any queries should be addressed to Lyn McDonald, International Division, Melbourne House, Aldwych, London WC2B 4LL (telephone number 020 7438 6860).

Commentary—*Simon's Direct Tax Service* **F1.302**.

RI 80 (August 1994) *Rent a room—accommodation for trade or business purposes*

F(No 2)A 1992 s 59, Sch 10 contain rules for determining whether rent a room relief may be due in respect of income which would otherwise be chargeable under Schedule D Case I or VI (or both those Cases).

There have been some suggestions in the professional press that relief could be available where a residence, or part of a residence, is used as an office or for other trade or business purposes (other than the business of providing furnished living accommodation) and sums are paid in respect of that use. [The Revenue] take the view that such claims are inadmissible since—

- *the words of the legislation, in [the Revenue's] opinion, do not permit such claims, and*
- *the legislation was never intended to give relief in such circumstances.*

Where a room is used exclusively as an office or as other trade or business premises, it is no longer occupied or intended to be occupied as a separate residence—one of the conditions for rent a room relief. As such, it is no longer, for rent a room purposes, part of the "residence" because Sch 10 para 7, permits the identification of parts of buildings which are occupied or intended to be occupied as a residence.

Rent a room relief can only apply where "relevant sums" accrue in respect of the use of "furnished accommodation" in a "qualifying residence". The Act does not define "accommodation" which should therefore take its everyday meaning. The dictionary meaning of "accommodation" is "lodgings" or "a place to live" and in [the Revenue's] opinion, the normal unqualified meaning of "accommodation" is "living accommodation". Consequently, even if an entire residence, or part of a residence, is used as trade or business premises and payments are made in respect of that use, [the Revenue] take the view that rent a room relief will not be due. The payments will not have been made in respect of the use of living accommodation as such.

The Standing Committee debate in Parliament on rent a room indicates that the context in which rent a room was being considered was that of providing additional residential accommodation and not office or business accommodation. [The Revenue] do not think that the legislation is ambiguous or obscure. However, should Commissioners, for example, consider that it is, then following the decision in the case of Pepper v Hart *[[1992] STC 989, HL] it may be possible for them to refer to relevant Parliamentary material. This material supports [the Revenue's] interpretation that lettings other than furnished residential lettings are excluded from rent a room relief.*

The foregoing does not apply to genuine lodgers such as students who are provided with study facilities in their lodgings. In such cases, [the Revenue] would not want to deny relief where a lodger living in the home is provided with a desk, or the use of a room with a desk, which he or she uses for work or study.

Note—This interpretation has been superseded by PIM4002.
Commentary—*Simon's Direct Tax Service* **A4.108B; B7.206A**.

RI 81 (August 1994) *Bad and doubtful debts*

Entries for bad debts and bad debts reserves are common features within the accounts of most traders and many professionals.

[The Revenue's] view is that a deduction for bad or doubtful debts is to be made in arriving at the profits of the year in which the debts become bad or doubtful, provided that the amount reserved may reasonably be regarded as based on a separate valuation of each debt.

ACCOUNTANCY PRACTICE

This accepts that events arising after the balance sheet date and before accounts are finalised may need to be reflected in the provision for bad and doubtful debts if they furnish additional evidence of conditions that existed at the balance sheet date.

[The Revenue's] interpretation of this is that if—

- *a debt existed at the balance sheet date, and*
- *the creditor at that date had no reason to believe that he would not be paid, but*
- *before the accounts were finalised he discovered that the financial position of the debtor at the balance sheet date was such that he was, even at that time, unlikely to be paid,*

the creditor would be entitled to make a provision for the debt in computing his profit.

A common example of the above is where a debtor at the balance sheet date goes into administration or liquidation shortly after the balance sheet date and before the date on which the financial statements are approved by the trader. Whilst the administration or liquidation took place after the balance sheet date, its occurrence before the accounts were finalised normally sheds light on the financial position of the debtor at the balance sheet date. If the period since the balance sheet date is short it is unlikely that a debtor would go from financial good health to insolvency in that period. In these circumstances it would normally be reasonable for the trader to regard the debt as doubtful. The amount of the acceptable provision would depend upon the information available.

SLOW PAYERS

If the debtor is habitually a slow payer, and there are no grounds to believe his financial position has changed, then [the Revenue] would not accept that the length of time a debt has been outstanding is on its own sufficient reason to regard it as doubtful. [The Revenue] would therefore reject a provision made on these grounds as not being "estimated to be bad".

EVIDENCE REQUIRED

Where inspectors cannot satisfy themselves, from the information available to them, that a deduction for a bad debt or bad debt provision fulfils the above criteria, additional details will be sought. The inspector will need to identify each debt involved and establish—

- *how the extent of its doubtfulness was evaluated;*
- *when this was done;*
- *by whom; and*
- *what specific information was used in arriving at that valuation.*

Typically, this requires sight of all the evidence available, at the relevant date, to the taxpayer creditor regarding the credit worthiness of the debtor. This will include copies of all correspondence, both internal (such as memos and minutes of meetings at which the matter was considered) and external (correspondence with the debtor, solicitors, banks, factoring agencies, etc and any reports obtained concerning the financial position of the debtor), relating to the transactions in question covering the period up until the time a reserve for the debts was entered in the creditor's books.

Note—This interpretation is now obsolete.
Commentary—*Simon's Direct Tax Service* **B3.1461.**

RI 82 (August 1994) *Deduction for costs of secretarial assistance and childcare costs*

[The Revenue's] attention has been drawn to recent press articles which indicate that a new "concession" has been given to barristers in private practice for part of the costs of employing a nanny. [The Revenue] wish to make it clear that neither by law nor Revenue concession is tax relief available for a business person's own child-care costs.

THE LAW

Expenditure is not deductible in computing the profits of a trade, profession or vocation unless it is incurred wholly and exclusively for the purposes of the business. But where an outgoing is such that a definite part or proportion of it can be identified as being wholly and exclusively expended for business purposes a deduction may be due for that part. This widely held understanding of the law has been approved by the courts.

USE OF NANNY TO UNDERTAKE SECRETARIAL DUTIES

A nanny may be partly employed to carry out material secretarial duties in the business of her employer. If so, a deduction may be due for that part of the costs of employing her referable (on a time basis) to those duties.

What proportion of the employment costs may be deductible in this way depends on the facts and circumstances of individual cases. But, where a district inspector handles the returns of a number of businesses carried on in an essentially similar way, he or she may decide, as a matter of local practice, to set down guidelines regarding the treatment of particular items of expenditure.

In the case of a barrister's nanny it has been reported that the local inspector has accepted that a secretarial ''allowance'' can be claimed. This misrepresents the position. What the inspector has done is to give an indication of the maximum deduction he would ordinarily accept.

It remains the case that no deduction at all will be due if the employee does not undertake material secretarial duties. Conversely, in a case where detailed records showed that exceptionally heavy duties were undertaken, a contention that a greater sum should be deducted would have to be considered on its merits. And in any event the figures have no application to other businesses where the need for a nanny to undertake secretarial duties may be very different.

Commentary—*Simon's Direct Tax Service* **B3.1232**.

RI 83 (August 1994) *Motor dealers—stock valuation*

Basic principles

Accounting practice requires that stocks normally need to be stated at cost, or, if lower, at net realisable value. The computation of net realisable value should take into account events occurring between the balance sheet date and the date when the accounts are approved which may provide additional evidence of the value of stocks at the balance sheet date. The profit computed by the correct application of generally accepted accounting practice to the particular facts is the starting point for the computation of the taxable trading profit.

THE MOTOR DEALERS SITUATION

Accountancy

Subject to some adjustment to the price to reflect the age and condition of a used vehicle, a motor dealer will only pay the trade value, arrived at from trade publications, for a used car except where it is acquired in a part exchange transaction. In that situation the price paid may be more than the dealer would otherwise have been willing to pay for the used car in order to secure the sale of the new car. The documentation generally shows the inflated price of the used car as its cost, but arguably the excess of that cost over the trade value is in substance a discount on the new car. It is a widespread industry practice for dealers to arrive at the stock value of used cars acquired in part exchange transactions from the published ''bottom book'' trade value. The accountancy advice [the Revenue] have received is that the correct application of the accruals concept, stated in SSAP 2, requires the substance of the transaction rather than the form to be reflected in the accounts. In the situation described above the true substance is that the excess of the part exchange price over that derived from the trade publication is a discount on the new car and the cost of the used car is its appropriate published trade value at the date of acquisition. For stock valuation therefore correct accounting practice allows the consistent use of the appropriate trade price of a used car taken in such a part exchange transaction as its cost.

Tax

[The Revenue's] view was that notwithstanding the accountancy substance the legal form of the part exchange agreement was decisive and therefore for tax purposes the legal cost of the used vehicle should be used in arriving at the stock valuation. In the light of legal advice [the Revenue] have received following the Court of Appeal decision Gallagher v Jones; Threlfall v Jones [[1993] STC 537, CA] [they] now accept that the legal form of the part exchange agreement need not override the correct application of the accruals concept in these particular circumstances. Therefore [the Revenue] accept that for stock valuation purposes the published trade value at the time of acquisition may be used to arrive at the cost of used cars acquired in part exchange transactions.

Use of trade value at the balance sheet date

Some dealers arrive at the stock value of a used car acquired in a part exchange transaction from its published trade value at the balance sheet date (TVBS) rather than from its published trade value when it was acquired.

As a car tends to depreciate with age valuation on a TVBS basis will involve a write down below cost, in substance, as well as in legal form. That basis will be justifiable if that figure is a reasonable approximation of the car's net realisable value taking into account the market in which it is likely to be sold and the further costs to be incurred. In making that comparison the actual sale proceeds (and further costs) should be taken into account when these were known at the time the accounts were drawn up. The use of hindsight is in accordance with SSAP 17.

Sometimes cars which were not acquired in a part exchange transaction are automatically valued on a TVBS basis in the accounts. In that situation there is no justification for the cost of such vehicles for stock valuation purposes being regarded as anything other than the legal cost and again TVBS will only be acceptable if it provides an accurate appraisal of the net realisable value of a particular car.

Inspectors may challenge the use of the TVBS basis where it leads to a significant loss of tax or timing differential.

Other accounting bases

Where accounts are prepared using another different basis [the Revenue] will accept it provided that it reflects the correct application of generally accepted accounting practice, as interpreted by the courts to the particular facts and is consistently applied.

A trader who has settled his or her past Schedule D Case I liability in accordance with [the Revenue's] previous view may want to change to a basis [the Revenue] would now accept is appropriate for determining the Case I profits for unsettled and future years. Such a change would be acceptable provided that the new basis was consistently used in the accounts. Statement of Practice 3/90 para 3 would apply to the year of change.

Background papers

SSAP 2 (Disclosure of accounting policies), SSAP 9 (Stocks and long-term contracts) and SSAP 17 (Accounting for post balance sheet events). Statement of Practice 3/90.

Note—This interpretation is now obsolete.
Commentary—*Simon's Direct Tax Service* **B3.1011**.
Statement of Practice SP 3/90—(Stocks and long-term contracts).

RI 84 (August 1994) *Trading receipts of members' golf clubs*

[The Revenue] have been asked whether non-proprietary members' golf clubs are liable to tax on trading income such as visitors' green fees. This article gives [the Revenue's] views on when income received by members' clubs for the use of their facilities by non-members is taxable trading income.

Any surplus arising to a members' club from transactions with its members is not normally taxable. Payments by members in respect of their personal guests, even when these are described as "visitors' fees" are normally regarded as part of that surplus.

But receipts from visitors who, in return for payment on a commercial basis, are allowed to use a club's facilities will be receipts from a taxable trade in the club's hands. This applies to individuals who arrive at a club to use its facilities on a casual basis and to groups who may book in advance.

Such visitors may become "temporary members" of the club. But this will not prevent receipts from their use of the club's facilities from being taken into account for tax unless their rights as temporary members (such as rights to vote at meetings, participate fully in club activities and generally to exercise control over the running of the club), and the opportunities to exercise them, are similar to those of full members. In computing the taxable income derived from non-members in this way the related expenses will be deductible, including a reasonable proportion of course overheads.

Note—This interpretation has been superseded by the Business Income Manual BIM24230.
Commentary—*Simon's Direct Tax Service* **B3.240, 603**.
Cross reference—See *Carlisle & Silloth Golf Club v Smith* (1912) 6 TC 48.

RI 85 (August 1994) *Beneficial loans—exemption for commercial loans*

FA 1994 s 88(3) introduced an exemption from the benefit in kind charge on loans which are "commercial loans"—loans made to employees on the same terms and conditions as loans made by lenders to members of the public (TA 1988 s 161(1A), (1B)). [The Revenue] have been asked to give guidance on some of the expressions in the new provisions.

SUMMARY OF EXEMPTION

The exemption takes effect from 1994–95 and applies to existing as well as new loans which satisfy all the following conditions—

– the loan to the employee was made by a person in the ordinary course of a business which includes the lending of money;

- at the time the loan to the employee was made, comparable loans (loans made for the same or similar purposes, and on the *same terms and conditions* as the loan to the employee) were available to ordinary customers;
- *at or about the time the loan to the employee was made, a substantial proportion* of the relevant loans (the loan to the employee plus comparable loans) were made to *members of the public at large*, and
- all the relevant loans are held on the same terms, and where those terms are different from the original terms, the changes were made in the ordinary course of the lender's business.

COMMENTS

[The Revenue] have printed in bold above the expressions on which [they] have been asked to comment.

Same terms and conditions

For loans made *on or after 1 June 1994,* only loans made on the same terms and conditions as loans made to the general public will qualify for the new exemption. It is not sufficient for the terms and conditions to be similar or broadly the same.

A loan to an employee would *not* be on the same terms and conditions if for example—

(*a*) the lending criteria (eg loan-to-income ratio or loan-to-value ratio) were relaxed in favour of the employee; or

(*b*) fees or charges normally made in connection with the application for the loan (eg valuation fees, administration or arrangement fees, reservation or booking fees) or in connection with the loan itself (eg where the loan is greater than a certain percentage of the value of the security) were waived or reduced in favour of the employee.

For loans made *before 1 June 1994*, the waiver or reduction of the incidental costs of obtaining a loan (eg valuation, administration, arrangement, reservation or booking fees) can be ignored (s 88(5)). All the other terms and conditions of a loan to an employee made before that date must, however, be precisely the same as for loans to the general public if the loan to the employee is to come within the exemption.

At or about the time the loan to the employee was made

The timespan for comparing the loan to the employee and comparable loans is not specified in the legislation. This is to allow a reasonable, commonsense approach in determining whether loans to employees are genuinely ''commercial'' loans within the context of the provisions. Any fixed period would have produced arbitrary results. For example, a particular offer to the public might open on 1 April and close the following 31 March. In the period 1 April to 5 April the majority of loans might be made to employees. However, in the period 6 April to 31 March more members of the public take up the offer so that in the overall period from 1 April to 31 March it is clear that a substantial proportion of the loans were made to members of the public as opposed to employees. It would be reasonable in those circumstances to take the whole period 1 April to 31 March in deciding whether the loans to employees were exempt.

A substantial proportion

This condition requires lenders to make a large or considerable proportion of loans to members of the public rather than to employees. [The Revenue] will accept as a matter of course that 50 per cent or more of the total number of loans is a ''substantial proportion''. Whether something less than 50 per cent would qualify would depend on the circumstances in any particular case.

Members of the public at large

The public at large means here the public in general, as opposed to a particular section of the public. The purpose of the expression is to ensure that a substantial proportion of loans are made by the lender to ordinary customers at arm's length rather than to a selected group (eg suppliers or former employees). However, loans made by merchant banks or other specialised lenders can still come within the exemption, provided all of the conditions are met. The requirement does not mean that lenders have to make loans to everyone on the Clapham omnibus.

Commentary—*Simon's Direct Tax Service* **E4.632**.

RI 86 (October 1994) *Capital allowances—machinery and plant fixtures*

CAA 1990 s 53 enables a lessor and lessee to make an election which gives the lessor title to allowances on machinery and plant fixtures. Two points have been raised on the section.

1 ORDER IN WHICH EVENTS OCCUR

Section 53(1), lists five conditions, (a) to (e), which have to be met before the lessor can claim allowances. [The Revenue] have been asked whether the order in which these conditions are met matters. [The Revenue's] view since the legislation was enacted in 1985 is that the order does not matter. The main principal effect of this view is that the section can apply to an asset which is a fixture before it is leased (as well as to chattels which become fixtures after they are leased).

2 ELECTIONS NOT VALID BEFORE LESSEE BEGINS TO TRADE

One of the cases in which the election can be made is where a lease is entered into ''for the purposes of a trade carried on by the equipment lessee'' (s 53(1)(b)). [The Revenue] used to take the view that a valid election could be made before the lessee began to trade, although [the Revenue] also said that the lessor could only claim allowances from the time the lessee's trade began. [The Revenue] now take the view that a valid election cannot be made at all until the lessee's trade has started. This is because s 53(1)(b) makes it a condition that the trade is ''carried on''—present tense—by the lessee. CAA 1990 s 83(2) does not affect this condition because it only deems machinery and plant expenditure incurred before commencement to be incurred on the date trading starts. Thus, in the present situation, it could apply to the lessor (who incurs the capital expenditure) but not to the lessee (who has incurred no expenditure on which allowances are due).

[The Revenue] will, however, continue to accept claims on the old basis where the parties committed themselves to a deal in reliance on [the Revenue's] previous view.

Note—This interpretation is now obsolete.

RI 87 (October 1994) *Capital gains tax—apportionment for rollover relief*

[The Revenue's] practice is to allow rollover relief under TCGA 1992 s 152 on the acquisition of a building or structure even though only part of it is exclusively used for business. Relief will be due on the apportioned cost of that part. It has been suggested that this practice is concessionary. For the reasons set out in this note, [the Revenue's] view is that the practice is not concessionary.

TCGA 1992 s 155 lists the classes of assets which may qualify for rollover relief. Class 1, Head A includes ''any building or part of a building''. The implication is that a part of a building can be treated as a separate asset for the purpose of the relief.

This implication is reinforced by s 152(6) which applies where a part of a building or structure is used for the purposes of a business. That part is treated as if it ''were a separate asset'' and the acquisition cost of the building or structure is to be apportioned between that part and the rest. The manner in which the apportionment is to be made is set out in s 152(11).

The language used in s 152(6) has led some commentators to infer that the subsection applies only to the old assets disposed of and not to the new. In [the Revenue's] view this inference is incorrect—the language used can usefully be contrasted with the apportionment provision in s 152(7) which explicitly applies only to the old assets.

There is no equivalent apportionment provision for the other classes of assets listed in s 155. Such assets must be used (and in the case of land occupied) only for the purpose of the business if relief is to be obtained.

Commentary—*Simon's Direct Tax Service* **C3.303**.

RI 88 (October 1994) *Capital gains tax—meaning of machinery*

TCGA 1992 s 44(1)(*c*) treats all items of plant and machinery as having a predictable life of less than 50 years. Such assets are, therefore, treated as wasting assets.

TCGA 1992 s 45 exempts wasting assets from capital gains tax unless they have been used in a business where capital allowances were, or could have been claimed.

[The Revenue] have been asked how this affects such items as antique clocks, vintage cars etc which are owned privately and are not used in a business.

The word ''machinery'' is not defined in TCGA 1992 so [the Revenue] give it its normal meaning. This includes any machine or its parts, mechanism or works. A machine is any apparatus which applies mechanical power.

[The Revenue] accept that any asset which falls into one of the following categories will be machinery and, therefore, exempt where it is owned privately and not used in a business—

(*a*) antique clocks and watches such as ''Tompion'' clocks;

(*b*) motor vehicles which are not normal private passenger vehicles (TCGA 1992 s 263). These include—

- taxi cabs,
- racing cars,
- single seat sports cars,
- vans, lorries or other commercial vehicles,
- motor cycles, scooters or motor cycle/sidecar combinations,
- railway locomotives and tramway engines of whatever size or gauge and irrespective of the method of propulsion,
- traction engines,

(*c*) trawlers, fishing vessels, tankers and other vessels propelled by engines.

[The Revenue] do not regard vessels propelled by sail or oars as machinery. Such vessels may, however, on the facts of the particular case, have a predictable life of 50 years or less.

Commentary—*Simon's Direct Tax Service* **C2.901**.

RI 89 (October 1994) *Principal private residence relief—residences occupied under licence*

[The Revenue] have been advised that [their] view of the application of TCGA 1992 s 222(5) to residences occupied under licence is incorrect. The circumstances in which an election is now no longer appropriate are discussed below. These are likely to be very rare and the vast majority of elections under s 222(5) will not be affected.

Section 222(5) concerns the need for, and method of, determining which of two or more residences is an individual's main residence. [The Revenue] have previously taken the view that s 222(5) applies to all residences, including residences occupied under licence such as a hotel or club room where that was in fact a person's place of residence, and a house in which someone lived with relatives (where there is no tenancy). An individual had to make an election under s 222(5)(*a*) where he or she occupied a residence under licence, as well as an owned residence. If an election was not made and the owned residence was sold, the inspector had to make a determination under s 222(5)(*b*).

[The Revenue's] new advice is that s 222(5) is to be interpreted purposively, considering the aim of s 222 as a whole. The section gives relief from capital gains tax on disposals of residences in which an individual has a legal or equitable interest. A "legal or equitable interest" in a property includes all forms of ownership, from that of the sole owner of a fee simple absolute in possession to that of the co-owner of a minimal tenancy. It does not include a residence occupied under licence. Elections or determinations are not appropriate where an individual has a legal or equitable interest in only one property but occupies another property under licence.

Where an individual's main residence is a residence occupied under licence, in which no legal or equitable interest is held, relief will still be available on one other residence which is owned even though an election cannot be made. This is because the owned residence will be the only residence in which that individual has a legal or equitable interest. An election will still be appropriate whenever an individual owns more than one residence each of which consists of a dwellinghouse or an interest in a dwellinghouse.

Job-related accommodation may be occupied under either a service occupancy or a tenancy. Under a service occupancy any rights derive from the service contract and there is no legal or equitable interest in the property which is occupied under licence.

Any notice of election given under s 222(5) which relies on a residence occupied under licence for its effect and which is made after 16 October 1994 will not be regarded as valid. This change of view does not affect the need for an election under s 222(5) in the majority of cases where an individual owns one property and rents another property, since the rented property will normally be occupied under a tenancy rather than under a licence.

Existing elections in favour of residences which fall within s 222(1) will continue to be regarded as valid even if they relied on a residence occupied under licence for their effect. An example would be where the occupation under licence was at the time treated as a change in the combination of residences beginning a new period for which it was necessary to determine the main residence; and hence as beginning a new two-year period in which a notice of election could be and was made.

Existing elections made in respect of residences occupied under licence will be regarded as ceasing to have effect from 16 October 1994. Where there is only one residence in which a legal or equitable interest is held that residence will become the only or main residence for the purposes of s 222 from that date, and the normal rules of time apportionment etc (s 223) will apply accordingly.

Where an existing election is in favour of a residence occupied under licence and there are two other residences in which a legal or equitable interest is held, a new two-year period for making an election between them will be regarded as beginning when the existing election ceases to take effect on 16 October 1994. For this purpose only the lapsing of the existing election will be regarded as giving rise to a change in the combination of residences held. Any new election made as a result in this new two-year period can only be backdated to the beginning of the period. This does not mean that an election made now cannot be backdated further if there was an earlier change of residences giving rise to a two-year period which has not expired.

In any case where an assessment is not yet final and conclusive an individual may ask for an election which relied for its effect on a residence occupied under licence, and which is therefore not valid, to be disregarded completely. In that case the strict statutory rules will be applied in accordance with [the Revenue's] new view to the whole of the period affected. This might mean, for example, that an election could not be made between two residences in which a legal or equitable interest is held, because the time limit for doing so has expired.

Commentary—*Simon's Direct Tax Service* **C3.1303.**

RI 90 (October 1994) *Corporation tax—company purchase scheme*

BACKGROUND

Some UK companies have used a company purchase scheme to avoid payment of substantial amounts of corporation tax. In a typical case the scheme works as follows—

– a profitable company transfers its business to another group company, leaving itself only with cash sufficient to meet its unpaid corporation tax liability;
– the profitable company—which is now worthless—is sold for a share (typically half) of the unpaid tax;
– the new owner arranges for the company to participate in transactions which allegedly remove the company's corporation tax liability;
– the cash is extracted from the company, so that the company ends with little or no assets.

If the tax avoidance scheme were ultimately found to be ineffective so that the company did have tax to pay, there would be little prospect of the Revenue securing payment because the company has no funds.

In all cases seen to date the purchaser who has removed the cash has been outside the UK.

THE LEGISLATION

FA 1994 s 135 introduced TA 1988 ss 767A, 767B which seek to prevent use of the company purchase scheme. The broad thrust of the legislation is that it enables the Revenue to collect the unpaid tax from the persons who previously controlled the stripped company, or from companies under the control of such persons.

In detail, if—

(*a*) there is a change in ownership of a company (s 767A(1)(*a*)), and
(*b*) corporation tax liabilities arise in respect of accounting periods beginning before the change of ownership and are wholly or in part unpaid (s 767A(1)(*b*)), and
(*c*) one of the following is fulfilled—
  – the activities of a trade or business of the company cease or its scale becomes small or negligible during the three years before the change in the ownership and there is no significant revival before that change (s 767A(4));
  – the activities of a trade or business of the company cease or its scale becomes small or negligible after the change but under arrangements made before that change (s 767A(5));
  – there is a major change in the nature or conduct of a trade or business of the company during the period of six years beginning three years before the change in ownership; there is a transfer of assets directly or indirectly from the company to the person or persons who previously controlled it, another company which was under their control or a connected person; the major change is attributable to that transfer; and the transfer occurred during the three years before the change in the ownership or after that change but under arrangements made before the change (s 767A(6))

then the Revenue is able to collect the unpaid tax from those who previously controlled the company, or from any other company which was, at any time in the three years before the change in ownership, controlled by that person or persons (s 767A(1), (2)). The tax which the Revenue can collect in this way is limited to the unpaid corporation tax for accounting periods beginning before the change in ownership. Any assessment is subject to the usual right of appeal.

PARTICULAR POINTS

1 The Revenue's powers extend not only to collection from those who previously controlled the company, but also to collection from any other company previously under the same control (s 767A(2)(*b*)). The extension to other companies previously under the same control extends the opportunity of collection of tax in a case in which those previously in control are non-resident. Such other companies may have been sold before the sale of the company which has failed to meet its tax liability. Anyone buying a company will want to consider seeking an indemnity from the vendor in case the company purchased is faced with a liability under the new provision.

2 It is expected that the introduction of the legislation will curtail use of the company purchase scheme. However, if the Revenue does have to apply the legislation, it will seek to obtain the outstanding tax from those who previously controlled the company and from any companies which can be charged and which are still controlled by the vendor before looking to companies which are no longer under the vendor's control. It is unlikely that the Revenue will have to look to a company which has been sold, but if it has to do so it will not seek collection under the legislation from a company which was sold before 30 November 1993 (Budget day).

3 Section 767A(6) could apply where a target company has two or more trades, transfers one trade to another member of the vendor group prior to a change of ownership and subsequently fails to pay its corporation tax liability for an accounting period beginning before the change of ownership. While this is possible it is unusual for a company to be carrying on more than one trade for tax purposes. The legislation could also conceivably apply where the target company disposes of part of its trade or business to another group company. The legislation was introduced because of the need to counter avoidance. It is unlikely that it will apply where avoidance of tax is not an issue. However, if a situation does arise in which no benefit is obtained by the vendors of a company deriving from the non-payment of tax, and the vendors are unable to secure recompense under any indemnities or warranties held, the Revenue will have regard to the purpose of the legislation in deciding whether to make an assessment under s 767A. It would clearly be unwise for warranties and indemnities not to be sought in respect of all disposals of companies. Inspectors in districts will be asked to refer to Head Office any case in which the legislation appears to be applicable.

4 In the second condition (s 767A(5)) the arrangements referred to are arrangements to which the person who had control of the target company before the change of ownership is party, or of which that person is aware.

5 If, after the introduction of the legislation, the vendor makes a payment (not under s 767A) direct to the Revenue under a warranty with the purchaser in respect of the target company's tax liability, the payment will reduce the consideration for the disposal of the shares.

Commentary—*Simon's Direct Tax Service* **D2.521**.
Revenue Interpretation RI 107—Treatment of payment received under indemnity.

RI 91 (October 1994) *Farming—election for the herd basis*

Production animals are defined as trading stock by TA 1988 Sch 5 para 1 unless an election is made under Para 2 for the herd basis to apply.

Schedule 5 para 3 deals with the consequences of a herd basis election. The initial cost of the herd and the cost of any additions are not allowable as trading deductions. Where an animal dies or ceases to be part of the herd and is replaced then (except for cases to which the special rules relating to disposal of whole herds or substantial parts of herds in para 3(7),(8) apply) para 3(4) provides that any sale proceeds are to be included as a trading receipt and the cost of the replacement animal is an allowable expense. But if an animal is disposed of without replacement then para 3(10) provides that the profit or loss on disposal is to be included or deducted in arriving at trading profits. The Act does not set down any time limit within which replacement must take place. Whether a particular animal brought into the herd (by purchase or home bred) is an addition or a replacement is a question of fact to be decided in the circumstances of the case concerned.

It is sometimes suggested that there is a basic or notional herd size which, in any year, is the maximum number previously reached and that if numbers drop and later increase then animals entering the herd up to the previous maximum must be replacements. But there is nothing in Sch 5 which suggests such a concept; nor would it be possible to apply this idea in the context of the legislation.

By way of example consider a herd which comprised 100 animals from year 1 through to year 10 but which then fell to 85 in year 11, remained at that level through to year 19 and then increased to 100 in year 20. Could the 15 animals acquired in year 20 be replacements, in statutory terms, of those which left in year 11?

Income tax is an annual tax and liability is normally settled year by year. The sale of 15 animals in year 11 would clearly, at that time, fall within para 3(10). This is because para 3(4) operates only when an animal forming part of the herd dies or ceases to form part of the herd and is replaced by another animal. Unless therefore, as a matter of fact, an animal is replaced para 3(4) cannot be in point and para 3(10) will apply. The liability of year 11 has to be settled on that basis. [The Revenue] could not in year 20 go back and adjust the liability for year 11 in accordance with the provisions of para 3(4). The earlier year would be time barred and this suggests that such an interpretation would be incorrect as it lacks the necessary administrative machinery.

So the question of the size of the herd is looked at year by year as a matter of fact and not by reference to any notional or theoretical standard based on the ''high'' of earlier years. The actual number of animals in the herd at a particular accounting date is not of special significance since an animal disposed of before the accounting date may, as a matter of fact, be replaced in a later period. But, if an animal which enters the herd does not replace one which has left it, then the herd is increased in size and the new animal cannot be regarded as a replacement.

[The Revenue] accept animals acquired as replacements where the taxpayer can demonstrate that there is a causal connection between the disposal of the old animal and the acquisition of the new.

The farmer has to show a definite and identifiable intention that the animal disposed of should be replaced by the animal acquired. It is not enough to say that the position is being restored to what it was previously in terms of numbers, rather there must be a direct connection between the disposal and the later addition. Normally farmers will replace animals shortly after they die or are disposed of. As a practical way of approaching the question and in order to avoid detailed discussion, inspectors will accept that replacement treatment is applied where animals are brought into the herd within 12 months of the corresponding disposal.

But there are some special cases where replacement treatment may be appropriate even though the interval is more than 12 months. Where animals are bought in there is unlikely to be sufficient evidence to support the view that there was a direct connection between sale and purchase if the interval was greater than 12 months. But where animals are home bred and particularly in the case of small herds, there may be insufficient home bred young stock to replace unexpected disposals (which might arise through injury or illness) within 12 months, so a longer interval may be reasonable on the facts of the case.

The annual submission of herd reconciliations with accounts and tax computations prevents misunderstanding and is of great assistance to inspectors. Many practitioners adopt this very welcome practice and those who do not are encouraged to do so.

Note—This interpretation has been superseded by the Business Income Manual BIM55520.
Commentary—*Simon's Direct Tax Service* **B3.518**.

RI 92 (October 1994) *Termination payments and legal costs—Concession A81*

APPLICATION TO ACCOUNTANCY AND OTHER PROFESSIONAL COSTS

In Issue 9 of Tax Bulletin November 1993 (page 101) [RI 61] [the Revenue] explained the treatment of legal costs incurred by an employee in a court action to recover compensation for loss of office. A Press Release publicising the concession was issued on 2 September 1993.

[The Revenue] have now been asked whether this concession applies to professional costs other than legal costs.

[The Revenue] confirm that the concession applies only to legal costs which the employee recovers from the employer. (There is, of course, no question of any parallel relief for costs, legal or otherwise, which an employee has to bear himself.) When the legislation under which termination payments are charged to tax was in its infancy, doubts were expressed as to whether awards of such costs by courts were within the scope of the legislation. A practice of not charging tax on awards of costs built up and was later extended to reimbursement of legal costs of a similar nature where the matter did not reach court. ([The Revenue] were subsequently advised that reimbursed costs were strictly taxable and the concession now published as Concession A81 is recognition that not taxing them is a departure from the statutory position.)

The concession is not intended to allow the deduction of any unrecovered expenses which an employee may incur in obtaining compensation for the loss of his or her employment. They have never qualified for relief. Rather the object of the concession is to enable us to continue not to tax sums recovered in respect of substantial expenses that may be incurred where enforcement of the claim through the courts has to be considered. Advice on the enforcement of a legal claim will properly be the province of a solicitor rather than an accountant or other professional. However, [the Revenue] would accept that where, exceptionally, the employee's solicitor found it necessary to consult other professionals for the specific claim, the cost to the solicitor would represent a disbursement and would therefore, as legal costs, be within the concession. Similarly, if a dispute proceeded to court [the Revenue] would accept that any part of the court proceedings, which included the expenses of expert professional witnesses, were legal costs and therefore within the concession.

Commentary—*Simon's Direct Tax Service* **E4.805E**.
Concession A81—(Termination payments and legal costs).

RI 93 (December 1994) *Transfers of assets at undervalue to employees or directors—disposal consideration*

Where an asset is transferred by an employer to an employee or a director in connection with the employment or services. TCGA 1992 s 17(1)(*b*) deems the consideration for the transfer to be at market value. For capital gains tax therefore the employer is treated as disposing of the asset at market value and the employee as acquiring it at that value.

But where the consideration actually paid by the employee is less than market value the difference will usually be chargeable to income tax on him as a Schedule E emolument. In such circumstances it has been [the Revenue's] practice, in computing any capital gains tax payable by the employer on the disposal, and subject to certain conditions, to take the actual consideration paid, and not the market value of the asset, as the consideration for the transfer. The effect is to reduce the amount of the employer's chargeable gain. The employee continues to be regarded as having given market value consideration in calculating any gain on a subsequent disposal of the asset.

The Schedule E and the capital gains charges that can arise on such transfers at undervalue are quite distinct, arising on different taxpayers and separately calculated. [The Revenue] have concluded that there are no grounds for the continuance of this concessionary practice and it is therefore being withdrawn. The correct statutory treatment will apply to transfers of assets on or after 6 April 1995.

Commentary—*Simon's Direct Tax Service* **C2.109**.

RI 94 (December 1994) *Farming—timing issues relating to grants and subsidies*

The general principles for dealing with timing issues relating to grants and subsidies were set out in the article on arable area payments (page 108 of Tax Bulletin February 1993).

That article did not comment on animal grants as, at that stage, [the Revenue] were awaiting accounting evidence.

[The Revenue] have now received representations from accountancy bodies about the correct time to recognise the following animal grants/subsidies—

- suckler cow premium scheme
- beef special premium scheme
- sheep annual premium scheme
- hill livestock compensatory allowances
- extensification payments

After considering those representations [the Revenue] accept that, in most circumstances, correct accounting practice currently provides that it will be appropriate to recognise the grants listed above either—

- at the end of the retention period; or
- on receipt.

If either of these bases is consistently used in the accounts then inspectors will accept that it is a valid basis for tax purposes.

Other bases may be recognised by accountancy bodies as reflecting the correct application of generally accepted accounting practice to the facts in particular cases. Inspectors will accept that such bases are valid provided they do not violate the taxing statutes as interpreted by the courts.

A change from the basis of recognition that is currently being used should only be made where the need to change outweighs the requirement that accounts should be produced on a consistent basis. Where such change is justified it will be dealt with in accordance with Statement of Practice SP 3/90, but practitioners should note that a change in accounting policy is one of the "triggers" in the anti-avoidance proposals in connection with the transition to current year basis periods.

[The Revenue] are sometimes asked about the effect of animal grants/subsidies on valuations which are prepared on the basis of "deemed cost" as described in Business Economic Note 19 section 7. Where a grant/subsidy has been taken into account in full in a particular period then there is no effect on such valuations. Where a receipt has not been taken into account in a particular period but—

- the grant/subsidy has been applied for; and
- that application had a material effect on the market value of the animal,

then the grant should be taken into account as a supplement to the market value when deemed cost is computed.

Grants/subsidies which have been applied for but not recognised as income in the period concerned should also be taken into account in arriving at net realisable value for stock valuation purposes.

Commentary—*Simon's Direct Tax Service* **B3.507**.
Statement of Practice SP 3/90—(Stocks and long-term contracts).

RI 96 (December 1994) *Trading loss relief—late claims*

[The Revenue] have been asked to explain how [they] respond to taxpayers who seek loss relief under TA 1988 ss 380, 381 outside the statutory time limits.

Claims to relief under s 380(1), (2) and s 381 have to be made within two years (extended by statutory regulations for Lloyd's underwriters), except where TMA 1970 ss 36(3), 43(2) or 43A apply.

For s 380(2) claims, the normal time limit expires two years after the year for which relief is claimed; otherwise, it expires two years after the year of loss. For example, where a loss was sustained in 1993–94, any claims under ss 380(1) or 381 should be made by 5 April 1996; any claim under s 380(2) by 5 April 1997.

There is no provision in the Taxes Acts enabling claims to be admitted outside these time limits and the Board is unable to accept late claims as such. It is, however, prepared, in certain circumstances, to exercise its general powers of care and management under TMA 1970 s 1 to grant such relief as would have been due if the claim had been made within time. These circumstances were set out by the then Financial Secretary to the Treasury (John Moore MP) in a written reply to a Parliamentary Question on 10 December 1985. Broadly, they are where the taxpayer or agent—

- has been misled by some relevant and uncorrected error on the part of the Revenue;
- had made an informal claim within the time limit which fell short of a clear and unambiguous statement of what was being claimed but which he or she reasonably believed was an acceptable claim, and the need to formalise the claim was not, within the time limit, pointed out by the Revenue; or
- had effectively been prevented from making an in-date claim for reasons beyond his or her control.

All the other conditions for relief will, of course, still need to be satisfied; and the late claim must have been made within a reasonable period (not normally more than three months) after the expiry of the excuse.

What constitutes acceptable reasons for late claims will depend upon the facts of each individual case. However, there are a number of common explanations which the Revenue do not normally accept as falling within these criteria. These include—

- Delay in preparing the accounts disclosing the loss, unless the delay is itself outside the control of the taxpayer or his agent. Past delays will not be regarded as reasonable excuses even where efforts are being made to bring matters up to date.
- Delay by the Revenue agreeing the accounts. (But it should be noted that a valid claim can be made before the accounts have been either submitted or agreed. A valid claim must state the source of the loss, the year of loss and either the year of claim or the precise statutory provision under which relief is claimed, eg ss 380(1), 381, etc.)
- Misunderstandings between taxpayers and their agents, and failures to pass information between each other.
- Oversight or neglect by current or previous agents.
- Ignorance of the statutory time limits.
- Deliberate decisions to delay the making of the claim because it was unclear when the time limit expired whether the claim was advantageous.

Where a taxpayer or agent believes he or she is entitled to the benefit of this practice, a late claim should be made to the local tax inspector explaining why it was not made within the statutory time limit.

There is no statutory right of appeal against the Revenue's application of this practice but any taxpayer who disputes the decision of a local office can ask for it to be reviewed by the District Inspector or the Controller of the Executive Office concerned.

Commentary—*Simon's Direct Tax Service* **E1.602**.
Note—Both the years for which relief may be claimed under TA 1988 s 380 and the time limits under s 380 and s 381 are amended from 1996/97 under self-assessment.

RI 97 (December 1994) *Relief for trading losses and losses on unquoted shares—transition to new rules*

Relief for trading losses to be offset against total income may be claimed under TA 1988 s 380 in one year in respect of losses sustained in different years. For example, a 1991–92 loss claimed under s 380(2) and a 1992–93 loss claimed under s 380(1), both against 1992–93 income. Following the changes made by FA 1994 s 209, a 1996–97 loss may similarly be claimed under s 380(1)(a) and a 1997–98 loss under s 380(1)(b), both against 1996–97 income. Equivalent claims may be made under TA 1988 s 574 in respect of losses sustained on certain unquoted shares.

The legislation specifies the order in which these reliefs are to be given. Relief for a loss sustained in an earlier year is given before relief for a later year's loss. (Old ss 380(2), 574(2)(a); new ss 380(2), 574(2).)

During the transitional period, loss reliefs could be claimed against the same year's income under both the old and the new rules. For example, a 1993–94 loss may be claimed under old s 574(1) and a 1994–95 loss may be claimed under new s 574(1)(b). Both will be relieved against 1993–94 income.

There is no statutory order of priority between the relief due under the old rules and that due under the new rules. TA 1988 s 835(4) will therefore apply, ensuring the reliefs are given in the order which saves most tax. In practice, therefore, taxpayers can choose the order in which these reliefs are given.

Note—This interpretation is now obsolete.
Commentary—*Simon's Direct Tax Service* **E1.627**.

RI 98 (December 1994) *Formulae to compute stock provisions and write downs*

GENERAL BACKGROUND PAPERS

The Accounting Standards Committee published its revised Statement of Standard Accounting Practice No 9 on stocks and long-term contracts in September 1988. On 10 January 1990 the Revenue published Statement of Practice SP 3/90 which comments on aspects of stock valuation. SP 3/90 also deals with the treatment of long-term contracts—a subject not dealt with in this article.

BASIC PRINCIPLES

The profit computed by the correct application of generally accepted accounting practice to the particular facts is the starting point for the computation of the taxable trading profit. For stocks, generally accepted accounting practice, as detailed in SSAP9, is to calculate the profit or loss for an accounting period by matching costs with related income. Therefore at the accounting date the cost of unsold or unconsumed stocks should be identified and carried forward as the related income would not arise until a later year. At the accounting date, however, there may be a reasonable expectation that the proceeds of sale of some stock in future years will not produce enough income to cover its cost. If so, a loss on such stock should be recognised in the year under review by writing off the irrecoverable costs incurred. Thus, stocks normally need to be stated at cost, or, if lower, at net realisable value. Net realisable value may be less than cost because of deterioration, obsolescence or changes in demand.

APPLYING FORMULAE

Generally the stock should be valued item by item, but accounting practice permits groups similar items to be considered together and allows net realisable value to be arrived at by applying to the cost of similar stocks a formula based on predetermined criteria. Some of the factors that such a formula would normally take into account are the age and condition, past and anticipated future demand and the scrap value of those stocks. The results of applying the formulae should be reviewed to ensure that they are likely to give a reasonable approximation of net realisable value. In particular they should be adjusted for any additional special circumstances and to take into account events occurring between the balance sheet date and the date when the accounts are approved which provide additional evidence of the value of stocks at the balance sheet date.

SLOW MOVING STOCK

If stock is slow moving it may be a pointer that the net realisable value is likely to be less than cost, eg because it is likely to become obsolete before it can be sold. In some cases the formula adopted is that a percentage of the costs of each category of stock is written off depending upon its age. But the fact that stock is slow moving does not of itself mean that its net realisable value will be less than its cost. Therefore although age-related formulae may often give acceptable results that is not always the case.

[THE REVENUE] APPROACH

Inspectors will accept provisions and write downs arrived at using formulae, including age-related formulae, provided that each formula reflects a realistic appraisal of the future income from the particular category of stock and results in the stock being included at a reasonable estimate of its net realisable value. This is not an area where [the Revenue] expect pinpoint accuracy, but inspectors will challenge provisions based on unrealistic assumptions where the effect on the tax liability is significant.

After reviewing the position in a particular case an inspector may agree that certain formulae are appropriate and indicate that it is not intended to review the position for a specified number of years, though the inspector's right to review the position during that period would remain. For their part traders and their agents should check each year that the agreed formulae still give a reasonable approximation of the net realisable value of the stock.

When inspectors accept computations without enquiry it is on the assumption that traders and their agents have ensured that the taxable trading profits declared are arrived at in accordance with the above principles and SP 3/90.

Note—This interpretation is now obsolete.
Commentary—*Simon's Direct Tax Service* **B3.1012.**
Statement of Practice SP 3/90—(Stocks and long-term contracts).

RI 99 (December 1994) *Expenses rule—allowable business travel*

[The Revenue] have been asked whether, in order to qualify for tax relief on their travelling expenses, employees must always take the shortest route on a business journey. This question might arise, for

example, when it would be quicker for someone to travel more miles along a motorway than to take the shortest route across country, possibly through country lanes, or to go across a city or town where there might be heavy traffic.

When it comes to calculating allowable business miles [the Revenue's] responsibility under the law is that [they] must be satisfied the journey made by the employee actually was a business journey. That is that the travelling expenses were incurred necessarily in the performance of the duties.

Looking at the most straightforward position first. When an employee has to go from his or her normal place of work to visit a client, and then returns to that normal place of work, the expenses of a journey longer than the shortest route may be allowable, provided the alternative route has been selected for good business reasons.

Similar considerations apply in the "triangular travel" situation when applying the "lesser of" rule in Booklet 480 [1994 edition] para 8.4. [The Revenue] need to be satisfied that when an employee travels from home to a temporary place of work or returns home directly after such a visit, the journey was in fact a business journey. Having satisfied [themselves] that the journey undertaken was a business one, [they] would compare the cost of that journey with the cost of the journey from the normal place of work to the temporary place of work by the same mode of transport.

...

Note—This interpretation is now obsolete.
Commentary—*Simon's Direct Tax Service* **E4.708**.
Cross reference—TA 1988 s 198 (1) (travelling expenses) (amended from 1998/99 by FA 1997 s 62).

RI 100 (February 1995) *Relief for maintenance payments under FA 1988 s 38*

FA 1988 s 38 provides relief for maintenance payments made under "existing obligations" as defined in FA 1988 s 36(4). Broadly these are court orders, written agreements and oral agreements evidenced in writing made before 15 March 1988 and court orders and written agreements made subsequently which vary, supplement or replace such court orders or agreements.

Relief is limited by s 38(3) by reference to the amount of payments due in 1988–89 in respect of which the payer was entitled to relief for that year (or the payments due and made for the year of assessment if less).

In practice in some cases [the Revenue] have allowed relief for 1989–90 and subsequent years by reference to payments due and made for 1988–89 even where the payer's income for that year was insufficient to give him entitlement to relief on the full amount of the payments. [The Revenue] have received legal advice that this approach was not in accordance with the legislation and [they] have now decided the practice must be withdrawn. No claims from new claimants for 1989–90 or any subsequent year which rely on this practice will now be accepted.

However, claimants who are already receiving relief on this basis will not be affected by the withdrawal of the practice.

Commentary—*Simon's Direct Tax Service* **E1.514**.

RI 102 (February 1995) *Californian tax—tax credit relief*

The US Supreme Court decided in June 1994 to uphold California's right to impose its corporate franchise tax using a unitary (worldwide combined reporting) method. This decision has led [the Revenue] to review the basis on which tax credit relief may be allowed for the tax. [Their] view is that relief should be allowed as follows, whether the tax is charged using the unitary method or on the basis of a water's edge selection.

Where a UK resident company has a branch which pays Californian franchise tax, unilateral credit relief will be allowed for the lesser of—

– the actual Californian tax paid, and
– the amount of the tax that would have been paid on the basis of the profits of the branch which arise in the US and the profits arising in the US of any affiliated companies, to the extent that these latter are brought into the calculation of the tax as members of the unitary group or following a water's edge election.

The limit of credit for the Californian tax (plus any other taxes paid by the branch on its profits, including federal income tax) will be the UK tax on the profits of the branch which arise in the US.

Relief will also be allowed where the Californian tax is paid by a company resident outside the UK which pays a dividend to a UK company and the companies are related to each other within the meaning of TA 1988 s 801. In this situation [the Revenue] would regard as eligible for inclusion in the calculation of underlying tax the lesser of—

– the actual Californian tax paid by the overseas company, and

RIs

– the Californian tax that it would have paid on the basis of its profits arising in the US and on profits arising in the US of affiliated companies, to the extent that these latter are brought into the calculation of the tax as members of the unitary group or following a water's edge election.

Commentary—*Simon's Direct Tax Service* **F1.215; F5.102.**

RI 103 (February 1995) *Redundancy payments and provisions—Schedule D Cases I and II*

This article summarises [the Revenue's] current thinking on the treatment of redundancy costs in the computation of the taxable profits from a trade, profession or vocation.

WHETHER RELIEF AVAILABLE AT ALL

Under general Schedule D Case I and II rules, redundancy payments will normally be an allowable Case I and II deduction provided that—

– *they are laid out wholly and exclusively for business purposes; and*
– *the payments are not of a capital nature.*

In particular, redundancy payments made as an incident in the discontinuance of a trade are inadmissible on first principles. See IRC v Anglo Brewing Co Ltd, ((1925) 12 TC 803).

Where a sum is not deductible under the general rules TA 1988 ss 90, 579 nevertheless give a deduction for—

– *statutory redundancy payments; and*
– *additional payments, inadmissible on the Anglo-Brewing principle, up to three times the statutory payment made.*

TIMING OF DEDUCTION

If the right to a tax deduction is dependent on TA 1988 s 90 or 579 then relief is due for the period of account in which the payment is made. Where the payment is made after the discontinuance it is regarded for this purpose as made on the last day on which the business is carried on.

Where instead a deduction is due under the general rules [the Revenue's] view is that a provision for future payments may be allowed as a deduction so long as—

– *the provision appears in the commercial accounts of the business in accordance with generally accepted accounting principles, including those in Financial Reporting Standard 3 para 18 where that is applicable; and*
– *a definite decision was taken during the period of account to proceed with the redundancy programme; and*
– *the provision was accurately calculated using the degree of hindsight permitted by Statement of Standard Accounting Practice 17 (an accurate calculation will normally require the individual employees affected to be identified); and*
– *payment was made within nine months of the end of the period of account, as required by FA 1989 s 43.*

Note—This interpretation is now obsolete.

RI 104 (February 1995) *Qualifying indexed securities*

The use of indices in determining the amount payable on redemption

FA 1989 Sch 11 para 2 provides for qualifying indexed securities to be exempted from the deep gain legislation which would otherwise impose a charge on an investor on transfer or redemption.

The exemption generally applies to securities which are intended to provide long-term protection against inflation. Schedule 11 para 2 sets out a number of detailed conditions which must be satisfied.

One of these conditions is that the amount payable on redemption needs to be determined by reference to the movement in an index as described in Sch 11 para 2(2).

Paragraph 2(2)(a) allows the Retail Price Index to be used where sterling is the nominal currency and para 2(2)(b) allows the use of similar indices published by governments of other countries where the security is denominated in the currency of that country. So, for example, the United States' Consumer Prices Index would be acceptable for a US dollar denominated security.

Paragraph 2(2)(c) provides a similar rule for quoted securities where the amount payable on redemption is determined by reference to the movement in a published index of prices of shares quoted in the official list of a recognised stock exchange.

It is [the Revenue's] view that the recognised stock exchange whose published index is used in determining the amount payable on redemption should also be the stock exchange on which the security is quoted. Thus [the Revenue] would expect that an index of UK Stock Exchange Prices, eg the FT-SE-Actuaries All Share Index or the FT-SE 100 Index, should be used if para 2(2)(c) is to be satisfied where a sterling denominated security is quoted on the UK Stock Exchange.

The use of indices in determining the interest payable

Paragraph 2(4)(d) contains a condition that the interest payable is also to be determined by reference to the movement in the same index as is used to determine the amount payable on redemption.

Paragraph 2(5) contains a further condition that where the index is applied to determine interest, it must, under the terms of issue, "be applied precisely and without restriction".

It is [the Revenue's] view that this condition is not satisfied where the index is applied directly to the interest payable but, for example—

– *a formula is used to restrict the impact of the index on the interest paid, or*
– *the movement in the interest payable is in inverse proportion to the movement in the index itself.*

Commentary—*Simon's Direct Tax Service* **B5.421**.
Note—FA 1989 Sch 11 has been repealed as part of the "loan relationships" provisions of FA 1996 Pt IV Chapter II. For income tax purposes, the "deep gain" provisions are superseded by the "discounted securities" provisions of FA 1996 Sch 13.

RI 105 (February 1995) *Travelling expenses of directors and employees earning £8,500 a year or more—Concession A4*

Concession A4 modifies, in certain circumstances, the general rule that the costs to a taxpayer of travelling to or from his or her UK place of business are not allowable in computing his or her tax liability. [The Revenue] have been asked whether this concession applies to taxpayers who are not resident in the UK.

[The Revenue] confirm that the concession should be regarded as applying to any taxpayer who falls within one or other of the circumstances set out in Concession A4 paras (*a*)–(*d*), whether or not he or she is resident in the UK.

[They] also confirm that the provisions of A4 extend to the expenses of a husband who accompanies his wife on a business journey overseas in the circumstances set out in para (*d*).

Commentary—*Simon's Direct Tax Service* **E4.708, 710**.
Concession A4—(Travelling expenses of directors and employees earning £8,500 a year or more).

RI 106 (April 1995) *Capital allowances—meaning of colony*

[FA 1995] introduces a new section, 33E, to CAA 1990.

In providing a definition of the term "relevant register" used earlier in the legislation subsection (7) of the new section makes reference to a "colony".

[The Revenue] have received enquiries as to how this term will be interpreted by them, and to avoid any possibility of doubt, this note confirms that for the purposes of s 33E a colony is as defined by the Interpretation Act 1978 Sch 1.

In particular the following territories are considered to be covered currently by the term "colonies" in s 33E—

– *Anguilla*
– *Bermuda*
– *British Virgin Islands*
– *Cayman Islands*
– *Channel Islands*
– *Falkland Islands*
– *Gibraltar*

...

– *Isle of Man*
– *Montserrat*
– *St Helena*
– *Turks & Caicos Islands.*

Note—This interpretation has been superseded by the Capital Allowances Manual CA25230.
Commentary—*Simon's Direct Tax Service* **B2.353**.
Note—See now CAA 2001 s 154(4) for definition of "relevant register".
Hong Kong has been removed from the above list as it is no longer a colony—see RI 185 below.

RI 107 (April 1995) *Corporation tax: company purchase scheme*

Tax Bulletin Issue 13 (October 1994) [RI 90] contained an article on the new legislation at TA 1988 ss 767A and 767B which seek to prevent use of the company purchase scheme.

In the article [the Revenue] said it would be unwise for warranties and indemnities not to be sought in respect of all disposals of companies. Such an indemnity would supplement the statutory right of recovery given by s 767B(2), which provides that any person making a payment on an assessment under s 767A shall be entitled to recover an amount equal to the payment from the taxpayer company. Concern has been expressed about the treatment of the payment received from the purchaser (under a contractual indemnity) or from the taxpayer company (under s 767B(2)). Depending on which company is assessed by the Revenue, the payment could be made either to the vendor or to a member of the vendor's group (ie companies within s 767A(2)).

[The Revenue] can confirm that in these circumstances there would not be a charge to tax on the recipient of the payment made under an indemnity or under s 767B(2).

Commentary—*Simon's Direct Tax Service* **D2.521**.

RI 108 (April 1995) *Interest rates and currency swaps: reduced importance of Concession C17*

Tax Bulletin Issue 15 (February 1995) referred to the introduction of a new legislative package for exchange gains and losses and financial instruments. The new scheme applies to the corporate sector and will apply from the first day of a company's first accounting period to begin on or after 23 March 1995—its "commencement day".

Concession C17 is concerned with the concessionary tax treatment of swap fees paid by or to a recognised UK bank or swaps dealer in the ordinary course of its trade. This concession will no longer be of any relevance to annual swap fees payable by a company in respect of currency swaps, after its commencement day. However, where an interest rate swap is held by a company at its commencement day, the new regime will only apply to that swap from commencement if the company has made an election under FA 1994 s 148(3). Where such an election is not made, the concession will remain in force until 6 years have elapsed) or until the company no longer holds the swap, if earlier).

...

Commentary—*Simon's Direct Tax Service* **D2.1051**.
Note—Concession C17 is regarded by the Revenue as obsolescent because the number of people able to benefit from it is decreasing.

RI 109 (April 1995) *VAT repayments received by sports clubs*

Note—This interpretation has been superseded by the Business Income Manual 31610.
Commentary—*Simon's Direct Tax Service* **B3.240**.

RI 111 (April 1995) *Interest relief: provision of certificates of interest paid to borrowers*

Under TA 1988 s 353, claims may be made for relief for certain types of loan interest, and TA 1988 s 366(1) requires the borrower, when making such a claim, to provide a written statement from the lender with certain details about the loan.

The details the lender has to provide are—

– the date the debt was incurred,
– the amount of the debt when incurred,
– the interest paid in the year of assessment for which the claim is made, and
– the name and address of the debtor.

TA 1988 s 366(2) allows the borrower to ask the lender to supply these details where relief under TA 1988 s 353 is being claimed. It should be noted that the requirement to supply a certificate of interest paid applies only where relief for the interest is being claimed under TA 1988 s 353. For lenders other than building societies and local authorities, the Revenue currently provides two types of form which a lender can use to furnish these details to a borrower who is making such a claim.

LOANS FROM BUILDING SOCIETIES AND LOCAL AUTHORITIES

The requirements set out in TA 1988 s 366 for making claims under TA 1988 s 353 do not apply where interest is paid to building societies or local authorities, as the arrangements for providing details of interest paid to these concerns are different.

OTHER LENDERS

For other lenders, the form to be used depends on whether or not they are banks. For lenders other than banks, form 38E–1(1988) can be used to provide the borrower with the relevant details. This form is available on request from the Inspector that deals with the lender's tax affairs. The lender certifies the details set out above, and before signing and sending the form to the Revenue, the borrower is asked to state the purpose for which the loan was used.

BANK LOANS

For bank loans, form 38E–2(1988) can be used. As well as asking the borrower for the purpose of the loan, this form also asks the bank to certify that the interest is on a loan other than an overdraft (since relief under TA 1988 s 353 cannot be claimed for interest on an overdraft). This form is supplied centrally by the Revenue, direct to all recognised banks. As the reference to overdrafts is generally applicable only in the context of banks, forms 38E–2 are not made available to non-bank lenders.

ALTERNATIVE FORMS

The forms provided by the Revenue do not have to be used, so long as the lender provides in writing the details set out above. Where lenders are in any doubt as to the suitability of their proposed form, they should contact the Inspector who deals with their tax affairs.

MORTGAGES WITH MIRAS LENDERS

Borrowers eligible for Mortgage Interest Relief At Source (MIRAS) get relief by paying over the net amount of interest to the lender. Building societies provide interest details centrally to the Revenue and borrowers need only enter details of the lender and account/roll number on their tax return. In other cases, borrowers should ask for Certificates of Interest paid, form MIRAS 5, only if they have not been given tax relief at source on all their qualifying interest payments.

For deferred interest/low start mortgages, which operate outside the MIRAS arrangements, special substitute Certificates should be used which show—

- gross interest due in the year,
- gross interest paid in the year,
- amount of the initial advance,
- balance outstanding at the end of the year.

Commentary—*Simon's Direct Tax Service* **E1.556**.

RI 112 (April 1995) *Schedule E: relocation packages—Concession A85*

BACKGROUND

On 27 April 1994 [the Revenue] published Concession A85.

This has particular relevance to the guaranteed selling price schemes (GSP schemes) that employers, who are making a job related house move, to dispose of their existing homes. The background to this extra-statutory concession was explained more fully in Tax Bulletin Issue 11 (May 1994).

If the employee is a director or employee within TA 1988 Part V Chapter II, [the Revenue] take the view that the GSP scheme is a facility within the meaning of "benefits and facilities" in TA 1988 s 154(2). Tax is charged on an amount equal to the cash equivalent of such a facility. The cash equivalent of any facility or benefit is its cost less any amount made good by the employee. The cost of the benefit is the expense incurred in or in connection with its provision.

A strict application of the law would mean that an employee, whose property was purchased through a GSP scheme, could be taxable on the costs incurred by the employer or relocation company as purchaser of the property. Concession A85 was introduced to avoid that result.

Concession A85 works by providing a concessionary method of calculating the cash equivalent of the benefit which arises when an employee transfers an asset in circumstances in which TA 1988 s 154 applies.

In those circumstances, Concession A85 provides that "the cost for the purposes of the cash equivalent (TA 1988 s 156) will be taken as—

- the price paid for the asset by the purchaser and any other valuable consideration given for it; plus
- any costs which would normally be met by a vendor but are borne by someone other than the employee.

Other costs incurred by the person(*s*) providing the benefit in connection with the transfer will be ignored."

Since [the Revenue] announced Concession A85, concerns have been raised about potential differences in the tax treatment of employees whose homes are purchased by their employers using GSP schemes in Scotland. This is because under Scottish property law, beneficial interest passes at a later point in a property transaction as compared with the rest of the UK.

Commonly GSP schemes involve the exchange of contracts on the property between the employee and either the employer or the relocation company. The property is then sold on to a third party without title to that property being taken by the employer or relocation company. In that way only the third party purchaser incurs liability to stamp duty. In England and Wales, beneficial interest in the property passes on the exchange of contracts. The most recent Scottish case on the subject indicates that beneficial interest does not pass until the purchaser records their title to the property. So it would not be possible to transfer beneficial interest in Scotland without incurring stamp duty on the transaction.

PREVIOUS VIEW

[The Revenue's] original view was that the transfer of beneficial interest has to be taken into account in looking at the tax treatment of GSP schemes. There are two reasons why this might be relevant.

First, because [the Revenue] have to decide on the tax treatment of the GSP scheme sale proceedings. [They] took the view that if the beneficial interest in a property had not passed to the employer or relocation company at the time the employee received the GSP scheme proceeds, these would represent, not the sale proceeds of the property, but a beneficial loan. In these circumstances the benefit received by the employee would not be taxable under TA 1988 s 154 but under TA 1988 s 160. As a result, the concessionary basis of calculating the cash equivalent of a TA 1988 s 154 benefit, set out in Concession A85, would not apply.

Second, [the Revenue] need to be able to identify the point at which the benefit to the employee arising from the transfer of the property ends. This is so [they] can measure the cost of the benefit to the person who provides it. [They] took the view that the transfer of beneficial interest marked that point.

CURRENT VIEW

[The Revenue] have looked again at [their] interpretation of the law in this area. This has led [them] to change [their] view of the significance of the transfer of beneficial interest. [They] now think that the payment of the GSP scheme proceeds prior to the transfer of the beneficial interest does not necessarily constitute the provision of a beneficial loan, provided that the beneficial interest in the property is eventually transferred by the employee, and the contract between the employee and the employer or relocation company is one of sale and not of loan.

Accordingly, for the purposes of applying Concession A85, [the Revenue] will not regard the transfer of beneficial interest as the point at which the benefit ends. Instead [they] shall look at the point at which the benefit arising from the transfer of the property ends and consider this as a question of fact. The facts of each case may of course vary, but [they] shall accept that the benefit has come to an end when—

(*a*) the employee has entered into a binding contract to dispose of the property; and
(*b*) the employee has permanently surrendered possession of the property in accordance with the contract; and
(*c*) the sale proceeds have been paid in full or in part.

Because it is the facility given to employees to transfer their homes to their employer or a relocation company which comes within the terms of TA 1988 s 154, only costs incurred in connection with that transfer are covered by the concession. Costs incurred by an employer or relocation company in connection with a subsequent sale to a third party are not taxable on the employee under TA 1988 s 154 and so are not within the concession.

Concession A85 itself has not changed. Employers' ancillary costs incurred in providing the benefit remain within the concession. Those costs incurred after the benefit has come to an end are not taxable on the employee anyway. The significance of [the Revenue's] revised view is that cases, typically in Scotland, where the GSP is paid to the employee before the transfer of the beneficial interest may now come within the terms of Concession A85.

[Their] revised interpretation will apply from 6 April 1995 and for all earlier cases where tax liability has not yet been agreed.

Commentary—*Simon's Direct Tax Service* **E4.613**.
Concession A85—Transfers of assets by employees and directors to employers and others (now obsolete).

RI 113 (June 1995) *Foreign exchange and financial instruments: currency contracts—transitional rules*

A company may hold a currency contract for a period which straddles its commencement day (the first day of the company's first accounting period to start on or after 23 March 1995) and on which any profit or loss does not fall to be dealt with in computing trading profits. Here, the transitional provisions at FA 1994 s 175 enable FA 1994 s 153(4), (5) to operate to bring in unrealised pre-commencement foreign exchange gains or losses as a deemed forward premium or discount. This is intended to ensure that the commercial profit or loss over the life of the contract is recognised for tax purposes. Concern has, however, been expressed that the operation of these provisions alone might inappropriately result in a company becoming subject to a direction under the controlled foreign company (CFC) legislation. This is because, prior to the FOREX legislation, such a contract would have been subject to capital gains rules which do not apply to CFCs.

Paragraphs 2.27 and 6.34 of the Revenue's Explanatory Statement (published in December 1994) explain how the transitional provisions will apply to CFCs. Broadly, where a CFC would have been subject to a direction under TA 1988 s 747 (or would have been, had it not paid an acceptable distribution) in the accounting period prior to it becoming subject to the FOREX rules, it is treated in the same way as a UK resident company for the purposes of both the foreign exchange and the financial instrument transitional rules. However, where this is not the case, but the CFC might otherwise become subject to a direction under TA 1988 s 747 in the following accounting period, purely because of FA 1994 s 153(4), (5) operating to impute a deemed receipt in respect of pre-commencement exchange gains, then the Board will take this factor into account when considering whether a direction should be made.

Note—This interpretation is now obsolete.
Commentary—*Simon's Direct Tax Service* **D2.1054**.

RI 114 (June 1995) *Foreign exchange and financial instruments: grandfathering and other elections*

"Grandfathering" is a feature of both the new foreign exchange regulations supporting the FOREX legislation in FA 1993 and the new financial instrument legislation in FA 1994, both of which came into force on 23 March 1995.

Where a qualifying company holds "fluctuating" debts at its commencement day (the first day of its first accounting period to start on or after 23 March 1995), subject to certain conditions, these are kept out of the new FOREX tax regime for six years (ie they are "grandfathered"), unless the company elects otherwise (Exchange Gains and Losses (Transitional Provisions) Regulations, SI 1994/3226 reg 3(2), (5)). Similarly, if a qualifying company holds an interest rate contract or option at its commencement day, this is also kept out of the new financial instrument regime for six years, again unless the company elects otherwise (FA 1994 s 148(2), (3)).

Such elections should be made by the company concerned. However, it is appreciated that in the case of a controlled foreign company (CFC) this requirement may cause practical difficulties. Therefore, the Revenue will be prepared to accept an election made on behalf of the CFC, by a company resident in the UK which alone or jointly with other companies resident in the UK has a majority interest in the CFC, as long as the secretary or director of the CFC has given specific authority to this effect.

This same principle will be applied for elections under the Exchange Gains and Losses (Transitional Provisions) Regulations, SI 1994/3226 regs 6(2), 15(1). (Under reg 6(2), a company may elect to adopt the original cost price as the basic valuation for certain qualifying assets. Under reg 15(1), it can elect for certain pre-commencement exchange gains or losses to be treated as accruing over the six years following commencement.)

Note—This interpretation is now obsolete.

RI 115 (June 1995) *Loss relief: cessation adjustments—Concession A88*

Note—Concession A88 was declared obsolete by the Revenue in 1998.

RI 116 (June 1995) *Schedule D Case I: franchise payments*

Various forms of agreement are often described, somewhat loosely, as franchises, (for example licences, dealerships and concessions) but this article is particularly concerned with payments under "business system franchise agreements". Under such an agreement, the owner of an established business format (the franchisor) grants to another person (the franchisee) the right to distribute products or perform services using that system.

The terms of agreements vary considerably but, generally, the franchisee gets the use of the system, training and any necessary management back-up for a specified period, of perhaps five to ten years, in return for—

– *an initial fee (payable in one sum or in instalments); and*
– *continuing, usually annual, fees.*

FRANCHISEE—TREATMENT OF THE INITIAL FEE

The capital or revenue quality of the initial payment by the franchisee depends upon what it is for. Normally, it is paid wholly or mainly for substantial rights of an enduring nature to initiate or substantially extend a business. To that extent, the initial payment, whether payable in one sum or

RIs

instalments, is capital, as are any related professional fees. It is immaterial that the expenditure may prove abortive. Nor is the tax treatment of the receipt in the hands of the franchisor relevant.

In some instances, the franchisor also provides, under the terms of the franchise agreement, goods or services of a revenue nature at the outset, for instance, trading stock or services such as the training of staff (other than the franchisee—see below). Inspectors will accept that an appropriate part of the initial fee is for such revenue items, and hence allowable, where—

- *the sum claimed in respect of revenue items fairly reflects the actual goods and services provided; and*
- *it is clear that those services are not separately charged for in the continuing fees.*

Normally, the costs of the initial training of the franchisee are disallowable, [see Revenue Interpretation RI 1].

Generally, the annual fee payable by the franchisee will be a revenue expense.

Note—This interpretation has been superseded by the Business Income Manual BIM57620.
Commentary—*Simon's Direct Tax Service* **B3.911**.
Revenue Interpretation RI 1—Expenditure on training courses for business proprietors.

RI 117 (June 1995) *Schedule D Case I: pre-trading expenditure*

There was an article on this topic in Tax Bulletin Issue 5 ([Revenue Interpretation RI 32]). Since then the legislation governing relief for expenditure incurred prior to the commencement of a business has been amended in a number of ways—

- *the period in which the expenditure must be incurred has been extended to cover the seven years prior to commencement;*
- *unrelieved charges on income paid by a company wholly and exclusively for trading purposes, prior to the commencement of trading, are now treated for corporation tax purposes as if they were paid on the first day of trading;*

(both these changes apply in cases where the trade etc commenced after 31 March 1993)

- *in the case of a non-resident company, a payment made wholly and exclusively for the purposes of a trade which it plans to carry on in the UK through a branch or agency, can now qualify as a charge. (This applies to payments after 31 March 1993.)*

Thus, relief for pre-trading expenditure is extended to interest which could not have been regarded as a deductible Schedule D Case I expense incurred on the first day of trading under the rules as they stood prior to these amendments.

Finally, pre-trading expenditure will no longer be regarded for income tax purposes as giving rise to a separate business loss. Instead, where the business commences on or after 6 April 1995, pre-trading expenditure will be treated as if it had been incurred on the first day of business. In other words, the relief is now given as a deduction in computing the taxable profit or the allowable loss for the first period of business. It will no longer be necessary to make separate income tax loss relief claims for pre-trading expenditure.

[The Revenue] continue to hold the view expressed in the earlier article that no relief is available to a business for pre-trading expenditure incurred by another person.

Note—This interpretation has been superseded by the Business Income Manual BIM46351 and BIM46355.
Commentary—*Simon's Direct Tax Service* **B3.1204**.
Revenue Interpretation RI 32—Pre-trading expenditure: expenses incurred by another person.
Cross reference—TA 1988 s 401 (relief for pre-trading expenditure).

RI 118 (June 1995) *Unapproved retirement benefit schemes*

Prior to 1989, unapproved retirement benefit schemes were rare. This was because the conditions governing ''Exempt approved schemes'' prevented an employer operating the two different types of scheme in tandem for the same employees.

These restrictions were repealed by FA 1989 s 75, Sch 6. At the same time, unapproved schemes were given statutory recognition. The intention behind this was to give greater flexibility and freedom in providing for pensions. But, as was made clear at the time, tax advantages were restricted to those available for approved schemes. No tax advantages were to be conferred on unapproved schemes.

This intention was achieved by FA 1989 s 76.

Section 76 ensures that no relief is given for the cost of providing some retirement benefits and determines the time at which relief is given for others.

Section 76(1)–(3) provides that—

- *to the extent that benefits are provided by an employer under arrangements which count as a ''retirement benefit scheme''; and*
- *the arrangements are not approved by the Revenue's Pension Schemes Office; and*

- *the provision of the benefits does not give rise to any tax charge on the employee or former employee;*

the employer cannot obtain any relief (whether as a deduction in computing taxable profits from a trade, profession or vocation or as management expenses) for the expenses of providing the benefit.

The latter subsections of s 76 contain a timing rule. It applies to the provision of benefits which result in a charge to tax on the employee or former employee. In these circumstances s 76 does not prevent the employer from obtaining relief subject to the general rules on whether an expense is deductible. But it does ensure timing symmetry between the timing of relief and the charge to tax. Relief is not given to the employer before the period in which the expense of providing the benefit is actually laid out (see FA 1989 s 76(4)–(6)).

[The Revenue] have seen it suggested that the legislation does not achieve timing symmetry. [They] do not accept that there is any drafting ambiguity in the legislation.

But, in the absence of agreement, the Commissioners and the courts can consider the intentions of Parliament, as expressed in debates during the passage of the 1989 Finance Bill, on Pepper v Hart [1992] STC 898 principles. In introducing amendments to the Bill, including what is now FA 1989 s 76(4), the then Financial Secretary to the Treasury said—

> *"The amendments deal with drafting shortcomings in clause 73. The intention is that non-approved top-up pension schemes should not benefit from the tax advantages available to approved occupational schemes ... As drafted the clause disallows those costs unless the employee is chargeable ... but it says nothing about the timing of deductions where costs are allowable. The effect is that the employer could claim a deduction in advance of payments being made if, at some point in the future, the employee would be chargeable to tax on these payments. The amendments prevent an employer from obtaining such a timing advantage."*

[The Revenue] consider that the above puts the matter beyond doubt.

Note—This interpretation has been superseded by the Business Income Manual BIM46015.
Commentary—*Simon's Direct Tax Service* **E7.256**.

RI 119 (August 1995) *Capital gains tax: private residence relief—garden or grounds*

TCGA 1992 s 222(1)(*b*) provides for relief on the disposal of, or of an interest in, land which an individual has for his own occupation and enjoyment with his residence as its garden or grounds up to the permitted area.

The purpose of this article is to set out the Revenue's interpretation of this section following comment on a recent Special Commissioner's decision in the case of *Wakeling v Maidment*, now correctly named *Wakeling v Pearce* [[1995] STC (SCD) 96]. Mrs Wakeling succeeded in her appeals but the Revenue have decided not to test the matter in the High Court due to her particular circumstances. The facts of the case and the decision do not affect the Revenue's interpretation of this section.

To qualify for private residence relief, the land must meet certain conditions at the date on which it is disposed of. The words "land which he has for his own occupation and enjoyment with that residence as its garden or grounds" in s 222(1)(*b*) make this clear. They contrast with s 222(1)(*a*) which applies to a dwelling house, "which is, or has at any time in his period of ownership been his only or main residence" and thus looks both at the present and the past. This difference in interpretation was confirmed in the case of *Varty v Lynes* [[1976] STC 508 Ch D]. The use of the land other than that at the date of disposal is therefore irrelevant.

The conditions to be met are—

- it must be land which the owner has for occupation and enjoyment with the residence;
- it must be the garden or grounds of the residence;
- the area of land must not exceed the permitted area.

However, this does not mean that land which meets these conditions necessarily qualifies fully for relief. TCGA 1992 s 222(1)(*b*) determines land which may qualify, whilst the amount of relief is then determined by TCGA 1992 s 223.

It is for the inspector to agree whether land can be regarded as occupied and enjoyed with the residence as its garden or grounds. The determination of what constitutes the permitted area, if over 0·5 of a hectare, (for disposals prior to 19 March 1991, one acre), rests with the District Valuer. (The procedures relating to the determination of the permitted area were reported in detail in *Tax Bulletin* Issue 2 (February 1992) [p 10].)

The phrase "occupation and enjoyment" is understood by reference to the legal meaning of the words used. Occupation means possession of the land while enjoyment means possession without contested claims from third parties.

The phrase "garden or grounds" is not defined in the statute, nor is there judicial authority. The words must carry their everyday meaning and whether a piece of land can be regarded as the garden or grounds of a residence is a question of fact.

The word ''garden'' is taken to mean an enclosed piece of ground devoted to the cultivation of flowers, fruit or vegetables. The word ''grounds'' extends this and makes it more difficult to define. A useful dictionary definition of grounds is—

> ''Enclosed land surrounding or attached to a dwellinghouse or other building serving chiefly for ornament or recreation''.

In general, the Revenue accepts that land surrounding the residence and in the same ownership is the grounds of the residence, unless it is used for some other purpose. The Revenue would not regard land used for agriculture, commercial woodlands, trade or business as part of the garden or grounds. Also, land which has been fenced off from the residence to be sold for development is excluded. Land which has traditionally been part of the grounds of the residence but which, at the date of sale, is unused or overgrown is not excluded, nor are paddocks or orchards if there is no significant business use. Included in the definition is land which has a building on it, provided the building is not let or in use for a business, and also land which is not used exclusively for recreational purposes. For example, the owner-occupier of a guest house may allow guests to use the garden. The land would still qualify for relief providing the other conditions are satisfied.

Disposal of land which is physically separated from the residence may cause problems. The Revenue does not accept that land is garden or grounds merely if it is in the same ownership as the residence and is used as a garden. However, land which can be shown objectively, on the facts, to be naturally and traditionally the garden of the residence, so that it would normally be offered to a prospective purchaser as part of the residence, will be accepted. An example of this is where, as in some villages, it is common for a garden to be across the street from the residence. The separation itself would not be regarded as a reason for denying relief.

It must be stressed that these cases will be rare and if land is separated from the residence by other land which is not in the same ownership as the residence, it will usually not be part of the garden or grounds. For example, land bought some distance from the residence due to an inadequate garden at the residence and which is cultivated and regarded as part of the garden will not qualify for relief.

Commentary—*Simon's Direct Tax Service* **C2.1302**.

RI 120 (August 2001) *Enterprise investment scheme: qualifying trades (Section 297 ICTA 1988)*

For the purposes of the enterprise investment scheme (EIS), the requirements which a trade must meet if it is to be a qualifying trade are set out at TA 1988 s 297. TA 1988 s 297(2) provides that the trade must not consist of any of the various activities listed in that subs, neither may such activities, taken together, form a substantial part of the whole trade (these activities will be referred to below as ''excluded activities''). In order to decide whether a particular trade is a qualifying trade, it is therefore necessary to ascertain whether it includes any excluded activities.

This article focuses on the three types of excluded activity listed in TA 1988 s 297(2)(*e*)—leasing, receiving royalties and receiving licence fees. The article applies equally for the purposes of the corporate venturing scheme, enterprise management incentives and the venture capital trust scheme, for which the corresponding rules are found in FA 2000 Sch 15 paras 25, 26, FA 2000 Sch 14 paras 18, 19 and TA 1988 Sch 28B para 4, respectively.

LEASING

This is defined in the statute as including letting ships on charter (though this exclusion is subject to an exception, which is set out in TA 1988 s 29) and letting other assets on hire. It thus covers any trading activity which consists in allowing the customer the use of the trader's property. Examples are television rental, video hire and the provision of self-storage warehousing facilities. It applies where, subject to reasonable conditions imposed by the trader, the customer is free to use the property for the purpose for which it is intended.

One area which has been found to give rise to difficulty is what is, and what is not, car hire. The question to be considered here is whether the person using the car is the company or the company's customer. On the one hand the company may itself use the car to provide a transportation service for customers. On the other hand the company may provide the car to the customer as a transportation facility, for use by the customer. The latter activity constitutes hire of an asset. A taxi service is likely to be a transportation service. By contrast, what is offered by a company providing chauffeured car hire is likely to be a transportation facility; the fact that the customer is not personally driving the car does not mean that that person is not the person using the car. But what is important is not the label ''taxi service'' or ''chauffeured car hire'' but the true nature of the contract between the parties.

RECEIVING ROYALTIES AND LICENCE FEES

Royalties or licence fees will be received where property rights of certain kinds are exploited by granting permission to others to make use of that property. But there will be cases where, although the "sales" are made under licence, the receipts are nevertheless consideration for the supply of goods—for example, the retailing of CDs.

Where there is an activity of receiving royalties or licence fees there is one exception to the general exclusion. This is set out for the EIS at TA 1988 s 297(4)–(5C), as enacted by FA 2000. It applies, broadly speaking, in certain cases where the receipts are attributable to the exploitation of assets such as intellectual property which have been created by the company itself or a group company.

LICENCE FEES

Licences may be granted as a means of exploiting an interest in land. But in some situations the grant of the licence is merely incidental to an activity of supplying services. In such cases it is considered that TA 1988 s 297(2)(*e*) is not in point; for example, what the proprietor of a cinema offers in return for payment for a ticket, is not just to admit the customer and provide a seat but to show a film.

This principle can be illustrated by looking at activities concerned with the provision of sports and leisure facilities. At one extreme, a simple activity of making sports facilities available to the general public, with no provision of services, would consist of little more than charging a fee in return for the right to use property. This would be an activity of receiving licence fees. But such a situation would be exceptional. A more commonly encountered activity might be operating a health club which provides a high level of services, including active supervision and advice from qualified staff. Here the licence to enter the premises and use the equipment would be merely incidental.

In some cases where fees for admission are received, while is no direct provision of services to customers, continuous work is required to keep the property in a fit state for use by them. The main question to be considered in any such case is the extent to which the fees relate to the cost of such work.

Commentary—*Simon's Direct Tax Service* **E3.119, 126, 133, 623**.
Note—This is an updated version of the interpretation published in August 1995.

RI 122 (August 1995) *Schedule A: basis periods—partnerships*

Commentary—*Simon's Direct Tax Service* **A4.101**.
Note—This interpretation was relevant for 1995–96 and 1996–97 only.

RI 123 (August 1995) *Schedule D Case I: change of accounting date—transition to current year basis*

Note—This interpretation summarised the Revenue's views on the practice to be adopted when considering a case in which a basis period for 1995/96 (or earlier) had to be determined by reference to an account ending in 1995/96.

RI 124 (August 1995) *Venture capital trusts—funding of management buy-outs*

A venture capital trust (VCT) must, broadly within three years of being provisionally approved by the Revenue, have at least 70 per cent by value of its investments represented by qualifying holdings. These are shares or securities specifically issued to the VCT by companies which satisfy the conditions of TA 1988 Sch 28B, as introduced by FA 1995 s 70.

[The Revenue] have been asked in what circumstances it is possible for an acquisition of shares or securities in a company, which is to be used in a management buy-out, to give rise to a qualifying holding.

THE TAX LAW RELEVANT TO BUY-OUTS

There are no provisions in the VCT legislation which relate specifically to management buy-outs. However, among the various requirements set out in TA 1988 Sch 28B, there are two which are of special relevance to buy-outs generally and management buy-outs in particular. They are that—

- the company issuing shares or securities to a VCT (or, in the case where that company is a holding company, a subsidiary of that company) must be carrying on a trade or else preparing to carry on a trade (TA 1988 Sch 28B para 3); and
- the money raised by the issue of shares or securities to a VCT must be employed for the purposes of the trade (which include the purpose of preparing to carry on the trade).

(TA 1988 Sch 28B para 6.)

One effect of these requirements is that it is not possible for the company issuing the shares or securities to the VCT merely to acquire shares with limited liability; rather it must bear the full risks of carrying on the trade.

THE TAX CONSEQUENCES FOR BUY-OUTS

There are many ways in which a buy-out might be organised. In any particular case it will be the facts which determine whether the arrangements satisfy the requirements of TA 1988 Sch 28B. This article considers three basic outline scenarios. These are where a company is formed to acquire—

- a trade;
- another company and its trade; or
- a holding company with a number of trading subsidiaries;

and the funds obtained from the VCT are used by the company specifically to purchase the trade, company or group.

In the first scenario, [the Revenue] will usually accept that the application of the funds to purchase the trade satisfies the requirement that the funds are employed for the purposes of the trade.

The second scenario will often come about as the result of a refusal by the existing owners to sell the trade without selling the company. [The Revenue's] view is that, where shares are purchased, the money cannot normally be said to be employed for the purposes of a trade—rather it is employed in the making of an investment.

However, if the trade is hived up to the acquiring company, leaving the acquired company as a dormant subsidiary, as soon as possible after the acquisition, [the Revenue] will usually accept that the funds have been employed for the purposes of the trade.

In the third scenario, if all of the activities of the holding company and of *all* of its subsidiaries are hived up to the acquiring company, [the Revenue] will usually accept that the funds have been employed for the purposes of the trade. To the extent that the trades are not hived up to the acquiring company, [the Revenue] consider the acquisition of the group is the making of an investment and not all the funds provided by the VCT are employed for the purposes of a trade or trades. Therefore, under TA 1988 Sch 28B para 1(3) only part of the holding is a qualifying holding.

Commentary—*Simon's Direct Tax Service* **E3.629**.

RI 125 (August 1995) *Tax credit relief—South African secondary tax on companies*

The Revenue booklet IR 146 ''Double taxation relief—admissible and inadmissible taxes'' published in March 1995 records that the secondary tax on companies introduced in South Africa in 1993 is not regarded as admissible for tax credit relief. [The Revenue] have now reconsidered the matter in the light of further information and have concluded that secondary tax on companies qualifies for unilateral relief as underlying tax under TA 1988 s 790(6). [The Revenue] will apply the change of view to payments of secondary tax on companies since its introduction. The amount of the relief due in a particular case should be agreed in the usual way with Double Taxation (Rates) Section, Financial Intermediaries and Claims, Office (FICO) (International), Fitz Roy House, PO Box 46, Nottingham NG2 1BD.

Commentary—*Simon's Direct Tax Service* **F5.102**.
Cross reference—See Revenue booklet IR 146 (1995) Double taxation relief—admissible and inadmissible taxes.

RI 126 (October 1995) *Corporation tax: investment companies*

The legislation which is now in TA 1988 ss 75, 76 and 130 was originally conceived—back in 1915—with two objectives—

- *primarily to give relief to Life Assurance companies (where the Crown opted not to assess under Schedule D Case I), and*
- *to give relief to commercial concerns whose business consisted predominantly of making investments.*

Companies qualifying in the second category are defined in TA 1988 s 130 as those ''whose business consists wholly or mainly in the making of investments and the principal part of whose income is derived therefrom''.

It is perhaps surprising that there has not been a single tax case in the UK on the meaning of TA 1988 s 130 or its direct predecessors, although there are two cases on identical legislation (Income Tax Act 1918 s 33) in the Irish Republic. These cases are Howth Estate Company v Davies *(1934) 2 ITC 74 and* Casey v The Monteagle Estate Company Ltd *(1962) 3 ITC 313. The essential point that can be inferred from these cases is that it is not enough that a company has investments, but rather that its business must consist in the making of investments and that is a question of looking at the totality of its functions and activities.*

In the Monteagle Estate case, Mr Justice Teevan said, ''What has to be looked to is the nature of the operations or functions of the company. The search is not for a company making investments but for a company whose main business is the making of investments. That, to my mind, involves the purpose of the operations as well as their nature''.

It is not possible to give a list of conditions that must be satisfied if a company is to be regarded as an investment company within TA 1988 s 130. But whether a company's business consists wholly or mainly in the making of investments has recently been considered by a Special Commissioner in 12 similar cases, Tintern Close Residents Society Ltd (and others) v Winter *(1995) Sp C 7–Sp C 18. In the* Tintern Close *case [[1995] STC (SCD) 57] the company's activities were confined to the ownership and management of the estate which comprised 21 houses, 1 flat and 22 lock-up garages. Its income consisted of members' subscriptions, ground rent and interest.*

In reaching her decision, the Special Commissioner asked a number of questions—

- *was the company incorporated to acquire assets to turn them to account so that profit could be distributed to the shareholders?*
- *what are the activities of the company?*
- *if investments are held, was that in order to make money from them?*
- *do the purpose and nature of the operations indicate that its main business is the making of investments?*

The Special Commissioner said that, while the company was incorporated to acquire land, it was not for the purpose of turning that land to account for profit nor for making distributions to its shareholders. Moreover, the functions and activities of the company are the management and maintenance of the property on behalf of the residents who pay subscriptions to cover the cost. Its main business, in terms of the purpose of the operations, is the provision of maintenance services and not the making of investments.

The Revenue agrees with this approach of looking to see what constitutes the company's main business. It can be illustrated with a further example. A company which is a housing association, briefly stated, consists wholly or mainly in the provision of housing (usually for a particular category of persons) and not the making of investments. This was the view taken in an analogous case involving excess profits tax legislation, IRC v 1933 Housing Society Ltd *(1946, EPT Leaflet 47), where the company's object was stated to be the provision and management of housing. The question was whether the company was carrying on a business consisting ''wholly or mainly in the dealing in or holding of investments''. Mr Justice Atkinson said the holding of investments incidental to the real purposes of a company does not necessarily involve it carrying on a business of holding investments.*

Note—This interpretation is now obsolete.
Commentary—*Simon's Direct Tax Service* **D4.401**.

RI 128 (October 1995) *Schedule D Case I: video tapes acquired for rental*

[The Revenue] have received a number of enquiries about the correct tax treatment of video tapes used in the rental trade. Practitioners may also be aware of various articles and comments in the accountancy journals and in the trade press. This article summarises [The Revenue's] views on the subject.

INTRODUCTION

The tax treatment of pre-recorded video tapes will vary between traders because the way that the cost of tapes is written off for tax purposes depends on a number of variable factors, such as how the tape is used in the trade, its useful economic life and, to some extent, the trader's choice.

A video tape acquired primarily for resale at a profit is treated as stock in trade in the normal way. But most video tapes are acquired for hiring out to produce an income stream while in the trader's ownership. Even if tapes are to be sold at the end of their useful life, they should not be treated as stock but in the way described below.

USEFUL ECONOMIC LIFE

The useful economic life of a tape is important in establishing the correct tax treatment of the tape. Useful economic life is not necessarily the same as the physical life of the tape. It depends on the popularity of the tape and so the pattern of demand for it. Typically the useful economic life of a tape will be less than its physical life.

MEANS OF OBTAINING RELIEF

Relief for the cost of acquiring video tapes for hire may be obtained by way of—

- *capital allowances where the tapes are sufficiently durable and have a sufficiently long useful economic life to qualify as plant; or*
- *valuation basis where the tapes do not qualify for capital allowances; or*
- *renewals basis (whatever the life of the tapes).*

The appropriate basis should be established when trading begins and whatever basis is used, this should then be followed consistently from year to year. Tapes with similar useful economic lives should be grouped together.

CAPITAL ALLOWANCES

Tapes with a useful economic life of two years or more will qualify as plant. Where that condition is met, capital allowances may be claimed on the tapes that form the original library and replacements and additions to that library. A short life asset election may be made.

VALUATION BASIS

This basis can be used where the facts show that a tape has a useful economic life of two years or less. On this basis the cost of the tape is allowed as a revenue expense. At the end of the accounting period a valuation is made of the tapes held at that date and that becomes the opening valuation for the following period.

The result is similar to treating the tapes as stock in trade, except that the closing value is not measured by reference to the tape's secondhand value, but rather by the potential income stream it generates. The effect is to spread the cost of each tape over its economic life to match the cost with the income that arises from it.

RATE OF WRITE DOWN ON VALUATION BASIS

The rate of write down of a tape on valuation basis will normally be on a straight line between the cost of acquisition of the tape and the anticipated disposal proceeds. However, in a particular case the facts may establish that an alternative method is more appropriate.

EXAMPLE

Consider a trader who buys a batch of newly released "AA Blockbuster" tapes of a similar nature and a batch of secondhand and classic videos, again of a consistent nature, on the first day of a 12 month accounting period. The anticipated useful economic life of the tapes is just less than two years. The tapes are to be disposed of after two years by being scrapped.

Using a straight line write down, a deduction is due for the cost of each batch in the year of acquisition. This is subject to a countervailing valuation at the end of the first year of one half of the difference between the cost of acquisition and the anticipated disposal proceeds.

Alternatively, the trader may be able to establish by reference to the trade's records, that, perhaps, 75 per cent of the new film rentals arise in the first 12 months after acquisition with 24 per cent in the following six months and only 1 per cent thereafter. In such a case at the end of the first year a valuation of 25 per cent of the acquisition cost less disposal proceeds would be justified. At the end of the second accounting period the tapes would be valued at the estimated disposal proceeds.

The secondhand and classic films may have a more even rental profile over their useful economic life but, nevertheless, it might be demonstrated by reference to trading records, that they too should be written off at a faster rate than that provided for by the straight line method.

RENEWALS BASIS

Under the renewals basis a deduction is given for the cost of replacing tapes, net of the proceeds of the sale of the tapes replaced. Thus renewals basis does not provide relief for—

- *the initial cost of the library;*
- *additions (and improvements) to the tape library; and*
- *the cost of replacing a tape on which capital allowances have been given.*

For these reasons it is rarely adopted in practice even though it avoids the need for a valuation of tapes at the end of the year.

Note—This Interpretation is now obsolete.
Commentary—*Simon's Direct Tax Service* **B2.314**.

RI 129 (October 1995) *Schedule D Case I: timing of VAT refunds to opticians*

BACKGROUND

Legislation introduced on 1 September 1988 ended the exemption from VAT of the sale of spectacles by opticians. The supply of services of opticians remained exempt. Many opticians claimed that part of the price paid for spectacles or contact lenses was for their medical services and hence should be exempt. But Customs took the view that the sale of spectacles or contact lenses was a single supply of standard rated goods and there was no separate supply of services.

The VAT tribunal considered the issue in the appeals brought by Leightons Opticians (LON/92/2521) and Eye-Tech Opticians (LON/92/3012 and LON/92/3288) in August 1993 and August 1994 respectively and found that there were two separate supplies. Customs disagreed with this view and while they appealed to the High Court, opticians were allowed to apportion their supplies between standard rated goods and the services the VAT tribunal had found were exempt.

On 13 March 1995 the High Court upheld the decisions of the VAT tribunal. Customs decided not to appeal and issued a Business Brief on 5 May 1995 inviting opticians to submit claims for repayment of overpaid VAT and statutory interest dating back to 1 September 1988.

TAX CONSEQUENCES

The period of account in which the refund should be recognised for the purposes of computing the trading profits

[The Revenue] have received a number of enquiries about the time VAT refunds received by opticians should be recognised as part of their trading profits. In particular [The Revenue] have been asked whether they should fall in the period of account ending on or spanning 13 March 1995, the date of the High Court decision.

In this situation, the tax treatment would follow that in accounts prepared in accordance with the correct application of the principles of commercial accounting practice. In particular, computations for earlier years should not be reopened on the basis of case law relating to extra payment sought for goods or services supplied by the business, (rather than the late recovery of an expense) and decided without modern accounting input.

The optician's accountant will consider how to apply correctly to the facts in any particular case, the principles of commercial accounting, including those in Financial Reporting Standard No 3. As so much will depend on the facts, this is not an area in which [The Revenue] can make a general statement that the refund should be recognised at a particular point in time.

But [The Revenue] can say that it does not necessarily follow that the refund will be recognised in the period of account into which the High Court judgment fell. On the basis of the particular facts an accountant could reasonably conclude that it was appropriate to recognise the refund at an earlier point. Standard Statement of Accounting Practice 17 (dealing with post balance sheet events) is particularly relevant.

Further, as opticians were allowed to apportion their supplies from August 1994, some opticians may have been making provision in the accounts for the VAT liability payable if Custom's appeal had been successful. If so, accounts drawn up after it became clear that the High Court judgment was final but for periods ending earlier, would include the release of such a provision.

TRANSITIONAL RULES FOR THE INTRODUCTION OF CURRENT YEAR BASIS OF ASSESSMENT

If, on the basis of the principles outlined above, the VAT refund falls within the basis period for 1996–97, the transitional averaging rules in FA 1994 Sch 20 would apply to it as they would to other income and expenditure of that period.

POST-CESSATION REFUNDS

If the business has ceased before the refund is received then the refund will be assessed under TA 1988 s 103 at the time of receipt.

INTEREST

It is the Revenue's understanding that the interest payments received by opticians are made under VATA 1994 s 78. This provides for payments of interest in cases of official error, which are calculated on a basis which takes account of the time that has elapsed since the VAT payment was made. It is the Revenue's view that these payments constitute interest for tax purposes, and, as they are not specifically exempted from income tax or corporation tax, are therefore, subject to the normal tax rules which apply to interest payments.

This tax treatment should not be confused with the exemption from income and corporation tax that is provided by TA 1988 s 827(2) for payments made by way of supplement under VATA 1994 s 79. Such supplements are calculated as a fixed percentage of the VAT repaid, irrespective of the time that had elapsed between the payment of VAT and its subsequent repayment, and do not, therefore, have the character of interest.

It should also be distinguished from the tax treatment of supplement on repayments of certain Revenue taxes which are expressly exempted from income tax or corporation tax by TA 1988 s 824(8) or 826(7).

Interest on the refund will be assessable under Schedule D Case III for the basis period in which falls the date to which the interest is calculated. The interest will be assessable on the current year basis.

Note—This Interpretation has been superseded by the Business Income Manual BIM80715 et seq.
Commentary—*Simon's Direct Tax Service* **B3.914**.

RI 130 (October 1995) *Schedule D Case I: post-cessation business expenses—new relief*

BACKGROUND

FA 1995 s 90 introduced, with effect from Budget Day (29 November 1994), a new relief for certain post-cessation expenses of persons who formerly carried on a business either alone or in partnership. The relief does not extend to companies, but individuals may claim relief against income and gains generally, of the year in which the expense is regarded as arising.

Before the new legislation took effect, there was no relief for expenses incurred after a business ceased, unless it was possible to deduct a provision for them in the final accounts or there were post-cessation receipts, charged under Schedule D Case VI, against which the expenses could be set.

EXPENSES QUALIFYING FOR RELIEF

The relief is for specific qualifying expenses paid in the year for which the relief is claimed and for trade debts which unexpectedly go bad after the business is discontinued. The qualifying expenses are payments made wholly and exclusively—

(a) in remedying defective work done, goods supplied or services rendered while the business was continuing, or damages in respect of such work, goods or services;
(b) legal and other professional expenses connected with such costs;
(c) in insuring against such costs;
(d) for collecting trade debts of the discontinued business.

To qualify for relief, the payment must have been made on or after 29 November 1994 and within seven years from the discontinuance. A claim to relief must also be made within two years of the end of the year of assessment in which the payment was made.

Professional indemnity insurance premiums for work undertaken in the course of the business will now, in principle, almost always be allowable. If incurred while the business is continuing they will be allowed as a deduction in computing profits within the ordinary rules of Schedule D Cases I/II. If paid after the business has ceased they will be within the terms of the new relief, subject to the seven year rule. [The Revenue] would not seek to disallow such an insurance premium paid while the business continues on the grounds that the cover extends to claims lodged after it has ceased. This view supersedes that in Tax Bulletin Issue 4 (August 1992 p 32) [RI 25].

BAD DEBTS

The new relief also extends to bad debts. Trade debts which have been included in business incomings before discontinuance and which have not been the subject of an admissible bad debt provision sometimes turn out to be bad. Alternatively debts may be sometimes wholly or partly released under a post-cessation formal ''voluntary arrangement''. The new rules deem a payment equal to the amount of the bad debt to qualify for relief, as described above, at the time the debt is ''proved'' to be bad. That will normally be the date when the inspector is notified that the debt is irrecoverable.

The inspector must be notified that a debt has gone bad within seven years of the time the business is discontinued. He or she will need to be satisfied that the debt is irrecoverable, and may require further information for this purpose. In these circumstances the debt is proved to be bad when the inspector is first notified, provided that the debt is eventually shown to have been bad at that date.

The relief is not restricted to debts that have become bad on or after 29 November 1994. Relief is available for debts which otherwise qualify even if they were already bad at that date, so long as they are irrecoverable when they are subsequently notified to the inspector.

INSURANCE RECOVERIES

Expenses that qualify for relief under the new provision may be reimbursed or refunded as, for example, insurance proceeds or premium refunds. This means that the cost will not be ultimately borne by the former trader. To take account of this, any sums received as reimbursements or refunds of a qualifying expense will be brought into charge as post-cessation receipts.

UNPAID EXPENSES

In arriving at the taxable trading profits of the discontinued business, some expenses might have been deducted on normal accountancy principles, even though they had not been paid. If there are any expenses that remain unpaid at the end of a year of assessment for which the new relief is claimed, the amount of the relief is reduced by the amount of the unpaid expense. But if an unpaid expense that triggered such a restriction is later paid, relief will be given as if it were a qualifying post-cessation expense of the year in which it is paid.

LINK WITH EXISTING POST-CESSATION EXPENSES PROVISION

The new relief exists alongside the rules already on the statute book for post-cessation receipts and expenses. Those rules provide that any loss or expense which would have qualified as a trading deduction had the business not ceased is relieved against post-cessation receipts. But where the deductions exceed the post-cessation receipts for a year of assessment the excess can only be carried forward and relieved against any post-cessation receipts arising in later years. Where an expense qualifies for sideways relief under the new rules as well as for carry forward under the provision described above, the new rules thus take priority.

Note—This Interpretation has been superseded by the Business Income Manual BIM80715 et seq.
Commentary—*Simon's Direct Tax Service* **B4.225**.
Revenue Interpretation RI 25—Post-cessation professional indemnity insurance premiums.

RI 131 (October 1995) *Schedule E: employees' liability and indemnity relief*

FA 1995 ss 91, 92 introduce a tax relief (TA 1988 s 201AA) for employees for payments they make to secure indemnity insurance against liability claims arising from their job, or to meet uninsured work-related liabilities. The legislation also cancels out any tax charge on an employee where the employer or someone else pays for the insurance or meets the liability. The relief extends to payments made by or for ex-employees, for periods of up to six years after the year in which the employment ceases.

(The relief applies to employees, directors and office-holders, and the following references to "employees" should be read as covering these other categories as well.)

This article clarifies certain points on how the relief will operate.

INTERPRETATION OF THE REQUIREMENT THAT A LIABILITY INSURANCE CONTRACT IS NOT CONNECTED WITH ANY OTHER CONTRACT

TA 1988 s 201AA(3)(*b*) provides that a liability insurance contract will not generally be within the terms of the new relief if it is "connected" with any other contract. This restriction is to prevent abuse. For example, the possibility that two associated contracts may be taken out, only one of which relates to liability insurance and whose premiums are artificially weighted to inflate the amount which qualifies for relief.

It is not, however, the intention that this restriction should disqualify an insurance contract connected with an ordinary contract of employment. Thus, where a job contract specifies that the employer or employee has to take out a work indemnity policy, so that the two contracts may effectively be connected, such a connection will not by itself be regarded as preventing the insurance policy from being a policy which can qualify under TA 1988 s 201AA.

INTERPRETATION OF "UNLAWFUL"—TA 1988 S 201AA(8)

Section 201AA(8) denies relief where it would be "unlawful" for any employer to enter into a contract of insurance in respect of particular liabilities or costs. This provision excludes relief for costs such as fines and penalties imposed on an employee for a criminal or other offence, which are costs which cannot legally be insured against. (But the costs of *defending* a criminal case, whether the defence is successful or not, are lawfully insurable and are not excluded from relief.)

The term "unlawful" relates, in the Revenue's view, to the lawfulness of entering into the contract under UK law. Relief will not be denied in respect of a contract which is not unlawful in itself but which, for example, is not within the power of a particular employing company to effect or is not authorised by its articles of association.

OPERATION OF THE RELIEF WHERE GROUP INDEMNITY POLICIES ARE TAKEN OUT, OR THE LIABILITY IS MET BY SOMEONE WHO IS NOT THE EMPLOYER

Relief is available in respect of payments made, or received by, or made on behalf of, an employee, regardless of whether it is the employer or someone else who actually takes out the contract of insurance or pays the liability. This latter situation can arise notably where one company in a group takes out insurance covering the employees of another company or of all companies in the same group. Relief is equally available where an unrelated third party effects the contract of insurance.

Payments (other than under an insurance policy) made to or on behalf of, an employee in respect of a liability claim arising from his or her job, are emoluments of the employment in respect of which the liability claim arises, whether they are made direct by the employer or by someone else. So an employee working for several group companies, and on whose behalf sums are paid out for a liability incurred in relation to the employment with one particular company, would be treated as receiving emoluments of that amount from the employment with the company (in addition to any ordinary remuneration receivable by the employee from that employment). Under the terms of the relief this is matched by a tax deduction against those emoluments of an amount equal to the liability payment.

EXAMPLE 1

A director (X) holds directorships with a number of companies, A, B, C, and D, in the same group. His main emoluments, £80,000, come from his directorship with A; he receives remuneration of only £1,000 pa from each of his offices with B, C, and D.

X is the subject of a work liability claim in respect of his job with company C. All directors in the group are covered by a group indemnity policy the premiums on which are paid by group company E. The claim against X is met by a payment of £100,000 made by another group company F because the indemnity policy claims limit for that year has been reached.

This sum, whether paid direct to the claimant or passed to the director (whether or not through C) to meet the liability, constitutes chargeable emoluments of the director from his office with C. His total remuneration from this office will therefore be £101,000; but under the relief he will have an offsetting deduction for £100,000.

(The amounts of premium payable by company E which are attributable to X and to fellow directors in respect of work-related indemnity insurance also form part of their remuneration. The liability on these amounts will similarly be offset under the relief by a matching deduction.)

EXAMPLE 2

X is the subject of another claim of £100,000 in respect of company B later in the tax year. By then the group has ceased trading and is insolvent with the result that it is no longer able to meet the claim against X out of its own resources and X must pay this himself.

If the claim was settled after the cessation of X's directorship with company B there will be no relief under FA 1995 s 91. But in such a case the £100,000 can be relieved under FA 1995 s 92 against X's other income of the year. FA 1995 s 92 gives relief for payments made up to six years after the employment in respect of which the payment arises has ceased. It is irrelevant whether other directorships or employments have or have not continued.

The normal Schedule E rules apply to the timing of relief. Where FA 1995 s 91 applies, relief will be available in the year in which the payment is made, by the employee or on his/her behalf, against the emoluments of that year for the employment in respect of which the payment arises. Where FA 1995 s 92 applies, relief will be against the employee's total income (and, if that income is insufficient, against his/her excess chargeable gains over allowable losses) of the year.

Commentary—*Simon's Direct Tax Service* E4.718A.

RI 132 (October 1995) *Special Commissioners—publication of decisions*

Following the introduction of procedural rules for both the Special and the General Commissioners from 1 September 1994 (SI 1994/1811, SI 1994/1812), the Special Commissioners are now publishing their decisions (for appeals where the notice of the hearing was given on or after 1 September 1994). The decisions will be anonymised if necessary, where the hearing, or part of it, was in private.

It is the Revenue's view that—

- these decisions do not create any legally binding precedent but the conclusions reached may be relevant in other cases, particularly if no appeal is made to a higher court against their decision;
- where a decision is or may be the subject of an appeal to the High Court, it will not be appropriate to enter into any discussion of it in other cases pending the possible appeal.

The Special Commissioners have indicated that they will expect, in future, to have their attention drawn in appropriate cases, to any of their previous published decisions which are relevant (but not to unpublished decisions), where that decision has not been superseded by that of a higher court. In a practice note issued by the presiding Special Commissioner, His Honour Stephen Oliver, QC, indicated how the Commissioners will expect previous decisions to be cited. Decisions should be cited using the decision number preceded by the year in which the decision was released (the example used in the practice note was *Aproline Ltd v Littlejohn* [[1995] STC (SCD) 201].

The full text of any decision may be obtained on application from the Office of the Special Commissioners, 15–19 Bedford Avenue, London WC1B 3AS, on payment of the appropriate fee; it is also possible to subscribe to receive copies of all the decisions. The Revenue will not be publishing the decisions in tax leaflets or the reports of tax cases. A summarised version of decisions of general interest or application is being made available to inspectors.

Commentary—*Simon's Direct Tax Service* A2.516.
Regulations—Special Commissioners (Jurisdiction and Procedure) Regulations, SI 1994/1811 reg 20.

RI 133 (December 1995) *Capital gains tax: reinvestment relief*

Reinvestment relief was introduced by FA 1993. The scope of the relief was widened in FA 1994 and again in FA 1995.

The relief allows certain chargeable gains accruing to individuals, or to the trustees of certain settlements, to be deferred if the gains are reinvested in eligible shares in a trading company or in the holding company of a trading group.

[The Revenue] have recently issued two Press Releases that may be of interest to practitioners.

REINVESTMENT RELIEF AND QUALIFYING CORPORATE BONDS (QCBS)—TCGA 1992 S 116

Tax Bulletin issue 11 [RI 69] set out [The Revenue's] then view on the availability of reinvestment relief where shares have been exchanged for QCBs so that a gain is computed in accordance with TCGA 1992 s 116(10)(a).

...

In an Inland Revenue Press Release dated 27 September 1995 the Financial Secretary to the Treasury announced the Government's intention to make changes in the Budget. Reinvestment relief will be available to further defer gains computed in accordance with s 116(10)(a) when they accrue in accordance with s 116(10)(b). The legislation will be retrospective, so that any gain accruing under s 116(10)(b) on or after 16 March 1993 will be capable of deferral if the other statutory conditions for a claim to reinvestment relief are met.

The example below illustrates how the amended legislation will apply.

EXAMPLE

Shares with a market value of £50,000 are exchanged in June 1992 for QCBs. The gain computed in accordance with s 116(10)(a) is £20,000. In July 1995 half of the QCBs are redeemed. A gain of £10,000 accrues in accordance with s 116(10)(b).

A claim to reinvestment relief can be made to defer the gain if £10,000 is invested in an acquisition of eligible shares at some time between July 1994 and July 1998. This is achieved by treating the consideration to be reduced under TCGA 1992 s 164A as the market value taken into account under s 116(10)(a).

LOANS TO INVESTORS

An acquisition of shares in a qualifying company is not treated as an acquisition of eligible shares if there is a return of the whole or any part of the value of that investment to the individual who is to acquire or has acquired those shares. TCGA 1992 s 164L describes the circumstances that are to be treated as a return of value.

Section 164L(4) treats a loan made to the investor as a return of value if it would not have been made, or would not have been made on the same terms, if the investor had not acquired, or proposed to acquire, those shares.

Statement of Practice 3/94 explained how [the Revenue] would apply the similar rules relating to these loan-linked investments for the purpose of the enterprise investment scheme and the business expansion scheme [concerning holdings of shares issued before 6 April 1998]. An Inland Revenue Press Release dated 14 September 1995 introduced a revised version of the Statement of Practice and confirms that [the Revenue] would apply the same treatment to reinvestment relief and to Venture Capital Trusts.

Note—This Interpretation is now obsolete.
Statement of Practice SP 6/98—Enterprise investment scheme, venture capital trusts, CGT reinvestment relief and business expansion scheme, loans to investors.
Revenue Interpretation RI 69—Reinvestment relief.

RI 134 (December 1995) *Capital gains tax: retirement relief—definition of personal company*

Retirement relief is available if the qualifying conditions are met on gains on disposals of shares in an individual's "personal company". TCGA 1992 Sch 6 para 1(2) defines an individual's "personal company" as one in which he or she can exercise at least 5 per cent of the voting rights.

[The Revenue] have been asked whether in this context voting rights attached to shares held by trustees can be regarded as exercisable by the first named trustee in his or her capacity as an individual.

[The Revenue's] view is that such voting rights cannot be so regarded. There are two specific provisions in particular which point to this conclusion.

Firstly, TCGA 1992 s 69(1) requires trustees to "... be treated as a single and continuing body of persons (distinct from the persons who may from time to time be the trustees) ...".

Secondly, TCGA 1992 Sch 6 para 1(3) allowed "voting rights exercisable by trustees of a settlement to be treated as voting rights exercisable by a member of the family of an individual ...". This provision has been repealed in FA 1993, following the abolition of the "family company" test. But it still illustrates the basic principle that voting rights are exercisable by the trustees as a body of persons distinct from any individual trustee.

Commentary—*Simon's Direct Tax Service* **C3.602**.

RI 135 (December 1995) *Schedule A: transitional proposals*

Note—This interpretation is obsolete from 1996–97.

RI 136 (December 1995) *Schedule D Case I: changes of accounting date—transition to current year assessing*

Note—This interpretation is obsolete.

RI 137 (December 1995) *Schedule A: partnerships—self-assessment*

[The Revenue] have been asked to clarify the circumstances in which the income from jointly owned property constitutes partnership income within the terms of TA 1988 s 111 (as substituted by FA 1995 s 117(2)).

There are a number of possibilities. For example, consider Mr and Mrs Jackson who let a jointly owned property.

Where Mr and Mrs Jackson carry on a business in partnership, and that business comprises both a Schedule D Case I source and a Schedule A source, then TA 1988 s 111(7), (8) would apply. The income from the Schedule A source will be assessable using the basis periods that apply for the Schedule D Case I source.

But it may be that these two activities have been arranged in such a way that there are two separate businesses and two separate partnerships, albeit partnerships between the same two individuals. In such circumstances TA 1988 s 111(10) would apply to the partnership with the Schedule A source. The income from the Schedule A source will be assessable on a tax year (6 April to 5 April) basis.

There is a further possibility. Joint ownership of property does not, of itself, create a partnership. There will only be a partnership if, exceptionally, the exploitation of the property constitutes the carrying on of a business jointly with a view to profit. Where the letting income is not ancillary to a Case I or II partnership source, and the letting activity cannot be described as the carrying on of a business, the income arising is not assessable as partnership income. Instead, each share will be assessable as the personal income of Mr and Mrs Jackson. In this context there is a distinction between the term "business" as used in the Partnership Act 1890, and the new concept of a "Schedule A business" introduced by FA 1995.

Commentary—*Simon's Direct Tax Service* **E1.808**.

RI 138 (February 1996) *Exchange gains and losses—transitional provisions*

This article clarifies [The Revenue's] views on the treatment of deep discount and qualifying indexed securities under the transitional rules for the foreign exchange (FOREX) legislation in FA 1993.

Tax Bulletin Issue 15 (February 1995) referred to the introduction of a new legislative package for exchange gains and losses and financial instruments. It also gave details of an Explanatory Statement containing clarifications which had been given during the consultative process about the operation of the scheme.

The scheme applies to the corporate sector and will apply from the first day of a company's first accounting period beginning on or after 23 March 1995—its "commencement day". Under the scheme, exchange gains and losses are computed by reference to the "basic valuation" of an asset or liability. The Exchange Gains and Losses (Transitional Provisions) Regulations, SI 1994/3226 provide rules—

– *to establish the basic valuation of an asset or liability which was held or owed immediately before and at the beginning of a company's commencement day, and*
– *to deal with pre-commencement gains and losses on such assets and liabilities.*

Where a deep discount or qualifying indexed security held by a qualifying company would have given rise to a chargeable gain or allowable loss, had it been disposed of at market value immediately before the company's commencement day, then reg 6(3) of the transitional rules will apply—its basic valuation will be its market value immediately before commencement day. As a "reg 6(3) asset" any pre-commencement gain or loss will be dealt with under Part III of the Transitional

Provisions Regulations [SI 1994/3226] which provides rules for cumulative set-off against post-commencement exchange differences.

Where a deep discount or qualifying indexed security would not have given rise to a chargeable gain or allowable loss pre-commencement because, for example, it was a liability owed by the company or a qualifying corporate bond held by the company, then reg 6(3) will not be in point. Instead, the basic valuation will be established by reg 6(6). This will normally be the issue price (possibly net of issue costs) or cost of acquisition. Because such debts are defined in reg 3(9) as fixed debts for the purposes of the Transitional Provisions Regulations [SI 1994/3226], pre-commencement exchange differences will be dealt with under Part IV of those regulations which provides the rules for the operation of a ''kink test''.

Further detail of the treatment of deep discount and qualifying indexed securities outside reg 6(3) is included in para 2.8 of the Explanatory Statement.

Note—This Interpretation is now obsolete.
Commentary—*Simon's Direct Tax Service* **D2.975**.

RI 139 (February 1996) *Farmer's averaging and the transition to self-assessment*

[The Revenue] have been asked about farmer's averaging and the transition to self-assessment.

At present, farmer's averaging works by adding the profits before capital allowances assessable for two consecutive years of assessment and assessing half the total each year.

It is profits assessable which are averaged not profits for periods of account. So the first step is to work out the profit assessable. For cases where 1996–97 is the transition year for self-assessment, the profit will generally be based on the results of two years of account reduced by self-assessment transition averaging (under FA 1994 Sch 20 para 2(2)). For example, a farmer's results are—

- *Year ended 31 December 1994, Profit £55,000*
- *Year ended 31 December 1995, Profit £60,000*
- *Year ended 31 December 1996, Profit £10,000*

The profits assessable are—

1995–96

£55,000 previous year basis

1996–97

£35,000 half the total profit for the two years ended 31 December 1996.

The profits assessable differ by more than 30 per cent of the higher of them so farmer's averaging may be claimed. If a claim is made the profits assessable become—

1995–96 = £45,000

1996–97 = £45,000

[The Revenue] have seen it suggested that farmer's averaging can be claimed when the results shown by the accounts for the first of these two years (the year ended 31 December 1995 in the example) are known. This suggestion is incorrect. It is based on the misconception that it is profits for periods of account, rather than profits for years of assessment, which are averaged.

The way in which averaging is given will change fundamentally under self-assessment. This will be explained in detail in a later article and in a Help Sheet which will be available to farmers to assist them with their self-assessment tax returns.

If 1996–97 is averaged with 1997–98 then new rules will apply—

- *it is profits after capital allowances which are averaged, and*
- *claims will be at partner level not partnership level.*

By contrast, if 1996–97 is averaged with 1995–96 then the present rules apply—

- *profits before capital allowances are averaged, and*
- *if the farm is a partnership, averaging is dealt with at partnership level.*

For cases which commenced for tax purposes after 5 April 1994 the new rules apply straightaway.

For further information see pages 188, 189 of Inland Revenue Guide SAT 1 (1995) ''The new current year basis of assessment''.

Note—This Interpretation has been superseded by the Business Income Manual BIM73120 and 73125.
Commentary—*Simon's Direct Tax Service* **B3.541**.

RI 140 (February 1996) *Record-keeping equipment*

There has been an increasing number of queries over recent months about the Revenue's attitude towards the use of optical imaging systems to preserve taxpayers' records.

Until recently there were no specific requirements for either business or personal taxpayers to keep records or to retain them after their returns and accounts had been filed. Obviously, people have always needed to keep records in order to make a complete and correct return. Equally, it has always made sense for them to retain these records for a time afterwards. In that respect, nothing has changed.

However, legislation introduced in FA 1994 as part of the preparation for the self-assessment system for individuals (which will be introduced from the tax year 1996–97) has now helped to clarify the position by setting some clear rules. These rules will also apply in due course to companies, although the precise starting date has yet to be fixed.

The rules, drafted with computer held records in mind, say that the new duty to preserve records may be satisfied by preserving the information which they contain. In the Revenue's view, these rules will specifically permit for tax purposes the use of optical imaging systems, provided that what is retained on disc represents a complete and unaltered image of the underlying paper document.

Records relating to a taxpayer's obligations as an employer (for example, records of PAYE deductions etc) must still be retained in paper form and contractors in the construction industry must continue to keep the originals of subcontractor documents and vouchers (for example forms SC60).

Any vouchers which will be used as the basis of a claim to repayment (for example, dividend vouchers) must also be retained in the original paper form. However, there is no change for financial intermediaries which are already authorised to retain records on microfiche or similar media without retaining the originals.

The Revenue regards these rules as applying *now* to both individuals and companies.

Further information can be obtained from—Julia Hawkes, Room 538, SW Wing, Bush House, Strand, London WC2 4RD, telephone number [020 7438 6196].

Further information on the new record keeping requirement can be found in the leaflet SA/BK3 ''Self-assessment—a guide to keeping records for the self-employed''.

Commentary—*Simon's Direct Tax Service* **E1.809**.

RI 141 (February 1996) *Basis periods: partnerships with ancillary letting income—transition to new Schedule A*

Commentary—*Simon's Direct Tax Service* **A4.110**.
Notes—This Interpretation is not relevant for 1997/98 and later years.

RI 142 (February 1996) *Acquisition of new businesses*

[The Revenue] have been asked in what circumstances the Schedule D Cases I and II ''commencement'' provisions apply where an existing business acquires another business as a going concern. For example, suppose Ms Green runs three clothes shops and then acquires a fourth shop from Mr Brown. Should the ''commencement'' provisions be applied and if so to what profits? The same question arises whether the relevant commencement provisions are the ''old'' ones in the existing TA 1988 ss 60–62 or the ''new'' ones introduced in connection with self-assessment.

ISSUE 1—"SUCCESSION"

The first question [the Revenue] ask is whether Ms Green has ''succeeded'' to Mr Brown's trade. This will happen if what she has taken over is the whole of Mr Brown's trade (and not just part of it) and if the business at what was Mr Brown's shop is still being carried on in an identifiable form. [The Revenue] would look at all the circumstances in order to decide whether the business was still being carried on in an identifiable form: these might include whether any goodwill was transferred as part of the purchase, whether stock was transferred, whether the shop continues to stock the same lines and sell to the same sort of customers and whether its name stays the same. No single factor will necessarily be conclusive.

If Ms Green has ''succeeded'' to Mr Brown's trade then the long established rules in TA 1988 s 113(1) say that this must be regarded as the commencement of a new trade by Ms Green, regardless of whether it is in fact a new trade. (Section 113(1) actually talks about a ''change in the persons engaged in carrying on any trade'' but decided cases show that this means the same as the earlier wording of ''succeeds to any trade''.) This means that the ''commencement'' provisions will apply to her profits from the new shop. If Ms Green prepares one set of accounts for all four shops, the profits will have to be apportioned between the three old shops and the new shop until the commencement provisions no longer apply. Unless what Ms Green is doing at her new shop is in fact a new and separate trade (see below), there will be no need for any apportionment once the normal continuing basis applies to all four shops.

There is no change to this aspect of TA 1988 s 113 under self-assessment.

ISSUE 2—"NEW TRADE"

If Ms Green has not ''succeeded'' to a trade (either because Mr Brown's shop was not the whole of his trade or because she does not carry on his business in an identifiable form) the second question is whether what she does in her new shop is in fact a new trade separate from the trade she carries on at her old shops. Again [the Revenue] would look at all the circumstances in order to decide this. These might include the amount of central co-ordination and control of the four shops, whether stock and staff are moved between the shops, whether customers of the old shops might use the new one and geographical factors such as whether the old shops are all in one town and the new shop in another. Again no single factor will be conclusive.

If what Ms Green is doing at her new shop is in fact a new and separate trade then the ''commencement'' provisions will again apply to her profits from this shop and again if a single set of accounts is prepared the profits will have to be apportioned. It will then be a question of fact whether at some later time the two trades she is carrying on merge to form a single trade.

NO SUCCESSION AND NO NEW TRADE

If Ms Green has not ''succeeded'' to a trade and what she is doing at the new shop is not a new and separate trade, then for tax purposes she is continuing to carry on the same trade as before, so that she can prepare a single set of accounts bringing in the new shop's activities. The acquisition of the new shop in this case has no effect on the basis of assessment.

WHICH COMMENCEMENT PROVISIONS APPLY?

If Ms Green acquired her new shop before 6 April 1994 and it was either a ''succession'' or a ''new trade'', then the commencement provisions to be applied are those in the existing TA 1988 ss 60–62. If the acquisition takes place on or after 6 April 1994 (and is a ''succession'' or a ''new trade'') then the self-assessment commencement provisions apply. These are summarised in Chapter 1 of the Inland Revenue guide SAT 1 (1995) ''The new current year basis of assessment''.

The computational aspects of successions and mergers under self-assessment and the consequences for the ''transitional'' years from 1994–95 to 1996–97, are dealt with in Chapter 8 of SAT 1.

Commentary—*Simon's Direct Tax Service* **B3.301**.

RI 145 (April 1996) *Compensation payable to agricultural and business tenants*

CAPITAL GAINS TAX—COMPENSATION PAYABLE TO AGRICULTURAL AND BUSINESS TENANTS—AGRICULTURAL HOLDINGS ACT 1986 S 60—AGRICULTURAL TENANCIES ACT 1995 SS 16—LANDLORD AND TENANT ACT 1954 S 37

8This article sets out [the Revenue's] current views on the capital gains tax treatment of compensation payable to agricultural tenants under the Agricultural Holdings Act 1986 or under the Agricultural Tenancies Act 1995, and to business tenants under the Landlord and Tenant Act 1954.

Following *Davis v Powell* STC [lsqb;1977] 32, compensation payable under the Agricultural Holdings Act 1986 s 60 to a tenant who quits his or her holding in consequence of a notice to quit is not chargeable to capital gains tax. [The Revenue] have, however, previously taken the view that where a tenant did not serve out the period of notice, following the receipt of a notice to quit, and instead entered into a surrender agreement with the landlord, then the surrender agreement broke the chain of causation, so that the tenant was not quitting in consequence of the notice to quit, but in consequence of the surrender agreement. It was [the Revenue's] view that as a result, any payment made by the landlord was not statutory compensation payable under the Agricultural Holdings Act 1986 s 60 and that the whole of any such payment was therefore chargeable to capital gains tax.

This point was tested before the Special Commissioners in two appeals heard in 1995. *Davis v Henderson* [1995] STC (SCD) 308 and *Pritchard v Purves* [1995] STC (SCD) 316. In both cases a notice to quit had been issued by the landlord under the Agricultural Holdings Act 1986 s 25 and subsequently, the tenants quit their holdings before the expiry of the period of notice in return for payments made by their landlords under a surrender agreement. The Special Commissioners held that in both cases the tenants had quit their holdings in consequence of the notice to quit and that part or all of the payments made by the landlords in each case was accordingly statutory compensation payable under the Agricultural Holdings Act 1986 s 60 and not chargeable to capital gains tax.

[The Revenue] have now decided not to appeal against these decisions. In future [they] will accept that where a tenant receives a genuine notice to quit issued by the landlord under the Agricultural Holdings Act 1986 s 25 and then enters into a surrender agreement, any of the payments made by the landlord under the terms of the surrender agreement which relate to compensation payable under the Agricultural Holdings Act 1986 s 60 will not be chargeable to capital gains tax. This does not mean that all of the payments made under a surrender agreement in these circumstances will be exempt from capital gains tax, but only the amount that represents the statutory compensation payable. [The Revenue] will continue to seek to tax any amount that is not genuine statutory compensation. An example is where the notice to quit was issued after negotiations for a surrender had already begun and where the notice to quit was not the real cause of the termination of the tenancy. In such a case the whole of the surrender payment would be chargeable.

[The Revenue] also accept that the decision in *Davis v Powell* applies to compensation received for tenants' improvements under the Agricultural Holdings Act 1986 s 64 or under the Agricultural Tenancies Act 1995 s 16 and that such compensation is exempt from capital gains tax.

Following the Special Commissioners' decisions above, [The Revenue] have also reviewed [their] approach to compensation received by business tenants under the Landlord and Tenant Act 1954 s 37. [The Revenue] will now accept that a surrender of the tenancy before it comes to an end does not prevent a tenant from being entitled to such compensation if the grounds for entitlement are otherwise met.

Commentary—*Simon's Direct Tax Service* **C1.319**.

RI 146 (April 1996) *Foreign income dividends*

A UK company might want to elect for a dividend it is to pay to be a foreign income dividend so that the dividend obtains the special treatment in TA 1988 ss 246A–246Y. The company might want to pay the dividend on some of the shares in a currency other than sterling.

For example—if the company had shares held in the form of American Depositary Receipts, it might declare a dividend in sterling but make arrangements to pay the same dividend in US dollars in respect of those shares. Under such arrangements, the amount of the dividend paid in US dollars might be fixed by reference to the exchange rate between sterling and the dollar on the day the dividend was declared.

TA 1988 section 246A(3) states, amongst other things, that an election may not be made where there are arrangements for the shareholder to choose the form in which dividends are to be paid. [The Revenue] do not think arrangements of the kind described in the above example come within the scope of s 246A(3).

Certain other provisions also depend on whether dividends are paid on the same terms. [The Revenue] do not think that arrangements of the kind described in the above example involve payment of the dividend on different terms even where there was a movement in the exchange rate between the time the dividend was declared and the time it was paid.

Note—This Interpretation is now obsolete.
Commentary—*Simon's Direct Tax Service* **D1.702**.

RI 147 (April 1996) *Pay and file: interest on repayments resulting from relief carry-backs*

The pay and file legislation changes the regime for interest added to repayments of corporation tax. Repayments of tax overpaid for accounting periods ending after 30 September 1993 attract repayment interest under TA 1988 s 826. This replaces the supplement regime in TA 1988 s 825 which applies to repayments of tax overpaid for earlier accounting periods. While the rate of interest under TA 1988 s 826 is lower in relation to base rates than the rate of supplement under TA 1988 s 825, it is usually calculated from the tax due date—a year before supplement would normally become available. But both sections contain rules restricting the interest or supplement available where the repayment arises because of a carry-back of surplus advance corporation tax from any later period, or of trade losses from a period ending more than 12 months later.

[The Revenue] still receive queries about the effects of this legislation in transitional cases, where a trade loss or surplus of advance corporation tax in an accounting period ending after 30 September 1993 is relieved by carry-back to an accounting period ending on or before that date.

Section 825 or s 826?

TA 1988 ss 825 and 826 are mutually exclusive—

- *repayments of tax paid for accounting periods ending after 30 September 1993 cannot attract supplement because of the words of s 826(8);*
- *repayments of tax paid for accounting periods ending on or before 30 September 1993 cannot attract interest under s 826 because of the words of s 826(1). They can still attract supplement, though.*

The fact that a repayment results from a relief carry-back is not relevant in deciding whether it is s 825 or s 826 which applies.

The following example illustrates the point—

EXAMPLE

- *Surplus advance corporation tax paid for the year ended 31.12.94 is carried back under TA 1988 s 239(3) to the year ended 31.12.92.*

- *This gives rise to a repayment of tax paid for the year ended 31.12.92.*
- *No repayment interest can be due as s 826 does not apply to repayments of tax paid for periods ending before 1.10.93.*
- *Repayment supplement will be due if the repayment is made after 1.10.96—12 months after the "material date" (s 825(2)). The "material date" is 1.10.95—the tax due date of the accounting period for which the surplus advance corporation tax arose, following s 825(4)(a).*
- *Section 825(4)(a) treats the repayment as if it were a repayment of tax paid for the year to 31.12.94, but only for the purposes of calculating the supplement due under s 825. It does not bring s 826 back into play, as s 825(4) begins with the words "For the purposes of this section ...".*

It would make no difference to the example if the carry-back were of a trade loss under TA 1988 s 393A(1)(b) rather than surplus advance corporation tax except that s 825(4)(c)(ii) would replace s 825(4)(a).

Commentary—*Simon's Direct Tax Service* **A3.1331**.

RI 148 (April 1996) *Enterprise investment scheme: raising money for qualifying business activities*

ENTERPRISE INVESTMENT SCHEME—RAISING MONEY FOR QUALIFYING BUSINESS ACTIVITIES—TA 1988 SS 289, 312

The provisions of the enterprise investment scheme apply where a company issues shares in order to raise money for the purpose of a qualifying business activity and the money raised is employed for that purpose. The phrase "qualifying business activity" is defined in TA 1988 s 289(2); briefly, it covers carrying on a trade (or preparing to do so), carrying on research and development and carrying on oil exploration.

Where a company raises money partly for the activity of preparing to carry on a trade and partly for the subsequent carrying on of that trade, [the Revenue] regard that as a single qualifying business activity. But a company may wish to issue shares to raise money for more than one qualifying business activity—for example, for two trades carried on by different subsidiaries, or for a trade carried on by one subsidiary and research and development carried on by another. [The Revenue] accept that the rules allow this. The purpose of this article is to explain the practical consequences of it.

When providing a statement under TA 1988 s 306(3) on form EIS 1, a company is required to state the nature of the qualifying business activity for which the money has been raised. If it has raised money for more than one such activity it should report that fact. The company will then have to satisfy the rule in TA 1988 s 289(1)(*c*), (3), about using the money within a certain time, separately in respect of each part of the sum raised.

Reflecting TA 1988 s 289A(6), (7), form EIS 1 requires the company to declare that the activity for which the money was raised has been carried on for four months. Where this four month point is reached at two different dates—as will happen, for example, if part of the money is raised for an existing trade and part for a trade not yet commenced—[the Revenue's] view is that form EIS 1 cannot be submitted unless the second date has been reached. Similarly, the terminal date for making the statement, provided by TA 1988 s 306(3A), will likewise be postponed.

In addition, the duration of the company's relevant period, which is governed by TA 1988 s 312(1A)(*b*), depends on the nature of the qualifying business activity and, where there are two different dates, [the Revenue's] view is that the relevant period lasts until the second date has been reached.

Of course, these complications do not arise if the funds for the two activities are raised separately. This can be achieved simply by issuing the shares on two different dates.

It is sometimes suggested that a company can be both "preparing to carry on a qualifying trade" and "carrying on research and development from which it is intended that a qualifying trade will be derived"; in other words, its activity falls within both (*a*) and (*b*) of TA 1988 s 289(2). In [the Revenue's] view, however, this is unlikely. A company is not nominally in a position to prepare to carry on a trade until its invention has reached the stage where it can be patented.

Not all research and development falls within TA 1988 s 289(2)(*b*); a company which is already trading and which raises money for research and development with a view to inventing something which will extend its trade can only come within TA 1988 s 289(2)(*a*), because despite engaging in research and development, it does not intend to derive a new trade from that activity.

In the rare case where a qualifying business activity does come within both (*a*) and (*b*) (or (*a*) and (*c*)) of TA 1988 s 289(2), [the Revenue] are content for the company to choose, by means of reporting the nature of the activity on form EIS 1, how it wishes that activity to be regarded. In making that choice, the company will need to bear in mind the consequences for the earliest date for sending in form EIS 1, the time limit for using the money raised, and the duration of the relevant period.

(All references in this article to provisions in TA 1988 are to the versions of them which apply in respect of shares issued on or after 31 December 1993.)

Commentary—*Simon's Direct Tax Service* **E3.142**.

RI 149 (April 1996) *Foreign loan interest and tax credit relief*

TA 1988 s 798 provides specific rules limiting the amount of tax credit relief which may be claimed by financial traders whose interest income has already been taxed by an overseas tax authority. It makes it clear that the credit is limited to the UK tax attributable to the net income after deducting the lender's financial expenditure in relation to the loan.

The purpose of this article is to clarify the scope, rather than discuss the detailed provisions of TA 1988 s 798.

Section 798 will apply wherever interest—

- *arises from a loan made to a non-UK resident ("foreign loan interest"); and*
- *falls to be treated as a Case I receipt of any person ("the lender");*

and wherever foreign tax—

- *is chargeable on the interest; and*
- *the lender is entitled to claim tax credit relief for it.*

It has been suggested that s 798 applies only where the recipient of the interest actually made the loan. This is not so. The section applies in all cases where "foreign loan interest" is trading income. It will, for example, apply to interest received—

- *by a securities dealer on overseas debt securities purchased on the secondary market; and*
- *by a financial trader to whom a loan has been assigned.*

"Foreign loan interest" in principle includes manufactured interest on overseas debt securities ("manufactured overseas dividends") arising as a result of a transfer of such securities, where the "manufactured overseas dividends" are in respect of "foreign loan interest" to which s 798 would have applied. This would include transfers by way of a "repo" (a sale and repurchase agreement), a stock loan or an outright sale. In such cases, the lender's financial expenditure to be included by virtue of s 798(7) will be that relating to the provision or purchase of the securities which have been transferred.

The amount of the financial expenditure to be deducted from the interest in calculating the amount of tax credit relief will depend on the facts and circumstances of the particular case and may be the subject of negotiation between the lender and its Inspector (having regard to the regulations in SI 1988/88).

Note—This Interpretation is now obsolete.
Commentary—*Simon's Direct Tax Service* **F1.123**.

RI 150 (April 1996) *Incidental costs of loan finance: timing of deductions*

TA 1988 s 77 provides that in computing profits assessable under Schedule D Case I or II, there may be deducted, subject to certain conditions, the incidental costs of business borrowing. [The Revenue] have been asked about the timing of the tax deduction for these costs.

In [the Revenue's] view, s 77 is silent on the timing of any deduction (apart from preventing any deduction for the costs of certain convertible loans or loan stock until three years after the date of the loan or issue). The section merely operates to ensure that incidental costs (as defined in the section) are not disallowed as capital expenditure (as would often have been the case before what is now s 77 was introduced in 1980).

It follows that a deduction for incidental costs is due at the same time as any other deduction given in computing Case I or II profits. In matters of timing, recent case law, for example Threlfall v Jones *[1993] STC 199, has emphasised the importance of the accountancy treatment. In this context the effect will be that the treatment of incidental costs in the taxpayer's accounts must be followed for tax purposes, provided that the accounts are correctly drawn up in accordance with applicable UK accounting standards.*

For example, where Financial Reporting Standard No 4 (Capital instruments) requires an arrangement fee to be factored into the cost of borrowing and therefore charged against profits over the life of a loan, the tax deduction under s 77 would be due in the same way.

If the 1996 Finance Bill currently proceeding through Parliament is enacted in its present form then s 77 will be superseded, for companies only, by the new provisions on "loan relationships". These will apply for accounting periods ending after 31 March 1996. There will be a Tax Bulletin article about the new rules for incidental costs of loan finance after Royal Assent.

Note—This Interpretation has been superseded by the Business Income Manual BIM45815.
Commentary—*Simon's Direct Tax Service* **B3.1321**.
Revenue Interpretation RI 156—Explains new rules for incidental costs of corporate borrowing for accounting periods ending after 31 March 1996.

RI 151 (June 1996) *Donations of trading stock to charities*

SCHEDULE D CASES I AND II—DONATIONS OF TRADING STOCK TO CHARITIES—TA 1988 SS 84, 577

[The Revenue] have been asked about the tax treatment of trading stock donated to charities, for example, surplus sandwiches and other perishables which are given by retailers to charities for the homeless.

Except for trading stock given to ''designated educational establishments'' (see below) there are no special rules governing donations of trading stock, so normal Schedule D Case I principles apply. What are these principles?

Provided that the trading stock was originally manufactured and/or purchased for sale in the ordinary course of trade, its later donation will not cause its cost to be disallowed for tax purposes. Neither does TA 1988 s 577 (business entertaining expenditure and gifts) cause the cost to be disallowed.

Where a donation is made in the course of trade the amount to be credited in the trader's accounts for tax purposes will be the actual disposal proceeds, that is, nil. [The Revenue] would accept that a donation is made in the course of trade where donation represents the most effective commercial way of disposing of the stock (for example, where it would not be commercially effective to sell surplus perishable food).

Where a donation is not made in the course of trade the amount to be credited for tax purposes will be the market value of stock at the date of disposal. This follows the normal rule which applies when trading stock is disposed of otherwise than in the course of trade. ''Market value'' means the amount the stock could reasonably be expected to have realised in a market commercially available to the trader. It may be that there is no market for the stock commercially available to the trader, in which case the market value would be nil.

There is a special rule (in TA 1988 s 84) for trading stock given to ''designated educational establishments'' (broadly speaking, schools, colleges and universities) where the trading stock is used by the recipient as plant or machinery, for example, laboratory equipment given by a manufacturer of such equipment. The donor may claim within two years of the date on which the gift is made that (notwithstanding the normal tax rule) the amount to be brought into the donor's accounts for tax purposes should be nil.

RI 152 (August 1996) *Valuations for capital gains tax: applying Gray v IRC*

[The Revenue] have been asked whether the decision of the Court of Appeal in Gray (Surviving Executor of Lady Fox deceased) v IRC *[1994] STC 360 has any implications for the valuation of assets for the purpose of capital gains tax.*

The Gray case concerned the valuation of assets for what is now inheritance tax but was at the material time capital transfer tax. IHTA 1984 s 4 deems a transfer of value to have been made for the purpose of capital transfer tax/inheritance tax immediately before death equal to the value of the deceased's estate at that time. IHTA 1984 s 5 defines a person's estate as ''the aggregate of all the property to which he is beneficially entitled''. And IHTA 1984 s 160 provides that ''... the value of any property at any time is ... the price which the property might reasonably be expected to fetch if sold in the open market at that time ...''. The main question in Gray was whether two items of property comprised in the deceased's estate must be taken separately or whether they could be treated as one unit for valuation under IHTA 1984 s 160.

The principle that emerged from Gray is that two or more different assets comprised in an estate can be treated as a single unit of property if disposal as one unit was the course that a prudent hypothetical vendor would have adopted in order to obtain the most favourable price without undue expenditure of time and effort.

This principle will be applicable to capital gains tax valuations in which the statutory hypothesis on which the valuation is based deems two or more assets to be disposed of together. Examples will include—

- *an acquisition by personal representatives or legatees under TCGA 1992 s 62 of assets of which a deceased person was competent to dispose;*
- *an acquisition of settled property under TCGA 1992 s 71(1) on the occasion of a person becoming absolutely entitled to that settled property.*

Where the principle established in Gray is followed, so as to value a number of assets collectively to produce a total valuation in excess of the value of the assets valued separately, an apportionment will be required in accordance with TCGA 1992 s 52(4). The apportionment is to be made on a just and reasonable basis and so must reflect the value of each of the assets. Commonly this will require an apportionment of the total value in proportion to the value of each asset.

Where the statutory hypothesis requiring a valuation proceeds on the assumption of a disposal of a single asset by itself the principle established in Gray cannot apply, For example, in Henderson v Karmel's Executors *[1984] STC 572 the court held that even though at 6 April 1965 Mrs Karmel owned both the freehold interest in a farm and controlled the tenant company, so having the power*

RIs

one way or another to terminate the company's interest, that was insufficient to value the freehold interest on a vacant possession basis for capital gains tax rebasing to 6 April 1965.

Other examples of valuation hypotheses for which assets will continue to be valued singly include—

- *TCGA 1992 s 17 where there is a disposal of an asset for consideration deemed to be equal to its market value;*
- *TCGA 1992 s 35 when a valuation of an asset is required for the purpose of rebasing to 31 March 1982.*

The single asset valuation for TCGA 1992 s 17 is modified by TCGA 1992 s 19 where there is a series of linked transactions between connected persons. Each disposal in the series may be treated as being made for consideration equal to a proportion of the aggregate value of all the assets in the series.

Note—This Interpretation is now obsolete.
Commentary—*Simon's Direct Tax Service* **C2.120**.

RI 153 (August 1996) *Exchange Gains and Losses (Alternative Method of Calculation of Gain or Loss) (Amendment) Regulations 1996—SI 1996/1347*

These Regulations were laid before the House of Commons on 21 May 1996 and came into force on 30 June 1996. They introduce amendments to that part of the Exchange Gains and Losses (Alternative Method of Calculation of Gain or Loss) Regulations, SI 1994/3227, which deals with matched assets and liabilities ("the matching regulations"). One change—designed to block an avoidance loophole—has given rise to concern that its effects go further than intended.

The matching regulations are designed to enable tax treatment broadly to follow normal accounting practice. Normally exchange differences on monetary assets and liabilities (for instance, cash or debt) are dealt with for accounting purposes through a company's profit and loss account and generally this is followed for tax purposes. The off-set method permitted by Statement of Standard Accounting Practice (SSAP) 20 allows exchange differences on liabilities used to fund or hedge equity investments to be dealt with as a reserve movement set against exchange differences arising on the translation of the net investment. As a result the exchange differences are not recognised in the profit and loss account. Where the exchange movements on the liability are brought to account for tax purposes on a translation basis following FA 1993, but those on the asset are not because it is not a "monetary asset" (for example shares rather than debt) then without special provision, accountancy treatment and tax treatment would diverge. The matching regulations aim to mirror as far as possible the accounting treatment permitted by SSAP 20 by providing for an election to enable exchange differences on certain matched liabilities (ie certain debt and duties under currency contracts) to be deferred or in certain circumstances to be left out of account altogether. The regulations allow the whole or a specified part of an asset to be matched in this way.

SI 1996/1347 reg 4 inserts a new reg 5(3A) into SI 1994/3227. This is designed to prevent companies taking advantage of these matching regulations by using the time limits for making an election or increasing the proportion of an asset to be matched to defer the recognition of exchange gains for tax purposes but obtaining immediate tax relief for exchange losses. It does this by preventing companies gaining immediate relief for exchange losses where for accounting purposes they have been taken to reserves to offset exchange gains on an equity investment or foreign enterprise, but which would otherwise be recognised as they accrue for tax purposes. It is intended to operate where less than 100 per cent of an asset is the subject of a matching election. It is not intended to deny relief for losses arising on liabilities on which exchange differences are taken to reserves in accordance with SSAP 20 where no matching election has been made in respect of an asset.

Concern has been expressed that the new reg 5(3A) goes too far, that it—

- disallows completely those losses which would have been recognised on disposal of the matched asset under the original regulations;
- disallows exchange losses dealt with as an adjustment to reserves to offset exchange gains on long term loans, inter-company balances or other assets not subject to a matching election which have also been dealt with as a movement to reserves in accordance with normal accounting practice.

To allay these concerns, the Revenue can offer reassurance that in applying new reg 5(3A)—

(*a*) Where the matched asset is one to which SI 1994/3227 reg 7 would otherwise apply, so that deferred exchange differences on matched liabilities would have been recognised on disposal of the asset under the original regulations, then any exchange loss not recognised as it accrues as a result of reg 5(3A) will also be relieved on disposal of the asset.

(*b*) New reg 5(3A) will only be applied where an asset is partially matched. In that case, it will only be applied to deny immediate tax recognition for exchange losses on one or more liabilities matching that asset to the extent that such losses relate to the excess of—

- the amount of such liabilities which hedge or fund that asset (and in respect of which exchange differences are consequently taken to reserves in accordance with SSAP 20); over

– the amount of such liabilities matched for tax purposes.

(*c*) New reg 5(3A) will only be given effect where such exchange losses taken to reserves remain outside a matching election at a time on or after 30 June 1996. Where, for example, a revised matching election is made before 30 June 1996 bringing the proportion of the asset matched into line with accounting treatment, reg 5(3A) will have no effect.

This article sets out how the Revenue will apply new reg 5(3A) and will be followed in all circumstances where that regulation is applied.

Commentary—*Simon's Direct Tax Service* **D2.936**.
Regulations—Exchange Gains and Losses (Alternative Method of Calculation of Gain or Loss) Regulations, SI 1994/3227.

RI 154 (August 1996) *Locum and fixed costs insurance policies*

A Revenue Press Release dated 30 April 1996 explained that the premiums on a certain type of sickness insurance policies are a deductible business expense.

These insurance policies indemnify the policy holder against business costs such as payments to a locum tenens, or other fixed overheads, in the event of the policy holder's incapacity to carry on the business during a period of illness. These locum and fixed costs insurance policies are held mainly by medical professionals such as doctors and dentists who practise alone or in partnership.

The benefits received under the policies are taxable as business receipts because they diminish allowable business expenses. They are not within the exemption legislated in FA 1996 (TA 1988 s 580A(6)) and nor are they within the earlier Concession A83—the premiums are a deductible business expense.

The Revenue Press Release dated 30 April 1996 describes arrangements for the holders of locum and fixed costs insurance policies to claim repayments under the error or mistake provisions (TMA 1970 s 33). Any such claims will be subject to the general rules for error or mistake relief, in particular the six year time limit. A claim may be beneficial if premiums and benefits under the policies have been excluded in computing the profits for settled periods of account. But relief for the previously unallowed premiums will be reduced by any untaxed benefits for the earliest period of account to which the claim relates and any subsequent settled periods.

If an error or mistake claim is made, the premiums must also be deducted and benefits treated as taxable receipts for any periods of account for which the profits and assessments are not yet settled.

[The Revenue] have been asked how error or mistake relief claims should be made by persons who carry on business in partnership. Relief for the premiums paid on locum and fixed costs policies are a deduction in computing the taxable profit of the single trade or profession the partnership carries on, even if they have been paid personally by one partner (SAT 1 (1995) ''The new current year of assessment'' para 5.17). The claim must therefore take into account both the premiums paid and the benefits received on locum and fixed costs policies for all the members of the partnership for the period of the claim and subsequent periods, as explained in the [Revenue] Press Release. It is not possible to determine whether the profits of the partnership already taxed (and hence the share of any individual partner) have been excessive unless the premiums and benefits on all such policies held by the partners are given the same treatment.

Some partnerships may include partners who hold locum and fixed costs policies and other partners whose sickness insurance cover is under other permanent health insurance arrangements. The two types of policy must be distinguished in making error or mistake claims. There is no relief for premiums on policies that provide ordinary life, accident or sickness cover. For tax the premiums are a private expense of the individual and the benefits received under the policies are not business receipts.

Note—This Interpretation has been superseded by the Business Income Manual BIM45565 et seq.
Commentary—*Simon's Direct Tax Service* **B4.112**.

RI 155 (August 1996) *Self-assessment: extended time limits for assessment of partnership profits where there has been "fraudulent or negligent conduct" in connection with a TMA 1970 s 36(2), TA 1988 s 111 partnership return*

[The Revenue] have been asked to clarify the operation of TMA 1970 s 36(2) (as amended by FA 1994 Sch 19 para 11(2)) as it applies to the assessment of profits from a trade or profession carried on in partnership under self-assessment.

[The Revenue] can confirm that it was never the intention that TMA 1970 s 36(2) (as amended by FA 1994 Sch 19 para 11(2)) should preserve ''joint liability'' to the tax on the profits of a trade or profession carried on in partnership. [The Revenue] would add that in [their] view the revised subsection does not—indeed cannot—have that effect.

The purpose of TMA 1970 s 36 is to provide the Revenue with extended time limits for assessments to make good to the Crown a loss of tax attributable to ''fraudulent or negligent conduct''. Under

RIs

self-assessment a partnership return will be given to all the relevant partners, collectively, but (as now) a single partner will be required to complete the return for the partnership. Where the partnership return is made in circumstances such that there has been ''fraudulent and negligent conduct''—whether by the partner responsible for the return, or attributable to some other relevant partner—then TMA 1970 s 36 may apply. But clearly it would be quite inappropriate for the Revenue's right to collect the additional tax due to be limited to the additional tax due on the share of profit allocated to the partner who is actually ''the person in default''. In these circumstances ''new'' TMA 1970 s 36(2) simply allows the Revenue to make individual assessments on each of the partners who have additional tax to pay on their revised share of the partnership profit.

The original version of TMA 1970 s 36(2) operated in a regime in which the profits of a trade or profession carried on in partnership could only be assessed by means of a composite partnership assessment (TA 1988 s 11). In that context any assessment made on the authority of TMA 1970 s 36(2) must be a composite partnership assessment for which the partners have joint liability. The new version of TMA 1970 s 36(2) operates in a regime in which the profits of a trade or profession carried on in partnership can only be assessed by means of separate assessment of each partner's share of profit (TA 1988 s 111 as amended by FA 1995 s 117(2)). In this context any assessments made on the authority of TMA 1970 s 36(2) must be separate assessments of each partner's shares of partnership profit. There is no longer any mechanism by which a composite partnership assessment can be made and therefore no means of creating a joint liability to the tax due on the profits of a trade or profession carried on in partnership.

Commentary—*Simon's Direct Tax Service* **E1.815**.

RI 156 (October 1996) *Incidental costs of corporate borrowing—FA 1996 s 84*

An article explaining the timing of tax deductions for the incidental costs of business borrowing allowable under TA 1988 s 77 was contained in Tax Bulletin Issue 22. For companies, FA 1996 s 84 has replaced TA 1988 s 77 as from 1 April 1996. This article explains the operation of the new rules.

The new provisions on government and corporate finance contained in FA 1996 Part IV Chap II bring into account profits and gains on ''loan relationships'' (FA 1996 s 80). A loan relationship exists wherever a company stands as a debtor or creditor in respect of a money debt and that debt arises from a transaction for the lending of money (FA 1996 s 81).

The debts and credits which can be brought into account in respect of a loan relationship include all charges or expenses incurred by a company under or for the purposes of its loan relationships or related transactions—FA 1996 s 84(1)(*b*). Related transactions are any acquisitions or disposal of any of the rights or liabilities of a loan relationship. The term includes part disposals but not the original setting up of the loan relationship.

Section 84(3) requires that charges and expenses must be incurred directly—

- in bringing the loan relationship into existence;
- in entering into or giving effect to related transactions;
- in making payments under the loan relationships or in pursuance of the related transactions; or
- in pursuing payments due under the loan relationship or in accordance with a related transaction.

Expenditure may be incurred without a company finally entering into the loan relationship. In such cases abortive expenditure of the types shown above will still be allowable under FA 1996 s 84(4).

Following the introduction of the new legislation, [the Revenue] have received a number of enquiries about some specific types of incidental expenditure.

- [The Revenue] have confirmed that s 84 allows the costs directly incurred in varying the terms of a loan relationship to be taken into account as a debit.
- Guarantee fees incurred in connection with loan relationships are not considered to be allowable under FA 1996 s 84 as they do not relate directly to a loan relationship or related transaction. However, guarantee payments might be allowable as trading deductions where, when made, the payment was wholly and exclusively for the purposes of the trade and was not a payment in respect of capital.

Where the company has entered into the loan relationship for the purposes of its trade, any debits in respect of allowable incidental costs are taken into account in calculating the profits of the trade. Otherwise the costs will represent a debit in calculating either the Case III profit or the non-trading deficit relievable under FA 1996 s 83.

On the issue of the timing of a deduction, the April 1996 article noted the emphasis put on accountancy treatment in recent tax cases such as *Threlfall v Jones* [[1993] STC 199]. The loan relationships legislation operates on the basis of authorised accounting methods (FA 1996 s 85). Under an accruals basis of accounting the appropriate treatment of incidental costs would often be to accrue them over the life of the loan relationship. FA 1996 s 85(3) specifically requires payments to be allocated to the period to which they relate and, where they relate to two or more periods, to be apportioned on a just and reasonable basis. This treatment would also be in line with the guidance contained in Financial Reporting Standard No 4 (Capital Instruments) on issue costs.

However, where incidental costs have been allowed in full—perhaps because they were allowed on a paid basis before 1 April 1996—there is provision in the loan relationship legislation to ensure that they cannot be allowed again as they accrue (FA 1996 Sch 15 para 14).

Commentary—*Simon's Direct Tax Service* **D2.1116**.
Revenue Interpretation RI 150—Explains timing of deductions for incidental costs of business borrowing.
RI 161—Where loan would not be advanced without provision of guarantee, guarantee fees paid by debtor can be brought into account under FA 1996 s 84.

RI 157 (October 1996) *Deductions for interest payable*

INCOME TAX—DEDUCTION FOR INTEREST PAID BY COMPANY—TA 1988 S 337A

TA 1988 s 337A was introduced by FA 1996 Sch 24 para 15 as part of new provisions relating to corporate debt. Section 337A states that, in computing a company's income, no deduction is available for interest except in accordance with the new loan relationship rules in FA 1996 Part IV Chap II. [The Revenue] have been asked whether this precludes a deduction for interest payable by a company within the charge to income tax rather than corporation tax. Such companies are comparatively rare, but for example, non-UK resident companies, with only UK property income, would be chargeable to income tax rather than corporation tax.

It is [the Revenue's] view that s 337A can only apply for the purposes of corporation tax and therefore does not preclude a deduction for interest for companies within the income tax provisions.

Commentary—*Simon's Direct Tax Service* **D4.122**.

RI 158 (October 1996) *Hong Kong: from 1 July 1997*

INTERNATIONAL TAX—TRANSFER OF SOVEREIGNTY OVER HONG KONG—TA 1988 S 278

[The Revenue] have been asked to outline some of the tax consequences which will apply to Hong Kong after the transfer of sovereignty on 30 June 1997.

APPLICATION OF UK/CHINA DOUBLE TAXATION AGREEMENT

The existing double taxation agreement between the Government of the People's Republic of China and the Government of the UK, signed on 26 July 1984, will not apply to the Hong Kong Special Administrative Region which comes into existence from 1 July 1997.

TA 1988 S 278 RELIEF

Present Hong Kong residents who are British Dependent Territories citizens by virtue of connection with Hong Kong will lose that status from 1 July 1997. Along with the loss of status they will also lose their entitlement to claim UK personal allowances and reliefs under TA 1988 s 278.

By that date, however, it is expected that most Hong Kong British Dependent Territories citizens will have registered as British Nationals (Overseas) and will therefore continue to be Commonwealth citizens who may continue to claim under TA 1988 s 278. Those who have decided not to register will either become British Overseas citizens (also a form of Commonwealth citizenship) or, if a citizen of another state, will cease to hold any form of British nationality. Of this last group, only persons who are citizens of other Commonwealth countries (eg India) and/or EEA nationals will continue to benefit from the reliefs provided under TA 1988 s 278.

Commentary—*Simon's Direct Tax Service* **E6.202**.

RI 159 (December 1996) *Corporation tax on chargeable gains: transfers of shares within a group of companies in exchange for qualifying corporate bonds.*

This article concerns transfers of shares from one company to another in the same group in exchange for a new issue of qualifying corporate bonds (QCBs). It explains [the Revenue's] view of the interaction between two provisions of TCGA 1992 in relation to the capital gains treatment of the transferee company—

- TCGA 1992 s 116 (deferred charges where QCBs are issued on a reorganisation); and
- TCGA 1992 s 171(1) (the no gain/no loss rule for assets transferred between companies in the same group).

The following analysis deals with the case where companies A and C are members of the same group. Company A holds shares in company B which are transferred to company C.

If group company A exchanges the shares in company B for shares issued by group company C, and the no disposal fiction in TCGA 1992 ss 127, 135 applies to A, then the no gain/no loss rule in

RIs

TCGA 1992 s 171(1) does not apply to C's acquisition from A of the shares in B. This is the result of TCGA 1992 s 171(3) reversing the effect of the decision in *Westcott v Woolcombers Ltd* [STC [1986] 182].

The technical analysis is different where the consideration given by C for the shares in B is not shares but a new issue of QCBs. In this case, provided the relevant conditions are satisfied, the capital gains treatment is given by TCGA 1992 s 116. And the effect of TCGA 1992 s 116(5) is to disapply the rules in TCGA 1992 ss 127–130. This in turn means that TCGA 1992 s 171(3) may not apply to prevent the operation of the TCGA 1992 s 171(1) no gain/no loss rule.

In [the Revenue's] view, though, the no gain/no loss rule does not apply to C's acquisition, for a reason which stands independently of TCGA 1992 s 171(3). If A exchanges shares in B for QCBs issued by C, and TCGA 1992 s 116 applies, then the rule in TCGA 1992 s 116(10) is that "so far as it relates to the old asset and the new asset, the relevant transaction shall be treated for the purposes of this Act as not involving any disposal of the old asset ...". This is sufficient to disapply the s 171(1) no gain/no loss rule in relation to C's acquisition of the shares in B, since TCGA 1992 s 171(1) requires both an acquisition and a corresponding disposal. The result is that C's acquisition cost of the shares in B is governed by the general capital gains rules, unaffected by TCGA 1992 s 171(1) no gain/no loss rule.

Commentary—*Simon's Direct Tax Service* **C2.804; D2.654**.

RI 160 (December 1996) *Consortium relief: Steele v EVC International NV (formerly European Vinyls Corp (Holdings) BV)—TA 1988 ss 410(2)(b)(ii), 839(7)*

[The Revenue] have been asked to clarify the effect of the decision in *Steele v EVC International NV* [[1996] STC 785] on consortium claims to group relief.

A group relief (consortium) claim is prevented where—

> "Arrangements are in existence by virtue of which any person, other than a holding company of which the trading company is a 90% subsidiary, either alone or together with connected persons, holds or could obtain, or controls or could control the exercise of not less than 75% of the votes which may be cast on a poll taken at a general meeting of that trading company in that accounting period or in any subsequent accounting period" (TA 1988 s 410(2)(*b*)(iii)).

By virtue of s 410(5), "connected persons" are defined by TA 1988 s 839. Section 839(7) says that—

> "Any two or more persons acting together to secure or exercise control of a company shall be treated in relation to that company as connected with one another and with any person acting on the directions of any of them to secure or exercise control of the company."

In the High Court Mr Justice Lightman held in *EVC International* that the "acting together" requirement in s 839(7) was satisfied by the ongoing shareholders' agreement. He considered that the companies in question were acting together to *secure*, in the sense of safeguard and protect, their control of the company. Furthermore, although the occasions for the *exercise* of control were limited, so far as required it was duly exercised by the shareholders acting together. The Court of Appeal also concluded that control had been exercised by the shareholders "acting together" and in these circumstances found it unnecessary to reach a conclusion on whether they had also "acted together" to secure control.

It has been suggested that the affairs of most consortia are regulated by shareholders' agreements to as great an extent as in *EVC International*, that the consortium members will be "connected persons" by virtue of s 839(7) and hence s 410(2)(*b*)(iii) will apply to most consortia. In [the Revenue's] view, this goes too far. Section 410(2)(*b*)(iii) will only apply where there is a continuing commitment by two or more members of the consortium, holding at least 75% of the votes, to ensure the consortium company operates in accordance with their collective will. It is the fact that the agreement is ongoing that is crucial. A shareholders' agreement that for instance did no more than define the type of activities to be carried on by the company but which left the parties free to act independently would not by itself make the parties "connected".

Where a joint venture company is owned in equal shares by just two consortium members, there is a greater likelihood of the members continuing to act together. A deadlocked company can only continue to function effectively if its owners agree about how it will operate. They may rely on a coincidence of commercial interest and act independently of each other. However, if they act in accordance with a previous agreement, they are likely to be "acting together", even if their commercial interests would have led them to act in the same way without the agreement.

Section 839(7) could be less relevant where a consortium has more than two members, or where the only two members do not have equal shareholdings. In such circumstances, there may be no continuing commitment to ensure that the consortium continues to operate in a way which is acceptable to all the shareholders; instead, reliance may be placed on the commercial interests of sufficient members coinciding. The potentially dissenting shareholders' interests may be protected by, for example, a put option which would allow them to realise a satisfactory price for their shares.

Commentary—*Simon's Direct Tax Service* **D2.638**.

RI 161 (December 1996) *Incidental costs of loan finance: guarantee fees—loan relationships—FA 1996 s 84*

An article on incidental costs of loan finance in *Tax Bulletin* Issue 25 (October 1996) stated that guarantee fees were not considered to relate directly to the bringing of loan relationships into existence. Consequently, such fees were not considered to be allowable expenses within FA 1996 s 84(3).

Since publication of the article, correspondents have pointed out that it is often the case that loans will not be advanced without the provision of a guarantee. In such circumstances [the Revenue] would accept that fees paid by the debtor in respect of such a guarantee would relate directly to the bringing into existence of the loan. Relief would therefore be available under FA 1996 s 84(3)(*a*).

Commentary—*Simon's Direct Tax Service* **D2.116**.
Revenue Interpretation 156—Relief for incidental costs of corporate borrowing under the "loan relationships" provisions applicable for accounting periods ending after 31 March 1996.

RI 162 (December 1996) *Trusts: liability at the rate applicable to trusts—TA 1988 s 686*

[The Revenue] have found that some trustees have wrongly completed returns in the belief that they were liable under TA 1988 s 686 to tax at the rate applicable to trusts when they were in fact liable only at the lower or basic rate. The purpose of this article is to help trustees identify any trusts where they may have done this.

Where trustees have powers to pay income at their discretion or to accumulate it, they will generally be liable at the rate applicable to trusts under TA 1988 s 686(1). The rate applicable to trusts is 35% for 1995–96 and 34% for 1996–97. However, if the income belongs before distribution to some person other than the trustees, then the trustees will be chargeable only at the basic or lower rate of tax as the persons receiving the income.

The trusts affected are those where a beneficiary has an indefeasibly vested interest in the capital and there is no other person entitled to receive the income. A beneficiary will have an indefeasibly vested interest in capital where he/she has a complete right to receive it without having to satisfy any conditions. When such a beneficiary dies, any income remaining in the hands of the trustees at that date will fall into the beneficiary's estate. It is clear from dicta in the case of *Stanley v CIR* (26 TC 12) that income arising to the trust in such circumstances is to be treated as the beneficiary's income so long as he or she is alive. Such income is therefore outside the scope of TA 1988 s 686(1) and is not chargeable at the rate applicable to trusts.

This does not apply where a minor beneficiary has a vested interest in income, but not capital, under the law of England and Wales or Northern Ireland. In these circumstances, the Trustees Act 1925 s 31 (or its Northern Ireland equivalent) prevents the beneficiary from being entitled to the income as it arises (unless there is some contrary intention expressed in the instrument which creates the interest), and the income is correctly chargeable at the rate applicable to trusts.

Any trustees who think they may have been wrongly assessed and have overpaid tax, because, for example, income over which they had a discretion belonged to the beneficiary, should make a claim for error or mistake relief (subject to the statutory time limit which is six years after the end of the year of assessment in which the assessment was made) to their local trust office enclosing the trust deed.

Commentary—*Simon's Direct Tax Service* **C4.203**.

RI 163 (December 1996) *Tax relief for trustees on mineral leases and timber cropping*

INCOME TAX—TRUSTS: TAX AT RATE APPLICABLE TO TRUSTS ON CAPITALISED INCOME FROM MINERAL LEASES AND TIMBER CROPPING—SETTLED LAND ACT 1925 SS 47, 66, TA 1988 S 686

Under the terms of the Settled Land Act 1925 s 47 a proportion of the rent arising from a mineral lease is allocated to capital. The proportion depends on whether or not the tenant for life is impeachable for waste—in broad terms, whether the tenant is liable to make good any damage caused to the land. There are similar provisions in the Settled Land Act 1925 s 66 which where a tenant for life sells timber that is ripe and fit for cutting, requires that a proportion of the net proceeds be allocated to capital where the tenant for life is impeachable for waste.

Since the introduction of what is now TA 1988 s 686 [the Revenue] have taken the view that the provision for capitalisation in the Settled Land Act 1925 ss 47, 66 was an accumulation for the purposes of TA 1988 s 686.

The effect is that such capitalised income has been charged to tax at what is now the rate applicable to trusts. This view has generally been accepted as being correct.

In the light of recent legal advice, [the Revenue] now accept that the provision for capitalisation in the Settled Land Act 1925 ss 47, 66 is not an accumulation for the purposes of TA 1988 s 686. [They] will therefore settle future liabilities on that basis and also deal with any unsettled liabilities in the same way. [They] do not intend re-opening settled liabilities which were agreed in accordance with the prevailing accepted practice at the time.

Commentary—*Simon's Direct Tax Service* **C4.239**.

RI 164 February 1997 *Capital gains tax: meaning of "small" in TCGA 1992 ss 23, 116, 122, 133, 243*

The above sections all contain provisions which apply where certain receipts are "small" as compared to some other specified amount. Our long standing approach has been that "small" means 5% or less. This view has been published in the Capital Gains manual and (in relation to TCGA 1992 s 122) in [RI 34].

[The Revenue] have reconsidered [their] approach in these cases. The judgements in the case of *O'Rourke v Binks* [1992] STC 703 indicate that what is "small" is a question of fact and degree and has to be considered in the light of the circumstances in any particular case. The purpose of the legislation is to avoid the delay and expense of a full computation where this would be disproportionate, and to avoid the need for assessments in trivial cases.

The "5% test" continues to offer practical advantages and we will continue to accept that any case which meets that test can be regarded as small. To further reduce the likelihood of assessments in trivial cases, we will also now accept that these provisions can apply wherever the amount or value of the receipt is £3,000 or less—*whether or not* this would fall within the 5% test. This revised approach may be applied to existing cases where the point remains open at the date of publication of this article—24 February 1997—and to all future cases.

Exceptionally, taxpayers may wish to suggest that receipts above these limits should nevertheless be regarded as small, in the context of their particular circumstances; or, conversely, that receipts below these limits should not be so regarded. Any such cases will remain to be resolved on their merits, having regard to the dicta in *O'Rourke v Binks*.

Commentary—*Simon's Direct Tax Service* **C2.720**.

RI 165 February 1997 *Capital gains tax: retirement relief—extending the qualifying period—TCGA 1992 Sch 6 para 14*

[The Revenue] have received numerous enquiries about when TCGA 1992 Sch 6 para 14 can apply to extend an individual's qualifying period for retirement relief purposes. A simple example illustrates the query.

EXAMPLE

Mrs Black worked for seven years as a full time employee of a large trading company. She held no shares in the company, so it was not her "personal company". (The definition of "personal company" is in TCGA 1992 Sch 6 para 1(2).) She then resigned from the company and immediately started her own consultancy business. Two years later she sold that business.

Assuming that the sale of the consultancy meets all the retirement relief conditions, her qualifying period is the two years she owned the business.

The question [the Revenue] are asked is whether the previous period of employment can be counted as an "earlier business period" under TCGA 1992 Sch 6 para 14, so that it can be added on to the later business period to make an extended nine year qualifying period.

It has been suggested that extension is possible because Mrs Black was "...concerned in the carrying on of a business...as a full time working officer or employee..." (para 14(3)). The period of employment therefore qualifies as an "earlier business period".

[The Revenue] take the view that para 14 does *not* allow extension of the qualifying period in Mrs Black's circumstances.

Paras 14(1), (2) require the length of the qualifying period to be redetermined on certain assumptions. In particular, it must be assumed that the two businesses are the same business. All the qualifying conditions in TCGA 1992 s 163 have to be met throughout the extended qualifying period which is redetermined by reference to that assumed "same business".

If the relevant business is owned for some period by a company which is not the individual's personal company, the qualifying conditions will not all be met and the qualifying period cannot be extended.

Commentary—*Simon's Direct Tax Service* **C3.611**.

RI 167 February 1997 *Schedule D Cases I and II: employee share ownership trusts*

This article considers the treatment of an employer's contributions to an Employee Share Ownership Trust (ESOT). It is concerned with situations where—

- the trust is not a statutory ESOT, that is it is not one set up in terms of FA 1989 ss 67–74, Sch 5;
- applying ordinary Schedule D Case I / II principles, contributions are revenue in character (not capital);
- normal accounting practice requires Urgent Issues Task Force abstract No 13 (UITF 13) to be applied to treat the making of the contributions as giving rise to an asset in the employer's accounts.

[The Revenue] have been asked to say how contributions made by an employer in these circumstances should be dealt with for tax purposes.

BACKGROUND

An ESOT is part of the mechanism to give effect to an Employee Share Ownership Plan (ESOP), which has been defined—loosely—as an arrangement whereby an employee benefit trust (the ESOT) acquires a substantial quantity of employer shares or securities for subsequent distribution to some or all employees, with financial assistance provided directly or indirectly by the employer.

Urgent Issues Task Force abstract No 13 (UITF 13 Accounting for ESOP Trusts) explains how Financial Reporting Standard No 5 (FRS 5: Reporting the Substance of Transactions') applies to ESOTs. It is beyond the scope of this article to set out in detail the guidance in the UITF. But very briefly, under it, cash held and shares purchased by the trustees will normally remain assets of the employer for accounting purposes (in accordance with the definition of an asset in FRS 5) until the rights in the shares are transferred to employees. Consequently contributions to the trust by the employer will not necessarily be charged against profits as they fall due but in an earlier or later period.

[THE REVENUE'S] VIEW

As a matter of general Case I computational principle it is well established that—

- the starting point for the computation of taxable profits is the accounts of a trader drawn up in accordance with normal accounting practice;
- the profits shown by those accounts are then adjusted to give effect to specific statutory rules or to more general principles, derived by the courts from the need to compute "the full amount of the profits or gains" (TA 1988 ss 60 and 70).

Unlike statutory ESOTs, for which FA 1989 s 67 guarantees a Schedule D Case I deduction at the time of the company's contribution to the trustees, no specific statutory rules apply to contributions to non-statutory ESOTs.

Unless therefore, the treatment in the accounts is overridden by such a tax rule, it is followed in computing taxable profit. The point at issue here is whether the time at which contributions to "non-statutory" ESOTs are charged against profits under UITF 13 is overridden by some general tax principle.

Recent cases show that the courts are nowadays reluctant to discern general tax principles which override the time when income and expenses are recognised in accounts drawn up in accordance with normal commercial practice. See *Threlfall v Jones* (66 TC 77) and *Johnston v Britannia Airways Ltd* (67 TC 99).

The Revenue consider that no such principle overrides the accounting treatment required by UITF 13. In particular, the Court of Appeal judgements in *Threlfall* make it clear that there is no general tax principle that an expense should necessarily be deducted for tax when it is incurred or paid. Nor, in the Revenue's view, should UITF 13 be overridden for timing purposes on the grounds that it strays too far from the legal form of the transactions. A similar contention, that Statement of Standard Accounting Practice 21 (Accounting for leases and hire purchase contracts) should not be followed because it treated the hiring of an asset as a loan, failed in *Threlfall* (66 TC at 126I–127F).

By the same token, no general tax principle derived from case law would, in [the Revenue's] view, prevent a deduction for a properly calculated provision included in an employer's trading accounts for a period in respect of future contributions to an ESOT to reflect employees' accruing entitlement to benefits in that period.

RI 168 (February 1997) *Schedule D Cases 1 and II: expenditure on staff training and development—TA 1988 s 74*

Sometimes, the Government gets suggestions that employers should be given tax relief for the costs of training their employees. That surprises [the Revenue], since except in cases where the employee has some link with the employer outside the employment itself, the disallowance of expenditure by an employer on staff training and development will be extremely unusual indeed.

We are concerned here with the treatment of expenditure by an employer on the training and development of employees in computing the employer's profits under Case I or II of Schedule D where that expenditure is properly charged against profits in the employer's accounts drawn up in accordance with normal accounting practice. This article considers in what circumstances such expenditure may be disallowed either under TA 1988 s 74(1)(a) or because for tax purposes it counts as capital. Both issues ultimately depend of course on particular facts and circumstances but some general observations may nevertheless be helpful.

By way of preliminary, it should be noted that expenditure disallowable under the general rules mentioned above may nevertheless qualify for relief under other provisions. For example certain employee training costs qualify for a deduction under TA 1988 s 588(3) and capital expenditure on, say, permanent training facilities or equipment for the purposes of the business may qualify for capital allowances.

BUSINESS PURPOSES

Under TA 1988 s 74(1)(a) expenditure is disallowed if it is not incurred wholly and exclusively for the purposes of the business in question. It is important to realise that the test is framed in terms of the purpose of expenditure rather than its result. It does not enable the inspector to second guess the wisdom of decisions taken for purely business purposes by reference to the amount of business benefit ultimately obtained from the expenditure. For the same reason, the existence of some non-business benefit arising out of expenditure does not cause it to be disallowed if in fact the expenditure is incurred exclusively for business purposes.

Against this background it is not easy to see how s 74(1)(a) would lead to the disallowance of expenditure on the training and development of staff whose relationship with their employer is limited to the employment itself. This remains the case where the expenditure is on the development of an employee's skills and attributes which may not be directly related to his or her current job with the employer, for example training that would only become relevant if the trainee is successful in winning promotion. Nor would expenditure cease to satisfy the statutory test just because the employee may derive considerable personal enjoyment or satisfaction from the training or development in question.

Where on the other hand an employee or director of a company, on whom the expenditure is incurred, has a significant proprietary stake in the business or is a relative of those who do, there is obviously a much greater chance that expenditure may have been incurred not, or not wholly, for business purposes but to provide the employee with some personal benefit. If that is the case then the expenditure is not deductible—the business purpose has to be the exclusive purpose. To take an extreme example, there could be no allowance for the educational costs of the business proprietor's son who is employed in the business during university holidays. In such cases it is often helpful to ask whether the expenditure would have been incurred on an otherwise unconnected employee doing the same job.

Finally a caveat on the purpose of expenditure—where an employer carries on more than one trade or profession, either at the same time or consecutively, expenditure on training, like other expenditure, for the purpose of one such business (or partly for its purpose) cannot be deducted in computing the profits of the other.

CAPITAL

Some employers may also be concerned that expenditure, though incurred exclusively for business purposes, may be disallowed for tax purposes on the grounds that it is of a capital rather than revenue nature even though it has been charged as incurred against profits in the employer's commercial accounts. This would be on the basis that the benefit the employer obtains from the expenditure by way of better trained staff is of such a substantial and enduring nature that the expenditure can be viewed as incurred on an identifiable capital asset.

In principle this may be a possibility, but [the Revenue] find it difficult to imagine circumstances likely to occur in practice where the benefit which the employer obtains can be viewed as such an identifiable capital asset. Such factors as the pace of technological and commercial change and an employee's right to resign and seek work elsewhere militate against such a view.

On a particular point, [the Revenue] would not regard the cost of training staff to use new equipment or systems of a capital nature as itself capital.

OTHER ISSUES

In this article [the Revenue] have not sought to address the tax treatment of the costs incurred by a self-employed person on his or her own training and development. There was an article on this in Tax Bulletin Issue 1 (November 1991 page 4). Nor is this article concerned with the treatment under Schedule E of employees who benefit from training and development expenditure. Clause 64 of the current Finance Bill confirms the current practice of exempting the benefit-in-kind of genuine work-related training, while taxing employees on holidays and other rewards dressed up as "training". Budget Day Press Release REV 29 gave fuller details.

Note—This Interpretation has been superseded by the Business Income Manual BIM35660.
Commentary—*Simon's Direct Tax Service* **B3.1431**.

RI 169 (April 1997) *Capital gains tax: authorised unit trust umbrella schemes—TA 1988 s 468, TCGA 1992 ss 99, 102, 126, 127, 136*

This article discusses the CGT treatment of unit holders in authorised unit trust umbrella schemes, that is, where unit holders can switch from one sub-fund to another within the total pool of investments making up the umbrella scheme. The article explains [the Revenue's] present view in the context of past legislative changes affecting unit holders in such schemes.

This article uses the following statutory abbreviations,

FSA 1986	Financial Services Act 1986
CGTA 1979	Capital Gains Tax Act 1979
[TA 1988]	Income and Corporation Taxes Act 1988
TCGA 1992	Taxation of Chargeable Gains Act 1992
FA	Finance Act

GENERAL BACKGROUND AND LEGISLATIVE HISTORY

The general CGT provisions for unit trusts are in TCGA 1992 s 99. The CGT rules apply as if—

– the scheme were a company,
– the rights of the unit holders were shares in the company.

In 1985, the case of *Arbuthnot Financial Services Ltd v Inland Revenue Commissioners*, [1985] STC 211, established that each sub-fund of an umbrella unit trust is a separate unit trust scheme. But in the following year, FSA 1986 s 75(4) permitted an umbrella fund to be constituted as a single scheme. In relation to the CGT treatment of unit holders, the effect of this change made by FSA 1986 was reversed by F(No 2)A 1987 s 78.

F(No 2)A 1987 s 78 provided that the question of whether there was a single collective investment scheme, had to be determined for CGT purposes without regard to the investors' entitlement to switch between sub-funds. This restored the practical effect of the *Arbuthnot* decision that the interests of unit holders in the various sub-funds within an umbrella scheme were to be treated for CGT purposes as shareholder interests in different companies. In particular, an individual unit holder switching out of a continuing sub-fund into another would be treated as making a disposal for CGT purposes, on the basis that shares in one company were replaced by shares in another. But, if an entire sub-fund ceased to exist on being merged with another, the unit holders in the disappearing sub-fund would be able to benefit from the rollover provisions for company reconstructions and amalgamations, now in TCGA 1992 s 136, if the relevant conditions were satisfied.

The next relevant change in the statutory rules was FA 1989 s 140 (now TCGA 1992 s 102). This applied to collective investment schemes generally, including authorised unit trusts. For non-UK resident open-ended investment schemes in corporate form, FA 1989 s 140 stopped investors benefiting from share reorganisation treatment when they switched from one class of share to another within the same company. And in relation to a unit holder switching between sub-funds in an authorised unit trust umbrella scheme, without there being any merger of sub-funds, FA 1989 s 140 had the same kind of practical effect (treating the switch as a disposal) as was previously achieved by F(No 2)A 1987 s 78. F(No 2)A 1987 s 78 was accordingly repealed by FA 1989 s 140(6).

Following FA 1989, the merger of one sub-fund with another in the same authorised unit trust umbrella scheme was governed by the rule for share reorganisations of a single company in CGTA 1979 ss 77, 78 (now TCGA 1992 ss 126, 127) and not by the rules for company reconstructions and amalgamations in CGTA 1979 s 86 (now TCGA 1992 s 136). The unit holder was treated as having a shareholder interest in a company comprising the umbrella scheme as a whole. This effect of FSA 1986 s 75(4) was no longer overridden by F(No 2)A 1987 s 78, which was repealed in 1989. And although FA 1989 s 140 disapplied paper for paper rollover treatment in the case where an individual unit holder switched out of a continuing sub-fund into another, s 140 did not prevent rollover treatment on a merger of sub-funds affecting all the unit holders in a sub-fund which ceased to exist.

The statutory position changed again in 1994, when FA 1994 s 113 amended the rules for authorised unit trusts in TA 1988 s 468. In particular, TA 1988 s 468(7) modifies the definition of authorised unit trust in s 468(6) in such a way that each sub-fund of an authorised umbrella scheme is an authorised unit trust and the whole umbrella scheme is not an authorised unit trust. Applying the effect of these amendments for CGT purposes has caused [the Revenue] to change [their] view of the way TCGA 1992 s 99 works in relation to an authorised unit trust.

[THE REVENUE'S] VIEWS ON THE CURRENT LEGISLATION

The conclusion [the Revenue] draw from the interactions between the relevant statutory provisions is that TCGA 1992 s 99 now applies to an umbrella scheme which is an authorised unit trust in the following way—

- Each sub-fund is a separate company, and the umbrella scheme as a whole is effectively transparent for CGT purposes.
- The unit holder's interest is a deemed shareholder interest in a company corresponding to the sub-fund concerned, not in a company corresponding to the whole of the umbrella scheme.

This has the following consequences. If an individual switches out of a continuing sub-fund into another, there is a disposal for CGT purposes. This is on the basis that a shareholder interest in one company is replaced by a shareholder interest in a different company. But if one sub-fund disappears on being merged with another sub-fund, this is subject to the rules for company reconstructions and amalgamations. So paper for paper rollover treatment under TCGA 1992 s 136 is available if the relevant conditions are satisfied.

On a separate point, [the Revenue] have been asked to explain the CGT treatment where an investor switches between income units and accumulation units in the same sub-fund of an authorised unit trust umbrella scheme. TCGA 1992 s 102 does not apply in these circumstances. This is because both the old units and the new units (treated as shares by TCGA 1992 s 99) provide rights to participate in the same separately pooled part of the scheme property. So, where an investor switches between income units and accumulation units in a single sub-fund of an umbrella scheme, TCGA 1992 s 127 can apply. In a straightforward switch, where no consideration is given or received apart from the old units and the new units, the switch would be treated as not giving rise to any disposal for CGT purposes. The new units will be treated as having the same date of acquisition, and the same capital gains cost, as the old units.

RI 170 (April 1997) *Estates of deceased persons in the course of administration*

FA 1995 Sch 18 introduced some changes to the rules in TA 1988 Pt XVI under which residuary beneficiaries of estates of deceased persons are deemed to have received income from the estate. Income is now taxable in the year in which a payment is received from the estate, rather than on an accruals basis over the administration period. Where an estate was in administration both before and after the 5 April 1995, the old rules apply up to 1994–95 with the new rules applying for 1995–96 and later years. There are two common misunderstandings about the new provisions which [the Revenue] would like to correct.

First; it has been suggested that Sch 18 para 3(4) permits the pre FA 1995 versions of TA 1988 s 696(3) and (5) to be applied where the administration of the estate began before 6 April 1995 and a sum is paid to the beneficiary in 1995–96 or a later year. This is not so. The new versions of s 696(3) and (5), introduced by Sch 18, apply whenever payments are made to beneficiaries with absolute interests in residue after 5 April 1995. There are no circumstances in which such payments can be deemed to be the income of 1994–95 or any earlier year. The purpose of paragraph 3(4) of FA 1995 Sch 18 is to ensure that amounts which have already been treated as the income of the beneficiary for 1994–95 or any earlier year are taken into account in any later year in the same way as any other payment within TA 1988 s 696(3A).

Second; a person who has an interest in the residue of an estate is deemed to have received income when a sum is paid. It has been suggested that that term necessarily means a cash sum and that the beneficiary would not be deemed to have received income if assets were transferred. Again this is not so. The term "sum" is given a wider meaning by TA 1988 s 701(12) and includes both assets transferred to a beneficiary and debts set off or released.

Note—This Interpretation is now obsolete.
Commentary—*Simon's Direct Tax Service* **C4.118**.

RI 171 (June 1997) *Double taxation relief—bought in foreign tax—TA 1988 s 801A*

FA 1997 s 20 introduced a new TA 1988 s 801A. The new section restricts double taxation relief for underlying tax in cases where a claim to credit relief is made as part of an avoidance scheme. The following indications of Revenue practice in connection with the new legislation are intended to be of assistance to practitioners when considering transactions undertaken by clients who have interests in overseas companies.

Concerns have been expressed about the application of s 801A(7). [The Revenue] can confirm that [they] would not regard a company acquired "off the shelf" as not having been under the control of a UK company at any time by reason only of the fact that it was owned by a company formation agent throughout the period between its incorporation and its acquisition by the UK company. Also generally speaking, [the Revenue] accept that a company is not caught if there was a time before the doing of anything as part of, or in pursuance of, the avoidance scheme when it was under the control of the UK company. However, [they] will not necessarily be bound to adopt that approach in a case involving a company that was under the control of the UK company. However, [they] will not necessarily be bound to adopt that approach in a case involving a company that was under the control of the UK company in the past, which then ceased to be so and in which an interest is subsequently acquired as part of, or in pursuance of, an avoidance scheme.

The simple introduction of a new "mixer" company into an existing group would not of itself trigger the new legislation, assuming that it does not form part of an avoidance scheme within s 801A. Equally, the new rules will not apply in cases where the acquisition of an interest in a highly-taxed company is not, or is not part of, a scheme or arrangement having as its purpose, or as one of its main purposes, obtaining relief for underlying tax, even though the interest may, at the time of acquisition or later as a result of an intra-group reorganisation, be held through a "mixer" company.

Of course, each case must be examined by reference to its own particular facts. [The Revenue] may also have to reassess the position if new schemes come to light which are designed to circumvent s 801A, especially if they seek to take advantage of [Revenue] practice as set out above. [The Revenue] will publish any new or revised approach to the application of s 801A.

An enquiry where, in a particular case, there is concern that a bona fide commercial acquisition might lead to a restriction of relief under the new rules may be referred to—

> International Division, (Double Taxation), 3rd Floor, Strand Bridge House, 138–142 Strand, London, WC2R 1HH.

The enquiry must identify all the parties concerned, the full details and the purposes of the transactions that are the subject of the enquiry and the reasons why it might be thought that s 801A will apply.

RI 172 (June 1997) *Accrual of purchase discount on loans repayable on demand—FA 1996 s 87*

FA 1996 introduced new rules for taxing profits, gains and losses from loan relationships in the hands of companies. Loan relationships are, essentially, all debts apart from trade debts for goods and services. This article concerns the treatment of debt where the purchaser is connected with the debtor under FA 1996 s 87. Where there is a connection, the purchaser must assume that the debt is repayable in full (bad debt relief is not generally available between connected parties). The question arises of how the purchase discount ought to be treated where, as is often the case, the loan is repayable on demand.

[The Revenue} have amended [their] original view that all purchased loans repayable on demand had to be shown immediately at full value. This would have produced an immediate credit of the difference between acquisition cost and full value.

[The Revenue] now accept that in some circumstances the legislation does not require that the full amount of purchase discount on a loan repayable on demand should be brought into account as a credit in the accounting period of acquisition. The problem is in deciding the period to which the discount on a loan repayable on demand should be said to relate for the purposes of FA 1996 s 85(3)(*a*). [The Revenue] think it is reasonable to take into account the prospects of the demand for repayment being made. Where normal accountancy practice would not operate to recognise discount in the accounting period of acquisition, whether or not the debt was doubtful, immediate recognition of this profit for tax purposes may also be inappropriate. Where the parties to the loan relationship are connected persons the requirement remains that the accounting method must assume that all amounts will be paid in full without relief for bad or doubtful debts. This means that discount should start to be recognised on a time-scale which would be realistic for a loan repayable on demand which was neither bad nor doubtful.

Commentary—*Simon's Direct Tax Service* **D2.1119**.

RI 173 (June 1997) *Partnership changes and the herd basis*

[The Revenue] explained in Tax Bulletin Issue 3 (May 1992) that a fresh herd basis election is required after a change in the membership of a partnership if herd basis treatment is to continue. [They] have been asked whether the changes to TA 1988 s 113 introduced as part of the preparation for self-assessment remove this requirement.

TA 1988 Sch 5 (the herd basis) applies to "animals kept by a farmer". It is clear from paragraphs 2(3), 5 that in this context, where the farming is carried on in partnership, the partnership is the farmer. Moreover, a partnership before a change in its membership is not the same partnership as that after the change. An election applies to all production herds of the class concerned kept ''by the farmer making the election''.

Under the new Self Assessment rules, TA 1988 s 113(2) disapplies s 113(1) so that a change in the membership of a partnership does not trigger a cessation and recommencement of the trade. But this does not alter the fact that the farmer carrying on the trade before the change is not the same as the farmer after the change. So the herd is no longer kept by the farmer making the election. It follows that a fresh herd basis election by the new farmer is still required after a partnership change, if the new partnership wants the herd basis to apply. Thus there is no change from the view of the law set out [by the Revenue] in the May 1992 article.

There is no special form for making a herd basis election, nor is there a requirement that the election be signed by the farmer. Where it is clear from material submitted to the Revenue within the time limit that a farmer has applied the herd basis, then [the Revenue] would regard an election as having been made. For example, the Help Sheet IR 224 which assists farmers in completing the self-employed pages of their returns, suggests that the additional information space on the return is used to record an analysis of herds on the herd basis and details of any adjustments. If this information is provided [the Revenue] would not need a separate election. But if the new partnership wants the herd basis to apply and this is not obvious from the return or other information routinely submitted, a written election stating the class of herd should be made.

Note—This Interpretation has been superseded by the Business Income Manual BIM55610.

RI 175 (October 1997) *Furnished holiday lettings—TA 1988 ss 503, 504 and loss relief claims under TA 1988 s 381*

We have been asked, following the Special Commissioners Decision in *Brown v Richardson* [1997] STC (SCD) 233 for our views where losses are claimed in furnished holiday letting cases (TA 1988 ss 381, 503, 504).

BROWN V RICHARDSON

In Brown v Richardson, the taxpayer acquired, with his wife, a property in Cornwall which was funded—including the cost of furniture and fittings—entirely by a mortgage secured on his main residence. The mortgage application indicated that part of the advance was required to purchase a ''holiday home''. Under the terms of a partnership agreement, profits from the Cornwall property were to be split equally between husband and wife, but any losses were to be allocated wholly to the husband. Loss relief, which arose primarily because of the significant finance charges, was claimed for the years 1992–93 to 1995–96 inclusive under TA 1988 s 381.

The Special Commissioner rejected the argument advanced by the taxpayer that the word ''profits'' in s 504(2) means the profits as calculated for tax purposes. Instead he took the view that profits should be defined in commercial terms, as distinct from profits which may be charged to tax under a particular Schedule or Case in a Schedule. In this case, the Special Commissioner found that the taxpayer's expectation of making an income profit was unrealistic.

Furthermore, the Special Commissioner decided that the taxpayer bought the property primarily as a holiday home (for the years in question, he and his family occupied the property in Cornwall for periods not exceeding six weeks in any 365 day period). Although the letting of this property was ''commercial'' (a letting agent, for instance, was engaged at the outset), it was

> ''... effected, however, with a view to generating revenue to offset costs rather than with a view to the realisation of profits.''

Consequently, the letting failed to qualify for relief.

GENERAL APPROACH

Cases of this kind turn on their own particular facts. In this one, there was evidence on which the Special Commissioner could come to his decision. But the decision supports our view that—

- ''profits'' in s 504(2) means the ''commercial'' and not the ''tax adjusted'' profit;
- a taxpayer's expressed intentions are not necessarily conclusive. There may be evidence which points to a motive other than the income profit motive (such as a holiday or retirement home, or a long term capital profit on the disposal of the property);
- where there is evidence to suggest that a property or caravan was acquired primarily as a holiday or second home, the letting activity is likely to be carried on with a view to generating income to offset costs rather than with a view to the realisation of profits. This principle may apply equally to claims for losses incurred in some trading activities such as farming and other activities where there may be non-commercial considerations;
- claimants may fail the test in s 504(2) where, as in *Brown v Richardson*, the size of the mortgage used to purchase the property or caravan is so large that the projected profitability is jeopardised

or the commercial credibility of the scheme as a whole is, consequently, questionable even though individual lettings are on a commercial basis.

In these cases, we would expect a written business plan to be prepared *at the outset* as was so in the earlier Special Commissioners case of *Walls v Livesey* [1995] STC (SCD) 12. The figures in such a plan must be credible. In *Brown v Richardson*, the taxpayer made no formal projections of the expected income but said he had made projections which (as an accountant) he was able to carry in his head.

However, his projections did not take into account inflation or contingent expenses and showed a fall in general expenses after excluding agents commission.

TA 1988 S 381

Where the claim is under s 381 and s 504(2) *is* satisfied, the loss claim may fail the stricter test of s 381(4). For that test to be satisfied, there must be a reasonable expectation of profits in the period concerned or in a ''reasonable time thereafter''.

We take the view that this test must be considered for each year for which relief under s 381 is claimed and that it is necessary to look at the year of loss and whatever, on the facts, is a reasonable time thereafter. In *Walls v Livesey*, the Special Commissioner observed that relief under s 381 is available so long as profits may be expected not later than a reasonable time after the end of the four year period for which claims under this section are possible. We do not construe the section in this way, although on the particular facts in *Walls v Livesey*, relief may be available in those circumstances. Indeed, in that case, on the facts as found, a profit could reasonably have been expected in a significantly shorter period.

We consider that ''reasonable time'' depends on the facts and, particularly, the nature of the loss making activity. In general, our view is that this should be a fairly short period. But, in the context of capital intensive activities, such as furnished holiday lettings, we would normally expect there to be a reasonable and realistic expectation of profits emerging within five years from the date of the commencement of the activities.

Commentary—*Simon's Direct Tax Service* **A4.108A, B7.206.**

RI 176 (December 1997) *Loan relationships—Definition of "connected"*

This article clarifies our interpretation of the connected persons rules in FA 1996 s 87. It sets out details of some circumstances in which the two parties to a loan relationship will not be connected.

Where the only link between the two parties is the loan relationship the two parties will not be connected persons. This is true even where the size of the loan is such that it would give the loan creditor the greatest share of the assets in a winding up. FA 1996 s 87(8) applies so that the person is not regarded as a participator.

Where the loan creditor has—

- any shareholding in the debtor company; or
- has any rights; or
- has any rights attributed to it,

which would make it a participator in the debtor company then the loan relationship will be taken into account in determining whether it is connected with the debtor company.

FA 1996 s 87(8) applies when determining whether a particular loan creditor is connected with the debtor company. It does not apply to rule out all loan creditors when applying the tests in TA 1988 s 416. For example, Company X has issued share capital of 100 and loans of 100 each from Bank A, Company B, Company C and Individual D. Company B has also entered into a swap agreement with Company X. When looking at whether Company B is connected with Company X the rights of the other loan creditors are not excluded in computing the amounts that Company B would be entitled to on a winding up.

Commentary—*Simon's Direct Tax Service* **D2.1118.**

RI 177 (December 1997) *Members' sports clubs*

BACKGROUND

In the past the taxation of members' clubs has usually been a straightforward matter. However, the increasing commercialisation of sport, evidenced for example by substantial business sponsorship and media coverage of events, can generate a range of tax issues where the answers depend not on any specific statutory enactment but on the application of general principles developed by the courts. In particular, an issue which frequently arises in these circumstances is to what extent a club's increasingly commercial activities can give rise to taxable trading profits or allowable trading losses. In this article we attempt to outline the way this question needs to be answered.

THE TYPES OF CLUBS WE CONSIDER

We are concerned here with members' clubs constituted, for example, as unincorporated associations or as companies limited by guarantee. Whatever their constitution these clubs are all chargeable under the corporation tax regime.

On the other hand, this article is not concerned with clubs which take the form of companies incorporated with limited liability and ordinary share capital under the Companies Act. Their trading profits do not normally come within the mutuality exemption described later in this article.

MEMBERS' CLUBS COME IN ALL SHAPES AND SIZES

At one extreme there are small members' clubs used only by the members who come together for the non-commercial purpose of providing themselves with the facilities to play and watch a sport or for other recreational purposes. Any surplus such clubs generate from their transactions with members is unlikely to amount to a trading profit (and nor is any deficit tax deductible). It is sometimes said that the surplus in these circumstances is exempt on grounds of mutuality. However there is a simpler prior point here. Such activities do not normally amount to a trade because they lack the necessary commercial inspiration.

At the other extreme there are far more commercial concerns whose principal function is to offer the general public entertainment in watching the clubs' sporting activities as well as access to bar and catering facilities and so on. The whole of such a club's activities are likely to amount to a taxable trade.

Increasingly many members' clubs find themselves between these two extremes. For example, their primary purpose may remain non-commercial but they may also have ancillary forms of trading income. These might be bar and catering sales to non-members or income from non-members for the use of club facilities such as golf clubs' ''green fee'' income from visitors using the facilities.

In some cases a club's pricing policy may distinguish between members and non-members. For example, a golf club may charge one green fee to visitors (trading income) and a different (lower) green fee to members' guests (non-trading income). However, often the club will provide its services and facilities to members and non-members alike on the same terms. For example, members and non-members may be charged identical admission prices to watch a football or cricket match.

THE SIGNIFICANT ISSUES

The two issues which arise in this context are to what extent, if at all, a club carries on a trade and, if so, to what extent that trade is undertaken on a mutual basis. In practice we think it is helpful to consider the two points separately even if as a matter of strict law the two issues cannot be disentangled quite so cleanly.

TRADING

The first issue which clubs and their advisers need to consider here is whether any of a club's activities are undertaken in a sufficiently commercial way to constitute a trade. The well-known ''badges of trade'' are relevant here but one particularly useful question to consider is whether the activities in question are broadly similar to those of an admittedly commercial undertaking, even though they are, perhaps, conducted on a smaller scale.

If no trading activities can be identified, then the further issues considered in this article do not arise.

If trading activity is identified it is then necessary to address two points.

The first point is the boundary between trading activities and non-trading activities. For example, it may be that transactions between the club and subordinate classes of members lack the element of commerciality necessary for them to be regarded as trading. This might be the case if associate members are subject to a lower fee or admission charge than that charged to the general public for the same facility.

Second, it is necessary to consider whether any part of a trading profit is not taxable (or a loss not allowable) on the grounds that it is referable to activities undertaken on a mutual basis. This concept is discussed further below.

MUTUALITY

The mutuality doctrine is one which has been developed by the courts over a long period. Its origin has been ascribed to the principle that one cannot make a taxable profit out of oneself.

For mutuality to apply there must be a class of contributors to a common fund who are also entitled, as a class, to share in the surpluses of that fund. By this we mean that arrangements must be in place whereby surpluses always come back to the class of contributors/participators. Individuals may continually be joining and leaving such a class without prejudicing this requirement but there must be a reasonable relationship between the contributions a participator makes and what he or she is entitled to receive both during the course of the business and on a winding up. Direct ownership of the common fund by such a class is not required. For example, the fund may be owned by a separate legal person, typically a company limited by guarantee and having no share capital, so long as the class indirectly owns the fund through its control of the company.

The effect of the doctrine of mutuality is that any trading surplus which a club derives from transactions with such a class of contributor/participator is exempt from tax and, similarly, any loss or deficit cannot be relieved.

In considering whether all or some of the members of clubs with trading activities constitute such a class two particular points need to be borne in mind.

First, in the case of clubs constituted as unincorporated associations, general law may give members the right to a share in the common fund or surpluses on a winding up, even if the club's rules are silent on the matter. On the other hand, where the club takes the form of a company, the company is a separate legal person and the members' entitlement to return of surplus is not protected by general law. Therefore the entitlement must be explicit in the contract between the club and its members.

Secondly, while it may be clear that full members are within the circle of mutuality, it will be necessary to consider separately the position of subordinate classes of member, such as ''junior'' or ''associate'' members. The question is whether these people have the necessary rights to share in club surpluses so that any profits the club derives from commercial transactions with them (as noted earlier, some transactions with them may lack commercial inspiration and not be by way of trade) are also exempt.

CALCULATING TAXABLE PROFIT

Having determined that there is a trade and whether or not mutuality is in point so far as a class of contributors/participators in club surpluses are concerned it is finally necessary to calculate what part of the profit from a club's activities is taxable.

Only non-mutual trading profits are chargeable to tax under Case I of Schedule D. Hence, where a club carries on a trade which is wholly non-mutual it will be necessary to exclude any surplus attributable to non-trading transactions with members. In addition, where a club carries on a trade which is in part mutual and in part not, it will also need to exclude the surplus from mutual trading transactions. In the latter case the arithmetic can be done without seeking to distinguish any non-trading surplus from a mutual trading surplus because both are exempt from tax, albeit for different reasons.

APPORTIONMENT OF INCOME AND EXPENSES

To identify the taxable profit an allocation or apportionment of income and expenses is necessary. There are no hard and fast rules about how this should be done but the objective is to identify what is non-mutual trading income and to allow as a deduction the expenditure incurred in generating that income, calculated as accurately as possible. Some general guidance is given below.

INCOME

Some income will be wholly non-mutual trading income. Examples might include television fees and sponsorship income.

Other income such as club membership subscriptions may not be trading income and may also derive wholly from members within the mutual circle. It should be matched with members' club expenses and excluded from tax computations.

Match receipts, car parking receipts and general bar takings will normally be trading income and may need to be split between that which is mutual, being derived from club-members, and that which is non-mutual, deriving from non-members.

The tax treatment of income from some items, for example programme sales and outdoor catering, may depend on the arrangements put in place. If the club is itself responsible for the programme production and sale and outdoor catering at the event then the income should be apportioned as described in the previous paragraph. However, these and other functions are sometimes franchised to independent operators and in that case the whole of the franchise fee would be treated as trading income.

EXPENSES

Expenses may need to be split correspondingly to allocate an appropriate proportion against the taxable and non-taxable sources of income. The principle applies to all expenditure though there is also a specific statutory rule regarding interest. FA 1996 Sch 9 para 13 provides that no relief is available in respect of interest paid to the extent that the interest is attributable, on a just and reasonable basis, to that part of the company's business which is not within the charge to corporation tax.

If the same prices are charged to members and non-members, the expenses may be apportioned by reference to the income from the two sources where that is known or can be measured with reasonable accuracy. If different prices are charged then the apportionment would need to be weighted appropriately depending on the particular circumstances. For example, in the case of a members' golf club, the weighting might be based on the total number of rounds played and the proportion of those which generate chargeable trading income.

Any items of expenditure that relate solely to a specific category of income should be matched with that income.

Note—This Interpretation has been superseded by the Business Income Manual BIM24215.
Commentary—*Simon's Direct Tax Service* **B3.240.**

RI 178 (December 1997) *Compensation received by business*

It is an increasingly common practice, especially among the utility companies, to pay compensation to customers for interruptions and other deficiencies in the service to be provided. How the compensation is calculated varies. It may for example take the form of a standard amount or be paid at a daily or other periodical rate. We have been asked how such compensation should be treated for tax purposes in the hands of a recipient who carries on a trade, profession or vocation (a "business").

There are two principal questions which need to be addressed—

- *does the compensation arise from the business activities?*
- *is the compensation of an income nature or is it capital?*

The guidance below reflects the principles developed by the courts from the basic Schedule D taxing provisions where they have had to consider the treatment of compensation and related receipts.

Where the compensation relates to specific services used wholly by the recipient for business purposes, we consider that the compensation will almost invariably arise from the business so that the answer to the first question is yes. This remains the case even if the recipient has no prospect of any legal right to compensation, and even if a private customer of the utility would be entitled to similar compensation or where compensation paid exceeds the actual loss of business profits, for example because the compensation is paid at standard rates.

Where the services in question are partly used for business and partly for private purposes, the proportion of the compensation referable on the particular facts to the private element is not a business receipt nor taxable as income under another head of charge.

Where the compensation (or part of it) arises from the business it is then necessary to consider whether the compensation is of an income or capital nature. All the compensation will be of an income nature and therefore a taxable receipt of the business, unless the compensation is paid to make good damage to, or for the physical destruction of, a capital asset of the business.

Compensation for damage reduces otherwise deductible expenditure on the repair of the asset. Compensation for the physical destruction of a capital asset is a capital matter. The complete destruction of an item of machinery or plant is a disposal event for capital allowance and capital gains tax purposes.

Note—This Interpretation has been superseded by the Business Income Manual BIM40101.
Commentary—*Simon's Direct Tax Service* **C1.325**.

RI 179 (February 1998) *Schedule A: basis periods—Case I/II partnerships with ancillary letting income*

In Tax Bulletin Issue 21, we published an article on Schedule A basis periods for trading or professional partnerships with ancillary letting income. That article—which is reproduced at Appendix 3 to IR 150 ("Taxation of rents—a guide to property income")—dealt primarily with situations where "old" (pre-6 April 1994) trading or professional partnerships had ancillary letting income.

Tax Bulletin Issue 30 (August 1997) provided comment on various partnership transitional issues. But we have been asked specifically what adjustments should be made for Schedule A purposes where, in the case of a trading or professional partnership—

- the non-statutory accounts basis was used for years up to 1994–95 inclusive; and
- the statutory current year fiscal basis was used for 1995–96 and 1996–97 (TA 1988 s 21(2)); and
- the statutory current year accounts basis applies—as it must for *all* trading and professional partnerships—for 1997–98 onwards (TA 1988 s 111(7)).

CURRENT YEAR ACCOUNTS BASIS USED FOR 1996–97 ONWARDS

Where the current year accounts basis has been used by concession for 1996–97 (see RI 141—and Appendix 3 to IR 150), that basis should be used for all subsequent years and no further transitional adjustment is required.

CURRENT YEAR FISCAL BASIS USED FOR 1995–96 AND 1996–97

Where the strict current year fiscal basis has been used for 1995–96 and 1996–97, it is necessary to consider what adjustments are needed following the change to the current year accounts basis for 1997–98 since some Schedule A profits may otherwise be taken into account twice.

EXAMPLE

ABC is a trading partnership with the following ancillary Schedule A profits (divisible equally between the three partners A, B and C)—

1994–95—	
accounts basis for year ended 30 September 1994	£10,000
1995–96—	
year ended 5 April 1996	£12,000
1996–97—	
year ended 5 April 1997	£14,000
1997–98—	
accounts basis for year ended 30 September 1997	£15,000

For years up to 1994–95 inclusive, the current year accounts basis has been accepted for Schedule A. And the strict current year fiscal basis was adopted for 1995–96 and 1996–97.

For 1997–98, TA 1988 new s 111 applies and the partners' shares of Schedule A income are assessable on a current year accounts basis. This means that there is an overlap between the Schedule A basis periods for 1996–97 and 1997–98. And the Schedule A profits for the period 1 October 1996–5 April 1997 are brought into account twice. So the profits of this overlap period (£7,000, ignoring odd days, divisible equally between the partners) are treated as ''overlap profit'' giving rise to ''overlap relief'' in due course.

OVERLAP RELIEF

General guidance on overlap relief may be found at paras 1.81 onwards of SAT 1 (1995) and the same principles may be applied to the ancillary letting income of trading and professional partnerships. Overlap relief will be given in two situations—

- at a change of basis period given by TA 1988 s 62(2)(*b*); or
- on cessation of the trade or profession (*not* the cessation of the Schedule A business) when the basis period is given by TA 1988 s 63.

LOSSES

Where Schedule A losses occur, TA 1988 s 63A(4) applies (by virtue of TA 1988 s 111(8)) ensuring that the losses cannot be relieved more than once. If, in the above example, the accounts for the year ended 5 April 1997 showed a loss of £14,000 and the accounts to 30 September 1997 showed a loss of £15,000, the loss attributable to the period 1 October 1996–5 April 1997 of £7,000 (ignoring odd days) will have already been taken into account for 1996–97.

The Schedule A loss for 1997–98 (based on the accounts to 30 September 1997) must therefore be reduced from £15,000 to £8,000 (the Schedule A losses brought forward from 1996–97 amount to £14,000).

Note—See also Revenue Property Income Manual PIM 4600, PIM 4610.

RI 180 (April 1998) *Computation of trading profits—software development costs*

THE YEAR 2000 PROBLEM

Press reports continue to stress the potential problems for many computer systems in handling dates falling in the year 2000 and the re-programming work which will be needed. The expenditure involved may be large and questions have been raised about how we believe it should be treated in computing taxable trading profits.

Our view is that an in-house or contracted-out software project to ensure that existing systems can be adapted for the millennium will always be a revenue matter unless it is part of a major new project instituting other changes and the project is of a capital nature. For example, a concern may decide that for strategic reasons the need for the specific millennium conversion expenditure which would otherwise have been necessary should be pre-empted by a much more substantial undertaking, such as the development of an entirely new (and of course millennium-proof) business system.

Our thinking on the tax treatment where software is acquired under licence was the subject of an article in Tax Bulletin Issue 9 (November 1993,). In line with that we would normally expect expenditure on off the shelf software designed specifically to solve the year 2000 problem to be revenue.

ECONOMIC AND MONETARY UNION (EMU) CONVERSION COSTS

Work on modifying software in connection with EMU and the introduction of the Euro raises similar issues. Again we consider that purely conversion-driven costs required in adapting computer systems for the Euro are unlikely to be capital. But if changes of this nature are overtaken by, or form part of, the development of new business systems for strategic reasons, for example to exploit changes in the financial markets accompanying EMU to open up new trading opportunities, it may be that expenditure on such systems is capital.

FURTHER GUIDANCE

Paragraphs 663–664 of the Inspectors' Manual, published under the Open Government Initiative, provide guidance on whether, and if so to what extent, we would regard the costs of a major project as capital, including a project into which software modification for year 2000 or EMU purposes may be subsumed as mentioned above. Expenditure which is found to be capital will qualify for machinery and plant capital allowances.

Note—This Interpretation has been superseded by the Business Income Manual BIM35865.
Commentary—*Simon's Direct Tax Service* **B2.341.**

RI 181 (April 1998) *Employer provided childcare*

When is an employer "wholly or partly responsible for financing and managing the provision of the care"?

BACKGROUND

TA 1988 s 155A exempts some employer provided childcare from a tax charge under s 154 (benefits in kind). The exemption depends on satisfying sets of conditions which are specified in the statute. One of those sets is that the care must be provided—

– either on premises which are made available by the employer alone (s 155A(4))
– or under arrangements—
  – made by at least two persons (s 155A(5)(*a*)) including the employer and the person(*s*) who make(*s*) the premises available (s 155A(5)(*b*)).
  – which render the employer wholly or partly responsible for financing and managing the provision of the care (s 155A(5)(*c*)).

We have been asked to set out our view on what is required to satisfy the condition set out in s 155A(5)(*c*).

RESPONSIBILITY FOR FINANCING

This requires significantly more than merely buying-in places from a commercial nursery whether on an ad hoc or a more structured basis. There must be some real and substantial commitment to funding the facility or providing it with capital. Such a commitment may take the form of an agreement to meet a set proportion of the overall cost of providing the care or it may be a guarantee to indemnify against losses a primary care provider who would otherwise be at real risk of losses. In the case of a facility which was newly established or of doubtful financial viability the commitment may take the form of a long term undertaking to pay a fixed periodical contribution (possibly expressed as the price of a given number of places) where that contribution is calculated to ensure overall financial viability. Arrangements in which the employer's participation in financing is little more than a token gesture, purporting to meet the statutory test but without real responsibility falling on the employer, do not meet that test.

RESPONSIBILITY FOR MANAGING

This does not necessarily mean day-to-day management or direct responsibility for the care of the children. But it does mean much more than being occasionally consulted about the broad policies which should apply to the provision of the care or having a right to a place on a committee which has no particular brief and little or no power to influence the way in which the care is provided. It requires close involvement in such matters as—

– appointing and monitoring the performance of those engaged to look after the children;
– the extent of the care provided;
– the conditions under which that care is provided; and
– the allocation of places.

Employers must, in a real sense, play a part in management. Arrangements in which the employer's participation in management is little more than a token gesture, purporting to meet the statutory test but without real responsibility falling on the employer, will not meet that test. Where an employee with a child at a nursery is appointed to the management board of that nursery as agent of the employer we will expect to see evidence that the employee is fully empowered to act for the employer and does so.

SUMMARY

What this means is that to satisfy the condition set out at s 155A(5)(*c*) the employer's role in financing and managing the provision of the care must be a real one which renders the employer accountable for his actions and so liable to be called to account if things go wrong.

NOTE 1—COMMERCIAL CHILDCARE PROVIDERS

An employer, or a group of employers, may engage a contractor to undertake the day-to-day running of a childcare facility. Whether the responsibility for management test is then met will depend on the degree of oversight that the employer exercises over the contractor. Arrangements between the employer and the contractor may be such that the employer has no need to become actively involved in the provision of the childcare because his contractual responsibilities require a degree of oversight which ensures that the statutory condition is met. On the other hand, if the employer's responsibility is limited to ensuring broad compliance with the contract he would not be even partly responsible for managing the childcare. In other words it is not possible by an arrangement of this kind for an employer both to pass management responsibility to someone else and to satisfy s 155A(5)(*c*).

Similar considerations apply to the financing requirement. The important point is that the employer must be able to show that he has a financial responsibility for the provision of the childcare either through the contribution of capital and/or through a financial commitment to the costs of running the childcare facility. So if an employer agrees to provide a significant part of the capital which the contractor uses in providing the care the test will be met. Also if the contract between the employer and the contractor is on a "cost plus" basis (with the employer directly responsible for the amount, if any, by which income from fees falls short of costs and the contractor's profit and entitled to any excess of income from fees over the costs and the contractor's profit) then the test will be met. However if the contract provides for a fixed price to be paid to the contractor and the employer's only responsibilities are to agree what he will pay for a certain number of places and to pay that amount, that will not meet the financial responsibility test. The employer is doing no more than agreeing and paying a general subsidy and/or paying for places. He is not taking any financial responsibility for providing childcare.

NOTE 2—ARTIFICIAL ARRANGEMENTS

We have seen a number of instances where an employee's cash remuneration is purportedly cut in return for the employer's paying for care for that employee's child or children. It is asserted that the childcare is within the exemption enacted by s 155A. The substance of the situation is that the employee has paid for childcare and in effect is claiming tax relief on the cost. It will not surprise readers that we are taking a close interest in such arrangements. Those who enter into them should be aware that we are likely to make detailed enquiries into the matter.

Commentary—*Simon's Direct Tax Service* **E4.623.**

RI 182 (April 1998) *Waste site expenditure*

Background

We have been receiving a number of representations and enquiries relating to how, when and by whom relief might be obtained for expenditure on the preparation and restoration of landfill sites for waste disposal. The relief is obtained by virtue of TA 1988 s 91A, 91B for preparation and restoration expenditure respectively. In recent years much waste disposal has moved from the hands of local authorities, etc to private sector companies and the operation of the legislation has become a far more significant question. This is also an area where we have been developing and refining our views in recent months.

The purpose of this article is to explain the way in which we interpret the legislation and to deal with some of the particular points which arise most frequently.

PREPARATION EXPENDITURE—TA 1988 S 91B

Who can claim relief?

In order to obtain relief for preparation expenditure it is necessary for the same person to both incur preparation expenditure (s 91B(1)(*a*)) and to hold a relevant licence which is in force when that person first deposits waste (s 91B(1)(*b*)). It is not necessary to hold the licence when the expenditure is incurred. Indeed, given the nature of the expenditure, much of it will inevitably be incurred before a licence can be obtained.

We do not regard the requirement to incur expenditure as being satisfied where one person actually incurs the expenditure but recharges it to another person who holds the licence when first depositing waste. In that circumstance the two essential elements for relief are in two different hands and no relief will be available to either person.

What is preparation expenditure?

This question has previously been considered in an article in Tax Bulletin Issue 5 (November 1992). There it was made clear that capital expenditure, excluding the cost of acquiring the site itself, was covered provided that the expenditure does not qualify for capital allowances. Revenue expenditure is outside s 91B and subject to the usual rules.

Site preparation expenditure therefore includes the costs of assessing a site for suitability, surveying and soil testing, and the costs of obtaining planning permission and the waste disposal licence. Also included are the costs of providing the infrastructure and engineering a site to the point where waste can be deposited. All of this expenditure contributes to creating the total potential capacity of the site.

Modern practice is to create within a single site a series of cells each of which is filled with waste material before being sealed. As the original cells are filled further cells will be constructed vertically and horizontally such that, over a period of time, a ''honeycomb'' arrangement results. During the useful lifetime of a site a large number of cells will be constructed. Each of the cells may have a short economic life, that is the period during which they can receive waste.

This might suggest that expenditure on creating the cells is not capital and thus outside s 91B. However, since the expenditure results in the permanent modification of a capital asset, the site, it could be argued that the expenditure is capital notwithstanding that the income producing life of the cell is short.

We view the application of the capital/revenue divide in this context as essentially one of economic effect. Thus, in practice, we would not normally seek to distinguish between expenditure on an asset which will cease to exist within twelve months and expenditure where the asset continues to exist after twelve months but has no economic value at the end of that period. In that light, provided the individual cell which is the subject of the expenditure will be completely filled and sealed within a period of two years from the date of its construction, we accept that expenditure on creating the individual cells is revenue and not, therefore, within s 91B.

Where preparation expenditure is incurred in relation to a site for which planning permission or a licence are not ultimately granted (that is abortive expenditure) the expenditure cannot be relieved under s 91B because nobody holds a licence when waste is first deposited on the site. Similarly, where expenditure is incurred in creating the whole potential capacity of the site and, for whatever reason, the whole of the potential capacity is not ultimately used, some part of the preparation expenditure will not be relieved. This might, for example, occur where a series of licences or permissions, etc are required as development of a large site progresses. If such licences, permissions, etc are refused for part of the site, the fraction of the preparation expenditure relating to that part of the site will not be relieved.

RESTORATION EXPENDITURE—TA 1988 S 91A

Who can claim relief?

The requirement for relief is that a person makes a site restoration payment in the course of carrying on a trade. There is no statutory requirement that the person claiming relief either deposited waste on the site or that the trade being carried on is wholly of, or indeed includes, waste disposal. However, there must be a trade being carried on when the payment is made and thus, if trade has ceased at the time of the payment, it cannot be relieved under the section.

What is restoration expenditure?

The legislation defines a ''restoration payment'' as a payment made in connection with the restoration of a site or part of a site and in order to comply with the condition of a relevant licence or a relevant agreement. ''Restoration'' is not defined and it therefore takes its usual dictionary meaning of replacing, reconstructing or returning something to its original state.

We do not regard the legislation as applying to sites other than those where waste disposal activities within s 91A(5) have taken place. For example, the legislation does not apply to sites where contamination has occurred as a result of the ''on-site'' disposal of industrial, etc waste unless the disposal was under a relevant licence as defined in s 91A(6) or there is a relevant agreement within s 91A(7). Similarly, a local authority may require that contaminated land on a former industrial site be restored as a condition of their giving planning permission for development. However, that requirement is unlikely to be under Town and Country Planning Act 1990 s 106 or the other statute listed in s 91A(7). Unless it is under the specific statute, s 91A will not be in point. There are a number of different elements of expenditure, all of which are generally incurred after waste disposal has ceased and capable of being described as restoration expenditure.

One is the cost of covering the site with an impermeable layer, sub-soil and topsoil, contouring, drainage, seeding, tree planting and other similar activities directed to returning the site to a condition where it is suitable for alternative use. These activities can readily be identified as restoration. They are generally, but not necessarily, incurred after waste deposition at the site has ceased, are normally made "once and for all" and have the effect of changing the physical appearance of the site. This expenditure has all the marks of capital expenditure and relief is available in accordance with s 91A in so far as it cannot be relieved by way of capital allowances (s 91A(3)(*b*)).

Another type of expenditure is on the continuation of work which is first required while the site is being used for waste disposal. As soon as waste is deposited, unless it is totally inert, it begins to decompose, producing noxious liquids and potentially hazardous or flammable gases. Many sites will have pipes, pumps, and possibly treatment plant, etc installed to sample and deal with these potentially polluting substances. Waste disposal licences will generally require the site operator to undertake a programme of sampling and analysis to establish that no problems exist or arise. As a result, during the active life of the site when waste deposition is taking place, a programme of sampling, analysis and treatment, etc will begin. This will continue seamlessly into the period after waste disposal has ceased and might then be described as "aftercare".

We see no distinction between the costs of the routine monitoring and treatment, etc described above during the active life of the site and subsequently after waste deposition has ceased. Therefore, we accept that the costs of routine monitoring, analysis and treatment is revenue expenditure, whenever incurred, and, as such is outside s 91A. Such expenditure should be dealt with as ordinary revenue expenditure.

Provisions for restoration expenditure

We acknowledge that generally accepted accounting practice requires a provision be made for future restoration expenditure. The costs of restoration can only be matched against the income generated from waste disposal and are a charge against that income. Since the decomposition of waste and the resulting potential environmental problems can occur over many tens of years the waste site operator will have a long term commitment to carry out "restoration" work.

However, s 91A only permits a deduction for a site restoration payment in the period of accounts in which the payment is made.

It has been suggested that the wording of s 91A(3)(*a*) implies that provisions are allowable but that is not the case given the clear statement of the position in s 91A(1). In order to explain the wording of s 91A(3)(*a*) it is necessary to outline the background to the legislation. Until the decision in the tax case of Rolfe v Wimpey Waste Management Ltd (62 TC 399) restoration expenditure was in practice treated as a revenue deduction. However, the Wimpey decision established that both preparation and restoration expenditure (such as recovering the site and planting trees, etc) were capital and, therefore, no revenue deduction could be allowed. Subsequently, what is now s 91A was enacted to give relief for restoration expenditure. Since the new legislation gives relief on an "as paid" basis, without s 91A(3)(*a*) it would have been possible to claim a deduction for expenditure when paid "post-Wimpey" which had previously been allowed as a provision "pre-Wimpey". Thus s 91A(3)(*a*) does not allow a provision but denies a double deduction in the circumstances described.

In so far as a provision for restoration is for capital expenditure that provision is not allowable in computing Case I profits. It would not be allowable under the normal rules which prohibit a provision for expenditure, such as capital expenditure, which would be disallowable when incurred nor under s 91A which only permits a deduction when the (capital) expenditure is incurred.

However, where a provision for restoration costs is for revenue expenditure, the question of s 91A does not arise. Such a provision would be allowable as a Case I deduction, subject to the usual rules. In the context of provisions for expenditure which will be incurred scores of years in the future the questions of accuracy and appropriate discounting may be in point. Subject to those questions a provision for the future revenue costs of routine monitoring and treatment of gases and leachate are likely to be allowable.

Note—This Interpretation has been superseded by the Business Income Manual BIM67440.
Commentary—*Simon's Direct Tax Service* **B3.1345.**

RI 183 (June 1998) *Capital Allowances: notification of expenditure on machinery or plant under self assessment for income tax cases*

FA 1994 s 118 imposes an obligation to give notice of expenditure on machinery or plant. For income tax cases, the time limit is 31 January, 22 months after the end of the year of assessment.

Statement of Practice 6/94 sets out the form of notification and the general criteria which the Board would adopt in considering applications for extending the time limits. It was written before the self assessment provisions were finalised and we have been asked how expenditure on machinery and plant should be notified for income tax cases under self assessment.

We have previously accepted that the notification requirement will normally be met if the expenditure is included in a tax computation submitted within the time limits. This will usually be in the computation of capital allowances. However, under self assessment, there is no requirement to send in a capital allowances computation, nor is separate provision made in the return to notify expenditure.

For income tax cases under self assessment, we will accept that a claim for capital allowances incorporated in a self assessment return (or amended return) will give satisfactory notification of the expenditure on machinery and plant included in the underlying computation of the claim, provided that the return has been made within the time limit of FA 1994 s 118.

Note—This Interpretation is now obsolete.
Commentary—*Simon's Direct Tax Service* **B2.333**.

RI 184 (June 1998) *Capital Allowances: machinery and plant fixtures—election to determine disposal value*

This article explains the circumstances in which the Revenue will accept a single election made under CAA 1990 s 59B covering a number of different machinery or plant fixtures.

Where a person who has claimed capital allowances on a machinery or plant fixture disposes of the qualifying interest in the land or building to which it is fixed, either by the sale of that interest in land or by the grant of a lease in respect of which a CAA 1990 s 59B election is made, it is necessary to make an apportionment under CAA 1990 s 150 of the capital sum paid on the sale or grant of a lease to determine the proportion of that sum attributable to the fixture. The disposal value to be brought into account for capital allowances purposes is generally the lower of this amount and the original cost of the fixture to the vendor.

CAA 1990 s 59B was introduced by Finance Act 1997 to remove the burden and expense of making the apportionment. Where the vendor has to bring in a disposal value, section 59B allows the vendor and purchaser to make a joint election to determine how much of the capital sum is to be attributed to the fixture, subject to a limit of the lower of the original cost of the fixture to the vendor and the sale price. The form of the election is specified in section 59C CAA 1990.

In strictness, as the fixtures rules in Chapter VI, Part II, CAA 1990 work on an asset by asset basis, a section 59B election would need to be made in respect of each individual fixture. In practice, we accept that the fixtures rules may be applied to groups of assets provided that this does not distort the tax computation. In particular, we will normally accept a single Section 59B election covering a group of fixtures or all the fixtures in a single property, but we will not accept a single election covering fixtures in different properties, for instance where a portfolio of properties are sold together.

Note—This Interpretation is now obsolete.
Commentary—*Simon's Direct Tax Service* **B2.357**.

RI 185 (June 1998) *Update of earlier capital allowances articles*

There have been various articles on capital allowance issues in Tax Bulletin. Parts of these have been overtaken by later developments. This article explains the changes to the previous articles and some new points of interest.

GLASSHOUSES—ISSUE 5

The article gives the Revenue's view of the features that would need to be present before a sophisticated glasshouse might be treated as plant.

Such glasshouses are now considered in paragraph 5(2) Schedule AA1 CAA 1990. This provision does not automatically class them as plant, rather they are not statutorily prevented from being plant because they are fixed structures. Each case will continue to be considered on its own merits.

Paragraph 5(2) applies to expenditure incurred on or after 30 November 1993, unless incurred before

5 April 1996 in pursuance of a contract entered into before 30 November 1993. However, it does not alter the treatment of glasshouses, and the guidance in the Tax Bulletin article is still directly relevant.

GLASSHOUSES—LONG-LIFE ASSETS—ISSUE 30

In an article on long-life assets in Tax Bulletin 30, we invited industry-wide agreements on which assets are, or are not long-life assets. We have now reached the first such agreement, although it is not binding on individual taxpayers. We have agreed with the NFU that sophisticated greenhouses which qualify for allowances as machinery and plant are not long-life assets. The text of the agreement is as follows:

We pleased to inform you that, in the light of the information and explanations provided by you, the Inland Revenue accepts that such glasshouses built to current designs have a useful economic life not exceeding 25 years and will not therefore be long-life assets for the purposes of Sections 38A to 38H CAA 1990.

We will need to review the position in the future because designs and technology will not stand still. We therefore propose that this agreement should include only expenditure incurred up to 31 December 2005. Of course, if glasshouses are developed before that time which have a useful economic life exceeding 25 years, they will necessarily be outside this agreement.

MACHINERY AND PLANT FIXTURES—ISSUE 13

Part 2 of the article in Issue 13 explained that an election under Section 53(1)(b) CAA 1990 between an equipment lessor and lessee could not be made if the agreement for the lease were entered into before the lessee had started to trade.

Section 53 was amended by Paragraph 3(5) Schedule 16 Finance Act 1997 to remove this bar on the election. Part 2 of the article therefore no longer applies.

For agreements entered into on or after 19 March 1997, Section 53(1A) allows an election to be made where the agreement is entered into before the lessee has started to trade but, where this happens, the lessor is treated as not having incurred the expenditure, and therefore does not become entitled to allowances, until the lessee starts to trade.

MEANING OF "COLONY"—ISSUE 16

This article contains a list of colonies for the purposes of Section 33E CAA 1990 relating to the provisions for rollover relief for balancing charges arising on ship disposals. Hong Kong was included in the list. It should now be removed.

Following the transfer of sovereignty to China, Hong Kong is no longer a colony. This means that ships registered in Hong Kong after 30 June 1997 will not have been registered in a relevant register and will not be qualifying ships.

Ships registered in Hong Kong before the hand-over will still be qualifying ships for the purposes of Sections 33A to 33D if they remain on that register or any other relevant register for the whole of their qualifying period.

Note—This Interpretation is now obsolete.
Commentary—*Simon's Direct Tax Service* **B2.314, 353.**

RI 186 (June 1998) *Enterprise zones: industrial buildings allowances on partially completed buildings*

This article clarifies our interpretation of the industrial buildings allowances available where a partially completed building is acquired in an Enterprise Zone. All statutory references are to the Capital Allowance Act 1990 (CAA 1990).

If a person incurs capital expenditure on the construction of a qualifying building or structure under a contract entered into during the life of an enterprise zone, such expenditure will normally qualify for a 100 per cent allowance under Section 1.

Alternatively, if a person purchases the relevant interest in a qualifying building or structure before the building or structure is first used, the purchaser will normally qualify for a 100 per cent allowance under Section 1, through the provisions of Section 10A, based on the net price paid for the relevant interest.

In some cases, a person may acquire the relevant interest in a qualifying building or structure in an enterprise zone before the construction has been completed. We have accepted in the past that the payment by the purchaser should be divided between:

- the purchase of the relevant interest, in relation to the developer's construction expenditure already incurred, in a partially completed building or structure (referred to as the ''Section 10A element'' in this article), and
- the developer's obligation to complete the building (referred to as the ''pure Section 1 element'' in this article)

and, provided that the purchase is made before the expiry of the enterprise zone, the purchaser will normally be entitled to a 100 per cent allowance in respect of both elements.

Many of the schemes we have seen have been structured as the sale and purchase of the relevant interest in the partially constructed building or structure, with additional clauses and guarantees included obliging the developer to complete the construction. The contract may make no distinction in terms between the Section 10A and pure Section 1 elements.

We have recently received legal advice which suggests that such schemes may not be effective in regard to an entitlement to capital allowances on the pure Section 1 element as the contract is for the sale and purchase of an interest in a building or structure. The terms of the contract may be insufficient to enable the purchaser to ''step into'' the construction contract and thereby incur construction expenditure on the pure Section 1 element, for instance if the developer is required to complete the construction works at its own cost (even if ultimately met from funds from the purchase) or the developer is granted or retains an interest in the property during the construction period.

In order to ensure that the purchaser will be entitled to capital allowances on both the Section 10A and pure Section 1 element, it would be advisable to ensure the contractual separation of the purchaser's obligations to purchase the relevant interest in the partially completed building or structure from the purchaser's arrangements with the developer to secure the completion of the building or structure by incurring construction expenditure on the purchaser's own account.

In such cases, it will also be necessary to make an apportionment under Section 21(3) CAA 1990 to determine the proportion of the price paid by the purchaser attributable to qualifying and to non-qualifying assets (for example land). Notwithstanding any contractual separation of the elements, we consider that the scheme should be looked at as a whole, apportioning the total purchase price paid by the purchaser to determine the aggregate of the Section 1 and Section 10A elements.

This change of interpretation will apply to contracts entered into on or after the publication of this article (15 June 1998). We will not seek to apply it to contracts entered into before that date provided they do not include artificial features designed to inflate the amount qualifying for allowances or form part of a wider scheme of tax avoidance transactions.

Commentary—*Simon's Direct Tax Service* **B2.263A.**

RI 187 (June 1998) *Foreign income dividends and employee benefit trusts*

Note—The legislation to which this Interpretation refers (TA 1988 s 246A(3)) has now been repealed.

RI 188 (June 1998) *Intra-group interest and similar sums treated as distributions*

Issue 17 of Tax Bulletin included an article on this topic which set out our general approach to the legislation introduced by FA 1995 s 87. It indicated that a subsequent article would appear in due course dealing with some of the more detailed points of interpretation to which the, then new, law was giving rise. The intention was to identify topics where taxpayers and their advisers were finding difficulty in practice and to offer clarification of our views on these. In fact, to date, the rules have given rise to very few problems of which we are aware. Nonetheless, various representative bodies have indicated that they believe it would be useful to record in Tax Bulletin some of the explanations given to them when the rules were first introduced. What follows therefore is a selection of the main questions put to us about subsection (2)(da) of TA 1988 s 209 and the related changes to other parts of section 209 and section 212, together with our answers.

DOES THE LEGISLATION APPLY TO "UPSTREAM LOANS"—IE, BORROWING BY A PARENT FROM A SUBSIDIARY?

Section 209(2)(da) only applies where the issuing company (the borrower) is a 75 per cent subsidiary of the other company or both are 75 per cent subsidiaries of a third company. So, where the borrower is the ultimate parent of the world-wide group the legislation will not be in point. On the other hand, where the borrower is the parent of the lender but is a 75 per cent subsidiary of another company, the legislation will potentially apply. It should be borne in mind, however, that, normally, interest paid in such circumstances will only be characterised as a distribution where the entire UK grouping (excluding the lender) borrows more than would have been possible at arm's length, where the borrowing would not have happened between independents, or where terms or conditions exist which would not be found between independent persons.

The exceptional treatment for borrowings by the ultimate group parent mirrors the treatment under the legislation which existed before 1995. In this respect there was no intention to depart from the previous rules to any greater extent than was necessary in the course of providing a more level playing field for inward investment. Although section 209(2)(*da*) does not apply in such cases, it may nonetheless be necessary to consider the wording of any relevant tax treaty to determine how interest paid on the borrowings should be dealt with for tax purposes.

DO ANY OF THE UK'S TAX TREATIES PREVENT SECTION 209(2)(DA) APPLYING?

Although the 1995 rule was designed to provide as level a playing field as possible for intra-group inward investment, the individual wording of a few of the United Kingdom's tax treaties has the effect of limiting the extent to which this objective could be achieved.

The terms of our tax treaty with Spain are such as to prevent excessive intra-group interest being treated as a distribution. Moreover, our treaties with:

– Austria;
– Fiji;
– Israel;

- South Africa; and
- The Sudan

are worded in a way which allows section 209(2)(*da*) to characterise excessive interest as distributions but prevents the paying company being denied a deduction for such distributions. Otherwise, we believe the terms of our tax treaties are such as to enable the 1995 rules to apply unhindered.

IS TA 1988 S 808A NOW REDUNDANT?

Why does section 209(8a) apply section 209(8a) apply section 808a for the purposes of section 209(2)(da)?

Why is the list of matters outlined in section 209(8b) similar to, but differently worded from, the equivalent list in section 808a(2)?

TA 1988 s 808A is an aid to interpreting certain ''special relationship'' provisions in the interest article of a number of our treaties. An aim of the 1995 domestic legislation was to broaden the range of cases to which the approach provided for in these treaties applied. Consequently where section 209(2)(*da*) applies, it achieves the same result as a combination of the former domestic rules and treaty wording of the type dealt with in section 808A(2) to (4). Nonetheless, section 808A is not redundant since it continues to assist in construing the relevant treaty wording in cases where the 1995 distribution rules do not apply—ie, where the borrower is the ultimate group parent or where there is a special relationship between the parties which falls short of the 75 per cent shareholder connection specified in that law.

To ensure that the approach of section 808A was generalised in the 1995 domestic legislation, section 209(8A) provided that, for the purposes of section 209(2)(*da*), the section 808A rules are to apply in the same way as they apply for the purposes of a treaty special relationship provision. To make this effective it was necessary to do two things. First, the treaty term ''special relationship'' to which section 808A refers had to be aligned with the domestic law phrase ''relationship, arrangements or other connection'' which appears in section 209(2)(*da*). This is done in sub-paragraph (*a*) of subsection 209(8A). Secondly, it was necessary to ensure that the hypothetical special relationship provision introduced by subsection 209(8A) was one of the type to which subsections (2) to (4) of section 808A would apply in determining what impact, if any, relationships involving borrower, lender and other parties might have had on the existence, quantum, interest rate or other terms of the loan. Subparagraph (*b*) of subsection 209(8A) together with subsection (8B) identify the hypothetical special relationship provision as being of the relevant type and so set the stage for subsections (2) to (4) of section 808A to apply for the purposes of subsection 209(2)(*da*).

Although there appears to be a significant degree of overlap between (8B) and 808A(2), they are in practice doing different things. Subsection (8B) describes the subject matter of the hypothetical provision whereas subsection 808A(2) as amended indicates factors to be taken into account in applying that provision for the purposes of new subsection 209(2)(*da*).

What is the difference between the section 209(2)(da) relationship referred to in subsection 209(8A)(a) and the relationship referred to in sub-paragraph (b) of the subsection?

Subparagraph (*a*) refers to the relationship, arrangements or other connection between the borrower and the lender. Subparagraph (*b*) is concerned with any relationship, arrangements or connection between the borrower and any other person.

Where the borrower's trade involves dealing with the lender or other non-UK members of the group, does the legislation's emphasis on disregarding any relationship, arrangements or other connection (whether formal or informal) between the borrower and connected companies who are not part of the UK grouping mean that the borrower's trading income has to be disregarded for the purposes of the legislation?

We do not believe the legislation requires us to go so far. We are required to disregard the relationship, arrangements or connection with these other group companies, but not to disregard the fact that the borrower has a real source of income which an unrelated lender would take into account in considering whether, or how much, to lend. So, provided the intra-group trading is conducted on arm's length terms, we do not believe that the legislation requires us to assume that the borrower had no source of income whatsoever.

Will the revenue provide illustrations of how the ''UK grouping'' rules in subsection 209(8D) work?

The ''UK grouping'' may consist of—

- just the issuing company (or borrower) itself;
- the issuing company and its effective 51 per cent subsidiaries (wherever resident);
- the top UK holding company in respect of which the issuing company is a 51 per cent subsidiary [subject to subsection (8E)] together with all that holding company's 51 per cent subsidiaries (wherever resident)

Figures I–III illustrate these cases in turn.

Figure I

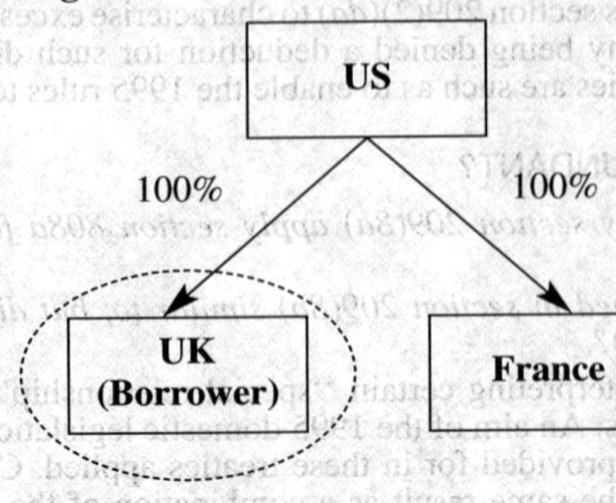

------------- UK Grouping for purposes of legislation

Figure II

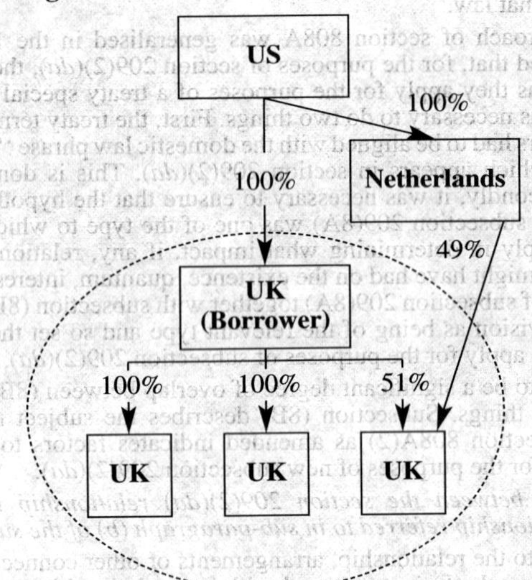

------------- UK Grouping for purposes of legislation

Figure III

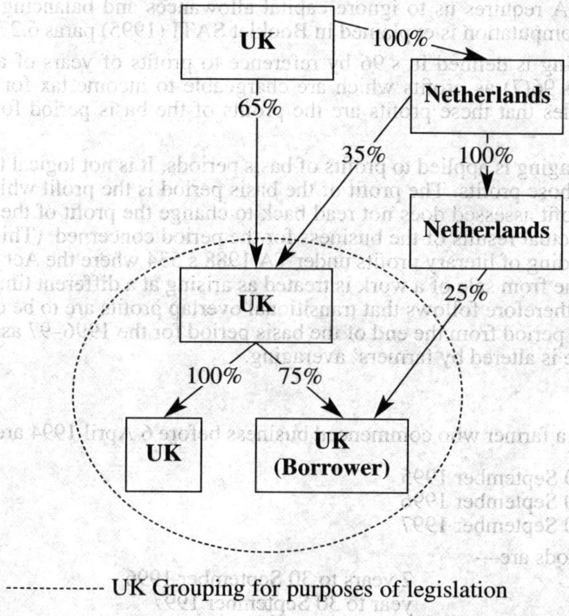

Commentary—*Simon's Direct Tax Service* **D1.128.**

RI 189 (August 1998) *Capital payments by offshore trusts to UK resident charities—change in Inland Revenue practice*

Following recent legal advice the Inland Revenue are changing their practice on the capital gains tax treatment of capital payments by offshore trusts to UK charities.

Under the provisions of TCGA 1992 s 87, where gains have been realised by the trustees of an offshore settlement, chargeable gains may be treated as accruing to beneficiaries who are resident in the UK to the extent that they receive capital payments from the trust.

Under TCGA 1992 s 256, gains accruing to charities are not chargeable to tax if they are applicable and applied for charitable purposes. Until now, however, the Inland Revenue have always taken the view that this exemption is not available for gains which are treated by TCGA 1992 s 87 as accruing to a charity as the beneficiary of an offshore settlement.

Following recent representations on the matter, the Inland Revenue have taken legal advice on the application of these provisions and, in the light of that advice, have now concluded that the better view is that TCGA 1992 s 256 may exempt gains which would otherwise be charged on UK charities under TCGA 1992 s 87.

Consequently, where a UK charity, as beneficiary of an offshore settlement, receives a capital payment, in respect of which a chargeable gain would be treated as accruing to it under s 87(4), the charity will now be entitled to exemption from tax provided by TCGA 1992 s 256(1) to the extent that the capital payment is applicable and applied for charitable purposes.

This change of practice will apply to capital payments made to charities in the circumstances outlined above on or after 10 August 1998, and to any such payments made before that date where the tax liability is still open.

Note—This Interpretation is now obsolete.
Commentary—*Simon's Direct Tax Service* **C1.220, C1.607; C4.442.**

RI 190 (August 1998) *Farmers' averaging and transitional overlap profits*

We have been asked whether transitional overlap profits, computed in accordance with FA 1994 Sch 20 para 2(4) as amended by FA 1995 s 122(2) are altered by farmers' averaging under TA 1988 s 96. The short answer is no. The long answer goes like this—

Transitional overlap profits are defined in FA 1994 Sch 20 para 2(4) as—

"the amount of profits or gains of the basis period for the year 1997–98 which arise after the end of the basis period for 1996–97 ... and before 6 April 1997."

Sub-paragraph 4A requires us to ignore capital allowances and balancing charges in this process. The method of computation is explained in Booklet SATI (1995) paras 6.27–6.32.

Farmers' averaging is defined in s 96 by reference to profits of years of assessment which are, in turn, defined in s 96(7) as profits which are chargeable to income tax for the year concerned. TA 1988 s 60 provides that these profits are the profits of the basis period for the year of assessment concerned.

So farmers' averaging is applied to profits of basis periods. It is not logical to suggest that it can alter the amounts of those profits. The profit of the basis period is the profit which is assessed but a later change to the profit assessed does not read back to change the profit of the basis period. That profit is based on the actual results of the business for the period concerned. (This may be contrasted with backwards spreading of literary profits under TA 1988 s 534 where the Act specifically provides that part of the income from sale of a work is treated as arising at a different time, normally in a different basis period). It therefore follows that transitional overlap profits are to be computed by reference to the profits of the period from the end of the basis period for the 1996–97 assessment to 5 April 1997 *before* that figure is altered by farmers' averaging.

EXAMPLE 1

The results of a farmer who commenced business before 6 April 1994 are as follows—

Year ended 30 September 1995	20,000
Year ended 30 September 1996	24,000
Year ended 30 September 1997	10,000

The basis periods are—

1996–97	2 years to 30 September 1996
1997–98	year to 30 September 1997

and the transitional overlap profit is the profit from 1 October 1997 to 5 April 1998—

ie 6/12 × 10,000 = 5,000

If farmers' averaging is not claimed the assessments are as follows—

1996–97	22,000 (12/24 × (20,000 + 24,000))
1997–98	10,000

If averaging is claimed the average profit for 1997–98 and 1996–97 is 16,000 ($\frac{1}{2}$ × (22,000 + 10,000)). The self-assessment for 1996–97 is not altered but an adjustment is made to the 1997–98 tax to take account of the reduction in profits for 1996–97 from 22,000 to 16,000. But there is no effect on the profit of the year ended 30 September 1997 so the transitional overlap profit is unaffected and remains as 5,000.

Capital allowances have been ignored so far. Including them emphasises that the transitional overlap profit is not changed by farmers' averaging.

EXAMPLE 2

The results are as before but there are capital allowances of 4,000 for 1996–97 and 8,000 for the basis period for 1997–98 (ie the year ended 30 September 1997).

So we have—

1996–97	Profits 22,000 less capital allowances 4,000 = 18,000
1997–98	Profits 2,000

If farmers' averaging is claimed the profits become 10,000 for each year.

Capital allowances must be ignored when computing transitional overlap profits. The Act provides no mechanism for unscrambling the capital allowances and incorporating unscrambled figures into revised transitional overlap computations. If Parliament had intended people to go through such a process there would have been rules. So the transitional overlap profit remains as £5,000 (2,000 + capital allowances 8,000 = 10,000 × 6/12)

In short transitional overlap profit is computed at an earlier stage in the process than farmers' averaging and the two do not interact at all. This is the way the law was intended to work and in our view it achieves that objective.

Commentary—*Simon's Direct Tax Service* **B3.541; E1.215.**

RI 191 (October 1998) *Self-assessment—(1) incomplete returns and (2) the use of provisional figures in returns*

We have been asked to clarify our position regarding "incomplete returns" and the use of provisional figures in self-assessment (SA) tax returns.

Statutory background

TMA 1970 s 8(1) allows the Revenue to issue a notice requiring the taxpayer to deliver a return of "such information as may reasonably be required" to establish the tax due for any year of assessment. TMA 1970 s 113(1) provides that any such return shall be "in such form" as the Board prescribes. And TMA 1970 s 8(2) requires that the taxpayer make a declaration to the effect that "the return is to the best of his knowledge correct and complete".

This means that whenever a tax return form is issued the statutory notice incorporated in that form places an obligation on the recipient to make a return of the information required, in the manner specified. If the completed tax return form delivered to the Revenue is not "correct and complete" the statutory notice has not been complied with and the relevant sanctions may apply. The relevant sanctions are penalties under either TMA 1970 s 93 or s 95, depending on the nature of the failure and the circumstances in which the failure is identified.

(1) INCOMPLETE RETURNS

In many cases it will be obvious that a tax return form is incomplete when it is received. For example, the signature required to satisfy the mandatory declaration may be missing. Or it may be that there is a tick, or note, to the effect that a particular set of pages have been attached to the form, but in fact they are missing. In such cases the return submitted by the taxpayer is clearly deficient in form and the taxpayer has clearly failed "... to comply with the notice ..." (TMA 1970 s 93(1)(*b*)). A failure of this sort should be identified during the initial screening of the return and in such cases we will send back the incomplete return almost immediately, to give the taxpayer the opportunity to rectify the omission.

In other cases the fact that the tax return form is incomplete may not come to light until the information in the return is being systematically transferred to our computer database. If so we may try to obtain the missing information from the taxpayer without sending back the return. This would be appropriate where, say, it is clear that there should be an entry in a particular box. But where there is a major omission we send the return back. This might be the case where, for example, we believe the necessary accounts information is incomplete. Whether we send the return back or not, the action we take has but a single purpose—to give the taxpayer the opportunity to rectify the omission.

Giving the taxpayer an opportunity to rectify an omission in such cases is a means of enhancing voluntary compliance. This is because by sending the incomplete tax return form back we are, in effect, opting to help taxpayers meet their obligations rather than penalising them for not doing so.

Incomplete returns delivered to the Inland Revenue on or before 31 January but sent back close to, or after, the 31 January filing deadline

One of the issues that arose during the first year of self-assessment was the treatment of returns delivered to the Inland Revenue on or before 31 January but sent back to taxpayers or their agents, as incomplete close to, or after, the 31 January deadline. If an incomplete return is sent back in these circumstances it may be too late for the omission to be rectified before the filing deadline. If so the taxpayer will face an automatic late filing penalty under TMA 1970 s 93(2).

In the Revenue Press Release of 3 February 1998, Dawn Primarolo, the Financial Secretary to the Treasury, announced a concession addressing this issue. The concession provided that taxpayers whose returns were sent back to them (or their agents) in the circumstances described above would still be treated as having met the filing deadline provided they sent back a corrected return within a specified period.

A similar concession will apply for 1997–98 returns. The concession will apply where—

- a return is delivered to the Inland Revenue on or before 31 January 1999, and
- the return is subsequently found to be incomplete, and
- it is sent back to the taxpayer (or agent) for completion on or after 18 January 1999.

In such circumstances the taxpayer will be given 14 days in which to complete the return and deliver it back to the Inland Revenue. If a completed return is delivered to us before the end of this 14 day period the taxpayer will be treated as having met the filing deadline.

The concession will also apply to those who file by electronic lodgement. Any rejection is carried out automatically. Accordingly, if a return is rejected shortly before the filing deadline and resubmitted successfully within the 14 day period, the agent will need to take a print-out of the rejection and send it to the office dealing with the return together with an explanation.

We will be monitoring the operation of the concession this year and, depending on the outcome, may recommend that it be established as a formal concession. For the avoidance of doubt it ought to be mentioned that the concession will only apply where the return is incomplete as a result of a genuine oversight. It will not apply where the return is deliberately incomplete, in an attempt to take advantage of the concession. For example, the concession will *not* apply if a return is deliberately sent in without a relevant set of pages, to buy a little more time to complete those pages. Nor will it apply if a return is deliberately sent in without a signature, to buy a little more time to obtain the signature.

EXAMPLES

Return submitted on 20 October 1998 and sent back to taxpayer as incomplete on 10 November 1998. Concession not relevant because taxpayer still has until 31 January 1999 to meet filing deadline.

Return submitted on 20 January 1999 and sent back to taxpayer as incomplete on 21 January 1999. Concession means that providing the completed return is sent back to the Revenue by 4 February 1999 the taxpayer will be treated as having met the filing deadline.

Return submitted on 20 January 1999 and sent back to taxpayer as incomplete on 10 February 1999. Concession means that providing the completed return is sent back to the Revenue by 24 February 1999 the taxpayer will be treated as having met the filing deadline.

Return submitted on 20 February 1999 and sent back to taxpayer as incomplete on 21 February 1999. *Concession not relevant* because return was not sent in on or before the 31 January 1999 filing deadline.

(2) USE OF PROVISIONAL FIGURES IN RETURNS

Given that the purpose of the SA tax return is to establish the tax chargeable for a particular year of assessment it is neither surprising, nor unreasonable, that taxpayers are asked to include correct and final figures of income and gains in their returns.

But it has long been realised that there is an unacceptable tension between an absolute requirement to provide correct and final figures and a requirement to provide such information by a certain date. Prior to self-assessment the courts supported the view that the paramount requirement was to comply with the statutory filing obligation and that this may require the taxpayer to use provisional figures in the return (*Dunk v General Commissioners for Havant* (1976) 51 TC 519; *Alexander v General Commissioners for Wallington* (1993) 65 TC 777). For example—

> "If a taxpayer finds particular circumstances that make the best of his knowledge more than usually unreliable, it is open to him to put against his figure for a particular item of income such words as "estimated—see accompanying memorandum", or something of that kind, and explain the circumstances. If he has done his best, and, of course, he is under a duty to use all proper sources of knowledge—he will not, in my view, be guilty of making a false statement, providing, as I say, he puts in a genuine estimate and, if necessary, explains that it is not very reliable." [Goulding, J, in *Dunk v General Commissioners* for Havant (1976) 51 TC 519 at 521].

Application of Dunk principles to self-assessment returns

We would argue that the time limits for filing an SA tax return are such that it is reasonable to expect the vast majority of taxpayers to be able to provide correct and final figures by the statutory filing date. Nonetheless, we recognise that there will still be some circumstances in which it is impossible for the taxpayer to provide final figures, despite their best efforts to do so. So it is the Inland Revenue's view that the "*Dunk* principles" apply equally well to SA returns. Indeed, these principles are clearly identifiable in the guidance published in 1994, at para 2.53 of SAT 2—

> "There will be occasions on which some information cannot be finalised within the formal self-assessment time limits despite the taxpayer's best efforts to do so. In such cases the taxpayer should include a "best estimate" of the information in the return and, if appropriate, a corresponding estimate of the tax due.... A return containing any such provisional figure will not be regarded as incomplete."

Our views on the use of the continuing application of the *Dunk* principles are also reflected in the guidance material provided with the SA tax return. For example, there is general advice on the use of provisional figures at page 27 of the main Tax Return Guide:

> "Do not delay sending your tax return just because you do not have all the information you need. You must do your best to obtain the information, but if you cannot provide final figures by the time you need to send your tax return, then estimate the amount."

Circumstances in which the Inland Revenue could regard a return containing provisional figures as "incomplete"

Despite the general guidance provided in the 1996–97 tax return there appears to have been some confusion as to the circumstances in which the Inland Revenue could regard a tax return as incomplete simply because it contains provisional figures.

The general guidance in the tax return guidance tells the taxpayer that "you must do your best to obtain the information" and goes on to say that we "... will not normally regard a tax return as incomplete simply because it contains provisional figures, provided you have taken all reasonable steps to get the final figures, and you ensure that they are sent as soon as they are available".

It should be clear from this that we expect the taxpayer to have done all they reasonably can to obtain the final figures, or, in the words of Goulding, J., the taxpayer must have "... done his best ...". If a taxpayer has made little or no effort to obtain the final figures before the filing deadline we would argue that a key element of the "*Dunk*" principles is absent and the taxpayer has failed to comply with the notice to make a return. Similarly, we would not accept that general pressure of work or the complexity of a taxpayer's affairs justifies the use of provisional figures. The onus is on the taxpayer (and his agent) to take such factors into account, for example, when considering how long it will take to complete the return.

There is further guidance on the use of provisional figures in the self-employment pages. This guidance (on page SEN3) allows for the return of a single figure of estimated profit, rather than standard accounts information—

> "If you cannot complete the income and expenses section of your self-employment pages because it is impossible to prepare the figures from which your taxable profit is to be calculated before the latest date for sending your tax return, you should provide an estimate of your taxable profit in box 3.88 ...".

As is made clear this guidance is to be read in conjunction with the general advice on the use of provisional figures in the main Tax Return Guide. It follows that we expect taxpayers to have done all they reasonably can to obtain the final figures. It was certainly not our intention to accept a single figure of profit when, for example, it was only "impossible" to prepare final figures because the taxpayer had made little or no effort to have the final figures prepared in time to meet the filing deadline. In such circumstances we would argue that a key element of the "*Dunk*" principles is absent and the taxpayer has failed to comply with the notice to make a return. In fact we would expect there to be very few circumstances in which, despite the taxpayer's best efforts, it is genuinely "impossible" for the taxpayer to provide us with accounts information. The only common circumstance would be where, in the case of a newly commenced business, the first accounting period does not end until close to, or after, the statutory filing date. (By "close to" we mean within three months of the filing date, so for the normal 31 January deadline, that means accounting periods ending on or after 1 November).

Even though there are relatively few circumstances in which it would be acceptable for a single provisional figure of profit to be returned there may be circumstances in which it is acceptable for some, or all, of the standard accounts information to be completed on a provisional basis. For example, there may have been a change of accounting date requiring two sets of accounts to be prepared. If only the earlier sets of accounts were final then provisional standard accounts information would be required, pending completion of the second set of accounts. In these and similar circumstances (that is where a provisional figure of profit is estimated by reference to an earlier period of account) we would expect provisional figures for each of the anticipated entries in the standard accounts information.

In practice it is unlikely that we will send back a 1997–98 tax return as incomplete simply because it contains provisional figures. We would prefer to process the return as received and then hold the taxpayer to the obligation to provide final figures as soon as they are available. We will do this by identifying all those returns, which contain provisional figures. If the final figures are not provided by the expected date we will take appropriate action to obtain them and in some cases this will mean opening an enquiry. (The guidance in the 1998–99 returns has been clarified along the lines described above).

Commentary—*Simon's Direct Tax Service* **E1.806.**

RI 192 (October 1998) *Schedule D Cases I and II—accountancy expenses arising out of self-assessment enquiries*

We have been asked to clarify the application of Statement of Practice SP 16/91 to accountancy expenses incurred in connection with self-assessment enquiries. We are currently considering the issues that have been raised and will consult with representative bodies before the statement is superseded. But there is one particular point that we would like to clarify immediately.

SP 16/91 identifies the circumstances in which we will treat any additional "accountancy expenses arising out of accounts investigations" as an allowable deduction. It will be obvious from the quote in the previous sentence that the language used in SP 16/91 does not reflect self-assessment concepts and terminology, and for that reason alone needs to be updated. But the text of SP 16/91 is deficient in one other important aspect. In practice we normally disallow accountancy expenses only where the additional profits arise out of negligent or fraudulent conduct. This is not stated explicitly in SP 16/91. Instead SP 16/91 simply refers to investigations which result in "... a charge to interest or interest and penalties". This phrase is intended to imply some degree of culpability on the part of the taxpayer (so that, for example, the additional profits attract interest under TMA 1970 s 88 and penalties under TMA 1970 s 95). But "... without a charge to interest." could be read as denying a deduction where there is a charge to interest under TMA 1970 s 86, a charge which could arise in circumstances where there is no suggestion of negligent or fraudulent conduct at all. This is not the intention. We have no reason to believe that this ambiguity has caused any difficulty in the operation of SP 16/91. But it becomes much more relevant in the context of self-assessment, because there is now just one interest charging provision, TMA 1970 s 86.

Until such time as SP 16/91 is superseded the text below should be regarded as a statement of our practice, as it applies to self-assessment enquiries.

ACCOUNTANCY EXPENSES ARISING OUT OF SELF-ASSESSMENT ENQUIRIES

It is the practice to allow, in computing profits assessable under Schedule D Case I and II, the normal accountancy expenses incurred in preparing accounts or accounts information and in assisting with the self-assessment of tax liabilities.

Additional accountancy expenses arising out of an enquiry into the accounts information in a particular year's return will *not* be allowed where the enquiry reveals discrepancies and additional liabilities for the year of enquiry, or any earlier year, which arise as a result of negligent or fraudulent conduct.

Where, however, the enquiry results in no addition to profits, or an adjustment to the profits for the year of enquiry only and that adjustment does not arise as a result of negligent or fraudulent conduct, the additional accountancy expenses *will* be allowable.

Commentary—*Simon's Direct Tax Service* **B3.1452.**

RI 193 (October 1998) *Use of apportionment in the calculation of transitional overlap profit—FA 1994 Sch 20 para 2(4)*

We have been asked to state our view on the use of apportionment's (under TA 1988 s 72) in the calculation of transitional overlap profit (FA 1994 Sch 20 para 2(4), as amended by FA 1995 s 122(2)).

Typically the examples referred to us concern a taxpayer who has made up accounts for the 12 months to 30-4-96, the 12 months to 30-4-97 and then the 11 months to 31-3-98. The basis period for 1997–98 is the 23 months to 31-3-98 and transitional overlap relief arises in respect of the period 1-5-96 to 5-4-97. Is the relief due 11/23rds of the profits of the basis period, or 11/12ths of the profit of the 12 month account to 30-4-97?

Our view is that the answer is 11/12ths of the profit of the 12 month account to 30-4-97 (or, more accurately, 340/365ths of that profit). In the absence of an account for the 11 months of the transitional overlap period itself a time-based apportionment of the 12 month account to 30-4-97 is the most accurate measure of the relevant profit available to us.

EXAMPLE

12 months to 30-4-96	£19,000
12 months to 30-4-97	£24,000
11 months to 31-3-98	£15,000

The profit of the basis period for 1997–98 (the 23 months 1-5-96 to 31-3-98) is £39,000 (TA 1988 s 62(2)(*b*)).

The profit of the transitional overlap period (the 340 days 1-5-96 to 5-4-97) is 340/365 × 24,000 = £22,356 (FA 1994 Sch 20 para 2(4)).

Strictly the overlap relief available on the change of accounting date to 31-3-98 is 335/340 × 22,356 = £22,027 (TA 1988 s 63A(1)). But if the 31 March concession is adopted, to treat the change of accounting dates as if a change to 5-4-98, the full £22,356 may be deducted.

Assuming the 31 March concession is adopted the taxable profit for 1997–98 is (39,000 – 22,356) = £16,644 (TA 1988 s 63A(1)).

[Note: There is a more detailed explanation of the general principles of apportionment in paras 1.17 to 1.20 of SAT1 (1995). The "31 March" concession is detailed at paras 1.98 to 1.99.]

Commentary—*Simon's Direct Tax Service* **E1.215.**

RI 194 (October 1998) *Recording overlap profit carried forward from 1997–98—TA 1988 s 63A*

The self-assessment returns for 1997–98 include boxes which taxpayers should use to record any overlap profit (including any transitional overlap profit) carried forward to 1998–99. The boxes in question are box 3.77 in the self-employment pages and boxes 4.11 and 4.66 in the partnership pages. (There are also boxes for overlap profit brought forward from the previous year, and for the overlap relief used in computing the profits of the year.)

The boxes for amounts of overlap profit were provided as a convenient means for taxpayers to maintain an accurate record of the amount of relief that will be available in a future year. We have received reports that some agents (and taxpayers) are failing to make entries in the overlap profit carried forward boxes in cases where we would expect entries to be appropriate. Failure to make an appropriate entry does not mean that the entitlement to relief is lost as it ought to be possible to establish the correct position in a future year. But it would be preferable for all concerned if the correct figures were established in the year in which the overlap arises. Where a return has already been sent in TMA 1970 s 9(4)(*b*) amendment should be considered.

Commentary—*Simon's Direct Tax Service* **E1.806A.**

RI 195 (October 1998) *Amendments to self-assessment returns: original return made negligently or fraudulently—TMA 1970 ss 9A(4), 12AB(2)*

There appears to be a mistaken belief in some quarters that amending a self-assessment under TMA 1970 s 9(4), or a partnership statement under TMA 1970 s 12AB(2), precludes penalty action by the Inland Revenue in relation to the incorrect figures included in the original return.

Self-assessment does not alter our policy of considering the imposition of a penalty under TMA 1970 s 95 or 95A whenever there is evidence that the taxpayer has acted negligently or fraudulently, even if the error first comes to light as a result of an amendment under TMA 1970 s 9(4), or TMA 1970 s 12AB(2), rather than as the result of an enquiry under TMA 1970 s 9A. Any such penalty would be based on the difference between the amount of tax correctly payable and the amount that would have been payable if the original return had been correct.

Commentary—*Simon's Direct Tax Service* **E1.826.**

RI 196 (October 1998) *Payments under charitable deeds of covenant*

Note—The legislation to which this interpretation refers (TA 1988 ss 347A and 339(8)) has now been repealed.

RI 197 (October 1998) *Flat management companies: new corporation tax Schedule A—residential service charges*

The Landlord and Tenant Act (LTA) 1987 s 42 provides that contributions to variable service charges (and to sinking funds) in respect of residential property should be paid into a trust fund.

Under the old corporation tax Schedule A rules (which applied up to 31 March 1998), the Revenue took the view that service charges received by flat management companies were normally within the scope of Schedule A notwithstanding the provisions of LTA 1987 s 42. This was because the charge under old Schedule A was based on the receipts to which a landlord was entitled in a chargeable period (old TA 1988 s 15(1) para 2). However, where service charges received by occupier controlled flat management companies were matched over a period of up to five years by admissible expenses, no Schedule A charge was normally imposed (see Property Income Manual para 5095 published externally under Open Government).

We have been asked whether the position has changed under the new Schedule A rules introduced by FA 1998 s 38, Sch 5. Under new Schedule A, it is necessary to consider the profits of the Schedule A business (calculated, in the first instance, in accordance with Schedule D Case I rules and correct accountancy principles). As from 1 April 1998, residential service charges received by occupier controlled flat management companies will ordinarily be outside the scope of Schedule A since, under correct accountancy principles, it will not usually be correct to include in the computation of profits sums to which the landlord is not beneficially entitled.

Consequently, where residential service charges are received by an occupier controlled flat management company for periods subsequent to 31 March 1998, such sums will ordinarily be received as capital in the landlord's capacity as trustee (under LTA 1987 s 42). Investment income arising on such sums held in a designated bank account will be chargeable on the trustee at the rate applicable to trusts (s 42 contains an implied power to accumulate).

Rents receivable by flat management companies (such as ground rents—other than peppercorn rents) are outside the scope of LTA 1987 s 42 and remain chargeable under Schedule A.

Note—This Interpretation has been superseded by the Property Income Manual PIM1070.
Commentary—*Simon's Direct Tax Service* **A4.102A.**

RI 198 (December 1998) *Offshore trusts: capital gains tax—FA 1998*

FA 1998: DEFINITION OF "PROTECTED SETTLEMENT" IN NEW TCGA 1992 SCH 5 PARAS 9(10A)–(10D).

FA 1998 s 132 brought trusts set up before 19 March 1991 within the scope of a capital gains tax charge, under TCGA 1992 s 86, on the settlor of the trust in respect of gains realised by the trust where the settlor, members of the settlor's immediate family, or companies they controlled, could benefit from the trust. For this purpose, ''members of the settlor's immediate family'' are the settlor's spouse, children of the settlor or of the settlor's spouse and their spouses. FA 1998 s 132 applies, generally, to chargeable gains realised on or after 6 April 1999.

A category of ''protected settlements'' will remain outside the scope of the charge on the settlor under TCGA 1992 s 86. ''Protected settlements'' are defined at new TCGA 1992 Sch 5 paras 9(10A)–9(10D) as untainted pre-19 March 1991 settlements where the only members of the settlor's immediate family who can benefit from the trust are, broadly—

– unborn children of the settlor or of the settlor's (current or future) spouse, or

– such children who are under the age of 18 at the end of the immediately preceding year of assessment. Future spouses of such children or of the settlor can also be included without jeopardising the "protected settlement" status, as can persons who are not counted as members of the settlor's immediate family for the purposes of the settlor charge.

However, FA 1998 s 131 treats grandchildren of the settlor or of the settlor's spouse as members of the settlor's immediate family for the purposes of the settlor charge in relation to trusts set up on or after 17 March 1998, or trusts set up before that date which become tainted. There is therefore some question over whether pre-1991 trusts where the beneficiaries, at 6 April 1999, include both children under 18 and grandchildren as the only members of the settlor's immediate family who can benefit from the trust would meet the definition of a "protected settlement".

In such cases the Inland Revenue will *not* regard the existence of the settlor's (or the settlor's spouse's) grandchildren of whatever age as beneficiaries of a relevant settlement as causing the settlement to fall outside the definition of a "protected settlement" for the purposes of new TCGA 1992 Sch 5 paras 9(10A)–(10D).

Commentary—*Simon's Direct Tax Service* **C4.438.**
Revenue Interpretation RI 232—Change of interpretation: Non-resident trusts—gains and losses accruing in the transitional period to trusts brought within the settlor charge by FA 1988—treatment for tax year 1999/2000.

RI 199 (February 1999) *The taxation of Schedule F income received by trustees after 6 April 1999*

In his Budget in July 1997 the Chancellor announced a major reform of the corporation tax system including the way in which Schedule F income (dividends, distributions and other similar income) is taxed. The principal legislation is in F(No 2)A 1997 ss 24–36.

We have received a number of enquiries about the effect of these changes on trusts, trustees and beneficiaries. This article provides some general guidance on the changes. It does not cover Schedule F income received by trustees of a UK unit trust scheme.

All references are to TA 1988 unless otherwise stated.

BARE TRUSTEES

Income received by bare trustees is treated as the income of the beneficiary for tax purposes. There have been no changes to that. So Schedule F income arising to such trusts will continue to be treated as the income of the beneficiary and be taxed as if they received the income direct.

TRUSTEES NOT SUBJECT TO TA 1988 S 686

Such trustees do not generally pay tax at the rate applicable to trusts and likewise will not normally be taxed at the Schedule F trust rate. But they will be liable at the Schedule F trust rate on share buybacks and other similar distributions in accordance with the new s 686A, just as at present they are taxable at the rate applicable to trusts on such distributions.

For other distributions received on and after 6 April 1999 the trustees will be chargeable at the Schedule F ordinary rate (10%). Since the distribution will have a non-payable tax credit of 10% attached to it, there will be no further tax to pay by the trustees just like under the current system.

TRUSTEES LIABLE UNDER TA 1988 S 686

At present such trustees are taxed at the rate applicable to trusts (34%) on all income they receive. From 6 April 1999 income falling within Schedule F is to be taxed at a new "Schedule F trust rate" of 25%. Schedule F income will have a non-payable tax credit of one-ninth of the amount or value of the dividend. So on a dividend of £900 the non-payable tax credit will be £100.

The Schedule F trust rate of 25% ensures that, in broad terms, the trustees will have to pay the same amount of tax on the same dividend under the new system as they do under the current system. This is demonstrated by the following example.

	Current System £	*New System* £
Dividend	900	900
Tax credit	225	100
Gross income	1125	1000
Tax at 34% / 25%	382.50	250
Income after tax	742.50	750
Tax due from trustees	382.50	250
Minus tax credit	225	100
Additional tax due	157.50	150

DISCRETIONARY PAYMENTS MADE BY TRUSTEES

Where trustees make payments to which s 687 applies, the beneficiary receives an annual payment which is treated as a gross payment from which tax at 34% has been deducted. Thus a payment of £750 is treated as a payment of £1136.36 from which tax of £386.36 has been deducted. The gross payment of £1136.36 is treated as the income of the beneficiary with further tax being due from them or tax being repaid to them as appropriate.

From 6 April 1999 as tax credits will be non-payable they cannot go into the s 687(3) "tax pool". So, using the example above, whereas at present £382.50 can go into the pool, under the new system only £150 will do so (£250 minus £100).

The example shows that the cash available to the trustees for distribution is £742.50 under the current system and £750 under the new. Under the current system, if the trustees distribute all the available cash (£742.50), the beneficiary's income is £1125 gross with a tax credit of £382.50. The credit is matched by the amount in the tax pool (see above).

Under the new system from 6 April 1999 if the trustees distribute all the cash available (£750) the beneficiary's income will be £1136.36 with a tax credit of £386.36. And, as at present, if there is insufficient tax in the tax pool to "frank" this tax credit there will be further liability on the trustees under s 687(2)(*b*). In the above example if the only tax in the pool is the £150 paid by the trustees on the dividend then there will be an s 687(2)(*b*) charge of £236.36 (£386.36 less £150).

If, in the above example, the trustees choose to rely only on the dividend income to fund both the payment to the beneficiary and the s 687(2)(*b*) liability then they only have sufficient funds to release 66% of the actual dividend, ie £900 × 66% = £594. This will translate to gross income of £900 with a tax credit of £306. The s 687(2)(*b*) liability will be £156 (£306 minus tax pool of £150). So, the trustees will pay £594 to the beneficiary and £156 to the Inland Revenue. This would equal the £750 cash they have in hand.

It has been suggested that the effect of s 687 has somehow been altered by the changes in legislation. This is incorrect. The current legislation works in exactly the same way where trustees receive a dividend without a tax credit such as a foreign income dividend (FID) as the following example shows. Assume a discretionary trust's only income in 1998–99 is a foreign income dividend of £900.

Dividend	£900
Notional tax treated as paid	£225
Gross income	£1125
Tax at 34%	£382.50
Income available after tax	£742.50
Tax due from trustees	£382.50
Minus notional tax treated as paid	£225.00
Additional tax due	£157.50

So far the computation is identical to that in the previous example.

However, because the notional tax is non-payable it cannot go into the tax pool so only the £157.50 paid by the trustees goes into the pool. If the trustees release the whole of the available cash of £742.50 the beneficiary's income is £1125 gross with a tax credit of £382.50. As the tax pool is only £157.50 the liability under s 687(2)(*b*) is £225.

Again if the trustees choose to rely only on the dividend income to fund the payment to the beneficiary and the s 687(2)(*b*) liability then they only have sufficient funds to release 66% of the actual dividend, ie £900 x 66% = £594. This will translate to gross income of £900 with a tax credit of £306. The s 687(2)(*b*) liability becomes £148.50 (£306 minus tax pool £157.50). So the trustees will pay £594 to the beneficiary and £148.50 to the Inland Revenue. This equals the £742.50 cash they have in hand.

TRUST MANAGEMENT EXPENSES

Sections 686(2AA), (2A), (2B), 689A, B contain the rules for trust management expenses. From 6 April 1999 s 689B has been amended so that the new Schedule F income is included in those types of income (ie income not carrying a payable tax credit) against which allowable expenses are set in priority to other income. Therefore allowable expenses will be set against income in the following order from 6 April 1999—

- first against Schedule F income and other income within ss 233(1A), (1B), 249(6), and 421(1)(*a*);
- next against foreign dividends as defined in s 1A(3)(*b*);
- next against savings income within s 1A; and
- finally against other income.

Commentary—*Simon's Direct Tax Service* **C4.203.**

RI 200 (February 1999) *Schedule D Cases I and II redundancy payments*

Tax Bulletin Issue 15 (February 1995, p 195) contained an article entitled "Redundancy payments and provisions". We have been asked how the decision of the Judicial Committee of the Privy

Council in IRC v Cosmotron Manufacturing Co Ltd [[1997] STC 1134] affects the views we expressed in that article.

The Cosmotron case concerned ''severance payments'' which the company was obliged under Hong Kong law to make to its employees when making them redundant. Cosmotron closed its factory and ceased business, so making all its employees redundant. The company claimed a deduction for the ''severance payments'' in computing its trading profits for tax purposes in the final period of trading. The Privy Council held that this deduction was allowable.

Although the relevant Hong Kong tax provisions were not identical to those in the UK, the Privy Council had UK case law cited to it, and expressly stated in its judgment that in applying the law to this case there was no difference between the test under Hong Kong law and the test in TA 1988 s 74(1)(a) that expenditure must be incurred wholly and exclusively for the purposes of the trade. The ''severance payments'' passed this test because they were a liability assumed when employees were taken on for the purposes of the trade. The obligation to make them was contingent, but was nonetheless incurred as a necessary condition of retaining the services of the employees concerned. It was immaterial that in this case it was the cessation of the trade that crystallised the liability.

Although decisions of the Privy Council are only of ''persuasive'' authority in UK tax law we have decided to be guided by the decision. Accordingly the Revenue will not argue that payments made—

- *to an employee taken on for the purposes of the trade;*
- *under a pre-existing contractual or statutory obligation which was a consequence of their being employed for the purposes of the trade;*

are disallowed by s 74(1)(a) just because it is the cessation of the trade that crystallises the liability to pay.

This does not apply to payments such as ex gratia payments which exceed an employee's pre-existing contractual or statutory entitlement and which are made for the purpose of closing down a business. Such payments continue to be inadmissible on general principles (IRC v Anglo Brewing Co Ltd), although they may be partly or wholly deductible by virtue of TA 1988 s 90.

There is a reference to this at paras 660a and 950 of the Inspector's Manual.

Note—This Interpretation is now obsolete.
Commentary—*Simon's Direct Tax Service* **B3.1429.**

RI 201 (April 1999) *Transfer of assets abroad—taxation of income under the provisions of TA 1988 ss 739–746*

INTRODUCTION

TA 1988 ss 739–746 are anti-avoidance provisions aimed at certain transactions involving transfers of assets abroad. These notes provide guidance on how the Inland Revenue interpret various aspects of this legislation at the time of writing, in cases where the courts have not given a definitive interpretation of particular statutory wording.

SECTION 739

It has been established by the courts (in *Lord Howard de Walden v IRC* [25 TC 121]) that ''power to enjoy'' the income of a person resident or domiciled outside the UK is not restricted to the income or benefit actually received. However, it has not been determined by the courts whether all the income of the overseas person should be assessed, or only the income of that person to the extent that it arose by virtue or in consequence of the relevant transfer of assets and any associated operation(*s*). It has been the Revenue's practice (since the decision in *Vestey v IRC* [[1977] STC 414]) to assess on the second of these two possible bases.

Section 739 can potentially apply not only to an individual who transfers assets but to someone who is ''associated with'' a transaction (according to the decision of the courts in *Vestey v IRC*). The Revenue regard this as including anyone who procured the transfer of assets.

Where the same assets are transferred by several individuals, the Revenue's practice is to assess the transferors in proportion to their share of the assets transferred. Thus where, for example, shares of a UK company are held by three shareholders in the proportion 40%, 40% and 20% and there is s 739 liability in respect of the income of an overseas person to which the shares are transferred, the liability is assessed on each of the three shareholders in proportion to their respective holdings.

SECTION 740

A non-UK domiciled individual who transfers assets but is outside the charge to tax under s 739 by virtue of the provisions of s 743(3), is not assessed under s 740.

Similarly, a transferor of assets who is outside the charge to tax under s 739 in respect of income arising before 26 November 1996 through being not ordinarily resident in the UK at the time of the transfer, is not assessed under s 740.

For the purposes of s 740(1)(*b*) a benefit is treated as not including either the giving of a life interest to a beneficiary or the receipt by a beneficiary of the proceeds of selling a life interest. But it is otherwise treated as including all benefits taken into account in determining whether an individual has power to enjoy income for the purposes of s 739. It therefore includes for example receipt of a loan at less than a commercial rate of interest, and the use of trust property at less than an open market rental.

For the purposes of s 740(3) the measure of ''relevant income'' is treated as not including such part of the income as has already been genuinely paid away to a beneficiary or to a *bona fide* charity.

Once relevant income has arisen and continues to be available to provide a benefit, it must in the Revenue's view be carried forward year by year until extinguished by such a benefit, even if it is capitalised in the accounts of the overseas person.

SECTION 741

The legislation places the onus on the taxpayer to demonstrate to the satisfaction of the Revenue that the conditions for relief under s 741 are met, or likewise to the satisfaction of the Special Commissioners in a case where the taxpayer has appealed against a decision by the Revenue that relief is not due. In either event the terms of s 741 in effect require the taxpayer to show that the transactions had a non-fiscal purpose, and did not also have a tax avoidance purpose. Where the taxpayer has been able to establish that at least one of the purposes for undertaking the transactions did not entail tax avoidance, the Revenue will regard it as incumbent on them to indicate why in their view tax avoidance may also have been involved. They will explain their reasons to the taxpayer, after considering fully all the arguments he or she have advanced and all the documents submitted in support of his or her contentions, and will do so prior to any Special Commissioners' hearing.

Although it is sometimes referred to as a ''motive test'', s 741 in fact refers to the ''purpose'' of a transfer and any associated operations. Consequently, it is only the purpose of a transaction that the Revenue consider in applying the section. ''Purpose'' is taken to be the end it is sought to achieve by the transaction. Furthermore, if a transaction involves tax avoidance, that is considered by the Revenue to be at least one of its purposes even if the transferor did not form the subjective intention of avoiding tax.

The law was amended in 1969 following a decision of the Courts (in *IRC v Herdman* [45 TC 394]) that only the transfer and any associated operations giving a power to enjoy at the outset were relevant for determining whether the terms of s 741 were satisfied. The amendment to the legislation sought to bring all associated operations into consideration when s 741 was invoked. Because of doubts expressed as to the effectiveness of this amendment, it has been the Revenue's practice in considering whether a defence under s 741 is available to consider only the transfer and any associated operations which directly establish a power to enjoy the income of the overseas person under any particular sub-head in s 742(2).

The role of advisers is taken into account in assessing the purpose of the transaction when considering the application of s 741.

The expression ''*bona fide* commercial'' in s 741(*b*) is taken to apply only to the furtherance of trade or business, and not to the making or managing of investments.

The Revenue's view is that one of the essential conditions of s 741(*b*) would not be satisfied where there was a significant element of tax avoidance purpose in the design of the transfer and any associated operations.

SECTION 742

The wording of s 742(1) is interpreted as meaning that an associated operation does not necessarily have to take place after a transfer of assets. A transaction undertaken ''in relation to'' a transfer of assets can precede the transfer.

SECTION 743

Unless transactions are part of a wider arrangement, Revenue practice is not to seek to assess a UK domiciled individual on the income of a non-UK domiciled spouse, where that income arises from a transfer of assets by that spouse and would be outside the charge to tax under s 739 by virtue of the provisions of s 743(3).

Where a non-UK domiciled individual transfers assets but is not chargeable to tax under the provisions of s 739 owing to s 743(3), there is no bar in the Revenue's view on the application of s 740 to others who did not themselves make the transfer but were beneficiaries of it.

SECTION 744

Where more than one person can be potentially assessable under ss 739, 740, the Revenue will seek to agree with the taxpayer under the terms of s 744 a ''just and reasonable'' division of liability.

SECTION 745

In the Revenue's view the introduction of a client to anyone responsible for establishing an overseas entity does not constitute the giving of professional advice to a client within s 745(3).

MISCELLANEOUS

Where income could be fully assessed under both s 739 and the settlements legislation in TA 1988 Part XV, it will not in practice be charged under both. Similarly, income will not in practice be charged on both the beneficiary under s 740 and the settlor under the settlements legislation, where an assessment could in strictness be made on each of them in a case involving income that is accumulated within a discretionary offshore trust in which the settlor retains an interest, and then paid to a beneficiary as capital. However, in both cases this is subject to the proviso that the Revenue may sometimes raise alternative assessments, for example where a taxpayer has not provided full information. Moreover, where income arises in an offshore company underlying a settlement and the income is not paid up immediately to that settlement, the provisions of s 739 will be invoked where necessary to assess the income of the underlying company.

The Revenue's practice is only to allow trading losses in an offshore company to be carried forward to be offset against future trading profits of that company. They cannot be offset against investment income of the same, previous or future years.

Because of their complex and specialised nature the provisions of ss 739–746 are applied in individual cases by the Revenue's Special Compliance Office and Financial Intermediaries and Claims Office (see Inspector's Manual IM4622). It is incumbent on taxpayers or their advisers to draw the Revenue's attention to the implications of the legislation when submitting details of transactions to which it may potentially apply (in the light of the decision of the courts in *Regina v IRC ex parte MFK Underwriting Agents Ltd* [[1989] STC 873]).

Taxpayers are required to disclose clearly in their self-assessment return if there is any income or benefit assessable under s 739 or 740, and whether reliance is being placed on s 741 to exclude income or benefit from assessment. Where such a disclosure has been made and exemption under s 741 claimed, the Revenue will make any necessary enquiries about that exemption in the statutory period allowed, and will not seek to reopen that year's return on discovery grounds if the s 741 exemption has to be reconsidered in later years.

Commentary—*Simon's Direct Tax Service* **E1.724.**

RI 202 (April 1999) *Capital gains tax—some retirement relief points*

This article covers—

- our present understanding of the meaning of full-time working officer or employee following the judgment in the case of *Palmer v Maloney and Shipleys* [71 TC 1983];
- the effect of the phasing out of retirement relief on claims for relief under Concession D31 [now obsolete];
- how we will treat disposals which are associated with other events which take place around 5 April 2003.

FULL-TIME WORKING OFFICER OR EMPLOYEE

We have had enquiries about our published view of the meaning of full-time working officer or employee for the purposes of TCGA 1992 Sch 6 para 1 following the judgment of Mr Justice Laddie in *Palmer v Maloney and Shipleys*.

This case concerns a claim for damages brought by Mr Palmer against his former accountants contending that he would have qualified for retirement relief if he had realised the profit in his company shareholding by way of a capital distribution, and that his accountants had been negligent in not advising him to that effect. The defendants stated that Mr Palmer did not qualify for retirement relief because he did not devote substantially the whole of his time to the service of the company. Judgment was given in favour of the defendants but the decision is subject to further litigation.

Our longstanding practice does not accord with the tests which Mr Justice Laddie applied to determine whether an individual is a full-time working officer or employee. For the moment however we can confirm that our interpretation of the definition of full-time working officer or employee for the purposes of capital gains tax retirement relief will remain unchanged pending the case becoming final. In particular we shall continue to abide by our published view in Capital Gains Manual CG63621 on the meaning of the words "substantially the whole of his time" contained in the definition of full-time working officer or employee at TCGA 1992 Sch 6 para 1.

This guidance is that one should consider whether someone devotes substantially the whole of his time to the service of the company by reference to the normal working week. For a company which has other full-time employees this can be taken to mean at least three quarters of the full normal working hours.

We will fully review, following finalisation of the litigation, whether or not it is necessary to re-appraise our understanding of the words ''substantially the whole of his time'' in the light of judicial observations. If reappraisal should prove necessary, we will determine what action needs to be taken in the light of a detailed study of the court judgments; a further announcement would then be made about our future approach.

CONCESSION D31 AND PHASING OUT OF RETIREMENT RELIEF

The effect of Concession D31 is to alter the date of disposal for retirement relief purposes where, pending completion of an unconditional contract, business activities continue beyond the date of that contract. Normally the date of disposal of an asset is determined by TCGA s 28, and will be the date of the unconditional contract. However when we are looking at the application of retirement relief we may consider the qualifying conditions by reference to the date of completion in accordance with Concession D31.

The result of this where the date of the unconditional contract and the date of completion span two tax years is described at Capital Gains Manual CG63291. If an individual is under the qualifying age at the time of the unconditional contract in one tax year, but continues in business until completion in the following tax year, and at completion has reached the qualifying age of relief, then we may accept that the individual is eligible for retirement relief in respect of the disposal in the earlier year (subject to all other provisions being fulfilled).

Where the date of completion is treated as the date of disposal in accordance with the Concession, then that date applies to all aspects of retirement relief including the amounts of relief available in the year of disposal when completion occurs.

This means that if an individual enters into an unconditional contract in the year ended 5 April 1999, but is only 49 at that date, and the contract is not completed until May 1999 when he is 50, then the retirement relief due will be calculated by reference to the lower amount of relief available in the year ended 5 April 2000.

It also means that where an unconditional contract is before 5 April 2003 and completion is not until after that date Concession D31 will not give access to retirement relief. This is because retirement relief would only be due by reference to the date of completion, and in the year ended 5 April 2004 retirement relief is no longer available.

Note—Concession D31 has been classified as obsolete.

SOME OTHER ASPECTS OF THE PHASING OUT OF RETIREMENT RELIEF

The final date for a disposal upon which retirement relief may be due is 5 April 2003. There are a number of situations where a disposal will qualify for retirement relief only if it can be associated with another event. The examples below illustrate some of the situations in which disposals will not qualify for relief because an associated event falls after 5 April 2003—

- Where there is an associated disposal before 5 April 2003, but the material disposal is after that date then for the purposes of TCGA ss 164(6)–(7) no retirement relief would be due on the gain on the earlier associated disposal. This is because no relief falls to be given on the material disposal which takes place at a time when retirement relief is no longer available.
- Where there is the cessation, or disposal of the whole or part of a business, prior to 5 April 2003, and there is a disposal of assets or an associated disposal after that date retirement relief will not be available in respect of any gain arising on that disposal because TCGA ss 163, 164 and Sch 6 shall not have effect in relation to disposals in 2003–04 and subsequent years of assessment by virtue of FA 1998 s 140(2).

Any questions on this guidance should be directed to—Jeffrey Davenport, Capital and Savings Division, Sapphire House, Streetsbrook Road, Solihull B91 1QU.

Commentary—*Simon's Direct Tax Service* **C3.602.**

RI 203 (April 1999) *Capital allowances on machinery or plant leased outside the UK*

CAA 1990 s 42 restricts the capital allowances available on machinery or plant leased outside the UK. Subsection (1) provides that the section applies where the asset is leased to a person who is neither resident in the UK nor using the asset exclusively for the purposes of a trade whose profits are chargeable to UK tax, unless the leasing is short-term or the leasing of a ship, aircraft or transport container which is used for a qualifying purpose as defined in CAA 1990 s 39(6)–(9). Subsection (2) provides that where the section applies, writing down allowances are given at 10% per annum, rather than at 25%. Where any of the conditions in sub-s (3) applies, no capital allowances are due.

It has previously been the view of the Inland Revenue, as explained in Capital Allowances Manual CA2832, that where there is a chain of leases, the tests in s 42(1) are applied to the end lessee only.

The Solicitor of the Inland Revenue has advised that this interpretation of the legislation is incorrect. The Solicitor has advised that s 42 should apply where any lessee in the chain, whether an intermediate lessee or the end lessee, meets the conditions in s 42(1).

We will accept the previous interpretation for leasing arrangements entered into—

- before the date of the publication of this Tax Bulletin, 19 April 1999;
- within three months after the date of publication of this Tax Bulletin where the principal terms of the leasing arrangement have been agreed in writing before the date of publication (for example in an agreed term-sheet or accepted offer letter) and have not materially altered since that date.

In all other cases, we will apply the revised view that s 42 will apply where any lessee or sub-lessee meets the conditions in s 42(1).

Commentary—*Simon's Direct Tax Service* **B2.345**.

RI 204 (June 1999) *Application of the long-life asset rules to jet aircraft*

In Tax Bulletin Issue 30 (August 1997) we explained how we interpret and plan to operate the rules for capital allowances on long-life assets in CAA 1990 Part II Chapter IVA. We said that we would welcome industry wide agreements on which assets are or are not long-life.

The large business offices (LBOs) dealing with the airlines (City B, Manchester and Nottingham) have reached an agreement with the British Air Transport Association (BATA) on the application of the long-life asset rules to jet aircraft capable of a configuration of 60 or more seats and used primarily for the carriage of passengers or freight for profit (referred to below as "jet aircraft") which make up the bulk of the aircraft operated by members of BATA. The agreement runs up until 31 December 2003. The LBOs and BATA have agreed to reconsider the issue before that date taking into account all the relevant information then available with a view to the renewal of the agreement on the same, or appropriately amended, terms.

The LBOs and BATA both recognise that the 25 year test is particularly difficult to apply to jet aircraft. From the evidence available, the LBOs consider that the useful economic life of a current generation jet aircraft would normally be more than 25 years. BATA consider that the evidence shows that it would be less than 25 years. Both sides remain convinced of the rightness of their views but have been unable to persuade the other of the correctness of the inferences they sought to draw from the evidence available. Both sides recognise that a test case is unlikely to resolve the issue for jet aircraft generally given the range of possible interpretations of the evidence and the extent to which the decision would depend on the facts of the particular case at the particular time.

The agreement also takes other factors into account. In Tax Bulletin Issue 30, we gave an example of the engines being treated as separate assets for tax purposes. BATA estimate that up to 50% of the cost of a jet aircraft can be made up of major components which are not in themselves long life and may be treated as separate assets. BATA estimate that only 39% by value of the original aircraft remains in existence at the end of its useful economic life.

In the light of these considerations and in order to resolve the treatment of aircraft on a basis which is—

- *simple and straightforward for the airline and the Inland Revenue to administer;*
- *fair to the airline and other taxpayers; and*
- *provides certainty for the airline,*

the LBOs have agreed with BATA that individual airlines may choose to enter into an arrangement with the Revenue. The arrangement will be open to the parent company of the airline and will apply to all its subsidiary companies. It will apply to all jet aircraft acquired by the airline under contracts entered into between the start of the long-life asset rules on 26 November 1996, other than ones excluded from the rules under the transitional provisions in CAA 1990 s 38H, and 31 December 2003.

For jet aircraft which come within the arrangement, the total expenditure on the aircraft in its ready for service configuration will be treated as made up of two equal sums, one of which is long-life and attracts allowances at 6% while the other is not long-life and attracts allowances at the normal rate for plant and machinery. Disposal proceeds will be apportioned in the same ratio.

Under the arrangement, the airline also undertakes to inform the Revenue of the details of any finance lease in respect of jet aircraft entered into up to 31 December 2003 within three months of so doing.

The arrangement will be open to lessors so that they too can have certainty in planning their transactions. In the case of finance lessors, we will accept an arrangement with an individual company which does not apply to other members of the leasing group.

In order to give airlines and lessors sufficient time to consider the consequences, we will allow them until 30 September 1999 to enter into an arrangement. Where an airline or lessor does not incur any expenditure to which the arrangement would apply until after that date, we will allow it to enter into the arrangement up until it makes its first claim to capital allowances in respect of such expenditure.

We will consider any claim for capital allowances on a jet aircraft not brought into an arrangement in the light of its particular facts, starting as explained above with the presumption that the aircraft will normally be a long-life asset.

Discussions are continuing with representative bodies on the treatment of other types of aircraft including regional jets below 60 seats configuration, corporate jets, turboprops and other aircraft used in general aviation. We hope to be able to issue a further Tax Bulletin article on the outcome of those discussions in the near future.

The details of the arrangement are contained in the text of formal agreements (one version for airlines, the other for lessors) and an explanatory statement agreed between the LBOs dealing with the airlines (City B, Manchester and Nottingham) and BATA. Copies of the agreements and explanatory statement are available from any of these LBOs or from—Business Tax Division, Room 301, 22 Kingsway, London, WC2B 6NR.

Any enquiries concerning the agreement can be made to any of these offices.

Note—This Interpretation has been superseded by the Capital Allowances Manual CA23781.
Commentary—*Simon's Direct Tax Service* **B2.344**.

RI 205 (June 1999) *Compulsory acquisition of freehold or extension of lease by tenant: tenant's right to buy: Statement of Practice SP 13/93—TCGA 1992 s 247*

TCGA 1992 s 247 allows rollover relief in certain circumstances where a landlord disposes of land to an ''authority exercising or having compulsory powers'' and acquires replacement land. ''Authority'' is defined in TCGA 1992 s 243(5) to mean a person or body of persons with compulsory purchase powers.

An existing statement of practice, SP 13/93, was issued to make it clear that relief under s 247 may be claimed by a landlord, if the conditions of the section are met, where tenants exercise their statutory right to acquire the freehold reversion or an extension of their lease under the Leasehold Reform, Housing & Urban Development Act 1993. It replaced SP 7/90 which applied the same treatment to cases under the Leasehold Reform Act 1967.

We have been asked to extend the statement of practice to deal with cases where a tenant's right to buy under the Housing Acts 1985 to 96 has been preserved following a transfer of housing stock into the private sector. This is of particular importance where there has been a large-scale voluntary transfer from a local authority to a registered social landlord. A revised statement of practice making it clear that s 247 can apply to the landlord in these circumstances is reproduced [see SP 13/93 Compulsory acquisition of freehold or extension of lease by tenant].

EXTENSION OF LEASES—CONCESSION D39

For convenience, a change to our practice in relation to capital gains tax on the extension of a lease, as embodied in Concession D39, is set out below.

Concession D39 applies where a lease is extended by the surrender of the old lease and the grant of a new lease. Where the lease is surrendered before its expiry and the conditions of the concession are met the tenant is treated as not having made a disposal or part disposal of the old lease.

One of the conditions is that the surrender and re-grant must be between unconnected parties bargaining at arms length. The concession has now been amended so that it can apply also to transactions between connected parties provided that the terms of the transaction are equivalent to those that would have been made between unconnected parties bargaining at arms length.

Commentary—*Simon's Direct Tax Service* **C2.1116**.
Concession D39—Extension of leases.
Statement of Practice SP 13/93—Compulsory acquisition of freehold or extension of lease by tenant.

RI 206 (June 1999) *Double taxation relief—adjustments to foreign tax paid*

FA 1998 s 107 introduced amendments to TA 1988 s 806. The new provisions require taxpayers (both individuals and companies) to notify the Revenue within one year of any adjustment to the amount of foreign tax in respect of which they have claimed credit relief against UK tax. This article seeks to clarify what is meant by an adjustment and when it should be considered to have been made for the purposes of s 107.

The requirement only applies however in circumstances where the adjustment is such that it results in a claim to relief becoming excessive.

The notice must be given in writing within one year from when the adjustment was made. A person who fails to give the required notice within the time limit is liable to a penalty of an amount not exceeding the amount by which the credit allowed has been rendered excessive by reason of the adjustment. Any penalty chargeable is subject to the provisions of TMA 1970 s 100, and to the normal abatement procedure.

WHAT IS AN ADJUSTMENT?

This new provision relates to foreign tax paid under a wide variety of systems and methods of collection. It is not possible therefore to define precisely what constitutes an adjustment of the tax paid. However, in most cases this will involve the foreign tax authority formally accepting that the amount of tax paid is excessive and agreeing to repay the excessive tax, either directly, or indirectly by setting it off against other liabilities that the taxpayer may have.

WHEN IS AN ADJUSTMENT MADE?

An adjustment should be considered to have been made when the foreign tax authority issues a notification, in writing to the person (or their advisers) who has paid the tax in respect of which the claim to relief has been made, that it accepts that the amount of tax paid is excessive. Where the foreign tax authority does not issue such a notification but simply repays or sets off the excessive tax, the date when the repayment was issued or the set off carried out should be taken as the date when the adjustment was made.

In some circumstances, for example where underlying tax is involved, claims may be made in respect of foreign tax paid by a person other than the person claiming relief in the UK. Notification of any adjustment to the amount of tax paid will normally be sent only to the person who has paid that tax. Persons who have claimed relief in the UK in respect of foreign tax paid by another person should therefore ensure that they will be made aware of any subsequent adjustment to the amount of foreign tax on which their claim is based.

Commentary—*Simon's Direct Tax Service* **F1.135.**

RI 207 (August 1999) *Deduction of tax at source—loan relationships for trading purposes*

We have been asked to clarify whether, or how, the obligation to deduct income tax from payments of yearly interest has been affected by the enactment of the loan relationships legislation at FA 1996 Part IV, Chapter II. In particular we have been asked to comment on the suggestion that, where interest received is being taxed as part of the Case I profit of a company, this removes the obligation to deduct tax imposed by TA 1988 s 349(2) on the payer.

TA 1988 s 349(2) provides that where annual interest chargeable to tax under Schedule D Case III is paid by a company, a partnership of which a company is a member, or any person to another person whose usual place of abode is outside the UK, the payer is obliged to deduct income tax. This obligation is subject to s 349(3) which provides that, in the case of certain specified payments (including payments to a person within the charge to corporation tax in respect of interest on an advance from a bank), there is no obligation to deduct tax on making the payment. Such exceptions to the rule in s 349(2) are not addressed further in this note.

Where interest is paid to a company within the charge to corporation tax the receipt will be taxed under the provisions of the loan relationships legislation. If the loan relationship is for trade purposes, yearly interest received will be a credit which falls to be taxed as part of the Case I profit of the company. It would not be taxed under Case III. It has been suggested that in such circumstances, where no Case III charge arises, there can be no obligation to deduct income tax in accordance with s 349. This is not the case.

The test in s 349(2) to establish whether there is an obligation to deduct tax is based on whether the yearly interest is—

> ''chargeable to tax under Case III of Schedule D (as that Schedule has effect apart from the modification made for the purposes of corporation tax by section 18(3A))''.

The payer of the interest therefore has to decide whether the interest falls into the categories of income referred to in TA 1988 s 18(3) under the heading ''Case III''. The test is carried out with no reference to the actual treatment of the interest in the hands of the recipient. Clearly it is possible for interest to be within the categories of income referred to in s 18(3) but actually to be taxed as part of the Case I profit of a corporate creditor. In such circumstances the obligation to deduct income tax remains.

Commentary—*Simon's Direct Tax Service* **D2.1138.**

RI 208 (August 1999) *Wines and spirits—the capital gains tax treatment*

We have received a number of enquiries recently about the capital gains tax treatment of bottles of wines, particularly ''fine'' wines, and spirits. This article sets out the position for transactions where the correct charge is to capital gains tax. It is written on the premise that any transactions by private individuals involving the acquisition and disposal of such wines are not regarded as ''trading'' or an ''adventure in the nature of trade'' within the charge to income tax under Schedule D Case I.

Where bottled wine is purchased, each bottle is a chattel for capital gains tax purposes. As gains on the disposal of chattels which are also wasting assets are generally exempt from capital gains tax, TCGA 1992 s 45(1), then the first question is whether bottled wine is a wasting asset or not.

For capital gains tax purposes a wasting asset is one whose predictable life, from the point of view of the person acquiring it, does not exceed 50 years, TCGA 1992 s 44(1). Whilst this definition would clearly apply to cheap table wine which may turn to vinegar within a relatively short period, even in unopened bottles, our view is that it would certainly not apply to port and other fortified wines which are generally recognised to have a very long storage life.

Between these extremes, there are a number of fine wines which are quite drinkable after a substantial period although of course the taste alters over that time. With these the basic consideration, in our view, is whether the wine has turned to vinegar or has merely matured. Of course in practice, most wine is drunk well below the age of 50 years and in that sense it is very difficult to consider the issue in isolation. However, where the facts justify it, we would normally contend that wine is not a wasting asset if it appears to be fine wine which not unusually is kept (or some samples of which are kept) for substantial periods sometimes well in excess of 50 years.

If a particular bottle of wine is not a wasting asset, then any gain accruing on its disposal may nevertheless be exempt where the disposal proceeds for that single bottle do not exceed £6,000, TCGA 1992 s 262(1). Where however, a number of bottles are sold to the same person in one or more transactions, then the question might arise as to whether the bottles themselves constitute a ''set''. If they do, then the £6,000 limit would apply to the overall sale proceeds rather than the price fetched for any individual bottle, TCGA 1992 s 262(4). This is a question of fact and would depend on—

(*a*) whether the bottles are ''similar and complementary''—which would require the wine in them to have been produced from the same vineyard in the same vintage year, and
(*b*) whether the bottles are of greater worth when sold collectively than when sold individually.

Commentary—*Simon's Direct Tax Service* **C2.902.**

RI 209 (August 1999) *Late Payment of Commercial Debts (Interest) Act 1998—whether interest payable under the Act is "yearly interest"*

The purpose of this article is to provide guidance on whether interest under the above Act is ''yearly'' interest within the meaning of TA 1988 s 349(2).

The Late Payment of Commercial Debts (Interest) Act 1998 came into force on 1 November 1998. It provides for statutory interest to run where payment is delayed on certain contracts for goods or services. It does not apply where there is a prior right to interest under the terms of the contract itself, or under statute.

The question arises as to whether interest under the Act is ''yearly'' interest and so subject to deduction of income tax by the payer in accordance with s 349(2). The leading case law authorities in this area explain that, in deciding whether interest is ''yearly'', it is of primary importance to establish whether the parties intend or contemplate that the debt will, or may, remain outstanding for a year or more. It is our understanding that the Late Payment Act was introduced primarily to encourage prompt payment, and that it is not its intention, nor will it normally be its effect, to provide interest of money over a long period. Accordingly we consider that interest payable under the Act will not constitute ''yearly'' interest, and that no obligation therefore arises to the payer to deduct tax from the payment under s 349(2). This same view extends to interest expressly provided for under the terms of a contract for goods or services, where that contract is one to which the Act would have applied but for the prior contractual right to interest.

More generally, all relevant provisions of the Taxes Acts will apply to interest payable under the Late Payment Act as they apply to any other interest chargeable under Schedule D Case III. This means for instance that, in the case of a company chargeable to corporation tax, the relevant interest will rank as interest on a ''money debt'' which by virtue of FA 1996 s 100(2) should be brought into account on an accruals basis in accordance with the loan relationships regime. Section 100(4) will apply to determine whether the corresponding debits or credits fall to be brought into account as trading or non-trading items. In the case of a business outside the scope of the corporation tax rules we will normally expect to follow the timing of recognition of receipts and payments given by correct accounting treatment. In such a case interest payable will normally qualify as a business expense on ordinary principles; interest receivable will be a component of the Case I profit where it is received in the course of an activity forming an integral part of a trade, otherwise it will be charged under Case III as it arises.

Commentary—*Simon's Direct Tax Service* **A3.409.**

RI 210 (October 1999) *Bookmakers' pitches and capital gains tax*

BACKGROUND

Up until October 1998, the pitch committee of the appropriate Bookmakers' Protection Association (BPA) allocated pitches at each horse racecourse on behalf of the racecourse authorities. BPAs covered all courses between them and combined formed the National Association of Bookmakers. On-course bookmakers obtained a "pitch"—a specified position in Tattersall's or the Silver Ring on which they erected a stand and traded. In each enclosure the pitches were arranged in rows, the front rows being regarded as the best from which to attract the most custom and the largest bets.

A bookmaker could only have one pitch at a racecourse at a time. A pitch was deemed to fall vacant if the occupant failed to regularly attend the course meetings. When a pitch fell vacant, the bookmaker with the longest satisfactory attendance in the ring concerned was given preference if they applied for it, except that in certain circumstances a member of the previous holder's family could obtain it.

Fundamental changes to the administration of on-course bookmakers and the allocation of pitches were introduced with effect from 8 October 1998, when the National Association of Bookmakers lost its control of racecourse betting rings to the National Joint Pitch Council, which is in turn administered by the Horse Race Betting Levy Board. Under the new regime, a number of changes to existing practices were introduced including the fact that although the seniority system used to determine pitch positions in the betting ring is maintained, transferring seniority by auction is now permitted. In addition, inherited seniority alone is no longer sufficient for a bookmaker to retain a ring position.

CAPITAL GAINS TAX

In our view, the right to occupy a particular "pitch" at a particular racecourse is an asset for capital gains tax purposes. TCGA 1992 s 21(1)(*a*) provides that—

> "All forms of property shall be assets ... including ... incorporeal property generally."

while the decision in *O'Brien v Benson's Hosiery (Holdings) Limited* [[1979] STC 735] established that incorporeal rights are assets where these could be "turned to account". A disposal of such a right by way of auction is therefore a disposal of a chargeable asset. The right is akin to a licence allowing the holder to occupy a particular position on a particular racecourse without the fear of action against them for trespass but would not amount to an interest in the particular racecourse.

DATE OF DISPOSAL

When a particular pitch is auctioned, the date of a disposal will be the date on which the purchaser's bid is accepted, TCGA 1992 s 28(1), rather than the date on which the new owner takes possession of that pitch by occupying it at the next race meeting.

ACQUISITION COSTS

Where a pitch has not previously changed hands by way of auction it is our view that there is no acquisition cost to deduct on a subsequent disposal. Under the pre-October 1998 system, a pitch which had fallen vacant was effectively forfeited by the previous occupant and then re-allocated. We therefore consider that the successor has acquired the pitch without any "corresponding disposal" of it to them, either by the previous occupant or the racecourse, so the market value rule would not apply, TCGA 1992 s 17(2).

In any event, if the particular pitch could not be put on the market before the October 1998 changes to the rules, there would be no market value. That would apply even where a member of the family could expect to acquire it through inheritance.

Similar comments would apply in the case of a bookmaker who occupied a particular pitch back on 31 March 1982 since even though it would have been an asset to which TCGA 1992 s 35(2) would apply, its market value on that date would again be nil.

INHERITED PITCHES

Where a pitch has been acquired by inheritance after the October 1998 changes to the rules came into effect, however, we consider that the position will be different. TCGA 1992 s 62(1) provides that—

> "The assets of which a deceased person was competent to dispose—
>
> (*a*) shall be deemed to be acquired on his death by the personal representatives or other persons on whom they devolve for a consideration equal to their market value at the date of death."

Clearly a particular pitch will now have a market value and as it was an asset "of which the deceased was competent to dispose" would fall within s 62(1).

A pitch will also be "property to which (the deceased) is beneficially entitled", IHTA 1984 s 5(1), and where it formed part of the deceased's business, its value may qualify for inheritance tax business property relief at 100% if the statutory conditions are met, IHTA 1984 ss 103–114.

If a member of the family acquires a pitch through inheritance then where its value has been ''ascertained'' for inheritance tax purposes, this will also be their acquisition cost, TCGA 1992 s 274.

TAPER RELIEF

As any sales would take place after 6 April 1998, the effect of taper relief, TCGA 1992 s 2A, has to be considered and we would accept that these pitches would fall within the meaning of ''business assets'' in Sch A1 para 5(2)(*a*). Where a bookmaker had acquired their pitch before 17 March 1998 and still held it then and on 6 April 1998, the additional ''bonus year'' would be due.

ROLLOVER RELIEF

While this might not apply in every case, we assume that a bookmaker might wish to put a particular pitch of theirs at one racecourse up for auction and then acquire one at another using the proceeds. We would not accept that these were transactions which qualified for rollover relief under TCGA 1992 ss 152–159. A pitch which is occupied by a particular bookmaker is neither ''land'' nor an ''interest in land'' so does not fall within s 155 class 1, head A2 and we would resist any argument that it represents ''goodwill'' within class 4.

While it is certainly an intangible asset it does not fall within the terms of Lord McNaughton's definition of goodwill in *IRC v Muller & Co (Margarine) Ltd* ([1901] AC217),as being the ''good name, reputation and connections of a business''.

Commentary—*Simon's Direct Tax Service* **C2.205, C3.303.**

RI 211 (October 1999) *FA 1999 s 76—concessions that defer a capital gains charge*

FA 1999 s 76 inserts two new sections, ss 284A, 284B, into TCGA 1992 with effect from 9 March 1999.

These sections provide for a statutory charge to be applied in certain circumstances where a capital gain has been relieved by way of a concession published before 9 March 1999 and the gain is not subsequently returned in accordance with the terms of the concession. We must emphasise, however, that the new charge does not apply where, as is normally the case, a taxpayer follows through the concession and returns the deferred gain in the later period.

The charge is based on the amount of the capital gain which has had the benefit of relief in the earlier period but it is not dependent upon whether that benefit was obtained before or after the passing of FA 1999. The important date is that on which the benefit of the relief falls to be recouped under the terms of the relevant concession. If that date falls on or after 9 March 1999, then a charge under TCGA 1992 s 284A applies if the deferred gain is not returned in the normal way.

Although we expect that charges under the new legislation will be very rare, we have been asked how we will apply TCGA 1992 ss 284A, 284B in practice. Guidance on this is now incorporated in the capital gains guidance manual at CG 13650–13662.

Commentary—*Simon's Direct Tax Service* **C1.424.**
Note—Concessions that defer capital gains charge include:
D15 Relief for the replacement of business assets: unincorporated associations.
D16 Relief for the replacement of business assets: repurchase of the same asset.
D22 Relief for the replacement of business assets: expenditure on improvements to existing assets.
D23 Relief for the replacement of business assets: partition of land on the dissolution of a partnership.
D24 Relief for the replacement of business assets: assets not brought immediately into trading use.
D25 Relief for the replacement of business assets: acquisition of an interest in an asset already used for the purposes of a trade.
D32 Transfer of a business to a company.
D39 Extension of leases.

RI 212 (December 1999) *Industrial buildings allowance: trade which consists of the storage of goods or materials—part of a trade*

The decision of the High Court in the case of Bestway (Holdings) Ltd v Luff *(70 TC 512) has altered our view on the meaning of ''part of a trade'' and a ''trade which consists in the storage of goods or materials'' in relation to industrial buildings allowances.*

PART OF A TRADE

To qualify for IBA the building or structure must be in use for the purposes of a qualifying trade. The qualifying trade does not need to be the whole of the trade carried on, it can be a part of the trade (CAA 1990 s 18(2)).

We previously took the view that anything done in the course of a trade is a part of the trade for this purpose.

Bestway shows that this view was too wide. The Court held that although the activities in question do not need to be self-contained, they must be a significant, separate and identifiable part of the trade carried on.

A TRADE WHICH CONSISTS IN THE STORAGE OF GOODS OR MATERIALS

A building or structure in use for the purposes of ''a trade which consists in the storage of goods or materials'' will qualify for IBA if one of the further conditions in s 18(1)(f)(i)–(iv) is satisfied.

Although we did not previously try to define what is meant by this phrase, we said that the main test was whether the further conditions in s 18(1)(f)(i)–(iv) were satisfied, for instance a warehouse used by a steel stockholder to store its stock would qualify for IBA if the goods stored would subsequently be used in the manufacture of other goods or materials.

The decision in Bestway clarifies the meaning of this phrase. The Court held that the determining factor in deciding whether the goods are stored is the purpose for which they are kept or held. A building is only used for storage if the purpose of keeping goods there is their storage as an end in itself. There is no such use for storage if the goods are kept there for some other purpose. Storage which is merely a necessary and transitory incident of the conduct of the business is not sufficient. The decision in Crusabridge Investments Ltd v Casings International *(54 TC 246) was distinguished as the collection and storage of tyres was an essential part of the business in that case.*

CONSEQUENCES OF THE DECISION IN BESTWAY

The main impact is likely to be on the wholesale trades where we have previously accepted, in the particular circumstances of the case, that there was a qualifying part trade of storage of goods or materials which would be used in the manufacture of other goods or materials or subjected in the course of a trade to a process. In order for the building or structure to continue to qualify for IBA, the storage must form a significant, separate and identifiable part of the trade and be conducted as a purpose and end in itself, not just a necessary and transitory incident of the conduct of the wholesale business.

Each case will have to be considered on its own facts. The sort of business which may be affected by the Bestway decision is a builders merchant where it has previously been accepted that a building or structure in use for the purposes of the trade which consists in the storage of building materials that are to be used in the manufacture of other goods or materials would qualify. Depending on the facts, such storage may no longer qualify the building or structure for IBA.

Where claims to IBA have been accepted for previous periods in accordance with our previous prevailing practice and IBA ceases to be due as a result of the revised view of the meaning of ''part of a trade'' and a ''trade which consists in the of storage of goods or materials'', the revised view should be applied to claims of that taxpayer for chargeable periods ending after 31 December 1999. Claims for periods ending on or before 31 December 1999 in respect of the expenditure that has been agreed as qualifying for IBA under our previous prevailing practice will be allowed subject to any other changes in the nature and conduct of the trade that may affect entitlement to IBA for those periods, such as the admission of retail customers or the outsourcing of supplies.

Note—This Interpretation has been superseded by the Capital Allowances Manual CA32224.
Commentary—*Simon's Direct Tax Service* **B2.209**.

RI 213 (December 1999) *Reverse Premiums—FA 1999 s 54 and Sch 6*

We have received a number of enquiries about the effect of the provisions for taxing reverse premiums now enacted as FA 1999 s 54 and Sch 6. To assist practitioners and the public, we publish the more commonly asked questions, and the Revenue's view of the answers. These break down into four areas—

(a) the meaning of ''payment or other benefit'';
(b) the distinction between fitting out and building costs;
(c) the types of transaction affected; and
(d) the commencement rule.

1 The legislation charges ''a payment or other benefit by way of inducement'' to take an interest in land. Do all inducements create a tax charge?

The most obvious form of inducement is a cash payment by the landlord to the tenant, but there are many others. A landlord may give a tenant some benefit other than cash or pay a sum to a third party to meet a liability of the tenant. The commonest forms of commercial inducement include—

- *allowing the tenant to occupy for a rent free period;*
- *a contribution to the tenant's costs, such as start up, fitting out or relocation;*
- *assumption by the landlord of the tenant's liabilities, such as any continuing obligation to pay rent under an old lease, or payment of a capital sum to terminate it.*

Not all these inducements create liability under Sch 6. The legislation brings into charge only benefits procured by actually laying out money. It does not, very broadly, catch inducements representing amounts foregone or deferred by the provider.

Apart from straightforward cash payments, the commonest forms of taxable inducements include—

- *contributions towards specified tenant's costs, such as fitting out, start up or relocation;*
- *sums paid to third parties to meet obligations of the tenant, such as rent to a landlord under an old lease, or a capital sum to terminate such a lease;*
- *the effective payment of cash by other means, for example, the landlord's writing off a sum which the tenant owes.*

Examples of inducements not caught, because they do not represent actual outlay, are—

- *the grant of a rent free period of occupation;*
- *replacement by agreement of an existing lease at a rent which a change in market conditions has made onerous by a new lease at a lower rent;*
- *replacement by agreement of an existing lease containing some other provision the tenant has found onerous by a new lease without the onerous condition.*

2 *You say a contribution towards a tenant's "fitting out costs" is a reverse premium charged by the legislation. What do you understand by "fitting out costs"?*

"Fitting out costs" are expenditure on equipping a building with tenant's or trade fixtures or chattels. The cost of these items is usually the responsibility of the tenant. If a landlord incurs them, either directly, by paying for their supply and installation, or indirectly, by reimbursing the tenant for its expenditure, the tenant has received either an "other benefit" or an actual payment charged by the legislation.

What if the landlord incurs the expenditure on fitting out, but charges a higher rent to reflect the enhanced value to the tenant of a fully fitted out building?

If the tenant effectively reimburses the landlord for trade or tenant's fixtures or chattels, he is not receiving any benefit, and so there is no charge under Sch 6.

What if the landlord reimburses the tenant for the cost of assets otherwise qualifying for capital allowances in the tenant's hands?

The new legislation does not charge any contribution which reduces the tenant's qualifying expenditure under CAA 1990 s 153. Such a contribution may still entitle the payer to claim capital allowances if he meets the terms of CAA 1990 s 154.

What if the parties agree that the tenant should be responsible for completing the building, and the landlord reimburses all or part of the cost? Say the tenant wants a specialised type of roof which it undertakes to have installed, and the landlord contributes in cash what it would have paid for a standard roof.

If a contribution is effectively towards the cost of completing the building, it is not chargeable under the new provisions. The issue of principle here is that the cost to the landlord of acquiring a building for letting is not a benefit by way of inducement to the tenant to take a lease. If, say, a landlord pays £1 million to a property developer to buy a finished building to rent out, that £1 million is clearly not an other benefit by way of inducement to any future tenant to take a lease. The same result must follow if the landlord pays the £1 million to a builder to construct the building on bare land; or pays £750,000 to the builder for a roofless structure, and £250,000 to the intended tenant which the latter must spend on installing a roof.

Would it make any difference to that answer if the landlord reimbursed the extra cost of the specialised roof?

No, because in either case the landlord is simply paying for the completion of the building. A roof, whether standard or specialised, is not a tenant's fixture, and hence the landlord's meeting its cost is not an inducement to the tenant to take a lease.

You say a landlord's contribution to fitting out costs is a reverse premium chargeable under Sch 6, whereas a contribution to permit the tenant to complete the building is not. How do you distinguish between the two types of expenditure?

It will normally be quite clear what expenditure completes the building, and what procures trade or tenant's fixtures or chattels. As a general guide, the former is likely to increase the value of the reversionary interest, while the latter will be valueless when the lease comes to an end. Another means of distinction may be that the former will fall to be taken into account in computing market rent on a rent review. The latter will not.

3 *The legislation applies where a payment is made or an other benefit is provided by way of inducement in connection with "a transaction". It defines a "relevant transaction" as one whereby a person becomes "entitled to an estate or interest in, or a right in or over, land". Does this mean there will be a charge if the transaction is, say, the sale of a freehold, or the assignment of an existing lease?*

The provisions you refer to are in Sch 6 para 1(1)(b). To determine whether you have a chargeable reverse premium, you must also consider para 1(1)(c). This makes clear that you will have a chargeable reverse premium only if the sum is paid or other benefit provided by the "grantor" of the estate etc, or by a person connected with the grantor, or by a nominee or person acting on the direction of either.

The use of the word "grantor" means there can be no charge when a freehold is conveyed. A lease or other subordinate interest in land is "granted" because it is created out of a superior interest in that land which the grantor holds. A freehold, however, is the highest interest in land a person may hold. Thus it cannot be granted, and there is no "grantor" for the purposes of the sub-para.

The most common occasion of charge will be a payment by way of inducement by a landlord (the "grantor") to a tenant to take a new lease. It may also apply, however, where an existing tenant pays a new tenant an inducement to take over the remaining term of an existing lease; but if and only if the old tenant is connected with the landlord ("the grantor") or acting as nominee or at the direction of the landlord, or of a person connected with the landlord.

***4** The provisions take effect from Budget Day 9 March 1999. The commencement rule in s 54 says the provisions of Sch 6 apply to a reverse premium received on or after 9 March 1999, unless it is a payment or other benefit to which the recipient was entitled immediately before that date. It goes on to say that in determining whether you are entitled to a payment before 9 March, you should take no account of arrangements made on or after that date. How does this work in practice?*

It may be helpful to consider three possibilities—

- *If an agreement for a lease were made on 8 March, without provision for a reverse premium, and the arrangements were varied on 9 March to incorporate a reverse premium of £1 million, that sum would be chargeable.*
- *If an original agreement of 8 March provided for a reverse premium of £1.5 million, but the arrangements as varied on 9 March increased the sum payable to £2 million, £0.5 million would be chargeable.*
- *If an agreement for a lease were in place by 8 March providing for payment of a reverse premium of £1 million, and the lease was granted and the premium of £1 million paid on 9 March, there would be no charge under the new provisions.*

Note—This Interpretation has been superseded by the Business Income Manual BIM41050 et seq.
Commentary—*Simon's Direct Tax Service* **A4.235.**

RI 214 (February 2000) *Shotguns—the capital gains tax treatment*

We have received a number of enquiries recently about the capital gains tax treatment of pairs of shotguns and this article sets out our views on the point. It is written on the premise that any transactions by private individuals involving the acquisition and disposal of such guns are not regarded as "trading" or an "adventure in the nature of trade" within the charge to income tax under Case I of Schedule D.

It is common for items such as shotguns to be purchased and sold in pairs, generally matched according to their maker. This does not, in our view, mean that a pair of guns should be treated as the asset (singular) for capital gains tax purposes rather than as two separate assets. The guns may well have been bought and sold together but they are still separate assets and any computation should apportion the figures for the disposal consideration and the cost or 31 March 1982 market value as appropriate, between the two guns.

This distinction could be important where the overall consideration for a pair of guns is £12,000 or less so that each single gun would have realised less than the £6,000 exemption, TCGA 1992 s 262(1). Where in such circumstances a loss arose by reference to the original cost or market value of each gun, that loss would then be restricted using a deemed disposal figure of £6,000 for each gun, TCGA 1992 s 262(3).

We accept that this raises a further question which is whether the pair formed a "set", TCGA 1992 s 262(4). Assuming that the requirement in that sub-section about the guns being sold to the same person would have been satisfied, that still leaves the question as to whether they would have been similar, complementary and worth more together than separately.

This will depend on the facts of the particular case but we would point out that while there is unlikely to be any doubt about the first two requirements given the nature of such sales, the third is likely to turn on the type of guns involved and whether these could be said to form a natural pair. While the limited number of cases we have seen suggest that this is likely to be the case where shotguns are concerned, there have been exceptions so the answer will turn on the facts of a particular disposal.

Assuming however that the "asset" was disposed of for more than £6,000, we then need to look at TCGA 1992 s 44 and the questions now become—

(i) is a gun, singular or plural, a "machine" or "machinery", given that we do not distinguish between these terms in this context?

or, if not—

(ii) did it have a predictable life not exceeding fifty years or less when it was acquired by the person making the disposal?

So far as question (i) is concerned, the word ''machinery'' is not defined for capital gains tax purposes so it must take its ordinary meaning. The Oxford English Dictionary defines a machine as—

> ''an apparatus for applying mechanical power, consisting of a number of interrelated parts, each having a definite function''.

In our article in *Tax Bulletin* Issue 13, October 1994, we set out our views on the various types of asset which we regard as ''machinery'' and those included antique clocks. However, in our view there has to be a subtle difference between clocks and shotguns. Once you have wound up a clock, it continues to tick more than once, whereas with a shotgun once you have pulled the trigger, you only get one discharge out of the barrel. That said, we accept that you then have to go on and consider what happens if you have an automatic weapon or machine gun which effectively fires continuously.

While we take the view that the matter is not free from doubt, we would generally accept the argument that all types of gun should be treated together under the general description of ''machinery'' so that they would have a predictable life of less than fifty years, TCGA 1992 s 44(1)(*c*).

In any event, assuming that these guns have been acquired for sporting or recreational purposes or by a farmer or gamekeeper as working guns, then the answer to question (ii) is, in our view, probably going to be that their predictable life by reference to the purpose for which they were acquired, TCGA 1992 s 44(1)(*b*), would not exceed fifty years.

It should however be borne in mind that, in the case of working guns particularly, where capital allowances had been or could have been claimed on the original acquisition cost of the gun, then any gain on its disposal would still be chargeable, TCGA 1992 s 45(2), notwithstanding its having a predictable life not exceeding fifty years.

Whether a particular chattel should be classed as ''machinery'' is very much a question of fact which can only be answered by looking at the state and nature of that chattel. Accordingly, we regret that it is not possible for us to issue a fully comprehensive list of those chattels which would, or would not, fall into this category. However, our capital gains tax manual looks at this and associated matters in the following paragraphs—

CG76870–76876—chattels generally, including antiques, militaria, medals & toys;
CG76880–76884—sets, including non-sterling coins and bank notes, stamps, books and magazines;
CG76900–76911—wasting assets, including clocks and watches, motor cars, locomotives and ships.

These paragraphs also set the general principles which we use to decide if a particular chattel was or was not an item of machinery.

Commentary—*Simon's Direct Tax Service* **C1.406**.

RI 215 (April 2000) *TA 1988 ss 765, 765A*

TA 1988 s 765 requires UK companies with overseas subsidiaries to obtain the consent of HM Treasury before certain transactions involving those subsidiaries are carried out. In line with European Union law, s 765A disapplies s 765 where the transactions are capital movements within the European Economic Area, substituting a reporting requirement instead. This article clarifies the position concerning three issues on which we have received questions from taxpayers and practitioners.

The first issue concerns a proviso that used to mean that the disapplication of s 765 by s 765A was relevant only where the transaction was carried out ''with a view to establishing or maintaining lasting economic links''. Its effect was that, if no such links existed, s 765 applied in the normal way. This was explained in paras 8, 9 of Inland Revenue Statement of Practice 2/92.

Changes made by the Maastricht Treaty removed the requirement for such links to exist. Paragraphs 8, 9 of SP 2/92 do not apply therefore to transactions carried out on or after 1 January 1994.

The second issue concerns the Treasury General Consents. To ease the administration of TA 1988 s 765, HM Treasury is empowered to give a general consent to transactions that might otherwise need its special consent. Known as the Treasury General Consents, these were last issued in 1988. One of them (at para 3(*c*)(ii)) is subject to conditions at para 7. One of the conditions (at sub-para (2)(*c*)), states that there should not be a loan associated with the transaction that has been made to a UK company by a non-UK company.

As a matter of practice, the loan condition is now regarded as being satisfied where a non-UK lender makes a loan from its UK branch, or where it is resident in a country within the European Economic Area.

The third issue also concerns the Treasury General Consents. Two of them (para 3(*b*)(i) and para 8(*c*)) apply to transactions between members of groups of companies wholly within another country. Definitions of these two types of group—an ''overseas group'' and ''territorial group'' respectively—are given at para 2. Very broadly, they rely on the definition of a UK group for group relief purposes at TA 1988 s 413.

South African groups did not previously satisfy either definition, because of the way they were taxed in South Africa. It has been put to us that changes to South African law in 1997 mean that such groups can now form an ''overseas group'' or a ''territorial group'' for the purposes of the General Consents. The matter is not free from doubt. But, as a matter of practice, the basis of taxation in South Africa is no longer regarded as preventing South African groups which otherwise fulfil the conditions set out in the respective definitions, from being able to form either an ''overseas group'' or a ''territorial group''.

Commentary—*Simon's Direct Tax Service* **D4.139.**

RI 216 (April 2000) *Restriction on allowable rental for hire of car costing more than £12,000: CAA 1990 s 35(2)—change of interpretation of "retail price when new"*

Where a trader hires a motor car the retail price of which when new exceeds £12,000, the deduction allowable for tax in respect of the rental for the hire of the car is reduced in the proportion which £12,000 plus half the excess bears to the retail price.

We have previously taken the view that the manufacturer's list of suggested retail prices, net of any discount available generally, should be used to establish the retail price when new.

Following discussions with the British Vehicle and Rental Leasing Association, we have revised our view. There have been considerable changes in the car market in recent years. In particular as discounts to private and fleet buyers are common and well known, the price paid is frequently lower than list price.

We now take the view that where the lessee knows the actual price paid by the lessor for the car when new, this can be used as the retail price when new. Where the lessee is not aware of the actual price paid by the lessor, the manufacturer's list price net of any discount available generally should be used as before. In either case, the price should be inclusive of extras and VAT.

This interpretation only applies to this rule. It does not affect other tax provisions on cars, including the benefit charges for employees, which use different definitions for the price of the car.

Note—This Interpretation has been superseded by the Business Income Manual BIM47717.
Commentary—*Simon's Direct Tax Service* **B2.342.**

RI 217 (June 2000) *CAA 1990 s 51: fixtures in buildings—licence to occupy land*

The provisions of CAA 1990 Part II Chapter VI link the ability to claim capital allowances on machinery and plant that are fixtures, to a qualifying interest in the land to which the fixtures are attached. CAA 1990 s 51(3)(e) provides that a licence to occupy land is such a qualifying interest. We have received a number of enquiries on what constitutes a licence to occupy, particularly where equipment is installed in a building under the terms of a wider agreement for the provision of services. The purpose of this article is to clarify when a licence to occupy exists for the purposes of s 51.

Our view is that a licence to occupy land within s 51(3)(e) will only arise where the claimant has an exclusive licence to occupy the land in question. A licence to occupy is a permission to enter and remain on land for such a purpose as enables the licensee to exert control over the land. It is this level of control that suggests that a licence to occupy must be an exclusive licence.

The idea of exclusive occupancy is also supported in part by ratings law that says that there can only be one occupier of land. It follows that where a person can enter onto land for a subordinate purpose, such licence of entry would be something less than a licence to occupy. This interpretation gains support from Melluish v BMI (No 3) Ltd (68 TC 1), where a right of entry into a building for the purpose of repossessing equipment was held not to amount to a licence to occupy land. The Special Commissioners' decision in J C Decaux (UK) Ltd v Francis (SpC 84) [[1996] STC (SCD) 281], where a right to enter land for the purpose of carrying out contractual obligations to repair and maintain equipment fell short of a licence to occupy, also supports this view.

Whether or not there is a licence to occupy will depend on the precise contractual terms between the parties where a licence is purported to exist. Where the provision of the fixtures is part of a larger contract incorporating such services as cleaning, maintenance, catering, security, etc, to another occupier of the building the service provider may not have the necessary exclusive rights of occupancy for the contract to amount to a licence to occupy.

For example, if a local authority grants a lease of land to a contractor who builds a school and then sub-leases the completed building to the school governors, the contractor will have the necessary qualifying interest in the land. If access to the site is by way of a licence, the subsequent occupation by the school governors may leave the contractor with an inadequate interest for the purpose of claiming capital allowances on the fixtures.

Note—This Interpretation has been superseded by the Capital Allowances Manual CA26100.
Commentary—*Simon's Direct Tax Service* **B2.355.**

RI 218 (August 2000) *Trust implications of flat management companies, service charge funds and sinking funds*

In *Tax Bulletin* Issue 37 (October 1998, p 598) we published some guidance entitled ''Flat management companies: new corporation tax Schedule A—residential service charges''. This article was primarily concerned with changes arising from the new Schedule A rules introduced by FA 1998 s 38 and Sch 5.

As the previous article made clear, the Landlord and Tenant Act 1987 s 42 (LTA 1987) provides that contributions to certain variable service charge funds (and to sinking funds) in respect of residential property should be paid into a trust fund. Investment income arising to that trust fund is chargeable on the trustee at the rate applicable to trusts, or the Schedule F trust rate, as LTA 1987 s 42 contains an implied power to accumulate.

Since the article was published we have received a number of inquiries about flat management companies and trusts created under LTA 1987 s 42. In many flat management companies LTA 1987 will not apply and so the tax treatment of the fund will depend on the general status of the fund. It has also become clear that there are some flat management companies holding funds on trust that have previously been dealt with under the corporation tax rules that should no longer be dealt with in that way.

This article provides some more detailed guidance on the scope of LTA 1987 s 42, what trustees should do where it applies and what to do where it does not apply.

BACKGROUND

Many tenants and owners of properties in the UK make contributions to management companies and various service charge funds or sinking funds. These funds pay for a variety of services and sometimes accumulate money for future repairs. Typically, residents of a block of flats will all pay a set amount each year into a fund. That fund will either pay for joint day to day running costs of the block, such as cleaners and minor repairs, or funds will be put aside to pay for future major expenditure such as a roof repair. Some funds may do both within one fund.

The charges may typically be paid to a management company which could manage just that block of flats or any number of blocks. Sometimes residents of a block will set up their own management company, residents' association or trust to receive the funds and carry out the work. Sometimes the landlord/freeholder holds the funds and organises the work.

SCOPE OF LTA 1987 S 42

The Landlord and Tenant Act 1987 applies only to England and Wales. LTA 1987 s 42 applies where the tenants of two or more dwellings are required under the terms of their lease to contribute to the same costs by the payment of service charges (as defined in LTA 1985 s (18)(1)). Such sums paid, or the investments representing those sums, or income accruing thereon, are held by the ''payee'' on trust to defray any expenses incurred in connection with service charge expenditure. Subject to such payments of service charge expenditure the funds are held on trust for the tenants for the time being. The ''payee'' can be the landlord or any other person to whom the service charges are payable by the tenants under the terms of the lease. LTA 1985 s 18(1) states that ''service charge'' means—

> ''an amount payable by a tenant of a dwelling as part of or in addition to rent—
>
> (*a*) which is payable, directly or indirectly, for services, repairs, maintenance or insurance or the landlord's costs of management, and
>
> (*b*) the whole or part of which varies or may vary according to the relevant costs''.

The ''relevant costs'' are the costs or estimated costs incurred or to be incurred by or on behalf of the landlord, or a superior landlord, in connection with the matters for which the service charges are payable (LTA 1985 s 18(2)).

If the landlord is an ''exempt landlord'' (as defined in LTA 1987 s 58(1)) then LTA 1987 s 42 does not apply. (See below.)

Therefore for LTA 1987 s 42 to apply—

- the landlord must not be an ''exempt landlord'', and
- tenants of two or more dwellings,
- under the terms of the lease,
- must be required to contribute directly or indirectly for repairs, maintenance, etc, and
- those charges, or part of them, must be variable.

If any of those elements are missing then LTA 1987 s 42 does not apply.

RIs

FUNDS CREATED

Typically there are two main types of fund to which LTA 1987 s 42 applies—

– *Sinking funds* involve the long term setting aside of funds for major repairs and renewals. Over a period, the fund can grow to a significant size and generate substantial investment income.
– *Service charge funds* are funds where the intention is to cover only the routine day to day costs of maintaining the communal areas and paying for minor repairs and decorations. The service charges are reviewed annually and set at a level to balance the actual expenditure and leave a ''no surplus–no deficit'' situation at the end of each year. In practise there may be a small amount held in reserve or carried over from the previous year. The trust will not accumulate any surplus charges or create any sort of contingency or sinking fund and any investment income is derived only from the short term deposit of temporarily surplus funds.

Some trusts will act both as a sinking fund and as a service charge fund, although usually the trustees would keep the two funds separate.

WHAT SINKING FUNDS OR SERVICE CHARGE FUNDS ARE WITHIN LTA 1987 S 42

There are a number of different situations in which sinking funds or service charge funds may be created. Not all of these will necessarily fall within the scope of LTA 1987 s 42.

TENANTS OF RENTED PROPERTY

Under the terms of a rental contract either the tenant or the landlord will be responsible for repairing the property. If the landlord includes in the rent payable some figure to cover his repairing obligations the fact that the payment by the tenant will be part of his rent will not preclude the operation of LTA 1987 s 42. However, in order to fall within the definition of ''service charge'' the amount must be variable according to the costs or estimated costs of repairs etc. So if the lease simply states that part of the rents payable will be used for servicing, repairs and maintenance etc for which the landlord is then responsible then the matter is outside LTA 1987 s 42 because the payments by the tenants do not amount to a ''service charge'' as defined in LTA 1985 s 18. The whole of the rent will be Schedule A income of the landlord.

LEASEHOLDER OWNERS OF PROPERTY

Under the terms of the lease the leaseholder may have to pay into a service charge fund or sinking fund. The funds may be paid to an individual, a company, a trust or an unincorporated association. As the owner owns the property under a lease, LTA 1987 will apply. If the lease specifies contributions are to be made to a service charge fund or sinking fund then an accumulation trust exists whether the funds are paid to an individual, a company, a trust or an unincorporated association.

The body holding the funds may not consider themselves to be trustees, for example a company. However if LTA 1987 s 42 applies then the company will be holding the funds as a trustee.

If the lease stipulates that tenants must pay a service charge for particular services to a service company which is not the landlord, connected with the landlord or stipulated by the landlord, this too is within LTA 1987 s 42. In that section ''the payee'' is defined as ''the landlord or other person to whom any such charges are payable by those tenants under the terms of their leases''.

If the lease states that the tenant should arrange for services, repairs and maintenance etc themselves but does not specify how this should be done, any arrangement made by the tenants with a service company is outside the scope of LTA 1987 s 42. The costs in respect of service charges are not made either to the landlord or to another person to whom such charges are payable under the terms of the lease.

Finally where there is no provision in the lease for the tenants to pay into a service charge fund, but nevertheless they decide to create one, then such an arrangement is not within LTA 1987 s 42 as the tenants are not ''required under the terms of their leases to contribute to the same costs by the payment of service charges''.

FREEHOLD OWNERS OF PROPERTY

Under the terms of sale of a freehold property (a covenant of some sort) the freeholders may have to pay into a service charge fund or sinking fund. The funds may be paid to an individual, a company, a trust or an unincorporated association. Such an arrangement does not come within LTA 1987 s 42 as it is not under the terms of a lease.

Alternatively there may be no provision to create a service charge fund or sinking fund but the freeholders together decide to form one. They may decide to pay those contributions to an individual, a company, a trust or an unincorporated association. Again this is a private arrangement not governed by LTA 1987 s 42 and the tax treatment depends on what the freeholders decide is going to hold the funds.

REGISTERED SOCIAL LANDLORDS AND OTHER "EXEMPT LANDLORDS"

Registered social landlords (RSLs) are, in England and Wales, independent, private sector, non-profit making bodies whose main purpose is to provide decent quality, affordable housing for people on low incomes. About three quarters of them are charities.

LTA 1987 s 42 does not apply to tenants of ''exempt landlords'' (LTA 1987 s 42(1)). In accordance with LTA 1987 s 58(1)(*g*) an RSL is an exempt landlord. There are other exempt landlords defined in LTA 1987 s 58(1), (1A) such as district councils and certain development corporations. (LTA 1987 s 58(1), (1A) is reproduced below.)

Whilst LTA 1987 s 42 does not apply to RSLs and other exempt landlords, as explained below, the terms under which sinking funds and/or service charge funds are held by exempt landlords may still create a trust.

Thus, in summary, reference must be made to the terms of the lease to determine the application of LTA 1987 s 42. A statutory trust will arise where the tenants of two or more dwellings are required under the terms of their leases to contribute to the payment of variable service charges to the landlord or other persons to whom such charges are payable under the terms of the leases. However, LTA 1987 s 42 does not apply where the landlord is an ''exempt landlord''.

FUNDS NOT WITHIN LTA 1987 S 42

Where a fund exists but it is not within LTA 1987 s 42, for example where freehold owners of property decide to create a sinking fund, or because the landlord is an RSL or other ''exempt landlord'', then the treatment of that fund will depend on what structure is used—

- where an individual holds the funds—The individual could be an employee, trading as a maintenance contractor or they could hold funds as trustee for the freeholders. If the latter then the sort of trust depends on the terms of the trust, not on LTA 1987 s 42.
- where a company holds the funds—Assuming the company was formed to hold funds for the freeholders who created it, then it could hold the funds as trustee. Alternatively it could trade as a flat management company receiving payments under a contractual arrangement to supply services and pay corporation tax. The status of the fund will depend on the terms under which the payments are made and the terms under which the funds are held by the company.
- where a trust holds the funds—It could be any sort of trust depending on the terms of the deed but it would not be within LTA 1987 s 42.
- where an unincorporated association holds the funds—such as a residents' association. It would be liable to corporation tax unless it was acting as a trustee. Again any trust would not be within LTA 1987 s 42.

Any funds held by trustees would be subject to the normal trust rules. It is possible for the funds to be held under a bare trust, interest in possession trust, discretionary trust or accumulation trust arrangement. The exact status will depend on the terms and nature of the trust agreement. (The Inland Revenue leaflet IR152 ''Trusts—an introduction'' provides some general information on trusts and how they are taxed.)

WHAT TRUSTEES SHOULD DO

As the October 1998 article made clear, in the past some flat management companies have been permitted to make returns in respect of investment income, arising on service charge funds and sinking funds, as part of their corporation tax returns. That is no longer appropriate where trustees are holding funds as trustees under LTA 1987 s 42. Likewise where LTA 1987 s 42 does not apply but the terms under which the funds are held creates a trust.

Trustees should write to the appropriate trust office, address below, enclosing a completed form 41G(Trust), or providing the following information for each trust—

- the full title of the trust fund;
- the names and addresses of the trustees;
- the name and address of any professional agents acting;
- the date the trust was established under the terms of the lease;
- the existing corporation tax reference, where appropriate;
- the gross amount of any investment income received each year which has not been included on a corporation tax return;
- whether the trust is a sinking fund, service charge fund or both as outlined above.

As the October 1998 article made clear, rents receivable by flat management companies (such as ground rents—other than peppercorn rents) are outside the scope of LTA 1987 s 42 and remain chargeable under Schedule A.

The October 1998 article explained the approach the Inland Revenue will take for all flat management companies as from 1 April 1998. However, because of the need to issue this further guidance, no action will ordinarily be taken to disturb any year or accounting period for which a corporation tax return has already been made and accepted. Where a trust return has not previously been made by a flat management company, or a trustee, of investment income arising from a fund within LTA 1987

RIs

s 42 (or from funds otherwise specifically held on trust), the trustees will have the normal obligation to notify chargeability.

LANDLORD AND TENANT ACT 1987 S 58

Sections 58(1), (1A) are reproduced below. They define ''exempt landlords'' for the purposes of the LTA 1987.

''(1) In this Act 'exempt landlord' means a landlord who is one of the following bodies, namely—

(*a*) a district, county or London borough council, the Common Council of the City of London, the Council of the Isles of Scilly, a police authority established under section 3 of the Police Act 1996 or a joint authority established by Part IV of the Local Government Act 1985;

(*b*) the Commission for the New Towns or a development corporation established by an order made (or having effect as if made) under the New Towns Act 1981;

(*c*) an urban development corporation within the meaning of Part XVI of the Local Government, Planning and Land Act 1980;

(*ca*) a housing action trust established under Part III of the Housing Act 1988;

(*dd*) the Broads Authority;

(*de*) a National Park Authority;

(*e*) the Housing Corporation;

(*f*) a housing trust (as defined in section 6 of the Housing Act 1985) which is a charity;

(*g*) a registered social landlord, or a fully mutual housing association which is not a registered social landlord; or

(*h*) an authority established under section 10 of the Local Government Act 1985 (joint arrangements for waste disposal functions).

(1A) In subsection (1)(*g*)—

'fully mutual housing association' has the same meaning as in the Housing Association Act 1985 (see section 1(1) and (2) of that Act); and 'registered social landlord' has the same meaning as in the Housing Act 1985 (see section 5(4) and (5) of that Act).''

INLAND REVENUE TRUST OFFICES

The UK resident trusts affected by this article are dealt with by one of five Inland Revenue offices.

For all trusts administered in Scotland or established under Scottish law—Edinburgh Haymarket District, Elgin House, 20 Haymarket Yards, Edinburgh EH12 5WS; telephone 0131 346 5600.

For trusts administered within the Greater London area (broadly within the M25)—London Trusts District, Charles House, 375 Kensington High Street, London W14 8QS; telephone 020 7605 9800.

Trusts administered within the Greater Manchester area—Manchester Castlefield District, Albert Bridge House, 1 Bridge Street, Manchester M60 9AF; telephone 0161 288 6000.

Trusts administered in the South West of England—Truro Tax District, Lysnoweth, Infirmary Hill, Truro, Cornwall TR1 2JD; telephone 01872 245300.

Trusts not dealt with by Edinburgh, London, Manchester, or Truro Districts, including trusts administered in Northern Ireland—Nottingham Trusts District, Huntingdon Court, 90–94 Mansfield Road, Nottingham NG1 3HG; telephone 0115 911 6500.

FURTHER INFORMATION

If you require further guidance on this topic please contact either the tax district that deals with the company tax file, where there is a company tax file, or where there is no company tax file, or where it appears a trust exists—the appropriate trust office as outlined above.

If you have any queries on the inheritance tax treatment of funds held on a discretionary trust, please contact the Capital Taxes Office, Ferrers House, PO Box 38, Castle Meadow Road, Nottingham NG2 1BB; telephone 0115 974 2400.

Commentary—*Simon's Direct Tax Service* **A4.102A**.

RI 219 (August 2000) *Carry back claims under self-assessment*

Claims for relief involving two or more years are now governed by TMA 1970 s 42 and Sch 1B. Such claims will most commonly arise from the carry back of losses or personal pension payments, and farmer's averaging. The same principles apply where farmer's averaging, literary spreading or the carry back of post-cessation receipts increases income in earlier years.

TMA 1970 Sch 1B says that such claims are given effect as claims of the year in which the event which gives the opportunity to claim occurs (the year of claim). The relief is quantified by reference to an earlier year, as if the amount claimed could be carried back and included in the self-assessment for that year. But the self-assessment for the earlier year is not actually revised at all.

The way the legislation does this is by making the amount of the claim the difference between—

- Amount A—"the amount in which the person is chargeable to tax for the earlier year"; and
- Amount B—"the amount which he would be so chargeable on the assumption that effect could be, and were, given to the claim in relation to that year".

And any reference to the amount in which a person is chargeable to tax is a reference to the amount in which they are so chargeable "after taking into account any relief or allowance for which a claim is made".

Some doubts have arisen about whether, because the earlier year's self-assessment is not reopened, taxpayers can still make (or revise) claims etc for the earlier year as a consequence of the loss etc in the later year (as they could do prior to self-assessment).

A typical example of this is where a person carries back a pension payment which reduces their total income. A result of the reduction in income for the earlier year may be that they would become entitled to claim, for example, age-related personal or married couple's allowance (MCA). Can such claims be made even though the earlier year's self-assessment is no longer reopened?

The answer to this question is yes. In calculating Amount B it is necessary to have regard to all reliefs and allowances. So Amount B is the net amount after taking into account all reliefs and allowances for which a claim is made.

Similarly, if the effect of a TMA 1970 Sch 1B claim is to free up some of the rate band below higher rate then that should be taken into account in computing the liability to CGT.

The same principle also applies where, for example, a loss carry back claim means that net relevant earnings for the purposes of relief for personal pensions or retirement annuity contributions would be reduced. A clawback of PPR/RAR is triggered and excessive personal pension contributions have to be refunded.

A slightly different situation arises where a carry back claim has a potential impact on someone else's liability to tax. The most common example of this is the transfer of surplus MCA under TA 1988 s 257BB. Where a person's income for an earlier year is reduced by the carry back of trading losses, such that they cannot use their entitlement to the allowance, can they still give notice that they wish to transfer surplus MCA to their husband or wife?

Again, our view is that TMA 1970 Sch 1B continues to permit this to happen. We think that the surplus allowance must be treated as a real consequence inevitably flowing from the claim process introduced by TMA 1970 Sch 1B. This will also apply to claims to transfer surplus blind person's allowance under TA 1988 s 265 and surplus children's tax credit (CTC) under TA 1988 Sch 13B when CTC commences on 6 April 2001.

If people have had consequential claims etc of this kind refused local tax offices will be pleased to reconsider them in the light of the views set out in this article.

Commentary—*Simon's Direct Tax Service* **E1.833**.

RI 220 (August 2000) *Employment status of set construction workers in the film and TV industries*

BACKGROUND

In 1983 the Inland Revenue reviewed the arrangements between companies in the film and TV industries and their casual and freelance staff. It was accepted by the industries and the Revenue that the relationships were generally that of employer and employee and as such earnings would be properly taxable under Schedule E from 6 April 1984. The only exceptions to this were the grades included on the Schedule D grading lists issued jointly by the Inland Revenue's film and television industry units. Services provided by set construction workers such as carpentry, rigging and painting do not appear on the Schedule D lists and, therefore, subject to any reviews of individual workers' employment status, income from such services is normally taxable under Schedule E. This is because typical contracts in the industry include such clauses that are typical of a contract of service and indeed the Special Commissioners, in an unreported decision, decided that the appellant set construction worker was an employee.

Under the principles of the common approach, the Contributions Agency generally adopted this line for national insurance purposes from 1992. However, in two Secretary of State's decisions in respect of cases for Hamilton Heritage (1997) and Southbrooke Studios Ltd (1997) it was held that the set construction workers concerned were self-employed rather than employees. Secretary of State decisions are not lawful precedent and relate to the named contributors only. Following publicity surrounding these decisions it has become apparent that some set construction companies were incorrectly advised by local Inland Revenue (national insurance) offices that their workers were now self-employed and many companies also wrongly assumed that the two Secretary of State decisions applied across the industry generally.

CONSEQUENCES

This has caused confusion within the industry because set construction workers can find themselves engaged on a self-employed basis with one studio and as an employee with another, whilst working under comparable terms and conditions for both. Consequently the Revenue has received representations from a number of employers in the industry requesting that it standardise the handling of these cases.

REVENUE POSITION

The Revenue still regards set construction workers as generally being employed earners because of the contractual arrangements mentioned and the Special Commissioner's case which found that the worker concerned was taxable under Schedule E. However, employment status can only be determined after establishing the individual facts and considering their relative importance. As the decisions in both of the Secretary of State cases mentioned above were found on their own facts it is reasonable to conclude they only relate to the named contributors.

REVENUE GUIDANCE TO STAFF

Guidance has been issued to all Revenue offices confirming the position on set construction workers. Any cases of doubt will be referred for advice to the film industry unit at Gateshead or the TV broadcasting group at Manchester to review the employment status as appropriate. Whatever the final outcome on individual reviews, the agreed status will apply for both tax and NICs. This will help to ensure a more consistent treatment for tax and NICs for set construction workers in the future.

Commentary—*Simon's Direct Tax Service* **E4.215**.

RI 221 (October 2000) *TA 1988 s 765*

TA 1988 s 765 requires UK companies with overseas subsidiaries to obtain the consent of the Treasury before certain transactions involving those subsidiaries are carried out.

Consent may be given specially or generally. For the former, application must be made to the Treasury. For the latter no application is necessary and the transactions to which consent is given generally are described in the ''the Treasury general consents 1988'' [which are reproduced in the *Miscellaneous* section of this publication].

The Treasury general consents adapt certain definitions used elsewhere in the Taxes Acts, including the definition of a group for group relief purposes. As a result of changes in FA 2000 to the definition of group for group relief purposes, a number of changes have been made to the definitions of groups for the purposes of the Treasury general consents. For transactions carried out on or after 28 July 2000—

''Overseas group'' means—

''Two or more companies, including the non-resident company, which are not resident in the United Kingdom and which—

(*a*) are liable to tax in the same territory outside the United Kingdom by reason of domicile, residence or place of management, and

(*b*) would be deemed to be members of a group of companies for the purposes of Chapter IV of Part X of the Income and Corporation Taxes Act 1988''.

''Territorial Group'' means—

''Two or more companies which are not resident in the United Kingdom and which—

(*a*) are liable to tax in the same territory outside the United Kingdom by reason of domicile, residence or place of management, and

(*b*) would be deemed to be members of a group of companies for the purposes of Chapter IV of Part X of the Income and Corporation Taxes Act 1998''.

''Resident Group'' means—

''Those companies, including the resident company, which are resident in the United Kingdom and which are deemed to be members of a group of companies for the purposes of Chapter IV of Part X of the Income and Corporation Taxes Act 1988''.

Additionally, reference to ''Section 258 of the Taxes Act'' at the ''Treasury general consents 1988'' para 2(3) is now a reference to ''Chapter IV of Part X of the Income and Corporation Taxes Act 1988''.

Full details were included in an Inland Revenue press release on 28 July 2000.

Commentary—*Simon's Direct Tax Service* **D4.130, 131, 135–139**.

RI 222 (December 2000) *Corporate trustees and hold-over relief*

FA 2000 s 90(4) amended TCGA 1992 s 165(3). As a result it has not been possible to claim hold-over relief under TCGA 1992 s 165 in respect of disposals of shares or securities to a company occurring on or after 9 November 1999.

We have been asked whether this applies in the case of disposals to a trust with a corporate trustee.

We are happy to confirm that this is not the case. Under TCGA 1992 s 69(1) the trustees of a settlement are treated for capital gains tax purposes as being a single and continuing body of persons distinct from the persons who may from time to time be the trustees. The transfer is therefore treated for all purposes of capital gains tax as a transfer to trustees and not a transfer to a company.

In the case of a transfer to a bare trust, by reason of TCGA 1992 s 60 it would be regarded as a transfer to the underlying beneficiaries.

Commentary—*Simon's Direct Tax Service* **C3.502**.

RI 223 (December 2000) *IRUs (indefeasible rights to use)—FA 2000 s 87 and Sch 23*

This article sets out the Revenue's views on a number of queries which have been put to us on the interpretation of FA 2000 Sch 23 in relation to IRUs.

DEFINITION OF IRUS

The legislation refers to "indefeasible rights to use a telecommunications cable system". Thus IRUs in any medium other than a cable will fall outside the relief. We have been asked whether IRUs in ducts would fall within the definition. If the IRUs are to use only the ducts, then in our view they are not IRUs in a telecommunications cable system.

The definition also covers derived rights. The aim is to give relief for the cost of acquiring an IRU from the grantor of it, and then to balance this by taxing the income derived from exploiting it or by disposing of it or derivative rights from it. Whether the acquirer of other rights is acquiring a "right derived from" an IRU or some other asset is a question of fact. If it is not an IRU or a right derived from an IRU, relief for the acquisition cost will of course follow general principles.

INTERNATIONAL PRIVATE LEASED CIRCUITS (IPLCS)

We have been asked whether these come within the definition. If they are IRUs, ie indefeasible rights to use the cable system, or are derived from them, then they would appear to be covered by Sch 23. If not, the tax treatment will follow normal principles.

MEANING OF "TAKEN INTO ACCOUNT"

We have been asked to clarify the meaning of "taken into account" in Sch 23 para 2. The aim of para 2 is to ensure that whatever treatment is followed is a correct accounting method, subject to the general override of the treatment not being more cautious than at any consolidated level.

DATE OF ACQUISITION

Sch 23 para 6 excludes IRUs acquired before 21 March 2000 from the scope of the relief. We have been asked how the date of acquisition is to be determined. For accounts purposes assets are defined as "rights or access to future economic benefits controlled by an entity as a result of past transactions or events". Accounts would generally record ownership of an IRU when the IRU is made available for use, which would normally be shown in the agreement. This view is based on the fact that accounts would recognise the IRU when it was available for use, not when an agreement was signed for the supply of rights some time in the future once the system had been built. The payment date if later is irrelevant. If payment was made before the IRU was available for use we would want to be sure that this was a genuine prepayment (akin to a deposit) in which case it would again not be relevant.

NON-TRADERS

The relief is available, by virtue of para 5, "for the purposes of calculating the amount of any profits chargeable to income tax or corporation tax". Thus, if the holder of the licence or IRU does not have a trading activity, it will still be able to claim the relief against the relevant income stream from exploiting the right. We would expect the income stream to be a Case VI source if it is not within Case I. We do not think the receipts from exploitation of the licence would be chargeable under Case III.

GRANT OF IRUS

We have been asked how the grant of an IRU by the owner of the cable system is affected by the new legislation. Schedule 23 only applies to acquisitions, disposals and revaluations of IRUs. This was because the original purpose was to address a "nothing", namely a business cost which currently did not qualify for tax relief. The aim of the new provision is to give relief for the cost of these particular intangible assets following depreciation shown in accounts. It was only logical to ensure that where the acquirer of the IRU disposed of it, or revalued it in his accounts, we could effectively claw back excessive tax relief by charging the disposal receipt or the revaluations.

The owner of a cable already qualifies for capital allowances on the cost of installing it. Granting an IRU might be considered to be disposing of a capital asset, and therefore liable to tax on the capital gain. It might, however, be part of his normal exploitation of the cable system and fall to be treated as part of his trading receipts. But in both cases he continues to own the cable, there is no part disposal, and he will continue to get capital allowances on its original cost.

Where the receipt for the granting of the IRU is a capital receipt, we have been asked whether it falls to be charged under TCGA 1992 s 21 or s 22. We do not think it comes within s 21(2)(*b*) as there is no part disposal of the network itself. The company owning the network grants a right of use of part of the cables to the person acquiring the IRU. Our view is that the receipt falls within s 22(1)(*d*) being for the exploitation of the rights to use the network. An agreement entered into for the disposal of the IRU appears to be a form of contractual licence containing contractual terms as to the costs of maintenance and repair during the period of the agreement. The disposal does not amount to the disposal of absolute ownership of the rights to use the cables. As there is no cost attributable to the rights themselves which are held by the company granting the IRU the only costs available to be set off against the capital receipt within TCGA 1992 s 38 are any incidental costs such as fees in drawing up the contracts.

ACCOUNTING APPROACH IN RELEVANT GROUP ACCOUNTS

Sch 23 para 4 provides that the accounting approach adopted by the taxpayer must not be more cautious than that adopted in any group accounts. This was designed to ensure that a taxpayer could not write the IRU down at an accelerated rate in its UK accounts (or revalue the IRU in the group accounts but not in the company accounts) in order to maximise the tax relief, while continuing to show a high value on its balance sheet at group level.

We have been asked what happens where an overseas accounting standard insists that an IRU is written down at a prescribed rate which differs from that under UK accounting standards, whether the balance of relief is lost. This will not be the case—we would expect the actual depreciation in the taxpayer's accounts to be added back in the computation and the amount charged in the group accounts to be deducted instead. Thereafter we would expect similar computational adjustments to be done each year, thus ensuring that over the life of the IRU the full cost is allowed, but on the less cautious approach.

CONTROLLED FOREIGN COMPANIES (CFCS)

We have been asked about the interaction with the CFC rules. The CFC rules are based on UK chargeable profits. If income from IRUs forms part of the chargeable profits of a UK company, it follows that it will form part of the chargeable profits of a CFC—which could potentially be apportioned back to the UK. The granting of an IRU seems fairly clearly to be the leasing of a property or right. As such, it would equally clearly come within the definition of investment business for the purposes of para 9(1)(*c*). The fact the business carried on would, if carried on in the UK, be taxed under Schedule D Case I, would make no difference here. For CFC purposes it will still be deemed to be "investment business" and, as such, outside the terms of the exempt activities test at TA 1988 Sch 25 para 6(2)(*a*)(*i*).

Commentary—*Simon's Direct Tax Service* **C1.319, C2.208.**

RI 224 (February 2001) *Delaware Limited Liability Companies (DLLCS)*

A number of practitioners and representative bodies have, over recent months, asked whether the Revenue regard US LLCs generally, and DLLCs in particular, as issuing "ordinary share capital" for the purposes of the rules in TA 1988 s 838 and TCGA 1992 ss 135, 136, 170–181.

In relation to DLLCs we understand that there is legal authority for such entities to issue "shares" under the Delaware Limited Liability Act s 18–702c. This provides that "a limited liability company agreement may provide that a member's interest in a limited liability company may be evidenced by a certificate of limited liability company interest issued by the limited liability company."

If a DLLC issues "shares" in this way then we will accept that these may be regarded as "ordinary share capital" for the purpose of TA 1988 s 838. Consequently such an LLC may be a "75% subsidiary" for the purposes of TA 1988 s 838 (1)(*b*). It follows that it is possible for an LLC to—

- be a member of a capital gains group (TCGA 1992 ss 170–181)
- be a party to share exchanges (TCGA 1992 ss 135–136), and
- be a member of the same group as another company for the purposes of group relief (TA 1988 ss 402–413).

It should be noted that it is not always the case that the DLLC issues shares. Regard must be had to the particular terms of the agreement by which the LLC has been created. In any case of doubt or difficulty we will advise in particular cases in line with Code of Practice 10. The contact point is Ben Newton, Inland Revenue Policy, Business Tax, Group Relief and Losses, Room 97, New Wing, Somerset House, London WC2R 1LB.

Commentary—*Simon's Direct Tax Service* **D2.621, 651**.

RI 225 (February 2001) *Waste site preparation expenditure—TA 1988 s 91B*

SUMMARY

The cost of engineering the base and sides of a waste disposal site to receive waste is capital expenditure, even though they may be constructed in sections that also form part of internal cells with an economic life of less than two years.

BACKGROUND

Tax Bulletin Issue 34 (April 1998, p 533 [see Simon's Weekly Tax Intelligence 1998 p 692]) looks at the question of what constitutes waste site preparation expenditure. The article details a number of the capital costs of site preparation, including engineering a site to the point where waste can be deposited. It also explains our view that the application of the capital/revenue divide to cell construction within a site is essentially one of economic effect. That is, we accept that the cost of constructing the honeycomb of internal cells within a waste disposal site is revenue expenditure, provided the cells are filled and sealed within two years.

As a result of that article, we have received a number of enquiries concerning the distinction between the capital costs of engineering a site to receive waste and the revenue costs of creating internal cells. The purpose of this article is to clarify that distinction.

PREPARATION EXPENDITURE

Engineering a modern waste disposal site to the point where waste can be deposited often includes constructing an impermeable clay layer, or laying an artificial lining, across the base and sides of the site. When the site has eventually been filled these elements, together with the final capping, create a containment structure for the whole site that is likely to fulfil that function for decades. We view the costs of creating such a containment structure as capital expenditure.

INTERNAL EARTHWORKS

For practical and financial reasons, the base and sides of site containment structures are often built in sections, with internal barriers, or ''bunds'', on the open sides to create the first level of internal cells. Provided these internal cells are filled and sealed within two years, we accept that the costs of the internal earthworks, ie the bunds and any internal caps, are revenue expenditure. However, the costs of the base and sides, which form part of the site containment structure, remain capital expenditure.

Note—This Interpretation has been superseded by the Business Income Manual BIM67445.
Commentary—*Simon's Direct Tax Service* **B3.1345.**

RI 226 (April 2001) *Capital gains tax: holdings of shares—matching acquisitions and disposals*

FA 1998 brought in a new set of CGT rules for matching disposals of shares (and similar fungible assets) with acquisitions. The basic rules are set out in our Help Sheet IR284 ''Shares and capital gains tax''. Since 1998 various questions have been raised as to how these rules apply in different situations. This article sets out the Revenue's views on some of the regular queries.

These new rules in TCGA 1992 do not apply to every share disposal. Most obviously, they do not apply to disposals by companies charged to corporation tax on their capital gains. But they are also overridden by special rules in various cases, for instance, where the shares are subject to relief under the enterprise investment scheme, or if they are shares in a venture capital trust.

We have been asked whether the new rules, and particularly the ''bed and breakfasting'' rule discussed below, apply in one specific circumstance. Do they apply when acquisitions and disposals take place whilst the person concerned is not resident in the UK? The short answer is ''Yes, they do apply''. So if, for example, an individual ''bed and breakfasts'' shares before coming (or returning) to the UK, the ''B&B'' rule applies in the normal way, just as all the other rules do when matching that person's disposals of shares with his/her disposals.

The rest of this article assumes that the normal CGT matching rules apply in the situations described. In particular it assumes that shares are all of the same class, in the same company, and held by the same individual, trustees of a settlement or personal representatives, in the same capacity.

SAME DAY TRANSACTIONS

The first query relates to the ''same day'' rules in TCGA 1992 s 105. TCGA1992 s 105(1)—

– treats all acquisitions on one day as a single acquisition;
– treats all disposals on one day as a single disposal;

– matches, as far as possible, disposals with acquisitions on the same day.

Some concern has been expressed that these rules prevent TCGA 1992 s 24(2), which allows ''negligible value'' claims, operating as intended. When someone makes a negligible value claim they are treated as having ''sold, and immediately reacquired'' the asset that is the subject of the claim. If the asset was a holding of shares and the same day rules applied to the disposal and reacquisition, neither a gain nor a loss would arise. The purpose of a negligible value claim, to crystallise a loss from the deemed disposal, would be frustrated.

The same day rule in TCGA 1992 s 105 is not new. In fact it goes back to FA 1971. The Revenue's long-held view, based on legal advice, is that the same day rule, which matches ''securities of the same class'', does not apply in any case where a particular shareholding (the asset) is deemed to be disposed of and the same asset reacquired. So if a negligible value claim is made the loss is calculated by reference to the original cost of the shares for which the claim is made.

BED AND BREAKFASTING (B&B)

The B&B matching rule (TCGA 1992 s 106A(5)) takes second priority after the same day rule, but before other matching rules. It matches disposals with acquisitions of securities of the same class ''within the period of 30 days after the disposal''. If there is more than one acquisition in this period you take the earliest acquisitions first.

It has been suggested that a deemed disposal and reacquisition might be within the B&B rule, because the acquisition falls within the 30 day period after the disposal. If that were so a deemed disposal and reacquisition would still be matched to result in no gain/no loss, even though the same day rule did not apply. This result would again frustrate the purpose of any claim for negligible value in respect of shares.

Like the same day rule, the B&B rule applies to match securities of the same class. So we consider that the same result follows. The B&B rule cannot apply where the same asset is deemed to have been disposed of and reacquired. In addition, we do not regard an acquisition as falling ''within the period of 30 days after the disposal'' if it falls on the same day as the disposal.

Another doubt has arisen where the B&B rule applies. That is, what are the consequences of the B&B rule for shares which were acquired before the relevant disposal? Take the following example—

Example 1

An individual makes the following purchases and sales of shares in XYZ plc—

- 1 June 1998 buys 5,000;
- 1 July 2001 sells 3,000;
- 15 July 2001 buys 3,000;
- 1 August 2001 sells 5,000

The B&B rule matches the sale of 3,000 shares with the purchase a fortnight later. But how should we regard the 5,000 shares sold a fortnight after that, for example, when working out what taper relief is available?

The sale on 1 August 2001 is matched with the acquisition on 1 June 1998, because the B&B rule applies to the earlier sale. The result for CGT purposes is that the individual is regarded as having held the 5,000 shares continuously from the time he/she acquired them until they are treated as sold under the relevant matching rule. So in Example 1 the individual will have held the 5,000 shares for three whole years. The gain on disposal of those shares will therefore attract three years' worth of taper relief (assuming that all other taper relief conditions are met).

A similar point arises in relation to shares held by trustees. TCGA 1992 s 80 creates a deemed disposal of trust assets if the trustees leave the UK and become non-resident (and not ordinarily resident). It has been suggested that the B&B rule can be used to nullify the gains which would otherwise arise on emigration. Take the following example—

Example 2

As at 31 January 2001 UK resident trustees hold 100,000 shares in a company. These shares have risen greatly in value and a large gain would arise if they were sold, or were deemed to be disposed of under the provision in s 80. Then on—

- 1 February 2001 the trustees sell the 100,000 shares;
- 3 February 2001 they leave the UK and become non-resident;
- 5 February 2001 they buy another 100,000 shares in the same company (using the proceeds from the earlier disposal).

The B&B rule matches the disposal on 1 February with the acquisition on 5 February and in all probability only a very small gain or loss will arise. Under TCGA 1992 s 80 trustees are deemed to dispose on 3 February of ''assets constituting settled property of the settlement immediately before'' they emigrated. But at that time they do not actually hold any shares. The suggestion is that there are therefore no assets which can be deemed to have been disposed of under TCGA 1992 s 80(2).

However this is not the right way to look at this situation. For CGT purposes the shares sold on 1 February are regarded as the ones bought on 5 February. It must follow that the shares held before 1 February had not been disposed of (again, for CGT purposes) by the time the trustees left the UK. Those shares still constitute settled property immediately before the emigration, and must be treated as disposed of and reacquired at that time under TCGA 1992 s 80(2).

Commentary—*Simon's Direct Tax Service* **C2.701A**.

RI 227 (April 2001) *Capital gains tax: Matrimonial Causes Act 1973 s 31(7B) as enacted by the Family Law Act 1996—court orders for payments of lump sums*

Matrimonial Causes Act 1973 (MCA 1973) s 31 gives the court power to vary, discharge or suspend an order for financial provision for a party to a marriage or former marriage. Where under MCA 1973 s 31(7A) the court has discharged an order for periodical payments or varied such an order, MCA 1973 s 31(7B) provides that the court has power to make a supplementary provision including an order for the payment of a lump sum.

We have been asked what the position is for capital gains tax where, in effect, a court replaces in whole or in part its order for periodic payments by an order for a lump sum payment.

In exercising its powers under MCA 1973 s 31 the court is required to have regard to all the circumstances of the case and in particular whether any of the criteria listed in MCA 1973 s 25(2)(*a*)–(*h*) have changed since the original order was made. It is making a fresh exercise of its discretionary powers. The order under MCA 1973 s 31(7B) is not derived from the discharge or variation of the order for periodical payments, even though that is the occasion which enables it to exercise this power.

In our view the lump sum derives from the exercise of the court's discretion in making its order and therefore is not a capital payment derived from an asset. Therefore in this situation TCGA 1992 s 22(1) is not in point and the recipient of the lump sum payment would have no liability to capital gains tax on the receipt.

Commentary—*Simon's Direct Tax Service* **C1.202, 319.**

RI 228 (June 2001) *Capital gains tax: taper relief—meaning of "trading company" and related issues*

We have received a number of enquiries from taxpayers and their advisers about the meaning of a "trading company" and "holding company of a trading group" (as defined in TCGA 1992 Sch A1 para 22) for the purposes of capital gains tax taper relief.

FA 1998 introduced taper relief for chargeable gains accruing to individuals, trustees and personal representatives on or after 6 April 1998. Generally, the amount of taper relief will depend on the length of time the asset has been held and whether or not it is a "business asset". This article is relevant to when shares may qualify as business assets or a company may be a qualifying company.

FA 2001 contains provisions to extend the business rate of taper relief to some employee shares in non-trading companies from 6 April 2000. The question of the trading status of the company may therefore concern fewer persons.

THE LEGISLATION

Shares as business assets and qualifying companies

TCGA 1992 Sch A1 para 4 sets out the conditions for shares to qualify as business assets and TCGA 1992 Sch A1 para 6 (as amended by FA 2000 s 67) the companies which are qualifying companies in relation to the person making the share disposal. Where a company is a qualifying company in relation to that person the business rate of taper relief may be due wholly or in part on any chargeable gains arising on the disposal. This question as to what is a qualifying company may also be relevant to persons who dispose of assets used in a trade carried on by their qualifying company.

INTERPRETATIONS

Trading company

TCGA 1992 Sch A1 para 22 states that a trading company is a company which is either "a company existing wholly for the purpose of carrying on one or more trades" or a company that would fall within that definition "apart from any purposes capable of having no substantial effect on the extent of the company's activities". The various elements which make up this definition are discussed in further detail below.

Wholly

In the context of the definition of a trading company we would take "wholly" to mean that the company had no purpose other than to trade. Wholly therefore means solely.

Whether something is wholly for a trading purpose can only be considered in light of the requirements of the company's trade. One common situation is where a company sets aside funds and receives investment income. The fact that investment income is generated does not automatically lead to the conclusion that a company's purpose is not wholly trading. Whether the generation of income from investments is or is not evidence of a non-trading purpose must ultimately depend on the nature of the company's trade and whether the holding of the investment is closely related to the conduct of that trade. If it can be shown that holding any investment is integral to the conduct of the trade or is a short-term lodgement of surplus funds held to meet demonstrable trading liabilities, then this is unlikely to be taken as evidence of non-trading purposes. For example, if a company has surplus funds which it intends to use for an expansion of the trading business in the near future, and it invests these in equities in the short term, then it may be that the company's purpose continues to be wholly trading during the period those equities are held.

A company which makes an investment falling outside the categories above (which may include acquiring and retaining a holding of shares in another company as part of a wider business strategy beyond that related to the requirements of the trade) still has the safety net of the "substantial test" (see below). Examples of such investments include those made in the expectation of a return in the longer term and those offering unrelated, indirect or non-specific benefits to the company's trade.

Purpose

Companies will usually have wide powers to carry on activities but will often only engage in a few. We can confirm that only those purposes which are reflected in the activities, or intended activities, of the company fall to be taken into account. The comparison will be of actual circumstances at a particular point in time and not of the scope of a company's powers under its articles and ambitions not seriously in contemplation.

In order to establish purpose we have to look at the taxpayer's "object" in mind at any point in time (see, for example, *Morgan v Tate and Lyle* 35 TC 367). Subsequent events are irrelevant except as a reflection of the taxpayer's state of mind at the time the expenditure was made. Purposes, in the case of companies, can probably only be established by looking at the intentions of the directors at a particular moment as well as looking at the transactions themselves. This is important because similar transactions by different companies (eg buying shares) may be for different purposes.

A company might cease being dormant and be actively preparing to trade but not actually trading. We would accept that such a company was a trading company from the point at which it had substantially trading purposes, even if this was before it commenced to trade. However, in the case of close companies, TCGA 1992 Sch A1 para 11(3) would deny taper relief before trading commenced, if it did in fact commence.

Trade

"Trade", for taper relief purposes, means anything which is a trade, profession or vocation within the meaning of the Income Tax Acts and is conducted on a commercial basis and with a view to the realisation of profits. It also includes any Schedule A business (within the meaning of TA 1988) which consists in the commercial letting of holiday accommodation in the UK as defined in TA 1988 s 504. We can confirm that activities, such as farming, that are treated as a trade by TA 1988 s 53, will also be trades for the purpose of para 22.

Capable and activities

In the case of trading companies the question is whether non-trading purposes are "capable" of having no substantial effect. In our view this requires an objective assessment at any point in time as to whether it can be shown that this is the case rather than that it is theoretically possible.

Substantial

TCGA 1992 Sch A1 para 22 refers to a "substantial effect on the extent of the company's activities". The word substantial is used in various sections of the Act to provide some flexibility in interpreting a section without opening the door to widespread abuse of a relieving provision. We consider that substantial here means "more than 20%". It is therefore necessary to consider what should form the basis for measuring whether a company's non-trading purposes are capable of having a substantial effect. We consider that this will vary according to the facts in each case but some or all of the following might be taken into account in reviewing a particular company's status—

- *Turnover receivable from non-trading activities;*
- For example, a company may have a trade but also let an investment property. If receipts from the letting were substantial in comparison to the combined trading and letting income then, on this measure, this would probably not be a trading company for taper relief purposes.
- *The asset base of the company;*

- If the value of non-trading assets was substantial in relation to trading and non-trading assets then again, on this measure, this would not be a trading company for taper relief purposes. In other cases holding on to an asset which had increased in value may indicate non-trading purposes if the company lacks liquid resources to develop it or too much time is spent looking after it (but see below regarding surplus trading premises). In some cases it might be appropriate to take account of intangible assets (eg goodwill) that are not shown on a balance sheet in considering a company's purpose. Current market value, cost and amounts given by way of consideration for assets may all be appropriate measures of the value of assets.
- *Expenses incurred by, or time spent by, officers and employees of the company in undertaking its activities;*
- For example, if a substantial proportion of the expenses of a company were incurred on non-trading activities then, on this measure, the company would not be a trading company.

The historical context of the company may be relevant. For example, it is quite possible that at an instant in time certain receipts may not be insubstantial but, if looked at on a longer timescale, they may. Looking at the historical context therefore a company might be able to show that it was a trading company at a particular point in time.

It may be that some measures point in one direction and others in the opposite direction. We would weigh up the impact of each of the measures to balance the effects of measures that point in different directions in coming to a view. If, at the end of the day, the inspector was unable to agree the status of a particular company for a period then this matter could only be ultimately established as a question of fact before the Commissioners. However, we anticipate that these cases will be relatively rare.

Holding company of a trading group

TCGA 1992 Sch A1 para 22(1) defines a holding company as "a company whose business (disregarding any trade carried on by it) consists wholly or mainly of the holding of shares in one or more companies which are its 51% subsidiaries". The fact that such companies may be investment companies for the purpose of corporation tax does not mean that they cannot also be classed as holding companies for taper relief purposes.

We can confirm that "wholly or mainly", in this context, means more than half of whatever measure is reasonable in the circumstances of the case.

A company that is the holding company of a group may let properties it holds to subsidiaries for use in the subsidiaries' trades. We can confirm that the fact that rent is paid by the tenant company would not in itself be a transaction to bring into account when considering whether or not a company is a holding company, even if a market rent were charged. Other intra-group transactions, such as inter-company lending and the use of intellectual property, are equally within this approach. This approach would not extend to transactions with qualifying joint venture companies (other than 51% subsidiaries).

Trading group

TCGA 1992 Sch A1 para 22 defines a trading group as "a group of companies the activities of which (if all the activities of the companies in the group are taken together) do not, or not to any substantial extent, include activities carried on otherwise than in the course of, or for the purposes of, a trade". The focus here will be on the actual activities of the group in determining non-trading purposes rather than those activities that a group might be permitted to engage in.

The expression "all the activities taken together" in the definition of trading group should be taken as meaning that all intra-group activities are disregarded for the purpose of the financial tests. So, for example, where one group company lets a property to another group company, the letting activity would be disregarded. However, this netting off approach would not be extended to transactions with qualifying joint venture companies (other than 51% subsidiaries), so letting property to a JVC would be an investment activity.

Qualifying joint venture investments

Where a company is treated by TCGA 1992 Sch A1 para 23 (FA 2000 s 67(6)) as having a qualifying shareholding in a qualifying joint venture company (as defined) the holding of these shares is disregarded. The investing company shall be treated as carrying on an appropriate proportion of the activities of the joint venture company. Similar provisions apply to determine if a company is the holding company of a trading group.

Shares and other assets held otherwise than as investments

Companies may acquire shares or other assets for reasons other than investment. For example, companies may be paid in shares instead of cash as fees for services rendered or work carried out. Once such shares have been acquired the reasons for retaining them will need to be considered and whether or not their retention means that a company has non-trading purposes. Among other issues, regard would be had to the reasons why the shares were taken instead of cash or credit, whether they can reasonably be turned into cash or otherwise exchanged to meet trading requirements.

A company may have to hold shares in another company as a pre-requisite to trading (for example, companies may be expected to own shares in a trade organisation). In such cases regard may be had to the reasons for holding the shares in deciding if a company had non-trading purposes.

Corporate venturing scheme (CVS)

The CVS is aimed at companies considering direct investment, in the form of a minority shareholding, in small independent higher-risk trading companies or groups of such companies. It provides tax incentives for corporate equity investment in the same types of companies as those qualifying under the enterprise investment scheme (EIS) and venture capital trust (VCT) scheme. The incentives are available in respect of qualifying shares issued between 1 April 2000 and 31 March 2010.

We have been asked if a company making corporate venturing investment(*s*) could be considered to have ceased to be a trading company, or, where appropriate, the holding company of a trading group, for the purpose of business asset taper. Regardless of the purpose for which the investing company exists, the holding of investments will not have any bearing on a company's status as a trading company for taper purposes unless, together with other non-trading purposes, it is capable of having a substantial effect on the extent of the investing company's activities.

The scheme works in such a way that it is very unlikely that making CVS investments will prevent a company being a trading company for taper relief purposes. This is because to qualify as a CVS investing company (there are equivalent provisions in respect of group companies)—

- the company must exist wholly for the purpose of carrying on one or more non-financial trades, apart from any incidental purposes which have no significant effect on the extent of the company's activities; and
- a holding of shares to which CVS investment relief is attributable would be significant where it amounted to a substantial part of the investing company's business;
- so an investing company that qualifies for CVS is very unlikely to have more than the 20% investment activity that would stop it being a trading company for taper relief.

In addition, when assessing for taper relief whether the investment element relating to a CVS shareholding contributes to exceeding 20% of a company's activities on various measures, companies should be careful to distinguish between activity in connection with the investment element and that which relates to the ''partnership'' element. The whole of the value of the CVS shareholding will be an investment purpose when looking at an assets-based measure. But when looking at a measure such as directors' time spent, only that part of the investing company's directors' time that is spent in connection with the share-holding itself (buy, sell, value monitoring) is an investment purpose; the time spent on the closer working relations between the two companies' trades that is the policy purpose of CVS should normally be seen as in support of trading purposes.

Where companies are in doubt as to their entitlement to relief as an investing company under CVS, and as to their trading status for taper relief, they should raise both issues with their inspector as set out below.

Companies moving in and out of being a trading company or holding company of a trading group

If a company moves in and out of ''trading company'' status it may be necessary for any gain on the disposal of shares to be apportioned for the periods when the company was and was not a trading company. This may not be necessary where the taper provisions in FA 2001 apply to relevant employees.

In the case where a company goes into liquidation it is unlikely to be trading during the period of the liquidation. If so, it may be necessary to apportion the gain on the shares.

Surplus trading property

We have been asked how property owned by a company and surplus to its immediate business requirements should be dealt with. Each case would need to be considered in light of the facts. We would not, for example, regard the following as necessarily indicating a non-trading purpose—

- letting part of the trading premises;
- letting properties that are no longer required for the purpose of the trade, where the objective is to sell those properties;
- subletting property where it would be impractical or uneconomic in terms of the trade to assign or surrender the lease. For example, the benefit derived from disposing of the lease may be outweighed by the reverse premium payable;
- the acquisition of property (whether vacant or already let) where it can be shown that the intention is that it will be brought into use for the purpose of the trade.

What to do if you want to know if a company is a trading company or the holding company of a trading group

Our advice to taxpayers is that in the first instance they should contact the company in which they hold the shares. If they cannot obtain an answer from the company, they should submit their tax returns using their own judgement.

Where a company wishes to establish its status for any accounting period that has ended, we have asked that districts should respond positively to requests for a view.

Any assurance given that a company is or is not a trading company can relate only to the period under consideration. It is possible for a company to change its status at any time, as its business position changes. It will be important for the company to continue to reappraise its position in future and to come back to the inspector if it is in doubt because of changed circumstances.

Commentary—*Simon's Direct Tax Service* **C2.1422**.

RI 229 (June 2001) *Meaning of "carrying on a business of holding investments" in TCGA 1992 Sch A1 para 11(4)*

TCGA 1992 Sch A1 para 11 is an anti-avoidance rule which may restrict the qualifying holding period of shares in close companies for taper relief purposes. It is designed to prevent any advantage being obtained from activities that could otherwise artificially increase the amount of taper relief given. One such restriction is imposed by TCGA 1992 Sch A1 para 11(4) where, ''at the time of disposal of the shares, the close company was carrying on a business of holding investments'' and, within a specified period prior to that disposal, it was either not carrying on that business at all or the business was comparatively small. We have been asked how the meaning of ''carrying on a business of holding investments'' for the purposes of TCGA 1992 Sch A1 para 11 should be interpreted. All the interpretations below will be used by the Revenue in applying para 11.

MEANING OF "BUSINESS"

The concept of a business is central to parts of the capital gains code. For example, TCGA 1992 s 162 concerns the transfer of a business to a company as a going concern and TCGA 1992 s 163 provides for retirement relief on the disposal of a business or business assets. In the case of s 163, relief is, for example, restricted to assets used in a trade, profession, etc and does not include lettings within Schedule A.

We can draw on case law to understand the meaning of ''business''. As Lord Diplock said in *Town Investments Ltd v Department of the Environment* [1978] AC 359, ''the word 'business' is an etymological chameleon; it suits its meaning to the context in which it is found. It is not a term of legal art and its dictionary meanings...embrace almost anything which is an occupation as distinguished from a pleasure—anything which is an occupation or duty which requires attention is a business''.

The next point to note is that ''business'' and ''trade'' are not synonymous whilst all trades are businesses, there are many businesses that are not trades. Property letting, as opposed to the provision of services to tenants, may be a business though not a trade. The holding of investments can also amount to a business. Indeed, there is judicial support for the view that this does not have to be actively carried on to be a business of making investments (see, for example, *IRC v The Korean Syndicate Ltd* 12 TC 181).

On the other hand, there are several cases where it has been held that a trading company which has ended its main activities but has retained its investment portfolio is not carrying on a business of holding investments. The most recent case is *Jowett v O'Neill and Brennan Construction Ltd* 70 TC 566.

In that case, Mr Justice Park acknowledged that whilst the normal conclusion, when a company lays out its assets and earns an income return, is that it is carrying on a business there will, as a matter of law, be exceptional cases where the facts indicate that no business is being carried on by the company. It is the exception rather than the rule that means a company is not carrying on a business when it puts its money on deposit.

WHAT "BUSINESS" IS WITHIN TCGA 1992 SCH A1 PARA 11 (4) IF A COMPANY IS TRADING?

Companies that trade may also carry on a business of holding investments. It is however provided by TCGA 1992 Sch A1 para 11(6)(*b*) that such a business shall not be taken to include the placing of money on deposit, the holding of shares in 51% subsidiaries and the making of loans to associated companies or participators.

We conclude from the above that activities which include holding shares in another company or making loans outside of the exceptions mentioned above may amount to a business of holding investments. However, where such activities are undertaken by a company which also carries on a trade, the trading context must be reviewed to establish whether a separate business of holding investments exists.

Where a company carries on a trade the question to ask is whether certain transactions are integral to that trade. This depends on the purpose for which a fund or asset is held. Where the holding of investments is to meet current trading liabilities, and forms capital of the trade, it is unlikely that any investments will be within the meaning of carrying on a business of holding investments. However, there will be companies where the holding of investments forms no part of its trade or in any sense represents capital employed in the trade. This is a question that can only be answered in the light of the particular facts in each case.

We can confirm that where a company does no more than invest funds surplus to its immediate trading requirements it will not be regarded as carrying on a business of holding investments under TCGA 1992 Sch A1 para 11(4). In consequence, neither the initial making of an investment with surplus funds, nor a change in the way the funds are invested subsequently, can constitute a ''relevant change of activity'' of the company within the legislation.

Whether particular investments are of funds of a company ''surplus to its immediate trading requirements'' is a question of fact. In understanding this expression some assistance may be found in the case of *Nuclear Electric plc v Bradley* 68 TC 670. This case concerned a claim to set off trading losses and whether interest received constituted part of the trading income for the purposes of the set-off. It was held that the question as to whether income from investments held by a business was trading income depended ultimately upon the nature of the business and the purpose for which the fund was held. At one end of the scale were insurance companies and banks part of whose business was the making and holding of investments to meet current liabilities. At the other end of the scale were businesses of which the making and holding of investments formed no part. In between those two ends there would no doubt fall other types of business whose position was not so clear.

This issue as to whether particular investments are part of a business of holding investments is similar to the ''excepted assets'' requirement of IHTA 1984 s 112(2). Excepted assets are those not used wholly or mainly for the purposes of the ''business concerned'' in the two years up to the relevant date, nor are they required at that time for future use in the business. In *Barclays Bank Trust Co Ltd* (SpC 158) the Special Commissioners considered the future use test. The Special Commissioner said—

> ''I do not accept that 'future' means at any time in the future nor that 'was required' includes the possibility that the money might be required should an opportunity arise to make use of the money in two, three or seven years' time for the purposes of the business. In my opinion and I do so hold that 'required' implies some imperative that the money will fall to be used upon a given project or for some palpable business purpose.''

Where funds are, for the immediate future, surplus to current trading requirements then the question will be whether it can be shown that there will be a foreseeable need to use those funds in the trade in the future. If so, then it is unlikely that these will be part of a business of holding investments. If not, then the question has to be asked, at the time of the disposal of the shares, whether the company in question was carrying on a business of holding investments and, if so, whether there has been a previous time when it wasn't or the business was small in comparison to the business at the time of the share disposal. Small, in this context, is taken to mean less than 5% of the size that the business of holding investments has at the time of the disposal.

PROPERTY LETTINGS

We have been asked how property owned by a company should be dealt with. The Capital Gains Manual at CG17919 confirms that we would not, for example, regard the following in themselves as amounting to a business of making investments where they are carried out by a trading company—

- letting part of the trading premises;
- letting properties that are no longer required for the purposes of the trade, where the long term objective is to sell those properties;
- subletting property where it would be impractical or uneconomic to assign or surrender the lease.

We can also confirm that where a company acquires property which is let to other companies in the same group for use in a lessee company's trade then this will not be taken into account in deciding if the lessor company is within TCGA 1992 Sch A1 para 11.

LIQUIDATION

Where a liquidator is appointed to wind up a company which at the time was not carrying on a business of holding investments, the company will not be regarded as commencing such a business for the purposes of para 11 by reason of a temporary investment which the liquidator makes pending a distribution to creditors and/or shareholders of funds arising in the winding up.

ASSETS ACQUIRED AND HELD OTHER THAN AS INVESTMENTS

Sometimes companies acquire shares in another company or other assets for reasons other than investment. For example, companies may be paid in shares instead of cash as fees for services rendered or work carried out. Once such shares have been acquired the reasons for retaining them will need to be considered and whether or not their retention means that a company has a business of holding investments. Among other issues, the reasons why the shares were taken in lieu of cash or credit, whether they can reasonably be turned into cash or otherwise exchanged to meet trading requirements would all need to be considered.

A company may have to hold shares in another company as a pre-requisite to trading (for example, companies may be expected to own shares in a trade organisation). In deciding if a company had a business of holding investments the reasons for holding the shares would all need to be considered.

TCGA 1992 Sch A1 para 13 also contains particular provisions relating to the holding of shares in joint venture companies. Where such shares are a ''qualifying shareholding'' within the meaning of that paragraph, then this investing activity is disregarded in favour of an appropriate proportion of the activities of the joint venture company in which the shares are held. A qualifying shareholding in a joint venture company cannot therefore, of itself, constitute a business of holding investments. TCGA 1992 Sch A1 para 23(9) also provides that the acquisition of a qualifying shareholding is not to be treated as a relevant change of activity for the purposes of para 11.

IF THE COMPANY HAS A BUSINESS OF HOLDING INVESTMENTS, WILL TCGA 1992 SCH A1 PARA 11 APPLY TO ITS SHARES?

Where the circumstances are such that the company has a business holding investments, there are a number of points to consider which may remove shares held in the company from scope of TCGA 1992 Sch A1 para 11. Firstly, the investing company must be a close company for para 11 to apply. Secondly, TCGA 1992 Sch A1 para 11(4) looks at the size of the business being conducted at the time of the disposal of the shares as compared with an earlier period when the level of activity was small or non-existent. Where a company has an ongoing and constant level of investment business it is unlikely that para 11 will need to be considered. Para 11 is concerned with increases in the size of an investment business, measured with reference to twelve monthly periods, rather than the existence of that business. Also, para 11 would not apply where the company's business was not being conducted at the time of the share disposal.

It is also appropriate to bear in mind that, even where the provisions of TCGA 1992 Sch A1 para 11 apply to exclude a period of share ownership from the qualifying holding period, sufficient time may have elapsed since the last relevant change of activity for the disposal of shares to attract full taper relief.

CORPORATE VENTURING SCHEME

The principles set out above apply equally where a company holds shares under the CVS, introduced by FA 2000 s 63 with effect from 1 April 2000.

So, in many situations, it is likely that the holding of shares which have attracted CVS reliefs will not prejudice the company's shareholders from claiming business asset taper relief for a period.

Commentary—*Simon's Direct Tax Service* **C2.1422**.

RI 230 (June 2001) *Capital gains tax: taper relief—meaning of "security"*

We have received a number of enquiries about the meaning of ''securities'' for taper relief purposes. In particular, we have been asked whether company debentures deemed to be securities by TCGA 1992 s 251(6) and earn-out rights within TCGA 1992 s 138A are securities for taper relief purposes.

The more generous taper relief for business assets may be due where an individual, the trustees of a settlement, an individual's personal representatives or a legatee disposes of shares that qualify as business assets. The definition of shares in relation to a company in TCGA 1992 Sch A1 para 22 includes any securities of that company. The meaning of what is a security for taper relief purposes is not further defined by Sch A1, nor does TCGA 1992 contain a general definition of what is a security.

It is our view that not all debentures will be securities. A security is more than an acknowledgement of indebtedness by a company. Any question as to whether a particular instrument was a security would, in the first instance, be a matter for the relevant inspector of taxes to consider.

TCGA 1992 s 132, which deals with conversions of company securities, gives limited guidance on the meaning of security in the definition in subsection (3)(*b*). We accept that a security within the meaning of TCGA 1992 s 132 is a security for the purposes of taper relief.

The meaning given to ''security'' TCGA 1992 in s 132 is also adopted by TCGA 1992 s 251(1), which refers to ''...the debt on a security (as defined in s 132)''. We think it follows that a company debenture possessing the characteristics of ''the debt on a security'' will be a security in the context of TCGA 1992 s 132. We therefore accept that any such debenture will also be a security for taper purposes.

The courts have held that a debenture issued by a company will have the characteristics of ''the debt on a security'' if it is capable of being realised at a profit by the person to whom it was first issued. Our views on the characteristics necessary for this to be possible are at paras CG53420 to CG53435 of the Capital Gains Manual.

A debenture issued by a company on or after 16 March 1993, which is not a security, can be deemed to be a security by TCGA 1992 s 251(6). But this treatment is only for the purposes of s 251. Schedule A1 does not extend the meaning of security for taper relief purposes to include such debentures. In contrast, TCGA 1992 s 117A(10) does provide such an extension in the context of assets that are not qualifying corporate bonds for corporation tax purposes. We do not therefore consider that a company debenture which is only deemed to be a security by s 251(6) is a security for taper relief purposes.

We have also considered whether earn-out rights can be securities for taper purposes. Where an earn-out right is the subject of a valid election under TCGA 1992 s 138A, the Act has effect on the assumption that it is a security within the definition in s 132 (see s 138A(2) and (3)(*a*)). Although this matter is not free from doubt we accept that such earn-out rights count as securities for the purposes of taper relief.

Commentary—*Simon's Direct Tax Service* **C2.1422.**

RI 231 (June 2001) *Interaction of tax and accountancy—"deferred revenue expenditure"*

BACKGROUND

In February 1999 we published an article on deferred revenue expenditure (Tax Bulletin 39). We did this as we had been asked to clarify the tax treatment of this kind of expenditure following an earlier article (Tax Bulletin 32 issued in December 1997). These articles set out our understanding of how the law was changing in this area as a result of court decisions, and how they had led to a closer alignment of tax and accounting.

"Deferred revenue expenditure" in this context means allowable revenue expenditure which has been accounted for by posting the expense somewhere on the balance sheet—whether to fixed or current assets—rather than writing it off immediately to the profit and loss account as it is incurred. The expenditure is then usually written off to the profit and loss account over a period of time, by being charged as an expense or depreciated.

We have become aware that this issue is still being dealt with in different ways. This article aims to clarify the position and re-affirm how the law operates in this area. It also details how we aim to resolve current enquiries on this point, and to cater, as far as practically possible, for any inconsistencies that have arisen. A number of amendments have been made already to Inland Revenue guidance to reflect the views detailed in this article. We will make further changes to ensure that all published material reflects those views.

The Department has given very careful consideration to the manner in which remaining inconsistencies should be resolved. We have concluded that where we have issued incomplete advice on how to deal with deferred revenue expenditure, the most appropriate course is to apply a cut off date, after which all businesses should consistently adopt the correct treatment in law as described below. The intended approach will also enable any past inconsistencies to be minimised as far as practically possible.

(Note 1—Revenue guidance that has been or will be revised to reflect our view of the law includes IM605f, IM608b, IM608d, IM990a, IM990b, PIM2020 and IR150 para 157).

OUR UNDERSTANDING OF THE LAW

Recent court decisions have presented an evolving view of the interaction of tax and accountancy. It has been well established that there is no rule of law stating that expenditure is tax deductible as it is paid or incurred. For timing purposes, the starting point for tax is the measure of accounting profits as shown by accounts drawn up under generally accepted accounting practice.

This means that expenditure which is revenue in terms of tax law, but which is deferred (or "capitalised") and shown somewhere on the balance sheet under correct accounting practice, can only be relieved for tax purposes as and when it is posted to the profit and loss account in accordance with generally accepted accountancy practice. Generally this will be when the expenditure is amortised or depreciated. (FRS15, "Recognition, measurement and depreciation of tangible fixed assets", may be relevant.)

So a computational adjustment to obtain earlier relief on a paid or incurred basis for this kind of expenditure, which is posted to the balance sheet, is no longer acceptable. This treatment, of course, only applies to bona fide revenue expenditure. It is well established in law that capital expenditure is inadmissible for tax purposes, whatever the accounting treatment might be.

Where a depreciation charge includes both revenue and capital elements, any reasonable method of identifying the revenue element will be accepted, provided it is consistently applied, and excludes amounts for which relief has already been given.

The article in Tax Bulletin Issue 39 (February 1999) will have alerted people to the impact of these developments. In addition, the judgement in the Herbert Smith case 72 TC 130 was delivered in February 1999. This case was about provisions, but the judgement also supports the trend in aligning tax and accounting. We issued a press release PR138/99 in July 1999 following the Herbert Smith case which explained that, broadly, deductions (for provisions for allowable revenue expenditure) were to be allowed for tax, if they followed generally accepted accounting practice, but that no expenditure could be relieved more than once [see Simon's Weekly Tax Intelligence 1999 p 263].

PRACTICAL MEASURES

We want to get everybody on the same footing because differing practices have grown up over the years on how to deal with deferred revenue expenditure. But we recognise that there can be practical difficulties in achieving this. Specifically, there may have been doubt over how to deal with revenue expenditure that is posted to fixed assets, as opposed to current assets. We now know that it is irrelevant for tax purposes where revenue expenditure, that is deferred, is held on the balance sheet.

The rest of this article sets out the approach we will adopt to move forward and reach consistency as quickly as possible. It details how we propose to deal with this particular point for all categories of returns.

THE CUT OFF

We propose to treat 30 June 1999 as the cut off date from which the correct view of the law should be applied. By this date we think that it is reasonable to assume that details of the new approach would have become known. So we would expect any income tax or corporation tax return, to the extent that it includes profits or losses shown in accounts for periods starting after 30 June 1999, to be settled in accordance with the law, and not to reflect computational adjustments to give relief for deferred revenue expenditure before it is deducted in the profit and loss account.

DETAIL

The detail of how this cut off applies is set out in the following paragraphs.

The term "accounts period" refers to a period for which accounts are drawn up.

A return and an accounts period "relate to" each other, if the return includes business profits or losses of the accounts period (disregarding losses and other amounts which for tax purposes can be carried forward or back between one period and another).

A return is "open" in the following circumstances—

(a) for periods preceding self-assessment:

- *the accounts have not yet been agreed, or*
- *an appeal has not yet been determined, or*
- *a return has not yet been made.*

(b) for periods where self-assessment applies:

- *the period for starting enquiries, or window for taxpayer amendment, has not yet expired, or*
- *an enquiry has been opened, whether or not the specific issue of deferred revenue expenditure is under consideration, or*
- *a return has not yet been made.*

Otherwise a return is "closed".

OPEN RETURNS RELATING WHOLLY TO ACCOUNTS PERIODS BEGINNING AFTER 30 JUNE 1999

If a return related to an accounts period beginning after 30 June 1999 is open, then the tax liability in respect of the profits in the accounts period should be settled in accordance with the correct legal position on deferred revenue expenditure (see above). But where a deduction for the expenditure has already been allowed on an incurred basis the expenditure cannot be allowed again.

OPEN RETURNS RELATING WHOLLY TO ACCOUNTS PERIODS BEGINNING ON OR BEFORE 30 JUNE 1999

If a return related to an accounts period beginning on or before 30 June 1999 is open, then the tax liability in respect of the profits in the accounts period will depend on whether the expenditure has been posted to fixed or current assets.

- *Where expenditure is posted to fixed assets we will accept any related computational adjustment that accompanied the original return thus allowing relief for the expenditure on the old incurred basis. This caters for earlier uncertainty about the law, which gave rise to potentially ambiguous guidance.*
- *Where the expenditure is posted to current assets the return should conform to the correct legal position (see above). There should have been no doubt at all as to the correct way in law that this expenditure should have been dealt with.*

SPECIAL CASES

There may be cases where an open return relates both to an accounts period beginning on or before 30 June 1999, and to one beginning after that date. An example would be an income tax return where the profits for the year of assessment are those of a period straddling a 30 June 1999 accounting date.

In this situation, the two accounts periods are dealt with separately, applying the general principles described in this article for open returns related to periods of account beginning respectively on or before, or after, the 30 June 1999 cut off date.

CASES WHERE THE RETURN IS CLOSED

If the return is closed, the treatment of deferred revenue expenditure can only be raised if the Inspector makes a discovery. In practice a discovery is unlikely as deferred revenue expenditure is usually clearly shown on the face of the computations.

INFORMAL UNDERSTANDINGS

In the case that an informal understanding has been reached with the Inspector on the treatment of deferred revenue expenditure, this should be reviewed and unwound as soon as practicable. This may involve negotiation with the Inspector depending upon the particular circumstances. The aim is to ensure that all taxpayers are brought onto the proper footing as quickly as possible.

If, owing to exceptional circumstances in any particular case, there are difficulties in applying the approaches detailed in this article, taxpayers should contact their local inspector for further advice. This article does not affect any other technical points under enquiry.

Note—This Interpretation has been superseded by the Business Income Manual BIM42215.

RI 232 (August 2001) *Change of interpretation: Non-resident trusts—gains and losses accruing in the transitional period to trusts brought within the settlor charge by FA 1998—treatment for tax year 1999/2000*

SUMMARY

This change of view is applicable only to non-resident trusts which were outside the scope of the TCGA 1992 s 86 settlor charge until the enactment of FA 1998 s 132.

As a consequence of recent legal advice, the Revenue has changed its position on the availability of net losses realised by non-resident trustees in the ''transitional period'' from 17 March 1998 to 5 April 1999 for set off against capital gains accruing to such trustees during 1999/2000, in respect of which a settlor is chargeable under TCGA 1992 s 86. Until now we have taken the view that net capital losses incurred in the transitional period are not available for set off against 1999/2000 gains. However we now accept that such losses can in fact be set off in this way.

Similarly, the Revenue now accepts that net losses incurred by non-resident trustees in 1999/2000 can be set against gains arising in the transitional period in respect of which a settlor is chargeable under section 86.

ACTION

Settlors affected by the transitional provisions whose capital gains position for 1999/2000 has been settled on the basis of our previous interpretation may now amend their self assessments for 1999/2000 in order to put into effect our changed interpretation. The amended self assessment must be submitted before the time limit for amending self assessments expires. In most cases this will be 31 January 2002.

BACKGROUND

Section 86, TCGA 1992, which charges certain UK domiciled and resident settlors in respect of gains realised by non-resident, or dual resident trustees, was first enacted in FA 1991. This 'settlor charge' taxes settlors of trusts in respect of the capital gains accruing from disposals of trust assets by the trustees, where the settlor or certain members of his family has an interest in the trust and certain other conditions are met. The 1991 legislation excluded from the charge all non-resident trusts created before Budget day, 19 March 1991, subject to certain conditions. Trusts whose gains are within the scope of section 86 are known as 'qualifying settlements'.

Under FA 1998 s 132, all trusts created before 19 March 1991 and otherwise meeting the conditions in section 86, were brought within the definition of qualifying settlements. This was announced on Budget Day 1998 (17 March) and took effect from 6 April 1999. The period from 17 March 1998 to 5 April 1999 was covered by transitional provisions. These are at FA 1998 Sch 23.

The aim of the transitional provisions was to allow time for trustees not wishing their trusts to become qualifying settlements to remove them from the scope of the settlor charge (eg by removing beneficiaries from the trust, or by certain other means). There were also anti-avoidance provisions to stop trustees realising gains in the transitional period and then removing their trusts from the scope of the settlor charge before 6 April 1999. For those trusts where the requisite steps to remain outside TCGA 1992 s 86 were not taken by 6 April 1999, paragraph 1(2)(*a*) of FA 1998 Sch 23 applied to treat gains and losses arising between 17 March 1998 and 5 April 1999 as accruing on 6 April 1999 for the purposes of the settlor charge.

Until now our interpretation of the transitional provisions has been that a settlor is taxable in 1999/2000 on any net gain arising in the transitional period, but any net loss arising in the transitional period cannot be set off against any actual gains accruing in 1999/2000. Equally, we considered that losses incurred in 1999/2000 were not available for setting off against net gains which arose during the transitional period. This view was seen as consistent with the general basis of the settlor charge, which attributes only net gains, and not losses, to settlors, and with FA 1998 s 132(5), which prohibits gains and losses arising before 6 April 1999 from being taken into account for the purposes of TCGA 1992 s 86.

However, following recent legal advice we now accept that the wording of paragraph 1(2)(*a*) FA 1998 Sch 23 allows for both net gains, and net losses, to be treated as accruing on 6 April 1999.

CONSEQUENCES

In cases falling within the provisions of paragraph 1(2)(*a*) of FA 1998 Sch 23:

1. Net capital losses arising on disposals made between 17 March 1998 and 5 April 1999 are available for set off against net capital gains accruing on disposals made between 6 April 1999 and 5 April 2000, for the purposes of calculating the amount on which a settlor is chargeable for 1999/2000 under section 86. To the extent that such losses are not so utilised, they will be available for carry forward in accordance with paragraph 1(6) TCGA 1992 Sch 5, and so may reduce the amount on which a settlor is charged under TCGA 1992 s 86 for a later year.
2. Net capital losses arising on disposals made between 6 April 1999 and 5 April 2000 are available for set off against net capital gains arising on disposals made between 17 March 1998 and 5 April 1999, for the purpose of calculating the amount on which a settlor is chargeable under TCGA 1992 s 86 for 1999/2000.

This interpretation will apply to all current open and future self assessments for 1999/2000. As noted above self assessments for 1999/2000 already settled on the basis of our previous view may be reopened, but the amended self assessment must be submitted to the Revenue before the time limit under TMA 1970 s 9(4)(*b*) expires.

Commentary—*Simon's Direct Tax Service* **C4.437–439**.

RI 233 (August 2001) *Capital gains tax (CGT): holdings of shares—matching acquisitions and disposals—a second instalment*

An article on matching share acquisitions and disposals in Inland Revenue *Tax Bulletin* Issue 52 published in April 2001, set out the Revenue's views on how the matching rules work in some circumstances. The points concerned the "same day" rule in TCGA 1992 s 105 and the "bed and breakfasting" rule in s 106A(5). This second article discusses how the matching rules work when shares are transferred between a married couple and TCGA 1992 s 58(1) applies so that the transfer is treated as being made at no gain/no loss to the transferor.

Whenever necessary, this article assumes that—

- section 58(1) applies to the transfer between husband and wife;
- the normal share matching rules in s 106A apply; and
- purchases and sales are at arm's length to unconnected persons.

The first point in relation to husbands and wives is that a transfer under s 58(1) of shares, or any other asset, is still a disposal by one spouse and an acquisition by the other one for CGT purposes. Section 58(1) does not change the date on which either spouse's disposal or acquisition are made. It simply fixes the disposal and acquisition value at whatever amount results in there being neither gain nor loss on the transfer.

From the point of view of the spouse making the disposal, this means that the shares transferred are identified with acquisitions under the normal s 106A rules, and the deemed amount of consideration for the transfer follows from that. From the other spouse's angle, those shares are treated as a single acquisition and will be matched with disposals by him/her under the normal rules by reference to the date on which they were acquired on the transfer.

If and when the transferee spouse comes to dispose of the shares and needs to work out what taper relief is available, he/she will have to take into account TCGA 1992 Sch A1 para 15. This lays down that, where there is a transfer within s 58(1), the transferee spouse is treated for the purposes of taper relief as acquiring the asset at the time when the other spouse originally acquired it. This is relevant to determining the transferee spouse's qualifying holding period and the relevant period of ownership. There is therefore a tension between—

- the basic identification rule, which treats the shares as acquired at the date of the transfer, and
- the taper rule, which looks back to the date of original acquisition by the first spouse.

This tension does not matter either if the shares transferred were originally acquired on the same day, or if they were acquired on different days but the transferee spouse disposes of them all in one go. In this latter case the different holding periods or relevant periods of ownership are simply applied to the relevant parts of the total holding. But if the shares transferred were originally acquired on different days, and the spouse receiving the shares disposes of only some of them, it is not immediately clear how to work out the holding period(*s*) and relevant period(*s*) of ownership of the shares disposed of on that occasion.

Our view is that in these circumstances—

– the spouse receiving the shares is treated as acquiring them as a single asset;
– a disposal of some of those shares is therefore a part-disposal and the cost of the shares is apportioned under the normal part-disposal formula in s 42;
– the s 42 apportionment does not attribute to the cost of the holding to any particular shares within it; and
– for taper purposes you apply the normal LIFO (last in, first out) rule in working out the period for which the shares disposed of have been held by both spouses overall.

A simple illustration of how this works out in practice is as follows—

– on 1 June 1998 Jack buys 3,000 shares in XYZ plc at £2.50 = total cost £7,500;
– on 1 July 1999 Jack buys another 1,000 shares in XYZ plc at £3.00 = total cost £3,000;
– on 1 January 2000 Jack transfers 1,500 of the total 4,000 shares to his wife Jill;
– on 1 August 2001 Jill sells 1,200 of her 1,500 shares at £4.00 = total proceeds £4,800.

Jack's position is simple. The 1,500 shares he gave to Jill on 1 January 2000 comprised the 1,000 shares acquired on 1 July 1999 and 500 of the 3,000 shares acquired on 1 June 1998, under the LIFO rule. His disposal proceeds under the no gain/no loss rule in s 58(1) are—

– 1,000 shares at £3 = £3,000
– + 500 shares at £2.50 = £1,250
– deemed disposal proceeds = £4,250

Jill's disposal on 1 August 2001 produces a gain as follows—

– disposal proceeds (ignoring disposal costs) = £4,800
– cost £4,250 × [1,200*/1,500] = £3,400
– chargeable gain = £1,400

*the pragmatic method of apportionment under s 42 by reference to the number of shares disposed of and retained, adopted in the capital gains manual at paragraphs CG50727–8.

For taper relief purposes Jill must look through her acquisition to the original purchases by Jack in order to work out her total holding period. These shares were originally acquired by Jack as follows, again applying the LIFO rule—

– 1,000 were acquired on 1 July 1999
– 500 were acquired on 1 June 1998.

5/6ths (1,000/1,200) of the chargeable gain arises on an asset that was held for two whole years and 1/6th on an asset held for three whole years. Taper relief will be calculated accordingly.

Commentary—*Simon's Direct Tax Service* **C1.202.**

RI 234 (August 2001) *Anticipated income tax loss claims*

We have been asked why we do not process income tax loss claims under TA 1988 s 380, 381 which are made before the end of the accounting period giving rise to the loss. In this article, the term "accounting period" is used to refer to a period for which accounts are drawn up.

In the help sheet IR227 on IT losses we say that people can claim loss relief as soon as they know how big the loss is. Normally that will be when the accounts have been prepared. But we do not insist that loss relief claims should be quantified precisely. A "best estimate" claim could be made in advance of accounts being prepared, with the final figure following as soon as possible.

However, our view is that it is not possible to anticipate a loss by claiming it before the end of the accounting period.

In most cases a taxpayer will not be able to establish with any certainty until the accounting period is finished that they have made a loss. It would be unusual for a trader to know that a loss had been made before having evidence for it, in the form of their accounts.

But in some rare situations it may be possible to say even before the end of the accounting period that there has been a loss, and to quantify it with some accuracy. One example is where a partnership is set up to invest in UK films. The only transaction in an accounting period may be an investment in a single qualifying film, giving a very high certainty that a loss will be made. And the approximate size of the loss may be quantifiable at a very early stage.

Even if we are satisfied that there would be an economic loss (ie the outgoings will exceed all possible income for the period) it is not possible to say that a loss has arisen for tax purposes until the accounting period is complete.

In the case of Jones v O'Brien (60 TC 706), involving Case V income, Hoffman J as he then was held that the Revenue could not raise an in-year estimated assessment on income assessed on a current year basis:

> *"Schedule D charges annual profits or gains and tax chargeable under Case V on profits or gains arising in Ireland is computed on the full amount of the income arising in the year of assessment. There is no charge to tax on the income per diem in diem as it arises during the year. In my view the imposition of liability to tax on the full amount of the income arising in a year necessarily entails that the year has elapsed. Until then the profits in respect of which he is liable to tax will not exist and therefore no charge to tax can attach."*

TA 1988 s 382(3) provides that losses shall be computed "in like manner and in respect of the same period" as profits. This means that the comments in the O'Brien case are equally applicable to anticipated loss claims.

The same principle applies where the results of more than one accounting period are required to compute the profit/loss for a year of assessment.

For example, a trader's first accounting period may run from 1 December 2000 to 31 January 2001 and give rise to a loss. But they cannot claim loss relief until all of the accounting periods which will contribute to the profit/loss for 2000–01 are complete. Only then is it possible to say whether a loss exists for 2000–01.

This is in contrast to what happens with a continuing business. A trader might contact their tax office on 28 February 2002, claiming to carry back losses from their accounts to 31 October 2001 (2001–02) against other income for 2000–01. In those circumstances there would be no problem with our processing the request as a stand-alone claim (TMA 1970 Sch 1B) immediately. We would not need to know the business results for the rest of 2001–02 because they relate to the following year of assessment.

It may be worth reminding readers about another related matter concerning loss carry back claims. A claim to carry back relief relates to the later year. So although relief is given in terms of the reduced liability of the earlier period, the self assessment for the earlier period is not affected. Payments on account for the later year will be based on the liability for the earlier year before the carry back claim was made.

It may be appropriate however to make a claim to reduce the payments on account for the later year because the total income tax and Class 4 NICs payable for the later year (less any tax deducted at source) will be less than the total of the payments on account based on the liability for the previous year.

Take the case of someone who draws up their accounts to 31 March, and who has net income tax and Class 4 liability for 1999–00 of £10,000. This is payable as follows—

- *1st payment on account 31 January 2000 £4,000;*
- *2nd payment on account 31 July 2000 £4,000;*
- *balancing payment 31 January 2001 £2,000.*

The payments on account have been paid but the balancing payment remains outstanding.

Payments on account of £5,000 each are set up for 2000–01, payable on 31 January 2001 and 31 July 2001. These have not been paid.

On 20 April 2001 they make a claim to carry back losses from the year 2000–01 to 1999–00, based on a "best estimate" of their loss for the year to 31 March 2001. At the same time, they claim to reduce the payments on account for 2000–01 to £1,000 each on the grounds that their net liability for that year will be less than the payments on account based on 1999–00.

The estimated loss relief amounts to £5,000. They will get the relief as follows—

- *£2,000 is set off against the balancing payment due on 31 January 2001 with an effective date of 20 April 2001;*
- *£1,000 is set off against the (revised) first payment on account due on 31 January 2001 with an effective date of 20 April 2001 (interest under TMA s 86 is due on both these charges, from 31 January 2001 to 20 April 2001);*
- *£2,000 is repaid (no repayment supplement is payable);*

The 2nd payment on account due on 31 July 2001 is £1,000.

The same principle applies to all types of claim covered by Sch 1B.

Note—This Interpretation has been superseded by the Business Income Manual BIM75050.
Commentary—*Simon's Direct Tax Service* **A2.605, E1.601, E1.832.**

RI 235 (October 2001) *Foot and mouth disease*

This article supplements the material in the special foot and mouth edition of *Tax Bulletin* issued in May this year.

HERD BASIS AND PARTNERSHIP CHANGES

It is fairly well known that a herd basis election comes to an end when there is a change in the membership of a partnership. This is because the new partnership is a different farmer for the purposes of the herd basis from the old one. So a genuine partnership change between the compulsory slaughter of a herd and replacement may serve to crystallise a tax free gain on the sale of the herd. But the cost of the new herd will not, of course, be allowable.

We have been asked whether a herd basis election lapses if a partnership converts to a limited liability partnership (LLP) without a change in membership. The answer in our view is no. This is because the LLP is deemed to be a partnership, has the same members, and so is not a different farmer.

SLAUGHTER OF IMMATURE ANIMALS INTENDED TO BE REPLACEMENTS

Ministers have approved a new concession to help with a situation which was not contemplated when the herd basis rules were written. Where a farmer buys in or breeds replacements for ewes culled from his herd they do not normally (there are special rules for home bred replacements in hefted flocks) enter the herd until they bear their first lamb. That is because of the definition of maturity in the herd basis rules (TA 1988 Sch 5 para 8(2)–(4)). In some flocks slaughter took place this year during lambing with the result that some ewes were slaughtered before they gave birth but others from the same batch of intended replacements may have had lambs at foot when they were slaughtered.

This may lead to an unexpected profit because animals which were slaughtered before they enter the herd are treated as trading stock. The concession, which applies to animals slaughtered as a result of the present outbreak of foot and mouth disease, enables farmers to treat such animals as if they had entered the herd before slaughter. Similar situations may arise with animals other than sheep so the concession is written in general terms. The text is as follows:

Where—

– a farmer has disposed of production animals subject to a herd basis election with the intention of replacing them with young animals which would have qualified as replacements when they gave birth to their first young; and
– the intended replacements did not give birth to their first young because they were slaughtered while pregnant as a result of the 2001 foot and mouth disease outbreak;
– the intended replacements may be regarded as mature for the purposes of TA 1988 Sch 5 para 8(4).

The concession does not apply to animals which were intended to be additions to a herd but any profit arising on the slaughter of such animals may be spread under ESC B11.

FORWARD SPREADING UNDER ESC B11

The Inspectors Manual at IM2268b says that spreading under concession B11 applies to mature animals which do not constitute the whole, or a substantial part, of a production herd. This may be incorrect on a strict reading of the concession but we do not propose to change it while the current outbreak of foot and mouth continues.

Later IM2268b suggests that for animals borne in the year of slaughter profit can be computed as compensation less 75%. That figure is correct for sheep and pigs but the figure for cattle in BEN19 is 60%. The use of 60% for cattle will be acceptable to the Revenue here as well.

If the trade is carried on in partnership, spreading under ESC B11 applies at partner rather than partnership level (IM2268c). Where a partner wishes to claim, the reduction should be made in box 4.8 of the partnership pages of the partner's personal tax return. An explanatory note should be included in the additional information box 4.79. We are grateful to people who have pointed out that there is nowhere obvious for partners to include the profit spread forward in subsequent returns. We will deal with this point in the guidance to next year's returns.

FOOT AND MOUTH DISEASE—QUALITY OF REPLACEMENT ANIMALS

Where animals which are part of a production herd on the herd basis are slaughtered because of the present outbreak of foot and mouth disease a special provision in the herd basis rules may be relevant.

When animals on the herd basis rules are replaced the normal rules provide that the proceeds of the old animal are included and the cost (subject to an appropriate restriction if the replacement is of better quality) of the new animal is deducted in computing the farming profits. The special rule in TA 1988 Sch 5 para 3(6) (IM2305) says that if slaughtered animals are replaced by animals of lower quality then the amount included as a trading receipt shall not exceed the amount allowable as a deduction. The effect is that when a farmer replaces a herd with animals of lower quality which cost less than the compensation received for the old animals, the excess of the compensation over the cost of the new animals is not taxable.

We have been asked how we interpret the term ''quality'' in this context. The point may be of particular relevance when the animals concerned are expensive pedigree bulls or rams.

The quality of an animal is a question of fact. Farmers will generally have well informed views on the quality of their animals. It does not follow that if the cost of the replacement is lower or higher than the proceeds of the animal slaughtered then the quality is lower or higher for two reasons—

- Quality does not depend upon age. But the compensation might reflect the fact that the animal concerned was getting to the end of its productive life. A replacement might cost more because it was younger.
- Price depends upon the state of the market on the day. There is a strong correlation between quality and price so a good animal will fetch a better price than a poor one. But a poor one next month might cost more or less than a good one this month.

In many cases the amount of compensation for the slaughtered animals depended upon quality and professional valuers advised when compensation was quantified. In the event of doubt the farmer might instruct the same valuer to give an opinion as to whether the replacements were of different quality.

If there are disputes which cannot be settled by agreement they will be referred to the Commissioners who are arbiters on questions of fact. Our experience after the 1967 outbreak of foot and mouth disease is that such action was very seldom necessary.

Commentary—*Simon's Direct Tax Service* **Division B3.5**.

RI 236 (October 2001) *Sugar beet outgoers scheme*

INTRODUCTION

British Sugar and the NFU announced on 23 July 2001 a new, one-off, scheme that allows sugar beet growers to relinquish all or part of their contract tonneage entitlement. We have been asked about the taxation consequences for farmers who sell or buy contract tonneage entitlement. We consider that the transactions are on Revenue account, with the result that amounts received are taxable receipts of the trade and amounts paid are deductible in computing trading profits.

WHY TRANSACTIONS ARE ON REVENUE ACCOUNT

Sugar beet contracts are sometime described as sugar beet quota. This is a misnomer which can lead to misunderstandings and should be avoided. Sugar beet contracts are not quotas but may be best understood as annual personal contracts, between British Sugar and the farmer, for the supply and delivery of a maximum tonneage of sugar beet to an identified processing plant. As such they are part of the ordinary arrangements farmers make for disposing of their products.

There is a long succession of decided tax cases where sums derived from the disposal of such contracts have been held to be income. Taxpayers (or the Revenue when the case was about an expense) have argued that contracts were fundamental to the structure of the business and therefore capital assets following *Van den Berghs Ltd v Clark* (1935) 19 TC 390. But it is only where a contract is one the cancellation of which would effectively destroy or cripple the whole structure of the taxpayer's profit-making apparatus that it falls to be treated exceptionally as a capital asset. That is not the case here.

The decisions of the Special Commissioners in the cases of *Croydon Hotel & Leisure Co Ltd v Bowen* (1996) SpC 101 [see *Simon's Weekly Tax Intelligence* 1996 p 1635] and *A Consultant v H M Insp of Taxes* (1998) SpC 180 [see *Simon's Weekly Tax Intelligence* 1999 p 161] show how difficult it is for an argument based on the *Van den Burghs* case to succeed.

In farming cases it is also necessary to take account of the statutory definition of farming in TA 1988 s 832 as the occupation of land for the purposes of husbandry. It is the land that is fundamental to a farming business. Payments which result from changes in the way it is farmed are very unlikely to be on capital account. An example is the payments for conversion from dairying to beef production in *White v G & M Davies* [[1979] STC 415] and *IRC v Biggar* [[1982] STC 672].

TIMING OF REVENUE DEDUCTIONS

We understand that accounts prepared in accordance with generally accepted accountancy practice will show payments for contract tonneage entitlement on the balance sheet and amortise them over the period for which they may reasonably be expected to be of value to the business.

Where revenue expenditure is treated in this way the amortisation charged to profit and loss account is allowable. For a more detailed explanation of the principles involved please see the article ''Deferred revenue expenditure'' in the June 2001 edition of *Tax Bulletin* [see *Simon's Weekly Tax Intelligence* 2001 p 933] at www.inlandrevenue.gov.uk/bulletins.

LANDLORDS

Our understanding is that landlords do not have an interest in transactions in contract tonneage entitlement by their tenants unless there is a clause in the tenancy agreement or a separate agreement which gives them one. If there is such a provision then the tax treatment of sums received under it will depend upon its terms so we cannot make any general statement.

Commentary—*Simon's Direct Tax Service* **Division B3.5**.

RI 237 (December 2001) *Travel expenses of employees not domiciled in the UK*

TRAVELLING EXPENSES OF EMPLOYEE'S FAMILY

TA 1988 s 195 applies to the travelling expenses of employees who are not domiciled in the UK but perform the duties of an employment in this country. It permits a deduction from emoluments chargeable to tax under either Case I or Case II of Schedule E in circumstances where TA 1988 s 198 would not apply.

The expenses of an employee's family in travelling between the UK and their normal place of abode in another country will also qualify for a deduction under s 195 where the following conditions are satisfied—

- The employee must be domiciled in a state other than the UK and receive emoluments from duties of an office or employment performed in the UK.
- The cost of travel by family members must be borne or reimbursed by (or on behalf of) the employer and be an assessable emolument of the employee.
- The employee must be present in the UK for the purpose of performing the duties of one or more offices or employments for a continuous period of 60 days or more.
- The journey has to be undertaken by the family to either—
  - accompany the employee at the beginning of the continuous period of 60 days or more; or
  - visit the employee during such a period or to return afterwards.
- The journey must be made within five years of a qualifying arrival in the UK by the employee.

The deduction is limited to two outward and two return journeys by the same person in any year of assessment. For guidance on how these conditions apply in practice see SE35000 in the Inland Revenue *Schedule E Manual*.

MEANING OF A CONTINUOUS PERIOD OF 60 DAYS OR MORE

We have been asked about the requirement in s 195(6) that "the employee is in the UK for a continuous period of 60 days or more". Our current approach, described at SE35050, has been to ignore an occasional day's absence from the UK due to a genuine business trip abroad. However, an increasing number of non-domiciled employees who are based in the UK are required to travel extensively outside the UK. These employees are finding it increasingly difficult to satisfy the 60 days rule because they are outside the UK for more than one day at a time.

From the date of this publication, therefore, we are prepared to accept that, for the purposes of s 195(6) only, employees satisfy the 60 days rule where—

- they spend at least two thirds of their working days in the UK over a period of 60 days or more; and
- they are present in the UK for the purpose of performing the duties of their employment both at the start and at the end of this period.

This will make it easier for employees who are sent to work in the UK and who travel outside the UK on business to satisfy the conditions permitting a deduction for family travel expenses. We think that this more accurately reflects employment in international business whilst preventing a deduction for travelling expenses of an employee's family where the employee simply makes frequent short business trips to the UK. This will apply to any self-assessment made from now on or to any self-assessment that can be amended within the usual time limits.

This approach will also apply to liability to Class 1 national insurance contributions as the Social Security (Contributions) Regulations, SI 2001/1004 Sch 3 Part VIII para 5 was aligned with s 195 with effect from 6 April 2001.

The following three examples show how the new approach may work in practice.

EXAMPLE 1A

Anita has been sent to the UK to work for 12 months as a project manager based at the European headquarters of a multi-national corporation. Her family accompanies her at the start of her assignment. During the first 60 days of her assignment, she spends 20 days working at her UK office and 10 days working outside the UK.

Anita will be entitled to a deduction for the travelling expenses of her family. She has spent two thirds or more of her working days during a 60 day period in the UK.

EXAMPLE 1B

The facts are the same as in example 1A except that during the first 60 days of her assignment, Anita spent 10 days working at her UK office and 20 days working outside the UK.

Anita does not satisfy the 60 day rule at the 60 day point. However, if she spent her next 30 working days in the UK, she would be entitled to a deduction for the travelling expenses of her family as she would have spent more than two thirds of her working days in the UK during a period of 60 days or more.

EXAMPLE 2

Jack was sent to the UK to work for the UK subsidiary of a US finance house in January 2000. He is required to travel extensively outside the UK on business.

His employer pays the travelling expenses of his family who arrive in the UK to visit him for two weeks on 1 July 2000. At that time, Jack had just returned from a five day business trip to the Far East on 30 June and was later recalled to the US on business for three days arriving back in the UK on 29 July. Between 1 June and 30 July, Jack worked on 30 days of which 21 were spent working in the UK.

Jack will be entitled to a deduction because his family visited him during a period of 60 days when two thirds or more of his working days were days spent working in the UK.

EXAMPLE 3

Sonia is sent by her French employer to work in the UK to oversee the installation and testing of a new computer system at its UK subsidiary. She arrives in the UK on 1 May 2001. She completes her UK assignment on 15 June having spent 24 out of 33 working days in the UK. Sonia then stays on in the UK to visit friends and doesn't leave until 10 July.

Her employer pays the travelling expenses of her husband who arrives in the UK to join her on 10 June.

Sonia would not be entitled to a deduction for her husband's travelling expenses. The period when she is in the UK for the purpose of performing her duties is only 46 days ie 1 May to 15 June so the 60 day rule cannot be satisfied.

FURTHER INFORMATION

Martin Delnon, Personal Tax (Technical), Sapphire House, 550 Streetsbrook Road, Solihull, B91 1QU, tel: 0121 713 4634, fax: 0121 713 4620, email: Martin.Delnon@ir.gsi.gov.uk.

Commentary—*Simon's Direct Tax Service* **E4.604, 708, 709**.

RI 238 (December 2001) *Change of interpretation—taxability of trade debt written-back*

Note—This interpretation is no longer current; reference should be made instead to the Inspector's Manual paras IM 380 and IM 381 (Business income manual paras BIM 40201, 42740).

RI 239 (December 2001) *Tax credit relief: Chile—additional tax*

The Revenue consider that the additional tax (*impuesto adicional/tasa adicional*) charged in Chile is admissible for tax credit relief (see the *Double Taxation Relief Guidance Manual* at DT4851). But following a re-examination of the nature of this tax, we have modified our view of it. The tax is computed by reference to company profits and is charged when there is a distribution of those profits to a shareholder who is not resident in Chile. Although the tax charge arises as a result of the distribution, the tax is not a withholding tax. Therefore, whilst still accepting that the tax is an admissible tax, we have concluded that it qualifies for unilateral relief as underlying tax under TA 1988 s 790(6). This means that relief for it will be allowable only to a UK company which receives a dividend from a Chilean company, where the UK company directly or indirectly controls, or is a subsidiary of a company which directly or indirectly controls, 10% or more of the voting power in the Chilean company. The amount of relief due in a particular case (including any further claims arising from this change of view) should be agreed in the usual way with Revenue Policy International, Underlying Tax Group, Fitz Roy House, PO Box 46, Nottingham, NG2 1BD.

We will not seek to withdraw relief made in accordance with previous practice, which treated the tax as a withholding tax, for returns made prior to the publication of this change of view.

Commentary—*Simon's Direct Tax Service* **F1.103, F1.149.**

RI 240 (December 2001) *Turkey—compulsory fund surcharge*

The Revenue have also reconsidered their view on the compulsory fund contribution, which is a surcharge applied to Turkish corporation tax. This surcharge has the effect of raising the rate of corporation tax. We now consider the surcharge to be a substantially similar tax to corporation tax, thus coming within art 2(4) of the double taxation agreement between the UK and Turkey. When a company resident in Turkey pays a dividend to a company resident in the UK which controls directly or indirectly at least 10% of the voting power in the company paying the dividend, the surcharge will be available for credit as underlying tax.

Any further claims to credit arising from this change of view should be sent to the Underlying Tax Group, whose address is given above.

If you have any other queries arising from these changes please contact Kevin Madley, Revenue Policy International, Victory House, 30–34 Kingsway, London, WC2B 6ES, tel: 020 7438 6306, email: Kevin.Madley@ir.gsi.gov.uk.

Commentary—*Simon's Direct Tax Service* **F2.102, F2.106, F2.107**.

RI 241 (January 2002) *Modern printing equipment—application of long-life asset rules*

INTRODUCTION

We have been asked to explain how we apply the capital allowances rules for long-life assets to equipment used in the printing industry.

Historically, equipment used in the printing industry had a long expected economic life. This is evidenced by a strong second hand market in printing presses, and by the availability in that market of a significant amount of printing equipment manufactured in the 1970's and early 1980's.

We have received representations from the printing industry that changes in practices and advances in technology in recent years mean that equipment is more likely to become obsolete in a shorter time than was previously the case. The industry has expressed concern that the Inland Revenue, in applying the capital allowances rules for long-life assets, is not taking full account of the changes that have taken place.

This article outlines our approach to the long-life asset rules generally, and explains how we would expect the rules to apply to modern printing equipment in particular.

THE GENERAL APPROACH

The long-life asset rules apply to plant or machinery that, when new, it is reasonable to expect will have a useful economic life of at least 25 years. When applying this test each asset must be dealt with on its own facts. It is possible that two identical assets could have different expected economic lives because of the predicted use of the asset in the particular trade in which it is employed.

Where there is no established second hand market for a particular category of asset, the Inland Revenue will generally follow the depreciation policy for the asset used in the accounts, provided this is reasonable. Where, however, there is an active second hand market other factors are relevant. These include how long the particular business typically keeps that type of asset before it is replaced, whether the business has a history of selling assets into the second hand market or scrapping them, and whether there are rapid technological or market changes in the sector.

THE APPROACH TO MODERN PRINTING EQUIPMENT

We have had discussions with representatives of the printing industry and have looked at trends in the second hand market for printing equipment. We will continue to deal with each case on its own particular facts, but unless there are exceptional circumstances we accept that modern printing equipment purchased new and unused is unlikely to have an expected useful economic life of 25 years or longer. As a result, traders in the printing industry can expect to obtain the benefit of the standard writing down allowance of 25% and, if they are small or medium sized enterprises, a first year allowance of 40% of the cost.

PURCHASE OF SECOND-HAND PRINTING EQUIPMENT

Where second-hand printing equipment is acquired the treatment will depend on whether or not the seller claimed capital allowances on it. If it is acquired from a person who has claimed capital allowances on the asset the purchaser will obtain the same treatment as the seller. If the seller treated the asset as a long-life asset the purchaser will obtain relief at the 6% rate. If the seller received writing down allowance at 25% the purchaser will receive the same.

If the asset is acquired from a dealer in second-hand equipment, or another person who has not claimed capital allowances on the particular asset, then the general approach outlined above will be applied. A key additional factor to those outlined above will be the age of the equipment on acquisition.

EQUIPMENT COVERED BY THIS ARTICLE

Printing equipment broadly falls into three categories

– pre-press;

- printing presses; and
- finishing equipment.

Pre-press is a distinct function in the printing process. Pre-press equipment is used to prepare the text and images for imposition onto an image-carrying device, usually a printing plate that is then fitted to the printing press. Examples might be proofing devices, imagesetters and computer to plate devices. Advances in digital technology mean that the printing plate is becoming obsolete. Products that enable images to be sent electronically to a digital or quasi-digital press are coming onto the market. Rapid technological advances mean that pre press products on the market today are becoming obsolescent in an increasingly short time.

Printing presses are the means by which the images are transposed onto paper or some other medium. The largest sector of this market is for sheet-fed offset presses. Other types of presses include heat and cold set ''web offset'' used for magazine and long run commercial print; ''flexographic'' used for packaging and labels; ''gravure'' used for long run magazines and packaging; and ''digital'' used for short run colour and variable data printing.

Finishing equipment is used for such things as folding, cutting and binding the printed product. Although very often a stand-alone investment, finishing equipment is increasingly becoming computer controlled and more productive and is acquired as an integral part of a modern printing equipment package.

Commentary—*Simon's Direct Tax Service* **B2.344.**

RI 242 (June 2002) *Depreciation in trading stock*

We have been asked to explain how a recent judgement by the UK Law Lord Lord Millett in the Hong Kong Court of Final Appeal case of IRC v Secan (FACV 9/2000) affects the treatment for tax purposes of depreciation included in trading stock.

WHAT IS DEPRECIATION IN TRADING STOCK?

For financial statements properly to reflect business costs they have to take account of the wearing out or other reduction in the useful economic life of fixed assets. Depreciation is a measure of this and is charged against income in arriving at the commercial profit. For tax purposes depreciation of fixed assets is a capital matter and therefore should be added back.

Statement of standard accounting practice (SSAP) 9 sets out the principles governing the valuation of stock. Stock is valued at the lower of cost or net realisable value. Cost should include ''those overheads (including depreciation) which relate to production'' (para 20).

Where depreciation is taken into account in arriving at the stock valuation the taxpayer may argue that the commercial profit has not been reduced by the depreciation charged to stock. So the relevant depreciation should not be added back in the tax computations until it does reduce those profits. That will normally be when the stock is sold.

SECAN

The case concerned the capitalisation of interest into trading stock/work in progress. Secan was a property development company. It had been treating interest as a development cost and adding it to the cost of its property stock, so that it was carried forward each year. When it started making sales it decided that it wanted to rewrite the accounts retrospectively so that interest was set against profits of the year in which it was incurred. The case was about whether it could do that or not.

Towards the end of his judgement Lord Millett comments on the evidence given by Secan's accountant—

> *''Mr Fong Hup explained how he prepared the taxpayer's accounts. He said that he debited the interest payable to the development cost account and took the figure directly into the balance sheet without putting it through the profit and loss account. The Court of Appeal took this to confirm what they could see with their own eyes, viz. that the interest had not been deducted in the profit and loss account.*
>
> *In fact this evidence established that the interest was deducted in computing the taxpayer's financial results. It was debited, not to the profit and loss account, but to the development cost account, another revenue account, in which the costs of the development including interest were duly entered. Mr Fong Hup's statement that he took the figure straight to the balance sheet is an abbreviated version of the truth. It is true in the trivial sense that the development cost account was the source of the figure which he entered in the balance sheet for the value of property under development. But, as I have explained, although the two figures are the same they do not represent the same thing. The cost of the development is a debit—'property under development' in the balance sheet is an asset. Accountants do not possess a philosopher's stone which can turn a debit into an asset. The figure which Mr Fong Hup took from the development cost account represented the cost of the development; the figure which he entered in the balance sheet represented the value of the development. In the process he must be taken mentally to*

have set them off against each other, and because they cancelled each other out there was no net balance to bring into the profit and loss account.

The taxpayer's accounts contain a note explaining the treatment of interest. This is required by the Companies Ordinance. Shareholders are entitled to be told whether interest has been capitalised and if so how much. They are entitled to know how much of the value of the assets shown in the balance sheet is attributable to capitalised interest, since this is a very weak indication of value. It is dependent on the directors' belief that the market value of the asset has appreciated since its purchase by an amount at least equal to the amount of interest which the company has incurred, and this may be optimistic. In the present case the note correctly shows the amount of interest payable as a debit and a like sum of capitalised interest as a credit. One figure represents the cost of interest taken from the development cost account. The other figure represents the matching amount of value taken to the balance sheet.''

HOW THIS RELATES TO DEPRECIATION IN TRADING STOCK

Secan is not a precedent in UK law. But the relevant Hong Kong tax law is very close to UK tax law, and the relevant accountancy principles are pretty much the same. We believe that Lord Millett's judgement would have been in identical terms had the point arisen first in the House of Lords. So it is extremely persuasive.

In our view his analysis provides a complete answer to the assertion that, if depreciation of fixed assets is included in the valuation of stock, only the net amount of depreciation has been charged against profits, and so only that amount should be added back.

Where depreciation is included in trading stock taxpayers are deducting the full amount of depreciation in their profit and loss account and are bringing in a credit representing the value of the stock on the other side of the profit and loss account. The fact that the ''cost'' or fall in value of the fixed assets has been included as part of the value to the taxpayer of the stock carried forward does not mean that the full amount of depreciation has not been charged to the profit and loss account. Further, even if the accounts show only the ''net'' figure charged to profit and loss account, this is irrelevant. It is not a matter of accounting principle. Rather it is, in Lord Millet's words, ''merely a matter of presentation''.

Where an adjustment to the depreciation add-back in respect of depreciation in trading stock has been an accepted part of tax computations taxpayers will now have to move to the correct basis for computing taxable profits. The treatment for tax purposes of this ''change of basis'' is covered by proposed legislation in this year's Finance Bill (clause 63 and Sch 22).

Note—This Interpretation has been superseded by the Business Income Manual BIM33190.
Commentary—*Simon's Direct Tax Service* **Division B3.12.**

RI 243 (August 2002) *Private Finance Initiative (PFI) projects—scope of trade*

We have been asked to clarify the approach we take to establishing the scope of trades carried on by private sector entities involved in PFI projects. This article follows consultation with the PFI working group referred to in Tax Bulletin Issue 40 (April 1999).

SUMMARY

The scope of a particular trade is essentially a question of fact. In some PFI cases we have accepted that the scope of the trade includes design and construction services as well as other support services.

BACKGROUND

In a typical PFI transaction a private sector entity (the ''operator'') contracts to provide services to a public sector body (the ''purchaser'') for a period, in return for annual service charges (the unitary charges). This will often involve the operator in the design and construction of a facility, for example a prison, hospital, or road.

Previous Tax Bulletin articles on PFI (Tax Bulletin Issue 40 (April 1999) and Tax Bulletin Issue 43 (October 1999) were specifically concerned with projects where, on the facts, it was clear that the operator's design and construction costs were capital expenditure for tax purposes. That is, the facility was a fixed capital asset of the operator's business, irrespective of whether the accounting treatment showed it as ''off balance sheet to the operator''. For a brief review of the relevant accounting treatment anticipated when dealing with PFI contracts—see Tax Bulletin Issue 40 (April 1999).

PFI projects can be structured in a variety of ways and the trade of a PFI operator can cover a wide range of activities. At one end of the spectrum is the operator who builds a facility as the setting in which to carry on the trade. An example is the operator whose trade is running a prison and who constructs a prison on land acquired for that purpose. There is the operator who builds a facility in order to rent it out, with related support services. For example an operator acquires land to build a hospital, leases it to an NHS Trust and also provides non clinical support services to the lessee by way of trade. In both of these examples the construction costs are capital expenditure for tax purposes and relief is only available against Schedule A or Case I income to the extent that it qualifies for capital allowances.

At the other end of the spectrum is the PFI operator who does not acquire a major interest in land, such as a freehold or leasehold, and whose trade is the provision of design, construction and maintenance services. An example is the operator who contracts to build and maintain a road or hospital on land that belongs to the purchaser. In such circumstances the design and construction costs, together with the costs of any other services provided, are revenue expenditure for tax purposes. None of this expenditure will qualify for capital allowances.

SCOPE OF TRADE

The question of whether or not a PFI operator is carrying on a trade of providing services is, generally, not in dispute. The scope of such a trade is a separate question.

As noted above, this is essentially a question of fact. Each case will depend upon its own particular facts and it is not, therefore, possible to provide a definitive checklist of all the factors to consider. However, the intention of the operator, the terms of the PFI agreement, as well as what the operator actually does, are all relevant factors.

The operator's stated intention does not, by itself, resolve the question of the scope of the trade. As Lord Justice Atkin noted, in Collins v The Firth-Brearley Stainless Steel Syndicate Ltd (9 TC 520) at p. 573—

> *"In order to examine the facts you must look at what the company purported to do, and also at what it in fact did".*

Where the facts point to a different conclusion, as for example in the case of the Alianza Company Ltd v Bell (5 TC 60), the stated intention cannot prevail over what it is that the operator in fact does. The question is what trade is actually carried on, not what trade the operator claims to carry on. However, where the facts are equivocal, the intention of the operator may well be a relevant factor in reaching a conclusion.

Note—This Interpretation has been superseded by the Business Income Manual BIM64025.

RI 244 (August 2002) *Shares & share options—internationally mobile employees & other international issues*

FOLLOW-UP TO TB46, 55 AND 56

The articles in *Tax Bulletin* Issue 55 (October 2001) and *Tax Bulletin* Issue 56 (December 2001) generated considerable interest. This further article is in response. It clarifies certain aspects and also deals with other questions on international issues that have been raised on taxation and National Insurance Contributions (NIC) with regard to shares and share options.

Q1 Is relief by allocation of taxing rights ONLY available if the five factors detailed in Tax Bulletin Issue 55 are present?

Tax Bulletin Issue 55 stated—

To avoid double taxation, where an employee—

- was granted a share option in the UK during the course of an employment;
- exercised that employment in the other country during the period between the grant and exercise of the option;
- remains in that employment at the date of the exercise;
- would be taxed by both of them in respect of the option gain; and
- is not resident in the UK at the date of exercise;

then the UK will give relief in calculating the tax charge for the proportion of the option gain which relates to the period or periods between the grant and exercise of the option during which the employee exercised the employment in the other country.

The article was written to give certainty in the most common situation where double taxation arises, which is when all five factors are present. But this section has been interpreted as meaning that relief by time apportioning the gain will be due only when all of the factors are present. This is incorrect. There are other situations in which some relief by allocation of taxing rights may be appropriate, for example if the employment ceased shortly before the options were exercised. However there are many permutations possible and it would not have been constructive to try and deal with all of these in that article. Cases that do not fall within the circumstances described in *Tax Bulletin* Issue 55 will continue to be considered on their own facts.

Q2 Does an employment "continue" if the employee changes contractual employer on being relocated?

If the employers were in the same group of companies and the change did not affect the employee's stock option rights, then the UK would normally regard it as one employment for the purposes of apportioning the option gain attributable to the UK.

Q3 Tax Bulletin Issue 55 says that alternative methods of apportionment may only be used "very occasionally". Is this a change from previous policy?

No. The Inland Revenue has always maintained that time-apportionment should be the expectation and in practice few cases have been seen claiming another basis. We are continuing to look at such claims on their merits, if necessary consulting with the other country concerned. However, this is one area in which an international consensus is evolving.

Q4 Is it necessary for the country of residence to actually tax the gain?

The normal expectation would be that tax would actually be levied. *Tax Bulletin* Issue 55 was worded so that absolute certainty could be given to people in the most common situation. Relief may be due in some other cases, but this depends on the country and particular circumstances involved.

Q5 If the employee is resident and ordinarily resident in the UK both when the option is granted and when it is exercised, can the gain ever be time-apportioned in the UK? Example 4 of Tax Bulletin Issue 55 implies that it can.

The statement that "a claim may be relevant under the employment income Article" does not mean that relief would be due by leaving out of account a part of the gain that related to overseas employment. It was meant to reflect that relief by means of credit might be available if the UK recognised that another country had a valid claim to tax part of the gain because it could be said to be derived from employment performed there.

Q6 Does it matter whether the option is over shares in an overseas or a UK company?

In general, no. The source for double taxation treaty purposes will be the employment, and where it is carried on.

Q7 Is any relief due on an option gain if an employee were resident in the UK at the date of grant but resident in a non-treaty country at the date of exercise?

The whole gain is taxable in the UK under TA 1988 s 135. If there were overseas tax payable on any part of the share option gain, the UK would consider unilateral relief on a claim. However, unilateral relief may only be given by means of giving credit, not by time-apportioning a gain. The amount of unilateral relief may never exceed what would be available if a double taxation treaty with the country existed.

Q8 Why have some important issues, such as periods of residence in a third country, short-term business visitors, or what happens when an option vests before it is exercised, not been covered in Tax Bulletin Issue 55?

Tax Bulletin Issue 55 said that the UK is actively involved in work at the Organisation for Economic Co-operation and Development (OECD) to reach a common international consensus on the treatment of share option gains. The OECD has now published a discussion paper on the OECD website at www.oecd.org/pdf/M00026000/M00026818.pdf.

This paper covers many of these topics. In practice many have only been seen infrequently in the UK. They have been dealt with on an individual basis, sometimes when international dialogue was in the early stages. As common international practices develop the UK is likely to harmonise its own rules in line with these. It would therefore be premature for the UK to publish guidelines based on past practice if some realignment becomes necessary. In the meantime specific cases arising in practice should continue to be referred to Susan New at the address below.

Q9 Why are NICs payable on the full gain rather than the amount taxable under PAYE?

The NICs legislation is clearly underpinned to the amount of tax chargeable under TA 1988 s 135 on any gain, not what is eventually taxed after relief. There are no contribution relief provisions under Social Security legislation, European Union (EU) legislation, Reciprocal Agreements (RA) or Double Contribution Conventions (DCC).

Q10 Are UK NICs payable on any gain on exercise of a share option where the gain has already been subject to the legislation of another European Economic Area (EEA), RA or DCC country?

No. There can never be a dual liability on the same payment of earnings. We will usually seek to apply UK legislation on the amount of gain chargeable to tax under TA 1988 s 135 arising from exercise of a share option granted in the UK where that gain was not subject to legislation of the host country. This practice follows the 1997 European Commission Agreement referred to in *Tax Bulletin* Issue 56 example but may depend on the country and particular circumstances involved.

Q11 Can share options fall within the 1997 European Commission Agreement?

The agreement referred to payments of social security contributions on income. Generally, share option gains can fall within this category.

Q12 From what date does the European Commission Agreement take effect for share options?

On any gain chargeable to tax under TA 1988 s 135 arising from the exercise, assignment or release of a share option granted on or after 6 April 1999.

Q13 Is an individual, granted an option whilst in a Case II/III employment, still liable under TA 1988 s 162(1) if he has left that employment before the time that option is exercised?

No, for the following reasons—

(*a*) Section 162(1) taxes Case II/III employees who are ''employed or about to be in employment''. It makes no mention of those who used to be employed.

(*b*) If s 162(1) did apply, then s 160(1) would be applied and that section deems such a benefit to be an emolument.

(*c*) If it were an emolument, then s 19(1)(4A)(*b*) could be used to treat it as an emolument of last year of employment.

(*d*) However, the fatal flaw in this argument is that s 160(1) cannot be reached without complying with the condition in s 162(1)(*a*)+(*b*), and those conditions are not satisfied.

(*e*) Thus, when a Case II/III employee is granted an option whilst employed in UK, but exercises that option after ceasing employment there is no Schedule E liability, under s 162(1).

(*f*) It would still be possible for a NR/NOR individual to be within the charge to UK tax; the crucial test is one of employment.

(*g*) Similarly, where there is no s 162(1) liability there can be no subsequent liability under s 162(5) when the shares are sold.

(*h*) However, there will still be a potential liability under s 162(5) when the employment ceases between the time of exercise of the option and when the shares are sold, because of the provisions of s 160(3).

(*i*) There also continues to be a potential liability under the ''stop loss'' provisions of s 162(6) after employment ceases, because the employment is deemed to continue under s 162(7).

Q14 Can an interest in the shares of a foreign company gain exemption from the conditional shares legislation under TA 1988 s 140A, by virtue of the shares being only forfeitable through that company's "articles of association" under s 140C(3)?

Yes, we have changed our view of this section and what follows describes the reasons for that change and what we propose to do.

14.1 Background

Some share schemes use conditional shares, a common feature of which is shares being subject to forfeiture if certain conditions are not met. When such a condition is lifted the value of the share increases. FA 1998 introduced TA 1988 ss 140A–C to determine the tax treatment of such shares.

Section 140A exempts any direct charge under TA 1988 s 19 (Schedule E emoluments) and charges tax under Schedule E on the excess of the market value of the shares over any consideration given by the employee.

Section 140C describes the types of shares to be treated as conditional for the purposes of s 140A. Section 140C(1A) exempts shares or securities that are conditional only for the reasons set out in subsections (2) to (4).

Subsection (3) exempts shares that are conditional only by virtue of a clause in the articles of association. It does so in the following terms—

> ''This subsection applies in relation to a person if the articles of association of the company require him to offer the shares for sale or transfer them if he ceases to be an officer or employee of the company or of one or more group companies or of any group company.''

14.2 Previous Tax Bulletin Article 46

In April 2000 we published an article in Tax Bulletin 46, Employee Share Plans—Conditional Shares, which sought to explain the interpretation of TA 1988 ss 140A–H. Part of that article explained how we strictly construed the term ''articles of association'' in s 140C(3) and said that it did not extend to foreign company equivalents of UK ''articles of association''.

Since we wrote that article we have received further legal advice that has cast doubt on our strict line.

RIs

14.3 Articles of Association

Black's Legal Dictionary defines ''articles of association'' in a multi-jurisdictional context as—

> ''the document that sets forth the basic terms of a corporation's existence, including the number and classes of shares and the purposes and duration of the corporation.''

Black's also notes that in most states the articles of association are filed with the Secretary of State as part of the process of forming the corporation.

We have seen cases where foreign companies have documents called ''articles of association'', and other cases where there is a document that performs a similar function under a different (foreign) name. Failure to recognise the function that such a document serves rather than relying simply on its descriptive name could raise issues of discrimination.

14.4 Change of Revenue view

We have looked critically at s 140C(3) and now accept that our previous interpretation of the term articles of association was too narrow. Consequently we consider the exemption in s 140C(3) should also be available to non-UK companies—

– if the condition referred to in s 140C(3) is set out in a document broadly equivalent to UK articles of association and in line with the Black's definition above.

– It will be a question of fact whether the foreign document is of equivalent status and performs an equivalent function to UK articles of association.

14.5 Transitional issues

A number of issues arise where taxpayers followed our previous advice and accepted that there was no exemption under s 140C(3).

Under the previous practice they would be charged to tax (and National Insurance) for the year in which forfeiture was lifted rather than the year in which the shares were awarded.

Under the revised practice tax (and National Insurance) will be charged for the year in which the shares were awarded rather than the year in which forfeiture was lifted.

Adopting the previous practice could have led to either a higher or a lower tax/NIC charge at a later date. Taxpayers following our previous practice will not have been charged tax/NIC for the year in which the shares were awarded and would be expecting to pay (or have already returned and paid) tax/NIC when the risk of forfeiture was lifted.

As a consequence of following our previously stated practice the acquisition cost of such shares for capital gains tax purposes would be the amount on which Schedule E was charged when the risk of forfeiture was lifted. Our revised practice will give rise to a different acquisition cost for capital gains tax purposes based on the amount on which Schedule E is charged when the time the shares are awarded.

14.6 What we propose to do

We believe the number of people affected by this change is likely to be relatively small.

(a) *Where return already submitted on basis of previous advice*

We will take no action. Exceptionally, where the time limit has not yet expired for amending the return, the taxpayer will be able, should he/she so wish, to amend the return.

(b) *Where return not yet submitted*

The return, for whichever year, should be submitted in accordance with the new advice.

(c) *Error or mistake claims*

Employees who believe that they may have been overcharged to tax in an assessment, and which they have paid, because of the Revenue's previous advice may make a claim for error or mistake relief under TMA 1970 s 33. The usual conditions of that section will need to be satisfied for a claim to be accepted, including a reduction of the claim for any tax that would have been due under the new practice but which will now not be assessed (see (*a*) above). Claims should be made initially to the local inspector.

(d) *Capital gains tax*

Where a capital gain/loss on shares subject to this change of practice is or has been made, similar rules will apply to it as to the income tax gain described above.

The base cost for CGT purposes will be the value of the shares self-assessed for Income Tax purposes.

(e) *PAYE*

Where PAYE has been operated by the employer, it will not affect the operation of the self assessment rules described above, including time limits for amendment of returns. But see below regarding NIC.

(f) National Insurance Contributions

Employees and employers who believe that they may have overpaid Class 1 National Insurance, because of the Revenue's previous advice, may make a claim for a refund. Please see instructions at NIM37000 et seq. An offset for NIC that should have been paid at another time, but was not, should be made in the claim. Claims should be submitted to—National Insurance Contributions Office, Refund Group, Room BP1001, Benton Park View, Longbenton, Newcastle upon Tyne, NE98 1ZZ.

14.7 Tax Law Rewrite

In view of this Tax Bulletin article, the recently published draft Income Tax (Earnings and Pensions) Bill includes at Clause 419(5)—

> In subsection (2)(*b*) "articles of association" includes, in the case of a company incorporated under the law of a country outside the United Kingdom, any equivalent document relating to the company.

FURTHER INFORMATION

Further information on international aspects of share options may be obtained from—Susan New, Revenue Policy International, Victory House, 30-34 Kingsway, London, WC2B 6ES, telephone 020 7438 7250, email Susan.New@ir.gsi.gov.uk.

Further information on the interpretation of United Kingdom legislation on share options may be obtained from—Michael Staples, Share Schemes, New Wing, Somerset House, London, WC2 1LB, telephone 020 7438 6778, email Michael.Staples@ir.gsi.gov.uk.

Further information on liability to pay NICs on share options may be obtained from—Steve Hickson, Revenue Policy, Personal Tax, Room 75E, Benton Park Road, Newcastle Upon Tyne, NE98 1ZZ, telephone 0191 22 56029, email Steve.Hickson@ir.gsi.gov.uk.

RI 245 (October 2002) *Human rights and penalties*

Article 6 of the European Convention on Human Rights (ECHR) entitles everyone to a fair trial. Where the person is charged with a criminal offence, this includes a right to silence and a right not to self incriminate oneself. Whether any of our penalties are "criminal" for the purposes of Article 6 remains in issue. But if ultimately it is determined that some of them are, we want to be sure we have not accidentally infringed those rights. We have therefore decided to make it clear to customers that they do not have any obligation to incriminate themselves, whilst at the same time drawing their attention to the potential to reduce penalties by making a disclosure and co-operating with the enquiry.

We have issued guidance to Inland Revenue staff to cover what should be said to customers at meetings or in correspondence at the stage in a case where it becomes clear that penalties are likely to be considered.

It has been practice to issue leaflet (IR160) explaining penalties to customers at the point penalties were being considered, this leaflet will continue to be issued. We will however also offer the advice that the extent to which customers co-operate and provide us with information is entirely a matter for them. A new leaflet on Public Funding (previously Legal Aid) will also be provided at this time.

Further details of the guidance to our staff can be found on the Inland Revenue web site at www.inlandrevenue.gov.uk/specialist/humanrights.pdf.

Commentary—See *Simon's Direct Tax Service* **A3.1691.**

RI 246 (October 2002) *VAT—flat rate scheme*

An optional VAT flat rate scheme was introduced with effect from 24 April 2002 by FA2002/S23. The scheme is available to all businesses with a VAT exclusive annual taxable turnover of up to £100,000 in the year of entry to the scheme, and with a VAT exclusive turnover, including the value of exempt supplies and other non-taxable income, of up to £125,000.

A business that joins the scheme avoids having to account internally for VAT on all purchases and supplies, and instead calculates its net liability by applying a flat rate percentage to the tax inclusive turnover. The flat rate percentage depends upon the trade sector into which a business falls for the purposes of the scheme. Full details of the scheme are included in VAT Notice 733 "Flat rate scheme for small businesses", which is available on the internet at www.hmce.gov.uk/forms/notices/733.htm or in printed form by telephoning 0845 010 9000.

1 COMPUTATION OF PROFITS CASE I/II SCHEDULE D

Our view on how profits chargeable under Case I/II of Schedule D are to be computed by businesses who adopt the scheme is as follows.

RIs

Businesses draw up their accounts on the VAT exclusive or on the VAT inclusive basis. Which ever method is used will result in the same profits being charged under Case I/II of Schedule D over the lifetime of the business.

Where the exclusive accounting basis is used

All VAT on inputs and outputs, including the amount due under the flat rate scheme, is taken to a separate VAT account. In the financial statements any balance on that account at the accounting date in respect of VAT, which cannot be recovered from Customs & Excise, is debited to the profit and loss account (where it is likely to be included in either administration costs or with other operating costs). The VAT not recovered is an allowable expense in computing the business profits for the purposes of Case I and II of Schedule D.

Any balance on the account that is an excess of VAT that is not due to be paid over to Customs & Excise, is credited to the profit and loss account (where it is likely to be included with other operating income or deducted from expenses). This is a taxable receipt of the business for the purposes of Case I and II of Schedule D. The reason for this is that VAT is an incidental cost of being in business. The gross payments from customers are received in the course of business and any VAT element included in those payments that does not have to be paid over to Customs & Excise does not lose that business nature.

EXAMPLE 1

A business has sales, net of VAT, of £80,000, with VAT received from customers of £14,000 (£80,000 x 17.5%), giving gross sales of £94,000. Expenses, net of VAT, total £50,000, with VAT paid on expenses of £8,750 (£50,000 x 17.5%). A new machine is purchased (qualifying for capital allowances) at a cost of £2,350, including VAT of £350. Flat rate VAT is paid to Customs & Excise of £5,640 (£94,000 x 6%).

VAT account:

	DR £	*CR £*
VAT collected on sales		*14,000*
VAT paid on expenses	*8,750*	
Flat rate scheme VAT paid	*5,640*	
VAT paid on machine	*350*	
Profit and loss account		*740*
	14,740	*14,740*

Case I profit computation:

Sales	*£80,000*
Expenses (including 'irrecoverable' VAT £740)	*£50,740*
Case I profit	*£29,260*

Qualifying expenditure for capital allowances £2,000 (£2,350 – £350)

EXAMPLE 2

As Example 1 but expenses net of VAT, total £40,000, with VAT paid of £7,000 (£40,000 x17.5%).

VAT account

	DR £	*CR £*
VAT collected on sales		*14,000*
VAT paid on expenses	*7,000*	
Flat rate scheme VAT paid	*5,640*	
VAT paid on machine	*350*	
Profit and loss account	*1,010*	
	14,000	*14,000*

Case I profit computation

Sales	*£80,000*
Other operating income—surplus VAT	*£1,010*
	£81,010
Expenses	*£40,000*
Case I profit	*£41,010*

Qualifying expenditure for capital allowances £2,000

Where the inclusive accounting basis is used

Turnover will include all the VAT charged to customers but it should exclude the amount paid to Customs & Excise under the flat rate scheme. Expenses will include all VAT paid on those expenses.

For example, taking the same figures used in the previous Example 1 above

Sales	*£94,000*	*(£80,000 + VAT charged to customers of £14,000)*
Less flat rate VAT	*£5,640*	*(£94,000 x 6%)*
	£88,360	
Expenses	*£58,750*	*(£50,000 + VAT £8,750)*
Case I Profit	*£29,610*	

Qualifying expenditure for capital allowances £2,350.

2 SERVICE COMPANIES ("IR35") LEGISLATION—DEEMED PAYMENT CALCULATION

The amount to be included under step 1 of the deemed payment calculation is the VAT exclusive amount whether or not the flat rate scheme is adopted.

Note—This Interpretation has been superseded by the Business Income Manual BIM31585.
Commentary—*Simon's Direct Tax Service* **Division E4.10.**

RI 247 (December 2002) *Taxation of chargeable gains—taper relief and exemption for disposals by companies with substantial shareholdings*

Meaning of "trading company", "trading group", "trading sub-group", "holding group" and related issues—TCGA 1992 Sch A1 paras 22(1), 22A and 22B and Sch 7AC paras 20, 21, 22 and 26.

We have been asked to offer guidance on the meaning of certain statutory terms for the purposes of Capital Gains Tax taper relief and the new exemption for disposals by companies with substantial shareholdings. This article provides that guidance. The relevant legislation was enacted by Finance Act 2002. Words in italics in this article denote expressions that are defined in the legislation.

INTRODUCTION

Tax Bulletin 53 (June 2001) [TB53] included an article which explained the Inland Revenue's approach to interpreting the meaning of trading company and holding company of a trading group for the purposes of taper relief. FA 2002 Sch 10 paras 9, 10 have revised the definitions of trading company and trading group for taper relief purposes for periods of ownership from 17 April 2002. There is also a new definition of holding company (see FA 2002 Sch 10 para 4). Further, the qualifications for investment in a joint venture company as they affect the question as to whether a company or group was a trading company or trading group during a period have been relaxed (see FA 2002 Sch 10 paras 11 and 12). The definitions described in TB 53 therefore now apply only for periods of ownership before 17 April 2002 even where the disposal takes place on or after that date.

Finance Act 2002 also introduced Schedule 7AC into the Taxation of Chargeable Gains Act [TCGA] 1992. This brings in an exemption regime for disposals by companies with substantial shareholdings [SSE]. The SSE legislation employs some of the same concepts as taper relief (eg trading company, trading group). Other definitions (eg trading subgroup) are relevant only to SSE.

This article considers further the meanings of these and other expressions in the light of the legislation introduced by Finance Act 2002 and, in particular, confirms that—

– although the definition of company for taper relief is not identical to that used for SSE and the definition of a group of companies for taper relief is different from that of a group for SSE, the definitions of trading company and trading group are essentially common to both regimes.
– for taper relief, the changes to the wording of the definitions of trading company and trading group align the statute with existing practice. They are not intended to alter the substance of the original definitions, or to have different meanings before and on or after 17 April 2002.

Subject to the different meanings of company and group in the two regimes, the explanations in this article apply equally to both reliefs. They draw on the existing guidance in TB53, which continues to apply for taper relief in respect of periods of ownership before 17 April 2002. Because the essentials of the definitions of trading company and trading group for taper relief remain the same, much of what was said in TB53 is repeated here although the text has been updated to reflect the new wording of the legislation.

THE LEGISLATION

Taper relief—shares as business assets and qualifying companies

TCGA 1992 Sch A1 para 4 sets out the conditions for shares to qualify as business assets and Sch A1 para 6 (as amended by Finance Act 2000 s 67) sets out the rules for a company to be a qualifying company in relation to a person making a disposal of shares in a company. Where a company is a qualifying company in relation to that person the business assets rate of taper relief may be due wholly or in part on any chargeable gain arising on the disposal. The question as to whether a company is a qualifying company may also be relevant to persons who dispose of assets used for a trade carried on by a company.

Substantial shareholdings

The SSE legislation provides that from 1 April 2002 disposals of shares (or interests in shares or assets related to shares—as defined in TCGA 1992 Sch 7AC paras 29, 30) by companies with substantial shareholdings do not result in chargeable gains, or allowable losses, provided certain conditions are met. Two of these conditions are that, at certain times determined by reference to the date of the disposal in question

– the company making the disposal is a member of a trading group or, if not a member of a group, is a trading company;
– the shares are in a company that is itself a trading company, or the holding company of either a trading group or a trading subgroup.

DEFINITIONS AND INTERPRETATIONS

Trading company

A trading company is "... a company carrying on trading activities whose activities do not include to a substantial extent activities other than trading activities" (TCGA 1992 Sch A1 para 22A(1) and Sch 7AC para 20(1)).

Holding company, group and subgroup

For taper relief, TCGA 1992 Sch A1 para 22(1) defines a group of companies as "... a company which has one or more 51% subsidiaries, together with those subsidiaries". For periods of ownership from 17 April 2002, TCGA 1992 Sch A1 para 22(1) defines a holding company as "... a company that has one or more 51% subsidiaries". The previous definition, which applies for such periods prior to that date, makes it necessary to determine the extent of a company's business (excluding its own trade, if any) which consists of holding shares in its 51% subsidiaries. A company is a holding company at any time prior to 17 April 2002 when its business consists wholly or mainly of holding shares in its 51% subsidiaries. This test does not apply for periods of ownership from 17 April 2002. From that date, a company is a "holding company" at any time when it has a 51% subsidiary.

In the SSE regime a holding company is defined differently to encompass subgroups as well as groups. But holding companies are defined in essentially the same way for both taper and SSE purposes. FA 2002 Sch 7AC para 26 defines a group and membership of a group by reference to the normal capital gains group rules in TCGA 1992 s 170 except that references in TCGA 1992 s 170 to 75% subsidiaries are replaced by references to 51% subsidiaries. FA 2002 Sch 7AC para 26 defines a subgroup as a collection of companies that would themselves form an SSE group but for the fact that one of them is a 51% subsidiary of another company. A holding company is then defined—

– for an SSE group, as the company described in TCGA 1992 s 170 as the principal company of the group, and
– for a subgroup, as the company that would be the holding company of an SSE group but for the fact that it is a 51% subsidiary of another company.

The taper relief and SSE legislation define a 51% subsidiary by reference to the meaning given by the Income and Corporation Taxes Act (ICTA) 1988 s 838 (see TCGA 1992 Sch A1 para 22(1) for taper relief and Sch 7AC para 26(4) for SSE). A company is a 51% subsidiary of another company for taper relief and SSE purposes if the second company owns directly or indirectly more than 50% of the ordinary share capital of the first company.

Ordinary share capital is defined for the purposes of the Tax Acts (which includes the provisions relating to corporation tax) in ICTA 1988 s 832(1) (this is applied for the purposes of TCGA 1992 Sch A1 by TCGA 1992 Sch A1 para 22(1)). The meaning is extended for the purposes of the definition of 51% subsidiary which applies for SSE purposes (but not for taper relief purposes) to include any share capital of a registered industrial and provident society (see TCGA 1992 Sch 7AC para 26(4)). Some companies do not have ordinary share capital (eg. some limited liability companies in the United States, see Tax Bulletin 51). Such companies cannot therefore be 51% subsidiaries of other companies.

Trading group and trading subgroup

TCGA 1992 Sch A1 para 22B(1), for taper relief, and TCGA 1992 Sch 7AC para 21, for SSE, define what is a trading group in the same terms. The definition parallels that of a trading company so that a trading group is a group one or more of whose members carries on trading activities provided the activities of the group as a whole do not include, to a substantial extent, activities other than trading activities. The activities of the members of a group are treated as one business. Intra-group activities are disregarded for the purpose of determining whether the group is a trading group. So, for example, where one group company lets a property to another group company, the letting activity would be disregarded for this purpose. However, this netting off approach does not extend to transactions with joint venture companies that are not members of the group. So, letting property to such a joint venture company would count as an activity of the lessor.

In identifying companies whose shares might qualify for SSE exemption the concept of a trading subgroup is used to describe part of a group. It is defined in TCGA 1992 Sch 7AC para 22 in the same way as a trading group, but with references to trading group changed to trading subgroup where appropriate. Intra-subgroup activities are disregarded in the same way as intra-group activities when determining whether a subgroup is a trading subgroup. However, intra-group activities between a member of the subgroup and another group company that is not in the subgroup are not disregarded in considering the status of the subgroup.

Trading activities

TCGA 1992 Sch A1 paras 22A and 22B and Sch 7AC paras 20, 21 and 22 define trading activities. For a company/group/subgroup these are activities carried on by the company/a member of the group/subgroup—

(*a*) in the course of, or for the purposes of, a trade being carried on by it/any member of the group/subgroup,
(*b*) for the purposes of a trade that it/any member of the group/subgroup is preparing to carry on,
(*c*) with a view to its/any member of the group/subgroup acquiring or starting to carry on a trade, or
(*d*) with a view to its/any member of the group/subgroup acquiring a significant interest in the share capital of another company that—
    (i) is a trading company or the holding company of a trading group (or a trading subgroup in SSE), and
    (ii) if the acquiring company is a member of a group, is not a member of that group.

However, activities within (*c*) and (*d*) count as trading activities only if the company/group member/subgroup member starts to carry on the trade, or acquires the shares, as soon as is reasonably practicable in the circumstances. For the purposes of (*d*) a significant interest is such an interest as—

– would make the company acquired a member of the same group/subgroup as the acquiring company, or
– would result in the acquiring company having a qualifying shareholding in a joint venture company without making the two companies members of the same group (see TCGA 1992 Sch A1 para 23 for taper relief and TCGA 1992 Sch 7AC para 24 for SSE for definitions of qualifying shareholding and joint venture company).

The word ''activities'' is not defined in the statute but in this context we interpret it to mean what a company does. Activities will therefore include engaging in trading operations, making and holding investments, planning, holding meetings and so forth. The legislation makes explicit that a company may have trading activities both when it is trading and before it commences to trade.

Trade

The following are trades for the purposes of taper relief and SSE:

– anything that is a trade, profession or vocation within the meaning of the Income Tax Acts and is conducted on a commercial basis with a view to the realisation of profits (TCGA 1992 Sch A1 para 22(1) and Sch 7AC para 27), and
– any Schedule A business (within the meaning of ICTA 1988) which consists in the commercial letting of holiday accommodation in the United Kingdom (TCGA 1992 s 241(3) as amended by FA 2002 Sch 8 para 3).

We confirm that activities, such as farming, that are treated as a trade by section 53 ICTA 1988, are trades for the purposes of the Income Tax Acts.

In the course of, or for the purposes of, a trade

We accept that an activity is carried on in the course of, or for the purposes of, a trade if it is carried on in the process of conducting or preparing to carry on the trade. So, for example, where a company renegotiates an ongoing trading contract relating to its trade this will be an activity undertaken ''in the course of'' its trade. It will be clear in most cases whether an activity that a company undertakes is carried on in the course of, or for the purposes of, its trade or not. But similar transactions can be undertaken for different reasons depending on the facts.

For instance, a company may buy some land. If the company is a property developer and buys the land as trading stock, or a manufacturer and buys it to provide a site for a factory it intends to build to house its manufacturing process, the buying of the land would probably count as a trading activity. However, if a company buys the land so as to earn future rental income, or for potential capital growth, the buying of the land would not normally be a trading activity.

Normally, making an investment that yields investment income would not count as a trading activity. However, there are a number of circumstances where such activities could be undertaken in the course of, or for the purposes of, a company's trade.

An investment may be so closely related to the conduct of a trade that it effectively forms an integral part of the trade. For example, a travel agent may be required to keep a fixed level of cash on deposit for bonding requirements. Or a company might receive a large payment, perhaps from selling a shareholding or on the completion of a major contract, and earmark the funds for some particular trade purposes, such as to meet some demonstrable trading liability or expand the trade in the near future. The short-term lodgement of such surplus funds, for example in an interest-bearing deposit account or in bonds or equities, could count as a trading activity. Alternatively, the company may intend distributing the monies received to its members.

Depending on the facts, temporarily investing such funds until they can be distributed could count as being an activity undertaken for the purposes of the company's trade, since paying out the profits generated by a trade can count as a trading activity. This would be the case, for example, where the payment of an annual dividend depended on a meeting of the company's shareholders. Whether or not making and holding investments are part of a company's trading activities is a question of fact that can be determined only by reference to all the relevant circumstances.

Preparing to carry on a trade

The legislation specifically provides that trading activities include activities for the purposes of a trade that a company is preparing to carry on. This encompasses the situation where a particular trade is about to be started but the company has to carry out certain activities first. It also covers cases where an existing trade, which is currently being carried on by another person, will be acquired. The trading activities here may include one or more of: developing a business plan for carrying on the trade, acquiring premises, hiring staff, ordering materials and incurring pre-trading expenditure for the purposes of the trade to be carried on.

Acquiring or starting to carry on a trade, or acquiring shares in a trading company

Activities that a company undertakes with a view to acquiring or starting to carry on a trade, or acquiring a significant interest in the share capital of a trading company, may count as trading activities.

It is quite common for a company to dispose of its trade (or main trading subsidiary) and to invest (or put on deposit) the cash proceeds while it looks around to acquire a new trade or trading subsidiary. A company, group or subgroup temporarily in this position and actively seeking to acquire a new trade or trading subsidiary might still be a trading company, trading company or trading subgroup if it does not have substantial non-trading activities.

Trading activities here include assessing the potential viability of a trade which the company, group or subgroup is considering carrying on and other such activities even though they are not directly preparatory to the carrying on of the particular trade under consideration. So, a company, group or subgroup which has surplus cash that it intends to use to acquire a trade, or to start up one from scratch, which is actively evaluating a number of possible trades may be engaged in trading activities. However, such activities are trading activities only if an acquisition is made, or a new trade is commenced, as soon as is reasonably practicable in the circumstances.

Rather than impose a fixed time limit, the legislation allows companies whatever time is reasonable, having regard to the particular circumstances, to prepare to carry on a new trade or to acquire a trade or trading company. What is reasonably practicable in the circumstances will depend on the facts in each case. For example, a company may be in negotiations to acquire a trading company but owing to circumstances beyond its control the purchase is delayed. There might be, for example, a problem with the vendor proving title to the company's assets. In such a case we would not suggest that the acquisition had not been made as soon as was reasonably practicable in the circumstances where this was the reason for the delay.

Substantial

Most companies groups and subgroups will have some activities that are not trading activities. The legislation provides that such companies and groups still count as trading if their activities "... do not include to a substantial extent activities other than trading activities". The phrase substantial extent is used in various parts of the TCGA 1992 to provide some flexibility in interpreting a provision without opening the door to widespread abuse. We consider that substantial in this context means more than 20%. The numerical tests in the SSE legislation for a shareholding to be a substantial shareholding refer to 10% or more, but this use of the word substantial is specifically applied only for the purpose of deciding whether a company holds a substantial shareholding in another company (TCGA 1992 Sch 7AC para 8(1)).

How should a company's non-trading activities be measured to assess whether they are substantial? Some or all of the following are among the measures that might be taken into account in reviewing a particular company's status.

Income from non-trading activities

For example, a company may have a trade but also let an investment property. If the company's receipts from the letting are substantial in comparison to its combined trading and letting receipts then, on this measure in isolation, the company would probably not be a trading company.

The asset base of the company

If the value of a company's non-trading assets is substantial in comparison with its total assets then again, on this measure, this could point towards it not being a trading company. If a company retains an asset it previously used, but no longer uses, for the purposes of its trade, this may not be a trading activity (but see below regarding surplus trading premises). In some cases it might be appropriate to take account of intangible assets (e.g. goodwill) that are not shown on a balance sheet in considering a company's assets. Current market value and amounts given by way of consideration for assets may both be appropriate measures of the relative extents of a company's trading and other activities. Which measure is appropriate will depend on the facts in each case.

Expenses incurred, or time spent, by officers and employees of the company in undertaking its activities.

For example, if a substantial proportion of the expenses of a company were to be incurred on non-trading activities then, on this measure, the company would not be a trading company. Or a company may devote a substantial amount of its staff resources, by time or costs incurred, to non-trading activities.

The company's history may be relevant. For example, at a particular instant certain receipts may be substantial compared to total receipts but, if looked at on a longer timescale, they may not be substantial compared to other receipts over that longer period. Looked at in this context, therefore, a company might be able to show that it was a trading company over a period, even where that period may have included particular points in time when, for example, non-trade receipts amounted to a substantial proportion of total receipts.

It may be that some indicators point in one direction and others the opposite way. We would weigh up the impact of each of the measures in the context of an individual case. If the Inspector was unable to agree the status of a particular company for a period then the issue could be established only as a question of fact before the Commissioners. However, we anticipate that such cases will be relatively rare.

Surplus trading property

We have been asked how property owned by a company and surplus to its immediate business requirements should be dealt with. Each case would need to be considered in light of the facts. We would not, for example, regard the following as necessarily indicating a non- trading activity—

- letting part of the trading premises;
- letting properties that are no longer required for the purpose of the trade in question, where the company's objective is to sell those properties;
- subletting property where it would be impractical or uneconomic in terms of the trade to assign or surrender the lease. For example, the benefit derived from disposing of the lease may be outweighed by the reverse premium payable;
- the acquisition of property (whether vacant or already let) where it can be shown that the intention is that it will be brought into use for trading activities.

Investments in joint venture companies

Where a company has a qualifying shareholding in a joint venture company (as defined in TCGA 1992 Sch A1 para 23 for taper relief and in Sch 7AC para 24 for SSE) then, provided the joint venture company is not in the same group as the company,

- the holding of any shares or securities that the company holds in the joint venture company is disregarded, and
- the company is treated as carrying on a proportion of the activities of the joint venture company equal to the proportion of that company's ordinary share capital it holds

in determining whether: (*a*) the company is a trading company, (*b*) a group that the company is a member of is a trading group, and (*c*) the company is the holding company of a trading group or trading subgroup.

Shares and other assets held otherwise than as investments

Companies may acquire shares or other assets for reasons other than investment. For example, companies may be paid in shares instead of cash as fees for services rendered or work carried out. Once such shares have been acquired the reasons for retaining them will need to be considered in order to determine whether or not their retention means that a company has non-trading activities. Among other issues, we should need to know the reasons why the shares were taken in settling a trade debt and whether they can reasonably be turned into cash or otherwise exchanged to meet trading requirements.

A company may have to hold shares in another company as a pre-requisite to trading (for example, companies may be expected to own shares in a trade organisation). In such cases we should want to know the reasons for holding such a share in order to determine whether the holding was a trading activity.

Corporate Venturing Scheme [CVS]

Investments in shares made under the CVS are investments like any others and the holding of such shares is unlikely to count as a trading activity in its own right. However, the CVS works in such a way that a company that qualifies for CVS investment relief is unlikely to have more than the 20% non-trading activity that would stop it being a trading company for taper relief and SSE purposes.

What to do if you want to know if a company is a trading company or the holding company of a trading group or subgroup

If you want to establish whether a company in which you held shares was a qualifying company for taper relief purposes while you owned the shares, our advice is that, in the first instance, you should seek advice from the company. The company will usually be able to tell you if its activities were such that it was a trading company (or the holding company of a trading group) so that it could have been a qualifying company so far as you were concerned.

Similarly, if a corporate shareholder planning to sell shares in a company wants some indication of whether that company is a trading company (or the holding company of a trading group or trading subgroup) for SSE purposes, it should ask the company concerned.

In either case, the responsibility for ascertaining the status of a company referred to in your tax return rests with you and you will need to take a view and make your return on this basis: you may wish, where applicable, to point out in the return that you made an unsuccessful approach to the company for confirmation of its status. Alternatively, the Inspector dealing with your returns may be able to provide a post-transaction ruling under the Code of Practice 10 procedures. For reasons of confidentiality the Inspector dealing with the company's tax affairs will not be able to correspond with you regarding its status.

A company may wish to establish its status for various reasons—

- so that it can tell its non-corporate shareholders when it has been a trading company (or the holding company of a trading group) for taper relief purposes;
- when it is planning to sell shares, the gain on the disposal may be exempted by the SSE legislation and it wants to know if it may qualify as a sole trading company (or a member of a trading group) for SSE purposes during the period specified in TCGA 1992 Sch 7AC para 18(1);
- when its corporate shareholders are planning to sell shares in the company and the gain on the disposal may be exempted by the SSE legislation, the shareholders may want to know if the company may qualify as a trading company (or the holding company of a trading group or trading subgroup) for SSE purpose during the period specified in TCGA 1992 Sch 7AC para 19(1).

In these circumstances Inspectors will, where there is uncertainty as to the company's status, respond to requests for their view in accordance with Code of Practice 10 and this article.

Any opinion that a company is or is not a trading company, a group is a trading group or a subgroup is a trading subgroup can relate only to the period under consideration. It is possible for a company, group or subgroup to change its status at any time, as its business or activities change.

Inspectors will usually be able to give a firm opinion on the status of a company for periods that have ended where all the relevant facts have been provided. Any view expressed which relates to a time for which facts are not yet available will be subject to revision. Future events may put a different perspective on the true nature of the activities of a company, group or subgroup during a previous period.

Because of the inherent difficulty in giving a view based on uncertain information, in some cases those involved may prefer to wait until all the relevant facts are known before approaching the Inspector.

So that the company's Inspector can form a view, the company should set out for its Inspector—

- the reason why it is seeking the Inspector's opinion and the period over which the company wants the Inspector to consider its status;
- all the facts that the company considers relevant in measuring the extent of its trading and its non trading activities and, where appropriate, the assumptions it has made in describing what it expects its activities to comprise over the part of the period falling after the latest point for which data is available;
- why the company considers that there is uncertainty as to its status;
- the company's conclusion as to its status, and why it considers, if applicable, that the measures that point in that direction outweigh those pointing in the opposite direction; and
- (for SSE purposes) what disposal is being contemplated and when it is expected that the transaction will be completed.

The Inspector will offer his or her opinion whenever this is practicable and, if this differs from the company's view, explain the reasons for that difference.

Commentary—*Simon's Direct Tax Service* **D2.1533–1535.**

RI 248 (December 2002) *Partnerships and loan relationships*

FA 2002 inserted a new paragraph 19 into FA 1996 Sch 9 to deal comprehensively with cases where a company is a member of a partnership and a money debt (which includes a loan relationship) is owed by or to the partnership. Each company partner computes separately loan relationship debits and credits arising on the money debt.

For this purpose FA 1996 Sch 9 para 19(4) deems that the money debt is owed by or to the company partner, and that everything done by the partnership in relation to the debt has been done by the company.

The company then computes the debits and credits ("the gross debits and credits") that arise from applying the loan relationships rules to this deemed situation. The company partner brings into account a proportion of these gross debits and credits, the proportion being determined by reference to the partner's interest in the partnership.

We have been asked whether FA 1996 Sch 9 para 19(4) means that you effectively ignore the existence of the partnership. The question arises in two circumstances—

- the company partner and the partnership have different accounting dates, or
- the functional currency of the partnership differs from that of the company partner. For example, a company that prepares accounts in sterling may have an investment in a partnership that prepares financial statements in US dollars.

Our view is that FA 1996 Sch 9 para 19(4) requires the company partner to imagine itself as "standing in the shoes" of the partnership. The company is not required to substitute its own accounting date, or its own functional currency, for that of the partnership.

Case law on deeming provisions shows that the application of a "statutory fiction" should be carried only so far as is necessary for the purposes of the statute. The purpose of the deeming exercise in FA 1996 Sch 9 para 19(4) is to compute the debits or credits accruing to the company partner, in a way that takes account of the particular circumstances of that company. There is no need, in doing this, to pretend that the partnership does not exist at all.

Example 1 illustrates how a company partner's loan relationships debits and credits are calculated where its accounting date differs from that of the partnership. Example 2 illustrates the computation where the partnership has a different functional currency.

EXAMPLE 1

X Ltd is a trading company with an accounting date of 31 December. It is a partner in a partnership P, which prepares accounts to 31 March. It does not account for its investment in P on a mark to market basis.

On 1 May 2003, the partnership acquires a zero coupon bond (issued by an unconnected company). The partnership accounts for the bond on an accruals basis. Its accounts show a credit of £50,000 in the year to 31 March 2004 in respect of accrued discount on the bond, and a similar credit of £80,000 in the year to 31 March 2005.

X Ltd is entitled to 50% of the profits of P in the year to 31 March 2004, but to only 25% in the year to 31 March 2005.

Step 1—calculate gross credits

Under FA 1996 Sch 9 para 19(4), the "gross credits" are computed as if the zero coupon bond were a creditor loan relationship to which X Ltd is a party for the purposes of its own trade. The company must account for this deemed loan relationship on an authorised accruals basis (paragraph 19(10)). X Ltd (and any other company partner) computes "gross credits" for periods of account ending on 31 March.

X Ltd therefore has gross trading loan relationship credits of £50,000 in the year to 31 March 2004, and £80,000 in the year to 31 March 2005.

The company is not required to work out the discount that would accrue on the bond in year ended 31 December 2003, or subsequent accounting periods.

Step 2—compute the "appropriate share" of gross credits for each AP of X Ltd

FA 1996 Sch 9 para 19(6) says that apportionment of gross credits between partners is to be according to the shares that would be found by TA 1988 s 114(2). Although FA 1996 Sch 9 para 19(2) disapplies TA 1988 s 114(1) where loan relationships are concerned, the apportionment rules in TA 1988 s 114(2) continue to apply, including the provision for apportioning profits or losses to the corresponding accounting periods of the company.

X Ltd's apportioned credits are £25,000 (50% x £50,000) for the year to 31 March 2004, and £20,000 (25% x £80,000) for the year to 31 March 2005.

X Ltd will therefore need to time-apportion these sums between its own accounting periods, and bring in:

Year ended 31 December 2003: 275/366 x £25,000 = £18,784

Year ended 31 December 2004: (91/366 x £25,000) + (275/365 x £20,000) = £21,284

RIs

EXAMPLE 2

Y plc is entitled to 40% of the profits of a partnership, Q. Y plc accounts in sterling; partnership Q accounts in dollars. Both Y plc and Q prepare accounts to 31 December. Y plc uses the closing rate/net investment method to translate its investment in the partnership, using an average exchange rate for the year to translate its share of Q's profit into sterling.

In the year to 31 December 2004, Q borrows $5 million from a bank. The bank is not connected with Y plc or any other company partner. Interest of $200,000 is payable on the loan during the period.

During the year the partnership sold goods to a customer for €10,000. The invoice remained unpaid at the year end. Q translated the trade debt into dollars at the year end, bringing into its accounts an exchange gain of $500.

Step 1—calculate gross debits and credits

The gross debits and credits are calculated in the functional currency of the partnership. FA 1996 Sch 9 para 19(10) requires an authorised accruals basis to be used. Thus there is a debit of $200,000 in respect of the loan interest. FA 1996 s 100(1), (2) also requires exchange differences on the Euro trade debt (which is a money debt, but not a loan relationship) to be accounted for under the loan relationships rules. This gives rise to a gross credit of $500.

Step 2—apportion gross debits and credits to the company partner

Since Y plc is entitled to 40% of partnership profits, it must bring into account a debit of $80,000 and a credit of $200 (or a net amount of $79,800). In accordance with FA 1993 s 94AB(1), (2), this is translated into sterling at the rate used in Y plc's accounts to translate the partnership profits. If the average rate used is, say, $1.6/£, Y plc would show a loan relationship debit of £49,875 (79,800 divided by 1.6) in its tax computations.

Similar principles apply where a partnership is a party to a derivative contract (FA 2002 Sch 26 para 49).

Commentary—*Simon's Direct Tax Service* **D2.1144.**

RI 249 (February 2003) *Payments in lieu of notice ('Pilons')*

The Revenue's view on the tax treatment of PILONs was published in the August 1996 edition of Tax Bulletin (TB24B). Since that time the area has not stood still and the purpose of this article is to provide an update on subsequent developments. The current Revenue guidance on the IR website (www.inlandrevenue.gov.uk) is regularly updated and already reflects what follows.

RESERVED RIGHTS AND DISCRETION

The 1996 article explained that—

> ''Some contractual arrangements give the employer a reserved right, or discretion—as opposed to imposing an obligation—to make a PILON where due notice is not given on termination of employment. Where an employer exercises such a reserved right or discretion, we regard the contract as being terminated in accordance with its terms under the agreed contractual arrangements for the provision of services generally.''

The consequence is that the PILON is regarded as—

- an emolument from the employment chargeable under TA 1988 s 19; and
- earnings derived from an employment under SSCBA 1992 s 3(1)(*a*), and so liable for Class 1 NICs.

This view was subsequently confirmed for tax purposes by the Court of Appeal in July 1999 in *EMI Group Electronics v Coldicott* (71 TC 455). In that case it was common ground that the employer had exercised a reserved right to make a PILON on redundancy.

There have been subsequent developments outside tax law concerning the options available to an employer when considering whether to exercise such discretion.

In January 2001 the employment law case *Cerberus Software Ltd v Rowley* (2001 IRLR 160) considered a contractual clause providing that the employer ''may'' make a PILON. The Court of Appeal held that the word ''may'' meant that the employer was free to give neither notice nor a PILON but instead to breach the contract and pay damages for that breach. That conclusion clearly applies wherever the contractual clause is not prescriptive in requiring a payment where notice is not given.

Such action was financially beneficial to the employer in *Cerberus* because the sum payable as compensation for breach of contract, initially calculated by reference to lost remuneration in the notice period, could be reduced or ''mitigated'' to take account of the fact that the ex-employee had found alternative employment during what would have been the notice period. This reduced the loss caused by the employer's action and so lessened the sum due as damages. By contrast, if the employer had exercised the right to pay a PILON instead of giving notice (and so terminated the contract lawfully), the payment would need to have been equal to the gross salary that would have been payable during the notice period.

The relevance of the case for tax purposes is that compensation for breach of contract is not an emolument within TA 1988 s 19 but falls within TA 1988 s148 as a payment in connection with termination of employment. As such—

– it qualifies for the £30,000 exemption from tax available for all such payments (subject to aggregation with other payments and benefits within the Section); and
– as a compensation payment, it is not ''earnings'' for NICs purposes. So no Class 1 NICs liability arises on it.

It is therefore crucial to establish and examine the facts in such cases in order to decide whether the discretion has been exercised. The following are only guidelines indicating the type of factor that may be relevant—

– although each case will depend on its own facts, a settlement that is substantially the same in value as exercise of the discretion would have produced is likely to be viewed as made by exercise of the discretion. The June 2001 High Court decision in *Richardson v Delaney* (74 TC 167) is an example of this. In that case, it was asserted by the taxpayer that such a discretion had not been exercised. The Court agreed with the Revenue's contention that, in the absence of any identifiable breach of contract, the source of the payment lay in the employer's discretion to make a payment for the remaining notice period. The *Richardson* case also demonstrates that a payment made by exercise of the employer's discretion need not be made precisely in either the sum, or in the form, provided for by the contract.
– a payment resulting from a decision not to exercise discretion could be expected to have characteristics normally associated with compensation or damages for breach of contract rather than those associated with a contractual payment.
– One such characteristic is apparent in *Cerberus*, where the payment was reduced (or ''mitigated'') to reflect the fact that the employee had secured alternative employment before the end of the notice period and by doing so had reduced the loss or damage caused by the employer's breach.
– Other adjustments are common when calculating such payments, for example to reflect the difference in tax and NIC consequences between an emolument from employment (taxed and liable for Class 1 NICs) and a payment of damages (taxed only after a £30,000 exemption and not subject to NICs).
– A damages payment will normally take into account all salary and benefits that would have been available in the notice period;
– a decision by an employer not to exercise its discretion might be evidenced in writing.

All factors need to be weighed in the balance in deciding whether the discretion has been exercised. Essentially the matter is a question of fact.

Problems in deciding the correct position, and so costs for taxpayer and Revenue, are often caused by incomplete documentation of the events surrounding termination and the calculation of the payment made.

THE RELEVANCE OF THE CERBERUS DECISION TO THE EMI CASE

It has been argued that the *Cerberus* decision means that the *EMI* case has effectively been overruled. The basis of this view is that *Cerberus* means that an employee has no right to sue for a payment and so it cannot be an emolument from employment.

The Revenue does not accept this analysis. TA 1988 s 131 which defines an emolument for the purpose of TA 1988 s 19 is not expressed in contractual terms. There are many taxable payments that are not dependent on any contractual obligation.

In *EMI* itself the employee equally had no right to sue for the PILON, but it was nevertheless held to be taxable as an emolument from employment because the employer had exercised its discretion and so ensured that the source of the payment was the employer-employee relationship, as evidenced in that case by the contractual terms.

THE RELEVANCE OF CONTRACTUAL STATUS

In the 1996 article, it was stated that—

> ''...even where there is no such contractual arrangement, an employer may regularly make a PILON instead of giving whatever notice is due. It is then possible that an implied contractual term of service may come into being, and where it does the payment is also properly regarded as made under contractual arrangements. All the facts of an individual case, including the employee's knowledge of an established practice, would need to be considered in deciding whether this was so.''

The Revenue now accepts that it is unlikely that an implied contractual term in relation to PILONs can exist. Contract law suggests that if something conflicts with an express or written contractual term, then it cannot be implied. Since contracts generally include a right to receive notice of termination of employment (whether directly or through ERA 1996) then an implied right to receive a PILON would appear to conflict with the express term that the employee is entitled to receive notice of termination.

Despite that, the Revenue maintains that a non-contractual PILON may in some circumstances fall within TA 1988 s 19 and be liable for NICs. This view affects those cases where, as a response to the *EMI* decision, PILON clauses were deleted from contractual arrangements as well as other cases where no contractual provision for PILON exists. In such cases it is commonly asserted that any PILON made is in breach of contract and so liable to tax only under TA 1988 s 148 and not liable to NICs.

What this approach overlooks is that the definition of ''emoluments'' in TA 1988 s 131 is, as explained above, not expressed in contractual terms. Something can be an ''emolument'' even though non-contractual—for example, tips or a discretionary bonus. So removal from contractual terms is not the final test of liability, although it is accepted that such a removal means that any subsequent payment is unlikely to be contractual in nature (either express or implied).

Where a PILON is paid as an automatic response to a termination, it may be within the scope of TA 1988 s 19 and liable for NICs. For example, every time there is a redundancy, all employees receive a payment in lieu of any period of unworked notice. In such circumstances the payment is an integral part of the employer-employee relationship for the workplace, albeit non-contractual, and has its source in that relationship and nowhere else.

The employer may well have the option in such circumstances of breaching the contract by not giving notice and paying damages, but where a sum is paid automatically the suggestion is that that route has not been chosen. Instead, the employer has followed a different route. As with discretionary contractual PILONs above, that conclusion may be shown to be incorrect where a PILON bears the characteristics or hallmarks of a payment of damages mentioned above. Again, all the relevant factors need to be considered in an individual case.

Such cases as *Corbett v Duff* (23 TC 763) and *Laidler v Perry* (42 TC 351) are examples of non-contractual payments that are emoluments from employment within TA 1988 s 19. That all employees are not aware of the payment is not crucial in the Revenue's view; what matters is that the payment is an automatic response in respect of any period of unworked notice.

INCOME TAX (EARNINGS AND PENSIONS) BILL

The substance of this guidance will not be affected by any of the provisions of the Income Tax (Earnings and Pensions) Bill, currently before Parliament. That Bill is rewriting the existing Schedule E provisions without any major change in effect. The Bill will change the terminology used, but it will not alter the tax treatment of PILONs.

Commentary—*Simon's Direct Tax Service* **E4.805A.**

RI 250 (February 2003) *Avoidance via employee remuneration packages*

LOANS IN TURKISH LIRA AND OTHER "SOFT" CURRENCIES

In recent years, we have seen a variety of schemes involving the payment of remuneration to employees in non-cash form designed primarily to avoid income tax and NICs. Specific legislation to counter several types of scheme has been enacted and indeed an announcement was made in the pre-Budget report on 27 November 2002 that immediate legislation was to be introduced to counter the abuse of Employee Benefit Trusts.

One particular avoidance scheme has attracted considerable media attention recently. Under that scheme, instead of part of an employee's remuneration—for example, a bonus—being in cash, there is a loan to the employee in a soft currency such as the Turkish lira that is expected to depreciate substantially against sterling. The employee can expect to realise an exchange gain in sterling terms when the loan is repaid which represents his or her ''bonus'' while the employer makes an equivalent exchange loss.

The Revenue's view is that, for accounting periods beginning on or after 1 October 2002, the unallowable purpose provisions in FA 1996 Sch 9 para 13—which were extended in FA 2002 to cover exchange gains and losses—will normally apply to deny relief for the exchange loss. For earlier accounting periods, we believe that the anti-avoidance provisions in FA 1993 ss 135, 136 apply to disallow the exchange loss.

The tax and NICs treatment of payments made in this way will depend upon the precise contractual arrangements between employer and employee. A detailed investigation of all the facts surrounding the payment will be required in every case to determine the precise contractual arrangements.

Commentary—*Simon's Direct Tax Service* **D2.1151.**

RI 251 (February 2003) *Share options and awards and transfer pricing*

WATERLOO PLC, EUSTON & PADDINGTON V IRC (SPC 301) ("WATERLOO")

This article sets out the Revenue's view on the application of transfer pricing principles to share option and share award schemes following a recent Special Commissioners' decision on this subject and the publication on 19 December 2002 of the draft legislation relating to the new statutory corporation tax deduction for employee acquisitions.

The new statutory deduction will be available to a company within the charge to corporation tax for accounting periods beginning on or after 1 January 2003, where an employee of that company acquires shares in that or another company whose shares meet the requirements for relief. The deduction will be equivalent to the difference between the market value of the shares at the time they are acquired and the amount payable by the recipient, or another, in respect of the shares. No other deduction will be allowed for corporation tax purposes in respect of the cost of providing the shares. The draft legislation and a technical commentary are available on the Inland Revenue website at www.inlandrevenue.gov.uk/drafts/index.htm.

One result of the draft legislation is to override the requirement in certain circumstances for taxpayers to consider whether TA 1988 Sch 28AA requires a transfer pricing adjustment. For accounting periods beginning on or after 1 January 2003, where employees of a UK company acquire shares in a non UK affiliate by reason of their employment and the UK company is able to obtain the statutory deduction the transfer pricing legislation is otiose because whatever amount is recharged in the accounts will be disallowed by the new legislation.

Where a statutory deduction is not available, for example, because the shares are not of a qualifying type or the accounting period begins before 1 January 2003 the relevant transfer pricing legislation will apply and any corporation tax deduction must be based on arms length principles. The transfer pricing legislation will continue to apply to all accounting periods, whether starting before, on or after 1 January 2003, in respect of the cost to UK companies of providing shares for employees of non-UK affiliates. This is because the statutory deduction only applies where shares are acquired by reason of employment with a UK company and the costs will not otherwise be incurred for the purposes of the UK company's business. Transfer pricing legislation will also apply to expenses incurred by a UK company in establishing, administering or borrowing for the purposes of an employee share scheme (which are not affected by the statutory deduction) where that scheme provides shares for employees of non UK affiliates.

Where transfer pricing legislation does apply to the costs of providing share options, as set out above, then the Revenue's approach will be based on its interpretation of a recent Special Commissioners' decision concerning the application of the transfer pricing legislation to such share option schemes.

The case considered by the Special Commissioners involved a UK company, Waterloo, which allowed employees of non-UK subsidiaries to participate in its share schemes. The decision also clarifies a number of issues arising in the reverse situation—where UK subsidiaries are charged by non UK parent companies in respect of options granted to UK based employees. Prior to the Special Commissioners' decision, there was no generally prevailing practice as to how to establish the arm's length price of share options granted by a parent company to the employees of a subsidiary. In accordance with the principles set out in TB44D (generally prevailing practice) the Revenue regards the Special Commissioners decision as applying to earlier periods, subject to the statutory time limits for making assessments and opening enquiries, and the normal rules governing discovery.

There may, however, be a considerable period between the grant of an option and its exercise. Accordingly the Revenue will not seek to apply the Waterloo decision in place of whatever approach has been used in the computations in respect of deductions claimed for options exercised in accounting periods ended before 1 January 1997 except in exceptional circumstances. These circumstances will be, for example, where there are open transfer pricing enquiries (not necessarily explicitly about share options) for the earlier periods; or where enquiries into deductions for share options had been opened (for any period) prior to publication of the Special Commissioners' decision; or where such enquiries had been closed following the provision of misleading information by the company.

Where companies have in periods starting before 1 January 2003 claimed an amount based on the spread at the date of exercise, the transitional rules will not be relevant. This is because options which have been exercised no longer exist at the commencement of the new legislation, so no statutory deduction can be due for such options. Where, on the other hand, companies have made deductions in respect of unexercised options in accounts for periods beginning before 1 January 2003 the transitional rules will apply. In such circumstances a deduction will be allowed for the arms length price in the appropriate period pre 1 January 2003. When the options are exercised (or shares acquired) by the employee, the statutory deduction will be available, reduced by the arms length amount(*s*) allowed in earlier periods. This might reduce the new relief to nil but does not create a charge to tax if the earlier amounts exceed the statutory deduction.

WATERLOO PLC ETC

Facts

Waterloo established a trust in connection with its employee share option scheme and made an interest free loan to the trustees so that they could purchase shares and grant options in respect of those shares to employees of Waterloo's subsidiaries. When options were exercised the employees paid the option price to the trustees who then repaid the loan. Waterloo also undertook to issue shares to the trustees at the option price so that options could be satisfied in the event that the trustees exhausted their reserve of shares.

Point at issue

Whether business facilities were provided within the meaning of TA 1988 s 773(4).

Decision

The Commissioners found that there was a business facility which "was more than the grant of interest free loans by Waterloo to the trustee; what Waterloo gave was the total facility for giving benefits to employees in the form of options" (para 51). Waterloo devised, set up, funded and operated a facility whereby the employees of its subsidiary companies were able to receive valuable share options. The facility was not just the making of the interest free loan, nor was it just the selling of shares to employees at a price below market value. The facility was the total package and it is the total package that needs to be examined and priced. The distinction between the "total facility" and the constituent transactions such as the loan is important and has implications beyond share options though these are not the subjects of this article. It is consistent with the Revenue's submission that "the phrase 'business facility' is a commercial not a legal term, and ... that where a commercial term is used in legislation, the test of ordinary business might require an aggregation of transactions which transcended their juristic individuality" (para 57).

Waterloo concerned the award of shares by way of options but the principles are clearly applicable to any share based remuneration scheme. The relevant transfer pricing legislation for the years covered by the appeals was TA 1988 s 770, which was replaced by TA 1988 Sch 28AA for periods ending after 1 July 1999. The Revenue regards Sch 28AA as being of wider application than s770 so will be applying the decision to periods ending after 1 July 1999 as well as periods for which TA 1988 s770 applied

The arms length price

Although not asked to consider pricing, the Special Commissioners commented that "it would be relatively simple" to price the facility by reference to the costs of the provider of the facility; and went on to enumerate the types of costs to be included (para 102). The Revenue takes the view that the Commissioners would have been extremely unlikely to endorse pricing by reference to the employee's gain on exercise (the difference between the market value at the date of exercise and the exercise price—known as "the spread"). This is because the costs of Waterloo were related largely to interest rates not to the increase in share price over the period of the option.

Where Waterloo issued new shares there is an argument that, under accountancy standards applicable in the years of the appeals, the company did not incur a cost. Arguably no charge should be made. It might appear on such reasoning that where a non-UK company issues shares in support of options granted to employees of its UK subsidiaries then the full amount of any charge made to the subsidiaries would be disallowed. However, parties acting at arm's length are prepared to pay for something of value to them even if there is no cost to the provider. Indeed, the Special Commissioners allude to one example elsewhere in the decision when they accepted the giving of bank guarantees as the provision of a business facility (para 52).

The Revenue approach

Any enterprise which grants share options does so in the expectation that the value of the shares will rise. A prudent business would look to hedge in some way the exposure to the expected share price increases. This presumption is borne out by the difficulty in finding groups that wait till options are exercised before buying shares in the market, thereby exposing themselves to increases in the share price. It is sometimes argued that, since share price increases are linked to profit increases, there is no need for the prudent business to hedge actively—the correlation between share prices and profits supposedly providing its own natural hedge. If this proposition were valid -and the difficulty of finding groups who have acted upon it suggest otherwise—then any correlation that exists between share price and profits would be stronger at a group consolidated level than at the level of the individual operating entity. It follows that if the group as a whole adopts an active hedging strategy of some sort then so should the subsidiary, which does not have the same correlation between its stand-alone profits and the group's share price.

Using group policy in this way as a starting point for the subsidiary's policy is in line with OECD guidance on group hedging strategies for dealing with foreign exchange or interest rate exposures which states—

"When addressing the issue of the extent to which a party to a transaction bears any ... risk, it will normally be necessary to consider the extent, if any, to which the taxpayer and/or the MNE group have a business strategy which deals with the minimisation or management of such risks" (OECD 1995 1.27)

Where exceptionally the group as a whole does not have a hedging strategy, the Revenue will consider whether the same unhedged strategy is appropriate for the subsidiary, bearing in mind that individual entities may not have the same correlation between profits and the group's share price as the group as a whole has.

There are 3 hedging strategies open to a company granting options to employees over its shares—

(*a*) issue new shares;
(*b*) buy shares in the market at or around the time options are granted; and
(*c*) buy an option that mirrors the terms of the options granted to the employees.

Subsidiaries, whose employees are granted options over the parent company's shares, cannot use option a. Similarly, a company granting options over its own shares is unlikely to opt for c. However, option c. approximates to how a subsidiary could hedge its exposure if it did not buy shares in the market; and one measure of the amount a party acting at arm's length would be prepared to pay is the cost of obtaining the same benefit by a different route. This article considers the application of pricing by reference to options b and c.

Shares bought in the market (Market Purchase Price)

Where shares are bought in the market the Special Commissioners found that the facility was not simply the making of a loan. Pricing the facility is not therefore simply a matter of pricing the loan. Rather the pricing of the loan is one ingredient in establishing the price of the facility. In the Waterloo case there was not an exact match between the exercise price of the option and the price of the shares acquired for hedging. Instead shares were purchased during the year at propitious times in anticipation of the grant of options later, so the price of the shares could be more or less than the exercise price of the option. Other groups may buy some shares before the grant of options and some after. Provided the parent company does not have an ulterior motive (such as supporting its share price) the actual purchase pattern of the parent is a good starting point for determining an appropriate strategy for the subsidiary.

Table 1 sets out how a UK headed group might calculate the charge to its non UK affiliates for options granted to employees of those affiliates. For the sake of simplicity the example assumes that options are granted at the year end and the mid year point is when options are exercised and shares purchased in advance of the next tranche of options. The example also assumes that the costs of acquiring more shares than are required for hedging are costs of the parent company, and are not to be allocated to the subsidiaries. Thus the allocation of non-UK costs are determined by the ratio of non-UK shares needed (C to total shares needed (and not non UK shares needed to shares held). In practice how the costs of "excess" share purchases are allocated will depend on the precise circumstances. If the parent company routinely and persistently over purchases it may be that it is doing so for its own purposes. If, on the other hand, it is sometimes over and sometimes under it may be that this is a valid hedging strategy for the share option awards so that all costs are allocable.

Expected rate of exercise—if, historically, only say 60 per cent of options granted were actually exercised, one would expect a prudent business to purchase 60 shares for every 100 options granted. Expected rates of exercise may vary from group to group depending on such factors as staff turnover and performance conditions attaching to the options. For new schemes documentation about expected take up may have been produced internally or by remuneration consultants involved in setting up the scheme. Such documentation could form the basis of expected rates of exercise until more reliable data is available.

Rate of interest—as with any loan the arm's length rate of interest depends upon the facts and circumstances of the case. Interest is calculated from the date the shares are purchased, not the date the options are granted.

Dividends—typically dividends are waived on shares held by share scheme trusts so that dividends payable to other shareholders are not diluted. A subsidiary acquiring shares from a hypothetical third party for its employees would not care about the interest of the other shareholders. The only concern would be with minimising the costs of its hedging strategy. So in calculating the price of an arms length hedging strategy there would be no reason to waive the dividends.

Profits and losses on disposal of shares—the example at Table 1 does not include an explicit entry for profits or losses that might arise on the disposal of shares. Such profits and losses are, however, included implicitly in the calculation since disposal proceeds on the sale of shares affect the amount of debt left in the trust, which in turn determines the amount of interest to be allocated to the subsidiaries. Share option schemes tend to be enduring structures and one might expect profits and losses to balance out sufficiently over the life of the scheme so that all debt is repaid—shares purchased to hedge a tranche of options which lapse while the options are under the water become the hedge for a second tranche of options granted when the share price recovers. In a period of steep and prolonged decline in share prices, however, it may be that the group decides to sell surplus shares to prevent further losses arising. The losses incurred on selling surplus shares may be so great that part of the loan to the trust will never be repaid. In such circumstances it may be appropriate to include as an ingredient in the price of the facility an amount for loans permanently written off. Such an apportionment might not be straightforward. The objectives and actual pattern of disposal of surplus shares of the parent company (whose shares are held in the trust) may be different to the pattern of disposal that would have been chosen by a subsidiary whose only interest in the shares is as a hedge against its employee options.

Purchase of an option mirroring terms of options granted to employees

Another way to establish an arm's length price would be to calculate how much it would cost the subsidiary to purchase an option that mirrors the terms of the options granted to the employees (though legally such a transaction with the parent may not be permitted). Economic models such as Black-Scholes are used to value options and depend on a number of variables—volatility of shares, interest rates, dividend flows, maturity of options, etc. Such variables, moreover, may change over time. The Revenue understands that generally the price will be in the region of 25–35% of the value of the shares at time the option is granted but for nil-cost options could rise to 55–65%.

A hedging strategy priced on buying an option that mirrors the terms of the options granted to the employees should take account of the expected exercise rates. Again, if 60 per cent of employees are expected to exercise the subsidiary employer would only require an option over a reduced number of shares. The fair value of the option would be spread over the vesting period of the employees' share options.

When applying models such as Black-Scholes, companies should bear in mind that they were not primarily designed for pricing options with the long maturity dates typical of employee share options. As such, substantial adjustments must be made to the model with the result that it is not as accurate as it might otherwise be. Therefore companies using Black-Scholes as their primary pricing method may want to check the result using a market purchase price.

For companies without in-house expertise in pricing options pricing by reference to buying the shares in the market may be simpler than using Black-Scholes. Accordingly, even where the scheme is actually hedged by the issue of shares rather than buying them in the market, the Revenue is prepared to accept a market purchase price, calculated along the lines of Tables 1; but assuming that the shares were purchased on the same day as the options were granted. However, and as indicated above, the share purchase model can become complicated where loans need to be written off and could become very difficult to apply when there are no actual loans or share disposal patterns to work from.

Treatment of receipts by UK parent

As indicated above, where shares are bought in the market the facility is not the making of an interest free loan and any receipt by the UK parent would be payment for a business facility, not interest. Similarly, inclusion of fair value of the options at grant in the price of the facility does not mean that the provider of the facility has actually sold an option to the trust (or subsidiary) mirroring the terms of the options granted to employees. Rather the price of such an option is merely an ingredient in pricing the facility. Where the parent, as in Waterloo, supports the scheme by a combination of market purchased and newly issued shares any payment received cannot—in light of the Commissioners finding of what the facility was—be separated out into capital and revenue. The receipt is indivisibly on revenue account and taxable as income.

When groups adopt structures that dispense with the trust and interest free loans and issue shares directly to the employees when they exercise the options then there may be no transfer pricing issue. At arms length one would still expect a third party to pay the issuing company, but provided the issuing company has not obtained a P&L deduction in respect of the option any receipt is likely to represent an increase in capital account and would not be caught by transfer pricing.

The issues arising on the quantum and nature of receipts in respect of share option schemes are unaffected by the proposed legislation giving a CT deduction for share options.

TREATMENT OF PAYMENTS BY UK SUBSIDIARIES

Accounting periods starting before 1 January 2003

Following the Waterloo decision the Revenue will accept that an intra-group recharge paid by a UK subsidiary in respect of share options granted to its employees is allowable as a deduction for the period for which the recharge is made, if it is calculated on an arm's length basis as set out in this article and relates to employees who work exclusively for UK entities.

The Commissioners' analysis of the nature of the facility provided by the parent company in the Waterloo case means that the recharge is not capital expenditure and will be wholly and exclusively for the purposes of the subsidiary's trade if it relates to employees who work exclusively for it (TA 1988 s 74(1)). As the recharge is not a payment of emoluments or potential emoluments, but is payment for "the total facility for giving benefits to employees in the form of share options", FA 1989 s 43 will not apply to defer the timing of any deduction.

Accounting periods starting on or after 1 January 2003

If the shares concerned are within the scope of the proposed new statutory deduction for the costs of providing shares for employee share schemes, the new legislation will determine the timing and amount of any deductions for providing shares to employees of UK companies.

To the extent that the new legislation does not disallow ancillary costs (such as interest on loans to purchase shares in the market) Sch 28AA may still apply to recover such costs from non UK affiliates whose employees benefit from the scheme.

Cost plus and cost sharing arrangements

Pricing share options by reference to the gain made by the employee will not give the same result as applying general transfer pricing rules. It follows that transfer pricing methods which incorporate or rely upon profit made by the employee will not result in an arm's length price. Where, for example, a company is remunerated by affiliates on a cost plus basis, and those costs include a charge for share options based on the employee profit, the mark up has been applied to a non arm's length cost base. Similarly, where companies enter into cost sharing arrangements, and the costs include a charge for share options based on the employees' profit, the resulting sharing of costs will not be on an arm's length basis because a non arm's length cost was included in the pool. Cost Plus and Cost Sharing Arrangements must instead be based on an arm's length cost calculated according to one of the acceptable methods explained above. This will remain the case from 1 January 2003.

Summary

The Special Commissioners' decision has established that where a parent company allows the employees of its subsidiaries to participate in its share schemes, the arm's length principle requires that the subsidiaries make a contribution to the parent. The pricing of the facility is relatively straightforward for share award schemes (which are easier to value than options) and share options where the scheme is supported by purchasing shares in the market. The position is less clear cut where an option scheme is supported by the issue of new shares. Where new issue shares are used, the Revenues' view is that the fair value of the options at the date of grant, spread over the vesting period, is an appropriate arm's length price. As this could result in complex (and costly) calculations, pricing the facility as if it had been supported by market purchase of shares may also be acceptable.

Unless the group as a whole buys shares in the market at the date of exercise, charges based on the increase in market value of the shares over the vesting period are not arm's length, whether the charge is made at yearly rests or taken in full in the year of exercise.

The arms length principle will apply to the costs of all options exercised in accounting periods other than those starting on or after 1 January 2003. In addition the arms length principle will apply to the cost of options or other share awards or costs in connection with such awards when no statutory deduction is available on exercise in accounting periods starting on or after 1 January 2003.

		Year 1	*Year 2*	*Year 3*	*Year 4*	*Year 5*
Options						
Option b/f		0	1000	1100	850	850
Options granted		1000	600	0	0	150
Price granted		1·75	2·5	0	0	3
Options exercised		0	500	250		300
Options unexercised		1000	1100	850	850	700
Shares						
Non UK options		400	550	350	350	300
Exercise rate		75%	75%	75%	75%	75%
Shares needed non UK	(C)	300	413	263	263	225
Shares needed by trust	(D)	750	825	638	638	525
Shares held by trust		900	1100	850	700	600
Loans						
Opening loan	(A)	0	1485	2010	1573	1348
Shares acquired		900	700	0	0	200
Price		1·65	2	0	0	2·9
New loan		1485	1400	0	0	580
Shares sold		0	500	250	150	300
Price		0	1·75	1·75	1·5	2·5
Loan repaid		0	875	438	225	750
Loan end of year	(B)	1485	2010	1573	1348	1178
Rate of interest		5%	5%	5%	5%	5%
Interest (A+B)/2		37	87	90	73	63
Less div income		5	5	5	5	5
Net cost	(E)	32	82	85	68	58
Non UK =	E x C/D	13	41	35	28	25

Richard Gallacher, Revenue Policy International, Victory House, 30–34 Kingsway, London, WC2B 6ES, Telephone 0207 438 6309, email Richard.Gallacher@ir.gsi.gov.uk.

Commentary—*Simon's Direct Tax Service* **B3.927.**

RI 252 (April 2003) *Reimbursement of employee's training expenses-—training undertaken before employment begins*

1 ITEPA 2003 s 250 (formerly, TA 1988 s 200B) provides exemption from tax when an employer pays or reimburses the costs of an employee's "work-related training" (as defined). The exemption also applies for National Insurance contribution purposes via Social Security (Contributions) Regulations 2001 Sch 3 Part VII para 2.

2 We believe some inconsistency may have arisen regarding the application of this provision when an employer reimburses, to a new employee, the expense of a training or academic course begun or completed before the commencement of the employment. This article explains that such reimbursements will not, normally, qualify for exemption. It also sets out some limited circumstances in which the reimbursement of pre-commencement training expenses will qualify.

BACKGROUND

3 Without a specific exemption, an employer's reimbursement of training expenses paid out of an employee's own pocket would be taxable as "general earnings" within ITEPA 2003 s 6. The payment would constitute earnings within s 62, or would be treated as earnings by s 72. No deduction would be due under s 336 (formerly, TA 1988 s 198) because the expense will not have been incurred "in the performance of" the employee's duties (*Fitzpatrick v IRC*, 1994 STC 237,66 TC 407).

4 The situation outlined in the previous paragraph led to the publication of Concession (A63) under which training costs met or reimbursed by an employer were not taxed provided that certain conditions were met. For 1997–98 onwards the concession was replaced by TA 1988 s 200B, which was significantly wider in scope than the previous concession. Section 200B has now been rewritten as ITEPA 2003 ss 250, 251.

APPLICATION OF ITEPA 2003 S 250 TO PRE-EMPLOYMENT TRAINING

5 In order to qualify for exemption under ITEPA 2003 s 250 the reimbursement must relate to the cost of "work-related training". Work-related training is defined in ITEPA 2003 s 251 (formerly TA 1988 s 200B(5) and (6)). The definition includes, *inter alia*, training for a future job with the employee's employer but does not, except in very limited circumstances (see para 9 below) cover the reimbursement by a new employer of training expenses incurred by the employee before the employment began.

6 Looking first at the provisions of TA 1988, the exemption applied to expenditure incurred by the employer on providing such training for "a person ... who holds an office or employment under him" (s 200B(1)). That employment condition applied equally, as regards the employee, to the reference at s 200B(6)(*a*) to "any office or employment which he ... is to hold under the employer (or a related employer)". The condition is underscored by the words "in relation to the employee" in the introductory words of Section 200B(6).

7 That position is reproduced in ITEPA 2003 s 251 where work-related training is defined in terms of the employment which the employee holds, or another employment with the same employer (or a person connected with the employer).

8 The legislation does not provide a general exemption for reimbursements of training costs incurred by individuals before they commenced employment. The Special Commissioners' decision in *Silva v Charnock* (SpC 332), where the facts were somewhat unusual, does not provide support for any such general proposition.

9 We recognise, however, that cases will arise where the link between the employment and the pre-commencement training is so strong that the reimbursement should also qualify for exemption. For example, if an individual has accepted an employment offer from a new employer, to start work in the reasonably near future, and the individual then pays for work related training (within s 251(1)) for that job, exemption will not be denied if the employer agrees to reimburse those costs after the employment has begun. If there is no such demonstrable link between the individual's undertaking the training and the particular employment that they subsequently obtain, the reimbursement of the pre-employment training costs will continue to be outside the exemption.

THE WAY FORWARD

10 It is possible that some inconsistency in treatment may have arisen in this area. Some employers may, on tax office advice, be taxing (and NIC-ing) the reimbursement of pre-employment training or academic fees, whilst others are not. We apologise for any discrepancies in treatment that may have arisen as a result.

11 In some cases tax offices may have told employers, or practitioners, that the reimbursement of pre-employment training or academic fees can always be paid tax and NIC free by virtue of TA 1988 s 200B(1) (now, ITEPA 2003 s 250). In those cases the tax office will write to the employer or practitioner concerned letting them know that payments in circumstances which are clearly outside the criteria mentioned in para 9 will be subject to both PAYE and National Insurance contributions. But they will also make it clear that the Revenue will not pursue arrears of tax, or NICs, in cases where—

- payment has been made gross in accordance with specific Revenue advice; or
- an employer who has received incorrect Revenue advice makes payments ''gross'' in fulfilment of an existing undertaking given in reliance on that advice.

12 Individuals who believe that their National Insurance contribution record may be adversely affected by the Revenue's decision not to recover arrears in the circumstances mentioned above should contact their National Insurance Contributions Office. Employers and employees who think, in the light of this article, that exemption has been wrongly withheld in the past should contact their own tax office.

Commentary—*Simon's Direct Tax Service* **E4.717A**.

RI 253 (April 2003) *Flat rate scheme for small businesses*

In Tax Bulletin issue 61 we published an article on the implications of the VAT flat rate scheme for the computation of profits under Schedule D Cases I and II. Subsequent comment on that article has pointed up problems with the views we expressed.

We will include new revised material on the VAT flat rate scheme in our published guidance manuals for Revenue staff. An advance copy of this revised material is set out below, and the Tax Bulletin article in issue 61 is accordingly superseded.

An optional flat rate scheme was introduced with effect from 24 April 2002 by FA 2002 s 23. At the introduction date the scheme was available to all small businesses—

- *with a VAT exclusive annual taxable turnover of up to £100,000; and*
- *with a VAT exclusive annual turnover, including the value of exempt supplies and other non taxable income, of up to £125,000.*

Both the above requirements apply at the point of entry into the scheme. Businesses check turnover each anniversary of joining the scheme, if it is over £150,000 VAT inclusive they must leave the scheme.

A business that joins the scheme avoids having to account internally for VAT on all purchases and supplies, and instead calculates its net liability by applying a flat rate percentage to the tax inclusive turnover. The flat rate percentage depends on the trade sector into which a business falls for the purposes of the scheme. There is a wide spread of applicable percentages ranging (on introduction of the scheme) from 5 percent to 14.5 percent.

Under the flat rate scheme businesses—

- *continue to charge their customers the normal rate for the supply (ie not the flat rate percentage) on all taxable supplies of goods or services;*
- *issue tax invoices to their VAT registered customers, and also to all other customers if the business chooses to do so (these invoices show the normal rate for the supply and are used for the customers VAT reclaim).*

They do not have to record all the details of the invoices issued or purchase invoices received to calculate the amount of VAT they must pay to Customs.

CAPITAL ASSETS

If capital assets are purchased with a VAT inclusive value of £2,000 or more, the VAT can be recovered in the normal way. This concession, however, cannot be used where the assets were—

- *acquired for resale, or for incorporation in goods to be sold;*
- *acquired to be hired out, leased or let;*
- *for consumption within one year; or*
- *covered by the capital goods scheme.*

FURTHER INFORMATION

Full details of the scheme are included in VAT Notice 733 ''Flat rate scheme for small businesses'', which is available on the internet at www.hmce.gov.uk/forms/notices/733.htm or in printed form by telephoning Customs' National Advice Service on 0845 010 9000.

COMPUTATION OF PROFITS CASE I/II SCH D

The flat rate scheme removes the necessity to calculate VAT on each individual input and output for the VAT account. Instead only the flat rate VAT will need to be passed to the VAT account. Where the concession for capital assets is adopted, the VAT reclaimed will also pass through the VAT account.

Expenses will probably be shown inclusive of VAT as it is irrecoverable (similar to a business not registered for VAT), and it is likely that turnover will be shown net of the flat rate VAT payment. You may however find that the flat rate VAT payment is shown as a profit and loss expense rather than deducted from total turnover.

Where there is irrecoverable VAT on capital items it will form part of the cost of the asset on the balance sheet and of the cost for capital allowances purposes.

EXAMPLE

A business has gross sales of £94,000 (including output VAT at 17.5% of £14,000), and expenses of £58,750 (including irrecoverable VAT). The flat rate VAT @ 6% is £5,640. A new machine is purchased (qualifying for capital allowances) at a cost of £2,350 including VAT of £350.

The accounts will show—

Turnover	*£88,360*	*(£94,000 less £5,640 flat rate VAT)*
Expenses	*£58,750*	
Profit	*£29,610*	

If VAT is not reclaimed on the asset the cost for capital allowances purposes will be £2,350. If VAT is reclaimed the cost will be £2,000.

SERVICE COMPANIES ("IR35") LEGISLATION—DEEMED PAYMENT CALCULATION

The amount to be included under Step 1 of the deemed payment calculation is the VAT exclusive amount whether or not the flat rate scheme is adopted. For the intermediary within the flat rate scheme in the example above the VAT exclusive amount would be £88,360. Irrecoverable VAT relating to allowable expenses met by the intermediary would be allowable as part of the expenses in the same way as if the intermediary was not VAT registered.

Note—This Interpretation has been superseded by the Business Income Manual BIM31585.
Commentary—*De Voil Indirect Tax Service* **V2.199B.**

RI 254 (April 2003) *Farming: herd basis—minor disposals without replacement*

The profit arising from minor disposals without replacement is chargeable by virtue of TA 1988 Sch 5 para 3(10). Following representations, we have reconsidered our interpretation of this legislation.

HERD BASIS COST

We no longer consider it necessary or appropriate to compute the profit on a minor disposal from a herd, without replacement, using what we have previously described as the "herd basis cost". In our previous interpretation of the herd basis provisions, the "herd basis cost" consisted of the initial cost of the herd and the cost of any improvement or increase in herd size. These costs were not and still are not deductible in the farm trading account. When an animal replaced another of the same quality it took on the "herd basis cost" of its predecessor.

MINOR DISPOSAL—NO REPLACEMENT

We consider a disposal amounting to less than 20 per cent of the herd to be minor. Profits on these disposals are taxable (paragraph 3(10)). In the past we computed this profit by reference to "herd basis cost". In old established herds the original animals would have been replaced, perhaps several times, and this brought into charge a profit largely due to inflation. On our revised view of the situation where a farmer sells, without replacement, a small part of the herd we accept the profit should be computed by reference to the actual cost of the animal or animals disposed of. The fact that an animal taken from the herd replaced an earlier one is no longer relevant.

The following example illustrates the practical effect—

Jim has been a dairy farmer since 1950. He started his herd with an initial purchase of 60 cows costing £100 each. Over the years he has maintained his herd by regularly replacing his stock with animals of the same quality.

In 2002, at the age of 70, he decided to sell 10 of his most recently purchased cattle without replacement. The sale proceeds were £5500 in total. As this disposal amounted to less than 20 per cent of the herd the profit needs to be included in the trading account of the farm by virtue of paragraph 3(10). The "herd basis cost" of these animals would have been £100 each, but they actually cost him £450 each.

Using the "herd basis cost" the profit would have been—

£5500 – (10 x 100) = £4500.

Using actual cost the profit becomes—

£5500 – (10 x 450) = £1000.

The computation of the profit at £1000 accords with our current interpretation of paragraph 3(10).

In a situation where the farmer's records are simply so bad that this identification is not possible, we will accept that the cost of the animals removed be computed by reference to the BEN19 formula applied to the sale price. In this case it would work out at £3300 (60% of £5500). The chargeable profit would then be £2200.

Our guidance to Inspectors is currently being rewritten to reflect this change of view. We will accept this revised interpretation both in returns received from the date of this Tax Bulletin article [Editor: 17 April 2003] and for returns already received where the liability can be recomputed under the normal self-assessment provisions.

Commentary—*Simon's Direct Tax Service* **B3.518.**

RI 255 (23 June 2003) *Revised special NIC rules for entertainers*

BACKGROUND

The NIC treatment of entertainers is different from that which applies for tax.

Following the Special Commissioner's case for *McCowen and West* the Revenue accepted that most performers/artistes in the entertainment sector were engaged under contracts for services and would generally be assessable to tax under Schedule D. However, it was acknowledged that to follow this line for NIC purposes would mean that the majority of entertainers who had previously paid Class 1 NICs would only be liable for Class 2 and Class 4 NICs which would not provide them with universal title to contributory benefits.

DSS Ministers decided to introduce regulations in 1998 which would treat the majority of entertainers as employed earners for NIC purposes. This would enable entertainers to build up entitlement to contribution based Jobseeker's Allowance and ensure that, in a precarious industry, new talent could be encouraged to weather long periods without work whilst they established themselves.

Prior to 1998, the main category of performer in the entertainment industry not paying Class 1 contributions were certain ''key talent'' stars who were generally regarded as having been engaged on productions because of their celebrity status. To try and ensure this practice continued The Social Security (Categorisation of Earners) (Amendment) Regulations 1998 were introduced from 17 July 1998 which created a liability for Class 1 NICs for entertainers whose earnings consisted ''wholly or mainly of salary''. Those who negotiated a fee or received rights and additional use payments higher than the salary element were not liable to pay Class 1 NICs but were regarded as self-employed as such payments did not come within the accepted description of ''salary''.

However, in all but a few exceptional cases it has become the usual practice for the majority of entertainers to receive as part of their remuneration package pre-purchase payments as compensation for the loss of future repeat fees and rights and royalties worth many times the salary element. Very few actors were, therefore, paid ''wholly or mainly'' by salary and the regulations did not achieve the object of bringing most entertainers into Class 1.

The Revenue, therefore, accepted that the 1998 regulations were not sustainable and new regulations were introduced from 6 April 2003. These are the Social Security (Categorisation of Earners) (Amendment) Regulations 2003/736. Equivalent regulations SI 2003/733 apply for Northern Ireland.

WHAT DO THE NEW REGULATIONS MEAN?

The new regulations reflect the fact that instead of a ''wholly or mainly'' salary test, those entertainers whose remuneration includes any element of salary would be treated as employed earners. Once subject to the regulations there will be liability for Class 1 NICs on all earnings from the engagement (including rights payments.)

Where the payment is a fee for the production, not a salary, and this would have to be made clear in the contract, the entertainer would remain self-employed and would be liable to Class 2 and Class 4 NICs.

The legislative definition of Salary requires that the remuneration satisfies the following four conditions—

- made for services rendered;
- paid under a contract for services;
- where there is more than one payment, payable at a specified period or interval; and
- computed by reference to the amount of time for which work has been performed.

The third bullet point includes those entertainers engaged on a single day or two day engagement. This means that the policy intention of ensuring that the regulations apply to film extras and walk-on parts is achieved. The last bullet point ensures that key talent artistes are excluded as they will be contracted to appear in productions for which their remuneration is not directly calculated according to the period of weeks or months they are assigned to the production.

WHAT IF THE ENTERTAINER IS ENGAGED THROUGH AN AGENCY?

The legislation also includes provisions which amend Sch 3 para 10 to the Social Security (Categorisation of Earners) Regulations 1978 to ensure that where an entertainer is engaged through a third party (an agency) the producer of the entertainment in respect of which the payments of salary are made is treated as the secondary contributor. However, this does not override the effect of the Intermediaries legislation (IR35) which provides that where an entertainer provides his services to a client through a personal service company it is the latter which is the secondary contributor.

EXCEPTIONS

In accordance with the Revenue's policy intention Session Musicians and Session Singers, who are generally engaged through Musicians Union approved contractors and whose earnings were not previously subject to Class 1 NICs, are excepted from the new regulations.

ARRANGEMENTS FOR CLAIMING REFUNDS OF CLASS 1 NICS PAID IN ERROR

Who can claim refunds

The 1998 Regulations have led to some entertainers being wrongly categorised as employed earners because their remuneration did not consist ''wholly or mainly of salary'' and therefore any primary or secondary Class 1 contributions which have been paid in relation to entertainers on the footing that they were employed earners may have been incorrectly paid. There is provision under National Insurance legislation for the return of contributions which have been paid in error and refund claims will be invited for appropriate periods between 17 July 1998 and 5 April 2003.

The restriction of refund claims to 2 years provided for in SSCBA 1992 s 19A will be waived for the purposes of this exercise until a cut-off point is announced. However, individuals can choose not to have their primary contributions refunded, but to let them count instead towards their Additional Pension (AP) entitlement, as if they had been correctly paid. This does not prevent the engager from seeking a refund of the wrongly paid secondary contributions or the individual notifying the Revenue that they wish to claim a refund before they reach pension age, subject to the appropriate time limits.

Primary NICs refunded to entertainers will be reduced by the amount of any Class 2 and 4 contributions which were due from them as self-employed earners, and of any contributory benefits paid on the basis of the incorrect Class 1 contributions.

How to make a claim

An engager or entertainer who considers that Class 1 NICs may have been incorrectly paid between 17 July 1998 and 5 April 2003 can apply for a refund. Claims for all tax years should be submitted together. Anyone who wishes to do so in the belief that workers previously treated as employed earners should have been regarded as self-employed should write to—Inland Revenue, National Insurance Contributions Office Refunds Group (Erroneous 4), Room BP1001, Benton Park View, Newcastle upon Tyne, NE98 1ZZ.

Alternatively they should telephone Refunds Group on 0845 912254042 [calls will be charged at BT local rates].

Claim forms will be available on request from the end of June 2003 and Refunds Group will begin dealing with refund applications shortly after that. As an alternative to the written application form some engagers may find it more convenient to submit claims for refunds by CD-Rom or floppy disk and this facility will be available on request.

What information is needed?

Engagers will need to give as much information as possible when making a claim ie Full name of individual / Stage Name (where appropriate)/ NINO/ Date of Birth/ Correct address. They will also be required to declare—

(i) All Basic and Rights Payments made in each tax year for which a claim is made.
(ii) Total earnings on which NICs were deducted and total amount of NICs paid.
(iii) Amounts of employers and employees contributions.
(iv) The type of contract under which the individual has been engaged; If it is either of the standard BBC/EQUITY, ITVA/EQUITY or PACT/EQUITY contracts then no other proof of payment will be required. Contracts and/or invoices will be required in all other cases.

What happens when claims are received?

On receipt the claim will be registered and if sufficient information is supplied, all secondary Class 1NICs confirmed as erroneously paid will be refunded. All claims will be dealt with in the order they are received and will be processed as soon as possible. Employees named on the claim form who, as a result of previous refund action, have already notified the Inland Revenue that they did not wish to claim a refund of primary NICs, will not be contacted but applications will be accepted from those individuals who choose not to allow their wrongly paid contributions to remain on their NI record.

How do applicants know if they are entitled to a refund?

If Class 1 NICs have been paid between 17 July 1998 and 5 April 2003 in respect of entertainers whose remuneration does not satisfy the ''wholly or mainly of salary'' criteria in the 1998 regulations then a refund of those contributions may be claimed. For example remuneration made up of 60% Rights Payments and 40% Salary would not be ''wholly or mainly of salary'' and there would have been no liability for Class 1 NICs. However, Class 1 NICs were properly payable in cases where, at the time of the engagement, it was known that the salary element of the remuneration exceeded any residuals. Therefore, any subsequent residual payments not quantifiable at the time of the original engagement will not change the nature of the original payment. The rule of thumb being that the status decision at the point of first contact is the deciding factor.

The following table indicates whether or not the various elements of remuneration under any of the standard BBC/Equity, ITVA/Equity or PACT/Equity contracts satisfy the case law definition of salary—

Type of payment salary	*Rights payment*
Engagement fee	salary or negotiable payment depending upon contract type
Attendance days	salary
Standby days	salary
Holiday pay	salary
Overtime	salary
Additional use fee	rights payment for pre-purchase
Retainer	salary—to ensure services available when needed
Secondary sales	rights payment—''one off'' for sale of programme
Repeat fees	rights payment—either pre-purchase or at each repeat
Option fee	rights payment—to ensure an engager has priority use of an entertainer's services

WHAT NOW?

If any entertainers, practitioners or engagers are in any doubt about the new regulations or whether they are entitled to a refund they should contact their nearest Inland Revenue office and ask to speak to a member of the Status team. Enquiries about entertainers engaged by TV Broadcasting Companies should be made to the TV Industry Unit on 0161 2613255.

Guidance notes on the new legislation and the arrangements for claiming refunds have been prepared for the entertainment industry and these will also be available at—www.inlandrevenue.gov.uk/publications/specialist from the end of June 2003.

RI 256 (23 June 2003) *Fee protection insurance*

1 This article is about premiums for fee protection insurance relating to the costs of possible future tax enquiries. We have been asked to clarify our views on whether such premiums are allowable as a deduction in computing the profits or losses chargeable to tax under Case I/II Sch D. In particular we have been asked whether our views on this issue are affected by the decision in *McKnight v Sheppard* (71 TC 419). The comments in this article apply equally to the computation of profits/losses of a Sch A business.

2 The Courts have approved the practice of allowing the normal accountancy expenses incurred in preparing accounts and establishing taxation liabilities (see *Smith's Potato Estates Ltd v Bolland*, 30 TC 267). Statement of Practice 16/91 as expanded by Tax Bulletin article 37 published in October 1998, sets out our view on the deductibility of additional accountancy expenses arising out of an enquiry into a tax return. It says that additional accountancy expenses incurred because of such an enquiry are not allowable if—

- the enquiry reveals discrepancies and additional liabilities for the year of enquiry, or any earlier year; and
- those discrepancies etc result from negligent or fraudulent conduct.

3 In relation to fee protection insurance, premiums paid to insure against the risk of incurring additional costs are allowable for tax purposes only if those additional costs would themselves have been allowable. This includes the requirement that those costs would, if incurred directly by the business, satisfy the test that they are incurred wholly and exclusively for the purposes of the business.

4 A premium on a fee protection policy, which entitles the policyholder, amongst other risks covered, to claim for the cost of accountancy fees incurred in negotiating additional tax liabilities resulting from negligent or fraudulent conduct, is not an allowable deduction. Furthermore it is not possible to apportion the premiums since it is impossible to identify a part that has been incurred wholly and exclusively for the purposes of the trade or profession.

5 This means that no deduction is allowable to those taxpayers who either make no claim under the policy or only claim against the policy for expenses that are allowable under SP 16/91. This is because the premiums covered some risks where the related costs are not allowable for tax purposes.

6 The decision in *McKnight v Sheppard* does not affect this analysis. That case concerned fines imposed in disciplinary proceedings and the associated legal expenses. In Lord Hoffman's judgement (71 TC 453) he made the point that tax fell into an entirely separate category from the set of issues concerning fines, penalties and damages dealt with in *McKnight v Sheppard* and earlier related cases. He said of *Smith's Potato Estates Ltd v Bolland*—

> "In that case, the taxpayer claimed to deduct the legal costs of contesting an assessment to tax. The dispute was about the computation of the taxpayer's profits. It assumed that those profits were ascertainable, one way or another, at the time when the dispute arose. The costs of the dispute could not therefore have been an element in the computation. They were logically as well as temporally subsequent to the profits having been earned."

7 Our view therefore remains that premiums for a fee protection insurance policy, which entitles the policyholder to claim for the cost of accountancy fees incurred in negotiating additional tax liabilities resulting from negligent or fraudulent conduct, are not an allowable deduction in computing taxable profits and losses under Sch D Cases I and II.

RI 257 (23 June 2003) *The interaction between the benefits code and payments or benefits received on a termination or change in the nature of employment*

From 6 April 2003 most of the provisions of TA 1988 relating to Income Tax chargeable under Schedule E ceased to have effect. They have been replaced by ITEPA 2003.

During the writing of ITEPA, a point arose concerning the interaction between TA 1988 ss 148, 154. Section 148 contained the tax charge on payments and benefits made either on termination of employment, or on a change in the nature of employment. Section 154 contained the rules for taxing general benefits.

NOT OTHERWISE CHARGEABLE TO TAX

Section 148 applied to payments and benefits "not otherwise chargeable to tax" whereas s 154 applied to benefits "not (apart from this section) chargeable to tax". From these conditions it was clear that both Sections applied only in the absence of more specific tax provisions and where there was a charge to tax under any other specific provision, for example TA 1988 s 19, that charge took precedence over both s 148 and s 154.

If there was no charge under any other provision it was normally apparent from the circumstances which of s 148 or s 154 should apply, but in a small number of instances there could be a potential overlap between the two Sections.

PAYMENT AND BENEFITS PAID ON TERMINATION OR CHANGE OF EMPLOYMENT

Where payments or benefits related to termination of employment there was no overlap because s 154 could not apply after termination. The tax charge on termination payments could arise under other provisions, such as s 19, but if none of these applied the payment on termination fell generally within s 148.

Where payments or benefits related to a change in the nature of employment, the position was not always so clear. If, exceptionally, the payment did not fall within s 19 it could potentially be taxed under either s 148 or s 154.

Where this potential overlap existed, the order of priority was not thought to be clear in all circumstances. The Revenue's practice, applied consistently over many years, was to treat the payment as taxable under s 148, in priority to s 154.

CHANGE OF PRACTICE FROM 6 APRIL 2003

In the light of advice received during the writing of ITEPA we now accept that, as a matter of law, and in circumstances where both sections potentially applied, s 154 did take precedence over s 148. That statutory position is maintained in ITEPA. The Revenue's practice has therefore been changed to reflect the statutory position.

From 6 April 2003, where there is a potential overlap between ITEPA s 401 (which replaces TA 1988 s 148) and ITEPA s 201 (which replaces TA 1988 s 154), the charge to tax arises under s 201, in priority to s 401.

It is anticipated that this change of practice will only affect a small number of cases but if you have any comments or views on this change of practice please write to—Revenue Policy Personal Tax (Technical) Room 131, Sapphire House, 550 Streetsbrook Rd, Solihull, West Midlands, B91 1QU.

RI 258 (23 June 2003) *National insurance contributions liability on payments into funded unapproved retirement benefits schemes*

INTRODUCTION

You may be aware that, as a result of the High Court decision in *Tullett & Tokyo Forex International Ltd and Others v the Secretary of State for Social Security* [2000] EWHC Admin 350, the Inland Revenue has been reconsidering its position on the National Insurance contributions (NICs) liability on payments into a Funded Unapproved Retirement Benefits Scheme (FURBS). This article sets out the conclusion of its deliberations. It confirms the Revenue's existing and published view that such payments are liable for Class 1 NICs.

All the legislative references mentioned in this article are those which apply in Great Britain. Northern Ireland has its own legislation which, in the main, is the same as that for Great Britain. But, for ease, we refer only to the latter in this article.

BACKGROUND

In May 1998 the Secretary of State for Social Security decided, under SSAA 1992 s 17, that bonuses made by way of additional payments in the form of short-dated gilts to life assurance policies were earnings and liable for Class 1 NICs.

The three employers involved appealed against the Secretary of State's decisions. In May 2000, the High Court gave judgement, when it decided in favour of the companies and allowed the appeals. Under SSAA 1992 s18(6), a decision of the High Court is final.

LEGISLATION

Subject to certain conditions, SSCBA 1992 s 6(1) provides that a Class 1 NICs liability arises when ''earnings are paid to or for the benefit of an earner [employee]''. ''Earnings'' are defined in SSCBA 1992 s 3(1) as including ''any remuneration or profit derived from an employment''.

THE HIGH COURT'S DECISION

The court decided that payments by the employers of the short-dated gilts to life assurance policies held by their employees were not earnings ''paid to or for the benefit of'' the employees in question within the meaning of SSCBA 1992 s 6(1). Mr Justice Collins held that, in construing SSCBA 1992 s 6(1), it was necessary to look at what the employee receives. As such, the ''earnings paid to or for the benefit'' of the employees was—

- the enhancement in the value of the life assurance policies held by the employees; and
- not the gilts paid into the assurance policies, which was merely the cost to the employers of making such payments.

The enhancement in the value of the policies was a payment in kind. As such, it fell to be disregarded, for the purposes of calculating the amount of the employees' gross earnings for Class 1 NICs purposes, by virtue of the Social Security (Contributions) Regulations 1979 reg 19(1)(*d*) (since 6 April 2001 Social Security (Contributions) Regulations, SI 2001/1004; Sch 3 Pt II para 1)).

NICS LIABILITY ON PAYMENTS INTO A FURBS

Since November 1997, the view has been that employer's cash payments into a FURBS are earnings ''paid to or for the benefit of'' an employee within the meaning of SSCBA 1992 s 6(1). Where such a payment is made in respect of two or more employees, Social Security (Contributions) Regulations, SI 2001/1004; Sch 2 para 13 sets out how the amount of earnings for each employee comprised in the payments into the FURBS must be calculated.

IMPLICATIONS OF THE TULLETT & TOKYO DECISION ON THE NICS LIABILITY ON PAYMENTS INTO A FURBS

The Revenue has been considering the effect of the *Tullett & Tokyo* judgement on the NICs liability on payments into a FURBS. After full and careful consideration, the Revenue does not accept the High Court's reasoning as applying to a payment into a FURBS.

We consider that—

- in reaching his decision, Mr Justice Collins put too much emphasis on Schedule E tax case law when the three appeals concerned the interpretation of NICs legislation;
- the definition of ''earnings'' in SSCBA 1992 s 6(1) is much wider than ''emoluments'' in TA 1988 s 131(1) (from 6 April 2003, ''earnings'' within ITEPA 2003 s 62);
- the wording of SSCBA 1992 s 6(1)—''...earnings...paid to or for the benefit of...''—further extends the meaning of ''earnings''
- so in some circumstances, as in the case of employer payments into a FURBS, ''earnings'' includes payments made to a third party for the benefit of the employee.

RIs

All of which means that there is no change to the Revenue's stated position that a payment into a FURBS is liable for Class 1 NICs. This position is set out—

- in booklet CWG2 (2003) ''Employer's Further Guide to PAYE and NICs''—
- in paragraph 81 on page 57;
- on page 76 under ''retirement benefits schemes''; and
- on pages 02155 to 02163 of the Revenue's internal guidance, the ''National Insurance Manual''.

UNPAID CLASS 1 NICS ON PAYMENTS INTO A FURBS

Where due, the Revenue will seek payment of any Class 1 NICs which have not been paid on payments into a FURBS. It will also seek interest on the unpaid amount.

REQUESTS FOR REFUNDS OF CLASS 1 NICS PAID ON PAYMENTS INTO A FURBS

As a result of the *Tullett & Tokyo* judgement, the Revenue has received a number of requests for refunds of the Class 1 NICs which have been paid on payments into a FURBS. These requests have been refused.

A refund can only be made if the NICs have been paid in error (regulation 52(1)(*a*) of the 2001 Regulations). ''Error'' is defined in reg 52(12) as meaning, and only meaning, an error which—

- is made at the time of payment; and
- relates to some present or past matter.

As explained above, the Revenue's view is that a payment into a FURBS is liable for Class 1 NICs. It follows that the NICs paid on a payment into a FURBS have not been paid in error within the meaning of regulation 52(12) of the 2001 Regulations. So the NICs cannot be refunded.

RI 259 (August 2003) *Taxation of chargeable gains—sale of trust interests and transfers linked to trustee borrowing (TCGA 1992 Schs 4A, 4B)*

We have been asked by representative bodies and individual firms of tax practitioners to offer guidance on the meaning of certain statutory terms and on the application of the legislation in TCGA 1992 Schs 4A, 4B. The relevant legislation was enacted in FA 2000. These schedules are part of a package of measures designed to prevent certain forms of avoidance of capital gains tax involving trusts.

DETAILS—SCHEDULE 4A

Schedule 4A is concerned with certain situations where there is a disposal of an interest in a UK resident settlement for consideration.

A1 Paragraph 3—"for consideration"

Under paragraph 3(1) ''A disposal is ''for consideration'' if consideration is given or received by any person for, or otherwise in connection with, any transaction by virtue of which the disposal is effected''. (Paragraph 3(3) restricts this to actual consideration.) Our view is that ''consideration'' in this context does not extend to the incidental costs of the transaction, in particular reasonable fees charged by professional advisers for giving guidance as to the legal and fiscal effects of the transaction or for drafting and executing the relevant paperwork. Therefore, if there are no payments other than in respect of the incidental costs, the transaction does not fall within Sch 4A.

A2 Paragraph 13(2)(b)—"for practical purposes"

This paragraph is concerned with the situation where there is a period between the beginning of the disposal of the interest in question and the ''effective completion'' of it in circumstances where Schedule 4A applies. In this situation the deemed disposal under para 4(1) of the relevant trust assets occurs at the moment of effective completion of the disposal of the interest. This is required for testing the conditions relating to the residence status of the trustees and settlor (paras 5 and 6) and the interest of the settlor in the settlement (para 7). It is also relevant for the purposes of paragraph 8 where the identity of the underlying assets changes during the period, and paragraph 9 where the value changes during the period.

The conditions as to the residence of the settlor and the trustees are met if they applied for

- the tax year in which the disposal of the interest began, or
- the tax year in which it was effectively completed, or
- any tax year in between.

The condition as to the interest of the settlor is met if it applied at any time between

- the beginning of the tax year two years before the tax year in which the disposal of the interest began; and
- the date of the effective completion of the disposal.

These two dates are inclusive.

The beginning of the disposal is defined by para 13(2)(*a*) as, in the case of a disposal involving the exercise of an option, the date of the grant of the option, and in any other case involving a contract, the date the contract was entered into.

The effective completion is defined by para 13(2)(*b*) as "the point at which the person acquiring the interest becomes for practical purposes unconditionally entitled to the whole of the intended subject matter of the disposal". The main purpose of the words "for practical purposes" is to cover cases where the buyer has the power to compel the trustees to transfer the property to him on giving due notice. Another example would be where the buyer has a right to enjoy the property now, but is not entitled to it until a particular contingency is fulfilled, and there is no real likelihood of its not being fulfilled.

DETAILS—SCHEDULE 4B

Schedule 4B is concerned with situations where the trustees of a settlement falling within TCGA 1992 s 77, 86 or 87 make a transfer of value which is treated as linked with trustee borrowing.

B1 Paragraph 2(1)(b)—cash distributions which are income

Where trustees of a discretionary trust make a distribution which is income of the recipient for UK tax purposes, this is not a "transfer of value" within para 2, which is concerned with capital transactions.

B2 Paragraph 2(1)(a)—beneficiary exercising rights under Trustee etc Act 1996 s 12

In certain circumstances a beneficiary's occupation of property, instead of being the consequence of the volition of the trustees, may result from personal rights under Trusts of Land and Appointment of Trustees Act 1996 s 12. Our view is that if the rights of the beneficiary arise as a consequence of the wording of the deed or will, then the occupation does not give rise to a transfer of value. It may be otherwise where the rights have arisen as a consequence of the exercise by the trustees of a power of appointment or advancement.

B3 Paragraph 2(1)(c)—"issue a security"

We have been asked what the expression "issue a security" covers. It caters for those exceptional circumstances where trustees issue to a beneficiary or to the trustees of another trust a document acknowledging liability. Schedule 4B para 13(2) provides that references to the transfer of an asset include everything that is or is treated as a disposal of an asset. The issue of a security is not in itself the disposal or part disposal of an asset. Therefore para 2(1)(*b*) does not apply to it, and it was necessary to have a specific provision to cover this possibility.

B4 Paragraph 4(1)—meaning of "borrowing"

It is not unusual for the trustees of a non-resident trust to borrow money from a non-resident company which they control. In this situation, if the company were resident in the UK, TA 1988 s 419 might well be applicable. It has been suggested that in this situation the trustees are effectively "borrowing" from themselves and therefore outside para 4(1). We consider this incorrect, particularly in the light of *Chamberlain v IRC*, 25 TC 357. It does not matter whether the borrowing is from a company controlled by the trustees or their associates, or from an entirely unconnected company. What matters is the use to which the borrowing is put.

The fact that money was borrowed before 21 March 2000 does not prevent it from being outstanding trust borrowing.

Where trustees are presented with a bill, for example for repairs to trust property, bona fide delay in payment would not convert this into a borrowing for the purposes of paragraph 4.

B5 Paragraph 6(4)—application of proceeds to meet current expenses

We have been asked whether trustee borrowings to meet payments on account or provision for future or past expenses are covered by the expression "current expenses". One circumstance in which borrowings are applied for "normal trust purposes" (para 6) is where they are applied by the trustees in making payments to meet bona fide current expenses incurred by them.

One may note that there are three tests to be met—

- The borrowings have been applied by the moment of the transfer of value (para 5(2)(*b*)(*i*)).
- They have been applied to meet bona fide "current expenses".
- The expenses are expenses of "administering" the settlement or any of the settled property.

In the case of borrowing to meet future expenses it is hard to see how the borrowings can be said to have been applied. But the time for making the test is not when the money is borrowed, but the time of the transfer of value (this is "the material time", as defined in para 2(2)). In the case of payments on account there would be the requisite application and the liability to pay would have been incurred.

We do not regard "current" as restricting qualification to expenditure which for accounting purposes must fall in the year of borrowing, but we should regard it as excluding borrowing to make a provision for future expenditure or to meet expenditure that was incurred long before but left unpaid.

In general where contracts for repairs of an ordinary kind have been entered into, we should regard the expenditure anticipated under those contracts to be current expenses at the moment of borrowing. Where trustees as the owner or tenant of a flat are obliged by contract or under the terms of the lease to make payments into a common fund to meet future maintenance or repair expenditure this would be regarded as a current expense.

The expression ''administering the settlement or any of the settled property'' should be construed widely to cover not only those expenses properly chargeable to income, or which would be so chargeable but for express provisions of the trust deed, but also capital expenditure such as capital taxes in the UK or elsewhere, or legal costs of a reorganisation, in particular the costs of an application under the Variation of Trusts Act. Other capital expenditure would often be expenditure on the asset itself, and therefore qualify under para 6(2). Contributions to the day-to-day running costs of a nominee company controlled by the trustees would also qualify.

B6 Paragraph 7—"ordinary trust assets"—futures contracts

We have been asked to say whether a futures contract relating to commodities is an ''ordinary trust asset''. Such a contract is not a tangible asset nor does it give the holder an interest in such an asset. Therefore, it is not an ''ordinary trust asset''.

B7 What happens when trustees put money into a conventional current or deposit account at a bank or building society?

Although in general law this is regarded as a loan from the customer to the bank, in the context of this legislation we do not consider that this comes within the meaning of ''lend'' for the purposes of para 2(1)(*a*). The currency in which the deposit is made is immaterial.

B8 What happens when money is borrowed to purchase the freehold interest of a property which is then rented on a commercial basis?

It is important to appreciate that the expression ''transfer of value'' equates to the three types of transaction described in para 2(1). It does not carry the kind of meaning that it has for inheritance tax purposes.

Under para13(2) references to the transfer of an asset include references to anything that is a disposal, and under TCGA 1992 s 21(2) references to a disposal include references to a part disposal. Paragraph 13(3) provides that references to a transfer of an asset do not include the transfer of an asset which is created by the part disposal of another asset. The grant of a lease is a part disposal of the freehold interest and therefore the grant of a lease is a transfer of the freehold interest for the purposes of para 2(1)(*b*) and is not regarded as the transfer simply of the lease. If the freehold interest was bought with borrowed money it meets the test in para 2(4)(*a*), and the amount of value transferred equals the market value of the freehold.

Assuming that there is outstanding trustee borrowing at ''the material time'', which is defined in para 2(2) as the time the transfer is effectively completed, it is then necessary to consider whether the transfer of value is linked with trustee borrowing. Under para 7 tangible property, and any interest in such property falls within the expression ''ordinary trust assets''. However the property concerned must under para 6(2)(*b*) either form part of the settled property immediately after the material time, or meet the alternative condition in para 8(1)(*b*) that it is represented by ordinary trust assets which form part of the settled property immediately after the material time. Paragraph 6(2)(*b*) and para 8(1)(*b*) may be looked at together. In this situation we say that the reversion to the lease is still part of the settled property, and the lease itself is represented by the right to the rental stream.

Therefore where trustees borrow money to acquire the freehold interest in a property which is then let commercially and, at the material time, there are no outstanding trustee borrowings other than those which have been applied for normal trust purposes, Sch 4B does not apply. But the position will be different if at that moment there are outstanding trustee borrowings applied for other purposes.

The same considerations apply where trustees acquire a long lease which is sublet, and where the asset in question is a chattel rather than land or buildings.

B9 What happens when money is spent unproductively, for example on a planning application that fails?

Under para 6(2) there are three conditions that must be met by a payment in respect of ''an ordinary trust asset'' if it is to be regarded as applied for normal trust purposes. The third, in para 6(2)(*c*), is that the sum is allowable under TCGA 1992 s 38 (or would be but for s 17 or 39) as a deduction in computing a gain accruing to the trustees on a disposal of the asset. If an application for planning permission fails, then when the land is actually sold the costs relating to the application are generally not allowable; this is because they are not ''reflected in the state or nature of the asset at the time of the disposal''. Paragraph 6(2)(*c*) however must be referring to a notional disposal not to a real one. In the context of para 6 we consider that the reference can only be to a notional disposal taking place at the time when the expenditure is incurred.

Although one could not lay down as a universal rule that the expenditure would always qualify, the test is whether the existence of the current application for planning permission is reflected in the state or nature of the asset at the time of the notional disposal.

B10 How should we compute the base cost of assets for future disposals?

The trustees are treated as disposing of the whole or a proportion of each of the chargeable assets continuing to form part of the settled property. Suppose that an asset cost £600, the trustees are treated as disposing of two thirds of the asset at the material time (paragraph 10(1)), and the respective values of two thirds and one third immediately after that time are £900 and £450. Leaving aside indexation, if any, the computation is—

Cost	2/3 of 600	400
Deemed Proceeds		900
Gain		500
Remaining original cost	600 – 400	200
Deemed Acquisition		900
Revised cost		1100

Commentary—*Simon's Direct Tax Service* **C4.331**; **C4.451**.

RI 260 (August 2003) *Capital gains—transfer of assets under a court order*

RESTRICTION OF GIFT HOLD-OVER RELIEF

We have been advised that our view, that we should apply TCGA 1992 s 165(7) to restrict gift hold-over relief on transfers of assets between spouses made under the provisions of a Court Order under the Matrimonial Causes Act 1973, is incorrect. This change in our prevailing practice follows legal advice we have taken in the light of the comments of Coleridge J. in *G v G* [2002] EWHC 1339 on the tax consequences of court orders made under the Matrimonial Causes Act 1973. We are therefore revising our guidance in the CG Manual as follows—

CG67192—GIFTS—HOLD-OVER RELIEF—CONSIDERATION

The disposal of an asset from one spouse to the other in the circumstances described in CG67191 is, where there is no recourse to the courts, usually made in exchange for a surrender by the donee of rights which they would otherwise be able to exercise to obtain alternative financial provision. In such cases we take the view that the value of the rights surrendered represents actual consideration of an amount which would reduce the gain potentially eligible for hold-over relief to nil. ''Consideration'' is not limited to money or money's worth.

Exceptionally, it may be possible for the parties concerned to demonstrate that there was a substantial gratuitous element in the transfer. It should be made clear that the onus is on the parties concerned to demonstrate that this was the case, and in particular that the amounts transferred were substantially in excess of what the recipient's spouse could reasonably have expected to have received as the result of a contested court case.

However, in cases where there is recourse to the courts and a court makes an order—

- for ancillary relief under the Matrimonial Causes Act 1973 which results in a transfer of assets from one spouse to another; or
- formally ratifying an agreement reached by the divorcing parties dealing with the transfer of assets,

we take the view that the spouse to whom the assets are transferred does not give actual consideration, in the form of surrendered rights, for their transfer. A Court Order, made in these circumstances, reflects the exercise by the court of its independent statutory jurisdiction and is not the consequence of any party to the proceedings agreeing to surrender alternative rights in return for assets.

This approach represents a change in the Revenue's prevailing practice, following consideration of judicial observations made in the case of *G v G* [2002] EWHC 1339 and applies with effect from 31 July 2002. Therefore, where assets are transferred between divorcing parties by reason of a Court Order as described above and a claim for gift hold-over relief is made, or remains unsettled, on or after that date, the relief should not be restricted in accordance with TCGA s 92, 165(7) on the grounds that actual consideration has been given by the donee.

This change of practice will apply from 31 July 2002 (the date of publication of the *G v G* judgment) to—

(*a*) relevant s 165 claims made on or after that date; and
(*b*) relevant s 165 claims previously made but unsettled at that date.

This change will also apply to similar orders made under the Family Law (Scotland) Act 1985.

RI 261 (27 August 2003) *Sale and repurchase agreements—"repo" tax changes in FA 2003*

The Finance Act contains a number of provisions relating to sale and repurchase agreements (repo). This article provides a brief overview of those changes and clarifies a few issues that have been raised since the legislation was introduced.

TAX CREDIT ADJUSTMENT

The Act removes an anomaly which dates back to the abolition of Advance Corporation Tax (ACT). It relates to manufactured dividends, deemed to be paid by TA 1988 s 737A and the consequent adjustment to the repurchase price under section TA 1988 s 737C. These provisions affect what are termed "net paying repos" where the parties agree that, instead of the interim holder making a manufactured payment to the original owner, the equivalent amount is netted off against the repurchase price.

When ACT was in force, the deemed payer of a manufactured dividend on a UK equity would have been liable to pay ACT, so that the amount of the deemed manufactured dividend plus the ACT made up the "gross amount". The objective for section 737C is to increase the repurchase price by the same amount, and hence the increase was defined to be equal to the "gross amount". However, this point was not corrected when ACT was abolished, so that a deemed manufactured dividend on a UK equity under s 737A became equal to just the dividend, but the deemed increase to the repurchase price remained at the higher amount of dividend plus tax credit.

The Finance Act corrects this anomaly so that the repurchase price is now increased by just the amount of the dividend. The change has effect where the repurchase under the repo takes place on or after Budget Day, 9 April 2003. TA 1988 s 737A deems the manufactured payment to be made on the repurchase date, and therefore the amended rules apply to any adjustment made under s 737C on or after 9 April 2003. In these cases, it will not be possible for a company to claim a deduction for any part of the higher s 737C adjustment "accrued" up to 9 April 2003.

EXCHANGE GAINS AND LOSSES

FA 2002 made significant changes to the loan relationships regime of FA 1996, and overhauled the tax treatment of foreign exchange gains and losses. It also brought sale and repurchase agreements for companies within the loan relationships rules, but made specific provision only for the price differential. This led to questions about the correct treatment of foreign exchange gains and losses in relation to the original sale price of the securities.

One possible interpretation was for any such gains or losses to be wrapped up in the overall repo price differential, but this could have led to unexpected results for tax. For example, the exchange movement could have been substantial, so that the overall amount of the price differential (deemed to be interest) in the accounting currency could have been regarded as giving rise to an excessive rate of return. This in turn could have triggered the distribution rules.

FA 2003 introduces a comprehensive scheme—TA 1988 s 730BB—which gives a clear and separate tax treatment for exchange gains and losses on the original sale price. The following example may help to demonstrate (all figures have been rounded off to the nearest £1000).

> *A company accounts in sterling. It sells securities for $900,000, with an agreement to buy them back for $918,000 after six months. At the start of the transaction the exchange rate is £1=$1·50 so the sterling value of the sale price is £600,000. At the repurchase date the exchange rate is £1=$1·45. Therefore the sterling value of the original sale price is £621,000. The original owner has therefore made an exchange loss of £21,000 in respect of the original sale price.*
>
> *The repurchase price in sterling is £633,000. The price differential under the repo agreement is £12,000 (£633,000 minus £621,000). This amount will be taxed and relieved under TA 1988 s 737A(2).*

Advisers have queried the timing of recognition of any exchange gain or loss where the repo crosses an accounting date. Advisers have suggested that the legislation requires that any such gain or loss can only be brought into account when the existence of a gain or loss is definite—at the end of the repo. This is not the intention. The whole thrust of the legislation is that recognised accounting principles should normally be followed. It is acceptable for a company to accrue an exchange gain or loss at its accounting date for tax purposes by reference to the information that it has in its possession at that time. Again, an example might help.

> *Take the same figures as in the above example, but assume that the accounting period ends after three months of the repo. At that time the exchange rate is £1 = $1·53. The sterling value of the original sale price is therefore £588,000. This would be recognised by the original owner as an exchange gain of £12,000 for that accounting period.*
>
> *If the exchange rate then moved to £1=$1·45, again using the original example, the original owner would recognise an exchange loss in the later accounting period of £33,000 under TA 1988 s 730BB.*

The Inland Revenue will not normally seek to disturb this approach, except in cases where there is attempted manipulation to avoid tax.

The Finance Act also contains a short amendment to FA 1996 s 100 to make sure that where a repo gives rise to a money debt, and the company stands as creditor or debtor in relation to that money debt, any exchange gains or losses will be dealt with only under TA 1988 s 730BB and not under FA 1996 s 100.

OPTIONS

There had been some uncertainty as to whether or not all of the repo tax rules applied where the repurchase was subject to either a put or a call option. Different provisions carried different forms of wording. The Finance Act standardises the wording and makes it clear that—

- The repo rules apply where the repurchase is subject to either a put option or a call option, or indeed cross options available to both parties; but
- The repo rules only apply if an option is actually exercised.

As with exchange gains and losses, this has also led advisers to question the timing for tax purposes when the repo crosses an accounting date. The Inland Revenue view is that normal accounting principles should be followed. This would usually involve the company taking a view at the accounting date of the likelihood that the option will or will not be exercised, and the consequences for tax will flow from that decision. Attention is also drawn to FA 1996 Sch 9 para 3, which sets out a prescribed treatment for determining (for tax purposes) whether or not an option will be exercised—but this should only be necessary where normal accounting principles have not been followed for whatever reason.

Advisers have questioned the boundary between the repo tax rules and the derivative contract tax rules in FA 2002 Sch 26—particularly where the repurchase is subject to an option. Should any question of overlap arise, FA 1996 s 101 provides a ''tie breaker'' giving the loan relationships rules precedence over derivative contracts. The FA 2002 changes made a repo subject to all the provisions of the loan relationships rules, which therefore includes FA 1996 s 101.

Finally, the Finance Bill provisions establish a consistent tax treatment for an option premium in a repo. The premium will fall to be accounted for, and therefore taxed, as part of the overall repo unless it is brought into account under the derivative contract rules in FA 2002 Sch 26. Persons not within the charge to corporation tax are not subject to FA 2002 Sch 26, and therefore the rules now specify that any option premium in a repo is to be taxed or relieved for such persons as part of the overall repo.

OTHER CLARIFICATIONS

The Finance Act also contains some changes which tidy up a few problem areas where there were potential mismatches between different parts of the repo rules. The overall thrust is to ensure that either all of the repo rules apply, or none of them. The changes include—

- Where TA 1988 s 730A(8) prevents a transaction from being treated as a repo for tax then the exclusion from the accrued income scheme (TA 1988 s 727A) will also not apply.
- Similarly, where TA 1988 s 730A(8) applies then the transaction will not be excluded from being a ''related transaction'' for loan relationships purposes (FA 1996 Sch 9 para 15).
- Where TA 1988 s 730A does not apply, for whatever reason, any repurchase price adjustment made under TA 1988 s 737C will be made for other relevant tax provisions.
- Changes to TA 1988 s 737A clarify that its provisions apply where a manufactured dividend rather than the real dividend is received by a person other then the original owner.

Commentary—*Simon's Direct Tax Service* **A7.2**.

RI 262 (August 2003) *First year allowances and plant hire*

This article describes a change of Revenue view concerning the exclusion from First Year Allowances (FYAs) of plant or machinery which is hired out.

Expenditure incurred by small or medium-sized enterprises on plant or machinery may qualify for FYAs. There are a number of exceptions, one of which is that the plant or machinery must not be acquired for the purposes of leasing (CAA 2001 s 46(2)). For the purposes of the legislation, leasing includes the letting of assets on hire. Much expenditure incurred by plant hire firms falls within this exclusion. But there is a distinction between the leasing of an asset and the provision of services that involve the use of an asset. We previously took the view that where an asset is provided with an operative and overall supervision and control lies with the customer then the asset is being hired out, but where control lies with the operator this is the provision of a service. In the construction industry it is commonplace to use the standard Construction and Plant Hire Association contract which contains the condition that where a driver is provided he ''shall be under the control of the hirer'', ie the person to whom the asset is hired out.

The judgement in the recent case of Baldwins Industrial Services PLC and Barr Ltd *considered whether the hire of a crane with an operative constituted a construction operation, and as such amounted to more than mere hire. Baldwins hired a 50 tonne crane to Barr to be used in the building of the new Southampton football stadium. An incident arose which led to a dispute as to which party was responsible for repairs to the crane. An essential element of the claim was whether the provision of the crane and driver was part of a construction contract within the ambit of Housing Grants, Construction and Regeneration Act 1996. A construction contract is one under which construction operations are carried out and it was accepted that a contract for mere plant hire is not a construction contract. The labour element was held to be crucial.*

The hire of the crane plus driver was held to be a contract for supply of plant and labour to be used as part of the operation to build the stadium. The contract for supply of the crane and driver was for an operation that formed an integral part of, was preparatory to, or was for rendering complete a work of construction. Following the judgement we accept that the supply of plant or machinery with an operator, by a business, is the provision of a service and not mere hire.

We take the supply of plant or machinery with an operator to mean that the operator remains with the equipment during its use and that it will be operated by him or her alone save for exceptional circumstances. It is not sufficient for the plant or machinery to be delivered or installed by the hire company.

For example, the delivery and installation of a generator would not be regarded as the provision of a service but the supply of a digger with driver would be so regarded.

Plant or machinery may be provided with an operator on some occasions and without on others. Where, at the time the expenditure is incurred, it is intended that the asset will be predominantly provided with an operator, the precise facts and use of the asset will have to be considered, but generally we accept that FYAs are due.

We also accept that the provision of building access services by the scaffolding industry amounts to a construction operation and is therefore more than mere hire. This does not apply to businesses that simply supply scaffolding poles etc for use by others.

Each case will have to be considered on its own facts. This change does not affect claims to capital allowances that have been agreed for past periods in accordance with our previous prevailing practice where those periods are now closed.

Note—This Interpretation has been superseded by the Capital Allowances Manual CA23115.
Commentary—*Simon's Direct Tax Service* **B2.325**.

RI 263 (August 2003) Swaps held by non-corporates

All statutory references are to TA 1988 unless otherwise stated.

1 Swap contracts, such as interest rate or currency swaps or certain kinds of credit derivative, are now widely used by traders and investors to hedge financial risks or to change their risk profile. Almost all swaps used by companies will fall within the derivative contracts rules of FA 2003 Sch 26 (for accounting periods beginning on or after 1 October 2002). But we have been asked to clarify our views on the tax treatment of swaps held by non-corporates. The term ''non-corporates'' includes individuals, whether trading or not; trusts (including approved and unapproved pension schemes and charitable trusts); and partnerships whose members include individuals or trusts.

2 More specifically, we have been asked—

– whether profits from swaps held by exempt approved retirement benefit schemes come within the exemption in section 592(2) for ''income derived from investments''; and
– whether, for a charity, a swap is capable of being a ''qualifying investment'' within Pt I Sch 20.

3 This article therefore deals both with the general position of non-corporates who hold swap contracts, and with the more specialised issues relating to approved pension schemes and to charities. It relates only to swaps (except in so far as it specifically refers to other sorts of derivatives). Different tax considerations may apply to other sorts of derivatives, such as futures and options.

4 The word ''swap'' is not found in the Taxes Acts. For the purposes of this article the term relates to any financial arrangement which would be regarded by the financial markets as a swap.

THE GENERAL POSITION OF NON-CORPORATES

5 Our general view is that profits or losses on a swap held by a non-corporate, if they are not within Case I of Schedule D, will fall within Case VI.

6 Case I takes priority over any other possible charge to tax. Receipts or payments under a swap contract are on trading account where either—

– the swap forms part of the circulating capital of a financial trade being carried on by the non-corporate; or
– the swap transaction is clearly ancillary to a trading transaction on current account. Swaps that hedge borrowing undertaken for trade purposes fall into this category, following the approach of example 10 in paragraph 17 of Statement of Practice 3/02.

7 Where a swap is taken out by a non-corporate to hedge interest payments which are deductible in computing the profits or losses of a Schedule A business, then profits or losses on that contract will normally be taxed or relieved as receipts or deductions of that Schedule A business. There is further guidance on this in the Property Income Manual (PIM2100).

8 Profits or gains that are not of a capital nature, and which are not within Case I or Schedule A, will constitute ''annual profits or gains not falling under any other Case of Schedule D'' and will therefore be chargeable under Case VI (unless, exceptionally, they are within Case V). Periodic payments under a swap are not annual payments within Case III because they are not pure income profit—the person who receives them has counter-obligations under the swap contract. It follows that such sums are payable without deduction of income tax.

9 The case of *Curtis Brown v Jarvis* (14 TC 744) makes it clear that in assessing receipts under Case VI it is permissible to deduct associated payments. And, under s 69, income tax under Case VI is charged on the full amount of profits or gains for the year of assessment. So the amount to be taxed under Case VI (or the Case VI loss) for a year of assessment will be the net amount receivable (or payable) under the swap contract in that year. If, however, the non-corporate prepares accounts and accounts for the swap on either an accruals or a mark to market basis, there is no objection to using the accounts figure as the measure of the ''full amount of profits or gains'', provided that the accounts bring in the full economic profit on the swap over the life of the contract.

10 Users of swaps may sometimes receive or pay lump sums. For example, one party may pay a premium to enter into a swap, or a lump sum representing the net present value of outstanding rights and obligations under the contract may change hands if a swap is assigned or terminated early. Such lump sums will also be within Case VI if they are on revenue account. Whether a receipt or payment is capital or income is a question of fact in any particular case. But in general all cashflows made or exchanged under or in connection with a swap will be income, whether they take the form of periodic payments or are rolled up into a lump sum payable at any point.

11 It is sometimes contended that certain swaps are ''financial futures'' that, if not within Case I, are taken out of Sch D by s 128(1) and are chargeable to capital gains tax by virtue of TCGA 1992 s 143. Statement of Practice 3/02 (or its earlier incarnation, SP 14/91) is sometimes quoted in support of this view.

12 We do not agree. Paragraph 4 of SP 3/02 makes the point that the statutory phrase ''financial futures'' is a wide term, encompassing cash-settled contracts as well as those settled by delivery, and over the counter contracts (including forward rate agreements) as well as exchange- traded contracts. But, wide as it is, it can only cover derivatives that are ''futures''. The word ''future'' must be interpreted in its normal commercial sense. And—while there is some fluidity in commercial usage—the market will generally see swaps as falling into a different category from futures.

13 SP 3/02 deals with the tax treatment of transactions in financial futures and options, not swaps. Nevertheless, when looking at a question of whether a swap transaction is within Case I, rather than Case VI, the Revenue will apply the general principles set out in SP 3/02.

APPROVED PENSION SCHEMES

14 Section 592(2) allows exempt approved retirement benefit schemes to claim exemption from income tax in respect of income from investments, provided those investments are held for the purposes of the scheme. There are similar exemptions for retirement annuity schemes (s 620(6)), approved personal pension schemes (s 643(2)), schemes approved before 6 April 1980 (s 608(2)(*a*)), Parliamentary pension funds (s 613(4)) and certain overseas pension schemes (s 614(3)). And TCGA 1992 s 271(1) contains related exemptions for capital gains accruing on the disposal of such investments.

15 Case law has established that the word ''investment'', where used in the Taxes Acts, is to be understood in its normal commercial meaning. In particular, it is not limited to an income-producing asset—in *Marson v Morton* (59 TC 381), it was emphasised that the interpretation of ''investment'' should reflect current commercial reality.

16 It is against this background that the question of whether a particular swap held by an approved pension scheme is an ''investment'' needs to be considered. Section 659A specifically provides that futures and options are investments for the purposes of s 592(2) and the related statutory provisions mentioned above. It was brought in by FA 1990 as a clarificatory measure; it is silent on swaps because, at that time, the use of swaps by investment funds was in its infancy. Section 659A therefore has no bearing on the tax status of swaps.

17 The question of whether a swap is held for the purposes of a trade is one of fact. Where a swap transaction by an approved pension scheme appears to fall close to the trading/investment borderline, the Revenue will look at the case on its merits.

18 However, where an approved pension scheme uses interest rate swaps, currency swaps, equity swaps, credit derivatives or similar instruments—

– to hedge risks inherent in its existing investment portfolio of shares, bonds or similar securities; or
– as part of an investment strategy to enhance the return from its existing investment portfolio; or

– to create a synthetic exposure to investments of a particular type or in a particular market, in line with the fund's normal policies of investing directly in such instruments,

the Revenue will normally regard such swaps as investments.

CHARITIES

19 The charity tax exemptions are subject to rules designed to restrict the exemptions where charities' income and gains are used for non-charitable purposes. These rules also apply where charities make ''non-qualifying'' loans or investments. Where a charity invests its funds in a ''non- qualifying investment'', the amount invested is treated as expenditure incurred for non-charitable purposes (s 506(1) and (4)). Part I Sch 20 lists those investments that are ''qualifying investments''. Sch 20 para 9 allows the Board to extend the ''qualifying investment'' designation to an investment not specifically listed, where such treatment is claimed. The Board must be satisfied that the investment is made for the benefit of the charity, and not for tax avoidance.

20 As outlined above in relation to approved pension schemes, ''investment'' takes its normal commercial meaning. It is capable of including a swap. While we cannot give advance confirmation that a particular swap will be a qualifying investment we can confirm that we will follow the Charity Commission guidance in their leaflet CC14 in deciding whether a particular swap is an investment. There is guidance in Annex III to the Detailed Guidance notes in the Charities pages on the Inland Revenue website that sets out the approach we adopt in deciding whether or not a particular investment is a qualifying investment.

21 However, even where the Board is satisfied that a swap contract held by a charity is a qualifying investment, profits arising on the swap will only be exempt from income or corporation tax if they fall within one of the categories listed in s 505(1).

22 The types of swap in normal commercial use will fall within the FA 2002 Sch 26 derivative contracts regime (for accounting periods beginning on or after 1 October 2002) where the charity concerned is a company or unincorporated association. In such cases, profits from the swap will normally give rise to non-trading loan relationship credits, taxable under Schedule D Case III. The exemption for Case III income in s 505(1)(*c*)(ii) will apply.

23 Where the swap is held by a charitable trust, however, profits will in many instances fall within Case VI (see the above discussion of the general position for non-corporates). Case VI income from such a source does not fall within any of the s 505 exemptions. But there is a *de minimis* exemption in FA 2000 s 46 which exempts most case VI income of charities below £5,000. It also exempts the lesser of £50,000 or the income if it is less than 25% of the charities' incoming resources for the chargeable period.

RI 264 (October 2003) *Capital Gains Tax: Mansworth v Jelley—Claims to increase capital losses for self-assessment tax years*

This article is intended to give wider circulation to a revision in our website guidance on the effects of the Court of Appeal decision in *Mansworth v Jelley*, which we made on 8 August 2003. The change, which may benefit a number of taxpayers, relates to the view we originally expressed in March 2003 on claims to increase capital losses for self-assessment tax years. This view was part of the general guidance we issued at that time to assist taxpayers following publication of the court decision.

We have revised our guidance following concerns expressed in an article in *Taxation*, which, after taking legal advice, we concluded were well founded. We now accept that taxpayers who have already settled claims to capital losses for self-assessment tax years are not barred from claiming an increase in such losses. The right to make any such claim does, of course, remain subject to the normal time limit laid down in TMA 1970 s 42.

The original guidance of March 2003, which was expressed in question and answer form, dealt with claims to increase capital losses at question and answer 13. That question and answer have been amended, as has the final section of the guidance headed ''Further details on the tax treatment of options following the decision in the case of *Mansworth v Jelley*''.

The amended question and answer 13 now read—

> **Q13.** I have already claimed a capital loss on the disposal of shares that I acquired by exercising an unapproved employee share option in the tax year 1998/99 and this was either set off against capital gains in the same tax year or carried forward. Can I now use the decision in *Mansworth v Jelley* to claim additional losses for that tax year?
>
> **A13.** Yes, provided you claim before the time limit expires on 31 January 2005. If you claim additional 1998/99 losses, you must first set them against any capital gains arising in 1998/99 that you could not cover with the loss you claimed earlier even though these capital gains may be less than the AEA for 1998/99. You carry forward any surplus loss and set it against the part of the capital gain that exceeds the AEA in the first subsequent year. Any CGT overpaid will be repaid.

The amended final section now reads—

Capital losses arising in self-assessment tax years following Mansworth v Jelley

The guidance below explains the position where a taxpayer has made a disposal which, following *Mansworth v Jelley*, gives rise to an allowable capital loss in a self-assessment tax year.

1.1 Where the taxpayer has made an Income Tax Self Assessment (ITSA) return for the tax year of disposal and the amendment window (12 months from the statutory filing date for that return) has not closed, the return may be amended to bring any capital gains computation into line with Mansworth v Jelley. If the return is under enquiry the taxpayer can ask the Inland Revenue officer to amend the return at the end of the enquiry to include the claim for a capital loss.

1.2 Where—

– the return was completed in accordance with the law as understood before *Mansworth v Jelley*, and
– the window for amending returns has closed, and
– the return is not under enquiry,

the return cannot be amended to reflect the consequences of the decision.

1.3 Where the taxpayer can no longer amend an ITSA return but a capital loss arises or is increased as a result of *Mansworth v Jelley*, the taxpayer can make a loss claim within 5 years from the first 31 January following the tax year of disposal—

– if the return showed an allowable loss on the disposal (which means that the loss has been claimed in the return), the taxpayer may make a free-standing supplementary claim for the increase in loss;
– if the loss was not claimed the taxpayer can make a free-standing claim for an allowable loss for the tax year of disposal. As the return cannot be amended, this may mean that the taxpayer has both a chargeable gain and an allowable loss for the disposal.

2.1 Where the taxpayer has not made an ITSA return for the tax year of disposal, a free-standing claim for an allowable loss can be made for that tax year, providing either that there has been no earlier claim for the loss on that disposal or that the earlier claim has not been settled.

For self-assessment, any free-standing claim has to be made within five years from the first 31 January following the tax year of disposal.

2.2 Where the taxpayer makes a valid free-standing claim to an allowable loss for the tax year of disposal:

– the loss is set against any gains for the tax year of disposal. If it exceeds those gains any surplus is carried forward and set against any gains for subsequent tax years. Losses brought forward to a tax year are set off against gains of that year only to the extent which reduces the taxable amount to the annual exempt amount for the year concerned;
– where the loss is set against a gain for the tax year of disposal or any subsequent tax year for which the ITSA return can no longer be amended, relief is given by repayment or discharge of the tax due (without amending the return);
– where the loss, or any part of it, is carried forward to a tax year for which an ITSA return has been made, and that return is under enquiry or in date for a taxpayer amendment, relief is given by amending the return for that later tax year.

3. Taxpayers should set off losses against gains before taper relief is applied. For examples see leaflet CGT1: *Capital Gains Tax an introduction*. The August 2002 version of CGT1 does not contain information about the position following *Mansworth v Jelley*.

RI 265 (October 2003) *Termination payments and benefits—repayment clauses in compromise agreements—application of ITEPA 2003 s 225–6*

In recent months, a question has arisen concerning whether the existence of a ''repayment clause'' in a compromise agreement made at termination of employment gives rise to a charge to tax and National Insurance Contributions under the legislation dealing with restrictive covenants (ITEPA 2003 s 225–6 (formerly TA 1988 s 313) and SSCBA 1992 s 4(4)(*b*)).

Typically, such a clause requires the employee to repay some or all of the sum settled by the agreement if he or she subsequently initiates litigation in respect of the employment or its termination.

The Revenue's view has been, and remains, that a compromise agreement by its very nature includes a restrictive covenant. This is because the employee agrees not to do something, namely not to commence or continue litigation.

Statement of Practice 3/96 advises that the Revenue will not attribute any of the settlement sum to such an undertaking, so there is nothing to charge under ITEPA 2003 s 225–6.

However, an employer could still make a payment specifically for an undertaking not to litigate, in which case SP 3/96 would not apply and a charge arises.

The question is whether a repayment clause entails attribution of some or all of the settlement sum to that undertaking since the sum is lost if litigation commences.

Following legal advice, the Revenue accepts that such a charge will not arise other than in very exceptional cases.

Vaughan-Neil v IRC (54 TC 223) confirmed that it is necessary to establish, realistically and as a matter of fact, what the settlement sum is actually paid for. Normally, a compromise agreement made at termination deals with genuine claims and the settlement sum is paid in consideration for settling those claims. Where that is the case, the settlement sum is exhausted by reference to those claims and no sum remains to be attributable to the undertaking not to litigate. That remains the case whether or not a repayment clause exists.

Consequently, enquiries will not normally be raised on this point alone. The Revenue will raise the question only if the claims appear spurious, for example the amounts are clearly in excess of a reasonable sum for settlement of the claims.

Practitioners should bear in mind that there are no tax or NIC provisions allowing adjustment to charges if such a repayment in fact happens.

All the NICs legislative references mentioned in this article are those which apply in Great Britain. Northern Ireland has its own NICs legislation which, in the main, is the same as that for Great Britain.

RI 266 (October 2003) *Companies—relief for underlying tax paid by overseas subsidiaries*

TA 1988 S 803A AND US LIMITED LIABILITY COMPANIES

In some countries the law may provide that one company may pay tax in respect of the aggregated profits of itself and others as if they were a single entity. The provisions at TA 1988 s 803A apply for dividends paid to the UK on or after 21 March 2000. Subject to certain conditions, for the purposes of calculating credit relief the relevant profits of these companies are regarded as a single aggregate figure in respect of a single company and the foreign tax paid by the responsible company as paid by that single company. The s 803A provisions are framed so that only companies that are resident in the country concerned may be included in the calculations of relevant profits and foreign tax for the deemed single entity. A question has been put to us in connection with Limited Liability Companies in the USA.

In Tax Bulletin 29 the Inland Revenue considered the treatment of LLCs under the UK/US Double Taxation Convention then in force and concluded—

- those LLCs so far considered were regarded as taxable entities, even if they were regarded as fiscally transparent in the US;
- but in the UK's view an LLC could not be said to be a resident of the US within the terms of the Convention;
- nevertheless as a matter of practice we would accept claims to relief from an LLC to the extent that the income in question was subject to US tax in the hands of those members who were residents of the US.

Since Tax Bulletin 29 the new UK/US DTC has come into effect—

- the Revenue continues to regard LLCs as taxable entities;
- the residence position of LLCs also remains unchanged, but
- Article 1(8) now provides that that an item of income, profit or gain derived through an LLC—so long as it is treated as fiscally transparent under the laws of the US—shall be considered to be derived by a resident of the US to the extent that the item is treated for the purposes of the taxation law of the US as the income, profit or gain of a resident of the US. Consequently the practice set out in Tax Bulletin 29 is now contained within the new UK/US DTC.

As stated above, s 803A specifically states that the entities to be included must be resident in the country concerned. But in many cases an LLC is included as part of a US grouping for US tax purposes.

In such cases, as a matter of practice, the profits and tax of the LLC should not be excluded from the s 803A calculation. This is in line with both Tax Bulletin 29 and the terms of the new Convention.

RI 267 (December 2003) *Assignment on divorce of life insurance policies, capital redemption policies and purchased life annuities*

This article explains about a change of view that may affect the income tax implications when there is a transfer on divorce of all or part of the rights under a life insurance policy, life annuity contract or capital redemption policy. [All further references in this article to life insurance policies should be read as also being references to purchased life annuities and capital redemption policies.]

BACKGROUND

Life insurance policies can give rise to "chargeable events" on which "chargeable event gains" can arise. These gains are taxable as income. Gains normally only arise when the policyholder receives value from the policy. There is no chargeable event and so no gain when the owner assigns all of the policy rights to another person but receives no money or money's worth in return. A gift of part of the policy rights could have given rise to a gain before the 2001–02 tax year, but cannot do so now. When the owner sells a policy for cash to an unconnected third party it is obvious that the owner receives money or money's worth. But there may also be circumstances in which there is money or money's worth received in return for the change of ownership even when no cash changes hands.

PREVIOUS VIEW OF THE LAW

Until recently the Inland Revenue took the view that the transfer by one spouse to the other of all or some of the rights under a policy as part of a divorce settlement was invariably for money or money's worth. It is for example not uncommon for a jointly owned mortgage endowment policy to change hands on divorce. This view was based on legal advice that an assignment as part of a divorce settlement involved a valuable "exchange" of rights. The policy rights in such cases were understood to be transferred in return for the surrender by the transferee of rights over other property, which he or she would otherwise have been able to exercise to obtain alternative financial provision. As a consequence the assignment of all or part of the policy rights was potentially within the charge to tax.

REVISED VIEW OF THE LAW

The Inland Revenue has now received further legal advice that the relevant matrimonial legislation, and the nature of the court orders following proceedings under that legislation, means that it must revise its view. This follows judicial observations by Coleridge J in *G v G* [2002] EWHC 1339 about capital gains tax gift hold-over relief (see article in August 2003 Tax Bulletin). The advice is that where there is recourse to the courts and a court makes an order—

- for ancillary relief under the Matrimonial Causes Act 1973 (or for financial provision under the Family Law (Scotland) Act 1985) which results in a transfer of rights under a life insurance policy from one spouse to another, or
- formally ratifying an agreement reached by the divorcing parties that deals with the transfer of assets including a life insurance policy,

the spouse to whom the rights under the life insurance policy are transferred does not give money or money's worth, in the form of surrendered rights, for their transfer. A Court Order made in these circumstances reflects the exercise by the court of its independent statutory jurisdiction. The transfer of ownership is not therefore the consequence of any party to the proceedings agreeing to surrender alternative rights that they might have in return for receiving rights under the life insurance policy.

This new approach represents a change in the previous view and prevailing practice. One consequence is that transferring ownership of the rights conferred by a life insurance policy under a Court Order is not for money or money's worth and no gain can arise because of it.

In the past insurers may have issued chargeable event certificates reporting gains as a result of assignments on divorce. The self-assessment (SA) tax return guide for 2002–03 income also says that such assignments are to be treated as being for money or money's worth for tax purposes.

As a consequence of this new approach, anybody—

- who has included a gain in box 12.2 or box 12.5 of the SA return (or box 6.8 of the foreign pages), **and**
- the gain arose as a result of assigning some or all of the rights under a policy as part of a divorce settlement, **and**
- the transfer took place in the circumstances described above,

may be entitled to amend their SA return **provided** they are within the normal time limits for doing so.

Years affected and time-limits for amending a self-assessment—chargeable event gains

As this revised interpretation represents a change of view and of prevailing practice, there is no right for taxpayers to go back to years that are not in-date for an amendment to the SA return. The in-date years are as follows—

- SA returns for years of assessment before 2001–02 may only be amended where a life insurance policy has been the subject of a **full assignment*** on divorce, a court order was made and, exceptionally, the returns are either still within the time limit for amendment by the taxpayer (because the notice requiring a return was issued later than normal) or are under enquiry;
- All SA returns for 2001–02 may be amended before 31 January 2004, where a life insurance policy has been the subject of a **full assignment*** on divorce where a court order was made;
- SA returns for 2002–03 may be amended before 31 January 2005 where the gain arose as a result of a **full or part assignment** on divorce where a court order was made.

(*The new interpretation does not normally alter the tax treatment of **part assignments** taxable in years prior to 2002–03. Before changes to the taxation of part assignments were made in Finance Act 2001, they were potentially taxable whether or not they were made for money or money's worth. The way in which the FA 2001 commencement rule operates means that part assignments made during the year ended 5 April 2002 are generally not taxable until 2002–03.)

Taxpayers who want to amend their SA return and are within the time limit for doing so should send the amendment to their tax office. If that time limit has passed but the return is under enquiry this matter should be brought to the attention of the officer conducting the enquiry.

LIFE ASSURANCE PREMIUM RELIEF ("LAPR")

Some people may have had LAPR removed from the premiums they pay because a change of life assured took place at the same time as an assignment to change the beneficial ownership of the policy as part of a divorce settlement. LAPR is only available for qualifying policies taken out before 14 March 1984.

One of the necessary conditions for retaining entitlement to LAPR in these circumstances is that there is no consideration given in connection with the change of life assured. Under the revised view the Inland Revenue acknowledges that there is no consideration for the assignment where there is recourse to the courts and a court makes an order—

– for ancillary relief under the Matrimonial Causes Act 1973 (or for financial provision under the Family Law (Scotland) Act 1985) which results in a transfer of rights under a life insurance policy from one spouse to the other, or
– formally ratifying an agreement reached by the divorcing parties that deals with the transfer of assets including a life insurance policy.

The change of view may mean that the new owner of the policy should have continued to receive LAPR but did not do so. The policyholder may therefore be eligible to apply now to the insurer to restore tax relief at source from future payments of premium. However, if the change of life assured on the policy took place when there was less than ten years to run before the maturity of the policy, it may not be possible to have LAPR reinstated.

The insurance company will know the details of a policy and is best placed to be able to say whether a policy is a qualifying policy. A qualifying policy is a regular premium policy with a life of at least 10 years. The most common type of qualifying policy is a mortgage endowment policy. There is normally no income tax charge when a qualifying policy pays out.

YEARS AFFECTED AND TIME-LIMITS FOR MAKING A CLAIM—LAPR

Policyholders are entitled to claim relief for all past years that are in-date for claims. They have to claim relief from the Inland Revenue, not from their insurer. The statutory time limit for making such a claim is longer than for making an amendment to an SA Return. Policyholders have five years from the 31 January following the year of assessment to which the claim relates to claim LAPR. The earliest in-date year of assessment is at present 1997/98. The time-limit for a claim to relief for 1997/98 is 31 January 2004. If you think that you or your client can make such a claim, you should write to Savings and Pensions Schemes (SPS), Team 1 Repayments, 3rd Floor, St John's House, Merton Road, Bootle, Merseyside, L69 9BB with the name of the insurer, policy number and other relevant details.

QUALIFYING POLICIES

Another consequence of the previous view was that a policy might exceptionally have ceased to be treated as a qualifying policy because of a change of life assured on divorce, whether or not LAPR was previously given. This is only likely to be the case when the change of life assured took place with less than ten years to run to the maturity of the policy. If you think that this may apply to you or your client, you should contact the insurer, whether or not it has already been made aware of the facts, to tell it about the order or ratification of an agreement issued by the divorce court. This will enable the insurer to update its records and administer the policy as a qualifying policy in future where that would be appropriate.

CAPITAL GAINS TAX ("CGT")

In the majority of cases there are no CGT implications when a policy or contract is transferred on divorce. This is because—

– TCGA 1992 s 210 takes life insurance policies and deferred life annuity contracts, which have not changed hands for actual consideration, outside the scope of CGT,
– TCGA 1992 s 237 excludes other annuities from CGT,
– TCGA 1992 s 204 excludes capital redemption policies from CGT.

Finance Act 2003 changed the rules in TCGA 1992 s 210. There is guidance on the new rules in the Capital Gains manual at paragraphs CG69040 to CG69071.

RI 268 (February 2004) *Businesses, individuals and the settlements legislation—Part II*

INTRODUCTION

In Tax Bulletin 64 we provided some information and examples on the settlements legislation in Part XV of Income and Corporation Taxes Acts (ICTA) 1988 [see the *Revenue & Other Press Releases section* for this article]. Publication of that article was welcomed but many people have asked us for some further information on examples 3, 4 and 5. These were cases where the settlements legislation applied to small companies and partnerships. We have also been asked for guidance on completing a SA return where the settlements legislation applies.

As with the original article in Tax Bulletin 64, this article sets out the Inland Revenue's view of the way the legislation applies. That view is not accepted by many accountants and tax practitioners.

Unless otherwise stated all references are to ICTA 1988 in this article.

The existing guidance on the settlements legislation is found in the Inland Revenue's Trusts, Settlements and Estates Manual which is available on our website at ''www.ir.gov.uk/manuals/tsemmanual/''. That manual will be updated to incorporate this further information shortly.

GENERAL

The feedback we have received on the Tax Bulletin 64 article was that the examples were particularly helpful so below we have provided some more examples. However there are some general principles that might also be of use.

SHARES

Much of the feedback we have received on the Tax Bulletin 64 article concerned ordinary shares and the rights that they carry. Whilst the rights and obligations associated with a share are relevant they are only part of the issue. We have not suggested that, for the legislation to apply, an ordinary share itself must be wholly or substantially a right to income. We look at the whole arrangement, as the legislation requires. The relevant questions are: What has been invested? What assets, trade, profession have been placed in the company and by whom? Who does what to earn the income of the company? Is the remuneration paid at a commercial rate for the job? Is someone getting a disproportionate return on the capital they have invested because of their relationship with the settlor? All these issues must be considered and if the shares are being used as a vehicle for diverting income then the legislation may apply.

It has also been argued that as the shares in *Young v Pearce* [1996] STC 743, were preference shares, ordinary shares cannot also be caught by the settlements legislation. We do not accept that. The *Young v Pearce* case was determined on the facts in that case and the question whether the settlements legislation can apply to situations involving ordinary shares was not considered.

PARTNERSHIPS

We have also received feedback on the application of the legislation to partnerships where some argue that the unlimited liability of the partners means the settlements legislation cannot apply. We do not accept that. It is important, in relation to partnerships, to look at the whole arrangement to see whether someone is getting a disproportionate return on their contribution because they are related to, or friends with, the settlor. If they are then the legislation applies even if a partnership is being used.

FAMILY COMPANY/PARTNERSHIPS

We have been asked to reconsider the application of the settlements legislation to family/company arrangements as it has been suggested these involve special factors. We consider this is a misunderstanding of the settlements legislation which was enacted specifically to prevent individuals avoiding tax by diverting income to a family member or friend. An outright gift of money is a bounteous act but does not create a settlement. But an arrangement for one spouse to receive the other's income via dividends is caught by the settlements legislation. There is a substantial body of case law on ''bounty'' and the suggestion that the rules should be applied differently in a family situation is not consistent with that case law.

GOODWILL

It has been suggested that we have ignored the value of goodwill in a company in determining whether a gift of shares is substantially a right to income. We agree that goodwill can be a valuable asset of a business and each case will depend on its particular facts. In the typical service company scenario to which the settlements legislation may apply, goodwill is personal to the individual who earns the income for the company and does not attach to the company itself. In such circumstances goodwill would not be an asset for distribution in the winding up of the company and it will not enhance the value of the shares.

SPOUSES

There has been some misunderstanding about how the legislation applies when spouses are involved. We have not suggested that a ''non fee-earning'' spouse makes no contribution to a business. The question, in the context of the settlements legislation, is ''What contribution does that spouse make and how commercial is the reward for it?''. The settlements legislation applies not only where there is a benefit to the settlor's spouse but also where the settlor retains an interest in the settlement whoever the beneficiary may be. In a service company it is usually the person with the specialist knowledge who retains the interest because s/he controls the source of income.

THE WHOLE ARRANGEMENT

It is essential to look at the whole arrangement when considering whether the settlements legislation applies. Sometimes the whole arrangement will not be clear until sometime after the company, for example, is set up. So we might need to wait until dividends or remuneration are paid before we can say the legislation applies.

WHAT IS A DISPROPORTIONATE RETURN ON CAPITAL?

We have said that one of the factors we look at when deciding whether or not the settlements legislation applies is whether someone is receiving a disproportionate return on capital invested. In deciding what is disproportionate we look at the return on the actual capital invested and also any risks. So, for example, someone who invests £1 in an ordinary share and gets £35,000 a year in dividends is getting a disproportionate return on the capital. If that £1 had been invested in the stock market or a bank the return would have been much less. On the other hand if an individual is admitted to a partnership they may take on considerable personal financial risk, and the partnership share of the profits might be a fair return for that risk (see example 14 below).

WHAT IS AN UNCOMMERCIAL SALARY?

Likewise we have said we look at individuals drawing an uncommercial salary. In deciding what is uncommercial we look at the going rate for the job and also an individual's previous earnings. So if an IT consultant was earning £80,000 a year when employed by a plc and she then sets up her own IT consulting company and earns fees of £120,000 a year with expenses of £20,000 we would expect to see her drawing a salary of around £80,000. If instead her total salary is only £40,000 with £40,000 going to a non-working spouse then that is uncommercial.

Similarly if one spouse undertakes an average of 8 hours secretarial work a week for a company, and the going rate for a secretary in that area is £6 an hour (£2,496 per year), then we would consider it uncommercial if the spouse was in fact receiving £5,000 a year from the company.

Deciding on what is and is not a commercial salary is not an exact science. It is impossible to give definitive guidance as each case depends on the facts. When in doubt it is useful to consider whether an individual employed at arms length would have accepted the same salary if their friend / relative was not also benefiting from the arrangement.

COMPLETING THE SA RETURN

As TA 1988 s 660C(1), (1A) sets out, income to which the settlements legislation applies is taxable either at Schedule F rates where it is dividends and dividend type income or under Schedule D Case VI for all other income.

When an individual completes a SA return and has to include income caught by the settlements legislation that income needs to go on the ''Trusts etc.'' pages (page T1) under ''Income from Trusts and Settlements'', unless it is foreign income which should be returned on the foreign pages (Box 6.2 on FI for foreign dividends and box 6.4 on F2 for other foreign income). For UK source income the boxes to use on page T1 will depend on the type of income:

- For dividends and other Schedule F type income use boxes 7.10, 7.11 and 7.12.
- For all other income (taxed under Schedule D Case VI) use boxes 7.4, 7.5 and 7.6. Where the income is not taxed in the recipient's hands then box 7.5 should be left blank.

We would also suggest individuals include suitable explanations in the ''Additional Information'' box. For example an individual receiving a dividend might not be required to include that dividend on the SA return as another person is taxable under the settlements legislation. If they both include a brief explanation about this it helps prevent unnecessary enquiries. (The figures in the returns will not necessarily agree with other information we might hold—for example from the company accounts.)

PREVIOUS EXAMPLES IN TAX BULLETIN 64

In Tax Bulletin 64 we provided fifteen examples of where the settlements legislation did and did not apply. We have been asked to make clear for those examples how the income should be returned on the individuals' SA returns. The fifteen examples are therefore reproduced below with an additional section explaining how SA returns should be completed.

EXAMPLE 1—ISSUED SHARES WITH RESTRICTED RIGHTS

An engineering company has 100 ordinary £1 shares. Mr A and Mr B own 50 ordinary shares each. They create a new class of B shares which carry no voting rights and no assets in a winding up. They then issue 50 B shares to each of their wives. Dividends voted on those B shares would be treated as the income of Mr A and Mr B rather than their wives as the B dividends are from shares that are wholly or substantially a right to income and so not exempted from TA 1988 s 660A by s 660A(6). (This example is based on the High Court case of *Young v Pearce; Young v Scrutton* [1996] STC 743).

Completing the SA return

Any dividends paid to Mrs A on the B shares are treated as Mr A's income under the settlements legislation and so he should return those dividends at boxes 7.10 to 7.12 on page T1 of his SA return and include a brief note in the ''Additional Information'' box.

Mrs A should not include any of the dividends received on the B shares on her SA return, if she gets one, but a brief note in the ''Additional Information'' box would be helpful.

The situation is the same for Mr and Mrs B.

EXAMPLE 2—GIFTED SHARES WITH RESTRICTED RIGHTS

Mr C is the sole director and owns all the 1000 ordinary £1 shares in C Limited. His aunt, Mrs D, has always been very kind to him and he wants to thank her for this. He subscribes, at par, for 100 B shares, with no voting rights and restricted rights to capital of £10 per share in the event of winding up. He gifts the shares to Mrs D. Mr C then declares a dividend of £100 per share with Mrs D receiving dividends of £10,000.

This is a bounteous arrangement and we would apply the settlements legislation to the dividends. The property giving rise to the dividends cannot be looked at too narrowly as the shares alone. The wider arrangement must be considered. Because he is in effective control of the company Mr C retains an interest in the underlying property as he could simply pay all future income arising to himself as director's salary or as dividends on the ordinary shares.

Completing the SA return

All of Mrs D's dividends of £10,000 are treated as Mr C's income under the settlements legislation. He should return that £10,000 at boxes 7.10 to 7.12 on page T1 of his SA return and include a brief note in the ''Additional Information'' box. His own dividends should be returned in the normal way.

Mrs D should not include any of the £10,000 of dividends on her SA return, if she gets one, but a brief note in the ''Additional Information'' box would be helpful.

EXAMPLE 3—SUBSCRIBED SHARES

E Ltd was incorporated in October 1997 to provide the services of Mr E as an IT consultant to a number of clients working in the pharmaceutical industry. The company's share capital is £2 consisting of 2 £1 shares. Mr E is the sole director of the company, and his wife Mrs E is company secretary but takes no other active part in the company. From the beginning each subscribed for one share. The company has no significant capital assets. The figures for the first year's trading are—

Turnover	100,000
Expenses	5,000
Salary (Mr E)	10,000
Salary (Mrs E)	5,000
Dividends	70,000

In this case Mrs E receives a salary for her duties as company secretary, but the whole arrangement whereby Mrs E invests £1 and in return gets a dividend of £35,000 is bounteous. There is nothing to suggest that the dividend is a commercial return on her investment. As there is no significant capital in the company, what has passed from Mr E to Mrs E is substantially a right to income and the whole of the dividend is taxed on Mr E.

In reaching this conclusion, the legislation allows us to look at the whole arrangement. It is the work that Mr E carries out which creates the company's profits which in turn enable the dividends to be paid. Mrs E's investment of £1 does not enable the company to make profits and the company itself has minimal capital value. In accepting a salary below the market rate from the company, and thereby allowing some of the income earned to pass to Mrs E as a dividend, Mr E has entered into a bounteous arrangement to divert income to his spouse with the aim of avoiding tax.

Completing the SA return

Mrs E has received a salary of £5,000 which is a commercial salary for the work she does. All of Mrs E's dividends of £35,000 are treated as Mr E's income under the settlements legislation. He should return that £35,000 at boxes 7.10 to 7.12 on page T1 of his SA return and include a brief note in the ''Additional Information'' box. His own dividends should be returned in the normal way.

Mrs E should not include any of the £35,000 of dividends on her SA return, if she gets one, but a brief note in the ''Additional Information'' box would be helpful. She should include the £5,000 salary on her return.

EXAMPLE 4—SUBSCRIBED SHARES WITH LITTLE CAPITAL VALUE THEN GIFTED

As in example 3 but in October 1997 Mr E was not married and subscribed for both £1 shares himself. Mr E's solicitor was acting as company secretary. A year later he got married and gave his wife one of his shares in the company. At this point Mrs E took over the role of company secretary. In the following year Mrs E receives a wage of £5,000 and the company pays a dividend of £35,000 per share.

Since the capital value of the company is insignificant the gift of the share from Mr E to his wife is not exempt from TA 1988 s 660A by virtue of section 660A(6) as the shares are ''wholly or substantially a right to income''. Accordingly the settlements legislation applies in relation to Mrs E's £35,000 dividend payment and the income would be treated as Mr E's for tax purposes.

Completing the SA return

As in example 3 all of Mrs E's dividends of £35,000 are treated as Mr E's income under the settlements legislation. He should return that £35,000 on page T1 his SA return at boxes 7.10 to 7.12 and include a brief note in the ''Additional Information'' box. His own dividends should be returned in the normal way.

Again Mrs E should not include any of the £35,000 of dividends on her SA return, if she gets one, but a brief note in the ''Additional Information'' box would be helpful. She should include the £5,000 salary on her return.

EXAMPLE 5—PARTNERSHIPS

Mr F and Mr G are in partnership as second hand car dealers. They do not have any premises but buy and sell cars through auctions and the classified adverts of local papers. The partnership's only assets are some office equipment worth less than £1,000 and they usually have a couple of cars in stock at any one time. They are successful and the profits of £80,000 a year are split equally between them. They decide to admit their wives to the partnership and amend the partnership agreement in order to split profits equally four ways. Mrs F and Mrs G do no work in the partnership and the partnership has no employees.

This is a bounteous arrangement transferring income from one spouse to the other. The settlements legislation will apply and Mr F and Mr G continue to be taxable on half the profits each.

Completing the SA return

Mr F and Mr G are taxable on half the partnership profits each. So each should include £40,000 on their SA return. The £20,000 not caught by the settlements legislation is returned as partnership profits in the normal way. The £20,000 caught by the settlements legislation goes on page T1 in boxes 7.4 and 7.6. A note explaining this should be included in the ''Additional Information'' box.

Mrs F and Mrs G should not include the £20,000 from the partnership on their SA returns. However they should each include in the ''Additional Information'' box a note explaining that although they received £20,000 of profits from the partnership this is taxable on their husbands under the settlements legislation and has therefore been excluded from their individual return.

The partnership return should show overall partnership profits of £80,000. The partnership allocation should show £20,000 to Mr F, £20,000 to Mr G, £20,000 to Mrs F and £20,000 to Mrs G. The partners should add a note to the ''Additional Information'' box explaining that the £20,000 attributable to Mrs F and the £20,000 attributable to Mrs G are taxable on Mr F and Mr G respectively under the settlements legislation and are being returned on Mr F and Mr G's individual SA returns.

EXAMPLE 6—DIVIDEND WAIVERS

Where a company with few shareholders declares a final dividend when one or more of the shareholders has waived their right to a dividend in circumstances where other shareholders may benefit, it is possible the settlements legislation could apply.

For example Mrs H owns 80 ordinary shares in H Limited. Mr H owns 20 shares. In 2000 the company made a profit of £25,000. Mrs H waived her right to any dividend. The company then declared a dividend of £1,000 per share, and Mr H, who had no other income, received a dividend of £20,000.

We would apply the settlements legislation in these circumstances. Clearly a dividend of this amount could not have been paid from the company's profits on all the shares, so the waiver arrangement enhanced the dividend paid to Mr H. £16,000 of the dividend paid to Mr H is attributed to Mrs H under TA 1988 s 660A because the waiver was a bounteous arrangement.

Completing the SA return

£16,000 of Mr H's dividends of £20,000 are treated as Mrs H's income under the settlements legislation. Mrs H should return that £16,000 at boxes 7.10 to 7.12 on page T1 of her SA return and include a brief note in the "Additional Information" box.

Mr H should include only £4,000 of the £20,000 dividends on his SA return in the normal way and add a note to the "Additional Information" box explaining why only £4,000 is being returned even though £20,000 was received.

EXAMPLE 7—DIVIDENDS ON CERTAIN SHARES

As in example 6, but in this case Mrs I owns A shares and Mr I owns B shares. Both A and B shares rank equally. Again profits of £25,000 are made and a dividend of £20,000 is voted on the B shares while no dividend is voted on the A shares.

Clearly by not voting dividends on the A shares (which rank equally with the B shares) this is a bounteous arrangement as the dividend paid on the B shares could only be paid if no dividend was declared in respect of the A shares. £16,000 of the dividend paid to Mr I is attributed to Mrs I under TA 1988 s 660A because the decision to vote dividends only on certain shares was a bounteous arrangement.

Completing the SA return

£16,000 of Mr I's dividends of £20,000 are treated as Mrs I's income under the settlements legislation. Mrs I should return that £16,000 at boxes 7.10 to 7.12 on page T1 of her SA return and include a brief note in the "Additional Information" box.

Mr I should include only £4,000 of the £20,000 dividends on his SA return in the normal way and add a note to the "Additional Information" box explaining why only £4,000 is being returned even though £20,000 was received.

EXAMPLE 8—CHILDREN: GIFT OF SHARES FROM PARENT

Mr J owns all 100 issued £1 shares in J Limited. Mr J is the sole company director and is the person responsible for making all the company's profits because of his knowledge, expertise and hard work. Mr J gives each of his four children 10 shares. Dividends are paid.

TA 1988 s 660B applies and attributes the dividends paid to the children to Mr J for tax purposes. This is because Mr J has paid the income to his unmarried minor children.

Completing the SA return

Any dividends paid to his four children are treated as Mr J's income under the settlements legislation. He should return those dividends at boxes 7.10 to 7.12 on page T1 of his SA return and include a brief note in the "Additional Information" box. His own dividends should be returned in the normal way.

The four children do not need to return the dividends or inform the Inland Revenue they have received them. If they do receive a SA return, a note should be included in the "Additional Information" box explaining that although they received dividends during the year these have not been returned as they are taxable as Mr J's income under the settlements legislation.

EXAMPLE 9—CHILDREN: GIFT OF SHARES OTHER THAN FROM PARENT

As in example 8, but the 40 shares held by the children were originally owned by their grandmother who had subscribed for them at par when the company was set up but shortly afterwards had gifted them to her grandchildren.

TA 1988 s 660B applies and attributes the dividends received by the children to Mr J for tax purposes. Since Mr J is the person responsible for making the company's profits and decides on the level of dividends paid, it is Mr J who is the settlor rather than the children's grandmother.

The legislation could apply in a similar way if the children had subscribed for the shares themselves with money received from a third party or even from bank accounts in their own names.

Completing the SA return

Any dividends paid to his four children are treated as Mr J's income under the settlements legislation. He should return those dividends at boxes 7.10 to 7.12 on page T1 of his SA return and include a brief note in the "Additional Information" box. His own dividends should be returned in the normal way.

The four children do not need to return the dividends or inform the Inland Revenue they have received them. If they do receive a SA return then a note should be included in the "Additional Information" box explaining that although they received dividends during the year these have not been returned as they are taxable as Mr J's income under the settlements legislation.

EXAMPLE 10—AN OUTRIGHT GIFT TO A SPOUSE

Mrs L owns 10,000 ordinary shares in a FTSE 100 company. Those shares are worth £40,000. Mrs L gives those shares to her husband. Mr L is now entitled to all the dividends from the shares and can sell the shares if he wants and keep the proceeds. This is an outright gift of shares that are not wholly, or substantially, a right to income since they have a capital value and can be traded, so the settlements legislation does not apply.

Completing the SA return

As the settlements legislation does not apply all income should go in the normal boxes on the SA return.

EXAMPLE 11—SUBSCRIBED SHARES

Mr M is the sole director and owns all the 100 ordinary shares in M Limited, a small manufacturing company. The company employs 10 people and owns a small factory, a high street shop, tools fixtures and fittings and 3 delivery vehicles. Mr M draws a salary of £30,000 each year and receives dividends of £20,000. Mr M then gifts 50 shares to his wife who plays no part in the business. Mr and Mrs M then each receive dividends of £10,000.

We would not seek to apply the settlements legislation to the dividends received by Mrs M. This is because the outright gift of the shares cannot be regarded as wholly or substantially a right to income. The shares have capital rights and the company has substantial assets so on the winding up or sale of the business the shares would have more than an insubstantial value.

Completing the SA return

As the settlements legislation does not apply all income should go in the normal boxes on the SA return.

EXAMPLE 12—SUBSCRIBED SHARES

Mr N wants to set up in business as a bookseller. He needs at least £100,000 to buy premises, equipment and stock. He sets up a company and he and Mrs N each subscribe for 40,000 ordinary £1 shares at par and the company borrows £20,000 from the bank. Mr N draws a salary which after four years is £40,000. Mrs N does not work for the company. Company profits are used to repay debt and expand the business. The business does well and after 6 years the profits are sufficient to pay a dividend of £10,000.

We would not seek to apply to apply the settlements legislation to the dividend of £5,000 received by Mrs N. There is no bounty as Mr N draws a commercial salary for his efforts and the dividend is a commercial return on the initial investment which was vital at the commencement of the business and contained a clear element of risk.

Completing the SA return

As the settlements legislation does not apply all income should go in the normal boxes on the SA return.

EXAMPLE 13—A PARTNERSHIP

Mr and Mrs O and their friend Mr P have a business idea. They want to open a Cycle Repair Shop. Mrs O does not want to work but agrees to invest in the business without taking an active part, that is to say she is a sleeping partner. Each partner invests £10,000 and the £30,000 is used to lease a shop, buy equipment and stock and keep the business going until trade builds up. Under the partnership agreement Mr O and Mr P receive £500 a week with all the remaining profits split three ways between the partners.

The business is a huge success and makes large profits and continues to grow. Within five years Mrs O is receiving £50,000 a year as her share of the partnership profits. Although Mrs O does not work in the business, and her initial investment has turned out to be very successful, the settlements legislation would not apply to treat her share of the partnership profits as Mr O's. Mrs O's original investment was vital to get the business started and she risked losing it if the business failed.

Completing the SA return

As the settlements legislation does not apply all income should go in the normal boxes on the SA return.

EXAMPLE 14—A PARTNERSHIP

Mr P is a self-employed engineer engaged on specialist work for a number of clients in the construction industry. Mr P employs his wife, who plays an active part in the business including ordering and collecting specialist parts. Mrs P is paid a salary of £20,000. The profits of the business are £40,000. Mrs P owns a substantial property inherited from her mother.

Because of a number of claims made against Mr P, his insurers want to raise premiums by £20,000. He doesn't think he can afford this so his insurers agree to not increase the premiums if Mr P agrees to pay the first £25,000 of any claim. Mr P and Mrs P enter into an equal partnership. Accordingly Mrs P no longer draws a salary but is entitled to a share of the profits as well as being exposed to the liabilities of the partnership. The property she owns is therefore potentially at risk.

Mrs P's share of the profits is £30,000. Mrs P therefore has extra overall income of £10,000 because she has taken on the risk of the partnership liabilities including that associated with the £25,000 excess on the insurance policy. There is therefore no bounty and the settlements legislation would not apply.

Completing the SA return

As the settlements legislation does not apply all income should go in the normal boxes on the SA return.

EXAMPLE 15—GIFT OF SHARES OTHER THAN FROM PARENT

In 1960 Mr & Mrs Q and Mr & Mrs R set up a small family cleaning company. In total there were, and still are, 100 £1 ordinary shares in the business. Initially Mr Q and Mr R each subscribed at par for 40 shares and Mrs Q and Mrs R each subscribed at par for 10 shares.

When Mr & Mrs Q died they each left their shares in the company (50 in total) to their daughter, Miss Q. When Mr R also died he left his 40 shares in the company to his daughter Mrs S. Miss Q and Mrs S are both directors of the company and carry out its day to day running. The current turnover of the company is approximately £1,000,000 per year and its capital value is over £250,000. Miss Q and Mrs S each receive a salary of £60,000 per year. Each year a dividend of £500 per share is paid.

Mrs R has retained her original 10 shares in the company since 1960. Without discussing the matter in advance with either Miss Q or Mrs S, Mrs R decides to give her shares to her five year old granddaughter who is also Mrs S's daughter. Mrs R makes the gift on her granddaughter's next birthday.

The settlements legislation would not apply to this case since Mrs R retains no interest in the shares which she gives to her granddaughter and is therefore not a settlor within the meaning of TA 1988 s 660G. Nor is Mrs R's decision to gift the shares to her granddaughter part of a wider arrangement with Mrs S to settle income on the child.

Completing the SA return

As the settlements legislation does not apply all income should go in the normal boxes on the SA return.

ADDITIONAL EXAMPLES INVOLVING A COMPANY

Examples 3, 4 & 5 plus examples 11, 12 & 13 explained circumstances in which the settlements legislation did and did not apply to some company and partnership situations. We have been asked to provide further examples like these, which are below. These examples also have guidance on completing the SA return:

EXAMPLE 16—SUBSCRIBED SHARES

T Ltd was incorporated in October 1997 to provide a consultancy service to the health sector. Mr T is an IT specialist with a number of years experience in the health sector and Mrs T is an ex-nurse who specialises in producing computer based learning materials for hospitals. The company's share capital is £10,000 consisting of 10,000 £1 shares. Mr and Mrs T are both full time working directors of the company. From the beginning each subscribed for 5,000 shares. The first year's accounts show that each director received remuneration of £30,000 and that profits available for distribution were £50,000. £30,000 profits are retained in the company to build up the business. A dividend of £2 per share is declared and paid—each shareholder receiving £10,000.There is no bounty here and no arrangement to which the settlement legislation can apply.

Completing the SA return

As the settlements legislation does not apply all remuneration and dividends should go in the normal boxes on the SA return.

EXAMPLE 17—SUBSCRIBED SHARES

Mr U is a self-employed IT consultant. He reads an advert on a specialist website and as a result he decides to offer his services through a ''composite'' company set up by another company specialising in taxation services. Under an agreement he will subscribe for a special class of share (a £1 ''U'' share) which has rights to all his earnings less a ''commission'' paid to the organisers. When the agreement is sent to him for signature there is a box to tick if he wants a share issued to anyone else. He ticks the box and asks for an additional share to be issued to Mrs U. Apart from subscribing £1 for the share, Mrs U takes no part in the business. During year one his efforts contribute income of £68,000 to the company. The company retains sufficient to cover expenses and tax and the balance remaining of £54,000 is paid to Mr and Mrs U as dividends who each receive £27,000.

This is a bounteous transaction caught by the settlements legislation. In reaching this conclusion it is necessary to look at the whole arrangement. The substance of what has happened is that part of Mr U's earnings have been paid to Mrs U.

Completing the SA return

Mr U should return his own dividend income of £30,000 (£27,000 + tax credit of £3,000) on his SA return in the normal way. He should include his wife's £30,000 on page T1 of his return at boxes 7.10, 7.11 and 7.12 and include a brief note in the ''Additional Information'' box.

Mrs U should not include any of the £30,000 of dividends on her SA return, if she gets one, but a brief note in the ''Additional Information'' box would be helpful.

EXAMPLE 18—GIFTED SHARES

Mrs V carries on a trade as a designer through a company V Ltd. She is the sole director and sole shareholder of 100 £1 shares subscribed for at par on the company's formation. The company's accountant acts as company secretary. The company has insignificant capital. In a typical year the company's gross income is in the region of £60,000 p.a. After expenses (including Director's remuneration of £25,000) and providing for tax, the profits available for distribution are £24,000. Dividends of £20,000 are paid to Mrs V. In the following year Mr V, who worked for another company, is made redundant and loses his source of income. Mrs V gifts half her shares to Mr V. Mr V carries out some part-time secretarial work for the company for which he is paid £5,000 p.a. At the end of the year gross income is £65,000, Mrs V votes herself £10,000 remuneration and after other expenses and tax the balance of £40,000 is paid out as dividends—each spouse receiving £20,000.This is a bounteous arrangement, whereby Mrs V has transferred part of her income to her spouse, and it is caught by the settlements legislation. In reaching this conclusion it is necessary to look at the whole arrangement. What has happened is that part of Mrs V's earnings have been paid to Mr V. Two of the key elements in the arrangement are that the expertise and earning capacity of Mrs V have been provided to the company at undervalue and Mr V is paid a market rate for his work.

Completing the SA return

Mrs V should include her husband's dividend income of £20,000 on page T1 of her SA Return at boxes 7.10, 7.11 and 7.12 and include a brief note in the ''Additional Information'' box. Her own dividend income of £20,000 goes on the main return in the normal way and her £10,000 of remuneration goes on the Employment pages.

Mr V should include the £5,000 of remuneration in his SA return, if he gets one, in the normal way but should not include the £20,000 of dividends. A brief note in the ''Additional Information'' box explaining why the £20,000 of dividends received are not on the return would be helpful.

EXAMPLE 19—GIFTED SHARES

The facts are as above but Mrs V continued to pay herself a commercial rate of remuneration of £25,000 leaving only £20,000 to be distributed to the two shareholders. The gift of shares is a bounteous transaction which diverts £10,000 of income to Mr V and in the absence of any capital in the company those shares represent substantially a right to income. So the exemption in TA 1988 s 660A(6) for gifts between spouses does not apply and the dividends are assessable on Mrs V.

Completing the SA return

Mrs V should include her husband's dividend income of £10,000 on page T1 of her SA Return at boxes 7.10, 7.11 and 7.12 and include a brief note in the ''Additional Information'' box. Her own dividend income of £10,000 goes on the main return in the normal way and the £25,000 of remuneration goes on the Employment pages.

Mr V should include the £5,000 of remuneration in his SA return, if he gets one, in the normal way but should not include the £10,000 of dividends. A brief note in the ''Additional Information'' box explaining why the £10,000 of dividends received are not on the return would be helpful.

EXAMPLE 20—GIFTED SHARES

Mr W & Mr X are founder shareholders and directors of a successful hardware shop run through a company called DIY Ltd. The company was set up to acquire the partnership trade carried on by the two shareholders. At the time there was a single shop, the trade plus assets were worth about £50,000 which were transferred to the company and the company issued 10,000 £1 shares to the partners in return. Over the years the company has grown. It now owns a chain of 8 DIY stores. Some premises are owned and others rented. The company owns a number of delivery vans and employs 50 staff. The shares have increased in value from £5 per share to £75 per share. Mr W and Mr X respectively gift some of their shares to their wives. Mrs W & Mrs X are given 2000 shares each. Dividends are paid on all shares. Although this is a bounteous transaction it is an outright gift that is not substantially a right to income, because the company has significant capital assets, and is therefore excluded from the definition of settlement by TA 1988 s 660A(6).

Completing the SA return

As the settlements legislation does not apply all income should go in the normal boxes on the SA return.

FURTHER EXAMPLES INVOLVING A PARTNERSHIP

EXAMPLE 21

Mr Y, an architect, commences business as a sole trader. The business is successful and a few years later annual profits are in the region of £80,000. The business has insignificant capital and there are no employees. The business is transferred to a new partnership of Mr & Mrs Y. A deed is created under which profits are to be shared equally. Mrs Y subscribes no new capital and carries out no work whatsoever for the partnership. Profits for the year are £80,000 and £40,000 belong to Mrs Y. This is a bounteous arrangement transferring income from one spouse to another. The settlements legislation will apply and Mrs Y's share of the profits will continue to be assessed on Mr Y.

Completing the SA return

Mr Y should include Mrs Y's partnership income of £40,000 on page T1 of his SA Return at boxes 7.4 and 7.6. His own share of £40,000 is returned as partnership profits in the normal way. A note explaining this should be included in the ''Additional Information'' box.

Mrs Y should not include the £40,000 from the partnership on her SA return. However she should include in the ''Additional Information'' box a note explaining that although she received £40,000 of profits from the partnership this is taxable on Mr Y under the settlements legislation and has therefore been excluded from her individual return.

When completing the partnership return this needs to show overall partnership profits of £80,000. The partnership allocation should show £40,000 to Mr Y and £40,000 to Mrs Y. The partners should add a note to the ''Additional Information'' box explaining that the £40,000 attributable to Mrs Y is taxable on Mr Y under the settlements legislation and is being returned on Mr Y's individual SA return.

EXAMPLE 22

Mr Alpha and Mr Beta are in partnership as second hand car dealers. They own the freehold premises through which the partnership trades (valued at £200,000) and routinely carry a stock of 50 used cars. The business is successful and has established goodwill in the locality as a reliable trader. It employs a number of salesmen and office staff. Profits of £100,000 a year are split equally between the partners. They decide to admit their wives to the partnership and amend the partnership agreement in order to split profits and capital equally four ways. Mrs Alpha and Mrs Beta do no work in the partnership. Although this is a bounteous transaction it is an outright gift that is not substantially a right to income and is excluded from the definition of settlement by TA 1988 s 660A(6).

Completing the SA return

As the settlements legislation does not apply all income should go in the normal boxes on the SA return.

SUMMARY

Whether or not the settlements legislation applies to an arrangement depends on the particular facts of the case. It is necessary to look at the arrangement as a whole. If there is a bounteous arrangement which effectively transfers income earned by one person to another resulting in a reduction in overall tax liability the arrangement will be liable to challenge under the settlements legislation.

When considering whether or not the settlements legislation applies it is worth remembering that Parliament introduced the settlements legislation to prevent individuals transferring their income to a relative or friend in order to avoid tax. It therefore follows that a simple test to indicate whether or not the legislation might apply is to consider whether the same arrangements would have been made with a third party at arms length.

If you have any comments on this article and the issues raised you can contact the Editor of Tax Bulletin at the Inland Revenue (Somerset House, Strand, London WC2R 1LB).

Commentary—*Simon's Direct Tax Service* **C4.302, 303, 310.**

RI 269 (February 2004) *Licences and other rights to use telecommunications cable systems*

In Tax Bulletin 50 we set out our views on a number of issues on the interpretation of Schedule 23 to the Finance Act 2000. The Schedule is about the tax treatment of certain licences granted under the Wireless Telegraphy Act 1949 and more generally to ''indefeasible rights'' (IRUs) to use telecommunications cable systems.

One issue concerned the head of charge where the holder of the licence or IRU did not exploit the asset in the course of a trade. We said we would expect the income stream to be a source within Case VI of Schedule D if it is not within Case I. We did not think the receipts from exploitation of the asset would be chargeable under Case III.

For companies within the charge to corporation tax in respect of these licences and rights the rules in FA 2000 are superseded by those in Schedule 29 to Finance Act 2002. This change takes effect for accounting periods ending on or after 1st April 2002. In applying the rules in Schedule 29 to these periods sums brought into account earlier under the FA 2000 rules are treated as if they had been brought into account under Schedule 29 itself.

Unlike the FA 2000 legislation, Schedule 29 provides specifically that sums relating to assets within its scope which are held for the purposes of (broadly) non-trading activities are to be brought into account under Case VI.

We now think that the expectation we expressed in our earlier Tax Bulletin article that Case VI would be the appropriate head of charge for non-trading assets within Schedule 23 is misleading. We consider that it is quite possible on the facts of a particular case that Case III would be the appropriate head of charge. That is where the royalties received from the licensing of the rights within Schedule 23 have a UK source and take the form of ''pure income profit''. Royalties, other than those arising in the course of a trade, may fall into this category where for example the licensing agreement under which they are paid does not impose any further obligation on the licensor to provide related services.

Where royalties fall within Case III in the hands of the recipient, Schedule 23 does not in strictness permit sums written off the related licence or rights in a company's accounts (on an impairment review or by way of amortisation under Finance Reporting Standard 10) to be deducted in computing the sum chargeable to tax. This is because the Schedule merely deems the sums written off to be on revenue account, which is insufficient to override the prohibition on deductions in computing Case III income in TA 1988 s 64.

We do not of course propose to apply our corrected view of the law retrospectively. This means that where the recipient of royalties is a company within the charge to corporation tax in respect of the relevant licence or rights our change of view will have no practical consequences. Accounting periods to which the rules in Schedule 23 applied will have ended at the latest on 31st March 2002.

The rules in Schedule 23 will continue to apply to a recipient of these royalties who is within the charge to income tax. In such cases we do not propose to apply the change of view to royalties arising under an agreement entered into by the payer and recipient prior to 20 February 2004 but our revised view will apply to royalties payable under other agreements.

INLAND REVENUE DECISIONS

LIST OF DECISIONS

Notes—The Revenue decisions were published in early editions of Inland Revenue Tax Bulletin. The decisions report conclusions that were reached on the facts of individual cases, but do not necessarily include all the detailed facts which may have been relevant to the decision. They provide an indication of the approach the Revenue has adopted in the past, but have not been drafted as generally applicable statements of the Revenue's position. It cannot be assumed therefore, that interpretations of the law contained or implicit in these decisions will necessarily be applied in other cases.

No new decisions have been published since February 1994.

The number before each decision (eg RD 1) does not appear in the official publications. It has been added by the publishers to distinguish "decisions" from "interpretations" (printed *ante*) and to facilitate identification for the purpose of cross references.

RD 1 (November 1991) *Company cars: payments by employees*

SCHEDULE E—BENEFITS IN KIND—PAYMENT BY EMPLOYEE TOWARDS THE COST OF MORE EXPENSIVE CAR—TA 1988 SCH 6 PARA 4

A company operated a car scheme under which it made leased cars available for the private use of its employees. The model allocated to an employee depended on his seniority within the company. Employees who accepted a car appropriate to their grade were not required to contribute anything to the employer for the private use of the car. However, an employee could obtain a more expensive car by making a monthly payment to the employer equal to the additional leasing costs. In such a case the rules of the scheme required these payments to be made—

- as a condition of the car being made available for the employee's private use; and
- specifically for that private use.

The employees concerned sought to deduct the monthly payments from the car benefit scale charge under TA 1988 Sch 6 para 4.

The deduction was allowed. While it might be argued that the payment in such a case was really for a more expensive car, rather than for the private use of the car, the Revenue accepted that the arrangement was not inconsistent with the payment being made as a condition of that particular car being made available for the private use of that particular employee. The requirements of TA 1988 Sch 6 para 4 were therefore satisfied.

Commentary—*Simon's Direct Tax Service* **E4.614**.

RD 2 (November 1991) *Controlled foreign companies: test of a trading company*

INTERNATIONAL TAX—CONTROLLED FOREIGN COMPANIES—ACCEPTABLE DISTRIBUTION POLICY—DISTRIBUTION STANDARD—TA 1988 SCH 25 PARA 2(2)

A controlled foreign company received 80 per cent of its income as fees from supplying personnel for other group members trading outside the UK. The remaining 20 per cent was from investment income. However, the company paid out 99 per cent of the personnel fees received to another management company within the group. It was claimed to be a trading company, as defined at TA 1988 s 756(1), on the grounds that its business consisted mainly of the carrying on of a trade so that distribution of 50 per cent of its available profits would be sufficient to prevent liability under the controlled foreign company provisions. The company's business did not consist mainly of the carrying on of a trade and a 90 per cent distribution standard was therefore appropriate. The key features were that the company's trading activities were very limited (it was merely acting as a conduit for management fees) and the bulk of its net profits arose from investments.

Commentary—*Simon's Direct Tax Service* **D4.138**.

RD 3 (February 1992) *Interest relief: director's overdrawn loan account*

SCHEDULE E—BENEFITS IN KIND—BENEFICIAL LOANS—DIRECTOR'S LOAN ACCOUNT USED TO FINANCE PURCHASE OF DIRECTOR'S PRIVATE RESIDENCE—TA 1988 S 353, SCH 7

A director of a close company had, for many years, an account with the company designated as a loan account. The account usually remained in credit. However, in one particular year a substantial debit balance was created by the withdrawal of money for the purchase of the director's main residence.

No interest was payable on this loan, and no specific terms were laid down for its repayment. Whilst accepting that the overdrawn balance attracted Schedule E liability under TA 1988 s 160 the director sought to mitigate the charge on the grounds that had interest been paid on the loan it would have been partly "eligible for relief". The benefit calculation should therefore be modified in accordance with TA 1988 Sch 7 para 8.

The loan did not fall within Sch 7 para 8. The term "eligible for relief" was defined in Sch 7 para 6 (now Sch 7 para 19(2)) in terms of eligibility under TA 1988 s 353. TA 1988 s 353(3)(*a*) says that relief is not given for interest on "a debt incurred by overdrawing an account ... or under similar arrangements". Whilst the passage quoted is more commonly applied to bank current accounts it applies equally to a director's current account with his company. It follows that interest on such an account—if any were paid—cannot be eligible for relief irrespective of the use to which the director puts the money.

Commentary—*Simon's Direct Tax Service* **E4.633**.

RD 4 (February 1992) *PAYE: agency workers*

A limited company had been interposed in the contractual arrangements between a worker and an employment agency. Even though all the other circumstances were such that TA 1988 s 134 would apply, the Revenue accepted that it was not necessary for the employment agency to operate PAYE. This was because the Revenue were satisfied that the contract with the employment agency for the worker's services was genuinely entered into by the company and not by the individual.

The company then paid out fees to the worker and described them as "consultancy fees" claiming that they were not paid to the worker for acting as a director or employee of the company.

The Revenue were able to recover PAYE from the company on the fees. This was because when it paid the worker, the company was itself an agency within TA 1988 s 134(1)(b).

Note—This Decision is now obsolete.
Commentary—*Simon's Direct Tax Service* **E4.225**.

RD 5 (May 1992) *Approved share option schemes: linked bonus schemes*

EMPLOYEE SHARE SCHEME—LINKAGE BETWEEN APPROVED DISCRETIONARY SHARE OPTION SCHEME AND "PHANTOM" SHARE SCHEME—TA 1988 S 185, SCH 9 PARA 1

A company operated a discretionary share option scheme which had received approval under TA 1988 Sch 9. The directors wished to operate a bonus scheme described as a "phantom" share scheme alongside the approved scheme.

The intention of the "phantom" scheme was to provide employees with cash with which they would subscribe for shares under the option scheme. Employees selected would be notionally allocated a number of shares in the company. On the fifth anniversary of that notional allocation the company would pay to the employees, as a bonus, the increase in value in the shares. The payment would be conditional upon the employees using the net amount (after deduction of tax and national insurance contributions) to acquire shares in the company in exercise of the option.

The question which arose was whether the linkage of the "phantom" scheme to the approved scheme removed the benefit of relief under TA 1988 s 185 in respect of the issue of shares under that scheme.

The existence of the "phantom" scheme did not affect either the approval of the discretionary share option scheme or the availability of tax relief on exercise of the option. On the other hand, if the "phantom" scheme had, for example, effectively given a participant a choice between exercising an option and receiving a cash payment, the arrangements would not have met the conditions for approval.

Commentary—*Simon's Direct Tax Service* **E4.592**.

RD 6 (August 1992) *Transactions in securities: counteraction of tax advantages: directors' pension scheme*

PENSION FUND—COUNTERACTION OF TAX ADVANTAGES—TRANSACTIONS IN SECURITIES—EXPLOITATION OF EXEMPT STATUS OF SMALL SELF-ADMINISTERED PENSION FUND—TA 1988 SS 590–612, 703–709

A company set up a pension scheme for the benefit of its four directors each of whom held 25 per cent of the company's issued share capital. The scheme was approved as an exempt scheme in accordance with TA 1988 ss 590–612 and contributions of £100,000 per annum made by the company to the scheme were allowed as deductions in computing its Schedule D Case I profits in accordance with TA 1988 s 592(4).

In each of three successive tax years each director sold to the pension fund small parts of his holding in the company for cash which, between the four directors, totalled £120,000 for 4·8 per cent of the company's shares. Clearance under TA 1988 s 707 from s 703 counteraction was applied for retrospectively and refused.

This was because the directors had obtained income tax advantages by receiving cash from the company in capital form which, if they had not first arranged for it to be paid to the pension fund, could have reached them as dividends. The tax advantages had arisen in consequence of transactions in securities and the Revenue were not satisfied that those advantages were not the main objects of the transactions or that they should not be subject to s 703 counteraction.

A financial settlement was negotiated with the directors who also agreed to repurchase the shares previously sold to the pension fund.

In Statement of Practice SP 3/80 the Board explained that, in practice, clearance under what is now s 707 would not be withheld unless, on the information available, counteraction if the transactions were effected could be expected. In this case the transactions had already taken place and so the Board commenced counteraction proceedings under s 703.

Commentary—*Simon's Direct Tax Service* **B3.703**.
Statement of Practice SP 3/80—(TA 1988 s 707: cancellation of tax advantages from certain transactions in securities: procedure for clearance in advance).

RD 7 (November 1992) *Additional personal allowances for children*

The children of a divorced couple normally lived with their mother but occasionally visited their father. The father claimed additional personal allowance in respect of one of the children, contending that if she slept at his house for only one night in the year she was "resident with him for ... part of the year" in accordance with TA 1988 s 259(2).

There is no statutory definition of the term "resident with" so the expression is given its normal meaning. The main entry in the Oxford Dictionary definition of "reside" is "to dwell permanently or for a considerable time, to have one's settled or usual abode, to live, in or at a particular place".

Put another way, a child is "resident with" a claimant if the child has his or her home with the claimant. [The Revenue] accept that it is possible to have more than one home and that a child can be resident with different people at each place. But [they] do not accept that any short visit necessarily meets the test. Nobody would say that during a brief stay in a holiday hotel, that hotel became their home. Equally, the fact that a child stayed with her father for a holiday or for short visits did not mean that that was her home.

Since, on the facts of this case, the child clearly had no home with her father the claim for additional personal allowance was rejected.

Note—This Decision is now obsolete.
Commentary—*Simon's Direct Tax Service* **E2.502**

RD 8 (February 1993) *Late partnership continuation election*

SCHEDULE D CASES I AND II—LATE PARTNERSHIP CONTINUATION BASIS ELECTION—TA 1988 S 113(2)

Two doctors submitted separate accounts. Whilst it could have been argued that in the circumstances of the case they acted in partnership, the inspector agreed with the accountants acting that the doctors should be treated as sole traders. The accountants mistakenly believed that the agreement meant that the doctors would be treated as sole traders indefinitely, irrespective of future changes. Consequently, when, after the death of one of the doctors, the remaining doctor took on two partners, the accountants continued to prepare sole accounts.

The existence of the partnership finally came to light and it was agreed that it should be taxed on the correct basis. But this was more than two years after the new partners had joined the practice and so was outside the statutory period for making an election for the continuation basis under TA 1988 s 113(2). A request was made for the Board to accept a late election in exercise of its care and management function.

The late election was accepted. In the circumstances of the case there was quite reasonably, some uncertainty and misunderstanding about the existence of the partnership for tax purposes and the basis upon which it was to be assessed. As soon as it was agreed that a partnership had in fact come into existence and that continuation basis elections were therefore competent they were made and it was thus considered reasonable to accept the late elections.

Commentary—*Simon's Direct Tax Service* **E5.312**

RD 9 (February 1994) *Letting surplus business accommodation*

A company received rents of £62,000 per year from the letting of property as follows—

- £27,000 related to the letting of premises which had formerly been in use as business premises but were vacated on becoming surplus to requirements. No part of these premises was retained by the company for its own use;
- £10,000 related to surplus land at factory premises. The company still used the factory and the remainder of the site;
- the balance of £25,000 related to premises which the company had built four years previously intending to occupy them themselves, but which, in the event, they found surplus to requirements before occupation and so were wholly let.

The company sought to include the rents received from the letting and associated expenses in their Schedule D Case I computations.

The case of *Salisbury House Estate Ltd v Fry* is authority for the proposition that the income tax schedules are mutually exclusive so that any rent from property should in law be excluded from the computation of liability under Schedule D Cases I or II and assessed to tax under Schedule A.

If the law was strictly applied this would mean that rent received from letting surplus business accommodation and the related expenses would have to be separately identified in each and every case even where there would be no overall effect on the ultimate tax liability.

To avoid the need to apportion outgoings on accommodation which is partly used for the business and partly let, between trading and Schedule A the Revenue has in practice allowed the rents receivable to be included in the Case I or II computations in certain limited circumstances as follows—

1 The accommodation must be temporarily surplus to current business requirements.

In other words the accommodation must previously have been used or intended to be used in the business. Also, Case I or II treatment is not appropriate where it is evident that the premises have become surplus to business requirements other than temporarily.

2 The individual premises must be used partly for the business and partly let.

As noted above the inclusion of rents within Case I or II avoids the need to apportion outgoings on the premises between trading and Schedule A expenses. The treatment cannot be applied to whole buildings which are let because there is no question of any apportionment of expenses being necessary.

3 The rental income is comparatively small.

Where a substantial amount of rent is receivable the strict basis should be applied because otherwise the tax liability resulting may not approximate to the strict statutory liability.

4 The rents must be in respect of the letting of surplus business accommodation only and not of land.

Since on the facts of this case it was clear that the company did not satisfy the above conditions in respect of any part of the rental income receivable the company's application for Case I treatment was refused.

Commentary—*Simon's Direct Tax Service* **A4.104, B3.620**.

PRESS RELEASES ETC

CONTENTS

LIST OF PRESS RELEASES, ETC

Date / Source	Subject
April 1964. IR booklet No 490 (1964)	Patents [TA 1988 ss 520, 522]
June 1965. CCAB	Meaning of "small" in connection with capital distributions [TCGA 1992 s 122(2)]; sums derived from assets not lost or destroyed [TCGA 1992 s 23(1) (*c*)]; part disposals of land [TCGA 1992 s 243(1) (*a*)]
June 1967. CCAB	Shares in close company transferring assets at undervalue [TCGA 1992 s 125]
June 1967. CCAB	Distribution of assets to legatees [TCGA 1992 s 62(4)]
June 1967. CCAB	Group of companies—company not treated as leaving a group
June 1967. CCAB	Quoted securities held on 6 April 1965—election under [TCGA 1992 Sch 2 para 4]
June 1968. CCAB	Associates—unitholders [TA 1988 s 417(3)]
June 1968. CCAB	Transfer of assets by group in liquidation [TCGA 1992 ss 170–181]
June 1968. CCAB	Bonus issues following reduction of capital [TA 1988 s 210]
June 1968. CCAB	Part disposals—single or multiple assets [TCGA 1992 s 42]
June 1969. CCAB	Non-resident companies [TCGA 1992 s 13]
June 1969. CCAB	Debt on a security) [TCGA 1992 s 132(3)(*b*) and s 251(1)]
10 November 1969. Hansard	Overseas British nationals (publication fees)
June 1970. CCAB	Transfers of assets and liabilities within a group [TA 1988 s 209]
June 1971. CCAB	Balancing adjustments (FA 1971 s 44(6) [CAA 1990 s 26(1)])
June 1970. CCAB	Meaning of negligible
22 June 1972. Hansard	Payment of tax by instalments: undue hardship [TA 1988 s 34(8)]; [TCGA 1992 s 280]
June 1972. CCAB	Availability of writing down allowances on liquidation of supplier of plant or machinery [CAA 1990 s 25]
October 1972. IR Leaflet CA 2	Industrial building and structures: meaning [CAA 1990 s 18]
26 June 1973. CCAB	Termination payments to directors and employees [TA 1988 ss 188, 209]
19 February 1974. CCAB	Taxation anomalies and practical difficulties 1973 TR 127
4 April 1974. IR letter	Industrial buildings allowance—garages
June 1975. CCAB	Distribution of asset in specie by liquidator of subsidiary company [TCGA 1992 s 171]
12 February 1976. IR	[Inheritance tax]—settled property—interest in possession
June 1976. CCAB	Gardens: loss of exemption [TCGA 1992 s 222]
June 1976. CCAB	Demolition of plant [CAA 1990 s 26(1)]
1 November 1976. Hansard	Schedule E: travelling expenses: overseas employment
August 1977. CCAB	New hotels: capital allowances
7 February 1978. IR	Double Taxation: United Kingdom and United States of America
16 February 1978. Hansard	Wife allowance
24 February 1978. IR letter	Election under [TA 1988 s 247]
2 March 1978. IR	Double Taxation: exchange of information with the United States of America
2 March 1978. Hansard	Parliamentary question: co-operation between UK and other countries' tax authorities
12 April 1978. IR letter	1977 Memorandum on taxation anomalies and practical difficulties, paragraph 31—Form P11D [TA 1988 s 156]
June 1978. CCAB	Hotels [CAA 1990 ss 7, 19]
June 1978. CCAB	Loans to traders—relief [TCGA 1992 s 253]
27 June 1978. IR letter	Double taxation relief—limitation of credit [TA 1988 s 797(1)]
29 June 1978. Hansard	Parliamentary proceedings: armed forces pensions [TA 1988 ss 19, 315]

17 July 1978. IR letter	Artificial transactions in land [TA 1988 s 776]—loss
6 September 1978. Law Society's Gazette (see also BTR, December 1978, p 477)	Key man insurance [TA 1988 s 74]
17 October 1978. IR letter	Capital gains tax: [TCGA 1992 Sch 6 para 7 (2)]: definition of ''chargeable asset''
23 October 1978. IR letter	Partners' chargeable gains [TCGA 1992 ss 152–158 and 165]
23 November 1978. IR letter	Capital gains tax: definition of chargeable asset [TCGA 1992 Sch 6 para 7 (2)]
30 November 1978. IR letter	Payments for group roll-over relief
December 1978. BTR 422	Goodwill: written off: loss relief: [TCGA 1992 s 24(2)]
22 January 1979. IR letter	Waiver of rent [TA 1988 s 41]
26 April 1979. IR letter	Capital allowances: plant and machinery [CAA 1990 s 24]
16 May 1979. CCAB TR 340	Elections to pay dividends as group income and annual payments and interest without deduction of tax
23 May 1979. Hansard	Benefits in kind [TA 1988 s 131]
18 June 1979. IR	Goods sold subject to reservation of title
29 June 1979. IR letter	Apportionment of benefit in kind [TA 1988 s 156(2)]
10 July 1979. IR letter	Ordinary residence ([TA 1988 s 336])
1 August 1979. Association of British Chambers of Commerce	Tax appeals and postal delays
15 September 1979. Taxation	Arts Council: awards and bursaries
25 September 1979. CCAB	Inland Revenue clarify position on use of gross profit margins
19 October 1979. CCAB	Accountants clarify calculations of double taxation relief
30 October 1979. IR letter	Capital gains deferment: holdover relief
31 December 1979. BTR 343, 431	Valuation: Lands Tribunal [TCGA 1992 Sch 2, para 17]
31 December 1979. BTR 393	Branch or agency: Brussels Convention on Jurisdiction (TMA 1970 s 79)
31 December 1979. BTR 398	Domicile: effect of Domicile and Matrimonial Proceedings Act 1973
31 December 1979. BTR 417	Plant: painting in office [CAA 2001 s 57]
22 January 1980. IR letter	[TA 1988 s 353] (Relief for payment of interest)
31 January 1980. IR letter	[TA 1988 s 410] (Group relief: effect of arrangements for transfer of company to another group, etc)
12 February 1980. IR letter	[TA 1988 s 193(1)] (Earnings from work done abroad)
14 February 1980. IR letter	Capital gains tax: trusts [TCGA 1992 s 72]
9 May 1980. IR letters	Agricultural buildings allowance
20 June 1980. IR	Demergers
22 July 1980. IR letter	Voyage or journey outside the UK
26 January 1981. IR	The transfer pricing of multinational enterprises: Notes by the UK Inland Revenue
3 February 1981. IR letter	Payment for surrender of group relief
25 March 1981. IR Letter	Industrial buildings allowances
20 October 1981. IR letter	Mineral depletion allowances [CAA 2001 ss 394, 417, 418]
10 November 1981. IR letter	Relief on replacement of business assets [TCGA 1992 ss 155, 157]
17 February 1982. IR letter	Interest on non-resident loan to UK resident [TA 1988 ss 18, 349]
1 February 1983. Hansard	Tax payments (interest charges)
10 March 1983. CCAB TR 500	Guidance note on taxation: points of practical interest
31 May 1983. IR letter	Transfer of a trade to a connected company
7 July 1983. IR letter	[TA 1988 s 146] (living accommodation provided for employee)
21 October 1983. IR letter	Associated companies—[TA 1988 s 416(3)]
5 December 1983. Hansard	Tax Status (Contract Workers)
20 December 1983. IR letter	Industrial buildings allowances [CAA 2001 s 283]
16 January 1984. IR letter	[TA 1988 s 410] (Arrangements for transfer of company to another group or consortium)
15 February 1984. Hansard	Corporation tax (allowances)

15 February 1984. Hansard	Capital gains tax
6 March 1984. Hansard	Gratuities (Taxation)
15 March 1984. IR	Cable television: capital allowances [CAA 2001 s 57]
17 May 1984. IR	Furnished holiday lettings and caravans
11 June 1984. Hansard	Taxation
19 June 1984. Hansard	Taxpayers and Inspectors (Transcripts of Meetings)
18 July 1984. Hansard	Farmers (Outgoers' Scheme)
2 November 1984. IR	Incentive awards and prizes for employees: taxed award schemes
21 March 1985. Hansard	Houseboats
28 March 1985. IR	Tips and tax
15 April 1985. Hansard	Outgoers' scheme
11 June 1985. IR	Approved employee share option schemes: Revenue revise practice on some share restrictions [TA 1988 Sch 9 paras 12, 13]
25 September 1985	ICAEW TR 588: *Furniss v Dawson*
28 November 1985. Hansard	Firemen (bounty payments)
31 January 1986. Hansard	Police rent allowances
10 February 1986. Hansard	Police rent allowances
20 March 1986. IR	Future Budget day tax changes
27 October 1986. IR	Capital allowances: changes in accounting practice for plant and machinery under lease or subject to hire purchase
6 November 1986. Hansard	Nurses' registration fees
17 November 1986. Hansard	Income tax—payment of bank giro
24 November 1986. ICAEW (TR 637)	Memorandum TR 637: expenditure for which tax relief is not available
27 January 1987. IR letter	Settlements: dividend waiver as disposition
10 April 1987. ICAEW	Memorandum TR 657: Company reconstructions and amalgamations clearances under [TCGA 1992 s 138]
15 January 1988. Hansard	Enterprise zones
30 March 1988. IR	Cutting the cost of handling claims for repayment of tax [TMA 1970 s 42]
14 April 1988. IR	Unapproved employee share schemes [FA 1988 s 78]
13 June 1988. IR letter	Small companies' rate: non-trading holding company [TA 1988 s 13]
25 January 1989. IR letter	Living accommodation: deemed director
11 May 1989. Institute of Taxation letter to IR	Living accommodation: deemed director
14 July 1989. IR letter	Living accommodation: deemed director
6 September 1989. ICAEW	Memorandum TR 760: Taxation procedural matters
5 October 1989. IR letter to Institute of Taxation	Gains from share options: non-residents
8 January 1990. ICAEW	Memorandum TR 788: Inland Revenue procedural matters: independent taxation and reimbursement of taxpayers' expenses
18 January 1990. IR	Incentives for employees—improvements to the taxed award scheme
23 February 1990. ICAEW	TR 781: Guidance on ownership of documents and records
15 March 1990. ICAEW	TR 786: Tax position on examination prizes
30 March 1990. Hansard	Professional bodies (membership)
19 April 1990. IR	Benefits in kind: valuation of living accommodation provided for employees in England and Wales
June 1990. ICAEW	TR 799: Tax aspects of the Insolvency Act 1986
July 1990. ICAEW	TR 800: Auditing standard 102—the audit report
27 July 1990. IR	Insurance companies and friendly societies: transfers of long term business—clearance applications
16 August 1990. ICAEW	TR 806: Inland Revenue procedural matters
18 October 1990. IR letter	Requests from practitioners for information or guidance
21 November 1990. IR	Independent taxation—capital gains tax on jointly owned assets
22 November 1990. IR	Benefits in kind—employer provided living accommodation
19 December 1990. IR	New trust deeds—change of practice

16 January 1991. Ministry of Agriculture, Fisheries and Food	Simpler tax arrangements for seasonal work by overseas farm students
27 March 1991. The Law Society	Notification of clearances—[TCGA 1992 s 138]
11 April 1991. ICAEW	Memorandum TR 830: Inland Revenue—technical guidance
29 May 1991. IR	PAYE: casual harvest workers
29 May 1991. The Law Society	Inland Revenue information powers—TMA 1970 s 13
31 October 1991. Institute of Taxation	Capital gains tax—replacement of business assets [TCGA 1992 ss 152–158]
6 November 1991. ICAEW	Memorandum TR 851: Taxation of ex gratia payments
18 November 1991. IR	Capital gains tax valuations of unquoted shares at 31 March 1982—new arrangements at the Shares Valuation Division
19 December 1991. Country Landowners Association	Share farming
29 January 1992. Law Society	Overseas retirement benefits
18 March 1992. Law Society	Tax returns—signature under enduring powers of attorney
18 March 1992. Law Society	Valuation of agricultural tenancies
31 March 1992. Lloyd's of London Market Bulletin	Guidance on the tax treatment of Lloyd's underwriters' compensation
16 June 1992. ICAEW Tax 13/92 (extract)	Offsetting overpayments against underpayments
7 October 1992. Law Society	Ex gratia payments—Statement of Practice SP 13/91
16 November 1992. ICAEW	Taxation representations (miscellaneous matters)—1992 (TAX 15/92)
14 December 1992. ICAEW	Guidance note—non-resident settlements (TAX 20/92)
21 January 1993. IR	Taxation of in-house benefits in kind
15 February 1993. Law Society	Company taxation—equity notes and thin capitalisation
19 March 1993. ICAEW	Equity notes and thin capitalisation—Guidance note (TAX 5/93)
1 April 1993. IR	Payments to the Inland Revenue by electronic funds transfer
12 May 1993. Hansard	Company cars
14 May 1993. Hansard	Company cars—provision of chauffeur
18 May 1993. IR	Business tax computations rounded to nearest £1,000
3 November 1993: Law Society	Legal costs relating to termination payments—Inland Revenue concession
17 December 1993. IR	Lloyd's: basis of assessment for individual names—transitional administrative arrangements
9 February 1994. IR	European Economic Area Agreement
31 March 1994. IR	Self-assessment: transition to current year basis—anti-avoidance provisions
August 1994. Taxation Practitioner: IR letter	Finance Act 1994: Capital allowance provisions
9 November 1994. IR	Clearance procedure for non-trading controlled foreign companies
20 February 1995. ICAEW	Incorporation of professional partnerships: tax implications of certain aspects—Guidance note (TAX 7/95)
20 February 1995. IR	Stock Exchange alternative investment market (AIM)—tax reliefs for investment in companies joining AIM
5 April 1995. Law Society's Gazette	1995 Finance Bill: clauses 54 [FA 1995 s 56], 83 [FA 1995 s 91]—Revenue's response to Revenue Law Committee's representations
12 April 1995. ICAEW	Relationship between accountancy practice and the tax computation in the light of *Gallagher v Jones and Johnston v Britannia Airways Ltd*—Guidance note (TAX 10/95)
24 April 1995. IR	Self-assessment—transitional arrangements for self-employed taxpayers
26 April 1995. Law Society's Gazette	1995 Finance Bill: clause 78 [FA 1995 s 86]—Revenue's response to Revenue Law Committee's representations

26 April 1995. Law Society's Gazette	Assignment of debts between members of a group of companies—TCGA 1992 s 251
16 May 1995. IR	Personal incidental expenses—guidance for employers
24 May 1995. IR	Administration of gilt-edged stock (Fotra securities)
6 June 1995. Hansard	Self-employment—classification
17 July 1995. Share Scheme Lawyers Group	Share option cancellation payments—PAYE
21 March 1996. IR	Carry-back of personal pension contributions made in 1996–97
21 March 1996. IR	Capital gains tax treatment of cashbacks and certain other lump sum payments by banks or building societies
1 April 1996. IR	Interest and repayment interest—effective date of payment of tax and NICs
4 April 1996. IR	Self assessment—early settlement of a deceased taxpayer's tax affairs or those of a trust or estate following cessation
30 April 1996. IR	Tax treatment of premiums and benefits under locum and fixed practice expenses insurance policies
31 May 1996. IR	Disclosure and discovery under self-assessment
29 July 1996. IR	Self-assessment—provision of information from taxpayer statements of account to authorised agents
31 July 1996. IR	Repayments to sub-contractors in the construction industry
26 September 1996. IR	Rulings
19 November 1996. IR/CA	Inland Revenue and Contributions Agency provide more help for the construction industry on employment status
2 December 1996. IR	Capital gains tax reinvestment relief—new clearance scheme
4 December 1996. IR	Consequences of Budget changes—deduction of tax and relief at source
20 January 1997. IR	Self-assessment—the tax obligations of trustees and beneficiaries of certain bare trusts
27 January 1997. IR	Self-assessment—payments on account for 1996–97 calculation of interest following late issue of statements of account
4 February 1997. IR	Self-assessment—valuations for capital gains tax
17 March 1997. IR	Employment termination settlements—taxation of benefits received after the year of termination
27 March 1997. IR	Capital gains tax—cash payments to investors in Cheltenham and Gloucester Building Society on takeover by Lloyds Bank
28 July 1997. IR	Taxation of sub-contractors in the construction industry—implementation of new scheme
29 August 1997. IR	Pension schemes and self-assessment for 1996–97
21 January 1998. IR	Economic and monetary union (EMU)—tax consequences
29 July 1998. HM Treasury	Preparing British business for the euro—consultation on tax consequences of the introduction of the single currency
16 February 1999. IR	Corporation tax reform—regulations for relief of past surplus advance corporation tax
8 June 1999. IR	A modern system for corporation tax payments—guidance on use of information and penalty powers in instalment payments regulations
25 January 2000. IR	Deregulatory change setting official rate of interest on beneficial loans in advance
February 2000. Tax Bulletin article	Provision of personal services through intermediaries
23 March 2000. IR Budget Note	Group relief rules
April 2000. Tax Bulletin article	Employee share plans—conditional shares and related topics
11 April 2000. IR	Electronic commerce—tax status of websites and servers
19 April 2000. IR	Pension sharing on divorce to begin on 1 December 2000
31 May 2000. IR	Inland Revenue helps to launch voluntary tax savings scheme for share fishermen

June 2000. Tax Bulletin article	Provision of personal services through an intermediary—FAQs
August 2000. Tax Bulletin article	Amending an income tax self assessment (ITSA) after an enquiry—TMA 1970 ss 28A, 28B
8 August 2000. IR	Recognised stock exchanges overseas
25 September 2000. IR	Venture capital schemes and enterprise management incentives—new centralised service for small companies
October 2000. Tax Bulletin article	Schedule E benefits in kind—calculating the cash equivalent of a benefit when there is part business use and part private use
October 2000. Tax Bulletin article	New criminal offence for tax fraud
October 2000. Tax Bulletin article	Finance Act 2000—modernisation of group relief
December 2000. Tax Bulletin article	Limited liability partnerships
February 2001. Tax Bulletin article	Providing services through an intermediary—IR 35, what happens next?
April 2001. Tax Bulletin article	Corporation tax—large companies: quarterly instalment payments and group payment arrangements
June 2001. Tax Bulletin Issue 53	Income tax self-assessment (ITSA) returns for 2000–01
August 2001. Tax Bulletin Issue 54	Gross payments of interest
October 2001. Tax Bulletin Issue 55	The taxation of share options: internationally mobile employees
15 November 2001. IR	CGT—more debentures to qualify for business assets taper relief
December 2001. Tax Bulletin Issue 56	Liability to pay Class 1 National Insurance Contributions—Internationally mobile employees
January 2002. Tax Bulletin Issue 57	Double Taxation Relief—Tax consolidations falling within Section 803A of TA 1988
April 2002. Tax Bulletin Issue 58	Revenue Accountants
June 2002. Tax Bulletin Issue 59	Taxation of Foreign Nationals: Schedule E—Tax Equalisation
August 2002. Tax Bulletin Issue 60.	Review of links with business—international tax issues
October 2002. Tax Bulletin Issue 61.	Capital gains tax—taper relief: anti-avoidance: TCGA 1992 Sch A1 paras 11 and 11A
October 2002. Tax Bulletin Issue 61.	Capital gains tax—capital sums derived from assets: reliefs and Extra-Statutory Concession D33
December 2002. Tax Bulletin Issue 62.	Changes to the ''Hansard'' Procedure.
February 2003. Tax Bulletin Issue 63.	Important changes to the filing of employer end-of-year returns.
April 2003. Tax Bulletin Special Edition.	UK/US double taxation agreement
April 2003. Tax Bulletin Issue 64.	Businesses, individuals and the settlements legislation
June 2003. Tax Bulletin Issue 65	Access to link papers or how the figures in the accounting records feature in the return
August 2003. Tax Bulletin Issue 66	Deceased estates—new procedures for income tax and capital gains tax
21 October 2003. IR Press Release	Capital gains tax—gifts relief
December 2003. Tax Bulletin Issue 68	Teleworkers—reimbursed expenses and benefits for employees working at home
February 2004. Tax Bulletin Issue 69	Self-assessment returns
February 2004. Tax Bulletin Issue 69	Tips, gratuities, service charges and troncs: income tax, national insurance contributions, national minimum wage issues and VAT
24 March 2004. IR Guidance Notes	Budget 2004—tax treatment of small companies
April 2004. Tax Bulletin Issue 70	Money Laundering Regulations 2003

April 1964. Inland Revenue booklet No 490 (1964)

Patents [TA 1988 ss 520, 522]

Expenditure and receipts in respect of patents may be either of an income or a capital nature. ''Royalties or other sums paid in respect of the user of a patent''—a term that is regarded as covering broadly payments in respect of past user or future limited user, restricted as to amount or quantity, where there is no acquisition of a defined portion of the property in the patent—are treated as income. There are provisions enabling certain reliefs to be claimed by inventors and others in respect of patent income.

Other payments in respect of patents (eg for outright acquisition; for exclusive user during the whole of the unexpired life; or for the future unlimited user within a defined area or for a term of years) are, in general, treated as capital. With certain exceptions, such payments qualify for tax allowances in the hands of the payer and are taxed as income of the recipient.

June 1965. CCAB

Meaning of "small" in connection with capital distributions [TCGA 1992 s 122(2)]; sums derived from assets not lost or destroyed [TCGA 1992 s 23(1)(*c*)]; part disposals of land [TCGA 1992 s 243(1)(*a*)]

The Revenue will normally regard one amount as small in comparison with another if the first amount does not exceed 5 per cent of the second. (CGT 8 (1980), paras 118 and 127).

Cross references—See TCGA 1992 s 242.
See also Revenue Interpretation RI 164.

June 1967. CCAB

Shares in close company transferring assets at undervalue [TCGA 1992 s 125]

The Revenue have intimated that, where a close company transfers assets at an undervalue and the amount thereof is treated as a distribution under what is now [TA 1988 s 209(4)] so that the grossed up amount is treated as income of the shareholder, it is agreed that the acquisition cost of his shares in the company should not be reduced and, in practice, TCGA 1992 s 125 will not be applied to such cases.

June 1967. CCAB

Distribution of assets to legatees [TCGA 1992 s 62(4)]

The Revenue stated that in their view [TCGA 1992 s 62(4)] does not apply in all cases where assets are transferred to beneficiaries *in specie*. Where assets are appointed by personal representatives to satisfy a legacy in circumstances where such appropriation requires the legatee's consent, *ie* where the personal representatives do not have (whether by the terms of the will or under the Administration of Estates Act 1925 s 41) powers of appropriation without consent, the Revenue are advised that the acquisition of the asset has a contractual basis and is not strictly an acquisition qua legatee. In practice, however, the disposal of appropriated assets by the personal representatives to a legatee in these circumstances is not treated as an occasion of charge on the personal representatives provided that both they and the legatee agree that the legatee should be treated as acquiring the assets concerned as legatee for the purposes of [TCGA 1992 s 62(4)].

Where settled property becomes distributable on the death of a life tenant the remainderman is not regarded as taking the property as legatee but as a beneficiary under a trust and the trustees are charged under [TCGA 1992 s 71(1)]. Where, however, a beneficiary who has a life interest in property under a will or intestacy dies before the end of the period of administration, so that the property never becomes settled property, a remainderman who then becomes absolutely entitled to the property is regarded as acquiring it as a legatee.

June 1967. CCAB

Group of companies—company not treated as leaving a group

The Revenue have confirmed that what is now [TCGA 1992 s 170(10)] provides that a company is not to be treated as leaving a group if it is transferred by its immediate parent company to the principal company or to another subsidiary of the principal company.

June 1967. CCAB

Quoted securities held on 6 April 1965—election under [TCGA 1992 Sch 2 para 4]

The Revenue confirm that the rights of election conferred by [TCGA 1992 Sch 2 para 4] may be exercised where appropriate by the taxpayer's legal personal representatives.

June 1968. CCAB

Associates—unitholders [TA 1988 s 417(3)]

The Revenue have confirmed that in their view holders of units in a unit trust are not "associates" merely by reason of their common membership of the trust.

June 1968. CCAB

Transfer of assets by group in liquidation [TCGA 1992 ss 170–181]

The Revenue state that in their view the decision in *IR Comrs v Olive Mill Ltd* (41 TC 77) has no application to the above provisions and consequently the Revenue consider that a transfer of assets by a group company in liquidation is covered by what are now [TCGA 1992 ss 170–181].

June 1968. CCAB

Bonus issues following reduction of capital [TA 1988 s 210]

Where on the reorganisation of a company's share capital an issue of shares is treated as income of the shareholder, the net amount of the distribution is treated as an addition to the acquisition price of the new holding *ie*, the net amount of the dividend is allowed as the cost of the bonus issue.

June 1968. CCAB

Part disposals—single or multiple assets [TCGA 1992 s 42]

Our general view is that unless it appears from the facts at the time of acquisition that more than one asset (given its natural meaning) was acquired, a single acquisition of land (with or without buildings) whether obtained by purchase under one contract at an inclusive price or by gift or inheritance as a whole, should be regarded as a single asset (even though it comprises distinguishable elements such as a house and garden, farmhouses, buildings, woodlands, cottages, etc).

On the other hand, in the case of acquisition by purchase, there may be contemporary evidence showing that the acquisition comprised more than one asset. For example, correspondence etc during negotiations leading up to a purchase may show that the contract price was based upon the sum rounded up or down of a number of valuation units; the land may have been offered for sale by auction in lots: or the rent roll of an estate may show separate tenants paying substantial rents for individual properties such as farms. In such cases it may be possible to make a satisfactory apportionment of the purchase price.

Where estates of small properties (*eg* terraced urban dwellinghouses) are acquired, blocks of a size convenient to hold as investments are normally regarded as single assets, but in practice no objection is taken to treating individual dwellinghouses as separate assets and apportioning the cost of the larger unit on the basis of such evidence as is available. As a general rule single buildings in multiple occupation such as blocks of flats or office suites are regarded as single assets, but again no objection is normally taken to treating individual flats, etc as separate assets if it appears that similar flats etc in the same ownership or in the locality have commonly been sold singly as independent dwellings.

June 1969. CCAB

Non-resident companies [TCGA 1992 s 13]

Where a UK shareholder in a non-resident company which would be a close company if resident in the UK is chargeable to capital gains tax on a proportion of a capital gain accruing to that company, the appropriate proportion of any overseas tax payable by the company in the country where it is resident in respect of its gain is regarded as deductible in computing the shareholder's capital gain [TCGA 1992 s 278]. Alternatively, tax credit relief may be allowable for the overseas tax [TCGA 1992 s 277].

June 1969. CCAB

Debt on a security [TCGA 1992 s 132(3)(*b*) and s 251(1)]

The definition of "security" in [TCGA 1992 s 132(3)(*b*)] which applies also for the purpose of [TCGA 1992 s 251(1)] is regarded as exhaustive so that the debt must be a loan stock or a similar security of a government, public or local authority or company. The view is also taken that the reference to loan "stock" implies in general a class of debt the holdings in which are transferable by purchase and sale and the words "whether secured or unsecured" in the definition made the existence of a charge immaterial.

Note—Confirmed as current in 1989, but in the light of case law (see *W T Ramsay Ltd v IR Comrs* [1981] STC 174) the Revenue take a less restrictive view than they did in 1969.

10 November 1969. Hansard

Overseas British nationals (publication fees)

The following parliamentary question was included in the House of Commons Written Answers.

Mr Ashton asked the Chancellor of the Exchequer what steps he takes to recover tax on fees paid to British nationals living abroad by publishers in this country.

Mr Roy Jenkins: [TA 1988 s 536] requires any person making such payments to deduct income tax at the standard rate and to pay it over to the Revenue. I am advised that this does not apply to payments made to those who are authors by profession, nor does it apply if the recipient is living in a country with which we have a double taxation agreement requiring us to exempt such payments.

HC Written Ans, 10 November 1969 Vol 791 col 31

PRs etc

June 1970. CCAB

Transfers of assets and liabilities within a group [TA 1988 s 209]

Where an amount is not to be treated as a distribution by reason of [TA 1988 s 209(5)], it will not be treated as a distribution under any of the other provisions of [TA 1988 s 209].

June 1971. CCAB

Balancing adjustments (FA 1971 s 44(6) [CAA 1990 s 26(1)])

The Revenue explained that where assets are not likely to be sold for a long time after the end of trading, inspectors were instructed to finalise on the basis of market value at the time of permanent cessation.

Note—See now CAA 2001 ss 61(2), 72(3), 423(1).

June 1970. CCAB

Meaning of negligible

As regards the interpretation of the word "negligible" in the context of [TCGA 1992 s 24(2)] this was viewed in percentage terms of the nominal value of each share. "Negligible" is not defined for this purpose, but as "small" is taken as 5 per cent, "negligible" should be considerably less.

22 June 1972. Hansard

Payment of tax by instalments: undue hardship [TA 1988 s 34(8)]; [TCGA 1992 s 280]

In considering whether undue hardship would arise, the Revenue would look primarily to the question whether the vendor or disponer could reasonably be expected to pay the tax on the full amount immediately, in the light of the resources made available by the particular transaction involved. Regard would not normally be paid to the other resources of the taxpayer if it could be shown that the instalment arrangement was in the circumstances, and apart from any tax considerations, a normal commercial arrangement and reflected a genuine deferment of the enjoyment of the consideration. The Revenue practice would, of course, be kept under review, in the light of its effect on actual cases arising.

(HC Debates, Standing Committee E, col 1358)

Revenue & other press releases—HL Written Answer, 17 March 1988. (IHT and family companies), see *IHT* section.

June 1972. CCAB

Availability of writing down allowances on liquidation of supplier of plant or machinery [CAA 1990 s 25]

In their 1971 memorandum, the allied accountancy bodies drew attention to the position whereby writing down allowances are denied if, for example, expenditure is incurred towards the fabrication of plant and, before delivery, the supplier goes into liquidation. The Revenue agreed to examine this point, and make the following comments.

In the case of a contract providing that the trader should become the owner of the plant on performance of the contract, [CAA 1990 s 25] would normally apply so as to give the same result as if the trader had sold the plant at a loss before putting it into use. If so, he would receive an addition to his pool of qualifying expenditure for the purpose of writing-down allowances equal to the excess of his capital payment over anything he received in respect of his rights under the contract.

Note—See now CAA 2001 ss 52, 57, 58, 220, 229, 231.

October 1972. IR Leaflet CA 2

Industrial building and structures: meaning [CAA 1990 s 18]

The expression ''building or structure'' is not defined but, in general, it includes a part of a building or structure. Hence, an addition, or extension or improvement to a building can rank for allowance purposes as though it were a separate building [CAA 1990 s 161(7)].

The word ''structure'' embraces artificial works which might not properly be described as buildings; examples of ''structures'' are walls, bridges, dams, roads, culverts and tunnels.

EXPENDITURE ON AGRICULTURAL BUILDINGS AND WORKS: DEFINITION [CAA 1990 S 124]

It must be expenditure on the construction, reconstruction, alteration or improvement of farmhouses, farm or forestry buildings, cottages, fences or other works.

The term ''works'' is regarded as including such things as drainage and sewerage works, water and electricity installations, walls, shelter belts of trees, glass-houses on market garden land, and the reclamation of former agricultural land.

Note—See now CAA 2001 ss 52, 57, 58, 220, 229, 231.

26 June 1973. CCAB

Termination payments to directors and employees [TA 1988 ss 188, 209]

Certain payments to directors and employees arising in connection with the termination of an office or employment are not chargeable to income tax by virtue of the provisions of [TA 1988 s 188]. However, where the director or employee concerned is a member of the paying company, it would appear that the payment might constitute a distribution in view of the provisions of [TA 1988 s 209].

The Inland Revenue state that they give sympathetic consideration to cases where a terminal payment is made by a continuing company to an arm's length director or employee, and where the sum is both reasonable in amount having regard to past services and length of service, and admissible as a deduction for corporation tax purposes.

19 February 1974. CCAB

Taxation anomalies and practical difficulties 1973 TR 127

[TA 1988 ss 349, 350, 43]—Schedule A Clarification is sought regarding the position of a lessee who pays rent into his landlord's bank account without deduction of tax in ignorance of the fact that the landlord has moved and that his usual place of abode is consequently outside the UK. The landlord may be unwilling to authorise the lessee to deduct the accrued liability from future payments of rent. It is assumed that no attempt would be made to hold the lessee liable for not having deducted tax at source whilst he was unaware of his landlord's change of abode but confirmation is sought that this is the case.

The Revenue confirmed that the lessee would not be held liable for not deducting tax at source if unaware of his landlord's change of abode. The Revenue could still assess the non-resident landlord, with the property as security.

4 April 1974. Inland Revenue letter

Industrial buildings allowance—garages

If a garage business carries on a trade of servicing and maintaining vehicles for the public then it is carrying on a qualifying trade and the premises used for the purpose of this trade *eg* a repair bay or a repair workshop used wholly or mainly for this purpose will qualify for industrial buildings allowance. Many garages carry on other trades such as the sale of cars, or the sale of spare parts. These are not qualifying trades and the premises used for the purposes of those trades do not qualify for allowance. Some garages carry on a trade of hiring vehicles. This is again not a qualifying trade and any premises used for the purpose of the vehicle hire (including a repair workshop used to maintain and service the hired vehicles) would not qualify for industrial buildings allowance.

June 1975. CCAB

Distribution of asset in specie by liquidator of subsidiary company [TCGA 1992 s 171]

The Revenue stated that capital gains relief was generally available under [TCGA 1992 s 171] where an asset was distributed by a liquidator *in specie*.

12 February 1976. Inland Revenue

[Inheritance tax]—settled property—interest in possession

The Board of Inland Revenue are aware that doubts have been expressed in the legal press and elsewhere concerning the precise scope of the term ''interest in possession'' as used in [IHTA 1984], and in particular about its application where an interest in settled property is subject to a discretion or power to accumulate the income of the property or to divert it elsewhere.

The Board therefore feel it appropriate, in view of the importance of the expression in [IHTA 1984 ss 43–93], to make known their understanding of the meaning of the expression. This is that an interest in possession in settled property exists where the person having the interest has the immediate entitlement (subject to any prior claim by the trustees for expenses or other outgoings properly payable out of income) to any income produced by that property as the income arises; but that a discretion or power, in whatever form, which can be exercised after income arises so as to withhold it from that person negatives the existence of an interest in possession. For this purpose a power to accumulate income is regarded as a power to withhold it, unless any accumulations must be held solely for the person having the interest or his personal representatives.

On the other hand the existence of a mere power of revocation or appointment, the exercise of which would determine the interest wholly or in part (but which, so long as it remains unexercised, does not affect the beneficiary's immediate entitlement to income) does not in the Board's view prevent the interest from being an interest in possession.

CAPITAL GAINS TAX

This understanding of the expression equally applies for the purposes of [TCGA 1992 s 72].

June 1976. CCAB

Gardens: loss of exemption [TCGA 1992 s 222]

The Revenue stated that they would not take the point established by *Varty v Lynes* [1976] STC 508 that the private residence exemption might be lost in respect of the garden if the taxpayer ceased to occupy the house before he sold it, unless the garden had development value.

June 1976. CCAB

Demolition of plant [CAA 1990 s 26(1)]

The Revenue assured the CCAB that in their view the cost of demolition was taken into account in calculating ''the net amount received'' for the purposes of CAA 1990 s 26(1)(*c*).

Note—See now CAA 2001 ss 61(2), 423(1) Table Item 3(2).

1 November 1976. Hansard

Schedule E: travelling expenses: overseas employment

Mr Peter Rees asked the Chancellor of the Exchequer whether directors and employees ordinarily resident in the UK of foreign subsidiaries of UK resident companies are permitted to deduct in the computation of their emoluments under Schedule E the expense of the board and lodging when visiting in the course of their duties those foreign subsidiaries.

Mr Robert Sheldon: Yes, unless the duties of the employment were performed wholly outside the UK, in which case the director or employee would instead be entitled to a deduction under [TA 1988 s 192] and to freedom from tax on the reimbursement of expenses—including reasonable hotel expenses—necessarily incurred by him in travelling to and from the country where the duties were performed.

HC Written Ans, Vol 918 col 482

Cross reference—See TA 1988 ss 193–195.

August 1977. CCAB

New hotels: capital allowances

As a result of the recent case of *St John's School (Mountford and Knibbs) v Ward* [1975] STC 7 the Consultative Committee of Accountancy Bodies had asked whether any change of practice is intended.

The reply from the Chairman of the Board of Inland Revenue was as follows:

> "You have asked about the treatment of expenditure on the installation of the 'main services' in new hotels. You said that hitherto the Revenue had regarded such expenditure as expenditure on plant and machinery which therefore qualified for capital allowances, but that recently, in the light of a Court case about school buildings, inspectors of taxes had begun to challenge this view and to suggest that no relief was due as such expenditure could be regarded as part of the cost of the building.
>
> There has, in fact, been no recent change of Revenue practice in this area. What has happened is that the recent case to which you refer—*St John's School v Ward*—has focused fresh attention on the distinction which has always had to be drawn for the purposes of capital allowances between expenditure on plant and machinery and expenditure on buildings. As a result, inspectors of taxes have no doubt recently been looking forward more critically at borderline expenditure. But there has been no change in our view of what falls on either side of the dividing line, and there is, of course, no question of any 'attack' on the hotel industry. It is our job to apply the law as we understand it, and the treatment of hotels and restaurants is in this respect no different from that of any other business.
>
> It may be helpful if I summarise our practice in this area, which is based on the views expressed by the Courts over the years. Expenditure on the provision of main services to buildings such as electrical wiring, cold water piping and gas is regarded as part of the cost of the building, and therefore as not qualifying for capital allowances. We do, however, regard as eligible for capital allowances expenditure on *apparatus* to provide electric light or power, hot water, central heating, ventilation or air-conditioning, and expenditure on alarm and sprinkler systems. Relief is also given on the cost of all hot water pipes, and on the cost of baths, wash basins, etc, although the *St John's School* case suggests that the Courts might regard such expenditure as part of the cost of the building. We do not, however, propose any change of practice in this respect. Finally, to complete the picture, and since you mentioned modernisation, I should say that expenditure on alterations to *existing* buildings which is incidental to the installation of plant or machinery qualifies for relief under a separate provision [CAA 2001 s 25]."

7 February 1978. Inland Revenue

Double Taxation: United Kingdom and United States of America

It has come to the attention of the Revenue that there are misunderstandings about the effect of a provision of the revised Double Taxation Convention with the United States of America, which was published on 14 April 1976 as a draft Order in Council, has been approved by Parliament and awaits approval by the United States Senate. The provision concerned is paragraph 1 of Article 19 (Government Service) and the question is what effect it would have in the case of remuneration paid by the United States Government to individuals resident in the UK in respect of services rendered to the United States. In particular misunderstandings have occurred among members of the United States forces and civilian personnel employed by the United States Department of Defense who are serving in the UK

Under the Article the remuneration would be taxable only by the United States except where the individual:

(i) is a national of the UK or

(ii) did not become a resident of the UK solely for the purpose of performing the services to the United States.

In cases where these exceptions apply the UK would have the sole right to tax remuneration.

The Revenue wish to make clear that in the case of the second exception, individuals who are United States nationals (without also being UK nationals) would not in fact be subject to UK tax in respect of the remuneration by reason of the special exemption provisions in [TA 1988 s 323] or, if that section does not apply, in [TA 1988 s 321].

There is a proviso in [TA 1988 s 321], that the special exemption does not apply where the remuneration is paid by a department or agency of a foreign state which carries on any trade, business or other undertaking for the purposes of profit. Broadly similar provisions also apply under both the existing Convention and the proposed new Convention. Cases subject to these provisions would, however, be exceptional.

Cross references—See TA 1988 ss 321, 323, 788 (consular staff and officers).

16 February 1978. Hansard

Wife allowance

Mr Brotherton asked the Chancellor of the Exchequer what account the Inland Revenue takes to assessing allowances for personal taxes of whether the taxpayer has more than one wife.

Mr Robert Sheldon: For income tax purposes a marriage is accepted as valid if it is valid under the law of the country in which it was performed and of the country of domicile of the parties. But a married man is entitled to claim only one married [couple's] allowance.

HC Written Ans, 16 Feb. 1978 Vol 944 col 355

Cross references—See TA 1988 s 257A (married couple's allowance).
Simon's Tax Cases—*Nabi v Heaton* [1981] STC 375.

24 February 1978. Inland Revenue letter

Election under [TA 1988 s 247]

The Revenue view is that the use of the word "may" in [TA 1988 s 247(4)] does not enable a company to make the payment in question with deduction of tax whilst the election is in force and it is not the practice to permit this. If it is desired that a particular payment should be made with deduction of tax either party may revoke the election in accordance with the provisions in s 248(4). This does not prevent the subsequent making of a new election.

2 March 1978. Inland Revenue

Double Taxation: exchange of information with the United States of America

In reply to the Parliamentary Question:

> "To ask Mr Chancellor of the Exchequer if there have been any recent changes in the administrative arrangements for co-operation between the United Kingdom and the United States of America in ensuring that the proper tax is paid on the income and profits of individuals and companies operating internationally, and if he will make a statement."

The Minister of State, Treasury, Mr Denzil Davies, gave the following Written Answer today:

> "The Inland Revenue have recently entered into a working arrangement with the United States Internal Revenue Service for the simultaneous examination of the affairs of related taxpayers with substantial operations in both countries. I have arranged for a copy of it to be placed in the Library.

Our Double Taxation Convention with the United States provides for the exchange of information in order to carry out the purposes of the Convention, to prevent fiscal evasion and to administer the statutory provisions against legal avoidance, under rules which protect the confidentiality of information about the affairs of taxpayers. The working arrangement was made under the terms of these provisions. Under it each country's tax authority will separately examine the affairs of taxpayers within its own jurisdiction but the tax authorities will co-ordinate their examination of important cases in order to make more efficient and effective use of their powers to exchange information. This will help them for example in considering the transfer prices adopted in transactions between affiliated companies in multinational groups."

Explanatory Note

The text of the working arrangement is reproduced below and is also available for inspection in the Inland Revenue Library at Somerset House, Strand, London WC2R 1LB.

The Double Taxation Convention with the United States of America, like most double taxation agreements, contains provisions which enable the tax authorities of the two countries to exchange information in certain circumstances about the affairs of particular taxpayers. (This is the case both for the existing Convention and for the revised Convention which is awaiting ratification by the United States of America.)

A previous statement about co-operation in this field between the United Kingdom tax authorities and those of other countries including the United States of America was made in answer to a Parliamentary Question by Mr Jeff Rooker, MP on 16 November 1977—which is produced below.

WORKING ARRANGEMENT BETWEEN THE UNITED STATES INTERNAL REVENUE SERVICE AND THE UNITED KINGDOM BOARD OF INLAND REVENUE UNDER THE TERMS OF THE EXCHANGE OF INFORMATION PROVISIONS OF THE CONVENTION FOR THE AVOIDANCE OF DOUBLE TAXATION AND THE PREVENTION OF FISCAL EVASION WITH RESPECT TO TAXES ON INCOME

Objectives

To:

1 Determine taxpayers correct tax liabilities particularly where costs are shared, or charged, and profits are allocated between taxpayers resident or operating in different taxing jurisdictions.

2 Improve the procedures for exchanging information which can be used by each country in accordance with the treaty in its examinations of *inter alia*, multinational enterprises having intra-group transactions which may include arrangements involving tax haven countries.

3 Exchange of information on new or apparent patterns or techniques of tax avoidance that significantly affect the tax administration of each country.

4 Study transfer pricing practices.

This approach should help to achieve the objective of effective, comprehensive and proper administration of our tax laws and tax treaties.

Case selection and examination procedures general

The following selection procedures will apply in the following sequence:

1 Appropriate taxpayers will be independently identified for simultaneous examination by tax administration officials of each country.

2 Each country will inform the other of its choice of potential cases using the selection criteria described below.

3 Each country will determine whether it wishes to participate in a particular simultaneous examination. Neither country, however, is obliged to co-operate in all examinations undertaken by the other country.

4 In those cases where there is agreement to conduct a simultaneous examination, the competent authority of each country will formally request of the other competent authority exchange of specific information pursuant to the tax treaty.

5 Representatives of the competent authorities will designate areas and periods to be examined in the particular cases selected, the timetable for the examinations and approaches to be taken. They will initiate exchange of specific information in accordance with formal written requests.

6 The information which may be requested under this arrangement must:

(*a*) be obtainable under the respective taxation laws of the two countries;
(*b*) be related to an income tax, corporation tax or capital gains tax matter.

7 Whenever possible, the Internal Revenue Service representative in London will be used to channel the information between the United Kingdom and the United States.

Criteria for selecting cases

Any case selected for simultaneous examination will involve related taxpayers with substantial operations in both countries. The factors considered in determining whether such a case is selected will mainly be, but will not be limited to:

1 the scale of its worldwide operations;
2 the extent of intragroup transactions; and
3 compatible tax years.

Personnel

Examinations will be conducted separately within the framework of national law and practice solely by tax administration officials of each country in a way which maximises the advantages obtainable from treaty exchanges of information. There will be no interchange of personnel between the countries.

Planning the examination

Before the start of the examination, the tax administration personnel in charge of the case will consider with their counterparts from the other country, within the framework of the tax treaty, the plans of each country, possible issues to be developed and target dates. However, there will be no exchange of formal examination plans between the countries.

Conducting the examinations

This procedure requires a measure of co-operation between personnel of each country who will independently examine the taxpayer within its jurisdiction. The country in which the parent or base company is located will usually have primary responsibility for co-ordinating the examination and exchanges of information, and all exchanges must be within the terms of the relevant provisions of the Double Taxation Treaty. If the parent company is outside the United States and the United Kingdom, tax administration officials of each country will together decide which country should function as co-ordinator.

Discontinuing simultaneous examinations

If either country concludes that it is no longer beneficial to continue the simultaneous examination of a case it may withdraw and notify the other country of its withdrawal.

Concluding the examination

The examination will be concluded after co-ordination and consultation between the two countries, in accordance with the existing procedures of each country.

Cross reference—See TA 1988 s 788 (relief by agreement).

2 March 1978. Hansard

Parliamentary question: co-operation between UK and other countries' tax authorities

Mr Rooker asked the Chancellor of the Exchequer if he will make a statement about co-operation between the United Kingdom and other member countries of the Organisation for Economic Co-operation and Development, in particular France, West Germany and the United States of America, in ensuring that the proper tax is paid on the income and profits of individuals and companies operating internationally.

Mr Denzil Davies: The agreements between the United Kingdom and other countries for the relief of double taxation on profits and income provide for the exchange of information, in order to carry out the purposes of the agreements and to prevent fiscal evasion, under rules which protect the confidentiality of information about the affairs of taxpayers. Double taxation agreements between other OECD member countries contain similar provisions.

The growth of international operations by both countries and individuals has made it necessary for the United Kingdom and other countries to make more effective use of these facilities for exchanging information by co-ordinating bilateral exchanges.

Regular meetings therefore take place between senior officials of the tax authorities of the United Kingdom, France, Germany and the United States to improve their Administrations' co-operation in practical ways. These include the study of more effective methods of avoiding double taxation, the simplification of arrangements for the assistance of taxpayers by way of mutual consultation between tax authorities and also the exchange, under the authority of tax treaties, of information needed for ascertaining the liability of taxpayers with interests and activities in the respective countries. Under these arrangements each tax authority separately examines the accounts and returns of the taxpayer within its own jurisdiction but they may meet to co-ordinate the exchanges of information made under the provisions of the relevant tax treaties.

HC Written Ans, 16 November 1977 Vol 939 cols 269–270

Cross reference—See TA 1988 s 788 (relief by agreement).

12 April 1978. Inland Revenue letter

1977 Memorandum on taxation anomalies and practical difficulties, paragraph 31—Form P11D [TA 1988 s 156]

The following sets out the legislation underlying the requirement on Form P11D that the amount to be returned should include the full amount of VAT paid, whether or not it might be recovered in whole or in part by the employer.

[TA 1988 s 156(1)] provides that the cash equivalent of any benefit chargeable to tax under [s 154] shall be an amount equal to the cost of the benefit, and [TA 1988 s 156(2)] defines the cost of the benefit as the amount of any expense incurred in or in connection with its provision. We are advised that the "expense incurred" for this purpose must be taken as the cost incurred regardless of any subsequent reduction in the employer's overall VAT bill, in the same way as the "expense incurred" by a body corporate was interpreted under the precedent legislation contained in TA 1970 s 196(1) [repealed]. This advice is based in part on the judgment of Lord Atkin in *Corporation of Birmingham v Barnes* 19 TC 196, where he said (p 217) that "the actual cost to that person is the same thing as the amount expended by the person" (regardless of whether the burden of that cost was borne wholly or partly by some third party).

The practice of taking the VAT-inclusive cost as the measure of benefits was announced by the Chief Secretary to the Treasury in reply to a Parliamentary Question on 17 July 1974 and has been applied from the year 1974–75 onwards [see SP/A6]. The decision of the VAT Tribunal in the case of *Pye of Cambridge Ltd v C & E Comrs* on 3 February 1977, to which reference was made at our meeting, does not seem to us to contain anything which should lead us to reconsider our practice.

It also seems to us that this practice achieves the right result, in that the measurement of the benefit proceeds broadly on the same basis as if the employee had met the cost himself and does not vary according to the VAT status of the employer, which would be very difficult to justify.

June 1978. CCAB

Hotels [CAA 1990 ss 7, 19]

The Revenue confirmed the following points:

(*a*) in practice 120 days would be regarded as equivalent to four months [CAA 1990 s 19(1)(*a*)];

(*b*) the availability of services would *not* satisfy the test in [CAA 1990 s 19(1)(*b*)(iii)]: there had also to be reasonable use [as to meals see SP 9/87];

(*c*) [CAA 1990 s 19(5)(*a*)] covered hostels which the workers occupied but was not intended to give relief for flats and houses provided for individual workers;

(*d*) where accommodation was excluded by [CAA 1990 s 19(5)(*b*)] there would be no restriction of allowances provided the [25] per cent rule in [CAA 1990 s 18(7)] was satisfied.

Note—See now CAA 2001 ss 271, 279, 285, 317.

June 1978. CCAB

Loans to traders—relief [TCGA 1992 s 253]

The Revenue confirmed that the term "guarantee" would cover the case where a person's property was charged as security for a qualifying loan. An indemnity as such normally created a primary liability and therefore plainly was not a guarantee.
TCGA 1992 s 253(4) applies to overdrafts but not to hire purchase agreements.

27 June 1978. Inland Revenue letter

Double taxation relief—limitation of credit [TA 1988 s 797(1)]

I can confirm that [TA 1988 s 790(4), (5)] applies to unilateral relief only. However the legislation in [TA 1988 s 788] which relates to agreement relief is governed partly by the agreements themselves and partly by the limits on credit provided for in [TA 1988 s 797(1)]. The work-out of this legislation can be complex but the general effect is that foreign tax on overseas income may only be set against UK tax payable on the same income.

29 June 1978. Hansard

Parliamentary proceedings: armed forces pensions [TA 1988 ss 19, 315]

Mr Ovenden asked the Chancellor of the Exchequer if he will list those pensions payable to former members of the Armed Forces in respect of service or disability which are tax-free and those which are liable to tax; and what are the conditions under which pensions which are normally taxable can be exempted when paid in combination with a tax-free pension.

Mr Robert Sheldon: The following pensions paid to former members of the Armed Forces in respect of disability are exempt—

– Wounds pensions granted to members of the forces.
– Officer's disability retired pay attributable to conditions of service.

- Pensions in respect of disablement or disability attributable to conditions of service granted to members of the forces other than commissioned officers.
- Disablement pensions attributable to conditions of service granted to persons who have been employed in the nursing services of the forces.
- War disability pensions administered by DHSS.

The following pensions paid to former members of the Armed Forces in respect of long service are taxable—

- Service career pensions.
- Illness or disability pensions other than those attributable to conditions of service.

Where a member of the Armed Forces is invalided out of the forces on account of a disability attributable to his service and is awarded a combined long-service and disability pension, the whole of that pension is exempted from tax because it is not possible to distinguish between the parts of the pension attributable to disability and to long service.

HC Written Ans, 29 June Vol 952 cols 654, 655

17 July 1978. Inland Revenue letter

Artificial transactions in land [TA 1988 s 776]—loss

In theory a loss could arise under [TA 1988 s 776] by virtue of [TA 1988 s 392], but no such case has in fact been recorded here. I am inclined to think that the reason for this is that if a loss occurred on the sale of an asset which was acquired wholly or mainly for the purpose of realising a gain from disposal (to use the words at [TA 1988 s 776(2)(*a*)]) the first inclination of an informed taxpayer would be to claim a Case I loss, with all its benefits.

6 September 1978. Law Society's Gazette (see also BTR, December 1978, p 477)

Key man insurance [TA 1988 s 74]

When a company insures the life of its key employees to protect itself against loss of profits resulting from the death of the employee within a specified term of years, I believe I am correct in saying that the policy premiums are deductible for corporate tax purposes, and that any proceeds of the policy are regarded as income for corporation tax purposes.

However, I would like also to be able to give *Gazette* readers guidance concerning the situation where a parent company which has guaranteed the bank borrowings of one of its subsidiary companies takes out a term insurance policy on the life of the key man in that subsidiary with the object of safeguarding the guarantee which it has given. Am I correct in thinking that in such a situation the policy premiums payable by the parent company in respect of the key employee of the subsidiary company would not be deductible by the parent company for corporation tax purposes, and that any policy proceeds received by the parent company on the death of the subsidiary's key man would not be subject to corporation tax?

Dear Mr Nelson-Jones,

In reply to your second paragraph you will no doubt be familiar with the several cases highlighting the separate identity of members of groups of companies, the most recent of which was *Milnes v J. Bean Group Ltd.* [(1975) 50 TC 675]. The force of these is that expenses incurred by parent companies on behalf of their subsidiaries and *vice versa* cannot be regarded as having been made for the purposes of the payers' trade and are not therefore allowable for tax purposes. Following the generality of this argument the expenses of Key Man Insurance incurred by a parent in the circumstances which you mention would not be allowable, but as a corollary, and as you surmise, any recoveries under such a policy would not be taxable.

Perhaps you would let me add a few general comments on the tax treatment of Key Man Insurance since relief is not so widely available as you imply in your first paragraph. Normal income tax considerations do apply but if the policy is "whole life" or "endowment" assurance then it is considered that the premiums are not admissible on the grounds that they fall within the dictum in *Earl Howe v IRC* (7 TC at p 300): "They are in truth instalments of purchase money for a capital sum payable on death." The deduction is thus disallowable generally as being on capital account and specifically as being prohibited by [TA 1988 s 74 (*f*)].

Even if the policy does not have a surrender value, as in the case of a term assurance, for the premiums to be an allowable trading expense the company must show that the policy was taken out "wholly and exclusively" for the purposes of the trade [TA 1988 s 74(*a*)]. Clearly there may be other motives, particularly where the director or employee whose life is insured has, or is associated with, a significant proprietorial interest in the company. This view is supported by the dictum in *Samuel Dracup & Sons Ltd. v Dakin* (37 TC at p 382) where Harman J. said: "You were laying out this money for your own advantage and not for that of the company, or, at any rate, your own advantage came into it."

In these cases also, of course, where the cost of premiums has been admitted as an allowable deduction in computing trade profits, then any receipts under the policy will be treated as trading income. If the cost of the premiums is not allowable then, as a general rule, the proceeds will not be taxed as a trading receipt of the company.

Yours sincerely,

CR Massingale, Inland Revenue Policy Division, Somerset House.

Note—As to policies held by companies issued or varied after 13 March 1989 see TA 1988 ss 540(5A) (Life policies: chargeable events) and 547(1)(*b*) (Method of charging gain to tax).

17 October 1978. Inland Revenue letter

Capital gains tax: [TCGA 1992 Sch 6 para 7 (2)]: definition of "chargeable asset"

[TCGA 1992 Sch 6 para 7 (2)] is interpreted as meaning that, on the hypothesis that a gain would accrue on the disposal of the asset at the stated time, if that gain would be a chargeable gain then the asset would be a chargeable asset. The important point to be ascertained is not whether a gain (as opposed to a loss) would accrue but whether a gain accruing in those circumstances would be a chargeable gain. In this context, therefore, it is equally appropriate to say that it is necessary to ascertain whether a loss arising on the disposal would be an allowable loss.

Revenue & other press releases—IR 23-11-78 (Definition of a chargeable asset). See below.

23 October 1978. Inland Revenue letter

Partners' chargeable gains [TCGA 1992 ss 152–158 and 165]

It is considered that a partner is entitled to claim relief under these provisions in respect of the disposal of an asset owned by himself but used for the purposes of the trade or profession carried on by the partnership of which he is a member, subject to the normal conditions for relief being satisfied, whether or not a rent is charged to the firm for the use of the asset.

Statement of Practice D11—Partnership: assets owned by a partner.

23 November 1978. Inland Revenue letter

Capital gains tax: definition of chargeable asset [TCGA 1992 Sch 6 para 7 (2)]

I can confirm that a single item of plant or machinery (other than an exempt motor vehicle) with a capital gains tax cost of more than [£6,000] and a market value at the relevant date which is less than that cost would be regarded as a chargeable asset whether the market value of that item at the relevant date was more than [£6,000] or less than [£6,000].

Revenue & other press releases—IR 17-10-78 (CGT: definition of chargeable asset). See above.
Cross reference—See TCGA 1992 s 262 (Chattel exemption).

30 November 1978. Inland Revenue letter

Payments for group roll-over relief

It is considered that the payments passing from one company to the other in respect of group roll-over relief (TCGA 1992 s 175) should not be taken into account in computing the profits of either company for corporation tax purposes.

December 1978. BTR 422

Goodwill: written off: loss relief: [TCGA 1992 s 24(2)]

It is understood that in a case where partners had written off goodwill, the City General Commissioners held that the value of a partner's share or interest had become negligible, being unsaleable under the terms of the agreement. See *New Law Journal*, p 269, March 1978

Statements of Practice—SP D12 (Partnerships) and SP 1/89 (Further extension of SP D12).

22 January 1979. Inland Revenue letter

Waiver of rent [TA 1988 s 41]

[TA 1988 s 41] is a relieving section which comes into play where a sum has become chargeable to tax under Schedule A by virtue of [TA 1988 s 15]. That charge is on the rents that the landlord is entitled to demand on rent days falling in the chargeable period. If there is a prior agreement to reduce that rent, the entitlement is consequently reduced when the rent day arrives. If there is any consideration for the deduction, a charge might arise under [TA 1988 s 34(5)].

26 April 1979. Inland Revenue letter

Capital allowances: plant and machinery [CAA 1990 s 24]

I agree with your first proposition, viz that where an asset is purchased by a company in order bona fide to provide welfare facilities for the staff, the company has incurred capital expenditure for the purposes of its trade. Whether [capital allowances] can then be claimed under [CAA 1990 s 24] depends upon the nature of the asset. Normally of course [they] can; but where, for example, the asset is a yacht which instead of being put to sea is used by employees as a kind of waterside hotel (and from what we hear, this is not a far-fetched possibility), the Revenue would consider it strongly arguable that such a yacht was no more than a part of the company's business setting (see *Benson v The Yard Arm Club Ltd.* [1979] STC 266.

As to possible distinctions between large public and small private companies, this raises questions of fact and degree rather than of law, and I can only say that the Revenue would not accept in all circumstances that assets provided for use exclusively or predominantly by controlling directors were necessarily fixed assets of the business. If for example the directors of a family company bought a yacht for their own use and enjoyment, the Revenue would certainly not feel debarred by the provisions of [TA 1988 ss 153–168] from contending, on the principle in *Samuel Dracup & Sons Ltd. v Dakin* (1957) 37 TC 377, that the yacht had not been provided for the purposes of the company's trade and that no [capital allowances were] therefore due.

16 May 1979. CCAB TR 340

Elections to pay dividends as group income and annual payments and interest without deduction of tax

Relaxation in the rules for making elections to pay group dividends without accounting for advance corporation tax, and making annual payments and interest without deducting tax, has been obtained from the Inland Revenue by the Consultative Committee of Accountancy Bodies.

In a guidance note published below the accountancy bodies refer to correspondence with the Inland Revenue concerning elections under [TA 1988 ss 247, 248]. The Revenue have agreed to accept one election covering several companies provided all the relevant facts are stated and the election is signed by the proper officer. Attention is also drawn to a means by which a named person may be authorised to make such elections.

1–5 ...

6 The Revenue will not take a hard line where there is an accidental failure to make an election due to some genuine reason provided that acceptance of a late election will not have the effect of disturbing settled claims or assessments which have become final and conclusive. The Revenue will be issuing instructions to Tax Districts to make sure that inspectors adopt a consistent practice.

7 On the question of signing elections:

(*a*) Where only two companies are involved a single election is acceptable provided it is signed by the person duly authorised to act on behalf of each company (in some cases this may be the same person);

(*b*) the Revenue will also accept one election covering three or more companies in a group provided that all the necessary facts are shown, that the election is signed on behalf of each company concerned, and that the application of the election between any two companies is clearly shown.

(*c*) The Revenue will accept that any company which is a member of the group may, by resolution of its board, appoint a named person as authorised to make a joint election on behalf of that company for the purposes of [TA 1988 s 247]. Thus if all the companies in the group appoint the same person, or some substitute, then one signature would suffice on the notice of election. In that case the Revenue would require that each company in the group should send the Revenue a certified copy of that resolution and another certified copy when the appropriate officer is changed. It is not, however, the Revenue practice to insist on the authorisation issuing directly from the board of directors; in this respect the Revenue will accept a delegation of authority by the company secretary where that can properly be made.

PRs etc

8 In other words one piece of paper may be used for multiple elections provided an appropriate officer of each company has signed the paper and the election is clearly enough worded to show the extent to which it applies between any two companies. Whilst no statutory form of election is laid down the Revenue have expressed themselves satisfied with the following:

HM Inspector of Taxes
(to be sent to the Inspector of Taxes for each Tax District concerned.)

Dear Sir,

XYZ Limited and Subsidiaries

Election under [TA 1988 s 247]

We the companies listed below (''the group'') elect under [TA 1988 s 247] that:

(i) payments of dividends referred to in subsection [1] of that section may be made within the group without giving rise to payments of advance corporation tax; and

(ii) payments of interest and other annual payments referred to in subsection [4] of that section may be made within the group without deduction of income tax.

Company	*Tax District and Reference*	*Percentage Shareholding*	*Signed Director/ Secretary*
Parent:			
(XYZ Ltd)	....		....
Subsidiaries			
(X Ltd)	....	....	....
(Y Ltd)	....	....	....
(Z Ltd)	....	....	....

23 May 1979. Hansard

Benefits in kind [TA 1988 s 131]

Mr Denzil Davies asked the Chancellor of the Exchequer whether he will itemise all those benefits in kind which are either wholly or partly exempt from the normal rates of income tax.

Mr Peter Rees: The following benefits in kind are wholly exempt from income tax for all employees: the provision of living accommodation where certain conditions are satisfied: the provision of death or retirement benefits: the provision of meals in a canteen: meal vouchers up to the value of 15p a day: free coal received by miners or cash allowances paid to them in lieu: the use of a pooled car available to more than one employee when the private use is incidental: and cheap or interest-free loans, the interest on which would have qualified for tax relief.

Employees who are not covered by the special rules for benefits in kind, applying to [employees earning £8,500 or more and] directors, are also wholly exempt on benefits—other than medical insurance—which cannot be converted into cash, do not represent the meeting of a pecuniary liability or are not provided by means of a voucher exchangeable for goods, services or money.

HC Written Ans, 23 May 1979, Vol 967, col 147

18 June 1979. Inland Revenue

Goods sold subject to reservation of title

Certain traders sell goods on special terms whereby they retain the title to the goods until payment is made. The accountancy bodies have advised their members that, for accountancy purposes, if the circumstances indicate that the reservation of title is regarded by the parties as having no practical relevance except in the event of the insolvency of the buyer, the goods should, notwithstanding the strict legal position, normally be treated as purchases in the accounts of the buyer and sales in the accounts of the supplier.

The Inland Revenue have agreed that for sales subject to reservation of title the above recommended accountancy treatment will be accepted for tax purposes provided that both parties to the contract follow it.

The sale of goods subject to reservation of title as described above is to be distinguished from the supply of goods as consignment stocks eg on a sale or return basis. Goods supplied as consignment stocks are normally to be treated as stock in the hands of the supplier until disposed of by the consignee.

Revenue & other press releases—CCAB 22-9-76 (Not reproduced).

29 June 1979. Inland Revenue letter

Apportionment of benefit in kind [TA 1988 s 156(2)]

By way of general background you will see that the wording of [TA 1988 s 156(2)] effectively repeats the substance of TA 1970 s 196(6) [repealed] and—where the facts properly justify it—would permit the apportionment of an expense incurred in the provision of a benefit chargeable under [TA 1988 s 154]. I should perhaps add that in the last resort, any question of apportionment would be a matter for the appropriate body of Commissioners and would depend upon questions of both fact and degree.

Thus, if an asset—*eg* a yacht—was made available to one director for six months of the tax year and to a fellow director for the remaining six months (and assuming there was no business use of the asset) the expectation is that the ''cash equivalent'' assessable upon each director would comprise the total of:

(i) one-half of the ''annual value'' of the yacht for a full 12 months (or the annual rental charge if this were greater), plus

(ii) all expenses incurred by the employer—or the provider of the yacht—in the way of maintenance, insurance, mooring charges etc of the yacht for the period during which it was made available for the use of the respective director.

Note. Where there is any genuine business use of the yacht, a deduction would be due in respect of the proportion of the total expense (*ie* the ''annual value of the use of'' the yacht plus all running costs) attributable to business use.

10 July 1979. Inland Revenue letter

Ordinary residence ([TA 1988 s 336])

I would point out that residence is a question of fact and a decision in any one case depends entirely on its own particular facts.

I can confirm that where an employee left the UK on 4 April 1979 and did not return until 6 April 1980 and was on a full time service contract during that period, he would be regarded as not resident and not ordinarily resident in the UK throughout the year 1979–80.

However this practice would not be extended to a taxpayer who was only partly in employment and partly self-employed during a similar period. In such circumstances the normal rules for determining an individual's residence status would apply and on the basis that no visits were made during the intervening period, the taxpayer would be regarded as not resident but ordinarily resident for the year 1979–80 in these circumstances.

For the purposes of [TA 1988 s 739], the normal rules used in determining residence or ordinary residence status apply.

1 August 1979. Association of British Chambers of Commerce

Tax appeals and postal delays

In our memorandum to the Revenue about the Finance Bill, we wrote under the heading ''Postal Delays''—

> ''Delays of up to and indeed sometimes exceeding 3 weeks are being reported even in respect of first class post. This seriously affects the time limits for appeals against assessments and may give rise to interest charges where remittances are delayed in the post. We suggest that until the position is rectified, a concession should be made whereby an additional 30 days should be added to the period in which appeals must be made and a similar extension should be made to the due date for payment of tax.''

Mr A. H. Dalton CB, Deputy Chairman of the Board of Inland Revenue, wrote on 20 July to the Chairman of our Taxation Committee as follows—

> ''We discussed last week the points raised under the head of postal delays in the ABCC's memorandum about the Finance Bill.

As regards appeals, I draw attention to [TMA 1970 s 49] which gives inspectors of taxes discretion to accept late appeals. This should avoid problems when appeals are out of time because of postal delays. Turning to the question of interest on delayed remittances, problems should also not arise in practice since in such cases Collectors of Taxes are authorised to allow the date of posting to be treated as the effective date of payment ...''

15 September 1979. Taxation

Arts Council: awards and bursaries

For some time there has been considerable uncertainty of the taxation liability arising on awards and grants made by the Arts Council to artists, writers, photographers, musicians and performing artists. The payments made fall into two broad categories. First, awards in respect of training schemes, or to enable creative artists to devote time to research and development. Secondly, grants offered in respect of specific non-training projects.

The treatment of awards and grants was agreed between the Arts Council and the Board of Inland Revenue in 1968, but the introduction of new awards subsequently has given rise to many problems of interpretation. Happily, a new procedure has now been agreed which becomes effective immediately. This agreement does not, of course, limit the rights of a recipient of an award or grant to appeal against an assessment should he or she so wish to do.

Those items which are taxable or non-taxable under the agreed procedure are as follows.

Category A—Awards and bursaries which are chargeable to tax

(1) Direct or indirect musical, design or choreographic commissions and direct or indirect commissions of sculpture and paintings for public sites.
(2) The Royalty Supplement Guarantee Scheme.
(3) The Contract Writers' Scheme.
(4) Jazz bursaries.
(5) Translators' grants.
(6) Photographic awards and bursaries.
(7) Film and video awards and bursaries.
(8) Performance Art awards.
(9) Art Publishing grants.
(10) Grants to assist with a specific project or projects (such as the writing of a book) or to meet specific professional expenses made to a composer, or to an artist's studio expenses.

Category B—Awards and bursaries which are not chargeable to tax

(1) Bursaries to trainee directors.
(2) In-service bursaries for theatre directors.
(3) Bursaries for associate directors.
(4) Bursaries to people attending full-time courses in arts administration (the practical training course).
(5) In-service bursaries to theatre designers and bursaries to trainees on the theatre designers' scheme.
(6) In-service bursaries for administrators.
(7) Bursaries for actors and actresses.
(8) Bursaries for technicians and stage managers.
(9) Bursaries made to students attending the City University arts administration courses.
(10) Awards, known as the Buying Time Awards, made, not to assist with a specific project or professional expenses, but to maintain the recipient to enable him to take time off to develop his personal talents. These at present include the following awards and bursaries known as the Theatre Writing Bursaries, Awards and Bursaries to composers, Awards and Bursaries to painters, sculptors and print makers, Literature Awards and Bursaries.

It will be open to the Arts Council to make both a grant in category A.10 and an award in category B.10 to an individual and accordingly, in such a case part only of the sum received by the individual concerned will be treated as taxable. However, it is agreed in relation to these cases that if the expenditure incurred by the individual in connection with the matters covered by the A.10 grant and the B.10 award exceeds the amount of the A.10 grant the excess up to and including the amount of the B.10 award will be regarded as covered by the B.10 award, and to this extent will not be allowable as a deduction in arriving at his or her taxable profits. The remainder of any of the expenditure will be subject to the normal Schedule D expenses rules.

The arrangements will be followed by the Inland Revenue, whilst the law remains as it is, in cases involving awards both for future assessments and in settlement of appeals now open. The Arts Council will, in making future awards, inform the recipient of the category applicable for tax purposes.

25 September 1979. CCAB

Inland Revenue clarify position on use of gross profit margins

The Revenue have confirmed that guidance notes issued to inspectors of taxes usually include a range of gross profit margins likely to be achieved by various businesses and that some people may have been misled by an earlier statement on this subject which the Revenue authorised.

In the memorandum printed below the Consultative Committee of Accountancy Bodies amplify their publication in September 1978 entitled ''Inland Revenue Procedures'', issued with the approval of the Inland Revenue, which includes a statement about lists of gross profit percentages.

The memorandum explains the use made by inspectors of guidance notes issued to them, and provides further information as to the reasons for his starting an ''in-depth'' enquiry.

Examination of business accounts—gross profit margins

1 Paragraph 18 of the Notes of a meeting held in June 1978 between representatives of the Inland Revenue and CCAB entitled ''Inland Revenue Procedures'' states that the Inland Revenue do not issue lists of gross profit margins appropriate to various types of businesses.

2 The discussion which gave rise to paragraph 18 took place at a time when it had been suggested that inspectors had lists showing the ''acceptable'' rate of gross profit for each trade—indeed one publication purported to reproduce such a list. The Revenue said that they did not and would not issue to inspectors lists of ''official'' gross profit rates. Their assurances on this matter were accepted and condensed into paragraph 18 of the guidance note referred to above.

3 However, many practitioners are aware that the Inland Revenue have, for some time, incorporated in guidance notes to inspectors information about the practice and economics of particular types of business. A further meeting has therefore been held with the Inland Revenue to discuss the nature and contents of this guidance issued to inspectors. In the course of that meeting the CCAB asked the Revenue to say more about the material supplied to inspectors since it is clear that the belief that lists of gross profit margins exist has grown up out of the knowledge of the existence of these guidance notes.

4 The Revenue have explained that the notes they issue cover many types of businesses and are intended to give inspectors a broad appreciation of the way these businesses operate, including various factors which could affect business results such as wastage and discounting practices. Where it is relevant, information is given about pricing policies and the range of margins commonly obtained on products or groups of products, and advice is given on the interpretation of gross profit rates.

5 Nevertheless the Revenue now accept that some people may have been misled by the statement which they authorised in paragraph 18. The statement that ''they do not issue lists of official gross profit percentages'' was intended to refer to a list showing a notional gross profit percentage for various types of businesses and which the inspectors would expect to be achieved for the business concerned. As stated in paragraph 2 above, such lists do not exist, but the guidance notes do include information of this nature albeit in the form referred to in paragraphs 3 and 4 above. Quite apart from this inspectors are, of course, at liberty to compile lists based on their own experience.

6 The Revenue state that the main use that the inspectors make of gross profit rates—and other business ratios—is as part of their review when considering whether to accept accounts without enquiry. One reason for starting an enquiry will be a discrepancy between the gross profit percentage shown by the accounts and the percentage the inspector would have expected to find in the light of his knowledge of the trade and of local conditions. His judgment may be influenced by information in his guidance notes—and for some trades this will include reference to gross profit rates—but he is expected to reach his own conclusions and rely mainly on his own experience and local knowledge. If an enquiry is started the inspector will usually want to know more about the way the business is conducted but there is no question of applying a single notional gross profit rate and insisting that this rate should have been achieved. The inspector will have regard to the particular circumstances of the business and should give the taxpayer or his adviser the opportunity to explain any apparent discrepancy.

7 The CCAB have asked the Revenue to publish the guidance notes they issue to inspectors—or edited versions of them—and the Revenue have undertaken to consider what might be done. The CCAB believe that these notes would be of considerable value to practitioners and would promote greater understanding between the Inland Revenue and accountants, although it is accepted that the published versions could not include those parts relating to procedural guidance to inspectors.

19 October 1979. CCAB

Accountants clarify calculations of double taxation relief

In the guidance note printed below the Consultative Committee of Accountancy Bodies clarifies the method of calculating the underlying rate for the purposes of double taxation relief.

In response to representations by the accountancy bodies the Inland Revenue have confirmed that they follow the spirit of the *Bowater* case in determining ''relevant profits'' of overseas companies for double tax relief purposes.

In further clarification the Revenue have indicated that realised gains on currency realignments are not regarded as available for distribution unless used for a dividend or included in the accounts as being distributable. Realised gains are regarded as distributable.

Realised capital profits credited to capital reserves are regarded by the Revenue as part of ''relevant profits'', although the accountancy bodies do not accept this view where the directors do not regard the profits as available for distribution.

The Revenue have also confirmed that the fraction used in calculating the underlying rate of overseas tax takes account of deferred tax charged and of adjustments to prior year tax charges.

Double taxation relief on dividends paid by overseas companies to UK companies: calculation of underlying rate of overseas tax

1 In their submission to the Inland Revenue in January 1978 on taxation anomalies and practical difficulties, the Consultative Committee of Accountancy Bodies requested clarification of two points concerning the calculation of the underlying rate of overseas tax applicable to the profits of an overseas company paying a dividend to a UK resident company, namely:

(*a*) confirmation that the Revenue were following the spirit of the House of Lords' decision in *Bowater Paper Corporation Limited v Murgatroyd* (1969) 46 TC 37 which laid down that ''relevant profits'' for double taxation relief purposes are the profits available for distribution as shown by the accounts, and

(*b*) clarification as to the correct denominator to be used in the actual calculation, *ie* profit before tax or profit after tax plus actual tax paid.

2 At a meeting between the Inland Revenue and the accountancy bodies in March 1978 the Revenue stated that they were following both the spirit and letter of the House of Lords' decision in the Bowater case and that there were bound to be some anomalies with any formula for computing the underlying tax.

There were, however, many complex questions which rested on the circumstances of particular cases and it was agreed that the accountancy bodies should first let the Revenue see examples of their points.

3 Examples were submitted to the Revenue for comment covering unrealised and realised profits on exchange and capital profits credited direct to capital reserves. The Revenue's comments and views on the definition of ''relevant profits'' (*ie* profits available for distribution) in the illustrative cases were as follows:

(*a*) Where the accounts profit includes unrealised gains on exchange differences, the Revenue say that there has been a change in practice. In a letter to the accountancy bodies the Revenue have stated:

> ''Since July 1978 the Inspector of Foreign Dividends provisionally treats unrealised gains on currency realignments as not available for distribution for the purposes of [TA 1988 s 799] unless the unrealised gains are in fact used for a dividend or put to a reserve of a general nature which is considered distributable or left in the retained earnings account.''

To the extent that the gains are realised gains, the Revenue's view is that such gains are regarded as available for distribution.

(*b*) Where realised capital profits are credited direct to capital reserves the Revenue regard such profits as being part of the ''relevant profits'' for double taxation relief purposes. The accountancy bodies do not agree with this view in circumstances where the capital profits referred to above are not regarded by the directors as available for distribution in the year under review. In this context the Revenue have written as follows:

> ''...the method adopted by the Department is considered to be correct and in no way inconsistent with the *Bowater* decision. In that case the argument for the taxpayer was that the profits were those assessed to foreign tax whereas the Revenue maintained that the profits available for distribution were those which were shown to be available by the accounts (whether on revenue or capital account).
>
> It is of no significance that the capital profit was taken in the accounts directly to a capital reserve. Such profit remains available for distribution to shareholders and it is immaterial whether it reaches capital reserve after first being credited to profit and loss account (or for that matter left in the profit and loss account).
>
> Where it is contended that [TA 1988 s 799(3)(*b*)] applies, full evidence including relevant minutes of meetings to establish as a fact that the dividend was paid out of specified profits must be supplied.''

4 With regard to the denominator to be used when calculating the underlying rate of overseas tax, the Revenue have written as follows:

> ''It is confirmed that the Inspector of Foreign Dividends accepts and applies the following calculation:

$$\frac{\text{Actual tax paid} \times 100}{\text{Actual tax paid} + \text{relevant profit*}} = \text{x per cent}$$

(*Relevant profit being profit after tax per accounts subject to any adjustments.)

It is confirmed too that the above calculation automatically takes into account any deferred taxation charged plus under and over provisions for any tax in previous years. However, in any case where any charge to deferred tax has not been deducted to arrive at relevant profit it is suggested that the matter should be referred to the Inspector of Foreign Dividends' Double Taxation (Rates) Section for attention.''

5 The above formula can be illustrated by the following example:

A UK resident company received a dividend of £8,500 (after withholding tax of £1,500) from its wholly-owned overseas subsidiary. The profit and loss account of the subsidiary expressed in sterling was as follows:

	£	£
Operating profit before taxation		30,000
Deduct:		
Taxation:		
Provision for income tax	10,000	
Deferred taxation	5,000	
Over provision for tax in prior years	(1,000)	
		14,000
Profit after taxation		16,000
Proposed dividend		10,000
Retained profit		£6,000

The actual tax paid by the subsidiary on the above profit was £9,500.

The profit after tax of £16,000 is the ''relevant profit'' for double taxation relief purposes.

The calculations of the underlying rate of overseas tax applicable to the above profit is therefore:

$$\frac{£9{,}500}{£9{,}500 + £16{,}000} \times 100 = 37{\cdot}25 \text{ per cent}$$

The Schedule D Case V income and double taxation relief arising to the UK resident company are as follows:

	£
Cash received	8,500
Add: Withholding tax	1,500
	10,000
Add: Underlying tax (*ie* £15,937 at 37·25 per cent)	5,937
Schedule D Case V income	£15,937
Double taxation relief available £1,500 + £5,937	£7,437

(It has been assumed that the rate of UK tax on the Case V income is 52 per cent.)

30 October 1979. Inland Revenue letter

Capital gains deferment: holdover relief

We shall be grateful for your comments with regard to the maximum time interval between the disposal of asset No 1 and the acquisition of Asset No 3 which is not a depreciating asset—please see [TCGA 1992 s 154(4) and (5)].

Subsection (5) states that the non-depreciating asset (No 3) should be acquired not later than the time when the chargeable gain postponed under subsection (2) would accrue. The latest date provided by sub-s (2) is ten years beginning with the acquisition of the depreciating asset [TCGA 1992 s 154(2)(*c*)]. It would seem from subsection (5) that the maximum time interval between the acquisition of asset No 2 and the replacement non-depreciating asset No 3 is ten years. For this purpose we are assuming that the non-depreciating asset No 3 is acquired before the disposal of asset No 2 but within ten years of the acquisition of asset No 2.

Revenue reply:

Where asset No 3 is acquired in such circumstances that a claim is possible under [TCGA 1992 s 154] then sub-s (5) specifically provides that the claim is to be accepted as if the time between the disposal of asset No 1 and the acquisition of asset No 3 was within the normal roll-over relief time limit and so it is unnecessary to consider the actual time interval between the disposal of asset No 1 and the acquisition of asset No 3. The important point is that asset No 3 must be acquired not later than the earliest of the events mentioned in subsection (2).

31 December 1979. BTR 343, 431

Valuation: Lands Tribunal [TCGA 1992 Sch 2, para 17]

Between 1971 and 1973 some 375 acres of agricultural land were compulsorily acquired from the taxpayer. He elected that for capital gains tax purposes valuation should be made as at 6 April 1965. The valuation of the land was referred to the Lands Tribunal which heard evidence from both the taxpayer and the Revenue, the taxpayer contending for a figure of approximately £1,000,000, and the Revenue for the District Valuer's figure of £650,000, which allowed, in particular, £100,000 for abnormal drainage costs. *Held*, that a prudent developer would have allowed for drainage costs, and the costs of acquiring necessary incidental easements, and that the value of the land should be determined at the District Valuer's figure of £650,000: *Halley v Weightman* (1978) 249 E.G. 547, Lands Tribunal.

31 December 1979. BTR 393

Branch or agency: Brussels Convention on Jurisdiction (TMA 1970 s 79)

The European Court has decided that the words ''branch or agency'' in Article 5 (5) of the Brussels Convention on Jurisdiction 1968 require an international interpretation common to all contracting states. They imply a place of business which has the appearance of permanency, such as the extension of a parent body, has a management and is materially equipped to negotiate business with third parties, so that they do not have to deal directly with the parent body but may transact business at the place of business constituting the branch or agency. *Etablissements Somafer S.A. v Saar—Ferngaz A.G.* (Case 33/79) [1979] 1 CMLR 490.

31 December 1979. BTR 398

Domicile: effect of Domicile and Matrimonial Proceedings Act 1973

In the course of an action for a declaration as to the validity of a marriage it was contended that the effect of the Domicile and Matrimonial Proceedings Act 1973 was that a married woman could avoid taking a dependent domicile if she did not want it but that she could still take it if she wished. Sir George Baker P. held that the effect of the Act was that dependent domicile had been abolished. If for example an English girl married an American she would not acquire an American domicile unless and until she went to America. ''Of course, a marriage as normally understood would be strong evidence that a woman had acquired the same domicile as her husband, for example, when a foreign woman comes here and marries an Englishman and they settle down as a married couple, have children and so on; but it is only one factor in her choice.'' *Puttick v Attorney-General*, 8 May 1979, [1979] 3 WLR 542; [1979] 3 All ER 463.

Note—See also IR 20 (explanation of Revenue practice as to residence).

31 December 1979. BTR 417

Plant: painting in office [CAA 2001 s 57]

It is understood that the Special Commissioners have decided that a painting in the reception room of a company's office does not constitute plant.

22 January 1980. Inland Revenue letter

[TA 1988 s 353] (Relief for payment of interest)

Whether interest is within the scope of [TA 1988 s 18] so that it is chargeable under Schedule D Case III depends upon the location of the source of the interest payment. This is not a straightforward point and there is little guidance in the statute or case law. However, following the tax case of *I.R. Comrs v Viscount Broome's Executors* (1935) 19 TC 667, the residence of the debtor is regarded as the most important factor. Broadly, where any UK debtor borrows under a simple contract or under a contract governed by English law, the Inland Revenue will regard the interest as within [TA 1988 s 353 (1) (*a*)]. *As a separate matter* from the question of relief under [TA 1988 s 353], because the interest is yearly or annual interest, [TA 1988 s 349] obliges the payer to deduct income tax unless authority is given under an appropriate double taxation agreement for payment of interest gross or for deduction of tax at a reduced rate.

In certain circumstances the Inland Revenue regard interest paid by a UK resident as outside the scope of Schedule D Case III so that there is no deduction under [TA 1988 s 353(1)(*a*)] and no obligation to deduct income tax under [TA 1988 s 349]. Broadly, if interest paid by a UK resident is payable abroad, to a non-resident, in foreign currency, under a foreign specialty contract and the loan is not secured on UK real property, the interest will be regarded as outside the scope of Schedule D Case III.

31 January 1980. Inland Revenue letter

[TA 1988 s 410] (Group relief: effect of arrangements for transfer of company to another group, etc)

The reference to accounting periods in [TA 1988 s 410] is a reference to accounting periods as defined in [TA 1988 s 12] not a period for which a company has prepared accounts. I can confirm that an arrangement coming into existence in the second accounting period will not affect the entitlement to group relief for the first accounting period.

Statement of Practice—SP 3/93 (Groups of companies—arrangements).

12 February 1980. Inland Revenue letter

[TA 1988 s 193(1)] (Earnings from work done abroad)

I confirm that, for a taxpayer to whom [TA 1988 s 193(1)] applies, where the conditions in [TA 1988 Sch 12 para 3(2)] are met, the 100 per cent deduction will be due on the whole of the emoluments for the period despite the fact that the return visits to the country are spent in the performance of his duties and that some of the emoluments relate to those duties.

In these circumstances it would be possible, as you suggest, to apply [TA 1988 Sch 12 para 2(2)] but in practice the Revenue would not do so unless there was any question of artificiality in the employee's arrangements with the employer. [TA 1988 Sch 12 para 2 (2)] would, however, apply where, for example, in one year of assessment a taxpayer receives some emoluments which would be relieved under [TA 1988 s 193(1)] and some which would not be so relieved. In determining the amount of the emoluments to which the 100 per cent deduction would apply consideration would be given to [TA 1988 Sch 12 para 2 (2)] in order to ensure that an excessive deduction was not given.

It is perhaps worth adding that [TA 1988 Sch 7 para 6] will operate to deny a 100 per cent deduction against the earnings of an employment the duties of which are in substance performed in the UK.

14 February 1980. Inland Revenue letter

Capital gains tax: trusts [TCGA 1992 s 72]

The problem on the termination of an annuity which is regarded as a life interest by virtue of [TCGA 1992 s 72(4)] is to determine the ''corresponding part'' of the annuity fund which is deemed to be disposed of under s 72(1). The same problem arises on the death of an annuitant where s 72 (4) does not apply, the termination being treated as the termination of a life interest by virtue of s 75. You will appreciate that s 72 (1) does not apply to assets ceasing to be settled property on the termination of the annuity, which are within s 71(1). Where s 72 (1) applies we normally take the ''corresponding part'' of the relevant assets to be the proportion, up to 100 per cent, which the amount of the annuity bears to the income of the s 72(4) fund (or the income of the whole settlement on the death of an annuitant). For this purpose we would consider the income of the 12 months up to the termination of the annuity, or at the trustees' option the income of the last trust accounts year ending before the termination, although difficulties such as widely fluctuating income might have to be looked at specially. The same procedure can be followed whether or not the terminating annuity is the only one.

9 May 1980. Inland Revenue letters

Agricultural buildings allowance

1 I agree that there is no provision similar to that contained in [CAA 2001 s 12] which is relevant to agricultural buildings allowances, but where the immediate purpose as opposed to future intentions satisfies the term ''for the purposes of husbandry'' in [CAA 2001 s 361(1)] expenditure would normally qualify for relief. This test of purpose must be applied at the time the relevant expenditure was incurred.

2 On the meaning of husbandry, I would refer you to the cases of *Lean and Dickson v Ball* (1925) 10 TC 341; *Jones v Nuttal* (1926) 10 TC 346 and *I.R. Comrs. v Cavan Central Co-op Agricultural & Dairy Society Ltd.* (1917) 12 TC 10.

Where bulbs [flowers, plants, shrubs] etc, are grown on the land this would normally be regarded as for the purposes of husbandry...

The question of whether expenditure qualifies for relief under [CAA 2001 ss 361–393] in these instances can only be determined in the light of the facts and the Inspector dealing with the case is, of course, in the best position to judge.

20 June 1980. Inland Revenue

Demergers

[TA 1988 s 214 is] concerned to prevent the new relief subsequently being used as a vehicle for tax avoidance. The provisions impose a charge to income tax (under Schedule D, Case VI), where, within five years after the demerger, any of the companies concerned makes a payment to the then shareholders in respect of their shares, otherwise than for bona fide commercial reasons, or for purposes of tax avoidance. Examples (the illustrations are not intended to be exhaustive—for example, much the same effect could be achieved if the roles were reversed and the ''demerged'' company bought back the shares of its original parent, or arranged for that to be liquidated) of the type of abuse which [section 214] seeks to prevent are where, as part of an avoidance operation,

1 A company has under [section 213] distributed to its shareholders the shares in a subsidiary company free of tax; but
2 It, or companies connected with it, (the definition of ''connected with'' is necessarily wide in the first instance but its practical application is then limited by the provisions in [section 214] below) subsequently buy the shares back, or arrange for the subsidiary to be liquidated or otherwise to pass cash out in a form not subject to income tax—in effect, using the demerger operation to pass to the shareholders cash or other assets which would have been subject to ACT and income tax, if paid as a straightforward dividend.

These anti-avoidance provisions do not of course apply where a shareholder sells his shares at arm's length to a third party not ''connected with'' (the definition of ''connected with'' is necessarily wide in the first instance but its practical application is then limited by the provisions in [section 214] below) the demerger operations (*eg* on the Stock Exchange). Similarly (though the provisions in [section 213(11)] will deny the new relief in a case where the original demerger is part of a scheme or arrangement whose sole or main purpose is to sell the demerged company or trade into another company group), the anti-avoidance provisions in [section 214] do not apply when subsequently—and without pre-arrangement—the shares concerned are the subject of a takeover bid by an arm's length third party.

22 July 1980. Inland Revenue letter

Voyage or journey outside the UK

[TA 1988 Sch 12 para 5] covers two types of voyage or journey;

(*a*) covers a voyage or journey beginning or ending outside the UK, and
(*b*) covers a voyage or journey beginning and ending in the UK

The question where a ''voyage'' begins and ends must be one of fact, but an example of a voyage within [TA 1988 Sch 12 para 5 (*a*)] would be a voyage from Newcastle–Tilbury–Antwerp. This ends outside the UK, so that the duties performed on the vessel are treated as performed outside the UK (excluding the part of the voyage which begins and ends in the UK, *ie* Newcastle–Tilbury). The result is, therefore, that the part of the voyage from Tilbury to Antwerp qualifies as outside the UK

An example of a voyage within [TA 1988 Sch 12 para 5 (*b*)] would be a voyage from Newcastle–Tilbury–Antwerp–Tilbury–Newcastle. This voyage begins and ends in the UK, but parts of the voyage begin and end outside the UK, *ie* the part from Tilbury–Antwerp ends outside the UK and the part from Antwerp–Tilbury begins outside the UK Duties performed on the vessel from Tilbury–Antwerp–Tilbury would therefore be treated as performed outside the UK

With regard to the example quoted by you, the Revenue view is that a voyage from the UK to the UK, not entailing a *scheduled* call at an overseas port is a voyage beginning and ending in the UK of which no part ends or begins outside the UK, so that [TA 1988 Sch 12 para 5] would not apply.

Finally, it should be remembered that whilst [TA 1988 Sch 12 para 5] specifies certain duties which are to be treated as performed outside the UK, where the number of qualifying days is relevant for the purposes of [TA 1988 Sch 12 para 4] provides that a person shall not be regarded as absent from the UK on any day unless he is so absent at the end of it, *ie* at midnight. For this purpose, the casting off from a UK berth (allied to passage for overseas port) would be taken as the time of departure from the UK, and equally a ship would be regarded as arriving in the UK at the time of berthing.

26 January 1981. Inland Revenue

The transfer pricing of multinational enterprises: Notes by the UK Inland Revenue

1 Introduction

These notes are primarily designed for the guidance of overseas companies which have, or may be thinking of setting up, subsidiaries in the UK; but the law and practice described apply to UK resident companies generally.

2 General—the arm's length principle

Prices charged in transactions between connected companies in a multinational group (transfer prices) may be designed to meet the convenience of the group as a whole. They will not necessarily produce a figure of profit or loss which can be accepted for tax purposes. The UK law therefore, in common with that of many other countries, provides that these prices may be adjusted in arriving at the taxable profit or allowable loss of a UK taxpayer. The price to which they may be adjusted is the ''arm's length price''. This is the price which might have been expected if the parties to the transaction had been independent persons dealing at arm's length *ie* dealing with each other in a normal commercial manner unaffected by any special relationship between them.

3 Circumstances in which adjustments may be made to transfer prices

The relevant law is largely contained in [TA 1988 s 770]. This provides the Inland Revenue with power, for example, to adjust a transfer price to the arm's length price in transactions between a resident and a non-resident body of persons when one controls the other or both are under common control.

4 Body of persons

A ''body of persons'' includes a partnership as well as a company.

5 Residence of a company

The general rule is that a company is resident where the central control and management of its trade or business is carried on. The application of the rule is a question of fact. [But see SP 1/90].

6 Control of a company

Control of a company has to be distinguished from the control and management of its trade or business. For the purposes of [TA 1988 s 770] it is defined in particular to mean, as in [TA 1988 s 840], the power of a person to secure that the affairs of the company are conducted in accordance with his wishes, *inter alia*, by holding shares or possessing voting power in relation to that company (or any other company) or by virtue of any powers conferred by the articles of association or other document regulating that or any other company.

7 Scope of UK transfer pricing law

[TA 1988 s 770] applies to sales of goods and other property, lettings or hiring of property, grants and transfers of rights, interests and licences and the giving of business facilities of whatever kind. Loan interest, patent royalties, management fees, and payments for services are thus within its scope as well as payments for goods. Contributions by a subsidiary towards costs incurred by the parent company are similarly within its scope.

8 Tax returns—assessment of profits—onus of proof—rights of appeal

The UK system of taxing profits requires the taxpayer to make a return of his profits each year to the appropriate inspector of taxes. It is normal for his return to be accompanied by accounts and computations in some detail in order to substantiate the return. But the inspector, if no return is made or if he is dissatisfied with a return which has been made, is however empowered to assess the liability to tax on the basis of his own estimate of the profits. The taxpayer has a right of appeal to independent Commissioners (and from the Commissioners, on a point of law, to the High Court and beyond) but it is for him in the first instance to disprove the correctness of the assessment in such an appeal and not for the inspector to prove that it is correct.

9 Adjustment by agreement

If, however, the inspector takes the view that it may be necessary to assess the profits on the basis of his own estimate he will normally seek, in any case where substantial amounts are at stake, to come to an agreement on the matter with the taxpayer either by correspondence or, very probably in a case where the adjustment of transfer prices is in point, by discussion round the table as well.

10 Requests for information

If it seems to the inspector that it may be necessary to adjust a company's transfer prices for tax purposes he will normally, therefore, in the first place, ask the UK company for the information necessary to decide whether adjustments should be made and what sort of adjustments. There is no standard list of questions—each case will need to be looked at in the light of its own special features. But the inspector will generally be interested in such matters as who owns or controls the company, what the nature of the trade is, how any group of which the company is a member is organised, what are the functions of particular companies in the group, what the results of the UK companies have been, how far they have come up to expectations and so on. The need for answers to more detailed questions may emerge as the discussions proceed.

11 Powers to require information

The Revenue have power in certain circumstances to require the production of information for tax purposes and, in particular under [TA 1988 s 772], they may require a company to produce information which is relevant to the adjustment of transfer prices (not necessarily its own transfer prices) under [TA 1988 s 770]. Powers provided under [TA 1988 s 772] also include in certain circumstances the power to require the production of information (including books and accounts) from a UK resident company, which is relevant to transactions with a 51 per cent. subsidiary resident outside the UK including books and accounts of the subsidiary. This also applies where the transactions are between UK resident and non-resident companies both of which are 51 per cent. subsidiaries of the UK resident company. (The UK parent company may however appeal against the requirement to an independent body of Commissioners.) In addition, in certain circumstances the Board may require books and accounts and other documents or records which are relevant to a transfer pricing adjustment under [s. 770] to be produced for examination by an inspector of taxes on the taxpayer's premises.

12 Confidentiality

Officers of the Revenue are governed by very strict rules about the confidentiality of information received by them in the course of their duties. They are prohibited from disclosing such information except for tax purposes and, within that limitation, in very limited circumstances strictly defined by law.

13 Exchange of information with other countries

Disclosure is permitted (under strict safeguards) to other countries tax authorities under agreements for the relief of double taxation and under the Directive concerning mutual assistance between tax authorities of the member States of the European Communities. (The Inland Revenue may also receive information from other countries under these instruments.)

14 Inland Revenue Organisation

The Revenue maintains a network of local tax offices spread over the whole of the UK and normally the affairs of a taxpayer will be mainly dealt with by a local inspector of taxes. But transfer pricing problems involving substantial amounts of money or important matters of principle may be dealt with instead by a section of the central head office in London. (The affairs of oil companies including matters of transfer pricing are dealt with by a centralised Oil Taxation Office in London.)

15 Objectives and methods of approach in adjusting transfer prices for tax purposes

The objectives of both central and local offices are however the same. The principal objective is to ensure that the UK taxpayer is paying the proper UK tax on its profits under the law. The Inland Revenue recognise, however, that answering the many detailed questions which may be necessary for the achievement of this objective may impose an onerous burden on the senior staff of companies or their advisers and they aim to keep these questions to a minimum by concentrating on the main pricing issues involved.

16 Methods of and considerations taken into account in arriving at arm's length prices

In ascertaining an arm's length price the Revenue will often look for evidence of prices in similar transactions between parties who are in fact operating at arm's length. They may however find it more useful in some circumstances to start with the re-sale of the goods or services etc and arrive at the relevant arm's length purchase price by deducting an appropriate mark up. They may find it more convenient on the other hand to start with the cost of the goods or services and arrive at the arm's length price by adding an appropriate mark up. But they will in practice use any method which seems likely to produce a satisfactory result. They will be guided in their search for an arm's length price by the considerations set out in the OECD Report on Multinationals and Transfer Pricing. (This Report examines the considerations which need to be taken into account in arriving at arm's length prices in general and also in particular in the context of sales of goods, the provision of intra group services, the transfer of technology and rights to use trademarks within a group and the provision of intra group loans.)

17 Settlement of problems

The Revenue recognise, as does the OECD Report, that the evidence needed to establish an arm's length price may be hard to come by and difficult to interpret and they recognise also that decisions on pricing in the arm's length situation would have had to be taken in the light of the facts which could have been known at the time when the decision was made. It is with considerations like this in mind that they are concerned to settle transfer pricing adjustments as far as possible by discussion and agreement with the companies concerned. They would hope as a result also to establish a reasonable basis of understanding with the companies for the future (possibly on the basis of a review after a number of years).

18 Consultation with other countries

The Revenue recognise that transfer pricing adjustments may have a consequence not only for UK tax but also for foreign tax. They are able, under the terms of some seventy agreements for the relief of double taxation and the prevention of fiscal evasion, to exchange information with the tax authorities of their partner countries on transfer pricing matters among others and they often do this for the purpose of ensuring that tax is adequately charged in the UK On the other hand, they are also able to consult and do consult with partner countries with a view to preventing unrelievable double taxation arising from (among other causes) the adjustment of transfer prices. A taxpayer who fears that unrelievable double taxation may result in his own case from some action of the tax authorities of a treaty partner may ask the UK Inland Revenue to enter into such consultations and they will do so whenever the need arises. All that such a taxpayer need do is to write a letter putting his request, and giving the relevant details, to the International Tax Policy Division of the Inland Revenue in Somerset House, London. For such consultation to be effective however it will usually be necessary for the request to be made in good time so as not to be frustrated by the expiry of legal time limits for tax adjustments either in the UK or in the other country.

19 Time limits for claims for credit

So far as concerns claiming relief for foreign tax against UK tax the normal rule is that a claim in respect of any income, must be made not later than six years from the end of the chargeable period for which the income is chargeable to UK tax. However where such credit has been rendered insufficient by reason of an adjustment to the other country's tax the time limit for a claim to additional credit is six years from the time when the adjustment was made—[TA 1988 s 806].

20 Status of these notes

These notes are for guidance only. They express the Inland Revenue's view of the law but they have no legal force and they do not affect any rights of appeal on points concerning a taxpayer's liability. Similarly any description in these notes of Inland Revenue approaches to the problem of transfer pricing or practices in dealing with this problem are not to be taken as limiting the Department to such approaches or practices in any particular case.

3 February 1981. Inland Revenue letter

Payment for surrender of group relief

I can confirm that it is not the Board's practice to seek any adjustment under [TCGA 1992 s 176(4)] in respect of the surrender of losses by way of group relief where no payment is made for the surrender, or where the payment made is less than the tax value of the group relief received.

Similarly I can confirm that in these circumstances, and on the assumption that there are no tax avoidance arrangements, the Board would not regard [TCGA 1992 s 30] as applying.

25 March 1981. Inland Revenue Letter

Industrial buildings allowances

1 The term ''process'' is a word of wide import given the case of *Kilmarnock Equitable Co-operative Society Ltd. v I.R. Comrs.* and now *Buckingham v Securitas Properties Ltd.* Securitas' activities in the words of the judge were:

> ''Large and complex involving a number of stages and as a result may afford additional grounds for arguing that a process was involved.''

...I think it is arguable, therefore, whether the repackaging of fruit/vegetable amounts to the subjection of goods to a process.

2 Where part of a company's trade [CAA 2001 s 276(1), (2)] is a qualifying trade then buildings or structures in use for that part trade will qualify for industrial buildings allowances. But where there is no identifiable part trade which qualifies and this would seem to be the position as regards the traders to whom you refer whom I imagine could not contend that part of the trade was, for example, a transport undertaking, then such items as vehicle loading bays will not qualify for Industrial Buildings Allowances.

3 *In our view, [CAA 1990 s 18(1)(f)(iv)] and in particular the phrase ''on their arrival by sea or air'' requires that the building qualifying under this provision should be located in the vicinity of the dock or airport. Consequently, where the relevant building is a few miles from the dock/airport we would not regard the provisions of [CAA 1990 s 18(1)(f)(iv)] as being satisfied.*

Cross reference—*Copol Clothing Ltd. v Hindmarch* [1984] STC 33.

The words in para 3 above from CAA 1990 s 18(1)(*f*)(iv) substituted by FA 1995 s 101. For the substantive law see now CAA 2001 s 274(1) Table A Item 3(*d*).

20 October 1981. Inland Revenue letter

Mineral depletion allowances [CAA 2001 ss 394, 417, 418]

Of the items listed in your letter deposits of the following would be considered to fall within the meaning of mineral asset in [CAA 2001 s 397]:

Chalk
Clay

Peat
Coal
Granite
Marble
Limestone
Natural gas
Oil.

The foregoing is on the basis that the deposits concerned are part of the land, as distinct from lying on the surface of the land as, for example, dumped materials.

10 November 1981. Inland Revenue letter

Relief on replacement of business assets [TCGA 1992 ss 155, 157]

Section 157 is silent on the question of payment by the company for the use of the asset owned by the individual. The same may be said of s 165 which is of contemporaneous origin and in connection with which it is necessary to determine whether an asset was 'used for the purposes of a trade...carried on by...his [personal] company'. Useful parallels have been drawn between the s 165 test and the definition of chargeable business asset in Sch 6, para 12(2) which definition specifically excludes assets held as investments.

On examining the structure of s 155, it is apparent that it is the 'asset' which must be a qualifying asset, that is, in the case of land or buildings, 'occupied (as well as used) only for the purposes of the trade'. The disposal and, acquisition referred to in s 152(1) may however be of the asset itself or of an interest in such a qualifying asset. Both s 157 and s 165 similarly refer to 'an asset, or an interest in, an asset'. Interests in assets may take the form of leaseholds, freehold reversions or fractional shares.

Under the generality of s 152(1) therefore a taxpayer may claim roll-over relief on disposal of a leasehold interest in land occupied as well as used only for the purposes of his trade. On the other hand if the property was let by the freehold reversioner it would not normally be occupied as well as used only for the purposes of his trade. Indeed, the grant of a lease suggests that the property is occupied by the lessee. Section 157 treats the trade of a [personal] company as having been carried on by the individual who owned the assets (or an interest in them) so that if in relation to the company the assets are qualifying assets the s 155 test may be satisfied by the individual.

If the company occupies land or buildings under a lease from the individual his reversionary interest is nevertheless an interest in a qualifying asset. It is conceivable that such a company might itself have entitlement to roll-over relief if it received consideration for the disposal of its interest which it reinvested in new qualifying assets. It follows that if the individual is treated as carrying on the trade in which the old assets (and the new assets) are used, he may, under s 152(1), claim to have reinvested the consideration for the disposal of his interest in those assets in new qualifying assets, but only if the new assets are again used in the trade (or trades) of a company which on the occasion of both disposal and acquisition is his [personal] company.

These requirements are not satisfied if the old assets or the new assets (owned by him) were used in the trade of his [personal] company; he is brought within s 152(1) only where both assets were so used. His ownership and the company's use must apply throughout. Similarly, the company must be his [personal] company on the occasion both of the disposal of the old assets and the acquisition of the new assets, although it could carry on one trade using the old assets and another trade using the new assets. See s 152(8).

It is considered that the words 'a company' in s 157(*b*) are deliberately phrased in the singular and that despite (or perhaps, because of) the provisions of the Interpretation Acts substitution of 'a company (or companies)' is not permissible. The degree of precision with which the section was enacted particularly the provision of alternative words, where appropriate; 'of, or of his interest in...assets', 'trade or trades in question' and the imposition of dual requirements that both old and new assets must be used in the trade of the [personal] company; that the company must be his [personal] company both at the time of disposal and acquisition of assets—seems to lead naturally to the conclusion that the context in which the words 'a company' are used requires them to be read literally. Whilst it is accepted that a construction which replaces 'a company' by 'any company' is possible, consequential amendments would make the section read very awkwardly. The 'plural' interpretation also renders irrelevant or at least meaningless the requirement that the company must be his [personal] company both at the time of disposal of old assets and the time of acquisition of new assets. If a second [personal] company used the new assets in its trade it would seem odd that it had to be his [personal] company at the time of disposal of the old assets, perhaps up to three years earlier.

17 February 1982. Inland Revenue letter

Interest on non-resident loan to UK resident [TA 1988 ss 18, 349]

In the past, before the ending of exchange control, the Revenue normally accepted that interest on a loan from a non-resident to a UK resident could have a foreign source if certain criteria were present, *ie*, if the interest was paid and payable abroad in a foreign currency under a foreign specialty contract and where there were no contaminating features such as the security on real assets in the UK The effective disappearance of any difference between borrowing in sterling and borrowing in a foreign currency and the ready availability of foreign loans to UK residents since the dismantling of the controls has altered the situation. We are advised that there can now be no confidence that the courts would attach sufficient significance to the foreign specialty contract in itself as being a decisive factor.

The practice of evaluating criteria has not changed, it is the criteria which have changed. The Revenue view therefore is that a loan from a non-resident to a company resident in the UK will normally give rise to interest within the charge to Case III and the machinery provisions will apply accordingly.

1 February 1983. Hansard

Tax payments (interest charges)

Mr Iain Mills asked the Chancellor of the Exchequer if he will introduce legislation to give discretionary powers to Her Majesty's Inland Revenue on the application of interest generated by late payment of tax where the late payment was due to delays caused by prolonged assessment by the district valuer.

Mr Ridley: Where a substantial delay on the part of the Inland Revenue gives rise to an interest charge, the Revenue has discretion to mitigate or remit the interest charge otherwise due. Such consideration is also given to cases involving the valuation office.

Cross reference—See TMA 1970 s 86 (Interest on overdue tax).

10 March 1983. CCAB TR 500

Guidance note on taxation: points of practical interest

1 In the notes of their meeting with the Inland Revenue in January 1982, published as TR 471, the accountancy bodies stated that they had compiled a list of unpublished practical points. This guidance note, which has been agreed with the Inland Revenue, sets out some of the more important points, mostly of interpretation, which are regarded as being of general interest. A number of other points have been discussed which will be published separately in due course.

PART I: INCOME TAX AND CORPORATION TAX

Schedule D: Losses and group relief

Relief for trading losses—interest deemed to be trading income [TA 1988 s 393(8)]

2 [TA 1988 s 393(8)] provides that for the purposes of [s. 393], any interest or dividends on investments which would fall to be taken into account as trading receipts in computing that trading income but for the fact that they have been subjected to tax under other provisions should be treated for the purpose of [s. 393(1)] as if they were trading income of the trade.

3 The Inland Revenue have commented that they are normally prepared to accept that interest on current account and trade interest can qualify for relief under [s 393(8)]. The Revenue also accept that interest from the temporary lodgement of part of the current working capital in a bank deposit account may qualify where:

(*a*) the investment is for a short term.

(*b*) it is an integral part of the trading activity to make such an investment, and

(*c*) the funds deposited can be regarded as continuing to be employed in the business and to form part of the current working capital.

4 It is the Revenue's view that the investment represents capital temporarily surplus to requirements or, although short term, is part of a series of investments which together constitute a long-term setting aside of part of the capital, the interest cannot qualify for relief under [s 393(8)].

Capital allowances: transfer of trade or part of trade under [TA 1988 s 343] part way through accounting period

5 The transfer of trade may take place during the currency of the accounting periods of the companies concerned. In those circumstances, the Inland Revenue take the view that [TA 1988 s 343] should normally be applied as follows:

(*a*) Writing down allowances are calculated on the ''pool'' of qualifying expenditure held by the transferee at the end of its accounting period, and those allowances are apportioned on a time basis for the period in which each company carried on the trade.

(*b*) First year allowances are given to the company which actually incurred the expenditure, no apportionment being necessary.

(*c*) Any balancing adjustments (whether charges or allowances) are made on the company carrying on a trade in the relevant time, without any apportionment.

6 Where there is a transfer of part of a trade, any necessary apportionment of the ''pool'' of qualifying expenditure should be made on a just and reasonable basis.

Schedule D and corporation tax: accounting date

7 Complications can arise where a business makes up accounts to slightly varying accounting dates, for example, the nearest Saturday to a month end. Where this happens and the terminal date does not vary by more than four days from a mean date, the Inland Revenue will not normally object to the treatment of each account as an account for a period of twelve months ended on the mean date provided that the taxpayer has agreed in writing to adopt this treatment. In the case of a company there are a number of other conditions concerning the accounting period for the purpose of [TA 1988 s 234, Schs 13, 16], and the application of [TA 1988 s 239] to which the company must agree in writing. Full details may be obtained from the inspector dealing with the company's tax affairs.

Treatment of interest payments

9 The Inland Revenue have confirmed that Extra-statutory concession B13 (1992) (under which no action is taken to recover income tax on untaxed interest paid to non-residents) applies to discounts on bills of exchange received by non-residents. In practice, the Inland Revenue also apply the concession to disposals on certificates of deposit in the hands of non-residents.

10, 11 *Spent.*

PART II: CAPITAL GAINS

Time apportionment

12 The Inland Revenue are prepared to accept the period of tenancy prior to the period of ownership as part of the time apportionment denominator. For example, where farm land was gifted from the father at say £4,000 (stamping value) in 1956 and sold for say £74,000 in 1975 but the son had been a tenant since 1937 a time apportionment factor of 10/20+10 would apply rather than 10/9+10. The Inland Revenue have said that the existence of an ordinary tenancy is quite sufficient to allow the extended time apportionment formulae to apply even though no formal lease or tenancy agreement was in existence. As long as rent was paid that is sufficient. Any sale of land, including buildings, where there was a tenancy prior to the period of ownership, follows the same pattern. Any ''wasted'' cost of a lease has, of course, to be added to the cost of the ''freehold reversion''. [See TCGA 1992 Sch 2 para 16].

Private residences

13 The Inland Revenue take the view that where absences from the dwelling-house exceed the three years or four years mentioned in [TCGA 1992 s 223(3)] then it is only the excess which does not qualify for the exemption. Where the other conditions are satisfied the three or four years out of the longer period of absence would qualify as the ''period of absence'' for which exemption under s 223(2) would be available.

PART III: DOUBLE TAXATION RELIEF AND OTHER OVERSEAS MATTERS

14 [TCGA 1992 s 13] can impose a charge on a UK parent company on capital gains arising from disposals by its overseas subsidiary if the latter would be a close company if it were resident in the UK The Inland Revenue have confirmed that, where the overseas subsidiary is resident in a territory with which the UK has a double taxation agreement and there is an article exempting residents of that territory from a charge to UK capital gains, then such an article may prevent the imposition of a charge under s 13.

15 In connection with the application of the small companies rate to UK branches of companies resident overseas, the Inland Revenue confirm that, in general, the small companies rate will be available where there is a non-discrimination clause in a double tax treaty on the basis that the overseas company is treated as if it were notionally resident in the UK for the purpose of [TA 1988 s 13]. Relief is of course governed by the worldwide profits of the company, not just the UK branch profits. Associated companies wherever they may be resident are taken into account in determining the lower and upper relevant maximum amounts for [TA 1988 s 13] purposes.

31 May 1983. Inland Revenue letter

Transfer of a trade to a connected company

In the circumstances you have outlined the period 6 April 1982 to 30 June 1983 would not in strictness form part of the basis period for any year of assessment.

In practice we would normally be prepared to extend the basis period for the final year of assessment of the trader to include the period 6 April 1982 to 30 June 1983 and give first year allowance for expenditure incurred in that period to the trader on the grounds that this gives the allowance to the person who actually incurred the expenditure. Similarly of course we would take account of any disposal values in this period in the computation of allowances for the trader's final year of assessment.

7 July 1983. Inland Revenue letter

[TA 1988 s 146] (living accommodation provided for employee)

We shall be grateful for your comments with regard to the situation where an excessive charge to tax could arise in the case of living accommodation situated outside the UK where [TA 1988 ss 145, 146] are relevant.

[TA 1988 s 146] refers to annual value being computed by reference to [TA 1988 s 145]. Whilst that value may very well be less than the commercial rent in the case of UK situated property it would seem that in the case of living accommodation situated outside the UK that the annual value for the purposes of the said [TA 1988 s 145] will equal or approximate the open market rent. Where this is the case then the additional benefit of 12 per cent of the cost of providing the accommodation in excess of £75,000 mentioned in [TA 1988 s 146] would represent an excessive amount to be taxed. It would seem that the purpose of [TA 1988 s 146] was to take account of the fact that the gross annual value for rating purposes of UK situated residential property is significantly less than the commercial rent and therefore in such a case the benefits falling to be assessed under the two sections together would start to approach what would be a commercial rent. However, in the situation where the living accommodation is outside the UK it would appear that the [TA 1988 s 145] benefit represents the full commercial rent and therefore in such a case there is placed upon the taxpayer an onerous tax burden which it would not seem that Parliament had in mind.

Having regard to the foregoing we shall be grateful for your comments with regard to our understanding of the legislation. Also, would you please let us know whether or not in such a situation the Revenue Authorities are prepared to ensure that the amounts assessable under the two sections together do not exceed what would be a full commercial rent, thereby preventing what would otherwise clearly be an injustice.

Revenue reply

May I thank you for raising this particular point. I can confirm your understanding both of the purpose of the new section and of the way that on present wording it would apply in relation to living accommodation situated outside the UK

It would greatly assist us in our consideration of the point you raise if you could give brief (if you prefer, anonymised) details of any particular cases you have in mind, indicating the cost and location of the property, the use to which it is put and the method adopted for computing the current charge under [TA 1988 s 145].

21 October 1983. Inland Revenue letter

Associated companies—[TA 1988 s 416(3)]

The situation posed was of a company X and a company Y the shareholdings of which are comprised as shown below.

	X Ltd	*Y Ltd*
A	15%	30%
B	51%	30%
C	14%	—
D	20%	—
E	—	20%
F	—	20%

As I understand it company X would not be associated with company Y because the minimal control group in company X would be B and that of company Y would be A and B together. Control would therefore not be by the same persons. I understand that other matters may be relevant in determining control but on the basis that no other elements are present the companies would not be associated.

PRs etc

Revenue reply

The Revenue practice is to regard two companies as under the control of the same person or persons only if an irreducible group of persons having control of A Limited is identical with an irreducible group of person which has control of B Limited. By ''an irreducible group of persons'' I mean a group of persons which has control of the company but which would not have control of the company if any one of them were excluded.

Looking solely at the possession of issued share capital and ignoring the alternative tests of control in [TA 1988 s 416(2)] the only minimum controlling group in X Limited is B. B is not a minimum controlling group in Y Limited and therefore the two companies are not associated.

Incidentally, Y Limited has three minimum controlling groups, namely A and B or A E and F or B E and F but, of course, none of these forms a minimum controlling group in X Limited.

As you will appreciate, the result may well be very different if any of the shareholders are associates within [TA 1988 s 417(3)].

5 December 1983. Hansard

Tax Status (Contract Workers)

Mr Neil Hamilton asked the Chancellor of the Exchequer what income tax status the Inland Revenue applies to taxpayers whose sole source of income arises from their being (*a*) contract crop pickers and (*b*) contract dairy herdsmen.

Mr Moore: An individual's employment status for taxation purposes depends on whether the terms and conditions of his engagement amount to a contract of service or a contract for services. The forms of engagement of most casual crop pickers are such that they will generally be employees assessable under Schedule E; those of dairy herdsmen vary in practice and the employment status of any individual herdsman will depend on the particular facts.

Mr Neil Hamilton asked the Chancellor of the Exchequer what income tax status the Inland Revenue applies to taxpayers whose sole source of income arises from their being (*a*) contract club musicians and (*b*) contract National Health Service doctors.

Mr Moore: An individual's employment status for taxation purposes will depend on whether the conditions and terms of his engagement amount to a contract of service or a contract for services. The forms of engagement of musicians working in clubs vary, and the employment status of any individual musician will depend on the particular facts. National Health Service doctors holding hospital appointments are office-holders assessable under Schedule E while independent general practitioners in practice on their own account are self-employed and assessable under Case II of Schedule D.

HC Written Answer, 5 December 1983 Vol 50 col 26

20 December 1983. Inland Revenue letter

Industrial buildings allowances [CAA 2001 s 283]

We shall be grateful if you will kindly let us know how the Inland Revenue interpret [CAA 2001 s 283] where the undermentioned circumstances apply:

1 In connection with the same building more than one person may have a relevant interest in relation to capital expenditure incurred by him. For example, a company owns the freehold of a building plot and erects a factory which the Inland Revenue accept as giving entitlement to industrial buildings allowances. Should the freeholder grant a lease, and no election is made under [CAA 2001 s 290] the freeholder remains entitled to the claim for industrial buildings allowances so long as the building remains in use for a qualifying purpose. If the freeholder incurs capital expenditure on the building of a non-qualifying nature then under [CAA 2001 s 283] the expenditure is deemed to qualify for relief so long as the relevant percentage, currently 25 per cent, is not exceeded. However, should the lessee incur the non-qualifying capital expenditure on the building we wonder whether, in attempting to ascertain whether or not the relevant percentage is exceeded, it is necessary to aggregate the capital costs incurred by both the freeholder and the lessee. It may assist you if you are given an illustration:

Freeholder—qualifying expenditure on the building	£100,000
—non-qualifying expenditure	20,000
TOTAL	£120,000

The freeholder would be entitled to industrial buildings allowances relief on the full cost of £120,000 (no land element is included) because the relevant percentage, which in this illustration is assumed to be 25 per cent, is not exceeded. However, if the freeholder did not incur the non-qualifying expenditure but rather the lessee spent the £20,000 would that lessee be entitled to industrial buildings allowances relief on the £20,000 no other facts changing.

2 As already mentioned capital expenditure of a non-qualifying nature may be deemed to qualify by virtue of [CAA 2001 s 283] where the relevant percentage is not exceeded. However, if in a later accounting period further non-qualifying capital expenditure is incurred which causes the relevant percentage to be exceeded clearly that further expenditure cannot qualify. However, we wonder whether the earlier non-qualifying capital expenditure which was deemed to be available for relief will cease to qualify for insertion in the capital allowances computation and if so whether or not any adjustment is appropriate to the computations for earlier years. Again, a simple illustration may be of help:

Qualifying capital expenditure	£100,000	(Freeholder)
Add: Non-qualifying capital expenditure	25,000	(Freeholder)
Total for year 1	£125,000	(Freeholder)

It is clear that assuming the percentage that is relevant is 25 per cent. then the full expenditure of £125,000 will be deemed to qualify for relief assuming that all the other conditions of the Capital Allowances Act are fully met. If in a subsequent period (say) year 5 a further £25,000 capital expenditure were incurred on the same building of a non-qualifying nature the aggregate non-qualifying expenditure of £50,000 would then exceed the 25 per cent. limit and the second £25,000 would not be available for relief. Would the first £25,000 incurred in year one continue to be eligible for relief.

May we take this opportunity of thanking you for your assistance.

Revenue reply

[CAA 2001 s 571(1)] defines building as including part of a building and so in the first example which you give we would look at the part of the building on which the lessee had incurred the expenditure and only give industrial buildings allowance to the lessee if the part of the building on which he had incurred the expenditure was in use for a qualifying trade .... If therefore the lessee only incurred expenditure on offices which are within [CAA 2001 s 277(1), (5)] he would not be entitled to any industrial buildings allowance.

In the second example you give where, initially the limit in [CAA 2001 s 283], is not exceeded but further non-qualifying expenditure is added later on, we would take into account the whole of the expenditure on the building in considering whether the limit in [CAA 2001 s 283] is now exceeded and if that limit is now exceeded no further industrial buildings allowance will be given on the expenditure on the non-qualifying part. Any allowances given in earlier years before the limit was exceeded will not however be withdrawn. In other words in your example the initial non-qualifying expenditure of £25,000 would qualify for initial and writing down allowances until the further expenditure was incurred. When the further expenditure on the non-qualifying part of the building was incurred, writing down allowance would no longer be given on the initial non-qualifying capital expenditure.

16 January 1984. Inland Revenue letter

[TA 1988 s 410] (Arrangements for transfer of company to another group or consortium)

We shall be grateful for your clarification of the entitlement to group relief where a subsidiary company has issued "fixed rate preference shares" as defined in [TA 1988 Sch 18]. The shares in question we have in mind are cumulative and carry no right to vote. However, in common with many preference shares they carry the right to vote should the preference dividend fall into arrear—once the position has been rectified then again they no longer have a right to vote. We wonder whether the fact that the preference shares could conceivably have a right to vote in the future would bring into play [TA 1988 s 410(1)(*b*)(ii)] thereby debarring entitlement to group relief.

Alternatively, is it the practice of the Revenue to ignore such fixed rate preference shares when considering possible future changes of control—it being appreciated that should entitlement to vote occur because the dividend is in arrear then at that moment in time the group relationship could be broken for the relevant accounting periods during which there was the right to vote?

Revenue reply

Where preference shares carry voting rights in the event of the preference dividend falling into arrear and the voting power of these shares is such that common control over the claimant and surrendering company could be broken, [TA 1988 s 410(1)(*b*)(ii)] will apply. [TA 1988 s 410] will apply to all accounting periods in which "arrangements" exist and not just the accounting periods in which there was an entitlement to vote.

15 February 1984. Hansard

Corporation tax (allowances)

Dr. Twinn asked the Chancellor of the Exchequer if he will enable computer rooms and export offices to be eligible for the 100 per cent. first year allowance against corporation tax for new lighting installations currently applying to pubs, discos and restaurants.

Mr Moore: Basic lighting systems do not qualify for first year allowances as machinery or plant, but the cost of installation may rank for industrial buildings allowance if they form part of a qualifying building or structure. Specialised lighting systems may qualify as plant and machinery where they perform a specific function and are not merely part of the setting in which the trade is carried on. These conditions are of general application.

HC, 15 February 1984 Vol 54 col 203

15 February 1984. Hansard

Capital gains tax

Lord James Douglas-Hamilton asked the Chancellor of the Exchequer if he will issue a directive to all relevant officers of the Inland Revenue on the application of [TCGA 1992 s 165] to a farmer or farmers who bring his or their own land into a business partnership of which he or they are partners; if he will arrange for a statement of practice in this matter to be available to professional advisers and taxpayers on request; and if he will make a statement.

Mr Moore: The general practice is that in the circumstances outlined, capital gains tax relief is not available to the extent that consideration is received by the transferor of the land. The usual avenues of appeal are, of course, available to any taxpayer who wishes to dispute the application of these provisions to the facts of a particular case.

HC, 15 February 1984 Vol 54 col 206

6 March 1984. Hansard

Gratuities (Taxation)

Mr Rowe asked the Chancellor of the Exchequer under what powers the Inland Revenue requires answers from employers to its standard letter concerning gratuities received where the employer is not the troncmaster.

Mr Moore: If a tronc is in operation and the employer is not the troncmaster, inquiries concerning tips would normally be made to the troncmaster. However, if the troncmaster has failed to operate PAYE, the Commissioners of Inland Revenue have power to direct the employer to operate PAYE on tips paid to the troncmaster through the employer.

Mr Rowe asked the Chancellor of the Exchequer (1) if, where the actual tips received and declared by an individual are different from the standard amount which the Inland Revenue considers it may be expected to have received, it is the policy of the Inland Revenue to assess the actual amount received and not the amount the Inland Revenue considers to be the standard;

(2) What is the policy of the Inland Revenue on altering employee codings in respect of gratuities where information on the level of gratuities is not forthcoming and the employer is not the troncmaster.

Mr Moore: The amount of tips declared by the individual is accepted unless the Inland Revenue has reason to believe the figure is inadequate. In the absence of satisfactory information on the levels of tips, the Inland Revenue estimates the amount to the best of its judgment. An employee can appeal against a PAYE code or assessment if he considers that any estimate of tips included is excessive. A code will be adjusted if a better estimate can be agreed. If an appeal is made, an assessment will be adjusted to show the actual amount when that information is provided.

Mr Rowe asked the Chancellor of the Exchequer what is the reason for, and the scope of, the investigation of the tips received by employees in hairdressing salons which is being conducted by the Inland Revenue.

Mr Moore: Tips received by employees in the course of their employment are taxable as emoluments. Employees receiving tips must show the full amount received in their income tax returns, whether or not they are received through a tronc scheme. It is the duty of the Inland Revenue to satisfy itself as to the accuracy and completeness of tax returns and to take steps to recover any tax that should have been deducted by employers or troncmasters. Investigations are generally conducted by local tax offices or by local PAYE auditors although where an employer has a large number of different establishments the matter may be handled centrally by a special office.

Mr Rowe asked the Chancellor of the Exchequer if he will publish what the Inland Revenue considers to be the likely amount of tips that various grades of hairdressing employees will receive according to the status of the salon in which they work and what is the basis on which the Inland Revenue have arrived at those numbers.

Mr Moore: No central guidance on this matter has been issued to inspectors of taxes who exercise their judgment in the light of individual circumstances. It is open to an employee who disagrees with the amount determined by an inspector to appeal and, where agreement cannot be reached, the matter may be heard by the commissioners, who are an independent tribunal.

HC, Written Answers, 6 March 1984 Vol 55 col 405

15 March 1984. Inland Revenue

Cable television: capital allowances [CAA 2001 s 57]

The Chief Secretary to the Treasury, the Rt. Hon. Peter Rees, QC, MP, announced yesterday that the Inland Revenue were writing to representatives of the cable television industry to inform them that, on the basis of legal advice received by the Revenue, the cost both of the provision and of the installation of ducting in connection with the construction of cable television networks, is to be regarded as expenditure qualifying for capital allowances as machinery or plant.

Note

1 This announcement concerns a point at issue between the cable television industry and the Inland Revenue regarding the eligibility of certain cable installation costs to capital allowances. The costs in question relate to the provision of protective ducting into which the cable is inserted, and the cutting and covering of trenches in which the ducting will be laid in the ground. Following representations from the industry, the Revenue sought the opinion of counsel. The outcome is that the Revenue are now advised that the costs in question are allowable as expenditure on the provision of machinery or plant, and therefore qualify for the appropriate rate of first-year and writing-down allowances.

2 There has never been any dispute that other capital expenditure involved in setting up cable network systems—such as studio and transmission equipment, and the cable itself—qualifies for machinery or plant allowances.

3 The rates of allowances will be those generally in force at the time when the expenditure is incurred (in accordance with the proposals contained in the Chancellor of the Exchequer's Budget Statement on 13 March).

17 May 1984. Inland Revenue

Furnished holiday lettings and caravans

In reply to the following Parliamentary Question about the tax treatment of caravan letting—

> "To ask Mr Chancellor of the Exchequer if he will clarify his proposals for the tax treatment of income from letting caravans and pitches and the application to holiday caravan parks of the proposals on furnished holiday letting in Clause 49 and Schedule 11 of the Finance Bill"

the Financial Secretary to the Treasury, Mr John Moore MP, gave the following Written Answer yesterday—

> "The letting of caravans is regarded as an activity of leasing chattels which may amount to a trade if it is on a sufficient scale and organised and operated on a commercial basis.
>
> This can only be determined on the facts of each case and there can be no hard and fast rule of general application. Where the scale, organisation and operation is such that it does amount to a trade, the income is assessable under Case I of Schedule D; in other cases under Case VI.
>
> Income from letting pitches, that is site rents, is assessable under Schedule A to the extent that it arises from exploiting an interest in land. However, where the provision of associated services assessable under Case I of Schedule D, such as, for example, shops, accounts for a substantial part of the income, in practice the whole income will be included in the Case I computation.
>
> Clause 49 defines furnished holiday accommodation in terms which include caravans. Caravan park operators who let caravans and who are correctly assessed under Case I of Schedule D as traders will not be affected by the clause which would offer them no additional reliefs. But those assessed under Case VI, and whose lettings meet the qualifying conditions, will be able to benefit from the capital gains tax reliefs and earned income treatment the clause provides in the same way as anyone letting other forms of self-catering holiday accommodation.
>
> The clause does not apply to the letting of pitches or of residential caravans for long-term occupation."

Note

The Financial Secretary's answer makes it clear that the Finance Bill Clause 49 now before Parliament is a wholly relieving provision. It does not change the basis on which furnished holiday

PRs etc

lettings are assessed to tax but simply provides additional reliefs where the lettings are assessable under Schedule D, Case VI. Case I will continue to apply where the activities amount to a trade.

This answer should allay the concern which has been expressed that the effect of the clause may be that holiday caravan lettings can no longer qualify as a trade within Case I and will instead be taxable under Case VI.

The Government announced last year that it would be making a change in the tax treatment of furnished holiday lettings. Clause 49 accordingly provides that income from the letting of furnished holiday accommodation which meets the qualifying conditions will be treated as earned income and that the assets used in the business will be eligible for capital gains tax retirement relief and for the relief on the replacement of business assets.

Further details were given in the Inland Revenue press releases of 31 January and 15 March 1984 (see *Simon's Tax Intelligence* 1984 p 118 and p 262 respectively).

Note—FA 1984 s 50, Sch 11 have been partially re-enacted in TA 1988 ss 503, 504 (Letting of furnished holiday accommodation treated as a trade).

11 June 1984. Hansard

Taxation

Mr Heddle asked the Chancellor of the Exchequer if he will allow for deductions from revenue for tax purposes where it does not result in the benefit of profit or the production of a business asset, expenditure wholly exclusively and necessarily incurred in the following categories: (*a*) preparing and presenting planning applications where planning permission is subsequently refused, (*b*) entering architectural competitions for the design of buildings and (*c*) tendering of contracts which are not obtained; and if he will make a statement.

Mr Moore: The general rule is that expenditure of a revenue nature which is wholly and exclusively for the purposes of a trade or profession is allowable for tax. This includes the expenses of entering architectural competitions or tendering for contracts, regardless of whether these are successful and lead to profit but not the costs of abortive planning permissions which are generally of a capital nature.

HC, 11 June 1984 Vol 61 col 334

19 June 1984. Hansard

Taxpayers and Inspectors (Transcripts of Meetings)

Mr Neil Hamilton asked the Chancellor of the Exchequer what guidelines the Board of Inland Revenue gives to Her Majesty's Inspectors of Taxes regarding the use of tape recorders by taxpayers for the purposes of making accurate transcripts of meetings held between taxpayers and inspectors.

Mr Moore: The Board of Inland Revenue has issued instructions to Her Majesty's Inspectors of Taxes that the use of tape recorders by taxpayers to record meetings between taxpayers and inspectors may be agreed provided the taxpayer undertakes to provide at his own expense a full and typed transcript of the proceedings to the Inland Revenue.

HC, 19 June 1984 Vol 62 col 149

18 July 1984. Hansard

Farmers (Outgoers' Scheme)

Mr Forth asked the Chancellor of the Exchequer whether payment made to farmers under the outgoers' scheme will be subject to taxation.

Mr Moore: Under the Milk Supplementary Levy (Outgoers) Scheme 1984, details of which were announced on 16 July by my right hon. Friend the Minister of Agriculture, Fisheries and Food, any farmer claiming payment under that scheme may apply either for compensation for loss of profits in the five years immediately after ceasing to produce milk, or for compensation for the surrender of his milk quota. Payments in respect of loss of profits will be treated as receipts of the farming business and therefore liable to tax as income. Payments in respect of surrender of quota will be treated as capital and liable to capital gains tax accordingly.

HC, 18 July 1984 Vol 64 col 218

Revenue & other press releases—Hansard 15-4-85 (Outgoers' scheme). See below.
Cross reference—See TCGA 1992 s 155 (Relevant classes of assets for the purpose of transferring business assets).

2 November 1984. Inland Revenue

Incentive awards and prizes for employees: taxed award schemes

The Board of Inland Revenue has recently approved new voluntary arrangements for collecting tax on non-cash incentive prizes awarded to employees. These arrangements will be open to the providers of non-cash awards and provide an alternative and simpler method of collecting tax on such awards than the existing procedure of collecting the tax directly from the recipient.

Under the new scheme providers of such awards to their own employees or to the employees of third parties, will be able, if they wish, to arrange with the Inland Revenue to cover the recipients' *basic rate* tax liability on the grossed-up value of the award by entering into a legally binding contract which provides for the grossing-up arrangement and the payment of the related tax together with simplified reporting arrangements. The arrangements do not cover any higher-rate liability which may arise from the receipt of the award (which tax will continue to be collected directly from the taxpayer) nor do they cover the award of cash prizes or cash vouchers assessable under PAYE in accordance with the instructions in paragraph 28 of the *Employers Guide to PAYE*. Recipients of any award should continue to include details of the award on their own tax returns.

These arrangements are voluntary and are intended only for award schemes which are designed for employees. A special Valuation Unit has been established to deal with the valuation of incentive awards and to set up Taxed Award Schemes.

A note designed to give producers further details of the Taxed Award Scheme arrangements may be obtained from Inland Revenue, Incentive Valuation Unit, 4th Floor, 27 Broadwick Street, London W1V 2AE. Telephone 0171–734 1696.

Notes

1 Incentive prizes awarded to employees for reaching sales or performance targets, etc, are assessable to tax under Schedule E. Where the prize is other than cash or a cash voucher the measure of the liability to tax will usually be the cost of providing the award. The exact figure may however depend on the details of the scheme and whether the recipient is "higher-" or "lower-paid" for the purposes of the benefits in kind provisions contained in [TA 1988 Part V, Ch II (ss 153–168)].

2 At present the liability on non-cash awards is collected directly from the recipient on the basis of a notification from the provider. Cash awards and cash vouchers are paid under deduction of tax through the PAYE system.

3 The new arrangements which are made by the Board of Inland Revenue under their statutory powers for the care and management of the tax system are designed to provide an alternative and simpler method of collecting tax on non-cash awards made to employees. The new arrangements are entirely voluntary and are restricted to providers making such awards through schemes designed for employees.

4 Under the new arrangements providers will be able, if they so wish, to cover the recipients' basic rate tax liability on the grossed-up value of the award. Any higher rate tax liability will be collected from the recipient in the usual manner. The scheme also includes a simplified reporting procedure for providers and enables the recipient to receive notification of the value of the award and the tax paid on his behalf.

Revenue & other press releases—IR 18-1-90 (Improvements to the taxed award scheme). See below.

21 March 1985. Hansard

Houseboats

Mr Jessel asked the Chancellor of the Exchequer in what circumstances houseboats, whether moving or stationary, are treated by his Department as houses rather than boats in respect of (*a*) value added tax, (*b*) tax relief on interest on loans for purchase and (*c*) capital gains tax.

Mr Moore:...

For mortgage interest relief purposes a houseboat, whether moving or stationary, is treated like any other property provided it is designed or adapted for use as a place of permanent habitation [see TA 1988 s 367(1)].

For capital gains tax a houseboat will normally be an exempt asset, but if this is not the case, it may, exceptionally, qualify as a dwellinghouse.

HC, 21 March 1985 Vol 75 col 597

28 March 1985. Inland Revenue

Tips and tax

In reply to the Parliamentary Question from Mr Piers Merchant, MP:

"To ask Mr Chancellor of the Exchequer what is the Inland Revenue practice in relation to the tax treatment of tips and if he will make a statement"

the Financial Secretary to the Treasury, Mr John Moore, MP, yesterday gave the following Written Answer:

"In law, tips are part of an employee's taxable income in the same way as his other earnings. In some businesses tips can form a substantial part of an employee's take-home pay. Unfortunately not all employees return details of the tips they receive. In these circumstances inspectors of taxes may have to make an estimate of the tips earned on the basis of the facts available to ensure that the correct amount of tax is paid. Any employee who disagrees with the estimate may, however, appeal in the usual way. If agreement on the correct figure cannot be reached, the matter may be considered at an informal meeting before the independent General Commissioners.

Before making an estimate for tips, inspectors of taxes are, however, instructed to establish first who is and who is not in a position to receive them. Wherever possible, they are asked to negotiate agreed figures with the employees concerned, or with their representatives.

In the case of postmen's tips, some Tax Offices did not follow all the instructions of the Inland Revenue's Head Office. The Inland Revenue apologise for this and have reminded the Offices concerned of the need to establish the facts with local Post Office management and staff.

In the many instances where correct procedures have been followed, however, substantial amounts of tips have subsequently been returned. A recent exercise over a period of about a year was conducted by Tax Offices in one of the 14 tax regions in relation to the hotel and catering industry. In a review of employees at 500 or so establishments, amounts averaging from £750 to £1,500 per annum per employee depending on the size of the establishment were agreed upon once the facts had been established, yielding additional revenue for one year alone of some £650,000. The negotiations leading to these agreements involved discussions with individual employees in many cases; or with their representatives where large numbers were employed at a particular establishment. The lowest average agreed tips per full time employee at any one of the establishments involved was £750 per annum; and some individuals at the larger, well-known establishments agreed they received tips of up to £7,500 per annum. Such investigations are carried out by the Inland Revenue as part of their duties to counter evasion wherever it may occur."

15 April 1985. Hansard

Outgoers' scheme

Mr Knox asked the Minister of Agriculture, Fisheries and Food if he will make a statement on progress made on the outgoers' scheme for dairy farmers.

Mr Jopling: Milk producers are being given a second chance to enter the outgoers' scheme....

Outgoers' payments can be either:

(i) For loss of profits in the five years immediately after the date on which production of milk for sale ceases. Such payments will be made at the rate of 2·6p a year for each litre of quota which are to be given up under the scheme; or

(ii) As compensation for the surrender of quota at the rate of 13p per litre, with a total lump sum due being paid out in five equal annual instalments.

Payments under the scheme will be taxed as income if they are made in respect of loss of profits, or as capital if they are made as compensation for the surrender of quota. In each case the first payment will be made as soon as possible after the date on which milk sales have ceased and subsequent payments will be made at yearly intervals thereafter.

When outgoers submit their claims they will have to give several undertakings. The most important of these are that they will give up their quota allocation in its entirety and that they will not be involved with the production of milk for sale as long as the Community milk quota regulations last.

HC, 15 April 1985 Vol 77 col 27

Revenue & other press releases—Hansard 18-7-84 (Farmers Outgoers' Scheme). See above.
Cross reference—See TCGA 1992 s 155 (Relevant classes of assets for the purpose of transferring business assets).

11 June 1985. Inland Revenue

Approved employee share option schemes: Revenue revise practice on some share restrictions [TA 1988 Sch 9 paras 12, 13]

Following legal advice the Revenue has revised its practice concerning the admissibility of employee share option schemes under FA 1980 and FA 1984 [now both in TA 1988 Sch 9], where the shares are subject to a directors' discretionary veto on share transfer. In future, if a company declares that the discretionary power will not be used to discriminate against the transfer of shares acquired under the scheme, the scheme will be approved provided the other statutory conditions are met. Otherwise the Revenue's practice on approving employee share option schemes is unchanged.

1 Under the approved share option provisions the shares which a company uses in its scheme must not be subject to restrictions other than restrictions which attach to all shares of the same class. The Revenue has in the past refused to give approval to a share option scheme if the shares in question are subject either to a directors' discretionary veto on share transfer or to employee pre-emption arrangements.

2 On the question of *discretionary veto* the Revenue is *modifying* its interpretation of the legislation. In future, it will therefore be acceptable for a company to have in its Articles of Association a provision authorising the directors to refuse to register a transfer of shares. However, since its legal advice is that the exercise of such a veto in a discriminatory way could offend the statutory requirement, the Revenue will be asking any company whose Articles contain such a provision to complete a declaration. The declaration should confirm that the discretionary power of the directors will not be exercised so as to discriminate against the transfer of shares acquired under the scheme and its existence should be made known to employees participating in the scheme.

3 On the question of *employee pre-emption arrangements* the Revenue *confirms* its current interpretation of the law. In consequence, it will continue to refuse approval to any share option scheme where a company could compel an employee who leaves his job to sell his shares to another shareholder.

PRs etc

Notes

1 Under FA 1980 a company can set up a savings-related share option scheme which attracts relief from the normal income tax Schedule E charge for employees who participate in the scheme. An employee granted an option over shares under one of these schemes will be liable to CGT when he disposes of his shares, on the gain over the option price. (There would otherwise be liability to income tax on the gain as soon as the option was exercised.) To qualify for this treatment the scheme must be approved by the Board of Inland Revenue and the shares must be purchased out of the proceeds of savings derived from a special SAYE contract with either the Department for National Savings or a building society. The current upper limit on monthly contributions is £100.

2 A share option scheme approved by the Revenue under FA 1984 gives similar CGT treatment to participating employees, provided certain conditions are satisfied, but differs from a scheme approved under FA 1980 in a number of important respects. For example, it may be approved without the necessity for it to be open to all employees and it need not depend on participants taking out SAYE contracts to fund the eventual exercise of options.

3 Before giving approval to a *share option scheme* either under FA 1980 or under FA 1984 the Revenue must be sure that certain statutory requirements, relating, for example, to the scheme shares, are met. Inter alia, the provisions stipulate that any restrictions attaching to the scheme shares must also attach to all the other shares of the same class.

4 As a separate matter, the wording of FA 1978 which provides relief from income tax for approved *profit sharing schemes*, is less specific about what constitutes a restriction. The Revenue's view has always been that a more liberal interpretation is therefore possible. They have therefore accepted, and will continue to accept, that under the FA 1978 legislation a company's Articles of Association can require an employee who has ceased to work for the company to transfer his shares, but only *after* their legal ownership has passed to him from the scheme trustees. This will be either at the specific and voluntary direction of the employee concerned or after the period during which shares are held in trust has expired. (This period is currently seven years but a Budget proposal reduces it to five years.)

Note—This practice was made statutory by FA 1986 s 22(4).

25 September 1985. ICAEW

TR 588: Furniss *v* Dawson

Guidance note TR588 was issued in September 1985 by the Institute of Chartered Accountants in England and Wales, comprising—

- Text of a letter dated 8 July 1985 to the Inland Revenue following a meeting between representatives of the Institute of Chartered Accountants in England and Wales, The Law Society and the Inland Revenue.
- Text of a reply dated 20 September 1985 from the Board of Inland Revenue.

The Revenue reply is reproduced in full below, following the corresponding paragraphs from the Institute's letter.

From the text of a letter dated 8 July 1985 from the Institute of Chartered Accountants in England and Wales—

Furniss v Dawson

We are grateful to you and your colleagues for meeting representatives of the Institute and The Law Society on 10 June 1985.

Introduction

1 The meeting can conveniently be divided into two parts: the need for short-term guidance and the longer-term aspects. As explained at the meeting, although both we and The Law Society are concerned with both aspects it was felt appropriate for us to concern ourselves primarily with the former and for The Law Society to cover the latter aspect. We identified certain areas which are of immediate concern, although as stated at the meeting this is by no means intended to be exhaustive.

2 We agreed to write further on certain aspects of the matters to which we referred and, for the sake of completeness, all of the areas which we mentioned are set out in paragraphs 4–21 below. We have also referred to the need for clarification as to the instructions given to inspectors.

3 As we mentioned at our meeting the areas which we have identified below arise from no more than a quick review of topics which have been raised following the *Furniss v Dawson* decision ([1984] STC 153, HL). The fact that they have been raised is indicative of their importance but, as stated at the meeting, the list is not exhaustive and further areas might need to be covered in due course....

Note

The rest of this letter (paras 4–29) is reproduced below, before the corresponding paragraphs of the Revenue's reply.

From the text of a reply dated 20 September 1985 from the Board of Inland Revenue

I am writing in reply to your letter of 8 July.

As you know, the Board very much welcomed the recent opportunity to discuss with the Institute of Chartered Accountants and The Law Society the implications of the judgements handed down by the House of Lords in the cases of *Ramsay, Burmah* and *Dawson.*

Clearly, the interpretation of the *Ramsay* and *Dawson* judgements is a matter for the courts. It will be for the courts, not for officials, to determine the law. However, you have explained that, meanwhile, there are a number of points on which practitioners and businesses would find it helpful to have a note of how the Revenue understands the position, and in this letter I try to respond accordingly.

We start with much common ground between us. Perhaps the shortest and simplest explanation of the ''new approach'' was given by Lord Wilberforce, when he said that ''legislation cannot be required...to enable the courts to arrive at a conclusion which corresponds with the parties' own intentions''. I think many of us accept that this ''new approach'' brings interpretation of the law in this area closer to the reality, or if you like the substance, of the transactions with which it has to deal. We are also conscious that it has also brought with it a measure of uncertainty: partly because by its nature it requires us all to take a rather broader view of the legal implications of a transaction or series of transactions; but partly also because the approach is ''new'' and (as the House of Lords themselves have emphasised) will no doubt be refined further, as the courts come to consider more cases.

I do not want to get this out of proportion. It is commonplace that the courts in North America and a number of European countries have been following somewhat similar approaches for many years. And even in this country a number of fundamental questions for tax purposes—for example, the existence of a ''partnership'', of ''employment'', of ''income'' itself—have always been left undefined in the taxing statutes: there is such a wide and complex variety of facts and real-life relationships that, accepting some inevitable uncertainty at the margin, the tax code does not attempt to capture them in a mechanical formula but leaves them to be determined in the last resort by the courts, having regard to the actual facts of the particular case. Having said that, we are all agreed that the line of reasoning in *Ramsay* and subsequent cases represents a new and important development. When we discussed these issues with the Institute and the Society, we in the Revenue confirmed our readiness to co-operate with you in reducing uncertainties of this kind and (where possible) removing them. Taxpayers should not be burdened by unnecessary uncertainty in judging the likely tax consequences of their actions; and I might add that uncertainty of this kind can also make more difficult the work of those who are responsible for administering the Taxes Acts.

On your side, the Institute recognised that, whilst we could try to help with guidance and clarification of the Revenue's attitude in the normal or more straightforward case, we are not in a position to give categorical assurances. In particular, we might well take one view of a transaction standing on its own; we might take another view—and I think this follows necessarily from the approach described by Lord Wilberforce—where a similar transaction was one step in a series of transactions apparently designed to avoid tax. You have therefore said that the Institute appreciates that any response which we are able to give must be subject to the caveat that, even where it is agreed that the Revenue would not as a rule seek to invoke the *Ramsay* and *Dawson* principle, there may well be individual cases where, because of the circumstances, the Revenue would nevertheless feel it was obliged to follow the *Ramsay* and *Dawson* approach. In particular, we may need to look at all the facts of the case in order to establish the nature and legal implications of the transaction. What follows is to be read in that spirit.

I thought that it would be helpful to spell out all this, even at the cost of some length. And it is against this background that I now try to give you as positive and helpful a response as we can, at this stage, to the 10 specific questions which the Institute has raised with us....

Capital losses

4 This is perhaps the most important area; it was referred to in the Ministerial statement which mentioned "straightforward transfers of, assets between members of the same group" and there is also earlier guidance following the *Ramsay* case [*W T Ramsay Ltd v IRC* [1981] STC 174, HL] where it was stated at our meeting on 6 January 1982 that the decision would not generally be applied to "the routing of assets through a company within the same Group which has allowable capital losses and had not been acquired after these had arisen". You indicated at the meeting that this statement is still regarded as valid following *Furniss v Dawson*.

5 Although this guide is of considerable help in a clear cut case problems can still arise. We touched upon some at our meeting. For example, a significant group might be acquired for demonstrably commercial reasons but one of the companies in that group has capital losses. We remain unclear whether the routing of assets from a member of the acquiring group to use that loss would be attacked.

6 We indicated in our discussions that we would have preferred the *Furniss v Dawson* doctrine to be identified as applicable under this heading only where a company with a capital loss was acquired with that loss being its sole or main asset and with a motive of acquisition to utilise the loss in question. We believe that confirmation of this approach would do much to clarify the area of what constitutes "straightforward transfer of assets between members of the same group".

Revenue response: I agree that this is an important area where, in our view, the *Ramsay* principles are likely to have considerable application. Let me say at once that the Board stands by the assurance given on 6 January 1982, about straightforward transfers of assets between members of the same group. By contrast, as you are no doubt aware, inspectors have advanced *Ramsay* contentions in a number of cases where the effect of a series of transactions has been to transfer the benefit of capital losses from one group to another. Whether the "new approach" is thought to be applicable will depend on the facts of particular cases bearing in mind, for example, the relationship between the amounts of the loss involved, the period for which the company with the loss has been within the group and on the circumstances in which the losses have arisen. On this approach it would seem unlikely that the judgment would be invoked where the losses were a relatively insubstantial element in the acquisition, as evidenced by the circumstances in which they were utilised and the commerciality of the circumstances surrounding the acquisition.

Hive-downs

7 One of the first priorities of a receiver appointed under a floating charge is to establish whether part or the whole of the business can be disposed of as a going concern. If this is viable it will invariably produce a greater return (and incidentally, preserve jobs) than a piecemeal sale of the assets. It will also, subject to the provisions of [TA 1988 ss 343, 768] enable the tax losses of the business to be preserved and made available to the purchaser, the value of which will be taken into account in arriving at the sale price.

8 For this purpose it is the normal practice, having established the position, to hive down part or all of the business and relevant assets into a newly-formed subsidiary the shares in which are disposed of. There are sound commercial reasons for disposing of the business in this way, and it is of course important to effect the hive-down as soon as possible and certainly before a liquidator is appointed; once that happens the company is no longer the beneficial owner of its assets and [TA 1988 s 343] will not apply.

9 The reasons for the hive-down are therefore founded on sound insolvency practice so that the benefit of the tax losses, representing additional funds, is available to creditors. We have encountered cases where inspectors have stated that they will seek to apply [TA 1988 s 768] but if this fails invoke the doctrine in *Furniss v Dawson.* Since the disposal of a business by a receiver is governed by commercial considerations it would be helpful if an assurance could be given that the *Furniss v Dawson* principle will not be applied and that the transaction only requires consideration under existing law and practice as outlined above.

Revenue response: This is one of the topics on which it is particularly difficult to see at present where exactly the new approach might apply, if at all. On the face of it, the new approach might have some relevance in cases where little more than the tax losses are being hived down, though even then it would be necessary to demonstrate that there was a composite transaction and the insertion of a ''non-commercial'' step in that transaction. However, we would not normally expect the new approach to be relevant in cases where an entire trade, or part trade, together with its related assets and liabilities, are hived down with a view to its being carried on in other hands—although of course in those circumstances [TA 1988 s 768] might apply.

Dividends paid before sale of a company

10 If a subsidiary company is to be disposed of outside the group it is often normal practice, prior to disposal, to declare a dividend, to eliminate the undistributed profits of the subsidiary. This reduces the value of the shares for the purposes of arriving at the chargeable gain on disposal and effectively avoids double taxation since the profits which are being distributed have already been subject to corporation tax. Furthermore, the depreciatory transactions provisions contained in [TCGA 1992 s 176] only prohibit the creation of capital losses in this way—they do not apply to the reduction of capital gains. Again, in some groups it is normal practice to pay as dividend to the parent each year the distributable profits of each subsidiary. We consider that the *Furniss v Dawson* principle should not apply to the payment of intra-group dividends as described above.

Revenue response: We would not normally expect the new approach to apply here. There is, of course, nothing objectionable about a parent taking out profits of a subsidiary as a dividend. And, as regards [TCGA 1992 s 176] which you specifically mention, we would not regard there being a depreciatory transaction under that provision where dividends are paid out of post-acquisition profits.

Capital transfer tax

11...

Charities

12 We referred to two aspects under this heading: the use of advance payments and separate companies.

(*a*) Under the first a loan is made to the charity which is allocated by the charity to each of the (normally) three succeeding years to satisfy the terms of a deed of covenant in its favour made at the same time.

(*b*) The second arises where a charity wishes to carry on a trade the profits on which are to be used for the benefit of the charity but which do not meet the requirements of [TA 1988 s 505(1)]. In these circumstances it would be arranged that the trading activity is carried on by a separate company the profits of which are covenanted to the charity so that no tax liability arises.

13 We understand that you would not seek to invoke the *Furniss v Dawson* doctrine in 12(*a*) above and indeed this follows from the Minister's statement that the doctrine would not apply to the tax treatments of covenants. With regard to 12(*b*) above you indicated you would have no concern if the trading activities in question followed the normal ''Christmas card'' type approach but you might wish to examine any more widespread trading activity. It would be helpful, in the meantime, to define what is regarded as an unobjectionable ''Christmas card'' type trading activity.

Revenue response: I can confirm that we would not normally seek to challenge a claim for relief where a loan or other advance payment is made to a charity to satisfy the terms of a deed of covenant drawn up in that charity's favour at the same time.

Similarly, we would not normally challenge the covenanting to a charity of the profits of its trading subsidiary—provided, of course, that no circularity was involved, such as the charity providing an interest-free loan back to the trading entity or the trader effectively controlling the charity and using it as a tax-free money box.

Leasing

14 This an area mentioned in the Ministerial statement which referred to ''leasing transactions''. As stated at our meeting, by their very nature, most leases are unlikely to be ''straightforward'' and many have a tax motive while also being based upon sound commercial principles.

15 Leases vary widely in their purpose and content. They are covered by a detailed tax code which should be capable of dealing adequately with any tax avoidance schemes. We therefore took the view that it is difficult to see how *Furniss v Dawson* can apply, but if there are any areas where it is considered that the present law is inadequate, we should be grateful if you could state which areas fall within that category.

Revenue's response: Perhaps it would be helpful to make two preliminary points. First, straightforward commercial leasing transactions—no doubt the vast majority—and especially those involving hire and operating lease, are unlikely to be called into question by *Ramsay*; and second, the phasing out of accelerated depreciation may in any event reduce the extent in practice to which *Ramsay* needs to be considered in the context of leasing.

As you say, leases, or arrangements involving leasing, may very well not be straightforward. Where this is so and just like any other complicated transaction, it may be necessary for the Revenue to make sure in appropriate cases that it understands precisely what is happening before being satisfied that claims to allowances or reliefs are validly based—especially where the claims are large.

Against this background we would be concerned for example about arrangements which have the appearance of a finance lease but where there are doubts about whether a person claiming capital allowances is genuinely at risk for the financing of the activity or has actually incurred the capital expenditure concerned; where it appears that no earnings (or substantially none) flowing from the investment on which allowances are being claimed will materialise in the UK; where the lessee has directly or indirectly financed the lessor's expenditure; where there is doubt about whether expenditure has been incurred for the purposes of the claimant's trade; and generally where a composite transaction appears artificially to have been structured so as to bring it within the provisions, about claiming allowances, of the Finance Acts. In one or more of these areas it is possible that *Ramsay* could apply to the particular arrangements—certainly it is not possible to say that it would not apply.

"Bed and Breakfast"

16 It seems that, as a result of the Finance Bill 1985, ''bed and breakfast'' will revert to the pre-April 1982 procedure of sale and repurchase on consecutive days. We sought confirmation that the *Furniss v Dawson* doctrine would not be applied, although it might be necessary to limit this to transactions in shares.

Revenue response: The share identification rules introduced as part of the indexation provisions in 1982 made bed and breakfast more difficult and expensive to carry out. This year's Finance Bill reinstated the pre-1982 position. A technical amendment at Report stage to the provisions in FA 1985 Sch 19 para 18 made it clear that the provisions were not designed to make bed and breakfast transactions more difficult. But a number of provisions already apply to circumscribe such operations and it will remain necessary to make sure that the transactions involved are effective in (for instance) transferring beneficial ownership of the shares. Assets other than shares and securities may need special consideration in this context.

Husband and wife

17 In addition to the CTT aspects referred to above we referred to the practice whereby inter-spouse transfers are made to ensure that the relevant assets are owned by the spouse carrying on the trade in order to obtain rollover or retirement relief for capital gains tax purposes. We suggest that such transfers should not be subject to the *Furniss v Dawson* principle, which would be in line with the theme of the legislation that, in general, husband and wife are treated as one for capital gains tax purposes.

Revenue response: Most transactions in this area obviously would not give rise to question. However, this is an instance where it will be necessary to consider the nature of the relevant transaction as a whole and its consequences. For example, if a wife owned assets which had been used in a business carried on by the husband and genuinely transferred the beneficial ownership of those assets to the husband before the disposal of the business, it would be necessary to consider, inter alia, whether the relief claimed by the husband (whether rollover or retirement relief) exceeded the relief which would have been due had the wife herself carried on the business for the whole of the period concerned and disposed of the assets. You will see that this approach is reflected in the case of retirement relief in FA 1985 Sch 20 para 16 [TCGA 1992 Sch 6 para 16] (previously Concession D7).

Year end stock adjustments

18 One of the adjustments made in arriving at group accounts figures is the elimination of profit on intra-group sales in respect of stock held by the purchasing company at the year end since although the profit is realised by one group company it is unrealised as regards the group. The adjustment is made on consolidation so it does not appear in the books or accounts of either company, and there is therefore no tax relief on the profit which has been eliminated.

19 It is common practice, instead of making the adjustment on consolidation, for the selling company at the year end to issue a credit note to the purchasing company so that the transaction is eliminated from the accounts of both companies and treated as stock at cost to the selling company. The credit note is, of course, reversed at the commencement of the following financial year so that for tax purposes the impact is no more than a timing difference representing the commercial reality of the group profit.

20 We suggested that the *Furniss v Dawson* principle should not be applied in such cases.

Revenue response: We do not anticipate that the new approach would apply to these adjustments. However, arrangements of this nature have always had to be considered on ordinary principles, and if you find any problems in practice we should be happy to discuss them separately.

Creation of UK holding company

21 Where the shares in UK-resident companies are held by an overseas-resident company no group relief is available because the definition in [TA 1988 s 413(5)] applies only to companies resident in the UK The formation of a UK-resident holding company enables group relief to be obtained for UK companies. The same practice is often followed where an individual or family controls more than one company, since otherwise there could be no group relief between those companies. We took the view that the setting up of a holding company in these circumstances should not involve the application of the *Furniss v Dawson* principle.

Revenue response: In itself, the setting up of a UK holding company will not normally be objectionable where all the companies are resident in the UK Generally speaking, therefore, the new approach is unlikely to apply here.

...

28 November 1985. Hansard

Firemen (bounty payments)

Sir David Price asked the Chancellor of the Exchequer why the Inland Revenue has decided that bounty payments for long service for retained firemen on the completion of 10, 15, 20, 25, 30 and 35 years of qualifying service should be taxable, when comparable bounty payments to members of the Territorial Army Volunteer Reserve are free of tax.

Mr Moore: If a retained fireman or any other employee receives a bounty payment, it is part of the income from his employment and taxed accordingly.

Exceptionally, the training bounty paid to members of the Territorial Army Volunteer Reserve is exempted from tax by legislation introduced in 1947 [TA 1988 s 316].

HC Written Answer, 28 November 1985 Vol 87 cols 660, 661

31 January 1986. Hansard

Police rent allowances

Mr Deakins asked the Secretary of State for the Home Department if he will introduce legislation to remove tax on police rent allowances.

Mr Giles Shaw: Tax legislation is a matter for my right hon Friend the Chancellor of the Exchequer. But under regulation 50 of the Police Regulations 1979, the tax paid on rent allowance is reimbursed by police authorities in the following financial year by means of compensatory grant. Rent allowance is thus effectively tax free.

HC Written Answer, 31 January 1986 Vol 90 col 634

10 February 1986. Hansard

Police rent allowances

Mr Deakins asked the Chancellor of the Exchequer whether it is the practice of the Inland Revenue to seek to raise an assessment on grant paid to police officers by police authorities to compensate for tax on rent allowance paid in the previous year; and if he will make a statement.

Mr Moore: I can confirm that the grant to which the hon Member refers is chargeable to income tax and is assessed accordingly.

HC Written Answer, 10 February 1986, Vol 91, col 330

20 March 1986. Inland Revenue

Future Budget day tax changes

In the course of his speech during the Budget debate last night, the Financial Secretary to the Treasury, the Right Hon. John Moore MP, said—

> "I have now a slightly technical matter that concerns arrangements for bringing Budget changes into operation, which affect income tax and corporation tax. Every year, some changes have to take effect more or less immediately. For those which work to the taxpayers' advantage, the normal rule is that they take effect on or after Budget day, but for those changes that work the other way—by imposing or increasing tax—the practice has been to apply the changes after Budget day. In most cases, this works well enough, but there may be occasions when some people engage in forestalling, which could be costly to the Exchequer, by doing business very quickly on Budget night. To allow this would be neither fair nor sensible, and it may be

necessary in future to make changes effective from the start of Budget day. I thought it right to draw the attention of the House to this change, which may be used in a future Budget.''

HC 19 March 1986, Vol 94, cols 377–378

27 October 1986. Inland Revenue

Capital allowances: changes in accounting practice for plant and machinery under lease or subject to hire purchase ...

1 The Revenue today confirmed that the 1984 SSAP on leases and hire purchase contracts (SSAP 21) did not alter the tax position: lessees are not entitled to obtain capital allowances in respect of leased machinery or plant.

2 The lessor, by incurring the capital expenditure and retaining ownership of the assets, will normally be entitled to capital allowances.

This continues to be so even where the leased machinery etc, is capitalised in the lessee's accounts.

3 Following discussions with the Revenue the Equipment Leasing Association is recommending to its members that new leases should include a clear statement of the tax position, *ie*, that irrespective of the accounting treatment adopted, the lessee is not entitled to capital allowances on leased equipment.

Note

1 In August 1984 the Accounting Standards Committee of the six major accountancy bodies in the UK and Ireland issued SSAP 21: Accounting for leases and hire purchase contracts.

2 The standard requires, amongst other things, that the lessor under a finance lease should show the lease in his business accounts in the same way as a loan made by him, rather than as a fixed asset subject to depreciation. In the business accounts of the lessee the lease should be capitalised, *ie* it should be recorded in the balance sheet both as an asset and as an obligation to pay future rentals.

3 For lessors, the accounting practices set out in SSAP 21 are to be adopted as soon as possible and regarded as standard for financial statements relating to accounting periods beginning on or after 1 July 1984. For lessees, the accounting practices are also to be adopted as soon as possible and regarded as standard in respect of financial statements relating to accounting periods beginning on or after 1 July 1987.

4 With the growth of leasing in recent years, the way in which various types of lease should be dealt with in business accounts has become increasingly important. SSAP 21, which distinguishes operating from finance leases, sets out a standard practice for each. In particular, it requires that assets held under finance leases together with the related leasing obligations should be capitalised in the lessee's balance sheet.

5 Publication of the accounting standard has not in any way altered entitlement under present statute to capital allowances in respect of the machinery or plant which is the subject of the lease or the hire purchase contract. Two of the main rules for capital allowances—incurring capital expenditure and ownership of the assets concerned—will normally continue to be met by the lessor even though the leased machinery or plant may be capitalised in the lessee's balance sheet. [Para 28 of exposure draft 29 published in October 1981 comments on the taxation rules.] Similarly, the special rules in [CAA 2001 ss 67, 229] will continue to give entitlement to capital allowances to the hirer under a hire purchase contract.

6 The Revenue discussed with the Equipment Leasing Association what steps might be taken to reduce any misunderstandings about entitlement to capital allowances as the accounting practices in SSAP 21 are more widely adopted by lessees.

7 Although dealing with the differences between the requirements of the accounting standard and the taxing statutes is primarily a matter for lessees and their advisers, the Revenue and the Equipment Leasing Association believe that the practice which the Association is recommending to its members will be helpful to all concerned. This is aimed at minimising the possibility of lessees inadvertently seeking capital allowances to which they are not entitled.

Note—SSAP 21 is also dealt with in Statement of Practice SP 3/91 (tax treatment of rentals payable by lessee under finance lease in cases where SSAP 21 has/has not been applied).

6 November 1986. Hansard

Nurses' registration fees

Mr Dobson asked the Chancellor of the Exchequer if he will introduce legislation to enable nurses to set against tax their compulsory initial and recurrent registration fees; and if he will make a statement.

PRs etc

Mr Brooke: The Revenue has already agreed the tax relief is allowable from 1 January 1987 for the recurrent registration fees payable by nurses to the UK Central Council for Nursing, Midwifery and Health Visiting, under existing legislation dealing with fees and subscriptions payable to professional bodies [TA 1988 s 201]. No relief is allowable, however, under these provisions for initial registration fees. This follows the general principle of the Schedule E expenses rules that relief is not given for expenses incurred to put a person in a position to perform the duties of an employment, and I do not think it would be appropriate to make a special exception for nurses.

HC Written Answer, 6 November 1986 Vol 103 col 519

17 November 1986. Hansard

Income tax—payment of bank giro

Mr Stern asked the Chancellor of the Exchequer whether, in view of the fact that the new form of income tax assessment incorporates a demand note in the form of a bank giro credit, it is the intention of the Revenue to treat the tax as paid when it is paid into the payer's bank, or when the amount of tax is received by the collector of taxes.

Mr Norman Lamont: Where a taxpayer makes a payment of tax at a branch bank using the bank giro system, the Revenue treats the date stamped on the payslip by the bank cashier as the date of payment.

HC Written Answer, 17 November 1986 Vol 105 col 81

24 November 1986. ICAEW (TR 637)

Memorandum TR 637: expenditure for which tax relief is not available

In submission to the Revenue released today the Institute draws attention to a number of areas where no tax relief is available for revenue and capital expenditure (known as "nothings").

In general the Institute believes that, except where there is a specific enactment made for known reasons, all expenditure which a person is obliged to incur in connection with his trading activities should be allowable either as revenue or by way of capital allowances.

The submission sets out a number of categories under the headings of revenue and capital as follows:

Revenue

1 *Post-cessation expenses, except to the extent that relief is available under [TA 1988 s 105] against post-cessation receipts* [*Now see FA 1995*].

2 Expenses of closing down a business (except to the extent of specific relief for redundancy payments under [TA 1988 s 579]).

3 Expenditure incurred by one company in a group for the purposes of a trade carried on by another.

4 Interest (and possibly penalties) on overdue tax. If, as has been stated, the charge is intended to represent commercial restitution, the denial of tax relief cannot be justified.

5 Lump sum payments for the variation of a lease to secure a lower future rental (as in *Tucker v Granada Motorway Services Ltd.* [1979] STC 393).

6 Charges on income payable prior to the commencement of trading.

7 Abortive capital expenditure, which by definition is not of an enduring nature and must therefore be charged to revenue when incurred.

8 *Pre-trading expenditure incurred more than three [now seven] years before commencement of trade.*

9 Payments in lieu of rent where a tenant spends money on dilapidations which, because of the proviso to [TA 1988 s 34(2)], cannot be treated as a premium.

10 Expenses, other than management expenses, of an investment company (*eg* short-term interest other than bank interest).

11 Dilapidations payments generally.

12 Payments to terminate a lease of premises used for trading purposes.

13 Initial repairs deemed to be capital following the decision in *Law Shipping Co Ltd. v Jones* (48 TC 257).

14 Formation expenses.

15 Costs and duty arising on raising share capital, and share reorganisation costs (including demergers and share buy-ins).

16 *Professional costs of setting up share incentive schemes and pension schemes.* [Now see FA 1991.]

17 Incidental costs of obtaining finance to the extent not allowed under [TA 1988 s 77] (*eg* equity finance).

18 Payments for variation of loan agreements.

19 Legal expenses on acquisition and disposals of leases.

20 *The tax treatment of exchange gains and losses*...[Now see FA 1993.]

Capital

1 Expenditure on commercial buildings, which are not industrial buildings, other than those in enterprise zones and those covered by special provisions such as agricultural buildings and hotels. It should be emphasised that improvement to leasehold properties are often of little value to the lessee.

2 Expenditure on plant and machinery in buildings, particularly installation work, where there may be difficulty in obtaining capital allowances because of the lack of an adequate definition of plant and machinery. See, for example, *Cole Brothers Ltd. v Phillips* (55 TC 188).

3 Premiums on leases of over 50 years.

4 Capital expenditure on wasting assets which do not rank for capital allowances, for example, copyrights, trade marks, goodwill, purchase of mailing lists.

5 ''Know-how'' purchased as part of a trade, including franchise fees and other payments for ''know-how'' which fall outside [TA 1988 ss 530, 531].

6 Premium for the assignment of a lease.

7 Purchase of ''holes in the ground'' for rubbish tipping purposes. The value of the infilled site is usually minimal compared with the original cost (see para 16 of 1984 submission on taxation anomalies—TR 581). [See *Rolfe v Wimpey Waste Management Ltd.* [1989] STC 454 and TA 1988 ss 91A, 91B.]

8 *Lump sum payments for licences to use computer software for say a five year term. Such payments are probably of a capital rather than a revenue nature, but since the asset remains the property of the computer company capital allowances are not available to the licensee. [See 9.]*

9 *Payments for computer software generally, which may not be eligible either as revenue or as plant and machinery. ....*

Copies of the Memorandum are available from the Publications Department, The Institute of Chartered Accountants in England and Wales, Gloucester House, 399 Silbury Boulevard, Witan Gate East, Milton Keynes MK9 2HL quoting reference TR 637. Please send a stamped addressed envelope.

27 January 1987. Inland Revenue letter

Settlements: dividend waiver as disposition

Letter from the Legal Practice Directorate of the Law Society

The justification for treating [a dividend waiver] as a disposition of income by the person effecting the waiver depends upon there being an ''arrangement'' within the meaning of [TA 1988 s 670 or s 681], and it implies therefore collaboration between the shareholder(*s*) waiving the dividends and the other shareholder(*s*). While there may be collaboration between the various shareholders for the purpose of tax avoidance, the usual situation in which waivers occur is that which is found where a major shareholder is also remunerated as a director or employee of the company and decides, possibly in agreement with his fellow shareholders, that the interests of the company require that he should content himself with that remuneration to ensure that the other shareholders, not so remunerated, continue to get a commercial return on their investment. Without such a return, the investment of the other shareholders may be in question, and thus the future of the company's undertaking.

Revenue reply

Whilst we agree that to come within the settlement legislation a dividend waiver has to be part of an ''arrangement'', and therefore a settlement as defined in [TA 1988 ss 670, 681], and that there must be an element of bounty such as enhanced dividends, we cannot accept that there must necessarily have been collaboration between the shareholder(*s*) waiving the dividend and the other shareholder(*s*). There is no ''commercial motive'' test in [TA 1988 Part XV (ss 660–694)] and if as a result of the situation outlined in the third paragraph of your letter [quoted above], the other shareholders receive more by way of dividend than they would if there had been no waiver, we would need to consider the application of [Part XV]. In practice, bounty is more likely to be present where the other shareholders are trustees, minors or members of the immediate family of the shareholder(*s*) waiving dividends; but is not necessarily confined to these cases.

10 April 1987. ICAEW

Memorandum TR 657: Company reconstructions and amalgamations clearances under [TCGA 1992 s 138]

The Institute of Chartered Accountants in England and Wales issued a guidance note in April 1987 comprising the text of a letter sent to the Revenue in November 1986 and the text of a reply dated February 1987.

LETTER TO THE INLAND REVENUE

In the course of assembling, through our district society network, submission on practical difficulties and anomalies, we have become aware of a number of concerns regarding aspects of clearances under [TCGA 1992 s 138]. The purpose of this letter is to draw attention to those areas which are causing difficulty. We accept that some of the points made would involve legislative change.

BACKGROUND

1 [TCGA 1992 s 137] provides that, subject to the 5 per cent. *de minimis* rule, the relief from tax on chargeable gains available under [TCGA 1992 ss 135 and 136] apply only if the transaction is effected for *bona fide* commercial reasons and does not form part of a scheme or arrangement of which the main purposes, or one of the main purposes, is the avoidance of tax.

2 The anti-avoidance provisions of [TCGA 1992 s 137] and the procedure for advance clearance under [TCGA 1992 s 138] were introduced almost ten years ago by FA 1977 s 40 at which time a Ministerial assurance was given by Mr Joel Barnett who said:

> "We are seeking to stop major tax avoidance schemes. That is all we are about. We are not seeking to catch the innocent taxpayer."

DIFFICULTIES ENCOUNTERED

3 Our understanding of the intention of the legislation was that the government were anxious to stop schemes under which transactions were entered into which resulted in a deferral of capital gains tax but with the benefit of the sale proceeds being made indirectly available to the shareholders. However it appears to us that [TCGA 1992 s 137] is in practice being applied to deny the benefit of "roll-over" in circumstances where no cash is released directly or indirectly to a shareholder, and there is a genuine deferral of the conversion of his shares into money.

4 In particular it appears that the Board are reluctant to grant clearance under [TCGA 1992 s 138] where a company acquires another with part of the consideration being satisfied by the issue of loan stock that is redeemable within a relatively short period, if the Board consider that the company has sufficient cash reserves that it could have bought the shares for cash had the parties chosen to so structure the transaction.

5 We would be grateful for confirmation that it is not in fact the Board's policy to seek to use the section to inhibit transactions solely because they consider that a different transaction with different tax effects could have been entered into had the parties so chosen. If a person who disposes of his business is prepared to wait for several months or even several years before he can realise the value of his investment in money it does not seem unreasonable for the CGT charge not to arise until he can receive that money, even though this may be in a different year of assessment to that in which the business is sold.

6 If the Board cannot give this assurance is it possible to issue a Statement of Practice indicating the circumstances in which the Board do not consider it appropriate to grant clearance? We appreciate that this could be only a rough guide, but it would nevertheless be helpful to those responsible for the submission of clearance applications.

7 A letter granting clearance frequently ends with a statement pointing out that the clearance cannot be regarded as confirmation that [TCGA 1992 s 135] will apply in practice but is concerned solely with the question of whether or not the conditions of [TCGA 1992 s 137(1)] are satisfied. Whilst it is appreciated that this is all that the Board are required to comment on by [TCGA 1992 s 138]—and in practice where the Board take the view that a transaction does not fall within [TCGA 1992 s 135] they frequently indicate why they consider the conditions are not satisfied—the object of a clearance procedure should be to enable a taxpayer to enter into a transaction with confidence. We believe that it would be in the interest of both the taxpayer and the Revenue for any clearances under [TCGA 1992 s 138] to encompass whether or not the transaction falls within [TCGA 1992 s 135].

8 As specific consideration is given to a transaction at the time clearance is applied for it would seem sensible for the Revenue to consider the applicability of [TCGA 1992 ss 135 and 136] at that stage, rather than this being left to the local inspector after the transaction has been carried out. This would greatly assist taxpayers and we would have thought that it would be in the interest of the Revenue for a transaction to be considered once only, rather than on two separate occasions.

9 Where the Board refuse an application for clearance the right of appeal granted by [TCGA 1992 s 138(4)] is unsatisfactory as it does not give either the taxpayer or the Revenue the right to appear or produce further points before the Special Commissioners. Indeed it has been suggested to us that the evidence going to the Special Commissioners is unbalanced since it concludes with a letter from the Revenue refusing to grant clearance and setting out the detailed reasons therefore which may not have been debated with the taxpayer.

10 It will normally be the case that a transaction which is refused clearance will not be proceeded with. Clearly the existence of any anti-avoidance provision ought not to inhibit commercially-desirable amalgamations and reorganisations. Under FA 1980 s 114 a procedure was introduced for DLT purposes under which, with safeguards for the Revenue, a taxpayer could elect to be assessed on a projected transaction with the assessment becoming void if the transaction did not take place. This gave him the right to appeal to the Commissioners. If it is felt that a right of appeal against refusal of a clearance as such is likely to set an undesirable precedent it may be that some similar procedure can be adopted for CGT purposes to enable a taxpayer who is refused clearance to appeal to the Special Commissioners in relation to a projected transaction.

11 As [TCGA 1992 s 135] can apply where a shareholder owns as little as 25.1 per cent of a company it should be possible for the shareholder himself to apply for a clearance, as the company may not always be concerned to ensure that rollover applies.

12 Some inspectors of taxes seem to assume that where clearance has not been sought [TCGA 1992 s 137] will automatically apply. The clearance procedure is voluntary even for the companies and as pointed out above, is not open to an individual shareholder. We would welcome confirmation that the absence of a clearance application has no bearing either on the determination of the position under [TCGA 1992 s 135] and more importantly the attitude of the inspector of taxes thereto.

13 Considerable difficulty is often encountered where a company is sold and part of the consideration is ascertainable later and, at that time, will be satisfied by the issue of further shares in the acquiring company. In these circumstances the Revenue say that the shares comprised in the deferred consideration payment may not fall within the rollover provisions of [TCGA 1992 s 135]. We suggest that this matter should be considered further with a view to confirming that [TCGA 1992 s 135] does apply to the issue of further shares to satisfy deferred consideration arrangements.

14 Clearance under [TCGA 1992 s 138] is not forthcoming where, for example, two companies are owned equally by two individuals, and they each wish to exchange their shares so that one individual owns the whole of one of the companies, and the other individual the whole of the other. If they merely exchange their shares, capital gains tax arises and they may not have the cash to pay the tax. Therefore, a holding company can be placed over the two companies on a share for share basis [TCGA 1992 s 138] clearance being required, following which a Companies Act 1985 s 582 reconstruction is carried out and at the end of the day all the shares in one of the companies are owned by one shareholder, and all the shares in the other company are owned by the remaining shareholder. However, the Revenue refuse [TCGA 1992 s 138] clearance to this type of transaction. We consider that this matter should be reconsidered.

15 Applications under [TCGA 1992 s 138] are frequently accompanied by applications under [TA 1988 s 703]. We would welcome a simplified working procedure which enabled a joint application to be made. Given the requirement for *bona fide* commercial transactions of the two clearance areas, we assume that the form of the response to the clearance application under both headings is likely to be the same.

REPLY FROM THE INLAND REVENUE

Paragraph 3

With respect, I am not sure that this argument follows from your (perfectly correct) quotation in paragraph 2. [TCGA 1992 s 137(1)] was certainly intended to counter the abuse flowing from a share exchange accompanied by transactions which give the shareholder effective access to cash equal to the value of his original shares. But that is not the only possible form of serious abuse, and the Section is not drafted in terms that limit its application accordingly.

Paragraph 4

The Board would not, indeed could not, refuse clearance simply because the acquiring company has sufficient cash to enable it to make the acquisition for cash. If clearance is refused where the scheme envisages the exchange of the original shares for short-dated stock, it is normally because it is difficult to discern any bona fide commercial reason for the exchange or to be satisfied that avoidance is not the main purpose, or one of the main purposes, of the scheme. For fairly obvious reasons, the distinction between cash and (in effect) a post-dated cheque can be one of form rather than substance. This is not to suggest that the Board can never be satisfied that the tests in [TCGA 1992 s 137(1)] are met where the exchange will involve the issue of short-dated stock. The Board looks at each scheme individually taking account of the information and explanations given, including any explanations given for the presence of short-dated stock in the scheme.

Paragraph 5

I can, of course, confirm that the Board does not seek to use [TCGA 1992 s 137(1)] to inhibit transactions solely because a different transaction with different tax effects could have been entered

PRs etc

into had the parties so chosen. If I may say so, I should be surprised if you had any serious doubts on this point. It is for the parties involved to select the route and for the Board to determine whether the tests laid down in [TCGA 1992 s 137(1)] are satisfied. I think that my comment on your fourth paragraph is relevant also to the second half of this paragraph.

Paragraph 6

As I read your letter, you do not see a need for a Statement of Practice, unless the Board is unable to give the assurance which I have given in my previous paragraph.

However, it might be helpful if I were to say a little more by way of explanation. As you would expect, there would be severe practical difficulties in trying to draw up a comprehensive schedule or ''blacklist'' of all the circumstances in which the Board would not consider it appropriate to grant clearance. The problem of defining every kind of device capable of being used for tax avoidance was one of the reasons why the legislation was enacted in the form that it was. The second sentence in paragraph 5 of your letter illustrates the difficulty. You give as an example the situation in which a person disposes of his business and is prepared to wait for several months or years before he can realise the value of his investment in money. It is only by looking at the facts of the particular case that one can determine whether the scheme will give him effective access to the sale consideration.

The whole purpose of the clearance procedure is to afford the companies involved in an exchange the opportunity to obtain the Board's response to a specific set of proposals. It may perhaps help to reassure you—and set the matter in context—if I give you some figures. In 1986 the Board refused clearance in only 61 out of the 3,000 plus applications received—or less than 3 per cent of the total. In the specific case of short-dated stock the Board would not normally take exception to stock which has a life of more than six months.

Paragraphs 7 and 8

You recognise that the clearance procedure is limited to the question of whether the Board is satisfied that the exchange will be effected for bona fide commercial reasons and will not form part of a scheme or arrangements of which the main purpose, or one of the main purposes, is the avoidance of liability to CGT or corporation tax. Most applicants are aware of this, but where an applicant specifically asks for confirmation that [TCGA 1992 s 135] will apply, the Board are obliged to point out that the clearance does not cover this aspect.

[TCGA 1992 s 137(1)] is concerned with motives or purposes, and judgements about these can be made in advance of the transactions being effected. Whether the particular conditions in [TCGA 1992 s 135] are satisfied can only be determined after the scheme including the share exchange has been carried out.

I should perhaps explain that the Board does not give detailed consideration to the question of whether [TCGA 1992 s 135] will apply on every clearance application involving a share exchange; and the Board is therefore not in a position necessarily to confirm the applicability of [TCGA 1992 s 135] at the time that the clearance application is considered. The section lists the relevant conditions for relief, and I think that it must be for the taxpayer and his advisers to satisfy themselves here (as elsewhere in the legislation) that the statutory conditions are met. Again, however, it may be helpful if I confirm that where it is apparent to the Board that [TCGA 1992 s 135] will not apply we, as you say, advise the applicant of our view.

I hope that it will be helpful if I add a further word of explanation about motive and tax avoidance—and the relevance in this context of the *Ramsay* principle.

The *Ramsay* principle is essentially concerned with the process of analysing and characterising a given factual situation for the purpose of determining whether or how a particular set of statutory provisions applies to it. In this context it will be relevant not only in determining whether what has taken place constitutes or includes an exchange, within the meaning of [TCGA 1992 s 135(1)], but also in deciding whether avoidance is one of the main purposes. In other words, the *Ramsay* principle does not stand apart from or in addition to the statutory conditions, but it is a principle to which the Courts will have regard, when appropriate, in interpreting, the statutory conditions. It follows that, while the Board cannot, in advance of the transactions being carried out, confirm that [TCGA 1992 s 135] will apply, it would not expect, where the Board itself has granted clearance, to involve the *Ramsay* principle to deny relief afforded by [TCGA 1992 s 135] unless facts emerge that had not been disclosed in the application.

Paragraphs 9 and 10

I note your view that the present review arrangements are unsatisfactory because they do not give either the taxpayer or the Revenue the right to appear or produce further points before the Special Commissioners. An application for clearance involves an assertion that one kind of purpose (a bona fide commercial) does exist and that another (tax avoidance) does not. The view taken when the legislation was introduced was that a satisfactory judicial review of this assertion could not be carried out before anything had happened against which it could be tested. In addition, [TCGA 1992 s 138(5)] provides that a clearance is void if it is obtained on material that is not full and accurate. If the applicant was entitled to produce further points at a hearing before the Commissioners at which both parties offered arguments on the considerations, there would be room for dispute afterwards about precisely what "facts and considerations" had been disclosed. It was also considered that such a hearing would be inappropriate while the taxpayer had a further right of appeal against any assessment after the transactions had taken place.

The present procedure enables Special Commissioners to provide a speedy and impartial second opinion on the Board's decision. You say that it has been suggested to you that the evidence going to the Special Commissioners is unbalanced because it concludes with the letter of refusal in which the Board sets out its reasons for refusing clearance. The "evidence" is, I have to say, provided solely by the applicant who, as [TCGA 1992 s 138(5)] makes clear, is expected to "disclose all facts and considerations material for the decision of the Board or the Special Commissioners". The Board does not add to the corpus of evidence. The Board does, as you say, set out its reasons for refusing clearance and I assume that you would welcome this. These comments serve only to enable the Special Commissioners to identify the features that prompted the Board to refuse clearance. The evidence on which the Special Commissioners make their decision remains that provided by the applicant. You will of course be aware that the Board is required by [TCGA 1992 s 138(4)] to transmit the "notice given" along with the application and any further particulars furnished under [TCGA 1992 s 138(2)] to the Special Commissioners.

Paragraph 11

[TCGA 1992 s 138] looks to the applicant fully and accurately to disclose all the material facts and considerations. [TCGA 1992 s 138(1)] confines the right to make an application to those who can be expected to be in a position to do this. The underlying thought is that it is unlikely that the shareholders of the target company would have the full information. There would thus be the prospect of the individual shareholder being unable to comply with the request by the Board for further particulars. Even if clearance were given it could transpire that there were relevant transactions of which he was unaware which might result in the clearance becoming void. In addition, extending the right to apply to individual shareholders could lead to multiple applications which would render the procedure impracticable.

For these reasons the legislation gives all the right to apply for clearance to those who can be expected to be in a position to disclose all the material factors and considerations. It could be argued that often only the acquiring company will have full knowledge of all the relevant transactions and on this basis the right to make application should be confined to this company. It was recognised that this would be too restrictive. Allowing an application by the target company represents a reasonable compromise, which in our experience has avoided the problems which I have tried to outline.

Have you any evidence to suggest that this is a serious problem in practice?

Paragraph 12

I am a little puzzled by what you say about the attitude of some inspectors. Inspectors in District Offices are required to submit such cases to Head Office where they are considered by the same inspectors who are responsible for reviewing the clearance applications. The object of this procedure is, of course, precisely to ensure consistent treatment. It carries, and can carry, no implications on the merits of any case.

Paragraph 13

[TCGA 1992 s 135] requires that the shares or debentures be issued to a person in exchange for his original shares or debentures. The Board has been advised that that condition is not met, if the shares are issued in satisfaction of a right obtained on disposal of the shares. There are certainly therefore cases where [TCGA 1992 s 135] will not apply to shares issued to satisfy deferred consideration arrangements. The whole subject of deferred consideration is a difficult one and the problems are not confined to [TCGA 1992 s 138]. Many of the difficulties revolve around the issue of whether the right to the deferred element constitutes a debt or, as was found to be the case in *Marren v Ingles* [1980] STC 500, a chose in action other than a debt. There is the possibility of litigation on this point and this is a subject which the Board will be keeping under review. [See also Extra-statutory concession D27.]

Paragraph 14

I understand the point that you are making here. However, I have to say that, in cases which we have seen here, it is difficult to see how they can be brought within the statutory provisions.

Paragraph 15

The tests in [TCGA 1992 s 137(1)] and [TA 1988 s 703] are different and must be considered separately. Where applicants believe that they can deal with both applications in one letter they do so, making the letter one application and a copy the other. The Board has no objection to this, and in these circumstances can see no real case for formally introducing provision for a joint application.

15 January 1988. Hansard

Enterprise zones

Mr Anderson asked the Secretary of State for the Environment whether he proposes an immediate or tapered cut-off of benefits when the enterprise zone period comes to an end; and if he will make a statement.

Mr Trippier: When the period for which an area is designated as an enterprise zone comes to an end, the financial benefits arising from enterprise zone status will cease immediately.

HC Written Answer, 15 January 1988 Vol 125 col 430

Cross reference—See CAA 2001 ss 299–304.

30 March 1988. Inland Revenue

Cutting the cost of handling claims for repayment of tax [TMA 1970 s 42]

The Financial Secretary to the Treasury, the Rt. Hon. Norman Lamont MP, announced today a change in the Revenue's practice for handling claims for small tax repayments that will be introduced on 6 April 1989.

The announcement was made in response to a Parliamentary Question. In his Written Answer, the Financial Secretary said:

> ''Individuals who are not liable to tax can claim payment of the tax credit attached to dividends; they can also claim repayment of tax deducted from certain interest and other payments. Whether or not an individual is liable to tax cannot be finally settled until the end of the tax year when his or her actual income and personal allowances and reliefs for the year are known. Nevertheless the Revenue's practice has been to allow individuals to claim provisional repayment by instalments during the course of a tax year rather than waiting until the end of the year. In very many cases these involve repayment of comparatively small amounts of tax at a disproportionate cost. With effect from 6 April 1989, therefore, there will be a change in the Revenue's practice. With my approval after that date the Revenue will repay tax claimed during the course of the tax year only when the amount of tax involved exceeds a limit of £50. Where the tax repayable is less than this, the Revenue will not process the claims but instead will be asking individuals to wait until either the amount exceeds the £50 limit or the end of the tax year, whichever is the earlier, before claiming repayment.
>
> This change in practice may affect the timing of repayments, but it will not affect the amount repaid.''

Notes

1 The Revenue's practice for handling claims for repayment of tax by individuals during the course of the year is to be changed with effect from 6 April 1989. There is to be a limit of £50 below which tax repayments will not be made during the course of a tax year.

2 Examples of the kind of the claims that may be affected are claims for:

(*a*) payment of the tax credit attached to dividends;

(*b*) repayment of tax deducted from some interest payments (but not composite rate tax on bank and building society interest which is not refundable);

(*c*) repayment of tax deducted from payments made under covenants entered into between individuals before 15 March 1988.

3 Individuals will be asked not to claim until either the amount of tax repayable exceeds £50 or the end of the tax year, whichever is the earlier. Claim forms received during the course of the year where the tax involved does not exceed £50 will be returned to claimants with a request to reapply either when the amount of tax involved exceeds £50 or after the end of the tax year, whichever is the earlier. Where the amount of tax payable is less than £50 it will still be repaid but at the end of the tax year rather than during the course of it.

4 Like any large organisation the Revenue must constantly strive to keep down its costs, particularly as the cost of running the Revenue falls on taxpayers. At present the cost of handling small claims during the course of a year can be a high proportion of—or in some cases even exceed—the amount of the repayment.

5 The change is being announced well in advance to facilitate a smooth introduction, by allowing adequate time for claim forms to be revised to clarify when individuals should claim repayment.

14 April 1988. Inland Revenue

Unapproved employee share schemes [FA 1988 s 78]

...

Performance-related rights or restrictions

Under the proposed new regime there will in most cases be a charge only if, when and to the extent that value is actually shifted preferentially in to the employee shares as a result of manipulation of rights or restrictions attaching to the shares. There was concern in some representations, however, that this might also catch certain kinds of performance-related right or restriction (sometimes known as ''equity ratchets'') which are commonly to be found in management buy-outs, and under which the portion of the company's equity represented by the managers' shares is increased on some predetermined basis by reference to the company's performance.

Subject to the precise facts in each particular case, the Revenue agree that a charge should not normally arise on the triggering of such a right or restriction on achievement of the predetermined performance level, where the right or restriction attached to the shares from the outset. Obviously, the Revenue will still, for normal Schedule E purposes, need to ensure that the price paid for the shares reflects their true value including the effect of any such rights relating to them.

13 June 1988. Inland Revenue letter

Small companies' rate: non-trading holding company [TA 1988 s 13]

For the purposes of the small companies' rate (and the marginal relief) we disregard in practice a non-trading holding company if it has no assets (other than shares in its subsidiaries), no income (other than group income within the meaning of TA 1988 s 247 (2) which it has distributed in full to its own shareholders) and no expenses in respect of which it makes claims to loss or group relief.

The Revenue continue to apply the law on this basis, and the possibility of publishing it was still under consideration on 29 June 1993.

25 January 1989. Inland Revenue letter

Living accommodation: deemed director

Someone who directly or indirectly controls the company (including control through some intermediary body such as a trust) which has provided him with living accommodation will generally be a director as defined in TA 1988 s 168. He will therefore be chargeable to income tax...under TA 1988 ss 145, 146. This treatment would apply to any other benefits similarly provided. It applies whether or not the individual receives other emoluments from the company.

11 May 1989. Institute of Taxation letter to Inland Revenue

Living accommodation: deemed director

It is, of course, a question of fact as to whether the non-domiciled individual is a ''deemed'' director within the meaning of TA 1988 s 168 (8) *ie* whether he is a ''person in accordance with whose directions or instructions the directors of the company...are accustomed to act''.

It would in our experience, be unusual for *bona fide* directors of a non-resident company to effectively rubber stamp ''directions or instructions'' of the non-domiciled individual. Indeed, such actions might call into question the residence status of the company. Accordingly, we find it difficult to imagine many cases where TA 1988 s 168 (8) will be in point.

However, even if the individual is found to be a ''deemed'' director under the above provisions he still cannot in our view be chargeable to income tax under Schedule E by reason of s 168(8) alone. This is because under TA 1988 s 19 (1) tax is ''...charged in respect of any office or employment on the emoluments therefrom...''.

It seems clear to us that a ''deemed'' director cannot be liable to tax under TA 1988 s 145 and 146 (see, for example, the article ''UK homes of foreign domiciliaries'' by Robert Venables, *Taxation,* 16 February 1989, Vol 122, No 3187, pp 468–471) but whether correct or not, they are in our opinion unnecessary in view of the comments above.

14 July 1989. Inland Revenue letter

Living accommodation: deemed director

We agree, of course, that it will depend on the facts of each particular case whether someone who is not domiciled in the UK is a ''deemed'' director within TA 1988 s 168(8); and that the precise way in which a company is managed and controlled may well affect its residence status. But there would be circumstances where a resident but non-domiciled individual would be ''deemed'' director of a non-resident company. I do not think that this is in any way inconsistent with the view that such cases are not likely to be frequent.

The main point you raise, however, is the question of whether, as a matter of law, a ''deemed'' director can be charged to tax under Schedule E because in your view there is no office for such a charge to attach to within TA 1988 s 19. Our view is that s 19(1), para 5 relaxes the charging provision so that it is necessary in these cases only to show that the charge under s 145 and s 146 can be applied.

We are aware, of course, that our view has been questioned by some commentators, including recently Mr Robert Venables in the *Taxation* article to which you refer. We have looked at the arguments, but our legal advice continues strongly to support the view that a ''deemed'' directorship can lead to income tax charges under s 145 and s 146 on the value of provided accommodation.

6 September 1989. ICAEW

Memorandum TR 760: Taxation procedural matters

INLAND REVENUE PROCEDURAL MATTERS

Note of a meeting in April 1989 between representatives of the Inland Revenue and the Institute of Chartered Accountants in England and Wales.

BACKGROUND

1 The meeting in April 1989 was the latest in a series of meetings to consider a number of procedural difficulties brought to the attention of the Institute by its members.

2 The previous meeting of a similar kind was held in March 1988, the agreed note which was issued in July 1988 as TR 708.

...

GENERAL COMMISSIONERS

7 The Institute accepted that the Revenue have no jurisdiction over the General Commissioners and complaints must be addressed to the Council on Tribunals or the Lord Chancellor's Department. Their points were therefore confined to cases largely involving conduct by inspectors.

CONFIRMATION OF ESTIMATED ASSESSMENTS

8 They referred to a standard letter issued by certain inspectors stating that from 30 June 1988 they would ask the General Commissioners to confirm estimated assessments, in the absence of accounts, at the first hearing. They asked whether this represents a general Revenue policy.

9 The Revenue considered this to be reasonable and helpful for the inspector to state in advance what his general attitude would be. It was then entirely a matter for the Commissioners to accept or reject the inspector's request. There is no central policy in this matter because inspectors must follow the wishes of their local Commissioners. Accountants could ask the clerks what the General Commissioners were likely to accept. And of course accountants could contact the inspector if there was difficulty in supplying the required information. The Institute pointed out that clerks are often not easy to contact.

CASE STATED

10 The Institute raised the question of preparation of a case stated. The Revenue said that the means of preparation is up to the clerk: he would normally consult both parties. Sometimes the clerk may be inexperienced and ask the inspector to help prepare the initial draft but this is very rarely the case. Internal instructions allow it, but emphasise that an inspector must ensure that he is impartial. When the case has been drafted, both parties to an appeal have an opportunity of commenting before the Commissioners finally approve it. Within the Revenue the draft is referred to their solicitor and Head Office.

NOTICES BY CLERKS

11 The Institute referred to a lack of consistency as to the notice given for dates of hearings. Notice given is often far too short and it would be helpful if the times of hearings could be staggered instead of all being stated to start at the same time.

12 The Revenue agreed that there is inconsistency, but this is a matter for the Commissioners. It is their normal practice to hear first the cases of those who have attended: staggering may be inconvenient because of the non-attendance by taxpayers or their agents.

13 The Institute referred to a change of practice in the Bournemouth area under which, from April 1989, notices of appeal hearings, based on the Inland Revenue computer listing, will be issued to the taxpayer but a copy of the notification will not be sent to the accountant.

14 They expressed concern at this since clients assume that copies of correspondence relating to their tax affairs, including notices of appeal hearings, will be sent to their accountants. Considerable difficulties will therefore arise to taxpayers, their advisers, and the Revenue since clients will not always advise their accountant when a notice of appeal hearing is received.

15 Furthermore this change has not been widely published and may well apply in other districts unbeknown to taxpayers or their accountants in these areas.

16 The Revenue said that there had recently been a change in practice. Using the CODA system, Districts could with the clerk's agreement now arrange for the computer production of notices for issue to taxpayers and their agents. However the issue of these notices still remain the responsibility of the clerk to Commissioners.

17 Districts have encouraged clerks to make full use of these arrangements in the interests of overall economy and they understood that this was generally the case. Commissioners and their clerks are independent of the Revenue and their decision on the procedures and arrangements to be adopted was a matter for them alone.

18 The legal requirement is for the clerk to issue a notice to the appellant. In the Bournemouth area one clerk has not agreed to issue copy notices to agents. This had led to the position outlined by the Institute.

19 The matter was of course one which should in the first instance be raised by local accountants with their local Commissioners. But where the position still remained unsatisfactory, local arrangements might well be made with local Districts if this was found to be of mutual benefit both to inspectors and accountants.

20 The running of Commissioners' meetings was a matter solely for them and arrangements differ throughout the country. Whilst the Revenue encourage local Districts to make local arrangements where this was beneficial to all concerned, they felt it would not be appropriate or indeed possible to issue standardised guidelines to all local offices.

21 In the particular instance raised, the Revenue understood that discussions were taking place between the local inspector and local accountants and they trusted that the matter could be resolved to both parties' satisfaction.

...

COPY CORRESPONDENCE

36 The Institute referred to difficulties which arise especially under the present erratic postal service where there is a dispute as to whether an election has been made: where the accountant states that it was but the inspector states that it was not.

37 They suggested that it would be appropriate to issue guidance as to how such disputes might be resolved especially as the legislation (such as TA 1988 s 288) often merely says that the election must be ''made'' within the time stated. For example, would a copy of the correspondence or the election form held by the accountant or the taxpayer be accepted and does the inspector have a register of post received?

38 The Revenue said that an election must be received: it will be accepted as having been received within the time limit if it is posted in the reasonable expectation that it will be received in time.

39 No register of post received is kept in tax districts: to do so would be very expensive administratively as it would involve 150 million documents per annum.

40 If there is a dispute the inspector will ask for evidence such as recorded delivery receipts or a well maintained post book, but inspectors have to be careful as there have, for example, been cases of people forging carbon copies.

DEDUCTION OF INCOME TAX

41 The Institute referred to the case where interest is paid by a company on a loan from its pension fund. This is subject to deduction of tax, which must be accounted for on form CT 61: the pension scheme then has to reclaim the tax. They understood that sometimes informal consent can be obtained on a discretionary basis to pay gross and suggested that it would be helpful if a more formal consent procedure could be adopted.

PRs etc

42 The Revenue said that they are aware of a 1979 concession which applies where a pension fund sets up an insured scheme direct with a life office. The life office then makes a loan to the pension fund trustees who in turn make a corresponding loan to the company. In these circumstances the Revenue accept a gross payment of interest to the pension fund. Following a review in 1985, it was decided this concession should not be extended to other pension schemes.

SHARE VALUATION DIVISION DISTRICT VALUERS

43 The Institute referred to considerable delays at the Share Valuation Division and referred to complaints received about excessive delays in the District Valuers Office in respect of valuations of land and property.

44 The Revenue said that the first priority of valuers must be non-domestic property. On the valuation of shares considerable efforts have been made, including overtime working, and 65–70 per cent of cases are dealt with within twelve months, but there have been considerable staff losses. A note has been issued to inspectors reminding them that valuation requests should be made to the Share Valuation Division as early as possible.

REPAYMENT OF TAX DEDUCTED AT SOURCE

45 The Institute referred to cases brought to their attention where repayments of tax deducted at source are not made until the Revenue have satisfied themselves that the tax has been paid over by the person making the payment. A similar point arises in respect of payments deducted by contractors from payments to sub-contractors. They suggested that repayments should be made or credit allowed provided an apparently valid R185 or SC60 is produced.

46 The Revenue confirmed that repayments are made or credit allowed provided that an apparently valid R185 or SC60 is produced. But there are exceptions, for example, when the taxpayer or sub-contractor is not resident in the UK

LIAISON BETWEEN INSPECTORS AND HEAD OFFICE

47 The Institute suggested that inspectors sometimes appear to be reluctant to contact Head Office about administrative weaknesses and by way of example they referred to a case where a bank notified an incorrect amount of interest as having been credited to the account of a client, which led to considerable problems. Extensive delay arose because the inspector was not permitted to communicate directly with the bank. He agreed that it would have been better had he been able to do so, but refused to make this suggestion to Head Office.

48 The Institute enquired as to whether it is Revenue practice to encourage inspectors to put suggestions for administrative improvements to Head Office.

49 The Revenue said that it is right that the inspector should not contact the bank concerned: that complies with Head Office instructions. He should obtain clarification through the taxpayer by reference to his bank statement or his bank.

50 This is because the banks provide a considerable number of slips giving the required information and it is not easy for them to backtrack. Furthermore, the slips are provided to districts in which the branch is situated and liaison with the bank has to be through that district. The inspector making the enquiry could go back to the district concerned to whom the slips had been distributed, but this takes a long while.

51 Regarding the general point the Revenue confirmed that there is a thriving administrative suggestions scheme. Some 4,000 suggestions are put forward each year, all of which are circulated: such a system has been in force for many years. In 1988 £43,000 was paid out in awards.

...

5 October 1989. Inland Revenue letter to Institute of Taxation

Gains from share options: non-residents

It is our view that, in general, Schedule E liability does arise under TA 1988 s 135 on the exercise of a share option by a director or employee who has ceased to be resident in the UK, provided that the requirement of TA 1988 s 140(1)(*a*) (that the office or employment by reason of which the option was granted was within Schedule E Case I at the date of grant) is satisfied and that the share option contract constitutes a UK source.

The Board of Inland Revenue does, however, have a duty under TMA 1970 to exercise its ''care and management'' role impartially and efficiently. It does not, therefore, pursue liability in particular cases where the circumstances in which the liability arises and the sums in question would not justify the costs and difficulties of collection of a charge to tax.

It is against this background that para 5.2 was included in booklet IR25 (1977) making the general comment that the question of charging to tax the s 135 liability of non-residents would not normally arise in practice.

We confirm that the domicile of the individual is not relevant to the point at issue. The purpose of the two examples in Chapter 5 of booklet IR25 was to illustrate the inter-relationship of foreign income deductions available under FA 1974 against "foreign emoluments" and under FA 1977 against "other emoluments", with share option gains which, as explained in para 5.3, would for this purpose be "treated as emoluments".

The domicile of the individual is only of importance in determining whether the deemed emoluments on the exercise of share options are "foreign emoluments" or "other emoluments" for the purpose of considering if any foreign income deduction is available.

Example 1 in Chapter 5 highlights the fact that the option holder is employed by a UK resident company, to illustrate that the emoluments concerned are "other emoluments" and that a special foreign income deduction under FA 1977 is being considered.

Example 2 is concerned with foreign emoluments (the requirements of which are that the employee must be non-domiciled and the employer non-resident in the UK) and the availability of the standard FA 1974 deduction against those emoluments.

It is not our view that the guidance and information in para 5.2 of booklet IR25 and example 1 only apply to foreign nationals.

In recent years, with the increase in share values and the share option gains which have resulted, we have been asked by taxpayers and their professional advisers to clarify how in practice we apply the general comments made in para 5.2 of IR25 (1977). As each case must be considered on its own facts, it is obviously difficult to comment in general and yet be more specific. When asked, we have, therefore, illustrated our approach by considering extremes:

(*a*) At one extreme we would not seek to charge to tax an employee who is normally resident and employed outside the UK, who whilst working in the UK for a brief period is within Schedule E Case I and is granted an option over shares in the overseas parent company by the UK subsidiary for which he is working, if that employee realises a share option gain—*eg*: by exercise of that option when he is not resident and not ordinarily resident in the UK

That situation, or a variation of it, is what has been considered to be the normal case involving the exercise of share options within s 135 by non-residents. In such a case the share option gain would probably be related to the employment for the whole group, the duties of which would mainly have been carried on outside the UK To pursue liability in those circumstances would be both unrealistic and uneconomic.

(*b*) At the other extreme, we should certainly seek to assess tax on an employee who is normally resident and employed in the UK, whose share option gain relates primarily to an employment carried on in the UK, who although non-resident at the time of exercise etc of that option, nevertheless retained significant UK connections—*eg*: by way of property and other investments.

A foreign national may be the prime example of an employee who is normally resident and employed outside the UK, but it is not the only example. We would not therefore seek to distinguish the citizenship of the non-resident employee in question in deciding whether his share option gain should be charged to UK tax under TA 1988 s 135.

Note—Booklet IR25 (1977) has been withdrawn. As to approved schemes see IR99, IR100.

8 January 1990. ICAEW

Memorandum TR 788: Inland Revenue procedural matters: independent taxation and reimbursement of taxpayers' expenses

NOTE OF A MEETING IN NOVEMBER 1989 BETWEEN REPRESENTATIVES OF THE INLAND REVENUE AND THE INSTITUTE OF CHARTERED ACCOUNTANTS OF ENGLAND AND WALES

INDEPENDENT TAXATION

[Paragraphs 1 and 2 concerned the timing of publication of guidance for practitioners—now available as booklet IR 83.]

3 As regards tax returns the Revenue stated that the returns will not be sent to all married women in April 1990. They will concentrate on those where it seems likely that the Revenue will be required to make an assessment, but they emphasised that all married women will be responsible for notifying chargeability of income whether or not a return is received.

4 The Revenue also referred to the effect of independent taxation on investigations. Under independent taxation there will be a right to confidentiality between husband and wife in financial matters. Inspectors will respect this right to confidentiality in all cases, including investigation cases. Spouses will not, for example, be questioned about their personal finances in each others presence without prior agreement.

5 But the underlying inter-dependence which has existed between husband and wife in many cases will remain and inspectors may, in the course of investigating one spouse, need information concerning or from the other. Every effort will be made by inspectors to obtain such information without unwarranted disclosure and to ensure that information provided by one spouse is not gratuitously given to the other. However, it remains open to the inspector to take such action as is necessary and reasonable to enable him to perform his duties.

6 They said that, in effect, following the introduction of independent taxation, where either husband or wife is being investigated, married persons will be in the same position with regard to confidentiality as are single persons.

7 Husbands will remain liable for tax, interest and penalties on the income or gains of their wife for years prior to independent taxation. But if a wife should wish to settle any such liability personally, the inspector will normally agree.

8 A national programme of training has been carried out to ensure that all inspectors are aware of the rights of husband and wife with regard to confidentiality and of the approach expected of them.

9 The Institute wished to ensure that the position is adequately monitored and that inspectors are properly trained to operate the system. The Revenue confirmed that programmes are already in hand to achieve this.

REIMBURSEMENT OF TAXPAYER'S EXPENSES

10 The Revenue referred to the practice of the Board with regard to the reimbursement of taxpayers' expenses on investigations which had been set out in the letter of 16 June 1975 from Sir Norman Price, KCB, the then Chairman of the Board. This had been issued as SP/A31.

11 They pointed out that, in general, the Board does not reimburse the taxpayer for the costs of an unsuccessful investigation. The exception is when the taxpayer's costs arise out of a serious error on the part of the department, either an initial error of judgment, or an error of judgment which becomes serious because it is persisted in. Claims under these heads are paid where appropriate.

12 They said that there has been a tendency in recent months for claims to be submitted, just because the investigation is settled for nil. It is not accepted that a nil settlement means that there has been a serious error of judgment on the part of the inspector.

13 Nil income tax settlements, at 7 to 8 per cent of the annual total, have not varied for some years. The inspector has to justify the reason for his enquiry. There is a distinction between not being satisfied and raising a sequence of enquiries to seek clarification. If an inspector were to persist in his enquiries, having been given facts or reason to be satisfied, then such persistence might amount to a serious error of judgment such that payment would be entertained.

14 In the cases which they had seen recently, this is not the situation. The inspector's actions have been appropriate in the circumstances of the case. The Revenue believes that a nil settlement will sometimes be the proper outcome of an investigation. In these circumstances, the accountancy fees are generally allowable as a Case I deduction (Statement of Practice A28), but the costs would not be reimbursed.

15 The Institute said that inspectors often appeared to move in an over zealous way and refuse to give up when it seems clear that there is nothing wrong. In such cases clients become annoyed and blame their accountant. It would be helpful were the inspector, at the end of a case which had resulted in nil adjustments, to acknowledge the problem in a pleasant way at the conclusion of the investigation.

16 The Revenue said that if a case is settled for nil, then inspectors are encouraged to write a letter at the conclusion of their enquiries setting out why the case was taken up and expressing gratitude for the explanations provided which have satisfied the initial doubts. It is hoped that such actions will help to overcome the understandable concern caused by the enquiries.

17 The Revenue confirmed that, although Statements of Practice A28 and A31 are in the section of the Press Release of 18 June 1979 applicable to income tax, they are equally applicable to corporation tax and capital gains tax.

18 January 1990. Inland Revenue

Incentives for employees—improvements to the taxed award scheme

Employers and others who provide non-cash incentive awards or prizes for employees have since 1984 been able to meet the recipients' income tax liability at the basic rate under the Revenue's taxed award scheme. From today, such schemes can also cover higher rate liability.

Commenting on the new arrangements, Mr Peter Lilley, MP, Financial Secretary to the Treasury said—

> "The taxed award scheme introduced in 1984 [see Inland Revenue Press Release, 2 November 1984] has proved popular with employers because it is simple to operate. And it is popular with employees who would otherwise have to pay the basic rate tax due on incentive awards and prizes, like cameras or holidays. Now we are responding to requests from employers that they should be able to meet higher tax rate liabilities too, so that they can be sure that the employee has no further tax to pay. This should be a very useful development of the scheme."

DETAILS

1 Those employers who provide non-cash incentive awards and prizes for their own employees, and most of those who provide such prizes for employees of third parties, can operate the Revenue's taxed award schemes.

2 These schemes have two objectives. First to allow the provider of the incentive to pay the tax due on the award, so that the incentive for the recipient is not blunted by having to pay tax on the award. Second, to provide an economical means of collecting the tax due—in bulk, instead of from individual recipients.

3 Before an incentive campaign beings, the provider enters into a contract with the Inland Revenue's Incentive Valuation Unit to pay the tax on the total value of the awards to be made. From today the provider can pay tax at the basic rate or at the higher rate or both. There are separate contracts for the basic rate and the higher rate schemes.

4 The amount of tax payable is worked out on the ''grossed up'' value of the award to the recipient. This takes into account the income tax due on the tax paid by the provider which is strictly the liability of the recipient.

5 The administration has been kept to a minimum. Providers must give award recipients certificates giving details of tax paid, so that they can complete their tax returns correctly, or claim repayment if appropriate. For basic rate schemes providers give the Revenue details of award recipients so that any higher rate tax can be collected. For higher rate schemes only a summary of the awards made and tax due are required.

6 If too much tax is paid (because, for example, tax is paid at the higher rate when the award recipient is liable only at basic rate) award recipients can make repayment claims to their own tax office.

7 Liability to NIC can arise on the tax which providers pay on behalf of their own employees. The taxed award scheme does *not* cover this liability. Further information is given in the Employer's Manual on National Insurance Contributions (NI 269) available from Local Department of Social Security Offices.

8 In the year to 5 April 1989 600 schemes were operated for basic rate tax covering awards valued at over £42 million. The tax paid came to more than £14 million.

9 Details of the taxed award scheme arrangements including an application form, sample contracts and forms are available from Inland Revenue, Incentive Valuation Unit, Room 135, New Wing, Somerset House, London WC2R 1LB (telephone: 0171–438 7329 or 7253).

23 February 1990. ICAEW

TR 781: Guidance on ownership of documents and records

The Institute of Chartered Accountants in England and Wales have issued a statement giving guidance to its members on the considerations involved in determining whether documents and records are the property of the client or the accountant. The question of ownership may be of particular relevance in considering requests made by tax authorities for the production of documents following the changes made by FA 1989. Copies of the statement may be obtained from the Publications Department, The Institute of Chartered Accountants in England and Wales, Gloucester House, 399 Silbury Boulevard, Central Milton Keynes MK9 2HL, quoting reference TR 781. Please enclose a stamped addressed envelope.

Note—The statement appears in *Accountancy*, May 1990, pp 134–136 and the Members Handbook section 1.302.

15 March 1990. ICAEW

TR 786: Tax position on examination prizes

The Institute of Chartered Accountants in England and Wales have released an exchange of correspondence with the Revenue in which they express concern about two aspects of the decision to tax examination prizes as benefits: the lack of public announcement and its wider implications. They also suggest that there should be an extra-statutory concession.

In their reply the Revenue outline the background pointing out that initially there was little impact because of the earnings threshold [£8,500] but subsequently they wrote to all those who had previously sought guidance and they have responded to subsequent specific enquiries. They do not consider there is any case for an extra-statutory concession.

30 March 1990. Hansard

Professional bodies (membership)

Mr Cartwright asked the Chancellor of the Exchequer if he had any plans to allow unemployed professional people to claim tax relief on their membership of professional bodies as if they were employed.

Mr Lilley: The general position is that, under TA 1988 s 201, an employee may have tax relief for annual subscriptions to a professional body if the subscription is paid out of the employee's pay, it is paid to a body approved by the Inland Revenue under TA 1988 s 201 (3) and the activities of the body are relevant to the duties of employment. A professional subscription paid during a period of unemployment would not normally satisfy the conditions for relief, but where a subscription is paid during a period of unemployment and the individual was employed during the same tax year (in a job to which membership of the professional body was relevant) tax relief would usually be given against the income from that employment. We have no plans for changing the rules of this tax relief.

(HC Written Answer, 30 March 1990 Vol 170 cols 333, 334)

19 April 1990. Inland Revenue

Benefits in kind: valuation of living accommodation provided for employees in England and Wales

With the approval of Treasury Ministers, the Revenue have today explained how the benefit of new living accommodation provided for employees will be valued for income tax purposes following the ending of domestic rating in England and Wales from April 1990.

The value of the benefit for income tax purposes is at present generally taken as the gross annual value for rating purposes. This will continue for properties on existing rating lists. For new properties estimated values will be used. This practice already applies for properties in Scotland, where domestic rating ended in April 1989.

DETAILS

1 Most properties are included on the existing domestic rating list. Where there has been no material change of circumstances the existing valuation of properties will continue to be used as the basis of the income tax charge where accommodation is provided for an employee by virtue of his employment.

2 Following the introduction of the community charge in England and Wales domestic rating lists are no longer being maintained. For new properties, therefore, and those where there has been a material change of circumstances, employers will be asked to provide an estimate of what the gross annual value would have been had rates continued. The tax office will agree such estimates with assistance from the local District Valuer's Office.

NOTES

1 Where an employee is provided with living accommodation by reason of his employment he is (unless qualifying for a specific statutory exemption) liable to tax on the value of the accommodation provided. A Revenue press release of 10 November 1989—''Income Tax: Abolition of domestic rates and introduction of community charge'' announced a similar basis to that described in this press release for establishing the value of new accommodation in Scotland, where domestic rating ended in April 1989.

2 The Government has already announced that, because domestic rating lists will become increasingly outdated, it is reviewing the long term basis of the tax charge on living accommodation with a view to introducing in due course new rules for the future.

3 The present main income tax charge is in TA 1988 s 145 which provides that the measure of the benefit is the annual value of the property occupied (or the outlay on rent if that is greater) less any rent paid by the employee. In practice the annual value has generally been measured by reference to the property's rating value.

4 FA 1983 introduced from 1984–85 a supplementary charging provision for more expensive accommodation in what is now TA 1988 s 146. Where the living accommodation plus improvements cost more than £75,000, there is an additional income tax charge which is determined by applying the ''official rate'' of interest (which is used for taxing the benefit of cheap loans and is currently 16·5 per cent.) to the amount by which that cost or, in certain circumstances, market value exceeds £75,000. A press release of 18 August 1988 explained that properties whose actual cost (plus improvements) was less than £75,000 are not within the scope of the additional charge even if their market value exceeds £75,000.

5 The domestic rating system is continuing in Northern Ireland. The annual value as appears on the domestic rating lists will therefore continue to be used to value living accommodation for both new and existing properties.

June 1990. ICAEW

TR 799: Tax aspects of the Insolvency Act 1986

Guidance note issued in June 1990 by the Institute of Chartered Accountants in England and Wales comprising a memorandum submitted to the Revenue and the text of their response. [Only the Revenue response is printed below].

INTRODUCTION

(*a*) The Inland Revenue deal with every administration order and voluntary arrangement proposal on its own individual merits, taking into account all known features of the case. When deciding how to vote, the Revenue give consideration to, amongst other things, the way in which the taxpayer has attended to his tax obligations, the level of uncertainty over assets and liabilities and whether a voluntary arrangement is the appropriate course for the Revenue to approve as a creditor. The Revenue are also very much aware of the interests of other parties and of the purpose of the voluntary arrangement procedure.

(*b*) Both the Inland Revenue's enforcement office and its collector's offices have instructions on how to deal with matters within their own areas of responsibility. But because every case is different, rather than adhering to strict guidelines, these instructions provide for the exercise of judgment upon the facts and background of each particular case. There have been no Inland Revenue Press Releases or statements of practice dealing with any aspects of the new insolvency legislation.

(*c*) The Revenue are presently liaising with the Department of Trade and Industry over revised regulations and notes for guidance of insolvency practitioners on the lines of those issued in 1977.

PRs etc

DETAILED COMMENTS

Administrators—liability to tax

(*a*) In most circumstances tax remains the company's liability.

(*b*) However, notwithstanding this, the administrator can discharge the liability of the company under:

- (i) his general powers in the Insolvency Act 1986 s 14(1);
- (ii) his specific power 13 in Sch 1 of that Act.

(*c*) Moreover, he is liable to account for PAYE/NIC deductions. As agent of the company (s 14(5)) he pays emoluments to its employees. He thereby becomes an employer within the 1973 PAYE regulations (reg 2; also SI 1973/334 reg 3) and thus liable to deduct the appropriate tax.

(*d*) Although, under s 20(2), the administrator is discharged from liability arising post his release and from liability outstanding at the date of his release, if a winding up order is made he may be liable under s 212(1)(*b*) in respect of the period for which he was, effectively, the employer.

Accounting period

(*a*) TA 1988 s 12 sets out the circumstances in which an accounting period ends. These include the commencement of a liquidation (s 12(7)); the cesser of a trade (s 12(3)(*c*)).

(*b*) It is considered that neither the filing of an administration order petition, nor the making of an administration order, would bring about the end of an accounting period.

Beneficial ownerships tests

(*c*) Whilst the Revenue would not normally regard an administration order itself as affecting the beneficial ownership tests of the various group relationships of a parent company, it is possible that proposals by the administrator which are approved under the Insolvency Act 1986 s 24 might well do so.

(*d*) Arrangements by the administrator for the sale of the shares in subsidiaries, even if they did not have the effect that the company subject to the order lost beneficial ownership of the shares in the subsidiaries, would by virtue of TA 1988 ss 240(11), 410(1)(*b*) respectively cut off entitlement to group relief and to set off by the subsidiaries of surrendered advance corporation tax.

VOLUNTARY ARRANGEMENTS

Tax treatment of the debtor

(*a*) The taxation treatment of debts which have been released is dealt with by TA 1988 s 94. This provides that where, in computing for tax purposes the profits or gains of a trade, profession or vocation, a deduction has been allowed for any debt incurred for the purposes of the trade etc, then if the whole or any part of the debt is later released the amount released is to be treated as a receipt of the trade etc arising in the period in which the release is effected.

(*b*) TA 1988 s 94, originated in FA 1960 s 36, the aim of which was to rectify an anomaly whereby a trader incurred a debt, obtained a tax deduction for the amount of the debt, and subsequently got his creditor to release him from all or part of the debt. The courts had held that the amount released could not be taxed even though the trader had obtained a deduction for the debt. The legislation in what is now s 94 therefore imposes a charge in these circumstances.

(*c*) It is a feature of the legislation that it only applies where a debt is formally released by the creditor. Thus the mere failure to pay or even the bankruptcy or liquidation of the debtor will not give rise to a charge under s 94.

(*d*) There is a release where there is a formal arrangement with creditors. The position is similar where there is a scheme approved by the court, notwithstanding that there were some creditors who did not want to agree but were obliged to do so because the necessary majority agreed. A compromise in satisfaction of debt under a voluntary arrangement would therefore give rise to a ''release'' which would be treated as a taxable receipt of the debtor by virtue of s 94.

Tax treatment of the creditor

(*e*) The creditor will not be entitled to relief in respect of any part of a debt which is to be paid to him under the terms of an arrangement. But the release of a debt (or part of a debt) by virtue of a voluntary arrangement may not necessarily entitle the creditor to a deduction. In particular, a deduction may only be allowed by virtue of s 74(*j*) for bad debts proved to be such and doubtful debts to the extent that they are respectively estimated to be bad. A release in excess of an amount arrived at on that basis is unlikely to be an allowable deduction.

(*f*) Inspectors will usually need to consider all the facts of a particular case before deciding whether a deduction is due in respect of any part of a debt which has been released.

Status of tax liability (TA 1988 s 94)

(*g*) Both rules 1.28(*b*) (company voluntary arrangements) and 5.28 (individual voluntary arrangements) provide what ''fees, costs, charges and expenses'' may be incurred for the purpose of a voluntary arrangement. Apart from those sanctioned by the voluntary arrangement itself, those permitted are defined as those which either would be payable, or would correspond to those which would be payable, (1) in an administration or winding up (companies); or (2) in the debtor's bankruptcy (individuals)—see rule 1.28(1)(*b*)(ii) and rule 5.28(*b*)(ii). The relevant rules for this purpose are rules 4.218 and 6.224—order of payment of costs etc out of estate. The only relevant provision in rule 4.218 is at rule 4.218(1)(*b*) ''expenses incurred or disbursements made by the Official Receiver or under his authority, including those incurred or made in carrying on the business of the company''. Clearly the release of a debt by a creditor giving rise to a taxable receipt under s 94 cannot be within rule 4.218(1)(*b*). The same applies to the corresponding rule for individuals at rule 6.224(1)(*b*) which is in similar terms. The s 94 tax liability, therefore, is outside the ambit of the Insolvency Rules.

INTEREST PAYMENTS UNDER INSOLVENCY ACT 1986 S 189

Deduction of tax and charges on income Inland Revenue response

(*a*) In normal circumstances interest paid under the Insolvency Act 1986 s 189 is not considered to be annual interest. There would, therefore, be no obligations or right for the payer to deduct tax.

(*b*) However, it is possible for the interest to constitute annual interest. This is on the basis that the period for which the interest is payable is known at the time it is paid, *ie* the period from the date of liquidation to the final date interest can run is ascertainable. Therefore, if interest is payable for less than a year it is short interest, but if it is payable for one year or more it is annual interest.

(*c*) Interest is allowable as a charge if it meets the conditions of TA 1988 s 338. Charges on income, so far as paid out of the company's profits brought into charge to corporation tax, are allowed only as deductions from the profits for the period in which they are paid.

Disclaimer

The charge to tax under Schedule D Case III is on the income arising. Income arises when it is paid or made available. Therefore, provided that the interest is not paid or made available there would prima facie be no Case III charge.

The interaction of Insolvency Act 1986 and TMA 1970

(*a*) Interest under TMA 1970 will not accrue beyond the date of commencement of the liquidation (compulsory/members voluntary liquidation). Interest under the Insolvency Act 1986 s 189, may arise on tax debts claimed in the liquidation, and in addition on interest under TMA 1970.

(*b*) Where tax is claimable in a liquidation, interest under the Insolvency Act 1986 s 189, may arise from either the date of the liquidation or the reckonable date for interest under TMA 1970 whichever is the later.

(*c*) Interest under the Insolvency Act 1986 s 189 may arise from the relevant date (as in (*b*) above) to the date of payment of the liability, no matter what the method of payment.

(*d*) The Revenue's view would remain the same for assessments made after the liquidation date. For post-liquidation accounting periods, interest under the Insolvency Act 1986 s 189 would not be applicable.

LIQUIDATION OF NON-RESIDENT UK COMPANIES

The test of residence

(*a*) The statement of practice SP 6/83 should not be read as implying that, as a general rule, the Revenue have moved in any way from the test enunciated by Lord Loreburn. A company is regarded as resident for tax purposes where central management and control is to be found because that, according to Lord Loreburn, is where the real business is carried on. (The Statement of Practice has now been superseded by SP 1/90 but the relevant paragraph is unchanged).

(*b*) The word ''business'' may have different connotations according to the context in which it is used. The Revenue does not consider that a company normally ceases to have a residence under Lord Loreburn's test on going into liquidation.

Application of the test

(*c*) In law, the liquidator has management and control of the company's affairs. It is therefore not possible to confirm that a company, whether solvent or insolvent, which has hitherto been non-resident, will not become resident in the UK on the appointment of a UK resident liquidator.

(*d*) However, the exercise of central management and control is a question of fact. If it is exercised abroad by the liquidator or if the liquidator acts in accordance with the wishes of non-resident shareholders so that management and control is not in fact in the UK, the company will not become resident here.

LIQUIDATION OF FOREIGN COMPANIES

The Revenue has no stated policy with regard to the application of TMA 1970 s 108(2) to liquidators of foreign companies. Where a foreign company owes tax it is the Revenue practice to proceed against the company itself, invoking the procedure in the Insolvency Act 1986 Part V for winding up unregistered companies.

OTHER MATTERS

Notes for guidance

(*a*) As mentioned earlier, amendments to the Department of Trade Regulations 1977 are currently under consideration by the Inland Revenue and Department of Trade and Industry.

Liaison arrangement

(*b*) Because of the extremely wide-ranging nature of matters affected by the Insolvency Act, it is not considered practicable for the Revenue to have clearly-identified technical or policy specialists. However, if any points of difficulty are referred, in the first instance, to compliance and collection division, they will consult with the necessary specialists to ensure that a reply is sent.

July 1990. ICAEW

TR 800: Auditing standard 102—the audit report

Guidance note issued in July 1990 by the Institute of Chartered Accountants in England and Wales.

1 Concern has been expressed by members as to the reaction by inspectors of taxes to the format of audit reports following the issue of auditing standard 102 (''The audit report'').

2 In particular it was suggested that inspectors may misinterpret the meaning of the replacement of the old ''Example 6'' report by one of the more specific audit reports of which examples are set out in the appendix to auditing standard 102.

3 Following discussions between the Revenue and the Institute of Chartered Accountants in England and Wales, the Revenue have circulated a copy of the standard to all tax districts together with an explanatory note prepared by the Revenue following these discussions.

4 The note refers to the concern by accountants that inspectors will misinterpret what has happened and use the change in audit report to justify an investigation, especially in respect of small companies. It explains the reasons for introducing the standard and states that it will continue to be a matter of judgment for local inspectors as to the part a qualified audit report will play in deciding whether to register a company for investigation. It emphasises, however, that there should be no fundamental change of practice by inspectors merely because one of the new style audit reports has been adopted.

5 The note explains that a qualification under the new arrangements does not necessarily mean that, although perforce the wording of the report has been changed, the auditing standards adopted or the reliability of the accounts have been impaired. In other words qualification is not, in itself, cause for investigation. The audit report is but one factor in deciding whether the accounts should be set down for investigation, although clearly a report which is heavily qualified or qualified in an important specific area is a factor which an inspector can reasonably take into account in deciding whether or not he is satisfied with the results shown by the accounts.

Revenue & other press releases—ICAEW 28-3-95 (Relaxation of statutory audit requirements for small companies—Guidance note). See below.

27 July 1990. Inland Revenue

Insurance companies and friendly societies: transfers of long term business—clearance applications

The Inland Revenue has announced details of how insurance companies and friendly societies can seek clearance that proposed transfers of long term business will be covered by the tax reliefs introduced by Sch 9 of the Finance Act 1990 [TCGA 1992 s 25(4), 211].

Clearance applications should be made to the Inland Revenue's Insurance Group by the company or society to which the business is transferred. Where clearance is refused, or a decision is not given within 30 days, the company or society can have the application considered by the special commissioners.

DETAILS

Finance Act 1990, Sch 9 [TCGA 1992 s 25(4), 211]

1. In cases where a court sanctions the transfer of long term insurance business from one insurance company or friendly society to another (or between an insurance company and friendly society or vice versa), the new measures introduced by FA 1990 Sch 9 [TCGA 1992 s 25(4), 211] provide, broadly, that the transfer may be made without immediate tax consequences. Provided that various conditions are met:

– business assets will be treated as having been transferred at a value which produces no gain and no loss for chargeable gains purposes;

– unrelieved expenses of management, and some losses, will be carried forward to the transferee; and

– the computation of capital allowances will continue broadly as if no change had occurred.

Note—TCGA 1992 s 25(4) repealed by FA 2000 with effect for cases where s 139 (reconstruction or amalgamation involving transfer of business) has effect as amended by FA 2000 Sch 29.

2. The first two of these reliefs (chargeable gains, and management expenses and losses) only apply if the transfer of the business is effected for bona fide commercial reasons and does not form part of a scheme or arrangement of which the main purpose, or one of the main purposes, is the avoidance of tax. To remove any uncertainty that this anti-avoidance rule could create, the legislation allows insurance companies and friendly societies to obtain an advance decision from the Board of Inland Revenue as to whether or not the rule will apply to a particular transfer.

Clearance procedure

3. Clearance applications in relation to—

– chargeable gains, are to be made under ICTA 1970, s 267(3A) [TCGA 1992 s 139(5)] (as amended by a new ICTA 1970, s 267A [TCGA 1992 s 211]). This is an existing provision which relates to certain company reconstructions and amalgamations; and

– management expenses and losses, are to be made under a new TA 1988 s 444A.

4. Applications should be made by the company or society to which the business is transferred. Apart from that the procedural rules which apply are those at CGTA 1979 s 88 [TCGA 1992 s 138]. These rules govern the way in which applications are to be made to the Board, [and] give the taxpayer the right to have the application considered by the special commissioners if the Board refuses clearance, or fails to make a decision within 30 days.

5. Applications should be sent to:

– Inland Revenue, Insurance Group, Room 130 New Wing, Somerset House, London, WC2R 1LB

6. Applications in respect of gains and management expenses and losses may be made in the same letter.

7. Where clearance is sought under other provisions in relation to a transaction associated with the transfer of business, separate applications should be made to the appropriate Inland Revenue office. It would be helpful if copies of such applications were sent to the Insurance Group.

Other clearance applications

8. Existing arrangements for dealing with other ICTA 1970 s 267 [TCGA 1992 s 139] clearance applications are not affected by the arrangements described above. Applications should continue to be sent to Solihull. These will include applications which relate to transactions which are associated with a transfer of long term insurance business, but which do not form part of the transfer.

9. Such applications should be sent to—

– Inland Revenue, Capital and Valuation Division (CGT), Sapphire House, 550 Streetsbrook Road, Solihull, West Midlands, B91 1QU

10. This address takes account of the recent transfer of responsibility for the work from Insurance and Specialist Division to Capital and Valuation Division.

16 August 1990. ICAEW

TR 806: Inland Revenue procedural matters

Note of a meeting in June 1990 between representatives of the Inland Revenue and the Institute of Chartered Accountants in England and Wales.

BACKGROUND

1 The meeting in June 1990 was the latest in a series of meetings to consider a number of procedural difficulties brought to the attention of the Institute by its members.

2 The previous meeting of a similar kind was held in November 1989 the agreed note of which was issued in January 1990 as TR 778.

INLAND REVENUE FORMS AND RETURNS

3 The Institute said that they had previously raised various aspects as to the design and use of forms, and continued to express their concern. They gave a number of examples, set out below.

FORM P1

4 Although forms 11 and 11P provide for claiming relief for free standing additional voluntary contributions to pension schemes, there is no such provision in form P1.

5 The Revenue said that this is intentional. Basic rate tax is given at source; a claim is required only for higher rate. Only basic rate taxpayers get P1, and the point therefore applies only to such taxpayers who come into the higher rate. It is necessary to balance the need for a simple form with catering for the few cases which fall within that category. They agreed to monitor the position and consider it at a future date, but most of those who contract for free standing AVCs will be advised of the position by those with whom the policies are taken out.

FORM P45

6 Form P45 should include the amount of NIC paid since the DOE often make enquiries of the employer on form UB77. This point has been raised with the DSS who have stated that it is a matter for the Inland Revenue.

7 The Revenue agreed to liaise with the DSS and the DOE but this is really a matter for those departments. The Revenue have taken the matter up with the DSS.

FOLDING OF FORMS

8 Many forms are of an awkward size and folding is difficult: for example form 300(CODA) can be folded without encroaching on the body of the form, but form P70(T) cannot.

9 The Revenue said that they had received no other complaints. Form P70(T) contains a lot of information and has to be separately folded by an "output machine" but they agreed to consider the point further.

COMPUTER ERRORS ON CODING NOTICES

10 ICAEW referred to an example where P2(T) was arithmetically incorrect. The Revenue explained that this had arisen as a result of incorrect computer procedures in the early part of the year which had now been corrected.

SCHEDULE E UNDERPAYMENTS

11 Institute suggested that form P70 should state how an underpayment is to be dealt with.

12 The Revenue said that form P70 is necessarily cramped and is issued automatically. The underpayment will either be coded in or a demand note issued. Sometimes a note stating which method is to be used is typed on the form: sometimes the information is given in a subsequent letter, but this may take some time. The Collector is contacted if the overpayment exceeds £350 for higher rate taxpayers. They agreed that there may be a lacuna and would look at departmental instructions.

FORM P11D

13 The Institute said they intend to prepare a separate paper on form P11D and this may also cover forms and returns generally: in February 1990 they had responded (TR 784) to the Deregulation Unit's request for comments.

14 The Institute referred to the difficulty in complying with the 6 June deadline. The Revenue explained that the due date for forms P11D has already been relaxed from 6 May to 6 June *ie* so that it comes after the revised due date of 18 May for the main end of year return from employers.

15 The Institute said that there is a considerable difference between the requirements of small companies and others; the former rely heavily on their auditors and regard completion of P11D forms as part of the annual audit/accounts exercise. Forms P35 are the first priority. Their suggestion that P11D be submitted with the accounts was not accepted by the Revenue.

CONSTRUCTION INDUSTRY TAX DEDUCTION SCHEME

16 The Institute referred to delays where a partnership is dissolved and the business continued by the former partners as sole traders. It can take up to six weeks for an exemption certificate to be issued, thus giving rise to cash flow problems.

17 The Revenue said that they do not get many complaints; a six weeks period should be the maximum. The issue of a certificate does depend on the applicant's tax affairs being up to date at the time of the application. This includes settlement of the tax liabilities of the partnership that had become due for the period up to the time that it was dissolved—but not those that became due for later periods. Once authorised for issue, the certificate will be sent to the applicant within three weeks.

LLOYD'S NAMES

18 The Institute referred to what appear to be unnecessary procedures in the reporting of the relevant information for Lloyd's External Names. Form 11 (Lloyd's) is submitted to the Leeds (Underwriters) Unit ("the Unit") who, after extraction of the relevant information, forward the return to the taxpayer's normal tax office.

19 However, the required information is usually not available by the time the return has to be submitted and it is therefore invariably necessary to complete this part of the form with the words "to be advised".

20 When the information is ultimately available it is notified to the Name by the Agent, who also provides the same information to the Unit.

21 They had been informed by the Unit (for whose capabilities and co-operation they had the very highest regard) that any attempt to include provisional figures in Form 11 (Lloyd's) would only cause confusion and it is better merely to state "to be advised".

22 They therefore suggested that, at best, the information as to Lloyd's income should be excluded from the return, leaving this to be obtained from the agent. Alternatively, the return should be sent direct to the taxpayer's normal tax office.

23 The Revenue accepted the special circumstances applicable to Lloyd's Names, which had been recognised by extended time limits for claims and elections. The Revenue accepted that there would be circumstances in which the underwriter could not do more than enter "to be agreed" and in such a case they would not argue that there had been a "failure to complete the return". However they could never accept that any body of taxpayers should be exempt from making a return of their income. If this were left to the Agent the essential responsibility of the taxpayer would be negated and thereby fall outside the enforcement regime should the question of penalties arise.

24 They said that they are at present carrying out a study with a view to possible improvement in procedures and they would bear in mind the suggestion that the return should be sent direct to the taxpayer's normal tax office.

ASSESSMENTS UNDER TA 1988 S 419

25 The Institute referred to a case where an assessment under TA 1988 s 419 (loans to participators etc) was issued before the end of the accounting period. It was made by reference to the quarter in which the loan was made rather than for the accounting period. They asked for confirmation that this was an isolated case which does not represent current practice.

26 The Revenue said that in their view an assessment under s 419 is not restricted to an accounting period, but assessments which are not are very rare. Those cases where they do occur do not constitute a change in practice.

RESIDENCE

27 The Institute referred to a case where the Revenue had stated that it was not their practice to give a definitive ruling for a person not working full time abroad until he had been resident abroad for three complete tax years, and that in this respect it is not the practice to follow the last sentence of para 16 of IR 20.

28 The Revenue confirmed that it is their practice to give confirmation as stated in para 16 of IR 20. However, the last sentence of that paragraph commences with the word "normally"; the exception applies to cases where there are good reasons for not giving confirmation, usually where insufficient evidence is available.

OVERPAYMENT OF ACT

29 The Institute asked for confirmation that where ACT is overpaid as a result of an error in completing form CT61, the Inland Revenue will allow the payment of a refund. The error or mistake provisions (TMA 1970 s 33) strictly do not apply unless an assessment has been raised by the Revenue.

30 They also sought confirmation that where a dividend is paid illegally, and repaid, the ACT thereby paid will be refunded. They had in mind the payment of a dividend on the basis of management accounts when, in the event, insufficient profits proved to be available.

31 The Revenue stated that a refund will be made where there is a genuine error: this can only be done by the inspector raising an assessment, in the correct figure, under TA 1988 Sch 13 para 3(3).

32 On the second point the Revenue stated that if the company had not parted with title the shareholders hold the dividend as constructive trustees and the ACT will be repaid. They pointed out, however, that TA 1988 s 419 might apply.

INTENSIVE TELEPHONING

33 The Institute referred to the "intensive telephoning" practice recently introduced by the Revenue. They said that it is unfortunate that the expectation of obtaining an answer early morning or late at night does not apply to calls made to the Revenue even where such calls are not especially early in the morning or late in the afternoon.

34 The self-employed may find it embarrassing to contact the Collector during working hours and would appreciate the ability to approach the Revenue outside such times.

35 The Revenue said that early or late calls would be taken at Shipley from those whom the Accounts Office had been trying to contact.

36 The Institute pointed out that they were more concerned with local offices. The Revenue said that they would like this facility to be also available there but given that some 6,500 staff are involved the cost would be prohibitive.

37 The Revenue agreed with the Institute suggestion that local offices should have fax machines, but cost constraints might not allow it. More generally the Revenue said that the experiment of telephoning delinquent taxpayers in the London area had been well received by taxpayers and accountants. VDU screens will be available to local Collection Offices at a later date, and this will help to reduce problems of communication.

RELATIONS BETWEEN INSPECTORS AND ACCOUNTANTS

38 The Institute said that most districts and local groups had held meetings with local inspectors although there were isolated cases where inspectors had shown a reluctance to participate.

39 The Revenue said they welcome and encourage such meetings either on an "open forum" basis or linked to particular subjects. In any case where there was difficulty in arranging participation by local inspectors M4 Head Office would be glad to help with the arrangements. The Revenue emphasised that they are always prepared to provide senior staff to speak at meetings organised by Chartered Accountants on a national or local basis.

COMPLIANCE STRATEGY

40 The Revenue said that their compliance policy includes helping taxpayers to meet their obligations and they would welcome comments on how matters can be better arranged so as to facilitate this compliance.

41 The Institute agreed to have particular regard to this aspect in their representations.

18 October 1990. Inland Revenue letter (ICAEW TR 830)

Requests from practitioners for information or guidance

You may recall that in April 1986 my predecessor, Barry Pollard, wrote to you and to other professional bodies saying that he had advised inspectors of taxes at Head Office that they should respond to requests for information or guidance from practitioners only if the enquiry involved recent legislation or changes in practice. The background against which this change was being made was the continuing loss of experienced inspectors from the Department and the priority which we had to give to giving advice for policy purposes and to local offices.

We have been reviewing experience over the four years since Barry Pollard wrote, particularly in the light of the judgment in the case of *R v IR Comrs., ex parte MFK Underwriting Agencies Ltd* [1989] STC 873. One of the factors which lay behind the matters in this case was the pressure on Head Office inspectors at the time in giving advice to practitioners. With the benefit of hindsight the case can be seen to have justified to the hilt the change which we made in 1986. Nevertheless we are, of course, aware that the professional bodies were unhappy that we had changed the practice and with that in mind we have recently looked at it again.

In considering this matter we have found that the practice has varied a little and that in some areas we have been able to respond to a slightly wider range of questions than Barry Pollard indicated we would. We have therefore now told our Head Office staff that they should be prepared when they can to answer requests for guidance on the Revenue's interpretation of tax law, not only where they involve the interpretation of recent legislation, Statements of Practice and other published information, but also in cases where there is a major public interest in developments in an industry or in the financial sector but where the operation of the law is uncertain. In addition, local inspectors of taxes will of course continue where practicable to inform practitioners about the Revenue's interpretation of tax law as it applies to any case which falls within the responsibility of that office.

In no case, however, whether at Head Office or local Office, would a member of the Department seek to advise a taxpayer or a practitioner on the arrangement of a person's own affairs: that must remain the responsibility of his professional advisers. Still less of course could we advise in the area of tax planning.

Where guidance is sought, the enquirer will doubtless bear in mind the principles set out by Bingham LJ in the MFK case. In addition to providing details such as the tax district and the reference, the enquirer should bear in mind that if he wishes to rely on Revenue guidance he must:

(*a*) put all his cards face upwards on the table;
(*b*) indicate the guidance sought;
(*c*) make it plain that it is fully considered guidance that is being sought; and
(*d*) indicate the use which it is intended to make of the guidance, and in particular whether he proposes to tell others of it.

Where guidance is given it should not be relied on to the extent of any qualification it contains. Moreover the actual application of the law will depend on the precise way in which the transaction is carried out and of course on the precise terms of the law at the time.

There may occasionally be cases, in particular where a representative body would find it helpful to be given an informal view of the interpretation of new legislation, where it would be appropriate for a reply to be given on an explicitly non-binding basis. Such cases will of course be quite different from Statements of Practice on the one hand or the more formal guidance with which this letter is otherwise concerned.

I hope you will find this letter helpful. As you know, the Revenue have for a long time—as confirmed by the Taxpayer's Charter—been anxious to help taxpayers know their rights as well as their obligations. It was welcome that in the MFK case the Court did not dissent from our view that we should do so where possible, subject to the clear rules which Bingham LJ enunciated as necessary if advice is sought on which the Revenue is to be bound. Even with the welcome reduction in the loss of fully trained inspectors to the professions and to industry, there remain limits on what we can do, but within these limits we shall continue to develop our services to the public.

I should have no objection to your circulating this letter to your members if you so wish.

Yours sincerely, L J H Beighton, Director General

Revenue & other press releases—ICAEW 11-4-91 (Memorandum TR 830: Inland Revenue—technical guidance). See below.

21 November 1990. Inland Revenue

Independent taxation—capital gains tax on jointly owned assets

In order to remove any uncertainty about the capital gains tax treatment of assets owned jointly by a husband and wife, the Revenue have today issued the following clarification.

Under independent taxation, husbands and wives are charged to capital gains tax independently. Where a married couple hold an asset in their joint names, any gain is apportioned between the husband and wife in accordance with their respective beneficial interests in the asset at the time of disposal. So if the husband owns 70% of the asset, and the wife 30%, the husband is chargeable on 70% of the gain, and the wife on 30%.

Where it is clear that there is a particular split of ownership between husband and wife, gains should be reported to the Revenue on that basis. A couple may for instance have agreed that one partner is merely a nominee and has no beneficial interest in the asset; and where land and buildings are jointly owned, there may be a legal agreement between the partners about their respective rights.

Where the split of ownership is not clearcut (as will often be the case with investments such as shares and securities) the Revenue will normally accept that the couple hold the asset in equal parts.

The capital gains tax treatment of jointly held assets will not necessarily be the same as the income tax treatment. For income tax, there is special treatment of the income from assets held in the names of a husband and wife who are living together. The law generally assumes that they are equally entitled to the income (even if in fact they are not) and so each is taxable on half of the income. However, where the assets and the rights to income from them are owned in the same unequal shares (including where one of the couples has complete ownership), the couple can, *if they wish*, declare to the Revenue that this is the case and be charged to income tax on the actual split of the income between them. Where a couple make such a declaration there is a presumption that the same split applies for capital gains tax purposes.

22 November 1990. Inland Revenue

Benefits in kind—employer provided living accommodation

The Inland Revenue announced today a change in the way in which the taxable benefit of living accommodation provided by an employer for an employee is calculated in cases where employees are provided with more than one property. The change applies from 6 April 1989.

Employees who have the benefit of free or cheap housing by virtue of their jobs are (subject to certain exemptions) taxed on the annual value of the property. An additional charge applies for accommodation costing more than £75,000, and hitherto employees provided with more than one property have been subject to the additional charge where the combined cost of the properties exceeded £75,000. The £75,000 threshold is now to be applied separately to each property so that a charge only arises in respect of properties which individually cost more than £75,000.

Where they can identify taxpayers affected by the change, tax offices will invite claims for repayment and adjust PAYE codings for 1990–91.

However, tax offices may not always be able to identify these cases, or to identify them quickly. Taxpayers who believe they are affected by the change should therefore contact their tax office, giving their name and address, tax reference, national insurance number and the name and address of their employer.

NOTES

1 TA 1988 s 145 charges the benefit of living accommodation provided by an employer. The measure of the benefit is the annual value of the property occupied, less any rent paid by the employee. The annual value is generally taken as the property's gross annual value for rating purposes.

2 TA 1988 s 146 imposes an additional charge in respect of accommodation which cost (with expenditure on improvements before the year of assessment) more than £75,000. The "official rate" of interest (15·5% from 6 November 1990) is applied to the amount by which that cost or, in certain circumstances market value, exceeds £75,000.

3 The new practice of applying the £75,000 threshold to each property separately follows legal advice received by the Revenue.

4 Assessments made from now on for 1988–89 and subsequent years will be on the basis of the new understanding of the law. For 1988–89 and 1989–90 a repayment of tax already paid may be due under the "error or mistake" provisions in TMA 1970 s 33. These provide for relief to be claimed where, by reason of an error or mistake in a return, there is an overcharge to tax in an assessment which is final. But no relief is due where the return was made on the basis of the practice generally prevailing at the time the return was made. Relief is thus available for 1988–89, because returns for that year will not normally have been made until after 5 April 1989, the date after which the change of practice applies. No relief will be due for 1984–85 to 1987–88 if returns for these years were made before 6 April 1989.

5 Where no assessment has been made for 1987–88 or earlier years, TA 1988 s 206 requires any assessment made now to be on the basis of the practice generally prevailing at 5 April 1989–that is on the old practice. But in some exceptional circumstances the new practice may apply for years before 1988–89, *eg* where an appeal remains open against a 1984–85 assessment made before 6 April 1986 or a 1985–86 assessment made before 6 April 1987, and so on.

19 December 1990. Inland Revenue

New trust deeds—change of practice

The Inland Revenue have decided to change the way in which they handle new trusts for income tax and capital gains tax. From 6 April 1991 tax offices will in general no longer ask, as they do at present, for a copy of every new trust document. Instead they will rely on the information shown by trustees, settlors and beneficiaries in their annual tax returns or repayment claims.

The Inland Revenue will seek further information only where necessary, and only exceptionally will they ask to see trust deeds, wills or other documents. That may happen if, for example, an inspector is not satisfied with a tax return or repayment claim, or if the taxpayer is unsure of the effect of the document and the issue cannot be resolved in some other way.

When a new trust is created, trustees will be sent a form which asks them to give some basic factual information about the identities of the trustees and settlor and whether the trustees have power to accumulate income or to distribute it at their discretion.

The change of practice is concerned only with ordinary family trusts where the documents are currently sent to local tax offices. It does not affect any arrangements for special types of trust such as unit trusts, charitable trusts and employee trusts. Nor does it alter the examination of deeds for inheritance tax purposes by the capital taxes offices.

NOTES

1 At present the Inland Revenue examine every new trust document and consider its validity under general law as well as its tax consequences. This examination is normally made by the specialist claims branches in Bootle and Edinburgh. There may then be correspondence with the trustees or their professional advisers. Trustees are also asked to inform their tax offices of any later supplementary deeds, so that they can be examined in a similar way.

2 This practice is being changed for a number of reasons. It began at a time when the Inland Revenue considered every business account and tax return in detail. Tax offices have, however, generally moved away from the detailed examination of every case so the practice is no longer consistent with the treatment of other taxpayers. It places unnecessary burdens on trustees and does not make the most efficient use of the Inland Revenue's resources. And it can lead to delays in the repayment of income tax to beneficiaries.

3 The new procedure should generally be simpler and involve less work for both trustees and the Inland Revenue.

16 January 1991. Ministry of Agriculture, Fisheries and Food

Simpler tax arrangements for seasonal work by overseas farm students

The Inland Revenue have simplified tax arrangements for overseas students coming to the UK to work in one of the six Home Office approved Seasonal Agricultural Workers' Schemes. In future these students, who in general are not liable for tax, will not have to pay income tax at source and recover it later. In a letter to the National Farmers Union, Baroness Trumpington, Minister of State at the Ministry of Agriculture, Fisheries and Food, welcomed the simplification of the new arrangements which will benefit farmers, growers and students.

Overseas students will be supplied with a form P38(S) by the scheme operator, which should be completed and handed to the farmer employing them. Receipts of the P38(S), which the farmer should retain, will enable the farmer to pay students without deducting tax. If students change employers during their stay, they will need to apply to the scheme for a second P38(S) to enable subsequent employers to pay them without deducting income tax.

This procedure only covers PAYE. The normal rules for deducting NICs will still apply.

NOTES

1 Form P38(S) is available from the Inland Revenue.

3 In 1990, 4,000 students, mainly from Eastern Europe took part in the Home Office approved Seasonal Agricultural Workers' Scheme.

27 March 1991. The Law Society

Notification of clearances—[TCGA 1992 s 138]

Notification of capital gains clearance under [TCGA 1992 s 138] is normally sent by letter from the Inland Revenue Insurance and Specialist Division at Solihull, West Midlands B91 1QU.

In cases of genuine urgency, where it has not been possible to deal with an application until close to the time when the clearance letter is required, the Revenue is prepared to consider a request that an expedited means of sending the letter be used, including arranging for a copy to be faxed to Somerset House, Strand, London WC2 for collection.

Where the application is submitted from outside London, the Revenue will try to give appropriate assistance in cases of particular urgency. Although the possibility of faxing the letter direct to the applicant would not be ruled out, the Revenue's fax capacity is limited and clearances will only be notified in this way in cases of real urgency when the Revenue is persuaded that there are particular reasons for doing so and fax capacity and staff resources are available (Practice note published in the *Law Society's Gazette*, 27 March 1991).

11 April 1991. ICAEW

Memorandum TR 830: Inland Revenue—technical guidance

TR 818 issued in October 1990 set out the text of a letter dated 18 October 1990 from the Inland Revenue regarding their practice in responding to requests for information or guidance.

The following sets out extracts from subsequent correspondence clarifying certain aspects of this practice.

EXTRACT OF A LETTER FROM THE INSTITUTE TO THE INLAND REVENUE

Committee members and others have questioned the extent to which, in practice, there will continue to be some limitation on the guidance available. Perhaps I can explain this by an analysis of the new arrangements as I understand them.

Barry Pollard's letter of 26 April 1986 [see *Simon's Tax Intelligence* 1986, p 407] said "our Technical Division will, as regards enquiries from tax practitioners, in future be able to respond only to those involving recent legislation and changes in practice"

Your letter refers to "requests for guidance on the Revenue's interpretation of...recent legislation, Statements of Practice and other published information, but also in cases where there is a major public interest in developments in an industry or in the financial sector but where the operation of the law is uncertain". It goes on to refer to the continuing practice to be adopted by local inspectors as regards particular cases and states that neither Head Office nor local inspectors will advise on the arrangement of a person's own affairs.

Finally, the letter refers to the need to have regard to the principles set out by Bingham LJ [in the case of *R. v I.R. Comrs., ex parte MFK Underwriting Agencies Ltd. and related applications*, [1989] STC 873] and sets out the information which the enquirer must make available.

Our first concern is that the first part of your letter quoted above (up to "published information") effectively restates the area in which Barry Pollard said that guidance would be continued: the second part ("but also...uncertain") represents the relaxation now made. This second part is, however, limited to those areas in which there is a "major public interest" in an industry or in the financial sector. On reconsideration, we have difficulty in seeing precisely what you have in mind here, and in particular whether this will in fact represent a meaningful extension to the assistance the Revenue currently gives. We should appreciate your comments.

Our second area of concern is the extent to which the pre-1986 practice is further limited by the need to have regard to the "Bingham principles" if the enquirer wishes to rely on the Revenue guidance (which will naturally always be the case). We do not dissent from conditions (*a*) to (*d*) (which I think are intended to summarise these principles as set out in the judgment [see [1989] STC 873 at p 892 f]), but the need to give the tax district and reference seems to make it clear that all enquiries are limited to specific cases rather than points of general application, even if they are of "major public interest".

There is, of course, what appears to be a relaxation in the paragraph towards the end of your letter which states "There may occasionally be cases...is otherwise concerned". It seems that in such cases, as implied in the last sentence, the information outlined above would not be required, since the response is to be informal and non-binding. This seems to be more in the nature of the pre-1986 practice, although it appears to be confined to an interpretation of new legislation with the exception that it is limited to views sought by representative bodies, although we are not aware that there has been any reluctance by the Revenue in this respect since 1986.

It is, incidentally, not clear whether "new legislation" means the most recent Finance Act or whether it extends to earlier, but recent, legislation, and whether the paragraph is intended to apply only infrequently as implied by the words "There may occasionally be cases..."

I would agree that guidance of this kind should not be regarded as tantamount to legislation, or even a Statement of Practice, and it may seem inappropriate to subject it to the above analysis, but it is a matter of considerable importance to our members.

EXTRACT OF A REPLY FROM THE INLAND REVENUE

I have delayed my response to your letter of 8 January until I could obtain comments from my colleagues on their expertise so far in handling enquiries for guidance since my letter to you (and the other representative bodies) of 24 October. I am glad to say that they reported little difficulty so far. In one respect their responses were varied as I had expected. As I said in my letter, we had found that some parts of Head Office had found it possible to give guidance on a less restrictive basis than Barry Pollard had foreshadowed in April 1986. So while in many areas the practice set out in my letter has led to an extension of the types of case in which guidance has been given, in other areas it has led to little change. But what it does mean is first, that there should now be a consistent approach

PRs etc

across Head Office, and second that practitioners and their representative bodies should know what the position is.

I find it difficult to explain what I meant by ''a major public interest in developments in an industry or in the financial sector'' without repeating those words: broadly, however, while I would expect it to exclude most transactions which any company was contemplating, I would expect it to include an industrial or financial development likely to be of importance to the country generally, going well beyond the circumstances of the particular company in question; in appropriate circumstances it might cover matters such as developments in the oil industry with consequences for the development of the North Sea; novel and major engineering projects; the application of the capital allowances legislation to projects involving leading-edge technology; and of course major issues arising from Government policy. But of course in any individual case the interpretation of my letter must be left to the individual who is responsible for handling the matter: it is, I think, self evident that not every transaction in the area covered by this list would be likely to be of major public interest, but equally nor would anything not listed above be necessarily excluded. And, as I made clear, we are not covering tax dodges, nor are we setting out to offer an alternative service to that provided by your members in giving guidance (let alone advising) on matters which should be within their competence or that of their legal advisers.

As to your second point, in the large majority of cases what practitioners want is guidance on our understanding of the application of the law in its relation to a specific case. To say anything in such circumstances without knowing which was the case involved would be rash to say the least. If we are going to go wider and give general guidance on certain types of transaction, then a Statement of Practice would probably be appropriate so that our view of the law would be available to every practitioner and not just to one who wrote and asked for it. When consultation seems appropriate there is of course a wide range of options between the extremes of formality and informality: as you say, these are matters which we are well used to discussing with the representative bodies rather than with individual practitioners.

On your final point I would expect most enquiries from representative bodies to relate to the most recent Finance Act but if issues remain unclear there is no hard and fast rule which would prevent a view being expressed on earlier legislation.

There is perhaps one point which I might mention myself while I am writing. That is that some of our people have found that quite a lot of their time is being taken up in dealing with these issues on the telephone. While in some cases practitioners (particularly those who are less used to our ways) may find it helpful to have a brief discussion on the telephone to find out how best to go about seeking a request for guidance, for the most part these are I think issues which can only be satisfactorily handled in writing.

29 May 1991. Inland Revenue

PAYE: casual harvest workers

Following recent legal advice the Inland Revenue has reviewed its interpretation of an agreement with the National Farmers' Union (NFU) about the application of Pay As You Earn (''PAYE'') to casual harvest workers. When deciding whether tax under PAYE should be deducted from a daily casual harvest worker's pay farmers will no longer need to consider whether they expect to offer the worker further employment.

DETAILS

1 Under an agreement made in 1984 between the Inland Revenue, the then Department of Health and Social Security, the Ministry of Agriculture, Fisheries and Food and the NFU, PAYE need not be applied to wages paid to daily casual harvest workers. A daily casual is defined as a worker who is employed for a period not exceeding a day, whose employment ends that day with no agreement for further employment, and who is paid off in cash at the end of the day.

2 The Inland Revenue has until now regarded the words ''agreement for further employment'' as including not only contractual arrangements but also cases where both the farmer and the employee expect there to be further employment. This view is reflected in Paragraph C1 of the Employer's Further Guide to Pay As You Earn (P7 (1991)).

3 Following recent legal advice the Inland Revenue will in future regard an agreement for further employment as existing only if there is a contract (not necessarily in writing) for further employment. This interpretation will also be applied to existing cases which have not been settled.

NOTES

1 The 1984 agreement recognised the special difficulties for farmers of applying PAYE to a large and changing group of casual harvest workers. But a farmer who under the agreement does not apply PAYE is required to tell the Inland Revenue after the end of the tax year about each individual employed and the amount paid, if it exceeds £100 in total for the year. This enables the Inland

Revenue to collect income tax directly from the employee if he or she has sufficient income to be liable.

2 The 1984 agreement also says that PAYE need not be applied to harvest workers who are not daily casuals but are taken on for two weeks or less (this concession can only be applied once a year for any particular worker by any one employer).

3 The parties to the 1984 agreement intend to review its operation later this year.

29 May 1991. The Law Society

Inland Revenue information powers—TMA 1970 s 13

Following discussions with the Society's revenue law committee, the Inland Revenue have indicated that instructions on the following lines would be issued to inspectors of taxes concerning the issue of notices (under TMA 1970 s 13) requiring returns of information from persons in receipt of taxable income on another's behalf.

> "The form of return is the [form] 8–2 (new) which should usually be issued at the beginning of May. Inspectors should be discriminating in their issue, however, and forms should not normally be sent to people who provide the information satisfactorily in another manner.
>
> A return should be obtained annually from each agent. But where a nil return has been received for two consecutive years, later returns need only be issued every five years until a return showing receipts is received. (In practice, inspectors may use their discretion to dispense with returns altogether if there does not seem any likelihood of there being receipts.)
>
> If the records maintained by the agent do not suit completion of the form issued, then the inspector may agree to accept a substitute return which provides the required information.
>
> In practice, the return may be restricted to receipts of the following nature:
>
> (*a*) those arising from sources chargeable under schedules a or d which have not suffered deduction of tax;
> (*b*) those exceeding £250 in the aggregate in respect of any one person or estate;
> (*c*) those which have not been included on any other return or repayment claim;
> (*d*) those received by an agent acting on behalf of an individual who is not domiciled in, or is a British subject not ordinarily resident in the UK
>
> The return should not be issued to persons who are unlikely to be in receipt of sums falling within (*a*) to (*d*) above. For example, whilst solicitors may be sent a return, the form should not normally be issued to a solicitor whose practice is known to comprise little else than transfers and mortgages of small properties. Further, the form should not be issued for purposes for which it is not intended, for example, to obtain particulars of receipts of sums passing through solicitors' hands under trading contracts of clients."

31 October 1991. Institute of Taxation

Capital gains tax—replacement of business assets [TCGA 1992 ss 152–158]

In May 1990 the Institute wrote to the Inland Revenue with a request that a review be instigated into the operation of [TCGA 1992 ss 152–158]. The Institute's paper on the subject, which raised a number of policy and technical issues concerning these provisions, was published in the Institute's magazine, Taxation Practitioner, in July 1990. Following further correspondence between the Institute and the Inland Revenue, The Institute is able to publish its understanding of the Inland Revenue's view on a number of technical issues arising from these provisions.

1 REINVESTMENT OF THE CONSIDERATION

1.1 The Inland Revenue has indicated that in its view the wording of [TCGA 1992 s 152(1)] which states that "if the consideration which a person obtains for the disposal of assets is applied by him in acquiring other assets" simply requires the taxpayer to reinvest an amount equal to the proceeds received.

1.2 The Inland Revenue has also indicated that, following a review of its practice in the area of time limits under [TCGA 1992 s 152(3)], it will in certain circumstances be prepared to extend the time limit beyond the statutory time limits.

1.3 Previously where a taxpayer invested all the proceeds in a new qualifying asset within the statutory time limit but chose not to make a rollover relief claim, the Board regarded that asset as the replacement asset and so refused to extend the time limit to enable the taxpayer to rollover a gain into a new asset acquired outside the normal time limits.

PRs etc

1.4 The Board will now be prepared to extend the time limit to allow a gain to be rolled over into a new asset acquired outside the statutory time limit provided certain conditions are met. In particular, the taxpayer will need to satisfy the Board that—

(*a*) he had a firm intention to acquire within the statutory time limit a qualifying asset or qualifying assets of the kind later acquired and requested to be treated as new assets (or the actual asset later acquired),

(*b*) he was prevented from doing so by reasonable cause (that is, as a result of something outside his control), and

(*c*) he did in fact do so as soon as possible thereafter.

1.5 The Institute also sought clarification as to whether, in the Inland Revenue's view, it is possible to claim rollover relief in the following circumstances—

(*a*) where a gain arises on a simple gift;

(*b*) where an asset is appropriated from "capital" to "trading stock" within [TCGA 1992 s 161(1)];

(*c*) where a company satisfies the consideration due on the acquisition of an asset by issuing shares to the vendor.

1.6 The Inland Revenue has confirmed that in its view gifts are within [TCGA 1992 s 152(10)]. Where the other conditions for rollover relief have been met, relief will be available based on the amount of the consideration deemed to have been received under other provisions of [TCGA 1992]. The Inland Revenue does *not*, however, regard rollover relief as available where there is a deemed disposal and reacquisition of the *same* asset. However, the Inland Revenue sees no reason why in principle the relief should not be available where the consideration is satisfied by an issue of shares.

2 ASSETS PROVIDED TO A FAMILY COMPANY

2.1 [TCGA 1992 s 157] deals with the case in which an individual disposes of assets used by his family company and reinvests the proceeds in replacement assets which will be used by the same family company. The Inland Revenue has confirmed that [TCGA 1992 s 157] requires both the old and the new assets to be used by the family company.

2.2 The Institute also drew attention to the fact that currently the relief is not available where the asset is used by a 100% subsidiary of a holding company since such a subsidiary cannot be a family company within the relevant definition of "family company" contained in [TCGA 1992 Sch 6]. This is notwithstanding the fact that [TCGA 1992 s 175] operates to treat all trades carried on by a group of companies as a single trade.

2.3 Commenting on this point the Inland Revenue has stated that although [TCGA 1992 s 175] treats all the trades carried on by a group of companies as a single trade, the section does not go as far as deeming all the trades to be carried on by a single company. The Inland Revenue's view, therefore, is that relief may be available under [TCGA 1992 s 157] where the assets are used by two or more group companies and any one of those companies is the individual's family company, but only in relation to the use of the assets by the family company and subject to the normal restrictions and conditions of relief.

2.4 The Institute noted that the payment of rent by a family company to an individual will not preclude a claim under [TCGA 1992 s 157]. The Institute's understanding was that this represented the Inland Revenue's practice rather than an entitlement under the legislation. In addition, the Institute understood that in some cases inspectors would look for the payment of rent as evidence of occupation by the company.

2.5 The Inland Revenue has indicated that in its view rollover relief may be claimed under [TCGA 1992 s 157] where rent is paid by a family company, not by concession but under the statute. As [TCGA 1992 s 157] is silent on the question of rent, it is not a relevant factor in deciding whether or not relief may be claimed.

3 INTERACTION WITH [TCGA 1992 S 162]

3.1 The Institute drew attention to the relationship of [TCGA 1992 ss 152 and 162]. It was concerned as to the availability of the relief under [s 152] where the taxpayer is also entitled to relief under [s 162] on incorporation of a business. The mandatory nature of the [s 162] relief might be thought to preclude a claim for relief under [s 152] where, for example, the taxpayer received shares on the incorporation of a business as a going concern and then, within the three year limit, also acquired assets which qualify under [s 155].

3.2 The Inland Revenue has stated that, although [TCGA 1992 s 162] is not subject to a claim procedure, in practice the Inland Revenue would not object if a taxpayer did not want [s 162] treatment.

4 PROVISIONAL CLAIMS

4.1 The Institute expressed its concern at the lack of statutory provision relating to provisional claims by taxpayers given the length of time (three years) within which the taxpayer is permitted to reinvest in qualifying assets. Experience has shown an apparent lack of consistency in the way in which inspectors deal with provisional claims.

4.2 The Inland Revenue has stated that, so far as provisional claims to rollover relief are concerned, inspectors have a responsibility to assess gains at the normal time. Given the long interval that may occur between the time when the gain arises and the latest date on which a claim could be made, not to assess timeously could deprive the Inland Revenue of the interest on unpaid tax should a competent rollover claim not be made in the event. Furthermore, with the elapse of several years the gain may be overlooked entirely.

4.3 However, once an assessment has been made, the taxpayer may apply for postponement of tax on production of satisfactory evidence of his intention to acquire a qualifying asset within the time limit. Where an inspector does not agree to the postponement, the taxpayer has the option of having his application heard by the commissioners.

5 NEW TRADES

5.1 The Institute had understood that it might be the Inland Revenue's view that only the first new trade commenced after the cessation of the old trade could be regarded as the successor trade for the purposes of [TCGA 1992 s 152(8)]. The Inland Revenue indicated that this was not so. It would generally have no difficulty in regarding a second or subsequent new trade as being carried on successively.

5.2 This means rollover relief would be available where a gain arises from the old trade and new assets are acquired in the second or subsequent new trade, provided that the other conditions for the relief are met and the gaps between the old and new trades are within the limits in statement of practice SP8/81.

The Institute is grateful to the Inland Revenue for the guidance that it has provided in relation to this topic. As with any such guidance, it represents the Inland Revenue's view of the law, as currently formulated, and how it proposes to operate it. It is naturally open to any taxpayer to take a different view in particular circumstances and, where appropriate, to exercise his rights of appeal if agreement cannot be reached on the matter with the Inland Revenue.

The Institute raised a number of other issues on rollover relief with the Inland Revenue where the Institute believes that some amendment of the legislation may be required. These have been noted by the Inland Revenue but are ultimately matters for Ministerial decision. The Institute will continue to press the case for change with the Government in this, as in other areas.

NOTE

Under [TCGA 1992 ss 152–157], a trader is entitled to claim that a capital gain arising on the disposal of specified classes of business asset may be rolled over or deferred where the proceeds of disposal are reinvested in new assets of the specified classes within the relevant time limits.

6 November 1991. ICAEW

Memorandum TR 851: Taxation of ex gratia payments

The Institute has published a memorandum containing further Inland Revenue guidance on the tax treatment of ex gratia payments made to employees on termination of their employment.

The first part of the memorandum repeats guidance set out in the Superannuation Funds Office Memorandum 111 following the issue of SP13/91.

The second part deals with the situation where a company car is transferred to an employee as part of an ex gratia severance package as follows.

Where an employee or office holder receives a company car as part of an ex gratia severance package on retirement or removal from an office or employment, both the cash and the car fall within TA 1988 s 148. The car is "valuable consideration other than money" under s 148(3) and its value is therefore aggregated with the cash payment when applying the £30,000 exemption in s 188(4).

But TA 1988 s 148 applies only to payments which are not otherwise chargeable to tax, and there are two circumstances in which liability could arise without the benefit of the £30,000 exemption.

First, the gift of a car would attract liability under TA 1988 s 19 where it was a reward for past services even though the recipient may have no entitlement to receive it on termination of his office or employment. The criteria for determining whether a s 19 charge arises on the value of such a gift would follow long established Schedule E principles and would be identical to those applicable to a cash payment made in similar circumstances.

Second, the gift of a car would attract liability under TA 1988 s 596A where it was received under a non-approved retirement benefits scheme set up to provide "relevant benefits". The criteria set out above for determining whether ex gratia payments constitute "relevant benefits" would also be used to determine whether s 596A should apply to the gift of a car.

18 November 1991. Inland Revenue

Capital gains tax valuations of unquoted shares at 31 March 1982—new arrangements at the Shares Valuation Division

The Inland Revenue Shares Valuation Division (SVD) announced today new arrangements in relation to valuations of unquoted shares for capital gains tax purposes at 31 March 1982. These are frequently needed so that capital gains tax computations can take account of indexation and the rebasing of capital gains tax to 1982.

In future, where 31 March 1982 values are needed and shareholders with similar holdings agree, SVD will begin valuation negotiations in advance of a formal request to do so from the tax office.

This responds to suggestions that have been made to SVD. It should mean that valuations, typically involving a number of minority shareholders, can be started sooner by SVD. Taxpayers will be able to approach SVD before making their tax returns or before their tax offices have asked SVD for assistance. This will have advantages for taxpayers, practitioners and the Inland Revenue alike.

DETAILS

1 The function of SVD is to provide a valuation service for other parts of the Inland Revenue. At present it undertakes valuations of shares in unquoted companies only when asked to do so by other Inland Revenue offices. In the case of capital gains tax, valuation requests will normally come from a tax office.

2 However, SVD is sometimes asked by taxpayers, before a formal request has been received from the tax office, to agree a valuation of shares in a company at 31 March 1982. Often, the valuation is of a minority shareholding in circumstances where it is apparent that valuations of similar holdings held by a number of shareholders have become necessary—for instance, following a takeover of the company.

3 In the following circumstances SVD, on application from taxpayers or a practitioner acting on their behalf, will begin valuation negotiations in advance of a formal request from a tax office. The intention is to arrive at an agreement of the value of all similar minority holdings of shares in the company as at 31 March 1982.

4 The circumstances are that:

– the request concerns the valuations of unquoted shares at 31 March 1982 for capital gains tax purposes;
– valuations are required for a number of shareholders;
– all shareholders with similar holdings requiring valuation at 31 March 1982 are prepared to be bound by the value agreed;
– SVD is provided with a full list of the company's shareholders and the size of their shareholdings at both 31 March 1982 and the date of disposal together with, if available, details of the tax offices involved.

5 Shareholders will still need to make a return to their own tax office of the gain which gives rise to the need for a valuation of their holdings at 31 March 1982. They should mention when doing so that valuations are being negotiated or, as the case may be, have been agreed with SVD.

6 Applications for the commencement of valuation proceedings in these circumstances and for further details of the arrangement should be made to Inland Revenue, Shares Valuation Division, Fitz Roy House, PO Box 46, Castle Meadow Road, Nottingham NG2 1BD.

Or in the case of companies incorporated in Scotland to Inland Revenue, Shares Valuation Division, Mulberry House, 16 Picardy Place, Edinburgh EH1 3NB.

7 All telephone enquiries about the arrangements can be made to SVD Information Room on 0115 974 2222. Correspondence should be headed "Application for advance negotiations of values at 31 March 1982".

19 December 1991. Country Landowners Association

Share farming

The Inland Revenue have concluded that both parties in a share farming agreement may now be considered to be carrying on a farming business as far as taxation is concerned.

In August 1991 the Inland Revenue suggested that a landowner involved in a share farming agreement would not normally be regarded as a farmer for tax purposes. But following further consideration the Inland Revenue have now agreed that the landowner in an agreement based upon the Country Landowners Association model may be regarded as a trading farmer, provided he takes an active part in the share farming venture, at least to the extent of concerning himself with details of farming policy and exercising his right to enter onto his land for some material purpose, even if only for the purposes of inspection and policy-making.

The Country Landowners Association expects to be able to issue a statement on the detailed tax arrangements for share farming in the near future.

NOTE

In August 1991, the Inland Revenue informed the Country Landowners Association that, contrary to an earlier-expressed opinion, a landowner involved in a share farming agreement would not normally be regarded as a farmer for tax purposes. Consequently, the landowner would not normally qualify for roll-over or retirement relief on any capital gains tax liability.

The Country Landowners Association, as an interim measure, advised its members not to enter into new share farming agreements because the fiscal penalties were too severe. The latest Inland Revenue opinion follows lengthy discussions with the Association's tax department.

29 January 1992. Law Society

Overseas retirement benefits

On 8 October 1991 the Revenue published new and revised extra-statutory concessions relating to pension schemes for service overseas.

The Revenue is now reported to have confirmed to the Law Society's Revenue Law Committee that lump sums paid under foreign pension schemes which would be chargeable to income tax under TA 1988 s 596A (as a benefit provided under a non-approved scheme) but for the operation of the revised concession A10, will not be treated as capital payments for the purposes of [TCGA 1992 s 87] (gains of non-resident settlements).

Further, if the facts of a particular case show clearly that the pension scheme is part of the normal arrangements for remunerating employees, the Revenue would not normally regard either the employer or the employees as a settlor or settlors for the purposes of [TCGA 1992 s 86, Sch 5] (non-resident settlements where the settlor has an interest).

18 March 1992. Law Society

Tax returns—signature under enduring powers of attorney

The following letter from B Cleave, Solicitor of Inland Revenue amplifies SP/A13.

> "The Revenue's general position on the signing of returns is that they must be signed by the taxpayer in person. That is considered to be the effect of TMA 1970 s 8 which displaces the common law rule that a person sufficiently signs a document if it is signed in his or her name and with his or her authority.
>
> TMA 1970 s 8(1) enables an inspector, for the purposes of assessing a person to income tax, to require him or her by a notice given to him or her to make and deliver a return to the inspector containing such information as may be required in pursuance of the notice. This is considered to put the burden of making the return personally on the taxpayer and TMA 1970 s 8(2) completes the picture by providing that every return made under the section is to include a declaration by the person making it to the effect that it is to the best of his or her knowledge correct and complete.
>
> So if the taxpayer is personally responsible for making the return, it follows that he or she must make the declaration required by s 8(2) personally.
>
> In practice...there are circumstances in which it is impossible to comply with the strict requirements of s 8. The circumstances in which the Revenue is, in principle, prepared to accept the signature of an attorney are those of physical inability to sign and mental incapacity.
>
> Where the reason given for signature by an attorney is the physical inability of the taxpayer to sign, inspectors will accept a return signed by an attorney acting under a general or an enduring power, provided the attorney confirms that he or she has full knowledge of the taxpayer's affairs. On the first occasion that he or she receives a return signed by an attorney in any such case, the inspector will want to see the original power or a copy certified on every page to be a true and complete copy of the original. If an enduring power has been stamped by the Court of Protection, the inspector will treat the case as one of mental incapacity.
>
> Where the reason given for signature by an attorney is the mental incapacity of the taxpayer, the inspector will accept the return if the attorney was appointed under an enduring power and the power has been registered with the Court of Protection on the taxpayer becoming of unsound mind.
>
> Again, on the first occasion that a return signed by an attorney is received in such a case, the inspector will need to see the power or copy bearing the stamp of the Court of Protection. In the case of mental incapacity, the inspector will also accept a return signed by a receiver or committee appointed by the Court of Protection on sight of the court order."

18 March 1992. Law Society

Valuation of agricultural tenancies

The following is an agreed summary of a meeting between representatives of the Law Society of England and Wales, the Law Society of Scotland and the Inland Revenue held on 3 February 1992 to discuss the specific issue of valuation of agricultural tenancies.

For the purposes of the meeting there was a common acceptance by both Law Societies and the Inland Revenue (including the Valuation Office Agency) that under the existing law, the principles of *Crossman* [[1937] AC 26; [1936] 1 All ER 762] apply in general to valuation exercises where an asset is subject to restrictions on its disposition.

In valuing an agricultural tenancy, there are several special factors which need to be considered:

– the benefits attaching to the tenancy, *eg* residential accommodation, rights of compensation for disturbance, waygoing (Scotland), dilapidations claims, improvements, manurial rights, and the fact that the rent might currently be less than the market rent;
– the principle that there should be no automatic presumption that the value of a tenancy could be arrived at by a method based upon a standard percentage of the vacant possession premium or value;
– the consideration of who might be in the hypothetical market for the tenancy; and
– the weight to attach to the various factors relevant in valuing the tenancy, which would be a matter of fact and for negotiation in each case.

In principle it appeared that there was only one area of dispute between the two sides, namely had the Revenue been correct to use as a starting point for valuing tenancies a percentage of the vacant possession value of the land or the vacant possession premium? It was very difficult for the Revenue to depart from this position since it obviously had a responsibility to both the Exchequer and the government. If it started from a point which was lower than the final value which might be agreed upon, it would be open to the criticism that it had not carried out its duty properly.

It was open to the taxpayer to adduce evidence at an early stage if the character of the landlord was to be a factor in determining the value, namely that there was evidence that the landlord was likely to make a bid for vacant possession of the land, or not, as the case might be. If the issue had arisen, for example, on the death of a tenant farmer within seven years of transferring his tenancy, such evidence could be submitted at the same time as the accounts for the estate were sent in. The Revenue would then be on notice from the outset that the question of a bid by the landlord was a matter that the taxpayer believed was not a factor to take into account.

The Law Societies agreed that if taxpayers were given an opportunity to adduce such evidence, this would resolve many difficulties. However, there was the practical problem of a sizeable backlog of cases, where it had been impossible to agree a value for transfers which had taken place several years ago and it would clearly not be viable to take advantage of the opportunity to adduce evidence ''at any early stage''. For cases which were open and where it was still possible to adduce evidence as to the landlord's intention, would the Revenue consider such evidence if now submitted and give due weight to it as a factor?

Mr Cayley [for the Inland Revenue] said that he would have no objection in principle to this. However, he emphasised that by agreeing to give due weight to evidence of a landlord's intention, the Revenue would be unable to guarantee that it would always modify its approach to the valuation. The Law Societies understood this.

Cross reference—See TCGA 1992 s 272 (Valuation: general).

31 March 1992. Lloyd's of London Market Bulletin

Guidance on the tax treatment of Lloyd's underwriters' compensation

Many Names are currently engaged in actions for compensation and damages for losses and some of these actions have already been settled by the payment of compensation. The taxation consequences for individual Names are dealt with by Leeds (Underwriters Unit). The Inland Revenue has written providing general guidance on the approach it will adopt in dealing with compensation receipts and this is reproduced below.

CHARACTER OF RECEIPT

The Revenue's view is that where a member receives a payment of compensation in settlement of a claim for damages in respect of a loss suffered in his underwriting business, the payment should be regarded as a receipt of the business. It should therefore be included as a trading receipt in computing the profit or loss of the underwriting trade. We think there is ample guidance from tax cases to support this view, including *Gray v Lord Penrhyn* (1937) 21 TC 252 and most recently, *Donald Fisher (Ealing) Ltd v Spencer* [1989] STC 256.

CAPITAL SUM

Some members may contend that the compensation is a capital sum derived from an asset, the right of action, and claim that it is exempt from capital gains tax by virtue of Extra-statutory concession D33. They may base this claim on the fact that the offer of compensation usually requires the member to waive or discontinue any rights of action. The Revenue does not accept this contention. "Capital sum" [TCGA 1992 s 22] is defined in s 22(3) as "any money or money's worth which is not excluded from the consideration taken into account in the computation [of the gain]".

[TCGA 1992 s 37(1) excludes consideration forming part of trading profits from the capital gains disposal proceeds.]

It follows that the first question to be asked is whether the compensation is a receipt of the trade which falls to be taken into account in computing the profits or losses of the trade. If it is, and the Revenue says it is, the question of capital gains tax does not arise.

DISCLOSURE

If the compensation falls to be regarded as a receipt of a syndicate which has not closed when it is received or entitlement to it becomes established, it should be included in the managing agent's return of the syndicate's profit or loss. The member is required to disclose any compensation received which has not otherwise been disclosed; failure to do so may render him liable to penalties.

UNDERWRITING YEAR

The underwriting year to which a compensation receipt should be attributed is regarded as a question of fact. One cannot therefore lay down a universal rule, but it appears that a receipt is unlikely to fall to be included for any underwriting year before that in which entitlement to it may be said to have become firmly established. It follows that the vigour with which a claim is resisted is a relevant factor, and where a claim is contested almost to the point of settlement, one would expect the compensation to be included as a receipt of the underwriting year in which settlement is reached.

YEAR OF ASSESSMENT

There appear to be various possibilities here, depending on the circumstances of the recipient.

Continuing member of Lloyd's: if the compensation relates to a syndicate which has closed, it should be included as a receipt of the year of assessment corresponding to the underwriting year of which it is a receipt. If the compensation is a receipt of a syndicate which is running off, it is carried back two years under SI 1974/896 reg 7. If it is not a syndicate receipt but a personal receipt of the individual member, it should be assessed in the year of assessment corresponding to the underwriting year for which it is a receipt.

Members who have ceased underwriting before receipt: a member is regarded as continuing to trade as long as he is a member of at least one syndicate which has not closed. If he is not a member of such a syndicate, and has resigned from Lloyd's, the compensation will be liable to income tax under Case VI by virtue of TA 1988 s 103(2), for the year of assessment in which it is received. If it is received within six years of the discontinuance, the former member may elect under TA 1988 s 108 to have it treated as if it were received on the date on which trading ceased.

Deceased members: the compensation will be assessable under Case VI by virtue of s 103(2). The election referred to above is available, where the compensation is received within six years of discontinuance.

Legal fees: legal fees incurred in connection with an action are likely to be deducted for tax purposes, where there is a continuing source. Where the source has ceased, they may be allowed against post-cessation receipts in accordance with TA 1988 s 105.

Whilst the above provides general guidance on the position, each case will be reviewed separately and settled on its own merits. However, there are some important points which Names and their accountants should be aware of. Names must notify the Inland Revenue of all sums that they receive by way of compensation following actions for damages. This holds true even where relief is sought under Extra-statutory concession D33—before relief under the concession can be granted, the Inland Revenue has to be aware of the full facts. Where tax is lost because of a failure to notify the Inland Revenue of a compensation receipt, then the Name concerned may be liable to interest and penalties.

If a member receiving compensation has to refund a previous stop loss recovery to his or her insurers, the Inland Revenue should be informed of the full amount of the compensation due together with the amount of the refund to the stop loss insurers.

16 June 1992. ICAEW Tax 13/92 (extract)

Offsetting overpayments against underpayments

Inland Revenue procedural matters: note of a meeting in March 1992 between representatives of the Inland Revenue and the Faculty of Taxation of the ICAEW (extract).

PRs etc

26 The Revenue said that the general policy is to set off overpayments in a way that is most advantageous to the taxpayer. However, the interest rules themselves are laid down in the statute and have to be followed.

27 When a payment is received the collector will allocate it to the taxpayer's best advantage at that time. Normally the taxpayer specifies the liabilities which a particular payment is to meet, and the collector must comply with any such allocation.

28 The Revenue explained the policy governing whether overpayments were reallocated against underpayments, and the order of set off which would be applied. (The details are set out in Appendix A).

29 The Revenue explained the interest consequences where overpaid tax was set against underpayments, and illustrated the position graphically. (Appendix B gives the explanations and illustrations for that and also for the situations where tax is initially held in suspense and where tax is met by certificates of tax deposit.)

30 Regarding the position where technical issues take a long time to resolve, the Revenue said that: the taxpayer can choose when to pay any liability which is in dispute: the consequences of delayed payment are clearly stated; the Revenue cannot predict how any disputed issues will be resolved; and the taxpayer has the use of any money which is retained and paid later.

APPENDIX A: REALLOCATION OF OVERPAYMENTS AGAINST UNDERPAYMENTS

Policy

The collector will automatically reallocate overpayments as follows:

(*a*) to any charge which is overdue;

(*b*) from a Schedule D first instalment to a Schedule D second instalment if it is after 1 June;

(*c*) from a Schedule D first instalment to a Schedule D second instalment prior to 1 June if the amount which could be reallocated is less than £1,000.

Reallocations will not be made automatically if the taxpayer has asked for them not to be. However, if there is an overdue charge against which the overpayment could be set, then the collector will suggest to the taxpayer that the overpayment be reallocated, and will go ahead unless it is confirmed that the money should not be reallocated.

Order

The general policy is that overpayments should be set off in the way which is most advantageous to the taxpayer.

The order for Schedule D payments is as follows:

Payment before 2nd instalment date	*Payment after 2nd instalment date*
Tax 1st instalment collectible	Tax 1st instalment collectible
NIC 1st instalment collectible	Tax 2nd instalment collectible
Tax 2nd instalment collectible	NIC 1st instalment collectible
NIC 2nd instalment collectible	NIC 2nd instalment collectible
Tax 1st instalment postponed	Tax 1st instalment postponed
NIC 1st instalment postponed	Tax 2nd instalment postponed
Tax 2nd instalment postponed	NIC 1st instalment postponed
NIC 2nd instalment postponed	NIC 2nd instalment postponed

If a payment relates to a particular instalment, the above table applies with all references to the other instalment removed.

APPENDIX B: INTEREST CONSEQUENCES OF REALLOCATIONS

Tax paid against assessments

The set-off is done in a way which gives the same result as if the overpaid tax had been repaid and then paid back against the other liability. In other words supplement will run from the relevant date of the original payment up to the set-off date, and late payment interest will run from the reckonable date of the underpaid charge up to the date of set-off. Diagrams (*a*) and (*b*) below illustrate the position graphically.

Payments held in suspense

Unallocated payments are held in a suspense account.

When the appropriate charge has been identified, the money is allocated to that charge and treated just as if it had been allocated on the original date of payment. If that date was before the reckonable date for the receiving charge, then no late payment interest will arise on that amount. See (*c*) and (*d*) below.

Certificates of tax deposit (CTDs)

If a CTD was purchased before the reckonable date for a charge against which it is set, then no late payment interest will be charged on the amount of CTD set-off. The amount available for set-off will in fact be the amount of the CTD purchased together with interest added from the purchase date up to the reckonable date for the charge it is used to satisfy. See (*e*) below.

Interest illustrations

These are graphical representations with time plotted across the page from left to right.

In each example the upper line represents the source of a set-off payment. The lower line represents a liability which is met by set-off. The vertical line at the right represents the set-off.

Key		
	Rel. D	Relevant date for repayment supplement
	Reck. D	Reckonable date for late-payment interest
	———	Period over which no interest is added/charged
	- - - - -	Period over which interest is added/charged

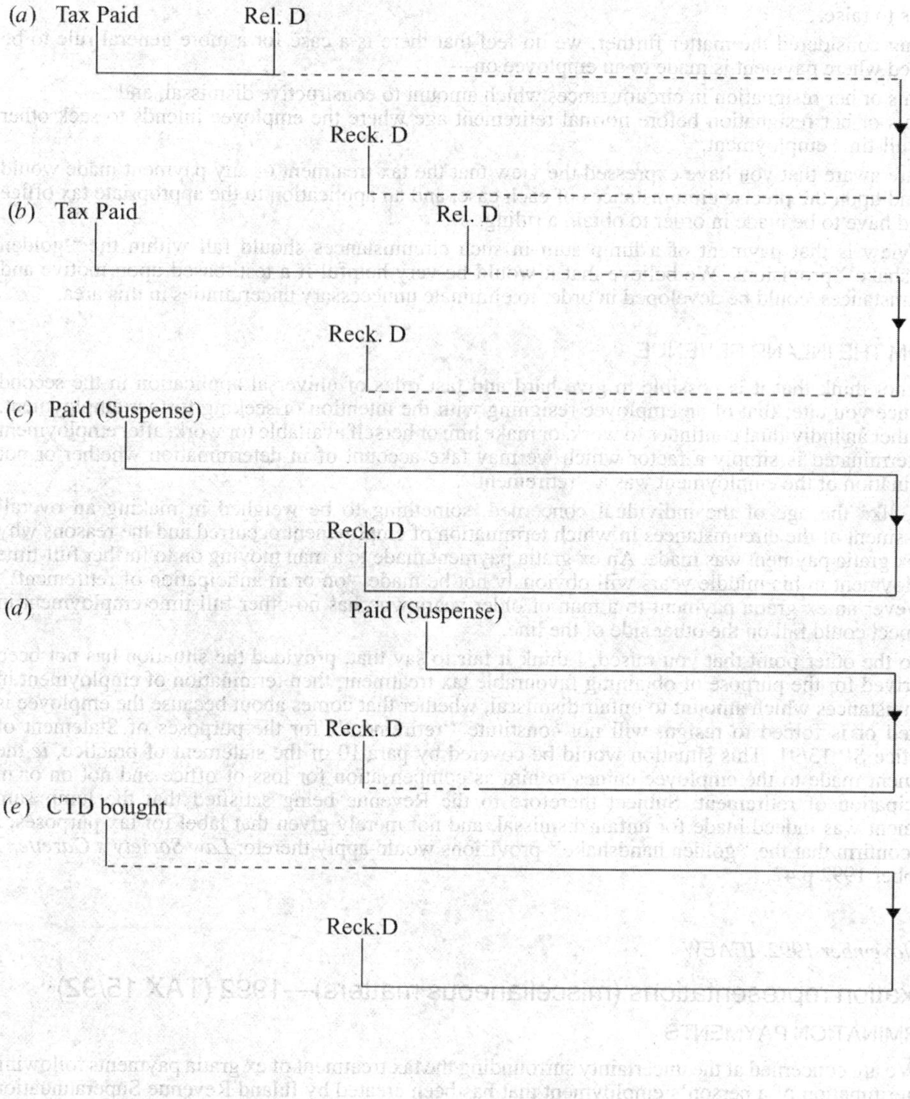

7 October 1992. Law Society

Ex gratia payments—Statement of Practice SP 13/91

The Inland Revenue issued a statement of practice in October 1991 (SP 13/91) announcing a change of practice in its treatment of ex gratia payments made to members of a retirement benefit scheme on retirement or death. The Revenue previously took the view that ex gratia payments made on an employee's retirement or death would fall outside the scope of the rules applying to taxation of pension schemes, and would thus only be taxable, if at all, under the ''golden handshake'' provisions.

As a result of legal advice obtained by the Revenue, this view was revised and fresh guidance issued in the form of the statement of practice. The Society's Revenue Law Committee was concerned over the application of the new rule to particular circumstances, and took up the matter with the savings and investment division of the Inland Revenue. The exchange of correspondence is set out below.

FROM THE LAW SOCIETY

When Statement of Practice SP 13/91 was issued in October 1991, it was read by members of the Law Society's Revenue Law Committee with interest although we had at that time no particular points to raise.

Having considered the matter further, we do feel that there is a case for a more general rule to be applied where payment is made to an employee on—

(*a*) his or her resignation in circumstances which amount to constructive dismissal, and

(*b*) his or her resignation before normal retirement age where the employee intends to seek other full-time employment.

We are aware that you have expressed the view that the tax treatment of any payment made would depend upon the precise circumstances of each case, and an application to the appropriate tax office would have to be made in order to obtain a ruling.

Our view is that payment of a lump sum in such circumstances should fall within the ''golden handshake'' provisions. We believe that it would be very helpful if a test, based upon motive and circumstances, could be developed in order to eliminate unnecessary uncertainties in this area.

FROM THE INLAND REVENUE

I do not think that it is possible to give hard and fast rules of universal application in the second instance you cite; that of an employee resigning with the intention of seeking further employment. Whether an individual continues to work, or make him or herself available for work, after employment has terminated is simply a factor which we may take account of in determination whether or not termination of the employment was a ''retirement''.

It is, like the age of the individual concerned, something to be weighed in making an overall assessment of the circumstances in which termination of employment occurred and the reasons why the ex gratia payment was made. An ex gratia payment made to a man moving on to further full-time employment in his middle years will obviously not be made ''on or in anticipation of retirement''. However an ex gratia payment to a man of older years who has no other full-time employment in prospect could fall on the other side of the line.

As to the other point that you raised, I think it fair to say that, provided the situation has not been contrived for the purpose of obtaining favourable tax treatment, then termination of employment in circumstances which amount to unfair dismissal, whether that comes about because the employee is sacked or is forced to resign, will not constitute ''retirement'' for the purposes of Statement of Practice SP 13/91. This situation would be covered by para 10 of the statement of practice, *ie* the payment made to the employee comes to him as compensation for loss of office and not on or in anticipation of retirement. Subject therefore to the Revenue being satisfied that the lump sum payment was indeed made for unfair dismissal, and not merely given that label for tax purposes, I can confirm that the ''golden handshake'' provisions would apply thereto: *Law Society's Gazette*, 7 October 1992 p 42.

16 November 1992. ICAEW

Taxation representations (miscellaneous matters)—1992 (TAX 15/92)

TERMINATION PAYMENTS

22 We are concerned at the uncertainty surrounding the tax treatment of ex gratia payments following the termination of a person's employment that has been created by Inland Revenue Superannuation Funds Office Memorandum 111 and Statement of Practice SP 13/91. We suggest that there should be further clarification of the Revenue's views as to what is meant by a payment made in connection with an employee's ''retirement''. It is appreciated that each case must to an extent depend on its facts, but we seek clarification as to whether the Revenue would normally seek to contend that a payment is made in connection with an employee's retirement in any of the following circumstances—

(*a*) A person who has worked for the company for 20 years leaves at age 45 to take a senior executive position in another company.
(*b*) A long-service employee leaves to take a senior executive position in another company at the age of 60.
(*c*) A division of the company is sold and the 55 year old manager responsible for running it leaves to take a job with the purchaser.
(*d*) A person in his 50's has a heart attack and is advised by his doctor to leave and seek a less stressful position.
(*e*) An employee aged 35 is involved in an accident and suffers disabilities that make him unable to continue with his job.
(*f*) An employee aged 50 leaves to take a job nearer home to be able to nurse her aged parents.

REVENUE RESPONSE

We would not accept that the issue last year of SP 13/91 and Memorandum 111 has created uncertainty about the tax treatment of *ex gratia* payments made on the termination of a person's employment. Whether, in a particular case, the termination of employment constitutes "retirement" must depend on the facts of the case, as you acknowledge. So I am afraid the statement of practice and memorandum could not lay down an exhaustive list of criteria which would define "retirement". But we do believe they provide useful guidelines on our approach in this difficult area of the law.

We can provide some indication of how we would view each of the hypothetical scenarios you postulate though, again, with the caveat that actual cases would need to be decided on their own facts. All statutory references are to TA 1988.

(*a*) A senior executive changing jobs at age 45, obviously as part of his or her normal working career, is not retirement. Any payment would fall within s 148.
(*b*) This is a borderline case which would depend very much on the precise circumstances. But, given the age, this might well be regarded as retirement, despite the new appointment. Any payment might well fall within s 596A.
(*c*) The action of the employee does not look to be consistent with retirement but with maximising his opportunities to continue working until normal retirement age. So any payment would fall within s 148.
(*d*) The circumstances set out may well be viewed as retirement. But if the *ex gratia* payment made is purely consolation for the loss of health which results in the premature termination of employment, it would not be regarded as made in connection with retirement. So s 148 would apply.
(*e*) As para 10 of SP 13/91 indicates, a lump sum paid on retirement solely by reason of disability from an accident is excluded from the definition of a "relevant benefit" in s 612. Section 148 would apply.
(*f*) This again is a borderline area. The example described probably would not be regarded as retirement bearing in mind the age of the employee, and the fact that she obtained further work. But the decision might well go the other way of the employee left to nurse a relative without seeking a further job, especially if she was nearer the normal retirement age for her job.

14 December 1992. ICAEW

Guidance note—non-resident settlements (TAX 20/92)

INTRODUCTION

1 FA 1991 ss 83–92, Sch 16–18 introduced new rules for capital gains of certain offshore trusts. The relevant legislation is now in TCGA 1992 ss 80–98, Sch 5.

2 In January 1992 the Inland Revenue invited various professional bodies to comment on a draft statement of practice explaining the practice to be followed in applying the new rules. Comments on the draft statement of practice were submitted by the Tax Faculty in February 1992 following which the statement of practice (SP5/92) and two new extra-statutory concessions (D40 and D41) were issued in May 1992 [Revenue Press Release dated 21 May 1992].

3 This guidance note sets out the text of some of the correspondence between the Tax Faculty and the Inland Revenue in respect of the statement of practice in both draft and final form. Correspondence quoted has been confined to matters which have not been clarified in the statement of practice or the extra-statutory concessions and has been amended to refer to the final version of statement of practice SP5/92 and to TCGA 1992 a consolidating Act which came into force on 6 April 1992.

4 The paragraphs which follow are set out under the relevant headings and paragraph numbers in statement of practice SP5/92. The point made by the Tax Faculty is followed by the Inland Revenue response.

PARAGRAPHS IN THE STATEMENT OF PRACTICE

IV Charge on the settlor: settlor's right to repayment from the trustees

Paragraph 8

5 The reference in para 8 to "any companies in which they are participators" implies that TA 1988 ss 660–694 could apply if a company can benefit from a trust if the settlor/settlor's spouse has a small shareholding in the company. Is this intended?

Revenue response: The reference to which you refer in para 8 is intended to imply that TA 1988 ss 660–694 could be invoked in circumstances where a company in which the settlor or the settlor's spouse has a small shareholding is a beneficiary of the trust.

Paragraph 9

6 As regards para 9, we note that a claim under IHTA 1984 s 3 (3) may arise if the settlor does not exercise his right of reimbursement. The drop in value in the settlor's estate will occur when the right to reimbursement expires. We shall therefore be grateful for guidance as to when the right expires.

Revenue response: The duration of the settlor's right to reimbursement is governed by the general law Limitation Act, which prescribes a six-year limit (unless the settlor indicates to the trustees before the expiration of this period that he does not intend to exercise his right to reimbursement, at which point the right would expire). The six-year period would begin when the settlor pays the tax.

V Charge on the settlor: trusts created before 19 March 1991

(a) TCGA 1992 Sch 5 para 9(3): transactions entered into at arm's length

Paragraphs 13 to 15

7 Paragraphs 13 to 15 deal with adjuster clauses so as to ensure that values are in accordance with what is finally agreed by the Revenue. It may not be appropriate in some circumstances for such a clause to deal only with the provision of compensating interest at a commercial rate but rather for there to be a provision for issued shares to be cancelled (*eg* in a situation where a company owned by the settlor has acquired shares in a company owned by an offshore trust on a share for share basis).

Revenue response: The practice does not encompass situations to which you refer. It would, of course, be possible for the parties to the transaction to show that the transaction was carried out on arm's length terms.

(d) TCGA 1992 Sch 5 para 9 (3): loans made to settlements

(i) Loans made before 19 March 1991

Paragraph 19

8 We seek confirmation that the words "directly or indirectly" in the first line of para 19 covers the position of a loan to an underlying company owned by the trustees.

Revenue response: The phrase "directly or indirectly" would, inter alia, cover the case of a loan made to a company owned by the trustees.

9 The extra-statutory concession does not deal with the case of a fixed term loan where the period expired after 18 March 1991 but repayment was not made immediately, and this may prove anomalous in a number of cases. There is very little difference between, on the one hand, a loan to trustees which, at 18 March 1991, was repayable on demand and, on the other, a loan which was then fixed term and which fell due shortly thereafter, but where repayment was not made immediately. In both cases, trustees would not have been capable of comprehending the full implications of TCGA 1992 Sch 5 para 9(3). We therefore remain of the view that there are strong grounds for saying that the concessionary treatment should extend to fixed term loans which have become repayable on demand loans at sometime between 18 March 1991 and 31 July 1992.

Revenue response: It is, in our experience, unusual for there to be a fixed-term loan to the trustees on better than commercial terms. But where such loans were in existence at 19 March 1991 and were not prepaid on a subsequent due date, the lender was effectively making a new repayable on demand loan. The extra-statutory concession is concerned only with repayable on demand loans which were entered into before the introduction of the legislation—on the basis that borrowers and lenders entering into such loans after that date were in a position to take the effects of the legislation fully into account. In those circumstances, it would in our view be inequitable to extend the concession to fixed term loans which became repayable on demand loans after 19 March 1991.

10 The Revenue accept in para 19 that a fixed period loan made before 19 March 1991 is generally to be treated as a provision of property in pursuance of a liability incurred before that date, but they do not accept this for a demand loan or similar terms. It is difficult to see the logic of this since a demand loan remains a liability unless and until it is called. There is nothing in the wording of TCGA 1992 Sch 5 para 9(3) to suggest that the failure to exercise a right constitutes the provision of property whether directly or indirectly.

Revenue response: The Revenue considers that the failure to exercise a right is a direct or indirect provision of property within TCGA 1992 Sch 5 para 9(3). The continued provision of the loan on better than commercial terms after it could have been recalled and the "benefit" to the settlement terminated is clearly within the ambit of para 9(3).

11 As the Revenue have hitherto strongly argued, there can be no such thing as past consideration if, as they now suggest, the terms of an interest-free demand loan be retrospectively amended. What is the status of the "interest" from the period 6 April 1991 to the date of variation? It cannot be interest and we hesitate to suggest that it is contractually enforceable. It presumably constitutes a distribution of trust assets to the lender. It is not income in his hands: is it therefore a capital payment?

Revenue response: You will note that, as it was not possible to issue the statement before 6 April, this treatment has been reclassified as a concession, and the text has been expanded to spell out how payments made under an arrangement to make the terms of a demand loan fully commercial will be treated in the hands of the recipient. I trust that this answers your comments on the status of such amounts. Similarly, because it was not possible to issue the concession before the end of the last tax year, and because the deadline has been extended to 31 July 1992, we have had to give some further consideration to the possible effects of the treatment of such amounts. As a result, the concessionary treatment has been extended to disapply the provisions of TCGA 1992 ss 92–95, Sch 5 para 9 (6) when considering certain payments for the year ended 5 April 1992.

12 Confirmation is sought that payment of "interest" or a sum in lieu of interest, will have no inheritance tax implications, and that there is no requirement for any inheritance tax return.

Revenue response: We do not consider the payment of a sum in lieu of interest, such as that envisaged in concession D41, to have any inheritance tax implications.

13 We would also like confirmation that such interest would qualify for a tax deduction where "real" interest would have been deductible, and that directors' loan accounts in respect of companies underlying trusts would be subject to the same Inland Revenue practice as other loans.

Revenue response: The treatment here will, of course, depend upon whether the sum is paid as interest, or as a sum in lieu of interest. Credit balances on director's loan accounts with underlying companies will be subject to the same treatment as other loans unless, exceptionally, paras 16 and 17 of the redrafted statement apply.

14 Further clarification is sought on five points with regard to the income tax implications of the payment of "interest"—

(*a*) This paragraph states that "the treatment here will, of course, depend upon whether the sum is paid as interest, or as a sum in lieu of interest". In the circumstances envisaged, there will necessarily have been a loan outstanding at 18 March 1991 which was either interest free, or bearing interest at less than a full rate. Any payment by the trustees to "make good" the interest must therefore be a payment in lieu of interest. We shall be grateful for confirmation that such payments will qualify for deduction for income tax purposes in determining the amount of income due to a life tenant, and for other income tax purposes (for example TA 1988 ss 660–694, 739, 740).

(*b*) Can the Revenue confirm that where a payment in lieu of interest is made to a lender, who is not a beneficiary, the amount paid will be treated as a capital payment.

(*c*) The final paragraph of the extra-statutory concession refers to the circumstances where an agreement to pay interest has been entered into by trustees before 6 April 1992 "or in respect of periods after 5 April 1992". We shall be grateful to have confirmation that the words in parenthesis are intended to refer to interest payable in respect of any period subsequent to the date of the agreement.

(*d*) If the lender is the settlor, or the settlor's spouse, confirmation is requested that payment of interest in lieu does not bring into play the provisions in TA 1988 ss 660–694 or TA 1988 ss 739, 740.

(*e*) What is the tax treatment of a sum in lieu of interest paid by an underlying company?

Revenue response:(*a*) I confirm that the payments in lieu of interest will qualify as a deduction, both in determining the income of a life tenant and for the purposes of TA 1988 s 740. Since both TA 1988 ss 660–694 and s 739 impose a charge on income *arising,* no deduction would be due where these provisions are applicable.

(*b*) I confirm that this is the effect of the concession.

(*c*) The basic point here is that amounts paid in respect of the fiscal year in which the agreement was made (or in fiscal years after the agreement was made) are treated as interest.

(*d*) Where funds have been lent to the trustees at less than a commercial rate of interest, it is the Revenue's view that the lender is a settlor and, by virtue of his right to revoke the loan agreement or arrangement by demanding repayment, is taxable under TA 1988 ss 672, 674 on income arising from the investment of the loaned monies. These provisions would, therefore, be in point *before* the question of a repayment in lieu of interest arose. Similarly, as TA 1988 s 739(3), (4)(*a*) specifically include repayments of loans, the provisions of s 739 would also already be in play *before* any possibility of payments within concession D41 could arise.

(*e*) The payment would not qualify as a deduction from profits in the hands of the company.

Paragraph 21 and the extra-statutory concession

15 It is suggested in the concession that if the terms of an interest-free demand loan are retrospectively amended so as to impose from 6 April 1991 a commercial rate of interest, that loan will not be treated as tainting the settlement. However, in most circumstances it would be a breach of trust for the trustees to accede to such a variation in the terms.

Revenue response: The other option available to the trustees is, of course, to repay the loan.

(ii) Loans made after 19 March 1991

(e) TCGA 1992 Sch 5 para 9(3): loans made by trustees

Paragraph 23

16 There are other issues concerning TCGA 1992 Sch 5 para 9(3) where it would be helpful for the statement of practice to provide clarification. Perhaps the most important point is confirmation that if the trustees make a loan to a beneficiary and the beneficiary pays interest at less than an arm's length rate, the payment of such interest does not fall within para 9(3). Similarly if the trustees lease property to a beneficiary and the beneficiary pays less than arm's length rental. While we believe it is clear that this does not fall within para 9(3), albeit that the undercharge of interest/rent is a capital payment within TCGA 1992 s 97, one leading counsel has expressed a contrary view. This is, therefore, a most important point where clarification is required.

Revenue response: Paragraph 23 of the redrafted statement sets out the position under TCGA 1992 Sch 5 para 9(3) where the trustees make a loan on better than commercial terms. The case of other benefits provided by the trustees, *eg* provision of property on beneficial terms, would be subject to the same principles.

(f) TCGA 1992 Sch 5 para 9(3): failure to exercise rights to reimbursement

Paragraph 24

17 A settlor of a trust may be liable to income tax on income arising to the trustees under, for example, TA 1988 ss 672, 674, 674A. Other provisions (such as TA 1988 s 675(3)) give the settlor a right of recovery of that income tax from a trustee. It would be helpful if the statement of practice could confirm that a failure by the settlor to exercise such a right of recovery is not regarded as a breach of the TCGA 1992 Sch 5 para 9(3) condition. If this confirmation cannot be given, clarification is needed on how far the settlor would have to go to seek recovery before demonstrating that he had ''done his best'' to obtain recovery from overseas trustees.

Revenue response: Paragraph 24 of the statement now covers the position where there is a failure to exercise rights to reimbursement against the settlement. Whether there had been a genuine, but unsuccessful attempt to enforce such rights could only be determined on the facts of the particular case.

18 Paragraph 24 of the statement of practice refers to the rights to reimbursement in TA 1988 ss 660–694. Could the Revenue please advise—

(*a*) when does the time limit for rights to reimbursement under TA 1988 ss 661, 667, 675(3), 685(5) expire;

(*b*) whether the Inland Revenue are operating a concession where the time limit expires after 18 March 1991 and, if so, the period during which the concessionary treatment is to apply.

Revenue response: The main point here is that the failure by the settlor to pursue his right to reimbursement within a reasonable period (and each case must be looked at in the light of its own facts) would, in itself, be a provision of property for the purposes of the settlement.

(g) TCGA 1992 Sch 5 para 9(3): administrative expenses

Paragraph 29

19 Paragraph 29 is rather unhelpful. The first alternative (*ie* payment of capital expenses out of income) would not normally be permitted where it is sought to have a qualifying interest in possession for inheritance tax purposes. The second alternative (the trustees borrowing money from the income account, which is subsequently restored with notional interest) requires further clarification. In particular, what does ''notional interest'' mean? Does it give rise to a liability to income tax on the income beneficiary? In this context, it would also be helpful to have the Revenue's view as to whether such interest constitutes relevant income for the purposes of s 740.

Revenue response: I confirm that interest credited to the income account will constitute taxable income in the hands of the beneficiary (either when it is credited in the case of a life tenant, or when it is paid or applied for the benefit of a discretionary beneficiary). It would also be treated as ''relevant income'' for TA 1988 s 740 purposes.

20 May we have confirmation that, where such a power exists and is exercised, then the Revenue will not regard the exercise as removing a qualifying interest in possession for inheritance tax purposes.

Revenue response: If the trust deed contains a power to pay capital expenses out of income, exercise of this power will not cause the trust to lose interest in possession status for inheritance tax purposes.

21 Where it becomes necessary to apply income to meet an expense on capital account for a year of assessment (see para 29 in the statement of practice), it of course follows that the income will not be available for distribution to the income beneficiary. Confirmation is sought that, in those circumstances, the income beneficiary is taxable only upon the amount of income, if any, which is available to be distributed to him. An income beneficiary is normally assessable upon the amount of trust income net of expenses charged against that income. If trustees properly apply trust income to meet a shortfall in respect of expenses on capital account relating to administration or taxation, the same reasoning should apply; the beneficiary should be taxed only upon that amount of income to which he is presently entitled. If that is correct, it would seem to follow that when the borrowing from income account is made good in a subsequent year, the relevant amount will become taxable upon the income beneficiary in that year. If the income that originally arose to the trustees had suffered deduction of tax at source, in either the UK or overseas, is credit to be given to the income beneficiary for such tax, when he becomes taxable upon the trust income in a later year?

Revenue response: I confirm that an income beneficiary will only be taxable on the net amount of income available after deduction of any income which has been applied to meet trust expenses on capital account and, when the income account is made good, that income will become taxable on the income beneficiary. The amount which is used to restore the income account is, however, no longer the same item as the income originally borrowed. It would not, therefore, retain the tax credit attached to the original income.

(i) TCGA 1992 Sch 5 para 8(3): indemnities and guarantees

Paragraph 35

22 Paragraph 35 of the statement of practice is causing concern. When a private company is being sold, and some or all of the shares in the private company are held by trustees of an offshore trust, it is normal for the purchaser to seek warranties and indemnities (at least in relation to tax) from all the vendors. Normally professional trustees will rightly resist the giving of warranties and indemnities by them, and if they give such warranties/indemnities, trustees will normally require some protection such as—

(*a*) a counter indemnity from the other shareholders (if any), or the beneficiaries;

(*b*) a restriction on the liability of the trust to the assets held in the trust from time to time, whereas there would not be a similar restriction applying to other shareholders who are selling their shares.

The statement of practice does not address this issue, and we shall be grateful to have the Revenue's views on this.

Revenue response: A decision on the issues raised in this paragraph could only be made in the light of all the facts of a particular case. Our general approach however would be on the lines that where the trustees sought to limit their liability on the warranty or indemnity to the value of the trust assets, and the warranty or indemnity was in all other respects identical to that of other vendors, the para 9(3)(*a*) exception would be regarded as satisfied. But this would not be the case where the trust assets were not exposed to the same risk that the other vendors accept.

(j) TCGA 1992 Sch 5 para 9(5): variations

Paragraph 36

23 Clarification is sought as to whether the Revenue accept that if a trust power is extant before 19 March 1991 any (proper) exercise of that power by the donee will not taint that trust under TCGA 1992 Sch 5 para 9(5).

Revenue response: The practice outlined at para 36 would apply regardless of whether the power was exercisable by the trustees, or by or at the consent or nomination of some other person.

OTHER MATTERS

Charge on the settlor: other issues

24 There are a number of further important issues on TCGA 1992 s 86, Sch 5, where it would be helpful for the statement of practice to contain clarification. TCGA 1992 Sch 5 specifies the test as to whether the settlor has an interest. Each of sub-paragraphs 2(1)(*a*) and(*b*) uses the words "may...in any circumstances whatever". Interpreted literally, it appears virtually impossible to define a trust where the settlor does not have an interest, because any beneficiary may become a relative of the settlor as a result of subsequent marriages (or indeed subsequent births if necessary to imagine all conceivable possibilities). This issue has given rise to litigation in a different context (inheritance tax), and it would be helpful if the Inland Revenue could indicate their practice in this context.

Revenue response: If the terms of a settlement are so framed that a clearly defined person can benefit, *eg* the class of beneficiaries includes "any spouse of the settlor" or "spouses of the settlor's children", or such persons could be added to the class of beneficiaries, then the settlor will be treated as having an "interest" in the trust. However, where there is no prima facie possibility of a defined person benefiting, the Revenue will not treat the settlor as having an "interest", unless the terms of the settlement and the circumstances of the case indicate an intention to benefit a person who is likely to become a defined person in the future, *eg* a settlement in favour of the fiancé of the settlor or of the settlor's child.

25 Also on the question of whether a settlor has an interest in a trust, it would be helpful if the statement of practice could confirm that a separated spouse would not be regarded as the settlor's spouse for this purpose.

Revenue response: A separated spouse would be regarded as a spouse for the purposes of these provisions unless, in accordance with existing practice (see para 13(*a*) Appendix B of the Resident trusts consultative document [19 March 1991]) on other provisions having a bearing on "settlor interest" trusts, the separation is permanent.

26 Finally on TCGA 1992 s 86, Sch 5, it would be helpful for the statement of practice to confirm that, in ascertaining the "amount on which the trustees would be chargeable to tax" as specified in TCGA 1992 s 86(1)(*e*), the overseas trustees are entitled to make all normal claims and elections available to UK taxpayers.

Revenue response: The trustees are entitled to make all elections and claims where they meet the particular requirements of the legislation. We did not think it necessary to include this in the statement.

21 January 1993. Inland Revenue

Taxation of in-house benefits in kind

The Inland Revenue announced today how it intends to deal with in-house benefits in kind following the House of Lords judgment in the case of *Pepper v Hart* [1992] STC 898.

The House of Lords decided the value for tax purposes of in-house benefits in kind is only the marginal or additional cost to the employer.

This does not affect the taxation of company cars, beneficial loans, living accommodation or the majority of benefits in kind which are bought by employers.

The judgment does affect the tax treatment of "in-house benefits":

- goods and services which employers provide free or at a discount from within their business; and
- some assets which are used both in the business and privately.

Treasury Ministers are considering the future tax treatment of these benefits in the light of the House of Lords' judgment and representations from employers and employees. In the meantime the Inland Revenue, with Ministers' approval, will now:

- settle in accordance with the House of Lords' decision the liabilities of employees whose tax affairs have been held open to await that judgment
- repay on request any excess tax paid in past years on in-house benefits in kind
- as tax offices or employees identify cases, repay any excess tax currently being deducted through PAYE
- adjust employees' PAYE codes to collect the tax (if any) due on the basis of marginal cost in 1993–94.

Employees who have paid tax based on more than the marginal cost of their in-house benefits should apply to their tax office for repayments. Current employees and retired pensioners of British Rail and London Regional Transport should *not* contact their tax offices: the Inland Revenue will send them details of how to get a repayment.

DETAILS

House of Lords judgment in Pepper v Hart

1 The cash equivalent of benefits in kind for tax purposes is determined by

- special rules for company cars and fuel, beneficial loans, living accommodation and mobile phones; and
- general rules for other benefits (in TA 1988 s 156).

2 The question before the House of Lords was how the general rule applied to the benefit to school staff of reduced school fees. The particular question was whether the cost to the employer was the average cost of educating a child at the school or the marginal costs attributable to the education of the children of staff. The decision was that in the case of all in-house benefits the cost of the benefit to the employer is the additional or marginal cost only.

Effects of the judgment

3 The judgment does not affect the tax treatment of—

- company cars and fuel, beneficial loans and provided accommodation;

- the majority of goods and services which are bought by employers to provide benefits for their employees.

4 The judgment does in principle change the tax treatment of benefits provided from within the employer's business— ie ''in-house'' benefits in contrast to those which are ''bought in''.

5 This applies both to benefits provided direct and to vouchers which employees exchange for in-house goods or services.

In-house benefits

6 In-house benefits include—

- goods and services sold in the normal course of the employer's business and provided free or at a discount to employees
- services and facilities provided in-house
- assets used in the business and made available for an employee's private use, and such assets if subsequently transferred to employees.

Who does this change affect?

7 The Inland Revenue have previously collected tax on some ''in-house'' benefits based on amounts greater than the marginal cost to the employer. Tax has been collected by assessments, and by adjustments to PAYE codes.

8 Employees who have paid tax include—

- railway employees;
- some teachers;
- employees who have the use of company vans.

Repayments

9 Employees who have paid tax on in-house benefits on the basis of more than the marginal cost to the employer can now seek a repayment. Repayments will be made with repayment supplement.

10 The Inland Revenue will make repayments of tax paid through PAYE or by assessment for 1986–87 and subsequent years. Taxpayers who had assessments for earlier years made after 5 April 1986 are also entitled to seek repayment for those earlier years. Requests for repayments should be made by 5 April 1993.

11 The repayment will be calculated on the difference between—

- the figure used previously for cost to the employer; and
- the marginal cost.

12 Employees will not be entitled to a repayment where the marginal cost to the employer of providing the benefit is greater than or equal to the figure adopted for tax in previous years. In these circumstances the Inland Revenue will not seek to disturb for 1992–93 or earlier years whatever arrangements tax offices have agreed or accepted in practice for valuing in-house benefits.

What taxpayers should do to get a repayment

13 The Inland Revenue is making arrangements to contact current employees and retired pensioners of British Rail and London Regional Transport about repayments.

14 Other employees (and former employees) who wish to seek a repayment should contact their current tax office. Tax offices will be able to deal with requests more speedily if employees give—

- their national insurance number; and
- the years in which they paid tax on in-house benefits.

What is the marginal cost of in-house benefits?

15 The marginal cost of in-house benefits depends on each employer's particular circumstances. But, as a general guide, the Inland Revenue accept that—

- rail or bus travel by employees on terms which do not displace fare-paying passengers involves no or negligible additional costs
- goods sold at a discount which leave employees paying at least the wholesale price involve no or negligible net benefit
- where teachers pay 15 per cent or more of a school's normal fees there is no net benefit
- professional services which do not require additional employees or partners (eg legal and financial services) have no or negligible cost to the employer (provided the employee meets the cost of any disbursements).

16 The treatment of other benefits (*eg* airline travel for airline staff) is being discussed with representative bodies.

Assets with business and private use

17 The Inland Revenue's view is that the House of Lords judgment also affects the calculation of the cash equivalent of some assets which are *both* used in the business *and* placed at the disposal of employees. Some fixed costs (eg the road tax for a fitter's van) will no longer need to be taken into account where the private use of the asset is incidental to its business use. The cash equivalent is the *additional* expense incurred in or in connection with its provision (TA 1988 s 156(5)(*b*)) together with a proper proportion of the annual value of the asset (TA 1988 s 156(5)(*a*)).

18 The Inland Revenue will continue to seek tax on the full costs of assets provided solely for private purposes.

Mobile phones

[These paragraphs are no longer relevant].

Employers' responsibilities

22 Employers should continue to include on forms P11D ... information about in-house benefits.

23 Employers should contact their tax office if they have questions about the need to report benefits or the calculation of marginal cost.

NOTES

1 The House of Lords gave their judgment in the case known as *Pepper v Hart* on 26 November. They decided—

– to change their previous practice and have regard to the debates reported in Hansard as an aid to interpretation of the law; and
– the law on benefits in kind required the inland revenue to take marginal cost as the cost to the employer of in-house benefits.

2 The Inland Revenue will continue to discuss with employers and representative bodies arrangements to deal with in-house benefits in other industries—eg airlines.

3 The Inland Revenue are grateful for the help they are receiving from employers to make these repayments.

15 February 1993. Law Society

Company taxation—equity notes and thin capitalisation

The International Tax Sub-Committee of the Revenue Law Committee has been in correspondence with the Inland Revenue International Division in order to seek clarification of certain aspects of TA 1988 ss 209, 808A which were amended and introduced respectively by F(No 2)A 1992 ss 31, 52. The questions put by the Law Society and [the] Revenue's answers are set out below.

EQUITY NOTES—TA 1988, S 209

Law Society: We understand that the legislation is aimed at attempts to obtain a deduction for interest payments in the UK where that interest, when received by an overseas affiliate, is treated for tax purposes as a dividend or return on an equity investment. Concern has been expressed that these provisions can be applied as a means of denying a deduction in other circumstances—for instance where a double taxation agreement disapplies TA 1988 s 209(2)(*e*)(iv) but there is no (or only a limited) exception for "special relationship" loans. We should be grateful if you would confirm that it is not intended to seek to apply the legislation in this way.

Revenue: The object of the legislation was not merely to deal with cases where payments were characterised as something other than interest in the hands of the overseas recipient company. The legislation is intended to lay down the rule that instruments with the characteristics described in TA 1988 s 209(9) shall be treated in all cases as giving rise to distributions. TA 1988 s 209(*e*)(vii) does not relate only to interest paid to a non-resident company and is not therefore affected by the "override" of s 209(2)(*e*)(iv) and (v) contained in many of our treaties.

Law Society: TA 1988 s 209(9) uses the term "security". In establishing whether an equity note exists, will s 209(9) be construed without regard to the extended definition of security contained in s 254(1) so that normal inter-company indebtedness, bank overdrafts and deposits accounts will not fall within the scope of these provisions?

Revenue: We confirm that TA 1988 s 209(9) defines those securities which are to be treated as equity notes. TA 1988 s 254(1) applies to the extent that the term "security" includes securities not creating or evidencing a charge on assets. But to the extent that interest paid in the circumstances dealt with in the remainder of the definition is not paid in respect of a security we can confirm that it will not be so treated by s 209(9). This is because the effect of s 254(1) is to treat the interest concerned as being paid in respect of a security but [that provision] does not define the underlying advance etc as being a security. In normal circumstances intercompany loans, bank overdrafts and bank deposits will not therefore be treated as equity notes.

Law Society: Although a demand loan might, in theory, not be repaid within the permitted period we understand that the Inland Revenue's view is that such a loan is not within the meaning of "equity note".

Revenue: We can confirm that a demand loan, whether or not it is evidenced by a security, will not be regarded as an equity note because it contains terms capable of giving rise to a particular date or dates by which it is to be repaid.

Law Society: In determining whether a security is an equity note s 209(9)(*d*) refers to circumstances where the issuing company "can secure that there is no particular date by which the security is to be redeemed". Could the Revenue confirm that the fact that the issuing company holds shares in the company holding the security (or controls it within TA 1988 s 840) will not, of itself, be regarded as sufficient for the issuing company to be treated as being able to secure that there is no particular date for redemption.

Revenue: We can confirm that the ownership of shares in a company will not of itself be treated as a "power to secure" within s 209(9)(*d*).

Law Society: TA 1988 s 209 (11) refers to "arrangements" involving a company being put in funds by the issuing company or a company associated with it. It may happen that an otherwise unconnected third party. *eg* a bank, is a holder of a deposit from a company and also the holder of securities capable of constituting equity notes in circumstances where there is no causal or other link between the deposit (*ie* the putting in funds) and the issue of the equity notes. We should be grateful if you could confirm that you would not treat a situation such as this as one to which s 209(11) would apply.

Revenue: A company which incidentally holds an equity note issued by a company with which it (directly or indirectly) has a business relationship will not be treated for that reason alone as a "funded company". The term "arrangements" involves in our view more than a mere capricious happening. In particular the taking of a deposit by a bank from an unconnected customer who may himself hold an equity note issued by that bank will not be treated of itself as such an arrangement.

PRs etc

THIN CAPITALISATION—TA 1988 S 808A

Law Society: Loan documentation negotiated between a third party lender and a company which is a member of a group will normally contain cross-default, cross-guarantee and other provisions relating to other members of the group. Such provisions will not normally be contained in an intra-group loan even though the terms for the payment of interest and principal are, otherwise, identical to those negotiated at arm's length. We should be grateful if you could confirm that the absence of such cross-default and cross-guarantee provisions will not of itself be taken into account in answering the questions of (i) whether the amount of interest exceeds that which would have been paid in the absence of a special relationship; or (ii) whether the loan would have been made at all.

Revenue: We can confirm that the absence of such provision will not of itself be taken into account for the purposes you refer to.

Law Society: Claims for treaty relief are made on forms issued by the Inspector of Foreign Dividends. We understand that no amendment will be made to those forms as a result of the introduction of s 808A. We should be grateful if you could confirm that applicants are not required to make any changes in the way they complete such forms or in the information provided when making such an application.

Revenue: TA 1988 s 808A is intended to restore the position to what the Inland Revenue understood it to be before recent decisions of the Special Commissioners. Accordingly, it does not in our view impose any additional requirement on applicants for claims to treaty relief. As a separate matter TMA 1970 s 42 provides that "a claim shall be in such form as the Board may determine".

Law Society: TA 1988 s 808A(3) refers to "the taxpayer". Is this intended to be a reference to the applicant for treaty relief (ie the recipient of interest) or to the paying company?

Revenue: The taxpayer in the context of s 808A(3) is the person making the claim under the treaty and is therefore normally the recipient of the interest. It is often the case however that the paying company (or his agent) will be asked to provide information in connection with the treaty claim. As a separate matter, the paying company may also need to take the provisions of the article into account when justifying a claim that interest is not within the scope of s 209 and therefore deductible either directly or as a charge.

19 March 1993. ICAEW

Equity notes and thin capitalisation—Guidance note (TAX 5/93)

FOREWORD

1 Following the laying on 18 June 1992 of the new clauses on equity notes and thin capitalisation referred to in the Inland Revenue Press Release dated 15 May 1992 (and at paras 44–47 "Clauses not yet published" of TAX 10/92: Memorandum submitted in June 1992 to the Chancellor of the Exchequer commenting on the Finance Bill 1992), representatives of the Tax Faculty met the Inland

Revenue in June 1992 to discuss the clauses, which were subsequently enacted as F(No 2)A 1992 ss 31, 32.

2 The legislation seeks to counteract the tax advantages of equity notes. Equity notes were developed to exploit the US tax treatment of certain types of debt which in the US could essentially be characterised as equity. Thus, interest paid would be deductible for UK tax purposes but for US tax purposes would be treated as a return on equity—providing the company had no earnings and profits for US tax purposes, then the receipts would be tax free in the US.

3 This guidance note covers certain points raised with the Revenue by the Tax Faculty and includes, where applicable, the substance of assurances given by Mr Stephen Dorrell, Financial Secretary to the Treasury during the Standing Committee debate reported in Hansard, 30 June 1992, cols 437–452 as to how the Revenue will apply the provisions. The Inland Revenue have seen this note and have confirmed that it correctly sets out their understanding of the meaning of the legislation. The Inland Revenue have made it clear that the law will be applied according to the facts and circumstances of each particular case.

DETAILED COMMENTS

4. The Tax Faculty sought confirmation of the following:

Point 1

ICAEW

5 That a security payable on demand will be treated for the purposes of TA 1988 s 209(9) as having a particular date by which it is to be redeemed, namely the demand date.

Revenue response

6 A loan repayable on demand has a date for redemption, namely the date of the demand, and, as a liability repayable on demand contains an indefinite number of particular dates by which it is to be redeemed, such a loan cannot be treated as falling within the new provisions.

7 The definition of ''equity notes'' in TA 1988 s 209 does not encompass bank overdrafts, normal inter-company balances or other similar loans where the lender can demand repayment by reasonable notice.

8 This accords with the assurance given by the Financial Secretary to the Treasury in the Standing Committee debate (Hansard, 30 June 1992, col 444).

Point 2

ICAEW

9 That an ordinary inter-company account which would not under general law constitute a security would not fall to be treated as an equity note, because it would not constitute a security for the purpose of TA 1988 s 209(9) despite the definition of ''security'' in TA 1988 s 254.

Revenue response

10 The definition of ''security'' in TA 1988 s 254 provides for two things. First it says that the term includes securities that do not create a charge on assets. Second it says that interest paid on a loan without the issue of a security will be treated as if it were paid in respect of a security.

11 The new provision in context reads—

> ''Section 209(2)...distribution, in relation to any company, means...
>
> (*e*) any interest or other distribution out of assets of the company in respect of securities of the company...where the securities are...
>
> (viii) equity notes issued by the company...''

TA 1988 s 209(9) defines an equity note.

12 It follows that an equity note is a particular form of security and TA 1988 s 254 cannot be used to deem that interest is paid in respect of an equity note if it is not in fact so paid. Most bank deposits or bank overdrafts and inter-company accounts will not normally be securities. Section 254 deems interest in respect of such loans to be paid in respect of securities but not in respect of equity note securities. Therefore such loans are beyond the scope of new TA 1988 s 209(9).

Point 3

ICAEW

13 That the word ''arrangement'' in the proposed TA 1988 s 209(11) will normally be taken only to apply to a preordained transaction where there is a link between the putting in funds of a company and the holding of the equity note. In other words, if a member of a banking group were to loan money to a company which as a separate matter happened to acquire equity notes issued by the group, then the provision would not apply.

Revenue response

14 A company which in the ordinary course of its business incidentally holds an equity note issued by a company with which it (directly or indirectly) has a business relationship or with whom it has banking facilities will in practice not be treated for that reason alone as a ''funded company''. An assurance confirming this practice was given by the Financial Secretary to the Treasury during the Standing Committee debate (Hansard, 30 June 1992, col 445).

15 TA 1988 s 209(11) is aimed at payments between associated companies which may insert another company in a chain between them in order to frustrate the legislation. If such arrangements exist the holder of the equity note will be regarded as a ''funded company'' and payments made under that note will be treated as distributions (subject to s 212).

16 To fall within the definition there must be ''arrangements involving the company being put in funds''. These provisions will not be invoked unless the ''arrangements'' in question clearly involve more than a mere happening. The term ''arrangements'' is often used in the Taxes Acts in conjunction with ''scheme or'' which gives a flavour of the Revenue's view as to the term's meaning. It is unlikely that wholly capricious business arrangements between non-associated companies can meet the definition of ''arrangements''.

Faculty comment

17 The Faculty welcomes the Revenue's indication (confirmed by ministerial assurance given to Parliament) that they will not seek to characterise any arrangements of whatever kind as falling within these provisions but will in practice only consider arrangements which have a purposive connection as falling within their scope. This is particularly welcome given the much wider construction placed on ''arrangements'' in other contexts, eg Inland Revenue Statement of Practice SP13/91 para 2: ''Ex gratia awards made on termination of an office or employment by retirement or death''.

Point 4

ICAEW

18 That where a loan is made to a company at a rate of interest lower than that which might have been set by an independent party, the special relationship provision in the relevant treaty will not prevent the interest article from overriding TA 1988 s 209(2)(*e*)(iv), (v).

Revenue response

19 If an equity note as defined is in issue, then interest may be regarded as a distribution regardless of the rate of interest charged on the note.

20 The application of TA 1988 s 209(2)(*e*)(iv), (v) depends on the facts and circumstances of each case, but if a loan is made on arm's length terms with the only exception that the interest rate is lower than the market rate, then it would be expected that the interest would be protected by the treaty in which case it would not be treated as a distribution by s 209(2)(*e*)(iv), (v).

21 The inter-relationship between the treaty and TA 1988 s 209(2)(*e*)(iv), (v) is of course governed by the precise terms of the treaty. In, for example, the UK/US double taxation agreement, art 11(7) effectively overrides TA 1988 s 209(2)(*e*)(iv), (v) by providing that ''any provision in the law of (the UK) relating only to interest paid to a non-resident corporation shall not operate so as to require such interest paid to a resident of the (US) to be treated as a distribution...''. However, art 11(5) then denies the benefit of art 11, including art 11(7), to the extent that interest paid ''exceeds for whatever reason the amount which would have been paid in the absence of such (special) relationship''. If therefore interest was paid at a lower rate than arm's length there would not normally be any excess interest caught by art 11(5).

22 However, the test is not only what the rate of interest is but also whether the loan would have been made at all so that it is conceivable that there will be cases where, despite the fact that interest is paid below an arm's length rate, the facts and circumstances are such that the whole of the interest may fail the test provided by art 11(5) as spelt out in the new legislation.

Point 5

ICAEW

23 That the new TA 1988 s 808A will be disapplied, by s 808A(5) in any case where the special relationship provision expressly requires regard to be had to the debt on which the interest is paid (as in the OECD Model), and that the phrase in brackets in s 808A(5) does not impose an additional requirement for further express wording in the special relationship provision.

Revenue response

24 TA 1988 s 808A(5) is designed to do no more than take the treaties which use the OECD Model ''special relationship provision'' outside the scope of the legislation in s 808A. The OECD Model article differs from the UK/US article and indeed from many other of our treaty articles by providing (art 11(6)) that the special relationship exclusion from benefit shall be applied "having regard to the debt claim for which it is paid". It is to this wording that s 808A(5) makes particular reference.

1 April 1993. Inland Revenue

Payments to the Inland Revenue by electronic funds transfer

The Financial Secretary to the Treasury, Stephen Dorrell, MP, today announced a new Inland Revenue practice when tax is paid by electronic funds transfer. In reply to a Parliamentary Question, Mr Dorrell said—

> "From today where a payment of tax is made by electronic funds transfer, an effective date of payment of the tax of one working day immediately before the date value is received by the Inland Revenue will be allowed."

NOTES

1 Electronic funds transfer is made through BACS (bankers' automated clearing services) and CHAPS (clearing house automated payment system). Details of how to make such payments to the Inland Revenue can be obtained from the accounts office to which payments are normally made.

Enquiries to the accounts office at Shipley should be sent to Angela Norfolk, S3/A, First Floor, Accounts Office, Shipley, West Yorkshire BD98 8AA (telephone 01274 589579 direct line or 01274 594141 ext 3579 or 3776).

Enquiries to the accounts office at Cumbernauld should be sent to Mary Hope, Credit Processing, Accounts Office, St Mungo's Road, Cumbernauld, Glasgow G70 5TR (telephone 01236 783717 direct line or 01236 36121 ext 3717).

2 The Inland Revenue currently treat the date on which value is received as the effective date of payment where an electronic transfer is used. The new treatment aims to encourage payment of tax by electronic funds transfer as this has added advantages of speed and security.

12 May 1993. Hansard

Company cars

Mr Beith asked the Chancellor of the Exchequer if he will list the circumstances when home-to-work travel in a car made available by an employer is not regarded as private use.

Mr Dorrell: Home-to-work travel in a car made available by an employer is not regarded as private use—

- where the employee has a travelling appointment;
- where the employee travels from home to a temporary place of work and the distance travelled is less than the distance between the normal place of work and the temporary place of work;
- where, exceptionally, the home qualifies under tax law as a place of work and the employee travels from home to another place of work in the performance of his duties.

There are also circumstances where home-to-work travel in a car provided by an employer is regarded as private use but is ignored for tax purposes. These are—

- where a disabled person is provided with a car from home-to-work travel and there is no other private use;
- where a car is provided for home-to-work travel when public transport is disrupted;
- where a car is provided for late night journeys work-to-home, within the terms of Inland Revenue Concession A66 [now obsolete];
- where the car is a pooled car and any home-to-work travel is merely incidental to its business use.

HC Written Answer, 12 May 1993, Vol 224, col 472

14 May 1993. Hansard

Company cars—provision of chauffeur

Mr Beith asked the Chancellor of the Exchequer what benefits in kind an employer should report on the form P11D in respect of an employee who is driven from home to his normal place of employment in a chauffeur-driven car provided by his employer.

Mr Dorrell: If the car is a pooled car and the journeys are merely incidental to the business use of the car, the employer should make no return.

In other circumstances, the employer should return on form P11D the benefit of the car and the costs of the chauffeur.

Whether or not an employee's private use of a car is incidental to its business use will depend on the facts of each particular case. If employers or employees are in any doubt about the correct treatment, they should consult their tax office.

HC Written Answer, 14 May 1993, Vol 224, cols 585, 586

18 May 1993. Inland Revenue

Business tax computations rounded to nearest £1,000

The Financial Secretary to the Treasury, Stephen Dorrell MP, today announced the criteria on which the Board of Inland Revenue will be prepared to accept tax computations rounded to the nearest £1,000. The intention of this practice is to reduce the compliance burden on large businesses which produce their statutory accounts in round thousands but have to repeat the accounting work in exact pound units solely for tax purposes.

In a written reply to a Parliamentary Question [HC Written Answer, 18 May 1993, Vol 225, cols 110, 111] Mr Dorrell said:

"**1** The Inland Revenue are prepared to accept computations of business profits for tax purposes in figures rounded to the nearest £1,000 from single businesses or companies with an annual turnover of not less than £5 million, where rounding at least to that extent has been used in preparing their accounts. (The turnover of members of a group will not be aggregated for applying this £5 million threshold.) Where turnover fluctuates either side of the threshold, rounding can be used for a period of account if the turnover for either that year or the immediately previous year is above the limit. (Turnover comprises gross receipts including investment and estate income, as well as trading receipts.)

2 The Inland Revenue will only accept rounding in any particular case if the basis adopted is satisfactory. Rounded computations from such businesses must be accompanied by a certificate made by the person preparing the computations which—

- states the basis on which the rounding has been done;
- confirms that this basis is unbiased, that it has been applied consistently and that it has been used in a manner which, in all the circumstances, produces a fair result for tax purposes; and
- if the rounding was done by computer, states the program or software used.

In subsequent years if there have been no charges in the basis or in the software, the certificate need only confirm that the rounding has been done on the same basis as before.

3 The Inland Revenue are prepared to accept rounded figures only in relation to the computation of the profits of the business, including in the case of companies, non-Case I items. They cannot accept rounded figures in relation to the computation of tax payable or of any other figure of tax.

4 Nor can they accept rounded figures, in relation to any other aspect of the tax computations, where rounding would impede the proper application of the relevant legislation or where it would normally be necessary to go back to the underlying records to do the computation, and thus there would be no reduction in the compliance burden in allowing the use of round sums. Rounding is not therefore acceptable in—

- computations of chargeable gains (since precise dates on which expenditure is incurred are needed for indexation allowance purposes); rounding can however be accepted in relation to the incidental costs of acquisition and disposal;
- computations of tax credit relief—while individual terms of foreign income (including profits of overseas branches and, for the purpose of calculating underlying tax rates, dividends paid by overseas companies and the profits of those companies) may be rounded, computations of credit relief must continue to distinguish the individual items of income and to show the exact amounts of foreign tax for which credit is claimed so that the rules for limiting the credit can be properly applied;
- computations required for purposes of the accrued income scheme (TA 1988 ss 710–728);
- aspects of capital allowances computations where precise figures are required, for example by the statute or where rounding might work unfairly because more than one taxpayer is involved and different bases could be used by each. One case where the statute requires the use of precise figures is the expensive car provisions in [CAA 2001 ss 74–80]. However in any capital allowances apportionment case it would be open to the taxpayer to demonstrate to the inspector that, taking all the circumstances into account, including those of any other party, the use of rounded figures did not lead to a result that was materially different from the statutory position. For example, in the case of the industrial buildings one-quarter rule (CAA 2001 s 283(2)), the inspector would want to be satisfied that the use of rounding alone did not reduce the non-qualifying expenditure to one-quarter or less of the total expenditure (and thereby enable the whole of the expenditure to attract allowances).
- the application of the statutory amount in TA 1988 s 748(1)(*d*) in relation to a controlled foreign company.

PRs etc

5 Exceptionally other circumstances may arise where rounding would not satisfy the tests in para 4. In those circumstances the inspector may insist that roundings are not used.

6 These arrangements will continue into pay and file. Subject to the exceptions provided in the two previous paragraphs, rounded figures from the accounts may be used in the computation of trading profits and losses, each category of income, management expenses and charges. Where appropriate, these figures will of course require adjustment to the ''received'' or ''paid'' basis. Group relief or relief for losses from other periods should be on the actual sums surrendered or brought forward (or carried back). No rounding should take place in the return form itself (for example, in the allocation of profits to financial years) or in any arithmetic that precedes such entries (for example, a computation of marginal small companies relief).

7 Where arrangements on the use of rounding have already been agreed locally with inspectors these may continue to operate in the short term, but must come to an end for all periods ending after 31 May 1995.''

NOTES

1 Generally tax computations are presented in precise figures and this generates additional work for the large companies which prepare their statutory and management accounts in rounded thousands.

2 This announcement sets out the criteria on which tax computations in rounded thousands will be accepted by the Board of Inland Revenue.

3 November 1993. Law Society

Legal costs relating to termination payments—Inland Revenue concession

The Law Society's Revenue Law Committee had correspondence with the Personal Tax Division of the Inland Revenue earlier this year on the subject of the tax treatment which the Revenue applied, on a concessionary basis, to the payment by an employer of the legal costs incurred by a former employee in connection with the termination of the employment.

In an extra-statutory concession published on 2 September 1993, the Revenue gave details of their practice and outlined the circumstances in which they would not seek to tax payment of legal costs including disbursements and VAT by the employer.

Where a dispute is settled without recourse to the courts, tax will not be charged where payments are made direct to the former employee's solicitor and in full or partial discharge of the solicitors' bill of costs incurred by the employee only in connection with the termination of his or her employment and under a specific term in the settlement agreement providing for that payment.

The Revenue has subsequently confirmed in correspondence that the requirement for the costs to be incurred ''only'' in connection with the termination of employment does not mean that the solicitors' bill must relate exclusively to costs so incurred, but the concession would only apply to those costs and it follows that accordingly, they should be clearly identifiable in the solicitors' bill: *Law Society's Gazette* 3 November 1993 p 34.

Commentary—Simon's Direct Tax Service **E4.805**.
Concession A81—(Termination payments and legal costs).
Revenue Interpretation RI 61—Termination payments and legal costs.

17 December 1993. Inland Revenue

Lloyd's: basis of assessment for individual names—transitional administrative arrangements

The Financial Secretary to the Treasury, Stephen Dorrell MP, has today announced the publication of the transitional administrative arrangements that will apply in moving from the present basis of assessing individual members to the new basis.

In reply to a Parliamentary Question [HC Official Report, 17 December 1993, Vol 234 col 972], the Financial Secretary said—

> ''The transitional administrative arrangements that will apply in the move from the present basis of assessing individual members to the new basis have now been finalised: these arrangements are subject to the legislative proposals being enacted in due course. The detail is set out in a note which is being placed in the House of Commons Library.''

DETAILS

1 Subject to Parliamentary scrutiny of the proposals in Finance Bill 1994, from Account 1994 onwards there will be a change in the basis of charging to tax profits that arise to a Lloyd's underwriter as a result of participation in one or more syndicates for a specific underwriting year.

The intention is that the profits of Account 1994 will be assessed not in 1994–95, as would have been the case, but in the year that those profits are declared and distributed, namely 1997–98.

2 The transitional arrangements needed to achieve such a change involve alterations in—

- the precise dates on which tax becomes payable in respect of syndicate profits;
- when information should be returned to the Inland Revenue;
- when loss relief claims can be made.

The transitional arrangements in these areas are set out below.

3 Currently tax is payable in respect of underwriting profits on the 1 January and the 1 July three years after the end of the underwriting year. Under present arrangements tax in respect of Account 1992 (1992–93) would have been due on 1 January 1996 (basic rate) and 1 July 1996 (higher rate).

As part of the transitional arrangements the higher rate assessment for this year will fall due on 31 January 1997; the basic rate assessment will remain at 1 January 1996. For Account 1993 the same pattern of payment dates will apply with basic rate tax due on 1 January 1997 and higher rate on 31 January 1998.

4 Under the proposed distribution year basis of assessment for Account 1994 onwards, tax on the profits will then fall due at the same dates as are envisaged for self-assessment generally, ie for 1997–98 tax will be due on 31 January 1998, 31 July 1998 and 31 January 1999.

5 Changing the basis of assessment in respect of syndicate profits results in there being three years of assessment (1994–95 to 1996–97) in which no syndicate profits fall to be assessed. There will, however, be personal receipts (such as ancillary fund income) and personal expenses (such as bank interest) to be assessed under Case I for those years. For these years, therefore, there will be just one tax payment date which will also be set at 31 January 1998.

6 Information relating to underwriting Account 1992 will be sought in conjunction with the income tax return to be issued in April 1996 and for Account 1993 that to be issued in April 1997. These dates are a year later than would have been the case had present arrangements continued.

7 Information relating to the years of assessment 1994–95 to 1996–97 will also be sought in conjunction with the income tax return to be issued in April 1997. In practice this information will be available to underwriters well before that date. Because of this, a form will be provided in April 1994 on which they can record the relevant information much closer to the time that it actually arises; it will, therefore, be readily accessible to them when it has to be returned formally in 1997.

8 If it is clear that any of the years 1994–95 to 1996–97 result in a loss (because personal expenses exceed personal receipts) the Inland Revenue will give effect to loss claims, subject to normal checking, on submission of a claim as soon as the figures are available. In some instances the tax adjusted results for 1992–93 and 1993–94 may also be available to an underwriter before the date he is required to return them to the Inland Revenue. If these results show a loss, the Inland Revenue will similarly be prepared to give effect to loss claims based on those results, subject to normal checking, provided all the information that would have been provided in the income tax return relating to that return of profit or loss is supplied with the loss claim.

9 The transitional arrangements will come to an end with the return of underwriting profits for 1997–98. For that year onwards the proposed self-assessment filing and payment dates will apply. No extended time limits for claims and elections will be required and members' agent accounting will not apply after Account 1993.

10 The transitional arrangements are summarised in the [table reproduced below].

NOTES

1 The Government's proposals were announced in an Inland Revenue Press Release 14 October 1993 entitled "Lloyd's: tax arrangements for corporate members—basis of assessment for individual members".

2 These proposals appear in the Finance Bill which will be published on 11 January 1994.

3 The administrative transitional arrangements are being publicised now so that the individual members can have adequate notice of the procedures. Also, it will enable those who might be considering acceptance of the Lloyd's Settlement Offer published on 6 December 1993 to know when tax on payments under that offer would be payable.

LLOYD'S UNDERWRITERS—ASSESSMENT OF LLOYD'S PROFITS DATES FOR PAYMENT OF TAX

The table sets out details of the information that will be asked for in each tax return from 1994 to 1998, as well as details of when Lloyd's profits will be assessed and the dates on which the tax on those profits will be due.

	1994	*1995*	*Return* *1996*	*1997*	*1998*
Syndicate income					
Account	1991	—	1992	1993	1994
Year of assessment	1991–92		1992–93	1993–94	1997–98
Tax payable					
Basic rate	[1]		1.1.96	1.1.97	
Expenses incurred, personally and income arising on personal funds					
Period	year to 5.4.92	—	year to 5.4.93	6.4.93– 31.12.93[2] year to 31.12.94 year to 31.12.95 year to 31.12.96	year to 31.12.97
Year of assessment	1991–92	—	1992–93	1993–94 1994–95 1995–96 1996–97	1997–98
Tax payable					31.1.98
Payment on account					31.7.98
Sweep up assessment	1.7.95		31.1.97	31.1.98	31.1.99
Gains on personal fund assets					
Period	year to 5.4.94	year to 5.4.95	year to 5.4.96	year to 5.4.97	year to 5.4.98
Year of assessment	1993–94	1994–95	1995–96	1996–97	1997–98

Commentary—*Simon's Direct Tax Service* **Division E5.4.**

Notes—[1] Members' Agent Accounting suspended for Account 1991 in light of losses.

[2] Expenses incurred in the period 1 January to 5 April 1993 that prior to Finance Act 1993 would have been allowable against 1993–94 profits will also be reported; and allowed for 1993–94.

9 February 1994. Inland Revenue

European Economic Area Agreement

The European Economic Area (EEA) Agreement which came into force on 1 January 1994 extends the principles of the Single Market to five states of the European Free Trade Association (Austria, Finland, Iceland, Norway and Sweden). [NB Austria, Finland and Sweden were admitted to the EU on 1 January 1995.]

The EEA Agreement covers the free movement of goods, services, capital and people and rules on competition and state aids. There are a number of direct tax consequences (described in detail below) concerning—

- private medical insurance;
- maintenance payments;
- European economic interest groups;
- company migrations; and
- deposit takers.

DETAILS

Private medical insurance

1 Tax relief is available on premiums paid under certain private medical insurance contracts for the over 60s. One condition for relief is that the insurer must be authorised to carry on insurance business either in the UK or in another European Union (EU) member state of which it is a national. From 1 January 1994 this will be extended to include all states within the European Economic Area.

Maintenance payments

2 The EEA Agreement extends tax relief to maintenance payments under new or existing EEA court orders or written agreements made and enforceable under the law of an EEA state. Relief will be available for payments due and made on or after 1 January 1994.

3 As with maintenance payments made under UK and other EU court orders or written agreements, to qualify for relief payments must be—

- made to a divorced or separated husband or wife who has not remarried; and
- for his or her own maintenance or for the maintenance by him or her of a child of the family aged under 21.

There is no relief for payments made directly to children.

4 Relief is available on maintenance payments up to a limit equal to the married couple's allowance (£1,720 for 1993–94, 1994–95 and 1995–96). [FA 1994 s 79] provides for the restriction of the relief to 20 per cent, for 1994–95 and to 15 per cent for 1995–96 in line with similar restrictions in the married couple's allowance.

5 Anyone wishing to claim relief should contact their tax office and provide a copy of the court order or written agreement under which payments are made.

European economic interest groupings (EEIGs)

6 EEIGs—an optional form of business entity for businesses looking to co-operate internationally—may be set up under Council Regulation (EEC) No 2137/85 of 25 July 1985 which came into effect on 1 July 1989. For tax purposes EEIGs are fiscally transparent in that profits are taxable and losses allowable only in the hands of their members. The relevant legislation was introduced by FA 1990 s 69, Sch 11. As a result of the extension of the 1985 Regulation under EEA Agreement, these provisions will apply to all EEIGs established within the European Economic Area.

Company migrations

7 TA 1988 s 765A removed the requirement under TA 1988 s 765 to obtain Treasury consent before carrying out certain transactions in securities where the transaction was a movement of capital between persons resident in member states of the EC, within the meaning of Council Directive No 88/361/EEC of 24 June 1988. The company is required instead to provide information to the Board of Inland Revenue within six months of carrying out the transaction as set out in The Movements of Capital (Required Information) Regulations 1990 [SI 1990/1671]. As a result of the EEA agreement, these provisions will apply to movements of capital between persons resident in member states of the EEA made on or after 1 January 1994.

Deposit takers

8 The EEA Agreement means that the provisions of the Second Banking Co-ordination Directive [86/646/EEC] will apply throughout the EEA. Any EU or EEA deposit taker operating a branch in the UK will be subject to the rules for deducting tax on interest paid to individual investors which apply to UK banks and building societies.

NOTES

1 The European Area Economic (EEA) Agreement was signed at Oporto on 2 May 1992 and entered into force on 1 January 1994. The Agreement extends the principles of the EC single market and some other EC rules to five states of the European Free Trade Association [EFTA] (Austria, Finland, Iceland, Norway and Sweden).

2 Switzerland, also an EFTA member, decided in a referendum in December 1992 not to participate in the EEA. The need to amend the Agreement to exclude Switzerland (in a Protocol signed on 17 March 1993) delayed the original target date for entry into force of 1 January 1993. Liechtenstein will join the EEA at a date after 1 January 1994 yet to be decided due to the need to make special arrangements arising from its close trading ties with Switzerland (with which it has a customs union).

3 The EEA Agreement covers the free movements of goods, services, capital and people and rules on competition and state aids. The Agreement also provides for enhanced co-operation on "flanking policies" such as the environment and research and development. The participating EFTA states have taken on relevant Community legislation and established new institutions to ensure that the EEA rules are observed.

4 The EEA Agreement does not extend to either Community legislation on direct tax (ie the Directives on Mutual Assistance, Mergers and Parent/Subsidiary companies) or the Arbitration Convention on transfer pricing.

Commentary—*Simon's Direct Tax Service* **E2.902, E5.104–109.**

31 March 1994. Inland Revenue

Self-assessment: transition to current year basis—anti-avoidance provisions

The Financial Secretary to the Treasury, Stephen Dorrell MP, today announced the broad scope of provisions that the Government intends to introduce in the next Finance Bill. These are intended to counter avoidance of tax through manipulation of the rules for the transition from the preceding year basis to the current year basis of income tax.

In reply to a written Parliamentary question today [HC Written Answer, 31 March 1994, Vol 240, cols 960, 961], the Financial Secretary said—

> "The Inland Revenue have today published, in a Press Release, details of the rules that the Government intends to introduce in the next Finance Bill concerning the anti-avoidance provisions for the transition from the preceding year basis to the current year basis.
>
> The transitional rules are set out in the 1994 Finance Bill Sch 19. They apply to businesses that commence before 6 April 1994 and to other sources from which income first arises before that date. Broadly for the year 1996–97 they allow a catching up process by averaging the profits for the two years ending in that year. Income in that period is therefore effectively taxed (in most cases) at half of the normal marginal rate for that year. And business profits arising in the period from the latest accounting date in 1996–97 to 5 April 1997 ultimately drop out of account altogether.
>
> The purpose of the transitional rules is broadly to ensure that there is no double taxation of business profits and other income, presently taxed on the preceding year basis under Schedule D, which the change to the current year basis of assessment might otherwise cause. But because of the way that the rules work, and the certainty that profits or income arising in a particular period will be taxed at a reduced rate (and in some cases will drop out of account altogether), it is necessary to counteract the effect of artificially moving profits or income into these periods. The Government's intention is to deter such avoidance.
>
> The proposals also deal with the treatment of other income, including interest, assessed on the preceding year basis, and with the treatment of interest paid on borrowings to finance trades, professions and businesses carried on in partnership.
>
> The proposed legislation will have effect in respect of all periods which affect the amount of income assessed in 1996–97. For businesses taxed under Schedule D Case I or II this could commence as early as 7 April 1994. The legislation will also affect the period before 6 April 1997 which is taxed in 1997–98. The new rules do not affect limited companies.
>
> The Inland Revenue have consulted on the proposals and will publish draft legislation later this year."

DETAILS

Self-employed trades, professions and vocations (including partnerships)

1 At present income taxed under Schedule D is assessed on a preceding year basis except in the first and last years of trading. Under the rules in the Finance Bill 1994, such income will from 1997–98 be taxed on a current year basis. Businesses commencing after 5 April 1994—or deemed to commence under TA 1988 s 113(1) following a change after that date in the membership of a partnership—will be immediately taxed on the new current year basis.

2 1996–97 will be a transitional year for which the rules for computation are set out in the Finance Bill 1994 Sch 19. Tax for this year will normally be assessed on the profits from the end of the 1995–96 basis period (the accounting date ending in 1994–95) to the latest accounting date ending in 1996–97 (the "transitional basis period"). In the normal case that will be a 24 month period, and one half of the profits will be taxed. In cases where the accounting date is changed, the period may be longer or shorter.

3 Under the new rules, the 1997–98 assessment will normally be based on the 12 months accounts ending in that year. That proportion of the profits which arises before 5 April 1997 will be available—as transitional relief—for deduction from the profits of the final period of trading, or, if earlier, when the accounting date of the business moves to 5 April. This means that eventually the profits arising in the period immediately preceding 5 April 1997 (the "transitional relief period") will drop out of account.

4 The proposed provisions will cancel any tax advantage that might accrue from artificial movement of profits into periods of account that form the transitional basis period or the transitional relief period. In certain circumstances such counteraction will extend to taxing in full, as well as in a proportionate amount, profits which are artificially moved into the 1996–97 period. Similarly the amount of transitional relief may be reduced by the full amount of the profits shifted into the basis for 1997–98 of which the transitional relief period forms a part.

5 In some circumstances, businesses will be taxed for 1996–97 on the actual profits arising in the year to 5 April 1997. Such businesses will not be affected by the proposed provisions set out in this Press Release.

Proposals identifying the avoidance and cancelling the benefit

6 The legislation will take a four-step approach. The first step is to identify the type of transaction, event or change in practice—referred to collectively as "triggers"—which may bring taxpayers within the scope of the anti-avoidance rules. Those triggers are—

- change of one accounting policy for another or a modification within one policy;
- transactions with persons with whom the taxpayer has some family or proprietorial link (typically "connected" persons) including partnerships;

- arrangements with unconnected persons which are wholly or partly reciprocal or self-cancelling, for example the sale of stock immediately before the end of the transitional basis period and re-purchase immediately afterwards;
- changes in business behaviour, which need not involve any changes in accounting policy. This would mean any change in a settled practice of a trade, profession or vocation as to the timing of any of the following—
  - on the incoming side of a business—the supply of goods or services, the invoicing of customers or clients and the collection of debts (including payments on account);
  - on the expenditure side of a business—the obtaining of goods or services, the incurring of business expenses and the settlement of outstanding debts (including making payments on account).

7 Any case that falls into one of these four categories will be regarded as raising a prima facie case for challenge that avoidance has taken place unless either—

(*a*) the obtaining of a tax advantage arising from an increase in the profits of the transitional basis period, or as the case may be of the transitional relief period, is not the main benefit or one of the main benefits that can reasonably be expected to arise from the trigger; or

(*b*) the business can show that the triggering transaction was undertaken solely for bona fide commercial reasons. Obtaining a tax advantage will not be such a reason; or

(*c*) the absolute and relative amounts of profits shifted into particular periods fall below a prescribed limit, or the turnover of the business is less than a prescribed amount. The legislation will provide powers to make Regulations to set these amounts which will be announced by 5 April 1997. The Government's intention is to deter people from undertaking triggering transactions; it is therefore not appropriate at this stage to indicate the level at which these limits will be set.

8 If the business is not excluded by any one of the tests in para 7 above, the increase in profits identified for the transitional basis period will be charged in full in addition to the profits averaged down, without any adjustments to the profits for any other year of assessment. For the transitional relief period, the transitional relief will be reduced by the full amount of the profits moved into the basis period for 1997–98. The effect is demonstrated in Examples 1 and 2 respectively in the Annex [reproduced below].

Other income taxed on the preceding year basis

9 Income taxed under Schedule D Cases III–V on the preceding year basis will, under the transitional rules, be assessed for 1996–97 on half of the income arising in the two years to 5 April 1997. Broadly similar rules to those applying for trades, professions and vocations will apply to income—other than interest—which is artificially moved into these periods. Such income is not subject to transitional relief.

Interest received

10 Where an account exists on which interest is paid gross, the law requires that new deposits and withdrawals should strictly be treated on the current year basis under the commencement and cessation provisions respectively. In practice all deposits into bank accounts are usually treated as a single source, unless the taxpayer asks for the strict basis to apply. Additions to existing holdings of National Savings Income Bonds are also usually treated as a single source.

11 New accounts are at present put directly onto the preceding year basis where there is an existing account taxed on that basis. With the move to the current year basis for new sources of income arising after 5 April 1994, such income will be taxed in accordance with the new basis period rules contained in the 1994 Finance Bill, even where there already exists one or more accounts assessed on the preceding year basis.

12 Deposits into or withdrawals from accounts, or additions to or withdrawals from existing holdings of National Savings Income Bonds on which interest first arose before 6 April 1994 that are made in the period from 6 April 1994 to 5 April 1997, will as now generally be treated on the preceding year basis. However the Revenue reserve the right to apply the strict basis (current year) where it appears that pre-existing sources of interest taxed on the current year basis have been depleted and such a source taxed on the preceding year basis has been correspondingly increased in such a way as to avoid tax that would otherwise be due by taking advantage of the transitional provisions. This practice will apply only to deposits made on or after 31 March 1994.

13 Legislation will be brought forward in the next Finance Bill to deal with variations made on or after 31 March 1994 in the terms of an account taxed on the preceding year basis. Where such variations provide for interest to arise at irregular intervals or at rates that do not reflect the underlying accrual rate in the period from 31 March 1994 to 5 April 1998 in such a way that a tax advantage might be expected to arise, the interest will be treated as arising on each day during the period of the deposit in the amount accruing to that day.

Interest paid

14 Payments of interest on borrowings to finance a trade or profession carried on in partnership may presently be relieved in one of two ways. Either there can be a deduction in the partnership accounts, if the interest is paid by the partnership on a partnership loan, or individual partners can get a deduction under TA 1988 s 353 for their own borrowings used to finance the partnership. For the transitional year 1996–97 partnerships choosing the first method would get relief only on a proportion of the interest paid, corresponding to the fraction applied to the basis period for that year. But if they claimed relief under s 353 the partners would be eligible for relief on the full amount of interest paid on a fiscal year basis. The Revenue are aware that partnerships are being advised to obtain new personal loans to ensure they get relief under s 353.

15 The Government intends to legislate to ensure that, unless there are bona fide commercial reasons for the re-financing, and the main or one of the main purposes is not to obtain a tax advantage, TA 1988 s 353 relief will be reduced proportionately. Any interest which qualifies for relief under s 353 and is paid in the period between the end of the 1995–96 basis period and 6 April 1997 (exclusive) will be reduced to the fraction of which the numerator is 12 and the denominator the number of months in that period. The effect of these proposals is shown in Example 3 in the Annex [reproduced below]. They will not apply to any re-financing arrangements completed before 31 March 1994.

Notes

1 The introduction of self-assessment and simplification of personal tax was announced by the Chancellor in his November Budget and the main legislation to give effect to this is contained in the Finance Bill 1994 Part IV Chs III, IV.

2 A key element of the proposals which will make the tax system for the self-employed and those in receipt of investment income both simpler and fairer is the introduction of the current year basis of assessment for all types of income. To permit the move from the preceding year basis to the current year basis, without doubly taxing businesses and income, it is necessary to tax profits and income arising in the transitional period at a lower average rate and the profits of some periods may drop out of account altogether.

3 In the consultative document "A simpler system for assessing personal tax" published on 5 November 1992, the Revenue stated that it would be necessary to have an anti-avoidance rule to prevent manipulation of the transitional rules for tax avoidance purposes. It was further announced at para 35 of a Press Release dated 11 January 1994 headed "Self-assessment and simplification of personal tax", that such rules would be brought forward in the Finance Bill 1995.

4 Further details about the operation of the transitional provisions can be found in the February 1994 edition of Tax Bulletin.

ANNEX

EXAMPLE 1

Transitional basis period avoidance (para 8)

Geoffrey returns profits as follows—

Year ended 5 April 1995	£10,000
2 years ended 5 April 1997	£30,000

The assessments are—

1995–96	£10,000
1996–97	£30,000 × 12/24 = £15,000

Profits of £5,000 were shifted from the year ended 5 April 1995 to the following period by means of one of the triggers. If Geoffrey is unable to demonstrate that either of the exclusions in para 7(*a*) or (*b*) applies, £5,000 will be added to the returned assessment for 1996–97, making £20,000 in all. The assessment for 1995–96 will remain unchanged.

EXAMPLE 2

Transitional relief period avoidance (para 8)

Helen returns profits as follows—

Year ended 5 October 1997	£36,000
Year ended 5 October 1998	£24,000

The assessments are—

1997–98	£36,000
1998–99	£24,000

Transitional relief in respect of the apportioned profits for the period from 6 October 1996 to 5 April 1997 would be £36,000 × $\frac{6}{12}$ = £18,000.

Profits of £6,000 were shifted from the year ended 5 October 1998 to the previous year by means of one of the triggers. If Helen is unable to demonstrate that either of the exclusions in para 7(*a*) or (*b*) applies, the transitional relief will be reduced by £6,000 to £12,000. There will be no further adjustments.

EXAMPLE 3

Re-financing of partnership borrowing (para 15)

Ian is a partner in ABC & Co which draws up accounts to 5 April. In 1994–95, he borrows £100,000 and introduces it into the partnership to reduce the partnership overdraft. In each of the years 1995–96 and 1996–97 he pays interest of £7,500, for which he claims relief under TA 1988 s 353. He is unable to demonstrate that the re-financing is undertaken for bona fide commercial reasons. The relief is reduced in the ratio 12/24: he is given relief of £3,750 in each of these years.

Janet is a partner in DE & Co which draws up accounts to 5 May. On 6 May 1994, she borrows £240,000 and introduces it into DE & Co to enable a term loan to be paid off early. In 1994–95 she pays interest of £16,500, and in each of the years 1995–96 and 1996–97 interest of £18,000. She claims relief each year under s 353. She is unable to demonstrate that the re-financing is undertaken for bona fide commercial reasons. The relief is reduced in the ratio 12/35 ie an average 12 month measure of interest paid is spread over the entire period from the start of the transitional basis period (6 May 1994) to the end of the transitional relief period (5 May 1997). This is to ensure that some relief is given for 1996–97. She is given relief of £5,658 in 1994–95 and £6,172 in both 1995–96 and 1996–97.

Commentary—*Simon's Direct Tax Service* **E1.201–212.**

August 1994. Taxation Practitioner: Inland Revenue letter

Finance Act 1994: Capital allowance provisions

[FA 1994 SECTION 117]. EXPENDITURE ON MACHINERY OR PLANT

You feel that [s 117] introduces a complex hybrid system for distinguishing building from plant. You also consider that the new rules will make the position more uncertain than it is at the moment.

As you know, court cases have, over the years, increasingly reclassified expenditure on buildings and structures as being expenditure on plant. This erosion in the plant/structure boundary has affected Exchequer receipts and has in itself created continuing uncertainty.

The intention behind the legislation is therefore to strengthen the current boundary, and to ensure that no further erosion takes place. It would of course be difficult for the new rules to replicate past treatment in every case. Nevertheless, the broad aim is to provide exclusions for assets currently regarded as plant as a result of court decisions, so as to leave the present position unchanged... It remains our view that, in practice, the tax treatment of specific assets should be less uncertain than it is at the moment.

On prescribed lists, you make the point that construction techniques are constantly being improved and over time, the lists would become out of date. We appreciate that there are continuing developments in building styles and that these will need to be kept under review.

You sought clarification on a number of specific points, on which our views are as follows.

[CAA 1990 SCH AA1 PARA 1(2)]

The broad proposition is that buildings were never intended to be plant and the clause aims to bring everything which is a part of a building within its scope except where, as I have explained, there is case law to the contrary.

The words "moveable or otherwise" are not intended to describe a category of assets. They are simply saying that it does not matter whether, as a matter of fact, the asset in question can be moved. The words are aimed at modern building techniques which, for example, permit an entire room (such as a toilet) to be placed in a building as a complete module.

[TABLE 1(2)]

I can confirm that references to "the trade" will apply where the asset is actually used in the course of businesses deemed to be trade by CAA 1990 s 27 (eg professions) and to the lessors of such assets in the normal way.

Table 1(2)(1) protects sewerage systems and Table 1(2)(9) protects sprinkler etc equipment.

[TABLE 1(2)(12)]

In practice, we have only accepted that strong rooms in banks or building societies can be plant (and not necessarily in every case). The precise facts are, as always, crucial, but, generally, we have not accepted that an ordinary room becomes plant because, say, better locks are fitted, bars are put on the windows and it is called a "strong room". Most claims for strong rooms outside the banking sector fall into this category and, for simplicity, the clause focuses on this instead of attempting to define the ingredients of a qualifying strong room. You will note that "safes" are protected in all cases.

[TABLE 1(2)(14)]

The use of decorative assets in trades other than hotels and restaurants have not previously been accepted as plant. The new rules therefore maintain the status quo.

You suggest that milk parlours, which have no alternative use as a building, should be included in the exclusions listed in Table 1. The test we have used has not been whether a structure has any alternative use, but whether it has been treated as plant under existing case law. The new rules let out structures which may have qualified in the past. Incidentally, you say that the Table treats certain items as plant. This is not correct—[it] continues to let existing case law apply. Not all cold stores are plant, for example.

Table 2, Note 2, is intended to let out from item G, column 1 of Table 2, assets which are within the definition in CAA 1990 s 18 (subject to additions for the purpose of FA 1994 s 117 only). Such assets will still be within the scope of the clause if they come within other headings in column 1 and are not let out by column 2 or any of the other provisions.

The definition of industrial buildings is not being extended for the purposes of industrial buildings allowances. These provisions are only for the purpose of excluding certain assets within the item G, column 1, Table 2 catch all.

[SECTION 118]: NOTIFICATION OF EXPENDITURE

You are generally concerned about the new rules for notifying expenditure on machinery and plant, and their application to periods ending before 30 November 1993. It may be helpful if I explain some of the background to these proposals.

It is the case that the reclassifications over the years of expenditure on buildings and structures have a retrospective effect. This means that under current legislation taxpayers would be able to make claims for plant allowances for assets purchased in the past, and later reclassified, in any tax year which is still open. This is despite the fact that when the assets were purchased they will often not have been thought to qualify for such allowances. Backdating of claims could represent a substantial windfall gain for taxpayers and, of course, a corresponding loss for the Exchequer. The new rules are intended to limit the extent to which such claims can be backdated by introducing a general time limit for notification of expenditure.

I should mention that where the new time limits have not been met, entitlement to the allowances will not usually be lost. These will normally be claimable in the next period for which the time limit has not expired. No relief will be available for assets which have been disposed of before the commencement of the chargeable period (or its basis period) in which notification takes place. But the normal balancing adjustments required on disposal would in any event have limited, if not removed completely, the net amount of relief which would have been claimed...

Finally, I can confirm that where expenditure is originally claimed as a revenue deduction but is subsequently recategorised as plant or industrial buildings, the original computation will be regarded as notice for the purposes of the new rules.

9 November 1994. Inland Revenue

Clearance procedure for non-trading controlled foreign companies

The Inland Revenue have today announced details of a new clearance procedure for companies which might be affected by changes to the controlled foreign companies legislation made by FA 1994 s 134.

DETAILS

1 This new procedure is intended to help controlled foreign companies to keep down their compliance costs. In future, the Revenue will be prepared to confirm, on the facts provided, that such a company will not be subject to a direction under the controlled foreign companies legislation, because it meets either the ''exempt activities'' or ''motive'' tests in TA 1988 s 748.

2 Clearance applications will be considered in respect of non-trading controlled foreign companies for accounting periods ending on or after 30 November 1993. Details of how to make an application and guidance on the information which the Revenue will require can be obtained by writing to International Division 4/2, Room 311, Melbourne House, Aldwych, London WC2B 4LL or by telephoning 0171 438 6945.

NOTES

Controlled foreign company legislation

1 A controlled foreign company is a company which is not resident in the UK but is controlled by individuals or companies who are. It must also be subject to a level of taxation which is less than three-quarters of what it would have paid had it been resident in the UK. UK resident corporate shareholders with a minimum 10% shareholding are chargeable to UK tax on the income of controlled foreign companies in which they have an interest. The amount assessable is usually the proportion of the controlled foreign company's income which is equal to the proportion of shares owned. A tax charge can be raised only following the issue of a formal direction by the Board of Inland Revenue. The relevant legislation can be found in TA 1988 Part XVII Ch IV and Sch 25, 26.

Exclusions

2 No charge is made on most controlled foreign companies' income because of a variety of exclusions within the legislation. There is no charge if any of the following applies—

- the controlled foreign company pursues an acceptable distribution policy, so that the required proportion of its profits finds its way to the UK;
- the controlled foreign company's activity is specifically exempted (the "exempt activities" test);
- subject to certain conditions, the controlled foreign company is publicly quoted;
- the controlled foreign company's chargeable profits fall below £20,000 in a full year (chargeable profits are calculated as for UK tax purposes, but exclude capital gains and losses); or
- the arrangements under which the controlled foreign company operates were not made to avoid UK tax (the "motive" test).

3 The Revenue have also issued a list of those countries in which residence and the carrying on of a business will not trigger a charge under the legislation.

FA 1994 s 134

4 In order to pursue an acceptable distribution policy, trading controlled foreign companies have had to distribute 50% of their accounting profits and non-trading companies 90%. However, some companies exploited the mismatch between the profits shown by their accounts and the profits which would have been chargeable to tax had they been resident in the UK to avoid a charge under the controlled foreign company legislation. To counter this practice, FA 1994 s 134 changed the measure of profits for non-trading controlled foreign companies from accounting profits to chargeable profits less foreign taxes. In future, non-trading controlled foreign companies will therefore need to calculate what their taxable profits would be if they wish to pursue an acceptable distribution policy.

Clearance procedure

5 The new Revenue clearance procedure has been introduced to give a measure of certainty and save compliance costs for those companies which believe that they would be excluded under the "exempt activities" or "motive" tests. It will therefore apply only to non-trading controlled foreign companies.

6 In most cases it should be possible for the Revenue to give an advance ruling about the application of the tests which covers a number of years, provided that all the relevant facts have been accurately disclosed and there is no change in the nature and conduct of the business of the controlled foreign company.

Commentary—*Simon's Direct Tax Service* **D4.138, 139.**

20 February 1995. ICAEW

Incorporation of professional partnerships: tax implications of certain aspects—Guidance note (TAX 7/95)

INTRODUCTION

The incorporation of a professional partnership by means of the transfer of its business as a going concern to a company owned by the former partners gives rise to a number of potential tax problems. Some are recognised by the tax legislation, some dealt with by concession and others not dealt with at all.

The Tax Faculty has been in correspondence with the Inland Revenue about certain aspects of this matter the text of which is set out in the following pages. It included references to the problems arising from the two points referred to in the last paragraph below and the statements mentioned were issued by the Revenue during the course of this correspondence.

For convenience this has been divided in sections as follows—

- A transfer of work in progress and debtors
- B interest relief
- C partnership annuities
- D corporate partnerships and TCGA 1992 s 162.

Particular attention is drawn to the issue on 20 June 1994 of the revised text of Concession A43 referred to at section B and to the article on page 151 of *Tax Bulletin* No 12 (August 1994) in respect of paragraph 5(*a*) of section C.

INCORPORATION OF PROFESSIONAL PARTNERSHIPS—TAX IMPLICATIONS

A Transfer of work in progress and debtors [ICAEW]

Partnership on earnings basis

1 The first potential problem is that there will practically always be an uplift in the basis of valuation because, for a variety of reasons, the partnership basis of valuation will fall short of a full earnings basis of a company. An example is when work in progress (WIP) excludes partners' time in the partnership, but will include their salaries as employees of the company. The rate of tax and its timing will depend upon which of three treatments applies—

(*a*) transfer at partnership valuation, following which the uplift is taken in the company on revaluation of its opening WIP. (This would not normally be good accounting practice, but might nonetheless be adopted.);

(*b*) transfer at partnership valuation but, since the asset is purchased, the company does not revalue its opening WIP; and

(*c*) transfer at company valuation, so the uplift is taken in the closing WIP of the partnership.

2 If there is a revaluation of opening WIP in the company as under (*a*), confirmation is sought that the uplift would fall within Case I, not Case VI. In that event, the only difference from the company not revaluing its WIP as under (*b*) would be that the profit would be deferred to the extent that the work is unbilled at the end of the company's first accounting period.

3 Please confirm that you would normally accept any of these three treatments as valid for taxation purposes provided that in cases (*a*) and (*b*) partnership valuation should be on the basis consistently used in the partnership accounts.

Revenue response

TA 1988 s 102(2) determines that if s 101(1)(*a*) applies the same figure is to be used for both parties to the agreement. If the terms of the transfer agreement are accepted and they provide that the WIP is transferred to the company at the partnership's closing valuation, scenario(*a*), then we will accept that s 101(1)(*a*) will apply. If the company revalues the WIP on acquisition the legislation overrides the company's accounts treatment so the uplift and the eventual profit arising out of that WIP will be assessed Case I on the company. Therefore the uplift could not be assessed Case VI at the Revenue's instigation. But under s 101(2) the partnership could elect that the difference between the original cost of the WIP and the s 101(1) valuation, in (*a*) the partners' closing valuation, should be assessed Case VI. With (*b*) the position is similar.

As the above is likely to apply in most cases we can generally provide the confirmation sought. Inspectors, however, will look closely at the application of s 101(1)(*a*), the transfer valuation basis adopted and the terms of the transfer agreement where the transfer valuation basis is not consistent with the basis previously used by the partnership, which itself must be acceptable. Subject to that we would accept that all three treatments are valid bases for transfer under s 101(1)(*a*).

[ICAEW]

4 Please also confirm that the transfer of the WIP in exchange for shares where TCGA 1992 s 162 rollover applies does not necessarily determine the transfer price of the WIP at market value for Case I/II purposes, and that inspectors will normally accept the price allocated to it in the sale agreement where it follows the basis of valuation consistently used in the partnership accounts.

Revenue response

Where an agreement for the sale of a professional business to a company in consideration for the issue of shares provides for an apportionment of the overall value of the business as between the various assets transferred, inspectors will normally accept such an apportionment unless it is clearly illusory, colourable or fraudulent. The value apportioned to professional WIP would therefore be accepted for TA 1988 s 101(1)(*a*) purposes if it represented the cost of the work on the basis consistently used to value the work for accounting purposes.

Partnership on conventional (eg bills delivered or cash) basis [ICAEW]

5 Where the partnership does not account for WIP, the consideration (if any) paid for it by the company is assessable under Case VI (TA 1988 s 104(6)). Please confirm, in consistency with [para] 4 above, that no consideration is assessable where the partnership assets are transferred for shares and a nil consideration is allocated to the WIP in the same agreement.

6 Similarly, where the partnership does not account for debtors, please confirm that no consideration is assessable if the debtors are transferred in consideration for shares and a nil consideration is allocated in the sale agreement.

7 Please confirm that the same principles apply to any other conventional basis, ie one which is not an earnings basis.

Revenue response

If, as seems to be the case in cash or conventional bases cases, the consistent basis adopted has been not to value WIP and if the terms of the bargain are that the WIP is transferred for nil consideration then we would not seek to challenge the agreement. Then s 101(1) would not apply because "in computing for any tax purpose the profits or gains of a profession" (this would not include the capital gains of the partners or the individual proprietor) there would not be "a valuation...taken of the work...in progress at the discontinuance" (s 101(1)). TA 1988 ss 104(2), 106(2) (see our next two paras) have similar effect.

TA 1988 s 104 applies to tax the partners under Case VI on any sums received on or after discontinuance unless the sums were "otherwise chargeable to tax" (s 104(2)). If all the profit on the partnership's closing WIP is assessable on the company we would accept it would be excluded from Case VI charge by s 104(2). Thus if for the Company's tax purposes the opening WIP of the company is nil then there will be no Case VI charge on the WIP. TA 1988 s 106(2) (see our next para) has a similar effect.

If the terms of the bargain are that all the rights to the debts of the partnership are transferred to the company then under s 106(2), sums received which would otherwise be chargeable on the predecessor under Schedule D, Case VI by virtue of s 104(1) are to be treated as business receipts of the successor. Therefore if the terms of the bargain are that nil consideration is given then for the company's tax purposes all receipts from those debtors would be the taxable business receipts.

INCORPORATION OF PROFESSIONAL PARTNERSHIPS—TAX IMPLICATIONS

B Interest relief [ICAEW]

1 Unless the company is close, the lack of interest relief on the working shareholders' borrowings for subscription or purchase of shares or for lending money to the company is a major bar to incorporation. The size of many professional companies will be such that they will not, in the normal way, be close.

2 Most professions restrict the amount of equity that may be held by non-members. For instance, an accountancy business carrying out a regulated audit has to have 75% of its equity owned by regulated individuals. Outside finance is generally limited by the lack of tangible asset cover. Accordingly, a professional company will tend to be under-capitalised if it cannot look to its shareholders for funds on a tax-effective basis. An owner-managed company of this sort cannot be compared with a quoted company that has institutional and portfolio investors and can offer good security. Under-capitalisation also reduces the ability of clients and the investing public to have effective redress when professional indemnity claims are made, particularly as insurance capacity in this market is severely limited. As the company would be owner-managed there is no good reason in principle why interest relief should not be given to working shareholders. Otherwise, it will make it very difficult for the equivalent of new partners to share in the ownership by becoming shareholders unless they have substantial private wealth—a retrogressive step.

3 In previous correspondence we asked if you would accept the case for an extension of Concession A43 so that partners who became the working shareholders of an owner-managed professional company would continue to obtain interest relief even if the company was not close. You rejected this request (which itself would not help new working shareholders) on the grounds that it would introduce a radical extension to interest relief.

4 As an alternative, we asked if you would grant concessionary relief where the company is employee-controlled and the loan would satisfy TA 1988 s 361. You responded that s 361 was designed to cover an employee *buy-out*, involving a change of control, so extending Concession A43 would be too far removed from the aims of the legislation. This would, incidentally, introduce an anomaly—new working shareholders of the incorporated firm would gain relief for the first 12 months after incorporation under s 361, whereas their colleagues who were partners before, and working shareholders after, the incorporation, or who became shareholders more than 12 months after incorporation, would not.

5 We appreciate that the political climate is presently unsympathetic to any extension of interest relief, however deserving the cause. We therefore invite you to consider another approach to the problem. This is that given that it is not difficult to make a company close, you should be prepared to agree that certain methods of doing this would not be challenged.

6 Broadly speaking, a company is close if it is controlled by five or fewer individuals or by its directors, with shareholdings of associates of the relevant individuals being counted in. There are three basic ways in which this test might be met—

(*a*) have all the working shareholders (or sufficient of them to give voting control) as directors. Because the definition of a director contained in TA 1988 s 417 is not exclusive, someone formally appointed director would be a director for the purpose of s 414(1), even if there was an inner core of directors who had real responsibility for the company's policy;

(*b*) have all the working shareholders associates of one another by making them partners in a parallel partnership carrying on a segment of the business (although in this event care would have to be taken not to jeopardise s 162 relief in its entirety);

(*c*) have all the working shareholders associates of one another by making them trustees of a settlement of which they are themselves settlors, which holds shares in the company (see s 417(3)(*b*)). An example is an employee share trust.

The above solutions are artificial and conflict with commercial objectives. Nevertheless there will be a strong incentive for the larger firms to use one of them. Please would you confirm, therefore, that in the absence of any relieving provision you would not find them intrinsically objectionable.

Revenue response

Whether a company is close, for the purpose of s 414, depends on the particular facts. It is not necessarily the case that everyone who is styled a director is actually a director for these purposes. It is possible, however, for a company to have directors who, within the powers bestowed by the Articles of Association, exercise different degrees of power and responsibility within the company. Similarly, whether someone is actually a member of a partnership is a question of fact. As far as trustees are concerned, a participator in a company can be attributed with the rights and powers of the trustees of a settlement of which he or she is the settlor. The attribution is, however, only of those rights and powers which the trustees hold as trustees of that settlement and does not extend to those they hold in a personal capacity or as trustees of another settlement.

Note

As stated above, in earlier correspondence the Institute requested that Concession A43 (issued in 1985) should be extended to meet the difficulties outlined above. This was not accepted by the Revenue and subsequent correspondence sought to explore other means of overcoming these difficulties.

On 20 June 1994, after the above exchange of correspondence, the Revenue issued a revised version of Concession A43 which extends the concession to cover cases where a partnership is incorporated into an employee controlled company.

This matter has, therefore, now been satisfactorily resolved in nearly all cases.

INCORPORATION OF PROFESSIONAL PARTNERSHIPS—TAX IMPLICATIONS

C. Partnership annuities [ICAEW]

Partners already retired

1 Please confirm your view that—

(*a*) where TCGA 1992 s 162 rollover applies on incorporation (assets exchanged for shares), the undertaking by the company to pay annuities, although strictly non-share consideration which would restrict the relief, by concession is treated as a payment for liabilities and therefore excluded from the consideration given for the chargeable assets; and

(*b*) where TCGA 1992 s 165 holdover is claimed (gift of business assets), the value of the undertaking to pay annuities (valued by reference to the cost of purchasing them from an insurance company) would produce a gain to the extent that it exceeded the base cost of the goodwill. In this connection we are unclear why it cannot be treated as payment for liabilities, as where s 162 applies.

Partners still working

2 You have told us that—

(*a*) under s 162, the undertaking by the company to pay annuities that commence in the future is not payment for an existing liability but part of the consideration given for the business transferred, thus restricting relief; and

(*b*) under s 165, there is also consideration so that relief is restricted.

3 This is regrettable. We have pointed out that in a typical situation the value of an annuity might be such that rollover relief is restricted by two-thirds—by contrast, if incorporation did not take place, Statement of Practice D12, para 8 would normally prevent capital gains tax being chargeable on retirement.

4 Very many professional practices still undertake to pay annuities to partners when they retire. If such a practice were to incorporate today, it would have substantial goodwill for which, typically, two forms of consideration would be regarded as having been given—the issue of shares and the undertaking to pay annuities in the future. If deferment of the gain on the second element is denied, this will be a serious impediment to incorporation. The fact that you have not seen cases in which these give rise to a difficulty suggests either that partnerships have been prevented from incorporating, or—much more seriously—that the point has not been noticed by either the firm or the Revenue. It seems to us inevitable that the point does exist and is potentially damaging.

Revenue response

Where a business is transferred in exchange for shares, any gains are deferred by reducing the acquisition cost of those shares, but relief is restricted where any other consideration is given. An undertaking to pay an annuity involves taking on a liability, and in strictness s 162(4) will apply, since taking over a liability represents other consideration. This is, of course, amended by Concession D32. Concession D32, however, only applies where relief is due under s 162, and is not relevant for s 165 purposes.

It is worth noting although s 162 is automatically applied against any chargeable gain where the conditions are met, if a taxpayer makes a claim to, or is entitled to, relief under ss 152, 163 and 164, such relief will be given in priority to s 162.

A claim may also be made under s 165 although, in practice, this would not apply where full consideration was given for the assets or the transfer was by way of a bargain at arm's length. In those circumstances, and subject to any relief being given under s 152 etc, the only relief would be under s 162.

In the circumstances you describe, an agreement to pay an annuity would probably restrict relief under s 165 in practice.

Where the annuity relates to future payments to existing partners, there is no existing liability, and Concession D32 does not apply, but represents consideration within either s 162 or 165. Statement of Practice D12, to which you refer, relates to the payment of annuities to retiring partners and has no relevance to gains made on incorporation by the continuing partners.

Post-incorporation annuity payments [ICAEW]

5 Please confirm your view that—

(*a*) the payment of annuities is allowable as an annual charge of the company under s 338;

(*b*) the payment of an annuity to a former member of a partnership is excluded from TA 1988 s 125 (annual payments for non-taxable consideration) similarly, annuities payable by the company as a result of having taken over the obligation to pay them are in practice so excluded.

Revenue response

Item (a)

An annuity is not treated as a charge for the purpose of s 338 if it is not made under a liability incurred for a valuable and sufficient consideration. Where a company undertakes to pay an annuity as part of the deal whereby it acquires the business of a partnership, there is no reason in principle why such an annuity should not be treated as a charge on these grounds.

Item (b)

We can confirm that annuities paid by a partnership to a former member for the acquisition of a business or a share in a partnership are excluded from the scope of s 125.

Where a company takes over an obligation to pay the annuities, provided the payments are made in respect of bona fide commercial transactions, we can confirm that it is our practice to regard the payments as outside the scope of s 125.

INCORPORATION OF PROFESSIONAL PARTNERSHIPS—TAX IMPLICATIONS

D Corporate partnerships and TCGA 1992 s 162 [ICAEW]

1 Capital gains tax rollover under s 162 depends upon the *whole* of the business being transferred by an individual. Having one or more corporate partners is not uncommon in professions such as those of surveyors and consulting engineers. Strictly, s 162 cannot apply to the individuals who are partners in such a partnership because part of the business is carried on by a company. Please confirm that the Revenue continue to apply the concession...[reproduced below] that s 162 relief is available to partners who are individuals where the partnership includes a company.

Revenue response

We can confirm that this applies to individuals. (Corporate partners are excluded under s 162(1).)

EXTRACT REFERRED TO UNDER SECTION D

Rollover relief—incorporation of business with individual and corporate partners

Where a sole trader or partnership incorporates a business, CGTA 1979 s 123 provides relief where the whole of the business is transferred by a person who is not a company for shares and cash. Where one of the partners is a company, s 123 could strictly not apply because those partners who are individuals are not transferring the whole business, but only their collective shares.

Somerset House have confirmed however, that provided the whole of the business has been transferred to a company, the Revenue will view each partner separately, thus enabling the individuals to have relief, but not the company. In addition, relief will be granted where one partner takes cash and another shares. This means a degree of flexibility could exist over the proportion of shares and cash which is taken in exchange for the business, so long as the whole of the business is exchanged wholly or partly for shares.

20 February 1995. Inland Revenue

Stock Exchange alternative investment market (AIM)—tax reliefs for investment in companies joining AIM

In a speech today to representatives of the venture capital industry the Financial Secretary to the Treasury, Sir George Young Bt, MP, said—

> "Last week the Stock Exchange announced details of the new securities market which it is launching in June, the alternative investment market (AIM). AIM hopes to attract a wide range of new, small and growing companies.
>
> The Exchange and market professionals have been concerned about the availability of the various tax reliefs for unquoted securities and for investment in unquoted companies—these reliefs include inheritance tax relief, capital gains tax reinvestment relief, and reliefs under the enterprise investment scheme and the new venture capital trust scheme.
>
> I am now pleased to be able to confirm that these unquoted reliefs will be available for AIM securities; the Revenue will be issuing a Press Release to publicise this point. We will monitor the progress of the new market carefully."

DETAILS

1 There are a large number of references in tax legislation to securities which are listed or quoted on the Stock Exchange or other recognised stock exchanges. As the Financial Secretary's speech makes clear, securities on AIM will not fall to be treated as quoted or listed for tax purposes. They will therefore qualify for the various tax reliefs available for unquoted securities.

2 It follows that AIM securities will not be eligible to be held directly by individual investors in PEPs. They will, however, count towards unit trusts' and investment trusts' own qualifying investments for PEP purposes.

3 The reliefs for unquoted securities include—

- inheritance tax business property relief (IHTA 1984 Part V Ch 1);
- income relief for losses on shares subscribed for (TA 1988 ss 573–576);
- capital gains tax reinvestments rollover relief (TCGA 1992 ss 164A–164N);
- capital gains tax holdover relief for gifts of business assets (TCGA 1992 ss 165–169);
- the enterprise investment scheme (FA 1994 s 137 Sch 15);
- venture capital trusts [FA 1995 ss 70–73 Sch 14–16].

Commentary—*Simon's Direct Tax Service* **D1.501, D2.416.**

5 April 1995. Law Society's Gazette

1995 Finance Bill: clauses 54 [FA 1995 s 56], 83 [FA 1995 s 91]—Revenue's response to Revenue Law Committee's representations

The *Law Society's Gazette* has published the Inland Revenue's response to the Revenue Law Committee's representations on the 1995 Finance Bill. The text of the article is reproduced below—

> "*Taxation of foreign life policies—clause 54 [FA 1995 s 56]*
>
> ...
>
> *Employee liabilities and indemnity insurance—clause 83 [FA 1995 s 91]*
>
> ...
>
> The Finance Bill included legislation intended to remove the existing charge to income tax on employees when employers pay for employees' liability insurance or meet work-related uninsured liabilities, and to give relief for employees' own expenditure on liability insurance and work-related uninsured liabilities.
>
> The provisions would apply in relation to liabilities 'imposed' on employees or directors. In its representations on the Bill, the Revenue Law Committee commented that it was unclear, in the proposed new TA 1988 s 201AA(2)(*b*), by whom a qualifying liability for the purposes of the legislation was to be 'imposed'. Did this refer to a liability imposed only by a judgment of the court?
>
> In the Committee's view, the legislation appeared to be designed to deal with compromise payments to settle legal proceedings, but since such payments would not be imposed by any court, it might be said to fail the test of 'qualifying liability'.
>
> The Committee sought confirmation from the Revenue whether it was intended that negotiated compromise payments should only qualify if court proceedings have been commenced and a court order (albeit a consent order) is made. If this were the case, this could have the detrimental effect of encouraging the commencement of legal proceedings and might prevent payment qualifying where legal procedures in a foreign jurisdiction do not provide for consent orders.

The Revenue have responded that, in its view, the expression 'imposed' would certainly cover the situation where liabilities or costs are incurred by order of a court, but the term would also be apt to cover any situation where the employee or office holder is under an obligation to discharge a liability, whether this arises as a result of a court order or of a compromise to which the employee has, in practice, been compelled to agree in order to settle legal proceedings.

The Committee asked the Revenue to comment specifically on the situation where a payment was made to settle a claim without the claimant having commenced legal proceedings. The Revenue's view is that it is implicit in such a situation that the person making the payment (for example, an employee or his employer) would do so because it could be shown that there was an obligation to meet the claim.

If the Revenue were satisfied that this was the case, and it could be established to the inspector's satisfaction that the liability giving rise to the payment was a type mentioned in s 201AA(2)(*a*) (a work-related act or omission), the liability would be regarded as a qualifying liability. In such a case, relief would be available.''.

12 April 1995. ICAEW

Relationship between accountancy practice and the tax computation in the light of *Gallagher v Jones* and *Johnston v Britannia Airways Ltd*—Guidance note (TAX 10/95)

INTRODUCTION

Recent decisions of the courts have dealt with the significance of accountancy practice in computing taxable profits *Gallagher v Jones; Threlfall v Jones* in the Court of Appeal ([1993] STC 537) and *Johnston v Britannia Airways Ltd* in the High Court ([1994] STC 763).

The Institute met with the Inland Revenue in November 1994 to discuss the approach which the Revenue could be expected to adopt in various common situations, in the light of these decisions. The conclusions are summarised below in question and answer form. The Revenue have seen the text of this release and have confirmed that their position is correctly stated.

PROVISIONS

Question 1

It is a fundamental accounting requirement that proper provision be made for future expenditure in certain circumstances. See for example SSAP 17 (Accounting for post balance sheet events) and SSAP 18 (Accounting for contingencies). However disagreements frequently arise as to the deductibility of such provisions, with inspectors citing *James Spencer & Co v IRC* (32 TC 111) as authority.

In the light of *Britannia Airways* what is the Revenue's view on the deductibility of provisions for the following items, for the purposes of Schedule D Cases I and II—

(*a*) warranty claims;
(*b*) closure costs, including redundancies;
(*c*) disputed legal actions; and
(*d*) the full amount of foreseeable losses on long-term contracts recognised in accordance with SSAP 9 (rather than the restricted relief under SP 3/90 para 7)?

Revenue response

A provision would of course not be deductible in any event if the underlying expense is non-deductible, being excluded for example by the ''wholly and exclusively'' test or because it is capital. Subject to that, the Revenue's view is as follows.

(a) Warranty claims

Commercial accounting principles should be applied and the provision assessed based on the tests in *Owen v Southern Railway of Peru Ltd* (36 TC 602). *James Spencer* will not normally be relevant.

(b) Closure costs

Where the underlying expense is deductible under the general rules a provision for future payments will be allowable, regardless of whether the redundancy notices are issued before or after the end of the relevant period of account, provided that—

(i) it appears in the commercial accounts of the business in accordance with generally accepted accounting principles;
(ii) a definite decision was taken during the period of account to proceed with the redundancy programme;
(iii) the provision was accurately calculated using the degree of hindsight permitted by SSAP 17 (which will normally require the individual employees affected to be identified); and

(iv) payment was made within nine months after the end of the period of account.

Where the payments are not deductible under the general rules because they are made as an incident in the discontinuance of the trade, a deduction may nevertheless be given under TA 1988 ss 579 or 90. In that event relief is allowed for the period of account in which the payments are made; where they are made after the discontinuance they are treated for this purpose as made on the last day of trading.

These views will be set out more fully in a forthcoming article in the Revenue's Tax Bulletin. [This has subsequently been published, in the February 1995 edition.]

(c) Disputed legal actions

The best (rather than the most prudent) estimate of the likely cost should be acceptable, subject to meeting the *Southern Railway of Peru* test on accuracy. *James Spencer* is now seen simply as an answer, on a specific set of facts and reached without the benefit of accountancy input, to the question of whether a provision is sufficiently accurate to be acceptable for tax.

(d) Losses on long-term contracts

The Revenue would regard the SSAP 9 treatment (recognising the whole of the loss on a contract as soon as it could be foreseen) as anticipating a loss. This would not normally be acceptable for tax purposes. SP 3/90 remains an accurate statement of the Revenue's practice.

Question 2

Consideration of provisions of this nature inevitably involves an attempt to quantify the outcome of uncertain events. For example a warranty provision will be statistically based upon prior claims experience. By contrast, consider a company which has received a specific claim for damages of say £1 million. The company's legal advice is that the claim will probably be settled for around £500,000 but there is an outside chance of getting away without liability or of having to pay the full claim. The company provides £500,000 in accordance with SSAP 18.

Would the Revenue accept that both approaches (using a statistical analysis or a value judgement as appropriate) could in principle provide sufficiently reliable figures to enable the provisions to be deducted for tax purposes?

Revenue response

A correct understanding of *James Spencer* should result in the provision being acceptable in principle in both cases. Obviously there could on the facts still be debate as to quantum, or indeed as to whether any reliable estimate could be made at all.

ALTERNATIVE ACCOUNTING POLICIES

Question 3

Britannia Airways illustrates the fact there are many cases where different accounting policies may be applied to the same situation, matching revenue and expense in different ways.

Specific examples of the type of situations which could arise include the following—

(i) where a business gains the benefit of a rent-free period, rent could either be charged to profit and loss account only in respect of years following this rent-free period or the total rent could be spread over the life of the lease including the rent-free period; and

(ii) where a trader incurs expense in Year 1 on an advertising campaign to launch a new product he could either spread the expense over say Years 1–3 or charge the whole amount in Year 1.

Where there is more than one view as to how the accruals and prudence concepts should be applied, in what circumstances, if at all—

(*a*) will the Revenue seek to challenge the view taken by the taxpayer in preparing his accounts; and

(*b*) will the taxpayer be able to produce a Case I computation based on a more prudent view than he has taken in the accounts?

Revenue response

In general the Revenue will accept a generally accepted accounting practice which does not violate any rules of tax law. In the area of timing, the Revenue will particularly wish to consider whether the treatment adopted, though in accordance with commercially-acceptable accountancy, violates the tax principle that losses must not be anticipated. They may consider this to be the case where the matching of income and expenditure to give effect to the accruals concept is overridden by the application of the prudence concept. For example, in situation (i) above, the policy of spreading rent over the whole period of the lease, including the rent-free period, would be acceptable if it was based on the matching principle, ie if the business was generating income. On the other hand, if the rent-free period had been agreed to enable the company to get established, ie whilst it was not generating income, there could be a problem.

If in situation (ii) above, the trader chose to spread the expense over three years, the Revenue would regard the trader as bound by the *Gallagher* and *Britannia Airways* decisions and would therefore not permit a tax deduction for the whole cost in Year 1.

Question 4

Do the Revenue agree that the same principles apply to revenue recognition such as where payments are received subject to a need to provide a facility or service over a number of accounting periods (eg a warranty fee for cover over several years)?

Revenue response

In short, yes. There is in principle no difference between revenue and expense recognition.

CAPITAL/REVENUE

Question 5

Where expenditure is "capitalised" (for example that on the advertising campaign mentioned at question 3(ii) above), does the Revenue agree that such expenditure retains its inherent nature and would be allowable or not dependent upon whether the expenditure was capital or revenue?

Revenue response

As noted above the application of generally accepted accounting practice cannot displace tax rules. A fundamental rule is that it is necessary to determine whether an expense is capital or revenue and the accounting treatment (which may need to meet other objectives) has little effect on the legal analysis (*ECC Quarries Ltd v Watkis* (51 TC 153)).

UNINCORPORATED BUSINESSES

Question 6

Is it the view of the Revenue that no distinction should be drawn between companies on the one hand and unincorporated associations, partnerships and sole traders on the other, in ascertaining the profit or loss of the business?

Revenue response

Broadly, yes. Clearly certain accounting requirements are not applicable to all business enterprises. However, the fundamental accounting concepts are relevant to determining the "full amount of profits". In *Gallagher v Jones* the Special Commissioner found that the application of SSAP 21 was required in order to meet that objective. There was no evidence that the alternative, a payments basis, was generally accepted or satisfied the accruals concept.

CHANGE OF ACCOUNTING POLICY

Question 7

Where there is a change from one valid accounting policy to another valid policy are the Revenue prepared to apply the same principles as apply to changes in stock valuation policy as set out in SP 3/90 paras 2–4?

Revenue response

Generally, yes. The approach underlying SP 3/90 is applicable whenever there is a change in the basis on which items of income or expenditure are brought into account from one valid basis to another. Thus adjustments to the tax computations for the year of change should be made, where necessary, to ensure that, over the life of the trade, the income will be brought into charge, or the expenditure will be allowed, once only. Different considerations may apply to changes in timing bases determined by statute, where there is a complete change from an earnings basis to a cash basis or where there is a change of conventional basis.

Commentary—*Simon's Direct Tax Service* **B3.904.**

24 April 1995. Inland Revenue

Self-assessment—transitional arrangements for self-employed taxpayers

The Inland Revenue today announced details of the information they will need from self-employed taxpayers for the tax years 1995–96 and 1996–97.

Self-assessment will apply to those people who receive tax returns, starting for the tax year 1996–97. It is a more straightforward system that will give taxpayers greater clarity about their tax affairs.

PRs etc

DETAILS

1 Under self-assessment, profits will be calculated on a current year basis. This means for example that profits earned in 1997–98 will be assessed at the end of 1997–98 rather than at the end of 1998–99.

2 To achieve this change simply and fairly, the transitional year (1996–97), taxable profits will be based on *half* of the profits for the *two* years ending in the year to 5 April 1997. Self-employed taxpayers should therefore wait for the results for the whole two year period before working out their taxable profits for 1996–97.

3 Taxpayers can either prepare a single account for the whole two year period, or draw up separate figures for each year. In the latter case, they should aggregate the accounts to arrive at a single figure for the taxable profits. Drawing up separate accounts may be beneficial where a loss is incurred, because losses arising in this period will be allowed in full.

Tax return for 1995–96

4 The transitional arrangements described above will apply to most self-employed taxpayers. However, some self-employed taxpayers will need to make a return of their business profits for 1995–96. This applies where—

- the taxpayer's income is assessable for 1995–96 on a current year basis (this will normally only be the case if the business started after 5 April 1994, or ceases in 1995–96); or
- a claim is made to offset trading losses suffered in a period ending in the tax year 1995–96 against other income in that or earlier years.

5 In April 1996, the Revenue will issue notes detailing the circumstances in which a return of business profits for 1995–96 should be made. Full details of the method of computing the taxable profits for 1996–97 will be given with the new tax return to be issued in April 1997. If however taxpayers would like to clarify their position in advance, they should contact their local tax enquiry centre. (Details can be found in the telephone directory under "Inland Revenue".)

Confirmation of income or earnings

6 Self-employed taxpayers sometimes ask the Revenue to confirm figures of business profits that have been agreed for assessment, for example to support applications for mortgage advances and educational grants. Under self-assessment the Revenue will continue to respond to requests by the taxpayer to confirm details of either the business profits or total taxable income returned, but without signifying whether the figures have been agreed.

NOTES

For businesses assessable under Schedule D Cases I and II which commenced trading before 6 April 1994, 1996–97 will be a year of transition from the existing preceding year basis of assessment to the new current year basis. The transitional arrangements will apply to up to four million self-employed taxpayers. The special rules that apply for 1996–97 were introduced in FA 1994, and ensure that all relevant accounting periods feature in the tax computation. Profits will be averaged but losses and capital allowances will be preserved in full.

Commentary—*Simon's Direct Tax Service* **E1.215, 216.**

26 April 1995. Law Society's Gazette

1995 Finance Bill: clause 78 [FA 1995 s 86]—Revenue's response to Revenue Law Committee's representations

The Law Society's Gazette has published the Inland Revenue's response to the Revenue Law Committee's representations on [FA 1995 s 86]. The text of the article is reproduced below—

> "*Deduction of tax from interest on deposits*
>
> Since 6 April 1991, interest paid by banks and building societies to UK individuals (to which the individual is beneficially entitled) or to personal representatives has in general been subject to deduction of basic rate tax at source.
>
> For guidance on the application of the deduction of tax at source rules to solicitors' client accounts, please see annex 27H to the Guide to the Professional Conduct of Solicitors, sixth edition.
>
> [FA 1995 s 86] extends the provisions of TA 1988 so that the rules will also apply to interest arising to the trustees of discretionary or accumulation trusts.
>
> The new rules would not affect trusts where there were no UK resident beneficiaries, so that the trustees of such trusts would be entitled to make a declaration under [TA 1988] s 481(5)(*k*) which allows bank or building society interest to be received gross.
>
> In its representations on the 1995 Finance Bill, the Revenue Law Committee expressed concern that the definition of 'beneficiaries' in the proposed new legislation (TA 1988 s 482(5A)) was

extremely wide, so that trusts which included a power to add to the class of beneficiaries would be precluded from making a declaration, since they would be brought within the terms of the new rules on the basis that a UK resident could be a potential beneficiary.

The committee's fear was that the result in practice would be that trustees of any discretionary or accumulation trust which was likely to be affected would automatically move their investments away from UK banks, to the disadvantage of the UK's financial community.

The Revenue has confirmed in correspondence, and the Financial Secretary has stated in the standing committee debate that they take the view that the reference in new s 482(5A) to 'beneficiaries' extends only to people who, at the time the definition is applied, are identified as beneficiaries under the terms of the particular trust deed.

New s 481(5)(*k*)(iii) specifically authorises trustees to make a declaration provided that, at the time, there are no reasonable grounds to believe that any of those identified beneficiaries of the trust is an individual who is ordinarily resident in the UK or a company which is resident in the UK.

The fact that a UK resident might, at some future time, be made a beneficiary because an addition is made to the class of beneficiaries is not a bar to the trustees making the declaration.

To fall within the scope of the new provision, all 'actual or potential' beneficiaries who are identifiable and known at the time the declaration is made must be not ordinarily resident in the UK.''.

Commentary—*Simon's Direct Tax Service* **D4.1105.**

26 April 1995. Law Society's Gazette

Assignment of debts between members of a group of companies—TCGA 1992 s 251

The Law Society's Gazette has published an article detailing the correspondence between the Revenue Law Committee and the Inland Revenue concerning the assignment of debts between members of a group of companies. The text of the article is reproduced below—

"The Revenue Law Committee has had correspondence with the Inland Revenue's capital and valuation division relating to the application of TCGA 1992 s 251 to the transfer within groups of companies of debts which are not qualifying corporate bonds.

In the course of that correspondence, the Revenue commented on, inter alia, the effect of s 251(4) in relation to debts which constitute debts on a security.

Section 251(1) provides that, except in the case of the disposal of a debt on a security, no chargeable gain or allowable loss arises where a debt is disposed of by the original creditor. However, if the debt is transferred to a third party, any gain (or loss) arising to the third party purchaser is generally chargeable (or allowable).

Section 251(4) is an anti-avoidance provision which provides that if a loss arises to the acquirer of a debt on the disposal of a debt which was acquired from a connected person, that loss is not an allowable loss.

One circumstance in which s 251(4) can apply is where one member of a group of companies transfers a debt to another member of the group. In such a case, under TCGA 1992 s 171(1), the transferee company is treated as acquiring the debt at the same base cost (with indexation allowance if applicable) at which it was held by the transferor regardless of the actual consideration given for the debt.

If the transferee company disposes of the debt at a loss, s 251(4) applies with the effect that the loss is not an allowable loss. In other words, the transferee company cannot claim an allowable loss in circumstances where the original creditor could not have claimed an allowable loss if it had disposed of the debt itself.

In its memorandum on revenue law reform 1994–95, the Revenue Law Committee pointed out that if TCGA 1992 s 251(4) also applied to debts which are debts on a security, its effect would be that a member of a group of companies which purchased the relevant debt from another group member would be prevented from claiming an allowable loss if that debt were disposed of at a loss, even though the original creditor would have been able to claim an allowable loss if it had disposed of the debt.

In the course of the correspondence mentioned above, however, the Revenue stated that it was its view that s 251(4) does not apply to debts which are debts on a security. In other words, if there has been an intra-group transfer of a debt on a security (which is not a qualifying corporate bond) a loss realised on a disposal by a group transferee is capable of being an allowable loss.

..."

Commentary—*Simon's Direct Tax Service* **D2.623.**

16 May 1995. Inland Revenue

Personal incidental expenses—guidance for employers

The Inland Revenue have today issued guidelines for employers on the practical application of the new exemption for personal incidental expenses. The exemption covers payments by employers, up to specified limits, of employees' miscellaneous personal expenses when they stay away from home overnight on business. A copy of the guidelines is [reproduced below].

The issue of these guidelines fulfils a commitment made by the Financial Secretary during debates on the 1995 Finance Bill.

The legislation is a deregulatory measure which will reduce employers' compliance costs.

DETAILS

1 When employees stay away from home overnight on business, they often incur personal incidental expenses. The most common are newspapers, telephone calls home and laundry. Employers often pay for these expenses.

2 Further information on the background to this legislation was given in Budget Press Release IR 20—''Exemption for personal incidental expenses paid by employers.''

PERSONAL INCIDENTAL EXPENSES—GUIDANCE NOTES FOR EMPLOYERS

These notes provide general guidance on the tax treatment of personal incidental expenses (PIEs). They have been produced following legislative changes in FA 1995. They will be incorporated in the existing general guidance available for employers at the next opportunity (Booklet 480 and Employers' guide to PAYE).

The notes are for guidance only and reflect the tax position at the time of writing. If you need more detailed information please ask your local tax office or consult your professional tax adviser.

1 *What is the general rule for the treatment of Schedule E expenses?*

Under general income tax law, a director or employee is taxable on the full amount of emoluments received and this generally includes reimbursed expenses he or she may receive. He or she may, however, claim a deduction from those emoluments under TA 1988 s 198, for qualifying expenses. That is to say, the level of income is reduced by the amount of the qualifying expenditure in calculating the tax due.

To qualify under s 198, the expenditure needs to be incurred wholly, exclusively and necessarily in the performance of the duties of employment. For travelling expenses, there is a deduction for expenditure necessarily incurred in travelling in the performance of the duties. These tests have been interpreted very strictly by the Courts over the years.

2 *Which subsistence expenses are deductible under the general rule?*

The expenses rule which applies to travel costs also covers related subsistence costs. This type of expenditure qualifies for a deduction where it is part of the cost of travel necessarily incurred in the performance of the duties. So, in general, payments by an employer for an employee's accommodation and subsistence when staying away from home overnight on business are not taxed.

Allowable expenses can include the cost of a meal, the cost of a reasonable level of refreshments (both alcoholic and non-alcoholic) with the meal and refreshments such as tea, coffee or soft drinks taken between meals.

3 *What are PIEs?*

Employees staying away from home overnight on business often incur additional expenses of a personal nature. Examples include newspapers, laundry and telephone calls home.

Although expenditure may arise as a consequence of working away from home, it is not incurred necessarily nor in the performance of the employee's duties. Under the Schedule E expenses rule this type of expenditure would not be allowable as a deduction. If this expenditure was met either wholly or in part by the employer, tax would be due under the general rule for taxing income.

4 *What is the new special exemption for PIEs?*

A new special exemption (FA 1995 s 93) provides that employers can pay for PIEs relating to a qualifying absence up to a de minimus limit, without any tax consequences for the employee.

5 *What is a qualifying absence?*

A qualifying absence from home is a continuous period throughout which an employee has to stay away from home, including at least one overnight stay away from home, and where the expense of travelling qualifies for tax relief under the normal rules.

6 *What types of payments are covered?*

The exemption covers all possible ways in which employers pay for employee's PIEs. These include—

- payment by non-cash vouchers;
- expenses paid by the employee by means of a credit card in the employer's name;

- benefits in kind—for example, where the employer arranges directly with a hotel to pay the bill;
- cash payments—such as allowances or reimbursed expenses.

7 *When does the new exemption become effective?*

The exemption has effect for all qualifying payments from 6 April 1995. Expenditure arising before this date but reimbursed on or after this date will be covered by the exemption.

8 *What are the tax free limits?*

The maximum amounts of PIEs an employer may pay for tax free are—

- £5 per night for overnight stays anywhere within the UK (Great Britain and Northern Ireland); and
- £10 per night for overnight stays outside the UK.

9 *Do these limits include VAT?*

Yes. In calculating the total amount paid, all expenditure, inclusive of VAT, needs to be included.

10 *Is there relief for employees' unreimbursed PIEs?*

No. The special exemption for PIEs is essentially a deregulatory measure designed to reduce the burden on employers of identifying and reporting to the Inland Revenue what would otherwise be taxable expenses.

11 *What if payments for PIEs are over the limit?*

Where an employer exceeds these limits, the *whole* of the payment becomes taxable—not just the excess.

12 *What if the employee later refunds the excess?*

Employers are encouraged to introduce clear policies on the payments of PIEs and the refunding of overpaid amounts. Where a policy requiring repayment of any amounts in excess of the exemption limits is in force, an employee would have no entitlement to the excess. In these circumstances, the employee would not be taxed on the payment provided the excess was paid back. However, if the refund by the employee is not made within a reasonable time of the overpayment (whether in the same tax year or soon after the end of the tax year) there may be reporting consequences. (Details may need to be returned on the P11D—if in doubt, ask your local tax office.)

13 *What if an employee spends several nights away from home?*

The total of the exemptions for each night away is simply compared to the total of the payments for that period.

For example, where an employee claims PIEs of £20 for a four night stay away from home in the UK on the basis of £5, £5, £6 and £4 for the four nights involved, the exemptions would apply to all repayments because the total does not exceed £20 (four nights at £5 exemption per night).

This aggregation rule needs to be applied to an unbroken run of consecutive nights in its entirety. An employer may not choose to break up a period of say five nights into one consecutive period of four plus one stand alone night.

14 *What about national insurance contributions?*

National insurance contributions are not payable on any payments of PIEs qualifying for the income tax exemption.

15 *Should payments for PIEs be included in a dispensation?*

Employers will be able to get dispensations for their travelling and subsistence payments—as at present. Payments for PIEs within the exemption would be taken out of tax—and so would not need to be included in a dispensation.

16 *What if payments for PIEs are already included in a dispensation?*

Some dispensations agreed in the past may include an element for PIEs—for example, if the travelling and subsistence payments include an allowance for PIEs. It is not necessary for those dispensations to be reviewed solely with a view to excluding the PIEs element. Such dispensations will be reviewed at the normal date.

17 *What about working rule agreements?*

Employees in the construction and allied industries in receipt of payments under a working rule agreement, are not normally undertaking journeys qualifying within the terms of the general s 198 rule (see Question 1 above). Employers wishing to make payments of PIEs to employees in addition to tax free lodging allowances under a working rule agreement will have to identify those journeys qualifying under TA 1988 s 198. Only in such cases will the PIEs exemption apply.

18 *What if the PIEs of several employees are aggregated on to one bill?*

The payment of PIEs should be made to the individual employees within the limits of the individual exemptions. Sometimes a number of employees' hotel bills are aggregated and paid directly by the employer. Where, in such cases, individual expenditure cannot readily be identified, a reasonable apportionment will be accepted.

19 *What should I do to check that the payments are tax free?*

You should satisfy yourself that the amounts paid do not exceed the maximum amounts payable tax free. You should also ensure that there is no double payment of PIEs—for example, by paying the standard allowance for PIEs *and* reimbursing in full a hotel bill already including such charges (eg telephone calls home).

20 *What do I put on P11Ds?*

If you have a dispensation *and* any PIEs are covered by the dispensation or within the exemption—nothing.

If you do not have a dispensation, you should show on the P11D the amount excluding any exempt PIEs. For example, if you reimburse a hotel bill for £87 including £4 PIEs you should show £83 on the P11D.

If you do not have a dispensation and any PIEs are not within the exemption, you should show the whole amount on the P11D.

General advice about completing form P11D is given in the guide which accompanies the form.

Commentary—*Simon's Direct Tax Service* **E4.612.**

24 May 1995. Inland Revenue

Administration of gilt-edged stock (Fotra securities)

The Inland Revenue have today announced that banks and approved stockbroking firms in the UK will be able to obtain block exemption from UK income tax on behalf of certain overseas customers in respect of income from—

- British government securities issued with the conditions for exemption specified in TA 1988 s 47(1) (Fotra securities); and
- holdings of overseas securities where there is a UK paying agent

irrespective of whether the relevant securities are to be held for at least two dividend dates.

The Financial Secretary to the Treasury, Sir George Young Bt MP, commented today—

> "This administrative change should increase the international attractiveness of the UK gilt market. I therefore very much welcome this development."

This change takes effect from 25 May 1995, and will apply to securities held in existing gross payment accounts.

NOTES

1 Persons not ordinarily resident in the UK may obtain exemption from income tax on interest from certain gilt holdings (Fotra securities) by making a claim to the Board of Inland Revenue. A similar exemption applies to persons not resident in the UK on income from holdings of overseas securities where there is a UK paying agent.

2 There are existing arrangements which enable banks and approved stockbroking firms in the UK to obtain block exemption from UK income tax on behalf of their customers/clients who meet the conditions for exemption, thus avoiding the necessity for individual claims. These arrangements apply only to—

- Fotra securities; and
- holdings of overseas securities where there is a UK paying agent.

The securities/shares must be registered in the name of a nominee approved for the purpose by the Board of Inland Revenue. Until now these arrangements have been intended only for long-term investments and it has not been possible to transfer into a gross payment account any holding which was not likely to satisfy that condition. A long-term holding has been defined as one that will be held for at least two and preferably three successive dividend dates. From 25 May 1995 this rule will no longer apply.

Commentary—*Simon's Direct Tax Service* **E6.208.**

6 June 1995. Hansard

Self-employment—classification

Mr French asked the Chancellor of the Exchequer in what ways the criteria applied by the Inland Revenue in deciding whether a person is employed or self-employed differ from those applied by the Contributions Agency.

Sir George Young: The criteria applied by the Inland Revenue and the Contributions Agency in deciding whether a person is employed or self-employed are based on the same body of general case law. They are set out in the Inland Revenue leaflet IR 56/N 139. An updated version of this leaflet is to be published shortly. There are a very limited number of groups of workers where statutory provisions may result in different tax and national insurance treatment.

HC, Written Answers, 6 June 1995 Vol 261 col 89.

17 July 1995. Share Scheme Lawyers Group

Share option cancellation payments—PAYE

In a letter to the Chairman of the Share Scheme Lawyers Group the Inland Revenue has confirmed that payments to employees as consideration for the surrender, cancellation, assignment or release of share options do not need to have tax deducted through the PAYE system irrespective of whether any payment was made for the grant of the option and whether the payment was made by the employer or by a third party.

NOTES

1 If a person is granted a share option pursuant to an employment opportunity and subsequently gives up the option in return for cash compensation, the compensatory payment, less any amount paid for the grant of the option, will be subject to income tax pursuant to TA 1988 s 135.

2 A possible implication of the decision of the House of Lords in *IRC v Herd* [1993] STC 436 was that payments taxable under s 135 were subject to deduction of tax under the PAYE system but only if the entire payment was taxable. This appeared to create an artificial distinction between those options granted under deed without payment and those granted for a purely nominal consideration.

3 After a period of uncertainty, the Revenue, having considered the *Herd* decision, has now confirmed that PAYE does not apply to option cancellation payments.

4 The membership of the Share Scheme Lawyers Group comprises approximately 60 lawyers in private practice who are specialists in the area of employee share schemes... For further information contact David Cohen, telephone number 0171 353 0299.

Commentary—*Simon's Direct Tax Service* **E4.524.**

21 March 1996. Inland Revenue

Carry-back of personal pension contributions made in 1996–97

The Inland Revenue have announced that where qualifying personal pension contributions are paid in the tax year 1996–97 but are carried back for relief to 1995–96, the Department will take those contributions into account when setting the level of any payments on account required for 1996–97 under self-assessment. This change responds to representations from the pensions industry and others about the interaction between the personal pension rules and the introduction of self-assessment.

DETAILS

1 Tax relief is available for contributions to personal pension schemes and retirement annuity contracts up to a fixed proportion of earnings. To give greater flexibility, and to encourage contributions up to the full amount allowed, taxpayers can elect to have contributions made in a later year treated as if they had been made in an earlier one. Currently, relief is given by amending the taxpayer's assessment to reflect the later contributions with consequential changes to the amount of tax that is due.

2 Under self-assessment—which begins on 6 April 1996—tax for a year of assessment will be due automatically on set dates and will be calculated on the basis of figures provided by the taxpayer. The self-assessment will then be used to set the level of payments on account for the subsequent year. For the system to work effectively, the amount of any payments needs to be firmly established and remain unchanged; but the present rules for the "carry-back" of personal pension payments from a later year would not allow this.

3 The new rules for self-assessment therefore retain the current provisions for calculating the relief available, but give effect to the relief in a way which does not alter the assessment for the earlier year. The rules come into effect for all pension payments made on or after 6 April 1996. This means that personal pension payments made in the tax year 1996–97, and carried back to 1995–96 would not affect the assessment made for 1995–96. Consequently the relief for these contributions would not be reflected in setting the level of the payments on account for 1996–97. By contrast, payments made before 6 April 1996, and set against income for 1995–96 would result in the reduction of payments on account for 1996–97.

4 Recent representations from the pension industry and from financial advisers have pointed out that the cash flow changes that the new rules would introduce were not generally expected and that the date from which the new rules apply has frequently been misinterpreted.

5 The Revenue have concluded that in the light of the misunderstanding about the proper treatment of pension contributions made in 1996–97 it would be appropriate for them to take into account any qualifying personal pension payments made in 1996–97, and carried back to 1995–96, when setting the levels of payments on account for 1996–97.

Commentary—*Simon's Direct Tax Service* **E4.524.**

21 March 1996. Inland Revenue

Capital gains tax treatment of cashbacks and certain other lump sum payments by banks or building societies

The Inland Revenue wish to make it clear following legal advice that they no longer regard ''cashbacks'' paid by banks and building societies, and other similar lump sum payments offered as an inducement to purchase goods or services, as chargeable to capital gains tax. Lump sum cash payments made by building societies in a variety of other situations, however, remain potentially chargeable to capital gains tax if an income tax liability does not arise.

DETAILS

Cashbacks

1 It is becoming increasingly common for a cash lump sum payment to be offered as an inducement to purchase goods, services or financial products. The payer may either be the provider of the goods etc (for example, a building society offering a mortgage) or a third party (for example, a car manufacturer). Such payments are commonly referred to as ''cashbacks''.

2 The Revenue have received legal advice that when such a payment, offered as an inducement to take out a mortgage or purchase particular goods etc, is received as a direct consequence of having entered into that transaction, the payment does not derive from a chargeable asset for capital gains tax purposes. No chargeable gain therefore arises in respect of the payment.

3 Previously the Revenue took the view that these payments—where they did not count as part of taxable income—were potentially chargeable to capital gains tax. Taxpayers will have been expected to include payments of this kind on their tax return as a chargeable gain, subject to the usual reporting relaxations. In future these payments will not need to be included in returns unless they are chargeable as income. Normally an income tax liability will only arise if payments constitute receipts of a taxable business of the customer or arise by reasons of his or her employment.

The circumstances in which an income tax liability may arise on cashbacks will be set out in a Statement of Practice covering ''Commissions and cashbacks'' which will be issued shortly. This Statement, which will replace SP 5/95, is currently being discussed between the Revenue and various representative bodies. Taxpayers who are uncertain of the tax treatment of any payment of this nature should contact their tax office.

4 As cashbacks are a fairly recent development it is unlikely that many taxpayers will have been assessed to capital gains tax on them. Any taxpayers who have should contact their tax office to establish how the assessment and any appeal will be dealt with.

Takeovers or conversions of building societies

5 The Revenue's legal advice is that investors, borrowers or depositors in a society who receive a cash payment when the society is taken over are chargeable to capital gains tax. These payments are not chargeable to income tax. This analysis applies to payments made to investors and depositors on the takeover of Cheltenham and Gloucester Building Society by Lloyds Bank plc, and it is expected that the result will be the same in similar takeovers.

6 The sum received derives from a chargeable asset for capital gains purposes. The identify of the asset depends upon the rights of the investor, borrower or depositor by virtue of which the payment is made. These may be contractual, statutory or under trust. In certain circumstances, rights of more than one kind may exist.

7 As no expenditure will have been incurred in acquiring the chargeable asset which gives rise to the gain the whole of the payment will be chargeable. Payments should therefore be included on tax returns for the year 1995–96 if, together with other chargeable gains for the year, they exceed the annual exempt amount of £6,000 or the total proceeds from all disposals exceed £12,000.

8 This analysis would also apply to cash payments on the conversion of a society from mutual status to a company.

Mergers of building societies

9 Cash payments made on the merger of two or more societies are chargeable to income tax.

Issue of shares

10 Where shares are issued on the transfer of the whole of a building society's business to a successor company no capital gains liability arises on the receipt of those shares. A capital gains liability may, however, arise on the sale of the shares. For the purpose of computing the liability the shares are treated as acquired for the amount of any consideration given by members. If no consideration is given, the acquisition cost will be nil.

11 In cases where both shares and cash are received the tax treatment will be determined according to the nature of the receipt.

12 Anyone who receives a payment in this kind of situation and is uncertain how it should be treated should contact their tax office.

Commentary—*Simon's Direct Tax Service* **C1.319.**
Note—For the Revenue's updated view on takeovers and conversions of building societies, see IR press release of 27 March 1997.

1 April 1996. Inland Revenue

Interest and repayment interest—effective date of payment of tax and national insurance contributions

The Inland Revenue have today announced details of when payments made to them in respect of tax and Class 4 NICs will be treated as received for the purpose of calculating interest.

The main changes will take effect from 6 April 1996. Certain other changes, introduced by regulations, will take effect from 19 April 1996.

Similar provisions in respect of Class 1 and Class 1A NICs will be introduced shortly by the DSS, to take effect from 19 April 1996.

DETAILS

1 Payments to the Revenue are made in a variety of ways. The following information identifies the different methods of payment and gives details of when payment will be deemed to have been made. The details reflect changes included in FA 1994 in relation to self-assessment, and changes included in regulations laid today amending the PAYE regulations, the construction industry sub-contractor regulations and the gilt interest quarterly accounting regulations.

2 These rules will apply to all payments of income tax, corporation tax, capital gains tax, and Class 4 NICs. The changes included in the regulations will apply to payments by cheque received after 19 April 1996. All other changes will apply to payments received on or after 6 April 1996. The payment dates will be used to calculate interest on late payments of tax and Class 4 NICs, and also repayment supplement and repayment interest.

3 Amendments to DSS regulations will introduce similar rules for Class 1 and Class 1A NICs with effect from 19 April 1996.

4 Payment method	Effective date of payment
Cheques, cash, postal orders	
— handed in at the Revenue office or received by post (except as below);	day of receipt by the Revenue,
— received by post following a day when the office has been closed for whatever reason (including a weekend).	the day the office was first closed (for payments received on Monday the effective date will be the previous Saturday).
Electronic funds transfer (EFT)—payment by BACS or CHAPS (clearing house automated payment system)	One working day immediately before the date that the value is received. (A working day is defined as a Bank of England working day.)
Bank Giro or Girobank	Three working days prior to the date of processing by the Revenue.

5 To avoid a charge to interest, payment of tax should be made by the due date.

Commentary—*Simon's Direct Tax Service* **A3.1313; E1.824; E4.954.**
Cross reference—See TMA 1970 s 70A.

4 April 1996. Inland Revenue

Self-assessment—early settlement of a deceased taxpayer's tax affairs or those of a trust or estate following cessation

The Inland Revenue have always been prepared, when asked to do so by the personal representatives or trustees of a deceased person, to issue a tax return before the end of the tax year to which it relates and to agree liabilities quickly. They have done this to minimise delays in winding up an estate and distributing estate or trust property.

The time limit for enquiring into tax returns under self-assessment, however, means that personal representatives may not know for some time whether the deceased's tax affairs can be regarded as settled. That could result in delays winding up an estate.

To help personal representatives settle the affairs of the deceased as quickly as possible, the Revenue have today announced that, under self-assessment they will, on request, issue a tax return before the end of the tax year in which death occurred and give early written confirmation if they do not intend to enquire into that return. Personal representatives can also request such confirmation at any time before the expiry of the normal enquiry time limit.

A similar situation may arise where the administration of a deceased person's estate is completed or a trust is wound up during a tax year. The Revenue will, on request, adopt the same approach to the tax affairs of personal representatives and trustees.

DETAILS

1 Self-assessment comes in for the tax year 1996–97 onwards for around 9 million taxpayers.

2 If one of those taxpayers dies after 5 April 1996 and the Revenue needs to send a tax return to the deceased's personal representatives, covering the period to the date of death, they will usually do this *after* the end of the tax year in which death occurred.

3 Under self-assessment, however, the Revenue can enquire into a tax return up to 12 months after the fixed filing date—that is up to 12 months after 31 January following the end of a year of assessment.

4 This could mean that if a taxpayer died in, say, early April 1996 the personal representatives of the deceased could not be sure, until after 31 January 1999, whether the Revenue were going to enquire into the return for the period to the date of death.

5 Representations have been made that this could delay the winding up of estates.

6 To help personal representatives settle the tax affairs of the deceased quickly the Revenue will, on request, issue a tax return *before* the end of the tax year in which death occurred; and whether issued before or after the end of that tax year, they will also give early written confirmation if they do not intend to enquire into that return.

7 This confirmation would not preclude, in exceptional circumstances, the Revenue enquiring into the tax return at a later date if they discovered that the return had been incomplete or incorrect.

8 But, in the vast majority of cases, receipt of this written confirmation will signify the end of the Revenue's interest in the income and capital gains tax affairs of the deceased and, where that is the only open matter, will enable the deceased's personal representatives to finalise the estate.

9 Where administration of a deceased person's estate is completed or a trust is wound up in a tax year, the personal representatives or trustees will similarly be able to request the issue of a tax return before the end of the tax year. And confirmation that the Revenue does not intend to enquire into that return will be given on the same basis. This will enable personal representatives and trustees to finalise tax liabilities and distribute estate or trust property.

Commentary—*Simon's Direct Tax Service* **C4.102–110.**

30 April 1996. Inland Revenue

Tax treatment of premiums and benefits under locum and fixed practice expenses insurance policies

The Inland Revenue today announced revised arrangements covering the way in which premiums paid for insurance policies to cover the cost of engaging a locum tenens, and benefits paid out under such policies, will be treated for tax purposes in the future.

This change of practice has been the subject of detailed consultation with the main parties likely to be affected, and the particulars set out below reflect their views.

DETAILS

1 Some professional people who practise alone or in partnership, in particular medical professionals, take out insurance policies to indemnify themselves against the cost of engaging a locum tenens, or against other practice expenses, in the event of the policyholder's illness or other incapacity. In the past the Revenue's view has been that premiums and benefits under these policies should be excluded from the calculation of taxable professional profits in the same way as other permanent health insurance premiums and benefits are excluded.

Change of view

2 The Revenue have now received legal advice that this view is incorrect. Premiums on policies of indemnification of this nature are deductible in computing profits under Schedule D Case II. Equally, benefits payable under the policies should be regarded as Case II receipts on the basis that they diminish the allowable expenses of the profession.

3 This treatment of both the premiums and the benefits holds good whether a person is obliged to insure (because of partnership obligations or National Health Service regulations) or does so as a matter of commercial prudence.

4 Where, however, the particular policy also includes insurance against other, non-business, risks such as the cost of medical treatment for accident or sickness of the insured, the premiums will be incurred partly for a personal purpose. Only the proportion of the premium relating to practice expenses cover, calculated on a reasonable and consistent basis, will then be deductible.

How the change of view will be put into effect

5 In calculating profits for periods of account that begin on or after 1 October 1996, the premiums on locum/fixed practice expenses policies will be deductible and the benefits treated as taxable business receipts.

6 Where the profits for a period of account beginning before 1 October 1996 have *not* been agreed with the Inspector and assessments have *not* otherwise become final, premiums should be deducted and benefits treated as taxable business receipts. Alternatively, where premiums and benefits have been excluded from the computation of taxable profits for earlier settled periods this practice may be continued for unsettled periods of account beginning before 1 October 1996 subject to para 7 below.

7 Where figures for periods of account beginning before 1 October 1996 have become final and premiums and benefits have been excluded from the computation of taxable profits for those periods, claims to repayment under the error or mistake provision (TMA 1970 s 33) may be made subject to the general rules for error or mistake relief, in particular the six year time limit. Under such a claim tax relief may be obtained for previously unallowed premiums but the total unallowed relief will be reduced by any untaxed benefits relating to the earliest period of account to which claims relate and all subsequent settled periods.

8 If an error or mistake claim is made premiums must also then be deducted and benefits treated as taxable business receipts for the unsettled periods mentioned in para 6 above.

NOTES

1 Tax assessments currently become final after 30 days after being raised unless the taxpayer makes an appeal, or when the appeal is determined.

2 There is, however, provision in TMA 1970 s 33 for a taxpayer to seek to re-open a final assessment for a year of assessment if there has been any error or mistake in a return. Such claims have to be made within six years of the end of the year of assessment in which the assessment for the year in question is raised. Claims for 1990–91 and subsequent years of assessment would always be within this time limit so long as they are made by 5 April 1997.

3 This change of view would provide an opportunity for any taxpayer who so wished to invoke that facility and have his or her liability revised in the light of the new view of the law.

Commentary—*Simon's Direct Tax Service* **B4.203, 211.**

31 May 1996. Inland Revenue

Disclosure and discovery under self-assessment

The Inland Revenue have today issued a paper about the operation of the discovery and disclosure rules under self-assessment. This follows discussions with representatives of accountants, tax advisers, businesses and other professional bodies. The paper addresses the concerns that have been expressed about the circumstances in which the Revenue will make assessments on the discovery of profits that have not been assessed or were inadequately assessed, or where excessive relief has been given.

It makes it clear that where a taxpayer has made a self-assessment for the relevant chargeable period, the Revenue may raise an assessment if there would otherwise be a loss of tax resulting from the taxpayer's failure to make a complete disclosure of all the relevant facts relating to his liability to tax.

The statement also makes it clear that while the new self-assessment return has been designed to enable the vast majority of taxpayers fully to disclose their liability without the need to submit accounts or computations, the Revenue will accept any additional information sent in with the return.

The paper is reproduced [below].

DISCOVERY AND DISCLOSURE UNDER SELF-ASSESSMENT

Introduction

1 The introduction of self-assessment and the electronic lodgement services (ELS) heralds a new approach to the handling of tax returns, with more realistic filing dates and streamlined procedures. In particular, the new return has been designed to enable full disclosure to be made without the need to send in accounts or computations in most cases. But concerns have been expressed that reliance on the self-assessment return, without additional information, such as accounts, might expose taxpayers to a greater risk of ''discovery'' assessments under (new) TMA 1970 s 29. This paper addresses the concerns that have been raised during the Revenue's discussions with representative bodies.

Discovery

2 New TMA 1970 s 29 introduced by FA 1994 s 19 is designed to reproduce the current mix of law, practice, and concession on discovery set out in the Revenue's Statement of Practice SP8/91 as it applies for self-assessment.

3 The foundation of the principle of discovery is that the Revenue should be able to recover tax which has been under-assessed (or over-relieved) where there is fraudulent or negligent conduct or where the Revenue officer could not be reasonably expected to be aware of the under-assessment (or excessive relief) from the information provided in or with the tax return.

Disclosure

4 This paper is concerned only with the second of these two aspects, the concept of "disclosure". Where all relevant facts are disclosed to the Revenue, taxpayers can be certain (except in the case of fraud or neglect) they have gained finality at the end of the enquiry period.

5 Section 29 sets out the ways in which information is made available for the purpose of making a disclosure. These include providing details in the return or claim, or in any material accompanying the return or claim, for the year in question or the two preceding years. In addition, it is open to the taxpayer or agent to write to the Revenue explaining the existence and relevance of any particular material for the purposes of making an adequate disclosure.

A change of opinion on information that has previously been made available to the Revenue will not be grounds for a discovery assessment.

The self-assessment return and standard accounts information

6 Additional information takes more time to process and store, costs which all taxpayers bear by extension. The new return is designed to enable full disclosure to be made without the need to send in accounts or computations in most cases. Taxpayers and practitioners are entitled to send in additional material if they consider that it adds information of relevance to the tax liability which cannot be contained within the return. The Revenue will accept any additional information sent in with the return; see para 13 (accompanying documents) below.

7 The self-assessment return requires comprehensive information regarding each taxpayer's affairs. With the exception of partnerships whose annual turnover exceeds £15 million (see para 10 below), separate accounts and computations are not required to be submitted with the return. Instead specific details, including standard accounts information (SAI), are required within the return.

8 The majority of income tax cases involve reasonably straightforward accounts. In these cases the fully completed return and SAI will enable a full and fair picture of the taxpayer's affairs including any business to be presented. In otherwise straightforward cases there may be the odd point of difficulty which needs further explanation. Such aspects may be dealt with by providing extra information within the areas provided on the return.

9 In some of the larger or more complex cases the SAI details and the space provided in the return for additional information may not by themselves provide a means of adequate disclosure. The submission of further information, including perhaps the submission of accounts, may be considered appropriate by the taxpayer or agent. Such cases would include, for example, large partnerships with substantial turnovers or cases where, although not large, the business is complex—perhaps because it is a highly specialised trade, or where accounts or computations are required for a proper understanding of the figures.

10 The SAI will have to be completed in order for the return to be accepted, even where the accounts are submitted. To leave this information to the discretion of the taxpayer would seriously undermine its value to the Revenue. The only exception is for the very largest partnerships (ie annual turnover over £15 million) where taxpayers are required to submit accounts and computations as well as the return instead of completing SAI. This difference in treatment is justified because the Revenue are likely, anyway, to require to see the accounts and computations of these large cases every year, on account of their size and inherent complexity. Tax returns will be considered to be incomplete where, at the filing date, the SAI boxes have not been completed or, in cases where partnership turnover exceeds £15 million per annum, the accounts have not been submitted.

The submission of additional material

11 Taxpayers and agents should be aware that the submission of accounts and computations or other documents may not provide protection against a discovery assessment beyond that arising from the submission of the return alone. The information contained in the additional material may have been fully covered within the return or, alternatively, there may be so much material that the Revenue officer "could not have been reasonably expected, on the basis of the information made available to him before that time, to be aware" (TMA 1970 new s 29(5)) of the particular point of liability, unless the taxpayer or agent had explained its relevance. Where voluminous information beyond the accounts and computations is sent with the return, therefore, it is recommended that there should be a brief indication of the relevance of the material.

Electronic lodgement service

12 The electronic lodgement service (ELS) will accommodate all the information which may be given on the self-assessment return, including any additional details in the "white space". Furthermore, recent developments in the design of the ELS system mean that the service will be able to cope with substantial amounts of additional information such as accounts or computations should their submission be considered appropriate by the taxpayer or accountant.

Accompanying documents

13 The s 29 definition of disclosure includes information in "any accounts, statements or documents accompanying the return". The Revenue consider that any material sent in support of a return "accompanies" the return for that purpose. Although advised that, in strictness, statutory time-limits for filing a return apply equally to any documents intended to accompany it, the Revenue will accept that any documents submitted within one month of the return "accompany" it for the purpose of making a disclosure within TMA 1970 s 29 if the return indicates that such documents have been, or are to be, submitted. Where documents have been sent outside that time limit, the Revenue will consider sympathetically any request for them to be treated as supporting the return in question for that purpose.

Conclusion

14 It is in everyone's interests that the new self-assessment system enables taxpayers to disclose their affairs fully. The Revenue believe that this can be achieved through the return and SAI, explanations in the space provided in the return for additional information, or the submission of accounts or computations where appropriate. The self-assessment return and the guidance notes will help taxpayers to be aware of matters which should be disclosed and, where there are doubts, taxpayers can consult their tax adviser or the Revenue.

Commentary—*Simon's Direct Tax Service* **D2.733, E1.810, 812.**

29 July 1996. Inland Revenue

Self-assessment—provision of information from taxpayer statements of account to authorised agents

Following discussions with representatives of accountants, tax advisers, businesses and other professional bodies, the Inland Revenue have today announced that they will provide agents who are currently authorised by their clients to receive copies of assessments, etc with details of the relevant information contained in taxpayer statements of account. This will enable agents to help their clients to comply with their obligations under self-assessment.

DETAILS

1 The information detailed below will be supplied to agents' client offices for individual taxpayers for whom the Revenue hold details of the taxpayer's authority on form 64–8 for information to be copied to the agent. It will not be necessary for agents to ask clients to complete a new form 64–8 in order to receive this information.

2 In October/November 1996, the Revenue will provide agents with advance notice of the information contained in the first self-assessment statements of account. These will be sent to taxpayers in November/December 1996, and include details of the first payment on account. The details to agents will include details of both payments on account the taxpayer is required to make for the year 1996–97.

3 Early in February 1998, where the return has been processed the Revenue will provide agents with details of any balancing payment for 1996–97 due from their client on 31 January 1998, and of the first payment on account due at the same time in respect of the self-assessment liability for the year 1997–98.

4 Agents will also be provided with particulars of any payments made by their client which have already been allocated against their liability to tax, and of any payments awaiting allocation. The information provided will include details of all liabilities and payments recorded on the taxpayer's account up to the date the information is extracted for the issue of the notification to the agent.

5 In April 1998, the Revenue will send agents details of their clients' outstanding liabilities. It will also include details of any movements on the account up to shortly before the issue of the note to the agents, including any new charges or payments of tax since the date on which the previous note was issued to the agent.

6 This information will be provided in the form of a separate note for each taxpayer the agent represents. The note will contain details of—

– the agent's name and address;
– the taxpayer's name and address;
– the agent's client reference;

PRs etc

– the taxpayer's tax reference.

7 Agents will be supplied information on the same basis and in a similar format in February and April 1999 and in subsequent years.

8 When the electronic lodgement service becomes operational in April 1997, agents who are registered to file returns electronically will automatically receive electronic copies of taxpayer statements of account provided the Revenue holds the authority for information to be copied to the agent. (It will not be necessary for a fresh form 64–8 to be completed specifically for this purpose.) Registered electronic lodgement filers will also receive information on the same basis as described above.

9 Taxpayers can elect for their agent to receive their copy of the taxpayer statement of account by completing a revised form 64–8. Agents who have been authorised to do so will begin receiving their client's taxpayer statement of account from April 1997.

10 The Revenue are continuing work on the design and content of the various self-assessment forms to make them as accessible and helpful as possible for taxpayers and their agents.

NOTES

1 In November and December 1996, the Revenue will be sending notifications (taxpayer statements of account) and guidance to taxpayers who are required to make payments of account under self-assessment due for payment on 31 January 1997.

2 Most of these taxpayer statements of account will go to self-employed taxpayers who are represented by accountants or other tax advisers (''agents'').

3 Agents who have been authorised to receive such information will be sent details of the information contained in the taxpayer statements of account sent to their clients to enable them to help them comply with their obligations under self-assessment.

Commentary—*Simon's Direct Tax Service* **E1.821.**

31 July 1996. Inland Revenue

Repayments to sub-contractors in the construction industry

Following the introduction of self-assessment, the Inland Revenue have produced new guidelines explaining the circumstances in which repayments will be made to sub-contractors in the construction industry before the end of a tax year. The new procedures which will take immediate effect will be kept under review. A copy of the guidelines is attached as an annex to this press release.

New forms have also been prepared on which individuals and partners who are sub-contractors may claim these repayments. These forms are available from tax offices.

Accountancy and industry representatives who have been consulted on this matter have responded positively to the new procedure and clearer guidelines.

NOTES

Those sub-contractors working in the construction industry who do not possess an exception (714) certificate have deductions made from their earnings on account of tax and Class 4 NICs. A repayment of these deductions will be due where they exceed the sub-contractor's liability to tax and national insurance for the year.

ANNEX

SUB-CONTRACTORS IN THE CONSTRUCTION INDUSTRY—GUIDELINES FOR REPAYMENTS OF SC60 DEDUCTIONS

Introduction

Deductions on account of tax and Class 4 NICs are made from the construction industry earnings of those sub-contractors who do not hold 714 certificates. Where these deductions exceed the sub-contractor's liability to tax and national insurance for the year, the excess may be repaid. Where the sub-contractor calculates that he is due a repayment before the end of the year in question, the Revenue will make a repayment on a provisional basis, pending the receipt of the full tax return after the end of the year.

However, it is in the interests of both the Revenue and sub-contractors that the provisional repayment does not exceed the actual amount of the overpayment for the year. The following procedures are designed, as far as is reasonable, to ensure that no part of the repayment needs to be recovered at a later date.

Procedure

- A repayment may be claimed by a sub-contractor when he is able to show that the amount of the deductions made under the construction industry scheme in a year exceed his liability to income tax and national insurance for that year.
- Where a claim is made before the end of the tax year, it should be made on form SC70 (or, in the case of a partner, form SC71) which can be obtained from local tax offices. Where the claim is made after the end of the year, it should be made using the tax return form.
- The claim must be accompanied by form SC60 showing the full amount of the deductions included in the calculation for the year.
- In making a repayment during the year to which it relates, Revenue officers will examine the sub-contractor's tax affairs in general to ensure that they are up to date before making a repayment. No repayment will be made where tax returns for earlier years remain outstanding.
- Where any tax or national insurance for earlier years remain unpaid, the overpayment will be used first to satisfy these amounts.
- Where a repayment is claimed by a partner, all the partners in that firm will be expected to confirm their agreement to the apportionment of the profit and tax deductions before repayment is made.

26 September 1996. Inland Revenue

Rulings

Following the recent consultation on pre-transaction rulings, Ministers have decided not to proceed at present with the introduction of a formal, comprehensive scheme for giving pre-transaction rulings. Instead, they have decided to introduce a comprehensive scheme for giving *post*–transaction rulings early next year in time for self-assessment. The Inland Revenue will also write to interested parties with a view to exploring the possibility of introducing a selective scheme for giving ''product rulings'', for which the Revenue would charge.

DETAILS

1 A pre-transaction ruling is a ruling given by the Revenue on the tax treatment of a particular transaction before the transaction takes place. In November last year the Revenue published a consultative document on the possible introduction of a scheme for giving such rulings for which they would charge [see *Simon's Weekly Tax Intelligence* 1995 p 1718]. Responses to this consultation indicated there was support for the Revenue developing its giving of certainty of tax treatment, but concerns were expressed about charging, the level of information required to obtain a ruling and the impact of a formal scheme on existing informal arrangements for obtaining advice on the application of the law [see *Simon's Weekly Tax Intelligence* 1996 pp 512, 685, 686, 993].

2 Given this response, Ministers have decided not to proceed for the time being with the introduction of a formal scheme. Instead, they have asked the Revenue to explore the possibility of introducing a selective scheme for giving product rulings. These have many of the characteristics of a pre-transaction ruling, but are given where—

- a pre-transaction ruling would not be appropriate because it is not practicable to identify the taxpayers who may enter into the arrangement; and
- the characteristics of the taxpayers who may enter into the arrangement would not affect the content of the ruling.

3 Product rulings therefore would apply to primarily retail products sold to a range of taxpayers. Financial instruments or savings plans marketed by insurance companies are examples of arrangements that could come within this category.

4 The aim of such a scheme would be to give greater certainty to potential investors in new products, while at the same time ensuring that any such system of rulings was not exploited by those wanting to develop products involving tax avoidance. The idea of product rulings was strongly welcomed in the responses to the consultative document—and there was considerably less opposition to the Revenue charging for giving them.

5 Ministers have also decided to introduce next year a formal scheme for giving post-transaction rulings as a taxpayer support for the introduction of self-assessment. A post-transaction ruling is a ruling given by the Revenue after the transaction has occurred and before the taxpayer makes his tax return. The scheme would be similar to that piloted last year in the Bristol and Swindon tax offices, and it is *not* intended that the Revenue would charge for these. Further details on this scheme will be published later this year.

NOTES

1 There is currently no formal comprehensive scheme in the UK for providing rulings—as there is in a number of other countries. But there are a number of circumstances where taxpayers can obtain certainty of tax treatment from the Revenue. These broadly fall into two categories—

- statutory clearances; and
- informal advice and rulings given in accordance with guidelines published last year in the Revenue Code of Practice No 10—''Information and advice''.

2 In order to help taxpayers and the business community cope with developments like pay and file for companies and self-assessment, Ministers have asked the Revenue to develop their giving of rulings in two ways—

- last year, the Revenue piloted a scheme for giving post-transaction rulings; and
- in November last year the Revenue published a consultative document on pre-transaction rulings for which there would be a full cost recovery charge.

3 Responses to the latter were mixed. There was support for the idea of the Revenue giving greater certainty of tax treatment. But there were strong concerns about—

- the possible impact of any formal scheme on the current arrangements for giving informal advice on the application of the law;
- the additional amount of information required to obtain a ruling; and
- the charging of a fee for the ruling sufficient to recover the Revenue's costs in providing the ruling.

4 For this reason Ministers have decided not to proceed with the introduction of a formal scheme for giving pre-transaction rulings. Instead, they have asked the Revenue to explore the possibility of introducing a selective scheme for giving product rulings, for which they would charge.

19 November 1996. Inland Revenue/Contributions Agency

Inland Revenue and Contributions Agency provide more help for the construction industry on employment status

The Financial Secretary to the Treasury, Michael Jack MP, and the Parliamentary Under Secretary of State for the Department of Social Security, Oliver Heald MP, have today announced the further steps the Inland Revenue and Contributions Agency are taking to help the construction industry review the employment status of their workers.

These steps, which include a new telephone helpline, are being taken in response to the construction industry's request for additional guidance on whether workers are employed or self-employed.

DETAILS

1 In October 1995, and at the request of the industry, the Revenue and Contributions Agency jointly published a leaflet ''Are your workers employed or self-employed?'' (IR 148/CA 69). The leaflet is designed to help contractors determine whether their workers are self-employed or employees.

2 In recent discussions with the Revenue and DSS, representatives of the construction industry have asked for more information about when contractors should complete their reviews of the employment status of their workers and make necessary changes. They have requested more time to implement those changes and help in explaining to their workers what a change in employment status means. The industry also sought an assurance that, by a given date, all construction firms must have made any necessary changes in the employment status of their workers and be deducting PAYE and NICs so that there is a level playing field when firms compete for contracts.

3 In response the Revenue and Contributions Agency will be taking the following steps—

(*a*) contractors will be given a reasonable time in which to review the employment status of their workers and set up PAYE arrangements where these are necessary but all contractors will be expected to have completed their reviews by 5 April 1997 at the latest and, where appropriate, to be accounting for PAYE and NICs by that date;

(*b*) where, after that date, contractors are found not to be accounting for PAYE and NICs in respect of payments to employees, the Revenue and Contributions Agency will normally seek payment of arrears back to 5 April 1997. Payment will be sought for earlier years only where there has been clear evidence of evasion;

(*c*) the present level of compliance visits to review contractors' records will be maintained in order to help them with employment status issues and ensure arrangements are being made to operate PAYE and NICs;

(*d*) from 2 December 1996, the following telephone helpline will be available for contractors and workers who need general assistance with employment status queries. Telephone Helpline—0345 33 55 88.

(*e*) a leaflet will shortly be published by the Revenue, to help construction workers understand how a change of employment status may affect their tax and national insurance liabilities. The leaflet will also provide guidance on self-assessment.

4 A number of common issues have emerged from the discussions with the construction industry. These are dealt with in an annex [reproduced below].

NOTES

1 The advice and guidance being issued by the Revenue and the Contributions Agency are in response to requests from representative bodies in the construction industry for help in deciding whether their workers are employed or self-employed.

2 Whether someone is employed or self-employed depends on the terms and conditions of their engagement. The same general rules apply to the construction industry as to other industries and are set out in leaflet IR 56/NI 39 ''Employed or self-employed''. Leaflet IR 148/CA 69, ''Are your workers employed or self-employed'' explains how the general rules on employment status apply to the particular circumstances of the construction industry.

3 Leaflet IR 148/CA 69 was sent to most contractors in April 1996. Since then, there has been some uncertainty about what contractors need to do and when. The Revenue and Contributions Agency have explained that their approach is to help the industry get employment status right. Many sub-contractors are genuinely self-employed and will continue to be handled within the construction industry tax deduction scheme. But where it is clear that the terms of a worker amount to employment, the contractor must operate PAYE and deduct NICs.

ANNEX

Does this mean you are ending self-employment in the construction industry?

Absolutely not. Contractors will continue to be free to take on workers as self-employed where the terms and conditions of engagement reflect genuine self-employment.

Will contractors be faced with large bills for back tax and national insurance if they have treated employees as self-employed in the past?

Where a contractor has reviewed the employment status of his workforce and made any necessary changes by 6 April 1997, the Revenue and Contributions Agency will not normally seek to recover tax and NICs for earlier years unless there is evidence of evasion. But where a contractor has not taken this action and PAYE and Class 1 contributions are found to be due, the Revenue and Contributions Agency will normally seek arrears back to 5 April 1997 (and earlier if there has been evasion).

How will the Revenue and Contributions Agency ensure that all contractors review the employment status of their workers and make necessary changes?

It is for contractors to decide whether their workers are employed or self-employed. The Revenue and Contributions Agency will be considering employment status issues as part of their normal compliance reviews. A contractor who has not reviewed the employment status of his workers and made necessary changes by 6 April 1997 may have his liability for PAYE and national insurance in respect of those workers reassessed back to that date. And in appropriate cases, the contractor may have to pay interest and penalties.

Commentary—*Simon's Direct Tax Service* **E4.202, 203.**

2 December 1996. Inland Revenue

Capital gains tax reinvestment relief—new clearance scheme

The Financial Secretary to the Treasury, Michael Jack MP, today announced the introduction of new arrangements by the Inland Revenue to help companies establish whether investment in their shares will qualify for capital gains tax reinvestment relief.

Reinvestment relief allows a charge to capital gains tax to be deferred if an individual reinvests the gain on the disposal of an asset in shares in a qualifying unlisted company. There are restrictions on the type of company which can qualify. This has led to uncertainty in particular cases as to whether proposed investment in a company will be eligible. Today's announcement sets out new procedures under which companies can approach the Revenue for guidance about their status.

DETAILS

1 Reinvestment relief is aimed at encouraging investment in unlisted, high-risk companies that trade or, broadly, are holding companies of a trading group. Such companies may find it difficult to attract equity investment, while the holders of shares in such companies may find it difficult to find buyers when they want to sell their holdings.

2 The relief operates by deferring the charge to capital gains tax on the sale of an asset if the gain is reinvested in shares in a qualifying company. Where a qualifying investment is made, liability to capital gains tax is deferred until the shares in the company are sold.

3 Because the relief is targeted at specific types of company, rules are needed to ensure that relief is given only for investment in those companies. These rules can make it difficult for investors to know whether investment in a particular company would qualify.

4 To help, the Revenue have introduced a new system under which companies can establish their status. The system has two stages. The first stage is a questionnaire which companies will be able to obtain from any tax office and which they should be able to complete themselves without difficulty. The questionnaire contains a check list of key requirements which all companies must meet if investment in them is to qualify. A copy of the questionnaire is [reproduced below].

5 If, after completing the questionnaire, a company considers it can qualify, it will progress to stage 2. This involves giving the Revenue details of its activities so that it can provide a ruling about whether it is eligible. The company can then advise potential investors of this ruling.

6 In order to give an informed ruling, the Revenue will require a company to supply, where it is not already held, all information which may be relevant, including—

- a copy of the latest accounts, if applicable;
- an up-to-date copy of the memorandum and articles of association, with details of any changes proposed;
- a copy of the draft of any prospectus or similar document to be issued to potential investors;
- details of the trade or activities carried on or proposed to be carried on;
- any further information which the company believes is necessary for an informed decision, or which the inspector may ask for.

Where the company is the parent company of a group, details of the group's structure, including any anticipated changes, should also be supplied together with details of the trade or activities carried on, or proposed to be carried on, by each subsidiary.

These requirements are very similar to those which currently apply to the clearance scheme which operates for the Enterprise Investment Scheme.

7 Where clearance is given this will be on the basis that the Revenue believe, on the facts supplied, that the company qualifies. Inevitably, however, such clearance must always be provisional. Whether investment in a company will qualify cannot ultimately be determined until the investment has been made and the Revenue have been able to confirm that the information supplied by the company still applied at the time of the investment.

8 Any ruling can be based only on the information supplied. If the company's circumstances change materially, it will need to draw the Revenue's attention to any changes which might influence the availability of relief.

9 Participation in the scheme will be entirely voluntary. But the scheme should mean that eligible companies will be able to advertise the likely availability of relief and so attract potential investors. Similarly, investors will be able to make a more informed choice when seeking to use the relief.

10 As now, potential investors will still be able to approach their own tax inspectors for advice on reinvestment relief. In such cases inspectors will give whatever help they can in answering questions. However, guidance given as a result of such approaches will inevitably be less reliable than a ruling obtained after a formal approach by a company itself since companies will hold the information on which the Revenue ruling will be based. The Revenue are also bound by the normal rules of confidentiality when providing any information to a potential investor concerning a company's qualifying status.

REINVESTMENT RELIEF—TESTS FOR THE COMPANY

Is the company a ''Qualifying Company'' (TCGA 1992 ss 164G, 164I)?

(This guide describes the tests which apply on or after 26 November 1996 only. If you need to consider the company's situation prior to 26 November 1996 for any reason, ask your tax office to help.)

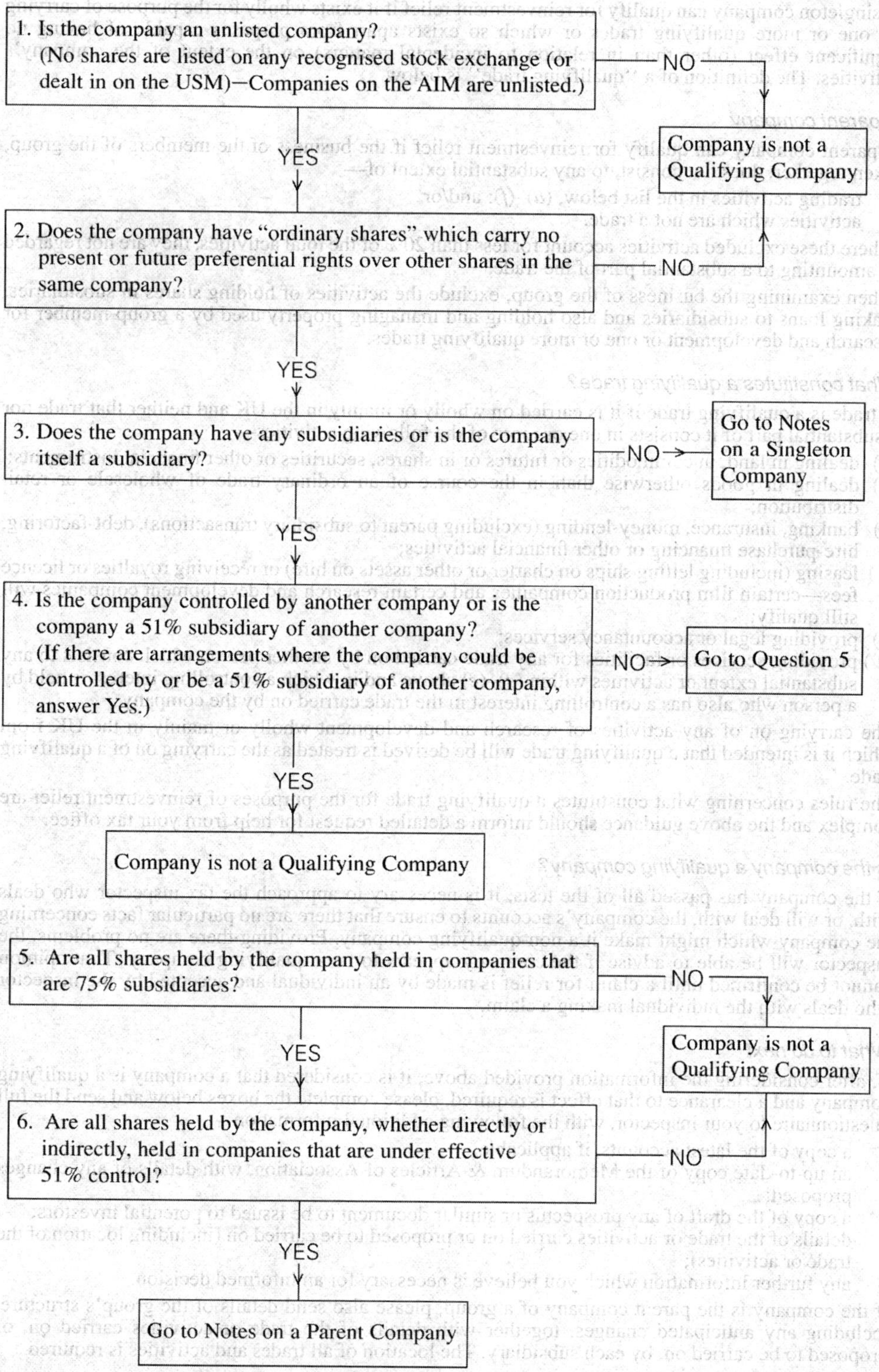
1. Is the company an unlisted company?
(No shares are listed on any recognised stock exchange (or dealt in on the USM)—Companies on the AIM are unlisted.)
NO
Company is not a Qualifying Company
YES
2. Does the company have "ordinary shares" which carry no present or future preferential rights over other shares in the same company?
NO
YES
3. Does the company have any subsidiaries or is the company itself a subsidiary?
NO
Go to Notes on a Singleton Company
YES
4. Is the company controlled by another company or is the company a 51% subsidiary of another company?
(If there are arrangements where the company could be controlled by or be a 51% subsidiary of another company, answer Yes.)
NO
Go to Question 5
YES
Company is not a Qualifying Company
5. Are all shares held by the company held in companies that are 75% subsidiaries?
NO
Company is not a Qualifying Company
YES
6. Are all shares held by the company, whether directly or indirectly, held in companies that are under effective 51% control?
NO
YES
Go to Notes on a Parent Company

A singleton company

A singleton company can qualify for reinvestment relief if it exists wholly for the purpose of carrying on one or more qualifying trades or which so exists apart from purposes capable of having no significant effect (other than in relation to incidental matters) on the extent of the company's activities. The definition of a "qualifying trade" is below.

A parent company

A parent company can qualify for reinvestment relief if the business of the members of the group, taken together, does not consist, to any substantial extent of—

- trading activities in the list below, (*a*)–(*f*); and/or
- activities which are not a trade.

Where these excluded activities account for less than 20% of the total activities, they are not regarded as amounting to a substantial part of the trade.

When examining the business of the group, exclude the activities of holding shares in subsidiaries, making loans to subsidiaries and also holding and managing property used by a group member for research and development or one or more qualifying trades.

What constitutes a qualifying trade?

A trade is a qualifying trade if it is carried on wholly or mainly in the UK and neither that trade nor a substantial part of it consists in one or more of the following activities—

(*a*) dealing in land, in commodities or futures or in shares, securities or other financial instruments;
(*b*) dealing in goods otherwise than in the course of an ordinary trade of wholesale or retail distribution;
(*c*) banking, insurance, money-lending (excluding parent to subsidiary transactions), debt-factoring, hire-purchase financing or other financial activities;
(*d*) leasing (including letting ships on charter or other assets on hire) or receiving royalties or licence fees—certain film production companies and certain research and development companies will still qualify;
(*e*) providing legal or accountancy services;
(*f*) providing services or facilities for any trade carried on by another person which consists to any substantial extent of activities within (*a*)–(*e*) above and in which a controlling interest is held by a person who also has a controlling interest in the trade carried on by the company.

The carrying on of any activities of research and development wholly or mainly in the UK from which it is intended that a qualifying trade will be derived is treated as the carrying on of a qualifying trade.

The rules concerning what constitutes a qualifying trade for the purposes of reinvestment relief are complex and the above guidance should inform a detailed request for help from your tax office.

Is the company a qualifying company?

If the company has passed all of the tests, it is necessary to approach the tax inspector who deals with, or will deal with, the company's accounts to ensure that there are no particular facts concerning the company which might make it a non-qualifying company. Providing there are no problems, the inspector will be able to advise if the company appears to be a qualifying company. That opinion cannot be confirmed until a claim for relief is made by an individual and accepted by the inspector who deals with the individual making a claim.

What to do next

If, after considering the information provided above, it is considered that a company is a qualifying company and a clearance to that effect is required, please complete the boxes below and send the full questionnaire to your inspector, with the following additional information—

- a copy of the latest accounts, if applicable;
- an up-to-date copy of the Memorandum & Articles of Association, with details of any changes proposed;
- a copy of the draft of any prospectus or similar document to be issued to potential investors;
- details of the trade or activities carried on or proposed to be carried on (including location of the trade or activities);
- any further information which you believe is necessary for an informed decision.

If the company is the parent company of a group, please also send details of the group's structure, including any anticipated changes, together with details of the trade or activities carried on, or proposed to be carried on, by each subsidiary. The location of all trades and activities is required.

Signature

Date

Capacity in which signed

(This form may be signed by the "proper officer" of the company or any person authorised by it (see TMA 1970 s 108)).

This signature confirms that the company intends to meet all the conditions of the relief that apply to the company and to its shares until the end of a relevant period. (The relevant period is the period of three years from the date a holding of shares is acquired.)

If this request for a clearance is not the first request for the company, please advise the name of the Tax Office and reference to which the previous request was submitted.

4 December 1996. Inland Revenue

Consequences of Budget changes—deduction of tax and relief at source

On 26 November the Chancellor proposed in his Budget to reduce the basic rate of income tax to 23%.

This change will affect some of the arrangements under which payments have to be made under deduction of tax, as well as some of the relief at source schemes under which payments are made net of tax relief. This press release sets out the rates applicable next year.

Most of the Chancellor's Budget proposals apply from 6 April 1997, before the Finance Bill giving statutory effect to them is likely to receive Royal Assent. Provisional statutory authority is given to these measures by resolutions under the Provisional Collection of Taxes Act 1968 passed yesterday by the House of Commons.

DETAILS

1 The rates to be used next tax year in the deduction of tax and relief at source schemes are set out below. Not all forms of income are affected by the reduction in the basic rate, however, and some of the rate changes will not have effect from the start of the tax year.

Deduction of tax

2 From 6 April 1997 (except where indicated) where any person is required, or entitled, under the Taxes Acts to deduct income tax from any payment, tax should be deducted at the rate set out below. Where at present payments may be made without deduction of tax, payments may continue to be made without deduction from 6 April—deduction of tax has not been extended to any new areas.

3 Interest on taxable National Savings investments will continue to be paid gross, apart from interest on first option bonds which will continue to be paid after deduction of tax.

Payment	*Rate*
Interest paid by banks, building societies and other deposit-takers	20%
Interest on UK Government and other securities	20%
Interest on National Savings first option bonds	20%
Interest distributions by authorised unit trusts	20%
Interest on cash deposits withdrawn from PEPs	20%
Other annual interest paid (including by companies) under deduction of tax	20%
Annual payments (including charges on income, such as payments under deeds of covenants to charities, and distributions by unauthorised unit trusts)	23%
Purchased life annuities (income element)	20%
Other annuities (where PAYE does not apply)	23%
Certain payments made by paying and collecting agents	20%
Rents paid to non-resident landlords	23%
Patent royalties	23%
Payments made before 1 July 1997 to sub-contractors who do not hold valid exception (714) certificates	24%
Payments made on or after 1 July 1997 to sub-contractors who do not hold valid exception (714) certificates	23%
Payments to foreign entertainers and sportsmen (subject to any application for a reduced tax payment)	23%
Payments out of pension scheme AVC surpluses made by scheme administrators (see para 14)	33%

4 Under the Budget proposals rents paid in respect of wayleaves will generally no longer be paid under deduction of tax. Except where rents fall within the arrangements for non-resident landlords, payers who currently deduct tax from wayleave payments should not do so for payments made on or after 6 April 1997.

Payments to charity under deed of covenant

5 Most covenants provide for a "net" payment, that is a sum which after deduction of tax at the basic rate is equal to £X. The change in the basic rate will not affect this amount. However, a payment of £76 which, at present, represents £100, less tax at 24%, will from 6 April 1997 represent £98·70, less tax at 23%. Any higher rate tax relief due will be given on £98·70.

6. Some covenants provide for payment of a "gross" amount, for example £Y, less tax. If the payment is £100 the payer must at present deduct £24. From 6 April 1997 he or she must deduct £23, increasing the payment to the charity from £76 to £77. Higher rate relief will continue to be given on the gross amount (£100 in this example).

7 For individuals the rate at which tax is to be deducted from a payment under a covenant is the basic rate for the year in which the payment is *due*. So where payments due in 1996–97 are paid on or after 6 April 1997 the 24% rate will apply.

8 For companies (including companies owned by charities making covenanted donations to their parents) the tax rate is the basic rate which applies for the year in which a payment is *made*.

Relief at source schemes

9 From 6 April 1997 where any person is entitled to tax relief on making any payment, relief should be deducted at the following rates.

Payment	*Rate*
Interest on a home loan (under MIRAS)	15%
Interest on a loan used to buy a life annuity (under MIRAS)	23%
Private medical insurance	23%
Vocational training relief	23%
Life assurance premium relief	12·5%
Free-standing additional voluntary contributions	23%
Contributions to approved personal pension schemes	23%

ACT—dividends and other distributions

10 The value of the tax credit accompanying a dividend or other distribution made by a UK company will continue to be 20% of the value of the distribution plus the tax credit. Companies should continue to account for ACT of 20/80 on dividends and other distributions.

Tax-exempt special savings accounts (TESSAs)

11 For interest paid or credited on or after 6 April 1997 the amount of interest that may be withdrawn from a TESSA "net" of tax will continue to be 80%.

The rate applicable to trusts

12 The income and capital gains of discretionary and accumulation trusts are chargeable to tax at the rate applicable to trusts (34% for 1996–97). When trustees make income payments to beneficiaries, the beneficiaries are chargeable to income tax at their normal rates and get credit for the tax paid by the trustees at the rate applicable for trusts. For 1997–98 the rate applicable to trusts remains at 34%.

Income treated as paid under deduction of tax

13 Certain forms of income are treated as though tax has been deducted from (or paid on) them, but the tax is not repayable. From 6 April 1997 tax will be treated as deducted (or paid) at the following rates.

Payment	*Rate*
Foreign income dividends (including deemed foreign income dividends)	20%
Stock dividends	20%
Certain chargeable event gains	23%
Loans to participators which are waived	20%
Payments out of pension scheme AVC surpluses received by employees (see para 14)	23%

Surplus employee additional voluntary contributions

14 Payments by occupational pension schemes of surplus employee additional voluntary contributions are currently subject to a special tax charge on the scheme administrator at the rate of 34%. The scheme member is then deemed to have received the payment net of basic rate tax. From 6 April 1997 the pension scheme administrator should deduct tax at a rate of 33% from such payments. The amount received by the scheme member will be treated as if tax at 23% has been deducted.

Gross gilt scheme—quarterly accounting

15 Companies and Lloyd's syndicates may, if they wish, receive interest on gilts gross. If they do, they have to account for tax on a quarterly basis. Where gilt interest is received gross tax will continue to be accounted for at the lower rate of 20%.

Commentary—*Simon's Direct Tax Service* **C3.921.**

20 January 1997. Inland Revenue

Self-assessment—the tax obligations of trustees and beneficiaries of certain bare trusts

Beneficiaries of certain types of bare trusts, who are within self-assessment, must ensure that all trust income and gains are included in their tax returns, and that any income tax or capital gains tax due is properly accounted for.

The changes outlined below will lead to a simplification of the responsibilities which beneficiaries and trustees of bare trusts previously had to meet.

This press release is concerned only with bare trusts which are treated as such for tax purposes, and not with bare trusts such as those unit trust schemes, whose trustees are chargeable to income or corporation tax on income that arises to them.

DETAILS

1 Prior to 6 April 1996, the trustees of some bare trusts accounted for income tax at the appropriate rate on the income which they paid over to the beneficiaries. These amounts became taxed income in the hands of the beneficiaries, who were required to give full details of that income in their tax returns, but were liable to pay further tax only if they were higher rate taxpayers. Conversely, they were entitled to a repayment of the tax paid by the trustees if they had no personal liability.

2 Under self-assessment, the Revenue will no longer expect trustees to account for tax in such circumstances because there is no entitlement in law for trustees to deduct tax from income arising to bare trusts. Any income which is received gross by the trustees must be paid gross to the beneficiaries. The only exception to this rule is that UK resident trustees may be required under the non-resident landlords scheme, to deduct and account for tax on the rental income of beneficiaries whose usual place of abode is outside the UK.

3 Trustees of bare trusts will not be required to complete self-assessment tax returns, or to make any payments on account. Beneficiaries will still be required to give details of all their income and gains from bare trusts in their own tax returns, and in addition will be required to account to the Revenue for the full amount of any tax due.

4 Although the Revenue are endeavouring to identify those bare trusts where trustees have previously made annual returns and accounted for the tax, in order to notify them of this change, there will be some cases which will not be recognised in time to prevent the 1996–97 payment on account notices and self-assessment tax returns from being issued to the trustees.

5 Any trustees receiving a payment on account notice should return it to the issuing trust office with a brief explanation so that the records can be amended. Any trustees receiving a self-assessment tax return after 6 April 1997 should complete the final three questions on the return form in accordance with the notes given in step 1 on the form.

6 There are a number of collective investment schemes which are constituted as bare trusts, but only two kinds of them are treated as such for tax purposes. These are enterprise zone property unit trusts (EZPUTs), and pension fund pooling vehicles (PFPVs). The trustees of such schemes will not receive self-assessment tax returns. That is because the income and gains which arise under EZPUTs and PFPVs belong to the unit holders of the schemes, and if any expenditure is incurred by the trustees which give rise to capital allowances, those allowances are made to the unit holders and not the trustees.

7 The trustees of EZPUTs and PFPVs will, however, remain responsible for agreeing the amounts of the schemes' income, profits, gains, capital expenditure, capital allowances, and balancing adjustments with their own tax inspectors in accordance with the rules laid down in the relevant income tax regulations, and for providing the unit holders of the schemes with certificates giving details of the parts of those amounts that are, in each case, attributable to them.

NOTES

1 A ''bare trust'', also known as a ''simple trust'', exists where the beneficial owner of the property held in trust is fully entitled to both the capital and income from that property. The property will be held in the name of the trustee, but the trustee will have no discretion over what income to pay the beneficiary. The trustee is in effect a nominee in whose name the property is held. The beneficial owner is the person who benefits from, and is entitled to, the property and any income it produces.

2 EZPUTs, which first became available in 1984, are unauthorised unit trust schemes which provide tax incentives for individuals to invest collectively in properties in enterprise zones.

3 Regulations providing tax rules for PFPVs were announced in an Inland Revenue Press Release on 19 June 1996 and came into force on 11 July [see *Simon's Weekly Tax Intelligence* 1996 p 1029]. These vehicles are pooled investment funds specialising in managing the assets of UK exempt approved pension schemes and their overseas equivalents.

4 Further information about the non resident landlords scheme can be found in leaflet IR 140 ''Non resident landlords, their agents and tenants''

Commentary—*Simon's Direct Tax Service* **E1.806.**

27 January 1997. Inland Revenue

Self-assessment—payments on account for 1996–97 calculation of interest following late issue of statements of account

The Inland Revenue have today announced details of a practice which will ensure that taxpayers will not be charged interest as a result of delay by the Revenue in issuing statements of account. Only a small number of taxpayers may be affected, for example those who started trading recently and have not yet been in business for a full 12 months. Where taxpayers have received a statement of account they should pay the tax due on 31 January 1997.

The practice applies where the taxpayer provided the Revenue in good time with all the information needed to calculate the payment on account due on 31 January, but a statement of account was not issued in time for the payment to be made. This approach is a modification of existing practice, to reflect the fixed timetable for the payment of tax under self-assessment.

DETAILS

1 Some people who will be getting self-assessment tax returns in April need to make tax payments on account for 1996–97. These are due on 31 January 1997 and 31 July 1997. Most people who need to make these payments on account were notified by the Revenue in November and December 1996, when statements were sent out showing the amounts due.

2 Where a taxpayer provided the Revenue in good time with the information needed to calculate the payment on account due on 31 January a statement of account should normally have been issued to the taxpayer in November or December 1996 advising them of the amount of tax to pay. But there will be a small number of taxpayers who will need to make payments on account and who have not yet been sent a statement.

3 If a statement of account was not issued in time for the correct payment to be made, even though the taxpayer had provided all relevant information at the appropriate time, then no interest will be charged for the period of delay arising from the late issue of the statement by the Revenue. In such cases the Revenue will, as a matter of practice, seek payment of the tax due within 30 days of the date of notification of the amounts due to that taxpayer. This date, rather than the original date of 31 January, will be the relevant date for interest purposes. Providing the tax due is paid by the date notified no interest will be charged.

4 A taxpayer may not have been sent a statement of account because, for example, during the period in which the statements were issued the taxpayer's records were being transferred from one office to another.

5 Statements may also be issued late where businesses commenced in 1995–96. Prior to self-assessment it was Revenue practice to delay the issue of the first assessment for a newly commenced business until 13 months after the date on which the business commenced. As a result there will be some taxpayers whose statements of account are issued late, not because of unnecessary delay but simply because the relevant amounts were not established in time. The practice described in para 3 above will also apply in such cases.

6 There are a variety of other circumstances in which the taxpayer may not have received a statement of account, only some of which will be covered by this practice. For example, it will not apply where the 1995–96 assessment was under appeal, at the time the payments on account for 1996–97 were calculated, and the amount of tax postponed was subsequently shown to be excessive. Taxpayers and agents should, therefore, seek clarification of the correct position from their tax office in any case in which they are in doubt, rather than assume that the practice will apply.

7 A similar practice will apply in subsequent years. It will apply where the taxpayer submits a return by 30 September and asks the Revenue to calculate the tax due on their behalf, but the Revenue fail to issue a statement of account in time for the payment to be made on 31 January. Details of the practice will be incorporated in Code of Practice 1 ''Mistakes by the Inland Revenue''.

Commentary—*Simon's Direct Tax Service* **E1.821.**

4 February 1997. Inland Revenue

Self-assessment—valuations for capital gains tax

The Inland Revenue are introducing a new valuation service to help taxpayers with capital gains complete their self-assessment tax returns. From 1 April 1997 taxpayers liable to capital gains tax may, if they wish, submit valuations to their tax office for checking before they make their returns.

The new service will be of great benefit to individuals and trustees who have to value assets in preparing their capital gains tax computations.

DETAILS

1 From 1 April 1997 taxpayers (individuals and trustees) will be able to ask their tax office to check valuations used to compute their capital gains liability for the purpose of completing their self-assessment returns.

2 Full information about the transactions to which the valuations relate, together with any relevant tax computations, must be submitted to the tax office with the valuations. A new form (CG34), setting out the information and documents which need to be furnished, will be available from 10 March from tax enquiry centres or tax offices.

3 Further details of the new arrangement are [reproduced below] and will also form an annex to a revised booklet, CGT 14, entitled ''Capital gains tax—an introduction''. Copies of the revised booklet will be available from tax enquiry centres or tax offices, or from the Public Enquiry Room, West Wing, Somerset House, Strand, London WC2R 1LB, in April.

POST-TRANSACTION VALUATION CHECKS FOR CAPITAL GAINS TAX

Introduction

If you use any valuations to work out the gain or loss on a disposal, there is a free service from the Revenue to help you complete your self-assessment tax return. From 1 April 1997 you may ask your tax office to check valuations after you have made the disposal but before you make your return.

If we agree your valuations we will not challenge your use of those valuations in your return unless there are any important facts affecting the valuations that you have not told us about. Agreement to your valuations may not mean that we agree the gain or loss. We will not consider the other figures you have used until you make your return.

If we cannot agree your valuations we will suggest alternatives. We use specialist valuers to value some assets, mainly shares, land, goodwill and works of art. You will also be able to discuss your valuations with our valuers. But you must file your return by the filing date printed on the return even if we have not been able to agree your valuations or to suggest alternatives. You must also tell us in your return about any valuations that we have checked but been unable to agree.

If we cannot reach agreement after discussion on any valuations you use in your return you will be able to appeal to an independent tribunal.

How do you get your valuations checked?

If you want us to check your valuations, ask your tax office or any tax enquiry centre for one copy of Form CG34 for each valuation you want us to check. Return the completed form to your tax office together with the information and documents requested on the form. You can also attach any other information that will help us understand your valuations.

If you do not provide all of the information requested on the form your tax office may be unable to check your valuations. If you have difficulty getting all of this information, or you are not sure how to prepare a capital gains tax computation, ask your tax office for help.

How long will it take?

Your tax office, or our specialist valuers, will contact you as soon as possible after you make your application. Valuation is an exercise of judgment that can be a difficult and lengthy process, particularly if discussion is necessary. We are more likely to be able to reach agreement with you before you need to make your return if you contact us as soon as possible after you have made a disposal.

We expect that it will take a minimum of 56 days to agree your valuations or to provide you with an alternative. In more complex cases it may take longer. In a few very complex cases we may not be able to provide you with any alternative valuation before the filing date for your return.

Further information

Further information about the operation of this scheme can be obtained from your tax office or from your nearest tax enquiry centre.

Commentary—*Simon's Direct Tax Service* **C2.120, 126.**

17 March 1997. Inland Revenue

Employment termination settlements—taxation of benefits received after the year of termination

The Financial Secretary to the Treasury, Michael Jack MP, has authorised the Inland Revenue to undertake consultations on amending the law on the taxation of settlements, made to employees when their job is terminated, which include benefits in kind that continue to be paid or made available after the year of termination.

A consultation paper will be issued later this year with the aim of bringing forward proposals for legislation.

In the meantime the Financial Secretary has authorised the Revenue to apply special arrangements for employment termination agreements entered into from 6 April 1996, which will offer taxpayers a simpler approach to taxing such continuing benefits.

DETAILS

1 Payment and benefits which an employee receives from an employer in compensation for the loss of his employment (other than those which are taxable in full as income from the employment) are generally taxable as income under TA 1988 s 148 on the excess above a certain limit, currently £30,000.

2 The application of s 148 to lump sums and benefits provided in full at or just after termination is generally straightforward. But difficulty can arise where the termination settlement involves benefits which continue after termination, such as the use of a car or a beneficial loan.

3 Section 148 taxes all payments and benefits, whenever received, as income of the year of termination. For continuing benefits the amount taxable for the year of termination is the value of the right to receive future benefits. It can be very difficult to value this right, particularly when it may not be known at the outset how long the benefit will in fact last. There is no provision for the amount assessed to be adjusted subsequently if the benefit is actually available for a shorter period than that on which the tax charge was originally based. The consultation document to be issued later this year will address these issues.

4 Those receiving termination settlements in tax year 1996–97 onwards who are liable to tax under s 148 will normally receive self-assessment returns for the year of termination. Pending legislation, and following discussions with bodies representing employers and others, to ease the difficulties arising in dealing with such benefits, the Revenue will operate the following arrangements to help taxpayers in completing their returns for the year in which the termination occurs—

(*a*) taxpayers can follow the strict interpretation of s 148 and provide an estimate of the value of the right to receive future benefits in the return. That amount will be final unless the Revenue decide to look at the figure by opening an enquiry within the normal time limit provided for enquiry into returns.

Alternatively taxpayers can adopt a basis whereby—

(*b*)

(i) the benefits enjoyed year-by-year will not be taxed until they are actually received or enjoyed;

(ii) the extent of the benefit each year will be calculated by reference to the provisions of TA 1988 s 596B (which largely follow the "cash equivalent" valuation rules in TA 1988 ss 154–168) for the year in which the benefit is received;

Where the taxpayer decides to adopt this alternative basis—

(iii) The self assessment return for the year of termination should include the benefit enjoyed in the year calculated as in (ii) above; thereafter the Revenue will make separate assessments for the year of termination in respect of benefits enjoyed in subsequent tax years, with the benefits being calculated as in (ii) above;

(iv) where a taxpayer who has chosen Alternative (*b*) can show that the total amount of benefits assessed under this method for the year of termination will exceed the amount that would have been taxable if he had opted for the strict basis under (*a*), the Revenue will not collect the excess.

5 Alternative (*b*) will be available to taxpayers in receipt of employment termination payments involving continuing benefits under a termination agreement entered into on or after 6 April 1996. Taxpayers concerned are advised to contact their tax office setting out the payments and benefits provided for under such agreements and to obtain fuller details of how the tax arrangements will apply to their circumstances.

Commentary—*Simon's Direct Tax Service* **E4.805**

27 March 1997. Inland Revenue

Capital gains tax—cash payments to investors in Cheltenham and Gloucester Building Society on takeover by Lloyds Bank

The Revenue have decided to accept a recent decision of the Special Commissioners which affects the capital gains tax liability of investors in the Cheltenham and Gloucester Building Society who received cash bonuses on the takeover of the Society by Lloyd's Bank plc in August 1995. As a consequence—

- *depositors* in the former Society are not liable to capital gains tax on the cash payments received in respect of their deposit accounts;
- *share account holders* remain liable to capital gains tax on the cash payments received in respect of their share accounts but entitled to an allowance for inflation based on the balances in their accounts.

DETAILS

The decision

1 The decision of the Special Commissioners concerned appeals by two investors in the Cheltenham and Gloucester Building Society against assessments to capital gains tax on cash payments they received on the takeover of the Society by Lloyds Bank plc in August 1995. The Special Commissioners decided the appeals in favour of the taxpayers and the Inland Revenue have decided to accept that decision.

2 As a result, former depositors with the Society who received cash payments following the takeover are not liable to capital gains tax in respect of payments received in respect of their deposit accounts.

3 The decision also affects former share account holders with the Society. Share account holders remain liable to capital gains tax in the cash payments (bonuses) they received in respect of their share accounts. However, a consequence of the Special Commissioners' decision is that share account holders are entitled to indexation allowance—based on allowable expenditure equal to the balance in their account(*s*) at the time of the takeover—in calculating the chargeable gain resulting from the cash payment.

Indexation allowance

4 Indexation allowance is an adjustment in calculating gains on an asset, for the effects of inflation since 31 March 1982 in calculating gains. Effectively it increases the expenditure on the asset in line with the Retail Prices Index (RPI) over the period the asset is held. The allowance is computed by multiplying the cost of the asset by the percentage increase in the RPI between the month in which the allowable expenditure was incurred and the month of disposal.

5 To calculate the indexation allowance for former share account holders in the Building Society, it is necessary to multiply the amount in the share account on 31 March 1982 (or the opening balance if later)—plus any subsequent deposits and less any withdrawals—by the percentage increase in the RPI between 31 March 1982 (or the relevant month of deposit if later) and the month of the takeover (August 1995). In principle, therefore information on the account back to 1982 or, of opened later, the whole period of the account, is needed to compute the indexation allowance. In practice, however, for many cases it may not be necessary to have all this information. The calculation has to be made separately for each share account.

Implications for investors

6 If, after applying the indexation allowance, the resulting gain(*s*), when added to any other chargeable gains for the year ended 5 April 1996, do not exceed the annual exempt amount for that year (£6,000), no capital gains tax will be payable. Where the total chargeable gains exceed the £6,000 threshold capital gains tax will be due on the amount of the excess.

7 Any investors who have been assessed to capital gains tax for 1995–96 in respect of any cash bonuses received on the takeover should contact their tax office to establish how the assessment and any appeal should be dealt with. Investors who have received cash payments as a result of the takeover but are uncertain as to the tax consequences may also wish to contact their tax office to resolve the matter.

8 Taxpayers may compute their indexation allowance, with any appropriate help from their tax advisers, and send revised computations to their tax office to have any capital gains assessment adjusted to the correct figure. If they prefer, however, they may ask their tax office to advise on the computation of the indexation allowance. The tax office will need certain information to do this.

9 The tax office will need to know the name and type of accounts with the former Building Society in respect of which the bonuses were received. (The tax office will be able to determine whether accounts were share or deposit accounts if investors are not sure which they were.)

10 Where the cash bonus received by an investor plus any other chargeable gains they may have for 1995–96 does not exceed £6,000 the investor will have no tax liability and need take no action. In any other case where investors have received cash bonuses in excess of £6,000 on their share accounts, or have other chargeable gains in 1995–96, they will need to let their tax office see their building society passbook(*s*) for the relevant accounts. If all such passbooks have not been retained, then investors should send the latest passbook(*s*) still held, together with any other information detailing transactions on those accounts. In cases where complete records have not been retained, it may nevertheless be possible for the tax office to establish whether or not a liability to tax arises. However, there will be situations where investors are asked to provide further information relating to share accounts before the extent of any liability to tax can be established.

Other building society takeovers or conversions

11 The Special Commissioners' decision will also apply to cash payments already received by investors as a result of the conversion or takeover of other building societies. Investors may contact their tax office for help in working out their indexation allowance for the purpose of completing their self-assessment returns.

12 The Special Commissioners' decision does not affect the capital gains treatment of *shares* issued on a takeover or conversion of a building society (as opposed to any cash bonuses). Where shares are issued to building society members in these circumstances legislation provides that no capital gains liability arises on receipt of the shares. For the purpose of computing any gain or a subsequent sale of the shares they are treated as acquired for the amount paid for them. If nothing is paid for the shares the acquisition cost will be nil and no indexation allowance will be due.

Commentary—*Simon's Direct Tax Service* **C1.319.**
Note—The Revenue's previous view of the tax treatment of cash payments was set out in IR press release of 21 March 1996.

28 July 1997. Inland Revenue

Taxation of sub-contractors in the construction industry—implementation of new scheme

The Revenue are now able to confirm that the changes to the construction industry tax scheme, involving the restriction of exemption certificates (714s) to more substantial businesses and the introduction mandatory registration cards, will take place on 1 August 1999. This will give the industry and the Revenue a firm date to work to in preparing suitable systems for the administration of the new scheme.

DETAILS

In August last year the Revenue announced that the implementation of the changes to the construction industry tax scheme set out in FA 1995 and FA 1996 would not take place before 1 August 1999. Following detailed reviews, in conjunction with their strategic partner EDS, of the new systems and procedures which will be required under these changes the Revenue are now able to confirm that the system will be in place for the implementation of the scheme on 1 August 1999.

NOTES

1 Under new rules in FA 1995 and FA 1996 the availability of 714 certificates will be restricted an mandatory registration cards will be introduced for those sub-contractors who would not be entitled to hold 714s.

2 The Revenue are continuing to discuss the development of the project with industry representatives.

Commentary—*Simon's Direct Tax Service* **E5.501, 502.**

29 August 1997. Inland Revenue

Pension schemes and self-assessment for 1996–97

Where the trustees of an occupational pension scheme have income or capital gains for 1996–97 which are chargeable to tax, they should tell their tax office by 5 October 1997. A tax return will then be issued to them for completion.

The completed tax return and the tax payable should be sent back to the tax office by 31 January 1998.

DETAILS

1 In previous years returns were not routinely sought from the trustees of pension schemes. But from 6 April 1996 the trustees of tax approved occupational pension schemes are within the scope of self-assessment.

2 As an interim measure, for 1996–97 the Inland Revenue do not intend issuing self-assessment tax returns to the trustees of all schemes. However the trustees of some schemes (mainly those where tax may be chargeable) will be sent tax returns from September 1997. Trustees also have a legal obligation to tell the Revenue when they have a liability to income tax or capital gains tax. For 1996–97 they must do this by 5 October 1997. Where the trustees know that there is tax to pay, they should therefore ask their tax office for a tax return as soon as possible.

3 If a trustee wishes the Revenue to calculate the tax due the completed return should be sent back within two months of the date of its issue. Returns sent back after 31 January 1998 will attract automatic penalties. Payments made after 31 January 1998 will attract interest and possibly a surcharge.

4 If the trustees of a scheme have no liability to tax on income or capital gains for 1996–97 (or any liability is fully covered by tax paid, or tax credits due, to the trustees on other income) they do not need to ask for a tax return.

5 Self-assessment applies to the income and capital gains tax liability of a scheme. The trustees are responsible for these tax liabilities. A self-assessment tax return is not normally needed to report the tax payable by the administrator of a scheme on—

- refunds of employee contributions;
- refunds of surplus additional voluntary contributions; or
- certain lump sum benefits paid in commutation of pensions.

These payments should not be included on the trustees' return unless the administrator for any reason has failed to pay the tax due. Administrators should already have told their tax office about any such payments for 1996–97, but if this has not been done a report should be made without further delay.

NOTES

1 The Revenue are consulting with representatives of pension schemes and taxation specialists about the design of a tax return to be issued for tax approved pension schemes from April 1999. In the meantime, for 1996–97 and for 1997–98 a provisional return form will be in use.

2 Not all schemes are within the self-assessment system. It applies only to those that are established as trusts and which arrange for funds to be invested outside of insurance policies. It is likely that self-assessment will apply to less than 50,000 schemes in total. For 1996–97, completion of a tax return will generally be required only by those schemes that have a net liability to tax (ie the amount of tax due from non-exempt income is greater than any repayments that arise from tax exemptions available). This is likely to be a very small proportion of the total number of schemes.

3 To supplement this press release, the Pension Schemes Office (PSO) are issuing an Update about self-assessment to all pension schemes and their advisors who subscribe to the PSO mailing list [see below]. A copy of the Update can be obtained from the Pension Schemes Office, Yorke House, PO Box 62, Castle Meadow Road, Nottingham NG2 1BG (Telephone number 0115 974 1630).

Commentary—*Simon's Direct Tax Service* **E1.806**.

21 January 1998. Inland Revenue

Economic and monetary union (EMU)—tax consequences

The Government proposes to introduce legislation in the next Finance Bill to deal with some technical tax issues arising out of EMU. In his speech to the Bank of England Symposium "London as an international financial centre for the euro" the Chancellor of the Exchequer, Gordon Brown MP, said—

> "I can announce a further step that the Government is taking to help business prepare. We propose to introduce legislation in the next Finance Bill to help businesses by dealing with technical tax issues arising out of EMU. The introduction of the euro in January 1999 will have implications for some UK businesses and there are some tax obstacles which business has identified and which we propose to remove. The Inland Revenue are today issuing a press release setting out some proposals for change."

This press release

- describes some consequences for the calculation of direct taxes which will arise as a result of the start of the single currency in January 1999, despite the UK not joining on that date;
- sets out the Government's proposals for some legislation in the next Finance Bill (which might take the form of an enabling power for appropriate secondary legislation); and
- invites written comments from interested parties on these proposals or other tax issues arising out of EMU, to be sent to the co-ordinator for EMU for the Revenue—Julian Reed, Inland Revenue, Room 507, 22 Kingsway, London, WC2B 6NR.

DETAILS

1 The Revenue have been holding discussions with the Bank of England and certain representative bodies about the tax consequences of EMU. An agreed statement is [reproduced below] which sets out how the Government proposes that the tax system will apply in certain circumstances.

2 When dealing with foreign currency, the corporate tax system broadly follows the accounting treatment. The Government proposes to adopt this approach when dealing with the introduction of the euro. Some technical changes are needed to achieve this result. The Government proposes to bring forward legislation to make the following changes—

- Under existing law a trading company can, subject to certain conditions, elect for its corporation tax liability to be computed on the basis of accounts drawn up in a foreign currency. The Government will bring forward legislation to convert automatically an existing election for a currency which joins EMU into an election for the euro.

- Bonds in currencies which join EMU may be redenominated into the euro. It is the Government's intention that a straightforward redenomination will not normally give rise to a tax charge that would not otherwise have arisen. The Government is considering what legislation will be needed to achieve this result.
- There are special rules applying, for the purposes of the legislation on foreign exchange gains and losses and financial instruments, to contracts involving two currencies ("currency contracts"). The Government proposes to introduce legislation to allow these rules to continue to apply to existing contracts if the currencies both join EMU.

SOME TAX ISSUES ARISING AS A RESULT OF ECONOMIC AND MONETARY UNION

The following is a summary of some tax issues arising as a result of EMU, whether or not the UK participates. The issues addressed are not comprehensive, but are those of immediate concern which have been raised with and agreed by the Revenue.

Discussions on remaining issues continue between the Revenue, the Bank of England and representatives of the following bodies—the International Swaps & Derivatives Association, the London Investment Banking Association, the British Bankers' Association, the International Primary Markets Association, the International Securities Markets Association, the Institutional Fund Managers' Association and the American Banking & Securities Association in London.

Foreign exchange legislation

Q The foreign exchange legislation allows a trading company which satisfies certain conditions (an "eligible company") to adopt a currency other than sterling as its functional currency for tax purposes by making a local election (under FA 1993 ss 92–94 and the Local Currency Elections Regulations, SI 1994/3230). Will eligible companies be allowed to make local currency election for the euro?

1.1 Yes. The euro will be allowed as the subject of a local currency election.

Q Will an existing local currency election in respect of a participating currency effectively carry over into the euro without any action or consequence for taxpayers?

1.2 The Government proposes to introduce legislation in the next Finance Bill to ensure the continuity of a local currency election for a participating currency.

Q Will a company which has an existing local currency election for non-participating currency be able to re-elect for the euro following monetary union?

1.3 Yes, if it satisfies the conditions in the normal way (that is, if the euro becomes an eligible currency and the existing currency becomes ineligible).

Q When will the revised local currency elections described at 1.2 and 1.3 above become effective?

1.4 The election for a participating currency (1.2) will switch automatically (as a result of the legislation proposed in 1.2) from that currency to the euro for the first accounting period ending after 1 January 1999 when the company in question prepares its accounts in euros.

An election for the euro which replaces an election for a non-participating currency (1.3) will only be effective from the beginning of the next accounting period after it is received. So companies must make an election before the start of the first accounting period to which they want the election to apply.

Q The foreign exchange legislation contains the anti-avoidance legislation in FA 1993 ss 135, 136 which may be applied at the direction of the Board. Respectively, the sections apply where the main benefit of the asset or liability is the accrual of a loss and where the transactions are entered into otherwise than at arm's length. In cases where the conversion of assets or liabilities occurs, or the main economic purpose of the transaction has fallen away, as a result of the introduction of the euro, will the Board seek to apply these provisions?

1.5 No. FA 1993 ss 135, 136 will not be invoked as a result of the introduction of the euro, provided that the Board believes that no abuse is taking place. It should also be noted that the Consultative Document on the Modernisation of Transfer Pricing Legislation proposes that under self-assessment the requirement for the Board's direction would be removed, so taxpayers would have an obligation to declare when these provisions applied. If these reforms proceed, then taxpayers may rely on this statement in the preparation of their tax returns.

Q Unrealised exchange gains on debts which are considered "long-term capital assets or liabilities" may be deferred under FA 1993 s 139. If the assets or liabilities are redenominated in such a way as to appear to give rise to a different asset or liability will such gains or losses be considered realised and therefore ineligible for deferral?

1.6 The Government proposes to introduce legislation to prevent the relief in FA 1993 s 139 being lost as a result of redenomination.

Q A company may choose to hedge a foreign currency asset with a foreign currency liability or currency contract. Under FA 1993 Sch 15 and the Exchange Gains and Losses (Alternative Method of Calculation of Gain or Loss) Regulations, SI 1994/3227 exchange movements on an eligible liability or currency contract may, in the circumstances prescribed, be deferred eg until the disposal of the matched asset. If such a matched asset is redominated in such a way as to appear to give rise to a different asset will it cause the crystallisation of any deferred exchange movements on hedging liabilities or currency contracts?

1.7 It is not the Government's intention that redenomination should cause matching elections to become ineffective. Views are invited on whether legislation is needed to achieve this in practice.

Financial instruments legislation

Q The financial instruments legislation provides inter alia for the taxation of "currency contracts". It contains a definition (FA 1994 s 150) of "currency contract" which requires payment in different currencies. Will currency contracts involving two currencies that convert to the euro no longer be currency contracts as only the euro will be involved?

2.1 No. The Government proposes to introduce legislation to ensure that such contracts will continue to be currency contracts for all purposes of the legislation.

Q The financial instruments legislation provides that "qualifying payments" may be paid gross by a "qualifying company" (FA 1994 s 174). Will fixed rate swaps of two currencies which convert to the euro lose this protection, becoming subject to withholding as an annuity or annual payments for tax purposes?

2.2 No. The Government's intention is that such contracts will continue to be within the financial instruments legislation provided that no abuse is taking place (eg where a transaction is entered into immediately before conversion to exploit this relief).

Q The financial instruments legislation prescribes the payments which may be made under a "currency contract". A contract may allow for other transfers of money or money's worth and still be a "currency contract" provided that the conditions in FA 1994 s 152 are met, which broadly seek to ensure that the relative value of these transfers at the "relevant time" is small. Will conversion constitute a "relevant time" for FA 1994 s 152, causing the issue of whether or not a contract is a "currency contract" to be re-considered?

2.3 No. Conversion, regardless of how it is achieved, will not be a "relevant time" for these purposes. (Council Regulation (EC) No 1103/97 under art 235[1] of the Treaty provides for continuity of contract on the introduction of the euro. However conversion may also be achieved through bilateral legal agreement.)

Q The financial instruments legislation contains anti-avoidance provisions, dealing with transfers of value, transactions not at arm's length and qualifying contracts with non-residents (FA 1994 ss 165–168). If conversion to the euro causes there be a new contract, will there be a re-consideration of FA 1994 ss 165–168 potentially causing adjustments to taxable income to arise under these anti-avoidance provisions?

2.4 No. Conversion to the euro of itself will not cause anti-avoidance provisions to apply, provided the Board believes that no abuse is taking place. (The removal of the requirement for a Board's direction which is referred to in 1.5 above also applies to this legislation.)

Commentary—See *Simon's Direct Tax Service* **Division B3.17; B3.18.**
Note—[1] Article 235 renumbered article 308 by the Treaty of Amsterdam (OJ C340 10.11.97 p 1).

29 July 1998. HM Treasury

Preparing British business for the euro—consultation on tax consequences of the introduction of the single currency

The Government will be consulting British businesses and other taxpayers on how transactions involving participating currencies will be treated for tax purposes following the introduction of the single currency on 1 January 1999, Economic Secretary Helen Liddell has announced.

Announcing the proposals, Mrs Liddell said—

> "The introduction of the single currency on 1 January 1999 will change the way in which business is conducted for many British companies, even though the UK will not be a member of EMU.
>
> The Government is determined to assist British business to adjust to these changes as effectively as possible. We are working together with business representatives whenever possible to find out what their requirements are and how we can assist them.
>
> Following earlier consultations, we have already identified some technical changes which need to be made to prevent unintended taxes consequences arising from the introduction of the euro in other EU countries. Today's proposals will be embodied in draft regulations to be published in the Autumn. The consultation will enable British business to ensure that these changes meet their requirements."

DETAILS

1 In the light of consultations held to date between the Inland Revenue and certain representative bodies, the Government has agreed that technical changes should be made to certain tax provisions.

Decisions made after an earlier round of consultations with these bodies were announced in the Revenue Press Release dated 21 January. The summary below covers both new points and those announced earlier. More details, in a set of "questions and answers" are available in the Annex.

2 The changes proposed will deal with four broad sets of questions—

(i) the treatment of assets/contracts denominated in participating foreign currencies where re-denomination into euros might otherwise give rise to a disposal or transfer or bring forward a tax charge; and the treatment of derivatives over re-denominated assets;
(ii) the treatment of financing transactions involving re-denominated assets;
(iii) the treatment of the costs of re-denomination; and
(iv) the interpretation of the special rules allowing for accounting in foreign currencies for tax purposes.

In general, the Government's approach is to try to ensure as far as possible that the introduction of the single currency in other member states is tax neutral and therefore does not give rise to a charge of a loss which would not otherwise have arisen.

3 In relation to continuity of assets and contracts—subheading (i)—the Government proposes to introduce regulations to—

- ensure that, where assets are subject to a straightforward re-denomination, there is continuity for the purposes of tax on capital gains both for the assets and any related derivative contracts within the scope of TCGA 1992;
- provide for the appropriate treatment of any cash payments received as a result of the re-denomination of bonds in the hands of investors;
- ensure that re-denomination does not disturb the relief on unrealised exchange gains under FA 1993 s 139;
- provide for continuity of currency contracts and options involving two currencies which convert to the euro.

4 For financing transactions—subheading (ii)—such as stock loans and sale and repurchase agreements, involving straightforward re-denominations (of bonds), the Government intends to ensure, by regulation if necessary, that the re-denominated bonds will count as the "same" or "equivalent" assets for the relevant tax provisions. The Government also intends to introduce a regulation to ensure that intermediaries obtain the appropriate deduction for any charge arising on passing on a cash-payment arising from a re-denomination.

5 On costs of re-denomination—subheading (iii)—the Government proposes to introduce a regulation to allow the costs of re-denomination into euros of existing non-sterling capital assets so long as the re-denomination involves only the replacement of existing stock and not the issue of increased amounts or of greater value. The Government also proposes to make clear in regulations what costs will be allowable in relation to the re-denomination of investments.

6 Finally, in relation to accounting for tax purposes in euro—subheading (iv)—the Government proposes regulations to ensure the continuity of local currency elections for participating currencies and to allow companies to make a local currency election for the euro before the euro comes into existence, but only for accounting periods commencing on or after 1 January 1999. In addition, it proposes a regulation amending the special rules for computing the chargeable profits of controlled foreign companies (CFCs). The rules lock a CFC into computing profits in the currency used by it in its first relevant accounting period. The proposed regulation will ensure that, where that currency is replaced by the euro, the currency to be used in computing future profits will switch automatically to the euro.

OTHER ISSUES

7 Although the consultation with representative bodies has focused mainly on the corporate sector, the Government also intends to use the regulations to deal with any tax issues that may specifically affect other taxpayers, including individuals. It will, for example, take the opportunity to ensure in the regulations that the conversion by UK resident individuals of cash holdings of a foreign participating currency into euro will not give rise to a capital gain or loss.

8 The Government encourages those who have comments or questions relating to these proposals, or to other areas which they think may need to be addressed, whether by regulation or otherwise, to write to Bridget Micklem, Inland Revenue, Room S23, West Wing, Somerset House, Strand, London WC2R 1LB.

NOTES

1 Clause 163 of the Finance Bill made provision for the introduction of an enabling power which would allow tax changes that are needed as a result of the introduction of the single currency in other member states to be made by regulation.

2 The enabling power covers all taxes for which the Inland Revenue is responsible and provides scope to change the law to prevent unintended tax consequences arising when the single currency starts in other member states.

3 Regulations made under the enabling power will be put into statute by a statutory instrument subject to negative resolution of the House of Commons. This is the normal method used for tax regulations.

4 The consultations which have taken place so far on the content of the regulations have been between the Revenue, the Bank of England and representatives of the following bodies—

- the International Swaps and Derivatives Association,
- the London Investment Banking Association,
- the British Bankers' Association,
- the International Primary Market Association,
- the American Banking & Securities Association in London.

5 Alongside the work on technical tax questions arising from the introduction of the single currency in other member states, the Inland Revenue has been working with Customs and the Treasury to consider practical arrangements relating to the payment of taxes in euro. More detail on these questions will be provided separately in a joint Inland Revenue/Customs press release.

ANNEX

FURTHER TAX ISSUES ARISING AS A RESULT OF THE INTRODUCTION OF THE SINGLE CURRENCY IN OTHER MEMBER STATES

The Question and Answer statement below on tax issues arising as a result of the introduction of the single currency in other member states should be read in conjunction with the Revenue Press Release of 21 January 1998 entitled "Some tax issues arising as a result of economic and monetary union". The statement deals with certain further tax issues arising as a result of EMU that have been raised with and agreed by the Inland Revenue.

The statement is not intended to address comprehensively all the issues that might arise as a result of the introduction of the single currency in other member states and does not cover possible tax issues that might arise if the UK were to join the single currency.

Continuity of assets

1.1 In what circumstances will the fact of monetary union and/or the re-denomination of an asset (ie a debt security, instruments or contracts) from a participating currency into euro be regarded as giving rise to a disposal, transfer, etc of the asset (or a derivative over the asset) and an acquisition of a new asset (or derivative) by a taxpayer and in what circumstances will the taxpayer receive continuity of treatment, ie so that the taxpayer is treated as still holding the same asset or derivative that it has always held?

Answer

The issue should not be relevant to a company to the extent that it is taxed in relation to the asset or derivative under the foreign exchange, financial instruments or loan relationship legislation. In those circumstances, the Inland Revenue would expect the accounts to be followed (subject to the specific rules in those provisions).

In other circumstances, under the application of the existing law on capital gains, the re-denomination could give rise to a taxable gain or loss. However, the Government accepts that it is not desirable for a charge to arise on a straightforward re-denomination of an asset consequent on the introduction of the single currency.

It therefore proposes to introduce a regulation to ensure that if an asset is re-denominated in euros and the post re-denomination asset is in all material respects the same as the pre re-denomination asset (ignoring the changes reasonably required to give effect to the re-denomination), then, where this would not otherwise be the case, the re-denomination will not be regarded as involving a disposal or acquisition, and the asset will be regarded as the same for capital gains purposes.

If other changes are simultaneously made to the asset beyond those associated with a straightforward re-denomination, then the question of whether those other changes give rise to a transfer or disposal and an acquisition of a different asset or derivative will need to be considered in accordance with existing principles.

1.2 How will cash-outs received as a result of a re-denomination of bonds be treated in the hands of investors?

Answer

Any cash received as the result of a re-denomination will need to be recognised by the taxpayer. In the case of a person holding the asset as part of its trade or of a company taxed in relation to the asset for example, under the loan relationship or financial instrument provisions, the treatment should follow existing rules.

Where the asset falls under the capital gains regime, under current law cash received may fall to be treated as a part-disposal. However, the Government is willing to accept that small amounts deriving from a straightforward re-denomination should not be taxed, and therefore proposes to introduce a regulation to provide a *de minimis* exemption for cash payments received on re-denomination as a result of the introduction of the single currency. This should tie in with the proposed regulation on continuity of assets and with current provisions such as the part-disposal provisions on the conversion of securities in TCGA 1992 s 133. The Government is still considering the question of the appropriate treatment of cash-outs derived from the repackaging of odd-lots and would welcome comments on this subject.

Note: Question & Answer **1.1** and **1.2** do not cover the re-denomination of equities and equity-related instruments, since detailed consideration of this issue can only be given once it becomes clearer how the re-denomination of equities is to be achieved and since it is not likely that many companies will re-denominate their shares in the early days of the single currency. At present, it does not seem that any new capital gains issues are likely to arise in this area, since the UK has existing legislation which deals with the capital gains consequences of reorganisations of share capital.

Equities

2 If a UK company were to re-denominate any of its share capital during the transitional period on the introduction of the single currency into euro and, due to rounding, a payment of cash or an issuance of new stock is required to be made to [a] shareholder, will that payment of cash or issuance of stock give rise to a dividend or distribution?

Answer

The consequences of re-denomination of equities (ordinary shares), preference shares and convertibles, can all be dealt with under the normal rules. A cash payment in respect of shares would therefore constitute a distribution except where and to the extent that it fell to be treated as a repayment of share capital.

A cash payment in respect of securities within TA 1988 s 209(2)(*e*)(ii) would also more than likely fall to be treated in whole or in part as a distribution. This treatment will apply equally for conversions of any non-£ and £ shares, preference shares or convertibles.

Options and other derivatives

3.1 In paras **2.1** and **2.3** of the Press Release of 21 January, certain guidance is given in relation to "currency contracts" as defined in FA 1994 s 150. Will the same guidance apply to "currency options" as defined in that section?

Answer

Yes

3.2 An interest rate contract (within FA 1994 s 149) must include the right to receive or a duty to make a variable rate payment. A variable rate is one based on a rate the value of which at any time is the same as that of the variable rate of interest specified in the contract, for example PIBOR. Will an interest rate contract, or an option to enter into such a contract which specifies a variable interest rate by reference to a currency which converts to euro such that the original specified rate no longer exists, be regarded as having termination and been replaced by a new contract or option?

Answer

Such a change to the subject matter of a contract may cause the contract to be void, voidable, or possibly frustrated. However, the contract may continue to exist for a number of reasons. The changes may be insufficient to cause the contract to be frustrated, by reason of the law under which it is written. Similarly, the change in questions may have been anticipated and be successfully provided for in the original agreement. Alternatively, the contract may remain operative by reason of the bilateral agreement of the counterparties to maintain it, which may or may not technically give rise to a new contract.

It is the Government's intention that a contract which "continues" for whatever reason (including when the new bilateral agreement gives rise to what is technically a new contract) will not give rise to a taxable event provided that the economic substance of the contract is not materially altered. As for assets in **1.1** above, the economic substance will be considered to be unaltered where there have been no material changes in the relevant factors.

It should be noted that the contract may be in respect of an underlying instrument which itself is not considered to have continued. In these circumstances the contract will be considered in its own right; the question will be whether, in economic substance, the contract has the same effect as before conversion.

In any event, if the contract falls within the FA 1994 regime for derivative financial instruments, and so is accounted for on an acceptable accruals or mark to market basis of accounting, it is likely that the tax consequences of a taxable event will be exactly the same as those arising if there had been no such event.

3.3 There may be transactions in futures or options in foreign currencies or in foreign currency denominated equities/debts/other financial instruments which are denominated in foreign currencies which do not fall within TA 1988 Sch 5AA. However, the effect of the introduction of the single currency and/or the re-denomination of assets may be to give rise from that time to a fixed return which is from that point a "guaranteed return". Will the provisions of Sch 5AA apply in these circumstances?

Answer

TA 1988 Sch 5AA applies where the main or one of the main purposes of the transaction in question is the production of a return that is guaranteed. It follows that one looks to the purposes of the parties at the time of entering into the transaction. Accordingly, the mere fact that the return from a future or option becomes fixed as a result of and from the time of the introduction of the single currency would not result in the provisions of Sch 5AA being applied, unless, in entering into the transaction in question, that was an intended result within the meaning of Sch 5AA.

3.4 TA 1988 Sch 5AA deals with the taxation of the profits and gains arising from transactions in futures and options that are designed to produce guaranteed returns. Will conversion constitute a disposal for the purposes of Sch 5AA, causing any inherent profits and gains to be realised for tax purposes at that time?

Answer

The treatment of a conversion for the purposes of Sch 5AA will follow that proposed at **1.1**.

3.5 TCGA 1992 ss 143–148 provides, *inter alia*, for the taxation of option contracts which are not taxable under Schedule D (broadly option contracts which do not fall within the financial instruments rules set out in FA 1994, or within the anti-avoidance rules set out in TA 1988 Sch 5AA, and which are not held on trading account). TCGA 1992 s 144 will apply for example to an investment company holding an option over shares which qualifies as a financial option. The basic approach (under TCGA 1992 s 144) is to treat an option as a separate asset for capital gains purposes except where it is exercised, in which case, its grant (or acquisition) and the acquisition or disposal of the underlying subject matter are treated as one transaction. Will the start of the single currency and/or the re-denomination of either the option or the subject-matter of the option be regarded as giving rise to settlement or lapse without exercise of an existing option and the entering into a new one?

Answer

The regulation referred to in para 1.1 will provide for the continuity treatment for capital gains purposes, where appropriate, both for assets and for derivatives (including options) over assets.

Financing transactions

4.1 Where a debt security denominated in a participating currency is re-denominated into euros, will the re-denominated security be regarded as similar to/equivalent to/the same description as the original security for repo/stock-lending and related purposes (ie for the purposes of the following provisions—

- FA 1986 ss 80C, 89AA;
- TA 1988 ss 730A, 730B, 737A, 737C;
- TCGA 1992 s 263B;
- FA 1996 Sch 9 para 15).

Answer

In the case of straightforward re-denominations—see **1.1**—the Government will ensure (by regulation if necessary) that re-denominated securities will count as similar to/ equivalent to/the same description as the original securities for the tax provisions relating to repo and stock lending for all taxpayers covered by **1.1**. The Government is still considering how the law should apply for financing transactions involving re-denominations which would not meet the proposed "same asset" tests.

4.2 Where "cashing out" takes place on re-denomination, for example, due to rounding, will payments representative of the cash amounts be treated as manufactured payments?

Answer

The starting position would be that we would expect the characterisation of the representative payments to mirror that of the payments they represent. To the extent therefore that cash amounts themselves are capital payments, the payments representative of them would not count as manufactured payments.

However, where the person making the representative payment is not taxed on a trading basis, the tax liability may not correspond to the economic effect of his action in receiving cash payment and passing it on.

The Government will introduce a regulation so that where cash-outs due as a result of a re-denomination are passed on, the intermediary obtains the appropriate deduction from any charge. This will only apply, however, where it is clear that no abuse is taking place in relation to credits for tax withheld (if any) or underlying tax relief.

Note: **4.1** and **4.2** do not cover financing transactions involving equities which are re-denominated into euro. The treatment of financing transactions involving re-denominated equities will be addressed, along with continuity questions, when it becomes clearer how share re-denominations are to be achieved. However, insofar as similar issues arise, the Government will wish as far as possible the principles established for transactions involving re-denominated bonds to carry over to equities so that in the case of straightforward re-denominations, the provisions referred to above will apply.

Costs of re-denomination

5.1 Will costs incurred by a company upon re-denomination, as a result of the introduction of the single currency, of securities and equities issued by it be deductible for tax purposes?

Answer

The costs incurred upon re-denomination of a company's loan relationships are already provided for in the existing legislation and will be regarded as charges and expenses within FA 1996 s 84(3)(*a*)–(*d*).

For other non-sterling securities or equities, which are re-denominated as a result of the start of the single currency, the Government believes there is a case for legislating a special relief. Accordingly the Government proposes to introduce a regulation to allow the costs of re-denomination into euros of existing non-sterling capital assets (both for traders and investment companies) so long as the re-denomination involves only the replacement of existing stock and not the issue of increased amounts or of greater value. This regulation will not apply to costs attributable to any other factor—eg to other changes made to a security or equity at the same time as re-denomination. To the extent that such costs are not attributable to the start of the single currency, their deductibility will be determined in accordance with existing principles.

5.2 Will costs incurred by an investor as a consequence of its investments being re-denominated as a result of the introduction of the single currency be deductible for tax purposes?

Answer

As far as the costs of re-denomination of investments is concerned, some costs may be allowable under current law as a trading expense or as an expense of management of an investment company, but others would not. The Government therefore proposes to make explicit in regulations exactly what will be allowable.

In the particular case of costs attributable to changes to computer software, the Revenue has already given guidance at para IM 664 of the Inspectors' Manual.

Foreign exchange

6.1 Will non-trading companies be able to make a local currency election to adopt the euro as their functional currency rather than sterling?

Answer

No. Non-trading companies will not be able to make a local currency election to adopt the euro as their functional currency.

6.2 It may not be apparent to a trading company that the inauguration of the single currency has made the euro the most appropriate currency for the company's accounts until some time after 1 January 1999 or even the start of its first post-January 1999 accounting period. Are there any plans to introduce a ''window period'' (of, say, 92 days, by analogy with the transitional provisions for the commencement of the FOREX provisions) for the making of an election for euro to take effect from the start of the accounting period of the company in which the single currency begins falls or of the first post-January 1999 accounting period of the company?

Answer

The Government does not intend to introduce a window period in respect of the timing rules on local currency elections. However, to facilitate the making of elections for the euro, the Government proposes to introduce a regulation which would amend the existing local currency rules to allow companies to elect, prior to 1 January 1999 (ie before the euro actually exists), for the euro for accounting periods commencing on or after that date. This will put beyond doubt the ability of companies with 31 December year-ends to elect for the euro for accounting periods beginning on 1 January 1999. The Government has already announced that it intends to introduce a regulation to ensure that existing local currency elections in participating currencies are converted automatically to the euro.

6.3 Are there any plans to allow a company with euro-denominated share capital and euro-denominated assets to match these under FA 1993 Sch 15 or any extension thereto?

Answer

No. There are no plans to extend the circumstances in which a matching election may be made.

Authorised unit trusts—stamp duty and stamp duty reserve tax

7 The start of the single currency is likely to give rise to an opportunity for or commercial desire for significant rationalisation of unit trusts. However, the existing provision (contained in FA 1997 s 95) for rationalisations of authorised unit trusts to take place without any stamp duty or stamp duty reserve tax charge arising on the relevant transfer of assets expires on 30 June 1999. Are there any plans to postpone that expiration date?

Answer

An extension of the deadline for these reliefs would require legislation. The Association of Unit Trusts and Investment Funds have asked Ministers to consider an extension, for a variety of reasons of which EMU is one, but no decision has yet been taken.

Commentary—*Simon's Direct Tax Service* **B7.204, B3.738, 739, B3.1007, B3.1706, B3.1746, B3.1807**.

16 February 1999. Inland Revenue

Corporation tax reform—regulations for relief of past surplus advance corporation tax

Regulations which introduce the detailed rules for the relief of past surplus advance corporation tax (ACT) from 6 April 1999 were laid before Parliament by the Treasury today.

After 6 April 1999 ACT no longer be generated, and most companies will not need to deal with advance corporation tax at all. The regulations will affect only companies and groups containing companies with surplus ACT at April 1999, and will substantially preserve their existing expectations in respect of the recovery of past surplus ACT.

Copies of the regulations will be available shortly from the Stationery Office. They will also be available on the Inland Revenue website.

DETAILS

1 The regulations are The Corporation Tax (Treatment of Unrelieved Surplus Advance Corporation Tax) Regulations (SI 1999/358).

2 The detailed rules governing the relief of surplus ACT for accounting periods ending on or after 6 April 1999 are set out in these regulations. Draft regulations were published for consultation on 13 May 1998. The Government is grateful to all those who commented on those draft regulations.

3 The rules are based on, and so far as possible replicate, the existing rules governing relief for ACT. Only those companies with surplus ACT at 6 April 1999 will be affected by the regulations. And companies can opt out of making the computations required under the relief of surplus ACT system if they decide not to recover any past surplus advance corporation tax.

4 The regulations provide for notional amounts of ACT, called shadow ACT, to arise when companies make a distribution of profits (for example, the payment of a dividend) on or after 6 April 1999. Shadow ACT does not mean that a company will have to pay something equivalent to ACT after its abolition. It merely governs the recovery by companies of surplus ACT once ACT has been scrapped.

5 Shadow ACT will work by—

- retaining the existing limit on the set-off of ACT, so a company will be able to use ACT to meet its corporation tax liability up to a limit of 20% of its corporation tax profits, even on or after 6 April 1999;
- prescribing that the space for relieving ACT in this way will have to be filled first by shadow ACT, computed on the same basis and at the same rate as now, but without allowing that shadow advance corporation tax to result in any reduction in the corporation tax due;
- restricting the set-off of surplus advance corporation tax, which will lead to a real reduction in the company's corporation tax liability, to any space remaining in the 20% limit after shadow ACT has used it up; and
- carrying forward any shadow ACT in excess of the space available for relieving ACT.

EXAMPLE

A company has surplus advance corporation tax of £100,000 at 6 April 1999. It has a 12 month accounting period ending on 5 April 2000, during which it pays dividends of £40,000 and has taxable profits of £120,000. In that case—

- the limit on the set-off of ACT is £24,000 (that is 20% of £120,000);
- there is shadow ACT of £10,000 (25% of £40,000) on account of its dividend payments;
- the effect is to restrict the set-off of past surplus ACT to £14,000 (£24,000 less £10,000); and
- its corporation tax liability is therefore reduced by £14,000, as is the figure for past surplus ACT carried forward to the next accounting period.

NOTES

1 In his pre-Budget report in November 1997, Chancellor Gordon Brown put forward proposals to solve permanently the problems connected with advance corporation tax (ACT), and particularly surplus advance corporation tax, by abolishing ACT altogether and replacing it with a modern system of quarterly payments of corporation tax for larger companies. The Inland Revenue published a consultative document "A modern system for corporation tax payments" dated 25 November 1997 which set out the framework for the proposed changes and invited companies and others to make representations.

2 In his March 1998 Budget the Chancellor confirmed the proposals set out in the consultative document, subject to some changes arising out of the consultation process. These changes are described in the document "A modern system for corporation tax payments: Outcome of consultation" which was published by the Inland Revenue in April 1998. The document also provides a summary of the responses received to the consultative document, and a regulatory appraisal of the change.

3 On 13 May 1998 the Inland Revenue published draft regulations on the shadow ACT system to give tax practitioners, business and others an opportunity to comment on them.

4 FA 1998 s 32 empowers the Treasury to make regulations in relation to the relief of unrelieved surplus advance corporation tax. These regulations are made under those powers.

Commentary—*Simon's Direct Tax Service* **D1.310–312**.
Regulations—The Corporation Tax (Treatment of Unrelieved Surplus Advance Corporation Tax) Regulations, SI 1999/358.

8 June 1999. Inland Revenue

A modern system for corporation tax payments—guidance on use of information and penalty powers in instalment payments regulations

Guidance published today outlines the way in which the Revenue will use the information and penalty powers contained in the instalment payments regulations. The regulations govern the payment of corporation tax by some 20,000 large companies.

The guidance—

– explains that the information powers are not for routine use; and
– confirms that the majority of cases of late or inadequate payment will attract only an interest charge, not a penalty.

The text of the guidance is attached as an annex to this press release.

DETAILS

1 The Revenue will use the information powers only where there are indications that a company may have deliberately or recklessly failed to comply with its payment obligations under the regulations, or fraudulently or negligently made a claim for repayment. In such a case, all the necessary evidence will be requested from the company in respect of its instalment payments, (or absence of them), or claim.

2 The penalty provision is in reg 13 of the instalment payments regulations. It provides for a penalty (under TMA 1970 s 59E(4)) of not more than twice the amount of interest on any unpaid amount in respect of the total liability of the company for that accounting period. Total liability includes liability to corporation tax, and tax under TA 1988 ss 419, 747 (provisions dealing with loans by a close company to its participators, and controlled foreign companies, respectively).

3 A penalty under TMA 1970 s 59E(4) will be sought in only the most serious cases involving flagrant abuse of the regulations. The normal appeal rights of TMA 1970 s 100B(1) will apply to any such penalty.

NOTES

1 The detailed rules governing the payment by large companies of their corporation tax by instalments are set out in the instalment payment regulations (SI 1998/3175). They provide for large companies (broadly those with profits of more than £1·5 million, or less if a company is associated with others) to pay their corporation tax in quarterly instalments for accounting periods ending on or after 1 July 1999.

2. The change is being phased in over a four year period, with companies paying a gradually increasing percentage of their tax by instalments (with the balance in a lump sum nine months and one day after the end of their accounting period). Transition to the new system will be completed in the year 2002, when companies with accounting periods ending on or after 1 July 2002 will pay all their tax by instalments.

3. A leaflet, "A modern system for corporation tax payments—a guide to quarterly instalment payments" contains more details, and is available free from tax offices.

ANNEX

GUIDANCE ON USE OF INFORMATION AND PENALTY POWERS IN QUARTERLY INSTALMENT PAYMENTS CASES

These guidance notes explain how the Revenue will use the information and penalty powers in the Corporation Tax (Instalment Payments) Regulations, SI 1998/3175.

Use of information powers

The information powers are in regs 10, 11 and 12 of the instalment payments regulations. They require a company to provide the Revenue with information to support the payments made on the instalment due dates, or the lack of such payments, or to support a claim for repayment. They are described in more detail below.

Where companies file their returns by the statutory filing date, a review of the quarterly instalment payment (QIP) position will be undertaken at the same time as the review of the return. Information about the basis upon which QIPs have been estimated will not be sought as a matter of routine.

Where the amounts paid on the instalment dates do not correspond to the amounts required under the regulations interest will be charged or paid accordingly. In cases where the Revenue make a determination of the tax payable because a company has failed to file its return on time, the Revenue also have the power to make a determination of the dates on which amounts should have been paid under the regulations.

The Revenue will seek to make use of the information powers in regs 10, 11 and 12 only where there are indications that a company may have deliberately or recklessly failed to comply with its payment obligations under the regulations, or fraudulently or negligently made a claim for repayment. In such a case, all the necessary evidence will be requested from the company in respect of its instalment payments (or absence of them) or claim. This will enable the Revenue to establish the extent to which the company failed to pay in accordance with its most recent estimate of its total liability, and to form a judgment as to whether the company, or persons acting on its behalf, acted deliberately or recklessly in failing to make its payments as they fell due, or in later failing to correct the position as newer and more accurate information became available.

Application of penalty regulation

The penalty power is in reg 13 of the instalment payments regulations. It provides for a penalty (under TMA 1970 s 59E(4)) of not more than twice the amount of interest charged in respect of the total liability of the company for that accounting period.

Total liability includes liability to corporation tax, and tax under TA 1988 ss 419, 747 (provisions dealing with loans by a close company to its participators, and controlled foreign companies, respectively).

The majority of cases of inadequate or late payments, or the miscalculation of a repayment, will involve only an interest charge—

– Inadequate payments—a penalty position will apply where there is evidence that the company failed to pay in accordance with its most recent estimate of its total liability, (including failing to make a top-up payment) or failed to pay the right amount at the right time. Such a failure by a company or by a person acting on its behalf must be more than negligent—it must be deliberate or reckless.
– Claims to repayment—a penalty will apply in respect of a claim to repayment under reg 6 if the company or a person acting on its behalf has acted fraudulently or negligently.

A penalty under TMA 1970 s 59E(4) will be sought in only the most serious cases involving flagrant abuse of the regulations. Before seeking a penalty the case must be submitted to Head Office for approval. The normal appeal rights of TMA 1970 s 100B(1) will apply to any such penalty.

Interest

New interest rates have been introduced for tax over and underpaid during the instalment payments period. This is provided for in the Taxes (Interest Rate) (Amendment No 2) Regulations, SI 1998/3176. The new rules are more generous to companies than those which apply outside that period. The rates also have a smaller spread and are more sensitive to base rate movements than the ordinary rates. Interest on underpaid corporation tax is also deductible in arriving at a company's chargeable profits. The interest represents no more than compensation for the Exchequer's (or the company's) loss of use of the money.

Information powers

The Corporation Tax (Instalment Payments) Regulations, SI 1998/3175, reg 10 requires a company to furnish information to the Board of the Revenue, and reg 11 requires a company to produce books, documents and other records in its possession or power, relating to—

– the estimation of amounts paid in respect of the company's total liability for an accounting period in accordance with SI 1998/3175 reg 5;
– the non-payment of any amount in respect of the company's total liability for an accounting period in accordance with SI 1998/3175 reg 5; and
– a claim for repayment under SI 1998/3175 reg 6(2).

Such details can be required within a period of not less than 30 days, by notice, at any time following the fixed filing date for the company.

In addition, reg 12 requires a company to make available for inspection all such books documents and other records in its possession or power as could be required to be produced under reg 11. Where such records are maintained by computer, the company must provide the officer making the inspection with all the facilities necessary for obtaining information from them.

Penalty

Regulation 13 provides for a penalty under TMA 1970 s 59(E)(4) where—

– a company, or a person acting on its behalf, deliberately or recklessly fails to pay the right amount on a particular instalment date in accordance with the regulations; or
– a company, or a person acting on its behalf, fraudulently or negligently makes a claim for repayment under the regulations.

The amount of the penalty is a sum not exceeding twice the amount of interest charged in respect of the total liability of the company for that accounting period.

Commentary—*Simon's Direct Tax Service* **D2.842, 846.**
Regulations—The Corporation Tax (Instalment Payments) Regulations, SI 1998/3175.
The Taxes (Interest Rate) (Amendment No 2) Regulations, SI 1998/3176 (amend SI 1993/743).

25 January 2000. Inland Revenue

Deregulatory change setting official rate of interest on beneficial loans in advance

Employees earning £8,500 a year or more (including gross expenses payments and the value of benefits in kind) and directors are taxed on benefits in kind received by virtue of their employment.

If the benefit in kind is in the form of a loan repayable at an advantageous rate of interest, tax is chargeable on the difference between the interest paid by the employee (if any) and the interest which would have been paid on the loan at the ''official rate'' of interest.

Fixing the official rate in advance for the whole of the following tax year will simplify record-keeping, valuation and reporting requirements.

Therefore as a deregulatory measure, the ''official rate'' is set to remain at 6·25% for both the current (1999–00) tax year and the 2000–01 tax year. This will make it simpler for employers to work out the value of beneficial loans which they need to report on behalf of their employees for income tax purposes and on which they will be liable to pay Class 1A national insurance contributions (NICs) from April 2000.

In future, the official rate will continue to be set in advance for the whole of the following tax year and will not be increased during that tax year, even if typical mortgage rates, on which the official rate is based, do increase. However, the Inland Revenue recognise that this policy would need to be reviewed if typical mortgage rates were to fall sharply during a future tax year—the advantages, in terms of lower regulatory burdens, of leaving the official rate unchanged for the whole tax year could in those circumstances be outweighed by the need to reduce the official rate so as not to overtax the benefit.

DETAILS

1. Where interest on a beneficial loan wholly qualifies for relief, the employee is entitled to an offsetting deduction against the taxable benefit. On 19 November, the Paymaster General, Dawn Primarolo, announced in response to a Parliamentary Question, that these fully qualifying beneficial loans are to be exempted from both tax and Class 1A NICs from April 2000 (see Inland Revenue press release dated 19 November ''Reform of Class 1A national insurance to include exemption of tax and NICs charges on some employee benefits'') so that employers will no longer have to report them.

2. Employers will, however, still have to report other beneficial loans for both tax and (from April 2000) Class 1A NICs purposes.

3. Regulations which came into force on 6 March 1999 (S1 1999/419) set the ''official rate'' of interest at 6·25% from that date, at the lower end of the range of bank and building society mortgage rates.

NOTES

1. TA 1988 s 160 charges the benefit of a loan provided by an employer to an employee by reason of the employment where either no interest is paid on the loan or the rate of interest chargeable is less than interest at the ''official rate''. It provides that the amount of the benefit shall be equal to the cash equivalent.

2. TA 1988 Sch 7 defines the cash equivalent for the purposes of s 160 as the amount of interest which would have been payable for the year on the loan at the ''official rate'' of interest less any interest actually paid on the loan for the year.

Commentary—*Simon's Direct Tax Service* **E4.633**.

February 2000. IR Tax Bulletin Issue 45

Provision of personal services through intermediaries

WOULD THE WORKER HAVE BEEN AN EMPLOYEE IF ENGAGED DIRECTLY BY THE CLIENT?

A broad outline of the new rules was given in a Press release dated 23 September 1999. They are intended to apply where a worker supplies his or her services to a client through an intermediary such as a service company or partnership. One of the central questions in deciding whether the new rules apply to an engagement is to establish whether the worker would have been an employee of the client if engaged directly. This article addresses this issue in detail. More details of the proposals can be found on the Inland Revenue website at http://www.inlandrevenue.gov.uk/ir35.

THE APPROACH TO BE ADOPTED

Whether a worker would have been an employee if engaged directly by the client depends on a range of factors, set out in this article. But the final decision is not reached by adding up the number of factors pointing towards employment and comparing that result with the number pointing towards self-employment. The Courts have specifically rejected that approach. In *Hall v Lorimer* Mummery J made the following comment which was quoted with approval by Nolan LJ in the Court of Appeal:

> ''In order to decide whether a person carries on business on his own account it is necessary to consider many different aspects of that person's work activity. This is not a mechanical exercise of running through a checklist to see whether they are present in, or absent from, a given situation. ... It is a matter of evaluation of the overall effect, which is not necessarily the same as the sum total of all the individual details. Not all details are of equal weight or importance in any given situation. The details may also vary in importance from one situation to another.''

When the detailed facts have been established the right approach is to stand back and look at the picture as a whole, to see if the overall effect is that of a person in business on his own account or a person working as an employee in somebody else's business. If the evidence is evenly balanced the intention of the parties may then decide the issue (*Massey v Crown Life Insurance Co*).

ESTABLISHING THE FACTS

In deciding whether a worker would have been an employee if engaged directly by the client it is firstly necessary to establish the terms and conditions of the engagement. In a simple case involving one intermediary (eg where a worker works through a service company) these will normally be established mainly from the contract between the client and the intermediary. It is that contract that will usually reflect the terms that would have applied had the worker been engaged directly by the client. The contract may be written, oral or implied – or a mixture of all three.

Having established the terms and conditions it is then necessary to consider any surrounding facts that may be relevant – eg whether the worker has other clients and a business organisation. In this context other contracts the company has under which the worker's services are supplied and any business organisation of the company which is relevant to the supply of the worker's services will be taken into account as relevant surrounding facts.

DECIDING EMPLOYMENT STATUS

There is no statutory definition of ''employment''. However, the question of employment status has come before the Courts on numerous occasions. The approach taken by the Courts has been to identify factors which help to determine if a particular contract is a 'contract of service' (employment) or a 'contract for services' (self-employment). Relevant factors are:

CONTROL

A worker will not be an employee unless there is a right to exercise 'control' over the worker. This may be a right to control 'what' work is done, 'where' or 'when' it is done or 'how' it is done. Actual control of this sort is not necessary – it the right of control that is important.

Where a client has the right to determine 'how' the work is done this is a strong pointer to employment. But it is not an essential feature of employment – many 'experts' who are employees are not necessarily subject to such control (for example, ship's captain, consultant brain surgeon, etc).

Equally, a right to determine 'what' work is carried out is a strong pointer to employment. It will normally be a feature whenever a client needs a worker to undertake whatever tasks are required at any particular time or where the worker is required to work as part of a co-ordinated team.

A working relationship which involves no control at all is unlikely to be an employment (*Ready Mixed Concrete (South East) Ltd v Minister of Pensions and National Insurance* (1968) 2 QB 497).

THE RIGHT TO GET A SUBSTITUTE OR HELPER TO DO THE JOB

Personal service is an essential element of a contract of employment. A person who has the freedom to choose whether to do the job himself or hire somebody else to do it for him, or who can hire someone else to provide substantial help is probably self-employed (*Australian Mutual Provident Society v Chaplin* (1978) 18 ALR 385 and *Express and Echo Publications Ltd v Tanton* (1999) IRLR 367). However, this must be viewed in the context of the arrangements overall. For example, a worker may choose to pay a helper to take phone messages and deal with invoicing and general book-keeping work for the intermediary. But this would not be directly relevant when considering an engagement where the worker is engaged to lay bricks for a client.

PROVISION OF EQUIPMENT

A self-employed contractor generally provides whatever equipment is needed to do the job (though in many trades, such as carpentry, it is common for employees, as well as self-employed workers, to provide their own hand tools). The provision of significant equipment (and/or materials) which are fundamental to the engagement is of particular importance. For example, where an IT consultant is engaged to undertake a specific piece of work and must work exclusively at home using the worker's own computer equipment that will be a strong pointer to self-employment. But where a worker is provided with office space and computer equipment that points to employment. The fact that a worker might occasionally choose to do some of the work at home using his or her own computer does not change that (many employees do just that). (*Ready Mixed Concrete (South East) Ltd v Minister of Pensions and National Insurance*).

FINANCIAL RISK

An individual who risks his own money by, for example, buying assets needed for the job and bearing their running costs and paying for overheads and large quantities of materials, is almost certainly self-employed. Financial risk could also take the form of quoting a fixed price for a job, with the consequent risk of bearing the additional costs if the job overruns. Another example of a financial risk is where a skilled worker incurs significant amounts of expenditure on training to provide himself with a skill which he uses in subsequent engagements. This can be treated in the same way as investment in equipment to be used in a trade, as a pointer to self-employment, if there is a real risk that the investment would not be recovered from income from future engagements (*Market Investigations Ltd v The Minister of Social Security* (1968) 2 QB 173).

BASIS OF PAYMENT

Employees tend to be paid a fixed wage or salary by the week or month and often qualify for additional payments such as overtime, long service bonus or profit share. Independent contractors, on the other hand, tend to be paid a fixed sum for a particular job. Payment ''by the piece'' (where the worker is paid according to the amount of work actually done) or by commission can be a feature of both employment and self-employment.

OPPORTUNITY TO PROFIT FROM SOUND MANAGEMENT

A person whose profit or loss depends on his capacity to reduce overheads and organise his work effectively may well be self-employed (*Market Investigations Ltd v The Minister of Social Security*). People who are paid by the job will often be in this position.

PART AND PARCEL OF THE ORGANISATION

Establishing whether a person becomes 'part and parcel' of a client's organisation can be a useful indicator in some situations. For example, someone taken on to manage a client's staff will normally be seen as part and parcel of the client's organisation and is likely to be an employee.

RIGHT OF DISMISSAL

A right to terminate an engagement by giving notice of a specified length is a common feature of employment. It is less common in a contract for services, which usually ends only on completion of the task, or if the terms of the contract are breached.

EMPLOYEE BENEFITS

Employees are often entitled to sick pay, holiday pay, pensions, expenses and so on. However, the absence of those features does not necessarily mean that the worker is self-employed – especially in the case of short-term engagements where such payments would not normally feature.

LENGTH OF ENGAGEMENT

Long periods working for one engager may be typical of an employment but are not conclusive. It is still necessary to consider all the terms and conditions of each engagement. Regular working for the same engager may indicate that there is a single and continuing contract of employment (*Nethermere (St Neots) Ltd v Gardiner* (1984) ICR 612). Where an engagement is covered by a series of short contracts, or an initial short contract subsequently extended for a longer period, it is the length of the engagement that is relevant, rather than the length of each contract.

PERSONAL FACTORS

In deciding a person's employment status it may sometimes be necessary to take into account factors which are personal to the worker and which have little to do with the terms of the particular engagement being considered. For example, if a skilled worker works for a number of clients throughout the year and has a business-like approach to obtaining his engagements (perhaps involving expenditure on office accommodation, office equipment, etc) this will point towards self-employment (*Hall v Lorimer* 66 TC 349). Personal factors will usually carry less weight in the case of an unskilled worker, where other factors such as the high level of control exercised by the contractor are likely to be conclusive of employment.

INTENTION

It is the reality of the relationship that matters. It is not enough to call a person ''self-employed'' if all the terms and conditions of the engagement point towards employment. However, if other factors are neutral the intention of the parties will then be the decisive factor in deciding employment status (*Massey v Crown Life Insurance Co* (1978) ICR 590).

REVENUE GUIDANCE

In most cases the question of whether a worker would have been an employee of the client if engaged directly will be obvious from a careful consideration of the terms and conditions of the engagement and the surrounding facts. However, where a worker is in doubt about whether an engagement would have been employment or self-employment then he may ask for an opinion from the Inland Revenue. Full details of how to contact us can be found on our website at www.inlandrevenue.gov.uk/ir35. In such cases a copy of the relevant contract setting out the full terms and conditions of the engagement will have to be provided, together with details of any fact that he considers relevant to the status position. An opinion will only be given on signed contracts and not on draft agreements.

The terms of contracts used by service company workers who obtain engagements through agencies tend to be of a standard form. Such contracts typically require the worker to work on the client's premises, use the client's equipment, work standard hours, be paid at an hourly rate and be subject to a high level of control. In such cases, the opinion of the IR about the engagement is likely to be that it would be employment.

Where a worker is engaged on this type of contract for a period of one month or more, and cannot demonstrate a recent history of work including engagements which have the characteristics of self-employment (see the third example below) then we will say that the engagement would have been employment and therefore be covered by the new rules. Where the contract is for less than a month, then, although the engagement may still have been one of employment, the status position will be considered on a case by case basis.

EXAMPLES

The examples which follow illustrate the process for deciding whether an engagement is employment or self-employment. These examples are purely illustrative. They do not indicate the IR's view of the employment status of particular groups of workers. The role of the IR is to provide advice and guidance about the employment status resulting from a given set of circumstances, not to impose any particular status. The terms and conditions of any engagement are entirely a matter for the parties involved.

EXAMPLE 1 – GORDON – AN IT CONTRACTOR WORKING THROUGH HIS OWN SERVICE COMPANY

FACTS	COMMENTS
Job description/Control	
Client is a large retail concern. The contract was obtained through an agency. The terms and conditions of the engagement are set out in the contracts between the client and the agency and the agency and Gordon's company.	The fact that the engagement has been obtained through an agency has no bearing on whether Gordon would have been an employee or not
Gordon works as part of a support team for the client's payroll system. The team leader (another IT contractor) tells Gordon what work he is to carry out at any particular time (eg help-desk work, specific maintenance tasks, etc).	The extensive right of control that exists here is a very strong pointer to employment. The more important features are the client's ability to shift Gordon from task to task and to specify how the work should be done – but in addition the client can control where and when the work is carried out.
The client has the right to tell Gordon 'how' the work should be carried out – although in practice such control is not normally necessary.	
Gordon must work a regular forty-hour week on the client's premises.	
Payment basis/risk	
Gordon's company is paid an hourly rate for Gordon's services. Any extra hours worked (by mutual agreement) are paid at 1.5 times the normal hourly rate. The client makes payment monthly following submission of an invoice by the agency. Gordon's service company invoices the agency.	The company is paid an hourly rate for Gordon's services and the only financial risk comes from invoicing. There is no opportunity to profit from sound management of the work covered by the contract. Overall this points to employment.
Holiday pay/sick pay	
No sick pay or holiday pay paid under the terms of the inter-company contract.	The engagement runs for six months and holiday pay/sick pay might be expected had there been a direct engagement. But both parties see the actual company/client contract as a contract for services and this is probably why no such payments are made. A minor pointer to self-employment.
Length of contract and personal factors	
The contract is for six months.	Gordon's company has a limited 'business organisation' consisting of an office and associated equipment at his home. This is a pointer to self-employment – but not an overly important one in the context of a six- month contract of this sort.
Gordon uses a computer, telephone, fax, etc at home to seek and negotiate contracts for his company.	
Gordon has worked through his company for two other clients in the last two and a half years – one for three months and one for two years. Prior to that he was a direct employee of another engager.	
Other factors	
The company is contracted to supply Gordon to do the work personally	Both point to employment
All equipment and materials are supplied by the client	
Neither side can terminate the contract early.	Neutral factor (no right to terminate is common in engagements of this length – whether employment or self-employment)
There is no restriction imposed by the contract that prevents either Gordon or his company providing services to others during the engagement.	Mild pointer towards self-employment
Both parties never intended Gordon to be an employee of the client.	Pointer to self employment, but will only be relevant if the other factors are neutral.

Overall picture

The engagement is fairly long term and there is an extensive right of control over Gordon. He must carry out the services personally. The client provides equipment and accommodation and there is no significant financial risk to the company.

The only pointers to self-employment are the minimal financial risk (from invoicing), the ability to work for others (again, a minor point) and the existence of a business organisation/work for other clients.
Standing back from the detail therefore the engagement is one which would have been an employment had it been direct between Gordon and the client. The common intention for self-employment does not alter that. Whilst it would have proved decisive in a 'borderline' situation a review of other factors points strongly to employment here. The new rules would apply to the engagement.

EXAMPLE 2 – HENRY – A CONSULTANT ENGINEER WORKING THROUGH HIS OWN SERVICE COMPANY

FACTS	COMMENTS
Job description/Control	
Client is a large manufacturing company. Under a previous contract Henry has undertaken a broad review of a 15 year old production line and established that significant improvements could be made to the line to increase productivity. Under the current contract Henry is to produce a further report with detailed and costed proposals on the improvements and how they might be carried out with minimum disruption to production.	A specific task has been agreed and the client cannot shift the worker to another task. Henry has the major say over how the work is carried out and when. The clients does have some right to ongoing control over the work in that regular reports are required and changes in Henry's proposals can be sought.
Henry has a free hand over how his work is carried out and when (although there is a deadline of three months for completion). However, Henry is required to keep the client fully informed about progress and the client can require Henry to modify proposals if any aspect seems unsuitable to them.	Overall, control is limited.
Payment basis/risk/opportunity to profit	
Henry is paid £70 an hour but there is a ceiling of 300 hours on the work. If Henry takes longer than this he will only be paid extra if unforeseen difficulties arise or the client insists on unreasonable changes. If the work takes less than 300 hours Henry is only paid for the hours worked.	Henry is being paid an hourly rate and there is no real prospect of his making a loss. Nevertheless he is subject to a ceiling and must complete the work in the time allowed for otherwise he will have to finish the work in his own time without further payment. This is a mild pointer to self-employment.
Holiday pay/sick pay	
No sick pay or holiday pay paid under the terms of the inter-company contract.	Pointer to self-employment
Length of contract and personal factors	
The contract has a deadline of 3 months.	The company has a business organisation and many different clients. This is a significant pointer to self-employment.
Henry has worked through his company as an engineer for many years and it is accepted that the company is 'in business'. The company has had many engagements similar to the current one and is generally engaged to provide an 'expert' service by clients with little engineering expertise. Henry has an office and computer at home which he uses for work extensively.	
Equipment	
Henry visits the client's factory regularly to examine the production line and processes. The only significant equipment he uses is his own computer (to prepare the report). 70% of the work is done in his office.	Significant and fundamental equipment is provided by the company as is office accommodation. This points to self-employment.
Other factors	
Engagement cannot be terminated 'early' other than following a breach of contract	Neutral factor (no right to terminate is common in engagements of this length – whether employment or self-employment)
There is no restriction imposed by the contract that prevents either Henry or his company providing services to others during the engagement.	Mild pointer towards self-employment
Both parties intend that the company is engaged to carry out the work and that Henry is not an employee of the client.	Pointer to self employment, but will only be relevant if the other factors are neutral.

Overall picture
Henry is a skilled worker who has been engaged to carry out a specific task and control over him is limited. He is paid based on an hourly rate but there is an over-riding limit within which the work agreed must be completed. There is a contract deadline of three months and the company has many other clients. Some important equipment is supplied by the company and the work is mainly carried out away from the client's premises.
Henry would have been self-employed if engaged directly by the client and the new rules will not apply. Even if the contract had been expected to last for a longer period – say, nine months – the other factors would still have led to a conclusion of self-employment.

EXAMPLE 3 – CHARLOTTE – AN IT CONSULTANT WORKING THROUGH HER OWN SERVICE COMPANY

FACTS	COMMENTS
Job description/Control Charlotte's client for this engagement is a software company. She has been engaged for her programming skills to work on a specific project as part of a team developing a new piece of software. She works to the client's project manager who allocates particular sub programs to Charlotte that she writes. The client expects the project to last for around three months. The manager specifies the way in which the sub-program is to be structured and can require changes to be made to make the work fit in with other parts of the program as it is developed, to rectify overall design faults, etc. Charlotte works a set number of hours but actual working times are flexible in line with the company's flexi-time arrangements for its employees. She is required to work at the client's premises.	There is an extensive right of control over Charlotte. The more important features are the client's ability to shift Charlotte from task to task and to specify how the work should be done. In addition the client can control to some extent where and when the work is carried out. But control is not total. Charlotte is engaged to work on a specific project so cannot be told to work on something completely different – and she cannot be required to work elsewhere. Overall, this is a strong pointer to employment.
Payment basis/risk/sick pay/holiday pay Charlotte is paid £3600 every four weeks in return for working a 40-hour week. Extra payments are made at the equivalent hourly rate for any additional hours agreed. Payment is made 14 days after the company has invoiced the client. No sick pay or holiday pay is paid; under the contract Charlotte has with her company she is paid an on-going, but much lower, salary which includes provision for holiday pay and sick pay.	It is the arrangements between the service company and the client that are important here. The company is paid the equivalent of a salary—with overtime payments—but no sick pay or holiday pay. Although the invoicing arrangements result in a small financial risk this is minor. Overall there is no significant financial risk and no opportunity to profit from sound management of the task. This points to employment.
Length of contract and personal factors The contract is for 12 weeks – but there is provision for an extension if the project overruns and all parties agree to the extension. Charlotte does some work for another client at weekends and has worked for various clients in the past—always through her company and often through employment agencies. Her contracts have usually lasted for between one and three months. Most have been similar to this one but some have involved her in specific tasks for a fixed fee using her own equipment and working at home.	Charlotte and her company have a 'business organisation' – including an office and associated equipment based at Charlotte's home. She has a variety of clients and all her contracts have been fairly short term. This is a strong pointer to self-employment.

FACTS	COMMENTS
Charlotte has an office at home and a computer and other office equipment that is used for some of her other work. These contribute to her company's business organisation—which she uses to obtain work, keep records, prepare invoices, etc.	
Other factors	
The company is contracted to supply Charlotte to do the work personally	Both point to employment
All equipment is supplied by the client	
The engagement cannot be terminated "early" other than following a breach of contract	Neutral factor (no right to terminate is common in engagements of this length – whether employment or self-employment)
There is no restriction imposed by the contract that prevents either Charlotte or her company providing services to others during the engagement.	Pointer to self-employment.
All parties intended that the company/client engagement would be self-employment.	Pointer to self employment, but will only be relevant if the other factors are neutral.

Overall picture

This is a borderline case. On balance, given all the facts, Charlotte would have been self-employed had she been engaged directly by the client. The new rules will not apply to the engagement.

The following point towards self-employment:

– existing business and a variety of different engagements, some of which would clearly count as self-employed if she had been engaged directly by her client.
– overall business organisation (office and equipment at home, business like approach to obtaining engagements and carrying them out, etc). Charlotte would clearly be regarded as being 'in business on her own account' for those engagements where she carried out of a specific task for a fixed fee using her own accommodation and equipment.
– risk from invoicing
– the lack of an exclusivity clause.

Other factors point to employment:

– There is fairly extensive control over Charlotte. The client can dictate 'what' work is carried out on the project and 'how' the work is done. But control is not total. Charlotte cannot be directed to work on another project or undertake some quite different work. Nor is there control in other areas (eg she subject to the clients normal staff rules/disciplinary procedures);
– There is virtually no financial risk in the engagement and no opportunity to profit from sound management of the task;
– Charlotte must carry out the work herself;
– All equipment and accommodation is provided by the client.

What can then have more significance is the extent to which the individual is dependant upon, or independent of, a particular paymaster for the financial exploitation of his or her talents (see *Hall v Lorimer*). The fact that Charlotte's company is also engaged in contracts which involve carrying out a specific task for a fixed fee, using her own equipment, suggests that it is a genuine business and neither she nor her company rely on a single client for the exploitation of her talents. These factors balance the control and other employment factors that exist in this particular context and put the matter near the borderline where the mutual intention for self-employment becomes decisive.

However, the overall picture would have been rather different had the engagement been longer. For example, had the engagement been for twelve months the 'personal factors' would have been far less significant and the employment pointers would have predominated. Just because a person has an established business does not automatically make them self-employed for all engagements (see *Fall v Hitchin* (49 TC 433) – also referred to in *Hall v Lorimer*). Also, if she had not also had contracts of a type which would clearly have fallen within the definition of self-employment, employment pointers would have dominated and the contract at issue would have been one of employment. The same could apply to shorter contracts.

21 March 2000. Inland Revenue Budget Note

Group relief rules

SUMMARY OF MEASURES

The group relief rules for companies will be modernised to allow groups and consortia to be established through companies resident anywhere in the world, it was announced today. The changes respond to the increasing globalisation of business and will give multinational groups of companies greater flexibility in structuring their commercial activities in the UK.

The changes will take effect from 1 April 2000. Group relief will also be extended from that date to UK branches of overseas companies.

DETAILS

1 From 1 April 2000, it will be possible to establish a group or consortium for group relief purposes through a company resident anywhere in the world. Examples of what this will mean in practice are given in the annex attached.

2 The Inland Revenue announced in February 1999 that, following the decision of the European Court of Justice in the case of *ICI v Colmer*, group relief would be available where the existence of a group or consortium was established through companies resident in the EU or the EEA The changes announced today go much further, by completely removing any restriction on the residence of companies through which a group or consortium is established.

3 Group relief will also be extended, from 1 April 2000, to UK branches of overseas companies. Under the new rules, a UK branch of an overseas company will be able to claim losses surrendered by other group companies as group relief, to reduce its profits chargeable to corporation tax. A UK branch will also be able to surrender its losses as group relief, where those losses are not relievable (other than against profits within the charge to UK corporation tax) in the overseas country.

4 The rules for overseas branches of UK companies will be brought into line with those for UK branches of overseas companies. A UK company will be able to surrender losses which are attributable to an overseas branch if those losses are not relievable (other than against profits within the charge to UK corporation tax) in the overseas country.

5 Two other minor technical amendments are also being made. These will provide for further simplification of the administrative arrangements for claiming group relief under existing regulatory powers, and will correct a minor defect in the rules determining the maximum amount of a consortium claim to group relief.

NOTES

Group relief

1 Group relief allows a company to claim the benefit of trading losses and certain other reliefs of another company if both companies are members of the same group. Its objective is to make the tax treatment of a group carrying on a variety of activities through different companies closer to what it would have been if those activities had been carried on by a single company. A group exists, broadly, where one company owns 75% of the other, or a third company owns 75% of both of them.

2 Simplified administrative arrangements for claiming group relief for accounting periods within corporation tax self assessment were provided by the Corporation Tax (Simplified Arrangements for Group Relief) Regulations, SI 1999/2975. These regulations reduce the paperwork involved in making and revising group relief claims.

Consortium claims to group relief

3 Group relief is extended to consortia. A consortium exists where companies (the consortium members) each own at least 5%, and together own at least 75%, of the share capital of—

– a trading company; or
– a holding company whose business is wholly or mainly the holding of shares in trading companies of which it owns 90% of the ordinary share capital.

Branches

4 UK branches of non-resident companies are subject to UK corporation tax on their trading profits. Before the changes announced today, their trading losses could be set off only against other profits of the branch or carried forward against future trading profits of the branch.

5 UK-resident companies are subject to corporation tax on their world-wide profits, including any profits made by their overseas branches (though overseas tax paid by the branch can be set against the company's corporation tax liability). Where an overseas branch makes a loss, that loss will be reflected in the results of the company as a whole. And to the extent that a branch loss forms part of an overall loss made by the company, it may be surrendered as group relief under the current rules. The new rules will restrict the surrender of losses which are attributable to an overseas branch where they are relievable in the overseas country (other than against profits within the charge to UK corporation tax). But otherwise the position will remain unchanged.

Previous press release

6 A press release was issued on 26 February 1999 following the decision of the European Court of Justice in *ICI v Colmer*. It explained how the Revenue would settle open cases where the establishment of a group or consortium relied on a company or companies resident within the EU or EEA.

Related press release

7 Modernisation of the rules affecting groups of companies for the purposes of chargeable gains has also been announced today. Details are given in REVBN2B [not reproduced].

Costs

8 The costs of extending the group relief rules are estimated to be £50 million in 2000–01, £100 million in 2001–02 and £65 million in 2002–03, but the ongoing annual cost is likely to be small. These costs take account of behavioural effects.

ANNEX
ESTABLISHING A GROUP OR CONSORTIUM—EXAMPLES

EXAMPLE 1 – NON-UK RESIDENT PARENT

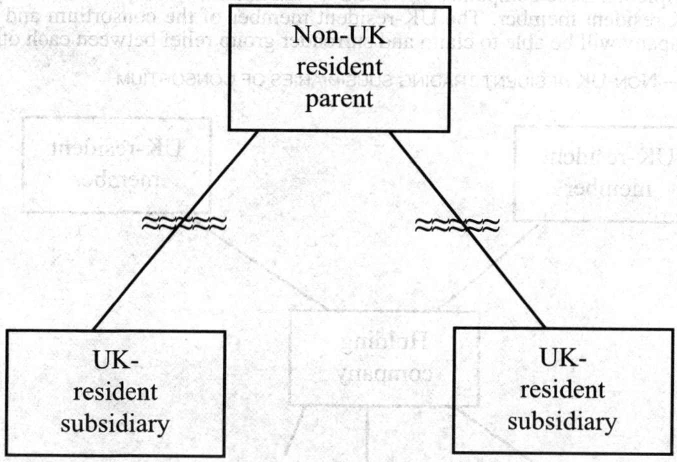

In this example the two UK subsidiaries will now be members of the same group, whatever the country of residence of the parent. The two UK subsidiaries will therefore be able to claim and surrender group relief between each other.

EXAMPLE 2 – NON-UK RESIDENT MEMBER OF CONSORTIUM

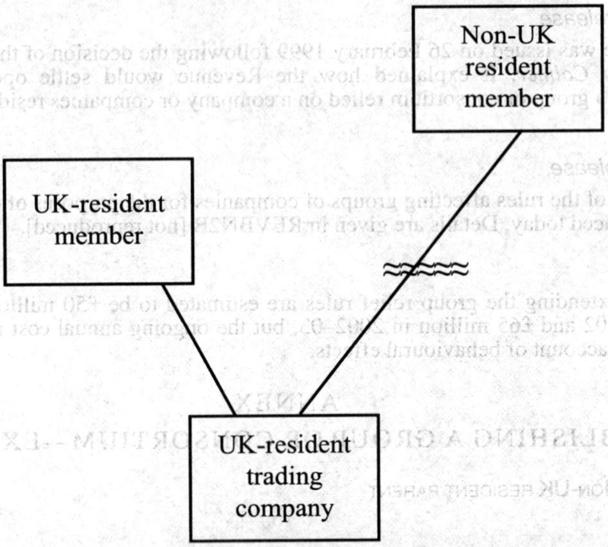

In this example the three companies will form a consortium, whatever the country of residence of the non-UK resident member. The UK-resident member of the consortium and the UK-resident trading company will be able to claim and surrender group relief between each other.

EXAMPLE 3 – NON-UK RESIDENT TRADING SUBSIDIARIES OF CONSORTIUM

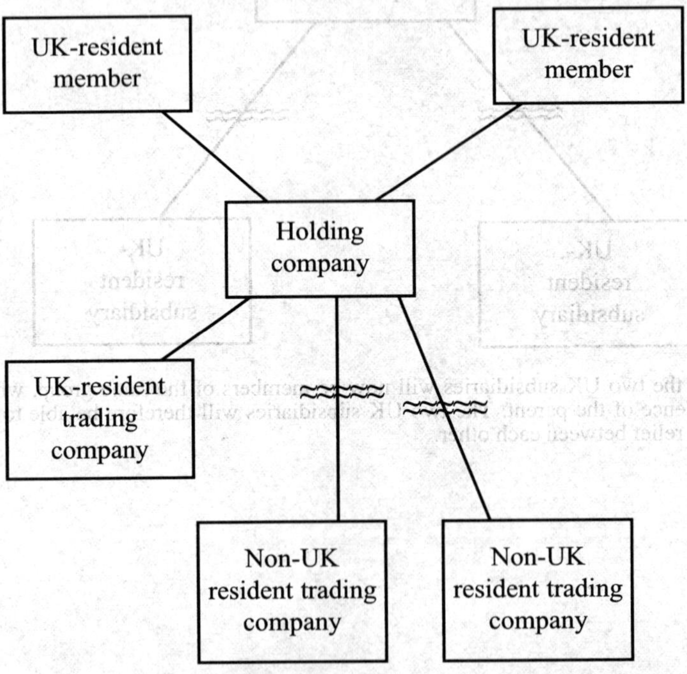

In this example a consortium will now exist, whatever the country of residence of the non-UK resident trading companies. Group relief will therefore be available between the UK-resident companies in the consortium.

April 2000. IR Tax Bulletin Issue 46

Employee share plans—conditional shares and related topics

The provision of shares or options over shares by corporate employers, as part of their remuneration strategy for their employees and directors, is a well-established practice. Where shares are provided directly to an employee or director there is normally a Schedule E income tax charge under TA 1988 s 19(1) on the value of those shares. Sometimes restrictions are placed on the shares at the time they are provided. A common restriction is the risk of forfeiture, so that the employee has an interest in the shares but that interest can be lost. These shares have a reduced value while they are subject to the risk of forfeiture but the value increases when the risk is lifted.

Legislation was introduced in FA 1998 in relation to the treatment of these restricted shares (also known as 'conditional shares'). This can be found at TA 1988 ss 140A–H. There were further changes in FA 1999 that were incorporated into those sections of ICTA.

Where an employee receives shares that are subject to the risk of forfeiture the normal income tax charge is exempted by Section 140A(3) TA 1988, unless the shares can still be subject to the risk of forfeiture more than five years after they were acquired. When the risk of forfeiture is lifted, or the shares are disposed of, a Schedule E charge arises on the value of the shares less any amounts paid for them or already charged to income tax. S140C defines the cases where the interest in shares is to be treated as only conditional.

Previous articles on these topics can be found in Tax Bulletins Issues 35 (June 1998) and 36 (August 1998). Since then we have been asked a number of questions about ss 140A–H TA 1988 as they now stand. We consider that these are of general interest and publish our answers to them here.

We are also taking this opportunity to deal with some other questions of general interest in the area of employee share remuneration, within the existing legislation; including PAYE, National Insurance and Capital Gains.

PRs etc

CONDITIONAL SHARES (TA 1988 SS 140A–H)

Comparison between TA 1988 ss 140C(3) and 140C(3A)

Q1. To fall within TA 1988 s 140C(3), it is necessary for the articles of association to require that an employee who leaves employment must offer the shares for sale. This implies that it is not possible to differentiate between different classes of leavers. For example, some employers will want all leavers to sell their shares while others will be content to allow employees who leave through ill health, disability etc. to retain theirs. In contrast, the wording of TA 1988 s 140C(3A) appears to allow some discretion in this matter. Does the Inland Revenue allow the same discretion as to which employees must sell their shares under both subsections of the Act?

A. We do not draw any distinction between the 'requirement' tests in TA 1988 ss 140C(3) and 140C(3A) and accept that both subsections allow for the possibility of differentiating between classes of leavers.

Misconduct

Q2. The term 'misconduct' is used in TA 1988 s 140C(3A). Many share plan rules refer to 'termination for cause'; does the Inland Revenue interpret 'misconduct' to include 'termination for cause' for this purpose?

A. We would agree that the term 'termination for cause' falls within the scope of TA 1988 s 140C(3A).

Bankruptcy

Q3. Many companies require that employees who own shares must sell them for a price determined by a formula if they cease employment. Provided these provisions are contained in the articles of association, this alone will not make the shares conditional. However, such companies often provide that the shares must be sold if the employee becomes bankrupt. This would not, on the face of it, fall within any of the exemptions of S140C(3) TA 1988. A director who was made bankrupt would have to cease to be a director, because of the prohibition in the Company Directors Disqualification Act of 1986, but could normally continue as an employee of the company.

This means that if shares owned by an employee were conditional solely because of a bankruptcy condition, they would not be conditional if the employee were also a director, because they would now fall within the exemption of S140C(3).

Would the Inland Revenue propose an amendment or introduce a concession that a bankruptcy provision contained in the articles of association would be ignored for the purposes of determining whether the shares were conditional for an employee who is not also a director?

A. We can confirm this interpretation of the legislation. There are no plans to introduce a concession or to amend the legislation.

Drag-along rights

Q4. Some shares are subject to ''drag-along'' rights. These rights typically require that a minority shareholder must sell some or all of his shares if other shareholders sell their shares to a third party. The price for such a sale is normally the price paid by the third party and, as such, is not normally discounted to take account of a minority interest, for example. Would such 'drag-along' rights, on their own, make the shares conditional?

A. Conditions may apply which potentially require shareholders to sell their shares when the majority shareholders sell out and at the same price as those shareholders. Where that requirement is, in effect, a requirement to offer shares at a genuine arms length price then the test in S140C(1)(*b*) would not be met so that the provisions of S140A would not apply.

Articles of association

Q5. The term ''articles of association'' is used in TA 1988 s 140C. How does the Inland Revenue interpret this term in relation to foreign companies that may not have articles of association, but have other documents such as 'bye-laws'? How does this interpretation fit with the Treaty of Rome?

A. The Inland Revenue does not treat agreements outside articles of association as if they were in articles of association for the purposes of TA 1988 s 140C. The exemption in TA 1988 s 140C(3) is not extended to foreign company equivalents.

With regard to the Treaty of Rome, the Revenue treats EU resident companies no differently from UK resident companies that have forfeiture rules outside of Articles of Association.

Q6. The term ''articles of association'' is also found in paragraph 12 of Schedule 9 of TA 1988, in the context of the approved share scheme legislation. The Inland Revenue interprets the term to include equivalent foreign documents for this purpose. What is the reason for this difference between the two circumstances?

A. The reason for the difference between the interpretation for TA 1988 s 140A and approved scheme legislation purposes is the difference in rationale for these two parts of the Taxes Act.

If employees receive shares on terms that mean those shares may be forfeit, it is right that the full value of the shares should be treated as remuneration and charged to income tax when that risk is subsequently removed. The Government was, however, concerned that employees in many small private companies, which have for a number of years been awarding shares, would be caught by TA 1988 s 140A because of pre-emption rights in the articles of association. Where this represented the only risk of forfeiture, it has always been accepted that the income tax charge arose on the value of the shares when they were received. As a result it was decided to exclude from the new provisions the situation where an employee acquires shares that are conditional solely as a result of conditions contained in the employing company's articles of association. The limits of the exemptions in TA 1988 s 140C as interpreted by the Inland Revenue do, generally speaking, exempt those small private companies with pre-emption rights.

The purpose of paragraph 12 Schedule 9 is to ensure that the shares that employees receive through approved schemes are normal shares on normal terms. This is reflected by the requirement that they must not be subject to restrictions, unless those restrictions attach to all shares of the same class. For this purpose the restrictions are not only those included in the articles of association but also those imposed by other documents or agreements (paragraph 13 Schedule 9). This applies equally to UK and foreign companies.

Company leaving the group

Q7. Some companies have articles of association that require employees to sell their shares if the subsidiary that they work for is sold or ceases to be a 51% subsidiary. This does not appear to fall within the exemption in TA 1988 s 140C(3), since the employee does not cease to be an employee. Instead the company that he works for ceases to be a group company. Would this situation mean the shares were conditional for the purposes of TA 1988 s 140A?

A. Where the requirement is, in effect, a requirement to offer shares at a genuine arms length price, the test in TA 1988 s 140C(1)(*b*) would not be met so that the provisions of S140A would not apply. It would be unusual for the requirement to meet the test in TA 1988 s 140C(1)(*b*), but where that happens, the acquisition of shares would fall outside the exemption in TA 1988 s 140C(3) and therefore within the scope of S140A.

Interaction between TA 1988 ss 140A and 162

Q8. Section 140A(3) of TA 1988 contains a reference to TA 1988 s 162. Does this apply to the difference between the full market value of the conditional shares and the amount paid, or merely act to retain the charge which would otherwise apply under S162?

A. The provisions at TA 1988 s 140A do not extend the circumstances in which a s 162 charge can apply to shares acquired at an undervalue.

The normal rules charge which arises under TA 1988 s 19 takes priority over any s 162 charge because of the operation s 162(11). TA 1988 s 140A then goes on to displace the S19 charge in certain circumstances but it does not extend the scope of TA 1988 s 162. It merely retains the S162 charge that would apply in normal circumstances.

Interaction between TA 1988 s 140A and FA 1988 ss 78, 79

Q9. Many share plans operate over shares in subsidiary companies. These share plans may be operated for genuine commercial reasons and in some cases the shares that the employees own will be conditional.

If an employee sells the shares then an income tax charge would appear to be due under both FA 1988 s 79 and TA 1988 s 140A. Each of these sections contains provision to allow a tax charge under the other in calculating the tax charge. What is the correct treatment when the tax charge arises at the same time under both sections?

A similar situation can arise in respect of a tax charge under S78 FA 1988, where share rights are altered. For example, a company's share capital may be changed on a flotation. This may give rise to a S140A TA 1988 charge, if the shares cease to be conditional, and a S78 FA 1988 charge on a variation in the rights attaching to those shares. How does the legislation apply such a case?

A. Section 79 (6A) FA 1988 provides that the s 79 charge will be reduced by any amount charged under TA 1988 s 140A if the TA 1988 s 140A event occurs before the time of the S79 chargeable increase.

The deductible amounts for the TA 1988 s 140A charge in respect of events for which there is a charge under FA 1988 s 79 (and s 78) are for those events which have occurred not later than the event giving rise to the TA 1988 s 140A charge. This order of priority is found at s 140A(7)(*c*).

Therefore, where a FA 1988 s 79 charge arises at the same time as the TA 1988 s 140A charge, the full s 79 charge will be taken, and that charge will be deductible in computing the TA 1988 s 140A charge.

Where a chargeable event for FA 1988 s 78 purposes occurs at the same time as the risk of forfeiture is lifted, the full s 78 charge will be taken and that charge will then be deductible in computing the amount for TA 1988 s 140A.

PAYE, NICS & TA 1988 S 144A

Section 144A of TA 1988

Q10. Why can't tax not recovered from an employee within the 30-day time limit under TA 1988 s 144A be treated as a beneficial loan, rather than a taxable benefit in kind. Alternatively, can the 30-day time limit be extended to 60 days?

A. A tax charge arises under Section 144A if the employer was obliged to account for PAYE tax, which could not be deducted from actual pay, and the employee has not made good to the employer the tax within 30 days. TA 1988 s 144A was introduced in Finance Act 1994 in association with ss 203B–L. Following representations from employers and advisers, own company shares were granted an exemption when these rules took effect in May 1994.

Subsequently the Inland Revenue saw much evidence that the shares exemption was being used for avoidance purposes and hence the exemption was lifted in November 1996.

There are no plans to issue concessions on TA 1988 s 144A, such as an extension of the 30-day period, nor to treat tax not recovered by an employer as a loan rather than a benefit-in-kind.

An employer who is properly advised will ensure the PAYE tax is recovered within the 30 day period and it would be neither equitable nor consistent for the Inland Revenue to introduce concessions for less well advised, or less compliant, employers/employees.

Right of the employer to recover PAYE from the employee

Q11. When a notional payment is made, SI 1994 No 1212 Regulation 7 allows an employer to recover PAYE from any other cash payments made in the remaining part of the tax month. The employer does not have a statutory right to recover the PAYE from payments made in, say, the following tax months.

This could cause practical problems, for example where an employee exercises an option after the payroll cut off date for the month. Could the recovery period be extended indefinitely so that PAYE paid by the employer (and not recovered) is effectively treated as a loan? This would not change the timing of the PAYE paid by the employer or the TA 1988 s 144A tax charge.

Failing this, could the period for the recovery of the PAYE be aligned with National Insurance, where the employer can recover the National Insurance from the employee at any time in the same tax year?

A. The Inland Revenue does not advise employers how to organise their internal procedures but employers are required to meet obligations which arise under the PAYE regulations.

As already stated in the context of TA 1988 s 144A, there are no plans to extend the recovery period for PAYE from the employee, nor to align with recovery of National Insurance. That would only be a partial solution because it would not solve difficulties that could arise towards the end of the tax year.

When FA 1994 legislation was enacted, and the Notional Payment regulations laid, it was made clear that employers and employees were free to adjust their relationships to allow the employer to recover the PAYE from the employee. The Inland Revenue sees no need to change the present position.

If the recovery arrangements are expressed as a formal loan there will be no TA 1988 s 144A charge but a beneficial loan charge will apply, if interest is paid at less than the official rate and the other limits have been exceeded.

Tax return

Q12. How should the employee complete her self-assessment tax return when tax on a share related benefit has been deducted under PAYE? The P60 will not show the PAYE deducted in respect of the share-related benefit and the employee will not necessarily know the amount of tax that has been deducted. What should the employee do if the employer has failed to operate PAYE?

A. If the employer operated PAYE, on the correct amount of the share income, the income and the associated PAYE tax will be included in the figures on the P60. If required to submit a return, the employee does not need to separate the share income and the PAYE on it from other income or tax, which should be entered in boxes 1.8 and 1.11 on the employment page. In these circumstances, if there is nothing else to go on a share schemes page, the employee should tick the 'no' box on the SA return about a share schemes supplementary page. She should also explain in the additional information box at the end of the return that all the share income has been taxed through PAYE and is declared on the employment page.

However, if the employee considers that the 'best estimate' on which PAYE was operated is not correct, she should—

- deduct the 'best estimate' from the P60 income figure
- put the balance in box 1.8 on the employment page, and
- enter the correct figure in the share pages.

All the tax should still go into box 1.11 on the employment page and an explanation should be given in the additional information space on that page.

If the employer does not operate PAYE on the share income, that income and the tax on it is not included in the P60 and the employee must return the income in the Share Pages of an SA return.

If the employee considers that tax should have been deducted in accordance with S 203J (so that there has been a PAYE failure by the employer), the PAYE regulations permit the employee to claim a tax credit. This should be entered in box 1.11 on the Employment page with an explanation in the additional information box.

If accurate information about the amount chargeable, or the associated tax charge, is not available by the filing date the employee should not delay submitting the return but should include best estimates for the figures with an explanation in the additional information boxes. The employee should ensure accurate information is submitted as soon as it becomes available.

Readily convertible assets (RCAs)—long stop provisions

Q13. Many new start up companies contain provisions in their articles of association or other agreements that if there has not been a flotation or sale by a 'long stop' date then—

- The minority shareholders can require that the majority shareholders purchase their shares, and
- The majority shareholders can require that the minority shareholders sell their shares.

This long stop date is typically five to ten years from the date when the original shares were acquired. Would this arrangement for a long stop provision on its own make the shares readily convertible assets?

A. The definition of an RCA in S203F(2) includes—

> '(*g*) an asset for which trading arrangements are likely to come into existence in accordance with any arrangements of another description existing when the asset is provided or with any understanding existing at that time'.

Long stop provisions are trading arrangements because the share award is made subject to a provision requiring them to be purchased/sold at a particular point in the future. This represents an arrangement or understanding likely to give rise to trading arrangements. Consequently the shares are RCAs.

Tax Bulletin Issue 36 (August 1998) advised that Shares Valuation Division (PAYE valuations) will assist private companies in the valuation of their shares for PAYE. SVD will consider the precise facts of any case. The long stop provision may be reflected in a lower valuation relative to shares capable of sale immediately after award.

RCAs and delayed sale

Q14. There are share plans that operate in such a way as to prohibit employees from selling the shares for, say, one year from the date of acquisition. This is a feature of some US stock purchase plans. However, the same class of shares will often be traded on a stock exchange and so those awarded to the employees will be readily convertible assets. This means that PAYE will be due when the shares are acquired but the employee will not be able to sell the shares to reimburse the PAYE.

Would it be possible to allow the employee to elect to defer the tax due if the shares cannot be sold in genuine commercial situations?

A. If an employee acquires shares under an arrangement that allows for sale of the shares one year later, the shares will be RCAs either—

- because the shares are traded on a recognised investment exchange or the New York Stock Exchange; or
- because the understanding that the shares can be sold in one year is an understanding likely to lead to trading arrangements.

Before the RCA rules were introduced in FA 1998, when employees were awarded shares whose sale was restricted for a given period, some employers were unsure about the date, and the correct amount, on which PAYE should be operated.

FA 1998 simplified this process and introduced a single method of calculating PAYE, based on a best reasonable estimate of the income chargeable to tax. This provides employers with certainty over the timing of the operation of PAYE, and feedback from employers and advisers has been positive.

A system where the employer's obligation to operate PAYE could be deferred until some later event would re-introduce the type of uncertainty removed in FA 1998. On a practical note, if the sale was delayed 12 months or more, the income would arise in one tax year and the obligation to operate PAYE in a later year. Since PAYE operates on an annual cycle, this would create considerable, and possibly insurmountable, operational problems.

Recovery of PAYE and NICs—Finance Act 1999 s 43

Q15. Section 43 FA 1999 introduced exclusions to TA 1988 s 140C and made those exclusions retrospective to 17 March 1998, when TA 1988 s 140C originally took effect. The result is that some companies may have operated PAYE and NICs when, for example, an employee ceased employment.

Can the employer recover National Insurance paid in this situation, now that the tax charge has been removed?

What action should be taken to remove any TA 1988 s 144A benefit and allow the employee to recover any income tax over paid?

A. There is no legislative provision that allows for a refund of NICs that may have been paid on the basis that the amounts were properly payable at the time. In this case, this applies to payments made between 9 April 1998 and 27 July 1999 (the date of Royal Assent of FA 1999).

The first year affected by S140A is 1997-98 for which the Self Assessment filing date was 31 January 1999 and the taxpayer was free to amend this return before 31 January 2000. Therefore any Self Assessment that included—

- a charge on shares now affected by FA 1999 s 43;
- a TA 1988 s 144A charge;
- a PAYE credit

could have been amended.

If there is an open SA enquiry, these points can be adjusted when that enquiry is closed.

If the taxpayer missed the 31 January 2000 deadline, or was not in SA in 1997–98, the matter can be dealt with via a claim under TMA 1970 s 33. This is because the retrospective nature of FA 1999 s 43 means the return was filed on the basis of a misunderstanding of the law.

National Insurance on option rollovers

Q16. SI 1979/591 Regulation 19(1)(*zm*) includes provisions to exempt from National Insurance gains on the exercise of certain 'rolled-over' options. How does the Inland Revenue interpret this provision in practice?

A. There are two things to consider when an option originally granted before 6 April 1999 is rolled over after 5 April 1999.

- Regulation 19(1)(*zl*) considers whether there should be any NICs on the event of the rollover itself, by reference to the values prevailing at the time.
- Regulation 19(1)(*zm*) considers whether there should be any NICs on the subsequent gain made on the new option, by reference to whether the rollover was conducted at parity.

The first consideration is whether there is any NIC on the event of the rollover itself. Regulation 19(1)(*zl*) exempts such rollovers from liability provided there is no increase in the total discount. Regulation 19(11) defines 'total discount' as—

> 'the difference between the total value of the exercise price of the shares that are the subject of the right in question and the total market value of that right'.

If the total discount on the new option is substantially greater, then NICs will be due on the best estimate of the amount of the increase at the time of the rollover. The basis of assessment is given in Regulation 18(17) of the Social Security (Contributions) Regulations 1979. Where the old option has gone underwater since grant and the new option has a nil discount, we do not consider that the 'total discount' has increased. Consequently no NICs would be due on the event of the rollover itself.

The second consideration is whether any NICs will arise on the subsequent gain made on the new option. The intention of Regulation 19(1)(*zm*) is to exempt from liability the gain made on an option rolled over after 5 April 1999, where the first option was granted before 6 April 1999, provided the consideration given for the old option was not in excess of the total market value of the old option, at the time of the rollover.

In summary, National Insurance will not be due on the gain on a rolled-over option where—

- the original option was granted before 6 April 1999
- the rollover happens after 5 April 1999
- the discount, at the time of the rollover, on the new option is not more than on the old option, and
- the total market value of the shares under the new option, at the time of the rollover, is not more than under the old option.

There have been a few queries on the operation of 19(1)(*zm*) and we will be clarifying this, by way of an amendment to ensure that it achieves the policy intention. If you are still in doubt you should contact your local Inland Revenue National Insurance Office with the scheme documentation.

Note—The 1979/591 regulations have now been consolidated into SI 2001/1004.

CAPITAL GAINS

Qualifying employee share ownership trusts ('QUESTS')

Q17. Section 69(3A) FA 1989 allows the transfer of shares by a QUEST for the purpose of a S135(1) TCGA 1992 reorganisation to be regarded as a qualifying transfer. Many reorganisations qualify for favourable capital gains tax treatment under S136 TCGA 1992. However, a transfer of shares for the purpose of such a reorganisation does not appear to be regarded as a qualifying transfer. As such, the transfer of shares in such circumstances would give rise to a chargeable event.

Can a reorganisation under S136 TCGA 1992 be treated in the same way as a reorganisation under S135 TCGA 1992?

A. A Section 135 TCGA 1992 reorganisation involves a transfer of shares by the shareholders in one of the companies involved, even though the new shares and /or securities are treated as if they were the old shares for capital gains purposes by virtue of Section 127–131 TCGA 1992.

Section 136 TCGA 1992 deals with an arrangement between a company and its shareholders in connection with a scheme of reconstruction or amalgamation under which another company issues shares to the shareholders in the first company. The shares in the first company are retained by the shareholders in the first company or cancelled. 'Shares' in this context includes debentures. There is no need for the shareholders in the first company to transfer their shares in the situations covered by Section 136 TCGA. In these circumstances there is no reason for Section 69(3A) FA 1989 to mention Section 136 TCGA 1992 and it therefore deals only with transactions within Section 135(1) TCGA 1992.

Section 69(3A) FA 1989 was introduced as a result of the European Union Mergers Directive to remove possible tax obstacles to community-wide business activities and cross-border expansion. The relief was targeted at cross-border transactions as UK companies already had wide scope to reorganise their commercial operations without triggering burdensome tax charges.

Extra-statutory Concession D35

Q18. Extra-statutory concession D35 provides relief from capital gains tax where an employee trust transfers an asset to an employee where the value in that transfer is subject to Schedule E. Does ESC D35 apply where the shares that are transferred are conditional, for the purpose of S140A TA 1988, and where no income tax is due on the acquisition of the shares by virtue of S140A(3) TA 1988?

A. An employee becoming absolutely entitled to the shares is an event giving rise to a deemed disposal under Section 71(1) TCGA and a charge under Section 140A(4)(*a*) TA 1988. Assuming that the employee is assessable on the full value of the shares on that date, because there is no deduction for the cost of those shares, then the trustees would be exempt from CGT.

Q19. Does ESC D35 apply to assets transferred following the exercise of a share option where the exercise price is nil or a nominal amount?

A. The ESC can apply where exceptionally the employee gives no consideration for the share option and for the shares he acquires on exercise—assuming that the case does not fall within the last paragraph of the concession. This disapplies ESC D35 where special statutory rules restrict either the liability to capital gains tax or the Schedule E liability. On the face of it, nominal consideration would take the case outside the concession.

Q20. Can ESC D35 be extended to cover situations where an employee has to pay something for the cost of the asset (for example, a nominal amount or an amount equal to the original cost of the asset)?

A. The intention was to keep the ESC as simple as possible. We consider that anything other than a straight exemption would almost certainly require legislation.

The ESC was introduced to help a simple employee benefit or welfare trust which could not in itself be subject to any of the statutory income tax or CGT reliefs where the company in question was to be floated on the Stock Exchange or taken over. The trust's shares would be distributed gratuitously in advance of this event. In this way the employees could take the maximum benefit from the shares. In this situation one would not expect the employees to pay anything to the trustees for the shares. If however the trustees did require some cash to meet expenses or repay loans, it would be a simple matter for them to retain sufficient shares to meet such liabilities net of tax.

OTHER ISSUES

Employee share plans & pensions

Q21. Can an employee's profits in respect of shares and share options be included in 'relevant earnings' for determining the limits on how much can be paid into a personal pension plan?

A. The definition of 'relevant earnings' for this purpose is found in Section 644 TA 1988. S644(4)(*a*) excludes—

'anything in respect of which tax is chargeable under Schedule E and which arises from the acquisition or disposal of shares or an interest in shares or from a right to acquire shares.'

Therefore the employee's profit on the shares cannot be taken into account as relevant earnings for a personal pension plan. This reflects S612 TA 1988 which was introduced to prevent the artificial manipulation of remuneration for occupational pension schemes for the purposes of boosting both employee contributions and benefit levels.

However, from April 2001, there will be extra scope to contribute to a personal pension plan at desired levels. Under the proposals for defined contribution schemes, members of personal pension plans will be able to contribute up to £3,600 per year without regard to relevant earnings. This is of potential benefit to the vast majority of personal pension scheme members who currently contribute at a far lower level.

Savings-related share plans—high value shares

Q22. Some companies have very high share prices and this means that employees saving relatively modest amounts each month would be unable to buy shares in an approved plan. For example, with a share price in excess of £1,000, an employee saving less than £25 per month under a 3 year savings-related share plan would not have sufficient to buy one share. Would the Inland Revenue consider allowing options to be granted over a fraction of a share to allow companies with high share prices to operate savings-related share option plans?

A. Our understanding of the law, as it currently stands in the UK, is that there is no concept of a fraction of a share and therefore the existing approved share schemes have been unable to accommodate such arrangements.

Reporting of share-related benefits

Q23. What are the time limits for an employer to report share-related benefits to the Inland Revenue? Could the time limits for reporting share-related benefits be aligned with the P11D return deadlines?

A. The time limits for notification are explained in booklet IR16. In summary they are—

Approved schemes—30 days from the date of the notice issued by the Board (paragraph 6 Schedule 9 TA 1988).

Other awards, including unapproved schemes—Generally these are 30 days from the end of the tax year in which the acquisition of the shares, interest in shares, grant of option or conversion occurs (S136(6) and 140G TA 1988 and S85(1) FA 1988).

Chargeable events and special benefits—60 days after the date of the event for those amounts chargeable under ss 78 and 80 FA 1988 (S85(2) FA 1988).

We do not consider that changing to the P11D reporting timetable would be appropriate because of the nature of the information, and the different way in which it is dealt with in the Revenue.

General guidance on share and share option schemes is available in leaflets in the IR series. We also provide guidance and news of current developments on our website at www.inlandrevenue.gov.uk/shareschemes.

11 April 2000. Inland Revenue

Electronic commerce—tax status of websites and servers

The UK today set out its views on the tax status of websites and servers.

Speaking at a conference in Lisbon, the director of the Inland Revenue's international division, Gabs Makhlouf, said—

> "The OECD has been reviewing with the business community the long term future of the 'permanent establishment' concept—the threshold in the OECD's model tax treaty below which a country will not tax non-residents carrying on a business in that country. This is crucial work.

And it is important that it is carried out with due consideration, and in partnership between representatives of Government and business.

'Permanent establishment' is a long standing concept. It is tried and tested. And it is widely supported. As yet, we do not know enough about how e-commerce will develop for anyone to make reasoned decisions on whether or not to move away from it. But now is clearly the time for the debate to begin.

In the meantime, early decisions are needed on the status of websites and servers under the existing rules of permanent establishment. Businesses need to know where they stand in order to make investment decisions and calculate their tax liabilities.

A particularly important policy objective is that the outcome is a practical one. One that works in the real world as well in the heads of lawyers. Governments and businesses need an outcome that allows e-commerce to flourish, that keeps down compliance costs, and that is enforceable.

In the UK, we take the view that a website of itself is not a permanent establishment. And we take the view that a server is insufficient of itself to constitute a permanent establishment of a business that is conducting e-commerce through a website on the server. We take that view regardless of whether the server is owned, rented or otherwise at the disposal of the business."

NOTES

1 The Government's goal is for the UK to be the best environment in the world in which to trade electronically by 2002.

2 The Inland Revenue and Customs & Excise published on 26 November 1999 a comprehensive review of the tax issues concerning e-commerce "Electronic commerce—the UK's taxation agenda". Chapter 8 highlighted a number of outstanding issues to do with the application of international tax rules to e-commerce, including the application of the permanent establishment concept in double taxation treaties.

3 Under the OECD's model tax treaty, a non-resident business is only taxable in a foreign country to the extent that it is carrying on business there through a permanent establishment. A permanent establishment is defined as being "a fixed place of business through which the business of an enterprise is wholly or partly carried on".

4 The OECD published a second draft of a consultation note clarifying the position on the status of websites and servers. It concerns the legal interpretation of the existing art 5 of the model treaty and records that there are differing views among OECD member countries on whether a server may be a permanent establishment. It is available on the OECD's website at http://www.oecd.org/daf/fa/treaties/art5rev_3March.pdf.

Commentary—*Simon's Direct Tax Service* **F1.206**.

19 April 2000. Inland Revenue

Pension sharing on divorce to begin 1 December 2000

Following the Government's decision that pension sharing will be available in respect of divorce and marriage annulment proceedings that begin on or after 1 December 2000, the Inland Revenue have laid Regulations today to bring into effect the pension sharing provisions contained in FA 1999.

From the first appointed day any retirement benefit scheme seeking tax approval (or continued approval in the case of an approved scheme that is being amended) must include the pension sharing provisions in their rules.

Copies of the regulations will be available shortly from the Stationery Office. They will be available on the Inland Revenue website at www.inlandrevenue.gov.uk.

DETAILS

1. FA 1999 included provisions amending the pensions scheme tax approval rules to enable pension sharing to be introduced. The main changes to the pension scheme tax approval rules are to—

- ease the current restriction on the assignment or surrender of benefits so that pension rights can be shared;
- set out the effect of pension sharing on the maximum benefits a tax approved pension scheme can give to a scheme member; and
- specify the form and timing of benefits that a tax approved pension scheme can give to a former spouse of a scheme member following a pension share.

These changes to the tax approval pension scheme rules will, in general, come into force at the same time as the Welfare Reform and Pensions Act provisions have effect.

2. The following regulations have now been made to complement the provisions of FA 1999.

The Finance Act 1999, Schedule 10, Paragraph 18, (First and Second Appointed Days) Order, SI 2000/1093

This Order announces that from 10 May 2000, the first appointed day, the approval or continued approval of a retirement benefit scheme is dependant on the inclusion of the provisions contained in FA 1999 Sch 10 paras 2, 3(*b*) and that pension sharing will come into force throughout the UK on 1 December 2000.

The Retirements Benefits Schemes (Restriction on Discretion to Approve) (Small Self-administered Schemes) (Amendment) Regulations, SI 2000/1086

These Regulations make changes to the tax rules for small self-administered pension schemes. These are occupational pension schemes that generally have less than 12 members. The regulations ensure that the special rules for schemes of this type will still apply when an ex-spouse becomes a scheme member because of a pension share.

The Retirements Benefits Schemes (Restriction on Discretion to Approve) (Additional Voluntary Contributions) (Amendment) Regulations, SI 2000/1088

These Regulations will ensure that, subject to an easement offered to scheme members on moderate earnings (defined as someone earning less than $\frac{1}{4}$ of the earnings cap, currently £22,950 per annum), a pension share does not affect the calculation of the maximum benefits that a tax approved occupational pension scheme can pay to an ex-spouse who pays additional voluntary contributions.

The Retirements Benefits Schemes (Restriction on Discretion to Approve) (Excepted Provisions) Regulations, SI 2000/1087

These Regulations are consequential to the preceding two sets of regulations. They disapply a feature of tax approval legislation that would require existing approved pension schemes to amend their rules within three years if they are not to lose automatically their tax approval status. (For existing tax approved schemes, FA 1999 included provisions, which overrode the trust deeds and rules, and so this three year time limit is not relevant.)

The Retirements Benefits Schemes (Sharing of Pensions on Divorce or Annulment) Regulations, SI 2000/1085

These Regulations will in certain circumstances modify the effect of FA 1999 Sch 10 para 18(5) which overrides the rules of all retirement benefit schemes approved before the first appointed day and which continue to be approved on or after 1 December 2000. In particular it will allow scheme members on moderate earnings (currently defined as £22,950 per annum) to rebuild some or all of their lost pension rights.

NOTES

1. Since the 1970s, courts have been able to take account of the value of pension rights in divorce and nullity of marriage settlements so that these can be offset against other assets in financial settlements. Additions in the Pensions Act 1995 to existing earmarking provisions allow courts—

– in England and Wales (and Northern Ireland under a separate order), to require occupational and personal pension schemes to pay maintenance from a member's pension to their former spouse;
– throughout the UK to order part or all of a lump sum payable on the death or retirement of a member to be directed to their former spouse.

2. Earmarking has limitations and as yet has been little used. It does not allow a clean break in most cases; title to the pension rights remains with the spouse in whose name the rights have accrued. It also leaves the person receiving the payment at risk of losing the intended retirement income if their former spouse dies or defers retirement.

3. The Government's manifesto included a commitment to implement pension sharing. Pension sharing provisions were included in FA 1999 Sch 10, which received Royal Assent on 27 July 1999 and the Welfare Reform and Pensions Act 1999, which received Royal Assent on 11 November 1999.

4. Draft regulations consequent on the provisions of FA 1999 were set out in consultative documents issued to pension scheme representative bodies and others on 15 December 1999 and 26 January 2000. The Government is grateful to all those who have provided comments on those draft regulations. The regulations that have now been made take account of comments received to the consultative process.

Commentary—*Simon's Direct Tax Service* **Division E7.1**.

31 May 2000. Inland Revenue

Inland Revenue helps to launch voluntary tax savings scheme for share fishermen

Share fishermen in England, Wales and Northern Ireland are being helped to save money towards their tax bills. The Inland Revenue have helped the fishing industry launch a special voluntary savings scheme with Barclays Bank.

Fishermen can now decide to have money deducted from their earnings and paid directly into a special, interest bearing account with Barclays. That money will be used to pay their tax and Class 4 national insurance liability. Fishermen will still have to pay their Class 2 national insurance contributions separately, a weekly amount of £2·65 (reduced from £7·20 from 6 April 2000).

Dawn Primarolo, the Paymaster General said—

> ''This excellent scheme will give share fishermen the security of knowing that their tax and NI bills are provided for when they are away at sea. The Inland Revenue want to make it easier for all taxpayers to meet their obligations, and this scheme will help share fishermen do that. A special helpline—0845 0789 789—has been set up to provide advice and answer any queries from those wishing to take part.''

Barry Deas of the National Federation of Fishermen's Organisations said—

> ''We wanted to provide fishermen with the opportunity to prepare in advance for their tax bills. Because they are away at sea so often it is difficult for them to contact the Inland Revenue and it is often their families that have to speak to the taxman. Using the scheme, they will be kept up to date with their tax affairs and know that they are well prepared to pay their tax and NI bills.''

This scheme is similar to one that has been working successfully in Scotland for about ten years, involving 98% of Scottish share fishermen.

DETAILS

1. The Inland Revenue are pleased to launch this new scheme at the request of the fishing industry. The launch follows detailed consultation with the National Federation of Fishermen's Organisations and representatives of a highly successful similar scheme in Scotland.

2. Share fishermen work in the fishing industry and are paid from a share of the profits of their boat.

"Sea-going" share fishermen

– normally work as a master or crew member of a British fishing boat manned by more than one person, and
– are paid some or all wages from a share of the boat's profits or earnings.

"On-shore" share fishermen

– used to work as above, but have stopped due to age or infirmity, and
– now normally work ashore, for example, making or mending gear for a British fishing boat, and
– are paid some or all wages from a share of the boat's profits or earnings.

3. The money paid into the special Barclays account will be used solely to pay tax and Class 4 national insurance contributions. Money can not be withdrawn from this account.

4. Twice a year some or all of this money will be transferred from the Barclays account to the Inland Revenue to pay income tax, Class 4 national insurance contributions and any capital gains tax liability, including arrears.

5. By the middle of January and July each year, before any money is transferred, the Inland Revenue will issue statements of liability to fishermen in the scheme. These will set out what is owed. Shortly thereafter Barclays will issue a statement showing amounts being transferred.

6. Fishermen remain responsible for their tax and national insurance and for either paying any balance due or claiming a refund. If refunds are not claimed any excess money paid will be retained by the Inland Revenue to set against any future liabilities incurred.

7. As this is a new scheme for the tax year 2000–01 the first transfer from accounts will be made in January 2001. Fishermen must still complete and send in their 1999–00 self-assessment returns. If people return their self-assessment forms by the end of September the Inland Revenue will calculate their tax liability for them and will be able to include the correct amount owed on those people's statements; otherwise an estimated payment amount will be transferred from the Barclays account in January.

8. At July 2000 fishermen should still make arrangements to pay the second instalment of their 1999–00 tax in the normal way. Any balance in the account after the January 2001 transfer will be available to set against any arrears.

9. Share fishermen are under no obligation to join the new scheme—membership is entirely voluntary. Fishermen who decide not to join will be required to pay tax and Class 4 NICs as normal, when payment falls due.

1.0. The Inland Revenue have opened the fishing industry unit at Paignton District to help administer the scheme. Fishermen and settling agents can contact them at Fishing Industry Unit, Concord House, 266–268 Torquay Road, Paignton, Devon TQ3 2HG; telephone 01803 697700.

1.1. There is also a special helpline—0845 0789789. Calls will be charged at 1·9p per minute from anywhere in the UK.

1.2. National fishing representative bodies and all settling agents know about the scheme; they should also be able to give advice and answer fishermen's queries.

Commentary—*Simon's Direct Tax Service* **E1.820**.

June 2000. IR Tax Bulletin Issue 47

Provision of personal services through intermediaries—frequently asked questions

The new rules which apply to workers who supply their services to clients through intermediaries such as service companies or partnerships came into effect on 6 April 2000. Details about how to decide when the new rules apply were published in Tax Bulletin Issue 45 (February 2000) [see above].

All our published information about this measure has been included on our website at—www.inlandrevenue.gov.uk/ir35, but some of the more frequently asked questions are being duplicated here for ease of reference.

Further information can also be obtained from our new leaflet, IR175 'Supplying services through a limited company or partnership', available from Inland Revenue Enquiry Centres, Tax Offices, Inland Revenue National Insurance Contribution Offices, or our website.

GENERAL QUESTIONS

What is IR 35 about?

Budget day 1999 press release IR35 announced the Chancellor's intention to tackle tax and NICs avoidance through the use of intermediaries such as service companies or partnerships.

Intermediaries such as service companies can be set up to provide the services of a single worker to a client in circumstances where, if it were not for the service company, the worker would be an employee of the client. The use of service companies in this way allows the client to make payments to the company rather than the individual, without deducting PAYE or NICs.

The worker can then take the money out of the service company in the form of dividends instead of salary. Dividends are not liable to NICs so the worker will pay less in NICs than either a conventional employee or a self-employed person.

The Chancellor believes that avoidance of PAYE and NICs in this way needs to be tackled in the interests of fairness.

Who will be affected by the proposals?

Anyone supplying their services through an intermediary such as a service company or partnership will need to think about the new rules.

But only those contracts which would have been contracts of employment with the client if the worker had worked directly to them instead of through an intermediary will be affected.

The most usual sorts of intermediary are service companies or partnerships which are normally under the control of the worker. The worker can then take the money out of the service company in the form of dividends instead of salary. Dividends are not liable to NICs so the worker will pay less in NICs than either a conventional employee or a self-employed person.

If there is more than one intermediary between the client and the worker, any intermediary which makes payments direct to the worker may be affected. However, the intermediary with the direct link with the worker will normally be the intermediary responsible for complying with the legislation.

Individuals not in business and contracting with an intermediary on a personal basis (eg a householder engaging a plumber to fix the kitchen sink) will be specifically excluded from these new rules.

Please see Inland Revenue Press Release of 23/9/99 for further details.

How are 'service companies' defined?

The legislation may affect any kind of intermediary so no particular intermediary will be defined in the legislation.

What are the existing rules used to determine the boundary between employment and self-employment (the 'D/E tests')?

The rules are based on a long history of case law. The same rules apply for both tax and NICs purposes. An overview of those rules is available in the Inland Revenue February 2000 Tax Bulletin.

PRs etc

Some professions (eg nurses working through nursing banks) have case law to define their employment status, but the IT and engineering industries have none.

Case law on employment status does not apply only in the industries where particular cases have been taken—it establishes principles which apply in all industries. Those principles are applied in every case, to nurses in the same way as to IT professionals. So a nurse has no more certainty, and no less, than any other worker. The principles are explained in the Tax Bulletin Issue 45 (February 2000).

In deciding whether I would have been an employee of my client, will you only look at the contract I have signed, or the contract between the client and an agency?

The Inland Revenue will take account of all relevant contracts in order to discover whether the relationship between a worker and a client would have been one of employment, if there had been no intermediary. This would include any contracts between the client and an agency, and between the agency and the worker's service company.

How will the Revenue determine the facts after the contract has finished? Will you go back and look at past contracts?

The Revenue will review the facts in the same way as it does for all employment status work. This will include going back and looking at past contracts if appropriate.

You say the Revenue will give an opinion on signed contracts but I do not have a written contract as the terms were agreed orally. What supporting documentation do I need to provide in order to receive an opinion from the Revenue?

You will need to provide whatever supporting evidence you consider will be helpful in demonstrating the terms and conditions under which you work. You should write to the Inland Revenue, in accordance with the existing guidance on obtaining opinions on contracts, setting out full details of the terms and conditions, which you have agreed with the client and the services which you are providing.

You should also obtain a letter from the client confirming that the terms and conditions are as agreed. If necessary the Inspector may need to speak to both you and your client in order to properly understand the working arrangements and to formulate an opinion on the contract.

I hear that the Revenue have approved a model contract—how could this happen if each case is decided on its merits?

The Inland Revenue has not approved a model contract.

A version of a model contract was sent to us for an opinion, according to the arrangements for giving advice on existing contracts announced in the Inland Revenue Press Notice on 7 February. An opinion was then given in relation to one person's particular circumstances.

Although we are unable to comment on the circumstances of individual cases we should confirm that a decision on employment status will depend on the circumstances of each case. We can also confirm that new rules will not apply in cases where the relationship with the client does not fall within the accepted definition of employment.

My contract specifies that I am allowed to hire a substitute. Will the Inland Revenue take this at face value? If not will I need to provide evidence to prove that this right is genuine?

The Inland Revenue will want to ensure that the right to send a substitute is a genuine right before it can be taken into account in deciding employment status.

A right of substitution is only likely to exist where the client does not mind, from one day to the next for the duration of the contract, who carries out the work, provided that whoever does so is suitably qualified and experienced.

Where the service company's contract is not with the client but with an agency, and there is a claimed right of substitution, the Inland Revenue would normally require a copy of the written contract between the agency and the client.

If you are unable to get access to that contract then you should ask the agency to send a copy to the Inland Revenue direct. If this is not possible you may be asked to provide alternative evidence. This could take the form of a letter from the client which confirms that it has agreed to your service company providing a substitute.

What will happen if someone fails to follow the new rules?

Where the Inland Revenue discover the new rules have not been followed, they will follow the normal approach to cases of PAYE/NICs failure set out in Inland Revenue leaflet IR 109—'Employer compliance reviews and negotiations'. The Revenue will seek to collect any unpaid tax or NICs, and any interest due. In addition penalties may be sought in cases of negligent or fraudulent conduct.

If I work through my own service company on 'relevant' engagements will my client have to provide me with employment rights such as sick pay, holiday pay etc?

No. Under this legislation, the client will not become your employer. What the legislation does is to treat your service company as making a payment to you chargeable to income tax under Schedule E and on which national insurance contributions are payable. All employer responsibilities fall on the service company as they have always done.

If I work through my own service company on relevant engagements will I be entitled to unemployment benefit?

People who work through their own service companies are unable to claim benefits between contracts if they are still employees of their own service companies.

Individuals who are no longer employed by their service company may claim benefits on the same basis as any other employee.

Why do I have to pay both employer's and employee's NICs when a conventional employee does not have to?

Service companies are already liable to pay employer's NICs on salary paid to their employees. The legislation does not change that.

A service company and its worker/director are two separate legal entities with separate legal responsibilities. Where the worker is employed by the service company the employer responsibilities rest with the service company and not the client. This is why the service company's client does not have to pay employer's NIC on the payment it makes for the worker's services and the service company does.

If my company is incorporated or resident abroad will the rules affect me?

If you would have been treated as an employee of the client had you provided services under a contract between yourself and that client, rather than under a contract between your company and the client, then the rules will apply to you wherever your company is incorporated or resident.

Can I avoid the legislation by using an offshore service company?

No. If you would have been liable to UK tax and NICs if you had been employed directly by the client, there will be a liability for UK tax and NICs under the new legislation, whether or not your service company is located in the UK.

If an offshore service company fails to deduct and account for PAYE tax and NICs due under the legislation, liability to pay tax and NICs can be transferred to the worker. Action to recover employer's NICs not paid by an offshore service company could also include action against any assets of that company located in the UK.

The Inland Revenue has powers to obtain details of payments to offshore companies from the records of clients and agencies.

COMPUTATIONAL QUESTIONS

When will the first 'deemed' payments have to be calculated?

For an ongoing business it is likely that the first deemed payments will have to be calculated by 5 April 2001.

If a business ceases before that date a deemed payment may need to be calculated sooner.

Does the service company have to pay a salary on 5 April?

No. The legislation will not force the service company to pay salary at any time. It will require a calculation of tax and NICs to be done on 5 April. If the service company has already paid enough salary to the worker during the year, no further tax or NICs will be payable on 5 April.

Nothing in the legislation will prevent a service company from paying money to the worker or others in the form of dividends, or retaining cash in the company. It will simply mean that an extra payment of PAYE tax and NICs will be calculated on 5 April. To calculate that payment an amount of salary will be deemed to have been paid on that date, whether or not any payment is actually made.

What happens if I cannot calculate the tax and NICs due on 5 April in time to pay it to the Inland Revenue by the normal date of 19 April?

Most of the information needed to calculate the deemed payment should be available before 5 April, and it should be possible to make a good estimate of the tax and NICs due at that point. It will be important to keep records of relevant income and expenditure so that you can do this.

If you are not able to calculate the amount of tax and NICs due on the deemed payment by 19 April, we will accept a payment at that date of a lower amount on account of the tax and NICs due, as long as the Revenue is notified on the Employer's Annual Return that the amount is provisional. This should mean that the worker need not necessarily consult his accountant before making the payment on 19 April.

You should submit your Employer's Annual Return (Form P35) by 19 May. If you are able at that time to finalise the calculation, you should show the correct figure and pay the difference or request a repayment. Otherwise, you should make it clear that the figure is still provisional.

You should seek to finalise matters as soon as possible thereafter, and send in a supplementary return with a final payment, or request for repayment.

Interest will be charged, calculated from 19 April when the original payment was due, but no penalties will be sought for late filing if—

(i) an Employer's Annual Return is received by 19 May, showing remuneration paid during the year, plus an amount on account of the deemed payment, with tax and NICs correctly calculated on the aggregate figure, and,

(ii) a supplementary return including the correct final figure for the deemed payment is sent in to the Revenue by 31 January following the end of the tax year.

What is the position where, in addition to making payments to the limited company/agency, a client makes payments to or in respect of the consultant direct? For example, where the client reimburses travelling expenses to the consultant direct? Could the client be held liable for PAYE?

If a client makes payments to a worker in connection with duties being performed, either for direct reward, as a round sum expense allowance, or a specific reimbursement of travel which was not business travel, and the worker is an employee of another, the payments are assessable on the worker and the client should deduct tax through PAYE from payments to the worker. If a client provides non-cash benefits in connection with the employment these are also assessable on the worker. If the client makes payments of this kind to a worker in respect of a contract with a partnership, the client will not have to operate PAYE, but the amounts should be included in the calculation of the deemed payment.

QUESTIONS ABOUT EXPENSES

Will travel expenses be allowed?

The rules that currently apply to employees of service companies which allow them to claim a deduction for travel from their home to place of work will be used to determine the travel expenses that can be deducted in calculating the salary on which tax and NICs must be paid. For example—

- a computer contractor provides his or her services through a limited company (which he or she owns);
- he or she has a series of contracts with different clients around the country;
- he or she regularly travels from home to work at the premises of the company's clients.

Provided the contractor does not expect to spend more than 40% of his or her working time at any one site he or she is entitled to a deduction for all journeys from home to the client's premises. If he or she does spend more than 40% of his time at a single site, but the engagement is both expected to, and actually does, last for no more than 2 years, a deduction for travel costs will also be available. The examples set out in Tax Bulletin Issue 33 (February 1998), along with the more extensive coverage provided in Booklet 490 (Employee Travel, A Tax and NIC's Guide for Employers), provide further guidance on the application of the travel rules.

Workers cannot obtain relief for their travel and subsistence where the period at the temporary workplace comprises 'all or almost all of the period for which the employee is likely to hold the employment'. There have been concerns that this rule will be used to prevent the personal service company worker obtaining tax relief. However, the 'employment' of the worker is with his or her Personal Service Company, not with the client; the new rules do not change this. They simply deem the income from relevant engagements to be taxable under Schedule E; they do not deem the worker to be an employee of the client.

Thus the 'period for which the worker is likely to hold the employment' refers to employment with the service company, not the engagement with the client. Thus the treatment of travel and subsistence for workers will be no different under the new rules than it is today.

We are grateful to Anne Redston of the CIOT for suggesting amendments to this answer to make it clearer.

How will company car expenses be treated?

In calculating the deemed payment on which PAYE tax and NICs must be paid, expenses which would be allowable under section 198 TA 1988 can be deducted. This will include travelling expenses, and if a car owned by the company is used for business travel then a deduction can be made for the costs of that business travel in the same way as if the worker had used his own car. For example, it would be possible to use the Inland Revenue's authorised mileage rates, which include an element for depreciation. Expenses incurred in the course of private use of the car cannot be deducted in calculating the deemed payment.

A car provided by the service company for the worker's private use will give rise to a car benefit charge on which the worker will be taxed in the normal way. The amount of the car benefit charge can be deducted in calculating the deemed payment.

The service company will be able to set any costs of providing the car, including capital allowances, against its taxable profits.

Class 1A NICs paid on the company car benefit will be deductible in the calculation of the deemed payment, alongside other employer's NICs.

What sort of capital allowances can be deducted when working out the deemed payment?

A deduction will only be given for capital allowances in working out the deemed payment where the plant or machinery is necessarily provided for use in the performance of the duties of the relevant engagement. This is a strict test and means that relief will only be given where the duties of the engagement meant that the company had to provide the equipment in question. If the company purchases the equipment out of choice then no deduction will be given. For example, where an IT contractor is required to use the client's computer equipment then no relief will be due for expenditure on computers owned by the service company. Neither will any relief be due where the client makes all the equipment necessary to do a job available but the worker uses his or her own computers, out of choice.

Where cars are concerned the test is less rigorous since there is no "necessarily" test. As an alternative to claiming capital allowances relief will be given using the Inland Revenue Authorised Mileage Rates.

Where during the tax year there is mixed qualifying and non-qualifying use then any capital allowance claim should be apportioned on a just and reasonable basis. Apportionment is normally by reference to the actual use in the year. Non-qualifying use would be where the asset in question is used for private use, on contracts not covered by the IR35 rules and on IR35 contracts where the Schedule E rules are not satisfied.

How do I apportion expenses between engagements that are affected by the new rules and those which are not?

Where an engagement falls within the new rules the proposed legislation will allow for two types of deduction to be made in calculating the salary on which tax and NICs must be paid.

First, a deduction may be given for expenses paid by the service company which you would have been allowed to claim, under the normal Schedule E rules, had you paid them as part of an employment. These are, broadly, certain travel expenses, other expenses wholly, exclusively and necessarily incurred in the performance of the duties of the relevant engagement; and certain specific items such as some professional subscriptions and premiums for professional indemnity insurance. You will need to keep records to identify expenses which qualify. More details are in Inland Revenue booklets 480 (Expenses and Benefits, Guide Tax Guide) and 490 (Employee Travel, A Tax and NIC's Guide for Employers).

Secondly, the company will also be allowed to deduct a flat rate amount of 5% of receipts from relevant engagements, in calculating the minimum salary on which tax and NICs must be paid. This will be allowed automatically, and need not be set against specific expenses.

How do I apportion the expenses when working out the deemed payment where a contract straddles the end of the tax year?

When working out the deemed payment, relief should be given for all allowable expenses met by the intermediary in the tax year, in respect of relevant engagements, as set out at Step 3. Relief for the expense should be given by reference to the date when the intermediary meets the liability. This is the date when the bill is paid. There should therefore be no need to apportion any expenses.

For example, an intermediary has a relevant engagement that runs from 1 January to 30 June 2001, during which the worker is required to work at a temporary workplace. In the course of this engagement the worker stays in bed and breakfast accommodation. The bill is settled on a monthly basis in arrears, with 14 days to pay. At the end of March a bill for £400 is issued which the intermediary pays on 12 April. The liability was met in the tax year 2001-2002. Therefore, relief for the expense will be given when working out the deemed payment payable.

Service company workers will be worse off than ordinary employees under the legislation because they will only be able to claim 5% of their expenses.

This is not correct. Service companies will be able to claim a flat rate deduction of 5% of the gross fees receivable for any relevant engagements. This 5% deduction is not available to employees but will be allowed for service companies to enable them to meet the additional costs of providing their services in this particular way.

In calculating the salary on which they are obliged to deduct Schedule E tax and NICs, workers will also be able to deduct all expenses that would normally be available to direct employees.

What sort of expenses will be covered by the 5%?

There is no restriction on the use of the allowance. There will be no requirement to demonstrate expenditure—the 5% deduction will be allowed in all cases.

EXAMPLE CALCULATION

What tax and NICs liabilities arise (tax year 2000–01)?

Mr and Mrs A work through a service company in which they own all the shares. They each carry out some engagements during the year which fall within the new rules ('relevant engagements') and some which do not.

Assume the service company receives £20,000 in respect of relevant engagements for Mr A and £40,000 in respect of relevant engagements for Mrs A and that there is a further £40,000 income from other business activities which do not fall within the new rules.

Assume the service company also incurs the following expenses during the course of the year:

Expense	*Mr A*	*Mrs A*	*Notes*
Salaries	£20,000	£20,000	Paid in year. PAYE and NICs deducted and accounted for under normal provisions.
Employer's NICs	£1,905	£1,905	Paid in year. NICs calculated on an annual earnings period, as for directors. Assumes that the employer's threshold (£4,385) has been set against these earnings, and 12.2% paid on remainder.
Employer's pension contributions	£4,000	£4,000	To an approved scheme.
Travel costs related to relevant engagements	£2,000	£500	All would be deductible under normal provisions relating to employees.
Other expenses	£10,000 business expenses, all allowable for Corporation Tax purposes.		
Under the new proposals, at the end of the tax year, the service company will have to calculate the amount of PAYE and NICs due on Mr and Mrs A's earnings. If they have not paid enough PAYE and NICs during the year, then PAYE and NICs will be payable on a 'deemed payment' on the last day of the tax year.			

Calculation of deemed payment

	Mr A	*Mrs A*
Income from relevant contracts	20,000	40,000
Less		
Expenses	2,000	500
Employer's NICs paid in year	1,905	1,905
Pension contributions	4,000	4,000
Flat rate 5% of gross relevant contract income, for general running expenses of intermediary	1,000	2,000
	11,095	31,595
Deduct		
Salary paid in year	20,000	20,000
	No deemed payment	11,595
Employer's NICs on deemed payment		1,261
Deemed payment		**10,334**

Company accounts

	Mr A	*Mrs A*
Turnover		100,000
Less		
Salaries	40,000	
Employer's NICs on salaries	3,810	
Pension contributions	8,000	
Expenses	12,500	
		64,310
Accounting Profit		35,690
Deemed Payment	10,334	
Employer's NICs on dp	1,261	
		11,595
Profits for Corporation Tax purposes		24,095

Summary

Mr A brought in £20,000 from relevant contracts during the course of the year. The service company paid the whole of that amount onto him in salary and deducted and accounted for full PAYE and NICs. No further action is required.

Mrs A brought in £40,000 from relevant contracts during the course of the year and the service company paid £20 000 onto her in salary and deducted and accounted for PAYE and NICs on that salary. This left £20,000 from her relevant contracts on which PAYE and NICs were not been deducted and accounted for during the course of the year. Under the new rules this £20 000, less the deductions allowed, will be deemed to be paid to Mrs A as salary at the year end (on 5 April).

August 2000. IR Tax Bulletin Issue 48

Amending an Income Tax Self Assessment (ITSA) after an enquiry—TMA 1970, ss 28A and 28B

The Special Commissioners' decisions in ''*Holly and Laurel*'' (SpC 225) and ''*Self Assessed*'' (SpC 207) related to notices opening an enquiry and notices requiring the production of documents and particulars. Both involved the application of time limits. It is clear from those decisions that we must use the test of receipt when we operate ITSA time limits.

We sought specific legal advice about the two 30-day time limits in S28A and S28B. Detailed guidance has been issued to our staff. This article explains our view of how S28A and S28B operate. It will refer to S28A (individuals) but applies equally to S28B (partnerships).

SECTION 28A(5)

- S28A(5) says that an enquiry is completed when we inform the taxpayer, by notice, that our enquiries are complete and of the amount of tax we believe should be contained in the self assessment.
- Our view is that *the day of completion* is the day the taxpayer receives this notice.
- If we hand the notice to the taxpayer that is the day of completion.
- If we have evidence of the day on which the notice was received through the post then that is the day of completion.
- In other cases (applying S7 of the Interpretation Act 1978) we shall assume that a notice is received 2 working days after being posted first class and 4 working days after being posted second class.

SECTION 28A(3)

- This gives the taxpayer 30 days from the day of completion (see above) in which to amend their self assessment.
- The amendment must be *received* by the Revenue within those 30 days.
- The 30 days start on the day of completion and end 29 days later.
- For example, where we calculate that the day of completion is Monday 16 October, this is day 1 of the taxpayer's 30-day period.
- Day 30 is Tuesday 14 November.
- If we receive a taxpayer's amendment on 15 November it is not valid.

SECTION 28A(4)

- S28A(4) allows the Revenue to amend the self assessment in the 30-day period immediately following the first 30-day period.

- Where we do not receive any amendment, or we disagree with an amendment made in time, or we receive a taxpayer's amendment too late, we will issue a Revenue amendment.
- If we use the same example as above, day 1 of this period is Wednesday 15 November.
- Day 30 is Thursday 14 December.
- Our amendment has to reach the taxpayer within that 30-day period to be valid.

8 August 2000. Inland Revenue

Recognised stock exchanges overseas

The phrase ''recognised stock exchange'' occurs throughout the Taxes Acts and in various tax regulations. For example it is used in the definition of a close company in TA 1988 s 415, and in the definition of investments which may be held in PEPs and ISAs.

The definition of a recognised stock exchange is at TA 1988 s 841. It includes the London Stock Exchange and any such stock exchange outside the UK as is approved by an Order of the Board of the Inland Revenue.

The current list of recognised stock exchanges is set out below.

The Board's policy is to consider recognition on receipt of a request made by an overseas stock exchange. So, the fact that a particular exchange is not recognised may simply mean that recognition has not been requested.

Note—Recognition under TA 1988 s 841 is for tax purposes only—it does not imply recognition or approval for regulatory or other purposes.

LIST OF STOCK EXCHANGES DESIGNATED AS "RECOGNISED STOCK EXCHANGES" BY ORDER OF THE BOARD UNDER TA 1988 S 841(1)(*B*) AS AT CURRENT DATE; AND DATE OF RECOGNITION

[Not reproduced: see the current list of recognised stock exchanges in the *Miscellaneous* section, post.]

Commentary—*Simon's Direct Tax Service* **A1.160**.

25 September 2000. Inland Revenue

Venture capital schemes and enterprise management incentives—new centralised service for small companies

A new centralised service for companies using the enterprise investment scheme, the venture capital trust scheme and enterprise management incentives becomes operational today.

A single point of contact, supported by four specialist offices, will streamline the handling of enquiries from companies newly raising money under the venture capital schemes, or granting options under enterprise management incentives.

The specialist offices will also deal with the corporation tax affairs of these companies and also those companies using the new corporate venturing scheme.

This initiative will support companies using the new enterprise management incentives and will improve the service to those raising finance under the venture capital schemes.

DETAILS

1 From today all enquiries about whether a small company meets the requirements of the enterprise investment scheme (EIS), the venture capital trust (VCT) scheme and enterprise management incentives (EMI) should be directed to—Small Company Enterprise Centre, TIDO, Ty Glas, Llanishen, Cardiff CF14 5ZG; telephone 029 2032 7400; fax 029 2032 7398; email enterprise.centre@ir.gsi.gov.uk.

2 All new work on the companies using these tax incentives will be dealt with at four specialist units which become operational from today. These are located in Cardiff, Maidstone, Middlesborough and Dundee.

3 The small company enterprise centre will deal with—

- enquiries from companies about whether they meet the conditions of the EIS, VCT scheme and EMI;
- requests from companies for informal advance clearance that they will meet the requirements of the EIS or the VCT scheme;
- checking whether EMI options meet the qualifying requirements, monitoring to ensure that the options continue to qualify, and controlling the issue and review of EMI returns;
- the corporation tax liability of companies using the EIS, VCT scheme, CVS and EMI and the monitoring of these companies during the qualifying period applicable to the relevant scheme.

4 The small company enterprise centre will not deal with—

- companies which have raised money under the EIS or VCT scheme in the past (unless that company raises further funds under either of those schemes or CVS in the future);
- investors in the EIS, VCTs or CVS or individuals holding options under EMI;
- statutory advance clearances and compliance statements under the corporate venturing scheme. (These will be dealt with by the corporate venturing unit);
- the approval and corporation tax affairs of venture capital trusts themselves—these matters will continue to be dealt with by the financial intermediaries and claims office (FICO).

NOTES

1 The enterprise investment scheme (EIS) provides a range of tax reliefs for investors to subscribe for new ordinary shares in small unquoted higher risk trading companies including income tax relief at 20% on investments up to £150,000 per tax year.

2 The venture capital trust (VCT) scheme offers similar reliefs to individuals investing up to £100,000 per tax year in VCTs, which are quoted companies that invest in the same sort of small companies as can qualify under the EIS.

3 The corporate venturing scheme (CVS) provides for corporation tax relief at 20% and other tax incentives to encourage companies to invest in the same sorts of small companies and to form wider corporate venturing relationships with those companies. The scheme applies to shares issued on or after 1 April 2000 and before 1 April 2010. A statutory advance clearance is available to companies using the scheme to obtain investment. Details of how to apply for clearance were published in a statement of practice attached to Press Release 133. Enquiries can be addressed to the Corporate Venturing Unit, Somerset House, Strand, London WC2R 1LB; telephone 020 7438 4485.

4 Enterprise management incentives (EMI) help small independent higher-risk trading companies to recruit and retain key employees. They will be able to reward up to 15 key employees with tax-advantaged share options, each employee receiving options worth up to £100,000 at the time of grant. Companies have been able to offer their employees EMI options since 28 July 2000.

5 The purpose of all these tax incentives is to foster growth in small higher-risk trading companies.

6 Work on the EIS and the VCT scheme of the kind which is to be dealt with by the small company enterprise centre has previously been done in local tax offices throughout the country.

Commentary—*Simon's Direct Tax Service* **Division E3.6, E3.1, U6.6822, U6.6823**.

October 2000. Tax Bulletin, Issue 49

Schedule E benefits in kind—calculating the cash equivalent of a benefit when there is part business use and part private use

This article deals with benefits in kind chargeable under the general benefits rules in Section 154 Income and Corporation Taxes Act (ICTA) 1988, for which the cash equivalent is calculated under Section 156. It sets out the Revenue's views—

- on how the extension to the workplace benefit exemption, contained in this year's Finance Act and included in TA 1988 as S155ZA, will operate in practice.
- on the treatment of reimbursements for, and provision of, a telephone at the employee's home.
- about when an apportionment under Section 156(2) is appropriate when there is mixed use of the "benefit", and when a deduction under Section 156(8) is due under the rules for expenses.
- on the circumstances in which the decision of the House of Lords in *Pepper v Hart* applies to "mixed use" benefits.

The views apply equally to Class 1A NICs. Further advice on Class 1A is in the guide, CWG5. The article does not deal with motor cars and vans available for private use, living accommodation, beneficial loans or any of the other benefits for which special rules apply. The reader should consult Booklet 480 about these matters.

EXEMPTION FOR BENEFITS PROVIDED FOR WORK PURPOSES—SECTION 155ZA TA 1988 INTRODUCED BY SCHEDULE 10 OF FA 2000

Since the start of the Schedule E benefits legislation in 1948, there has been an exemption for the benefit

> "in premises occupied by the employer... of accommodation, supplies and services used by the employee solely in performing the duties of the employment."

The need for this exemption demonstrates the scope of Section 154(1), which brings to charge "benefits or facilities of whatsoever nature". Without the exemption desks, chairs, telephones, photocopiers, computers and all the usual office equipment would have to be reported on a P11D with the employee making an expenses claim for work use, or a dispensation sought.

This year's Finance Act extends the exemption to situations where "any use of (the benefit) for private purposes by the employee... is not significant."

Exemption is also allowed for benefits provided other than on the employer's premises provided that private use is not significant and

"the sole purpose of providing the benefit is to enable the employee to perform the duties of his employment."

These changes recognise that employers face practical difficulty in policing the "solely" test, and that working practices have changed since 1948. It is now relatively common for office equipment to be supplied for work use other than on the employer's premises.

"Not significant" private use has not been statutorily defined. It will depend on all the circumstances of the case but an important factor will be the employer's policy for allowing employees to make occasional private use of work items. Employers will not be expected to keep detailed records of every instance of actual use in order to substantiate a claim for exemption. If the employer's policy is—

- clearly stated to the employees and sets out the circumstances in which occasional private use may be made, and
- any policy of the employer not to recover the costs of such private use is a commercial decision because the administrative costs of doing so would exceed the amounts involved, rather than a desire to reward the employee, and
- there are reasonable checks to ensure that the policy is actually followed in practice

then provided that the amount of private use is small compared to work use, we will accept that the test is met.

Some benefits are excluded from the possibility of exemption. These are motor vehicles, boats, aeroplanes and benefits which involve improvements to living accommodation or any structure on land adjacent to and enjoyed with such accommodation. Such benefits must continue to be reported on form P11D whatever the extent of "business" use of the benefit by the recipient. A deduction from the reportable amount, in respect of the use of the benefit by the employee in performing his duties, may be due. If the employee completes a Self Assessment tax return, the deduction should be made on that return.

TELEPHONES

An employer may pay for or provide a telephone line in an employee's home so that the employee may make outgoing and receive incoming calls for work purposes.

EMPLOYER PAYS TOWARDS OR REIMBURSES THE COST OF AN EMPLOYEE'S HOME TELEPHONE.

If the employer pays a cash allowance towards, or reimburses the employee's telephone costs, then the amount paid or reimbursed is chargeable to tax and the employee may get a deduction under the expenses rules for the actual cost of calls made in the course of the duties of the employment. Class 1 NICs are payable on the amount paid by the employer towards the cost of the rental and all private calls.

EMPLOYER IS THE SUBSCRIBER FOR THE TELEPHONE LINE AND RESPONSIBLE FOR PAYING THE TELEPHONE BILL.

If the benefit to the employee of the employer providing the telephone is not exempt from income tax (see below), then the employee is chargeable to tax on the expense incurred by the employer (the cost of the line rental and the cost of all calls) less any sum that the employee may make good to the employer for, say, private use of the telephone. The employee may get a deduction under the expenses rules for the actual cost of calls made in the course of the duties of the employment. Class 1A NICs are payable by the employer on the cost of the line rental, and, unless the cost of private calls are made good by the employee, the cost of the calls.

The benefit of the telephone line will be exempt from tax, and from Class 1A NICs if—

- The employer's **sole purpose** in providing the telephone is to enable the employee to perform their duties, **and**
- the employee's private use of the benefit of the telephone is **not significant**.

The exemption will apply where—

- there is a clear business need for the employer to provide the employee with a telephone, and
- the employer has internal controls to monitor, control and minimise the cost to him/her of private use, and
- the employer has no intention to reward the employee.

Examples where the exemption is likely to apply include cases where an employer provides a telephone line so that employee may make or receive calls which are a vital and central part of the duties of the employment, such as—

- ministers of religion, where there is an imperative need for contact with their parishioners and congregations 24 hours a day.

- teleworkers, where a telephone line at home is provided for remote computer working or telephone business.
- employees such as care workers in residential homes for the elderly, or disabled, or hospices, whose daily duties may require contact with the emergency services or contacting relatives of those they care for.

RELIEF FOR TELEPHONE LINE RENTAL

Section 198 of TA 1988 permits relief for qualifying travelling expenses and for other expenses that are incurred wholly, exclusively and necessarily in carrying out the duties of a person's employment. The decision in *Lucas v Cattell* (48TC353) denied a claim for relief for telephone line rental for a telephone installed in an employee's home where the telephone was available for private use as well as for use in carrying out the duties of the employment.

In practice the Inland Revenue has allowed relief for a proportion of telephone line rental in certain defined circumstances set out in the old SE Manual at SE4331. These are cases in which there is a clear business need to have a telephone available to carry out the duties of the employment, for example where it is genuinely part of someone's duties to deal with emergencies. The extension of TA 1988 s 155ZA, described above, now covers this sort of situation by providing exemption from the benefit charge where an employer provides a telephone line and all the relevant conditions are met. In view of this reform, we intend to discontinue the practice at SE4331. Relief will still be available for the actual cost of business calls.

We recognise that there may be some employees who have organised their affairs on the assumption that the practice at SE4331 would continue to apply. For that reason the practice will not be withdrawn until 5 April 2001.

APPORTIONMENT UNDER SECTION 156(2) AND DEDUCTION UNDER SECTION 156(8)

Section 156(2) of TA 1988 allows for apportionment if the employer's expense in or in connection with providing a benefit for an employee relates partly to the benefit and partly to "other matters". This will apply if, for instance, the asset or service comprising the benefit is used in the employer's business in a way other than as the provision of a benefit for the employee. In deciding whether this is so then, unless the statutory context indicates otherwise (as used to be the case with mobile telephones, where the tax charge related to provision of the phone for private use), provision for use by the employee in performing his or her duties is just as much a benefit within Section 154 as provision for the employee's private use. The employee's avenue of relief for use in performing the duties of employment is by deduction under s 156(8), not apportionment under s 156(2). If there is an "other matter" which calls for a proper apportionment, s 156(2) works by reducing the chargeable cash equivalent of the benefit.

Section 156(8) allows for a deduction, from the chargeable cash equivalent of a benefit, for—

- qualifying travel expenses and other expenses that are incurred wholly, exclusively and necessarily in the course of the duties of the employment (Section 198), and for other matters treated as falling within Section 198 (for instance expenses within Section 193(3))
- professional subscriptions (Section 201)))
- directors' and officers' liabilities (Section 201AA)
- expenses deductible by ministers of religion (Section 332(3)).

Any relief due is given by deduction from the chargeable cash equivalent. Unless such relief has been taken into account in a dispensation (if it fully matches the chargeable benefit) the benefit should be reported by the employer on form P11D. The employee gets relief due under TA 1988 s 156(8) by claiming a deduction, usually on his/her self-assessment tax return.

Class 1A NICs are payable on the chargeable cash equivalent of the benefit before any deduction is made under s 156(8). The one exception to this is if the deduction due under s 156(8) fully matches the chargeable cash equivalent of the benefit. If that is the case no Class 1A is payable, even though the benefit concerned may not have been included in a dispensation.

PEPPER V HART AND MIXED USE BENEFITS

The House of Lords decision in *Pepper v Hart* 65 TC 420 (that the expense of providing a benefit was the marginal additional expense of its provision) was based on the opening words of what is now TA 1988 s 156(2) "the amount of any expense in or in connection with" the provision of a benefit. Our view is that the decision also applies to the similar words in s 156(5)(*b*). So if the employer's sole motive for the purchase and continued ownership of an asset is for use it in its business, other than by provision as a benefit to an employee or employees, and the exemption in s 155ZA does not apply for any reason, the *Pepper v Hart* marginal additional cost principle will apply to "running" expenses within s 156(5)(*b*). The chargeable cash equivalent of the benefit for an employee to whom the asset is provided will therefore be a proper proportion of its annual value plus the marginal additional running expenses relating to its provision as a benefit. This is the amount that the employer should report on form P11D. If the employee uses the benefit, in whole or in part,

PRs etc

in circumstances which attract relief under s 156(8), any relief due should usually be claimed on his/her self-assessment tax return.

Commentary—*Simon's Direct Tax Service* **E4.611–613**.

October 2000. Tax Bulletin, Issue 49

New criminal offence for tax fraud

INTRODUCTION

Section 144 of Finance Act 2000 introduces a specific criminal offence aimed at tax fraud and punishable by up to seven years in prison. This fits with the Chancellor's commitment in his Budget Speech to implement the recommendations of the review of the informal economy he asked Lord Grabiner QC to undertake last November.

Lord Grabiner considered that at present we concentrate too much on prosecuting the largest frauds to the exclusion of smaller, but still serious, tax frauds. To address this point fifty extra staff will be drafted into Special Compliance Office (SCO) to join existing criminal investigators there. As at present, local office staff will not carry out criminal investigations.

The Grabiner report made some further recommendations—

– That there should be more joint investigations involving the Benefits Agency, HM Customs & Excise and the Revenue. He singled out as a particular target, so called ''collusive employers''. That is employers who evade the tax due under PAYE and national insurance contributions (and sometimes VAT), by paying their work-force wholly or partly in unrecorded cash; at the same time employees are encouraged to claim income-related benefits (and tax credits) on the strength of their understated earnings.

– That there should be a confidential helpline for advice on putting tax and benefits affairs in order. This can be reached on 0845 608 6000.

FEATURES OF NEW OFFENCE

The new offence is to be ''knowingly concerned in the fraudulent evasion of income tax''. The detail of the new offence reflects its genesis in the Grabiner review in several respects—

– It applies only to the fraudulent evasion of income tax; that was the particular area of tax fraud on which the review concentrated.

– It can be tried either summarily or before a jury. That is a feature of similarly worded offences concerned with VAT and NIC fraud and of the general law offences the Benefits Agency uses in serious cases. Lord Grabiner considered the absence of a suitable ''either way'' offence as a hindrance to the change in our approach he recommended. It will not be for the Revenue to decide on the mode of trial.

– It applies to offences committed from the beginning of 2001; participants in the informal economy are therefore given the opportunity to regularise their affairs under current law and practice.

CONDUCT AMOUNTING TO THE NEW OFFENCE

In general and subject to the point about Scots law below, the new offence does not criminalise conduct which is not already an offence under current law. Case-law suggests that the ambit of the new offence is similar to that of the existing common law offence in England and Wales of cheating the public revenue, an offence used for the prosecution of many existing income tax frauds. (But, as Lord Grabiner noted, ''cheat'' cannot be tried summarily, unlike other offences which often go hand in hand with tax and contribution frauds.)

DISHONESTY

Dishonesty is a necessary feature of conduct which can amount to an offence under a number of provisions relevant to fraud in the widest sense. But dishonesty is the very essence of ''cheat'' and will be for the new offence. The criminal courts have never sought to define as such the conduct which counts as dishonest but they have provided guidance which is likely to apply in this context (the leading case is *Ghosh*, [1982] QB 1053). Conduct is dishonest if—

– by the ordinary standards of reasonable and honest people it is dishonest; and

– the person whose conduct is under consideration must have realised that the conduct was dishonest by those standards.

A positive act of deception (such as completing a tax return known to be false) is not a necessary element either of ''cheat'' or of the new offence. Deliberately refraining from notifying chargeability to tax or from submitting tax returns, in circumstances where the person concerned must have known tax should be paid, may well in itself amount to dishonest conduct and therefore to either offence.

The new offence, unlike ''cheat'', applies to offences committed in Scotland as well as elsewhere in the UK. Under current Scottish law, however, there is no precise equivalent of ''cheat''. The nearest, the Scottish common law offence of ''fraud'', requires some positive act of deception. So the new offence does entail an extension in the conduct which counts as criminal north of the border.

"KNOWINGLY CONCERNED" IN AN INCOME TAX FRAUD

During the debate in the Finance Bill Standing Committee, the Paymaster General was asked in what circumstances a customer of a business could become ''knowingly concerned'' in a fraud by that business. She explained that the test was one requiring both knowledge (rather than mere suspicion) of an offence and also actual involvement in it. Simply paying for services in cash was unlikely to satisfy this test.

THE BORDERLINE BETWEEN AVOIDANCE AND EVASION

In the same debate at least one Member raised the subject of the impact of the new offence on tax advisers, especially those involved in advising on arrangements which could be characterised as tax avoidance. We do not consider that the new offence has led to any change in the law in this area.

Where a scheme labelled as ''avoidance'' by its participants and their advisers admittedly fails, the key issue as a matter of criminal law would be whether they have been dishonest in the unsuccessful effort to reduce the relevant tax liability. It would be for the courts to decide as a question of fact whether that is the case.

Concern has been expressed in some quarters that as a result the decision will not normally be taken by those with professional experience of tax matters and, given the highly technical nature of much tax law, that state of affairs may lead to injustice. That is an issue well beyond the scope of this article, but it may be helpful to remember that possible dishonesty becomes a consideration in this context only in certain circumstances. That is where there is some suggestion that the participants in an avoidance scheme are not merely relying on the intrinsic technical soundness of the arrangements actually put in place to reduce the liability, but also on concealment of the true facts from the inspector. If so, then, if the scheme fails, it is perfectly possible that the criminal courts may find there has been an offence. But, conversely, where there is no trace of any concealment of the true facts of arrangements for which there is a respectable technical case, it is hard to imagine how a criminal offence can have been committed.

Commentary—*Simon's Direct Tax Service* **A3.1502A**.

October 2000. Tax Bulletin, Issue 49.

Finance Act 2000—s 97 and Sch 27, Modernisation of group relief

The changes to the group relief rules in this year's Finance Act allow groups and consortia to be established for group relief purposes through companies resident anywhere in the world. Group relief has also been extended to UK branches of non-resident companies, and the rules for the surrender of losses attributable to overseas branches of UK-resident companies have been brought into line.

The new rules apply for accounting periods ending on or after 1 April 2000. But periods straddling 1 April will be apportioned so that the changes take effect only in respect of losses arising from that date.

Companies and their advisers may find it helpful, in submitting claims for group relief, to have some guidance on the operation of the new ss 403D and 403E of TA 1988, which contain the rules for branch losses. The following summary outlines the basic principles of these new rules and gives examples of how they will apply in practice.

These examples represent the Revenue's current understanding of the law in the various countries mentioned but should not be taken as definitive statements on the foreign law. It was not possible in the time available to check each statement with the relevant overseas fiscal authorities.

SECTION 403D—LOSSES OF UK BRANCHES OF NON-RESIDENT COMPANIES

New s 403D of TA 1988 allows for the surrender of losses of UK branches, but not where that loss is deductible or allowable, in any period, against non-UK profits (ie profits outside the scope of UK corporation tax) of that or another person for the purposes of any foreign tax. The purpose of the rule is to prevent relief being obtained twice—once for UK tax and once for overseas tax.

Companies in territories which operate a credit system in relation to UK branch income and which allow UK branch losses to reduce the total profits taxable will generally not be able to surrender losses. This will still apply where the overseas company also makes a loss on its domestic activities as long as the total loss is, as in the UK system, available to carry forward against future profits. Only where it is clear at the time of the claim that the loss can never be used (eg because the company is in liquidation and any possibility of an overseas form of group relief has been ruled out), will the UK branch loss be available for surrender. It is not sufficient that relief available overseas is not in fact claimed.

PRs etc

Countries which operate a credit system for UK branch profits and which allow UK branch losses to reduce non UK profits **include Finland, Denmark, Norway, Sweden, Spain, Italy, Austria, USA, Ireland, Canada** (other than for companies carrying on life assurance business, where an exemption system operates) and **New Zealand**. (Some of these countries may apply an exemption system to profits or losses arising through branches in territories other than the UK depending on the terms of the treaty between the two countries.)

Group relief is available where the company is resident in an exemption territory, but only where the loss arising in the permanent establishment cannot be set against other profits (whether or not it is recouped at a later date).

In **France** a loss in a UK permanent establishment cannot be relieved against French taxable profits unless (*a*) the company has elected to join one of the consolidation systems and calculates its tax base by including the results of foreign operations or (*b*) the company benefits from the special provision for overseas investment, whereby a provision equal to the first four years of branch tax losses is relievable against the company's other profits. Where neither of the above applies group relief is available.

Although the **Netherlands** operates an exemption system, losses of overseas permanent establishments are nevertheless available for set-off against domestic income of the company after being set first against non-taxable foreign source income. If the loss in the UK branch is entirely set against such non-taxable income in the Netherlands, group relief will be available in the UK. However, if the loss in the UK branch is available against domestic income (ie it exceeds profits in other foreign branches) group relief is not due.

While **Switzerland** does not tax foreign profits it allows branch losses against domestic profits. Under both the Dutch and Swiss systems the tax relieved may eventually be recouped when the branch becomes profitable, but that will not make the losses available for UK group relief. In Switzerland a company can claim a lower rate on domestic income in lieu of deducting branch losses. A company that has elected to be taxed under that particular system can surrender the losses of its UK branch as group relief.

Although profits arising through a UK permanent establishment of a **German** company are exempt from German tax, any losses arising are deductible from the company's profits (as long as the branch is engaged exclusively in the active conduct of a business). Any loss which is relievable in this way is not available for UK group relief. The fact that the losses must be recouped when the permanent establishment subsequently realises profits does not affect the position.

Under **Australian** law losses in UK permanent establishments are not relievable against other income, so UK group relief is available.

Luxembourg neither taxes UK branch profits nor allows losses. **Belgium** does not tax UK branch profits but allows losses against taxable income after they have been set first against other non-taxable foreign income. Group relief will therefore be available for Luxembourg companies, but for Belgian companies it will only be available where no part of the loss is, or ever can be, set against taxable sources of income in Belgium.

Under **US** law a company is taxed on its world-wide income and cannot therefore make a UK group relief claim on branch losses. Where, however, a US group has elected to make a consolidated return, a branch loss cannot be consolidated into the return if the company is permitted to use those losses elsewhere. The effect of the tie-breaker at s 403D(6) is that, where deductibility of a loss overseas depends on whether the loss is deductible in the UK, the loss is treated as deductible overseas. So the loss is not available for surrender as group relief. This is in line with the internationally recognised principle that the country of residence has primary responsibility for relieving losses.

SECTION 403E—OVERSEAS BRANCHES OF UK-RESIDENT COMPANIES

New s 403E of TA 1988 acts as a mirror provision to s 403D. A UK-resident company trading through an overseas branch cannot claim group relief on that part of the loss that arises in the branch if it is deductible or otherwise allowable against the non-UK profits of another person. We are aware of only a few countries which do allow relief for the losses of the branch of a non-resident company against the profits of resident companies.

In applying s 403E, the question of whether the losses will be relievable overseas will be decided without hypothesising entities and structures which do not exist at the time of the claim. So, for example, where an overseas country allows the losses of a branch to be carried forward when the branch is incorporated, that will not prevent the losses from being surrendered as group relief if the branch has not in fact been incorporated.

Ireland allows a relief similar to UK group relief for branches of non-resident companies, and as in the UK that relief cannot be carried forward. So where there are group members resident in Ireland which have profits for the year in which a claim can be made, the branch loss will not be available for surrender in the UK.

Where a **French** group has elected to be taxed under a consolidation system which allows losses in French branches of UK subsidiaries to be offset against group profits (of that period or a later one), that part of the UK company's loss that arises in France must be excluded from the UK group relief claim.

Where a **German** Organschaft includes the German branch of a UK company, no UK group relief will be available for any loss attributable to the branch.

UK group relief will also be restricted where a UK company is a member of a loss-making partnership trading in a territory where that partnership is treated as a corporate body (for example, an **Australian** or **US** limited partnership) and within local group relief provisions.

Commentary—*Simon's Direct Tax Service* **D2.633**.

December 2000. IR Tax Bulletin Issue 50

Limited Liability Partnerships

This article sets out the Revenue's views on how the members of a Limited Liability Partnership (''LLP''), regulated by the Limited Liability Partnership Act 2000 (''the LLP Act''), **which carries on a trade or profession**, will be taxed.

In this article the following expressions are used—

''Ordinary Partnership'' means a partnership within the meaning of the Partnership Act 1890.

''Limited Partnership'' means a partnership regulated by the Limited Partnership Act 1907.

''Old Partnership'' includes both an ''ordinary'' and a ''limited partnership''.

During the passage of the LLP Act, Ministers announced that the tax treatment would be reviewed for those LLPs used for businesses for which the LLP structure was not originally intended. Legislation would be brought forward in the Finance Bill 2001 after appropriate consultation. This review was prompted by concerns that some businesses, particularly investment businesses, could be motivated to adopt LLP structure for tax reasons rather than to obtain limited liability. Further details of the tax treatment of LLPs were announced by the Chancellor in his Pre Budget Report (PBR) on 8 November 2000. Details and an invitation to comment were given in the PBR Press Release—Inland Revenue 5. An announcement will be made in due course of the further changes to the tax treatment of LLPs (if any) which are required because of points raised during this consultation.

GENERAL

LLPs are in law regarded as ''bodies corporate'' and will be subject to aspects of company law. But for tax they will generally be treated as ''partnerships''. As mentioned above **this guidance covers LLPs carrying on a trade or profession**. It does not cover the detailed tax treatment of investment businesses for which the LLP structure was not originally intended.

Section 10 of the LLP Act ensures that where an LLP carries on a ''business with a view of profit'' the members will be treated for the purposes of income tax, corporation tax and capital gains tax as if they were partners carrying on business in partnership.

That is to say the LLP will be regarded as transparent for tax purposes and each member will be assessed to tax on their share of the LLPs income or gains. For members liable to income tax their share of the partnership's profits to be charged to tax will be calculated in accordance with the rules set out in TA 1988 s 111 and for those members liable to corporation tax in accordance with the rules set out in TA 1988 s 114.

This article deals with the UK tax treatment of LLPs formed under the LLP Act (ie UK LLPs as opposed to overseas LLPs). It would be for the tax authorities of other countries to decide how to tax UK LLPs under their own tax codes.

COMPUTATION OF TAXABLE PROFITS OF PROFESSIONAL BUSINESSES

In Tax Bulletin, Issue 38 (December 1998, page 606) the Revenue set out guidance on what is meant by ''true and fair view'' for the purposes of calculating the taxable profits of a professional business. It is confirmed that those rules will apply equally to the computation of the Case II Schedule D profit of a LLP which carries on a professional business for the purposes of calculating the Income Tax liability of the members of the LLP.

CAPITAL ALLOWANCES

Where a LLP succeeds to a business previously carried on by an old partnership this will not of itself give rise to a balancing event for the purposes of the Capital Allowance provisions.

INTEREST RELIEF

Members of a LLP, who are individuals, will be entitled to claim interest relief on the loans they obtain in order to defray money applied in the circumstances set out in TA 1988 s 362(1); provided that they otherwise meet the conditions of the relief.

ESC A43 covers interest for investments in partnerships. Where an ordinary partnership converts to a LLP, the existing terms of the extra-statutory concession are not appropriate, to preserve existing relief. To rectify this we are currently considering what changes should be made to the text. (A 1907 limited partner would not have been entitled to such relief in the first place, so it would be inappropriate to extend ESC A43 to those circumstances.)

LOSS RELIEF

a. Unlike Section 117 ICTA, the undrawn profits of a member of a LLP cannot normally be added to their subscribed capital in order to calculate the limit of their entitlement to sideways loss relief. This is because, subject to any agreement between them, a member's undrawn profits will normally be regarded as a debt of the LLP. This means that the member ranks, for that sum, alongside the other creditors in the event of liquidation. If however the terms of the agreement between the members specifically provide that the undrawn profit stands as part of a member's capital contribution and that agreement is unconditional then that amount can be taken into account in calculating the limit.

b. The following is an example of how the provisions of ss 118C–D will apply:

> Mr A becomes a member of a LLP on 6 April 2003. He introduces capital of £10,000 into the partnership. The LLP carries on a trade. During the year ended 5 April 2006 he makes a further capital contribution of £6,000.
> His share of the LLP's Case I loss is as follows and he claims relief under Section 380 ICTA for those losses against his other income.
> Ye 5 April 2004 £6,000
> Ye 5 April 2005 £6,000
> Ye 5 April 2006 £3,000
> Mr A is entitled to Section 380 relief as follows:
> 2003/2004 £6,000 (unrelieved capital contribution £4,000)
> 2004/2005 £4,000(1) (unrelieved loss £2,000)
> 2005/2006 £5,000(2) (unrelieved capital contribution £1,000)
> 1) sideways loss relief is restricted to the unrelieved capital contribution brought forward of £4,000. The balance of the loss of £2,000 (£6,000—£4,000) is carried forward.
> 2) sideways loss relief of £5,000 available ie loss of year £3000 + unrelieved loss brought forward £2,000. Unrelieved capital contribution carried forward is £1,000 ie total contributions £16,000 less total sideways loss relief given £15,000)

Where a member of a LLP makes a capital contribution to a partnership in order to meet a liability for negligence for which they are personally responsible then that amount will be taken into account in determining the amount of their capital contribution to the partnership for the purposes of Section TA 118ZC. Provided that the conditions for relief are otherwise met then that partner will be entitled to relief up to a maximum of the amount of that additional contribution either under the normal sideways loss relief provisions, or under TA s 109A if he/she has left the partnership, or the partnership has ceased business.

c. The provisions in ss 118C–D ICTA (restriction of sideways loss relief to members of a LLP) do not apply to a LLP which carries on a profession; only to one which carries on a trade. Provided that the conditions for relief are otherwise met; a member of a LLP, which carries on a profession rather than a trade, will be entitled to loss relief, either under the normal sideways loss relief provisions, or under TA 1988 s 109, if he/she has left the partnership, or the partnership has ceased business.

OVERLAP RELIEF

Where a partnership carries on a trade or profession each partner is deemed to carry on a personal trade or profession. The basis period rules are applied to that deemed trade or profession and any overlap profit is personal to each partner.

If, on conversion, a LLP succeeds to the business previously carried by an old partnership then a partner's personal trade or profession will be regarded as continuing. He/she will be entitled to a deduction for overlap relief at the time they finally retire from the LLP (or perhaps earlier if the LLP changes its accounting date).

DEMERGERS

Where a LLP takes over only part of the old partnership's trade, such an event constitutes a ''demerger'' to which Statement of Practice 9/86 applies. Unless it can be shown that on the demerger the part of the business carried on by the LLP is recognisably ''the business'' previously carried on by the old partnership then the cessation provisions will apply. In that event each member of the old partnership will be entitled to their personal overlap relief. Equally the commencement provisions will apply to all the members of the LLP.

But if it can be shown that the LLP does carry on ''the business'' previously carried on by the old partnership then, as it will have succeeded to the old partnership's business, the cessation provisions will not be applied to the old partnership and any overlap relief will be carried forward. Equally the commencement provisions will not be applied to the members of the LLP. But the old partnership will be assumed to have commenced a new business in relation to the part of the trade it retains.

Whether or not the business carried on by the LLP is recognisably ''the business'' previously carried on by the old partnership is a question of fact.

CASH BASIS – CATCHING UP CHARGE

Again if on conversion the LLP succeeds to the business previously carried on by an old partnership then the spreading rules for the catching up charge will continue to apply as if the conversion had not occurred.

CESSATION

Where a LLP succeeds to a business previously carried on by an old partnership this will not of itself involve the cessation of the old partnership's trade or profession.

TAX RETURNS

Where an old partnership incorporates as a LLP during an accounting period then if the partners so wish a single partnership return need only be made for the one tax year. They may do this even if the partnership changes its accounting date. Single PAYE returns may also be made for the tax year in which an old partnership incorporates as a LLP.

UK BRANCHES OF OVERSEAS LLP'S

The tax treatment of a UK branch of an overseas Limited Liability Partnership, and the members of such an LLP, will depend on how the foreign entity is regarded for the purposes of the UK taxation provisions. Where the foreign LLP is regarded as a ''body corporate'' for the purposes of the UK Taxes Acts the profits of the UK branch will be chargeable to corporation tax. On the other hand if it is regarded as a partnership then members will be separately liable to tax on their share of the branch's profits under the existing legislation for partnerships rather than under the LLP Act. The latter act only applies to UK registered LLPs.

DOUBLE TAXATION RELIEF

Where an overseas tax authority regards a foreign branch of a UK LLP as a ''body corporate'' the UK members will be entitled to claim Tax Credit Relief in respect of their proportionate share of the foreign tax paid on the overseas branch's profits.

DIVIDENDS

A UK LLP is not itself ''liable to tax'' in the UK as the LLP tax provisions identify other persons (ie the members) as the persons who are to be taxed. Accordingly for the purposes of the Double Taxation Agreements (DTA) the LLP it is not regarded as being resident in the UK and cannot itself therefore claim relief from foreign taxes under such Agreements. As is now the case with ordinary and limited partnerships the members must make the claim.

Assuming they are UK residents in accordance with the provisions of the relevant DTA the members of an LLP will be entitled to relief for any withholding tax on overseas dividends. Normally a DTA provides for withholding tax of a maximum of 15% to be deducted and relief for that tax will be given. Where a partner is an individual then no relief will be due in respect of the taxes paid (the underlying taxes) on the profits out of which the dividend is paid.

In the very narrow circumstances where the LLP is not treated as transparent, but instead as a body corporate for tax purposes (such as when the LLP is in liquidation or being wound up in circumstances where transparency cannot be retained in the manner explained below under ''Capital Gains—Liquidation /Winding Up''), we can confirm the LLP could itself claim relief for foreign taxes, including if appropriate underlying tax.

PARTNERSHIP ANNUITIES

Where an obligation to pay an annuity is transferred from the old partnership to the LLP then the members of the LLP will be entitled to higher rate income tax relief for their share of the ongoing payments; and incoming LLP members who assume part of that obligation will also be entitled to such relief for their share.

If an obligation to pay an annuity is not transferred to the LLP and the members of the old partnership continue to pay it they will be entitled to higher rate income tax relief for their share of those payments until such time as they cease to be a member of the LLP or until the business originally carried on by the old partnership ceases, whichever is the earlier.

CAPITAL GAINS

Partners capital interests

So long as the LLP carries on a trade or profession with a view to profit a partner's capital interest as a member of a LLP will not be regarded as a chargeable asset in its own right. In these circumstances the members of the LLP will be directly taxable on their share of the chargeable gains arising on the disposal of the LLP's assets and there will be no concurrent charge on a non-transparent basis.

Temporary cessation of trading

The transparency of a LLP, for capital gains purposes, is not disturbed by reason of temporary periods of time during which no trade or profession is carried on by it. For example, if the LLP ceases to carry on one business and disposes of its assets in order to realise funds to commence another business then those asset disposals, and any gains or losses arising in consequence, will be treated as those of the members.

Transfer of a business to a LLP

Where a business, previously carried on by an old partnership, is transferred to a LLP then, for the purposes of the Capital Gains legislation, this will not of itself constitute a disposal by the partners in their interests in the old partnership's assets. This applies equally to the members of partnerships in Scotland as it does to those in England and Wales.

Furthermore such a transfer will not affect—

a) the availability of indexation allowance.

b) the ownership period for retirement relief.

c) the holding period for taper relief.

Application of Statement of Practice D12

The rules set out in Statement of Practice D12 apply equally to the members of a LLP as they do to members of an old partnership. When D12 is next updated it will be amended to incorporate this confirmation.

LIQUIDATION/WINDING UP

Liquidations

Where a LLP ceases to carry on a trade or profession then it will no longer be regarded as a ''partnership'' for the purposes of the taxation provisions and will instead be regarded as a ''body corporate''. The LLP will thus cease to be transparent (Section 59A(2) TCGA).

Where a LLP goes into liquidation, chargeable gains on the disposal of the LLP's assets by the liquidator will be computed by reference to the date on which they were first acquired by the LLP and their cost at that date. In the liquidation period, the LLP's capital gains will be treated in precisely the same way for tax purposes as those for any other body corporate (Section 8(6) TCGA).

LLP members will be taxed on any gain (or given relief for any loss) that arises on the disposal of their capital interests in the LLP. The base cost of a partner's capital interest is not equal to the market value of that interest at the time when transparency is lost. The allowable acquisition cost of each partner's interest will be determined according to the historical capital contributions made as if the LLP had never been transparent. This treatment does not affect preliquidation asset disposals, which remain undisturbed.

Informal winding up

Where the members of a LLP proceed to wind up its affairs in an orderly way, without the formal appointment of a liquidator, by settling outstanding liabilities and realising the assets following or in the course of a cessation of commercial activity, then it will be accepted that the transparency of the LLP will be preserved during the period in which the assets are being disposed of provided the conditions set out below are met.

Those conditions are—

- that the LLP is not being wound up for reasons connected in whole or in part with the avoidance of tax, and
- that, following the termination of the LLP's business, the period of winding up is not unduly protracted taking account of the LLP's assets and liabilities.

If these conditions are not met, then the transparency of the LLP may be regarded as coming to an end before the informal winding up process has been completed. It is also emphasised that, whatever the circumstances, transparency cannot continue beyond any date on which a liquidator is formally appointed (whether or not that liquidator is charged for a period with completing any outstanding business transactions).

CGT roll-over relief

Where, as a result of claiming business asset roll-over relief (Sections 152-154 TCGA 1992) a LLP member postpones a chargeable gain through their acquisition of a share in a LLP asset, there is the potential for that gain to fall out of charge in the future by reason of the LLP ceasing to be transparent. This could occur, for example, where the LLP asset remains unsold when the LLP goes into liquidation and vests in the liquidator (who will compute the gain arising on the disposal of the asset in the course of liquidation without regard to past roll-over relief claims by any LLP member). Accordingly, there is a tax liability on the member, at the point in time when the LLP ceases to be transparent, which is based on an amount equal to the postponed gain or gains which have not then come back into charge (Section 156A TCGA 1992). Gains which accrue to a member in consequence of this special provision do not attract taper relief.

Annuities

Provided that the rights remain substantially the same then—

- the transfer of a partner's annuity rights and/or
- the transfer of annuity obligations to former members

from an ordinary partnership to a LLP will not be regarded as a chargeable disposal.

Similarly where an annuitant agrees to the substitution of the LLP for the predecessor partnership as the payer of the annuity, and the terms otherwise remain substantially the same, then the annuitant will not be regarded as making a chargeable disposal.

INHERITANCE TAX

Business property relief and agricultural property relief

Where an old partnership incorporates as a LLP a partner's period of ownership for both reliefs will not be regarded as being interrupted.

Deemed transfers by close companies

Because Section 267A(*d*) IHTA 1984, inserted by Section 11 of the LLP Act, deems transfers of value to be made by the members of the LLP and not by the LLP itself, liability under Section 94 IHTA 1984 cannot arise even if the LLP might otherwise be a close company.

Availability of reliefs

The normal reliefs and exemptions available to partners in an old partnership will equally be available to members of a LLP. In particular Section 10 IHTA 1984, which provides an exemption for dispositions not intended to confer gratuitous benefit, will apply.

STAMP DUTY

Transfer of property to a LLP

Section 12 of the LLP Act requires that for the stamp duty exemption to apply the proportions of property conveyed or transferred into a LLP must either be unchanged "before" and "after" the transfer, or the proportions must not have been changed for tax avoidance reasons. Strictly under property law the partners' interest in the LLP will replace their interests in the old partnership's assets. In determining whether the stamp duty exemption applies the Revenue will not, however take this point.

The Revenue will accept that any property transferred to the LLP within one year of its incorporation will qualify for relief from stamp duty under Section 12 of the LLP Act, provided that the conditions for that relief are met.

Section 12(2) of the LLP Act prevents stamp duty exemption being available if property is transferred at the time of the LLP's incorporation and also there are retirements of former partners and/or admission of new partners to the LLP.

Provided that all the other conditions for the exemption are met the Revenue accepts that this charge can be averted by arranging matters so that the change of partners takes place the instant before or after incorporation. To confirm that matters were organised in this way the Stamp Office will need to see all associated documents effecting any change in the membership of the old partnership and of the LLP prior to and/or after incorporation, as well as evidence that any stamp duty appropriate to those documents has been paid. It may be necessary to call for further information once these documents have been reviewed.

Transfers of interests in a LLP

An interest in a LLP is not a chargeable security for Stamp Duty purposes. So if stamp duty is due on the transfer of such an interest it will be payable at the 1%, 3% or 4% rate, as appropriate, rather than the 0.5% rate applicable to shares. This is in line with the intention behind the LLP Act that the treatment of LLPs should be the same as for partnerships. Since the sale of an interest in any other type of partnership bears duty at the property rates, the sale of an interest in a LLP will be charged in the same way.

General

As with all transactions potentially liable to stamp duty, the Technical Services Unit Manager at any Stamp Office will be happy to assist customers in connection with any enquiries regarding the operation of the stamp duty relief in the Act.

NATIONAL INSURANCE CONTRIBUTIONS

The National Insurance Contributions (NICs) position of members of a LLP is the same as that of partners in an ordinary partnership. Thus the members of a LLP will be liable to Class 2, Class 3 and Class 4 NICs as appropriate.

February 2001. Tax Bulletin Issue 51

Providing services through an intermediary—IR35—what happens next?

The IR35 legislation has been in force since 6 April 2000. Although much of the public interest has related to workers in the IT and engineering industries, it could affect people in any industry who use a limited company or partnership to provide their services to others.

Advisers with clients who may be affected will need to take action before the end of the tax year. This article explains who is affected and what you need to consider before 5 April.

This article is not intended to provide a detailed analysis of the legislation, which is contained in Schedule 12 Finance Act 2000 and the Social Security Contributions (Intermediaries) Regulations 2000. Copies of this legislation and all of the other documents and publications referred to in this article can be accessed through the Inland Revenue's web site at www.inlandrevenue.gov.uk/ir35.

WHO DOES IR35 AFFECT?

There is a common misconception that IR35 only applies to people working in the IT sector. This is not correct. The legislation is not targeted at any particular occupation or business sector. It can apply in any business sector where—

- an individual (known as a worker) provides services to another person (known as the client);
- under arrangements involving an intermediary (such as a company or a partnership);
- in circumstances such that if the contract had been made directly then the worker would have been an employee of the client.

Anyone who structures their working arrangements in this way could be affected by the legislation. Examples of occupations where people work through service companies run right across the board, including medical staff, chief executives of large plc's, legal and accountancy staff, construction industry workers, clerical workers, press officers, night club bouncers and many others.

Advisers need to be aware that IR35 can apply to anyone working through an intermediary, regardless of occupation. If they are giving advice to those working in this way they need to decide whether their clients are affected by the legislation and find out what action they need to take over the coming months.

The intermediary is normally a limited company, commonly referred to as a service company. However, a partnership could also be an intermediary. The vast majority of intermediaries are companies so this article is aimed principally at how the legislation applies to companies. There are, however, some differences in the treatment of partnerships and further guidance on these aspects can be found in the Inland Revenue's Employment Status Manual at ESM3000 onwards.

HOW DO I KNOW IF THE LEGISLATION APPLIES IN A PARTICULAR CASE?

We have already produced a lot of information to help people decide whether the legislation applies in a particular case. These include—

- Leaflet IR175 'supplying services through a limited company or partnership'.
- a series of Frequently Asked Questions.
- Tax bulletin No 47 issued in July 2000 [reproduced above].

The Inland Revenue has also undertaken to give opinions on whether a particular contract would have been considered to be employment or self-employment. Where someone is in doubt about whether an engagement would have been employment or self- employment, then he or she may ask us for an opinion. Our opinion will be based upon the existing case law tests for determining employment status. An opinion will only be given on contracts that are in force and not on draft agreements.

The opinion is given in accordance with the Revenue's overall commitment under Code of Practice 10. It does not of itself create a decision subject to appeal. Taxpayers are entitled to rely on our opinion in completing tax returns (including the intermediary's P35 and related documentation) provided that the information given to enable us to reach that opinion is complete and correctly reflects the true relationship. They are also at liberty to adopt their own alternative view in completing those returns and, if we cannot reach agreement, can ask us for a formal NICs decision against which there is a right of appeal to the General or Special Commissioners.

The Inland Revenue will take account of the circumstances in which the services are provided, including all of the contracts forming part of the overall arrangements in order to decide whether the relationship between the worker and the client would have been one of employment, if there had been no intermediary. This will include any contracts between the client and an agency and between the agency and a worker's service company.

PROCEDURE FOR OBTAINING AN OPINION

If you want the Inland Revenue to give an opinion then we will need to establish the facts relating to the engagement and will need to see copies of any contracts involved in the relationship. You should send us copies of these contracts when asking for an opinion together with any other information that you consider might be relevant.

You should send the contracts to:
IR35, Penhaligon House Trinity Street, St Austell Cornwall, PL25 5BA, Fax—0845-302-3535

You should also provide the worker's National Insurance number, the company's Inland Revenue reference number and the company's postcode. Workers in the TV and Radio field should put 'TV' instead of the postcode. Workers in the film industry should replace postcode with 'FILM'.

We will often not be able to give you an opinion based solely on the contracts and may have to ask you for further information about the working relationship. This may mean that we will have to speak to the worker and to someone representing the client. Therefore, when submitting any contract for consideration please let us have details of someone who can speak on behalf of the client, whom we can contact and also details of how we can speak to the worker.

It would also help us to provide an opinion as quickly as possible if you enclose any other information relevant to the particular engagement when submitting the contract. This might include, but not be limited to:

- details of how the engagement was obtained and the recruitment procedure together with a copy of any adverts for the work in question;
- a description of the nature of the services to be performed together with any job or work specifications for the contract;
- copies of any tenders made by the intermediary;
- details of any additional contractual terms not included within the written contracts, whether oral, written or implied;
- details of how and who allocates the work and the role the worker plays in the client's organisation ie does he/she work alone or as part of a team.

Further guidance on the Revenue's views on employment status and the intermediaries legislation can be found in the February 2000 Tax Bulletin and in the Employment Status Manual.

WHAT HAPPENS WHEN THE LEGISLATION APPLIES?

When the legislation applies, then tax and NICs must be paid on a minimum amount of salary. This may be either in the form of actual payments during the year or as a notional payment deemed to have been paid to the worker by the intermediary. This deemed payment is usually treated as made on the last day of the tax year, although it is accelerated in certain situations, such as when an individual leaves the service company, see *Specific points* at the end of this article.

In broad terms the effect of the IR35 rules is as follows—

- the client – is not affected and continues to make gross payments to the service company as before;
- the service company – is treated as making a payment to the worker which is taxable under Schedule E and subject to Class 1 NICs. For NICs purposes, the service company is treated as the secondary contributor. The company's corporation tax position is not affected other than that it will obtain a deduction for the deemed payment and associated secondary NICs;
- the worker – is treated as receiving a payment chargeable to income tax under Schedule E (with a credit for tax deducted under PAYE) and subject to PAYE and to Class 1 NICs from the service company. For NICs purposes, the worker is treated as an employed earner of the service company.

EXAMPLE

Mr Adams is a draughtsman. He negotiates a contract with Client plc. Under this contract, which will last for 12 months starting on 1 May 2000, he is engaged on terms and conditions that would make him an employee of Client plc if taken on directly. However, the agreement for the supply of Mr Adams' services is made between Client plc and Mr Adams' company, Adams Services Ltd, in which he owns all of the shares. There is no contract between Mr Adams and Client plc.

All of the income from the contract with Client plc will be covered by the intermediaries legislation.

– Mr Adams (the worker) is under an obligation to personally perform services for the purposes of a business carried on by another person, Client plc (the client);
– the services are provided not under a contract directly between the client and the worker but under arrangements involving a third party, Adams Services Ltd (the intermediary);
– if the services had been provided under a contract directly between Mr Adams and Client plc, he would be regarded as an employee of the client for tax and NICs purposes;
– the work done under the contract starts on or after 6th April 2000.

In addition:

– Mr Adams owns shares in the intermediary and is entitled to receive dividends from the company. He therefore has rights entitling him to receive a payment from the intermediary that is not chargeable to tax under Schedule E.
– Mr Adams owns all of the shares in the intermediary. He therefore has a material interest in the intermediary and thus the conditions of liability where the intermediary is a company are satisfied.

Therefore a deemed Schedule E payment will be treated as paid.

WHAT DO ADVISERS HAVE TO DO BEFORE THE END OF THE TAX YEAR?

The first step will be to work out which, if any, of the engagements undertaken by the service company will be caught by the IR35 rules. Assuming some are caught, there will only be a deemed payment if a minimum amount of salary and secondary NICs has not been paid. If you want to avoid having a deemed payment, you therefore need to work out how much salary needs to be paid. This means you need to know what the income for the tax year is likely to be and what the allowable deductions are. Note that these are both on a cash, and not an accruals, basis. Also, a deduction will only be given for the amount of salary actually paid during the tax year, so your client needs to make arrangements for this before it is too late, if he wishes to avoid having to pay tax and NICs on a deemed payment.

ACTION TO TAKE BEFORE THE END OF THE TAX YEAR

If you have any clients whom you think could be affected you need to:

– decide whether the client is affected by the legislation;
– find out what the income and allowable expenditure for the year is likely to be;
– work out how much salary the company needs to pay the worker, if you wish to avoid a deemed payment;
– ensure the salary is paid before the end of the tax year if a deduction is to be given in the deemed payment calculation for that year.

Provided the calculation of the minimum amount of salary to pay is reasonably accurate then any deemed payment is likely to be nil, or no more than a small balancing amount.

If the minimum amount of salary and NICs is not paid then there will be a deemed payment. In this event you will need to work out the amount of that deemed payment and the secondary NICs and ensure this is included on the relevant returns and paid to the Inland Revenue. Detailed guidance on the deemed payment calculation is provided at the end of this article.

WHAT DOES THE SERVICE COMPANY HAVE TO DO AT THE END OF THE TAX YEAR?

The legislation requires a calculation of tax and NICs to be made, normally, on 5 April. If the intermediary has already paid enough salary to the worker during the year, no further tax or NICs will be payable.

If there is a deemed payment this simply means that an extra payment of PAYE tax and NICs has to be calculated and accounted for. To calculate that payment, an amount of salary is deemed to have been paid, whether or not any payment is actually made.

If the company is treated as making a deemed payment then the legislation ensures that the net amount of money remaining after PAYE and employer's NICs can be paid out as dividends, up to the amount of that deemed payment, without further tax or NICs becoming due. The dividends can be paid during the same tax year as the deemed payment or in a subsequent year. The dividends can be paid to someone other than the worker.

If money, which has been included in the calculation of a deemed payment is paid out by the company after the end of the tax year, it will often be advantageous to pay it in the form of a dividend, and take advantage of this provision, rather than in the form of a salary, see Specific points below.

The service company that has been treated as making a deemed payment makes the claim to effect that the dividend is treated as non-taxable in the hands of the recipient. Once the claim has been accepted the dividend does not have to be returned on the recipient's self-assessment.

HOW TO MAKE A CLAIM

The company should make any claim to its own Inland Revenue office and tell us about any dividends it has paid which it wants to be exempted. We will need the following information:

- the name and tax reference of the company making the claim;
- the name(*s*) and tax reference(*s*) of the person(*s*) who received the dividend;
- the amount of the dividend paid to each person and the total amount paid;
- the date the dividend was paid;
- the amount of the deemed payment and date on which it was treated as paid.

HOW DO YOU ACCOUNT FOR THE DEEMED PAYMENT AND SECONDARY NICS?

The deemed payment and any tax and NICs due on it should be entered in the normal way on the deductions working sheet. *The Employers Further Guide to PAYE* (*CWG2*) explains how to work out PAYE and NICs.

For NICs purposes only—

- the amount of the deemed payment should be aggregated with any other earnings derived from employed earner's employment (in effect, any salary paid in-year by the service company to the worker, but not drawings from a partnership); and
- the amount of Class 1 NICs calculated on that aggregate amount using an annual earnings period, whether or not the worker is a director of a company during the year.

Any tax and NICs due at the end of a year as a result of the calculation of the deemed payment should be sent to the collector by 19 April following the end of the tax year in which the deemed payment arises, along with any other tax and NICs due to be paid at that date.

The deemed payment and the tax and NICs due on it should be included in the totals of pay, tax and NICs in the end of year PAYE returns (forms P35 and P14) which should be sent to us by 19 May. Any tax and NICs due on the deemed payment do not have to be identified separately from any other pay, tax and NICs included in the end of year forms. On the P35, the tax and the NICs can simply be included in the total tax and total NICs boxes. But there is a question to answer at box 6 of the checklist on the front of form P35 to tell us whether or not PAYE and NICs on a deemed payment are included in the total figures.

If you are unable to complete the deemed payment calculation by 19 April we will accept a payment on account at that date of the tax and NICs due on the deemed payment. However, the company will need to tell us in a note accompanying the form P35 by 19 May that the amount paid on 19 April and reflected in the end of year forms sent in by 19 May is provisional.

Interest will be due in the normal way on any of the tax or NICs due on the deemed payment that is not paid to us by 19 April. But, as long as the company tells us by 19 May that the figures are provisional, no penalties will be charged, provided it sends us a correction to the form P35 and P14 figures by the following 31 January and pays any balance of tax and NICs due in respect of the deemed payment by that date. The company will also need to issue a corrected P60 to the employee. This procedure will apply for the tax year 2000–01 and will be reviewed to establish whether it should continue to apply for subsequent years.

WHAT FIGURES ARE RECORDED ON THE WORKER'S SELF ASSESSMENT RETURN?

The deemed payment is treated as income from employment with the company, and the tax is treated in exactly the same way as other PAYE tax.

The pay and tax details should therefore be recorded on the Self Assessment (SA) return on the supplementary employment page relating to the worker's work through the company. But as the pay and tax details on the P60 given to the worker by the company should include the deemed payment and the tax, there is no need to enter the figures separately on the employment page. Simply enter the total P60 pay and tax figures in the relevant boxes. If, however, only a provisional amount of tax had been paid by the time P60 was issued, the worker may receive a revised one when the correct deemed payment is calculated and tax accounted for. In such a case, use the pay and tax figures on the revised P60.

HOW ARE THE COMPANY'S TAX COMPUTATIONS AFFECTED?

The company may deduct the whole of the deemed payment and any employer's NICs due on it in calculating its corporation tax liability. The deemed payment includes the primary employee's NICs, PAYE tax and the net amount remaining after the tax and NICs have been deducted. There is no need for the net amount to be paid out to the worker either as salary or dividend for a corporation tax deduction to be claimed. However, no other deductions are allowed for these amounts and if anything has already been claimed through the accounts an appropriate adjustment must be made.

This deduction is only allowable in calculating the taxable profits for the accounting period in which the deemed payment is treated as paid.

The deemed payment is normally treated as paid at the end of the tax year. However, companies are taxed on an accounts basis and can choose which date to make their accounts up to. Advisers will need to consider which is the best accounting date for their client since this will determine when relief is given for the deemed payment. Significant differences can arise where different accounting dates are used.

However, the timing of the accounting date is not likely to be material if the company pays the worker sufficient salary during the tax year so that there is no, or only a small, deemed payment.

EXAMPLES OF THE CONSEQUENCES OF USING DIFFERENT ACCOUNTING DATES

EXAMPLE 1

Locost Services Ltd makes up its accounts to 31 March. In the year ending 31 March 2001 it earned £50,000 supplying the services of Mary Brown. All of these engagements during the accounting period are within the IR35 rules.

The company had a taxable profit of £45,000. Locost is treated as making a deemed payment of £40,000 with associated secondary NICs of £4,454 on 5 April 2001.

The deemed payment is treated as paid during Locost's accounting period ending 31 March 2002. Therefore Locost's corporation tax profits for the year ending 31 March 2001 will remain as £45,000. Mary Brown will be treated as receiving a taxable payment of £40,000 on 5 April 2001.

EXAMPLE 2

Swift Services Ltd makes up its accounts to 30 April. In the year ending 30 April 2001 it earned £50,000 supplying the services of Michael Green. All of these engagements during the accounting period are within the IR35 rules.

The company had a taxable profit of £45,000. Swift is treated as making a deemed payment of £40,000 with associated secondary NICs of £4,454 on 5 April 2001.

The deemed payment is treated as paid during Swift's accounting period ending 30 April 2001. Therefore Swift's corporation tax profits for the year ending 30 April 2001 are reduced to £546. Michael Green is treated as receiving a taxable payment of £40,000 on 5 April 2001.

SPECIFIC POINTS

What if the money is paid as a salary after the end of the tax year, rather than as dividends?

Any money paid as salary will be subject to the normal PAYE and NICs rules, whenever that salary is paid. The legislation only provides for a dividend to be paid without further tax liability.

Any salary paid in a later year will reduce the amount of the deemed payment in the tax year in which it is paid. It cannot be used to frank a deemed payment in an earlier or subsequent tax year.

More tax and NICs may be paid than is needed, if the company pays a salary after the end of a tax year in which tax has been paid on a deemed payment, and the salary in the later year is more than the amount the company receives from engagements covered by the legislation, after deductions. In these circumstances it may be more advantageous for the company to pay a dividend, rather than salary.

What if the worker stops working through the service company or partnership before the end of the year (an in-year event)?

The deemed payment is normally treated as made on 5 April. However, it is treated as made at an earlier date when one of the following events occurs—

Where the intermediary is a company—

- the worker disposes of his/her shares in the company;
- the worker ceases to hold office with the company;
- the worker ceases to be employed by the company.

Where the intermediary is a partnership—

- the partnership is dissolved or ceases to trade;
- the partner ceases to act as such or ceases to be employed by the partnership.

Where one, or more, of these events occur the deemed payment is treated as being made at the date of the earliest of the events.

It is important to be aware that where the intermediary is a company the cessation of trade does not mean a deemed payment is treated as paid on that date unless one of the other events occurs at the same time. However, where someone working through their service company continues to work for the company as an employee or a director the Revenue will not normally seek to argue for this purpose that the trade has ceased at an earlier date.

Where there is an in year event, the intermediary will need to calculate the deemed payment at that time and arrange for any tax and national insurance contributions to be paid to the Revenue in the normal way, as for any payment of salary. The form P45 should also be completed in the usual way.

What happens if the service company's income has tax deducted under the Construction Industry Scheme (CIS)?

The deemed payment is based upon the amount the company receives from the engagement. However, where the company receives monies from which tax at the current rate of 18% has been deducted under the CIS, the gross amount before deduction of the 18% tax is the amount to be used in the deemed payment calculation. The CIS deduction is a payment on account of the corporation tax due. It is not therefore available for offset against the liability in respect of the deemed payment and secondary NICs. If the company has no corporation tax liability, submission of the accounts and tax return promptly after the end of the tax year will enable the Revenue to make any repayment that is due at an early date.

What is happening about the Judicial Review of the legislation being brought by the Professional Contractors Group and others?

The Professional Contractors Group has been given permission by the Administrative Court to proceed to a full hearing of their case. The Government is confident that at the full hearing, the Court will decide that the legislation is fair, proportionate, and compatible with all the UK's obligations under EU law. We expect the full hearing to take place in March 2001.

FURTHER INFORMATION

Further guidance and information about the IR35 legislation can be obtained from the following sources—

- Leaflet IR175 entitled "Supplying Services Through a Limited Company or Partnership".
- Leaflet IR2003 entitled "Supplying Services—How to calculate the deemed payment", (to be published in March).
- Accessing our website at www.inlandrevenue.gov.uk/IR35.
- Telephoning the IR hotline on 0845 303 3535
- E-mailing us at IR35@inlandrevenue.gov.uk.
- Faxing us on 0845 302 3535.
- Writing to us at IR35, Penhaligon House, Trinity Street, St Austell, Cornwall PL25 5BA.

APPENDIX 1

The deemed payment is based upon the income from relevant engagements less certain deductions. It is calculated as follows—

Step One

The starting point for working out the deemed payment is the amount received by the intermediary in the tax year in respect of engagements to which the legislation applies. This includes any non-cash benefits.

Non-cash benefits might include things like the provision of living accommodation, the use of an asset such as a car, gifts of assets, and any other benefit or facility provided by the client. Further guidance about benefits can be found in *Booklet 480—Expenses and Benefits—a tax guide.*

From this amount a flat rate 5% is deducted, to cover other unspecified expenses, such as running costs of the intermediary.

This deduction is given automatically, but only affects the calculation of the deemed payment. You cannot deduct it when you are working out the taxable profits of the company or partnership.

Step Two

Add any payments or benefits received by the worker, or his family, in respect of the relevant engagements from anyone other than the intermediary which are not otherwise chargeable to income tax under Schedule E but would be if the worker were employed by the client.

Step Three

Deduct any expenses met by the intermediary, which could have been claimed as expenses against income tax if the worker had been an employee of the client and had paid for them himself.

Employees are only allowed to deduct expenses which are wholly, exclusively and necessarily incurred in the performance of their duties. These will not include some common items which are deductible in company accounts.

For example, where a spouse is employed by the intermediary to carry out administrative work for the company it is unlikely that his or her wages will be allowed when working out the deemed payment. This is because an employee would not have been allowed to deduct those wages when working out his or her taxable earnings from employment.

The worker may, however, be able to claim for—

– travel and related meal and accommodation costs incurred in doing the job or in travelling to a temporary workplace he or she had to attend to perform the job (see leaflet IR175, 'Common Questions'), and
– other necessary expenses incurred solely in doing the job.

Further guidance about what expenses may be claimed can be found in *Booklet 480—Expenses and Benefits -a tax guide* and *Booklet 490—Employee Travel – a tax and NICs guide for employees*.

Any such deduction made in working out the deemed payment does not affect the expenses that can be deducted in the company or partnership accounts.

Step Four

Deduct any capital allowances in respect of expenditure incurred by the intermediary that the worker could have claimed if employed by the client and he or she had incurred the expenditure.

Equipment or machinery is regarded as necessary if the worker could not do the job without it. The equipment and machinery must be things that each and every person doing that job would have to provide.

For example, an intermediary may own computer equipment. However, the client provides all of the equipment necessary to complete the job and the worker only uses the intermediary's equipment out of choice. In this case capital allowances will not be allowed for the intermediary's equipment.

The 'necessary' test does not apply for cars, motor bikes and bicycles. Therefore, it may be possible to claim capital allowances for a car, motorbike or bicycle that was used for work or in travelling to a temporary workplace the worker had to attend to perform the job.

Further guidance about claiming capital allowances can be found in Leaflet *IR125—Using your own car or motor bike for work* and in *Helpsheet IR206 – Capital allowances for employees and office holders*.

Any such capital allowances claimed in working out the deemed payment do not affect the capital allowances that can be deducted in the company or partnership accounts.

Step Five

Deduct any contributions to an approved pension scheme by the company for the benefit of the worker in the year.

Step Six

Deduct any employer's Class 1 and Class 1A NICs paid by the intermediary for that year in respect of salary or benefits in kind provided to the worker during the year.

The NICs should be calculated on an annual basis, whether or not the worker is a director of the company (see *CWG1 'Employer's Quick Guide to Pay As You Earn and National Insurance Contributions', Card 12 Company Directors – National Insurance Contributions*).

Step Seven

Deduct the amount of any salary and benefits in kind received during the same tax year by the worker from the intermediary which are already taxable under Schedule E. This does not include anything for which a deduction has already been given at Step Three. If the figure reached at Step Seven is nil or a negative number, then there is no deemed payment and no further tax or NICs are payable. If the result is positive, move on to Step Eight.

Step Eight

Deduct the amount of the Employer's NICs on the deemed payment. It is therefore necessary to calculate the amount, which, together with the employer's NICs on it, equals the result of Step Seven.

Step Nine

The amount that you are left with is the deemed payment on which tax and NICs are payable.

Examples of deemed payment calculations can be found on the Inland Revenue website at www.inlandrevenue.gov.uk/ir35.

April 2001. Tax Bulletin Issue 52

Corporation tax—large companies: quarterly instalment payments and group payment arrangements

We are approaching the end of the first annual cycle under the new corporation tax self assessment (CTSA) rules. Two significant changes for large companies have been the requirement to pay corporation tax by quarterly instalments (QIPs) and the option to pay on a group-wide basis through a group payment arrangement (GPA).

This article addresses some practical issues in relation to QIPs and GPAs. It does not attempt to outline the rules and practicalities of QIPs and GPAs. For this background, see—

– leaflet CTSA/BK3 ''A modern system for corporation tax payments'' available from the CTSA Orderline (telephone 0845 300 6555), and
– Chapters 12 and 13 of CTSA BK2 ''A guide to corporation tax self assessment for tax practitioners and Inland Revenue staff'' a copy of which was issued to all tax practitioners in April 1999 (now out of print).

Both of these guides are available on the Internet at www.inlandrevenue.gov.uk.

The scope of this article is limited to practical advice on specific technical and operational matters.

ANSWERS TO SOME PRACTICAL QUESTIONS

1. What difference should QIPs and GPAs make to the entries on a company's CT600 tax return form?

A company is required to show in its return if it considers that it was liable to pay by quarterly instalments on the basis of its self assessment. It must do this by putting an ''X'' in box 79 at the foot of page 5 (short calculation) or page 8 (detailed calculation).

We have seen a number of cases where a company has paid instalments but failed to put an ''X'' in Box 79. It is essential to make this entry **whether or not the company actually made the necessary payments**. We apply the normal ''Process Now, Check Later'' principle of self assessment to all aspects of the return, and the liability to pay by QIPs is no exception. Our computer system will initially calculate, charge and credit interest on the basis of the entry (or lack of an entry) in Box 79.

In particular, it makes no difference to the entry required in Box 79 that the company's instalment payments have been paid through a group payment arrangement. A large company participating in a GPA must still put a cross in Box 79.

A company whose corporation tax has been paid through a GPA—

– must indicate this by putting an ''X'' in Box 80. It should also
– enter ''£0.00p'' at Box 75 (''Tax already paid (and not repaid)'') except in the rare circumstance that the return is being filed after money has been allocated down to it from the GPA. And it should also
– leave Box 76 blank (''Tax Outstanding''). This is perfectly acceptable provided an ''X'' is present in Box 80.

In all other respects, it should complete the CT600 return form in exactly the same way as it would if there were no GPA in force. In particular, at Box 72 it must show its self assessment of the correct amount of tax payable by the company. The fact that this liability is actually paid through a GPA should not affect this entry.

We will not issue payment applications until the GPA is closed and the monies paid under the arrangement have been allocated out to the individual participating companies.

[Illustration of worked example not reproduced]

2. How can companies help to ensure that the payments they make are correctly allocated by the Inland Revenue?

The introduction of QIPs has highlighted the problems that can occur if the correct payslip or payment reference number is not used.

Our Accounts Offices handle many thousands of payments each day and most are processed automatically, using the reference number on the payslip enclosed with a cheque payment or quoted in the transmission with an electronic payment. All payslips that we issue are encoded to tell our computer—

– the taxpayer reference, and
– the appropriate accounting period.

Each payslip is intended for a specific taxpayer and a specific accounting period. The payment reference shown on your payslip will be in the following format:

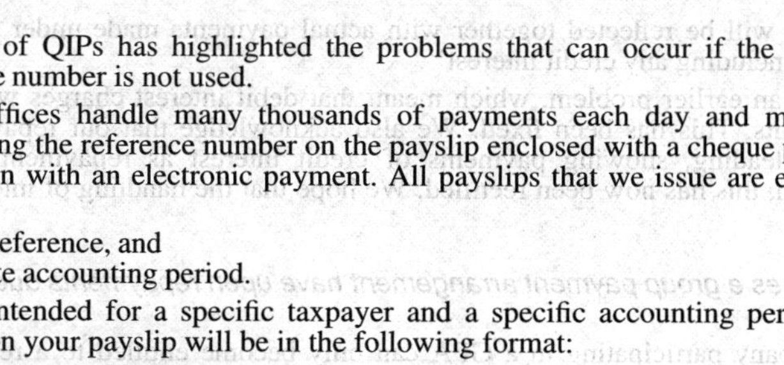

1234567890A00102A

1234567890 — This part is the company's taxpayer reference

02 — This part tells the computer the period to which the payment relates

It is important that you use the correct payslip or quote the correct reference for each payment you make.

We have seen a number of cases where a company has used the wrong payslip or quoted the wrong reference, leading to payments being allocated automatically to the wrong period. This is not easy for us to spot and we cannot guarantee to correct such errors before the return is filed. So if you make a mistake, it can lead to incorrect interest calculations and even incorrect repayments.

It is particularly important that you take care to use the correct payslip during the QIP transitional period, when you may need to make payments for more than one accounting period at much the same time. And if you intend to pay electronically by either CHAPS or BACS, please ensure that the reference you give to your bank is both correct and complete.

3. How does the Inland Revenue deal with interest in relation to a company's QIP liability?

We pay ''credit interest'' on all overpaid balances between the due date of the first QIP and the normal due date (nine months and one day after the end of the accounting period). We charge ''debit interest'' on all underpaid balances during this same period. Credit and debit interest are calculated on a daily basis on the positive or negative balance for each day of the period. There are some worked examples at paragraph 12.10.7 of CTSA/BK2.

We calculate credit and debit interest retrospectively, once the normal due date has passed and the tax charge is established—normally from the self assessment in the company's tax return.

For a company which is **not part of a group payment arrangement**, this means that we normally credit or charge the interest to its account as soon as we process the return form (or when the normal due date passes, if the return is filed before then).

For a company which is a **participator** in a GPA, we credit or charge the interest to its account when we allocate out to individual participating companies the payments made into the arrangement. We do this when the group returns its allocation instructions in response to the ''Closure Notice'' (Form CT630) or, if the group does not specify an allocation, 30 days after we send out our proposed allocation on Form CT631.

We immediately post the credit or debit to the company's account with us for the accounting period and it is set against, or added to, any unpaid tax for the period.

If the corporation tax paid (either directly by the company, or allocated to it from a GPA) as at the normal due date is less than the company's corporation tax liability, we charge late payment interest on the unpaid amount until the date it is paid. This is charged at a higher rate than the debit interest applicable to underpaid balances before the normal due date.

If we repay corporation tax to a company after the normal due date, we add repayment interest to the repayment. This repayment interest is calculated from the normal due date (or the date the repaid tax was paid, if that is later) to the date of repayment. It is paid at a lower rate than the credit interest rate applicable to overpaid balances before the normal due date.

4. How can one tell what interest has been credited or charged to a company's account?

By the time you read this article, repayment notifications will include—

- both credit interest and repayment interest under the heading ''Interest payable to you'', and
- both debit interest and late payment interest under the heading ''Interest payable by you''.

Reconciliation statements, applications for payment and the like will show

- ''Interest accrued, including any debit interest'' as an element within the total amount chargeable, and
- credit interest will be reflected together with actual payments made under the heading ''less already paid, including any credit interest''.

We apologise for an earlier problem, which meant that debit interest charges were being omitted from certain outputs. This has been fixed. We also acknowledge that our repayment notification outputs were misleading, showing payments of credit interest as repayments of tax, without explanation. Again, this has now been rectified. We hope that the handling of interest on our forms is now clearer.

5. What effect does a group payment arrangement have upon repayments due to a participating company?

Normally, a company participating in a GPA can only become entitled to a repayment once the appropriate proportion of the payments made for the group as a whole have been allocated to it, following Closure. But once that has happened, the money allocated to an individual company from the arrangement is treated for all purposes as having been paid by the company on the dates it was actually paid into the GPA.

If the money allocated to a company, plus any credit interest to which it is entitled, exceeds its total liabilities (corporation tax, interest and any penalty) for the accounting period, the company becomes entitled to a repayment as if it had paid the tax directly. We will normally process this automatically, without claim. So if you want us to deal with such an overpayment in a specific way, it is important that you tell the Inspector who deals with the company, in advance. Equally, the company can give notice that any such balance is to be surrendered under Finance Act 1989 Section 102, subject to the normal conditions of such a surrender.

However, a company may be entitled, without awaiting the closure of the GPA for the period, to immediate payment of certain surpluses revealed by its return where there is no net corporation tax liability. In particular, this may apply to income tax deducted at source from gross income, construction industry deductions or a payable research and development tax credit. You should make the relevant claims in the company's return in the normal way.

6. What effect does a GPA have on the operation of FA 1989 s 102?

A group payment arrangement is clearly not itself a company. So neither FA 1989 s 102 itself, nor its extension under the Corporation Tax (Instalment Payments) Regulations, SI 1998/3175 reg 9 (''the QIP regulations'') can apply to any transfer of money between a GPA and an individual company, whether or not that company is a participator in the arrangement. But there will generally be an alternative way of dealing with any overpayment which will be equally efficient in mitigating the group's overall interest exposure.

EXAMPLE 1

A Ltd files its return for its accounting period 1.1.2000–31.12.2000. The bulk of the company's income is investment income from which income tax has been deducted. After set-off against A Ltd's corporation tax liability, there is an income tax repayment due to it of £50,000. The company wishes to surrender this amount under FA 1989 s 102 to other members of its group, all of whom are participators in a GPA.

It is not possible to ''pay'' this surrender ''into the GPA''. (It makes no difference whether A Ltd is itself a participator in the GPA or not.) However, it is perfectly possible, subject to the rules of FA 1989 s 102, for A Ltd to surrender the repayment to the individual companies in the usual way. A Ltd should give notice in its return and make the relevant entries in Section 7 of the return form in the usual way. The group will then need to take the surrendered amounts into account when allocating money from the group payment arrangement to the participating companies at closure.

EXAMPLE 2

B Ltd is a member of a GPA for its first CTSA accounting period, 1.4.1999–31.3.2000.

B Ltd's liability for its last Pay and File accounting period, 1.4.1998–31.3.1999, has just been settled and the company is entitled to a repayment of £20,000 for that period. There are no outstanding liabilities of other group members for this year against which it can surrender this repayment under S.102.

As in Example 1, the company cannot ''pay'' this money into the GPA. However, it may be advantageous from an interest point of view to set this repayment against its liability for the next period and for the group to reduce the payments it makes into the GPA on B Ltd's behalf accordingly. This is perfectly acceptable, and the company should tell the Inspector if it wants this to happen. Again, the group will need to take this into account when allocating the payments made into the GPA between the participators at closure.

EXAMPLE 3

C Ltd is the nominated company in relation to the ''Sea Activities'' GPA for the period 1.4.2000–31.3.2001. Management accounts show that payments into the GPA for this period have been excessive and C Ltd is in a position to claim a repayment from the GPA of £1.5 million.

D Ltd is a 75% subsidiary of C Ltd, but is not in the Sea Activities GPA. It has not paid any quarterly instalments for its accounting period 1.4.2000–31.3.2001, but its circumstances changed during the latter part of the year and management accounts show, in retrospect, that it should have done so.

The group has a choice:

– C Ltd can claim the full repayment under Clause 4 of the GPA contract and ask for the necessary amount to be credited to D Ltd's account for the period. However, this will not be interest-efficient. At this stage FA 1989 s 102 cannot apply, as no individual company is entitled to a repayment. The credit to D Ltd's account will only be effective from the date on which it is agreed, not on the original dates of payment into the GPA.

Alternatively

– C Ltd can leave all or part of the potential repayment in the GPA and distribute it as a surplus to one or more of the participating companies at closure. That company (or companies) can then give joint notice with D Ltd under FA 1989 s 102 and SI 1998/3175 reg 9. This is likely to prove more effective in mitigating the interest effects of D Ltd's failure to pay by QIPs.

Either way, D Ltd should write immediately to the Inspector who deals with its affairs to explain the reasons for the original error in relation to its instalment payment obligations, and to set out the intended course of action. We would not seek a penalty for non-payment under the Regulations in such a case, where it is clear that the group has acted in good faith and taken action to correct its failure to pay by QIPs at the first opportunity.

7. How should a group decide, at closure, the allocation of payments made into a GPA between the individual participating companies?

A group payment arrangement clearly simplifies the making of payments. But the real advantage of a GPA comes at closure. Paying through a GPA allows the group benefit of hindsight in allocating payments made on behalf of many companies between the individual companies. By tailoring the division of each individual payment made between the participating companies, the group can optimise the overall interest position. This is entirely legitimate and is the point of the arrangement.

We have seen instances of groups allocating payments in a way which does not appear to be advantageous. This may be based upon a misconception. For example, one group allocated each payment in proportion to the tax liabilities of the participating companies, even though some are not liable to pay by QIPs, and the allocation results in a higher than necessary overall debit interest liability for the group. There are no restrictions of this kind.

It is only advisable to allocate instalment payments to non-QIP companies if either—

- the payment being allocated is in excess of the overall liability of the participating companies liable to pay by QIPs as at the next instalment date, or
- there is likely to be an uplift in the tax charge of the company in question for the period beyond its original self assessment, for example where we have its return under enquiry at the point of closure.

On the other hand, we have also seen a number of notices of apportionment in which the group has asked to allocate a negative amount to a particular participating company from one or more payment- for example, allocating a payment of £500,000 between 3 companies: £300,000 to A; £400,000 to B; (minus £200,000) to C.

This is not permissible. The group's power of apportionment under Clause 8 of the GPA contract relates to "payments made"–that is, actual amounts of money, not notional figures. Clearly a negative payment is not possible.

8. Does it matter if there is a delay in informing the Revenue that a company participating in a GPA has left the group?

Yes. Clause 13.1 says that "The Nominated Company shall immediately remove any of the Participating Companies (other than the Nominated Company) from the Arrangement, by giving notice in writing to that effect to the Board, if such company has ceased to be a member of the ... Group..."

A group which fails to do so with reasonable speed is in default of its obligations under the contract. And failure to remove such a company expeditiously can lead to real practical problems.

EXAMPLE

A group has a GPA for the period 1.4.2000–31.3.2001.

In December 2000, one of the participating companies is sold out of the group, so is no longer eligible to be a member of the GPA.

If the group does not remove the company from the arrangement before 31.3.2001, the effect of Clause 14(*a*) of the contract is that the Nominated company remains liable to pay the liabilities of the sold company for the period. And if the company is only removed from the arrangement when the Revenue exercises its power under Clause 13.2 of the contact, the Nominated company is likely to retain the obligation to pay the company's tax for the following accounting period as well.

9. Does a GPA have to fall if the nominated company draws up accounts for a period exceeding 12 months?

On the basis of the standard contract, yes. The contract is structured around the concept of a "Period of Account", which is defined in Clause 1.(1) as "any period **not exceeding 12 months** for which the Nominated company draws up its accounts".

On the face of it, this invalidates any contract, and so any GPA, where the Nominated company draws up an account for a period exceeding 12 months. This can be a problem, for example, where a group is taken over and required to bring its reporting date into line with the new parent.

To overcome this difficulty, we have introduced an Annex to the contract which the group can choose to adopt if it wishes, rather than allowing the GPA to lapse. The effect of the Annex is to treat the long period of account as two periods of account for the purposes of the GPA.

Groups affected by this sort of situation should seek advice from the Group Payment Team at the Inland Revenue Accounts Office to which they make payments.

CREDIT AND DEBIT INTEREST, AND THE LOAN RELATIONSHIP RULES

All interest paid by the Inland Revenue to companies is now taxable, following changes in FA 1998 ss 33 and 34. Similarly, interest charged by us from a company is allowable for tax purposes in the same way as other interest paid by a company.

Of itself, this change simplifies the tax computation, as ''Inland Revenue interest'' no longer needs to be adjusted for. However, we do recognise that some practical difficulties are associated with the change, particularly in relation to debit and credit interest accruing during the period prior to the accounting date.

This interest falls within the scope of the loan relationships legislation, in the same way as any other kind of interest receivable and payable. Under the loan relationship rules the interest should be taxed/relieved in accordance with an accepted accruals method of accounting—a receipts/payments basis is not acceptable.

In practice, this may be hard to do with certainty. We expect Inspectors to take a pragmatic view, recognising the inherent practical problems.

June 2001. Tax Bulletin Issue 53

Income Tax Self-Assessment (ITSA) Returns for 2000–01

As we start to receive the 2000–01 income tax return forms we have tried to identify areas which have caused concern in the past, to see how we can help avoid any problems this year. This article gives a brief outline of our position on three issues—

– signatures on ITSA return (and other) forms;
– using provisional figures in returns;
– rejecting unsatisfactory return forms.

1. SIGNATURES

TMA 1970 s 8(2) requires that every return should include a declaration by the person making the return to the effect that the return is to the best of his knowledge correct and complete. We consider that the obligation to make this declaration is one which the person making the return cannot delegate. Accordingly, it is normal practice to insist that a paper return should be signed by the taxpayer personally. Similarly, where the taxpayer makes a return using the Internet service for Self Assessment the return should be personally authenticated by the taxpayer using their confidential password and User ID. Where an agent sends in the return electronically the taxpayer must sign a copy of the return before the electronic version is sent. The exceptions to this are where, because of the age, physical infirmity or mental incapacity of the taxpayer, they are unable to cope adequately with the management of their affairs or where their general health might suffer if they were troubled for a personal signature. In such special circumstances we accept the signature of an attorney who has full knowledge of the taxpayer's affairs.

In all other cases we expect the return to be signed by the taxpayer. If the signature does not appear to be that of the taxpayer we will reject the return form as not satisfying the requirements of TMA 1970 s 8. The form will be sent back to whoever submitted it (taxpayer or agent) with an explanation. If this is close to the filing deadline there is a risk of incurring a late filing penalty (see ''unsatisfactory returns'' below). Where the taxpayer is travelling a lot, working or living abroad, we expect them to make arrangements with their agent to ensure that they do sign the return form in time to file by the statutory deadline.

It is worth noting that we also need the taxpayer's signature on the form 64-8, giving an agent authority to receive Revenue documents on their behalf. We cannot pass any information to, or discuss the client's tax matters with, the agent without the taxpayer's signed authority. We may ask for another form 64-8 to be completed if it is not clear that an authority we have already received has been signed by the taxpayer.

2. PROVISIONAL FIGURES

Our approach to handling returns containing provisional figures evolved over the first couple of years of income tax self assessment. We explained our position on the use of provisional figures in returns in Tax Bulletins Issue 37 (October 1998) and Issue 44 (December 1999). The first addressed the issue in detail for 1997–98, and TB44 reiterated the message for 1998–99 returns.

We are now in the fifth year of self-assessment. Our view of the legal position has not changed. There are limited circumstances in which we can accept provisional figures as meeting the obligation to file a return and these were set out in detail in TB37 (pages 593-6). But we are now clear that a return containing unjustified provisional figures should be returned to the taxpayer or agent. Our guidance to staff (for example in Enquiry Handbook at EH260) has been updated to explain this approach as appropriate for current and future self-assessment returns.

Where a provisional figure is used we require the taxpayer to tick box 23.3 (for 2000–01 return) and to use the additional information section on the last page of the core return to give—

– an acceptable explanation for the delay in providing final figures, AND
– a date by which they expect to provide the final figure.

Unless both of the above are given we will reject the return as not satisfying the requirements of TMA 1970 s 8.

We will not regard pressure of work either on the taxpayer or their tax adviser, or the complexity of the taxpayer's affairs, as reasons for accepting a return containing provisional figures.

3. REJECTING UNSATISFACTORY RETURN FORMS

In the past we have allowed a 14-day period of grace (when we do not charge a fixed late-filing penalty) where we have sent back an ITSA return form, received on or before the filing deadline, because something is missing. Tax Bulletin 37 said "we will be monitoring the operation of the concession this year and, depending on the outcome, may recommend that it is established as a formal Extra-Statutory Concession". We have reviewed the operation of the period of grace and have decided to continue the practice for 2000–01 returns. We have not decided, at this stage, to establish the period of grace as an Extra-Statutory Concession. Instead we are including this within wider options under consideration to help and encourage people to file on time.

In Tax Bulletin 37, and in other places, we have referred to these returns as "incomplete returns". We now believe this could be misleading. A return from which income has been omitted is "incomplete" but it is still a return under TMA 1970 s 8. We would deal with the omission by opening an enquiry and not by sending the form back to the customer. We are sorry to introduce new terminology but in future we shall refer to returns we reject at the processing stage as "unsatisfactory returns", because they fail to satisfy TMA 1970 s 8.

We will send back a return form when it fails to satisfy the requirements of TMA 1970 s 8. Some examples of an unsatisfactory return form are those—

- not in the prescribed form (standard Revenue form or agreed alternative);
- not signed by the person making the return;
- with a box ticked on page 2 (to say a supplementary page is needed) but the relevant pages not attached;
- containing unjustified provisional figures (see requirements above).

Unsatisfactory returns (those failing to satisfy TMA 1970 s 8) will be sent back to whoever submitted them (taxpayer or agent) with an explanatory letter. Where an unsatisfactory return form is received before the filing deadline the customer has until the normal filing date to send back a satisfactory return. In past years we have applied the 14-day period of grace to all unsatisfactory returns received on or before the filing date. We realise this is unnecessary and could be viewed as coercive because until we are within a fortnight of the filing date the customer has longer (up to the filing date) in which to file.

If we receive an unsatisfactory return form on the filing date, or within the previous 13 days we will not charge a late-filing penalty if a satisfactory return is then received within 14 days from the date of our letter sending back the unsatisfactory return. We will also allow a 14-day period of grace where an unsatisfactory return was received earlier but not sent back until on or after the date 13 days before the filing date.

For example: an unsatisfactory return form, to which the 31 January filing date applies, received on any day from 18 January to 31 January will be sent back with a letter allowing the 14 days period of grace. An unsatisfactory return form received on 10 January but not sent back until the 20 January will also be given the benefit of the 14 days. An unsatisfactory return form received and sent back on 11 January would not be given the 14 day period of grace because it is not needed (the customer has 20 days to 31 January). An unsatisfactory return form received on 1 February, or on any day after, is already late and the customer will be asked to send a satisfactory return as soon as possible. We will not give the 14 day period of grace in these cases.

Our aim in doing this is not to penalise someone who has genuinely forgotten something, such as signing the return. The 14-day period of grace will not be given in cases where the taxpayer appears to be using deliberate delaying tactics (for example, unjustified provisional figures put into a last-minute return year on year).

Returns received after the statutory filing date will not have the benefit of any period of grace.

August 2001. Tax Bulletin Issue 54

Gross payments of interest

This article outlines changes made by Finance Acts 2000 and 2001 to the rules requiring deduction of tax at source from certain payments of interest. Although the types of interest payment involved differ, both sets of new rules came into force on **1 April 2001**. From that date companies have been able to make many more payments of interest without deducting income tax and, as a consequence, both individuals and companies have received more payments of interest gross. The Inland Revenue has received enquiries about these changes and this article is intended to clarify the position for payers, for those who may now be receiving payments gross, and for any tax professionals asked to explain why some interest payments have begun to be made without income tax having been deducted.

CHANGES MADE BY FA 2000

Amongst other things FA 2000—

- repealed TA 1988 ss 118A–118K which placed an obligation on UK paying and collecting agents to deduct tax from foreign dividends (including interest);
- repealed TA 1988 s 124 which deals with interest on quoted Eurobonds, and
- amended TA 1988 s 349 by bringing UK public revenue dividends into the general provisions for the deduction of tax at source, and incorporating within the section an updated definition of a Eurobond.

PUBLIC REVENUE DIVIDENDS

The inclusion of public revenue dividends within TA 1988 s 349 ensures that, unless there are specific provisions to the contrary elsewhere in the Taxes Acts, tax will be deducted from gilt interest, or other public revenue dividends.

The rule for interest on UK gilt edged securities (gilts) is set out at TA 1988 s 50. This provides that interest on bearer and registered gilts flows gross. A holder of registered gilts can, however, continue to request net payment under the provisions of TA 1988 s 50(2). These specific provisions override the general provisions for deduction of tax in TA 1988 s 349.

PAYMENTS OF INTEREST ON A QUOTED EUROBOND

Under TA 1988 s 349(3)(*c*) payments of interest on a quoted Eurobond are excluded from the general requirement to deduct income tax. The updated definition of a quoted Eurobond can be found in TA 1988 s 349(4). A ''quoted Eurobond'' now means any security that:

- is issued by a company;
- is listed on a recognised stock exchange, and
- carries a right to receive interest.

This definition is more widely drawn than the definition in TA 1988 s 124 so that now all **listed** securities issued by companies will pay interest gross both to individuals and to companies.

CHANGES MADE BY FA 2001

FA 2001 made more changes which impact on TA 1988 s 349. Again these changes have increased the likelihood of interest being paid and received gross.

FA 2001 inserted new TA 1988 ss 349A to 349D. Under these provisions companies (or partnerships with at least one member which is a company) will be able to pay interest as well as certain royalties, annuities and annual payments without deducting income tax when the person beneficially entitled to the income is:

- a UK resident company;
- a partnership where all the members are UK companies; or
- a UK branch of a non resident company, where the income will be charged to CT.

The normal TA 1988 s 349 requirement to deduct tax is switched off when the payer 'reasonably believes' that the recipient is within one of these categories. It should be noted that the provisions refer to a 'company' which, as defined by TA 1988 s 832, means:

> ''any body corporate or unincorporated association but does not include a partnership, a local authority or a local authority association.''

Thus payments made by and to local authorities are not included in the new provisions while payments made to a charity might be. They are included if the payments are made by a company and the recipient charity is constituted as a UK resident company.

REASONABLE BELIEF

Basing the obligation to deduct income tax on ''reasonable belief'' rather than an objective test enables companies to make gross payments even when it is not possible to verify the circumstances of the recipient directly. For instance, where the payment will be made through a series of intermediaries it should be possible for the payer to reach a reasonable belief based on the evidence provided by an intermediary.

What would constitute grounds for ''reasonable belief'' will vary depending on the relationship between the payer and payee. Where, for example, a payment is made between associated companies, the payer is in a good position to know whether the recipient is the beneficial owner and meets the conditions to receive the payment gross. Where the payer and payee are not known to each other, the payer may want to obtain documentary evidence of the status of the recipient, perhaps in the form of a statement signed by the appropriate officer of the company. Such a statement might contain either—

- confirmation that the recipient is beneficially entitled to the income and meets the conditions to receive the payment gross; or

– if the recipient is a nominee, confirmation that the beneficial owner meets these conditions.

The Revenue is willing to work with market operators and support them in drawing up their market-sector specific guidance.

If the payer is in doubt as to the accuracy or trustworthiness of the evidence provided by the payee then the payer will not have reasonable grounds for believing the payee is entitled to receive the payment gross and should therefore make the payment under deduction of income tax.

WHAT IF A REASONABLE BELIEF PROVES INCORRECT?

The right to make a payment gross based on the payer's reasonable belief does not affect the Revenue's right to recover tax and interest from the payer where it is subsequently found that the recipient was not within any of the categories of recipient to which the new gross payments rule applies. It is for this reason that some payers may wish to seek indemnities as protection from the risk of paying gross where this is not appropriate.

There will not normally be any question of a penalty being imposed on a company which makes a mistake. If, however, the company makes a payment without deducting tax when it does not believe (or could not reasonably believe) that the beneficial owner is in one of the relevant categories, the Revenue will consider seeking a penalty.

October 2001. Tax Bulletin Issue 55

The taxation of share options: internationally mobile employees

SHARE OPTIONS

Share incentives available to internationally mobile employees can take various forms. This article is about share and stock options.

Employees can be granted options to acquire shares in their employing company or a company in the same group. Typically the employee is granted options to acquire a specified number of shares at a price fixed at grant — the ''option price''. This may be set at the market value of the shares at the date of grant or at a lower figure. The option will then be exercised some years later, when the employee buys shares at the option price. The shares then belong to the employee and can usually be immediately sold.

DOMESTIC LEGISLATION

The UK tax treatment of such options in the hands of the employee depends on factors such as:

- Whether or not it was granted under a plan providing income tax advantages-the Inland Revenue approved Company Share Option Plan or a SAYE share option plan within TA 1988 Schs 9 and 10, or an Enterprise Management Incentive (EMI) option within FA 2000 Sch 14;
- The employee's residence status at the dates of grant and exercise;
- The period over which the option can be exercised;
- Whether the option was granted at a price below the market value of the shares at the time of grant.

This article is concerned only with options granted under an unapproved share option plan and non-qualifying exercises of options granted under an Inland Revenue approved plan. A ''non-qualifying'' exercise here means one where the conditions for income tax relief have not been followed, such that there is an income tax charge. An EMI also provides income tax exemption on the exercise of certain share options, but income tax may be due if the options were issued at a discount to the share price or there has been a disqualifying event. To the extent that gains on such options remain in charge to income tax, this article applies to them in the same way as to unapproved share options.

Further information on approved plans and EMI can be found at www.inlandrevenue.gov.uk/shareschemes

There will normally be UK income tax implications only if the individual was resident in the UK at the date of grant, or the option was granted in respect of duties carried out in the UK. As the option over the shares is acquired by reason of employment a tax charge may arise under Schedule E at:

- The date the option was granted;
- The date the option was exercised; or
- The date the shares acquired at exercise are disposed of.

Capital gains tax may be due where gains on the disposal of shares are greater than the gain chargeable to tax under Schedule E. Examples are where:

- The sale price exceeds the exercise price, or
- The individual was not resident in the UK at the date of the event.

Capital gains tax may arise where individuals are either resident or ordinarily resident in the UK at the date of disposal or if they are within the scope of the temporary non-residents rules contained in TCGA 1992 s 10A. There are special rules for the tax year of commencement or cessation of residence and for non-UK domiciliaries.

A UK tax charge may be triggered by other events, such as the assignment or release of an option to acquire shares, or the conversion of shares acquired by reason of employment from one class of share into another class of share. This article cannot cover every possible situation but guidance about circumstances not dealt with here is available from the contacts listed at the end.

INTERACTION WITH DOUBLE TAXATION AGREEMENTS

If the employee moves between countries a tax charge may also arise in another country when the option is exercised, assigned or released. This article sets out the Revenue's current practice for dealing with possible double taxation in the most common scenarios.

The UK is actively involved at the Organisation for Economic Co-operation and Development (OECD) with their work on reaching a common international consensus on the treatment of share option gains.

If there is no Double Taxation Agreement (DTA) with the other country then both countries are free to tax income in accordance with their domestic laws. In some circumstances, however, the United Kingdom will grant its residents unilateral relief in respect of foreign tax suffered on income that arises in another country but is taxed in the UK on the basis of residence.

However if a comprehensive DTA exists it will normally have an employment income Article along the lines of Article 15 of the OECD Model Tax Convention. Gains realised from the exercise of options granted to an employee fall within the provisions of this Article rather than those Articles that deal with other income or capital gains.

Article 15(1) provides that if a resident of one country performs the duties of his employment in the other country, then the latter country retains any domestic rights to taxation of remuneration and benefits from that portion of the employment.

To avoid double taxation, where an employee:

- was granted a share option in the UK during the course of an employment,
- exercised that employment in the other country during the period between the grant and exercise of the option,
- remains in that employment at the date of the exercise and,
- would be taxed by both of them in respect of the option gain; and
- is not resident in the UK at the date of exercise;

then the UK will give relief in calculating the tax charge for the proportion of the option gain which relates to the period or periods between the grant and exercise of the option during which the employee exercised the employment in the other country.

The gain will normally be time-apportioned on a straight-line basis. Periods not in that particular employment are left out of account so that the apportionment is still made on the basis of relative periods of employment in each country. Very occasionally this may not provide a sufficiently accurate apportionment. If so, another method may be used provided this does not produce double taxation or lead to income going untaxed in either country.

In other cases credit relief may be appropriate.

In the following examples:

- All the share option plans are unapproved;
- All references are to the Income and Corporation Taxes Act 1988 (ICTA) unless otherwise stated;
- There is a comprehensive DTA with the overseas country containing a provision along the lines of Article 15 of the OECD Model.

Example 1

Mr A is resident and ordinarily resident in the UK and working here on 1 January 1997. On that day he is granted an option to purchase 1,000 shares in the company in four years' time at the 1 January 1997 market price of £1. On 1 January 2001 he is moved to another country and is still in the employment there when the option is exercised on 1 January 2002. At that date the shares are worth £5 each.

A is resident and ordinarily resident in the UK at the date of grant and is therefore liable to income tax under Section 135 on any gain realised at exercise. The gain is calculated as the difference between (*a*) the value of the shares at the date of exercise and (*b*) the option price paid plus any consideration given for the option itself; in this case the gain is 1,000 x £4 = £4,000. The charge falls to Schedule E generally [Section I35(1),] rather than through any of the Cases of Schedule E and, as such, it arises regardless of the individual's residence status at the date of exercise.

Since the date of grant the employment has been performed in the UK for 4 years and in the other country for one year. 80% of the gain (£3,200) will therefore be assessed in the UK and 20% (£800) will be regarded as attributable to the other country.

The exercise of the option will be within the scope of PAYE by virtue of Section 203FB if the shares are readily convertible assets (see Tax Bulletin Issue 36, August 1998). Under Section 203F(3) the amount on which PAYE should be operated is the amount which, on the basis of the best estimate that can reasonably be made, is the amount of income likely to be chargeable to UK income tax. So if the employer has sufficiently accurate information on periods of employment spent abroad they may be able to operate PAYE for the non-resident employee only on the UK proportion.

EXAMPLE 2

The facts are the same as for example 1 except that A takes the whole of 1998 as a sabbatical year when he does not exercise his employment anywhere.

Four years have been spent in employment over the period between the grant and exercise of the option. The total gain in value of £4,000 is apportioned 75% to the UK and 25% to the other country.

EXAMPLE 3

Mr B is resident and ordinarily resident in the UK and working here on 1 December 1996 when he is granted a share option. He works overseas during 1997. He returns to the UK on 1 January 1998 and is still in the employment here when he exercises the option on 1 January 2001.

As B is not resident in the other country either when the option is granted or when it is exercised it is very unlikely that any tax could be charged there in respect of the share option. As he is resident in the UK at both grant and exercise, the UK will tax the whole gain. If any tax has been paid in respect of the option in the other country for the year spent working there then the UK will give credit for this against the Section 135 charge.

EXAMPLE 4

Mrs C is resident but not ordinarily resident in the UK when an option is granted. She is still resident in the UK when she exercises the option and sells the shares.

At the time of grant the UK charge in respect of the employment is not under Case I of Schedule E therefore Section 135 will not apply. C will be liable to UK income tax under Section 162(5) at the time of disposal of the shares. The charge is on the difference between the market value of the shares at the time of exercise less any amounts paid. This is treated as a notional loan written off within Section 160(2) and as emoluments of the employment.

If an individual is resident in the UK at both the date of grant and the date of exercise the UK will have primary taxing rights even where a treaty partner country wishes to tax the gain under its own domestic legislation. However a claim under the employment income Article of the DTA may be relevant if the duties of the employment have been carried out in the other country during the period between grant and exercise of the option and double taxation has occurred.

C may, however, be liable to UK capital gains tax on any gain she makes on selling the shares acquired by exercising the option. Her allowable cost will be the total of the amounts she paid for the option and shares together with any amount charged to UK income tax under Section 162(5). There are special capital gains rules for non-domiciliaries at Section 12, TCGA 1992.

EXAMPLE 5

Mrs D is not resident and not ordinarily resident in the UK when her employer grants her an option to purchase shares. At some time before exercise she moves to the UK and performs the duties of the employment there. She exercises the option when working in the UK and sells the shares.

D will not be liable to UK income tax on any gain realised at exercise, unless the grant of the option is clearly related to duties performed in the UK. In this case there could be a liability under Section 162 although all relevant facts and circumstances would need to be considered before determining whether or not a liability arises.

She may, however, be liable to UK capital gains tax on any gain realised as a result of selling the shares acquired following the exercise of the option. This would be so if she is either resident or ordinarily resident in the UK at the date of disposal or if she is within the scope of the temporary non-residents rules contained in Section 10A, TCGA 1992. There are special capital gains rules for the tax year she commences UK residence and for the case where she is a non-UK domiciliary. D's allowable capital gains cost would be the total of her payments for the option and shares together with any amount charged to UK income tax under Section 162(5).

Even though exercise will not normally trigger a UK income tax liability in this case, it may well give rise to a tax charge in another country. Strictly, the exercise of the option and the subsequent disposal of the shares are two distinct events and the UK is not obliged to allow a foreign tax credit for any foreign tax paid on exercise against any UK capital gains tax payable on disposal. Nevertheless, where tax has been paid in a treaty partner country, we will treat all or part of the gain as falling within the provisions of the employment income Article of the relevant double taxation agreement and allow the relevant proportion of the foreign tax paid as a credit against the UK capital gains tax:

If the options are exercised and the shares sold on the same day, the whole gain is treated as falling within the provisions of the employment income Article of the relevant DTA.

If the shares are disposed of at a later date, part of the gain may be treated as falling within the employment income Article of the agreement. All the facts and circumstances in a particular case will be considered and the tax treatment will depend on such factors as whether the share price has increased or decreased, or whether there have been significant changes in the share price since exercise.

We will allow a proportion of the foreign tax paid as a credit against UK capital gains tax normally calculated on a time apportionment basis by reference to periods of employment abroad. It does not matter whether the foreign tax was charged on grant, exercise or some other occasion. The credit for foreign tax can never exceed the UK tax payable on the relevant proportion of the total gain.

FURTHER ADVICE

We intend to publish a further article shortly covering other issues around share incentives for internationally mobile employees, principally National Insurance Contributions.

For further advice on domestic legislation governing the charge to tax on share options, contact:

Martin Randall, Revenue Policy, Savings, Pensions and Share Schemes, 111 New Wing, Somerset House, Strand, London WC2R 1LB. Tel: 020 7438 6778; e-mail: Martin.Randall@ir.gsi.gov.uk.

For further advice on the PAYE treatment of share options, contact:

Peter Walker, Personal Tax (Solihull), 550 Streetsbrook Road, Solihull, West Midlands B91 1QU. Tel: 0121 713 4602; e-mail: Peter.Walker@ir.gsi.gov.uk.

And for further advice on international aspects, contact:

Susan New, Revenue Policy International, Victory House, 30–34 Kingsway, London WC2B 6ES. Tel: 020 7438 7250; e-mail: Susan.New@ir.gsi.gov.uk.

15 November 2001. Inland Revenue

CGT—more debentures to qualify for business assets taper relief

More assets are to qualify for business assets taper relief, and capital gains tax will be simplified, as the ways in which certain debentures benefit from taper relief and are treated in other capital gains tax provisions are aligned, Paymaster General Dawn Primarolo announced today.

DETAIL

1. Legislation will be introduced so that debentures that are deemed to be securities for certain purposes by TCGA 1992 s 251(6) will also be treated as securities for capital gains tax (CGT) taper relief.

2. Companies may merge, be taken over, reorganise their share capital, convert their securities, or reorganise in other ways.

3. Subject to conditions, special provisions ensure that there is no immediate CGT charge when a company reorganisation occurs and shares or debentures are exchanged for, or converted to, other shares or debentures. Instead, investors are treated as holding a single continuous asset consisting of the old and new shares etc.

4. Debentures may or may not be securities. Gains on debentures are normally liable to CGT only if the debentures are securities.

5. TCGA 1992 s 251(6) provides that all debentures that are received in company reorganisations are deemed to be securities for certain purposes. One consequence is that if debentures which would not otherwise be securities are issued in exchange for shares, any chargeable gains on the shares will be taken into account when the debentures are disposed of.

6. CGT taper relief was introduced in 1998. It reduces the amount of a gain that is charged to tax the longer an asset is held. The business assets rate of CGT taper relief is available on certain shares and securities, including all shares and securities in unlisted trading companies.

7. To simplify CGT, all debentures that are deemed to be securities under TCGA 1992 s 251(6) will now also be treated as securities for taper relief. Holders of such instruments will therefore not have to address the question whether the debentures actually are securities when considering the rate of taper relief. Holders will still need to consider whether the debentures meet the other conditions for business assets taper relief.

8. The legislation will take effect for disposals from 6 April 2001 and for holding periods from 6 April 1998.

9. The measure is wholly relieving.

NOTES

10. On 18 June 2001, as part of the ''Enterprise for all initiative'', the Chancellor of the Exchequer launched a consultation seeking good value for money ways to simplify CGT within the existing policy framework. Today's decision is the first change to be announced as a result of that initiative. Others are being considered. For more information see www.hm-treasury.gov.uk.

11. The announcement was made by the Paymaster General in response to a written Parliamentary Question.

Commentary—*Simon's Direct Tax Service* **C1.408, C2.1422, C2.804A**.

December 2001. Tax Bulletin Issue 56

Liability to pay Class 1 National Insurance Contributions: Internationally mobile employees

INTRODUCTION

This article sets out the Revenue's current practice for dealing with questions of Class 1 National Insurance Contributions ('NICs') liability in the most common scenarios when options are granted by employers to and subsequently exercised by an internationally mobile workforce.

Share incentives available to internationally mobile employees can take various forms. This article is about share and stock options and is concerned only with:

– options granted under an unapproved share option plan; and
– non-qualifying exercises of options granted under an Inland Revenue approved plan.

Employees can be granted options to acquire shares in their employing company or a company in the same group. Typically the employee is granted options to acquire a specified number of shares at a price fixed at grant-the "option price". This may be set at the market value of the shares at the date of grant or at a lower figure. The option will normally then be exercised at a later date, when the employee buys shares at the option price. The shares then belong to the employee and can usually be immediately sold.

LIABILITY TO PAY

The NICs treatment of such options in the hands of the employee depends on such factors as:

– whether the worker is a EC national and falls within UK legislation under Council Regulation European Economic Community (EEC) 1408/71;
– whether the worker falls within UK legislation under a Social Security Reciprocal Agreement or Double Contribution Convention;
– whether or not it was granted under a plan providing income tax advantages – the Inland Revenue approved Company Share Option Plan or a SAYE share option plan within Schedules 9 and 10 Income and Corporation Taxes Act (TA 1988), or an Enterprise Management Incentive (EMI) option within Schedule 14 Finance Act (FA) 2000;
– the employee's residence status at the dates of exercise;
– the period over which the option can be exercised;
– whether the option was granted at a price below the market value of the shares at the time of grant; and
– whether there is a charge to income tax under Section 135 TA 1988 on exercise.

Enterprise Management Initiative (EMI) also provides income tax exemption on the exercise of certain share options, but NICs may be due if the options were issued at a discount to the share price or there has been a disqualifying event. To the extent that gains on such options remain in charge to NICs, this article applies to them in the same way as to unapproved share options. [Further information on approved plans and EMI can be found at: www.inlandrevenue.gov.uk/shareschemes]

A liability to pay Class 1 NICs may be triggered by other events, such as the assignment or release of an option to acquire shares, or the conversion of shares acquired by reason of employment from one class of share into another class of share. This article does not cover every possible situation but guidance about circumstances not dealt with here is available from the contacts listed at the end.

INTERACTION WITH COUNCIL REGULATION EUROPEAN ECONOMIC COMMUNITY (EEC) 1408/71 AND RECIPROCAL AGREEMENTS/DOUBLE CONTRIBUTION CONVENTIONS

The objectives of the EC legislation and Reciprocal Agreement (RAs) are to:

– prevent a dual contribution liability;
– prevent payment of contributions to systems where employees are unlikely to receive benefits; and
– to reduce administrative burdens.

If the employee moves between EC and RA countries a NIC liability may arise whilst working in a different EC or RA country when the option is exercised, assigned or released-subject to certain conditions being satisfied. There are currently 18 RAs, listed as an appendix to this article and, although the general principles of each agreement regarding liability to pay contributions are broadly similar to EC legislation, each RA must be checked individually.

Where a liability to pay Class 1 NICs arises the amount of earnings to be included for the calculation of NICs is the same as that chargeable (not what is eventually charged) to Schedule E tax.

UK DOMESTIC LEGISLATION

If EC legislation or a RA do not apply for employees coming from or going to 'rest of the world' ('ROW') countries, NIC liability will be determined in accordance with UK NICs legislation.

EXAMPLES

In the following examples:

- all the share option plans are unapproved; and
- all tax references are to the Income and Corporation Taxes Act 1988 (ICTA) unless otherwise stated.

Example 1: European Economic Area (EEA) – Option granted in UK and exercised while on short secondment to France (EEA)

Alan is resident and ordinarily resident and working in the UK on 1 June 1999. On that date his UK employer grants an option to purchase 1000 shares in the company in two years' time at the 1 June 1999 market price of £1. On 1 July 2000 Alan is seconded to France for 12 months only and is still in the employment there when the option is exercised on 1 June 2001. At that date the value of the shares is £5 each.

Alan is resident and ordinarily resident in the UK at the date of grant and is therefore liable to income tax under Section135 on any gain realised at exercise.

Under Article 14.1(*a*) of Council Regulation (EEC) 1408/71 Alan is a 'posted worker' and remains subject to UK legislation. Under Section 4(4)(*a*) Social Security Contributions and Benefits Act (SSCBA) 1992 a liability to pay NICs arises on exercise of the option. The gain is calculated as the difference between (*a*) the value of the shares at the date of exercise and (*b*) the option price paid plus any consideration given for the option itself; in this case the gain is 1,000 x (£5-£1) £4 = £4,000.

Example 2: EEA – Option granted in the UK by UK employer and exercised when on long secondment to Netherlands (EEA)

Peter is resident and ordinarily resident and working in the UK on 1 June 1999. On that date his UK employer grants an option to purchase 1000 shares in the company in two years' time at the 1 June 1999 market price of £1. On 1 July 2000 Peter is seconded to Netherlands for 3 years and is still in the employment there when the option is exercised on 1 June 2001. At that date the value of the shares is £5 each.

Peter is resident and ordinarily resident in the UK at the date of grant and is therefore liable to income tax under Section 135 on any gain realised at exercise.

Although a posted worker, no application is made to subject Peter to UK legislation for the period of the secondment. Peter is therefore subject to Netherlands legislation under Article 13.2(*a*) of Council Regulation (EEC) 1408/71. On date of exercise Peter would not normally fall within UK legislation.

However, in 1997 the EC Administrative Commission concluded that a person should normally be subject to the legislation of the Member State where the income related to a period of employment in the Home State rather than be subject to the legislation of the Member State at the actual time of payment. As the gain on the share option was realised from a period of employment in the UK a liability to pay Class 1 NICs on that gain arises under UK legislation in the normal way.

The gain is calculated as the difference between (*a*) the value of the shares at the date of exercise and (*b*) the option price paid plus any consideration given for the option itself; in this case the gain is 1,000 x (£5-£1) £4 = £4,000.

Example 3: EEA – Option granted in the UK by UK employer and exercised when in different employment in Germany

The facts are similar to example 2 except that Barbara leaves her UK employment on 1 July 2000 to work permanently for a German employer for 3 years. Barbara is resident and ordinarily resident in the UK at the date of grant and is therefore liable to income tax under Section 135 on any gain realised at exercise.

Under Article 13.2(*a*) of Council Regulation (EEC) 1408/71 Barbara would be liable to pay social security contributions under the legislation of the EC country of employment. On date of exercise Barbara would not normally fall within UK legislation. As in example 2 the EC Administrative Commission concluded that a person should normally be subject to the legislation of the State where income related to a former period of employment.

As the gain on the share option was realised from a former period of employment in the UK a liability to pay Class 1 NICs on that gain arises under UK legislation in the normal way and on the same amount as for Alan.

EXAMPLE 4: RECIPROCAL AGREEMENT (RA) – USA NATIONAL WORKING FOR UK EMPLOYER AND OPTION GRANTED BY UK EMPLOYER

Caroline is a USA national working for an UK employer. She is resident but not ordinarily resident for tax purposes in the UK when the option is granted on 1 June 1999 over 1000 shares. Caroline is still resident and working in the UK when she exercises the option and sells the shares on 1 July 2000. The option price is £1 per share and the value and sale price at 1 July 2000 is £5 per share.

Under Article 4 of The Social Security (United States of America) Order 1997 ('USA RA') Caroline is subject to UK legislation. At the time of the grant the UK tax charge in respect of the employment, she is resident but not ordinarily resident and is liable to income tax under Case II of Schedule E, not under Case I of Schedule E. Section 135 does not apply. As Section 135 does not apply there can be no liability to pay Class 1 contributions on exercise.

Caroline will be liable to UK income tax under S162(5) at the time of disposal of the shares. The charge is on the difference between the market value of the shares at the time of exercise less any amounts paid. This is treated as a notional loan written off within S160(2) and as emoluments of the employment. The emolument is (1000 @ £5)-(1000 @ £1) = £4000. There will also be a Class 1A NICs liability on the same amount.

EXAMPLE 5: RA – USA NATIONAL AND OPTION GRANTED BY USA EMPLOYER; SUBSEQUENTLY SECONDED TO UK AND OPTION EXERCISED

David is a USA national working for a US employer. David is neither resident nor ordinarily resident in the UK when a stock option over 1000 shares in the US employer is granted. He is subsequently seconded to work in the UK for 6 years. David exercises the US stock option when working in the UK and sells the shares. The price of the option is £1 per share and the price on exercise is £4 per share.

At the time of the grant there is no UK tax charge in respect of the employment. David will not be liable to UK income tax on any gain realised at exercise, unless the grant of the option is clearly related to duties performed in the UK.

As Section 135 does not apply there is no liability to pay Class 1 contributions on exercise.

There could be a liability under Section 162 and Class 1A NICs may be payable although all relevant facts and circumstances would need to be considered before determining whether or not a liability arises.

{Had the secondment been for no more than 5 years David would have been subject to US legislation under Article 4.2 of the USA RA and there would be no liability for any class of contribution under UK legislation, whether or not there was any liability to UK income tax}

EXAMPLE 6: RA – UK NATIONAL, OPTION GRANTED BY UK EMPLOYER; SUBSEQUENTLY SECONDED TO USA AND OPTION EXERCISED

Elena is resident and ordinarily resident in the UK and working here on 1 June 1999. On that date her UK employer grants an option to purchase 1,000 shares in the company in two years' time at the 1 June 1999 market price of £1. On 1 July 2000 she is seconded to the US for 6 years and is still in the employment there when the option is exercised on 1 June 2001. At that date the shares are worth £5 each.

Elena is resident and ordinarily resident in the UK at the date of grant and is therefore liable to income tax under Section135 on any gain realised at exercise. Under Article 4.1 of the Social Security (United States of America) Order 1997 she is subject to US legislation. On date of exercise there is no liability to pay UK contributions.

[Had the secondment been for no more than 5 years Elena would have been subject to UK legislation under Article 4.2 and Class 1 NICs would have been payable.]

EXAMPLE 7: REST OF THE WORLD (ROW) – UK NATIONAL, OPTIONS GRANTED BY UK EMPLOYER; SUBSEQUENTLY SECONDED TO NIGERIA AND OPTION EXERCISED

Frank is resident and ordinarily resident in the UK and working here on 1 June 1999. On that date his UK employer grants an option to purchase 1,000 shares in the company in two years' time at the 1 June 1999 market price of £1. On 1 July 2000 he is seconded to Nigeria on secondment for 3 years and is still in the employment there when the option is exercised on 1 September 2001. At that date the shares are worth £5 each.

Frank is resident and ordinarily resident in the UK at the date of grant and is therefore liable to income tax under Section135 on any gain realised at exercise.

Under regulation 146 Social Security (Contributions) Regulations (SSCR) 2001 a liability to pay UK social security contributions continues for the period of 52 weeks from the date of leaving the UK. As the exercise of the option is after the period of continuing contribution liability no further Class 1 NICs are payable.

EXAMPLE 8: ROW – PERUVIAN NATIONAL; ON SECONDMENT FROM ROW COUNTRY TO UK EMPLOYER. OPTION GRANTED BY UK EMPLOYER

Nolberto is a Peruvian national who arrives in the UK on 1 May 1999 on secondment from his Peruvian employer to work for a UK employer. He is resident but not ordinarily resident for tax purposes in the UK when the option is granted on 1 May 1999 over 1000 shares. Nolberto is still resident and working in the UK when he exercises the option and sells the shares on 29 April 2000. The option price is £1 per share and the value and sale price at 29 April 2000 is £5 per share.

Nolberto will be liable to UK income tax under S162(5) at the time of disposal of the shares. The charge is on the difference between the market value of the shares at the time of exercise less any amounts paid. This is treated as a notional loan written off within S160(2) and as emoluments of the employment. The emolument is (1000 @ £5)-(1000 @ £1) = £4000.

No Class 1A is payable. Under regulation 145(2) SSCR there is a 52 week period of exemption from liability to pay a Class 1, Class 1A or Class 1B contribution beginning from the date of entry into the UK.

EXAMPLE 9: ROW – ARGENTINE NATIONAL AND OPTION GRANTED BY ARGENTINE EMPLOYER; SUBSEQUENTLY SECONDED TO UK AND OPTION EXERCISED IN UK EMPLOYMENT

Eva is a Argentine national working for a Argentine employer. Eva is neither resident nor ordinarily resident in the UK when a stock option over 1000 shares in the Argentine employer is granted. She is subsequently seconded to work in the UK for a UK employer for 3 years. Eva exercises the Argentine stock option when working in the UK and sells the shares. The price of the option is £1 per share and the price on exercise is £4 per share.

At the time of the grant there is no UK tax charge in respect of the employment. Eva will not be liable to UK income tax on any gain realised at exercise, unless the grant of the option is clearly related to duties performed in the UK.

As Section 135 does not apply there is no liability to pay Class 1 contributions on exercise.

There could be a liability under Section 162 and Class 1A NICs may be payable if the option is exercised after the 52 week exemption period although all relevant facts and circumstances would need to be considered before determining whether or not a liability arises.

Further advice

For further advice on this bulletin governing the liability to pay NICs on share options, contact:

Steve Hickson, Revenue Policy, Personal Tax, Room 75E, Benton Park Road, Newcastle Upon Tyne NE98 1ZZ, Tel 01912256029 E-mail: Steve.Hickson@ir.gsi.gov.uk

And for further advice on international tax aspects, contact:

Susan New, Revenue Policy International, Victory House, 30-34 Kingsway, London WC2B 6ES, Tel: 020 7438 7250 E-mail: Susan.New@ir.gsi.gov.uk

APPENDIX

Barbados	Israel	Mauritius
Bermuda	Jamaica	Philippines
Canada (DCC)	Japan (DCC)	Switzerland
Cyprus	Jersey	Turkey
Guernsey	Korea (DCC)	USA
* Isle of Man	Malta	Yugoslavia (including former Republics)

* The Agreement with the Isle of Man is limited and liability is generally determined under place of residence.

January 2002. Tax Bulletin Issue 57

Double Taxation Relief: Tax consolidations falling within Section 803A of TA 1988

Paragraph 15 of Schedule 30, Finance Act (FA) introduced a new Section 803A into Income and Corporation Taxes Act (ICTA) 1988. In some countries the law may provide that one company may pay tax in respect of the aggregated profits of itself and others as if they were a single entity. The new provisions at Section 803A provide that, for the purposes of calculating credit relief:

- the relevant profits of these companies are regarded as a single aggregate figure in respect of a single company; and
- the foreign tax paid by the responsible company as having been paid by that single company.

Tax Bulletin Issue 54 published in August 2001 brought together guidance previously published on the Inland Revenue website concerning additional situations on which we had given individual guidance. Since then we have been able to look at how tax consolidations work in various countries, and the implications for treatment under Section 803A. If entities other than companies resident in the relevant territory are included in the group then the appropriate amounts of relevant profits and foreign tax will need to be excluded from the calculation of underlying tax for the S803A entity.

NETHERLANDS

A fiscal entity can be formed if one company owns at least 99% of a subsidiary. Neither parent nor subsidiary need be Dutch incorporated or resident, but all companies involved should be subject to the same Dutch tax regime. The formation of a fiscal entity is deemed to be a merger of the subsidiaries into the parent and all tax is assessed on the parent. However all companies within the fiscal unity are jointly and severally liable for the tax, although strictly the liability of subsidiaries is secondary. The fiscal unity is within Section 803A, even if the parent company is a company that is not resident in the Netherlands, because tax is payable by any other company any may be the ''responsible company'' and the fiscal unity will be within Section 803A.

USA

A US resident entity and its 80% subsidiaries may elect to file a consolidated federal income tax return. This may include non-corporate entities e.g. single member LLCs and non-US resident single member companies, if (re the latter) transparency has been elected under check-the-box. Each company is jointly and severally liable for the tax of the group.

Any company in the consolidated return may be the ''responsible company''. Section 803A applies, even if the parent company is a non-resident company or a non-corporate entity. This point is covered more fully in Tax Bulletin Issue 54.

GERMANY

From 1 January 2001 an ''Organschaft'' can exist for federal tax if an entity and its subsidiaries:

a. are integrated financially with the dominant entity having more than 50% of the voting rights in each subsidiary; and
b. have a profit or loss pooling arrangement in place.

It is also possible to have an Organschaft for trade tax purposes but, until 31/12/01 only if the dormant entity and its subsidiaries are economically and organisationally integrated. So a group may have either a federal or a trade tax Organschaft, or both.

The dominant entity may be a German company or partnership, or a German branch of a non-German company. It is liable for the Organschaft's tax. This is in respect of its own profits as augmented by those of subsidiaries, in other words the aggregate profits of all the companies.

From 1/1/02, only financial integration is required for trade tax organschaft.

Both federal and trade Organschaften are within Section 803A. Provided a group forms an Organschaft for one tax, Section 803A will apply in respect of both. This follows the principle set out in Tax Bulletin 54 for federal and state taxes in the USA.

Where a federal organschaft is headed by a KG, OHG or branch, as the subsidiaries' profits will move up by way of profit pooling payment, there will be no dividend in practice in respect of which S803A can apply. In that case Section 801B, which deals with profits transferred other than by way of a dividend, will apply.

FRANCE

Any entity which either:

a. is subject to French corporation tax; or
b. can elect to be taxed as a company; or
c. is a permanent establishment of a non-French company

can form an ''Intégration Fiscale'' with its 95% subsidiaries. Each group entity completes a tax computation on a stand-alone basis. These are then consolidated with adjustments made for intra-group dividends, etc.

Tax on the net consolidated profits is assessed on the top company. Although the subsidiaries are in principle jointly liable for the group's tax liability, this is statutorily limited to the stand-alone tax that a subsidiary would have paid if it had not been a member of the Intégration Fiscale.

As the parent entity is responsible for paying French tax in respect of all members of the Intégration Fiscale the tax grouping will fall within Section 803A unless the parent entity is a non-corporate entity or a French branch of a non-French company.

Tax is always assessed on the ''top'' company. Therefore examples A and C included in Tax Bulletin 54 cannot in practice arise for a French tax consolidation.

Two other consolidation systems are available in France, 'Bénéfice Consolidé'' and ''Bénéfice Mondial''. However these are usually only available to a French company that heads an international group. The Section 803A position has not therefore been considered.

LUXEMBOURG

A fiscal unity can be formed between Luxembourg resident companies where a fully taxable company and one or more fully taxed subsidiaries are integrated financially, economically and organisationally. The parent company is responsible for paying the consolidated tax liability.

Effective 1/1/02, only financial integration (now 95% ownership, rather than 99%, previously) is required. Moreover, Luxembourg branches of non-resident companies (which themselves are fully liable to a tax corresponding to Luxembourg tax) may now head a Luxembourg fiscal unity.

Such a tax consolidated group will fall within Section 803A, the parent company begin the ''responsible company''. As this will always be a Luxembourg-resident company, there will be no exceptions.

NEW ZEALAND

Groups of resident companies with 100% common ownership may elect to be subject to the consolidated companies' regime. The group files a single return and receives a single tax assessment. This may be issued to any company in the group and all other group members remain liable for their share of the group tax liability.

The company to which the group tax assessment is issued is the ''responsible company'' and Section 803A applies. As this will always be a New Zealand-resident company, there will be no exceptions.

SPAIN

A Spanish resident company may elect to file a consolidated return on behalf of itself and its 90% Spanish resident subsidiaries. The tax is assessed on the parent company, but each company is jointly and severally liable for the tax.

Section 803A applies. Any company may be the responsible company although this will normally be the parent company.

FUTURE CHANGES

Changes are proposed to the consolidation arrangements in the Netherlands from 1/1/03. The potential implications of these for Section 803A will be considered later once they are implemented and become relevant.

CONTACT POINTS

Further advice in a particular case may be obtained from

Paul West, International (External Relations Group), (Underlying Tax Group), Fitzroy House, PO Box 46, Castle Meadow Road, Nottingham, NG2 1BD Tel: 0115 974 2020

Or more general policy advice from

Susan New, International (External Relations Group), Victory House, 30-34 Kingsway, London WC2B 6ES, Tel: 020 7438 7250 E-mail: Susan.New@ir.gsi.gov.uk

Although the Inland Revenue is responsible for the conclusions reached, we are grateful to PricewaterhouseCoopers for their assistance in gathering information about the legislation in other countries.

April 2002. Tax Bulletin Issue 58

Revenue accountants

In Tax Bulletin Issue 47 (June 2000) we explained that we had recruited over forty accountants for deployment on compliance work. This article gives further information on the current position. We now employ approximately ninety accountants mainly based in the Area Offices, Large Business Office (LBO) and Special Compliance Office (SCO). They are there to advise inspectors on accountancy and related commercial matters. In particular they advise on whether accounts comply with UK generally accepted accounting practice (GAAP) and show a true and fair view.

The accountants who have been recruited are all members of ICAEW, ICAS, ICAI or ACCA. They have a number of years experience in practice and have worked for a range of firms from the small practice to the top five. Many of them have worked at senior manager or partner level prior to joining the Revenue. They are recruited because of their wide audit and accounting experience, and as such they are not tax specialists.

The work they do covers all situations where the tax liability depends on the accounts. At one extreme this could be because amounts may have been omitted from the records and the accounts based on them. At the other extreme it could involve highly technical issues on the correct application of accounting standards. The Revenue accountants deal with all of the accountancy profession from the top five firms to sole practitioners and also unqualified agents.

A senior local inspector generally manages the area accountants and SCO accountants. The LBO accountants are managed centrally by a senior accountant.

Accountancy queries are referred to the Revenue accountants by inspectors at various stages in the selection and enquiry process. In the majority of these referrals they are able to assure the inspector that no further enquiries are required. This is seen as an important function of their work in that it saves valuable inspector time and further saves time and money for the taxpayers and their agents in dealing with what might otherwise have been fruitless enquiries. On occasions, however, they do have to make further enquiries in order to establish the facts before they can be satisfied that the accounts have been prepared in accordance with UK GAAP. Sometimes the explanations provided prolong the enquiries. As a simple example a tax partner explained that a stock provision was justified under FRS 12. Further enquiries established that the provision was indeed correct but of course it had nothing to do with FRS 12.

In some cases there may be a dispute as to what is correct accounting practice in the particular circumstances and facts of the case. Accountancy is not an exact science and occasionally it is possible for different accountants to come to different conclusions, both of which are within the bounds of UK GAAP. However the advent of FRS 18 should reduce the number of occasions on which this occurs, as preparers of accounts are now required to choose those policies and estimation techniques that are most appropriate to the particular circumstances. In these difficult areas it will be necessary for the Revenue accountants to establish all of the facts and to ensure that both sides have considered the alternatives before they are able to come to a conclusion one way or another. If they conclude that the accounts have been prepared on a tenable basis in accordance with FRS 18 then they will not try to substitute an alternative basis that they may prefer. Where they do not feel that the accounts have been prepared in accordance with UK GAAP they will pursue the matter.

In reaching their conclusions the Revenue accountants have to follow certain procedures. They are encouraged to discuss more complex or difficult accounting issues with their accountant colleagues at an early stage. They are required to submit the case to the Board's Advisory Accountant, based in the Inland Revenue Solicitor's Office, at the earliest possible stage of the enquiries, where a matter is potentially contentious. Naturally it would be premature to submit the case for a formal decision before all the facts are known. However, informal discussions can take place with the Board's Advisory Accountant at any time.

It is in the Revenue's interest that it should make best use of its accountancy resource. Thus, a further quality assurance/quality control procedure has been set up whereby senior accountants in the region will review other Revenue accountants' work and be available to give advice at an early stage in proceedings. This will ensure that we get the best use of our accountants so that all cases are tackled in the most efficient manner to the benefit of both taxpayers and the Revenue.

The Revenue accountants will not normally be corresponding direct with practitioners. Accountancy aspects will be dealt with by inspectors with relevant input from the Revenue accountant, in the course of dealing with all the tax aspects of a case. However, if the practitioner feels that a meeting with the Revenue accountant would help to resolve the matter more efficiently then the Revenue accountant will be happy to take part in such a meeting. Indeed on occasions they will suggest that such a meeting is the best way forward.

June 2002. Tax Bulletin Issue 59

Taxation of Foreign Nationals: Schedule E—tax equalisation

EMPLOYEES RESIDENT BUT NOT ORDINARILY RESIDENT IN THE UNITED KINGDOM—LIABILITY UNDER CASES II AND III OF SCHEDULE E

An employee resident but not ordinarily resident in the UK is liable to UK tax under Case II Schedule E on emoluments in respect of duties performed in the UK. Such employees are also liable under Case III Schedule E on emoluments for duties performed outside the UK but only to the extent that the emoluments are received in the UK.

Paragraph 2 of Statement of Practice 5/84 (SP5/84) states that where the duties of a single office or employment are performed both in and outside the UK, an apportionment is required to determine how much of the emoluments are attributable to UK duties and therefore liable to tax under Case II Schedule E. Apportionment of emoluments is essentially a question of fact and the Inland Revenue accepts time apportionment based on the number of days worked abroad and in the UK except where this would clearly be inappropriate.

In addition to salaries and benefits, employers may also provide their employees with the benefit of tax equalisation. This usually means that the employer undertakes to meet on the employee's behalf any additional tax payable above the tax that the employee would have paid in his home country. It is well established that such payments made on behalf of employees form part of their emoluments. But there has been a difference of view between the Revenue and a number of accountancy firms about the extent to which such tax equalisation emoluments are attributable to Case II or Case III Schedule E.

The Inland Revenue's view is that tax equalisation emoluments are wholly referable to duties performed in the UK where the underlying tax liability is similarly wholly referable to duties performed in the UK. Therefore, where an employer pays liability under Case II Schedule E on an employee's behalf, the resulting tax equalisation emolument will itself be wholly chargeable under Case II Schedule E.

The Revenue's view was approved recently by a Special Commissioner in the case of *Perro v. Mansworth* (SPC286). The Special Commissioner stated that it was an inescapable fact that the payment of tax by the appellant's employer was an emolument in respect of UK duties since that tax was only payable because of the performance of duties in the UK.

Ms Perro's net emoluments were time apportioned in accordance with SP5/84 in order to find the net attributable to UK duties. The Inland Revenue's approach was to gross up this net figure of Case II Schedule E income on the basis that the payment of the tax was itself an additional emolument wholly referable to duties performed in the UK and chargeable to tax under Case II Schedule E.

The Special Commissioner did not consider the treatment of reimbursement of tax on income other than employment income chargeable under Case II Schedule E. The employer of a tax-equalised employee may reimburse UK tax on investment income or capital gains. Employers may also pay foreign tax liabilities on the employee's behalf. We have been asked for our view on the treatment of such reimbursements.

In the *Perro* case, time apportionment was the appropriate method for attributing the appellant's net emoluments to Case II Schedule E, as there was no specific attribution of salary or other benefits between UK and overseas duties. However, the tax equalisation emolument was in that case as a matter of fact wholly referable to duties performed in the UK, so time apportionment was clearly inappropriate. We consider that the approach approved by the Special Commissioner in *Perro* is in harmony with SP5/84.

When apportioning emoluments between Cases II and Cases III Schedule E, it is necessary first to consider whether those emoluments are wholly referable to UK or non-UK duties on the facts. Clearly if this is so, there is no need to consider time apportionment. If the emoluments are not wholly referable either to UK or non-UK duties, then time apportionment will be necessary in accordance with SP5/84.

If an employer reimburses personal tax liability arising on non employment income such as bank interest, dividends or capital gains, then the first question is whether that reimbursement is an emolument that relates wholly to either UK or non-UK duties. We do not consider that the physical presence of the employee in the UK in order to perform employment duties is sufficient justification for treating such reimbursements as wholly in respect of duties performed in the UK. In the absence of unusual facts, we believe that such emoluments should be time apportioned. This will produce a net Case II emolument that will then need to be grossed up. The gross up will be on the basis that the payment of tax on an emolument within Case II of Schedule E is itself an emolument wholly chargeable under Case II Schedule E.

With regard to foreign tax reimbursements, the attribution between Cases II and III Schedule E will depend upon the facts and circumstances. If the foreign tax relates solely to overseas duties, then the payment of that tax by the employer will comprise an emolument wholly referable to duties performed outside the UK that cannot be charged to tax under Case II Schedule E. Alternatively, the foreign tax may be charged on worldwide income so that time apportionment is likely to provide the only practical mechanism for determining the attribution between Cases II and III Schedule E.

We have also been asked about the treatment of reimbursements of tax chargeable under Case III Schedule E. SP5/84 states that provided the emoluments assessable under Case II Schedule E are arrived at in a reasonable manner, the Inland Revenue are prepared to accept that Case III Schedule E liability will arise only where the aggregate of emoluments received in the UK exceeds the amount assessable under Case II Schedule E for that year. The amount assessable under Case III Schedule E is therefore restricted to the excess of the aggregate over the amount assessable under Case II Schedule E. We do not intend to depart from this practice.

Where the employer meets Case III Schedule E liability, the payment of that tax to the Inland Revenue will clearly be received in the UK. We believe that it is logical that the payment of the Case III Schedule E liability will itself be a Case III Schedule E emolument and as the tax payment will be received in the UK, the related gross up will also be wholly chargeable under Case III Schedule E.

We recognise that there can be significant practical difficulties in identifying whether an emolument relates solely to non-UK duties and therefore falls within Schedule E Case III. In such cases, we would not generally dispute time apportionment between Cases II and III Schedule E on the basis of working days. If any emoluments were allocated solely to Case III Schedule E as attributable wholly to non-UK duties, we would expect evidence to be available to justify the attribution, in the event of a Revenue enquiry.

NON RESIDENT EMPLOYEES

Some tax-equalised employees are not resident in the UK. They may perform substantive duties of their employment in this country. Unless the specific terms of a Double Taxation Agreement (DTA) confer an exemption from UK tax on UK source employment income, such employees will remain liable under Case II of Schedule E on emoluments in respect of duties performed in the UK. Emoluments for duties performed outside the UK will fall outside of the scope of Schedule E except in very limited circumstances. We believe that the same approach to attributing tax equalisation

PRs etc

emoluments should be adopted for non-resident employees as for those resident but not ordinarily resident employees whose emoluments are apportioned between Cases II and III Schedule E.

The following simple examples are intended to illustrate the basic approach to tax equalisation emoluments described in this article. It is recognised that many cases will have much more complex facts and that the ensuing calculations will be similarly complex.

EXAMPLES

Tanya has been sent to the UK to work at her employer's UK branch for two years from 1 January 2002. She is resident but not ordinarily resident in the UK from the day of her arrival. In addition to her UK duties, her employer requires her to make regular and extensive visits to an overseas branch of its business in order to monitor an important project. Whilst assigned to the UK, Tanya is subject to her employer's policy on tax equalisation which provides for her to receive the same net salary and benefits as if she had remained in her home state.

During 2002–03, Tanya performed the duties of her employment on 225 days. She spent 158 days working in the UK and 67 days working overseas. Net salary and benefits from her employment were £100,000 of which £60,000 was received in the UK. Her employer was obliged to pay her tax liabilities in accordance with its tax equalisation policy. For simplicity, all calculations assume that Tanya's income is chargeable to UK tax at 40%

Scenario 1

Tanya's only tax liability was incurred in the UK on the emoluments from her employment.

CALCULATION OF UK TAX FOR 2002–03

Net salary and benefits	100,000
Less amount attributable to overseas workdays – 67/225 (30%)	(30,000)
Net attributable to the performance of UK duties	70,000
Tax equalisation emolument – gross up for UK tax at 4/6	46,666
Gross Case II Schedule E	116,666
Tax at 40%	46,666
Net Case II Schedule E	70,000
Liability under Case III Schedule E Case II	116,666
Received in the UK – 60,000 plus Case II tax of 46,666	106,666
Case III – SP5/84	Nil

Scenario 2

Facts as above but Tanya's employer also paid UK tax liability of £5,000 on her investment income. As the £5,000 is not directly referable to the performance of duties inside or outside the UK, it falls to be time apportioned in accordance with SP5/84. Therefore, the £5,000 has been added to net salary and benefits before calculating and deducting the amount attributable to overseas workdays.

CALCULATION OF UK TAX FOR 2002–03

Net salary and benefits – as before	100,000
Plus UK tax liability on investment income	5,000
Revised net salary and benefits	105,000
Less amount attributable to overseas workdays – 67/225 (30%)	(31,500)
Net attributable to the performance of UK duties	73,500
Tax equalisation emolument – gross up for UK tax at 4/6	49,000
Gross Case II Schedule E 122,500 Tax at 40%	49,000
Net Case II Schedule E	73,500
Liability under Case III Schedule E Case II	122,500
Received in the UK – 60,000 plus Case II tax 49,000 & other UK tax 5,000	114,000
Case III – SP5/84	Nil

Scenario 3

Additionally, Tanya's employer pays overseas tax liability of £5,000 direct to an overseas tax authority. The overseas tax is referable solely to the performance of duties outside the UK and is therefore excluded from the Case II calculation.

CALCULATION OF UK TAX FOR 2002–03

Net salary and benefits – as before	100,000
Plus UK tax liability on investment income	5,000
Plus overseas tax liability on overseas duties	5,000
Revised net salary and benefits	110,000
Less overseas tax	(5,000)
Amount to be time apportioned	105,000

Less amount attributable to overseas workdays – 67/225 (30%)	(31,500)
Net attributable to the performance of UK duties	73,500
Tax equalisation emolument – gross up for UK tax at 4/6	49,000
Gross Case II Schedule E	122,500
Tax at 40%	49,000
Net Case II Schedule E	73,500
Liability under Case III Schedule E Case II	122,500
Received in the UK – 60,000 plus Case II tax 49,000 & other UK tax 5,000	114,000
Case III – SP5/84	Nil

Scenario 4

Facts are the same as in Scenario 2 except that £70,000 out of the £100,000 net salary and benefits has been received in the UK.

CALCULATION OF UK TAX FOR 2002–03

Net salary and benefits – as before	100,000
Plus UK tax liability on investment income	5,000
Revised net salary and benefits	105,000
Less amount attributable to overseas workdays – 67/225 (30%)	(31,500)
Net attributable to the performance of UK duties	73,500
Tax equalisation emolument – gross up for UK tax at 4/6	49,000
Gross Case II Schedule E	122,500
Tax at 40%	49,000
Net Case II Schedule E	73,500
Liability under Case III Schedule E Case II	122,500
Received in the UK – 70,000 plus Case II tax 49,000 & other UK tax 5,000	124,000
Net Case III – SP5/84	1,500
Tax equalisation emolument – gross up for UK tax at 4/6	1,000
Gross Case III	2,500
Total gross emoluments – Cases II & III	125,000
Tax at 40%	50,000

FURTHER INFORMATION

Martin Delnon, Personal Tax (Technical), Sapphire House, 550 Streetsbrook Road, Solihull B91 1QU Tel: 0121 713 4634; Fax: 0121 713 4620; E-mail: Martin.Delnon@ir.gsi.gov.uk

August 2002. Tax Bulletin Issue 60

Review of links with business—international tax issues

The Review of links with business, published in November 2001, recommended (R35) that the Revenue should publish guidance that would—

- better focus transfer pricing enquiries by giving more advice on the nature of the risk assessment to be carried out before the decision to embark on an enquiry is made.
- facilitate the timetabling of the course of an enquiry, by setting out what could reasonably be expected of each side in terms of the time to provide information and to examine what is provided.

This article is concerned with transfer pricing enquiries into an enterprise's fundamental pricing structure for cross-border transactions with associated enterprises. These include enquiries into such areas as royalty rates, distributor margins, manufacturer margins, pricing methodologies (for example cost plus versus profit split). This article is not concerned with enquiries into such areas as thin capitalisation, imputation of interest on outward loans; guarantee fees, or management fees where such an area is the only cross border transaction. Such enquiries do not generally require the level of analysis of other transfer-pricing enquiries and do not normally take as long.

Representations received by the Revenue clearly favoured a collaborative approach to timetabling rather than a prescriptive or inflexible approach. This article sets out a collaborative approach. It is hoped that this will meet the best interests of both companies and the Revenue. Where it is not possible to pursue a collaborative approach enquiries will need to be based on what is specifically provided for in UK legislation supplemented by exchange of information powers in tax treaties. Such an approach is likely to be longer and less flexible than collaboration.

This article addresses Recommendation 35. It does not address Recommendation 34 (Transfer Pricing documentation requirements). However, the Revenue recognises that some taxpayers are anxious to know the level of documentation to be submitted with a CTSA return. In that context, we can reaffirm that, although there is a requirement that appropriate documentation needs to exist at the time the return is made, there is no requirement to provide such documentation as a routine matter along with a CTSA return.

RISK ASSESSMENT PROCESS

Transfer pricing enquiries can be enormously resource intensive for both companies and the Revenue, so a transfer pricing enquiry should not be contemplated without first undertaking a detailed risk assessment.

In view of the potential resource cost of a full enquiry, transfer pricing risk assessments should be conducted to a greater level of detail than risk assessments in many other potential enquiry areas.

It is recommended that risk assessment should ideally include—

- A review of any previous transfer pricing papers
- A detailed examination of six years' consolidated group accounts and of accounts of individual UK and appropriate non-UK entities
- Consideration of the group structure and identification of haven/shelter countries
- A review of industry trends, details of the company's place in its sector, and recent developments within the group (new acquisitions, new locations, etc)
- A review of databases for multiple year data and potential comparables
- A review of company returns in other jurisdictions
- Liaison with PAYE office for details of highly-paid UK staff
- Possibly liaison with Customs & Excise.

If such pre-enquiry work seems excessive in a particular case this may be an indication either that the case is not suitable for a transfer-pricing enquiry, or that any enquiry should have limited scope.

The mere presence of cross-border transactions between associated entities is not in itself sufficient reason to initiate a transfer-pricing enquiry, even if the amounts involved in the transactions are substantial. For example, a car distributor may purchase £1bn of cars from its foreign parent company, but if a net profit in line with commercial experience in car distribution is achieved on UK activities, there may be no substantial transfer pricing risk.

OBTAINING INFORMATION FOR RISK ASSESSMENT

There may be difficulties obtaining some of the information outlined above; particularly with foreign owned small or medium sized groups. Such cases sometimes are not (even on a world-wide basis) large enough to feature on data bases, websites, sector commentaries, etc.

If the group as a whole does not feature in the above sources, this may be an indication that the UK operation is small: the potential tax at risk may not justify the resource cost of a transfer pricing enquiry for either the Revenue or the business.

In a large multi-national enterprise (MNE) the high value-adding activities can be located in any part of the group. There is a risk that UK companies within the group might be rewarded as if they were performing routine functions with low added value that understate the economic reality. With smaller firms, the high value-adding parts of the enterprise are more likely to be found in the home territory and this should be borne in mind when conducting risk assessments. Of course if the evidence of the accounts (eg large bonuses to staff) or other sources suggests otherwise then a different view of the risk may need to be taken.

Depending on the functions and role of the UK business, it may not always be necessary to know a lot about the rest of the group. For example if the UK business is a distributor, it may be appropriate to establish the arm's length price by examination of comparable uncontrolled transactions of independent UK distributors which would not necessarily involve analysing the results of the world-wide group.

EXCHANGE OF INFORMATION

Information powers under domestic UK law are not suitable for dealing with information not in a UK resident's power and possession.

UK subsidiaries can often legitimately say that some of the information requested in transfer pricing enquiries is in the power and possession only of a foreign associate. Where a double tax treaty with the UK exists and contains an Exchange of Information article, the UK Competent Authority can request the information about associated entities via his/her opposite number in the associate company's territory.

In the light of this alternative power, businesses may want to volunteer the information, in the knowledge that the Revenue can obtain it eventually anyway, and that failure to do so would hold up the enquiry. Many Multi National Enterprises already volunteer the information where they are persuaded that it is relevant.

There are no de minimis limits for an Exchange of Information request. However the Revenue will not generally burden other tax administrations with routine requests where the amount of tax at stake is either small or speculative.

PARTICULAR RISK AREAS

Existence of tax haven entities outside the CFC rules that are profitable despite the absence of significant activities carried out in their bases.

Instances of mismatches between the likely scale of tax haven operations and the level of profits allocated to them; (Although the existence of transactions with affiliates in low tax areas may act as an important indicator, potential transfer pricing issues should not be ignored simply because the other party is in a normal or even high tax rate jurisdiction).

Profit margins in the UK are lower than in the group generally AND there are reasons to believe that this should not be the case.

UK company possesses the resources to generate high margin profits yet produces only a routine low margin profit. The Revenue will look for presence of eg—

- heavy investment
- highly skilled and remunerated technical or R&D workforce
- intangibles eg trade names, know-how, patents etc.

Royalty or management fee payments that don't appear to make commercial sense AND which substantially impact on UK bottom line eg—

- for a brand name unknown in the UK
- for technology to which significant value has been added by complex processes carried out in the UK
- for nebulous bundles of intangibles.

Poor performance over a number of years when there is no obvious prospect of super profits in later years to justify the risk of continuing losses.

Any period in which changes in intra group contractual arrangements purport to adjust the risk profile, and hence the reward, of the UK group; eg—

- distributor becomes commissionaire (AND net profits fall away)
- full manufacturer becomes contract manufacturer
- R&D activities that once generated royalties move to contract basis
- cost sharing arrangements introduced.

There are no de minimis limits or safe harbours in UK transfer pricing legislation, but regard should be given to both the potential tax at risk and the level of difficulty in establishing the arm's length price.

Where, for example, the cost base is agreed to be £5m, in a case where exceptionally an arm's length cost plus percentage is agreed to be the appropriate method, each 1% increase in the mark up adds only £50,000 to profits. Given the difficulties that can sometimes arise in establishing an arm's length mark up, an enquiry into whether the cost plus percentage should be, for example, 11% rather than 10% may well not be appropriate.

Where on the other hand a company makes an interest free loan of £1m to a well capitalised affiliate, the potential adjustment may still only be in the order of £50–£100,000, but such a case could well merit enquiry because of the relative ease of identifying an arm's length price.

TIMETABLING

A timetabling framework already exists for transfer pricing cases where applications are accepted for Advance Pricing Agreements (APAs). Further details are set out in Tax Bulletin 43E(part 3) and Statement of Practice 3/99. There, the Inland Revenue aims to complete the APA process in 18 months. An important feature of an APA is that the process is initiated by the company and the timetable does not start until the company has submitted a comprehensive formal proposal. APA formal proposals often contain information that may not be in the power and possession of a UK resident, and hence possibly go beyond the requirements of CTSA. As business operations become more globally integrated a functional analysis of the counterparty to a transaction or details of how the business is structured globally may be relevant in establishing the arms length price. In such circumstances a company may have complied with its obligations under CTSA but still not be in a position to produce readily all the information requested by the Revenue.

A transfer pricing enquiry, unlike an APA, is initiated by the Revenue and the timetable may well need to be longer than 18 months to enable the company to collate the information prepared for CTSA purposes and to obtain any further information requested by the Revenue.

Transfer pricing enquiries can be broken down into four stages

Stage 1 Initial enquiry following risk assessment by the Revenue
Stage 2 Provision by the company of response to Revenue initial enquiries
Stage 3 Revenue's consideration of company's response
Stage 4 Negotiation and agreement

As a result of the risk assessment the Revenue may decide not to make enquiries. Similarly the conclusion of the Revenue's consideration may be that the company's transfer pricing need not be challenged and the enquiry will be closed. A typical analysis of the full enquiry process is illustrated at the end of this article.

Whilst the structure afforded by an APA style timetable can have benefits both for companies and the Revenue, other transfer pricing enquiries may need to be more flexible. In particular, it may not be in the interests of anyone for the timetable for the whole enquiry to be set in stone at the outset.

There are advantages in ongoing discussion to agree a timetable for the next stage of the enquiry. So, for example, when the initial enquiry is made there will be an agreement as to how long the company would have to make a response. When the company responds the Revenue will agree with the company a reasonable time for the Revenue response, and so on. Where the agreed timeframe for a particular stage exceeds three months it may be appropriate to agree an interim meeting to discuss progress.

INITIAL ENQUIRY (FOLLOWING RISK ASSESSMENT)

The initial enquiry should be both focused and comprehensive.

The risk assessment may show that it is not appropriate or feasible to review all cross border transactions in a single enquiry, particularly for large complex groups.

In a pharmaceutical company for example, it may be appropriate to focus on the transfer pricing issues arising from a single drug. In a financial concern it may be appropriate to focus on a single business stream, say fund management, but not capital markets. In an industrial conglomerate there may be little overlap between different businesses so it may be appropriate to deal with them separately.

If there is an existing agreed procedure for reviewing risks with a company this may be particularly helpful in questions of transfer pricing. But once having identified an area of concern, the initial enquiry should be comprehensive, the objective being to procure from the company a justification for its transfer pricing in the relevant area comparable to that of an APA formal proposal. So, for example, where the risk assessment identifies a royalty rate as a concern, the opening enquiry will generally extend to include other cross border transactions such as management fees or purchases of goods.

Requests by the Revenue for information should avoid placing an unnecessary or disproportionate burden upon the company. Sometimes putting the company to considerable trouble is unavoidable but an early meeting to discuss the practicalities of producing and presenting the information could be beneficial. For example—

- A request for information in a particular format that was particularly difficult or incompatible with the way that the company keeps its records could be avoided.
- The Revenue and the company would have an opportunity to ensure that the Revenue's concerns were clear and that the company understood what information was required to address those concerns.

COMPANY'S RESPONSE TO INITIAL ENQUIRY

When a company makes a return under CTSA there is a statutory requirement to prepare and retain documentation that demonstrates that its transfer pricing satisfies the arm's length standard. This documentation needs to exist at the time the return is made. This is discussed further in Tax Bulletin 37A (Part 2) published in October 1998.

In response to an initial enquiry, a company will need to make use of the documentation that existed at the time the return was made. Such documentation ought to be capable of being produced quickly. The company might, however, want to provide material going beyond what is contained in the required documentation or going into that material issues in greater detail. Such material might or might not exist at the time the initial enquiry is made. Where it does exist, it can be produced quickly. Where it does not exist, the time necessary to produce it will vary with the nature of the material. Depending on the circumstances and complexity of the issues, it would be reasonable for the company and the Revenue to agree a period of anything up to 6 months to produce the material.

In the event that the company is able to respond within a month, because all the requested documentation exists at the time the return is made, the Revenue does not then have an extra five months to complete its own consideration. Nor has the company gained five months grace for some later stage in the process. The response times for each stage of the process whatever they are agreed to be are determined independently of response times in other stages of the process.

Depending on the nature of the transactions under enquiry some of the information requested might not be in the power and possession of UK subsidiaries. The Revenue may be able to obtain such information under the Exchange of Information article of the relevant Double Taxation Treaty, but this will inevitably introduce delay. If the process is to be speeded up the company will need to volunteer such information.

REVENUE'S CONSIDERATION OF COMPANY'S RESPONSE

The Revenue will aim to conclude its initial review of the company's position within a timeframe agreed with the company. In the APA model this initial review phase can take up to six months, with a further six months for obtaining and reviewing additional information. This phase of the transfer pricing enquiry needs to be carefully handled and the time needed will vary greatly from case to case. It is not sensible to be prescriptive but the following is indicative of the steps and timeframes that may be achievable.

Within six months the Revenue aims to conclude its initial review and to share its preliminary conclusions with the company. The Revenue may decide at this stage to close the enquiry. If not the Revenue will say what the concerns are and explain what further information is required and why.

The company and the Revenue may agree to schedule an interim meeting, for example after three months, to discuss the Revenue's preliminary findings and report on progress.

The Revenue's request for supplementary information will often include arrangements for site visits and the opportunity to meet key employees of the company. The purpose of such visits and meetings would be to obtain information required by the Revenue to complete its consideration of the company's position.

In the next six months the company produces the requested information, arranges any site visits and makes further representations in support of the appropriateness of its transfer pricing. Representations and information may be presented at meetings, in writing or through any other convenient and secure media. Again interim meetings to discuss progress can be agreed.

Following receipt of the supplementary information the Revenue will present its position, either in writing or at a meeting. The enquiry may be closed at this stage. The Revenue may request further information if appropriate (again giving reasons) but ideally the enquiry should be narrowing by now.

In practice there may be more or fewer steps in this phase, and depending on the facts and circumstances of the particular case, one step may take longer than another. The important point is that the Revenue will explain its reasons for any supplementary information requests and for its decision to continue with the enquiry.

NEGOTIATION AND SETTLEMENT

The Revenue and companies have a mutual interest in settling transfer pricing enquiries by negotiation rather than through litigation. The combination of well directed risk assessment and an agreed timetable for enquiries should mean that the negotiating stage is reached after a reasonable period with the disputed areas clearly identified.

MUTUAL AGREEMENT PROCEDURES

In the event that an adjustment to UK profits results from the enquiry, then the company may be exposed to double taxation. Where Mutual Agreement Procedures are invoked the respective tax administrations will endeavour to eliminate that double taxation. At present the Revenue has an agreed timetable framework for dealing with Mutual Agreement Procedure cases involving the USA and is seeking to extend that framework to other treaty partners. More details about Mutual Agreement Procedures will be published in due course.

CONTACT NAMES

Richard Gallacher Tel: 020 7438 6309 Email: Richard.Gallacher@ir.gsi.gov.uk

Hazel Preece Tel: 020 7438 6823 Email: Hazel.Preece@ir.gsi.gov.uk

October 2002. Tax Bulletin Issue 61

Capital gains tax—taper relief: anti-avoidance—TCGA 1992 Sch A1 paras 11 and 11A

This article covers:

- The implications of the repeal of TCGA 1992 Sch A1 para 11
- The purpose and scope of TCGA 1992 Sch A1 para 11A
- The application of TCGA 1992 Sch A1 para 11A in some common situations

THE IMPLICATIONS OF THE REPEAL OF TCGA 1992 SCH A1 PARA 11

TCGA 1992 Sch A1 para 11 does not apply to disposals of shares on or after 17 April 2002, even if there was a relevant change of activity involving a close company before that date. The paragraph only needs to be considered on a disposal of shares of a close company before that date.

THE ENACTMENT OF TCGA 1992 SCH A1 PARA 11A

FA 2002 s 47, Sch 10(3) enacted TCGA 1992 Sch A1 para 11A (periods of share ownership not to count if company is not active) for disposals of shares in companies from 17 April 2002. For taper relief, ''shares'' includes securities and certain debentures. The full text of paragraph 11A is [reproduced in Part 1b of this publication].

THE PURPOSE OF TCGA 1992 SCH A1 PARA 11A

The Government had two purposes in mind when introducing TCGA 1992 Sch A1 para 11A as part of the Finance Bill 2002:

– That the paragraph should provide continued revenue protection against transactions arranged to secure excessive taper relief. For example, where an individual sets up a company in year 1; does nothing with it until year 8 when it is used to acquire an asset; and disposes of the company's shares in year 11. Without TCGA 1992 Sch A1 para 11A, the individual would obtain ten years of taper relief on the gain from the shares, even though that gain would be wholly attributable to the increased value of the asset acquired by the company only three years previously.

– That the paragraph should ensure that people are not inadvertently disadvantaged if they use a long-held dormant company to conduct a trade. Without TCGA 1992 Sch A1 para 11A, the company's shares would be classed as non-business assets during the period of dormancy, leading to less taper relief than expected on a future disposal of those shares, even though the only activity ever actually conducted by the company prior to the disposal was trading.

HOW TCGA 1992 SCH A1 PARA 11A WORKS

The paragraph applies where, on or after 17 April 2002, there has been a disposal of shares in a company which was both close and ''inactive'' at any time from 6 April 1998 to the date of disposal. If so, then the period during which the company was both close and inactive will not count for the purposes of taper relief. So the paragraph 11A test should be applied before considering whether an asset is a business asset or not. The examples below show how paragraph 11A works.

> Mary acquires shares in a company on 1 July 1998. These are disposed of on 1 September 2002. The company was both close and inactive from 1 July 1998 to 31 December 1998 (inclusive). On 1 January 1999 the company started to trade (ie it became ''active''). It continued trading until 1 September 2002 and remained close in that period.
>
> Under FA 2002 Sch 10 para 8(3)(*d*), certain debentures are now treated as securities for the purposes of taper relief for disposals on or after 6 April 2001 and for all holding periods. However, TCGA 1992 Sch A1 para 11A (like certain other revenue protection provisions) does not apply to any such debentures in relation to any time before 17 April 2002.
>
> Mary's qualifying holding period for taper relief purposes will be the period from 1 January 1999 (rather than 1 July 1998) to 1 September 2002. There are three (rather than four) whole years in this period. This will also be Mary's relevant period of ownership. If the shares qualified as business assets throughout the relevant period of ownership full taper relief at the business rate will be due in computing the chargeable gain.
>
> John acquires shares in an active close company on 1 May 1999. The company is inactive from 1 August 2002 but becomes active again on 1 August 2004. John disposes of his shares on 1 December 2005. The company remained close throughout. John's qualifying holding period will be the combined period from 1 May 1999 to 31 July 2002 and 1 August 2004 to 1 December 2005, or four years and seven months. This is also the relevant period of ownership of the shares. There are four whole years in the qualifying holding period. John will need to work out if the company was his qualifying company during the two parts of the relevant period of ownership in order to see if business assets taper is due. (The period 1 August 2002 to 31 July 2004 is a period that ''does not count'' for taper purposes. It is not therefore taken into account in working out either the qualifying holding period or the relevant period of ownership.)

RELEVANT PERIOD OF OWNERSHIP

Where TCGA 1992 Sch A1 para 11A applies, the start point of the relevant period of ownership can be more than ten years before the date of disposal. But the relevant period of ownership cannot be more than ten years, nor can the start date precede 6 April 1998 or the date of acquisition of the asset (TCGA 1992 Sch A1 para 2). This can be illustrated by a simple example.

> Amarjeet acquired shares in an active close company on 15 February 1999. These are disposed of on 15 May 2010. The company was close throughout but inactive between 15 June 2001 and 15 March 2002 and this period will not count in working out the relevant period of ownership. The relevant period of ownership will therefore be the combined periods from 16 March 2002 to 15 May 2010 and 15 August 1999 (not 15 February 1999) to 14 June 2001, being 10 years ending with 15 May 2010.

The way in which periods that do not count affect the qualifying holding period and relevant period of ownership for paragraph 11A purposes is therefore the same as for TCGA 1992 Sch A1 para 10 (see CG17928).

REQUIREMENT TO BE CLOSE

Whether or not a company is close at any time for the purposes of TCGA 1992 Sch A1 para 11A is to be determined in accordance with the normal rules found in TA 1988 ss 414 and 415.

Note that the assessment of whether a company is both close and inactive needs to be made for all times that shares were owned and may involve more than one company if there has been a share reorganisation (see below). That is different from TCGA 1992 Sch A1 para 11, where the assessment whether a company was close needed only to be made in respect of the position on a disposal and only in relation to the company in which the shares were held at the time of the disposal.

A period when a company is inactive but not close will still count for taper relief purposes. So, in John's case above, if the company had been a non-close company at all times then paragraph 11A would not apply and John's qualifying holding period and relevant period of ownership would be 1 May 1999 to 1 December 2005.

COMPANY RECONSTRUCTIONS AND REORGANISATIONS

A person eligible for taper relief may exchange shares or debentures for other shares or debentures when a company is reorganised, reconstructed or amalgamated. Where the relevant conditions are met, TCGA 1992 s 127 applies and the reorganisation is treated as not involving any disposal of the original shares or any acquisition of a new holding. The original shares and the new holding are treated as the same asset acquired as the original shares were acquired. Where, as a result, there is but one asset—represented at certain points in time during the holding period by the original shares and at other points in time by the new holding of shares—the tests in TCGA 1992 Sch A1 para 11A are applied, at any particular time during the holding period and the relevant period of ownership, by an examination of the status of the company in which the shares were then held. For example—

> Ali holds shares in a close trading company A, which he acquired on 18 November 1999. On 7 July 2002 the trade of that company is transferred to a newly formed close company B. The shareholders of A receive shares in B in consideration for the transfer of the trade. Company A is then liquidated. This whole transaction is treated as a reorganisation of shares for capital gains tax purposes. There is no disposal of the A shares as a result of the reconstruction, and the shares in company B are treated as acquired when the A shares were acquired. Ali disposes of his B shares on 1 October 2007. B was a trading company throughout. The assessment for paragraph 11A is made in respect of the shares actually held at the time. So for the period 18 November 1999 to 6 July 2002, Ali looks at company A; for the period 7 July 2002 to 1 October 2007, Ali looks at company B. Whilst Ali held shares in company A it was close but active throughout. The same applies to the times he held shares in Company B. Therefore paragraph 11A will not apply. Ali's qualifying holding period and relevant period of ownership will be from 18 November 1999 to 1 October 2007.

BONUS YEAR

The bonus year is available for assets that had been acquired before 17 March 1998 and held on 6 April 1998. TCGA 1992 Sch A1 para 11A has no effect on the availability of the bonus year.

MEANING OF ACTIVE

TCGA 1992 Sch A1 para 11A(2) details when a company is "active" for the purposes of the paragraph but this is subject to TCGA 1992 Sch A1 para 11A(4).

A company is regarded as active at any time when it is carrying on a business of any description. Business has a wider meaning than trade and may include property investment and rental. Any time when a company is a trading company, or the holding company of a trading group, will be a time when that company is active, for TCGA 1992 Sch A1 para 11A purposes.

A company will also be regarded as active when it is preparing to carry on a business of any description. Whether or not it is preparing to carry on a business is a question of fact. At one extreme the directors of a company may simply get together once a year to agree that the company will do nothing in the coming year unless a business opportunity arises. That company would not be "active" for TCGA 1992 Sch A1 para 11A purposes. By comparison, the directors of another company may have identified a specific business opportunity and be in negotiation to finance and start up or acquire a business. This would be an active company for TCGA 1992 Sch A1 para 11A purposes.

A company will also be active when it or another person is winding up the affairs of a business of any description that it has ceased to carry on. This will include the formal winding up of the company by a liquidator. But a company that is in liquidation and where there are no winding up activities is unlikely to be active. It will also include cases where the directors, or some other person, are dealing with the post-cessation business affairs of the company but the company remains in being. This will usually involve paying off creditors, closing bank accounts, selling off assets etc. And it will include cases where the company is intended to remain in being in order to start another business later, but there is to be a gap between winding up the first business and starting the next: the time spent winding up the affairs of the first business counts as active. Alternatively, a company previously engaged in one trade or business, may do nothing for a time and subsequently start a new trade or business. Only the middle period, during which the company is neither settling the affairs of the earlier business nor preparing to start the later business, is "inactive".

TCGA 1992 Sch A1 para 11A(4) describes certain activities which will not count as activities for the purposes of TCGA 1992 Sch A1 para 11A(2) where all or any of these are the company's only activities. These activities are explained in the next section of this article.

FURTHER SITUATIONS WHEN A COMPANY IS TREATED AS ACTIVE

TCGA 1992 Sch A1 para 11A treats a company as active in certain specific situations where groups and/or joint ventures are involved. These are—

– Where the company is the holding company of a group of companies that contains at least one active company; or,
– Where the company has a qualifying shareholding in a joint venture company or is the holding company of a group of companies any member of which has a qualifying shareholding in a joint venture company.

By definition a joint venture company will be active, as it has to be a trading company or the holding company of a trading group (TCGA 1992 Sch A1 para 23(2)).

CERTAIN ACTIVITIES ARE NOT ENOUGH TO MAKE A COMPANY ACTIVE

A company will not be regarded as active where all it does is one or more of the following—

– Holding money (in any currency) in cash or on deposit;
– Holding other assets whose total value is insignificant;
– Holding shares in or debentures of a company that is not active;
– Making loans to an associated company or to a participator or an associate of a participator; and
– Carrying out of certain statutory administrative functions.

For example, a company may issue 100 £1 ordinary shares (fully paid). If that is all the company has done to date it will not be active. Or, it may simply be a repository for funds which are held in cash or on deposit without indulging in any other activity.

Only where there is a structured commercial activity beyond the holding of money on deposit which the company is carrying on, or is preparing to carry on, would it count as active.

In another case a company may have invested the £100 it received on the issue of the ordinary shares in an option to buy an asset. The value of the option would normally be insignificant at that time.

Finally, the company may simply make an annual return of accounts to Companies House.

In all these cases the company will be inactive.

MEANING OF INSIGNIFICANT

The word "insignificant" must be given its normal dictionary meaning of trifling or completely unimportant. Thus in most cases it is unlikely to cover any assets with a value in excess of £1000. Ultimately, whether or not the holding of assets is insignificant is a question of fact.

MEANING OF BUSINESS

The meaning of business was discussed in Tax Bulletin 53 in the context of TCGA 1992 Sch A1 para 11 and its use in TCGA 1992 generally. There we explained that the concept of a business is central to parts of the capital gains code. For example, TCGA 1992 s 162 concerns the transfer of a business to a company as a going concern and TCGA 1992 s 163 provides for retirement relief on the disposal of a business or business assets. In the case of TCGA 1992 s 163, for example, relief is restricted to assets used for a trade, profession, etc and this does not include assets used for a lettings business within Schedule A. However, a lettings business will be a business for the purposes of TCGA 1992 Sch A1 para 11A.The meaning of business is not defined for the purposes of TCGA 1992 Sch A1 para 11A. Generally it should not be difficult to identify whether or not a business is being carried on. Inevitably there will be a few cases on the margin where the facts will have to be considered carefully. The first point to note is that 'business' and 'trade' are not synonymous. Whilst all trades are businesses, there are many businesses that are not trades. Property letting, as opposed to the provision of services to tenants, may be a business though not a trade. The holding of investments can also amount to a business. Indeed, there is judicial support for the view that this does not have to be actively carried on to be a business of making investments (see, for example, *IRC v The Korean Syndicate Ltd* 12 TC 181). But TCGA 1992 Sch A1 para 11A will apply where the "business" is not regarded as active because of the restrictions in TCGA 1992 Sch A1 para 11A(4). On the other hand, there are several cases where it has been held that a trading company which has ended its main activities but has retained its investment portfolio is not carrying on a business of holding investments. The most recent case is *Jowett v O'Neill and Brennan Construction Ltd* 70 TC 566. In that case, Mr Justice Park acknowledged that whilst the normal conclusion, when a company lays out its assets and earns an income return, is that it is carrying on a business there will, as a matter of law, be exceptional cases where the facts indicate that no business is being carried on by the company. As Park J pointed out in the *O'Neill* case, it is the exception rather than the rule that means a company is not carrying on a business when it puts its money on deposit. But—because of the restrictions in TCGA 1992 Sch A1 para 11A(4)—there needs to be business activities beyond just holding money on deposit for a company to count as active.

The new legislation in TCGA 1992 Sch A1 para 11A makes clear that it is not necessary for the business to be conducted on a commercial basis or with a view to the realisation of a profit. References to carrying on a business include holding assets and managing them (TCGA 1992 Sch A1 para 11A(3)(*b*)). Simply holding assets will not necessarily amount to carrying on a business.

...

Commentary—*Simon's Direct Tax Service* **C2.1414A**.

October 2002. Tax Bulletin Issue 61

Capital gains tax—capital sums derived from assets: reliefs and Extra Statutory Concession D33

INTRODUCTION

This article sets out how reliefs are calculated when a capital sum is derived from an asset and when ESC D33 (the Zim concession) is applied. In particular this note deals with some common situations where taper relief is due. The Revenue's Capital Gains Manual provides guidance on general capital gains tax (CGT) principles where capital sums are derived from assets at CG12940 onwards and for ESC D33 at CG13010 onwards.

OVERVIEW

For CGT purposes, a reference to a ''disposal'' of an asset includes not only a reference to the actual disposal (or an actual part-disposal) of the asset: it also includes reference to certain occasions where a ''capital sum'', in money or ''money's worth'', is ''derived from assets'' (TCGA 1992 s 22). Accordingly, a person who receives a capital sum derived from an asset is treated for CGT purposes as though he or she had made a disposal of that asset. The date of the deemed disposal is the date the capital sum is received (TCGA 1992 s 22(2)).

There is a deemed disposal of an asset where a capital sum is received as compensation

- for any kind of damage or injury to the asset, or
- for the loss, destruction or dissipation of the asset, or
- for any depreciation or risk of depreciation of the asset.

Identifying the asset from which a capital sum is derived can sometimes be a problem in the application of TCGA 1992 s 22. The case of *IRC v Montgomery* (49 TC 679) explores the meaning of the phrase ''derived from assets'' and is also a useful illustration of the problems associated with identifying the correct asset for TCGA 1992 s 22 purposes. Other cases are discussed at CG12985 onwards. The question will often be whether the sum derives from the asset itself or from a right to take action for compensation or damages. This point was considered in the case of *Zim Properties Ltd v Proctor* (58 TC 371). In that case the asset disposed of was held to be the ''right to take action'' rather than the land which, owing to the alleged negligence of the company's solicitors, was not sold.

Where a capital sum is derived from an asset, and TCGA 1992 s 22 applies, we look at the history of the use of the asset from the time it was acquired to the time the capital sum is received to determine what reliefs are due and how they should be calculated. We confirm that in these circumstances ''reliefs'' includes taper relief.

TAPER RELIEF AND TCGA 1992 S 22

Taper relief reduces a chargeable gain after losses according to how long an asset has been held before its disposal (the qualifying holding period). The amount of the reduction depends on the number of whole years in that period and whether or not the asset was a business asset during the relevant period of ownership. TCGA 1992 Sch A1 para 2 explains how to determine the qualifying holding period and the relevant period of ownership. Neither period can begin before 6 April 1998 or, if later, the time the asset is acquired. In the case of the relevant period of ownership this can not be longer than ten years ending in the disposal of the asset. The rules to determine if shares qualify as business assets can be found in TCGA 1992 Sch A1 para 4. TCGA 1992 Sch A1 para explains when other assets qualify as business assets.

EXAMPLE 1: CAPITAL SUM DERIVED FROM ASSET

Joan is a sole trader and on 1 June 1998 she purchased land that she occupied and used wholly for the purposes of her trade from that date. On 1 October 1999 part of the land was damaged by a chemical spillage from a factory adjoining her land. Despite the spillage, Joan was able to continue using the land in her trade. The land was disposed of on 1 September 2001. Joan therefore ceased to occupy and use the land for the purposes of her trade from that date. It was then occupied by a another sole trader and used for the purposes of his trade.

PRs etc

On 1 May 2002 Joan received compensation from the factory owners for the damage to her land: this is chargeable to capital gains tax in accordance with TCGA 1992 s 22 as a capital sum derived from the land. Where a sum is recovered as compensation for physical damage to an asset, identification is not a problem because it is inevitably the asset, rather than any right of action, from which the sum derives.

From 1 September 2001 the land did not qualify as a business asset in relation to Joan. For the purposes of calculating taper relief on the compensation payment, Joan's qualifying holding period and relevant period of ownership will be the period from 1 June 1998 to 1 May 2002 (inclusive). In relation to Joan, the asset will be a business asset between 1 June 1998 and 1 September 2001 (inclusive) but not thereafter.

EXAMPLE 2: CAPITAL SUM DERIVED FROM RIGHT OF ACTION

If, however, Joan's capital receipt did not derive from the land but from a right of action, for example because of her solicitor's negligence, the statutory position would be different. All applicable reliefs would be calculated by reference to the asset being the right of action. It is difficult to see how the right of action could be an asset that can be used for the purposes of a trade and it is therefore unlikely that the right would qualify as a business asset at any time. The result is that only non-business asset taper relief would be available on the chargeable gain.

In such a case it would be to Joan's advantage to apply ESC D33. We show how this would work in her case later in this article.

ESC D33

This concession provides that damages or compensation which derive from a right of action in respect of an underlying asset are treated for the purposes of tax on chargeable gains as though they derive from that underlying asset. So applying ESC D33 means that the calculation of chargeable gains is made in exactly the same way as if TCGA 1992 s 22 applied. If any relief or exemption would be available on a disposal of the underlying asset, the concession allows that relief or exemption to be available on the disposal of the right of action. The usual conditions for the availability of the relief in question, such as those relating to use, employment or voting rights, have to be met at the relevant times.

For taper relief purposes, for any disposal of a right of action to which the concession applies—

- the qualifying holding period includes not only the period after 5 April 1998 when the underlying asset was held but also the period after that date when the right of action was held until the time at which the capital sum in question is received, and
- the relevant period of ownership is the period after 5 April 1998 during which the underlying asset was held and also the period after that date when the right of action was held until the time at which the capital sum in question is received or, if shorter, the period of ten years ending when the capital sum is received.

Once the chargeable gain on the disposal of the right has been calculated it will be necessary to determine whether that gain arises on the disposal of a business asset or a non-business asset in order to work out the amount of taper relief due. The taper rules will be applied to determine if an asset is a business asset for any part of the relevant period of ownership when the underlying asset is held. They will also apply for any period when the right of action, but not the underlying asset, is held as if the underlying asset were still held. However, this does not mean that the conditions relating to use in a trade, or voting rights and so forth will be deemed to be satisfied when the underlying asset is no longer held. The normal rules for assets to qualify as business assets will apply for any period when the right of action is held but the underlying asset is no longer held.

We now consider how ESC D33 would apply in the circumstances described in Example 2. Its effect is that, instead of non-business asset taper relief applying to the total chargeable gain, the non-business rate of taper applies only to the proportion of the gain which corresponds to the period from 2 September 2001 to 1 May 2002 (inclusive). The business asset rate of taper will be applied to the proportion corresponding to the period from 1 June 1998 to 1 September 2001 (inclusive).

It may help if we provide further examples of the application of taper relief in some typical scenarios where ESC D33 is applied.

EXAMPLE 3: NO DISPOSAL OF UNDERLYING ASSET-ASSET OTHER THAN SHARES

Jack owns the freehold of premises which he uses wholly for the purposes of his trade from 2 January 1997. On 1 July 2000 he instructed an estate agent to sell the premises. He continued to trade from the premises. Owing to the agent's negligence the sale of the building fell through on 31 January 2001. The estate agent paid Jack compensation on 1 September 2001.

Jack applies ESC D33 in computing a gain on the disposal of the right of action, which is chargeable to capital gains tax for the tax year 2001/02. Because the compensation is treated as being derived from the underlying asset, part of the acquisition cost of the premises, using the normal part disposal rules, (TCGA 1992 s 42), is allowed in computing the gain.

For taper relief purposes, the qualifying holding period is from 6 April 1998 to 1 September 2001 (inclusive). There are three complete years in that period. The part disposal is of an asset that has been wholly a business asset throughout the relevant period of ownership from 6 April 1998 to 1 September 2001 (inclusive) by reference to the use of the underlying asset—the land including the premises.

Business assets taper relief for three whole years will therefore be due on any chargeable gain arising on the disposal.

EXAMPLE 4: DISPOSAL OF UNDERLYING ASSET—ASSET OTHER THAN SHARES

John owned the freehold of premises which he used wholly for the purposes of his trade from 20 June 1996. On 1 May 2000 he instructed his solicitor to sell the premises. He continued to trade from the premises until they were disposed of on 1 November 2000. John made a capital loss on the disposal.

It later transpired that owing to a surveyor's negligence the sale of the building was at undervalue. The surveyor paid compensation to John on 1 December 2001. John applies ESC D33 in computing the gain arising on the disposal of the right of action chargeable to capital gains tax for the tax year 2001–02.

For taper relief purposes the qualifying holding period is from 6 April 1998 to 1 December 2001 (inclusive). There are three complete years in that period. The relevant period of ownership is also the period from 6 April 1998 to 1 December 2001 (inclusive).

The gain arises on an asset that was a business asset in relation to John for taper relief purposes from 6 April 1998 to 1 November 2000. From 2 November 2000 the land was not used in a trade carried on by John, by a partnership of which he was a member, or by a company which is a ''qualifying company'' (TCGA 1992 Sch A1 para 6) in relation to him. It was, therefore, not a business asset in relation to him from 2 November 2000 until 1 December 2001 (inclusive). The part of the gain relating to the time when the asset was a business asset will qualify for business assets taper relief applying to an asset held for three whole years. The other part will be a gain on a non-business asset and will qualify for four whole years of non-business asset taper relief, as the bonus year is available.

EXAMPLE 5: DISPOSAL OF UNDERLYING ASSET—SHARES

Jennifer acquired 1000 shares in an unlisted trading company on 1 July 1998. On her accountant's advice, which proved to be negligent, she sold 400 of the shares at a significant undervalue on 1 May 2000. The 400 shares qualified as business assets throughout the period they were held. On 10 May 2000 she instructed her solicitor to take action against her accountant and on 1 December 2001 she received a capital sum to compensate her for the sale of the 400 shares.

Applying ESC D33, for taper relief purposes the qualifying holding period in computing any chargeable gain after taper relief on the capital sum is the period from 1 July 1998 to 1 December 2001 (inclusive). There are three complete years in that period. The relevant period of ownership is also the period from 1 July 1998 to 1 December 2001 (inclusive).

By applying the concession the capital sum is treated as deriving from the shares. In Jennifer's case the gain arises on shares that were business assets for taper relief purposes throughout the period from 1 July 1998 to 1 December 2001 (inclusive) since the shares were held in a company that was a qualifying company in relation to her throughout that period.

The reason the company continued to be a qualifying company in relation to Jennifer after she sold the shares is that for trading companies the definition of a qualifying company in TCGA 1992 Sch A1 para 6(1) from 6 April 2000 does not require the individual concerned to be a shareholder or an employee of the company if it is unlisted.

RELIEFS OTHER THAN TAPER RELIEF

For completeness, here are two examples where the reliefs in question are other than taper relief.

EXAMPLE 6: DISPOSAL OF UNDERLYING ASSET OTHER THAN SHARES—ROLL-OVER RELIEF

Jake owned the freehold of premises that he occupied and used wholly for the purposes of his trade from 1 August 1992. On 1 October 1999 he instructed an estate agent to sell the premises. The disposal occurred on 1 July 2000 when Jake moved his trade elsewhere.

Jake then realised that the estate agent had undervalued his property. Compensation for negligence was paid on 1 February 2002. Jake applies ESC D33 in computing the gain arising on the disposal of the right of action chargeable to CGT for the tax year 2001–02.

For the purpose of calculating what part of the compensation qualifies for roll-over relief, the period of ownership of the premises is deemed to be 1 August 1992 to 1 February 2002 (inclusive). The gain on the compensation must be apportioned between the period from 1 August 1992 to 1 July 2000 (the last day when the premises were occupied and used for the purposes of the business) and 2 July 2000 to 1 February 2002. The amount of the gain for the period 1 August 1992 to 1 July 2000 (inclusive) is available for roll-over relief if re-invested in an asset acquired within three years after 1 February 2002. No roll-over relief is available against the remainder of the gain as the premises were not occupied and used for the purposes of Jake's trade from 2 July 2000.

Detailed guidance on ''roll-over'' relief can be found at CG60250 onwards.

EXAMPLE 7: DISPOSAL OF UNDERLYING ASSET OTHER THAN SHARES-PRIVATE RESIDENCE RELIEF

Jasmine owned a house that was her only private residence from purchase on 1 December 1989. On 1 March 1997 she instructed her solicitor to arrange the disposal of the house. The disposal was due to take place on 1 October 1997 but the sale fell through owing to delays by the solicitor. Another solicitor was instructed and the disposal occurred on 1 March 1998 but at a lower sale price. Jasmine moved out on that day.

Jasmine sued the first solicitor and received compensation on 1 February 2002. Since there is no base cost associated with the disposal of the right of action, the whole of the gain is chargeable to CGT for the tax year 2001–02. However, Jasmine applies ESC D33 in calculating the reliefs to which she is entitled to reduce the gain.

For the purpose of calculating what part of the compensation qualifies for private residence relief, the period of ownership of the house is deemed to be 1 December 1989 to 1 February 2002 (inclusive). It was Jasmine's only residence from 1 December 1989 to 1 March 1998 (inclusive). In addition, the three years 2 February 1999 to 1 February 2002 qualify for relief in accordance with TCGA 1992 s 223(2). The proportion of the gain relating to these periods is fully covered by private residence relief. Private residence relief is not available for the remainder of the gain relating to the period 2 March 1998 to 1 February 1999 (inclusive) but non-business assets taper relief will be due. The qualifying holding period will be the period from 6 April 1998 to 1 February 2002 and there are three whole years in that period. The bonus year will also be due as the residence was owned by Jasmine before 17 March 1998.

Detailed guidance on ''private residence'' relief can be found at CG64200.

Commentary—*Simon's Direct Tax Service* **C1.328**.

December 2002. Tax Bulletin Issue 62

Changes to the "Hansard" procedure

INTRODUCTION

You may be familiar with the term, the ''Hansard'' procedure. For those who are not, this is a process by which the Inland Revenue offers a taxpayer suspected of serious tax fraud an opportunity to confess to all, if any, of the irregularities in their tax affairs. The term ''Hansard'' is used, because the practice of the Board of Inland Revenue is set out in a statement by the Chancellor of the Exchequer in the Parliamentary Hansard records.

Hansard is a long established concept and its origins can be traced back to the latter part of the First World War. It first appears in Hansard by way of a lengthy written answer by Sir W. Johnson Hicks, in the House of Commons 19 July 1923. Over the years there have only been minor changes and the Hansard practice has survived a number of challenges in the Courts.

From time to time the Chancellor of the day updates the Hansard statement to reflect the latest practice of the Inland Revenue. This article reports that the Chancellor has recently made a revised statement; it looks at the main changes and the reasons behind these. It also announces changes in the Inland Revenue's Code of Practice number 9, which provides further information about these types of investigations.

BACKGROUND

The Hansard procedure was last updated by the then Chancellor, the Rt Hon John Major MP, on 18 October 1990. In answering a Parliamentary Question about the practice of the Board of Inland Revenue with regard to instituting criminal proceedings in case of suspected tax fraud, he gave the following statement—

> ''The practice of the Board of Inland Revenue in cases of tax fraud is as follows—
>
> The Board may accept a money settlement instead of instituting criminal proceedings in respect of fraud alleged to have been committed by a taxpayer.
>
> They can give no undertaking that they will accept a money settlement and refrain from instituting criminal proceedings even if the case is one in which the taxpayer has made a full confession and has given full facilities for investigation of the facts. They reserve to themselves full discretion in all cases as to the course they pursue.
>
> But in considering whether to accept a money settlement or to institute criminal proceedings, it is their practice to be influenced by the fact that the taxpayer has made a full confession and has given full facilities for investigation into his affairs and for examination of such books, papers, documents or information as the Board may consider necessary''.

This statement includes an indication that a taxpayer who makes a full confession and who co-operates fully with the Inland Revenue during their investigations can expect that the matter will be dealt with on a civil basis, rather than criminal proceedings being taken against them. But the statement is not explicit on the matter and the taxpayer is left with no absolute assurance that the Board of the Inland Revenue will not institute criminal proceedings even in these circumstances.

STATEMENTS BY THE LORDS

More recently, the House of Lords has considered the case of *R v Allen*. In this case the appellant claimed that the admission into evidence of statements made in response to the Hansard procedure breached his right to a fair trial under Article 6(1) of the European Convention of Human Rights. This, he claimed, was because he had been subjected to an inducement at the time when the statements were made. The inducement in question was said to be the assurance implicit in the Hansard statement that if the taxpayer makes a full confession criminal proceedings would not be instituted against him.

There was, however, a flaw in the argument advanced by the appellant. As Lord Hutton explained—

> ''To the extent that there was an inducement contained in the Hansard statement, the inducement was to give true and accurate information to the Revenue, but the accused ... did not respond to that inducement and instead of giving true and accurate information gave false information. Therefore, in my opinion, the appellant's argument ... that he was induced by the hope of non-institution of criminal proceedings held out by the Revenue to provide the schedule and that its provision was, therefore, involuntary is invalid''.

In other words, the whole basis of the appellant's argument was founded on a false premise. The facts of the appellant's case did not engage the legal argument advanced on his behalf because the appellant had not made full disclosure in accordance with the terms of the Hansard statement.

Lord Hutton pointed out that the position would have been different if the appellant had made full disclosure to the Inland Revenue in response to the Hansard statement.

> ''If, in response to the Hansard statement, the appellant had given true and accurate information which disclosed that he had earlier cheated the Revenue and had been prosecuted for that earlier dishonesty, he would have had a strong argument that the criminal proceedings were unfair and an even stronger argument that the Crown should not rely on evidence of his admission, but that is the reverse of what actually occurred''.

A FULL CONFESSION

The conclusion to be drawn from Lord Hutton's remarks is that a taxpayer invited under the Hansard procedure to make a full confession, who unlike the appellant in this case actually did so, would be hard done by if the Revenue then subsequently prosecuted him or her anyway. This would be particularly true if the Revenue used his confession as evidence in court.

These remarks are significant in terms of the Hansard statement. The Board of the Inland Revenue had previously reserved to itself full discretion as to the course of action it would take in any case. Lord Hutton took the view, however, that in cases of a full confession under Hansard, the Revenue would be unfair to prosecute, effectively placing a limit on the full discretion of the Revenue in this matter.

As significant as these points are, in practical terms there is no record of any case in which a taxpayer who has made a full confession under Hansard being prosecuted for these offences later. The substantive point is how assured the taxpayer can be that the Revenue will not prosecute in these circumstances.

It is important to stress that the Hansard procedure invites a full and complete confession. Deliberate failure to disclose errors or omissions may result in criminal prosecution. Depending upon the facts of the particular case and the admissibility of evidence before the Courts, it is possible that someone who only admits to part of the irregularities could face criminal charges not only in relation to the matters undisclosed or misrepresented but also the matters disclosed.

FULL CO-OPERATION

A further element to be taken into account according to the previous version of Hansard is whether the taxpayer had given full co-operation to the Revenue during the investigation. This includes the giving of full facilities for investigation into his affairs and for examination of such books, papers, documents or information as the Board may consider necessary. A taxpayer could conclude from this, that even in cases of a full confession, if the right amount of co-operation is not offered, then he or she remains at the risk of prosecution.

Again in practice there have been no cases of the Revenue prosecuting in these circumstances. It has considered instead the fullness of the confession made under Hansard when deciding on subsequent prosecution action. It is a matter for the taxpayer to decide whether or not to co-operate with the investigation and the extent of that co-operation. If the matter remains civil, the Revenue will, however, take the degree of co-operation into account in determining any penalties which may be applicable.

It must however be made clear that the Board does not hold out the opportunity of Hansard indefinitely. So, for example, if a taxpayer who had been given Hansard took an unreasonable amount of time in making their full disclosure, the Inland Revenue may decide to commence its own investigation. Depending upon the information held or obtained by the Inland Revenue, this may lead at any time to the withdrawal of Hansard and the start of an investigation with a view to criminal prosecution. If this happened a full confession subsequently made by the taxpayer would not by itself prevent the Board from continuing to pursue the prosecution.

A REVISED HANSARD STATEMENT

There has been a revised statement about the Board of the Inland Revenue's policy on these matters. The response to a Parliamentary Question to the Chancellor on 7th November 2002 was—

> ''Further to the statement made on 18th October 1990 at column 882 by the then Chancellor, the Rt. Hon. John Major, the practice of the Board of Inland Revenue in cases of suspected serious tax fraud is as follows—
>
> The Board reserves complete discretion to pursue prosecutions in the circumstances it considers appropriate.
>
> Where serious tax fraud has been committed, the Board may accept a money settlement instead of pursuing a criminal prosecution.
>
> The Board will accept a money settlement and will not pursue a criminal prosecution, if the taxpayer, in response to being given a copy of this Statement by an authorised officer, makes a full and complete confession of all tax irregularities''.

The significant points to note are that a taxpayer making a full confession under this procedure may now be assured that the Inland Revenue will not pursue a criminal prosecution. The term ''pursue'' is used because the Revenue is a prosecuting body in its own right only in England and Wales. In Scotland and in Northern Ireland it refers cases to the Procurator Fiscal and the Director of Public Prosecutions, respectively, for their consideration.

The revised text refers to a copy of the Statement being given by an authorised officer. For these purposes, an authorised officer is a current serving member of the Inland Revenue Special Compliance Office. A copy of the Hansard Statement will normally be given at the first meeting with the taxpayer after the case has been taken up for investigation under Code of Practice 9.

The Hansard procedure is explained in the Inland Revenue Code of Practice 9. This has been substantially updated as a result of the revised Statement. (There have also been some consequential changes to Code of Practice 8, which deals with cases where serious fraud is not suspected). One of the key changes is to make clear that it is for the taxpayer to decide whether to co-operate with the investigation and that in making this decision the taxpayer may seek the help of a professional advisor. The Code of Practice also makes clear that any information that the taxpayer does provide may be used in any subsequent proceedings to determine tax, interest and penalties. As stated above, if the case is concluded by way of a money settlement, the level of co-operation will be one of the factors taken into account in deciding the amount of any penalties.

These changes will have immediate effect and so taxpayers subjected to the Hansard procedure will be read the revised text from now on. Copies of the revised Codes of Practice will be available soon from the Inland Revenue.

Commentary—*Simon's Direct Tax Service* **A3.1665**.

February 2003. Tax Bulletin Issue 63

Important changes to the filing of employer End of Year returns

The Government believes that encouraging employers to make greater use of new technology is the best way to help them deal with their payroll tasks.

As part of the measures to support this change all employers will be required to file their End of Year returns electronically (e-file) by 2010, either directly or through an intermediary, such as a payroll bureau or agent.

All employers with 250 or more employees will be required to e-file End of Year forms by May 2005.

DETAIL

The compulsory electronic filing date will depend on the number of employees an employer has:

Number of Employees	*First compulsory electronic Return*	*Deadline*
250 or more	2004/05 End of Year	May 2005
Between 50 and 249	2005/06 End of Year	May 2006
Fewer than 50	2009/10 End of Year	May 2010

The primary legislation for compulsory electronic filing is in FA 2002 ss 135, 136 FA 2002. The draft regulations are expected to be published on the Inland Revenue website in March 2003. Copies may also be obtained from Press Office.

WHAT IS E-FILING?

E-filing means employers will have to send their End of Year returns (both forms P35 and P14 together) by—

- Internet service for PAYE or
- Electronic Data Interchange (EDI) service or
- using an intermediary, such as a payroll bureau or agent, who will submit End of Year returns on the employers behalf using one of the above.

Please note: Magnetic media (CD ROM, flexible disk, data cartridge and open reel tape) are not considered electronic.

PENALTIES

There will be a new penalty of up to £3000 per annum per PAYE scheme for the employer's failure to make an electronic End of Year return when they should have done so. This is in addition to the existing late filing penalty.

FINANCIAL INCENTIVES

There will be financial incentives for employers with fewer than 50 employees to encourage them to make the transition from paper to e-filing earlier. All qualifying employers who successfully e-file for these years will receive the payment shown in the table, including those who are already e-filing.

End of Year Return	2004-05	2005-06	2006-07	2007-08	2008-09
Incentive £	250	250	150	150	75

WHAT NOW

- Most agents are employers, so will have to prepare to meet their own obligation to e-file as well as considering how they will help their employer clients with e-filing.
- Agents can also help their clients by letting them know that this change is coming.
- Agents should establish that they will meet the electronic submission requirements (as shown on previous page).
- Agents who want to e-file and are already using payroll software should contact their software provider to ascertain which of the two services it will support and from what date, and the range of electronic forms and returns it will support (eg forms P14, P35, P6, P9 etc).
- Agents who do not already have payroll software should start considering their options now. If they use an IT payroll product they should find it will help and enable them to deal more easily with their payroll obligations. When employers, intermediaries or agents decide to file electronically they need to consider:
  - which service to use; and
  - what software or hardware they need to buy. Employers and agents will need to make sure that the payroll software that they choose include an electronic submission capability.

Details of software which is formally accredited by IR can be found at: http://www.inlandrevenue.gov.uk/ebu/acclist.htm. The IR accreditation process checks that the payroll software accurately calculates tax, NICs, student loan deductions etc and also ensures that it incorporates one of the two electronic transmission service requirements.

Details of software which is EDI certificated can be found at: http://www.inlandrevenue.gov.uk/ebu/eb4_paye_edi.pdf

Details of software which has been IR checked as meeting the requirements of Internet transmissions can be found at: http://www.inlandrevenue.gov.uk/efiling/paye/paye_software_forms.htm.

Agents and Employers can find more information about EDI, the Internet service for PAYE and all the other services available on the Inland Revenue Website at: http://www.inlandrevenue.gov.uk/ebu/emp_index.htm

Additional information about the compulsory filing of employers End of Year returns, including financial incentives available, can be found on the Inland Revenue website at http://www.inlandrevenue.gov.uk/employers/ppip/index.htm

April 2003. Tax Bulletin Special Edition

UK/US Double Taxation Agreement

The new UK/US Double Taxation Agreement was signed on 24 July 2001 with an amending protocol being signed a year later on 19 July 2002. The treaty came into force on 31 March 2003.

Since signature the treaty has generated much comment and analysis in the professional press and we have received many enquiries about how we will interpret and apply the various articles in the treaty. Because many of these enquiries covered common ground we decided to issue a Tax Bulletin edition dedicated solely to the treaty and, in particular, to those articles in it that are new or that have been substantially altered from the corresponding articles in the previous UK/US treaty.

What follows is not intended as an exhaustive commentary on the provisions of the new treaty. It reflects the understanding of the Inland Revenue on how certain provisions will be interpreted and applied in certain circumstances. In the interests of brevity it has sometimes been necessary to paraphrase the wording of the treaty. In interpreting and applying the treaty in a particular case, it will be necessary to consider the facts of the case and the detailed wording of the treaty.

INTRODUCTION TO THE NEW UK/US DOUBLE TAXATION AGREEMENT

What does the treaty do?

The treaty seeks to eliminate double taxation of income and gains for UK and US residents, to protect those residents from fiscal discrimination, to provide them with certainty about the tax treatment of income and gains, and to prevent tax evasion and avoidance. The treaty also seeks to ensure that its benefits go to those UK and US residents that are entitled to them and it contains measures to prevent its being abused by residents of third countries who are not entitled to those benefits.

Does the treaty follow the OECD Model?

The new treaty, like the previous (1975) treaty, is firmly founded on the OECD Model Tax Convention. Consequently, a number of articles remain substantially unchanged from the previous treaty and are immediately recognisable from the OECD Model (for example the permanent establishment article (Article 5) and the associated enterprises article (Article 9)).

What has changed?

Other articles have been modernised in line with current OECD thinking. For example, the independent personal services article in the previous treaty has been deleted in accordance with the 2000 update of the OECD Model so that income derived from professional services or other services of an independent character is now dealt with as business profits under Article 7.

Other articles, whilst remaining broadly unchanged, now include additional provisions addressing issues that in the past may have led to uncertainty of treatment under the treaty. For example, the residence article (Article 4) now includes a tie-breaker for dual resident companies (residence to be determined by the UK and US competent authorities) and the business profits article (Article 7) includes new language governing the attribution of business profits to a permanent establishment (''the business profits to be attributed to the permanent establishment shall include only the profits derived from the assets used, risks assumed and activities performed by the permanent establishment'').

Some articles have changed significantly from the corresponding articles in the previous treaty. These are the articles relating to dividends, gains, pensions, mutual agreement and the exchange of information.

What is new?

Some articles and provisions are completely new: the article on pension schemes; the limitation on benefits article; the conduit arrangement provisions (defined in the general definitions article and found in the dividend, interest, royalties, and other income articles); a provision restricting relief where the tax treatment of the income is different in each country (in the relief from double taxation article); and the Exchange of Notes, which gives, for example, authoritative guidance on how the UK and the US will seek to eliminate double taxation of share option gains.

THE PROTOCOL TO THE TREATY

An amending protocol to the treaty was signed on 19 July 2002.

What does it do?

The protocol makes clear the date on which UK tax credits will cease to be payable under the old treaty and corrects an oversight that would otherwise have denied UK pension funds the benefit of zero withholding tax if they held US equities through certain pooled investment vehicles. It also reinstates a teachers article and amends the definition of ''equivalent beneficiary'' in the limitation on benefits article (Article 23(7)(*d*)).

Tax credits

The new treaty, as originally signed, contained a possible ambiguity over the date on which the previous treaty terminated and ceased to have effect in relation to the entitlement to tax credits of US resident recipients of UK dividends.

Article V of the protocol put the matter beyond doubt, providing that, for tax credits in respect of dividends paid by UK resident companies, the previous treaty will terminate and cease to be effective for dividends paid on or after the first day of the second month following the date on which the new treaty enters into force (Article 29(3) of the treaty as replaced by Article V of the protocol).

UK pension funds holding US equities through pooled investment vehicles

Article II of the protocol amended Article 10(4) of the treaty so that tax exempt UK pension funds entitled to zero US withholding tax on dividends paid by US companies will also be entitled to zero US withholding tax on dividends where they invest in US equities through either US regulated investment companies or US real estate investment trusts. This means that it is immaterial whether the pension fund holds the US investments direct or through these pooled investment vehicles.

Teachers article

Article III of the Protocol inserted a teachers article at Article 20A of the treaty.

The article is identical to the teachers article in the previous treaty and provides a two year tax exemption for UK and US resident professors or teachers who visit the other country for not more than two years for the purpose of teaching or engaging in public interest research at a university, college or other recognised educational institution. The exemption relates only to remuneration derived from such teaching and public interest research.

One of the conditions of receiving the exemption is that the teacher or professor may stay in the other country for only two years. If they stay longer, they will be treated in the same way as any other group of employees, and tax will be payable for the full period, starting from the first day of the visit.

THE DEFINITION OF "EQUIVALENT BENEFICIARY"

The definition of "equivalent beneficiary" at Article 23(7)(*d*)(ii) of the treaty was amended by Article IV of the protocol.

The definition now includes a resident of a Member State of the European Community or of a European Economic Area state or of a party to the North American Free Trade Agreement provided that resident is a specified "qualified person".

Broadly, from the UK perspective, the "qualified persons" specified by the new Article 23(7)(*d*)(ii) are UK resident individuals, qualified UK governmental entities, UK resident UK or US listed companies whose shares are regularly traded on a recognised stock exchange, UK resident UK or US listed entities other than individuals or companies whose units are regularly traded on a recognised stock exchange, UK pension schemes, UK employee benefit funds and UK charities.

The protocol also added a paragraph which provides that for the purposes of applying Article 10(3) (the dividends article) in order to determine whether a person, owning shares, directly or indirectly, in the company claiming the benefit of the treaty is an "equivalent beneficiary", that person will be deemed to hold the same voting power in the company paying the dividend as the company claiming the benefit of the treaty holds in such company. For details of how this provision works, see the section on Article 23.

GENERAL SCOPE—ARTICLE 1

"Saving clause"—Article 1(4)

Under this provision, and subject to some exceptions which are set out below, the contracting states reserve their rights to tax their residents and citizens in accordance with their domestic laws, notwithstanding anything in the treaty to the contrary.

As indicated, there are exceptions to the clause so that some of the benefits provided by the treaty are available to all citizens and residents of the contracting states.

The following are some examples:

(*a*) the benefit of non-discrimination on the grounds of nationality;

(*b*) the benefit of exemptions for certain pension distributions and social security payments;

(*c*) the benefit of double taxation relief for certain income taxes paid in the other contracting state even where such relief may not be available under domestic tax law;

(*d*) the benefit of access to the mutual agreement procedure for resolving issues of taxation not in accordance with the treaty;

(*e*) the benefit of host country exemption for the income of diplomatic agents and consular officials;

(*f*) the benefit of host country exemption from tax for certain income of students, business apprentices and teachers.

Special rule for former long-term residents—Article 1(6)

This rule prevents residents of either country changing their residence status in order to avoid UK or US tax liabilities. It provides that each country reserves for 10 years the right to tax former citizens and long-term residents whose loss of citizenship or long-term resident status had as one of its principal purposes the avoidance of tax.

A ''long-term resident'' of a state is defined in the Exchange of Notes as an individual (other than a citizen of that state) who is a lawful permanent resident of that state in at least 8 of the 15 taxable years ending with the taxable year in which the individual ceased to be a long-term resident.

Currently this provision has no effect in the UK.

How does the treaty fit with UK rules on residence and domicile—Article 1(7)?

Individuals who are UK resident but not UK domiciled are only taxed on non-UK income and gains to the extent that the income or gains are remitted to the UK. The provision overrides other terms of the treaty to preserve the taxing rights of the US where the effect of UK domestic law might otherwise allow double exemption. Where the provision applies, treaty relief in the US is limited to the income or gain remitted and taxed in the UK.

Fiscally transparent persons—Article 1(8)

This provision provides that income derived through a person that is a fiscally transparent entity under the laws of either the US or the UK will be treated as the income of a resident of a contracting state if the taxation laws of either country treat it as such. In those circumstances treaty benefits will be available to the resident of either the US or the UK, not the fiscally transparent entity.

The new rule addresses problems presented by fiscally transparent entities such as partnerships and certain estates and trusts that are not taxed at the entity level but rather are taxed at the level of partner or trustee.

The provision applies to any resident of the UK or US who is entitled to income derived through an entity that is treated as fiscally transparent under the laws of either State. In the US this will include, for example, general partnerships, limited partnerships (LPs), limited liability partnerships (LLPs) and US limited liability companies (LLCs) that are treated as partnerships for US tax purposes. In the UK it includes all partnerships, including UK LLPs, and certain trusts.

For example, where UK interest is paid to a US limited liability company, treaty benefits will be available to the extent that US tax law treats a US resident as deriving that income. Entitlement to treaty benefits is dependent on various criteria such as residence, being a qualified person, and satisfying the particular conditions in the relevant income article.

The new rule does not impose a ''subject to tax'' test in addition to the test contained in the various income articles for obtaining benefits. It simply looks through fiscally transparent entities to the ultimate beneficial owners of the income and asks the questions relating to entitlement of them rather than of the transparent entity.

The Exchange of Notes sets out rules for taxing income, profits or gains:

(*a*) preserving the right of both States to tax income, profits or gains derived through a fiscally transparent person under the respective domestic laws of each State;
(*b*) providing that where both contracting states consider an item of income, profit or gain to have been derived by one of their residents, both States can tax that person in respect of the item of income, profit or gain;
(*c*) (in the UK) treating some items of income, profit or gain arising to a person as falling within the paragraph where another person is charged to UK tax in respect of them under specific anti-avoidance legislation.

The relevant UK domestic law is specified in the Note.

US LLCs—relief for US tax

The Revenue take the view that for UK tax purposes LLCs should be regarded as taxable entities and not as fiscally transparent. Accordingly, the UK taxes a UK member of an LLC by reference to distributions of profits made by the LLC and not by reference to the income of the LLC as it arises. If tax is paid in the US on the profits of the LLC—and irrespective of by whom that tax is paid—the UK regards that tax as underlying tax. Credit is available for it if, and only if, the member is a UK company which controls, directly or indirectly, at least 10 per cent of the voting power of the LLC.

It follows that relief for underlying tax is not available to an individual UK member of an LLC. This is consistent with the purpose of the elimination of double taxation provisions contained in the previous treaty at Article 23. Article 23(2)(*b*) provides that, in the case of dividends paid by an ordinary US corporation, relief for underlying tax is only available to a UK company. There is no authority to allow relief for what is underlying tax to a UK individual member of an LLC.

There is no difference in substance between Article 23(2)(*b*) of the previous treaty and Article 24(4)(*b*) in the new treaty. Relief for underlying tax will only be available to a UK company which has at least a 10 per cent interest in the US LLC.

General definitions—Article 3

Article 3 contains definitions of words and phrases used in the Convention.

CONDUIT ARRANGEMENTS—ARTICLE 3(1)(*N*)

Introduction

Bilateral double taxation treaties provide benefits for residents of the two contracting states. The ''conduit arrangement'' provision is designed to ensure that the benefits of the treaty go only to those residents and not to residents of third countries who have deliberately arranged their transactions in such a way as to obtain treaty benefits to which they would not otherwise be entitled. The provision is therefore an anti-treaty abuse measure and like similar measures found in other UK double taxation treaties is transaction-based.

Whilst the UK has traditionally favoured such transaction- based measures in its double taxation treaties the US prefers entity-based rules. This treaty contains both: the ''anti- conduit'' rule, which focuses on transactions, and the limitation on benefits article, which focuses on entities. The two approaches are complementary, providing clear objective tests for determining entitlement to benefits and strong protection against treaty abuse.

This is the first time a UK double taxation treaty has included a limitation on benefits article and the transaction-based anti-abuse measure needed to be framed in such a way as to complement the operation of that article. The provision is therefore somewhat different from the UK's usual anti-treaty shopping provision. However, the UK will apply the new provision in a manner consistent with its practice under those other treaties. This means that a resident of a third country will be denied the benefits of the treaty if he deliberately attempts to secure them by entering into a conduit arrangement as defined in the treaty.

Whether the provision will apply in any given situation will depend on the particular facts and circumstances.

How will the Revenue apply the "conduit arrangement" rule?

Every case will be considered on its particular facts and circumstances to determine whether the transaction or series of transactions meets the definition of a conduit arrangement. The definition contains an objective test (defining a conduit) and a subjective test (a motive test). Only if both tests are satisfied so that the transactions or series of transactions constitute a conduit arrangement will the relief provided by the relevant article be denied.

When making such a determination it is important that the Revenue is able to put a transaction or series of transactions into their proper context.

It will be necessary to consider all of the arrangements involving payments between UK and US taxpayers, and between US taxpayers and a taxpayer of a third country before the true pattern and purpose of the transaction or series of transactions can be established.

When this level of understanding has been achieved, the Revenue will be able to determine whether or not the transaction or series of transactions meets the objective part of the conduit test and whether the obtaining of treaty benefits was a main purpose or merely an incidental consequence.

Given this, it is difficult to be prescriptive as to what type of transaction might constitute a conduit arrangement. But here are two examples of what might meet the definition:

1. A company resident in a country which does not have a tax treaty with the UK makes a loan to its UK subsidiary, but instead of lending the money direct it makes the loan indirectly via a wholly unconnected but accommodating US bank by providing a matching collateral deposit to the bank as security for the loan the bank then makes to the UK subsidiary company.

   The objective test contained in the definition of a conduit would be satisfied as a US resident (the US bank) entitled to zero UK withholding tax on interest under the treaty receives interest arising in the UK and pays that interest to another person (the parent company) who is not resident in either the UK or the US but who is resident in a third country which doesn't have a treaty with the UK that provides for zero UK withholding tax on interest.

   The fact that treaty benefits are available if the UK subsidiary borrows from the US bank but would not be available if it borrowed from its parent suggests that a main purpose of the transactions might be to obtain the increased benefit of the treaty. So the motive test might also be satisfied. This will have to be determined by reference to the particular facts and circumstances.

   If examination of the facts supported this interpretation, then the series of transactions would be a conduit arrangement as defined in the treaty and the relief provided for by the Interest article would be denied. Full UK withholding tax on the interest paid by the UK subsidiary company would then be due.

2. A company organised in a country that does not have a tax treaty with the UK loans £1,000,000 to its wholly-owned UK subsidiary in exchange for a note issued by the UK company. The parent company later realises that it can avoid UK withholding tax by assigning the note to another wholly-owned subsidiary in the US. Accordingly, the parent assigns the note to its US subsidiary in exchange for a note issued by the US company. The UK company note pays 7% and the US company note pays 6.3/4%.

   The loan note was assigned to avoid UK income tax on the payment of interest. The transaction constitutes a conduit arrangement as defined in the treaty as both the objective definition and the motive test at Article 3(1)(*n*)(i) and (ii) respectively are met.

PRs etc

Can a pre-existing structure constitute a "conduit arrangement"?

A ''conduit arrangement'' is defined as a ''transaction or a series of transactions''. Therefore, provided all the other criteria are met to make the provision applicable, it makes no difference whether a structure through which the transactions flow pre-dates the entry into force of the treaty.

The previous treaty contains no transaction-based provisions for addressing abusive conduit arrangements or treaty shopping. To give an ''amnesty'' for pre-existing structures would undermine the effectiveness of the new rule.

Where a notice has been issued allowing the UK source income to be paid gross and it is thought that the anti-conduit rule may apply, the non-resident should set out the relevant details in a letter to the Centre for Non-Residents. There is further guidance later in this article (see Entry into Force—Article 29) about directions given under the previous treaty.

How will the UK interpret "substantially all"?

In determining whether ''substantially all'' of an item of income has been paid directly or indirectly to a resident of a third state the Revenue will consider all the relevant facts and circumstances of the case.

What does "at any time or in any form" mean?

An example might be US dividends received by a UK resident company in 2003 paid on to a resident of a third country in the form of interest in 2004. However, there is no presumption in the words ''at any time'' that the payment to the resident of the third country must take place after the payment from the source state.

Are there any plans for an advance clearance procedure for determining whether transactions constitute a "conduit arrangement"?

There are no plans for an advance clearance procedure. To obtain the benefits of the treaty a person has to make a claim. It is incumbent on that person to ensure that all the conditions for entitlement to those benefits are met. That includes, where applicable, that the transaction or series of transactions does not constitute a conduit arrangement. However, in formulating claims, claimants can refer to published guidance.

PENSION SCHEMES DEFINITION—ARTICLE 3(1)(*O*)

What schemes will be entitled to treaty benefits?

Treaty benefits are for approved schemes only. As TA 1988 s 615 schemes, which are UK established trusts for non-residents, are not approved they do not come within the definition of ''pension scheme'' in Article 3(1)(*o*) because they are not ''generally exempt from income taxation in that State''. They are therefore not included in the list in the Exchange of Notes.

Are section 401(k) plans included within the definition of a pension scheme?

Yes, they are within the definition of a pension scheme in Article 3(1)(*o*) as they are a type of section 401(*a*) plan.

Interpretation—Article 3(2)

The treaty provides that any term not defined in the treaty shall have the meaning that it has under the law of the contracting state whose tax is being applied. If the term has different definitions under tax and non-tax laws in that state the treaty makes it clear that the tax law definition will apply.

But if the meaning of a term cannot be determined in this way, or if there is a difference in meaning under the laws of each contracting state that leads to difficulties in applying the treaty, the competent authorities may agree a common meaning under the mutual agreement procedure.

Residence—Article 4

Article 4 defines the meaning of the term ''resident of a contracting state'' for the purposes of the treaty and sets out rules for resolving the residence status of individuals or other persons who are dual resident under that definition.

The rules for dual resident individuals follow the OECD Model Tax Convention, whereas the rule for dual resident companies is that the UK and US competent authorities will endeavour to determine by mutual agreement how the treaty will apply to the dual resident. The article also provides that, if the competent authorities do not reach agreement, the dual resident person will not, with some exceptions, be able to claim the benefits of the treaty.

The previous treaty did not have a mechanism for determining the residence status of dual resident companies. The inclusion of this provision will therefore mean that such companies will now have certainty about their residence status for the purposes of the treaty.

The absence of a specific test for determining the residence status of such companies allows the two competent authorities to consider all the facts and circumstances before determining whether treaty benefits should be granted.

Application of FA 1994 s 249

A UK/US dual resident company will only cease to be resident for UK tax purposes under FA 1994 s 249(1) if the company has made a claim under the new treaty and the competent authorities have awarded residence to the US. Each case will depend on its own facts and circumstances. Whenever the competent authorities come to an agreement they will also agree the date from which residence in either the UK or the US is appropriate.

THE TAXATION OF BUSINESS PROFITS—ARTICLE 7

Article 7 follows very closely the business profits article in the OECD Model Tax Convention. However it does include new language concerning the attribution of business profits to permanent establishments and the Exchange of Notes to the treaty comments on the attribution of capital to permanent establishments. Both have generated comment, particularly in the context of the measure announced in Budget 2002 and to be introduced in Finance Bill 2003 relating to the attribution of capital to branches.

Does the new language signify a change in the way the UK will attribute business profits to UK permanent establishments of US corporations?

The new language in paragraph 2 (''the business profits to be attributed to the permanent establishment shall include only the profits derived from the assets used, risks assumed and activities performed by the permanent establishment'') does not signify a change in the UK's current approach to attributing profits to permanent establishments. It clarifies that approach by describing the characteristic features of profit generating activity that are typically taken into account when determining attributable profits.

It also makes clear that only profits derived from the assets used, risks assumed and activities performed by the particular permanent establishment will be attributed to that permanent establishment.

Consequently, profits derived from assets used, risks assumed and activities performed by the head office of a US corporation or by a second UK permanent establishment of the US corporation of which the first UK permanent establishment is part, will not form part of the first UK permanent establishment's attributable profits. Again, this does not represent a change in the UK's current approach.

Does the treaty pre-empt the OECD discussion draft paper on the attribution of profits to a permanent establishment?

No, the treaty is a bilateral agreement between the UK and the US. But it should be of little surprise that OECD thinking is reflected in it, given that both countries have contributed to discussion of the issue at the OECD.

In view of what is said in the Exchange of Notes, will the UK now attribute capital to permanent establishments of US corporations when determining their attributable profits?

At present the UK does not have the domestic law to allow it to attribute capital to branches, in order to arrive at the profits of the branch, in anything other than a very limited set of circumstances.

However, the treaty provides that, in arriving at the amount of profits to be attributed to the permanent establishment, the permanent establishment shall be treated as having the same amount of capital that it would need to support its activities if it were a distinct and separate enterprise engaged in the same or similar activities under the same or similar conditions

This does not at present impact on how UK branches of US corporations will be taxed in the UK as we do not have the domestic legislation to enable us to attribute capital in this way. Such legislation, applying from 1 January 2003, will be introduced in Finance Bill 2003 (see below).

Does the treaty pre-empt the measure announced in Budget 2002 and to be introduced in Finance Act 2003 relating to the attribution of capital to branches?

The measure announced in 2002 is about modernising the UK's rules for taxing foreign companies operating in the UK through branches, with effect from 1 January 2003. The present rules are out of line with international practice and the measure would create a level playing field between foreign companies, mainly banks, with UK branches and their UK-incorporated competitors.

The measure, if enacted in Finance Bill 2003, will provide that a UK branch of a foreign company will be assumed to have, for the purpose of determining the amount of profits for tax purposes, the amount of equity capital and loan capital that it would have if it were a distinct and separate company trading in the UK engaged in the same or similar activities under the same or similar conditions.

By contrast the treaty does not of itself create a domestic taxing right to attribute capital to UK branches of US corporations. Rather it provides that if and when the UK has that taxing right (as will be the case if the measure described is enacted) then any capital attributed to a UK branch of a US corporation for the purposes of determining branch profits will be attributed on the basis that the branch is treated as a distinct and separate enterprise engaged in the same or similar activities under the same or similar conditions.

Does the treaty provide a choice between a "thin capitalisation" and a regulatory capital approach to the measurement of profits attributable to a permanent establishment of a financial institution?

The treaty is not prescriptive. The Exchange of Notes cites allocation of regulatory capital as a method either country may use to determine the amount of capital to be attributed to the permanent establishment of a financial institution (other than an insurance company). But other methods, including one based on the amount of equity capital that the entity would have if it were an independent enterprise acting at arm's length, engaged in the same or similar activities under the same or similar conditions, may be used.

ZERO WITHHOLDING TAX ON US DIVIDENDS—ARTICLES 10 AND 23

The treaty allows both the US and the UK to tax dividends paid to a resident of the other country but, subject to certain conditions, limits the tax the source country may impose to 5 per cent or 15 per cent of the gross amount of the dividend. In other circumstances, it removes entirely the right of the source country to tax dividends.

As the UK does not have a withholding tax on dividends, the limitations are only applicable to US dividends beneficially owned by and paid to UK residents.

This section considers the circumstances in which such UK residents may be entitled to receive US source dividends free of withholding tax. Reference is made to Article 1 (General Scope), Article 10 (Dividends) and Article 23 (Limitation on Benefits).

Who will be entitled to zero US withholding tax ("zero") on dividends?

UK resident companies that beneficially own the dividend and that have owned shares representing 80 per cent or more of the voting power of the US company paying the dividend for a 12 month period ending on the date the dividend is declared will be entitled to zero (Article 10(3)(*a*)), provided that the UK company either:

(*a*) owned those shares, directly or indirectly, before 1 October 1998 (Article 10(3)(*a*)(i)) and it passes either an ''ownership and base erosion'' test (Article 23(2)(*f*)) or an ''active conduct of a trade or business'' test (Article 23(4));

(*b*) is a company whose principal class of shares is listed or admitted to dealings on a recognised UK or US stock exchange and whose shares are regularly traded on a recognised stock exchange (Article 23(2)(*c*)(i));

(*c*) is a company which is at least 50 per cent owned (by reference to the aggregate voting power and value of its shares) directly or indirectly by five or fewer such companies (Article 23(2)(*c*)(ii));

(*d*) is a company at least 95 per cent owned (by reference to the aggregate voting power and value of its shares) directly or indirectly by seven or fewer ''equivalent beneficiaries'' and which passes a ''base erosion'' test (Article 23(3)); or

(*e*) is accepted by the US competent authority as being entitled to the benefits of the treaty on the basis that the establishment, acquisition or maintenance of the company and the conduct of its operations did not have as one if its principal purposes the obtaining of treaty benefits (Article 23(6)).

UK tax exempt pension schemes will also be entitled to zero, provided that the dividends in question are not derived from the carrying on of a business, directly or indirectly, by the pension scheme and that more than 50% of the beneficiaries, members or participants of the scheme are individuals who are residents of either the UK or the US (Article 10(3)(*b*) and Article 23(2)(*e*)).

In summary therefore, in order to obtain zero a person must be a UK resident, must satisfy the conditions at Article 10(3)(*a*) or (*b*), must satisfy one of the relevant tests in the limitation on benefits article and must satisfy all the other specified conditions for obtaining the benefit.

The 1 October 1998 ownership test and the subsequent interposition of intermediate holding companies

In order to qualify for zero under Article 10(3)(*a*)(i) the beneficial owner of the US dividend must be a UK resident company that has owned shares representing 80 per cent or more of the voting power of the US company paying the dividend for at least 12 months before the dividend is declared and must have owned shares representing, directly or indirectly, 80 per cent or more of the voting power of the US company paying the dividend before 1 October 1998.

In the case of direct ownership a UK company that owned the requisite shares before 1 October 1998 and continues to hold them will be entitled to zero when a dividend is declared by the US company.

In the case of indirect ownership, where before 1 October 1998 a UK ultimate group parent company owned the US subsidiary through an intermediate holding company and subsequently reorganises so that it assumes direct ownership of the US subsidiary, entitlement to zero is preserved because the UK ultimate parent company will be the beneficial owner of the dividend and it held the requisite shares in the US company, albeit indirectly, before 1 October 1998.

However, in the case where before 1 October 1998 a UK ultimate group parent company owned the US company directly, but subsequently reorganises so that a newly incorporated company is interposed between it and the US company paying the dividend, entitlement to zero (by virtue of this test) will not be preserved. This is because (in the case where the interposed intermediate holding company is a UK resident) although the new intermediate holding company will be the beneficial owner of a US dividend it did not hold the requisite shares in the US company before 1 October 1998, directly or indirectly, as they were held by the UK ultimate group parent company at that date.

In an alternative situation (where the interposed intermediate holding company is a US resident) the UK ultimate group parent company, whilst being the beneficial owner of a US dividend, did not hold the requisite shares in the US company paying the dividend at 1 October 1998 because this company did not exist at that date.

The "active conduct of a trade or business" test

A UK resident company seeking to obtain zero under Article 10(3)(*a*)(i) must, in addition to satisfying the 1 October 1998 ownership condition, satisfy either the "base erosion" and ownership test at Article 23(2)(*f*) or the "active conduct of a trade or business" test at Article 23(4).

The "active conduct of a trade or business" test has three main conditions: the UK resident must be engaged in the active conduct of a trade or business in the UK; the dividend derived from the US must be derived in connection with or be incidental to that trade or business; and the trade in the UK must be substantial in relation to the activity in the US.

The meaning of a "trade or business"

In the context of entitlement to zero withholding on US dividends, the terms, not being defined in the treaty, have the meaning they have in US law, in accordance with Article 3(2) (General Definitions).

The meaning of "in connection" with

In accordance with the Exchange of Notes to the treaty a dividend is to be considered as derived "in connection" with an active trade or business in the UK if the US activity that produces the dividend is a line of business which forms a part of, or is complementary to, the trade or business conducted in the UK.

A US trade or business activity will generally be considered to "form part of" a UK trade or business activity if, for example, it provides inputs to a manufacturing process carried on in the UK or if it sells the output of UK manufacturing operations or if it sells in the US the same sorts of products that are being sold by the trade or business carried in the UK.

A US trade or business activity may be considered "complementary" to a UK trade or business if its activities are part of the same overall industry and the two activities are economically and commercially interdependent.

The meaning of "incidental to"

A US dividend would be considered to be "incidental" to a UK trade or business if the dividend, though not produced by a line of business which forms part of, or is complementary, to the UK trade or business, nevertheless facilitates the conduct of the UK trade or business.

The meaning of "substantial"

To pass the "active conduct of a trade or business" test, the UK trade or business has to be substantial in relation to the trade or business activity in the US that gives rise to the dividend. Whether a trade or business activity is "substantial" will depend on all the facts and circumstances. Factors such as the nature of the activities carried on in each country and the comparative sizes of the trades or businesses carried on in each country will be taken into account.

Will a UK resident company that is owned by seven or fewer EC resident companies be entitled to zero?

A UK resident company that is at least 95 per cent owned by seven or fewer "equivalent beneficiaries" will be entitled to zero if the company also meets a base erosion test (Article 23(3)) and satisfies any of the other specified conditions for obtaining zero.

Assuming it meets those other conditions the question is whether EC resident companies are "equivalent beneficiaries" as defined by the treaty.

What is an "equivalent beneficiary"?

An "equivalent beneficiary" is defined in Article 23(7)(*d*) (as amended by Article IV of the protocol to the treaty) as a resident of a Member State of the European Community or of a European Economic Area state, but only if either:

(*a*) that resident is entitled to all the benefits of a comprehensive convention for the avoidance of double taxation (which includes a comprehensive limitation on benefits article) between any Member State of the EC or a EEA state and the US and would, under that convention, be entitled to zero US withholding tax on dividends or,

(*b*) that resident is a specified "qualified person".

At present the US has not entered into any other double taxation treaties with EC or EEC States which provide for zero US withholding tax on dividends. Therefore EC companies currently do not meet the first definition of "equivalent beneficiary".

Neither do they meet the various specified definitions of "qualified person" (UK resident individuals, qualified UK governmental entities, UK resident UK or US listed companies whose shares are regularly traded on a recognised stock exchange, UK resident UK or US listed entities other than individuals or companies whose units are regularly traded on a recognised stock exchange, UK pension schemes, UK employee benefit funds or UK charities).

Therefore such a UK resident company would not automatically be entitled to the benefit of zero US withholding on dividends by virtue of Article 23(3).

However, assuming the UK resident company met all the other conditions for obtaining zero, it could apply to the US competent authority for the benefit of zero under Article 23(6).

Are unquoted UK companies entitled to zero?

Assuming an unquoted UK resident company is the beneficial owner of the dividend and has owned shares representing 80 per cent or more of the voting power of the US company paying the dividend for at least 12 months before the declaration of the dividend it may be entitled to zero US withholding tax on the dividend if it is owned by seven or fewer "equivalent beneficiaries" and it passes a so-called "base erosion" test (Article 10(3)(*a*)(iii) and Article 23(3)).

The definition of "equivalent beneficiaries" includes UK resident individuals (Article 23(7)(*d*)(ii) (as amended by Article IV of the protocol to the treaty)).

The "base erosion" test requires that less that 50 per cent of the unquoted UK resident company's gross income for the taxable year or chargeable period in which the dividend arises is paid, directly or indirectly, to persons who are not "equivalent beneficiaries", in the form of payments that are tax deductible.

The company must, of course, also satisfy the other conditions of the dividends article.

If the company did not qualify by this route it could apply to the US competent authority for the benefit of zero under Article 23(6).

What is the procedure for applying to the US competent authority for zero under Article 23(6) and how long will it take?

A taxpayer that is not otherwise entitled to benefits under Article 23 but believes it may be entitled to such benefits under the discretionary provision of Article 23(6) should submit that request to: Director International, Internal Revenue Service, Attn: LM:IN:TT, 1111 Constitution Avenue, NW, Washington, DC 20224.

For guidance in preparing requests for discretionary benefits, taxpayers should consult the U.S. Treasury Technical Explanation of Articles 10 and 23 of the Treaty (see http://www.ustreas.gov/offices/tax-policy/library/teus-uk.pdf), and the US Internal Revenue Service's Revenue Procedure 2002-52, with particular reference to Sections 3.08 and 4 (see http://www.irs.gov/individuals/article/0,,id=96945,00.html). The IRS Internal Revenue Manual Exhibit 4.60.3-3, at http://www.irs.gov/irm/page/0,,id%3D21706,00.html#ss5 7, provides detailed guidance regarding information that should be submitted in connection with any request for a discretionary determination.

The US has provided assurances that the competent authority office will consider any requests received as expeditiously as possible. In the case of a favourable determination, benefits will be allowed retrospectively to the later of the effective date of the relevant treaty provision or the time of establishment of the structure in question.

On what basis will the US competent authority decide whether a UK resident company is entitled to zero?

Zero will be granted if the US competent authority is satisfied that the establishment, acquisition or maintenance of the UK resident company and the conduct of its operations did not have as one of its principal purposes the obtaining of benefits under the treaty.

The Exchange of Notes to the treaty sets out in some detail, with reference to specific circumstances, how the US competent authority will approach this task.

What is the purpose of the consultation requirement?

The US competent authority is required to consult the UK competent authority before refusing zero to a UK resident under Article 23(6). This requirement gives the UK competent authority the opportunity to provide any further facts, arguments or interpretations in favour of the claimant that might be material to the determination of the claim.

However, it is for the US competent authority to have the final say.

Can a UK resident company that is treated as fiscally transparent for US tax purposes obtain zero?

Assuming all the other conditions for obtaining zero are met, a UK resident company which is treated for US tax purposes as fiscally transparent due to a ''check the box'' election will be entitled to zero in respect of a dividend paid by its wholly owned US company if, and to the extent that, the UK treats the dividend as the income of a UK resident.

The rule governing how the treaty applies to persons who are regarded as fiscally transparent by either the UK or the US is at Article 1(8).

TAXATION OF GAINS—ARTICLE 13

Generally the previous treaty allows each country to tax gains in accordance with its domestic laws. As such it offers no protection against the double taxation of gains.

By contrast, the new treaty provides that gains will be taxable only in the country in which the person disposing of the property is resident, except for gains arising from the disposal of real property situated in the other country or from the disposal of the business property of a permanent establishment, in which case the country in which the real property or permanent establishment is situated has the primary right to tax.

Relief from double taxation will therefore be afforded by the award of exclusive taxing rights to the residence country or, where the source country taxes the gain, by the residence country giving credit relief.

The article is based on the OECD Model article but includes additional provisions to deal with specific types of gains such as those arising on the disposal of shares deriving their value or the greater part of their value from real property situated in the UK or the US (the ''securitised land'' provision) and those realised by temporary non-residents.

The "securitised land" provision

In accordance with the OECD Model Tax Convention the article provides that the UK has the primary taxing right over gains arising from the alienation of real property situated in the UK. Thus, a US resident individual owning real property in the UK would, under the terms of the treaty, be taxable in the UK on any gain arising from the sale of that property.

However, if that US resident individual arranged for the property to be held by a company in which he was the sole shareholder and then arranged for the sale of the shares in that company, the OECD Model wording would give the result that any gain on the sale of the shares would be taxable only in the country of which he was a resident—the US.

To prevent this, the Article provides at paragraph (2)(*c*)(i) that shares which derive their value or the greater part of their value directly or indirectly from real property situated in the UK will be treated as real property situated in the UK, thereby preserving taxing rights over gains substantively derived from real property. The provision is reciprocal.

The "temporary non-residents" provision

Paragraph 6 of the article aligns the treaty with the UK's rules in section 10A of the Taxation of Chargeable Gains Act 1992.

Those rules aim to stop long term UK residents avoiding UK capital gains tax by becoming temporarily non-UK resident and realising gains while abroad before resuming UK residence.

The provision works by allowing the UK to tax gains arising to US residents who were previously UK residents and who, after having realised gains while being temporarily US resident, return to the UK.

This does not prevent the US taxing the gains of its residents. The primary taxing right always remains with the residence country. But it allows the UK to tax such gains as well, giving credit for US tax paid on those gains.

STOCK OPTIONS—ARTICLE 14 EXCHANGE OF NOTES

This is the first time the UK has specifically covered share/stock options in a treaty and we believe this clear statement of mutual practice will be very valuable. The circumstances itemised cover the most frequently found situations and will inform the majority of cases we see.

In line with existing practice ''that proportion of the option gain'' will normally be determined by reference to the periods of employment in each country using a straight-line time apportionment.

PRs etc

This is simple, clear and avoids distortions arising from short-term fluctuations in share values. More details of UK current practice, together with examples, can be found in Tax Bulletins 55, 56 and 60.

The Exchange of Notes represents the views of both the UK and the US that a gain in the value of share options granted while in employment before those options are exercised is correctly within the income from employment article. Occasionally time-apportionment or other circumstances may not produce an appropriate result and the Exchange of Notes provides that the competent authorities will then endeavour to resolve the difficulty.

PENSIONS AND PENSION SCHEMES—ARTICLES 17 AND 18

Article 17

Article 17 is a fairly standard pensions article, which provides for the taxation of pensions and other similar remuneration only in the state of residence of the beneficial owner. There are two provisions that have generated particular interest.

Paragraph 1(*a*) sets out the general rule above. For this purpose, a payment is treated as a pension or other similar remuneration if it is a payment under a pension scheme, as defined at Article 3(1)(*o*).

However, the residence state, under paragraph 1(*b*), must exempt from tax any amount of such pensions or other similar remuneration that would be exempt from tax in the State in which the pension scheme is established if the recipient were a resident of that State. Thus, for example, a distribution from a US ''IRA'' to a UK resident will be exempt from tax in the UK to the same extent the distribution would be exempt from tax in the US.

Under the previous treaty, a lump-sum payment from a pension scheme was taxable only in the country of residence. So if an individual moved from the US to the UK before receiving a lump sum from a US pension scheme, they would be taxable on the lump sum neither in the US (because of the treaty) nor in the UK (which does not tax lump sums anyway).

The new provision prevents this occurring by providing that a lump-sum payment derived by a resident of one State from a pension scheme established in the other State shall be taxable only in that other State.

The provision preserves the exemption from income tax of a lump sum relevant benefit where it is paid by a UK approved pension scheme to a beneficial owner who is a US resident. However, Article 1(4) will apply in respect of US citizens as the provisions of Article 17(2) are not amongst those listed at Article 1(5).

Article 18

This article is concerned primarily with the tax treatment of contributions to pension schemes. It also touches on the taxation of the income, profits and gains accruing to pension schemes. As indicated in the note on Article 17 the term ''pension scheme'' is defined for the purposes of the treaty at Article 3(1)(*o*).

It is a feature of several recent UK treaties that pension contributions made in one country are recognised for tax purposes in the other.

If a member of a pension scheme established in one country goes to work (as an employee or in a self-employed capacity) in the other country, the state of residence will not tax the scheme member on income earned by the scheme unless it is paid to him (or for his benefit). Nor will tax be payable if income is transferred to another pension scheme until the benefits are actually received.

Contributions to the scheme by that member (or those paid on his behalf) shall be tax-deductible in the state of residence. In the same way, benefits accrued under the scheme, or employer contributions to the scheme, will not be treated as part of his taxable income and those contributions will be tax-deductible for the employer. The reliefs available cannot exceed those allowed by the state of residence for contributions of the same amount to a scheme established in the state of residence.

The conditions for getting the relief are as follows

(*a*) contributions were made by or on behalf of the individual or (in the case of an employee) his employer to the pension scheme (or to a similar scheme for which it was substituted) before the individual began to exercise an employment or self-employment in the other contracting state, and

(*b*) the competent authority of the other State agrees that the pension scheme generally corresponds to a pension scheme established in that other State.

Where someone comes to work in the UK we will regard the first condition as having been met if the individual was a member of the US scheme before beginning to exercise an employment or self-employment in the UK.

The types of scheme that would be accepted as ''generally corresponding'' are those listed in the Exchange of Notes.

Relief will be restricted where contributions to a pension scheme are deductible or excludable in computing a person's taxable income in the host country if he is subject to tax there not on his total income but only on amounts remitted to that country. Relief is available only on a corresponding proportion of the pension contributions.

EXAMPLE

Individual's total income, profits and gains – £100,000

Income, profits and gains remitted to the UK – £90,000

Individual's contributions to US pension scheme – £5,000

Contributions deductible in computing individual's UK taxable income – £4,500 (ie 90% of individual's total contributions)

Guidance on the procedures for claiming relief from UK income tax on contributions to US pension schemes under Article 18 will be provided in an Update that will be issued by the Inland Revenue's Audit and Pension Schemes Services in the near future.

LIMITATION ON BENEFITS—ARTICLE 23

This is the first time the UK has included a limitation on benefits article in one of its double taxation treaties, though such articles are a common feature of recent US treaties.

The purpose of the article

The purpose of the article is to ensure that UK and US residents benefit from the treaty, whilst ensuring that residents of third countries who establish legal entities in either the UK or the US, not for legitimate commercial and economic reasons, but with the principal purpose of obtaining benefits under the treaty, do not benefit.

To achieve this the article poses a number of tests for UK and US residents, one of which must be satisfied if entitlement to treaty benefits is to be established.

The Technical Explanation to the US Model Income Tax Convention of September 20, 1996 comments that the assumption underlying each of these tests "is that a taxpayer that satisfies the requirements of any of the tests probably has a real business purpose for the structure it has adopted, or has a sufficiently strong nexus to the other contracting state (eg a resident individual) to warrant benefits even in the absence of a business connection, and that this business purpose or connection outweighs any purpose to obtain the benefits of the treaty." In other words, the assumption is that a taxpayer who satisfies one of the tests is not "treaty shopping".

As such, any UK or US resident who satisfies one of the tests in the article will, provided they satisfy any other specified conditions for obtaining the relevant benefit, be entitled to treaty benefits.

How it works

The article provides that residents of the UK and the US are entitled to all the benefits of the treaty only if they are a "qualified person" (paragraph 2). If a resident is not a "qualified person" they may be entitled to benefits in respect of specific items of income, profits or gains under the "derivative benefits test" (paragraph 3), the "active conduct of a trade or business" test (paragraph 4) or at the discretion of the competent authority of the country that is giving up its taxing right under the treaty (paragraph 6).

For the majority of UK residents the article will provide clear rules and certainty of treatment about entitlement to treaty benefits without recourse to either the Inland Revenue or the US Internal Revenue Service.

"Qualified persons"

In broad terms, a "qualified person" is a UK or US resident who is either:

(*a*) an individual;
(*b*) a qualified governmental entity (as defined in Article 3);
(*c*) a publicly traded company (listed in the UK or US);
(*d*) a 50%+ subsidiary of five or fewer publicly traded companies (that are listed in the UK or US);
(*e*) a publicly traded trust (listed in the UK or US);
(*f*) a trust 50%+ owned by publicly traded companies or by publicly traded trusts (that are listed in the UK or the US);
(*g*) a pension scheme (where more than 50% of beneficiaries, members or participants are individuals who are UK or US resident);
(*h*) a tax exempt employee benefit scheme (where more than 50% of beneficiaries, members or participants are individuals who are UK or US resident);
(*i*) a religious, charitable, scientific, artistic, cultural or educational organisation;
(*j*) a legal entity that satisfies an ownership and a "base erosion" test;
(*k*) a trust, or trustee of a trust in their capacity as such, if the trust is more than 50% owned by certain "qualified persons" or by "equivalent beneficiaries" provided it satisfies a "base erosion" test.

These tests, which determine whether a particular category of UK or US resident is a "qualified person", are all based on the concept that a substantial commercial and economic connection must exist between the taxpayer and the UK or the US to warrant entitlement to treaty benefits. If the standard set by any one of the tests in paragraph 2 is met, then entitlement to all treaty benefits is

PRs etc

established (subject to conditions in the articles dealing with the type of income concerned being met).

How is the "base erosion" test satisfied?

The base erosion test is satisfied if less than 50% of the person's gross income for the relevant taxable or chargeable period is paid or accrued, directly or indirectly, to persons who are not UK or US residents in the form of payments that are tax deductible for the purposes of the taxes covered by the treaty in the country in which the person is resident.

The "derivative benefits" test

Paragraph 3 of the article provides that, even if a company is not a ''qualified person'' as defined by the treaty, it shall nevertheless be entitled to the benefit of the treaty with respect to an item of income, profit or gain, if it satisfies any other specified condition for obtaining such benefit, and it is at least 95 per cent owned by seven or fewer persons who are ''equivalent beneficiaries'' as defined by the treaty, and less than 50 per cent of the company's gross income for that period is paid to non-UK or non-US persons in the form of tax deductible payments. The conditions set out in paragraph 3 of the article are commonly known as the ''derivative benefits'' test, though this is not a term employed in the treaty.

Passing this test relies on the third country resident owners of the UK company being ''equivalent beneficiaries''. From the UK perspective, broadly, an ''equivalent beneficiary'' is a resident of a Member State of the European Community (EC) or of a European Economic Area (EEA) state, but only if either:

(*a*) that resident is entitled to all the benefits of a comprehensive treaty for the avoidance of double taxation (which includes a comprehensive limitation on benefits article) between any Member State of the EC or a EEA state and the US and would be entitled under that treaty to a rate of tax with respect to the particular class of income for which the benefits are being claimed under the UK/US treaty that is at least as low as the rate applicable under the UK/US treaty or;

(*b*) that resident is a specified ''qualified person''.

The definition of ''equivalent beneficiary'' is at paragraph 7(*d*) of the article as amended by Article IV of the protocol to the treaty.

Paragraph 7(*d*) also provides, that for the purposes of applying Article 10(3) (the dividends article), in order to determine whether a person, owning shares, directly or indirectly, in the company claiming the benefit of the treaty is an ''equivalent beneficiary'', that person will be deemed to hold the same voting power in the company paying the dividend as the company claiming the benefit of the treaty holds in such company

The purpose of the provision is as follows. Suppose a UK company (UKCo) receiving dividends from a US subsidiary company (USCo) is 80 per cent owned by a company (ECCo) resident in an EC or EEA state that also has a comprehensive tax treaty with the US that provides for zero on dividends. Under Article 23(7)(*d*)(i), ECCo will be an ''equivalent beneficiary'' and, the other conditions being met, UKCo will receive its dividends from USCo free of US withholding tax. That is the result achieved by the treaty as originally signed, and is not changed by the protocol.

But suppose instead that UKCo was owned 50:50 by another UK company and ECCo. Without this protocol provision, UKCo could not get zero. ECCo is not an equivalent beneficiary because, had it owned USCo directly, it would hold less than the 80 per cent required by Article 10(3). But by deeming ECCo to own the same proportion of USCo that UKCo owns, the 80 per cent test is satisfied, and UKCo can receive its dividends from USCo gross.

The provision therefore prevents the anomalous situation where a UK resident company that owned 80 per cent of the voting power in the US company paying the dividend would be denied zero on US dividends because its joint owners owned individually less than 80 per cent in it, despite the fact that together they owned 100 per cent of it and both the UK treaty with the US and the EC/EEA country treaty with the US provided for zero withholding tax on dividends.

At present, the provision has no effect because no EC or EEA country has a comprehensive double taxation treaty with the US that provides for zero US withholding tax on dividends.

What is the rationale for the "derivative benefits" test?

This is best demonstrated by an example.

If a UK resident company in receipt of income from the US is substantially owned by residents of a third country and that third country has a tax treaty with the US that provides for the same benefits for that type of income as the treaty between the UK and the US, then there should be no objection to those third country residents getting that benefit indirectly under the UK/US treaty as opposed to directly under the third country/US treaty.

This is because (i) the US in this instance has, as a matter of policy, already decided that the residents of the third country should receive that benefit and (ii) prima facie the residents of the third country are not treaty shopping through the UK as the same benefits are available in their home country.

Which individuals can be "qualified persons" under Article 23(7)(d)(ii)?

As it relates to individuals, the term ''equivalent beneficiary'' is defined in Article 23(7)(*d*) as including ''a resident of a Member State of the European Community or of a European Economic Area state or of a party to the North American Free Trade Agreement but only if that resident ... is a qualified person by reason of sub-paragraph (*a*) ... of paragraph 2 of this Article''.

Article 23(2) defines the term ''qualified person'' by listing seven categories of person who will automatically be a ''qualified person'' for the purposes of the treaty. Individuals are included at paragraph 2(*a*).

As provided by the opening words of paragraph 2, only a resident of one of the two contracting states can be a ''qualified person'' by reason of paragraph 2(*a*). It follows that only such residents can be qualified persons for the purpose of the definition of equivalent beneficiary in Article 23(7)(*d*).

The "active conduct of a trade or business" test

What conditions does a UK resident have to fulfil to pass this test?

Paragraph 4 of the article provides that even if a UK resident is not a ''qualified person'' as defined by the treaty it shall nevertheless be entitled to the benefit of the treaty with respect to an item of income, profit or gain, if it satisfies any other specified condition for obtaining such benefit, and it is engaged in the active conduct of a trade or business in the UK.

Paragraph 4(*a*), (*b*) and (*c*) set out the conditions for passing the ''active conduct of a trade or business'' test and guidance on the meaning of some of the specific terms used in the paragraph is provided in the Exchange of Notes to the treaty. Essentially however, there are three main conditions: the UK resident must be engaged in the active conduct of a trade or business in the UK; the income derived from the US must be derived in connection with or incidental to that trade or business; and the trade must be substantial in relation to the activity in the US.

Comment on the meaning of ''trade or business'', ''in connection with'', ''incidental to'' and ''substantial'' is given in the section entitled ''Zero Withholding Tax on US Dividends—Articles 10 and 23'' earlier in this Tax Bulletin.

What is the rationale for the ''active conduct of a trade or business'' test?

To quote again from the Technical Explanation to the US Model Income Tax Convention of September 20, 1996, the assumption underlying this test ''is that a third country resident that establishes a 'substantial' operation in the other State and that derives income from a similar activity in the US would not do so primarily to avail itself of the benefits of the treaty; it is presumed in such a case that the investor had a valid business purpose for investing in the other State, and that the link between that trade and or business and the US activity that generates the treaty-benefited income manifests a business purpose for placing the US investments in the entity in the other State. It is considered unlikely that the investor would incur the expense of establishing a substantial trade or business in the other State simply to obtain the benefits of the Convention.''

In such circumstances there can be no objection to granting entitlement to treaty benefits in respect of the relevant item of income, profit or gain.

Competent authority discretion

Paragraph 6 provides that a UK or US resident who is neither a ''qualified person'' nor entitled to treaty benefits with respect to an item of income, profit or gain under the ''derivative benefits'' test or the ''active conduct of a trade or business'' test shall nevertheless be granted treaty benefits by the competent authority of the other country if the competent authority determines that the establishment, acquisition or maintenance of the person claiming the benefit and the conduct of its operations did not have as one of its principal purposes the obtaining of benefits under the treaty.

The Exchange of Notes to the treaty sets out in detail, with reference to specific circumstances, how the competent authority will approach this task.

Why have competent authority discretion in addition to the other tests?

The tests at paragraphs 2, 3 and 4 of the article, whilst providing clarity and certainty regarding entitlement to treaty benefits, are nevertheless essentially mechanical and cannot account for every situation.

As such, competent authority discretion allows taxpayers who do not meet the objective criteria set by those tests, but who were nevertheless not engaged in treaty shopping, to obtain the benefits of the treaty. (For details on how to apply to the US Competent Authority see Zero Withholding Tax on US Dividends—Articles 10 and 23 and to the UK Competent Authority see Entry into force—Article 29)

MUTUAL AGREEMENT PROCEDURE—ARTICLE 26

This article authorises the competent authorities of the two countries to endeavour, by mutual agreement, to resolve cases of taxation not in accordance with the treaty and to settle points of doubt or difficulty in its application or interpretation.

Specifically it provides that, where a person considers that the actions of one or both countries will result in taxation not in accordance with the treaty, he may present his case to the competent authority of the country of which he is a resident or national. This right applies irrespective of any remedies provided by domestic law.

Time limits

The article sets out time limits for the presentation of a case: a case must be presented within three years of the first notification of the action resulting in taxation not in accordance with the treaty or, if later, within six years from the end of the taxable or chargeable period in respect of which that taxation is imposed or proposed. This provides certainty and consistency of treatment for applicants and contributes to the effective administration of the mutual agreement procedure.

The time limits in the treaty are compatible with the time limits in UK law. TA 1988 s 815AA(6) provides that cases may be presented for consideration under the mutual agreement procedure before the expiration of six years following the end of the chargeable period to which the case relates.

Implementation of agreements reached

Agreements reached between the competent authorities will be implemented notwithstanding the countries' domestic time limits or other procedural limitations (except such limitations as apply for the purposes of giving effect to such an agreement).

This time limit is the 12 month period stipulated in UK law for making a claim to relief following mutual agreement (TA 1988 s 815AA(3)).

The presentation of a case for consideration under the mutual agreement procedure does not in itself constitute a claim to relief. In the absence of a claim the Revenue cannot give relief. TA 1988 s 815AA(3) provides that once mutual agreement has been reached by the competent authorities a claim to relief may be made within 12 months of the notification.

EXCHANGE OF INFORMATION AND ADMINISTRATIVE ASSISTANCE—ARTICLE 27

The article provides that the UK and US competent authorities will exchange information and assist each other administratively for the purposes of carrying out the provisions of the treaty and their respective domestic tax laws.

Can information relating to residents of third countries be exchanged?

Generally, unless otherwise provided for in the treaty, the treaty only applies to residents of either or both the UK and the US (Article 1(1)). However, paragraph 1 of the exchange of information and administrative assistance article provides that the exchange of information is not restricted by Article 1(1) of the treaty. Therefore the UK and the US competent authorities may exchange information relating to residents of third countries.

For example, the US competent authority will be able to ask the UK competent authority for information relating to the UK source income of a US national (who may be taxable in the US in respect of that income) even though that person may be resident in a third country.

Another example might be where a company, resident in a third country, has a permanent establishment in the US which is transacting with UK taxpayers and the UK competent authority wants information about those transactions in order to determine the profits of the UK taxpayers concerned. The article permits the US competent authority to exchange information about the US permanent establishment even though the company of which it represents a part is not a US resident.

Exchanging information about residents of third countries in this way is in line with OECD thinking and reflects the wider and growing international consensus that effective exchange of information represents one of the best ways of combating tax avoidance and evasion—particularly in view of increasing economic and commercial internationalisation.

What is the extent of the obligation imposed by the article on the UK competent authority to obtain and exchange information?

Paragraph 2 of the article provides that if one of the competent authorities requests information, the other competent authority will obtain that information in the same manner and to the same extent as it would for its country's own tax purposes.

This reflects the fact that the powers that exist under UK domestic tax law to call for documents relevant to liability to UK income tax, corporation tax or capital gains tax (TMA 1970 s 20) may, by virtue of Finance Act 2000 s 146, be used in a case where the liability is to the tax of a treaty partner provided that tax is covered by the relevant treaty.

What safeguards are there to protect those about whom information is exchanged?

Information may only be exchanged between the US and UK competent authorities and the exchange must:

(*a*) be necessary for carrying out the provisions of the treaty or of UK or US domestic tax law;
(*b*) relate to the taxes covered by the treaty; and

(*c*) be treated as secret.

The obligation to exchange information does not require either country to carry out administrative measures at variance with its existing practice; or to supply information that is not obtainable under domestic law; or to supply any information that would disclose any trade, business, industrial, commercial, or professional secret or trade process, or whose disclosure would be contrary to public policy.

ENTRY INTO FORCE—ARTICLE 29

From when does the treaty have effect?

The instruments of ratification were exchanged on 31 March 2003 and the treaty entered into force on that date. It will have effect for UK taxes covered from the following dates:

(*a*) taxes withheld at source 1 May 2003;

(*b*) income tax and capital gains tax 6 April 2003;

(*c*) corporation tax 1 April 2003; and

(*d*) petroleum revenue tax 1 January 2004.

For the purposes of Article 29(2)(*b*)(iii), ''financial year'' is defined at TA 1988 s 834. It is the 12 months commencing on the 1 April in any given calendar year, so the financial year 2003 is the year beginning on 1 April 2003.

How will US residents be able to claim relief?

The Centre for Non-Residents (CNR) in Nottingham is the office primarily responsible for giving relief from UK income tax to residents of the USA in receipt of relievable UK source income tax under tax treaties.

The main types of income that may be relieved under the treaty are interest (Article 11), royalties (Article 12) and pensions, annuities, alimony, social security and child support entitlements (Article 17). The other income article (Article 22) may operate to relieve items of income not dealt with under any other article of the treaty, but specifically excludes from its scope any income paid out of trusts or the estates of deceased persons in the course of administration.

Article 10 deals with dividends. Unlike its predecessor, the article does not contain a provision granting US residents entitlement to tax credits in respect of UK dividends. And as there is no withholding tax on UK dividends, there will generally be no relief for a US resident to claim under this article.

A claim for relief from UK tax may be made in two ways. A US resident can claim repayment of tax already deducted from UK source income. It is also possible to make an application to CNR asking it to direct that future payments of income be made without deduction of tax (or after deduction of tax at the rate specified in the treaty).

Which form should a US resident use to claim relief?

Individuals will need to complete form US/Individual 2002.

All other types of claimant will need to complete form US/Company 2002.

How do I obtain a form to claim relief?

Both forms can be downloaded from CNR's website at http://www.inlandrevenue.gov.uk/cnr/app_dtt.htm or by contacting CNR by telephone on 0845 070 0040 or from outside the UK on +44 151 210 2222. Each form has a set of guidance notes attached.

The forms follow the pattern of those published in 2001 for claims under the previous treaty, but with appropriate additions and amendments.

How do I claim relief?

The method of claiming relief has not altered with the introduction of the new treaty.

The completed form should be sent to the US Residency Certification Unit of the IRS (whose full address is given on the form), which will certify the claimant's US tax status and forward the form direct to CNR. It is not CNR's practice to process a form that has not been certified by the IRS in this manner, although it is open to claimants to send CNR an advance copy of their claim, and CNR may consider it without prejudice, dependent upon receipt of the certified form.

Why does the form have so many questions?

The questions on the forms are designed to ensure that CNR has all the information necessary to determine whether the claimant is entitled to treaty benefits. But as the new treaty contains provisions not found in the previous treaty (such as the ''conduit arrangement'' provision in the dividends, interest, royalties and other income articles and the provisions in the limitation on benefits article) there are inevitably more questions than on the previous claim forms. But we have done all we can to keep the number of extra questions to a minimum consistent with the need to ensure that a claimant establishes entitlement to treaty benefits.

How do I make a claim under Article 23(6)?

There is no form or set form of words for making a claim under the competent authority discretion provision at Article 23(6). Claims, detailing the reasons why the claimant thinks they are entitled to treaty benefits, should be made by letter to either of the UK competent authority contacts listed at the end of this Tax Bulletin. In addition claimants should complete the appropriate CNR claim form and send it in the normal way to the United States Internal Revenue Service (see "How do I claim relief?" above). Please attach a copy of the competent authority contact letter to the claim form.

How do I claim repayment of UK tax that was deducted before the new treaty came into effect?

You should complete the claim form appropriate to the previous treaty. This form can be downloaded from CNR's website at http://www.inlandrevenue.gov.uk/cnr/app_dtt.htm or by contacting CNR by telephone on 0845 070 0040 or from outside the UK on +44 151 210 2222. Each form has a set of Guidance Notes attached.

Will Directions under the previous treaty for interest or royalties to be paid gross continue to apply under the new treaty?

Some people may already have received clearance from the Inland Revenue for interest or royalties to flow gross between the UK and US following an application under the previous treaty. Clearance under the previous treaty will normally have been granted for the duration of the loan or licensing agreement or until a review date has been reached. With the introduction of the new treaty, some of these clearances may need to be reviewed to ensure that the claimant continues to be entitled to the benefit of the interest or royalty article.

The Revenue expects both the UK payer and the overseas applicant to consider whether they are still entitled to make and receive the payments without deducting income tax. If they believe they might not be, they should tell CNR.

What if a claimant is fiscally transparent?

Article 1(8) deals with entities that are "fiscally transparent" for taxation purposes and directs the taxation authorities to "look through" such concerns to establish eligibility to relief. This is not so different from the provisions of the previous treaty, and CNR will apply broadly the same tests as it did with partnerships, LLCs and similar concerns that made claims under the previous treaty. (See Tax Bulletin 29 available at www.inlandrevenue.gov.uk/bulletins/tb29.htm).

With partnerships and LLCs (where the latter are taxed in the US on a non-corporate basis), CNR will continue to take claims in the name of the transparent concern signed by a senior, general or managing partner or member, as appropriate. However, the claim should be accompanied by particulars of all the individual beneficial owners of the income, whether natural or legal persons. In the first instance, the name and address (residential or registered business addresses only are acceptable) may be given, subject to enquiry and verification.

If any participants are not US residents, the schedule of beneficial owners should show each beneficial owner's percentage share of the income.

Where there are multiple layers of investors, especially if some of them are themselves transparent concerns, CNR will look sympathetically at the compliance difficulties the above procedure may cause claimants, and if necessary will consider specific proposals to provide adequate and effective verification arrangements.

In cases of multiple ownership or where a non-US element is involved, CNR will need to decide whether to authorise relief at source. In such cases, relief may be possible only by way of meeting discrete payment claims made after a UK-source payment has been made, and tax deducted from it.

What is "grandfathering"?

"Grandfathering" (though not a term found in the treaty itself) is the process whereby a claimant can elect, under the provisions of Article 29(3), to have the provisions of the previous treaty apply in their entirety for a period of 12 months from the date on which the new treaty otherwise would have effect under Article 29(2). A claimant may wish to make such an election because the previous treaty provides them with greater benefits than they would be entitled to under the new treaty.

There is no form or set form of words provided for such an election. Instead, CNR will consider the provision invoked only where the claimant has expressly asked for it to apply, or has demonstrated a clear and unmistakable intention that it is to apply. The question will need to be determined on the making of the first claim to relief to which Article 29(3) could have relevance. If such an election is made, it will apply to all of the income arising in that 12-month period.

A claimant making such an election will need to make any claim to which it relates using the appropriate form for the previous treaty. These forms will continue to be available on CNR's website, or obtainable from them on request, until the statutory time limit for making a claim under UK tax law (TMA 1970 s 43) expires. Claims relating to income paid in the period from 1 May 2003 to 5 April 2004 will have to be made no later than 31 January 2010; claims for the period from 6 April to 30 April 2004 will have to be made no later than 31 January 2011.

WHERE CAN I FIND OUT MORE?

Visit CNR's website at http://www.inlandrevenue.gov.uk/cnr/app_dtt.htm to find out more about how it processes claims for relief under the UK's tax treaties.

April 2003. Tax Bulletin.

Businesses, individuals and the settlements legislation

Note—See also RI 268 which provides further information on this subject.

INTRODUCTION

We have been asked by the Chartered Institute of Taxation (CIOT) if we would provide some further information and examples on the settlements legislation in Part XV of Income and Corporation Taxes Acts (ICTA) 1988 especially in the context of its application to businesses and individuals. We are happy to do so. We have incorporated a number of comments made by the CIOT on a draft of this article and the examples it contains, but the article remains an expression of the views and practice of the Inland Revenue and the CIOT does not necessarily agree with all the points made.

Unless otherwise stated all references are to TA 1988 in this article.

The settlements legislation was originally enacted in the 1930's. The legislation was brought up to date in 1995, further amended in 1999 and can now be found at sections 660A to 660G. The legislation not only applies to trusts but can also apply to other situations involving individuals, companies and partnerships. It is these non-trust situations where we have been asked to provide further information.

The existing guidance on the settlements legislation is found in the Inland Revenue's Trusts Estates and Settlements Manual which is available on our website at www.ir.gov.uk/manuals/tsemmanual/. That manual will be updated to incorporate this additional information shortly.

The settlements legislation is intended to prevent an individual from gaining a tax advantage by making arrangements which divert his or her income to another person who is liable at a lower rate of tax or is not liable to income tax.

DEFINITIONS

There are two key definitions when considering the settlements legislation, both set out in section 660G(1):

- **Settlement** includes any disposition, trust, covenant, arrangement or transfer of assets. Settlement may include a series of transactions which taken together are regarded as an arrangement. The courts have limited the scope of a settlement to where there is some element of bounty, see *IRC v Plummer* [1979] STC 793: 54 TC 1;
- **Settlor** means any person by whom the settlement was made.

There are some important statutory exemptions from the legislation:

- Section 660A(6) exempts situations where the property passed to a spouse is an outright gift, unless;
  - the gift does not carry the right to the whole of the income arising, or
  - the property given is wholly or substantially a right to income.
- Section 660A(9)(*a*) exempts annual payments made by an individual for bona fide commercial reasons in connection with their trade, profession or vocation.
- Section 660A(9)(*b*) exempts certain donations made to charities.
- Section 660A(9)(*c*) exempts income consisting of a benefit under approved pension schemes.

So, in general, the settlements legislation can apply where an individual enters into an arrangement to divert income to someone else and in the process tax is saved. So long as those arrangements are:

- bounteous, or
- not commercial, or
- not at arm's length, or
- in the case of a gift between spouses, wholly or substantially a right to income.

DOES THE LEGISLATION ONLY APPLY TO TRANSFERS TO SPOUSES AND MINOR CHILDREN?

It is a common misconception that the settlements legislation applies only to arrangements involving a settlor's spouse or minor children. However, section 660A(2) makes it clear the settlor is treated as having an interest in property if "that property or any derived property is, or will or may become, payable to or applicable for the benefit of the settlor or his spouse in any circumstances whatsoever." It is not necessary for the settlor's spouse or children to be the people to whom the income is transferred. If the settlor or their spouse retains an interest in the property then the legislation can apply. See example 2 below.

PRs etc

Section 660A applies to arrangements where the settlor, or their spouse, retain an interest in the settlement. Section 660B applies to situations where income not caught by section 660A is paid or made available to a minor unmarried child of the settlor. The 1999 amendments extended the legislation to include income otherwise treated as that of the child with regard to settlements made on or after 9 March 1999. For example a settlor who invests money in a savings scheme which is held on bare trust for their child will find the income treated as theirs under this section if the child's relevant settlement income exceeds £100 (section 660B(5)). There are further examples involving children below at examples 8 and 9.

HOW DOES THE LEGISLATION APPLY TO NON-TRUST SITUATIONS?

A very small percentage of the enquiries we currently undertake each year involve the settlements legislation and non-trust situations. However we do seek tax, interest and penalties in appropriate cases. It is not possible to provide a definitive list of the issues we look for when deciding which cases to take up for enquiry, but some of the factors that the Revenue is looking for might include:

– Main earner drawing a low salary leading to enhanced profits from which dividends can be paid to shareholders who are friends or family members.
– Disproportionately large returns on capital investments.

Differing classes of shares enabling dividends to be paid only to – shareholders paying lower rates of tax.

Dividends being waived so that higher dividends can be paid to – shareholders paying lower rates of tax.

– Income being transferred from the person making most of the profits of a business to a friend or family member who pays tax at a lower rate.

There are a wide range of arrangements that can potentially be caught by the settlements legislation which do not involve a trust. Each case will depend on the facts but some of the most common situations which we see are:

– Shares subscribed at par that carry only restricted rights.
– Shares given away that carry only restricted rights.
– Shares subscribed at par in a company by someone else where the income of the company derives mainly from a single employee.
– A share in a partnership gifted or transferred below value.
– Dividend waivers.
– Situations where dividends are paid only on certain classes of shares.
– Dividends paid to the settlor's minor children.

These lists are by no means definitive of situations to which the settlements legislation can be applied.

The best way to illustrate how the legislation applies is by using the following examples although it should be noted that these are by no means exhaustive.

Note—The original examples are not reproduced here. See instead RI 268, which provides more extensive versions of the same examples.

SUMMARY

Whether or not the settlements legislation applies to an arrangement depends on the particular facts of the case. It is necessary to look at the arrangement as a whole. If there is a bounteous arrangement which effectively transfers income earned by one person to another resulting in a reduction in overall tax liability the arrangement may be liable to challenge under the settlements legislation.

A purely commercial transaction or series of transactions at arms length is outside the meaning of ''settlement''. Most commonly the legislation will apply where individuals seek to divert income to members of their family or to friends. A good test of whether or not the legislation could apply is to consider would the same payments be made to a person who acquired shares in a company or a share of a partnership at arms length. Or whether income is being paid simply because the recipient is your spouse or child or some other individual you might wish to benefit.

If you have any comments on this article and the issues raised you can contact the Editor of Tax Bulletin at the Inland Revenue or at the CIOT contact Liz Lathwood, Technical Officer, Chartered Institute of Taxation, 12 Upper Belgrave Street, London, SW1X 8BB.

Commentary—*Simon's Direct Tax Service* **C4.302, 303, 310.**

June 2003. Tax Bulletin Issue 65

Access to link papers or how the figures in the accounting records feature in the return

During the course of an enquiry it may be necessary to examine part or all of the books and records of a business. Sometimes it may not be clear exactly how the figures in the accounting records feature in the return. This is usually because accounting adjustments or journals have been made to those figures. So as to understand better how the business records reconcile with the final accounts/ tax return the enquiry officer may sometimes request access to the accountants' ''link papers''. This can often reduce the time and costs of an enquiry. ''Link papers'' is a Revenue term defined in Tax Bulletin Special Edition 2 August 1997—

> ''Those papers which show how the figures in the return are derived from the figures in the prime records, are held by the agent, but are available to the taxpayer''.

A request for ''link papers'' does not go against the principles of SP 5/90, which specifically refers to an accountants' ''working papers''. SP 5/90 notes that three classes of documents are still excluded from the papers which may be called for from a third party. First, there is no change in the protection given to documents brought into existence specifically to support the conduct of a pending appeal. Second, audit papers are protected from disclosure by an auditor. Third, communications relating to giving or obtaining tax advice are protected from disclosure by a tax adviser. However, the protection given to audit papers and tax advice is limited where the papers contain essential information about the origin of figures in accounts, returns and other information submitted to the Revenue or the relationship of those figures with the books and records of the taxpayer.

It should also be borne in mind that where the business under enquiry is a limited company that the ICAEW Guidance for Members in Practice—Documents and records: ownership, lien and rights of access provides guidance in this area. In particular paragraph 11 says that where a company has not kept accounting records in accordance with section 221 of the Companies Act 1985, and the court took a view that such schedules had been prepared for the company in order to comply with s 221 then the schedules would belong to the company. Where an informal request is refused by the business under enquiry the enquiry officer will be able to use paragraph 27 to require production of the papers by the company.

Where the business is unincorporated and access to the papers is refused the enquiry officer will be able to proceed by way of a section 19A notice to the taxpayer.

If the taxpayer cannot produce the papers because they haven't got them or cannot get them the enquiry officer will be able to consider the use of section 20(3) to require delivery of the papers from the accountant.

At all times the enquiry officer is aiming to understand the figures in the return and how they have been derived. A review of the linking documents between the books and records and the return will greatly assist in this process and will generally lead to reduced time and costs in an enquiry.

August 2003. Tax Bulletin Issue 66

Deceased estates—new procedures for income tax and capital gains tax

BACKGROUND

When somebody dies, their assets pass to their estate. The estate is then administered by their personal representatives, whose main duties are to—

- gather in the assets left by the deceased individual,
- settle their debts,
- pay out any legacies, and then
- distribute any remaining assets to the beneficiaries.

The personal representatives are also responsible for paying tax on any income or capital gains the state receives during the administration period. (That is, the period from the date of death until they distribute the assets.)

Strictly, personal representatives should—

- notify the Inland Revenue that they are liable to tax within 6 months of the end of the year they became liable,
- complete a Self-assessment return and pay any tax due on the estate income and gains.

INFORMAL PROCEDURES—CURRENT PRACTICE

In practice, the tax due on many estates is either already covered by tax deducted from the income, or so small that it is impractical to deal with under normal self-assessment procedures. So to minimise costs and administrative burdens for personal representatives and their agents, the Inland Revenue has allowed tax liabilities for the smallest estates to be settled by a one-off payment. These ''informal procedures'' apply where the probate value of an estate is below £400,000.

As part of our drive to provide a better service for all our customers, we are extending these informal procedures to many more estates.

INFORMAL PROCEDURES—NEW PRACTICE

For estates where the date of death was on or after 6 April 2003, we will normally accept a simple computation of the estate's self-assessment liability if—

– the estate is not regarded as complex (see below), and
– the tax arising during the whole of the administration period is less than £10,000.

In these cases, we will provide the personal representative with a payslip to allow them to pay the tax due.

In all cases where the tax liability for the whole of the administration period is £10,000 or more, or where the estate is one we regard as complex, we will still require self-assessment returns. (IR Trusts offices will normally issue these, not local service offices.)

COMPLEX ESTATE

We regard an estate as complex where—

– there is a very high probate/confirmation value, generally over **£2.5 million**, or
– the administration of the estate is continuing and has entered the third income tax year from the date of death, or
– the personal representatives have disposed of a chargeable capital asset, and the proceeds of sale exceed **£250,000**.

WHICH OFFICE WILL DEAL WITH THE ESTATE

a) Trust created

In all estates, large or small, where the terms of the will or intestacy provide for a trust to be created, the responsible office will be the IR Trusts office that deals with the address of the trustees. The IR Trusts offices will deal with the administration period liability for all estates where a trust is created, regardless of whether the case is to be dealt with under the informal procedures or via the self-assessment regime.

b) No trust created—informal procedures

Where the informal procedures apply, the local service office that dealt with the deceased individual's tax affairs will also deal with the estate. If the deceased did not have a tax office at the date of death, the responsible office will be the office that deals with the personal representatives' address.

c) No trust created—normal self-assessment procedures

If no continuing trust is established under the terms of the will or intestacy, but self-assessment returns are needed, the estate's tax affairs will be dealt with by IR Trusts (usually from its Edinburgh office).

The only exceptions are—

– if Public Departments 1 handled the deceased individual's affairs, it will also deal with the estate
– if the deceased individual was a Lloyds underwriter, West Yorkshire Personal Tax Unit will deal with the estate.

Large or complex estates will be expected to complete a trust and estate self-assessment return, and may also be asked to provide certain information about the distribution of sums to the beneficiaries of the estate.

Statements of residuary income (Forms 922)

IR Trusts Edinburgh currently issues forms 922 (Statement of residuary income) annually for a large number of estates. This form is used to calculate and allocate estate income to the beneficiaries of the estate.

We are reviewing the need for these forms, and will issue fewer of them in future. We are also looking at whether the detailed information we currently request can be summarised.

OUTCOME OF THESE CHANGES

We expect that personal representatives will benefit from these changes as they will ensure consistency of approach throughout the Inland Revenue. We intend this simplification of our procedures to allow personal representatives' income tax and capital gains tax liabilities to be satisfied easily and with the minimum of delay.

We will publicise any further changes to our procedures for the tax liabilities of deceased estates as soon as we have developed them.

QUERIES

To Charlie Kerr or Roger Willoughby at—
IR Trusts Edinburgh

Meldrum House
15 Drumsheugh Gardens
Edinburgh
EH3 7UB.
Tel: 0131 777 4099 or 0131 777 4143.

21 October 2003. IR Press Release, 86/03.

Capital gains tax—gifts relief

The Paymaster General announced today that legislation will be introduced in next year's Finance Bill to correct the effect of an oversight which has led to the unintended repeal of legislation introduced in 2000 to prevent capital gains tax gifts relief being exploited in certain tax-avoidance schemes.

The correction will have effect in relation to disposals of shares or securities to companies on or after today.

DETAILS

The rules in section 165 of the Taxation of Chargeable Gains Act 1992 (TCGA) provide for charges to capital gains tax (CGT) to be postponed in certain circumstances where business assets are transferred from one person to another on non-arm's length terms.

Action was taken in Finance Act 2000 to counter a large number of tax avoidance schemes which involved the transfer of shares or securities to a company and which relied upon gifts relief being available on the transfer.

Gifts relief ceased to be available in these circumstances with effect for disposals of shares or securities on or after 9th November 1999. The relevant change to the legislation was made by way of amendment to TCGA 1992 s 165(3)(*b*), a provision which was otherwise concerned with the interaction of gifts relief with CGT retirement relief.

CGT retirement relief was phased out over a five-year period following the introduction of CGT taper relief in April 1998, and is not available for disposals of business assets on or after 6th April 2003. Provision was made in Finance Act 1998 for the retirement relief legislation, including the measure in TCGA 1992 s 165(3)(*b*), to be repealed with effect for such disposals. This prospective repeal was overlooked when s 165(3)(*b*) was amended in Finance Act 2000. The effect is that the gifts relief anti-avoidance provision introduced in that Act does not apply to disposals of shares or securities to companies after 5th April 2003.

The measure announced today will reinstate this anti-avoidance provision with effect for disposals of shares or securities on or after today.

NOTES

1. Where gifts relief is allowed:

- the donor is not charged any tax on the gain;
- the recipient is treated for capital gains tax purposes as acquiring the asset for the current market value less the amount of the chargeable gain on the gift; and
- as a consequence, the gain is effectively brought into charge when the recipient disposes of the asset.

2. The main purposes of the relief are to prevent erosion of business capital when a business is handed down within the family and to prevent the break-up of small businesses.

3. Finance Act 2000 introduced legislation that ended the availability of gifts relief for transfers of shares or securities to companies. This was done in order to counter widespread abuse of the relief in schemes whose primary purpose was to avoid CGT on a anticipated sale, rather than simply defer the liability on a genuine gift. The legislation protects more than £50 million of tax per annum.

4. Finance Act 1998 introduced taper relief as part of the Government's reform of CGT. This relief provides for a progressive reduction in the effective rate of CGT on the disposal of assets by reference to the time they have been owned. As a consequence, the same Act contained legislation providing for the gradual phasing out of CGT retirement relief on the disposal of business assets.

December 2003. Tax Bulletin Issue 68

Teleworkers—reimbursed expenses and benefits for employees working at home

Increasing numbers of employees are working wholly or partly at home. A recent report by The Work Foundation (''Time to go home: embracing the homeworking revolution'' by Tim Dwelly and Yvonne Bennion) suggested that 2.2 million employees in the UK (about 7.4% of all employees)

PRs etc

work at home at least one day a week using a telephone or computer. Around one million employees work mainly at home. The number of employees working at home is increasing by around 13% a year.

The great majority of these home workers are employees who are sometimes referred to as teleworkers; workers who rely on the use of computers and telecommunications to carry out office work at home. Government policy aims to support employers that seek to provide better work-life balance opportunities.

In the last few years a number of changes to legislation have been made to help employers support teleworkers and other employees who agree to work at home without incurring a tax charge or liability for NICs. This article looks at that legislation and also at tax relief for expenses incurred by teleworkers as a result of working at home.

EMPLOYER PROVIDED EQUIPMENT

Employers can now provide all of the computing facilities, telecommunications links, office furniture and supplies that a teleworker needs to work at home, without a tax charge. This is achieved by—

- ITEPA 2003 s 316, which provides an exemption for provided furniture, equipment, supplies and services where the employer's sole purpose in providing them is to enable the employee to perform the duties of the employment and any private use is not significant,
  - an article in Tax Bulletin 49 (''Schedule E benefits in kind—part business use and part private use'') provides further guidance,
  - this exemption can extend to the provision of a telephone line in the employee's home and to broadband Internet access in the circumstances described in EIM21615 in the Inland Revenue's Employment Income Manual;
- ITEPA 2003 s 320, which permits a limited exemption for provided computer equipment up to the first £500 of cash equivalent. Where this limit is exceeded the exemption in ITEPA 2003 s 316 can apply to the excess.

Where benefits are exempted from tax there is no liability for Class 1A NICs (SSCBA 1992 Section 10(1)(*a*)).

EXPENSE PAYMENTS TO THE EMPLOYEE

New legislation in ITEPA 2003 s 316A applies with effect from 6 April 2003 to prevent any tax charge where an employer makes payments to employees to reimburse the additional household expenses that they incur in working at home. There is further guidance on this at EIM01472. Such payments could already be made without a NICs liability arising.

Exempt payments can be made where there are arrangements between the employee and the employer under which the employee regularly works at home. This covers employers' homeworking policies but will not cover employees who work at home informally and not by arrangement with the employer. So, for example, the new exemption will not apply to employees who simply take additional work home in the evenings.

The exemption applies to employees who do some or all of their work at home with the agreement of the employer instead of working on the employer's premises. For example, the new exemption could apply to payments made to an employee who arranges to spend two days each week working at the office and the other three days working at home.

The additional expenses that the employer may reimburse are those connected with the day to day running of the employee's home. This might include additional costs of heating and lighting the work area, or the metered cost of increased water use. There might also be increased charges for Internet access or telephone use. In some cases work at home may lead to an increase in household contents insurance or to a liability for business rates. It might be difficult for employers to calculate the exact amount of additional costs that an employee is incurring as a result of working at home. So we have published a guideline rate of £2 per week that can be paid to employees working regularly at home without the employer having to justify the amount paid or the employee having to keep any records to demonstrate the additional expenditure.

The £2 per week figure is not a maximum, and greater amounts can be paid where the employer provides evidence to justify them. There are two ways to do this. The employer can agree in advance with their Inland Revenue office on a scale rate payment that is calculated to do no more than reimburse the average additional costs that the employees are meeting while working at home. It may be useful to agree that the scale rate payment can be increased annually in line with inflation. If the employer has agreed a scale rate payment based on reasonable estimates of additional household costs derived from records of costs kept by employees it is not necessary for employees to keep subsequent evidence of costs incurred.

Alternatively, an employer may prefer to reimburse the actual additional costs incurred by each employee. In such cases we would expect the employer to keep records to show how the payments have been computed. In turn this will depend on evidence retained by the employee about the amount of additional costs.

EXPENSE DEDUCTIONS

Travel expenses

The rules on travel for necessary attendance in ITEPA 2003 ss 338 and 339 assist teleworkers. Relief is available for home to work travel unless that travel is ordinary commuting. Many teleworkers do not have an ordinary commuting journey and are entitled to tax relief for all of their business travel. Where those costs are met by the employer, they can be covered by a dispensation in the normal way.

In this context the facts of the recent case of *Kirkwood v Evans* (74TC481) are slightly unusual. Mr Evans worked mainly at home but travelled regularly on one day each week to his employer's office. There was no evidence that he would do so for a limited duration or for a temporary purpose. So his employer's office was a permanent workplace and he was not entitled to tax relief for his travel. This simply shows that a teleworker might still have an ordinary commuting journey.

Many teleworkers no longer use the employer's office as a permanent workplace. Visits to the employer's office become irregular or self-contained, so that the employer's office becomes a temporary workplace. For example, teleworkers may occasionally need to visit the office to attend team meetings or similar events. Irregular visits, or regular but self-contained visits, do not make the office a permanent workplace. Where the employer meets the cost of such visits they can be covered by a dispensation.

Where a teleworker who was previously office based begins to work from home the status of the employer's office as a permanent workplace needs to be reconsidered in the light of the new working pattern. The fact that the employer's office was once a permanent workplace does not mean that it must remain one.

Household expenses

The exemption for payments by employers in ITEPA 2003 s 316A is wider than the existing relief for employees' expenses in ITEPA 2003 s 336. So the fact that an employer could make exempt payments to an employee for additional household expenses does not mean that the employee would be entitled to relief for unreimbursed expenses.

The principal difference between the rules for exemption and those for deduction is that the exemption applies wherever an employee works at home under homeworking arrangements with the employer. By contrast an employee is only entitled to a deduction for expenses incurred in working at home where the nature of the employment itself would require any employee to work at home.

This distinction can be illustrated by *Kirkwood v Evans*. Mr Evans worked at home out of choice under his employer's voluntary scheme. If his employer had met the additional household costs he incurred then the payments would now be within the scope of the exemption in Section 316A. However, there was nothing about the nature of his work that dictated working at home and so he was not entitled to a deduction under ITEPA 2003 s 336.

We anticipate that most employees who work at home under homeworking schemes will be doing so by choice and so will not be entitled to a deduction for any unreimbursed additional household expenses.

NON-RESIDENTS WORKING IN THE UK FOR SHORT PERIODS: THE "60-DAY" RULE

Most of the United Kingdom's double taxation agreements contain a provision which may enable an employee who comes to work here on a short-term basis to be taxed only in his or her home country. An employee must show that he or she fulfils a series of conditions specified in the agreement to make a valid claim to exemption from UK tax. One of those conditions will be that the employee's remuneration must be 'paid by or on behalf of an employer' who is not resident in the United Kingdom. In many cases, it is clear that the employer is the non-resident company for whom the taxpayer was working before he or she came to the UK. In other cases, the employee may have been seconded by his or her overseas employer to work for a UK company, or the overseas employer may carry on a business of hiring out staff to other companies. A formal contract of employment remains with the overseas employer, but the employee works in the business of the UK company, which obtains the benefits and bears any risks in relation to the work undertaken by the employee. In economic terms, this state of affairs is recognised by the overseas employer recharging the cost of the employee's earnings to the United Kingdom and the UK company might be described as the ''economic employer''. In such a case, the exemption from UK tax for short-term visitors will not be available. This was explained in Tax Bulletin 17, published in June 1995.

However, the position of very short-term visitors caused concern, and Tax Bulletin 25 dealt with this in October 1996. This reproduced a statement by the Financial Secretary to the Treasury (FST) that the Inland Revenue would not consider that a short term business visitor was sufficiently integrated into the business of a UK company for it to be regarded as the employer where—

- the employee concerned is in the UK for less than 60 days in a tax year; and
- that period does not form part of a more substantial period when the taxpayer is present in the UK.

This has become known as the ''60-day rule''. This article gives further guidance on common situations where it may be an issue.

Does the worker have to be from a country with which we have a full double tax agreement for the 60-day rule to apply?

The 60-day rule is framed in terms of accepting without enquiry that the conditions in a DTA for short-term business visitors to be solely taxed in their country of residence have been satisfied. That exemption, and consequently the 60 day rule, is therefore only relevant if the person is resident in a country with which we have signed a comprehensive double tax agreement. If not, domestic legislation will apply in full.

Is the 60-day exemption available if the employee is on the UK payroll?

No. The FST's statement was made in the context of workers who were paid via a non-resident employer's payroll but whose economic employer might be in the UK.

How do you count the days for the 60-day rule?

It is based on physical presence in the UK in the same way as the 183 days are counted for the purposes of Article 15(2) of the OECD model Tax Convention.

Is the 60 days a fixed limit? For example, an employer has a succession of people who work for him and he bears their wages, but they may be in the UK up to 90 days.

The 60-day rule represents a balance between a loss of tax revenue which may be due to the UK and the compliance costs to both employers and the Revenue of ascertaining and collecting such tax for very short-term visitors. There are no plans for it to be altered. However individuals working in the UK may be exempt under the relevant DTA anyway, for example if their earnings are paid by an overseas company, not recharged in any form to a UK company or permanent establishment and no UK company acts as their employer.

Is the 60-day rule available where the earnings have been recharged to a UK permanent establishment rather than a UK-resident company?

Although not covered in the actual wording of the 1996 statement, the Revenue accepts the 60-day rule should apply in these circumstances also.

How should the phrase "part of a more substantial period" be interpreted?

The aim is to provide consistency—

- Between very short-term workers, regardless of the particular dates involved; and
- Between short-term workers seconded from overseas and the normal workforce of the UK employer.

The most obvious example met is where less than 60 days are worked up to 5th April and less than 60 days after, but the overall period is more than 60 days. In these circumstances, the 60-day exemption will not be available, to be consistent with periods of more than 60 days worked over, say, November to January.

What if there is a gap between two shorter periods of employment?

To consider whether the 60-day period has been exceeded, the following factors may be relevant:

- Is there an expectation that the employee will return to the UK when they depart initially?
- How long is the gap between visits in comparison to the length of those visits?
- How frequently does the employee return to the UK?
- How integral to the business are the duties performed?

It is impossible to give an exact formula that will cover all circumstances. However, the following examples should assist in seeing how the Revenue will approach this question.

Example 1: Alain visits the UK for 35 days in Feb/March 2003, then returns to Austria for a fortnight's holiday, and returns again to the same contract for 40 days in April/May.

The 75 days would be regarded as one period. The gap here is insignificant compared to the two periods either side and liability to UK tax would be consistent with a person who works for 75 days here continuously. As the periods are part of the same contract, the employer would be expected to operate PAYE from day one. If there had been no expectation of returning during the first 35 days we would expect PAYE to be operated only for the second period even though liability to UK tax would exist for both for Alain. This is because the 60 days is an objective test whilst PAYE is based on ''reasonable expectation'' that payments are liable to UK tax.

Example 2: Beatrice visits the UK for 35 days in Year 1. She returns to Belgium but unexpectedly is asked to return in Year 2, after a 7 month gap, and does so for 40 days.

Each episode in the UK would be regarded as separate periods of less than 60 days. Beatrice's return was unexpected, and after a relatively long gap. So there is no UK liability for either and no PAYE is due.

Example 3: Cedric is the financial controller for a Canadian group. Each year he visits the UK subsidiary for 55–59 days.

Once there is an expectation that this will be the work pattern, the Revenue would consider that the episodes of work here were part of a more substantial period. A financial controller will be significantly integrated into the business, whether this is of the UK subsidiary or possibly a permanent establishment of the parent company. PAYE will apply from when it is clear that visits will recur as part of a regular and integrated pattern, although Cedric may have to consider whether he is also liable under self-assessment to UK tax for an earlier period of work, as for Alain in Example 1. Cedric and the group will then be able to decide the duration and timing of visits to the UK on business grounds rather than for individual tax considerations.

Example 4: Danielle spends 50 days working in UK between 10 April and 15 January, with visits averaging 3 days each. Then from 1 June to 6 October a further 15 days are spent visiting UK for business meetings on the same piece of work.

Although Danielle is taxable from the very start, we would not expect either her or the company to be able to recognise this. However, the Revenue would expect PAYE to be operated in Year 2.

For guidance on any particular case, the first approach should be to the tax office that deals with the individual. For further information on the Revenue's general approach to taxation for internationally mobile employees working in the UK, please contact—

Susan New (for double taxation relief aspects)
Revenue Policy International
Victory House
30-34 Kingsway
London
WC2B 6ES
Tel: 0207 438 7250
e-mail Susan.New@ir.gsi.gov.uk.

—or—

Martin Delnon (for domestic taxation aspects)
Revenue Policy Personal Tax
Sapphire House
550 Streetsbrook Road
Solihull
B91 1QU
Tel: 0121 713 7634

February 2004. Tax Bulletin Issue 69

Self-assessment returns

Three new measures to improve self-assessment (SA) for taxpayers and agents are being taken forward.

1. SHORT TAX RETURN

A new four page short tax return (STR) for people with simple tax affairs has already been piloted with 50,000 taxpayers in four Area offices. Interim results of independent research with taxpayers and agents involved in the pilot has shown widespread and positive support for the STR and accompanying simplified guide.

In April 2004 we plan to introduce the form to more taxpayers over a wider area. Tax agents are therefore more likely to find some of their clients receive the STR. Our aim is to roll the STR out nationwide in April 2005.

As well as being shorter than the main return, the STR is also simpler. For example, there is no facility to include a self-calculation. Taxpayers are encouraged to file by 30 September so we can calculate their tax position for them and let them know how much to pay in good time for January. For those who want to make a rough calculation for their own purposes, a simple guide will be included in the 2004 version.

To be able to use the STR, a person's affairs have to fit a tightly drawn set of criteria. People will therefore be selected automatically on the basis of the information from their previous year's return. However, returns filed close to the January filing date are less likely to be captured onto the Revenue's systems in time for a STR to be selected for the following year. In those cases people will receive a main tax return. Filing earlier in the year will ensure that the STR is sent to an eligible person the following year.

The STR has been designed so that the information provided on it can be captured automatically on to the Revenue's systems, using automated data capture technology. This will ensure the processing

PRs etc

of these returns is more efficient and accurate. This places great importance on the use of the printed form we issue, to ensure the precise accuracy of print format and coloration. We therefore do not have plans to produce a substitute of the form for 2004. We appreciate that tax agents who use software may not wish to complete a STR manually and they can, of course, use their normal software to complete a main return or file on-line.

People qualifying for a STR will be those with simple affairs, for example some employees (other than company directors) with P11D benefits, self-employed with a turnover less than £15,000 (three line account cases), pensioners in receipt of state retirement pension, an occupational pension or a retirement annuity. In addition, they may have straightforward investment income, or a modest amount of income from property.

The STR will not be available from the IR website, Orderline, or local offices (except where the original is lost or destroyed).

Although the Revenue will issue STRs based on information from the preceding year's return, it remains the taxpayer's responsibility to check their eligibility to complete the form. Their circumstances may have changed during the year which might mean a STR is no longer appropriate. Details of eligibility are set out clearly at the front of the guide.

During this year's pilot we have also been testing ''telefiling'', which allows people to file STR information over the telephone using a voice recognition system. Callers needing further advice during the process are connected to the Revenue helpline. Although the take-up is still fairly limited, those using the service have found it to be helpful. We therefore plan to continue the small pilot next year.

2. NEW CRITERIA FOR THOSE WHO NEED TO COMPLETE A SELF-ASSESSMENT TAX RETURN

Many people will no longer need to complete a SA return under new criteria to be published in April. With the help of Working Together colleagues and others we have concluded that there are certain groups of people, who currently receive returns, whose affairs can be adequately dealt with using the PAYE system. We have consulted widely on these proposals and the new rules will be introduced in April 2004. The new criteria will also be published on our website around the same time. Generally the types of people who will no longer need to complete a SA return are those with very straightforward affairs.

The changes mean—

- higher rate employees with simple affairs will no longer automatically be sent a SA return;
- the limit for claims to professional fees/expenses dealt with outside a SA return will rise to £2,500 (from the current limit of £500);
- the investment income limit will rise to £10,000 (from the current limit of £8,500);
- some relaxation to the rules for pensioners (where any further liability can be recovered through the PAYE coding).

After 6th April 2004 when a 2003/4 return is filed and captured onto our systems it will be automatically checked against the new rules. Where appropriate, the process will automatically—

- Stop the issue of any further returns if the person no longer meets the new SA criteria.
- Send a letter to the taxpayer and agent (where authority held) explaining the change in procedure and setting out the taxpayer's responsibilities.
- Notify the PAYE coding record of any changes required for the following year.
- Identify those cases where taxpayers need to return certain information (ie investment income) affecting their coding, on a Coding Review Form (the ''P810'') which will be sent the following April.

The system will identify likely candidates, such as pensioners and individuals on low incomes, for a manual review. Because these cases are likely to be more involved, they will be checked by staff to see whether they meet the new criteria. If so, the record will be noted that a return need not be issued and a letter issued to the taxpayer (and agent).

Some taxpayers may prefer, for varying reasons, to continue to receive a SA return. As long as we are notified we can override the signals on the system and the taxpayer will continue to receive returns.

Keeping the taxpayer better informed of his or her tax situation is a key part of this initiative. The letters sent to people no longer receiving a return set out the circumstances in which they may need to request a return in the future. And, from next year, where employees become liable to higher rate tax, but do not meet the new criteria, we will send them a letter informing them what they are required to do if they have any additional liability. Furthermore, all taxpayers that are newly set up in SA will receive a letter explaining why they will be receiving a return and how to get help.

3. MINOR QUERIES

Increased use of the telephone will help resolve problems that arise where staff have difficulty in understanding the customer's entries on the form. Up until now we have adhered closely to the amendment of a return either on the basis of an ''obvious error'' or following an enquiry. But we have become increasingly aware of many situations where a simple conversation with the customer can resolve minor issues.

These issues include incorrect completion of the gross, net and tax boxes in respect of investment income, confusion over claims to married couple's allowance or the amount of the state pension, or a clear misunderstanding of the employment benefit figure provided by the employer.

The new way of handling 'minor queries' by telephone contact with the taxpayer or their agent has been successfully piloted for over a year. Staff, customers and agents have all welcomed the exercise, which helps to improve the accuracy of our processing and saves unnecessary correspondence. Following the success of the pilots we plan to roll this out nationally in April 2004, for the capture of the 2003/04 and subsequent tax returns.

February 2004. Tax Bulletin Issue 69

Tips, gratuities, service charges and troncs: income tax, national insurance contributions, national minimum wage issues and VAT

Feedback from employers and representations from industry bodies has identified a need for additional guidance for employers regarding tips, gratuities and service charges. This was felt to be particularly necessary in respect of National Insurance contributions because of the increasing incidence of payments made by means of credit or debit card or cheque.

A new booklet (E24) "Tips, Gratuities, Service Charges and Troncs: A guide to Income Tax, National Insurance contributions, national minimum wage issues and VAT" will be published in February. The booklet will be distributed to employers through industry bodies and will be on the 2004 Employer's CD-ROM. It will also be on the employer's website from 2nd February 2004 at www.inlandrevenue.gov.uk/employers.

The booklet does not signal any changes to PAYE, national insurance, national minimum wage or VAT procedures or to our view of the legislation relating to tips, gratuities, service charges or troncs. Rather, its aim is to provide in one place, clearer and more detailed guidance to enable employers and troncmasters to deal with these areas correctly.

This article provides additional explanation on issues where there may have been a degree of uncertainty on the part of some employers and though not essential, we suggest it is read in conjunction with the booklet E24. In this guidance and the booklet, the word "tips" refers to payments of tips, gratuities and voluntary service charges.

INCOME TAX AND TRONCS

Where there is a tronc the employer must (from 6 April 2004) notify the Inland Revenue of the name of a new troncmaster. The troncmaster is responsible for operating PAYE on all distributions from the tronc and is personally liable for tax which he/she fails to deduct (example 3 in the booklet refers).

If an employer, business partner or an official of the company, which operates the business, performs the role of troncmaster the tronc will not be accepted by the Inland Revenue as a tronc for PAYE purposes. Payments made from the tronc in this situation are considered to be made by the employer and must be taxed under the employer's PAYE scheme (example 4 refers).

Where there is a tronc with an independent troncmaster but the employer is involved in the distribution of monies from the tronc, the responsibility for PAYE rests with the employer.

Where an employer arranges for cash tips to be collected and distributed to staff by a trusted employee in accordance with a formula set by the employer, PAYE responsibility rests with the employer as the trusted employee is acting on the employer's behalf (example 5 refers).

NATIONAL INSURANCE CONTRIBUTIONS

Tips passed to an employee by an employer are liable for both employer and employee National Insurance contributions.

Legislation at paragraph 5, Part 10 of Schedule 3 to the Social Security (Contributions) Regulations 2001 provides that any amount paid to an employee which is a gratuity or is in respect of a gratuity will be exempt from National Insurance contributions if it meets one of the following two conditions—

- it is not paid, directly or indirectly, to the employee by the employer and does not comprise or represent monies previously paid to the employer by a customer;
- it is not allocated, directly or indirectly, to the employee by the employer.

Example 6 of the new booklet shows how a payment of tips distributed to employees might fail to satisfy either of the conditions for exemption.

In that example the proprietor of a restaurant passes all tips paid by cheque and credit or debit card to his employees. Because the tips were included in cheque, credit or debit card payments made to the restaurateur it follows that they can never satisfy the first condition for exemption set out above, since that includes a requirement that the money must not have been paid to the employer by the customer.

The alternative condition will also not be satisfied because the restaurateur (the employer) has directly allocated the payments to the employees.

As neither of the conditions for exemption is satisfied the payments will all be liable for the payment of National Insurance contributions.

It might be useful here to make brief mention of the decision in the European Court of Human Rights in the case of *Nerva and others v United Kingdom*. The main finding in that case was that where a customer pays a tip by means of a credit card or cheque this constitutes a payment to the employer and he attains legal title to it. If he then pays it to his employees through the payroll it can be counted as remuneration paid by him for the purpose of complying with legislation relevant to the national minimum wage.

Legal advice secured following this decision confirmed that, where an employer pays a waiter a sum equivalent to the tips included in credit or debit card or cheque payments, then he is paying a sum ''in respect of '' a gratuity. Such payments therefore fall to be considered against the conditions in paragraph 5, Part 10 of Schedule 3 in the normal way.

The payments can never satisfy the first condition for exemption (contained in paragraph 5(2) of Part 10) although they may satisfy the alternative condition in paragraph 5(3). But that condition will not be satisfied if the employer decides how much is allocated as in example 6 outlined above. A similar outcome would arise if the employer were to try to satisfy his national minimum wage obligations by arranging things so that tips are used to top up the earnings to the level of the national minimum wage; or if he deducted charges imposed by the credit card company and therefore paid into the tronc less than the total amount of tips paid by credit or debit card and cheque. It is our view that in all these situations the employer is influencing or determining the amount to be allocated. The conditions for exemption will accordingly not be satisfied and national insurance contributions will be due on all payments received by employees.

A payment made by an employer as part of a contractual arrangement or undertaking with an employee cannot be accepted as a tip and cannot therefore be disregarded for national insurance contribution purposes.

A contractual payment includes any payment which—

- forms part of the terms and conditions of the employment, or
- is promised, guaranteed or underwritten by the employer even if the payment (or some part of it) is paid by a third party.

This is highlighted in the booklet by example 13. In that example, the employer agrees with his employees a minimum each will receive in tips from the tronc. If necessary he makes a payment into the tronc at the end of each week to make sure there is enough to meet the promised payments. All payments from the tronc are contractual because they are promised by the employer. They cannot satisfy the exemption at paragraph 5 of Part 10 of Schedule 3 because they are not payments of gratuities-they are promised/expected rather than being spontaneous and unexpected. National Insurance contributions are therefore due on all payments made by the tronc.

NATIONAL INSURANCE CONTRIBUTIONS AND TRONCS

A troncmaster is not required to pay national insurance contributions on payments made from the tronc. Where payments from a tronc attract National Insurance contributions responsibility for calculating and paying the contributions due to the Inland Revenue rests with the employer because he is the secondary contributor as provided for by section 7 of the Social Security Contributions and Benefits Act 1992.

Payment of tips by a troncmaster will not attract National Insurance contributions where—

- they are not distributing money that was originally paid to the employer and the employer does not pay the money directly or indirectly to their employees; or
- the employer does not influence, directly or indirectly, the distribution of those tips.

Examples 9 to 14 of the booklet illustrate the Department's interpretation of the legislation by considering various scenarios. Some of these are covered here in a little more depth to aid your understanding of our position.

Example 9

A restaurateur passes all tips paid by cheque, credit or debit card to a troncmaster who has been elected by members of staff. The troncmaster is responsible for distributing tips to staff in accordance with an allocation framework determined by a staff committee. The employer has no control over the election of the troncmaster or the allocation arrangements.

No National Insurance contributions are due on the tips received by employees. The first condition for exemption is not satisfied because the payments were initially made to the employer. But the alternative condition is satisfied because the employer can in no way (directly or indirectly) be said to be allocating the tips because the allocation is totally independent of the employer and he has no involvement in it or influence over it.

Examples 11 and 12

These concern situations where we would hold that neither of the conditions for exemption is satisfied.

In example 11 the employer passes tips paid by cheque, credit or debit card to a troncmaster elected by the other staff but retains a portion of the tips to cover some of his expenses. The troncmaster distributes the tips passed to her and the distribution is in accordance with rules determined by a staff committee.

In example 12 the employer includes in the employment contract all of his employess a right to participate in the tronc.

The first condition for exemption is not satisfied in either example because we are concerned here with tips paid by cheque, credit or debit card and these are initially paid to the employer so can never satisfy this condition.

The second condition for exemption—that the employer does not allocate the payments, directly or indirectly—is also not satisfied in either scenario.

In example 11 this is because the employer has reduced the amount of tips available for distribution to staff from the tronc by retaining some tips to cover his costs. He has therefore been responsible (albeit indirectly) for the amounts disbursed to employees.

Eg: If tips totalling £100 are received and the tronc determines that it will allocate equal shares to all of the 10 staff then each employee would expect to get £10. If, however, the employer retains £10 this will impact on the distribution and mean that each employee will get only £9.

In such circumstances it is our view that the employer has indirectly allocated the tips and the condition for exemption is therefore not satisfied. National insurance contributions will be due on all payments out of the tronc.

In example 12 the situation is different but the outcome is the same and National Insurance contributions will be payable on all payments out of the tronc. In that example the employer provides in each employee's contract a right to share in the tronc. The employer has accordingly indirectly impacted the allocation of tips because he has promised a share of tips to all employees. Even though he may not have specified any amounts, his actions will have an effect on the amount of tips each employee will receive because his actions mean every employee will get a share of the tips. Given a free hand the troncmaster/tronc committee might have decided that only some employees would participate in the tronc. In these circumstances it is our view that the employer has indirectly allocated the tips and the alternative condition for exemption is accordingly not satisfied.

Example 13

This example concerns a situation where an employer promises their employees—either orally or in a written contract—a minimum amount from the tronc. In such circumstances all payments out of the tronc are contractual payments. As stated above, contractual payments are not gratuities because they are in no way unexpected or spontaneous—rather, they are promised or guaranteed by the employer. They are therefore not covered by the exemption from national insurance contributions provided for by paragraph 5 of Part 10 of Schedule 3 and national insurance contributions will accordingly be due.

There is a flowchart on page 7 of the booklet, which provides a quick guide to how tips are dealt with for national insurance contributions purposes.

NATIONAL MINIMUM WAGE

Only money that is paid by the employer through an employer's payroll counts for national minimum wage (NMW) purposes. Tips that are not paid through the employer's payroll, for example tips paid by a tronc, do not count for NMW purposes.

Increasingly, tips are paid by cheque or credit card and following the decision in Nerva, such payments will initially belong to the employer. However, if the employer gives them away, for example to a tronc, then if the troncmaster or a person other than the employer distributes them, they will not be included in the minimum wage calculation.

Examples 15 to 17 in the booklet illustrate how the NMW legislation operates in regard to tips. It also demonstrates in examples 15 and 16 that payments which do not count for NMW purposes (because they are not paid by the employer through the employer's payroll) may nonetheless attract National Insurance contributions. If an employer influences the allocation of the tronc then he will be liable to pay National Insurance contributions on the tronc payments.

In example 15, the employer combines tronc money with house pay to bring pay up to the NMW. But, as the NMW Regulations (Reg 31(1)(*e*)) only allow payments that have been paid by the employer through the employer's payroll to count as pay for NMW purposes, the employer will fail to meet the NMW criteria. And, having influenced the distribution of tips from the tronc, the employer will be liable for National Insurance contributions on all payments from the tronc.

In example 16 the facts are the same as in example 15 except that the troncmaster arranges for the employer to pay the tronc payments in with the employer's cheque. This may be done for convenience or to bring pay up to NMW levels. But although the pay cheque comes from the employer it does so

PRs etc

after it has been through the tronc payroll. The employer is effectively acting as agent for the troncmaster. The tips have not been paid through the employer's payroll-they have already been allocated through the tronc payroll. The troncmaster will remain responsible for PAYE and the employer for operating National Insurance contributions.

Example 17 in the booklet illustrates the effect on the treatment of tips for NMW and National Insurance contributions purposes if the employer retains some of the cheque or credit card payments to meet his wages bill. Following the decision in Nerva, these monies belong to the employer and in the scenario described have been paid by him through his payroll. The payments will count as pay for NMW purposes and the employer will be liable for National Insurance contributions on these amounts. The employer has interfered with the amount of tips available for distribution by the tronc and has therefore indirectly effected the allocation of the tips. He will therefore be liable for National Insurance contributions on all payments made by the tronc.

There is a flowchart on page 8 of the booklet, which shows how tips are dealt with for NMW purposes.

24 March 2004. Inland Revenue Guidance Notes (updated in April)

Budget 2004—tax treatment of small companies

Following the 2003 Pre-Budget Report announcement about reviewing the way in which companies and their directors/managers are taxed, the Government has announced in Budget 2004 [REV BN 34] that—

- Company profits paid out as distributions (usually dividends) to non-company shareholders will be subject to a minimum rate of corporation tax of 19%.
- The new minimum rate will apply to profits that are distributed to persons other than companies on or after 1 April 2004. The minimum rate will not apply to distributions made to other companies.
- There will be special rules to cover groups and to cover the situation where distributions in an accounting period exceed the profits of that accounting period.

The information in the question and answer brief below is based on the current proposed design of the measures announced in the Budget. The precise detail may be subject to change and cannot be treated as final until the Finance Bill has received Royal Assent.

Mini glossary

CT: Corporation Tax
PCTCT: profits chargeable to corporation tax
NCD: non-corporate distributions

Q1 Will the new rate affect my company?

A This will affect companies who are liable to the starting rate of CT or those receiving marginal relief from the small companies rate if they make distributions of profits other than to companies.

Q2 We are a large company (or group). Are we affected?

A This affects those companies within the group who are liable to the starting rate of CT or those receiving marginal relief from the small companies rate if group companies make distributions of profits other than to companies.

Q3 Will this measure affect groups?

A The measure will affect groups where a company within a group makes a distribution to a non-company shareholder and that company has profits chargeable to CT at the starting rate, or receives marginal relief from the small companies' rate (see also question 19).

Q4 Will this affect any other liability of the company or its directors (such as PAYE and NIC)?

A No.

Q5 Does this replace the IR35 legislation?

A No. Measures to tackle service companies were introduced in 2000 to ensure that employees could not avoid tax and NI contributions by using a company as an intermediary between them and their employer.

Q6 If this doesn't replace the IR35 legislation is there a double charge?

A The interaction of the new non-corporate distribution rate with the ''IR35 legislation'' creates a double charge.

- Where the company has engagements that are within the intermediaries legislation and is treated as having made a ''deemed payment'' under that legislation there will not be a double charge on either the individual or on the company arising from the non-corporate distribution rate.
- Under the existing legislation the individual is prevented from suffering a double charge. Where a company is treated as making a deemed payment and it makes a distribution in the same tax year or in a subsequent year, it can claim relief in order to avoid a double charge to tax on the individual.
- Relief is given by setting the amount of the deemed payment against the relevant distribution so as to reduce the distribution that is taxable on the individual. This is by virtue of the intermediaries legislation found in section 58(4) of the Income Tax (Earnings and Pensions) Act 2003 (ITEPA).
- As the relief provided in section 58(4) reduces the distribution it also ensures that for the purposes of assessing corporation tax due, the amount of the distribution taken into account to assess the corporation tax payable will be net of the deemed payment arising from the intermediaries legislation.
- In addition of course, where the company has engagements that are within the intermediaries legislation and is treated as having made a ''deemed payment'' under that legislation, that deemed payment and the employers national insurance contributions thereon is deductible against the company's profits for CT purposes. This is provided for by paragraph 17 of Schedule 12 to the Finance Act 2000.

Q7 How do I work out whether or not I have got to apply the new rate?

A. If your company pays corporation tax at an underlying rate of less than 19% and you make a distribution eg pay a dividend to someone other than a company then this new rate is likely to apply.

Example A

Assume that PCTCT for an accounting period are £8,000. These profits are distributed by way of a dividend to individuals. The tax computation would be—

PCTCT	£8,000 @ 0%	=	£0.00
Corporation Tax due		=	£0.00
the underlying rate: (tax/PCTCT x 100)	0.00/8,000 x 100	=	0%
Non corporate distribution	£8,000 @ 19%	=	£1,520.00
Remaining PCTCT			NIL
Total CT due			£1,520.00

Example B

Assume that PCTCT are £40,000. The distributions made in the accounting period totalled £35,000 of which £10,000 were made to a company. The tax computation would be—

PCTCT £40,000 @ 19%	=	£7,600.00
Less: Marginal Relief (£50,000 – 40,000 x 19/400)	=	£ 475.00
Corporation Tax due on basic profits	=	£7,125.00
the **underlying rate** is 7125.00/40000 x 100	=	17.8125%
Non corporate distribution £25,000 @ 19%	=	£4,750.00
Remaining PCTCT £15,000 @ 17.8125%	=	£2,671.87
Total CT due		£7,421.87

Q8 What is meant by "underlying rate"?

A Underlying rate can be calculated as follows—

$$\frac{tax \times 100}{profits}$$

(See examples at question 7).

Q9 What help is available to work it out?

A You may obtain help through our special ''Distribution Rate Helpline'' by phoning 0845 3021418. For the hard of hearing, deaf, blind and speech impaired customers assistance is available from the Typetalk service. The number to dial for this service is 18001 0845 302 1418. There will also be full guidance on the calculation in the Company Tax Return Guide. And for those companies delivering their returns on-line the calculation will be done automatically.

Q10 If I get the tax due wrong will the company be charged interest or penalties?

A The normal interest and penalty provisions will apply.

Q11 Where do we make a return of the extra tax?

A On your corporation tax self-assessment return.

Q12 When is the tax due to be paid?

A On the normal due date for the payment of corporation tax for small companies, nine months and one day after the end of the accounting period.

Q13 When does the new rate start—which distributions—what profits?

A The new rate when distributions are made to non company shareholders on or after 1 April 2004. Where an accounting period begins before 1 April 2004 and ends on or after that date the profits are apportioned (see examples).

Example

Company has AP for the year to 30 June 2004
PCTCT for AP £40000
Distributions: £15000 on 1 November 2003[1]
£20000 on 1 May 2004 of which: 20% (£4000) to a company[2]
80% (16000) to individuals[3]

£40000 x 9/12 = £30000 pre 1/4/2004
£40000 x 3/12 = £10000 post 1/4/2004[4]
Distributions (£20000) exceed basic PCTCT of the relevant part of the AP (£10000)
Proportion of PCTCT which can be matched is £10000 x 80% (NCDs as a percentage of total relevant distributions) = £8000
Underlying rate of CT for the AP is 17.8125% (see working 1)

Working 1

£40000 @ 19%		=	7,600
Less-Marginal relief 50000–40000 x 19/400		=	475
CT on profits		=	7,125
Underlying Rate:	Tax / Profit = 7,125 x 100 / 40,000	=	17.8125%

The total tax for the AP is therefore:

non-corporate distributions (NDR) applies to £8000 @ 19%	=	1,520
remaining PCTCT at underlying rate £32000 @ 17.8125 %	=	5,700
Total CT Due	=	7,220

Excess NCDs to be carried forward to next AP is £16,000-£8,000 (matched this AP) = £8,000.

[1] Does not come into the calculation of the NDR as before 1 April 2004.
[2] NDR rate will not apply to that part.
[3] New rate will apply.
[4] Only post 1/4/2004 profits fall to be considered for NDR.

Q14 What happens if the distributions in an accounting period are more than the profits?

A Where distributions exceed PCTCT for the accounting period, the excess is taken forward to the next or subsequent accounting periods to be ‘‘franked’’ against future PCTCT.

Q15 Is there any carry back of excess distributions or losses?

A The excess will not be carried back and the normal rules apply to losses.

Q16 What happens if the company makes a profit but no distribution?

A The normal rates of CT apply.

Q17 What happens if we pay distributions to other companies?

A. These distributions are disregarded for the purpose of working out whether the new rate applies. Where there is an excess of distributions over PCTCT only that part of the excess related to distributions to companies is disregarded.

Q18 What do I do about dividends received from other companies when working out the corporation tax due?

A There is no change to the way profits are calculated for corporation tax purposes. This change only affects the rate at which profits are charged.

Q19 What happens if my company is part of a group of companies?

A. Each company in the group needs to consider if it has made a distribution to a non-company shareholder and what rate of tax applies to its profits for that accounting period.

Where there are insufficient PCTCT in the company to cover non-company distributions (NCDs), there will be rules for allocating the excess to other companies within the group that can absorb the excess. These rules will include—

– The procedure for allocating excess NCDs;
– Carry forward of excess NCDs;

- Allocations of excess NCDs proving to be excessive;
- Degrouping—to cover situations where a company leaves a group.

Where there are insufficient PCTCT within the group to cover the distribution the remaining excess is carried forward to subsequent accounting periods. (see examples).

Example

Company A

Company A is 75% owned by an individual Mr X and 25% owned by another company.

It has no income other than the distribution received from company B (£12,000 x 80% = £9,600).

Company A makes a distribution of £9,600 of which (£9,600 x 75%) £7,200 is an NCD.

Company A has no PCTCT so no CT liability.

Company A's excess NCD is therefore £7,200 to be allocated as far as is possible within the group.

Company B

The recipient company B is 20% owned by an individual Mrs Y, the remaining shares held by holding company A.

It has profits of £10,000 and makes a distribution of £12,000.

Amount of NCD's matched in company B			
total NCD £12,000 x20%		=	£2,400
less matched in this accounting period £10,000 x 20%		=	£2,000
own NCDs carried forward		=	£400
Remaining unmatched profits in company B are £10,000-£2,000		=	£8,000

The maximum capacity to absorb unmatched excess NCD's from company A are £8,000 x 75% = £6,000.

Company A therefore allocates £6,000 to Company B and carries forward £1,200 (£7,200 – £6,000) excess NCD's.

Limits for Marginal relief:	£50,000/2	=	£25,000
	£10,000/2	=	£5,000
PCTCT £10000 @ 19 %		=	1,900.00
Marginal relief (£25000 – £10000) x 19/400		=	712.50
Tax		=	1,187.50
Underlying rate therefore	$\frac{1,187.50}{10,000}$ x 100	=	11.875%
Corporation Tax chargeable:			
NCD rate on 2000 @ 19%		=	£380.00
NCD rate on 6,000 allocated from Company A @ 19%		=	£1,140.00
remaining PCTCT (10,000 – {2,000 +6,000}) x 11.875%		=	£237.50
Total CT Due		=	£2,137.50

Q20 My company has paid a distribution but made a loss. Is it correct that the company will not pay tax?

A If you are part of a group, another company within the group may have the excess distributions allocated to it and that company will pay the appropriate rate of tax. Otherwise the excess will be carried forward the appropriate rate will apply when you have chargeable profits.

Q21 If companies wish to disincorporate so that the owner once again becomes self employed, what will the tax consequences be?

A The normal rules relevant to the transfer of assets and the winding up of a company will apply.

April 2004. Tax Bulletin 70

Money Laundering Regulations 2003

The Money Laundering Regulations 2003 came into force, in the main, from 1st March 2004. The regulations were accompanied by Orders to amend the provisions on money laundering and terrorist finance in the Proceeds of Crime Act 2002 and the Terrorism Act 2000.

This legislation imposes some important new obligations upon professionals from a wide range of sectors, including Tax advisers, Accountants, Auditors, Insolvency Practitioners and Legal advisers. These obligations relate to the need of such professionals to make reports to the authorities on money laundering and the need to have systems in place to train staff and keep records.

INTRODUCTION

Under Section 330 of the Proceeds of Crime Act 2002 (POCA 2002) individuals carrying on ''relevant business'' may be guilty of an offence of failing to disclose knowledge or suspicion of money laundering where they know or suspect, or have reasonable grounds for knowing or suspecting, that another person is engaged in laundering the proceeds of crime. This concerns the proceeds of all crime including all acts of tax evasion and fraud.

In addition to the obligation to report, there are three further money laundering offences—

- concealing criminal proceeds;
- assisting another person to retain criminal proceeds; and
- acquiring, possessing or using criminal proceeds.

These ''principal money laundering offences'' have been in force since 24 February 2003, and apply to any individual or business.

CONSENT

The legislation also contains provisions whereby consent may be necessary from NCIS to proceed with a transaction. Where consent is required, time limits have been introduced for the handling of applications. From the working day after consent has been sought, NCIS have undertaken a seven working day notice period in which to either issue or withhold consent. If consent is withheld, law enforcement have a further 31 calendar day moratorium period in which to obtain a restraint order. If neither deadline is met, the person who made the disclosure may proceed with the transaction or continue with the arrangement without committing an offence.

RELEVANT BUSINESS

The Money Laundering Regulations 2003 and accompanying Orders expanded the categories of those carrying on relevant business and falling within the Regulated sector. With effect from 1st March 2004, these categories now include—

- Estate Agency work;
- Casino operators;
- Insolvency practitioners;
- Tax advisers (providing by way of business advice about the tax affairs of another person);
- Accountants (providing by way of business accountancy services);
- Auditors (providing by way of business audit services by a person who is eligible for appointment as a company auditor under section 25 of the Companies Act 1989(*c*) or Article 28 of the Companies (Northern Ireland) Order 1990(*d*));
- Legal advisers (providing by way of business legal services which involve participation in a financial or real property transaction);
- Company formation agents (providing by way of business services in relation to the formation, operation or management of a company or trust). This has not been intended to include anyone who assists in the management or operation of that company;
- Dealers in high value goods (by way of business whenever a transaction involves accepting a total cash payment of 15,000 Euro or more). Please note that for high value dealers the regulations will not come into force until 1 April 2004.

In practice a wide variety of business has been brought in the regulated sector such as certain jewellers and car dealers. Businesses may need to seek legal advice to understand the implications of the new legislation for their activities, notably whether or not they fall within the expanded Regulated Sector.

Reports, including those concerning suspicion of tax evasion, are to be made to the National Criminal Intelligence Service (NCIS) on a Suspicious Activity Report form(*s*).

SUSPICIOUS ACTIVITY REPORT FORMS (SAR)

With effect from 1st March NCIS have updated and improved the SAR form(*s*). These can be downloaded from their website at www.ncis.co.uk/disclosure.asp.

In particular a Limited Intelligence Value report has been introduced for use in circumstances where the information being reported is likely to be of limited intelligence value. The NCIS website provides guidance on the types of circumstances where this abbreviated report can be used.

INLAND REVENUE ENQUIRIES AND HANSARD

Reports that concern evasion of direct tax or NICs, and that are not linked to wider criminality, will be forwarded by NCIS to the Inland Revenue as the investigating body and, in England and Wales, the prosecuting body for these offences. (In Scotland the Procurator Fiscal and in Northern Ireland the Director of Public Prosecutions are the prosecuting bodies).

Inland Revenue enquiries that result will be carried out in the same manner as any other Inland Revenue enquiry. In particular reporting a case to NCIS ahead of notifying the Revenue will have no bearing on how the Revenue may treat a case, if the taxpayer is actively seeking to set their affairs straight. This also applies to cases dealt with under the Inland Revenue approach to civil settlements known as 'Hansard'.

MARKER LETTERS

Where an Agent is acting for a client who wishes to make a voluntary disclosure to the Revenue of their tax evasion the Agent is still required to submit a Suspicious Activity Report to NCIS. As the requirement to submit the Suspicious Activity Report is ''as soon as is practicable'' (PCA 2002 s 330) this is likely to be before the Agent is in a position to approach the Revenue, on behalf of their client, with full details of the extent of the tax evasion committed.

A number of the professional accountancy and taxation bodies have suggested that Agents in these circumstances, having obtained their client's permission, may wish to send a ''marker letter'' to the Revenue. This is so that the Revenue knows of their client's intention to make a voluntary disclosure. The ''marker letter'' will be sent at the same time or shortly after making the report to NCIS. It will provide a date by which the Agent expects, on behalf of the taxpayer, to provide the Revenue with a full disclosure.

In order to ensure that these letters are properly dealt with, Agents sending a ''marker letter'' are requested to send these to—

SDS Compliance Centre for Revenue Intelligence
Financial Investigation Unit
Ground Floor
Ty Glas Road
Llanishen
Cardiff
CF14 5ZG

An acknowledgement letter will be sent to the Agent to confirm receipt.

FURTHER GUIDANCE

Further guidance on the Proceeds of Crime Act 2002 can be found in Issue 13 (June 2003) of Working Together magazine. Guidance is also available on the Home Office (www.homeoffice.gov.uk/crimpol/oic/proceeds/index.html), Treasury (www.hm-treasury.gov.uk/moneylaundering) and NCIS (www.ncis.gov.uk) websites.

In addition the professional accountancy and taxation bodies and the Law Society have published extensive guidance in this area.

MISCELLANEOUS NON-STATUTORY MATERIAL

CONTENTS

Note—The number before each publication (eg Misc I) does not appear in the official version. It has been added by the publishers to facilitate identification.

Misc I. Prospectus for certificates of tax deposits (series 7)

1

(i) The Commissioners of Inland Revenue are authorised by the Lords Commissioners of Her Majesty's Treasury to accept from persons liable to certain UK taxes and other liabilities deposits under the terms of this prospectus. Certificates to be known as certificates of tax deposit will be issued by the Treasury in respect of these deposits under the National Loans Act 1968 s 12.

(ii) The deposits will be paid into the National Loans Fund and the principal of and interest on deposits will be a charge on the National Loans Fund with recourse to the UK Consolidated Fund.

(iii) Deposits under the terms of this prospectus will be accepted from 1 October 1993 and thereafter until the Treasury give notice in the manner prescribed in paragraph 8 below (''the prescribed manner''). The Treasury may, on giving such notice, temporarily suspend the taking of deposits under this prospectus.

2 LODGING OF DEPOSITS

(i) Deposits may be made by individuals, trustees, companies or other persons or bodies for the payment of any taxes or liabilities listed in the Schedule hereto (hereinafter referred to collectively as ''scheduled liability'' or ''scheduled liabilities'') assessed on or due from them. Partnerships may make deposits for the payment of scheduled liabilities assessed on the partnership. Personal representatives may make deposits for payment of scheduled liabilities due on or from the estate of a deceased person.

(ii) Deposits of £100,000 or more, or such sum as the Treasury may determine on giving notice in the prescribed manner, must be remitted direct to the Bank of England (Drawing Office) in London for credit to the General Account of the Commissioners of Inland Revenue, No 23411007.[1] Such remittances should indicate that they are intended for a certificate of tax deposit and a confirmatory letter should be sent without delay to the Central Accounting Office (CTD), Inland Revenue (A), Barrington Road, Worthing, West Sussex BN12 4XH, stating the name and address of the depositor and the date and amount of the remittance. Deposits of less than £100,000, or such other figure as the Treasury may determine on giving notice in the prescribed manner, may be made at any Inland Revenue tax collecting office in the UK, but may not be made by direct remittance to the Bank of England.

(iii) The first deposit made by a depositor under this prospectus must be of an amount which will bring the balance which he has on deposit under this prospectus and Series 1–6 prospectuses up to a minimum of £2,000. The Treasury may from time to time, on giving notice in the prescribed manner, vary the minimum balance figure. Such a variation will not affect a deposit which has already been made but any subsequent deposit, whether made by a new or existing depositor, must bring the depositor's balance under Series 1–7 prospectuses up to the new minimum. No deposit may be made of less than £500 or such other figure as may be notified by the Treasury from time to time in the prescribed manner.

(iv) A certificate of tax deposit will be issued to the depositor for each deposit, specifying the amount and the date on which the deposit was received at the relevant Revenue tax collecting office (hereinafter referred to as ''the certificate date''). In the case of a deposit remitted direct to the Bank of England in London, the certificate date will be the date on which the funds are credited to the Inland Revenue's General Account at the Bank of England. It should be noted that a direct remittance to the Bank of England by cheque may take some days to clear and there will be a corresponding delay in the crediting of the funds to the Revenue's General Account.

3 TENDER OF DEPOSITS IN PAYMENT OF TAX ETC

(i) A certificate of tax deposit may be tendered by the depositor (which expression shall where appropriate include the personal representatives of the depositor) in or towards payment of any scheduled liability. The Treasury may add taxes or other liabilities to the Schedule by giving notice in the prescribed manner and any certificate of tax deposit issued under this prospectus may be tendered in respect of any tax or liability listed in the Schedule current at the date of tender (hereinafter called ''the current Schedule''). The Treasury may also delete taxes or other liabilities from the Schedule on giving notice in the prescribed manner. However, deposits having a certificate date prior to the date from which a deletion is effective will be accepted in or towards settlement of a deleted liability. Updated copies of the Schedule may be obtained from any Revenue tax collecting office, or from the Financial Services Office (CTD), Inland Revenue, on demand.

(ii) A certificate of tax deposit tendered in payment of a scheduled liability must be presented to the office prescribed in relation to that scheduled liability in the current Schedule and be accompanied by any documents specified therein; the tender must comply with any other requirements so specified. The Treasury may vary or add to any of these requirements by giving notice in the prescribed manner.

(iii) If a deposit is duly tendered in respect of any scheduled liability that liability will be treated as paid, to the extent of the deposit and any accrued interest, on the date which for the purposes of this prospectus is the due date in relation to that scheduled liability, or on the certificate date, whichever is the later. For all purposes of certificates of tax deposit the date (hereinafter called "the deemed due date") on which the relevant scheduled liability is deemed to be due is the date shown in the current Schedule in relation to that liability. In general, the date shown in the current Schedule in relation to a liability is or relates to the date on which the scheduled liability normally becomes due and payable under the relevant legislation and does not change if for any reason an assessment is made late or the scheduled liability is not payable until later (for example on the settlement of a tax appeal). If the date on which the scheduled liability normally becomes due and payable under the relevant legislation is at any time altered by statute then the deemed due date will automatically be modified accordingly for all purposes of this prospectus.

(iv) The tendering of a certificate of tax deposit will not preclude the charge of interest which has accrued prior to the certificate date on any part of the scheduled liability or the charge of interest on any part of the scheduled liability not satisfied by the deposit and any accrued interest thereon.

(v) Deposits will be applied in payment of scheduled liabilities in such order as the depositor may require. Neither the Revenue nor any other Government Department can advise on the order in which the deposits should be applied.

(vi) If a deposit is applied in payment of a scheduled liability and part of the principal remains unused it may, if not withdrawn for cash, be applied in or towards payment of a future scheduled liability. A balance certificate will be issued to the depositor for the remaining principal, which will bear the same date as the original certificate for the purposes of this prospectus.

4 INTEREST ON DEPOSITS

(i) Interest will accrue on deposits on a daily basis for the interest period and will not be compounded. This period, which will not in any case exceed six years, will run from the certificate date until the deemed due date of the scheduled liability in payment of which it is applied or the date on which the deposit is withdrawn for cash (as to which see para 6(v) below).

(ii) The rate of interest applicable to a deposit during each year of the interest period will be the rate in force on the first day of that year, namely the certificate date or an anniversary thereof. If more than one rate is in force on that day, the rate applicable to an individual deposit will be determined by one or more of the following factors—

(*a*) the number of calendar months for which the deposit is held in the relevant year;

(*b*) whether the deposit is ultimately applied in payment of a scheduled liability or withdrawn for cash, and

(*c*) whether or not the deposit on the first day of the relevant year is less than £100,000, or such other amount as the Treasury may specify, on giving notice in the prescribed manner.

(iii) The rate or rates of interest in force on any day will be notified by the Treasury from time to time in the prescribed manner.

(iv) Though it will attract no further interest or other increment a deposit may, subject to para 7 below, be maintained after the end of six years.

(v) Interest will be allowed, or in the case of withdrawals for cash will be paid, without deduction of tax, but in all cases will be itself income of the depositor or his estate for tax purposes.

5 DEPOSITS APPLIED IN PAYMENT OF TAX ETC

Interest will be allowed on the full amount of a deposit applied in payment of a scheduled liability so long as the principal together with accrued interest does not exceed the amount of the scheduled liability in respect of which the deposit is to be applied. If the deposit is so applied, and the principal together with accrued interest would exceed the amount of the scheduled liability, interest will be allowed only on such part of the principal as with interest on that part is equal to the amount of the scheduled liability—and that part of the principal with interest will be applied in payment of the scheduled liability. Any balance of the deposit, after payment of the scheduled liability, will be subject to the terms of para 3(vi) above.

6 WITHDRAWALS FOR CASH

(i) A deposit or part of a deposit, together with accrued interest, may be withdrawn for cash at any time. Deposits may be withdrawn for cash in such order as the depositor shall require. A request for such withdrawal should be accompanied by the relevant certificate of tax deposit. If a deposit is partly withdrawn for cash a balance certificate will be issued to the depositor for the remaining principal, which will bear the same date as the original certificate for the purposes of this prospectus.

(ii) Subject to sub-para (iii) below, requests for deposits to be withdrawn for cash should be made to the Financial Services Office (CTD), Inland Revenue (A), Barrington Road, Worthing, West Sussex, BN12 4XH. Repayment will normally be made within ten working days of receipt of the request.

(iii) If a deposit is to be applied partly in payment of a scheduled liability and the balance immediately to be withdrawn for cash a request for both application in payment of the scheduled liability and withdrawal of the balance should be made to the office prescribed in relation to that scheduled liability in the Schedule.

(iv) Repayments will be made by a payable order drawn in favour of the depositor and will, unless the depositor or his personal representatives instruct otherwise, be sent to the address given on the certificate of tax deposit. However, in the case of deposits made by remittance direct to the Bank of England in London for credit to the Revenue's General Account repayments will, if requested, be made direct to a bank for credit to the depositor's bank account.

(v) For interest purposes, the day on which a payable order for repayment is issued or the day on which instructions are given to the Bank of England to debit the Revenue's General Account and directly to credit the depositor's bank account, as the case may be, will be deemed to be the date on which the deposit, or part of the deposit, is withdrawn for cash.

7 TERMINATION OF SCHEME

(i) If, as provided in para 1(iii) above, the Treasury give notice that no further deposits are to be received under the terms of this prospectus, deposits held after the giving of such notice must be applied in satisfaction of a scheduled liability or withdrawn for cash within the period (if any) specified in the notice. This period will be not less than six years.

(ii) Temporary suspension of deposit-taking, as provided in para 1(iii), will not affect existing deposits in any way.

8 NOTICE

For the purposes of para 1(iii), (ii), (iii), 3(i), (ii), 4(ii) and (iii) above the Treasury will give notice to depositors by the issue of a Treasury Press Notice to Reuters. The Treasury reserve the right, if circumstances prevent the issue of a Press Notice or would prevent such a Press Notice from receiving publicity which is in their view adequate, to make the notification in any other manner which they think fit. Notification will as soon as reasonably possible thereafter be recorded in the Edinburgh and London Gazettes.

9 OTHER TERMS

(i) Deposits will not be transferable, except that a company's deposits may be applied in payment of a scheduled liability payable by a company which is either the first company's holding company or its subsidiary or another subsidiary of its holding company, these terms having the meanings given to them in the Companies Act 1985 s 736.

(ii) Neither the Revenue nor any other Government Department will, except as ordered by a court of competent jurisdiction, be bound to recognise any transfer, charge, trust or equity affecting the ownership of a deposit or a certificate of tax deposit. Save as aforesaid depositors will be regarded by the Revenue or any other Government Department as exclusively entitled to the benefit of deposits and the obligations created by them.

Copies of this prospectus may be obtained from any Revenue tax collecting office or from the Financial Services Office (CTD) Inland Revenue (A), Barrington Road, Worthing, West Sussex, BN12 4XH. Updated copies of the Schedule to the prospectus may also be obtained individually from these offices.

HM Treasury, London SW1P 3AG

1 October 1993

SCHEDULE

TAX	DUE DATES
Income tax (except PAYE tax, amounts deducted from payments to sub-contractors, and as specified below)	
If payable in one sum	1 January in the year of assessment for which the tax is payable.
If payable in two instalments (Cases I & II of Schedule D)	1st Instalment—1 January in the year of assessment for which the tax is payable. 2nd Instalment—1 July next following the end of the year of assessment for which the tax is payable.
Income tax charged at a rate other than the basic rate on income from which income tax has been deducted (otherwise than under TA 1988 s 203) or from or on which income tax is treated as having been deducted or paid, or income chargeable under Schedule F	1 December next following the end of the year of assessment for which the tax is payable.

TAX	DUE DATES
Surtax	1 January next following the end of the year of assessment for which the tax is payable. (Note: As surtax ceased to be charged for years after 1972–73 no interest can accrue on deposits applied in payment of that tax.)
Capital gains tax	1 December next following the end of the year of assessment for which the tax is payable
Inheritance tax	
— on death and on lifetime transfers not chargeable when made	6 months after the end of the month in which the death occurs or, as regards tax paid by personal representatives on delivery of their account, on the date of delivery of that account, if earlier.
— on lifetime gifts when made, and on occasions of charge under IHTA 1984 Pt III Ch II	6 months after the end of the month in which the chargeable transfer is made or if the transfer is made after 5 April and before 1 October in any year, at the end of April in the next year.
Development land tax	(not reproduced)
Income tax payable by building societies Income tax payable by banks	1 January in the year of assessment for which the tax is payable.
Advance corporation tax on payments which are "qualifying distributions"(TA 1988 ss 14, 238) Income tax on payments by companies which are "relevant payments" (TA 1988 s 350(4))	14 days after the end of the return period.
Petroleum revenue tax Advance petroleum revenue tax Petroleum royalty Gas levy	(not reproduced)

Note

Depositors are reminded that under para 3(iii) of the prospectus the dates shown above as the due dates are (subject to amendment of the relevant legislation) the dates on which the relevant scheduled liabilities are deemed to be due for all purposes of certificates of tax deposit. The deemed due date does not change if for any reason an assessment is made late or the scheduled liability is not payable until later (for example on the settlement of a tax appeal).

HM Treasury, London SW1P 3AG;

1 October 1993.

Notes—Rates of interest on certificates of tax deposit can be found in *Simon's Direct Tax Service*, Binder 1, Tax Tables and *Simon's Weekly Tax Intelligence*. Rates of interest can also be obtained from Inland Revenue Financial Accounting Office at Worthing, telephone 01903 700222 ext 2064/2065.

[1] An amendment issued by the Inland Revenue Compliance Division states that deposits of £100,000 or more should be forwarded to the Bank of England by telegraphic transfer or CHAPS (Clearing House Automated Payment System) for the credit of the Inland Revenue Miscellaneous Receipts Account, account number 23430788, sort code 10—00—00.

Misc II. Inland Revenue booklet IR 20

RESIDENTS AND NON-RESIDENTS—LIABILITY TO TAX IN THE UK

PREFACE

The notes in this booklet reflect the law and practice at October 1999. They are not binding in law and do not affect rights of appeal about your own tax.

You should bear in mind that the booklet offers general guidance on how the rules apply, but whether the guidance is appropriate in a particular case will depend on all the facts of that case. If you have any difficulty in applying the rules in your own case, you should consult an Inland Revenue Tax Office—see paragraphs 7 9 of the Introduction on contacting the Inland Revenue.

Some practices explained in this booklet are concessions made by the Inland Revenue. A concession will not be given in any case where an attempt is made to use it for tax avoidance. Where the booklet mentions a concession, the reference given (for example 'extra-statutory concession A11') is the number of the concession in booklet IR1 'Extra-statutory concessions', which provides further details.

INTRODUCTION

General

1 Broadly, the United Kingdom (UK) charges tax on—

- income arising in the UK, whether or not the person to whom it belongs is resident in the UK
- income arising outside the UK which belongs to people resident in the UK
- gains accruing on the disposal of assets anywhere in the world which belong to people resident or ordinarily resident in the UK.

2 Special rules apply in some circumstances, but generally the amount of income tax and capital gains tax you have to pay depends on whether you are resident and/or ordinarily resident in the UK, and in some cases on your domicile.

3 The first part of this booklet explains what is meant by 'residence', 'ordinary residence' and 'domicile'. The second part explains how these factors affect how much income tax and capital gains tax you have to pay in the UK, and how the normal rules of taxation may be modified in some cases where a double taxation agreement applies.

4 The third part of the booklet outlines the rules for payment of UK National Insurance contributions for individuals going abroad or coming to the UK.

5 The booklet is only concerned with individuals. It does not cover the position of companies, trusts, clubs, societies or other legal persons. Nor does it deal with inheritance tax. Booklet IHT 18 'Inheritance tax. Foreign aspects' explains how your domicile can affect the inheritance tax position if you transfer property, normally on or within seven years of death.

Definitions used in this booklet

6 Several terms used in this booklet have a particular meaning, as follows—

Tax Year	The 12 months starting with 6 April in one year and ending with 5 April in the following year. For example, the tax year 1999–2000 runs from 6 April 1999 to 5 April 2000.
United Kingdom	England, Wales, Scotland and Northern Ireland, including the territorial sea (that is, waters within 12 nautical miles of the shore).
Abroad/overseas	Anywhere outside the UK. The Channel Islands and the Isle of Man are abroad (except in the limited context of certain bilateral Social Security Agreements—see paragraph 11.1).

Contacting the Inland Revenue

7 If you have any queries on your tax position, you should contact your Tax Office. Your employer will normally be able to tell you the address. If you have just come to the UK, or for any other reason you do not know which office deals with your tax affairs, you should write to your local Tax Office—the address is in the phone book under 'Inland Revenue'. If you have a National Insurance number, please give it in your letter.

8 A system of self-assessment applies to individuals from 1996–97. This requires you to work out for yourself what tax you owe (calculating your own tax is, however, optional if you submit your tax return by a certain date, normally 30 September following the tax year). Initially, we will accept and process the figures in your return—except for any obvious mistakes, which we will correct. After processing, we will check all cases and select some for further examination.

We will provide guidance to help you calculate your tax liability or make any claim. We will ask you to give sufficient detail of your income and circumstances to allow us to check your tax return.

9 In a number of places this booklet refers to matters that are dealt with by specialist offices of the Inland Revenue. These offices and their addresses are as follows—

Financial Intermediaries and Claims Office (FICO), Bootle (Residence Advice and Liabilities—Unit 373), St John's House, Merton Road, Bootle, Merseyside, England, L69 9BB (Telephone number 0151–472 6196. If phoning from abroad, 44 151 472 6196)

Financial Intermediaries and Claims Office (FICO), (Non Resident Claims), Fitz Roy House, PO Box 46, England, NG2 1BD (Telephone number 0115–974 2000. If phoning from abroad, 44 115 974 2000)

HM Inspector of Taxes Cardiff 4 (Foreign Section), Ty-Glas, Llanishen, Cardiff, Wales, CF4 5GN, (Telephone number 01222 325000)

Foreign Compliance, Compliance Centre 1, Queensway House, East Kilbride, Glasgow, Scotland, G79 1AA (Telephone number 01355 275877/ 275733/ 275795)

Foreign Entertainers Unit, Prince's Gate, 2–6 Homer Road, Solihull, West Midlands, England, B91 3WG (Telephone number 0121–606 2861/2/3)

HM Inspector of Taxes Cardiff 1, Phase 2 Building, Ty-Glas, Llanishen, Cardiff, Wales, CF4 5FN (Telephone number 01222 326077/8/9)

National Insurance Contributions Office, International Services, Benton Park Road, Newcastle upon Tyne, NE98 1ZZ (Telephone number 06451–54811. If phoning from abroad, 44 191 2254811)

Commentary—*Simon's Direct Tax Service* **Part E6**.

PART I

MEANING OF 'RESIDENCE', 'ORDINARY RESIDENCE' AND 'DOMICILE' FOR TAX PURPOSES

1 Residence and ordinary residence

1.1 The terms 'residence' and 'ordinary residence' are not defined in the Taxes Acts. The guidelines to their meaning in this Chapter and in Chapters 2 (residence status of those leaving the UK) and 3 (those coming to the UK) are largely based on rulings of the Courts. This booklet sets out the main factors that are taken into account, but we can only make a decision on your residence status on the facts in your particular case.

As mentioned in paragraph 1.4, even if you are resident (or ordinarily resident) in the UK under these rules, the terms of a double taxation agreement with another country might affect your final tax position if, for example, you are resident in both that country and the UK.

Residence

1.2 To be regarded as resident in the UK you must normally be physically present in the country at some time in the tax year. You will always be resident if you are here for 183 days or more in the tax year. There are no exceptions to this. You count the total number of days you spend in the UK—it does not matter if you come and go several times during the year or if you are here for one stay of 183 days or more. If you are here for less than 183 days, you may still be treated as resident for the year under other tests (see Chapter 3, and in particular paragraph 3.3).

The normal rule is that days of arrival in and departure from the UK are ignored in counting the days spent in the UK, in all the various cases where calculations have to be made to determine your residence position—see for example paragraphs 2.2, 3.3 and 3.4 and the examples in 2.10 and 3.6. (This rule is not relevant to the concessionary split year treatment described in paragraphs 1.5–1.6, where a person coming to or leaving the UK part way through a tax year is resident from the date of arrival or to the date of departure.)

Ordinary residence

1.3 If you are resident in the UK year after year, you are treated as ordinarily resident here. You may be resident but not ordinarily resident in the UK for a tax year if, for example, you normally live outside the UK but are in this country for 183 days or more in the year. Or you may be ordinarily resident but not resident for a tax year if, for example, you usually live in the UK but have gone abroad for a long holiday and do not set foot in the UK during that year.

Residence in both the UK and another country

1.4 It is possible to be resident (or ordinarily resident) in both the UK and some other country (or countries) at the same time. If you are resident (or ordinarily resident) in another country, this does not mean that you cannot also be resident (or ordinarily resident) in the UK. Where, however, you are resident both in the UK and a country with which the UK has a double taxation agreement, there may be special provisions in the agreement for treating you as a resident of only one of the countries for the purposes of the agreement (see paragraph 9.2).

Leaving or coming to the UK part way through a tax year

1.5 Strictly, you are taxed as a UK resident for the whole of a tax year if you are resident here for any part of it. But if you leave or come to the UK part way through a tax year, the year may, by concession (extra-statutory concession A11), be split. Where this applies, your tax liabilities on income which are affected by tax residence will be calculated on the basis of the period of your actual residence here during the year (see also paragraph 5.4). This has the same effect as splitting the tax year into resident and not resident periods.

1.6 Split year treatment applies where

- you have been not ordinarily resident in the UK and you come to live here permanently or to stay for at least two years. You are taxed as a resident only from the date of your arrival; or
- you have been resident in the UK* and you leave to live abroad permanently or for a period of at least three years, and on your departure are not ordinarily resident in the UK. You are taxed as a resident only up to and including the date of your departure; or
- you have been resident in the UK* and you leave to take up full-time employment abroad, and you meet certain conditions (see paragraphs 2.2–2.3). You are taxed as a resident only up to and including the date of your departure (and from the date when you return to the UK).

* other than resident only as a short term visitor—see paragraph 3.3.

1.7 For certain types of income of a non-resident the UK tax charged is limited to any tax deducted before payment (see paragraphs 5.15, 6.3 and 6.11). This only applies, however, to complete years of non-residence. Where the tax year is split, the limitation does not apply to the part of the year for which you are treated as though you were not resident.

Split year treatment does not apply if you come to the UK as a short term visitor, or if you come for only limited periods with no intention to live here permanently or to stay for at least two years. (See paragraph 3.3 for details of the rules that apply in this case.)

Commentary—*Simon's Direct Tax Service* **Part E6.**

2 Leaving the UK

Short absences

2.1 You are resident and ordinarily resident in the UK if you usually live in this country and only go abroad for short periods—for example, on holiday or on business trips.

Working abroad

2.2 If you leave the UK to work full-time abroad under a contract of employment, you are treated as not resident and not ordinarily resident if you meet all the following conditions

- your absence from the UK and your employment abroad both last for at least a whole tax year
- during your absence any visits you make to the UK
  - total less than 183 days in any tax year, and
  - average less than 91 days a tax year. (The average is taken over the period of absence up to a maximum of four years—see paragraph 2.10. Any days spent in the UK because of exceptional circumstances beyond your control, for example the illness of yourself or a member of your immediate family, are not normally counted for this purpose.)

2.3 If you meet all the conditions in paragraph 2.2, you are treated as not resident and not ordinarily resident in the UK from the day after you leave the UK to the day before you return to the UK at the end of your employment abroad. You are treated as coming to the UK permanently on the day you return from your employment abroad and as resident and ordinarily resident from that date.

If there is a break in full-time employment, or some other change in your circumstances during the period you are overseas, we would have to review the position to decide whether you still meet the conditions in paragraph 2.2. If at the end of one employment you returned temporarily to the UK, planning to go abroad again after a very short stay in this country, we may review your residence status in the light of all the circumstances of your employment abroad and your return to the UK.

If you do not meet all the conditions in paragraph 2.2, you remain resident and ordinarily resident unless paragraphs 2.8–2.9 apply to you. Special rules apply to employees of the European Community (see paragraph 2.14).

2.4 The treatment in paragraph 2.3 will also apply if you leave the UK to work full-time in a trade, profession or vocation and you meet conditions similar to those in paragraph 2.2.

Meaning of 'full-time'

2.5 There is no precise definition of when employment overseas is 'full-time', and a decision in a particular case will depend on all the facts. Where your employment involves a standard pattern of hours, we will regard it as full time if the hours you work each week clearly compare with those in a typical UK working week. If your job has no formal structure or no fixed number of working days, we will look at the nature of the job, local conditions and practices in the particular occupation to decide if the job is full-time.

If you have several part-time jobs overseas at the same time, we may be able to treat this as full-time employment. That might be so if, for example, you have several appointments with the same employer or group of companies, and perhaps also where you have simultaneous employment and self-employment overseas. But if you have a main employment abroad and some unconnected occupation in the UK at the same time, we will consider whether the extent of the UK activities was consistent with the overseas employment being full-time.

Accompanying spouse

2.6 If you are the husband or wife of someone who leaves the UK within the terms of paragraph 2.2 or 2.4 and you accompany or later join your spouse abroad, you may also by concession (extra-statutory concession A78) be treated as not resident and not ordinarily resident from the day after your departure to the day before your return, even if you are not yourself in full-time employment abroad. This applies where—

- you are abroad for a complete tax year, and

– during your absence any visits you make to the UK
  – total less than 183 days in the tax year
  – average less than 91 days a tax year. (The average is taken over the period of absence up to a maximum of four years—see paragraph 2.10. Any days spent in the UK because of exceptional circumstances beyond your control, for example the illness of yourself or a member of your immediate family, are not normally counted for this purpose.)

Where the tax years of your departure or return are split in this way, your tax liabilities which are affected by residence status are calculated on the basis of the period you are treated as resident in the UK.

Concession A78—Residence in the UK: accompanying spouse.

Leaving the UK permanently or indefinitely

2.7 If you go abroad permanently, you will be treated as remaining resident and ordinarily resident if your visits to the UK average 91 days or more a year—see paragraph 2.10. Any days spent in the UK because of exceptional circumstances beyond your control, for example the illness of yourself or your immediate family, are not normally counted for the purposes of averaging your visits.

2.8 If you claim that you are no longer resident and ordinarily resident, we may ask you to give some evidence that you have left the UK permanently, or to live outside the UK for three years or more. This evidence might be, for example, that you have taken steps to acquire accommodation abroad to live in as a permanent home, and if you continue to have property in the UK for your use, the reason is consistent with your stated aim of living abroad permanently or for three years or more. If you have left the UK permanently or for at least three years, you will be treated as not resident and not ordinarily resident from the day after the date of your departure providing—

– your absence from the UK has covered at least a whole tax year, and
– your visits to the UK since leaving
  – have totalled less than 183 days in any tax year, and
  – have averaged less than 91 days a tax year. (The average is taken over the period of absence up to a maximum of four years—see paragraph 2.10. Any days spent in the UK because of exceptional circumstances beyond your control, for example the illness of yourself or a member of your immediate family, are not normally counted for this purpose.)

2.9 If you do not have this evidence, but you have gone abroad for a settled purpose (this would include a fixed object or intention in which you are going to be engaged for an extended period of time), you will be treated as not resident and not ordinarily resident from the day after the date of your departure providing—

– your absence from the UK has covered at least a whole tax year, and
– your visits to the UK since leaving—
  – have totalled less than 183 days in any tax year, and
  – have averaged less than 91 days a tax year.

If you have not gone abroad for a settled purpose, you will be treated as remaining resident and ordinarily resident in the UK, but your status can be reviewed if—

– your absence actually covers three years from your departure, or
– evidence becomes available to show that you have left the UK permanently,

providing in either case your visits to the UK since leaving have totalled less than 183 days in any tax year and have averaged less than 91 days a tax year.

Calculating annual average visits

2.10 If it is necessary to calculate your annual average visits to the UK, the method is as follows:

$$\frac{\text{Total visits to the UK (in days)}}{\text{Total period since leaving (in days}} \times 365 = \text{annual average visits}$$

For this purpose, days spent in the UK in the tax year before the date of your original departure are excluded.

Suppose, for example, you leave the UK on 5 October 1997. The first review of the average of your visits is made after 5 April 1999, and takes account of your visits between those two dates. If you visited the UK for 30 days between 6 October 1997 and 5 April 1998 and for 50 days in 1998–99, the annual average is—

[(30 + 50)/(182+365)] × 365 = 53.38 days

If you continue to remain outside the UK, the annual average is calculated as follows in reviews after 5 April in subsequent years—

– after 5 April 2000—include visits from 5 October 1997 to 5 April 2000
– after 5 April 2001—include visits from 5 October 1997 to 5 April 2001
– after 5 April 2002—include visits from 6 April 1998 to 5 April 2002.

After the third review the year of departure is dropped from the calculation. At each subsequent review the oldest year is dropped, so that there is a rolling period of four years being reviewed.

However, if during your absence the pattern of your visits varied substantially year by year, it might be appropriate to look at the absence as being made up of separate periods for the purpose of calculating average visits. This might be necessary if, for example, a shift in the pattern of your visits suggested a change of circumstances, which altered how we viewed your residence status.

Contacting the Inland Revenue

2.11 You should let us know when you leave the UK (other than for short trips as in paragraph 2.1). You will normally be asked to complete form P85, which will help to determine your residence status.

Tax treatment after leaving the UK

2.12 For details of the tax treatment of your earned income (such as earnings from employment) after you have ceased to be resident in the UK, see Chapter 5 and in particular paragraphs 5.1–5.3 and the tables at 5.19–5.21. For similar details in the case of any investment income you may have (for example, interest arising in the UK), see Chapter 6 and in particular paragraph 6.3.

2.13 Some special provisions applying to those who leave the UK are dealt with as follows—

earnings of those who come to the UK part way through a tax year:	paragraph 5.4
earnings of those who leave the UK part way through a tax year:	paragraph 5.4
UK Government securities; interest arising in year of departure from UK:	paragraph 6.7
investment income of those leaving the UK part way through a tax year:	paragraphs 6.14–6.16
tax allowances:	paragraph 7.4
capital gains:	paragraphs 8.3–8.6

Special classes of employees

2.14 Special rules apply to some employees working abroad. If one of the classes shown below applies to you, write to the Inland Revenue office shown—the addresses appear in paragraph 9 of the Introduction. Please give your National Insurance number and details of your employment abroad. We will advise you of your tax position.

Class	**Write to Inland Revenue**
Crown employees (eg civil servants, diplomats, members of the armed forces, etc.)	HM Inspector of Taxes Cardiff 4 (Foreign Section)
European Union (EU) employees	FICO, Bootle
Employees working in oil and gas exploration and extraction industries (where the employer is not resident in the UK)	Foreign Compliance, Compliance Centre 1
Merchant Navy seafarers	HM Inspector of Taxes Cardiff 1

Commentary—*Simon's Direct Tax Service* **Part E6**.

3 Coming to the UK

Coming to the UK permanently or indefinitely

3.1 You are treated as resident and ordinarily resident from the date you arrive if your home has been abroad and you intend

– to come to the UK to live here permanently, or
– to come and remain here for three years or more.

You 'remain' in the UK if you are here on a continuing basis and any departures are for holidays or short business trips. (The same applies for the other references in this Chapter to 'remaining' in the UK.)

Visitors to the UK

3.2 If you come to the UK other than to live here permanently as in paragraph 3.1, the guidelines in the rest of this Chapter will govern your residence and ordinary residence position in the UK.

The Chapter deals in turn with two main groups coming to this country

- short term visitors—where you visit the UK for only limited periods in one or more tax years, without any intention to remain for an extended period
- longer term visitors—where you come to the UK intending to remain indefinitely or for an extended period, perhaps stretching over several tax years.

At first you may fall within one of these categories and later move to the other, depending on your precise circumstances.

Short term visitors

Residence

3.3 You will be treated as resident for a tax year if—

- you are in the UK for 183 days or more in the tax year (see paragraph 1.2), or
- you visit the UK regularly and after four tax years your visits during those years average 91 days or more a tax year—see paragraph 3.6. You are treated as resident from the fifth year.

However—

- any days spent in the UK for exceptional circumstances beyond your control, for example the illness of yourself or a member of your immediate family, are not counted for this purpose;
- you are treated as resident from 6 April of the first year, if it is clear when you first come to the UK that you intend making such visits and you actually carry out your intention;
- you are treated as resident from 6 April of the tax year in which you decide that you will make such visits, where this decision is made before the start of the fifth tax year and you actually carry out your decision.

For example

- you come to the UK with no definite intentions, but your visits during the tax years 1999–2000 to 2002–2003 average at least 91 days a tax year; you are resident from 6 April 2003;
- you first come to the UK during 1999–2000, intending that between then and 5 April 2003 your visits will average at least 91 days a tax year; you are resident from 6 April 1999, provided that your visits in fact reach that level;
- you first come to the UK during 1999–2000 with no definite intentions and you spend, say, 60 days here; you come again during 2000–2001 and decide you will come regularly in future years and your visits will average at least 91 days a tax year; you are resident from 6 April 2000, provided that your visits in fact reach that level.

Ordinary residence

3.4 You will be treated as ordinarily resident if you come to the UK regularly and your visits average 91 days or more a tax year—see paragraph 3.6. Any days spent in the UK for exceptional circumstances beyond your control, for example the illness of yourself or a member of your immediate family, are not normally counted for this purpose.

3.5 The date from which you are treated as ordinarily resident depends upon your intentions and whether you actually carry them out. You will be ordinarily resident—

- from 6 April of the tax year of your first arrival, if it is clear when you first come here that you intend visiting the UK regularly for at least four tax years;
- from 6 April of the fifth tax year after you have visited the UK over four years, if you originally came with no definite plans about the number of years you will visit;
- from 6 April of the tax year in which you decide you will be visiting the UK regularly, if that decision is made before the start of the fifth tax year.

For example

- you first come to the UK during 1999–2000, you intend visiting regularly until at least 5 April 2003 and your visits will average at least 91 days a tax year. You are ordinarily resident from 6 April 1999;
- you come to the UK with no definite intentions, but you visit regularly during the tax years 1999–2000 to 2002–2003 and your visits average at least 91 days a tax year. You are ordinarily resident from 6 April 2003;
- you first come to the UK during 1999–2000 with no definite intentions; you come again in 2000–2001 and 2001–2002; during 2001–2002 you decide you will come regularly in future years, and your visits will average at least 91 days a tax year. You are ordinarily resident from 6 April 2001.

Calculating annual average visits

3.6 Where it is necessary to calculate your annual average visits, the method is as follows—

$$\frac{\text{Total visits to the UK (in days)}}{\text{Relevant tax years (in days)}} \times 365 = \text{annual average visits}$$

For example, suppose you visited the UK for 80 days in 1995–96, 100 days in 1996–97, 85 days in 1997–98 and 105 days in 1998–99. The annual average is—

$$\frac{80+100+85+105}{366+365+365+365} \times 365 = \frac{370}{1461} \times 365 = 92.44 \text{ days}$$

Longer term visitors—residence

3.7 You are treated as resident in the UK from the day you arrive to the day you leave (see paragraphs 1.5–1.6) if you come to the UK for a purpose (for example, employment) that will mean you remain here for at least two years. The same treatment will apply if you own or lease accommodation in the UK in the year you arrive here (see paragraph 3.11, first bullet).

In all other cases you will be treated as resident for the tax year if—

– you spend 183 days or more in the UK in the tax year, or
– you own or lease accommodation in the UK (see paragraph 3.11, second bullet).

Ordinary residence

3.8 You will be treated as ordinarily resident in the UK from the date you arrive, whether to work here or not, if it is clear that you intend to stay for at least three years.

If you come to the UK as a student for an extended period of study or education, see paragraph 3.13.

3.9 You will be treated as ordinarily resident from the beginning of the tax year after the third anniversary of your arrival if you come to, and remain in, the UK, but you

– do not originally intend to stay for at least three years, and
– do not buy accommodation or acquire it on a lease of three years or more.

For example, if you arrive in the UK on 21 November 1999 and are still living in the UK on 6 April 2003, you are ordinarily resident from 6 April 2003.

3.10 If, after you have come to the UK, you decide to stay for at least three years from the date of your original arrival, you will be treated as ordinarily resident from—

– the day you arrive if your decision is made in the tax year of arrival, or
– the beginning of the tax year in which you make your decision when this is after the year of arrival.

For example—

– you arrive in the UK on 4 January 2000 and decide on 16 May 2000 to stay permanently. You are ordinarily resident from 6 April 2000;
– you come to the UK to work on 14 July 1999 on a 2 year contract of employment, but in December 2001 your assignment is changed and your contract is extended until after July 2002*. You are ordinarily resident from 6 April 2001.

* If there is a change in the circumstances of your assignment, but no formal change to the terms of a contract, whether you are treated as ordinarily resident—and from what date—will depend on the precise facts.

3.11 If you come to, and remain in, the UK, you will be treated as ordinarily resident

– from the day you arrive, if—
  – you already own accommodation here;
  – you buy accommodation during the tax year of arrival, or
  – you have or acquire accommodation on a lease of three years or more during the tax year of arrival; or
  – from 6 April of the tax year in which such accommodation becomes available, when this occurs after the year of arrival.

3.12 If you are treated as ordinarily resident solely because you have accommodation here (paragraph 3.11) and you dispose of the accommodation and leave the UK within three years of your arrival, you may be treated as not ordinarily resident for the duration of your stay if this is to your advantage.

3.13 If you are a student who comes to the UK for a period of study or education and you will be here for less than four years, you will be treated as not ordinarily resident, providing—

– you do not own or buy accommodation here, or acquire it on a lease of three years or more, and
– on leaving the UK you do not plan to return regularly for visits which average 91 days or more a tax year.

Contacting the Inland Revenue

3.14 You should let us know when you come to the UK. You will normally be asked to complete form P86, which will help to determine your residence status.

Tax treatment after arrival in the UK

3.15 For details of the tax treatment of your earned income both in the UK and abroad (such as earnings from employments) after you have become resident in the UK, see Chapter 5 and in particular paragraphs 5.1–5.3, 5.9–5.12 and the tables at 5.19–5.21. For details of the treatment of any investment income you may have, see Chapter 6 and in particular paragraph 6.2.

3.16 Some special provisions applying to those coming to the UK are dealt with as follows—

earnings of those who come to the UK part way through a tax year:	paragraph 5.4
lump sums from overseas pension schemes and provident funds:	paragraph 5.16
UK Government securities: interest arising in year of arrival in UK:	paragraph 6.7
investment income of those coming to the UK onwards part way through a tax year:	paragraphs 6.17
tax allowances:	paragraph 7.4
capital gains:	paragraphs 8.3–8.6

Commentary—*Simon's Direct Tax Service* **Part E6**.

4 Domicile

4.1 Domicile is a general law concept. It is not possible to list all the factors that affect your domicile, but some of the main points are explained in this Chapter.

4.2 Broadly speaking, you are domiciled in the country where you have your permanent home. Domicile is distinct from nationality or residence. You can only have one domicile at any given time.

Domicile of origin

4.3 You normally acquire a domicile of origin from your father when you are born. It need not be the country in which you are born. For example, if you are born in France while your father is working there, but his permanent home is in the UK, your domicile of origin is in the UK.

Domicile of dependency

4.4 Until you have the legal capacity to change it—see paragraph 4.5—your domicile will follow that of the person on whom you are legally dependent. If the domicile of that person changes, you automatically acquire the same domicile (a domicile of dependency), in place of your domicile of origin.

Domicile of choice

4.5 You have the legal capacity to acquire a new domicile (a domicile of choice) when you reach age 16. To do so, you must broadly leave your current country of domicile and settle in another country. You need to provide strong evidence that you intend to live there permanently or indefinitely. Living in another country for a long time, although an important factor, is not enough in itself to prove you have acquired a new domicile.

Married women

4.6 Before 1974, when you married you automatically acquired your husband's domicile. After marriage this domicile would change at the same time as your husband's domicile changed. If your marriage ended, you kept your husband's domicile until such time as you legally acquired a new domicile.

This rule is modified by the terms of the double taxation agreement between the UK and the USA. A marriage before 1974 between a woman who is a US national and a man domiciled within the UK is deemed to have taken place on 1 January 1974 for the purpose of determining her domicile on or after 6 April 1976 for UK tax purposes.

4.7 From 1 January 1974 your domicile is not necessarily the same as your husband's domicile. It is decided by the same factors as for any other individual who is able to have an independent domicile. If, however, you were married before 1974 and had acquired your husband's domicile (see paragraph 4.6), you retain this after 1 January 1974 until such time as you legally acquire a new domicile.

Overseas electors

4.8 From 6 April 1996 registering and voting as an overseas elector is not normally taken into account as one of the factors for determining whether you are domiciled in the UK, for the purpose of establishing your tax liability here.

Tax treatment of those not domiciled in the UK

4.9 Those who are resident in the UK but not domiciled here receive special tax treatment in respect of income and gains arising outside the UK. For details, see paragraphs 5.12 and 6.2 (income tax) and 8.8 (capital gains tax). We will consider the question of your domicile only where this will affect your current tax liability.

For inheritance tax purposes, see booklet IHT 18 ''Inheritance tax. Foreign aspects''.

Commentary—*Simon's Direct Tax Service* **Part E6**.

PART II

LIABILITY TO UK TAX

5 Earned income

Basis of liability

5.1 If you are resident in the UK under the rules in Part I of this booklet, you will normally pay UK tax on all your earned income, wherever it arises. As well as earnings for employment, earned income includes items such as pensions and income from a trade, profession or vocation. You may, however, be entitled to a reduction in the UK tax you have to pay if you receive overseas earnings and spend long periods abroad (see paragraphs 5.9–5.10) or if you receive an overseas pension (see paragraph 5.11). In certain cases where you are resident but not ordinarily resident in the UK, or resident but not domiciled here, we will deal with your overseas income on the 'remittance basis' (see paragraphs 5.9, 5.11–5.12).

5.2 If you are not resident in the UK, we will generally tax you on any UK pensions or on earnings from employment the duties of which are carried on in this country. Where your duties are carried on partly in the UK and partly abroad, an allocation, based on days worked in the UK and days worked abroad, will normally be made to ascertain the earnings for duties carried on in this country which are liable for UK tax. We will not tax you on earnings from an employment which is carried on wholly abroad (see paragraph 5.5). See paragraph 5.4 for the position if you become resident in the UK part way through a tax year and 5.9 regarding overseas earnings taxable on the remittance basis. In some cases you may make a claim under a double taxation agreement for exemption from UK tax on your UK pension, or on earnings arising in this country (see Chapter 9 and in particular paragraphs 9.3, 9.4 and 9.6).

We will tax you on the profits of a trade, profession or vocation which is not carried on wholly outside the UK.

5.3 The tables at the end of this Chapter show in more detail how your pensions, earnings from any office or employment or profits from a trade, profession or vocation will be taxed, depending on your residence status and the place where your duties are performed. You should ask your Tax Office if you need further information or advice about your own tax position (paragraph 7 of the Introduction).

Special rules apply in the case of Crown employees—see paragraph 2.14.

Earnings of those who come to, or leave, the UK part way through a tax year

5.4 If you come to the UK during a tax year and are treated as resident here from the date of your arrival, by concession (extra-statutory concession A11) you will not pay tax on earnings for the part of the year before you arrive here, where these are from an employment carried on wholly abroad.

A similar concession applies if you leave the UK during a tax year and are treated as resident here up to and including the date of your departure. You will not pay tax on earnings for the part of the year after you leave the UK, where these are from an employment carried on wholly abroad.

In the case of earned income other than earnings from employment, the rules are the same as those for unearned income—see paragraphs 6.14–6.24.

If you are paid for a period of leave spent in the UK following work abroad, we treat this 'terminal leave pay' as arising during the period to which it relates even if your entitlement to it was built up over a period of overseas employment. Leave pay is normally taxable in the UK where an individual is resident here. It may, however, be covered by the 'foreign earnings deduction' if the leave immediately follows a period abroad which is a 'qualifying period' (see paragraphs 5.9–5.10, and footnote 2 to the table at 5.19, on the foreign earnings deduction).

Concession A11—Residence in the UK: year of commencement or cessation of residence.

Where your duties are performed

5.5 The table at 5.19 shows that the place where your duties are performed is a key factor in deciding the tax treatment of your earnings. If your work is usually done abroad but some duties are performed in the UK, we will treat these as though they had been performed abroad as long as they are merely incidental to your overseas duties (see paragraphs 5.7 and 5.8).

5.6 Where you are a seafarer or a member of an aircraft crew, we normally treat your duties as performed in the UK if—

– the voyage or flight does not extend to a place outside the UK, or

– you are resident in the UK and the voyage or flight begins or ends in the UK, or
– you are resident in the UK and embarked on part of a voyage or flight which begins or ends in the UK.

A different rule applies for the purposes of the foreign earnings deduction (see paragraphs 5.9–5.10 and footnote 2 to the table at 5.19).

Incidental duties

5.7 Whether duties you perform in the UK are 'incidental' to your overseas duties (paragraph 5.5) depends on all the circumstances. If the work you do in the UK is of the same kind as, or of similar importance to, the work that you do abroad, it will not be merely incidental unless it can be shown to be ancillary or subordinate to that work. It is normally the nature of the duties performed in the UK rather than the amount of time spent on them that is important, but if the total time you spend working in the UK is more than 91 days in a year, the work will not be treated as incidental. Examples of duties which we do not normally regard as incidental are—

– attendance at directors' meetings in the UK by a director of the company who normally works abroad
– visits to the UK as a member of the crew of a ship or aircraft
– visits to the UK in the course of work by a courier.

5.8 If the work you do in the UK has no importance in itself, but simply enables you to do your normal work abroad, it may be treated as incidental. We will decide after looking at all the circumstances in your case. Examples of duties which we regard as incidental are—

– visits to the UK by an overseas representative of a UK employer to report to the employer or to receive fresh instructions
– training in the UK by an overseas employee as long as
  – the total time spent in the UK for training is not more than 91 days in a year, and
  – no productive work is done in the UK in that time.

Earned income arising outside the UK

5.9 In the case of earnings from employment, the table at 5.19 sets out the tax position. If you are resident in the UK, we will normally tax you on all earnings you receive from sources abroad. In certain circumstances, however, you may be entitled to a deduction of 100% on certain earnings from an employment performed wholly or partly overseas, if you are resident (and ordinarily resident) in the UK but spend a sufficient number of days abroad (see paragraph 5.10).

We tax you on the earnings from your overseas employment on the remittance basis (see paragraph 5.12) if you are

– resident but not ordinarily resident in the UK, or
– resident and ordinarily resident but not domiciled in the UK—but only in the case of 'foreign emoluments' where the duties of the employment are performed wholly outside the UK (see footnote 1 to the table at 5.19).

5.10 The foreign earnings deduction in certain circumstances provides a deduction of 100% from the amount of earnings chargeable where the following conditions are met—

– the duties of your employment are performed wholly or partly overseas;
– you remain resident and ordinarily resident in the UK while working abroad;
– the earnings are for a period which is part of a qualifying absence lasting 365 days or more.

Up to 16 March 1998 the Foreign Earnings Deduction could be claimed by all employees, but after that date it is only available to seafarers. 'Seafarers' are individuals who perform the duties of their employment on a ship. A 'ship' would not include offshore installations such as mobile offshore drilling rigs.

For further details of the current rules—

– seafarers may contact HM Inspector of Taxes Cardiff 1 (see paragraph 9 of the Introduction);
– workers in the oil and gas industry may obtain further information from Foreign Compliance, Compliance Centre 1 (see paragraph 9 of the Introduction and paragraph 5.17).

5.11 In the case of other types of earned income, such as overseas pensions and income from an overseas trade, profession or vocation, the tables at 5.20 and 5.21 set out the position. We will normally tax you on all the income you receive from overseas sources if you are resident in the UK. You may, however, be entitled to a 10% deduction from the amount chargeable in the case of overseas pensions.

We tax you on your other earned income from overseas sources on the remittance basis (see paragraph 5.12) if you are—

– resident but not domiciled in the UK, or
– resident but not ordinarily resident in the UK, and either a Commonwealth citizen (which includes a British citizen) or a citizen of the Republic of Ireland.

The remittance basis does not apply to other types of earned income arising in the Republic of Ireland.

5.12 Where the remittance basis applies, you are liable to UK tax on the amount of your overseas income that is remitted to the UK. Income is remitted if it is paid here or transmitted or brought to the UK in any way. In working out your tax liability, we include all income remitted to the UK.

Where you are taxed on the remittance basis, you will not be able to claim either the 100% deduction for foreign earnings (see paragraphs 5.9–5.10) or the deduction for overseas pensions (see paragraph 5.11).

The remittance basis may also apply to any overseas investment income you receive (see paragraph 6.2) and to capital gains arising overseas (see paragraph 8.8).

Change of location of a trade, profession or vocation

From 6 April 1997 (or from 6 April 1995 for businesses which started on or after 6 April 1994)

5.13 If you have been carrying on a business wholly or partly outside the UK and you either become resident in the UK or cease to be resident in the UK, we will treat you at that point as having discontinued one business and started a new one. This means that the special cessation provisions will apply up to the date of 'deemed' cessation and the special commencement provisions from the date of deemed commencement. These provisions are described in booklet CWL1 'Starting your own business?'.

Cessation and commencement of residence (and therefore deemed cessation and commencement of trade) usually take place at the start of the tax year in which your change of residence occurs. However, if you satisfy the conditions set out in paragraphs 1.5–1.6, the deemed cessation and commencement will take place on your actual date of arrival or departure.

Despite the deemed cessation and commencement, any losses incurred before the change of residence can be carried forward and set against profits of the business, as long as it would have been the same business under the rules in paragraph 5.14.

Before 6 April 1997 (or, where appropriate, 6 April 1995)

5.14 Whether a change of residence triggers the discontinuance of one business and the commencement of another is a question of fact. It depends on where the business is carried on rather than where the proprietor resides. Most trades and professions are carried on in a particular location (for example a shop, office or factory), so that a significant change of business location (such as from one country to another) will normally mean that the new business is a different one from the old business. This means that the cessation provisions will apply to your old business and the commencement provisions to the new one. It also means that losses from your old business cannot be carried forward and set against profits of the new business.

A few businesses, mainly of professional people, are not localised in this way, but are carried on wherever in the world the person happens to be. Examples are international actors, musicians, authors and sportsmen/women. If you are carrying on this kind of profession and continue to carry it on in the same way after a change of residence, it will be the same profession, and neither the cessation nor the commencement provisions will apply. However, for the year of change of residence, we will only assess you on a proportion of your profits for the full year, reflecting the profits made in the period from the date of your arrival in the UK to the following 5 April (or in the period from the preceding 6 April to the date of departure from the UK).

UK social security benefits

5.15 Various UK social security benefits including, for example, National Insurance Retirement Pension and widow's payments, are liable to UK tax. However, some relief from UK tax may be due under the terms of a double taxation agreement if you are not resident in the UK (see also paragraph 9.3).

From the year 1996–97, if you are not resident in the UK for the whole of a tax year and do not claim relief under the terms of a double taxation agreement, your liability on taxable UK social security benefits is limited to the tax, if any, deducted before payment.

Lump sums from overseas pension schemes and provident funds

5.16 By concession (extra-statutory concession A10), we will not charge income tax (or we will charge it only on a reduced amount) if you receive lump sum retirement benefits, relating to an employment overseas, under an overseas pension scheme or provident fund.

The level of relief will depend on the extent of your overseas service. You qualify for full exemption where in that employment—

- at least 75% of your total service was overseas, or
- your total service exceeds 10 years and the whole of the last 10 years of service have been overseas, or
- your total service exceeds 20 years and not less than 50% of total service, including any 10 of the last 20 years, was overseas.

If you do not meet the conditions for full exemption, we will charge income tax only on that percentage of the lump sum equivalent to your non-overseas service in that employment.

Concession A10—Lump sums paid under overseas pension schemes.

Offshore oil and gas workers

5.17 If you work offshore in connection with the exploration or exploitation of UK oil or gas, the rules set out in the first part of this Chapter still normally apply to you. In this context 'offshore' means—

- the territorial sea of the UK (see paragraph 6 of the Introduction), and
- the UK continental shelf outside the territorial sea.

If, however, you are a resident of a country with which the UK has a double taxation agreement, the normal rules may be affected by that agreement (see Chapter 9 on agreements generally). Some of these include provisions specific to offshore oil and gas activities. You should put any queries about your tax liabilities to your Tax Office, if your employer is resident in the UK; or to Foreign Compliance, Compliance Centre 1, if your employer is not resident in the UK.

Partnerships

5.18 If you carry on a trade or profession in a partnership, the table at 5.21 sets out the position. In those circumstances, the remittance basis (see paragraph 5.12) may apply to your overseas profit, where the trade—

- is carried on wholly abroad, or
- is carried on partly abroad and the partnership is managed and controlled abroad,

and in either case you are a UK resident partner and are—

- not domiciled in the UK, or
- not ordinarily resident in the UK, and a Commonwealth citizen or a citizen of the Irish Republic.

5.19 Scope of liability to income tax of earnings

		Duties of employment performed wholly or partly in the UK		Duties of employment performed wholly outside the UK
		in the UK	outside the UK	
Foreign emoluments [1]	Employee resident and ordinarily resident in the UK	Liable—less possible deduction [2]	Liable—less possible deduction [2]	Liable if received in the UK [3]
	Resident but not ordinarily resident	Liable	Liable if received in the UK [3]	Liable if received in the UK [3]
	Not resident	Liable	Not liable	Not liable
Other earnings	Resident and ordinarily resident	Liable—less possible deduction [2]	Liable—less possible deduction [2]	Liable—less possible deduction [2]
	Resident but not ordinarily resident	Liable	Liable if received in the UK [3]	Liable if received in the UK [3]
	Not resident	Liable	Not liable	Not liable

Notes[1] ''Foreign emoluments'' is the term used in the Taxes Acts to mean the earnings of someone who is not domiciled in the UK and whose employer is resident outside, and not resident in, the UK (nor resident in the Republic of Ireland).

[2] There may be a foreign earnings deduction of 100% in these cases from the amount chargeable, if the earnings are for a period which is part of a qualifying absence lasting 365 days or more—this means that such earnings for that period will be free from UK tax. See paragraphs 5.9–5.10 for further details, and a summary of the changes that were introduced from 17 March 1998.

[3] See paragraph 5.12 for details of the remittance basis which applies in these cases.

5.20 Scope of liability to income tax on individuals receiving pensions

	Paid by or on behalf of a person	
Residence status and domicile	*in the UK*	*outside the UK (overseas*
Resident and ordinarily resident, and domiciled	Liable	Liable [1]
Resident and ordinarily resident, not domiciled	Liable	Liable if received in the UK (paragraph 5.12) [2]
Resident but not ordinarily resident, domiciled	Liable	Liable [1, 3]
Resident but not ordinarily resident, not domiciled	Liable	Liable if received in the UK (paragraph 5.12) [2]
Not Resident	Liable [4, 5]	Not Liable

Notes[1] Less 10% deduction.

[2] You are taxable on the whole of a pension arising in the Republic of Ireland, less 10% deduction; but if the pension is from the Irish Government, you are taxable only if you are a UK national without also being an Irish national.

[3] If you are a Commonwealth (this includes a British) citizen or an Irish citizen, the remittance basis applies and the 10% deduction is not due, unless the pension arises in the Irish Republic, in which case note 2 applies.

[4] See Chapter 9 about possible relief under a double taxation agreement.

[5] See paragraph 5.15 in the case of UK social security benefits such as National Insurance Retirement Pension.

5.21 Scope of liability to income tax on profits of individuals carrying on a trade or profession

Residence status and domicile	*Trade or profession carried on wholly or partly in the UK*	*Trade or profession carried on wholly outside the UK*
Resident and ordinarily resident, and domiciled		
Resident and ordinarily resident, not domiciled	Liable	Liable if received in the UK (paragraph 5.12) [1]
Resident but not ordinarily resident, domiciled	Liable	Liable [2]
Resident but not ordinarily resident, not domiciled	Liable	Liable if received in the UK (paragraph 5.12) [1]
Not Resident	Liable [3]	Not Liable

Commentary—*Simon's Direct Tax Service* **Parts E4, E6.**

Notes—[1] You are taxable on the whole of the income from a trade or profession carried on wholly in the Republic of Ireland.

[2] If you are a Commonwealth (this includes a British) citizen or an Irish citizen the remittance basis applies, unless the trade or profession is carried on wholly in the Irish Republic, in which case note 1 applies.

[3] You are liable on the profits of the part of the trade or profession carried on the UK.

6 Investment income

General

6.1 Broadly, investment income means any income which is not a pension and is not earned by you as an employee, or from carrying on your profession or from running your own business. Among the more common types are—

– interest from bank and building society accounts;
– dividends on shares (see also paragraphs 9.11–9.13);
– interest on stocks;
– rental income (unless your business amounts to a trade).

6.2 If you are resident in the UK, you will normally pay UK tax on all your investment income, wherever it arises. The remittance basis will apply to overseas investment income (other than investment income arising in the Republic of Ireland) if you are—

– resident but not domiciled in the UK, or
– resident but not ordinarily resident in the UK, and either a Commonwealth citizen (this includes a British citizen) or a citizen of the Republic of Ireland.

Where the remittance basis applies, you are liable to UK tax on the amount of your overseas investment income that is remitted to the UK. Income is remitted if it is paid here or transmitted or brought to the UK in any way. In working out your tax liability, we include all income remitted to the UK.

6.3 If you are not resident in the UK, we will only charge UK tax on investment income arising in the UK. Except in the case of UK rental income, if you are not carrying on a trade, profession or vocation through a UK branch or agency, your liability on investment income from 1996–97 will be limited to the tax, if any, deducted at source. However, if you have other UK income which is fully taxable, any personal allowances will be set against your investment income first.

If you are a resident of a country with which the UK has a double taxation agreement (see Chapter 9), you may in some cases be able to claim exemption or partial relief from UK tax on investment income (other than rental income from property in the UK).

Investment income arising in the UK

Income from property in the UK

6.4 Any profits you make from letting property situated in the UK are taxable in the UK, even if you cease to be resident in the UK. New rules apply to the taxation of UK rental income from 6 April 1996.

Before 6 April 1996

6.5 If you were not resident in the UK (or if your usual place of abode was outside the UK)

– where you received rental income direct from the tenant, the tenant first deducted tax at the basic rate and paid it to the Inland Revenue. If the tax deducted exceeded your tax liability you could claim a repayment of tax overpaid
– where a letting agent collected the property income for you, the Inland Revenue assessed the letting agent, who was responsible for paying the tax. The letting agent was entitled to recover the tax out of the rental income collected on your behalf.

Your Tax Office or an Inland Revenue Enquiry Centre will be able to give you more information.

From 6 April 1996

6.6 If your usual place of abode is outside the UK

– where you receive rental income direct from the tenant, the tenant must first deduct tax at the basic rate and pay it to the Inland Revenue
– where a letting agent collects the rental income for you, the letting agent must deduct tax at the basic rate from the income received less the allowable expenses paid on your behalf.

In either case you can set off the tax against your UK income tax liability when you complete your tax return.

You can, however, apply to FICO at Bootle (see paragraph 9 of the Introduction) for approval for your property income to be paid without tax being deducted providing—

– your UK tax affairs are up to date, or
– you have never had any UK tax obligations, or
– you do not expect to be liable to UK income tax

and in all cases you undertake to comply with all your UK tax obligations.

More information can be found in leaflet IR140 ‘Non-resident landlords, their agents and tenants’. You can obtain a copy from FICO at Bootle (see paragraph 9 of the Introduction) or from any Tax Office or Inland Revenue Enquiry Centre.

UK Government securities

6.7 UK tax is not chargeable on interest arising on UK Government ‘FOTRA’ securities, if you are not ordinarily resident in the UK. ‘FOTRA’ stands for ‘Free of Tax to Residents Abroad’. Where we treat you as becoming, or ceasing to be, ordinarily resident in the UK part way through the tax year, no tax will normally be charged on interest payable while you are not ordinarily resident—that is, before the date you arrive here or after the date you leave.

Before 6 April 1998 FOTRA status only applied to certain UK Government securities. Please write to FICO at Nottingham (see paragraph 9 of the Introduction) if you want a list of the securities that had FOTRA status before 6 April 1998, or a form to claim repayment of tax.

6.8 UK tax is, however, charged if the interest forms part of the profits of a trade or business carried on in the UK. It is also charged in cases where laws to prevent tax avoidance provide that the income is to be treated as belonging to another person.

6.9 If you hold securities with a nominal value of more than £5,000 during a tax year in which you are resident in the UK at any time, special tax provisions (known as the ‘accrued income scheme’) normally apply when the securities are transferred. You are charged income tax on the interest that has built up over the period you owned the securities following the last interest payment, even if you were not resident in the UK for part of that period. Leaflet IR68 ‘Accrued income scheme. Taxing securities on transfer’ gives further details.

Interest from building societies and banks

6.10 Building societies, banks and other deposit takers in the UK normally deduct UK tax from interest paid or credited to your account. But if you are not ordinarily resident in the UK, you may be able to have the interest paid or credited without tax deducted. You can arrange this—assuming it is an option under the terms and conditions of your account—by completing a 'not ordinarily resident' declaration.

Any interest you receive without tax deducted is still liable to UK tax, but see paragraph 6.11 if you are not resident in the UK for a whole tax year.

If your account includes the facility to make a 'not ordinarily resident' declaration and you want to arrange for your interest to be paid or credited without deduction of tax

- ask the building society, bank or deposit taker for a declaration form R105
- if your account is a joint account, you can complete the declaration only if all the people who are beneficially entitled to the interest are not ordinarily resident in the UK
- give the completed declaration form to your building society, bank or deposit taker
- the declaration will have effect from the date on which your building society, bank or deposit taker receives it. It cannot be backdated to cover earlier interest payments
- if you later become ordinarily resident in the UK (or, in the case of a joint account, if any of the people who are beneficially entitled to the interest becomes ordinarily resident in the UK), you must notify your building society, bank or deposit taker without delay.

6.11 For years up to and including 1995–96, by concession (extra-statutory concession B13, obsolete for later tax years), no UK tax would be charged if, for the whole of any tax year, you were not resident in the UK and you received interest from a UK source without tax being deducted. This concession would not, however, apply if—

- the tax due could be recovered by setting it off against any tax relief in respect of your other UK income (unless the relief arose because the other UK income is exempt under the Taxes Acts or is relieved under a double taxation agreement, in which case the concession would still apply), or
- an agent or branch in the UK had management or control of the interest (in which case the agent or branch would be charged).

From the year 1996–97, where you are not resident for the whole tax year, your liability on interest from a UK bank or building society is limited to the tax, if any, deducted before payment, unless you carry on a trade, profession or vocation through a UK branch or agency.

Investment income arising outside the UK

6.12 Special rules apply where foreign dividends and interest are paid to you through a paying agent in the UK, or are received by a collecting agent in the UK, for example a bank acting on your behalf. The paying or collecting agent will normally deduct tax before paying the income to you. If you are not resident in the UK, you can claim repayment of the tax deducted, or in some circumstances arrange for the paying or collecting agent to pay the income to you without deducting tax (see also paragraphs 6.14 and 6.17).

6.13 Some income from overseas sources may not have UK tax deducted before it is paid to you. If you are resident in the UK, you will have to pay the tax due. From 6 April 1997 the tax due will be calculated on the whole amount arising or, if the remittance basis applies (see paragraph 6.2), the amount received in the UK in the year concerned. For years before 6 April 1997 different rules may apply; for further advice, contact your Tax Office.

Investment income of those who leave, or come to, the UK part way through a tax year

Leaving the UK

6.14 If you leave the UK during a tax year and cease to be resident here from the day after the date of your departure, we will only charge you tax on overseas income you receive through a paying or collecting agent (see paragraph 6.12) up to and including the date of your departure.

However, if you wish to receive overseas income without deduction of tax from a paying or collecting agent after you have ceased to be resident here, you will need to complete a declaration and give it to the paying or collecting agent. You should make the declaration on form PA1 (in the case of a paying agent) or form CA1 (in the case of a collecting agent). The forms are available from paying and collecting agents.

6.15 For all other overseas investment income where you are not taxed on the remittance basis, you will pay tax on the smaller of—

- the actual overseas investment income arising for the period from 6 April to the date of your departure, and
- the same fraction of your total overseas income for the year of departure (or, for years before 6 April 1997, for the previous year, if that is the proper basis of assessment) as the fraction of the full tax year for which you are resident in this country. For example, if you are resident in the UK from 6 April until 6 October in the same tax year, ie 6 months, the fraction is 6/12.

6.16 For overseas investment income where you are taxed on the remittance basis (see paragraph 6.2), you will pay tax on the smaller of—

- the actual overseas investment income remitted to the UK in the period from 6 April to the date of your departure, and

– the same fraction of the total overseas income you remit to the UK in the year of departure (or, for years before 6 April 1997, in the previous year, if that is the proper basis of assessment) as the fraction of the full tax year for which you are resident in this country.

Coming to the UK

6.17 If you come to the UK during a tax year and become resident here from the date of your arrival, we will only charge tax on overseas income you receive through a paying or collecting agent in the UK (see paragraph 6.12) from the date of your arrival.

6.18 Paragraphs 6.19 and 6.20 apply for years before 6 April 1996 and after 5 April 1997. There are special rules for the tax year 1996–97 which are explained at paragraphs 6.21–6.24.

Years before 6 April 1996 and after 5 April 1997

6.19 For the tax year of your arrival, where you receive overseas investment income from which tax has not been deducted and you are not taxed on the remittance basis, the following rules apply—

- you will not have to pay tax on income from a source which ceases before the date of your arrival;
- where the source continues after your arrival, but ceases in the same tax year, you will only pay tax on the income arising from the date of your arrival to the date the source ceased;
- where the source ceases in the tax year following the year of your arrival, you may be charged to tax for both years—
  - for the year of arrival, you will pay tax on the greater of—
    (*a*) the same fraction of your overseas investment income for the year of arrival as the fraction of the full tax year for which you are resident in this country, and
    (*b*) for years before 6 April 1996 the same fraction as in a. of your overseas income for the year preceding the year of arrival if the source was in existence at 5 April 1994
  - for the year following the year of arrival, you will pay tax on the overseas income arising from 6 April in that year to the date when the source ceased
- where the source continues to the end of the tax year of your arrival and beyond, and income first arose—
  - in the tax year of your arrival but before you became resident here, or
  - for years up to and including 1995–96, in the previous tax year if the source was in existence at 5 April 1994

you will only pay tax on the same fraction of your total overseas income for the year of arrival as the fraction of the full tax year for which you are resident in this country.

Suppose, for example, you come to the UK on 6 August 1993, and are resident for the rest of the tax year of your arrival (ending 5 April 1994). Your investment income continues beyond 5 April 1994, and first arose at some time between 6 April 1992 and 5 August 1993 (that is, in the tax year 1992–93 or the first part of the year of your arrival). You are resident for 8 months during 1993–94, and are therefore taxed on 8/12 of the whole of your investment income for that year

- for years up to and including 1995–96 where the source continued as in the previous example, but income first arose earlier than the tax year before the year of your arrival, the fraction of income on which tax was chargeable was worked out in the same way as in the previous example, but the income in question was that of the year before the year of your arrival if the source was in existence at 5 April 1994.

Suppose the facts are as in the previous example, but your investment income first arose before 6 April 1992. You are taxed in the year of your arrival, 1993–94, on 8/12 of your investment income for the tax year 1992–93.

6.20 For the tax year of arrival, where you receive overseas investment income from which tax has not been deducted and you are taxed on the remittance basis (see paragraph 6.2), the following rules apply

- you will not have to pay tax on overseas investment income you remit from a source which ceased before the date of your arrival (for example, a bank account which you have closed)
- where the source continues after your arrival but ceases in the same tax year, you will pay tax on the lesser of—
  - the total overseas investment income that you remit to the UK in the year, and
  - the overseas income arising from the date of your arrival to the date the source ceased
  - where the source ceases in the tax year following the year of your arrival, you may be charged to tax for both years—
  - for the year of arrival, you will pay tax on the lesser of—
    (*a*) the overseas investment income you remit to the UK in that year (if the source was already in existence at 5 April 1994, the income remitted to the UK in the previous year if this is greater), and
    (*b*) the same fraction of your total overseas income for the year of arrival (if the source was already in existence at 5 April 1994, the income remitted to the UK in the previous year if this is greater) as the fraction of the full tax year for which you are resident in this country

- for the year following the year of arrival, you will pay tax on the overseas income you remit to the UK in that year, but reduced if necessary so that the sum taxed for the two years does not exceed the total of—
  (*a*) an amount worked out on the lines of b. above for the year of your arrival, and
  (*b*) the amount of income arising from 6 April in the following year up to the date the source ceased.

Coming to the UK during the tax year ended 5 April 1997

6.21 You will not have to pay tax on income from a source which ceases before the date of your arrival.

6.22 If the source of income ceases during the year ended 5 April 1997 but after the date of your arrival in this country, you will pay tax on income as follows—

- if you are not taxed on the remittance basis, on the income arising from the date of your arrival to the date the source ceased
- if you are taxed on the remittance basis, on the lesser of—
  - the total overseas income you remit to the UK during the year ended 5 April 1997, and
  - the overseas income arising from the date of your arrival to the date the source ceased.

6.23 If the source of income ceases during the year ended 5 April 1998, you will pay tax on income as follows for the year ended 5 April 1997—

- if you are not taxed on the remittance basis, on the same fraction of your total overseas income for the year ended 5 April 1997 as the fraction of the full tax year for which you are resident in this country
- if you are taxed on the remittance basis, on the lesser of—
  - the total overseas income you remit to the UK during the year ended 5 April 1997, and
  - the same fraction of your total overseas income for the year ended 5 April 1997 as the fraction of the full tax year for which you are resident in this country.

6.24 If the source of income continues beyond 5 April 1998, you will pay tax on income as follows for the year ended 5 April 1997—

- if you are not taxed on the remittance basis, on the proportion on a time basis, from the date of your arrival to 5 April 1997, of the sum of 50% of the income arising in each of the years ended 5 April 1996 and 5 April 1997. However, where income from the source first arose after 5 April 1994, you will pay tax on the proportion on a time basis, from the date of your arrival to 5 April 1997, on the full amount of the income arising in the year ended 5 April 1997
- if you are taxed on the remittance basis, on the sum of 50% of the amounts you remit to the UK in the years ended 5 April 1996 and 5 April 1997. However, where income from the source was first received in the UK after 5 April 1994, you will pay tax on the whole of the income you remit to the UK in the year ended 5 April 1997 or, if less, on the amount worked out on the lines of the first bullet above.

	Investment income		*UK Government "FOTRA" securities (see para 7.7)*
	Arising in the UK	*Arising outside the UK*	
Residence status and domicile			
Resident and ordinarily resident, and domiciled	Liable	Liable	Liable
Resident and ordinarily resident, not domiciled	Liable	Liable if received in the UK [1]	Liable
Resident but not ordinarily resident, domiciled	Liable	Liable [2]	Not Liable
Resident but not ordinarily resident, not domiciled	Liable	Liable if received in the UK [1]	Not Liable
Not resident but ordinarily resident, domiciled	Liable [3, 4]	Not Liable	Liable
Not resident but ordinarily resident, not domiciled	Liable [3, 4]	Not Liable	Liable
Not resident and not ordinarily resident, domiciled	Liable [3, 4]	Not Liable	Not Liable
Not resident and not ordinarily resident, not domiciled	Liable [3, 4]	Not Liable	Not Liable

Misc

Notes to table[1] You are taxable on the whole of the income arising in the Republic of Ireland.
[2] If you are a Commonwealth (this includes a British) citizen or an Irish citizen, the remittance basis applies, unless the income arises in the Irish Republic, in which case note 1 applies.
[3] See Chapter 9 about possible relief under a double taxation agreement.
[4] The charge to tax may be limited—see para 6.11.
Commentary—*Simon's Direct Tax Service* **Part E6**.

7 Tax allowances and reliefs

Allowances for UK residents

7.1 If you are resident in the UK, you are entitled to certain allowances and reliefs, based on your personal circumstances, which reduce the amount of tax charged on your income. Leaflet IR90 'Tax allowances and reliefs' explains in more detail.

7.2 UK residents who are employees have tax deducted at source from their wages or salaries under the 'Pay As You Earn' (PAYE) system. The employer deducts tax on the basis of code numbers issued for each employee by the Inland Revenue. These codes take account of the tax allowances and reliefs to which each individual is entitled. For more details, ask your Tax Office for leaflet IR34 'PAYE. Pay As You Earn'.

Allowances for non-UK residents

7.3 If you are not resident in the UK, you may claim tax allowances if you are any one of the following

- a Commonwealth citizen (this includes a British citizen)
- a citizen of a state within the European Economic Area (EEA), that is Austria, Belgium, Denmark, Finland, France, Germany, Greece, Iceland, Italy, Liechtenstein, Luxembourg, Netherlands, Norway, Portugal, Republic of Ireland, Spain, Sweden and the United Kingdom
- a present or former employee of the British Crown (including a civil servant, member of the armed forces, etc.)
- a UK missionary society employee
- a civil servant in a territory under the protection of the British Crown
- a resident of the Isle of Man or the Channel Islands
- a former resident of the UK and you live abroad for the sake of your own health or the health of a member of your family who lives with you
- a widow or widower of an employee of the British Crown
- a national and/or resident of a country with which the UK has a double taxation agreement which allows such a claim.

Allowances for those coming to, or leaving, the UK part way through a tax year

7.4 If you either become, or cease to be, resident in the UK during a tax year, you will be able to claim full allowances and reliefs for the year of arrival or departure.

Mortgage interest relief

7.5 Tax relief for mortgage interest on a loan to buy your home in the UK is available for interest paid up to 5 April 2000. Relief is commonly given under the Mortgage Interest Relief At Source (MIRAS) scheme. If you have to move away from your home temporarily because of your employment, tax relief may continue, by concession (extra-statutory concession A27), provided that you expect to be away for no more than four years and you expect to live in your home again on your return. There is no relief for mortgage interest paid after 5 April 2000.

Concession A27—Mortgage interest relief: temporary absence from mortgaged property.

How to claim tax allowances

7.6 If you wish to make a claim for tax allowances, you must do so—

- for years before 1996–97, within six years from the end of the tax year to which the claim relates. For example, if you wish to claim for the tax year 1995–96 (6 April 1995 to 5 April 1996), you have until 5 April 2002 to make your claim;
- from the year 1996–97, within 5 years 10 months from the end of the tax year to which the claim relates. For example, if you wish to claim for the tax year 1996–97 (6 April 1996 to 5 April 1997), you have until 31 January 2003.

7.7 UK residents may be sent a tax return. If you get one, you can use it to claim your allowances and reliefs. If you do not get a tax return, you can write to your Tax Office to claim allowances and reliefs.

7.8 If you are not resident in the UK, you should contact FICO at Bootle, unless you are an employee of the British Crown or receive a pension for Crown service, when you should contact HM Inspector of Taxes Cardiff 4 (Foreign Section). The addresses are in paragraph 9 of the Introduction.

Commentary—*Simon's Direct Tax Service* **Part E6**.

8 Capital gains tax

Basis of liability

8.1 If you are either resident or ordinarily resident in the UK, you may be liable to capital gains tax on gains arising when you dispose of assets situated anywhere in the world. Disposing of an asset means selling, exchanging or transferring it, or giving it away, or realising a capital sum from it. Usually you will not pay capital gains tax—

- on the transfer of an asset to your spouse;
- on disposing of private motor vehicles;
- on disposing of household goods and personal effects up to a value of £6,000 per item;
- on disposing of a private home which has been treated as your only or main residence throughout the time you have owned it;
- on gains arising from certain other assets—for example Save-As-You-Earn (SAYE) terminal bonuses, National Savings Certificates, Premium Bonds and investments held within an Individual Savings Account or Personal Equity Plan. Leaflet CGT1 'Capital gains tax. An introduction' contains a fuller list.

If you have two or more residences, you can nominate one of them as your main residence for capital gains purposes by notifying your Tax Office. The residence you nominate need not be the same one as your main residence for mortgage interest tax relief purposes.

No tax is charged on the gains (after reliefs) you receive in any one year up to a certain amount. The 'annual exempt amount' is set at £7,100 for the tax year 1999–2000. Husbands and wives are both entitled to their own annual exempt amount.

8.2 If you dispose of an asset you acquired before 31 March 1982, only the change in value since that date will generally be taken into account for determining the gain or loss. You may be able to make an election for this to apply in every case. An allowance is made for the effects of inflation up to April 1998 when computing gains. Taper relief, which reduces the amount of a gain which is chargeable to tax by reference to whole years of ownership, may be due for disposals on or after 6 April 1998. Leaflet CGT1 'Capital gains tax. An introduction' gives more details.

Gains by those who leave, or come to, the UK part way through a tax year

8.3 If you leave the UK during a tax year and cease to be resident or ordinarily resident in the UK, you may, by concession (extra-statutory concession D2), not be liable to capital gains tax on gains arising to you from disposals made after the date of your departure. However, if you leave the UK on or after 17 March 1998, you can qualify for this concession only if you were neither resident nor ordinarily resident in the UK for the whole of at least four of the seven tax years immediately preceding the tax year in which you leave the UK.

If you become resident in the UK during a tax year, having been neither resident nor ordinarily resident in the UK at any time during the five tax years immediately preceding that year, you are, by concession (extra-statutory concession D2), liable to capital gains tax only on gains arising from disposals made after the date of your arrival. If you arrived in the UK before 6 April 1998, the concession applied if you were neither resident nor ordinarily resident throughout the whole of the 36 months before the date of your arrival.

There is normally no charge to capital gains tax on your assets when you leave the UK if you do not actually make a disposal, nor is there any revaluation of assets when you come to the UK. However, in some cases, gains on which a charge has been held over or deferred, or which have been subject to a claim to reinvestment relief, may be brought back into charge if you become neither resident nor ordinarily resident in the UK. This charge will not apply if the reason you become neither resident nor ordinarily resident in the UK is that you are working abroad, provided that you become resident or ordinarily resident in the UK again within three years.

Concession D2—Residence in the UK: year of commencement of residence.

Temporary non-residence

8.4 If you have left the UK and dispose of assets while you are temporarily non-resident, special rules may apply for gains that would have been chargeable, and losses that would have been allowable, if you had been resident or ordinarily resident in the UK for the tax years in question. You are 'temporarily' non-resident if you have been neither resident nor ordinarily resident in the UK for fewer than five complete tax years.

The special rules have the effect of treating these gains and losses as though they arise in the tax year in which you return to the UK.

The special rules do not apply for gains and losses arising from disposals of any assets you acquired while you were temporarily non-resident, provided that the assets were not derived in some part from assets you held while you were resident or ordinarily resident in the UK.

8.5 The special rules apply only if all the following conditions are met—

- there is a tax year (the 'year of return') for which you satisfy the residence requirements*;
- you did not satisfy the residence requirements* for one or more tax years immediately preceding the year of return;

- no more than four tax years fell between the most recent tax year for which you satisfied the residence requirements* (the 'year of departure') and the year of return;
- you satisfied the residence requirements* for at least four of the seven tax years immediately preceding the year of departure.

  * You satisfy the 'residence requirements' for a tax year if you are ordinarily resident in the UK during that year or if you are resident in the UK for any part of it.

If any of these conditions is not **met**, there is no charge to capital gains tax on gains arising on the disposal of assets during your temporary non-residence. Similarly, losses arising in these circumstances will not be allowable losses for capital gains tax purposes.

8.6 Where the special rules apply, you may be able to claim relief from tax in the year in which you resume residence in the UK, if at the time you disposed of the assets you were a resident of a country with which the UK has a double taxation agreement. Any such relief (which may take the form of credit for the overseas tax or, in some cases, exemption from UK tax) will depend on the terms of the relevant agreement. In certain circumstances you may also be able to claim credit for overseas tax against UK tax where there is no double taxation agreement.

Non-residents with a UK branch or agency

8.7 If you are neither resident nor ordinarily resident in the UK and carry on a trade, profession or vocation through a branch or agency in the UK, you will be liable to capital gains tax on any gains on the disposal of assets in the UK which were used in the trade, profession or vocation, or by the branch or agency. You may also be liable to capital gains tax if the activity ceases or you transfer the assets outside the UK.

Overseas assets

8.8 An overseas asset is one situated outside the UK under the capital gains tax rules. For assets such as land and most types of movable property the asset is situated where it is located. For other assets (for example shares and securities) the rules are more complex. Your Tax Office will be able to advise you further.

If you are resident or ordinarily resident in the UK, and dispose of overseas assets, you will normally be liable to capital gains tax on any gains arising. But if you are not domiciled in the UK, you are taxed on such gains only to the extent that they are received in or remitted to the UK in a tax year for which you are resident or ordinarily resident in the UK. There is no capital gains tax charge on gains remitted to the UK before you become resident in the UK. (See also paragraph 5.12 on the remittance basis.) Where the proceeds of a disposal are remitted, an appropriate proportion of the proceeds is treated as a remittance of the gain.

Gains in a foreign currency

8.9 Where prices are expressed in a currency other than sterling, we calculate gains on the basis of sterling equivalents of the considerations for acquisition and disposal, converted at the date of purchase or sale as appropriate. Except where it is for personal expenditure outside the UK, foreign currency is a chargeable asset for capital gains tax purposes. Its disposal in return for any other asset will normally give rise to a chargeable gain or allowable loss.

Exempt assets

8.10 Gains on the disposal of gilt-edged securities and qualifying corporate bonds are exempt from capital gains tax.

Further information

8.11 In the space available in this Chapter it is only possible to offer general guidance on some of the more important topics. For more detailed information about capital gains tax you can obtain leaflet CGT1 'Capital gains tax. An introduction' from any Tax Office.

	Gains on disposal of	
	UK assets	overseas assets
Residence status and domicile		
Resident and ordinarily resident, and domiciled	Liable	Liable
Resident and ordinarily resident, not domiciled	Liable	Liable if received in the UK
Resident but not ordinarily resident, domiciled	Liable	Liable
Resident but not ordinarily resident, not domiciled	Liable	Liable if received in the UK

	Gains on disposal of	
	UK assets [1]	overseas assets
Not resident but ordinarily resident, domiciled	Liable [2]	Liable
Not resident but ordinarily resident, not domiciled	Liable [2]	Liable if received in the UK [2]
Not resident and not ordinarily resident, domiciled	Not Liable [3, 4]	Not Liable [4]
Not resident and not ordinarily resident, not domiciled	Not Liable [3, 4]	Not Liable [4]

Notes[1] There is no liability if the disposal is of certain UK Government Securities.
[2] See Chapter 9 about possible relief under a double taxation agreement.
[3] Liability will arise if the assets were used or held for the purposes of a trade, profession or vocation carried on in the UK through a branch or agency or by the branch or agency.
[4] Gains arising during a period of temporary non-residence may be chargeable (see paragraphs 8.4–8.6).
Commentary—*Simon's Direct Tax Service* **Parts C1, C2**.

9 Double taxation relief

9.1 If you have income or gains from a source in one country and are resident in another, you may be liable to pay tax in both countries under their tax laws. To avoid 'double taxation' in this situation, the UK has negotiated double taxation agreements with a large number of countries. A list of these is given at paragraph 9.16.

Non-residents, and residents of more than one country

9.2 If you are a resident of a country with which the UK has a double taxation agreement, you may be able to claim exemption or partial relief from UK tax on certain types of income from UK sources. You may also be able to claim exemption from capital gains tax on the disposal of assets. The precise conditions of exemption or relief can be found in the relevant agreement. It is not possible to give full details here as they vary from agreement to agreement. If you are resident both in the UK and a country with which the UK has a double taxation agreement, there may be special provisions in the agreement for treating you as a resident of only one of the countries for the purposes of the agreement.

9.3 Normally, you will receive some relief from UK tax on the following sources of income under an agreement—

- pensions and some annuities (other than UK Government pensions)
- royalties
- dividends (paid before 6 April 1999)
- interest

Some agreements state that you must be subject to tax in the other country on the income in question before you get relief from UK tax.

9.4 If you receive a pension paid by the UK for service to the UK Government or to a local authority in the UK, you will usually be taxed only by the UK.

9.5 If you are carrying on a trade or running a business through a permanent establishment in the UK, you may not qualify for any relief from UK tax on royalties, interest or dividends connected with the permanent establishment. A 'permanent establishment' includes, for example, a place of management, a branch or an office.

Earnings from employment and professional services

9.6 Under many double taxation agreements you may be able to claim exemption from UK tax on—

- earnings from an employment, and—
- profits or earnings for independent, personal or professional services

carried on in the UK, if you are a resident of the overseas country for the purposes of the agreement (see paragraph 9.2). The usual conditions to be met are—

- in the case of employments
  - you must not be in the UK for more than 183 days in the period (often, twelve months) specified in the agreement, and
  - your remuneration must be paid by (or on behalf of) an employer who is not resident in the UK, and it must not be borne by a UK branch of your employer
- in the case of independent, personal or professional services, you must not operate from a fixed base in the UK (or, in the case of some agreements, spend more than a specified number of days in the UK).

Teachers and researchers

9.7 Under some agreements, if you are a teacher or professor who comes to the UK to teach in a school, college, university or other educational establishment for a period of two years or less, you

Misc

are exempt from UK tax on your earnings from the teaching post. Temporary absences from the UK during this period normally count as part of the two years.

Some agreements cover persons who engage in research. Where this is so, the rules are normally the same as for teachers.

9.8 If you stay for more than two years you cannot claim exemption and you will be liable to tax on the whole of your earnings from the date you arrived. Some agreements only allow exemptions to be given if the earnings are liable to tax in your home country. If you have already received exemption for a visit (or visits) of up to two years, some agreements will not allow you to claim the exemption again if you make a further visit at a later date.

Students and apprentices

9.9 Under most agreements, if you are an overseas student or apprentice visiting the UK solely for full-time education or training, you will not pay tax on payments from sources outside the UK for your maintenance, education or training.

A number of agreements also provide that students or apprentices visiting this country will be exempt from UK tax on certain earnings from employment here. Individual agreements impose various restrictions on this relief, including, for example, monetary limits and conditions as to the type of employment.

Entertainers and sportsmen/women

9.10 Under most agreements, if you are not resident in the UK and you come here as an entertainer or sportsman/woman, any payments you receive will be liable to UK tax. The exemption described in paragraph 9.6 will not apply. You should contact the Foreign Entertainers Unit (see paragraph 9 of the Introduction) for advice on how your income as an entertainer or sportsman/woman will be treated for tax purposes.

This includes, for example, actors and musicians performing on stage or screen and those participating in all kinds of sports.

Dividends

9.11 If you are resident in the UK, you are entitled to a tax credit when you receive a dividend from a company resident in the UK. We charge income tax on the total of the dividend and the tax credit. The tax credit is available to reduce your tax liability. The rate of the tax credit was reduced from 20% to 10% from 6 April 1999, reflecting the reduction in the rate of tax on dividend income from that date.

For dividends paid up to 5 April 1999, if all or any part of your dividend income is not taxable (for example, because you are a non-taxpayer), you may make a claim for the tax credit to be paid to you. However, payment of tax credits cannot be claimed in respect of dividends paid after 5 April 1999. (Tax credits will continue to be paid on dividends within an individual savings account or personal equity plan, up to 5 April 2004.)

Prior to 6 April 1999 companies with dividends paid wholly out of foreign source income could opt to have them treated as 'foreign income dividends' (FIDs). FIDs do not carry any tax credit, and are treated as paid to shareholders with notional income tax already deducted. This notional tax cannot be repaid to you.

9.12 If you are not resident in the UK, the normal rule is that you are not entitled to a tax credit when you receive a dividend from a UK company. From 6 April 1996 you do not pay UK tax (and before that date you would have paid UK tax, if at all, only at the higher rate) on any dividends.

You may, however, be entitled to a tax credit if you are a resident of a country with which the UK has a double taxation agreement, and the agreement provides for payment of the same tax credit as a UK resident would be entitled to receive. In that case, you are liable to income tax on the total of the dividend and tax credit, at the rate of tax laid down in the agreement. For periods up to 5 April 1999, you may claim payment of the tax credit in excess of the amount which the UK is entitled to retain.

From 6 April 1999, all double taxation agreements that provide for payment of a tax credit on dividends paid by UK companies continue to give that right. However, because the rate of tax credit has been reduced (see paragraph 9.11), the amount which the UK is entitled to retain under those agreements will in practice cover the whole of the tax credit. So if you make a claim under an agreement where a dividend has been paid on or after 6 April 1999, there will be no balance of tax credit left for us to pay to you.

9.13 You may also have the right to a tax credit if you receive UK tax allowances and reliefs through a claim in accordance with paragraph 7.3. But if you can only claim these allowances because of the terms of a double taxation agreement (the final category in paragraph 7.3), whether you are entitled to the tax credit will depend on the terms of the agreement.

Capital gains

9.14 Under many agreements, if you are a resident of another country for the purposes of the agreement, you will often be liable to tax only in the other country on any gains you make from disposing of assets. In that case, you will be exempt from capital gains tax in the UK even if you are ordinarily resident here. If, however, you are carrying on a trade or running a business through a permanent establishment in the UK, any gains you make from disposing of assets connected with the permanent establishment will continue to be chargeable to capital gains tax in the UK.

UK residents

9.15 If you are resident in the UK and have overseas income or gains which are taxable in both the UK and the country of origin, you may qualify for relief against UK tax for all or part of the overseas tax you have paid. Even if there is no double taxation agreement between the UK and the other country concerned, you may still be entitled to relief under special provisions in the UK's tax legislation.

List of the UK's double taxation agreements

9.16 Countries with which the UK has double taxation agreements in force covering taxes on income and/or capital gains (other than limited agreements concerned solely with air transport and shipping) at October 1999 were as follows—

Antigua and Barbuda	Iceland	Pakistan
Argentina	India	Papua New Guinea
Australia	Indonesia	Philippines
Austria	Ireland (Republic of)	Poland
Azerbaijan	Isle of Man	Portugal
Bangladesh	Israel	Romania
Barbados	Italy	Russian Federation
Belarus [1]	Ivory Coast (Côte d'Ivoire)	St Kitts and Nevis
Belgium	Jamaica	Sierra Leone
Belize	Japan	Singapore
Bolivia	Jersey	Slovak Republic (Slovakia)
Botswana	Kazakhstan	Slovenia [2]
Brunei	Kenya	Solomon Islands
Bulgaria	Kiribati	South Africa
Canada	Korea (Republic of)	Spain
China	Latvia	Sri Lanka
Croatia [2]	Lesotho	Sudan
Cyprus	Luxembourg	Swaziland
Czech Republic	Macedonia [2]	Sweden
Denmark	Malawi	Switzerland
Egypt	Malaysia	Thailand
Estonia	Malta	Trinidad and Tobago
Falkland Islands	Mauritius	Tunisia
Fiji	Mexico	Turkey
Finland	Mongolia	Tuvalu
France	Montserrat	Uganda
Gambia	Morocco	Ukraine

Misc

Germany	Myanmar (Burma)	USA
Ghana	Namibia	Uzbekistan
Greece	Netherlands	Venezuela
Grenada	New Zealand	Vietnam
Guernsey	Nigeria	Yugoslavia (Federal Republic) [2]
Guyana	Norway	Zambia
Hungary	Oman	Zimbabwe

Notes[1] The UK's agreement with the Soviet Union is to be regarded as in force between the UK and the former Soviet Republic marked. The position with regard to former Soviet Republics not listed is less clear, but the UK will in all cases apply the provisions of the agreement on the basis that it is still in force (until such time as new agreements take effect with particular countries).

[2] The UK's agreement with Yugoslavia is to be regarded as in force between the UK and the former Yugoslav states marked. The position with regard to the remainder of what was Yugoslavia is undetermined.

Commentary—*Simon's Direct Tax Service* **Parts E6, F1**.

10 Appeals

10.1 If you have any dispute with the Inland Revenue about your residence, ordinary residence or domicile, or about any claim for relief from UK tax, and agreement cannot be reached, you have the right to have your case considered by an independent tribunal.

10.2 If the Inland Revenue write to you giving a formal decision, they will explain to you how you may appeal and how long you have for this purpose. You may choose to have an appeal heard by either the General Commissioners or the Special Commissioners in connection with your residence status and claims for relief. All appeals in connection with your ordinary residence status and domicile are heard by the Special Commissioners.

10.3 Both the General Commissioners and the Special Commissioners are independent of the Inland Revenue. Their decisions on questions of fact are final, but you can appeal against their decisions on questions of law to the High Court. Leaflet IR37 'Appeals against tax, National Insurance contributions, Statutory Sick Pay and Statutory Maternity Pay' explains the procedures in full. It can be obtained from any Tax Office or Inland Revenue Enquiry Centre.

Commentary—*Simon's Direct Tax Service* **E6.106**.

PART III

PAYMENT OF UK NATIONAL INSURANCE CONTRIBUTIONS

11 National Insurance contributions

General

11.1 This chapter deals briefly with the rules for payment of National Insurance contributions (NICs) for individuals leaving or coming to the UK. The position broadly depends on whether you are going to or arriving from an EEA country, a country with which the UK has a bilateral Social Security Agreement covering NICs, or some other country.

The EEA countries are Austria, Belgium, Denmark, Finland, France, Germany, Greece, Iceland, Italy, Liechtenstein, Luxembourg, Netherlands, Norway, Portugal, Ireland (Republic of), Spain and Sweden.

The countries with which the UK 1 has a bilateral Social Security Agreement in force covering NICs at October 1999 were as follows—

Barbados	Jersey
Bermuda	Macedonia [2]
Bosnia Herzegovina [2]	Malta
Canada (excluding Quebec)	Mauritius
Croatia [2]	Philippines
Cyprus	Slovenia [2]

Guernsey	Switzerland
Isle of Man	Turkey
Israel	USA
Jamaica	Yugoslavia (Federal Republic) [2]

Notes[1] Some agreements include the Isle of Man, Guernsey and Jersey as part of the UK; where that is the case the benefits and obligations of the agreement apply also to those countries.
[2] The UK's agreement with Yugoslavia is to be regarded as in force between the UK and the former Yugoslav states marked.

11.2 The terms 'resident' and 'ordinarily resident' in relation to NICs do not have the same meaning as they do for tax purposes. The tax rules set out in the first part of this booklet are not therefore relevant. Leaflet NI38 'Social Security abroad' gives guidance on the rules that apply for NI purposes.

11.3 If you want further information about paying UK NICs, or copies of leaflets mentioned in this Chapter, you should contact the Inland Revenue's National Insurance Contributions Office, International Services (see paragraph 9 of the Introduction), or your local National Insurance Contributions Office.

Going abroad

EEA countries

11.4 If you are going to another EEA country, the European Community Social Security Regulations apply. The general rule is that you will be subject to the social security legislation of the country in which you work; but there are some exceptions, as explained in the following paragraphs. Leaflet SA29 'Your social security insurance, benefits and health care rights in the European Community, and in Iceland, Liechtenstein and Norway' gives further details.

11.5 If your UK employer sends you to work in another EEA country for not more than 12 months at the outset, you and your UK employer will usually continue paying UK NICs as if you were still in the UK. Your employer will need to apply on your behalf to the National Insurance Contributions Office, International Services, for form E101. This confirms that you will continue to pay UK NICs while working in the other country and will ensure that you are not required to contribute to the other country's social security scheme.

Form E128 (which will be issued with form E101) provides healthcare cover abroad for you and any family members who accompany you for the period of your employment in the other country. This form will cover the same period as form E101.

11.6 If your job in the other EEA country lasts longer than 12 months—even though you did not expect it to—you and your UK employer may continue paying UK NICs, for not more than another 12 months. However, the social security authorities in the other country must first agree to this. Your UK employer must, before the end of the first 12 months, apply on forms E102 to the social security authorities in the other country. These forms can be obtained from the National Insurance Contributions Office, International Services. If the social security authorities in the other country agree to the request, another form E128 will be issued to provide cover for healthcare.

There are also special arrangements that allow you to continue paying UK NICs for longer periods, but usually for no more than five years. The social security authorities in the other country must agree to this.

11.7 Similar rules apply if you are self-employed. You must obtain forms E101/E102/E128 from the National Insurance Contributions Office, International Services.

11.8 Different rules apply if you belong to one of the following groups

– those who work in more than one country
– mariners
– transport workers
– civil servants
– members of the staff of diplomatic or consular posts
– those who work for a member of the staff of a diplomatic or consular post
– members of the staff of the European Communities
– members of Her Majesty's forces
– civilians who work for Her Majesty's forces in Germany, or for an organisation like NAAFI which serves Her Majesty's forces.

In many of these cases, you will continue to pay UK NICs.

11.9 If you work in another EEA country in any other circumstances (for example, for a foreign employer) or you intend to remain abroad indefinitely, you will probably have to pay social security contributions to the other country's scheme. If so, you will not be required to pay UK NICs. However, it may be possible for you to pay UK voluntary NICs to protect your UK basic pension rights. There are more details in leaflet NI38, which contains an application form to pay UK voluntary NICs.

Misc

Agreement countries

11.10 If you are going to a country with which the UK has a bilateral Social Security Agreement covering NICs, the position will depend on the terms of the particular agreement. The general rule is that you will be subject to the social security legislation of the country in which you work; but there are some exceptions to this rule, as explained in the following paragraphs. There are information leaflets for each country (see paragraph **11.3** on how to obtain copies).

11.11 If your UK employer sends you to work in a country with which the UK has an agreement, you may be required to continue paying UK NICs as if you were still in the UK. How long you continue to pay UK NICs depends on the particular agreement. Your employer will need to apply on your behalf to the National Insurance Contributions Office, International Services for a certificate confirming that UK NICs continue to be paid while you are working in the other country. This will ensure that you are not required to contribute to the other country's social security scheme.

Unlike the EEA, there is no general provision for healthcare arrangements in most of the bilateral agreements.

Some agreements include provisions which may allow you to continue paying UK NICs for longer than the normal period under the agreement.

11.12 Not all agreements cover the self-employed. In the case of those that do, similar rules apply as for those in employment.

Certain agreements contain special rules for particular groups, such as civil servants, mariners or transport workers.

11.13 If you work in a country with which the UK has an agreement in any other circumstances, for example, for a foreign employer, or you intend to remain abroad indefinitely, you will probably have to pay social security contributions to the other's country scheme. If so, you will not be required to pay UK NICs. However, it may be possible for you to pay UK voluntary NICs to protect your UK basic pension rights. There are more details in leaflet NI38, which contains an application form to pay UK voluntary NICs.

Other countries

11.14 If you are going to any other country, the position will depend on the domestic rules there. Leaflets NI38 and NI132 'National insurance for employers of people working abroad' give information.

11.15 If your UK employer sends you to work in a country outside the EEA and not covered by a bilateral agreement, you will be required to continue paying UK NICs for the first 52 weeks of employment in the other country where all the following conditions apply

- your employer has a place of business in the UK
- you are ordinarily resident in the UK
- you were resident in the UK immediately before starting the work abroad.

11.16 No certificate is required to confirm that you continue to pay UK NICs. Some countries will require you, in addition to your UK NICs, to contribute to their social security scheme. After 52 weeks you are not required to continue paying

UK NICs, but you may pay voluntary NICs to protect your UK basic pension rights. There are more details in leaflet NI38, which contains an application form to pay UK voluntary NICs.

Should you decide not to pay voluntary UK NICs, your UK National Insurance record will still be protected for certain social security benefits (but not retirement pension or widow's benefit) on your return to the UK.

Arriving from abroad

11.17 If you arrive here from abroad and take up employment with a UK employer, or take up self-employment, you will generally be required to pay UK NICs; but there are some exceptions to this rule, as explained in the following paragraphs.

EEA countries

11.18 If an employer in another EEA country sends you to work in the UK for up to 12 months (longer in special cases), you may be able to continue paying foreign social security contributions. If form E101 is issued by the foreign social security institution, confirming that you continue to contribute to the foreign scheme, you will not have to pay UK NICs. Similar provisions apply to self-employed people who are working temporarily in the UK. Leaflet SA29 gives further information.

Agreement countries

11.19 If you are sent to work temporarily in the UK by an employer in a country with which the UK has a bilateral Social Security Agreement covering NICs, you may be able to continue paying foreign social security contributions. If a certificate is issued by the foreign social security institution, confirming that you continue to contribute to the foreign scheme, you will not have to pay UK NICs.

The information leaflet for each country (see paragraph 11.10) gives further details, and also explains if there are provisions for the self-employed in a particular agreement.

Other countries

11.20 If you are sent to work temporarily in the UK by an employer in a country which is outside the EEA and not covered by a bilateral Social Security Agreement, the general rule is that neither you nor your employer has to pay UK NICs for the first 52 weeks of your employment in the UK. NICs are payable from the 53rd week. If the foreign employer does not have a place of business in the UK, NICs are due from the UK 'host' employer (if the posting began on or after 6 April 1994).

These notes are for guidance only and reflect the position at the time of writing. They do not affect any right of appeal.

Issued by the External Communications Unit of the Inland Revenue

December 1999

Misc III. Revenue booklet IR 56

EMPLOYED OR SELF-EMPLOYED? A GUIDE FOR TAX AND NATIONAL INSURANCE

[Preface]

This leaflet is to help you find out if you are employed or self-employed.

Your employment status affects the tax and national insurance you have to pay, so it is important you know which heading your job falls under.

The law doesn't define "employment" and "self-employment". You or your employer can't simply call your job "employment" or "self-employment". The questions [below] should help you to decide your employment status, although they are only a brief guide and don't cover every situation. It is not possible to list all the factors which may be relevant or provide a precise guide to their relative importance. For each engagement the whole picture needs to be looked at in the light of all the facts.

If you are unsure, or you have any questions, ask at your local Inland Revenue Enquiry Centre or Tax Office, or Inland Revenue (NI Contributions) Office. Each office has someone responsible for all enquiries and decisions about employment status.

In most cases it will be obvious whether you are employed or self-employed. For example, if you work for a company on a production line in its factory, you are almost certainly employed. It may be clear that you are an employee because you have been given a written statement of your employment terms, or you may be a member of a pension scheme open only to employees.

You are self-employed if you are in business on your own, for example if you run your own shop, or are buying and selling goods, or providing services direct to the public from your own office premises.

However, sometimes it isn't so easy to decide. You'll need to look at your job as a whole, taking into account all the conditions you work under in the light of the guidelines below.

As well as applying for tax and national insurance purposes, these considerations may apply in employment law matters such as unfair dismissal and redundancy. However, other considerations may also be relevant in these areas, so your position under employment law will not necessarily be the same as under tax and national insurance law. For employment protection purposes the industrial tribunals, which are independent judicial bodies, will decide whether someone who makes a complaint is employed or self-employed.

Bear in mind that because you are self-employed in one job doesn't necessarily mean you will be in your next job.

Employed or self-employed?

Employed

If you can answer "Yes" to the following questions, you are probably **employed**.

- Do you yourself have to do the work rather than hire someone else to do it for you?
- Can someone tell you at any time what to do or when and how to do it?
- Are you paid by the hour, week, or month? Can you get overtime pay?
- Do you work set hours, or a given number of hours a week or month?
- Do you work at the premises of the person you work for, or at a place or places he or she decides?

Self-employed

If you can answer "Yes" to the following questions, it will usually mean you are **self-employed**.

- Do you have the final say in how the business is run?
- Do you risk your own money in the business?
- Are you responsible for meeting the losses as well as taking the profits?

Misc

- Do you provide the main items of equipment you need to do your job, not just the small tools many employees provide for themselves?
- Are you free to hire other people on your own terms to do the work you have taken on? Do you pay them out of your own pocket?
- Do you have to correct unsatisfactory work in your own time and at your own expense?

Special rules

These may apply to certain jobs or positions. If for instance—

- your work is arranged through an agency;
- you are a company director or the secretary of a club or the holder of any other office;

you will normally have to pay tax and national insurance contributions as if you are an employee.

There are also special rules which apply to national insurance contributions but not tax. These may affect you if—

- you are an office cleaner;
- you are a minister of religion;
- you are an examiner, moderator or invigilator of an examining board;
- you are a school teacher, lecturer or instructor;
- you work for someone in your family.

Ask at your local Inland Revenue (NI Contributions) Office for advice.

Casual, short term, temporary or part-time working

The same considerations to determine employment status will apply even if you work part-time or for a short period. Unless you can answer ''Yes'' to the self-employed questions, you will normally be an employee.

If—

- you have more than one job, or
- you work for a number of different people for a few days or weeks at a time;

you will need to answer the questions [above] for each job. Remember, because you are self-employed in one job, it doesn't necessarily mean you will be self-employed in any other job you take on. Where, however, you provide services to many different persons and do not work regularly for one person to the exclusion of others, this may be relevant to the decision whether your work for each is as an employee, or a self-employed person.

You can even be employed and self-employed at the same time in different jobs. For example, you could be employed as a part-time shop assistant and spend the rest of your time running your own business from home. You could work full time in a factory as an employee, and run a part time business in the evening or weekends. You may have a number of short term or part-time activities, some of which may amount to employments and others to self employment. It all depends on the facts.

What about my tax and national insurance?

Employed

It will normally be your employer's responsibility to deduct tax and national insurance from your pay under PAYE and pay it over to the Inland Revenue. The Inland Revenue leaflet IR34 ''PAYE – Pay As You Earn'' explains this in more detail.

Self-employed

You are responsible for your own tax and national insurance. This means—

- telling your Tax Office and Inland Revenue (NI Contributions) Office if you haven't already done so, that you are in business;
- telling your Tax Office about all your income. Once you have told the Tax Office that you are in business, they will normally send you a Tax Return each year to enable you to do this. However, you must still tell the Inland Revenue about income you have in any tax year, even if the Tax Office doesn't send you a Return for that year;
- paying the tax;
- paying Class 2 national insurance contributions. You will be sent a bill every 13 weeks, in arrears unless you choose to pay monthly by direct debit;
- paying Class 4 national insurance contributions—see Inland Revenue leaflet IR24 ''Class 4 National Insurance Contributions'' or leaflet CA03 [NP18] ''National Insurance for Self-Employed People Class 2 and 4'' for more information.

Being self-employed also affects—

- the social security benefits you can claim, such as unemployment benefit;
- other rights, for example those under employment legislation, such as the right to maternity leave, or to a redundancy payment, notice rights and so on;

– your liability to the public for the work you do for them.

If you would like to know more about how the tax and national insurance systems affect the self-employed, there are a number of leaflets to help you. These are listed on the [Revenue website].

Still not sure?

If you are not sure whether you are employed or self-employed, or if you have any other questions, please get in touch with your local Inland Revenue Enquiry Centre, Tax Office or Inland Revenue (NI Contributions) Office of the DSS for advice. They can give you a written decision about your employment status for tax and National Insurance purposes. If you can't agree with their decision, you can appeal against it. Leaflet IR37 ''Appeals against tax'' gives you more information about how to appeal against an Inland Revenue decision.

If you are not sure whether employment protection rights apply to you, an industrial tribunal would decide whether you were employed or self-employed if you complained that these rights had been infringed.

If you are paying someone to work for you and are not sure if you are the employer responsible for deducting PAYE/national insurance from his or her pay, your local Tax Enquiry Centre, Tax Office or Inland Revenue (NI Contributions) Office can also advise you. You may also find the Inland Revenue leaflet IR53 ''Thinking of taking someone on?'' helpful.

...

Issued by the Inland Revenue

April 1999

Misc IV. Revenue booklet IR 124

USING YOUR OWN VEHICLE FOR WORK

Introduction

This leaflet is for employees who use their own car, van, motor cycle or bicycle when they travel on business from 6 April 2002.

For details of the rules before 6 April 2002 please ask for leaflet IR125 ''Using your own car or motor bike for work''.

If you use a bicycle ask your Tax Office for leaflet IR176 ''Tax, National Insurance contributions and Green Travel''.

This leaflet tells you—

- which journeys qualify as business travel
- how using your own vehicle for business travel can affect the amount of tax and national insurance contributions (NICs) you pay
- about taxable profit and tax relief
- about keeping records of allowances and business mileage
- the information your employer will give you
- what information you should give the Inland Revenue.

It also provides you with detailed examples and a work sheet to help you to calculate your own tax position.

If there is something we have not covered, or you are in doubt about anything in this guide, please contact any Inland Revenue Enquiry Centre or Tax Office. Details are in your phone book under ''Inland Revenue''.

If you are VAT registered, the VAT rules on motoring expenses are set out in Notice 700/64, which is available from the Customs and Excise website www.hmce.gov.uk

Using your own vehicle for business travel

What journeys qualify as business travel?

Journeys that count as business travel for both tax and NICs are—

- those you **have to make** in the course of doing your job. For example, if you travel from your office to visit a client and use your own car, van, motor cycle or bicycle
- those you make to or from a place you **have to attend** in order to do your job. For example, if you travel directly from home to visit a client (unless the journey is practically the same as your ordinary commuting journey, because the client's premises are just down the road from your office).

What journeys do not qualify as business travel?

Journeys that do not count as business travel include—

– ordinary commuting – travel between your home, or any other place you attend for personal reasons (such as the home of a friend or relative) and your usual workplace, or
– private travel – any other travel where the purpose is not for business.

If you are paid an allowance for any journey that is ordinary commuting or private travel, your employer should deduct tax and NICs from it. See our leaflet IR34 ''PAYE. Pay As You Earn'' for more information.

Most employees who use their own car, van, motor cycle or bicycle to travel on business are paid an allowance by their employer to cover some or all of the costs. It can be in the form of a lump sum or periodic payments, but usually the allowance is based on an amount per mile.

How does it affect my tax and national insurance contributions?

From 6 April 2002, there is a new system for working out whether you have to pay tax and NICs on any payments your employer makes to you for using your own vehicle for business journeys. Under the new rules, there is a maximum amount that you can receive without paying tax. This is called an ''approved mileage allowance payment'' (AMAP) and is calculated by using approved mileage rates.

The approved mileage rates are also used to work out whether you have to pay NICs on your business motoring expenses. See [national insurance contributions] for more information.

The approved mileage rates

From 6 April 2002, the approved mileage rates are—

	First 10,000 business miles in the tax year	*Each mile over 10,000 miles in the tax year*
Cars and vans	40p	25p
Motor cycles	24p	24p
Bicycles	20p	20p

How much can I receive without paying tax and NICs?

This depends on the type of vehicle that you use and, for cars and vans, on the number of business miles you drive in the year.

What if I am paid more than the AMAP rate?

If your employer pays you more than the AMAP rate you will be liable to pay tax on the excess. Tax will normally be dealt with through your PAYE tax code or your Self Assessment tax return, if you receive one (see *Tax*).

Your employer will work out whether you need to pay NICs on any motoring expenses you receive (see *Calculating NICs on motoring expenses*)

What if I am paid less than the AMAP rate?

If you are not paid a mileage allowance or your employer pays less than the AMAP rate you can get tax relief against your earnings for the difference. This is called 'mileage allowance relief' (MAR). If you want to claim relief you will have to keep a record of—

– your business miles, and
– the mileage allowance payments made by your employer.

You cannot claim tax relief for any costs above the AMAP rate.

What about payments made for passengers?

If your employer pays you an allowance for business passengers the maximum amount you can get without paying tax and NICs is 5p per mile per passenger. You will be liable to pay tax and NICs on any amount over that.

For payment to be free of tax and NICs the passenger must also be an employee on business travel.

If your employer pays less than 5p per mile per passenger or does not pay you an allowance for passengers you cannot claim tax relief on the difference.

What about my car insurance?

It is a good idea to check the position with your insurance provider, especially if your employer pays a passenger rate to encourage car sharing on business journeys. You will need to check that—

– the insurance company is satisfied that no profit or reward is involved, and
– your insurance remains valid.

Tax

Keeping records of allowances and business travel for tax purposes

To work out if the allowances you have received from your employer come to more or less than the new AMAP, you first need to know

- what allowances* you were paid in recognition of the use of your vehicle for business travel during the tax year (a tax year runs from 6 April in one year to 5 April in the next)
- your total business mileage during the year.

*Excluding amounts from which your employer has deducted PAYE tax.

What records do I need to keep?

It is important that you keep records of your allowances and business mileage so you can—

- check your PAYE tax code
- complete a tax return fully and accurately, if you get one
- claim tax relief for business travel
- answer any enquiries from your Tax Office.

To help you, we have included a log sheet which you can use to keep a record of your allowances and business mileage.

What if I travel on business for more than one employment?

If you have two or more employments that are associated then your business travel for both is added together to work out when you have travelled 10,000 business miles.

Employments are associated if they are—

- with the same employer, or
- with different employers who are under the same control, for example, two different companies in the same group of companies.

If the employments are not associated a separate 10,000 mile limit is applied to each.

How do I work out the tax position on my business travel?

You need to

- work out how many business miles you have travelled in the tax year
- multiply the number of business miles you travelled by the AMAP rate, to give you your total approved mileage allowance payments
- add up all the allowances you received from your employer
- compare the difference between that and your total AMAP.

The three examples on the following pages show you how to calculate the tax position on business travel.

Example

Ann uses her own car for business travel. In the tax year 2002–2003 (6 April 2002 to 5 April 2003) Ann travels 5,000 miles on business. Her employer pays her 44p a mile for all her business miles.

Step 1
Total business miles travelled 5,000

Step 2
5,000 business miles at 40p a mile £2,000
Total approved mileage allowance payments **£2,000** **(A)**

Step 3
Allowances received from employer
5,000 at 44p per mile **£2,200** **(B)**

Step 4
Difference between A and B **£200** **(C)**

If A is bigger than B, C is the amount on which Ann can claim tax relief. If B is bigger than A, C is the amount of taxable profit.

In this example, B is bigger than A so Ann has to pay tax on the profit of £200.

Example

Jack uses his own car for business travel. He is paid a mileage allowance of 44p a mile. Whenever he drives directly from home to a business appointment, away from his usual office, his employer does not pay for the first 20 miles that Jack would have driven if he had made his usual commuting journey.

In 2002–03, Jack travels 12,000 miles on business, but his employer pays him a mileage allowance for only 10,000 miles so he receives £4,400 (10,000 x 44p). Jack's tax position is calculated as follows—

Step 1
Total business miles travelled — 12,000

Step 2
First 10,000 business miles at 40p a mile — £4,000
Next 2,000 business miles at 25p a mile — £500
Total approved mileage allowance payments — **£4,500** (A)

Step 3
Allowances received from employer
10,000 at 44p per mile — **£4,400** (B)

Step 4
Difference between A and B — **£100** (C)

In this example, A is bigger than B so Jack can claim tax relief on £100.

Example

Steve uses his own car for business travel. He has two employments that are not associated. ABC Ltd pays him a mileage allowance of 30p a mile while XYZ Ltd pays him a mileage allowance of 45p a mile.

In 2002–03, Steve travels 12,000 miles on business for ABC Ltd and 4,000 business miles for XYZ Ltd. Steve's tax position is calculated as follows—

ABC Ltd

Step 1
Total business miles travelled — 12,000

Step 2
First 10,000 business miles at 40p a mile — £4,000
Next 2,000 business miles at 25p a mile — £500
Total approved mileage allowance payments — **£4,500** **(A)**

Step 3
Allowances received from employer
12,000 at 30p per mile — **£3,600** **(B)**

Step 4
Difference between **A** and **B** — £900 **(C)**

For his employment with ABC Ltd, A is bigger than B so Steve can claim tax relief on £900.

XYZ Ltd

Step 1
Total business miles travelled — 4,000

Step 2
4,000 business miles at 40p a mile — £1,600
Total approved mileage allowance payments — **£1,600** **(A)**

Step 3
Allowances received from employer
4,000 at 45p per mile — **£1,800** **(B)**

Step 4
Difference between **A** and **B** — **£200** **(C)**

For his employment with XYZ Ltd, B is bigger than A so Steve has to pay tax on the profit of £200.

Overall, Steve will be able to claim tax relief on the difference between his two employments.

Tax relief due from ABC Ltd	£900
Less taxable profit from XYZ Ltd	£200
Total relief due	**£700**

Work sheet

Use this work sheet to calculate your tax position using the approved mileage allowance payment (AMAP) rates.

Step 1
Total business miles travelled ________

Step 2
First 10,000 business miles at ..... p.a. mile £ ________
Next .... business miles at ...... p.a. mile £ ________
Total approved mileage allowance payments £ ________ **(A)**

Step 3
Allowance received from employer £ ________ **(B)**

Step 4
Difference between A and B £ ________ **(C)**

If A is bigger than B, C is the amount on which you can claim tax relief

If B is bigger than A, C is the profit you have to pay tax on.

For **all** your business mileage travelled

– by motor cycle, use the 24p rate,
– on your bicycle, use the 20p rate.

Claims for mileage allowance relief

What records do I need to support a claim for mileage allowance relief?

If you are going to claim MAR, you will need to keep records of your business mileage for the year and the mileage allowances you were paid by your employer. You can use the log sheet to record this information.

Can I get relief for the costs of cleaning my vehicle?

No.

Can I get separate tax relief for loan interest to buy my vehicle?

No.

Can I get help towards the cost of travelling to a training course?

If your employer pays or reimburses you for travel to work-related training* you will not have to pay tax or NICs on the amount paid or reimbursed. Mileage allowances can be paid tax free up to the AMAP limit. But, unlike business travel, you cannot get relief for any part of the cost of travel that exceeds the amount paid or reimbursed by your employer.

*Work-related training does not include any training you receive as a reward or inducement. For example, you cannot claim the costs of travelling to a conference in Paris if it is your reward for being one of the top ten sales people.

Can I claim for capital allowances?

No. You will not be able to claim capital allowances for your vehicle after the end of the 2001–02 tax year.

Reporting information

What information does my employer provide?

Your employer will—

– report to us the excess of any business mileage allowances paid to you over the tax free AMAP rate, and
– give you details of what has been reported (or let you have a copy of the P11D report form) by 6 July after the end of the tax year.

If the payments you receive for business mileage do not exceed the tax free AMAP rate your employer does not need to report to us.

What information do I need to keep?

If your employer pays less than the AMAP rate, you need to keep records of all your business mileage and any mileage allowances you are paid if you want to get tax relief on the shortfall (see *Tax*). Use the log sheet to help you record the details of each business journey you make.

Misc

What information do I give the Inland Revenue?

It depends on whether or not you get a tax return.

What if I do not receive a tax return?

Your employer will tell us if the mileage allowances they paid you exceed the tax free AMAP rate and we will usually collect any tax that is due through your PAYE tax code.

However, if you think you should get tax relief, send us your calculation or ask for the Expenses Claim form P87.

What if I receive a tax return?

Your employer will tell you if you have a taxable profit on your allowances. You should enter the amount in box 1.15 of the Employment Pages on your tax return.

If your employer pays less than the AMAP rate you should work out the amount of tax relief that is due and enter that amount in box 1.32 of the Employment Pages on your tax return.

Log sheet—business mileage and allowances

You can use this log sheet to keep a record of your business mileage for the year and the mileage allowances you are paid by your employer.

Date of journey details business journey	Total business miles	Mileage allowances received

National Insurance contributions

Calculating NICs on motoring expenses

Your employer will work out the amount of NICs you have to pay each time they pay you. In most cases this will be weekly or monthly.

Your employer will also work out whether you have to pay NICs on the business motoring expenses they pay you. If you do have to pay NICs on these expenses, your employer will add them to your normal weekly or monthly pay and will work out the total amount of NICs you must pay.

To work out whether you have to pay NICs on your business motoring expenses, your employer will—

- multiply the total number of business miles that you have travelled by the approved mileage rate, to find out how much of your motoring expense can be paid free of NICs;
- compare that figure to the amount they have paid you.

If the amount your employer has paid you is more than the NICs free amount you will have to pay NICs on the excess.

If you use your own car or van for business travel your employer will use the higher, first 10,000 mile, approved rate in all NICs calculations, irrespective of the actual number of business miles you travel.

In calculating the NICs free amount, your employer will include all payments made to you for using your own vehicle for business purposes. This will include mileage allowances that are based on a set rate per mile, regular lump sum payments and one-off payments which are paid in recognition of the use of your vehicle for business travel.

The following three examples show you how your employer will calculate whether NICs are due on your business motoring expenses.

Example

Gita uses her own car for business travel. In June 2002 Gita travels 100 miles on business. Her employer pays her 44p a mile for all her business miles.

NICs free amount	
100 business miles at 40p a mile	£40.00
Allowances received from employer	
100 at 44p per mile	£44.00
NICs due on	**£4.00**

In this example, the mileage allowances Gita received from her employer are more than the NICs free amount so she has to pay National Insurance contributions on £4.00.

Example

Fred uses his own car for business travel. He is paid £45 per month towards the costs of using his car for business travel and also 20p a mile for every business mile travelled. In September 2002 Fred travels 300 miles on business.

NICs free amount		
300 business miles at 40p a mile		£120.00
Allowances received from employer		
Monthly payment	£45.00	
300 at 20p per mile	£60.00	
Total allowances received		£105.00
Difference		**£15.00**

Here, the mileage allowances Fred received from his employer are less than the NICs free amount so he doesn't have to pay National Insurance contributions.

Example

Simon's employer pays 50p a mile for business journeys but requires Simon to deduct his normal home to office mileage from the total business miles travelled for each journey. In January 2003 Simon drives 500 business miles but his employer only pays him for 400 miles.

NICs free amount	
500 business miles at 40p a mile	£200.00
Allowances received from employer	
400 at 50p per mile	£200.00
Difference	**NIL**

In this final example, the NICs free amount and the mileage allowances Simon received from his employer are the same so he doesn't have to pay any National Insurance contributions.

...

Issued by Inland Revenue Marketing and Communications
April 2002

Misc V. IR175: Supplying services through a limited company or partnership

October 2001

Do you use a limited company or a partnership to provide your services to clients? If so, you need to know about new tax and national insurance contributions (NICs) rules introduced from 6 April 2000.

This leaflet will help you find out—

- whether the new rules apply to you, and
- what to do if they do apply.

It also answers some common questions and tells you where to get advice if you are still unclear on any point.

Do the rules apply to me?

The rules will apply to you if you answer ''yes'' to both the following questions—

- Would you be an employee if you worked for your client directly and not through your company or partnership?
- Does the company or partnership you work through meet the conditions set out below?

These questions are explained in more detail below.

Misc

Would I have been an employee of my client?

The rules only apply if you would have been an employee of your client, had it not been for the existence of your company or partnership.

If you can answer ''yes'' to the following questions, you would probably have been an employee of your client for the contract in question and therefore within the new rules—

- Do you work set hours, or a given number of hours a week or a month?
- Do you have to do the work yourself rather than hire someone else to do the work for you?
- Can someone tell you at any time what to do or when and how to do it?
- Are you paid by the hour, week or month?
- Can you get overtime pay?
- Do you work at the premises of the person you work for, or at a place or places he or she decides?
- Do you generally work for one client at a time, rather than having a number of contracts?

If you can answer ''yes'' to the following questions, you would probably **not** have been an employee of your client and therefore outside the new rules—

- Do you have the final say in how you do the work for the client?
- Can you make a loss on the contract?
- Do you provide the main items of equipment you need to do the job for the client, not just the small tools many employees provide for themselves?
- Are you free to hire other people on your own terms to do the work you have taken on? Do you pay them out of your own pocket?
- Do you have to correct unsatisfactory work in your own time and at your own expense?
- Do you have a number of customers at the same time?

You will have to think about each contract individually. Some people will find that they have some contracts which would have been employment and so come within the rules, and others which do not.

The number of clients you have **may** be relevant to the decision whether your work for each is as an employee, or as a self employed person. If you have many different clients this **may** indicate self employment, and be a factor that should be considered in addition to the actual details of each contract. If you have a number of different clients, but are unsure whether you are within or outside the rules, you may wish to talk to your local Tax Office.

More information about employment status can be found in leaflet IR56, ''Employed or self-employed'' [see Misc. III above], the February 2000 edition of ''Tax Bulletin'' [see *Revenue and Other Press Releases* ante], the Employment Status Manual as published on the Inland Revenue website www.inlandrevenue.gov.uk, or by contacting your local Tax Office.

Does the company or partnership I work through meet the following conditions?

If your services are supplied through a company.

The rules apply if—

- you (or your family*) control more than 5 per cent of the ordinary share capital of the company, or
- you (or your family*) are entitled to receive more than 5 per cent of any dividends from the company, or
- you receive, or could receive, payments or benefits from the company which are not salary, but could reasonably be taken to represent payment for the services you provide to clients.

If your services are supplied through a partnership of which you are a partner.

The rules apply if—

- you (or your family*) are entitled to 60 per cent or more of the profits of the partnership, or
- all or most of the partnership's income comes from providing services to a single client, or
- the profit sharing arrangements in the partnership are designed to ensure that you receive an amount based on the payments received for your services to clients.

(* family includes an unmarried partner)

What happens if the rules apply to my contract?

Your company/ partnership should operate Pay As You Earn (PAYE) and pay NICs on any payments of salary during the year in the usual way.

You may also have to pay an additional amount of tax and NICs, based on the payments received by your company or partnership for your services, at the end of the tax year or earlier, if you break your connection with the company or partnership during the year (see ''Common questions''). Your company or partnership will also pay employer's NICs on the same amount. The following section tells you how to calculate any end of year payment.

What should I do at the end of the tax year?

At the end of the tax year you will need to check that you have paid the correct amount of tax and NICs. If not, you may have to pay additional tax and NICs.

To calculate if any tax or NICs are due at the end of the year—

1 Add up all the payments your company or partnership has received for your services, under contracts to which the rules apply.

2 Deduct 5 per cent from this total. This is to allow for the costs involved in running your company or partnership. There is no need to show how this money is used.

3 Add any other payments and the value of any benefits in kind (such as the use of a car) you have received directly, not through your company or partnership, for services provided under the contract, if they are not already taxable.

4 Deduct any allowable expenses met by your company or partnership (see ''Common questions'').

5 Deduct any earnings that you have received from your company or partnership in the tax year on which PAYE has been operated and NICs have been paid, and the value of any benefits in kind (such as a car) provided by your company or partnership on which tax and NICs are payable.

6 Deduct the employer's NICs that your company or partnership has paid on the earnings (but not employee NICs) and Class 1A contributions due on the benefits in kind. NICs should be calculated on an annual basis, whether or not you are a director of the company, (see CWG1. ''Employer's Quick Guide to Pay As You Earn and National Insurance Contributions'', Card 12 Company Directors – National Insurance contributions).

7 Work out the amount which, together with the employer's NICs due on it, comes to the amount calculated after Step 6. The result is known as the ''deemed payment''. If the deemed payment is greater than zero you will need to pay more tax and NICs and you should include it in the calculation of PAYE and NICs for the pay period in which it falls. (See ''Common questions''). There is an example of how to calculate a deemed payment at the end of this leaflet.

Common questions

Does the deemed payment have to be paid as salary on 5 April?

No. The deemed payment is simply a means to calculate the tax and NICs due, whether or not any payment is actually made to the worker. It can be paid as salary, but the rules do not require this to happen. It may be given to the worker (or others) in the form of dividends, or may be retained in the company.

You will not have to pay tax twice on the deemed payment if it is paid as dividends. Your Tax Office can explain to you how the tax payable on the dividends can be offset.

The deemed payment and employer's NICs due on it can be deducted when calculating your company's corporation tax.

Companies should be aware an extra payment of tax and NICs may be due at the end of the tax year and budget accordingly.

When must I pay any additional tax and NICs?

Any tax and NICs due at the end of the tax year as a result of the calculation of the deemed payment should be paid according to the normal PAYE and NIC payment rules. The amount of the deemed payment and the tax and NICs due on it should, if possible, be included in the PAYE return by 19 April and in the Employer's Annual Return (Form P35), which has to be sent to the Inland Revenue by 19 May.

Most of the information needed to calculate the final tax and NICs liability should be available before 5 April and it should be possible to make an estimate of the tax and NICs due at that point. It will be important to keep records of relevant income and expenditure so that you can do this.

However, if it is not possible to calculate the correct amount by 19 April, the Inland Revenue will accept a payment of a lower amount on account of the tax and NICs due, as long as it is made clear on the Employer's Annual Return (P35) that the amount is provisional.

There will be an interest charge on any of the tax or NICs due on the deemed payment, if it is paid after 19 April. But, if you make it clear on the P35 that the amount is provisional, no penalties will be charged if you pay the correct amount by the following 31 January.

This concession on penalties will apply for the tax year 2000/ 01 and will be reviewed to establish whether it should continue to apply for subsequent years.

If you do not send the final amount by 31 January following the end of the tax year, the Inland Revenue will take steps to collect any unpaid tax or NICs, and any interest due. In addition penalties may be sought in cases of negligent or fraudulent conduct.

What if I stop working through my service company or partnership before the end of the year?

If you stop working through your service company or partnership before the end of the year, the deemed payment should be calculated in the normal way, and will be treated as having been made immediately before you stop. Please contact your Tax Office for further advice.

What expenses can I deduct in calculating the deemed payment?

In addition to the flat rate deduction of 5 per cent, the following expenses can be deducted in the calculation.

- Any expenses met by your company or partnership that an employee of the client would have been able to claim against income tax if he or she had spent the money personally (such as certain travel expenses, professional subscriptions and premiums for professional indemnity insurance). Inland Revenue booklet 480 ''Expenses and Benefits. A tax guide'' provides full details. More details about travelling expenses are given in the next section.
- Any pension contributions paid by the company to an approved pension scheme for your benefit (but not for anyone else).

What travelling expenses are allowed in calculating the deemed payment?

This will depend on your pattern of working. If you work through your company or partnership for a series of clients in different places, you may be able to deduct the costs of travelling to your clients' places of business. Provided you do not expect to spend more than 40 per cent of your working time at any one site you are entitled to a deduction for all journeys from home to the clients' premises.

If you do spend more than 40 per cent of your time at a single site, but the engagement is both expected to, and actually does, last for no more than 2 years, a deduction for travel costs will also be available. Further details are in Booklet 490 ''Employee Travel – a tax and NICs guide for employers''.

What about company cars?

If you use a car owned by your company or partnership for business travel, a deduction can be made in the calculation of the deemed payment for the costs of that business travel met by your company. You may use the actual costs or the Inland Revenue's authorised mileage rates. Expenses incurred in the course of private use of the car cannot be deducted in calculating the deemed payment.

If the company or partnership provides you with a car for your private use, you will have to pay tax on this benefit according to the rules which apply to other employees. The amount of the car benefit charge can be deducted (at Step 5) in calculating the deemed payment. See sections 11 and 12 of booklet 480 – ''Expenses and benefits. A tax guide'' for further details.

Class 1A NICs paid on the company car benefit will be deductible in the calculation of the deemed payment, alongside other employer's NICs.

Your company or partnership will be able to set any costs of providing the car, including capital allowances, against its taxable profits.

What do I need to put on my Self Assessment return?

The deemed payment is treated as income from employment with the company or partnership. It should be recorded on your Self Assessment return on the supplementary employment pages. If you have any other income from employment with the same company or partnership you should record the total amount, including the deemed payment.

How do I apportion expenses between engagements that are affected by the new rules and those which are not?

In calculating the deemed payment, you can deduct expenses paid by the company or partnership which you would have been allowed to claim against tax if you had been an employee of the client, and spent the money yourself. These expenses must relate specifically to your engagement with that client. You will have to keep suitable records to be able to identify the correct amounts.

For example, this could be by reference to car mileage to work out what part of the motoring expenses related to engagements affected by the new rules.

If a client makes a single payment in respect of two or more workers, how will the income be split between them?

This will depend on the particular facts and circumstances. If a company or partnership receives a payment in respect of services provided by more than one worker, the payment should be apportioned between them, by the company or partnership, on a reasonable basis. The Revenue will re- apportion any payment if it appears the company's or partnership's basis of apportionment is unreasonable. The company can appeal against the decision of the Inland Revenue.

What are my tax and NICs liabilities if I work overseas?

If you work overseas your tax and NICs liabilities are the same as if you were employed directly by the overseas client. Further information on liability and the rules about residency can be found in the Inland Revenue booklet IR20 ''Residents and non-residents – liability to tax in the United Kingdom'' [see Misc II above] or from your local Tax Office.

Can I avoid the legislation by using an offshore service company?

No. If you would have been liable to UK tax and NICs had you been employed directly by the client, you must pay UK tax and NICs under these rules, whether or not your service company is located in the UK.

If an offshore company fails to deduct and account for PAYE tax and NICs under the legislation, liability to pay tax and NICs can be transferred to you. Action to recover employer's NICs not paid by an offshore company could also include action against any assets of that company located in the UK.

The Inland Revenue has powers to obtain details of payments to offshore companies from the records of clients and agencies.

Where can I get advice about whether the legislation applies to my contracts?

Advice can be given on existing contracts only. If you are not sure whether the new legislation applies to a particular engagement, advice will be available from local Tax Offices. They will give a written opinion about employment status for tax and NICs purposes.

The Inland Revenue will review the facts. This will involve looking at whether the relationship between a worker and a client would have been one of employment, if there had been no company or partnership. In order to do this, the Inland Revenue will review the contract or contracts which establish the relationship. They may also talk to you and to others. If you do not agree with the opinion given by the Inland Revenue, and further discussion has failed to achieve agreement, you can request a formal decision against which you can appeal.

If you would like our opinion on a particular engagement you should send your contract(*s*) to

LP10, IR35 Unit, 1st Floor, Tyne Bridge Tower, Church Street, Gateshead, Tyne & Wear NE8 2DT
e-mail: IR35@inlandrevenue.gov.uk Tel: 0845 303 3535 Fax: 0845 302 3535.

*Example of a calculation of the deemed payment under the service provision rules **

Mr Worker works through his own limited company. He provides services to Mr Client under a contract which falls within the new rules. Mr Client pays £40,000 to Mr Worker's limited company for the services provided by Mr Worker.

Mr Worker does no other work in the year in question. He pays himself a salary of £20,000 during the course of the year and operates PAYE and deducts NICs from that salary in the usual way.

The limited company buys Mr Worker a travel card for £500 to allow him to get to Mr Client's business premises. It also pays £4,000 into Mr Worker's pension scheme.

	£**
Total amount from client (all subject to new rules)	**40,000**
Deduct	
5% to reflect the costs involved in running a company or partnership	2,000
Schedule E expenses related to contract	500
Employer's pension contributions, to an approved scheme, on behalf of worker	4,000
Earnings paid to Mr Worker in year (subject to tax under Schedule E)	20,000
Employer's NICs paid in year	1,840
Total deductions	**28,340**
Balance (£40,000–£28,340)	**11,660**
Deemed payment = Balance x 100 ÷ (100 + 11.9)*** (see Step 7)	**10,420**
Schedule E tax and NICs are due on the total of the earnings paid in year plus the deemed payment.	
Employer's NICs due on the deemed payment	1,240
Extra tax and employee's NICs may be due on the deemed payment	

* The calculation assumes the NICs contribution rates, thresholds and earnings limits for 2001/02.

** Rounded to the nearest whole number.

*** The employer's contribution rate can vary, contracted out or in rates are different. The figure you add to 100 to get the correct divisor should be the contributions rate that is applicable to you. See Inland Revenue National Insurance tables CA38 and Employer's Annual Pack.

Where can I get more information?

The Inland Revenue's web site has more information about the tax and NICs consequences where services are supplied through a limited company or partnership, a copy of the legislation and a list of frequently asked questions with answers. The address is www.inlandrevenue.gov.uk/ir35.

Misc

Misc VI. The Treasury General Consents 1988

NON-RESIDENT COMPANIES: GENERAL CONSENTS AND PROCEDURE FOR OBTAINING CONSENT

The Treasury, in exercise of the powers conferred on them by TA 1988 s 765(4) hereby gives the following consents:

Citation and commencement

1 These consents may be cited as the Treasury General Consents 1988 and apply to transactions on and after 15 March 1988.

Interpretation

2—(1) In these consents unless the context otherwise requires—

''company'' means a body corporate;
''non-resident company'' means the body corporate referred to in section 765(1)(*c*) or (*d*) which is not resident in the UK;
[''overseas group'' means two or more companies, including the non-resident company, which are not resident in the United Kingdom and which—

(*a*) are liable to tax in the same territory outside the United Kingdom by reason of domicile, residence or place of management, and
(*b*) would be deemed to be members of a group of companies for the purposes of Chapter IV of Part X of the Income and Corporation Taxes Act 1988][1];

''redeemable'', in relation to shares, means that the shares satisfy one or both of the following conditions:

(*a*) that, by virtue of the terms of their issue, the exercise of a right by any person or the existence of any arrangements, they are liable to be redeemed, cancelled or repaid, in whole or in part;
(*b*) that, by virtue of any material arrangements, the holder has a right to require another person to acquire the shares or is obliged in any circumstances to dispose of them or another person has a right or is in any circumstances obliged to acquire them;

and arrangements are material arrangements if the company which issued the shares or a company connected with that company is a party to the arrangements;

''resident company'' means the body corporate resident in the UK referred to in section 765(1)(*c*) or (*d*);
[''resident group'' means those companies, including the resident company, which are resident in the United Kingdom, and which are deemed to be members of a group of companies for the purposes of Chapter IV of Part X of the Income and Corporation Taxes Act 1988][1];
''section 765(1)(*c*)'' and ''section 765(1)(*d*)'' mean section 765(1)(*c*) and section 765(1)(*d*) of the Taxes Act, as the case may be;
''the Taxes Act'' means the Income and Corporation Taxes Act 1988;
[''territorial group'' means two or more companies which are not resident in the United Kingdom and which—

(*a*) are liable to tax in the same territory outside the United Kingdom by reason of domicile, residence or place of management, and
(*b*) would be deemed to be members of a group of companies for the purposes of Chapter IV of Part X of the Income and Corporation Taxes Act 1988][1];

''transaction'' means a transaction of one of the classes described in section 765(1)(*c*) or (*d*) as the case may be;
and other expressions have the same meaning as in TA 1988 s 765.

(2) The Interpretation Act 1978 shall apply to these consents as it applies to an Act of Parliament.

(3) In applying the provisions of [Chapter IV of Part X of the Income and Corporation Taxes Act 1988][1] for the purposes of the definitions of ''overseas group'', ''resident group'' and ''territorial group'' in sub-paragraph (1) above, the words ''51 per cent subsidiary'' and ''51 per cent subsidiaries'' shall be substituted for ''75 per cent subsidiary'' and ''75 per cent subsidiaries'' as the case may be, wherever they occur in that section.

(4) For the purposes of these consents, any question whether a person is connected with another shall be determined in accordance with the provisions of TA 1988 s 839(2) to (8) (any provision that one person is connected with another being taken to mean that they are connected with one another).

Amendments—[1] Definitions of ''overseas group'', ''resident group'' and ''territorial group'' in para (2) and words in para (3) substituted by Inland Revenue press release dated 28 July 2000.

Revenue Interpretations RI 215—South African groups can now form an ''overseas group'' or a ''territorial group'' for the purposes of these General Consents.

Consent to transactions within section 765(1)(*c*)

3 The Treasury consent generally to transactions of the class described in section 765(1)(*c*) which consist of—

(*a*) the creation of shares by the non-resident company;
(*b*) the issue of shares by the non-resident company:
  (i) to another member of the overseas group, or
  (ii) subject to the conditions prescribed by para 4, to the resident company or to another member of the resident group, or
  (iii) subject to the conditions prescribed by para 5, to a person not connected with the resident company, or
  (iv) subject to the conditions prescribed by para 6, to all persons who are its shareholders at the time of the issue;

(*c*) the creation of debentures by the non-resident company and their issue:
  (i) to another member of the overseas group, or
  (ii) subject to the condition prescribed by paragraph 7, to the resident company or to another member of the resident group, or
  (iii) subject to the conditions prescribed by paragraph 5, to persons not connected with the resident company;

(*d*) transactions of any kind described in subsection (1)(*c*) where the non-resident company:
  (i) was incorporated after 31st December 1951,
  (ii) is liable to tax in a Commonwealth territory other than the UK by reason of domicile, residence or place of management, and
  (iii) was incorporated for the purpose of starting and carrying on a new industrial activity in that Commonwealth territory,

and in this sub-paragraph "industrial activity" means any productive, extractive or manufacturing industry, any public utility, fisheries or any form of husbandry.

4 The conditions prescribed by this paragraph are that the issue:

(*a*) is of shares that are not redeemable; and
(*b*) is made either:
  (i) for full consideration paid in cash to the non-resident company, or
  (ii) in or towards payment for any business undertaking or property acquired by the non-resident company for full consideration.

5 The conditions prescribed by this paragraph are:

(*a*) that the issue:
  (i) is for full consideration paid to the non-resident company, and
  (ii) is not to a nominee or trustee for a person who is connected with the resident company;
(*b*) that no arrangements exist as a consequence of which the resident company or a person connected with the resident company, or a nominee or trustee for that person or that company, is or may become entitled to the shares or debentures so issued or to any of them or to any interest in them or in any of them.

6 The conditions prescribed by this paragraph are that the issue:

(*a*) is in respect of and in proportion to the shares held by the shareholders in the non-resident company at the time of the issue; and
(*b*) is either:
  (i) of shares that are not redeemable, or
  (ii) where no shares are issued to a company which is resident in the UK or to a nominee or trustee for such a company, for full consideration paid in cash to the non-resident company.

7—(1) The condition prescribed by this paragraph is that none of the circumstances set out in sub-paragraph (2) below are associated with, or are present in connection with, the issue of the debentures.

(2) Those circumstances are:

(*a*) that the debentures are issued at a discount;
(*b*) that arrangements exist as a result of which the non-resident company acquires property of any description from a company which is resident in the UK and the consideration, or some part of the consideration, for the acquisition remains unpaid;
(*c*) that a loan, whether or not of the same amount as that secured by the debentures, is made by a company which is not resident in the United Kingdom to a company which is resident in the UK;
(*d*) that any amount payable in respect of the debentures is determined by reference to the movement of an index of prices, earnings or any other indicator of an economic nature published in the UK or elsewhere.

Consent to transactions within section 765(1)(*d*)

8 The Treasury consent generally to transactions of the class described in section 765(1)(*d*) which consist of:

(*a*) the transfer by the resident company of shares or debentures of the non-resident company to another member of the resident group;

(*b*) subject to the conditions prescribed by para 9, the transfer by the resident company or by a company which is not resident in the UK (in para 9 referred to in either case as "the transferor company") of shares or debentures of the non-resident company to a person not connected with the resident company;

(*c*) the transfer by a company which is not resident in the UK of shares or debentures of the non-resident company to a company which is a member of a territorial group of which the first-mentioned company is also a member.

9 The conditions prescribed by this paragraph are:

(*a*) that the transfer:

(i) is for full consideration paid to the transferor company, and

(ii) is not to a nominee or trustee for a person who is connected with the resident company;

(*b*) that no arrangements exist as a consequence of which:

(i) the resident company, or

(ii) a nominee or trustee for the resident company, or

(iii) a person connected with the resident company, or

(iv) a nominee or trustee for a person connected with the resident company,

is or may become entitled to the shares or debentures transferred or to any of them or to any interest in them or in any of them.

Revocation of previous consents

10 All consents previously given generally by the Treasury to transactions of the classes described in section 765(1)(*c*) and (*d*) are hereby revoked.

Notes for guidance (20 September 1988)

Applications for consent under TA 1988 s 765(1)(c), (d)

1 An application for consent to a transaction which does not fall within the "General Consents" should be made by letter addressed to: The Secretary, HM Treasury (AP), Parliament Street, London SW1P 3AG.

Please send three copies of all letters concerning any application but only one copy of accounts or other supporting documents. [Copies of the Treasury General Consents may be obtained either by personal application or letter from the Inland Revenue Public Enquiry Room, West Wing, Somerset House, Strand, London WC2R 1LB or by letter only from The Secretary, HM Treasury (AP), Parliament Street, London SW1P 3AG.]

2 The Treasury obtains the advice of the Revenue on all applications. If the application is urgent, two copies of the letter with all the accounts and other supporting documents may be sent direct to: Inland Revenue, International Division, Room 311, Melbourne House, Aldwych, London WC2B 4LL. The one letter sent to the Treasury should indicate clearly whether copies have been sent to the Revenue.

3 The application should give sufficient information to enable the Treasury to form a view on the transaction proposed; in doing that it is guided by the terms of reference of the Chancellor's Advisory Committee which are as follows:

> "They will take into account the significance of any new factors or circumstances which are represented to require a proposed change and any compelling reason for such application based on the efficiency and development of the applicant's operations. The Committee will weigh against considerations of this kind the prospective loss of revenue or of foreign exchange to the country which the transaction, if permitted, would entail, and they will inform the Chancellor whether, on a balance of considerations, it would, in their opinion, be in the national interest that permission should be granted".

As a result of the removal of Exchange Control, loss of foreign exchange is not a factor which is currently taken into account.

4 The commercial reasons for the proposed transactions should therefore be fully explained and relevant background information given so as to enable the transactions to be understood in their proper context.

5 The application need not be made in any particular form. The Appendix to these notes lists the information which is normally needed, according to the circumstances of the application and the nature of the transaction. In some cases, particularly where the company or group has made other applications, a brief letter may be sufficient. In other cases information additional to that suggested by the Appendix may be needed, including copies of the accounts of the non-resident company and of other group companies involved in the transaction.

6 The letter of the application should authorise the Commissioners of Inland Revenue to disclose particulars of the company's tax affairs to the Advisory Committee, and, insofar as they are not disclosed by the application, to the Treasury.

APPENDIX—RELEVANT INFORMATION

First applications

1 Name of applicant company and name of ultimate UK parent if applicant is a member of a group.

2 Nature of business of the applicant company (and the group) and the place where the main activities are carried on.

3 Whether the company and, if appropriate, its parent is a public or private company.

4 The extent of the shareholdings by non-residents (in the company or its parent as appropriate) if these exceed 20 per cent

5 The Tax District and reference to which the company makes its corporation tax returns.

6 A copy of the latest accounts of the applicant and, if appropriate, of the UK parent.

Subsequent applications

7 Name of applicant company and name of ultimate UK parent if applicant is a member of a group.

8 The date of the last application relating to the overseas company to which the current application refers or, if there is no such application, the date of the latest application by the company or other member of the same group. The Treasury reference number should be quoted.

9 Significant changes in the information previously given at 2–5 above, including the latest accounts.

All applications

10 A description of the proposed transactions.

11 Name, country of incorporation and of tax residence of the non-resident company.

12 Nature of the business of the non-resident company.

13 Extent of applicant's control over the non-resident company (*a*) at present and (*b*) after the proposed transactions. (See TA 1988 ss 767 (5), 840.)

14 The name(*s*) and country or countries of residence of the person(*s*) to whom the issue (other than a public issue) or transfer is to be made and full details of any direct or indirect connection by shareholdings or otherwise between such person(*s*) and the applicant.

15 Full details of the consideration for the issue or transfer.

16 Where an issue is of redeemable shares (as defined for the purposes of the General Consents), the terms of issue and of redemption.

17 If applicable, the reasons why any sale is not at market value.

18 The reasons for the transactions—see paras 3 and 4.

19 An estimate of the effect, if any, on UK tax. This should indicate any difference in the tax payable at any time by the applicant company or any member of the same group as a direct or indirect result of the proposed transaction(*s*) compared with that payable under existing arrangements.

Cross reference—As to the movements of capital between residents of EC member states, see TA 1983 s 765A.

Misc VII. Notes for parties to appeals and other proceedings before the special commissioners

APPEALS AND OTHER PROCEEDINGS BEFORE THE SPECIAL COMMISSIONERS

Lord Chancellor's Department

The office of the Special Commissioners of Income Tax is part of the Court Service Agency and administrative responsibility for the Special Commissioners rests with the Lord Chancellor. The Special Commissioners are not connected with the Inland Revenue, or any other department.

CONTENTS

I.
INFORMATION YOU NEED TO KNOW

1 What is the purpose of the Special Commissioners?

Special Commissioners deal with appeals against assessments made by the Inland Revenue authorities and against certain decisions of the Inland Revenue. They are an alternative Tribunal to the General Commissioners in relation to many appeals but in some appeals the Special Commissioners have exclusive jurisdiction and in a small number of appeals the General Commissioners also have exclusive jurisdiction. The Special Commissioners cannot hear appeals against decisions of the General Commissioners.

Unlike the General Commissioners, who are unpaid laymen, the Special Commissioners are salaried legally qualified judicial officers. The Special Commissioners and the Tribunal staff are entirely independent of the Inland Revenue. They are not part of the Inland Revenue and are quite separate from it. They cannot therefore deal with complaints against Inland Revenue officials.

This leaflet explains how you may bring a case before the Special Commissioners. It does not try to list legal references and is not itself part of the law. Should you or your advisor wish to consult the law, it will be found in the Taxes Acts.

Procedure before the Special Commissioners is regulated by the Special Commissioners (Jurisdiction and Procedure) Regulations 1994 (SI 1994 No. 1811). Those regulations apply in respect to appeals and other proceedings where notice of the hearing was given after 31 August 1994.

2 How much will it cost me to appeal?

The Special Commissioners do not charge any fee for dealing with appeals. Your own costs in preparing your appeal will depend on the difficulty of your case and whether you decide to handle your appeal yourself or instruct a representative. You have the right to be represented by a barrister, a solicitor, or a qualified accountant. Other agents or representatives may appear for you but in an exceptional case the Tribunal may refuse to permit an unqualified representative to appear on your behalf.

Legal aid is not available for appeals to the Special Commissioners.

You should also read paragraph 20 which deals with the award of costs (expenses in Scotland).

II
PRELIMINARY MATTERS

3 What happens first?

Hearings are arranged wherever possible to suit the convenience of the parties. You will usually be approached therefore by the Clerk to the Special Commissioners about the time, date and place for the hearing of your appeal. If the date of the hearing subsequently becomes inconvenient for you, you should immediately notify the Clerk to the Special Commissioners, preferably in writing. (See paragraph 9 below). If it becomes apparent to you that the time allotted for the hearing of your appeal is too long or too short you should also inform the Clerk to the Special Commissioners.

4 Where will my appeal be heard?

English appeals are normally heard in London. Scottish appeals are normally heard in Edinburgh. Northern Ireland appeals are normally heard in Belfast. However the Special Commissioners will consider applications to hear appeals in any city or town if suitable accommodation is available and the need for a local hearing is shown (eg. because a large number of witnesses all reside at or near a particular city or town or you are not well enough to travel). If you wish your appeal to be heard away from London, Edinburgh or Belfast you should make an application in writing to the Clerk to the Special Commissioners, giving the reasons why you wish to have your appeal heard locally.

5 Should I continue to negotiate with the Inland Revenue before the hearing?

You may continue or commence to negotiate with the Inland Revenue concerning your appeal right up to the day of the hearing. Many appeals are settled in this manner with the result that a hearing before the Special Commissioners is made unnecessary.

Where you cannot reach agreement with the Inland Revenue before the hearing on the outcome of your appeal it is helpful to the Special Commissioners if you can agree with the Inland Revenue the points of disagreement between you. It will also shorten the appeal hearing and save time and money if you can agree with the Inland Revenue in advance—

(*a*) a statement of facts which are agreed,
(*b*) what documents are agreed,
(*c*) what matters are not agreed,
(*d*) what decided cases and statutes you intend to reply upon.

6 How can I make sure a witness will turn up at the hearing?

If you wish to make sure that someone who you wish to give evidence for you at the hearing comes to court at the right time you may apply to the Clerk to the Special Commissioners in writing for a witness summons. Your application should say why you require that particular witness to attend. If your application is granted you will receive through the post a witness summons and you must serve it on the witness and be responsible for the witness' reasonable travelling expenses to and from the appeal. It is your responsibility to serve the summons on the witness and to pay all reasonable expenses: it is not the task of the Special Commissioners or their staff.

7 What happens if the Inland Revenue and I cannot agree what the dispute is about?

Occasionally it happens that the parties to an appeal cannot agree what the appeal is about. In such cases you can apply to the Clerk to the Special Commissioners for a preliminary hearing. The Inland Revenue may also make such an application and occasionally the Tribunal may itself decide that a preliminary hearing is required.

Preliminary hearings are arranged in order to identify what matters are in dispute and to arrange for the procedure at an appeal hearing. A Special Commissioner will hear both parties to an appeal and give directions on some or all of the following matters—

(*a*) when an appeal is to be heard,
(*b*) how long the hearing is to take,
(*c*) if there is to be a statement of agreed facts, when it is to be produced,
(*d*) when documents are to be exchanged,
(*e*) whether expert evidence is to be given and if so when their reports are to be exchanged (see paragraph 8 below),
(*f*) whether two or more appeals are to be heard together or in succession,
(*g*) whether some person other than the Inland Revenue and the taxpayer should be made a party to the appeal.

8 Can I use the opinion of an expert in my appeal?

Sometimes it is helpful to the hearing of an appeal for an expert to give his opinion to the Tribunal on certain matters. For example an accountant may give evidence as to how, in his opinion, certain matters should be dealt with in a set of accounts. If you propose to call an expert to give evidence you should notify the Clerk to the Special Commissioners and the Inland Revenue in advance and agree with the Inland Revenue the date on which a copy of your expert witness' report is to be produced to the Inland Revenue in advance of the hearing.

9 What do I do if I wish to postpone a Tribunal hearing?

A Tribunal is usually reluctant to postpone a hearing, but if it is essential for you to seek a postponement—

(*a*) you or your representative should request a postponement, if necessary by telephone or fax, to the Clerk to the Special Commissioners seeking an adjournment,
(*b*) you should give your reasons, in writing, for asking for a postponement,
(*c*) you should be prepared to agree an alternative hearing date when you and your witnesses will be ready,
(*d*) if your reason for seeking a postponement includes illness you should be ready to supply a medical certificate to the Tribunal,
(*e*) an engagement elsewhere is not normally sufficient reason to justify a postponement; you should be ready to explain why the other engagement takes priority over the tribunal hearing.

You should not assume a hearing will be cancelled because you have asked. Once a hearing has been arranged it is not cancelled until you are notified of cancellation by the Clerk to the Special Commissioners.

10 Can I withdraw my appeal?

You can withdraw your appeal at any time before the hearing date by notice in writing to the Inland Revenue. The Inland Revenue is not obliged to accept the withdrawal of your appeal and if they refuse to accept the withdrawal the appeal hearing will not be cancelled. If the Inland Revenue accept the withdrawal of your appeal they will notify the Clerk to the Special Commissioners.

III
THE HEARING

11 What happens if I fail to attend a Tribunal hearing?

If for any reason you do not attend on the hearing date the Tribunal can hear the case in your absence. If the Tribunal decides the appeal in favour of the Inland Revenue in your absence you may, within fourteen days of the date of the written decision, apply to have the Tribunal decision set aside and your case reconsidered. Your application must give the reasons for your failure to attend. The Tribunal will consider your application and, if necessary, arrange for a hearing to decide the issue.

12 Do I have to prove the Inland Revenue are wrong?

In almost all appeals at the start, the "burden of proof" is upon you. This means that it is up to you to show why the disputed assessment or decision is wrong. You will need to put evidence before the Tribunal which will establish the facts, figures, dates etc. If you need to call witnesses or produce documents it is up to you to see to it that they are all available at the hearing of the appeal. You must persuade the Special Commissioner that the Inland Revenue's view of your affairs is wrong.

13 What documents will I need?

Any documents which you intend to refer to or to rely on in support of your case must be available at the hearing. These may include invoices, books of accounts, bank statements, contracts, company reports etc. Original documents should be brought if possible, together with copies for the Inland Revenue and for the Special Commissioner to refer to.

If you are in doubt about whether a document will be needed, your best course is to bring it with you. You should not assume that the hearing will be adjourned to another occasion to enable the documents to be produced.

14 Do the documents have to be disclosed in advance?

The Tribunal will sometimes give a direction to provide documents in advance. Otherwise you are not required to do so. It is always an advantage if you can agree with the other side what documents are to be used at the hearing. This saves time at the hearing, and showing documents to the Inland Revenue beforehand may persuade the Inspector of Taxes that he is wrong and you are right, thus avoiding the necessity of a hearing of the appeal.

15 I need the evidence of a witness to prove my case; what do I do?

Normally it is up to you to arrange for your witnesses to attend the hearing ready to give their evidence. If a witness is reluctant to attend, the Tribunal has power to compel attendance by means of a witness summons; the Tribunal centre can tell you how this can be obtained. (See also paragraph 6 above.)

If the Inland Revenue does not dispute the evidence of a witness, it can be presented in writing ("a witness statement") but all disputed evidence must be given in person at a hearing. Contact the Inland Revenue if you think a witness statement might be acceptable to them and likewise they may contact you about the evidence of their witnesses.

16 What happens if some of the evidence is agreed, but some is disputed?

If you wish, you may approach the Inland Revenue to discuss the case with them and possibly produce an agreed statement of facts, an agreed bundle of documents, agreed accounts, a summary of those matters not agreed etc. This would simplify preparations for the hearing and save time and money. The Tribunal finds agreed statements helpful. If you do reach such agreement, you should notify the clerk to the Special Commissioners in writing well before the date of the hearing.

17 What happens at an appeal hearing?

Appeal hearings are normally in public, but you have the right to have your appeal, or some part of it, heard in private if you wish. Usually the appeal will be heard by one Special Commissioner. Exceptionally, in long or difficult cases, two or more Special Commissioners may hear your appeal.

You or your representative must bring all the documents on which you intend to rely in support of your case and arrange for the attendance of your witnesses if applicable, on the appropriate dates.

The party upon whom the burden of proof rests (normally you) will begin. You should introduce the case by explaining what it is about, giving a summary of the facts and indicating how the law applies to the facts.

You will need to explain what is already agreed, what is disputed, what evidence you are putting forward and the basic points you are making. It is important for each party, in the course of presenting the case, to bring out the essential facts. You should state quite clearly why the Inland Revenue's assessment or decision is wrong.

When the first party to an appeal has introduced its case and called its evidence, the other party will open its case, call evidence (if any) in the same way and make submissions including its answers to the first party's case. The first party then has a right of reply, but may not raise new issues unless the Tribunal allows.

Witnesses may give evidence on oath or affirmation. After being examined (questioned) by the party calling him, the witness may be cross-examined by the other party, then re-examined by the first party and perhaps questioned also by the Special Commissioner. Except in cross-examination, leading questions are not permitted. A leading question is one which suggests the required answer to the witness.

18 Will the Tribunal help me to put forward my case?

If you are not used to court proceedings, the Special Commissioner will help you with your case where appropriate. But the Special Commissioner, being independent of the Inland Revenue, will be new to the case and so will have had no knowledge of it before the hearing and will not have seen correspondence between you and the Inland Revenue. If it helps, the Special Commissioner may ask the Inland Revenue representative to explain initially the basis of the dispute.

19 What happens at the end of the hearing?

The Tribunal may announce its decision there and then, or may reserve it to be given in writing later. In either case the reasons for the decision will be given and a copy of the written decision, signed by the Special Commissioner, will be sent to you.

20 Can I ask for an award of costs if my appeal succeeds? And what about costs if I lose?

The Tribunal has a limited power to award costs to either party to an appeal but only if the Tribunal is of the opinion that the party against whom costs are to be awarded has acted wholly unreasonably in connection with the hearing in question.

21 How do I appeal against the Tribunal's decision?

If the Tribunal decides your appeal in favour of the Inland Revenue in whole or in part you have the right in England to appeal to the High Court. In Scotland appeals lie from the Tribunal to the Court of Session. In Northern Ireland appeals from the Tribunal lie to the Northern Ireland Court of Appeal. Appeals from the Tribunal are on points of law only. Special Commissioners are final judges of fact.

IV

OTHER INFORMATION

22 Address of Special Commissioners

The name of the Clerk to the Special Commissioners, together with his address and telephone number, is given below—

R P LESTER,
15–19 Bedford Avenue,
London
WC1B 3AS
Telephone: 020 7612 9700
Fax: 020 7436 4151

The Clerk to the Special Commissioners cannot enter into correspondence about the merits of individual cases nor give advice on evidence. He deals only with the arrangements for hearings but will be glad to give any help or guidance which he can in relation to matters referred to in this leaflet.

Misc VIII. Taxable Social Security Benefits—Rates for 2004–05

The table below shows the rates of the main taxable social security benefits for 2004–05.

	Weekly 12.4.04 onwards	*Total 2004–05 (52 weeks)*
	£	£
Retirement pensions		
Single person	79.60	4,139.20
Married couples		
both contributors—each	79.60	4,139.20
wife not contributor—addition	47.65	2,477.80
Age addition (over 80)—each	0.25	13.00
Bereavement benefits		
Bereavement allowance—standard	79.60	4,139.20
Widowed parent's allowance	79.60	4,139.20
Non-contributory retirement pension		
Single person (category C or D)	47.65	2,477.80
Married couple (category C)	76.15	3,959.80
Married couple (category D—over 80)	95.30	4,955.60
Age addition	0.25	13.00
Incapacity benefit		
Long term:	74.15	3,855.80
Increased for age—Higher rate	15.55	808.60
Lower rate	7.80	405.60
Short-term (under pension age)		
higher rate	66.15	—
(over pension age)		
higher rate	74.15	—
Invalidity allowance when paid with retirement pension		
Higher rate	15.55	808.60
Middle rate	10.00	520.00
Lower rate	5.00	260.00
Industrial death benefit		
Widow's pension—		
Higher permanent rate	79.60	4,139.20
Lower permanent rate	23.88	1,241.76
Widower's pension	79.60	4,139.20
Invalid care allowance		
Each qualifying individual	44.35	2,306.20
Adult dependency increase	26.50	1,378.00
Jobseekers allowance		
Single person under 18	33.50	—
Single person 18–24	44.05	—
Single person 25 and over	55.65	—
Statutory adoption pay		
Lower rate	102.80	—
Statutory maternity pay		
Lower rate	102.80	—
Statutory paternity pay		
Lower rate	102.80	—
Statutory sick pay		
Standard rate	66.15	—

Misc IX.A Tax treatment of R&D expenditure

CONTENTS

Commentary—*Simon's Direct Tax Service* **Division B2.7, B3.1421.**

SCOPE OF THESE GUIDANCE NOTES

These notes outline the changes to the tax relief available for spending on R&D from April 2000. Previously, Scientific Research Allowances were available for such expenditure. The notes cover four main areas—

– Capital allowances for R&D expenditure
– R&D tax credit scheme
– Revenue spending on R&D—special provision
– Payments to Scientific Research Associations.

These guidance notes are not intended to be an authoritative statement of the law and have no legal force. References to statute are to Capital Allowances Act 1990 unless specified otherwise.

Any enquiries about these notes should be addressed to:

Chris Orchard or Ivor Graham

Room 301
Business Tax
22 Kingsway
London
WC2B 6NR
Telephone: 020 7438 7491 or 020 7438 6784

INTRODUCTION AND OVERVIEW

There are long established reliefs, available to persons carrying on a trade, for expenditure incurred on scientific research. The legislation at CAA 1990 ss 136–139 provided relief in two ways.

– Revenue expenditure on scientific research and payments to approved bodies are treated as trading expenses if they would not otherwise be allowed in arriving at the profits of the trade.
– Capital expenditure on scientific research qualified for a 100% capital allowance. This allowance is given as a one off up front deduction. No writing down allowances or balancing allowances are available to give relief for the balance if the 100% deduction is not taken, or is only partly taken; there are balancing charges to recover excess relief when an asset is sold.

Scientific Research Allowances were only given to traders, as the legislation did not include any provisions to extend the relief to professions, vocations, etc, unlike the provisions relating to plant and machinery allowances for example.

Scientific Research was defined in the statute as:

> ''Any activities in the fields of natural or applied science for the extension of knowledge''.

Activities were on scientific research if they involved:

– the application of new scientific principles in an existing area of research, or
– the application of existing principles in a new area of research.

The application of existing principles in an existing area, however, is not regarded as scientific research, but rather as technological development. The essential test is innovation.

Finance Act 2000 changes

Finance Act 2000 introduced changes and additions to the reliefs available to businesses carrying out research and development (R&D).

The following changes have been introduced:

– A new definition of ''research and development'' replaces the existing definition of ''scientific research'' for most tax purposes. The definition is underpinned by new guidelines on the meaning of R&D, but the scope remains unchanged.
– ''Scientific Research Allowances'' (SRA) have been renamed ''Research and Development Allowances'' R&DA, but their scope and application are otherwise unchanged, except
– Appeals on R&D issues will now be heard by the tax Commissioners and the Courts, in line with other tax appeals, rather than by the Secretary of State for Trade and Industry.
– Small and medium-size companies can claim enhanced relief on qualifying current R&D spending. This new R&D tax relief is given at a rate of 150%. This means the company can deduct £150 in its profit and loss account for each £100 of qualifying spending.
– Small and medium-sized companies not in profit will be able to surrender the R&D tax relief for a cash payment called the payable R&D tax credit. The payment is equivalent to £24 for each £100 of qualifying R&D spending.
– Small and medium-sized companies that have not yet started to trade for tax purposes can also claim R&D tax relief and the payable R&D tax credit.

THE DEFINITION OF RESEARCH AND DEVELOPMENT

A new definition of R&D for tax purposes is introduced by FA 2000 s 68 and Sch 19. These insert the new definition into TA 1988 s 837A. It replaces the existing definition of ''scientific research'' in CAA 1990 s 139(1)(*a*) for most purposes. The new definition applies to—

– income tax cases—for 2000/01 and later years of assessment
– corporation tax cases—for accounting periods ending on or after 1st April 2000. However, in practice the new definition of R&D covers the same range of activities that qualified under the existing definition of scientific research.

An activity will qualify as R&D for tax purposes if it would be treated as R&D under normal accounting practice for companies in the UK (Statement of Standard Accountancy Practice 13, SSAP13), as qualified by the ''Guidelines on the Meaning of Research and Development for Tax Purposes'' issued by the Secretary of State for Trade and Industry on 28 July 2000 [updated March 2004; see *Misc IX.B* below].

The Guidelines have statutory force. They discuss in detail the meaning of R&D, and illustrate through explanation and examples the boundary between those activities that are, and are not R&D.

Broadly speaking, an activity may qualify as R&D if it is characterised by work that contains an appreciable element of innovation and creativity in the fields of science and technology. The work can range from research into purely theoretical areas to applied research and experimental development directed towards a practical aim or product. It is research that aims to break new ground or to resolve scientific or technological uncertainties. R&D can include the development of prototypes and pilot plant to test the R&D, but commercial development without such scientific or technological investigation, or after the resolution of such uncertainties, is not R&D for tax purposes.

Oil and gas exploration and appraisal

Schedule 19 of Finance Act 2000 introduces a new definition of ''oil and gas exploration and appraisal'' as TA s 837B. Oil and gas exploration and appraisal is defined as activities carried out for the purpose of:

- searching for petroleum anywhere in an area, or
- ascertaining the extent or characteristics of any petroleum bearing area, or what the reserves of petroleum of any such area are, so that it may be determined whether the petroleum is suitable for commercial exploitation.

Oil and Gas exploration and appraisal activities do not qualify as R&D under normal accounting practice (SSAP 13) and are expressly excluded from being R&D in the new definition in TA 1988 s 837A. But oil and gas exploration and appraisal, as defined in the new TA 1988 s 837B, is expressly brought within the definition of R&D for the purposes of research and development allowances (Section 139(1)(*a*) as amended by FA 2000 Sch 19, para 10).

The scope of oil and gas exploration and appraisal remains unchanged for tax purposes. Activities that would have qualified as scientific research under the old rules will qualify as R&D under the new rules.

The Inland Revenue Oil Taxation Office deals with oil and gas exploration and appraisal.

Application of the new definition of R&D

The new definition of research and development applies to a range of tax measures that are designed to encourage innovation and investment in R&D.

The definition as extended to include oil and gas exploration applies to

- research and development allowances (previously called scientific research allowances) – these allow a business to write off against its taxable profits the full cost of its capital investment in R&D in the period during which the investment is made
- a deduction for revenue expenditure on R&D related to the trade of the person incurring it that would not otherwise be allowed for tax purposes.

The definition excluding oil and gas exploration applies to R&D tax credits, and also

- The Enterprise Investment Scheme (EIS) – in relation to shares and securities issued on or after 6 April 2000. The aim of the scheme is to encourage equity investment in small higher risk unquoted trading companies by giving various tax reliefs on the investment
- Venture Capital Trusts (VCT) in relation to shares issued on or after 6 April 2000. These are quoted companies that also invest in small high risk unquoted trading companies. Tax reliefs are available to individual investors in the VCT
- Corporate Venturing Scheme – the scheme provides tax reliefs incentive to encourage companies to make equity investments in the same sorts of companies as those qualifying for EIS and VCTS, and through this to form corporate venturing relationships with these companies
- Enterprise Management Incentives – aimed at small higher risk trading companies, whether quoted or not, EMI's will enable young growing businesses to recruit and retain key employees by allowing companies to grant options worth up to £100,000 normally without any income tax or national insurance charge .

It does not apply to payments to Scientific Research Associations.

CAPITAL ALLOWANCES FOR RESEARCH AND DEVELOPMENT EXPENDITURE

Who can claim Research & Development Allowances?

All businesses, regardless of size or whether incorporated or unincorporated can claim capital allowances on their capital investment in R&D. The allowances were previously called ''scientific research allowances'' (SRA). They are now renamed ''research and development allowances'' (R&DA) in line with the new definition of research and development for tax purposes.

R&DA are only given to traders. A person who carries on a profession, vocation, etc, does not qualify for R&DA. The reason for this is that the legislation only refers to 'trades' and there are no provisions which extend 'trade' to include other activities unlike, for example, the provisions relating to capital allowances on machinery and plant.

The cost of land and dwellings

No allowances are due for expenditure on the acquisition of, or of rights in or over, land. Where expenditure has been incurred on the cost of the site of a building, structure or fixed machinery or plant a just apportionment of the expenditure is made to exclude the part relating to the land.

Misc

Allowances are also not due for expenditure on the provision of a dwelling. Where, however, a dwelling is part of a larger building and the building is used for R&D, the expenditure on the dwelling is ignored if it is not more than one quarter of the cost of the whole building (CAA 1990 s 137(3)). In applying the one-quarter test to the building, any additional VAT incurred or any additional VAT rebates that would be taken into account in arriving at the amount of R&DA are ignored. More details on VAT aspects are available on the section on Allowances for VAT.

R&D must be related to the trade

The R&D expenditure must be related to the trade being carried on. R&D related to a trade or class of trades includes:

– any R&D which may lead to or facilitate an extension of the trade, or of trades of that class (CAA 1990 s 139(1)(*d*)(i)); and
– medical research which has a special relation to the welfare of workers employed in that trade or trades of that class, for example, research into an occupational disease (s 139(1)(*d*)(iii)).

Medical research does not include research undertaken for the benefit of the community as a whole that may fall within the first category above. For example, medical research undertaken by a drug company for the purpose of its trade.

It is possible for a trader to have a trade which consists solely of R&D. For example, a group of companies may set up a company to carry out R&D on behalf of the group. In such a case all the assets of the trade are used for, or provide facilities for, R&D and so expenditure on them qualifies for R&DA unless it is specifically excluded.

Mixed use of an asset

If part of an asset is used for R&D and part is not, only the part of the expenditure on the provision of the asset that is used for R&D qualifies for R&DA. Where an asset is used partly for R&D and partly for other purposes, and no part is used exclusively for one or the other, the expenditure on the asset should be apportioned on a just basis to arrive at the part of the expenditure that relates to use for R&D.

For example, a trader may invest in a building part of which is used as a research facility and part as offices used for general administration. The cost should be apportioned on a just basis to reflect the proportion of use of the asset for R&D purposes, as opposed to administration purposes.

Expenditure in respect of more than one trade

Allowances must not be given on the same expenditure in respect of more than one trade. For example, if the research leads to the setting up of two trades, R&DA must only be given against one of them. CAA 1990 s 139(2) prevents expenditure qualifying for relief in relation to more than one trade. It applies whether the expenditure is capital or revenue expenditure. This is in addition to the general capital allowances rule at CAA 1990 s 147 that prevents double allowances on the same expenditure.

Appeals

The appeals procedure for R&DA has now been brought into line with the general rules for resolving disputes. They will be heard by the tax Commissioners and Courts. Under the old SRA rules, a dispute over whether activities constituted scientific research or whether an asset was being used for scientific research had to be referred to the Secretary of State at the Department of Trade and Industry.

However, appeals concerning payments to scientific research associations and universities, colleges, research institutes and similar institutions, [will] remain with the Secretary of State at the DTI, who also retains responsibility for decisions regarding Scientific Research Associations.

In the event that there is a dispute that still requires determination by the Secretary of State the case must be submitted by the Inspector to Business Tax (Capital Allowances). This is because the case has to be referred by the Board of Inland Revenue to the Secretary of State of Trade and Industry for his decision. If the taxpayer or agent wishes to make a direct submission to the Secretary of State it must be pointed out that this may cause inconvenience and delays for all parties. The determination by the Secretary of State in these cases is final.

Where there is a dispute the Inspector and taxpayer should establish the facts and arguments of both sides as comprehensively as possible. It often happens that this process provides both the Inspector and the taxpayer with a fuller understanding of the case and this leads to agreement. The submission to Business Tax (Capital Allowances) should only be made when the parties are satisfied that an agreement cannot be reached and all the facts and arguments have been fully established.

Grants and subsidies etc

Most grants, contributions and subsidies towards R&D expenditure are deducted from the expenditure in order to arrive at the net amount on which relief is due. No allowances are due for expenditure that is met, or is to be met, either directly or indirectly by any of the following:

- the Crown
- any Government
- any public or local authority
- any person other than the person incurring the expenditure.

However, expenditure met by any of the following does qualify for allowance:

- a regional development grant made under Part II of the Industrial Development Act 1982
- a regional development grant made under Part I of the Industry Act 1972
- a corresponding Northern Ireland grant.

Research undertaken directly by the trader or on his behalf

Expenditure incurred by a person on R&D only qualifies for R&DA if the research is either:

- directly undertaken by that person, or
- directly undertaken on his behalf by someone else

Research is only undertaken on behalf of a person if there is a clear link between him and the research undertaken. The relationship between the person claiming the allowances and the person undertaking the research need not be contractual, but if it is not, it must be one of agency or something similar to agency. The fact that research undertaken by someone else is for a trader's benefit, or is in his interest, is not enough to make the expenditure qualify for R&DA (see *Gaspet Ltd v. Elliss*, 1987, 60 TC 91).

Treatment of capital expenditure

Section 137 of CAA 1990 gives a 100% allowance for capital expenditure incurred on R&D. The expenditure that qualifies is:

- capital expenditure incurred by a trader on R&D related to his trade and directly undertaken by him or on his behalf, and
- capital expenditure incurred by a person on R&D directly undertaken by him or on his behalf before trading starts provided that person then starts a trade connected with that R&D.

Allowances are only due where the expenditure is incurred on R&D. No R&DA are due where an asset acquired for ordinary business use later begins to be used for R&D. The asset may continue to qualify in the ordinary way for other capital allowances, such as machinery or plant allowances or industrial buildings allowance, if they are due.

On the other hand, there is no balancing adjustment where an asset has properly qualified for R&DA and later begins to be used for other purposes. The adjustment is made when the taxpayer ceases to own the asset. See details [below] on *Balancing Adjustments*.

There are no R&DA writing-down or balancing allowances. This means that the taxpayer who chooses not to take the full 100% allowance in the first year cannot claim writing-down allowance on the unrelieved expenditure in later years.

Period for which allowances given

An allowance for capital expenditure is given for the relevant chargeable period. This is defined by CAA 1990 s 137(5) as the chargeable period in which the expenditure was incurred or, if it was incurred before the setting up and commencement of the trade, the chargeable period beginning with that setting up and commencement.

For Corporation Tax the chargeable period is the Accounting Period in which the expenditure is incurred, or for pre-trading expenditure, the accounting period in which the trade is set-up and commences.

For Income Tax the chargeable period is defined by CAA 1990 s 160 as the period of account in which the expenditure is incurred, or for pre-trading expenditure, the period of account that commences when the trade begins.

Double allowances

It is possible that expenditure may qualify for more than one type of allowance, for example, a building may qualify for both R&DA and IBA. Once a claim for one sort of allowance has been made, the taxpayer is prevented from making a claim under another part of the capital allowances code for the same asset.

The practical effect of CAA 1990 s 147 is to enable the taxpayer to choose which allowance to claim where alternatives are available but, once a claim has been made for one type of allowance, the taxpayer is barred from claiming another. It is for the taxpayer to choose which allowance to take advantage of.

Claims procedure

A claim for R&DA is to be made in a return under ITSA or CTSA in the same manner as for other assets. R&DA are given as an expense in computing profits.

Time when expenditure is incurred

The definition of the time when expenditure is incurred is contained in CAA 1990 s 159. The basic rule is that expenditure is incurred on the date that the obligation to pay becomes unconditional.

Balancing adjustments

The balancing adjustment rules for R&DA only provide for the recovery of excess allowances. They do this by treating the excess as a trading receipt. There are no balancing allowances. Hence, there are no further reliefs if the trader does not take the full 100% allowance available at the outset.

A balancing adjustment is made where the asset ceases to belong to the trader. Where the cessation of ownership is as a result of a sale, the asset is treated as ceasing to belong to the taxpayer at the earlier of:

– the time of completion; or
– the time when possession is given.

Where the asset is destroyed, the asset is deemed to have been sold immediately before destruction.

In other cases, such as a gift, it is the time when the asset actually ceases to belong to the taxpayer.

There is no balancing adjustment merely because the asset ceases to be used for R&D. If an asset ceases to be so used shortly after allowances have been given it may be necessary for the Inspector to look closely at the facts to determine the intentions of the trader when the asset was acquired.

The disposal proceeds to be brought into account will be determined by the nature of the disposal event. If it is the sale of the asset then it will be the net proceeds of the sale. If it is the destruction of the asset it will be any insurance monies or other compensation received as a result plus any sums received for the remainder of the asset. In any other case it will be the open market value of the asset.

It is possible that where the asset is disposed of to a connected party, an election under CAA 1990 s 158 could be made to treat the asset as being disposed of at its tax written down value. For R&DA this will always be nil because of the once and for all nature of the relief.

Any capital expenditure that was previously treated as spending on scientific research is treated as if it were spending on research and development for the purpose of calculating balancing adjustments on disposals on or after 1 April 2000.

Demolition costs

Relief is available for the cost of demolishing the asset provided it was not used for non-R&D purposes before demolition; for example, where a research building was later used as ordinary offices, there is no relief for demolition costs. If the building is left completely unused for a period before demolition the relief will still be available.

When an asset is demolished it is treated as sold immediately before the demolition. The cost of qualifying demolition expenditure is treated as part of the cost of the asset when calculating the balancing adjustment. This can only be done by:

– reducing the amount of excess allowances brought back into charge as a trading receipt by the amount of the demolition costs; or
– providing a deduction as an expense of the trade for the demolition costs; or
– a combination of these two.

The demolition rule does not provide relief for any part of the original cost of the asset for which allowances were not claimed in the first place. The relief is given in the chargeable period in which the asset is treated as sold. Where the trade has ceased before the deemed date of sale the receipt or deduction is brought in for the last chargeable period in which the trade was carried on.

Connected person and control sales

The legislation in CAA 1990 ss 157, 158 about connected person sales, control sales and sole or main benefit sales applies to disposals of assets that qualify for R&DA. The effect is for the sale to be deemed to have occurred at open market value unless the parties can elect under s 158 for tax written down value to be used instead.

Allowances for VAT

Normally, VAT presents no special problems for R&DA. Where capital expenditure on an asset qualifies for the 100% allowance, any VAT finally borne by the trader on that asset also qualifies. Where the trader can recover the VAT that is paid it is the amount net of VAT that qualifies.

The situation is slightly complicated by the VAT Capital Goods Scheme, which allows additional VAT to be charged for a period of up to ten years after the asset was acquired. There may also be repayments of VAT under the scheme.

S137 CAA 1990 permits allowances to be given or recovered where additional VAT liabilities or rebates arise in relation to assets that have qualified for R&DA.

Any additional VAT incurred by a person qualifies for R&DA if that VAT:

– relates to expenditure on an asset that qualified for R&DA, and

– is incurred while the asset belongs to him.

Any additional VAT rebates received while the asset belongs to the trader are assessed as trading receipts.

The additional VAT incurred and VAT rebates received while the asset belongs to the trader are taken into account when calculating the balancing adjustment when the asset cease to belong to him.

R&D TAX CREDIT SCHEME

Introduction

The R&D Tax Credits scheme was introduced in FA 2000 to encourage small and medium-sized companies to invest in research and development. The legislation is found in s 69 and Schs 19 and 20, and applies to qualifying R&D expenditure incurred on or after 1 April 2000.

Under the scheme

- the company can increase the amount that it deducts for qualifying R&D spending when it computes its profits for tax purposes from the normal 100% to 150%. This is called R&D tax relief,
- a company that is not in profit can surrender its qualifying R&D losses (including the R&D tax relief) to the Exchequer in exchange for a cash payment, worth 24% of the spending on R&D. This is called the payable R&D tax credit. The Inland Revenue makes the payment,
- R&D tax relief and the payable R&D tax credit can be claimed by a company even though it has not started to trade for tax purposes.

Summary of Entitlement to R&D Tax Relief

Not everyone can claim R&D tax credits, and not all expenditure qualifies. The most important conditions are:

- only companies can claim R&D tax credits. R&D tax relief and the payable R&D tax credit are not available to individuals or partnerships
- the company must be a small or medium-sized enterprise (SME) as defined by the European Commission for State Aid purposes
- the spending qualifying for relief must
  - not be less than £25,000 a year
  - be revenue expenditure
  - be attributable to relevant research and development directly undertaken by the company or on its behalf
  - be incurred only on the costs of staff directly involved in carrying out the R&D, the costs of consumable stores used in the R&D effort, and certain costs where R&D is subcontracted to another person
  - the company must be entitled to the ownership rights of any intellectual property arising from the R&D
  - the spending must not be incurred in carrying out activities contracted to it by another person
  - the expenditure cannot be met by another person. Also, if the R&D project is funded in whole or in part by a State aid such as a Government grant, eg Smart and LINK, none of the spending on that project can qualify for R&D tax credits

Definition of Small or Medium-sized Enterprise

A company must be a small or medium-sized enterprise (SME) for the accounting period to qualify for R&D tax relief for that period. The definition used is that adopted by the European Commission for State aids purposes in the Commission Recommendation 96/280/EC of 3rd April 2000.

Broadly speaking, a company is a SME if, in the current or previous year it, together with any company in which it holds 25 per cent or more of the capital or voting rights has

- fewer than 250 employees, and either, or both, of
- an annual turnover not exceeding Euro 40 million (about £25 million)
- and an annual balance sheet total not exceeding Euro 27 million (about £17 million), and
- it has less than 25 per cent of its capital or voting rights owned by an enterprise (or jointly by several enterprises) that fall outside the definition of an SME.

The company will only need to calculate its turnover or balance sheet totals in Euros if it is close to the threshold. The balance sheet total should be calculated at the accounting date. The rules do not specify any particular formula for translating turnover. Any method can be used provided it gives a reasonable result, for example using the average exchange rate for the accounting period.

A company will not be excluded from being treated as a SME under the rules that says it must have less than 25 per cent of its capital or voting rights owned by an enterprise that is not a SME, if:

- the enterprise is held by public investment corporations, venture capital companies or institutional investors and no control is exercised either individually or jointly, or
- the company cannot determine by whom its capital is held, but can legitimately presume that this 25% ownership test will not apply.

Public investment corporations are public entities controlled by central or local government or independent agencies that provide funds for companies, without direct involvement. Venture capital companies invest in small companies in return for shares. Institutional investors include major investment businesses, such as pension funds, and unit trusts.

Example

Able Controls Ltd is a UK resident company that draws up accounts up to 31 March. It is agreed it is a SME in the period to 31 March 2002. In the year to 31 March 2003, it has a turnover of €34M, a balance sheet total of €25M and 225 employees. In the following year to 31 March 2004 turnover is €45M, the balance sheet total is €26M and the employees number 260. In the year to 31 March 2005 the turnover has reduced to €39M, the balance sheet total is €28M and the employees remain 260.

The status of the company is as follows:

– Accounting period to 31 March 2003: the company is below the SME thresholds in this, and the preceding period. It is a SME during this period. Accounting period to 31 March 2004: the company exceeds both the employee and turnover limits during the period. But it satisfied the tests in the preceding period, so it remains a SME during this period.
– Accounting period ended 31 March 2005: The company exceeds the employee limit again and the balance sheet limit. It also failed to satisfy the criteria in the preceding year. It is not a SME in this period.

Minimum expenditure for R&D tax relief

A company must have qualifying expenditure on R&D that it is entitled to deduct when it computes its profits of a period of £25,000 or more in a 12 month period before it can claim R&D tax relief for that period. This amount is reduced or increased proportionally if the accounting period is shorter or longer than 12 months. There is no tapering of the relief so a company that is only entitled to deduct £24,875 in its 12-month period of accounts cannot claim R&D relief. But they will still be entitled to the normal 100% revenue deduction.

There is a special rule for companies that have not yet started to trade (but which are entitled to claim R&D tax relief and the payable R&D tax credit). The relevant minimum expenditure is based on that which would have been deductible for the period had the company been carrying on a trade consisting of the activities represented by the qualifying R&D spending.

The minimum expenditure test does not include any spending on R&D of earlier accounting periods during which the company was not trading, but which is treated as incurred for tax purposes in the later period under the special rules for pre-trading expenditure in TA 1988 s 401. But the company may be able to claim R&D tax relief for a pre-trading period if the minimum spend of that period exceeds the minimum threshold.

The expenditure must be revenue expenditure

R&D tax relief can only be claimed in respect of revenue expenditure. Capital expenditure does not qualify for R&D tax relief. This includes amounts that the company might capitalise. However, capital expenditure can still qualify for the 100% capital allowances under the rules for research and development allowances (previously called scientific research allowances).

Specific costs qualify for R&D tax relief

R&D tax relief can be claimed in respect of spending by the company on:

– the costs of staff directly involved in the R&D activity
– the costs of consumable stores used in the R&D activity
– certain costs incurred by the company if it subcontracts R&D to another person.

Qualifying staff

The costs of certain staff can qualify for R&D tax relief. The qualifying staff are those staff directly and actively involved in carrying out the R&D activity. These people are the researchers, managers and directors who directly plan and organise the programme of research, and technical and other staff who directly provide support for the research effort. Broadly speaking, all staff directly involved in running and maintaining a research facility or laboratory will normally qualify.

The employment costs of people who are only indirectly involved in R&D do not qualify for R&D tax relief. Such people include general clerical staff, those in general management and administration even if they support the R&D staff (including those involved in the financial administration of R&D projects).

Qualifying staff costs

There are three sorts of staff costs that can qualify for R&D tax relief, provided they are incurred in respect of qualifying staff. They comprise:

- all money payments such as salaries, wages, fees and bonuses before deductions for PAYE, National Insurance, or other agreed sums (such as season ticket loans etc). But they do not include the costs of providing benefits in kind.
- the employer's National Insurance contributions paid in respect of the employee insofar as they relate to the money payments (Class 1 NIC). However, NIC on benefits in kind (Class 1A, Class 1B NIC) are excluded.
- all payments to a pension fund by the employer in respect of the company's directors or employees directly engaged in R&D to provide those R&D staff with a pension, retirement annuity or other superannuation benefits.

It is not unusual for staff to have mixed duties, some of which are directly related to the R&D activity (which costs do qualify for the R&D tax relief) and other more remote duties which do not qualify. For example, a director of a medical research company may spend 75% of her time on administration and the rest actively involved in research. In such a case, her staff costs are apportioned to give R&D tax relief on the appropriate amount attributable to the R&D activity. This apportionment need not necessarily be made on a time basis, if this would give an unreasonable result.

To simplify matters, there are two de minimis rules. Where an employee spends more than 80% of his or her total working time on qualifying R&D activities, all of his or her costs can qualify for R&D tax relief. Conversely, where a person spends less than 20% of his or her total working time on qualifying activities, none of his or her costs will qualify for R&D tax relief.

R&D consumable stores

These comprise supplies such as materials and equipment used up in the direct conduct of the R&D, but which are not in themselves incorporated or reflected in the product of the R&D.

Consumable stores are, by their nature comparatively short-lived, and spending on them will be revenue expenditure. Capital expenditure on more durable assets does not qualify for R&D tax relief. But it could still qualify for 100% research and development allowances.

For example, the consumable stores of a chemistry-based R&D project may include such items as disposable laboratory equipment (flasks, test tubes) and chemicals used in the R&D process, etc. This spending could qualify for R&D tax relief. But expenditure on a centrifuge will usually be on capital account, and will not qualify.

Supplies, materials, or equipment used only indirectly in the R&D effort eg related to general overheads such as administration will not qualify. There is no de minimis rule for consumable stores as there is for staff costs.

Some consumable stores are recyclable; for example, it may be economically viable to sell the waste products from chemicals used in an R&D activity. The whole cost of such items can be claimed as qualifying for the R&D tax credit.

Qualifying costs of subcontracted research

A company may subcontract out part or all of its R&D to another person. The work is done by the sub-contractor in return for payment, but the ownership rights of any intellectual property that may be created rests with the company. The company can claim R&D relief in respect of its payments for the subcontracted R&D up to certain limits. The sub-contractor cannot claim R&D tax relief on its spending to fulfil the subcontract

The company that claims R&D tax relief for subcontracted R&D must be a small or medium-sized enterprise. But there are no restrictions on who carries out the work under the subcontract The sub-contractor could be a company of any size, or an unincorporated business. Similarly, the company can claim R&D tax relief even though the subcontracted work might be carried on outside the UK.

The actual work carried out by the sub-contractor need not, in isolation, be R&D. For example a company might, as part of its R&D activities need to subcontract analytical testing of a material to another person who has the specialised machinery needed for the test. The test is well-established and routine and on its own would not be R&D. But the subcontracted work will count as R&D from the perspective of the company because it is one component of a larger project that is R&D.

The rules are different, depending on whether or not the company and sub-contractor are connected. However, parties that are not connected can jointly elect for the connected person's treatment.

Company and sub-contractor are connected

If the company and the sub-contractor are connected persons, as defined in TA 1988 s 839, the company can claim R&D tax relief on the lower of:

- the amount brought into the sub-contractor's accounts, in respect of the costs of R&D staff and consumable stores to fulfil the work to which the company's payment relates, in any period ending not more than 12 months from the end of the company's accounting period in which its payment is brought into account for that work, and

– the amount of the company's payment to the sub-contractor.

The relevant sub-contractor's costs are calculated as if it could have claimed R&D tax relief. They are the qualifying revenue staff costs, and R&D consumable stores. However, no R&D tax relief is given on the costs of work that the sub-contractor itself may further subcontract to another person.

Example

Ragham Chemicals Ltd, a qualifying SME, and Raglan Road Ltd are connected. Ragham Chemicals draws up its accounts to 31 December, and Raglan Road draws up accounts to 30 June.

During the year ended 31 December 2005, Ragham Chemicals subcontracted part of its R&D to Raglan Road. It brought in the whole of its expenditure for the subcontracted R&D of £73,000 as a deduction in its profit and loss account for the period ended 31 December 2005.

Raglan Road incurred the following expenditure fulfilling the contract, £22,000 overheads, £43,000 on the salaries of the two research chemists who carried out the work, and £3,000 on consumable stores for the R&D. The balance was the profit on the contract. All amounts were brought into its accounts in accordance with normal accounting practice for the year ended 30 June 2006.

Ragham Chemicals can claim R&D tax relief on the lower of:

– the amount it brought into account for the sub-contractor payment (£73,000), and
– the revenue costs of R&D staff and consumable stores brought into the profit and loss by Raglan Road in a period of account ending not more than 12 months after the period of accounts in which Ragham Chemicals deducts its payment in its profit and loss. This is £46,000.

This means Ragham Chemicals Ltd has qualifying R&D spending of £46,000 on which it can claim R&D tax relief. It can thus increase the deduction in its profit and loss by a further 50% i.e. £23,000, bringing the relief to £69,000. It can also claim the normal 100% deduction on the balance of its expenditure of £27,000 (i.e. £73,000 – £46,000).

Company and sub-contractor are not connected

If the company and sub-contractor are not connected, then they may elect to follow the connected person's treatment. The joint election, which is irrevocable, must be made in writing, within 2 years of the end of the company's accounting period during which the contract or arrangement was entered into.

If no election is made then the company is entitled to claim R&D tax relief on 65% of the payment made to the sub-contractor

Example

If, in the above example Ragham Chemicals Ltd and Raglan Road Ltd were not connected, and no election was made, Ragham Chemicals would be able to claim RT&D tax relief on 65% of its sub-contractor payment of £73,000. The total deduction, including R&D tax relief will be £73,000 x 65% = £47,450 x 150% = £71175. It can also claim the normal 100% deduction on the balance of its expenditure of £25,550 (£73,000 – £47,450).

R&D must be related to the trade

Only expenditure on the relevant R&D qualifies. To be relevant the R&D must be related to a trade carried on by the company. This will include R&D that is intended to lead to or to facilitate a development of the trade. For companies that have not commenced trading relief will be due if the R&D is relevant to the intended trade. Medical R&D, where it is connected with the welfare of the workers employed in the trade is included.

Company must own the Intellectual Property in the R&D

R&D tax relief is available for expenditure on R&D provided that the ownership of the fruits of the R&D will vest in the claimant company. This does not mean that the R&D must be successful, or that it must result in the creation of intellectual property. Indeed, R&D is inherently risky, and may end in failure. A company can still claim R&D tax relief on its qualifying R&D spending if the R&D is unsuccessful, provided that it would have owned any intellectual property that could have been created had the R&D been successful.

Joint ventures

Not all companies exploit the fruits of the R&D for the purposes of their own trade. They may turn the rights to account by licensing them to another party. This can happen at any time during the R&D process. The company can still claim R&D tax relief on its continued research expenditure provided it retains ownership of the intellectual property.

Joint ventures and other collaborative arrangements are common between R&D companies. There are various arrangements that R&D companies may adopt but it must be remembered that the relief only applies to SMEs.

Where two or more companies simply collaborate on an R&D project the individual companies may account for their own share of R&D spending in their accounts. The usual arrangement is for each company to become the owner of the intellectual property it generates, but there are cross-licensing agreements to allow the other collaborators to exploit it as part of the larger R&D effort. Alternatively, they could simply share the intellectual property. In these situations, each SME company receives the R&D tax credit on the R&D expenditure it incurs in creating the intellectual property that it owns, or co-owns.

Two or more companies might carry out their collaborative R&D through a separate company set up for that purpose. Any intellectual property that is created rests in the new joint venture company and is exploited through that vehicle. In this situation, the R&D tax credit will follow the rules above and to go to the person who owns the intellectual property as it is created—the joint venture company, provided that it is an SME.

Grants, subsidies etc

There are situations where companies receive assistance with the cost of their R&D. Relief is limited depending on the assistance received.

If part or all of the costs of a company's research project is met by a notified State Aid then none of the cost of the project's R&D qualifies for R&D tax relief, even if the aid only meets part of the cost. The restriction applies where a State aid is received for any expenditure attributable to the R&D project.

Examples of notified State aid for a R&D project are the Smart and LINK awards given by the Department of Trade and Industry. If, for example, 30% of the cost of a company's R&D project is funded by a Smart award, the company cannot claim R&D tax relief for any costs associated with that project. But it could still claim R&D tax relief on qualifying R&D spending on a different project it may be carrying on at the same time that is not part of the award.

If the subsidy, grant or other payment is not a notified State aid, then R&D tax relief cannot be claimed on that part of the qualifying expenditure which is met by the subsidy etc. For example, a subsidy, which meets 30% of the costs of a project, would limit the R&D tax relief based on to the remaining 70% of the costs. Thus, in so far as the R&D expenditure is met by a person other than the company the relief is restricted accordingly.

It is quite common for subsidies and grants to be for specific projects and so they can be readily identified as can the expenditure they cover. But where the subsidy etc is not specifically allocated to particular expenditure then it is to be allocated on a just and reasonable basis.

Consortium relief

If the company is owned by a consortium, at least one of the members of which is not a small or medium sized enterprise and it makes a claim to R&D tax relief or R&D pre-trading relief, a restriction is placed on the surrender of consortium relief under TA 1988 s 402. No sum may be surrendered to any other company that is not a small or medium sized enterprise.

Giving effect to R&D tax relief

Where a company is entitled to R&D tax relief and is carrying on a trade in that period, it can claim 150% of the qualifying sum incurred on R&D.

Example

Cable Ltd incurs £37,000 on qualifying staff costs and consumable stores on R&D. The amount that can be deducted in computing profits/losses is £37,000 x 150% = £55,500.

Payable R&D tax credit

A company may claim R&D tax relief in a period, but make a trading loss in that period. The R&D tax relief is simply incorporated into that loss enabling it to be used in the normal way. For example, it can be set sideways against other income of the period, carried backwards to the preceding accounting period, carried forwards to be set against future profits of the trade, or surrendered as group relief.

Alternatively, the company can claim the payable R&D tax credit. Where a company has made a loss in an accounting period attributable to qualifying R&D expenditure and the R&D tax relief, it may surrender that loss in exchange for a cash payment. Such losses are known as 'surrenderable losses'.

The maximum 'surrenderable loss' of an accounting period is the lower of:

1. the total 150% deduction for qualifying expenditure and the claim for R&D tax relief, and
2. the total loss of the trade of the period in which the R&D is undertaken reduced by—

Misc

- any claim made, or which could be made, to set the loss against other profits or gains of the same accounting period (TA 1988 s 393A(1)(*a*)); and
- any other relief successfully claimed in respect of the losses, including losses carried back to earlier accounting periods (TA 1998 s 393A(1)(*b*)) and amounts surrendered as group or consortium relief (TA 1998 s 403).

No account is taken of any losses carried forward from an earlier accounting period or carried back from a subsequent accounting period in calculating this limit.

Example

Buckton Chemicals Ltd incurs a trading loss of £85,500 in the year ended 30 September 2005. This includes qualifying R&D expenditure and its R&D tax relief of £68,000. It has other income amounting to £19,000 and losses brought forward of £12,000. No claim is made for the trading loss to be set against any other income.

The surrenderable loss is the lower of:

- the R&D relief of £68,000 and
- the total loss of the trade(ignoring losses brought forward) less the amount that could be set against the other profits of the accounting period; £66,500 (£85,500 less £19,000)

The maximum surrenderable loss is £66,500.

The amount of the payable R&D tax credit that can be claimed for an accounting periods is the lower of

- 16% of the surrenderable loss of the accounting period (ie 24% of the actual qualifying R&D expenditure), and
- the total amount of the relevant PAYE and Class 1 National Insurance contributions paid by the company for the accounting period.

In the example above, Buckton Chemicals Ltd may claim a payable R&D tax credit of £10,640 (£66,500 x 16%), provided its relevant PAYE and Class 1 National Insurance contributions are not less than this amount.

Companies that have not yet started trading for tax purposes

A company may begin a programme of R&D before it starts to trade for tax purposes. Under the existing rules, any pre-trading expenditure is treated as being incurred for tax purposes when the taxable trade actually commences and relief given in accordance with TA 1988 s 401.

But a new rule has been introduced for qualifying R&D expenditure incurred by companies that have not yet started to trade in relation to those R&D activities.

The company may elect to have the expenditure treated as if it were a trading loss of the period in which it was incurred. It can then claim R&D tax relief on this R&D expenditure. The resulting enhanced ''trading'' loss can be used in the normal way. The loss can be:

- set against other profits of that period, such as interest (TA 1988 s 393A(1)(*a*)) or,
- carried back and set against profits of the preceding 12 months (TA 1988 s 393A(1)(*b*)) provided the company would have been entitled to R&D tax relief had it incurred qualifying expenditure in that earlier period, or,
- it may be surrendered as group relief or,
- cashed in for the payable R&D tax credit.

Any unused losses are carried forward as if they were losses of the trade to be set against future trading income in accordance with TA 1988 s 393.

The election must be made in writing within 2 years of the end of the accounting period of the loss. A separate election is needed for each accounting period. A company will normally have an accounting period for tax purposes even though it has not started to trade, because it will often have other income such as interest on its working capital. In the rare case in which there is no existing accounting period, R&D tax relief is calculated as if the company had started, and then carried on a trade consisting of the R&D activities in respect of which the qualifying R&D expenditure is incurred.

The claim for R&D tax relief must be for all qualifying R&D expenditure incurred in the period. A company cannot claim R&D tax relief on part of the qualifying R&D expenditure under the special pre-trading rules, and treat the balance as incurred when the company starts to trade under the rules in TA 1988 s 401.

These special rules apply only to the qualifying R&D spending. The normal pre-trading rules apply to all other expenditure.

Example

Clemons Ltd incurs £48,000 on qualifying R&D expenditure in its first accounting period, ended on the 30 April 2004. The company does not trade during this first year. It also incurs £29,000 on other revenue expenditure. The enhanced R&D relief is £72,000 (£48,000 x 150%) The total loss is £101,000

With a valid election, the whole of the £72,000 is treated as a trading loss arising in the year ended 30 April 2004. The balance of £29,000 is treated as incurred on the first day of trading under the pre-trading rules in TA 1988 s 401.

There are special rules to prevent the double counting of qualifying R&D spending where a company claims R&D tax relief for a pre-trading period.

Any expenditure covered by an election for the pre-trading R&D tax relief cannot qualify for relief under TA 1988 s 401. This means that qualifying R&D expenditure and R&D tax relief claimed during a pre-trading period which is not surrendered for the payable R&D tax credit or otherwise used, is carried forward to the time when trading actually begins. It is then treated as a trading loss brought forward.

The enhanced expenditure brought forward is not treated as incurred on the first day of trading under the rules in S401 TA 1988 and the losses cannot be set sideways, or surrendered for group relief.

A company which has not claimed R&D tax relief during a pre-trading period cannot use the rules in TA 1988 s 401 to claim R&D tax relief on R&D expenditure of earlier accounting periods. This is deemed to be incurred for tax purposes when the actual trade begins. The R&D expenditure is treated like any other pre-trading expenditure. However, a company may start to trade part of the way through its accounting period. In this case, it can claim R&D tax relief for the trading period on all its qualifying R&D expenditure of the accounting period (including spending before the trade actually started), but not for earlier accounting periods.

The PAYE/NIC limit

A claim for the payable R&D tax credit for an accounting period cannot exceed the PAYE/NIC liabilities of the company for the accounting period. This PAYE/NIC cap is the total of the PAYE and Class 1 NIC the company is required to pay in the period in respect of all employees. It is not restricted to those people engaged in R&D activity.

The PAYE is the gross amount, ignoring any reductions for Working Families Tax Credit or Disabled Persons Tax Credit.

The NICs are the total gross Class 1 contributions, ignoring any reductions for statutory sick pay, statutory maternity pay, Working Families Tax Credit, or Disabled Persons Tax Credit. Class 1A and Class 1B NICs are not included.

The limit is the total of the gross PAYE/NICs due for each of the return periods that end on the 5th of the month in the company accounting period. For example, if the company has an accounting period of a year to 31 March 2005, the PAYE/NIC limit is the total payable for the 12 monthly periods ended on the 5 March 2005. Payment of PAYE/NIC is to be made within 14 days of the 5th of the month and thus the amount paid in the accounting period month may not tally with the amount due.

Small employers may opt to pay over their PAYE/NICs quarterly. In these cases, the limit is based on the payments due for the quarterly periods that end in the accounting period.

If the company is in arrears with PAYE/NIC liabilities for the accounting period in which a claim to repayable tax credit is made the repayment may be withheld until the outstanding amounts are paid.

Where there are arrears of tax/NIC liabilities the payable tax credit can be set off against them.

How to claim R&D tax relief and R&D tax credit

Claims for R&D tax relief may be made at any time within 6 years of the end of the accounting period to which the claim relates. A company must claim R&D tax relief in its tax return or in an amended return if a notice to file a return has been issued. The company will show the 150% enhanced expenditure on R&D in Section 5 of the revised print of the CT600 return form. Where the time limit for notifying amendments to the company's return has passed, it may make a new claim or amend the claim outside the return.

A claim for the payable R&D tax credit must:

- always be made in the company's tax return, or amended return (it will be in boxes 149 and 150 in Section 4 of the new CT600 return form)
- be quantified at the time it is made
- be made within one year of the filing date for the return for the accounting period for which the claim is made.

The Revenue has powers to extend the time limit. The normal rules apply. In general terms, a late claim should only be admitted if, for reasons beyond the company's control, it could not have been made within the statutory time limit.

Interest

Interest is payable on the payable R&D tax credit from the later of the filing date for the accounting period of the claim and the date of delivery of the return to the Revenue in which the claim is made, to the date of payment. The interest is paid gross and forms part of the taxable income of the company.

Interest can also be charged where an assessment or amended assessment is made to recover an excessive payment of the payable R&D tax credit.

Enquiries

There are no special rules and enquiries into claims for R&D tax relief fall within the normal CTSA compliance regime. However, unlike CTSA generally, the Revenue can withhold part or all of a tax credit payment if an enquiry has been opened into the company's accounts for that period. A penalty may be charged where a fraudulent or negligent claim is made for an R&D tax credit.

A penalty may also be charged where a company discovers a claim is incorrect and fails to remedy the error without unreasonable delay. The maximum penalty is the difference between the relief claimed and that actually due.

Artificially inflated claims

There are rules to counteract arrangements where the object, or one of the main objects is to enable a company to obtain, or inflate the amount of R&D relief or payable tax credit. In such cases, the amount of the relief or payable R&D tax credit attributable to the arrangement will be disregarded. Arrangements include any scheme, agreement, or understanding, whether it is legally enforceable or not.

Cases in which it is suspected a claim has been artificially inflated should be submitted to Business Tax (Capital Allowances) once the facts have been established, but before any challenge is made.

Commencement

R&D tax relief and the payable tax credit may be claimed in respect of qualifying R&D expenditure incurred on or after 1 April 2000. This does not include expenditure made before 1 April 2000, which could be treated as incurred on or after that date under the pre-trading rules in TA 1988 s 401.

If the company's accounting period straddles the 1 April 2000, the minimum threshold for R&D spending is calculated by reference to the length of the accounting period falling on or after 1 April 2000. For example, a company with an accounting period ending on the 31 December 2001 must incur at least £18,750 of qualifying expenditure in the 9 months from 1 April to 31 December 2001.

REVENUE SPENDING ON R&D

There could be rare situations in which a business incurs revenue expenditure on R&D which would not otherwise be deductible because of the action of TA 1988 s 74.

TA 1988 s 82A allows a business to claim a deduction for such expenditure provided it is on R&D related to the trade and directly undertaken by the trader or on its behalf, but is not incurred in the acquisition of rights in, or arising out of R&D.

The legislation previously applied to expenditure incurred on scientific research, and was contained in CAA 1990 s 136(*a*). The basic rules are unchanged, except that they have been up-dated to refer to R&D and all related appeals will be heard by the tax Commissioners and Courts. The rules apply to all businesses (and not just the corporate SMEs that can claim R&D tax credits).

SCIENTIFIC RESEARCH ASSOCIATIONS

A trader may make a payment for scientific research to a scientific research association, or a university, college research institute or other similar institution that would, without special rules, not be deductible when it computes its profits for tax because of TA 1988 s 74.

Section 82B of TA 1988 allows a deduction to be made provided that:

- a scientific research association to which the sum is paid has as its object the carrying out of R&D, or
- the university, college research institute or similar institution is approved for this purpose by the Secretary of State for Trade and Industry.

In each case, the scientific research must be related to the class of trade carried on by the trader. This includes scientific research which may lead to or facilitate an extension of trades of that class, or scientific research of a medical mature which has a special relation to the welfare of workers employed by trades of that class. Disputes as to whether the activities constitute scientific research are referred to the Secretary of State for Trade and Industry through the Revenue. The Secretary of State's decision is final. Any other disputes relating to the relief that cannot be resolved are dealt with by the usual appeal procedures.

The legislation was previously contained in CAA 1990 s 136(*b*) and (*c*). Although now moved to TA, its scope and operation is unchanged.

Misc IX.B Guidelines on the meaning of Research and Development for tax purposes

These Guidelines are issued by the Secretary of State for Trade and Industry for the purposes of TA 1988 s 837A. They replace the previous Guidelines issued on 28 July 2000.

1 Research and development (''R&D'') is defined for tax purposes TA 1988 s 837A[1]. This says the definition of R&D for tax purposes follows generally accepted accounting practice. SSAP 13 ''Accounting for research and development'' is the Statement of Standard Accounting Practice which defines R&D. The accountancy definition is then modified for tax purposes by these Guidelines, which are given legal force by Parliamentary Regulations. These Guidelines explain what is meant by R&D for a variety of tax purposes, but the rules of particular tax schemes may restrict the qualifying expenditure[2].

Note—[1] For the purposes of research and development allowances (CAA 2001 Pt 6) this definition is extended to include oil and gas exploration and appraisal as defined in TA 1988 s 837A. These Guidelines apply to this extended definition as well.

[2] Note (not forming part of the Guidelines)—for example, the qualifying indirect activities listed at para 31 are R&D, as para 5 indicates, but they do not attract R&D tax credits; see for example FA 2000 Sch 20 para 5(4)).

2 In these Guidelines a number of terms are used which are intended to have a special meaning for the purpose of the Guidelines. Such terms are **highlighted** on first appearance and defined later.

THE DEFINITION OF RESEARCH & DEVELOPMENT

3 R&D for tax purposes takes place when a **project** seeks to achieve an **advance in science or technology**.

4 The activities which **directly contribute** to achieving this advance in science or technology through the resolution of **scientific or technological uncertainty** are R&D.

5 Certain **qualifying indirect activities** related to the project are also R&D. Activities other than qualifying indirect activities which do not directly contribute to the resolution of the project's scientific or technological uncertainty are not R&D.

ADVANCE IN SCIENCE OR TECHNOLOGY

6 An advance in science or technology means an advance in **overall knowledge or capability** in a field of **science** or **technology** (not a company's own state of knowledge or capability alone). This includes the adaptation of knowledge or capability from another field of science or technology in order to make such an advance where this adaptation was not readily deducible.

7 An advance in science or technology may have tangible consequences (such as a new or more efficient cleaning product, or a process which generates less waste) or more intangible outcomes (new knowledge or cost improvements, for example).

8 A process, material, device, product, service or source of knowledge does not become an advance in science or technology simply because science or technology is used in its creation. Work which uses science or technology but which does not advance scientific or technological capability as a whole is not an advance in science or technology.

9 A project which seeks to, for example—

(*a*) extend overall knowledge or capability in a field of science or technology; or

(*b*) create a process, material, device, product or service which incorporates or represents an increase in overall knowledge or capability in a field of science or technology; or

(*c*) make an **appreciable improvement** to an existing process, material, device, product or service through scientific or technological changes; or

(*d*) use science or technology to duplicate the effect of an existing process, material, device, product or service in a new or appreciably improved way (eg a product which has exactly the same performance characteristics as existing models, but is built in a fundamentally different manner);

will therefore be R&D.

10 Even if the advance in science or technology sought by a project is not achieved or not fully realised, R&D still takes place.

11 If a particular advance in science or technology has already been made or attempted but details are not readily available (for example, if it is a trade secret), work to achieve such an advance can still be an advance in science or technology.

12 However, the routine analysis, copying or adaptation of an existing product, process, service or material, will not be an advance in science or technology.

SCIENTIFIC OR TECHNOLOGICAL UNCERTAINTY

13 Scientific or technological uncertainty exists when knowledge of whether something is scientifically possible or technologically feasible, or how to achieve it in practice, is not readily available or deducible by a competent professional working in the field. This includes **system uncertainty**. Scientific or technological uncertainty will often arise from turning something that has

Misc

already been established as scientifically feasible into a cost-effective, reliable and reproducible process, material, device, product or service.

14 Uncertainties that can readily be resolved by a competent professional working in the field are not scientific or technological uncertainties. Similarly, improvements, optimisations and fine-tuning which do not materially affect the underlying science or technology do not constitute work to resolve scientific or technological uncertainty.

OTHER DEFINITIONS

Science

15 Science is the systematic study of the nature and behaviour of the physical and material universe. Work in the arts, humanities and social sciences, including economics, is not science for the purpose of these Guidelines. Mathematical techniques are frequently used in science, but mathematical advances in and of themselves are not science unless they are advances in representing the nature and behaviour of the physical and material universe.

16 These Guidelines apply equally to work in any branch or field of science.

Technology

17 Technology is the practical application of scientific principles and knowledge, where ''scientific'' is based on the definition of science above.

18 These Guidelines apply equally to work in any branch or field of technology.

Project

19 A project consists of a number of activities conducted to a method or plan in order to achieve an advance in science or technology. It is important to get the boundaries of the project correct. It should encompass all the activities which collectively serve to resolve the scientific or technological uncertainty associated with achieving the advance, so it could include a number of different sub-projects. A project may itself be part of a larger commercial project, but that does not make the parts of the commercial project that do not address scientific or technological uncertainty into R&D.

Overall knowledge or capability

20 Overall knowledge or capability in a field of science or technology means the knowledge or capability in the field which is publicly available or is readily deducible from the publicly available knowledge or capability by a competent professional working in the field. Work which seeks an advance relative to this overall knowledge or capability is R&D.

21 Overall knowledge or capability in a field of science or technology can still be advanced (and hence R&D can still be done) in situations where—

- companies are working at the cutting edge in the same field, and are doing similar work independently; or
- has already been done but this is not known in general because it is a trade secret, and another company repeats the work; or
- is known that a particular advance in science or technology has been achieved, but the details of how are not readily available.

22 However, the routine analysis, copying or adaptation of an existing process, material, device, product or service will not advance overall knowledge or capability, even though it may be completely new to the company or the company's trade.

Appreciable improvement

23 Appreciable improvement means to change or adapt the scientific or technological characteristics of something to the point where it is ''better'' than the original. The improvement should be more than a minor or routine upgrading, and should represent something that would generally be acknowledged by a competent professional working in the field as a genuine and non-trivial improvement. Improvements arising from the adaptation of knowledge or capability from another field of science or technology are appreciable improvements if they would generally be acknowledged by a competent professional working in the field as a genuine and non-trivial improvement.

24 Improvements which arise from taking existing science or technology and deploying it in a new context (eg a different trade) with only minor or routine changes are not appreciable improvements. A process, material, device, product or service will not be appreciably improved if it simply brings a company into line with overall knowledge or capability in science or technology, even though it may be completely new to the company or the company's trade.

25 The question of what scale of advance would constitute an appreciable improvement will differ between fields of science and technology and will depend on what a competent professional working in the field would regard as a genuine and non-trivial improvement.

Directly contribute

26 To directly contribute to achieving an advance in science or technology, an activity (or several activities in combination) must attempt to resolve an element of the scientific or technological uncertainty associated with achieving the advance.

27 Activities which directly contribute to R&D include—

(*a*) activities to create or adapt software, materials or equipment needed to resolve the scientific or technological uncertainty, provided that the software, material or equipment is created or adapted solely for use in R&D;
(*b*) scientific or technological planning activities; and
(*c*) scientific or technological design, testing and analysis undertaken to resolve the scientific or technological uncertainty.

28 Activities which do not directly contribute to the resolution of scientific or technological uncertainty include—

(*a*) the range of commercial and financial steps necessary for innovation and for the successful development and marketing of a new or appreciably improved process, material, device, product or service;
(*b*) work to develop non-scientific or non-technological aspects of a new or appreciably improved process, material, device, product or service;
(*c*) the production and distribution of goods and services;
(*d*) administration and other supporting services;
(*e*) general support services (such as transportation, storage, cleaning, repair, maintenance and security); and
(*f*) qualifying indirect activities.

System uncertainty

29 System uncertainty is scientific or technological uncertainty that results from the complexity of a system rather than uncertainty about how its individual components behave. For example, in electronic devices, the characteristics of individual components or chips are fixed, but there can still be uncertainty about the best way to combine those components to achieve an overall effect. However, assembling a number of components (or software sub-programs) to an established pattern, or following routine methods for doing so, involves little or no scientific or technological uncertainty.

30 Similarly, work on combining standard technologies, devices, and/or processes can involve scientific or technological uncertainty even if the principles for their integration are well known. There will be scientific or technological uncertainty if a competent professional working in the field cannot readily deduce how the separate components or sub-systems should be combined to have the intended function.

Misc

Qualifying indirect activity

31 These are activities which form part of a project but do not directly contribute to the resolution of the scientific or technological uncertainty. They are—

(*a*) scientific and technical information services, insofar as they are conducted for the purpose of R&D support (such as the preparation of the original report of R&D findings);
(*b*) indirect supporting activities such as maintenance, security, administration and clerical activities, and finance and personnel activities, insofar as undertaken for R&D;
(*c*) ancillary activities essential to the undertaking of R&D (eg taking on and paying staff, leasing laboratories and maintaining research and development equipment including computers used for R&D purposes);
(*d*) training required to directly support an R&D project;
(*e*) research by students and researchers carried out at universities;
(*f*) research (including related data collection) to devise new scientific or technological testing, survey, or sampling methods, where this research is not R&D in its own right; and
(*g*) feasibility studies to inform the strategic direction of a specific R&D activity.

32 Activities not described in paragraph 31 are not qualifying indirect activities.

COMMENTARY ON PARTICULAR QUESTIONS WHICH ARISE

Start and end of R&D

33 R&D begins when work to resolve the scientific or technological uncertainty starts, and ends when that uncertainty is resolved or work to resolve it ceases. This means that work to identify the requirements for the process, material, device, product or service, where no scientific or technological questions are at issue, is not R&D.

34 R&D ends when knowledge is codified in a form usable by a competent professional working in the field, or when a prototype or pilot plant with all the functional characteristics of the final process, material, device, product or service is produced.

35 Although the R&D for a process, material, device, product or service may have ended, new problems which involve scientific or technological uncertainty may emerge after it has been turned over to production or put into use. The resolution of these problems may require new R&D to be carried out. But there is a distinction to be drawn between such problems and routine fault fixing.

Planning as part of R&D

36 Scientific or technological planning activities associated with a project directly contribute to resolving the scientific or technological uncertainty associated with the project, and are therefore R&D. These include defining scientific or technological objectives, assessing scientific or technological feasibility, identifying particular scientific or technological uncertainties, estimating development time, schedule, and resources of the R&D, and high-level outlining of the scientific or technical work, as well as the detailed planning and management of the work.

37 Elements of a company's planning activity relating to a project but not directly contributing to the resolution of scientific or technological uncertainty, such as identifying or researching market niches in which R&D might benefit a company, or examination of a project's financial, marketing, and legal aspects, fall outside the category of scientific or technological planning, and are therefore not R&D.

Abortive projects

38 Not all projects succeed in their aims. What counts is whether there is an intention to achieve an advance in science or technology, not whether ultimately the associated scientific or technological uncertainty is completely resolved, or resolved to the degree intended. Scientific or technological planning activities associated with projects which are not taken forward (eg because of insurmountable technical or commercial challenges) are still R&D.

Prototypes, pilot plants

39 A prototype is an original model on which something new or appreciably improved is patterned, and of which all things of the same type are representations or copies. It is a basic experimental model possessing the essential characteristics of the intended process, material, device, product or service. The design, construction, and testing of prototypes generally fall within the scope of R&D for tax purposes. But once any modifications necessary to reflect the test findings have been made to the prototypes, and further testing has been satisfactorily completed, the scientific or technological uncertainty has been resolved and further work will not be R&D.

40 Similarly the construction and operation of pilot plants while assessing their operations is R&D until the scientific or technological uncertainty associated with the intended advance in science or technology has been resolved.

Design

41 When achieving design objectives requires the resolution of scientific or technological uncertainty within a project, work to do this will be R&D. Design activities which do not directly contribute to the resolution of scientific or technological uncertainty within a project are not R&D.

Cosmetic and aesthetic effects

42 Cosmetic and aesthetic qualities are not of themselves science or technology, and so work to improve the cosmetic or aesthetic appeal of a process, material, device, product or service would not in itself be R&D. However, work to create a desired cosmetic or aesthetic effect through the application of science or technology can require a scientific or technological advance, and resolving the scientific or technological uncertainty associated with such a project would therefore be R&D.

Content delivered through science or technology

43 Information or other content which is delivered through a scientific or technological medium is not of itself science or technology. However, improvements in scientific or technological means to create, manipulate and transfer information or other content can be scientific or technological advances, and resolving the scientific or technological uncertainty associated with such projects would therefore be R&D.

EXAMPLES/ILLUSTRATIONS

Examples in these Guidelines are illustrative, designed to cast light on the principles explained in the Guidelines, and should be read in that context.

A The R&D process

A1 A company conducts extensive market research to learn what technical and design characteristics a new DVD player should have in order to be an appealing product. This work is not R&D (paragraph 37). However, it does identify a potential project to create a DVD player incorporating a number of technological improvements which the company's R&D staff (who are competent professionals) regard as genuine and non-trivial. This project would be seeking to develop an appreciably improved DVD player (paragraphs 23–25) and would therefore be seeking to achieve an advance in science or technology (paragraph 9).

A2 The company then decides on a detailed specification for the desired new product, and devises a plan for developing it. Some elements of this plan involve planning of activities which directly contribute to resolving the project's scientific or technological uncertainties (such as the system uncertainty associated with an improved control mechanism for the laser that ''reads'' the DVD). This element of planning is R&D (paragraph 36), as are the activities themselves (paragraph 4). Other elements of the plan focus on obtaining intellectual property protection or cosmetic design decisions, for example, which do not directly contribute to resolving the project's scientific or technological uncertainties and are not qualifying indirect activities (paragraph 31) and are therefore not R&D. Neither this planning (paragraph 37) nor these activities (paragraph 28) are R&D.

A3 The scientific or technological work culminates in the creation of a series of prototype DVD players, and ultimately a ''final'' prototype is produced and tested which possesses the essential characteristics of the intended product (circuit board design, performance characteristics, etc). All the activities which directly contributed to resolving the scientific or technological uncertainty of creating the DVD player up to this point (such as the testing of successive prototypes) are R&D (paragraphs 34 and 39).

A4 Several copies of this prototype are made (not R&D; paragraphs 4–5 and 26–28) and distributed to a group of consumers to test their reactions (not R&D; paragraph 28(*a*)). Some of these consumers report concerns about the noise level of the DVD player in operation. Additional work is done to resolve this problem. If this involves a routine adjustment of the existing prototype (ie no scientific or technological uncertainty) then it will not be R&D (paragraph 14); if it involves more substantial changes (ie there is scientific or technological uncertainty to resolve) then it will be R&D.

B Equal applicability in any branch or field of science or technology

B1 The Guidelines apply equally to work in any branch or field of science or technology (paragraphs 15–18). This means that work in software engineering, for example, is subject to the same fundamental criteria for being R&D as work in textile science, or nanotechnology, or anything else.

B2 This equality also applies to the methods used to resolve scientific or technological uncertainty. For example, it is sometimes possible to implement functionality in a product or process by means of software or of hardware. As long as the scientific or technological uncertainty cannot readily be resolved by a competent professional working in the field, hardware and software methods are both equally R&D in these circumstances.

C Abortive projects

C1 Not all projects achieve the advance in science or technology they are seeking. For example, work to insert a particular gene into a gene sequence may simply fail, while an attempt to appreciably increase the life of a battery may only yield a marginal improvement. In both cases, the project seeks to achieve an advance in science or technology and work to resolve the scientific or technological uncertainty would be R&D (paragraph 10).

D Advance in science or technology

D1 Searching for the molecular structures of possible new drugs would be an advance in science or technology, because it applies existing knowledge of science (which compounds are known to cause particular physiological effects) in search of new or improved active compounds (paragraph 9 (*b*)). This is true even if the method used to search for those molecular structures (eg running a computer program on a particular set of data) is itself entirely routine; the activity directly contributes to the resolution of scientific or technological uncertainty (paragraph 27 (*c*)) and so would be R&D (paragraph 4). Work to identify new uses of existing compounds would also be creative work in science or technology, because it seeks new scientific knowledge about those molecules (paragraph 9 (*a*)).

D2 However, the development of software intended for the analysis of market research data (which is not scientific or technological knowledge; paragraphs 15–18) which was not expected to result in the development of a scientific or technological advance in the field of software as a whole (such as an algorithm which extends overall knowledge or capability in the field of software) would not be R&D (paragraph 8). Work to adapt such software to analyse, say, customer spending patterns would also not be R&D.

D3 An advance in science or technology need not imply an absolute improvement in the performance of a process, material, device, product or service. For example, the existence of high-fidelity audio equipment does not prevent a project to create lower-performance equipment from being an advance in science or technology (for instance, if it incorporated technological improvements leading to lower cost through more efficient circuit design or speaker construction) (paragraph 9 (*d*)).

E Scientific or technological uncertainty

E1 A firm's project involves finding a new active ingredient for weed-killer (an advance in overall knowledge or capability in the particular field of science or technology; paragraphs 6, 20), and developing a formula incorporating the new active ingredient for use in a commercial product (paragraph 9 (*b*) or (*c*)). Both of these would constitute an advance in science or technology.

E2 In order to achieve this advance, a programme of investigation by computer to pick likely ingredients and the systematic testing of possible ingredients and products based on those "trial" ingredients is undertaken. The work involves the adaptation of existing software to tackle the specific problem, and product formulation and testing using established methods. This investigation and testing evaluates the weed-killing performance and other relevant characteristics of the formulations (for example, toxicity to humans and wildlife, water solubility, adhesion to weeds, damage done to other plants). All of these activities would therefore be R&D (paragraphs 4, 26, 27).

E3 The company also does work to assess what characteristics a new weed-killing product should have in order to appeal to consumers. This activity does not directly contribute to the resolution of scientific or technological uncertainty (paragraph 28 (*a*)) and is not a qualifying indirect activity (paragraph 31), and is therefore not R&D (paragraph 4).

F Direct contribution to the resolution of scientific or technological uncertainty

F1 Work to compare the effectiveness of two possible designs for controlling part of a new manufacturing process would directly contribute to resolving the scientific or technological uncertainty inherent in the new process, and hence the activity would be R&D (paragraphs 4, 26). But work to raise finance for the project, while *indirectly* contributing to the resolution of scientific or technological uncertainty (eg by paying for work) does not of itself help resolve the uncertainty, and hence is not R&D (paragraph 28 (*a*)). Human Resources work to support the R&D is a qualifying indirect activity (paragraph 31) and hence is also R&D (paragraph 5), though it does not directly contribute to the resolution of scientific or technological uncertainty (paragraph 28 (*e*) and (*f*))[1].

[1] Note (not forming part of the Guidelines)—as noted in para 1, the rules of particular tax schemes may restrict what expenditure qualifies. For example, expenditure on qualifying indirect activities does not attract R&D tax credits; see for example FA 2000 Sch 20 para 5(4).

G Testing as part of R&D

G1 Scientific or technological testing and analysis which directly contributes to the resolution of scientific or technological uncertainty is R&D (paragraph 26). So for example if testing work is carried out as part of the development of a pilot plant, this would be R&D, but once the design of the 'final' pilot plant had been finalised and tested, any further testing would not be R&D (paragraph 39). However, if flaws in the design became apparent later on, then work to remedy them would be R&D if they could not readily be resolved by a competent professional working in the field (in other words, if there was scientific or technological uncertainty around how to fix the problem; paragraph 14).

H Cosmetic and aesthetic effects

H1 A company is seeking to make a water-breathable fabric for use in hiking gear. A test fabric with the required physical characteristics is produced through R&D. This new fabric is then produced in small quantities (not R&D) and market tested with a number of trial users. The user tests are not R&D, because they are concerned with testing the commercial potential of the new material and assessing its appeal to users (paragraph 42).

H2 One of the results of these tests is that users do not like the feel of the new fabric against their skin, and dislike its shiny appearance. The company decides to investigate variants of its new fabric, which require significant changes to the material's weave and physical structure, to overcome these problems. Because there is scientific and technological uncertainty around whether a material with the desired physical characteristics can be made, the R&D continues.

J Project, prototype and end of R&D

J1 A company develops new spark plugs for use in an existing petrol engine. The scientific or technological uncertainty associated with this work is resolved once prototype plugs have been fully tested in the engine. The activities directly contributing to this work, including the construction of prototypes and their testing in the engine, would be R&D.

J2 The same company decides to design a new engine to incorporate the new spark plugs, involving a new combustion chamber design, lighter materials and other improvements such that the overall engine is appreciably improved (it uses less petrol to achieve slightly greater power output performance, and generates less pollution than current models). The activities directly contributing to this work, including the design of the separate components (not all of which need be different from those used in previous models) and their integration into a new engine, are R&D. The uncertainty associated with this work is resolved, and R&D is complete. once a functionally final prototype has been tested.

Inland Revenue, March 2004

Commentary—*Simon's Direct Tax Service* **D2.1201.**

Misc X. Recognised stock exchanges

The following is a list of exchanges which have been designated as recognised stock exchanges by Order of the Board under TA 1988 s 841(1)(*b*), as at October 2003. Current Inland Revenue policy is to consider recognition of stock exchanges on receipt of a request from the exchange concerned, so the fact that an exchange is not included in the list may simply mean that it has not sought recognition.

The Revenue provides an updated list of recognised stock exchanges on its website at: http://www.inlandrevenue.gov.uk/fid/rse.htm.

Country	*Effective date*
Australia	
Any stock exchange which is a member of the Australian Associated Stock Exchanges, being a prescribed stock exchange within the meaning of the Australian law relating to stock exchanges	14 December 1970
The Australian Stock Exchange and any of its stock exchange subsidiaries	22 September 1988
Austria	
Any stock exchange which is a stock exchange within the meaning of the Austrian law relating to stock exchanges	22 October 1970
Belgium[1]	
Any stock exchange which is a stock exchange within the meaning of the Belgian law relating to stock exchanges	22 October 1970
Brazil	
Rio de Janeiro Stock Exchange	17 August 1995
São Paulo Stock Exchange	11 December 1995
Canada	
Any stock exchange prescribed for the purposes of the Canadian Income Tax Act	22 October 1970
The Cayman Islands	
The Cayman Islands Stock Exchange	4 March 2004
China	
Any stock exchange in Hong Kong which is recognised under section 2A(1) of the Hong Kong Companies Ordinance	26 February 1971
Denmark	
Copenhagen Stock Exchange	22 October 1970
Finland	
Helsinki Stock Exchange	22 October 1970
France	
Any stock exchange set up in accordance with the French legislation	22 October 1970
Germany	
Any stock exchange approved under the laws relating to stock exchanges in the Federal Republic of Germany	5 August 1971
Greece	
Athens Stock Exchange	14 June 1993
Guernsey	
Any stock exchange which is a stock exchange within the meaning of Guernsey law relating to stock exchanges	10 December 2002
Ireland (Republic of)	
Any stock exchange which is a stock exchange within the meaning of the Irish law relating to stock exchanges	22 October 1970
Italy	
Any stock exchange which is a stock exchange within the meaning of the Italian law relating to stock exchanges	3 May 1972
Japan	
Any stock exchange which is a stock exchange within the meaning of the Japanese law relating to stock exchanges	22 October 1970
Korea	
Korea Stock Exchange	10 October 1994

Misc

Country	*Effective date*
Luxembourg	
Any stock exchange which is a stock exchange within the meaning of the Luxembourg law relating to stock exchanges	21 February 1972
Malaysia	
Kuala Lumpur Stock Exchange	10 October 1994
Mexico	
Mexico Stock Exchange	10 October 1994
Netherlands[2]	
Any stock exchange which is a stock exchange within the meaning of the Netherlands law relating to stock exchanges	22 October 1970
New Zealand	
New Zealand Stock Exchange	22 September 1988
Norway	
Any stock exchange which is a stock exchange within the meaning of the Norwegian rules relating to stock exchanges	22 October 1970
Portugal	
Any stock exchange which is a stock exchange within the meaning of the Portuguese law relating to stock exchanges	21 February 1972
Singapore	
Singapore Stock Exchange	30 June 1977
South Africa	
Johannesburg Stock Exchange	22 October 1970
Spain	
Any stock exchange which is a stock exchange within the meaning of the Spanish law relating to stock exchanges	5 August 1971
Sri Lanka	
Colombo Stock Exchange	21 February 1972
Sweden	
Stockholm Stock Exchange	16 July 1985
Switzerland	
Swiss Stock Exchange[3]	12 May 1997
Thailand	
Stock Exchange of Thailand	10 October 1994
United Kingdom	
London Stock Exchange[4]	6 April 1965
United States	
Any stock exchange registered with the Securities and Exchange Commission as a national securities exchange[5]	22 October 1970
Nasdaq Stock Market[6]	10 March 1992

Notes—[1] This includes EASDAQ.
[2] This includes the European Options Exchange.
[3] Formerly the Basle, Geneva and Zurich Stock Exchanges.
[4] Formerly the International Stock Exchange, previously The Stock Exchange.
[5] This includes the Chicago Board Options Exchange. The term ''national securities exchange'' does not include any local exchanges registered with the Securities and Exchange Commission.
[6] As maintained through the facilities of the National Association of Securities Dealers Inc and its subsidiaries.

Misc XI. Recognised futures exchanges

The following is a list of exchanges which have been designated as recognised futures exchanges under TCGA 1992 s 288(6). By concession, the UK exchanges designated before the end of 1985 can be treated as having been designated with effect from 6 April 1985—

Country		*Effective date*
Australia		
	Sydney Futures Exchange	31 October 1988
Canada		
	Montreal Exchange	29 July 1987
China[1]		
	Hong Kong Futures Exchange	15 December 1987
Sweden		
	OM Stockholm	18 March 1992
United Kingdom		
	Baltic International Freight Futures Exchange[2]	6 August 1985

Country	Effective date
International Petroleum Exchange of London	6 August 1985
London Cocoa Terminal Market[2]	6 August 1985
London Coffee Terminal Market[2]	6 August 1985
London Commodity Exchange[3]	18 March 1992
London Futures and Options Exchange[3]	18 March 1992
London Gold Futures Market[4]	6 August 1985
London Gold Market	12 December 1985
London Grain Futures Market[2]	6 August 1985
London International Financial Futures Exchange[5]	6 April 1985
London International Financial Futures and Options Exchange	18 March 1992
London Meat Futures Market[2]	6 August 1985
London Metal Exchange	6 August 1985
London Potato Futures Market[2]	6 August 1985
London Rubber Market[2]	6 August 1985
London Silver Market	12 December 1985
London Soya Bean Meal Futures Market[2]	6 August 1985
London Sugar Terminal Market[2]	6 August 1985
London Wool Terminal Market	6 August 1985
OM London [6]	18 March 1992
OMLX	18 March 1992
United States	
Chicago Board of Trade	24 April 1987
Chicago Mercantile Exchange	19 December 1986
Citrus Associates of the New York Cotton Exchange[7]	25 August 1988
Coffee, Sugar and Cocoa Exchange, New York[7]	15 December 1987
Commodity Exchange	25 August 1988
Mid America Commodity Exchange	29 July 1987
New York Board of Trade[8]	—[8]
New York Cotton Exchange[7]	25 August 1988
New York Mercantile Exchange	19 December 1986
Philadelphia Board of Trade	19 December 1986

Notes—[1] Now the Hong Kong Special Administrative Region of China, following the transfer of sovereignty on 30 June 1997.
[2] Came under the umbrella of the London Commodity Exchange.
[3] Name changed to London Commodity Exchange from 1 July 1993. (The name London Futures and Options Exchange (London FOX) was adopted in June 1987 in place of the original name, London Commodity Exchange.) Merged with the London International Financial Futures and Options Exchange in 1996.
[4] Closed in 1985.
[5] Merged with the Stock Exchange's London Traded Options Market from 23 March 1992, to form the London International Financial Futures and Options Exchange.
[6] Name changed to OMLX in 1994.
[7] Merged into the New York Board of Trade in 1998.
[8] Formed by the merger of the Coffee, Sugar and Cocoa Exchange, New York, and the New York Cotton Exchange in 1998.

Misc XII. Recognised investment exchanges

The following exchange has been designated as a recognised investment exchange (under the Financial Services Act 1986 s 37(3)) for the purposes of TA 1988 s 841(3) and TCGA 1992 s 285.

Country	Effective date
United Kingdom	March 1992
London International Financial Futures Exchange (Administration and Management)(LIFFE (A&M))	

Misc

DESTINATION TABLES FOR CONSOLIDATION AND TAX LAW REWRITE STATUTES

TA 1988: DESTINATION TABLE

This table lists the provisions of the Income and Corporation Taxes Act 1970 and subsequent Finance Acts and other Acts which were re-enacted in the Income and Corporation Taxes Act 1988. Where no corresponding provision appears under the 1988 Act in the third column, the former enactment may be spent or may have been repealed as indicated in the ''Remarks'' column. The table does not reflect any subsequent amendment history after 1988.

For the operative date of the re-enacted provisions, please see sections 843 and 844 of the 1988 Act.

Finance Acts are referred to in this table by their years only, *eg* 1971 means Finance Act 1971. References to other Acts are abbreviated as shown in the abbreviation list below.

Abbreviations used in this table are—

1970 or 1970(F)	=	Finance Act 1970
1971	=	Finance Act 1971 and so on as respects subsequent years
1975(2)	=	Finance (No 2) Act 1975 and so on as respects subsequent years
§	=	paragraph
AFA 1981	=	Armed Forces Act 1981
AJA 1982	=	Administration of Justice Act 1982
Am	=	Amended by
BA 1987	=	Banking Act 1987
BNA	=	British Nationality Act 1981
BSA 1986	=	Building Societies Act 1986
CGTA 7	=	Capital Gains Tax Act 1979 Sch 7 and so on
CCCPA	=	Companies Consolidation (Consequential Provisions) Act 1985 Sch 2
CCA 1974	=	Consumer Credit Act 1974
CCA 1984	=	County Courts Act 1984
CUA 1979	=	Credit Unions Act 1979
CJA 1975	=	Criminal Jurisdiction Act 1975
DCA 1969	=	Decimal Currency Act 1969
EP(C)A	=	Employment Protection (Consolidation) Act 1978
FA	=	Finance Act
FSA	=	Friendly Societies Act
HSA 1984	=	Health and Social Security Act 1984
HCPA 1985	=	Housing (Consequential Provisions) Act 1985
IDA 1982	=	Industrial Development Act 1982
ITA	=	Inheritance Tax Act 1984
IA 1986	=	Insolvency Act 1986
ICA	=	Insurance Companies Act
IA 1978	=	Interpretation Act 1978
J(NI)A	=	Judicature (Northern Ireland) Act 1978
LGA	=	Local Government Act 1972
LRTA	=	London Regional Transport Act 1984
NHS 1977	=	National Health Service Act 1977
NHS 1978	=	National Health Service (Scotland) Act 1978
NICA	=	Northern Ireland Constitution Act 1973
OTA	=	Oil Taxation Act
OPA 1973	=	Overseas Pensions Act 1973
para	=	paragraph
PPA 1972	=	Parliamentary and other Pensions Act 1972
PPA 1987	=	Parliamentary and other Pensions Act 1987
PPA 1976	=	Parliamentary and other Pensions and Salaries Act 1976
Pt	=	Part
Rep	=	Repealed
Sch	=	Schedule
s	=	section
SSA	=	Social Security Act
SSCPA	=	Social Security (Consequential Provisions) Act 1975
SI	=	Statutory Instrument
Subst	=	Substituted by
SBA 1976	=	Supplementary Benefits Act 1976
TA	=	Income and Corporation Taxes Act
TA 1984	=	Telecommunications Act 1984
TSB 1985	=	Trustee Savings Banks Act 1985

The above abbreviations are also used as applicable in the annotations under the sections and the schedules paragraphs of the 1988 Act.

The statutory instruments are referred to in this table by their numbers only. The following list shows their full titles—

1970/1537 = Secretary of State for Trade and Industry Order 1970
1970/1681 = Secretary of State for the Environment Order 1970
1971/2099 = Minister for the Civil Service Order 1971
1977/2158 = Supplementary Benefits etc (Consequential Provisions) (Northern Ireland) Order 1977
1979/1573 = Statutory Rules (Northern Ireland) Order 1979
1979/1574 = Industrial Assurance (Northern Ireland) Order 1979
1979/1576 = Tax, Consumer Credit and Judicature (Northern Ireland Consequential Amendments) Order 1979
1980/1171 = Income Tax (Construction Operations) Order 1980
1981/157 = Building Societies and Tax (Northern Ireland Consequential Amendments) Order 1981
1981/1670 = Transfer of Functions (Minister for the Civil Service and the Treasury) Order 1981
1982/338 = The Departments (Northern Ireland) Order 1982 (SI No 338 (NI 6))
1983/50 = Companies (Northern Ireland) Order 1983
1985/1205 = Credit Unions (Northern Ireland) Order 1985
1985/1598 = Income Tax (Cash Equivalents of Car Benefits) Order 1985
1986/702 = Income Tax (Cash Equivalents of Car Fuel Benefits) Order 1986
1986/703 = Income Tax (Cash Equivalents of Car Benefits) Order 1986
CCCP(NI) = Companies Consolidation (Consequential Provisions) (Northern Ireland) Order 1986
1986/771 = Income Tax (Composite Rates) (Relevant Deposits) Order 1986
1986/1888 = Social Security (Northern Ireland) Order 1986
1987/434 = Income Tax (Indexation) Order 1987
1987/898 = Income Tax (Interest on Unpaid Tax and Repayment Supplement) (No 2) Order 1987

INCOME AND CORPORATION TAXES ACT 1970
(c 10)

TA 1970	Subject Matter	Re-enacted in TA 1988	Remarks
s 1	The charge to income tax.	s 1(1), (2)	
s 2	Fractions of a pound, and yearly assessments.	s 2	Am 1970(F) Sch 4 §11; partly spent.
s 3	Certain income charged at basic rate.	s 3	Subst 1971 Sch 6 §2.
s 4	Dates for payment.	s 5	Rep in part 1971 Sch 14 Pt II; am 1971 Sch 6 §3; 1975(2) s 44(1); 1972 Sch 24 §15; 1980 s 61(1).
s 5	Personal reliefs: general.	s 256	Am 1975(2) s 31(3); 1976 Sch 4 §18.
s 6	—	—	Rep 1971 Sch 14 Pt II.
s 7	—	—	Rep 1975(2) Sch 14 Pt IV.
s 8(1)	Personal relief.	s 257(1)	Am 1971 Sch 6 § 5; 1987/434.
s 8(1A)		s 257(2)	Added 1975(2) s 31(1); am 1977 s 22(1); 1987/434.
s 8(1B)		s 257(5)	Added 1975(2) s 31(1); am 1987/434.
s 8(2)		s 257(6), (7)	Am 1971 Sch 6 §5; 1979(2) Sch 2 §1; 1981 s 27(9); 1987 s 27(1); 1987/434; rep in part 1981 Sch 19 Pt VI; 1982 Sch 22 Pt IV.
s 8(3)		s 257(8)	Am 1970(F) s 14(1).
s 9	—	—	Rep 1971 Sch 14 Pt II.
s 10	—	—	Rep 1982 Sch 22 Pt XI.
s 11(1)–(3), (6)	—	—	Rep 1982 Sch 22 Pt XI.
s 11(4), (5)	Apportionment of relief.	s 263(5), (6)	Applied by 1970 s 16(3).
s 12	Widow's or widower's housekeeper.	s 258	Rep in part 1978 Sch 13 Pt III; 1971 Sch 14 Pt II; am 1971 s 15(5), Sch 6 §7; 1978 s 19(2).
s 13	—	—	Rep 1979(2) Sch 5 Pt II.
s 14	Relief in respect of children.	s 259	Rep in part 1970(F) Sch 8 §6; am 1976 s 36(4); 1979(2) Sch 1 §2; 1980 s 24(6); 1987 Sch 15 §2(2).
s 14A	Apportionment of relief.	s 260	Added 1979(2) Sch 1 §3; am 1980 s 24(6).
s 15	Claims under ss 12–14 for year of marriage.	s 261	
s 15A	Widow's bereavement allowance.	s 262	Added 1980 s 23; am 1980 s 24(6); 1983 s 15(1).
s 16(1), (2)	Dependent relatives.	s 263(1), (2)	Am 1973 s 12(2).
s 16(2A)		s 263(3)	Added 1979(2) Sch 2 §2.
s 16(3)		s 263(4)	Am 1973 s 12(2).
s 16(4)		s 263(7)	
s 16(5)		—	Spent.
s 17	Claim for services of son or daughter.	s 264	Am 1971 Sch 6 §11; 1978 s 19(5).
s 18(1), (2)	Relief for blind persons.	s 265(1), (2)	Am 1978 s 19(6); 1981 s 23(2), (3); 1987 s 28; rep in part 1981 Sch 19 Pt VI.
s 18(3), (4)		—	Rep 1978 Sch 13 Pt III.
s 18(5), (6)		s 265(3), (4)	Am 1978 s 19(5); 1987 Sch 15 §2(3); rep in part 1981 Sch 19 Pt VI.
s 19(1)	Relief for certain premiums.	s 266(1)	Am 1976 Sch 4 §3(1).
s 19(2)		s 266(2)	Am 1976 s 36(5), Sch 4 §3(2); ICA 1982 Sch 5 §10.
s 19(3)(*a*), (*b*)		s 266(3)(*a*), (*d*)	
s 19(3)(i), (ii)		s 266(11)	
s 19(4)		s 266(3)(*b*), (10)	Rep in part 1971 Sch 14 Pt I; am 1971 Sch 3 §11.

TA 1970	Subject Matter	Re-enacted in TA 1988	Remarks
s 19(5)		Sch 14 §8(1), (2)	
s 19(6)		s 267	
s 19(7), (8)		—	Rep 1971 Sch 14 Pt II; 1976 Sch 15 Pt IV.
s 20(1)	Further relief for premiums and other payments.	s 273	Rep in part 1972 Sch 28 Pt IV; 1976 Sch 15 Pt IV; 1987 Sch 15 §2(4).
s 20(2)–(5)		—	Rep 1987 Sch 16 Pt VII.
s 21(1)	Limits on relief under ss 19 and 20.	s 274(1)	Am 1976 Sch 4 §21.
s 21(1A), (2)		—	Rep 1976 Sch 4 §21(3); 1975 Sch 13 Pt II.
s 21(3)		s 274(2)	Am 1976 Sch 4 §21; 1975 Sch 2 §6.
s 21(4)		s 274(3)	Am 1975 Sch 2 §6; 1980 s 29; 1987 Sch 15 §2(5); rep in part 1976 Sch 15 Pt IV.
s 21(5)		s 274(4)	Rep in part 1975 Sch 13 Pt II.
s 22	—	—	Rep 1970(F) Sch 8 Pt IV.
s 23	Meaning of relative.	s 275	
s 24	—	—	Rep 1977 Sch 9 Pt IV; 1976 Sch 15 Pt III.
s 25	Effect on relief of charges on income.	s 276	Subst 1971 s 33(5); rep in part 1976 Sch 15 Pt IV.
s 26	Partners.	s 277	Rep in part 1970(F) Sch 8 Pt VII.
s 27(1), (2)	Non-residents.	s 278(1)–(3)	Am BNA s 51(1)(*b*), (2); rep in part 1971 Sch 14 Pt II.
s 27(3)–(5)		s 278(5)–(8)	Rep in part 1972 Sch 28 Pt VI.
s 28, 29	—	—	Rep 1971 Sch 14 Pt II.
s 30	—	—	Rep 1985 Sch 27 Pt VIII.
s 31, 32	—	—	Rep 1971 Sch 14 Pt II.
s 33	—	—	Rep 1985 Sch 27 Pt VIII.
s 34(1)	Tax on consideration for certain restrictive covenants.	s 313(1)–(3)	Am 1971 Sch 16 §15; rep in part 1980 Sch 20 Pt V.
s 34(2)–(5)		s 313(4)–(6)	Rep in part 1987 Sch 16 Pt VII.
s 35	—	—	Rep 1971 Sch 14 Pt II.
s 36	Recovery from trustees of tax due from certain beneficiaries.	s 689	Am 1971 Sch 6 §16; 1978 Sch 2 §3; rep in part 1980 Sch 20 Pt V; 1984 Sch 23 Pt VI.
s 37(1)	Aggregation of wife's income with husband's.	s 279(1), (2)	Am 1976 s 36(2), (9); 1978 s 30(7)(*e*).
s 37(2)		s 279(3), (4)	
s 37(3)		s 279(5)	Subst 1971 Sch 6 §17.
s 37(4)		s 279(6)	
s 37(5)		—	Rep 1971 Sch 14 Pt II.
s 38(1)	Options for separate assessment.	s 283(1)	Rep in part 1971 Sch 14 Pt II; 1976 Sch 15 Pt III; am 1976 s 36(3).
s 38(2)		s 283(2)	Subst 1971 Sch 6 §18; rep in part 1984 Sch 23 Pt VI.
s 38(3)–(5)		s 283(3)–(5)	Rep in part 1971 Sch 14 Pt II.
s 39(1)(*a*), (*b*)	Separate assessments and personal reliefs.	—	Rep 1971 Sch 14 Pt II.
s 39(1)(*c*)–(*e*)		s 284(1), (5)	Rep in part 1971 Sch 14 Pt II; 1982 Sch 22 Pt XI; am 1978 s 19(5); 1971 Sch 6 §19.
s 39(1) proviso		s 284(2)	Am 1971 Sch 6 §19.
s 39(2)		s 284(3)	Rep in part 1971 Sch 14 Pt II.
s 39(3)		s 284(4)	
s 39(4)		—	Rep 1971 Sch 14 Pt II.

TA 1970	Subject Matter	Re-enacted in TA 1988	Remarks
s 40	Collection from wife of tax on her income.	s 285	Rep in part 1971 Sch 14 Pt II.
s 41	Husband's disclaimer of tax on dead wife's income.	s 286	Rep in part 1971 Sch 14 Pt II.
s 42	Interpretation.	s 282	Rep in part 1971 Sch 14 Pt II.
s 43–48	—	—	Rep 1971 Sch 14 Pt VII.
s 49	Residence: temporary absence.	s 334	Am BNA s 51(1)(*b*), (2).
s 50(1)	Working abroad.	s 335(1)	
s 50(2)		s 335(1)(*b*)	
s 50(3)		s 335(2)	
s 51	Temporary residents in UK.	s 336	
s 51A	Annual payments	s 347A	Added 1988 s 36(2).
s 51B	Qualifying maintenance payments	s 347B	Added 1988 s 36(2).
s 52(1)(*a*)	Deduction of tax: payments out of profits etc brought into charge to income tax.	—	Rep in part 1971 Sch 14 Pt II.
s 52(1)(*b*)		s 348(1)(*a*)	
s 52(1)(*c*)		s 348(1)(*b*)	Rep 1971 Sch 14 Pt II.
s 52(1)(*d*)		s 348(1)(*c*)	
s 52(1)(*e*)		s 348(1)(*d*)	Added 1971 Sch 6 §20(*c*).
s 52(2)		s 348(2)	Rep in part 1971 Sch 14 Pt II.
s 53(1)	Payments not out of profits etc brought into charge to income tax.	s 349(1)	Rep in part 1971 Sch 14 Pt II.
s 53(2)		s 350(1)	Am 1971 Sch 6 §21.
s 53(3)		s 350(3)	
s 53(4)		s 350(4)(*a*)	Am 1972 Sch 24 §16.
s 54(1)	Annual interest.	s 349(2)	Am 1971 Sch 1 §22.
s 54(2)		s 349(3)(*a*), (*b*)	
s 54(3)		s 350(1), (3), (4)	
s 55(1)	Certificates of deduction of tax.	s 352(1)	Am 1973 s 17(4); 1986 s 29(3).
s 55(2)		s 352(2)	
s 56	Interpretation.	s 350(2)	
s 57–64	—	—	Rep 1972 Sch 28 Pt V.
s 64A	Employee share schemes.	s 688	Added 1970(F) Sch 4 §9(5); am CCCPA.
s 65(1), (1A)	Small maintenance payments.	s 351(1), (2)	Subst 1982 s 33(2); am Income Tax (Small Maintenance Payments) Order 1986 (SI No 328).
s 65(2)		s 348(3), 349(3)(*d*), 351(3)	
s 65(3), (4)		s 351(4), (5)	
s 65(5)		s 351(6)	Am 1982 s 33(3).
s 65(6)		s 351(7)	Am 1982 s 33(4).
s 65(7)		s 351(8)	
s 66	—	—	Rep 1977 Sch 9 Pt V.
s 67	Schedule A.	s 15	
s 68	Persons chargeable.	s 21	
s 69(1)	Assessments.	s 22(1)	
s 69(2)		s 22(2), (3)	
s 70(1)	Collection from lessees and agents.	s 23(1)–(6)	
s 70(2)		s 23(7), (8)	
s 71(1)	Deductions from rents etc.	s 25(1), 28(1), 29(1), 31(1)	
s 71(2)	Interpretation.	s 24(6), (7)	
s 72(1)	Deductions from rents: general rules.	s 25(1), (2)	
s 72(2)		s 25(3), (4)	
s 72(3)		s 25(5), (6)	
s 72(4)–(6)		s 25(7)–(9)	
s 72(7)		s 25(2)	

Dest. Tables

TA 1970	Subject Matter	Re-enacted in TA 1988	Remarks
s 73(1)	Deductions from rents: land managed as one estate.	s 26(1), (2)	
s 73(2)		s 26(3)	
s 73(3)		s 26(4), (5)	Am 1987 Sch 15 §2(6).
s 73(4)		s 26(6)	
s 74	Deductions from receipts other than rent.	s 28	
s 75(1)	Sporting rights.	s 29(1), (2)	
s 75(2), (3), (4)		s 29(3), (4), (5)	Am 1976 Sch 9 §12.
s 76	Expenditure on sea walls.	s 30	
s 77	Interpretation.	s 31(2)–(7)	
s 78(1)	Capital allowances for machinery etc.	s 32(1), (2)	Am 1971 s 47(2).
s 78(2)		s 32(3), (4)	Am 1971 s 47(2).
s 78(3)–(6)		s 32(5)–(8)	Partly spent; am 1971 s 47(2).
s 79(1)	Agricultural land.	s 33(1), (2), (4)	
s 79(2)		s 33(3)	
s 80(1)	Premiums as rent or Schedule D profits.	s 34(1)	
s 80(2)		s 34(2), (3)	Am 1987 Sch 15 §13.
s 80(3), (4)		s 34(4), (5)	
s 80(5)		s 34(6), (7)	
s 80(6), (7)		s 34(8), (9)	Am 1972 s 81(1).
s 81(1)	Assignment of lease granted at an undervalue.	s 35(1), (2)	
s 81(2)		s 35(3)	
s 82(1), (2)	Sale of land with right to reconveyance.	s 36(1), (2), (5)	
s 82(3)		s 36(3), (4), (5)	
s 83(1)	Deductions from premium and rents received.	s 37(1)–(3)	Am 1978 s 32(2); rep in part 1972 Sch 28 Pt XII.
s 83(2)		s 37(4)	Rep in part 1978 Sch 13 Pt III.
s 83(3)		s 37(5), (6)	
s 83(4)(*a*)		s 37(7)(*a*)	
s 83(4)(*b*)(i), (ii)		s 37(7)(*b*)	
s 83(4)(*b*)(iii)		—	Rep 1978 Sch 13 Pt III.
s 83(5)		s 37(8)	
s 83(6)		—	Rep 1978 Sch 13 Pt III.
s 83(7)		s 37(9)	
s 84(1)(*a*)	Rules for ascertaining duration of leases.	—	Rep 1972 Sch 28 Pt XII.
s 84(1)(*b*)–(*d*)		s 38(1)	Am 1972 s 81(2).
s 84(2)		s 38(2), (3), (4)	Am 1972 s 81(2).
s 84(3)		s 38(6)	Am 1972 s 81(2).
s 84(3A)		s 38(5)	Added 1972 s 81(5).
s 84(4)		s 38(7)	
s 85(1)	Pre-1963 leases and special relief for individuals.	s 39(1), (2)	
s 85(2)		s 39(3)	Rep in part 1972 Sch 28 Pt XII.
s 86	Receipts and outgoings on sale of land.	s 40	
s 87(1)	Relief for rent not paid.	s 41(1), (2)	
s 87(2)		s 41(3)	
s 88	—	—	Rep 1971 Sch 14 Pt III.
s 89	Non-residents.	s 43	
s 90(1)	Interpretation.	s 24(1)	Am 1972 s 81(3).
s 90(2)		s 24(2)	
s 90(2A), (2B)		s 24(3), (4)	Added 1972 s 81(4).
s 90(3)		s 24(5)	
s 91	Schedule B.	s 16(1)	
s 92(1)–(3)	Supplementary provisions.	s 16(2)–(5)	
s 92(4)		s 16(6)	Added 1984 s 51.
s 93	Schedule C.	s 17	Am DCA 1969 s 10.
s 94	Mode of charge.	s 44	
s 95–97	—	—	Rep 1981 Sch 19 Pt VI.
s 98	Tax reserve certificates.	s 46(2)	
s 99	UK government securities.	s 47	
s 100	Securities of foreign states.	s 48(1)–(3)	

TA 1970	Subject Matter	Re-enacted in TA 1988	Remarks
s 101(1)	Payment of interest without deduction of tax.	s 50(1)	
s 101(2)		s 50(2), (3)	
s 101(3)–(6)		s 50(4)–(7)	
s 102	Northern Ireland securities.	s 51	Am NICA Sch 5 §8(1); 1982/338.
s 103	Information.	Sch 29	Am 1987 Sch 15 §2(7).
s 104	Converted government securities.	s 52	
s 105	War loans.	—	Rep 1987 Sch 16 Pt VII.
s 106(1), (2)	Treasury and Crown holdings etc.	s 49	
s 106(3)		Sch 29	
s 107	Interpretation.	s 45	
s 108	Schedule D.	s 18(1), (4)	Rep in part 1973 Sch 22 Pt II; am BNA s 51(1), (2).
s 109	The six Cases.	s 18(2)–(4)	Rep in part 1971 Sch 14 Pt IV.
s 110(1), (2)	Farming etc.	s 53(1), (2)	
s 110(3)		s 53(3), (4)	
s 111	Woodlands.	s 54	
s 112	Mines etc.	s 55	
s 113	Foreign pensions.	s 58	
s 114	Persons chargeable.	s 59	
s 115(1)	Case I and II assessments on preceding year basis.	s 60(1)	
s 115(2)		s 60(2)–(4)	
s 115(3)–(6)		s 60(5)–(8)	
s 116(1)	Special basis on start of business.	s 61(1), (2)	Am 1985 s 47.
s 116(2)		s 61(3)	
s 117(1)	Special basis for two years after start.	s 62(1)	Am 1985 s 47.
s 117(2)		s 62(2), (3)	
s 117(3)		s 62(6)–(8)	Am 1987 Sch 15 §2(8).
s 117(4), (5)		s 62(9), (10)	Am 1987 Sch 15 §2(8).
s 118	Special basis on discontinuance.	s 63	
s 119	Case III assessments.	s 64	
s 120	Special rules for fresh income.	s 66(1)–(4)	
s 121(1), (2)	Special rules where source of income ceases.	s 67(1), (2)	
s 121(3)		s 67(4), (5)	
s 121(4), (5)		s 67(7), (8)	
s 122(1)(*a*), (*b*)	Case IV and V assessments.	s 65(1)	
s 122(1)(*c*)		—	Rep 1987 Sch 16 Pt VII.
s 122(2)(*a*)		s 65(4)	Am BNA s 51(1), (2).
s 122(2)(*b*), (*c*)		—	Rep 1974 Sch 14 Pt VI.
s 122(3)–(7)		s 65(5)–(9)	
s 123(1)–(3)	Special rules for fresh income.	s 66(1)–(3)	
s 123(4), (5)		s 66(5), (6)	
s 124(1)	Special rules where source of income ceases.	s 67(1)	
s 124(2)		s 67(3)	
s 124(3)		s 67(4), (5)	
s 124(4)–(6)		s 67(6)–(8)	
s 125	Case VI assessments.	s 69	
s 126	Taxation where no profits.	s 71	
s 127	Apportionments for Cases I, II and VI.	s 72	
s 128	Single assessments.	s 73	
s 129(1)	Corporation tax.	s 70(1)	
s 129(2)		s 72(1)	
s 129(3)		s 73	
s 129(4), (5)		s 70(2), (3)	
s 130(*a*)–(*m*)	Deductions not allowable.	s 74(*a*)–(*n*)	Am 1987 Sch 15 §2(9).
s 130(*n*), (*o*)		s 74(*p*), (*q*)	

Dest. Tables

TA 1970	Subject Matter	Re-enacted in TA 1988	Remarks
s 131(1)–(5)	Interest paid to non-residents.	s 82(1)–(5)	S 131(2)(*c*)(ii) am 1982 s 64(1).
s 131(6)		—	Rep 1982 Sch 22 Pt IV.
s 131(7)		s 82(6)	
s 132	Patent fees etc.	s 83	
s 133	Payments for technical education.	s 84	Am 1987 Sch 15 §2(10).
s 134(1)	Taxable premiums etc.	s 87(1), (9)	Rep in part 1972 Sch 28 Pt XII, 1978 Sch 13 Pt III; am 1978 s 32.
s 134(2)		s 87(2)	Am 1978 s 32; rep in part 1978 Sch 13 Pt III.
s 134(3)		s 87(3)	
s 134(4)		s 87(4), (5), (6)	
s 134(5), (6)		s 87(7), (8)	Am 1986 Sch 13 §26.
s 134(7)		—	Rep 1978 Sch 13 Pt III.
s 135	Irrecoverable debts.	s 89	
s 136	Released debts.	s 94	
s 137(1)	Valuation of trading stock.	s 100(1)	
s 137(2), (3)		s 102(1), (2)	
s 137(4)		s 100(2)	
s 138(1)	Valuation of work in progress.	s 101(1)	
s 138(2)		s 102(1)	
s 138(3)		s 101(2)	
s 138(4)		s 102(2)	
s 138(5)		s 101(3)	
s 139	Treatment of farm animals etc.	s 97	
s 140	Tied premises.	s 98	
s 141(1)	Cemeteries.	s 91(1)	
s 141(2)		s 91(2), (3)	
s 141(3)–(8)		s 91(4)–(9)	
s 142(1)	Dealers in land.	s 99(1), (4)	
s 142(2)		s 99(2)	
s 142(3)		—	Rep 1972 Sch 28 Pt XII.
s 142(4)		s 99(2), (3)	
s 143	Receipts after discontinuance.	s 103	
s 144(1)		s 104(1)–(3)	
s 144(2)		s 104(4), (5)	
s 144(3), (4)		s 104(6), (7)	
s 144(5)		—	Unnecessary.
s 145	Allowable deductions.	s 105	
s 146	Permanent discontinuance of business.	s 110(2)	
s 147	Transfer of rights to certain payments.	s 106	Partly spent.
s 148	Receipts as earned income.	s 107	
s 149	Election for carry-back.	s 108	
s 150	Relief for individuals over 71.	s 109	
s 151	Interpretation.	s 110(1), (3)–(6)	
s 152	Partnership assessments.	s 111	
s 153	Foreign partnerships.	s 112	Am 1987(2) s 62.
s 154	Change in ownership of business.	s 113	Am 1971 s 17.
s 155(1)	Partnerships involving companies.	s 114(1)	Am 1980 s 39(3).
s 155(2)		s 114(2)	Subst 1972 s 107(2).
s 155(3), (4)		s 114(3), (4)	
s 155(5)		s 115(1), (2), (3)	
s 155(6)–(9)		s 115(4)–(7), 6(4)	Am 1971 Sch 8 §16; 1986 s 56(7)(*a*), Sch 13 §2(5).
s 156	Mining rents etc.	s 119	
s 157	Rent for certain wayleaves.	s 120	Am DCA 1969 s 10(1).
s 158(1)	Management expenses of mine owners.	s 121(1), (2)	
s 158(2)		s 121(3)	
s 158(3)		—	Rep 1971 Sch 14 Pt III.
s 159	Foreign dividends.	s 123	Am 1986 s 48(2).

TA 1970	Subject Matter	Re-enacted in TA 1988	Remarks
s 160–167	—	—	Rep 1971 Sch 14 Pt IV.
s 168(1), (2)	Set off of losses against general income.	s 380(1), (2)	
s 168(3)		s 382(1)	Subst 1971 s 16(2)(*a*).
s 168(4)		s 382(2)	Rep in part 1971 Sch 14 Pt VII.
s 168(5)		s 382(3)	
s 168(6)		s 380(3)	
s 168(7)		s 382(4)	Am 1987 Sch 15 §2(11).
s 168(8)		s 380(4)	
s 169(1)–(3)	Extension of right of set off to capital allowances.	s 383(1)–(3)	
s 169(4)–(7)		s 383(5)–(8)	
s 169(8)		s 383(9), (10)	
s 169(9)		s 383(11)	
s 169(10)		s 383(12)	
s 170(1)	Restrictions on right of set-off.	s 384(1), (2)	
s 170(2)–(4)		s 384(3)–(5)	
s 170(5), (6)		s 384(9), (10)	
s 171(1)	Carry-forward against subsequent profits.	s 385(1), (2)	
s 171(2)–(6)		s 385(3)–(7)	
s 171(7)		s 385(8)	Partly spent.
s 172	Carry-forward where business transferred to a company.	s 386	
s 173(1), (2)	Carry-forward as losses of amounts taxed under 1970 s 53.	s 387(1), (2)	
s 173(3)(*aa*)		s 387(3)(*a*)	Added 1970(F) Sch 4 §9(6).
s 173(3)(*a*)–(*e*)		s 387(3)(*b*)–(*f*)	
s 174(1)	Carry-back of terminal losses.	s 388(1), (2)	
s 174(2)–(6)		s 388(3)–(7)	
s 174(7)–(11)		s 389(1)–(5)	Am 1986 Sch 13 §27.
s 174(12)		s 389(6), (7)	Am 1971 Sch 8 §16(5).
s 174(13)		s 389(8)	
s 175(1)	Treatment of interest as a loss.	s 390	
s 175(2)(*a*)		s 390	New para (*a*) subst. for paras (*a*) & (*b*) by 1972 Sch 11 §3; am 1974 Sch 1 §28.
s 175(2)(*b*)		—	
s 175(2)(*c*)		—	Rep 1977 Sch 9 Pt V.
s 175(2)(*d*)		—	Rep 1987 Sch 16 Pt VII.
s 175(3)		—	Unnecessary.
s 176	Case VI losses.	s 392	
s 177(1)–(3)	Losses other than terminal losses: corporation tax.	s 393(1)–(3)	
s 177(3A)		s 393(4)	Added 1971 Sch 8 §16; am & rep in part 1972 s 67(2)(*c*); am 1985 s 60.
s 177(4)–(10)		s 393(5)–(11)	
s 178(1)	Terminal losses: corporation tax.	s 394(1), (2)	
s 178(2)–(5)		s 394(3)–(6)	
s 179	Case VI losses: corporation tax.	s 396	
s 180(1)–(7)	Loss relief in case of farming and market gardening.	s 397(1)–(7)	Am 1971 Sch 8 §16(5); 1986 s 56(7)(*a*), Sch 13 §2(5).
s 180(8)		s 397(8), (9)	
s 180(9)		s 397(10)	
s 181(1)	Schedule E.	s 19(1), 192(1)	Am 1974 s 21(1); 1977 s 31(3)(*a*); BNA Sch 7.
s 181(2)		s 19(2)	
s 182	Voluntary pensions.	s 133	
s 183	Taxable emoluments.	s 131	Partly spent.

Dest. Tables

TA 1970	Subject Matter	Re-enacted in TA 1988	Remarks
s 184	Place of performance etc.	s 132(1), (2), (4), (5)	Am 1977 s 31(3)(*b*); 1986 s 34(7).
s 185	—	—	Rep 1977 Sch 9 Pt VI.
s 186(1)–(3)	Gains by directors etc from share options.	s 135(1)–(4)	
s 186(4), (5)		s 135(6), (7)	
s 186(5A), (5B)		s 135(8), (9)	Added 1986 s 26(1).
s 186(6)–(8)		s 136(1)–(4)	
s 186(9)		s 140(1)	
s 186(10)		s 140(2), (3), 136(5)	
s 186(11)		s 136(6)	Am 1986 s 26(2).
s 186(12)(*a*)		Sch 29	Am CGTA 7.
s 186(12)(*b*)		—	Rep 1971 Sch 14 Pt IV.
s 187	Payments on retirement etc.	s 148	
s 188(1)	Exemptions from s 187.	s 188(1)	Am 1971 Sch 6 §24; 1970(F) Sch 5 Pt III §12(1).
s 188(2)(*a*)		—	Rep 1984 s 30(7).
s 188(2)(*b*)		—	Rep 1974 Sch 14 Pt VI.
s 188(2)(*c*)		s 188(3)	1974 s 21(3) altered §(*c*) to (*b*); rep in part 1974 Sch 14 Pt VI.
s 188(3)		s 188(4), (5)	Am 1981 s 31(1).
s 188(4), (5)		s 188(6), (7)	
s 188(6)		s 188(8)	Rep in part 1981 Sch 19 Pt VI.
s 189	Relief for necessary expenses.	s 198	Am 1971 s 47(1)(ii); 1984 s 28(2).
s 190	—	—	Rep 1972 Sch 28 Pt V.
s 191	Expenses: official emoluments.	s 199	Am 1971/2099 Art 4(1).
s 192	Fees to professional bodies etc.	s 201	
s 193	—	—	Rep 1971 Sch 14 Pt II.
s 194(1), (2)	Expenses etc of Minister of religion.	s 332(1), (2)	Am 1977 Sch 8 §3(2), (3); 1987 Sch 15 §2(12).
s 194(3), (4)		s 332(3), (4)	
s 195–203	—	—	Rep 1976 Sch 15 Pt III.
s 204(1)	PAYE.	s 203(1)	
s 204(2)		s 203(2), (3), (5)	Am 1971 Sch 6 §25; 1987(2) s 92(2).
s 204(3)		s 203(6)–(8)	Rep in part 1971 Sch 14 Pt II.
s 204(3A)		s 203(4)	Added 1987(2) s 92(3).
s 204(4)		s 828	
s 205(1)	Assessments unnecessary in certain cases.	s 205(1), (2)	
s 205(2)	Additional provision for certain assessments. s 205(3)		
s 206		s 206	
s 207	Disputes as to domicile or ordinary residence.	s 207	
s 208, 209	—	—	Rep 1971 Sch 14 Pt I.
s 210		—	Rep 1972 Sch 28 Pt IV.
s 211(1)	Parliamentary pension funds.	s 613(1), (2)	
s 211(2)		s 613(4)	Am PPA 1972 Sch 3; 1981 s 50(1); PPA 1987 Sch 3 §2(1).
s 211(3)		Sch 29	Rep in part 1971 Sch 14 Pt IV.
s 211(4)		s 613(3)	
s 211(5)		—	Rep 1971 Sch 14 Pt I.
s 212(1)	National insurance supplementary schemes.	s 614(1)	Subst SSCPA Sch 2 §28.
s 212(2)		—	Rep 1987 Sch 16 Pt VII.
s 212(3)		s 614(6)	
s 212(4)		Sch 29	Rep in part 1971 Sch 14 Pt IV.

TA 1970	Subject Matter	Re-enacted in TA 1988	Remarks
s 213(1)	Indian pensions.	s 614(2)	Am OPA 1973 s 2; 1987 Sch 15 §2(13).
s 213(2)		Sch 29	Rep in part 1971 Sch 14 Pt IV; am OPA 1973 s 2.
s 214(1)	Colonial pensions.	s 615(1), (2)(*a*)–(*d*), (4)	Am BNA Sch 7; 1973 s 53(1); rep in part 1987 Sch 16 Pt VII.
s 214(2)		s 614(3)	Am 1973 s 53(1).
s 214(3)		s 614(6), 615(1)	
s 214(4)		Sch 29	Am 1973 s 53(1); rep in part 1971 Sch 14 Pt IV.
s 214(5)		s 615(7), (8)(*a*)	
s 214(6)		s 615(5)	Added BNA Sch 7; am 1987 Sch 15 §2(14).
s 215(1), (2)	Overseas Service Act 1958 pensions.	s 615(1), (2)(*e*)	Am OPA 1973 s 2.
s 215(3)		s 615(7), (8)(*b*)	
s 216(1)	Central African Pension Fund.	s 615(1), (2)(*f*)	
s 216(2)		s 614(3)	Am 1987 Sch 15 §2(13).
s 216(3)		Sch 29	Rep in part 1971 Sch 14 Pt IV.
s 216(4)		s 615(2)(*f*), (7)	
s 217(1)	Overseas Service Pensions Fund.	s 615(1), (2)(*g*)	
s 217(2)		s 614(4)	Am 1987 Sch 15 §2(13).
s 217(3)		Sch 29	
s 217(4)		s 614(4), 615(2)(*g*), (7)	
s 218(1)	Pension funds for overseas employees.	s 614(5), (6)	Rep in part 1971 Sch 14 Pt IV.
s 218(2)		Sch 29	
s 218(3), (4)		s 615(3), (6)	
s 219(1)(*a*)	Social security benefits etc.	s 617(1)	Am SSCPA Sch 2 §39; 1979(2) Sch 1 §4(1), Sch 2 §3; 1981 s 27(1); 1982 s 30(1); HSA 1984 Sch 4 §2; rep in part 1979(2) Sch 5 Pt II; SSA 1986 Sch 11.
s 219(1)(*b*)		—	Rep 1977 Sch 9 Pt IV.
s 219(2)		s 617(2)	Subst 1987 s 29(1).
s 219(3)		s 617(3), (4)	Am SSCPA Sch 2 §39; rep in part Social Security Pensions Act 1975 c 60 Sch 5.
s 219A	Job release scheme allowances etc.	s 150	Added 1982 s 31(1); am & rep in part SSA 1986 Sch 10 §71, Sch 11.
s 220–225	—	—	Rep 1971 Sch 14 Pt I.
s 226(1)	Tax exemption for qualifying premiums.	s 619(1), 620(1)	Am 1971 s 20(1).
s 226(2)		s 620(2), (3)	Am 1971 s 20(3); 1976 s 30(2); rep in part 1980 Sch 20 Pt VII.
s 226(3)		s 620(4)	Rep in part 1983 Sch 10 Pt II.
s 226(4)		s 619(1)	
s 226(5)		s 620(5)	
s 226(6)		s 620(6), Sch 29	Rep in part 1971 Sch 14 Pt IV.
s 226(7)		s 620(7)	
s 226(8)–(10)		s 623(1)–(4), 624(3)	Am 1972 Sch 24 §17; 1970(F) Sch 5 Pt III §12(7); 1976 s 30(2); rep in part 1987 Sch 16 Pt VII.
s 226(11)		s 624(1), (2)	
s 226(12), (13)		s 620(8), (9)	Am 1987(2) Sch 2 §1.
s 226A	Other approved contracts.	s 621, Sch 29	Added 1971 Sch 2 §1; am 1976 s 30(2); rep in part 1980 Sch 20 Pt VII.

TA 1970	Subject Matter	Re-enacted in TA 1988	Remarks
s 227(1), (1A), (1B)	Qualifying premiums.	s 619(1)–(3)	Subst 1971 s 20(2); am 1980 s 31(1), (2).
s 227(1BB)		s 619(4)	Added 1980 s 33(2).
s 227(1C), (2), (2A), (2B), (3)		—	Rep 1980 Sch 20 Pt VII.
s 227(4)		s 623(5)	
s 227(5)(*a*)		s 623(6)(*a*)	Subst 1980 s 33(3); rep in part 1971 Sch 14 Pt II; 1980 Sch 20 Pt VII.
s 227(5)(*aa*)		s 623(6)(*b*)	Added 1980 s 33(3).
s 227(5)(*b*)		s 623(6)(*c*)	Rep in part 1987 Sch 16 Pt VII.
s 227(6)		s 623(7)	
s 227(7)		—	Rep 1980 Sch 20 Pt VII.
s 227(8), (9)		s 623(8), (9)	Partly spent; rep in part 1987 Sch 16 Pt VII.
s 227(10), (11)		s 619(5), (6)	
s 227(12)		—	Rep 1987 Sch 16 Pt VII.
s 227(13)		s 619(7)	
s 227A	Carry-forward of unused relief.	s 625	Added 1980 s 32(1).
s 228	Increased relief in certain cases.	s 626	Subst 1987(2) s 54(2).
s 229(1), (1A), (1B)	Annuity premiums for Ministers etc.	s 629	Rep in part 1980 Sch 20 Pt VII; am PPA 1972 s 32; PPA 1976 s 1(3); PPA 1987 Sch 3 §2(2).
s 229(2)		—	Rep 1987 Sch 16 Pt VII.
s 230(1)	Purchased life annuities.	s 656(1)	
s 230(2)		s 656(3)(*a*)–(*d*)	
s 230(2A)		s 656(2), (3)(*e*)	Added 1970(F) Sch 4 §8.
s 230(3)–(5)		s 656(4)–(6)	
s 230(6), (7)		s 657	Rep in part 1976 Sch 15 Pt IV; am 1978 s 26(4); 1987(2) s 41(3).
s 231	Supplementary provisions.	s 658, 828	
s 232(1)	Schedule F.	s 20	Subst 1972 s 87(2).
s 232(2), (3)		—	Rep 1972 Sch 28 Pt VI.
s 232(4)		s 234(1), (2)	Subst 1972 Sch 24 §18.
s 233(1)	Meaning of "distribution".	s 209(1)	Am 1980 s 45(2).
s 233(2)(*a*)		s 209(2)(*a*)	
s 233(2)(*b*)		s 209(2)(*b*)	Am 1972 Sch 22 §1.
s 233(2)(*c*)		s 209(2)(*c*)	Subst 1972 Sch 22 §2(1).
s 233(2)(*d*)(i)		s 209(2)(*e*)(i)	
s 233(2)(*d*)(ii)		s 209(2)(*e*)(ii)	Subst 1972 Sch 22 §3(1).
s 233(2)(*d*)(iii)		s 209(2)(*d*), (*e*)(iii)	Am 1972 Sch 22 §3(2).
s 233(2)(*d*)(iv)(*aa*)		s 209(2)(*e*)(iv)	
s 233(2)(*d*)(iv)(*bb*)		s 209(2)(*e*)(iv)	Subst 1970(F) Sch 4 §6(1).
s 233(2)(*d*)(iv)(*cc*)		s 209(2)(*e*)(v)	Subst 1970(F) Sch 4 §6(1).
s 233(2)(*d*)(v)		s 209(2)(*e*)(vi)	
s 233(2)(*e*)		s 209(2)(*f*)	
s 233(3)		s 209(4), (5)	
s 233(4)		s 209(7)	
s 234(1)	Bonus issue following repayment of capital.	s 210(1)	Rep in part 1972 Sch 28 Pt VI.
s 234(2)		s 210(2)	
s 234(3)		s 210(4)	Rep in part 1972 Sch 28 Pt VI.
s 235(1)	Matters to be treated or not to be treated as repayments of share capital.	s 211(1)	Am 1972 Sch 22 §6(1), (3).
s 235(2)–(5)		s 211(3)–(7)	
s 236	—	—	Rep 1972 Sch 28 Pt VI.
s 237(1)		s 254(1), (5)	
s 237(2)		s 254(9)	
s 237(3)		s 254(1)	
s 237(4)		s 254(10)	
s 237(5)		s 254(1)	
s 237(6)		s 254(11)	
s 237(7)		s 254(12)	

TA 1970	Subject Matter	Re-enacted in TA 1988	Remarks
s 238	Charge to corporation tax.	s 6(1)–(4)	Rep in part 1971 Sch 14 Pt II. Subsection (4) not repealed.
s 239	Certain distributions not chargeable to corporation tax.	s 208	
s 240(1)–(3), (6)	—	—	Rep 1972 Sch 28 Pt VI.
s 240(4), (5), (7)	Payments exempt from income tax.	s 7(1), (2), (4)	Rep in part 1972 Sch 28 Pt VI.
s 240A	—	—	Added 1971 Sch 4 §§1, 5; rep 1972 Sch 28 Pt VI.
s 241	Claims for repayment etc.	s 7(5)	
s 242	Information to be attached to dividend warrants etc.	s 234(3), (4)	Am 1972 Sch 24 §19; CCCPA; CCCP(NI).
s 243(1)–(3)	General scheme of corporation tax.	s 8(1)–(3)	Am 1974 s 36; 1987(2) s 90(1)(*a*).
s 243(4)		s 10(1)	Rep in part 1987 Sch 16 Pt V; am 1975(2) s 44(2); 1987(2) s 90(1)(*b*).
s 243(5)–(7)		s 8(4)–(6)	
s 244		—	Rep 1987 Sch 16 Pt V.
s 245(1)	Tax on company in liquidation.	s 342(1)	
s 245(2), (3)		s 342(2), (3)	Subst 1974 s 37(1).
s 245(4)–(6)		s 342(4)–(6)	
s 245(7)–(9)		s 342(7)–(9)	Subst 1974 s 37(1).
s 246	Non-resident companies.	s 11(1)–(3)	Am CGTA 7.
s 247	Basis of and periods for assessment.	s 12	Am 1972 s 107(1); CCCPA.
s 248(1), (2)	Allowance of charges on income and capital.	s 338(1), (2)(*a*)	Am 1981 s 38(1); 1973 s 54(1).
s 248(3)		s 338(3)	
s 248(4)		s 338(4)	Am 1972 Sch 24 §20; 1984 s 35(4).
s 248(5)		s 338(5)	Am 1981 s 38(2).
s 248(6)		s 338(6)	Am 1974 Sch 1 27; rep in part 1987 Sch 16 Pt VI.
s 248(7)		—	Rep 1977 Sch 9 Pt V.
s 248(8)		s 339(6)	Am 1972 Sch 24 §20.
s 248(8A)		s 339(7)	Added 1986 s 30(2).
s 248(9)		s 339(8)	Am 1980 s 55(3).
s 249(1)–(4)	Interest payable to non-residents.	s 340	Am 1982 s 64(1).
s 249(5)		—	Rep 1982 Sch 22 Pt IV.
s 250	Computation of income: general.	s 9	Rep in part 1971 Sch 14 Pts II, IV.
s 251	Computation of income: special rules.	s 337	
s 252	Company reconstructions without change of ownership.	s 343	Am 1971 Sch 8 §16; 1986 s 42, 56(7)(*a*), Sch 10 §1, Sch 13 §2(5); 1987(2) s 64(2).
s 253(1)–(4)	Supplemental.	s 344(1)–(4)	
s 253(5)–(12)		s 344(5)–(12)	Added 1986 Sch 10 §2.
s 254(1)	Set-off of losses etc against franked investment income.	s 242(1)	Section 254 subst by 1972 Sch 15 Pt I.
s 254(2)		s 242(2)	Am 1981 s 37; 1984 Sch 9 §13.
s 254(3)		s 242(3)	
s 254(4)		s 242(4)	Am 1981 s 37.
s 254(5)		s 242(5)	
s 254(6)		s 242(6), (7)	Am 1981 s 37.
s 254(7)		s 242(8)	Am 1981 s 37; 1984 Sch 9 §13.
s 254(8)		s 242(9)	
s 255	Set-off of loss brought forward etc.	s 243	Subst 1972 Sch 15 Pt I.
s 256(1)	Group income.	s 247(1)–(3)	Subst 1972 Sch 15 Pt II.
s 256(2)		s 247(4)	

Dest. Tables

TA 1970	Subject Matter	Re-enacted in TA 1988	Remarks
s 256(3)		s 247(5)	Am 1973 s 24.
s 256(4), (4A)		s 247(6), (7)	Subst 1972 Sch 15 Pt II.
s 256(5)		s 247(8)	
s 256(6)		s 247(9)	Rep in part 1984 s 46(1).
s 256(7)		s 247(10)	
s 257	Election for group income etc.	s 248	
s 258(1)	Group relief.	s 402(1), (2)	
s 258(2)		s 402(3), (4)	Subst 1981 s 40(2).
s 258(3), (4)		s 402(5), (6)	
s 258(5)		s 413(3)	
s 258(6), (7)		s 413(4), (5)	
s 258(8)		s 413(6)	Subst 1984 s 46(2).
s 259(1)–(7)	Kinds of group relief.	s 403(1)–(8)	
s 259(8)		s 403(9)	Subst 1981 s 40(3).
s 260(1)	Relation to other relief.	s 407(1)	
s 260(2)		s 407(1)(*b*)	
s 260(3)(*a*)		s 407(2)(*a*)	
s 260(3)(*b*)		s 407(2)(*b*)	
s 260(3)(*c*)		—	Spent.
s 260(3)(*d*)		s 407(2)(*a*)	
s 260(4)		s 407(3)	Partly spent.
s 261	Corresponding accounting periods.	s 408	
s 262(1)	Companies joining groups etc.	s 409(1)	
s 262(2)		s 409(2)	Rep in part and am 1984 s 47(1).
s 262(3)		s 409(3)	
s 262(4)		s 409(4)	Am 1984 s 47(2).
s 263	Exclusion of double allowances etc.	s 411	Am 1985 Sch 9 Pt II.
s 264	Claims and adjustments.	s 412	Am 1981 s 40(4).
s 265(1)	Computation of chargeable gains.	s 345(1)(*a*)	
s 265(2)		s 345(2)	
s 265(3)(*a*)		s 345(3)(*a*)	Am CGTA 7.
s 265(3)(*b*)		—	Rep 1978 Sch 13 Pt IV.
s 265(3)(*c*)		s 345(3)(*b*)	
s 265(4), (5)		s 345(4), (5)	Am CGTA 7; CCCPA; CCCP(NI).
s 266	Corporation tax attributable to chargeable gains.	s 346	Am CGTA 7; 1987(2) Sch 6 §1.
s 277	Tax on one member of group recoverable from another.	s 347(1)–(4)	Am 1987(2) Sch 6 §3.
s 282(1)	Meaning of close company.	s 414(1)	Partly spent (1970 s 343(9) rep 1985).
s 282(2)		s 414(2), (3)	Subst 1972 Sch 17 §1(2).
s 282(3)		s 414(4)	
s 282(4), (5)		s 414(5), (6)	Subst 1972 Sch 17 §1(3).
s 283(1)–(3)	Certain companies with quoted shares not to be close companies.	s 415(1)–(3)	
s 283(4)(*a*)		s 415(4)(*a*)	
s 283(4)(*b*)		—	Rep 1971 Sch 14 Pt I.
s 283(4)(*bb*)		s 415(4)(*b*)	Added 1970(F) Sch 5 Pt III §12(3).
s 283(4)(*c*)		s 415(4)(*c*)	
s 283(5)–(8)		s 415(5)–(8)	
s 284(1)(*a*), (*b*)	Payments to participators and associates.	—	Rep 1972 Sch 28 Pt VI.
s 284(1)(*c*)		s 418(1)	
s 284(2)		s 418(2), (3)	Am 1976 Sch 9 §15; 1977 s 35(4); 1980 s 51(4).
s 284(3)		s 418(4)	Subst 1976 Sch 9 §16.
s 284(4)–(7)		s 418(5)–(8)	
s 285(1)–(5)		—	Rep 1980 Sch 20 Pt VIII.
s 285(6)	Persons materially interested in companies.	s 187(3)	Rep in part 1980 Sch 20 Pt VIII; am 1971 Sch 6 §30; 1978 Sch 9 §11(3); 1980 Sch 10 §26(2); 1984 Sch 10 §4(4).

TA 1970	Subject Matter	Re-enacted in TA 1988	Remarks
s 286(1)	Loans to participators etc.	s 419(1)	Am 1972 Sch 17 §3(2).
s 286(2)		s 419(2), 420(1)	
s 286(3)		s 420(2)	Am 1971 s 25(5)(*c*); 1972 Sch 17 §3(3).
s 286(3)(*a*)		—	Rep 1971 s 25(5)(*a*).
s 286(3)(*b*)		s 420(2)(*a*)	Subst 1971 s 25(5)(*b*).
s 286(3)(*c*), (*d*)		s 420(2)(*b*), (*c*)	
s 286(4)		s 419(3)	Am 1986 s 43.
s 286(5)		s 419(4)	Am 1972 Sch 17 §3(4); 1976 s 44(1); 1986 s 43.
s 286(6)		—	Rep 1972 Sch 28 Pt VI.
s 286(7)		s 419(5)	Rep in part 1971 Sch 14 Pt II; 1972 Sch 28 Pt VI.
s 286(8)		s 419(6)	
s 286(9)		s 419(7), 420(2)	
s 287(1)(*a*), (*b*)	Release of debt in respect of loan under s 286.	s 421(1)(*a*), (*b*)	Am 1971 Sch 6 §32(1).
s 287(1)(*c*)		s 421(1)(*c*)	Am 1971 Sch 6 §32(1); 1978 Sch 2 §4; rep in part 1980 Sch 20 Pt V.
s 287(1)(*d*)		s 421(1)(*d*)	Am 1971 Sch 6 §32(1).
s 287(2)		s 421(2)	Am & rep in part 1971 Sch 6 §32(2), Sch 14 Pt II.
s 287(3), (4)		s 421(3), (4)	
s 287A	Loans by controlled companies.	s 422	Added 1976 s 44.
s 288–301	—	—	Rep 1972 Sch 28 Pts V & VI.
s 302(1)	"Associated company" and "control".	s 416(1)	Am 1972 Sch 24 §21; rep in part 1972 Sch 28 Pt VI.
s 302(2)–(4)		s 416(2)–(4)	Added 1972 Sch 17 §5.
s 302(5), (6)		s 416(5), (6)	
s 303(1), (2)	"Participator" etc.	s 417(1), (2)	
s 303(3)		s 417(3)	Am 1970 Sch 5 Pt III §12(4); rep in part 1971 Sch 14 Pt I; 1987 Sch 16 Pt V.
s 303(4)		s 417(4)	
s 303(5)(*a*)		s 417(5)(*a*)	
s 303(5)(*b*)		—	Rep 1972 Sch 28 Pt VI.
s 303(5)(*c*)		s 417(5)(*b*)	
s 303(6)		s 417(6)	Rep in part 1987 Sch 16 Pt V.
s 303(7)		s 417(7), (9)	
s 303(8)		s 417(8)	Added 1972 Sch 17 §7.
s 304(1)	Expenses of management: investment companies.	s 75(1), (2)	Am 1984 s 54(2)(*b*); 1987 s 41.
s 304(2)–(4)		s 75(3)–(5)	
s 304(5)		s 130	Am 1980 Sch 11 §1; Trustee Savings Bank Act 1981 c 65 Sch 6; TSB 1985 Sch 2 §6.
s 305(1)	Insurance companies.	s 76(1)	
s 305(2)		s 76(2), (5), Sch 29	Rep in part 1972 Sch 28 Pt VI; am CGTA 7.
s 305(3)		s 76(8)	
s 307	Insurance business.	s 432	
s 308		s 434(1), (2)	
s 309		s 433	
s 310(1)–(4)		—	Rep 1984 Sch 23 Pt V; 1972 Sch 28 Pt VI.
s 310(5)		s 434(3)	Subst 1972 Sch 18 §2(3).
s 310(6)		s 434(4), (5)	
s 310(7)		s 434(7)	Added 1984 s 18(5).
s 311	—	—	Rep 1972 Sch 28 Pt VI.
s 312(1)	Annuity business.	s 436(1), (2)	Am 1970(F) Sch 5 Pt III §11(3).
s 312(2), (3)		s 436(3)(*a*)–(*c*), (4)	Am 1970(F) Sch 5 Pt III §11(6); rep in part 1987 Sch 16 Pt VII.
s 312(4)		Sch 30	

Dest. Tables

TA 1970	Subject Matter	Re-enacted in TA 1988	Remarks
s 313(1)	General annuity business.	s 437(1)	
s 313(2)		s 437(2)	Am 1985 Sch 25 §7.
s 313(4)		s 437(4)	Am 1972 Sch 18 §3.
s 313(5), (6)		s 437(5), (6)	
s 314(1)	Pension annuity business.	s 438(1)	Rep in part 1972 Sch 18 Pt VI; am 1970(F) Sch 5 Pt III §11(3), (6).
s 314(2)		s 438(2)	
s 314(3)		s 438(3)	Rep in part 1972 Sch 18 Pt VI.
s 314(4)		s 438(6), (7)	Am 1970(F) Sch 5 Pt III §11(3); rep in part 1972 Sch 28 Pt VI.
s 314(5)		s 436(3)(*d*)	
s 315(1)–(6)	Foreign life assurance funds.	s 441(1)–(6)	
s 315(7), (8)		—	Rep 1976 Sch 15 Pt III.
s 315(9)		s 441(7)	
s 316(1)	Overseas life assurance companies.	s 445(1)	Am 1970(F) Sch 5 Pt III §11(6).
s 316(1A)		s 445(2)(*a*)	Subst 1985 Sch 25 §8.
s 316(2)		s 445(3)	Am 1972 Sch 18 §5.
s 316(3)		s 445(4)	Am 1970(F) Sch 5 Pt III §11(6).
s 316(4)–(6)		s 445(5)–(7)	
s 317	Management expenses.	s 76(6)	
s 318(1)	Overseas life assurance companies.	s 446(1)	Am 1970(F) Sch 5 Pt III §11(3); 1972 Sch 18 §5.
s 318(2)–(4)		s 446(2)–(4)	
s 319	Set off of income tax against corporation tax.	s 447(1)–(3)	Am 1971 Sch 6 §39.
s 320(1)	Double taxation agreements.	s 449(1)	Am 1970(F) Sch 5 Pt III §11(6).
s 320(2)		s 449(2), (3)	Am 1970(F) Sch 5 Pt III §11(6); 1972 Sch 18 §5.
s 321(1)(*b*), (2)	Life policies.	s 443	
s 321(1)(*a*)		Sch 29	
s 321(1)(*c*)		—	Rep 1971 Sch 14 Pt IV.
s 322	Pre-5/8/65 life policies.	s 444	
s 323(1), (2)	Interpretation.	s 431(1), (2)	Am ICA 1973 s 54(2); 1970(F) Sch 5 Pt III §11(4); ICA 1974 Sch 1; ICA 1982 Sch 5 §10(*b*); rep in part ICA 1981 Sch 5.
s 323(3)		s 431(3)	Subst 1970(F) Sch 5 Pt III §11(5).
s 323(4)		s 431(4), (6)	Rep in part & am 1970(F) Sch 5 Pt III §11(1)–(3); am 1978 s 26(5); 1987(2) s 39(3), Sch 3 §16.
s 324	Capital redemption policies.	s 458	
s 325		—	Rep 1987 Sch 16 Pt VII.
s 326(1)	Exchange of certain securities.	s 471(1), (2)	
s 326(2), (3)		s 471(3), (4)	
s 327	Distribution of certain securities.	s 472	
s 328(1), (2)	Tax-free income.	s 474	Am 1970(F) Sch 5 Pt III §11.
s 328(3)		s 445(8)	
s 329	Tax-free Treasury securities.	s 475	
s 330		—	Unnecessary.
s 331	Unregistered friendly societies.	s 459	
s 332(1)	Registered friendly societies.	s 460(1), 461(1)	
s 332(2)		s 460(2)(*b*), (*c*), (*d*)	Am 1984 s 73(1), (2); 1987 s 30(2); 1987(2) Sch 2 §2.
s 332(3)		s 460(3), (4)	Am 1984 s 73(1), (2); FSA 1984 s 2; 1987 s 30(3).
s 332(4)–(9)		s 460(5)–(10)	Added 1975(2) s 52(1); am 1980 s 57(1); 1984 s 73(3).

TA 1970	Subject Matter	Re-enacted in TA 1988	Remarks
s 332(10)		s 460(11)	Added 1976 s 48(1).
s 332(11)		s 461(4)	Added 1976 s 48(1).
s 332(12)(*a*)		s 460(12)	Added 1976 s 48(1).
s 332(12)(*b*)		s 461(5)	Added 1976 s 48(1).
s 333(1)(*a*)	Distinction between old and new societies.	s 460(2)(*a*)	
s 333(1)(*b*), (2)		—	Rep 1985 Sch 27 Pt V.
s 334	Tax exempt business.	s 462(1), Sch 15 §3, 4	Am 1985 s 41(6); 1979/1576; rep in part 1985 Sch 27 Pt V.
s 335(1)	Life or endowment business.	s 463, 828	
s 335(2)–(5)		—	Rep 1985 Sch 27 Pt V.
s 336	Pre-3/5/66 contracts.	s 462(2)	Partly spent.
s 337(1)	Interpretation.	—	Unnecessary.
s 337(2)		s 466(1)	Am FSA 1974 Sch 9 §23; 1985 s 41(7)(*b*), (*c*); 1987(2) Sch 2 §2.
s 337(3)		s 466(2), 832	Am 1985 s 41(7)(*d*); 1987(2) Sch 2 §2.
s 337(4)		s 466(3), (4)	Am 1975(2) s 52(2); 1985 s 41(7)(*e*); rep in part 1985 Sch 27 Pt V.
s 337(5)		s 832, Sch 15 §3	Am 1979/1576; FSA 1974 Sch 9 §23.
s 338(1)	Trade unions.	s 467(1)	Am 1982 s 36.
s 338(2)		s 467(2)	Rep in part 1974 Sch 14 Pt VI.
s 338(3)		s 467(3)	Am 1982 s 36.
s 339	Savings banks.	s 484(1)	Am 1980 Sch 11 §5; TSB 1985 Sch 2 §6(6); partly spent.
s 340	Industrial and provident societies.	s 486	Am CUA 1979 s 25(2); NICA Sch 5 §8.
s 340A(1)–(4), (7)	Credit unions.	s 487	Added CUA 1979 s 25(1); am Credit Unions (Northern Ireland) Order 1985 (SI No 1205).
s 340A(5), (6)		—	Spent.
s 341	Co-operative housing associations.	s 488	Am 1972 Sch 11 §6; 1981/157; HCPA 1985 Sch 2 §18; 1979/1573 Art 4; 1970/1681.
s 341A	Self-build societies.	s 489	Added Housing Act 1974 c 44 s 120; am HCPA 1985 Sch 2 §18; 1984 s 56(1).
s 343(1)	Building societies.	—	Spent: rep in part 1984 s 26(5); am 1985 s 40(2).
s 343(1A), (1B)		s 476(1), (2), 828	Added 1985 s 40(3); am 1986 s 47(1).
s 343(2)		s 476(3), 477(3)	Rep in part 1971 Sch 14 Pt II; 1985 Sch 27 Pt V; am 1985 s 40(4); 1986 s 47(2).
s 343(3)(*a*)		s 476(5)(*a*)	Am 1985 s 40(5).
s 343(3)(*b*)		s 476(5)(*b*)	Am 1971 Sch 6 §40(*c*).
s 343(3)(*c*)		s 476(5)(*c*)	Subst 1971 Sch 6 §40(*d*); am 1978 Sch 2 §5(8); rep in part 1980 Sch 20 Pt V.
s 343(3)(*d*)		s 476(5)(*d*)	Am 1971 Sch 6 §40(*e*).
s 343(3)(i)		s 476(6)	Subst 1971 Sch 6 §40(*f*).
s 343(3)(ii)		s 476(8)	Subst 1971 Sch 6 §40(*f*); rep in part 1975(2) Sch 14 Pt IV.
s 343(3)(iii), (iv)		—	Rep 1985 Sch 27 Pt V.
s 343(4)		s 476(9)	Am 1985 s 40(6).
s 343(5)		Sch 29	Rep in part BSA 1986 Sch 19 Pt I.
s 343(6)		—	Rep 1985 Sch 27 Pt V.
s 343(7)		s 476(11)	Am 1985 s 40(7); 1986 s 47(3).
s 343(8)		s 832(1)	Am BSA 1986 Sch 18.

Dest. Tables

TA 1970	Subject Matter	Re-enacted in TA 1988	Remarks
s 343(8A)–(9)		—	Rep 1985 Sch 27 Pt V.
s 344(1)	Time for payment of tax.	s 478(1)	See 1987 s 36(2), Sch 6 Pt II.
s 344(2)		s 478(2), (3)	Am 1975(2) s 45(2).
s 345	Companies trading with members etc.	s 486(10), (11)	Rep in part 1987 Sch 16 Pt VII.
s 346	Companies carrying on mutual business etc.	s 490	
s 347	Distribution of assets.	s 491	
s 348	Agricultural marketing boards etc.	s 509	Subst 1971 s 28; am NICA Sch 5.
s 349(1)–(3)	Electricity Council etc.	s 511(1)–(3)	
s 349(4)		s 511(6)	
s 350(1), (2)	Gas Council etc.	—	Rep Gas Act 1986 c 44.
s 350(3)		s 511(7)	
s 351	Atomic Energy Authority etc.	s 512, Sch 29	
s 352(1)–(3)	Harbour re-organisation schemes.	s 518(1)–(3)	
s 352(4)		s 518(4), (5)	Am 1971 Sch 8 §16(5); 1986 s 56(7)(*a*), Sch 13 §2(5).
s 352(5), (6)		s 518(6), (7)	Partly spent.
s 352(7)		Sch 29	Am CGTA Sch 7.
s 352(8), (9)		s 518(8), (9)	
s 352(10)		—	Rep 1987 Sch 16 Pt VII.
s 352(11)		s 518(10)	
s 353(1)	Local authorities.	s 519(1), (2), Sch 29	
s 353(2), (3)		—	Rep 1974 Sch 14 Pt VI.
s 353(4)		s 519(3)	
s 354	Authorised unit trusts.	s 468(1)–(4), (6)	Subst 1987 s 38.
s 354A	Other unit trusts.	s 469	Added 1987 s 39.
s 355	—	—	Rep 1980 Sch 20 Pt X.
s 356	—	—	Rep 1972 Sch 28 Pt VI.
s 357	—	—	Rep 1972 Sch 28 Pt X.
s 358	Interpretation.	s 832(1)	Subst 1987 s 40(1).
s 359	Investment trusts.	s 842	Am CGTA Sch 7.
s 360(1)	Charities.	s 505(1)	Rep in part 1971 Sch 14 Pt VI.
s 360(2)		—	Unnecessary.
s 360(3)		s 506(1)	Am CGTA 7.
s 361	Agricultural societies.	s 510	
s 362(1)–(3)	Scientific research organisations.	s 508, Sch 29	Am 1970/1537.
s 362(4)		—	Rep 1987 Sch 16 Pt VII.
s 363	British Museum.	s 507(2), Sch 29	
s 364	National Debt.	s 514, Sch 29	
s 365(1), (2)	Wounds & disability pensions.	s 315	
s 365(3)		—	Rep 1979(2) Sch 5 Pt II.
s 366	Allowances, bounties & gratuities.	s 316	Am 1981/1670; rep in part AFA 1981 Sch 5 Pt I.
s 367(1)–(6)	Visiting forces.	s 323, Sch 29	Am BNA s 51(3)(*a*).
s 367(7)		—	Unnecessary: see IA 1978 s 14.
s 368	Victoria Cross etc.	s 317	Am 1980 s 26.
s 369	Foreign service allowance.	s 319	Am 1981/1670.
s 370	Non-resident central banks.	s 516	
s 371	Issue departments of certain banks.	s 517, Sch 29	
s 372	Commonwealth Agents General.	s 320, Sch 29	Am BNA Sch 7.
s 373	Consuls.	s 321	Am BNA s 51(1)(*b*), (2).
s 374(1)	Consular officers etc.	s 322(1)	Am BNA s 51(3)(*a*); rep in part 1971 Sch 14 Pt IV.
s 374(2)		Sch 29	
s 374(3)–(7)		s 322(2)–(6)	Am BNA s 51(3)(*a*).
s 375	Scholarship income.	s 331	Rep in part 1987 Sch 16 Pt VII.
s 375A(1)	Interest on damages.	s 329(1)	Am AJA 1982 s 74.

TA 1970	Subject Matter	Re-enacted in TA 1988	Remarks
s 375A(1A)		s 329(3)	Added 1981 s 39.
s 375A(1B)		s 329(2)	Added 1971 s 19; am CCA 1984 Sch 2 §37; AJA 1982 s 74.
s 375A(2)		s 329(4)	Added 1971 s 19.
s 376	Housing grants.	s 578	
s 377	Certain compensation.	s 330	Subst 1986 s 51.
s 378(1), (2)	Writing down allowances in respect of patent rights.	s 520(1)–(3), 522(1)–(6)	Am 1985 s 64(1), (2)(*a*)–(*c*).
s 378(3)		s 522(7)	
s 379	Effect of lapses of patent rights.	s 523	Am 1985 s 64(2)(*c*).
s 380	Taxation of receipts from sale of patent rights.	s 524	Rep in part 1970(F) Sch 8 Pt VII; 1971 Sch 14 Pt II.
s 381	Capital sums: death etc.	s 525	Rep in part 1971 Sch 14 Pt II.
s 382	Relief for expenses.	s 526	
s 383	Patent income.	s 529	
s 384	Spreading of royalties.	s 527	Rep in part 1971 Sch 14 Pt II.
s 385	Manner of making allowances etc.	s 528	Am 1985 s 64(2)(*d*)–(*f*).
s 386(1)	Disposal of know-how.	s 530(1), (6), (7)	Am 1985 s 65(1).
s 386(2)–(6)		s 531(1)–(7)	Am 1985 s 65(3).
s 386(7)		s 533(7)	
s 386(8)		s 531(8)	
s 386(9)		s 530(8)	
s 387	Application of 1968 Act.	s 532	
s 388	Interpretation.	s 533(1)–(6)	Am 1985 s 64(2)(*g*); rep in part 1987 Sch 16 Pt VII.
s 389	Copyright.	s 534	
s 390	Sale of copyright ten years after first publication.	s 535	Rep in part 1971 Sch 14 Pt II.
s 391	Owner resident abroad.	s 536	
s 392	Artists' receipts.	s 538	
s 393(1)	Life policies etc: general.	s 539(1)	Am 1971 Sch 6 §41; 1972 Sch 24 §23.
s 393(2)(*a*)		s 539(2)(*a*)	
s 393(2)(*b*)		—	Rep 1971 Sch 14 §1.
s 393(2)(*c*)		s 539(2)(*b*)	Added 1971 Sch 3 §11.
s 393(2A)		s 539(2)(*c*)	Added 1971 Sch 2 §6.
s 393(3)		s 539(3)	Am 1985 s 41(8).
s 393(4), (5)		s 539(5)–(7)	
s 394(1)	Life policies: chargeable events.	s 540(1)	Rep in part 1975 Sch 13 Pt II; am 1975 Sch 2 §9.
s 394(2)		s 540(1)(*b*)	
s 394(3)		s 540(2)	Am 1984 s 75.
s 394(4)		s 540(3)	Am 1983 s 18(1); 1975 Sch 2 §10.
s 394(5), (6)		s 540(4), (5)	Rep in part 1975 Sch 13 Pt II.
s 395(1)	Computation of gain.	s 541(1)	Am 1975 Sch 2 §11(1); rep in part 1975 Sch 13 Pt II.
s 395(2), (3)		s 541(2), (3)	
s 395(3A)		s 541(4)	Added 1975 Sch 2 §11(2).
s 395(4)		s 541(5)	Rep in part 1975 Sch 13 Pt II.
s 396(1)	Life annuity contracts.	s 542(1), (2)	Rep in part 1975 Sch 13 Pt II; am 1975 Sch 2 §§9(3), 12(1).
s 396(2), (3)		s 542(3), (4)	Am 1975 Sch 2 §12(2); 1983 s 18(2).
s 397(1)	Computation of gain.	s 543(1)	Rep in part 1975 Sch 13 Pt II; am 1975 Sch 2 §13(1).
s 397(2), (3)		s 543(2), (3)	Am 1975 Sch 2 §13(2), (3).
s 398(1)	Capital redemption policies.	s 545(1)	Rep in part 1975 Sch 13 Pt II; am 1975 Sch 2 §§9(4), 14.
s 398(2)–(4)		s 545(2)–(4)	

TA 1970	Subject Matter	Re-enacted in TA 1988	Remarks
s 399(1)	Charge to tax.	s 547(1), (2)	Rep in part 1971 Sch 14 Pt II; am 1972 Sch 24 §24.
s 399(2), (3)		s 547(3), (4)	
s 399(4)		s 547(5)	Added 1971 Sch 6 §42; 1978 Sch 2 §6; rep in part 1980 Sch 20 Pt V.
s 400(1)–(3)	Relief for higher rate tax payer.	s 550(1)–(4)	Am 1971 Sch 6 §43; 1978 Sch 2 §7; rep in part 1980 Sch 20 Pt V.
s 400(4), (5)		s 550(6), (7)	Am 1971 Sch 6 §43.
s 401	Recovery of tax from trustees.	s 551	
s 402	Information.	s 552(1), (2)	
s 403, 404		—	Rep 1987 Sch 16 Pt VII.
s 405	Certain loans treated as income.	s 554	
s 406	Deduction of contributions to schemes for rationalizing industry.	s 568	Am 1970/1537.
s 407	Repayment of contributions.	s 569	Am 1971 Sch 6 §45.
s 408	Other payments.	s 570	Am 1970/1537.
s 409	Cancellation of certificates.	s 571	Am 1970/1537.
s 410	Statutory redundancy schemes.	s 572	
s 411(1)	Business entertaining expenses.	s 577(1)	Am 1971 s 50(8).
s 411(2)–(7)		s 577(2)–(7)	
s 411(8)		s 577(8)	Am 1985 s 43.
s 411(9)		s 577(10)	
s 412(1)–(6)	Statutory redundancy schemes.	s 579	Am EP(C)A Sch 16 §9.
s 412(7), (8)		s 580	Am EP(C)A Sch 16 §9.
s 413(1), (2)	Funds in court.	s 328(1)	Am AJA 1982 s 46(2).
s 413(3)		s 328(5)	
s 413(4), (5)		s 328(6), (7)	Am AJA s 46(2).
s 413(6)		s 328(8)	Am Supreme Court Act 1981 c 54 s 1(1); Judicature (Northern Ireland) Act 1978 c 23 Sch 5.
s 414(1)(*a*)	Savings bank interest.	s 325	Rep in part 1971 Sch 14 Pt II; am 1977 s 29; 1980 s 59.
s 414(1)(*b*)		—	Rep 1980 Sch 20 Pt IX.
s 414(1)(*c*)		—	Rep Merchant Shipping Act 1970 c 36 Sch 5.
s 414(2)		—	Rep 1971 Sch 14 Pt II.
s 414(3)–(7)		—	Rep 1980 Sch 20 Pt IX.
s 415(1)–(3)	Contractual savings schemes.	s 326, Sch 29	
s 415(4)		s 476(4)	
s 415(5)		s 832	
s 416(1)–(3)	Borrowings in foreign currency.	s 581(1)–(3)	Am 1982 s 64(2).
s 416(4)		s 581(6)	Rep 1982 Sch 22 Pt IV.
s 417	Funding bonds.	s 582	Am 1971 Sch 6 §47.
s 418(1), (2)	Relief for unremittable overseas income.	s 584(1), (2)	Am 1987(2) Sch 6 §6(2).
s 418(2A), (2B)		s 584(3), (4)	Added 1987(2) Sch 6 §6(3).
s 418(3)–(6)		s 584(6)–(9)	
s 418(7)		—	Rep 1971 Sch 14 Pt IV.
s 419	Delayed remittances.	s 585	
s 420	War risk premiums.	s 586	Rep in part 1987 Sch 16 Pt VII.
s 421	War injuries.	s 587	
s 422–424	—	—	Rep 1987 Sch 16 Pt VII.
s 425	Payments of interest less tax.	s 818	Am 1971 Sch 6 §51.
s 426	Limited interests in residue.	s 695	Am 1971 Sch 6 §52.
s 427	Absolute interests in residue.	s 696, 701(14)	Rep in part 1975 Sch 13 Pt I; am 1971 Sch 6 §53; 1974 Sch 7 §9(3).

TA 1970	Subject Matter	Re-enacted in TA 1988	Remarks
s 428	Supplementary provisions.	s 697	Am 1971 Sch 6 §54.
s 429	Special provisions.	s 698, 701(14)	Am 1971 Sch 6 §55; 1974 Sch 7 §9(4).
s 430	Inheritance tax.	s 699	Am 1971 Sch 6 §56; 1975 Sch 12 §16; 1978 Sch 2 §11; 1986 s 100; rep in part 1975 Sch 13 Pt I; 1980 Sch 20 Pt V; 1984 Sch 23 Pt VI.
s 431	Adjustments etc.	s 700	Rep in part 1971 Sch 14 Pt II; am 1971 Sch 6 §57.
s 432	Interpretation.	s 701	Rep in part 1971 Sch 14 Pt II; 1972 Sch 24 §25; 1975 Sch 13 Pt I; am 1972 Sch 24 §25; 1975(2) s 34(5).
s 433	Scotland.	s 702	Am 1987 Sch 15 §2(15).
s 434(1)	Dispositions for short periods.	s 660(1)	Am 1980 s 55(1).
s 434(1A)		s 660(2)	Added 1980 s 55(1); subst 1987 Sch 15 §2(16).
s 434(2)		s 660(3)	Am 1980 s 55(1).
s 435	Adjustments between disponor and trustees.	s 661	Rep in part 1971 Sch 14 Pt II.
s 436	Cases involving more than disponor.	s 662	
s 437(1)	Settlements on children: general rule.	s 663(1)	Am 1971 s 16(2)(*b*).
s 437(2), (3)		s 663(3), (4)	Am 1971 s 16(2)(*d*).
s 437(4)			Rep 1971 s 16(2)(*d*).
s 437(5)		s 663(5)	
s 438(1)	Accumulation settlements.	s 664(1)	
s 438(2)		s 664(2), (3)	Am 1971 s 16(2)(*c*); 1987 Sch 15 §2(17).
s 438(3)		—	Unnecessary.
s 439(1)	Meaning of ''irrevocable''.	s 665	
s 439(2)		—	Spent.
s 440(1)–(3)	Interest paid by trustees.	s 666(1)–(3)	Rep in part 1971 Sch 14 Pt II; am 1971 s 16(2).
s 440(4)		s 666(4), (5)	
s 441	Adjustments between settlor and trustees.	s 667	Rep in part 1971 Sch 14 Pt II.
s 442(1)	Cases involving more than settlor.	s 668(1)	
s 442(2)		s 668(2), (3)	
s 442(3)–(5)		s 668(4)–(6)	
s 443	Power to obtain information.	s 669	Rep in part 1971 Sch 14 Pt II; am 1971 Sch 6 §62.
s 444(1), (2)	Interpretation.	s 670	Rep in part 1971 Sch 14 Pt VII.
s 444(3), (4)		—	Rep 1971 Sch 14 Pt IV.
s 445(1)	Revocable settlements allowing release of obligation.	s 671(1), (2)	
s 445(1A)		s 671(2)(*b*)	Added 1980 s 55(2).
s 445(2)		s 671(3)	
s 445(3)		Sch 30	
s 446(1)	Revocable settlements allowing reversion of property.	s 672(1), (2)	
s 446(2)		s 672(3)	
s 446(3)		Sch 30	
s 447(1)	Settlements where settlor retains an interest.	s 673(1)	
s 447(2)		s 673(2), (3)	
s 448(1)	Discretionary power for benefit of settlor etc.	s 674(1), (2)	
s 448(2), (3)		s 674(3), (4)	
s 448(4)		Sch 30	
s 449	Supplementary provisions.	s 675	Rep in part 1971 Sch 14 Pt II.

Dest. Tables

TA 1970	Subject Matter	Re-enacted in TA 1988	Remarks
s 450	Disallowance of certain deductions from total income.	s 676	Rep in part 1971 Sch 14 Pt II.
s 451(1)	Capital sums paid to settlor.	s 677(1)	Am 1981 s 42(2)(*a*), (*b*); 1982 s 63(3).
s 451(2)(*aa*)		s 677(2)(*a*)	Added 1981 s 42(3).
s 451(2)(*a*)		s 677(2)(*b*)	
s 451(2)(*b*)		s 677(2)(*c*)	Am 1981 s 42(3).
s 451(2)(*c*)		s 677(2)(*d*)	
s 451(2)(*d*)		s 677(2)(*e*)	
s 451(2)(*dd*)		s 677(2)(*f*)	Added 1981 s 42(3).
s 451(2)(*ddd*)		s 677(2)(*g*)	Added 1981 s 42(3).
s 451(2)(*e*)		s 677(2)(*h*)	Am 1973 s 16(7); 1981 s 42(3)(*d*); 1971 Sch 6 §64.
s 451(3)		s 677(3)	
s 451(3A), (3B)		s 677(4), (5)	Added 1981 s 42(4).
s 451(4)		—	Rep 1981 Sch 19 Pt VI.
s 451(5)		s 677(6)	Am 1973 s 16(7); 1971 Sch 6 §64.
s 451(6)		s 677(7)	Rep in part 1971 Sch 14 Pt II; am 1981 s 42(5).
s 451(7)		s 677(8)	
s 451(8)		s 677(9)	Am 1981 s 42(6)(*a*), (*b*).
s 451(9)		s 677(10)	Added 1981 s 42(7).
s 451A	Capital payments by connected bodies.	s 678	Added 1981 s 43(2).
s 452	Cases involving more than one settlor.	s 679	
s 453	Power to obtain information.	s 680	Rep in part 1971 Sch 14 Pt II; am 1971 Sch 6 §65.
s 454(1)	Interpretation.	s 681(1), (2)	Am 1972 Sch 24 §26; 1981 s 44(1); partly spent.
s 454(1A)		s 681(3)	Added 1981 s 44(1).
s 454(2)		—	Rep 1971 Sch 14 Pt IV.
s 454(3)		s 681(4)	
s 454(4)		s 681(5)	Subst 1981 s 44(2).
s 454(5)		—	Spent.
s 454(6)		s 681(6)	
s 455	Ascertainment of undistributed income.	s 682(1)	
s 456		s 682(2)–(6)	Rep in part 1971 Sch 14 Pt II.
s 457(1)	Post-6th April 1965 settlements.	s 683(1), (2)	Am 1971 Sch 6 §67; 1978 Sch 2 §12; 1980 s 56(1); rep in part 1980 Sch 20 Pt V; 1984 Sch 23 Pt VI.
s 457(1A)		s 683(3)	Added 1980 s 56(2); am 1985 s 49(1); 1986 s 32(2); rep in part 1986 Sch 23 Pt V.
s 457(1B), (1C)		s 683(4), (5)	Added 1986 s 32(2).
s 457(2)–(4)		s 683(6)–(8)	
s 457(4A)		s 683(9)	Added 1980 s 34(4).
s 457(5)		s 683(10)	Am 1980 s 56(3).
s 457(6)		s 685(1), (2)	
s 458(1)	Pre-7th April 1965 settlements.	s 684(1)–(3)	Am 1971 Sch 6 §68; 1978 Sch 2 §13; rep in part 1980 Sch 20 Pt V; 1984 Sch 23 Pt VI.
s 458(2)		s 685(1), (2)	
s 459	Interpretation.	s 685(4), (5)	
s 460(1)–(3)	Cancellation of tax advantage.	s 703(1)–(3)	Rep in part 1987 Sch 16 Pt VII.
s 460(4), (4A), (4B)		s 703(4)–(6)	Added 1973 Sch 11 §1.
s 460(5)–(9)		s 703(7)–(12)	
s 461	The prescribed circumstances.	s 704	Am 1973 s 54, Sch 11 §2; rep in part 1973 Sch 22 Pt II.
s 462	Appeals.	s 705(1)–(5)	
s 462A	Appeals.	s 705(6)–(8)	Added 1973 Sch 11 §3.

TA 1970	Subject Matter	Re-enacted in TA 1988	Remarks
s 463	The tribunal.	s 706	Am 1982 Sch 21 §3(1).
s 464	Advance clearance.	s 707	
s 465	Information.	s 708	
s 466(1)	"Tax advantage".	s 709(1)	Am 1973 Sch 11 §4.
s 466(2)		—	Rep 1973 Sch 22 Pt II.
s 467	Interpretation.	s 709(2)–(6)	Am 1973 Sch 11 §5; rep in part 1987 Sch 16 Pt VII.
s 468		—	Rep 1987 Sch 16 Pt VII.
s 469(1)	Sale and repurchase of securities.	s 729(1)	Rep in part 1971 Sch 14 Pt II; am 1971 Sch 6 §70.
s 469(2)–(6)		s 729(2)–(6)	
s 469(6A), (6B), (6C)		s 729(7)–(9)	Added 1986 Sch 18 §1(1).
s 469(7)		s 729(10)	Am 1986 Sch 18 §1(4).
s 469(8)		s 729(11)	
s 470	Transfers of income.	s 730	Am 1971 Sch 6 §71.
s 471	Application of sections 472–474.	s 731	Am 1973 Sch 11 §6; 1986 Sch 18 §2(1).
s 472(1)	Dealers in securities.	s 732(1)	
s 472(2)		s 732(2)	Subst 1986 Sch 18 §3(1).
s 472(3), (4)		s 732(3), (4)	Am 1986 Sch 18 §1(3).
s 472(5)		s 732(5)	Added 1982 s 57.
s 472(6)		s 732(6)	Added 1986 Sch 18 §3(2).
s 473(1)	Persons entitled to exemptions.	s 733	
s 473(2)		—	Rep 1986 Sch 15 Pt III.
s 474(1), (2)	Persons other than dealers in securities.	s 734(1), (2)	Am 1978 s 30(7); CGTA 7. Added 1973 Sch 11 §7.
s 474(3)		s 734(3)	
s 475(1)–(5)	"Appropriate amount" in respect of interest.	s 735	Am 1973 s 54, Sch 21 §7.
s 475(6)		—	Rep 1986 Sch 23 Pt VIII.
s 476	Company dealing in securities.	s 736	
s 477(1)–(6)	Manufactured dividends.	s 737(1)–(6)	Am 1973 Sch 11 §8; 1982 s 59(1); 1986 Sch 18 §5, 6(2), (3); rep in part 1973 Sch 22 Pt IV.
s 477(6A)		s 737(7)	Added 1973 Sch 11 §8.
s 477(7)		s 737(8)	
s 478(1), (2)	Transfer of assets abroad.	s 739(1)–(4)	Am 1981 s 46(3).
s 478(2A), (2B)		s 739(5), (6)	Added 1981 s 46(3).
s 478(3)		s 741	
s 478(4)–(6)		s 742(1)–(3)	Am 1981 s 46(5).
s 478(7), (8)		s 742(8), (9)	Am 1972 Sch 24 §27; rep in part 1971 Sch 14 Pt II.
s 478(9)		s 742(10)	Added 1981 s 46.
s 479	Irish residents.	s 746	
s 480	Supplemental.	s 743	Am 1971 Sch 6 §72; 1981 s 46(7); rep in part 1971 Sch 14 Pt II.
s 481	Information.	s 745	Rep in part 1971 Sch 14 Pt II; am 1972 Sch 24 §28.
s 482(1)–(4)	Migration of companies.	s 765	
s 482(5)		s 766(1), (2)	
s 482(6)		s 766(3)	See Criminal Law Act 1977 c 45 s 32(1), Criminal Procedure (Scotland) Act 1975 c 21 s 193A, Fines and Penalties (Northern Ireland) Order 1984 (SI No 703 (NI 3)).
s 482(7)		s 767(1), (2)	
s 482(8)–(10)		s 767(3)–(5)	Am CCCPA.
s 482(11)		s 766(4)	Rep in part CJA 1975 Sch 6 Pt I.
s 482(12)		s 767(6)	
s 483	Change in ownership of company.	s 768	

TA 1970	Subject Matter	Re-enacted in TA 1988	Remarks
s 484	Rules for section 483.	s 769	Partly spent.
s 485(1)	Sales at an undervalue etc.	s 770(1), (2)(*a*)	Am 1975 s 17(2).
s 485(2)		s 770(1), (2)(*b*)	Am 1975 s 17(2).
s 485(3)		s 770(2)(*d*), (3)	
s 485(4), (5)		s 773(1), (2)	Am 1971 Sch 8 §16(5).
s 485(5A)		s 773(3)	Added 1975 s 17(1).
s 485(6)		s 773(4)	
s 486	Dealing company and associated companies.	s 774	
s 487(1)–(7)	Sale of certain income.	s 775	
s 487(8)		—	Spent.
s 488(1)–(13)	Artificial transactions in land.	s 776	
s 488(14)		—	Spent.
s 489	Supplemental.	s 777	Am CGTA 7; rep in part 1971 Sch 14 Pt III.
s 490	Information.	s 778	
s 491	Limitation of tax reliefs.	s 779	
s 492(1)–(5)	Assets leased to traders etc.	s 781(1)–(6)	
s 492(6)		s 785	
s 492(7)–(9)		s 781(7)–(9)	Am 1971 Sch 8 §16(7).
s 493	Special cases.	s 782	Am 1971 Sch 8 §16(8).
s 494	Supplemental.	s 783	
s 495	Hire-purchase agreements.	s 784	Am CCA 1974 Sch 4 §29; rep in part 1987 Sch 16 Pt VII.
s 496	Credit transactions.	s 786	Rep in part 1971 Sch 14 Pt II.
s 497(1)–(8)	Double taxation relief.	s 788	Am 1972 ss 100(1), 98(2); 1976 s 50(2); 1987 s 70(1).
s 497(9), (10)		s 789	Am 1971 Sch 6 §74; partly spent.
s 498(1)–(4)	Unilateral relief.	s 790(1)–(6)	Rep in part 1976 Sch 15 Pt III; 1971 Sch 14 Pt VII; am 1972 s 83, 100(1); 1971 s 26.
s 498(5), (6)		s 790(11), (12)	Am 1972 s 100(1).
s 499	—	—	Rep 1972 Sch 28 Pt VI.
s 500	Interpretation of credit code.	s 792	Rep in part 1971 Sch 14 Pt VII.
s 501	Relief by way of credit.	s 793	Am 1972 s 100(1).
s 502	Requirements as to residence.	s 794	Am 1982 s 67.
s 503	Computation of certain income.	s 795	Am 1972 s 100(1); 1987 Sch 15 §2(18).
s 504	Limits on credit.	s 796	
s 505	Limits on credit.	s 797(1)	Am 1972 s 100(3)–(7).
s 506(1)	Underlying tax.	s 799(1)	
s 506(1A)		s 799(2)	Added 1976 s 50(3).
s 506(2), (3)		s 799(3), (4)	
s 507(1)	Related companies' dividends.	s 800	Am 1971 s 26(4).
s 507(2), (3)		—	Rep 1971 Sch 14 Pt VII.
s 508		s 801	Subst 1971 s 26(2).
s 509	Insurance companies.	s 802	
s 510	Relief against income tax.	s 804	Am 1971 Sch 6 §75.
s 511	Elections against credit.	s 805	Am 1972 s 100(1).
s 512	Time limit for claims etc.	s 806	Am 1972 s 100(1).
s 513	—	—	Rep 1976 Sch 15 Pt III.
s 514	—	—	Rep 1987 Sch 16 Pt VII.
s 515	Capital allowances.	s 810	Am 1971 s 54(1); 1982 s 78(1); rep in part 1970(F) Sch 8 Pt VII.
s 516	Deductions for foreign tax.	s 811	Am 1973 s 40(1); 1987 Sch 15 §2(19).
s 517(1)	Regulations.	s 791, 828	
s 517(2)		—	Rep 1972 Sch 28 Pt VI.
s 518	Information.	s 816	
s 519(1), (2)	Deductions not allowed.	s 817	
s 519(3)		—	Rep 1987 Sch 16 Pt VII.

TA 1970	Subject Matter	Re-enacted in TA 1988	Remarks
s 520	Income tax provisions.	s 820	
s 521(1), (2)		s 821(1), (2)	Rep in part 1972 Sch 28 Pt VI.
s 521(3)(*a*)		—	Rep 1972 Sch 28 Pt VI.
s 521(3)(*b*), (*c*), (*d*)		s 821(3)	Am 1983 s 27.
s 521(4)		s 821(4)	Added 1972 Sch 24 §29.
s 522		s 822	Am 1971 Sch 6 §76; 1972 Sch 24 §30; rep in part 1972 Sch 28 Pt VI.
s 523		s 823	
s 524		s 829(1)–(3)	
s 525(1)		s 829(4)	
s 525(2)		Sch 29	Am CGTA 7.
s 526(1), (2)	Interpretation.	s 831(1), (2)	
s 526(3), (4)		s 832(3), (4)	
s 526(5)		s 832(1)	Am NICA Sch 5; 1971 Sch 8 §(3); CGTA 7; 1972 Sch 24 §31; 1974 Sch 12 §10; 1979(2) Sch 2 §4; 1987 Sch 15 §2(20); rep in part 1972 Sch 28 Pt VI.
s 526(5A)		s 832(5)	Added 1987 Sch 15 §2(21).
s 526(6)		s 832(2)	
s 527	Interpretation.	s 834	Am 1980 s 45(2).
s 528(1), (2)		s 835(1), (2)	Am 1971 Sch 6 §78.
s 528(3)–(5)		s 835(6)–(8)	Am 1971 Sch 6 §78; 1972 Sch 11 §8, Sch 24 §32; rep in part 1971 Sch 14 Pt II.
s 529		s 833(3)	
s 530		s 833(4)–(6)	Am 1982 s 31(2); 1981 s 27(10); rep in part 1977 Sch 9 Pt IV.
s 531		s 837	
s 532		s 838	
s 533		s 839	Rep in part 1987 Sch 16 Pt VII.
s 534		s 840	
s 535		s 841	Am 1973 s 54, Sch 21 §9.
Sch 1	Qualifying policies.		
para 1(1)–(4A)		Sch 15 §1(1)–(5)	Am 1975 Sch 2 §4.
para 1(5)–(7)		Sch 15 §1(7)–(9)	Am 1975 Sch 2 §4.
para 2		Sch 15 §2(1)–(3)	Am 1975 Sch 2 §4.
para 3, 3A		Sch 15 §3, 4, 6(1)	Subst 1985 Sch 10 Pt I; 1985 s 41(4).
para 4		Sch 15 §7	Am 1976 Sch 4 §12; rep in part 1976 Sch 15 Pt IV.
para 5		Sch 15 §9	
para 6, 7		Sch 15 §12, 13	
para 8		Sch 15 §15	
para 9		Sch 15 §17(1)–(3)	Am 1984 s 76(3), (6).
para 10		Sch 15 §18	
para 11		Sch 15 §22(1)–(3)	Rep in part 1978 Sch 14 Pt III; am 1975 Sch 2 §2; 1976 s 33(2); 1978 Sch 3 §13.
Sch 2	Restrictions on Schedule A deductions.		
para 1–3		Sch 1 §1–3	
para 4		—	Rep 1977 Sch 9 §5.
Sch 3	Taxable premiums.	Sch 2	Rep in part 1971 Sch 14 Pt II; 1970(F) Sch 8 Pt VI.
Sch 4	—	—	Rep 1971 Sch 14 Pt III.
Sch 5	Tax under Schedule C.		
para 1–13		Sch 3 §1–13	Am 1971 Sch 6 §80; DCA 1969 s 10; 1975(2) s 44(3).
para 14		s 45, Sch 3 §14	
Sch 6	Farm animals etc.		
para 1–11		Sch 5 §1–11	

TA 1970	Subject Matter	Re-enacted in TA 1988	Remarks
Sch 7	—	—	Rep 1971 Sch 14 Pt IV.
Sch 8	Schedule E: retirement benefits etc.		
para 1		Sch 11 §1	
para 2		Sch 11 §2	Rep in part 1971 Sch 14 Pt II.
para 3–5		Sch 11 §13	Am 1978 s 24; 1970(F) Sch 5 Pt III §12(6); 1971 Sch 3 §12(6); 1981 s 31(7); rep in part 1973 Sch 22 Pt II.
para 6		Sch 11 §3, 14	Rep in part 1971 Sch 14 Pt VI; 1981 Sch 19 Pt VI.
para 7		Sch 11 §4, 15	Am 1981 s 31(3); 1982 s 43(1).
para 7A		Sch 11 §5	Added 1982 s 43(1).
para 8, 9		Sch 11 §16	See 1981 s 31(7).
para 10		Sch 11 §6, 7	Rep in part 1981 Sch 19 Pt VI; see 1981 s 31(7); am 1986 s 45(2).
para 11		Sch 11 §7, 18	Rep in part 1981 Sch 19 Pt VI; see 1981 s 31(7).
para 12		—	Rep 1986 Sch 23 Pt V.
para 13		Sch 11 §19	Rep in part 1981 Sch 19 Pt VI; see 1981 s 31(7).
para 14		Sch 11 §8	Am 1971 Sch 8 §16.
para 15		Sch 11 §9	
para 16		Sch 11 §10	Am 1974 s 21; 1977 s 31.
para 17		Sch 11 §11	
Sch 9	—	—	Rep 1972 Sch 28 Pt VI.
Sch 10	Underwriters.		
para 1		s 452(1)	Rep in part 1973 Sch 22 Pt III; 1987 Sch 16 Pt VII.
para 2–4		—	Rep 1973 Sch 22 Pt III.
para 5		s 452(2), (3)	
para 6		s 452(4)(*a*)	
para 7(1)–(3)		s 452(5)–(9)	Am 1973 Sch 16 §10; 1985 Sch 23 §29; rep in part 1973 Sch 22 Pt III; 1987 Sch 16 Pt VII.
para 7(4)		—	Rep 1971 Sch 14 Pt IV.
para 8		s 453(1)–(4)	
para 9		s 453(5)–(7)	
para 10		s 452(4)(*b*)	
para 11		s 454	Rep in part 1973 Sch 22 Pt III; 1971 Sch 14 Pt II; am 1973 Sch 16 §§8, 11, 12.
para 12		s 455	Rep in part 1971 Sch 14 Pt II.
para 12A		s 456(1), (2)	Added 1973 Sch 16 §§8, 13.
para 13		s 456(3)	
para 14(*a*)		—	Rep 1973 Sch 22 Pt III.
para 14(*b*)		s 456(4)	Rep in part 1987 Sch 16 Pt VII.
para 15		—	Rep 1971 Sch 14 Pt IV.
para 16		s 457	Partly spent; am 1987 Sch 15 §2(22); rep in part 1987 Sch 16 Pt VII.
Sch 11	Tax relief in connection with certain schemes.	Sch 21	
Sch 12			
Pt I, II	—	—	Rep 1976 Sch 15 Pt III.
Pt III			
para 1		—	Rep 1976 Sch 15 Pt III.
para 2	Double taxation relief: Republic of Ireland.	s 68(1)–(4)	Am 1974 Sch 1 §§27, 29; 1976 s 49(4); rep in part 1984 Sch 23 Pt VII; partly spent.
para 3(1), (2)		—	Rep 1976 Sch 15 Pt III.

TA 1970	Subject Matter	Re-enacted in TA 1988	Remarks
Sch 12 Pt III (contd)			
para 3(3)		s 192(1)	Am 1974 s 21(6).
para 4, 5		—	Rep 1976 Sch 15 Pt III.
para 6		Sch 3 §15	Am 1987 Sch 15 §2(23).
Sch 13	Returns of total income.	s 836	
Sch 14	Transitionals.		
para 1, 2		—	Spent.
para 3, 4		Sch 30	
para 5		—	Spent.
para 6		Sch 30	
para 7, 8		—	Rep 1971 Sch 14 Pt IV.
para 9		Sch 30	
para 10		—	Rep 1972 Sch 28 Pt V.
para 11			Not repealed.
para 12		—	Rep 1980 Sch 20 Pt VIII.
para 13–17		—	Spent.
para 18		Sch 30	
para 19(1)		—	Rep 1972 Sch 28 Pt VI.
para 19(2), 20–22		—	Spent.
para 23		—	Rep in part 1972 Sch 28 Pt VI; spent.
para 24–27		—	Spent.
para 28		—	Rep 1971/2099.
para 29		—	Rep 1970(F) Sch 8 Pt VII.
Sch 16	Repeals.	—	

FINANCE ACT 1970
(c 24)

FA 1970	Subject Matter	Re-enacted in TA 1988	Remarks
s 11–13	IT, CT & surtax rates.	—	Spent; rep in part 1971 Sch 14 Pt II.
s 14(1)(*a*)(i)–(iii)	Personal reliefs.	—	Rep 1971 Sch 14 Pt II.
s 14(1)(*a*)(iv)		s 257(8)	
s 14(1)(*b*)–(*e*)		—	Rep 1971 Sch 14 Pt II, VII.
s 14(1)(*f*)		—	Spent.
s 14(2)		—	Spent.
s 16(1)	Passenger transport executives.	—	Rep Transport Act 1985 c 67 Sch 8.
s 16(2), (3)		Sch 30	
s 16(4)		—	Unnecessary.
s 17		—	Rep 1972 Sch 28 Pt V.
s 19(1)	Occupational pension schemes.	s 590(1)	Subst 1971 s 21(2).
s 19(2)(*a*)–(*e*)		s 590(2)(*a*)–(*e*)	
s 19(2)(*f*)		—	Rep 1973 Sch 22 Pt II.
s 19(2)(*g*)		s 590(2)(*f*)	
s 19(2A)		s 590(3), (4)	Added 1971 s 21(3).
s 19(2B)		s 590(3)	Added 1987(2) Sch 3 §1.
s 19(3)		s 590(5)	Am 1987(2) Sch 3 §2.
s 19(4)		s 590(6)	Subst 1971 Sch 3 §12(1).
s 19(5)		s 590(7)	
s 19(6)	Commencement.	—	Spent.
s 20(1)		s 591(1)	Am 1987(2) Sch 3 §3.
s 20(2)(*a*)–(*f*)		s 591(2)(*a*)–(*f*)	Subst 1971 s 21(4).
s 20(2)(*g*), (*h*)		s 591(2)(*g*), (*h*)	Added 1981 s 32; subst 1987(2) Sch 3 §3.
s 20(2A)		s 591(3)	Added 1981 s 32; am ICA 1982.
s 20(3)		s 591(4)	
s 20(4), (5)		s. 591(5), (6)	Added 1987 Sch 15 §3.
s 20(6)		s 612(3), 828	
s 21(1), (2)		s 592(1), (2)	
s 21(2A)		s 592(3)	Added 1971 s 21(5).
s 21(3)		s 592(4)–(6)	

FA 1970	Subject Matter	Re-enacted in TA 1988	Remarks
s 21(4)		s 592(7)	Rep in part 1987(2) Sch 9 Pt I.
s 21(4A)		s 592(8)	Subst 1987(2) Sch 3 §4.
s 21(5)		s 592(9)	
s 21(6)		—	Rep 1971 Sch 14 Pt IV.
s 21(7)		Sch 29	
s 21(7A), (7B)		s 592(10), Sch 29	Added 1987(2) Sch 3 §5.
s 21(8), (9)		s 592(11), (12)	
s 21(10), (11)		—	Rep 1971 Sch 14 Pt I.
s 22(1), (2), (2A)	Statutory schemes.	s 594	Am 1972 s 74(3); 1987(2) Sch 3 §6.
s 22(3)		—	Rep 1972 Sch 28 Pt IV.
s 22(4)		—	Rep 1971 Sch 14 Pt I.
s 23(1)–(5)	Payments by employer etc.	s 595	
s 23(6)		—	Rep 1971 Sch 14 Pt I.
s 24(1)	Exceptions from s 23.	s 596(1)	
s 24(2)		s 596(2)	Subst 1974 s 21(7).
s 24(3)		s 596(3)	
s 25	Definitions.	s 611(1)–(4)	
s 26(1)	Further interpretation.	s 612(1)	Rep in part 1971 Sch 14 Pt I; 1973 Sch 22 Pt II; am 1971 Sch 3 §12(4); NICA Sch 5; 1987(2) Sch 3 §7.
s 26(2)		s 612(2)	Am 1987(2) Sch 3 §8.
s 26(3)		—	Unnecessary.
s 29(1), (2)	Mineral royalties.	s 122(1), (2)	Rep in part 1971 Sch 14 Pt II, III; am CGTA 7.
s 29(3)(*a*)		s 122(1)(*b*), (3)	See 1971 Sch 9 §4.
s 29(3)(*b*), (*c*)		—	Rep 1971 Sch 14 Pt III.
s 29(4)		s 122(4)	Rep in part 1971 Sch 14 Pt II.
s 29(6)–(9)		s 122(5)–(7), Sch 29	Not wholly repealed.
Sch 3	London transport authorities.		
para 2–7		Sch 30	Partly spent.
Sch 4	Amendments.		
para 1–5		—	Rep 1972 Sch 28 Pt VI.
para 6		s 209(2)(*e*)(iv), (v)	
para 7		—	Not repealed.
para 8		s 656(2), (3)(*e*)	
para 9(1)–(5), (7)–(9)		—	Rep 1972 Sch 28 Pt V.
para 9(6)		s 387(3)(*a*)	
para 10		—	Not repealed.
para 11		—	Unnecessary.
Sch 5	Occupational pensions schemes.		
Pt I		—	Rep 1971 Sch 14 Pt I.
Pt II para 1		s 597	
para 2		s 598, 828	Subst 1971 Sch 3 §7.
para 3(1)–(5)		s 599	Subst 1971 Sch 3 §7; am 1987(2) Sch 3 §9.
para 3(6)		—	Spent.
para 4		s 601(5), (6)	Am 1971 Sch 3 §12(5).
para 5		—	Rep 1971 Sch 14 Pt I.
para 6		s 604	Am 1987(2) Sch 3 §11.
para 6A		s 593	Added 1987(2) Sch 3 §12.
para 7, 8		s 605	Am 1987(2) Sch 3 §13, 14.
para 9		s 606	Am 1987(2) Sch 3 §15.
para 10		s 612(3)	
Pt III para 11, 12	Amendments.		See destinations of enactments amended.

INCOME AND CORPORATION TAXES (NO 2) ACT 1970
(c 54)

T (No 2) A 1970	Subject Matter	Re-enacted in TA 1988	Remarks
s 1	IT rates.	—	Spent.
s 2	—	—	Rep 1973 Sch 22 Pt II.
s 3	CT rates.	—	Spent.
s 4	—	—	Unnecessary.

FINANCE ACT 1971
(c 68)

FA 1971	Subject Matter	Re-enacted in TA 1988	Remarks
s 13, 14	IT & CT rates.	—	Spent.
s 15(1)	—	—	Unnecessary.
s 15(2)–(4)	Personal reliefs.	—	Rep 1974 Sch 14 Pt VI, VII.
s 15(5)		s 258(2)(*c*)	
s 15(6)		—	Rep 1973 Sch 23 Pt II.
s 15(7)		—	Rep 1977 Sch 9 Pt IV.
s 16(1)	Settlements.	—	Unnecessary.
s 16(2)(*a*)		s 382(1)	
s 16(2)(*b*)		s 663(1)	
s 16(2)(*c*)		s 664(2)(*b*), 666(1)	
s 16(2)(*d*)		s 663(4)	
s 17(1)	Partnerships.	s 113(2)	
s 17(2)		—	Spent.
s 18(1)	Social security benefits.	s 617(1)(*a*)	
s 18(2)		—	Rep 1973 Sch 22 Pt II.
s 19	Damages for personal injuries.	s 329	Am NICA Sch 5 §4(1); AJA 1982 s 74; 1981 s 39; CCA 1984 Sch 2 §37.
s 20(1)	Annuities.	s 620(1)	
s 20(2)		s 619(2), (3)	Rep in part 1980 Sch 20 Pt VII; am 1980 s 31(1), (2).
s 20(3)		s 620(3)	
s 20(4)		—	Unnecessary.
s 21(1)	—	—	Unnecessary.
s 21(2), (3)	Occupational pensions schemes.	s 590(1), (3)	
s 21(4)		s 591(2)	Am 1981 s 32.
s 21(5)		s 592(3)	
s 21(6)		—	Not repealed.
s 22(1)–(3)	Pensions.	s 610	
s 22(4)–(10)		—	Rep SSA 1973 Sch 28.
s 23(1)	Taxation of wife's earnings.	s 287(1)	
s 23(2)–(5)		s 288	Am 1976 s 36(10).
s 24	—	—	Spent.
s 25(1)–(4)(*a*)	—	—	Rep 1972 Sch 28 Pt VI.
s 25(4)(*b*)	—	—	Spent.
s 25(5)	Close companies.	s 420(2)	
s 25(6)		s 414(7)	
s 25(7)		—	Unnecessary.
s 26(1)	DTR.	—	Unnecessary.
s 26(2)		s 801	
s 26(3)		s 790(6)(*a*)	
s 26(4)		s 800	
s 26(5)		—	Spent.
s 27	—	—	Spent.
s 28	Marketing boards.	s 509	
s 29–31	—	—	Rep 1975(2) Sch 14 Pt IV.
s 32(1)(*a*)	Basic and higher rates.	s 1(2)(*a*)	
s 32(1)(*aa*)		—	Added 1978 s 14(1); rep 1980 Sch 20 Pt V.
s 32(1)(*b*)		s 1(2)(*b*)	
s 32(1)		s 832(1)	Am 1984 Sch 7 §1.
s 32(1A), (1B), (1C)		—	Added 1978 s 14(2); rep 1980 Sch 20 Pt V.

FA 1971	Subject Matter	Re-enacted in TA 1988	Remarks
s 32(1D)		s 832(1)	Added 1978 s 14(1); rep in part 1980 Sch 20 Pt V.
s 32(2)		—	Spent.
s 32(3), (4)		—	Rep 1984 Sch 23 Pt VI.
s 33(1)		—	Spent.
s 33(2), (3)	Amendments.		See destinations of enactments amended.
s 33(4)		—	Rep 1977 Sch 9 Pt IV.
s 33(5)		s 276	
s 34(1)–(3)	Deductions.	s 835(3)–(5)	Am 1975(2) s 31(4).
s 34(4)		—	Rep 1984 Sch 23 Pt VI.
s 35	Surtax.	—	Spent.
s 36	Deduction of tax.	s 4	Am 1975(2) s 44(6).
s 39	IT rate.	—	Spent.
s 54(1)	DTR: capital allowances.	s 810(4)(*b*)	
s 54(2)		—	Spent.
Sch 2	Amendments.		
para 1		s 621, Sch 29	Am 1976 s 30(2); rep in part 1980 Sch 20 Pt VII.
para 2–5		—	Rep 1980 Sch 20 Pt VII.
para 6		s 539(2)(*c*)	
para 7	Commencement.	—	Spent; rep in part 1980 Sch 20 Pt VII.
Sch 3	Occupational pension schemes.		
para 1–3		—	Spent.
para 4		—	Spent.
para 5		s 611(5)	
para 6		—	Spent.
para 7		s 598, 599	
para 8		—	Not repealed.
para 9		s 600	
para 10		—	Rep CGTA 8.
para 11, 12			See destinations of enactments amended.
para 13		—	Unnecessary.
Sch 4	Separate taxation of wife's earnings.		
para 1, 2		s 287(2), (3)	Am 1979(2) Sch 2 §5; 1987 s 27(3).
para 3		s 287(4)–(6)	Rep in part 1971 Sch 4 §8; 1979(2) Sch 5 Pt II; 1982 Sch 22 Pt XI; am 1975(2) s 31(5); 1987 s 26(5).
para 4, 5		s 287(7)–(9)	
para 6		—	Rep 1971 Sch 4 §8.
para 7		s 287(10)	
para 8		—	Spent.
Sch 5	—	—	Rep 1975(2) Sch 14 Pt IV.
Sch 6	Amendments.		
Pt I			See destinations of enactments amended.
Pt III			
para 91, 92		—	Rep CGTA 8; 1972 Sch 28 Pt VI.
para 93		—	Spent.
Sch 7	Income tax provisions.		
para 1		—	Spent.
para 2–4		s 819	Am 1978 Sch 2 §14; rep in part 1980 Sch 20 Pt V; 1984 Sch 23 Pt VI.
Sch 9	Development value.		
para 4		s 122	

FINANCE ACT 1972
(c 41)

FA 1972	Subject Matter	Re-enacted in TA 1988	Remarks
s 62–64	IT, CT & surtax rates.	—	Spent.
s 65	—	—	Rep 1973 Sch 23 Pt II; 1974 Sch 14 Pt VI, VII.
s 66	IT rates.	—	Spent.
s 70	Grants for the disabled.	s 327	Am NHS 1977 Sch 15 §57; NHS 1978 Sch 16 §37.
s 71	—	—	Spent.
s 72	Terminal grants to Members of Parliament.	s 190	
s 73	Compensation for early retirement etc.	s 188(2)	
s 74(1), (2)	—	—	Spent.
s 74(3)	Pensions.	s 594	
s 75(1)	Relief for payment of interest.	s 353(1)	Am 1974 s 19(1)(*a*); 1973 s 54.
s 75(1A)		s 353(3)(*a*)	Added 1974 s 19(1)(*b*).
s 75(2)		s 353(3)(*b*)	
s 75(3)–(5)		—	Rep 1974 Sch 14 Pt I.
s 75(6)		s 353(1)(*b*)	Subst 1976 s 49(5).
s 75(7)		s 353(1)	Am 1974 s 19(1)(*d*).
s 75(8)		—	Unnecessary.
s 76	Securities.	—	Rep 1987 Sch 16 Pt VII.
s 77(1)	Share options.	s 135(2), (5)	
s 77(2), (3)		s 135(5)	
s 78	—	—	Rep 1974 Sch 14 Pt II.
s 79(1)	Share incentive schemes.	s 138(1)	
s 79(1A), (1B)		s 139(1), (2)	Added 1984 s 41(1).
s 79(2)(*a*)		—	Rep 1974 Sch 14 Pt II.
s 79(2)(*b*)		s 138(2)(*a*)	Rep in part 1974 Sch 14 Pt II.
s 79(2)(*bb*)		s 138(3)(*b*)	Added 1984 s 40(1).
s 79(2)(*c*)		s 138(3)(*a*), (5)	Subst 1973 Sch 8 §4(1)(*a*).
s 79(2A)		s 138(6)	Added 1973 Sch 8 §4(1)(*b*).
s 79(2B)		s 138(7)	Added 1984 s 40(2).
s 79(3)		s 138(2)(*a*), (12)	Rep in part 1974 Sch 14 Pt II.
s 79(4)		s 138(1)(*a*)	
s 79(4A)		s 139(14)	Added 1984 s 40(3).
s 79(5)		s 138(8)	
s 79(5A), (5B)		s 138(10), (11)	Added 1986 s 26(3).
s 79(6)		s 138(9)	Am 1973 Sch 8 §4(1)(*c*); 1986 s 26(4).
s 79(6A)		s 139(13)	Added 1986 s 26(5).
s 79(7)		s 138(1)(*b*)	
s 79(8)		s 138(2)(*a*)	
s 79(9)		Sch 29	Am CGTA 7.
s 79(10), (11)		s 139(3), (4)	
s 79(12)		—	Unnecessary.
s 80	Sale & lease-back of land.	s 780	
s 81(1)	Premiums for and duration of leases.	s 34(8)	
s 81(2)(*a*), (*b*)		s 38(1)	
s 81(2)(*c*)		s 38(2), (3), (4)	
s 81(2)(*d*)		s 38(6)	
s 81(3)		s 24(1)	
s 81(4)		s 24(3), (4)	
s 81(5)		s 38(5), Sch 29	
s 81(6)		Sch 30	Partly spent.
s 82	Appeals against certain determinations.	s 42	
s 83	Double taxation relief.	s 790(6)–(10)	
s 84(1)	Advance corporation tax.	s 14(1)	Partly spent.
s 84(2)		s 14(3)	Am 1986 s 17(1).
s 84(3)		s 238(1)	
s 84(4)		s 14(2)	
s 84(5)		s 238(5)	

Dest. Tables

FA 1972	Subject Matter	Re-enacted in TA 1988	Remarks
s 85(1), (2)	Set-off of ACT against liability to corporation tax.	s 239(1), (2)	Am 1987(2) s 74(2).
s 85(3)		s 239(3)	Am 1984 ss 52(1), 53(2); 1987(2) s 74(2).
s 85(4), (5)		s 239(4), (5)	
s 85(6)		s 239(6)	Am 1974 Sch 7 §3(1); 1987(2) s 74(2).
s 85(7)		s 239(7)	Partly spent.
s 86	Tax credits.	s 231	
s 87(1)	Schedule F.	—	Unnecessary.
s 87(2), (3)		s 20(1), (2)	
s 87(4)		—	Spent.
s 87(5), (6)		s 233	Rep in part 1984 Sch 23 Pt VI.
s 88(1)	Franked investment income.	s 238(1)	
s 88(2)		—	Unnecessary.
s 89(1)–(5)	Calculation of ACT.	s 241	
s 89(6)		s 238(1)	Partly unnecessary.
s 90(1)	Set-off of losses etc against franked investment income.	—	Unnecessary.
s 90(2), (3)		s 244	Am 1973 Sch 13 §9.
s 91(1), (2)	Group income.	—	Spent.
s 91(3)		s 248(1), (6), 828	
s 91(4)		—	Effect preserved by IA 1978 s 17(2)(*b*).
s 92(1)	Setting of company's surplus ACT against subsidiary's liability.	s 240(1)	Am 1973 Sch 13 §2.
s 92(2)		s 240(2)	Am and rep in part 1973 Sch 13 §§3, 4.
s 92(3)		s 240(3)	
s 92(3A)		s 240(4)	Added 1973 Sch 13 §5.
s 92(4)		s 240(5)	
s 92(5)		s 240(6)	Am 1973 Sch 13 §6.
s 92(6), (7)		s 240(7), (8)	
s 92(7A)		s 240(9)	Added 1982 s 55.
s 92(8)		s 240(10)	Am 1973 Sch 13 §7.
s 92(9)–(11)		s 240(11), (13)	Added 1973 Sch 13 §8.
s 93	—	—	Rep 1987(2) Sch 9 Pt I.
s 94	Close companies.	—	Unnecessary.
s 95	Small companies' relief.	s 13	Am 1973 Sch 14 §2; 1983(2) s 2(2); 1987(2) s 74(4).
s 96	—	—	Rep 1984 Sch 23 Pt V.
s 97	—	—	Unnecessary.
s 98(1), (3), (4)	Tax credits for non-UK residents.	s 232	
s 98(2)		s 788	
s 99	—	—	Spent.
s 100(1)	Double taxation relief.	Pt XVIII	
s 100(2)		—	Spent.
s 100(3)–(6)		s 797(1)–(4)	Am 1984 s 53; 1986 s 49(2); rep in part 1986 Sch 23 Pt V; 1987(2) s 77(2).
s 100(6A)		s 797(5)	Added 1986 s 49(3); am 1987(2) s 77(2).
s 100(7), (8)		—	Spent.
s 101	Calculation of ACT etc on change of ownership of company.	s 245	Am 1987(2) s 74(5).
s 102	Rectification of excessive set-off of ACT or tax credit.	s 252	Am 1987(2) s 88(5)–(7).
s 103(1)–(3)	Charge of ACT at old rates.	—	Rep 1986 Sch 23 Pt V.
s 103(4), (5)		s 246(5), (6)	Am 1973 Sch 14 §5; 1987(2) s 74(5).
s 104	Liability to account for income tax.	s 350(4)	
s 105	—	—	Unnecessary.

FA 1972	Subject Matter	Re-enacted in TA 1988	Remarks
s 106	—	—	Unnecessary.
s 107	Amendments.		See destinations of enactments amended; rep in part 1986 Sch 23 Pt V.
s 108	Power to modify 1972 Sch 14, 20 or 21.	s 253, 350(4)–(7)	
s 109	—	—	Spent.
s 110(1)–(4)	Interpretation.	s 238(1)–(4), 231(5)	
s 110(5)		—	Spent.
s 111(1)	—	—	Unnecessary.
s 111(2)	Relationship between provisions about ACT and corporation tax.	s 14(4)	
s 111(3)		—	Spent.
s 111(3)		—	Spent.
s 124(1)	Payments to ECGD.	s 88	Rep in part CGTA 8.
s 124(2)(*a*)		s 584(5)	
s 124(2)(*b*)		s 441(9)	
Sch 9	Relief for payment of interest.		Am 1974 Sch 1 §§1, 2; 1983 s 17(5).
para 1		s 354(1)	
para 2		s 367(2)	
para 3, 4		s 354(2)	
para 5		s 354(1), (3)	Am 1974 Sch 1 §1.
para 5A		s 354(1), 367(1)	Added 1974 Sch 1 §3.
para 6		s 354(4)	
para 7		s 354(7)	
para 8		s 355(5)	
para 9		s 367(1)	
para 10–13		s 359(1)–(4)	Am 1974 Sch 1 §1.
para 14		s 367(3)	
para 15		s 367(4)	Am 1974 Sch 1 §1.
Sch 10	Relief for interest: supplementary provisions.		
para 1–6		s 368	
para 7		s 366(1)	Am 1974 Sch 1 §25(1).
para 8, 9		s 366(2), (3)	
para 10, 11		—	Spent.
Sch 11	Amendments.		Rep in part 1974 Sch 14 Pt I; see destinations of enactments amended.
Sch 12	Share option and share incentive schemes.		
Pts I to VI		—	Rep 1974 Sch 14 Pt II.
Pt VII para 1, 2		—	Rep 1974 Sch 14 Pt II.
para 3(1)		s 139(5)	
para 3(2)		s 139(5)	Added 1984 s 41(2).
para 3A		s 139(6)	Added 1984 s 40(4).
para 4		—	Rep 1974 Sch 14 Pt II.
para 5		Sch 40	
para 6		s 139(11), 140(3)	Rep in part 1974 Sch 14 Pt II; am CGTA 7.
para 7		s 140(1)	Rep in part 1974 Sch 14 Pt II.
para 8		s 139(12)	
para 9		s 140(2)	Rep in part 1974 Sch 14 Pt II.
Sch 13	Leases.		
para 1–5		—	Spent.
para 6, 7		Sch 30 §3	
Sch 14	Collection of ACT.	Sch 13	
Sch 15	Loss relief.		
Pt I		s 242, 243	
Pt II		s 247	
Sch 16	Apportionment of income etc of close companies.		
para 1(1)		s 423(1)(*a*)	Am 1987(2) s 61(3).
para 1(2)		s 424(1)(*a*), 423(7)	Am 1974 Sch 1 §26.
para 1(3)		s 424(1)(*b*)	
para 1(4)		s 423(3)	Am 1987(2) s 61(3).
para 1(5)		s 423(6)	

FA 1972	Subject Matter	Re-enacted in TA 1988	Remarks
Sch 16 (contd)			
para 2		s 424(2)	
para 3(1)		s 423(1)(*b*)	Am 1980 s 56(4); 1987(2) s 61(4).
para 3(2)		s 424(3)	
para 3(3)		s 423(2), 424(1)	
para 3A(1)		s 423(1)(*c*)	Para 3A added 1974 Sch 1 §26; am 1987(2)s 61(1).
para 3A(2)		s 424(4)	
para 3A(3)		s 424(6)	
para 3A(4)		s 423(4)	
para 3A(5)		s 423(2), 424(1)	
para 3A(6)		s 423(5)	
para 3A(7)		s 424(5)	
para 4	Manner of apportionment.	s 425	
para 5(1)–(3)	Consequences of apportionment: income tax.	s 426	Rep in part 1980 Sch 20 Pt V.
para 5(4)		s 427(1)	Am 1984 s 32.
para 5(5)		s 427(2)	
para 5(5A)		s 427(3)	Added 1980 s 56(5); am 1986 s 32(3).
para 5(6)		s 427(4)	Am 1973 Sch 9 §1(2).
para 5(6A)		s 427(5)	Added 1973 Sch 9 §1(3); 1978 Sch 2 §16(*b*); rep in part 1980 Sch 20 Pt V; 1984 Sch 23 Pt VI.
para 5(7)		s 428(1)	Am 1974 Sch 1 §26; rep in part 1973 Sch 22 Pt II.
para 5(8)		s 428(2)	
para 6	Payment and collection of income tax.	s 429	Am 1976 s 45; 1980 s 61(4).
para 7(1)	Consequences of apportionment: ACT.	s 430(1)	
para 7(2)–(5)		s 430(3)–(6)	
para 7(6)(*a*)		s 430(7)(*a*)	
para 7(6)(*aa*)		s 430(7)(*b*)	Added 1975(2) s 46(6).
para 7(6)(*b*)		s 430(7)(*c*)	
para 7(7)		—	Rep 1973 Sch 22 §2.
para 7(8), (9)		s 430(8), (9)	
para 8(1)	''Relevant income''.	Sch 19 §1(1)	Am 1980 Sch 9 §1.
para 8(2)		Sch 19 §1(2)	
para 8(3)–(5)		Sch 19 §1(3)–(5)	Added 1978 Sch 5 §1.
para 9(1)		Sch 19 §2(1)	
para 9(2)		Sch 19 §2(2)	Subst 1980 Sch 9 §2.
para 9(3)		Sch 19 §2(3)	Am 1978 s 35(1).
para 9(4)		Sch 19 §2(4)	Am 1978 s 35(2).
para 9(5), (6)		Sch 19 §2(5), (6)	
para 10(1)	Distributions and distributable income.	Sch 19 §3(1), (2)	
para 10(2)		Sch 19 §4(1)	Am 1980 Sch 9 §3.
para 10(3)		Sch 19 §4(2)	Am 1978 s 35(3); 1980 s 44(2).
para 10(4), (4A)		Sch 19 §5(1), (2)	Subst and added 1980 Sch 9 §4.
para 10(5)		Sch 19 §5(3)	Am 1980 Sch 9 §5.
para 10(6)		Sch 19 §5(4)	
para 10(7)		Sch 19 §6(1)	
para 10(8)		Sch 19 §6(2)	Am 1985 Sch 25 §9.
para 10(9)		Sch 19 §6(3)	Added 1980 Sch 9 §6; am1987 Sch 15 §4.
para 10A		Sch 19 §3(3)–(5)	Added 1973 Sch 9 §3.
para 11	Trading company.	Sch 19 §7	
para 12(1)		Sch 19 §8(1)	Am 1974 Sch 9 §4; rep in part 1987 Sch 16 Pt VII.
para 12(2)		Sch 19 §8(2)	
para 12(2A)		Sch 19 §8(3)	Added 1973 Sch 9 §4.
para 12(2B)		Sch 19 §8(4)	Added 1982 s 56(2).
para 12(3)		Sch 19 §8(5)	
para 12A		Sch 19 §9	Added 1978 Sch 5 §2.
para 13		Sch 19 §10	Am 1980 Sch 9 §7.

FA 1972	Subject Matter	Re-enacted in TA 1988	Remarks
Sch 16 (contd)			
para 14		Sch 19 §11	
para 14A		—	Rep 1985 Sch 27 Pt X.
para 15–18	Procedure.	Sch 19 §13–16	Am 1987(2) s 61(5).
para 19		Sch 19 §17	Am 1976 s 44(3).
para 20		Sch 19 §18	Am 1987(2) s 61(6).
Sch 17	Close companies.		
paras 1, 3, 5, 7	Amendments.		See destinations of enactments amended.
paras 2, 4, 6		—	Spent.
para 7	Commencement.	—	Spent.
Sch 18	Insurance companies.		
para 1		s 76(2)–(4)	
para 2(1)		—	Rep 1984 Sch 23 Pt V.
para 2(2)		—	Spent.
para 2(3)		s 434(3)	
para 2(4)		s 434(6)	Am 1987(2) s 75(1)(*b*).
para 2(5)		s 434(8)	
para 3		s 437(4)	
para 4(1)		s 438(4)	
para 4(2)		s 438(5), (6)	
para 4(3)		—	Spent.
para 4(4)		—	Spent.
para 5		s 436(3)(*e*), 445(2)(*a*), 449(2)	
para 6		s 447(4)	
Sch 19		—	Spent.
Sch 20	Collection of income tax on payments which are not distributions.	Sch 16	
Sch 21	Returns of non-qualifying distributions.	s 234(5)–(9)	
Sch 22	Meaning of ''distribution''.		
para 1		s 209(2)(*b*)	
para 2(1)		s 209(2)(*c*)	
para 2(2)		s 209(8)	
para 3(1)		s 209(2)(*e*)(ii)	
para 3(2)		s 209(2)(*d*)	
para 3(3)		s 209(3)	
para 4(1), (2)		s 209(6)	
para 4(3)		s 209(5)	
para 5(1)		—	Spent.
para 5(2), (3)		s 210(3)	
para 6		s 211(1), (2)	
para 7		—	Spent.
para 8(1), (2)		s 254(6), (7)	
para 9		s 254(8)	
para 10(1)–(3)		s 254(1)–(4)	
para 10(4)		s 254(1)	
para 11		—	Unnecessary.
Sch 23	Transitional provisions.		
paras 1–17		—	Spent.
para 18	References to gross distributions etc.	s 255	Am 1976 s 46(1).
para 19		—	Spent.

FINANCE ACT 1973
(c 51)

FA 1973	Subject Matter	Re-enacted in TA 1988	Remarks
s 10, 11	IT & surtax rates.	—	Spent.
s 12(1)	Personal reliefs.	—	Rep 1974 Sch 14 Pt VI.
s 12(2)		s 263	Rep in part 1979(2) Sch 5 Pt II.
s 13	—	—	Rep 1977 Sch 9 Pt VI.

Dest. Tables

FA 1973	Subject Matter	Re-enacted in TA 1988	Remarks
s 14	Retirement benefits.	s 189	Am 1987(2) Sch 2 §3.
s 15			Spent.
s 16(1)–(6)	Additional rate tax on certain income from discretionary trusts.	s 686	Am 1986 s 47(4)(*a*).
s 16(7)		s 677(2)(*h*), (6)	
s 16(8)		Sch 29	
s 17(1)	Payments under discretionary trusts.	s 687(1), 348(3), 349(1)	
s 17(2)		s 687(2)	
s 17(3)		s 687(3)	Am 1975(2) s 34(6); 1984 s 100(2); 1985 Sch 23 §8(3); 1974 Sch 7 §8.
s 17(4)		s 352(1)	
s 17(5)		s 687(4)	
s 18	Discretionary trusts.	s 809	
s 19		—	Unnecessary; rep in part 1974 Sch 14 Pt II.
s 20		—	Rep 1974 Sch 14 Pt II.
s 21		—	Spent.
s 22(1)–(5)	Distribution to exempt funds etc.	s 235	
s 22(6)		—	Unnecessary.
s 23	Bonus issues: disallowance of reliefs.	s 237	
s 24	Group income.	s 247(5)	
s 25	—	—	Unnecessary.
s 26(1)	Certificates of deposit.	s 56(1)–(3)	Am 1975(2) s 50.
s 26(2)		s 398	
s 26(3), (4)		s 56(5), (6)	
s 27	Discounted Treasury securities.	s 126	
s 28(1)	Group relief.	—	Unnecessary.
s 28(2)–(5)		s 413(7)–(10)	Am 1981 s 40(5).
s 28(6)(*a*)		—	Rep 1981 Sch 19 Pt VI.
s 28(6)(*b*)		—	Spent.
s 28(7)		s 413	
s 29	Group relief.	s 410(1)–(6)	Am 1981 s 40(6); 1973 s 32(6).
s 30	Leasing contracts.	s 395	
s 31(1)–(5)	Partnerships involving companies.	s 116	
s 31(6)–(8)		—	Rep 1987 Sch 16 Pt VII.
s 31(9)		s 834(1), 116(7)	
s 32(5)	Amends TMA s 98.	Sch 29	
s 32(6)		s 116, 240(11), 395, 410, Sch 18	
s 33	—	—	Unnecessary.
s 34	—	—	Unnecessary.
s 35	Election for herd basis.	Sch 5 §12	
s 36(1)		s 513(1)	
s 36(2)		—	Spent.
s 37	—	—	Rep CGTA 8.
s 38(6)	Territorial sea etc.	s 830(5)	
s 39	—	—	Unnecessary.
s 40(1)	Overseas life assurance companies.	s 811	
s 40(2)–(6)		s 448	
s 40(7)		s 431	
s 43	Chevening House.	s 147	Am 1977 Sch 8 §4.
s 51	—	—	Rep CGTA 8.
s 52	Charities.	—	Spent.
s 53(1)	Overseas pensions.	s 614(3), 615(2)(*d*), (4), Sch 29	
s 53(2)		s 615(2)(*e*)	Rep in part 1975 Sch 13 Pt I.
s 53(3)–(5)		s 616	
s 53(6)–(8)		—	Rep 1975 Sch 13 Pt I.
s 53(9)		s 616	Rep in part 1975 Sch 13 Pt I.
s 54	The Stock Exchange.	Passim	

FA 1973	Subject Matter	Re-enacted in TA 1988	Remarks
Sch 8	Share option and share incentive schemes.		
para 1		s 138(2)	Am 1974 s 20(2).
para 2		s 138(4)(*b*)	
para 3		s 138(4)(*a*)	
para 4(1)		s 138(3)(*a*), (5)	
para 4(2)		—	Unnecessary.
para 5		s 139(7)	Rep in part 1974 Sch 14 Pt II.
para 6		s 139(8)	
para 7		s 139(9)	Rep in part 1974 Sch 14 Pt II; am 1982 s 41.
paras 8–34		—	Rep 1974 Sch 14 Pt II.
para 35		s 139(11), (12), 140	
para 36		—	Unnecessary.
Sch 9	Close companies.		
Pt I	Amendments.		See destinations of enactments amended.
Pt II	Transitionals.	—	Spent.
Sch 10	Exempt funds.	s 236	
Sch 11	Amendments.		See destinations of enactments amended.
Sch 12	Group relief.		
Pt I		Sch 18	Am 1987 Sch 15 §5.
Pt II			
paras 8, 9		—	Spent.
paras 10, 11		Sch 30	Partly spent.
Sch 13, 14	Amendments.		See destinations of enactments amended.
Sch 15	Territorial sea etc.		
paras 1, 3		Sch 29	
Sch 16	Underwriters.		
para 1		s 457	
para 2		s 450(1)	
paras 3–5		s 450(3), (4), (6)	
paras 6, 7		Sch 29	
paras 8–14	Amendments.		See destinations of enactments amended.
para 15		—	Rep CGTA 8.
para 16		s 450(2)	
para 17(1)(*a*)		s 451(1)(*a*), Sch 29	
para 17(1)(*b*)		s 451(4)	
para 17(1)(*c*)		s 451(1)(*b*), Sch 29	
para 17(1)(*d*)		Sch 29	
para 17(1)(*e*)		s 451(1)(*c*)	
para 17(2)		s 828	
Sch 16A	Underwriters: assessment and collection of tax	Sch 19A	Inserted 1988, s 58(4)(*b*) and Sch 5.
Sch 21 paras 6–9	Amendments.		See destinations of enactments amended.

FINANCE ACT 1974
(c 30)

FA 1974	Subject Matter	Re-enacted in TA 1988	Remarks
s 7–13	IT, CT & ACT rates.	—	Spent; rep in part 1984 Sch 23 Pt V.
s 14	—	—	Spent; rep in part 1975(2) Sch 14 Pt IV; 1980 Sch 20 Pt VI; 1977 Sch 9 Pt IV.
s 15	—	—	Rep 1984 Sch 23 Pt VI.

Dest. Tables

FA 1974	Subject Matter	Re-enacted in TA 1988	Remarks
s 16(1)	Annuities.	s 628(1)	Rep in part 1984 Sch 23 Pt VI.
s 16(2)		s 628(2)	
s 16(2A)		s 628(3)	Added 1982 s 39(1).
s 16(3), (4)		s 628(4), (5)	Added 1980 s 34(3).
s 18	—	—	Rep 1976 Sch 15 Pt III.
s 19(1)(*a*)	Relief for payment of interest.	s 353(1)	
s 19(1)(*b*)		s 353(3)(*a*)	
s 19(1)(*c*)		—	Spent.
s 19(1)(*d*)		s 353(1)	
s 19(2)		—	Unnecessary.
s 19(3)–(7)		—	Spent.
s 20(1)		—	Spent.
s 20(2)		s 138(4)(*a*)	
s 21(1)	Amends Sch E.	s 19	
s 21(2)		—	Rep 1977 Sch 9 Pt VI.
s 21(3)	Amends 1970 s 188(2).	s 188(3)	Partly spent.
s 21(4)	Amends 1970 Sch 8.	Sch 11 §10	
s 21(5)		—	Spent.
s 21(6)	Amends 1970 Sch 12.	s 192(1)	
s 21(7)	Amends 1970(F) s 24(2).	s 596(2)	
s 21(8)		—	Unnecessary.
s 21(9)		—	Spent.
s 22(1)	Foreign pensions.	s 65(2)	
s 22(2)		—	Rep 1986 Sch 23 Pt V.
s 22(3)		s 196	
s 22(4), (5)		—	Spent.
s 23(1)	Income from foreign trade etc.	s 65(3)	
s 23(2)(*a*)		s 391(1)	
s 23(2)(*b*)		Sch 29	
s 23(3)		—	Rep 1984 Sch 23 Pt VII.
s 23(4)		s 391(2)	Am 1984 s 30.
s 23(5)		—	Spent.
s 23(6)(*a*)		Sch 29	
s 23(6)(*b*)		s 65(3)	
s 23(7)		—	Spent.
s 25	—	—	Rep 1975(2) Sch 14 Pt IV.
s 26(1)	Life insurance companies.	s 435(1)	
s 26(2), (3)		s 435(2), (3)	Am CGTA 7; 1987(2) s 75(2), (3).
s 26(4)		s 435(1)	
s 26(5)		—	Unnecessary.
s 27(1)(*a*)	Friendly societies.	s 461(1)	
s 27(1)(*b*)		s 461(3)	
s 27(2)		s 461(2)	
s 27(3)–(7)		s 461(6)–(10)	Am 1985 s 41(10); 1987 Sch 15 §6.
s 27(8)		s 466(1), (2), (5)	
s 27(9)		—	Spent.
s 28(1)(*a*)	Trade unions.	s 467(4)(*a*)	
s 28(1)(*b*)		s 467(2)	
s 28(2)		—	Spent.
s 30(1)	Transactions in deposits without certificate or in debts.	s 56(1), (2), (6)	CGTA 7.
s 30(2)		s 398, 56(5), (6)	
s 30(3)		—	Spent.
s 31–33	—	—	Rep CGTA 8.
s 34	—	—	Rep 1978 Sch 13 Pt IV.
s 35	—	—	Rep 1980 Sch 20 Pt VIII.
s 36	CT.	s 8	
s 37(1)	CT.	s 342	
s 37(2)		—	Rep 1986 Sch 23 Pt V.
Sch 1	Relief for payment of interest.		
para 1		s 354(1), 359, 367(4)	
para 2		s 354(1)	
para 3		s 354(1), 367(1)	

FA 1974	Subject Matter	Re-enacted in TA 1988	Remarks
Sch 1 (contd)			
para 4(1)–(3)		s 355(1)–(3)	
para 4(4)		s 367(1)	
para 4A(1), (2)		s 356(1), (2)	Para 4A added 1977 s 36(1).
para 4A(3)		s 356(3)(*a*)	
para 4A(3A)		s 356(3)(*b*)	Added 1984 s 25.
para 4A(3B)		s 356(5)	Added 1984 s 25.
para 4A(4), (5)		s 356(4)	
para 4A(6)		s 356(6)	
para 4A(7)		—	Unnecessary.
para 5(1)		s 357(1)	Am 1977 Sch 8 §8(2); 1984 s 22(1)(*a*), (*b*).
para 5(1A)		s 367(5)	Added 1984 s 22(1)(*c*).
para 5(2)(*a*)		s 357(1)	
para 5(2)(*b*), (*c*)		—	Spent.
para 5(3)		s 357(2)	Am 1977 Sch 8 §8(3).
para 5(4), (5)		s 357(3), (5)	
para 5(6)		s 357(6)	Added 1982 s 25(2).
para 6(1)		s 354(5)	
para 6(1A)		s 357(4)	Added 1984 s 22(2).
para 6(2)		s 354(6)	
para 7		s 355(4)	Am 1977 Sch 8 §9.
para 8		s 358	Subst 1977 Sch 8 §10.
para 9(1)		s 360(1)	Am 1982 s 49(2).
para 9(2)		—	Spent.
para 10(1)		s 360(2)	Am 1982 s 49(3).
para 10(1)(*a*)		s 360(2)(*a*)	
para 10(1)(*b*)		—	Rep 1980 Sch 20 Pt IX.
para 10(1)(*c*)		s 360(2)(*b*)	Am 1980 s 28(1)(*b*).
para 10(1)(*d*)		s 360(2)(*c*)	Added 1980 s 28(1)(*c*).
para 10(2)		s 360(3)	Added 1982 s 49(3).
para 10A(1)		s 361(1)	Added 1981 s 25(3).
para 10A(2)		s 363(5)	Added 1981 s 25(3).
para 10B		s 361(2)(*b*)–(*d*)	Added 1981 s 25(3).
para 10C		s 361(3)	Added 1983 s 24(1).
para 10D(1)		s 361(4)	Added 1983 s 24(1).
para 10D(2)		s 361(5)	Am 1984 s 24(2).
para 10D(3)		s 361(6)	Am 1984 s 24(3).
para 10D(3A)		s 361(7)	Added 1984 s 24(4).
para 10D(4)		s 361(8)	
para 11(1)		s 362(1)	
para 11(2)		—	Spent.
para 12		s 362(2)	Am 1981 s 25(2).
para 13		s 363(1)	
para 14(1)		s 363(2)	Am 1981 s 25(4); 1983 s 24(2)(*a*); rep in part 1984 Sch 23 Pt V.
para 14(2)		s 363(3)	
para 15		s 363(4)	Am 1981 s 25(4); 1983 s 24(2)(*b*).
para 16		s 360(4)	
para 17(1)		s 364(1)	Am 1975 Sch 12 §19(2); 1986 s 100(1).
para 17(2)		—	Spent.
para 18		s 364(2)	
para 19		—	Rep 1975 Sch 13 Pt I.
para 20		s 364(3)	Subst 1975 Sch 12 §19(3).
para 21		s 364(4)	Am 1975 Sch 12 §19(4).
para 22		—	Rep 1975 Sch 13 Pt I.
para 23		s 367(2)–(4)	
para 24		s 365	Am 1984 s 22(3).
para 25(1)		s 366(1)	
para 25(2)		—	Spent.
para 26–29	Amendments.	—	See destinations of enactments amended and notes on clauses.
Sch 2	Foreign emoluments.		
paras 1, 2		—	Rep 1977 Sch 9 Pt VI.
para 3		s 192(4)	Rep & am 1984 s 30(9)–(12), Sch 23 Pt VII.
para 4		s 192(2)	

Dest. Tables

FA 1974	Subject Matter	Re-enacted in TA 1988	Remarks
Sch 2 (contd)			
para 5		s 192(5)	
para 6		s 192(3)	
Sch 12	Amendments.		
paras 7–12			See destinations of enactments amended.

FRIENDLY SOCIETIES ACT 1974
(c 46)

FSA 1974	Subject Matter	Re-enacted in TA 1988	Remarks
s 64	Limits on benefits.	s 464, Sch 15 §6(2)	Am 1985 s 41(1), (2); 1980 s 57(2)(*b*); FSA 1984 s 2; rep in part FSA 1984 s 2(5).
Sch 9 para 23	Amendments.	s 466	

FINANCE ACT 1975
(c 7)

FA 1975	Subject Matter	Re-enacted in TA 1988	Remarks
s 5	IT rates.	—	Spent.
s 6	Pension funds.	s 476(7)	Am 1987(2) s 39(4).
s 7	Life policies.	s 268	Am 1976 Sch 4 §19(1); 1984 s 72(5).
s 8		s 269, 832	Am 1976 Sch 4 §19(2); 1984 s 72(5).
s 9(1)–(4)		s 270	Am 1976 Sch 4 §19(3); rep in part 1976 Sch 15 Pt IV.
s 9(5)		—	Unnecessary.
s 10		—	Unnecessary.
s 11		—	Rep 1981 Sch 19 Pt VI.
s 12	Borrowing in foreign currency.	s 581(4)	Am 1987 Sch 15 §7.
s 16	Trade unions.	—	Spent.
s 17(1)	Sales at undervalue etc.	s 773(3)	
s 17(2)		s 770(1)(*a*)	
s 17(3)–(8)		s 772	
s 17(9)		Sch 29	
Sch 1	Life policies.	s 272	
Sch 2	Qualifying policies.		
para 1		Sch 15 §21	Am 1987 Sch 15 §7.
para 1A		Sch 15 §24	Added 1984 Sch 15 Pt I.
para 2(1), (2)		Sch 15 §22	
para 3		Sch 15 §19	
para 4(1)		—	Unnecessary.
para 4(2)		Sch 15 §1(1)	
para 4(3)		Sch 15 §1(5)	
para 4(4)		Sch 15 §1(6)	
para 4(5)–(8)	Amendments.		See destinations of enactments amended.
para 5		Sch 15 §17(4)	
para 6		s 274	
para 7		Sch 15 §8	Am SI 1979/1576; 1976 Sch 4 §19(4).
para 8		—	Unnecessary.
para 9(1)–(4)	Amendments.		See destinations of enactments amended.
para 9(5)–(9)		s 546	

FA 1975	Subject Matter	Re-enacted in TA 1988	Remarks
Sch 2 (contd)			
paras 10–14	Amendments.		See destinations of enactments amended.
para 15		s 539(4)	
para 16(1)		s 548(1), 271(1)	
para 16(2)		s 548(2)	
para 16(3)		s 548(3)(*a*), 271(2)(*a*)	
para 16(4)		s 548(4)	
para 17		s 547(6)	
para 18		s 550(5)	
para 19		s 549	Am 1975(2) s 40; 1978 Sch 2 §18; rep in part 1980 Sch 20 Pt V; 1984 Sch 23 Pt VI.
para 20		s 552(3)–(5)	
Sch 12			
para 16		s 699	
para 19		s 364(1), (3), (4)	

OIL TAXATION ACT 1975
(c 22)

OTA 1975	Subject Matter	Re-enacted in TA 1988	Remarks
s 13(1)	Taxation relating to oil extraction activities etc.	s 492(1)	
s 13(2)		s 492(2), (3)	Am 1978 s 30(7)(*d*); 1984 s 79(5).
s 13(2A)		s 492(4)	Added 1982 s 136(1).
s 13(3)		s 492(5), (6)	Am 1984 s 79(5).
s 13(4)		s 492(7)	
s 13(5)		s 492(8)	Am 1984 s 79(5).
s 13(6)		—	Spent.
s 14(1)–(4)	Valuation of oil.	s 493(1)–(3)	Am 1985 s 53; 1987 Sch 11 §6; rep in part 1987 Sch 16 Pt X.
s 14(4A)		s 493(4)	Added 1985 s 53(1); rep in part 1987 Sch 16 Pt X.
s 14(5)		s 493(5)	Am 1984 s 79(5); 1985 s 53(2).
s 14(6)		s 770(2)(*c*)	
s 15(1)–(3)	Charges on income.	s 494(1)–(3)	Am 1984 s 79(5).
s 15(4)		—	Spent.
s 15(5)		s 494(4)	Added 1982 s 136(2).
s 16	ACT: restrictions on set-off.	s 497	Am 1987 s 46; 1987(2) s 76(2).
s 17(1), (2)	Deduction of PTR.	s 500(1)–(4)	Am 1981 s 120.
s 17(3)		—	Rep 1984 Sch 23 Pt V.
s 17(4)		s 502, 500(5)	
s 18(1)	Interest on PRT.	s 501	
s 18(2)		s 502	
s 19(1)–(3)	Interpretation.	s 502(1)–(3)	
s 19(4)		s 502(4)	Added 1986 s 54(1).
s 20(1)	Miscellany.	s 771	
s 20(2)		s 772(8)	
s 20(3)		—	Unnecessary.
Sch 9	Extension of 1970 s 485.	s 771	Am 1987 Sch 11 §7.

FINANCE (NO 2) ACT 1975
(c 45)

F(No 2)A 1975	Subject Matter	Re-enacted in TA 1988	Remarks
s 25–29	IC, CT & ACT rates.	—	Spent.
s 30	—	—	Rep 1976 Sch 15 Pt III; 1981 Pt VI.
s 31	Amendments.		See destinations of enactments amended.
s 32	—	—	Rep 1976 Sch 15 Pt III.
s 33	—	—	Spent.
s 34(1)–(6)	Stock dividends.	s 249(1)–(6), 687(3)(*b*), 701	
s 34(7)		—	Unnecessary.
s 34(8)		s 251(1)	
s 34(9)–(11)		s 249(7)–(9)	
s 35	—	—	Rep 1976 Sch 15 Pt III.
s 36(1)	Non-cash vouchers.	s 141(1), (2)	Am 1982 s 44(2).
s 36(2)		s 141(3)	Subst 1982 s 44(3).
s 36(2A)		s 141(4)	Added 1981 s 70(2).
s 36(3)		s 141(5)	
s 36(3A)		s 141(6)	Added 1982 s 44(4).
s 36(4)		s 141(7), 144(5)	Added 1982 s 44(5); am CCCPA.
s 36(5)(*a*)		—	Rep 1982 Sch 22 Pt IV.
s 36(5)(*b*)		s 144(3)	Am 1981 s 70(5)(*b*).
s 36(5)(*c*)		s 144(4)(*a*)	
s 36(5)(*d*)		s 144(4)(*b*)	Am 1981 s 70(5)(*b*); rep in part 1981 Sch 19 Pt VI.
s 36(5A)		s 144(1), (2)	Added 1982 s 44(6).
s 36(6)		—	Unnecessary.
s 36A	Credit tokens.	s 142	Added 1981 s 71.
s 36A(1)(*a*)		—	Rep 1982 Sch 22 Pt IV.
s 36A(1)(*b*)		s 142(1)(*a*)	Am 1982 s 45(2).
s 36A(1)(*c*)		s 142(1)(*b*)	Rep in part 1982 Sch 22 Pt IV.
s 36A(2), (3)		s 142(2), (3)	Am 1982 s 45(2).
s 36A(4)		s 142(4)	Subst 1982 s 45(3).
s 36A(4A)		s 142(5)	Added 1982 s 45(3).
s 36A(4B)		s 142(4), 144(5)	Added 1982 s 45(3).
s 36A(5)		s 144(3), (4)	
s 36A(6), (7)		s 144(1), (2)	
s 37(1)–(4)	Cash vouchers.	s 143(1)–(4)	
s 37(5)		s 143(5)	Am 1976 s 71(2).
s 37(6)		s 144(4), (5)	Rep in part 1976 Sch 15 Pt III.
s 37(7)		—	Unnecessary.
s 38(1)–(6)	Agency workers.	s 134(1)–(6)	
s 38(7)		Sch 29	
s 38(8)		s 134(7), Sch 29	
s 38(9), (10)		—	Unnecessary.
s 39	—	—	Rep 1975(2) Sch 14 Pt IV.
s 40	Amendments.	s 549	
s 41	—	—	Rep 1987 Sch 16 Pt VII.
s 42(1)	Insurance companies.	s 440(1)	
s 42(2)		—	Spent.
s 42(3)–(11)		s 440(2)–(10)	Am CGTA 7; 1987 Sch 15 §8.
s 42(12)		—	Spent.
s 43	Oil losses.	Sch 30	
s 44(1)–(3), (6)	Amendments.		See destinations of enactments amended; rep in part 1987 Sch 16 Pt V.
s 47(1)(*a*)	Repayment supplements.	s 824(1)	(Not repealed); rep in part 1987 Sch 16 Pt VII; am 1987/1988.
s 47(1)(*b*)		—	Rep 1987 Sch 16 Pt VII.
s 47(2)		—	Rep 1987 Sch 16 Pt VII.
s 47(3)(*a*)		s 824(2)	
s 47(3)(*b*)		—	Rep 1987 Sch 16 Pt VII.

F(No 2)A 1975	Subject Matter	Re-enacted in TA 1988	Remarks
s 47(4)(*a*), (*c*)		s 824(3)	(Not repealed.)
s 47(4)(*b*)		—	Rep 1987 Sch 16 Pt VII.
s 47(5)–(7)		s 824(4)–(6)	
s 47(8)		s 824(7)	(Not repealed.)
s 47(9)		s 824(8)	
s 47(10)		s 828	
s 47(11), (12)		s 824(9), (10)	(Not repealed.)
s 48(1), (2)	Repayment supplements.	s 825(1), (2)	Am 1987/1988.
s 48(3)		—	Spent.
s 48(4), (5)		s 825(3), (4)	
s 48(6)		s 825(5), 828	
s 48(7)–(9)		s 825(6)–(8)	Rep in part 1987 Sch 16 Pt V.
s 50	Certificates of deposits.	s 56	
s 51		—	Rep 1980 Sch 20 Pt IX.
s 52(1)	Friendly societies.	s 460(5)–(10)	
s 52(2)		s 466(1)	
s 52(3)		—	Spent.
s 52(4)		—	Unnecessary.
s 53	Employers' associations.	s 467(4)(*b*)	
s 68		—	Spent.
s 69(1)	Sub-contractors in the construction industry.	s 559(1), (2)(*a*)	
s 69(2)		s 560(1)	
s 69(3)		s 560(2)(*a*)–(*e*)	Rep in part HCPA 1985 Sch 1.
s 69(3A)		s 560(2)(*f*)	Added 1980 Sch 8 §1.
s 69(3B), (3C)		s 560(3), (4)	Added 1980 Sch 8 §1.
s 69(4), (5)		s 559(3), (4)	Am 1979(2) s 15; 1987 s 23.
s 69(6)		s 566(1)	
s 69(7)		s 559(5)	
s 69(8)		Sch 29	
s 69(9)		s 828	
s 69(10)		s 559(7)	
s 70(1)–(6)		s 561(1)–(3), (6)–(9)	Am 1982 Sch 8 §1, 2; 1987(2) s 93; rep in part 1980 Sch 20 Pt IX.
s 70(7)		s 566(2)	Am 1982 Sch 8 §§3, 4; 1987(2) s 93.
s 70(8)		s 828	
s 70(9)–(11)		s 561(8)–(10)	
s 70(12)		Sch 29	
s 70A		s 561(3), (4)	Added 1982 Sch 8 §5.
s 71(1)		—	Unnecessary.
s 71(2)		—	Rep 1980 Sch 20 Pt IX.
s 71(3)		s 560(5)	Am & rep in part HCPA 1985 Sch 1, 2 §28.
s 71(4)		s 561(4)	
s 71(5)		s 559(7)	Subst 1982 Sch 8 §6.
s 71(6)		s 559(6)	Rep in part Insolvency Act 1985 c 65 Sch 10; Bankruptcy (Scotland) Act 1985 c 66 Sch 8.
s 71(7)		—	Rep 1980 Sch 20 Pt IX.
s 71(8)		s 567(1)	
s 71(9), (10)		s 567(5), (6)	
Sch 8	Stock dividends.		
para 1		s 251(2)–(4)	Rep in part CGTA 8.
para 2(1)		s 251(3)	
para 2(2), (3)		s 251(5), (6)	Am CGTA 7.
para 3(1)–(3)		Sch 19 §12(1)–(3)	
para 3(4)		s 430(2)	
para 4		Sch 19 §12(4)	
para 5		—	Rep CGTA 8.
para 6		s 230	
para 7(1)–(6)		s 250	
para 7(7)		—	Spent.
para 8		Sch 29	

F(No 2)A 1975	Subject Matter	Re-enacted in TA 1988	Remarks
Sch 12	Sub-contractors in the construction industry.		
Pt I			
para 1		s 562(2)	
para 2(1)		s 562(3)	Am 1980 Sch 8 §4(2); 1982 Sch 8 §7; rep in part 1980 Sch 20 Pt IX.
para 2(2), (3)		s 562(5), (6)	Added 1980 Sch 8 §4(3); am 1982 Sch 8 §8.
para 2(4)		s 562(14)	Added 1980 Sch 8 §4(3).
para 2(5)		s 562(7)	Added 1982 Sch 8 §9.
para 2A		s 562(4)	Added 1982 Sch 8 §10.
para 3(1)		s 562(8)	Am 1982 Sch 8 §11.
para 3(1A)		s 562(9)	Added 1982 Sch 8 §12.
para 3(2)		s 562(10)	Am 1982 Sch 8 §13; 1980 Sch 8 §7.
para 3(3)		s 562(11)	Subst 1980 Sch 8 §6(1).
para 4		s 562(12)	Partly spent.
para 5		—	Rep 1982 Sch 22 Pt XI.
para 6		—	Rep 1980 Sch 20 Pt IX.
para 7		s 562(13)	
Pt II			
para 1(1)		s 563(2)	Rep in part 1980 Sch 20; am 1982 Sch 8 §14.
para 1(2), (3)		s 563(3), (4)	Added 1980 Sch 8 §§4, 5.
para 1(4)		s 563(10)	Added 1980 Sch 8 §5.
para 2		s 563(5)–(7)	Am 1980 Sch 8 §6, 7.
para 3		s 563(8)	Partly spent.
para 4		s 563(9)	
Pt III			
para 1, 2		s 564(2)–(4)	Am 1980 Sch 8 §7.
para 3		—	Rep 1982 Sch 22 Pt XI.
para 4		—	Rep 1980 Sch 20 Pt IX.
para 5		s 564(5)	
Pt IV			
para 1		s 565(2)	
para 2(1), (2)		s 565(3), (4)	Am 1982 Sch 8 §15; 1980 Sch 8 §7.
para 2(3)		s 565(9)	
para 3		s 565(5)	Partly spent.
para 4		—	Rep 1982 Sch 22 Pt XI.
para 5		—	Rep 1980 Sch 20 Pt IX.
para 6		s 565(6), (7)	Am & rep in part CCCPA; CCCP(NI); 1987 Sch 15 §8.
para 7		s 565(8)	
Sch 13	Construction operations.		
Pt I		s 567(2), (4)	Am TA 1984 Sch 4 §62.
Pt II		s 567(3)	Am 1980/1171.

FINANCE ACT 1976
(c 40)

FA 1976	Subject Matter	Re-enacted in TA 1988	Remarks
s 24–27	IC, CT & ACT rates.	—	Spent.
s 28	—	—	Rep 1977 Sch 9 Pt VI.
s 29	—	—	Rep 1977 Sch 9 Pt VI; 1979(2) Sch 5 Pt II; 1980 Sch 20 Pt VI; 1982 Sch 22 Pt XI.
s 30(1)	—	—	Rep 1977 Sch 9 Pt VI.
s 30(2)		s 620(2), 621(1), (3), 623(3)	
s 30(3)	—	—	Spent.

FA 1976	Subject Matter	Re-enacted in TA 1988	Remarks
s 31	—	—	Rep 1979(2) Sch 5 Pt VI.
s 32	—	—	Rep 1977 Sch 9 Pt IV; partly spent.
s 33	Certification of life policies.	Sch 15 §22(2)	Rep in part 1987 Sch 16 Pt VII.
s 34	—	—	Unnecessary.
s 35	Loan annuity contracts by elderly.	s 271(2)(*b*)	
s 36(1)–(6)	Amendments.		See destinations of enactments amended.
s 36(7), (8)		s 280	Am 1983 s 15(2).
s 36(9)		s 279(7)	
s 36(10)		s 288(1), (3)	
s 37	—	—	Rep 1981 Sch 19 Pt VII.
s 38(1)–(3)	Interest payments.	s 787	
s 38(4), (5)		—	Spent.
s 44, 45	Amendments.		See destinations of enactments amended.
s 46(1)	ACT.	s 255	
s 46(2)–(6)		—	Spent.
s 47	Levies on insurance companies.	s 76(7)	
s 48	Amendments.		See destinations of enactments amended.
s 49(1)–(3)	DTR: Ireland.	—	Spent & Order in Council saved by IA 1978.
s 49(4)		s 68(4)	
s 49(5)		s 353(1)(*b*)	
s 49(6)		s 68(5)	
s 49(7), (8)		—	Spent.
s 50(1)	DTR.	s 808	
s 50(2)		s 788	
s 50(3)		s 799	
s 60(1)–(3)	Payments in respect of expenses.	s 153	
s 60(4)	Commencement.	—	Unnecessary.
s 61(1)–(3)	Benefits in kind: general charging provision.	s 154	Am 1977 Sch 8 §5; 1981 s 30(3), 72(3).
s 61(4)	Commencement.	—	Unnecessary.
s 62(1)	Exceptions from the general charge.	s 155(1)	Subst 1980 s 48(1).
s 62(2)		—	Rep 1980 s 48(1).
s 62(3)		s 155(2)	
s 62(4)		s 155(3)	Subst 1977 Sch 8 §6; am HCPA Sch 2 §31.
s 62(5)		—	Rep 1977 Sch 8 §6.
s 62(6), (7)		s 155(4), (5)	
s 62(8)		s 155(6)	Subst 1981 s 72.
s 62A(1)–(3)	Scholarships.	s 165(1)–(3)	Added 1983 s 20(1); am 1984 s 31(1).
s 62A(4)		s 165(6)	Added 1983 s 20(1); am 1984 s 31(2).
s 63(1)–(3)	Cash equivalents of benefits in kind.	s 156(1)–(3)	
s 63(3A)		s 156(4)	Added 1980 s 49(2).
s 63(4)		s 156(5)	Added 1980 s 51(1)(*a*).
s 63(5)(*a*)		s 156(6)(*a*)	
s 63(5)(*b*)		—	Rep 1980 Sch 20 Pt IX.
s 63(5)(*c*)		s 156(6)(*b*)	Am 1980 s 49(3).
s 63(6)		s 156(7)	Am 1980 s 51(1)(*b*).
s 63(7)		—	Rep 1977 Sch 9 Pt VI.
s 63(8)		s 156(8)	
s 63A	Expenses connected with living accommodation.	s 163	Added 1977 s 34.
s 64(1)	Cars available for private use.	s 157(1)	
s 64(2)		s 157(2)	Am 1985/1598.
s 64(2A)		s 157(3)	Added 1981 s 68(3); am 1982 s 46(2).
s 64(2B)		—	Spent.
s 64(3)	Commencement.	—	Unnecessary.

FA 1976	Subject Matter	Re-enacted in TA 1988	Remarks
s 64(4)		s 157(4)	Am 1980 s 51(2).
s 64(5)		s 157(5)	
s 64A(1)	Car fuel.	s 158(1)	Subst 1981 s 69(1); am 1982 s 46(4).
s 64A(2)		s 158(2)	Subst 1981 s 69(1); am 1986/702.
s 64A(3)		s 158(3)	Subst 1981 s 69(1).
s 64A(4)		s 158(4)	Subst 1981 s 69(1); partly spent.
s 64A(5), (6)		s 158(5), (6)	Subst 1981 s 69(1).
s 64A(7), (8)		—	Subst 1981 s 69(1); rep 1982 Sch 22 Pt IV.
s 65	Pooled cars.	s 159	
s 66(1)	Beneficial loan arrangements.	s 160(1)	
s 66(2)		s 161(1)	Am 1980 s 50(1).
s 66(3)		s 160(2)	
s 66(4), (5)		s 161(4), (5)	
s 66(6)		s 160(3)	
s 66(7)		s 161(6)	
s 66(8)–(11)		s 160(4)–(7), 161(7)	Partly spent; am 1982 s 26(9)(*a*).
s 66A	Tax paid by employer.	s 164	Added 1983 s 22.
s 67(1)–(12)	Employee shareholdings.	s 162	Am CGTA 7.
s 67(13)		Sch 29	
s 67(14)	Commencement.	—	Unnecessary.
s 68	—	—	Rep 1981 Sch 19 Pt VI.
s 69	''Director's or higher paid employment''.	s 167	Subst 1977 s 35; am 1978 s 23(1); 1981 s 71(2); 1982 s 46(2).
s 70	Notice of nil liability.	s 166(1), (2)	
s 71(1)	—	—	Spent.
s 71(2)	Cash vouchers.	s 143	
s 72(1)–(12)	Interpretation of 1976 Pt III Ch II.	s 168	Am 1980 s 51(3).
Sch 4	Life policies etc.		
para 1		—	Unnecessary.
para 2		Sch 15 §10	
para 2A		Sch 15 §11	Added 1978 Sch 3 §4; am 1982 s 35(1); ICA 1982 Sch 5 §17.
para 3		s 266(1), (2)	
para 4(1)		s 266(4)	
para 4(2)		s 266(8)	
para 5		s 266(5)	Am 1980 s 29(2)(*b*).
para 5A		s 266(9)	Added 1978 Sch 3 §5; am AFA 1981 Sch 3 §1.
para 6		—	Rep 1978 Sch 13 Pt III.
para 7		—	Spent.
para 8–10		Sch 14 §1	
para 11		Sch 14 §2, cl 832	Am 1979/1576; 1982 s 35(2).
para 12		Sch 15 §7	
para 13		Sch 14 §3	Am 1978 Sch 3 §7(1); 1980 s 28(2)(*c*); 1987 Sch 15 §9.
para 14		Sch 14 §4	Am 1978 Sch 3 §8.
para 14A		Sch 14 §5	Partly spent; added 1978 Sch 3 §9.
para 15		Sch 14 §6	
para 16(1), (2)		Sch 14 §7(1), (2)	Am 1978 Sch 3 §10.
para 16(3)		Sch 29	
para 16(4)		Sch 14 §7(3)	
para 17		Sch 29	
para 18–21	Amendments.		See destinations of enactments amended.
Sch 7	Taxation of directors etc in respect of cars.	Sch 6	
Pt I		Pt I	Subst 1987/1897.
Pt II para 1		Pt II §1	Am 1985/1598.

FA 1976	Subject Matter	Re-enacted in TA 1988	Remarks
Sch 7 (contd)			
Pt II para 2		§2	
para 3		§3	Am 1980 s 48(2).
para 4		§4	
para 5		§5	Added 1980 s 48(3).
Sch 8	Taxation of benefit of loans.	Sch 7	
para 1(1)		§1(1), (2)	
para 1(2)		§1(5)	
para 2		§1(3)	
para 3		§1(4)	
para 4		§2	
para 5–7		§3–5	
para 8(1)		§6	Subst 1982 s 26(9)(*b*).
para 8(2)		—	Spent.
para 9–11		§7–9	
para 12–14		§10–12	Added 1983(2) s 4.
Sch 9	Consequential amendments.		
para 3, 4		—	Spent.
para 8, 9		Sch 29	
para 12, 13	Amendments.		See destinations of enactments amended.
para 14(1)		—	Spent.
para 14(2)–(4)		s 166(4)	
para 15, 16		s 418(3), (4)	

FINANCE ACT 1977
(c 36)

FA 1977	Subject Matter	Re-enacted in TA 1988	Remarks
s 17–20	IT, CT & ACT rates.	—	Spent.
s 21	MIR.	—	Rep 1978 Sch 13 Pt III.
s 22(1)	Personal reliefs.	s 257(2)	Rep in part 1978 Sch 13 Pt III; 1979(2) Sch 5 Pt II.
s 22(2), (3)		—	Rep 1980 Sch 20 Pt IX.
s 23(1)	Child benefit etc.	—	Spent.
s 23(2), (5)		—	Spent.
s 23(3), (4)		—	Rep 1979(2) Sch 5 Pt II.
s 24	—	—	Rep 1978 Sch 13 Pt III.
s 25	—	—	Rep 1982 Sch 22 Pt XI.
s 26	—	—	Rep 1980 Sch 20 Pt VI; 1978 Sch 13 Pt III.
s 27	—	—	Rep in part 1980 Sch 20 Pt VII; spent.
s 28	—	—	Rep 1978 Sch 13 Pt III.
s 29	Savings bank interest.	s 325	
s 30	Job release scheme allowances.	s 191	Am Departments (No 2) (Northern Ireland) Order 1982 (SI No 846 (NI 11)) Art 3.
s 31(1)	Earnings from work done abroad.	—	Unnecessary.
s 31(2)		s 192(5)	Rep in part & am 1984 s 30(14).
s 31(3)(*a*)	Amends Sch E.	s 19	
s 31(3)(*b*)	Amends 1970 s 184(3).	s 132(4)	
s 31(3)(*c*)	Amends 1980 Sch 8 § 16.	Sch 11 §10	
s 31(3)(*d*)	—	—	Spent.
s 31(4)	—	—	Spent.
s 32(1)	Expenses in connection with work done abroad.	s 193(2)	
s 32(2)		s 193(3)	Am 1986 s 34(2).
s 32(3)–(5)		s 193(4)–(6)	
s 32(6)		s 194(2)	Added. 1986 s 34(3).
s 32(6A)–(6D)		s 194(3)–(6)	Added 1986 s 34(4).
s 32(7)		s 194(1)	Am 1986 s 34(5).
s 32(7A)–(7C)		s 194(7)–(9)	Added 1986 s 34(6).
s 32(8)		s 193(7), 194(10)	

FA 1977	Subject Matter	Re-enacted in TA 1988	Remarks
s 32(9)		—	Unnecessary.
s 33(1)–(8)	Living accommodation for employees.	s 145	
s 33(9)		—	Unnecessary.
s 33A	Additional charge in certain cases.	s 146	Added 1983 s 21(1).
s 34(1)	Expenses connected with living accommodation.	s 163	
s 34(2)		—	Unnecessary.
s 35(1)	Miscellaneous amendments.	s 167	
s 35(2), (3)		—	Unnecessary.
s 35(4)		s 418	
s 36(1)	Interest relief.	s 356	
s 36(2)		—	Unnecessary.
s 37(1), (2)	Leave travel for services.	s 197	
s 37(3)		—	Unnecessary.
s 38	Maintenance funds.	s 691	Am 1980 s 88(7); 1982 Sch 10 §1; ITA Sch 8; 1987 Sch 15 §10.
s 39	—	—	Spent.
s 45(1)–(4)	Insurance companies.	s 442	Am CGTA 7.
s 45(5)		—	Unnecessary.
s 46(1)–(7)	Conversion of certain securities.	s 473	Am CGTA 7.
s 46(8)		—	Unnecessary.
s 47(1)	Police provident benefits.	s 467(4)(*c*)	
s 47(2)		—	Unnecessary.
s 48	Annual payments.	s 125	
Sch 7	Foreign earnings.		
para 1(1)		s 193(1)	
para 1(2)–(4)		Sch 12 §3	
para 1(5)		—	Spent.
para 2, 3		—	Rep 1984 Sch 23 Pt VII.
para 4(1), (2)		Sch 12 §2(1), (2)	
para 4(3), (4)		—	Rep 1984 Sch 23 Pt VII.
para 4(5)		Sch 12 §2(3)	
para 5		—	Rep 1984 Sch 23 Pt VII.
paras 6–8		Sch 12 §4–6	
para 9		s 132(3)	
para 10		—	Rep 1984 Sch 23 Pt VII.
para 11		Sch 12 §7	
Sch 8	Amendments.		See destinations of enactments amended.

FINANCE ACT 1978
(c 42)

FA 1978	Subject Matter	Re-enacted in TA 1988	Remarks
s 13	IT rates.	—	Spent.
s 14		—	Spent; rep 1980 Sch 20 Pt V.
s 15–17	CT rates.	—	Spent.
s 18	Mortgage interest relief limit.	—	Rep 1979(2) Sch 5 Pt II.
s 19(1)	Personal reliefs.	—	Rep 1979(2) Sch 5 Pt II.
s 19(2)		s 258(2)	
s 19(3), (4)		—	Rep 1979(2) Sch 5 Pt II.
s 19(5)		s 264, 265(3), 284	
s 19(6)		s 265	
s 20	—	—	Rep 1979(2) Sch 5 Pt II; 1980 Sch 20 Pt VI; 1982 Sch 22 Pt XI.
s 21	—	—	Spent.
s 22(1)–(4)	Tax repayments.	s 281(1)–(4)	
s 22(5)		—	Spent: see 1982 s 149(2).
s 22(6)–(9)		s 281(5)–(8)	

FA 1978	Subject Matter	Re-enacted in TA 1988	Remarks
s 22(10)		—	Spent.
s 23	Benefits in kind.	s 167	
s 24		—	Rep 1981 Sch 19 Pt VI.
s 25	—	—	Unnecessary.
s 26(1)–(3)	Annuities.	s 622	Am 1987(2) Sch 2 §4.
s 26(4)		s 657	
s 26(5)		s 431(4)(*a*)	
s 27	—	—	Rep 1984 s 30(2).
s 28(1)–(4)	Farming and market gardening.	s 96(1)–(4)	
s 28(5)		s 96(5)	Rep in part 1981 Sch 19 Pt VII.
s 28(6)–(12)		s 96(6)–(12)	Am 1981 s 35(4).
s 29(1), (2)	Divers and diving supervisors.	s 314	
s 29(4)		—	Spent.
s 30(1)–(6)	Loss relief.	s 381(1)–(6)	
s 30(7)(*a*)		s 382, 734(1)	
s 30(7)(*b*)		s 391(1)	
s 30(7)(*c*)		Sch 29	Am 1987 Sch 15 §11(1).
s 30(7)(*d*)		s 492(2)	
s 30(7)(*e*)		s 279(7)	
s 30(7)(*f*)		—	Spent.
s 30(8)(*a*)		s 383(4)	
s 30(8)(*b*)		s 383(7)(*b*)	
s 30(8)(*c*)		s 383(9)	
s 30(9)		—	Spent.
s 30(10)		s 381(7)	
s 30(11)		—	Spent.
s 31	Commodity futures.	s 399(2)–(4)	Am 1987 Sch 15 §11(2).
s 32(1)	—	—	Unnecessary.
s 32(2)(*a*)		s 37(1)	
s 32(2)(*b*), (*c*)		—	Spent.
s 32(3)(*a*)		s 87(1)(*a*)	
s 32(3)(*b*), (*c*)		—	Spent.
s 32(3)(*d*)		s 87(2)	
s 32(4)		—	Unnecessary.
s 33, 34	—	—	Spent.
s 35	Amendments.		See destinations of enactments amended.
s 36	—	—	Unnecessary.
s 41, 42	—	—	Spent.
s 53(1)	Profit sharing schemes.	s 186(1)	
s 53(2)		s 187(2)	
s 53(3)		s 186(2)	
s 53(4)		Sch 9 §30(4)	
s 53(5)		Sch 29	
s 53(6)		s 186(11), Sch 29	
s 53(7)		Sch 9 §6	
s 53(8)		Sch 29	
s 54(1)	Supplementary provisions.	Sch 9 §2(2)	Am 1986 s 24(3)(*a*).
s 54(1A)		Sch 10 §1(2)	Added 1980 s 46(2).
s 54(2)		Sch 10 §1(1), s 187(2)	
s 54(3)		Sch 10 §1(3)	
s 54(4), (5)		Sch 10 §2	Am 1980 s 46(3); 1986 s 24(3)(*b*).
s 54(6)		s 187(2)	Am 1980 s 46(4); 1985 s 45(2).
s 54(7)		Sch 10 §3	Am 1980 s 46(5); 1985 s 45(3).
s 55(1)–(5)	Disposal of scheme shares.	s 186(4)–(8)	
s 55(6)		s 187(8)	
s 55(7), (8)		s 186(9), (10)	
s 55(9)		s 186(8)	
s 56(1)	Capital receipts.	s 186(3)	Am 1982 s 42(1).
s 56(2)–(5)		Sch 10 §4	
s 56(6)		s 186(12)	Added 1980 s 46(6); subst 1982 s 42(2); am 1985 s 45(4).

FA 1978	Subject Matter	Re-enacted in TA 1988	Remarks
s 57	Company reconstructions etc.	Sch 10 §5	Am CGTA 7.
s 58(1)	Excess shares etc.	Sch 10 §6(1)(*a*), (2)	Am 1982 s 42(3); 1983 s 25(1).
s 58(2)		Sch 10 §6(3)	Am 1982 s 42(3); 1983 s 25(1).
s 58(3)		Sch 10 §6(1)(*b*), (2)	
s 58(4)–(7)		Sch 10 §6(4)–(7)	
s 59(1)	PAYE deduction of tax.	Sch 10 §7(1)	
s 59(1A)		Sch 10 §7(2)	Added 1980 s 46(8).
s 59(2)–(7)		Sch 10 §7(3)–(8)	Am 1987 Sch 15 §11(3).
s 60	Schedule D deductions.	s 85	
s 61(1)	Interpretation.	s 187(2)	Am CGTA 7; 1983 s 25(1); 1982 s 42(3).
s 61(2)		s 187(9)	
s 61(3)		Sch 29	
s 61(4)		s 187(5)	Added 1983 s 25(2).
Sch 2	Amendments		Partly spent; see destinations of enactments.
Sch 3			
para 1		—	Unnecessary.
para 2		s 266(4)	
para 3–10, 13	Amendments.		See destinations of enactments amended.
para 11, 12		s 266(6), (7)	Am 1981 s 33.
Sch 4	—	—	Rep 1984 Sch 23 Pt VIII.
Sch 5	Close companies.	Sch 19 §1, 9	
Sch 9	Profit sharing schemes.		
para 1(1)		Sch 9 §1(1), 2(1)	
para 1(2)		Sch 9 §1(3), (4)	
para 1(3)		Sch 9 §30(1)	
para 1(4)		Sch 9 §30(3)	Am 1983 s 25(1).
para 1(5)		Sch 9 §1(2)	
para 2		Sch 9 §36, 2(3), (4)	Am 1983 s 25(4), (5).
para 3(1)		Sch 9 §3(2)	Am 1983 s 25(6).
para 3(2)		Sch 9 §4, 30(2)	
para 3(3)		Sch 9 §3(3)	
para 4		Sch 9 §5	
para 5		Sch 9 §10	
para 6		Sch 9 §11	Am 1980 s 46(10).
para 7		Sch 9 §12	Am 1986 s 22(1), (4), (5), 24.
para 8		Sch 9 §14	Am 1980 s 46(11); 1986 s 23(2), (3).
para 9		Sch 9 §35(1)	
para 10		Sch 9 §35(2)	
para 11(1), (2), (3)(*a*)		Sch 9 §8, cl 832	
para 11(3)(*b*)		s 187(3)	
para 11(3)(*c*)		—	Rep 1987 Sch 16 Pt V.
para 12		Sch 9 §31	
para 13		Sch 9 §32	Am 1980 s 46(13).
paras 14, 15		Sch 9 §§33, 34	
para 16		s 187(2)	
para 17		s 187(7)	
para 18		s 187(10)	Added 1986 s 24(1).

Capital Gains Tax Act 1979
(c 14)

CGTA 1979	Subject Matter	Re-enacted in TA 1988	Remarks
s 155(5)	Chargeable gains.	s 833(1)	

CREDIT UNIONS ACT 1979
(c 34)

CUA 1979	Subject Matter	Re-enacted in TA 1988	Remarks
s 25(1)	Credit unions.	s 487	

FINANCE (NO 2) ACT 1979
(c 47)

F (No 2) A 1979	Subject Matter	Re-enacted in TA 1988	Remarks
s 5–7	IT & CT rates.	—	Spent.
s 8	Personal reliefs.	—	Spent.
s 9	War service pensions.	s 318	
s 10		—	Spent.
s 11, 12	—	—	Unnecessary.
s 13	—	—	Rep 1981 Sch 19 Pt VII.
s 15	—	—	Spent.
s 16	DTR.	Sch 30	
s 17	—	—	Spent.
Schs 1, 2	Amendments.		See destinations of enactments amended.

FINANCE ACT 1980
(c. 48)

FA 1980	Subject Matter	Re-enacted in TA 1988	Remarks
s 18–21	IT, CT & ACT rates.	—	Spent.
s 22	Personal reliefs.	—	Spent.
s 23	Widow's bereavement allowance.	s 262	Am 1983 s 15(1).
s 24(1)	Indexation.	—	Spent.
s 24(2)(*a*)		s 1(2)(*b*)	
s 24(2)(*b*)		—	Spent.
s 24(3)		s 1(3)	Am & rep in part 1984 Sch 7 §3(5), Sch 23 Pt VI.
s 24(4)		s 1(4)	
s 24(5)		s 257(9)	
s 24(6)	Amendments.		See destinations of enactments amended.
s 24(7)		s 1(5), 257(10)	
s 24(8)		s 833(2), Sch 29	
s 24(9)		s 1(6), 257(11)	
s 25	—	—	Rep 1982 Sch 22 Pt XI.
s 26	Amendments.		See destinations of enactments amended.
s 27	Mortgage interest relief limit.	—	Spent.
s 28, 29	Amendments.		See destinations of enactments amended.
s 30	Life policies.	Sch 15 §14	Am 1984 s 74.
s 31	Amendments.		See destinations of enactments amended.
s 32(1)	Adds s 227A to ICTA 1970.	s 625	
s 32(2)–(4)		—	Spent.
s 33, 34	Amendments.		See destinations of enactments amended.

Dest. Tables

FA 1980	Subject Matter	Re-enacted in TA 1988	Remarks
s 35	Pilots' benefit fund.	s 607	Am Pilotage Act 1983 (c. 21) Sch 3 §10; Pilotage Act 1987 (c 21) Sch 2 §4.
s 36(1), (2)	Old approved funds.	s 608(1), (2)	Rep in part 1987 Sch 16 Pt VII.
s 36(3)		Sch 29	
s 36(4)		s 608(3)	
s 36(5)		s 431(5)	
s 36(6)		s 608(4)	
s 37(1)–(4)	Relief for certain losses.	s 574	Rep in part 1981 Sch 19 Pt VIII.
s 37(5)		s 576(4)	
s 37(6)–(8)		s 575	
s 37(9)–(11)		s 576(1)–(3)	
s 37(12)		s 576(5)	Am 1981 s 36(7); 1987(2) s 71.
s 37(13)		—	Spent.
s 38(1)	Incidental cost of obtaining loan finance.	s 77(1)	Am 1984 s 43(1)(*a*).
s 38(2)		s 77(2)(*a*)	Am 1984 s 43(1)(*b*).
s 38(3)		s 77(3)	Am 1984 s 43(1)(*c*).
s 38(3A), (3B)		s 77(4), (5)	Added 1984 s 43(2).
s 38(4), (5)		s 77(6), (7)	
s 38(6)		—	Unnecessary.
s 39(1), (2), (4)	Relief for pre-trading expenditure.	s 401	Am 1982 s 50.
s 39(3)		s 114(1)(*b*)	
s 40	—	—	Rep 1981 Sch 19 Pt VII.
s 41	Redundancy payments.	s 90	
s 42	Grants under Industrial Development Act 1982 etc.	s 93	Am IDA 1982 Sch 2 Pt II §16; 1984 s 55.
s 43	—	—	Unnecessary.
s 44, 45	Amendments.		See destinations of enactments amended.
s 46(1)	Profit sharing schemes.	—	Unnecessary.
s 46(2)		Sch 10 §1(2)	
s 46(3)		Sch 10 §2	
s 46(4)		s 187(2)	
s 46(5)		Sch 10 §3(1)	
s 46(6)		s 187(12)	Subst 1982 s 42(2).
s 46(7)		—	Spent.
s 46(8)		Sch 10 §7	
s 46(9)		—	Spent.
s 46(10)		Sch 9 §11	
s 46(11)		Sch 9 §14	
s 46(12)		—	Rep 1987 Sch 16 Pt V.
s 46(13)		Sch 9 §32	
s 46(14)		—	Spent.
s 47(1)	Savings-related share option schemes.	s 185(1)–(3)	See Finance Act 1980 (Savings-related Share Option Schemes) Commencement Order 1980 SI 1980/1546; am 1981 s 90(3)(*a*); 1984 s 39(1).
s 47(2)		s 185(4)	
s 47(2A)		Sch 29	Added 1987 Sch 4 §4; am 1987(2) s 59(1).
s 47(3)		—	Spent.
s 48(1)	Cars available for private use.	s 155(1)	
s 48(2)		Sch 6 §3	
s 48(3)		Sch 6 §5	
s 48(4)		—	Unnecessary.
s 49(1)	Cash equivalents.	—	Unnecessary.
s 49(2)		s 156(4)	
s 49(3)		s 156(6)	
s 49(4)		s 156(9)	
s 50(1)	Beneficial loans.	s 161(1)	

FA 1980	Subject Matter	Re-enacted in TA 1988	Remarks
s 50(2), (3)		s 161(2), (3)	
s 50(4)		—	Unnecessary.
s 51(1)	Benefits in kind.	s 156(5), (7)	
s 51(2)		s 157(4)	
s 51(3)		s 168(5)	
s 51(4)		s 418	
s 51(5)		Sch 29	
s 52	Maintenance funds.	s 694	Am 1982 Sch 10 §2; ITA Sch 8 §17.
s 53	Maintenance funds.	s 27	Am 1982 Sch 10 §3; ITA Sch 8 §18; 1987 Sch 15 §13(1).
s 54	Charitable gifts by traders.	s 577(9)	
s 55(1)	Charitable dispositions.	s 660	Subst 1987 Sch 15 §2(16).
s 55(2)		s 671(2)	
s 55(3)		s 339(8)	
s 55(4)		—	Spent.
s 56, 57(1), (3), (4)	Amendments.		See destinations of enactments amended.
s 59	Trustee Savings Banks.	—	Spent.
s 60	Authorised unit trusts.	s 468(4)	Rep in part 1987 Sch 16 Pt VI.
s 61(1)	Amendment.	s 5(4)	
s 63	INMARSAT.	s 515, Sch 29	
s 70(1), (2)	Loss relief.	s 384(6), (7)	
s 109(11)	Oil.	Sch 30	
s 118(1)	National Heritage Memorial Fund.	s 507(1)	
s 118(2)		Sch 29	
s 119(1)–(3)	British Airways etc.	s 513	Partly spent.
s 119(4)		—	Rep 1981 Sch 19 Pt VI.
s 121	Penalties.	Sch 29	
Sch 8, 9	Amendments.		See destinations of enactments amended.
Sch 10	Savings related share option schemes.	Sch 9	
para 1(1), (1A)		Sch 9 §1(1), (3), 2	Am 1984 s 39(2), (3); 1987 Sch 15 §13(2).
para 1(2)		Sch 9 §1(2)	
para 1(3)		Sch 9 §1(3), (4)	
para 2		—	Rep 1986 Sch 23 Pt V.
para 3(1)		Sch 9 §3(1)	
para 3(2)		Sch 9 §4	
para 4		Sch 9 §5	
para 5(*a*)		Sch 9 §9(1)	
para 5(*b*)		Sch 9 §16(1), cl 187(2)	
para 6, 7		Sch 9 §17, 18	
para 8		Sch 9 §19	Am 1986 s 25(3).
para 9		Sch 9 §20	
para 10		Sch 9 §21	Am 1986 s 25(4).
para 10A		Sch 9 §15(1)–(4)	Added 1987 Sch 4 §1; am 1987(2) s 59.
para 11		Sch 9 §22	
para 12		Sch 9 §23	Am 1986 s 25(5).
para 13		Sch 9 §24	Am 1984 s 39(5).
para 14		Sch 9 §25	
para 15		Sch 9 §10	
para 16		Sch 9 §11	
para 17		Sch 9 §12	Am 1986 s 22(2).
para 18		Sch 9 §13(1)	Am 1982 s 41; 1986 s 23(4).
para 19		Sch 9 §14	Am 1986 s 23.
para 20		Sch 9 §26(1), (2)	Am 1984 s 39(6).
para 21		Sch 9 §26(3)	Am 1986 s 25(6).
para 22		—	Rep 1986 Sch 23 Pt V.
para 23		Sch 9 §8	
para 24		Sch 9 §16(2), (3)	
para 25		Sch 9 §6	
para 26(1)		s 187(2)	Am 1982 s 40(8).
para 26(2)		s 187(3)	

FA 1980	Subject Matter	Re-enacted in TA 1988	Remarks
Sch 10 (contd)			
para 26(3)		—	Rep 1987 Sch 16 Pt V.
para 26(4)		s 187(6)	
para 26(5)		s 187(7)	Am 1986 s 23(5).
Sch 11	Trustee savings banks.		
para 1(1)		s 130	
para 1(2)		—	Unnecessary.
para 2(1)		Sch 30	
para 2(2)		—	Spent.
para 2(3)–(6)		s 484	Am TSB 1985 Sch 2 §6(3); partly spent.
para 3, 4		—	Spent.
para 5		s 484	
para 6(1)		Sch 30	
para 6(2)–(4)		s 485	
para 7, 8		—	Spent.
Sch 18	Demergers.		
para 1–8		s 213	
para 13		s 214(2)–(6)	
para 14		s 214(1)	
para 17		s 215(1)–(4)	
para 18		s 215(5)–(8)	
para 19		s 216(1)	
para 20		s 216(2)–(4)	
para 21		s 217(1)	
para 22		s 217(2)–(4)	
para 23		s 218(1), 213(10), 214	Not wholly repealed.

FINANCE ACT 1981
(c 35)

FA 1981	Subject Matter	Re-enacted in TA 1988	Remarks
s 19–22	IT, CT & ACT rates.	—	Spent.
s 23(1)	Personal reliefs.	—	Spent.
s 23(2)		s 265(1)	
s 23(3)		s 265(2)	
s 23(4)		—	Spent.
s 24		—	Rep 1982 Sch 22 Pt IV.
s 25	Amendments.		See destinations of enactments amended.
s 26		—	Spent.
s 27	—	—	Rep 1987 Sch 16 Pt V.
s 28	Notification of taxable amounts.	s 152	Am 1987 Sch 3 §6.
s 29	PAYE repayments.	s 204	Am 1987 Sch 3 §7.
s 30(1), (2)	Sick pay.	s 149(1), (2)	
s 30(3)		s 154(2)	
s 30(4)		s 149(3)	
s 30(5)		—	Unnecessary.
s 31(1)	Payments for loss of employment etc.	s 188(4)	
s 31(2), (4), (7)		Sch 11 Pt II	
s 31(3)		Sch 11 §4	
s 31(5), (6), (8)		—	Spent.
s 32	Occupational pension schemes.	s 591	
s 33	Police provident benefits.	s 266(7)	
s 34	Savings certificates.	s 46, 832	
s 35	Stock relief.	s 96(7)(*c*)	
s 36(1)–(5)	Relief for losses.	s 573(1)–(5)	
s 36(6)		s 573(6), 575, 576	
s 37	Amendments.		See destinations of enactments amended.
s 38(1), (2)	Interest charged to capital.	s 338	

FA 1981	Subject Matter	Re-enacted in TA 1988	Remarks
s 39	Damages for personal injuries.	s 329(3)	
s 40	Amendments.		See destinations of enactments amended.
s 41	Insurance companies.	s 439(1)–(5)	Am ICA 1982 Sch 5 §25.
s 42(1)–(7)	Amendments.		See destinations of enactments amended.
s 42(8)		s 677(11)	
s 43, 44	Amendments.		See destinations of enactments amended.
s 45(1)–(6)	Transfer of assets abroad.	s 740	
s 45(7)		s 741, 742	
s 45(8)		s 745, Sch 29	
s 45(9)		s 740	
s 46(1), (2)	Transfer of assets abroad.	s 744	
s 46(3)–(7)	Amendments.		See destinations of enactments amended.
s 46(8)		—	Rep ITA Sch 9.
s 47	Assets of statutory bodies.	s 410, 240(12)	
s 48	Write-off of government investment.	s 400	Am 1987 Sch 15 §14(1).
s 49	National Heritage Memorial Fund.	s 339(9)	
s 50(1)	Northern Ireland.	s 613(4)	
s 50(2)		—	Spent.
s 50(3), (4)		s 511(4), (5)	
s 51	—	—	Spent.
s 52(1)–(6)	Relief for investment in new corporate trades: the Business Expansion Scheme.	—	Spent, but see 1983 Sch 5 & 1986 Sch 9 for application with amendments of ss 52 to 67 and Sch 11 & 12.
s 52(7), (8)		s 289(14), (15)	Am 1983 Sch 5 §2(9).
s 52(8A)		Sch 29	Added 1982 s 51(1); rep 1986 Sch 9 §19.
s 52(9)		—	Spent.
s 53		—	Spent.
s 54(1)		—	Spent.
s 54(2)–(8)		s 291(2)–(8)	Applied 1983 Sch 5 §4(2).
s 54(9)		—	Spent.
s 55		—	Spent.
s 56(1)		—	Spent.
s 56(2)		s 297(2)(*a*)–(*c*), (*e*)–(*g*)	Applied 1983 Sch 5 §6(2).
s 56(3)		s 297(3)	Applied 1983 Sch 5 §6(2).
s 56(4)–(7)		—	Spent.
s 56(8)–(10)		s 298(1)–(3)	Applied 1983 Sch 5 §5(9), 6(4).
s 57(1)–(3)		—	Spent.
s 57(4)		s 299(5)	Am 1983 Sch 5 §7(3).
s 58(1)		—	Spent.
s 58(2)–(4)		s 300(2)–(4)	Am 1983 Sch 5 §8(2); 1986 Sch 9 §10.
s 58(5)		s 301(1)	Am 1983 Sch 5 §8(2).
s 58(6)–(9)		s 301(3)–(6)	Applied 1983 Sch 5 §8(2); 1986 Sch 9 §10(3); 1987 Sch 15 §14(2).
s 59(1), (2)		—	Spent.
s 59(3)–(8)		s 303(2)–(7)	Am 1983 Sch 5 §10(2); rep in part 1983 Sch 10 Pt II.
s 60(1)		—	Spent.
s 60(2)		s 284(1)(*a*), (5), 287(7)(*a*), 283(2)	Am 1983 Sch 5 §12(2).
s 60(3)		s 280	Am 1983 Sch 5 §12(2).
s 60(4)–(7)		s 304(2), (3), (5), (6)	Am 1983 Sch 5 §12(2).
s 61(1)–(5), (7)		—	Spent.
s 61(6)		s 306(8)	Applied 1983 Sch 5 §13(8).
s 62(1)		—	Spent.
s 62(2)–(7)		s 307(2)–(7), (9)	Am 1983 Sch 5 §14(2).
s 63		s 310(7)–(9)	Am 1983 Sch 5 §15(6).

FA 1981	Subject Matter	Re-enacted in TA 1988	Remarks
s 64		Sch 29	Am 1982 s 52(1); partly spent.
s 65(1)		—	Spent.
s 65(2), (3)		s 308(6)	Applied 1983 Sch 5 §17(1).
s 65(4)		—	Spent.
s 66		—	Spent.
s 67		s 312	Applied 1983 Sch 5 §20.
s 68(1)	Cars available for private use.	—	Unnecessary.
s 68(3)		s 157(3)	
s 68(6)		Sch 6 Pt II §5	
s 68(7)		—	Unnecessary.
s 68(2), (4), (5)		—	See 1982 s 46(1).
s 69(1)	Car fuel.	s 158	Am 1986/702.
s 69(2)		—	Unnecessary.
s 70(1)	Transport vouchers.	—	Unnecessary.
s 70(2)		s 141(4)	
s 70(3), (4)		—	Spent.
s 70(5)(*a*)		—	Rep 1982 Sch 22 Pt IV.
s 70(5)(*b*)		s 144(4)	
s 70(6)		—	Unnecessary.
s 71(1)	Credit-tokens.	s 142, 144	
s 71(2)		Sch 29	
s 71(3)		—	Unnecessary.
s 72(1)	Medical insurance etc.	s 155(6)	
s 72(2)		—	
s 72(3)		Sch 29	
s 72(4)		—	Unnecessary.
s 138		Sch 29	Partly spent.
Sch 9	Stock relief.	Sch 30	
Sch 10	Stock relief.	—	Spent.
Sch 11	Relief for investment in new corporate trades.	s 297(3)(*d*)	Applied 1983 Sch 5 §6(2).
Sch 12			
para 1		—	Spent.
para 2		s 309(5)–(7)	Am 1982 s 52(2); 1983 Sch 5 §18(5).
para 3		—	Spent.
para 4		s 309(8)	Am 1982 s 52(3); 1983 Sch 5 §18(5).
para 4A, 5		—	Spent; am 1982 s 52(4).
para 6, 7		s 310(11)	

FINANCE ACT 1982
(c 39)

FA 1982	Subject Matter	Re-enacted in TA 1988	Remarks
s 20–23	IT, CT & ACT rates.	—	Spent.
s 24	Personal reliefs.	—	Spent.
s 25(1)	Mortgage interest relief limit.	—	Spent.
s 25(2)		s 357(6)	
s 26(1)	MIRAS.	s 369(1), 349(3)(*d*), 353(2), 476(10)	
s 26(2)		s 369(2)	
s 26(3)		—	Unnecessary.
s 26(4)–(6)		s 369(3)–(5)	
s 26(7)		s 7(3), 11(4), 369(6)	
s 26(8)		s 74(*o*)	
s 26(9)		s 160(4), Sch 7 §6	
s 28(1)–(3)	Variation of loan agreements.	s 377(1)–(3)	
s 28(4)		s 377(4), (5)	Am 1984 s 23(1), (2).

FA 1982	Subject Matter	Re-enacted in TA 1988	Remarks
s 28(4A)		s 377(6)	Added 1984 s 23(3).
s 28(5)		s 377(8), 832	Am BSA 1986 Sch 18 §15.
s 28(6)		s 377(9)	
s 28(7)		s 377(10), 379	
s 29(1)	Supplementary regulations.	s 378(1), (4)(*a*)	Am 1984 s 56(2); HCPA 1985 Sch 2 §54(2).
s 29(2), (3)		s 378(2), (3)	
s 29(4)		s 378(4), (6)	
s 29(5)		s 828	
s 30(1)	Amends 1970 s 219.	s 617	
s 30(2), (3)	—	—	Spent.
s 31	Income taxable under Schedule E.	s 150	
s 32		—	Rep 1987 Sch 16 Pt V.
s 33	Small maintenance payments.	s 351	
s 34	Qualifying policies.	Sch 15 §20	
s 35, 36	Amendments.		See destinations of enactments amended.
s 37	Annuities.	s 627	
s 38	—	—	Spent.
s 39	Annuities.	s 628(3)	
s 40(1)–(7)	Share options.	s 137	Am and rep in part 1984 s 39(7), (8).
s 40(8)		s 187(2)	
s 41	Share options etc: insider dealing.	s 139(10), Sch 9 §13	Am 1986 s 23(4).
s 42(1)	Approved profit sharing schemes.	s 186(3)	
s 42(2)		s 186(12)	
s 42(3)–(5)		—	Spent.
s 43(1)	Payments for loss of employment etc.	Sch 11 §4, 5	
s 43(2)		—	Unnecessary.
s 44	Non-cash vouchers.	s 141(1)–(3), (6), (7), 144(1), (2), (5)	
s 45(1)	Credit tokens.	—	Unnecessary.
s 45(2)		s 142(1), (3)	
s 45(3)		s 142(4), (5)	
s 45(4)		—	Unnecessary.
s 46(1)	Cars and car fuel.	—	Spent.
s 46(2)		s 157(3), 167(2)	
s 46(3)		—	Spent.
s 46(4)		s 158(1)	
s 46(5)–(7)		—	Spent.
s 47	—	—	Unnecesssary.
s 48(1)–(4)	Contributions to local enterprise agencies.	s 79(1)–(4)	
s 48(5)		s 79(5)–(7)	
s 48(6)–(9)		s 79(8)–(11)	
s 49–52	Amendments.		See destinations of enactments amended.
s 53	Purchase by company of own shares: distributions.	s 219	Am 1986 s 100.
s 54	Dealer's receipts.	s 95	
s 55–57	Amendments.		See destinations of enactments amended.
s 58(1)	Index-linked Treasury stock.	s 439(6)	
s 58(2)		—	Spent.
s 58(3)		s 439(6)	
s 58(4)		s 439(7)(*a*)	
s 58(5)		s 439(7)(*b*)	
s 58(6)		s 439(8)	
s 58(7)		s 431	
s 59	Manufactured dividends.	s 737	
s 60(1)	Meaning of ''distribution''.	s 212(1)	
s 60(2)		s 209(2)(*d*)	
s 60(3), (4)		s 212(2), (3)	
s 60(5), (6)		—	Unnecessary.

FA 1982	Subject Matter	Re-enacted in TA 1988	Remarks
s 61	Maintenance funds.	s 692	
s 62(1), (2)		s 693	
s 62(3)		—	Unnecessary.
s 63	Amends ICTA 1970 s 451.	s 677, Sch 30	
s 64	Amendments.		See destinations of enactments amended.
s 65	DTR.	s 798	Am 1987(2) s 67.
s 66		s 803	
s 67		s 794	
s 136(1)	Oil activities.	s 492(3)	
s 136(2)		s 494(4)	
s 136(3)		Sch 30	
s 137(4)–(6)	Regional development grants.	s 495(1), (2), (7)	Am IDA 1982 Sch 2 Pt II §18.
s 138		s 495(3)–(7)	
s 142(3), (4)		—	Rep 1987 Sch 16 Pt VII.
Sch 7	MIRAS.		
para 1		s 379	Partly unnecessary.
para 2(1)		s 370(1)	
para 2(2)		s 370(2)	Partly spent.
para 2(3)		s 370(3)	
para 2(4)–(6)		—	Spent.
para 2(7)		s 370(4)	
para 3(1)–(3)		s 370(5)–(7)	
para 3(4)–(6)		s 371	
para 4(1)(*a*), (*b*)		s 372(1), 379	Am BSA 1986 Sch 18 §15.
para 4(1)(*c*)		s 372(1)	Added 1983 s 17(1).
para 4(2)–(4)		s 372(2)–(4)	
para 5(1)–(3)		s 373(1)–(3)	Am 1985 s 37(2).
para 5(3A)		s 373(4)	Added 1983 s 17(2).
para 5(4)		s 373(5)	Am 1983 s 17(2); 1985 s 37(3).
para 6(1), (2)		s 373(6), (7)	
para 7(1)–(3)		s 374(1)–(3)	
para 7(4)		s 374(1)(*d*)(iii)	
para 7(5)		s 374(1)(*d*)(i)	
para 8		s 375(1)–(4), 74(*o*)	
para 9(1)		s 375(5)	
para 9(2)		Sch 29	
para 10		s 375(6), (7)	
para 11		s 375(8)	
para 12		s 375(9), (10)	
para 13(1)		s 376(1), 379	
para 13(2), (3)		s 376(2), (3)	
para 14(1)		s 376(4), 379	Am ICA 1982 Sch 5 §28(*b*); 1983 s 17(3); TSB 1985 Sch 2 §7(1); BSA 1986 Sch 18 §15; BA 1987 Sch 6 §13.
para 14(2)		s 376(5)	Am 1983 s 17(4); 1985 s 37(4).
para 15		s 376(6)	
Sch 8	Amendments.		See destinations of enactments amended.
Sch 9	Distributions: purchase of own shares.		
para 1, 2		s 220	
para 3(1)		s 221(1)	
para 3(2)–(7)		s 221(4)–(8)	Am CCCPA.
para 4		s 221(2), (3)	
para 5(1), (2)		s 222(1), (2)	
para 5(3)–(10)		s 222(5)–(12)	
para 6(1), (2)		s 222(3)	
para 6(3)		s 222(4)	
para 6(4)		s 222(9)	
para 7		s 223(1)	
para 8		s 223(2), (3)	
para 9		s 224	
para 10(1)		s 225(1)(*a*)	
para 10(2)		s 225(1)(*b*)	
para 10(3)–(6)		s 225(2)–(5)	

FA 1982	Subject Matter	Re-enacted in TA 1988	Remarks
Sch 9 (contd)			
para 11		s 226(1), (2)	
para 12		s 226(3), (4)	
para 13		Sch 29	
para 14		s 227	
para 15		s 228	
para 16		s 229	
Sch 10	Amendments.		See destinations of enactments amended.
Sch 21 para 3(1)	Amendments.	s 706	

FINANCE ACT 1983
(c 28)

FA 1983	Subject Matter	Re-enacted in TA 1988	Remarks
s 10–13	IT, CT & ACT rates.	—	Spent; rep in part 1983(2) Sch 2 Pt I.
s 14	Personal reliefs.	—	Spent.
s 15(1)		s 262	
s 15(2)		s 280	
s 15(3)		—	Spent.
s 16		—	Rep 1983(2) Sch 2 Pt I.
s 17(1)	MIRAS.	s 372(1)	
s 17(2)		s 373(4), (5)	
s 17(3)		s 376(4)(*o*), (*p*)	
s 17(4)		s 828	
s 17(5)		s 354(1)(*c*)	
s 17(6)		—	Spent.
s 18(1)		s 540(3)	
s 18(2)		s 542(3)	
s 18(3)–(5)		—	Unnecessary.
s 19	Repeals.	—	Spent.
s 20(1)	Scholarships.	s 165	
s 20(2)		s 165(4)	
s 20(3)(*a*), (*b*)		s 165(4)(*a*), (*b*)	
s 20(3)(*c*)		s 165(4)(*c*)	Subst 1984 s 31(3).
s 20(3A)		s 165(5)	Added 1984 s 31(3).
s 20(4)		—	Rep 1984 Sch 23 Pt V.
s 21	Additional charge for living accommodation.	s 146	
s 22	Director's tax paid by employer.	s 164	
s 23		—	Spent.
s 24, 25	Amendments.		See destinations of enactments amended.
s 26	Business expansion scheme.	s 289	Am 1986 s 40(2).
s 27(*a*)	Public lending right.	Sch 29	
s 27(*b*)		s 103(3), 537, 821(3)(*a*)	
s 28(1), (2)	Employees seconded to charities.	s 86(1), (2)	
s 28(2A), (2B)		s 86(1), (2)	Added 1984 s 33.
s 28(3)		—	Unnecessary.
s 46(1)	Historic Buildings and Monuments Commission for England.	s 507(1)	
s 46(2)		Sch 29	
s 46(3)(*a*), (*b*)		s 339(9), 577(9), 660(4)	
Sch 4	Life policies etc.	s 544	
Sch 5	*Business expansion scheme.*		Abolished with effect from 1.1.94 and replaced by Enterprise investment scheme.
para 1		—	Unnecessary.

Dest. Tables

FA 1983	Subject Matter	Re-enacted in TA 1988	Remarks
Sch 5 (contd)			
para 2(1)		s 289(1)(*a*)	
para 2(2), (3)		s 289(4), (5)	
para 2(4)		s 289(8)	
para 2(4A), (4B)		s 289(6), (7)	Added 1987 s 42(1).
para 2(5)		s 289(9)	
para 2(6)		s 289(10)	
para 2(7), (8)		s 289(12), (13)	Am 1986 Sch 9 §2.
para 2(9), (10)		s 289(14), (15), Sch 29	Applies 1981 s 52(7); subst 1987 s 42(2).
para 2A(1)		—	Unnecessary; added 1985 s 44(2); am 1986 Sch 9 §3(*a*).
para 2A(2)		s 289(1)(*b*), (*c*)	Added 1985 s 44(2); am 1986 Sch 9 §3(*b*).
para 2A(3)		s 289(8)(*b*)	Added 1985 s 44(2); am 1986 Sch 9 §3(*c*).
para 2A(4)		s 289(9)	Added 1985 s 44(2); am 1986 Sch 9 §3(*d*).
para 2A(5)		s 289(12)(*b*)	Added 1985 s 44(2).
para 2B		s 289(1)(*d*), (2), (3), (8)(*c*), (9), 12(*b*), 297(9)	Added 1986 Sch 9 §4.
para 3		s 290	Am 1987 s 42(3).
para 4(1)		s 291(1)	Am 1983(2) Sch 1 §2.
para 4(2)		s 291(2)–(8)	Applies 1981 s 54(2)–(8).
para 4(3), (4)		s 291(9), (10)	
para 4(5)		s 291(1)	Added 1986 Sch 9 §5.
para 5(1)–(7)		s 293(1)–(8)	Am 1983(2) Sch 1 §3; CCCPA; CCCP(NI); 1986 Sch 9 §6; IA 1986 Sch 14.
para 5(9)		s 298	Applies 1981 s 56(8), (9).
para 5(8), (10), (11)		s 293(9)–(11)	Am 1983(2) Sch 1 §3; rep 1986 Sch 9 §6.
para 5A		s 294, 307(8), 828	Added 1986 Sch 9 §7.
para 5B		s 295	Added 1986 Sch 9 §7.
para 5C		s 296	Added 1986 Sch 9 §7.
para 6(1)		s 297(1)	
para 6(2)		s 297(2)(*a*)–(*h*), 298(5)	Subst 1986 Sch 9 §8(2); am 1984 s 37(1); 1985 s 44(3).
para 6(2A)		s 297(4)	Added 1984 s 37(2).
para 6(2AA)		s 297(5)	Added 1985 s 44(4).
para 6(2B)		s 297(6), 298(5)	Added 1984 s 37(2); subst 1986 Sch 9 §8(3).
para 6(2C)		s 297(7)	Added 1986 Sch 9 §8(3).
para 6(3)		s 297(8)	
para 6(4)		ss 297(3), 298(3)	Subst 1986 Sch 9 §8(4).
para 6(5)–(10)		s 298(1)–(5), 828	Added 1986 Sch 9 §8(4).
para 7(1)		s 299(1)	
para 7(1A)		s 299(2)	Added 1986 Sch 9 §9(2).
para 7(2)		s 299(3)	Am 1983(2) Sch 1 §4(2); 1986 Sch 9 §9(3).
para 7(2A)		s 299(4)	Added 1983(2) Sch 1 §4(3); am 1986 Sch 9 §9(4).
para 7(3)		s 299(5)	Applies 1981 s 57(4); am 1983(2) Sch 1 §4(4).
para 7(4)		s 299(6)	Added 1983(2) Sch 1 §4(5); subst 1986 Sch 9 §9(5).
para 8(1)		s 300(1)	
para 8(2)		s 300(2)–(4), 301	Subst 1986 Sch 9 §10(3); applies 1981 s 58(2)–(9).
para 8(3)		s 300(5)	Am 1983(2) Sch 1 §5.
para 8(4)		s 301(2)	Added 1986 Sch 9 §10(4).
para 9		s 302	Am 1983(2) Sch 1 §6.
para 10(1)		s 303(1)	Am 1986 Sch 9 §11(2).
para 10(2)		s 303(2)–(7)	Applies 1981 s 59(3)–(8).
para 10(3), (4)		s 303(8), (9)	Am 1987 Sch 15 §15(1).
para 10(5)		—	Am 1983(2) Sch 1 §7; spent.
para 10(5A)		s 303(10)	Added 1983(2) Sch 1 §7; subst 1986 Sch 9 §11(3).

FA 1983	Subject Matter	Re-enacted in TA 1988	Remarks
Sch 5 (contd)			
para 10A		s 292	Added 1986 Sch 9 §12.
para 11		s 289(11)	
para 12(1)		s. 304(1)	
para 12 (2), (3)		s 280(2), 283(2), 284(1), (5), 287(7), 304(2)–(5)	Applies 1981 s 60(2)–(7); am 1987 s 42(4).
para 13		s 306	Am 1986 Sch 9 §13.
para 14(1), (1A)		s 307(1)	Am 1987 s 42(5).
para 14(2)		s 307(2)–(7), (9)	Applies & amends 1981 s 62(2)–(7); am 1983(2) Sch 1 §8; 1986 Sch 9 §14.
para 15(1), (2)		s 310(1), (2)	
para 15(3)–(5)		s 310(4)–(6)	
para 15(6)		s 310(7)–(9)	Applies 1981 s 63(7)–(9).
para 15A		s 310(3), (4)	Added 1986 Sch 9 §15.
para 16		Sch 29	Am 1986 Sch 9 §16.
para 16A(1)		s 305(1)	Added 1986 Sch 9 §17.
para 16A(2)		Sch 29	Added 1986 Sch 9 §17.
para 16A(3), (4)		s 305(2), (3)	Added 1986 Sch 9 §17.
para 16A(5)		Sch 29	Added 1986 Sch 9 §17.
para 17(1)–(1D)		s 308(1)–(5)	Subst 1986 Sch 9 §18; am 1987 Sch 15 §15(2).
para 17(2)		s 309(1)	
para 18(1)–(3)		s 309(2)–(4)	
para 18(4)		s 310(5), (6)	
para 18(5)		s 309(5)–(8)	Applies 1981 Sch 12 §§2, 4; am 1982 s 52(2).
para 19		s 311(1), (3)–(6)	
para 19A		s 311(2)	Added 1986 Sch 9 §20.
para 20		s 312	Am 1985 s 44(6); CCCPA; 1986 Sch 9 §21.
paras 21–23		—	Spent.

FINANCE (NO 2) ACT 1983
(c 49)

F(No 2)A 1983	Subject Matter	Re-enacted in TA 1988	Remarks
s 1, 2	IT & CT rates.	—	Spent.
s 3	Mortgage interest relief limit.	—	Spent.
s 4	Loans.	Sch 7 §§10, 11	
s 5	—	—	Unnecessary.
Sch 1	Amendments.		See destinations of enactments amended.

OIL TAXATION ACT 1983
(c 56)

OTA 1983	Subject Matter	Re-enacted in TA 1988	Remarks
s 11	Tariff receipts.	s 496	

Dest. Tables

FINANCE ACT 1984
(c 43)

FA 1984	Subject Matter	Re-enacted in TA 1988	Remarks
s 17, 18(1)–(4)	IT & CT rates.	—	Spent.
s 18(5)		s 434(7)	
s 18(6)		—	Spent.
s 19, 20	ACT & CT rates.	—	Spent.
s 21	Personal reliefs.	—	Spent.
s 22(1)	MIRAS.	s 357(1), 367(5)	
s 22(2)		s 357(4)	
s 22(3)		s 365(3)	
s 22(4), (5)		—	Spent.
s 23	Variation of loan agreements.	s 377(4)–(6), 379	
s 24(1)–(4)	Relief for interest.	s 361(4)–(7)	
s 24(5)		—	Spent.
s 25(1)	Job-related accommodation.	s 356(3)(*b*), (5)	
s 25(2)(*a*)		—	Spent.
s 25(2)(*b*)		Sch 29	
s 26(1)–(4)	The composite rate.	s 483(1)–(4)	
s 26(5)		—	Spent.
s 26(6), (7)		s 483(5), 832	
s 26(8)		Sch 29	
s 26(9)		s 483(5)	
s 27(1)	Interest paid on bank deposits etc.	s 479(1)	
s 27(2)		s 349(3)(*d*)	
s 27(3), (4)		—	Unnecessary.
s 28(1)	MPs' allowances.	s 200	
s 28(2)(*a*)		s 198(4)	
s 28(2)(*b*)		Sch 29	
s 29	Grant to MEPs.	s 190(*b*), (*c*)	
s 30(1)–(3)	Foreign emoluments.	—	Spent.
s 30(4)		Sch 29, Sch 30	
s 30(5)		—	Spent.
s 30(6)		Sch 29	
s 30(7), (8)		—	Spent.
s 30(9)–(12)		s 192(4)	
s 30(13)		s 391	
s 30(14)(*a*)		—	Spent.
s 30(14)(*b*)		s 192(5)	
s 30(15)			Unnecessary.
s 31–33	Amendments.		See destinations of enactments amended.
s 34		—	Rep 1985 Sch 27 Pt V.
s 35(1)–(3)	Eurobonds.	s 124(1)–(3)	
s 35(4)		s 338(4)(*b*)	
s 35(5)–(8)		s 124(4)–(7)	
s 35(9)		Sch 29	
s 35(10)		—	Unnecessary.
s 36(1)	Deep discount securities.	s 57	
s 36(2)		Sch 4 §1(1)	
s 36(3), (4)		Sch 4 §1(2), (3)	
s 36(5)		Sch 4 §1(1)	
s 37(1)	Business expansion scheme.	s 297(2)(*j*)	
s 37(2)		s 297(4), 298(5)	Am 1985 s 44(5); 1986 Sch 9 §3.
s 37(3)		s 298(6)(*b*)	
s 38(1)–(3)	Share option schemes.	s 185(1)–(3)	
s 38(4)–(9)		s 185(5)–(8)	Am 1987 Sch 4 §5.
s 38(10)		Sch 29	
s 39–41	Amendments.		See destinations of enactments amended.
s 42	Discounted bills of exchange.	s 78	
s 43	Loan finance.	s 77	
s 45	Pension funds.	s 659	Am 1987(2) Sch 2 §5.
s 46(1)	Group relief etc.	—	Spent.
s 46(2)		s 413(6)	
s 46(3)–(5)		—	Spent.
s 47(1), (2)		s 409	

FA 1984	Subject Matter	Re-enacted in TA 1988	Remarks
s 47(3)		—	Spent.
s 48, 49	—	—	Spent.
s 50(1)	Furnished holiday lettings.	—	[Not repealed].
s 50(2)–(9)		s 504(2)–(9)	[Not repealed].
s 50(10)(*a*)		—	Spent.
s 50(10)(*b*)		—	[Not repealed].
s 50(10)(*c*)		—	Spent.
s 51	Woodlands.	s 16	
s 52(1)	ACT.	s 239(3)	
s 52(2), (3)		—	Spent.
s 53	DTR: amendments.		See destinations of enactments amended.
s 54	Regional development grants.	s 92	
s 55	Other grants.	s 93	
s 56, 57	Amendments.		See destinations of enactments amended.
s 56(1)	Northern Ireland self-build societies etc.	s 489(11), (12)	
s 56(2)		s 378(1)(*b*), (4)(*a*)	
s 72(1)	Premium relief.	s 266(3)(*c*)	
s 72(2)–(4)		Sch 14 §8(3)–(5)	
s 72(5)		s 268(7)(*a*), 269(5)(*a*)	
s 72(6), (7)		Sch 14 §8(6), (7)	
s 72(8)		—	Spent.
s 72(9)		Sch 15 §16, s 541(6), 546(5)	
s 73(1)	Friendly societies.	s 460(2)	
s 73(2), (3)		s 460(6)	
s 73(4)		—	[Not repealed].
s 73(5), (6)		s 464(1)	
s 74	Life policies.	Sch 15 §14(1)–(7)	
s 75, 76	Amendments.		See destinations of enactments amended.
s 77		—	Spent.
s 79(5), (10)	Oil taxation.	s 492, 494, 502	
s 82	Foreign controlled companies.	s 747	
s 83	Limits on directions.	s 748	
s 84	Residence etc.	s 749	
s 85	Lower level of tax.	s 750	
s 86	Accounting periods etc.	s 751	
s 87	Apportionment of profits etc.	s 752	
s 88	Notices etc.	s 753	
s 89(1), (2)		s 754(1), (2)	
s 89(3)		Sch 29, s 754(3)	
s 89(4)		s 754(4)	
s 89(5), (6)		Sch 29	
s 89(7)–(11)		s 754(5)–(9)	
s 90(1)–(7)	Information.	s 755	
s 90(8)		Sch 29	
s 91	Interpretation.	s 756	
s 92(1)–(6)	Offshore funds.	s 757(1)–(6)	Partly spent.
s 92(7)		s 757(1)	Rep in part 1987 Sch 16 Pt VI.
s 92(8)		s 757(7)	
s 93	Equalisation arrangements.	s 758	
s 94	Material interests.	s 759	Rep in part 1987 Sch 16 Pt VI.
s 95	Non-qualifying funds.	s 760	
s 96(1)–(7)	Charge to tax.	s 761	Am 1987 Sch 15 §16(1).
s 96(8)		—	Rep ITA Sch 8.
s 97	Foreign residents etc.	s 762	
s 98	Deductions.	s 763	
s 99(1)	Insurance companies.	s 441(8)	
s 99(2)		s 437(2)(*a*)	Rep in part and superseded 1985 Sch 25 §7, Sch 27 Pt X.

FA 1984	Subject Matter	Re-enacted in TA 1988	Remarks
s 99(3)		—	Rep 1985 Sch 27 Pt X.
s 99(4)		s 431	
s 100(1)	Trustees.	s 764	
s 100(2)		s 687(3)	
s 100(3)		s 663(2)	
s 126(1)–(3)(*a*)	International organisations.	s 324	Only s 126(3)(*a*) repealed; am 1985 s 96.
Sch 7	The additional rate: amendments.		See destinations of enactments amended.
Sch 8	Interest on bank deposits etc.		
para 1(1)		—	Unnecessary.
para 1(2)		s 482(1)	
para 2(1)		s 481(1), (2)	Am 1985 s 38(2); 1987 Sch 15 §16(2); BA 1987 Sch 6 §16.
para 2(2)		s 482(10)	Subst 1985 s 38(2).
para 2(3)		s 828	
para 3(1)–(3)		s 481(3)–(5)	Am 1985 s 38(3), (4).
para 3(4)–(9)		s 482(2)–(7)	Am 1985 s 38(5), (6); Income Tax (Composite Rate) (Relevant Deposits) Order 1986 SI No 771.
para 3A		s 481(6), 482(11), (12), 828	Added 1985 s 38(7).
para 4		s 479(2)–(4)	
para 5		s 479(5)–(7)	
para 6(1)		—	Spent.
para 6(2), (3)		s 482(8), (9)	
para 6(4)		—	Spent.
para 6(5)–(8)		s 480	
para 7		Sch 29	
Sch 9	Deep discount securities.		
para 1(1)(*a*), (*b*)		Sch 4 §4(1)	
para 1(1)(*c*)		Sch 29	
para 1(2)–(6)		Sch 4 §4(2)–(6)	
para 1(7)		Sch 4 §1(1)	Am 1985 Sch 11 §4.
para 1(8)		Sch 4 §13(1)	
para 1(9)		Sch 4 §4(7)	
para 2		Sch 4 §7(1), (2)	
para 3(1)–(5)		Sch 4 §5(1)–(5)	
para 3(6), (7)		s 77	
para 3(8)		—	Spent.
para 3(9), (10)		Sch 4 §5(6), (7)	
para 4		Sch 4 §6	
para 5–7		Sch 4 §9–11	
para 8(1), (2)(*a*)		Sch 4 §7(3)	
para 8(2)(*b*), (*c*)		Sch 29	
para 8(3)		Sch 4 §7(4)	
para 9		Sch 29	
para 10		Sch 4 §8	
para 11(1)		Sch 4 §12	
para 11(2)		Sch 29	
para 12		Sch 4 §14	Subst 1987 Sch 15 §16(3).
para 13		s 242	
para 14		—	Rep ITA Sch 9.
Sch 10	Approved share option schemes.		
para 1(1)		Sch 9 §1(1), 2(1)	
para 1(2)–(4)		Sch 9 §1(2)–(4)	
para 1(5)		s 185(9)	
para 2(1)		Sch 9 §3(1)	
para 2(2)		Sch 9 §4	
para 3		Sch 9 §5	
para 4(1)(*a*), (2)		Sch 9 §27(1)	
para 4(1)(*b*), (3)		Sch 9 §8	
para 4(4)		s 187(3)(*c*)	Rep in part 1987 Sch 16 Pt V.
para 4A		Sch 9 §15(1)–(4)	
para 5		Sch 9 §28	
para 6		Sch 9 §9(1)	

FA 1984	Subject Matter	Re-enacted in TA 1988	Remarks
Sch 10 (contd)			
para 7–11		Sch 9 §10–14	Am 1986 s 22, 23.
para 12		Sch 9 §27(2), (3)	
para 13		Sch 9 §29	
para 14		Sch 9 §6	
para 15		s 187(2), (3), (6), (7), Sch 9 §27(4)	
Sch 11	Furnished holiday lettings.		
para 1(1)		s 503(1)	Not repealed; am 1987(2) Sch 2 §6.
para 1(2)(*a*)–(*e*)		s 503(1)	
para 1(2)(*f*)–(*i*)		—	Not repealed.
para 1(2)(*j*)		s 503(1)	
para 2		s 503(2)–(4)	
para 3		s 503(5)	
paras 4, 5		—	Not repealed.
para 6		s 503(6)	Not repealed.
para 7		s 503(7)	Not wholly repealed.
Sch 15	Life policies.		
Pt I		Sch 15 §24	
Pt II		Sch 15 Pt III	
Pt III		s 553	Am 1985 s 51.
Sch 16	Controlled foreign companies.		
para 1–11, 13		Sch 24	Am 1985 Sch 14 §16.
para 12		—	Spent.
Sch 17	Exceptions from directions.	Sch 25	Am 1987(2) s 65.
Sch 18	Relief from tax.	Sch 26	
Sch 19	Offshore funds.	Sch 27	Am 1986 s 50; 1987(2) s 66.
Sch 20	Offshore income gains.	Sch 28	

FINANCE ACT 1985
(c 54)

FA 1985	Subject Matter	Re-enacted in TA 1988	Remarks
s 34, 35	IT & CT rates.	—	Spent.
s 36	Personal reliefs.	—	Spent.
s 37(1)	Relief for interest.	—	Spent.
s 37(2)		s 373(2)	
s 37(3)		s 373(5)	
s 37(4)		s 376(5)	
s 38(1)	Interest on bank deposits.	—	Unnecessary.
s 38(2)		s 482(10)	
s 38(3)		s 481(4)(*b*)	
s 38(4)		s 481(5)(*e*), (*f*)	
s 38(5)		s 482(2)(*b*)	
s 38(6)		s 482(6)	
s 38(7)		s 481(6), 482(11), (12), 828	
s 38(8), (9)		—	Spent.
s 38(10)		Sch 29	
s 39	Group relief.	—	Unnecessary.
s 40(1)	Building societies.	—	Unnecessary.
s 40(2)		—	Spent.
s 40(3)		s 476(1), (2), 828	
s 40(4)		s 476(3)	
s 40(5)		s 476(5)	
s 40(6)		s 476(9)	
s 40(7)		s 476(11)	
s 40(8), (9)		—	Spent.
s 40(10)		Sch 29	
s 41(1)	Friendly societies.	s 464, Sch 15 §6	
s 41(2)		—	Unnecessary.
s 41(3)		—	Spent.
s 41(4)		Sch 29, Sch 15 §3–6	

FA 1985	Subject Matter	Re-enacted in TA 1988	Remarks
s 41(5)		—	
s 41(6)		s 462	
s 41(7)		s 466	
s 41(8)		s 539(3)	
s 41(9)		s 547(7)	
s 41(10)		s 461(6)	
s 42(1)	Class 4 contributions.	s 617(5)	
s 42(2)		Sch 29	
s 43	Business entertaining expenses.	s 577(8)(*b*)	
s 44(1)	Business expansion scheme.	—	Unnecessary.
s 44(2)		s 289(1), (8), (9), (12)(*b*)(i)	
s 44(3)		s 297(2)(*h*)	
s 44(4)		s 297(5)	
s 44(5)		s 298(5)	
s 44(6)		s 312(1)	
s 44(7)		s 289(1)(*c*), 298(6)(*a*)	
s 45(1)	Profit sharing schemes.	—	Unnecessary.
s 45(2)		s 187(2)	
s 45(3)		Sch 10 §3(1)	
s 45(4)		s 186(12)	
s 45(5)		—	Spent.
s 46		—	Unnecessary.
s 47	Partnerships.	s 61(4), 62(1), (4), (5)	
s 48	—	—	Unnecessary.
s 49	—	—	Rep 1986 Sch 23 Pt V.
s 51	Offshore life assurance.	s 553(5)	
s 52	London Transport.	Sch 30	
s 53	Oil taxation.	s 493(4), (5)	
s 54	Companies connected with unitary states.	s 812	
s 60	Loss relief.	s 393(4)	
s 64, 65	Amendments.		See destinations of enactments amended.
s 72(1)(*b*)	Commodity futures.	s 128, 399(5)	
s 72(7)		s 436(5)	
s 73	Bondwashing.	s 713(1)–(6)	
s 74		s 714	
s 75(1)		s 715(1)(*a*)–(*c*), (*e*)–(*j*)	
s 75(2)		s 715(2)	
s 75(3), (4)		s 715(4), (5)	
s 75(5), (6)		s 715(8)	
s 76		—	Spent.
s 77		—	Unnecessary.
Sch 9	Group relief.		
para 1		s 413(2)	
para 2		s 405(1)–(3)	
para 3		s 405(4)–(6)	
para 4		s 403(10), (11)	
para 5		s 406(1)–(4)	
para 6		s 406(1), (5)–(8)	
para 7(1), (2)		s 409(5), (6)	
para 7(3)		s 409(8)	
para 8(1), (2)		s 409(7)	
para 8(3)		s 409(8)	
para 9		s 411(3)	
para 10		s 411(4), (5)	
para 11		s 411(6)	
para 12		s 411(7), (8)	
para 13		s 411(9)	
Sch 10	Friendly societies.		
Pt I		Sch 15 §§3, 4	
Pt II		s 462(3), (4)	
Pt III		s 465	
Sch 11	Deep discount securities.		
para 1		Sch 4 §1, 2	
para 2(1)–(3)		Sch 4 §3	

FA 1985	Subject Matter	Re-enacted in TA 1988	Remarks
Sch 11 (contd)			
para 2(4)		Sch 4 §4(1)(*a*)	
para 2(5)		Sch 4 §7	
para 2(6)		Sch 29	
para 2(7)		Sch 4 §11(2)	
para 2(8)		—	Rep 1987 Sch 16 Pt VII.
para 2(9)		Sch 4 §1	
para 3		Sch 4 §13	
para 4		Sch 4 §1(1)(*f*)(ii)	
Sch 12	Limited partners.		
para 1		s 117(2)	
para 2(1)–(3)		s 117(1)	
para 2(4)		s 117(2)	
para 2(5)		s 117(4)	
para 3(1)–(3)		s 118(1)	
para 3(4)		s 118(2)	
para 4		s 117(3)	
Sch 13	Companies connection with unitary states.		
para 1		s 813	
para 2		—	Unnecessary.
para 3		s 814	
para 4		s 815	
para 5		s 812(2), (5), (6)	
Sch 14			
para 16	Amendments.	Sch 24 §10	
Sch 18	Writing-down allowances.		
para 1		s 520(4)–(6)	
para 2		s 521(1)	
para 3		s 521(2)–(4)	
para 4		s 521(5)	
para 5		s 530(2), (3)	
para 6		s 530(4)	
para 7		s 530(5)	
para 8		s 533	
Sch 22		—	Spent.
Sch 23	Bondwashing.		
para 1		s 710(1)–(4)	
para 2		s 710(5)–(10)	
para 3		s 711(1)–(5), (7)–(9)	
para 4		s 712	
para 5		s 710(11)	
para 6		s 720(1), (2)	
para 7		s 720(4), 711(6)	
para 8(1), (2)		s 720(5)	
para 8(3)		s 687(3)(*f*)	
para 8(4)		s 720(5)	Am 1986 Sch 17 §1(1).
para 8(5), (6)		s 328(2)–(4)	Added 1986 Sch 17 §1(1).
para 9		s 720(6)–(8)	
para 10(1)–(3)		s 713(7), (8)	
para 10(4), (5)		—	Spent.
para 10(6)		s 710(12)	Partly spent.
para 10(7)		s 713(9), 710(12)	
para 11		s 723	
para 12		s 721(1)–(4), 711(6)	Partly spent.
para 13		s 722, 711(6)	
para 14		s 710(13), 711(6)	
para 15(1)–(4)		s 716(1)–(4)	
para 15(5)		s 716(5)	Subst 1986 Sch 17 §2(2).
para 15(6)		s 720(1)	
para 15(7)		Sch 29	
para 15(7A)		Sch 29	Added 1986 Sch 17 §3.
para 15(8)		s 716(6)	
para 15A, 15B		s 717, 718	Added 1986 Sch 17 §3.
para 15C		s 719, Sch 29	Added 1986 Sch 17 §3.
para 16		s 724(1)	Partly spent.
para 17		s 724(2)	Partly spent.
para 18(1), (2)		s 724(3), (4)	
para 18(3)		—	Spent.

FA 1985	Subject Matter	Re-enacted in TA 1988	Remarks
Sch 23 (contd)			
para 19(1), (2)		s 724(3), (4)	
para 19(3)		—	Spent.
para 19(4), (5)		s 724(3), (4)	
para 19(6)		—	Spent.
para 20(1)		s 445(2)	
para 20(2)–(6)		s 724(5)–(8)	
para 21		s 710(14)	Rep in part 1987 Sch 16 Pt VII.
para 22		s 720(3)	Rep in part 1987 Sch 16 Pt VII.
para 23		—	Spent.
para 24		s 725(1)–(3)	
para 25		s 725(4)–(6)	
para 26		s 725(7)–(9)	
para 27		s 721(5), (6)	Rep in part 1987 Sch 16 Pt VII.
para 28		—	Spent.
para 29		s 452(9)	Partly spent.
para 30(1)		s 715(1)(*d*)(i)	
para 30(2)		s 715(2)(*b*)	
para 30(3)		—	Spent.
para 30(4)		s 715(1)(*d*)(ii)	
para 30(5)		s 715(2)(*b*)	
para 30(6)		—	Spent.
para 31		s 715(3)	
para 32(1), (2)		s 715(1), (2)	
para 32(3)		—	Spent.
para 32A		s 726(1)–(6), Sch 29	Added 1986 Sch 17 §4.
para 32B		s 726(7)	Added 1986 Sch 17 §4.
para 32C		s 727	Added 1986 Sch 17 §4.
para 33–35		Sch 29	
para 36		—	Spent.
para 37, 38		s 807	
para 39		s 742(4)–(7)	
para 40		—	Spent.
para 41, 42		—	Rep 1986 Sch 23 Pt VIII.
para 43		s 715(6), (7)	Am 1986 Sch 17 §5.
para 44(1)–(5A)		s 728	Am 1986 Sch 17 §6.
para 44(6)		Sch 29	
Sch 25	Amendments.		
para 7		s 437(2)(*a*)	
para 8		s 445(2)(*a*)	
para 9		Sch 19 §6(2)	

FINANCE ACT 1986
(c 41)

FA 1986	Subject Matter	Re-enacted in TA 1988	Remarks
s 16	IT rates.	—	Spent.
s 17(1)	ACT rate.	s 14(3), 246(4)	
s 17(2)–(4)		s 246(1)–(3)	
s 17(5)		s 14(3)	
s 17(6), (7)		—	Spent.
s 18	CT rates.	—	Spent.
s 19	PAYE.	—	Spent.
s 20	—	—	Spent.
s 21–23	Amendments.		See destinations of enactments amended.
s 24(1)–(3)	Amendments.		See destinations of enactments amended.
s 25(1)–(7)	Amendments.		See destinations of enactments amended.
s 25(8), (9)		Sch 9 §21(3)	

FA 1986	Subject Matter	Re-enacted in TA 1988	Remarks
s 26(1)	Shares acquired by directors etc.	s 135(8)(*a*)	
s 26(2)		s 136(6)	
s 26(3)		s 138(10), (11)	
s 26(4)		s 138(9)	
s 26(5)		s 139(13)	
s 26(6)		s 138(10)	Partly spent.
s 27(1)–(7)	Payroll deduction scheme.	s 202(1)–(7)	
s 27(8)		s 202(11)	
s 27(9)		—	Spent.
s 28(1), (2)		s 202(8)	
s 28(3)		s 202(9)	
s 28(4)		s 202(10)	
s 28(5)		s 202(9)	
s 28(6)		Sch 29	
s 28(7)		s 828	
s 29(1)	Company gifts to charity.	s 338(1), 339(2)	
s 29(2)		s 339(1)	
s 29(3)		s 339(3), 352	
s 29(4), (5)		s 339(4), (5)	
s 29(6)		s 339(9)	
s 29(7)		—	Spent.
s 30(1)	Charities.	s 505(2)	
s 30(2)		s 505(6)	
s 30(3)		s 506	
s 31(1), (2)	Charities.	s 505(3), (4)	
s 31(3)(*a*)		s 506(1)	
s 31(3)(*b*)		s 339(8)	
s 31(3)(*c*)		s 505, 506	
s 31(3)(*d*)		s 505(5)	
s 31(4)–(6)		s 506(4)–(6)	
s 31(7)–(9)		s 505(6)–(8)	
s 31(10), (11)		—	Spent.
s 32(1)	Payments to charities.	s 683(3)	
s 32(2)		s 683(4), (5)	
s 32(3)		s 427(3)	
s 34	Amendments.		See destinations of enactments amended.
s 35	Expenses.	s 80	
s 36		s 81	
s 37		s 195(1)–(12)	
s 38(1)–(3)		—	Spent.
s 38(4)		s 195(13)	
s 38(5)		—	Spent.
s 39		—	Unnecessary.
s 40	Business expansion scheme.	s 289	
s 41(1)–(3)	Enterprise allowance.	s 127	
s 41(4)		Sch 29	
s 41(5)		—	Spent.
s 42	Company reconstructions.	s 343(4)	
s 43	Close companies.	s 419(3), (4)	
s 44	—	—	Unnecessary.
s 45	Amendments.		See destinations of enactments amended.
s 46		—	Unnecessary.
s 47(1)	Building societies.	s 476(1)	
s 47(2)		s 476(3)	
s 47(3)		s 476(11)	
s 47(4)(*a*)		s 686(5)	
s 47(4)(*b*)		s 476(7)	
s 47(5), (6)		s 477(1), (2)	
s 47(7)		—	Spent.
s 47(8)		s 477(3)	
s 47(9)		—	Spent.
s 48(1)	Foreign dividends.	s 48(4)	
s 48(2)–(5)		s 123(1)(*b*), (2), 832	
s 49	DTR.	s 797(4), (5)	
s 50	Offshore funds.		See destinations of enactments amended.
s 51	Foreign pensions etc.	s 330	

Dest. Tables

FA 1986	Subject Matter	Re-enacted in TA 1988	Remarks
s 52	—	—	Spent.
s 53	VAT penalties etc.	s 827	
s 54	Oil taxation.	s 502(4)	
s 56(7)(*a*)	Amendments.		See destinations of enactments amended.
s 61	Stock lending.	s 129, Sch 29, s 828	
s 62, 63		—	Unnecessary.
Sch 7 Pt I	Private indirect charities.	s 506(1)–(3)	
Pts II–IV		Sch 20	Am BA 1987 Sch 6 §24.
Sch 8	Personal equity plans.	s 333, Sch 29, s 828	
Sch 9	Business expansion scheme.		See destinations of enactments amended.
Sch 10	Amendments.		See destinations of enactments amended.
Sch 11	Entertainers and sportsmen.		
para 1		s 555(1)	
para 2(1)		s 555(2)	
para 2(2)		s 555(4)	
para 2(3)		s 555(3)	
para 2(4)		s 555(4)	
para 2(5)		s 555(5)(*a*)	
para 2(6)		s 555(5)(*b*)	
para 2(7)		s 555(6)	
para 3(1)		s 555(7)	
para 3(2)		Sch 29	
para 4		s 555(8)–(11)	
para 5		s 558(4)	
para 6		s 556(1), (4), (5)	
para 7		s 556(2)–(5)	
para 8		s 557	
para 9		s 558(1)–(3)	
para 10–12		s 558(5), (6), 828	
Sch 12	Pension scheme surpluses.		
para 1(1)		s 601(1)	
para 1(2)		s 601(2)	
para 1(3)		s 601(1)	
para 1(4)		s 601(5)	
para 1(5)		s 601(3)(*a*)	
para 1(6)		s 601(4)	
para 1(7)		s 601(3)(*c*)	
para 1(8)		s 601(3)(*b*)	
para 1(9)		s 601(6)(*a*)	
para 1(10)		s 612(1)	
para 1(11)		—	Unnecessary.
para 1(12)		s 601(3)(*d*)	
para 1(13)		s 601(3)(*e*)	
para 2		s 602, Sch 29	
para 3		s 601(6), 602(1), 828	
para 4–11		Sch 22, s 828	
Sch 17	Amendments.		See destinations of enactments amended.
Sch 18	Securities.		
para 1(1)		s 729(7)–(9)	
para 1(2)		—	Unnecessary.
para 1(3)		s 732(3)	
para 1(4)		s 729(10)(*b*)	
para 1(5)		s 729(12)	
para 2(1)		s 731(9)	
para 2(2)		—	Spent.
para 3(1)		s 732(2)	
para 3(2)		s 732(6)	
para 3(3)		—	Spent.
para 4		s 738(1)	
para 5		s 737	
para 6(1)		—	Unnecessary.
para 6(2)		s 737(3)	
para 6(3)		s 737(6)	

FA 1986	Subject Matter	Re-enacted in TA 1988	Remarks
Sch 18 (contd)			
para 6(4)		—	Spent.
para 6(5), (6)		s 738(2), (4)	
para 9(1)(*a*)		s 738(3)	
para 9(2)		s 738(4)	

FINANCE ACT 1987
(c 16)

FA 1987	Subject Matter	Re-enacted in TA 1988	Remarks
s 20, 21, 22	IT & CT rates.	—	Spent.
s 23	Sub-contractors.	s 559(3)	
s 24	—	—	Spent.
s 25	—	—	Spent.
s 26(1), (2)	Personal reliefs.	s 257(3)	
s 26(3)		s 257(4)	
s 26(4)		s 257(3)	
s 26(5)(*a*)		s 257(5)	
s 26(5)(*b*)		s 259(2)	
s 26(5)(*c*)		s 287(5)	
s 26(6)		s 280(2)(*b*)(i)	
s 26(7)		s 257(9)	
s 26(8)		—	Spent.
s 27(1)	Wife's earnings.	s 257(7)(*b*)(iii)	
s 27(2)		s 287(2)(*b*)	
s 27(3)		—	Spent.
s 28	Blind persons.	s 265	
s 29(1)	Social security benefits.	s 617(2)	
s 29(2)–(4)		s 151(1)–(4)	
s 29(5)		s 151(9)	
s 29(6)			Unnecessary.
s 29(7)–(9)		Sch 30	
s 30(1)	Friendly societies.	—	
s 30(2)		s 460(2)(*c*)(i)	
s 30(3)		s 460(3)	
s 30(4)		s 464(2)–(4)	
s 30(5)		s 464(5)(*d*)	
s 30(6)		Sch 15 §6(2)	
s 30(7)		s 464(7)	
s 30(8)		s 547(7)	
s 31	Trade unions.	s 467(1), (3)	
s 32	Charities.	s 202(7)	
s 33(1), (2)	Employee share schemes.	s 187, Sch 9	
s 33(3)		s 360(4)(*a*)	
s 33(4)		—	Unnecessary.
s 34(1), (2)	Charities.	s 86(3)	
s 34(3)		—	Spent.
s 35(1)–(7)	Training costs.	s 588	
s 35(8)		Sch 29	
s 36(1)	Corporation tax.	—	Spent.
s 36(2)		s 478(1)	
s 36(3)(*a*)		Sch 30	
s 36(3)(*b*)		s 478(4)–(7)	
s 37(1)	Associates.	s 417(3)(*c*)	
s 37(2)		s 360(4)(*b*)	
s 37(3)		—	Spent.
s 38(1)	Authorised unit trusts.	s 468(1)–(4), (6)	
s 38(2)		—	Spent.
s 39	Other unit trusts.	s 469, 828	
s 40(1), (2)	Definitions.	s 468(6), 832	Subsections (4), (5), (6) not repealed.
s 41	Expenses of management.	s 75(1)	
s 42(1)	Business Expansion Scheme.	s 289(6), (7)	
s 42(2)		s 289(14), (15)	

Dest. Tables

FA 1987	Subject Matter	Re-enacted in TA 1988	Remarks
s 42(3)		s 290(2)	
s 42(4)		s 304(4)	
s 42(5)		s 307(1)	
s 42(6)		—	Spent.
s 43(1)		s 297(4)	
s 43(2)		s 298(8)	
s 44, 45	Oil: ACT.	s 498, 499	Am 1987(2) s 76(4), (5).
s 46(1)		s 497(2)	
s 46(2)		s 497(3), (4)	
s 46(3)		s 497(6), (7)	
s 70(1)		s 788(2)	
s 71		—	Unnecessary.
Sch 3	Income support.		
para 7		s 151(5)	
para 1(2)		s 151(2)	
para 2–4		s 151(6)–(8)	
para 5		s 833(5)(*c*)	
para 6		s 152(1)	
para 7		s 204(*b*)	
Sch 4	Employee share schemes.		
para 1, 2		Sch 9 §15(1)–(4)	Am & rep in part 1987(2) s 59(2), (3), Sch 9 Pt I.
para 3		Sch 9 §15(5)–(8)	
para 4, 5		Sch 29	Am 1987(2) s 56.
para 6–8		Sch 9 §37–39	
Sch 5	Training costs.	s 589	
Sch 6	Corporation tax.		
para 1–8		Sch 30 §1	
para 9–12		s 478(4)–(7)	
Sch 15	Pre-consolidation amendments.		See destinations of enactments amended.

FINANCE (NO 2) ACT 1987
(c 51)

F(No 2)A 1987	Subject Matter	Re-enacted in TA 1988	Remarks
s 1	Profit-related pay.	s 169	
s 2		s 170	
s 3		s 171	
s 4		s 172	
s 5		s 173	
s 6		s 174	
s 7		s 175	
s 8		s 176	
s 9		s 177	
s 10		s 178	
s 11		s 179	
s 12		s 180	
s 13		s 181	
s 14		Sch 29	
s 15		s 182	
s 16		s 183	
s 17		s 184	
s 18	Personal pension schemes.	s 630	
s 19		s 631(1)–(4)	
s 20		s 632, 828	
s 21		s 633	
s 22		s 634	
s 23		s 635, 828	
s 24		s 636	
s 25		s 637(1)	
s 26		s 637(2)	
s 27		s 638(1)	
s 28		s 638(2), 828	
s 29		s 638(3)–(5)	

F(No 2)A 1987	Subject Matter	Re-enacted in TA 1988	Remarks
s 30		s 638(6), (7)	
s 31		s 639(1)	
s 32		s 640	
s 33		s 641	
s 34		s 642	
s 35		s 644	
s 36		s 645	
s 37		s 646	
s 38		s 643(1)	
s 39(1)		s 643(2)	
s 39(2)		Sch 29	
s 39(3)		s 431(4)(*c*), 438(8)	
s 39(4)		s 476(7)	
s 40		s 468(2), Sch 29	
s 41(1), (2)		s 643(3), (4)	
s 41(3)		s 657(2)(*e*)	
s 42		s 649, 828	
s 43		s 650	
s 44		s 647	
s 45		s 639(2)–(5), 828	
s 46		s 639(1)	
s 47		s 651	
s 48		s 639(6)	
s 49		s 639(7), (8)	
s 50		s 652	
s 51(1)		s 653	
s 51(2)		Sch 29	
s 52		s 654	
s 53		s 648	
s 54(1)		s 618	
s 54(2)		s 626	
s 54(3)–(6)		s 618	
s 55		s 655(1)–(3)	
s 56		s 655(4), (5), 828	
s 57, 58		—	Unnecessary.
s 59(1)	Employee share schemes.	Sch 29	
s 59(2), (3)		Sch 9 §15	
s 60	Payments between related companies.	s 341	
s 61(1), (2)	Close companies.	—	Unnecessary.
s 61(3), (4)		s 423(1), (3)	
s 61(5), (6)		Sch 19 §15(1), 18	
s 62(1)	Partnerships.	s 112(4), (5)	
s 62(2)		—	Spent.
s 63	Group relief.	s 404	
s 64(2)		s 343(2)	
s 65	Controlled foreign companies.	Sch 25 §2(1)(*c*), 4(1)(*c*)	
s 66	Offshore funds.	Sch 27 §1(1)(*c*), 14	
s 67	DTR.	s 798(1), (2), (5)(*b*), (6)–(11)	
s 68		s 803(2)–(5), (11)	
s 70	Lloyd's underwriters.	s 450(5)	
s 71	Loss relief.	s 576(5)	
s 74(1)	Companies' chargeable gains.	—	Unnecessary.
s 74(2)		s 239	
s 74(3)		—	Spent.
s 74(4)		s 13	
s 74(5)		s 245(2), 246(5)	
s 75(1)		s 434(6)	
s 75(2), (3)		s 435(2), (3)	
s 75(4)		—	Spent.
s 76(1)	Oil.	—	Unnecessary.
s 76(2)		s 497(5)	
s 76(3)		s 497(1)	
s 76(4)		s 498	
s 76(5)		s 499(4)	
s 77(2)		s 797(4), (5)	
s 77(3)–(5)		—	Spent.
s 87	Interest on overpaid tax.	s 826	

F(No 2)A 1987	Subject Matter	Re-enacted in TA 1988	Remarks
s 90(1)	Payment of corporation tax.	s 8(3), 10(1)	
s 90(2), (3)		s 419(1), (3)	
s 90(4)–(7)		s 10(2)–(5)	
s 92	PAYE.	s 203	
s 93	Sub-contractors.	s 561, 566	
Sch 1	Profit-related pay schemes.	Sch 8	
Sch 2	Amendments.		See destinations of enactments amended.
Sch 3	Occupational pension schemes.		
Pt I	Amendments.		See destinations of enactments amended.
Pt II	Pre-19th March 1987 schemes.	Sch 23	
Sch 4	Dual resident investing companies.	Sch 17	
Sch 5	—	—	Spent.
Sch 6	Management provisions.		
para 1		s 346	
para 2		—	Not repealed.
para 3		s 347	
para 4, 5		—	Not repealed.
para 6		s 584	
para 7		—	Not repealed.
para 8		s 451(2), 828	

TCGA 1992: DESTINATION TABLE

This Table lists the provisions of the Capital Gains Tax Act 1979 the Income and Corporation Taxes Acts 1970 and 1988 and various Finance Acts which are re-enacted in the Taxation of Chargeable Gains Act 1992.

For the operative date of the re-enacted provisions, see TCGA 1992 s 289. The table does not take account of amendments and repeals made to TCGA 1992 after its date of Royal Assent.

	Re-enacted in TCGA 1992 (unless otherwise stated)	*Remarks*
Income and Corporation Taxes Act 1970		
s 238(4)	s 170(1)	
s 267(1), (2)	s 139(1), (2)	
s 267(2A)	s 139(3)	Added by FA 1990 s 65.
s 267(3)	s 139(4)	Amended by FA 1980 s 81; repealed in part by FA 1980 Sch 20 Part X.
s 267(3A)–(3C)	s 139(5)–(7)	Added by FA 1977 s 41; F(No 2)A 1987 Sch 6 para 2.
s 267(4)	ss 139(9), 288(1)	
s 267A	s 211	Added by FA 1990 Sch 9.
s 268A	s 140	Added by FA 1977 s 42.
s 269	s 40	Amended and repealed in part by FA 1981 s 38.
s 270(4)–(6)	—	Inserted in TA 1988 as s 126A: see Sch 10 para 14(6).
s 272(1)	s 170(2)	Amended by FA 1989 s 138; FA 1990 s 70(2)(*a*).
s 272(1A)–(1F)	s 170(3)–(8)	Added by FA 1989 s 132; amended by FA 1990 s 86.
s 272(2)	s 170(9)	Amended by the Companies Consolidation (Consequential Provisions) Act 1985 Sch 2; F(No 2)A 1987 s 79; partly spent.
s 272(3), (4)	s 170(10), (11)	Amended by FA 1989 s 138.
s 272(5)	s 170(12), (13)	
s 272(6)	s 170(14)	Repealed in part and amended by the London Regional Transport Act 1984 Sch 3 para 7.
s 273(1), (2)	s 171(1), (2)	Amended by FA 1980 s 81(4); F(No 2)A 1987 s 64(3); FA 1990 s 65.
s 273(2A)	s 171(3)	Added by FA 1988 s 115.
s 273(3)	s 171(4)	
s 273A	s 172	Added by FA 1990 s 70.
s 274	s 173	
s 275(1), (1A), (1B)	s 174(1)–(3)	Added by FA 1990 s 70.
s 275(2)	s 174(4)	
s 275(3)	s 174(5)	Amended by FA 1980 s 81(5).
s 276(1)	s 175(1)	Amended by F(No 2)A 1987 s 64(4).
s 276(1A)	s 175(2)	Added by F(No 2)A 1987 s 64(4); amended by FA 1990 s 65.
s 276(2)	s 175(3)	
s 277	—	Repealed by TA 1988 Sch 31.
s 278(1)–(3)	ss 178(1)–(3), 179(1)–(3)	
s 278(3A)	s 179(4)	Added by F(No 2)A 1987 Sch 6 para 4.
s 278(3B)–(3D)	ss 178(4)–(6), 179(5)–(7)	Added by FA 1989 s 138(5).
s 278(3E)	s 179(8)	Added by FA 1989 s 138(5).
s 278(3F)	ss 178(7), 179(9)	Added by FA 1989 s 138(5).
s 278(4)	ss 178(8), 179(10)	
s 278(5)	ss 178(9), 179(11)	
s 278(5A)	s 179(12)	Added by F(No 2)A 1987 Sch 6 para 4.
s 278(6)	ss 178(1), 179(13)	Repealed in part by F(No 2)A 1987 Sch 6 para 4.
s 278(7)	—	Spent.
s 278(8)	s 180(1)	
s 278A	s 181	Added by FA 1970 s 27.
s 279	—	Spent.

Dest. Tables

	Re-enacted in TCGA 1992 (unless otherwise stated)	*Remarks*
Income and Corporation Taxes Act 1970		
s 280	s 176	Amended by the Companies Consolidation (Consequential Provisions) Act 1985 Sch 2; FA 1988 Sch 8 para 6; repealed in part by FA 1988 Sch 14 Part VII; FA 1974 Sch 14 Part VI.
s 281	s 177	Amended by FA 1990 s 70.
s 342	s 218	Amended by the Housing (Consequential Provisions) Act 1985 Sch 2; FA 1991 ss 95, 96; repealed in part by FA 1991 Sch 19 para 6.
s 342A	s 219	Added by the Housing Act 1974 s 11; amended by the Housing (Consequential Provisions) Act 1985 Sch 2; FA 1991 ss 95, 96.
s 342B	s 220	Added by FA 1984 s 56.
Finance Act 1970		
s 27	s 181	
s 28	Sch 10	See TA 1988 s 126A.
s 29(5)	s 202(1), (2)	
s 29(6)–(9)	s 203(1)	
Sch 3		
paras 1, 8	Sch 11 paras 26, 27	
Sch 6		
paras 3–9	ss 202, 203	Repealed in part by FA 1971 Sch 14 Part III.
Finance Act 1973		
s 38(1)–(3)	s 276(1)–(3)	Repealed in part by TA 1988 Sch 31.
s 38(3A)–(3C)	s 276(4)–(6)	Added by FA 1984 s 81; amended by FA 1989 s 130; repealed in part by FA 1989 Sch 17 Part VII.
s 38(4)	s 276(7)	Substituted by TA 1988 Sch 29 para 12. Partly spent.
s 38(5)	s 276(8)	Amended by FA 1984 s 81.
Finance (No 2) Act 1975		
s 47(1), (4), (8), (11), (12)	s 283	Repealed in part by FA 1988 Sch 14 Part IV; amended by FA 1989 s 179.
s 47(2), (3), (5)–(7), (9), (10)	—	Repealed by FA 1988 Sch 14 Part IV; FA 1989 Sch 17 Part X.
s 58	s 106	Repealed in part by FA 1990 Sch 19 Part IV.
Finance Act 1976		
s 54		Spent.
s 131	s 266	
Finance Act 1977		
s 41	s 139(5)–(7), (10)	
s 42	s 140	
Capital Gains Tax Act 1979		
s 1	s 1	
s 2	s 2(1)	
s 3	—	Repealed by FA 1988 Sch 14 Part VII.
s 4(1)	s 2(2)	
s 4(2)	—	Repealed by FA 1988 Sch 14 Part VIII.
s 5(1)	s 3(1)	Substituted by FA 1980 s 77(2); amended by FA 1982 s 80(1).
s 5(2), (3)	—	Replaced by sub-s (1) substituted by FA 1980 s 77.
s 5(1A), (1B), (1C)	s 3(2)–(4)	Added by FA 1982 s 80(2); £5,500 fixed for 1991–92 by SI 1991/736.

	Re-enacted in TCGA 1992 (unless otherwise stated)	*Remarks*
Capital Gains Tax Act 1979		
s 5(4), (5)	s 3(5), (6)	Amended by FA 1980 s 77(3); FA 1982 s 80(1); repealed in part by FA 1988 Sch 14 Part VIII.
s 5(6)	s 3(8)	
s 6	—	Repealed by FA 1984 Sch 23 Part VIII.
s 7	s 7	Amended by FA 1980 s 61(2).
s 7A	s 281	Added by FA 1989 Sch 14 para 5.
ss 8, 9	—	Repealed by FA 1984 Sch 23 Part VIII.
s 10	s 277	
s 11	s 278	
s 12(1)	s 10(1)	
s 12(1A)	s 10(2)	Added by FA 1989 s 128(2).
s 12(2)	s 10(4)	
s 12(2A)	s 10(5)	Added by FA 1989 s 126(2).
s 12(3)	s 10(6)	
s 13	s 279(1)–(6)	Amended by FA 1991 s 97.
s 14	s 12	Amended by TA 1988 Sch 29 para 15.
s 15(1)–(9)	s 13(1)–(9)	
s 15(10)	s 13(11)	
s 16	s 14	
s 17	—	Repealed by FA 1981 Sch 19 Part VIII.
s 18(1)–(3)	s 9	
s 18(4)	s 275	Amended by FA 1984 s 69; Copyright, Designs and Patents Act 1988 Sch 7 para 26.
s 18(5)–(8)	s 11	Added by TA 1988 Sch 29 para 16.
s 19(1), (2)	s 21	
s 19(3)	—	Repealed by FA 1981 Sch 19 Part VIII.
s 19(4), (5)	s 51	
s 20	s 22	
s 21(1)–(5)	s 23(1)–(5)	
s 21(6)	s 35(9)	
s 21(7)	s 23(6)	
s 22	s 24	
s 23	s 26	
s 24	s 27	
s 25	s 29	
s 26	s 30	Amended by FA 1989 s 135.
s 26A	s 31	Added by FA 1989 s 136.
s 26B	s 32	Added by FA 1989 s 136.
s 26C	s 33	Added by FA 1989 s 136.
s 26D	s 34	Added by FA 1989 s 137.
s 27	s 28	
s 28(1), (2)	s 15	Amended by FA 1982 s 86(4).
s 28(3)	s 35(9)	
s 29(1)–(4)	s 16	
s 29(5)	s 2(3)	
s 29A(1), (2)	s 17	Added by FA 1981 s 90.
s 29A(3)–(5)	—	Spent.
s 30	s 15(1)	
s 31	s 37	Amended by TA 1988 Sch 29 para 17; CAA 1990 Sch 1 para 3.
s 32	s 38	Repealed in part by FA 1984 Sch 23 Part VIII.
s 32A	s 120(2)–(7)	Added by TA 1988 Sch 29 para 18.
s 33	s 39	Amended by TA 1988 Sch 29 para 19.
s 33A	s 119	Added by TA 1988 Sch 29 para 20.
s 34	s 41	Amended and repealed in part by CAA 1990 Sch 1, 2; FA 1988 Sch 13 para 16.
s 35	s 42	
s 36	s 43	
s 37	s 44	
s 38	s 46	
s 39	s 47	

	Re-enacted in TCGA 1992 (unless otherwise stated)	*Remarks*
Capital Gains Tax Act 1979		
s 40(1)	s 280	
s 40(2)	s 48	
s 41	s 49	
s 42	s 50	
s 43	s 52	
s 44	s 58	
s 45	—	Repealed by FA 1988 Sch 14 Part VIII.
s 46	s 60	
s 47	s 64	
s 48	s 65	
s 49	s 62	Amended by FA 1981 s 90.
s 50	s 63	
s 51	s 68	
s 52	s 69	
s 53	s 70	Amended by FA 1981 s 86.
s 54	s 71	Amended by FA 1981 s 87.
s 55(1)	s 72	Amended by FA 1982 s 84.
s 55(2)	—	Repealed by FA 1982 Sch 22 Part VI.
s 55(3)–(6)	s 72(2)–(5)	
s 56(1)	s 73(1)	Amended by FA 1981 s 87.
s 56(1A), (1B)	s 73(2), (3)	Added by FA 1982 s 84.
s 56(2)	—	Repealed by FA 1982 Sch 22 Part VI.
s 56A	s 74	Added by FA 1982 s 84; amended by FA 1989 Sch 14 para 6.
s 57	s 75	
s 58	s 76	
s 59	s 282	
s 60	s 59	
s 61	s 66	
s 62	s 18	Amended by FA 1981 s 90.
s 63	s 286	Amended by TA 1988 Sch 29 para 15.
s 64	s 288(1), (5), (8)	
s 65	Sch 2 para 4	Partly spent.
s 66(1), (2)	s 105	Amended by FA 1985 Sch 19 para 17(2).
s 66(3), (4)	s 104(3)	Repealed in part by FA 1985 Sch 27 Part VII.
s 67	s 115	Substituted by FA 1986 s 59.
ss 68–70	—	Repealed by FA 1985 Sch 27 Part VII.
s 71	s 121	
s 72	s 122	
s 73	s 123	Sub-s (2) spent.
s 74	s 124	
s 75	s 125	Amended by FA 1988 Sch 8 para 7.
s 76	—	Spent.
s 77	s 126	
s 78	s 127	
s 79(1)	s 128(1)	
s 79(1) proviso 1	s 128(2)	
s 79(1) proviso 2	s 128(2)	Added by FA 1981 s 91.
s 79(2), (3)	s 128(3), (4)	
s 80	s 129	
s 81	s 130	
s 82	s 132	
s 83	s 133	
s 84(1)	s 134(1)	
s 84(2)	s 134(2)	
s 84(3)	s 134(2)	Repealed in part by FA 1985 Sch 27 Part VII.
s 84(4)	s 134(3)	Amended by FA 1985 s 67(2).
s 84(5)–(7)	s 134(4)–(6)	
s 84(8)	—	Spent.
s 85	s 135	
s 86	s 136	
s 87	s 137	Amended by F(No 2)A 1987 Sch 6 para 5.

	Re-enacted in TCGA 1992 (unless otherwise stated)	*Remarks*
Capital Gains Tax Act 1979		
s 88	s 138	
s 89	s 141	Amended by FA 1981 s 91; repealed in part by FA 1989 Sch 17 Part V.
s 90	s 142	
s 91	—	Unnecessary.
s 92(1)	s 99(2), 288(1), (8)	Amended by FA 1987 s 40.
s 92(2), (3)	s 99(3)	Amended by FA 1987 s 40.
s 93	s 99(1)	
ss 94, 95	—	Repealed by FA 1980 Sch 20 Part X.
s 96	s 100(2)	
s 97	—	Repealed by FA 1980 Sch 20 Part X.
s 98	s 101	Amended by FA 1981 s 81(3).
s 99	s 61	Amended by the Administration of Justice Act 1982 s 46(2)(*f*).
s 100	—	Repealed by FA 1980 Sch 20 Part X.
s 101	s 222	Amended by TA 1988 Sch 29 para 21; FA 1991 s 93.
s 102(1), (2)	s 223(1), (2)	Amended by FA 1980 s 80; FA 1991 s 94.
s 102(3)	s 223(3), (7)	
s 102(4)	s 223(7)	Amended by FA 1988 Sch 8 para 8.
s 102(5), (6), (7)	s 223(5), (6), 287	Added by FA 1991 s 94.
s 103	s 224	
s 104	s 225	
s 105	s 226	Amended by FA 1988 s 111.
s 106	s 240	
s 107	s 242	Amended by FA 1984 s 63; FA 1986 s 60; TA 1988 Sch 29 para 15.
s 108	s 243	
s 109	s 244	
s 110	s 245	
s 111	s 246	
s 111A	s 247	Added by FA 1982 s 83.
s 111B	s 248	Added by FA 1982 s 83.
s 112	s 249	
s 113	s 250	Amended by FA 1988 Sch 6 para 6.
s 114	—	Repealed by FA 1985 Sch 27 Part X.
s 115(1), (2)	s 152(1), (2)	
s 115(3)	s 152(3), (4)	
s 115(4)–(7)	s 152(5)–(8)	
s 115(7A)	s 152(9)	Added by FA 1988 Sch 8 para 9.
s 115(8), (9)	s 152(10), (11)	
s 116	s 153	
s 117(1), (2)	s 154(1), (2)	Amended by FA 1990 s 40(2).
s 117(2A)	s 154(3)	Added by FA 1990 s 40(3).
s 117(3)–(6)	s 154(4)–(7)	Amended by FA 1990 s 40(4).
s 118	s 155	Amended by FA 1988 s 112.
s 119	s 156	
s 120	s 157	Amended by FA 1985 s 70(9).
s 121	s 158	
s 122	s 161	
s 123	s 162	
s 123A	s 221	Added by TA 1988 Sch 29 para 22.
ss 124, 125	—	Repealed by FA 1985 Sch 27 Part VII.
s 126(1), (1A)	s 165(1), (2)	Substituted by FA 1989 Sch 14 para 1.
s 126(2)–(8)	s 165(3)–(9)	Amended by FA 1981 s 90; FA 1985 s 70(9); FA 1989 Sch 14 para 1; repealed in part by FA 1989 Sch 17 Part VII.
s 126(9), (10)	s 165(10), (11)	Added by FA 1989 Sch 14 para 1.
s 126A	s 166	Added by FA 1989 Sch 14 para 2.
s 126B	s 167	Added by FA 1989 Sch 14 para 2.
s 126C	—	Repealed by FA 1991 Sch 19 Part VI.
s 127	s 45	
s 128	s 262	Amended by FA 1989 s 123.

	Re-enacted in TCGA 1992 (unless otherwise stated)	*Remarks*
Capital Gains Tax Act 1979		
s 129	s 240	
s 130	s 263	
s 131	s 268	
s 132	—	Unnecessary.
s 132A	s 118	Added by TA 1988 Sch 29 para 23; amended by FA 1989 s 96(3).
s 133	s 269	
s 134	s 251	
s 135	s 252	
s 136(1)–(5)	s 253(1)–(5)	
s 136(5A)–(5C)	s 253(6)–(8)	Added by FA 1990 s 83.
s 136(6)–(9)	s 253(9)–(12)	Amended by FA 1990 s 83.
s 136(9A)	s 253(13)	Added by FA 1990 s 83.
s 136(10), (11)	s 253(14), (15)	Amended by FA 1989 Sch 12 para 6.
s 136A	s 254	Added by FA 1990 s 84.
s 136B	s 255	Added by FA 1990 s 84.
s 137(1)–(4)	s 144(1)–(4)	Amended by F(No 2)A 1987 s 81.
s 137(5)	—	Spent.
s 137(6)–(8)	s 144(5)–(7)	
s 137(9), (10)	ss 144(8), (9), 287	Added by F(No 2)A 1987 s 81.
s 138	s 146	Amended by FA 1980 s 84; F(No 2)A 1987 s 81.
s 139	s 147	
s 140	s 204(1), (2), (4)	
s 141	s 205	
s 142	s 206	Amended by FA 1988 s 101.
s 142A(1)–(3)	s 207(1)–(3)	Section 142A was added by TA 1988 Sch 29 para 24.
s 142A(4)	s 207(6)	
s 142A(4A), (4B)	s 207(4), (5)	Added by FA 1989 s 91.
s 142A(5)	s 209(2)	Repealed in part by FA 1989 Sch 17 para 7.
s 142A(6), (7)	s 209(6)	Added by FA 1989 s 92.
s 143	s 210	
s 144	s 237	
s 144A	s 238	Added by TA 1988 Sch 29 para 25.
s 145	s 256	
s 146	s 257	Amended by FA 1981 s 90; IHTA 1984 Sch 8 para 9; repealed in part by FA 1982 Sch 22 Part VI.
s 146A	s 259	Added by FA 1989 s 125.
s 147	s 258	Amended by FA 1985 s 95; IHTA 1984 Sch 8 para 10.
s 147A	s 260	Added by FA 1989 Sch 14 para 4.
s 147B	s 261	Added by FA 1989 Sch 14 para 4.
s 148	—	Repealed by FA 1984 Sch 23 Part VIII.
s 149	s 239	Amended by FA 1981 s 90(3); IHTA 1984 Sch 8 para 11; Companies Consolidation (Consequential Provisions) Act 1985 Sch 2.
s 149A	ss 204(3), 215	Added by TA 1988 Sch 29 para 26.
s 149B	s 271	Added by TA 1988 Sch 29 para 26; amended by FA 1988 Sch 13 para 17; FA 1990 ss 28(3), 81, Sch 18 para 3; FA 1991 s 57(4).
s 149C	s 150	Added by TA 1988 Sch 29 para 26; amended by FA 1990 Sch 14 para 17.
s 149D	ss 151, 287	Added by TA 1988 Sch 29 para 26; amended by FA 1988 s 116.
s 150	s 272	Repealed in part by FA 1987 Sch 16 para XI.
s 151	—	Repealed by FA 1985 Sch 27 Part VII.
s 152	s 273	
s 153	s 274	
s 154	s 284	

	Re-enacted in TCGA 1992 (unless otherwise stated)	*Remarks*
Capital Gains Tax Act 1979		
s 155	s 288	Amended by FA 1990 s 127(2); FA 1989 Sch 14 para 6; TA 1988 Sch 29 para 27; FA 1985 s 72(6).
ss 156–160	—	Commencement, savings etc: for corresponding provisions see ss 289–291 and Sch 11 Part IV.
Sch 1		
paras 1–3	—	Repealed by FA 1988 Sch 14 Part VIII.
para 4	s 3(7)	Amended by FA 1980 s 77(4)(*c*).
paras 5, 6	Sch 1	Amended by FA 1980 s 77(4)(*c*); FA 1981 s 89; FA 1982 s 80; Mental Health Act 1983 Sch 4 para 49; FA 1980 s 78.
Sch 2	Sch 9	Repealed in part by Gas Act 1986 Sch 9 para 2; FA 1989 Sch 17 Part XIV; FA 1989 (Repeal of Tithe Redemption Enactments) (Appointed Day) Order, SI 1989/1788; Electricity Act 1989 Sch 18.
Sch 3	Sch 8	
Sch 4	Sch 7	Amended by IHTA 1984 Sch 8 para 12; FA 1989 Sch 14 para 3; repealed in part by FA 1981 Sch 19 Part VIII; FA 1989 Sch 17 Part VII.
Sch 5	Sch 2	
Sch 6	Sch 11	
para 1	para 1	
para 2	para 7, 8	
para 3	para 6	
para 4	para 1	
paras 5, 6	para 3	
para 7	para 4	
para 8	para 5	
para 9	para 9	
para 10	para 26	
para 11	para 10(1)	
paras 12, 13	paras 11, 12	
paras 14–16	—	Spent.
paras 17–20	paras 13–16	
para 21	para 17	
para 22	—	Unnecessary.
para 23	—	Spent.
paras 24–26	paras 20–22	
para 27	—	Spent.
paras 28, 29	paras 23, 25	
Finance Act 1980		
s 61(2)	s 7	
ss 77, 78	—	See destinations of enactments amended.
s 79	—	Repealed by FA 1989 Sch 17 Part VII.
s 80(1)	s 223(4)	Amended by FA 1991 s 94.
s 80(2)	—	Spent.
s 81(1)	s 100(1)	
s 81(2)–(6)	—	See destinations of enactments amended.
s 81(7)	—	Spent.
s 82	—	Repealed by FA 1984 Sch 23 Part VIII.
ss 83, 84	—	See destinations of enactments amended.
s 117	s 192(1)	
Sch 18		
paras 9, 10, 15, 23	s 192	
paras 1–8, 11–14	—	Repealed by FA 1985 Sch 27 Part X; FA 1986 Sch 23 Part IX; FA 1988 Sch 4 Part XI; TA 1988 Sch 31.
Finance Act 1981		
s 38(3), (4)	s 40	

	Re-enacted in TCGA 1992 (unless otherwise stated)	*Remarks*
Finance Act 1981		
s 78	—	Spent.
s 79	s 168	Amended by FA 1989 Sch 14 para 6; FA 1991 s 92.
s 80(1), (2)	s 87(1), (2), (10)	
s 80(2A)	s 87(3)	Added by FA 1991 s 89.
s 80(3)–(6)	s 87(4)–(7)	
s 80(6A)	s 87(8)	Added by FA 1991 Sch 18 para 1.
s 80(7), (8)	s 87(9), (10)	Partly spent.
s 80A	s 88	Added by FA 1991 Sch 1 para 2.
s 81	s 89	Amended by FA 1991 Sch 1 para 3.
s 82	s 90	
s 82A	s 96	Added by FA 1991 Sch 1 para 4.
s 83	s 97	Amended by FA 1984 s 71; FA 1990 Sch 14 paras 18, 19; FA 1991 Sch 1 paras 5, 6.
s 84	s 98	
s 85	s 13(10)	
s 86	s 70	
s 87	ss 71, 73	
s 88(1)	s 85(1)	
s 88(2)–(6)	—	Repealed by FA 1991 Sch 19 Part VI.
ss 89–91		See destinations of enactments amended.
s 135	s 270	
Finance Act 1982		
s 80		See destinations of enactments amended.
s 83	ss 247, 248	
s 84	ss 72–74	
s 85	—	Repealed by FA 1984 Sch 23 Part VIII.
s 86(1)	—	Repealed in part by FA 1985 Sch 27 Part VII.
s 86(2), (3)	s 53(2), (3)	Amended by FA 1985 Sch 19 Part I.
s 86(4)	s 53(1)	Amended by FA 1985 Sch 19 Part I.
s 86(5)	—	Repealed by FA 1985 Sch 27 Part VII.
s 86(6)	s 53(4)	
s 87	s 54	Amended by FA 1985 Sch 19 Part I; repealed in part by FA 1985 Sch 27 Part VII.
s 88	s 108	Amended by FA 1985 Sch 19 Part I; repealed in part by FA 1985 Sch 27 Part VII.
s 148	—	Spent.
Sch 13		
paras 1, 2	s 56(1), (2)	Amended by FA 1985 Sch 19 Part I; repealed in part by FA 1985 Sch 27 Part VII.
para 3	—	Repealed by FA 1985 Sch 27 Part VII.
para 4	s 57	Repealed in part by FA 1985 Sch 27 Part VII.
para 5	ss 126, 131, 132	
para 6	s 113	Amended by FA 1985 Sch 19 Part I.
para 7	s 145	Repealed in part by FA 1985 Sch 27 Part VII.
paras 8–10	s 109	
para 11	Sch 2 para 2(2)	
Finance Act 1983		
s 34, Sch 6	—	Spent.
Finance (No 2) Act 1983		
s 7	s 264	Amended by the Parliamentary Constituencies Act 1986 Sch 3 para 6.
Finance Act 1984		
s 44	—	Spent.
s 50	s 241(1), (2)	

	Re-enacted in TCGA 1992 (unless otherwise stated)	*Remarks*
Finance Act 1984		
s 56(3), (4)	s 220	
s 63		See destinations of enactments amended.
s 64(1)	—	Unnecessary.
s 64(2)	s 117(1)	Repealed in part by FA 1989 Sch 17 Part VII.
s 64(2A)	s 117(1)	Added by FA 1991 s 98.
s 64(3)	s 117(2)	
s 64(3A)–(3C)	s 117(3)(*a*)–(*c*)	Added by FA 1989 s 139.
s 64(3D)	s 117(3)(*d*)	Added by FA 1990 Sch 10 para 28.
s 64(3E)–(3G)	s 117(4)–(6)	Added by FA 1991 Sch 10 para 1.
s 64(4), (5)	s 117(7), (8)	Amended by FA 1989 Sch 14 para 6.
s 64(5A)–(5C)	s 117(9)(*a*)–(*c*)	Added by FA 1989 s 139.
s 64(5D)	s 117(9)(*d*)	Added by FA 1990 Sch 10 para 28.
s 64(6)	s 117(10)	Amended by FA 1989 s 139.
s 64(7)	s 116(1)	
s 64(8)	s 117(11)(*a*)	
s 64(9)–(12)	s 117(11)(*b*), (12), 287	Added by FA 1991 Sch 10 para 1.
s 65	—	Repealed by F(No 2)A 1987 Sch 9 Part II.
s 66	—	Spent.
ss 67, 68	—	Spent.
s 69	s 275	
s 70	Sch 11 para 18	
s 71	s 97	
s 79(1)–(4)	s 197(1)–(4)	
s 79(5)	Sch 10, TA 1988 s 502	Repealed in part by F(No 2)A 1987 Sch 9 Part II; TA 1988 Sch 31.
s 79(6)–(9)	s 197(5)–(8)	
s 79(10)		Unnecessary.
s 80	s 198	Amended by FA 1988 Sch 13 para 22.
s 81	s 276	
s 126	s 265	
Sch 11	s 241	Repealed in part by TA 1988 Sch 31.
Sch 13		
paras 1–4		See destinations of enactments amended.
para 5	—	Repealed in part by TA 1988 Sch 31.
para 6	—	Spent.
para 7	s 116(2)–(4)	
para 8	s 116(5)–(8)	
para 9	s 116(9)	Repealed in part by FA 1985 Sch 27 Part VII.
para 10	s 116(10), (11)	Amended by FA 1985 s 67; FA 1989 s 139.
para 11	s 116(12), (13), (14)	
para 12	s 116(15)	Added by FA 1990 s 85.
Sch 14	Sch 11 para 18	
Finance Act 1985		
s 67		See destinations of enactments amended.
s 68(1)–(3)	—	Unnecessary.
s 68(4)	s 55(1)	Repealed in part by FA 1988 Sch 14 Part VII.
s 68(5)	s 55(2)	Substituted by FA 1988 Sch 8 para 11.
s 68(5A)	s 55(3)	Added by FA 1988 s 118.
s 68(6), (7)	s 55(4), (5)	Amended by FA 1988 s 118.
s 68(7A)	s 55(5)	Added by FA 1988 s 118; amended by FA 1989 Sch 15 para 4; FA 1990 s 70(7); FA 1991 ss 78(6), 99.
s 68(8)	s 55(6)	
s 68(9), (10)	s 104(3)	
s 69	s 163	Amended by FA 1991 s 100.
s 70(1)–(8)	s 164	Amended by FA 1991 s 100.
s 70(9), (10)		See destinations of enactments amended.
s 71(1)–(4)	s 19(1)–(4)	
s 71(5)	—	Spent.
s 71(6), (7)	s 19(5), (6)	
s 71(8)	—	Spent.

	Re-enacted in TCGA 1992 (unless otherwise stated)	*Remarks*
Finance Act 1985		
s 72(1), (2)	s 143(1), (2)	Amended by F(No 2)A 1987 s 81; repealed in part by TA 1988 Sch 31.
s 72(2A), (2B)	s 143(3), (4)	Added by F(No 2)A 1987 s 81.
s 72(3), (4)	s 143(5), (6)	
s 72(5), (7)	—	Repealed by F(No 2)A 1987 Sch 9 Part II; TA 1988 Sch 31.
s 72(6)	s 288(6), (7)	
Sch 19		
Part I		See destinations of enactments amended.
Part II para 6(1), (2)	s 109(1)	
para 6(3), (4)	s 109(4), (5)	
para 7(1)	s 109(2)	
para 7(2), (3)	s 109(6)	
Part III para 8	s 104(3)–(5)	
para 9	s 104(1)	
para 10	s 104(6)	
para 11	s 110(1)–(3)	
para 12	s 110(4)	
para 13	s 110(5)–(9)	
para 14	s 110(10), (11)	
para 15	s 114	
Part IV para 16	ss 107(1), (2), 150(5)	
para 17	ss 104(2)(*b*), 105(2)	
para 18, 19	s 107(3)–(9)	
Part V paras 20, 21	s 112	Partly spent.
Part VI paras 22, 23	s 208	
Sch 20	Sch 6	Amended by FA 1988 s 110; FA 1991 s 100.
Sch 21		
para 1	s 20(1), (2)	
para 2	s 20(3)	
para 3	s 20(4), (5)	
para 4	s 20(6)–(9)	
Finance Act 1986		
s 58	s 169	Amended by FA 1989 Sch 14 para 6; repealed in part by FA 1989 Sch 17 Part VII; FA 1991 Sch 19 Part VI.
s 59	s 115	
s 60	s 242	
Finance Act 1987		
s 40	s 99	Repealed in part by TA 1988 Sch 31.
s 68(3)	Sch 11 para 7	
Finance (No 2) Act 1987		
s 64	ss 171(2), 175(2)	Partly spent.
s 73	ss 285, 287	
s 79	s 170(9)	
s 80	s 193	
s 81(1)–(3)	s 143	In force on 29.4.88: F(No 2)A 1987 (Commencement) Order, SI 1988/744.
s 81(4), (5)	s 144	
s 81(6)	s 146	
Sch 6		
para 2	s 139	
para 4	s 179	
para 5	s 137	
Income and Corporation Taxes Act 1988		
s 122(1)(*b*), (3), (8)	s 201	
s 345	s 8	
s 346	s 189	
s 347	s 190	
s 761(4)	Sch 10 para 14(47)(*b*)	

	Re-enacted in TCGA 1992 (unless otherwise stated)	Remarks
Income and Corporation Taxes Act 1988		
Sch 28		
para 8(4), (5)	—	Spent.
Finance Act 1988		
s 62	s 194	
s 63	s 195	
s 64	s 196	Amended by FA 1991 s 67.
s 96	s 35	
s 97	s 36	
s 98	s 4	
s 99	—	Spent.
s 100	s 5	
s 101	s 206	
s 102(1)	s 6(1)	
s 102(1A)	s 6(1)	Added by FA 1991 Sch 6 para 6.
s 102(2)–(4)	s 6(2)–(4)	Section 102(2)(*a*) was repealed by FA 1989 Sch 17 Part V.
s 103	—	Spent.
s 104(1), (2)	—	Spent.
s 104(3)	s 279(7)	
s 105	s 185	Partly spent.
s 106	s 186	
s 107	s 187	
s 108	—	Spent.
s 109	—	Unnecessary.
s 110	Sch 6	
s 111	s 226	
s 112	s 155	
s 113	s 111	
s 114	—	Unnecessary.
s 115	s 171(3)	
s 116	s 151	
s 118	s 55	
Sch 6		
para 6(5)	s 250	
Sch 8	Sch 3	And see destinations of enactments amended.
Sch 9		
paras 1, 2	Sch 4 paras 1, 2	Amended by FA 1991 s 101.
para 2A	Sch 4 para 3	Added by FA 1991 s 101.
para 3	Sch 4 para 4	Amended by FA 1989 Sch 15 para 2; FA 1991 s 101; repealed in part by FA 1991 Sch 19 Part VI.
paras 4–7	Sch 4 paras 5–8	
para 8	Sch 4 para 9	Amended by FA 1991 s 101.
Sch 10		
paras 1–4	s 77	
para 5	s 78	Amended by FA 1991 s 89; repealed in part by FA 1989 Sch 14 Part VIII.
paras 6–9	s 79	
Sch 11		
paras 1, 2	s 182	
para 3	s 183	
paras 4–6	s 184	Amended by FA 1990 s 70.
para 7	—	Spent.
Sch 12		
para 4	s 216	
para 5	s 217	
para 7(*b*)	s 271(4)	
Sch 13		
para 16	s 41	
para 17	s 271(1)(*c*)	
para 18	s 288(3)	
Finance Act 1989		
s 81(2)	—	Spent.
s 91(2)	s 207	
s 92(3)	s 209	
s 96(3)	s 118	
s 122	—	Spent.
s 123	—	See destinations of enactments amended.
s 124	s 67	And see destinations of enactments amended.
s 125	s 259	
s 126	s 10	Partly spent.

	Re-enacted in TCGA 1992 (unless otherwise stated)	*Remarks*
Finance Act 1989		
s 127	s 25	Amended by FA 1990 Sch 9 para 2.
s 128	s 10	
s 129	s 159	
s 130	s 276	
s 131	s 199	
s 132	s 188	
s 133	s 160	
s 134	s 191	
s 135	s 30	
s 136	ss 31–33	
s 137	s 34	
s 138	ss 170, 178, 179, 180	
s 139	s 117	
s 140	s 102	
s 141	—	Unnecessary.
Sch 14		See destinations of enactments amended.
Sch 15		
para 1	Sch 4 para 4(5)	
para 2	Sch 4 para 4(1)	
para 3	Sch 3 para 4(2)	
paras 4, 5		See destinations of enactments amended.
Finance Act 1990		
s 28(3)	s 271(4)	
ss 31–39	ss 227–235	
s 40(1)–(4)	s 154	
s 40(5)–(8)	s 236	
s 46	s 212	Amended by FA 1991 Sch 7 para 14.
s 47	s 213	
s 54	s 103	
s 63	Sch 3 para 7	
s 64	s 200	
s 65		See destinations of enactments amended.
s 70		See destinations of enactments amended.
s 81	s 271(10), (11)	
s 83	s 253	
s 84	ss 254, 255	
s 85	s 116	
s 86	s 170	
s 127(2)	s 288	
Sch 8	s 214	Amended by FA 1991 Sch 7 para 15.
Sch 9		
paras 1, 2	ss 25, 211	
Sch 10		
paras 28, 29	s 117, Sch 11 para 16	
Sch 14		
paras 17, 18	ss 97, 150	
para 19(2), (3), (4)	—	Spent.
Sch 18		
para 3	s 271	
Finance Act 1991		
s 57(4)	s 271(9)	
s 67	Sch 10 para 21	
s 77	—	Spent.
s 78(1)–(3), (8)	s 267	And see destinations of enactments amended.

	Re-enacted in TCGA 1992 (unless otherwise stated)	*Remarks*
Finance Act 1991		
s 83	s 80	
s 84	s 81	
s 85	s 82	
s 86	s 83	
s 87	s 84	
s 88	s 85(2)–(9)	
s 89(1)	—	Unnecessary.
s 89(2)	s 87(3)	
s 89(3)	s 78(3)	
s 90	—	Unnecessary.
s 91	—	Unnecessary.
s 92(1)	—	Spent.
s 92(2)	s 168	
s 92(3)–(7)	—	Spent.
s 93	s 222	
s 94	s 223	
ss 95, 96	ss 218, 219	
s 97	s 279	
s 98	s 117	
s 99		See destinations of enactments amended.
s 100	ss 163, 164, Sch 6	
s 101(1)	—	Spent.
s 101(2)	Sch 4 para 1(*b*)	
s 101(3)	Sch 4 para 2(1)	
s 101(4)	Sch 4 para 2(3),(4)	
s 101(5)	Sch 4 para 3	
s 101(6)	Sch 4 para 4(1)	
s 101(7)	Sch 4 para 4(2)	
s 101(8)	Sch 4 para 4(4)	
s 101(9)	Sch 4 para 9	
s 101(10)	—	Spent.
s 102	s 148	
Sch 6		
para 6	s 6(1)	
Sch 10		
para 1(1), (2)	s 117(4)–(6)	
para 1(3)	ss 117(11), (12), 287, 288	
para 1(4)	—	Spent.
para 1(5)	s 117(13)	
para 4	s 149	
Sch 16		
paras 1, 2	s 86(1)–(4)	
paras 3–16	Sch 5	
para 17	Sch 10 para 2	
Sch 17		
para 1	s 97	Partly spent.
para 2	s 92(1), (2)	
para 3	s 92(3)–(6)	
para 4	s 91	
para 5	s 93(1), (2)	
para 6	s 93(1), (3)	
para 7	s 93(4)	
para 8	s 94	
para 9	s 95	
Sch 18		
para 1	s 87(8)	
para 2	s 88	
para 3	s 89(1)	
para 4	s 96	
para 5	s 97(1), (8)–(10)	
para 6	s 97(1)–(7)	

CAPITAL ALLOWANCES ACT 2001 DESTINATION TABLE

This Table shows how enactments proposed to be repealed are dealt with by the Capital Allowances Act.

The following abbreviations are used in this Table—

Acts of Parliament

ICTA	Income and Corporation Taxes Act 1988 (c 1)
FA 1988	Finance Act 1988 (c 39)
FA 1989	Finance Act 1989 (c 26)
CAA 1990	Capital Allowances Act 1990 (c 1).
FA 1990	Finance Act 1990 (c 29)
FA 1991	Finance Act 1991 (c 31)
TCGA 1992	Taxation of Chargeable Gains Act 1992 (c 12)
F(No 2)A 1992	Finance (No 2) Act 1992 (c 48)
FA 1993	Finance Act 1993 (c 34).
FA 1994	Finance Act 1994 (c 9)
VATA 1994	Value Added Tax Act 1994 (c 23)
FA 1995	Finance Act 1995 (c 4)
FA 1996	Finance Act 1996 (c 8)
FA 1997	Finance Act 1997 (c 16)
F(No 2)A 1997	Finance (No 2) Act 1997 (c 58)
FA 1998	Finance Act 1998 (c 36)
FA 1999	Finance Act 1999 (c 16)
FA 2000	Finance Act 2000 (c 17).

FINANCE ACT 1982 (C 39)

Existing provision		Rewritten provision	Remarks
137	Expenditure met by regional development grants to be disregarded for certain purposes		
	(2), (3)	534(2), (3)	
	(4)	Sch 3 para 89	
	(6)	—	Unnecessary.
	(7)		

INCOME AND CORPORATION TAXES ACT 1988 (C 1)

Existing provision		Rewritten provision	Remarks
83A	Gifts in kind to charities etc		
	(2)(*b*)	63(2)	
	(3)(*b*)	63(2)	
84	Gifts to educational establishments		
	(1)(*b*)	63(2)	
	(3)(*b*)	63(2)	
198	Relief for necessary expenses		
	(2) (words)	20(2), (3)	Amended CAA 1990 Sch 1 para 8(10).
434D	Capital allowances: management assets		Inserted FA 1995 Sch 8 para 23(1).
	(1)	544(2)	
	(2)	544(1)	
	(3)	255(3), 256(3), (4)	
	(4)	255(1)	
	(5)	256(3), (4)	
	(6)	256(1), (2)	
	(7)	544(3)	
	(8)	257(1), (2)	Repealed in part FA 1996 Sch 41 Pt V(24).
434E	Capital allowances: investment assets		Inserted FA 1995 Sch 8 para 23(1).
	(1)	19(5), 545(1), (2)	Substituted FA 1998 Sch 5 para 40(2).
	(2)	19(5)	Amended FA 1997 Sch 15 para 8.
	(3)	—	Repealed FA 1998 Sch 5 para 40(3).

Dest. Tables

Existing provision		*Rewritten provision*	*Remarks*
434E	(4)	545(3)	
	(5)	545(4), (5)	
	(6)	261	Amended FA 1998 Sch 5 para 40(4).
520	Allowances for expenditure on purchase of patent rights: post-31st March 1986 expenditure		
	(1)	468(1), (2)	
	(2)	468(1), 469, 474(2) to (4)	
	(3)	468(3), (4)	
	(4)	470, 471(1), (2), (4) to (6), 472(1) to (3), (6)	Amended FA 1994 s 214(4).
	(5)	471(6)	
	(6)	470, 471(1), (3), 472(5)	
521	Provisions supplementary to section 520		
	(1)	473, 474(2) to (4), 475(1), (2)	Repealed in part FA 1994 s 214(5)(*a*).
	(2)	476(2), (3)	Repealed in part FA 1994 s 214(5)(*a*).
	(3)	477(1)	
	(4)	477(2), (3), 575(1)	
	(5)	481(1) to (3)	Amended and repealed in part FA 1989 Sch 13 para 27(2).
	(6)	481(4) to (6), 577(1)	Inserted FA 1989 Sch 13 para 27(3).
	(7)	575(1)	Inserted FA 1989 Sch 13 para 27(3).
522	Allowances for expenditure on purchase of patent rights: pre-31st March 1986 expenditure		
	(1)	Sch 3 paras 92, 95, 96(1)	
	(2)	Sch 3 para 94(1), (2)	
	(3) to (6)	Sch 3 para 95	
	(7)	Sch 3 paras 94(3), 95, 96(1)	Amended CAA 1990 Sch 1 para 8(25).
523	Lapses of patent rights, sales etc		
	(1)	Sch 3 paras 92, 97	
	(2)	Sch 3 paras 92, 99	
	(3)	Sch 3 paras 92, 100(1) to (3)	
	(4)	Sch 3 para 98	
	(5)	Sch 3 para 93	
	(6)	Sch 3 paras 99, 100(4), (5)	
528	Manner of making allowances and charges		
	(1)	468(1), 474(2) to (4), 478, Sch 3 paras 94(1), (2), 101	Amended FA 1998 s 46(3), Sch 7 para 1, repealed in part FA 1994 s 214(5)(*b*).
	(4)	479(1), (4), 480(1), (4), Sch 3 para 101	
530	Disposal of know-how		
	(1)	454(1), (2), 455(1)	
	(2)	456, 457(1), (2), (4), (5), 458(1) to (3), (6)	Amended FA 1994 s 214(6).
	(3)	456, 457(1), (3), 458(5)	
	(4)	459, 460(2), (3), 461(1), (2)	Repealed in part FA 1994 s 214(5)(*c*).
	(5)	462(1), (2)	Repealed in part FA 1994 s 214(5)(*c*).
	(6)	—	Unnecessary.
	(7)	454(3), (4)	
	(8)	—	Amended CAA 1990 Sch 1 para 8(27); unnecessary.
531	Provisions supplementary to section 530		
	(3) (words)	454(1)	
	(7) (words)	455(2), (3)	
533	Interpretation of sections 520 to 532		
	(1) (words)	483, Sch 3 paras 95, 101	
577	Business entertaining expenses		
	(1)(*c*)	269(1)	
	(7)(*a*) (words)	269(2)	
	(10) (words)	269(4)	
828	Orders and regulations made by the Treasury or the Board		
	(4) (words)	82(4)	
834			
	(2) (words)	2(4), 260(8)	Amended CAA 1990 Sch 1 para 8(37).
SCH 19AC	MODIFICATION OF ACT IN RELATION TO OVERSEAS LIFE INSURANCE COMPANIES		
	para 9C	255(2)	Inserted FA 1995 Sch 8 para 42.

FINANCE ACT 1989 (C 26)

Existing provision		Rewritten provision	Remarks
SCH 13	CAPITAL ALLOWANCES: MISCELLANEOUS AMENDMENTS		
	para 27(1)	—	Introductory words
	para 27(2)	481(1)	Amends and repeals in part ICTA s 521(5).
	para 27(3)	481(4) to (6), 575(1)	Inserts ICTA s 521(6), (7).
	para 27(4)	Sch 3 para 102	Commencement.

CAPITAL ALLOWANCES ACT 1990 (C 1)

Existing provision		Rewritten provision	Remarks
PT I	INDUSTRIAL BUILDINGS AND STRUCTURES		
CH I	INITIAL ALLOWANCES		
1	Buildings and structures in enterprise zones		
	(1)	271(1), (3), 294, 298(1), 299, 301(3), 303(3), 305(1), 306(1)	
	(1A)	346(1) to (3), (5), Sch 3 paras 75, 76	Inserted FA 1991 Sch 14 para 1.
	(2)	271(1)	Amended FA 1990 Sch 13 para 1(1).
	(3)	305(2)	
	(4)	305(1), (2), Sch 3 para 64	
	(5)	306(2), 346(4)	Repealed in part FA 1990 Sch 17 para 2.
	(6)	307(1) , (2), (4)	
	(7)	308(1), (2), Sch 3 para 65	
	(8)	308(3), (4)	
	(9)	308(5), (6)	
	(10)	306(4)	Repealed in part F(No 2)A 1992 Sch 13 para 3.
	(11)	298(1)	Inserted F(No 2)A 1992 Sch 13 para 11.
2	Transitional relief for regional projects		Unnecessary.
	(1)	—	Amended FA 1991 Sch 14 para 2(1), repealed in part FA 1991 Sch 19 Pt V.
	(2)	—	
	(3)	—	
	(3A)	—	Inserted FA 1991 Sch 14 para 2(2).
	(4)	—	
2A	Initial allowances: contracts entered into between October 1992 and November 1993		Inserted FA 1993 s 113(1).
	(1) to (5)	Sch 3 paras 75 to 77	
	(6)	—	Unnecessary.
Ch II	Writing-down Allowances, Balancing Allowances and Balancing Charges		
3	Writing-down allowances		
	(1)	271(1), (3), 294, 301(3), 303(3), 309(1)	Repealed in part FA 1994 s 213(1).
	(2)	310(1), (2), Sch 3 para 66	Amended FA 1994 s 213(2).
	(2A)	347(1), (2)	Inserted FA 1991 Sch 14 para 3(1).
	(2B)	311(1) to (3), 347(3)	Inserted FA 1991 Sch 14 para 3(1), repealed in part FA 1994 s 213(1).
	(2C)	311(1) to (3), 349(1), (2)	Inserted FA 1991 Sch 14 para 3(1), repealed in part FA 1994 s 213(1).
	(3)	311(1) to (3), Sch 3 para 67	Amended FA 1991 Sch 14 para 3(2), repealed in part FA 1991 Sch 19 Pt V, FA 1994 s 213(1).
	(4)	312(1), (2)	Repealed in part FA 1994 s 213(1).
	(5)	—	Inserted FA 1991 s 60(3), amended FA 1995 s 99(2); unnecessary.
4	Balancing allowances and balancing charges		
	(1)	314(1) to (3), 315(1), 328(1), 343(1), 350(1)	Amended FA 1991 Sch 14 para 4(1), FA 1994 s 120(2)(*a*), FA 1995 s 99(3).
	(2)	314(4), (5), Sch 3 para 68	Amended FA 1991 Sch 14 para 4(2).
	(2AA)	343(1), 344(5)	Inserted FA 1995 s 99(4).
	(2AB)	342(3), 344(1) to (4), 575(1)	Inserted FA 1995 s 99(4).

Dest. Tables

Existing provision		Rewritten provision	Remarks
4	(2A)	350(2) to (4)	Inserted FA 1991 Sch 14 para 4(3).
	(3)	318(2), (3)	
	(4)	318(4), (5)	
	(5)	318(1), 319(1)	Amended FA 2000 Sch 19, para 8.
	(6)	319(4), (5)	
	(7)	319(2), (3), (6), (7)	
	(8)	569(5)	
	(9)	321, 322, 323, 350(5)	Amended FA 1991 Sch 14 para 4(4), F(No 2)A 1992 Sch 13 para 13, FA 1993 s 113(2), FA 2000 Sch 19, para 8.
	(9A)	328(2) to (4)	Inserted FA 1994 s 120(2)(*b*).
	(10)	320, 324, Sch 3 para 69	Amended FA 1991 Sch 14 para 4(5), FA 2000 Sch 19, para 8, repealed in part FA 1994 s 213(1).
	(11)	Sch 3 para 70	
	(12)	Sch 3 para 69	
4A	Realisation of capital value		Inserted FA 1994 s 120(3).
	(1)	328(5) to (7), 330(1)	
	(2)	329(1)	
	(3)	331(1)	
	(4)	329(2), 331(4)	
	(5)	329(4), (5), 331(4)	
	(6)	329(3), 331(4)	
	(7)	330(3), (4)	
	(8)	329(6)	
	(9)	331(2), (3)	
	(10)	331(4)	
	(11)	330(2)	
	(12)	330(1)	
	(13)	331(5), 360(2)	
5	Restriction of balancing allowances on sale of industrial buildings or structures		
	(1)	325(1) to (3), 575(1)	
	(2)	325(4), (5)	
	(2A)	328(4)	Inserted FA 1994 s 120(4).
	(3)	325(7)	
	(4)	326(1), (2)	
	(5)	325(6)	
6	Buildings and structures (including hotels) in enterprise zones		
	(1)	271(1), 281, 285(1), (2), 294, 298(1), 299, 301(3), 303(3)	
	(2)	310(1)	
	(3)	317(5)	
	(4)	—	Amended FA 1994 s 120(5); unnecessary.
	(4A)	298(1)	Inserted F(No 2)A 1992 Sch 13 para 12.
	(5)	—	Repealed F(No 2)A 1992 Sch para 4.
7	Other hotels		
	(1)	271(1), 285(1), (2), 317(1), (2), 577(1)	Amended FA 1990 Sch 13 para 1(2), in part unnecessary (see s 7(3)).
	(2)	317(3), (4)	Repealed in part FA 1994 s 213(1).
	(3)	—	Repealed in part FA 1994 s 213(1), remainder spent.
CH III	PROVISIONS SUPPLEMENTARY TO CHAPTERS I AND II		
8	Writing off of expenditure and meaning of ''residue of expenditure''		
	(1)	313, 332	
	(2)	333, 348	Substituted FA 1991 Sch 14 para 5(1).
	(3)	334(1)	Repealed in part FA 1994 s 213(1).
	(4)	334(2)	
	(5)	335(1)	Amended FA 1990 Sch 13 para 2(1), FA 2000 Sch 19 para 8, repealed in part FA 1994 s 213(3)(*a*); paragraph (*b*) not rewritten.
	(6)	335(2)	
	(7)	336(1) to (4)	
	(8)	Sch 3 para 72	
	(9)	337(1), (2)	
	(10)	337(1), (3)	

Existing provision		*Rewritten provision*	*Remarks*
8	(11)	337(1), (4)	
	(12)	340(1) to (4)	
	(12A)	351	Inserted FA 1991 Sch 14 para 5(2).
	(12B)	338	Inserted FA 1994 s 120(6)(*a*).
	(13)	339(1) to (4)	Amended FA 1991 Sch 14 para 5(3), FA 1994 s 120(6)(*b*), s 213(3)(*b*).
	(14)	339(1) to (4), Sch 3 para 73	
9	Manner of making allowances and charges		Substituted FA 1998 Sch 5 para 47.
	(1)	352(1), 353(2) to (4)	
	(2)	353(1) to (4)	
	(3)	353(5)	
	(4)	353(1)	
10	Purchases of buildings and structures		
	(1)	271(3), 294, 295(2) to (4), 296(1), 307(3)	Amended F(No 2)A 1992 Sch 13 para 5.
	(1A)	—	Inserted F(No 2)A 1992 Sch 13 para 6; unnecessary.
	(2)	295(4)	
	(3)	271(3), 293, 295(1), 296(1) to (3)	
	(3A)	—	Inserted F(No 2)A 1992 Sch 13 para 7, amended FA 1993 s 113(3); unnecessary.
	(4)	293, 297(1), (3), 301(6), Sch 3 para 60	Amended F(No 2)A 1992 Sch 13 para 9.
	(5)	297(2)	
10A	Purchases of buildings and structures: special provisions for enterprise zones		Inserted F(No 2)A 1992 Sch 13 para 2.
	(1)	294, 295(1). 298(1), 300, 302(1)	
	(2)	271(3), 294, 295(2), (3), 296(2) to (4), 300, 307(3)	
	(3)	302(2)	
	(4)	302(3)	
	(5)	302(3)	
	(6)	302(2)	
	(7)	298(1)	
	(8)	295(4), 299, 300	
	(9)	292(3), 293, 295(1), 296(1) to (3), 300, 302(1)	
	(10)	298(1)	
10B	Purchases of buildings and structures in enterprise zones within two years of first use		Inserted F(No 2)A 1992 Sch 13 para 8.
	(1)	298(1), 301(1), 303(1)	
	(2)	271(3), 301(2), (3), (8), 303(2), (3), (5)	
	(3)		
	(4), (5)	301(4), 303(4)	
	(6), (7)	303(4)	
	(8)	271(3), 301(5) to (7), 304(1) to (3)	
	(9), (10)	298(1)	
10C	Purchases of buildings and structures: allowances under section 2A		Inserted FA 1993 s 113(4).
	(1) to (11)	Sch 3, para 77	
10D	Arrangements affecting the value of the purchased interest		Inserted FA 1995 s 100(1).
	(1)	357(1), (2)	
	(2)	357(1), (2)	
	(3)	357(1) to (3)	
	(4)	357(4), (5)	
	(5)	357(1), (2)	
11	Long leases		
	(1)	290(1), (2)	
	(2)	290(3)	
	(3)	291(4), (5)	
	(4)	290(1), 291(3)	
	(5)	288(2)	
	(6)	291(1), (2), 575(1)	
12	Expenditure on repair of buildings		
		272(2), (3)	Amended FA 1998 Sch 7 para 4.
13	Expenditure on sites for machinery and plant		
		273(1), (2)	Para (*b*) unnecessary (refers to

Existing provision		Rewritten provision	Remarks
			s 148 which does not apply relation to chargeable periods ending after 26th July 1989).
14	Sports pavilions		
		271(1), 280	
15	Temporary disuse of industrial buildings or structures		
	(1)	285(1), (2)	
	(2), (2A), (3)	—	Repealed FA 1998 Sch 5 para 48.
15ZA	Temporary disuse: manner of making allowances and charges in certain cases		
			Inserted FA 1998 Sch 5 para 49.
	(1)	354(1)	
	(2)	354(1), (2)	
	(3)	354(3), (4)	
	(4)	354(5)	
	(5)	354(1), (5)	
15A	Balancing charge after cessation of trade		
		—	Repealed FA 1998 Sch 5 para 50.
16	Requisitioned land, holding over of leased land and other special cases		
	(1)	358(1) , (2), (4), (5)	
	(2)	358(3) to (5)	
	(3)	358(1)	
	(4)	359(1), (2)	
	(5)	359(1), (3)	
	(6)	359(1), (4)	
	(7)	359(1), (5)	
17	Mining structures etc: balancing allowances carried back to earlier chargeable periods		
	(1)	355(1) to (4)	Amended FA 1998 Sch 7 para 4.
	(2)	355(5), (6)	Amended FA 1991 Sch 15 para 28.
	(3)	3(4)	Amended FA 1999 Sch 11 para 4.
17A	Enterprise zones: exclusion of expenditure		
		298(1)	Inserted F(No 2) 1992 Sch 13 para 10, amended FA 1993 s 113(5).
18	Definition of ''industrial building or structure''		
	(1)	271(1), 274(1) Tables A and B, (2), 275	Amended FA 1991 s 60(4), FA 1995 s 99(5), s 101, in part unnecessary.
	(2)	276(1), (2)	
	(3)	274(1), Table A, item 2, 276(3)	
	(4)	277(1), (5)	
	(5)	277(2), (3)	
	(6)	278, Sch 3 para 57	
	(7)	283(1), (2), Sch 3 para 59	
	(8)	284	Repealed in part FA 1994 s 213(1); in part unnecessary.
	(9)	274, 277(1), (2), 360(1)	Amended Water (Consolidation) (Consequential Provisions) Act 1991 (c 60) Sch 1 para 53.
	''crops''	274(1), Table A, items 4 and 5	
	''dock''	274(1), Table A, item 10	
	''electricity undertaking''	274(1), Table B, item 1	
	''foreign plantation''	274(1), Table A, item 5, 277(2)	
	''hydraulic power undertaking''	274(1), Table B, item 3	
	''retail shop''	277(1)	
	''sewerage undertaking''	274(1), Table B, item 4	
	''undertaking''	274(1)(*b*)	
	''water undertaking''	274(1), Table B, item 2	
	(10)	274(1), Table A item 5, 277(2)	
	(11)	—	Unnecessary.
	(12)	Sch 3 para 56	
	(13)	282	Amended FA 1998 Sch 7 para 4.
	(14)	282, 283	Amended FA 1993 s 113(6).
19	Meaning of ''qualifying hotel''		
	(1)	279(1), (9)	
	(2)	279(1), (8), (9)	
	(3)	279(2) to (4), (6)	Repealed in part FA 1994 s 213(1).
	(4)	279(5)	
	(5)	279(7), (8)	
	(6)	Sch 3 para 58	
20	Meaning of ''the relevant interest''		
	(1)	286(1),(2)	
	(2)	286(3)	

Existing provision		Rewritten provision	Remarks
20	(3)	288(1), 289	
	(4)	—	Spent.
	(5)	342(1)	Inserted FA 1991 s 60(5), amended FA 1995 s 99(6)(*a*).
	(6)	342(2)	Inserted FA 1991 s 60(5), amended FA 1995 s 99(6)(*b*).
21	Other interpretation of Part I		
	(1)	272(1)	
	(2)	287	
	(3)	356(1) to (3)	
	(4)	272(1), 298(3)	
	(5)	281	
	(5AA)	274(1), Table B, item 6, 341(4)	Inserted FA 1995 s 99(7).
	(5A)	341(1)	Inserted FA 1991 s 60(6), amended FA 1995 s 99(8).
	(5B)	341(2)	Inserted FA 1991 s 60(6), amended FA 1995 s 99(8).
	(6)	573(1), (2), (3) 577(1)	
	(7)	573(3)	
	(8)	—	Repealed in part FA 1994 s 213(1); unnecessary.
	(9)	Sch 3, para 79	
	(10)	—	
PT II	MACHINERY AND PLANT		
CH I	ALLOWANCES AND CHARGES: GENERAL PROVISIONS		
22	First-year allowances: transitional relief for regional projects		
	(1)	11(4), 15(1)(*a*), 39, 52(1) to (3), Sch 3 para 46(3)	Amended FA 1993 s 115(1), F(No 2)A 1997 s 42(1), FA 1998 s 84(1).
	(1AA)	Sch 3 para 46(3)	Inserted F(No 2)A 1997 s 42(2).
	(1A)	236(1)	Inserted FA 1991 Sch 14 para 6(1).
	(1B)	236(2), (3)	Inserted FA 1991 Sch 14 para 6(1).
	(2)	—	Spent.
	(3)	—	Spent.
	(3A)	—	Inserted FA 1991 Sch 14 para 6(2); spent.
	(3B)	50, Sch 3 paras 46(1), 47(1), (2)	Inserted FA 1993 s 115(2).
	(3C)	50, Sch 3 paras 46(1), 48(1) to (3)	Inserted F(No 2)A 1997 s 42(3), amended FA 2000 s 70(2)(*a*).
	(3CA)	40(1), (2), 237(2)	Inserted FA 1998 s 83(1), amended FA 2000 s 70(2)(*a*).
	(3CB)	40(1), 50, Sch 3 para 50	Inserted FA 1998 s 83(1).
	(3CC)	41(1), (2)	Inserted FA 1998 s 83(1), amended FA 1999 s 78(1).
	(3CD)	41(2), (5)	Inserted FA 1999 s 78(2).
	(3CE)	41(3), (4)	Inserted FA 1999 s 78(2).
	(3D)	44(1), (2), 50, Sch 3 para 50	Inserted FA 1998 s 84(2), amended FA 2000 s 70(1), (2)(*a*).
	(3E)	45(1), 50, Sch 3 paras 14, 50	Inserted FA 2000 s 71(1).
	(3F)	45(2)	Inserted FA 2000 s 71(1).
	(3G)	45(2)	Inserted FA 2000 s 71(1).
	(3H)	45(3)	Inserted FA 2000 s 71(1).
	(4)	Sch 3 para 47(6)	Amended FA 1993 s 115(3), F(No 2)A 1997 s 42(4), FA 1998 s 85(1), FA 2000 s 71(2).
	(5)	Sch 3 para 47(6)	
	(6)	82(4), Sch 3 para 47(6)	Amended Disability Living Allowance and Disability Working Allowance Act 1991 (c21) Sch 2 para 20, amended and repealed in part Disability Living Allowance and Disability Working Allowance (Northern Ireland Consequential Amendments) Order 1991 S I.1991/2874 art 6(2)(*a*), (*b*), Social Security (Consequential Provisions) Act 1992 (c 6) Sch 2 para 109(*a*), Social Security (Consequential Provisions) (Northern Ireland) Act 1992 (c 9) Sch 2 para 38(*a*).
	(6A)	237(1), Sch 3 para 47(3) to (5)	Inserted FA 1993 s 115(3).

Existing provision		Rewritten provision	Remarks
22	(6B)	46(2), 237(1), Sch 3 para 48(4)	Inserted F(No 2)A 1997 s 42(5), amended FA 1998 s 85(1), FA 2000 s 71(2).
	(6C)	46(2), Sch 3 para 48(4)	Inserted F(No 2)A 1997 s 42(5), amended FA 1998 s 85(1), FA 2000 s 71(2).
	(6D)	42(1)	Inserted FA 1998 s 83(2).
	(6E)	42(1), (2)	Inserted FA 1998 s 83(2).
	(7)	52(4)	Substituted FA 1990 Sch 17 para 3(2).
	(8)	—	Repealed in part FA 1990 Sch 17 para 3(3); unnecessary.
	(9)	—	Repealed FA 1990 Sch 17 para 3(4).
	(10)	41(5)	Amended FA 1998 s 83(3), FA 1999 s 78(3).
	(11)	Sch 3 para 47(6)	
22A	Expenditure of a small company or small business		
			Inserted F(No 2)A 1997 s 43(1).
	(1)	47(1), (2)	Amended FA 2000 s 70(2)(*b*).
	(2)	48(1), (3), (5), (6)	Amended FA 2000 s 70(2)(*b*).
	(3)	48(5), (8)	
	(4)	49(2)	Amended FA 1998 s 85(2)(*a*).
	(5)	49(4)	
	(6)	47(4) to (6), 48(2), (8), (9), 49(6) to (8)	Amended FA 1998 s 85(1)(*b*).
	(7)	47(2), (4), (5), 48(8), (9)	
	(8)	49(5), (6)	Amended FA 1998 s 85(3).
	(9)	49(7)	
22AA	Expenditure of a small enterprise		
			Inserted FA 2000 s 72.
	(1)	47(1), (3)	
	(2)	48(1), (4), (5), (7)	
	(3)	48(5), (8)	
	(4)	49(3)	
	(5)	49(4)	
	(6)	47(4) to (6), 48(2), (8), (9), 49(7), (8)	
	(7)	47(3), (4), 48(8), (9)	
	(8)	49(5), (6)	
	(9)	49(7)	
22B	Withdrawal of first-year allowance on change of use		
			Inserted FA 1998 s 83(4).
	(1)	43(1), 237(2)	
	(2)	43(2), 575(1)	Amended FA 1999 s 78(4).
	(2A)	43(3)	Amended FA 1999 s 78(4).
	(3)	43(4)	
	(4)	43(5), (6)	
22C	Disclosure of information in connection with first-year allowances		
			Inserted FA 1999 s 78(5).
	(1)	51(1), (2)	
	(2)	51(3)	
23	Information relating to first-year allowances		
			Spent.
	(1)	—	Amended FA 1998 Sch 7 para 4, repealed in part FA 1990 Sch 17 para 4(2).
	(2)	—	Repealed in part FA 1990 Sch 17 para 4(3), FA 1994 s 213(1).
	(3) to (5)	—	
	(6)	—	Amended FA 1993 Sch 13 para 2, FA 1998 s 85(4), FA 2000 s 71(2).
24	Writing-down allowances and balancing adjustments		
	(1)	11(4), 15(1)(*a*), 59(3)	
	(1A)	235	Inserted FA 1991 Sch 14 para 7(1).
	(2)	55(1), (2), (4), 56(1), (3), (4), (7), 65(1), 102(4), 109(4)	Amended FA 1994 s 213(4).
	(3)	56(5)	Repealed in part FA 1990 Sch 17 para 5(2).
	(4)	—	Repealed FA 1990 Sch 17 para 5(3).
	(5)	55(3), 56(6)	

Existing provision		Rewritten provision	Remarks
24	(6)	58(6), 60(3), 61(1), (2), 63(1), 64(1), (2), 65(2), 70(3), 132(2), 220(2)	Amended FA 1991 Sch 14 para 7(2), F(No 2)A 1992 s 68(2), repealed in part FA 1994 s 213(1).
	(6A)	72(1), (2)	Inserted F(No 2)A 1992 s 68(3), repealed in part FA 1994 s 213(1).
	(7)	238(1) to (3)	Inserted FA 1991 Sch 14 para 7(2), repealed in part FA 1994 s 213(1).
	(8)	58(6), 70(3), 132(2), 220(2)	Inserted FA 1991 Sch 14 para 7(2), amended F(No 2)A 1992 s 68(4).
25	Qualifying expenditure		
	(1)	57(1), 58(2), (3), (5), 59(1), (2)	Repealed in part FA 1990 Sch 17 para 6(2), FA 1994 s 213(1).
	(2)	—	Repealed FA 1990 Sch 17 para 6(3).
	(3)	58(5)	Amended FA 1996 Sch 21 para 26(2) , repealed in part FA 1990 Sch 17 para 6(4).
	(3A)	—	Inserted FA 1996 Sch 21 para 26(3); unnecessary.
	(4)	52(4), 58(5)	Repealed in part FA 1990 Sch 17 para 6(5).
	(5)	58(6)	
	(5A)	220(1), (2)	Inserted F(No 2)A 1997 s 44(2).
	(5B)	220(2)	Inserted F(No 2)A 1997 s 44(2).
	(5C)	220(2)	Inserted F(No 2)A 1997 s 44(2).
	(6)	229	Amended F(No 2)A 1997 s 44(3).
	(7)	—	Repealed in part FA 1994 s 213(1); unnecessary.
	(8)	231	Amended F(No 2)A 1997 s 44(4).
	(9)	—	Unnecessary.
26	The disposal value		
	(1) (opening words)	61(2), 72(3), 423(1)	
	(1)(*a*)	61(2), Table, item 1, (3), 423(1), Table, item 1, (2)	
	(1)(*b*)	61(2), Table, item 2, (4), 88, 423(1), Table, item 2, (3), 575(1), 577(1) (''dual resident investing company'')	
	(1)(*c*)	61(2), Table, item 3, (3), 423(1), Table, item 3, (2)	
	(1)(*d*)	61(2), Table, item 4, (3), 423(1), Table, item 4, (2)	
	(1)(*e*)	61(2), Table, item 6, 423(1), Table, item 5	Repealed in part FA 1991 Sch 19 Pt V.
	(1)(*ea*)	72(3), Table, item 1	Inserted F(No 2)A 1992 s 68(5).
	(1)(*eb*)	72(3), Table, item 2, (5), 575(1), 577(1) (''dual resident investing company'')	Inserted F(No 2)A 1992 s 68(5).
	(1)(*ec*)	72(3), Table, item 3, (4)	Inserted F(No 2)A 1992 s 68(5).
	(1)(*ee*)	238(2), (3)	Inserted FA 1991 Sch 14 para 8(1).
	(1)(*ef*)	171(1), (2)	Inserted FA 2000 s 81(2).
	(1)(*eg*)	171(1), (3)	Inserted FA 2000 s 81(2).
	(1)(*f*)	61(2), Table, item 7, 196(1), Table, item 6, 423(1), Table, item 6	
	(2)	62(1), (3), 73(1) to (3), 239(2), (5)	Amended FA 1991 Sch 14 para 8(2).
	(2AA)	73(1) to (3)	Inserted F(No 2)A 1992 s 68(6).
	(2A)	239(3), (4)	Inserted FA 1991 Sch 14 para 8(2).
	(3)	62(2), (3), 64(3), 239(5), 575(1)	
	(4)	62(4), 239(5), (6)	Inserted FA 1991 Sch 14 para 8(3).
27	Professions, employments, vocations etc		
	(1)	15(1)(*e*), (i), (4), 20(1), 251, 262	Amended FA 1990 s 87(1); s 27(1)(*b*) repealed from 6th April 1993 by CAA 1990 s 27(3).
	(2)	20(2), 36(2)	
	(2A)	80(2)	Inserted FA 1990 s 87(2).
	(2B)	80(1), (4)	Inserted FA 1990 s 87(2), amended FA 1999 s 50(2).
	(2C)	80(1)	Inserted FA 1990 s 87(2).
	(2D)	80(3)	Inserted FA 1990 s 87(2).

Existing provision		Rewritten provision	Remarks
27	(2E)	80(3)	Inserted FA 1990 s 87(2).
	(3)	—	Transitional provision; spent.
28	Investment companies and life assurance companies		
			Substituted FA 1995 Sch 8 para 24.
	(1)	15(1)(*g*), 18(2), 253(1)	
	(2)	253(2), (3)	
	(3)	253(4)	
	(4)	18(1)	
	(5)	253(5)	
	(6)	253(6)	
28A	Schedule A cases		
			Inserted FA 1997 Sch 15 para 3.
	(1)	15(1)(*b*), (*d*), 16, 33(8), 248	
	(2)	—	Repealed FA 1998 Sch 27 Pt III.
	(3)	15(3), 35(1), (2)	
	(4)	35(3)	
29	Furnished holiday lettings		
	(1)	15(1)(*c*), 16, 17(1), 33(8), 249(1)	Substituted FA 1997 Sch 15 para 4, repealed in part FA 1998 Sch 5 para 51(*a*)
	(1A)	—	Inserted FA 1997 Sch 15 para 4, repealed FA 1998 Sch 5 para 51(*b*).
	(2)	17(2), (3), 249(2)	
	(3)	17(4)	Amended FA 1996 Sch 20 para 44.
CH II	SHIPS		
30	First-year allowances		
	(1)	52(4), 130(1), (3) to (5)	Amended FA 1996 Sch 21 para 27(2), repealed in part FA 1990 Sch 17 para 7. para 27(2), repealed in part FA 1990 Sch 17 para 7.
	(1A)	130(4), (5), 577(1)	Inserted FA 1996 Sch 21 para 27(3).
	(2)	131(1), (2), (4)	Amended FA 1993 Sch 13 para 3.
	(3)	157(1)	
	(4)	131(7)	Amended FA 1998 Sch 5 para 52.
	(5)	130(6)	
31	Writing-down allowances		
	(1)	127(1), (2), 128(1), (2), 130(2), 133(1)	
	(2)	65(2), 127(1), (2), 132(1)	
	(3)	130(2) to (5)	Amended FA 1996 Sch 21 para 28.
	(3A)	130(4), (5), 577(1)	Inserted FA 1996 Sch 21 para 28.
	(4)	131(1), (3), (4)	
	(5)	131(6)	
	(6)	130(7)	Substituted FA 1990 Sch 17 para 8.
	(7)	132(2), (3)	
	(8)	—	Not rewritten (old expenditure).
	(9)	157(9)	
	(10)	131(7)	Amended FA 1998 Sch 5 para 52.
	(11)	128(3), 132(4)	
	(12)	—	Not rewritten (old expenditure).
32	Ships not used in the actual trade		
	(1)	133(1) to (4)	
	(2)	—	Unnecessary.
33	Exclusion of section 31		
	(1)	129(1)	Amended FA 1996 Sch 21 para 29(2); unnecessary in part.
	(2)	—	Unnecessary.
	(3)	129(1)	Repealed in part FA 1994 s 213(1).
	(4)	129(1)	Substituted FA 1996 Sch 21 para 29(3).
	(5)	129(1), 132(3)	
	(5A)	129(2), (3), 577(1)	Inserted FA 1996 Sch 21 para 29(4).
	(6)	—	Unnecessary.
33A	Deferment of balancing charge		
			Inserted FA 1995 s 94.
	(1)	135(1), 136	
	(2)	135(1), (2), 137, 138(1)	
	(3)	138(1), (2)	Amended FA 1996 Sch 35 para 2(1), FA 1998 Sch 7 para 4.
	(4)	144(1), (2)	Amended FA 1996 Sch 35 para 2(2).

Existing provision		Rewritten provision	Remarks
33A	(5)	140(1) to (5)	Substituted FA 1996 Sch 35 para 2(3).
	(5A)	140(6)	Inserted FA 1996 Sch 35 para 2(3).
	(6)	138(1)	
	(7)	136	
	(8)	140(4), 150(1), 158	Inserted FA 1996 Sch 35 para 2(4).
33B	Amount brought into account in respect of the old ship		
			Inserted FA 1995 s 94.
	(1)	139(1), (2)	
	(2)	139(1), (3)	
	(3)	139(3), (4)	
	(4)	139(5)	
	(5)	—	Unnecessary.
33C	Reimposition of deferred charge		
			Inserted FA 1995 s 95.
	(1)	143(1), (2)	Amended FA 1996 Sch 35 para 3(1).
	(2)	143(1), (2)	Amended and repealed in part FA 1996 Sch 35 para 3(2).
33D	Expenditure to which deferments attributed		
			Inserted FA 1995 s 96.
	(1)	146(1) to (3)	Amended FA 1996 Sch 35 para 4(1).
	(2)	149(1), (2)	Amended FA 1996 Sch 35 para 4(2).
	(2A)	150(1), (2), (4), 158	Inserted FA 1996 Sch 35 para 4(3).
	(2B)	150(3), (5), (6)	Inserted FA 1996 Sch 35 para 4(3).
	(3)	149(1)	
	(4)	147(1), 148	Amended FA 1996 Sch 35 para 4(4).
	(5)	147(2)	
	(6)	141(1), (2)	Amended FA 1996 Sch 35 para 4(5).
	(7)	155(1), (2)	Amended FA 1996 Sch 35 para 4(6).
	(8)	156(1) to (3)	Substituted FA 1996 Sch 35 para 4(7).
33E	Qualifying ships		
			Inserted FA 1995 s 96.
	(1)	151(1), (2)	
	(2)	152(1) to (3)	
	(3)	153(1)	
	(4)	153(2), (3)	
	(5)	154(1), Sch 3 para 24	
	(6)	154(2)	
	(7)	154(4), (5)	
	(8)	154(3), 156(1) to (3)	
	(9)	154(1) to (3)	Inserted FA 1996 Sch 35 para 5.
33F	Procedural provisions relating to deferred charges		
			Inserted FA 1995 s 97(1).
	(1)	135(5)	Amended FA 1999 Sch 11 para 5.
	(2)	135(3), (4), 577(1)	
	(3)	—	Spent.
	(4)	142(1) to (5)	Amended FA 1996 Sch 35 para 6(1).
	(4A)	142(6)	Inserted FA 1996 Sch 35 para 6(2).
	(5)	145(1) to (3)	
	(6)	145(4), (5), 157(1), (2)	
	(7)	155(1), (2)	
CH III	EXPENSIVE MOTOR CARS		
34	Writing-down allowances etc		
	(1)	74(1), (2)	Amended F(No 2)A 1992 s 71(2).
	(2)	65(2), 74(1)	
	(3)	75(1), (2), 76(1), (2), (5)	Amended FA 1994 s 213(5).
	(4)	79(1) to (3), 577(1)	
	(5)	77(1) to (3), (5), 78(1), (2), (4), (5)	
35	Contributions to expenditure, and hiring of cars		
	(1)	74(1), (2), 76(3), (4), (5)	Amended F(No 2)A 1992 s 71(4), FA 1994 s 213(6).
	(2)	Sch 2, para 52 [ICTA s 578A(1) to (4)]	Amended FA 1991 s 61(2), F(No 2)A 1992 s 71(5), FA 1998 Sch 7 para 4.
	(2A)	Sch 2, para 52 [ICTA s 578A(5)]	Inserted FA 1996 Sch 39 para 1(3).
	(3)	Sch 2, para 52 [ICTA s 578B(2)]	Inserted FA 1991 s 61(3).
	(4)	Sch 2, para 52 [ICTA s 578B(2)]	Inserted FA 1991 s 61(3).

Dest. Tables

Existing provision		*Rewritten provision*	*Remarks*
36	Definition of "motor car", etc		
	(1)	74(3), 81, 82(1), Sch 2, para 52 [ICTA s 578B(1)]	
	(2)	82(2), (3)	
	(3)	82(5), 575(1), Sch 2 para 52 [ICTA s 578B(2)]	
	(4)	82(4)	Amended Disability Living Allowance and Disability Working Allowance Act 1991 (c 21) Sch 2 para 21, amended and repealed in part Disability Living Allowance and Disability Working Allowance (Northern Ireland Consequential Amendments) Order 1991 S I.1991/2874 art 6(3)(*a*), (*b*), Social Security (Consequential Provisions) Act 1992 (c 6) Sch 2 para 109(*b*), Social Security (Consequential Provisions) (Northern Ireland) Act 1992 (c 9) Sch 2 para 38(*b*).
	(5)	74(4), Sch 2 para 52 [ICTA s 578B(4)]	
CH IV	SHORT-LIFE ASSETS		
37	Election for certain machinery or plant to be treated as short-life assets		
	(1)	83, 84, 85(1)	Amended FA 1997 Sch 14 para 3.
	(2)	85(1) to (4)	Amended FA 1996 Sch 21 para 30(2), repealed in part FA 1994 s 213(1), FA 1996 Sch 21 para 30(2).
	(2A)	85(2), (3), 577(1)	Inserted FA 1996 Sch 21 para 30(3).
	(3)	65(2), 86(1)	
	(4)	85(5)	
	(4A)	240	Inserted FA 1991 Sch 14 para 9(1).
	(5)	86(2) to (4)	Amended FA 1991 Sch 14 para 9(2), F(No 2)A 1992 s 68(7), repealed in part FA 1994 s 213(1).
	(6)	87(1),(2)	Repealed in part FA 1994 s 213(1).
	(7)	—	Unnecessary.
	(8)	89(1) to (5), 575(1)	
	(9)	89(6), (7)	Repealed in part FA 1994 s 213(1).
	(10)	88, 577(1)	
38	Assets which cannot be treated as short-life assets		
		84	Amended FA 1993 Sch 13 para 4; unnecessary in part.
CH IVA	LONG-LIFE ASSETS		
38A	Application of Chapter		Inserted FA 1997 Sch 14 para 2.
	(1)	90	
	(2)	91(1)	
	(3)	91(3)	
	(4)	92(1)	
	(5)	92(2)	
38B	Expenditure excluded from the application of the Chapter		Inserted FA 1997 Sch 14 para 2.
	(1)	93	
	(2)	46(2), 96	
	(3)	46(2), 94	
	(4)	46(2), 95(1)	
	(5)		
	"fixture"	93(2)	
	"goods"	95(6)	
	"light maintenance depot"	95(6)	
	"railway"	95(5)	
	"railway asset"	95(2)	
	"railway business"	95(3)	
	"railway station"	95(6)	
	"railway track"	95(6)	
	"retail shop"	93(2)	
	(6)	95(4)	

Existing provision		*Rewritten provision*	*Remarks*
38C	Exclusion of Chapter where limit for individuals and partners not exceeded		
			Inserted FA 1997 Sch 14 para 2.
	(1)	97, 98(2), 100(1), (2)	
	(2)	98(1), (2), 100(1), (2)	
	(3)	98(1)	
	(4)	98(2)	
	(5)	98(4)	
	(6)	99(1)	
	(7)	99(2)	
	(8)	100(3), (4)	
	(9)	—	Unnecessary.
38D	Exclusion of Chapter where company's limit not exceeded		
			Inserted FA 1997 Sch 14 para 2.
	(1)	97, 98(3), 100(1), (2)	
	(2)	98(3)	
	(3)	99(1)	
	(4)	99(3)	
	(5)	99(4)	
	(6)	99(5)	
	(7)	98(4), 100(3), (4)	
38E	Separate pools for expenditure on long-life assets		
			Inserted FA 1997 Sch 14 para 2.
	(1)	101(2)	
	(2)	65(1)	
	(3), (4)	—	Unnecessary.
	(5)	101(1)	
	(6)	101(2)	
38F	Modifications applying to pools for long-life assets		
			Inserted FA 1997 Sch 14 para 2.
	(1)	102(1), (4)	
	(2)	102(2)	
	(3)	103(1), (2)	
	(4)	103(3)	
	(5)	3(3)	
	(6)	102(3)	
38G	Disposal value of long-life assets		
			Inserted FA 1997 Sch 14 para 2.
	(1)	104(1), (2)	
	(2), (3)	104(3)	
	(4)	577(4)	
38H	Transitional provisions		
			Inserted FA 1997 Sch 14 para 2.
	(1) to (5)	Sch 3 para 20	
CH V	LEASED ASSETS AND INEXPENSIVE CARS		
39	Meaning of ''qualifying purpose''		
	(1)	122(1), (2), 125(1)	
	(2)	125(4)	Amended FA 1993 Sch 13 para 5(1), FA 1998 s 85(6), FA 2000 s 71(4), in part unnecessary.
	(3)	122(1), (2)	
	(4)	122(1), (2)	
	(5)	125(2), (3)	
	(6)	123(1), (3)	
	(7)	123(2)	
	(8)	123(4), Sch 3 para 23	Amended FA 1993 Sch 13 para 5(2).
	(9)	124	
	(10)	122(2), 125(3)	
40	Meaning of ''short-term leasing'' and ''the requisite period''		
	(1)	121(1), (2)	
	(2)	121(2)	
	(3)	121(3), (4)	
	(4)	87(1)(*c*), 106(1), (2), 132(1)(*b*)	Amended FA 1993 s 116(1); in part unnecessary.
	(5)	106(3), (4), 122(2), (3), 125(3), (5)	
41	Writing-down allowances etc for leased assets and inexpensive cars		
	(1)	107(2)	Repealed in part FA 2000 s 74(1).
	(2)	107(1)	
	(3)		Repealed in part FA 1990 Sch 17 para 9.
	(4)	65(4)	Repealed in part FA 2000 s 74(1).
	(5)	108, 577(1)	
	(6)	107(2)	Substituted FA 1997 Sch 14 para 4.

Dest. Tables

Existing provision		*Rewritten provision*	*Remarks*
42	Assets leased outside the United Kingdom		
	(1)	105(2), (3), 109(2)	Amended FA 1993 s 116(2), FA 1998 Sch 7 para 4.
	(2)	109	Amended FA 1997 Sch 14 para 5.
	(3)	110	
	(4)	114(1) to (3)	Repealed in part FA 1994 s 213(1).
	(5)	114(4)	
	(6)	115(1), (3)	
	(7)	115(2)	
	(8)	—	Unnecessary.
	(9)	114(1), (3)	Inserted FA 1993 Sch 13 para 6, amended FA 1998 s 85(4), FA 2000 s 71(2).
43	Joint lessees: new expenditure		
	(1)	116(1)	Amended FA 1993 Sch 13 para 7(1); s 43(1)(*b*) unnecessary.
	(2)	116(2), (3)	Amended FA 1998 Sch 7 para 4.
	(3)	116(4) to (6)	Amended FA 1997 Sch 14 para 6.
	(4)	Sch 3 para 47(7), (8)	Inserted FA 1993 Sch 13 para 7(2).
	(5)	—	Inserted F(No 2)A 1997 s 42(8), amended FA 1998 s 85(7), FA 2000 s 71(3); unnecessary.
44	Further provisions relating to joint lessees in cases involving new expenditure		
	(1)	117(1)	
	(2)	117(1), 120(3) to (5)	Amended FA 1998 Sch 7 para 4.
	(3)	117(2), 120(3) to (5)	
	(4)	117(3) to (6)	
	(5)	117(2), Sch 3 para 22	Inserted FA 1993 Sch 13 para 8, amended FA 1998 s 85(5), FA 2000 s 71(3).
45	Joint lessees: old expenditure		
	(1) to (7)	—	Amended FA 1998 Sch 7 para 4.
46	Recovery of excess relief: new expenditure		
	(1)	111(1) to (4), 237(1)	Repealed in part FA 1994 s 213(1).
	(2)	111(2), (4), (6)	
	(3)	111(2), (4)	
	(4)	111(5)	
	(5)	112	
	(6)	112(1)	Repealed in part FA 1990 Sch 17 para 10.
	(7)	113	Amended FA 1997 Sch 14 para 7.
	(8)	111(1), (4), 112(1), (2), 113(1)	Inserted FA 1993 Sch 13 para 9, amended FA 1998 s 85(5), FA 2000 s 71(3).
47	Recovery of excess relief: old expenditure		
	(1)	—	Repealed in part FA 1994 s 213(1).
	(2) to (5)	—	
	(6)	—	Repealed in part FA 1990 Sch 17 para 11.
	(7) to (10)	—	
48	Information relating to allowances made in respect of new expenditure		
	(1)	118(1), (2)	Repealed in part FA 1990 Sch 17 para 12.
	(2)	119(1), 120(3)	
	(3)	119(3), 120(5)	Repealed in part FA 1994 s 213(1).
	(4)	118(2), 119(2)	Repealed in part FA 1994 s 213(1).
	(5)	120(1), (2), (5)	Repealed in part FA 1994 s 213(1).
	(6)	119(3), 120(5)	
	(7)	118(3), (4), 119(1)	Inserted FA 1993 Sch 13 para 10, amended FA 1998 s 85(5), FA 2000 s 71(3).
49	Information relating to allowances made in respect of old expenditure		
	(1)	—	
	(2)	—	Repealed in part FA 1990 Sch 17 para 13, FA 1994 s 213(1).
	(3), (4)	—	
50	Interpretation of Chapter V		
	(1)	105(1)(*b*)	
	(2)	46(2),105(1)(*a*)	
	(3)		
	''new expenditure''	—	Unnecessary.
	''non-resident''	—	Unnecessary.

Provision		Destination	Remarks
			Amended FA 1997 Sch 14 para 8.
			Amended FA 1993 Sch 13 para 11(1), FA 1998 s 85(4), FA 2000 s 71(2); unnecessary.
	…ing''	105(5)	Label changed to ''protected leasing''.
	…ifying purpose''	—	Unnecessary.
	''requisite period''	106(1), (2)	Label changed to ''designated period''.
	''short-term leasing''	—	Unnecessary.
	(3A)	105(3), (4)	Inserted FA 1993 s 116(3).
	(4)	126(2)	
	(4A)	126(3)	Inserted FA 1993 Sch 13 para 11(2), amended FA 1998 s 85(4), FA 2000 s 71(2).
	(5)	—	Unnecessary.
	(6)	575(1)	
CH VI	FIXTURES		
51	Application and interpretation of Chapter VI		
	(1)	172(1), (2)	Amended FA 2000 s 78(2).
	(2)		
	''equipment lessor'', ''equipment lessee''	174(3)	
	''equipment lease''	174(1)	
	''fixture''	173(1)	Inserted FA 2000 s 78(3).
	''interest in land'' and ''lease''	174(4), 175(1)	
	''relevant land''	173(2)	
	''return''	3(3), 201(4)(*b*), 202(3), 203(1), (3), 577(1)	Amended FA 1997 Sch 16 para 2(1).
	(2A)	173(1), (2)	Inserted FA 2000 s 78(4).
	(3)	174(4), 175(1), Sch 3 para 29	Amended Abolition of Feudal Tenure etc Scotland Act 2000, Sch 12, para 51.
	(4)	175(2)	
	(5)	202(1), (2)	Amended FA 1997 Sch 16 para 2(2).
	(5A)	202(3)	Inserted FA 1997 Sch 16 para 2(3).
	(6)	203(4)	
	(6A)	203(1) to (3)	Inserted FA 1997 Sch 16 para 2(4).
	(7)	204(1) to (3)	
	(8)	172(5)	Substituted FA 2000 s 78(5).
52	Expenditure incurred by holder of interest in land		
	(1)	172(3), (4) 176(1), (4)	Amended FA 1998 Sch 5 para 53.
	(2)	172(4), 176(2), (3)	
53	Expenditure incurred by equipment lessor		
	(1)	172(3), (4), 174(2), (3), 177(1), (2), 178	Amended FA 1997 Sch 16 para 3(1) to (4), amended and repealed in part FA 1998 Sch 5 para 54(2), (3), repealed in part FA 2000 s 75(5).
	(1A)	177(3)	Inserted FA 1997 Sch 16 para 3(5).
	(1B)	177(1), (2), 179(1)	Inserted FA 1997 Sch 16 para 3(5), amended FA 1998 Sch 5 para 54(4), FA 2000 s 75(5).
	(1C)	179(1), (2)	Inserted FA 1997 Sch 16 para 3(5).
	(1D)	177(1), (2), 180(1)	Inserted FA 2000 s 79(1).
	(1E)	180(1)	Inserted FA 2000 s 79(1).
	(1F)	180(2)	Inserted FA 2000 s 79(1).
	(1G)	180(3), 203(4)	Inserted FA 2000 s 79(1).
	(1H)	203(1) to (3)	Inserted FA 2000 s 79(1).
	(2)	177(1), (5), 575(1)	Amended FA 1996 Sch 21 para 31(2).
	(2A)	177(5), (6), 577(1)	Inserted FA 1996 Sch 21 para 31(3).
	(3)	172(4), 177(4)	
	(4)	174(1)	
54	Expenditure included in consideration for acquisition of existing interest in land		
	(1)	172(3), (4), 181(1), 182(1)	Amended and repealed in part FA 1997 Sch 16 para 4(2).
	(2)	181(4), 182(1)	

Existing provision		*Rewritten provision*	
55	Expenditure incurred by incoming lessee: transfer of allowances		
	(1)	172(3), (4), 183(1)	
	(2)	183(1)	
	(3)	183(2)	
	(4)	183(1), 575(1)	Repealed in part FA 1997 Sch 18 Pt VI(12).
56	Expenditure incurred by incoming lessee: lessor not entitled to allowances		
		172(3), (4) 184(1), 575(1)	Amended and repealed in part FA 1997 Sch 16 para 4(3).
56A	Restriction on duplicate allowances under sections 54 and 56		
			Inserted FA 1997 Sch 16 para 4(1).
	(1)	181(2), 182(2), 184(2)	
	(2)	172(4), 181(2), (3), 182(2), (3), 184(2), (3)	Unnecessary in part.
	(3)	181(3), 182(3), 184(3)	
56B	Fixtures on which a former owner had an allowance		
			Inserted FA 1997 Sch 16 para 4(1).
	(1)	172(4), 185(1), (2)	
	(2)	185(1), Sch 3 para 38	
	(3)	185(5)	
	(4)	185(3)	
	(5)	185(4)	
	(6)	185(6), (7)	
	(7)	185(7), 575(1)	
56C	Fixtures on which an allowance has been given under Part I		
			Inserted FA 1997 Sch 16 para 4(1).
	(1)	172(4), 186(1), (2), (4), Sch 3 para 39	
	(2)	186(3)	
	(3)	186(3)	
	(4)	186(5)	
56D	Fixtures on which an allowance has been given under Part VII		
			Inserted FA 1997 Sch 16 para 4(1).
	(1)	187(1), (2), (4), Sch 3 para 40	Amended FA 2000 Sch 19 para 8.
	(2)	187(3)	
	(3)	187(3)	
	(4)	—	Unnecessary.
57	Fixtures treated as ceasing to belong to particular persons		
	(1)	196(5)	
	(2)	172(4), 188(1), (2), (4)	
	(3)	188(3), 189(1)	
	(4)	188(2) to (5)	
	(5)	172(4), 190(1), (2)	
	(6)	172(4), 193	
	(7)	172(4), 191	
58	Equipment lessors: special provisions		
	(1)	172(4), 192(1), (2)	
	(2)	172(4), 194(1), 196(1) Table, item 7	
	(3)	172(4), 194(2)	
	(4)	172(4), 195(1), 196(1), Table, item 8	
	(5)	192(3), 195(2), 196(4)	
59	Disposal value of fixtures in certain cases		
	(1)	196(1), Table, items 1, to 3, 5, (3), (6)	Amended FA 1997 Sch 16 para 5(1).
	(2)	196(1), Table, item 1	
	(3)	196(1), Table, item 5	
	(4)	196(1), Table, item 3, 577(1)	
	(5)	196(1), Table, item 3, 577(1)	
	(6)	196(1), Table item 2, (2), 577(1)	
	(7)	196(1), Table, item 4	
	(8)	196(1), Table items 9 to 11	
	(9)	196(1), Table, item 12	
	(10)	—	Repealed FA 1997 Sch 18 Pt VI(12).
	(11)	Sch 3 para 41	
59A	Disposal values in avoidance cases		
			Inserted FA 1997 Sch 16 para 5(2).
	(1)	197(1), (2)	
	(2)	197(3)	
	(3)	197(3)	
	(4)	577(4)	
59B	Election to use alternative apportionment		
			Inserted FA 1997 Sch 16 para 6(1).

Existing provision		*Rewritten provision*	*Remarks*
59B	(1)	198(1), 199(1)	
	(2)	198(2), (5), 199(2), (5)	
	(3)	198(3), 199(3)	
	(4)	198(4), 199(4)	
	(5)	200(2)	
	(6)	—	Unnecessary.
59C	Elections under section 59B: supplemental		
			Inserted FA 1997 Sch 16 para 6(1).
	(1)	201(1)	
	(2)	201(3)	
	(3)	200(4), 201(2)	
	(4)	201(1)	
	(5)	201(4)	
	(6)	200(3)	
	(7)	201(5)	Substituted FA 1999 Sch 11 para 6.
	(8)	204(4) to (6)	
	(9)	201(4)	Unnecessary in part.
	(10)	201(6)	
CH VII	MISCELLANEOUS EXPENDITURE		
60	Machinery and plant on hire-purchase etc		
	(1)	67(1) to (3)	
	(2)	67(4), 68(1), (2), (4)	
	(2A)	229(3)	Inserted F(No 2)A 1997 s 45(1).
	(3)	Sch 3 para 15	
	(4)	67(5)	Inserted FA 2000 s 80(1).
60A	Machinery and plant on hire-purchase etc : fixtures		
			Inserted FA 2000 s 80(2).
	(1)	69(1)	
	(2)	69(2)	
	(3)	69(3)	
61	Machinery and plant on lease		
	(1)	15(1)(*h*), 19(1), (2), (4), 65(1)	In part unnecessary.
	(2)	15(3), 35(1), (2)	
	(3)	—	Unnecessary.
	(4)	70(1) to (5), Sch 3 para 17	
	(5)	258(4)	Repealed in part FA 1994 s 213(1).
	(6)	—	Repealed FA 1998 Sch 5 para 55(2).
	(7)	260(7)	Amended FA 1998 Sch 5 para 55(3).
	(8)	70(6)	Unnecessary except in relation to subsection (4).
62	Treatment of demolition costs		
	(1)	26(1) to (3), (5), 163(4)	Amended FA 1990 s 60.
	(2)	26(4)	
62A	Special allowance for demolition costs related to offshore machinery or plant		
			Inserted FA 1990 s 60.
	(1)	163(1), (2), (4), (5)	
	(2)	162(2)	
	(3)	163(3), (5)	Amended Petroleum Act 1998 (c 17) Sch 4 para 27(2).
	(4)	164(1), (4), (5)	
	(5)	164(2), (3)	
	(6)	Sch 3 para 26	Repealed in part FA 1994 s 213(1).
62B	Treatment of post-cessation abandonment expenditure related to off-shore machinery or plant		
			Inserted FA 1990 s 60.
	(1)	165(1), (2), Sch 3 para 27	
	(2)	165(3), (4)	
	(3)	165(3)	
	(4)	165(5)	
	(5)	162(2)	
63	Mineral extraction		
	(1)	161(1) to (5)	
	(2)	Sch 3 para 25	
64	Transfers of interests in oil fields		
	(1)	166(1)	
	(2)	166(2), (3)	
	(3)	166(4)	
	(4)	166(5)	
64A	Production sharing contracts		
			Inserted FA 2000 s 81(1).
	(1)	167(1), 168(1)	
	(2)	168(2)	
	(3)	167(1), 169(1)	
	(4)	169(2)	

Existing provision		Rewritten provision	Remarks
64A	(5)	167(1), 170(1)	
	(6)	170(2)	
	(7)	170(3)	
	(8)	170(4), (5)	
	(9)	170(5)	
	(10)	170(6)	
	(11)	167(2)	
	(12)	167(3), 556(2)	
65	Partnership using property of a partner		
	(1)	264(1), (2)	
	(2)	264(3)	
	(3)	264(4)	Amended FA 1998 Sch 7 para 4.
66	Building alterations connected with installation of machinery or plant		
		25	
67	Expenditure on thermal insulation		
	(1)	27(2), 28(1), 63(5)	
	(2) to (3A)	—	Repealed FA 1998 Sch 5 para 56.
	(4)	28(3)	
	(4A)	28(2)	Inserted FA 1997 Sch 15 para 5(3).
	(5)	—	Unnecessary.
	(6)	—	Repealed in part FA 1994 s 213(1); unnecessary.
67A	Computer software		
			Inserted F(No 2)A 1992 s 68(1).
	(1)	71(2)	
	(2)	71(1)	
68	Exclusion of certain expenditure relating to films, tapes and discs		
	(1)	Sch 2, para 82 [F(No 2)A 1992 s 40A(1)]	Substituted FA 2000 s 113(1).
	(2)	Sch 2, para 82 [F(No 2)A 1992 s 40A(5)]	Substituted FA 2000 s 113(2).
	(3)	Sch 2, para 82 [F(No 2)A 1992 s 40B(1), (2), (3), s 40D(5)]	
	(4)	Sch 2, para 82 [F(No 2)A 1992 s 40B(4)]	
	(5)	Sch 2, para 82 [F(No 2)A 1992 s 40B(5)]	Amended FA 1996 Sch 21 para 32(2).
	(5A)	Sch 2, para 82 [F(No 2)A 1992 s 40B(6)]	Inserted FA 1996 Sch 21 para 32(3).
	(6)	Sch 2, para 82 [F(No 2)A 1992 s 40B(7)]	
	(6A)	Sch 2, para 82 [F(No 2)A 1992 s 40C(1)]	Inserted F(No 2)A 1992 s 69(2).
	(6B)	Sch 2, para 82 [F(No 2)A 1992 s 40C(1)]	Inserted F(No 2)A 1992 s 69(2).
	(7)	Sch 2, para 82 [F(No 2)A 1992 s 40C(2)]	Amended FA 1998 Sch 7 para 4.
	(8)	Sch 2, para 82 [F(No 2)A 1992 s 40A(2), (3)]	
	(9)	Sch 2 para 82 [F(No 2)A 1992 s 40D(1), (2)]	Amended F(No 2)A 1992 s 69(3).
	(9A)	Sch 2 para 82 [F(No 2)A 1992 s 40D(3), (4)]	Inserted F(No 2)A 1992 s 69(4), amended FA 1996 Sch 21 para 32(4).
	(9AA)	Sch 2 para 82 [F(No 2)A 1992 s 40D(4)]	Inserted FA 1996 Sch 21 para 32(5)
	(9B)	Sch 2 para 82 [F(No 2)A 1992 s 40D(6)]	Inserted F(No 2)A 1992 s 69(4), amended FA 1996 Sch 21 para 32(6).
	(9C)	Sch 2 para 82 [F(No 2)A 1992 s 40D(7)]	Inserted F(No 2)A 1992 s 69(4).
	(10)	Sch 2, para 82 [s 40A(4) F(No 2)A 1992]	Amended FA 1998 Sch 7 para 4.
69	Expenditure on fire safety		
	(1)	27(1), (2), 29(1), (2), 63(5)	Amended FA 1998 Sch 7 para 4.
	(2)	27(1), (2), 29(1), (3), (4)	Amended FA 1998 Sch 7 para 4.
70	Expenditure on safety at sports grounds		
	(1)	27(1), (2), 30(1) to (3), 31(1) to (3), 63(5)	Amended FA 1998 Sch 7 para 4.
	(2)	27(1), (2), 32(1), (2), 63(5)	
	(3)	30(1)	
	(4)	32(3)	
	(5)	30(1) to (3), 31(1) to (3), 32(1), (2), (4)	

Existing provision		Rewritten provision	Remarks
71	Security		
	(1)	27(1), 33(1), (8)	Amended FA 1998 Sch 7 para 4.
	(2)	27(2), 63(5)	
	(3), (4)	33(2)	
	(5), (6)	33(5)	
72	Security: supplementary		
	(1)	33(6)	
	(2)	33(3)	
	(3)	33(4)	
	(4)	33(6)	
	(5)	—	
CH VIII	SUPPLEMENTARY PROVISIONS		
73	Manner of making allowances and charges		
	(1)	247	Amended FA 1998 Sch 5 para 57(*a*).
	(1A)	—	Repealed FA 1998 Sch 5 para 57(*b*).
	(2)	258(2)	Repealed in part FA 1998 Sch 5 para 57(*c*).
	(3)	258(4)	Repealed in part FA 1994 s 213(1).
	(4)	—	Repealed FA 1997 Sch 18 Pt VI(11).
74	Allowances not available: expenses of MPs and others		
		34(1), (2)	Substituted FA 1999 Sch 5 para 2(3).
75	Further restrictions on allowances		
	(1)	213(1), (2), 214 to 218, 221 to 224, 241 to 243	Amended FA 1991 Sch 14 para 11(1), F(No 2)A 1997 s 46(1)(*a*), FA 2000 s 77(2).
	(2)	213(1), (2), 214 to 218, 221 to 224, 241 to 243	Amended FA 1991 Sch 14 para 11(2), F(No 2)A 1997 s 46(1)(*a*), FA 2000 s 77(2).
	(3)	213(1), (2), 214 to 218, 221 to 224, 241 to 243	Amended FA 1991 Sch 14 para 11(3), F(No 2)A 1997 s 46(1)(*a*), FA 2000 s 77(2).
	(4)	232(1)	
	(5)	231, 246(1)	
76	Extension of section 75		
	(1)	216, 221, 223, 241	
	(2)	218(3), 222(1), (2), 224(1) to (3), 242(5), 577(1)	
	(2A)	218(4), 224(4), 242(6), 243(7)	Inserted FA 1991 Sch 14 para 11(4).
	(2B)	218(3), 242(5)	Inserted FA 1991 Sch 14 para 11(4).
	(3)	—	Repealed FA 1998 s 85(8)(*a*).
	(4)	218(3), (4), 224(4), 242(5), (6), 243	Amended FA 1991 Sch 14 para 11(5), FA 1998 s 85(8)(*b*).
	(5)	230	
	(6)	232(1), 577(1)	
	(7)	218(4)	Inserted F(No 2)A 1997 s 46(1)(*b*).
76A	Special provisions for finance lease cases		Inserted F(No 2)A 1997 s 46(2).
	(1)	221, 223, 241	
	(2)	221, 222(1), (2), 224(1) to (4), 243(2) to (5)	
	(3)	226	
	(4)	226	
	(5)	224(1) to (3), 243(2) to (5)	
	(6)	222(4), 224(5), 225(1), (3), 244	
	(7)	222(5), 224(5), 225(2), 226(1), 244	
	(8)	225(2)	
	(9)	222(1) to (3), 224(4), 243(6)	
	(10)	222(3), 224(4), 243(6)	
	(11)	232(1), (2), (4), 246(2)	
	(12)	221(2), 225(1), 232(3)	
76B	Special provision for sale and leaseback cases		Inserted FA 2000 s 77(1).
	(1)	227(1)	
	(2)	227(2)	
	(3)	228(1) to (5), 245(1), (2)	
	(4)	227(4)	
	(5)	227(4), (5)	
	(6)	227(2), (6)	
	(7)	227(2), (3), (6)	
	(8)	3(2)	

Dest. Tables

	Existing provision	*Rewritten provision*	*Remarks*
77	Successions to trades: connected persons		
	(1)	—	Unnecessary.
	(2)	—	Unnecessary.
	(3)	266(1), (2), (4)	
	(4)	266(3), 267(1) to (4)	
	(5)	266(5)	
	(6)	266(6), 574	
	(7)	267(5)	
	(8)	266(7), Sch 3 para 52	Amended FA 1997 Sch 14 para 9.
78	Succession to trades where no election made under section 77		
	(1)	265(1) to (4), 268(1), 577(1)	
	(2)	268(1) to (4)	
	(2A)	268(5) to (7)	Inserted FA 1990 Sch 13 para 3(1).
	(3)	263(1) to (4)	
	(4)	263(1), (2), (5), (6)	
	(5)	263(7), 265(4), 268(8)	
79	Effect of use partly for trade etc and partly for other purposes		
	(1)	11(4), 205(1), (2)	
	(2)	11(4), 206(1), (2), 207(1)	
	(3)	206(3)	Repealed in part FA 1994 s 213(1).
	(4)	65(2), 206(4), 575(1)	
	(5)	207(2), (3)	Repealed in part FA 1994 s 213(1).
	(6)	207(5)	Repealed in part FA 1990 Sch 17 para 14.
79A	Reduction in qualifying use		Inserted FA 2000 s 75(2).
	(1)	208(1)	
	(2)	208(2)	
	(3)	208(2)	
	(4)	577(1)	
80	Effect of subsidies towards wear and tear		
	(1)	37(1), (2), 209	Amended FA 1998 Sch 7 para 4; in part unnecessary.
	(2)	209, 210(1)	
	(3)	209, 211(2), 212(1)	
	(4)	211(3)	
	(5)	65(2), 211(1), (4), 212(2)	
	(6)	212(4)	Repealed in part FA 1990 Sch 17 para 15.
	(7)	211(5)	In part unnecessary.
81	Effect of use after user not attracting capital allowances, or after receipt by way of gift		
	(1)	13(1) to (3), (7), 14(1) to (3), (5), 46(2), 577(1)	
	(1A)	13(2), (3), (7), 14(2), (3), (5), 46(2)	Inserted FA 1993 Sch 13 para 12(1), in part unnecessary.
	(2)	13(6), 14(4)	
	(2AA)	13(4)	Inserted FA 2000 s 75(3).
	(2AB)	13(5)	Inserted FA 2000 s 75(3).
	(2A)	—	Inserted FA 1993 Sch 13 para 12(2); unnecessary.
	(3)	213(3)	
	(4)	Sch 3 para 12	
82	Capital expenditure to which this Part does not apply		
	(1)	Sch 3 para 55	Repealed in part FA 1994 s 213(1); provisions of s 82 renumbered as ss(1) FA 2000 s 76(1).
	(2)	38	Inserted FA 2000 s 76(1).
82A	Meaning of ''finance lease''		Inserted F(No 2)A 1997 s 47(1).
	(1)	219, 226(1)	
	(2)	219, 226(1), 232(1), (4)	
83	Other interpretative provisions		
	(1)		
	''income''	259(3)	Unnecessary as a general definition.
	''mineral exploration and access'' and ''trade of mineral extraction''	159	
	''motor car''	—	
	''new''	91(2), 227(2)(*b*)	
	(2)	12	

Existing provision		Rewritten provision	Remarks
83	(2A)	15(1), 105(6), 168(1), 169(1), 216(2), 221(2), 263(2), 265(5), 268(8)	Inserted FA 2000 s 75(1).
	(3)		
	(4)	270(1), (2)	
	(5)	269	
	(6)	160	
	(7)	—	Inserted FA 1994 s 117(1); introduces Sch AA1; unnecessary.
PT III	DWELLING-HOUSES LET ON ASSURED TENANCIES		
84	Application of Part III		
	(1)	490(1), 491(1)	
	(2)	491(1) to (3)	
	(3)	491(2), (3)	
85	Writing-down allowances		
	(1)	501, 507(1)	Repealed in part FA 1994 s 213(1).
	(2)	501, 508(1), (2)	Amended FA 1994 s 213(7).
	(3)	509	Repealed in part FA 1994 s 213(1).
	(4)	510(1), (2)	Repealed in part FA 1994 s 213(1).
86	Qualifying dwelling-houses		
	(1)	490(2), 491(1)	
	(2)	490(2), (4), 491(1) to (3)	
	(3)	491(2), (3), 504(1), 505(1), (2), 531(1), 575(1)	
	(4)	490(5)	
	(5)	504(2)	
87	Balancing allowances and charges and withdrawal of initial allowances in certain cases		
	(1)	501, 513(1) to (3), 514	
	(2)	513(4)	
	(3)	516(2), (3)	
	(4)	516(4), (5)	
	(5)	573(1), (2), (3)	
	(6)	518	Repealed in part FA 1994 s 213(1).
	(7)	519(1), (2)	
	(8)	519(1)	
88	Dwelling-houses not continuously qualifying dwelling-houses		
	(1)	516(1), 517(1)	
	(2)	517(4), (5)	
	(3)	517(4), (5)	
	(4)	569(5)	
	(5)		
	''the relevant period''	520	
	''the capital expenditure''	521	
	''the allowances given''	517(8)	
	''the adjusted net cost''	522	
89	Supplementary provisions where dwelling-house ceases to be a qualifying dwelling-house		
	(1)	506(1)	
	(2)	506(2)	
90	Writing off of expenditure and meaning of ''residue of expenditure''		
	(1)	512(1), 523	
	(2)	524	
	(3)	525(1)	
	(4)	525(2)	
	(5)	526(1) to (4)	
	(6)	527(1), (2)	
	(7)	527(3)	
	(8)	527(4)	
	(9)	528(1) to (4)	
91	Buildings bought unused		
	(1)	502(1) to (3), 503(1) to (4)	
	(2)	502(4)	
	(3)	503(2) to (5)	
92	Manner of making allowances and charges		
	(1), (2)	529	Substituted FA 1998 Sch 5 para 58.
93	Repairs, and double allowances		
	(1)	493(2)	
	(2)	—	Spent.
	(3)	—	Repealed in part FA 1994 s 213(1); spent.

Existing provision		Rewritten provision	Remarks
94	Holding over by lessees, etc		
	(1)	499(1)	
	(2)	499(2)	
	(3)	497, 498, 499(3)	
	(4)	499(4)	
	(5)	499(5)	
95	The relevant interest		
	(1)	495(1), (2), 500	
	(2)	495(3)	
	(3)	497, 498	
96	The appropriate capital expenditure		
	(1)	511(1) to (3)	
	(2)	511(4), (5)	
	(3)	491(1)	
97	Interpretation		
	(1)		
	"approved body"	492	
	"assured tenancy"	490(3)	
	"building"	571	
	"dwelling-house"	531(1)	
	"expenditure appropriate to a dwelling-house"	—	Unnecessary.
	"qualifying dwelling-house"	—	Unnecessary.
	(2)	493(1)	
	(3)	496	
	(4)	530	
PT IV	MINERAL EXTRACTION		
CH I	ALLOWANCES AND CHARGES		
98	Writing-down and balancing allowances		
	(1)	394(1), 400(1), 403(1), 414(1)	
	(2)	417(1), (2), 419(1), (2)	
	(3)	417(1), (2), 419(1), (2)	
	(4)	418(5)	
	(5)	418(1)	
	(6)	418(2), (3)	Substituted FA 1994 s 213(8).
99	Disposal receipts		
	(1)	421(1), (2), 422(1), 430(1)	Repealed in part FA 1994 s 213(1).
	(2)	422(1) to (4)	
	(3)	423(1) to (3), 424(1)	
	(4)	425(1), (2)	Repealed in part FA 1994 s 213(1).
100	Balancing charges: excess of allowances etc over expenditure		
	(1)	417(1), (3)	
	(2)	418(4)	
	(3)	418(4)	
101	Occasions of balancing allowances		
	(1)	431	
	(2)	428(1)	Repealed in part FA 1994 s 213(1).
	(3)	428(2), (3)	
	(4)	430(1)	
	(5)	426	
	(6)	427	Repealed in part FA 1994 s 213(1).
	(7)	429	Repealed in part FA 1994 s 213(1).
	(8)	430(2)	Repealed in part FA 1994 s 213(1).
102	Treatment of qualifying expenditure on mineral exploration and access		
		400(2)	
103	Demolition costs		
	(1)	433(1)	
	(2)	433(3)	
	(3)	433(2)	
104	Manner of making allowances and charges		
		432	
CH II	QUALIFYING EXPENDITURE		
105	General provisions		
	(1)	394(1), 395(1), (2), 400(1), 403(1), 414(1)	
	(2)	400(3)	
	(3)	395(3), 403(2)	
	(4)	399(1)	
	(5)	399(2) to (6), 414(2)	
	(6)	396(2), (3)	
	(7)	398	
106	Pre-trading expenditure on machinery or plant which is sold etc		
	(1)	402(1)	

Existing provision		Rewritten provision	Remarks
106	(2)	400(4), 402(3)	In part duplicates s 120(2).
	(3)	402(3) to (5)	
	(4)	402(2), (4)	
107	Pre-trading exploration expenditure		
	(1)	401(1)	
	(2)	401(2), (3)	
	(3)	400(4), 401(2), (4)	In part duplicates s 120(2).
	(4)	401(5)	
	(5)	401(2)	
108	Contributions by mining concerns to public services etc outside the United Kingdom		
	(1)	415(1), (2)	
	(2)	415(1)	
	(3)	415(3)	
109	Restoration expenditure		
	(1)	394(1), 416(1) to (3), (6)	Amended FA 1998 Sch 7 para 4.
	(2)	416(6)	
	(3)	416(5)	
	(4)	416(7)	
	(5)	416(4)	
	(6)	416(8)	
CH III	LIMITATIONS ON QUALIFYING EXPENDITURE ETC		
110	Expenditure on the acquisition of land		
	(1)	404(1)	In part unnecessary (see definition of ''mineral asset'' in s 121(1)).
	(2)	404(2) to (4), 424(2)	
	(3)	404(5), 422(4), 424(5)	
	(4)	405(1), (2)	
	(5)	405(3), Sch 3 para 84	
	(6)	404(6), 405(4)	
111	Reduction of qualifying expenditure for premium relief	406(1), (2)	
112	Restriction of disposal receipts		
	(1)	424(1), (2)	
	(2)	424(2) to (5)	
113	Assets formerly owned by traders		
	(1)	407(1), 411(1)	
	(2)	Sch 3 para 87	
	(3)	407(3), 411(1), Sch 3 para 87	
	(4)	407(6), 411(5)	
	(5)	407(7), 411(6)	
	(6)	411(7)	
114	Assets previously acquired		
	(1)	407(2), 411(2)	
	(2)	411(3)	
	(3)	411(3)	
	(4)	411(4)	
	(5)	411(7)	
	(6)	411(4) to (6)	
115	Expenditure partly attributable to mineral exploration and access		
	(1)	407(3)	
	(2)	407(3), (5)	Paragraph (*b*) unnecessary.
	(2A)	407(4), Sch 3 para 85	Inserted FA 1997 s 66(2), amended FA 1998 Sch 7 para 4.
	(3)	407(2), (6), (7)	
116	Oil licences etc		
	(1)	410(1), (2)	
	(2)	410(2), (3), 552(2)	Amended Petroleum Act 1998 (c 17) Sch 4 para 27(3).
	(3)	410(3)	
117	Transfer of mineral assets within a group		
	(1)	412(1), 413(1)	
	(2)	413(2), (3)	
	(3)	412(2)	
	(4)	412(2)	
	(5)	412(4) to (6)	
	(6)	412(7)	
118	Assets formerly owned by non-traders		
	(1)	409(1)	Provisions of s 118 re-numbered ss(1), FA 1996 s 180(3).
	(2)	408	Inserted FA 1996 s 180(3), amended FA 2000 Sch 19 para 8.
118A	Disposal of oil licences relating to undeveloped areas		
			Inserted TCGA 1992 Sch 10 para 21(1).

Dest. Tables

Existing provision		*Rewritten provision*	*Remarks*
118A	(1)	553(1), (2)	
	(2)	553(3)	
	(3)	553(4)	
	(4)	552(2) to (4), 553(3), (5), (6), 554(1) to (5),556(1), (2)	
CH IV	SUPPLEMENTARY PROVISIONS		
119	Transitional provisions relating to old expenditure		
	(1) to (6)	Sch 3 para 88	
120	Time when expenditure is incurred		
	(1)	434	
	(2)	400(4)	
121	Interpretation of Part IV		
	(1)		
	''development'', ''development order''	436(1)	
	''mineral asset''	397	
	''mineral exploration and access''	396(1)	
	''planning permission''	436(1)	
	''pre-trading expenditure on machinery or plant''	—	Unnecessary.
	''pre-trading exploration expenditure''	—	Unnecessary.
	''qualifying expenditure''	—	Unnecessary.
	''the relevant planning enactment''	436(2)	Amended Planning (Northern Ireland) Order 1991 S I. 1991/1220 (NI 11) Sch 5, Planning (Consequential Provisions) (Scotland) Act 1997 (c 11) Sch 2 para 45.
	''source of mineral deposits''	394(5)	
	''trade of mineral extraction''	394(2)	
	(2)	394(4), Sch 3 para 87	
	(3)	409(3)	
	(4)	—	Repealed in part FA 1994 s 213(1); unnecessary.
	(5)	435(1), (2)	
PT V	AGRICULTURAL BUILDINGS ETC		
CH I	AGRICULTURE		
122	Allowances for expenditure incurred before 1st April 1986		
	(1) to (7)	—	Unnecessary.
123	Allowances for expenditure incurred after 31st March 1986		
		361(1), 369(1) to (5), 370(1), 372(1), (2), Sch 3 para 82	
124	Expenditure qualifying for allowances		
	(1)	361(1), 369(1) to (5)	Amended FA 1993 Sch 12 para 2(1).
	(2)	374(1) to (3)	Amended FA 1993 Sch 12 para 2(2).
	(3)	—	Repealed in part FA 1994 s 213(1); applies to chargeable periods ending after 26th July 1989; unnecessary.
124A	Initial allowances: contracts entered into between October 1992 and November 1993		
	(1) to (7)	—	Inserted FA 1993 Sch 12 para 3; unnecessary.
124B	Restriction on writing-down allowance where initial allowance made		
		—	Inserted FA 1993 Sch 12 para 3; unnecessary.
125	Meaning of ''major interest'' and ''the relevant interest''		
	(1)	361(1), 364(1), (3), 393(1), (2), Sch 3 para 81	Amended Abolition of Feudal Tenure etc (Scotland) Act 2000 Sch 12, para 51.
	(2)	364(1), (2)	
	(3)	364(3)	
	(4)	365, 367(1), (3)	

Existing provision		Rewritten provision	Remarks
126	Transfers of relevant interest		
	(1)	372(1), 375(1) to (4)	Amended FA 1993 Sch 12 para 4(1).
	(2)	375(3) , (4), 376(6)	Substituted FA 1993 Sch 12 para 4(2); repealed in part FA 1994 s 213(1); paragraph (*a*) unnecessary.
	(3)	375(5)	
	(4)	367(2)	
	(5)	368(1) to (4)	
	(6)	379(1), (2), (3)	Amended FA 1993 Sch 12 para 4(3).
	(7)	—	
127	Buildings etc bought unused		
	(1)	370(1), 374(2)	
	(2)	370(2), (5), 374(2), (3)	
	(3)	370(2)	
	(3A)	370(1), (3)	Inserted FA 1993 Sch 12 para 5(1); paragraph (*b*) unnecessary.
	(3B)	370(2)	Inserted FA 1993 Sch 12 para 5(1).
	(4)	370(6)	Amended FA 1993 Sch 12 para 5(2).
127A	Purchases of buildings and structures: cases involving initial allowances		
	(1) to (9)	—	Inserted FA 1993 Sch 12 para 6; unnecessary.
128	Balancing allowances and charges		
	(1)	377, 380(1) to (3)	Amended FA 1993 Sch 12 para 7(1); repealed in part FA 1994 s 213(1).
	(2)	383(1), 386	Amended FA 1993 Sch 12 para 7(2).
	(3)	384(2)	Amended FA 1993 Sch 12 para 7(3).
	(4)	385(1), (2)	
	(5)	385(3), (4)	
	(6)	387	Amended FA 1993 Sch 12 para 7(4).
	(7)	388(1) to (3)	
	(8)	Sch 3 para 80	
129	Balancing events		
	(1)	376(1), 381(1), (2)	Amended FA 1993 Sch 12 para 8.
	(2)	381(1), 382(6), (7)	Amended FA 1996 Sch 21 para 33.
	(3)	376(1), (2), (4)	Repealed in part FA 1994 s 213(1).
	(4)	382(1)	
	(5)	382(2), (3), (5), 577(3)	
130	Restriction of balancing allowances on sale of buildings		
	(1)	389(1) to (3), 575(1)	
	(2)	389(4), (5)	
	(3)	376(5), 389(7)	
	(4)	390(1), (2)	
	(5)	389(6)	
CH II	FORESTRY		
131	Forestry: transitional provisions		
	(1) to (6)	—	Ss(2) amended FA 1993 Sch 12 para 9; unnecessary.
CH III	SUPPLEMENTAL		
132	Manner of making allowances and charges		
			Substituted FA 1998 Sch 5 para 59.
	(1)	392(1)	
	(2)	392(2), (3)	
133	Interpretation of Part V		
	(1)		
	"agricultural land"	361(1)	
	"agricultural income"	—	Unnecessary.
	"forestry land"	—	Unnecessary: see CAA 1990 s 133(2).
	"forestry income"	—	Unnecessary: see CAA 1990 s 133(2).
	"husbandry"	362(1)	
	(2)	—	Unnecessary.
	(3)	Sch 3 para 82	
	(4)	366	
	(5)	—	Unnecessary.
	(6)	363	

Existing provision		*Rewritten provision*	*Remarks*
133	(7)	370(3), (4), 384(1), (3)	
	(8)	573(1), (2), (3)	
	(9)	573(3)	
PT VI	DREDGING		
134	Allowances for expenditure on dredging		
	(1)	485(1), 487(1), (2), Sch 3 para 103	Repealed in part FA 1994 s 213(9).
	(2)	488(1), (2)	
	(3)	Sch 3, para 104	
	(4)	488(1), (3) to (5)	
	(5)	489	
	(6)	485(2)	
	(7)	486(1), (2)	
	(8)	532(2), 533(1), 543	
135	Interpretation of Part VI		
	(1)	484(2), 485(3)	
	(2)	486(1), (2)	Unnecessary in part.
	(3)	484(3), (4)	
PT VII	RESEARCH AND DEVELOPMENT		
136	Allowances for expenditure on scientific research not of a capital nature, and on payments to research associations, universities etc		
		—	Repealed FA 2000 Sch 40 Pt II (7).
137	Allowances for capital expenditure on research and development		
	(1)	2(1), 437(1), 439(1), 441(1), 450	Amended FA 2000 Sch 19 paras 8, 9; the words ''subsections (5) to (7) below'' spent in part.
	(1A)	447(1), (2)	Inserted FA 1991 Sch 14 para 12(1), amended FA 2000 Sch 19 para 8.
	(2)	440	
	(3)	438(3), (4), (5), (6)	Amended FA 1991 Sch 14 para 12(2), FA 2000 Sch 19 para 8.
	(4)	439(4), Sch 3 para 89	
	(5)	441(2), 447(3)	Substituted FA 1994 s 213(10).
	(6), (7)	—	Repealed FA 1994 s 213(10).
138	Assets ceasing to belong to traders		
	(1)	442(1), 443(1), 449(1), 447(2)	Amended FA 2000 Sch 19 para 8.
	(2)	441(1), 442, (1) to (3), 443(1), 444, 449(2), 450	
	(2A)	449	Inserted FA 1991 Sch 14 para 13(1).
	(3)	—	Unnecessary.
	(3A)	443(6), 448	Inserted FA 1991 Sch 14 para 13(2), amended FA 2000 Sch 19 para 8.
	(4)	443(4), 577(1)	
	(5)	445(1) to (5), 442, 443(4) to (6), 444, 450	Amended FA 2000 Sch 19 para 8.
	(6)	443(3)	
	(7)	—	Repealed in part FA 1994 s 213(1); unnecessary.
	(7A)	443(5)	Inserted TCGA 1992 Sch 10 para 21(2).
	(8)	—	Inserted FA 1991 Sch 14 para 13(3); unnecessary.
138A	Disposal of oil licences etc		Inserted FA 1996 s 180(1).
	(1)	408(1), (2), 443(2), (5), 555(1)	
	(2)	408(1), (2), 555(1), (2), (3)	
	(3)	555(4)	Amended FA 2000 Sch 19 para 8.
	(4)	408(3), 552(1) to (4), 555(4), 556(2)	Amended Petroleum Act 1998 (c 17) Sch 4 para 27(4).
138B	Disposal of oil licences: election for alternative tax treatment		
		Sch 3 para 91	Inserted FA 1996 s 180(1); unnecessary.
139	Supplemental		
	(1)	437(2), 438(1), (2), 439(5), 571	Amended FA 2000 Sch 19 paras 8, 10, repealed in part FA 2000 Sch 40 Pt II (7); in part unnecessary.
	(2)	439(2)	
	(3)	—	Repealed FA 2000 Sch 40 Pt II (7).
	(4)	451	
	(5)	445(6)	

Existing provision		Rewritten provision	Remarks
PT VIII	SUPPLEMENTARY PROVISIONS		
140	Income tax allowances and charges in taxing a trade etc		Substituted FA 1994 s 211(1).
	(1)	2(1)	
	(2)	247, 352(1), 391, 392, 432, 450, 463, 478, 489, 529, Sch 3 para 101	
	(3)	3(2), (3)	
	(4)	251, 262	
	(5)	2(1), 450	
	(6)	352(2)	
141	Other income tax allowances		
	(1)	3(4), 258(1)	
	(2)	258(2), (3), (5), (7)	Repealed in part FA 1997 Sch 18 Pt VI(11).
	(3), (4)	—	Repealed FA 1997 Sch 18 Pt VI(11).
	(5)	3(4)	
	(6)	—	Repealed FA 1997 Sch 18 Pt VI(11).
142	Restriction of set-off of allowances against general income		
	(1)	Sch 2 para 30 [ICTA s 384A(1), (2)]	
	(2)	Sch 2 para 30 [ICTA s 384A(1), (4), (5), (7)]	
	(3)	Sch 2 para 30 [ICTA s 384A(6)]	
	(4)	Sch 2 para 30 [ICTA s 384A(3)]	
	(5)	Sch 2 para 30 [ICTA s 384A(8), and passim]	
143	Tax agreements		
	(1)	565(1), (2), (4)	
	(2)	565(3)	
144	Corporation tax allowances and charges in taxing a trade		
	(1)	2(1)	
	(2)	247, 352(1), 391, 392, 432, 450, 463, 478, 489, 529, Sch 3 para 101	
	(3)	2(1), 450	
	(4)	352(2)	Inserted FA 1991 s 60(9).
145	Other corporation tax allowances		
	(1)	259(1) to (3)	
	(2)	260(1), (2)	
	(3)	260(3)	Amended FA 1999 Sch 11 para 7.
	(4)	260(4), (5)	
	(5)	260(6)	
	(6)	—	Unnecessary.
145A	Corporation tax allowances: claims	—	Repealed FA 1998 Sch 27 Pt III (28).
146	Writing-down allowances under Parts V and VI		
	(1)	373(2), 487(4)	
	(2)	373(2), 375(4), 487(4), Sch 3 para 96(1)	
	(3)	378(1), 487(5), Sch 3 para 94(3)	Amended FA 1993 Sch 12 para 10.
	(4)	Sch 3 paras 83, 105	
147	Exclusion of double allowances		
	(1)	7(1), (2), 8(3) to (5), 10(2)	Amended FA 1993 Sch 13 para 13(1).
	(2)	7(1), (2), 8(1), (2), (5), 10(2)	Amended FA 1993 Sch 13 para 13(2).
	(2A)	9(1), 10(2)	Inserted FA 1997 Sch 16 para 7(1).
	(2B)	9(2)	Inserted FA 1997 Sch 16 para 7(1).
	(2C)	9(3), 10(2)	Inserted FA 1997 Sch 16 para 7(1).
	(2D)	9(4), 202(3)	Inserted FA 1997 Sch 16 para 7(1).
	(3)		
	''asset''	—	Unnecessary.
	''capital expenditure''	10(1)	
	''return''	3(3)	Inserted FA 1997 Sch 16 para 7(2).
	references, etc	10(2)	
	(4)	—	Unnecessary.
148	Double allowances: transitional provisions	—	Repealed in part FA 1994 s 213(1);

Dest. Tables

Existing provision		*Rewritten provision*	*Remarks*
			does not apply in relation to chargeable periods ending after 26th July 1989; unnecessary.
149	Companies not resident in the United Kingdom		
	(1)	566	
	(2)	—	Repealed FA 1990 Sch 13 para 4(1).
150	Apportionment of consideration, and exchanges and surrenders of leasehold interests		
	(1)	562(1), (3)	
	(2)	562(2)	
	(3)	562(4)	
	(4)	572(1) to (3)	
	(5)	562(5)	Paragraph (*a*) unnecessary.
151	Procedure on apportionments		
	(1)	563(1) to (6), 564(1)	Amended FA 1996 s 180(2).
	(1A)	564(3)	Inserted FA 1995 s 100(2).
	(2)	564(1) to (6)	
	(3)	—	Unnecessary.
152	Succession to trades etc		
	(1)	557, 559(1) to (3), (5), 577(1)	
	(2)	559(4)	
	(3)	557, 558(1) to (4)	
	(4)	—	Repealed.
152A	Insurance companies: transfers of business		
			Inserted FA 1990 Sch 9 para 5.
	(1)	560(1)	Substituted FA 1995 Sch 9 para 3.
	(1A)	560(2)	Inserted FA 1995 Sch 9 para 3; unnecessary in part.
	(1B)	560(5), (6)	Inserted FA 1995 Sch 9 para 3; unnecessary in part.
	(2)	560(4)	
152B	Transfer of a UK trade		
			Inserted F(No 2)A 1992 s 67.
	(1) to (3)	561(1)	
	(4) to (6)	561(2)	
	(7)	561(3)	
	(8), (9)	564(4)	
	(10)	266(8), 560(3), 561(5), 567(5), 573(4)	
153	Subsidies, contributions etc		
	(1)	532(1), (2), 534(1), Sch 3 para 106	
	(2)	535, 536(1) to (3)	Amended FA 1998 Sch 7 para 4.
	(3)	536(4)	
	(4)	532(3)	
	(5)	Sch 3 para 107	
154	Allowances in respect of contributions to capital expenditure		
	(1)	537(1) to (3), 538(1), (2), 539(1), (2), 540(1), (2), 541(1), (2)	
	(2)	538(1), (2)	Amended FA 1990 Sch 13 para 5(1).
	(3)	537(2), 575(1)	
	(4)	537(2), (3)	
	(5)	537(5), Sch 3 para 108	
155	Further provisions relating to capital contributions		
	(1)	539(3), 540(3)	Unnecessary.
	(2)	538(2), 539(2), 540(2), 541(2)	
	(3)	538(4) to (6), 542(1) to (3)	
	(4)	539(3) to (5), 540(3) to (5)	
	(5)	539(6)	
	(6)	538(3)	
	(7)	Sch 3 para 110	
	(8)	540(5)	
156	Meaning of "sale, insurance, salvage or compensation moneys"		
		316(1), (2), 343(2), 383(1), (2), 402(5), 443(3)	Para (*e*) inserted FA 1995 s 99(9).
157	Sales between connected persons etc		
	(1)	567(1), (2), (4), 568(1), 575(1)	
	(2)	567(3)	
	(3)	Note 73.	
	(4)	567(1), 568, 573(3), 577(1)	
	(5)	567(1)	
158	Further provisions relating to sales without change of control or between connected persons		
	(1)	569(1) to (3), (6), 570(5), 577(1)	
	(2)	569(3), (4)	Amended FA 1993 s 117(2), (3), FA 2000 Sch 19 para 8.

Existing provision		Rewritten provision	Remarks
158	(3)	570(2) to (4)	Amended FA 1993 s 117(4).
	(4)	569(7)	
	(5)	570(1)	
	(6)	—	Unnecessary.
159	Capital expenditure, capital sums and time when capital expenditure was incurred		
	(1)	4(1) to (4)	
	(1A)	4(2)(*a*), (3)(*a*)	Inserted FA 1997 Sch 15 para 7, repealed in part FA 1998 Sch 5 para 60.
	(2)	5(7)	Amended FA 1991 Sch 14 para 14.
	(3)	5(1) to (3)	
	(4)	5(4)	Repealed in part FA 1994 s 213(1).
	(5)	5(5)	
	(6)	5(6)	Repealed in part FA 1994 s 213(1).
	(7)	5(7)	
	(8)	—	Repealed in part FA 1994 s 213(1); unnecessary.
159A	Additional VAT liabilities and rebates		
			Inserted FA 1991 Sch 14 para 14.
	(1), (2)	548(1), (2)	
	(3)	235(2), 236(2), 238(2), (3), 240(2), 346(5), 347(2), (3), 348, 349(2), 350(3), 351, 549(1), Sch 3 para 46(2)	
	(4)	549(1), (2)	Repealed in part FA 1994 s 213(1).
	(5)	550	
	(6)		
	''additional VAT liability''	547(1)	Unnecessary in part.
	''additional VAT rebate''	547(2)	Unnecessary in part.
	''VAT capital items legislation''	548(2), 551(1) to (4)	Amended VATA 1994 Sch 14 para 11.
	''VAT period of adjustment''	548(2)	
	(7)	549(2), 551(4)	Amended VATA 1994 Sch 14 para 11.
160	Meaning of ''period of account''		
			Substituted FA 1994 s 212(1).
	(1)	—	Unnecessary.
	(2)	6(2), (3)	
	(3)	6(4), (5)	
	(4)	6(6)	
	(5)	6(2)	
	(6)	6(4)	
161	Other interpretative provisions		
	(1)	571(2)	
	(2)		
	''the 1968 Act''	—	Unnecessary.
	''the Board''	576(3)	
	''chargeable period''	2(1), 6(1), 247, 306(3), 314(1) to (3), 352(1), 391, 432, 433(1), 450, 463, 478, 489	Substituted FA 1994 s 212(2).
	''control''	574	
	''dual resident investing company''	577(1)	
	''foreign concession''	277(4), 315(2), 414(3)	
	''income''	—	Unnecessary.
	''lease''	360(1), 393(3), 531(2)	
	''mineral deposits''	274(1), Table A, item 7, 394(3), 452(3)	
	''notice''	577(1)	
	''the principal Act''	—	Unnecessary.
	''research and development allowance''	—	Amended FA 2000 Sch 19 paras 8, 11.
	''tax''	—	Unnecessary (see ICTA s 832(3)).
	''writing-down allowance''	—	Unnecessary.
	concluding words	—	Unnecessary.
	(2A)	4(2)(*a*), (3)(*a*), 15(1)(*d*), 33(8), 35(1), 353(3)	Substituted FA 1998 Sch 5 para 61.
	(3)	27(1), 468(1)	

Dest. Tables

Existing provision		Rewritten provision	Remarks
161	(4)	—	Unnecessary (see ICTA s 832(1)).
	(5)	247, 352(1), 391, 392, 432, 450, 463, 478, 489	Amended FA 1994 s 213(11).
	(6)	577(3)	
	(7)	571(1)	
	(8)	572(4)	
	(9)	577(2)	Reference to FA 1965 Sch 16 para 7 spent.
	(10)	—	Repealed in part FA 1990 Sch 13 para 6(1); unnecessary.
	(11)	—	Unnecessary.
162	Application to Scotland	360(2), 393(4), 531(3), 572(1)	
163	Continuity and construction of enactments etc		
164	Commencement, amendments and repeals		
165	Short title		
SCH AA1	EXCLUSIONS FROM EXPENDITURE ON MACHINERY OR PLANT		
			Inserted FA 1994 s 117(1).
	para 1(1)	21(1)	
	para 1(2)	21(3), 23(3)	
	para 1(3)	23(3), List C, items 18 to 21	
	para 1(4)	22(3)	
	Table 1, col.(1)	23(3), List A	
	Table 1, col.(2)	23, List C, items 1 to 16	
	Note 1 to Table 1	23(4)	
	Note 2 to Table 1	23, List C, item 2	
	para 2(1), (2)	22(1)	
	para 2(3)	23(3)	
	para 2(4)	22(1)	
	Table 2, col.(1)	22, List B	
	Table 2, col.(2)	23, List C, items 22 to 33	
	Note 1 to Table 2	22, List B, item 5	
	Note 2 to Table 2	22, List B, item 7	
	para 3(1)	24(1)	
	para 3(2)	24(2)	
	para 4	23(1), (2)	
	para 5(1)	21(2), 22(2), (3)	
	para 5(2)	23, List C, item 17	
	para 5(3)	22(3), 24(2), (3)	
SCH A1	CORPORATION TAX ALLOWANCES: CLAIMS		
		—	Repealed FA 1998 Sch 27 Pt III (28).
SCH 1	CONSEQUENTIAL AMENDMENTS		
	para 1(1)	Sch 2 paras 2, 3	Amends TMA s 57(8)(3)(*b*), s 58(3)(*b*).
	para 1(2)	Sch 2 para 4(1)	Amends TMA s 98, Table, col 1.
	para 1(3)	Sch 2 para 4(2)	Amends TMA s 98, Table col 2.
	para 1(4)	—	Repealed FA 1996 Sch 41 Pt V(12).
	para 2	—	Repealed Social Security (Consequential Provisions) Act 1992 Sch 1.
	para 3	—	Repealed TCGA 1992 Sch 12.
	para 4	534(2), (3)	Amends FA 1982 s 137.
	para 5	Sch 3 para 65	Amends London Regional Transport Act 1984 (c 32) Sch 5 para 5.
	para 6	Sch 2 paras 8, 9	Amends Films Act 1985 (c 21) s 6(1), Sch 1 paras 2, 3.
	para 7	Sch 2 para 10	Amends Trustee Savings Bank Act 1985 (c 58) Sch 2 para 1.
	para 8(1)	—	Introductory words
	para 8(2)	—	Repealed FA 1997 Sch 18 Pt VI(11).
	para 8(3)	—	Repealed FA 1998 Sch 27 Pt III.
	para 8(4)	Sch 2 para 15	Amends ICTA s 75(4).
	para 8(5)	Sch 2 para 18	Amends ICTA s 87(7).
	para 8(6)	Sch 2 para 19	Amends ICTA s 91(9).
	para 8(7)	Sch 2 para 21	Amends ICTA s 116(4)(*b*).
	para 8(8)	Sch 2 para 22	Amends ICTA s 117(1), (2).
	para 8(9)	Sch 2 para 23	Amends ICTA s 118(1), (2).
	para 8(10)	20(2), (3)	Amends ICTA s 198(2).
	para 8(11)	—	Repealed F(No 2)A 1997 Sch 8 Pt II(4).
	para 8(12)	Sch 2 para 27	Amends ICTA s 359(3)(*a*).

Existing provision	*Rewritten provision*	*Remarks*
Sch 1 (cont) para 8(13)	—	Amends ICTA s 583, which is repealed FA 1994 s 214(1)(*b*).
para 8(14)	Sch 2 para 29(2)	Amends ICTA s 384(10).
para 8(15)	Sch 2 para 31	Amends ICTA s 389(2), (6).
para 8(16)	—	Repealed FA 1991 Sch 19 Pt V.
para 8(17)	Sch 2 para 33	Amends ICTA s 395(1).
para 8(18)	Sch 2 para 34(1), (3)	Amends ICTA s 397(5), (7).
para 8(19)	Sch 2 para 35	Amends ICTA s 400(2)(*c*), (4), (6).
para 8(20)	Sch 2 para 37	Amends ICTA s 407.
para 8(21)	Sch 2 para 38	Amends ICTA s 411(10).
para 8(22)	Sch 2 para 41	Amends ICTA s 492(5), (6), (7).
para 8(23)	Sch 2 para 42	Amends ICTA s 495(1)(*b*), (3)(*b*), (7).
para 8(24)	—	Amends ICTA s 497 which is repealed FA 1998 Sch 3 para 29.
para 8(25)	—	Amends ICTA s 522(7), which is repealed by Sch 2 para 44.
para 8(26)	Sch 2 para 45	Amends ICTA s 525(3).
para 8(27)	Sch 2 para 47	Amends ICTA s 530(8).
para 8(28)	4(5), 452(3), 453, 463, 468(1), 478, 532(1), 534(1), 535(1), 536(1) to (3), 563(1), 567(1), 568(1), 570(3), (4), Sch 3 para 101	Amends ICTA s 532(1) to (5).
para 8(29)	Sch 2 para 54	Amends ICTA s 646(3).
para 8(30)	Sch 2 para 51(1)	Amends ICTA s 577(1)(*c*).
para 8(31)	Sch 2 para 55	Amends ICTA s 768(6).
para 8(32)	—	Repealed FA 1998 Sch 27 Pt III(25).
para 8(33)	Sch 2 para 57	Amends ICTA s 781(9).
para 8(34)	Sch 2 para 58	Amends ICTA s 828(4).
para 8(35)	Sch 2 para 59	Amends ICTA s 831(3).
para 8(36)	Sch 2 para 60	Amends ICTA s 832(1).
para 8(37)	2(4), Sch 2 para 61	Amends ICTA s 834(2).
para 8(38)	Sch 2 para 62	Amends ICTA s 835(8).
para 8(39)	—	Repealed FA 1998 Sch 27 Pt III(9).
para 8(40)	Sch 2 para 63	Amends ICTA Sch 18 para 1(6)(*b*).
para 8(41)	Sch 2 para 65	Amends ICTA Sch 21 para 6(1)(*a*).
para 8(42)	Sch 2 para 66	Amends ICTA Sch 24, paras 10(1), (2), (11).
para 8(43)	Sch 3 para 114	Inserts ICTA Sch 30 para 18A.
para 9(1) to (3)	—	Repealed TCGA 1992 Sch 12
para 9(4)	Sch 2 para 69	Amends FA 1988 Sch 12 para 3(1).
para 10	—	Amends FA 1989 s 121(2).
para 11	Sch 2 para 71	Amends Electricity Act 1989 Sch 11 para 5.
SCH 2 REPEALS	—	SPENT.

FINANCE ACT 1990 (C 29)

Existing provision	*Rewritten provision*	*Remarks*
60 Allowance for abandonment expenditure related to offshore machinery plant		
	26(5), 162(2), 163, 164, Sch 3 paras 26, 27	Amends CAA 1990 s 62(1), inserts CAA 1990 s 62A, s 62B.
87 Capital allowances: vehicles provided by employees		
(1)	15(4)	Amends CAA 1990 s 27(1).
(2)	80	Inserts CAA 1990 s 27(2A) to (2E).
(3)	Sch 3 para 53	Transitional.
(4)	Sch 3 para 53	Commencement (year 1990-91 and subsequent years of assessment).
103 Capital allowances: assimilation to claims by individuals		
(1)		Introduces Schedule 17.
(2)	—	Commencement (chargeable periods after the day appointed for pay and file; unnecessary).
SCH 9 INSURANCE COMPANIES: TRANSFERS OF LONG TERM BUSINESS		
para 5	560(1), (2), (5), (6)	Inserts CAA 1990 s 152A.
SCH 13 CAPITAL ALLOWANCES: MISCELLANEOUS AMENDMENTS		
para 1(1)	271(1)(*b*)	Amends CAA 1990 s 1(2).
para 1(2)	271(1)(*b*)	Amends CAA 1990 s 7(1).

Existing provision		*Rewritten provision*	*Remarks*
Sch13 (cont)	para 1(3)	—	Commencement of para 1 (any chargeable or its basis period ending on or after 6th April 1990; unnecessary).
	para 2(1)	335(1)	Amends CAA 1990 s 8(5).
	para 2(2)		Commencement.
	para 3(1)	268(5) to (7)	Inserts CAA 1990 s 78(2A).
	para 3(2)	Sch 3 para 53	Commencement.
	para 4(1)	—	Repeals CAA 1990 s 149(2).
	para 4(2)	—	Commencement of para 4 (chargeable periods beginning on or after 6th April 1990; unnecessary).
	para 5(1)	537(2), 538(2)	Amends CAA 1990 s 154(2).
	para 5(2)	Sch 3 para 109	Commencement.
	para 6(1)	—	Repeals in part CAA 1990 s 161(10).
	para 6(2)	—	Commencement.
	para 7(1)	—	Repeals words in ICTA s 832(1).
	para 7(2)	—	Commencement (chargeable periods beginning on or after 6th April 1990; unnecessary).
SCH 17	CAPITAL ALLOWANCES: ASSIMILATION OF CLAIMS BY COMPANIES TO CLAIMS BY INDIVIDUALS		
	para 1	—	Introductory words
	para 2	—	Repeals words in CAA 1990 s 1(5).
	para 3(1)	—	Introductory words
	para 3(2)	52(7)	Substitutes CAA 1990 s 22(7).
	para 3(3)	—	Repeals in part CAA 1990 s 22(8).
	para 3(4)	—	Repeals CAA 1990 s 22(9).
	para 4(1)	—	Introductory words
	para 4(2)	—	Repeals in part CAA 1990 s 23(1).
	para 4(3)	—	Repeals in part CAA 1990 s 23(2).
	para 5(1)	—	Introductory words
	para 5(2)	—	Repeals in part CAA 1990 s 24(3).
	para 5(3)	—	Repeals CAA 1990 s 24(4).
	para 6(1)	—	Introductory words
	para 6(2)	—	Repeals in part CAA 1990 s 25(1).
	para 6(3)	—	Repeals CAA 1990 s 25(2).
	para 6(4)	—	Repeals in part CAA 1990 s 25(3).
	para 6(5)	—	Repeals in part CAA 1990 s 25(4).
	para 7	—	Repeals in part CAA 1990 s 30(1).
	para 8	130(7)	Substitutes CAA 1990 s 31(6).
	para 9	—	Repeals in part CAA 1990 s 41(3).
	para 10	—	Repeals in part CAA 1990 s 46(6).
	para 11	—	Repeals in part CAA 1990 s 47(6)(*a*).
	para 12	—	Repeals in part CAA 1990 s 48(1).
	para 13	—	Repeals in part CAA 1990 s 49(2).
	para 14	—	Repeals in part CAA 1990 s 79(6).
	para 15	—	Repeals in part CAA 1990 s 80(6).

DISABILITY LIVING ALLOWANCE AND DISABILITY WORKING ALLOWANCE ACT 1991 (C 21)

Existing provision		*Rewritten provision*	*Remarks*
SCH 2	DISABILITY LIVING ALLOWANCE AND ATTENDANCE ALLOWANCE: AMENDMENTS		
	paras 20, 21	82(4)	Amends CAA 1990 s 22(6)(*a*), s 34(6)(*a*).

FINANCE ACT 1991 (C 31)

Existing provision		*Rewritten provision*	*Remarks*
59	Interaction with VAT capital goods scheme		
	(1)	—	Introduces Schedule 14.
	(2)	—	Commencement (any chargeable period or its basis period ending on or after 6th April 1990; unnecessary).

Existing provision		*Rewritten provision*	*Remarks*
60	Toll roads		
	(1)	—	Introductory.
	(2)	—	Introductory.
	(3)	—	Inserts CAA 1990 s 3(5); unnecessary.
	(4)	274(1), Table B, item 6	Amends CAA 1990 s 18(1).
	(5)	342(1), (2)	Inserts CAA 1990 s 20(5), (6).
	(6)	341(1), (2)	Inserts CAA 1990 s 21(5A), (5B).
	(7)	—	Introductory.
	(8)	—	Inserts s 140(11); spent following substitution of s 140 by FA 1994 s 211(1).
	(9)	352(2)	Inserts s 144(4).
	(10)	—	Commencement (any chargeable period or its basis period ending on or after 6th April 1990; unnecessary).
61	Hiring motor cars		
	(1)	—	Introductory.
	(2)	Sch 2, para 52 [ICTA s 578A(1) to (4)]	Amends CAA 1990 s 35(2).
	(3)	Sch 2, para 52 [ICTA s 578A(1) to (4)]	Inserts CAA 1990 s 35(3), (4).
	(4)	—	Commencement (any chargeable period or its basis period ending on or after day on which FA 1991 passed; unnecessary).
SCH 14	CAPITAL ALLOWANCES: VAT CAPITAL GOODS SCHEME		
	para 1	346(1), (2)	Inserts CAA 1990 s 1(1A).
	para 2(1)	—	Amends CAA 1990 s 2(1) (not rewritten).
	para 2(2)	—	Inserts CAA 1990 s 2(3A) (not rewritten).
	para 3(1)	347(1) to (4), 349	Inserts CAA 1990 s 3(2A) to (2C).
	para 3(2)		Amends CAA 1990 s 3(3).
	para 4(1)	350(1)	Amends CAA 1990 s 4(1).
	para 4(2)		Amends CAA 1990 s 4(2).
	para 4(3)	350(2) to (4)	Inserts CAA 1990 s 4(2A).
	para 4(4)	350(5)	Amends CAA 1990 s 4(9).
	para 4(5)	324(1), (2)	Amends CAA 1990 s 4(10).
	para 5(1)	333, 348	Substitutes CAA 1990 s 8(2).
	para 5(2)	351	Inserts CAA 1990 s 8(12A).
	para 5(3)	—	Amends CAA 1990 s 8(13); superseded by amendment made FA 1994 s 120(6).
	para 6(1)	236	Inserts CAA 1990 s 22(1A), (1B).
	para 6(2)	—	Inserts CAA 1990 s 22(3A); s 22(3A) not rewritten.
	para 7(1)	235	Inserts CAA 1990 s 24(1A).
	para 7(2)	238	Amends CAA 1990 s 24(6), inserts CAA 1990 s 24(7), (8).
	para 8(1)	238	Amends CAA 1990 s 26(1).
	para 8(2)	239(3), (4)	Amends CAA 1990 s 26(2), inserts CAA 1990 s 26(2A).
	para 8(3)	239(6)	Inserts CAA 1990 s 26(4).
	para 9(1)	240	Inserts CAA 1990 s 37(4A).
	para 9(2)		Amends CAA 1990 s 37(5).
	para 10	—	Repealed FA 1997 Sch 18 Pt IV(12).
	para 11(1)	241, 242(1) to (4).	Amends CAA 1990 s 75(1).
	para 11(2)	241, 242(1) to (4).	Amends CAA 1990 s 75(2).
	para 11(3)	241, 242(1) to (4).	Amends CAA 1990 s 75(3).
	para 11(4)	242(5), (6), 243(7).	Inserts CAA 1990 s 76(2A), (2B).
	para 11(5)	242(5), (6), 243(7).	Amends CAA 1990 s 76(4).
	para 12(1)	447(1)	Inserts CAA 1990 s 137(1A).
	para 12(2)	438	Amends CAA 1990 s 137(3).
	para 13(1)	449	Inserts CAA 1990 s 138(2A).
	para 13(2)	443(6)	Inserts CAA 1990 s 138(3A).
	para 13(3)	—	Inserts CAA 1990 s 138(8) (not rewritten).
	para 14	5(7), 548, 549, 550, 551	Amends CAA 1990 s 159(2), inserts CAA 1990 s 159A.
SCH 15	RELIEF FOR COMPANY TRADING LOSSES		
	para 28	355(6)	Amends CAA 1990 s 17(2).

WATER CONSOLIDATION (CONSEQUENTIAL PROVISIONS) ACT 1991 (C 60)

Existing provision		*Rewritten provision*	*Remarks*
SCH 1	para 53	274(1), Table B, item 4	

SOCIAL SECURITY (CONSEQUENTIAL PROVISIONS) ACT 1992 (C 6)

Existing provision		*Rewritten provision*	*Remarks*
SCH 2	CONSEQUENTIAL AMENDMENTS		
	para 109	82(4)	Amends CAA 1990 s 22(6)(*a*), s 34(6)(*a*).

SOCIAL SECURITY (CONSEQUENTIAL PROVISIONS) (NORTHERN IRELAND) ACT 1992 (C 9)

Existing provision		*Rewritten provision*	*Remarks*
SCH 2	CONSEQUENTIAL AMENDMENTS		
	para 38	82(4)	Amends CAA 1990 s 22(6)(*a*), s 34(6)(*a*).

TAXATION OF CHARGEABLE GAINS ACT 1992 (C 12)

Existing provision		*Rewritten provision*	*Remarks*
SCH 10	CONSEQUENTIAL AMENDMENTS		
	para 21(1)	552(2) to (4), 553, 554, 556(1), (2)	Inserts CAA 1990 s 118A.
	para 21(2)	443(5)	Inserts CAA 1990 s 138(7A).

FINANCE (NO 2) ACT 1992 (C 48)

Existing provision		*Rewritten provision*	*Remarks*
43	Interpretation of sections 41 and 42		
	(1) (part)	—	Unnecessary.
67	Transfer of a UK trade		
		560, 561, 564(4), 567, 573, 568, 569	Inserts CAA 1990 s 152B.
68	Computer software		
	(1)	71	Inserts CAA 1990 s 67A.
	(2)	—	Amends CAA 1990 s 24(6).
	(3)	72(1), (2)	Inserts CAA 1990 s 24(6A).
	(4)	—	Amends CAA 1990 s 24(8).
	(5)	72(2) to (4)	Amends CAA 1990 s 26(1).
	(6)	73	Inserts CAA 1990 s 26(2AA).
	(7)	—	Amends CAA 1990 s 37(5).
	(8) to (10)	Sch 3 para 18	Commencement.
69	Films etc		
	(1)	—	Introductory.
	(2)	Sch 2 para 82	Inserts CAA 1990 s 68(6A), (6B).
	(3)	Sch 2 para 82	Amends CAA 1990 s 68(9).
	(4)	Sch 2 para 82	Inserts CAA 1990 s 68(9A) to (9C).
	(5)	Sch 3 para 117	Commencement.
70	Enterprise zones		
		—	Introduces Sch 13.
71	Expensive motor cars		
	(1)	—	Introductory.
	(2)	74(2)	Amends CAA 1990 s 34(1).
	(3)	—	Amends CAA 1990 s 34(3); spent following amendment of s 34(3) FA 1994 s 213(5).
	(4)	74(2)	Amends CAA 1990 s 35(1).

Existing provision		Rewritten provision	Remarks
71	(5)	Sch 2 para 52	Amends CAA 1990 s 35(2).
	(6), (7)	Sch 3 para 19	Commencement.
	(8)	Sch 3 para 113(1)	
SCH 13	CAPITAL ALLOWANCES: ENTERPRISE ZONES		
	para 1	—	Introductory words
	para 2	271, 294, 295, 296, 298, 299, 302, 307	Inserts CAA 1990 s 10A.
	para 3	—	Repeals in part CAA 1990 s 1(10).
	para 4	—	Repeals CAA 1990 s 6(5).
	para 5	—	Amends CAA 1990 s 10(1).
	para 6	—	Inserts CAA 1990 s 10(1A).
	para 7	—	Inserts CAA 1990 s 10(3A).
	para 8	271, 298, 301, 303, 304	Inserts CAA 1990 s 10B.
	para 9	297	Amends CAA 1990 s 10(4).
	para 10	298(1)	Inserts CAA 1990 s 17A.
	para 11	298(1)	Inserts CAA 1990 s 1(11).
	para 12	298(1)	Inserts CAA 1990 s 6(4), (4A).
	para 13	322(2)	Amends CAA 1990 s 4(9) ("the capital expenditure").
	para 14	Sch 3 para 61	Commencement.
	para 15	Sch 3 para 62	
	para 16		
	para 17		

FINANCE ACT 1993 (C 34)

Existing provision		Rewritten provision	Remarks
113	Initial allowances: industrial buildings and structures		
	(1)	Sch 3 paras 75 to 77	Inserts CAA 1990 s 2A.
	(2)	322(2)	Amends CAA 1990 s 4(9) ("the capital expenditure").
	(3)	—	Amends CAA 1990 s 10(3A).
	(4)	Sch 3 para 77	Inserts CAA 1990 s 10C.
	(5)	298(1)	Amends CAA 1990 s 17A.
	(6)	282	Amends CAA 1990 s 18(14).
	(7)	—	Commencement (any chargeable period or its basis period ending after 31st October 1992; unnecessary).
114	Initial allowances: agricultural buildings etc		
	(1)	—	Introduces Schedule 12.
	(2)	—	Commencement of s 114 and Sch 12 (any chargeable period or its basis period ending after 31st October 1992; unnecessary).
115	First year allowances: machinery and plant		
	(1)	Sch 3 para 46(3)	Amends CAA 1990 s 22(1).
	(2)	Sch 3 paras 46(1), 47(1), (2)	Inserts CAA 1990 s 22(3B).
	(3)	Sch 3 para 47(6)	Amends CAA 1990 s 22(4), inserts s 22(6A).
	(4)	—	Introduces Schedule 13.
	(5)	—	Commencement of s 115 and Sch 13 (subject to para 12(3), any chargeable period or its basis period ending after 31st October 1992; unnecessary).
116	Leasing		
	(1)	87(1)(*c*), 132(1)(*b*)	Amends CAA 1990 s 40(4).
	(2)	105(2), (3)	Amends CAA 1990 s 42(1).
	(3)	105(4)	Inserts CAA 1990 s 50(3A).
	(4)	Sch 3 para 21	Commencement.
117	Transactions between connected persons etc		
	(1)	—	Introductory.
	(2)	569(3)	Amends CAA 1990 s 158(2).
	(3)	569(3), (4)	Amends CAA 1990 s 158(2).
	(4)	570(2), (3), (4)	Amends CAA 1990 s 158(3).
	(5)	Sch 3 para 112	Commencement.
SCH 12	INITIAL ALLOWANCES AND AGRICULTURAL BUILDINGS		
	para 1	—	Introductory.
	para 2(1)	—	Amends CAA 1990 s 124(1).
	para 2(2)	374(1), (2), (3)	Amends CAA 1990 s 124(2).
	para 3	—	Inserts CAA 1990 s 124A, s 124B.

Existing provision		Rewritten provision	Remarks
Sch12 (cont)	para 4(1)	375(1)	Amends CAA 1990 s 126(1).
	para 4(2)	375(3), (4), 376(6)	Substitutes CAA 1990 s 126(2).
	para 4(3)		Amends CAA 1990 s 126(6).
	para 5(1)	370(1) to (3)	Inserts CAA 1990 s 127(3A), (3B).
	para 5(2)		Amends CAA 1990 s 127(4).
	para 6		Inserts CAA 1990 s 127A.
	para 7(1)		Amends CAA 1990 s 128(1).
	para 7(2)	386	Amends CAA 1990 s 128(2).
	para 7(3)		Amends CAA 1990 s 128(3).
	para 7(4)	387	Amends CAA 1990 s 128(6).
	para 8		Amends CAA 1990 s 129(1).
	para 9		Amends CAA 1990 s 131(2).
	para 10		Amends CAA 1990 s 146(3).
SCH 13	FIRST-YEAR ALLOWANCES FOR MACHINERY AND PLANT		
	para 1	—	Introductory.
	para 2	—	Amends CAA 1990 s 23(6).
	para 3	—	Amends CAA 1990 s 30(2).
	para 4	—	Amends CAA 1990 s 38(m).
	para 5(1)	—	Amends CAA 1990 s 39(2)(*a*).
	para 5(2)	Sch 3 para 23	Amends CAA 1990 s 39(8).
	para 6	114(1), (3)	Inserts CAA 1990 s 42(9).
	para 7(1)	—	Amends CAA 1990 s 43(1).
	para 7(2)	Sch 3 para 47(7), (8)	Inserts CAA 1990 s 43(4).
	para 8	117(2), Sch 3, para 22	Inserts CAA 1990 s 44(5).
	para 9	111(1), (4), 112(1), (2), 113(1)	Inserts CAA 1990 s 46(8).
	para 10	118(3), (4), 119(1)	Inserts CAA 1990 s 48(7).
	para 11(1)	—	Amends CAA 1990 s 50(3).
	para 11(2)	126(3)	Inserts CAA 1990 s 50(4A).
	para 12(1)	13(2), (3), (7), 14(2), (3), (5)	Inserts CAA 1990 s 81(1A).
	para 12(2)	—	Inserts CAA 1990 s 81(2A); s 81(2A) not rewritten.
	para 12(3)	—	Commencement.
	para 13(1)	7(1)	Amends CAA 1990 s 147(1).
	para 13(2)	7(1)	Amends CAA 1990 s 147(2).

FINANCE ACT 1994 (C 9)

Existing provision		Rewritten provision	Remarks
117	Expenditure on machinery or plant		
	(1)	21, 22, 23, 24	Inserts CAA 1990 s 83(7), Sch AA1.
	(2)	Sch 3 para 13	Commencement.
118	Expenditure on machinery or plant: notification		
	(6)(*a*)	58(4)	Amended FA 2000 s 73(1)(*b*).
120	Balancing charge on realisation of capital value		
	(1)	—	Introductory.
	(2)	328(1) to (3)	Amends CAA 1990 s 4(1), inserts CAA 1990 s 4(9A).
	(3)	328(5) to (6), 329, 330, 331	Inserts CAA 1990 s 4A.
	(4)	328(4)	Inserts CAA 1990 s 5(2A).
	(5)	—	Amends CAA 1990 s 6(4).
	(6)	338	Inserts CAA 1990 s 8(12B), amends CAA 1990 s 8(13).
	(7)	327, Sch 3 para 71	Commencement.
	(8)	327, Sch 3 para 71	Commencement.
121	Used buildings etc in enterprise zones		
	(1)	Sch 3 para 63	
	(2)	—	
211	Income tax allowances and charges in taxing a trade etc		
	(1)	2(1), 3(2), (3), 352(1), (2), 262, 251, 247, 432, 391, 489, 450, 478, Sch 3 para 101	Substitutes CAA 1990 s 140.
	(2)		Commencement.
212	Chargeable periods for income tax purposes		
	(1)	6(2) to (6)	Substitutes CAA 1990 s 160.
	(2)	2(1), 6(1)	Substitutes CAA 1990 s 161(2), definition of ''chargeable period''.
213	Other amendments of Capital Allowances Act 1990		
	(1)	—	Amends CAA 1990 passim.
	(2)	310(1), (2)	Amends CAA 1990 s 3(2).
	(3)	335, 339(4)	Amends CAA 1990 s 8(5), (13).

Existing provision		Rewritten provision	Remarks
213	(4)	55(2), (4), 56(3), (4)	Amends CAA 1990 s 24(2).
	(5)	75(1), (2), 76(1), (2), (5)	Amends CAA 1990 s 34(3).
	(6)	76(5)	Amends CAA 1990 s 35(1).
	(7)		Amends CAA 1990 s 85(2).
	(8)	418(2), (3)	Substitutes CAA 1990 s 98(6).
	(9)	—	Repeals in part CAA 1990 s 134(1).
	(10)	441(2), 447(3)	Substitutes CAA 1990 s 137(5), repeals CAA 1990 s 137(6), (7).
	(11)	247, 352(1), 391, 432, 450, 463, 478, 489	Amends CAA 1990 s 161(5).
214	Amendments of other enactments		
	(4)	472(2), (3)	Amends ICTA s 520(4)(*a*).
	(5)	—	Repeals ''or its basis period'' ICTA s 521, s 528, s 530.
	(6)	458(2), (3)	Amends ICTA s 530(2)(*a*).

VALUE ADDED TAX ACT 1994 (C 23)

Existing provision		Rewritten provision	Remarks
SCH 14	CONSEQUENTIAL AMENDMENTS		
	para 11	—	Amends CAA 1990 s 159A(6), (7); specific references to sections 4 and 24 of VATA not reproduced.

FINANCE ACT 1995 (C 4)

Existing provision		Rewritten provision	Remarks
94	Deferment of balancing charges in respect of ships		
		135, 136, 137, 138, 139, 140, 144, 150, 158	Inserts CAA 1990 s 33A, s 33B.
95	Reimposition of deferred charge		
		143	Inserts CAA 1990 s 33C.
96	Ships in respect of which charge may be deferred		
		141, 146, 147, 148, 149, 150, 151, 152, 153, 154, 155, 156, 158	Inserts CAA 1990 s 33D, s 33E.
97	Procedural provisions relating to deferred charges		
	(1)	135, 142, 145, 155, 157, 577(1)	Inserts CAA 1990 s 33F.
	(2)		Amends TMA s 42(7).
	(3)		Amends TMA s 98.
98	(1) to (8)	—	Commencement (chargeable periods ending on or after 21st April 1994, subject to special provisions for a transitional year; unnecessary).
99	Highway concessions		
	(1)	—	Introductory words
	(2)	—	Amends CAA 1990 s 3(5); unnecessary.
	(3)	343(1)	Amends CAA 1990 s 4(1).
	(4)	342(3), 343(1), 344(1), (5)	Inserts CAA 1990 s 4(2AA), (2AB).
	(5)	274(1), Table B, item 6	Amends CAA 1990 s 18(1)(*da*).
	(6)	342(1), (2)	Amends CAA 1990 s 20(5), (6).
	(7)	274(1), Table B, item 6, 341(4)	Inserts CAA 1990 s 21(5AA).
	(8)	341(1), (2)	Amends CAA 1990 s 21(5A), (5B).
	(9)	343	Amends CAA 1990 s 156.
	(10)	Sch 3 para 74	Commencement.
100	Arrangements affecting the value of a relevant interest		
	(1)	357(1) to (5)	Inserts CAA 1990 s 10D.
	(2)	564(3)	Inserts CAA 1990 s 151(1A).
	(3)	Sch 3 para 78	Commencement.
101	Import warehouses etc		
		274(1), Table A, item 3(*d*)	Amends CAA 1990 s 18(1)(*f*)(iv).
SCH 8	LIFE ASSURANCE BUSINESS		
	para 23(1)	19(5), 255, 256, 257, 261, 544, 545	Inserts ICTA s 434D, s 434E.
	para 24	15(1)(*g*), 18, 253	Substitutes CAA 1990 s 28.

Existing provision		*Rewritten provision*	*Remarks*
SCH 9	TRANSFER OF LIFE INSURANCE BUSINESS		
	para 3	560	Substitutes CAA 1990 s 152A(1), inserts CAA 1990 s 152A(1A), (1B).

FINANCE ACT 1996 (C 8)

Existing provision		*Rewritten provision*	*Remarks*
135	Time limits for claims etc		
	(3)	—	Commencement of capital allowance amendments in Sch 21.
	(4)	—	Amends CAA 1990 s 25(3), s 30(1), s 31(3), s 33(1), (4), s 37(2), s 53(2), s 68(5), s 68(9A), s 129(2), s 141(3) (but s 141(3) repealed FA 1997 Sch 18 Pt VI(11) and rest spent).
	(5)	—	Amends FA 1994 s 118(3); superseded by repeal of s 118(3) by FA 2000 s 73(1).
179	Roll-over relief in respect of ships		
		—	Introduces Schedule 35.
180	Scientific research expenditure: oil licences		
	(1)	408(1) to (3), 552(1) to (4), 555(1) to (5), 556(2)	Inserts CAA 1990 s 138A, s 138B.
	(2)	—	Amends CAA 1990 s 151(1).
	(3)	408	Re-numbers provisions of CAA 1990 s 118 as ss(1) and inserts ss(2).
	(4)	Sch 3 para 86	Commencement of s 180(3).
	(5)	—	Retrospective provision.
SCH 20	SELF-ASSESSMENT: DIRECTIONS EXERCISABLE BY THE BOARD ETC		
	para 44	17(4)	Amends CAA 1990 s 29(3).
SCH 21	SELF-ASSESSMENT: TIME LIMITS		
	para 26(1)	—	Introductory.
	para 26(2)	—	Amends CAA 1990 s 25(3).
	para 26(3)	—	Inserts CAA 1990 s 25(3A).
	para 27(1)	—	Introductory.
	para 27(2)	130(4)	Amends CAA 1990 s 30(1).
	para 27(3)	130(4), (5), 577(1)	Inserts CAA 1990 s 30(1A).
	para 28	130(2) to (5), 577(1)	Substitutes CAA 1990 s 31(3), inserts CAA 1990 s 31(3A).
	para 29(1)	—	Introductory.
	para 29(2)	129(1)	Substitutes CAA 1990 s 33(1).
	para 29(3)	129(1)	Substitutes CAA 1990 s 33(4).
	para 29(4)	129(2), (3), 577(1)	Inserts CAA 1990 s 33(5A).
	para 30(1)	—	Introductory.
	para 30(2)	85(2), (3)	Amends CAA 1990 s 37(2).
	para 30(3)	85(2), (3)	Inserts CAA 1990 s 37(2A).
	para 31(1)	—	Introductory.
	para 31(2)	177(1), (5), 576(1)	Amends CAA 1990 s 53(2).
	para 31(3)	177(5), (6), 577(1)	Inserts CAA 1990 s 53(2A).
	para 32(1)	—	Introductory.
	para 32(2)	—	Amends CAA 1990 s 68(5).
	para 32(3)	Sch 2 para 82	Inserts CAA 1990 s 68(5A).
	para 32(4)	Sch 2 para 82	Amends CAA 1990 s 68(9A).
	para 32(5)	Sch 2 para 82	Inserts CAA 1990 s 68(9AA).
	para 32(6)	—	Amends CAA 1990 s 68(9B).
	para 33	382(6), (7)	Amends CAA 1990 s 129(2).
	para 34	—	Repealed FA 1997 Sch 18 Pt VI(11).
SCH 35	ROLL-OVER RELIEF IN RESPECT OF SHIPS		
	para 1	—	Introductory
	para 2(1)	138(1)	Amends CAA 1990 s 33A(3).
	para 2(2)	144	Amends CAA 1990 s 33A(4).
	para 2(3)	140	Substitutes CAA 1990 s 33A(5), inserts CAA 1990 s 33A(5A).
	para 2(4)	140(4), 141(1), 158	Inserts CAA 1990 s 33A(8).
	para 3(1)	140(4)	Amends CAA 1990 s 33C(1).
	para 3(2)	—	Amends and repeals in part CAA 1990 s 33C(2).

Existing provision		Rewritten provision	Remarks
Sch 35 (cont)	para 4(1)	146(3)	Amends CAA 1990 s 33D(1).
	para 4(2)	149(2)	Amends CAA 1990 s 33D(2).
	para 4(3)	150	Inserts CAA 1990 s 33D(2A), (2B).
	para 4(4)	147(1)	Amends CAA 1990 s 33D(4).
	para 4(5)	141(1)	Amends CAA 1990 s 33D(6).
	para 4(6)	155	Amends CAA 1990 s 33D(7).
	para 4(7)	156	Substitutes CAA 1990 s 33D(8).
	para 5	—	Inserts CAA 1990 s 33E(9).
	para 6(1)	142(1) to (5)	Amends CAA 1990 s 33F(4).
	para 6(2)	142(6)	Inserts CAA 1990 s 33F(4A).
	para 7(1) to (3)	—	Commencement.
SCH 39	ENACTMENT OF CERTAIN EXTRA-STATUTORY TAX CONCESSIONS		
	para 1(1)	—	Introductory.
	para 1(3)	Sch 2 para 52	Inserts CAA 1990 s 35(2A).
	para 1(4)	Sch 3 para 113(2)	Commencement.

PLANNING (CONSEQUENTIAL AMENDMENTS) (SCOTLAND) ACT 1997 (C 11)

Existing provision		Rewritten provision	Remarks
Sch 2	Consequential amendments		
	para 45	436(2)(*b*)	Amends CAA 1990 s 121(1) ("the relevant planning enactment").

FINANCE ACT 1997 (C 16)

Existing provision		Rewritten provision	Remarks
66	Expenditure on production wells etc		
	(2)	407(4), Sch 3 para 85	Inserts CAA 1990 s 115(2A).
	(5)	Sch 3 para 85	Commencement of s 66(2).
84	Writing-down allowances on long-life assets		
		—	Introduces Schedule 14.
86	Capital allowances on fixtures		
		—	Introduces Schedule 16.
SCH 14	CAPITAL ALLOWANCES ON LONG-LIFE ASSETS		
	para 1	—	Introductory.
	para 2	3(3), 65(1), 90 to 104, Sch 3 para 20	Inserts CAA 1990 s 38A to 38H.
	para 3	84	Amends CAA 1990 s 37(1).
	para 4	107(2)	Substitutes CAA 1990 s 41(6).
	para 5	109(2)(*b*)	Amends CAA 1990 s 42(2).
	para 6	116(5)	Amends CAA 1990 s 43(3).
	para 7	113	Amends CAA 1990 s 46(7).
	para 8	126(1)	Amends CAA 1990 s 50(3), definition of "normal writing-down allowance".
	para 9	266(7), Sch 3 para 52	Amends CAA 1990 s 77(8).
	para 10	—	Commencement (chargeable periods ending on or after 26th November 1996; unnecessary).
SCH 15	CAPITAL ALLOWANCES: SCHEDULE A CASES ETC		
	para 3	15(1)(*b*), (*d*), (3), 16, 35(1), (2), (3), 248	Inserts CAA 1990 s 28A.
	para 4	15(1)(*c*), 17(1), 249(1)	Substitutes CAA 1990 s 29(1), inserts CAA 1990 s 29(1A).
	para 5(3)	28(2)	Inserts CAA 1990 s 67(4A).
	para 7	4(2)	Inserts CAA 1990 s 159(1A).
	para 8	19(5)	Amends ICTA s 434E(2).
	para 9(2)	Sch 3 para 9	Commencement of para 7.
SCH 16	CAPITAL ALLOWANCES ON FIXTURES		
	para 1	—	Introductory.
	para 2(1)	3(3), 577(1)	Amends CAA 1990 s 51(2).
	para 2(2)	202(2)	Amends CAA 1990 s 51(5).
	para 2(3)	202(3)	Inserts CAA 1990 s 51(5A).
	para 2(4)	203(1) to (3)	Inserts CAA 1990 s 51(6A).
	para 2(5)	172(1)	Repeals in part CAA 1990 s 51(8).
	para 2(6) to (8)	—	Commencement.
	para 3(1)	172(3), (4), 174(2), (3)	Amends CAA 1990 s 53(1).

Existing provision	Rewritten provision	Remarks
Sch 16 (cont) para 3(2)	172(3), (4), 178	Amends CAA 1990 s 53(1).
para 3(3)	172(3), (4), 177(1), (2), 178	Amends CAA 1990 s 53(1).
para 3(4)	178	Amends CAA 1990 s 53(1).
para 3(5)	177(3)	Inserts CAA 1990 s 53(1A), (1B), (1C).
para 3(6), (7)	Sch 3 paras 30 to 32	Commencement.
para 4(1)	181(2), (3), 182(2), (3), 184(2), (3), 172(4), 185(1) to (7), 186(1) to (5), 187(1) to (4), 575(1), Sch 3 paras 38 to 40	Inserts CAA 1990 s 56A to 56D.
para 4(2)	172(3), (4), 181(1), 182(1)	Amends and repeals in part CAA 1990 s 54(1).
para 4(3)	172(3), (4), 184(1), 575(1)	Amends and repeals in part CAA 1990 s 56.
para 4(4) to (6)	Sch 3 paras 34, 35, 37	Commencement.
para 5(1)	196(1), (3), (6)	Amends CAA 1990 s 59(1).
para 5(2)	197(1) to (3), 577(4)	Inserts CAA 1990 s 59A.
para 5(3)	—	
para 6(1)	198(1) to (5), 199(1) to (5), 200(2) to (4), 201(1) to (6), 204(4) to (6)	Inserts CAA 1990 s 59B , 59C.
para 6(2)	—	
para 7(1)	9(1) to (4), 10(2), 202(3)	Inserts CAA 1990 s 147(2A) to (2D).
para 7(2)	3(3)	Amends CAA 1990 s 147(3).
para 7(3)	Sch 3 para 10	Commencement of para 7 amendments
para 8	—	Construction of enactments
para 9		Amends TMA s 98.

FINANCE (NO 2) ACT 1997 (C 58)

Existing provision		Rewritten provision	Remarks
42	Temporary first-year allowances		
	(1)	Sch 3 para 46(3)	Amends CAA 1990 s 22(1).
	(2)	Sch 3 para 46(3)	Inserts CAA 1990 s 22(1AA).
	(3)	Sch 3 paras 46(1), 48(1) to (3)	Inserts CAA 1990 s 22(3C).
	(4)	—	Amends CAA 1990 s 22(4).
	(5)	46(2), 237(1)	Inserts CAA 1990 s 22(6B), (6C).
	(6)	—	Repealed FA 1998 Sch 27 Pt III(18).
	(7)	—	Repealed FA 1998 Sch 27 Pt III(18).
	(8)	—	Inserts CAA 1990 s 43(5); unnecessary.
	(9)	—	Commencement (chargeable periods ending on or after 2nd July 1997; unnecessary).
43	Expenditure of a small company or small business		
	(1)	47(1), (2), (4) to (6)	Inserts CAA 1990 s 22A.
	(2)	—	Commencement (chargeable periods ending on or after 2nd July 1997; unnecessary).
44	Writing-down allowances for finance lessors		
	(1)	—	Introductory.
	(2)	220(1), (2)	Inserts CAA 1990 s 25(5A) to (5C).
	(3)	—	Amends CAA 1990 s 25(6).
	(4)	231	Amends CAA 1990 s 25(8).
	(5)	Sch 3 para 44	Commencement.
45	Hire-purchase by finance lessors		
	(1)	229(3)	Inserts CAA 1990 s 60(2A).
	(2)	Sch 3 para 44	Commencement.
46	Sale and leaseback etc using finance leases		
	(1)	217(3), 218(4)	Amends CAA 1990 s 75(1), (2), (3), inserts CAA 1990 s 76(7).
	(2)	221, 222, 223, 224, 225, 226, 232, 241, 243(1) to (6), 244	Inserts CAA 1990 s 76A.
	(3)	Sch 3 paras 45, 51	Commencement.
47	Meaning of ''finance lease''		
	(1)	219	Inserts CAA 1990 s 82A.
	(2)		Commencement.

PETROLEUM ACT 1998 (C 17)

Existing provision		Rewritten provision	Remarks
SCH 4	CONSEQUENTIAL AMENDMENTS		
	para 27(1)	—	Introductory.
	para 27(2)	163(5)	Amends CAA 1990 s 62A(3)(*a*).
	para 27(3)	552(2)	Amends CAA 1990 s 116(2).
	para 27(4)	552(3)	Amends CAA 1990 s 138A(4).

FINANCE ACT 1998 (C 36)

Existing provision		Rewritten provision	Remarks
83	First-year allowances for investment in Northern Ireland		
	(1)	40(1), (2), 237(2)	Inserts CAA 1990 s 22(3CA) to (3CC).
	(2)	42(1), (2)	Inserts CAA 1990 s 22(6D), (6E).
	(3)	41(5)	Amends CAA 1990 s 22(10).
	(4)	43(1) to (6), 575(1)	Inserts CAA 1990 s 22B.
	(5)		Amends TMA s 98.
	(6)	—	Commencement.
	(7)	—	Limitation on commencement subject to appointed day; spent on exercise of power by SI 1999/2119.
84	First-year allowances for small businesses etc		
	(1)	52(3)	Amends CAA 1990 s 22(1).
	(2)	44(1), (2), 50	Inserts CAA 1990 s 22(3D).
	(3)	—	Commencement (chargeable periods ending on or after 2nd July 1997; unnecessary)
85	First-year allowances: consequential amendments etc		
	(1)		Amends CAA 1990 s 22(4), (6B), (6C).
	(2)	49(2), (8)	Amends CAA 1990 s 22A(4), (6).
	(3)	49(5)	Amends CAA 1990 s 22A(8).
	(4)	114(1), (3), 126(3)	Amends CAA 1990 s 23(6), s 42(9), s 50(3), (4A).
	(5)	111(1), (4), 112(1), (2), 113(1), 114(1), 117(2), 118(3), 119(1), Sch 3 para 22	Amends CAA 1990 s 44(5), s 46(8), s 48(7).
	(6)	125(4)	Amends CAA 1990 s 39(2).
	(7)	—	Amends CAA 1990 s 43(5).
	(8)		Repeals CAA 1990 s 76(3), amends CAA 1990 s 76(4).
	(9)	—	Commencement (chargeable periods ending on or after 12th May 1998; unnecessary).
	(10)	Sch 3 para 49	Commencement.
	(11)	—	Commencement.
117	Company tax returns, assessments and related matters		
	(1)(*d*)	—	Read together with Sch 27 Pt III (28) repeals CAA 1990 Sch A1.
SCH 5	RENT AND OTHER RECEIPTS FROM LAND—MINOR AND CONSEQUENTIAL AMENDMENTS		
	para 40(1)	—	Introductory.
	para 40(2)	19(5), 545(1), (2)	Substitutes ICTA s 434E(1).
	para 40(3)	—	Repeals ICTA s 434E(3).
	para 40(4)	261	Amends ICTA s 434E(6).
	para 47	352, 353	Substitutes CAA 1990 s 9.
	para 48	—	Repeals CAA 1990 s 15(2), (2A), (3).
	para 49	354	Inserts CAA 1990 s 15ZA.
	para 50	—	Repeals CAA 1990 s 15A.
	para 51	—	Repeals in part CAA 1990 s 29(1), repeals s 29(1A).
	para 52	131(7)	Amends CAA 1990 s 30(4), s 31(10).
	para 53	176(1)	Amends CAA 1990 s 52(1).
	para 54(1)	—	Introductory.
	para 54(2)	—	Repeals in part CAA 1990 s 53(1).
	para 54(3)	—	Substitutes CAA 1990 s 53(1)(bb), which is repealed FA 2000 s 75(5).

Dest. Tables

Existing provision		Rewritten provision	Remarks
Sch 5 (cont)	para 54(4)	—	Amends CAA 1990 s 53(1B).
	para 55(1)	—	Introductory.
	para 55(2)	—	Repeals CAA 1990 s 61(6).
	para 55(3)	260(7)	Amends CAA 1990 s 61(7).
	para 56	—	Repeals CAA 1990 s 67(2), (3), (3A).
	para 57	—	Amends CAA 1990 s 73(1), repeals CAA 1990 s 73(1A), repeals in part CAA 1990 s 73(2).
	para 58	529	Substitutes CAA 1990 s 92.
	para 59	392	Substitutes CAA 1990 s 132.
	para 60	—	Repeals in part CAA 1990 s 159(1A).
	para 61	4(2)(*a*), (3)(*a*), 15(1)(*d*), (3), 33(8), 35(1)	Substitutes CAA 1990 s 161(2A).
SCH 7	REMOVAL OF UNNECESSARY REFERENCES TO GAINS		
	para 1 (words)	Sch 3 para 101	Read with s 46(3), amends ICTA s 528(1).
	para 4	37(2), 116(3), 138(1), 117(1), 264(4), 272(3), 282, 355(1), (4), 536(3)	Read with s 46(3), amends CAA 1990 s 12, s 17(1), s 18(13), s 23(1)(*c*), s 33A(3), s 35(2), s 42(1)(*b*), s 43(2), s 44(2), s 45(2), (4), (5), s 65(3), s 68(7), (10), s 69(1), (2), s 70(1), s 71(1), s 80(1), s 109(1), s 115(2A), s 136, s 153(2).

FINANCE ACT 1999 (C 16)

Existing provision		Rewritten provision	Remarks
50	Cycles and cyclist's safety equipment		
	(2)	80(1), (4)	Amends CAA 1990 s 27(2B).
77	Extension of first-year allowances		
		—	Amends CAA 1990 s 22(3D).
78	First-year allowances for investment in Northern Ireland		
	(1)	41(1)(*c*), (2)	Amends CAA 1990 s 22(3CC).
	(2)	41(2) to (5)	Inserts CAA 1990 s 22(3CD), (3CE).
	(3)	41(5)	Amends CAA 1990 s 22(10).
	(4)	43(2), (3)	Amends CAA 1990 s 22B(2)(*a*), inserts CAA 1990 s 22B(2A).
	(5)	51(1) to (3)	Inserts CAA 1990 s 22C.
	(6)	—	Commencement (chargeable periods ending on or after 12th May 1998; unnecessary).
SCH 5	SCOTTISH PARLIAMENT AND DEVOLVED ASSEMBLIES: EXEMPTIONS AND RELIEFS		
	para 2(3)	34(1), (2)	Substitutes CAA 1990 s 74.
SCH 11	COMPANY TAX RETURNS, ETC: MINOR AND CONSEQUENTIAL AMENDMENTS		
	para 4	3(4)	Amends CAA 1990 s 17(3).
	para 5	135(5)	Amends CAA 1990 s 33F(1).
	para 6	201(5)	Substitutes CAA 1990 s 59C(7).
	para 7	—	Repeals in part CAA 1990 s 145(3).
	para 8	—	Substitutes FA 1994 s 118(7); superseded following repeal s 118(7) by FA 2000 s 73(1).

FINANCE ACT 2000 (C 17)

Existing provision		Rewritten provision	Remarks
70	First year allowances for small or medium-sized enterprises		
	(1)	—	Amends CAA 1990 s 22(3D), unnecessary.
	(2)	40(1)(*b*), 44(1), 47(1), (2), 48(1), (3)	Amends CAA 1990 s 22(3C)(*a*), (3CA), (3D)(*a*), s 22A.
71	First year allowances for ICT expenditure by small enterprises		
	(1)	45(1) to (3)	Inserts CAA 1990 s 22(3E) to (3H).

Existing provision		*Rewritten provision*	*Remarks*
71	(2)	46(2), 114(1), (3), 126(3)	Amends CAA 1990 s 22(4), (6B), (6C), s 23(6), s 42(9), s 50(3), (4A).
	(3)	111(1), (4), 112(1), (2), 113(1), 117(2), 118(3), 119(1)	Amends CAA 1990 s 43(5), s 44(5), s 46(8), s 48(7).
	(4)		Amends CAA 1990 s 39(2)(*a*).
72	Expenditure of a small enterprise		
		47(1), (3) to (6), 48(2), (4), (5), (7), (8), 49(3), (4) to (8)	Inserts CAA 1990 s 22AA.
75	Machinery and plant allowances for non-residents		
	(1)	15(1), 105(6), 168(1), 169(1), 216(2), 221(2), 263(2), 265(5), 268(8)	Inserts CAA 1990 s 83(2A).
	(2)	208	Inserts CAA 1990 s 79A.
	(3)	13(4), (5)	Inserts CAA 1990 s 81(2AA), (2AB).
	(5)	—	Repeals in part CAA 1990 s 53(1), amends CAA 1990 s 53(1B)(*b*).
	(6) (*b*) and (*c*)	Sch 3 paras 11, 42	Commencement.
76	Production animals		
	(1)	38	Inserts CAA 1990 s 82(2).
77	Sale and leaseback		
	(1)	227, 228, 245	Inserts CAA 1990 s 76B.
	(2)	—	Amends CAA 1990 s 75(1) to (3).
78	Meaning of "fixture"		
	(1)	—	Introductory words
	(2)	172(1)	Amends CAA 1990 s 51(1)
	(3)	173(1)	Amends CAA 1990 s 51(2)
	(4)	173(1), (2)	Inserts CAA 1990 s 51(2A).
	(5)	172(1)	Substitutes CAA 1990 s 51(8).
	(6)	—	Retrospective application of amendments
79	Leased Assets under the Affordable Warmth Programme		
	(1)	177(1), (2), 180(1) to (3), 203(1) to (4)	Inserts CAA 1990 s 53(1D) to (1H).
	(2)		Amends Taxes Management Act 1970 s 98
	(3)	Sch 3 para 33	Commencement of amendments
80	Fixtures and machinery or plant on hire-purchase		
	(1)	67(5)	Inserts CAA 1990 s 60(4).
	(2)	69	Inserts CAA 1990 s 60A.
	(3)	Sch 3 para 16	Application of amendments
81	Production sharing contracts		
	(1)	167, 168, 169, 170	Inserts CAA 1990 s 64A.
	(2)	171	Amends CAA 1990 s 26(1).
	(3)	Sch 3 para 28	Application of amendments
113	Tax treatment of expenditure on acquisition of films		
	(1)	Sch 2, para 82 [F(No 2)A 1992 s 40A(1)]	Substitutes CAA 1990 s 68(1).
	(2)	Sch 2, para 82 [F(No 2)A 1992 s 40A(5)]	Substitutes CAA 1990 s 68(2).
	(5), (6)	Sch 3 para 116	
SCH 19	MEANING OF "RESEARCH AND DEVELOPMENT"		
	para 7	—	Introductory words
	para 8	319(1), 437, 439(1), (5), 438(1), (2), (4), 445(4), 442(1), 443(1), 555(4), 449(1), 447(1), 448(1), 569(3), (4)	Amends CAA 1990 s 4(5), (9), (10), s 8(5), s 56D(1)(*a*), s 118(2), s 137(1), (1A), (3), s 138(1), (3A)(*a*), (5)(*b*), s 138A(3), s 139(1)(*b*), (*c*), (*d*), s 158(2)(*d*), s 161(2).
	para 9	439(1)	Amends CAA 1990 s 137(1)(*b*).
	para 10	437(2)	Amends CAA 1990 s 139(1).
	para 11	437(1)	Amends CAA 1990 s 161(2).

ITEPA 2003: DESTINATION TABLE

This Table shows how enactments proposed to be repealed are dealt with by the Income Tax (Earnings and Pensions) Act.

The following abbreviations are used in this Table—

Acts of Parliament

TMA 1970	Taxes Management Act 1970 (c 9)
IHTA 1984	Inheritance Tax Act 1984 (c 51)
TA 1988	Income and Corporation Taxes Act 1988 (c 1)
FA 1986	Finance Act 1986 (c 41)
FA 1988	Finance Act 1988 (c 39)
FA 1989	Finance Act 1989 (c 26)
FA 1990	Finance Act 1990 (c 29)
FA 1991	Finance Act 1991 (c 31)
TCGA 1992	Taxation of Chargeable Gains Act 1992 (c 12)
F(No 2)A 1992	Finance (No 2) Act 1992 (c 48)
FA 1993	Finance Act 1993 (c 34)
FA 1994	Finance Act 1994 (c 9)
FA 1995	Finance Act 1995 (c 4)
FA 1996	Finance Act 1996 (c 8)
FA 1997	Finance Act 1997 (c 16)
FA 1998	Finance Act 1998 (c 36)
FA 1999	Finance Act 1999 (c 16)
FA 2000	Finance Act 2000 (c 17)
CAA 2001	Capital Allowances Act 2001 (c 2)
FA 2002	Finance Act 2002 (c 23)
ESSA 2002	Employee Share Schemes Act 2002 (c 34)

Other Abbreviations

Annex 1, Change 1 etc	Annex 1 of the Explanatory Notes to the Act.
Annex 2, Note 1 etc	Annex 2 of the Explanatory Notes to the Act.

PART 1
ACTS OF PARLIAMENT

In this Table section 5(1) (application of the employment income Parts to offices) is not always acknowledged as the destination of a provision repealed by the Act. The provisions upon which that section is based are very numerous

TAXES MANAGEMENT ACT 1970 (C 9)

Existing provision	*Rewritten provision*	*Remarks*
s 98 Special returns, etc		
(Entries in Table)	—	Inserted FA 1988 s 85(3), FA 1998 s 52(2), FA 2000 Sch 8 para 117(4), Sch 14 paras 64(3), 65(3). Unnecessary: see Sch 6 paras 15, 18, 28(*c*), 30, 39 and 137.

INCOME AND CORPORATION TAXES ACT 1988 (C 1)

Existing provision	*Rewritten provision*	*Remarks*
s 19 Schedule E		
s 19(1)		
para 1, opening words	6(1), 7(2), (3), 10(2)	
Case I	10(2), 15(1), 21(1), 22(1)	Substituted FA 1989 s 36(2), repealed in part FA 1998 s 63(3).
Case II	10(2), 25(1), 27(1)	Substituted FA 1989 s 36(2).
Case III	10(2), 22(1), (2), 26(1)	Substituted FA 1989 s 36(2).
concluding words	—	Unnecessary.
para 2	569(1), 577(1), (2)	Amended FA 1996 Sch 7 paras 5, 32.
para 3	569(1)	
para 4	615(1)–(6)	

Dest. Tables

Existing provision	*Rewritten provision*	*Remarks*
para 4A	17(1)–(3), 30(1)–(3)	Inserted FA 1989 s 36(3).
para 5	6(1), 7(6)	
s 19(2)	—	Unnecessary.
s 19(3)	—	Unnecessary.
s 58 Foreign pensions		
s 58(1)	573(1)	
s 58 (2)	574, 633	
s 65 Cases IV and V assessments: general		
s 65(2) (words)	—	Unnecessary: see commentary on clause 642.
s 131 Chargeable emoluments		
s 131(1)	10(2), 62(2), 327	
s 131(2)	—	Unnecessary. Repealed in part FA 1989 s 42(2).
s 132 Place of performance and meaning of emoluments received in the UK		
s 132(1)	38	Amended FA 1996 Sch 20 para 6.
s 132(2)	39(1), (2)	
s 132(3)	39(3), 383(4)	Amended FA 1998 s 63(3).
s 132(4)	25(1), 27(1), 28(1)–(3), 40	
s 132(5)	33(1)–(6), 34(2)–(7)	
s 133 Voluntary pensions		
s 133(1)	570, 633	
s 133(2)	570, 615(7)	
s 134 Workers supplied by agencies		
s 134(1)	7(5), 44(1), (2), 47(1)	
s 134(2)	46(1)	
s 134(3)	46(1), (2)	
s 134(4)	44(2)	
s 134(5)	44(1), 47(2)	Repealed in part FA 1998 s 55(1).
s 134(6)	45	
s 134(7)	47(3)	
s 135 Gains by directors and employees from share options		
s 135(1)	7(6), 10(3), 471(1), (2), 476(1),(2), (4), 478(1)	
s 135(2)	474 Amended FA 1998 s 49(1).	
s 135(3)	479(1), (2), 480(1), (2), 484(2)	
s 135(4)	479(3), 480(3), 484(3)	
s 135(5)	475(1), (2), 478(2)	Amended FA 1998 s 49(1); amended FA 2002 Sch 6 para 1.
s 135(6)	471(1), 477(1), (2), 478(1), 479(2), 480(2)	
s 135(7)	477(5), (6)	Part unnecessary: see commentary on clause 477.
s 135(8)	483(1)	
s 135(9)	—	Unnecessary: see commentary on clause 484.
s 136 Provisions supplementary to section 135		
s 136(1)	485(1)–(4)	
s 136(2)	485(5)	
s 136(3)	485(6)	
s 136(4)	—	Spent.
s 136(5)	483(2), 487(1) ("director", "employee", "shares")	Part unnecessary: see commentary on clauses 434, 446 and 487.
s 136(6)	486(1)–(3)	Amended FA 2000 s 56(3).
s 136(7)	486(5)	Inserted FA 2000 s 56(4).
s 136(8)	486(4)	Inserted FA 2000 s 56(4).
s 137 Payment of tax under section 135 by instalments		Amended TCGA 1992 Sch 10 para 14(9); spent.
s 140 Further interpretation of sections 135–139		
s 140(1)	471(1), (3), 473	
s 140(2)	718	
s 140(3)	475(3), 487(1) ("shares")	Amended TCGA 1992 Sch 10 para 14(11).

Existing provision	*Rewritten provision*	*Remarks*
s 140A Conditional acquisition of shares		Inserted FA 1998 s 50(1).
s 140A(1)	422(1)	
s 140A(2)	—	Repealed FA 1999 s 42(2).
s 140A(3)	426	Amended FA 1999 s 42(3).
s 140A(4)	7(6), 10(3), 427(1)–(3)	Amended FA 1999 s 42(4).
s 140A(5)	7(6), 10(3), 428(1)	
s 140A(6)	434(1) (''market value'')	
s 140A(7)	428(2), (3)	
s 140A(8)	431	
s 140A(9)	428(4), 434(1) (''shares'')	
s 140B Consideration for shares conditionally acquired		Inserted FA 1998 s 50(1).
s 140B(1)	429(1)	
s 140B(2)	429(2)	
s 140B(3)	429(3)	
s 140B(4)	429(4)	
s 140B(5)	429(5)	
s 140B(6)	429(6)	
s 140B(7)	430(1)–(5)	
s 140C Cases where interest to be treated as only conditional		Inserted FA 1998 s 50(1).
s 140C(1)	424(1), (4), 434(1) (''market value'')	
s 140C(1A)	424(2)	Inserted FA 1999 s 43(2).
s 140C(2)	424(2)	Amended FA 1999 s 43(3).
s 140C(3)	424(2), (6)	Amended FA 1999 s 43(3), (4).
s 140C(3A)	424(2), (6)	Inserted FA 1999 s 43(5).
s 140C(4)	424(2)	Amended FA 1999 s 43(3).
s 140C(5)	424(3)	
s 140C(6)	424(7)	Inserted FA 1999 s 43(6).
s 140D Convertible shares		Inserted FA 1998 s 51(1).
s 140D(1)	435(1)	
s 140D(2)	435(2)	
s 140D(3)	7(6), 10(3), 438(1), (2)	
s 140D(4)	7(6), 10(3), 438(2), (3)	
s 140D(5)	439(1)	
s 140D(6)	439(2), (3)	
s 140D(7)	439(6)	
s 140D(8)	440(1)	
s 140D(9)	440(2), (3)	
s 140D(10)	441	
s 140E Consideration for convertible shares		Inserted FA 1998 s 51(1).
s 140E(1)	442(1)	
s 140E(2)	442(2)	
s 140E(3)	442(3)	
s 140E(4)	442(4)	
s 140E(5)	442(5)	
s 140E(6)	442(6)	
s 140E(7)	443(1)–(5)	
s 140F Supplemental provisions with respect to convertible shares		Inserted FA 1998 s 51(1).
s 140F(1)	444	
s 140F(2)	435(3)	
s 140F(3)	439(5)	
s 140F(4)	440(5)	
s 140F(5)	440(4)	
s 140F(6)	435(1), 439(2), 442(1), (2)	
s 140F(7)	719	
s 140G Information for the purposes of sections 140A–140F		Inserted FA 1998 s 52(1).
s 140G(1)	432(1), (2)	Part unnecessary: see commentary on clause 432.
s 140G(2)	433(1), (2)	

Existing provision	*Rewritten provision*	*Remarks*
s 140G(3)	445(1), (2)	
s 140G(4)	432(2), 433(2), 445(2)	
s 140G(5)	432(3), 433(3), 445(3)	
s 140G(6)	434(1) (''shares''), 435(2), 445(1), (2)	
s 140H Construction of sections 140A–140G		Inserted FA 1998 s 53.
s 140H(1)	423(1), 434(1) (''shares''), 436(1)	
s 140H(2)	423(2), 436(2)	
s 140H(3)	425, 437	
s 140H(4)	423(3), (4), (5), 434(1) (''shares''), 436(3), (4), (5)	
s 140H(5)	424(1), 435(2)	
s 140H(6)	434(1) (''terms''), 446(1) (''terms'')	
s 140H(7)	423(1), (2), (3), 436(1)–(3), 437(1)	
s 140H(8)	430(6), 434(1) (''director'', ''employee'', ''shares''), 443(6), 446(1) (''director'', ''employee'', ''shares'')	Part unnecessary: see commentary on clauses 434 and 446.
s 140H(9)	718	
s 141 Non-cash vouchers		
s 141(1)	7(5), 82(1), 87(1)–(3), 88, 95(1)–(3)	Amended and repealed in part FA 1994 s 89(2).
s 141(2)	88	
s 141(3)	328(1), 329(1), (5), 353(4), 362	Amended FA 1995 s 91(2). See Annex 1, Change 81 and Annex 2, Notes 36 and 37.
s 141(4)	87(2)	
s 141(5)	82(3)	
s 141(6)	86(1), (2)	Amended FA 1988 s 46(1).
s 141(6A)	266(1)	Inserted FA 1988 s 46(1). Part unnecessary: see commentary on clause 95.
s 141(6B)	266(1)	Inserted FA 1988 s 47(1), amended FA 1994 s 89(3). Part unnecessary: see commentary on clause 95.
s 141(6C)	268(1)–(5)	Inserted FA 1995 s 93(1). Part unnecessary: see commentary on clause 95.
s 141(6D)	268(2), (3), (6)	Inserted FA 1995 s 93(1).
s 141(7)		
''cheque voucher''	84(4)	
''passenger transport undertaking''	86(3)	
''subsidiary''	86(3)	Amended Companies Act 1989 (c 40) Sch 18 para 46.
''transport voucher''	84(3), 87(4), 95(4)	
''non-cash voucher''	84(1), (2), 721(1)	
s 142 Credit-tokens		
s 142(1)	7(5), 90(1), 94(1)–(3), 95(1)–(3)	Amended FA 1994 s 89(5).
s 142(2)	328(1), 329(1), 363	Amended FA 1995 s 91(2).
s 142(3)	94(1)–(3), 329(5), 353(4)	Amended FA 1994 s 89(6). See Annex 1, Change 81 and Annex 2, Notes 36 and 37.
s 142(3A)	267	Inserted FA 1988 s 46(2). Part unnecessary: see commentary on clause 95.
s 142(3B)	267	Inserted FA 1988 s 48(1), amended FA 1994 s 89(7). Part unnecessary: see commentary on clause 95.

Existing provision	*Rewritten provision*	*Remarks*
s 142(3C)	268(1)–(5)	Inserted FA 1995 s 93(2). Part unnecessary: see commentary on clause 95.
s 142(3D)	268(2), (3), (6)	Inserted FA 1995 s 93(2).
s 142(4)	92(1), (2), (4), 721(1) (''credit token'')	
s 142(5)	92(3)	
s 143 Cash vouchers taxable under PAYE		
s 143(1)	7(5), 73(1), 81, 95(1), (2)	Amended FA 1994 s 89(9).
s 143(2)	73(3)	
s 143(3)	75, 80	Amended FA 1994 s 89(10). Part unnecessary: see commentary on clause 80.
s 143(4)	76	Amended FA 1994 s 89(11).
s 143(5)	79	
s 144 Supplementary provisions		
s 144(1)	96(1)–(4)	Amended FA 1994 s 89(13).
s 144(2)	96(5)–(8)	
s 144(3)	77, 87(6), 94(4)	Amended FA 1994 s 89(14).
s 144(4)	73(2), 74, 82(2), 83, 90(2), 91	
s 144(4A)	91, 95	Inserted FA 2002 Sch 6 para 2.
s 144(5)		
''cash voucher''	75	
''credit-token''	92(1)	
''employee''	66	
''non-cash voucher''	84	
''relation''	721(4)	
s 144A Payments etc received free of tax		
		Inserted FA 1994 s 132.
s 144A(1)	7(5), 222(1), (2)	Amended FA 2002 Sch 6 para 4.
s 144A(2)	222(3)	Amended FA 1998 s 69(4).
s 145 Living accommodation provided for employee		
s 145(1)	7(5), 97(1), 102(1), 105(2)	Repealed in part FA 1996 s 106(1).
s 145(2)	105(3), (4)	
s 145(3)	328(1), 329(1), (5), 353(4), 364	See Annex 1, Change 81 and Annex 2, Notes 36 and 37.
s 145(4)	99(1), (2), 100, 314	
s 145(5)	99(3), (4)	
s 145(6)	97(1)	
s 145(7)	97(2), 98	Repealed in part FA 1996 Sch 20 para 7.
s 145(8)	66, 67, 68, 69, 99(5), 721(5)	
s 146 Additional charge in respect of certain living accommodation		
s 146(1)	97(1), 98, 99(1), (2), 100, 102(1), 105(1), 106(1)	
s 146(2)	7(5), 106(2), (3)	
s 146(3)	106(2)	
s 146(4)	104, 106(2), 107(3)	
s 146(5)	104, 106(2), 107(3)	
s 146(6)	107(2), (3)	
s 146(7)	112	
s 146(8)	Sch 7 para 21	
s 146(9)	328(1), 329(1), 364	
s 146(10)	66, 97	
s 146(11)		
''the appropriate percentage''	106(2)	Amended FA 1989 s 179(5).
''market value''	107(3), (4)	
''property''	113	
''tenancy''	104, 107(3)	
	concluding words	718
s 146A Priority of rules applying to living accommodation		
	64(1), (2), 109	Inserted FA 1996 s 106(2).
s 147 Occupation of Chevening House		
		101

Dest. Tables

Existing provision	Rewritten provision	Remarks
s 148 Payments and other benefits in connection with termination of employment etc		Substituted FA 1998 s 58(1).
s 148(1)	401(1), (3), 403(1), (4), 404	
s 148(2)	402(1)	Substituted FA 2002 Sch 6 para 5.
s 148(2A)	239(1), (2), 310(1), 402(2), (3), 405	Inserted FA 2002 Sch 6 para 5.
s 148(3)	7(6), 10(3), 402(4), 403(1), (2)	
s 148(4)	403(3)	
s 148(5)	—	Unnecessary—see Annex 2, Note 42.
s 148(6)	401(1), (4), 403(5), 404, 406, 407, 411, 412, 413(1), (3)–(6), 414(1)–(5), 415, 416	
s 148(7)	5(1), (2)	
s 149 Sick pay		
s 149(1)	7(5), 221(1)–(3), (5)–(7)	Repealed in part FA 1989 s 42(3).
s 149(2)	221(4)	
s 149(3)	221(5)–(7), 721(4)	
s 150 Job release scheme allowances, maternity pay and statutory sick pay		
s 150(*a*)	—	Spent.
s 150(*b*)	—	Repealed Employment Rights Act 1996 (c 18) Sch 3 Pt I.
s 150(*c*)	660	
s 150(*d*)	660	
s 150(*e*)	660	Inserted FA 2002 s 35.
s 151 Income support etc		
s 151(1)	660, 665(1)	
s 151(2)	665(2), 669(1)	
s 151(3)	667	
s 151(4)	—	Spent.
s 151(5)	668	
s 151(6)	—	Spent.
s 151(7)	668, 669(1)	
s 151(8)	—	Spent.
s 151(9)	669(2)	
s 151A Jobseeker's allowance		Inserted Jobseekers Act 1995 (c 18) Sch 2 para 12.
s 151A(1)	660	
s 151A(2)	671	
s 151A(3)	672	
s 151A(4)	673(3)	
s 151A(5)	674(3)	
s 151A(6)	673(2)	
s 151A(7)	674(2)	
s 151A(8)	673(4)	
s 151A(9)	675(1), (2)	
s 153 Payments in respect of expenses		
s 153(1)	7(5), 70(1), (3)–(5), 72(1)	Amended FA 1989 s 53(2)(*b*), FA 2001 Sch 12 Pt 2 para 1.
s 153(2)	72(2), (3)	Amended FA 1995 s 91(2), FA 2001 Sch 12 Pt 2 para 1.
s 153(3)	70(2)	
s 154 General charging provision		
s 154(1)	7(5), 201(1), (2), (4), 203(1)	Amended FA 1989 s 53(2)(*b*).
s 154(2)	201(2), 202	Amended FA 1990 s 21(2), FA 1993 Sch 4 para 2, FA 1999 s 44(3), s 45(2), FA 2000 Sch 10 paras 2(2), 3(2).
s 154(3)	209	Amended FA 2000 Sch 10 para 2(2).
s 155 Exceptions from the general charge		
s 155(1)	239(4), (5), 240(3)	Amended FA 1993 Sch 4 para 3.
s 155(1A)	237(1), (3)	Inserted FA 1988 s 46(3).
s 155(1B)	240(2), (4), 241(1)	Inserted FA 1995 s 93(3).
s 155(1C)	240(4), 241	Inserted FA 1995 s 93(3).
s 155(2)	—	Repealed FA 2000 Sch 40 Pt II(2).
s 155(3)	313	

Existing provision	Rewritten provision	Remarks
s 155(4)	307(1), (2)	
s 155(5)	317(1)	
s 155(6)	325	
s 155(7)	265, 718	Inserted FA 1988 s 49(1).
s 155ZA Accommodation, supplies or services used in performing duties of employment		Inserted FA 2000 Sch 10 para 2(1).
s 155ZA(1)	316(1)	
s 155ZA(2)	316(2)	
s 155ZA(3)	316(4)	
s 155ZA(4)	316(6), (7)	
s 155ZA(5)	316(5)	
s 155ZA(6)	316(3)	
s 155ZB Power to provide for exemption of minor benefits		Inserted FA 2000 Sch 10 para 3(1).
s 155ZB(1)	210(1)	
s 155ZB(2)	210(2)	
s 155ZB(3)	266(4), (5)	Inserted FA 2002 s 36(1).
s 155AA Mobile telephones		Inserted FA 1999 s 44(1).
s 155AA(1)	319(1)	
s 155AA(2)	319(2), (3)	
s 155AA(3)	—	Unnecessary: see Annex 2, Note 35.
s 155AA(4)	319(3)	
s 155AA(5)	319(3)	
s 155AA(6)	—	Unnecessary.
s 155A Care for children		Inserted FA 1990 s 21(1).
s 155A(1)	318(1), (2)	
s 155A(2)	318(3)–(6)	
s 155A(3)	318(3)	
s 155A(4)	318(6)	
s 155A(5)	318(7)	
s 155A(6)	318(4), (5)	Amended Care Standards Act 2000 Sch 4 para 13.
s 155A(7)	318(3)	
s 155A(8)		
"care"	318(8)	
"child"	318(3)	
"domestic premises"	318(4)	
"parental responsibility"	318(3)	
s 156 Cash equivalent of benefits charged under section 154		
s 156(1)	203(2)	
s 156(2)	203(3), 204	
s 156(3)	203(3), 206	
s 156(4)	203(3), 206	
s 156(5)	203(3), 205	
s 156(6)	203(3), 205, 207(1)	
s 156(7)	203(3), 205	
s 156(8)	328(1), 329(1), (5), 353(4), 365(1), (2)	Amended FA 1995 s 91(2). See Annex 1, Change 81 and Annex 2, Notes 36 and 37.
s 156(9)	205, 206	
s 156A Limited exemption for computer equipment		Inserted FA 1999 s 45(1).
s 156A(1)	320(1), (4), (5)	
s 156A(2)	320(4)–(6)	
s 156A(3)	320(1)–(5)	
s 156A(4)	320(7)	
s 156A(5)	320(7)	
s 157 Cars available for private use		
s 157(1)	7(5), 114(1),(3), 120	Amended FA 1989 s 53(2)(*b*).
s 157(2)	121(1)	Substituted FA 1993 Sch 3 para 2(1).
s 157(3)	239(1), (2), 269(1), 721(4)	Amended FA 2002 Sch 6 para 3.
s 157(4), (5)	—	Repealed FA 1993 Sch 3 para 2(2).
s 157A Cars available for private use: cash alternative, etc	119	Inserted FA 1995 s 43(1).

Existing provision	*Rewritten provision*	*Remarks*
s 158 Car fuel		
s 158(1)	7(5), 149(1)	Amended FA 1989 s 53(2)(*b*), FA 1995 s 43(2).
s 158(2)	150(1), (2)	Inserted FA 2002 s 34(2).
s 158(3)	149(3), 721(1) (''credit-token'', ''non-cash voucher'')	
s 158(4)	170(5), (6)	Amended FA 2002 s 34(3).
s 158(5)	152(1)	Substituted FA 2002 s 34(4).
s 158(6)	151	Part unnecessary; repealed in part FA 1998 Sch 27 Pt 3(10).
s 158(6A)	152(2)	Inserted FA 2002 s 34(5).
s 158(6B)	152(3)	Inserted FA 2002 s 34(5).
s 158(7)	—	Repealed FA 1998 Sch 27 Pt 3(10).
s 158(8)	152(4)	Inserted FA 2002 s 34(6).
s 158(9)	149(4)	Inserted FA 2002 s 34(7).
s 159 Pooled cars		
s 159(1)	167(1)	Substituted FA 1996 Sch 20 para 8.
s 159(2)	167(3)	
s 159(3)	167(2)	
s 159(4)–(6)	—	Repealed FA 1996 Sch 20 para 8.
s 159AA Vans available for private use		
		Inserted FA 1993 Sch 4 para 4.
s 159AA(1)	7(5), 114(1), (3), 154	
s 159AA(2)	—	Introduces TA 1988 Sch 6A.
s 159AA(3)	239(1), (2), 269(1), 721(4)	Amended FA 2002 Sch 6 para 3.
s 159AB Pooled vans		
	168	Inserted FA 1993 Sch 4 para 4.
s 159AC Heavier commercial vehicles available for private use		
		Inserted FA 1993 s 74(1).
s 159AC(1)	238(1)–(3)	
s 159AC(2)	238(1), 239(4),(5)	
s 159AC(3)	239(1), (2), 269(1), 721(4)	Amended FA 2002 Sch 6 para 3.
s 159AC(4)	238(4) (''heavy goods vehicle'')	
s 159AC(5)	238(4) (''private use'')	
s 160 Beneficial loan arrangements		
s 160(1)	7(5), 174(1), 175(1), (2), 184(1), (2), (3)	Amended FA 1989 s 53(2)(*b*); FA 1994 s 88(1).
s 160(1A)	184(2)–(5)	Inserted FA 1994 s 88(1).
s 160(1B)	187(1), (2), (3), (5)	Substituted FA 1996 s 107(1).
s 160(1BA)	187(1), (4)	Inserted FA 1996 s 107(1)
s 160(1C)	—	Repealed FA 2000 Sch 10 para 4(2).
s 160(2)	7(5), 174(1), 188(1)	Amended FA 1989 s 53(2)(*b*).
s 160(3)	188(2)	Substituted FA 1989 s 53(2)(*c*).
s 160(3A)	188(3)	Inserted FA 1995 s 45(3).
s 160(4)	174(1), 175(3), (4)	Repealed in part FA 1994 Sch 26 Pt V(5).
s 160(4A)	191(1), (2), (5)	Inserted FA 1991 Sch 6 para 1(2); part unnecessary.
s 160(5)	173(2), 181	Amended FA 1989 s 179(1)(*g*), FA 1994 s 88(2), FA 2000 Sch 10 para 4(2), 5(3). Repealed in part FA 1995 s 45(2).
s 160(6)	174(6)	
s 160(7)	Sch 7 para 25	
s 161 Exceptions from section 160		
s 161(1)	180(1)–(3)	Substituted FA 1994 s 88(3).
s 161(1A), (1B)	—	Repealed FA 2000 Sch 10, para 5(4).
s 161(2)	177(1), (2), (5)	
s 161(3)	177(3), (4), (5), 718	Repealed in part FA 1996 Sch 20 para 9.
s 161(4)	174(5)	Repealed in part FA 1996 Sch 20 para 9.
s 161(5)	189	
s 161(6)	190	

Existing provision	Rewritten provision	Remarks
s 161(7)	Sch 7, para 25	
s 161A Treatment of qualifying loans		Inserted FA 2000 Sch 10 para 4(1).
s 161A(1)	180(5)	
s 161A(2)	178	
s 161B Beneficial loans: loans on ordinary commercial terms		Inserted FA 2000 Sch 10 para 5(1).
s 161B(1)	176(1)	
s 161B(2)	176(2)	
s 162 Employee shareholdings		
s 162(1)	7(5), 192(1), (2), 193(1)–(4), 197(1) (''employee''), 198(3), 200(1) (''employee''), Sch 7 para 28	Amended FA 1988 Sch 13 para 3, FA 1989 s 53(2)(*b*).
s 162(2)	193(1), (2), (5), 194(1), (2)	
s 162(3)	194(1)–(3), 195(1)	
s 162(4)	195(1)	Part unnecessary: see commentary on clause 195.
s 162(5)	195(2), (3)	Amended FA 1989 s 53(2)(*d*).
s 162(6)	198(1), (3), 199(1), (3), Sch 7 para 30	Part unnecessary: see commentary on clause 199.
s 162(7)	199(4)	Substituted FA 1989 s 53(2)(*e*).
s 162(8)	199(2)	Part unnecessary: see commentary on clause 199.
s 162(9)	192(1), (2), 193(1), (2), 194(1), 197(1) (''interest in shares''), 198(1), 199(5), 200(1) (''interest in shares'')	
s 162(10)	197(1) (''market value'', ''shares''), (2), (3), 200 (1) (''market value'', ''shares''), (2), 718	Amended TCGA 1992 Sch 10 para 14(11).
s 162(11)	64(1), (2), 194(2), 196	
s 163 Expenses connected with living accommodation		
s 163(1)	315(1), (2)	Amended FA 1989 s 53(2).
s 163(2)	315(1), (3)	
s 163(3)	315(3)	
s 163(4)	315(4), (5)	Amended FA 2001 Sch 12 Pt 2 para 2.
s 163(5)	315(4), (5)	
s 164 Director's tax paid by employer		
s 164(1)	7(5), 223(1)–(4), (6)	
s 164(2)	223(7)	
s 164(3)	223(5), (6)	
s 165 Scholarships		
s 165(1)	215	
s 165(2)	212	
s 165(3)	213	
s 165(4), (5)	Sch 7 para 32	
s 165(6)	212, 213, 718	Amended FA 1989 s 53(2).
s 166 Notice of nil liability under this Chapter (1)	65(1)–(3), (5)	
s 166(2)	65(6)–(9)	
s 166(3), (4)	Sch 7 para 15	
s 167 Employment to which this Chapter applies		Substituted FA 1989 s 53(1).
s 167(1)	216(1)–(4), 217(1), 218(1)	
s 167(2)	218(1), (3), (4), 219(5), (6)	Amended FA 1995 s 43(3), FA 2001 Sch 12 Pt 2 para 3.
s 167(2A)	—	Repealed FA 1994 Sch 26 Pt V(5).
s 167(2B)	218(1), 219(1)–(4)	Inserted FA 1995 s 43(3).
s 167(2C)	219(2)–(4)	Inserted FA 1995 s 43(3).
s 167(2D)	218(1)	Inserted FA 1995 s 43(3).
s 167(3)	220	
s 167(4)	220(3)	
s 167(5)	216(3)	

Dest. Tables

Existing provision	*Rewritten provision*	*Remarks*
s 168 Other interpretative provisions		
s 168(1)	—	Introductory.
s 168(2)	66	
s 168(3)	71, 192(3), 198(4), 201(3)	Amended FA 1996 Sch 20 para 10.
s 168(4)	721(5)	
s 168(5)	115(1) (''car'') (2) (''goods vehicle'', ''invalid carriage'', ''motor cycle''), 118(2), 171(1) (''business travel''), (2), (3), 329(5), 353(4)	Amended FA 1993 Sch 3 para 3, VERA 1994 Sch 3 para 22, FA 1997 s 62(4), FA 2001 Sch 12 Pt 2 para 4. See Annex 1, Change 81 and Annex 2, Notes 36 and 37.
s 168(5A)	115(1) (''van''), (2) (''design weight'', ''goods vehicle'', ''motor cycle''), 118(2), 171(1) (''business travel''), (2), (3)	Inserted FA 1993 Sch 4 para 6(1), amended VERA 1994 Sch 3 para 22, FA 1997 s 62(4), FA 2001 Sch 12 Pt 2 para 4.
s 168(6)	117, 118(1)	Amended FA 1993 Sch 4, para 6(2), FA 1996 Sch 20 para 10.
s 168(7)	208	
s 168(8)	67(1), 223(8)	
s 168(9)	67(2), 223(8)	
s 168(10)	67(3)	
s 168(11)	68, 223(8)	Amended FA 1989 Sch 12 para 8.
s 168(12)	69	
s 168(13)	721(1) (''tax year'')	Part unnecessary.
s 168A Price of a car as regards a year		Inserted FA 1993 Sch 3 para 4.
s 168A(1)	122, 126(5)	Amended FA 1998 s 60(1).
s 168A(2)	123	
s 168A(3)		Unnecessary: see commentary on clause 126.
s 168A(4)	126(1), (2), 127(1), 128(1)	
s 168A(5)	126(1), (4), 127(1)	
s 168A(6)	126(1), (2), (4), 127(1)	
s 168A(7)	126(2), 127(1)	
s 168A(8)	124	
s 168A(9)	123, 124, 125(4), 128, 171(1)(''relevant taxes'')	
s 168A(10)	125(1)	
s 168A(11)	125(2)	Amended FA 1995 s 44(1), FA 1998 s 60(2), FA 1999 s 44(4).
s 168A(12)	116(2)	
s 168AA Equipment to enable disabled person to use car		Inserted FA 1995 s 44(2).
s 168AA(1)	172(1)	
s 168AA(2)	172(1), (2)	
s 168AA(3)	171(4)	
s 168AA(4)	116(2)	
s 168AB Equipment to enable car to run on road fuel gas		Inserted FA 1998 s 60(3).
s 168AB(1)	125(2)	
s 168AB(2)	146(1), (2)	
s 168AB(3)	171(1)	
s 168AB(4)	125(3), 146(1)	Inserted FA 2000 Sch 11 para 2.
s 168B Price of a car: accessories not included in list price		Inserted FA 1993 Sch 3 para 4.
s 168B(1)	126(1), (2)	
s 168B(2)	126(1), 127(1)	Amended FA 1998 s 60(4).
s 168B(3)	126(4)	
s 168B(4)	129(1)	
s 168B (5)	130(1)	
s 168B(6)	129(2), 130(2)	
s 168B(7)	129(2), 130(2)	
s 168B(8)	116(2), 125(1), (2)	
s 168C Price of a car: accessories available after car first made available		Inserted FA 1993 Sch 3 para 4.

Existing provision	Rewritten provision	Remarks
s 168C(1)	126(3)	
s 168C(2)	126(1), 127(2)	Amended FA 1998 s 60(5).
s 168C(3)	116(2), 125(1), (2)	
s 168C(4)	126(4), 129, 130	
s 168C(5)	170(1), (2)	
s 168D Price of a car: capital contributions		Inserted FA 1993 Sch 3 para 4.
s 168D(1)	132(1)	
s 168D(2)	132(2)	
s 168D(3)	132(3)	
s 168D(4)	132(3)	
s 168D(5)	125(1), (2)	
s 168D(6)	170(1), (2)	
s 168E Price of a car: replacement accessories	—	Inserted FA 1993 Sch 3 para 4; unnecessary: see commentary on clause 131.
s 168F Price of a car: classic cars		Inserted FA 1993 Sch 3 para 4.
s 168F(1)	147(1)	
s 168F(2)	147(2)	
s 168F(3)	147(3), (4)	
s 168F(4)	147(3)	
s 168F(5)	147(2), (5), (6)	
s 168F(6)	147(6)	
s 168F(7)	147(7)	
s 168F(8)	147(7)	
s 168F(9)	125(1), (2)	
s 168F(10)	116(2)	
s 168F(11)	170(1), (2)	
s 168G Price of a car: cap for expensive car		Inserted FA 1993 Sch 3 para 4.
s 168G(1)	121(1)	
s 168G(2)	170(1), (2)	
s 185 Approved share option schemes		
s 185(1)	517, 522	See also Sch 6 para 221.
s 185(2)	518, 523	Amended FA 1996 s 114(4), (5).
s 185(3)	519(1), 520(1), (2), 524(1), 525	Amended FA 1988 s 89, TCGA 1992 Sch 10 para 14(12). Part unnecessary: see Annex 1, Change 129. See also Sch 6 para 221.
s 185(4)	519(2), (3), 520(1)	Amended FA 1991 s 39(2), (4), (8). See also Sch 6 para 221.
s 185(5)	524(1)–(3), 525(1)	See Sch 6 para 221.
s 185(6)	7(6), 10(3), 526(1)–(3)	Substituted FA 1996 s 114(4), (6), (7). Part unnecessary: see commentary on clause 526.
s 185(7)	—	Amended TCGA 1992 Sch 10 para 14(12), FA 1996 s 114(4), (7). See Sch 6 para 221.
s 185(8)	194(2), 479(2), 480(2)	Amended FA 1996 s 114(4), (7).
s 185(9)	—	Spent.
s 185(10)	—	Unnecessary.
s 186 Approved profit sharing schemes		
s 186(3) (words)	—	See Sch 6 para 26(2).
s 186(4) (words)	—	See Sch 6 para 26(3).
s 187 Interpretation of sections 185 and 186 and Schedules 9 and 10		
s 187(1)	—	Provisions relating to approved profit sharing schemes ("APSS provisions") are not being repealed. Some APSS provisions Otherwise unnecessary.
s 187(2)	516(4), 521(4), 719, Sch 3 paras 35, 47, 48, Sch 4 paras 35, 36	Some APSS provisions Definition of "market value" amended TCGA 1992 Sch 10 para 14(13).

Dest. Tables

Existing provision	Rewritten provision	Remarks
s 187(3)	Sch 3 paras 11, 12, 14, Sch 4 paras 9, 10, 12	Amended FA 1989 Sch 12 para 9. Part unnecessary: see commentary on Sch 3 para 12, Sch 4 para 10. Some APSS provisions
s 187(4)	Sch 3 para 11, Sch 4 para 9	Some APSS provisions
s 187(6)	718	Some APSS provisions
s 187(7)	Sch 3 para 48, Sch 4 para 36	Some APSS provisions
s 187A Relief for contributions in respect of share option gains		Inserted FA 2000 s 56(1).
s 187A(1)	481(1)	
s 187A(2)	481(2)	
s 187A(3)	481(3)	
s 187A(4)	478(1), (2), 481(1)	
s 187A(5)	—	Unnecessary: see commentary on clauses 481 and 482.
s 187A(6)	481(1), (5)	
s 187A(7)	481(5), 487(1) ("secondary Class 1 contributions", "the Contributions and Benefits Act")	
s 189 Lump sum benefits on retirement		
	637	Amended FA 1988 s 57, FA 1994 s 108(7)(*b*), FA 1998 Sch 9 Part II para 1.
s 190 Payments to MPs and others		Substituted FA 1999 Sch 5 para 1.
s 190(1)	291(1)	
s 190(2)	291(2)	
s 190(3)	291(2)	
s 190(4)	291(3)	
s 191 Job release scheme allowances not to be treated as income		
s 191(1)	—	Spent.
s 191(2)	—	Spent.
s 191A Removal expenses and benefits		
	—	Introduces TA 1988 Sch 11A; inserted FA 1993 Sch 5 para 1.
s 191B Removal benefits: beneficial loan arrangements		Inserted FA 1993 Sch 5 para 1.
s 191B(1)	288(1), (2)	
s 191B(2)	288(1), (2)	
s 191B(3)	288(5)	
s 191B(4)	288(5)	
s 191B(5)–(7)	288(1), (3)	
s 191B(8)	288(1), 289(1)–(3)	
s 191B(9)	288(1)	
s 191B(10)	288(4)	
s 191B(11)	288(4)	
s 191B(12)	288(4)	
s 191B(13)	191(4), (5), 288(6), 289(4)	
s 191B(14)		Repealed FA 1994 Sch 26 Part V(5).
s 191B(15)	274(1), (2)	
s 191B(16)	5, 276, 721(5)	
s 192 Relief from tax for foreign emoluments		
s 192(1)	22(1), 23(2), 355(2), (3), 390, 721(1) ("foreign employer")	
s 192(2)	22(1), 23(2)	
s 192(3)	328(1), 329(1), 334(1), 355(1), (4)–(6)	
s 192(4)	—	Spent.
s 192(5)	23(3), 24 (1), (2), (3), (5), (6), 329(1), 331(2)	Amended FA 2001 Sch 12 Pt 2 para 5.
s 192A Foreign earnings deduction for seafarers		Inserted FA 1998 s 63(2).

Existing provision	*Rewritten provision*	*Remarks*
s 192A(1)	328(4), (5), 329(1), 378(1), (2), 379(1)	
s 192A(2)	40(3)–(6), 384	
s 192A(3)	40(3)–(6), 385	
s 192A(4)	329(1), 330(1), 331(2), 380, 381, 382, 383(1)–(3)	
s 193 Foreign earnings and travel expenses		
s 193(1)	—	Repealed FA 1998 s 63(1).
s 193(2)	341(1)–(4), 376(1), 721(1) (''foreign employer'')	
s 193(3)	341(1)–(6)	
s 193(4)	328(1), 329(1), 369(1), 376(1)–(3)	
s 193(3)		
s 193(5)	342(1)–(7), 721(1) (''foreign employer'')	
s 193(6)	342(1)–(8)	
s 193(7)	—	The destinations for this subsection are very numerous and so are not separately acknowledged.
s 194 Other foreign travel expenses		
s 194(1)	328(4), (5), 329(1), 369(1), 370(1), (2), 371(1), (2)	
s 194(2)	371(3)–(7)	
s 194(3)	370(4)	
s 194(4)	370(4), (5)	
s 194(5)	370(3)	
s 194(6)	370(3)	
s 194(7)	372	
s 194(8)	370(5)	
s 194(9)	330(1)	
s 194(10)	—	The destinations for this subsection are very numerous and so are not separately acknowledged.
s 195 Travel expenses of employees not domiciled in the United Kingdom		
s 195(1)	373(1), 374(1)	
s 195(2)	373(2), (3), 374(2), (3), 375(1)	
s 195(3)	375(2), (3), (4)	
s 195(4)	375(3), (4)	
s 195(5)	373(1), (4)	
s 195(6)	374(1), (3)–(5), (8)	
s 195(7)	328(4), (5), 329(1), 369(1), 373(1), (2), (5), 374(1), (2), (6), (9)	
s 195(8)	373(6), 374(7)	
s 195(9)	373(4), 374(3)	
s 195(10)	374(9)	
s 195(11)	—	The destinations for this subsection are very numerous and so are not separately acknowledged.
s 195(12)	330(1)	
s 195(13)	—	Spent.
s 196 Foreign pensions		
		617
s 197 Leave travel facilities for the armed forces		
s 197(1)	228(2), 296(1)	
s 197(2)	266(3), 296	
s 197A Car parking facilities		
	237(2), (3), 266(1)	Inserted FA 1988 s 46(4).
s 197AA Works bus services		
		Inserted FA 1999 s 48.
s 197AA(1)	242(1)	Amended FA 2001 s 60(2).
s 197AA(2)	242(2) (''works transport service'')	Amended FA 2001 s 60(3).
s 197AA(3)	242(3) (''bus''), 249 (''qualifying journey'')	Amended FA 2001 s 60(4).

Dest. Tables

Existing provision	Rewritten provision	Remarks
s 197AA(4)	242(1)	
s 197AA(5)	242(1), (2) (''children'')	
s 197AA(6)	266(2), (5)	Amended FA 2001 s 60(5).
s 197AA(7)	249 (''workplace'')	
s 197AA(8)	242(5)	
s 197AA(9)	242(4), (6)	Inserted FA 2001 s 60(6).
s 197AB Support for public transport bus services		
		Inserted FA 1999 s 48.
s 197AB(1)	243(1), (2)	
s 197AB(2)	243(5), 249 (''qualifying journey'')	Amended FA 2002 s 33(2).
s 197AB(3)	243(1)	Substituted FA 2002 s 33(3).
s 197AB(3A)	243(3)	Inserted FA 2002 s 33(3).
s 197AB(4)	5, 243(4), (5), 249 (''workplace'')	Amended FA 2002 s 33(4).
s 197AB(5)	266(2), (5)	Inserted FA 2002 s 33(5).
s 197AC Provision of cycle or cyclist's safety equipment		
		Inserted FA 1999 s 50(1).
s 197AC(1)	244(1), (2)	
s 197AC(2)	244(5)	
s 197AC(3)	244(4)	
s 197AC(4)	244(3), 249 (''qualifying journey'')	
s 197AC(5)	266(2), (5)	
s 197AC(6)	5, 249 (''workplace'')	
s 197AD Mileage allowance payments		
		Inserted FA 2001 s 57(1).
s 197AD(1)	229(1)	
s 197AD(2)	229(2)	
s 197AD(3)	229(3)	
s 197AD(4)	229(4)	
s 197AE Passenger payments		
		Inserted FA 2001 s 57(1).
s 197AE(1)	233(1), (2)	
s 197AE(2)	233(3)	
s 197AE(3)	233(4)	
s 197AE(4)	233(5)	
s 197AF Mileage allowance relief		
		Inserted FA 2001 s 57(1).
s 197AF(1)	231(1)	
s 197AF(2)	231(3)	
s 197AF(3)	231(2)	
s 197AF(4)	—	Unnecessary.
s 197AG Giving effect to mileage allowance relief		
		Inserted FA 2001 s 57(1).
s 197AG(1)	232(1)	
s 197AG(2)	232(2)	
s 197AG(3)	232(3), (4)	
s 197AG(4)	232(5)	
s 197AG(5)	232(6)	
s 197AH Interpretation of sections 197AD–197AG		
		Inserted FA 2001 s 57(1).
	—	Unnecessary.
s 197B Limit on chargeable mileage profit		
	—	Repealed FA 2001 Sch 33 Pt 2 (1).
s 197C Definition of mileage profit		
	—	Repealed FA 2001 Sch 33 Pt 2 (1).
s 197D Definition of taxed mileage profit		
	—	Repealed FA 2001 Sch 33 Pt 2 (1).
s 197E Exception from section 197B		
	—	Repealed FA 2001 Sch 33 Pt 2 (1).
s 197F Other interpretative provisions		
	—	Repealed FA 2001 Sch 33 Pt 2 (1).
s 197G Sporting and recreational facilities		
		Inserted FA 1993 s 75.
s 197G(1)	261(1), 266(3)	

Existing provision	Rewritten provision	Remarks
s 197G(2)	261(2), (3)	
s 197G(3)	261(2), (4), (5), 262(1), 263	
s 197G(4)	261(6)	
s 197G(5)	263	
s 197G(6)	262(2), 263, 721(1), (5)	
s 198 Relief for necessary expenses		
s 198(1)	328(1), 329(1), 330(1), 333(1), (2), 334(1), 336(1), (3), 337(1), 338(1)	Substituted FA 1998 s 61(1).
s 198(1A)	337(1), 338(1)–(5), 339	Substituted FA 1998 s 61(1).
s 198(1B)	340(1)–(7)	Substituted FA 1998 s 61(1).
s 198(2)	328(4), (5), 335 (2), (3), 354(1), (2)	Repealed in part CAA 2001 Sch 2 para 25.
s 198(3)	328(1), (4), (5), 329(1), 330(1), 335(3), 353(1)–(3), 354(2)	
s 198(4)	360	Substituted FA 1999 Sch 5 para 2(2).
s 198(5)	359	Inserted FA 2001 Sch 12 Pt 2 para 6.
s 199 Expenses necessarily incurred and defrayed from official emoluments		
s 199(1)	328(3), 329(1), 368(1), (2)	
s 199(2)	330(2), 368(3)	
s 200 Expenses of Members of Parliament		
s 200(1)	292	
s 200(2)	228(2), 294(1)	Inserted FA 1993 s 124(1), amended FA 1999 s 51.
s 200(3)	294(2)	Inserted FA 1999 s 51, amended FA 2002 s 41(2).
s 200(4)	294(3)	Added FA 2002 s 41(3).
s 200(5)	294(4)	Added FA 2002 s 41(3).
s 200ZA Expenses of members of Scottish Parliament, National Assembly for Wales or Northern Ireland Assembly		Inserted FA 1999 Sch 5 para 2(1).
s 200ZA(1)	293(2), 294(1)	
s 200ZA(2)	228(2), 293(1), 294(1)	
s 200ZA(3)	293(3), 294(2)	Amended FA 2002 s 41(2).
s 200ZA(4)	294(3)	Added FA 2002 s 41(3).
s 200ZA(5)	294(4)	Added FA 2002 s 41(3).
s 200AA Incidental benefits for holders of certain offices etc		Inserted FA 1996 s 108.
s 200AA(1)	228(2), 295(1), (2)	
s 200AA(2)	295(3), (4)	Amended FA 1999 Sch 5 para 3.
s 200AA(3)	—	Repealed FA 1999 s 44(5).
s 200AA(4)	721(5)	
s 200AA(5)	295(5)	
s 200AA(6)	295(6)	
s 200A Incidental overnight expenses		Inserted FA 1995 s 93(4).
s 200A(1)	240(1), 329(5), 353(4)	Amended FA 2001 Sch 12 Pt 2 para 7. See Annex 1, Change 81 and Annex 2, Notes 36 and 37.
s 200A(2)	240(3), 241(1)	
s 200A(3)	240(4)–(7), 329(5), 353(4)	Amended FA 1997 s 63(2), FA 2000 s 58(2). See Annex 1, Change 81 and Annex 2, Notes 36 and 37.
s 200A(4)	241(3)	
s 200A(5)	241(1), (2)	
s 200A(6)	716(1)–(3)	
s 200B Work-related training provided by employers		Inserted FA 1997 s 63(1).
s 200B(1)	250(1)	
s 200B(2)	250(1)	
s 200B(3)	250(1)	
s 200B(4)	250(2)	
s 200B(5)	251(1)	
s 200B(6)	251	
s 200B(7)	718	

Existing provision	*Rewritten provision*	*Remarks*
s 200C Expenditure excluded from section 200B		
		Inserted FA 1997 s 63(1).
s 200C(1)	253(1), (2), (4)	
s 200C(2)	252(1)–(3)	Substituted FA 2001 Sch 12 Pt 2 para 8.
s 200C(2A)	252(4), 329(5), 353(4)	Inserted FA 2001 Sch 12 Pt 2 para 8. See Annex 1, Change 81 and Annex 2, Notes 36 and 37.
s 200C(3)	254(1), (2)	
s 200C(4)	—	Unnecessary: see Annex 2, Note 30.
s 200C(5)	—	Unnecessary: see commentary on clause 253.
s 200C(6)	253(3)	
s 200C(7)	252(5), 253(2), 254(3)	
s 200C(8)	718	
s 200D Other work-related training		
		Inserted FA 1997 s 63(1).
s 200D(1)	250(1)	
s 200D(2)	250(1)	
s 200E Education and training funded by employers		
		Inserted FA 2000 s 58(1).
s 200E(1)	255(1)	
s 200E(2)	255(1)	
s 200E(3)	255(3)	
s 200E(4)	256	
s 200E(5)	255(2)	
s 200E(6)	255(2)	
s 200F Section 200E: exclusion of expenditure not directly related to training		
		Inserted FA 2000 s 58(1).
s 200F(1)	258(1), (2)	
s 200F(2)	257(1)–(3)	Substituted FA 2001 Sch 12 Pt 2 para 9.
s 200F(2A)	257(4), 329(5), 353(4)	Inserted FA 2001 Sch 12 Pt 2 para 9. See Annex 1, Change 81 and Annex 2, Notes 36 and 37.
s 200F(3)	259(1), (2)	
s 200F(4)	258(3)	
s 200F(5)	257(5), 259(3)	
s 200G Section 200E: exclusion of expenditure if contributions not generally available to staff		
		Inserted FA 2000 s 58(1).
s 200G(1)	260(1), (2)	
s 200G(2)	260(1)	
s 200G(3)	260(3)–(5)	
s 200H Section 200E: exclusion of expenditure otherwise relieved		
	—	Inserted FA 2000 s 58(1). Unnecessary: see Annex 2, Note 30.
s 200J Education or training funded by third parties		
	255(1), 260(1)	Inserted FA 2000 s 58(1).
s 201 Fees and subscriptions to professional bodies, learned societies etc		
s 201(1)	328(1), 329(1), 333(1), (2), 334(1), 343(1), 344(1)	
s 201(2)	343(2)	
s 201(3)	344(2), (3)	
s 201(4)	344(5), (6)	
s 201(5)	343(1), 344(1)	
s 201(6)	344(7), 345(1)	
s 201(7)	345(2), (3)	
201AA Employee liabilities and indemnity insurance		
		Inserted FA 1995 s 91(1).
201AA(1)	328(1), 329(1), 333(1), (2), 334(1), 346(1), 347(1), 558(1)	
201AA(2)	348, 559	
201AA(3)	349(2)–(5), 560(2)–(5)	
201AA(4)	349(2)	
201AA(5)	350(1)–(3), 561(1)–(3)	

Existing provision	*Rewritten provision*	*Remarks*
201AA(6)	350(4)–(6), 561(4)–(6)	
201AA(7)	346(3), 558(3)	
201AA(8)	346(2), 558(2)	
201AA(9)	346(3), 558(3)	
s 201A Expenses of entertainers		
		Inserted FA 1990 s 77.
s 201A(1)	328(1), 352(1)	Amended FA 1991 s 69(2).
s 201A(2)	329(1), 333(1), (2), 334(1), 352(1), (5)	Repealed in part Deregulation and Contracting Out Act 1994 Sch 17.
s 201A(2A)	329(1), 333(1), (2), 334(1), 352(1), (5)	Inserted FA 1991 s 69(3).
s 201A(3)	352(6)	Repealed in part Deregulation and Contracting Out Act 1994 s 81(1).
s 201A(3A)	352(6)	Inserted FA 1991 s 69(4).
s 201A(4)	352(2)	
s 201A(4A)	352(1)	Inserted FA 1991 s 69(5).
s 201A(5)	352(4)	
s 201A(6)	—	Commencement.
s 202 Donations to charity: payroll deduction scheme		
s 202(1)	713(1), (2)	
s 202(2)	713(3)–(5)	
s 202(3)	714(1), (2)	
s 202(4)	714(2), (3)	
s 202(5)	713(1), 714(1)	
s 202(6)	714(1)	Amended FA 2000 s 38(5), (7).
s 202(7)	—	Amended FA 1993 s 68, FA 1996 s 109, repealed FA 2000 s 38(5), (7).
s 202(8)	715(1), (2)	
s 202(9)	715(3)	
s 202(10)	715(3)	
s 202(11)	714(2)	Amended FA 2000 s 38(5), (7).
s 202A Assessments on receipts basis		
		Inserted FA 1989 s 37.
s 202A(1)	10(2), 15(2), 21(2), 22(2), 25(2), 26(2), 27(2)	
s 202A(2)	15(3), 21(3), 22(3), 25(3), 26(3), 27(3)	
s 202A(3)	13(4), (5)	
s 202A(4)	—	Unnecessary.
s 202B Receipts basis: meaning of receipt		
		Inserted FA 1989 s 37.
s 202B(1), (2)	18(1), 31(1)	
s 202B(3)	18(2), 31(2)	
s 202B(4)	18(1), 31(1)	
s 202B(5)	18(3), (4), 31(3), (4), 686(3)	
s 202B(6)	18(3), (4), 31(3), (4), 686(4)	
s 202B(7)	19(1), 32(1)	
s 202B(8)	19(2), (3), 32(1)–(3)	Amended FA 1998 Sch 9 Part 2 para 3.
s 202B(9)	19(2), 32(1), (2)	
s 202B(10)	19(2), 32(1), (2)	
s 202B(11)	19(4), 32(1), (4)	
s 203 PAYE		
s 203(1)	684(6).	Part unnecessary; see Annex 2, Note 57.
s 203(2)	684(1), (2), (7)	Amended FA 1988 s 128(1), repealed in part FA 1994 Sch 19 para 38; see Annex 2, Note 56.
s 203(3)	684(3)	
s 203(3A)	—	Spent; inserted FA 1988 Sch 3 para 4.
s 203(4)	—	Repealed FA 1989 s 45(3).
s 203(5)	684(5)	
s 203(6)	685(1)	
s 203(7)	685(2)	

Dest. Tables

Existing provision	*Rewritten provision*	*Remarks*
s 203(8)	685(3)	
s 203(9)	684(4)	Inserted FA 1988 s 128(2).
s 203(10)	684(2)	Inserted FA 1998 s 119, prospective repeal in part by FA 1999 Sch 20 Pt 7.
s 203A PAYE: meaning of payment		
		Inserted FA 1989 s 45(2).
s 203A(1)	686(1)	
s 203A(2)	686(1)	
s 203A(3)	686(2)	
s 203A(4)	686(1)	
s 203A(5)	686(3), (4)	
s 203B PAYE: payment by intermediary		
		Inserted FA 1994 s 125.
s 203B(1)	687(1)	
s 203B(2)	687(2)	See Annex 2, Note 58.
s 203B(3)	687(3)	
s 203B(4)	687(4)	
s 203B(5)	718	
s 203C PAYE: employee of non-UK employer		
		Inserted FA 1994 s 126.
s 203C(1)	689(1)	Amended FA 1998 s 69(1); see Annex 2, Note 58.
s 203C(2)	689(2)	
s 203C(3)	689(3)	
s 203C(3A)	689(4)	Inserted FA 1998 s 69(2).
s 203C(3B)	689(5)	Inserted FA 1998 s 69(2).
s 203C(4)	689(6)	
s 203C(5)	689(5), 718	
s 203D PAYE: employee non-resident, etc		
		Inserted FA 1994 s 126.
s 203D(1)	690(1)	
s 203D(2)	690(2)	See Annex 1, Changes 148 and 149.
s 203D(3)	690(3)	
s 203D(4)	690(4)	
s 203D(5)	690(5)	
s 203D(6)	690(6)	
s 203D(7)	690(7)	
s 203D(8)	690(8)	
s 203D(9)	690(9)	
s 203E PAYE: mobile UK workforce		
		Inserted FA 1994 s 126.
s 203E(1)	691(1)	See Annex 2, Note 58.
s 203E(2)	691(2)	
s 203E(3)	691(3)	
s 203E(4)	691(4)	
s 203E(5)	691(5)	
s 203F PAYE: tradeable assets		
		Inserted FA 1994 s 127.
s 203F(1)	696(1)	Amended FA 1998 s 65(2).
s 203F(2)	702(1)	Substituted FA 1998 s 65(3).
s 203F(3)	696(2)	Substituted FA 1998 s 65(3).
s 203F(3A)	702(2)	Inserted FA 1998 s 65(3).
s 203F(3B)	702(4)	Inserted FA 1998 s 65(3).
s 203F(3C)	702(5)	Inserted FA 1998 s 65(3).
s 203F(4)	701(2), 721(1) (''cash voucher'', ''credit-token'', ''non-cash voucher'')	Amended FA 1998 s 65(4).
s 203F(5)	701(1)	Amended FA 1998 s 65(4).
s 203F(6)	702(6), 721(5)	Inserted FA 1998 s 65(5); see Annex 2, Note 59.
s 203FA PAYE: enhancing the value of an asset		
		Inserted FA 1998 s 66(1).
s 203FA(1)	697(1), (2)	
s 203FA(2)	697(2)	
s 203FA(3)	697(3)	

Existing provision	*Rewritten provision*	*Remarks*
s 203FA(4)	697(5)	
s 203FA(5)	—	Unnecessary.
s 203FB PAYE: gains from share options etc		
		Inserted FA 1998 s 67(1).
s 203FB(1)	698(1), 699(1), 700(1)	
s 203FB(2)	700(2)	Amended FA 2000 s 56(2).
s 203FB(3)	700(3)	Amended FA 2000 s 56(2); see Annex 1, Change 151.
s 203FB(4)	698(3)	
s 203FB(5)	699(3)	
s 203FB(6)	699(4)	
s 203FB(6A)	700(4)	Inserted FA 2000 s 56(2); see Annex 1, Change 151.
s 203FB(7)	698(4), 699(5)	Amended FA 2000 s 56(2).
s 203FB(8)	700(5)	
s 203FB(9)	700(6), 721(1) (''cash voucher'', ''credit-token'', ''non-cash voucher'')	See Annex 1, Change 152.
s 203FB(10)	698(2), (5), 699(2), (6), 700(7), (8)	
s 203G PAYE: non-cash vouchers		
		Inserted FA 1994 s 128.
s 203G(1)	694(1)	
s 203G(2)	694(2), 721(1) (''non-cash voucher'')	
s 203G(3)	694(3)	Substituted FA 1998 s 68(1).
s 203G(4)	694(4)	Substituted FA 1998 s 68(1).
s 203G(5)	694(7)	Substituted FA 1998 s 68(1).
s 203H PAYE: credit-tokens		
		Inserted FA 1994 s 129.
s 203H(1)	695(1)	Amended FA 1998 s 68(2).
s 203H(2)	—	Repealed FA 1998 s 68(2).
s 203H(3)	695(3)	
s 203H(4)	721(1) (''credit-token'')	
s 203I PAYE: cash vouchers		
		Inserted FA 1994 s 130.
s 203I(1)	693(1)	
s 203I(2)	693(4)	
s 203I(3)	693(5)	Inserted FA 1998 s 68(3).
s 203J s 203B to s 203I: accounting for tax		
		Inserted FA 1994 s 131.
s 203J(1)	710(1)	
s 203J(2)	710(2)	
s 203J(3)	710(3), (4)	
s 203J(4)	710(5)	
s 203J(5)	710(6)	See Annex 1, Change 153.
s 203K Trading arrangements		
		Inserted FA 1994 s 131.
s 203K(1)–(3)	—	Repealed FA 1998 Sch 27 Pt 3(12).
s 203K(4)	702(3)	
s 203L s 203B to s 203K: interpretation, etc		
		Inserted FA 1994 s 131.
s 203L(1)	712(1)	Substituted FA 1998 s 69(3).
s 203L(1A)	688(1)	Inserted FA 1998 s 69(3).
s 203L(1B)	688(2)	Inserted FA 1998 s 69(3).
s 203L(1C)	688(3), 718	Inserted FA 1998 s 69(3).
s 203L(2)	—	Unnecessary; substituted FA 1998 s 69(3).
s 203L(3)	684(8)	
s 203L(4)	684(2)	
s 204 PAYE repayments		
	708(1), (2)	Amended Jobseekers Act 1995 Sch 2 para 14; see Annex 2, Note 60.
s 205 Assessments unnecessary in certain circumstances		
		Substituted FA 1995 s 111(1).
s 205(1) to (3), (5)	—	Unnecessary: see Annex 2, Note 62.

Dest. Tables

Existing provision	*Rewritten provision*	*Remarks*
s 205(4)	711	
s 206 Additional provision for certain assessments		
	709	Amended FA 1995 s 111(2); see Annex 2, Note 61.
s 206A PAYE settlement agreements		
		Inserted FA 1996 s 110.
s 206A(1)	703	
s 206A(2)	704(1)	
s 206A(3)	705	
s 206A(4)	706	
s 206A(5)	—	Unnecessary.
s 206A(6)	684(2)	
s 206A(7)	—	Unnecessary.
s 206A(8)	704(2)	
s 206A(9)	707	
s 207 Disputes as to domicile or ordinary residence		
		42, 43
s 313 Taxation of consideration for certain restrictive undertakings		
s 313(1)	7(5), 225(1), (3), (8)	Substituted FA 1988 s 73(1).
s 313(2)	225(1), (2), (4)	Substituted FA 1988 s 73(1).
s 313(3)	225(5)	Substituted FA 1988 s 73(1).
s 313(4)	226(1)	Substituted FA 1988 s 73(1).
s 313(5)	—	Repealed FA 1988 s 73(1).
s 313(6)	225(6), (7), 226(2)	
s 315 Wounds and disability pensions		
s 315(1)	641(1)	
s 315(2)	641(1)	
s 315(3)	641(2)	Amended Transfer of Functions (Health and Social Security) Order 1988 (S I. 1988/1843) Sch 3 para 2.
s 316 Allowances, bounties and gratuities		
s 316(1)	—	Spent; see commentary on clause 297.
s 316(2)	—	Spent; see commentary on clause 297.
s 316(3)	228(2), 297	
s 316(4)	228(2), 298	
s 316(5)	—	Spent; see commentary on clause 297.
s 317 Victoria Cross and other awards		
		638
s 318 Other pensions in respect of death due to war service etc		
s 318(1)	639	
s 318(2)	639 Amended Transfer of Functions (Health and Social Security) Order 1988 (S I. 1988/1843).	
s 318(3)	640	
s 319 Crown servants: foreign service allowance		
s 319(1)	228(2), 299(1)	Amended Transfer of Functions (Foreign Service Allowance) Order 1996 (S I. 1996/313).
s 319(2)	299(2)	Inserted Transfer of Functions (Foreign Service Allowance) Order 1996 (S I. 1996/313), amended Transfer of Functions (Lord Advocate and Secretary of State) Order 1999 (S I. 1999/678).
s 321 Consuls and other official agents		
s 321(1)	228(2), 300(1), (2), 301(1), (2), (4)	
s 321(2)	300(1), (2), 301(1)–(3)	
s 321(3)	300(3), 301(5), (6)	
s 322 Consular officers and employees		
s 322(2)	228(2), 302(1), (2), (3), (8)	Amended FA 1990 Sch 14 para 4(1).

Existing provision	*Rewritten provision*	*Remarks*
s 323 Visiting forces		
s 323(1)	228(2), 303(1)	Amended FA 1990 Sch 14 para 4(1).
s 323(6)(*b*)	303(3)	
s 323(7)	303(4)	Amended FA 1990 Sch 14 para 4(2).
s 330 Compensation for National-Socialist persecution		
		642
s 332 Expenditure and houses of ministers of religion		
s 332(1)	290(4), (5) ("full-time minister"), 351(3)	
s 332(2)	290(1)–(3)	Amended FA 1989 s 53(2).
s 332(3A)	359(1)–(3)	Inserted FA 2001 Sch 12 Pt 2 para 10.
s 332(3B)	359(1)–(3), (4) ("company vehicle", "mileage allowance payment")	Inserted FA 2001 Sch 12 Pt 2 para 10.
s 332(4)	290(5)	
s 577 Business entertaining expenses		
s 577(1)(*a*) (words)	—	Inserted CAA 2001 Sch 2 para 51(1)(*a*).
s 577(1)(*b*)	356(1)	
s 577(3) (words)	357	
s 579 Statutory redundancy payments		
s 579(1)	309(1), (3), (4)	
s 580 Provisions supplementary to section 579		
s 580(3)	309(2), (3)	
s 585 Relief from tax on delayed remittances		
s 585(1) (words)	35	
s 585(9)(*b*)	35	
s 588 Training courses for employees		
s 588(5)(*a*)	312(1)	
s 589 Qualifying courses of training etc		
s 589(1)	311(3)	Part affected by Annex 1, Changes 72 and 74.
s 589(2)	311(3), (4)	
s 589(3), (4)	311(4)	
s 589(5)	311(2)	
s 589(6)	311(5), 329(5), 353(4)	Substituted FA 2001 Sch 12 Pt 2 para 12. See Annex 1, Change 81 and Annex 2, Notes 36 and 37.
s 589(6A)	311(6)	Inserted FA 2001 Sch 12 Pt 2 para 12. See Annex 1, Change 81.
s 589(7)	5	
s 589A Counselling services for employees		
		Inserted FA 1993 s 108.
s 589A(2), (3)	—	Spent.
s 589A(4)	310(1)	
s 589A(5)	—	Spent.
s 589A(6)	310(1)	
s 589A(10)	—	Spent.
s 589B Qualifying counselling services etc		
		Inserted FA 1993 s 108.
s 589B(1)	—	Spent.
s 589B(2)	310(2) to (5)	Part affected by Annex 1, Change 72.
s 589B(3)	—	See Annex 1, Change 72.
s 589B(4)	310(6), 329(5), 353(4)	Substituted FA 2001 Sch 12 Pt 2 para 13. See Annex 1, Change 73 and Annex 2, Notes 36 and 37.
s 589B(4A)	310(7)	Inserted FA 2001 Sch 12 Pt 2 para 13. See Annex 1, Change 81.
s 589B(5) (words)	5	
s 591D Section 591C: supplementary		
s 591D(6)	397(9)	Inserted FA 1995 s 61(1).
s 595 Charge to tax in respect of certain sums paid by employer		
s 595(1)	7(6), 10(3), 386(1)–(4)	Amended FA 2002 Sch 6 para 6. See Sch 6 para 36.

Existing provision	*Rewritten provision*	*Remarks*
s 595(2), (3)	—	Repealed FA 1989 Sch 6 para 7.
s 595(4)	388	See Sch 6 para 36.
s 595(5)	386(6)	Amended FA 1999 Sch 10 para 4. See Sch 6 para 36.
s 596 Exceptions from section 595		
s 596(1)	386(1), 387(2)	Amended FA 1989 Sch 6 para 8(2). See Sch 6 para 36.
s 596(2)	389, 390, 721(1) ("foreign employer")	Amended FA 1989 Sch 6 para 8(3). See Sch 6 para 36.
s 596(3)	392(1)–(5)	Repealed in part FA 1989 Sch 6 para 8(4).
s 596(4)	392(6), (7)	Inserted FA 1999 Sch 10 para 5.
s 596A Charge to tax: benefits under non-approved schemes		
		Inserted FA 1989 Sch 6 paras 9, 18(7).
s 596A(1)	393(1), 394(1), (2), (3), 400(1)	
s 596A(2)	7(6), 10(3), 393(1), 394(1), (3)	
s 596A(3)	394(2), (3)	
s 596A(4)	398	Amended FA 1994 s 108(2), FA 1998 s 93(1).
s 596A(5)	394(3), (4)	
s 596A(6)	393(2)	Substituted FA 1994 s 108(3).
s 596A(7)	—	Amended FA 1994 s 108(4); see Annex 2, Note 40.
s 596A(8)	395(2)–(4), 396(1), 397(2)–(5), 400(1)	Substituted FA 1994 s 108(5), amended FA 1999 Sch 10 para 6.
s 596A(9)	395(3)–(4), 397(1)	Substituted FA 1994 s 108(5).
s 596A(10)	397(2)–(4)	Inserted FA 1994 s 108(5).
s 596A(11)	397(5), 400(1)	Inserted FA 1994 s 108(5).
s 596A(12)	397(6)	Inserted FA 1994 s 108(5).
s 596A(13)	397(6)	Inserted FA 1994 s 108(5).
s 596A(14)	397(7)	Inserted FA 1994 s 108(5).
s 596A(15)	395(5), 396(2), 397(8)	Inserted FA 1994 s 108(5).
s 596A(16)	718	Inserted FA 1994 s 108(5).
s 596A(17)	397(10)	Inserted FA 1994 s 108(5).
s 596B Section 596A: supplementary provisions		
	398, 415(3)–(7), 718	Inserted FA 1989 Sch 6 paras 9, 18(7), amended FA 1998 s 93(2).
s 596C Notional interest treated as paid if amount charged in respect of beneficial loan	399	
		Inserted FA 1998 s 93(3).
s 597 Charge to tax: pensions		
s 597(1)	580(*a*)	
s 597(2)	—	Unnecessary: see commentary on clause 580.
s 597(3)	580(*b*)	Inserted FA 1994 s 110.
s 599A Charge to tax: payments out of surplus funds		
s 599A(5)	624, 625, 626(1)	
s 599A(6)	626(2)	Repealed in part FA 1996 s 122(7)((*b*).
s 599A(8)	625	
s 600 Charge to tax: unauthorised payments to or for employees		
s 600(1)	583(3), (4), (5), 586(1), 593(1)	Amended FA 1989 Sch 6 paras 13(1), (2) and 18(9), FA 1999 Sch 10 para 8.
s 600(2)	583(3), 584, 585, 593(1)	Amended FA 1989 Sch 6 paras 13(1), (3) and 18(9), FA 1999 Sch 10 para 8.
s 600(3)	583(6)	
s 600(4)	583(7), 584, 593(3)	
s 607 Pilots' benefits fund		
s 607(3)(*b*)(iv)	—	Unnecessary: see Annex 1 Change 136. See also clause 683(4).
s 608 Superannuation funds approved before 6th April 1980		
s 608(4)	590, 591	
s 613 Parliamentary pension funds		

Existing provision	Rewritten provision	Remarks
s 613(1), (2)	—	Unnecessary: see commentary on clause 619.
s 613(3)	619, 621	
s 615 Exemption from tax in respect of certain pensions		
s 615(1)	647(1), (2), 648(1), 649(1), 650(1), 651(1), 652(1), 653(1), 654(1)	
s 615(2)	648, 649(1)–(3), 650, 651(1), 652(1), (2), (4), (5), 653(1), (2), 654(1), (2)	Amended Oversea Superannuation Act 1991 s 2.
s 615(4)	651(2), (4), 654(3)	
s 615(5)	649(3)	
s 615(7)	647(3), 649(5), 651(3), (4), 653(3), 654(4)	
s 615(8)	649(4), 650(2), 652(4)–(7), 654(2)	
s 616 Other overseas pensions		
s 616(1), (2)	643	
s 616(3)	629(1), (2), 630(2)	
s 616(4)	630(1), 643	
s 617 Social security benefits and contributions		
s 617(1)	577(1), (2), 645, 660, 664(1), 676, 677(1) Table B	The provisions which amended TA 1988 s 617 are too numerous to list. But they have all been repealed by the Bill.
s 617(2)	666, 670, 677(1) Table B	See above.
s 617A Tax credits under Part 1 of Tax Credits Act 2002		
	677(1) Table B	Inserted TCA 2002 Sch 3 para 14.
s 638 Other restrictions on approval (13) (words)		
	—	See Sch 6 para 90(5)(*b*).
s 643 Employer's contributions and personal pension income etc		
s 643(1)	308(1)	
s 643(5) (words)	598, 599	Inserted FA 1995 Sch 11 paras 1, 11.
s 647 Unauthorised payments		
s 647(1)	601(2)	
s 647(2)	601(4), (5), (6)	
s 647(3)	602, 603	
s 647(4)	601(7)	
s 648 Contributions under unapproved arrangements		
	7(5), 224(1),(2)	
s 648A Annuities: charge under Schedule E		
s 648A(1)	595	Inserted FA 1994 s 109.
s 648A(2)	—	Unnecessary: see commentary on clause 595.
s 830 Territorial sea and designated areas		
s 830(5)	41(1)	
Sch 6 Taxation of directors and others in respect of cars		
		Substituted FA 1993 Sch 3 para 5.
para 1	121(1)	Substituted FA 2000 Sch 11 para 1(2).
para 2	133(2), (3)	Substituted FA 2000 Sch 11 para 1(2).
para 3(1)	134(1), 135(1), 136(1)	Substituted FA 2000 Sch 11 para 1(2).
para 3(2)	134(1), 135(2), (3), 136(2), (3)	Substituted FA 2000 Sch 11 para 1(2).
para 3(3)	139(2)	Substituted FA 2000 Sch 11 para 1(2).
para 3(4)	139(3)	Substituted FA 2000 Sch 11 para 1(2).
para 3(5)	139(6)	Substituted FA 2000 Sch 11 para 1(2).
para 4(1)	139(4)	Substituted FA 2000 Sch 11 para 1(2).
para 4(2)	170(3)	Substituted FA 2000 Sch 11 para 1(2).

Existing provision	*Rewritten provision*	*Remarks*
para 4(3)	139(5)	Substituted FA 2000 Sch 11 para 1(2).
para 5	134(1), 137	Substituted FA 2000 Sch 11 para 1(2).
para 5A(1)	138(1), (5)	Inserted FA 2000 Sch 11 para 1(2).
para 5A(2)	138(2)	Inserted FA 2000 Sch 11 para 1(2).
para 5A(3)	138(3)	Inserted FA 2000 Sch 11 para 1(2).
para 5A(4)	138(4)	Inserted FA 2000 Sch 11 para 1(2).
para 5A(5)	171(4)	Inserted FA 2000 Sch 11 para 1(2).
para 5B	171(1) (''EC certificate of conformity'', ''EC type-approval certificate'', ''UK approval certificate'')	Inserted FA 2000 Sch 11 para 1(2).
para 5C(1)	134(2)	Inserted FA 2000 Sch 11 para 1(2).
para 5C(2)	140(2)	Inserted FA 2000 Sch 11 para 1(2).
para 5C(3)	140(3)	Inserted FA 2000 Sch 11 para 1(2).
para 5C(4)	140(5)	Inserted FA 2000 Sch 11 para 1(2).
para 5D(1)	141(1), (3)	Inserted FA 2000 Sch 11 para 1(2).
para 5D(2)	141(2)	Inserted FA 2000 Sch 11 para 1(2).
para 5D(3)	171(1) (''diesel'')	Inserted FA 2000 Sch 11 para 1(2).
para 5D(4)	141(4)	Inserted FA 2000 Sch 11 para 1(2).
para 5E	170(4)	Inserted FA 2000 Sch 11 para 1(2).
para 5F(1)	142(1)	Inserted FA 2000 Sch 11 para 1(2).
para 5F(2)	142(2)	Inserted FA 2000 Sch 11 para 1(2).
para 5F(3)	142(3)	Inserted FA 2000 Sch 11 para 1(2).
para 5G	140(4), 142(4)	Inserted FA 2000 Sch 11 para 1(2).
para 6	143(1), (3)	Amended FA 2000 Sch 11 para 1(3).
para 7(1)	144(1)–(3)	
para 7(2)	144(1)–(4)	
para 8	—	Unnecessary: see commentary on clause 145.
para 9	143(2)	
para 10	116(1), (3)	Amended FA 2000 Sch 11 para 1(4).
Sch 6A Taxation of directors and others in respect of vans		Inserted FA 1993 Sch 4 para 7.
para 1(1)	155(2), (4)	
para 1(2)	157	
para 2(1)	157, 158(1), (3)	
para 2(2)	158(4)	
para 2(3)	158(2)	
para 3(1)	157, 159(1)–(3)	
para 3(2)	159(1), (2), (3), (5)	
para 3(3)	159(4)	
para 4(1)	155(3), (4)	
para 4(2)	156(1), (2)	
para 4(3)	156(1), (3)	
para 4(4)	156(4)	
para 4(5)	156(5)	
para 5(1)	161(1)	
para 5(2)	162(1), (2)	
para 5(3)	162(3)	
para 5(4)	161(2)	
para 5(5)	161(1)	
para 5(6)	155(3), (4), (7)	
para 6(1)	163(1)	
para 6(2)	163(1)	
para 6(3)	163(3)	
para 6(4)	163(2)	
para 7	161(1)	
para 8(1)	164(1)	Part unnecessary: see commentary on clause 164.
para 8(2)	164(2)	
para 8(3)	164(3)	
para 8(4)	164(4)	
para 9(1)	161(1), 164(2), 165(1)–(3)	
para 9(2)	165(4)	

Existing provision	*Rewritten provision*	*Remarks*
para 9(3)	165(5)	
para 10	155(4), (7)	
para 11	166	
para 12	116(1)	
Sch 7 Taxation of benefit from loans obtained by reason of employment		
para 1(1)	174(1), (2)	
para 1(2)	174(2)	
para 1(3)	174(2)	
para 1(4)	174(2)	
para 1(5)	174(5)	Amended and repealed in part FA 1994 s 88(4); repealed in part FA 1996 Sch 20 para 41.
para 2	174(2), (3), (4)	
para 3(1)	175(3), (4)	Amended FA 1991 Sch 6 para 3.
para 3(2)	—	Repealed FA 1991 Sch 6 para 3.
para 3(3)	—	Repealed FA 1991 Sch 6 para 3.
para 4(1)	182	
para 4(2)	186(1), (2)	Inserted FA 1995 s 45(4).
para 4(3)	186(1), (2)	Inserted FA 1995 s 45(4).
para 4(4)	186(4), 718	Inserted FA 1995 s 45(4).
para 5(1)	183(1)	Amended FA 1996 s 107(2).
para 5(2)	183(2)	Substituted FA 1996 s 107(3).
para 5(3)	183(3)	
para 5A(1)	185	Inserted FA 2000 Sch 10 para 6.
para 5A(2)	183(4)	Inserted FA 2000 Sch 10 para 6.
paras 6–12	—	Repealed FA 1994 s 88(4).
Sch 7A Beneficial loans: loans on ordinary commercial terms		Inserted FA 2000 Sch 10 para 5(2).
para 1	176(2)	
para 2(1)	176(3)	
para 2(2)	176(3)	
para 2(3)	176(4)	
para 2(4)	176(3)	
para 2(5)	176(8)	
para 3(1)	176(5), (7)	
para 3(2)	176(5)	
para 3(3)	176(7)	
para 4(1)	176(6), (7)	
para 4(2)	176(6)	
para 4(3)	176(6)	
para 4(4)	176(6)	
para 4(5)	176(6)	
para 4(6)	176(7)	
para 5	176(8), (9)	
para 6	176(10)	
Sch 9 Approved share option schemes and profit sharing schemes		
para 1(1)	Sch 3 paras 4, 9, 23, 27, 40, Sch 4 paras 4, 7, 21, 28	Provisions relating to approved profit sharing schemes ("APSS provisions") are not being repealed.
para 1(2)	Sch 3 para 40, Sch 4 para 28	Some APSS provisions
para 1(3)	Sch 3 para 3, Sch 4 para 3	Some APSS provisions
para 1(4)	Sch 3 para 3, Sch 4 para 3	Some APSS provisions
para 2(1)	Sch 3 para 5, Sch 4 para 5	Some APSS provisions
para 2(3)	Sch 3 paras 6, 8	
para 2(4)	Sch 3 para 8	
para 3(1)	Sch 3 para 42, Sch 4 para 30	
para 4	Sch 3 para 43, Sch 4 para 31	Some APSS provisions
para 5	Sch 3 paras 41, 44, Sch 4 paras 29, 32	Part unnecessary: see commentary on Sch 3 para 44. Some APSS provisions
para 6	Sch 3 para 45, Sch 4 para 33	Some APSS provisions
para 7	Sch 3 paras 9, 17, Sch 4 paras 7, 15	Some APSS provisions
para 8	Sch 3 paras 2, 11, Sch 4 paras 2, 9	Some APSS provisions

Existing provision	*Rewritten provision*	*Remarks*
para 8A	Sch 3 para 31	Inserted FA 1991 s 38(1), (5), (6). Some APSS provisions
para 9(1)	Sch 3 para 17, Sch 4 para 15	Amended FA 2000 s 52(1), (2), (5). Some APSS provisions
para 10	Sch 3 para 18, Sch 4 para 16	Part repealed FA 1989 s 64. Some APSS provisions
para 11	Sch 3 para 19, Sch 4 para 17	Amended FA 1996 Sch 38 para 6(1), (2), (10). Some APSS provisions
para 12(1)	Sch 3 paras 20, 21, Sch 4 paras 18, 19	Amended FA 2000 s 52(1), (4), (5). Some APSS provisions
para 12(1A)	Sch 3 para 21, Sch 4 para 19	Inserted FA 2000 s 52(1), (4), (5). Some APSS provisions
para 12(2), (3)	Sch 3 para 21, Sch 4 para 19	Some APSS provisions
para 13(1), (2)	Sch 3 para 21, Sch 4 para 19	
para 13(3)	Sch 4 para 19	Inserted FA 1988 s 69(1).
para 14(1)	Sch 3 para 22, Sch 4 para 20	Some APSS provisions
para 14(3)	Sch 3 para 22, Sch 4 para 20	Some APSS provisions
para 15(1)	Sch 3 paras 2, 38, 39, Sch 4 paras 2, 26, 27	
para 15(2)	Sch 3 para 38, Sch 4 para 26	
para 15(3)	Sch 3 para 39, Sch 4 para 27	
para 15(4)	Sch 3 para 39, Sch 4 para 27	
para 15(5)–(8)	—	Transitional provisions
para 16(1)	Sch 3 para 24	Part unnecessary: see commentary on Sch 3 para 24.
para 16(2), (3)	—	Spent.
para 17	Sch 3 paras 26, 30	
para 18	Sch 3 paras 2, 32	
para 19	Sch 3 paras 2, 34	Amended FA 1991 s 38 (2), Employment Rights Act 1996 Sch 1 para 35(1), (4).
para 20	Sch 3 paras 2, 33	Amended FA 1991 s 38 (2).
para 21(1)	Sch 3 paras 2, 34, 36, 37	Amended FA 1996 s 113(1).
para 21(2)	Sch 3 para 37	
para 21(3)	—	See Sch 7 para 71.
para 21(4)	—	Inserted FA 1996 s 113(2). See Sch 7 para 71.
para 22	Sch 3 paras 2, 29, 30, 33, 34	
para 23	Sch 3 paras 2, 35	Part unnecessary: see commentary on Sch 3 para 35.
para 24	Sch 3 para 25	Amended FA 1991 s 40.
para 25	Sch 3 para 28	Amended FA 1989 s 62(3).
para 26(1)	Sch 3 paras 6, 7	Amended FA 1995 s 137(2).
para 26(2)	Sch 3 para 7	
para 26(3)	Sch 3 para 10	Amended FA 1996 s 113(3).
para 27(1)	Sch 4 paras 8, 24	
para 27(2)	Sch 4 paras 2, 23, 25	
para 27(3)	—	See Annex 1, Change 129.
para 27(4)	Sch 4 para 8	Part repealed FA 1995 s 137(3).
para 28(1)	Sch 4 para 6	Amended FA 1996 s 114(2).
para 28(2)	—	Repealed FA 1996 s 114(2).
para 28(3)	Sch 4 para 6	
para 28(4)	—	Repealed FA 1996 s 114(2).
para 29(1)	Sch 4 para 22	Para substituted FA 1991 s 39(1). Sub-para substituted FA 1996 s 114(3).
para 29(2)–(6)	—	Replaced FA 1996 s 114(3).
para 29(7)	Sch 4 para 22	
para 29(8)	—	Repealed FA 1996 Sch 41 Part 5(5).
para 37(1)	Sch 3 para 16, Sch 4 para 14	Some APSS provisions
para 37(2)	—	Spent.
para 37(3)	Sch 3 para 16, Sch 4 para 14	Part unnecessary: see commentary on Sch 3 para 16, Sch 4 para 14. Some APSS provisions
para 37(4)	Sch 3 para 16, Sch 4 para 14	Some APSS provisions

Existing provision	Rewritten provision	Remarks
para 37(5)	—	Unnecessary. See commentary on Sch 3 para 16, Sch 4 para 14.
para 38(1)–(3)	Sch 3 para 13, Sch 4 para 11	Some APSS provisions
para 38(4)	—	Commencement. Some APSS provisions
para 39	—	See Sch 7 para 87. Some APSS provisions
para 40	549–554, Sch 3 para 15, Sch 4 para 13	Inserted FA 1989 s 65. Some APSS provisions
Sch 10 Further provisions relating to profit sharing schemes		
para 7 (a word)	—	See Sch 6 para 113(3)(*c*).
Sch 11 Payments and other benefits in connection with termination of employment, etc		
		Substituted FA 1998 s 58(2), Sch 9 Part I.
para 1	—	Introductory.
para 2(1)	401(1)	
para 2(2)	401(4)	
para 3	406	
para 4(1)	407(1), (2)	
para 4(2)	407(1)	
para 4(3)	407(1), (3)	
para 5	411	
para 6(1)	412(1)	
para 6(2)	412(2)	Amended International Development Act 2002 Sch 3 para 10.
para 7(1)	404(1), (4), (5)	
para 7(2)	403(4), 404(1)	
para 7(3)	404(4)	
para 7(4)	404(5)	
para 8(1)	404(2), (3)	
para 8(2)	404(3), 719	
para 9(1)	413(1), 414(1)–(5)	
para 9(2)	413(3)–(6)	
para 10	413(1)	
para 11(1)	414(1), (2)	
para 11(2)	414(3)	
para 11(3), (4)	414(4), (5)	
para 12(1)	415(1), (2)	
para 12(2)	415(2)–(7)	
para 13(1)	416(1)	
para 13(2)	416(2)	
para 13(3)	416(4)	
para 13(4)	416(3)	
para 13(5)	416(2)	
para 14(1)	403(1)	
para 14(2)	403(5)	
para 15	684(2)	
para 16	404(2), (3), 413(1), 414(3)	
Sch 11A Removal expenses and benefits		
		Inserted FA 1993 Sch 5 para 2.
para 1(1)	271(1), (2)	
para 1(2)	271(3)	
para 2	—	Unnecessary: see commentary on clause 271.
para 3	272(3)	
para 4	272(1)	
para 5(1)	273(2)	Part unnecessary: see commentary on clause 273.
para 5(2)	273(3)	
para 5(3)	273(4)	
para 6(1)	274(1)	
para 6(2)	274	
para 7	272(3)	
para 8(1)	279(1), (3)	
para 8(2)	279(3)	
para 8(3)	279(4)	

Existing provision	Rewritten provision	Remarks
para 8(4)	279(5)	
para 9(1)	277(1), (3)	
para 9(2)	277(1)	
para 9(3)	277(4)	
para 9(4)	277(2)	
para 9(5)	277(5)	
para 10	278	
para 11(1)	280(2)	
para 11(2)	280(3)	
para 11(3)	280(3)	
para 12(1)	281(1)–(4)	
para 12(2)	281(1), (2), (6)	
para 12(3)	281(6)	
para 12(4)	282(1), (2)	
para 13(1)	284(1)	
para 13(2)	284(1)	
para 13(3)	284(3)	
para 13(4)	284(2)	
para 13(5)	284(2)	
para 13(6)	284(6)	
para 13(7)	284(6)	
para 13(8)	284(6)	
para 14(1)	285(1)	
para 14(2), (3)	—	See Annex 1, Change 65.
para 14(4)	285(2)	
para 15(1)	286(1)	
para 15(2)	286(2), (3)	
para 15(3)	286(4)	
para 16	272(1)	
para 17(1)	279(1), (2)	
para 17(2)	279(2)	
para 17(3)	279(4), (5)	
para 18(1)	277(1), (2)	
para 18(2)	277(1), (2), (4)	
para 19	278	
para 20(1)	280(1)	
para 20(2)	280(3)	
para 21(1)	281(1)–(3)	
para 21(2)	283(1)	
para 21(3)	281(1), (6)	
para 21(4)	283(2)	
para 21(5)	283(2)	
para 21(6)	283(1)	
para 21(7)	282(1), (2)	
para 21(8)	282(3)	
para 22(1)	285(1)	
para 22(2)	285(2)	
para 23(1)	286(1)	
para 23(2)	286(2), (3)	
para 23(3)	286(4)	
para 24(1)	287(1)	
para 24(2)	287(3)–(5)	
para 24(3)	287(4), (5)	
para 24(4)	287(5)	
para 24(5)	287(5)	
para 24(6)	287(5)	
para 24(7)	287(5)	
para 24(8)	287(5)	
para 24(9)	287(1)	
para 24(10)	716(1), (2)	
para 24(11)	716(4)	
para 25	276	
para 26	721(5)	
para 27	5	
para 28	281(6)	
para 29	—	Spent.

Existing provision	Rewritten provision	Remarks
Sch 12 Foreign earnings		
para 1	—	Introductory; amended FA 1998 s 63(3).
para 1A	24(2), (3), 329(1), 330(1), 331(2), 381	Inserted F(No.2)A 1992 s 54, amended FA 1998 s 63(3), amended FA 2001 Sch 12 Pt 2 para 15.
para 2(1)	24(1), 380(1)	Amended FA 1998 s 63(3).
para 2(2)	24(2), (3), 380(1), (2)	Amended FA 1989 s 42(5), repealed in part FA 1996 Sch 20 para 42.
para 2(3)	24(5), (6), 380(3), (4)	Part unnecessary: see commentary on clause 380.
para 3(1)	378(2)	Amended FA 1998 s 63(3).
para 3(2)	378(3)	Amended FA 1998 s 63(4).
para 3(2A)	—	Repealed FA 1998 Sch 27 Part III(11).
para 3(3)	379(2)	Amended FA 1998 s 63(3).
para 4	378(4)	
para 5	40(3)–(5), 382	Amended FA 1998 s 63(3), (4).
para 6	383(1)–(3)	Amended FA 1998 s 63(3).
para 7	—	Repealed FA 1998 Sch 27 Part III(11).
Sch 12AA Mileage allowances: interpretation		Inserted FA 2001 s 57(2), Sch 12 Pt 1.
para 1(1), (2)	—	Unnecessary.
para 1(3)	236(1)	
para 2	236(1)	
para 3(1)	235(1)	
para 3(2)	235(2)	
para 3(3)	235(3)	
para 3(4)	235(4)	
para 3(5)	235(5)	
para 3(6)	235(6)	
para 4(1)	230(1)	
para 4(2)	230(2)–(5), 719	
para 4(3)	230(6)	
para 5(1)	234(1)	
para 5(2), (3)	234(2)	
para 5(4)	234(3)	
para 6(1)	236(2)	
para 6(2)	236(3)	
para 7	—	Unnecessary.
para 8	—	Unnecessary.
Sch 12A Ordinary commuting and private travel		Inserted FA 1998 s 61(2), Sch 10.
para 1(1)	—	Unnecessary.
para 1(2)	5(1)	
para 2(1)	338(3)	
para 2(2)	338(5)	
para 2(3)	339(1)	
para 3	338(2), (4)	
para 4	339(2), (3)	
para 5(1)	339(5)	
para 5(2)	339(6)	
para 5(3)	339(7)	
para 6	339(4)	
para 7	339(8)	
Sch 29 Consequential amendments		
para 6	—	Inserts TMA s 16A. See Sch 6 para 127.

Dest. Tables

SOCIAL SECURITY ACT 1988 (C 7)

Existing provision	*Rewritten provision*	*Remarks*
Sch 4 Minor and consequential amendments		
para 1	—	Inserts TA 1988 s 617(2)(*aa*).

FINANCE ACT 1988 (C 39)

Existing provision	*Rewritten provision*	*Remarks*
s 46 Car parking facilities		
s 46(1)	—	Amends TA 1988 s 141(6), inserts TA 1988 s 141(6A).
s 46(2)	—	Inserts TA 1988 s 142(3A).
s 46(3)	—	Inserts TA 1988 s 155(1A).
s 46(4)	—	Inserts TA 1988 s 197A.
s 46(5)	—	Commencement.
s 47 Entertainment: non-cash vouchers		
s 47(1)	—	Inserts TA 1988 s 141(6B).
s 48 Entertainment: credit-tokens		
s 48(1)	—	Inserts TA 1988 s 142(3B).
s 49 Entertainment of directors and higher-paid employees		
s 49(1)	—	Inserts TA 1988 s 155(7).
s 57 Lump sum benefits paid otherwise than on retirement		
	—	Amends TA 1988 s 189.
s 68 Priority share allocations for employees etc		
s 68(1)	542(1), (2), 544(1), (2)	Amended FA 1989 s 66(2), FA 1991 s 44(2).
s 68(1ZA)	544(1)	Inserted FA 1991 s 44(3).
s 68(1ZB)	544(1), (2), (3), (4), 545(1), 547(2)	Inserted FA 1991 s 44(3).
s 68(1A)	543(1), (2), 545(1), (2)	Substituted FA 1991 s 44(4).
s 68(2)	542(3), (5), (6), 544(3), (5), (6)	Amended FA 1989 s 66(4).
s 68(2A)	542(3), 544(3)	Inserted FA 1989 s 66(5).
s 68(2B)	542(3), (4), 544(3), (4)	Inserted FA 1989 s 66(5).
s 68(2C)	544(3), (4)	Inserted FA 1991 s 44(5).
s 68(3)	546(2)	
s 68(3A)	546(3), (4), (5), (6), (7)	Inserted FA 1990 s 79(1), amended FA 1991 s 44(6).
s 68(4)	—	Amended TCGA 1992 Sch 10 para 16(3). See Sch 6 para 212.
s 68(5)	548(1) (''director'', ''employee'', ''the employee offer'', ''the public offer'')	Amended FA 1991 s 44(7).
s 68(5A)	547	Inserted FA 1991 s 44(8).
s 68(5B)	545(3), (5)	Inserted FA 1991 s 44(8).
s 68(5C)	545(4), (6)	Inserted FA 1991 s 44(8).
s 68(6)	—	Spent.
s 69 Share options		
s 69(1)	—	Inserts TA 1988 Sch 9 para 13(3).
s 69(2)	—	Spent.
s 73 Consideration for certain restrictive undertakings		
s 73(1)	—	Amends TA 1988 s 313.
s 77 Scope of Chapter		
s 77(1)	447(1), (4), 452(2), 456(2), Sch 7 para 55	Amended FA 1991 s 44(9), FA 1998 s 50(2).
s 77(2)	448(1)	
s 77(3)	448(2)	
s 77(4)	448(3), (4), Sch 7 para 58	Inserted FA 1991 s 44(9).
s 78 Charge where restrictions removed etc		
s 78(1)	449(1), 452(4)	
s 78(2)	449(5), 450(2), (3)	
s 78(3)	7(6), 10(3), 449(2), (3), 451	
s 78(4)	452(3)	
s 78(5)	450(4)	

Existing provision	*Rewritten provision*	*Remarks*
s 78(6)	450(4), (5), 469	Part unnecessary: see commentary on clause 450.
s 78(7)	450(6)	
s 79 Charge for shares in dependent subsidiaries		
s 79(1)	453(1)	
s 79(2)	454(2), (3)	
s 79(3)	453(5), 454(4), (5)	
s 79(4)	7(6), 10(3), 453(2), (3), 455(1), (4)	
s 79(5)	455(2)	
s 79(6)	455(3)	
s 79(6A)	455(2)	Inserted FA 1998 s 50(3).
s 79(6B)	455(2)	Inserted FA 1998 s 51(2).
s 79(7)	456(3)	
s 80 Charge on special benefits		
s 80(1)	457(1), (2)	
s 80(1A)	458(4)	Inserted F(No.2)A 1992 s 37(2).
s 80(2)	458(3), (5)	Substituted F(No.2)A 1992 s 37(2).
s 80(3)	458(6), 469	Amended F(No.2)A 1992 s 37(3), (4).
s 80(3A)	458(7)	Inserted F(No.2)A 1992 s 37(5).
s 80(4)	7(6), 10(3), 457(3), (4), 459	
s 80(5)	460	
s 80(6)	457(6)	
s 81 Changes in interest		
	464	
s 82 Company reorganisations etc		
s 82(1)	461(1)	
s 82(2)	461(2), (3)	
s 82(3)	462	Amended TCGA 1992 Sch 10 para 16(1), (4).
s 83 Connected persons etc		
s 83(1)	447(5)	
s 83(2), (3)	463	
s 83(4)	457(2), 460	
s 84 Capital gains tax		
	—	Amended TCGA 1992 Sch 10 para 16(1), (5). See Sch 6 para 210.
s 85 Information		
s 85(1)	465(1), (3), (4)	Amended FA 2000 s 56(3).
s 85(2)	466	
s 85(3)	—	Amends TMA 1970 s 98. See Sch 6 para 137(4)(*d*).
s 86 Meaning of ‘‘dependent subsidiary’’		
s 86(1)	467(1)–(5)	
s 86(2)	467(6), (7)	
s 86(3)	467(8)	
s 87 Other interpretation provisions		
s 87(1)	448(2), 450(4), 458(7) 459, 467(8), 470(1)	
s 87(2)	468, 718	
s 87(3)	719	
s 87(4)	447(4)	
s 88 Transitional provisions		
s 88(1)	Sch 7 para 57	
s 88(2)	—	Spent.
s 88(3)	Sch 7 para 55	
s 88(4)	Sch 7 para 56	
s 89 Consequential amendments		
s 89(*a*) (words)	—	Amends TA 1988 s 185(3).
s 89(*b*)	—	Spent.
s 128 Interest on overdue or overpaid PAYE		
s 128(1)	—	Amends TA 1988 s 203(2).
s 128(2)	—	Inserts TA 1988 s 203(9).

Existing provision	Rewritten provision	Remarks
Sch 3 Married couples: amendments of TA 1988		
para 4	—	Inserts TA 1988 s 203(3A).
Sch 13 Post-consolidation amendments		
para 3	—	Amends TA 1988 s 162(1).

FINANCE ACT 1989 (C 26)

Existing provision	Rewritten provision	Remarks
s 36 Schedule E: revised Cases		
s 36(1)	—	Introductory.
s 36(2)	—	Substitutes TA 1988 s 19(1) Sch E, Cases I to III.
s 36(3)	—	Inserts TA 1988 s 19(1) Sch E para 4A.
s 36(4), (5)	—	Commencement.
s 37 Schedule E: assessment on receipts basis		
s 37(1)	—	Inserts TA 1988 ss 202A, 202B.
s 37(2), (3)	—	Commencement.
s 38 Schedule E: unpaid emoluments		
	—	Spent.
s 39 Schedule E: unremitted emoluments		
		Sch 7 para 8(3)
s 40 Schedule E: emoluments already paid		
	—	Spent.
s 41 Schedule E: pensions etc		
s 41(1)	571, 578, 581, 616, 634(2), 661	
s 41(2)	571, 578, 581, 616, 634(2), 661	
s 41(3)	—	Commencement.
s 42 Schedule E: supplementary		
s 42(1)	—	Introductory.
s 42(2)	—	Repeals in part TA 1988 s 131(2).
s 42(3)	—	Repeals in part TA 1988 s 149(1).
s 42(4)	—	Repeals TA 1988 s 170.
s 42(5)	—	Amends TA 1988 Sch 12 para 2(2).
s 42(6)	—	Commencement.
s 45 PAYE: meaning of payment		
	—	Inserts TA 1988 s 203A, repeals TA 1988 s 203(4).
s 50 Security assets and services		
s 50(1)	377(1)	
s 50(2)	328(1), 329(1), 369(1), 377(1), (2), (6)	
s 50(3)	328(1), 329(1), 369(1), 377(1), (2), (6)	
s 50(4)	377(1)	
s 50(5)	377(1)	
s 50(6)	377(6)	
s 50(7)	377(2)	
s 51 Assets used partly for security		
s 51(1)	377(4)	
s 51(2)	377(4)	
s 51(3)	377(4)	
s 51(4)	377(4)	
s 52 Security: supplementary		
s 52(1)	377(3)	
s 52(2)	377(7)	
s 52(3)	377(8)	
s 52(4)	377(5)	
s 52(5)	377(5)	
s 52(6)	—	Commencement.
s 53 Employees earning £8,500 or more and directors		
s 53(1)	—	Substitutes TA 1988 s 167.

Existing provision	Rewritten provision	Remarks
s 53(2)(*a*)	—	Amends heading of Pt 5 Ch.2 TA 1988.
s 53(2)(*b*)	—	Amends TA 1988 s 153(1), s 154(1), s 157(1), s 158(1), s 160(1), (2), s 162(1), s 163(1), s 165(6)(*b*).
s 53(2)(*c*)	—	Substitutes TA 1988 s 160(3).
s 53(2)(*d*)	—	Amends TA 1988 s 162(5).
s 53(2)(*e*)	—	Substitutes TA 1988 s 162(7).
s 53(2)(*f*)	—	Amends TA 1988 s 332(2)(*c*), s 418(3)(*a*). See Sch 6 para 55(2) and 159.
s 53(2)(*g*)	—	See Sch 6 para 126(3).
s 62 Savings-related share option schemes		
s 62(1)	—	Introductory.
s 62(2)	—	Repealed FA 1991 Sch 19 Pt 5.
s 62(3)	—	Amends TA 1988 Sch 9 para 25.
s 62(4)	—	Commencement.
s 64 Share option and profit sharing schemes: shares of consortium member		
	—	Repeals in part TA 1988 Sch 9 para 10.
s 66 Priority share allocations for employees etc		
s 66(1)	—	Commencement.
s 66(2)	—	Amends FA 1988 s 68(1).
s 66(3)	—	Spent (superseded amendment of FA 1988 s 68(1A)).
s 66(4)	—	Amends FA 1988 s 68(2).
s 66(5)	—	Inserts FA 1988 s 68(2A), (2B).
s 178 Setting of rates of interest		
s 178(2)(m) (words)	—	See new s 178(2)(r) in Sch 6 para 162(*d*).
s 178(2)(p) (words)	—	See new s 178(2)(r) in Sch 6 para 162(*d*).
s 179 Provisions consequential on section 178		
s 179(1)(*g*)	—	Amends TA 1988 s 160(5)(*d*).
s 179(5)	—	Amends TA 1988 s 146(11).
Sch 6 Retirement benefits schemes		
para 7	—	Repealed TA 1988 s 595(2), (3).
para 8	—	Amends TA 1988 s 596.
para 9	—	Inserts TA 1988 s 596A, s596B.
para 13	—	Amends TA 1988 s 600.
para 18(1) (words)	—	Commencement.
para 18(5)–(7)	—	Commencement.
Sch 12 Close companies		
para 8	—	Amends TA 1988 s 168(11).

COMPANIES ACT 1989 (C 40)

Existing provision	*Rewritten provision*	*Remarks*
Sch 18 ''Subsidiary'' and related expressions: consequential amendments and savings		
para 46	—	Amends TA 1988 s 141(7) (''subsidiary'').

FINANCE ACT 1990 (C 29)

Existing provision	*Rewritten provision*	*Remarks*
s 21 Care for children		
s 21(1)	—	Inserts TA 1988 s 155A.
s 21(2)	—	Amends TA 1988 s 154(2).
s 21(3)	—	Commencement.
s 77 Expenses of entertainers		
	—	Inserts TA 1988 s 201A.
s 79 Priority share allocations for employees etc		
s 79(1)	—	Inserts FA 1988 s 68(3A).

Existing provision	*Rewritten provision*	*Remarks*
s 79(2)	—	Commencement.
Sch 14 Amendments correcting errors in TA 1988		
para 4(2)	—	Amends TA 1988 ss 323(7); see Sch 6 para 167.

OVERSEA SUPERANNUATION ACT 1991 (C 16)

Existing provision	*Rewritten provision*	*Remarks*
s 2 Continuation of tax exemption for non-resident pensioners		
	—	Amends TA 1988 s 615(2).

DISABILITY LIVING ALLOWANCE AND DISABILITY WORKING ALLOWANCE ACT 1991 (C 21)

Existing provision	*Rewritten provision*	*Remarks*
Sch 2 Disability Living Allowance and Attendance Allowance: amendments		
para 18	—	Inserts TA 1988 s 617(1)(*a*).

FINANCE ACT 1991 (C 31)

Existing provision	*Rewritten provision*	*Remarks*
s 38 Employee share schemes: non-discrimination		
s 38(2)	—	Amends TA 1988 Sch 9 paras 19,20.
s 39 Approved share option schemes: price at which shares may be obtained		
s 39(1)	—	Substitutes TA 1988 Sch 9 para 29.
s 39(2)–(6)	—	Amended TA 1988 s 185 as from 1.1.1992.
		Superseded in part by FA 1996 s 114(4)–(7) from 29.4.1996.
s 39(7)	—	Commencement. See Sch 6 para 221.
s 39(8)	—	Commencement.
s 40 Savings-related share schemes		
s 40(1)	—	Amends TA 1988 Sch 9 para 24.
s 40(2)	—	Commencement.
s 44 Priority share allocations for employees etc		
s 44(1)	—	Commencement.
s 44(2)	—	Amends FA 1988 s 68(1).
s 44(3)	—	Inserts FA 1988 s 68(1ZA), (1ZB).
s 44(4)	—	Substitutes FA 1988 s 68(1A).
s 44(5)	—	Inserts FA 1988 s 68(2C).
s 44(6)	—	Amends FA 1988 s 68(3A).
s 44(7)	—	Amends FA 1988 s 68(5).
s 44(8)	—	Inserts FA 1988 s 68(5A)–(5C).
s 44(9)	—	Amends FA 1988 s 77.
s 44(10)	—	Commencement.
s 69 Expenses of entertainers		
s 69(1)	—	Introductory.
s 69(2)	—	Amends TA 1988 s 201A(1).
s 69(3)	—	Inserts TA 1988 s 201A(2A).
s 69(4)	—	Inserts TA 1988 s 201A(3A).
s 69(5)	—	Inserts TA 1988 s 201A(4A).
s 69(6)	—	Commencement.
s 69(7)	—	Spent.
Sch 6 Restriction of higher rate relief: beneficial loans etc		
para 1(1)	—	Spent (superseded amendment of TA 1988 s 160(4)).
para 1(2)	—	Inserts TA 1988 s 160(4A).
para 3	—	Amends and repeals in part TA 1988 Sch 7 para 3.

SOCIAL SECURITY CONTRIBUTIONS AND BENEFITS ACT 1992 (C 4)

Existing provision	*Rewritten provision*	*Remarks*
s 10 Class 1A contributions: benefits in kind etc		
s 10(10)	—	Unnecessary: see Schedule 6 para 178(2).
s 150 Interpretation of Part 10		
s 150(2) (words)	—	Unnecessary: see Schedule 6 para 180(2)(*a*).

SOCIAL SECURITY (CONSEQUENTIAL PROVISIONS) ACT 1992 (C 6)

Existing provision	*Rewritten provision*	*Remarks*
Sch 2 Consequential amendments		
para 93	—	Amends TA 1988 s 617(1), (2)(*a*), (2)(*aa*).

SOCIAL SECURITY CONTRIBUTIONS AND BENEFITS (NORTHERN IRELAND) ACT 1992 (C 7)

Existing provision	*Rewritten provision*	*Remarks*
s 10 Class 1A contributions: benefits in kind etc		
s 10(10)	—	Unnecessary: see Schedule 6 para 199(2).
s 146 Interpretation of Part 10		
s 146(2) (words)	—	Unnecessary: see Schedule 6 para 201(2)(*a*).

SOCIAL SECURITY (CONSEQUENTIAL PROVISIONS)(NORTHERN IRELAND) ACT 1992 (C 9)

Existing provision	*Rewritten provision*	*Remarks*
Sch 2 Consequential amendments		
para 33	—	Amends TA 1988 s 617(1), (2)(*a*), (2)(*aa*).

TAXATION OF CHARGEABLE GAINS ACT 1992 (C 12)

Existing provision	*Rewritten provision*	*Remarks*
s 120 Increase in expenditure by reference to tax charged in relation to shares etc		
s 120(6)	—	Amended FA 1993 s 105(1), (2); FA 1996 s 114(8). Unnecessary: see commentary on Sch 6 paras 210, 221.
Sch 10 Consequential amendments		
para 14(9)	—	Amends TA 1988 s 137(1), (2).
para 14(10)	—	Amends TA 1988 s 139(14) but s 139 repealed FA 1988 Sch 14 Pt VI.
para 14(11)	—	Amends TA 1988 s 140(3), s 162(10)(*d*).
para 14(12)	—	Amends TA 1988 s 185(3), (7). See Sch 6 para 221.
para 16(3)	—	Amends FA 1988 s 68(4).
para 16(4)	—	Amends FA 1988 s 82.
para 16(5)	—	Amends FA 1988 s 84.

FINANCE (NO 2) ACT 1992 (C 48)

Existing provision	*Rewritten provision*	*Remarks*
s 37 Employee share schemes: special benefits		
s 37(1)	—	Introductory.
s 37(2)	—	Substitutes FA 1988 s 80(1A), (2).
s 37(3), (4)	—	Amends FA 1988 s 80(3).
s 37(5)	—	Inserts FA 1988 s 80(3A).
s 37(6)	—	Commencement.
s 54 Foreign earnings		
	—	Inserts Sch 12 para 1A.
s 54(172)		

FINANCE ACT 1993 (C 34)

Existing provision	*Rewritten provision*	*Remarks*
s 68 Payroll deduction schemes		
s 68(1)		Amends TA 1988 s 202(7).
s 68(2)		Commencement.
s 73 Vans		
	—	Introduces FA 1993 Sch 4.
s 74 Heavier commercial vehicles		
s 74(1)	—	Inserts TA 1988 s 159AC
s 74(2)	—	Repealed FA 1999 Sch 20 Pt III(9).
s 74(3)	—	Commencement.
s 75 Sporting and recreational facilities		
	—	Inserts TA 1988 s 197G.
s 76 Removal expenses and benefits		
	—	Introduces FA 1993 Sch 5.
s 105 Expenditure on shares		
s 105(1), (2)	—	Amends TCGA 1992, s 120(7).
s 124 Expenses of Members of Parliament		
s 124(1)	—	Inserts TA 1988 s 200(2).
s 124(2)	—	Commencement.
s 124(3)	—	Spent.
Sch 3 Car and car fuel benefits: 1994–95 onwards		
para 1	—	Introductory.
para 2(1)	—	Substitutes TA 1988 s 157(2).
para 2(2)	—	Repeals TA 1988 s 157(4), (5).
para 3	—	Amends TA 1988 s 168(5).
para 4	—	Inserts TA 1988 s 168A, s 168B, s 168C, s 168D, s 168E, s 168F, s 168G.
para 5	—	Substitutes TA 1988 Sch 6.
para 6	—	Spent (superseded amendment of TA 1988 s 158(2) & (5)).
para 7	—	Commencement.
Sch 4 Vans		
para 1	—	Introductory.
para 2	—	Amends TA 1988 s 154(2).
para 3	—	Amends TA 1988 s 155(1).
para 4	—	Inserts TA 1988 s 159AA, s 159AB.
para 5	—	Spent (superseded amendment of TA 1988 s 159A).
para 6(1)	—	Inserts TA 1988 s 168(5A).
para 6(2)	—	Amends TA 1988 s 168(6).
para 7	—	Inserts TA 1988 Sch 6A.
para 8	—	Commencement.
Sch 5 Removal expenses and benefits		
para 1	—	Inserts TA 1988 ss 191A, 191B.
para 2	—	Inserts TA 1988 Sch 11A.

FINANCE ACT 1994 (C 9)

Existing provision	*Rewritten provision*	*Remarks*
s 88 Beneficial loan arrangements		
s 88(1)	—	Amends TA 1988 s 160(1), inserts TA 1988 s 160(1A).
s 88(2)	—	Amends TA 1988 s 160(5).
s 88(3)	—	Substitutes TA 1988 s 161(1).
s 88(4)	—	Amends and repeals in part TA 1988 Sch 7 para 1(5), repeals paras 6–12.
s 88(5)	—	Spent.
s 88(6)	—	Commencement.
s 89 Vouchers and credit tokens		
s 89(1)	—	Introductory.
s 89(2)	—	Amends and repeals in part TA 1988 s 141(1).
s 89(3)	—	Amends TA 1988 s 141(6B).
s 89(4)	—	Introductory.
s 89(5)	—	Amends TA 1988 s 142(1).
s 89(6)	—	Amends TA 1988 s 142(3).
s 89(7)	—	Amends TA 1988 s 142(3B).
s 89(8)	—	Introductory.
s 89(9)	—	Amends TA 1988 s 143(1).
s 89(10)	—	Amends TA 1988 s 143(3).
s 89(11)	—	Amends TA 1988 s 143(4).
s 89(12)	—	Introductory.
s 89(13)	—	Amends TA 1988 s 144(1).
s 89(14)	—	Amends TA 1988 s 144(3).
s 108 Taxation of benefits of non-approved schemes		
s 108(1)–(5)		Amends TA 1988 s 596A.
s 108(6)	Sch 7 para 41	Commencement.
s 108(7)(*b*)	—	Amends TA 1988 s 189(1)(*b*).
s 109 Annuities derived from personal pension schemes		
s 109(1)	—	Inserts TA 1988 s 648A.
s 109(2)	—	Commencement.
s 110 Annuities derived from retirement benefits schemes		
s 10(1)	—	Inserts TA 1988 s 597(3).
s 10(2)	—	Commencement.
s 125 PAYE: payment by intermediary		
	—	Inserts TA 1988 s 203B.
s 126 PAYE: employees working for persons other than their employers etc		
	—	Inserts TA 1988 ss 203C–203E.
s 127 PAYE: tradeable assets		
	—	Inserts TA 1988 s 203F.
s 128 PAYE: non-cash vouchers		
	—	Inserts TA 1988 s 203G.
s 129 PAYE: credit-tokens		
	—	Inserts TA 1988 s 203H.
s 130 PAYE: cash vouchers		
	—	Inserts TA 1988 s 203I.
s 131 PAYE: supplementary		
	—	Inserts TA 1988 ss 203J–203L.
s 132 PAYE: Payments etc received free of tax		
	—	Inserts TA 1988 s 144A.
s 139 Taxation of incapacity benefit		
s 139(1)	660, 664(1), 676	
s 139(2)	663	
s 139(3)	661	
s 139(4)		Unnecessary—see Annex 2, Note 56.
s 139(5)	660, 663, 664(1)	Amended FA 1995 s 141(2).
s 139(6)	664(2)	Inserted FA 1995 s 141(3).

VEHICLE EXCISE AND REGISTRATION ACT 1994 (C 22)

Existing provision	*Rewritten provision*	*Remarks*
Sch 3 Consequential amendments		
para 22	—	Spent in part (superseded amendment of TA 1988 s 158(2B)); amends TA 1988 s 168(5), (5A).

FINANCE ACT 1995 (C 4)

Existing provision	*Rewritten provision*	*Remarks*
s 43 Cars available for private use		
s 43(1)	—	Inserts TA 1988 s 157A.
s 43(2)	—	Amends TA 1988 s 158(1).
s 43(3)	—	Amends TA 1988 s 167(2), inserts TA 1988 s 167(2B), (2C), (2D).
s 43(4)	—	Commencement.
s 44 Cars: accessories for the disabled		
s 44(1)	—	Amends TA 1988 s 168A(11).
s 44(2)	—	Inserts TA 1988 s 168AA.
s 44(3)	—	Commencement.
s 45 Beneficial loan arrangements: replacement loans		
s 45(1)	—	Introductory.
s 45(2)	—	Repeals in part TA 1988 s 160(5).
s 45(3)	—	Inserts TA 1988 s 160(3A).
s 45(4)	—	Inserts TA 1988 Sch 7 para 4(2)–(4).
s 45(5)	—	Commencement.
s 91 Employee liabilities and indemnity insurance		
s 91(1)	—	Inserts TA 1988 s 201AA.
s 91(2)	—	Amends TA 1988 s 141(3), s 142(2), s 153(2), s 156(8).
s 91(3)	—	Commencement.
s 92 Post-employment deductions		
s 92(1)	555(1)–(3), 564(1)	
s 92(2)	556(1), 558, 559, 560(2)–(5), 561(1)–(6)	
s 92(3)	—	Unnecessary.
s 92(4)	557(1), (2), 563, 718	
s 92(5)	555(1), 557(3), (4)	
s 92(6)–(8)	—	See Sch 6 para 217.
s 92(9)	563	
s 92(10)	409(1), (3)–(5), 410(1), (3)–(5)	Substituted FA 1998 Sch 9, Part 2 para 5.
s 92(11)	—	Commencement.
s 93 Incidental overnight expenses etc		
s 93(1)	—	Inserts TA 1988 s 141(6C), (6D).
s 93(2)	—	Inserts TA 1988 s 142(3C), (3D).
s 93(3)	—	Inserts TA 1988 s 155(1B), (1C).
s 93(4)	—	Inserts TA 1988 s 200A.
s 93(5)	—	Commencement.
s 111 Assessments in respect of income taken into account under PAYE		
	—	Substitutes TA 1988 s 205, amends TA 1988 s 206.
s 137 Part-time workers: miscellaneous provisions		
s 137(2)	—	Amends TA 1988 Sch 9 para 26(1).
s 137(3)	—	Part repeals TA 1988 Sch 9 para 27(4).
s 137(8)	—	Commencement.
s 141 Incapacity benefit		
s 141(1)	—	Commencement.
s 141(2)	—	Amends FA 1994 s 139(5).
s 141(3)	—	Inserts FA 1994 s 139(6).

JOBSEEKERS ACT 1995 (C 18)

Existing provision	*Rewritten provision*	*Remarks*
Sch 2 Consequential Amendments		
para 12	—	Inserts TA 1988 s 151A.
para 14	—	Amends TA 1988 s 204.
para 16	—	Inserts TA 1988 s 617(2)(*ab*), (2)(*ac*).

CHILD SUPPORT ACT 1995 (C 34)

Existing provision	*Rewritten provision*	*Remarks*
Sch 3 Minor and consequential amendments		
para 1	—	Inserts TA 1988 s 617(2)(*ad*), (2)(*ae*).

FINANCE ACT 1996 (C 8)

Existing provision	*Rewritten provision*	*Remarks*
s 106 Living accommodation provided for employees		
s 106(1)	—	Repeals in part TA 1988 s 145(1).
s 106(2)	—	Inserts TA 1988 s 146A.
s 106(3)	—	Commencement.
s 107 Beneficial loans		
s 107(1)	—	Substitutes TA 1988 s 160(1B), inserts TA 1988 s 160(1BA).
s 107(2)	—	Amends TA 1988 Sch 7 para 5(1).
s 107(3)	—	Substitutes TA 1988 Sch 7 para 5(2).
s 107(4)	—	Commencement.
s 108 Incidental benefits for holders of certain offices etc		
	—	Inserts TA 1988 s 200AA.
s 109 Charitable donations: payroll deduction schemes		
s 109(1)	—	Amends TA 1988 s 202(7).
s 109(2)	—	Commencement.
s 110 PAYE settlement agreements		
	—	Inserts TA 1988 s 206A.
s 113 Exercise of rights by employees of non-participating companies		
s 113(1)	—	Amends and part repeals TA 1988 Sch 9 para 21(1).
s 113(2)	—	Inserts TA 1988 Sch 9 para 21(4).
s 113(3)	—	Amends TA 1988 Sch 9 para 26(3).
s 114 Requirements to be satisfied by approved schemes		
s 114(1)	—	Introductory.
s 114(2)	—	Amends TA 1988 Sch 9 para 28.
s 114(3)	—	Amends TA 1988 Sch 9 para 29.
s 114(4)–(7)	—	Amends TA 1988 s 185 from 29.4.1996. See Sch 6 para 221.
s 114(8)	—	Amends TCGA 1992, s 120(6). See Sch 6 para 221.
s 114(9)	—	Introduces Sch 16.
s 114(10)	—	Commencement. See Sch 6 para 221.
s 115 Transitional provisions		
	—	See Sch 7 para 76.
s 120 Grant and exercise of share options		
s 120(11)(*b*)	—	Spent. See Sch 6 para 163(4).
s 152 Jobfinder's grant		
	—	Spent.
Sch 7 Transfer of charge under Schedule C to Schedule D		
para 5	—	Amends TA 1988 s 19(1) Sch E para 2.
Sch 16 Share option schemes approved before passing of this Act		
paras 1–3	—	See Sch 7 para 75.
para 4	—	Spent.
para 5	—	See Sch 7 para 75.

Dest. Tables

Existing provision	*Rewritten provision*	*Remarks*
Sch 20 Self-assessment: discretions exercisable by the Board etc		
para 6	—	Amends TA 1988 s 132(1).
para 7	—	Repeals in part TA 1988 s 145(7).
para 8	—	Amends TA 1988 s 159(1), repeals TA 1988 s 159(4)–(6).
para 9	—	Repeals in part TA 1988 s 161(3), (4).
para 10	—	Amends TA 1988 s168(3), (6).
para 41	—	Repeals in part TA 1988 Sch 7 para 1(5).
para 42	—	Repeals in part TA 1988 Sch 12 para 2(2).

FINANCE ACT 1997 (C 16)

Existing provision	*Rewritten provision*	*Remarks*
s 62 Travelling expenses etc		
s 62(1)–(3)	—	Repealed FA 1998 Sch 27 Part 3(10).
s 62(4)	—	Amends TA 1988 s 168(5), (5A).
s 62(5)	—	Commencement.
s 63 Work-related training		
s 63(1)	—	Inserts TA 1988 s 200B, s 200C, s 200D.
s 63(2)	—	Amends TA 1988 s 200A(3).
s 63(3)	—	Commencement.
Sch 18 Repeals: profit-related pay		
Pt 6(3), Note 3(*b*)	—	Saves TA 1988 Sch 8 para 7 for the operation of TA 1988 Sch 9, para 40(2) and (4). See clauses 549 to 554.

FINANCE ACT 1998 (C 36)

Existing provision	*Rewritten provision*	*Remarks*
s 49 Employee share options		
s 49(1)	—	Amends TA 1988 s 135(2), (5).
s 49(2)	Sch 7 para 62	Commencement.
s 50 Conditional acquisition of shares		
s 50(1)	—	Inserts TA 1988 s 140A–140C
s 50(2)	—	Amends FA 1988 s 77(1).
s 50(3)	—	Inserts FA 1988 s 79(6A).
s 50(4)	Sch 7 para 44	Commencement.
s 51 Convertible shares provided to directors and employees		
s 51(1)	—	Inserts TA 1988 s 140D to s 140F.
s 51(2)	—	Inserts FA 1988 s 79(6B).
s 51(3)	Sch 7 para 49	Commencement.
s 52 Information powers		
s 52(1)	—	Inserts TA 1988 s 140G.
s 52(2)	—	Amends TMA 1970 s 98.
s 53 Provision supplemental to sections 50–52		
	—	Inserts TA 1988 s 140H.
s 55 Construction workers supplied by agencies		
s 55(1)	—	Repeals in part TA 1988 s 134(5).
s 58 Payments and other benefits in connection with termination of employment, etc		
s 58(1)	—	Substitutes TA 1988 s 148.
s 58(2)	—	Substitutes TA 1988 Sch 11.
s 58(3)	—	Introduces FA 1998 Sch 9.
s 58(4)	—	Unnecessary: see Sch 7 para 42.
s 60 Reductions for road fuel gas cars		
s 60(1)–(5)	—	Amends TA 1988 s 168A(1), (11), s 168B(2), s 168C(2), inserts TA 1988 s 168AB.
s 60(6)	—	Commencement.

Existing provision	Rewritten provision	Remarks
s 61 Travelling expenses		
s 61(1)	—	Substitutes TA 1988 s 198(1)–(1B).
s 61(2)	—	Inserts TA 1988 Sch 12A.
s 61(3)	—	Commencement.
s 63 Withdrawal (of foreign earnings deduction) except in relation to seafarers		
s 63(1)	—	Repeals TA 1988 s 193(1).
s 63(2)	—	Inserts TA 1988 s 192A.
s 63(3)	—	Repeals in part TA 1988 s 19(1) Sch E Case I, amends TA 1988 s 132(3), Sch 11 para 10, Sch 12 paras 1, 1A, 2(1), 3(1) and (3), 5, 6.
s 63(4)	—	Amends TA 1988 Sch 12 paras 3(2), (5).
s 63(5)–(7)	—	Commencement.
s 64 Transitory provision relating to tradeable assets		
s 64(1)–(7)	—	Spent.
s 65 PAYE: payment in the form of a readily convertible asset		
s 65(1)–(5)	—	Amends TA 1988 s 203F.
s 65(6), (7)	—	Spent.
s 66 PAYE: enhancing the value of an asset		
s 66(1)	—	Inserts TA 1988 s 203FA.
s 66(2), (3)	—	Spent.
s 67 PAYE: gains from share options etc		
s 67(1)	—	Inserts TA 1988 s 203FB.
s 67(2), (3)	—	Spent.
s 68 PAYE: Vouchers and credit-tokens		
s 68(1)	—	Amends TA 1988 s 203G.
s 68(2)	—	Amends TA 1988 s 203H.
s 68(3)	—	Amends TA 1988 s 203I.
s 68(4), (5)	—	Spent.
s 69 Intermediaries, non-UK employers, agencies etc		
s 69(1)	—	Amends TA 1988 s 203C(1).
s 69(2)	—	Inserts TA 1988 s 203C(3A), (3B).
s 69(3)	—	Substitutes TA 1988 s 203L(1), inserts TA 1988 s 203L(1A), (1B), (1C), substitutes TA 1988 s 203L(2).
s 69(4)	—	Amends TA 1988 s 144A(2).
s 69(5), (6)	—	Spent.
s 93 Benefits received under non-approved retirement benefits scheme		
s 93(1)	—	Amends TA 1988 s 596A(4).
s 93(2)	—	Amends TA 1988 s 596B(9).
s 93(3)	—	Inserts TA 1988 s 596C
s 93(4)	—	Commencement.
Sch 9 Payments in connection with termination of employment etc		
pt 1	—	Substitutes TA 1988 Sch 11.
pt 2 para 1	—	Amends TA 1988 s 189.
para 2	—	Spent (superseded amendment of TA 1988 s 190).
para 3	—	Amends TA 1988 s 202B(8).
para 4	—	Amends TA 1988 s 833(3)(*a*): see Sch 6 para 108(2).
para 5	—	Substitutes FA 1995 s 92(10).
Sch 10 Ordinary commuting and private travel		
	—	Inserts TA 1988 Sch 12A.

TAX CREDITS ACT 1999 (C 10)

Existing provision	*Rewritten provision*	*Remarks*
Sch 1 Provision consequential on renaming of benefits		
para 6(*c*)	—	Amends TA 1988 s 617(2)(*a*).

FINANCE ACT 1999 (C 16)

Existing provision	*Rewritten provision*	*Remarks*
s 42 Conditional acquisition of shares		
s 42(1)	—	Introductory.
s 42(2)	—	Repeals TA 1988 s 140A(2).
s 42(3)	—	Amends TA 1988 s 140A(3).
s 42(4)	—	Amends TA 1988 s 140A(4).
s 42(5)	—	Spent.
s 43 Meaning of conditional interests in shares		
s 43(1)	—	Introductory.
s 43(2)	—	Inserts TA 1988 s 140C(1A).
s 43(3)	—	Amends TA 1988 s 140C(2), (3), (4).
s 43(4)	—	Amends TA 1988 s 140C(3).
s 43(5)	—	Inserts TA 1988 s 140C(3A).
s 43(6)	—	Inserts TA 1988 s 140C(6).
s 43(7)	—	Commencement.
s 44 Exemption for mobile telephones		
s 44(1)	—	Inserts TA 1988 s 155AA.
s 44(2)	—	Repeals TA 1988 s 159A.
s 44(3)	—	Amends TA 1988 s 154(2).
s 44(4)	—	Amends TA 1988 s 168A(11).
s 44(5)	—	Repeals TA 1988 s 200AA(3).
s 44(6)	—	Commencement.
s 45 Limited exemption for computer equipment		
s 45(1)	—	Inserts TA 1988 s 156A.
s 45(2)	—	Amends TA 1988 s 154(2).
s 45(3)	—	Commencement.
s 48 Provision and support of bus services		
s 48(1)	—	Inserts TA 1988 s 197AA, s 197AB.
s 48(2)	—	Commencement.
s 49 Provision of motor cycle or cycle parking facilities		
s 49(1)	237, 266(1), 267	
s 49(2)	237, 266(1), 267	
s 49(3)	—	See Annex 2, Note 29.
s 49(4)	—	Commencement.
s 50 Cycles and cyclist's safety equipment		
s 50(1)	—	Inserts TA 1988 s 197AC
s 50(2)	—	Repealed CAA 2001 Sch 4.
s 50(3)	—	Commencement.
s 51 EU travel expenses		
s 51(1)	—	Amends TA 1988 s 200(2), inserts TA 1988 s 200(3).
s 51(2)	—	Commencement.
Sch 5 Scottish Parliament and devolved assemblies: exemptions and reliefs		
para 1	—	Substitutes TA 1988 s 190.
para 2(1)	—	Inserts TA 1988 s 200ZA.
para 2(2)	—	Substitutes TA 1988 s 198(4).
para 2(3)	—	Repealed CAA 2001 Sch 4.
para 3	—	Amends TA 1988 s 200AA(2).
Sch 10 Sharing of pensions etc on divorce or annulment		
para 4	—	Amends TA 1988 s 595(5).
para 5	—	Inserts TA 1988 s 596(4).
para 6	—	Amends TA 1988 s 596A(8).
para 8	—	Amends TA 1988 s 600(1), (2).

WELFARE REFORM AND PENSIONS ACT 1999 (C 30)

Existing provision	*Rewritten provision*	*Remarks*
Sch 8 Welfare benefits: minor and consequential amendments		
para 1(2)	—	Amends TA 1988 s 617(1)(*a*).
Sch 12 Consequential amendments		
para 75	—	Inserts TA 1988 s 617(2)(*af*).

CARE STANDARDS ACT 2000 (C 14)

Existing provision	*Rewritten provision*	*Remarks*
Sch 4 Minor and consequential amendments		
para 13	—	Amends TA 1988 s 155A(6).

FINANCE ACT 2000 (C 17)

Existing provision	*Rewritten provision*	*Remarks*
s 38 Payroll deduction scheme		
s 38(5)	—	Amends and repeals in part TA 1988 s 202.
s 38(7)	—	Commencement of subs (5).
s 47 Employee share ownership plans		
	—	Introduces FA 2000 Sch 8.
s 56 Further provisions about share options		
s 56(1)	—	Inserts TA 1988 s 187A.
s 56(2)	—	Amends TA 1988 s 203FB.
s 56(3)	—	Amends TA 1988 s 136(6), FA 1988 s 85(1).
s 56(4)	—	Inserts TA 1988 s 136(7), (8).
s 57 Benefits in kind: deregulatory amendments		
s 57(1)	—	Introduces FA 2000 Sch 10.
s 57(2)	—	Commencement.
s 58 Education and training		
s 58(1)	—	Inserts TA 1988 s 200E, s 200F, s 200G, s 200H, s 200J.
s 58(2)	—	Amends TA 1988 s 200A(3).
s 58(3)	—	Commencement.
s 59 Cars available for private use		
	—	Introduces FA 2000 Sch 11.
s 60 Provision of services through intermediary		
	—	Introduces FA 2000 Sch 12.
s 62 Enterprise management incentives		
	—	Introduces FA 2000 Sch 14.
Sch 8 Employee share ownership plans		
para 1(1)	488(4), Sch 2 para 2	
para 1(2), (3)	Sch 2 para 3	
para 1(4)	Sch 2 para 2	
para 2	Sch 2 para 4	
para 3	Sch 2 paras 5, 53	Part unnecessary: see commentary on Sch 2 para 5.
para 4	Sch 2 para 81	
para 5	Sch 2 para 82	
para 6	Sch 2 para 6	
para 7	Sch 2 para 7	
para 8	Sch 2 para 8	
para 9	Sch 2 para 9	
para 10	Sch 2 para 10	
para 11	Sch 2 para 11	
para 12	Sch 2 para 12	
para 13	Sch 2 para 14	
para 14(1)	Sch 2 para 15	Amended FA 2001 Sch 13 para 2.
para 14(1A), (1B)	Sch 2 para 17	Inserted FA 2001 Sch 13 para 2.
para 14(2)–(5)	Sch 2 para 16	
para 15	Sch 2 para 19	
para 16	Sch 2 para 18.	See Annex 1, Change 160.
para 17	Sch 2 para 20	
para 18	Sch 2 para 21	
para 19	Sch 2 para 21	See also Sch 7 para 87.
para 20	Sch 2 para 22	
para 21	549–554, Sch 2 para 23	
para 22	Sch 2 para 24	
para 23	Sch 2 para 34	
para 24	Sch 2 para 35	
para 25	Sch 2 para 34	

Existing provision	*Rewritten provision*	*Remarks*
para 26	Sch 2 para 38	
para 27	Sch 2 para 39	
para 28	Sch 2 para 40	
para 29	Sch 2 para 41	
para 30	Sch 2 para 42	
para 31	Sch 2 para 36	
para 32	Sch 2 para 37	
para 33	Sch 2 para 43	
para 34	Sch 2 para 44	
para 35	Sch 2 para 45	
para 36	Sch 2 para 46	
para 37	Sch 2 para 47	
para 38	Sch 2 para 48	
para 39(1)	Sch 2 para 49	
para 39(2)	Sch 2 para 43	
para 39(3)	Sch 2 para 49	Amended Financial Services and Markets Act 2000 (Consequential Amendments) (Taxes) Order 2001 (S I. 2001/3629) Art.107.
para 39(4)	Sch 2 para 49	
para 40	Sch 2 para 50	
para 41	Sch 2 para 51	
para 42	Sch 2 para 52	
para 43	Sch 2 para 53	
para 44	Sch 2 para 54	
para 45	Sch 2 para 55	
para 46	Sch 2 para 56	
para 47	Sch 2 para 57	
para 48	Sch 2 para 43	Amended FA 2001 Sch 13 para 3(1).
para 49	Sch 2 para 58	
para 50	Sch 2 para 59	
para 51	Sch 2 para 60	
para 52	Sch 2 para 61	
para 53(1), (2)	Sch 2 para 62	
para 53(3)	Sch 2 para 69	
para 53(4)	Sch 2 para 62	
para 54	Sch 2 para 64, para 55	Sch 2 para 65
para 56(1)–(4)	Sch 2 para 66 Sub-para (2)	Part unnecessary: see commentary on Sch 2 para 66.
para 56(5)	Sch 2 para 62	
para 57	Sch 2 para 67	
para 58	Sch 2 para 68	
para 59	Sch 2 para 25	
para 60	Sch 2 para 26	
para 61	Sch 2 para 27	
para 62	Sch 2 para 28	Part unnecessary: see commentary on Sch 2 para 28.
para 63	Sch 2 para 30	
para 64	Sch 2 para 31	
para 65(1)–(5)	Sch 2 para 32	
para 65(6)	Sch 2 para 99	
para 66	Sch 2 para 33	
para 67	Sch 2 para 29	
para 68	Sch 2 para 71	Amended ESSA 2002 s 1(2).
para 69	Sch 2 para 76	
para 70	Sch 2 para 75	
para 71(1), (2)	Sch 2 para 72	
para 71(3)	Sch 2 para 73	
para 71(4)	Sch 2 para 74	
para 72(1)	Sch 2 para 77	
para 72(2)	Sch 2 para 99	
para 73	Sch 2 para 79	
para 74	—	See Sch 6 para 221.
para 75	Sch 2 para 80	
para 76	Sch 2 para 78	
para 77(1)	489(1), 500(2), (3)	See Sch 6 paras 10, 34 and 100.

Existing provision	*Rewritten provision*	*Remarks*
para 77(2)	489(1), 500(2), (3)	See Sch 6 paras 10 and 34.
para 78(1)	490	
para 78(2)	491	Part unnecessary: see commentary on clause 491.
para 78(3)	499	Inserted FA 2001 Sch 13 para 4.
para 79(1)	7(6), 10(3), 501(1)–(5)	
para 79(2)	502(2), (3)	
para 79(3)	502(4)	
para 79(4)	502(5), Sch 2 para 99	
para 79(5)	501(6)	
para 80(1), (2)	494	
para 80(3)	495	
para 81(1)	505(1)	
para 81(2)–(3)	7(6), 10(3), 505(2),(3)	
para 81(4)	505(4)	
para 81(5), (6)	505(6)	
para 81(7)	497(1)	
para 82(1)	7(6), 10(3), 505(6), 507(1), (2)	
para 82(2)	—	Repealed FA 2001 Sch 13 para 5.
para 83	492	
para 84	7(6), 10(3), 503	
para 85	7(6), 10(3), 504(1), (2)	
para 86(1)	506(1)	
para 86(2)–(3)	7(6), 10(3), 506(2),(3)	
para 86(4)	506(4)	
para 86(5)	506(6)	
para 86(6)	497(2)	
para 87(1)	498(1)	
para 87(2)	498(2), Sch 2 para 32	
para 87(3)	Sch 2 para 99	
para 87(4)	498(2), Sch 2 para 98	
para 88(1)–(4), (5)–(7)	—	See Sch 6 para 100; amended FA 2001 Sch 13 para 6(1).
para 88(4A)	—	Inserted ESSA 2002 s 3(2); see Sch 6 para 100.
para 89	493	
para 90	Sch 2 para 80	
para 91	496	
para 92(1)	—	See Sch 6 paras 10 and 34.
para 92(2)	—	See Sch 6 para 34.
para 92(3)	Sch 2 para 80(4)	
para 93(1)	Sch 2 para 80(5)	See Sch 6 paras 10, 34.
para 93(2)	—	See Sch 6 para 34; amended FA 2001 Sch 13 para 7.
para 93(3)	—	See Sch 6 paras 10, 34.
para 93(4)	Sch 2 para 80(4)	
para 93(5)	—	See Sch 6 paras 10, 34.
para 93(6)	497(3)	
para 94	509(1), (2), (3)	Amended FA 2002 s 39(2).
para 95(1)–(6)	510	Amended FA 2002 s 39(3).
para 95(7), (8)	511	
para 95(9)	512	
para 95(10)	488(4)	
para 96(1)	513(1)–(5)	
para 96(2)	513(5)	Amended FA 2002 s 39(4).
para 96(3)	514(1)–(5)	
para 96(4)	514(6)	
para 96(5)	488(4)	
para 97	Sch 7 para 86	See Sch 6 para 221.
para 98	—	See Sch 6 para 221; amended FA 2001 Sch 13 para 8, ESSA 2002 s 3(3).
para 99	—	See Sch 6 para 221.
para 100	—	Amended ESSA 2002 s 3(4); see Sch 6 para 221.
paras 101–102	—	See Sch 6 para 221.

Existing provision	*Rewritten provision*	*Remarks*
para 103	—	See Sch 7 para 86.
para 104	—	See Sch 6 para 221.
paras 105–107	—	See Sch 6 para 109.
para 108	—	Amended ESSA 2002 s 2(2); see Sch 6 para 109.
paras 109–112	—	See Sch 6 para 109.
para 112A	—	Inserted ESSA 2002 s 1(3); see Sch 6 para 109.
para 112B	—	Inserted ESSA 2002 s 1(4); see Sch 6 para 109.
para 113	—	Amended ESSA 2002 s 2(3); see Sch 6 para 109.
para 114	—	See Sch 6 para 109.
para 115(1), (2)	Sch 2 para 86	
para 115(3)–(8)	Sch 2 para 87	
para 116(1)–(4)	Sch 2 para 88	
para 116(5)	Sch 2 para 99(1)	
para 116A	—	Inserted FA 2001 s 95. See now s 95 as substituted by Sch 6 para 257.
para 117(1)–(3)	Sch 2 para 93	
para 117(4)	—	Amends TMA 1970 s 98. See Sch 6 para 137(2)(*b*).
para 118(1)	Sch 2 para 83	
para 118(2)	Sch 2 paras 42, 84	
para 118(3)	Sch 2 para 84	
para 118(4)	Sch 2 para 42	
para 118(5), (6)	Sch 2 para 84	
para 118(7)	Sch 2 para 83	
para 119	Sch 2 para 85	
para 120	Sch 2 para 89	
para 121(1)	Sch 2 para 90 See also Sch 6 para 109.	
para 121(2)–(9)	Sch 2 para 90 Sub-para (3)	Part unnecessary: see commentary on Sch 2 para 90.
para 121(10), (11)	—	Inserted ESSA 2002 s 2(4); see Sch 6 para 109.
para 122(1), (2)	Sch 2 para 96	
para 122(3)–(5)	Sch 2 para 97	
para 122(6)	508(1)	
para 122(7)	Sch 2 para 97	
para 123	Sch 2 para 95	
para 124	720(1)	
para 125	Sch 2 para 92	See Sch 6 para 221.
para 126	Sch 2 para 94	
para 127	Sch 2 para 91	Amended FA 2002 s 39(5).
para 128	509(4), (5)	Amended FA 2002 s 39(6); see Sch 6 paras 100, 221.
para 129(1)	719 (''control'') 721(1) (''tax year''), Sch 2 paras 75, 99(1)	See also Sch 6 paras 10, 34, 100, 221.
para 129(2)	718	
para 129(3), (4)	Sch 2 para 99(2), (3)	
para 130	—	Index.
Sch 10 Benefits in kind: deregulatory amendments		
para 1	—	Introductory.
para 2(1)	—	Inserts TA 1988 s 155ZA.
para 2(2)	—	Amends TA 1988 s 154(2), (3).
para 3(1)	—	Inserts TA 1988 s 155ZB.
para 3(2)	—	Amends TA 1988 s 154(2).
para 4(1)	—	Inserts TA 1988 s 161A.
para 4(2)	—	Repeals TA 1988 s 160(1C), amends TA 1988 s 160(5).
para 5(1)	—	Inserts TA 1988 s 161B.
para 5(2)	—	Inserts TA 1988 Sch 7A.
para 5(3)	—	Amends TA 1988 s 160(5).
para 5(4)	—	Repeals TA 1988 s 161(1A), (1B).

Existing provision	Rewritten provision	Remarks
para 6	—	Inserts TA 1988 Sch 7 para 5A.
Sch 11 Cars available for private use		
para 1(1)	—	Introductory.
para 1(2)	—	Substitutes TA 1988 Sch 6 paras 1–5, inserts TA 1988 Sch 6 paras 5A–5G.
para 1(3)	—	Amends TA 1988 Sch 6 para 6.
para 1(4)	—	Amends TA 1988 Sch 6 para 10.
para 2	—	Inserts TA 1988 s 168AB(4).
Sch 12 Provision of services through an intermediary		
para 1(1)–(4)	49	
para 1(5)	—	See Annex 2, Note 12.
para 2	7(5), 50	
para 3	51	See Annex 1, Changes 12 and 157.
para 4	52	
para 5	53	
para 6	48	
para 7	54(1)	Amended CAA 2001 Sch 2 para 107; see Annex 1, Change 13.
para 7A	54(3)	Inserted FA 2002 s 38(2).
para 7B(1), (2)	54(4), (5)	Inserted FA 2002 s 38(2).
para 7B(3)	54(7)	Inserted FA 2002 s 38(2).
para 8	54(2)	
para 9	54(8)	
para 10	55	See Annex 1, Change 14.
para 11(1)	56(1)	
para 11(2)	56(2)	
para 11(3)	56(4), (5)	
para 11(4)	56(3)	Unnecessary (in part): see section 218(1), Step (1)(*d*); amended FA 2001 Sch 12 Pt 2 para 16.
para 11(5)	56(6)	
para 11(6)	56(7)	
para 11(7)	56(8)	
para 12	57	Amended FA 2002 s 38(3).
para 13	58	
para 14(1)	59(1)	
para 14(2)	59(7)	
para 14(3)	59(6)	
para 15(1)	59(4)	
para 15(2)	59(5)	
para 16(1)	59(2)	
para 16(2)	59(3)	
para 19 60,	718	See Annex 1, Change 157.
para 20	720(1)	
para 21 61,	721(5)	
para 22	—	Unnecessary.
para 23	—	Spent.
para 24	48	
Sch 14 Enterprise management incentives		
para 1(1)	527(4), Sch 5 para 1	
para 1(2)	Sch 5 para 1	
para 1(3)	Sch 5 para 2	
para 2	Sch 5 para 44	Amended FA 2001 Sch 14 para 2.
para 3	Sch 5 para 45	
para 4	Sch 5 para 46	Amended FA 2001 Sch 14 para 3.
para 5(1)–(5)	Sch 5 para 47	
para 5(6)–(9)	Sch 5 para 48	
para 6	Sch 5 para 49	
para 7	Sch 5 para 50	
para 8	Sch 5 para 3	Amended FA 2001 Sch 14 para 4.
para 9	Sch 5 para 4	Amended FA 2001 Sch 14 para 5.
para 10(1)–(3)	Sch 5 para 5	
para 10(4), (5)	Sch 5 para 6	
para 10(6)–(8)	Sch 5 paras 5, 6	
para 11	Sch 5 para 7	Substituted FA 2001 Sch 14 para 6.

Existing provision	*Rewritten provision*	*Remarks*
para 12	Sch 5 para 8	
para 13	719, Sch 5 para 9	
para 14	Sch 5 para 10	
para 15	719, Sch 5 para 11	
para 16	Sch 5 para 12	Amended Enterprise Management Incentives (Gross Asset Requirement) Order 2001 (S I. 2001/3799).
para 17(1)	Sch 5 para 13	
para 17(2), (3)	Sch 5 para 14	
para 17(4)	Sch 5 paras 13, 14	
para 17(5), (6)	Sch 5 para 14	
para 17(7)	Sch 5 paras 13, 14	
para 18	Sch 5 para 15	
para 19	Sch 5 para 16	
para 20	Sch 5 para 17	
para 21	Sch 5 para 18	
para 22	Sch 5 para 19	Amended FA 2002 s 103(4)(*f*).
para 23	Sch 5 para 20	
para 24	Sch 5 para 21	
para 25	Sch 5 para 22	
para 26	Sch 5 para 23	
para 27	Sch 5 para 24	
para 28	Sch 5 para 25	
para 29(1)–(3)	Sch 5 para 26	
para 29(4)	Sch 5 para 26	
para 29(5),(6)	Sch 5 para 27	
para 30(1),(2)	Sch 5 para 28	
para 30(3)	Sch 5 para 30	
para 30(4)	Sch 5 para 28	
para 31	Sch 5 para 29	
para 32	Sch 5 para 30	
para 33	Sch 5 para 30	See also Sch 7 para 87
para 34	Sch 5 para 31	
para 35	549–554, Sch 5 para 32	
para 36	Sch 5 para 33	
para 37	Sch 5 para 34	
para 38	Sch 5 para 35	
para 39	Sch 5 para 36	
para 40	Sch 5 para 37	
para 41	Sch 5 para 38	
para 42(1)	528, 529(1)	
para 42(2), (3)	529(2), (3)	
para 43	528	
para 44	530	
para 45(1)	531(1)	
para 45(2)	531(2), (4)	Substituted FA 2001 Sch 14 para 7.
para 45(3)	531(3)	Substituted FA 2001 Sch 14 para 7.
para 45(4)	420	Substituted FA 2001 Sch 14 para 7.
para 45(5)	531(5)	
para 46(1)	531(1)	
para 46(2)	531(2), (3), (4)	Substituted FA 2001 Sch 14 para 8.
para 46(2A)	420	Substituted FA 2001 Sch 14 para 8.
para 46(3)	531(5)	
para 47(1)	534(1), 535(1),536(1), 537(2), (3)	Amended FA 2001 Sch 14 para 9.
para 47(2)	534(3)–(5) Sub-para (2)	Part unnecessary: see commentary on clause 534.
para 47(3)	535(2), (4)	
para 47(4)	—	Drafting.
para 48	534(2)	
para 49	537	Amended FA 2001 Sch 14 para 10.
para 50	538	
para 51(1)	539(1)	
para 51(2)	536(2), 539(4)	
para 51(3)	539(2)	

Existing provision	*Rewritten provision*	*Remarks*
para 51(4)	539(3)	
para 51(5)	536(2)	
para 52(1)	535(3)	
para 52(2)–(5)		See Annex 1, Change 130.
para 52(6)	535(6)	
para 53(1)	532(1)	
para 53(2)	532(2), (4), (5)	Substituted FA 2001 Sch 14 para 11.
para 53(2A)	532(3)–(5)	Substituted FA 2001 Sch 14 para 11.
para 53(2B)	532(3)–(5)	Substituted FA 2001 Sch 14 para 11.
para 53(2C)	532(4), (5)	Substituted FA 2001 Sch 14 para 11.
para 53(2D)	420	Substituted FA 2001 Sch 14 para 11.
para 53(3)	532(6)	Amended FA 2001 Sch 14 para 11.
para 54(1)	540	
para 54(2)	541(1)	
para 55	541	
para 56	—	See Sch 6, para 221.
para 57	—	See Sch 6, para 221.
para 58	—	See Sch 6, para 221.
para 59	719, Sch 5 para 39	
para 60	Sch 5 para 40	
para 61	Sch 5 para 41	
para 62	Sch 5 para 42	
para 63	Sch 5 para 43	Amended FA 2001 Sch 14 para 12.
para 64(1), (2)	Sch 5 para 51	
para 64(3)	—	Amends TMA 1970 s 98. See Sch 6 para 137(2)(*c*), (3).
para 65(1), (2)	Sch 5 para 52	
para 65(3)	—	Amends TMA 1970 s 98. See Sch 6 para 137(4)(*e*), (5).
para 66(1)	Sch 5 para 55	
para 66(2)	Sch 5 para 56	
para 67(1)	Sch 5 para 56	
para 67(2), (3)	Sch 5 para 57	
para 67(4)	Sch 5 para 56	
para 67(5)	Sch 5 paras 56, 57	
para 68	720(1)	
para 69	Sch 5 para 54	
para 70	Sch 5 para 53	
para 71(1)	721(1) (''tax year''), Sch 5 para 58	
para 71(2)	718	
para 72	—	Index.

CAPITAL ALLOWANCES ACT 2001 (C 2)

Existing provision	*Rewritten provision*	*Remarks*
Sch 2 Consequential amendments		
para 24	—	Spent.
para 25	—	Repeals in part TA 1988 s 198(2).
para 51(1)	—	Spent in part; see Sch 6 para 62.
para 107	—	Amends FA 2000 Sch 12 para 7.

FINANCE ACT 2001 (C 9)

Existing provision	*Rewritten provision*	*Remarks*
s 57 Mileage allowances: exemptions and relief		
s 57(1)	—	Inserts TA 1988 s 197AD–197AH.
s 57(2)	—	Inserts TA 1988 Sch 12AA.
s 58 Mileage allowances: nil liability notices		
		Sch 7 paras 16, 20
s 60 Exemption for works bus services: extension to minibuses		
	—	Amends TA 1988 s 197AA.

Dest. Tables

Existing provision	Rewritten provision	Remarks
s 61 Employee share ownership plans		
	—	Introduces FA 2001 Sch 13.
s 62 Enterprise Management incentives		
	—	Introduces FA 2001 Sch 14.
Sch 12 Mileage allowances		
pt 1	—	Inserts TA 1988 Sch 12AA.
pt 2, para 1	—	Amends TA 1988 s 153.
pt 2, para 2	—	Amends TA 1988 s 163(4)(*b*).
pt 2, para 3	—	Amends TA 1988 s 167(2)(*b*).
pt 2, para 4	—	Amends TA 1988 s 168(5), (5A).
pt 2, para 5	—	Amends TA 1988 s 192(5).
pt 2, para 6	—	Inserts TA 1988 s 198(5).
pt 2, para 7	—	Amends TA 1988 s 200A(1)(*b*).
pt 2, para 8	—	Amends TA 1988 s 200C
pt 2, para 9	—	Amends TA 1988 s 200F.
pt 2, para 10	—	Inserts TA 1988 s 332(3A), (3B).
pt 2 para 12	—	Amends TA 1988 s 589.
pt 2 para 13	—	Amends TA 1988 s 589B.
pt 2, para 14	—	Amends TA 1988 s 646(2)(*b*). See Sch 6 para 94.
pt 2, para 15	—	Amends TA 1988 Sch 12 para 1A.
pt 2, para 16	—	Inserts FA 2000 Sch 12 Pt 2 para 11(4)(*ab*).
Sch 13 Employee share ownership plans: amendments		
para 1	—	Introductory.
para 2(1)	—	Amends FA 2000 Sch 8, para 14.
para 2(2)	—	Spent.
para 3(1)	—	Amends FA 2000 Sch 8, para 48.
para 3(2), (3)	—	Spent.
para 4	—	Adds FA 2000 Sch 8, para 78(3).
para 5	—	Repeals FA 2000 Sch 8, para 82(2).
para 6(1)	—	Amends FA 2000 Sch 8 para 88.
para 6(2), (3)	—	Commencement; see Sch 6 para 100.
para 7(1)	—	Amends FA 2000 Sch 8 para 93.
para 7(2)	—	Spent.
para 8(1)	—	Amends FA 2000 Sch 8 para 98.
para 8(2), (3)	—	Commencement; see Sch 6 para 221.
Sch 14 Enterprise Management Incentives: Amendments		
para 1	—	Introductory.
para 2	—	Amends FA 2000 Sch 14, para 2.
para 3	—	Amends FA 2000 Sch 14, para 4.
para 4	—	Amends FA 2000 Sch 14, para 8.
para 5	—	Amends FA 2000 Sch 14, para 9.
para 6	—	Substitutes FA 2000 Sch 14, para 11.
para 7	—	Substitutes FA 2000 Sch 14, para 45(2)–(4).
para 8	—	Amends FA 2000 Sch 14, para 46(2)–(2A).
para 9	—	Amends FA 2000 Sch 14, para 47.
para 10	—	Amends FA 2000 Sch 14, para 49.
para 11	—	Amends FA 2000 Sch 14, para 53.
para 12	—	Amends FA 2000 Sch 14, para 63.
para 13(1), (2)	—	Commencement.
para 13(3)	Sch 7 paras 79, 80.	
Sch 22 Remediation of contaminated land		
para 16(5) (words)	—	See section 684(7).

SOCIAL SECURITY CONTRIBUTIONS (SHARE OPTIONS) ACT 2001 (C 20)

Existing provision	Rewritten provision	Remarks
s 4 Consequential changes to tax relief provisions		
s 4(1)	482(2)–(4)	
s 4(2)	482(1)	

Existing provision	Rewritten provision	Remarks
s 4(3)	481(4), 482(5)	
s 4(4)		Unnecessary—see section 700(3)(*a*)(ii) and (4)(*b*).

INTERNATIONAL DEVELOPMENT ACT 2002 (C 1)

Existing provision	*Rewritten provision*	*Remarks*
Sch 3 Consequential amendments		
para 10	—	Amends TA 1988 Sch 11, para 6(2).

STATE PENSION CREDIT ACT 2002 (C 16)

Existing provision	*Rewritten provision*	*Remarks*
Sch 2 Minor and consequential amendments		
para 28	—	Inserts TA 1988 s 617(2)(*ag*).

TAX CREDITS ACT 2002 (C 21)

Existing provision	*Rewritten provision*	*Remarks*
s 25 Payments of working tax credit by employers		
s 25(6)	—	Unnecessary: see Sch 6 para 265(4).
Sch 3 Tax credits: consequential amendments		
para 14	—	Inserts TA 1988 s 617A.

FINANCE ACT 2002 (C 23)

Existing provision	*Rewritten provision*	*Remarks*
s 33 Employer-subsidised public transport bus services		
s 33(1)	—	Introductory.
s 33(2)	—	Amends TA 1988 s 197AB(2).
s 33(3)	—	Substitutes TA 1988 s 197AB(3) and inserts TA 1988 s 197AB(3A).
s 33(4)	—	Amends TA 1988 s 197AB(4).
s 33(5)	—	Inserts TA 1988 s 197AB(5).
s 33(6)	—	Commencement.
s 34 Car fuel: calculation of cash equivalent of benefit		
s 34(1)	—	Introductory.
s 34(2)	—	Amends TA 1988 s 158(2)–(2B).
s 34(3)	—	Amends TA 1988 s 158(4).
s 34(4)	—	Substitutes TA 1988 s 158(5).
s 34(5)	—	Inserts TA 1988 s 158(6A), (6B).
s 34(6)	—	Inserts TA 1988 s 158(8).
s 34(7)	—	Inserts TA 1988 s 158(9).
s 34(8)	—	Commencement.
s 35 Statutory paternity pay and statutory adoption pay	—	Inserts TA 1988 s 150(*e*).
s 36 Exemption of minor benefits: application to non-cash vouchers	—	Inserts TA 1988 s 155ZB(3).
s 37 Minor amendments to Schedule E charge	—	Introduces FA 2002 Sch 6.
s 38 Provision of services through an intermediary: minor amendments		
s 38(2)	—	Inserts FA 2000 Sch 12 paras 7A, 7B.
s 38(3)	—	Amends FA 2000 Sch 12 para 12(2).
s 39 Employee share ownership plans: minor amendments		
s 39(1)	—	Introductory.
s 39(2)	—	Amends FA 2000 Sch 8 para 94.
s 39(3)	—	Amends FA 2000 Sch 8 para 95(6).
s 39(4)	—	Amends FA 2000 Sch 8 para 96(2).
s 39(5)	—	Amends FA 2000 Sch 8 para 127.

Existing provision	*Rewritten provision*	*Remarks*
s 39(6)	—	Amends FA 2000 Sch 8 para 128(2).
s 39(7)	—	Commencement.
s 39(8)	Sch 7 para 70	
s 41 Parliamentary visits to EU candidate countries: tax treatment of members' expenses		
s 41(1)	—	Introductory.
s 41(2)	—	Amends TA 1988 s 200(3), s 200ZA(3).
s 41(3)	—	Adds TA 1988 s 200(4), (5), s 200ZA(4), (5).
s 41(4)	—	Spent.
s 103 References to accounting practice and periods of account		
s 103(4) (words)	—	Amends FA 2000 Sch 14 para 22(4).
Sch 6 Minor amendments to Schedule E charge		
para 1	—	Amends TA 1988 s 135(5).
para 2	—	Inserts TA 1988 s 144(4A).
para 3	—	Amends TA 1988 s 157(3)(*b*), s 159AA(3)(*b*), s 159AC(3)(*b*).
para 4	—	Amends TA 1988 s 144A(1).
para 5	—	Amends TA 1988 s 148.
para 6	—	Amends TA 1988 s 595(1).
Sch 13 Tax relief for expenditure on vaccine research etc		
para 27(1) (words)	—	See section 684(8).

EMPLOYEE SHARE SCHEMES ACT 2002 (C 34)

Existing provision	*Rewritten provision*	*Remarks*
s 1 Employee share ownership plans		
s 1(1)	—	Introductory.
s 1(2)	—	Inserts FA 2000 Sch 8 para 68(3).
s 1(3)	—	Inserts FA 2000 Sch 8 para 112A.
s 1(4)	—	Inserts FA 2000 Sch 8 para 112B.
s 2 Deductions: supplementary		
s 2(1)	—	Introductory.
s 2(2)	—	Inserts FA 2000 Sch 8 para 108(6).
s 2(3)	—	Amends FA 2000 Sch 8 para 113.
s 2(4)	—	Inserts FA 2000 Sch 8 para 121(10) and (11).
s 3 Deductions: income tax and capital gains tax		
s 3(1)	—	Introductory.
s 3(2)	—	Inserts FA 2000 Sch 8 para 88(4A).
s 3(3)	—	Inserts FA 2000 Sch 8 para 98(3A).
s 3(4)	—	Inserts FA 2000 Sch 8 para 100(4).
s 4 Short title		Unnecessary.
s 5 Commencement.	—	Commencement.

PART 2
SUBORDINATE LEGISLATION

Existing provision	*Rewritten provision*	*Remarks*
Disability Living Allowance and Disability Working Allowance (Northern Ireland Consequential Amendments) Order 1991 (S I. 1991/2874)		
Art.5	Amendment of TA 1988	
	—	Amends TA 1988 s 617(1)(*a*).

Existing provision	Rewritten provision	Remarks
Income Tax (Car benefits) (Replacement Accessories) Regulations (S I. 1994/777)	131	
Income Tax (Replacement Cars) Regulations (S I. 1994/778)	145	Amended Income Tax (Car Benefits) (Reduction of Value of Appropriate Percentage) Regulations 2001 (S I. 2001/1123) Reg.8(2).
Income Tax (Employments)(Notional Payments)Regulations (S I. 1994/1212)		
Reg.2	Interpretation	
Reg.2(1) (words)	694(6), 710(8)	Part unnecessary.
Reg.2(2)	—	Unnecessary.
Reg.3	Exclusion of property from section 203F TA 1988	
Reg.3(1)	701(2)	Amended Income Tax (Employments) (Notional Payments) (Amendment) Regulations 1998 (S I. 1998/1891) Reg.4.
Reg.3(2)	701(2), (3)	Substituted Income Tax (Employments) (Notional Payments) (Amendment)Regulations 1996 (S I. 1996/2969).
Reg.3(3)	701(4), (5)	Amended S I. 1998/1891 Reg.4. Part unnecessary: see Sch 1 (''company'', ''control'', ''ordinary share capital'')
Reg.3A	Specification of market for the purposes of section 203F(2)(*b*) TA 1988	
	702(1)	Inserted S I. 1998/1891 Reg.5.
Reg.3B	Exclusion of matters from section 203FA TA 1988	Inserted S I. 1998/1891 Reg.5.
Reg.3B(1), (2)	697(4), 701(3)	
Reg.3B(3)	701(4), (5)	Part unnecessary: see Sch 1 (''company'', ''control'', ''ordinary share capital'')
Reg.4	Exclusion of use of credit-token from section 203H TA 1988	
	695(2)	
Reg.5	Exclusion of cash vouchers from section 203I TA 1988	
	693(2), (3)	
Reg.6	Notional payments—non-cash vouchers—time of payment	
	694(5), (6)	
Reg.7	Notional payments—deduction of income tax	
	710(7)	Amended S I. 1998/1891 Reg.6.
Reg.8	Notional payments—accounting for income tax where inability to deduct	
	710(7)	Amended S I. 1998/1891 Reg.6.

Existing provision	Rewritten provision	Remarks
Reg.8A	Certain notional payments made between 6th April 1998 and 31st July 1998—accounting for income tax	
	—	Spent.
Income Tax (Employments) (Notional Payments) (Amendment) Regulations 1996 (S I. 1996/2969)	—	Substitutes Income Tax (Employments) (Notional Payments) Regulations 1994 (S I.1994/1212) Reg.3(2).
Income Tax (Employments) (Notional Payments) (Amendment) Regulations 1998 (S I. 1998/1891)		
Reg.4	Amendment to Reg. 3 S I. 1994/1212	Amends S I. 1994/1212 Reg.3.
Reg.5	Inserted Reg. 3A, 3 S I. 1994/1212	Inserts S I. 1994/1212 Reg.3A & 3B.
Reg.6	Amendment to Reg. 7 & 8 S I. 1994/1212	
	—	Amends S I. 1994/1212 Reg.7, 8.
Income Tax (Car Benefits) (Reduction of Value of Appropriate Percentage) Regulations 2001 (S I. 2001/1123)		
Reg.8	Amendment to S I. 1994/778	
Reg.8(1)	—	Introductory.
Reg.8(2)	—	Amends Income Tax (Replacement Cars) Regulations (S I. 1994/778) Reg.5.
Financial Services and Markets Act 2000 (Consequential Amendments) (Taxes) Order 2001 (S I. 2001/3629)		
Art.107	Employee share ownership plans	
	—	Amends FA 2000 Sch 8, para 39(3).
Enterprise Management (Gross Asset Requirement) Order 2001 (S I. 2001/ 3799)	—	Amends FA 2000 Sch 14 para 16.

INDEX

INDEX

INDEX

INDEX

B

C

INDEX

INDEX

INDEX

INDEX

INDEX

INDEX

INDEX

N

O

INDEX

INDEX

Z

WORDS AND PHRASES

Words in brackets indicate the context in which the word or phrase is used.